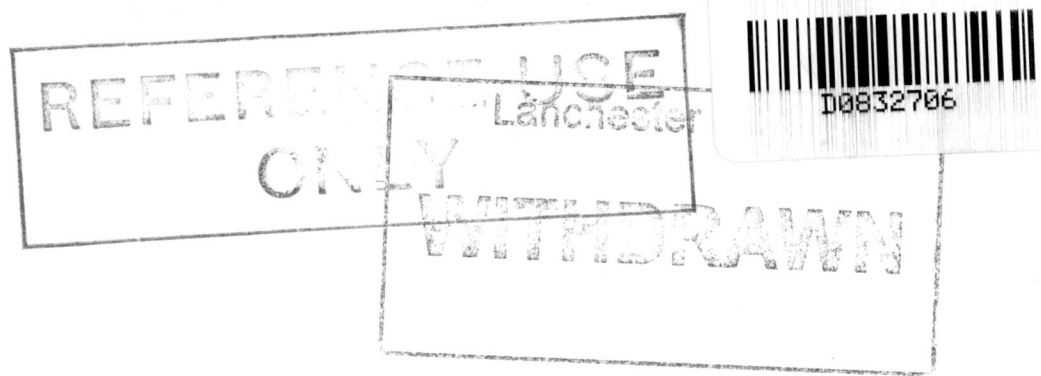

YEARBOOK OF THE
UNITED NATIONS
1982

Volume 36

YEARBOOK
OF THE
UNITED
NATIONS
1982

Volume 36

Department of Public Information
United Nations, New York

UNITED NATIONS PUBLICATION
SALES NO. E.85.I.1

07500

Foreword

W E LIVE in a time of rapid change, marked by recurrent crises and upheavals. This volatility lends further urgency to the need to employ international machinery to maintain peace and security, promote justice, encourage respect for human rights and accelerate economic and social development. The world's response to this need is described in the working of the United Nations.

No single year can furnish conclusive evidence of either the success or the failure of the response. All it can record is the continuity and the dynamism of an enterprise which covers the entire spectrum of collective concerns, some of them perennial, others relatively transitory but no less pressing. As the United Nations is not a world government, it can impose no solutions of its own and achieve no spectacular, quick results. Its principal instrument is multilateral negotiations; its main aim to secure agreements on how nations can jointly solve the complex problems confronting them all.

The experiences of 1982 recounted in the *Yearbook of the United Nations* indicate the efforts made to serve the great ideals of the Charter. A strong focus was maintained on all the objectives—political, economic, social and humanitarian—essential for creating conditions of stability and well-being for all peoples. The task of defining these common ends and spelling out the means of their attainment acquires added significance against the discouraging background of parochial attitudes and unilateralist trends. Perseverance in this task is the essence of the strategy to counter the degeneration of international life. There is no other way to avert anarchy and no other means to build and fortify the unifying sense of common interests which can lead to a brighter future for humanity.

Javier PÉREZ DE CUÉLLAR
Secretary-General

Contents

Part One: United Nations

POLITICAL AND SECURITY QUESTIONS

ECONOMIC AND SOCIAL QUESTIONS

TRUSTEESHIP AND DECOLONIZATION

LEGAL QUESTIONS

ADMINISTRATIVE AND BUDGETARY QUESTIONS

Part Two: *Intergovernmental organizations related to the United Nations*

Appendices

Indexes

ABBREVIATIONS COMMONLY USED IN THE *YEARBOOK*

AALCC	Asian-African Legal Consultative Committee
ACABQ	Advisory Committee on Administrative and Budgetary Questions
ACC	Administrative Committee on Co-ordination
ACP	African, Caribbean and Pacific
ADB	African Development Bank
AMS	Administrative Management Service
ANC	African National Congress of South Africa
APDC	Asian and Pacific Development Centre
ARSAP	Agricultural Requisites Scheme for Asia and the Pacific
ASEAN	Association of South-East Asian Nations
BIS	Bank for International Settlements
CCAQ	Consultative Committee on Administrative Questions
CCIR	International Radio Consultative Committee (ITU)
CCITT	International Telegraph and Telephone Consultative Committee
CCOP/ SOPAC	Committee for Co-ordination of Joint Prospecting for Mineral Resources in South Pacific Offshore Areas
CDP	Committee for Development Planning
CELADE	Latin American Demographic Centre
CERD	Committee on the Elimination of Racial Discrimination
CFA	Committee on Food Aid Policies and Programmes
CGPRT	coarse grains, pulses, roots and tuber crops
CILSS	Permanent Inter-State Committee on Drought Control in the Sahel
CMEA	Council for Mutual Economic Assistance
COPAC	Joint Committee for the Promotion of Aid to Co-operatives
COPUOS	Committee on the Peaceful Uses of Outer Space
CPC	Committee for Programme and Co-ordination
CSDHA	Centre for Social Development and Humanitarian Affairs (DIESA)
DAC	Development Assistance Committee (OECD)
DIEC	Development and International Economic Co-operation
DIESA	Department of International Economic and Social Affairs
DIS	Development Information System (ISU)
DPI	Department of Public Information
DTA	Democratic Turnhalle Alliance (Namibia)
DTCD	Department of Technical Co-operation for Development
EC	European Community
ECA	Economic Commission for Africa
ECDC	economic co-operation among developing countries
ECE	Economic Commission for Europe
ECLA	Economic Commission for Latin America
ECOWAS	Economic Community of West African States
ECWA	Economic Commission for Western Asia
EEC	European Economic Community
ESC	Economic and Social Council
ESCAP	Economic and Social Commission for Asia and the Pacific
EURATOM	European Atomic Energy Community
FADINAP	Fertilizer Advisory, Development and Information Network for Asia and the Pacific
FALPRO	Special Programme on Trade Facilitation
FAO	Food and Agriculture Organization of the United Nations
FICSA	Federation of International Civil Servants' Associations
FRETILIN	Frente Revolucionária de Timor Leste Independente
GA	General Assembly
GAB	General Arrangement to Borrow (IMF)
GATT	General Agreement on Tariffs and Trade
GCO	Greeting Card Operation (UNICEF)
GDP	gross domestic product
GDPS	Global Data-Processing System (WMO)
GEMS	Global Environmental Monitoring System (UNEP)
GNP	gross national product
GOS	Global Observing System (WMO)
GSP	generalized system of preferences
GSTP	global system of trade preferences
GTS	Global Telecommunication System (WMO)
IAEA	International Atomic Energy Agency
IBI	Intergovernmental Bureau of Informatics
ICAO	International Civil Aviation Organization
ICARA	International Conference on Assistance to Refugees in Africa
ICCROM	International Centre for the Study of the Preservation and the Restoration of Cultural Property
ICITO	Interim Commission for the International Trade Organization
ICJ	International Court of Justice
ICM	Intergovernmental Committee for Migration
ICP	International Comparison Project
ICRC	International Committee of the Red Cross
ICRP	International Commission on Radiological Protection
ICSC	International Civil Service Commission
IDA	International Development Association
IDB	Industrial Development Board (UNIDO)
IEFR	International Emergency Food Reserve
IFAD	International Fund for Agricultural Development
IFC	International Finance Corporation
ILC	International Law Commission
ILMAC	Israel-Lebanon Mixed Armistice Commission
ILO	International Labour Organisation
ILPES	Latin American Institute for Economic and Social Planning
IMCO	Inter-Governmental Maritime Consultative Organization
IMF	International Monetary Fund
INCB	International Narcotics Control Board
INFOTERRA	International Referral System for Sources of Environmental Information (UNEP)
INSTRAW	International Research and Training Institute for the Advancement of Women
INTIB	Industrial and Technological Information Bank (UNIDO)
IOB	Inter-Organization Board for Information Systems
IOC	International Oceanographic Commission
IPC	International Pepper Community
IPDC	International Programme for Development of Communication (UNESCO)
IPF	indicative planning figure (UNDP)
IRIRC	International Refugee Integration Resource Centre
IRPTC	International Register of Potentially Toxic Chemicals (UNEP)
ISIP	Integrated Systems Improvement Project (UNDP)
ISU	Information Systems Unit (DIESA)
ITC	International Trade Centre (UNCTAD/GATT)
ITO	International Trade Organization
ITU	International Telecommunication Union
IUCN	International Union for Conservation of Nature and Natural Resources
IYDP	International Year of Disabled Persons
IYC	International Year of the Child
IYY	International Youth Year
JAG	Joint Advisory Group on the International Trade Centre
JIU	Joint Inspection Unit
JUNIC	Joint United Nations Information Committee
LDC	least developed country
LPG	liquefied petroleum gas
MFA	Multifibre Arrangement (Arrangement Regarding Trade in Textiles) (GATT)
MNLITD	Movimento Nacional para a Libertação e Independência de Timor-Díli
MULPOC	Multinational Programming and Operational Centre (ECA)
NATO	North Atlantic Treaty Organization
NEA	Nuclear Energy Agency (OECD)
NGO	non-governmental organization
NPT	Treaty on the Non-Proliferation of Nuclear Weapons
NSGT	Non-Self-Governing Territory
NUSS	Nuclear Safety Standards (IAEA)
OAPEC	Organization of Arab Petroleum Exporting Countries
OAS	Organization of American States
OAU	Organization of African Unity
ODA	official development assistance
OECD	Organisation for Economic Co-operation and Development
OPEC	Organization of Petroleum Exporting Countries
PAC	Pan Africanist Congress of Azania
PADIS	Pan-African Documentation and Information System
PANS	Procedure for Air Navigation Services (ICAO)
PCT	Patent Co-operation Treaty (WIPO)
PHC	primary health care
PLO	Palestine Liberation Organization
POLISARIO	Frente Popular para la Liberación de Saguia el-Hamra y de Río de Oro
POPIN	Population Information Network
RCA	Regional Co-operation Agreement for Research, Development and Training Related to Nuclear Science and Technology (IAEA)
RID	International Regulations concerning the Carriage of Dangerous Goods by Rail
SALT	strategic arms limitation talks
SC	Security Council

SCPDPM	Sub-Commission on Prevention of Discrimination and Protection of Minorities
SDR	special drawing rights
SG	Secretary-General
SIDFA	Senior Industrial Development Field Adviser (UNIDO)
SIS	Special Industrial Services (UNIDO)
SNA	United Nations System of National Accounts
SOLAS	International Convention for the Safety of Life at Sea (IMCO)
SPC	Special Political Committee
START	strategic arms reduction talks
SWAPO	South West Africa People's Organization (Namibia)
TC	Trusteeship Council
TCDC	technical co-operation among developing countries
TCP	Technical Co-operation Programme (FAO)
TDB	Trade and Development Board (UNCTAD)
TELECOM-83	World Telecommunication Exhibition
TIR	*transport international routier* (international road transport) (ECE)
TNC	transnational corporation
UN	United Nations
UNCDF	United Nations Capital Development Fund
UNCHS	United Nations Centre for Human Settlements (Habitat)
UNCITRAL	United Nations Commission on International Trade Law
UNCIVPOL	United Nations civilian police (UNFICYP)
UNCTAD	United Nations Conference on Trade and Development
UNDOF	United Nations Disengagement Observer Force (Golan Heights)
UNDP	United Nations Development Programme
UNDRO	Office of the United Nations Disaster Relief Co-ordinator
UNEF	United Nations Emergency Force
UNEP	United Nations Environment Programme
UNESCO	United Nations Educational, Scientific and Cultural Organization
UNFDAC	United Nations Fund for Drug Abuse Control
UNFICYP	United Nations Peace-keeping Force in Cyprus
UNFPA	United Nations Fund for Population Activities
UNHCR	United Nations High Commissioner for Refugees
UNICEF	United Nations Children's Fund

UNIDF	United Nations Industrial Development Fund (UNIDO)
UNIDIR	United Nations Institute for Disarmament Research
UNIDO	United Nations Industrial Development Organization
UNIDROIT	International Institute for the Unification of Private Law
UNIFIL	United Nations Interim Force in Lebanon
UNIPAC	UNICEF Packing and Assembly Centre
UNISPACE-82	Second United Nations Conference on the Exploration and Peaceful Uses of Outer Space
UNITAR	United Nations Institute for Training and Research
UNRFNRE	United Nations Revolving Fund for Natural Resources Exploration
UNRISD	United Nations Research Institute for Social Development
UNRWA	United Nations Relief and Works Agency for Palestine Refugees in the Near East
UNSCEAR	United Nations Scientific Committee on the Effects of Atomic Radiation
UNSDRI	United Nations Social Defence Research Institute
UNSO	United Nations Sudano-Sahelian Office
UNTAG	United Nations Transition Assistance Group
UNTSO	United Nations Truce Supervision Organization (Israel and neighbouring States)
UNU	United Nations University
UNV	United Nations Volunteers
UPU	Universal Postal Union
WAPA	weighted average of post adjustments
WCISP	World Climate Impact Studies Programme
WFC	World Food Council
WFP	World Food Programme
WFS	World Fertility Survey
WHO	World Health Organization
WIPO	World Intellectual Property Organization
WMO	World Meteorological Organization
WTO	World Tourism Organization
WWW	World Weather Watch (WMO)
YUN	*Yearbook of the United Nations*

EXPLANATORY NOTE ON DOCUMENTS

Documentary notes at the end of each article in Part One of this volume give the symbols of the main documents issued in 1982 on the topic, arranged by type of document—drafts not adopted, letters and notes verbales, publications (with titles), reports, resolutions, statements of administrative and financial implications, meeting records, etc. Items in these notes are linked by numerical indicators to the article text, as described on page xii. The following is a guide to the principal document symbols:

A/- refers to documents of the General Assembly, numbered in separate series by session. Thus, A/37/- refers to documents issued for consideration at the thirty-seventh session, beginning with A/37/1. Documents of special and emergency special sessions are identified as A/S- and A/ES-, followed by the session number: in 1982, A/S-12/- (twelfth special session), A/ES-7/- (resumed seventh emergency special session) and A/ES-9/- (ninth emergency special session).

A/C.- refers to documents of six of the Assembly's Main Committees, e.g. A/C.1/- is a document of the First Committee, A/C.6/-, a document of the Sixth Committee. The symbol for documents of the seventh Main Committee, the Special Political Committee, is A/SPC/-. A/BUR/- refers to documents of the General Committee. A/AC.- documents are those of the Assembly's *ad hoc* bodies and A/CN.-, of its commissions; e.g. A/AC.105/- identifies documents of the Assembly's Committee on the Peaceful Uses of Outer Space, A/CN.4/-, of its International Law Commission. Assembly resolutions and decisions since the thirty-first (1976) session have been identified by two Arabic numerals: the first indicates the session of adoption; the second, the sequential number in the series. Resolutions are numbered consecutively from 1 at each session. Decisions of regular sessions are numbered consecutively, from 301 for those concerned with elections and appointments, and from 401 for all other decisions. Decisions of special and emergency special sessions are numbered consecutively, from 11 for those concerned with elections and appointments, and from 21 for all other decisions.

E/- refers to documents of the Economic and Social Council, numbered in separate series by year. Thus, E/1982/- refers to documents issued for consideration by the Council at its 1982 sessions, beginning with E/1982/1. E/AC.-, E/C.- and E/CN.-, followed by identifying numbers, refer to documents of the Council's subsidiary *ad hoc* bodies, committees and commissions. For example, E/C.1/-, E/C.2/- and E/C.3/- refer to documents of the Council's sessional committees, namely, the First (Economic), Second (Social) and Third (Programme and Co-ordination) Committees, respectively; E/CN.5/- refers to documents of the Council's Commission for Social Development, E/CN.7/-, to documents of its Committee on Natural Resources. E/ICEF/- documents are those of the United Nations Children's Fund (UNICEF). Symbols for the Council's resolutions and decisions, since 1978, consist of two Arabic numerals: the first indicates the year of adoption and the second, the sequential number in the series. There are two series: one for resolutions, beginning with 1 (resolution 1982/1);

and one for decisions, beginning, since 1980, with 100 (decision 1982/100).

S/- refers to documents of the Security Council. Its resolutions are identified by consecutive numbers followed by the year of adoption in parentheses, beginning with resolution 1 (1946).

T/- refers to documents of the Trusteeship Council. Its resolutions are numbered consecutively, with the session at which they were adopted indicated by Roman numerals, e.g. resolutions 2173(XLIX) and 2174(S-XV) of the forty-ninth and fifteenth special sessions. The Council's decisions are not numbered.

ST/-, followed by symbols representing the issuing department or office, refers to documents of the United Nations Secretariat.

Documents of certain bodies bear special series symbols, including the following:

ACC/-	Administrative Committee on Co-ordination
CERD/-	International Convention on the Elimination of All Forms of Racial Discrimination
DC/-	Disarmament Commission
DP/-	United Nations Development Programme
HS/-	Commission on Human Settlements
ID/-	United Nations Industrial Development Organization
ITC/-	International Trade Centre
TD/-	United Nations Conference on Trade and Development
UNEP/-	United Nations Environment Programme
UNITAR/-	United Nations Institute for Training and Research

Many documents of the regional commissions bear special symbol series. These are sometimes preceded by the following:

E/CEPAL/-	Economic Commission for Latin America
E/CN.14/-, E/ECA/-	Economic Commission for Africa
E/ECE/-	Economic Commission for Europe
E/ECWA/-	Economic Commission for Western Asia
E/ESCAP/-	Economic and Social Commission for Asia and the Pacific

"L" in a symbol refers to documents of limited distribution, such as draft resolutions; "CONF." to documents of a conference; "INF." to those of general information. Summary records are designated by "SR.", verbatim records by "PV.", each followed by the meeting number.

United Nations sales publications each carry a sales number with the following components separated by periods: a capital letter indicating the language(s) of the publication; two Arabic numerals indicating the year; a Roman numeral indicating the subject category; a capital letter indicating a subdivision of the category, if any; and an Arabic numeral(s) indicating the number of the publication within the category. Examples: E.82.I.9; E/F.82.II.E.8; E.83.XVII.12.

PART ONE

United Nations

Report of the Secretary-General on the work of the Organization

Following is the text of the report of the Secretary-General on the work of the Organization, submitted to the General Assembly and dated 7 September 1982.[1] The Assembly took note of the report on 3 December.[2]

The past year has seen an alarming succession of international crises as well as stalemates on a number of fundamental international issues. The United Nations itself has been unable to play as effective and decisive a role as the Charter certainly envisaged for it. Therefore, in this, my first annual report to the General Assembly, I shall depart from the usual practice of surveying the broad range of the work of the United Nations; instead I shall focus on the central problem of the Organization's capacity to keep the peace and to serve as a forum for negotiations. I shall try to analyse its evident difficulties in doing so, difficulties related to conflicts between national aims and Charter goals and to the current tendency to resort to confrontation, violence and even war in pursuit of what are perceived as vital interests, claims or aspirations. The general international divisions and disorder which have characterized the past year have unquestionably made it even more difficult than usual for the Organization to be, as it was intended to be, a centre for harmonizing the actions of nations in the attainment of common ends.

The problems faced by the United Nations in fulfilling its mission derive in large measure from the difficulties which Governments appear to have in coming to terms, both within and outside the Organization, with the harsh realities of the time in which we live. This question is, of course, highly relevant to the use, misuse or non-use of the United Nations as an instrument for peace and rational change.

I am of the view that we now have potentially better means to solve many of the major problems facing humanity than ever before. For this reason I retain, in the last analysis, a sense of optimism. This basic optimism, however, is tempered by our apparent inability to make adequate use of these means. Instead we sometimes appear still to be in the grip of the dead hand of a less fortunate past. As a result we often lack the vision to differentiate between short-term advantage and long-term progress, between politically expedient positions and the indispensable objective of creating a civilized and peaceful world order. While such attitudes do not affect the validity of the ideals of the Charter, they seriously impair the proper utilization of the machinery of the United Nations for the purposes for which it was set up.

* * *

We live today in the presence of a chilling and unprecedented phenomenon. At the peak of world power there exist enough nuclear weapons to destroy life on our planet. It seems evident that nothing worthwhile would survive such a holocaust, and this fact, above all else, contains the nuclear confrontation—for the time being at least.

In the middle level of world power there exist vast quantities of sophisticated, so-called conventional weapons. Indeed we have seen some of them in devastating action this very year. These weapons are, by comparison with those of former times, immensely destructive, and they are actually being used. They are also the objects of a highly profitable international trade.

At yet another level we have the poverty of a vast proportion of the world's population—a deprivation inexplicable in terms either of available resources or of the money and ingenuity spent on armaments and war. We have unsolved but soluble problems of economic relations, trade, distribution of resources and technology. We have many ideas and plans as to how to meet the growing needs of the large mass of humanity, but somehow such human considerations seem to take second place to the technology and funding of violence and war in the name of national security.

It is for these reasons that our peoples, especially the young, take to the streets in their hundreds of thousands in many parts of the world to proclaim their peaceful protest against the existing situation and their deep fear of the consequences of the arms race and nuclear catastrophe. Who can say that these gentle protestors are wrong or misguided? On the contrary, they recall us to the standards and the duties which we set ourselves in the Charter of the United Nations. The States Members of this Organization should not ignore the significance of what they are trying to say.

* * *

What in reality is the role and the capacity of the United Nations in such a world? Our Charter was born of six years of global agony and destruction. I sometimes feel that we now take the Charter far less seriously than did its authors, living as they did in the wake of a world tragedy. I believe therefore that an important first step would be a conscious recommitment by Governments to the Charter.

Certainly we have strayed far from the Charter in recent years. Governments that believe they can win an international objective by force are often quite ready to do so, and domestic opinion not infrequently applauds such a course. The Security Council, the primary organ of the United Nations for the maintenance of international peace and security, all too often finds itself unable to take decisive action to resolve international conflicts and its resolutions are increasingly defied or ignored by those that feel themselves strong enough to do so. Too frequently the Council seems powerless to generate the support and influence to ensure that its decisions are respected, even when these are taken unanimously. Thus the process of peaceful settlement of disputes prescribed in the Charter is often brushed aside. Sterner measures for world peace were envisaged in Chapter VII of the Charter, which was conceived as a key element of the United Nations system of collective security, but the prospect of realizing such measures is now deemed almost impossible in our divided international community. We are perilously near to a new international anarchy.

I believe that we are at present embarked on an exceedingly dangerous course, one symptom of which is the crisis in the multilateral approach in international affairs and the concomitant erosion of the authority and status of world and regional intergovernmental institutions. Above all, this trend has adversely affected the United Nations, the instrument that was created specifically to prevent such a self-destructive course. Such a trend must be reversed before once again we bring upon ourselves a global catastrophe and find ourselves without institutions effective enough to prevent it.

* * *

While I do not propose here to review in detail specific situations and developments, it is, of course, my deep concern about them that leads me to examine the underlying deficiencies of our present system. The tragedy of Lebanon and the imperative need to resolve the problem of the Middle East in all its aspects, including the legitimate rights of the Palestinians and the security of all States in the region; the war between Iran and Iraq; the political situation relating to Afghanistan; the prevailing convulsion of Central America; questions relating to Kampuchea; painful efforts to reach a settlement in Cyprus; the situation in Western Sahara and in the Horn of Africa—these and other potential conflict situations, although often differing widely in their nature, should all be responsive to a respected international system for the peaceful settlement of disputes. Even in the sudden crisis over the Falkland Islands (Malvinas), despite the intensive negotiations which I conducted with the full support and encouragement of the Security Council and which endeavoured to narrow the differences between the parties, it nevertheless proved impossible in the end to stave off the major conflict.

Yet in all of these cases, all of the parties would have gained immeasurably in the long run from the effectiveness of a system for the peaceful settlement of disputes. In the case of Namibia we now see some signs of the possibility of a solution after many setbacks. Let us hope that this will prove a welcome exception to the general rule. But the lesson is clear—something must be done, and urgently, to strengthen our international institutions and to adopt new and imaginative approaches to the prevention and resolution of conflicts. Failure to do so will exacerbate precisely that sense of insecurity which, recently, cast its shadow over the second special session of the General Assembly devoted to disarmament. Despite present difficulties, it is imperative for the United Nations to dispel that sense of insecurity through joint and agreed action in the field of disarmament, especially nuclear disarmament.

I must mention here some of the other main sides of our work. There is the promotion and protection of human rights throughout the world, to which I intend to devote, as a matter of high priority, the attention that is called for by the Charter and made all the more imperative by the current state of world affairs. There are the great humanitarian challenges, often involving large numbers of refugees and displaced persons, whose plight in many parts of the world is the tragic reflection of political strife and economic distress. There is the grave and as yet unsolved problem of *apartheid*. There is, furthermore, the whole spectrum of issues related to social and economic development, which so vitally affect both present conditions and future prospects. My statement to the Economic and Social Council on 7 July of this year provided an opportunity to review the latter, to call for action and to express my concern on the stalemate in the North-South dialogue and the difficulties encountered in furthering global negotiations and measures to promote world economic recovery.

In our endeavour to carry out this extremely wide and demanding range of tasks, a fundamental requirement is the continued dedication, integrity and professionalism of the international civil service. I expect the highest standards from the staff of the Secretariat and, for my part, am determined to protect their independence and to ensure that performance and merit are the essential criteria for professional advancement. I have already defined as one of my first priorities the attainment of enhanced efficiency in the Secretariat, which must be worthy of the full confidence of Member States. I will continue to devote every effort towards an improved, unified and coherent administration.

* * *

It seems to me that our most urgent goal is to reconstruct the Charter concept of collective action for peace and security so as to render the United Nations more capable of carrying out its primary function. It was the lack of an effective system of collective security through the League of Nations that, among other factors, led to the Second World War. Although we now face a vastly changed world situation, Governments in fact need more than ever a workable system of collective security in which they can have real confidence. Without such a system, Governments will feel it necessary to arm themselves beyond their means for their own security, thereby increasing the general insecurity. Without such a system, the world community will remain powerless to deal with military adventures which threaten the very fabric of international peace, and the danger of the widening and escalation of local conflicts will be correspondingly greater. Without such a system there will be no reliable defence or shelter for the small and weak. And without such a system all of our efforts on the economic and social side, which also need their own collective impetus, may well falter.

* * *

There are many ways in which Governments could actively assist in strengthening the system prescribed in the Charter. More systematic, less last-minute use of the Security Council would be one means. If the Council were to keep an active watch on dangerous situations and, if necessary, initiate discussions with the parties before they reach the point of crisis, it might often be possible to defuse them at an early stage before they degenerate into violence.

Unfortunately there has been a tendency to avoid bringing critical problems to the Security Council, or to do so too late for the Council to have any serious influence on their development. It is essential to reverse this trend if the Council is to play its role as the primary world authority for in-ternational peace and security. I do not believe that it is necessarily wise or responsible of the Council to leave such matters to the judgement of the conflicting parties to the point where the Council's irrelevance to some ongoing wars becomes a matter of comment by word public opinion.

In recent years the Security Council has resorted increasingly to the valuable process of informal consultations. However, there is sometimes a risk that this process may become a substitute for action by the Security Council or even an excuse for inaction. Along the same line of thought, it may be useful for the Council to give renewed consideration to reviewing and streamlining its practices and procedures with a view to acting swiftly and decisively in crises.

Adequate working relations between the permanent members of the Security Council are a *sine qua non* of the Council's effectiveness. Whatever their relations may be outside the United Nations, within the Council the permanent members, which have special rights and special responsibilities under the Charter, share a sacred trust that should not go by default owing to their bilateral difficulties. When this happens, the Council and therefore the United Nations are the losers, since the system of collective security envisaged by the Charter presupposes, at the minimum, a working relationship among the permanent members. I appeal to the members of the Council, especially its permanent members, to reassess their obligations in that regard and to fulfil them at the high level of responsibility indicated in the Charter.

There is a tendency in the United Nations for Governments to act as though the passage of a resolution absolved them from further responsibility for the subject in question. Nothing could be further from the intention of the Charter. In fact resolutions, particularly those unanimously adopted by the Security Council, should serve as a springboard for governmental support and determination and should motivate their policies outside the United Nations. This indeed is the essence of the treaty obligation which the Charter imposes on Member States. In other words the best resolution in the world will have little practical effect unless Governments of Member States follow it up with the appropriate support and action.

Very often the Secretary-General is allotted the function of following up on the implementation of a resolution. Without the continuing diplomatic and other support of Member States, the Secretary-General's efforts often have less chance of bearing fruit. Concerted diplomatic action is an essential complement to the implementation of resolutions. I believe that in reviewing one of the greatest problems of the United Nations—lack of respect for its decisions by those to whom they are addressed—new ways should be considered of bringing to bear the collective influence of the membership on the problem at hand.

The same consideration applies to good offices and negotiations of various kinds undertaken at the behest of the Security Council. Very often a Member State or group of Member States with a special relationship to those involved in such negotiations could play an extremely important reinforcing role in promoting understanding and a positive attitude.

In order to avoid the Security Council becoming involved too late in critical situations, it may well be that the Secretary-General should play a more forthright role in bringing potentially dangerous situations to the attention of the Council within the general framework of Article 99 of the Charter. My predecessors have done this on a number of occasions, but I wonder if the time has not come for a more systematic approach. Most potential conflict areas are well known. The Secretary-General has traditionally, if informally, tried to keep watch for problems likely to result in conflict and to do what he can to pre-empt them by quiet diplomacy. The Secretary-General's diplomatic means are, however, in themselves quite limited. In order to carry out effectively the preventive role foreseen for the Secretary-General under Article 99, I intend to develop a wider and more systematic capacity for fact-finding in potential conflict areas. Such efforts would naturally be undertaken in close co-ordination with the Council. Moreover, the Council itself could devise more swift and responsive procedures for sending good offices missions, military or civilian observers or a United Nations presence to areas of potential conflict. Such measures could inhibit the deterioration of conflict situations and might also be of real assistance to the parties in resolving incipient disputes by peaceful means.

* * *

Peace-keeping operations have generally been considered to be one of the most successful innovations of the United Nations, and certainly their record over the years is one of which to be proud. They have proved to be a most useful instrument of de-escalation and conflict control and have extended the influence of the Security Council into the field in a unique way. I may add that United Nations peace-keeping operations have traditionally shown an admirable degree of courage, objectivity and impartiality. This record, which is a great credit to the Organization, is sometimes overlooked in the heat of partisanship.

The limitations of peace-keeping operations are less well understood. Thus when, as happened recently, a peace-keeping operation is overrun or brushed aside, the credibility both of the United Nations and of peace-keeping operations as such is severely shaken.

It is not always realized that peace-keeping operations are the visible part of a complex framework of political and diplomatic efforts and of countervailing pressures designed to keep the peace-keeping efforts and related peace-making efforts effective. It is assumed that the Security Council itself and those Member States in a position to bring influence to bear will be able to act decisively to ensure respect for decisions of the Council. If this framework breaks down, as it did for example in Lebanon last June, there is little that a United Nations peace-keeping force can by itself do to rectify the situation. Indeed in such circumstances it tends to become the scapegoat for the developments that follow.

Peace-keeping operations can function properly only with the co-operation of the parties and on a clearly defined mandate from the Security Council. They are based on the assumption that the parties, in accepting a United Nations peace-keeping operation, commit themselves to co-operating with it. This commitment is also required by the Charter, under which all concerned have a clear obligation to abide by the decisions of the Council. United Nations peace-keeping operations are not equipped, authorized, or indeed made available, to take part in military activities other than peace-keeping. Their main strength is the will of the international community which they symbolize. Their weakness comes to light when the political assumptions on which they are based are ignored or overridden.

I recommend that Member States, especially the members of the Security Council, should again study urgently the means by which our peace-keeping operations could be strengthened. An increase in their military capacity or authority is only one possibility—a possibility which may well give rise in some circumstances to serious political and other objections. Another possibility is to underpin the authority of peace-keeping operations by guarantees, including explicit guarantees for collective or individual supportive action.

In recent months, two multinational forces were set up outside the framework of the United Nations to perform peace-keeping tasks, because of opposition to United Nations involvement either within or outside the Security Council. While understanding the circumstances which led to the establishment of these forces, I find such a trend disturbing because it demonstrates the difficulties the Security Council encounters in fulfilling its responsibilities as the primary organ for the maintenance of international peace and security in the prevailing political conditions.

* * *

We should examine with the utmost frankness the reasons for the reluctance of parties to some conflicts to resort to the Security Council or to use the machinery of the United Nations. The fact is that the Council too often finds itself on the sidelines at a time when, according to the Charter, its possibilities should be used to the maximum. Allegations of partisanship, indecisiveness or incapacity arising from divisions among Member States are sometimes invoked to justify this sidetracking of the Council. We should take such matters with the utmost seriousness and ask ourselves what justifications, if any, there are for them and what can be done to restore the Council to the position of influence it was given in the Charter.

This last problem also applies to other organs of the United Nations and brings me to the question of the validity and utility of the United Nations as a negotiating forum. We have seen, in the case of the law of the sea for example, what remarkable results can be achieved in well-organized negotiations within the United Nations framework, even on the most complex of issues and even though there was no unanimous agreement. On the peace and security side, the Security Council has shown and continues to show that it is often capable of negotiating important basic resolutions on difficult problems. The General Assembly also has to its credit historic documents negotiated in that organ and in its subsidiary organs, not only on the political but also on the economic and social side.

But in spite of all this I am concerned that the possibilities of the United Nations, especially of the Security Council, as a negotiating forum for urgent international problems are not being sufficiently realized or used. Let us consider what is perhaps our most formidable international problem—the Middle East. It is absolutely essential that serious negotiations on the various aspects of that problem involve all the parties concerned at the earliest possible time. Far too much time has already elapsed, far too many lives and far too many opportunities have been lost, and too many *faits accomplis* have been created.

I feel that the Security Council, the only place in the world where all of the parties concerned can sit at the same table, could become a most useful forum for this absolutely essential effort. But if this is to be done, careful consideration will have to be given to what procedures, new if necessary, should be used and what rules should govern the negotiations. I do not believe that a public debate, which could well become rhetorical and confrontational, will be enough. Other means will have to be used as well if negotiations on such a complex and deeply rooted problem are to have any useful outcome. The devising of such means is certainly well within the ingenuity and capacity of concerned Member States.

A related question to which we should give more consideration concerns what are productive and what are counter-productive approaches to the different aspects of our work. Obviously, a parliamentary debate may generate rhetoric, and sometimes even a touch of acrimony. But negotiations and the resolution of urgent problems require a different approach. Debate without effective action erodes the credibility of the Organization. I feel that in the United Nations, if we wish to achieve results, we must make a more careful study of the psychological and political aspects of problems and address ourselves to our work accordingly. It is insufficient to indulge in a course of action that merely tends to strengthen extreme positions.

*   *   *

The United Nations is now 37 years old. It has survived a period of unprecedented change in almost all aspects of human life. The world of 1982 is vastly different from that of 1945, and that difference is reflected in the United Nations. In other words, the Organization has had to adapt to new circumstances to a quite unexpected extent. But it is not enough for the United Nations merely to reflect change or conflict. The Organization was intended to present to the world the highest common denominator of international behaviour and, in doing so, to develop a binding sense of international community. It was to that end that Governments drafted and ratified the Charter. Amid the various perils that now threaten the orderly progress of humanity, I hope that we can rally once again to the standards of the Charter, beginning with the peaceful settlement of disputes and steadily branching out towards the other objectives of that prophetic document.

Finally let me appeal to all Governments to make a serious effort to reinforce the protective and pre-emptive ring of collective security which should be our common shelter and the most important task of the United Nations. The will to use the machinery of the Charter needs to be consciously strengthened, and all Governments must try to look beyond short-term national interests to the great possibilities of a more stable system of collective international security, as well as to the very great perils of failing to develop such a system. For these reasons I would suggest that consideration be given to the usefulness of holding a meeting of the Security Council at the highest possible level, one object of which might be to discuss in depth some of the problems I have mentioned.

*   *   *

Member States will, I hope, understand if I end this report on a personal note. Last year I was appointed Secretary-General of this Organization, which embodies the noblest hopes and aspirations of the peoples of the world and whose functions and aims under the Charter are certainly the highest and most important ever entrusted to an international institution. This year, time after time we have seen the Organization set aside or rebuffed, for this reason or for that, in situations in which it should, and could, have played an important and constructive role. I think this tendency is dangerous for the world community and dangerous for the future. As one who has to play a highly public role in the Organization, I cannot disguise my deep anxiety at present trends, for I am absolutely convinced that the United Nations is indispensable in a world fraught with tension and peril. Institutions such as this are not built in a day. They require constant constructive work

and fidelity to the principles on which they are based.

We take the United Nations seriously when we desperately need it. I would urge that we also seriously consider the practical ways in which it should develop its capacity and be used as an essential institution in a stormy and uncertain world.

JAVIER PÉREZ DE CUÉLLAR
Secretary-General

7 September 1982

Report. [1]S-G, A/37/1.
Resolution (1982). [2]GA: A/37/67, 3 Dec.

Political and security questions

Chapter I

Disarmament

Contents

Related topics:

International peace and security. Africa: Military and nuclear relations with South Africa. Environment: Environmental aspects of the arms race. Human rights: and peace.

For resolutions and decisions of major organs mentioned but not reproduced, refer to INDEX OF RESOLUTIONS AND DECISIONS.

General aspects

The focus of United Nations concern with disarmament issues during 1982 was the twelfth special session of the General Assembly, its second devoted to disarmament, held from 7 June to 10 July at United Nations Headquarters. During those five weeks, the Assembly heard 134 delegations during the period of a general debate in plenary meetings, and 53 non-governmental organizations and 22 peace and disarmament research organizations in the *Ad Hoc* Committee of the Twelfth Special Session.

Except for the launching of the World Disarmament Campaign and a decision to expand the United Nations disarmament fellowship programme, the special session failed to reach agreement on substantive items, notably the proposed comprehensive programme of disarmament, which had been considered the centre-piece of the session. The Assembly, instead, adopted the largely descriptive report of the *Ad Hoc* Committee as its Concluding Document and requested the Committee on Disarmament to consider further and submit in 1983 a revised draft comprehensive programme.

The Preparatory Committee for the Second Special Session of the General Assembly Devoted to Disarmament, which began work in December 1980,[1] held its fourth and final session in New York from 26 April to 14 May 1982.

The 40-member Committee on Disarmament—the main intergovernmental negotiating body on disarmament—met at Geneva from 2 February to 23 April and from 3 August to 17 September, with substantially the same agenda as in 1981. The Disarmament Commission, composed of all United Nations Member States, held its 1982 substantive session from 17 to 28 May at United Nations Headquarters.

At its 1982 regular session, the General Assembly examined 23 disarmament items. Four of these had been added in 1982, concerning: a follow-up to the work of the special session, efforts to remove the threat of nuclear war and ensure the safe development of nuclear energy (proposed by the USSR) (p. 47), prohibition of nuclear-weapon tests (proposed by the USSR) (p. 75) and the relationship between disarmament and development (proposed by Sweden) (p. 141). A record number of 58 resolutions were adopted on these items in December. As in previous years, all disarmament items were considered by the Assembly's First Committee, which held a general debate on disarmament extending over 26 meetings between 18 October and 5 November.

Yearbook reference. [1]1980, p. 97.
Meeting records. GA: plenary, A/S-12/PV.1-29 (7 June–10 July), A/37/PV.98, 101 (9, 13 Dec.); *Ad Hoc* Committee, A/S-12/AC.1/PV.2-7, 8 & Add.1, 9-15 (14 June–9 July); 1st Committee, A/C.1/37/PV.3-45, 47, 48, 57, 58 (18 Oct.–8 Dec.).
Publication. The United Nations Disarmament Yearbook, vol. 7, *1982*, Sales No. E.83.IX.7.

Special session of the General Assembly on disarmament

Preparations for the session

The Preparatory Committee for the Second Special Session of the General Assembly Devoted to Disarmament held its fourth and final session in New York from 26 April to 14 May 1982.[2]

The 78-member Committee recommended that the Assembly President should launch the World Disarmament Campaign at the opening meeting of the special session and that the Assembly should adopt two documents, one containing the comprehensive programme of disarmament and a second encompassing all other agenda items.

Other recommendations concerned the duration of the general debate, allocation of agenda items to plenary meetings and to the session's *Ad Hoc* Committee, and the organization of the session's work. The Committee recommended that the heads of several United Nations organizations be invited to speak in the Assembly (p. 12), as well as representatives of the Inter-Parliamentary Union and the Independent Commission on Disarmament and Security Issues (p. 141). Further, the *Ad Hoc* Committee should allocate four meetings to hear statements by the representatives of 56 non-governmental organizations (NGOs) and 23 peace and disarmament research institutions that had been selected (see below). In that regard the Preparatory Committee took into consideration the recommendations of the *Ad Hoc* Liaison Group of the two NGO disarmament committees at Geneva and New York.

Also during the April/May session, working groups of the Preparatory Committee prepared two documents that were annexed to its report: a commentary on the comprehensive programme of disarmament and a composite paper reviewing the implementation of the recommendations made by the Assembly at its first special session on disarmament, in 1978.

At the first meeting of the special session, on 7 June,[1] the Assembly, acting without vote on an oral proposal of its President, endorsed the report and recommendations of the Preparatory Committee.

Decision (1982). [1]GA: S-12/22, 7 June, text following.
Report. [2]Preparatory Committee, A/S-12/1 & Corr.1.
Meeting record. GA: A/S-12/PV.1 (7 June).

General Assembly decision S-12/22

Adopted without vote

Oral proposal by President; agenda item 6.

Report of the Preparatory Committee for the Second Special Session of the General Assembly Devoted to Disarmament
    At its 1st plenary meeting, on 7 June 1982, the General Assembly endorsed the report of the Preparatory Committee for the Second Special Session of the General Assembly Devoted to Disarmament and the recommendations contained therein.

Work of the special session

The twelfth special session of the General Assembly, its second devoted to disarmament, opened on 7 June 1982 at United Nations Headquarters, marking the opening day with the launching of the World Disarmament Campaign. It ended on 10 July after approving without vote a Concluding Document detailing the work of the session and stating a number of broad conclusions (see below).

A general debate on disarmament took place at 24 meetings from 8 to 23 June. During that period, statements were made on behalf of 133 countries and the European Community (EC). Speakers included 18 heads of State or Government (p. 17), a deputy head of State and 44 Foreign Ministers. In addition, statements were made by the heads of five organizations in the United Nations system: the United Nations Educational, Scientific and Cultural Organization, the International Atomic Energy Agency, the United Nations Environment Programme, the United Nations Development Programme and the United Nations Institute for Training and Research.

Substantive items on the agenda concerned implementation of the recommendations and decisions adopted at the 1978 special session on disarmament, the proposed comprehensive programme of disarmament, implementation of the Assembly's Declaration of the 1980s as the Second Disarmament Decade[27] and consideration of initiatives and proposals of Member States, enhancement of the effectiveness of disarmament machinery and the possible convening of a World Disarmament Conference, and mobilization of world public opinion (p. 31). (For the agenda of the session, see APPENDIX IV.)

In his opening statement, the President of the General Assembly observed that not a single weapon had been destroyed as a result of a disarmament agreement in the four years since the first special session on disarmament. He noted the steady increase in global military expenditures, currently more than $600 billion a year; the stalled strategic arms negotiations, save for the agreement between the USSR and the United States to resume bilateral talks in June 1982; decreased prospects for a comprehensive nuclear-test-ban treaty; an alarming increase in the potential for the military use of outer space; and the growing tendency in some circles to accept such doctrines as limited or winnable nuclear war. He viewed as encouraging, however, the high-level political representation at the session, as well as the broad and impressive representation and activities of NGOs, and welcomed the growing assertive public movement against the arms race.

The United Nations Secretary-General stressed the extreme immediacy and urgency of the ponderous and difficult task facing the Assembly at a time when the modern technology of war was being displayed in all its virtuosity, short only of weapons of mass destruction. Annual military outlays world-wide came to about $112 per capita, more than the per capita gross domestic product of some developing countries, he observed. Unless restrained by political decisions backed by a moral will, the advance of military technology could never exhaust itself.

On 7 June, following the recommendations of its Preparatory Committee, the Assembly, by a decision adopted without vote,[1] established an *Ad Hoc* Committee of the Twelfth Special Session and decided that two documents should emerge from the session, one containing the comprehensive programme of disarmament and another encompassing all other agenda items.

As authorized by the Assembly, the *Ad Hoc* Committee, entrusted with all the substantive items except the general debate, established three working groups, each open to all United Nations Members. Working Group I, on the comprehensive programme of disarmament, was established on 14 June and held 4 meetings between 14 June and 7 July under the chairmanship of Alfonso García Robles (Mexico). Working Group II, on implementation of the recommendations of the 1978 special session, was established on 17 June and held 7 meetings between 18 June and 2 July, with David Sadleir (Australia) as Chairman. Working Group III, on the Second Disarmament Decade, consideration of Member States' proposals and mobilization of public opinion, was also established on 17 June and held 17 meetings between 18 June and 6 July, chaired by Gerhard Herder (German Democratic Republic).

Except for agreements in Working Group III on the United Nations programme of disarmament fellowships and on the World Disarmament Campaign, work at the session did not result in agreed texts. Consequently, the Assembly, on 10 July, adopted the report of the *Ad Hoc* Committee[24] as the Concluding Document of the special session.[2] In so doing, the Assembly endorsed the Committee's recommendation that the Assembly take up for further consideration at its regular session later in the year those items on which no decision had been reached at the special session.

The adoption of the Concluding Document—on an oral proposal by the President approved without vote—followed approval of an oral amendment by Mexico to clarify a passage in the conclusions listing types of actions taken during the preceding four years contrary to the Final Document of the Tenth Special Session of the General Assembly (1978).[26] The amendment added the word "other" in a sentence which then read: "The period has also witnessed other actions by States contrary to the Final Document" (paragraph 60).

In its chapter entitled "Conclusions", the Concluding Document stated the following:

"57.   The tenth special session of the General Assembly, the first special session devoted to disarmament, held in 1978, was an event of historic significance. The special session was convened in response to a growing concern among the peoples of the world that the arms race, especially the nuclear-arms race, represented ever-increasing threats to human well-being and even to the survival of mankind. At that session the international community of nations achieved, for the first time in the history of disarmament negotiations, a consensus on an international disarmament strategy, the immediate goal of which was the elimination of the danger of nuclear war and implementation of measures to halt and reverse the arms race. The final objective of the strategy was to achieve general and complete disarmament under effective international control. The conviction that all peoples had a legitimate right to expect early and significant progress in disarmament and a vital interest in its success led to the United Nations being given a central role and primary responsibility in the field of disarmament.

58.   The historic consensus embodied in the Final Document of the Tenth Special Session of the General Assembly (resolution S-10/2) was rooted in a common awareness that the accumulation of weapons, particularly nuclear weapons, constituted much more a threat to than a protection of mankind. It was also based on recognition that the time had come to put an end to that situation, to abandon the use of force in international relations and to seek security in disarmament, that is to say, through a gradual but effective process beginning with a reduction in the current level of armaments. The Final Document recognized that in the contemporary world, the security of States could be greatly enhanced by effective action aimed at preventing nuclear war, ending the arms race and achieving real disarmament. Progress in disarmament would significantly contribute to pursuing the goals of economic and social development, particularly of developing countries. The consensus embodied in the Final Document sought to place disarmament negotiations in a unified perspective and became a most significant and integral part of the context within which negotiations on disarmament have been pursued.

59.   In the course of the twelfth special session, the second special session devoted to disarmament, the General Assembly has noted that developments since 1978 have not lived up to the hopes engendered by the tenth special session. Despite the efforts that have been made by the international community to implement the decisions and recommendations of that session on a multilateral, bilateral and regional level, including action in the General Assembly and the Committee on Disarmament, and steps that have been taken on some specific measures contained in the Final Document, the objectives, priorities and principles there laid down have not been generally observed. The Programme of Action contained in the Final Document remains largely unimplemented. A number of important negotiations either have not begun or have been suspended, and efforts in the Committee on Disarmament and other forums have produced little tangible result. There has been some progress in certain negotiations and bilateral negotiations in the nuclear field have been initiated. The arms race, however, in particular the nuclear-arms race, has assumed more dangerous proportions and global military expenditures have increased sharply. In short, since the adoption of the Final Document in 1978, there has been no significant progress in the field of arms limitation and disarmament and the seriousness of the situation has increased.

60.   The Final Document stated that disarmament, relaxation of international tension, respect for the right to self-determination and national independence, the peaceful settlement of disputes in accordance with the Charter of the United Nations and the strengthening of international peace and security are directly related to each other. Progress in any of these spheres has a beneficial effect on all of them; in turn, failure in one sphere has negative effects on others. The past four years have witnessed increasing recourse to the use or threat of use of force against the sovereignty and territorial integrity of States, military intervention, occupation, annexation and interference in the internal affairs of States and denial of the inalienable right to self-determination and independence of peoples under colonial or foreign domination. The period has also witnessed other actions by States contrary to the Final Document. The consequent tensions and confrontations have retarded progress in disarmament and have in turn been aggravated by the failure to make significant progress towards disarmament.

61.   It was stressed that in a world of finite resources there is an organic relationship between expenditures on armaments and economic and social development. The vastly increased military budgets since 1978 and the development, production and deployment, especially by the States possessing the largest military arsenals, of new types of weapon systems represent a huge and growing diversion of human and material resources. Apart from the significant capital costs that these military expenditures represent, they have also contributed to current economic problems in certain States. Existing and planned military programmes constitute a colossal waste of precious resources which might otherwise be used to elevate living standards of all peoples; furthermore, such waste greatly compounds the problems confronting developing countries in achieving economic and social development.

62.   The General Assembly regrets that at its twelfth special session it has not been able to adopt a document on the Comprehensive Programme of

Disarmament and on a number of other items on its agenda. However, on two agenda items, relating to the United Nations programme of fellowships on disarmament and the World Disarmament Campaign, there are agreed texts (see annexes IV and V) for consideration and appropriate action by the General Assembly. The General Assembly was encouraged by the unanimous and categorical reaffirmation by all Member States of the validity of the Final Document of the Tenth Special Session as well as their solemn commitment to it and their pledge to respect the priorities in disarmament negotiations as agreed to in its Programme of Action. Taking into account the aggravation of the international situation and being gravely concerned about the continuing arms race, particularly in its nuclear aspect, the General Assembly expresses its profound preoccupation over the danger of war, in particular nuclear war, the prevention of which remains the most acute and urgent task of the present day. The General Assembly urges all Member States to consider as soon as possible relevant proposals designed to secure the avoidance of war, in particular nuclear war, thus ensuring that the survival of mankind is not endangered. The General Assembly also stresses the need for strengthening the central role of the United Nations in the field of disarmament and the implementation of the security system provided for in the Charter of the United Nations in accordance with the Final Document and to enhance the effectiveness of the Committee on Disarmament as the single multilateral negotiating body. In this regard the Committee on Disarmament is requested to report to the General Assembly at its thirty-seventh session on its consideration of an expansion of its membership, consistent with the need to enhance its effectiveness.

63.   Member States have affirmed their determination to continue to work for the urgent conclusion of negotiations on and the adoption of the Comprehensive Programme of Disarmament, which shall encompass all measures thought to be advisable in order to ensure that the goal of general and complete disarmament under effective international control becomes a reality in a world in which international peace and security prevail, and in which a new international economic order is strengthened and consolidated. To this end, the draft Comprehensive Programme of Disarmament is hereby referred back to the Committee on Disarmament, together with the views expressed and the progress achieved on the subject at the special session. The Committee on Disarmament is requested to submit a revised draft Comprehensive Programme of Disarmament to the General Assembly at its thirty-eighth session.

64.   The other items on the agenda on which the special session has not reached decisions should be taken up at the thirty-seventh session of the General Assembly for further consideration.

65.   The General Assembly is convinced that the discussion of disarmament problems, which it has undertaken at the special session and in which representatives of Member States—among them some heads of State or Government and many Foreign Ministers—have participated, and the active interest shown by peoples all over the world will provide a powerful impetus to Member States to redouble their efforts in the cause of disarmament. The General Assembly hopes that the World Disarmament Campaign, which it solemnly launched at the opening meeting of the special session, will further contribute to the mobilization of public opinion to the cause of disarmament and the strengthening of international peace and security. In this regard the campaign should provide an opportunity for discussion and debate in all countries on all points of view relating to disarmament issues, objectives and conditions.

66.   The third special session of the General Assembly devoted to disarmament should be held at a date to be decided by the General Assembly at its thirty-eighth session."

During the special session, five draft resolutions were submitted to the *Ad Hoc* Committee: one by India on nuclear disarmament and the prevention of nuclear war (p. 46); one by India and Mexico on the appointment of a group of eminent persons on the prevention of nuclear war (p. 49); one by India and another by Mexico and Sweden on a nuclear-arms freeze (p. 49); and one by India for a convention on prohibition of the use of nuclear weapons (p. 52). In the absence of action at the special session, the drafts were deferred for consideration by the Assembly later in the year. In addition, annex III of the Concluding Document contained the texts of three proposals on the prevention of nuclear war, submitted by Bulgaria, by India, and by the Federal Republic of Germany, Japan and the Netherlands.

Other proposals submitted by Member States were summarized in annex II of the Concluding Document. A number of these (summarized elsewhere in this chapter) dealt with specific aspects of disarmament. Others, more general, included the following proposals:

—By China, on measures for an immediate halt to the arms race and for disarmament.[15] It proposed that all nuclear Powers undertake not to be the first to use nuclear weapons and not to use them against non-nuclear-weapon States; that the USSR and the United States cease all tests, improvement and manufacture of such weapons and reduce their nuclear arsenals by 50 per cent, after which all nuclear-weapon States should undertake to reduce such weapons by agreed proportions; that conventional disarmament be undertaken in conjunction with nuclear disarmament; and that an international verification mechanism be set up.

—By Romania, proposing a number of measures including cessation of nuclear-weapon production, convening a conference on confidence-building and disarmament in Europe, freezing military expenditures at the 1982 level and their reduction by 10 to 15 per cent until 1985, and creating United Nations bodies to resolve disputes among States and monitor implementation of disarmament agreements.[11]

—By the USSR, reiterating proposals for averting the nuclear threat and curbing the arms race, including the elaboration, adoption and stage-by-stage implementation of a nuclear disarmament programme; limitation and reduction of strategic arms, as well as of nuclear weapons in Europe; prohibition of all nuclear-weapon tests; limitation and reduction of conventional weapons and armed forces; reduction of military budgets; and prohibition of the stationing of weapons in outer space.[13]

Several heads of Government submitted messages urging steps towards disarmament, including: the President of Guatemala[19] and the Chairman of the People's Redemption Council of Liberia,[21] who stressed that resources and skills used for military purposes could be utilized instead to improve social and economic conditions; the General Secretary of the Central Committee of the Socialist Unity Party and Chairman of the Council of State of the German Democratic Republic, who called for decisions to end the nuclear-arms race and stressed the need for negotiations;[6] the Prime Minister of India, who urged a five-point programme encompassing a convention on the non-use of nuclear weapons, a nuclear-weapon freeze, immediate suspension of all nuclear-weapon tests, a treaty on general and complete disarmament, and education of the public on the dangers of nuclear war;[20] and the General Secretary of the Central Committee of the Communist Party of the USSR and President of the Presidium of the Supreme Soviet, assuming the obligation not to be the first to use nuclear weapons, urging reciprocal steps by others, favouring the idea of a nuclear freeze, and calling for an accord to prohibit chemical weapons and destroy stockpiles.[12]

The views of Switzerland, stressing the need for confidence-building and security measures in Europe, were submitted on its behalf by Austria, Finland, Sweden and Yugoslavia.[14] Viet Nam transmitted a 5 June telegram from the Vice-President of the Council of Ministers and Minister for Foreign Affairs of the People's Republic of Kampuchea, condemning United States military policies and Chinese collusion, and supporting peace proposals by the USSR and the socialist and non-aligned countries.[23]

The Secretary-General transmitted to the special session a resolution adopted by the Commission on Human Rights on 19 February,[25] in which the Commission stressed the need for international efforts to strengthen peace, remove the threat of war and achieve general and complete disarmament under effective international control, thus contributing to assuring the inherent right to life (see ECONOMIC AND SOCIAL QUESTIONS, Chapter XVIII).

The Ministerial Meeting of the Co-ordinating Bureau of the Non-Aligned Countries (Havana, Cuba, 31 May–4 June), in a communiqué transmitted on 6 June by Cuba,[16] urged the resumption of disarmament negotiations without delay, recommended that the nuclear-weapon States submit practical suggestions for preventing a nuclear war, and stated that the arms race was incompatible with the search for economic and social development.

A number of messages and declarations by organizations and peoples addressed to the Assembly on the occasion of the special session were transmitted by their respective Governments, as follows: statement by the participants in a meeting of the Bulgarian public;[3] Declaration of the Bulgarian Inter-Parliamentary Group;[4] Declaration of the Ninth Congress of the Bulgarian Fatherland Front;[5] message from the Deputies of the Czechoslovak Group of the Inter-Parliamentary Union;[17] message from the participants in the International Seminar on Student Action for Peace and National Liberation (Addis Ababa, Ethiopia, 7-9 July);[18] statement by the Presidium of the League of the German Democratic Republic for the United Nations;[7] messages from the Hungarian Peace Movement and from a meeting of Hungarian intellectuals;[8] resolution of the Inter-Parliamentary Council (130th session, Lagos, Nigeria) on the proposed reduction of military budgets and its effect on the economic and social development of the third world;[22] and an appeal for disarmament from the people of Romania.[10]

Assessing the results of the special session in a statement transmitted by Hungary on 10 July, Bulgaria, the Byelorussian SSR, Czechoslovakia, the German Democratic Republic, Hungary, Mongolia, Poland, the Ukrainian SSR and the USSR said it had been impossible to act on concrete disarmament measures because of the obstructionist position of the United States and some other members of the North Atlantic Treaty Organization (NATO), which would not allow decisions impeding their arms build-up.[9]

Summing up the work of the special session, the Assembly President stated on 10 July that the cause of its failure to advance the areas of agreement on disarmament lay in the current world political climate. Nations could not resort to force in international relations and at the same time expect the United Nations, which they had weakened by their actions, to solve problems and create a disarmed world. Moreover, the United Nations could not be expected to insulate itself from reality and produce miracles. He viewed as positive developments at the session the participation by a large number of prominent world leaders and by NGOs world-wide, and the launching of the World Disarmament Campaign. Rather than despairing over the too few and too insubstantial achievements at the session, he stated, delegates should temper their justified feelings of disappointment and frustration with a rededication to peace.

During the two concluding meetings, disappointment or regret over the outcome of the special session was expressed by a large number of speakers, among them Austria, Bangladesh, Bulgaria, Canada, Cuba, Egypt, France, Indonesia, the Netherlands, Poland, Romania, Tunisia and the United Kingdom. India expressed a sense of deep sorrow and anguish at the complete failure of the session to fulfil any of the substantive tasks on the agenda. Australia, Finland and Italy had expected a more substantial outcome. Ireland said an important opportunity had been missed, while Pakistan and Yugoslavia asserted that expectations had been betrayed. Sri Lanka said the public's sense of loss and disillusionment was perhaps greater than that of the delegates. Sweden termed the session's outcome dismal and infinitesimal.

The Netherlands regarded the lack of results at the session as a temporary set-back, and Turkey did not wish to interpret the lack of points of understanding as an irreparable failure. New Zealand spoke similarly, though acknowledging the results as meagre and discouraging. A number of others, including Canada, the Federal Republic of Germany, Norway and Sri Lanka, said efforts should continue.

Some of the reasons advanced for the failure of the session to meet expectations included the deterioration of international relations, the attitudes of certain countries as regards disarmament in general or in relation to the priorities agreed upon in the 1978 Final Document, and differing security perceptions.

A number of speakers, including Denmark, Finland, Italy and Norway, observed that the special session had taken place at a time of deterioration in international relations, to which Egypt, France and the United States attributed the lack of substantial results at the session. Pakistan agreed that the grave and deteriorating international situation had eroded the prospects of progress on disarmament.

Canada considered it all the more important that the session had taken place at an unpropitious time in international relations. Sweden said that, with time running out, most countries deplored the fact that most of the leading Powers, and especially the super-Powers, had again shown themselves unprepared to make use of the United Nations as an instrument for genuine disarmament efforts.

The results of the session were also attributed to the attitude of certain countries. Hungary, speaking also on behalf of Bulgaria, the Byelorussian SSR, Czechoslovakia, the German Democratic Republic, Mongolia, Poland, the Ukrainian SSR and the USSR, asserted that efforts for concrete measures of nuclear disarmament and other important matters had been hindered by the obstructionist position of the United States and some other NATO members. The USSR said those countries had come to the session empty-handed and failed to submit a single specific proposal, in contrast to the socialist States of Eastern Europe, which had put forward a number of specific proposals. Hungary considered it alarming that certain delegations had defied the determination of the majority and blocked efforts to reach agreements. Poland said the session had proved the lack of political will on the part of those responsible for the arms race and for exacerbation of the international situation.

When the technique of non-negotiation took precedence over the painstaking search for agreement, when procedural means were used to challenge agreed principles and priorities, and when policies were designed to impede implementation of the 1978 Final Document, said Algeria, it was inevitable that all efforts and energies foundered before the strongholds of established positions. Brazil observed that the session might have been successful in revealing to the world the stark reality of a handful of nations clinging to the illusion of exclusive and absolute power in utter disregard of the vital interests of all nations. China asserted that the States with the largest arsenals had dodged their responsibility and had raised extraneous issues to obstruct agreement. Cuba said the session's outcome was due to the unchanging rhetorical and chauvinistic positions of those who disregarded the fundamental interest of peace and the legitimate interests of developing countries.

India attributed the results of the session to the attitude of the powerful nations, and to failure in admitting the divergences of views and searching together for new and more meaningful common ground. The Bahamas appealed to all States to shoulder their responsibilities for disarmament without recourse to lame excuses, blame-casting or delaying tactics.

Belgium, speaking for the EC members, said attempts had been made to shift the centre of gravity at the session towards matters whose unbalanced treatment was unlikely to win consensus, with the result that important items, such as proposed studies, ways of improving the effectiveness of disarmament machinery and fresh initiatives, could not be taken up substantively. The Federal Republic of Germany, the Netherlands and Norway agreed in retrospect that the goal of the session had been too ambitious, in view of the limited time to cope with the vast array of issues. In the view of Sweden, the work of the session had been impeded by unnecessary squabbles over procedure and organization, and Denmark believed that much time had been used up to discuss minor issues.

Indonesia said discussions on important items had been inconclusive owing to the inability to reconcile viewpoints based on conflicting security perceptions, coupled with the re-emergence of outdated concepts that made the cause of disarmament a casualty of the current climate of mistrust and suspicion. Australia remarked that recognition of national security was essential in disarmament, which did not operate in a political vacuum. The United Kingdom believed the session had contributed to a wider public understanding of the reality of the differences in the security concerns of Member States, which had made agreement so hard to achieve. The Federal Republic of Germany and New Zealand also observed that the session had provided an opportunity to understand better the security perceptions of others.

Commenting on the Concluding Document, China thought it reflected the highly complex and difficult situation faced by disarmament efforts rather than representing any modest progress. The Federal Republic of Germany said the reference in paragraph 60 (p. 13) should not be construed as a restriction of the right to self-determination and independence, which was endowed with a universal character under the Charter of the United Nations. India said the approved "Conclusions" failed to do even minimal justice to the depth of public concern and anxiety, and hence India dissociated itself from that text; the report merely provided a fig leaf to cover the Assembly's failure to address the issues. Norway, which regarded consensus as a necessary prerequisite for disarmament, considered it significant that a consensus report had been adopted at the session.

According to some delegations, the session was not entirely devoid of favourable aspects. Belgium, for the EC members, said the international community, at the session, had expressed its grave concern at the deterioration in the international situation and at the impact of that situation on disarmament efforts, reaffirmed the close link between disarmament and international security, and stressed the need for observance of the Charter. Cyprus and others noted that the session had given an opportunity to hear the voices of people from all over the world, as represented by NGOs, raised emphatically against continuation of the arms race. Denmark observed that many fruitful ideas had been put forward and some foundation for future disarmament initiatives had been laid. France considered that the general debate was of outstanding quality and the statements were an extremely interesting contribution to the consideration of disarmament and security problems.

Poland said the session had forcefully manifested that nations were gravely concerned about the arms race, that prevention of nuclear catastrophe remained the most acute task and that redoubled efforts towards disarmament should be continued.

During the general debate, Yugoslavia suggested that a decision be taken on convening a third special session; it believed the four-year interval between the first two sessions had proven practical and politically acceptable to all. Liberia suggested that the interval between special sessions on disarmament be made shorter. Cyprus suggested that the next special session be devoted to international security.

The following heads of State or Government spoke during the period while the general debate was in progress (except for the President of Guinea, who spoke on 29 June):

Lieutenant-General Hussain Muhammad Ershad, Chairman of the Council of Ministers and Head of Government of Bangladesh.
Pierre Elliot Trudeau, Prime Minister of Canada.
Spyros Kyprianou, President of Cyprus.
Anker Jorgensen, Prime Minister of Denmark.
Kalevi Sorsa, Prime Minister of Finland.
Helmut Schmidt, Chancellor of the Federal Republic of Germany.
Ahmed Sékou Touré, President of Guinea.
Charles J. Haughey, Prime Minister of Ireland.
Menachem Begin, Prime Minister of Israel.
Giovanni Spadolini, President of the Council of Ministers of Italy.
Zenko Suzuki, Prime Minister of Japan.
Andreas A. M. van Agt, Prime Minister of the Netherlands.
Aristides Royo Sánchez, President of Panama.
Thörbjörn Fälldin, Prime Minister of Sweden.
M. Otema Allimadi, Prime Minister of Uganda.
Margaret Thatcher, Prime Minister of the United Kingdom.
Ronald Reagan, President of the United States.
Petar Stambolic, President of Yugoslavia.

While the general debate proceeded in plenary meetings, representatives of the following 53 NGOs and 22 peace and disarmament research institutions addressed the *Ad Hoc* Committee:

Non-governmental organizations
Action Reconciliation/Service for Peace
Afro-Asian Peoples' Solidarity Organization
Asian Buddhists Conference for Peace
Bahá'i International Community
Campaign for Nuclear Disarmament
Christian Peace Conference
Commission of the Churches on International Affairs of the World Council of Churches
Friends of the Earth
Friends World Committee for Consultation
Hiroshima Peace Culture Foundation/Nagasaki Atomic Bomb Casualty Council
Inter-Church Peace Council
International Association for Religious Freedom
International Association for the Work of Dr. Albert Schweitzer
International Association of Democratic Lawyers
International Committee for European Security and Co-operation
International Confederation of Free Trade Unions

International Co-operative Alliance
International Fellowship of Reconciliation
International Organization of Journalists
International Peace Bureau
International Physicians for the Prevention of Nuclear
  War, Inc.
International Union of Students
International Youth and Student Movement for the
  United Nations
National Nuclear Weapons Freeze Campaign
Pacific Concerns Resource Center
Parliamentarians for World Order
Pax Christi, International Catholic Peace Movement
Project Ploughshares
Pugwash Conferences on Science and World Affairs
Russian Orthodox Church
SSOD II National Liaison Committee for Nuclear and
  General Disarmament
Soviet Peace Fund/Soviet Liaison Committee for Peace
  Forces
Swedish People's Parliament for Disarmament
Union of Arab Jurists
United Presbyterian Church in the United States of
  America
War Resisters International
Women for Peace
Women's International Democratic Federation
Women's International League for Peace and Freedom
World Association of World Federalists
World Confederation of Organizations of the Teach-
  ing Profession
World Conference on Religion and Peace
World Federation of Democratic Youth
World Federation of Scientific Workers
World Federation of Teachers' Unions
World Federation of Trade Unions
World Federation of United Nations Associations
World Jewish Congress
World Muslim Congress
World Peace Council
World Union of Catholic Women's Organizations
World Veterans Federation
Yugoslav League for Peace, Independence and Equal-
  ity of Peoples

Research institutions
Center for Defense Information
Centre for Conflict Studies
Council for Arms Control
Foundation for the Study of National Defense/French
  Institute of Polemology
French Institute of International Relations
Gandhi Peace Foundation
Heritage Foundation
Hungarian Institute of International Relations
Institute for Peace Research
Institute for Peace Science—Hiroshima University
Institute for World Economy and International Relations
Institute of Defense Studies and Analyses
International Institute for Peace
International Peace Academy
International Peace Research Association
Israeli Institute for the Study of International Affairs
Nigerian Institute of International Affairs
Peace Research Institute—Dundas
Romanian National Committee of Scientists for Peace

Stanley Foundation
Stockholm International Peace Research Institute
Tampere Peace Research Institute

Decisions (1982). GA: [1]S-12/21, 7 June, text following; [2]S-12/24, 10 July, text following.
Letters, note verbale (nv) and telegram (t).
  Bulgaria: [3]8 June, A/S-12/AC.1/7; [4]23 June, A/S-12/AC.1/36; [5]28 June, A/S-12/AC.1/48.
  German Democratic Republic: [6]8 June, A/S-12/AC.1/6; [7]9 Aug., A/37/380.
  Hungary: [8]7 June, A/S-12/AC.1/5; [9]10 July, A/S-12/33.
  Romania: [10]16 June, A/S-12/AC.1/14; [11]22 June, A/S-12/AC.1/24.
  USSR, 16 June: [12]A/S-12/AC.1/10 & Corr.1, [13]A/S-12/AC.1/11 & Corr.1.
  Others: [14]Austria, Finland, Sweden, Yugoslavia: 17 June, A/S-12/AC.1/15. [15]China: 21 June, A/S-12/AC.1/23. [16]Cuba: 6 June, transmitting communiqué of non-aligned countries, A/S-12/AC.1/1 *(t)* (superseded A/S-12/26). [17]Czechoslovakia: 11 June, A/S-12/AC.1/8. [18]Ethiopia: 9 July, A/S-12/AC.1/68 *(nv)*. [19]Guatemala: 29 June, A/S-12/AC.1/61. [20]India: 18 June, A/S-12/AC.1/22. [21]Liberia: 25 June, A/S-12/AC.1/60. [22]Nigeria: 7 June, A/S-12/AC.1/4. [23]Viet Nam: 23 June, A/S-12/AC.1/27.
Report. [24]*Ad Hoc* Committee, A/S-12/32.
Resolution (1982). [25]Commission on Human Rights (report, E/1982/12): 1982/7, 19 Feb. (transmitted by S-G note, A/S-12/AC.1/2).
Resolutions (prior). GA: [26]S-10/2, 30 June 1978 (YUN 1978, p. 39); [27]35/46, annex, 3 Dec. 1980 (YUN 1980, p. 102).
Meeting records. GA: plenary, A/S-12/PV.*1, 28, 29* (7 June, 10 July); *Ad Hoc* Committee, A/S-12/AC.1/PV.15 (9 July).
Publications. Disarmament, a Periodic Review by the United Nations. Second Special Session of the General Assembly Devoted to Disarmament, vol. V: No. 1, Sales No. E.82.IX.5; No. 2, Sales No. E.83.IX.1.

General Assembly decision S-12/21

Adopted without vote

Recommendations of Preparatory Committee (A/S-12/1); agenda item 5.

Establishment of the *Ad Hoc* Committee of the Twelfth Special Session

At its 1st plenary meeting, on 7 June 1982, the General Assembly:

(a) Decided to establish an *Ad Hoc* Committee of the Twelfth Special Session, which would be a committee of the whole with a Chairman, thirteen Vice-Chairmen and a Rapporteur, on the understanding that its Chairman would also be a member of the General Committee;

(b) Decided that the *Ad Hoc* Committee would establish a working group on the Comprehensive Programme of Disarmament, another working group on the review of the implementation of the recommendations and decisions of the tenth special session of the General Assembly, and any additional working groups as necessary;

(c) Decided that the General Assembly should adopt two documents, one containing the Comprehensive Programme of Disarmament and a second encompassing all other items on the agenda.

General Assembly decision S-12/24

Adopted without vote

Oral proposal by President; agenda items 9-14.

Concluding Document of the Twelfth Special Session of the General Assembly

At its 28th plenary meeting, on 10 July 1982, the General Assembly approved the report of the *Ad Hoc* Committee of the Twelfth Special Session as the Concluding Document of the Twelfth Special Session of the General Assembly.

Implementation of the recommendations of the special session

As explained in a September 1982 note by the Secretary-General to the General Assembly,[1] an item on review and implementation of the Concluding Document of the 1982 special session on disarmament was included in the agenda of the Assembly's 1982 regular session, in accordance with the Assembly's decision of 10 July (p. 12) that items on which decisions had not been taken at the special session should be taken up at the regular one.

Ten resolutions under this item were adopted by the Assembly on 13 December. Three concerned topics on which draft resolutions submitted at the special session—listed in an October note by the Secretary-General[2]—had been referred to the regular session: a proposed nuclear-weapon freeze (two resolutions) and a draft convention on prohibition of the use of nuclear weapons. Three concerned the World Disarmament Campaign. The others dealt with regional disarmament, confidence-building measures, disarmament and international security and United Nations fellowships.

Notes. S-G, [1]A/37/493, [2]A/37/494.

Proposed comprehensive programme of disarmament

A comprehensive programme of disarmament, covering all aspects of nuclear and non-nuclear weapons and forces as well as related topics such as confidence-building measures, was to have been a principal result of the General Assembly's 1982 special session on disarmament. The elaboration of such a document by the Committee on Disarmament had been envisaged in the Final Document of the Tenth Special Session, in 1978.[7] However, although the Committee began work on the draft in 1980, it was unable to submit an agreed text at the 1982 special session, and the Assembly itself, at that session, was unable to eliminate the large number of square brackets in the text, marking passages on which consensus could not be reached. Accordingly the Assembly, in July, referred the matter back to the Committee, with instructions to produce a further draft for Assembly consideration in 1983.

Consideration by the Committee on Disarmament (January-April). The *Ad Hoc* Working Group on the Comprehensive Programme of Disarmament, established in 1980 by the Committee on Disarmament[8] to initiate negotiations aimed at completing a draft before the General Assembly's second special session on disarmament, held a total of 59 meetings: 10 in 1980 to establish an outline of the programme,[9] 24 in 1981 to complete a preliminary examination of the chapters[10] and 25 in 1982 to elaborate the text.

At its 1982 session, held between 11 January and 8 April, the Working Group established four contact groups to elaborate the chapters of the programme, which were concerned with objectives, principles, priorities, measures and stages of implementation, and machinery and procedures. An introduction or preamble was left for later consideration.

However, beyond general agreement that the programme should be implemented in the shortest time possible, divergent views persisted on time-frames, the nature of the programme, and measures and stages of implementation. Those who favoured setting a time-frame for implementing each stage argued that that would be the only way to judge progress and political will, and that it could generate confidence by introducing an element of predictability into the disarmament process. Those opposed said the setting of time-frames was not compatible with the conditions of negotiation and that periodic reviews would provide a chance to judge progress. As to the programme's nature, some felt it should be in a legally binding instrument while others disagreed, saying that States could not be bound to the success of negotiations before they had begun.

Draft texts reflecting differing positions were placed in square brackets in the hope that the deliberations at the special session would contribute to the harmonization of positions. Of the five main chapters of the draft, only the shortest, on priorities, was free from square brackets. The resulting draft and the Working Group's report were included in the Committee's special report to the Assembly at its special session.[2]

Preparatory Committee consideration (April/May). An open-ended informal Working Group, established on 30 April by the Preparatory Committee for the Second Special Session of the General Assembly Devoted to Disarmament, submitted to the Committee on 12 May a commentary on the draft programme. Calling the elaboration of the programme one of the central tasks of the special session, the Working Group listed measures, time-frames and the nature of the programme as the three main problem areas and called for efforts to harmonize the different positions during the session. The report of the Working Group, which was chaired by Davidson L. Hepburn (Bahamas), was annexed to the Committee's report to the Assembly.[4]

General Assembly consideration (June/July). At the General Assembly's special session devoted to disarmament, Working Group I of the *Ad Hoc* Committee of the Twelfth Special Session, charged with consideration of the comprehensive programme of disarmament, held four meetings between 14 June and 7 July. Its work was divided among four drafting groups, each open to all

United Nations Members, which were instructed to proceed on the basis of the draft submitted by the Committee on Disarmament.

Progress was reported in Working Group I on a number of issues, particularly in the chapters on objectives and principles, but significant differences of opinion persisted on various aspects of the programme, notably as regards measures and stages of implementation. Informal consultations on time-frames and a review mechanism, led by the Group's Chairman, failed to reconcile divergent views.

Working Group I submitted texts for a seven-chapter programme, which were annexed to the *Ad Hoc* Committee's report to the Assembly[(1)] and thereby became part of the Concluding Document of the session. Chapter I, a six-paragraph introduction, was prepared by the Group's Chairman. Chapter II, consisting of three paragraphs of objectives, was unbracketed except for provisions on public opinion. Chapter III, on principles, contained 48 paragraphs, many of them in square brackets or in two or more alternative versions. Chapter IV, on priorities, though submitted without square brackets by the Committee on Disarmament, emerged in the Working Group's text with one proposed amendment in brackets, affecting one of its three paragraphs.

Chapter V, on measures and stages of implementation, was the longest part of the draft programme and contained many proposed alternatives for individual paragraphs. It was concerned entirely with the first stage of the programme; sections on an intermediate stage and a last stage, included in the draft of the Committee on Disarmament, were omitted from the Working Group's text. Its longest section set out proposed disarmament measures in five categories: nuclear weapons, other weapons of mass destruction, conventional weapons and armed forces, military expenditures and related measures. There followed sections on other measures (for confidence-building, reducing international tension, preventing the use of force in international relations and mobilizing world public opinion for disarmament), on disarmament and development, and on disarmament and international security.

Chapter VI, consisting of 13 paragraphs, was concerned with machinery and procedures and was described in a footnote as a tentative text. Chapter VII, on verification, contained five paragraphs; the draft from the Committee on Disarmament did not contain a separate chapter on this topic, and the chapter heading in the Working Group's text was within square brackets.

Procedures for implementation of the programme, and for review and monitoring of im-plementation, were set out in chapter VI. The portions not enclosed in square brackets provided that: the Committee on Disarmament should, as a rule, negotiate on disarmament measures susceptible to multilateral negotiations; bilateral and regional negotiations could also play an important role; and the General Assembly should conduct an annual review of implementation, aided by a report from the Secretary-General. A proposal for a special Assembly session to review implementation remained in square brackets.

In the absence of agreement on the text of the programme, the Assembly, in the conclusions adopted on 10 July as part of its Concluding Document, referred the draft programme back to the Committee on Disarmament, together with the views expressed and the progress achieved on the subject at the special session, and requested it to submit a revised draft programme to the Assembly in 1983.

In the general debate at the special session, many of those who spoke in favour of a comprehensive programme shared the view, as expressed for example by Algeria, that the programme should contain time-frames or a timetable that would co-ordinate the actions to be taken in successive stages. Those who spoke similarly included Bhutan, Ethiopia, Indonesia, Jamaica, the Libyan Arab Jamahiriya, Madagascar, Mongolia, Morocco, Nepal, Pakistan, the Philippines, Romania, the Sudan, Togo, the United Republic of Tanzania, Uruguay and Yugoslavia.

Brazil, while stating that precise time-frames would be difficult to determine in advance, said the total absence of any temporal indicator would render the programme frustratingly abstract. Without a fixed schedule for each stage, Egypt believed, there would be no incentive for progress, and political obstacles and technical problems would appear more complex than they actually were. Pakistan believed the end of the current century would be a politically feasible and symbolically important date for implementation of the programme. Kenya likewise called for a 20-year time-span up to the year 2000, with a five-year period of review and appraisal of the implementation of each stage.

For the European Community (EC) members, Belgium stated that the programme should be a realistic and flexible framework for negotiation on arms limitation; the international community should periodically examine its implementation without setting deadlines which would deprive the negotiations of flexibility. Ireland believed that, in addition to a programme, there was need to confirm the world's commitment to general and complete disarmament and to take the first steps that would give life to the programme. Portugal also thought it desirable to have flexible objectives allowing for a realistic adaptation to international developments.

Romania believed the programme should include a set of measures for bilateral and multilateral negotiations. Uruguay expected the programme to be a firm and accepted guide for disarmament.

Morocco, the Philippines, Romania and Venezuela said the programme should have legal, binding effect. Indonesia suggested that it be accompanied by a declaration to be signed by heads of delegations.

When the report of the *Ad Hoc* Committee was presented to the Assembly on 10 July without an agreed text for the comprehensive programme of disarmament, regret was expressed by many representatives. Speaking for the EC members, Belgium asserted that the breakdown of negotiations aimed at reconciling viewpoints on the programme had largely compromised the results of the entire session. Mexico said the Group of 21 had a clear conscience, having made numerous and far-reaching concessions during the session.

The Netherlands wondered, in view of the international climate, whether it had not been too ambitious to have tried to achieve among so many countries a comprehensive programme encompassing a wide spectrum of specific, complicated negotiations. Austria agreed that even in optimal conditions of an excellent international climate it would have been difficult to adopt such an ambitious and complex programme; the work done at the session, however, would serve as a good basis for future negotiations. Asserting that the session had lacked the time and perhaps the will to agree to formulae flexible enough to offer certain options, France said those who were called to enter into negotiations could not be bound to accept, in a disarmament programme, provisions that ran counter to their security needs.

Cuba said certain nuclear-weapon States and their allies had prevented the Assembly from adopting a comprehensive programme by questioning the objectives and priorities accepted in the Final Document of the 1978 special session. Indonesia blamed some countries for having attempted to turn upside-down the priority measures agreed upon in 1978 and insisting on a mere listing of measures, despite the fact that the comprehensive programme was not intended to tie the hands of States in negotiations.

Australia said the concept of a comprehensive programme of disarmament remained valid, and Egypt, Ireland, Italy and Pakistan urged continued negotiation on it. For Algeria, the lack of concrete results at the session made a comprehensive programme more necessary than ever. Yugoslavia viewed the outcome of the session as a warning for the international community to increase its efforts at overcoming difficulties and reaching consensus on the programme. Bangladesh urged all nuclear-weapon and other militarily significant States to chart a concrete and definitive course so as to ensure the programme's early conclusion.

Egypt and Tunisia expected the Committee on Disarmament to continue consideration of the comprehensive programme and present it to the Assembly in 1983 for adoption.

Consideration by the Committee on Disarmament (August). On 5 August 1982, the Committee on Disarmament[3] re-established its *Ad Hoc* Working Group on a Comprehensive Programme of Disarmament with a view to submitting a revised draft to the General Assembly in 1983. It was understood that the Group would meet only informally during the remainder of the Committee's 1982 session.

General Assembly action (December). Two General Assembly resolutions adopted on 9 December referred to the continuing work on the draft programme in the Committee on Disarmament. In a resolution on implementation of the recommendations of the 1978 special session on disarmament, the Assembly called on Committee members, particularly the nuclear-weapon States, to show readiness and flexibility in negotiations on the draft so that it could be submitted to the Assembly in 1983.[5] In a resolution on the Committee's work, the Assembly requested it to continue intensive work on the programme from the beginning of its 1983 session and repeated the request that the draft be submitted to the Assembly in 1983.[6]

Reports. [1]*Ad Hoc* Committee, A/S-12/32; Committee on Disarmament, [2]A/S-12/2, [3]A/37/27, [4]Preparatory Committee, A/S-12/1.
Resolutions (1982). GA: [5]37/78 F, para. 6, 9 Dec.; [6]37/78 G, para. 3, 9 Dec.
Resolution (prior). [7]GA: S-10/2, 30 June 1978 (YUN 1978, p. 39).
Yearbook references. 1980, [8]p. 27, [9]p. 28; [10]1981, p. 22.

Committee on Disarmament

Activities of the Committee. In 1982, the 40-member Committee on Disarmament—the main multilateral negotiating body on this subject—met at Geneva from 2 February to 23 April and from 3 August to 17 September. Holding 39 formal and 35 informal plenary meetings, it continued to devote much of its time to the preparation of a draft convention to prohibit chemical weapons. In addition, it worked on substantially the same agenda items as in 1981,[7] concerning the proposed comprehensive programme of disarmament, cessation of the nuclear-arms race and nuclear disarmament, a nuclear-test ban, security assurances to non-nuclear-weapon States, radiological weapons and new types of weapons of mass destruction. As requested by the General Assembly in December 1981,[8] it took up a new item on prevention of an arms race in outer space. It also discussed, but reached no decision on, the question of its membership.

The Committee adopted on 21 April a special report summarizing its work from January 1979 until April 1982,[2] for consideration at the Assembly's special session on disarmament. The Committee's annual report for 1982,[3] adopted at the close of its meetings for the year, was considered at the Assembly's regular session.

During the year, the Committee re-established the four *ad hoc* working groups it had established in 1980, on chemical weapons, security assurances to non-nuclear-weapon States, radiological weapons and the draft comprehensive programme of disarmament. It established a new *ad hoc* working group, on a nuclear-test ban. In addition, the *Ad Hoc* Group of Scientific Experts to Consider International Co-operative Measures to Detect and Identify Seismic Events continued its work in relation to verification of a prohibition of nuclear-weapon tests.

The Committee was unable to reach agreement on the establishment of further subsidiary bodies, such as working groups on prevention of nuclear war or on prevention of an arms race in outer space. In this connection, the "Group of 21" (Algeria, Argentina, Brazil, Burma, Cuba, Egypt, Ethiopia, India, Indonesia, Iran, Kenya, Mexico, Morocco, Nigeria, Pakistan, Peru, Sri Lanka, Sweden, Venezuela, Yugoslavia, Zaire) submitted a working paper for possible consideration at the 1983 session whereby the Committee's rules of procedure would be amended to specify that the consensus rule would not be used to prevent the establishment of subsidiary bodies.

General Assembly consideration (June/ July). The draft comprehensive programme of disarmament, as it stood at the close of the second special session of the General Assembly devoted to disarmament, stated, in its tentative section on machinery, that negotiations on disarmament measures susceptible to multilateral negotiations should as a rule be conducted in the Committee on Disarmament.[1]

In the general debate at the special session, several delegations urged that the effectiveness of the Committee be enhanced and some asked that its membership be expanded.

A number of speakers viewed the negotiating character of the Committee as less than fully realized. Among them, Algeria saw a growing trend to shift the Committee away from its role as a forum for negotiating specific agreements and towards limiting it to being a mere registration office. Burma observed that little had been accom-

plished beyond tackling procedural and peripheral issues. Kenya supported the establishment of subsidiary negotiating bodies within the Committee as a means of effective and efficient consideration of key disarmament issues; it said the Committee should never be deprived of its character as the single multilateral negotiating forum for disarmament.

Peru asserted that the Committee had been debating a great deal and negotiating little and badly, concentrating on a few secondary issues on which it was deadlocked by the nuclear Powers' reluctance to allow it to reach significant agreements. Sri Lanka also regretted the tendency to regard that body as yet another forum for deliberation, adding that its prospects for serious negotiations were almost non-existent because some members had made patently clear their opposition to negotiations on nuclear disarmament. Argentina held the United Kingdom and its unconditional ally responsible in that regard.

Indonesia likewise viewed with dismay the inability of the Committee to reach even one modest agreement due to the attitudes of certain nuclear-weapon States which claimed that issue to be their exclusive domain and beyond the ambit of decision-making by the international community. Jamaica regretted that the Committee, despite a new mandate, had made little progress with its agenda, and felt that full advantage had not been taken of its potential largely because the major Powers were unwilling to use it for negotiating meaningful disarmament proposals. Mauritius asserted that non-nuclear-weapon States had the right to participate in multilateral negotiations on nuclear disarmament. Mongolia said that, while the participation of all nuclear-weapon States in the Committee's negotiations was a positive factor, the growing obstructiveness of certain members had caused it to bog down in unnecessary procedural discussions. The United Republic of Cameroon attributed the insubstantial progress in the Committee to lack of political will on the part of the great Powers.

Nepal urged the General Assembly to examine the Committee's working to ensure full co-operation by all its members, especially the nuclear-weapon States. Yugoslavia called for the full and equal participation of all Committee members and countries concerned in negotiations on all questions considered in that body.

In Bulgaria's view, the Committee, in which five nuclear Powers participated, was fully in a position to serve as an effective multilateral negotiating body, and the existing organizational structure was perfectly appropriate.

Among ideas presented with a view to facilitating the Committee's work was one by the Netherlands suggesting that the Committee meet all year round. Brazil asserted that the Committee's agenda should remain restricted to the priority items on which treaties or international instruments were to be negotiated.

General Assembly action (December). By a resolution of 9 December on the work of the Committee on Disarmament,[5] the General Assembly urged the Committee to continue or undertake substantive negotiations in 1983 on priority issues on its agenda, providing its existing working groups with appropriate negotiating mandates and establishing a group on the cessation of the nuclear-arms race and on nuclear disarmament. The Assembly further requested the Committee to try to achieve concrete results within the shortest possible time and to prepare draft international agreements on the specific priority issues, above all on prohibition of nuclear-weapon tests and on prohibition and destruction of chemical weapons. The Committee was also asked to continue intensive work on a draft comprehensive programme of disarmament. The Assembly invited Committee members involved in separate disarmament negotiations to intensify their efforts and inform the Committee fully of the results.

The Assembly adopted the resolution by a recorded vote of 131 to none, with 17 abstentions. The text, sponsored by 29 States and introduced by Yugoslavia, had been approved by the First Committee on 24 November by a recorded vote of 113 to none, with 17 abstentions.

In another resolution adopted on 9 December, on implementation of the recommendations of the 1978 special session on disarmament, the Assembly called on the Committee on Disarmament to negotiate on nuclear disarmament and to elaborate drafts of international agreements on issues under negotiation for a number of years, particularly a treaty on a nuclear-weapon-test ban and another on prohibition of the development, production and stockpiling of chemical weapons and on their destruction.[4]

Further, in a 13 December resolution on institutional arrangements for disarmament,[6] the Assembly requested the Committee to report in 1983 on a review of its membership (p. 150).

Reports. [1]*Ad Hoc* Committee, A/S-12/32. Committee on Disarmament, [2]A/S-12/2, [3]A/37/27 & Corr.1.
Resolutions (1982). GA: [4]37/78 F, para. 5, 9 Dec.; [5]37/78 G, 9 Dec., text following; [6]37/99 K, sect. I, 13 Dec.
Yearbook references. 1981, [7]p. 31, [8]p. 80.
Meeting records. GA: *Ad Hoc* Committee, A/S-12/AC.1/PV.*10, 11* (29, 30 June); 1st Committee, A/C.1/37/PV.3-10, 12-28, *35, 42* (18 Oct.–24 Nov.); plenary, A/37/PV.98 (9 Dec.).

General Assembly resolution 37/78 G

9 December 1982   Meeting 98   131-0-17 (recorded vote)

Approved by First Committee (A/37/662) by recorded vote (113-0-17), 24 November (meeting 42); 29-nation draft (A/C.1/37/L.27); agenda item 50 *(b)*.

Sponsors: Algeria, Argentina, Bangladesh, Benin, Brazil, Burma, Colombia, Congo, Cuba, Egypt, Ethiopia, German Democratic Republic, Ghana, India, Indonesia, Iran, Madagascar, Mexico, Nigeria, Pakistan, Peru, Romania, Sri Lanka, Sudan, Sweden, United Republic of Cameroon, Venezuela, Yugoslavia, Zaire.

Report of the Committee on Disarmament

The General Assembly,

Recalling its resolutions 34/83 B of 11 December 1979, 35/152 J of 12 December 1980 and 36/92 F of 9 December 1981,

Recalling also the Final Document of the Tenth Special Session of the General Assembly and the Concluding Document of the Twelfth Special Session of the General Assembly,

Having considered the report of the Committee on Disarmament,

Reaffirming that the establishment of *ad hoc* working groups offers the best available machinery for the conduct of multilateral negotiations on items included in the agenda of the Committee on Disarmament and contributes to the strengthening of the negotiating role of the Committee,

Noting that the Committee on Disarmament has established, on 21 April 1982, an *Ad Hoc* Working Group under item 1 of its agenda, entitled "Nuclear-test ban",

Regretting that, despite the express wishes of the great majority of members of the Committee on Disarmament, the establishment of an *ad hoc* working group to undertake multilateral negotiations on nuclear disarmament was once again prevented during the session held by the Committee in 1982,

Expressing its deep concern and disappointment that the Committee on Disarmament has not thus far been able to reach concrete agreements on disarmament issues which have been under consideration for a number of years, particularly on those to which the United Nations has assigned greatest priority and urgency,

Convinced that the Committee on Disarmament, as the single multilateral negotiating body on disarmament, should play the central role in substantive negotiations on priority questions of disarmament and on the implementation of the Programme of Action set forth in section III of the Final Document of the Tenth Special Session,

Stressing that negotiations on specific disarmament issues conducted outside the Committee on Disarmament should in no way serve as a pretext for preventing the conduct of multilateral negotiations on such questions in the Committee,

1.   *Urges* the Committee on Disarmament to continue or undertake, during its session to be held in 1983, substantive negotiations on the priority questions of disarmament on its agenda, in accordance with the provisions of the Final Document of the Tenth Special Session of the General Assembly and other relevant resolutions of the Assembly on those questions, and, in order to reach that goal, to provide the existing *ad hoc* working groups with appropriate negotiating mandates and to establish, as a matter of urgency, an *ad hoc* working group on the cessation of the nuclear-arms race and nuclear disarmament;

2.   *Requests* the Committee on Disarmament to intensify its work, to make the utmost effort to achieve concrete results in the shortest possible period of time and to prepare draft international agreements on the specific priority issues of disarmament on its agenda, above all on a treaty on a nuclear-weapon-test ban and on the complete and effective prohibition of all chemical weapons and on their destruction;

3.   *Also requests* the Committee on Disarmament to continue as from the beginning of its session in 1983, in accordance with the Concluding Document of the Twelfth Special Session of the General Assembly, its intensive work on the elaboration of a comprehensive programme of disarmament and to submit the revised draft of such a programme to the General Assembly at its thirty-eighth session;

4.   *Invites* the members of the Committee on Disarmament involved in separate negotiations on specific priority questions of disarmament to intensify their efforts in order to achieve a positive conclusion of those negotiations without further delay and to submit to the Committee a full report on their separate negotiations and the results achieved in order to contribute most directly to the negotiations in the Committee, in accordance with paragraph 1 above;

5.   *Further requests* the Committee on Disarmament to submit a report on its work to the General Assembly at its thirty-eighth session;

6.   *Decides* to include in the provisional agenda of its thirty-eighth session the item entitled "Report of the Committee on Disarmament".

Recorded vote in Assembly as follows:

In favour: Afghanistan, Algeria, Angola, Antigua and Barbuda, Argentina, Austria, Bahamas, Bahrain, Bangladesh, Barbados, Belize, Benin, Bhutan, Bolivia,

Botswana, Brazil, Bulgaria, Burma, Burundi, Byelorussian SSR, Cape Verde, Central African Republic, Chad, Chile, China, Colombia, Comoros, Congo, Costa Rica, Cuba, Cyprus, Czechoslovakia, Democratic Kampuchea, Democratic Yemen, Djibouti, Dominican Republic, Ecuador, Egypt, El Salvador, Ethiopia, Fiji, Finland, Gabon, Gambia, German Democratic Republic, Ghana, Greece, Grenada, Guatemala, Guinea, Guinea-Bissau, Guyana, Haiti, Honduras, Hungary, India, Indonesia, Iran, Iraq, Ireland, Israel, Ivory Coast, Jamaica, Jordan, Kenya, Kuwait, Lao People's Democratic Republic, Lebanon, Liberia, Libyan Arab Jamahiriya, Madagascar, Malawi, Malaysia, Maldives, Mali, Malta, Mauritania, Mauritius, Mexico, Mongolia, Morocco, Mozambique, Nepal, Nicaragua, Niger, Nigeria, Oman, Pakistan, Panama, Papua New Guinea, Paraguay, Peru, Philippines, Poland, Qatar, Romania, Rwanda, Saint Lucia, Sao Tome and Principe, Saudi Arabia, Senegal, Sierra Leone, Singapore, Solomon Islands, Somalia, Spain, Sri Lanka, Sudan, Suriname, Swaziland, Sweden, Syrian Arab Republic, Thailand, Togo, Trinidad and Tobago, Tunisia, Uganda, Ukrainian SSR, USSR, United Arab Emirates, United Republic of Cameroon, United Republic of Tanzania, Upper Volta, Uruguay, Vanuatu, Venezuela, Viet Nam, Yemen, Yugoslavia, Zaire, Zambia.

Against: None.

Abstaining: Australia, Belgium, Canada, Denmark, France, Germany, Federal Republic of, Iceland, Italy, Japan, Luxembourg, Netherlands, New Zealand, Norway, Portugal, Turkey, United Kingdom, United States.

Disarmament Commission

Activities of the Commission. The Disarmament Commission, composed of all United Nations Member States, held its 1982 substantive session from 17 to 28 May at United Nations Headquarters. It later met on 14 October to adopt its 1982 report to the General Assembly, and again on 15 December to organize its work for the coming year.

Its agenda, identical to that of its 1981 session,[7] included items on aspects of the arms race, particularly the nuclear-arms race; South Africa's nuclear plans and capability; guidelines for a study on the conventional-arms race and disarmament; and reduction of military budgets. The Commission submitted reports to the Assembly at its special session on disarmament, covering the Commission's work from 1979 up to and including its 1982 substantive session,[3] and at the Assembly's regular session, covering the Commission's 1982 activities.[4]

The future role and functions of the Commission were also referred to during the session, but the suggestions made in that regard by delegations could not be considered due to lack of time. Some felt the issue should be left to the Assembly at its special session. The suggestions included calls for the Commission to concentrate on a manageably small number of subjects, prepare proposals to serve as a negotiating basis in disarmament bodies, consider proposals on establishing nuclear-weapon-free zones and have a role in the review mechanism for the comprehensive programme of disarmament. It was also suggested that the Commission be enabled to hold more than one annual substantive session, if necessary; that working groups should be able to work between sessions; and that the Commission should have its own annual work programme and not be dependent on the work of other disarmament bodies.

General Assembly consideration (June/July). At the special session on disarmament, Turkey, in a note verbale dated 28 June,[1] submitted a proposal aimed at improving the work of the Disarmament Commission; it suggested that the Commission should not duplicate the deliberations of the General Assembly's First Committee, that its agenda should have a very limited number of items, that all general debate should be avoided and that its decisions should continue to be taken by consensus.

The draft comprehensive programme of disarmament contained, in its tentative section on machinery, an incomplete provision on the Disarmament Commission which stated that that body should play an active role in preparing the ground for subsequent negotiations on concrete agreements and could also assist the Assembly in the review and appraisal of the programme's implementation.[2]

In the general debate at the special session, Belgium, on behalf of the European Community (EC) members, called for promoting the Commission's role, as did Bangladesh; Belgium also suggested that the Commission be given specific deliberative functions, particularly in following up disarmament studies prepared by the Secretary-General at the request of the Assembly. Brazil, which also believed in rendering the Commission's deliberations more practical, said it could be asked to examine the implementation of resolutions adopted by the Assembly on the recommendation of its First Committee or to supervise the recommendations of study groups established by the Assembly. Observing that the shorter sessions held by the Commission during the previous two years had been viewed by some as an effort to reduce its importance, Kuwait expressed support for any arrangement enabling that body to assume its full responsibilities.

Nepal suggested that the Assembly help the Commission find direction, and Spain felt a review of its functions would be appropriate. Yugoslavia called for more effective and substantive work by the Commission.

General Assembly action (December). By a resolution on the report of the Disarmament Commission, adopted without vote on 9 December,[6] the General Assembly, noting that the Commission had been unable to conclude consideration of several items on its agenda, requested it to direct its attention to specific subjects and to make concrete recommendations on them to the Assembly. The Commission was requested to meet for up to four weeks in 1983. The 14-nation text, introduced by Peru, had been approved by the First Committee on 26 November by a recorded vote of 125 to none.

In another resolution of 9 December,[5] on implementation of the recommendations of the 1978 special session on disarmament, the Assembly called on the Commission to intensify its work and to submit concrete recommendations in 1983 with a view to contributing to a solution of outstanding issues.

Note verbale. [1]Turkey, 28 June, A/S-12/AC.1/54.
Reports. [2]*Ad Hoc* Committee, A/S-12/32; Disarmament Commission, [3]A/S-12/3, [4]A/37/42.
Resolutions (1982). GA, 9 Dec.: [5]37/78 F, para. 7; [6]37/78 H, text following.
Yearbook reference. [7]1981, p. 29.
Meeting records. GA: 1st Committee, A/C.1/37/PV.3-10, 12-28, *36, 44* (18 Oct.–26 Nov.); plenary, A/37/PV.98 (9 Dec.).

General Assembly resolution 37/78 H

9 December 1982   Meeting 98   Adopted without vote

Approved by First Committee (A/37/662) by recorded vote (125-0), 26 November (meeting 44); 14-nation draft (A/C.1/37/L.42); agenda item 50 *(a)*.

Sponsors: Bahamas, Belgium, Czechoslovakia, Ecuador, Egypt, Germany, Federal Republic of, Liberia, Morocco, Pakistan, Peru, Poland, Sweden, Yugoslavia, Zaire.

Report of the Disarmament Commission

The General Assembly,

Having considered the report of the Disarmament Commission,

Emphasizing again the importance of an effective follow-up to the relevant recommendations and decisions contained in the Final Document of the Tenth Special Session of the General Assembly, the first special session devoted to disarmament,

Taking into account the relevant sections of the Concluding Document of the Twelfth Special Session of the General Assembly, the second special session devoted to disarmament,

Considering the important role that the Disarmament Commission has played and the significant contribution that it has made in examining and submitting recommendations on various problems in the field of disarmament and in the promotion of the implementation of the relevant decisions of the tenth special session,

Desirous of strengthening the effectiveness of the Disarmament Commission,

Recalling its resolutions 33/71 H of 14 December 1978, 34/83 H of 11 December 1979, 35/152 F of 12 December 1980 and 36/92 B of 9 December 1981,

1. *Takes note* of the report of the Disarmament Commission;

2. *Notes* that the Disarmament Commission again was not able to conclude its consideration of several items on its agenda;

3. *Requests* the Disarmament Commission to continue its work in accordance with its mandate, as set forth in paragraph 118 of the Final Document of the Tenth Special Session of the General Assembly, and, to that end, to direct its attention at each substantive session to specific subjects from among those which have been or will be under its consideration, taking into account the relevant resolutions of the General Assembly, and to make concrete recommendations on such subjects to the subsequent session of the Assembly;

4. *Requests* the Disarmament Commission to meet for a period not exceeding four weeks during 1983 and to submit a substantive report on its work to the General Assembly at its thirty-eighth session;

5. *Requests* the Secretary-General to transmit to the Disarmament Commission the report of the Committee on Disarmament, together with all the official records of the thirty-seventh session of the General Assembly relating to disarmament matters, and to render all assistance that the Commission may require for implementing the present resolution;

6. *Decides* to include in the provisional agenda of its thirty-eighth session the item entitled "Report of the Disarmament Commission".

Implementation of the recommendations of the 1978 special session on disarmament

General Assembly action (June/July). In the conclusions approved as part of the Concluding Document of its 1982 special session on disarmament,[2] the General Assembly observed that the objectives, priorities and principles, as well as the Programme of Action, contained in the Final Document of the Tenth Special Session of the General Assembly,[15] held in 1978, remained largely unimplemented. A number of important negotiations either had not begun or had been suspended, and efforts in the Committee on Disarmament and other forums had produced little tangible result. The arms race, in particular the nuclear-arms race, had assumed more dangerous proportions and global military expenditures had increased sharply; there had been no significant progress in arms limitation and disarmament. However, the Assembly was encouraged at the 1982 special session by the unanimous and categorical reaffirmation by Member States of the validity of, and their commitment to, the Final Document, and by their pledge to respect in disarmament negotiations the priorities agreed upon in the Programme of Action.

The *Ad Hoc* Committee of the Twelfth Special Session entrusted its Working Group II with a review of the implementation of the recommendations and decisions adopted at the 1978 session. The Group, which held seven meetings between 18 June and 2 July 1982, established two drafting groups to work on the basis of a composite paper prepared in May by a working group of the Preparatory Committee for the Second Special Session of the General Assembly Devoted to Disarmament, and annexed to that Committee's report.[3] That paper contained an analysis of the situation in respect of each main disarmament area, and included a number of conclusions and recommendations; however, it was a composite incorporating all the elements contained in different working papers and proposals, rather than an attempt to achieve an agreed text.

As much work remained to be accomplished by the time the drafting groups terminated their work, the *Ad Hoc* Committee established on 2 July a contact group, which in turn set up a small drafting group. On 7 July, the Committee Chairman reported that despite strenuous efforts the drafting group had been unable to conclude its work. The *Ad Hoc* Committee therefore recommended that the proposals submitted during the special session, which could not be considered, be forwarded to the Assembly at its regular session.

At the two concluding meetings of the special session, a large number of delegations welcomed the Assembly's reaffirmation of, or themselves reaffirmed, the validity of the 1978 Final Document. France called the unanimous reaffirmation a positive outcome, Canada termed it important, and the Netherlands found it encouraging. Others noting the reaffirmation of the Final Document included Algeria, Austria, Belgium (on behalf of the EC members), Bulgaria, Finland, the Federal

Republic of Germany, Ireland, Italy, Japan, New Zealand, Norway, Pakistan, Romania, Sweden and Yugoslavia.

As regards the review of implementation of the 1978 Final Document, however, China found it regrettable that the session had failed to reach a consensus even in that regard. Austria, Sri Lanka and Tunisia also regretted the failure at the session to find even the lowest common denominator of language to describe the current international situation.

Several delegations asserted that attempts had been made at the session to deviate from the Final Document. Sri Lanka was distressed to observe that some States believed they had given too much in 1978 and sought to retract commitments then undertaken. The Ukrainian SSR charged the United States and other countries of the North Atlantic Treaty Organization with having attempted to revise the priorities agreed to in 1978. The Byelorussian SSR said those countries had blocked the work of the session by rejecting previous decisions on such questions as nuclear disarmament.

In Indonesia's view, political bickering among delegations had prevented an early initiation of the work of Working Group II. Ireland considered it sad that the simple preservation of what had been agreed on four years previously should be counted as a positive result of the 1982 session.

During the general debate at the session, many speakers offered views as to why the goals of the Final Document had not been achieved and the arms race had in fact intensified. Most States blamed the fact that, as Morocco put it, the resort to force had replaced the resort to peaceful means to settle disputes. Disarmament was hampered, said Belgium on behalf of the EC members, by such unfavourable conditions as invasions, military occupations, interference in the internal affairs of States and human rights violations. The United States said that USSR aggression and support for violence around the world had eroded the confidence needed for arms negotiations; the United States refused to become weaker while potential adversaries remained committed to imperialist adventures.

Samoa observed that the 1982 special session was sharing the headlines with three wars; other speakers put the number at four or eight. Singapore remarked that disarmament could prosper only in an environment of political stability and mutual trust, whereas many events had occurred to destabilize the international order and poison the negotiating atmosphere.

Other speakers cited a spiral of fear and mistrust which led to an arms build-up that generated further mistrust. Every country thought its own intentions were good but believed it had good reason to mistrust the intentions of others, Ireland remarked; every country consequently built up its armaments and then failed to see why its potential rivals should be suspicious.

China ascribed the lack of progress to the attitude of the super-Powers which, it said, were not sincere about disarmament but instead were trying to gain supremacy over each other. The German Democratic Republic asserted that the socialist States of Eastern Europe had taken a number of unilateral steps aimed at opening the door to a scaling down of military confrontation, but these had not been matched by the other side. Poland said a group of States seemed to have subordinated the disarmament dialogue to their policy of confrontation; the major task of the special session was to overcome the obstacles originating in that trend.

Pope John Paul II, in a message read to the Assembly on behalf of the Holy See, declared that the production and possession of weapons was the consequence of a moral crisis gnawing at all aspects of society; to the extent that efforts at arms reduction and then total disarmament were not matched by parallel moral renewal, they were doomed to failure.

General Assembly action (December). Expressing regret that it had not been able, at its 1982 special session, to give further impetus to the outcome of the 1978 session, the General Assembly, by a resolution of 9 December,[9] expressed deep concern over the intensification of the arms race, particularly in the nuclear field. The Assembly called on all States, in particular nuclear-weapon and other militarily significant States, to take immediate steps aimed at promoting international security and leading to the effective halting and reversing of the arms race and to disarmament. Further, it invited them to implement without delay the recommendations and decisions contained in the Final Document, as well as the priority tasks listed in the 1978 Programme of Action and in the Concluding Document of the 1982 special session.

The Assembly urged Member States to stimulate and accelerate disarmament negotiations, called for results in nuclear disarmament negotiations between nuclear-weapon States, and called on the Committee on Disarmament and the Disarmament Commission to continue their work, including work by the Committee on a draft comprehensive programme of disarmament.

This resolution, sponsored by 31 States and introduced by Yugoslavia, was adopted by the Assembly by a recorded vote of 134 to none, with 12 abstentions. The First Committee had approved the draft on 26 November, as revised by the sponsors, by a recorded vote of 114 to none, with 10 abstentions.

Egypt introduced and later withdrew a draft resolution,[1] also on behalf of Colombia, Ecuador and Sierra Leone, which would have had the Assembly reaffirm the disarmament priorities contained in the 1978 Final Document, express concern over the arms-race escalation, reiterate the central role and primary responsibility of the United Nations in disarmament efforts, and call on the major nuclear Powers to take concrete and effective action to halt and reverse the arms race. In announcing that it would not press for a vote on this proposal, Egypt stated that many of the ideas contained in its draft had already been approved by the First Committee in the resolution on implementation of the recommendations of the 1978 special session.

Under the agenda item concerned with implementation of the 1978 recommendations the Assembly adopted 10 other resolutions on 9 December, concerning nuclear-arms negotiations between the USSR and the United States,[4] international co-operation for disarmament,[5] nuclear disarmament,[6] Disarmament Week,[7] proposed prohibition of the nuclear neutron weapon,[8] the work of the Committee on Disarmament[10] and the Disarmament Commission,[11] prevention of nuclear war,[12] non-use of nuclear weapons and prevention of nuclear war,[13] and a proposed international agency for the verification by satellite of disarmament agreements.[14]

Draft resolution withdrawn. [1]Colombia, Ecuador, Egypt, Sierra Leone, A/C.1/37/L.63.

Reports. [2]*Ad Hoc* Committee, A/S-12/32; [3]Preparatory Committee, A/S-12/1.

Resolutions (1982). GA, 9 Dec.: [4]37/78 A; [5]37/78 B; [6]37/78 C; [7]37/78 D; [8]37/78 E; [9]37/78 F, text following; [10]37/78 G; [11]37/78 H; [12]37/78 I; [13]37/78 J; [14]37/78 K.

Resolution (prior). [15]GA: S-10/2, 30 June 1978 (YUN 1978, p. 39).

Meeting records. GA: *Ad Hoc* Committee, A/S-12/AC.1/PV.*12, 14* (2, 7 July); 1st Committee, A/C.1/37/PV.3-10, 12-29, *36, 40, 44* (18 Oct.–26 Nov.); plenary, A/37/PV.98 (9 Dec.).

General Assembly resolution 37/78 F

9 December 1982   Meeting 98   134-0-12 (recorded vote)

Approved by First Committee (A/37/662) by recorded vote (114-0-10), 26 November (meeting 44); 31-nation draft (A/C.1/37/L.26/Rev.1); agenda item 50 *(h)*.

Sponsors: Algeria, Argentina, Bahamas, Bangladesh, Benin, Congo, Cuba, Czechoslovakia, Ecuador, Egypt, Ethiopia, German Democratic Republic, Ghana, India, Indonesia, Iran, Liberia, Madagascar, Mongolia, Nigeria, Pakistan, Peru, Qatar, Romania, Sierra Leone, Sri Lanka, Sudan, Venezuela, Viet Nam, Yugoslavia, Zaire.

Implementation of the recommendations and decisions of the tenth special session

The General Assembly,

Having reviewed the implementation of the recommendations and decisions adopted by the General Assembly at its tenth special session, the first special session devoted to disarmament, as well as the Concluding Document of the Twelfth Special Session of the General Assembly, the second special session devoted to disarmament,

Recalling its resolutions S-10/2 of 30 June 1978, 34/83 C of 11 December 1979, 35/46 of 3 December 1980, 35/152 E of 12 December 1980 and 36/92 M of 9 December 1981 and its decision S-12/24 of 10 July 1982,

Regretting that at its twelfth special session it was not able to achieve, despite the expectations of the international community and the efforts exerted by a large number of Member States, the main objectives of that session, namely, to adopt a comprehensive programme of disarmament and to give further impetus to, and assess the implementation of, the decisions and recommendations of the tenth special session, as well as certain urgent measures for the prevention of nuclear war and for nuclear disarmament,

Noting with deep concern that the recommendations and decisions of the tenth special session have not been implemented, that, between the two special sessions on disarmament, the arms race, particularly in its nuclear aspect, has gained in intensity, that urgent measures to prevent nuclear war and for disarmament have not been adopted and that open threats, pressures and military intervention against independent States and violations of the fundamental principles of the Charter of the United Nations have taken place, posing the most serious threat to international peace and security,

Convinced that one of the most urgent tasks is to halt and reverse the arms race and to undertake concrete measures of disarmament, particularly nuclear disarmament, and that, in this respect, the nuclear-weapon States and other militarily significant States have the primary responsibility,

Deeply concerned that negotiations on disarmament issues are lagging far behind the rapid technological development in the field of armaments and the relentless growth of military arsenals,

Considering it imperative to give a new impetus to negotiations on disarmament, in particular nuclear disarmament, at all levels and to achieve genuine progress in the immediate future,

Convinced that the success of disarmament negotiations, in which all the peoples of the world have a vital interest, can be achieved through the active participation of Member States in such negotiations, contributing thereby to the maintenance of international peace and security,

Reaffirming that the United Nations has a central role and primary responsibility in the sphere of disarmament,

Recalling with satisfaction that at the twelfth special session of the General Assembly, all Member States unanimously and categorically reaffirmed the validity of the Final Document of the Tenth Special Session, as well as their solemn commitment to it and their pledge to respect the priorities in disarmament negotiations, as agreed to in the Programme of Action contained in section III of the Final Document,

Recalling the commitment of States undertaken in various international agreements to negotiate on disarmament measures, in particular on nuclear disarmament,

1. *Expresses its deep concern* over the constant deterioration of international relations, as well as the intensification of the arms race, particularly the nuclear-arms race, which directly threatens international peace and security and increases the danger of outbreak of war, in particular nuclear war;

2. *Calls upon* all States, in particular nuclear-weapon States and other militarily significant States, to take immediate steps aimed at promoting international security and leading to the effective halting and reversing of the arms race and to disarmament;

3. *Invites* all States, particularly nuclear-weapon States and especially those which possess the most important nuclear arsenals, to take urgent measures with a view to implementing the recommendations and decisions contained in the Final Document of the Tenth Special Session of the General Assembly concerning nuclear disarmament, as well as to fulfilling the priority tasks listed in the Programme of Action set forth in section III of the Final Document and in the Concluding Document of the Twelfth Special Session;

4. *Urges* all Member States to exert the greatest effort to stimulate and accelerate disarmament negotiations in good faith at all levels and to achieve rapid progress in resolving various disarmament issues;

5. *Calls upon* the Committee on Disarmament to concentrate its work on the substantive and priority items on its agenda, to proceed to negotiations on nuclear disarmament without further delay and to elaborate, as soon as possible, drafts of international agreements on those disarmament issues which have been the object of negotiations over a number of years, particularly a treaty on a nuclear-weapon-test ban and on a complete and effective prohibition of the development, production and stockpiling of all chemical weapons and on their destruction;

6. *Calls upon* members of the Committee on Disarmament, particularly the nuclear-weapon States, to show a greater measure of readiness and flexibility in further negotiations on the elaboration of a draft comprehensive programme of disarmament and thus enable the Committee to submit, pursuant to the decision taken at the twelfth special session, a revised draft of such a programme to the General Assembly at its thirty-eighth session;

7. *Calls upon* the Disarmament Commission to intensify its work in considering various issues of disarmament on its agenda and to submit to the General Assembly at its thirty-eighth session concrete recommendations with a view to contributing to a solution of outstanding issues;

8. *Calls upon* nuclear-weapon States engaged in separate negotiations on issues of nuclear disarmament to exert the utmost effort with a view to achieving concrete results in those negotiations and thus contribute to the success of multilateral negotiations on nuclear disarmament;

9. *Invites* all States engaged in disarmament and arms limitation negotiations outside the framework of the United Nations to keep the General Assembly and the Committee on Disarmament informed of the results of such negotiations, in conformity with the relevant provisions of the Final Document of the Tenth Special Session;

10. *Decides* to include in the provisional agenda of its thirty-eighth session the item entitled "Implementation of the recommendations and decisions of the tenth special session".

Recorded vote in Assembly as follows:

In favour: Afghanistan, Algeria, Angola, Antigua and Barbuda, Argentina, Australia, Austria, Bahamas, Bahrain, Bangladesh, Barbados, Belize, Benin, Bhutan, Bolivia, Botswana, Brazil, Bulgaria, Burma, Burundi, Byelorussian SSR, Canada, Cape Verde, Central African Republic, Chad, Chile, China, Comoros, Congo, Costa Rica, Cuba, Cyprus, Czechoslovakia, Democratic Kampuchea, Democratic Yemen, Denmark, Djibouti, Dominican Republic, Ecuador, Egypt, El Salvador, Ethiopia, Fiji, Finland, Gabon, German Democratic Republic, Ghana, Greece, Grenada, Guatemala, Guinea, Guinea-Bissau, Guyana, Haiti, Honduras, Hungary, Iceland, India, Indonesia, Iran, Iraq, Ireland, Israel, Ivory Coast, Jamaica, Jordan, Kenya, Kuwait, Lao People's Democratic Republic, Liberia, Libyan Arab Jamahiriya, Madagascar, Malawi, Malaysia, Maldives, Mali, Malta, Mauritania, Mauritius, Mexico, Mongolia, Morocco, Mozambique, Nepal, New Zealand, Nicaragua, Niger, Nigeria, Norway, Oman, Pakistan, Panama, Papua New Guinea, Paraguay, Peru, Philippines, Poland, Portugal, Qatar, Romania, Rwanda, Saint Lucia, Sao Tome and Principe, Saudi Arabia, Sierra Leone, Singapore, Solomon Islands, Somalia, Spain, Sri Lanka, Sudan, Suriname, Swaziland, Sweden, Syrian Arab Republic, Thailand, Togo, Trinidad and Tobago, Tunisia, Uganda, Ukrainian SSR, USSR, United Arab Emirates, United Republic of Cameroon, United Republic of Tanzania, Upper Volta, Uruguay, Vanuatu, Venezuela, Viet Nam, Yemen, Yugoslavia, Zaire, Zambia.

Against: None.

Abstaining: Belgium, Colombia,[a] France, Germany, Federal Republic of, Italy, Japan, Lebanon, Luxembourg, Netherlands, Turkey, United Kingdom, United States.

[a]Later advised the Secretariat it had intended to vote in favour.

Implementation of the 1979 Declaration on International Co-operation for Disarmament

In a resolution adopted on 9 December 1982 on international co-operation for disarmament,[3] the General Assembly called on States to utilize the principles and ideas contained in its 1979 Declaration on International Co-operation for Disarmament[5] by actively participating in disarmament negotiations and refraining from developing new directions and channels of the arms race. It declared that doctrines justifying the unleashing of nuclear war intensified the arms race and stated that measures such as an obligation not to make first use of nuclear weapons (p. 54) would improve conditions for resolving disarmament issues. It appealed to members of military or political groupings to promote the gradual mutual limitation of their military activities. It called on Member States

to cultivate and disseminate the ideas of international co-operation for disarmament, particularly in connection with the World Disarmament Campaign, and called on the United Nations Educational, Scientific and Cultural Organization (UNESCO) to consider measures to strengthen such ideas.

The resolution was adopted by a recorded vote of 116 to 12, with 16 abstentions, following First Committee approval on 24 November by a recorded vote of 92 to 14, with 17 abstentions. Sponsored by 24 States, the text was introduced by Czechoslovakia, which described it as a measure for invigorating constructive co-operation among States to implement disarmament objectives and for mobilizing the political goodwill leading to effective disarmament agreements. Czechoslovakia added that the text was based entirely on the 1979 Declaration, proposed by Czechoslovakia and others; its main purpose was to facilitate implementation of the recommendations and decisions of the Assembly's 1978 special session on disarmament.[4]

Belgium, explaining its negative vote, asserted that the text omitted the primary factor of international co-operation in disarmament matters, namely, scrupulous respect for the Charter of the United Nations; the numerous hypotheses contained in the text did not constitute a guarantee of co-operation. Belgium and France, which also voted against, objected to the paragraphs on non-first use of nuclear weapons. France also opposed the provision on doctrines justifying nuclear war and voiced reservations about the role of UNESCO in relation to the World Disarmament Campaign.

Democratic Kampuchea, explaining why it did not take part in the vote, said the co-sponsorship of the resolution by Viet Nam, whose troops had occupied Democratic Kampuchea and massacred its people, was inconsistent with a resolution which declared the use of force in international relations to be incompatible with international co-operation for disarmament. Somalia said it had abstained in the Committee vote because it objected to some of the language but it would have voted in favour of the paragraph stating that the use of force in international relations and attempts to prevent decolonization were incompatible with international co-operation for disarmament. Despite its reservation on what it considered to be a slight imbalance in the text, Oman cast a positive vote in the belief that multilateral disarmament efforts should be intensified.

Two communications from peace movements in support of disarmament were transmitted by letters to the Secretary-General from the USSR and Viet Nam. By a letter dated 30 September,[2] Viet Nam transmitted a statement of 21 September at the conclusion of a nation-wide Campaign for

Peace and Disarmament, made by the Presidiums of the Central Committee of the Viet Nam Fatherland Front and the Viet Nam Peace Committee. The USSR, by a letter dated 11 October,[1] transmitted the text of an appeal to the General Assembly by participants in the Soviet peace movement.

Letters. [1]USSR, 11 Oct., A/C.1/37/4; [2]Viet Nam, 30 Sep., A/C.1/37/3.
Resolution (1982). [3]GA: 37/78 B, 9 Dec., text following.
Resolutions (prior). GA: [4]S-10/2, 30 June 1978 (YUN 1978, p. 39); [5]34/88, 11 Dec. 1979 (YUN 1979, p. 86).
Meeting records. GA: 1st Committee, A/C.1/37/PV.3-10, 12-28, 34, 42 (18 Oct.–24 Nov.); plenary, A/37/PV.98 (9 Dec.).

General Assembly resolution 37/78 B

9 December 1982   Meeting 98   116-12-16 (recorded vote)

Approved by First Committee (A/37/662 and Corr.1) by recorded vote (92-14-17), 24 November (meeting 42); 24-nation draft (A/C.1/37/L.19); agenda item 50.

Sponsors: Afghanistan, Angola, Benin, Congo, Cuba, Czechoslovakia, Democratic Yemen, Ethiopia, German Democratic Republic, Grenada, Guinea, Guyana, Hungary, Indonesia, Lao People's Democratic Republic, Madagascar, Mali, Mongolia, Mozambique, Poland, Syrian Arab Republic, Ukrainian SSR, Viet Nam, Yemen.

International co-operation for disarmament

The General Assembly,

Stressing again the urgent need for an active and sustained effort to intensify the comprehensive implementation of the recommendations and decisions unanimously adopted at its tenth special session, the first special session devoted to disarmament, as contained in the Final Document of that session, and confirmed in the Concluding Document of the Twelfth Special Session of the General Assembly, the second special session devoted to disarmament,

Recalling the Declaration on International Co-operation for Disarmament of 11 December 1979 and General Assembly resolution 36/92 D of 9 December 1981,

Deeply concerned over the danger of a nuclear war, the continued arms race and the danger of unleashing a further, qualitatively new round of the arms race, all of which have an extraordinarily negative impact on the international situation,

Stressing the vital importance of eliminating the danger of a nuclear war, halting the nuclear-arms race and attaining disarmament, particularly in the nuclear field, for the preservation of peace and the strengthening of international security,

Bearing in mind the vital interest of all nations in the attainment of effective disarmament measures, which would release considerable financial and material resources to be used for the economic and social development of all States, in particular developing countries,

Considering the importance of manifestations of popular peace and anti-nuclear movements against the arms race and the escalation of the danger of nuclear war throughout the world,

Convinced of the need to strengthen constructive international co-operation, based on the political goodwill of States, for successful negotiations on disarmament, in accordance with the Final Document of the Tenth Special Session,

Emphasizing the duty of States to co-operate for the preservation of international peace and security, in accordance with the Charter of the United Nations, as confirmed in the Declaration on Principles of International Law concerning Friendly Relations and Co-operation among States in accordance with the Charter of the United Nations, of 24 October 1970, the obligation to co-operate actively and constructively for the attainment of the aims of disarmament being an indispensable part of that duty,

Expressing the conviction that concrete manifestations of political goodwill, including unilateral measures, such as an obligation not to make first use of nuclear weapons, improve conditions for resolving disarmament issues in a spirit of co-operation among States,

Taking into consideration the central role and primary responsibility of the United Nations in combining efforts and in supporting and developing active co-operation among States aimed at the solution of disarmament problems,

1. *Calls upon* all States, in implementing the Final Document of the Tenth Special Session of the General Assembly, to make active use of the principles and ideas contained in the Declaration on International Co-operation for Disarmament by actively participating in disarmament negotiations, with a view to achieving concrete results, and by conducting them on the basis of equality and undiminished security and the non-use of force in international relations, refraining at the same time from developing new directions and channels of the arms race;

2. *Declares* that the elaboration and dissemination of any doctrines and concepts justifying the unleashing of nuclear war endanger world peace, lead to deterioration of the international situation and further intensification of the arms race and are detrimental to the generally recognized necessity of international co-operation for disarmament;

3. *Declares* that the use of force in international relations as well as in attempts to prevent the full implementation of the Declaration on the Granting of Independence to Colonial Countries and Peoples is a phenomenon incompatible with the ideas of international co-operation for disarmament;

4. *Appeals* to States which are members of military or political groupings to promote, on the basis of the Final Document, in the spirit of international co-operation for disarmament, the gradual mutual limitation of military activities of these groupings, thus creating conditions for their dissolution;

5. *Calls upon* all Member States to cultivate and disseminate, particularly in connection with the World Disarmament Campaign launched by the General Assembly at its twelfth special session, the ideas of international co-operation for disarmament, *inter alia* through their educational systems, mass media and cultural policies;

6. *Calls upon* the United Nations Educational, Scientific and Cultural Organization to consider, in order further to mobilize world public opinion on behalf of disarmament, measures aimed at strengthening the ideas of international co-operation for disarmament through research, education, information, communication and culture.

Recorded vote in Assembly as follows:

In favour: Afghanistan, Algeria, Angola, Antigua and Barbuda, Argentina, Bahamas, Bahrain, Bangladesh, Barbados, Belize, Benin, Bhutan, Bolivia, Botswana, Brazil, Bulgaria, Burundi, Byelorussian SSR, Cape Verde, Central African Republic, Chad, Chile, Colombia, Comoros, Congo, Costa Rica, Cuba, Cyprus, Czechoslovakia, Democratic Yemen, Djibouti, Dominican Republic, Ecuador, Egypt, El Salvador, Ethiopia, Fiji, Gabon, Gambia, German Democratic Republic, Ghana, Grenada, Guatemala, Guinea, Guinea-Bissau, Guyana, Haiti, Honduras, Hungary, India, Indonesia, Iran, Iraq, Ivory Coast, Jamaica, Jordan, Kenya, Kuwait, Lao People's Democratic Republic, Lebanon, Liberia, Libyan Arab Jamahiriya, Madagascar, Malawi, Malaysia, Maldives, Mali, Malta, Mauritania, Mauritius, Mexico, Mongolia, Morocco, Mozambique, Nepal, Nicaragua, Niger, Nigeria, Oman, Pakistan, Panama, Papua New Guinea, Peru, Poland, Qatar, Romania, Rwanda, Saint Lucia, Sao Tome and Principe, Senegal, Sierra Leone, Solomon Islands, Somalia, Sri Lanka, Sudan, Suriname, Swaziland, Syrian Arab Republic, Thailand, Togo, Trinidad and Tobago, Tunisia, Uganda, Ukrainian SSR, USSR, United Arab Emirates, United Republic of Cameroon, United Republic of Tanzania, Upper Volta, Vanuatu, Venezuela, Viet Nam, Yemen, Yugoslavia, Zaire, Zambia.

Against: Belgium, France, Germany, Federal Republic of, Italy, Japan, Luxembourg, Netherlands, New Zealand, Portugal, Turkey, United Kingdom, United States.

Abstaining: Australia,[a] Austria, Canada,[a] Denmark, Finland, Greece, Iceland, Ireland, Israel, Norway, Paraguay, Philippines, Saudi Arabia, Spain, Sweden, Uruguay.

[a]Later advised the Secretariat it had intended to vote against.

Disarmament negotiations

General Assembly consideration (June/July). At the General Assembly's second special session on disarmament, the German Democratic Republic, by a letter dated 24 June 1982,[2] submitted a working paper in which it urged the Assembly to declare it the responsibility of all States, in particular the nuclear-weapon and other militarily significant States, to live up to their commitment under international instruments to conduct without pre-conditions serious arms limitation and disarmament negotiations in good faith on the basis of equality and undiminished security; the proposal added that current negotiations should be intensified, suspended negotiations resumed and new negotiations started on effective international agreements on items of highest priority.

The draft comprehensive programme of disarmament contained a number of principles in relation to disarmament negotiations, including the following: they should be based on strict observance of the purposes and principles of the Charter of the United Nations; all States had the right to participate; it was important to secure the active participation of all nuclear-weapon States, particularly those with the most important nuclear arsenals and other militarily significant States; negotiations on partial disarmament measures should be conducted concurrently with those on comprehensive measures and should be followed by negotiations on a treaty for general and complete disarmament under effective international control; they should include negotiations to limit and halt qualitative improvement of armaments; in negotiating multilateral agreements, every effort should be made to ensure their universal applicability; bilateral and regional negotiations could play an important role.[3]

The chapter of the draft programme concerned with priorities for negotiation stated that effective measures of nuclear disarmament and the prevention of nuclear war had the highest priority. Along with negotiations on those measures, it added, effective measures should be negotiated to prohibit or prevent the development, production or use of other weapons of mass destruction, as well as on the balanced reduction of armed forces and conventional armaments. A proposal to insert the words "which maintain or enhance security" after the reference to nuclear disarmament measures was left in square brackets, signifying that its inclusion had not been agreed.

During the general debate at the special session, many delegations spoke of the importance of disarmament negotiations in general as well as in relation to specific types of weapons. Reference was made both to negotiations in the Committee on Disarmament and to those conducted outside the United Nations, especially between the USSR and the United States on strategic arms limitation and on intermediate-range ballistic missiles.

Austria believed that all current and envisaged disarmament negotiations on various weapons and regions should be co-ordinated in one programme, in recognition of the fact that their results were closely interrelated. Several States, including China, made the point that all States should be enabled to participate on an equal footing in the settlement of disarmament issues. The USSR said disarmament negotiations currently under way

should be revived, those that had been suspended should be resumed and new negotiations should be started in areas where the situation called for it.

General Assembly action (December). Disarmament negotiations were referred to in four resolutions adopted by the General Assembly on 9 December.

In its resolution on international co-operation for disarmament,[5] the Assembly called on States to participate actively in disarmament negotiations and to conduct them on the basis of equality and undiminished security and the non-use of force in international relations, while refraining from developing new channels of the arms race. In a resolution on implementation of the recommendations of its 1978 special session on disarmament,[6] the Assembly urged Member States to stimulate and accelerate disarmament negotiations in good faith at all levels, and invited States engaged in such negotiations outside the United Nations to keep the Assembly and the Committee on Disarmament informed of the results. In a resolution on the work of the Committee on Disarmament,[7] the Assembly invited the Committee members involved in separate negotiations to intensify their efforts and to provide the Committee with a full report on such negotiations. The Assembly also requested the USSR and the United States to report on their bilateral nuclear-arms negotiations.[4]

Further, in a resolution of 16 December on strengthening international security,[8] the Assembly urged all States, in particular the permanent members of the Security Council, to start serious negotiations to implement the recommendations and decisions of the 1978 special session and to fulfil the priority tasks identified by that session.

The German Democratic Republic did not press for a vote on a draft resolution it had submitted under the title "Obligation of States to contribute to effective disarmament negotiations".[1] Instead, it joined as a co-sponsor of the revised draft on implementation of the recommendations of the 1978 special session, adopted by the Assembly on 9 December.

The text not pressed to a vote would have had the Assembly express alarm about the continued escalation of the arms race while disarmament negotiations were being protracted, blocked or discontinued; refer to the obligation of States to live up to their commitments in international instruments to conduct such negotiations in good faith; urge them to bring current negotiations to a successful end and to resume or start others; and call on States to intensify efforts in negotiations outside the United Nations and to refrain from actions which might have negative effects on negotiations.

Draft resolution not pressed. [1]German Democratic Republic, A/C.1/37/L.11.
Letter. [2]German Democratic Republic, 24 June, A/S-12/AC.1/30.
Report. [3]*Ad Hoc* Committee, A/S-12/32.
Resolutions (1982). GA: [4]37/78 A, 9 Dec.; [5]37/78 B, para. 1, 9 Dec.; [6]37/78 F, paras. 4 & 9, 9 Dec.; [7]37/78 G, para. 4, 9 Dec.; [8]37/118, para. 6 *(b)*, 16 Dec.

World Disarmament Campaign

The World Disarmament Campaign, aimed at informing, educating and generating public understanding and support for the disarmament objectives of the United Nations, was launched by the General Assembly on 7 June 1982, at the start of its second special session devoted to disarmament. In December, the Assembly approved the general framework for the Campaign and a 1983 programme of activities. It also invited Member States to co-operate with the United Nations to ensure a better flow of information on disarmament and called on them to encourage their citizens to express their views on disarmament questions.

Recommendations on the Campaign's objectives and other particulars were initially prepared in 1981 by a Group of Experts on the Organization and Financing of a World Disarmament Campaign under the Auspices of the United Nations.[22] These were elaborated in a report which the Secretary-General submitted to the Assembly in June 1982, outlining a programme for the Campaign. After the launching of the Campaign at the special session, agreement was reached on a text setting out its objectives, contents and modalities. These were further refined in a November report by the Secretary-General on the general framework and 1983 programme for the Campaign, which the Assembly approved in December 1982. As at 31 December 1982, two Governments had paid a total of $59,524 into the Campaign's Trust Fund and nine others had pledged $2,624,170.

General Assembly action (June/July). The Assembly's decision on 7 June to launch the Campaign was made on the recommendation, approved on 14 May, of the Preparatory Committee for the Second Special Session of the General Assembly Devoted to Disarmament.[8] As recommended by the Committee, the Secretary-General submitted to the Assembly a report[11] outlining a proposed programme for 1982-1984, based primarily on the findings of the 1981 Group of Experts.

This report was examined by Working Group III of the *Ad Hoc* Committee of the Twelfth Special Session, which produced an agreed text defining the objectives, contents and modalities of the Campaign. In view of the need for additional resources, this text stated, the Secretary-General was urged to report at the Assembly's 1982 regular session on the possibilities of redeploying existing resources. Voluntary contributions were welcomed from Member States, non-governmental organizations (NGOs) and other sources. This text was annexed to the report of the *Ad Hoc* Committee,[6] which became the Concluding Document of the special session.

The Secretary-General presented two additional reports at the special session on measures to mobilize world public opinion in favour of disarmament. One report[9] contained or referred to the views of 21 States, requested by the Assembly in December 1981,[19] on how the recommendations for the Campaign made by the Group of Experts in 1981 might be implemented. The other report[10] contained the views of 14 States, also requested by the Assembly in December 1981,[20] on a suggestion advanced by Bulgaria[23] for a worldwide collection of signatures in support of measures to prevent nuclear war, to curb the arms race and for disarmament. On the latter topic, the Secretary-General said that, while it might be too early to formulate a specific position on the questions involved, he noted the possibility, raised in the replies of States, of relating the signature-collection idea to the objectives of the World Disarmament Campaign.

The draft comprehensive programme of disarmament contained some statements about public opinion and disarmament. Stressing the need for peoples to understand the dangers involved, it said the United Nations should increase the dissemination of information on the armaments race and disarmament with the full co-operation of Member States. In particular, it added, publicity should be given to the decisions of the Assembly's special sessions on disarmament. However, agreement was not reached on a proposed section of the text relating to the mobilization of public opinion.

Five States, in communications for consideration at the special session, submitted proposals relating to the World Disarmament Campaign.

Bulgaria, by a letter to the Secretary-General dated 24 June,[1] asked the Assembly to decide to carry out, in the framework of the Campaign, a world-wide action for collecting signatures, in order to ensure the broadest public support for the decisions and recommendations of the special session.

Egypt, in a letter to the Secretary-General dated 28 June,[2] said the Campaign's effectiveness depended on governmental assistance and co-ordination; suggested a world-wide ban on war movies, toy weapons and any other materials that made the public receptive to armaments; proposed that psychological methods be used to instil disarmament and peace concepts in children; and recommended a periodic assessment by the Disarmament Commission of the relevant activities of the United Nations Department of Public Information (DPI).

Norway suggested, in a letter dated 24 June to the Chairman of the *Ad Hoc* Committee,[3] that a proposed Advisory Board on Disarmament Research and Information be entrusted with assessing activities in connection with the Campaign.

By a note verbale dated 25 June addressed to the Secretary-General,[4] Sierra Leone proposed that the the Assembly request him, within existing resources, to strengthen a number of United Nations information centres in the developing areas of the world so as to enable them to generate understanding of disarmament issues.

The United States, in a statement of 23 June to Working Group III of the *Ad Hoc* Committee, subsequently transmitted by a letter to the Secretary-General dated 28 June,[5] asserted that mobilization of public opinion, as opposed to supplying facts, was an activity unsuited to the United Nations, and stressed the need for broad access to and the presentation of a variety of viewpoints in all societies; it proposed that the Campaign include multilateral and bilateral discussion, regional seminars and literature dissemination, and that an impartial group be appointed to assess its impact.

At the concluding meetings of the special session, many speakers welcomed the launching of the Campaign as a positive outcome of the session. Mexico expressed satisfaction that the Campaign, which it had proposed to the Assembly in 1980,[21] had been launched. Finland pledged its support, including financial support, to the Campaign. The Philippines remarked that the cost of the Campaign would be infinitesimal compared to the more than $600 billion a year being spent on armaments. Also welcoming or voicing support for the Campaign were Argentina, Bangladesh, Bhutan, Bulgaria, the Byelorussian SSR, Czechoslovakia, Hungary, India, Ireland, Jamaica, Kenya, Luxembourg, Mongolia, Nepal, Romania, Somalia, Sri Lanka, the Sudan, Venezuela, Zambia and Zimbabwe.

Belgium and Norway hoped the Campaign would be addressed impartially and in a non-discriminatory manner to all nations. The United Kingdom was pleased to see the Campaign guidelines recognize the need for its universal application and for unimpeded access for all to a broad range of information and opinions. The United States also considered as vital the open and universal availability, under the Campaign, of information on disarmament matters.

The Lao People's Democratic Republic said the peace movement should be encouraged within the

framework of the Campaign. If financing could be guaranteed, said Madagascar, the Campaign could give greater scope to popular movements that supported disarmament; it hoped too that the Campaign would help make the voices of the third world heard on a subject which the major information media treated as of interest to the militarily important countries only.

Hungary supported the proposal for a worldwide collection of signatures in support of disarmament as an important element of the Campaign. The Byelorussian SSR said such activities would provide world public opinion with an important lever to influence the efforts of States towards disarmament. The Ukrainian SSR suggested that a brief appeal, based on United Nations–adopted documents on the prevention of nuclear war and on disarmament, be recommended for dissemination in United Nations Member States and for organizing the signature collection.

Another suggestion, by Romania, was for a United Nations conference of the mass media to establish measures to put an end to propaganda for armaments and war and to educate peoples for peace and against war.

Several speakers, both in the general debate and during the closing meetings of the session, referred to mass demonstrations for disarmament organized in New York City and elsewhere at the time of the special session and in the months leading up to it.

In this connection, Australia said there was a risk that, by their popular appeal, mass peace movements might divert attention from real arms control and disarmament measures. Austria believed that genuine peace movements which were not instruments of propaganda and confrontation had a crucial role in preparing the ground for the political will essential for disarmament. Canada said the Warsaw Pact countries would be ill-advised to assume that public demonstrations in the West would weaken their negotiating position. Denmark thought it wrong to view such currents of opinion as indications of defeatism or capitulation; they represented a deeply felt popular reaction that viewed a balance of terror based on unlimited quantities of nuclear weapons as insane.

France, acknowledging the resurgence of the fear of war in Western European and United States public opinion, warned that the cause of peace was not served by awakening or exploiting a war psychosis or by multiplying unilateral proposals of a vague and spectacular nature with the aim of manipulating public opinion. Supporters of the peace movement should not be dismissed as lacking sufficient insight, said the Federal Republic of Germany; their driving force should be regarded as a motivation and a moral obligation for Governments. Greece viewed the emergence of a new popular consciousness about the real dangers of nuclear weapons as a hopeful sign.

Bolivia believed that what mattered above any other type of disarmament was disarmament of the mind; if any act of disobedience was acceptable in civilized life, it was anti-war disobedience. Democratic Yemen emphasized the importance of mass rallies and demonstrations against nuclear weapons and for peace which it said had been held in a number of capitalist countries. Kuwait said such demonstrations could put pressure on Governments to transfer part of their military allocations to finance projects for improved living standards.

Mexico saw the rebirth of a pacifist anti-nuclear movement, especially in Western Europe where the siting of the bulk of nuclear weapons had been permitted, as one of the few sources of encouragement since the 1978 special session on disarmament; it believed the 1982 session had strengthened the active public interest in peace and disarmament. Expressing a similar view, Sri Lanka and Uganda commended NGOs that had contributed effectively towards disarmament. That movement, said the Philippines, must be developed into a universal force working side by side with the United Nations towards the goal of universal and complete disarmament under effective international control.

New Zealand considered that the session had helped stimulate public consciousness of the need for genuine disarmament. Pakistan said it had served as the focal point for the widespread expression of public concern. Sweden asserted that the session should be remembered as having played a catalyst for one of the most impressive public manifestations of free popular movements.

Hungary, speaking also on behalf of Bulgaria, the Byelorussian SSR, Czechoslovakia, the German Democratic Republic, Mongolia, Poland, the Ukrainian SSR and the USSR, asserted that the anti-war movement of the popular masses was a powerful force against the attempts of imperialist forces. The growing peace movement, in the view of the German Democratic Republic, showed that the desire for disarmament reflected the peoples' will.

Bangladesh suggested that the Secretary-General be asked to launch a public relations campaign to apprise the world of the deleterious impact of the unrestricted arms race. Indonesia, on the other hand, remarked that the many demonstrations and petitions for disarmament were ample proof that the people were aware of the problems caused by the arms race; it was the Governments, especially those of the nuclear-weapon Powers and other militarily significant States, that needed a greater understanding of the problems they created by their armaments race.

The importance of public information about disarmament was also stressed during the general debate at the special session. Belgium, for the European Community (EC) members, thought the United Nations Centre for Disarmament could be an appropriate means of informing public opinion; EC members would support initiatives for impartial and objective information, devoid of propaganda. France, which stressed the importance of free access to information sources, asked that United Nations information centres make available, in national languages, highlights of the speeches on various disarmament issues made by delegations at the United Nations, which should then be taken up regularly in public forums, including television. The Netherlands also considered it vital for the United Nations to provide world-wide, impartial and factual information.

Iran favoured having the United Nations disseminate information on disarmament. The Niger suggested that this take the form of drawing up a data inventory on the arms race and determining the most effective means for ensuring the widest dissemination of the information. Sierra Leone agreed and thought the United Nations should work to that end with Governments, NGOs, educational institutions and community organizations, and through a strengthened network of information centres.

Japan expressed hope that documentation and materials it would supply concerning its atomic bomb experiences would be installed at the United Nations in support of nuclear disarmament.

General Assembly action (December). As requested in the text on the World Disarmament Campaign agreed upon at the special session, the Secretary-General submitted to the Assembly in November 1982 a report outlining a general framework for the Campaign and a programme of activities for 1983.[12] According to the report, the Campaign would be implemented world-wide in a balanced, factual and objective manner, with primary focus on elected representatives, media, NGOs, educational communities and research institutes. The United Nations, and particularly its Centre for Disarmament, would provide the substance of information for the Campaign and generally co-ordinate its implementation. Member States would be encouraged to co-operate with the Organization to ensure a better flow of disarmament-related information and to avoid dissemination of false and tendentious information. Universality would be guaranteed by such co-operation and by unimpeded access for all sectors of the public to a broad range of information and opinions.

The Secretary-General proposed a series of activities for 1983, selected on the basis of their immediate impact, their multiplier effect and their ability to be carried out without extensive preparation. This programme called for the production of United Nations publications and audio-visual materials, interpersonal communication through such means as seminars and training, special events including Disarmament Week activities, publicity for the Campaign, and activities by United Nations information centres and other field offices.

The Secretary-General also transmitted to the Assembly in November a report by the United Nations Educational, Scientific and Cultural Organization (UNESCO)[13] on its contribution to the Campaign, as supported by a 4 October decision of its Executive Board (annexed to the report) inviting the Director-General to make a specific contribution to the Campaign. The report described activities planned for 1983 in the areas of education, social sciences, communication and public information. These included an Intergovernmental Conference on Education for International Understanding, Co-operation and Peace and Education relating to Human Rights and Fundamental Freedoms; an African training seminar on disarmament education; a symposium on the media and disarmament; and a brochure explaining the main concepts and conditions of disarmament.

On 13 December 1982, the General Assembly adopted three resolutions dealing with the World Disarmament Campaign.

By one of these,[17] the Assembly approved the general framework of the Campaign as specified by the Secretary-General, including the submission of an annual report to the Assembly, as well as his proposals for a programme of activities for 1983. The Assembly again invited Member States to make voluntary contributions and decided to hold a pledging conference in 1983.

The Assembly adopted this resolution without vote, following its approval in the First Committee on 26 November by a recorded vote of 129 to none. The text, introduced by Mexico, was also sponsored by Bangladesh, Colombia, Ghana, India, Romania, Sri Lanka, Sweden and Yugoslavia.

By another resolution,[16] Member States were invited, in implementing activities for the Campaign, to take into account views expressed at the special session, including the proposal on a worldwide collection of signatures in support of disarmament. They were also invited to co-operate with the United Nations to ensure a better flow of disarmament information and to avoid disseminating false and tendentious information.

The Assembly adopted this resolution by a recorded vote of 108 to none, with 33 abstentions. The First Committee had approved it on 24 November by a recorded vote of 80 to none, with 38 abstentions, on an orally revised draft introduced by Bulgaria and also sponsored by Mongolia, Romania and Viet Nam.

By the third resolution,[18] adopted without vote, the Assembly called on Member States to facilitate the flow of a broad range of accurate information on disarmament matters, both governmental and non-governmental, to and among their citizens, so as to advance the objectives of the Campaign and of general and complete disarmament under effective international control. Member States were also called upon to encourage their citizens freely and publicly to express their views on disarmament questions and to organize and meet publicly for that purpose. The Secretary-General was requested to report to the Assembly annually on implementation of the resolution.

The 12-nation draft, introduced by the United States, had been approved by the First Committee on 24 November by a recorded vote of 119 to none, with 2 abstentions (Brazil, Ireland). This action followed a decision, by a recorded vote of 42 to 2 (Kenya, Singapore), with 11 abstentions, to incorporate the adjective "accurate" to qualify "information". This had been suggested by Nigeria as an alternative to an oral amendment by the USSR for the addition of the word "*pravdivy*" (translated as "truthful" or "authentic").

The World Disarmament Campaign was mentioned in two other resolutions adopted in December. The Assembly, in its 9 December resolution on international co-operation for disarmament,[14] called on Member States to cultivate and disseminate the ideas of international co-operation for disarmament, particularly in connection with the Campaign, through such channels as their educational systems, mass media and cultural policies. It also called on UNESCO to consider, in order further to mobilize world public opinion for disarmament, measures to strengthen international co-operation for disarmament through research, education, information, communication and culture.

In a 10 December resolution on United Nations public information activities,[15] based on the recommendations of the Committee on Information,[7] the Assembly requested the Secretary-General to ensure that the Campaign gave full consideration to the role of mass media as the most effective way to promote in world public opinion a climate of understanding, confidence and co-operation conducive to peace and disarmament. He was also asked to ensure that DPI fulfilled the role assigned to it within the Campaign.

France, which voted against the resolution on international co-operation for disarmament, expressed concern that the UNESCO plans for a $2-million peace research programme, which went far beyond what was contained in the Final Document of the 1978 special session, could duplicate some of the activities of the World Disarmament Campaign.

Letters and note verbale (nv). [1]Bulgaria, 24 June, A/S-12/-AC.1/31; [2]Egypt, 28 June, A/S-12/AC.1/63; [3]Norway, 24 June, A/S-12/AC.1/32; [4]Sierra Leone, 25 June, A/S-12/-AC.1/47 *(nv);* [5]United States, 28 June, A/S-12/AC.1/51.

Reports. [6]*Ad Hoc* Committee, A/S-12/32; [7]Committee on Information, A/37/21; [8]Preparatory Committee, A/S-12/1; S-G, [9]A/S-12/14 & Add.1-3, [10]A/S-12/15 & Add.1, [11]A/S-12/27, [12]A/37/548; [13]UNESCO Director-General, transmitted by S-G note, A/37/569.

Resolutions (1982). GA: [14]37/78 B, paras. 5 & 6, 9 Dec.; [15]37/94 B, para. 14, 10 Dec.; [16]37/100 H, 13 Dec., text following; [17]37/100 I, 13 Dec., text following; [18]37/100 J, 13 Dec., text following.

Resolutions (prior). GA: [19]S-10/2, 30 June 1978 (YUN 1978, p. 39); [20]36/92 C, 9 Dec. 1981 (YUN 1981, p. 110); [21]36/92 J, 9 Dec. 1981 *(ibid.,* p. 112).

Yearbook references. [22]1980, p. 112; 1981, [23]p. 109, [24]p. 111.

Meeting records. GA: plenary, A/S-12/PV.*1,* 2-26, 28, 29 (7 June–10 July), A/37/PV.101 (13 Dec.); *Ad Hoc* Committee, A/S-12/AC.1/PV.2, 9-13 (14 June–6 July); 1st Committee, A/C.1/37/PV.3-10, 12-28, *38, 39, 42, 43, 45* (18 Oct.–26 Nov.).

General Assembly resolution 37/100 H

13 December 1982   Meeting 101   108-0-33 (recorded vote)

Approved by First Committee (A/37/670) by recorded vote (80-0-38), 24 November (meeting 42); 4-nation draft (A/C.1/37/L.34), orally revised; agenda item 133 *(d).*

Sponsors: Bulgaria, Mongolia, Romania, Viet Nam.

World Disarmament Campaign

The General Assembly,

Aware of the public concern at the dangers of the arms race, particularly the nuclear arms race, and its negative social and economic consequences,

Noting that the World Disarmament Campaign, launched by the General Assembly at its twelfth special session, the second special session devoted to disarmament, is intended to promote public interest in and support for the goals set out in the Final Document of the Tenth Special Session of the General Assembly, the first special session devoted to disarmament, in particular for the reaching of agreements on measures of arms limitation and disarmament with a view to achieving the goal of general and complete disarmament under effective international control,

Reaffirming that the universality of the World Disarmament Campaign should be guaranteed by the co-operation and participation of all States and by the widest possible dissemination of information and unimpeded access for all sectors of the public to a broad range of information and opinions on questions of arms limitation and disarmament and on the dangers relating to all aspects of the arms race and war, in particular nuclear war,

Convinced that the United Nations system, Member States, with respect for their sovereign rights, and other bodies, in particular non-governmental organizations, all have their role to play in achieving the objectives of the World Disarmament Campaign,

Taking into account the report of the Secretary-General on worldwide action for collecting signatures in support of measures to prevent nuclear war, to curb the arms race and for disarmament,

Recalling its resolution 36/92 J of 9 December 1981 and the discussions thereon at the twelfth special session of the General Assembly,

Welcoming voluntary contributions made by some Member States to carry out the objectives of the World Disarmament Campaign,

Noting with satisfaction the report of the Director-General of the United Nations Educational, Scientific and Cultural Organization on its contribution to the World Disarmament Campaign,

1. *Invites* Member States, in the implementation of the activities within the framework of the World Disarmament Campaign, to take into account various views and opinions expressed at the twelfth special session, including the proposal on launching world-wide action for collecting signatures in support of measures to prevent nuclear war, to curb the arms race and for disarmament;

2. *Also invites* Member States to co-operate with the United Nations to ensure a better flow of information with regard to the various aspects of disarmament and to avoid dissemination of false and tendentious information;

3. *Takes note* of the programme of activities for 1983 for the World Disarmament Campaign proposed by the Secretary-General and requests the Secretary-General to inform the General Assembly at its thirty-eighth session of the progress made in the implementation of the present resolution.

Recorded vote in Assembly as follows:

In favour: Afghanistan, Algeria, Angola, Bahamas, Bahrain, Bangladesh, Barbados, Benin, Bhutan, Bolivia, Botswana, Bulgaria, Burundi, Byelorussian SSR, Cape Verde, Central African Republic, Chad, Chile, Comoros, Congo, Costa Rica, Cuba, Cyprus, Czechoslovakia, Democratic Yemen, Djibouti, Dominican Republic, Ecuador, Egypt, Equatorial Guinea, Ethiopia, Fiji, Gabon, German Democratic Republic, Ghana, Grenada, Guinea, Guinea-Bissau, Guyana, Haiti, Honduras, Hungary, India, Indonesia, Iran, Iraq, Jamaica, Japan, Jordan, Kenya, Kuwait, Lao People's Democratic Republic, Lebanon, Lesotho, Liberia, Libyan Arab Jamahiriya, Madagascar, Malawi, Malaysia, Maldives, Mali, Malta, Mauritania, Mauritius, Mexico, Mongolia, Morocco, Mozambique, Nepal, Nicaragua, Niger, Nigeria, Oman, Pakistan, Panama, Papua New Guinea, Peru, Philippines, Poland, Qatar, Romania, Rwanda, Saint Lucia, Sao Tome and Principe, Senegal, Sierra Leone, Solomon Islands, Somalia, Sudan, Swaziland, Syrian Arab Republic, Thailand, Togo, Trinidad and Tobago, Tunisia, Uganda, Ukrainian SSR, USSR, United Arab Emirates, United Republic of Cameroon, United Republic of Tanzania, Upper Volta, Vanuatu, Viet Nam, Yemen, Yugoslavia, Zaire, Zambia.

Against: None.

Abstaining: Argentina, Australia, Austria, Belgium, Brazil, Canada, Colombia, Denmark, El Salvador, Finland, France, Germany, Federal Republic of, Greece, Guatemala, Iceland, Ireland, Israel, Italy, Luxembourg, Netherlands, New Zealand, Norway, Paraguay, Portugal, Saudi Arabia, Spain, Sri Lanka, Sweden, Turkey, United Kingdom, United States, Uruguay, Venezuela.

General Assembly resolution 37/100 I

13 December 1982   Meeting 101   Adopted without vote

Approved by First Committee (A/37/670) by recorded vote (129-0), 26 November (meeting 45); 9-nation draft (A/C.1/37/L.50); agenda item 133 *(d).*

Sponsors: Bangladesh, Colombia, Ghana, India, Mexico, Romania, Sri Lanka, Sweden, Yugoslavia.

World Disarmament Campaign

The General Assembly,

Recalling that, in paragraph 15 of the Final Document of the Tenth Special Session of the General Assembly, the first special session devoted to disarmament, it declared that it was essential that not only Governments but also the peoples of the world recognize and understand the dangers in the present situation and stressed the importance of mobilizing world public opinion on behalf of disarmament,

Recalling also its resolutions 35/152 I of 12 December 1980 and 36/92 C of 9 December 1981, as well as the reports of the Secretary-General of 17 September 1981 and 11 June 1982,

Noting with satisfaction that the World Disarmament Campaign contemplated in the above-mentioned resolutions and reports was solemnly launched on 7 June 1982 at the opening meeting of the twelfth special session of the General Assembly, the second special session devoted to disarmament,

Bearing in mind that at the twelfth special session the General Assembly defined in general terms the objectives, contents, modalities and financial implications of the World Disarmament Campaign and requested the Secretary-General to submit to the Assembly at its thirty-seventh session the specifics of the programme outlined in his previous report,

Having examined the report of the Secretary-General of 3 November 1982, submitted in conformity with that request,

1. *Approves* the general framework of the World Disarmament Campaign specified by the Secretary-General in his report of 3 November 1982 relating to the programme of activities for the Campaign under the auspices of the United Nations, including the provisions of its paragraph 21 relating to the submission of an annual report to the General Assembly on the implementation of the Campaign during the preceding year, and the transmission to the Assembly of the relevant views of the Advisory Board on Disarmament Studies;

2. *Also approves* the programme of activities for 1983 for the World Disarmament Campaign proposed by the Secretary-General;

3. *Reiterates* its invitation to all Member States that have not yet done so to supplement available United Nations resources with voluntary contributions;

4. *Decides* that at the thirty-eighth session of the General Assembly there should be a pledging conference for contributions from Member States for the World Disarmament Campaign;

5. *Declares again* that voluntary contributions made by non-governmental organizations, foundations and trusts and other private sources would also be welcome;

6. *Decides* to include in the provisional agenda of its thirty-eighth session the item entitled "World Disarmament Campaign".

General Assembly resolution 37/100 J

13 December 1982   Meeting 101   Adopted without vote

Approved by First Committee (A/37/670) by recorded vote (119-0-2), 24 November (meeting 43); 12-nation draft (A/C.1/37/L.65), orally amended by Nigeria; agenda item 133 *(d)*.

Sponsors: Australia, Bahamas, Costa Rica, Germany, Federal Republic of, Indonesia, Japan, Kenya, Mali, Norway, Singapore, United States, Uruguay.

**World Disarmament Campaign:
peace and disarmament movements**

The General Assembly,

Recognizing that well-informed discussion and debate on all points of view relating to disarmament issues may exercise a positive influence on the attainment of meaningful arms limitation measures, progress in disarmament and the ultimate goal of general and complete disarmament under effective international control,

Convinced that the best way to build trust and confidence and to advance the conditions which contribute to the cause of disarmament is through the co-operation and participation of all States and by the widest possible dissemination of information and unimpeded access by all sectors of the public to a broad range of information and opinion on questions of arms limitation and disarmament,

Desirous of promoting the ability of all citizens to participate in an informed and free discussion of such matters,

Recalling that the World Disarmament Campaign was launched at the twelfth special session of the General Assembly, the second special session devoted to disarmament,

Noting with satisfaction that at its twelfth special session the General Assembly called, *inter alia*, for the World Disarmament Campaign to be carried out in all regions of the world in a balanced, factual and objective manner, for the universality of the Campaign to be guaranteed by the co-operation and participation of all States and by the widest possible dissemination of information, for unimpeded access by all sectors of the public to a broad range of information and opinions, and for the Campaign to provide an opportunity for discussion and debate in all countries on all points of view relating to disarmament issues, objectives and conditions,

1. *Calls upon* Member States to facilitate the flow of a broad range of accurate information on disarmament matters, both governmental and non-governmental, to and among their citizens, with a view to the furtherance of the objectives of the World Disarmament Campaign and in order to advance the final objective of general and complete disarmament under effective international control;

2. *Calls upon* all Member States to encourage their citizens freely and publicly to express their own views on disarmament questions and to organize and meet publicly for that purpose;

3. *Requests* the Secretary-General to report annually to the General Assembly on implementation of the provisions of the present resolution.

Financing

In his November 1982 report to the General Assembly on the World Disarmament Campaign,[1] the Secretary-General estimated that $760,000 in addition to the funds already available in the United Nations budget for 1982-1983 would be required to implement the proposed programme of Campaign-related activities for 1983. Funding had to be found from various sources, such as voluntary contributions from Member States and others, and through redeployment of resources within the budget.

The Assembly, by a 13 December resolution on the Campaign,[2] again invited Member States to make voluntary contributions to supplement avail-able United Nations resources and decided to hold at its 1983 session a pledging conference for contributions from Member States for the Campaign. At the same time, the Assembly said it would welcome voluntary contributions from NGOs, foundations, trusts and other private sources.

As at 31 December 1982, two States—Iraq ($10,000) and Mexico ($49,524)—had paid contributions to the Trust Fund for the Campaign, and the German Democratic Republic had made a pledge for 1982 ($40,000). Public donations totalled $5,924. Including interest, the total 1982 income of the Fund came to $105,859. In addition, pledges for future years totalling $2,584,170 had been made by Bulgaria ($23,474), the Byelorussian SSR ($134,228), Hungary ($7,026), India ($109,290), Mongolia ($1,000), Romania ($27,273), the Ukrainian SSR ($268,456) and the USSR ($2,013,423). (All amounts are United States dollar equivalents.)

Report. [1]S-G, A/37/548.
Resolution (1982). [2]GA: 37/100 I, paras. 3-5, 13 Dec.

Proposed Universal Conscience Council

By a note verbale to the United Nations Secretariat dated 24 June 1982,[1] during the General Assembly's special session on disarmament, France proposed the creation, within the framework of the World Disarmament Campaign, of a Universal Conscience Council, composed of eminent persons representing the main categories of spiritual life, science, culture, art and philosophy. In the view of France, the Council could respond to the growing public demand for information on disarmament questions and consider proposals submitted to it by the Assembly.

As with other proposals submitted at that session, no action was taken on the French initiative.

Note verbale. [1]France, 24 June, A/S-12/AC.1/40.

Observance of Disarmament Week
(24-30 October)

Disarmament Week—proclaimed by the General Assembly in 1978[6] to start on United Nations Day, 24 October—was marked in 1982 at United Nations Headquarters at a special meeting of the Assembly's First Committee on 26 October, where statements were made by the Assembly President and the Secretary-General as well as by representatives of regional groups.

The President said the international community had reason to worry that the Assembly's June/July 1982 special session on disarmament had concluded without agreement on substantive arms limitation and disarmament issues; under those circumstances, he hoped the World Disarmament Campaign and activities during Disarmament Week would help create a climate for progress in disarmament through negotiations and agreements between Governments.

The Secretary-General, while acknowledging that the 1982 special session on disarmament had fallen short of aspirations, identified as that session's positive aspects the high level of government representation, the fact that it was the occasion for unprecedented public support for disarmament, and the inauguration of the World Disarmament Campaign; he stressed the responsibility of the nuclear-weapon States in restoring restraint and sanity, and urged the international community to work for a return to the common perception of danger and the spirit of co-operation that had characterized the 1978 special session on disarmament.[7]

A text on the World Disarmament Campaign approved at the 1982 special session and annexed to the Concluding Document which the Assembly approved on 10 July stated that, since the observance had played a useful role in fostering disarmament objectives, the week starting 24 October should continue to be widely observed as Disarmament Week.

By a resolution of 9 December on Disarmament Week,[5] the Assembly expressed appreciation to States and international and national non-governmental organizations for their participation in Disarmament Week, and invited them to inform the Secretary-General of their pertinent activities. United Nations organizations were invited to intensify, and report to the Secretary-General on, their information dissemination activities on the consequences of the arms race. The Secretary-General was requested to prepare annually, within existing resources, a compilation of information on the observance collected by Secretariat departments and United Nations information centres.

The Assembly adopted the resolution without vote. The 14-nation text, introduced by Mongolia, had been approved by the First Committee in like manner on 22 November. Mongolia had proposed at the special session, in a working paper transmitted by a note verbale to the Secretary-General dated 23 June, the continuation of the annual observance of Disarmament Week.[1]

The Secretary-General submitted to the Assembly in an annual report the replies received from five Governments concerning activities in connection with Disarmament Week 1981.[4] Also submitted to the Assembly were a letter dated 11 October 1982 from the USSR transmitting an appeal to the Assembly by participants in the Soviet peace movement in which they pledged to observe the Week,[2] and a letter dated 29 October from Viet Nam forwarding a resolution adopted at a Disarmament Week observance at Hanoi on 25 October.[3]

Letters and note verbale (nv). [1]Mongolia, 23 June, A/S-12/AC.1/26 *(nv)*; [2]USSR, 11 Oct., A/C.1/37/4; [3]Viet Nam, 29 Oct., A/C.1/37/8.
Report. [4]S-G, A/37/455 & Add.1.
Resolution (1982). [5]GA: 37/78 D, 9 Dec., text following.
Resolution (prior). [6]GA: S-10/2, 30 June 1978 (YUN 1978, p. 39).
Yearbook reference. [7]1978, p. 17.
Meeting records. GA: 1st Committee, A/C.1/37/PV.3-10, *11*, 12-28, *34*, *39* (18 Oct.–22 Nov.); plenary, A/37/PV.98 (9 Dec.).

General Assembly resolution 37/78 D

9 December 1982   Meeting 98   Adopted without vote

Approved by First Committee (A/37/662) without vote, 22 November (meeting 39); 14-nation draft (A/C.1/37/L.24); agenda item 50 *(c)*.

Sponsors: Afghanistan, Byelorussian SSR, Congo, Cuba, Czechoslovakia, German Democratic Republic, India, Japan, Lao People's Democratic Republic, Mali, Mongolia, Mozambique, Ukrainian SSR, Viet Nam.

Disarmament Week

The General Assembly,

Gravely concerned over the continuing arms race,

Emphasizing the urgent need for and the importance of wide and continued mobilization of world public opinion in support of halting and reversing the arms race, especially the nuclear-arms race in all its aspects,

Noting with satisfaction the broad and active support by Governments and international and national organizations of the decision taken by the General Assembly at its tenth special session regarding the proclamation of the week starting 24 October, the day of the foundation of the United Nations, as a week devoted to fostering the objectives of disarmament,

Recalling the recommendations concerning the World Disarmament Campaign launched by the General Assembly at its twelfth special session, in particular the recommendation that, in view of the fact that Disarmament Week has played a useful role in fostering the objectives of disarmament, the week starting 24 October should continue to be widely observed as Disarmament Week,

Recognizing the important role which the mass information organs of the United Nations can play in promoting more active involvement of governmental and public organizations in Disarmament Week,

1. *Expresses its appreciation* to all States and international and national non-governmental organizations for their energetic support of and active participation in Disarmament Week;

2. *Takes note with satisfaction* of the report of the Secretary-General on the follow-up measures undertaken by governmental and non-governmental organizations in holding Disarmament Week;

3. *Invites* all States that so desire, in carrying out appropriate measures at the local level on the occasion of Disarmament Week, to take into account the elements of the model programme for Disarmament Week, prepared by the Secretary-General;

4. *Invites* the relevant specialized agencies and the International Atomic Energy Agency to intensify activities, within their areas of competence, to disseminate information on the consequences of the arms race and requests them to inform the Secretary-General accordingly;

5. *Invites* Governments, in accordance with General Assembly resolution 33/71 D of 14 December 1978, to inform the Secretary-General of activities undertaken to promote the objectives of Disarmament Week;

6. *Invites* international non-governmental organizations to take an active part in Disarmament Week and to inform the Secretary-General of the activities undertaken;

7. *Requests* the Secretary-General to prepare annually, within existing resources, a compilation of the information collected by the relevant departments of the Secretariat, as well as at United Nations information centres, pertaining to the holding of Disarmament Week in the preceding year;

8. *Requests* the Secretary-General, in accordance with paragraph 4 of resolution 33/71 D, to submit to the General Assembly at its thirty-eighth session a report containing the information referred to in paragraphs 4 to 7 above.

Nuclear weapons

Nuclear disarmament

The dangers of war, and nuclear war in particular, were a constant theme of resolutions and speeches in the General Assembly in 1982, at both its special session devoted to disarmament (June/July) and its regular session (September-December).

Most speakers in the general debate at the special session welcomed the commencement, on 29 June at Geneva, of the strategic arms limitation and reduction talks between the USSR and the United States, as well as the continuation of talks between them on medium-range nuclear-armed missiles in Europe, which began in November 1981. In December, the Assembly asked the two Powers to report in 1983 on the state of the negotiations.

The Assembly adopted two resolutions on a nuclear-weapon freeze, one addressed to all nuclear-weapon States and the other to the USSR and the United States, asking them to proclaim an immediate halt to the production, deployment and testing of nuclear arms. It also requested the Committee on Disarmament to undertake negotiations aimed at reaching conventions to prohibit the use or threat of use of nuclear weapons under any circumstances, the development, production, stockpiling, deployment and use of the neutron bomb, and the stationing of nuclear weapons on the territories of States where currently there were no such weapons.

In December, the Assembly welcomed declarations made by the USSR and reiterated by China at the second special session on disarmament that they would not be the first to use nuclear weapons; it said the pledges offered an important avenue to decrease the danger of nuclear war and expressed hope that the other nuclear-weapon States would consider making similar declarations.

A number of actions were taken to promote various aspects of the non-proliferation of nuclear weapons, including the establishment of nuclear-weapon-free zones in various regions.

With a view to prohibiting nuclear-weapon tests, the Assembly urged the start of multilateral negotiations for a test-ban treaty in a newly established working group of the Committee on Disarmament, and asked the Committee to determine the arrangements necessary for an international seismic monitoring network and a verification system to check compliance with a ban. The Assembly urged all nuclear-weapon States to declare a moratorium on nuclear-weapon testing until a treaty was concluded. It also called for the prohibition of fissionable materials production for nuclear weapons and for agreement on legal provisions to prohibit attacks on nuclear facilities.

With the aim of providing security guarantees to non-nuclear-weapon States, the Assembly called for declarations by nuclear-weapon States as a first step towards an international convention and recommended continued negotiations in the Committee on Disarmament to find a common approach or formula.

Consideration by the Committee on Disarmament. In its special report to the 1982 special session of the General Assembly on disarmament,[3] reviewing its work from 1979 to April 1982, the Committee on Disarmament said it had attempted to identify the prerequisites and elements for multilateral negotiations on nuclear disarmament and to delineate the course of action to achieve that objective. However, while the special responsibility of nuclear-weapon States was recognized as essential for attaining nuclear disarmament, an agreed basis for negotiations in the Committee had not been achieved. Moreover, there had been no consensus on the establishment by the Committee of a subsidiary body for negotiations on nuclear disarmament.

Summarizing the views of its members on cessation of the nuclear-arms race and nuclear disarmament, the Committee said certain nuclear-weapon States held that nuclear disarmament should take place as part of a general process of disarmament and considered deterrence an essential component in maintaining equilibrium between the two major military alliances and, thus, global stability. The Group of 21 (p. 22) opposed that view, arguing that doctrines of deterrence lay at the root of the nuclear-arms race and instability in international relations; it stressed the right of all States to participate in nuclear disarmament negotiations. A group of socialist States favoured a stage-by-stage and mutually acceptable cessation of production, reduction and elimination of nuclear weapons, to be taken in parallel with measures to strengthen political and legal guarantees of the security of States; during this process the balance of nuclear arms should remain undisturbed and the security of all States remain undiminished. Another view was that only after a radical reduction of armaments by the two major Powers could the other nuclear-weapon States accept similar undertakings.

When the Committee met for the second part of its 1982 session,[4] it resumed consideration of the question mainly from 3 to 6 August and again found no consensus for the establishment of working groups proposed by the Group of 21 and others for multilateral negotiations on nuclear disarmament (p. 44).

Disarmament Commission action. In a text adopted by consensus on 28 May,[5] the Disarmament Commission expressed its profound preoccupation over the danger of war, in particular nuclear war, the prevention of which, it said, remained the most acute and urgent task of the day.

The Commission regretted the marked lack of achievements on disarmament since its 1981 session. However, it noted with satisfaction the nuclear-arms negotiations initiated at Geneva in November 1981 between the USSR and the United States and their intention to engage in further negotiations on strategic arms. The Commission again called on all States, particularly the nuclear-weapon States, to facilitate speedy progress in the multilateral negotiating body; expressed hope that negotiations outside the United Nations framework, particularly in the nuclear field, would lead to agreements on halting and reversing the arms race and reducing the danger of war; recognized that all nations had a vital interest in the achievement of disarmament and in prevention of the further spread of nuclear weapons and of the nuclear-arms race, while acknowledging the different degrees of responsibility States bore in that task; and emphasized the need to respect in nuclear disarmament negotiations the security concerns of the non-nuclear-weapon States.

The Commission considered it urgent to initiate appropriate bilateral, regional or multilateral negotiations, especially in areas with a high concentration of armaments, and to intensify negotiations already under way in Europe, which had the highest arms concentration. It also stressed the importance of initiating multilateral negotiations on questions of vital interest to both nuclear-weapon and non-nuclear-weapon States.

General Assembly consideration (June/July). In his address of 18 June 1982 to the General Assembly's special session on disarmament, the Prime Minister of Canada reiterated a "strategy of suffocation" which that country had first proposed at the 1978 special session on disarmament.[6] The strategy sought to halt the technological momentum of the nuclear-arms race through a comprehensive test ban to impede the further development of nuclear explosive devices, a halt to flight-testing of new strategic delivery vehicles, prohibition of the production of fissionable material for weapons purposes, and limitation and reduction of military spending on new strategic nuclear-weapon systems. The proposal was subsequently transmitted by a letter to the Secretary-General dated 28 June.[1]

The draft comprehensive programme of disarmament contained a number of provisions on nuclear disarmament in general as well as on its specific elements, such as non-proliferation and weapons tests.[2] Many of them were within square brackets, indicating the absence of consensus. Provisions not in this category included the following:

The chapter defining principles stated that nuclear weapons posed the greatest danger to mankind and to the survival of civilization. Nuclear disarmament should be carried out in such a way as to ensure that the security of all States was guaranteed at progressively lower levels of nuclear armaments, taking account of the quality and quantity of existing arsenals.

The chapter on disarmament measures described the complete elimination of nuclear weapons as the ultimate goal. It said all nuclear-weapon States, in particular those with the most important arsenals, bore a special responsibility in achieving nuclear disarmament. Such achievement would require urgent negotiation of agreements, at appropriate stages and with adequate verification measures, for cessation of qualitative improvement and development of nuclear-weapon systems, cessation of production of all types of nuclear weapons and their means of delivery and of fissionable material for weapons purposes, and a programme for the progressive and balanced reduction of stockpiles leading to their complete elimination at the earliest possible time.

Agreement was not reached on a section of the document dealing in greater detail with multilateral negotiations on nuclear disarmament.

In the course of the general debate at the special session, Brazil, Japan and Mauritius were among a large number of States urging priority for nuclear disarmament in view of the imminent threat posed to all humanity by the nuclear-weapon build-up. Japan, recalling that it alone had experienced atomic bombs, appealed to all nuclear-weapon States to take effective measures to ensure that such weapons would never be used again.

Countries cited a variety of figures to stress the magnitude of the nuclear threat. Thus, the Byelorussian SSR mentioned an estimate that the aggregate yield of accumulated nuclear weapons was 500 times greater than the total amount of explosives used in the entire history of war, estimated at no more than 10 megatons of TNT. Ireland and Japan said the nuclear weapons currently available had an explosive power more than a million times that of the Hiroshima bomb which had killed 150,000 people in 1945. The German Democratic Republic asserted that nuclear stockpiles contained the equivalent of 3 tons of TNT for every human being on earth, and Jamaica said the total number of nuclear warheads was currently estimated at nearly 54,000, while new generations of nuclear weapons were being developed. Singapore ob-

served that the five nuclear-weapon States—
China, France, the USSR, the United Kingdom
and the United States—reportedly possessed a
stockpile of nuclear weapons estimated at between
40,000 and 50,000, and that the USSR was
thought to have in its nuclear arsenal at least 113
twenty-megaton bombs, each having 1,600 times
the explosive power of the Hiroshima bomb.

According to the United Republic of Cameroon, it was estimated that during the 1980s
some 30 countries would achieve nuclear-weapon
capability, and that the figure could double before the end of the century. Portugal cited an estimate that, by the year 2000, about 40 countries
on various continents would have achieved that
capability.

China said the USSR and the United States
should stop testing, improving and manufacturing nuclear weapons, and should reduce by 50 per
cent all types of nuclear weapons and means of
delivery in their arsenals; after that, all other
nuclear States should follow suit and should reduce
their nuclear arsenals according to an agreed scale
and procedure. Indonesia said a 1975 proposal to
reduce nuclear-weapon stockpiles by half remained
relevant and could be initiated through a mutually agreed moratorium on new weapons development. Iraq believed that reduction by one third
in the arsenals of the two super-Powers would create positive momentum towards nuclear disarmament.

Existing nuclear arsenals were unnecessarily
large, said Norway; military security and deterrence could be maintained at considerably lower
levels of armament. The largest arsenals—those
of the USSR and the United States—should be
reduced significantly as soon as possible, Pakistan
declared; it added that early consideration should
be given to tactical nuclear weapons, whose use
would precipitate a general nuclear exchange.
Romania also favoured a substantial reduction by
the two major Powers of their nuclear weapons,
for example by 50 per cent in the first stage, as
a step towards the total elimination of nuclear
weapons.

Czechoslovakia and Hungary called for an
agreement on halting the production of all types
of nuclear weapons and on the stage-by-stage
reduction of stockpiles leading to their complete
elimination, and the Ukrainian SSR said the Assembly should urge all nuclear Powers to begin
early negotiations to that end. Finland opposed the
development and deployment of all new nuclear
weapons, their spread to new owners and their
deployment on new territories. Maldives believed
that the only approach to preventing a nuclear war
was total nuclear disarmament, starting with a
freeze on the development and production of
nuclear weapons and their means of delivery.

Among three possible approaches to nuclear disarmament, Saint Vincent and the Grenadines
preferred strategic arms reduction to either limitation or a freeze, since it could lead by stages to
the total elimination of such weapons. Somalia
favoured a programme of mutual, balanced and
significant reduction of nuclear weapons and
weapon systems, along with a convention on the
non-use of nuclear and other weapons of mass destruction. Suriname urged a commitment by the
nuclear-weapon States to the speedy conclusion of
an agreement to halt the qualitative nuclear-arms
race. In the view of Togo, a test ban should be followed by commitments to reduce and subsequently
to destroy nuclear weapons on the basis of a
timetable and under international control. Zimbabwe called for the start of negotiations on a
progressive and balanced reduction of nuclear-
weapon stockpiles and their means of delivery,
ultimately leading to the total elimination and
destruction of nuclear arsenals.

France regarded total nuclear disarmament or
a universal commitment to non-first-use of nuclear
weapons as Utopian or misleading solutions that
compounded the threat of war as long as the imbalance in conventional arms existed in Europe.
The United Republic of Tanzania, on the other
hand, said conventional arms should not be used
as an excuse for lack of progress in nuclear-arms
control and nuclear disarmament.

Letter. [1] Canada, 29 June, A/S-12/AC.1/58.
Reports. [2]*Ad Hoc* Committee, A/S-12/32; Committee on Disarmament, [3]A/S-12/2, [4]A/37/27; [5]Disarmament Commission, A/S-12/3.
Yearbook reference. [6]1978, p. 23.

Negotiations between
the USSR and the United States

The General Assembly asked in December 1982
that the USSR and the United States keep it informed about the two sets of disarmament negotiations currently under way between them at
Geneva. These were the talks on medium-range
nuclear-armed missiles in Europe (covering such
devices as SS-18 and SS-20 missiles deployed by
the USSR and Pershing-2 and cruise missiles developed by the United States), taking place since
November 1981,[5] and talks on the limitation and
reduction of strategic arms, which began on 29
June 1982. (The talks were referred to by the
United States by the acronyms INF, for
intermediate-range nuclear forces, and START, for
strategic arms reduction talks.)

**General Assembly consideration (June/
July).** At the General Assembly's special session
on disarmament (June/July 1982), no agreement
was reached on the inclusion in the draft comprehensive programme of disarmament of texts
proposing a freeze or halt in the development of
nuclear weapons and delivery vehicles pending

the outcome of negotiations between the USSR and the United States, or on references to their negotiations on strategic and medium-range weapons. The only provision to which no amendments were proposed was a paragraph stating that, pending the conclusion of further nuclear disarmament agreements, the two States should reciprocally refrain from undercutting existing strategic arms agreements concluded between them.[1]

Many speakers in the session's general debate welcomed the commencement at Geneva on 29 June of the strategic arms reduction talks between the USSR and the United States. Malta commented that the dialogue should never have been interrupted in the first place. Bulgaria remarked that both sides must show good will if the talks were to succeed and to dispel the well-founded doubts about them to the effect that they were being used as camouflage for the arms race. China, endorsing the holding of bilateral talks on nuclear weapons, expressed hope that they would not repeat the pattern of past negotiations, which had left the two sides with room to improve and develop their nuclear arms instead of cutting them back.

Austria and Sierra Leone expected the talks to lead to substantial reductions in nuclear arsenals and significant limitations on their qualitative improvement. Belgium, on behalf of the European Community (EC) members, noted with satisfaction that the two Powers had agreed to have the negotiations cover not only limitations but also significant reductions in strategic weapons. For Canada, any attempt to secure strategic advantages at the expense of the other side was doomed to failure; the impact of the current and proposed negotiations, if they succeeded, would be to produce a stable balance at a lower level of armament. The Netherlands hoped the negotiators could agree on substantial reductions of strategic weapons leading to much lower but equal levels. Australia, Bhutan, Denmark, Finland, Iceland, Italy, Japan, Luxembourg, Madagascar, Norway, Oman, Pakistan, Portugal, Singapore, Spain and Turkey also stressed the element of reductions.

Zimbabwe thought the talks should be widened to other categories of strategic nuclear weapons, while India and Madagascar said they should be enlarged to cover all nuclear-weapon systems; further, India said, a commitment by both to abide by the treaties already entered into could open up prospects for more comprehensive efforts towards nuclear disarmament. Mali hoped the negotiations would go beyond nuclear matters to tackle all essential aspects of the maintenance of peace and security.

With regard to the substance of the talks, the USSR said the United States sought reductions in land-based intercontinental ballistic missiles, in which the USSR had a numerical advantage, while deliberately blurring the United States advantage in other strategic arms, such as long-range cruise missiles; the aim was to wreck the existing parity in nuclear arms, as determined by the totality of weapons possessed by each side rather than by quantities of individual types.

The German Democratic Republic said it would be encouraging if, at the start of the negotiations, as proposed by the USSR, a moratorium on strategic weapons and their modernization could be agreed upon; however, mutually acceptable agreements could not be reached if one side demanded drastic reductions from the other while leaving its own strategic weapons untouched. The Byelorussian SSR stated that such a freeze would facilitate movement towards the radical limitation and reduction of strategic arms. The negotiations, said Mongolia and Viet Nam, should be conducted on the basis of equality and equal security; any attempt to win military superiority, Viet Nam added, would produce a deadlock. Making the same point, the Ukrainian SSR said both sides should seek to maintain a military-strategic balance, with full regard for the national interest.

The United States outlined what it described as a two-phased approach to strategic arms reduction, originally announced on 9 May; in the first phase, the number of ballistic missile warheads on each side would be reduced to about 5,000—which it said was about half the current United States number—and no more than half of the remaining warheads would be on land-based missiles; in the second phase, each side's overall destructive power would be reduced to equal levels, including a mutual ceiling on ballistic missile throw-weight below the current United States level. The Federal Republic of Germany commented that it had become possible, as a result of the United States proposal for substantial reductions, to make a decisive contribution to future stability.

Nepal said an agreement setting a ceiling on the quality and quantity of strategic weapons was unacceptable; the two Powers should agree on a balanced and verifiable reduction leading ultimately to the total elimination of nuclear weapons. Pakistan said it seemed essential to hold in abeyance the qualitative development of nuclear-weapon systems, which could complicate the negotiations.

Finland considered that the strategic dialogue between the USSR and the United States constituted in itself an arms control measure of vital importance, but expressed regret that the Treaty known as SALT II (the Treaty between the United States of America and the Union of Soviet Socialist Republics on the Limitation of Strategic Offensive Arms), which had emerged from the second phase (1972-1979) of the strategic arms limitation talks, had not formally entered into force.

Ethiopia, Nigeria, Papua New Guinea and Sierra Leone also regretted that the Treaty remained unratified, Nigeria adding the hope that both sides would conduct themselves in line with its provisions until a more satisfactory agreement was reached. Ireland and Zimbabwe called for early ratification. Belgium (for the EC members), Ethiopia, the Federal Republic of Germany, Nepal, the Netherlands, New Zealand, Somalia, Sweden, Turkey and Uruguay were pleased that the two Powers had declared their intention to continue to respect SALT II. Honduras said the two Powers should be urged to maintain and comply with the measures negotiated at their past talks.

Sweden viewed the failure to ratify SALT II as a serious reversal for efforts to control development of strategic arms. The USSR asserted that the action by the United States to shelve SALT II had dealt a heavy blow to international confidence and security.

Ireland expressed hope that all of the nuclear Powers could eventually be brought to participate in such talks. Similarly, Brazil urged a firm commitment by the nuclear-weapon States to begin negotiations on nuclear disarmament questions without delay. While welcoming the resumption of talks, France said it could not participate directly or indirectly in negotiations that must for the time being remain bilateral; unlike the two super-Powers with excess armament, France had no choice but to rely on nuclear deterrence, limited to the absolute minimum, as a means of warding off the threat of vastly superior forces.

A number of speakers referred to the negotiations between the two Powers on intermediate-range nuclear-armed missiles in Europe. The dangers of deploying such missiles were referred to by some speakers. Austria noted that some of them were a particular threat to stability because their location and speed drastically reduced the warning-time in case of attack. Mexico observed that if agreement was not reached promptly, nearly 500 such missiles would be deployed in Western Europe in 1983, with no reduction in the number of SS-20 missiles.

The United States said it had proposed in February to cancel its deployment of Pershing-2 ballistic missiles and ground-launched cruise missiles in exchange for USSR elimination of its SS-20, SS-4 and SS-5 missiles. Supporting this proposal, the Federal Republic of Germany said the elimination of an entire category of weapons would be a major step towards genuine disarmament. Italy stated that the massive reinforcements of USSR intermediate-range missiles had created a nuclear imbalance in Europe which countries of the North Atlantic Treaty Organization (NATO)

had had to remedy by deciding to modernize their own forces while expediting negotiations for the reduction of such arms. Also supporting the United States proposal, Portugal said the alternative proposal of freezing the current situation seemed unacceptable; instead, it called for negotiations for the withdrawal of such weapons from Europe. Turkey and the United Kingdom also spoke favourably of the proposal.

Morocco thought the proposal for a one-third cut was bound to make a positive contribution to nuclear disarmament. Samoa saw it as a step in the right direction, though certainly not removing the threat of a nuclear holocaust. Norway hoped as a first step for the total elimination of land-based intermediate-range missiles.

The USSR said it had unilaterally ceased further deployment, and begun considerable reduction, of medium-range missiles in the European part of the country, and no additional missiles of that category would be deployed in areas where Western European countries would be within their range. Afghanistan, Czechoslovakia and Poland welcomed the USSR initiative, which Afghanistan said the United States and other NATO countries should reciprocate. The German Democratic Republic asserted that the decision to station United States medium-range missiles in Western Europe was designed to tip the military balance in Central Europe decisively in favour of NATO.

Japan said the greatly increased deployment of USSR intermediate-range missiles had induced the plan to deploy such weapons in Western Europe and was also increasing security concerns in Asia; it appealed to the USSR to agree to abolish all ground-launched intermediate-range nuclear missiles throughout its territory and appealed to the United States to respond by not deploying its planned new missiles in Europe.

In Albania's view, the disarmament problem could not be resolved by the bilateral talks between the USSR and the United States, which disguised the deals they made at the expense of sovereign peoples and countries; their proposals were aimed not at disarmament but at guaranteeing supremacy over the other. Iran maintained that disarmament negotiations, such as SALT, achieved no results but simply wasted time and fell behind the rapid progress of technology. Mexico, referring to SALT as an attempt to institutionalize and control the nuclear-arms race, remarked that after 10 years of negotiations the super-Powers had not eliminated a single nuclear warhead from their arsenals but had merely transformed the chaotic arms race of the 1950s and 1960s into a more orderly and controlled race. Qatar said the adoption of the theory of a balance of nuclear terror had reduced humanity's dream of comprehensive disarmament to a mere attempt to agree on the limitation of strategic arms, and even that attempt had been deadlocked.

General Assembly action (December). By a resolution on bilateral nuclear-arms negotiations adopted on 9 December 1982,[2] the General Assembly requested the USSR and the United States to transmit to the Secretary-General by 1 September 1983 a joint report or two separate reports on the stage reached in their negotiations, to be considered by the Assembly as a new agenda item. It also requested the two negotiating parties to bear constantly in mind that not only their national interests but also the vital interests of all the peoples of the world were at stake.

The resolution was adopted by a recorded vote of 114 to 1, with 32 abstentions. The First Committee had approved the text on 23 November, as revised by its sponsors, by a recorded vote of 99 to 1, with 28 abstentions.

Also on 9 December, in a resolution on implementation of the recommendations and decisions of the 1978 special session,[3] the Assembly called on nuclear-weapon States engaged in separate negotiations on nuclear disarmament to exert the utmost effort to achieve concrete results and thus contribute to the success of multilateral negotiations on nuclear disarmament.

Mexico recalled when introducing the resolution on bilateral nuclear-arms negotiations—sponsored also by Colombia, Ghana, Indonesia, Sweden and Yugoslavia—that the Assembly, in the Final Document of the Tenth Special Session (1978),[4] had stressed the need for the United Nations to be kept informed of all disarmament developments, without prejudice to the progress of negotiations. However, no official information had been submitted to the United Nations concerning either set of bilateral talks taking place at Geneva. Mexico added that the resolution was similar to earlier ones requesting information on the SALT talks.

In explanation of its negative vote, the United States said that, while it had already provided the Committee with information on the negotiations and intended to continue that endeavour, the call for reports by a deadline and for their subsequent debate would only prove prejudicial or harmful to the progress of complex and difficult negotiations which, by their nature, required a degree of confidentiality. The USSR, which abstained, said it could not accept the obligation to submit a report, nor could it support the inclusion of the item on the 1983 Assembly agenda.

Belgium, France, the Federal Republic of Germany, Greece, Italy and Turkey abstained because they did not feel the request contained in the text could contribute positively to the negotiations; the relevant provision of the 1978 Final Document, they pointed out, clearly stated that the United

Nations should be kept duly informed without prejudice to the progress of negotiations. In the United Kingdom's view, it might be harmful to request the participants in such sensitive negotiations to transmit reports by arbitrary dates; although the text might have justified a negative vote, the United Kingdom abstained as the resolution was addressed directly to the two parties concerned. Belgium and Italy expressed regret that the Committee had not been given an opportunity to work on a text which could have been adopted by consensus.

Voting in favour, Argentina said that competent multilateral bodies, particularly the Committee on Disarmament, should receive adequate and reliable information on the progress of bilateral negotiations without prejudicing their confidential nature or their progress. Cyprus voted likewise to emphasize that the USSR and the United States could negotiate successfully to reduce armaments while the arms race was going on.

Regarding the substance of the talks, the USSR said the United States proposals on strategic arms concentrated on reducing land-based, multi-stage ballistic missiles such as the Soviet SS-18 missile—a type which accounted for about 70 per cent of USSR warheads—while allowing the United States to deploy new MX intercontinental ballistic missiles, Trident-1 and -2 submarine-based missiles, B-1-B strategic bombers and long-range cruise missiles. Instead, the USSR thought it essential to take a comprehensive look at all the strategic potentials of both sides so as to avoid a sharp disruption of the existing balance, detrimental to the security interests of one side. Regarding medium-range nuclear missiles, the USSR proposed to start with a major reduction of all types of medium-range missiles and aircraft, down to a level of 300 units on each side—NATO and the USSR. However, the United States proposals would leave the quantity of NATO weapons undiminished while those in the European part of the USSR would be cut by more than half.

The United States said the first objective of its nuclear-arms policy was to eliminate the destabilizing emphasis in the USSR arsenal on intermediate-range and intercontinental ground-based ballistic missiles, which were swifter, more accurate, more destructive and less vulnerable than other nuclear weapons. Accordingly, the United States proposed the complete elimination, on both sides, of intermediate-range missiles, and equal ceilings, at much lower levels, on intercontinental missiles, which would reduce the USSR lead in those weapons. However, the USSR proposed a moratorium on intermediate-range missiles for the duration of the negotiations, which would preserve its advantage and remove any Soviet incentive for agreeing to serious reductions, and its proposals for limitation sought to include the defensive British and French missiles while refusing to negotiate on USSR missiles in the Far East. The Soviet proposals for reductions and restrictions on modernization of intercontinental missiles would preserve the USSR advantage in those weapons as well.

Report. (1)*Ad Hoc* Committee, A/S-12/32.
Resolutions (1982). GA, 9 Dec.: (2)37/78 A, text following; (3)37/78 F, para. 8.
Resolution (prior). (4)GA: S-10/2, 30 June 1978 (YUN 1978, p. 39).
Yearbook reference. (5)1981, p. 38.
Meeting records. GA: plenary, A/S-12/PV.2-26, 28, 29 (8 June– 10 July), A/37/PV.98 (9 Dec.); 1st Committee, A/C.1/37/PV.3-10, 12, *13*, 14, *15*, 16-26, *27*, 28, *29, 39, 40* (18 Oct.–23 Nov.).

General Assembly resolution 37/78 A

9 December 1982   Meeting 98   114-1-32 (recorded vote)

Approved by First Committee (A/37/662) by recorded vote (99-1-28), 23 November (meeting 40); 6-nation draft (A/C.1/37/L.12/Rev.1); agenda item 50.

Sponsors: Colombia, Ghana, Indonesia, Mexico, Sweden, Yugoslavia.

Bilateral nuclear-arms negotiations

The General Assembly,

Recalling that at its tenth special session, the first special session devoted to disarmament, it approved by consensus a Declaration, contained in section II of the Final Document of that session, in which, *inter alia,* it proclaimed that, in order effectively to discharge the central role and primary responsibility in the sphere of disarmament which belong to the United Nations in accordance with its Charter, the United Nations should be kept appropriately informed of all steps in this field, whether unilateral, bilateral, regional or multilateral, without prejudice to the progress of negotiations,

Recalling also that at its twelfth special session, the second special session devoted to disarmament, Member States reiterated their solemn commitment to implement the Final Document of the Tenth Special Session, the validity of which received their unanimous and categorical reaffirmation,

Noting that the Union of Soviet Socialist Republics and the United States of America have been carrying out at Geneva two series of bilateral nuclear-arms negotiations, begun on 30 November 1981 and 29 June 1982 respectively,

1. *Requests* the Governments of the Union of Soviet Socialist Republics and the United States of America to transmit to the Secretary-General, not later than 1 September 1983, a joint report or two separate reports on the stage reached in their above-mentioned negotiations, for consideration by the General Assembly at its thirty-eighth session;

2. *Also requests* the two negotiating parties to bear constantly in mind that not only their national interests but also the vital interests of all the peoples of the world are at stake in this question;

3. *Decides* to include in the provisional agenda of its thirty-eighth session an item entitled "Bilateral nuclear-arms negotiations".

Recorded vote in Assembly as follows:

In favour: Afghanistan, Algeria, Angola, Antigua and Barbuda, Argentina, Austria, Bahamas, Bahrain, Bangladesh, Barbados, Belize, Benin, Bhutan, Bolivia, Botswana, Brazil, Burma, Burundi, Cape Verde, Central African Republic, Chad, Chile, China, Colombia, Comoros, Congo, Costa Rica, Cyprus, Democratic Kampuchea, Democratic Yemen, Djibouti, Dominican Republic, Ecuador, Egypt, El Salvador, Ethiopia, Fiji, Finland, Gabon, Gambia, Ghana, Guatemala, Guinea, Guinea-Bissau, Guyana, Haiti, Honduras, India, Indonesia, Iran, Iraq, Ireland, Ivory Coast, Jamaica, Jordan, Kenya, Kuwait, Lebanon, Liberia, Libyan Arab Jamahiriya, Madagascar, Malawi, Malaysia, Maldives, Mali, Malta, Mauritania, Mauritius, Mexico, Morocco, Mozambique, Nepal, Nicaragua, Niger, Nigeria, Oman, Pakistan, Panama, Papua New Guinea, Paraguay, Peru, Philippines, Qatar, Romania, Rwanda, Saint Lucia, Sao Tome and Principe, Saudi Arabia, Sierra Leone, Singapore, Solomon Islands, Somalia, Sri Lanka, Sudan, Suriname, Swaziland, Sweden, Syrian Arab Republic, Thailand, Togo, Trinidad and Tobago, Tunisia, Uganda, United Arab Emirates, United Republic of Cameroon, United Republic of Tanzania, Upper Volta, Uruguay, Vanuatu, Venezuela, Yemen, Yugoslavia, Zaire, Zambia.

Against: United States.

Abstaining: Australia, Belgium, Bulgaria, Byelorussian SSR, Canada, Cuba, Czechoslovakia, Denmark, France, German Democratic Republic, Germany, Federal Republic of, Greece, Grenada, Hungary, Iceland, Israel, Italy, Japan, Lao People's Democratic Republic, Luxembourg, Mongolia, Netherlands, New Zealand, Norway, Poland, Portugal, Spain, Turkey, Ukrainian SSR, USSR, United Kingdom, Viet Nam.

Proposed working group

The Committee on Disarmament, in its special report to the 1982 special session of the General Assembly on disarmament covering the period from 1979 to April 1982,(1) said in regard to its consideration of nuclear disarmament that there had been no consensus on the establishment by the Committee of a subsidiary body for negotiations on the subject.

When the Committee met for the second part of its 1982 session,(2) it resumed consideration of the question mainly from 3 to 6 August and again found no consensus on proposals by the Group of 21 (p. 22) and others for the establishment of working groups for multilateral negotiations on nuclear disarmament. It reported to the Assembly that some nuclear-weapon States saw a lack of suitable conditions for multilateral negotiations on nuclear disarmament in the Committee as a whole; they believed that in the first instance such negotiations should be undertaken by nuclear-weapon States, as was happening in the two sets of talks between the USSR and the United States. The Group of 21 disagreed with that view, holding that multilateral negotiations in the Committee were essential and reiterating that all States had the right to participate in negotiations.

By a resolution of 9 December,(3) the Assembly called on the Committee on Disarmament to proceed without delay to negotiations on the cessation of the nuclear arms race and nuclear disarmament. The Assembly asked the Committee especially to elaborate a nuclear-disarmament programme and to establish for that purpose an *ad hoc* working group. In the preamble of the resolution, the Assembly stated that the dangerous doctrines of limited or protracted nuclear war could lead to a new twist in the spiral of the arms race, thereby hampering agreement on nuclear disarmament.

The resolution was adopted by a recorded vote of 118 to 19, with 9 abstentions. The First Committee had approved the text on 24 November, as revised by its 13 sponsors, by a recorded vote of 94 to 18, with 10 abstentions.

In another 9 December resolution, on the work of the Committee on Disarmament,(4) the Assembly urged the Committee to establish, as a matter of urgency, an *ad hoc* working group on the cessation of the nuclear-arms race and nuclear disarmament.

Introducing the 13-nation draft by Eastern European States and others, the German Democratic Republic said the Assembly should oppose doctrines such as nuclear deterrence and support proposals to prevent nuclear war and achieve nuclear disarmament. The proposed multilateral negotiations, with all nuclear-weapon States participating to define the stages of nuclear disarmament, would complement rather than prejudice ongoing bilateral negotiations.

In explanation of its negative vote, Belgium maintained that the Committee on Disarmament should decide on how to approach the preparation of a programme; it added that the text failed to condemn the threat or use of force in international relations or recall the right to legitimate self-defence, and contained unilateral and polemical references in its preamble. Greece explained its abstention by saying that priority given to nuclear disarmament should not be at the expense of conventional disarmament; further, what was lacking was the political will, rather than another *ad hoc* group, to achieve disarmament.

Austria voted in favour because of its support for the basic thrust of the operative part of the resolution but said it did not agree with elements of the preamble. Brazil voted in favour on the understanding that the nuclear-disarmament programme mentioned in the resolution related to the comprehensive, phased programme referred to in the Final Document of the Assembly's 1978 special session on disarmament,[5] and that negotiations on such a programme should not be considered as a prerequisite for negotiations on cessation of the nuclear-arms race. Finland voted in favour as it believed that efforts to halt the nuclear-arms race should be intensified and that the nuclear-arms build-up, particularly in Europe, should be brought within the scope of negotiations; however, it would have preferred more general language in the preambular paragraphs referring to limited nuclear war, as it was concerned at all doctrines which might bring nearer the possibility of a nuclear war.

Reports. Committee on Disarmament, [1]A/S-12/2, [2]A/37/27.
Resolutions (1982). GA, 9 Dec.: [3]37/78 C, text following; [4]37/78 G, para. 1.
Resolution (prior). [5]GA: S-10/2, 30 June 1978 (YUN 1978, p. 39).
Meeting records. GA: 1st Committee, A/C.1/37/PV.3-10, 12-28, *33*, 38, 42, *43* (18 Oct.–24 Nov.); plenary, A/37/PV.98 (9 Dec.).

General Assembly resolution 37/78 C

9 December 1982   Meeting 98   118-19-9 (recorded vote)

Approved by First Committee (A/37/662) by recorded vote (94-18-10), 24 November (meeting 43); 13-nation draft (A/C.1/37/L.21/Rev.1); agenda item 50 *(d)*.

Sponsors: Bulgaria, Byelorussian SSR, Cuba, Czechoslovakia, German Democratic Republic, Hungary, Lao People's Democratic Republic, Mongolia, Poland, Romania, Ukrainian SSR, USSR, Viet Nam.

Nuclear weapons in all aspects

The General Assembly,

Recalling that at its twelfth special session, the second special session devoted to disarmament, it expressed its profound preoccupation over the danger of war, in particular nuclear war, the prevention of which remains the most acute and urgent task of the present day,

Reaffirming once again that nuclear weapons pose the most serious threat to mankind and its survival and that it is therefore essential to proceed with nuclear disarmament and the complete elimination of nuclear weapons,

Reaffirming also that all nuclear-weapon States, in particular those which possess the most important nuclear arsenals, bear a special responsibility for the fulfilment of the task of achieving the goals of nuclear disarmament,

Stressing again that existing arsenals of nuclear weapons alone are more than sufficient to destroy all life on earth, and bearing in mind the devastating results which nuclear war would have on belligerents and non-belligerents alike,

Recalling that at its tenth special session, the first special session devoted to disarmament, it decided that effective measures of nuclear disarmament and the prevention of nuclear war had the highest priority and that it was essential to halt and reverse the nuclear-arms race in all its aspects in order to avert the danger of war involving nuclear weapons,

Recalling further that, in its resolution 35/152 B of 12 December 1980, it noted with alarm the increased risk of a nuclear catastrophe associated both with the intensification of the nuclear-arms race and with the adoption of the new doctrine of limited or partial use of nuclear weapons giving rise to illusions of the admissibility and acceptability of a nuclear conflict,

Noting with alarm that to the doctrine of a limited nuclear war was later added the concept of a protracted nuclear war,

Noting also with alarm that these dangerous doctrines lead to a new twist in the spiral of the arms race, which may seriously hamper the reaching of agreement on nuclear disarmament,

Stressing the urgent need for the cessation of the development and deployment of new types and systems of nuclear weapons as a step on the road to nuclear disarmament,

Stressing again that priority in disarmament negotiations should be given to nuclear weapons, and referring to paragraphs 49 and 54 of the Final Document of the Tenth Special Session of the General Assembly,

Recalling its resolutions 33/71 H of 14 December 1978, 34/83 J of 11 December 1979, 35/152 B and C of 12 December 1980 and 36/92 E of 9 December 1981,

Noting that the Committee on Disarmament, during its session held in 1982, discussed the question of the cessation of the nuclear-arms race and nuclear disarmament and, in particular, the establishment of an *ad hoc* working group for negotiations on that question,

Regretting, however, that the Committee on Disarmament was unable to reach agreement on the establishment of an *ad hoc* working group for the purpose of undertaking multilateral negotiations on the question of the cessation of the nuclear-arms race and nuclear disarmament,

Considering that efforts will continue to be made in order to enable the Committee on Disarmament to fulfil its negotiating role with regard to the cessation of the nuclear-arms race and nuclear disarmament, bearing in mind the high priority accorded to this question in the Final Document of the Tenth Special Session,

Convinced that the Committee on Disarmament is the most suitable forum for the preparation and conduct of negotiations on nuclear disarmament,

1. *Calls upon* the Committee on Disarmament to proceed without delay to negotiations on the cessation of the nuclear-arms race and nuclear disarmament, in accordance with paragraph 50 of the Final Document of the Tenth Special Session of the General Assembly, and especially to elaborate a nuclear-disarmament programme, and to establish for this purpose an *ad hoc* working group on the cessation of the nuclear-arms race and on nuclear disarmament;

2. *Decides* to include in the provisional agenda of its thirty-eighth session an item entitled "Cessation of the nuclear-arms race and nuclear disarmament: report of the Committee on Disarmament".

Recorded vote in Assembly as follows:

In favour: Afghanistan, Algeria, Angola, Antigua and Barbuda, Argentina, Austria, Bahamas, Bahrain, Bangladesh, Barbados, Belize, Benin, Bhutan, Bolivia, Botswana, Brazil, Bulgaria, Burma, Burundi, Byelorussian SSR, Cape Verde, Central African Republic, Chad, Chile, Colombia, Comoros, Congo, Costa Rica, Cuba, Cyprus, Czechoslovakia, Democratic Yemen, Djibouti, Dominican Republic,

Ecuador, Egypt, El Salvador, Ethiopia, Fiji, Finland, Gabon, Gambia, German Democratic Republic, Ghana, Grenada, Guinea, Guinea-Bissau, Guyana, Haiti, Honduras, Hungary, India, Indonesia, Iran, Iraq, Ireland, Ivory Coast, Jamaica, Jordan, Kenya, Kuwait, Lao People's Democratic Republic, Liberia, Libyan Arab Jamahiriya, Madagascar, Malawi, Malaysia, Maldives, Mali, Malta, Mauritania, Mauritius, Mexico, Mongolia, Morocco, Mozambique, Nepal, Nicaragua, Niger, Nigeria, Oman, Pakistan, Panama, Papua New Guinea, Peru, Poland, Qatar, Romania, Rwanda, Saint Lucia, Sao Tome and Principe, Senegal, Sierra Leone, Singapore, Solomon Islands, Sri Lanka, Sudan, Suriname, Swaziland, Sweden, Syrian Arab Republic, Thailand, Togo, Trinidad and Tobago, Tunisia, Uganda, Ukrainian SSR, USSR, United Arab Emirates, United Republic of Cameroon, United Republic of Tanzania, Upper Volta, Vanuatu, Venezuela, Viet Nam, Yemen, Yugoslavia, Zambia.

Against: Australia, Belgium, Canada, Denmark, France, Germany, Federal Republic of, Iceland, Israel, Italy, Japan, Luxembourg, Netherlands, New Zealand, Norway, Portugal, Spain, Turkey, United Kingdom, United States.

Abstaining: Greece, Guatemala, Lebanon, Paraguay, Philippines, Saudi Arabia, Somalia, Uruguay, Zaire.

Prevention of nuclear war

General Assembly consideration (June/July). At the General Assembly's second special session devoted to disarmament, in June/July 1982, the prevention of nuclear war was discussed by Working Group III of the *Ad Hoc* Committee of the Twelfth Special Session.[7] That body considered three proposals by delegations and a report by the Secretary-General[10] containing replies received from 18 States in response to a December 1981 Assembly resolution[13] requesting their views on the subject.

Of the three proposals (annexed to the *Ad Hoc* Committee's report), one by Bulgaria called for outlawing the use of nuclear weapons and the waging of nuclear war and urged all nuclear-weapon States to assume an obligation not to be the first to use nuclear weapons. Measures proposed in a text by the Federal Republic of Germany, Japan and the Netherlands included greater openness on military budgets and other matters, expanded exchange of information on military strategy, improved communications between Governments by the establishment of "hot lines" and other methods, and agreement by the two major nuclear-weapon States on significant and verifiable reductions. An Indian proposal called for prohibition of the threat or use of nuclear weapons, a nuclear freeze to halt the growth of arsenals and an immediate suspension of all nuclear-weapon testing.

A drafting group established by the *Ad Hoc* Committee to continue consideration of the proposals failed to reach agreement, and the Assembly decided to transmit them for consideration at its regular 1982 session along with five draft resolutions submitted to the Committee. One of these was a text by India[2] which would have had the Assembly call for a convention to prohibit the use or threat of use of nuclear weapons, cessation of nuclear-weapon testing and a freeze on development, production and deployment. The other four proposals were more specific, two of them calling for a nuclear-weapon freeze and the others for the establishment of a group of eminent persons on methods

of avoiding nuclear war and for a convention to prohibit the use of nuclear weapons.

The draft comprehensive programme of disarmament referred to this issue in its chapter on principles, in an agreed paragraph saying that all States, in particular nuclear-weapon States, should consider various proposals for avoiding nuclear-weapon use and for preventing nuclear war. However, there was no consensus on specific provisions in this regard for inclusion in the chapter on disarmament measures.

In a 6 July note verbale to the Secretary-General,[5] the German Democratic Republic transmitted the text of an appeal for action against the threat of a nuclear catastrophe, adopted at Dresden on 29 June by the twentieth co-ordination meeting of national commissions of socialist countries for the United Nations Educational, Scientific and Cultural Organization.

The horrors of nuclear war were cited by many speakers during the general debate. Sweden said those directly involved in the hostilities would suffer enormous material and human losses; radioactive fall-out would spread death and destruction far from the theatre of war and long after the last charge had exploded; a nuclear war would cause economic collapse, and in the aftermath would come hunger, lack of necessities and shortage of usable water; the very prerequisites for human life would be extinguished over large areas.

The threat of nuclear war must be removed immediately, said Brazil; a task of such urgency could not await ideal political conditions or dramatically irreversible situations. Finland said an international agreement on the prevention of nuclear war could be envisaged as a confidence-building measure. Israel suggested a three-stage peace plan: first, all nations would sign a treaty renouncing aggressive war; second, the nuclear Powers would negotiate a nuclear non-aggression pact; and third, nuclear-weapon-free zones would be successively established. Although the nuclear Powers were directly responsible for the threatening situation, said Qatar, the other countries shared the responsibility for saving humanity from a war that could be triggered by a wrong evaluation or even by malfunction of the push-buttons at a missile site. Sierra Leone was among many States expressing the view that the Assembly must formulate practical and concrete measures to prevent a nuclear catastrophe.

Ghana, challenging the thesis that nuclear war was impossible because no one would start a conflict with such devastating consequences, said it must be recognized that the unprecedented scientific and technical advances had brought about no improvement in human nature; given the right conditions, nuclear war was just as possible as the conventional wars occurring with such abandon.

France regarded nuclear deterrence as an arm of peace between East and West; it saw two potential threats of major conflict—the possibility of a nuclear first-strike by one super-Power hoping thereby to prevent such an attack by the other, and aggression by means of conventional or chemical weapons in Europe initiated by a Power convinced that the level of its nuclear means sheltered it from the highest form of nuclear retaliation. The best way to avoid nuclear war, said Italy, was to avoid all conflicts through respect for international law, strengthening of United Nations machinery for security and dispute settlement, and general and complete disarmament. Declaring that nuclear weapons had kept the peace between East and West for 37 years, the United Kingdom said it would be a perilous pretence to suggest that a system better than nuclear deterrence currently existed between East and West; the United Kingdom's approach to the prevention of war was not through simple declarations of good intentions but to seek specific, balanced and verifiable arms control and disarmament agreements which conserved or enhanced existing levels of security.

The argument of the deterrent value of nuclear weapons was questioned by Burma, which said it presupposed a readiness to resort if necessary to the use or threat of nuclear weapons—an action contrary to the Charter of the United Nations—and would inevitably result in an endless process of balancing and competition among nations with a view to maintaining military superiority over an adversary, thereby setting in motion the vicious circle of distrust, suspicion, fear and insecurity, with a spiralling arms race. Although the enormity of nuclear war created an inhibiting mechanism that had preserved the world from catastrophe so far, said Colombia, no one could predict when or under what pressures a prudent statesman would become a pitiless aggressor or a powerful nation would place its fate and the fate of others in the hands of a dangerous bully or an unscrupulous fanatic.

Kenya rejected deterrence as a theory which promoted the super-Power arms race and increased opportunities for military confrontation between their alliances. Along the same lines, India said such an idea blocked nuclear disarmament and implied that peace should forever remain hostage to nuclear weapons and that the perceived security of some nations was to be equated with peace throughout the world; nuclear-war doctrines were essentially doctrines of terrorism practised by States.

A number of speakers saw a fallacy in the idea that nuclear war, once it began, could be limited to certain so-called tactical or battlefield weapons. Thus, Bulgaria said that any use of nuclear weapons, no matter where, would immediately lead to a world-wide thermonuclear conflict. Greece believed that any seemingly limited nuclear war would rapidly escalate into a more general nuclear war. Jordan believed that the use of any kind of nuclear weapon by one side would be countered by the other side, leading to an all-out nuclear conflagration. It was difficult, said Luxembourg, to believe in the possibility of a limited nuclear war. Malta stated that the detonation of even one nuclear weapon would unleash a military and psychological situation hardly anyone could begin to imagine. Similarly, Mozambique said a nuclear war would inevitably assume universal dimensions owing to its own dynamics and the high technological level of modern weapons.

The idea that a nuclear war was winnable was also mentioned during the debate as a factor adding to the threat that such a war could occur. Cyprus said such a misconception increased the temptation to strike first and raised the chances of nuclear war by miscalculation or accident. The world seemed to have become so used to the possibility that nuclear weapons would eventually be used, said Samoa, that preparation for survival after a nuclear holocaust was seen as a logical and legitimate exercise of man's ingenuity.

The USSR denounced such doctrines as first nuclear strike and a winnable nuclear war, which the Ukrainian SSR said were aimed at blurring the distinction between nuclear and conventional weapons, creating a psychological climate of acceptability for the use of nuclear weapons, reconciling people to nuclear war and the unprecedented arms race, and getting them to give up the struggle against the nuclear threat. Zaire remarked that the image of a powerful enemy presented in the mass media created feelings of fear and hatred, preventing rational debate and giving credence to such outrageous concepts as first-strike capability, the theory of deterrence, the indispensable balance of forces, the inevitability of armed peace, and limited and preventive nuclear war.

Bangladesh proposed that nuclear-weapon States make joint or individual declarations not to use nuclear weapons, and suggested that the Security Council consider practical measures to avert the danger of nuclear war through accident or miscalculation. Mauritius hoped that proposals to avoid the risks of an unintentional nuclear war would be considered by the Committee on Disarmament and other disarmament bodies. Guyana urged that all nuclear-weapon States agree on the complete prohibition of the use or threat of use of nuclear weapons under any circumstances. Pakistan hoped decisions would be taken, especially by the nuclear Powers, to reduce the danger that nuclear war could break out through miscalculation or technical failure.

Consideration by the Committee on Disarmament. During the August/September session of the Committee on Disarmament, in connection with its consideration of nuclear disarmament, India submitted a proposal for an *ad hoc* working group to negotiate practical measures for the prevention of nuclear war. However, the Committee stated in its report to the General Assembly[8] that despite intensive discussion, no consensus had been reached on the proposal and that further informal consultations would continue.

General Assembly action (December). By a resolution of 9 December,[12] the General Assembly requested the Committee on Disarmament to undertake, as a matter of the highest priority, negotiations with a view to achieving agreement on appropriate and practical measures for the prevention of nuclear war.

The resolution was adopted by a recorded vote of 130 to none, with 17 abstentions. The First Committee had approved the text on 24 November by a recorded vote of 111 to none, with 17 abstentions. The draft, sponsored by 19 nations, was introduced by Argentina.

Also on 9 December, in a resolution on international co-operation for disarmament,[11] the Assembly declared that the elaboration and dissemination of doctrines justifying the unleashing of nuclear war endangered world peace and led to deterioration of the international situation and further intensification of the arms race.

Explaining its vote against the latter resolution, France said the provision on nuclear-war doctrines, which it considered polemical, would be construed as a denunciation of the policy of nuclear deterrence, which was the foundation of its national security and a fundamental condition for the maintenance of balance and security in Europe.

Also on 9 December,[1] acting without vote on an oral proposal of its President, the Assembly took note of the First Committee's report[9] on an agenda item entitled "Intensification of efforts to remove the threat of nuclear war and ensure the safe development of nuclear energy", which had been added to the session's agenda on 8 October at the request of the USSR. That request was contained in a letter dated 1 October from the USSR addressed to the Secretary-General,[6] which stated that the need to ensure the safe development of nuclear energy was organically linked to the prevention of nuclear war, as attacks on peaceful nuclear installations (p. 86) would have disastrous consequences.

Annexed to the USSR letter was a draft resolution (subsequently issued as a First Committee document[3]) which would have had the Assembly declare that the deliberate destruction of peaceful nuclear installations even by conventional weapons was essentially equivalent to a nuclear attack, and call on all nuclear-weapon States, as a first step towards the reduction and ultimate elimination of their nuclear arsenals, to agree on a simultaneous suspension of the production and development of nuclear weapons and their delivery vehicles as well as the production of fissionable materials for weapons. The USSR later announced that it would not insist on a vote on the draft, stating that its provisions were reflected in other resolutions adopted in 1982.

India also submitted, and later withdrew for similar reasons, a draft resolution[4] reiterating the measures it had proposed at the special session earlier in the year—a convention to prohibit the use or threat of use of nuclear weapons, a test ban and a freeze.

Decision (1982). [1]GA: 37/423, 9 Dec., text following.
Draft resolution deferred. [2]India, A/S-12/AC.1/L.6.
Draft resolution not pressed. [3]USSR, A/C.1/37/L.7.
Draft resolution withdrawn. [4]India, A/C.1/37/L.5.
Letter and note verbale (nv). [5]German Democratic Republic, 6 July, A/S-12/AC.1/65 *(nv)*; [6]USSR, 1 Oct., A/37/242.
Reports. [7]*Ad Hoc* Committee, A/S-12/32; [8]Committee on Disarmament, A/37/27; [9]1st Committee, A/37/673; [10]S-G, A/S-12/11 & Add.1 & Add.1/Corr.1 & Add.2-5.
Resolutions (1982). GA, 9 Dec.: [11]37/78 B, para. 2; [12]37/78 I, text following.
Resolution (prior). [13]GA: 36/81 B, 9 Dec. 1981 (YUN 1981, p. 40).
Meeting records. GA: plenary, A/S-12/PV.2-26, 28, 29 (8 June– 10 July), A/37/PV.24, 98 (8 Oct., 9 Dec.); *Ad Hoc* Committee, A/S-12/AC.1/PV.9, 10, 13 (28 June–6 July); General Committee, A/BUR/37/SR.3 (8 Oct.); 1st Committee, A/C.1/37/PV.3-10, 12-28, *29, 36, 37, 42, 43* (18 Oct.–24 Nov.).

General Assembly resolution 37/78 I

9 December 1982   Meeting 98   130-0-17 (recorded vote)

Approved by First Committee (A/37/662) by recorded vote (111-0-17), 24 November (meeting 43); 19-nation draft (A/C.1/37/L.45); agenda item 50 *(f)*.

Sponsors: Algeria, Argentina, Bangladesh, Benin, Brazil, Colombia, Costa Rica, Ecuador, Egypt, German Democratic Republic, India, Indonesia, Mexico, Pakistan, Qatar, Romania, Sri Lanka, Venezuela, Yugoslavia.

Prevention of nuclear war

The General Assembly,

Alarmed by the threat to the survival of mankind posed by the existence of nuclear weapons and the continuing arms race,

Recalling that removal of the threat of a nuclear war is the most acute and urgent task of the present day,

Reiterating that it is the shared responsibility of all Member States to save succeeding generations from the scourge of another world war,

Recalling the provisions of paragraphs 47 to 50 and 56 to 58 of the Final Document of the Tenth Special Session of the General Assembly, the first special session devoted to disarmament, regarding the procedures designed to secure the avoidance of nuclear war,

Recalling also its resolution 36/81 B of 9 December 1981, in which it urged all nuclear-weapon States to submit to the Secretary-General by 30 April 1982, for consideration at the twelfth special session of the General Assembly, the second special session devoted to disarmament, their views, proposals and practical suggestions for ensuring the prevention of nuclear war and invited all other Member States that so desired to do likewise,

Having considered the report of the Secretary-General containing such views, proposals and practical suggestions, which was submitted at the twelfth special session,

Taking into account the deliberations held on this item during the twelfth special session, in particular in Working Group III of the *Ad Hoc* Committee of the Twelfth Special Session and in the drafting group established to continue consideration of the proposals concerning the question of the prevention of nuclear war, referred to in the Concluding Document of that session,

Convinced that the prevention of nuclear war and the reduction of the risks of nuclear war are matters of the highest priority and of vital interest to all peoples of the world,

1. *Requests* the Committee on Disarmament to undertake, as a matter of the highest priority, negotiations with a view to achieving agreement on appropriate and practical measures for the prevention of nuclear war, taking into account the documents referred to above, as well as other existing proposals and future initiatives;

2. *Requests* the Secretary-General to transmit to the Committee on Disarmament all relevant documents to facilitate the consideration of this item by the Committee;

3. *Decides* to include in the provisional agenda of its thirty-eighth session an item entitled "Prevention of nuclear war: report of the Committee on Disarmament".

Recorded vote in Assembly as follows:

In favour: Afghanistan, Algeria, Angola, Antigua and Barbuda, Argentina, Austria, Bahamas, Bahrain, Bangladesh, Barbados, Belize, Benin, Bhutan, Bolivia, Botswana, Brazil, Bulgaria, Burma, Burundi, Byelorussian SSR, Cape Verde, Central African Republic, Chad, Chile, China, Colombia, Comoros, Congo, Costa Rica, Cuba, Cyprus, Czechoslovakia, Democratic Kampuchea, Democratic Yemen, Djibouti, Dominican Republic, Ecuador, Egypt, El Salvador, Ethiopia, Fiji, Finland, Gabon, Gambia, German Democratic Republic, Ghana, Greece, Grenada, Guatemala, Guinea, Guinea-Bissau, Guyana, Haiti, Honduras, Hungary, India, Indonesia, Iran, Iraq, Ireland, Israel, Ivory Coast, Jamaica, Jordan, Kenya, Kuwait, Lao People's Democratic Republic, Lebanon, Liberia, Libyan Arab Jamahiriya, Madagascar, Malawi, Malaysia, Maldives, Mali, Malta, Mauritania, Mauritius, Mexico, Mongolia, Morocco, Mozambique, Nepal, Nicaragua, Niger, Nigeria, Pakistan, Panama, Papua New Guinea, Paraguay, Peru, Philippines, Poland, Qatar, Romania, Rwanda, Saint Lucia, Sao Tome and Principe, Saudi Arabia, Senegal, Sierra Leone, Singapore, Solomon Islands, Somalia, Spain, Sri Lanka, Sudan, Suriname, Swaziland, Sweden, Syrian Arab Republic, Thailand, Togo, Trinidad and Tobago, Tunisia, Uganda, Ukrainian SSR, USSR, United Arab Emirates, United Republic of Cameroon, United Republic of Tanzania, Upper Volta, Uruguay, Vanuatu, Venezuela, Viet Nam, Yemen, Yugoslavia, Zaire, Zambia.

Against: None.

Abstaining: Australia, Belgium, Canada, Denmark, France, Germany, Federal Republic of, Iceland, Italy, Japan, Luxembourg, Netherlands, New Zealand, Norway, Portugal, Turkey, United Kingdom, United States.

General Assembly decision 37/423

Adopted without vote

Oral proposal by President; agenda item 139.

Intensification of efforts to remove the threat of nuclear war and ensure the safe development of nuclear energy

At its 98th plenary meeting, on 9 December 1982, the General Assembly took note of the report of the First Committee.

Proposed group of eminent persons

At the General Assembly's special session on disarmament in June/July 1982, India and Mexico submitted a draft resolution[1] that would have had the Assembly request the Secretary-General to appoint a representative group of eminent public persons to advise on measures for the collective management and resolution of critical or confrontational situations which could escalate to nuclear war. The proposed group was to include statesmen, scientists, physicians, jurists, religious leaders, philosophers and others.

Along with four other draft resolutions on the prevention of nuclear war and prohibitions against nuclear weapons, this proposal was transmitted to the Assembly's 1982 regular session. There, a similar draft was submitted[2] and was later revised by the sponsors to have the Secretary-General solicit the views of Member States on the appointment of such a group, after which the Assembly would take up the question again in 1983 with a view to appointing the group. The text was introduced by India, also on behalf of Ecuador, Liberia and Mexico.

However, India subsequently informed the Committee that, in view of requests from a number of delegations for more intensive consultations, the sponsors had decided not to press the draft to a vote at the 1982 session.

Draft resolution deferred. [1]India, Mexico, A/S-12/AC.1/L.2 & Corr.1.
Draft resolution not pressed. [2]Ecuador, India, Liberia, Mexico, A/C.1/37/L.2/Rev.1.

Prohibitions against nuclear weapons

Proposed nuclear-weapon freeze

General Assembly consideration (June/July). At the General Assembly's second special session devoted to disarmament, its *Ad Hoc* Committee of the Twelfth Special Session received in July 1982 two draft resolutions calling for a nuclear-weapon freeze—one by India, addressed to all nuclear-weapon States,[1] and another by Mexico and Sweden, calling on the two major nuclear-weapon States to make freeze declarations.[2] As in the case of all draft resolutions submitted during that session, the Secretary-General was asked to transmit the texts to the Assembly at its 1982 regular session.

In a note verbale dated 25 June submitted to the Secretariat for distribution at the special session,[3] Ireland proposed that the USSR and the United States observe a two-year, renewable moratorium on the introduction of further strategic nuclear weapons or delivery vehicles, during which time the parties should negotiate on nuclear-arms reduction.

Proposals for a freeze on nuclear weapons were also made for inclusion in the draft comprehensive programme of disarmament, but no consensus was reached on them.[4]

During the session's general debate, India, referring to its proposal for a freeze, said it would enable the nuclear-weapon States to accept international safeguards against the military use of nuclear facilities, since no more nuclear weapons would be produced anywhere; the freeze would need to be immediately followed by a reduction in existing nuclear-weapon stockpiles. The idea of a freeze was endorsed by Argentina, Ireland, Madagascar, Maldives, Nigeria and Uganda. Seychelles appealed to States to decide, as a first step, to halt the production of all types of nuclear weapons.

Along with the German Democratic Republic, which called for an immediate freeze of nuclear-weapon potentials, Romania, the USSR and Zambia supported the idea of a mutual freeze of nuclear weapons as a first step towards their reduction and eventual elimination. Bangladesh called for a total freeze on the production, development, deployment, and research and development of nuclear weapons and their delivery systems, to be followed by the application of universal and non-discriminatory safeguards to all nuclear facilities world-wide. Fiji, noting that calls for a freeze had gone unheeded, urged that negotiations on the cessation of development and production of nuclear weapons be undertaken within the framework of the Committee on Disarmament.

Nicaragua welcomed the introduction in the United States Senate of a resolution calling for an immediate freeze in the production, deployment and testing of nuclear weapons and their subsequent reduction through negotiations. Sweden believed the super-Powers must agree on freezing nuclear-weapon arsenals and the number of delivery vehicles, thus paving the way for negotiations on balanced and verifiable reductions of various kinds of nuclear weapons, as well as on limitations on the development and production of new types of nuclear weapons and delivery vehicles. The Ukrainian SSR said the freeze idea was generally in keeping with its approach to the limitation, reduction and elimination of nuclear weapons.

Australia, on the other hand, said freeze proposals would only perpetuate the current overarmed state of the world unless they were accompanied by verifiable reductions in both conventional and nuclear weapons. France asserted that a commitment on the non-use of nuclear weapons would, in one region of the world, constitute a factor of destabilization and hence a serious threat to security. Italy said simple proposals to freeze imbalances could only aggravate East-West tension and make it more difficult to achieve disarmament agreements based on reciprocity. Saint Vincent and the Grenadines said a freeze would leave the *status quo* intact, with all its massive overkill of weaponry.

Mexico found unacceptable the argument for negotiation from a position of strength and said that, given the difficulty in achieving perfect nuclear symmetry between the two great Powers, the important thing was to accept the overall parity which had been achieved between them and move on to halt the development of new weapon systems such as the United States MX and cruise missiles and the Soviet SS-18 and SS-19 missiles; no breakthrough by one party would give it greater security.

General Assembly action (December). On 13 December, the Assembly adopted two resolutions on a nuclear-weapon freeze, one addressed to all nuclear-weapon States and covering production only, and the other to the USSR and the United States, covering production, deployment and a test ban. They were revised versions of the draft resolutions submitted at the special session.

By the resolution addressed to all nuclear-weapon States,[5] the Assembly called on them to agree to a freeze providing for a simultaneous total stoppage of further production of nuclear weapons and a complete cut-off in the production of fissionable material for weapons purposes.

The resolution was adopted by a recorded vote of 122 to 16, with 6 abstentions. The First Committee had approved the draft on 23 November by a recorded vote of 105 to 16, with 8 abstentions. The text contained the same wording as the one submitted by India at the special session, with an additional paragraph on inclusion of the item in the 1983 Assembly agenda.

By the second text, addressed to the USSR and the United States,[6] the Assembly urged them to proclaim an immediate nuclear-arms freeze, either through simultaneous unilateral declarations or jointly, and to report to the Assembly in 1983 on implementation of the resolution. According to the preamble, an overall rough parity in nuclear military power existed between the two countries, thus providing the most propitious conditions for a freeze. The proposed freeze embraced three elements: a comprehensive test ban; cessation of manufacture and a ban on further deployment of nuclear weapons and their delivery vehicles; and cessation of the production of fissionable material for weapons purposes. It would be subject to verification and its initial five-year duration was subject to extension in the event other nuclear-weapon States joined.

The resolution, essentially the same as the one proposed by Mexico and Sweden at the special session but with an added subparagraph on duration and extension, was adopted by a recorded vote of 119 to 17, with 5 abstentions. The First Committee had approved the draft on 23 November by a recorded vote of 103 to 17, with 6 abstentions.

Introducing the revised draft addressed to all nuclear Powers, of which the German Democratic Republic, Liberia and Mali were also sponsors, India stated that, although the text focused on production in order to facilitate speedy agreement, a freeze must be followed immediately by negotiations on reduction and subsequent elimination of all nuclear-weapon stockpiles. A production freeze would also permit the application of universal and non-discriminatory safeguards to all nuclear facilities throughout the world, so that the problem of verification and control cited in the case of a freeze on development or deployment would not arise. Nuclear-weapon testing was not included because other proposals addressed that problem.

Introducing the second text, also sponsored by Colombia, Ecuador and Sweden, Mexico asserted that the existence of rough parity between the two major nuclear Powers had been borne out by reliable sources, among them the Independent Commission on Disarmament and Security Issues (p. 141). The two super-Powers would set the example by applying a freeze, and their action should be followed by other nuclear Powers within a reasonable period of time. The problem of verification could not be legitimately invoked as an excuse not to agree on a freeze.

Among those voting against the two resolutions, Canada feared that a freeze, particularly a comprehensive one, could prove to be destabilizing and that it could be unilaterally abandoned; moreover, it prejudged the complex issues involved. The Federal Republic of Germany advanced the following arguments against a freeze: it could be justified if there was a genuine balance between the participants, but the USSR had in recent years deployed hundreds of nuclear warheads in Europe and substantially reinforced its conventional capability without any corresponding arms development on the other side; a freeze that codified imbalances destroyed the incentive for genuine nuclear reduction and left existing arsenals in place; without verification, a freeze would do nothing to allay fear and suspicion and would not be durable.

Also voting negatively, the Netherlands and Norway stated that a freeze would leave intact the imbalance caused by the recent massive growth in USSR missiles and that it could not be adequately verified, and they emphasized that the Geneva negotiations between the USSR and the United States sought reductions rather than a freeze; however, Norway supported a test ban and cessation of fissionable materials production. Portugal also believed that a freeze would consolidate existing imbalances in Europe and remove the incentive of the USSR to continue arms-reduction negotiations.

China, explaining its abstention on the first resolution, said that an indiscriminate demand for a freeze by all nuclear States would only legalize their nuclear superiority over other countries and perpetuate their nuclear threat and blackmail. Abstaining on both resolutions, Denmark said it sympathized with the freeze idea but feared a negative impact on the Geneva negotiations and a legitimizing of the massive growth in USSR nuclear weaponry.

Voting in favour of the two resolutions, Austria cited the exceptional dangers posed by nuclear weapons and said that, if there was a disequilibrium, it could be balanced by measures relating to other types of weapons. Finland saw the resolutions as a response to anxiety about the nuclear-war danger and concern at the lack of progress in negotiations, but it added that real results could be achieved only in serious and substantive negotiations among the parties principally concerned. Indonesia expressed support for concrete and practical measures for preventing a nuclear war, including a verifiable freeze in nuclear-weapons development and production. Ireland stated that both sides in the nuclear competition should halt the development and deployment of such weapons so as to create a climate conducive to negotiations.

Pakistan, explaining its positive votes, spoke of the special responsibility of the major nuclear-weapon States and said that efforts to eliminate the nuclear threat could be made at more than one level. Sweden viewed a freeze by all nuclear-weapon States as desirable, although not as urgent as a freeze by the two nuclear super-Powers.

The USSR said it viewed a freeze positively as a first step towards reduction, although it should be limited to a certain time-frame whose extension would be contingent on the actions of other nuclear States. Verification arrangements required further agreement through talks between the parties. Approximate parity continued to exist in nuclear and conventional forces, but that fact was being denied so as to cover up an unjustified build-up of nuclear weapons in the United States. The USSR defined its goal as military parity at the lowest level of arms.

During the First Committee's general debate on disarmament, the United States asserted that the USSR proposals for moratoriums in regard to both strategic and intermediate-range missiles, as presented at the current bilateral negotiations at Geneva, were designed to preserve the USSR advantage in ground-based missiles. The first nuclear-arms policy objective of the United States was to eliminate that factor of instability, preferably by reasonable agreements but by force modernization if necessary.

Draft resolutions deferred. [1]India, A/S-12/AC.1/L.1 & Corr.1; [2]Mexico, Sweden, A/S-12/AC.1/L.3.
Note verbale. [3]Ireland, 25 June, A/S-12/AC.1/46/Rev.1.
Report. [4]*Ad Hoc* Committee, A/S-12/32.
Resolutions (1982). GA, 13 Dec.: [5]37/100 A, text following; [6]37/100 B, text following.
Meeting records. GA: plenary, A/S-12/PV.2-26, 28, 29 (8 June–10 July), A/37/PV.101 (13 Dec.); *Ad Hoc* Committee, A/S-12/AC.1/PV.2, *10*, 12, 13 (14 June–6 July); 1st Committee, A/C.1/37/PV.3-10, 12-28, *36-40* (18 Oct.–23 Nov.).

General Assembly resolution 37/100 A

13 December 1982   Meeting 101   122-16-6 (recorded vote)

Approved by First Committee (A/37/670) by recorded vote (105-16-8), 23 November (meeting 40); 4-nation draft (A/C.1/37/L.1/Rev.1); agenda item 133.

Sponsors: German Democratic Republic, India, Liberia, Mali.

Freeze on nuclear weapons

The General Assembly,

Convinced that in this nuclear age lasting world peace can be based only on the attainment of the goal of general and complete disarmament under effective international control,

Further convinced that the highest priority objectives in the field of disarmament have to be nuclear disarmament and the elimination of all weapons of mass destruction,

Recognizing the urgent need to halt the arms race, particularly in nuclear weapons,

Recognizing further the urgent need for a negotiated reduction of nuclear-weapon stockpiles leading to their complete elimination,

1. *Calls upon* all nuclear-weapon States to agree to a freeze on nuclear weapons, which would, *inter alia*, provide for a simultaneous total stoppage of any further production of nuclear weapons and a complete cut-off in the production of fissionable material for weapons purposes;

2. *Decides* to include in the provisional agenda of its thirty-eighth session an item entitled "Freeze on nuclear weapons".

Recorded vote in Assembly as follows:

In favour: Afghanistan, Algeria, Angola, Argentina, Austria, Bahamas, Bahrain, Bangladesh, Barbados, Benin, Bhutan, Bolivia, Botswana, Brazil, Bulgaria, Burma, Burundi, Byelorussian SSR, Central African Republic, Chad, Chile, Colombia, Comoros, Congo, Costa Rica, Cuba, Cyprus, Czechoslovakia, Democratic Yemen, Djibouti, Dominican Republic, Ecuador, Egypt, El Salvador, Equatorial Guinea, Ethiopia, Fiji, Finland, Gabon, German Democratic Republic, Ghana, Greece, Grenada, Guinea, Guinea-Bissau, Guyana, Haiti, Honduras, Hungary, India, Indonesia, Iran, Iraq, Ireland, Jamaica, Jordan, Kenya, Kuwait, Lao People's Democratic Republic, Lebanon, Lesotho, Liberia, Libyan Arab Jamahiriya, Madagascar, Malawi, Malaysia, Maldives, Mali, Malta, Mauritania, Mauritius, Mexico, Mongolia, Morocco, Mozambique, Nepal, Nicaragua, Niger, Nigeria, Oman, Pakistan, Panama, Papua New Guinea, Paraguay, Peru, Philippines, Poland, Qatar, Romania, Rwanda, Saint Lucia, Sao Tome and Principe, Saudi Arabia, Senegal, Sierra Leone, Singapore, Solomon Islands, Sri Lanka, Sudan, Suriname, Swaziland, Sweden, Syrian Arab Republic, Thailand, Togo, Trinidad and Tobago, Tunisia, Uganda, Ukrainian SSR, USSR, United Arab Emirates, United Republic of Cameroon, United Republic of Tanzania, Upper Volta, Uruguay, Vanuatu, Venezuela, Viet Nam, Yemen, Yugoslavia, Zaire, Zambia.

Against: Australia, Belgium, Canada, France, Germany, Federal Republic of, Israel, Italy, Luxembourg, Netherlands, New Zealand, Norway, Portugal, Spain, Turkey, United Kingdom, United States.

Abstaining: China, Denmark, Guatemala, Iceland, Japan, Somalia.

General Assembly resolution 37/100 B

13 December 1982   Meeting 101   119-17-5 (recorded vote)

Approved by First Committee (A/37/670) by recorded vote (103-17-6), 23 November (meeting 40); 4-nation draft (A/C.1/37/L.3/Rev.2); agenda item 133.

Sponsors: Colombia, Ecuador, Mexico, Sweden.

Nuclear-arms freeze

The General Assembly,

Recalling that, in the Final Document of the Tenth Special Session of the General Assembly, in 1978, it expressed deep concern over the threat to the very survival of mankind posed by the existence of nuclear weapons and the continuing arms race,

Recalling also that, on the same occasion, it pointed out that existing arsenals of nuclear weapons were more than sufficient to destroy all life on earth and stressed that mankind was therefore confronted with a choice: halt the arms race and proceed to disarmament, or face annihilation,

Noting that the conditions prevailing today are a source of even more serious concern than those existing in 1978 because of several factors such as the deterioration of the international situation, the increase in the accuracy, speed and destructive power of nuclear weapons, the promotion of illusory doctrines of "limited" or "winnable" nuclear war and the many false alarms which have occurred owing to the malfunctioning of computers,

Believing that it is a matter of the utmost urgency to stop any further increase in the awesome arsenals of the two major nuclear-weapon States, which already have ample retaliatory power and a frightening overkill capacity,

Believing also that it is equally urgent to activate negotiations for the substantial reduction and qualitative limitation of existing nuclear arms,

Considering that a nuclear-arms freeze, while not an end in itself, would constitute the most effective first step for the achievement of the above-mentioned two objectives, since it would provide a favourable environment for the conduct of the reduction negotiations while, at the same time, preventing the continued increase and qualitative improvement of existing nuclear weaponry during the period when the negotiations would take place,

Firmly convinced that at present the conditions are most propitious for such a freeze, since the Union of Soviet Socialist Republics and the United States of America are now equivalent in nuclear military power and it seems evident that there exists between them an overall rough parity,

1. *Urges* the Union of Soviet Socialist Republics and the United States of America, as the two major nuclear-weapon States, to proclaim, either through simultaneous unilateral declarations or through a joint declaration, an immediate nuclear-arms freeze which would be a first step towards the comprehensive programme of disarmament and whose structure and scope would be the following:

(a) It would embrace:

(i) A comprehensive test ban of nuclear weapons and of their delivery vehicles;

(ii) The complete cessation of the manufacture of nuclear weapons and of their delivery vehicles;

(iii) A ban on all further deployment of nuclear weapons and of their delivery vehicles;

(iv) The complete cessation of the production of fissionable material for weapons purposes;

(b) It would be subject to all the relevant measures and procedures of verification which have already been agreed upon by the parties in the case of the SALT I and SALT II treaties, as well as those agreed upon in principle by them during the preparatory trilateral negotiations on the comprehensive test ban held at Geneva;

(c) It would be of an initial five-year duration, subject to prolongation in the event of other nuclear-weapon States joining in such a freeze, as the General Assembly expects them to do;

2. *Requests* the above-mentioned two major nuclear-weapon States to report to the General Assembly, prior to the opening of its thirty-eighth session, on the implementation of the present resolution;

3. *Decides* to include in the provisional agenda of its thirty-eighth session an item entitled "Implementation of General Assembly resolution 37/100 B on a nuclear-arms freeze".

Recorded vote in Assembly as follows:

In favour: Afghanistan, Algeria, Angola, Argentina, Austria, Bahamas, Bahrain, Bangladesh, Barbados, Benin, Bhutan, Bolivia, Botswana, Brazil, Bulgaria, Burma, Burundi, Byelorussian SSR, Central African Republic, Chad, Chile, Colombia, Comoros, Congo, Costa Rica, Cuba, Cyprus, Czechoslovakia, Democratic Yemen, Djibouti, Dominican Republic, Ecuador, Egypt, El Salvador, Equatorial Guinea, Ethiopia, Fiji, Finland, Gabon, German Democratic Republic, Ghana, Greece, Grenada, Guinea, Guinea-Bissau, Guyana, Haiti, Honduras, Hungary, India, Indonesia, Iran, Iraq, Ireland, Jamaica, Jordan, Kenya, Kuwait, Lao People's Democratic Republic, Lebanon, Lesotho, Liberia, Libyan Arab Jamahiriya, Madagascar, Malawi, Malaysia, Maldives, Mali, Malta, Mauritania, Mauritius, Mexico, Mongolia, Mozambique, Nepal, Nicaragua, Niger, Nigeria, Oman, Pakistan, Panama, Papua New Guinea, Paraguay, Peru, Poland, Qatar, Romania, Rwanda, Saint Lucia, Sao Tome and Principe, Saudi Arabia, Senegal, Sierra Leone, Singapore, Solomon Islands, Sri Lanka, Sudan, Suriname, Swaziland, Sweden, Syrian Arab Republic, Togo, Trinidad and Tobago, Tunisia, Uganda, Ukrainian SSR, USSR, United Arab Emirates, United Republic of Cameroon, United Republic of Tanzania, Upper Volta, Uruguay, Vanuatu, Venezuela, Viet Nam, Yemen, Yugoslavia, Zaire, Zambia.

Against: Australia, Belgium, Canada, France, Germany, Federal Republic of, Israel, Italy, Japan, Luxembourg, Netherlands, New Zealand, Norway, Portugal, Spain, Turkey, United Kingdom, United States.

Abstaining: Denmark, Guatemala, Iceland, Philippines, Somalia.

Draft convention

General Assembly consideration (June/ July). At the General Assembly's 1982 special session on disarmament, India submitted, by a letter dated 16 June addressed to the Secretary-General,[2] the text of a draft Convention on the Prohibition of the Use of Nuclear Weapons. This was subsequently presented to the *Ad Hoc* Committee, annexed to a draft resolution proposing that the Assembly adopt the text, which would prohibit the use or threat of use of nuclear weapons under any circumstances, pending nuclear disarmament.[1] As with other texts submitted at that session, the draft was transmitted for consideration by the Assembly at its regular 1982 session.[3]

During the general debate at the special session, India said it was strange that the banning of nuclear weapons had not been seriously considered when there was a treaty prohibiting the use of chemical and biological weapons and another one was being negotiated on radiological weapons. Madagascar agreed there was need for a convention prohibiting the use or threat of use of nuclear weapons.

General Assembly action (December). By a resolution adopted on 13 December,[4] the General Assembly requested the Committee on Disarmament to undertake, on a priority basis, negotiations aimed at achieving agreement on an international convention prohibiting the use or threat of use of nuclear weapons under any circumstances. The Committee was to take as a basis the text (by India) annexed to the resolution.

The draft convention contained a single substantive article, according to which the parties would undertake not to use or threaten to use nuclear weapons under any circumstances. Its three other articles specified that it was to be unlimited in duration and open to all States, and would enter into force when ratified by 25 Governments, including those of the five nuclear-weapon States.

The resolution was adopted by a recorded vote of 117 to 17, with 8 abstentions. The First Committee had approved the text on 23 November by a recorded vote of 103 to 17, with 9 abstentions, after it had been revised by its 21 sponsors to provide for consideration by the Committee on Disarmament rather than immediate adoption by the Assembly as in the June version.

Introducing the revised draft, India recalled that, as early as 1961,[5] the Assembly had declared that the use of nuclear weapons would be a violation of the Charter of the United Nations and a crime against humanity, and that two nuclear Powers, China and the USSR, had voted in December 1981 for a resolution reaffirming that statement.[6] It was appropriate and indispensable for the Committee on Disarmament, the sole multilateral negotiating body in the disarmament field, to consider effective measures for preventing a nuclear war and ensuring the collective survival of mankind. The annexed text was not intended to preclude consideration of other proposals with the same objective. A new preambular paragraph in the revised draft resolution stressed that prohibition of nuclear-weapon use was not an end in itself but a step towards total nuclear disarmament and ultimately general and complete disarmament.

In explanation of its abstention, Greece said the text should have foreseen a prohibition of any use of force, save in the common interest; as it stood, it could be misconstrued as legalizing the use of conventional weapons. Ireland abstained because of the reaffirmation in the fifth preambular paragraph of resolutions which it had been unable to support. Sweden said its affirmative vote reflected its support for the general thrust of the text, despite a reservation that the fifth preambular paragraph (stating that the use of nuclear weapons would be a violation of the United Nations Charter) contained a legally contestable interpretation of the Charter; it would have preferred deletion of that paragraph or parts thereof.

Draft resolution deferred. [1]India, A/S-12/AC.1/L.4.
Letter. [2]India, 16 June, A/S-12/AC.1/13.
Report. [3]*Ad Hoc* Committee, A/S-12/32.
Resolution (1982). [4]GA: 37/100 C, 13 Dec., text following.
Resolutions (prior). GA: [5]1653(XVI), 24 Nov. 1961 (YUN 1961, p. 30); [6]36/92 I, 9 Dec. 1981 (YUN 1981, p. 41).
Meeting records. GA: plenary, A/S-12/PV.2-26, 28, 29 (8 June–10 July), A/37/PV.101 (13 Dec.); *Ad Hoc* Committee, A/S-12/AC.1/PV.9 (28 June); 1st Committee, A/C.1/37/PV.3-10, 12-28, *33,* 37, *40* (18 Oct.–23 Nov.).

General Assembly resolution 37/100 C

13 December 1982   Meeting 101   117-17-8 (recorded vote)

Approved by First Committee (A/37/670) by recorded vote (103-17-9), 23 November (meeting 40); 21-nation draft (A/C.1/37/L.4/Rev.1); agenda item 133.

Sponsors: Algeria, Argentina, Bahamas, Bangladesh, Bhutan, Congo, Cyprus, Ecuador, Egypt, Ethiopia, Ghana, Guyana, India, Indonesia, Jamaica, Madagascar, Mali, Nigeria, Romania, Yugoslavia, Zambia.

Convention on the prohibition of the use of nuclear weapons
The General Assembly,

Alarmed by the threat to the survival of mankind and to the life-sustaining system posed by nuclear weapons and by their use, inherent in concepts of deterrence,

Convinced that nuclear disarmament is essential for the prevention of nuclear war and for the strengthening of international peace and security,

Further convinced that a prohibition of the use or threat of use of nuclear weapons would be a step towards the complete elimination of nuclear weapons leading to general and complete disarmament under strict and effective international control,

Recalling that, in paragraph 58 of the Final Document of the Tenth Special Session of the General Assembly, it is stated that all States should actively participate in efforts to bring about conditions in international relations among States in which a code of peaceful conduct of nations in international affairs could be agreed upon and which would preclude the use or threat of use of nuclear weapons,

Reaffirming the declaration that the use of nuclear weapons would be a violation of the Charter of the United Nations and a crime against humanity, contained in its resolutions 1653(XVI) of 24 November 1961, 33/71 B of 14 December 1978, 34/83 G of 11 December 1979, 35/152 D of 12 December 1980 and 36/92 I of 9 December 1981,

1. *Requests* the Committee on Disarmament to undertake, on a priority basis, negotiations with a view to achieving agreement on an international convention prohibiting the use or threat of use of nuclear weapons under any circumstances, taking as a basis the text of the annexed draft Convention on the Prohibition of the Use of Nuclear Weapons;

2. *Decides* to include in the provisional agenda of its thirty-eighth session an item entitled "Convention on the Prohibition of the Use of Nuclear Weapons".

ANNEX
Draft Convention on the Prohibition of the Use of Nuclear Weapons
The States Parties to this Convention,

Alarmed by the threat to the very survival of mankind posed by the existence of nuclear weapons,

Convinced that any use of nuclear weapons constitutes a violation of the Charter of the United Nations and a crime against humanity,

Convinced that this Convention would be a step towards the complete elimination of nuclear weapons leading to general and complete disarmament under strict and effective international control,

Determined to continue negotiations for the achievement of this goal,

Have agreed as follows:

Article 1

The States Parties to this Convention solemnly undertake not to use or threaten to use nuclear weapons under any circumstances.

Article 2

This Convention shall be of unlimited duration.

Article 3

1. This Convention shall be open to all States for signature. Any State which does not sign the Convention before its entry into force in accordance with paragraph 3 of this article may accede to it at any time.

2. This Convention shall be subject to ratification by signatory States. Instruments of ratification or accession shall be deposited with the Secretary-General of the United Nations.

3. This Convention shall enter into force on the deposit of instruments of ratification by twenty-five Governments, including the Governments of the five nuclear-weapon States, in accordance with paragraph 2 of this article.

4. For States whose instruments of ratification or accession are deposited after the entry into force of this Convention, it shall enter into force on the date of the deposit of their instruments of ratification or accession.

5. The depositary shall promptly inform all signatory and acceding States of the date of each signature, the date of deposit of each instrument of ratification or accession and the date of the entry into force of this Convention, as well as of the receipt of other notices.

6. This Convention shall be registered by the depositary in accordance with Article 102 of the Charter of the United Nations.

Article 4

This Convention, of which the Arabic, Chinese, English, French, Russian and Spanish texts are equally authentic, shall be deposited with the Secretary-General of the United Nations, who shall send duly certified copies thereof to the Governments of the signatory and acceding States.

IN WITNESS WHEREOF, the undersigned, being duly authorized thereto by their respective Governments, have signed this Convention, opened for signature at _____, on the _____ day of _____ one thousand nine hundred and _____.

Recorded vote in Assembly as follows:

In favour: Afghanistan, Algeria, Angola, Argentina, Bahrain, Bangladesh, Barbados, Benin, Bhutan, Bolivia, Botswana, Brazil, Bulgaria, Burma, Burundi, Byelorussian SSR, Central African Republic, Chad, Chile, China, Colombia, Comoros, Congo, Costa Rica, Cuba, Cyprus, Czechoslovakia, Democratic Yemen, Djibouti, Dominican Republic, Ecuador, Egypt, El Salvador, Equatorial Guinea, Ethiopia, Fiji, Gabon, German Democratic Republic, Ghana, Grenada, Guinea, Guinea-Bissau, Guyana, Haiti, Honduras, Hungary, India, Indonesia, Iran, Iraq, Jamaica, Jordan, Kenya, Kuwait, Lao People's Democratic Republic, Lebanon, Lesotho, Liberia, Libyan Arab Jamahiriya, Madagascar, Malawi, Malaysia, Maldives, Mali, Malta, Mauritania, Mauritius, Mexico, Mongolia, Morocco, Mozambique, Nepal, Nicaragua, Niger, Nigeria, Oman, Pakistan, Panama, Papua New Guinea, Peru, Philippines, Poland, Qatar, Romania, Rwanda, Saint Lucia, Sao Tome and Principe, Saudi Arabia, Senegal, Sierra Leone, Singapore, Solomon Islands, Somalia, Sri Lanka, Sudan, Suriname, Swaziland, Sweden, Syrian Arab Republic, Thailand, Togo, Trinidad and Tobago, Tunisia, Uganda, Ukrainian SSR, USSR, United Arab Emirates, United Republic of Cameroon, United Republic of Tanzania, Uruguay, Vanuatu, Venezuela, Viet Nam, Yemen, Yugoslavia, Zaire, Zambia.

Against: Australia, Belgium, Canada, Denmark, France, Germany, Federal Republic of, Iceland, Italy, Luxembourg, Netherlands, New Zealand, Norway, Portugal, Spain, Turkey, United Kingdom, United States.

Abstaining: Austria, Finland, Greece, Guatemala, Ireland, Israel, Japan, Paraguay.

First use

General Assembly consideration (June/July). The USSR declaration at the General Assembly's 1982 special session devoted to disarmament—that it assumed, effective immediately (15 June), an obligation not to be the first to use nuclear weapons—was welcomed by several speakers in the general debate at the session, among them Bulgaria, Cuba, Czechoslovakia, Grenada, the Lao People's Democratic Republic, Nicaragua and the Syrian Arab Republic. Benin called it a historic and positive commitment, and Bhutan, Bulgaria and the German Democratic Republic urged other nuclear-weapon States to follow suit; those who feared that this would favour the use of conventional weapons, the German Democratic Republic added, need only accept the proposal by the socialist States to renounce the first use of both types of weapons.

The Byelorussian SSR and the Ukrainian SSR supported the USSR view that assumption by other nuclear Powers of a non-first-use obligation would be tantamount in practice to a ban on the use of nuclear weapons altogether.

Also during the special session, China recalled and reaffirmed the declaration it had made 18 years previously of unconditional non-first-use and unconditional guarantee of non-use of such weapons against non-nuclear States, and urged all other nuclear States to take similar actions. The Philippines welcomed China's unconditional non-first-use guarantee. Argentina and Ecuador welcomed the non-first-use declarations by China and the USSR.

Guyana, Madagascar, Mexico, Mongolia, Romania, Suriname and Zambia were among those which hoped other nuclear-weapon States would unilaterally or jointly make similar declarations. Sharing that view, Jamaica urged, in the interim, a moratorium on further nuclear tests. Pakistan and Tunisia hoped those declarations would facilitate a general agreement on the matter among the nuclear Powers. Pending nuclear disarmament, Hungary supported any intermediate, partial measures such as outlawing the first use of nuclear weapons. Ireland said the nuclear Powers should seriously consider what methods or agreements they might work out providing against the first use of nuclear weapons by any of them. Sri Lanka urged the Assembly to demand declarations to that effect from the nuclear-weapon Powers, which Uruguay hoped would be reflected in binding legal instruments.

Some Western countries expressed misgivings about the value of such declarations. Observing that the United Nations Charter already prohibited the first use of any force, Canada considered it dangerous to create the impression that there was an order of priority among the various uses of force. The Netherlands said that, although the possibility of any use of nuclear weapons was horrifying, the right of individual and collective self-defence included the right to determine what level of force was needed to dissuade an aggressor; before non-first-use declarations, progress must be made in controlling and limiting nuclear weapons and creating a stable East-West balance in the conventional field.

For the United Kingdom, the key need was not for promises against the first use of any specific kind of weapon, but a credible assurance against starting military action at all. The United States said its policy went beyond a non-first-use pledge to the statement made at the June summit meeting of the North Atlantic Treaty Organization (NATO) that none of its weapons would ever be used except in response to an attack.

At the conclusion of the session, Pakistan said it would have liked to see the Assembly adopt proposals on nuclear disarmament, particularly one calling for non-first-use declarations by nuclear Powers. China reiterated its readiness to assume appropriate obligations with other nuclear States through negotiations. Hungary, speaking also on behalf of Bulgaria, the Byelorussian SSR, Czechoslovakia, the German Democratic Republic, Mongolia, Poland, the Ukrainian SSR and the USSR, urged other nuclear-weapon States to follow the USSR declaration with reciprocal steps. France asserted that, as the prevention of nuclear war could not be isolated from the prevention of war itself and the maintenance of security, a commitment on the non-use of nuclear weapons would, in one region of the world, constitute a destabilizing factor and hence a serious threat to security.

General Assembly action (December). By a 9 December resolution on non-use of nuclear weapons and prevention of nuclear war,[2] the General Assembly considered that the solemn declarations made or reiterated at the second special session on disarmament by two nuclear-weapon States on the non-first-use of nuclear weapons offered an important avenue to decrease the danger of nuclear war. The Assembly expressed hope that the other nuclear-weapon States would consider making similar declarations.

The resolution was adopted by a recorded vote of 112 to 19, with 15 abstentions. The First Committee had approved the draft on 23 November by a recorded vote of 87 to 19, with 18 abstentions.

Also on 9 December, in the preamble of a resolution on international co-operation for disarmament,[1] the Assembly expressed the conviction that concrete manifestations of political goodwill, including unilateral measures such as an obligation not to make first use of nuclear weapons, would improve conditions for resolving disarmament issues in a spirit of co-operation among States.

Sponsored also by Cuba, Romania and Viet Nam, the resolution on non-first-use was introduced by the German Democratic Republic, which expressed the belief that declarations on non-first-use by all nuclear-weapon States would create favourable conditions for nuclear disarmament negotiations and for conclusion of an international instrument such as that proposed by India to prohibit the use of nuclear weapons (p. 53).

Explaining their negative votes, Belgium, Denmark and the United States reiterated the commitment by their defensive alliance to the non-use of force except in response to an attack. Belgium added that singling out nuclear weapons would reduce the purport of the commitment by Member States under the United Nations Charter to refrain from the threat or use of force in their international relations. The United States advanced a similar argument and added that the right of self-defence could not be fettered in an atmosphere of flagrant and unremitting violations of the Charter, combined with large and growing forces; in view of the threat posed by the massive build-up of strategic and intermediate-range nuclear forces of one bloc of States, calls by that side for unenforceable unilateral pledges were hollow. Denmark said such declarations might be an important confidence-building measure at a given stage of disarmament but a real step forward would not be taken until there were substantial weapons reductions.

China abstained, asserting that its position differed from that of the USSR: as previously stated, the USSR declaration, which had been preceded by its vast nuclear build-up and preponderance in conventional arms, was conditional on action of other nuclear Powers and failed to refer to non-use against non-nuclear-weapon States or nuclear-weapon-free zones.

Also abstaining, Austria believed that early agreement on substantial limitations and reductions of nuclear arsenals, rather than mere declarations, would be the most significant contribution the nuclear-weapon States could make to international security. Finland's abstention was based on its reservations concerning the text's basic presumptions and the fact that it contained certain controversial elements linked to the most sensitive part of the doctrines guiding the defence policies of Member States.

Explaining its affirmative vote, Greece said it disapproved of any first aggressive use of any weapon, nuclear or conventional. The Sudan voted in favour, although it did not believe that declarations could by themselves constitute effective disarmament measures. It was joined by Egypt, which also voted affirmatively, in asserting that the principle of non-first-use should be viewed in the broader context of the inadmissibility of the use of force in international relations. Also referring to that principle, Costa Rica supported the proposal in the belief that, if no one used nuclear weapons first, no one would use them second.

Czechoslovakia, voting in favour, asserted that NATO members had not responded positively to the proposal by the Warsaw Treaty countries on the non-first-use of either nuclear or conventional weapons against each other, and a proposal for a world treaty on non-use of force in international relations had been on the negotiating table since 1976. Hungary supported the text in view of its importance and timeliness in regard to the urgent task of eliminating the danger of nuclear war. Voting similarly, India none the less believed that, pending nuclear disarmament, complete prohibition of the use or threat of use of nuclear weapons was the best means of preventing nuclear war. Mongolia believed the proposed measure would enhance confidence and create favourable conditions for nuclear disarmament efforts. Also voting in favour, Sweden attached importance to the establishment of rough parity in the balance of conventional and nuclear forces at lower levels, in order to facilitate non-first-use undertakings by all nuclear-weapon States.

Explaining their votes against the resolution on international co-operation for disarmament, Belgium stated that the concept of non-first-use of nuclear weapons was far from sufficient to meet the supreme requirement of preventing nuclear war, and France said an obligation not to make first use of nuclear weapons would not serve the cause of non-use of force, particularly in the part of the world where France was situated.

Resolutions (1982). GA, 9 Dec.: [1]37/78 B; [2]37/78 J, text following.
Meeting records. GA: plenary, A/S-12/PV.2-26, 28, 29 (8 June–10 July), A/37/PV.98 (9 Dec.); 1st Committee, A/C.1/37/PV.3-10, 12-28, *37*, 41 (18 Oct.–23 Nov.).

General Assembly resolution 37/78 J

9 December 1982   Meeting 98   112-19-15 (recorded vote)

Approved by First Committee (A/37/662) by recorded vote (87-19-18), 23 November (meeting 41); 4-nation draft (A/C.1/37/L.47); agenda item 50 *(f)*.

Sponsors: Cuba, German Democratic Republic, Romania, Viet Nam.

Non-use of nuclear weapons and prevention of nuclear war
The General Assembly,

Alarmed by the threat to the survival of mankind posed by the existence of nuclear weapons and the continuing arms race,

Recalling that, in accordance with the Final Document of the Tenth Special Session of the General Assembly, the first special session devoted to disarmament, effective measures of nuclear disarmament and the prevention of nuclear war have the highest priority,

Bearing in mind its resolutions 36/81 B, 36/92 I and 36/100 of 9 December 1981,

Reaffirming that the most effective guarantee against the danger of nuclear war and the use of nuclear weapons is nuclear disarmament and the complete elimination of nuclear weapons,

Recalling also that, in the Final Document of the Tenth Special Session, it is stated that all States should actively participate in efforts to bring about conditions in international relations among States in which a code of peaceful conduct of nations in international affairs could be agreed upon and which would preclude the use or threat of use of nuclear weapons,

1. *Considers* that the solemn declarations by two nuclear-weapon States made or reiterated at the twelfth special session of the General Assembly, the second special session devoted to disarmament, concerning their respective obligations not to be the first to use nuclear weapons offer an important avenue to decrease the danger of nuclear war;

2. *Expresses the hope* that the other nuclear-weapon States will consider making similar declarations with respect to not being the first to use nuclear weapons.

Recorded vote in Assembly as follows:

In favour: Afghanistan, Algeria, Angola, Antigua and Barbuda, Argentina, Bahrain, Bangladesh, Barbados, Belize, Benin, Bhutan, Bolivia, Botswana, Brazil, Bulgaria, Burma, Burundi, Byelorussian SSR, Cape Verde, Central African Republic, Chad, Chile, Colombia, Comoros, Congo, Costa Rica, Cuba, Cyprus, Czechoslovakia, Democratic Yemen, Djibouti, Dominican Republic, Ecuador, Egypt, El Salvador, Ethiopia, Fiji, Gabon, Gambia, German Democratic Republic, Ghana, Greece, Grenada, Guinea, Guinea-Bissau, Guyana, Haiti, Honduras, Hungary, India, Indonesia, Iran, Iraq, Ireland, Jamaica, Jordan, Kenya, Kuwait, Lao People's Democratic Republic, Lebanon, Liberia, Libyan Arab Jamahiriya, Madagascar, Maldives, Mali, Mauritania, Mauritius, Mexico, Mongolia, Morocco, Mozambique, Nepal, Nicaragua, Niger, Nigeria, Oman, Pakistan, Panama, Papua New Guinea, Peru, Poland, Qatar, Romania, Saint Lucia, Sao Tome and Principe, Senegal, Sierra Leone, Solomon Islands, Somalia, Sri Lanka, Sudan, Suriname, Swaziland, Sweden, Syrian Arab Republic, Thailand, Togo, Trinidad and Tobago, Tunisia, Uganda, Ukrainian SSR, USSR, United Arab Emirates, United Republic of Cameroon, United Republic of Tanzania, Upper Volta, Vanuatu, Venezuela, Viet Nam, Yemen, Yugoslavia, Zambia.

Against: Australia, Belgium, Canada, Denmark, France, Germany, Federal Republic of, Iceland, Israel, Italy, Japan, Luxembourg, Netherlands, New Zealand, Norway, Portugal, Spain, Turkey, United Kingdom, United States.

Abstaining: Austria, Bahamas, China, Finland, Guatemala, Ivory Coast, Malawi, Malaysia, Paraguay, Philippines, Rwanda, Saudi Arabia, Singapore, Uruguay, Zaire.

Proposed convention on prohibition of the neutron bomb

General Assembly consideration (June/July). During the General Assembly's 1982 special session on disarmament, the German Democratic Republic, by a letter dated 24 June to the Chairman of the *Ad Hoc* Committee,[1] submitted a working paper proposing that the Assembly request the Committee on Disarmament to negotiate a convention on the prohibition of the production, stockpiling, stationing and use of neutron weapons. The working paper stated that the introduction of that weapon constituted a qualitative improvement of nuclear-weapon systems, significantly lowered the threshold of nuclear war, increased the danger of such war and gave rise to illusions on the admissibility of a nuclear conflict.

The neutron bomb was defined in the Secretary-General's April report to the Assembly[2] on the protection of nature from the pernicious effects of the arms race as a low-yield nuclear weapon designed to kill or incapacitate people in armoured vehicles mainly by ionizing radiation rather than blast or heat.

In the special session's general debate, Czechoslovakia, Ethiopia and Romania were among those speaking of the need for an agreement prohibiting the development, manufacture and deployment of new systems of nuclear weapons or of weapons of mass destruction, particularly the neutron weapon. Ethiopia said the neutron weapon made a mockery of the sanctity of human life and lowered the nuclear threshold. The Netherlands noted that it had expressed itself against the deployment of this weapon in Europe.

Hungary, which urged the Assembly to adopt a declaration outlawing neutron weapons, was joined by Viet Nam in calling on the Committee on Disarmament to elaborate a treaty on their prohibition. The Ukrainian SSR asserted that talks on this subject in the Committee were being blocked by those actively working to start large-scale production of such weapons.

General Assembly action (December). By a 9 December resolution on prohibition of the nuclear neutron weapon,[3] the General Assembly reiterated its December 1981 request[4] that the Committee on Disarmament start without delay negotiations with a view to concluding a convention on the prohibition of the development, production, stockpiling, deployment and use of such weapons.

The Assembly adopted the resolution by a recorded vote of 81 to 14, with 52 abstentions. The First Committee had approved the text on 22 November by a recorded vote of 59 to 14, with 52 abstentions.

Presenting the 22-nation draft, the German Democratic Republic said a special agreement on banning the neutron weapon was imperative to prevent the creation of other new types of specialized nuclear weapons that could lead to a new round in the nuclear-arms race. The text did not condemn any party and proceeded from the belief that banning neutron weapons would serve the best interests of all States.

Argentina, Bangladesh, Brazil, Egypt, Greece, Ireland, Pakistan, the Sudan, Sweden and Venezuela abstained, as they opposed a selective approach that singled out one type of weapon when there were other similarly dangerous nuclear weapons, all of which they opposed. Costa Rica voiced a similar view in Committee, where it did not participate in the vote; it voted in favour in the Assembly. Sweden, in particular, regretted that the sponsors had not accepted its suggestion to have the resolution apply to "tactical nuclear weapons, in particular nuclear neutron weapons". Guyana abstained for similar reasons, although it considered the neutron weapon to be the ultimate capitalist weapon. Brazil also feared that including a specific item on neutron weapons in the agenda of the Committee on Disarmament would compound that body's difficulties with regard to the long-overdue nuclear-disarmament negotiations.

Also abstaining, Denmark and the Netherlands, neither of which intended to have neutron weapons on their territories, considered the text to be politically inspired: for Denmark, the draft was an undisguised attempt to split the Western allies in an important area of defence policy, while the Netherlands was not interested in a convention prohibiting that weapon specifically.

Voting affirmatively, Cyprus believed the neutron weapon contributed to the concept of a limited nuclear war; India called on the Committee on Disarmament to undertake without delay negotiations for the total elimination of all nuclear weapons; and Sierra Leone opposed the development, production and testing of all nuclear weapons, including the neutron weapon.

Letter. [1]German Democratic Republic, 24 June, A/S-12/AC.1/28.
Report. [2] SG, A/S-12/9.
Resolution (1982). [3]GA: 37/78 E, 9 Dec., text following.
Resolution (prior). [4]GA: 36/92 K, 9 Dec. 1981 (YUN 1981, p. 63).
Meeting records. GA: *Ad Hoc* Committee, A/S-12/AC.1/PV.10 (29 June); 1st Committee, A/C.1/37/PV.3-10, 12-28, *34, 39* (18 Oct.–22 Nov.); plenary, A/37/PV.98 (9 Dec.).

General Assembly resolution 37/78 E

9 December 1982   Meeting 98   81-14-52 (recorded vote)

Approved by First Committee (A/37/662) by recorded vote (59-14-52), 22 November (meeting 39); 22-nation draft (A/C.1/37/L.25); agenda item 50 *(g).*

Sponsors: Afghanistan, Angola, Bulgaria, Byelorussian SSR, Cuba, Czechoslovakia, Democratic Yemen, Ethiopia, German Democratic Republic, Grenada, Hungary, Jordan, Lao People's Democratic Republic, Mongolia, Mozambique, Poland, Romania, Sao Tome and Principe, Syrian Arab Republic, Ukrainian SSR, Viet Nam, Zimbabwe.

Prohibition of the nuclear neutron weapon

The General Assembly,

Recalling paragraph 50 of the Final Document of the Tenth Special Session of the General Assembly, in which it is stated that the achievement of nuclear disarmament will require urgent negotiations of agreements, *inter alia,* on the cessation of the qualitative improvement and development of nuclear-weapon systems,

Stressing that the nuclear neutron weapon represents a further step in the qualitative arms race in the field of nuclear weapons,

Reaffirming its resolution 36/92 K of 9 December 1981,

Sharing the world-wide concern expressed by Member States, as well as by non-governmental organizations, over the continued and expanded production and introduction of the nuclear neutron weapon in military arsenals, which escalates the nuclear-arms race and significantly lowers the threshold of nuclear war,

Aware of the inhuman effects of that weapon, which constitutes a grave threat, particularly to the unprotected civilian population,

Noting the consideration by the Committee on Disarmament during its session held in 1982 of issues connected with the cessation of the nuclear-arms race and nuclear disarmament, as well as the prohibition of the nuclear neutron weapon,

Regretting that the Committee on Disarmament was not able to reach agreement on the commencement of negotiations on the cessation of the nuclear-arms race and nuclear disarmament or on the prohibition of the nuclear neutron weapon in an appropriate organizational framework,

1. *Reiterates its request* to the Committee on Disarmament to start without delay negotiations within an appropriate organizational framework with a view to concluding a convention on the prohibition of the development, production, stockpiling, deployment and use of nuclear neutron weapons;

2. *Requests* the Secretary-General to transmit to the Committee on Disarmament all documents relating to the discussion of this question by the General Assembly at its twelfth special session and at its thirty-seventh session;

3. *Requests* the Committee on Disarmament to submit a report on this question to the General Assembly at its thirty-eighth session;

4. *Decides* to include in the provisional agenda of its thirty-eighth session the item entitled "Prohibition of the nuclear neutron weapon".

Recorded vote in Assembly as follows:

In favour: Afghanistan, Algeria, Angola, Antigua and Barbuda, Bahrain, Barbados, Belize, Benin, Botswana, Bulgaria, Burundi, Byelorussian SSR, Cape Verde, Central African Republic, Chad, Congo, Costa Rica, Cuba, Cyprus, Czechoslovakia, Democratic Yemen, Dominican Republic, Ecuador, Ethiopia, Fiji, Finland, Gabon, Gambia, German Democratic Republic, Ghana, Grenada, Guinea, Guinea-Bissau, Haiti, Honduras, Hungary, India, Indonesia, Iran, Iraq, Jordan, Kenya, Kuwait,[a] Lao People's Democratic Republic, Libyan Arab Jamahiriya, Madagascar, Mali, Malta, Mauritania, Mauritius, Mexico, Mongolia, Mozambique, Nicaragua, Oman,[a] Panama, Papua New Guinea, Poland, Qatar, Romania, Rwanda, Sao Tome and Principe, Senegal, Sierra Leone, Solomon Islands,

Suriname, Swaziland, Syrian Arab Republic, Togo, Trinidad and Tobago, Uganda, Ukrainian SSR, USSR, United Arab Emirates, United Republic of Cameroon, United Republic of Tanzania, Vanuatu, Viet Nam, Yemen, Yugoslavia, Zambia.

Against: Australia, Belgium, Canada, France, Germany, Federal Republic of, Israel, Italy, Japan, Luxembourg, New Zealand, Portugal, Turkey, United Kingdom, United States.

Abstaining: Argentina, Austria, Bahamas, Bangladesh, Bhutan, Bolivia, Brazil, Burma, Chile, Colombia, Comoros, Democratic Kampuchea, Denmark, Djibouti, Egypt, El Salvador, Greece, Guatemala, Guyana, Iceland, Ireland, Ivory Coast, Jamaica, Lebanon, Liberia, Malawi, Malaysia, Maldives, Morocco, Nepal, Netherlands, Niger, Nigeria, Norway, Pakistan, Paraguay, Peru, Philippines, Saint Lucia, Saudi Arabia, Singapore, Somalia, Spain, Sri Lanka, Sudan, Sweden, Thailand, Tunisia, Upper Volta, Uruguay, Venezuela, Zaire.

aLater advised the Secretariat it had intended to abstain.

Nuclear non-proliferation

The General Assembly continued to call in 1982 for measures to prevent the spread of nuclear weapons to countries other than the known nuclear-weapon Powers and to areas where none were currently located. This was the main objective of the 1968 Treaty on the Non-Proliferation of Nuclear Weapons[4] (NPT), to which there were 119 States parties as at 31 December 1982.

In December, the Assembly requested the Committee on Disarmament to hold talks aimed at elaborating an international agreement on the non-stationing of nuclear weapons on the territories of States where no such weapons currently existed. It continued to encourage agreement by States in the regions concerned on the establishment of nuclear-weapon-free zones. It authorized United Nations assistance to a 1983 review conference of the parties to the Treaty on the Prohibition of the Emplacement of Nuclear Weapons and Other Weapons of Mass Destruction on the Sea-Bed and the Ocean Floor and in the Subsoil Thereof.

General Assembly consideration (June/July). During the General Assembly's second special session devoted to disarmament, Denmark, Finland, Iceland, Norway and Sweden, by a letter of 10 May to the Secretary-General, submitted a working paper on the non-proliferation of nuclear weapons[1] in which they advocated the following: adherence to NPT by the largest possible number of States; acceptance by all non-nuclear-weapon States of full-scope safeguards of the International Atomic Energy Agency (IAEA) on all their current and future nuclear activities; requirement of full-scope safeguards as a condition for export of all nuclear material, equipment and technology; strengthening IAEA safeguards; early conclusion of a comprehensive test-ban treaty; renunciation of any act which would defeat the object of strategic arms limitation, and early resumption of negotiations on the topic; international arrangements to assure non-nuclear-weapon States against nuclear-weapon use or threat; and the creation of nuclear-weapon-free zones.

By a 28 June letter to the Secretary-General,[2] Viet Nam transmitted a 14 June message from its Minister for Foreign Affairs to his counterpart in the USSR—one of the depositary Governments for NPT—conveying its instrument of accession to the Treaty.

Paragraphs relating to nuclear non-proliferation were among the uncontested parts of the draft comprehensive programme of disarmament as it stood at the end of the special session.[3] In the chapter on principles it was stated that disarmament measures must be consistent with the inalienable right of all States to develop, acquire and use nuclear technology, equipment and materials for peaceful use and to determine their peaceful nuclear programmes in accordance with national priorities, needs and interests, bearing in mind the need to prevent nuclear-weapon proliferation. International cooperation in this area should be conducted under non-discriminatory safeguards. Full implementation of non-proliferation treaties would be an important contribution. The draft reproduced paragraphs from the Final Document of the Tenth Special Session of the General Assembly (1978) on the right to peaceful uses of nuclear energy under agreed safeguards.[5]

Agreement was not reached on more specific provisions concerning non-proliferation proposed for inclusion in the chapter of the draft programme concerned with disarmament measures.

In the general debate at the special session, Austria observed that States, particularly those with a potential nuclear capacity, must weigh the possible short-term advantages of possessing nuclear weapons against the disastrous international consequences of the further spread of such weapons.

Cyprus, Czechoslovakia, the Libyan Arab Jamahiriya, Poland, Turkey, the United States and Zimbabwe called for strengthening the international régime of nuclear non-proliferation as established by NPT. Belgium, on behalf of the European Community members, recognized the importance of new measures to make the régime more effective and to assure all States of respect for their inalienable right to the peaceful use of nuclear energy. Bhutan believed that NPT should be strengthened and made equitable so as to ensure its wider acceptance. Bolivia suggested that the militarily significant States study an agreement to control the flow of nuclear materials in support of NPT. Honduras also called for a strengthening, particularly through improved methods of monitoring and controlling the transfer of nuclear materials for peaceful purposes. Sierra Leone saw a need to enforce the régime on a universal and non-discriminatory basis.

Many other speakers stressed the importance of NPT as a major means of preventing the spread of nuclear weapons to States that did not possess them. Australia, Austria, Denmark, Fiji, Hungary, Iceland, Japan, Kenya, Malaysia, New Zealand, Somalia and Tunisia were among those calling for universal adherence to NPT, and Mongolia suggested that the Assembly should make that call at the special session.   In the view of Portugal, NPT would not attain its full moral and political dimensions until all States, particularly those with advanced technology, became parties and undertook to use nuclear technology only for peaceful purposes. Sweden viewed as a serious shortcoming of NPT the fact that many important non-nuclear-weapon States were not among its signatories and that two of the nuclear-weapon States had not acceded. The United Kingdom asserted that there had been no additional nuclear-weapon State since 1964.

Several States spoke of the need to reinforce IAEA functions in overseeing safeguards against the diversion of nuclear processes or materials to military purposes. Fiji saw the effectiveness of NPT as limited by the reluctance of some non-nuclear-weapon States to enter into safeguards agreements, and said the Agency's role in that regard should be enhanced if necessary in order to generate the confidence needed for the participation of all States. Finland said the refusal by some States to adhere to NPT and to accept international safeguards on all their nuclear activities hampered international co-operation in the peaceful uses of nuclear energy. The Netherlands and Sweden also noted the importance of having all States accept safeguards for their nuclear installations, and Denmark urged all States with non-military nuclear facilities to accept international safeguards for all fissionable materials.

Reaffirming its commitment to abide strictly by all the obligations it had entered into, Argentina expressly reserved its right regarding the so-called non-proscribed military uses of nuclear energy; at the same time, it would continue to develop unhindered its potential for peaceful uses. Chile said that, although the safeguards stipulated by NPT did not apply to non-parties, it was necessary to encourage the widest utilization, and political reinforcement, of IAEA safeguards.

Australia, Nepal and Panama urged a strengthening and extension of the IAEA safeguards system as a measure of practical operation of NPT and as a working international system of verification. In the view of Turkey, IAEA, which had proved its efficiency for verification, deserved to be strengthened and expanded, particularly to meet the requirements of promoting the peaceful uses of nuclear energy. The USSR said it was agreeable to placing part of its peaceful nuclear installations under IAEA control.

Kuwait reaffirmed the right of States to use nuclear energy for peaceful purposes, and Uruguay declared it the right of all non-nuclear-weapon States parties to NPT to benefit from the peaceful uses of nuclear energy, subject to inter-national control to prevent clandestine uses for military purposes. Also stressing the importance of promoting peaceful uses, Japan said nuclear-energy development must be made compatible with the prevention of nuclear proliferation. Morocco saw a need for international co-operation in the use of nuclear technology for the development of developing countries. Papua New Guinea said such co-operation should be conducted under agreed and appropriate international safeguards applied on a non-discriminatory basis. Pakistan asserted that the international community should respond to the legitimate security concerns of the non-nuclear-weapon States and their right to free and unhindered access to nuclear technology for peaceful purposes.

France urged the international community to support the establishment of zones of peaceful nuclear co-operation by reconciling guarantees of non-proliferation with the dissemination of all non-military nuclear technology, without discrimination; to that end, regional centres for the enrichment or reprocessing of nuclear fuels could be set up with the assistance of countries possessing the technology, to provide groups of States that had freely decided to form nuclear-free or nuclear co-operation zones with privileged access to all technology relating to the nuclear fuel cycle. The Netherlands advocated the establishment of new arrangements to improve the safety of the nuclear fuel cycle, such as an international plutonium storage régime.

Several developing countries regretted what they saw as lack of commitment by nuclear-weapon States to abide fully by NPT, and particularly its clause obliging parties to pursue negotiations in good faith on cessation of the nuclear-arms race. Brazil said the nuclear-weapon Powers had interpreted NPT as a licence to continue the proliferation of their nuclear arsenals in quality and quantity. Egypt thought compliance with that obligation on the part of the nuclear Powers would be a practical way of convincing additional non-nuclear-weapon States to adhere to NPT. Guyana, despite its regret over some imbalance inherent in NPT, was joined by the United Republic of Tanzania in urging those countries to act consistently with the objectives of that instrument.

Nepal and Nigeria asked the nuclear-weapon States parties to NPT to show tangible proof of their readiness to fulfil their moral and legal obligations under it. Peru said the nuclear Powers' lack of will to initiate disarmament would prompt countries to ask why what was indispensable for some should not be considered necessary for others.

Some speakers regarded NPT as discriminatory against non-nuclear-weapon States. India considered that it was based on the faulty notion of checking horizontal proliferation alone without placing simultaneous and equal curbs on the existing nuclear-weapon States. Indonesia observed that it was a party to NPT despite misgivings about the Treaty's discriminatory character and the unequal obligations it imposed on nuclear and non-nuclear States. Iran, though stating that it agreed with NPT, believed it vain to implement the Treaty without also eradicating all existing nuclear weapons, because nuclear weapons would otherwise remain at the disposal of the super-Powers.

Jamaica said the unrestrained vertical proliferation embarked upon by the nuclear Powers strengthened the contention that the Treaty's obligations as regards non-nuclear-weapon States were discriminatory. The Upper Volta said NPT had not offered the non-nuclear-weapon States the real guarantees they were entitled to expect from the nuclear-weapon States.

Australia mentioned two pressures challenging non-proliferation: the temptation to develop civilian nuclear facilities towards but stopping just short of the capacity to produce nuclear weapons, and the possible undermining of non-proliferation principles by the failure of some suppliers and customers to apply full-scope safeguards to all nuclear transactions. Botswana asserted that the two super-Powers had not restricted their race to themselves, as illustrated by the fact that nuclear reactors purportedly meant for the peaceful development of energy resources, but capable of producing nuclear bombs, were part of foreign aid.

Jordan, pointing to Israel's refusal to adhere to NPT and allow its nuclear facilities to be investigated, said the benefits derived by not adhering would encourage others to follow suit, with the result that NPT was contributing to nuclear proliferation instead of ending it. Samoa, expressing concern at what it saw as a runaway nuclear-weapon problem, said the build-up of such arms by the super-Powers in the name of self-protection and deterrence had legitimized such pursuits by other countries as a matter of national entitlement.

Disappointment was expressed by some over the results of the second Review Conference of the Parties to NPT, held in 1980.[6] Morocco regretted the failure of the Conference to take practical steps to implement all the Treaty's objectives, a failure which Nigeria regarded as a manifestation of a wide crack in the Treaty wall.

Several speakers pointed to the nuclear capabilities of Israel and South Africa as a threat to the non-proliferation régime.

Letters. [1]Denmark, Finland, Iceland, Norway, Sweden, 10 May, A/S-12/21; [2]Viet Nam, 28 June, A/S-12/AC.1/56. *Report.* [3]*Ad Hoc* Committee, A/S-12/32.
Resolutions. GA: [4]2373(XXII), annex, 12 June 1968 (YUN 1968, p. 17); [5]S-10/2, 30 June 1978 (YUN 1978, p. 39).
Yearbook reference. [6]1980, p. 51.

Non-placement of nuclear weapons in non-nuclear-weapon States

General Assembly consideration (June/July). In the general debate at the second special session of the General Assembly on disarmament, in June/July 1982, Czechoslovakia, Hungary and the Philippines expressed support for the principle that nuclear arms should not be stationed on the territory of States where such weapons were not currently placed. Mongolia urged the Assembly to favour speedy initiation of negotiations on an agreement to that effect. Zimbabwe also saw the need for an international agreement, and the Ukrainian SSR hoped the special session would promote its conclusion. To prevent the spread of nuclear weapons, said the Lao People's Democratic Republic, all imperialist military bases should immediately be dismantled.

General Assembly action (December). By a resolution of 13 December,[1] the General Assembly again requested the Committee on Disarmament to proceed without delay to talks aimed at elaborating an international agreement on the non-stationing of nuclear weapons on the territories of States where there were currently no such weapons. Expressing deep alarm over plans for nuclear-weapon build-up on the territories of other States, the Assembly called on all nuclear-weapon States not to station such weapons in States where there were none, to refrain from their further stationing in other States and to freeze qualitatively those that were already there.

The resolution was adopted by a recorded vote of 70 to 18, with 51 abstentions. The First Committee had approved the text on 24 November by a recorded vote of 55 to 19, with 44 abstentions.

Introducing the 17-nation draft, Hungary recalled that the Assembly's call for the non-stationing of nuclear weapons had been repeated annually since 1978[2] and the request to the Committee on Disarmament since 1980.[3] Prevention of further deployment, and subsequent withdrawal of nuclear weapons from the territories of other countries, would help strengthen the non-proliferation régime, contribute to the creation of nuclear-weapon-free zones and help prevent destabilization of the existing approximate strategic balance of nuclear power.

In explanation of its negative vote, Belgium said the proposal could deny States the exercise of their right of collective defence, while the declaration of a qualitative freeze would endorse existing inequalities between the arsenals of opposing parties. Voting similarly, Japan asserted that, under current circumstances, restriction of nuclear-weapon deployment might destabilize the international military balance and thereby prove detrimental to the maintenance of peace and security. For Belgium and Japan, the proposal was also unclear on effective verification measures.

Brazil, which abstained, felt that the non-stationing concept conferred legality on the presence of nuclear weapons where they already existed; similarly, the proposed qualitative freeze could leave the nuclear-weapon States free to improve their arsenals. Also abstaining, the United Republic of Cameroon questioned why the ban relating to nuclear weapons on the territories of other States was restricted to qualitative aspects. Noting that the sponsors were mainly members of one military alliance, Ireland abstained to remain neutral on the strategic issues between the two alliances.

Sweden abstained because, though it attached great importance to measures aimed at preventing the stationing of nuclear weapons in States where there were none, it had reservations about seeking to solve a complex problem by dealing with only one of its aspects in an international agreement. Yugoslavia, also abstaining, supported non-stationing but said the proposed framework was narrow and inadequate: the envisaged agreement should encompass the withdrawal of nuclear weapons from the territories of non-nuclear-weapon States where such weapons were already located and extend to all other areas and spaces as well.

Argentina, Finland, India and Indonesia voted affirmatively in expression of their support for nuclear disarmament, despite certain reservations. For Argentina, paragraph 3, on a qualitative freeze, introduced an extraneous element on which it would have abstained had there been a separate vote. Indonesia also would not have supported that paragraph. India's positive vote was not an endorsement of the polemical elements in the text, nor of the recommendation for an international agreement, since India believed the Committee on Disarmament should negotiate on cessation of the nuclear-arms race and nuclear disarmament. Finland asserted that each Government's right to interpret its own security needs should be kept in mind in examining the possibility of an international agreement; it also took exception to the last preambular paragraph and paragraph 2 (on the build-up and stationing of nuclear weapons in other States) on the ground that they tended to prejudge the outcome of the Geneva talks on intermediate-range nuclear forces.

Resolution (1982). [1]GA: 37/99 A, 13 Dec., text following.
Resolutions (prior). GA: [2]33/91 F, 16 Dec. 1978 (YUN 1978, p. 95); [3]35/156 C, 12 Dec. 1980 (YUN 1980, p. 68).
Meeting records. GA: 1st Committee, A/C.1/37/PV.3-10, 12-28, 33, 42 (18 Oct.–24 Nov.); plenary, A/37/PV.101 (13 Dec.).

General Assembly resolution 37/99 A

13 December 1982   Meeting 101   70-18-51 (recorded vote)

Approved by First Committee (A/37/667) by recorded vote (55-19-44), 24 November (meeting 42); 17-nation draft (A/C.1/37/L.18); agenda item 55 *(d)*.

Sponsors: Afghanistan, Angola, Bulgaria, Byelorussian SSR, Czechoslovakia, Democratic Yemen, Ethiopia, German Democratic Republic, Hungary, Lao People's Democratic Republic, Madagascar, Mongolia, Mozambique, Poland, Ukrainian SSR, USSR, Viet Nam.

Non-stationing of nuclear weapons on the territories of States where there are no such weapons at present

The General Assembly,

Conscious that a nuclear war would have devastating consequences for the whole of mankind,

Recalling its resolution 33/91 F of 16 December 1978, which contains an appeal to all nuclear-weapon States to refrain from stationing nuclear weapons on the territories of States where there are no such weapons at present and to all non-nuclear-weapon States that do not have nuclear weapons on their territories to refrain from any steps that would directly or indirectly result in the stationing of such weapons on their territories,

Recalling further its resolutions 35/156 C of 12 December 1980 and 36/97 E of 9 December 1981, in which it requested the Committee on Disarmament to proceed without delay to talks with a view to elaborating an international agreement on the non-stationing of nuclear weapons on the territories of States where there are no such weapons at present,

Noting with regret that the appeals by the General Assembly remain unheeded,

Considering that the non-stationing of nuclear weapons on the territories of States where there are no such weapons at present would constitute a step towards the larger objective of the subsequent complete withdrawal of nuclear weapons from the territories of other States, thus contributing to the prevention of the spread of nuclear weapons and leading eventually to the total elimination of nuclear weapons,

Bearing in mind the clearly expressed intention of many States to prevent the stationing of nuclear weapons on their territories,

Deeply alarmed by plans and practical steps leading to a build-up of nuclear-weapon arsenals on the territories of other States,

1. *Requests once again* the Committee on Disarmament to proceed without delay to talks with a view to elaborating an international agreement on the non-stationing of nuclear weapons on the territories of States where there are no such weapons at present;

2. *Calls upon* all nuclear-weapon States not to station nuclear weapons on the territories of States where there are no such weapons at present and to refrain from further action involving the stationing of nuclear weapons on the territories of other States;

3. *Calls upon* all nuclear-weapon States to freeze qualitatively nuclear weapons on the territories of other States;

4. *Requests* the Secretary-General to transmit to the Committee on Disarmament all documents relating to the discussion of this question by the General Assembly at its thirty-seventh session;

5. *Requests* the Committee on Disarmament to submit a report on the question to the General Assembly at its thirty-eighth session;

6. *Decides* to include in the provisional agenda of its thirty-eighth session the item entitled "Non-stationing of nuclear weapons on the territories of States where there are no such weapons at present: report of the Committee on Disarmament".

Recorded vote in Assembly as follows:

In favour: Afghanistan, Angola, Argentina, Bahrain, Barbados, Benin, Bhutan, Botswana, Bulgaria, Burundi, Byelorussian SSR, Central African Republic, Chad, Congo, Cuba, Czechoslovakia, Democratic Yemen, Dominican Republic, Ecuador, Egypt, Ethiopia, Fiji, Finland, German Democratic Republic, Ghana, Grenada, Guinea, Guyana, Honduras, Hungary, India, Indonesia, Iraq, Jordan, Kenya, Kuwait, Lao People's Democratic Republic, Lesotho, Libyan Arab Jamahiriya, Madagascar, Malaysia, Mali, Mauritania, Mauritius, Mexico, Mongolia, Mozambique, Nicaragua, Niger, Nigeria, Panama, Papua New Guinea, Poland, Qatar, Romania, Rwanda, Sao Tome and Principe, Swaziland, Syrian Arab Republic, Trinidad and Tobago, Uganda, Ukrainian SSR, USSR, United Arab Emirates, Upper Volta, Vanuatu, Venezuela, Viet Nam, Zambia.

Against: Australia, Belgium, Canada, Denmark, France, Germany, Federal Republic of, Iceland, Italy, Japan, Luxembourg, Netherlands, New Zealand, Norway, Portugal, Spain, Turkey, United Kingdom, United States.

Abstaining: Algeria, Austria, Bahamas, Bangladesh, Bolivia, Brazil, Burma, Chile, Colombia, Comoros, Costa Rica, Cyprus, Democratic Kampuchea, Djibouti, El Salvador, Gabon, Greece, Guatemala, Guinea-Bissau, Haiti, Ireland, Israel, Jamaica, Lebanon, Liberia, Malawi, Morocco, Nepal, Oman, Pakistan, Paraguay, Peru, Philippines, Saudi Arabia, Senegal, Sierra Leone, Singapore, Solomon Islands, Somalia, Sri Lanka, Sudan, Suriname, Sweden, Thailand, Togo, Tunisia, United Republic of Cameroon, United Republic of Tanzania, Uruguay, Yugoslavia, Zaire.

Establishment of nuclear-weapon-free zones

As in previous years, the General Assembly made recommendations in December 1982 on the establishment of nuclear-weapon-free zones in Africa, the Middle East and South Asia, as well as on consolidation of the existing zone in Latin America. Suggestions were made during Assembly debates for creating such zones in Europe, the Nordic region, the Balkans and the South Pacific (see below).

The Assembly repeated its call on all States to respect Africa as a nuclear-weapon-free zone. To that end, it called on States and corporations to terminate forthwith all military and nuclear collaboration with South Africa, including the provision of computers and other electronic equipment. Concerning the Middle East, it urged all parties directly concerned seriously to consider implementing the proposal to establish such a zone in that region. It reaffirmed its endorsement in principle of the concept of such a zone in South Asia. In regard to the one existing nuclear-weapon-free zone in a populated area—Latin America—the Assembly urged France not to delay any further in becoming a party to the Treaty for the Prohibition of Nuclear Weapons in Latin America.

Also in December, the Assembly requested the Secretary-General, with the assistance of an *ad hoc* group of governmental experts, to review and supplement a seven-year-old United Nations study of nuclear-weapon-free zones, covering all aspects of the question. On a related topic, it requested the Secretary-General to assist the 1983 Review Conference of the Parties to the 1970 Treaty on the Prohibition of the Emplacement of Nuclear Weapons and Other Weapons of Mass Destruction on the Sea-Bed and the Ocean Floor and in the Subsoil Thereof.

General Assembly consideration (June/ July). The establishment of nuclear-weapon-free zones on the basis of agreements or arrangements freely arrived at among the States of the zone and full compliance therewith, thus ensuring that the zones were genuinely free from nuclear weapons, and respect for such zones by nuclear-weapon States, constituted an important disarmament measure, according to an agreed paragraph in the "Principles" chapter of the draft comprehensive programme of disarmament, considered by the General Assembly at its 1982 special session on disarmament.[1] However, more detailed provisions, intended for inclusion in the chapter on disarmament measures, were not agreed upon.

In the general debate at the session, support for the principle and objectives of nuclear-weapon-free zones was expressed by many, among them Bangladesh, Burundi, Czechoslovakia, Democratic Kampuchea, Denmark, Ethiopia, Finland, Indonesia, Italy, Japan, the Libyan Arab Jamahiriya, Morocco, Mozambique, Nepal, the Netherlands, New Zealand, Nigeria, Oman, Papua New Guinea, Peru, the Philippines, Portugal, Romania, the Sudan, the Ukrainian SSR, the United Republic of Tanzania, Uruguay and Viet Nam. Several of these speakers emphasized that arrangements for such zones must be made with the free choice of the States concerned.

Belgium, on behalf of the European Community members, said the establishment of such zones in certain regions could be a major contribution to disarmament, in so far as all States concerned were prepared to co-operate on the basis of freely concluded arrangements. Bolivia thought the militarily significant States should promote regional denuclearization following the example of the nuclear-weapon-free zone in Latin America. France favoured such zones in areas where the balance of power did not rest on nuclear deterrent forces, but said they should be established only by the unanimous decision of the States concerned, with no imposition from outside; it also suggested that the international community study the possibility of making technical means of verification available to such groupings. Liberia believed the entire third world should be preserved as a nuclear-weapon-free zone.

Maldives believed the concept should be promoted by allowing the States of the region to take the necessary action free from outside pressure. Turkey was among those which asserted that the desire to create such zones should come from the countries in the regions concerned and should honour the principle of undiminished security.

The Bahamas said that initiatives of non-militarily-significant States were prerequisites for effective nuclear-weapon-free zones and zones of peace. Iraq supported the concept as complementary to efforts for comprehensive disarmament and as all the more important where States in a region possessed or had the capability of possessing nuclear weapons, since that would lead others in the region to seek the same capability. Kuwait viewed the concept as a means of reducing nuclear proliferation and as a guarantee of the security of the non-nuclear-weapon countries. Mongolia believed the General Assembly should support an expansion of the concept, including the creation of such zones in regions where nuclear weapons were already deployed. The United Republic of Cameroon deplored the problems impeding the creation of such zones. The USSR pledged its contribution to the search for generally acceptable solutions concerning the establishment of nuclear-weapon-free zones.

Asserting that the concept had become unrealistic, India said it opposed legitimization of the possession of nuclear weapons by a few Powers by agreeing to live under their professedly benign protection in the guise of a nuclear-weapon-free zone;

instead, the whole world should be free of nuclear weapons. Iran asked what the United Nations could do about countries that openly disregarded their international obligations and secretly produced and amassed nuclear arms. Saint Vincent and the Grenadines thought it too late to pursue the concept of nuclear-weapon-free zones, since a piece-by-piece approach merely made it easier to tolerate the danger when what was needed was the complete removal of the cause.

Views on such zones in various parts of the world, other than those traditionally discussed, were also heard in the general debate. Bulgaria, Czechoslovakia, the Libyan Arab Jamahiriya and Viet Nam voiced support for the creation of a nuclear-weapon-free zone in Europe, while Poland supported one for northern Europe. Denmark remarked that the Nordic countries were already nuclear-free and none of them would want to change that, but the global threat of nuclear war could not be removed solely by declaring parts of the world free of nuclear weapons. For Norway, the creation of a nuclear-weapon-free zone in northern Europe would be meaningful only if it contributed to mutual and balanced nuclear disarmament and thus served to enhance security, not diminish it. Finland, which had previously suggested the establishment of a Nordic nuclear-weapon-free zone, said the Nordic Foreign Ministers had agreed to maintain contacts on the issue. Sweden stated the position of its Parliament that the Government should keep in close contact with the other Nordic Governments on the issue and explore whether there was common ground.

Along with Bulgaria, Greece and Poland, which supported creation of a nuclear-weapon-free zone in the Balkans, Yugoslavia attached importance to the transformation of the Balkans into a zone of peace and co-operation, free from nuclear weapons. Endorsing that idea, Romania favoured a Balkan meeting of heads of State or Government. Albania thought the situation in the Balkans would be greatly improved if the States of the region took practical measures to prevent the super-Powers from intervening in that region.

New Zealand, although aware of the difficulties, favoured the establishment of a verifiable nuclear-weapon-free zone in the South Pacific, compatible with the rules of international law and the security arrangements to which New Zealand was a party. Iraq voiced support for such a zone, as did Papua New Guinea, which said it was the collective wish of the peoples of the region to keep the area free from all forms of nuclear activity.

Report. [1]*Ad Hoc* Committee, A/S-12/32.

Study by a group of experts

By a resolution of 13 December 1982,[3] the General Assembly decided that a study should be made to review and supplement the study on nuclear-weapon-free zones prepared for it in 1975 by a group of experts.[5] The Secretary-General was requested to conduct the study, with the assistance of an *ad hoc* group of governmental experts, and to report in 1984.

The resolution was adopted by a recorded vote of 141 to 1, with 2 abstentions. On 26 November, the First Committee had approved the draft, orally revised, by a recorded vote of 125 to 1, with 2 abstentions.

A proposal for such a study had been made by Finland in a letter dated 13 May to the Secretary-General,[1] followed by another dated 28 June containing a working paper.[2] Both were circulated at the Assembly's second special session on disarmament.

Introducing the 15-nation draft resolution to the First Committee in November, Finland reiterated what it had stated in its two letters as well as in the general debate at the special session: that a number of important developments had taken place since the completion of the 1975 study, including progress in regard to the one existing zone in Latin America, consideration by the Committee on Disarmament of the security of non-nuclear-weapon States, the discussion of proposals for such zones as well as for zones of peace in various regions, wide agreement that such zones would be effective against nuclear proliferation, and extensive analysis of regional disarmament approaches. Finland believed that a broader consensus could be reached on several aspects of the question than had been possible in 1975.

India cast a negative vote, reiterating what it had said at the special session, namely that the concept had become unrealistic and obsolete, that the nuclear-weapon-free zone was a guise to legitimize possession of such weapons by a few countries and that nuclear disarmament, like peace, could not be geographically piecemeal.

The USSR said its affirmative vote should not be interpreted as a change of its position on the 1975 Assembly declaration defining the concept of the zone and the obligations of nuclear-weapon States,[4] to which the current text referred (the USSR position was that it could not automatically assume obligations with regard to such zones[6]).

Letters. Finland: [1]13 May, A/S-12/19; [2]28 June, A/S-12/AC.1/50.
Resolution (1982). [3]GA: 37/99 F, 13 Dec., text following.
Resolution (prior). [4]GA: 3472 B (XXX), 11 Dec. 1975 (YUN 1975, p. 50).
Yearbook references. 1975, [5]p. 8, [6]p. 39.
Financial implications. ACABQ report, A/37/7/Add.16; 5th Committee report, A/37/734; S-G statements, A/C.1/37/L.72, A/C.5/37/84.
Meeting records. GA: *Ad Hoc* Committee, A/S-12/AC.1/PV.10 (29 June); 1st Committee, A/C.1/37/PV.3-10, 12-28, *37, 45* (18 Oct.–26 Nov.); 5th Committee, A/C.5/37/SR.62 (10 Dec.); plenary, A/37/PV.101 (13 Dec.).

General Assembly resolution 37/99 F

13 December 1982   Meeting 101   141-1-2 (recorded vote)

Approved by First Committee (A/37/667) by recorded vote (125-1-2), 26 November (meeting 45); 15-nation draft (A/C.1/37/L.52), orally revised; agenda item 55.

Sponsors: Colombia, Ecuador, Egypt, Finland, France, Ghana, Greece, Mexico, Morocco, Nigeria, Senegal, Sierra Leone, Sri Lanka, Sweden, Uruguay.

Review of and supplement to the *Comprehensive study of the question of nuclear-weapon-free zones in all its aspects*

The General Assembly,

Conscious of the need to make every effort towards achieving a cessation of the nuclear-arms race, nuclear disarmament and general and complete disarmament under strict and effective international control,

Recognizing, in pursuance of these ends, the urgent need to prevent the proliferation of nuclear weapons in the world,

Affirming that the establishment of nuclear-weapon-free zones is a contribution to disarmament,

Recalling its resolution 3472(XXX) of 11 December 1975 on the comprehensive study of the question of nuclear-weapon-free zones in all its aspects,

Recalling the views, observations and suggestions made on it by Governments, and by the International Atomic Energy Agency and other international organizations concerned, and the report of the Secretary-General containing them,

Considering that questions related to the establishment of nuclear-weapon-free zones in various parts of the world have been addressed in a number of recent studies undertaken by the United Nations in the field of disarmament,

Considering further that the experience of the Treaty for the Prohibition of Nuclear Weapons in Latin America (Treaty of Tlatelolco) would be of great value for the other regions of the world,

Recognizing that these developments should be recorded in a new complementary study of this subject,

1. *Decides* that a study should be undertaken to review and supplement the *Comprehensive study of the question of nuclear-weapon-free zones in all its aspects* in the light of information and experience accumulated since 1975;

2. *Requests* the Secretary-General, with the assistance of an *ad hoc* group of qualified governmental experts,* to carry out the study and to submit it to the General Assembly at its thirty-ninth session, bearing in mind the savings that may be made within existing budgetary appropriations;

3. *Calls upon* interested Governments and international organizations concerned to extend such assistance as may be required from time to time for the carrying out of the study;

4. *Decides* to include in the provisional agenda of its thirty-ninth session an item entitled "Study of the question of nuclear-weapon-free zones in all its aspects".

---

*Subsequently referred to as the Group of Governmental Experts on Nuclear-Weapon-Free Zones.

Recorded vote in Assembly as follows:

In favour: Afghanistan, Algeria, Angola, Argentina, Australia, Austria, Bahamas, Bahrain, Bangladesh, Barbados, Belgium, Benin, Bolivia, Botswana, Brazil, Bulgaria, Burma, Burundi, Byelorussian SSR, Canada, Central African Republic, Chad, Chile, China, Colombia, Comoros, Congo, Costa Rica, Cuba, Cyprus, Czechoslovakia, Democratic Kampuchea, Democratic Yemen, Denmark, Djibouti, Dominican Republic, Ecuador, Egypt, El Salvador, Equatorial Guinea, Ethiopia, Fiji, Finland, France, Gabon, German Democratic Republic, Germany, Federal Republic of, Ghana, Greece, Grenada, Guatemala, Guinea, Guinea-Bissau, Haiti, Honduras, Hungary, Iceland, Indonesia, Iran, Iraq, Ireland, Israel, Italy, Jamaica, Japan, Jordan, Kenya, Kuwait, Lao People's Democratic Republic, Lebanon, Lesotho, Liberia, Libyan Arab Jamahiriya, Luxembourg, Madagascar, Malawi, Malaysia, Maldives, Mali, Malta, Mauritania, Mauritius, Mexico, Mongolia, Morocco, Mozambique, Nepal, Netherlands, New Zealand, Nicaragua, Niger, Nigeria, Norway, Oman, Pakistan, Panama, Papua New Guinea, Paraguay, Peru, Philippines, Poland, Portugal, Qatar, Romania, Rwanda, Saint Lucia, Sao Tome and Principe, Saudi Arabia, Senegal, Sierra Leone, Singapore, Solomon Islands, Somalia, Spain, Sri Lanka, Sudan, Suriname, Swaziland, Sweden, Syrian Arab Republic, Thailand, Togo, Trinidad and Tobago, Tunisia, Turkey, Uganda, Ukrainian SSR, USSR, United Arab Emirates, United Kingdom, United Republic of Cameroon, United Republic of Tanzania, Upper Volta, Uruguay, Vanuatu, Venezuela, Viet Nam, Yemen, Yugoslavia, Zaire, Zambia.

Against: India.

Abstaining: Guyana, United States.

Africa

General Assembly consideration (June/ July). At the General Assembly's second special session on disarmament in 1982, support for a nuclear-weapon-free zone in Africa was expressed by a number of speakers in the general debate, among them Burundi, Democratic Kampuchea, Egypt, Honduras, Iraq, the Libyan Arab Jamahiriya, Maldives, Mauritania, Mozambique, Nepal, Oman, Rwanda, the Sudan, the United Republic of Tanzania and Viet Nam. Zimbabwe said nuclear testing or the stationing of nuclear weapons in any State on the continent would threaten the peace and security of all Africans. These and other delegations spoke of the zone largely in relation to the possible nuclear capability of South Africa.

France said it would support such a zone if African countries decided to create one in part or all of the continent.

General Assembly action (December). Noting with concern that South Africa's continued pursuit of a nuclear-weapon capability seriously jeopardized prospects for a denuclearized Africa, the General Assembly, by a resolution of 9 December 1982[1] on implementation of the Declaration on the Denuclearization of Africa adopted by the Organization of African Unity (OAU) in 1964, reiterated its call on all States to consider and respect Africa and its surrounding areas as a nuclear-weapon-free zone. It requested the Security Council, for the purpose of disarmament, to take enforcement measures to prevent any racist régimes from acquiring any arms or arms technology. By this resolution, which dealt mostly with nuclear weapons and South Africa, the Assembly condemned all forms of nuclear collaboration with South Africa and called on States to terminate all military and nuclear collaboration with that country.

This resolution, introduced by Kenya on behalf of the African Group, was adopted by a recorded vote of 134 to none, with 13 abstentions. The First Committee had approved it on 26 November by a recorded vote of 110 to none, with 13 abstentions, following a vote on paragraph 3, on termination of military and nuclear collaboration with South Africa. Another resolution of the same date dealt exclusively with the nuclear capability of South Africa.[2]

Resolutions (1982). GA, 9 Dec.: [1]37/74 A, text following; [2]37/74 B.

Meeting records. GA: 1st Committee, A/C.1/37/PV.3-10, 12-28, *37, 44* (18 Oct.–26 Nov.); plenary, A/37/PV.98 (9 Dec.).

General Assembly resolution 37/74 A

9 December 1982   Meeting 98   134-0-13 (recorded vote)

Approved by First Committee (A/37/656) by recorded vote (110-0-13), 26 November (meeting 44); draft by Kenya, for African Group (A/C.1/37/L.37); agenda item 44.

Implementation of the Declaration

The General Assembly,

Bearing in mind the Declaration on the Denuclearization of Africa adopted by the Assembly of Heads of State and Government of the Organization of African Unity at its first ordinary session, held at Cairo from 17 to 21 July 1964,

Recalling resolution 1652(XVI) of 24 November 1961, its earliest on the subject, as well as resolutions 32/81 of 12 December 1977, 33/63 of 14 December 1978, 34/76 A of 11 December 1979, 35/146 B of 12 December 1980 and 36/86 B of 9 December 1981, in which it called upon all States to consider and respect the continent of Africa as a nuclear-weapon-free zone, in particular resolution 33/63 in which it vigorously condemned any overt or covert attempt by South Africa to introduce nuclear weapons into the continent,

Noting with concern that South Africa's continued pursuit of a nuclear-weapon capability seriously jeopardizes the realization of the objective of a denuclearized Africa and poses a grave danger not only to the security of African States but also to international peace and security,

Taking note of the report of the Security Council Committee established by resolution 421(1977) concerning the question of South Africa on ways and means of making the mandatory arms embargo against South Africa more effective, in particular its recommendation that all forms of nuclear collaboration with South Africa should cease,

Expressing its indignation that certain Western States and Israel have, in flagrant and defiant violation of its relevant resolutions and in utter disregard of international concern on the subject, continued to collaborate with South Africa in the nuclear field, despite the risk and danger of proliferation of nuclear weapons which the nuclear programme of the racist régime represents and poses to the legitimate right of African States to live in peace within secure borders,

Recalling its decision, contained in the Final Document of the Tenth Special Session of the General Assembly, the first special session devoted to disarmament, that the Security Council should take appropriate steps to prevent the frustration of the objective of the Organization of African Unity for the denuclearization of Africa,

Recalling that in the Final Document it noted that the accumulation of armaments and the acquisition of armaments technology by racist régimes, as well as their possible acquisition of nuclear weapons, present a challenging and an increasingly dangerous obstacle to a world community faced with the urgent need to disarm,

1. *Once again reiterates* its call upon all States to consider and respect the continent of Africa and its surrounding areas as a nuclear-weapon-free zone;

2. *Condemns* all forms of nuclear collaboration by any State, corporation, institution or individual with the racist régime of South Africa since such collaboration enables it to frustrate, *inter alia*, the objective of the Declaration on the Denuclearization of Africa which seeks to keep Africa free from nuclear weapons;

3. *Calls upon* all States, corporations, institutions and individuals to terminate forthwith all military and nuclear collaboration with the racist régime of South Africa, including the provision to it of such related dual-purpose materials as computers, electronic equipment and related technology;

4. *Requests* the Security Council, for the purposes of disarmament, to take enforcement measures, through strict adherence by all States to its relevant decisions, to prevent any racist régimes from acquiring any arms or arms technology;

5. *Requests* the Security Council in this connection to conclude expeditiously its consideration of the recommendations of its Committee established by resolution 421(1977) concerning the question of South Africa with a view to blocking the existing loopholes in the arms embargo, rendering it more effective and prohibiting in particular all forms of co-operation and collaboration with the racist régime of South Africa in the nuclear field;

6. *Demands* that South Africa submit all its nuclear installations and facilities to inspection by the International Atomic Energy Agency;

7. *Decides* to include in the provisional agenda of its thirty-eighth session the item entitled "Implementation of the Declaration on the Denuclearization of Africa".

Recorded vote in Assembly as follows:

In favour: Afghanistan, Albania, Algeria, Angola, Antigua and Barbuda, Argentina, Australia, Austria, Bahamas, Bahrain, Bangladesh, Barbados, Belize, Benin, Bhutan, Bolivia, Botswana, Brazil, Bulgaria, Burma, Burundi, Byelorussian SSR, Cape Verde, Central African Republic, Chad, Chile, China, Colombia, Comoros, Congo, Costa Rica, Cuba, Cyprus, Czechoslovakia, Democratic Kampuchea, Democratic Yemen, Denmark, Djibouti, Dominican Republic, Ecuador,

Egypt, El Salvador, Ethiopia, Fiji, Finland, Gabon, Gambia, German Democratic Republic, Ghana, Greece, Grenada, Guinea, Guinea-Bissau, Guyana, Haiti, Honduras, Hungary, Iceland, India, Indonesia, Iran, Iraq, Ireland, Ivory Coast, Jamaica, Japan, Jordan, Kenya, Kuwait, Lao People's Democratic Republic, Lebanon, Liberia, Libyan Arab Jamahiriya, Madagascar, Malaysia, Maldives, Mali, Malta, Mauritania, Mauritius, Mexico, Mongolia, Morocco, Mozambique, Nepal, New Zealand, Nicaragua, Niger, Nigeria, Norway, Oman, Pakistan, Panama, Papua New Guinea, Peru, Philippines, Poland, Qatar, Romania, Rwanda, Saint Lucia, Saudi Arabia, Senegal, Sierra Leone, Singapore, Solomon Islands, Somalia, Spain, Sri Lanka, Sudan, Suriname, Swaziland, Sweden, Syrian Arab Republic, Thailand, Togo, Trinidad and Tobago, Tunisia, Turkey, Uganda, Ukrainian SSR, USSR, United Arab Emirates, United Republic of Cameroon, United Republic of Tanzania, Upper Volta, Uruguay, Vanuatu, Venezuela, Viet Nam, Yemen, Yugoslavia, Zaire, Zambia.

Against: None.

Abstaining: Belgium, Canada, France, Germany, Federal Republic of, Israel, Italy, Luxembourg, Malawi, Netherlands, Portugal, Sao Tome and Principe,[a] United Kingdom, United States.

[a]Later advised the Secretariat it had intended to vote in favour.

Nuclear weapons and South Africa

The nuclear capability of South Africa, especially in the military field, continued to be considered by the General Assembly and other United Nations bodies during 1982 in the context of disarmament and the call for a nuclear-weapon-free zone in Africa (see below), as well as in connection with military and nuclear relations with South Africa and their effects on that country's *apartheid* policies. In both contexts, the Assembly repeated previous calls for a cessation of foreign collaboration in the nuclear field with the South African régime.

As in 1981,[(12)] the Disarmament Commission, at its 1982 session,[(4)] was unable to reach agreed conclusions in regard to the nuclear plans and capability of South Africa. It therefore recommended on 28 May that consideration should continue at its subsequent substantive session on the basis of views and proposals made in 1981 and 1982 or submitted later.

A call for a Security Council decision to forbid any co-operation that would assist South Africa to manufacture nuclear weapons was proposed for inclusion in the comprehensive programme of disarmament as part of a section on measures to relax international tension, but consensus on the paragraph was not reached during the General Assembly's special session on disarmament.[(3)]

Circulated as documents of the session were two letters from the Special Committee against *Apartheid* addressed to the Secretary-General. The first, from the Committee Chairman dated 24 May,[(1)] transmitted a message to the session adopted by the International Conference on Women and *Apartheid* (Brussels, Belgium, 17-19 May) condemning military and nuclear collaboration with South Africa and appealing to the Assembly to take action for the imposition of sanctions against that country. The second letter, from the Committee's Acting Chairman and dated 15 June,[(2)] transmitted a statement adopted by the Committee on 14 June at the conclusion of a hearing on the "Threat to peace in southern Africa and the implementation of United Nations resolutions for an end to military, nuclear and other collaboration with South Africa'', in which the Committee made a similar appeal and stated that South Africa's frantic efforts to acquire nuclear capability were a grave threat to peace.

In the general debate at the special session, many African States, among them Burundi, Nigeria, Sierra Leone, Tunisia, Zaire and Zambia, viewed the military and nuclear activities of South Africa as frustrating implementation of the Declaration on the Denuclearization of Africa.

A number of countries, including Jamaica, Sierra Leone, Togo and Uganda, expressed concern over reported nuclear collaboration between South Africa and certain Western States, leading to the development of nuclear-weapon capability. In that regard, Ethiopia named the United States, while the Lao People's Democratic Republic and Mauritania named Israel as among South Africa's collaborators. Democratic Yemen said South Africa had already acquired nuclear weapons through such collaboration. The United Arab Emirates asserted that South Africa was acquiring nuclear weapons to intimidate the continent.

While Jamaica, Somalia, the Sudan and Zimbabwe expressed concern over the reported acquisition by South Africa of nuclear-weapon capability, Benin, Madagascar, Rwanda and the United Republic of Tanzania stated that South Africa had indeed acquired such capability. The Upper Volta added that South Africa had recently embarked on nuclear testing, with the complicity of some Western Powers.

Nigeria urged the General Assembly to enforce sanctions against South Africa and discourage Western countries from enabling it to destabilize Africa, while the United Republic of Cameroon called on the Security Council to adopt without delay the enforcement measures provided for in the Charter of the United Nations, in order to compel South Africa to co-operate with the Organization.

Senegal said the transfer of nuclear technology to South Africa should be prohibited until that country signed the Treaty on the Non-Proliferation of Nuclear Weapons[9] (NPT) and opened its facilities to inspection by the International Atomic Energy Agency (IAEA). Morocco called on the Security Council to act in view of South Africa's refusal to adhere to NPT.

In a resolution of 9 December on implementation of the OAU Declaration on the Denuclearization of Africa,[6] the General Assembly condemned all forms of nuclear collaboration with South Africa by any State, corporation, institution or individual, and called on them to terminate forthwith all military and nuclear collaboration,

including the provision of such related dual-purpose materials as computers, electronic equipment and related technology. It requested the Security Council to take enforcement measures to prevent racist régimes from acquiring any arms or arms technology and to block loopholes in the arms embargo against South Africa. It demanded that South Africa submit all its nuclear installations and facilities to IAEA inspection.

Paragraph 3 of this resolution, calling for the termination of all military and nuclear collaboration with South Africa including the provision of computers and electronic equipment, was adopted in the First Committee by a recorded vote of 99 to 8, with 15 abstentions.

By another resolution of 9 December, on the nuclear capability of South Africa,[7] the Assembly deplored the massive build-up of South Africa's military machine and its acquisition of a nuclear-weapon capability for repressive and aggressive purposes and as an instrument of blackmail. It reaffirmed that such action by South Africa gravely endangered international peace and security and increased the danger of nuclear-weapon proliferation, and requested the Disarmament Commission to consider the question. The Assembly requested the Security Council to take enforcement measures to prevent acquisition of arms or arms technology by any racist régime; called on States, corporations, institutions and individuals to terminate all military and nuclear collaboration with South Africa; and demanded that South Africa cease developing a nuclear-weapon capability and submit all its nuclear installations and facilities to IAEA inspection. The Secretary-General was asked to report in 1983 on South Africa's evolution in the nuclear field.

The resolution also mentioned a September 1982 report[5] in which the Secretary-General stated that he had followed closely South Africa's evolution in the nuclear field, as requested by the Assembly in December 1981,[10] but that he had neither received nor identified further information to add to his earlier reports. (The last full-scale report on the subject, prepared by a Group of Experts on South Africa's Plan and Capability in the Nuclear Field, had been submitted in 1980.[11])

The resolution was adopted by a recorded vote of 132 to 4, with 11 abstentions. The First Committee had approved it on 26 November by a recorded vote of 107 to 6, with 10 abstentions.

In a resolution of 16 December on the strengthening of international security, the Assembly called on the Security Council to take effective measures to promote the objective of Africa's denuclearization in order to avert the serious danger posed by South Africa's nuclear capability to the African States and to international peace and security.[8]

Introducing, on behalf of the African Group and Qatar, the text on South Africa's nuclear capability, Kenya said that a destabilized Africa was a danger to international peace and security, that the Security Council should prohibit effectively all forms of nuclear collaboration with South Africa, and that those countries which used the veto on issues of southern Africa should reconsider their policy and attitude. The resolution was not directed against any State or group of States.

The United States—although saying that it favoured an Africa free of nuclear weapons, strictly enforced the arms embargo against South Africa and did not sell nuclear fuel or sensitive nuclear materials except to signatories of NPT which accepted full-scope safeguards—abstained in the vote on the first of the 9 December resolutions and voted against the second on the ground that both texts contained intemperate language and discouraged South Africa from implementing a non-proliferation policy; moreover, it could not support language that prejudged a situation and attempted to commit it to a position prior to Security Council consideration.

Regarding the first resolution, the United Kingdom, which voted against paragraph 3 and abstained on the text as a whole, said it was wrong to seek limitation of the internationally recognized right of all States to the peaceful uses of nuclear energy; the United Kingdom did not collaborate with South Africa on nuclear weapons or supply it with nuclear material, facilities or equipment.

France, which abstained on the first resolution and voted against the one on nuclear capability, said it agreed that South Africa must submit all its nuclear installations to IAEA control but not with the assumption of the resolutions' sponsors that any form of international co-operation in the civilian nuclear field must inevitably lead to military uses; further, the texts were not in keeping with provisions of the United Nations Charter concerning the division of responsibilities and powers between the main organs of the Organization, and the ninth preambular paragraph in the resolution on South Africa's nuclear capability (expressing the Assembly's disappointment at what it called the ready use of the veto on the South African question by certain Western States) was a serious breach of the Charter and of respect for State sovereignty in that it challenged the votes of certain permanent members of the Security Council.

Despite its support for denuclearization of Africa, New Zealand abstained in Committee on both resolutions because of paragraphs whose intention it regarded as unclear and because of several elements with which it had difficulty; in the Assembly it voted for the first resolution. Also abstaining on both texts, Portugal, while supporting nuclear-weapon-free zones, found some of the

language in the operative part of the first text ill-advised, particularly the sweeping condemnation of any co-operation with South Africa in the nuclear field; it stressed the importance of accession by all States to NPT and the application of IAEA safeguards to all African countries.

Australia, voting in favour of the first resolution because of the overriding emphasis its Government placed on preventing nuclear proliferation and its growing concern about the attitude of some States on that question, nevertheless expressed serious misgivings about some of the wording, asserting that the expressions used in the text should be understood in the context of the resolution. Along with the United Kingdom, Australia urged South Africa to adhere to NPT. Japan said its positive vote did not indicate agreement with assertions in the text unbacked by conclusive evidence.

Although voting in favour of both resolutions, Argentina, Austria, Denmark, Finland, Ireland, Norway, Spain, Sweden and Turkey expressed reservations regarding paragraphs which, in their view, unnecessarily singled out certain countries or groups of countries or which failed to respect the respective competences of the General Assembly and the Security Council as laid down in the United Nations Charter.

As regards the first text, on implementation of the OAU Declaration, reservations were expressed by Denmark, Norway and Sweden on the fifth preambular paragraph, mentioning collaboration by certain countries; by Norway on paragraph 3, calling for termination of military and nuclear collaboration, on which it abstained in the vote; and by Denmark, Finland, Norway and Spain on paragraph 4, requesting Security Council enforcement measures to prevent racist régimes from acquiring arms.

As to the second resolution, on South Africa's nuclear capability, there were reservations by Denmark, Norway and Sweden on the fifth preambular paragraph, referring to support for South Africa's nuclear programme by certain Western States and Israel; by Finland, Norway and Spain on the ninth preambular paragraph, referring to the use of the veto in the Security Council; by Denmark, Finland, Spain and Turkey on paragraph 4, requesting enforcement measures by the Council; and by Finland and Norway on paragraph 5, calling for termination of military and nuclear collaboration.

Austria, without citing specific paragraphs, said it would have preferred to see a clearer distinction drawn between the responsibilities of the Assembly and those of the Council. Finland regretted the absence of a reference to adherence to NPT. Ireland objected to the contentious singling out of certain countries in the preambles of both resolutions and regretted the failure to distinguish in the texts between co-operation for peaceful and weapons purposes. Spain found the wording excessively polemical. Turkey voiced hesitation about paragraphs that placed certain interpretations on the functioning and methods of some United Nations bodies.

For reasons of principle, Argentina had reservations on those provisions supporting the application of full-scope IAEA safeguards to nuclear installations.

Also voting for both resolutions, the USSR said it supported the efforts of African States for a nuclear-weapon-free Africa, shared the indignation over the encouragement of South Africa's nuclear ambitions by certain Western countries and Israel, and advocated comprehensive sanctions to end military and nuclear co-operation.

Letters. Committee against *Apartheid* Chairman and Acting Chairman *(AC)*: [1]24 May, A/S-12/24; [2]15 June, A/S-12/AC.1/21 *(AC)*.
Reports. [3]*Ad Hoc* Committee, A/S-12/32; [4]Disarmament Commission, A/S-12/3; [5]S-G, A/37/432.
Resolutions (1982). GA: [6]37/74 A, paras. 2-6, 9 Dec.; [7]37/74 B, 9 Dec., text following; [8]37/118, para. 12, 16 Dec.
Resolutions (prior). GA: [9]2373(XXII), annex, 12 June 1968 (YUN 1968, p. 17); [10]36/86 A, 9 Dec. 1981 (YUN 1981, p. 47).
Yearbook references. [11]1980, p. 45; [12]1981, p. 46.
Meeting records. GA: plenary, A/S-12/PV.2-26, 28, 29 (8 June–10 July), A/37/PV.98 (9 Dec.); 1st Committee, A/C.1/37/PV.3-10, 12-28, *37, 44* (18 Oct.–26 Nov.).

General Assembly resolution 37/74 B

9 December 1982   Meeting 98   132-4-11 (recorded vote)

Approved by First Committee (A/37/656) by recorded vote (107-6-10), 26 November (meeting 44); 2-nation draft (A/C.1/37/L.38); agenda item 44.

Sponsors: Kenya (for African Group), Qatar.

Nuclear capability of South Africa

The General Assembly,

Recalling its resolutions 34/76 B of 11 December 1979, 35/146 A of 12 December 1980 and 36/86 A of 9 December 1981,

Bearing in mind the Declaration on the Denuclearization of Africa adopted by the Assembly of Heads of State and Government of the Organization of African Unity at its first ordinary session, held at Cairo from 17 to 21 July 1964,

Recalling that, in its resolution 33/63 of 14 December 1978, it vigorously condemned any overt or covert attempt by South Africa to introduce nuclear weapons into the continent and demanded that South Africa refrain forthwith from conducting any nuclear explosion in the continent of Africa or elsewhere,

Recalling also that in the Final Document of the Tenth Special Session of the General Assembly it noted that the accumulation of armaments and the acquisition of armaments technology by racist régimes, as well as their possible acquisition of nuclear weapons, presented a challenging and an increasingly dangerous obstacle to a world community faced with the urgent need to disarm,

Alarmed that South Africa's nuclear programme has enabled it to acquire a nuclear-weapon capability and that that capability has been enhanced by the continued support and active collaboration which certain Western States and Israel have readily given to it in pursuance of their economic interests and geostrategic designs, in gross violation of the relevant resolutions and decisions of the United Nations,

Taking note of the report of the Security Council Committee established by resolution 421(1977) concerning the question of South Africa on ways and means of making the mandatory arms embargo against South Africa more effective, as well as the report of the Secretary-General on the implementation of Security Council resolution 473(1980),

Having examined the report of the Group of Experts on South Africa's Plan and Capability in the Nuclear Field as well as the reports of the Secretary-General of 3 September 1981 and 20 September 1982 submitted pursuant to General Assembly resolutions 35/146 A and 36/86 A on the nuclear capability of South Africa,

Gravely concerned that South Africa, in flagrant violation of the principles of international law and the relevant provisions of the Charter of the United Nations, has continued its military attacks against independent States of southern Africa, in particular Angola, part of which still remains occupied by South African forces, and has increased its acts of subversion aimed at destabilizing those States,

Expressing its utter disappointment that certain Western States have continued to collaborate with the racist régime of South Africa in its nuclear and military build-up and have, by a ready recourse to the use of the veto, consistently frustrated every effort at the United Nations to deal with the South African question,

1.   *Deplores* the massive build-up of South Africa's military machine, including its frenzied acquisition of a nuclear-weapon capability for repressive and aggressive purposes and as an instrument of blackmail;

2.   *Reaffirms* that the acquisition of nuclear capability by the racist régime constitutes a very grave danger to international peace and security and, in particular, jeopardizes the security of African States and increases the danger of the proliferation of nuclear weapons;

3.   *Requests* the Disarmament Commission to consider substantively the question of South Africa's nuclear capability pursuant, *inter alia*, to the findings contained in section VII of the report of the Group of Experts on South Africa's Plan and Capability in the Nuclear Field;

4.   *Requests* the Security Council, for the purposes of disarmament, to take enforcement measures, through strict adherence by all States to its relevant decisions, to prevent any racist régimes from acquiring arms or arms technology;

5.   *Calls upon* all States, corporations, institutions and individuals to terminate forthwith all military and nuclear collaboration with the racist régime of South Africa, including the provision to it of such materials as computers, electronic equipment and related technology;

6.   *Demands* that South Africa respect international concern for peace and stability in Africa by terminating forthwith its development of the capability to produce nuclear weapons and that it submit all its nuclear installations and facilities to inspection by the International Atomic Energy Agency;

7.   *Requests* the Secretary-General to follow closely South Africa's evolution in the nuclear field and to report thereon to the General Assembly at its thirty-eighth session;

8.   *Decides* to include in the provisional agenda of its thirty-eighth session the item entitled "Implementation of the Declaration on the Denuclearization of Africa".

Recorded vote in Assembly as follows:

In favour: Afghanistan, Albania, Algeria, Angola, Antigua and Barbuda, Argentina, Austria, Bahamas, Bahrain, Bangladesh, Barbados, Belize, Benin, Bhutan, Bolivia, Botswana, Brazil, Bulgaria, Burma, Burundi, Byelorussian SSR, Cape Verde, Central African Republic, Chad, Chile, China, Colombia, Comoros, Congo, Costa Rica, Cuba, Cyprus, Czechoslovakia, Democratic Kampuchea, Democratic Yemen, Denmark, Djibouti, Dominican Republic, Ecuador, Egypt, El Salvador, Ethiopia, Fiji, Finland, Gabon, Gambia, German Democratic Republic, Ghana, Greece, Grenada, Guinea, Guinea-Bissau, Guyana, Haiti, Honduras, Hungary, Iceland, India, Indonesia, Iran, Iraq, Ireland, Ivory Coast, Jamaica, Jordan, Kenya, Kuwait, Lao People's Democratic Republic, Lebanon, Liberia, Libyan Arab Jamahiriya, Madagascar, Malaysia, Maldives, Mali, Malta, Mauritania, Mauritius, Mexico, Mongolia, Morocco, Mozambique, Nepal, Nicaragua, Niger, Nigeria, Norway, Oman, Pakistan, Panama, Papua New Guinea, Peru, Philippines, Poland, Qatar, Romania, Rwanda, Saint Lucia, Sao Tome and Principe, Saudi Arabia, Senegal, Sierra Leone, Singapore, Solomon Islands, Somalia, Spain, Sri Lanka, Sudan, Suriname, Swaziland, Sweden, Syrian Arab Republic, Thailand, Togo, Trinidad and Tobago, Tunisia, Turkey, Uganda, Ukrainian SSR, USSR, United Arab Emirates, United Republic of Cameroon, United Republic of Tanzania, Upper Volta, Uruguay, Vanuatu, Venezuela, Viet Nam, Yemen, Yugoslavia, Zaire, Zambia.

Against: France, Israel, United Kingdom, United States.

Abstaining: Australia, Belgium, Canada, Germany, Federal Republic of, Italy, Japan, Luxembourg, Malawi, Netherlands, New Zealand, Portugal.

Latin America

General Assembly consideration (June/July). In the general debate at the 1982 special session of the General Assembly devoted to disarmament, Belgium, speaking for the European

Community members, considered the 1967 Treaty for the Prohibition of Nuclear Weapons in Latin America (Treaty of Tlatelolco) exceptionally valuable despite the fact that its provisions had not come into force in all the States of the region. The Netherlands expressed hope that the Treaty would soon become fully effective. Guyana supported the Treaty's principles and objectives, although remarking that it was denied accession to that instrument by an exclusion clause which discriminated against it. Panama urged a collective effort to have States sign and ratify the Treaty.

Panama asserted that the United Kingdom had made a mockery of Additional Protocol I of the Treaty through introduction of its nuclear-powered submarines in the Falkland Islands (Malvinas) zone. Argentina called the action by the United Kingdom a violation of its commitment under signed agreements and declared guarantees. The Congo and Venezuela similarly spoke of the entry into that area by British submarines carrying nuclear warheads; Venezuela added that such actions, by a party to the Treaty, could lead to a reformulation of the concept of nuclear-weapon-free zones and a re-evaluation of their effectiveness for non-proliferation.

The United Kingdom replied that its use of nuclear weapons against Argentina was inconceivable, that the Treaty of Tlatelolco did not apply to nuclear-powered submarines and that, in any case, Argentina was not a party to the Treaty.

General Assembly action (December). By a resolution adopted on 9 December 1982,[1] the General Assembly, recalling that the Kingdom of the Netherlands, the United Kingdom and the United States had previously become parties to Additional Protocol I of the Treaty of Tlatelolco, expressed regret that its signature by France on 2 March 1979 had not been followed by ratification and urged France not to delay action any further. The Assembly noted that non-sovereign territories within the zone of application of the Treaty could receive the benefits of the Treaty if the States internationally responsible for them adhered to the Protocol.

The resolution was adopted by a recorded vote of 136 to none, with 7 abstentions, following its approval in the First Committee on 24 November by a recorded vote of 119 to none, with 7 abstentions. The text, sponsored by 20 parties to the Treaty and Ghana, was introduced by Mexico, the Treaty's depositary Government, and was approved with an oral amendment by the Netherlands, accepted by the sponsors, to use "Kingdom of the Netherlands", its legally correct nomenclature in international agreements.

France abstained, stating that it could not accept being called into question while certain countries in the Treaty's zone of application had neither

signed nor ratified it; France would act in due course, taking into account the status of ratifications.

The Netherlands and the United States, which voted in favour, urged all eligible States within the region to adhere to the Treaty. The Netherlands added that the resolution should have encompassed the Treaty as a whole rather than just the Procotol, and the United States regretted that one country had been singled out for not ratifying the Protocol.

Resolution (1982). [1]GA: 37/71, 9 Dec., text following.
Meeting records. GA: 1st Committee, A/C.1/37/PV.3-10, 12-28, *39, 43,* 48 (18 Oct.–30 Nov.); plenary, A/37/PV.98 (9 Dec.).

General Assembly resolution 37/71

9 December 1982   Meeting 98   136-0-7 (recorded vote)

Approved by First Committee (A/37/653) by recorded vote (119-0-7), 24 November (meeting 43); 21-nation draft (A/C.1/37/L.51), orally amended by Netherlands; agenda item 41.

Sponsors: Bahamas, Barbados, Bolivia, Colombia, Costa Rica, Dominican Republic, Ecuador, El Salvador, Ghana, Guatemala, Haiti, Honduras, Jamaica, Mexico, Nicaragua, Panama, Paraguay, Peru, Suriname, Trinidad and Tobago, Uruguay.

Implementation of General Assembly resolution 36/83 concerning the signature and ratification of Additional Protocol I of the Treaty for the Prohibition of Nuclear Weapons in Latin America (Treaty of Tlatelolco)

The General Assembly,

Recalling its resolutions 2286(XXII) of 5 December 1967, 3262(XXIX) of 9 December 1974, 3473(XXX) of 11 December 1975, 32/76 of 12 December 1977, S-10/2 of 30 June 1978, 33/58 of 14 December 1978, 34/71 of 11 December 1979, 35/143 of 12 December 1980 and 36/83 of 9 December 1981 concerning the signature and ratification of Additional Protocol I of the Treaty for the Prohibition of Nuclear Weapons in Latin America (Treaty of Tlatelolco),

Taking into account that within the zone of application of that Treaty, to which twenty-two sovereign States are already parties, there are some territories which, in spite of not being sovereign political entities, are nevertheless in a position to receive the benefits deriving from the Treaty through its Additional Protocol I, to which the States that *de jure* or *de facto* are internationally responsible for those territories may become parties,

Recalling that the United Kingdom of Great Britain and Northern Ireland, the Kingdom of the Netherlands and the United States of America became parties to Additional Protocol I in 1969, 1971 and 1981, respectively,

1. *Regrets* that the signature of Additional Protocol I by France, which took place on 2 March 1979, has not yet been followed by the corresponding ratification, notwithstanding the time already elapsed and the pressing invitations which the General Assembly has addressed to it;

2. *Urges* France not to delay any further such ratification, which has been requested so many times;

3. *Decides* to include in the provisional agenda of its thirty-eighth session an item entitled "Implementation of General Assembly resolution 37/71 concerning the signature and ratification of Additional Protocol I of the Treaty for the Prohibition of Nuclear Weapons in Latin America (Treaty of Tlatelolco)".

Recorded vote in Assembly as follows:

In favour: Afghanistan, Algeria, Angola, Australia, Austria, Bahrain, Bangladesh, Barbados, Belgium, Benin, Bhutan, Bolivia, Botswana, Brazil, Bulgaria, Burma, Burundi, Byelorussian SSR, Canada, Cape Verde, Central African Republic, Chad, Chile, China, Colombia, Comoros, Congo, Costa Rica, Cyprus, Czechoslovakia, Democratic Kampuchea, Democratic Yemen, Denmark, Dominican Republic, Ecuador, Egypt, El Salvador, Ethiopia, Fiji, Finland, Gabon, Gambia, German Democratic Republic, Germany, Federal Republic of, Ghana, Greece, Grenada, Guatemala, Guinea, Guinea-Bissau, Haiti, Honduras, Hungary, Iceland, India, Indonesia, Iran, Iraq, Ireland, Israel, Italy, Ivory Coast, Jamaica, Japan, Jordan, Kenya, Kuwait, Lao People's Democratic Republic, Lebanon, Liberia, Libyan Arab Jamahiriya, Luxembourg, Madagascar, Malaysia, Maldives, Malta, Mauritania,

Mauritius, Mexico, Mongolia, Morocco, Mozambique, Nepal, Netherlands, New Zealand, Nicaragua, Niger, Nigeria, Norway, Oman, Pakistan, Panama, Papua New Guinea, Paraguay, Peru, Philippines, Poland, Portugal, Qatar, Romania, Rwanda, Sao Tome and Principe, Saudi Arabia, Senegal, Sierra Leone, Singapore, Solomon Islands, Somalia, Spain, Sri Lanka, Sudan, Suriname, Swaziland, Sweden, Syrian Arab Republic, Thailand, Togo, Trinidad and Tobago, Tunisia, Turkey, Uganda, Ukrainian SSR, USSR, United Arab Emirates, United Kingdom, United Republic of Cameroon, United Republic of Tanzania, United States, Upper Volta, Uruguay, Vanuatu, Viet Nam, Yemen, Yugoslavia, Zaire, Zambia.

Against: None.

Abstaining: Argentina, Cuba, France, Guyana, Malawi, Mali, Venezuela.

Middle East

General Assembly consideration (June/July). At the General Assembly's 1982 special session on disarmament, support for the establishment of a nuclear-weapon-free zone in the region of the Middle East was voiced by many speakers in the general debate, among them Burundi, Democratic Kampuchea, Egypt, Honduras, Iraq, Israel, Kuwait, the Libyan Arab Jamahiriya, Maldives, Mauritania, Morocco, Nepal, Oman, Viet Nam and Zimbabwe.

Egypt recalled that it had been proposing such a zone since 1974, with three objectives: to move towards nuclear disarmament, to foster the objectives of the 1968 Treaty on the Non-Proliferation of Nuclear Weapons[2] (NPT), and to ease tension in the region and the world. Iraq listed what it viewed as necessary conditions for such a zone, including the conviction of the parties that denuclearization would bolster their security and that of the region, renunciation of aggressive or expansionist tendencies by all States of the region, commitments by nuclear Powers not to use or threaten to use nuclear weapons against any State in the zone and to protect those States from outside nuclear attacks, the participation of all States of the region, the establishment of international supervision machinery and the right of inspection, an absence of time-limits on the zone, and non-involvement of the parties with military alliances.

Qatar said the Middle East should be considered a nuclear-weapon-free zone by the imposition of international controls over countries in the region which had nuclear reactors, particularly Israel. The Syrian Arab Republic asserted that the Israeli project to set up a so-called nuclear-weapon-free zone in the region was only nuclear blackmail from a position of strength. Tunisia declared that Israel's arms potential, including its nuclear-weapon potential, made any idea of establishing a zone of peace in the Middle East illusory.

France suggested that, whatever difficulties might be involved, the Secretary-General might usefully make contacts in order to consider the best procedure for the establishment of a nuclear-weapon-free zone in the Middle East. Lebanon urged an end to aggression, a freeze of the conventional-arms race and elimination of the use of cluster bombs before proceeding to the establishment of such a zone in the region.

General Assembly action (December). By a 9 December resolution on the establishment of a nuclear-weapon-free zone in the Middle East,[1] adopted without vote, the General Assembly urged all parties directly concerned seriously to consider implementing the proposal to establish such a zone and, as a means of promoting that objective, invited them to adhere to NPT. The Assembly called on all countries of the region, pending the zone's establishment, to agree to place all their nuclear activities under International Atomic Energy Agency (IAEA) safeguards; invited them to declare their support for establishing such a zone in declarations to be deposited with the Security Council; and invited them not to develop, produce, test or otherwise acquire nuclear weapons or permit their stationing on their territories or territories under their control. It also invited the nuclear-weapon States and all others to assist in establishing the zone and to refrain from action counter to the resolution.

The First Committee had approved the text, also without vote, on 26 November, on a text sponsored and revised by Egypt.

Resolution (1982). [1]GA: 37/75, 9 Dec., text following.
Resolution (prior). [2]GA: 2373(XXII), annex, 12 June 1968 (YUN 1968, p. 17).
Meeting records. GA: 1st Committee, A/C.1/37/PV.3-10, 12-28, *38, 45* (18 Oct.–26 Nov.); plenary, A/37/PV.98 (9 Dec.).

General Assembly resolution 37/75

9 December 1982   Meeting 98   Adopted without vote

Approved by First Committee (A/37/657) without vote, 26 November (meeting 45); draft by Egypt (A/C.1/37/L.49/Rev.1); agenda item 45.

Establishment of a nuclear-weapon-free zone
in the region of the Middle East

The General Assembly,

Recalling its resolutions 3263(XXIX) of 9 December 1974, 3474(XXX) of 11 December 1975, 31/71 of 10 December 1976, 32/82 of 12 December 1977, 33/64 of 14 December 1978, 34/77 of 11 December 1979, 35/147 of 12 December 1980 and 36/87 of 9 December 1981 on the establishment of a nuclear-weapon-free zone in the region of the Middle East,

Recalling also the recommendations for the establishment of such a zone in the Middle East consistent with paragraphs 60 to 63, in particular paragraph 63 *(d)*, of the Final Document of the Tenth Special Session of the General Assembly,

Emphasizing the basic provisions of the above-mentioned resolutions, which call upon all parties directly concerned to consider taking the practical and urgent steps required for the implementation of the proposal to establish a nuclear-weapon-free zone in the region of the Middle East and, pending and during the establishment of such a zone, to declare solemnly that they will refrain, on a reciprocal basis, from producing, acquiring or in any other way possessing nuclear weapons and nuclear explosive devices and from permitting the stationing of nuclear weapons on their territory by any third party, to agree to place all their nuclear facilities under International Atomic Energy Agency safeguards and to declare their support for the establishment of the zone and deposit such declarations with the Security Council for consideration, as appropriate,

Reaffirming the inalienable right of all States to acquire and develop nuclear energy for peaceful purposes,

Emphasizing further the need for appropriate measures on the question of the prohibition of military attacks on nuclear facilities,

Bearing in mind the consensus reached by the General Assembly at its thirty-fifth session that the establishment of a nuclear-weapon-free zone in the region of the Middle East would greatly enhance international peace and security,

Desirous to build on that consensus so that substantial progress can be made towards establishing a nuclear-weapon-free zone in the region of the Middle East,

1. *Urges* all parties directly concerned to consider seriously taking the practical and urgent steps required for the implementation of the proposal to establish a nuclear-weapon-free zone in the region of the Middle East in accordance with the relevant resolutions of the General Assembly and, as a means of promoting this objective, invites the countries concerned to adhere to the Treaty on the Non-Proliferation of Nuclear Weapons;

2. *Calls upon* all countries of the region that have not done so, pending the establishment of the zone, to agree to place all their nuclear activities under International Atomic Energy Agency safeguards;

3. *Invites* those countries, pending the establishment of a nuclear-weapon-free zone in the region of the Middle East, to declare their support for establishing such a zone, consistent with the relevant paragraph of the Final Document of the Tenth Special Session of the General Assembly, and to deposit those declarations with the Security Council;

4. *Invites further* those countries, pending the establishment of the zone, not to develop, produce, test or otherwise acquire nuclear weapons or permit the stationing on their territories, or territories under their control, of nuclear weapons or nuclear explosive devices;

5. *Invites* the nuclear-weapon States and all other States to render their assistance in the establishment of the zone and at the same time to refrain from any action that runs counter to both the letter and spirit of the present resolution;

6. *Requests* the Secretary-General to report to the General Assembly at its thirty-eighth session on the implementation of the present resolution;

7. *Decides* to include in the provisional agenda of its thirty-eighth session the item entitled "Establishment of a nuclear-weapon-free zone in the region of the Middle East".

Nuclear weapons and Israel

In 1982, during the general debate at the General Assembly's second special session on disarmament, a number of countries in the Middle East expressed concern that Israel possessed nuclear-weapon capability.

Iraq said Israel had managed to have a reserve stock of nuclear weapons, which some United States sources had estimated as numbering between 10 and 20. For the Syrian Arab Republic, there was no doubt that Israel possessed nuclear capability. Jordan similarly asserted that Israel's nuclear capabilities as well as its nuclear collaboration with South Africa had been confirmed. Algeria saw that development as proof of the ineffectiveness of the nuclear non-proliferation régime as regards those against which it should above all have applied.

Democratic Yemen, Mauritania and Qatar said the Western countries had provided Israel with that capacity, and the Libyan Arab Jamahiriya named the United States as among those which had given Israel and South Africa assistance in this field. Zimbabwe condemned such collaboration.

Kuwait asserted that Israel and South Africa had collaborated in manufacturing scores of atomic bombs and had thus driven the Middle East towards a new arms race for the possession of nuclear weapons. Malaysia was concerned over the indication that the two countries might pos-

sess nuclear armaments outside any international control. Mauritania believed it the wish of most United Nations Members that IAEA exercise control over the nuclear installations of certain countries which were not parties to NPT,[3] such as Israel and South Africa. The Sudan expressed regret that the two countries had found the means to acquire and manufacture nuclear weapons. The Syrian Arab Republic said the peoples of Africa and the Middle East were the targets of the two countries' collaboration.

Egypt, remarking that it had unilaterally renounced the nuclear option by ratifying NPT in February 1981,[5] expressed hope that Israel would follow that example so that the Middle East could become a nuclear-weapon-free zone.

In a brief report submitted to the Assembly in September 1982[1] in accordance with a request it had made in December 1981,[4] the Secretary-General stated that he had given maximum publicity to the 1981 report by a Group of Experts on Israeli nuclear armament.[6] He had followed Israeli nuclear activities, taking into account information published by IAEA, but had received no new information to add to that report.

By a 9 December 1982 resolution on Israeli nuclear armament,[2] the General Assembly reaffirmed its demand that Israel renounce any possession of nuclear weapons and place all its nuclear activities under international safeguards. The Assembly called again on States and others to terminate all nuclear collaboration with Israel, and called on States to submit to the Secretary-General information on the Israeli nuclear programme or any public or private assistance thereto. Further, the Assembly again requested the Security Council to investigate Israel's nuclear activities and the collaboration of other parties therein, and to consider taking effective action to prevent Israel from pursuing its policy of aggression, expansion and annexation of territories. It condemned Israel's declared intention to repeat its armed attack against nuclear facilities. The Secretary-General was asked to keep Israeli nuclear activities under review and to follow its nuclear and military collaboration with South Africa.

The resolution was adopted by a recorded vote of 106 to 2, with 34 abstentions. The First Committee had approved the orally revised text on 24 November by a recorded vote of 91 to 2, with 30 abstentions, following approval of paragraph 2, calling for termination of all nuclear collaboration with Israel, by a recorded vote of 87 to 17, with 18 abstentions.

Iraq introduced the text in the name of 20 Arab and other States as a contribution to efforts to reduce tension in the region and to prevent the catastrophe that could result from Israel's possession of nuclear weapons. According to Iraq, the vast majority of Member States were convinced of Israel's intention to establish superiority through nuclear blackmail in the Middle East, in addition to its policies of aggression, annexation and occupation. Israel's nuclear activities were a growing cause of concern for the United Nations, other international bodies and for the countries of the Middle East.

In explanation of its negative vote, Israel stated that hostile and biased initiatives such as the Iraqi text, containing unwarranted and unacceptable demands, were not intended to serve peace in the Middle East. Israel objected to having been singled out for study under prejudicial terms. Israel had concluded that an effective non-proliferation régime could be established in the Middle East only if each State was contractually assured; it had therefore proposed the establishment by negotiation of a nuclear-weapon-free zone. It was Israel's adamant policy not to have governmental relations with South Africa in the nuclear field.

The United States also cast a negative vote, as it considered the text unbalanced and not conducive to collective non-proliferation efforts nor to the goal of Middle East peace and stability; singling out one State for condemnation was objectionable, as the problems in the region were much broader.

Ireland, Portugal and Sweden abstained in the vote on the text as a whole and voted against paragraph 2. Ireland could not support the inconsistency of urging Israel to submit its nuclear facilities to safeguards while calling for an end to co-operation with Israel in the nuclear field; all nations had the right to develop nuclear energy for peaceful purposes. Portugal found it unacceptable to allow any country to attack nuclear facilities subject to IAEA safeguards but it objected to comprehensive condemnation of all nuclear co-operation with Israel and it had reservations on paragraphs 3 (requesting a Security Council investigation) and 4 (calling on States to submit information). Sweden saw paragraphs 2 and 3 as at variance with the division of responsibilities between the Council and the Assembly as envisaged in the Charter of the United Nations and hoped all those supporting the resolution would themselves comply with the demand they made of Israel to accept IAEA safeguards.

Spain voted for the resolution out of concern at the consequences of introducing nuclear weapons into the Middle East but abstained in the vote on paragraph 2; regarding the sixth preambular paragraph (expressing concern at Israel's refusal to adhere to NPT and to place its nuclear facilities under IAEA safeguards), Spain reserved its position concerning the freedom of every State to adhere to the Treaty.

While voting for the resolution as well as paragraph 2, some delegations stated that they would have abstained on some paragraphs had separate votes been taken on them. Argentina and Brazil would have abstained on the sixth preambular paragraph; and Argentina and Ecuador would have abstained on paragraph 5 (requesting Security Council action to prevent Israel from endangering peace), which Ecuador viewed as disregarding the political prerogatives of other United Nations bodies.

Peru, which supported the resolution, said the requirement to submit to full IAEA safeguards should apply to all States which had not accepted them; it had reservations on those paragraphs which could not be reconciled with the Charter provisions on the division of responsibilities between the Assembly and the Security Council.

Report. [1]S-G, A/37/434.
Resolution (1982). [2]GA: 37/82, 9 Dec., text following.
Resolutions (prior). GA: [3]2373(XXII), annex, 12 June 1968 (YUN 1968, p. 17); [4]36/98, 9 Dec. 1981 (YUN 1981, p. 52).
Yearbook references: 1981, [5]p. 49, [6]p. 51.
Meeting records. GA: 1st Committee, A/C.1/37/PV.3-10, 12-28, 36, 37, 43 (18 Oct.–24 Nov.); plenary, A/37/PV.98 (9 Dec.).

General Assembly resolution 37/82

9 December 1982   Meeting 98   106-2-34 (recorded vote)

Approved by First Committee (A/37/668 and Corr.1,2) by recorded vote (91-2-30), 24 November (meeting 43); 20-nation draft (A/C.1/37/L.31), orally revised; agenda item 56.

Sponsors: Algeria, Bahrain, Democratic Yemen, Djibouti, Iraq, Jordan, Kuwait, Libyan Arab Jamahiriya, Mali, Mauritania, Morocco, Oman, Qatar, Saudi Arabia, Somalia, Sudan, Tunisia, United Arab Emirates, Viet Nam, Yemen.

Israeli nuclear armament

The General Assembly,

Recalling its resolutions 35/157 of 12 December 1980 and 36/98 of 9 December 1981 on Israeli nuclear armament,

Recalling also its relevant resolutions on the establishment of a nuclear-weapon-free zone in the region of the Middle East,

Recalling further its resolution 33/71 A of 14 December 1978 on military and nuclear collaboration with Israel,

Recalling its repeated condemnation of the nuclear collaboration between Israel and South Africa,

Recalling Security Council resolution 487(1981) of 19 June 1981 and taking note of the first special report of the Special Committee against *Apartheid* on recent developments concerning relations between Israel and South Africa,

Noting with grave concern Israel's persistent refusal to adhere to the Treaty on the Non-Proliferation of Nuclear Weapons, despite repeated calls by the General Assembly, the Security Council and the International Atomic Energy Agency, and to place its nuclear facilities under Agency safeguards,

Conscious of the grave consequences which endanger international peace and security as a result of Israel's nuclear-weapon capability and its collaboration with South Africa to develop nuclear weapons and their delivery systems,

Taking note of the report of the Secretary-General on Israeli nuclear armament,

1. *Reaffirms* its demand that Israel renounce, without delay, any possession of nuclear weapons and place all its nuclear activities under international safeguards;

2. *Calls again upon* all States and other parties and institutions to terminate forthwith all nuclear collaboration with Israel;

3. *Requests again* the Security Council to investigate Israel's nuclear activities and the collaboration of other States, parties and institutions in these activities;

4. *Calls upon* all States to submit to the Secretary-General all information in their possession concerning the Israeli nuclear programme or any public or private assistance thereto;

5. *Requests* the Security Council to consider taking effective action so as to prevent Israel from endangering international peace and security by pursuing its policy of aggression, expansion and annexation of territories;

6. *Condemns* Israel's officially declared intention to repeat its armed attack against nuclear facilities;

7. *Requests* the Secretary-General to keep Israeli nuclear activities under constant review and to report thereon as appropriate;

8. *Also requests* the Secretary-General, in co-operation with the Organization of African Unity and the League of Arab States, to follow closely the nuclear and military collaboration between Israel and South Africa and the dangers it constitutes to peace and security and to efforts aimed at the establishment of nuclear-weapon-free zones in Africa and the Middle East;

9. *Decides* to include in the provisional agenda of its thirty-eighth session the item entitled "Israeli nuclear armament".

Recorded vote in Assembly as follows:

In favour: Afghanistan, Albania, Algeria, Angola, Argentina, Bahamas, Bahrain, Bangladesh, Barbados, Belize, Benin, Bhutan, Bolivia, Botswana, Brazil, Bulgaria, Burundi, Byelorussian SSR, Cape Verde, Central African Republic, Chad, China, Comoros, Congo, Cuba, Cyprus, Czechoslovakia, Democratic Kampuchea, Democratic Yemen, Djibouti, Ecuador, Egypt, El Salvador, Ethiopia, Gambia, German Democratic Republic, Ghana, Greece, Grenada, Guinea, Guinea-Bissau, Guyana, Hungary, India, Indonesia, Iran, Iraq, Jordan, Kenya, Kuwait, Lao People's Democratic Republic, Lebanon, Liberia, Libyan Arab Jamahiriya, Madagascar, Malaysia, Maldives, Mali, Malta, Mauritania, Mauritius, Mexico, Mongolia, Morocco, Mozambique, Nicaragua, Niger, Nigeria, Oman, Pakistan, Panama, Peru, Philippines, Poland, Qatar, Romania, Rwanda, Sao Tome and Principe, Saudi Arabia, Senegal, Sierra Leone, Solomon Islands, Somalia, Spain, Sri Lanka, Sudan, Suriname, Syrian Arab Republic, Thailand, Togo, Trinidad and Tobago, Tunisia, Turkey, Uganda, Ukrainian SSR, USSR, United Arab Emirates, United Republic of Cameroon, United Republic of Tanzania, Upper Volta, Vanuatu, Venezuela, Viet Nam, Yemen, Yugoslavia, Zambia.

Against: Israel, United States.

Abstaining: Australia, Austria, Belgium, Burma, Canada, Chile, Colombia, Denmark, Dominican Republic, Fiji, Finland, France, Germany, Federal Republic of, Guatemala, Haiti, Iceland, Ireland, Italy, Ivory Coast, Jamaica, Japan, Luxembourg, Malawi, Nepal, Netherlands, New Zealand, Norway, Papua New Guinea, Paraguay, Portugal, Saint Lucia, Sweden, United Kingdom, Uruguay.

South Asia

Reports of the Secretary-General. In reports submitted to the General Assembly in June[1] and September 1982,[2] the Secretary-General said he had been in contact with States of the region with regard to a December 1981 request by the Assembly that he render any assistance required to promote a nuclear-weapon-free zone in South Asia,[5] but there had been no request by them for his assistance. In the course of those contacts, a view had been expressed that he should continue to be available for that purpose.

General Assembly consideration (June/July). At the 1982 special session of the General Assembly on disarmament, support for the creation of a nuclear-weapon-free zone in South Asia was expressed in the general debate by a number of speakers, among them Democratic Kampuchea, Honduras, Iraq, the Libyan Arab Jamahiriya, Maldives, Nepal, Oman and Pakistan. Burundi supported such a zone in South-East Asia. Maldives added that it looked forward to the day when all Asia could become such a zone. Nepal proposed to have itself declared a zone of peace. Pakistan said it was prepared to explore with its South Asian

neighbours any other means to ensure nuclear non-proliferation.

General Assembly action (December). On 9 December, by a resolution on the establishment of a nuclear-weapon-free zone in South Asia,[3] the General Assembly reaffirmed its endorsement in principle of the concept of such a zone in that region. The Assembly again urged States of the region and interested neighbouring non-nuclear-weapon States to continue making all possible efforts to establish such a zone, and to refrain in the mean time from any action contrary to that objective. It also called on nuclear-weapon States to respond positively to the proposal and to co-operate in efforts to establish the zone. The Secretary-General was requested to render such assistance as might be required to promote efforts for a zone and to report again in 1983.

The resolution was adopted by a recorded vote of 99 to 2, with 45 abstentions. The First Committee had approved the text on 23 November by a recorded vote of 79 to 2, with 39 abstentions.

The draft was sponsored by Pakistan, which stated in introducing it that declarations made by all the States of the region that they opposed the acquisition of nuclear weapons and their introduction into the region had prepared the stage for further action to establish a nuclear-weapon-free zone there. The proximity of nuclear-weapon Powers to a given region should serve as another reason for, rather than against, the creation of such zones. In both its preambular and operative paragraphs, the 1982 text followed the one adopted in 1981.

India explained its negative vote by stating that it had become clear over the years that countries of South Asia had no consensus on the creation of a nuclear-weapon-free zone in the area; it regretted the unnecessarily discordant note the annual submission of the proposal added to the spirit of harmony that the countries of the region were seeking to foster through gradual and painstaking efforts.

For Brazil, which abstained in the vote, the resolution did not adequately reflect such requirements as the consensus of the States involved and the commitment by nuclear-weapon States to respect the zone's status and to refrain from interfering in the negotiations; the establishment of such zones must not be allowed to lead to horizontal nuclear proliferation through legitimization of the existence of nuclear weapons in the territories of nuclear-weapon Powers or in the oceans and airspace all over the world. Indonesia and Sweden abstained on the ground that, although they supported the concept in principle, the resolution did not enjoy unanimous regional support; Sweden urged the States concerned to continue efforts to achieve the text's objectives.

Among those voting in favour, Bangladesh and Sri Lanka considered it essential to have close consultations among all States of the region, taking into account particular characteristics of the zone so that agreement could be reached on various issues including definition of its limits. Greece said that, in creating a nuclear-weapon-free zone, the States in a region should promote mutual confidence and security and abide by the principles of the non-use of force and the peaceful settlement of disputes. Japan recognized regional consensus as among the prerequisites for the establishment of such a zone and urged all countries in the region to adhere to NPT[4] and accept full-scope IAEA safeguards.

The Netherlands, supporting the text as a step in the right direction, also noted the need for regional consensus and reaffirmed that no distinction could be made from a disarmament viewpoint between nuclear-weapon explosions and so-called peaceful nuclear explosions. The United States said its affirmative vote was not directed against any particular State in the region but was an expression of its general support for nuclear-weapon-free zones, whose effectiveness depended on a number of conditions.

Reports. S-G, [1]A/S-12/17, [2]A/37/433.
Resolution (1982). [3]GA: 37/76, 9 Dec., text following.
Resolutions (prior). GA: [4]2373(XXII), annex, 12 June 1968 (YUN 1968, p. 17); [5]36/88, 9 Dec. 1981 (YUN 1981, p. 55).
Meeting records. GA: 1st Committee, A/C.1/37/PV.3-10, 12-28, 30, 41 (18 Oct.–23 Nov.); plenary, A/37/PV.98 (9 Dec.).

General Assembly resolution 37/76

9 December 1982   Meeting 98   99-2-45 (recorded vote)

Approved by First Committee (A/37/658) by recorded vote (79-2-39), 23 November (meeting 41); draft by Pakistan (A/C.1/37/L.14); agenda item 46.

Establishment of a nuclear-weapon-free zone in South Asia
The General Assembly,

Recalling its resolutions 3265 B (XXIX) of 9 December 1974, 3476 B (XXX) of 11 December 1975, 31/73 of 10 December 1976, 32/83 of 12 December 1977, 33/65 of 14 December 1978, 34/78 of 11 December 1979, 35/148 of 12 December 1980 and 36/88 of 9 December 1981 concerning the establishment of a nuclear-weapon-free zone in South Asia,

Reiterating its conviction that the establishment of nuclear-weapon-free zones in various regions of the world is one of the measures which can contribute most effectively to the objectives of non-proliferation of nuclear weapons and general and complete disarmament,

Believing that the establishment of a nuclear-weapon-free zone in South Asia, as in other regions, will strengthen the security of the States of the region against the use or threat of use of nuclear weapons,

Noting the declarations issued at the highest level by Governments of South Asian States reaffirming their undertaking not to acquire or manufacture nuclear weapons and to devote their nuclear programmes exclusively to the economic and social advancement of their peoples,

Recalling that in the above-mentioned resolutions it called upon the States of the South Asian region, and such other neighbouring non-nuclear-weapon States as might be interested, to make all possible efforts to establish a nuclear-weapon-free zone in South Asia and to refrain, in the mean time, from any action contrary to this objective,

Further recalling that, in its resolutions 3265 B (XXIX), 31/73 and 32/83, it requested the Secretary-General to convene a meeting for the purpose of the consultations mentioned therein and to render such assistance as might be required to promote the efforts for the establishment of a nuclear-weapon-free zone in South Asia,

Bearing in mind the provisions of paragraphs 60 to 63 of the Final Document of the Tenth Special Session of the General Assembly regarding the establishment of nuclear-weapon-free zones, including in the region of South Asia,

Taking note of the report of the Secretary-General on the establishment of a nuclear-weapon-free zone in South Asia,

1. *Reaffirms* its endorsement, in principle, of the concept of a nuclear-weapon-free zone in South Asia;

2. *Urges once again* the States of South Asia and such other neighbouring non-nuclear-weapon States as may be interested to continue to make all possible efforts to establish a nuclear-weapon-free zone in South Asia and to refrain, in the mean time, from any action contrary to this objective;

3. *Calls upon* those nuclear-weapon States that have not done so to respond positively to this proposal and to extend the necessary cooperation in the efforts to establish a nuclear-weapon-free zone in South Asia;

4. *Requests* the Secretary-General to render such assistance as may be required to promote the efforts for the establishment of a nuclear-weapon-free zone in South Asia and to report on the subject to the General Assembly at its thirty-eighth session;

5. *Decides* to include in the provisional agenda of its thirty-eighth session the item entitled "Establishment of a nuclear-weapon-free zone in South Asia".

Recorded vote in Assembly as follows:

In favour: Antigua and Barbuda, Bahrain, Bangladesh, Barbados, Belgium, Botswana, Burundi, Canada, Cape Verde, Central African Republic, Chad, Chile, China, Colombia, Comoros, Costa Rica, Democratic Kampuchea, Democratic Yemen, Djibouti, Dominican Republic, Ecuador, Egypt, El Salvador, Finland, Gabon, Gambia, Germany, Federal Republic of, Ghana, Greece, Guatemala, Guinea, Guinea-Bissau, Guyana, Haiti, Honduras, Iceland, Iran, Iraq, Ireland, Jamaica, Japan, Jordan, Kenya, Kuwait, Lebanon, Liberia, Luxembourg, Malawi, Malaysia, Maldives, Mali, Malta, Mauritania, Mexico, Morocco, Nepal, Netherlands, New Zealand, Niger, Nigeria, Oman, Pakistan, Panama, Papua New Guinea, Paraguay, Peru, Philippines, Portugal, Qatar, Romania, Rwanda, Saint Lucia, Saudi Arabia, Senegal, Sierra Leone, Singapore, Solomon Islands, Somalia, Spain, Sri Lanka, Sudan, Swaziland, Syrian Arab Republic,[a] Thailand, Togo, Trinidad and Tobago, Tunisia, Turkey, Uganda, United Arab Emirates, United Republic of Cameroon, United Republic of Tanzania, United States, Upper Volta, Uruguay, Venezuela, Yemen, Zaire, Zambia.

Against: Bhutan, India.

Abstaining: Afghanistan, Algeria, Angola, Argentina, Australia, Austria, Bahamas, Belize, Benin, Bolivia, Brazil, Bulgaria, Burma, Byelorussian SSR, Congo, Cuba, Cyprus, Czechoslovakia, Denmark, Ethiopia, Fiji, France, German Democratic Republic, Grenada, Hungary, Indonesia, Israel, Italy, Ivory Coast, Lao People's Democratic Republic, Libyan Arab Jamahiriya, Madagascar, Mongolia, Mozambique, Nicaragua, Norway, Poland, Sao Tome and Principe, Sweden, Ukrainian SSR, USSR, United Kingdom, Vanuatu, Viet Nam, Yugoslavia.

[a]Later advised the Secretariat it had intended not to participate in the vote.

Preparations for the 1983 Review Conference on the Treaty to prohibit the placement of nuclear weapons on the sea-bed

By a resolution of 13 December 1982,[2] adopted without vote, the General Assembly requested the Secretary-General to provide assistance and services for the second Review Conference of the Parties to the Treaty on the Prohibition of the Emplacement of Nuclear Weapons and Other Weapons of Mass Destruction on the Sea-Bed and the Ocean Floor and in the Subsoil Thereof. This assistance was to cover both the Conference, scheduled for 1983, and its preparation, to be handled by a preparatory committee. The Assembly noted that the first Review Conference, in 1977,[4] had decided that the second conference should be convened not later than in 1984. It also recalled its expressed hope for the widest possible adherence to the Treaty.

The First Committee approved this resolution on 24 November 1982, also without vote. Sponsored by 11 countries, the draft was introduced by Denmark.

The Treaty was concluded in 1970 by a non-United Nations conference and commended to United Nations Members by the General Assembly.[3] It entered into force on 18 May 1972. As at 31 December 1982, it had been ratified by 72 States.

A paragraph mentioning the need for further steps to prevent an arms race on the sea-bed was included in the draft comprehensive programme of disarmament considered earlier in the year at the Assembly's special session on disarmament,[1] but the final wording was not agreed upon.

During the general debate at that session, Zimbabwe stated that, despite the Treaty and the holding of the first Review Conference in 1977, the sea-bed continued to be used for hiding armaments.

Report. [1]*Ad Hoc* Committee, A/S-12/32.
Resolution (1982). [2]GA: 37/99 H, 13 Dec., text following.
Resolution (prior). [3]GA: 2660(XXV), annex, 7 Dec. 1970 (YUN 1970, p. 18).
Yearbook reference. [4]1977, p. 44.
Meeting records. GA: plenary, A/S-12/PV.2-26, 28, 29 (8 June–10 July), A/37/PV.101 (13 Dec.); *Ad Hoc* Committee, A/S-12/-AC.1/PV.9 (28 June); 1st Committee, A/C.1/37/PV.3-10, 12-28, *37, 43* (18 Oct.–24 Nov.).

General Assembly resolution 37/99 H

13 December 1982   Meeting 101   Adopted without vote

Approved by First Committee (A/37/667) without vote, 24 November (meeting 43); 11-nation draft (A/C.1/37/L.56); agenda item 55.

Sponsors: Australia, Belgium, Colombia, Denmark, Ecuador, Finland, German Democratic Republic, India, Japan, Norway, Romania.

Second Review Conference of the Parties to the Treaty on the Prohibition of the Emplacement of Nuclear Weapons and Other Weapons of Mass Destruction on the Sea-Bed and the Ocean Floor and in the Subsoil Thereof

The General Assembly,

Recalling its resolution 2660(XXV) of 7 December 1970, in which it commended the Treaty on the Prohibition of the Emplacement of Nuclear Weapons and Other Weapons of Mass Destruction on the Sea-Bed and the Ocean Floor and in the Subsoil Thereof,

Noting the provisions of article VII of that Treaty concerning the holding of review conferences,

Bearing in mind that the first Review Conference of the Parties to the Treaty on the Prohibition of the Emplacement of Nuclear Weapons and Other Weapons of Mass Destruction on the Sea-Bed and the Ocean Floor and in the Subsoil Thereof, held at Geneva from 20 June to 1 July 1977, decided, in its Final Declaration, that a further review conference should be held at Geneva in 1982, unless a majority of States parties indicated to the depositaries that they wished such a conference to be postponed, in which case it should be convened not later than in 1984,

Recalling its resolution 32/87 A of 12 December 1977, in which it made an assessment of the outcome of the first Review Conference,

Bearing in mind all the relevant paragraphs of the Final Document of the Tenth Special Session of the General Assembly,

1. *Notes* that, following appropriate consultations, a Preparatory Committee for the Second Review Conference of the Parties to the Treaty on the Prohibition of the Emplacement of Nuclear Weapons and Other Weapons of Mass Destruction on the Sea-Bed and the Ocean Floor and in the Subsoil Thereof is to be established prior to holding a further review conference in 1983;

2. *Requests* the Secretary General to render the necessary assistance and to provide such services, including summary records, as may be required for the Review Conference and its preparation;

3. *Recalls* its expressed hope for the widest possible adherence to the Treaty.

Proposed treaty on prohibition of nuclear-weapon tests

The Committee on Disarmament decided in April 1982 to establish an *ad hoc* working group under its agenda item on a nuclear-test ban and requested it, in the first instance, to discuss and define issues relating to verification and compliance with a proposed treaty to prohibit nuclear-weapon tests. The Working Group held an initial round of meetings in August and September. In December, the General Assembly adopted three resolutions calling for negotiations in the Committee on a comprehensive test-ban treaty, and also urged a suspension of all such tests (see below). Meanwhile, a Group of Scientific Experts under the Committee on Disarmament continued to study verification techniques that could identify seismic activity indicative of nuclear testing after a test ban was instituted.

General Assembly consideration (June/July). Agreement was not reached at the General Assembly's 1982 special session devoted to disarmament on provisions relating to a ban on nuclear-weapon tests proposed for inclusion in the comprehensive programme of disarmament.[2]

In the general debate at that session, a large number of countries spoke in favour of concluding a comprehensive test-ban treaty.

Many of these cited figures on the number of tests that had been conducted despite the 1963 Treaty Banning Nuclear Weapon Tests in the Atmosphere, in Outer Space and under Water, known as the partial test-ban Treaty.[8] Ireland stated that, in the period since the Treaty took effect, some 800 nuclear tests had taken place, significantly more than the total of 500 tests which had occurred in the preceding 1945-1963 period. In the view of the United Republic of Cameroon, the 1,300 tests carried out in the previous 36 years should have provided the nuclear Powers with more than sufficient data. The Congo, Japan and Sierra Leone observed that as many as 200 nuclear-test explosions had been conducted in the four years between the first and second special sessions on disarmament. Iceland noted that that was an average of one a week.

Others favouring the conclusion of a comprehensive test-ban treaty included Angola, Antigua and Barbuda, Australia, Bhutan, Czechoslovakia, Ecuador, the Federal Republic of Germany, Ireland, Malaysia, Mozambique, Norway, the Philippines, Poland, Romania, Spain, Togo, Trinidad and Tobago, the United Republic of Tanzania, Uruguay and Zaire. Such a treaty, said Italy, would increase mutual trust and signal an approach towards an effective and radical process of nuclear disarmament.

Gabon, Honduras and Zimbabwe called for an early start of negotiations on a comprehensive test-ban treaty. Kenya and Somalia asserted that, whatever the differences on the issue of verification, there were no insurmountable obstacles necessitating a delay in the conclusion of such a treaty. Expressing particular concern about the tests being conducted in the Pacific, New Zealand said that, the longer an agreement was delayed, the greater the risks of proliferation would become. Pakistan expected such a treaty to be equitable and universally acceptable to nuclear and non-nuclear States alike. Sierra Leone called for a comprehensive test-ban treaty under which verification measures would be applied on a universal and non-discriminatory basis.

Many States, including Denmark, Jamaica, Nepal, the Syrian Arab Republic and the Ukrainian SSR, welcomed the efforts of the Committee on Disarmament to elaborate a comprehensive test-ban treaty, and Mongolia said the Committee should speed its work in this area. New Zealand hoped the Committee's recent agreement to consider some of the most vexed problems would contribute to their solution and lead to an early resumption of negotiations for a test-ban treaty satisfactory to all. Sweden said that, in view of the long deadlock over the issue, it was encouraging that the nuclear-weapon Powers had at least been prevailed upon to enter into concrete negotiations in the Committee.

Bangladesh, the German Democratic Republic and Guyana called for an immediate halt to all nuclear-weapon tests pending conclusion of a comprehensive test-ban treaty, as did India pending nuclear disarmament. India said this would serve two objectives: to prevent radioactive pollution of the environment and to slow the nuclear-arms race. In the view of the Netherlands, the international community stood farther from the goal of a comprehensive test ban than in 1978, when it had appeared to be within reach; it believed the resumption of negotiations between the USSR, the United Kingdom and the United States, parallel with the multilateral negotiations, to be indispensable.

Some countries, among them Austria, Fiji, Iraq and Turkey, viewed cessation of nuclear-weapon testing as a vital element in preventing vertical and horizontal proliferation of such weapons. Pending nuclear disarmament, Burma and Norway considered a comprehensive test ban essential for halting the qualitative improvement of nuclear weapons and nuclear proliferation, while Finland believed it would serve at least as a partial remedy to the problem of qualitative development. In the view of Singapore, such a treaty would help narrow one channel of arms competition among the major Powers by making it difficult for them to be certain about the performance of weapons under development, and would also reinforce the 1968 Treaty on the Non-Proliferation of Nuclear Weapons[7] (NPT) by demonstrating the major Powers' awareness of their legal and moral obligations to halt the nuclear-arms race.

Cyprus feared that the continuation of nuclear testing might have an adverse impact on the will of the parties to NPT to maintain their adherence to it. Indonesia warned that further delay in the permanent cessation of tests would erode the value of a test ban in halting qualitative improvement of nuclear weapons and would hinder non-proliferation efforts.

Meanwhile, Denmark and Japan appealed to every State to participate in the 1963 partial test-ban Treaty. Brazil, recalling that that Treaty obliged the nuclear-weapon Powers to achieve the discontinuance of all test explosions of nuclear weapons for all time, said that official declarations 20 years later had relegated that objective from a first priority to a long-term goal. Kenya considered the 1963 Treaty to have served only as a licence for accelerating nuclear testing.

The USSR observed that the 1974 Treaty between the United States of America and the Union of Soviet Socialist Republics on the Limitation of Underground Nuclear Weapon Tests and the 1976 Treaty between the United States of America and the Union of Soviet Socialist Republics on Underground Nuclear Explosions for Peaceful Purposes remained to be ratified.

Some speakers called for an early resumption of the trilateral talks on complete and general prohibition of nuclear-weapon tests, between the USSR, the United Kingdom and the United States, held between 1977 and 1980. Fiji urged the remaining nuclear States to join in those negotiations. The Ukrainian SSR and the USSR asserted that the suspension had been caused by the Western participants; Poland joined those two States in calling for a resumption without delay.

Madagascar stated that a commitment by all States to respect a test moratorium would be very useful pending the conclusion of a properly prepared agreement. Bolivia, Fiji, Jamaica and Sri Lanka also favoured a moratorium, and Mexico said the great Powers could make a convincing contribution if during the special session they were unilaterally to declare a moratorium.

France said it could discern no real sign of a genuine readiness on the part of the two super-Powers to abandon testing and it could not, at the current time, cease conducting underground tests without endangering an essential element of its independence in that area.

A number of countries in the South Pacific expressed concern over continued nuclear-test explosions in the region. Australia, though noting that there had been no testing in the atmosphere since 1974, joined the other members of the South Pacific Forum in the strong condemnation of testing of nuclear weapons or dumping or storage of nuclear wastes in the Pacific by any Government. Fiji, asserting that France's statement reflected insensitivity to the concern of the people in the South Pacific, said it would seek assurances that States would refrain from testing, developing and manufacturing nuclear weapons or other nuclear explosive devices in the region, would not transfer such weapons or devices to any country of the region and would not use or threaten to use them against any country there.

Papua New Guinea urged those responsible to restrict the testing of catastrophic and inhuman weapons to their own soil. Samoa, urging a total ban, said there had been well over 200 explosions of nuclear devices in the Pacific, thousands of nuclear warheads were stored or deployed there, nuclear submarines roamed its waters and radioactive wastes abounded; it demanded that those responsible provide all the facts, although the damage was irreparable.

General Assembly action (December). On 9 December, the General Assembly adopted three resolutions asking for the prohibition of nuclear-weapon tests, in addition to its call of 13 December addressed to the USSR and the United States to declare a comprehensive test ban of nuclear weapons and of their delivery vehicles as part of a nuclear-arms freeze.[6]

By the first resolution, on cessation of nuclear-test explosions,[3] sponsored by 12 nations and introduced by Mexico, the Assembly urged all States to adhere to the partial test-ban Treaty and meanwhile to refrain from testing in all environments covered by that Treaty. It urged the three original parties to the Treaty (USSR, United Kingdom, United States) to abide by their undertaking therein to continue negotiations to achieve the discontinuance of all nuclear-weapon tests for all time, and it called on them to halt without delay all nuclear-test explosions, either jointly or unilaterally. Stating that the consensus rule in the Committee on Disarmament should not be used to prevent the approval of mandates for subsidiary bodies, the Assembly urged Committee members to ask its *Ad Hoc* Working Group on a nuclear-test ban to initiate, immediately after the beginning of the Committee's 1983 session, multilateral negotiation of a treaty to prohibit all tests and to do their best to enable the Committee to transmit the negotiated text to the Assembly in 1983.

This resolution was adopted by a recorded vote of 124 to 2, with 19 abstentions, following its approval by the First Committee on 23 November by a recorded vote of 104 to 2, with 19 abstentions.

By the second resolution,[4] on the urgent need for a comprehensive nuclear-test-ban treaty, sponsored by 27 States and introduced by Australia, the Assembly reiterated its grave concern at continued nuclear-weapon testing and reaffirmed its conviction that a treaty to prohibit all tests for all time was a matter of the greatest urgency and a vital element for the success of efforts to reverse the nuclear-arms race. It requested the Committee on Disarmament to initiate substantive negotiations with a view to submitting a draft treaty to the Assembly at the earliest possible date. The Committee was asked to determine, in the context of those negotiations, the institutional and administrative arrangements needed for establishing, testing and operating an international seismic monitoring network and an effective verification system.

The resolution was adopted by a recorded vote of 111 to 1, with 35 abstentions. The First Committee had approved the draft on 26 November by a recorded vote of 92 to 1, with 34 abstentions.

By the third resolution,[5] on the immediate cessation and prohibition of nuclear-weapon tests, sponsored by 10 Eastern European and other socialist countries and introduced by the USSR, the Assembly urged the Committee on Disarmament to proceed promptly to practical negotiations with a view to elaborating a draft treaty on the complete and general prohibition of nuclear-weapon tests, and referred to the Committee for consideration a USSR text on the basic provisions of such a treaty. The Assembly called on all nuclear-weapon States not to conduct any nuclear explosions, starting from a date agreed by them and until the treaty was concluded.

According to the basic provisions proposed by the USSR (annexed to the resolution), the treaty, in addition to prohibiting all nuclear-weapon testing, would provide for a moratorium on nuclear explosions for peaceful purposes until a procedure for carrying them out was agreed. Various measures were included for ensuring compliance with the treaty, which would enter into force upon ratification by 20 States, including all permanent members of the Security Council. It would be of unlimited duration, except that the States parties might agree on its entry into force for a limited period, given the participation of the USSR, the United Kingdom and the United States.

The Assembly adopted this resolution by a recorded vote of 115 to 5, with 25 abstentions. The First Committee had approved it on 23 November by a recorded vote of 98 to 4, with 24 abstentions.

Introducing the 12-nation resolution, as revised by its sponsors, Mexico said the text recapitulated some highly relevant facts which it believed the nuclear Powers concerned would have liked forgotten, among them the fact that the Assembly had adopted more than 40 resolutions in over 25 years of discussing the nuclear-weapon-test ban and that no valid reason existed for delaying the conclusion of a comprehensive test-ban agreement. Moreover, the three nuclear-weapon States that were depositaries of the partial test-ban Treaty had undertaken in that Treaty to seek the discontinuance of all tests for all time, and that undertaking had been reiterated in NPT. The corner-stone of the text, according to Mexico, was the call to members of the Committee on Disarmament to assign the negotiation of a treaty to its *Ad Hoc* Working Group.

Introducing the 27-nation draft, which was revised by its sponsors before adoption, Australia stated that the conclusion of a comprehensive test-ban treaty, covering explosions for both military and peaceful purposes, would contribute to limiting and perhaps stopping both vertical and horizontal nuclear-weapon proliferation. It would also strengthen NPT by leading to its fuller implementation as well as by helping overcome the objections of those that saw NPT as discriminatory in favour of existing nuclear-weapon States. Such a comprehensive treaty, however, would not be possible without full examination first of the issues of verification and compliance, and the sponsors hoped the Committee on Disarmament would speedily complete its current stage of work and initiate substantive negotiations on a treaty.

The third resolution had been submitted under an item entitled "Immediate cessation and prohibition of nuclear-weapon tests", which was included in the Assembly agenda at the request of the USSR, contained in a letter to the Secretary-General dated 1 October.[1] The letter stated that the complete cessation of tests would be a serious obstacle to the development of new weapons systems as well as to the emergence of new nuclear-weapon States. Annexed to the letter was the draft resolution later adopted by the Assembly, with its attached basic provisions of a treaty. The letter said of these basic provisions that they took account of what had been achieved in years of discussion and reflected the considerations of many States, in particular on verification of compliance.

Introducing the draft in the First Committee, the USSR said the text sought to have the Assembly endorse the adoption of concrete measures for the cessation and prohibition of nuclear-weapon tests. The proposed basic provisions created a new situation which should help States in emerging from the impasse on this item.

In explanation of vote on the first resolution, the United States, which cast a negative vote, voiced several objections: while a prohibition of all nuclear explosions remained a long-term objective, it would not reduce the threat implicit in the existing weapons stockpile; the verification issue remained a serious problem; the resolution was directed at weapon tests, ignoring the fact that weapon-related benefits were derived from any nuclear explosion; the proposed moratorium would not be subject to verification; and the text not only ignored the decision of the Committee on Disarmament to discuss verification and compliance issues but also told the Committee how to conduct its work.

Among those abstaining in the vote on this resolution, Canada expressed regret that the presentation of three competing resolutions on the subject reflected a falling off of the will to achieve consensus; the issue of verification and compliance should be resolved not by ignoring it but by reaching agreement. France was of the view that a comprehensive test ban should be part of, rather than a prerequisite for, nuclear disarmament; until the two principal nuclear Powers had created the necessary conditions, France would not work on, or sign, a test-ban treaty. Greece said the text contained several unbalanced elements concerning the doctrines and intentions of the nuclear-weapon States on such matters as verification. Japan abstained because the text called on only three nuclear-weapon States to halt their nuclear tests.

With regard to the provision opposing use of the consensus rule in determining the mandates of subsidiary bodies in the Committee on Disarmament, France did not believe a return to majority rule could contribute to progress in substantive negotiations; Greece feared the text could undermine a rule which was uncomfortable yet indispensable, and Japan opposed changing the rule.

Voting in favour of the first resolution, Brazil hoped the text would help secure the full participation and co-operation of the nuclear-weapon Powers in the Committee's negotiations on a test-ban treaty. Cuba and the German Democratic Republic supported the call for the beginning of concrete negotiations in the Committee but expressed the view that a test moratorium would be effective only if all nuclear-weapon States joined in; Cuba added that its favourable vote did not indicate a change in its position regarding its accession to the partial test-ban Treaty. The German Democratic Republic and the USSR welcomed the premise of the resolution that existing means of verification were sufficient and presented no cause for delaying the conclusion of a treaty; however, the USSR thought a trilateral moratorium should be linked to a specific timetable, the possible extension of which would depend on the conduct of other nuclear Powers.

While voting in favour, India reaffirmed its conviction that the appeal for test suspension should be addressed to all nuclear-weapon States without exception. Cuba and the German Democratic Republic also hoped all nuclear-weapon States would join in the suspension.

Explaining its vote against the second resolution, the United States said it believed negotiations on a test-ban treaty would currently be inappropriate; the Committee on Disarmament should focus on verification and compliance.

Cuba abstained because the text asked the Committee to continue consideration of verification and compliance, unlike the other resolutions, for which Cuba had voted, asking it to embark forthwith on urgent negotiations on a treaty; if the request in paragraph 7 for substantive negotiations did not mean their commencement at the Committee's spring 1983 session, Cuba would have voted against. The German Democratic Republic abstained as it believed the *Ad Hoc* Working Group should proceed to actual comprehensive test-ban negotiations rather than continue under its current limited mandate. The USSR called the text intrinsically contradictory in referring to the need for talks on a treaty in the Committee on Disarmament and at the same time asking the Committee to continue work on the basis of the limited mandate given to its *Ad Hoc* Working Group, which was not addressed to the preparation of a treaty; the USSR belived that Group should be given a new mandate.

Argentina abstained, stating that the resolution presented difficulties for the development and use of nuclear energy for peaceful purposes; moreover, it was not logical to adopt two resolutions on the same subject reflecting different views and approaches. France objected that by paragraphs 7 and 8 it was called on to participate in negotiations to draft a treaty, the conditions for which had not been met. India considered that paragraph 2 (reaffirming the Assembly's conviction as to the urgency of a treaty prohibiting all nuclear-test explosions by all States for all time) ran counter to the generally accepted scope of a nuclear-test-ban treaty, which should aim at the general and complete cessation of nuclear-weapon testing by all States in all environments for all time. Mexico ascribed its abstention to its dissatisfaction with that paragraph's description of the mandate for work on a treaty.

Pakistan, though voting for both the first and second resolutions to show its support of all initiatives for a comprehensive test-ban treaty, expressed difficulty with paragraph 2 of the second text on the ground that its language was not in line with past Assembly pronouncements. Algeria said its

vote for the second resolution did not change its position as reflected in the first text.

Voting against the text introduced by the USSR, China, while supporting the cessation of nuclear tests as part of comprehensive nuclear disarmament, asserted that the proposal, submitted by a Power which had conducted nearly 500 nuclear-test explosions including more than a dozen in 1982 alone, did not reflect a genuine desire for disarmament; when the two States with the largest arsenals had stopped all testing and reduced their nuclear arsenals by half, all nuclear States should stop testing, cease production and reduce their arsenals to reasonable proportions.

France, also voting negatively, said a moratorium on tests would have the primary effect of consolidating the qualitative and quantitative advantages that the two principal nuclear Powers had gained from previous tests. The United States said it had voted against the text because it contained a number of objectionable provisions.

Australia, which abstained, objected that the text dealt with a treaty applicable only to nuclear-weapon tests, whereas the world would not be free from the threat of proliferation of nuclear weapons as long as so-called peaceful explosions were not banned; moreover, since a treaty must have adequate provisions for verification and compliance, it would be logical for the Committee on Disarmament to begin work there. Canada abstained, stating that the text failed to come to grips with the critical area of verification and that its reference to a moratorium ruled out the possibility of full agreement.

Although supporting the underlying principle of the USSR-introduced text, Costa Rica did not participate in the vote in the First Committee (it voted affirmatively in the Assembly) on the ground that a proposal from one of the two major Powers, at a time when they were preparing for talks and when the Committee on Disarmament was conducting negotiations on the delicate issue, had a unilateral aspect.

Argentina, Colombia and India said their affirmative vote did not constitute an endorsement of the basic provisions of the draft treaty submitted by the USSR. India added that the Committee on Disarmament should take into account all existing and future proposals on an equal footing; also, the nuclear-weapon States should suspend all testing of such weapons pending conclusion of a comprehensive test-ban treaty.

Belgium abstained in the vote on the texts introduced by Mexico and by the USSR, but voted in favour of the one introduced by Australia; it expressed serious doubts about the possibility of distinguishing between weapon tests and tests for peaceful purposes, and asserted that the question of verification remained one of the main problems to be solved.

During the First Committee's disarmament debate, the United Kingdom, recalling that two sustained efforts to conclude a comprehensive test ban had been unsuccessful, said a third attempt could succeed only if there was greater confidence and if answers were found to the important question of verification.

Letter. [1]USSR, 1 Oct., A/37/243.
Report. [2]*Ad Hoc* Committee, A/S-12/32.
Resolutions (1982). GA: [3]37/72, 9 Dec., text following; [4]37/73, 9 Dec., text following; [5]37/85, 9 Dec., text following; [6]37/100 B, para. 1 *(a)* (i), 13 Dec.
Resolution (prior). [7]GA: 2373(XXII), annex, 12 June 1968 (YUN 1968, p. 17).
Yearbook reference. [8]1963, p. 137.
Meeting records. GA: plenary, A/S-12/PV.2-26, 28 (8 June–10 July), A/37/PV.24, 98 (8 Oct., 9 Dec.); *Ad Hoc* Committee, A/S-12/AC.1/PV.2 (14 June); General Committee, A/BUR/37/SR.3 (8 Oct.); 1st Committee, A/C.1/37/PV.3-10, 12-28, *29*, 34, 37, *38-41*, *45* (18 Oct.–26 Nov.).

General Assembly resolution 37/72

9 December 1982   Meeting 98   124-2-19 (recorded vote)

Approved by First Committee (A/37/654) by recorded vote (104-2-19), 23 November (meeting 41); 12-nation draft (A/C.1/37/L.32/Rev.1); agenda item 42.

Sponsors: Bangladesh, Colombia, Costa Rica, Ecuador, Ireland, Kenya, Mexico, Pakistan, Sri Lanka, Sweden, Venezuela, Yugoslavia.

Cessation of all test explosions of nuclear weapons
The General Assembly,

Bearing in mind that the complete cessation of nuclear-weapon tests, which has been examined for more than twenty-five years and on which the General Assembly has adopted more than forty resolutions, is a basic objective of the United Nations in the sphere of disarmament, to the attainment of which it has repeatedly assigned the highest priority,

Stressing that on seven different occasions it has condemned such tests in the strongest terms and that, since 1974, it has stated its conviction that the continuance of nuclear-weapon testing will intensify the arms race, thus increasing the danger of nuclear war,

Reiterating the assertion made in several previous resolutions that, whatever may be the differences on the question of verification, there is no valid reason for delaying the conclusion of an agreement on a comprehensive test ban,

Recalling that since 1972 the Secretary-General has declared that all the technical and scientific aspects of the problem have been so fully explored that only a political decision is now necessary in order to achieve final agreement, that when the existing means of verification are taken into account it is difficult to understand further delay in achieving agreement on an underground test ban, and that the potential risks of continuing underground nuclear-weapon tests would far outweigh any possible risks from ending such tests,

Recalling also that the Secretary-General, in his foreword to the report entitled "Comprehensive nuclear-test ban", submitted to the General Assembly at its thirty-fifth session, reiterated with special emphasis the opinion he had expressed nine years earlier and, after specifically referring to it, added: "I still hold that belief. The problem can and should be solved now",

Noting that in the same report, which was prepared in compliance with General Assembly decision 34/422 of 11 December 1979, the experts emphasized that non-nuclear-weapon States in general had come to regard the achievement of a comprehensive test ban as a litmus test of the determination of the nuclear-weapon States to halt the arms race, adding that verification of compliance no longer seemed to be an obstacle to reaching agreement,

Taking into account that the three nuclear-weapon States which act as depositaries of the Treaty Banning Nuclear Weapon Tests in the Atmosphere, in Outer Space and under Water undertook in that Treaty, almost twenty years ago, to seek the achievement of the discontinu-

ance of all test explosions of nuclear weapons for all time and that such an undertaking was explicitly reiterated in 1968 in the Treaty on the Non-Proliferation of Nuclear Weapons,

Deploring that neither the Committee on Disarmament nor the General Assembly at its the twelfth special session have been able to elaborate a comprehensive test-ban treaty,

1. *Reiterates once again its grave concern* that, despite the express wishes of the overwhelming majority of Member States, nuclear-weapon testing continues unabated;

2. *Reaffirms its conviction* that a treaty to achieve the prohibition of all nuclear-test explosions by all States for all time is a matter of the highest priority and constitutes a vital element for the success of efforts to prevent both vertical and horizontal proliferation of nuclear weapons and a contribution to nuclear disarmament;

3. *Urges* all States that have not yet done so to adhere without further delay to the Treaty Banning Nuclear Weapon Tests in the Atmosphere, in Outer Space and under Water and, meanwhile, to refrain from testing in the environments covered by that Treaty;

4. *Urges also* the three original parties to the Treaty Banning Nuclear Weapons Tests in the Atmosphere, in Outer Space and under Water to abide strictly by the undertakings contained therein to seek "to achieve the discontinuance of all test explosions of nuclear weapons for all time" and "to continue negotiations to this end";

5. *Urges likewise* all States members of the Committee on Disarmament:

*(a)*To bear in mind that, if the consensus rule should not be used in such a manner as to prevent the establishment of subsidiary bodies for the effective discharge of the functions of the Committee, neither should it be used to prevent the approval of appropriate mandates for such subsidiary bodies;

*(b)*To assign to the *Ad Hoc* Working Group under item 1 of its agenda, entitled "Nuclear-test ban", established on 21 April 1982 by the Committee, a mandate which should provide for the multilateral negotiation of a treaty for the prohibition of all nuclear-weapon tests, to be initiated immediately after the beginning of the session of the Committee to be held in 1983;

*(c)*To exert their best endeavours in order that the Committee may transmit to the General Assembly at its thirty-eighth session the multilaterally negotiated text of such a treaty;

6. *Calls upon* the States depositaries of the Treaty Banning Nuclear Weapon Tests in the Atmosphere, in Outer Space and under Water and the Treaty on the Non-Proliferation of Nuclear Weapons, by virtue of their special responsibilities under those two treaties and as a provisional measure, to bring to a halt without delay all nuclear-test explosions, either through a trilaterally agreed moratorium or through three unilateral moratoriums;

7. *Decides* to include in the provisional agenda of its thirty-eighth session the item entitled "Cessation of all test explosions of nuclear weapons".

Recorded vote in Assembly as follows:

In favour: Afghanistan, Algeria, Angola, Argentina, Austria, Bahamas, Bahrain, Bangladesh, Barbados, Belize, Benin, Bhutan, Bolivia, Botswana, Brazil, Bulgaria, Burma, Burundi, Byelorussian SSR, Cape Verde, Central African Republic, Chad, Chile, Colombia, Comoros, Congo, Costa Rica, Cuba, Cyprus, Czechoslovakia, Democratic Yemen, Djibouti, Dominican Republic, Ecuador, Egypt, El Salvador, Ethiopia, Fiji, Finland, Gabon, Gambia, German Democratic Republic, Ghana, Grenada, Guatemala, Guinea, Guinea-Bissau, Guyana, Haiti, Honduras, Hungary, India, Indonesia, Iran, Iraq, Ireland, Ivory Coast, Jamaica, Jordan, Kenya, Kuwait, Lao People's Democratic Republic, Lebanon, Liberia, Libyan Arab Jamahiriya, Madagascar, Malawi, Malaysia, Maldives, Mali, Malta, Mauritania, Mauritius, Mexico, Mongolia, Morocco, Mozambique, Nepal, Nicaragua, Niger, Nigeria, Oman, Pakistan, Panama, Papua New Guinea, Paraguay, Peru, Philippines, Poland, Qatar, Romania, Rwanda, Sao Tome and Principe, Saudi Arabia, Senegal, Sierra Leone, Singapore, Solomon Islands, Somalia, Sri Lanka, Sudan, Suriname, Swaziland, Sweden, Syrian Arab Republic, Thailand, Togo, Trinidad and Tobago, Tunisia, Uganda, Ukrainian SSR, USSR, United Arab Emirates, United Republic of Cameroon, United Republic of Tanzania, Upper Volta, Uruguay, Vanuatu, Venezuela, Viet Nam, Yemen, Yugoslavia, Zaire, Zambia.

Against: United Kingdom, United States.

Abstaining: Australia, Belgium, Canada, China, Denmark, France, Germany, Federal Republic of, Greece, Iceland, Israel, Italy, Japan, Luxembourg, Netherlands, New Zealand, Norway, Portugal, Spain, Turkey.

General Assembly resolution 37/73

9 December 1982   Meeting 98   111-1-35 (recorded vote)

Approved by First Committee (A/37/655) by recorded vote (92-1-34), 26 November (meeting 45); 27-nation draft (A/C.1/37/L.40/Rev.1); agenda item 43.

Sponsors: Australia, Austria, Bahamas, Bangladesh, Canada, Colombia, Denmark, Ecuador, Fiji, Finland, Ireland, Japan, Malaysia, Netherlands, New Zealand, Niger, Norway, Papua New Guinea, Philippines, Samoa, Sierra Leone, Singapore, Solomon Islands, Spain, Sweden, Thailand, Uruguay.

Urgent need for a comprehensive nuclear-test-ban treaty

The General Assembly,

Convinced of the urgent need for the negotiation of a comprehensive nuclear-test-ban treaty capable of attracting the widest possible international support and adherence,

Reaffirming its conviction that an end to nuclear-weapon testing by all States in all environments would be a major step towards ending the qualitative improvement, development and proliferation of nuclear weapons, a means of relieving the deep apprehension concerning the harmful consequences of radioactive contamination for the health of present and future generations and a measure of the utmost importance in bringing the nuclear-arms race to an end,

Recalling that the parties to the Treaty Banning Nuclear Weapon Tests in the Atmosphere, in Outer Space and under Water undertook not to carry out any nuclear-weapon-test explosion, or any other nuclear explosion, in the environments covered by that Treaty, and that in that Treaty and in the Treaty on the Non-Proliferation of Nuclear Weapons the parties expressed their determination to continue negotiations to achieve the discontinuance of all test explosions of nuclear weapons for all time,

Recalling also its previous resolutions on this subject,

Recognizing the indispensable role of the Committee on Disarmament in the negotiation of a comprehensive nuclear-test-ban treaty,

Taking into account that part of the report of the Committee on Disarmament concerning consideration of the item entitled "Nuclear-test ban" during its session in 1982,

Convinced that the Committee on Disarmament should commence negotiations on such a treaty at the earliest possible date,

Recognizing the importance to such a treaty of the work assigned by the Committee on Disarmament to the *Ad Hoc* Group of Scientific Experts to Consider International Co-operative Measures to Detect and Identify Seismic Events on a global network of stations for the exchange of seismological data,

Stressing the importance of further efforts by the Union of Soviet Socialist Republics, the United Kingdom of Great Britain and Northern Ireland and the United States of America to facilitate the conclusion of such a treaty,

1. *Reiterates its grave concern* that, despite the express wishes of the overwhelming majority of Member States, nuclear-weapon testing continues unabated;

2. *Reaffirms its conviction* that a treaty to achieve the prohibition of all nuclear-test explosions by all States for all time is a matter of the greatest urgency and highest priority;

3. *Expresses the conviction* that such a treaty would constitute a vital element for the success of efforts to halt and reverse the nuclear-arms race and the qualitative improvement of nuclear weapons, and to prevent the expansion of existing nuclear arsenals and the spread of nuclear weapons to additional countries;

4. *Notes* that the Committee on Disarmament, in the exercise of its responsibilities as the multilateral disarmament negotiating forum, established on 21 April 1982 an *Ad Hoc* Working Group under item 1 of its agenda, entitled "Nuclear-test ban", and, considering that discussion of specific issues in the first instance might facilitate progress towards negotiation of a nuclear-test ban, requested the *Ad Hoc* Working Group:

    (a) To discuss and define, through substantive examination, issues relating to verification and compliance, with a view to making further progress towards a nuclear-test ban;

    (b) To take into account all existing proposals and future initiatives and report to the Committee on the progress of its work before the conclusion of the session in 1982;

5. *Also notes* that the Committee on Disarmament agreed that it would thereafter take a decision on subsequent courses of action with a view to fulfilling its responsibilities in this regard;

6. *Further notes* that the *Ad Hoc* Working Group has initiated consideration of the issues under its mandate;

7. *Requests* the Committee on Disarmament to continue the consideration of those issues and to take the necessary steps to initiate substantive negotiations in order that the draft of a comprehensive nuclear-test-ban treaty may be submitted to the General Assembly at the earliest possible date;

8. *Urges* all members of the Committee on Disarmament, in particular the nuclear-weapon States, to co-operate with the Committee in fulfilling these tasks;

9. *Also requests* the Committee on Disarmament to determine, in the context of its negotiations on such a treaty, the institutional and administrative arrangements necessary for establishing, testing and operating an international seismic monitoring network and an effective verification system;

10. *Calls upon* the Committee on Disarmament to report on progress to the General Assembly at its thirty-eighth session;

11. *Decides* to include in the provisional agenda of its thirty-eighth session an item entitled "Urgent need for a comprehensive nuclear-test-ban treaty".

Recorded vote in Assembly as follows:

In favour: Algeria, Antigua and Barbuda, Australia, Austria, Bahamas, Bahrain, Bangladesh, Barbados, Belgium, Belize, Benin, Bhutan, Botswana, Burma, Burundi, Canada, Cape Verde, Central African Republic, Chad, Colombia, Comoros, Congo, Costa Rica, Cyprus, Democratic Kampuchea, Democratic Yemen, Denmark, Djibouti, Dominican Republic, Ecuador, Egypt, El Salvador, Ethiopia, Fiji, Finland, Gabon, Gambia, Germany, Federal Republic of, Ghana, Greece, Guatemala, Guinea, Guinea-Bissau, Guyana, Haiti, Honduras, Iceland, Indonesia, Iraq, Ireland, Italy, Ivory Coast, Jamaica, Japan, Jordan, Kenya, Kuwait, Lebanon, Liberia, Libyan Arab Jamahiriya, Luxembourg, Malawi, Malaysia, Maldives, Mali, Malta, Mauritania, Mauritius, Morocco, Nepal, Netherlands, New Zealand, Niger, Norway, Oman, Pakistan, Papua New Guinea, Paraguay, Philippines, Portugal, Qatar, Romania, Rwanda, Saint Lucia, Saudi Arabia, Senegal, Sierra Leone, Singapore, Solomon Islands, Somalia, Spain, Sri Lanka, Sudan, Suriname, Swaziland, Sweden, Syrian Arab Republic, Thailand, Togo, Trinidad and Tobago, Tunisia, Turkey, United Arab Emirates, United Republic of Cameroon, Upper Volta, Uruguay, Vanuatu, Yemen, Yugoslavia, Zaire, Zambia.

Against: United States.

Abstaining: Afghanistan, Angola, Argentina, Bolivia, Brazil, Bulgaria, Byelorussian SSR, Chile, China, Cuba, Czechoslovakia, France, German Democratic Republic, Grenada, Hungary, India, Israel, Lao People's Democratic Republic, Madagascar, Mexico, Mongolia, Mozambique, Nicaragua, Nigeria, Panama, Peru, Poland, Sao Tome and Principe, Uganda, Ukrainian SSR, USSR, United Kingdom, United Republic of Tanzania, Venezuela, Viet Nam.

General Assembly resolution 37/85

9 December 1982   Meeting 98   115-5-25 (recorded vote)

Approved by First Committee (A/37/672) by recorded vote (98-4-24), 23 November (meeting 40); 10-nation draft (A/C.1/37/L.6); agenda item 138.

Sponsors: Bulgaria, Byelorussian SSR, Czechoslovakia, German Democratic Republic, Hungary, Mongolia, Poland, Ukrainian SSR, USSR, Viet Nam.

Immediate cessation and prohibition of nuclear-weapon tests

The General Assembly,

Deeply concerned over the continuing nuclear-arms race and the growing danger of nuclear war,

Convinced that an immediate cessation of nuclear-weapon tests by all States in all environments and the prohibition of such testing in the future would be a serious obstacle to the development of ever-new types and systems of nuclear weapons, as well as to the emergence of new nuclear States,

Taking note of the "Basic provisions of a treaty on the complete and general prohibition of nuclear-weapon tests", submitted by the Union of Soviet Socialist Republics at the current session, the text of which is annexed to the present resolution,

1. *Urges* the Committee on Disarmament to proceed promptly to practical negotiations with a view to elaborating a draft treaty on the complete and general prohibition of nuclear-weapon tests;

2. *Refers* to the Committee on Disarmament, for its consideration, the basic provisions of such a treaty, submitted by the Union of Soviet Socialist Republics, the text of which is annexed to the present resolution, as well as the proposals and observations made by other States on this question in the course of the current session;

3. *Calls upon* all the nuclear-weapon States, as a gesture of goodwill and with a view to creating more favourable conditions for the formulation of a treaty on the complete and general prohibition of nuclear-weapon tests, not to conduct any nuclear explosions, starting from a date to be agreed among them and until the above-mentioned treaty

is concluded, after the appropriate declarations have been made by them to that effect well in advance;

4. *Decides* to include in the provisional agenda of its thirty-eighth session the item entitled "Immediate cessation and prohibition of nuclear-weapon tests".

ANNEX
**Basic provisions of a treaty on the complete and
general prohibition of nuclear-weapon tests**

The objective of averting nuclear war, towards which the efforts of the Union of Soviet Socialist Republics and of other peace-loving States are directed, makes it imperative to take such measures, *inter alia*, as would impede the development of ever-new types and systems of nuclear weapons.

One such effective measure would be the immediate cessation and prohibition of nuclear-weapon tests by all States and in all environments, which at the same time would promote the non-proliferation of nuclear weapons.

Motivated by these goals, the Soviet Union is submitting to States Members of the United Nations, for their consideration, the following basic provisions of a treaty on the complete and general prohibition of nuclear-weapon tests.

A. Scope of the prohibition

1. Each State party to this Treaty shall undertake to prohibit, to prevent and not to carry out any nuclear-weapon-test explosions at any place under its jurisdiction or control, in any environment—in the atmosphere, beyond its limits, including outer space, under water or under ground.

2. No party shall cause, encourage or in any way participate in the conduct of any nuclear-weapon-test explosions anywhere.

3. A moratorium shall be declared on nuclear explosions for peaceful purposes, under which the parties to this Treaty shall refrain from causing, encouraging, or in any way participating in carrying out such explosions until the relevant procedure has been evolved.

4. Promptly after the entry into force of this Treaty, consideration shall be given to the question of procedure for carrying out nuclear explosions for peaceful purposes. Such procedure, to be agreed upon, may take the form of a special agreement or agreements constituting an integral part of this Treaty.

B. Ensuring compliance with the Treaty

(1) *General provisions on verification*

5. The States parties to this Treaty shall base their activities in verifying compliance with the provisions of this Treaty on a combination of national and international measures.

6. For the purpose of verifying compliance by other States parties with the provisions of this Treaty, any State party shall have the right to use the national technical means of verification which it has at its disposal, in a manner consistent with generally recognized principles of international law.

7. States parties which possess national technical means of verification may, in case of necessity, place the information which they obtained through those means, and which is important for the purposes of this Treaty, at the disposal of other parties.

8. The States parties to this Treaty undertake not to interfere with the national technical means of verification of other States parties.

9. International measures of verification shall be carried out through international procedures within the framework of the United Nations, in accordance with the Charter, and through consultations and co-operation between States parties, as well as through the services of the Committee of Experts of States parties to this Treaty.

(2) *Consultations and co-operation*

10. The States parties to this Treaty shall, in case of necessity, consult each other, make inquiries and provide information in connection with such inquiries with a view to solving any questions that may arise with regard to compliance with the provisions of this Treaty.

11. The States parties shall exchange, bilaterally or through the Committee of Experts, information which they consider necessary to provide assurance of compliance with the obligations assumed under this Treaty.

12. Consultations and co-operation may also be undertaken through appropriate international procedures within the framework of the United Nations and in accordance with the Charter.

13. In the interests of increasing the effectiveness of this Treaty, the States parties to the Treaty shall agree in an appropriate way on the prevention of any actions aimed at deliberately falsifying the actual state of affairs with regard to compliance with this Treaty by other States parties.

(3) *International exchange of seismic data*

14. For the purposes of better assuring compliance with obligations under this Treaty, each party may participate in an international exchange of seismic data. Such international exchange shall be carried out in accordance with the following guidelines.

(4) *Guidelines for the international exchange of seismic data*

15. Each State party to this Treaty shall have the right to participate in the international exchange of seismic data, to contribute data from seismic stations on its territory which it designates for participation in the international exchange and to receive all the seismic data made available through the international exchange.

16. Each party that decides to participate in the international exchange shall designate an appropriate body through which it will communicate with the international exchange.

17. Seismic data will be transmitted through the Global Telecommunication System of the World Meteorological Organization or through any other agreed communication channels.

18. International seismic data centres shall be established in agreed locations, taking into account the desirability of appropriate geographical distribution. These centres shall receive all seismic data contributed to the international exchange by its participants, process seismic data without interpreting the nature of seismic events, make the processed seismic data available to all participants and maintain records of all seismic data contributed by participants and processed by the centre. Each centre shall be under the jurisdiction of the party on whose territory it is located.

19. The Committee of Experts, whose establishment is provided for in this Treaty, shall draw in its work upon the recommendations contained in the reports of the *Ad Hoc* Group of Scientific Experts to Consider International Co-operative Measures to Detect and Identify Seismic Events established by the Committee on Disarmament. Such measures include the elaboration of standards for the technical and operational characteristics of participating seismic stations and international seismic data centres, for the form in which data are transmitted to the centres, and for the form and manner in which the centres make seismic data available to participants and respond to their requests for additional seismic data regarding specific seismic events.

(5) *International Committee of Experts of States parties to the Treaty*

20. A Committee of Experts of States parties to this Treaty shall be established to consider questions related to the international exchange of seismic data. Any State party shall have the right to appoint a representative to this Committee.

21. The Committee, which will function on the basis of consensus, shall hold its first meeting not later than ninety days after the entry into force of this Treaty and shall meet thereafter as necessary.

22. The Committee shall develop, in accordance with the guidelines, detailed arrangements regulating the establishment and operation of the international exchange; it shall facilitate its implementation and co-operation between States parties to enhance the effectiveness of such exchange.

23. The Committee shall facilitate more extensive international consultations and co-operation, exchange of information and assistance in verification in the interests of compliance with the provisions of this Treaty.

24. Other questions relating to the organization and procedures of the Committee of Experts, its possible subsidiary bodies and their functions, rights, duties and proceedings, its role in promoting international exchange and in on-site inspection, as well as other matters, are to be elaborated.

(6) *Fact-finding procedure regarding compliance with the Treaty: on-site inspection*

25. Each State party to this Treaty, if it has doubts regarding an event on the territory of another State which may have been a nuclear explosion, may send that party a request for an on-site inspection. The request should state the reasons why it is being made, including relevant seismic and other physical data that could be associated with a possible nuclear explosion, its time and location.

26. The party which has received the request, being aware of the importance of providing assurance of compliance with the obligations under this Treaty, shall state whether or not it is prepared to agree to an inspection. If the party which has received the request is not prepared to agree to an inspection on its territory, it shall communicate the reasons for its decision to the requesting State and to the Committee of Experts.

27. If the requesting State party is not satisfied with the explanation received and the information provided on a bilateral basis, it may ask the Committee of Experts for additional information and consultation regarding that request and assistance in ascertaining the facts in the form of scientific and technical expertise.

28. For the purpose of conducting inspection on the territory of the States parties which may give their agreement, procedures shall be elaborated for such inspections and the manner in which they are to be conducted, including the list of rights and functions of the inspecting personnel and the definition of the role of the receiving party during the inspection.

29. This Treaty shall also contain a provision enabling any two or more of the States parties to agree, by mutual consent, in view of special interests or special circumstances, on additional measures which would facilitate verification of compliance with this Treaty.

(7) *Procedure for lodging complaints with the Security Council*

30. Any State party which has reason to believe that any other State party has acted or may be acting in violation of the obligations deriving from the provisions of this Treaty shall have the right to lodge a complaint with the Security Council. Such a complaint should include all relevant information, as well as all possible evidence supporting the validity of the complaint.

31. Each State party undertakes to co-operate in carrying out any investigation which the Security Council may initiate, in accordance with the provisions of the Charter of the United Nations, on the basis of a complaint received by the Security Council. The Security Council shall inform the States parties of the results of the investigation.

32. Each State party to this Treaty undertakes to provide or support assistance, in accordance with the provisions of the Charter of the United Nations, to any State party which so requests it, if the Security Council decides that such party has been exposed to danger or is perhaps being exposed to danger as a result of violation by another State party of the obligations assumed under this Treaty.

C.   Concluding provisions of the Treaty

33. This Treaty shall be of unlimited duration. It shall enter into force upon the deposit of instruments of ratification by twenty Governments, including the Governments of all States permanent members of the Security Council.

34. However, the States parties may agree that this Treaty should enter into force for an agreed limited period, given the participation of three States permanent members of the Security Council — the Union of Soviet Socialist Republics, the United Kingdom of Great Britain and Northern Ireland and the United States of America.

35. Provision should be made for the procedure for the signing and ratification of this Treaty, for the depositary, for accession by States to this Treaty and for amendments.

Recorded vote in Assembly as follows:

In favour: Afghanistan, Algeria, Angola, Argentina, Austria, Bahamas, Bahrain, Bangladesh, Barbados, Belize, Benin, Bhutan, Bolivia, Botswana, Brazil, Bulgaria, Burma, Burundi, Byelorussian SSR, Cape Verde, Central African Republic, Chad, Chile, Colombia, Congo, Costa Rica, Cuba, Cyprus, Czechoslovakia, Democratic Yemen, Djibouti, Dominican Republic, Ecuador, Egypt, El Salvador, Ethiopia, Fiji, Finland, Gabon, Gambia, German Democratic Republic, Ghana, Grenada, Guinea, Guinea-Bissau, Guyana, Haiti, Honduras, Hungary, India, Indonesia, Iran, Iraq, Ireland, Jamaica, Jordan, Kenya, Kuwait, Lao People's Democratic Republic, Liberia, Libyan Arab Jamahiriya, Madagascar, Malaysia, Maldives, Mali, Malta, Mauritania, Mauritius, Mexico, Mongolia, Morocco, Mozambique, Nepal, Nicaragua, Niger, Nigeria, Oman, Pakistan, Panama, Peru, Philippines, Poland, Qatar, Romania, Rwanda, Saint Lucia, Sao Tome and Principe, Senegal, Sierra Leone, Singapore, Sri Lanka, Sudan, Suriname, Swaziland, Sweden, Syrian Arab Republic, Thailand, Togo, Trinidad and Tobago, Tunisia, Uganda, Ukrainian SSR, USSR, United Arab Emirates, United Republic of Cameroon, United Republic of Tanzania, Upper Volta, Uruguay, Vanuatu, Venezuela, Viet Nam, Yemen, Yugoslavia, Zaire, Zambia.

Against: Australia,[a] China, France, United Kingdom[*], United States.

Abstaining: Belgium, Canada, Denmark, Germany, Federal Republic of, Greece, Guatemala, Iceland, Israel, Italy, Ivory Coast, Japan, Lebanon, Luxembourg,

Malawi, Netherlands, New Zealand, Norway, Papua New Guinea, Paraguay, Portugal, Saudi Arabia, Solomon Islands, Somalia, Spain, Turkey.

[a]Later advised the Secretariat it had intended to abstain.

Verification measures

Consideration by the Committee on Disarmament. Considering that discussion of specific issues might facilitate progress towards negotiation of a nuclear-test ban, the Committee on Disarmament decided on 21 April 1982[(2)] to establish an *ad hoc* working group under its agenda item on a nuclear-test ban and requested it, in the first instance, to discuss and define issues relating to verification and compliance with a view to making further progress towards such a ban. The Committee asked the working group to take into account all existing proposals and future initiatives, and to make a progress report before the end of the Committee's 1982 session so that it could decide on subsequent courses of action.

The mandate for the working group had been drawn up by a drafting group which the Committee established after receiving two proposals on the matter. The Group of 21 (p. 22) reiterated its April 1981 proposal for the establishment of an *ad hoc* working group to negotiate a treaty on a nuclear-test ban[(6)] and its view that, regardless of differing views on the question of verification, there was no valid reason for delaying the conclusion of such a treaty. A group of socialist countries (Bulgaria, Czechoslovakia, German Democratic Republic, Hungary, Mongolia, Poland, USSR) submitted in April 1982 a proposal for a working group to negotiate on a treaty prohibiting all nuclear-weapon tests, taking into account existing and future proposals.

The *Ad Hoc* Working Group, chaired by Curt Lidgard (Sweden), held 10 meetings between 13 August and 13 September. Although failing to agree on its work programme, the Group held an exchange of views on general aspects of the question of verification and compliance, on the scope of its mandate and on basic questions relating to a test ban. Two nuclear-weapon States (China, France) did not participate in the Group, whose report was incorporated in the Committee's report to the General Assembly.[(3)]

According to the Working Group's report, differing views were expressed on a number of points, including the following: whether verification issues could be considered before agreement was reached on the scope of a nuclear-test-ban treaty; whether nuclear explosions for peaceful purposes should be covered by the treaty and the associated verification system; whether laboratory testing should be subject to verification procedures; whether existing means of verification were sufficient to provide reasonable assurance of compliance; whether methods to detect airborne radioactivity should be examined; whether the system should rely largely on national verification and international exchange or on international verification providing equal access to all parties; whether voluntary on-site inspection would suffice to build confidence; whether the verification machinery should be guided solely by a committee of experts or whether a separate committee was needed to serve as a political forum for discussion of issues related to the treaty; and whether a recourse procedure should be limited to the Security Council.

The Working Group also considered aspects of the work of the *Ad Hoc* Group of Scientific Experts to Consider International Co-operative Measures to Detect and Identify Seismic Events (p. 85).

In response to questions by Working Group members as to the nature of obstacles to agreement on a verification system, one of the parties to the earlier tripartite negotiations on a comprehensive test ban (USSR) expressed the view that existing means were adequate to assure compliance, while the two others (United Kingdom, United States) said it could not be presumed that all technical problems had been solved and, in any case, a determination of adequacy was a matter for political decision by each Government in the light of its national requirements and of existing circumstances.

Regarding the Working Group's mandate, some delegations were of the view that it was inadequate in that it did not provide for negotiations leading to the conclusion of a treaty, while others felt that it should proceed on its existing mandate without prejudice to any future decision on the matter. Still others believed that the mandate did not preclude treaty negotiations. Some delegations held that the Group had completed its examination of verification and compliance issues and that its mandate should be revised so that it could negotiate a treaty, while others believed that considerable work remained to be done on verification and compliance.

Proposals submitted to the Committee on Disarmament during 1982 included one by Sweden (in March) on an international system for detecting airborne radioactivity from nuclear explosions, and an outline by the Netherlands (in August) for a work programme of the *Ad Hoc* Working Group on a nuclear-test ban, envisaging the establishment of an integrated international monitoring system and the subordination of the Group of Scientific Experts on seismic events to the Working Group.

General Assembly consideration (June/ July). At the second special session of the General Assembly devoted to disarmament, Sweden, in a letter of 27 June to the Secretary-General,[1] submitted a working paper which included the concept of "verification by challenge", which Sweden subsequently explained in the *Ad Hoc* Committee of the special session as a politically important tool—

along with technical means such as seismic methods and monitoring of airborne radioactivity—in allaying suspicions and unfounded accusations. Norway submitted in May a working paper on seismological verification of a comprehensive test ban.

In the general debate at the special session, New Zealand welcomed the Swedish proposal and expressed support of the activities of the Group of Scientific Experts on seismic events. Australia offered to provide the site of one of the future data centres, and Norway repeated its offer to make the Norwegian Seismic Array available as a station in a global seismic verification system. Similarly, Canada committed its resources to become a full participant in the international seismic data exchange which it expected to form part of the provisions of a comprehensive test-ban treaty.

General Assembly action (December). In one of the three resolutions on prohibition of nuclear-weapon tests adopted on 9 December,[4] the General Assembly noted the establishment of the *Ad Hoc* Working Group on a nuclear-test ban, entrusted with the task of defining issues relating to verification and compliance, and requested the Committee on Disarmament to continue consideration of those issues and to initiate substantive negotiations in order that the draft of a comprehensive nuclear-test-ban treaty could be submitted to the Assembly at the earliest possible date. At the same time, the Committee was asked to determine, in the context of its negotiations on such a treaty, the institutional and administrative arrangements necessary for establishing, testing and operating an international seismic monitoring network and an effective verification system.

Proposals for a verification system to ensure compliance with a comprehensive test-ban treaty were included in a set of basic provisions for a treaty submitted to the Assembly in October by the USSR and later annexed to another of the Assembly's resolutions of 9 December on the subject, which referred the draft to the Committee on Disarmament.[5] The proposals called for a system based on a combination of national and international measures, including consultations and co-operation among States parties, the international exchange of seismic data according to agreed guidelines, the establishment of an international committee of experts to consider questions relating to such exchange, a fact-finding procedure under which on-site inspections could be carried out on the territory of States which agreed to such a procedure, and a procedure for lodging complaints with the Security Council.

Letter. [1]Sweden, 27 June, A/S-12/AC.1/39.
Reports. Committee on Disarmament, [2]A/S-12/2, [3]A/37/27 (Committee documents, CD/335/appendix II).
Resolutions (1982). GA, 9 Dec.: [4]37/73; [5]37/85, annex, paras. 5-32.
Yearbook reference. [6]1981, p. 64.

Identification of seismic activity

In 1982, the Committee on Disarmament[2] received two further progress reports of its *Ad Hoc* Group of Scientific Experts to Consider International Co-operative Measures to Detect and Identify Seismic Events, which held its thirteenth session from 1 to 12 March and its fourteenth session from 9 to 20 August, both at Geneva. The Group continued to develop scientific and technical aspects of a proposed global exchange of seismological data that could assist States in national monitoring of a comprehensive nuclear-test ban, and to consider an experimental test of the whole global system. In particular, it examined recent developments in seismology and improvements in associated telecommunication and computer techniques to the extent that they were relevant to the envisaged international co-operative measures to detect and identify seismic events.

The Group reported in August that it needed more time to assess national investigations and co-operative studies before it could submit its next substantive report, which it envisaged doing in 1983. The Committee adopted the Group's recommendations on 30 March and 31 August.

The Chairman of the Group since its establishment in 1976,[4] Ulf Ericsson (Sweden), died in November 1982.

Acting on one of the Group's recommendations, and in line with a proposal by Japan, the Committee Chairman requested the World Meteorological Organization (WMO), through its Secretary-General, to arrange for the Group's continued utilization of the WMO Global Telecommunication System for seismic data transmission. In response, the WMO Deputy Secretary-General informed the Chairman by a letter of 6 September that the question would be submitted in 1983 to the WMO Commission for Basic Systems and to the ninth WMO Congress.

During the second special session of the General Assembly devoted to disarmament, Norway, by a letter to the Secretary-General dated 27 May,[1] submitted a working paper on seismological verification of a comprehensive test ban, based on experience provided by the Norwegian Seismic Array. In another working paper, submitted in August to the Committee on Disarmament, Norway reported on experiments which, it said, demonstrated the feasibility of rapid, flexible and inexpensive international exchange of seismological data, using standard telephone services; it suggested further experimentation and inclusion of that method of rapid data exchange in the global seismological system which might be established under a comprehensive nuclear-test-ban treaty.

Aspects of the work of the Group of Scientific Experts were discussed in August and September by the *Ad Hoc* Working Group set up by the Committee on Disarmament under its agenda item on a nuclear-test ban. According to the Working Group's report, annexed to the 1982 report of the Committee to the General Assembly, differing views were expressed on such matters as whether an international system for the exchange of seismic data should be established before or after a comprehensive test-ban treaty entered into force and whether it was time to consider institutional aspects of such a system. The Working Group reached no conclusions.

Among basic provisions proposed by the USSR for a draft treaty on the complete and general prohibition of nuclear-weapon tests, annexed to a 9 December General Assembly resolution referring them to the Committee on Disarmament, were paragraphs dealing with the international exchange of seismic data through international centres that would process the data and make it available to all parties.[3]

Letter. [1]Norway, 27 May, A/S-12/23.
Report. [2]Committee on Disarmament, A/37/27 (Committee documents, CD/335/Appendix II).
Resolution (1982). [3]GA: 37/85, annex, paras. 14-19, 9 Dec.
Yearbook reference. [4]1976, p. 6.

Prohibition of fissionable materials production for nuclear weapons

By a resolution of 13 December 1982,[1] the General Assembly, recalling similar requests it had made annually since 1978, asked the Committee on Disarmament, at an appropriate stage, to pursue the question of an adequately verified cessation and prohibition of the production of fissionable material for nuclear weapons and other nuclear explosive devices.

The resolution was adopted by a recorded vote of 121 to none, with 22 abstentions. On 24 November, the First Committee had approved the 17-nation draft, introduced by Canada, by a recorded vote of 104 to none, with 21 abstentions.

In two other resolutions, also adopted on 13 December, the Assembly called for the complete cessation of the production of fissionable material for weapons purposes as one element in a nuclear-arms freeze. One of these resolutions was addressed to all nuclear-weapon States[2] and the other to the USSR and the United States.[3]

In June, at the Assembly's special session on disarmament, the Netherlands, observing that the international community stood farther away from the goal of a comprehensive test ban than in 1978, called for urgent examination of a cut-off of production of fissionable material for weapons purposes, which it considered more fundamental than the test ban itself.

Resolutions (1982). GA, 13 Dec.: [1]37/99 E, text following; [2]37/100 A, para. 1; [3]37/100 B, para. 1 *(a)* (iv).

Meeting records. GA: 1st Committee, A/C.1/37/PV.3-10, 12-28, *37*, 38, 40, *43* (18 Oct.-24 Nov.); plenary, A/37/PV.101 (13 Dec.).

General Assembly resolution 37/99 E

13 December 1982   Meeting 101   121-0-22 (recorded vote)

Approved by First Committee (A/37/667) by recorded vote (104-0-21), 24 November (meeting 43); 17-nation draft (A/C.1/37/L.48); agenda item 55 *(e)*.

Sponsors: Australia, Austria, Bahamas, Bangladesh, Canada, Denmark, Greece, Indonesia, Ireland, Japan, Netherlands, New Zealand, Norway, Philippines, Romania, Singapore, Sweden.

Prohibition of the production of fissionable material for weapons purposes

The General Assembly,

Recalling its resolutions 33/91 H of 16 December 1978, 34/87 D of 11 December 1979, 35/156 H of 12 December 1980 and 36/97 G of 9 December 1981, in which it requested the Committee on Disarmament, at an appropriate stage of the implementation of the Programme of Action set forth in section III of the Final Document of the Tenth Special Session of the General Assembly, and of its work on the item entitled "Nuclear weapons in all aspects", to consider urgently the question of adequately verified cessation and prohibition of the production of fissionable material for nuclear weapons and other nuclear explosive devices and to keep the Assembly informed of the progress of that consideration,

Noting that the agenda of the Committee on Disarmament for 1982 included the item entitled "Nuclear weapons in all aspects" and that the Committee's programme of work for both parts of its session held in 1982 contained the item entitled "Cessation of the nuclear-arms race and nuclear disarmament",

Recalling the proposals and statements made in the Committee on Disarmament on those items,

Considering that the cessation of production of fissionable material for weapons purposes and the progressive conversion and transfer of stocks to peaceful uses would be a significant step towards halting and reversing the nuclear-arms race,

Considering that the prohibition of the production of fissionable material for nuclear weapons and other explosive devices also would be an important measure in facilitating the prevention of the proliferation of nuclear weapons and explosive devices,

Requests the Committee on Disarmament, at an appropriate stage of its work on the item entitled "Nuclear weapons in all aspects", to pursue its consideration of the question of adequately verified cessation and prohibition of the production of fissionable material for nuclear weapons and other nuclear explosive devices and to keep the General Assembly informed of the progress of that consideration.

Recorded vote in Assembly as follows:

In favour: Algeria, Angola, Australia, Austria, Bahamas, Bahrain, Bangladesh, Barbados, Belgium, Benin, Bhutan, Bolivia, Botswana, Burma, Burundi, Canada, Central African Republic, Chad, Chile, Colombia, Comoros, Congo, Costa Rica, Cuba,[a] Cyprus, Democratic Kampuchea, Democratic Yemen, Denmark, Djibouti, Dominican Republic, Ecuador, Egypt, El Salvador, Equatorial Guinea, Ethiopia, Fiji, Finland, Gabon, Germany, Federal Republic of, Ghana, Greece, Grenada, Guatemala, Guinea, Guinea-Bissau, Haiti, Honduras, Iceland, Indonesia, Iran, Iraq, Ireland, Israel, Italy, Jamaica, Japan, Jordan, Kenya, Kuwait, Lebanon, Lesotho, Liberia, Libyan Arab Jamahiriya, Luxembourg, Madagascar, Malawi, Malaysia, Maldives, Mali, Malta, Mauritania, Mauritius, Morocco, Nepal, Netherlands, New Zealand, Niger, Nigeria, Norway, Oman, Pakistan, Papua New Guinea, Paraguay, Peru, Philippines, Portugal, Qatar, Romania, Rwanda, Saint Lucia, Sao Tome and Principe, Saudi Arabia, Senegal, Sierra Leone, Singapore, Solomon Islands, Somalia, Spain, Sri Lanka, Sudan, Suriname, Swaziland, Sweden, Syrian Arab Republic, Thailand, Togo, Trinidad and Tobago, Tunisia, Turkey, Uganda, United Arab Emirates, United Republic of Cameroon, United Republic of Tanzania, Upper Volta, Uruguay, Vanuatu, Venezuela, Yemen, Yugoslavia, Zaire, Zambia.

Against: None.

Abstaining: Afghanistan, Argentina, Brazil, Bulgaria, Byelorussian SSR, Czechoslovakia, France, German Democratic Republic, Guyana, Hungary, India, Lao People's Democratic Republic, Mexico, Mongolia, Mozambique, Panama, Poland, Ukrainian SSR, USSR, United Kingdom, United States, Viet Nam.

[a]Later advised the Secretariat it had intended to abstain.

Protection of nuclear facilities

Consideration by the Committee on Disarmament. The *Ad Hoc* Working Group on Radiological Weapons of the Committee on Disarmament, established to seek agreement on a convention prohibiting the development, production, stockpiling and use of such weapons, devoted three meetings during its February-April 1982 session to the question of prohibition of attacks on nuclear facilities, which some delegations believed should be dealt with in the convention. When, on 15 March, the Group decided to hold separate meetings on this topic, some delegations expressed the view that the suggested procedure should not be interpreted as the commencement of negotiations on the prohibition of attacks on nuclear facilities, and others voiced doubts as to the Committee's (or the Working Group's) competence to negotiate on the question. On the other hand, some believed that the two subjects should be treated on a non-discriminatory basis for inclusion in the same legal instrument, while others were of the view that the number and form of the future legal instrument(s) on the subject could not be decided on at that stage.

According to the Working Group's April report, incorporated in the Committee's report to the General Assembly at its special session on disarmament,[2] divergent views emerged in the discussion, centring around the definition of facilities to be protected and the scope of prohibition. Some delegations asserted that the prohibition should be as comprehensive as possible, without distinction between civilian and military facilities, and that the proposed instrument should aim at restoring confidence among nations regarding their peaceful nuclear programmes. Others, seeing serious difficulties involved in granting protection to all nuclear facilities, considered it appropriate to introduce a threshold of minimum inventory of radioactivity so as to eliminate from the protection those facilities which, if attacked, would not cause mass destruction. Those opposing that approach asserted that such a partial ban could legitimize attacks on certain facilities, contravene the objective of the prohibition and increase the difficulties of compliance and verification.

In a working paper submitted to the Committee in September,[3] Japan proposed an outline of a draft protocol on the prohibition of attacks against nuclear facilities, in the form of an optional protocol to a radiological weapons treaty. Also in September, the Federal Republic of Germany submitted a working paper on prohibition of attacks against nuclear facilities in the framework of such a treaty.

General Assembly consideration (June/July). A paragraph on attacks against nuclear facilities was included in the disarmament measures chapter of the draft comprehensive programme of disarmament considered at the General Assembly's second special session on disarmament, but agreement was not reached on the wording.[1]

In the general debate at the session, Japan offered to contribute to international efforts to ensure the security of nuclear facilities for peaceful purposes. Morocco called for the prohibition of attacks on nuclear reactors and Sweden did likewise in regard to nuclear-power stations, while Pakistan called for an international instrument to that end.

Many speakers, including the Libyan Arab Jamahiriya, Morocco, the Niger, Oman, Qatar, the Syrian Arab Republic, Tunisia, the United Arab Emirates and the United Republic of Cameroon, condemned the Israeli attack on Iraqi nuclear installations on 7 June 1981.[8] Kuwait condemned the act as a severe blow to the Treaty on the Non-Proliferation of Nuclear Weapons[7] (NPT), which guaranteed the right of non-nuclear-weapon States to develop their own peaceful nuclear programmes. For Somalia, the incident emphasized the need to protect that right. Malaysia feared the action had undermined the nuclear safeguards régime of the International Atomic Energy Agency (IAEA). Egypt hoped the Israeli action had not aborted the resolution on establishing a nuclear-weapon-free zone in the Middle East.

General Assembly action (December). The question of protecting nuclear facilities from armed attack was dealt with in provisions of three 1982 General Assembly resolutions.

In a resolution of 16 November[4] on the consequences of the 1981 aerial attack by Israel on an Iraqi nuclear reactor, the Assembly called for continued international consideration of legal measures to prohibit armed attacks and threats against nuclear facilities, as a contribution to the safe development of nuclear energy for peaceful purposes. By a resolution of 19 November[5] on the work of IAEA, the Assembly considered Israel's threat to repeat its armed attack against nuclear facilities, as well as any other armed attack against such facilities, to be a serious threat to IAEA activities for the peaceful development of nuclear energy. In a resolution of 13 December on radiological weapons,[6] the Assembly requested the Committee on Disarmament to continue searching for a solution to the question of prohibition of military attacks on nuclear facilities, including the scope of such prohibition.

France said its positive vote on the 16 November resolution should not be interpreted as a change in its position with regard to the call for continued consideration of legal measures to prohibit armed attacks against nuclear facilities. The United Kingdom said it did not regard that call

as prejudicing the issue of whether further legal measures were needed or as prejudging the forum in which the discussion should take place.

A paragraph declaring that the deliberate destruction of peaceful nuclear installations, even by conventional weapons, was essentially equivalent to an attack using nuclear weapons, was included in a USSR draft resolution on prevention of nuclear war and on the safe development of nuclear energy, presented to the First Committee in November but not pressed to a vote.

Reports. [1]*Ad Hoc* Committee, A/S-12/32; Committee on Disarmament, [2]A/S-12/2, [3]A/37/27 (Committee documents, CD/335/appendix II).
Resolutions (1982). GA: [4]37/18, para. 7, 16 Nov.; [5]37/19, para. 3, 19 Nov.; [6]37/99 C, para. 2, 13 Dec.
Resolution (prior). [7]GA: 2373(XXII), annex, 12 June 1968 (YUN 1968, p. 17).
Yearbook reference. [8]1981, p. 275.

Strengthening the security of non-nuclear-weapon States

Activities of the Committee on Disarmament (February-April). In 1982, the Committee on Disarmament continued consideration of an agenda item entitled "Effective international arrangements to assure non-nuclear-weapon States against the use or threat of use of nuclear weapons", a type of arrangement also known as negative security guarantees. Discussion took place in both the Committee and an *Ad Hoc* Working Group set up in 1979[7] and re-established on 18 February 1982 with a mandate to continue to negotiate with a view to reaching agreement on such arrangements.

The *Ad Hoc* Working Group to Consider, and Negotiate on, Effective International Arrangements to Assure Non-Nuclear-Weapon States against the Use or Threat of Use of Nuclear Weapons held 10 meetings between 26 February and 19 April, and its report, adopted by the Committee on 21 April, became part of the Committee's special report to the General Assembly at its 1982 special session on disarmament.[2]

As in 1981,[8] the Working Group concentrated on finding a common approach to the wording of such assurances and in particular a common formula for inclusion in a binding international instrument. Under one suggested approach, highlighted in a working paper by China annexed to the Group's report, the nuclear-weapon States would provide assurances to all non-nuclear-weapon States without any conditions, qualifications or limitations. Under other approaches, various criteria would be provided to describe the conditions for including non-nuclear-weapon States in the scope of the assurances. In its working paper, China reiterated its security assurances (see below), attributed the lack of results in the Working Group to various conditions imposed by the major nuclear-weapon States and stated that their demand amounted to seeking for themselves security assurances from non-nuclear-weapon States.

The Working Group subsequently took up the idea of interim arrangements pending the conclusion of an international instrument, particularly proposals for a Security Council resolution. The Netherlands and Pakistan each proposed draft resolutions.

The draft by the Netherlands, embodying a common formula of assurances, would have the Council welcome the undertaking by nuclear-weapon States not to use or threaten to use nuclear weapons against any non-nuclear-weapon State that had committed itself not to manufacture or receive nuclear weapons or acquire control over them, provided that State did not undertake or partake in an attack on a nuclear-weapon State or its allies with the support of another nuclear-weapon State. Pakistan's proposal would have the Council urge the Committee on Disarmament to conclude without delay a binding international instrument of security guarantees, call on the nuclear-weapon States to undertake in such an instrument not to use or threaten to use nuclear weapons against non-nuclear-weapon States, and urge nuclear-weapon States in the mean time to confirm in a legally binding manner their assurance that they would not take such steps against non-nuclear-weapon States that were not parties to the nuclear security arrangements of the two major military alliances.

The Group of 21 (p. 22) attributed the marginal progress in the Working Group to positions by some nuclear-weapon States whose unilateral declarations of assurances, based on the doctrine of nuclear deterrence, contained conditions, limitations and exceptions that left no credible assurance to non-nuclear-weapon States that they would not be threatened or attacked with nuclear weapons. The Group set out five principles as the basis for international arrangements: (*i*) nuclear-weapon States had an obligation to assure non-nuclear-weapon States against the use or threat of nuclear weapons; (*ii*) non-nuclear-weapon States had the right to such assurances; (*iii*) the assurances should be provided in a legally binding and multilaterally negotiated international instrument; (*iv*) a common formula or approach in such an instrument should be clear, credible and responsive to the legitimate security interests of non-nuclear-weapon States; and (*v*) the agreement should encompass commitments by the nuclear-weapon States to achieve nuclear disarmament and, until then, to prohibit the use or threat of use of nuclear weapons.

In its conclusions and recommendations, the Working Group reaffirmed the need for effective security guarantees to non-nuclear-weapon States and noted that negotiations during the previous three sessions (1979-1981) had clarified many of the issues involved, although agreement on international arrangements remained elusive. The Group noted that specific difficulties related to differing perceptions of security interests of some nuclear-weapon States and to the complexity of the issues in evolving a common formula acceptable to all which could be included in a legally binding international instrument. It recommended that the Committee explore ways to overcome the difficulties encountered in the Working Group's negotiations.

General Assembly consideration (June/July). At its second special session on disarmament, the General Assembly did not reach agreement on the wording of a provision on security assurances to non-nuclear-weapon States to be included in the proposed comprehensive programme of disarmament.[1]

Many delegations in the general debate at the session mentioned the need for effective security assurances, among them Bangladesh, Burma, Czechoslovakia, Mali, Mauritania, Poland, Romania, Sierra Leone, the United Republic of Tanzania and Zaire. Gabon considered that all the non-nuclear-weapon States were entitled to obtain unconditional guarantees from the nuclear-weapon States responsible for tension and fear in the world.

Egypt and Panama said the guarantees should be finalized in a manner satisfactory to States that had renounced the nuclear option, with a view to reassuring them that they would not be blackmailed by the threat or use of nuclear weapons. Kenya, stating that the question of assurances should be seen as a step towards the elimination of nuclear weapons and not as an end in itself, called on the nuclear Powers to re-examine their unilaterally declared policies and positions regarding assurances to non-nuclear-weapon States.

In the view of Madagascar, a joint or unilateral declaration of guarantees by the nuclear Powers to non-aligned, neutral and other non-nuclear States having no affiliations with the two major alliances would help considerably to increase the security of those States as well as strengthen the nuclear non-proliferation régime. Bangladesh also called for a joint or individual declaration by the nuclear-weapon States.

Finland, Iraq, Kenya, Morocco, New Zealand, Nigeria, Oman, Pakistan, Uganda, the United Republic of Cameroon and Zimbabwe urged making such guarantees legally binding. Venezuela advocated the adoption of an international agreement banning the use or threat of use of nuclear weapons, as a means of restoring the balance of responsibilities and obligations between nuclear-weapon and non-nuclear-weapon States.

Somalia hoped the nuclear States would support the efforts of the Committee on Disarmament to establish such arrangements. Japan also called for further efforts by the Committee, while Jamaica regretted the lack of progress on the topic in that body.

Hungary, which favoured a multilateral agreement, considered acceptable, as a first step, identical declarations by the nuclear-weapon States, confirmed by a Security Council resolution. Nepal shared that view. Ireland urged the five nuclear Powers to use the Council and its procedures to give binding security guarantees to the non-nuclear-weapon States. Tunisia expected from the special session formal assurances that nuclear weapons would never be directed against them, and the Ukrainian SSR hoped the session would promote the conclusion of a convention. Viet Nam also favoured an international convention.

Belgium, on behalf of the European Community members, considered it legitimate for States which had renounced nuclear weapons to expect such security guarantees and added that it was important to find an effective solution to the question, taking into account the diversity of security situations. Portugal supported security assurances in accordance with formulae that could safeguard the legitimate interests of all parties, and the Netherlands said the nuclear-weapon States should elaborate a common formula for their guarantees.

China, reaffirming an earlier pledge, said it undertook unconditionally not to use nuclear weapons against non-nuclear-weapon States. Supporting security guarantees and the drafting of a Security Council resolution on the issue, France declared that it would not use nuclear arms against a State that did not have them and that had pledged not to seek them, unless an act of aggression was carried out in association or alliance with a nuclear-weapon State against France or against a State with which France had a security commitment. The USSR favoured an international convention but added that it was also prepared to conclude bilateral agreements.

Algeria said the desire to give security guarantees to non-nuclear-weapon States only in a discriminatory and selective manner seemed to indicate a lack of political will to support the objective of security for all. Democratic Yemen called for elimination of what it termed the difficulties created by the refusal of the United States and other Western States to provide such guarantees.

Ethiopia and Morocco were opposed to conditions which, in exchange for security commitments by nuclear-weapon States, would impose additional commitments on non-nuclear-weapon States beyond those they had already undertaken as parties to NPT. Sharing that view, Indonesia added that a convention offering categorical

assurances must also take into account the special characteristics and geography of certain non-nuclear States, such as protection of archipelagic States and their environment in the event of transit of nuclear weapons through their sea lanes.

Sri Lanka, calling existing assurances and unilateral declarations far from adequate, said the special session offered nuclear-weapon States an opportunity to submit proposals that could break a three-year deadlock on the issue.

At the conclusion of the session, Pakistan expressed disappointment at the Assembly's failure to adopt proposals on immediate and unconditional security assurances to non-aligned and other developing countries outside the major military alliances against the use or threat of use of nuclear weapons. Australia thought the issue of security guarantees might have to be temporarily downgraded in the priorities of the Committee on Disarmament.

Consideration by the Committee on Disarmament (August). At the start of the second part of the 1982 session of the Committee on Disarmament, on 3 August, the Chairman of the *Ad Hoc* Working Group on assurances to non-nuclear-weapon States told the Committee that two of the nuclear-weapon States had not responded at the Assembly's special session to the concerns expressed by the Group of 21, and that work on the item had reached an impasse. Having taken note of that assessment of the state of negotiations, the Committee said in its report to the Assembly[3] that it was generally understood that the Working Group would not meet during the latter part of 1982.

General Assembly action (December). On 9 December, the General Assembly adopted two resolutions concerning security guarantees to non-nuclear-weapon States—one calling for declarations by nuclear-weapon States as a first step towards an international convention and the other recommending continued negotiations to find a common approach or formula.

By the first resolution,[4] the Assembly reiterated its previous call that all nuclear-weapon States make declarations on the non-use of nuclear weapons against States having no such weapons on their territories, as a first step towards an international convention. The declarations, if they all met that objective, would be approved by the Security Council. Meanwhile, the Committee on Disarmament was requested to continue negotiations on the subject and participating States were called on to make efforts for the elaboration and conclusion of a convention. By the preamble, the Assembly welcomed the declarations made at the special session on disarmament concerning the non-first-use of nuclear weapons and expressed the conviction that, if all nuclear-weapon

States assumed such an obligation, that would be tantamount to banning nuclear-weapon use against all States, including the non-nuclear-weapon States.

The resolution was adopted by a recorded vote of 108 to 17, with 19 abstentions. The First Committee had approved the draft on 23 November by a recorded vote of 84 to 17, with 19 abstentions. The sponsors were Angola, Bulgaria, the Byelorussian SSR, Czechoslovakia, Democratic Yemen, Ethiopia, Mongolia, the USSR and Viet Nam.

By the second resolution,[5] the Assembly appealed to all States, especially the nuclear-weapon States, to demonstrate the political will to reach agreement on a common approach and particularly a common formula which could be included in a legally binding international instrument. The Assembly recommended a further search for such a common approach or formula, including continued negotiations in the Committee on Disarmament, taking into account the widespread support for an international convention and giving consideration to any other proposals designed to secure the same objective.

The resolution was adopted by a recorded vote of 144 to none, with 3 abstentions. On 23 November, the First Committee had approved the draft, submitted by Pakistan, by a recorded vote of 104 to none, with 3 abstentions.

Introducing the nine-nation text, Bulgaria said the non-nuclear-weapon States, especially those which had renounced the nuclear option and had not allowed such weapons to be stationed on their territory, were entitled to receive security guarantees against the use or threat of use of nuclear weapons. That goal would be served best by a legally binding international instrument such as a convention; at the same time, the draft's sponsors were convinced that renouncing the first use of nuclear weapons could contribute significantly to the strengthening of security guarantees.

Introducing its resolution, Pakistan said the non-nuclear-weapon States had the right to refuse to become victims of nuclear war which they had not sought and which they wanted to prevent. While the most effective assurance remained the complete prohibition of the use or threat of nuclear weapons and their eventual elimination, interim arrangements could play an important role in allaying concerns about threats to security. The unilateral declarations by some nuclear-weapon States were inadequate and reflected their own security concerns. To be effective, assurances must be unconditional and legally binding.

Several States explained their votes on the nine-nation text. The Netherlands, which cast a negative vote, expressed reservations as to the feasibility and desirability of incorporating such security assurances in a convention; further, the text prescribed and prejudged the result of negotiations in the Committee on Disarmament by placing non-first-use declarations in the context of security assurances to non-nuclear-weapon States and by dictating that an intermediate step be based on the principle of non-stationing of nuclear weapons. Turkey also voted against the text because its seventh and eighth preambular paragraphs (referring to escalation of the arms race and plans for stationing nuclear weapons on the territories of non-nuclear-weapon States) contained elements which related to the defence postures of the two major military alliances and which were alien to the concept of security assurances.

Austria, Ireland and Sweden abstained on the ground that the text failed to take into account different possible approaches to achieving arrangements on the matter and clearly favoured the idea of an international convention; for Ireland and Sweden, that seemed to imply further obligations for non-nuclear-weapon States, which they thought unnecessary. Also abstaining, Japan had reservations concerning the preambular paragraphs not included in the Assembly's December 1981 resolution on the subject[6] as well as the reference to a particular procedure (an international convention) that prejudged the work of the Committee on Disarmament.

Although voting in favour, Argentina, Brazil, Finland and Iraq expressed reservations. Argentina continued to hold the reservations it had expressed at previous sessions[9] and added that serious efforts should be made in the future to adopt a single text on this subject. Brazil said the question should not be approached from the narrow security perceptions of the nuclear-weapon States because it would then amount to legitimizing their possession of such weapons and ratifying vertical and horizontal nuclear-weapon proliferation. Finland believed that all approaches should continue to be explored, including further development of unilateral declarations as well as multilateral agreements; however, it regretted the introduction of new elements which did not contribute to the thrust of the text. Iraq had reservations on the wording of the third preambular paragraph which, it believed, presupposed one narrow formula for the establishment of nuclear-weapon-free zones—on the basis of arrangements freely arrived at among the States of the region—that disregarded conditions peculiar to the Middle East.

Reports. [1]*Ad Hoc* Committee, A/S-12/32; Committee on Disarmament, [2]A/S-12/2, [3]A/37/27 (Committee documents, CD/335/appendix II).
Resolutions (1982). GA, 9 Dec.: [4]37/80, text following; [5]37/81, text following.
Resolution (prior). [6]GA: 36/94, 9 Dec. 1981 (YUN 1981, p. 60).
Yearbook references. [7]1979, p. 23; 1981, [8]p. 58, [9]p. 59.
Meeting records. GA: 1st Committee, A/C.1/37/PV.3-10, 12-28, 30, 38, 41 (18 Oct.–23 Nov.); plenary, A/37/PV.98 (9 Dec.).

General Assembly resolution 37/80

9 December 1982 Meeting 98 108-17-19 (recorded vote)

Approved by First Committee (A/37/664) by recorded vote (84-17-19), 23 November (meeting 41); 9-nation draft (A/C.1/37/L.29); agenda item 52.

Sponsors: Angola, Bulgaria, Byelorussian SSR, Czechoslovakia, Democratic Yemen, Ethiopia, Mongolia, USSR, Viet Nam.

Conclusion of an international convention on the strengthening of the security of non-nuclear-weapon States against the use or threat of use of nuclear weapons

The General Assembly,

Convinced of the need to take effective measures for the strengthening of the security of States and prompted by the desire shared by all nations to eliminate war and prevent nuclear conflagration,

Taking into account the principle of non-use of force or threat of force enshrined in the Charter of the United Nations and reaffirmed in a number of United Nations declarations and resolutions,

Noting with satisfaction the desire of States in various regions to prevent nuclear weapons from being introduced into their territories, including through the establishment of nuclear-weapon-free zones, on the basis of arrangements freely arrived at among the States of the region concerned, and being anxious to contribute to the attainment of this objective,

Considering that, until nuclear disarmament is achieved on a universal basis, it is imperative for the international community to develop effective measures to ensure the security of non-nuclear-weapon States against the use or threat of use of nuclear weapons from any quarter,

Recognizing that effective measures to assure non-nuclear-weapon States against the use or threat of use of nuclear weapons can constitute a positive contribution to the prevention of the spread of nuclear weapons,

Mindful of the statements made and views expressed by various States on the strengthening of the security of non-nuclear-weapon States,

Concerned at the continuing escalation of the arms race, in particular the nuclear-arms race, and the increased danger of recourse to use or threat of use of nuclear weapons,

Deeply concerned at the plans for further stationing of nuclear weapons on the territories of non-nuclear-weapon States that could directly affect the security of non-nuclear-weapon States,

Desirous of promoting the implementation of paragraph 59 of the Final Document of the Tenth Special Session of the General Assembly, in which it urged the nuclear-weapon States to pursue efforts to conclude, as appropriate, effective arrangements to assure non-nuclear-weapon States against the use or threat of use of nuclear weapons,

Recalling its resolutions 33/72 of 14 December 1978, 34/84 and 34/85 of 11 December 1979, 35/154 and 35/155 of 12 December 1980, the relevant provisions of its resolution 35/46 of 3 December 1980 and its resolutions 36/94 and 36/95 of 9 December 1981,

Noting that the Committee on Disarmament considered in 1982 the item entitled "Effective international arrangements to assure non-nuclear-weapon States against the use or threat of use of nuclear weapons" and the work done by the *Ad Hoc* Working Group on this item,

Recalling the drafts of an international convention submitted on that item to the Committee on Disarmament in 1979 and noting with satisfaction that the idea of concluding such a convention has received widespread international support,

Taking note of the special report of the Committee on Disarmament, submitted to the General Assembly at its twelfth special session, including the report of the *Ad Hoc* Working Group to Consider, and Negotiate on, Effective International Arrangements to Assure Non-Nuclear-Weapon States against the Use or Threat of Use of Nuclear Weapons, as well as the report of the Committee on Disarmament,

Wishing to promote an early and successful completion of the negotiations on the elaboration of a convention on the strengthening of the security of non-nuclear-weapon States against the use or threat of use of nuclear weapons,

Noting that the idea of interim arrangements as a first step towards the conclusion of such a convention has also been considered in the Committee on Disarmament, particularly in the form of a Security Council resolution on this subject, and reaffirming the call made in that respect by the General Assembly in paragraph 6 of its resolution 35/154 and in paragraph 5 of its resolution 36/94,

Taking note of the recommendation contained in the special report of the Committee on Disarmament that ways and means should be explored by the Committee to overcome the difficulties encountered in the negotiations of the above-mentioned Working Group with a view to reaching agreement on effective international arrangements to assure non-nuclear-weapon States against the use or threat of use of nuclear weapons,

Convinced that abandoning policies of first use of nuclear weapons would, *inter alia*, constitute a substantive contribution to the efforts to achieve progress towards effective strengthening of the security guarantees for non-nuclear-weapon States,

Welcoming the solemn declarations concerning the non-first-use of nuclear weapons, in particular the obligation of nuclear-weapon States not to be the first to use nuclear weapons, assumed at the highest political level or confirmed at the twelfth special session of the General Assembly,

Convinced further that, if all nuclear-weapon States were to assume obligations not to be the first to use nuclear weapons, that would be tantamount, in practice, to banning the use of nuclear weapons against all States, including all non-nuclear-weapon States,

Bearing in mind that, in the search for a solution of the problem of security assurances, priority should be given to the legitimate security concerns of the non-nuclear-weapon States, which, by virtue of their forgoing the nuclear option and of not allowing nuclear weapons to be stationed on their territories, have every right to expect to be most effectively guaranteed against the use or threat of use of nuclear weapons,

1. *Welcomes once again* the conclusion of the Committee on Disarmament that there is continuing recognition of the urgent need to reach agreement on effective international arrangements to assure non-nuclear-weapon States against the use or threat of use of nuclear weapons;

2. *Notes with satisfaction* that in the Committee on Disarmament there is once again no objection, in principle, to the idea of an international convention on this subject;

3. *Requests* the Committee on Disarmament to continue the negotiations on the question of the strengthening of the security guarantees for non-nuclear-weapon States during its session in 1983;

4. *Calls once again upon* all States participating in these negotiations to make efforts to elaborate and conclude an international instrument of a legally binding character, such as an international convention, on this matter;

5. *Calls once again upon* all nuclear-weapon States to make solemn declarations, identical in substance, concerning the non-use of nuclear weapons against non-nuclear-weapon States having no such weapons on their territories, as a first step towards the conclusion of an international convention, and recommends that the Security Council should examine such declarations and, if they all meet the above-mentioned objective, should adopt an appropriate resolution approving them;

6. *Decides* to include in the provisional agenda of its thirty-eighth session the item entitled "Conclusion of an international convention on the strengthening of the security of non-nuclear-weapon States against the use or threat of use of nuclear weapons".

Recorded vote in Assembly as follows:

In favour: Afghanistan, Algeria, Angola, Antigua and Barbuda, Argentina, Bahamas, Bahrain, Bangladesh, Barbados, Belize, Benin, Bolivia, Botswana, Brazil, Bulgaria, Burundi, Byelorussian SSR, Cape Verde, Central African Republic, Chad, Chile, Colombia, Comoros, Congo, Costa Rica, Cuba, Cyprus, Czechoslovakia, Democratic Yemen, Djibouti, Dominican Republic, Ecuador, Egypt, El Salvador, Ethiopia, Fiji, Finland, Gabon, Gambia, German Democratic Republic, Ghana, Greece, Grenada, Guinea, Guinea-Bissau, Guyana, Haiti, Honduras, Hungary, Indonesia, Iran, Iraq, Jamaica, Jordan, Kenya, Kuwait, Lao People's Democratic Republic, Liberia, Libyan Arab Jamahiriya, Madagascar, Malaysia, Maldives, Mali, Mauritania, Mauritius, Mexico, Mongolia, Morocco, Mozambique, Nepal, Nicaragua, Niger, Nigeria, Oman, Pakistan, Panama, Papua New Guinea, Poland, Qatar, Romania, Rwanda, Saint Lucia, Sao Tome and Principe, Senegal, Sierra Leone, Solomon Islands, Sri Lanka, Sudan, Suriname, Swaziland, Syrian Arab Republic, Thailand, Togo, Trinidad and Tobago, Tunisia, Uganda, Ukrainian SSR, USSR, United Arab Emirates, United Republic of Cameroon, United Republic of Tanzania, Upper Volta, Vanuatu, Venezuela, Viet Nam, Yemen, Yugoslavia, Zambia.

Against: Australia, Belgium, Canada, Denmark, France, Germany, Federal Republic of, Iceland, Italy, Luxembourg, Netherlands, New Zealand, Norway, Portugal, Spain, Turkey, United Kingdom, United States.

Abstaining: Austria, Burma, Guatemala, India, Ireland, Israel, Ivory Coast, Japan, Lebanon, Malawi, Paraguay, Peru, Philippines, Saudi Arabia, Singapore, Somalia, Sweden, Uruguay, Zaire.

General Assembly resolution 37/81

9 December 1982   Meeting 98   144-0-3 (recorded vote)

Approved by First Committee (A/37/665) by recorded vote (104-0-3), 23 November (meeting 41); draft by Pakistan (A/C.1/37/L.13); agenda item 53.

Conclusion of effective international arrangements to assure non-nuclear-weapon States against the use or threat of use of nuclear weapons

The General Assembly,

Bearing in mind the need to allay the legitimate concern of the States of the world with regard to ensuring lasting security for their peoples,

Convinced that nuclear weapons pose the greatest threat to mankind and to the survival of civilization,

Deeply concerned at the continuing escalation of the arms race, in particular the nuclear-arms race,

Convinced that nuclear disarmament and the complete elimination of nuclear weapons are essential to remove the danger of nuclear war,

Taking into account the principle of the non-use of force or threat of force enshrined in the Charter of the United Nations,

Deeply concerned about the possibility of the use or threat of use of nuclear weapons,

Recognizing that the independence, territorial integrity and sovereignty of non-nuclear-weapon States need to be safeguarded against the use or threat of use of force, including the use or threat of use of nuclear weapons,

Considering that, until nuclear disarmament is achieved on a universal basis, it is imperative for the international community to develop effective measures to ensure the security of non-nuclear-weapon States against the use or threat of use of nuclear weapons from any quarter,

Recognizing that effective measures to assure the non-nuclear-weapon States against the use or threat of use of nuclear weapons can constitute a positive contribution to the prevention of the spread of nuclear weapons,

Recalling its resolution 3261 G (XXIX) of 9 December 1974,

Recalling also its resolution 31/189 C of 21 December 1976,

Bearing in mind paragraph 59 of the Final Document of the Tenth Special Session of the General Assembly, in which it urged the nuclear-weapon States to pursue efforts to conclude, as appropriate, effective arrangements to assure non-nuclear-weapon States against the use or threat of use of nuclear weapons,

Desirous of promoting the implementation of the relevant provisions of the Final Document of the Tenth Special Session,

Recalling its resolutions 33/72 of 14 December 1978, 34/85 of 11 December 1979, 35/155 of 12 December 1980 and 36/95 of 9 December 1981,

Further recalling paragraph 12 of the Declaration of the 1980s as the Second Disarmament Decade, contained in the annex to its resolution 35/46 of 3 December 1980, which states, *inter alia,* that all efforts should be exerted, therefore, by the Committee on Disarmament urgently to negotiate with a view to reaching agreement, and to submit agreed texts, where possible, before the second special session devoted to disarmament, on effective international arrangements to assure non-nuclear-weapon States against the use or threat of use of nuclear weapons,

Welcoming the in-depth negotiations undertaken in the Committee on Disarmament and its *Ad Hoc* Working Group to Consider, and Negotiate on, Effective International Arrangements to Assure Non-Nuclear-Weapon States against the Use or Threat of Use of Nuclear Weapons, with a view to reaching agreement on this item,

Noting the proposals submitted under that item in the Committee on Disarmament, including the drafts of an international convention,

Taking note of the decision of the Sixth Conference of Heads of State or Government of Non-Aligned Countries, held at Havana from 3 to 9 September 1979, as well as the relevant recommendations of the Islamic Conference, reiterated recently at the Thirteenth Islamic Conference of Foreign Ministers, held at Niamey from 22 to 26 August 1982, calling upon the Committee on Disarmament to elaborate and reach an agreement on an international basis to assure non-

nuclear-weapon States against the use or threat of use of nuclear weapons,

Further noting the support expressed in the Committee on Disarmament and in the General Assembly for the elaboration of an international convention to assure non-nuclear-weapon States against the use or threat of use of nuclear weapons, as well as the difficulties pointed out in evolving a common approach acceptable to all,

1.   *Reaffirms* the urgent need to reach agreement on effective international arrangements to assure non-nuclear-weapon States against the use or threat of use of nuclear weapons;

2.   *Notes with satisfaction* that in the Committee on Disarmament there is no objection, in principle, to the idea of an international convention to assure non-nuclear-weapon States against the use or threat of use of nuclear weapons, although the difficulties as regards evolving a common approach acceptable to all have also been pointed out;

3.   *Appeals* to all States, especially the nuclear-weapon States, to demonstrate the political will necessary to reach agreement on a common approach and, in particular, on a common formula which could be included in an international instrument of a legally binding character;

4.   *Recommends* that further intensive efforts should be devoted to the search for such a common approach or common formula and that the various alternative approaches, including in particular those considered in the Committee on Disarmament, should be further explored in order to overcome the difficulties;

5.   *Recommends* that the Committee on Disarmament should actively continue negotiations with a view to reaching early agreement and concluding effective international arrangements to assure non-nuclear-weapon States against the use or threat of use of nuclear weapons, taking into account the widespread support for the conclusion of an international convention and giving consideration to any other proposals designed to secure the same objective;

6.   *Decides* to include in the provisional agenda of its thirty-eighth session the item entitled "Conclusion of effective international arrangements to assure non-nuclear-weapon States against the use or threat of use of nuclear weapons".

Recorded vote in Assembly as follows:

In favour: Afghanistan, Algeria, Angola, Antigua and Barbuda, Argentina, Australia, Austria, Bahamas, Bahrain, Bangladesh, Barbados, Belgium, Belize, Benin, Bolivia, Botswana, Brazil, Bulgaria, Burma, Burundi, Byelorussian SSR, Canada, Cape Verde, Central African Republic, Chad, Chile, China, Colombia, Comoros, Congo, Costa Rica, Cuba, Cyprus, Czechoslovakia, Democratic Kampuchea, Democratic Yemen, Denmark, Djibouti, Dominican Republic, Ecuador, Egypt, El Salvador, Ethiopia, Fiji, Finland, France, Gabon, Gambia, German Democratic Republic, Germany, Federal Republic of, Ghana, Greece, Grenada, Guatemala, Guinea, Guinea-Bissau, Guyana, Haiti, Honduras, Hungary, Iceland, Indonesia, Iran, Iraq, Ireland, Israel, Italy, Ivory Coast, Jamaica, Japan, Jordan, Kenya, Kuwait, Lao People's Democratic Republic, Lebanon, Liberia, Libyan Arab Jamahiriya, Luxembourg, Madagascar, Malawi, Malaysia, Maldives, Mali, Malta, Mauritania, Mauritius, Mexico, Mongolia, Morocco, Mozambique, Nepal, Netherlands, New Zealand, Nicaragua, Niger, Nigeria, Norway, Oman, Pakistan, Panama, Papua New Guinea, Paraguay, Peru, Philippines, Poland, Portugal, Qatar, Romania, Rwanda, Saint Lucia, Sao Tome and Principe, Saudi Arabia, Senegal, Sierra Leone, Singapore, Solomon Islands, Somalia, Spain, Sri Lanka, Sudan, Suriname, Swaziland, Sweden, Syrian Arab Republic, Thailand, Togo, Trinidad and Tobago, Tunisia, Turkey, Uganda, Ukrainian SSR, USSR, United Arab Emirates, United Republic of Cameroon, United Republic of Tanzania, Upper Volta, Uruguay, Vanuatu, Venezuela, Viet Nam, Yemen, Yugoslavia, Zaire, Zambia.

Against: None.

Abstaining: India, United Kingdom, United States.

Other weapons of mass destruction

Chemical and biological weapons

The Committee on Disarmament continued in 1982 the preparation of a draft convention to prohibit chemical weapons and, in December, the General Assembly urged the Committee to accord high priority to this work so that agreement on a convention banning the development, production and stockpiling of all such weapons could be achieved as soon as possible. Meanwhile, the Group of Experts to Investigate Reports on the Alleged Use of Chemical Weapons visited Pakistan and Thailand to collect and examine evidence in connection with charges that such weapons were being used in neighbouring States; according to its final report to the Assembly, while the Group could not state that the allegations had been proven, it could not disregard circumstantial evidence suggestive of the possible use of some sort of toxic chemical in some instances.

With a view to strengthening existing multilateral treaties on chemical and biological weapons, the Assembly authorized a procedure under which the Secretary-General could investigate alleged violations of the 1925 Protocol prohibiting poison gas and bacteriological warfare (see below), and recommended that the States parties to the 1972 Convention against biological and toxin weapons meet as soon as possible to establish a procedure relating to compliance with that Convention.

Implementation of the 1925 Protocol

General Assembly consideration (June/July). Proposals to have the comprehensive programme of disarmament include a call for adherence to and compliance with the 1925 Geneva Protocol for the Prohibition of the Use in War of Asphyxiating, Poisonous or Other Gases, and of Bacteriological Methods of Warfare were considered during the General Assembly's 1982 special session devoted to disarmament, but agreement was not reached on the wording.[3]

Two proposals were submitted on monitoring compliance with the Protocol. Belgium, in a note verbale dated 16 June to the Secretary-General,[1] suggested asking the Committee on Disarmament to elaborate an *ad hoc* instrument, as a means of reinforcing the Geneva Protocol, that would set up two international committees and a technical secretariat to monitor compliance with the prohibition of the use in combat of chemical, bacteriological or toxin weapons; a suggested structure of such an instrument was attached to the note. France, in a note verbale to the Secretariat dated 25 June,[2] proposed specific fact-finding arrangements, utilizing the expertise of the World Health Organization, for verification of alleged violations of the Protocol.

During the general debate at the special session, Democratic Kampuchea called for an international conference on chemical warfare and stressed the importance of strict compliance with the Protocol. Indonesia urged the strengthening of that instrument. France suggested that procedures be established for rapid identification of symptoms by specialized medical techniques.

General Assembly action (December). By a resolution of 13 December 1982,[4] the General Assembly established provisional procedures to investigate reported violations of the 1925 Geneva Protocol. The Secretary-General was authorized to investigate, with expert assistance, information received from any United Nations Member State concerning possible violations of the Protocol or other relevant rules of international law, and promptly to report the results to all Member States and the Assembly. With the co-operation of Member States, he was to compile and maintain lists of experts and laboratories whose services could be enlisted for urgent investigations. He was also to devise procedures, and to assemble and organize documentation on identification of signs and symptoms of the use of prohibited chemical agents and on medical treatment. The Assembly called on all States to accede to the 1925 Protocol and comply with its provisions. It requested the Committee on Disarmament to expedite negotiations on a convention to prohibit chemical weapons.

The resolution was adopted by a recorded vote of 86 to 19, with 33 abstentions. The First Committee had approved the nine-nation draft on 29 November by a recorded vote of 70 to 18, with 31 abstentions.

The call for strict observance by all States of the objectives of the 1925 Geneva Protocol was repeated in another Assembly resolution of 13 December on the United Nations investigation of the alleged use of chemical weapons in two Asian regions.[5]

Introducing the nine-nation text—also sponsored by Belgium, Colombia, Costa Rica, Ecuador, the Federal Republic of Germany, the Netherlands, Sweden and Uruguay—France, the depositary of the 1925 Protocol, observed that the instrument's provisions had become part of customary international law. The resolution sought to maintain the authority of that Protocol by providing the international community, as a provisional measure pending future agreements, with an impartial and competent investigative mechanism which was flexible, practical and susceptible of rapid implementation. The proposal stood outside any political context, had no links to various allegations of chemical-weapons use, and was meant to serve as a confidence-building measure by obviating groundless accusations and propaganda use of doubtful information. France orally revised the title of the draft from "Chemical and bacteriological (biological) weapons" to "Provisional procedures to uphold the authority of the 1925 Geneva Protocol".

Several Eastern European and other countries voted against the proposal on the ground that it undermined the Protocol and diverted attention from the efforts aimed at concluding a convention on complete prohibition of chemical weapons. Such views were expressed by Bulgaria, Czechoslovakia, the German Democratic Republic, the Ukrainian SSR, the USSR and Viet Nam. They saw the resolution as poisoning the atmosphere by creating suspicion and hostility. The USSR said the proposal divided the States parties to the Protocol into those which would participate in the investigating mechanism and those which would not.

Further, the Byelorussian SSR and the USSR considered the proposal an attempt to institutionalize the Group of Experts to Investigate Reports on the Alleged Use of Chemical Weapons, while the Ukrainian SSR saw it as designed to legalize the practice of establishing a group of experts to investigate false charges against a State. Bulgaria called the creation of a separate body of investigation illegal, and India termed it inappropriate even on a temporary basis to set up an investigation machinery that went beyond the relevant treaty.

Also voting against the resolution, Hungary and the German Democratic Republic viewed the action as creating a dangerous precedent by modifying multilateral treaties without the express consent of the States parties concerned. Sharing that view, Czechoslovakia and the USSR said the action amounted to revising the Protocol by vote rather than by negotiations—the USSR adding that it was detrimental to the consensus principle that had guided disarmament negotiations.

Concurring with the observation of the German Democratic Republic that only the States parties to an agreement could review and assess compliance by other parties, Bulgaria and Viet Nam feared that the proposal sought to legitimize a right of non-parties—Viet Nam noting that the United States was in that category—to pass judgement on the conduct of others, while remaining outside the Protocol and thus being exempt from relevant legal responsibilities. The Byelorussian SSR and the USSR also objected to conferring rights on States not parties to the Protocol. For the Congo, the resolution established a dangerous precedent for forcing a State to comply with the provisions of a convention to which it was not a party or simply interfering in that State's internal affairs. In a similar vein, Czechoslovakia regretted that the Assembly and the Secretary-General had to be associated with a course of action that could be misused for such interference.

Hungary also stated that, while an Assembly resolution was no more than a recommendation, the text aimed at conferring treaty obligations and rights on an international organization as well. In this light, a number of countries, among them the Congo, Czechoslovakia, Hungary, the USSR and

Viet Nam, observed that the text asked the Secretary-General, who was not the depositary of the Protocol and hence devoid of legal authority in respect of it, to make highly controversial and political decisions.

Abstaining in the vote, a number of countries, among them Argentina, Finland, Mexico and Venezuela, asserted that a treaty could not be amended or improved by means of General Assembly resolutions. Argentina also had difficulty with the proposed role of non-parties and that of the Secretary-General, and added that the issue of compliance should be covered in the draft convention under negotiation at Geneva. Algeria said it was for the States parties to decide to alter an international instrument. Yugoslavia believed the proposal contained some elements not entirely in conformity with the goals of effective verification and control, and Brazil expressed regret, as did Finland, that the proposal had become confrontational or politically controversial.

Among those supporting the initiative, Australia and Norway saw it as an important and timely attempt to fill a void pending a permanent and negotiated solution to the current absence of a verification mechanism under the Protocol; Norway also mentioned the importance of rapid investigations because of the volatility of chemical agents. Canada considered verification a key to enforcement and asserted that the treaty would remain unimpaired as it incorporated peremptory norms of international law. Indonesia supported the text on the understanding that the procedure proposed was provisional.

Notes verbales. [1]Belgium, 16 June, A/S-12/AC.1/18; [2]France, 25 June, A/S-12/AC.1/41.
Report. [3]*Ad Hoc* Committee, A/S-12/32.
Resolutions (1982). GA, 13 Dec.: [4]37/98 D, text following; [5]37/98 E, para. 2.
Financial implications. ACABQ report, A/37/7/Add.16; 5th Committee report, A/37/733; S-G statements, A/C.1/37/L.75, A/C.5/37/75.
Meeting records. GA: plenary, A/S-12/PV.2-26, 28, 29 (8 June- 10 July); *Ad Hoc* Committee, A/S-12/AC.1/PV.9 (28 June); 1st Committee, A/C.1/37/PV.3-10, 12-28, 37, *38, 45, 47* (18 Oct.–29 Nov.); 5th Committee, A/C.5/37/SR.62 (10 Dec.); plenary, A/37/PV.101 (13 Dec.).

General Assembly resolution 37/98 D

13 December 1982   Meeting 101   86-19-33 (recorded vote)

Approved by First Committee (A/37/666) by recorded vote (70-18-31), 29 November (meeting 47); 9-nation draft (A/C.1/37/L.54), orally revised; agenda item 54.
Sponsors: Belgium, Colombia, Costa Rica, Ecuador, France, Germany, Federal Republic of, Netherlands, Sweden, Uruguay.

Provisional procedures to uphold the authority of the 1925 Geneva Protocol

The General Assembly,

Recalling the provisions of the Protocol for the Prohibition of the Use in War of Asphyxiating, Poisonous or Other Gases, and of Bacteriological Methods of Warfare, signed at Geneva on 17 June 1925, which entered into force on 8 February 1928,

Noting that States parties to the Convention on the Prohibition of the Development, Production and Stockpiling of Bacteriological (Biological) and Toxin Weapons and on Their Destruction have reaffirmed their adherence to the principles and objectives of that Protocol and called upon all States to comply with them,

Noting also that the Protocol does not provide for the establishment of procedures for investigating reports concerning activities prohibited by the Protocol,

Noting further that the Committee on Disarmament is currently engaged in the negotiation of a convention on the prohibition of chemical weapons, which should contain provisions to ensure its effective verification,

Believing it conducive to the continued authority of the Protocol that, pending eventual formal arrangements, procedures be established to make possible the prompt and impartial investigation of information concerning possible violations of the provisions of the Protocol,

1. *Calls upon* all States that have not yet done so to accede to the 1925 Protocol for the Prohibition of the Use in War of Asphyxiating, Poisonous or Other Gases, and of Bacteriological Methods of Warfare;

2. *Calls upon* all States to comply with the provisions of the Protocol;

3. *Calls upon* the Committee on Disarmament to expedite its negotiations on a convention on the prohibition of chemical weapons with a view to its submission to the General Assembly with the shortest possible delay;

4. *Requests* the Secretary-General to investigate, with the assistance of qualified experts, information that may be brought to his attention by any Member State concerning activities that may constitute a violation of the Protocol or of the relevant rules of customary international law in order to ascertain thereby the facts of the matter, and promptly to report the results of any such investigation to all Member States and to the General Assembly;

5. *Requests* the Secretary-General, with the co-operation of Member States, to compile, as a matter of priority, and maintain lists of qualified experts whose services could be made available at short notice to undertake such investigations, and of laboratories with the capability to undertake testing for the presence of agents the use of which is prohibited;

6. *Requests* the Secretary-General, in meeting the objectives of paragraph 4 above:

(a)To appoint, as necessary, groups of experts selected from the above-mentioned list to undertake urgent investigation of possible violations;

(b)To make the necessary arrangements for the experts to collect and examine evidence, including on-site, with the co-operation of the countries concerned, to the extent relevant to the investigation, and for such testing as may be required;

(c)To seek, in any such investigation, appropriate assistance and relevant information from all Governments and international organizations concerned, as well as from other appropriate sources;

7. *Further requests* the Secretary-General, with the assistance of qualified consultant experts, to devise procedures for the timely and efficient investigation of information concerning activities that may constitute a violation of the Geneva Protocol or of the relevant rules of customary international law and to assemble and organize systematically documentation relating to the identification of signs and symptoms associated with the use of such agents as a means of facilitating such investigations and the medical treatment that may be required;

8. *Requests* Governments, national and international organizations, as well as scientific and research institutions, to co-operate fully with the Secretary-General in this work;

9. *Requests* the Secretary-General to report to the General Assembly at its thirty-eighth session on the implementation of the present resolution.

Recorded vote in Assembly as follows:

In favour: Australia, Austria, Bahamas, Bangladesh, Barbados, Belgium, Botswana, Canada, Central African Republic, Chad, Chile, China, Colombia, Comoros, Costa Rica, Democratic Kampuchea, Denmark, Djibouti, Dominican Republic, Ecuador, Egypt, El Salvador, Fiji, France, Germany, Federal Republic of, Greece, Guatemala, Haiti, Honduras, Iceland, India,[a] Indonesia, Ireland, Israel, Italy, Jamaica, Japan, Kenya, Lebanon, Lesotho, Liberia, Luxembourg, Malawi, Malaysia, Maldives, Malta, Mauritania, Morocco, Nepal, Netherlands, New Zealand, Niger, Nigeria, Norway, Oman, Pakistan, Papua New Guinea, Paraguay, Philippines, Portugal, Romania, Rwanda, Saint Lucia, Saudi Arabia, Senegal, Singapore, Solomon Islands, Somalia, Spain, Sudan, Suriname, Swaziland, Sweden, Thailand, Togo, Trinidad and Tobago, Tunisia, Turkey, United

Kingdom, United Republic of Cameroon, United States, Upper Volta, Uruguay, Zaire, Zambia, Zimbabwe.

Against: Afghanistan, Bulgaria, Byelorussian SSR, Congo, Cuba, Czechoslovakia, Democratic Yemen, Ethiopia, German Democratic Republic, Grenada, Hungary, Lao People's Democratic Republic, Libyan Arab Jamahiriya, Mongolia, Poland, Syrian Arab Republic, Ukrainian SSR, USSR, Viet Nam.

Abstaining: Algeria, Argentina, Bahrain, Bhutan, Bolivia, Brazil, Burma, Burundi, Cyprus, Finland, Ghana, Guinea, Guinea-Bissau, Guyana, Iraq, Jordan, Kuwait, Madagascar, Mali, Mexico, Mozambique, Nicaragua, Panama, Peru, Qatar, Sierra Leone, Sri Lanka, Uganda, United Arab Emirates, United Republic of Tanzania, Venezuela, Yemen, Yugoslavia.

[a]Later advised the Secretariat it had intended to vote against.

Implementation of the 1972 Convention on biological weapons

General Assembly consideration (June-July). Calls for adherence to and compliance with the Convention on the Prohibition of the Development, Production and Stockpiling of Bacteriological (Biological) and Toxin Weapons and on Their Destruction were proposed for inclusion in the disarmament measures chapter of the comprehensive programme of disarmament, but the General Assembly, at its 1982 special session on disarmament, did not reach agreement on the wording.[1] The Convention was completed in 1971[4] and entered into force in March 1975.[5] It had 95 States parties as at 31 December 1982.

During the general debate at the special session, Democratic Kampuchea urged strict compliance with the Convention. France, announcing that its Government had sought parliamentary approval to accede to the Convention, stated that it intended to propose steps to meet obvious inadequacies in regard to consultations among parties and verification. Honduras called for universal accession to the Convention, while Singapore and the Syrian Arab Republic said the system provided for in the Convention should be extended and Somalia said the Convention should be strengthened.

General Assembly action (December). Reaffirming a 1970 resolution[3] in which it stated that an acceptable verification system should combine national and international measures, the General Assembly, by a resolution of 13 December 1982,[2] recommended the convening as soon as possible of a special conference of the States parties to the Convention on biological weapons for the purpose of establishing a flexible, objective and non-discriminatory procedure to deal with issues of compliance with that instrument. The Assembly requested the Secretary-General to provide the conference with assistance and services.

The resolution was adopted by a recorded vote of 124 to 15, with 1 abstention. The First Committee had approved the draft on 26 November by a recorded vote of 106 to 14, with 2 abstentions.

Introducing the 10-nation draft, Sweden called the Convention an important example of an international disarmament agreement concluded without the inclusion of a satisfactory complaint and verification mechanism. Although a partial improvement was made in that area at the 1980 Review Conference,[6] the resolution's sponsors thought it desirable to consider further the adequacy of the complaints procedure. Noting the role assigned by the Convention to the Security Council in carrying out investigations, the sponsors hoped that permanent members of the Council would not prevent an investigation or, alternatively, that the initiation of an investigation would be decided on by the Council in a manner prescribed for procedural matters.

In explanation of negative votes by a number of Eastern European and other socialist States, Czechoslovakia said on their behalf that the resolution constituted an attempt to undermine and revise existing agreements, led to the establishment of dubious mechanisms and amounted to the revision of international treaties through a vote in the Assembly in which States not parties to those treaties could also participate. The USSR added that the proposal for a conference was unjustified and served no useful purpose, that the mechanism provided in the Convention was neither inadequate nor ineffective and that the proposed review would do irreparable harm to the instrument.

Democratic Kampuchea, explaining its affirmative vote, said the resolution responded to its own appeal for an international conference to take effective measures against the chemical and bacteriological warfare being waged in Kampuchea, Laos and Afghanistan.

Report. [1]*Ad Hoc* Committee, A/S-12/32.
Resolution (1982). [2]GA: 37/98 C, 13 Dec., text following.
Resolutions (prior). GA: [3]2662(XXV), 7 Dec. 1970 (YUN 1970, p. 27); [4]2826(XXVI), annex, 16 Dec. 1971 (YUN 1971, p. 19).
Yearbook references. [5]1975, p. 64; [6]1980, p. 70.
Meeting records. GA: plenary, A/S-12/PV.2-26, 28, 29 (8 June–10 July), A/37/PV.101 (13 Dec.); *Ad Hoc* Committee, A/S-12/AC.1/PV.2 (14 June); 1st Committee, A/C.1/37/PV.3-10, 12-28, *38, 45* (18 Oct.–26 Nov.).

General Assembly resolution 37/98 C

13 December 1982   Meeting 101   124-15-1 (recorded vote)

Approved by First Committee (A/37/666) by recorded vote (106-14-2), 26 November (meeting 45); 10-nation draft (A/C.1/37/L.61); agenda item 54.

Sponsors: Austria, Colombia, Ecuador, Germany, Federal Republic of, Ireland, Mexico, Pakistan, Sweden, Uruguay, Yugoslavia.

Chemical and bacteriological (biological) weapons

The General Assembly,

Mindful of the continued importance of the Convention on the Prohibition of the Development, Production and Stockpiling of Bacteriological (Biological) and Toxin Weapons and on Their Destruction, signed in London, Moscow and Washington on 10 April 1972,

Deeply convinced that the effective implementation and functioning of the Convention, through the application of an adequate complaint and verification procedure, will enhance international peace and security as well as the prospect of realizing the goal of general and complete disarmament under effective international control,

Conscious of the need to maintain inviolate the Protocol for the Prohibition of the Use in War of Asphyxiating, Poisonous or Other Gases,

and of Bacteriological Methods of Warfare, signed at Geneva on 17 June 1925, and to ensure its universal application,

Recalling its resolution 2662(XXV) of 7 December 1970 on the question of chemical and bacteriological (biological) weapons, in which it stated, *inter alia*, that verification should be based on a combination of appropriate national and international measures which would complement and supplement each other, thereby providing an acceptable system that would ensure the effective implementation of the prohibition,

Recalling also resolution 35/144 A of 12 December 1980, by which it welcomed the Final Declaration of the Review Conference of the Parties to the Convention on the Prohibition of the Development, Production and Stockpiling of Bacteriological (Biological) and Toxin Weapons and on Their Destruction,

Noting that, in the Final Declaration, the States parties considered that various international procedures, including the right of any State party subsequently to request that a consultative meeting open to all States parties be convened at expert level, would make it possible to ensure effectively and adequately the implementation of the provisions of the Convention,

Taking into account that, in their Final Declaration, the States parties, having noted the concerns and differing views expressed on the adequacy of article V of the Convention, believed that this question should be further considered at an appropriate time,

1. *Reaffirms once again* its resolution 2662(XXV) on the question of chemical and bacteriological (biological) weapons;

2. *Recommends* that the States parties should hold a special conference as soon as possible to establish a flexible, objective and non-discriminatory procedure to deal with issues concerning compliance with the Convention on the Prohibition of the Development, Production and Stockpiling of Bacteriological (Biological) and Toxin Weapons and on Their Destruction;

3. *Requests* the Secretary-General to render the necessary assistance and to provide such services, including summary research, as may be required for the special conference of States parties to the Convention.

Recorded vote in Assembly as follows:

In favour: Algeria, Angola, Argentina, Australia, Austria, Bahamas, Bahrain, Bangladesh, Barbados, Belgium, Benin, Bhutan, Bolivia, Botswana, Brazil, Burma, Burundi, Canada, Central African Republic, Chad, Chile, Colombia, Comoros, Congo, Costa Rica, Cyprus, Democratic Kampuchea, Denmark, Djibouti, Dominican Republic, Ecuador, Egypt, El Salvador, Fiji, Finland, France, Gabon, Germany, Federal Republic of, Ghana, Greece, Guatemala, Guinea-Bissau, Guyana, Haiti, Honduras, Iceland, India,[a] Indonesia, Iran, Iraq, Ireland, Israel, Italy, Jamaica, Japan, Jordan, Kenya, Kuwait, Lebanon, Lesotho, Liberia, Libyan Arab Jamahiriya, Luxembourg, Madagascar, Malawi, Malaysia, Maldives, Mali, Malta, Mauritania, Mexico, Morocco, Nepal, Netherlands, New Zealand, Nicaragua, Niger, Nigeria, Norway, Oman, Pakistan, Panama, Papua New Guinea, Paraguay, Peru, Philippines, Portugal, Qatar, Romania, Rwanda, Saint Lucia, Sao Tome and Principe, Saudi Arabia, Senegal, Sierra Leone, Singapore, Solomon Islands, Somalia, Spain, Sri Lanka, Sudan, Suriname, Swaziland, Sweden, Syrian Arab Republic, Thailand, Togo, Trinidad and Tobago, Tunisia, Turkey, Uganda, United Arab Emirates, United Kingdom, United Republic of Cameroon, United Republic of Tanzania, United States, Upper Volta, Uruguay, Venezuela, Yemen, Yugoslavia, Zaire, Zambia, Zimbabwe.

Against: Afghanistan, Bulgaria, Byelorussian SSR, Cuba, Czechoslovakia, German Democratic Republic, Grenada, Hungary, Lao People's Democratic Republic, Mongolia, Mozambique, Poland, Ukrainian SSR, USSR, Viet Nam.

Abstaining: Guinea.

[a]Later advised the Secretariat it had intended to abstain.

Chemical weapons

Draft convention on prohibition of chemical weapons

Consideration by the Committee on Disarmament. In 1982, the Committee on Disarmament continued negotiations towards a multilateral convention on the total prohibition of the development, production and stockpiling of chemical weapons and on their destruction. As in previous years, much of the work was conducted in the Committee's *Ad Hoc* Working Group on Chemical

Weapons, originally established in 1980[12] and re-established on 18 February 1982. The Group, whose mandate in its first two years had been to examine and define issues to be dealt with in the negotiations on a convention, was given a new mandate in 1982: to elaborate a convention so as to enable the Committee to achieve agreement at the earliest date.

The Group held 42 meetings between 24 February and 15 September, under the chairmanship of Bogumil Sujka (Poland). It established nine open-ended contact groups, assigned to deal, respectively, with: the scope of the convention; definitions; declarations on stocks and production facilities; destruction, diversion, dismantling and conversion; general provisions on verification; preamble and final clauses of the convention; national implementation measures; national technical means of verification; and consultation and co-operation. The reports of the contact group co-ordinators were annexed to that of the Working Group, which was incorporated in the Committee's 1982 report to the General Assembly.[7]

In addition, the Chairman of the Working Group consulted delegations, between 2 and 6 August, on two specific sets of technical issues: possible standardized physical, chemical or biological methods to determine the toxicity of other harmful chemicals and products formed during the production of chemical warfare agents; and possible methods to monitor the destruction of chemical weapons.

On 14 September, the Working Group Chairman circulated his views on possible compromise wording of the elements of a future convention, having taken into account the views in the Committee debate as well as discussions in the Working Group and the contact groups. The Chairman's text included the following points (in summary):

> States parties would undertake never under any circumstances to develop, produce, otherwise acquire, stockpile, retain or transfer chemical weapons; they would commit themselves to destroy or divert to permitted purposes stocks of such weapons, to destroy or dismantle production facilities, and not to assist, encourage or induce anyone to engage in activities prohibited by the convention. Chemical weapons would be defined to include super-toxic lethal chemicals and their precursors, other lethal or harmful chemicals except those intended for permitted purposes, munitions or devices designed to cause death or harm through the toxic properties of chemicals they released, and equipment for use in connection with such munitions or devices.

> The prohibition of transfer would include the non-stationing of chemical weapons in the territories of other States and the withdrawal of all such weapons previously stationed there. Destruction of stocks of prohibited weapons, and destruction or dismantling of production facilities, would take place over a max-

imum period of 10 years and be carried out in such a way as to avoid harm to populations and the environment. States would have the right to retain, produce, acquire and use toxic chemicals for permitted activities—defined as non-hostile purposes and military purposes not connected with chemical-weapon use—in types and quantities consistent with such purposes; but stocks of super-toxic lethal chemicals would be limited in quantity and could be produced at only one facility in each producing country. The convention would be implemented in such a manner as to avoid hampering international co-operation for peaceful chemical activities.

States parties would be required to submit information in a series of declarations: initially, stating whether they had chemical-weapon stocks, their size, the existence of production facilities and the volume of transfers to anyone; at a subsequent time to be specified, presenting plans for destruction or diversion to permitted purposes; and periodically, notifying implementation of destruction/diversion plans, and submitting data on production and transfers of super-toxic lethal chemicals for permitted purposes.

Verification of compliance would be based on a combination of national and international measures. National measures to implement the convention and prohibit violations anywhere under their jurisdiction or control would be taken by States, which would submit information on such measures. National technical means of verification could be used to provide assurance of compliance, and States would be obliged not to impede such means, through deliberate concealment or otherwise.

States would undertake to consult and co-operate in solving any problems arising under the convention. A consultative committee composed of all States parties would be established to promote verification through information exchange, provision of expert opinions and other measures. International verification measures would include: a fact-finding procedure that could be invoked by any State party suspecting a violation; on-site inspection in such cases, which a State could accept or could turn down with an appropriate explanation; and on-site inspection of stock destruction and permitted production, on a basis to be agreed. Complaints of violations could be lodged with the Security Council, which could carry out an investigation and assist any party it found to have been exposed to danger as a result of a violation.

According to a review of its work since 1980, which the Working Group prepared for the General Assembly's 1982 special session on disarmament and which the Committee adopted on 21 April for inclusion in its special report for that session,[6] there was common understanding that the scope of the prohibition should include all existing and possible types of chemical weapons. In addition, a better understanding was reached of the need to ensure that verification of compliance with the convention was based on an adequate combination of national and international means.

The report added that the main differences regarding the scope concerned whether the convention should: include a prohibition of the use of chemical weapons; be applicable to animals and plants; prohibit planning, organization and training for the use of toxic chemicals in combat; and provide for the non-stationing of chemical weapons on the territories of other States. Also awaiting agreement were questions concerning the balance between national and international verification, the appropriateness of including a provision on the use of national technical means of verification, the organization and functions of a consultative committee of States parties and of the national verification or implementation system, the timing of on-site inspection, and verification of a ban on binary chemical weapons.

Proposed basic provisions for a convention submitted by the USSR in June at the General Assembly's special session on disarmament (see below) were also submitted to the Committee in July. The Federal Republic of Germany and the Netherlands, in August, submitted preliminary questions on the USSR paper, and in September the Federal Republic of Germany submitted a working paper on several aspects of the proposed convention.

On verification, working papers were submitted to the Committee by the following: Australia, United Kingdom and United States (technical evaluation of "recover" techniques for verification); Canada (proposed verification organization); Finland (relation of verification to the scope of a ban on chemical warfare agents; systematic identification of chemical warfare agents and identification of non-phosphorus agents); France (monitoring the destruction of stocks); Federal Republic of Germany (principles and rules for verifying compliance); Netherlands (verification of the presence of nerve agents, their decomposition products or starting materials downstream of chemical production plants); Norway (sampling and analysis of chemical warfare agents under winter conditions); Sweden (monitoring destruction of stockpiles); United Kingdom (verification and monitoring of compliance); and Yugoslavia (some aspects of verification).

In relation to the definition of chemical weapons and their toxic precursors in the production process, Sweden submitted a working paper on the concept of "precursor" and a suggested definition, and another paper on toxicity criteria for "key chemical-weapon precursors". Bulgaria, Czechoslovakia, the German Democratic Republic, Hungary, Mongolia, Poland and the USSR jointly submitted a working paper on binary weapons and the

problem of effective prohibition of chemical weapons, as did Yugoslavia concerning binary weapons and the problem of their definition and verification.

Sweden also submitted a working paper on measures to enhance confidence between the parties negotiating a comprehensive ban on chemical weapons. In addition, the Committee received a position paper by the United States on its programme to deter chemical warfare.

The Working Group recommended that it continue work in January 1983 through its contact groups and the Chairman's consultations on technical issues.

General Assembly consideration (June/July). During the General Assembly's 1982 special session on disarmament, proposals on a convention on chemical-weapons prohibition were made by the German Democratic Republic, the Federal Republic of Germany and the USSR.

The USSR, by a 16 June letter to the Secretary-General,[4] submitted a proposal containing basic provisions of a convention. These called for an undertaking by the parties never under any circumstances to develop, produce, otherwise acquire, stockpile, retain or transfer chemical weapons, to destroy any stocks or divert them to permitted purposes and to destroy or dismantle production facilities. They would require the submission of information, in the form of initial and periodic declarations, on stocks and facilities destroyed and chemicals diverted to permitted purposes. They envisaged compliance verification through national and international means—including on-site inspection carried out in response to complaints of violation, subject to the consent of the State concerned—and on a systematic basis to verify stock destruction and the production of super-toxic lethal chemicals for permitted purposes at specified facilities. A consultative committee of States parties would exchange information and promote verification, and complaints could be lodged with the Security Council.

The German Democratic Republic, in a working paper annexed to a letter dated 24 June to the Chairman of the *Ad Hoc* Committee of the Twelfth Special Session,[2] proposed that the Assembly call for an immediate cessation of the qualitative improvement and development of chemical weapons in order to guarantee an early ban, and urge States to refrain from acting in a manner that could impede negotiations on the prohibition of such weapons, including the production and deployment of binary and other new types of chemical weapons and the deployment of chemical weapons on the territories of States where there were none.

By a note verbale dated 24 June,[3] the Federal Republic of Germany submitted a proposal on principles and rules for verifying compliance with a chemical-weapons convention. It suggested four principles to guide a consultative committee entrusted with that task: confidentiality of deliberations, to prevent public controversy while they were in progress; readiness of all contracting parties to co-operate by such means as supplying information and permitting investigations and on-site inspections; rules to protect States against evidently unfounded allegations while ensuring that the committee's work would not be impeded by non-participation of a party; and strict impartiality and non-discrimination, allowing a State under inquiry to participate from the outset in monitoring. Of the two types of on-site verification envisaged—on-challenge and regular checks—the latter, based on a system of random selection of a proportion of installations in each State, could be used to verify that binary weapons were not being produced.

Agreement was not reached at the session on the wording of provisions calling for the conclusion of a convention, to be included in the disarmament measures chapter of the proposed comprehensive programme of disarmament.[5]

The early conclusion of an international agreement banning chemical weapons was urged by many speakers in the general debate at the special session, among them Angola, Australia, Belgium, Bhutan, Bolivia, Brazil, Burma, the Byelorussian SSR, Democratic Kampuchea, Democratic Yemen, Denmark, France, Iraq, Jamaica, Nepal, the Netherlands, New Zealand, Norway, Oman, Poland, Romania, Togo, the Ukrainian SSR and Uruguay. The Netherlands added that it did not possess chemical weapons, was not considering their introduction for its armed forces and rejected their stationing on its territory. Zimbabwe called for negotiations on a treaty to prohibit the possession of chemical and bacteriological weapons as well as their stationing on the territories of other States.

Bangladesh called for suspension of the production, development, deployment, and research on and development of new chemical weapons pending the conclusion of a chemical-weapons treaty. Further delay in the negotiations, said Pakistan, could add the spectre of general chemical warfare to the nuclear shadow that hung over humanity.

Democratic Yemen advocated measures to prevent the United States from proceeding with plans to produce chemical weapons. Ethiopia stated that the introduction of a new generation of chemical weapons undermined and complicated the achievement of a chemical-weapons convention, which, it said, had been within reach until recently. The German Democratic Republic and Hungary called for renewed efforts to negotiate an instrument in view of the recent decision on the manufacture and deployment of binary weapons in Western Europe.

Sierra Leone expressed distress at the decision to produce chemical weapons and appealed to all the Powers involved to refrain from such action. According to Mozambique, the imperialists had deliberately adopted delaying manœuvres aimed at gaining time for implementation of their plans to deploy such weapons. The Ukrainian SSR felt it was important for States to avoid actions that could complicate the talks and to renounce the deployment of chemical weapons in countries where none existed. The United Republic of Tanzania thought the arms scene could only be complicated by the argument that chemical weapons should be manufactured in retaliation against their alleged use by some Powers.

The role of the Committee on Disarmament in negotiating such a convention and moving towards chemical disarmament was reaffirmed by many, including Belgium (on behalf of the European Community (EC) members), Egypt, Fiji, Japan, Malaysia, Mongolia, Singapore, Somalia, the Syrian Arab Republic, the United Republic of Cameroon and the Upper Volta. Morocco, Sri Lanka, the United Kingdom and Viet Nam hoped the Committee would expedite negotiations on a convention.

Along with Thailand, which noted the lack of verification provisions in existing treaties, Portugal, Turkey and the United States said an agreement should include machinery and procedures for effective verification of its implementation. Belgium, for the EC members, said recent history had confirmed the importance of adequate verification measures. Also stressing the need for verification, France said it was unfortunate that a treaty was still obstructed by the USSR, which claimed not to understand the need for verification. Portugal considered the possibility of on-site inspections to be compatible with the sovereignty of States and absolutely essential for a chemical-weapons-ban agreement. The United Kingdom noted that the USSR seemed ready to accept the need for systematic on-site inspection in respect of a chemical-weapons treaty.

For New Zealand, persistent reports of the use of chemical weapons reinforced the need for setting up stand-by machinery to investigate such allegations pending the establishment of permanent arrangements for that purpose.

The Federal Republic of Germany, which had sponsored in 1978 an international seminar on verification in connection with a chemical-weapons ban, invited experts to a second such workshop in 1983 to pave the way for the conclusion of a treaty.

Japan hoped that the USSR and the United States would promptly resume their bilateral negotiations on chemical weapons.

Ethiopia and Guyana welcomed the draft convention submitted by the USSR during the special session, which Czechoslovakia and Mongolia believed should constitute the basis for further negotiations in the Committee on Disarmament. The draft, said the Ukrainian SSR, contained constructive new elements, particularly on verification. Australia and Ethiopia welcomed as an encouraging step the USSR declaration indicating its acceptance of the principle of on-site chemical-weapons inspection.

General Assembly action (December). Among five resolutions on chemical and bacteriological weapons which the General Assembly adopted on 13 December, two dealt specifically with the need to conclude a convention prohibiting the development, production and stockpiling of all such weapons. In a third resolution, on implementation of the 1925 Protocol prohibiting poison-gas and bacteriological warfare,[10] the Assembly urged the Committee on Disarmament to negotiate expeditiously, for submission to the Assembly within the shortest possible time, a convention on the prohibition of chemical weapons.

By the first of the two resolutions devoted to this topic,[8] the Assembly urged the Committee on Disarmament to intensify negotiations in the *Ad Hoc* Working Group on Chemical Weapons on the basis of its new mandate, to achieve accord on a chemical-weapons convention at the earliest possible date. The USSR and the United States were called on to resume soon their bilateral negotiations on the prohibition of such weapons, suspended in 1980, and to submit their joint proposal to the Committee. The Assembly also reiterated its call to all States to refrain from any action that could impede negotiations and specifically to refrain from producing and deploying binary and other new types of chemical weapons and from stationing chemical weapons on the territory of other States.

The resolution, with 11 sponsors from Eastern Europe and elsewhere, was adopted by a recorded vote of 95 to 1, with 46 abstentions. The First Committee had approved the draft on 24 November, as revised by its sponsors, by a recorded vote of 79 to 1, with 43 abstentions.

By the second resolution, adopted without vote,[9] the Assembly, expressing regret at the lack of-agreement, urged the Committee on Disarmament to intensify in 1983 the elaboration of a chemical-weapons convention as a matter of high priority, and to re-establish its *Ad Hoc* Working Group on Chemical Weapons with a view to achieving early agreement. The First Committee had approved the 18-nation draft on 26 November, also without vote, as orally revised by its sponsors.

Introducing the 11-nation text, the German Democratic Republic said the draft, based on a resolution adopted by the Assembly in December 1981,[11] supplemented the other proposal on the subject by providing for additional ways to further the quick achievement of a convention through halting the qualitative arms race in this field and curbing the geographical spread of chemical weapons. In their revised text, the sponsors dropped three paragraphs which would have had the Assembly appeal to States to consider the establishment of zones free from chemical weapons and invite their views on the subject, but they added a preambular paragraph taking note of proposals for such zones aimed at facilitating complete prohibition.

The 18-nation resolution, introduced by Poland, incorporated by an oral revision the idea contained in an amendment proposed by 11 members of the Group of 21,[1] adding to paragraph 3 the request that the Committee on Disarmament re-establish its *Ad Hoc* Working Group on Chemical Weapons. The amendment, introduced by Yugoslavia, was withdrawn after the resolution was revised to that effect.

In explanation of vote on the first resolution, Australia, Belgium, Colombia and the Netherlands said they had abstained as the text did not contribute to an early conclusion of the ongoing multilateral negotiations in the Committee on Disarmament; the Netherlands, in particular, considered the use of controversial language in the text counter-productive to that end.

Belgium considered the call for resumption of the bilateral talks incompatible with the Committee negotiations and said the notion of chemical-weapon-free zones should be considered only when there was no possibility of agreement on a convention. India opposed setting up such zones even as an interim measure, as it believed disarmament issues should be dealt with in a global framework. In a similar vein, the Sudan abstained in opposition to the preamble's reference to chemical-weapon-free zones, saying that it could not subscribe to legitimizing or linking with geographical considerations the possession of chemical weapons. France, which also abstained, opposed introducing the idea of non-stationing in the text, as did Brazil, which thought accepting the concepts of zones and non-stationing that had originated from confrontation between the two super-Powers would lead away from the conclusion of a convention.

In addition, Belgium, Brazil and France, referring to the mention of binary weapons, said it served no useful purpose to single out one specific type of weapon when all chemical weapons should be banned.

China abstained, stating that a convention should be comprehensive and include prohibition of use, and that resolutions on the subject should not be used to divert attention away from the development and use of such weapons. Although welcoming the call for non-stationing of chemical weapons on foreign territories, Democratic Kampuchea also abstained, citing what it called the cynicism demonstrated by one of the sponsors of the text, which had authorized the deployment of such weapons in warfare against the Kampucheans.

Canada's abstention was based on the value it placed on working by consensus, which, it believed, was exemplified by the other resolution on the subject. Costa Rica did not participate in the vote in Committee (it voted affirmatively in the Assembly) as it considered that the second resolution reflected the underlying principle in a more satisfactory manner.

Voting in favour despite its reservations regarding chemical-weapon-free zones, Argentina, which opposed according special treatment to certain kinds of weapons, asserted that the resolution requested no special treatment for binary weapons in the negotiations, nor did it ask for a separate convention on them. Algeria's affirmative vote reflected its continuing support for the chemical-weapon ban. Cuba and the USSR supported the text for its recognition of the need for all States to abstain from action which could complicate the negotiations.

During the First Committee's disarmament debate, the USSR said it attached particular importance to the prohibition, along with the traditional poisons and warheads, of binary (multi-component) weapons, which not only threatened to produce a qualitatively new stage in the chemical-arms race but would hamper monitoring of a chemical-weapon ban by making the problem of secret stocks more difficult to resolve. It was therefore important that States refrain from developing such weapons while talks on a prohibition were under way. Remarking that the output of agreed provisions in the Committee on Disarmament was minimal, the USSR said some delegations were taking up time with endless debate on all sorts of scientific or technical issues without allowing the Committee to discharge its role as a treaty-drafting forum.

The United States said effective verification procedures were of particular importance in a convention on chemical weapons. They should include systematic on-site inspection, including continuous monitoring while stockpiles were being destroyed, verification of declared production facilities until they were destroyed, and inspection of facilities permitted to manufacture any super-toxic lethal chemicals which the convention might allow. Also, to deal with the possibility of undeclared stockpiles or facilities, there should be provision for fact-finding investigations of suspicious activities, including a right of inspection of suspected

sites and an obligation by the parties to co-operate in resolving disputes over compliance. The USSR proposals submitted to the Assembly in June (see above), while showing a certain flexibility on verification, did not treat the problem adequately.

Amendment withdrawn. [1]Algeria, Cuba, Egypt, Ethiopia, India, Mexico, Nigeria, Pakistan, Sri Lanka, Venezuela, Yugoslavia, A/C.1/37/L.66.

Letters and note verbale (nv). [2]German Democratic Republic, 24 June, A/S-12/AC.1/29 & Corr.1; [3]Germany, Federal Republic of, 24 June, A/S-12/AC.1/37 & Corr.1 *(nv)*; [4]USSR, 16 June, A/S-12/AC.1/12 & Corr.1.

Reports. [5]*Ad Hoc* Committee, A/S-12/32; Committee on Disarmament, [6]A/S-12/2, [7]A/37/27 (Committee documents, CD/335/appendix II).

Resolutions (1982). GA, 13 Dec.: [8]37/98 A, text following; [9]37/98 B, text following; [10]37/98 D, para. 3.

Resolution (prior). [11]GA: 36/96 B, 9 Dec. 1981 (YUN 1981, p. 73).

Yearbook reference. [12]1980, p. 25.

Meeting records. GA: plenary, A/S-12/PV.2-26, 28, 29 (8 June–10 July), A/37/PV.101 (13 Dec.); *Ad Hoc* Committee, A/S-12/AC.1/PV.9, 10 (28, 29 June); 1st Committee, A/C.1/37/PV.3-10, 12-28, 31, 34, 37 39, 41, 42, 44 (10 Oct.–26 Nov.).

General Assembly resolution 37/98 A

13 December 1982   Meeting 101   95-1-46 (recorded vote)

Approved by First Committee (A/37/666) by recorded vote (79-1-43), 24 November (meeting 42); 11-nation draft (A/C.1/37/L.15/Rev.1); agenda item 54.

Sponsors: Afghanistan, Bulgaria, Byelorussian SSR, Czechoslovakia, German Democratic Republic, Hungary, Lao People's Democratic Republic, Mongolia, Poland, Ukrainian SSR, Viet Nam.

Prohibition of chemical and bacteriological weapons

The General Assembly,

Recalling paragraph 75 of the Final Document of the Tenth Special Session of the General Assembly, the first special session devoted to disarmament, in which it is stated that the complete and effective prohibition of the development, production and stockpiling of all chemical weapons and their destruction represents one of the most urgent measures of disarmament,

Recalling the unanimous and categorical reaffirmation by all Member States, at the twelfth special session of the General Assembly, the second special session devoted to disarmament, of the validity of the Final Document of the Tenth Special Session,

Convinced of the need for the earliest conclusion of a convention on the prohibition of the development, production and stockpiling of all chemical weapons and on their destruction, which would significantly contribute to general and complete disarmament under effective international control,

Recalling its resolution 36/96 B of 9 December 1981,

Expressing profound concern at the production and deployment of binary chemical weapons,

Taking into consideration the decision by the Committee on Disarmament on the new mandate for the *Ad Hoc* Working Group on Chemical Weapons, as well as the work of the Group during the session of the Committee in 1982,

Regretting that the bilateral negotiations between the Union of Soviet Socialist Republics and the United States of America have been suspended since 1980 and have not been resumed,

Deeming it desirable for States to refrain from taking any action that could delay or further complicate negotiations,

Aware that the qualitative improvement and development of chemical weapons complicate ongoing negotiations on the prohibition of chemical weapons,

Taking note of the proposals on the creation of chemical-weapon-free zones aimed at facilitating the complete prohibition of chemical weapons,

1. *Reaffirms* the necessity of the earliest elaboration and conclusion of a convention on the prohibition of the development, production and stockpiling of all chemical weapons and on their destruction;

2. *Appeals* to all States to facilitate in every possible way the conclusion of such a convention;

3. *Urges* the Committee on Disarmament to intensify the negotiations in the *Ad Hoc* Working Group on Chemical Weapons on the basis of its new mandate to achieve accord on a chemical-weapons convention at the earliest possible date;

4. *Calls upon* the Union of Soviet Socialist Republics and the United States of America to resume at the earliest possible date their bilateral negotiations on the prohibition of chemical weapons and to submit their joint proposal to the Committee on Disarmament;

5. *Reiterates its call* to all States to refrain from any action that could impede negotiations on the prohibition of chemical weapons and specifically to refrain from the production and deployment of binary and other new types of chemical weapons, as well as from stationing chemical weapons on the territory of other States.

Recorded vote in Assembly as follows:

In favour: Afghanistan, Algeria, Angola, Argentina, Bahamas, Bahrain, Bangladesh, Barbados, Benin, Bolivia, Botswana, Bulgaria, Burundi, Byelorussian SSR, Central African Republic, Chad, Congo, Costa Rica, Cuba, Cyprus, Czechoslovakia, Democratic Yemen, Dominican Republic, Ecuador, Egypt, Ethiopia, Fiji, Gabon, German Democratic Republic, Ghana, Grenada, Guinea, Guinea-Bissau, Guyana, Haiti, Hungary, India,[a] Indonesia, Iran, Iraq, Jamaica, Jordan, Kenya, Kuwait, Lao People's Democratic Republic, Lesotho, Liberia, Libyan Arab Jamahiriya, Madagascar, Malaysia, Maldives, Mali, Malta, Mauritania, Mexico, Mongolia, Mozambique, Nepal, Nicaragua, Niger, Oman, Pakistan, Panama, Papua New Guinea, Peru, Poland, Qatar, Romania, Saint Lucia, Sao Tome and Principe, Senegal, Sierra Leone, Singapore, Solomon Islands, Suriname, Swaziland, Syrian Arab Republic, Thailand, Togo, Trinidad and Tobago, Tunisia, Uganda, Ukrainian SSR, USSR, United Arab Emirates, United Republic of Cameroon, United Republic of Tanzania, Upper Volta, Venezuela, Viet Nam, Yemen, Yugoslavia, Zaire, Zambia, Zimbabwe.

Against: United States.

Abstaining: Australia, Austria, Belgium, Bhutan, Brazil, Burma, Canada, Chile, China, Colombia, Comoros, Democratic Kampuchea, Denmark, Djibouti, El Salvador, Finland, France, Germany, Federal Republic of, Greece, Guatemala, Honduras, Iceland, Ireland, Israel, Italy, Japan, Lebanon, Luxembourg, Malawi, Morocco, Netherlands, New Zealand, Nigeria, Norway, Paraguay, Philippines, Portugal, Saudi Arabia, Somalia, Spain, Sri Lanka, Sudan, Sweden, Turkey, United Kingdom, Uruguay.

[a] Later advised the Secretariat it had intended to abstain.

General Assembly resolution 37/98 B

13 December 1982   Meeting 101   Adopted without vote

Approved by First Committee (A/37/666) without vote, 26 November (meeting 44); 18-nation draft (A/C.1/37/L.44), orally revised; agenda item 54.

Sponsors: Argentina, Australia, Belgium, Canada, Colombia, Ecuador, Germany, Federal Republic of, Indonesia, Ireland, Japan, Kenya, Mongolia, Netherlands, Norway, Poland, Sweden, Ukrainian SSR, United Kingdom.

Chemical and bacteriological (biological) weapons

The General Assembly,

Recalling its previous resolutions relating to the complete and effective prohibition of the development, production and stockpiling of all chemical weapons and to their destruction,

Reaffirming the necessity of strict observance by all States of the principles and objectives of the Protocol for the Prohibition of the Use in War of Asphyxiating, Poisonous or Other Gases, and of Bacteriological Methods of Warfare, signed at Geneva on 17 June 1925, and of the adherence by all States to the Convention on the Prohibition of the Development, Production and Stockpiling of Bacteriological (Biological) and Toxin Weapons and on Their Destruction, signed in London, Moscow and Washington on 10 April 1972,

Having considered the report of the Committee on Disarmament, which includes, *inter alia*, the report of its *Ad Hoc* Working Group on Chemical Weapons,

Noting relevant proposals and initiatives, including those put forward at the twelfth special session of the General Assembly, the second special session devoted to disarmament,

Considering it necessary that all efforts be exerted for the resumption and successful conclusion of the bilateral and multilateral negotiations on the prohibition of the development, production and stockpiling of all chemical weapons and on their destruction,

1. *Takes note with satisfaction* of the work of the Committee on Disarmament during its session in 1982 regarding the prohibition of chemical weapons, in particular the progress in the work of its *Ad Hoc* Working Group on that question;

2. *Expresses its regret* that an agreement on the complete and effective prohibition of the development, production and stockpiling of all chemical weapons and on their destruction has not yet been elaborated;

3. *Urges* the Committee on Disarmament, as a matter of high priority, to intensify, during its session in 1983, the elaboration of such a convention, taking into account all existing proposals and future initiatives with a view to enabling the Committee to achieve agreement at the earliest date, and to re-establish its *Ad Hoc* Working Group on Chemical Weapons for this purpose;

4. *Requests* the Committee on Disarmament to report on the results of its negotiations to the General Assembly at its thirty-eighth session.

Investigation of the alleged use of chemical weapons

Communications. Letters and notes verbales sent to the Secretary-General during 1982 concerning the alleged use of chemical weapons included five communications from the United States, four each from the USSR and Viet Nam, three from Democratic Kampuchea, two from the Lao People's Democratic Republic and one from Canada. They related mainly to allegations of the current or recent use of chemical weapons in Afghanistan and Kampuchea (see Chapter VI of this section), and to denials of those allegations. Data were also submitted on the effects of toxic chemicals used in the 1960s during the Indo-China war.

Letters dated 19 January[2] and 19 April[4] from Democratic Kampuchea transmitted lists of instances between November 1981 and April 1982 in which Vietnamese forces were said to have engaged in chemical warfare in Kampuchea, including the firing of poison-gas shells and the addition of toxic substances to water supplies. Another letter from Democratic Kampuchea, dated 19 March,[3] transmitted a 9 March statement by its Ministry of Information condemning the continuation of chemical warfare by Viet Nam, including "yellow rain" discharged from aircraft, and calling on the United Nations to send a commission of inquiry.

The United States submitted, by notes verbales of 24 February[11] and 20 May,[13] information in its possession, based on analyses of blood samples, which it said tended to support the hypothesis that trichothecene-based agents (a type of mycotoxin, a poison produced by microscopic fungi) had been used by Viet Nam against Kampuchea in attacks in the autumn of 1981 and on 13 February 1982.

Viet Nam, in a letter dated 14 April,[16] transmitted the text of a 13 April statement by a spokesman for its Foreign Ministry, rejecting United States allegations about Viet Nam's use of chemical weapons in Kampuchea and the Lao People's Democratic Republic. By letters of 25 June,[17] 5 August[18] and 6 August,[19] it transmitted, for circulation at the General Assembly's special session on disarmament and at its regular 1982 session, extracts of a "Dossier on United States chemical warfare and its consequences", prepared by

Vietnamese and other scientists, on the effects on humans and the environment of herbicides and defoliants, notably "Agent Orange", used between 1961 and 1971 in what the paper described as a systematic chemical war in South Viet Nam conducted by the United States.

In a note verbale dated 22 March 1982,[12] the United States transmitted a report of the same date by its Secretary of State to its Congress on chemical warfare in South-East Asia and Afghanistan. Described as the most comprehensive compilation and analysis of information on the topic, based on data and evidence obtained by the Government from 1975 to January 1982, the report asserted that the USSR had used chemical warfare agents in Afghanistan and had provided lethal trichothecene mycotoxins and other agents to Lao and Vietnamese forces and had supervised their use.

The USSR, by a letter of 7 April,[7] transmitted a note dated 5 April addressed to the United States, protesting what it called a slanderous campaign against the USSR, which had never used chemical weapons anywhere or transferred them to other countries. Further, it transmitted by a letter of 30 April[8] the record of an 11 March press conference, given by USSR officials and academicians at its Ministry of Foreign Affairs, on the United States decision, announced on 8 February, to begin large-scale manufacture of toxic chemicals for military use.

The USSR, in a critique prepared by its experts and annexed to a letter of 20 May,[9] called the United States report an unsubstantiated fabrication intended to divert attention from United States preparations for chemical warfare and from its chemical "herbicide" war in Indo-China, involving over 90,000 tons of chemical agents dropped on Vietnamese soil. The Soviet report denied that there were USSR military chemical specialists in Kampuchea, Laos or Viet Nam, and said it maintained in Afghanistan only chemical-defence units, an integral part of its army, performing chemical reconnaissance in the face of the use by insurgents of American-made chemical weapons.

The Lao People's Democratic Republic, in a letter of 27 April,[5] transmitted a declaration of 6 April by its Ministry of Foreign Affairs spokesman, rejecting United States allegations on so-called chemical-weapons use in Laos. In a statement of 19 February attributed to the Ministry of Foreign Affairs spokesman of the People's Republic of Kampuchea, transmitted by a letter of 28 April from the Lao People's Democratic Republic,[6] the charge was made that Thailand, on 12 and 14 February, had fired toxic chemical artillery shells in the Phnom Melai region of Battambang province.

Canada, by a letter dated 23 June,[1] transmitted a report by Dr. Bruno Schiefer, described as one of Canada's foremost authorities on mycotoxins, who concluded after a fact-finding visit in February to Thailand, including visits to refugee camps on the Lao and Kampuchean borders with Thailand, that the events reported at the time of the alleged chemical-weapon attacks could not be explained on the basis of natural phenomena.

By a letter dated 28 June,[14] the United States proposed that the General Assembly, at its special session on disarmament, call on the USSR, the Lao People's Democratic Republic and Viet Nam to grant full and free access to areas of alleged chemical attacks so that the United Nations Group of Experts to Investigate Reports on the Alleged Use of Chemical Weapons could ascertain the facts in Afghanistan, Kampuchea and Laos.

The United States submitted, by a note verbale dated 29 November,[15] a follow-up report of the same date to the United States Congress and the United Nations, in which its Secretary of State asserted, among other things, that the USSR had continued the selective use of toxic agents in Afghanistan as late as October 1982 and that lethal and incapacitating chemical agents had continued to be used by Vietnamese and Lao troops against resistance forces in Kampuchea and Laos at least through June.

By a letter of 14 December,[10] the USSR transmitted the text of a 2 December *Pravda* article entitled "The latest falsification", stating that the November report by the United States, based on rumours and hearsay, followed the report by the United Nations Group (see below) which had found no confirmation of the United States version.

General Assembly consideration (June/July). In the general debate at the General Assembly's 1982 special session on disarmament, Australia, Morocco, Singapore and Somalia noted the persistent reports of the use of chemical weapons in Afghanistan and Indo-China, and Oman expressed concern over such reports. Somalia thought it all the more scandalous when such weapons, disgraceful in any circumstances, were directed against peoples fighting for liberation from colonial and foreign domination. For the United Kingdom, there was reason to doubt compliance by all signatories to the Convention on biological and toxin weapons; the disquieting and well-documented reports on the use of chemical weapons and toxins in Asia deserved urgent investigation.

The United States said there was conclusive evidence that the USSR had provided toxins for use in Laos and Kampuchea, and was using chemical weapons against freedom fighters in Afghanistan; it called on the Governments concerned to grant full and free access to their territories or to countries they controlled so that United Nations experts could investigate. Democratic Kampuchea stated that Vietnamese invaders had killed thousands of people in that country since early 1979 through the use of chemical weapons, including toxic gases, lethal mycotoxins and trichothecenes supplied by the USSR, and that the country currently served as a vast testing-ground for chemical and bacteriological weapons of the USSR; in addition, the Lao and Afghan peoples were victims of chemical warfare waged by Viet Nam and the USSR.

Malaysia and Singapore hoped the Group of Experts would be able to continue its investigation and present a more definitive conclusion. Thailand said it would continue to co-operate with the United Nations investigation.

Czechoslovakia dismissed as malicious propaganda the allegation of the use of chemical weapons by one or another of the socialist countries, and Mongolia condemned as indecent what it called the ill-intentioned and false reports by the United States about USSR involvement in alleged violations of the 1925 Geneva Protocol for the Prohibition of the Use in War of Asphyxiating, Poisonous or Other Gases, and of Bacteriological Methods of Warfare (p. 93). The Byelorussian SSR stated that the USSR had never used or transferred chemical weapons anywhere and that the anti-USSR slander was spouted by enemies of peace to conceal their unwillingness to conduct meaningful negotiations on banning chemical weapons. The USSR rejected as absurd the stories implicating it in the use of those weapons.

The Lao People's Democratic Republic said its forces had no reason to use chemical weapons against the meagre remnants of its opponents, which were eking out an existence only in uninhabited high mountain areas. Viet Nam, also rejecting the charges against it, said the United States was trying to involve the United Nations more deeply in its infamous propaganda operation despite the conclusions of the United Nations Group of Experts that the accusations were groundless; prevarications could not whitewash the imperialists' crime of having waged a chemical war of annihilation against the Indo-Chinese peoples, with immeasurable consequences for millions of Indo-Chinese, tens of thousands of United States military veterans and their families, and the environment.

Zimbabwe said its people had been victims of the use of chemical and bacteriological weapons during their struggle for national independence and asserted that South Africa had resorted to their use, especially in Angola. The Syrian Arab Republic said Israel and South Africa were developing chemical and biological weapons.

Report of the Group of Experts. The Group of Experts to Investigate Reports on the Alleged Use of Chemical Weapons, composed of four experts appointed by the Secretary-General, transmitted to him on 26 November 1982 a report[20] in response to a December 1981 General Assembly request[23] that the Group continue an impartial investigation to ascertain facts regarding the alleged use of chemical weapons and to assess the extent of damage caused by such use. The Group, which began work and submitted its first report in 1981,[24] held its fourth to sixth sessions in 1982: 4 to 22 February at Geneva, 21 to 30 July at Geneva, and 13 October to 22 November at Geneva and New York. During two of those sessions, the Group visited Pakistan from 9 to 22 February and Thailand from 25 October to 10 November to collect and examine evidence on site.

The Group's report included sections on sources of information on which the investigation was based, evaluation of written submissions, on-site collection and examination of evidence, samples obtained during on-site visits and conclusions. Annexed to the report were communications, analyses of samples and summaries of field interviews.

During its visits to Pakistan and Thailand, the Group met with alleged victims and eyewitnesses of alleged chemical attacks, as well as medical personnel at refugee camps and hospitals at Peshawar and Quetta, Pakistan, and at refugee camps and processing centres in Thailand close to its borders with the Lao People's Democratic Republic and Kampuchea. Despite a series of efforts by the Group to arrange for a visit to Democratic Kampuchea, which had invited it in a letter of 16 June, such a visit did not materialize. After its return to New York, the Group was informed by the Government's representative that technical, logistical and communications problems due to the hostilities in the country had prevented the visit.

The Group therefore reported that, due to circumstances beyond its control, it had not been able to proceed to the territories where chemical attacks had allegedly occurred and thus it had been unable to conduct any on-site investigations or collect samples in those territories. Nevertheless, the Group had received samples allegedly collected in some of the areas of conflict and it had also collected blood and urine samples from alleged victims during its visits to Pakistan and Thailand. Many of the medical signs and symptoms reported by alleged victims and medical personnel could be explained by trichothecene poisoning but, because of the vagueness of the symptoms described in most reports, other explanations could not be excluded. The results of analysis of body fluids collected were consistent with previous exposure to this type of mycotoxin, but the Group could not decide from the analytical results whether exposure was due to a chemical attack or to natural causes.

The results of chemical analysis of samples received or collected by the Group were inconclusive: in most cases, no presence of chemical warfare agents beyond the detection limits of the analytical methods could be demonstrated.

Evaluating the allegations mentioned in the course of its interviews, the Group noted that some charges had been supported only by scanty circumstantial evidence and that alternative explanations other than the use of chemical warfare agents were possible, and even likely. In some cases, however, more circumstantial evidence had been obtained, as of the possible use of harassing agents against persons seeking shelter in underground water canals in Afghanistan and the allegation of the use of toxic material in the area of Laos inhabited by the Hmong people. While the Group could not state that those allegations had been proven, it could not disregard the circumstantial evidence suggestive of the possible use of some sort of toxic chemical in some instances.

General Assembly action (December). By a resolution of 13 December,[22] the General Assembly took note of the report of the Secretary-General and of the Group's conclusion that, while it could not state that the allegations had been proven, nevertheless it could not disregard the circumstantial evidence suggestive of the possible use of some sort of toxic chemical in some instances. The Assembly expressed appreciation to the Group of Experts for its work and to the States that had co-operated with it. The Assembly called anew for strict observance by all States of the principles and objectives of the 1925 Geneva Protocol against poison-gas and bacteriological warfare and condemned all actions contrary to those objectives.

The resolution was adopted by a recorded vote of 83 to 22, with 33 abstentions. The First Committee had approved the text on 8 December, as orally revised by its sponsors, by a roll-call vote of 63 to 20, with 31 abstentions, following approval by 55 votes to 21, with 33 abstentions, of the preambular paragraph by which the Assembly noted the Group's conclusion concerning the possible use of some sort of toxic chemical. The sponsors were Australia, Canada, the Federal Republic of Germany, the Netherlands, New Zealand, Norway, Spain and Turkey. The vote on the preambular paragraph was requested by Ghana.

In another resolution of 13 December concerning the 1925 Protocol, the Assembly requested the Secretary-General to investigate alleged violations of the Protocol and to compile, with the co-operation of Member States, lists of experts and laboratories whose services he could enlist in carrying out such investigations.[21]

Introducing the resolution on the Group of Experts, New Zealand stated that the Group, which had set high standards for judging evidence, agreed that there were a number of incidents for which there was strong and well-supported evidence of chemical-weapon use. For nearly two years, the Group had pursued its investigation with integrity and objectivity; if its careful and responsible conclusions were incomplete, that was because the Group had been unable to secure approval for all the on-site investigations it had considered necessary. It was not proposed that the Group's mandate be extended.

In explanation of their negative votes, Bulgaria, the German Democratic Republic and Mongolia cited their opposition to an inquiry into what they regarded as false charges and stated that the exercise highlighted the absence of any evidence of the use of chemical weapons. Bulgaria also viewed the exercise as a purely political move to exacerbate tension and considered the resolution as a face-saving operation meant to give the impression that something useful had been successfully concluded. The German Democratic Republic and Mongolia regarded the study as a waste of United Nations resources.

Also voting against, Afghanistan asserted that the United States and some others had chosen to disregard its invitation for inspection of chemical grenades captured from terrorist counter-revolutionaries who had received their supplies from the same people who were making charges about chemical-weapons use; parts of the Group's report unveiled the baselessness of the United States allegations. The Lao People's Democratic Republic said the United States, which had waged a chemical war in Indo-China, had fabricated the allegations to justify its production of binary chemical weapons, for which a $54-million budget had been allocated for fiscal year 1983.

The USSR, recalling that it had opposed the Group of Experts from the beginning on the ground that it would be used to justify plans to build a chemical-weapons arsenal, also stated that the Group's report had not confirmed the false United States allegations on chemical-weapons use. Viet Nam stated that chemical weapons had never been used in either South-East Asia or Afghanistan except for those used in enormous quantities for an extended period by the United States in its war of aggression against Indo-China and the weapons produced by the United States and used by gangs of mercenaries in Afghanistan.

Observing that it had been the first victim of violation of the 1925 Geneva Protocol, Ethiopia, which voted against the resolution, asserted that undisguised political motivations and unfounded allegations could erode the moral and legal edifice of the Protocol.

Algeria abstained in the vote in view of what it regarded as the polemical nature of the discussion. Argentina abstained, as it had done in the previous two years on the same subject, for the reason that a verification machinery established under the General Assembly was alien to the framework of the solution which Argentina preferred—a convention negotiated between States. In the view of Ghana, which abstained on the text as a whole and voted against the second preambular paragraph, the Assembly should simply have thanked the Group for its work, without attempting to summarize the contents of the report in one sentence containing an insinuation when the Group itself had been careful not to assert that the circumstantial evidence was a sufficient basis for accusing anyone. Guinea, remarking that chemical and other forbidden weapons had been used against many oppressed peoples around the world, said the principle of international inquiry should be applied to all conflict areas and not just to those selected for ideological or political reasons; moreover, the Group's report was inconclusive.

Voting in favour despite many reservations on the report, Democratic Kampuchea supported the second preambular paragraph, paid tribute to the Group of Experts and expressed regret that the Group had failed to conduct an on-site investigation in the territory under its control due to what it called communications problems and lack of sufficient advance notice of the Group's intention to visit. Nigeria and the Sudan voted in favour as an expression of their continued belief in the need for universal observance of the 1925 Protocol and for impartial investigation of alleged violations; the Sudan added that its vote should not be construed as an endorsement of the Group's findings or as a comment on the allegations. Nigeria had reservations on the second preambular paragraph, and Tunisia, which also cast a positive vote, saw no link between the second preambular and operative paragraphs.

Also voting in favour, Singapore said it believed the evidence presented on this issue, including some that had been examined by the Group of Experts, pointed to the use of chemical weapons in Afghanistan and Kampuchea; in the light of that evidence, it was understandable why the occupying authorities there had not permitted the Group to investigate. The United States considered the resolution a careful and sombre commentary on the question of chemical-weapons use, noted that the reports of such use were continuing, stressed the importance of strict observance of the 1972 Convention on the Prohibition of the Development, Production and Stockpiling of Bacteriological (Biological) and Toxin Weapons and on Their Destruction (p. 95), and considered it highly significant that the Group had not been permitted to enter the areas where chemical-weapon attacks were taking place.

Letters and notes verbales (nv). [1]Canada: 23 June, A/37/308. Democratic Kampuchea: [2]19 Jan., A/37/72; [3]19 Mar., A/37/152-S/14915; [4]19 Apr., A/37/202-S/14986. Lao People's Democratic Republic: [5]27 Apr., A/37/210; [6]28 Apr., A/37/212. USSR: [7]7 Apr., A/37/173; [8]30 Apr., A/37/219; [9]20 May, A/37/233; [10]14 Dec., A/37/765. United States: [11]24 Feb., A/37/102 *(nv)*; [12]22 Mar., A/37/157 *(nv)*; [13]20 May, A/37/234 & Corr.1 *(nv)*; [14]28 June, A/S-12/AC.1/53; [15]29 Nov., A/C.1/37/10 *(nv)*. Viet Nam: [16]14 Apr., A/37/180; [17]25 June, A/S-12/AC.1/57; [18]5 Aug., A/37/376; [19]6 Aug., A/37/377.
Report. [20]S-G and Group of Experts, A/37/259.
Resolutions (1982). GA, 13 Dec.: [21]37/98 D, paras. 4-7; [22]37/98 E, text following.
Resolution (prior). GA: [23]36/96 C, 9 Dec. 1981 (YUN 1981, p. 76).
Yearbook reference: [24]1981, p. 74.
Meeting records. GA: General Committee, A/BUR/37/SR.2 (22 Sep.); 1st Committee, A/C.1/37/PV.3-10, 12-28, *57, 58* (18 Oct.-8 Dec.); plenary, A/37/PV.101 (13 Dec.).

General Assembly resolution 37/98 E

13 December 1982   Meeting 101   83-22-33 (recorded vote)

Approved by First Committee (A/37/666) by roll-call vote (63-20-31), 8 December (meeting 58); 8-nation draft (A/C.1/37/L.79), orally revised; agenda item 54.

Sponsors: Australia, Canada, Germany, Federal Republic of, Netherlands, New Zealand, Norway, Spain, Turkey.

Chemical and bacteriological (biological) weapons
The General Assembly,

Having considered the report of the Secretary-General to which was annexed the report of the Group of Experts to Investigate Reports on the Alleged Use of Chemical Weapons, appointed by the Secretary-General pursuant to General Assembly resolutions 35/144 C of 12 December 1980 and 36/96 C of 9 December 1981,

Taking note of the final conclusion of the Group of Experts that, while it could not state that the allegations had been proven, nevertheless it could not disregard the circumstantial evidence suggestive of the possible use of some sort of toxic chemical substance in some instances,

Recalling that the use of chemical and biological weapons has been declared incompatible with the accepted norms of civilization,

1. *Takes note* of the report of the Secretary-General and expresses its appreciation to the Group of Experts to Investigate Reports on the Alleged Use of Chemical Weapons for the work it has accomplished, as well as to the Member States that co-operated with the Group in fulfilling its mandate;

2. *Calls anew* for strict observance by all States of the principles and objectives of the Protocol for the Prohibition of the Use in War of Asphyxiating, Poisonous or Other Gases, and of Bacteriological Methods of Warfare and condemns all actions that are contrary to those objectives.

Recorded vote in Assembly as follows:

In favour: Australia, Austria, Bahamas, Barbados, Belgium, Bolivia, Botswana, Canada, Central African Republic, Chad, Chile, China, Colombia, Comoros, Costa Rica, Democratic Kampuchea, Denmark, Djibouti, Dominican Republic, Ecuador, Egypt, El Salvador, Fiji, France, Gabon, Germany, Federal Republic of, Greece, Guatemala, Guyana, Haiti, Honduras, Iceland, Ireland, Israel, Italy, Japan, Kenya, Lebanon, Lesotho, Liberia, Luxembourg, Malawi, Malaysia, Malta, Mauritania, Mauritius, Morocco, Netherlands, New Zealand, Niger, Nigeria, Norway, Oman, Pakistan, Papua New Guinea, Paraguay, Philippines, Portugal, Rwanda, Saint Lucia, Saudi Arabia, Senegal, Sierra Leone, Singapore, Solomon Islands, Somalia, Spain, Sudan, Suriname, Swaziland, Sweden, Thailand, Togo, Trinidad and Tobago, Tunisia, Turkey, United Kingdom, United States, Upper Volta, Uruguay, Zaire, Zambia, Zimbabwe.

Against: Afghanistan, Angola, Bulgaria, Byelorussian SSR, Congo, Cuba, Czechoslovakia, Democratic Yemen, Ethiopia, German Democratic Republic, Grenada, Hungary, Lao People's Democratic Republic, Libyan Arab Jamahiriya, Mongolia, Mozambique, Poland, Romania, Syrian Arab Republic, Ukrainian SSR, USSR, Viet Nam.

Abstaining: Algeria, Argentina, Bahrain, Bangladesh, Bhutan, Brazil, Burma, Burundi, Cyprus, Finland, Ghana, Guinea, Guinea-Bissau, India, Indonesia, Iraq, Jamaica, Kuwait, Mali, Mexico, Nepal, Nicaragua, Panama, Peru, Qatar, Sri Lanka, Uganda, United Arab Emirates, United Republic of Cameroon, United Republic of Tanzania, Venezuela, Yemen, Yugoslavia.

Radiological weapons

Consideration by the Committee on Disarmament. In considering its agenda item on "New types of weapons of mass destruction and new systems of such weapons; radiological weapons", the Committee on Disarmament re-established on 18 February 1982, for the duration of the 1982 session, its *Ad Hoc* Working Group on Radiological Weapons. The Group's mandate remained the same as when it was initially established in 1980:[6] to reach agreement on a convention prohibiting the development, production, stockpiling and use of radiological weapons. The Working Group held 14 meetings in 1982 (20 February–21 April, 2-8 September), in addition to informal consultations.

The Working Group reported to the Committee twice in 1982: an account of its work from 1980 through the first part of the 1982 session was included in the Committee's special report to the Assembly at the special session on disarmament[2] and its work throughout 1982 was described in the Committee's annual report to the Assembly.[3]

The Working Group agreed on 15 March, as a procedural hypothesis and without prejudice to later decisions, to conduct separate meetings on what it called the "traditional" radiological weapons, encompassing the scope of prohibition envisaged in a 1979 joint proposal by the USSR and the United States for a radiological-weapons treaty,[5] and on the prohibition of attacks on nuclear facilities (p. 86). During the first part of the 1982 session, the Working Group devoted three meetings each to issues relating to the so-called traditional radiological weapons and to those concerning attacks on nuclear facilities.

In an overview of the state of the negotiations as at April 1982, the Working Group said in its report for the Assembly's special session that divergencies persisted among delegations, particularly with regard to the definition of radiological weapons, the scope of a prohibition, verification of compliance, peaceful uses, and the relationship of a treaty on radiological weapons with other disarmament measures. For instance, some continued to believe that the most effective approach to definition was through maintaining a clause excluding nuclear weapons from the treaty, while others feared that such action would amount to legitimizing nuclear weapons. Doubts were expressed as to the feasibility of including certain radioactive materials in the definition. Differences also remained over whether the treaty should encompass radiological warfare and whether violations of the treaty should be reported to the Security Council—as proposed in the USSR–United States draft of 1979—or to a consultative committee of experts.

Among the working papers and other documents submitted during the 1982 session were two alternative texts by Australia on a definition of radiological weapons, one by Yugoslavia on a definition, a memorandum by Sweden on aspects of a convention, and a draft article by the Group of 21 (p. 22) which would commit parties to pursue negotiations for cessation of the nuclear-arms race. In the Working Group, some members felt that the latter article was inappropriate for inclusion in the convention.

Following further consideration in September, the Working Group stated in its report to the Committee that, despite differences of opinion, there was a general recognition that negotiations on an international convention should continue with a view to attaining rapid progress. The Group therefore recommended that a similar working group be established at the beginning of the Committee's 1983 session to continue negotiations.

General Assembly consideration (June/July). At the second special session of the General Assembly on disarmament, agreement was not reached on the wording of a clause on radiological weapons for inclusion in the disarmament measures chapter of the comprehensive programme of disarmament.[1]

In the general debate at the special session, Bhutan and the Ukrainian SSR were among those calling for the prohibition of radiological weapons. Conclusion of a treaty banning such weapons was also urged by Burma, Czechoslovakia, Democratic Yemen, Egypt, Hungary, Iraq, Nepal, Romania, Togo, the United Republic of Cameroon and Zimbabwe. Somalia hoped the militarily powerful States would co-operate with the Committee on Disarmament in multilateral negotiations on the treaty. Sri Lanka hoped the Committee would move faster towards drafting a convention.

Australia had no doubt that a treaty was achievable, though it thought new approaches might be needed. Morocco urged all parties to show flexibility in negotiating an agreement in the Committee and not accept an ambiguous prohibition deprived of specificity.

General Assembly action (December). By a resolution of 13 December,[4] adopted without vote, the General Assembly requested the Committee on Disarmament to continue negotiations with a view to early elaboration of a treaty prohibiting the development, production, stockpiling and use of radiological weapons, in order that it might be submitted to the Assembly in 1983. It also took note of the recommendation by the Committee's *Ad Hoc* Working Group that a similar group be established in 1983 to continue negotiations on the prohibition of such weapons. In addition, the Committee was requested to continue searching for a solution to the question of prohibiting military attacks on nuclear facilities (p. 86).

The First Committee had approved this text on 22 November, also without vote. It was introduced by the Federal Republic of Germany and also sponsored by Bangladesh, Colombia, Costa Rica, Hungary, Japan and Sweden.

Reports. [1]*Ad Hoc* Committee, A/S-12/32; Committee on Disarmament, [2]A/S-12/2, [3]A/37/27 (Committee documents, CD/335/appendix II).
Resolution (1982). [4]GA: 37/99 C, 13 Dec., text following.
Yearbook references. [5]1979, p. 25; [6]1980, p. 27.
Meeting records. GA: plenary, A/S-12/PV.2-26, 28, 29 (8 June-10 July), A/37/PV.101 (13 Dec.); 1st Committee, A/C.1/37/PV.3-10, 12-28, *35, 39* (18 Oct.-22 Nov.).

General Assembly resolution 37/99 C

13 December 1982   Meeting 101   Adopted without vote

Approved by First Committee (A/37/667) without vote, 22 November (meeting 39); 7-nation draft (A/C.1/37/L.33); agenda item 55 *(a)*.

Sponsors: Bangladesh, Colombia, Costa Rica, Germany, Federal Republic of, Hungary, Japan, Sweden.

Prohibition of the development, production, stockpiling and use of radiological weapons

The General Assembly,

Recalling the resolution of the Commission for Conventional Armaments of 12 August 1948, which defined weapons of mass destruction to include atomic explosive weapons, radioactive material weapons, lethal chemical and biological weapons and any weapons developed in the future which have characteristics comparable in destructive effect to those of the atomic bomb or the other weapons mentioned above,

Recalling its resolution 2602 C (XXIV) of 16 December 1969,

Recalling paragraph 76 of the Final Document of the Tenth Special Session of the General Assembly in which it is stated that a convention should be concluded prohibiting the development, production, stockpiling and use of radiological weapons,

Reaffirming its resolution 36/97 B of 9 December 1981 on the conclusion of such a convention,

Convinced that such a convention would serve to spare mankind the potential dangers of the use of radiological weapons and thereby contribute to strengthening peace and averting the threat of war,

Noting that negotiations on the conclusion of an international convention prohibiting the development, production, stockpiling and use of radiological weapons have been conducted in the Committee on Disarmament,

Taking note of those parts of the reports of the Committee on Disarmament to the General Assembly at its twelfth special session and its thirty-seventh session that deal with those negotiations, including the reports of the *Ad Hoc* Working Group on Radiological Weapons,

Recognizing that notwithstanding the progress achieved in those negotiations, divergent views continue to exist in connection with various aspects,

Taking into consideration the fact that the peaceful applications of nuclear energy involve the establishment of a large number of nuclear installations with a high concentration of radioactive materials, and bearing in mind that the destruction of such nuclear facilities by military attacks could have disastrous consequences,

Noting with satisfaction the wide recognition of the need to reach agreement on the comprehensive prohibition of radiological weapons,

1. *Requests* the Committee on Disarmament to continue negotiations with a view to an early conclusion of the elaboration of a treaty prohibiting the development, production, stockpiling and use of radiological weapons, in order that it may be submitted to the General Assembly at its thirty-eighth session;

2. *Further requests* the Committee on Disarmament to continue its search for a solution to the question of prohibition of military attacks on nuclear facilities, including the scope of such prohibition, taking into account all proposals submitted to it to this end;

3. *Takes note* of the recommendation of the *Ad Hoc* Working Group on Radiological Weapons, in the report adopted by the Committee on Disarmament, to establish, at the beginning of its session to be held in 1983, an *ad hoc* working group to continue negotiations on the prohibition of radiological weapons;

4. *Requests* the Secretary-General to transmit to the Committee on Disarmament all documents relating to the discussion by the General Assembly at its thirty-seventh session of the prohibition of the development, production, stockpiling and use of radiological weapons;

5. *Decides* to include in the provisional agenda of its thirty-eighth session the item entitled "Prohibition of the development, production, stockpiling and use of radiological weapons".

Proposed prohibition of new weapons of mass destruction

Consideration by the Committee on Disarmament. Discussion of the question of banning new weapons of mass destruction continued in 1982 in the Committee on Disarmament, at plenary meetings and two informal meetings, with the participation of experts from some member States.

The exchange of views, as summarized in the Committee's annual report to the General Assembly,[2] showed the continued presence of two differing approaches. One group of delegations favoured a general agreement prohibiting the development and production of all new types of weapons of mass destruction, to be exemplified in a list, and which would also provide for the conclusion of separate agreements to ban specific weapons. They maintained that the permanent members of the Security Council and other militarily significant States should first declare their refusal to create new types and systems of such weapons and that the Committee should establish an *ad hoc* group of governmental experts to draft agreements. This approach was suggested by Hungary in a working paper submitted in March. Another group of delegations believed it more appropriate to negotiate agreements case by case as such weapons might be identified. They observed that no such weapon had been identified so far and asserted that a general prohibitory agreement would be too ambiguous to be useful in concrete situations and would not permit the definition and implementation of verification measures.

General Assembly consideration (June/July). Several alternative texts concerning measures to prohibit new types of weapons of mass destruction were considered for inclusion in the disarmament measures chapter of the proposed comprehensive programme of disarmament, but no agreement on them was reached at the General Assembly's 1982 special session on disarmament.[1]

In the general debate at the session, Denmark and Sierra Leone called for prevention of the invention and deployment of weapons of mass destruction. Czechoslovakia, Hungary and Romania urged the speedy elaboration of treaties prohibiting new types of such weapons, while the

Ukrainian SSR called for intensified negotiations on the topic. Ethiopia made the same plea, observing that experience had repeatedly shown how difficult it was to eliminate weapons once they were developed and deployed. The latter point was also made by Ireland and Somalia. Mongolia urged the permanent members of the Security Council and other militarily significant States to accept a USSR proposal on the subject and to make, at the special session, identical declarations renouncing the creation of new types and systems of weapons of mass destruction and submit them to the Council for approval. China urged a ban on all weapons of mass destruction.

General Assembly action (December). By a resolution of 9 December,[3] the General Assembly requested the Committee on Disarmament to intensify negotiations, assisted by governmental experts, with a view to preparing a draft comprehensive agreement on the prohibition of the development and manufacture of new types of weapons of mass destruction and new systems of such weapons, and to draft possible agreements on particular types of such weapons. The Assembly again urged States to refrain from action which could adversely affect talks aimed at working out agreements on this subject. It also called on the permanent members of the Security Council, as well as other militarily significant States, to make identical declarations, to be approved by the Council, on the refusal to create new types and systems of such weapons, as a first step towards a comprehensive agreement.

The resolution was adopted by a recorded vote of 119 to none, with 26 abstentions. The First Committee had approved the text on 23 November by a recorded vote of 99 to none, with 26 abstentions. The 27-nation draft was introduced by the Byelorussian SSR.

In a related action of 9 December,[4] the Assembly called on all States to ensure that scientific and technological achievements were ultimately used solely for peaceful purposes.

Reports. [1]*Ad Hoc* Committee, A/S-12/32; [2]Committee on Disarmament, A/37/27 (Committee documents, CD/335/appendix II).
Resolutions (1982). GA, 9 Dec.: [3]37/77 A, text following; [4]37/77 B.
Meeting records. GA: plenary, A/S-12/PV.2-26, 28, 29 (8 June–10 July), A/37/PV.98 (9 Dec.); 1st Committee, A/C.1/37/PV.3-10, 12-28, *36, 41* (18 Oct.–23 Nov.).

General Assembly resolution 37/77 A

9 December 1982   Meeting 98   119-0-26 (recorded vote)

Approved by First Committee (A/37/659) by recorded vote (99-0-26), 23 November (meeting 41); 27-nation draft (A/C.1/37/L.43); agenda item 47.

Sponsors: Afghanistan, Angola, Benin, Bulgaria, Burundi, Byelorussian SSR, Congo, Cuba, Czechoslovakia, Democratic Yemen, Ethiopia, German Democratic Republic, Guinea, Hungary, Jordan, Lao People's Democratic Republic, Mongolia, Mozambique, Niger, Poland, Romania, Sao Tome and Principe, Syrian Arab Republic, Ukrainian SSR, USSR, Viet Nam, Yemen.

New types of weapons of mass destruction and new systems of such weapons

The General Assembly,

Recalling its resolutions 3479(XXX) of 11 December 1975, 31/74 of 10 December 1976, 32/84 A of 12 December 1977, 33/66 B of 14 December 1978, 34/79 of 11 December 1979, 35/149 of 12 December 1980 and 36/89 of 9 December 1981 concerning the prohibition of new types of weapons of mass destruction,

Bearing in mind the provisions of paragraph 39 of the Final Document of the Tenth Special Session of the General Assembly, according to which qualitative and quantitative disarmament measures are both important for halting the arms race and efforts to that end must include negotiations on the limitation and cessation of the qualitative improvement of armaments, especially weapons of mass destruction, and the development of new means of warfare,

Recalling the decision contained in paragraph 77 of the Final Document to the effect that, in order to help prevent a qualitative arms race and so that scientific and technological achievements might ultimately be used solely for peaceful purposes, effective measures should be taken to prevent the emergence of new types of weapons of mass destruction based on new scientific principles and achievements, and that efforts aimed at the prohibition of such new types and new systems of weapons of mass destruction should be appropriately pursued,

Expressing once again its firm belief, in the light of the decisions adopted at the tenth special session, in the importance of concluding an agreement or agreements to prevent the use of scientific and technological progress for the development of new types of weapons of mass destruction and new systems of such weapons,

Noting that in the course of its session in 1982 the Committee on Disarmament considered the item entitled "New types of weapons of mass destruction and new systems of such weapons; radiological weapons",

Noting with satisfaction that in the course of its session in 1982 the Committee on Disarmament held informal meetings on this item with the participation of qualified governmental experts,

Convinced that all ways and means should be utilized to prevent the development and manufacture of new types of weapons of mass destruction and new systems of such weapons,

Taking into consideration the part of the report of the Committee on Disarmament relating to this question,

1. *Requests* the Committee on Disarmament, in the light of its existing priorities, to intensify negotiations, with the assistance of qualified governmental experts, with a view to preparing a draft comprehensive agreement on the prohibition of the development and manufacture of new types of weapons of mass destruction and new systems of such weapons, and to draft possible agreements on particular types of such weapons;

2. *Once again urges* all States to refrain from any action which could adversely affect the talks aimed at working out an agreement or agreements to prevent the emergence of new types of weapons of mass destruction and new systems of such weapons;

3. *Calls upon* the States permanent members of the Security Council, as well as upon other militarily significant States, to make declarations, identical in substance, concerning the refusal to create new types of weapons of mass destruction and new systems of such weapons, as a first step towards the conclusion of a comprehensive agreement on this subject, bearing in mind that such declarations would be approved thereafter by a decision of the Security Council;

4. *Requests* the Secretary-General to transmit to the Committee on Disarmament all documents relating to the consideration of this item by the General Assembly at its thirty-seventh session;

5. *Requests* the Committee on Disarmament to submit a report on the results achieved to the General Assembly for consideration at its thirty-eighth session;

6. *Decides* to include in the provisional agenda of its thirty-eighth session the item entitled "Prohibition of the development and manufacture of new types of weapons of mass destruction and new systems of such weapons: report of the Committee on Disarmament".

Recorded vote in Assembly as follows:

In favour: Afghanistan, Algeria, Angola, Antigua and Barbuda, Argentina, Bahamas, Bahrain, Bangladesh, Barbados, Belize, Benin, Bhutan, Bolivia, Botswana, Brazil, Bulgaria, Burma, Burundi, Byelorussian SSR, Cape Verde, Central African Republic, Chad, Chile, Comoros, Congo, Costa Rica, Cuba, Cyprus,

Czechoslovakia, Democratic Yemen, Djibouti, Dominican Republic, Ecuador, Egypt, El Salvador, Ethiopia, Fiji, Finland, Gabon, Gambia, German Democratic Republic, Ghana, Grenada, Guinea, Guinea-Bissau, Guyana, Haiti, Honduras, Hungary, India, Indonesia, Iran, Iraq, Jamaica, Jordan, Kenya, Kuwait, Lao People's Democratic Republic, Lebanon, Liberia, Libyan Arab Jamahiriya, Madagascar, Malawi, Malaysia, Maldives, Mali, Malta, Mauritania, Mauritius, Mexico, Mongolia, Morocco, Mozambique, Nepal, Nicaragua, Niger, Nigeria, Oman, Pakistan, Panama, Papua New Guinea, Paraguay, Peru, Philippines, Poland, Qatar, Romania, Rwanda, Saint Lucia, Sao Tome and Principe, Senegal, Sierra Leone, Singapore, Solomon Islands, Somalia, Sri Lanka, Sudan, Suriname, Swaziland, Syrian Arab Republic, Thailand, Togo, Trinidad and Tobago, Tunisia, Uganda, Ukrainian SSR, USSR, United Arab Emirates, United Republic of Cameroon, United Republic of Tanzania, Upper Volta, Uruguay, Vanuatu, Venezuela, Viet Nam, Yemen, Yugoslavia, Zaire, Zambia.

Against: None.

Abstaining: Australia, Austria, Belgium, Canada, Denmark, France, Germany, Federal Republic of, Greece, Guatemala, Iceland, Ireland, Israel, Italy, Ivory Coast, Japan, Luxembourg, Netherlands, New Zealand, Norway, Portugal, Saudi Arabia, Spain, Sweden, Turkey, United Kingdom, United States.

Conventional weapons

General Assembly consideration (June/July). At the General Assembly's 1982 special session on disarmament, three written proposals were submitted with regard to two aspects of the problem of conventional weapons.

Italy, by a letter dated 17 June to the Chairman of the *Ad Hoc* Committee of the Twelfth Special Session,[1] proposed that the Centre for Disarmament keep a register of all international transactions in conventional weapons, with information to be provided regularly by Member States. The proposal suggested also that consideration be given, possibly by the Group of Experts on conventional disarmament, to proposals on controlling and limiting the volume of such transfers.

Sweden, by a letter of 27 June to the Secretary-General,[2] proposed that the Assembly call attention to the serious problems presented by the naval arms race, including developments in anti-submarine warfare capabilities that could increase the risk of nuclear war. Subsequently, in a note verbale dated 7 July,[3] Sweden resubmitted a proposal it had made to the Preparatory Committee for the Second Special Session of the General Assembly Devoted to Disarmament, suggesting that recent agreement on basic law-of-the-sea concepts had paved the way for a United Nations study of the naval arms race.

The draft comprehensive programme of disarmament considered at the special session included, in its chapter on principles, two paragraphs referring to conventional weapons.[4] The first called for the pursuit of bilateral, regional and multilateral agreements or other measures to strengthen security at a lower level of forces, by limiting and reducing armed forces and conventional weapons, taking into account the need of States to protect their security, bearing in mind the right of self-defence and without prejudice to the principle of equal rights and self-determination of peoples, and the need to ensure balance at each stage and undiminished security of all States. The second paragraph called for bilateral, regional and multilateral consultations and conferences to be held where appropriate conditions existed, to consider different aspects of conventional disarmament. Although there were no outstanding proposals to amend these two paragraphs, the Assembly was unable to choose among five alternative versions of another paragraph in this chapter, touching on the relative responsibility of militarily significant States in the conventional disarmament process.

A subsection on conventional weapons and armed forces, under the draft programme's chapter on disarmament measures, dealt in part with the need for agreements on a gradual reduction in weapons production, the need for a broadening of prohibitions or restrictions on the use of conventional weapons deemed to be excessively injurious or to have indiscriminate effects, and the question of international arms transfers.

In the general debate at the special session, many speakers, including Czechoslovakia, Denmark, Finland, New Zealand and Zaire, said conventional disarmament deserved greater attention than it had received in the past. Belgium, on behalf of the European Community (EC) members, hoped to see the Committee on Disarmament pay more attention to the question.

Nepal believed that conventional disarmament, both global and regional, must begin with the most heavily armed States. Romania favoured an agreement between the two main military alliances on a ceiling for the principal armaments—aircraft, tanks, battleships, missiles, heavy guns and others. Sierra Leone thought that States with the largest military arsenals had a special duty to pursue conventional disarmament, because they developed, produced, stockpiled and sold the largest share of such arms. Senegal, however, suggested that disarmament could begin in the third world, whose members could work within the Movement of Non-Aligned Countries to reduce armaments, assuming the existence of political will to settle any disputes that might arise between them through peaceful means and without outside interference.

Belgium (for the EC members), the Congo, Japan and Portugal were among those noting that conventional weapons had been the only kind used in all the more than 100 armed conflicts waged in the previous 35 years. They were joined by Denmark, Panama, Samoa, Tunisia and Zambia, among others, in pointing out that more than 80 per cent of total arms expenditures were absorbed by conventional armaments. Mali added that in all conflicts in the third world conventional weapons were used, and Pakistan and Zambia said those weapons posed the primary threat to small and medium-sized countries. In this regard,

Antigua and Barbuda cited the report of the Independent Commission on Disarmament and Security Issues (p. 141) to the effect that between 1945 and 1976 alone there had been 120 wars in 71 third world countries involving active participation of the armed forces of 84 countries. The use of conventional weapons since 1945, said Panama, had cost the lives of more than 10 million people.

The Dominican Republic and the Syrian Arab Republic remarked that, to the people killed by them, conventional armaments were no less devastating than nuclear arms.

Parallel efforts for nuclear and conventional disarmament were called for by a number of States in the general debate and at the concluding meetings of the session, among them Australia, China, Egypt, Greece, Japan, the Sudan, Trinidad and Tobago, Turkey and Yugoslavia. Togo favoured a freeze and the reduction of military budgets and the conventional arsenals of all countries, including the developing countries. The USSR thought that, to start with, agreement could be reached not to increase armed forces and conventional armaments, to be followed by negotiations on their reduction, both globally and in specific regions.

Many speakers saw a link between conventional and nuclear weapons. The Netherlands said conventional weapons could trigger the use of even more devastating categories of weaponry, while Luxembourg and Trinidad and Tobago saw a potential in all conventional conflicts for escalation into a nuclear war. Colombia said the threat of conventional warfare might be less notorious but it was much more immediate than nuclear weapons. In the words of the United Kingdom, nuclear war was a terrible threat, while conventional war was a terrible reality. Democratic Kampuchea urged that conventional disarmament be accompanied by the complete withdrawal of foreign forces from territories occupied by force.

In addition to the destructive power of conventional weapons, many speakers, among them Ecuador, Ghana, Indonesia and Italy, spoke of the economic and social burden of maintaining conventional arsenals which diverted resources essential to development (p.145). Samoa considered it ironic that the third world countries called for the reduction of military budgets while themselves increasing their military spending on conventional weapons at a far greater rate than the developed countries. Malaysia observed that the accumulation of conventional weapons could create conditions of instability and lead to a spiralling of the conventional-arms race beyond the level needed for self-defence.

Cuba, which said it had almost doubled its military capability in one year in response to threats by the United States, asserted that, while arming

to attack one's neighbours was reprehensible, arming in self-defence was necessary in the face of the philosophy of plunder. Nigeria said conventional disarmament must take account of the legitimate defence requirements of States, the defence of sovereignty and the inalienable right of peoples to self-determination and independence.

Similarly, Pakistan said negotiations for conventional disarmament should follow such guidelines as recognition of each State's right to acquire the means to safeguard its security, the need to maintain an acceptable military ratio of war potential, the need to reduce armament levels in the regional context consistent with the principle of undiminished security of States, and the institution of confidence-building measures pending conventional disarmament. Spain agreed that efforts for conventional disarmament should take full account of the legitimate right of self-defence.

Somalia, one of several States which remarked that the deployment of armed forces on foreign soil and in foreign military bases posed grave dangers to regional and international peace and security, said the deployment of more than 50,000 surrogate troops in various African countries to promote the strategic designs of a super-Power had serious destabilizing effects on African affairs.

Jamaica believed that conventional arms limitation and reduction should be promoted principally in the context of each region, especially in Europe, where a world-wide holocaust might be triggered. Austria likewise favoured a regional framework, seeing a particularly promising example in the Vienna negotiations on the mutual and balanced reduction of conventional forces in Europe (p. 126). Brazil, on the other hand, viewed the emphasis placed by certain military Powers and their allies on conventional disarmament as a disguise for a lack of political will to negotiate on nuclear disarmament, which had a greater priority.

Iceland expressed concern at the continuing naval arms race and remarked that some nuclear-armed submarines seemed to have no hesitation in stealthily entering the territorial waters of coastal States. The USSR believed the time was ripe for agreement to limit naval activities, especially those of powerful navies. Albania said countries should fight more vehemently against super-Power pressure and blackmail to obtain naval bases for their war fleets, which should not be allowed to enter and leave the ports of other countries even under the pretext of making friendly visits, refueling or making repairs; nor must the super-Powers be allowed to use other countries' airspace for their military aircraft.

The Libyan Arab Jamahiriya called attention to the loss of life and property still occurring in that country as a result of the occasional explosions of booby-trapped land-mines placed during the Second World War; it asked the United Nations to take a decision rewarding compensation for the losses caused (see ECONOMIC AND SOCIAL QUESTIONS, Chapter XVI).

The question of international transfer of conventional weapons occupied the attention of a large number of speakers.

Barbados quoted the report of the Independent Commission on Disarmament and Security Issues (p. 141) as saying that arms imports by developing countries had increased even more rapidly than overall military spending, having risen from $5.6 billion in 1970 to $16.1 billion in 1979. Recent annual expenditures for arms purchase by developing and developed countries were estimated at $20 billion by Saint Vincent and the Grenadines, and at some $26 billion by Bhutan and Trinidad and Tobago.

Guyana said that, according to information published in 1982 by the Stockholm International Peace Research Institute, world trade in general had grown by only 70 per cent over the past decade but the sales volume of major weapons to third world countries had increased by over 300 per cent; some third world countries were mortgaging the future of their needy populations for the acquisition of sophisticated military hardware. Fiji and Panama said 75 per cent of total global arms transfers went to the third world, while Tunisia estimated it at 70 per cent.

Bolivia observed that 12 countries were the major producers and suppliers of conventional weapons and 20 produced their own weapons and sold their surpluses, but 120 States did not produce weapons and had to satisfy their defence needs by investing resources needed for economic and social development. Fiji quoted the United States Arms Control and Disarmament Agency to the effect that the value of arms exported by developing countries and smaller industrialized countries had risen from $300 million in 1970 to $1.5 billion in 1980, while the value of arms produced in the third world had climbed from less than $1 billion to over $6 billion, representing 5 per cent of the world total. Uganda also observed that some developing countries had become significant arms producers and suppliers in their own right and called for greater efforts to halt production and sale. The USSR expressed readiness to resume talks with the United States on international arms transfers, which it said had been broken off by the other side.

Turkey said arms smuggling and illicit arms sales were conducive to the destabilization of the domestic political and social order of States and to the impairment of regional security.

Ghana said the conventional-arms race seemed to have become one of the cheapest means for the manufacturing States to make billions of dollars at the expense of poor developing countries. Iran argued likewise, holding the economic and military complexes of capitalism and socialism responsible for exploitation through the arms trade, while Yemen held the two super-Powers responsible for action that diverted resources desperately needed for development.

Panama said economic, technical, military and political dependency was being imposed on weaker nations through the network of sales, purchase and distribution of arms and military technology. The United Republic of Cameroon observed that third world countries faced interminable negotiations, intolerable pressures and sometimes even blackmail when seeking development loans but had only minor difficulties in procuring weapons. Zambia declared that the big Powers promoted tension around the world and then sold large quantities of arms to third world countries that felt themselves threatened or were actually engaged in combat with each other.

Malta said poor nations felt the pressure from advanced countries to accept costlier arms imports and the subsequent pressure to participate in regional military groupings indirectly encouraged the spread of super-Power conflict to previously untouched parts of the world. Papua New Guinea also spoke of the role of Governments of industrialized nations in aiding and abetting conventional-arms proliferation.

The Syrian Arab Republic asserted that the United States had made the Middle East a testing-ground for the sophisticated conventional weapons which it provided to Israel.

To deal with the problem, Bolivia suggested that the countries which were the largest producers and sellers of weapons regulate and limit the supply of conventional weapons to States, in accordance with regional balance and the true security needs of each country. Costa Rica called on the arms-producing countries to limit their production of conventional weapons. Singapore and the United Republic of Tanzania said action was required by both suppliers and consumers; Singapore noted, however, that there had been no follow-up to a 1978 conference of 20 Latin American countries to deal with conventional-arms control in that region. Australia said it imposed rigorous controls on arms exports to other countries and called on others to do likewise.

The need for action to curb arms transfers was mentioned by some, including Antigua and Barbuda and Uganda. Bangladesh said special levies should be imposed on all international sales of arms and the funds thus generated should be placed at the disposal of the United Nations for world-wide development purposes. The Federal Republic of Germany suggested that a possible agreement to limit arms transfers could be examined in connection with the planned study on conventional weapons (see below). Japan, expressing concern that the increasing international transfer of conventional weapons escalated the danger of regional conflicts, favoured restrictions on such transfers and proposed as a first step the international monitoring of inventories and analysis of transfers. Jamaica also urged a curb on the flow of arms to developing countries.

Letters and note verbale (nv). [1]Italy: 17 June, A/S-12/AC.1/20. Sweden: [2]27 June, A/S-12/AC.1/39; [3]7 July, A/S-12/AC.1/67 *(nv).*
Report. [4]*Ad Hoc* Committee, A/S-12/32.

Guidelines for a study by a group of experts

Following approval by the Disarmament Commission in May 1982 of guidelines for a study on conventional disarmament, the 23-member body that was to carry it out—the Group of Experts on All Aspects of the Conventional Arms Race and on Disarmament relating to Conventional Weapons and Armed Forces—was appointed by the Secretary-General and held its first two sessions. At the first of these (12-16 July), it agreed on an outline of its report and requested the Secretariat to prepare a first draft, which it reviewed at its second session (6-17 December). A final report on the study was due in 1983.

The Group had been asked to assist the Secretary-General in conducting the study in accordance with a General Assembly resolution of December 1981.[3] The decision to undertake the study had been approved in principle by the Assembly in December 1980,[2] but the Disarmament Commission had been unable to agree on the guidelines in 1981.[4]

Disarmament Commission action. Guidelines for the study on conventional disarmament were adopted by the Disarmament Commission on 28 May 1982.

The guidelines, annexed to the Commission's 1982 report,[1] outlined a general approach to the study and its scope and structure. Members of the Group of Experts were asked to include their assessments of the effects of the conventional-arms race on disarmament prospects, identify areas in which conventional disarmament ought to be pursued and make recommendations accordingly.

The guidelines stated a number of principles to be taken into account in the study's general approach, among them that: nuclear disarmament had highest priority; limitation and gradual reduction of conventional weapons should be pursued within the framework of progress towards general and complete disarmament; account should be taken of the need of all States to protect their security and the right of peoples under colonial or foreign domination to self-determination and independence; negotiations on arms reduction should have the objective of undiminished security at the lowest possible level of armaments and armed forces; the study should analyse the global dimension of the conventional-arms race while taking account of regional aspects, and should draw attention to the growing dangers of that race; disarmament agreements should include provisions for verification; and the Group should be guided by the consensus principle.

As to scope and structure, the Commission suggested that the study, among other things, identify the underlying cause and the effects of the conventional-arms race, give a factual account of all aspects, and consider the international transfer of conventional weapons, their impact in regions of tension, their use against State sovereignty and independence, the impact of technological advances, and the contribution of confidence-building measures.

General Assembly consideration (June/July). In the general debate at the General Assembly's 1982 special session on disarmament, a greater role for the United Nations in conventional disarmament was urged by New Zealand, which viewed the planned study on conventional disarmament as a useful first step in that direction. Nigeria and Portugal also expressed support for the proposed study. Belgium, for the EC members, thought the study could help in regard to problems for which the international community had not been able to find solutions; it expected to see the Committee on Disarmament pay more attention to the question of conventional weapons.

Report. [1]Disarmament Commission, A/S-12/3.
Resolutions. GA: [2]35/156 A, 12 Dec. 1980 (YUN 1980, p. 115); [3]36/97 A, 9 Dec. 1981 (YUN 1981, p. 88).
Yearbook reference. [4]1981, p. 85.

Ratification of the 1980 Convention on restrictions on certain conventional weapons

General Assembly consideration (June/July). In the general debate at the General Assembly's 1982 special session on disarmament, the 1980 Convention on Prohibitions or Restrictions on the Use of Certain Conventional Weapons Which May Be Deemed to Be Excessively Injurious or to Have Indiscriminate Effects, and its three annexed Protocols,[3] were cited by Madagascar and Somalia as the only tangible achievement in arms control since the 1978 special session, while Sweden, which ratified the instrument on 7 July 1982, called it one positive result achieved since 1978. Denmark announced that it would soon ratify and hoped all States would do likewise. Turkey welcomed the conclusion of the Convention, as did Belgium, on behalf of the EC members, which hoped that efforts would continue to complete its provisions, particularly by establishing a mechanism to ensure compliance. Egypt hoped that additional protocols would be concluded.

The Byelorussian SSR and Mongolia announced that they had ratified the Convention, and the Ukrainian SSR said the Assembly should appeal to those that had not done so to sign and ratify.

Somalia asserted that the use of napalm and other inhuman weapons against peoples struggling for their national rights in Namibia, the Horn of Africa and the Middle East was well documented. Zimbabwe expressed hope that the United Nations would establish machinery to help the victims of wars in which use was made of conventional weapons deemed to be excessively harmful or to have indiscriminate effects.

Mozambique considered the Convention and its Protocols as only a first step in the field of conventional disarmament, as did Uruguay, which saw the need to ban certain other conventional weapons not covered in the Convention.

General Assembly action (December). Recalling with satisfaction the adoption in 1980 of the Convention and its three Protocols, the General Assembly, by a resolution of 9 December 1982,[2] urged States that had not done so to become parties to the instruments so as to obtain their entry into force and, ultimately, their universal adherence. The Assembly took note of the fact that, under article 8 of the Convention, conferences might be convened to consider amendments or additional protocols for other categories of conventional weapons, or to review the scope and operation of the Convention and its Protocols. The Secretary-General, as their depositary, was requested to inform the Assembly from time to time of the state of adherence to those instruments.

The Assembly adopted this resolution without vote, following its approval by the First Committee on 23 November by a recorded vote of 123 to none. Nigeria had introduced the 23-nation draft, which was orally revised by its sponsors before approval.

An October report to the Assembly by the Secretary-General[1] contained a list of signatories and parties to the Convention and Protocols as at 31 August, as well as declarations and reservations submitted by France, Italy, Romania, the United Kingdom and the United States.

As at 31 December 1982, the following 16 States had ratified or accepted the Convention, all in 1982:

Bulgaria, Byelorussian SSR, China, Czechoslovakia, Denmark, Ecuador, Finland, German Democratic Republic, Hungary, Japan, Mexico, Mongolia, Sweden, Switzerland, Ukrainian SSR, USSR.

In addition, the following 37 States had signed but not ratified the Convention since it was opened for signature in April 1981[4] (italics indicate those signing in 1982):

Afghanistan, Argentina, *Australia*, Austria, Belgium, Canada, Cuba, Egypt, France, Germany, Federal Republic of, Greece, Iceland, India, Ireland, Italy, *Liechtenstein*, Luxembourg, Morocco, Netherlands, New Zealand, Nicaragua, *Nigeria*, Norway, *Pakistan*, Philippines, Poland, Portugal, *Romania*, Sierra Leone, Spain, Sudan, Togo, *Turkey*, United Kingdom, *United States*, Viet Nam, Yugoslavia.

All of the States which ratified or accepted the Convention also accepted each of the three Protocols.

The Convention and Protocols provided new rules for the protection of military personnel, civilians and civilian objects from injury or attack by means of incendiary weapons, land-mines, booby traps and other devices, as well as fragments that cannot be readily detected in the human body by X-rays. They were to enter into force six months after 20 States notified their consent to be bound by them through ratification, acceptance or equivalent action.

Report. [1]S-G, A/37/199 & Corr.1.
Resolution (1982). [2]GA: 37/79, 9 Dec., text following.
Yearbook references. [3]1980, p. 76; [4]1981, p. 84.
Meeting records. GA: 1st Committee, A/C.1/37/PV.3-10, 12-28, 37, *38, 41* (18 Oct.–23 Nov.); plenary, A/37/PV.98 (9 Dec.).

General Assembly resolution 37/79

9 December 1982   Meeting 98   Adopted without vote

Approved by First Committee (A/37/663) by recorded vote (123-0), 23 November (meeting 41); 23-nation draft (A/C.1/37/L.59), orally revised; agenda item 51.

Sponsors: Austria, Belgium, Cuba, Denmark, Ecuador, Egypt, Finland, France, German Democratic Republic, Greece, Ireland, Italy, Liberia, Mongolia, Netherlands, New Zealand, Nigeria, Norway, Spain, Sweden, United Kingdom, Viet Nam, Yugoslavia.

United Nations Conference on Prohibitions or Restrictions of Use of Certain Conventional Weapons Which May Be Deemed to Be Excessively Injurious or to Have Indiscriminate Effects

The General Assembly,

Recalling its resolutions 32/152 of 19 December 1977, 35/153 of 12 December 1980 and 36/93 of 9 December 1981,

Reaffirming its conviction that the suffering of civilian populations and of combatants would be significantly reduced if general agreement could be attained on the prohibition or restriction, for humanitarian reasons, of the use of specific conventional weapons, including any which may be deemed to be excessively injurious or to have indiscriminate effects,

Recalling with satisfaction the adoption, on 10 October 1980, of the Convention on Prohibitions or Restrictions on the Use of Certain Conventional Weapons Which May Be Deemed to Be Excessively Injurious or to Have Indiscriminate Effects, together with the Protocol on Non-Detectable Fragments (Protocol I), the Protocol on Prohibitions or Restrictions on the Use of Mines, Booby Traps and Other Devices (Protocol II) and the Protocol on Prohibitions or Restrictions on the Use of Incendiary Weapons (Protocol III),

Taking note with satisfaction of the report of the Secretary-General, in which indication was given that an increasing number of States had either signed or ratified the Convention, which was opened for signature in New York on 10 April 1981,

1. *Urges* those States that have not yet done so to exert their best endeavours to become parties to the Convention on Prohibitions or Restrictions on the Use of Certain Conventional Weapons Which May Be Deemed to Be Excessively Injurious or to Have Indiscriminate Effects and the Protocols annexed thereto, as early as possible, so as to obtain their entry into force and, ultimately, their universal adherence;

2. *Takes note* of the fact that, under article 8 of the Convention, conferences may be convened to consider amendments to the

Convention or any of the annexed Protocols, to consider additional protocols relating to other categories of conventional weapons not covered by the existing annexed Protocols, or to review the scope and operation of the Convention and the Protocols annexed thereto and to consider any proposal for amendments to the Convention or to the existing annexed Protocols and any proposals for additional protocols relating to other categories of conventional weapons not covered by the existing annexed Protocols;

3. *Requests* the Secretary-General, as the depositary of the Convention and its three annexed Protocols, to inform the General Assembly from time to time of the state of adherence to the said Convention and its Protocols;

4. *Decides* to include in the provisional agenda of its thirty-eighth session the item entitled "United Nations Conference on Prohibitions or Restrictions of Use of Certain Conventional Weapons Which May Be Deemed to Be Excessively Injurious or to Have Indiscriminate Effects".

Other aspects of disarmament and related matters

Military budgets and expenditures

The amount of the world's resources devoted to armaments and armed forces was examined from several angles during 1982, at the General Assembly's special session on disarmament and at its regular session. Formulae to reduce military expenditures were discussed and work continued towards a standardized reporting procedure intended eventually to give an internationally comparable picture of what each nation spends on its military sector (see below). These expenditures were also examined from the broader standpoint of ways in which disarmament could aid development, as well as the overall economic and social consequences of the arms race.

In the general debate at the special session in June and July, the magnitude of world military expenditures in comparison to other basic outlays and needs was stressed by many speakers. Antigua and Barbuda, Barbados and Panama cited the report of the Independent Commission on Disarmament and Security Issues (p. 141) to the effect that total military spending amounted to over $650 billion in 1982, or more than the entire income of 1.5 billion people living in the 50 poorest countries. Japan and Qatar observed that this was 6 per cent of total world product, Japan adding that the total had risen from the $400-billion level in 1978, when the first special session devoted to disarmament had been held. According to Iran, the military expenditures of the developing countries had increased four and a half times during the past 20 years, while their gross national product had not even tripled. Yemen quoted a World Bank estimate that, at the average annual increase of 3 per cent recorded during the previous 20 years, world military expenditure in the year 2000 would reach $940 billion at 1980 prices.

Botswana warned that there could be no security in a world of starving masses and escalating military expenditures. Fiji viewed it as a sign of moral decadence that so much was spent for military purposes in a world where basic human needs were denied to most of the population. Kenya saw no justification for a continued squandering of scarce resources on military expenditure, and Mauritania said the choice lay between a decent life for the poorest and death for all.

Cuba asserted that the United States military budget, $105 billion in 1978, had more than doubled and, according to announced plans, would almost double again within four years. The German Democratic Republic said it was a matter of alarm that the United States was planning to spend $1,600 billion on armaments over the following five years. The United States asserted that the decade of so-called détente had witnessed a 40 per cent increase in USSR military spending and a decline in the same real terms in the American counterpart.

Proposed reduction of military budgets

Disarmament Commission consideration. In 1982, the Disarmament Commission continued consideration of two aspects of the reduction of military budgets: harmonization of views on their gradual, agreed reduction and the reallocation to economic and social development of resources thus saved; and examination and identification of ways to achieve verifiable agreements to freeze, reduce or otherwise restrain military expenditures in a balanced manner.

Discussion in a working group, set up for that purpose on 17 May, revolved around a background paper containing a number of proposed guiding principles. Among other things, the paper—annexed to the Commission's May report to the General Assembly at its special session on disarmament[2]—called for concluding international agreements, with verification measures, to freeze and reduce military budgets at the lowest possible level of military forces and armaments. It asserted that the freezing and reduction should begin with militarily significant States, mentioned the importance of transparency of military budgets and a standardized expenditure-reporting system, and suggested that the United Nations play a central role in orienting and stimulating negotiations on this topic. The Commission did not have time to discuss a working paper of 20 May by India[4] which proposed that the Commission, rather than explore and elaborate governing principles, should identify specific steps for action on the basis of already established principles.

The exchange of views, as summarized in a text adopted by the Commission on 28 May and included in its report, revealed serious concern among States over the implications of the arms race and growing military expenditures, a general understanding of the need for international agreements on the reduction of such expenditures and a divergence of views on the way to achieve that goal. The Commission recommended that the General Assembly should request the Commission to continue, at its next substantive sessions, consideration of the reduction of military budgets, with a view to identifying and elaborating the principles which should govern further actions of States on freezing and reducing military expenditures, keeping in mind the possibility of embodying such principles in a suitable document at an appropriate stage.

General Assembly consideration (June/July). The draft comprehensive programme of disarmament, considered at the General Assembly's special session on disarmament, contained several references to military budgets and the need to reduce them.[1]

The introduction, prepared by a Working Group Chairman, contrasted the hundreds of billions of dollars spent annually on weapons with the poverty of two thirds of the world's people, and mentioned the diversion of technical and human resources to military purposes. In the chapter on disarmament measures, a section on military expenditures contained seven paragraphs, only one of which was without square brackets indicating text on which agreement had not been reached. The paragraph to which no objection had been raised said that the gradual reduction of military budgets on a mutually agreed basis, for example in absolute figures or percentages, particularly by nuclear-weapon and other militarily significant States, would contribute to curbing the arms race and would increase the possibility of reallocating resources to economic and social development, particularly of developing countries. Consensus was not reached on paragraphs proposing more specific measures, for which several alternative texts remained.

In the general debate at the special session, Egypt called for agreement on an annual percentage reduction of military expenditures and on transfer of the savings to development purposes. Fiji appealed for a freeze or cut-backs in military budgets by both developed and developing countries, with the savings directed to the world's neediest.

Nigeria believed that reductions should begin with the nuclear-weapon States, followed by other militarily significant States and then by others. Romania proposed the freezing of military expenditures at the 1982 level and their reduction by 10 to 15 per cent by 1985; 30 to 50 per cent of the funds thus saved should be used to support the efforts of the developing countries and the rest used to create new jobs and carry out economic and so-

cial measures in the countries making the reductions. Togo favoured a freeze and reduction of military budgets of all countries, including the developing countries, and the Upper Volta saw need for an effective control machinery for the reduction of such budgets. Calls for reduction of military budgets were also made by Angola, Hungary, Iraq and Mauritius.

Afghanistan supported, and Mozambique noted the importance of, proposals by the Eastern European socialist countries for reduction of the military budgets of States, especially the permanent members of the Security Council, in order to release resources for economic and social development.

Belgium favoured the limitation of military budgets to what was strictly needed for essential security. Portugal suggested that the more militarily powerful States set an example by agreeing to reduce military expenditures to levels compatible with their security, subject to verification.

General Assembly action (December). By a resolution adopted without vote on 13 December,[3] the General Assembly reiterated the need to reinforce action regarding reduction of military budgets, with a view to reaching international agreements to freeze, reduce or otherwise restrain military expenditures. It urged States, in particular the most heavily armed, pending agreement on reductions, to exercise self-restraint in their military expenditures with a view to reallocating the funds thus saved to economic and social development, particularly for developing countries. The Assembly requested the Disarmament Commission to continue consideration of the question in 1983, keeping in mind the possibility of embodying in a suitable document the governing principles for the freezing and reduction of military expenditures.

The First Committee had approved the 16-nation text without vote on 22 November, as introduced by Romania.

Reports. [1]*Ad Hoc* Committee, A/S-12/32; [2]Disarmament Commission, A/S-12/3.
Resolution (1982). [3]GA: 37/95 A, 13 Dec., text following.
Working paper. [4]India, A/CN.10/35.
Meeting records. GA: plenary, A/S-12/PV.2-26, 28, 29 (8 June-10 July), A/37/PV.101 (13 Dec.); *Ad Hoc* Committee, A/S-12/AC.1/PV.9, 10 (28, 29 June); 1st Committee, A/C.1/37/PV.3-10, 12-28, *34, 39,* 45 (18 Oct.-26 Nov.).

General Assembly resolution 37/95 A

13 December 1982   Meeting 101   Adopted without vote

Approved by First Committee (A/37/652) without vote, 22 November (meeting 39); 16-nation draft (A/C.1/37/L.20); agenda item 40.

Sponsors: Austria, Bangladesh, Colombia, Costa Rica, Ecuador, Indonesia, Ireland, Mali, Nigeria, Peru, Romania, Rwanda, Senegal, Sudan, Sweden, Uruguay.

The General Assembly,

Expressing its deep concern about the ever-spiralling arms race and growing military expenditures, which constitute a heavy burden for the economies of all nations and have extremely harmful effects on world peace and security,

Recalling that at its twelfth special session, the second special session devoted to disarmament, all Member States unanimously and categorically reaffirmed the validity of the Final Document of the Tenth Special Session of the General Assembly, the first special session devoted to disarmament, as well as their solemn commitment to it,

Reaffirming the provisions of the Final Document of the Tenth Special Session of the General Assembly, according to which the gradual reduction of military budgets on a mutually agreed basis, for example in absolute figures or in terms of percentage points, particularly by nuclear-weapon States and other militarily significant States, would be a measure that would contribute to curbing the arms race and would increase the possibilities for the reallocation of resources now being used for military purposes to economic and social development, particularly for the benefit of the developing countries,

Recalling also the Declaration of the 1980s as the Second Disarmament Decade, in which it is provided that during this period renewed efforts should be made to reach agreement on the reduction of military expenditures and the reallocation of resources thus saved to economic and social development, especially for the benefit of developing countries,

Recalling further its resolution 34/83 F of 11 December 1979, in which it considered that a new impetus should be given to endeavours to achieve agreements to freeze, reduce or otherwise restrain, in a balanced manner, military expenditures, including adequate measures of verification satisfactory to all parties concerned,

Having considered the report of the Disarmament Commission on the work accomplished during its session in 1982 on the question of the reduction of military budgets,

Convinced that the identification and elaboration of a set of principles that should govern further actions of States in freezing and reducing military budgets could contribute to harmonizing the views of States and create confidence among them conducive to achieving international agreements on the reduction of military budgets,

Considering that the identification and elaboration of the principles that should govern further actions of States in freezing and reducing military budgets and the other current activities within the framework of the United Nations related to the question of the reduction of military budgets should be regarded as having the fundamental objective of reaching international agreements on the reduction of military expenditures,

Aware of the various proposals submitted by Member States and of the activities carried out so far within the framework of the United Nations in the field of the reduction of military budgets,

1. *Declares once again its conviction* that it is possible to achieve international agreements on reduction of military budgets without prejudice to the right of all States to undiminished security, self-defence and sovereignty;

2. *Reaffirms* that human and material resources released through the reduction of military expenditures could be reallocated to economic and social development, especially for the benefit of the developing countries;

3. *Reiterates* the urgent need to reinforce the endeavours of all States and international action in the reduction of military budgets, with a view to reaching international agreements to freeze, reduce or otherwise restrain military expenditures;

4. *Urges* all States, in particular the most heavily armed States, pending the conclusion of agreements on the reduction of military expenditures, to exercise self-restraint in their military expenditures with a view to reallocating the funds thus saved to economic and social development, especially for the benefit of developing countries;

5. *Requests* the Disarmament Commission to continue, at its session in 1983, the consideration of the item entitled "Reduction of military budgets", including consideration of the background paper as well as other proposals and ideas on that subject, with a view to identifying and elaborating the principles that should govern further actions of States in freezing and reducing military expenditures, keeping in mind the possibility of embodying such principles in a suitable document at an appropriate stage;

6. *Also requests* the Disarmament Commission to consider, at its next substantive session, other proposals and ideas, as well as recommendations submitted by Member States, for reducing military budgets;

7. *Decides* to include in the provisional agenda of its thirty-eighth session the item entitled "Reduction of military budgets".

Reporting procedures

Report of the Group of Experts. The Group of Experts on the Reduction of Military Budgets, appointed by the Secretary-General at the request of the General Assembly in 1980,[7] submitted in March 1982 a report proposing steps to improve procedures followed by States in reporting their military expenditures to the United Nations.[3] The eight-member Group held four sessions between February 1981 and March 1982, the last of which was from 1 to 12 March 1982 in New York.

The report, which the Group adopted unanimously, consisted of a preface, summary conclusions and recommendations, an introduction, and three chapters dealing with reporting by States, intertemporal and international comparisons, and verification problems.

The Group considered that the initial reporting system devised in 1980 by the *Ad Hoc* Panel on Military Budgeting,[9] enabling Member States to report their military expenditures on a standard form, was viable and practical, and concluded that its wider and continuous use would permit a better assessment of its general usefulness with a view to future agreement on reduction of military expenditures. It suggested revised general guidelines for States to use in filling out the form.

The Group noted the need to develop price deflators applicable to the military sector in each country and a set of parities reflecting the relative purchasing power of different currencies, in order to facilitate estimates in constant prices and allow for accurate comparisons of military expenditures among different States. It believed that, given a common understanding on the construction of such a tool, it should be possible to resolve the technical problems in a way satisfactory to all parties.

Pointing to the need for a verification system to ensure compliance by all parties, the Group said verification might require the use of techniques applying to both physical quantities and financial outlays, and reliable assessments might involve a relatively high degree of political understanding and confidence. It added that negotiations on the reduction of military expenditures should proceed on the basis that no State's security would be diminished, and could lead to regional, subregional and global agreements.

In addition to recommending continued use of the reporting instrument by an increasing number of States from different geographic regions and with different budgeting and accounting systems, the Group recommended to the General Assembly that the Secretary-General, assisted by a group of experts and with the voluntary co-operation of States, should construct price indices and purchasing-power parities for the military expenditures of participating States.

General Assembly consideration (June/July). In the general debate at the General Assembly's 1982 special session on disarmament, the United States proposed an international conference on military expenditures that would build on United Nations work in developing a common accounting and reporting system; it urged the USSR to join that effort and to revise what the United States called the universally discredited official figures published by that country. Further details on this proposal were transmitted by a letter from the United States to the Secretary-General dated 28 June,[2] suggesting that the proposed conference consider modalities for encouraging wider participation in the United Nations reporting system, possible refinement of the standard reporting instrument, means for publicizing the submission of data, and ways in which accurate military expenditure information could be disseminated and used to promote peace and international stability.

Sweden, in a letter dated 27 June,[1] proposed that work continue on methods of comparing military expenditures, and that a study be made on the problem of constructing price indices and purchasing-power parities for the military expenditures of States, as recommended by the Group of Experts.

The draft comprehensive programme of disarmament, considered at the special session, contained a paragraph in its chapter on disarmament and development proposing that States make public data on their use of resources for military purposes.[4] However, agreement was not reached on the wording of this paragraph.

Several Western countries spoke during the general debate of the need for effective reporting procedures on military budgets. Belgium, on behalf of the European Community members, called for wider use and further improvement of the United Nations standard reporting instrument. The Federal Republic of Germany, joined by the Netherlands and Portugal, called for greater openness in disclosing military expenditure, as a first step on the path towards establishing comparability; otherwise, they argued, agreements on verifiable reductions in military budgets were inconceivable or would remain at a declaratory stage. Ireland said there was need to work out methods for calculating military budgets and arms expenditure on a common, universally accepted basis, leading to their reduction on all sides on a graduated basis. Mauritius proposed that further development of the United Nations reporting instrument be undertaken by the United Nations Institute for Disarmament Research (p. 154), which could also sponsor the conference proposed by the United States.

Norway hoped that more countries would make use of the United Nations reporting system. Portugal suggested that information be provided on military research and development expenditures and that ways be found to make such data comparable, with a view to limiting innovations in military technology.

Report of the Secretary-General. The second annual report by the Secretary-General containing information on military expenditures supplied on a voluntary basis by United Nations Member States was issued in 1982,[5] as requested by the General Assembly in December 1981.[8] Of the 23 countries which submitted information through early November, 17 did so by filling in a matrix, or table, which was the key element in the standard reporting instrument. This was designed to show how much each force group (such as land, naval and air forces) spent on each resource category (such as personnel and procurement).

General Assembly action (December). By a resolution of 13 December,[6] the General Assembly stressed the need to increase the number of reporting States with a view to the broadest possible participation from different geographic regions and budgeting systems. The Assembly requested the Secretary-General to solicit, and report to the Assembly in 1983, the views of Member States on means to that end. Reiterating its recommendation that all Member States report their military expenditures to the Secretary-General by 30 April of each year, it requested him to circulate, for their 1983 reporting, the instrument as revised according to the suggestions of the Group of Experts. Further, the Assembly requested him, with the aid of a group of experts, to construct price indices and purchasing-power parities for the military expenditures of participating States, and to ascertain the willingness of States to take part in the exercise. He was asked to make the collection and assembling of military expenditure data an integral part of United Nations statistical services.

The resolution was adopted by a recorded vote of 96 to 13, with 9 abstentions. The First Committee had approved the draft on 26 November, as revised by its 23 sponsors, by a recorded vote of 98 to 13, with 8 abstentions.

Introducing the text, Sweden stressed that the reporting exercise was aimed not at providing better statistics but at promoting international agreements to restrain military expenditures. To negotiate such agreements, States would need to know what military expenditures were and how they could be reported. It was therefore important to improve the system by a continuous and growing participation.

In explanation of its negative vote, the USSR said the resolution diverted attention from the increase in military budgets and brought the reduction of such budgets to an impasse; whereas the USSR was ready for specific reduction measures based on either percentages or absolute amounts, some States refused practical arrangements and sought instead to establish a control system over military budgets.

Brazil abstained in the belief that the nuclear-weapon and other militarily significant States had the primary responsibility to take concrete measures to reduce their military budgets and make use of the reporting instrument. Brazil's reservation as regards the $2-million estimate of costs relating to the project (mainly the value of conference services to be provided to the expert group) was shared by the Netherlands and the United Kingdom, both of which, none the less, voted in favour.

The Netherlands added that the question of adequately verifiable reduction of military budgets deserved serious consideration but did not command immediate urgency, as the measures envisaged could not focus on the most destabilizing and threatening weapons systems; the exercise should be reviewed, since it was clear that the States of one group refused to report their military expenditures. Noting with disappointment the lack of participation by any Warsaw Pact country, the United Kingdom saw the need for a generally accepted procedure for the comparison of military expenditures as a means of arriving at balanced and verifiable agreements to reduce such expenditures but thought it difficult to justify the proposed study unless there was more balanced participation in reporting.

Letters. [1]Sweden, 27 June, A/S-12/AC.1/39; [2]United States, 28 June, A/S-12/AC.1/52.
Publication. [3]*Reduction of Military Budgets. Refinement of International Reporting and Comparison of Military Expenditures* (A/S-12/7), Sales No. E.83.IX.4.
Reports. [4]*Ad Hoc* Committee, A/S-12/32. [5]S-G, A/37/418 & Corr.1 & Add.1.
Resolution (1982). [6]GA: 37/95 B, 13 Dec., text following.
Resolutions (prior). GA: [7]35/142 B, 12 Dec. 1980 (YUN 1980, p. 88); [8]36/82 B, 9 Dec. 1981 (YUN 1981, p. 92).
Yearbook reference. [9]1980, p. 78.
Financial implications. ACABQ report, A/37/7/Add.16; 5th Committee report, A/37/730; S-G statements, A/C.1/37/L.70, A/C.5/37/76.
Meeting records. GA: plenary, A/S-12/PV.2-26, 28, 29 (8 June–10 July), A/37/PV.101 (13 Dec.); *Ad Hoc* Committee, A/S-12/AC.1/PV.10, 12 (29 June, 2 July); 1st Committee, A/C.1/37/PV.3-10, 12-28, *34, 42, 45* (18 Oct.–26 Nov.); 5th Committee, A/C.5/37/SR.62 (10 Dec.).

General Assembly resolution 37/95 B

13 December 1982   Meeting 101   96-13-9 (recorded vote)

Approved by First Committee (A/37/652) by recorded vote (98-13-8), 26 November (meeting 45); 23-nation draft (A/C.1/37/L.22/Rev.2); agenda item 40.

Sponsors: Austria, Bangladesh, Belgium, Canada, Colombia, Costa Rica, Ecuador, Finland, France, Germany, Federal Republic of, Indonesia, Ireland, Italy, Malta, Mexico, New Zealand, Nigeria, Norway, Rómania, Rwanda, Sudan, Sweden, Uruguay.

The General Assembly,

Deeply concerned about the arms race and present tendencies to increase further the rate of growth of military expenditures, the deplorable waste of human and economic resources and the potentially harmful effects on world peace and security,

Considering that a gradual reduction of military expenditures on a mutually agreed basis would be a measure that would contribute to curbing the arms race and would increase the possibilities of reallocating resources now being used for military purposes to economic and social development, especially for the benefit of the developing countries,

Convinced that such reductions could and should be carried out on a mutually agreed basis without detriment to the national security of any country,

Reaffirming its conviction that provisions for defining, reporting, comparing and verifying military expenditures will have to be basic elements of any international agreement to reduce such expenditures,

Recalling that an international system for the standardized reporting of military expenditures has been introduced in pursuance of General Assembly resolution 35/142 B of 12 December 1980 and that annual reports on military expenditures are now being received from a number of Member States,

Considering that a wider participation in the reporting system would promote its further refinement and would, by contributing to greater openness in military matters, increase confidence between States,

Considering that new initiatives are called for to give a fresh impetus towards achievement of the broadest possible participation, by States from different geographic regions and representing different budgeting systems, in the reporting of military expenditures to the Secretary-General,

Noting that among such initiatives is a proposal to convene an International conference on military. expenditures,

Noting with appreciation that, in pursuance of resolution 35/142 B, the Secretary-General has submitted his report on the reduction of military budgets, which deals, *inter alia*, with the question of comparing and verifying military expenditures and contains several useful conclusions and recommendations for the promotion of further progress in this field,

Considering also that the study of this question should be followed by a practical exercise in order to explore it further with a view to facilitating future negotiations on the reduction of military expenditures,

Emphasizing that all the above-mentioned activities and initiatives, as well as other ongoing activities within the United Nations related to the reduction of military budgets, should have the fundamental objective of facilitating future negotiations aimed at the conclusion of international agreements on the reduction of military expenditures,

1. *Stresses* the need to increase the number of reporting States with a view to the broadest possible participation from different geographic regions and representing different budgeting systems and requests the Secretary-General to invite Member States to submit their views and suggestions on practical means of promoting this goal and to report to the General Assembly at its thirty-eighth session on the results of this consultation;

2. *Reiterates its recommendation* that all Member States should report annually, by 30 April, to the Secretary-General, using the reporting instrument, their military expenditures for the latest fiscal year for which data are available;

3. *Requests* the Secretary-General to modify the instructions of the reporting instrument in the manner suggested in paragraph 59 of his report and to circulate this revised instrument among all Member States so that they may use it in their reporting in 1983;

4. *Requests* the Secretary-General to make the collecting and assembling of data on military expenditures, reported by States on the basis of the reporting instrument, an integral part of his normal statistical services and to arrange and publish these data according to statistical practice;

5. *Requests* the Secretary-General, with the assistance of a group of qualified experts* and with the voluntary co-operation of States, to undertake the task of constructing price indices and purchasing-power parities for the military expenditures of participating States; this task should encompass a study of the problem as a whole, which would include the following:

*(a)*To assess the feasibility of such an exercise;

*(b)*To design the project and methodology to be employed;

*(c)*To determine the types of data required, such as product descriptions, prices and statistical weights;

*(d)*To construct military price indices and purchasing-power parities;

6. *Requests* the Secretary-General to ascertain the willingness of States to participate and to enlist their voluntary co-operation;

7. *Invites* Member States to participate in the above-mentioned exercise;

8. *Requests* the Secretary-General to submit progress reports to the General Assembly at its thirty-eighth and thirty-ninth sessions and a final report to the Assembly at its fortieth session;

9. *Also requests* the Secretary-General to provide the group of experts with the necessary assistance and secretariat services;

10. *Further requests* the Secretary-General to make the necessary arrangements for the report on the reduction of military budgets to be issued as a United Nations publication and to be widely distributed;

11. *Decides* to include in the provisional agenda of its thirty-eighth session the item entitled "Reduction of military budgets".

---

*Subsequently referred to as the Group of Experts on the Comparison of Military Budgets.

Recorded vote in Assembly as follows:

In favour: Australia, Austria, Bahamas, Bahrain, Bangladesh, Barbados, Belgium, Benin, Bhutan, Bolivia, Burundi, Canada, Chile, Colombia, Comoros, Cyprus, Democratic Kampuchea, Denmark, Djibouti, Dominican Republic, Ecuador, El Salvador, Fiji, Finland, France, Gabon, Germany, Federal Republic of, Greece, Guinea, Guyana, Haiti, Honduras, Iceland, Indonesia, Iraq, Ireland, Israel, Italy, Jamaica, Japan, Jordan, Kuwait, Lebanon, Lesotho, Liberia, Luxembourg, Madagascar, Malawi, Malaysia, Mali, Malta, Mauritania, Mexico, Morocco, Nepal, Netherlands, New Zealand, Nigeria, Norway, Oman, Pakistan, Panama, Papua New Guinea, Paraguay, Peru, Portugal, Qatar, Romania, Rwanda, Saudi Arabia, Senegal, Sierra Leone, Singapore, Somalia, Spain, Sri Lanka, Sudan, Suriname, Sweden, Syrian Arab Republic, Thailand, Togo, Trinidad and Tobago, Tunisia, Turkey, United Arab Emirates, United Kingdom, United Republic of Cameroon, United Republic of Tanzania, United States, Upper Volta, Uruguay, Venezuela, Yemen, Yugoslavia, Zaire.

Against: Afghanistan, Bulgaria, Byelorussian SSR, Cuba, German Democratic Republic, Grenada, Hungary, Lao People's Democratic Republic, Mongolia, Poland, Ukrainian SSR, USSR, Viet Nam.

Abstaining: Angola, Argentina, Brazil, China, Congo, Ghana, India, Mozambique, Zambia.

Environmental aspects of the arms race

A report by the Secretary-General entitled "Protection of nature from the pernicious effects of the arms race"[2] was presented to the General Assembly in April 1982 for consideration at its second special session on disarmament.

Prepared in response to Assembly requests of October 1980[5] and October 1981,[6] the report analysed the responses of 50 Governments, as at 30 March 1982, to a letter from the Executive Director of the United Nations Environment Programme (UNEP), who had solicited their views on international measures for the protection of nature. Also in the report was a summary of three studies on the environmental effects of military activity, which had been transmitted to Governments along with the letter, and the conclusions reached at a high-level expert group meeting, convened by the Executive Director at Geneva in 1982, on the historical responsibility of States for the preservation of the environment for current and future generations. The report concluded with some recommendations.

Views of Governments on the question varied widely. Most of the developed countries which responded opposed UNEP involvement, while the replies from developing countries visualized a role

for it. Some made specific comments on the studies transmitted to them, namely, a chapter on the environmental effects of military activity in the Executive Director's report on the state of the environment in 1980, a UNEP study entitled "Effects of weapons on ecosystems", and a draft chapter on peace, security and the environment from a report on the state of the world environment, 1972-1982.

These studies pointed out that, while the direct impact on man and his settlements, food and environment had in one form or another been familiar features of wars through the centuries, wars had become increasingly disruptive of the environment. The questions of disarmament, development and environmental protection were closely linked. A full-scale nuclear war would destroy all major cities in the northern hemisphere, would kill many millions in the southern hemisphere by radiation from fall-out and would also cause long-term consequences harmful to man and ecosystems. Chemical and biological weapons involved deliberate pollution by the release of toxic chemicals and disturbed the ecological balance, and the possibility existed of causing economic or other damage to the enemy population through environmental modification. Other threats to ecosystems and the environment were posed by the disposal of obsolete weapon stocks, including chemical weapons, and of high-level radioactive wastes, as well as by refugee migrations.

The expert group, meeting at Geneva, concluded that general and complete disarmament should remain the ultimate goal of arms control and disarmament negotiations. Of great concern was the military use of space for technologies which supported war-fighting capabilities with great potential for environmental destruction, and the pollution of outer space by increasing debris from military and other satellites. Other areas of concern included the waste of limited resources spent on the military, including raw materials, land, and scientific and intellectual effort; nuclear-weapon tests that vented radioactivity into the atmosphere; possible accidents involving military research into biological agents; and long-term effects on the sustainable resource base for development.

The Secretary-General suggested to the Assembly a number of measures, among them the possibility of demilitarizing ecologically important regions and converting them to protected areas, the establishment of a network of scientific institutions for information dissemination and evaluation of the impacts of military activity on the environment, a comprehensive nuclear-test ban, and consideration at the Review Conference of the Parties to the Convention on the Prohibition of Military or Any Other Hostile Use of Environmental

Modification Techniques, envisaged for 1983, of the possibility of banning anti-plant chemical warfare and of strengthening the Convention to ban all hostile uses of environmental manipulation techniques.

Also transmitted to the Assembly at its special session was the text of a resolution adopted by the UNEP Governing Council on 18 May 1982 on "Arms and the environment".[4] It contained an appeal to Governments and the international community to strive to halt the arms race and thereby prevent a major threat to the environment (see ECONOMIC AND SOCIAL QUESTIONS, Chapter XVI).

Sweden, in a working paper annexed to a letter to the Secretary-General dated 27 June,[1] proposed that the Secretary-General, in co-operation with UNEP, be requested to undertake continuing assessment, monitoring and evaluation of the impact of military activities on the environment.

A call for avoidance of military activities damaging to nature was contained in the World Charter for Nature,[3] adopted by the General Assembly on 28 October.

Letter. [1]Sweden, 27 June, A/S-12/AC.1/39.
Report. [2]S-G, A/S-12/9.
Resolutions (1982). [3]GA: 37/7, annex, para. 20, 28 Oct.; [4]UNEP Council (report, A/37/25): III, 18 May (transmitted by S-G note, A/S-12/AC.1/16).
Resolutions (prior). GA: [5]35/8, 30 Oct. 1980 (YUN 1980, p. 725); [6]36/7, 27 Oct. 1981 (YUN 1981, p. 836).

Preparations for the Review Conference on the Convention to prohibit the hostile use of environmental modification

By a resolution of 13 December 1982,[2] the General Assembly noted plans to convene, at the earliest practicable time after 5 October 1983, the Review Conference of the Parties to the Convention on the Prohibition of Military or Any Other Hostile Use of Environmental Modification Techniques. At that date, the Convention[3] would have been in force for five years. The Assembly further noted that the Secretary-General, as depositary of the Convention, would consult with the parties concerning the Conference and its preparation, including the establishment of a Preparatory Committee. While the Conference would make arrangements for meeting its costs, including those for the preparatory work, the Assembly requested the Secretary-General to provide assistance and services.

The resolution was adopted by a recorded vote of 135 to none, with 7 abstentions. The First Committee had approved on 26 November, by a recorded vote of 117 to none, with 7 abstentions, the 17-nation draft, introduced by Finland.

As at 31 December 1982, the Convention, which entered into force on 5 October 1978, had been ratified, acceded to or succeeded to by 38 States, as follows (States in italics adhered in 1982):

Bangladesh, *Belgium*, Bulgaria, Byelorussian SSR, Canada, Cape Verde, Cuba, Cyprus, Czechoslovakia, Democratic Yemen, Denmark, *Egypt*, Finland, German Democratic Republic, Ghana, Hungary, India, *Ireland*, Italy, *Japan*, Kuwait, Lao People's Democratic Republic, Malawi, Mongolia, Norway, Papua New Guinea, Poland, Sao Tome and Principe, Solomon Islands, Spain, Sri Lanka, Tunisia, Ukrainian SSR, USSR, United Kingdom, United States, Viet Nam, Yemen.

A review of the need for a further prohibition of military or any other hostile use of environmental modification techniques, with a view to adopting further measures to eliminate the danger to mankind from such use, was called for in the disarmament measures chapter of the draft comprehensive programme of disarmament transmitted to the Assembly at its special session on disarmament by the Committee on Disarmament.[1] The provision remained unchanged following its consideration at the special session.

Report. [1]Committee on Disarmament, A/S-12/2.
Resolution (1982). [2]GA: 37/99 I, 13 Dec., text following.
Resolution (prior). [3]GA: 31/72, annex, 10 Dec. 1976 (YUN 1976, p. 45).
Meeting records. GA: 1st Committee, A/C.1/37/PV.3-10, 12-28, 37, 45 (18 Oct.–26 Nov.); plenary, A/37/PV.101 (13 Dec.).

General Assembly resolution 37/99 I

13 December 1982   Meeting 101   135-0-7 (recorded vote)

Approved by First Committee (A/37/667) by recorded vote (117-0-7), 26 November (meeting 45); 17-nation draft (A/C.1/37/L.57); agenda item 55.

Sponsors: Bangladesh, Belgium, Bulgaria, Canada, Czechoslovakia, Denmark, Egypt, Finland, German Democratic Republic, Italy, Japan, Malawi, Norway, Sao Tome and Principe, Spain, United Kingdom, United States.

Review Conference of the Parties to the Convention on the Prohibition of Military or Any Other Hostile Use of Environmental Modification Techniques

The General Assembly,

Recalling its resolution 31/72 of 10 December 1976, in which it referred the Convention on the Prohibition of Military or Any Other Hostile Use of Environmental Modification Techniques to all States for their consideration, signature and ratification and expressed the hope for the widest possible adherence to the Convention,

Noting that paragraph 1 of article VIII of the Convention provides that:

"Five years after the entry into force of this Convention, a conference of the States Parties to the Convention shall be convened by the Depositary at Geneva, Switzerland. The conference shall review the operation of the Convention with a view to ensuring that its purposes and provisions are being realized, and shall in particular examine the effectiveness of the provisions of paragraph 1 of article I in eliminating the dangers of military or any other hostile use of environmental modification techniques",

Bearing in mind that the Convention will have been in force for five years on 5 October 1983,

1. *Notes* that the Secretary-General, as depositary of the Convention, intends to convene the Review Conference of the Parties to the Convention on the Prohibition of Military or Any Other Hostile Use of Environmental Modification Techniques called for in paragraph 1 of article VIII of the Convention at the earliest practicable time after 5 October 1983 and that, to that end, he will hold consultations with the parties to the Convention with regard to questions relating to the Conference and its preparation, including the establishment of a Preparatory Committee for the Conference;

2. *Requests* the Secretary-General to render the necessary assistance and to provide such services, including summary records, as may be required for the Review Conference and its preparation;

3. *Also notes* that arrangements for meeting the costs of the Review Conference and its preparation are to be made by the Conference.

Recorded vote in Assembly as follows:

In favour: Afghanistan, Angola, Australia, Austria, Bahamas, Bahrain, Bangladesh, Barbados, Belgium, Benin, Bhutan, Bolivia, Botswana, Brazil, Bulgaria, Burma, Burundi, Byelorussian SSR, Canada, Central African Republic, Chad, Chile, Comoros, Congo, Costa Rica, Cuba, Cyprus, Czechoslovakia, Democratic Kampuchea, Democratic Yemen, Denmark, Djibouti, Dominican Republic, Egypt, El Salvador, Equatorial Guinea, Ethiopia, Fiji, Finland, Gabon, German Democratic Republic, Germany, Federal Republic of, Ghana, Greece, Grenada, Guatemala, Guinea, Guinea-Bissau, Guyana, Haiti, Honduras, Hungary, Iceland, India, Indonesia, Iran, Iraq, Ireland, Israel, Italy, Japan, Jordan, Kenya, Kuwait, Lao People's Democratic Republic, Lebanon, Lesotho, Liberia, Libyan Arab Jamahiriya, Luxembourg, Madagascar, Malawi, Malaysia, Maldives, Mali, Malta, Mauritania, Mauritius, Mongolia, Morocco, Mozambique, Nepal, Netherlands, New Zealand, Nicaragua, Niger, Nigeria, Norway, Oman, Pakistan, Panama, Papua New Guinea, Paraguay, Philippines, Poland, Portugal, Qatar, Romania, Rwanda, Saint Lucia, Sao Tome and Principe, Saudi Arabia, Senegal, Sierra Leone, Singapore, Solomon Islands, Somalia, Spain, Sri Lanka, Sudan, Suriname, Swaziland, Sweden, Syrian Arab Republic, Thailand, Togo, Trinidad and Tobago, Tunisia, Turkey, Uganda, Ukrainian SSR, USSR, United Arab Emirates, United Kingdom, United Republic of Cameroon, United Republic of Tanzania, United States, Upper Volta, Uruguay, Vanuatu, Viet Nam, Yemen, Yugoslavia, Zaire, Zambia.

Against: None.

Abstaining: Argentina, Colombia, Ecuador, Jamaica, Mexico, Peru, Venezuela.

Prevention of an arms race in outer space and prohibition of anti-satellite systems

Consideration by the Committee on Disarmament. In 1982, the Committee on Disarmament inscribed on its agenda for the year a new item entitled "Prevention of an arms race in outer space". It acted in response to December 1981 requests by the General Assembly that it consider negotiating an agreement to prohibit anti-satellite systems[9] and begin negotiations on a treaty to prevent the spread of the arms race to outer space.[10] The Committee discussed the question at informal meetings on 30 March and 7 April 1982 and at plenary meetings from 30 August to 1 September.

Proposals before the Committee included the text of a nine-article draft treaty by the USSR to prohibit the stationing of weapons of any kind in outer space, originally submitted to the General Assembly in August 1981,[11] and a working paper by Canada on "Arms control and outer space", which took the position that, while it seemed desirable to prevent anti-satellite measures because most military satellites tended to have stabilizing effects, the difficulties in the way of a workable agreement were formidable, especially in respect of verification.

According to the Committee's 1982 report to the Assembly,[3] three different approaches were suggested during the discussions. Some (a group of Western countries) considered it necessary to establish priorities and suggested that, as a first step, the Committee should consider negotiating an effective and verifiable agreement prohibiting anti-satellite systems. Others (a group of socialist countries) called for the conclusion of agreements banning all types of weapons in outer space, not excluding only aggressive or offensive activities or devices such as anti-satellite systems. The Group of 21 believed that the aim of the negotiations should be to conclude an agreement or agreements to prevent an arms race in outer space in all aspects.

The Committee considered proposals for the establishment of an *ad hoc* working group on the subject. Several members supported a Mongolian proposal to have such a group negotiate and agree on a text for an international treaty on the prevention of an arms race in outer space. Others felt the group should begin by working on an agreement on anti-satellite systems. The Group of 21 proposed that the working group negotiate one or more agreements on the prevention of an arms race in outer space in all aspects. Still another view was that the Committee should continue discussing current and future proposals so as to sharpen its focus before deciding to establish a working group and fix its mandate. No consensus emerged on the establishment of a working group.

General Assembly consideration (June/July). Two alternative texts on prevention of an arms race in outer space, reflecting the differing approaches taken in the Committee on Disarmament, were submitted for inclusion in the disarmament measures chapter of the proposed comprehensive programme of disarmament, considered at the General Assembly's 1982 special session on disarmament.[2] No consensus text was arrived at during the session.

Concern over militarization of outer space was expressed by many in the general debate at the session. Malta said that, of the 3,000 or so satellites launched to date, about two thirds had either been entirely military in scope or had fed information into defence projects. Singapore cited an estimate in the Stockholm International Peace Research Institute's 1982 yearbook that at least 75 per cent of all satellites were used for military purposes.

Austria feared that a wasteful and destabilizing arms race in outer space could result from the research programmes in anti-satellite and anti-ballistic missile technology being pursued by both leading space Powers. Bangladesh called for the adoption of a declaration on outer space as a common heritage of mankind. Sierra Leone appealed for adherence to a policy of non-installation of nuclear and other weapons of mass destruction both in outer space and on the sea-bed, while Mozambique, making the same appeal, said those two spheres should be exploited for the benefit of all. Uruguay believed that armaments should be forbidden in both areas before they became further theatres of confrontation. In a similar vein, Ecuador drew attention to a joint declaration made by equatorial countries at Quito, Ecuador, in April 1982, reaffirming that outer space should remain a sphere of peace and co-operation for scientific and technical development.

Many countries, including Bhutan, Bolivia, Burma, Luxembourg, Sri Lanka, Sweden, and Trinidad and Tobago, called for action to secure the immediate and unconditional demilitarization of outer space before the arms race there became irreversible and made disarmament more complex and intractable. The Netherlands believed the prerequisites for arms control in outer space still existed since no State seemed to possess a commanding technological lead.

The conclusion of an international agreement or agreements to prohibit the use of outer space for non-peaceful purposes was urged by many, among them Czechoslovakia, Democratic Yemen, Egypt, Ethiopia and Zimbabwe, while others such as Chile, Nepal and Somalia said existing instruments should be strengthened or supplemented. Canada proposed an early start on a treaty to prohibit the development, testing and deployment of all weapons for use in outer space.

Hungary, Mongolia and the USSR urged consideration in the Committee on Disarmament, and the speedy conclusion, of a treaty on the prohibition of the stationing of weapons of any kind in outer space, the draft of which had been proposed by the USSR in 1981. Mongolia remarked that the United States had taken steps aimed at spreading weapons of mass destruction into outer space.

Speaking on behalf of the European Community (EC) members, Belgium mentioned the need for effective and verifiable agreements on weapons that could be used in outer space, among them anti-satellite weapons; it added that such agreements should be negotiated in the Committee on Disarmament under appropriate conditions. The Netherlands welcomed the Committee's discussion of the question, which Italy recalled having urged in 1981.[11] France also favoured an international convention banning anti-satellite weapons, to fill a gap in existing treaties and to prevent a qualitative leap in the arms race. Conclusion of an agreement on non-interference with other States' satellites was also urged by Egypt.

At the same time, the Netherlands and Singapore urged the USSR and the United States, which met once in 1978 and twice in 1979 to discuss limitation of their anti-satellite systems, to resume negotiations with a view to reaching agreement on banning the deployment of such weapons and dismantling all existing systems.

Action by the Conference on outer space. Meeting at Vienna, Austria, in August 1982, the Second United Nations Conference on the Exploration and Peaceful Uses of Outer Space declared in its report[4] that the extension of an arms race into outer space would be detrimental to humanity and should be prevented. It urged all nations to contribute actively to that goal and to adhere to the 1966 Treaty on Principles Governing the Activities of States in the Exploration and Use of Outer Space, including the Moon and Other Celestial Bodies[8] (which prohibited nuclear and other weapons of mass destruction from being placed in orbit or elsewhere in space). The Conference recommended that United Nations organs, particularly the General Assembly, and the Committee on Disarmament, when dealing with this topic, give priority attention to the concerns it had expressed.

General Assembly action (December). As it had done in 1981, the General Assembly adopted two resolutions in December 1982 aimed at preventing an arms race in outer space. On 9 December, it requested the Committee on Disarmament to negotiate an agreement or agreements covering all aspects and, on 13 December, it asked the Committee to accord priority to an agreement to prohibit anti-satellite systems.

By its 9 December resolution,[5] the Assembly reaffirmed that outer space should be used exclusively for peaceful purposes, emphasized that the international community should adopt further effective measures to prevent an arms race there and called on States to take immediate measures to that end. It requested the Committee on Disarmament to establish an *ad hoc* working group at the beginning of its 1983 session, with a view to negotiating for the conclusion of an agreement or agreements to prevent an arms race in all aspects in outer space.

The resolution was adopted by a recorded vote of 138 to 1, with 7 abstentions, following its approval in the First Committee on 26 November by a recorded vote of 118 to 1, with 8 abstentions.

The 35-nation text, introduced by Sri Lanka, was revised by its sponsors before adoption. With the revision, Bulgaria, the Byelorussian SSR, Cuba, Czechoslovakia, the German Democratic Republic, Hungary, Mongolia, the Ukrainian SSR and Viet Nam—which had sponsored an earlier draft resolution introduced by Mongolia[1]—announced that they would withdraw their draft since its main elements had been reflected in the revised text, which they then joined as co-sponsors. The withdrawn text would have had the Assembly request the Committee to activate work on the preparation of an international agreement, including the establishment of an *ad hoc* working group, and call on the USSR and the United States to renew bilateral talks on anti-satellite systems.

By its resolution of 13 December,[7] the Assembly reaffirmed the need for further effective measures to prevent an arms race in outer space, and requested the Committee on Disarmament to continue consideration of the question of negotiating effective and verifiable agreements to that end and, as a matter of priority, the question of negotiating such an agreement to prohibit anti-satellite systems. The Assembly expressed the hope that the Committee would take appropriate steps to that end, such as the possible establishment of a working group.

The resolution was adopted by a recorded vote of 112 to none, with 29 abstentions. The First Committee had approved the text on 26 November by a recorded vote of 92 to none, with 29 abstentions. The text, sponsored by 17 Western European and other States, was introduced by Italy.

In another action the Assembly, by a 10 December resolution on the Conference on outer space,[6] invited all Member States, in particular those with major space capabilities, to contribute actively to the prevention of an arms race in outer space, as an essential condition for the promotion of international co-operation in the exploration and uses of outer space for peaceful purposes.

Sri Lanka, introducing the first resolution, said it conveyed to the Committee on Disarmament, without intruding or imposing on that body, the Assembly's wish for it to take the first step on this issue. It provided for the Committee to develop its own approach and invited it to handle the issue on a comprehensive basis without limiting itself to a single aspect.

Italy, introducing the second resolution, said it singled out the most immediately threatening feature—the development of space weapons intended to damage, destroy or interfere with satellites. The text was drafted in such a way as to safeguard the Committee's autonomy on matters concerning the organization of its work, since it would not be appropriate for the Assembly to address requests to the Committee on procedural questions such as the establishment of a subsidiary body.

In explanation of its negative vote on the first resolution, the United States expressed objection to impractical or one-sided resolutions that might discourage progress on constructive initiatives in the Assembly or the Committee on Disarmament; it particularly objected to the text's unfortunate focus on an overly simplistic ban on all military devices in outer space, many of which were defensive and served vital stabilizing purposes.

The Netherlands abstained in the vote for similar reasons, adding that paragraphs 1 and 2 touched on issues that could not be solved by a majority vote; the question of preventing an arms race in outer space had come to the fore because of disturbing developments relating to anti-satellite weapons. That reservation was also shared by Turkey which, nevertheless, supported the text for its general thrust. Belgium, abstaining in the vote, had hoped the work of the Committee on Disarmament could proceed methodically on the basis

of a single consensus resolution that took into account the views of all States.

Although supporting the main thrust of the text and voting for it, France, the Federal Republic of Germany, Italy and Japan considered as inappropriate the reference in the last preambular paragraph to "overwhelming majority" support in the Committee on Disarmament for the establishment of a working group on outer space, when in fact that body worked on the basis of consensus. As regards paragraph 6, the four countries, along with Belgium, which abstained in the vote, stressed that it was within the competence of the Committee on Disarmament alone to organize its work; Japan added that the Committee should try to narrow existing differences before deciding on the establishment and mandate of a working group.

Reservations with regard to the use of the adverb "exclusively" in the phrase in paragraph 1 stating that outer space should be used "exclusively for peaceful purposes" were expressed by France, the Federal Republic of Germany and Italy on the ground that it introduced ambiguities and controversial interpretations. Further, the Federal Republic of Germany considered that it should be left to the parties to former bilateral discussions to weigh the merits and timeliness of embarking on further talks supplementary to multilateral efforts.

China, which also voted in favour, pointed out that it had not acceded to the outer space Treaty referred to in the text.

Draft resolution withdrawn. [1]Bulgaria, Byelorussian SSR, Cuba, Czechoslovakia, German Democratic Republic, Hungary, Mongolia, Ukrainian SSR, Viet Nam, A/C.1/37/L.8.

Reports. [2]*Ad Hoc* Committee, A/S-12/32; [3]Committee on Disarmament, A/37/27 (Committee documents, CD/335/appendix II); [4]Conference on outer space, A/CONF.101/10.

Resolutions (1982). GA: [5]37/83, 9 Dec., text following; [6]37/90, para. 4, 10 Dec.; [7]37/99 D, 13 Dec., text following.

Resolutions (prior). GA: [8]2222(XXI), annex, 19 Dec. 1966 (YUN 1966, p. 41); [9]36/97 C, 9 Dec. 1981 (YUN 1981, p. 83); [10]36/99, 9 Dec. 1981 (*ibid.*).

Yearbook references. [11]1981, p. 81.

Meeting records. GA: plenary, A/S-12/PV.2-26, 28, 29 (8 June–10 July), A/37/PV.98, 101 (9, 13 Dec.); *Ad Hoc* Committee, A/S-12/AC.1/PV.2 (14 June); 1st Committee, A/C.1/37/PV.3-10, 12-28, *36, 38, 43-45* (18 Oct.–26 Nov.).

General Assembly resolution 37/83

9 December 1982   Meeting 98   138-1-7 (recorded vote)

Approved by First Committee (A/37/669) by recorded vote (118-1-8), 26 November (meeting 45); 35-nation draft (A/C.1/37/L.64/Rev.1); agenda item 57.

Sponsors: Algeria, Argentina, Bangladesh, Benin, Brazil, Bulgaria, Byelorussian SSR, Colombia, Congo, Cuba, Czechoslovakia, Ecuador, Egypt, German Democratic Republic, Ghana, Hungary, India, Indonesia, Ireland, Liberia, Maldives, Mexico, Mongolia, Morocco, Nigeria, Peru, Romania, Singapore, Sri Lanka, Sudan, Sweden, Ukrainian SSR, Venezuela, Viet Nam, Yugoslavia.

Prevention of an arms race in outer space

The General Assembly,

Inspired by the great prospects opening up before mankind as a result of man's entry into outer space twenty-five years ago,

Recognizing the common interest of all mankind in the exploration and use of outer space for peaceful purposes,

Reaffirming that the exploration and use of outer space, including the Moon and other celestial bodies, shall be carried out for the benefit and in the interest of all countries, irrespective of their degree of economic or scientific development, and shall be the province of all mankind,

Reaffirming further the will of all States that the exploration and use of outer space, including the Moon and other celestial bodies, shall be exclusively for peaceful purposes,

Recalling that the States parties to the Treaty on Principles Governing the Activities of States in the Exploration and Use of Outer Space, including the Moon and Other Celestial Bodies, have undertaken, in article III, to carry on activities in the exploration and use of outer space, including the Moon and other celestial bodies, in accordance with international law and the Charter of the United Nations, in the interest of maintaining international peace and security and promoting international co-operation and understanding,

Reaffirming, in particular, article IV of the above-mentioned Treaty, which stipulates that States parties to the Treaty undertake not to place in orbit around the earth any objects carrying nuclear weapons or any other kinds of weapons of mass destruction, install such weapons on celestial bodies or station such weapons in outer space in any other manner,

Reaffirming also paragraph 80 of the Final Document of the Tenth Special Session of the General Assembly, in which it is stated that, in order to prevent an arms race in outer space, further measures should be taken and appropriate international negotiations held in accordance with the spirit of the Treaty,

Recalling its resolutions 36/97 C and 36/99 of 9 December 1981,

Gravely concerned at the danger posed to all mankind by an arms race in outer space,

Mindful of the widespread interest expressed by Member States in the course of the negotiations on and following the adoption of the above-mentioned Treaty in ensuring that the exploration and use of outer space should be for peaceful purposes, and taking note of proposals submitted to the General Assembly at its tenth special session and at its regular sessions and to the Committee on Disarmament,

Noting the grave concern expressed by the Second United Nations Conference on the Exploration and Peaceful Uses of Outer Space over the possible extension of an arms race into outer space and the recommendations made to the competent organs of the United Nations, in particular the General Assembly, and also to the Committee on Disarmament,

Convinced that further measures are needed for the prevention of an arms race in outer space,

Recognizing that, in the context of multilateral negotiations for preventing an arms race in outer space, the resumption of bilateral negotiations between the Union of Soviet Socialist Republics and the United States of America can play a positive role,

Taking note of the report of the Committee on Disarmament,

Noting that in the course of its session in 1982 the Committee on Disarmament considered this subject both at its formal and informal meetings as well as through informal consultations,

Aware of the various proposals submitted by Member States to the Committee on Disarmament, particularly concerning the establishment of a working group on outer space and its draft mandate,

Noting, in particular, the express wishes of the overwhelming majority of members of the Committee on Disarmament for the establishment, without delay, of a working group on outer space,

1. *Reaffirms* the will of all States that outer space shall be used exclusively for peaceful purposes and that it shall not become an arena for an arms race;

2. *Declares* that any use of outer space other than for exclusively peaceful purposes runs counter to the agreed objective of general and complete disarmament under effective international control;

3. *Emphasizes* that further effective measures to prevent an arms race in outer space should be adopted by the international community;

4. *Calls upon* all States, in particular those with major space capabilities, to contribute actively to the objective of the peaceful use of outer space and to take immediate measures to prevent an arms race in outer space;

5. *Requests* the Committee on Disarmament to consider as a matter of priority the question of preventing an arms race in outer space;

6. *Further requests* the Committee on Disarmament to establish an *ad hoc* working group on the subject at the beginning of its session in 1983, with a view to undertaking negotiations for the conclusion of an agreement or agreements, as appropriate, to prevent an arms race in all its aspects in outer space;

7. *Requests* the Committee on Disarmament to report on its consideration of this subject to the General Assembly at its thirty-eighth session;

8. *Requests* the Secretary-General to transmit to the Committee on Disarmament all documents relating to the consideration of this subject by the General Assembly at its thirty-seventh session;

9. *Decides* to include in the provisional agenda of its thirty-eighth session an item entitled "Prevention of an arms race in outer space".

Recorded vote in Assembly as follows:

In favour: Afghanistan, Algeria, Angola, Argentina, Austria, Bahamas, Bahrain, Bangladesh, Barbados, Belize, Benin, Bhutan, Bolivia, Botswana, Brazil, Bulgaria, Burma, Burundi, Byelorussian SSR, Cape Verde, Central African Republic, Chad, Chile, Colombia, Comoros, Congo, Costa Rica, Cuba, Cyprus, Czechoslovakia, Democratic Kampuchea, Democratic Yemen, Denmark, Djibouti, Dominican Republic, Ecuador, Egypt, El Salvador, Ethiopia, Fiji, Finland, France, Gabon, Gambia, German Democratic Republic, Germany, Federal Republic of, Ghana, Greece, Grenada, Guatemala, Guinea, Guinea-Bissau, Guyana, Haiti, Honduras, Hungary, Iceland, India, Indonesia, Iran, Iraq, Ireland, Italy, Ivory Coast, Jamaica, Japan, Jordan, Kenya, Kuwait, Lao People's Democratic Republic, Lebanon, Liberia, Libyan Arab Jamahiriya, Madagascar, Malawi, Malaysia, Maldives, Mali, Malta, Mauritania, Mauritius, Mexico, Mongolia, Morocco, Mozambique, Nepal, New Zealand, Nicaragua, Niger, Nigeria, Norway, Oman, Pakistan, Panama, Papua New Guinea, Paraguay, Peru, Philippines, Poland, Portugal, Qatar, Romania, Rwanda, Saint Lucia, Sao Tome and Principe, Saudi Arabia, Senegal, Sierra Leone, Singapore, Solomon Islands, Somalia, Spain, Sri Lanka, Sudan, Suriname, Swaziland, Sweden, Syrian Arab Republic, Thailand, Togo, Trinidad and Tobago, Tunisia, Turkey, Uganda, Ukrainian SSR, USSR, United Arab Emirates, United Republic of Cameroon, United Republic of Tanzania, Upper Volta, Uruguay, Vanuatu, Venezuela, Viet Nam, Yemen, Yugoslavia, Zaire, Zambia.

Against: United States.

Abstaining: Australia, Belgium, Canada, Israel, Luxembourg, Netherlands, United Kingdom.

General Assembly resolution 37/99 D

13 December 1982   Meeting 101   112-0-29 (recorded vote)

Approved by First Committee (A/37/667) by recorded vote (92-0-29), 26 November (meeting 44); 17-nation draft (A/C.1/37/L.41); agenda item 55 *(b)*.

Sponsors: Australia, Canada, Costa Rica, Denmark, France, Germany, Federal Republic of, Greece, Italy, Japan, Netherlands, New Zealand, Niger, Norway, Spain, Sweden, United Kingdom, Uruguay.

Prevention of an arms race in outer space and prohibition of anti-satellite systems

The General Assembly,

Inspired by the great prospects opening up before mankind as a result of man's entry into outer space,

Believing that any activity in outer space should be for peaceful purposes and carried on for the benefit of all peoples, irrespective of the degree of their economic and scientific development,

Recalling that the States parties to the Treaty on Principles Governing the Activities of States in the Exploration and Use of Outer Space, including the Moon and Other Celestial Bodies, have undertaken, in article III, to carry on activities in the exploration and use of outer space, including the Moon and other celestial bodies, in accordance with international law and the Charter of the United Nations, in the interest of maintaining international peace and security and promoting international co-operation and understanding,

Reaffirming, in particular, article IV of the above-mentioned Treaty, which stipulates that States parties to the Treaty undertake not to place in orbit around the earth any objects carrying nuclear weapons or any other kinds of weapons of mass destruction, install such weapons on celestial bodies or station such weapons in outer space in any other manner,

Reaffirming also paragraph 80 of the Final Document of the Tenth Special Session of the General Assembly, in which it is stated that, in order to prevent an arms race in outer space, further measures should be taken and appropriate international negotiations held in accordance with the spirit of the Treaty,

Aware of the need to prevent an arms race in outer space and in particular of the threat posed by anti-satellite systems and their destabilizing effects on international peace and security,

Recalling its resolutions 36/97 C and 36/99 of 9 December 1981,

Noting the grave concern expressed by the Second United Nations Conference on the Exploration and Peaceful Uses of Outer Space over the possible extension of an arms race into outer space and the recommendations made to the competent organs of the United Nations, in particular the General Assembly, and also to the Committee on Disarmament,

Noting also that in the course of its session in 1982 the Committee on Disarmament considered this subject both at its formal and informal meetings, as well as through informal consultations,

Taking note of the part of the report of the Committee on Disarmament relating to the item entitled "Prevention of an arms race in outer space",

1. *Reaffirms* that further effective measures to prevent an arms race in outer space should be adopted by the international community;

2. *Notes with appreciation* the contribution made by Member States to the discussion of the item in the Committee on Disarmament and in the General Assembly;

3. *Requests* the Committee on Disarmament to continue substantive consideration of:

(a) The question of negotiating effective and verifiable agreements aimed at preventing an arms race in outer space, taking into account all existing and future proposals designed to meet this objective;

(b) As a matter of priority, the question of negotiating an effective and verifiable agreement to prohibit anti-satellite systems as an important step towards the fulfilment of the objectives set out in subparagraph *(a)* above;

4. *Expresses the hope* that the Committee on Disarmament will take the appropriate steps, such as the possible establishment of a working group, in order to promote the objectives set forth in paragraphs 1 and 3 above;

5. *Requests* the Committee on Disarmament to report on the consideration given to this subject to the General Assembly at the thirty-eighth session;

6. *Decides* to include in the provisional agenda of its thirty-eighth session the item entitled "Prevention of an arms race in outer space and prohibition of anti-satellite systems".

Recorded vote in Assembly as follows:

In favour: Algeria, Australia, Austria, Bahamas, Bahrain, Bangladesh, Barbados, Belgium, Bhutan, Bolivia, Botswana, Brazil, Burma, Burundi, Canada, Central African Republic, Chad, Chile, Comoros, Congo, Costa Rica, Cyprus, Democratic Kampuchea, Democratic Yemen, Denmark, Djibouti, Dominican Republic, El Salvador, Equatorial Guinea, Ethiopia, Fiji, Finland, France, Gabon, Germany, Federal Republic of, Ghana, Greece, Grenada, Guatemala, Guinea, Guyana, Haiti, Honduras, Iceland, India, Indonesia,[a] Iran, Iraq, Ireland, Israel, Italy, Jamaica, Japan, Jordan, Kenya, Kuwait, Lesotho, Liberia, Libyan Arab Jamahiriya, Luxembourg, Malawi, Malaysia, Maldives, Mali, Malta, Mauritania, Mauritius, Morocco, Nepal, Netherlands, New Zealand, Niger, Nigeria, Norway, Oman, Pakistan, Papua New Guinea, Paraguay, Philippines, Portugal, Qatar, Romania, Rwanda, Saint Lucia, Senegal, Sierra Leone, Singapore, Solomon Islands, Somalia, Spain, Sudan, Suriname, Swaziland, Sweden, Thailand, Togo, Trinidad and Tobago, Tunisia, Turkey, Uganda, United Arab Emirates, United Kingdom, United Republic of Cameroon, United States, Upper Volta, Uruguay, Vanuatu, Venezuela, Yemen, Yugoslavia, Zaire, Zambia.

Against: None.

Abstaining: Afghanistan, Angola, Argentina, Benin, Bulgaria, Byelorussian SSR, Colombia, Cuba, Czechoslovakia, Ecuador, Egypt, German Democratic Republic, Guinea-Bissau, Hungary, Lao People's Democratic Republic, Lebanon, Madagascar, Mexico, Mongolia, Mozambique, Panama, Peru, Poland, Saudi Arabia, Sri Lanka, Ukrainian SSR, USSR, United Republic of Tanzania, Viet Nam.

[a]Later advised the Secretariat it had intended to abstain.

Regional disarmament

In December 1982, the General Assembly, reaffirming the right of each State to assess the conditions needed for its security and take measures in that respect, encouraged consultations among Governments on regional disarmament measures, including regional institutional arrangements capable of promoting their implementation.

The Assembly also took action in regard to the nuclear-weapon-free zone in Latin America and similar zones proposed for Africa, the Middle East and South Asia, and dealt with the broader concept of zones of peace in the Indian Ocean and other regions.

General Assembly consideration (June/July). In a note verbale to the Secretary-General dated 16 June 1982,[(1)] Belgium submitted to the General Assembly at its special session on disarmament a memorandum on regional disarmament, accompanied by the text of a draft resolution for Assembly action, suggesting steps the United Nations could take to promote joint disarmament measures by States in various regions; these included the provision of advice or assistance by the United Nations Centre for Disarmament, information reports to the Assembly from regional institutions and annual discussion of the subject by the Assembly.

Many speakers in the session's general debate pointed to the benefits that a regional approach to disarmament could bring. Maldives viewed regional disarmament as an effective measure for strengthening the security of the countries of a region while also strengthening international security and contributing to nuclear non-proliferation. Tunisia saw it as an important step towards general and complete disarmament. The big Powers had a responsibility to promote regional disarmament, said Zambia, by desisting from fomenting local conflicts and tensions and from using the third world as a market and testing-ground for their weapons.

The Bahamas believed that the non-militarily-significant States should explore initiatives to ensure the lowest possible level of armaments for their national defence systems and those of their region; such action would lead militarily significant States to think twice about maintaining the doctrines that inflated their legitimate security needs and led to arms escalation and transfers. Colombia praised defensive alliances such as the Inter-American Treaty for Reciprocal Assistance which, if properly implemented, constituted an optimum guarantee for preserving territorial integrity against unprovoked aggression, thereby preventing an arms escalation among the member States. France advocated regional security arrangements among developing countries, removed from the possibility of external interference, which would make it possible to set up local peace-monitoring forces or maintain permanent contingents to verify and even guarantee commitments among neighbouring States.

Albania, on the other hand, believed that the establishment of zones of peace or nuclear-weapon-free zones was practically impossible because regional peace and security could not be dissociated from international peace and security; the regions where attempts were being made to establish such zones were precisely those in which the super-Powers had concentrated huge military forces and where their alliances were operating.

Comments on possible zones of peace in specific regions—Asia and the Pacific, the Caribbean, Central America, Latin America, North Africa and Europe—were made during the debate.

The Lao People's Democratic Republic and Viet Nam expressed support for a Mongolian proposal, originally made in May 1981,[3] for a convention on non-aggression and the non-use of force in relations among the States of Asia and the Pacific.

Grenada and Jamaica, supported by Guyana, reiterated their call for the establishment of a zone of peace and tranquillity in the Caribbean. Grenada described this as a zone where the introduction of nuclear weapons would be prohibited, aggressive military manoeuvres banned, and foreign military and naval bases dismantled, and where machinery would be established to deal with all forms of aggression, including assassinations, propaganda destabilization, diplomatic and economic sabotage, and mercenary invasion. Guyana urged States to eschew policies which frustrated the development of that concept and to refrain from introducing into the region's politics the acquisition of new and sophisticated weapons.

Honduras recalled a peace plan for Central America it had proposed in March (see Chapter VII of this section) which included a proposal for disarmament measures such as the conclusion of agreements on the reduction of armaments and military forces; it also favoured the idea of a meeting of Central American Foreign Ministers to promote the reduction of conventional weapons in the region, an objective which should be pursued concurrently with the strengthening of dispute-settlement machinery and international action against arms traffic. Costa Rica added that there was a need to initiate demilitarization in Central America, while Nicaragua expressed a willingness to take part in a meeting of Central American leaders on the subject of arms.

Panama called for a conference of heads of State or Government of Latin American countries and, concurrently, of their chiefs of staff, to lay the foundations for establishing an institutional machinery for the collective defence and security of Latin America, with an exclusively regional character.

Morocco said it was willing to co-operate with its neighbours in the context of any organization established to achieve disarmament in North Africa.

A large number of European countries joined Belgium, on behalf of the EC members, in expressing hope that the impending resumption at Madrid, Spain, of the Conference on Security and Co-operation in Europe would lead to the adoption of a substantive and balanced document, including the mandate for and the convening of a conference on disarmament in Europe. They included Austria, Bulgaria, Czechoslovakia, Finland, France, the Federal Republic of Germany, Greece, Luxembourg, the Netherlands, Norway, Poland, Romania, Spain, Turkey, the USSR and Yugoslavia.

France added that, within all of Europe, from the Atlantic to the Urals, confidence must be restored by reducing the threat of surprise attack, and the current imbalance must be corrected by effective and verifiable reductions of offensive potential. Norway said that, as a first step, an effective system should be established to build confidence and security in order to achieve greater openness and transparency in military matters all over Europe. Sweden mentioned its offer to host a special European disarmament conference within the framework of the Conference on Security and Co-operation in Europe.

Several Western European countries expressed support for the Vienna negotiations, formally known as the Vienna Talks on Mutual Reduction of Forces and Armaments and Associated Measures in Central Europe. Belgium, for the EC members, said those talks, which had been bogged down too long, should resume, leading to reduction of forces based on agreed data and accompanied by adequate confidence-building and verification measures. The United Kingdom recalled having pursued nine years of negotiations at Vienna on mutual and balanced force reductions, and said it hoped to see some progress on fresh proposals that were currently being made.

The United States announced that the leaders of the North Atlantic Treaty Organization (NATO) had agreed in June to introduce a major initiative in the Vienna talks, calling for common collective ceilings for both NATO and the Warsaw Treaty Organization, totalling 700,000 ground forces and 900,000 ground and air force personnel combined, along with a package of measures to encourage co-operation and verify compliance. The aim of this initiative, said the Federal Republic of Germany, was to reach agreement on equal, collective ceilings on both sides in Central Europe. Norway hoped the proposals—introduced at the Vienna talks on 9 July—would create a new momentum in the talks and facilitate a breakthrough after nine years of negotiations. Turkey believed that an agreement of this nature would go a long way towards achieving a stable military balance in Europe and complementing limitations and reductions of nuclear weapons.

Poland said a first-stage agreement for the reduction of USSR and United States troops and the parallel freeze of force strengths in Central Europe could be reached soon if the Western States responded constructively to the proposals submitted at the Vienna talks in February by Poland on behalf of the socialist States. Unfortunately, said Czechoslovakia, despite signs of readiness to begin a dialogue, reactions from the West had been held up by the absence of a sincere interest in bringing about a just agreement.

General Assembly action (December). Reaffirming the right of each State to assess conditions for its security and to adopt measures which took account of United Nations objectives and principles as well as the specific conditions of each region, the General Assembly, by a resolution adopted without vote on 13 December,[2] expressed hope that Governments, regional circumstances permitting, would consult with each other on regional disarmament measures that could be taken at the initiative, and with the participation, of all the States concerned. Governments were encouraged to consider establishing or strengthening, where appropriate, regional institutional arrangements to promote the implementation of such measures, and the Assembly called on those that had already taken such steps so to inform the Secretary-General. It requested the Secretariat, in particular the Department for Disarmament Affairs, and the United Nations Institute for Disarmament Research to assist States and regional institutions which might so request in the context of regional disarmament measures.

The First Committee had approved the text on 22 November, also without vote, on a 31-nation draft introduced by Belgium and revised by the sponsors.

Note verbale. [1]Belgium, 16 June, A/S-12/AC.1/17.
Resolution (1982). [2]GA: 37/100 F, 13 Dec., text following.
Yearbook reference. [3]1981, p. 141.
Meeting records. GA: plenary, A/S-12/PV.2-26, 28, 29 (8 June–10 July), A/37/PV.101 (13 Dec.); *Ad Hoc* Committee, A/S-12/AC.1/PV.9 (28 June); 1st Committee, A/C.1/37/PV.3-10, 12-28, 37, *38, 39* (18 Oct.–22 Nov.).

General Assembly resolution 37/100 F

13 December 1982   Meeting 101   Adopted without vote

Approved by First Committee (A/37/670) without vote, 22 November (meeting 39); 31-nation draft (A/C.1/37/L.58/Rev.1); agenda item 133.

Sponsors: Austria, Bahamas, Bangladesh, Belgium, Bulgaria, Chile, Colombia, Costa Rica, Czechoslovakia, Denmark, Ecuador, Finland, France, Germany, Federal Republic of, Greece, Guatemala, Indonesia, Italy, Malta, Netherlands, Norway, Pakistan, Peru, Poland, Portugal, Romania, Singapore, Spain, Sweden, United Kingdom, Viet Nam.

Regional disarmament

The General Assembly,

Reiterating its concern over the arms race, particularly in its nuclear aspects, and the continuing increase in arms expenditure,

Recalling that all States, in particular nuclear-weapon States and other militarily significant States, have the responsibility for halting and reversing the arms race,

Reaffirming the right of each State to make a sovereign assessment of the conditions necessary for its security and to take all appropriate measures in this respect, taking into account the objectives and principles of the United Nations, as well as the specific conditions of each region,

Taking account of the decisions and recommendations of the Final Document of the Tenth Special Session of the General Assembly, *inter alia* in its paragraph 114,

Stressing the importance of the regional measures that have already been adopted, as well as of efforts of a regional nature undertaken in the field of nuclear and conventional disarmament,

Aware of the studies that have already been carried out and are of relevance to regional disarmament,

Recalling its resolutions 35/156 D of 12 December 1980 and 36/97 H of 9 December 1981 concerning the *Study on All the Aspects of Regional Disarmament* and the views of Member States on that study,

Recalling also that one of the aims of regional disarmament is to assist in promoting the ultimate goal of general and complete disarmament under effective international control,

Confirming the importance and the potential effectiveness of regional disarmament measures taken at the initiative and with the participation of all the States concerned, in that they can contribute to the realization of general and complete disarmament under strict and effective international control,

1. *Expresses the hope* that Governments, where the circumstances of the region permit, will consult with each other on appropriate regional disarmament measures that could be taken at the initiative, and with the participation, of all the States concerned;

2. *Encourages* Governments to consider the possible establishment or strengthening at the regional level, where appropriate, of institutional arrangements capable of promoting the implementation of such measures;

3. *Calls upon* Governments and the existing competent regional institutions which may have taken measures to that end so to inform the Secretary-General;

4. *Requests* the Secretariat, in particular the Department for Disarmament Affairs, and the United Nations Institute for Disarmament Research to lend assistance to States and regional institutions which may request it in the context of regional disarmament measures taken at the initiative and with the participation of all the States concerned;

5. *Requests* the Secretary-General to submit a progress report to the General Assembly at its thirty-eighth session;

6. *Decides* to include in the provisional agenda of its thirty-eighth session an item entitled "Regional disarmament: report of the Secretary-General".

Zones of peace

Further progress towards implementing the General Assembly's 1971 Declaration of the Indian Ocean as a Zone of Peace continued to be blocked in 1982 by failure to reach consensus on the dates for the proposed Conference on the Indian Ocean (see below). The *Ad Hoc* Committee on the Indian Ocean held three sessions on this subject in 1982. The Assembly renewed the Committee's mandate in December and requested it to make every effort to accomplish the preparatory work for the Conference, including consideration of its convening not later than the first half of 1984.

During discussions on disarmament in the Assembly, several speakers raised the possibility of creating zones of peace in other regions, including South-East Asia and the Mediterranean area.

Indian Ocean

Activities of the Committee on the Indian Ocean. In 1982, the *Ad Hoc* Committee on the Indian Ocean, established by the General Assembly in 1972,[10] held three sessions—from 1 to 12 March and from 20 to 28 May in New York, and from 3 to 20 August at Geneva—with an additional meeting on 23 November in New York to adopt its annual report to the Assembly.[6] Thirty formal meetings were held in addition to a number of informal ones.

As requested by the Assembly in December 1981,[12] the Committee continued its efforts to harmonize views relevant to the convening of the proposed Conference on the Indian Ocean, which the Assembly had decided in 1979[11] should be convened at Colombo, Sri Lanka, as a necessary step for implementing the Assembly's 1971 Declaration of the Indian Ocean as a Zone of Peace.[9] According to the Committee's 1982 report, its work proceeded on the understanding that substantive issues would be taken up before organizational issues.

As in previous years, two different approaches were advocated in the Committee. Most of the non-aligned and Eastern European members urged the Committee to proceed without delay to practical preparations for the Conference so that it could be held not later than the first half of 1983, a timing indicated in the Assembly's 1981 resolution. Other Committee members asserted that the lack of real progress on the harmonization of views, and the political and security climate in the region, were not currently conducive to the convening of the Conference.

Bulgaria and the German Democratic Republic submitted on 9 March 1982 a working paper outlining ideas for the Conference's possible structure and procedure, envisaging three successive stages leading to the adoption of a Declaration of Principles of the Zone of Peace.[14] Another working paper, containing a proposed set of principles on the Indian Ocean as a zone of peace, was introduced in the Committee on 25 May by Australia, also on behalf of Canada, the Federal Republic of Germany, Italy, Japan, the Netherlands, Norway, the United Kingdom and the United States.[13] On 16 August, Sri Lanka introduced a draft resolution, on behalf of the non-aligned States members of the Committee, calling for the convening of the Conference at Colombo on 9 May 1983.[2]

In a report to the General Assembly's special session on disarmament,[5] adopted on 28 May, the Committee summarized its work since 1973 and suggested that the Assembly at that session might make specific recommendations for the expeditious discharge of the Committee's mandate and for implementing the 1981 Assembly resolution.

In adopting its annual report on 23 November, the Committee recommended to the Assembly the adoption of a draft resolution requesting the Committee to continue work on harmonizing views and on preparatory work for the Conference, including consideration of its convening not later than the first half of 1984. In addition, it reported that it was unable, in the time available, to reach consensus on applications for participation in its work submitted by Cuba, Czechoslovakia, Democratic Kampuchea, Hungary, the Lao People's Democratic Republic, Mongolia and Viet Nam.

The World Conference on the Indian Ocean as a Zone of Peace (New Delhi, India, 23-25 April 1982), sponsored by the World Peace Council and others, adopted a declaration whose text was issued as a document of the Special Committee against *Apartheid*[1] by decision of that Committee.

General Assembly consideration (June/July). Two paragraphs on the Indian Ocean as a zone of peace were proposed for inclusion in the disarmament measures chapter of the draft comprehensive programme of disarmament considered at the second special session of the General Assembly devoted to disarmament.[4] However, consensus was not reached on the wording.

A large number of speakers in the general debate at the session reaffirmed their support of the 1971 Declaration and called for the convening, without further delay, of the Conference on the Indian Ocean, an area which Mauritius described as having 36 littoral and 11 hinterland nations, with a population of approximately 1,270 million, or 30 per cent of the world's total.

Afghanistan, Democratic Kampuchea, Egypt, Iran, the Libyan Arab Jamahiriya, Mauritania and Pakistan favoured the creation of a zone of peace in the region, and Democratic Yemen expressed appreciation for a USSR proposal to that end. Australia supported the objective of establishing a zone of peace there and pledged to continue contributing to the work of the *Ad Hoc* Committee. Maldives, Mozambique, Oman and Rwanda supported the establishment of a nuclear-weapon-free zone in the Indian Ocean. Kuwait and the Sudan supported the Declaration.

Madagascar deplored, and Malaysia regretted, that the Conference initially scheduled for 1981 at Colombo had had to be postponed. Several countries, among them Bangladesh, Democratic Yemen, Oman, Uganda, Viet Nam and Zambia, supported the holding of the Conference at Colombo in 1983. In a similar vein, Benin, Ethiopia, Indonesia, the Lao People's Democratic Republic and Nepal regarded such an undertaking as an important step towards implementing the Declaration. Sharing that view, Sri Lanka called on the Assembly to reaffirm the urgency of convening the Conference at Colombo as scheduled. France supported the principle of convening a Conference if thorough preparation indicated that it would be of value. For Yemen, it was important that all the major Powers participate in the Conference.

The United Republic of Cameroon was joined by a number of countries in deploring the problems delaying the creation of a nuclear-weapon-free zone in the Indian Ocean. Czechoslovakia held obstructive behaviour of the Western Powers responsible for delaying the Conference. The United Republic of Tanzania asserted that certain major Powers had obstructed the holding of the Conference by injecting extraneous issues of no concern to the littoral States. Indonesia, Mauritius and Thailand observed that recent developments in the Indian Ocean and in adjacent areas had added a sense of urgency for an early convening of the Conference.

For Seychelles, Somalia, Uganda, the United Republic of Tanzania and Zimbabwe, the military presence of one or more major Powers threatened peace and security in the Indian Ocean. Qatar expressed concern that, since the adoption of the Declaration in 1971, the great Powers had escalated their rivalry over zones of influence in South Asia and the Horn of Africa.

Democratic Yemen blamed imperialist forces led by the United States. Mozambique charged certain countries of the North Atlantic Treaty Organization which were members of the Committee on the Indian Ocean with systematically hindering efforts to secure a zone of peace in that region. The USSR said the United States, in installing a strategic military base on Diego Garcia, was developing another springboard to threaten the USSR and other countries. Ethiopia and Iran demanded the dismantling of all foreign military bases in the area; Iran also urged the elimination of the military presence and rivalries of foreign Powers from various regions, particularly the Indian Ocean and the Gulf.

Seychelles called on the Disarmament Commission to deal with the issue and hoped that the World Disarmament Campaign would make the international public aware of the dangerous situation.

The Sudan said it was seeking to promote the concept of the security of the Red Sea as a peaceful waterway exempt from great-Power rivalries. Yemen spoke of the need to eliminate the increasing strife between the two super-Powers around that sea.

General Assembly action (December). On 13 December, the General Assembly adopted without vote the resolution recommended to it by the Committee on the Indian Ocean.[7] By this text, the Assembly expressed regret at the lack of consensus in the Committee on the dates for the Conference on the Indian Ocean and emphasized its decision to convene the Conference. It requested the Committee to continue work on the harmonization of views on remaining issues related to convening the Conference and to make every effort

to accomplish the preparatory work, including consideration of convening the Conference not later than the first half of 1984. Renewing the Committee's mandate, the Assembly requested it to hold three two-week sessions in 1983, with the possibility of a fourth session as required. Further, the Assembly requested the Committee Chairman to continue consultations aimed at an early resolution of the question of participation in the Committee's work by States that were not members of it.

The First Committee had approved this text on 2 December, also without vote.

In a resolution of 16 December on strengthening international security,[8] the Assembly reiterated its support for the Declaration of the Indian Ocean as a Zone of Peace and expressed hope that the Conference on the Indian Ocean, an important stage in the realization of the Declaration's objectives, would be held not later than in the first half of 1984. To that end, it called on States to contribute to the success of the Conference.

In a joint statement transmitted by a note verbale of 30 November to the Secretary-General,[3] Bulgaria, the German Democratic Republic, Poland and the USSR held the Western States responsible for delaying the Conference, and expressed regret and dissatisfaction that the draft resolution recommended by the *Ad Hoc* Committee was far removed from the proposal submitted in August by Sri Lanka on behalf of the non-aligned countries for the convening of the Conference in May 1983.

Declaration. [1]World Conference on Indian Ocean as Zone of Peace, A/AC.115/L.570.
Draft resolution not pressed. [2]Sri Lanka, for non-aligned States, A/AC.159/L.47.
Note verbale. [3]Bulgaria, German Democratic Republic, Poland, USSR, 30 Nov., A/C.1/37/11.
Reports. [4]*Ad Hoc* Committee, A/S-12/32; Committee on Indian Ocean, [5]A/S-12/5, [6]A/37/29.
Resolutions (1982). GA: [7]37/96, 13 Dec., text following; [8]37/118, para. 13, 16 Dec.
Resolutions (prior). GA: [9]2832(XXVI), 16 Dec. 1971 (YUN 1971, p. 34); [10]2992(XXVII), 15 Dec. 1972 (YUN 1972, p. 29); [11]34/80 B, 11 Dec. 1979 (YUN 1979, p. 67); [12]36/90, 9 Dec. 1981 (YUN 1981, p. 95).
Working papers. [13]Australia, Canada, Germany, Federal Republic of, Italy, Japan, Netherlands, Norway, United Kingdom, United States, transmitted by letter from Australia, 20 May, A/AC.159/L.44; [14]Bulgaria, German Democratic Republic, A/AC.159/L.43.
Financial implications. 5th Committee report, A/37/731; S-G statements, A/C.1/37/L.76, A/C.5/37/86.
Meeting records. GA: plenary, A/S-12/PV.2-26, 28, 29 (8 June-10 July), A/37/PV.101 (13 Dec.); *Ad Hoc* Committee, A/S-12/AC.1/PV.9 (28 June); 1st Committee, A/C.1/37/PV.3-10, 12-28, *44, 47, 50* (18 Oct.-2 Dec.); 5th Committee, A/C.5/37/SR.61 (9 Dec.).

General Assembly resolution 37/96

13 December 1982   Meeting 101   Adopted without vote

Approved by First Committee (A/37/660) without vote, 2 December (meeting 50); draft by Committee on Indian Ocean (A/37/29); agenda item 48.

Implementation of the Declaration of the Indian Ocean as a Zone of Peace

The General Assembly,

Recalling the Declaration of the Indian Ocean as a Zone of Peace, contained in its resolution 2832(XXVI) of 16 December 1971, and recalling also its resolutions 2992(XXVII) of 15 December 1972, 3080(XXVIII) of 6 December 1973, 3259 A (XXIX) of 9 December 1974, 3468(XXX) of 11 December 1975, 31/88 of 14 December 1976, 32/86 of 12 December 1977, S-10/2 of 30 June 1978, 33/68 of 14 December 1978, 34/80 A and B of 11 December 1979, 35/150 of 12 December 1980 and 36/90 of 9 December 1981, and other relevant resolutions,

Recalling also that, in the Final Document of the Tenth Special Session of the General Assembly, it is stated that the establishment of zones of peace in various regions of the world under appropriate conditions to be clearly defined and determined freely by the States concerned in the zone, taking into account the characteristics of the zone and the principles of the Charter of the United Nations, and in conformity with international law, can contribute to strengthening the security of States within such zones and to international peace and security as a whole,

Recalling further the report of the Meeting of the Littoral and Hinterland States of the Indian Ocean,

Reaffirming its conviction that concrete action for the achievement of the objectives of the Declaration of the Indian Ocean as a Zone of Peace would be a substantial contribution to the strengthening of international peace and security,

Recalling its decision, taken at the thirty-fourth session in resolution 34/80 B, to convene a Conference on the Indian Ocean at Colombo during 1981,

Recalling further its decision, taken at the thirty-fifth session in resolution 35/150, to make every effort, in consideration of the political and security climate in the Indian Ocean area, particularly recent developments, as well as the progress made in the harmonization of views, to finalize, in accordance with its normal methods of work, all preparations for the Conference, including the date for its convening,

Recalling the exchange of varied views in the *Ad Hoc* Committee on the Indian Ocean in 1982 and noting that, while some progress has been made, a number of issues remain to be resolved,

Noting the exchange of views on the adverse political and security climate in the region,

Noting also that the *Ad Hoc* Committee has failed to reach consensus on the date for the convening, during 1983, of the Conference on the Indian Ocean at Colombo,

Convinced that the continued military presence of the great Powers in the Indian Ocean area, conceived in the context of their confrontation, gives urgency to the need to take practical steps for the early achievement of the objectives of the Declaration of the Indian Ocean as a Zone of Peace,

Considering that all other foreign military presence in the area, whenever it is contrary to the objectives of the Declaration of the Indian Ocean as a Zone of Peace and the purposes and principles of the Charter, further gives greater urgency to the need to take practical steps towards the early achievement of the objectives of the Declaration,

Considering also that the creation of a zone of peace in the Indian Ocean requires the active participation of and full co-operation among the littoral and hinterland States, the permanent members of the Security Council and the major maritime users to ensure conditions of peace and security based on the purposes and principles of the Charter as well as the general principles of international law,

Considering further that the creation of a zone of peace requires co-operation and agreement among the States of the region to ensure conditions of peace and security within the area, as envisaged in the Declaration of the Indian Ocean as a Zone of Peace, and respect for the independence, sovereignty and territorial integrity of the littoral and hinterland States,

Calling for the renewal of genuinely constructive efforts through the exercise of the political will necessary for the achievement of the objectives of the Declaration of the Indian Ocean as a Zone of Peace,

Deeply concerned at the danger posed by the grave and ominous developments in the area and the resulting sharp deterioration of peace, security and stability which particularly seriously affect the littoral and hinterland States, as well as international peace and security,

Convinced that the continued deterioration of the political and security climate in the Indian Ocean area is an important consideration bearing on the question of the early convening of the Conference and that the easing of tension in the area would enhance the prospect of success being achieved by the Conference,

1. *Takes note* of the report of the *Ad Hoc* Committee on the Indian Ocean and the exchange of views in the Committee;

2. *Regrets* that the *Ad Hoc* Committee has failed to reach consensus on the finalization of the date for the convening in 1983 of the Conference on the Indian Ocean, and takes note of the views expressed relating to the need for the convening of the Conference in the first half of 1984;

3. *Emphasizes* its decision to convene the Conference at Colombo as a necessary step for the implementation of the Declaration of the Indian Ocean as a Zone of Peace, adopted in 1971;

4. *Emphasizes also*, in pursuance of that decision and in consideration of the political and security climate in the Indian Ocean area, its decision to request the *Ad Hoc* Committee to continue its efforts for the necessary harmonization of views on the remaining issues related to the convening of the Conference;

5. *Requests* the *Ad Hoc* Committee to continue its work on the necessary harmonization of views on the relevant issues, including those set forth in paragraph 4 above, and to make every effort to accomplish the necessary preparatory work for the Conference, including consideration of its convening not later than the first half of 1984;

6. *Renews* the mandate of the *Ad Hoc* Committee as defined in the relevant resolutions;

7. *Requests* the *Ad Hoc* Committee to hold three further sessions in 1983 of a duration of two weeks each, with the possibility of holding a fourth session to be considered as required;

8. *Requests* the Chairman of the *Ad Hoc* Committee to continue his consultations on the participation in the work of the Committee by States Members of the United Nations which are not members of the Committee, with the aim of resolving this matter at the earliest possible date;

9. *Requests* the *Ad Hoc* Committee to submit to the General Assembly at its thirty-eighth session a full report on the implementation of the present resolution;

10. *Requests* the Secretary-General to continue to render all necessary assistance to the *Ad Hoc* Committee, including the provision of summary records.

Summary records for the Committee on the Indian Ocean

In a resolution of 16 November 1982,[3] the General Assembly decided that, for an experimental period of three years, none of its subsidiary organs should be entitled to summary records of its meetings, with seven exceptions including the *Ad Hoc* Committee on the Indian Ocean.

The original draft by the Committee on Conferences did not include the *Ad Hoc* Committee among the bodies to be entitled to that service. However, on 25 October, before approving the draft resolution, the Assembly's Fifth (Administrative and Budgetary) Committee adopted, by 87 votes to 1, with 18 abstentions, an amendment introduced by Sri Lanka, and co-sponsored by Egypt, Ethiopia, Guinea, Lebanon, Somalia, Togo and Tunisia, adding the *Ad Hoc* Committee to the list of exceptions.[1]

In its 13 December resolution on the work of the *Ad Hoc* Committee, the Assembly requested the Secretary-General to continue to assist it, including the provision of summary records.[4]

On the recommendation of the Committee on Conferences and of the General Committee of the General Assembly, the *Ad Hoc* Committee was among 11 bodies authorized to meet during the Assembly's regular 1982 session.[2]

Amendment adopted. [1]Egypt, Ethiopia, Guinea, Lebanon, Somalia, Sri Lanka, Togo, Tunisia, A/C.5/37/L.14 (to draft by Committee on Conferences, A/37/32).
Decision (1982). [2]GA: 37/403, para *(a)*, 24 Sep.
Resolutions (1982). GA: [3]37/14 C, para. 3 *(a)*, 16 Nov.; [4]37/96, para. 10, 13 Dec.

South-East Asia

By a resolution of 28 October 1982 on the Kampuchea situation,[2] the General Assembly urged the countries of South-East Asia, once a comprehensive political solution to the Kampuchean conflict was achieved, to exert renewed efforts to establish a zone of peace, freedom and neutrality in South-East Asia.

References to such a zone were to have been included in the proposed comprehensive programme of disarmament considered at the Assembly's special session on disarmament, but consensus was not reached on the wording.[1]

In the general debate at the special session, Indonesia, Malaysia and Thailand noted the continued efforts since 1971 by the Association of South-East Asian Nations (ASEAN) for the establishment of a zone of peace, freedom and neutrality in South-East Asia, which Australia and Democratic Kampuchea supported. Viet Nam said the dialogue with ASEAN countries proposed by the Indo-Chinese States (see Chapter VI of this section) would contribute to creating conditions for a zone of peace, stability and co-operation in South-East Asia.

Report. [1]*Ad Hoc* Committee, A/S-12/32.
Resolution (1982). [2]GA: 37/6, para. 12, 28 Oct.

Mediterranean area

By a note verbale to the Secretary-General dated 5 July 1982,[1] Yugoslavia submitted at the General Assembly's second special session devoted to disarmament a working paper endorsing efforts to transform the Mediterranean into a sea of peace, co-operation, good-neighbourliness and progress of all countries, irrespective of their social system, degree of development or size; the paper contained a suggestion for a United Nations study to provide the basis for a concrete programme to that end, to define specific measures of co-operation, confidence-building and military disengagement.

In the general debate at that session, Cyprus, Malta and Tunisia expressed support for the establishment of a zone of peace and co-operation in the Mediterranean, as did Greece, which envisaged the gradual reduction and ultimate withdrawal of foreign military forces from the region. The Libyan Arab Jamahiriya and Mauritania also called for the removal of the foreign military presence from the Mediterranean. Yugoslavia favoured the convening under United Nations auspices of an international conference on the subject.

On 16 December 1982, in a resolution on the strengthening of international security, the Assembly called on Governments to submit their views on the strengthening of security and co-operation in the Mediterranean, and decided to discuss that topic under a separate agenda item in 1983 (see Chapter VIII of this section).

Note verbale. [1]Yugoslavia, 5 July, A/S-12/AC.1/64.

Confidence-building measures

General Assembly consideration (June/July). During the 1982 special session of the General Assembly devoted to disarmament, Turkey, in a note verbale dated 24 June,[2] discussed the urgency for confidence-building measures that were militarily significant, verifiable and obligatory, so as to reduce the causes of mistrust, misunderstanding, fear, tensions and hostilities. By a note verbale of the same date,[1] the Federal Republic of Germany submitted a working paper on confidence-building measures, suggesting that the Committee on Disarmament prepare agreements on concrete measures and that a United Nations body elaborate a code of conduct containing guidelines on such matters as military manœuvres, notification of arms projects, publication of defence budgets and international incidents.

Texts examined at the special session for inclusion in the draft comprehensive programme of disarmament included two paragraphs on confidence-building measures proposed for the chapter on principles and a section for the chapter on disarmament measures listing a number of specific measures. There was general agreement on one of the paragraphs, which said that measures designed to build confidence should be undertaken to help create conditions for the adoption of additional disarmament measures and to further the relaxation of international tension. There was also at least partial agreement on a number of specific measures proposed for mention, including "hot lines" and other improved communications between Governments, other measures to help prevent the possibility of a surprise attack, promotion of economic co-operation, publication of information on military and security matters, scholarships to foreign military schools, exchange of military delegations and military attachés, information on military activities such as manœuvres, invitations to manœuvres, and limitation of certain military activities.

In the general debate at the special session, Austria attached importance to measures to reduce the danger of surprise attacks or misperceptions, including the provision of objective information on militarily relevant facts (see below) and electronic warning systems (p. 147). Bolivia suggested that the militarily significant States establish a standing committee, parallel to the Committee on

Disarmament, to study and implement ways of increasing confidence. Far from being a substitute for disarmament, said the Netherlands, confidence-building measures could help bring about a climate conducive to disarmament by reducing the misconceptions and uncertainties that were often a stimulus to the arms race.

Poland saw a need for economic confidence-building measures and a system of economic security that would prevent the use of economic pressure for obtaining political goals. Portugal, noting its participation in efforts to create a climate of confidence in Europe, said the adoption of similar measures in other regions, adapted to their specific conditions, could help strengthen international peace and security. Romania said it was of utmost importance for the strengthening of confidence that there be agreement on the withdrawal of all foreign troops to within their national borders and that every State make the firm commitment not to deploy troops on the territory of other States.

The Federal Republic of Germany announced that it was sponsoring an International Symposium on Confidence-building Measures, to take place in that country in the spring of 1983.

Thailand, while recognizing the importance of confidence-building measures, said that, in the face of military *faits accomplis* in countries occupied by foreign forces, any such measures were unrealistic and bound to fail.

General Assembly action (December). Stating that it was convinced of the need to reduce mistrust and fear among States through confidence-building measures, the General Assembly, by a resolution of 13 December 1982[(3)] adopted without vote, requested the Disarmament Commission to consider elaborating guidelines for appropriate types of such measures and for their global or regional implementation. It also invited States to consider the possible introduction of confidence-building measures in their particular regions and, where possible, to negotiate on them in keeping with the conditions and requirements in those regions. The Assembly further recommended that States consider including a reference to, or an agreement on, confidence-building measures when they made joint political statements or declarations. A new item on guidelines for confidence-building measures was included in the provisional agenda of the Assembly's 1983 session.

The First Committee recommended this resolution on 22 November, also without vote, on the basis of a 36-nation text introduced by the Federal Republic of Germany.

Notes verbales. [(1)]Germany, Federal Republic of, 24 June, A/S-12/AC.1/38 & Corr.1; [(2)]Turkey, 24 June, A/S-12/AC.1/34 & Corr.1.

Resolution (1982). [(3)]GA: 37/100 D, 13 Dec., text following.
Meeting records. GA: plenary, A/S-12/PV.2-26, 28, 29 (8 June–10 July), A/37/PV.101 (13 Dec.); *Ad Hoc* Committee, A/S-12/AC.1/PV.10, 13 (29 June, 6 July); 1st Committee, A/C.1/37/PV.3-10, 12-28, *35*, 37, 38, *39* (18 Oct.–22 Nov.).

General Assembly resolution 37/100 D

13 December 1982   Meeting 101   Adopted without vote

Approved by First Committee (A/37/670) without vote, 22 November (meeting 39); 36-nation draft (A/C.1/37/L.35); agenda item 133.

Sponsors: Austria, Bahamas, Bangladesh, Belgium, Bolivia, Canada, Chile, Colombia, Congo, Costa Rica, Denmark, Ecuador, Egypt, Finland, France, Germany, Federal Republic of, Ghana, Greece, Indonesia, Ireland, Italy, Mauritania, Netherlands, New Zealand, Norway, Pakistan, Peru, Philippines, Romania, Spain, Sweden, Turkey, United Kingdom, United States, Uruguay, Zaire.

Confidence-building measures

The General Assembly,

Recalling its resolution 36/97 F of 9 December 1981, in which it took note of the *Comprehensive Study on Confidence-building Measures*, prepared by the Secretary-General with the assistance of the Group of Governmental Experts on Confidence-building Measures appointed by him on an equitable geographical basis,

Expressing its concern about the deterioration of the international situation and the further escalation of the arms race, which both reflect and aggravate the unsatisfactory international political climate, tension and mistrust,

Desirous of strengthening international peace and security and, at the same time, creating and improving conditions conducive to further measures of disarmament,

Noting again the findings of the *Comprehensive Study on Confidence-building Measures* and in particular the important role that confidence-building measures can play with regard to regional and world-wide stability as well as to progress in disarmament,

Mindful of the fact that, while confidence-building measures cannot serve as a substitute for concrete disarmament measures, they play a very significant role in achieving disarmament,

Convinced of the usefulness of confidence-building measures freely arrived at by the States concerned and agreed upon, taking into account the particular conditions and requirements of the regions concerned,

Convinced of the need to reduce mistrust and fear among States through the realization of confidence-building measures, such as those recommended by consensus in the *Comprehensive Study on Confidence-building Measures*, including pertinent and timely information on military activities and other matters pertaining to mutual security, and on measures concerning the military conduct of States in peacetime, as well as through progress on concrete measures of disarmament,

Recalling that confidence reflects a set of interrelated factors of a military as well as of a non-military character and that a plurality of approaches is needed to overcome fear, apprehension and mistrust between States and to replace them by confidence,

1. *Urges* all States to encourage and assist all efforts designed to explore further the ways in which confidence-building measures can strengthen international peace and security;

2. *Invites* all States to consider the possible introduction of confidence-building measures in their particular regions and, where possible, to negotiate on them in keeping with the conditions and requirements prevailing in the respective regions;

3. *Requests* the Disarmament Commission to consider the elaboration of guidelines for appropriate types of confidence-building measures and for the implementation of such measures on a global or regional level;

4. *Further requests* the Disarmament Commission to submit a progress report on its deliberations on this item to the General Assembly at its thirty-eighth session;

5. *Further recommends* that all States consider the inclusion of a reference to, or an agreement on, confidence-building measures, as appropriate, in any joint statements or declarations of a political nature;

6. *Decides* to include in the provisional agenda of its thirty-eighth session an item entitled "Consideration of guidelines for confidence-building measures".

Information on military capabilities

General Assembly consideration (June/July).
During the second special session of the General Assembly devoted to disarmament, Austria, by a letter to the Secretary-General dated 28 June 1982,[1] submitted a memorandum on measures to improve the reliability and objectivity of information on military capabilities, suggesting that international mechanisms to evaluate the state of armaments on a regional, interregional and global level could help defuse international tension, build confidence and prepare the ground for disarmament measures. In the session's general debate, Austria, remarking that inadequate information was one of the main obstacles to arms control, suggested that the Security Council and the Assembly could decide to develop and apply regional, interregional or global mechanisms to establish an objective data base on specific types of weapons systems and military forces and their comparability.

The Federal Republic of Germany said it supported all efforts aimed at greater explicitness, since stability presupposed the openness and calculability of military potentials and activities. Japan asked the United Nations to carry out a study on the possibility of establishing a mechanism to monitor global and regional military situations and make them public as deemed proper. Malta saw a need for a United Nations panel of experts to unravel the technicalities and impact of military technology in a lucid and comprehensible manner so as to educate the public.

Nigeria, noting the rival super-Power claims about which of them retained the edge of superiority in weaponry, suggested that the Assembly decide on modalities for establishing the facts. Romania believed that, with a view to achieving reductions, States should co-operate by providing the elements necessary for measuring military budgets, forces and armaments. The United States said it would propose to the USSR reciprocal exchanges of information, to include strategic forces data as well as advance notification of major strategic exercises that might otherwise be misinterpreted and of intercontinental ballistic missile launches within and beyond national boundaries.

General Assembly action (December). By a resolution of 13 December,[2] the General Assembly called on all States, in particular nuclear-weapon and other militarily significant States, to consider additional measures to facilitate the provision of objective information on, and objective assessments of, military capabilities. The Assembly invited States to communicate to the Secretary-General their views and proposals on such measures, and asked him to submit in 1983 a report containing those views, along with a preliminary analysis of a possible United Nations role in the

provision of objective information on, and objective assessments of, military capabilities.

The resolution was adopted by a recorded vote of 121 to none, with 17 abstentions. The First Committee had approved the draft on 24 November by a recorded vote of 103 to none, with 18 abstentions. The text had 14 sponsors and was introduced by Austria.

Letter. [1]Austria, 28 June, A/S-12/AC.1/59.
Resolution (1982). [2]GA: 37/99 G, 13 Dec., text following.
Meeting records. GA: plenary, A/S-12/PV.2-26, 28, 29 (8 June–10 July), A/37/PV.101 (13 Dec.); 1st Committee, A/C.1/37/PV.3-10, 12-28, *38, 43* (18 Oct.–24 Nov.).

General Assembly resolution 37/99 G

13 December 1982   Meeting 101   121-0-17 (recorded vote)

Approved by First Committee (A/37/667) by recorded vote (103-0-18), 24 November (meeting 43); 14-nation draft (A/C.1/37/L.53); agenda item 55.

Sponsors: Austria, Bahamas, Bangladesh, Belgium, Colombia, Ecuador, France, Ghana, Indonesia, Ireland, Nigeria, Pakistan, Romania, Sweden.

Measures to provide objective information on military capabilities

The General Assembly,

Deeply concerned about the continuing escalation of the arms race, in particular the nuclear-arms race, its extremely harmful effects on world peace and security and the deplorable waste of human and material resources for military purposes,

Recalling paragraph 93 of the Final Document of the Tenth Special Session of the General Assembly, in which it is stated, *inter alia,* that, in order to facilitate the process of disarmament, it is necessary to take measures and to pursue policies to strengthen international peace and security and to build confidence among States, in accordance with the purposes and principles of the Charter of the United Nations,

Bearing in mind that it is also stated, in paragraph 34 of the Final Document, that disarmament, relaxation of international tension, respect for the right of self-determination and national independence, the peaceful settlement of disputes in accordance with the Charter of the United Nations and the strengthening of international peace and security are directly related to each other, that progress in any of these spheres has a beneficial effect on all of them and that, in turn, failure in one sphere has negative effects on others,

Recalling also that, in paragraph 105 of the Final Document, Member States are encouraged to ensure a better flow of information with regard to the various aspects of disarmament, to avoid dissemination of false and tendentious information concerning armaments and to concentrate on the danger of escalation of the arms race and on the need for general and complete disarmament under effective international control,

Noting that misperceptions of the military capabilities and the intentions of potential adversaries, which could be caused, *inter alia,* by lack of objective information, could induce States to undertake armaments programmes leading to the acceleration of the arms race, in particular the nuclear-arms race, and to heightened international tensions,

Aware that objective information on military capabilities, in particular among nuclear-weapon States and other militarily significant States, could contribute to the building of confidence among States and to the conclusion of concrete disarmament agreements and, thereby, help to halt and reverse the arms race,

1. *Calls upon* all States, in particular nuclear-weapon States and other militarily significant States, to consider additional measures to facilitate the provision of objective information on, and objective assessments of, military capabilities;

2. *Invites* all States to submit to the Secretary-General their views and proposals concerning such measures;

3. *Requests* the Secretary-General to submit to the General Assembly at its thirty-eighth session a report containing, first, the replies of Member States called for under paragraph 2 above, and, secondly, on the basis of these replies, a preliminary analysis of the possible role of the United Nations in the context of measures to facilitate the

provision of objective information on, and objective assessments of, military capabilities.

Recorded vote in Assembly as follows:

In favour: Algeria, Angola, Argentina, Australia, Austria, Bahamas, Bahrain, Bangladesh, Barbados, Belgium, Benin, Bhutan, Bolivia, Botswana, Brazil, Burma, Burundi, Canada, Central African Republic, Chad, Chile, Colombia, Comoros, Congo, Costa Rica, Cyprus, Democratic Kampuchea, Denmark, Djibouti, Dominican Republic, Ecuador, Egypt, El Salvador, Equatorial Guinea, Fiji, Finland, France, Gabon, Germany, Federal Republic of, Ghana, Greece, Grenada, Guatemala, Guinea, Guinea-Bissau, Haiti, Honduras, Iceland, Indonesia, Iran, Iraq, Ireland, Israel, Italy, Jamaica, Japan, Jordan, Kenya, Kuwait, Lebanon, Lesotho, Liberia, Luxembourg, Madagascar, Malawi, Malaysia, Maldives, Mali, Malta, Mauritania, Mauritius, Mexico, Morocco, Nepal, Netherlands, New Zealand, Niger, Nigeria, Norway, Oman, Pakistan, Panama, Papua New Guinea, Paraguay, Peru, Philippines, Portugal, Qatar, Romania, Rwanda, Saint Lucia, Saudi Arabia, Senegal, Sierra Leone, Singapore, Solomon Islands, Somalia, Spain, Sri Lanka, Sudan, Suriname, Swaziland, Sweden, Thailand, Togo, Trinidad and Tobago, Tunisia, Turkey, Uganda, United Arab Emirates, United Kingdom, United Republic of Cameroon, United Republic of Tanzania, United States, Upper Volta, Uruguay, Vanuatu, Venezuela, Yemen, Yugoslavia, Zaire.

Against: None.

Abstaining: Afghanistan, Bulgaria, Byelorussian SSR, Cuba, Czechoslovakia, German Democratic Republic, Guyana, Hungary, India, Lao People's Democratic Republic, Mongolia, Mozambique, Poland, Ukrainian SSR, USSR, Viet Nam, Zambia.

Group of governmental experts on military research

By a resolution of 13 December 1982,[3] the General Assembly requested the Secretary-General, assisted by governmental experts, to carry out a comprehensive study on the scope, role and direction of the military use of research and development, the mechanisms involved, its role in the arms race, and its impact on arms limitation and disarmament, with a view to preventing a qualitative arms race and to ensuring the use of scientific and technological achievements ultimately for peaceful purposes only. The Assembly invited States to submit their views on the subject to the Secretary-General by 15 April 1983 and to co-operate with him in pursuing the objectives of the study.

The resolution was adopted by a recorded vote of 137 to none, with 8 abstentions. On 30 November 1982, the First Committee had approved the 16-nation draft, introduced by Sweden and orally revised by its sponsors, by a recorded vote of 103 to none, with 8 abstentions.

Earlier in the year, by a note verbale to the Secretary-General dated 7 July,[1] Sweden forwarded to the Assembly at its special session on disarmament a resumé of a proposal it had previously submitted to the Preparatory Committee for that session for a study on military research and development and its impact on the arms race, with particular regard to the consideration of measures to prevent the further use of science and technology for military purposes.

In another action pertaining to the military use of science and technology, the Assembly, on 9 December, called on States to make efforts to ensure that ultimately scientific and technological achievements would be used solely for peaceful purposes.[2]

Note verbale. [1]Sweden, 7 July, A/S-12/AC.1/66.
Resolutions (1982). GA: [2]37/77 B, 9 Dec.; [3]37/99 J, 13 Dec., text following.

Financial implications. ACABQ report, A/37/7/Add.16; 5th Committee report, A/37/734; S-G statements, A/C.1/37/L.74, A/C.5/37/68.
Meeting records. GA: 1st Committee, A/C.1/37/PV.3-10, 12-28, *38, 44, 48* (18 Oct.–30 Nov.); 5th Committee, A/C.5/37/SR.62 (10 Dec.); plenary, A/37/PV.101 (13 Dec.).

General Assembly resolution 37/99 J

13 December 1982   Meeting 101   137-0-8 (recorded vote)

Approved by First Committee (A/37/667) by recorded vote (103-0-8), 30 November (meeting 48); 16-nation draft (A/C.1/37/L.62), orally revised; agenda item 55.

Sponsors: Argentina, Austria, Bangladesh, Colombia, Ecuador, France, Ghana, India, Indonesia, Ireland, Malta, Mexico, Pakistan, Romania, Sweden, Yugoslavia.

Military research and development

The General Assembly,

Mindful of the important task of the United Nations to evaluate the state of the arms race, in particular the nuclear-arms race, and to deliberate all relevant issues of disarmament,

Recalling the provisions of paragraph 39 of the Final Document of the Tenth Special Session of the General Assembly, the first special session devoted to disarmament, according to which qualitative and quantitative disarmament measures are both important for halting the arms race and efforts to that end must include negotiations on the limitation and cessation of the qualitative improvement of armaments, especially weapons of mass destruction, and the development of new means of warfare, so that ultimately scientific and technological achievements may be used solely for peaceful purposes,

Recalling further that, according to paragraph 103 of the Final Document, the Centre for Disarmament of the Secretariat should intensify its activities in the presentation of information concerning the armaments race and disarmament,

Noting the impact of military research and development on the arms race, in particular in relation to major weapons systems such as nuclear weapons and other weapons of mass destruction,

Concerned that, at present, a large proportion of all scientists and technicians in the world are involved in military programmes,

Noting also that in the arms race, particularly as regards nuclear weapons and other weapons of mass destruction, there is an increasing emphasis on the qualitative aspects,

Recognizing that research and development in certain fields may contribute to disarmament and have conflict-preventing effects,

Aware of the fundamental importance of research and development for peaceful purposes, and of the inalienable right of all States to develop, also in co-operation with other States, their research and development for such purposes,

Convinced of the need to focus attention on the military use of research and development and to prepare the ground for further substantial consideration of this matter,

Recalling the suggestions on military research and development submitted to the General Assembly at its twelfth special session, the second special session devoted to disarmament,

Convinced also that increased information on military research and development could contribute to promoting confidence between States and enhance the possibility of reaching agreements on arms limitation and disarmament,

Convinced further that a study on the military application of research and development would make a valuable contribution to increasing available knowledge on military research and development in all States, particularly research and development by the major military Powers, and to the dissemination of factual information on these issues, as well as the analysis thereof,

1. *Requests* the Secretary-General, with the assistance of qualified governmental experts,* bearing in mind the savings that might be made from the existing budgetary appropriations, to carry out a comprehensive study on the scope, role and direction of the military use of research and development, the mechanisms involved, its role in the overall arms race, in particular the nuclear-arms race, and its impact on arms limitation and disarmament, particularly in relation to major weapons systems, such as nuclear weapons and other weapons of mass destruction, with a view to preventing a qualitative arms race and to ensuring that scientific and technological achievements may ultimately be used solely for peaceful purposes;

2. *Invites* all States to submit to the Secretary-General, not later than 15 April 1983, their views on the subject of the study and to cooperate with the Secretary-General so that the objectives of the study may be achieved;

3. *Requests* the Secretary-General to report on this subject to the General Assembly at its thirty-ninth session.

---

*Subsequently referred to as the Group of Governmental Experts on Military Research and Development.

Recorded vote in Assembly as follows:

In favour: Afghanistan, Algeria, Angola, Argentina, Australia, Austria, Bahamas, Bahrain, Bangladesh, Barbados, Belgium, Benin, Bhutan, Bolivia, Botswana, Brazil, Bulgaria, Burma, Burundi, Byelorussian SSR, Canada, Central African Republic, Chad, Chile, China, Colombia, Comoros, Congo, Costa Rica, Cuba, Cyprus, Czechoslovakia, Democratic Kampuchea, Democratic Yemen, Denmark, Djibouti, Dominican Republic, Ecuador, Egypt, El Salvador, Equatorial Guinea, Ethiopia, Fiji, Finland, France, Gabon, German Democratic Republic, Ghana, Greece, Grenada, Guatemala, Guinea, Guinea-Bissau, Guyana, Haiti, Honduras, Hungary, Iceland, India, Indonesia, Iran, Iraq, Ireland, Israel, Jamaica, Jordan, Kenya, Kuwait, Lao People's Democratic Republic, Lebanon, Lesotho, Liberia, Libyan Arab Jamahiriya, Madagascar, Malawi, Malaysia, Maldives, Mali, Malta, Mauritania, Mauritius, Mexico, Mongolia, Morocco, Mozambique, Nepal, New Zealand, Nicaragua, Niger, Nigeria, Norway, Oman, Pakistan, Panama, Papua New Guinea, Paraguay, Peru, Philippines, Poland, Portugal, Qatar, Romania, Rwanda, Saint Lucia, Sao Tome and Principe, Saudi Arabia, Senegal, Sierra Leone, Singapore, Solomon Islands, Somalia, Spain, Sri Lanka, Sudan, Suriname, Swaziland, Sweden, Syrian Arab Republic, Thailand, Togo, Trinidad and Tobago, Tunisia, Uganda, Ukrainian SSR, USSR, United Arab Emirates, United Republic of Cameroon, United Republic of Tanzania, Upper Volta, Uruguay, Vanuatu, Venezuela, Viet Nam, Yemen, Yugoslavia, Zaire, Zambia.

Against: None.

Abstaining: Germany, Federal Republic of, Italy, Japan, Luxembourg, Netherlands, Turkey, United Kingdom, United States.

Verification measures for disarmament agreements

In 1982, during the second special session of the General Assembly devoted to disarmament, a number of States stressed the importance of ensuring that disarmament agreements were accompanied by adequate machinery to verify that the parties were complying with them. Three proposals to that end were placed before the Assembly.

Italy, by a letter dated 24 June to the Chairman of the *Ad Hoc* Committee of the Twelfth Special Session,[1] submitted a working paper outlining a series of functions for a permanent international body in the United Nations framework that would verify implementation of disarmament agreements and provide technical and legal support to arms-control negotiations.

In a working paper submitted by a note verbale of 25 June to the Secretary-General,[2] Japan proposed that the United Nations Centre for Disarmament establish a division to collect information on compliance with disarmament agreements, prepare lists of experts who could provide technical assistance in fact-finding and other areas, examine the possibility of giving the Secretary-General the authority to mediate and arbitrate on problems arising in the application of agreements, and study ways of assuring compliance with earlier agreements that lacked verification provisions.

A Swedish working paper, transmitted by a letter of 27 June to the Secretary-General,[3] mentioned the concept of "verification by challenge" as a tool for ensuring compliance with international agreements and for alleviating unfounded suspicions of non-compliance.

Several paragraphs on verification, proposed for inclusion in the chapters on principles and on machinery and procedures of the proposed comprehensive programme of disarmament, lacked consensus at the special session.[4]

In the general debate at the special session, many speakers made the point that appropriate and effective verification measures were indispensable in disarmament agreements. This was the view of Australia, Austria, Belgium (on behalf of the European Community (EC) members), Honduras, Japan, Luxembourg, Saint Vincent and the Grenadines, and Spain. China asserted that disarmament agreements should provide for strict and effective international verification as well as sanctions in the event of violation.

In a similar vein, Turkey said no disarmament measure could be effective unless it provided for undiminished security, and this involved adequate and appropriate verification. The United Kingdom regarded verification as the heart of arms control, not an optional extra; where national security was at stake, agreements could not be taken on trust, especially when some States had closed societies. The United States said it had instructed its representatives in the Committee on Disarmament to renew emphasis on verification and compliance; the building of mutual confidence in compliance could be achieved only through greater openness. The Netherlands and Norway saw little value in simple declarations of good intentions.

Several Western countries took note of the USSR stand on verification as expressed at the special session, notably with regard to the draft convention on prohibition of chemical weapons. On behalf of the EC members, Belgium noted that even those who had held a very restrictive attitude on the question had indicated the possibility of a change in their position. Canada saw as positive the approach taken by the USSR Foreign Minister.

Asserting that the international community should tackle verification as one of the significant factors in disarmament negotiations in the 1980s, Canada said that, ideally, the work on verification should prepare the way for arms-control agreements that still lay ahead, as problems of verification would, otherwise, inevitably prevent the conclusion of even well-advanced negotiations. France said it was ready to study proposals to give the United Nations a larger role in all international verification techniques—an idea also favoured by Nepal and New Zealand. Agreeing with Japan on the desirability of forming an international verification unit within the United Nations framework, Italy said such an international body could be established in successive stages, with a corresponding increase in responsibilities and functions, until it took over direct control procedures through a corps of international inspectors. Romania also favoured setting up a United Nations body to monitor and inspect the implementation of disarmament measures. The Netherlands and Zimbabwe favoured giving verification functions to an international disarmament organization (p. 157).

Egypt made the point that a perfect verification system was not possible and that it was necessary to accept a degree of risk for the cause of peace; nevertheless, such a risk was far less than would be entailed by allowing the arms race to continue to its inevitable end—war.

Letters and note verbale (nv). [1]Italy, 24 June, A/S-12/AC.1/19/Rev.1; [2]Japan, 25 June, A/S-12/AC.1/43 & Corr.1 *(nv)*; [3]Sweden, 27 June, A/S-12/AC.1/39.
Report. [4]*Ad Hoc* Committee, A/S-12/32.

Proposed international agency for verification by satellite

General Assembly consideration (June/July). At the 1982 second special session of the General Assembly devoted to disarmament, France, by a note verbale of 26 June,[1] transmitted a proposal that the Secretary-General report on arrangements for implementing institutional aspects of the conclusions of a study submitted in June 1981 by the Group of Governmental Experts on the Question of the Establishment of an International Satellite Monitoring Agency.[3] That study found such an organization feasible and suggested a three-stage plan for enabling it to acquire its own satellites and other technical facilities.

In the general debate at the special session, France said it would continue to work for acceptance of its proposal for such an agency, first made in 1978; it suggested that the activities of the proposed agency should be considered in the context of a restructured United Nations Centre for Disarmament.

Several countries spoke in favour of setting up an agency for arms-control verification, among them Belgium on behalf of the EC members. In a similar vein, Luxembourg thought it could make an important contribution towards eliminating mistrust. Senegal said that such an agency, whose establishment would require less than 1 per cent of annual world arms expenditures, would help to reduce considerably the difficulties involved in verifying disarmament agreements and would prove useful in crisis management. Malta, observing that the skies were criss-crossed by a web of military surveillance satellites, asserted that verification of arms-control

agreements by independent but sophisticated surveillance systems operated by the United Nations should be within the current capabilities of the international community; the study of such a system should become a major priority of disarmament negotiations.

Austria saw a need for an appropriate legal framework for international satellite monitoring.

General Assembly action (December). Referring to the contribution that artificial satellite technology could make in solving problems of monitoring compliance with disarmament agreements, the General Assembly, by a resolution of 9 December 1982,[2] took note of the 1981 study on the implications of establishing an international satellite monitoring agency. The Secretary-General was requested to have the study reproduced as a United Nations publication to ensure its widest possible dissemination, and to report to the Assembly in 1983 on practical modalities for implementing the study's conclusions on institutional aspects.

The resolution was adopted by a recorded vote of 126 to 9, with 11 abstentions, following its approval in the First Committee on 24 November by a recorded vote of 109 to 9, with 8 abstentions.

The 38-nation text, orally revised by its sponsors before approval, was introduced by France, which noted the unanimous conclusion of the experts responsible for the study that the agency should be an independent international body closely linked to the United Nations through the General Assembly. The proposals in the study needed further elaboration on such matters as membership, decision-making and the initial development phase of the agency. Other studies would have to be carried out before the Assembly decided on establishing the agency and called for negotiations to that end.

In explanation of its negative vote, the USSR expressed serious doubts as to the desirability of establishing a monitoring or control procedure without any link to actual disarmament measures, and which implied a review and subsequent adaptation of agreements to the work of the agency. Also voicing doubts, Cuba abstained in the vote.

Favouring the resolution, the Philippines, noting that the agency's budget could ultimately reach hundreds of millions of dollars, hoped an equitable financing formula would be devised which would allow developing countries to contribute to the agency's establishment and maintenance in a manner commensurate with their means, while the greater burden of supporting the agency should rest with the major Powers that had created the problems in the first place.

Note verbale. [1]France, 26 June, A/S-12/AC.1/55.
Resolution (1982). [2]GA: 37/78 K, 9 Dec., text following.
Yearbook reference. [3]1981, p. 104.
Meeting records. GA: plenary, A/S-12/PV.2-26, 28, 29 (8 June–10 July), A/37/PV.98 (9 Dec.); 1st Committee, A/C.1/37/PV.3-10, 12-28, *39, 41, 43* (18 Oct.–24 Nov.).

General Assembly resolution 37/78 K

9 December 1982   Meeting 98   126-9-11 (recorded vote)

Approved by First Committee (A/37/662) by recorded vote (109-9-8), 24 November (meeting 43); 38-nation draft (A/C.1/37/L.55), orally revised; agenda item 50 *(e)*.

Sponsors: Algeria, Argentina, Austria, Bahamas, Bangladesh, Belgium, Bolivia, Brazil, Canada, Central African Republic, Chile, Colombia, Costa Rica, Ecuador, Egypt, France, Ghana, Greece, India, Indonesia, Italy, Liberia, Malta, Mexico, Norway, Pakistan, Peru, Philippines, Portugal, Romania, Senegal, Sudan, Sweden, Togo, Tunisia, Turkey, United Republic of Cameroon, Yugoslavia.

Monitoring of disarmament agreements and strengthening of international security: proposal for the establishment of an international satellite monitoring agency

The General Assembly,

Reaffirming the essential role to be played by appropriate international monitoring measures satisfactory to all interested parties in establishing and implementing disarmament agreements and in strengthening international security and confidence,

Considering the progress made in the technology of earth observation by artificial satellites,

Aware of the important contribution that such technology can make to solving problems posed by monitoring, given, in particular, the need to provide for international measures of a non-discriminatory character which do not constitute interference in the internal affairs of States,

Recalling its resolutions 33/71 J of 14 December 1978, in which it requested the Secretary-General to undertake, with the assistance of a group of qualified governmental experts, a study on the technical, legal and financial implications of establishing an international satellite monitoring agency and to seek the views of Member States on this subject and 34/83 E of 11 December 1979, in which it took note of those views,

Noting with interest the report of the Secretary-General to which was annexed the very detailed study prepared by the Group of Governmental Experts appointed to study the implications of establishing an international satellite monitoring agency,

Emphasizing that technological advances increase the possibilities in this area and that Member States, as well as the international community represented by its competent organs, should be in a position to benefit, in the appropriate conditions, from adequate monitoring techniques, whether through the implementation of disarmament agreements or through the strengthening of international security and confidence,

Convinced that for these reasons consideration of the proposal for the establishment of an international satellite monitoring agency should be pursued in all of its aspects,

1. *Takes note* of the report of the Secretary-General to which was annexed the study on the implications of establishing an international satellite monitoring agency;

2. *Expresses its satisfaction* to the Secretary-General and to the Group of Governmental Experts on the Question of the Establishment of an International Satellite Monitoring Agency, which helped him, for the way in which the report was prepared;

3. *Takes note also* of the conclusions of the study regarding the possibilities of establishing an international satellite monitoring agency;

4. *Requests* the Secretary-General to take the necessary steps to have the report reproduced as a United Nations publication in order to ensure that it receives the widest possible dissemination;

5. *Requests* the Secretary-General to report to the General Assembly, at its thirty-eighth session, on the practical modalities for implementing those conclusions with respect to the institutional aspects of the draft examined in chapter II, part V, of the study.

Recorded vote in Assembly as follows:

In favour: Algeria, Antigua and Barbuda, Argentina, Australia, Austria, Bahamas, Bahrain, Bangladesh, Barbados, Belgium, Belize, Benin, Bhutan, Bolivia, Botswana, Brazil, Burma, Burundi, Canada, Cape Verde, Central African Republic, Chad, Chile, China, Colombia, Comoros, Congo, Costa Rica, Democratic Kampuchea, Denmark, Djibouti, Dominican Republic, Ecuador, Egypt, El Salvador, Fiji, Finland, France, Gabon, Gambia, Germany, Federal Republic of, Ghana, Greece, Guatemala, Guinea, Guinea-Bissau, Guyana, Haiti, Honduras, Iceland, India, Indonesia, Iran, Iraq, Ireland, Israel, Italy, Ivory Coast, Jamaica, Japan, Jordan, Kenya, Kuwait, Liberia, Libyan Arab Jamahiriya, Luxembourg, Madagascar, Malawi, Malaysia, Maldives, Mali, Malta, Mauritania, Mauritius, Mexico, Morocco, Nepal, Netherlands, New Zealand, Nicaragua, Niger, Nigeria, Norway, Oman, Pakistan, Panama, Papua New Guinea, Paraguay, Peru, Philippines, Portugal, Qatar, Romania, Rwanda, Saint Lucia, Saudi Arabia, Senegal, Sierra Leone,

Singapore, Solomon Islands, Somalia, Spain, Sri Lanka, Sudan, Suriname, Swaziland, Sweden, Syrian Arab Republic, Thailand, Togo, Trinidad and Tobago, Tunisia, Turkey, Uganda, United Arab Emirates, United Kingdom, United Republic of Cameroon, United Republic of Tanzania, Upper Volta, Uruguay, Vanuatu, Venezuela, Yemen, Yugoslavia, Zaire, Zambia.

Against: Bulgaria, Byelorussian SSR, Czechoslovakia, German Democratic Republic, Hungary, Mongolia, Poland, Ukrainian SSR, USSR.

Abstaining: Afghanistan, Angola, Cuba, Cyprus,[a] Democratic Yemen, Grenada, Lao People's Democratic Republic, Lebanon, Mozambique, United States, Viet Nam.

[a]Later advised the Secretariat it had intended to vote in favour.

Disarmament and international security

General Assembly consideration (June/July).

At the General Assembly's 1982 special session on disarmament, Japan, in a working paper submitted by a note verbale to the Secretary-General dated 25 June,[1] proposed technical studies by a group of experts on the role the United Nations might play in the prevention and peaceful solution of international conflicts, as well as in peace-keeping, with a view to promoting disarmament.

Also before the Assembly was a report of the Secretary-General[3] containing the views of nine States, submitted in response to a December 1981 request of the Assembly,[7] on an experts' study issued in November 1981 on the relationship between disarmament and international security.[8]

Measures aimed at achieving relaxation of international tension and preventing the use of force in international relations were proposed for inclusion in the disarmament measures chapter of the draft comprehensive programme of disarmament examined at the special session, but there was no agreement on the wording of most of them.[2]

There was a large measure of agreement on a chapter on disarmament and international security containing the following points, among others: disarmament and international security were directly related; the causes of the arms race and threats to peace must be reduced, and effective action taken to eliminate tensions and settle disputes peacefully; progress in disarmament should be accompanied by means to strengthen institutions for maintaining peace and settling disputes, including an international peace force; disarmament should take place in an equitable and balanced manner to ensure the right of each State to security and to ensure that no State or group of States could obtain advantages; progress in disarmament and the strengthening of international security should be pursued in parallel; and States should refrain from the threat or use of force in international relations, settle disputes without endangering peace and security or justice, and support a stronger United Nations role in action against threats to and breaches of the peace and in dispute settlement.

In the general debate at the special session, many speakers referred to the close link between disarmament and international security.

Bangladesh urged the Assembly to adopt an action programme to include a complete prohibition of the use and threat of force as a means of settling disputes. Lebanon recalled its earlier proposals for an international status of neutrality for countries where external conflicts projected into internal divisions, and for a permanent international peace-keeping force capable of guaranteeing the security of smaller nations unwilling to invest in armaments at the expense of more vital needs.

As long as aggression continued and a major Power could invade a neighbouring State to ensure ideological obedience, said Portugal, progress in disarmament would be difficult. The settlement of international disputes by force, which led to escalation of the arms race, was occurring because countries had lost confidence, said Qatar. Romania suggested that the Assembly adopt a declaration on the settlement of all disputes exclusively by peaceful means and create a special body that would attempt to organize negotiations and solve disputes by those means only; States which failed to make use of such a body or disregarded the fundamental requirement of peaceful settlement would be considered aggressors. Uruguay said the primary necessity was to lessen tensions through common efforts to create a climate of confidence, in which disarmament would be negotiated gradually and patiently.

A number of States cited the need to maintain defensive strength in response to an unsettled world. Referring to the arms race as more frequently a result than a cause of international tension, Belgium stated that, as long as tensions persisted, adequate defence would remain necessary to ensure security; security did not come with unilateral disarmament. As long as tyranny was armed, declared Israel, liberty must have and develop weapons for its defence. No disarmament measure could be effective, said Turkey, unless it provided for undiminished security. In the view of the United Kingdom, arms control carried out in such a way as to damage peace must be resisted; there had been occasions when the known or perceived military weakness of an opponent had been at least as potent a cause of war as military strength.

The absence of an effective collective security system was mentioned by many as contributing to the arms build-up. Fear of external threat was a major reason for arms purchases by developing countries, Antigua and Barbuda observed, and such threats existed only because the United Nations had not lived up to its commitment to provide collective security. Only after collective security had established confidence that States would not become victims of aggression could disarmament be tackled effectively, said Cyprus. If there had been an effective international security system, Jordan observed, the world would not have witnessed such a growth in military expenditures and destructive weapons.

Singapore said nations would continue to arm themselves as long as violence was a fact of life and as long as the collective security system embodied in the Charter of the United Nations had little or no efficacy. Zaire said that, in escalating the arms race, Governments were turning their backs on the system for the maintenance of international peace and security provided for in the Charter. Several countries made suggestions to strengthen United Nations machinery in this respect (p. 149).

Also speaking of how insecurity in international relations stimulated the arms race, Iran said the super-Powers were creating tension so as to force other countries to purchase weapons from them and take refuge under their protective umbrella, making them join the ranks of satellite countries to whose resources the super-Powers could have easy access.

The reverse of this relationship—the arms race as a stimulant to insecurity—was pointed out by a number of speakers. The theories that based national security on armament had proved erroneous, said Egypt, since the arms race had undermined international peace and security, particularly since the introduction of nuclear weapons. The existence of arms, declared Saint Vincent and the Grenadines, seemed to give psychological confidence and strength, sometimes leading to recklessness and adventurism. Sierra Leone remarked that the continued massive acquisition of arms had led to the denial of self-determination of peoples and allowed régimes to blackmail others with the threat of annihilation.

Austria and Japan said nations had been trapped in a vicious circle in which the military strength of one State led to insecurity and fear among others, causing them in turn to strengthen their military arsenals and leading to war and destruction. One way out of that circle, Austria added, would be to develop co-operation among States and thus create confidence and mutual dependence, as had happened in Western Europe since the Second World War. Japan saw three aspects to disarmament—reversal of the arms race, utilization of the resources thus released to alleviate the poverty and social instability that bred conflict, and strengthening United Nations peacekeeping functions. One of the major causes of deterioration in international security, in Yugoslavia's view, was the fact that the forces threatening freedom, as well as the instruments of military intervention, had been growing much faster than the national defence capabilities of threatened countries.

France remarked that those who were so virtuously astonished to see poor countries spend so much on armaments must admit that the worsening of economic inequalities and social injustices contributed to insecurity and tension.

Guyana suggested that the special session provided a unique opportunity to start searching for ways to explore the preventive security aspects of the Charter. Senegal suggested that the permanent members of the Security Council and representatives chosen from the various geographical groups at the United Nations participate together in a summit meeting which would deal exclusively with promoting international peace and security.

General Assembly action (December). By a resolution of 13 December 1982,[4] the General Assembly called on States to act promptly in implementing its 1981 resolution on disarmament and international security[6] and to co-operate in rendering more effective the system of security provided for in the United Nations Charter, thus facilitating substantial disarmament. The Assembly requested the Security Council, in particular its permanent members, to take measures for the effective implementation of its decisions for the maintenance of international peace and security.

The Assembly took this action by a recorded vote of 115 to none, with 28 abstentions, following approval by the First Committee on 24 November of an 18-nation text, introduced by Cyprus and revised by the sponsors, by a recorded vote of 103 to none, with 25 abstentions.

In a 16 December resolution on the strengthening of international security,[5] the Assembly called on States, in particular nuclear-weapon and other militarily significant States, to take immediate steps aimed at promoting the collective security system envisaged in the Charter, together with measures for halting the arms race and achieving general and complete disarmament under effective international control.

Note verbale. [1]Japan, 25 June, A/S-12/AC.1/45 & Corr.1.
Reports. [2]*Ad Hoc* Committee, A/S-12/32; [3]S-G, A/S-12/16 & Add.1.
Resolutions (1982). GA: [4]37/100 E, 13 Dec., text following; [5]37/118, para. 4, 16 Dec.
Resolutions (prior). GA, 9 Dec. 1981: [6]36/97 K (YUN 1981, p. 101); [7]36/97 L (*ibid.*, p. 102).
Yearbook reference. [8]1981, p. 99.
Meeting records. GA: plenary, A/S-12/PV.2-26, 28, 29 (8 June–10 July), A/37/PV.101 (13 Dec.); 1st Committee, A/C.1/37/PV.3-10, 12-28, *30, 38, 43* (18 Oct.–24 Nov.).

General Assembly resolution 37/100 E

13 December 1982   Meeting 101   115-0-28 (recorded vote)

Approved by First Committee (A/37/670) by recorded vote (103-0-25), 24 November (meeting 43); 18-nation draft (A/C.1/37/L.39/Rev.1); agenda item 133.

Sponsors: Algeria, Argentina, Bahamas, Bangladesh, Colombia, Congo, Costa Rica, Cyprus, Ecuador, Egypt, Greece, India, Kenya, Malta, Pakistan, Sri Lanka, Sudan, Yugoslavia.

Disarmament and international security

The General Assembly,

Recalling its resolutions 34/83 A of 11 December 1979, 35/156 J of 12 December 1980 and 36/97 K of 9 December 1981,

Viewing with concern the aggravation of the deteriorating world situation which has reached the lowest point of understanding and co-operation for peace and security, thus making the survival of mankind extremely precarious,

Alarmed at the present critical world situation and the incapacity of the United Nations to take decisive action, thus bringing into sharp focus the reality that the Security Council finds itself without the means to give effect to its decisions, even when they were unanimously adopted,

Gravely concerned over the continuing stagnation in the disarmament negotiating efforts, while the arms race has been rapidly escalating with threatening consequences and the danger of the outbreak of nuclear war has increased,

Conscious of the need for a new and more positive approach to the whole problem of disarmament based on rendering operable the collective security system provided for in the Charter of the United Nations in conjunction with efforts towards disarmament agreements,

Convinced that to this end the first step is to restore to the Security Council its meaningfulness by making effective its decisions for the maintenance of international security and peace, as required by the Charter,

Recognizing that this process would create the necessary conditions for the cessation of the arms race and would facilitate productive negotiations on a comprehensive programme of disarmament,

Recognizing further that implementation of such an approach would engender a climate of confidence in the United Nations, thereby initiating a stable détente that would harmonize the actions of nations—more significantly among the major Powers—for co-operation towards peace and survival,

Aware that the principles of disarmament embodied in the Charter are an integral part of the system of collective international security and flow from it,

Recalling paragraph 13 of the Final Document of the Tenth Special Session of the General Assembly, the first special session devoted to disarmament, in which it is recognized that genuine and lasting peace can only be created through the effective implementation of the security system provided for in the Charter and the speedy and substantial reduction of arms and armed forces by international agreement and mutual example,

Recalling further paragraph 62 of the Concluding Document of the Twelfth Special Session of the General Assembly, the second special session devoted to disarmament, in which it stressed the need for strengthening the central role of the United Nations in the field of disarmament and the implementation of the security system provided for in the Charter in accordance with the Final Document of the Tenth Special Session,

Noting with appreciation the report of the Secretary-General on the work of the Organization, in which he emphasized, *inter alia*, that "our most urgent goal is to reconstruct the Charter concept of collective action for peace and security so as to render the United Nations more capable of carrying out its primary function" and appealed to all Governments to make a serious effort for "a more stable system of collective international security",

Reaffirming its resolution 36/97 K of 9 December 1981, in which it called for the provisions of its resolution 35/156 J of 12 December 1980, adopted by consensus, to be carried out,

1. *Calls upon* all States to take prompt action for the implementation of General Assembly resolution 36/97 K and to co-operate towards making more effective the system of security provided for in the Charter of the United Nations, thus effectively facilitating substantial disarmament;

2. *Requests* the Security Council—and more significantly its permanent members—to proceed with a sense of urgency to the necessary measures for the effective implementation of the decisions of the Council, in accordance with the Charter, for the maintenance of international peace and security.

Recorded vote in Assembly as follows:

In favour: Algeria, Angola, Argentina, Australia, Austria, Bahrain, Bangladesh, Barbados, Benin, Bhutan, Bolivia, Botswana, Burma, Burundi, Central African Republic, Chad, Chile, China, Colombia, Comoros, Congo, Costa Rica, Cyprus, Democratic Kampuchea, Democratic Yemen, Denmark, Djibouti, Dominican Republic, Ecuador, Egypt, El Salvador, Equatorial Guinea, Ethiopia, Fiji, Finland, Gabon, Ghana, Greece, Guatemala, Guinea, Guinea-Bissau, Guyana, Haiti, Honduras, Iceland, India, Indonesia, Iran, Iraq, Ireland, Israel, Jamaica, Japan, Jordan, Kenya, Kuwait, Lebanon, Lesotho, Liberia, Libyan Arab Jamahiriya,

Madagascar, Malaysia, Maldives, Mali, Malta, Mauritania, Mauritius, Mexico, Morocco, Nepal, Nicaragua, Niger, Nigeria, Norway, Oman, Pakistan, Panama, Papua New Guinea, Paraguay, Peru, Philippines, Qatar, Romania, Rwanda, Saint Lucia, Sao Tome and Principe, Saudi Arabia, Senegal, Sierra Leone, Singapore, Solomon Islands, Somalia, Spain, Sri Lanka, Sudan, Suriname, Swaziland, Sweden, Syrian Arab Republic, Thailand, Togo, Trinidad and Tobago, Tunisia, Uganda, United Arab Emirates, United Republic of Cameroon, United Republic of Tanzania, Upper Volta, Uruguay, Vanuatu, Venezuela, Yemen, Yugoslavia, Zaire, Zambia.

Against: None.

Abstaining: Afghanistan, Belgium, Brazil,[a] Bulgaria, Byelorussian SSR, Canada, Cuba, Czechoslovakia, France, German Democratic Republic, Germany, Federal Republic of, Grenada, Hungary, Italy, Lao People's Democratic Republic, Luxembourg, Malawi, Mongolia, Mozambique, Netherlands, New Zealand, Poland, Portugal, Ukrainian SSR, USSR, United Kingdom, United States, Viet Nam.

[a]Later advised the Secretariat it had intended to vote in favour.

Report of the Independent Commission on Disarmament and Security Issues

By a resolution of 13 December 1982,[2] adopted without vote, the General Assembly requested the Secretary-General to transmit to the Disarmament Commission the report of the Independent Commission on Disarmament and Security Issues, entitled "Common Security—a programme for disarmament".[1] In so doing, the Assembly requested the Disarmament Commission to consider the disarmament-related recommendations and proposals in that report and to suggest to the Assembly effective follow-up measures within the United Nations system or otherwise.

The First Committee had approved this resolution on 24 November, also without vote, on a text introduced by Sweden and sponsored also by Ecuador, Indonesia, Mali, Mexico and Nigeria.

Although joining in the consensus, France, the Federal Republic of Germany, India, Japan, Turkey and the United States expressed reservations about requesting the United Nations, composed of Member States, to commend reports produced by a private group of individuals or to conduct follow-up work on them.

The report of the Independent Commission, adopted by it on 25 April, was introduced at the General Assembly's special session on disarmament by its Chairman, Olof Palme of Sweden. Mr. Palme stated that the Commission, in offering a practical programme of action, had rejected the doctrines of limited or winnable nuclear war, concluded that a doctrine of common security should replace the current expedient of deterrence through armaments, and recognized the United Nations as the most valuable tool for common security that should be used in a more determined way. The Commission, composed of prominent individuals from various parts of the world, had begun its work in September 1980.

The value of the Independent Commission and its report were hailed by several speakers during the general debate at the special session, among them Canada, Greece, Ireland, Malta, Nepal, Oman and Sweden. Antigua and Barbuda urged the Assembly to take account of the Commission's recom-

mendations to improve Security Council procedures for dealing with disputes between developing countries, and Denmark and Sweden called attention to its proposals to increase the role of the Secretary-General and the Security Council in preventing hostilities. Austria concurred with the Commission's conclusion on common security and said its proposal for a zone in Central Europe free of tactical nuclear weapons deserved consideration. Denmark and Poland also regarded as interesting the Commission's ideas on disarmament in Europe.

Report. [1]Independent Commission on Disarmament and Security Issues, A/CN.10/38.
Resolution (1982). [2]GA: 37/99 B, 13 Dec., text following.
Meeting records. GA: *Ad Hoc* Committee, A/S-12/AC.1/PV.4 (23 June); 1st Committee, A/C.1/37/PV.3-10, 12-28, *35, 42* (18 Oct.–24 Nov.); plenary, A/37/PV.101 (13 Dec.).

General Assembly resolution 37/99 B

13 December 1982   Meeting 101   Adopted without vote

Approved by First Committee (A/37/667) without vote, 24 November (meeting 42); 6-nation draft (A/C.1/37/L.30); agenda item 55.

Sponsors: Ecuador, Indonesia, Mali, Mexico, Nigeria, Sweden.

Report of the Independent Commission on Disarmament and Security Issues

The General Assembly,

Concerned over the alarming state of the arms race and the risks it causes to the very survival of humanity,

Recognizing the central role of the United Nations in reducing tension, in safeguarding and promoting confidence between States and in furthering common security and the cause of disarmament,

Having noted the report of the Independent Commission on Disarmament and Security Issues entitled "Common Security—a programme for disarmament", submitted to the General Assembly at its twelfth special session,

Convinced that the Commission has made an important contribution to the discussion and deliberation on disarmament and security issues and that its recommendations and proposals, embodied in its programme of action, should be further considered within the United Nations system,

Noting that the recommendations in the report were addressed to Governments and to the United Nations and its organs,

Convinced of the importance of ensuring an effective follow-up to the report in the United Nations system and in other relevant contexts,

1. *Requests* the Secretary-General to transmit the report of the Independent Commission on Disarmament and Security Issues to the Disarmament Commission;

2. *Further requests* the Disarmament Commission to consider those recommendations and proposals in the report that relate to disarmament and arms limitation and to suggest, in a report to the General Assembly, how best to ensure an effective follow-up thereto within the United Nations system or otherwise;

3. *Decides* to include in the agenda of its thirty-eighth session an item entitled "Independent Commission on Disarmament and Security Issues: report of the Disarmament Commission".

Disarmament and development

General Assembly consideration (June/July). In the Concluding Document of its second special session on disarmament,[6] approved on 10 July 1982, the General Assembly noted the organic relationship between arms expenditures and economic and social development, as well as the vast increase world-wide in military budgets since 1978, and stated that exisiting and planned military programmes constituted a colossal waste of precious resources which might otherwise be used to elevate living standards of all peoples.

This statement was included in the conclusions of the *Ad Hoc* Committee of the Twelfth Special Session (p. 12). Other passages on disarmament and development, many of them in square brackets indicating that consensus on them had not been reached, were included in the draft comprehensive programme of disarmament submitted by Working Group I of the *Ad Hoc* Committee (p. 19). One paragraph which was free from square brackets, included in the chapter on principles, stated that the continuation of the arms race was detrimental to and incompatible with the new international economic order. It added that resources released as a result of disarmament should be devoted to the economic and social development of all nations and contribute to bridging the economic gap between developed and developing countries.

A chapter of the draft programme was devoted to disarmament and development, but most of its provisions remained in square brackets or existed in alternative versions. The only paragraph without brackets stated that a comprehensive disarmament programme could make an effective contribution to economic and social development of all States, in particular the developing countries.

The draft chapter included a series of measures to achieve that aim, of which only four were without brackets. These stated that: effective follow-up on the disarmament-development perspective should be undertaken at different levels so that national and United Nations activities could reinforce each other; the Secretary-General, assisted by experts, should update periodically the study on the economic and social consequences of the arms race and of military expenditures; the Secretary-General should promote and co-ordinate the incorporation of the disarmament-development perspective in programmes and activities of the United Nations system; and States should endeavour when possible to transfer resources released by disarmament to purposes of internal and international development rather than to another type of military expenditure.

At the special session, a working paper by Denmark, Finland, Iceland, Norway and Sweden, submitted by a letter to the Secretary-General dated 19 April,[2] suggested steps to follow up the recommendations contained in the 1981 study by the Group of Governmental Experts on the Relationship between Disarmament and Development.[13]

The Nordic States subsequently proposed, by a note verbale dated 28 June,[3] specific measures, including the following: by the United Nations, a General Assembly discussion every fifth year of the conversion of resources from military to economic and social purposes, development of methods to identify and analyse the benefits of such conversion, exploration of methods for collecting and disseminating information on experiences with conversion, investigation of the nature and amount of information on military use of resources and arms transfers States ought to supply to the United Nations, publication of comparable data from all countries, investigation of the modalities for an international disarmament fund for development, and information activities on the economic and social consequences of the arms race and benefits of disarmament; and by individual countries, analysis and publicity of the economic and social consequences of military spending, work on methods to identify and analyse the benefits of reallocating such spending, and creation of prerequisites to facilitate conversion.

The views of 21 Member States on the United Nations study were contained in a report of the Secretary-General[7] submitted in response to a December 1981 request of the Assembly.[12]

The Assembly also received, by a letter dated 28 May from the Executive Director of the United Nations Children's Fund (UNICEF) to the Assembly President,[5] a message from the UNICEF Executive Board, adopted on 18 May, in which the Board appealed to the Assembly to take all appropriate steps to assure reduction of arms expenditures and the channelling of part of the funds thus saved towards meeting the minimum requirements of children everywhere—adequate nutrition, safe water, primary health care and suitable education. That appeal was supported by the national committees for UNICEF in Europe, in a 10 June message adopted at their twenty-eighth meeting at Sofia, Bulgaria, and forwarded to the Assembly in a letter to the Secretary-General dated 15 June from Bulgaria.[1]

In the general debate at the special session, a large number of speakers urged that resources released from disarmament be used to promote the well-being of peoples and to improve the economic conditions of the developing countries. France, recalling that it had proposed in 1978 the creation of an international disarmament fund for development, asserted that it was time to begin the transfer to development of the human and financial resources fuelling the arms race. Honduras thought the Assembly might recommend a programme for the reduction of arms expenditures by the most militarily advanced States, for the conversion of the industries involved, and for the transfer of released resources and technology to international economic and social co-operation programmes. Kenya called on those concerned to release resources being unwisely squandered on the arms race for reallocation to the socio-economic development of all, especially the poor. It was impossible, said Mexico, to spend astronomical sums on armaments while proceeding at the same time towards stable and equitable development. The USSR said that part of the savings produced by disarmament could be used to assist developing States.

Various statistics were cited to illustrate the discrepancy in the funds allocated for disarmament and for development, which Nigeria called scandalous and immoral in view of the abject poverty in which two thirds of the world population lived. Afghanistan, Ethiopia and Zaire asserted that annual armament expenditures of over $600 billion exceeded by about 30 times the $20 billion spent on aid to the developing countries. Bulgaria and Jamaica observed that $1 million were being squandered every minute on military preparations world-wide. Others, among them Iran, pointed out that 570 million people faced hunger and malnutrition, 800 million were illiterate and 1,500 million had insufficient medical services, while the amount spent for military purposes averaged $110 a year for each person on earth.

Portugal said the money spent on arms was roughly equal to the total investment in developing countries. Samoa observed that world public health expenditure was only 60 per cent of military expenditure and that resources devoted to medical research were only a fifth of the amount going to military research and development. Senegal asserted that, at the beginning of the Third United Nations Development Decade and the Second Disarmament Decade (the 1980s), the international community had continued to devote 4.5 per cent of its gross national product (GNP) to military budgets, as opposed to 0.3 per cent to development aid.

Burundi believed a mere fifth of world military expenditures, which it said had increased by 3 per cent a year since 1978, could ensure implementation of the International Development Strategy for the Third United Nations Development Decade,[11] while Uganda estimated that 5 per cent of such expenditures would be sufficient.

Zimbabwe and several others cited figures to the effect that some 500,000, or 20 per cent, of the world's scientists and technicians were involved in military research, instead of being used in the field of development for the good of humanity.

Statistics showing the extent to which development and welfare could be supported by channelling resources away from armaments had been reiterated time and again, with negligible impact, said India; those with vested interests in the production of weapons of mass destruction, and some of the Governments had helped sustain them, evidently could not care less about the immense costs.

Austria observed that enormous military expenditures were an important reason for the steadily declining willingness to provide appropriate resources for development. Similarly, Costa Rica and Ecuador lamented that the leading Powers were reducing their already modest contributions to programmes designed to promote the transfer of resources for development, while at the same time increasing their military budgets.

Senegal endorsed the idea put forward by the Group of Experts that an international disarmament fund for development should be set up, financed by a tax on military budgets; the proposal seemed feasible to the extent that the United Nations standardized system for reporting military expenditures (p. 117) helped solve the problem of measuring the real level of armament in the world. Costa Rica, urging serious consideration of that proposal, added that, in allocating resources through international co-operation programmes, special attention should be given not only to the comparative poverty of countries but also to the efforts they made towards disarmament. The United Republic of Cameroon also supported the idea of a development fund financed from money released by the reduction of military budgets and the armaments industries.

Denmark suggested that steps be taken to pave the way for reallocating resources from military to civilian purposes. Egypt said agreement must be reached on reducing military expenditures by a certain percentage yearly and allocating a portion of the resources thus saved for the purpose of the economic and social development of developing countries. Several other States made suggestions for the reduction of military budgets (p. 115).

Algeria, Greece, Mongolia, Morocco, Nepal and the Upper Volta spoke of the relationship among disarmament, development and international security, Algeria adding that it was necessary to carry out global economic negotiations and disarmament negotiations simultaneously. Egypt asserted that international security and economic development were but the two sides of the same coin. Illustrating this three-way relationship, Guinea said third world economies were becoming increasingly fragile because of the concern of the great Powers to stabilize régimes which assigned to military expenditure funds that should serve to raise living standards.

Belgium agreed with the recommendations of the 1981 study by the Group of Experts and its conclusion that social injustice and the economic gap between poor and rich countries was an important part of the concept of security. Also welcoming the study as unique and highly relevant, the Netherlands called for a positive follow-up.

Other States referring to the close relationship between disarmament and development included

Angola, Antigua and Barbuda, Argentina, Bangladesh, Bhutan, Brazil, Cuba, the Dominican Republic, Fiji, Gabon, Grenada, Guyana, Indonesia, Japan, Jordan, Kuwait, Madagascar, Maldives, Mali, Mauritania, Papua New Guinea, Singapore, Somalia, Spain, the Sudan, Suriname, Thailand, Togo, Trinidad and Tobago, Tunisia, Turkey, the United Republic of Cameroon, Yemen and Venezuela.

UNCTAD consideration. The Trade and Development Board of the United Nations Conference on Trade and Development (UNCTAD),[8] in September 1982, heard the views of several of its members on the trade and economic aspects of disarmament, a subject which the Board had decided in October 1981[14] that it would discuss in the light of the results of the General Assembly's special session. A representative of the UNCTAD Secretary-General told the Board that the UNCTAD secretariat planned to establish contacts with the United Nations Centre for Disarmament in regard to UNCTAD participation in the World Disarmament Campaign.

A chapter in the UNCTAD *Trade and Development Report, 1982* (see ECONOMIC AND SOCIAL QUESTIONS, Chapter IV) was devoted to some development consequences of armaments expenditure and disarmament. It began by citing rough and unofficial estimates of the resources used for military purposes—$510-630 billion a year for total annual military expenditures, at a growth rate of 3 per cent; more than 50 million persons in military uniforms or producing weapons; military production of about $125-150 billion; a 2-8 per cent share of total consumption of many minerals; rising land requirements for bases, airports and other installations; and an estimated 20-25 per cent of scientific and research activities devoted to military purposes.

The report stated that inflation and unemployment in developed market-economy countries had been aggravated by military spending, which increased demand without making more goods available to those whose income was derived from that expenditure and which created fewer jobs than the same amount spent for civilian purposes. Rechannelling resources to civilian ends could contribute substantially to accelerating long-term economic growth in the socialist countries of Eastern Europe, permit a faster rise in the standard of living, and help solve such problems as the need to speed science and technological progress, raise labour productivity, overcome labour scarcity, and save energy and materials. In the developing countries, whose growth rate of military spending between 1972 and 1981 was twice that of their gross domestic product, such outlays seriously restricted their investment possibilities, while the 12 per cent annual increase in military imports during the 1970s reduced their ability to import economic development goods and raised their external debt.

The chapter concluded by stating that a relaxation of international tension and of the arms race, and the redirection of armaments expenditure to civilian use, could play an important role in revitalizing the world economy and accelerating the development of developing countries.

General Assembly action (December). The relationship between disarmament and development was included in the agenda of the Assembly's 1982 regular session at the request of Sweden, which observed, in an explanatory memorandum annexed to a letter of 20 August to the Secretary-General,[4] that the Assembly at its special session had been unable to act on all of the proposals in the Nordic countries' working paper (see above).

By a resolution of 9 December,[9] the Assembly urged Member States, and requested the Secretary-General, to act on the recommendations made in 1981 by the Group of Governmental Experts. It determined that the question of reallocation and conversion of resources, through disarmament measures, from military to civilian purposes should be included in its provisional agenda at intervals to be decided upon, starting with its 1985 session. Further, the Assembly recommended that the United Nations Institute for Disarmament Research, in consultation with other international institutions, should investigate the modalities of an international disarmament fund for development.

The resolution was adopted by a recorded vote of 136 to none, with 10 abstentions. The First Committee had approved on 23 November the 35-nation draft, introduced by Sweden, by a recorded vote of 114 to none, with 11 abstentions.

In an 18 December resolution on human rights and scientific and technological developments,[10] the Assembly stressed the importance of implementing practical disarmament measures for the release of substantial additional resources, which should be used for social and economic development, particularly to benefit the developing countries.

Letters and note verbale (nv). [1]Bulgaria: 15 June, A/S-12/AC.1/9. Denmark, Finland, Iceland, Norway, Sweden: [2]19 Apr., A/S-12/18; [3]28 June, A/S-12/AC.1/49 *(nv)*. [4]Sweden: 20 Aug., A/37/195. [5]UNICEF Executive Director: 28 May, A/S-12/AC.1/3.
Reports. [6]*Ad Hoc* Committee, A/S-12/32; [7]S-G, A/S-12/13 & Add.1-4; [8]TDB, A/37/15, vol. II.
Resolutions (1982). GA: [9]37/84, 9 Dec., text following; [10]37/189 A, para. 3, 18 Dec.
Resolutions (prior). GA: [11]35/56, annex, 5 Dec. 1980 (YUN 1980, p. 503); [12]36/92 G, 9 Dec. 1981 (YUN 1981, p. 99).
Yearbook references. 1981, [13]p. 96, [14]p. 99.
Meeting records. GA: plenary, A/S-12/PV.2-26, 28, 29 (8 June-10 July), A/37/PV.98 (9 Dec.); *Ad Hoc* Committee, A/S-12/AC.1/PV.2, 4, 10 (14-29 June); General Committee, A/BUR/37/SR.2 (22 Sep.); 1st Committee, A/C.1/37/PV.3-10, 12-28, *31, 41* (18 Oct.-23 Nov.).

General Assembly resolution 37/84

9 December 1982   Meeting 98   136-0-10 (recorded vote)

Approved by First Committee (A/37/671) by recorded vote (114-0-11), 23 November (meeting 41); 35-nation draft (A/C.1/37/L.17); agenda item 136.

Sponsors: Austria, Bahamas, Bangladesh, Colombia, Congo, Costa Rica, Denmark, Ecuador, Egypt, Finland, France, Ghana, Greece, Iceland, Ireland, Jamaica, Kenya, Kuwait, Liberia, Mali, Malta, Mexico, Nepal, Norway, Pakistan, Romania, Rwanda, Senegal, Sierra Leone, Spain, Sri Lanka, Sweden, United Republic of Cameroon, Venezuela, Zaire.

Relationship between disarmament and development

The General Assembly,

Recalling the conclusions contained in chapter VII of the study entitled *The Relationship between Disarmament and Development,*

Recalling also resolution 36/92 G of 9 December 1981, in which the General Assembly, *inter alia,* commended the study, its conclusions and its recommendations to the attention of all Member States and decided to transmit the report to the Assembly at its twelfth special session for its substantive consideration and appropriate action,

Noting the proposals on the follow-up decisions regarding the study, circulated as official documents at the twelfth special session of the General Assembly,

Noting also that, in the Concluding Document of the Twelfth Special Session of the General Assembly, it is recommended that the items on the agenda on which the Assembly had not reached decisions should be taken up at its thirty-seventh session for further consideration,

Noting further that it has decided to include the question of the relationship between disarmament and development in its agenda as a separate item,

1. *Requests* the Secretary-General to take appropriate administrative action in accordance with the recommendations of the Group of Governmental Experts on the Relationship between Disarmament and Development, as specified in chapter VII of the study entitled *The Relationship between Disarmament and Development;*

2. *Urges* Member States to consider appropriate measures in accordance with all relevant recommendations of the Group of Governmental Experts;

3. *Determines* that the question of reallocation and conversion of resources, through disarmament measures, from military to civilian purposes should be included in the provisional agenda of the General Assembly at intervals to be decided upon, starting with its fortieth session, in 1985;

4. *Recommends* that an investigation—with due regard to the capabilities of existing agencies and institutions currently responsible for the international transfer of resources—of the modalities of an international disarmament fund for development should be undertaken by the United Nations Institute for Disarmament Research, in consultation with other relevant international institutions;

5. *Requests* the Secretary-General to report to the General Assembly at its thirty-eighth session on the measures taken in implementation of the present resolution.

Recorded vote in Assembly as follows:

In favour: Afghanistan, Algeria, Angola, Argentina, Australia, Austria, Bahamas, Bahrain, Bangladesh, Barbados, Belgium, Belize, Benin, Bhutan, Bolivia, Botswana, Brazil, Burma, Burundi, Canada, Cape Verde, Central African Republic, Chad, Chile, China, Colombia, Comoros, Congo, Costa Rica, Cuba, Cyprus, Democratic Kampuchea, Democratic Yemen, Denmark, Djibouti, Dominican Republic, Ecuador, Egypt, El Salvador, Ethiopia, Fiji, Finland, France, Gabon, Gambia, Germany, Federal Republic of, Ghana, Greece, Grenada, Guatemala, Guinea, Guinea-Bissau, Guyana, Haiti, Honduras, Iceland, India, Indonesia, Iran, Iraq, Ireland, Israel, Italy, Ivory Coast, Jamaica, Japan, Jordan, Kenya, Kuwait, Lebanon, Liberia, Libyan Arab Jamahiriya, Luxembourg, Madagascar, Malawi, Malaysia, Maldives, Mali, Malta, Mauritania, Mauritius, Mexico, Morocco, Mozambique, Nepal, Netherlands, New Zealand, Nicaragua, Niger, Nigeria, Norway, Oman, Pakistan, Panama, Papua New Guinea, Paraguay, Peru, Philippines, Portugal, Qatar, Romania, Rwanda, Saint Lucia, Sao Tome and Principe, Saudi Arabia, Senegal, Sierra Leone, Singapore, Solomon Islands, Somalia, Spain, Sri Lanka, Sudan, Suriname, Swaziland, Sweden, Syrian Arab Republic, Thailand, Togo, Trinidad and Tobago, Tunisia, Turkey, Uganda, United Arab Emirates, United Kingdom, United Republic of Cameroon, United Republic of Tanzania, United States, Upper Volta, Uruguay, Vanuatu, Venezuela, Yemen, Yugoslavia, Zaire, Zambia.

Against: None.

Abstaining: Bulgaria, Byelorussian SSR, Czechoslovakia, German Democratic Republic, Hungary, Lao People's Democratic Republic, Mongolia, Poland, Ukrainian SSR, USSR.

Economic and social consequences of the arms race

Study by the Group of Experts. A group of experts, appointed by the Secretary-General in pursuance of a 1980 General Assembly request[4] to update a 1977 report entitled *Economic and Social Consequences of the Arms Race and of Military Expenditure,*[5] completed its work and submitted a report in 1982.[1]

Known as the Group of Consultant Experts on the Economic and Social Consequences of the Arms Race and of Military Expenditures, the 12-member Group held three sessions in New York between July 1981 and July 1982, the last two of which were in 1982: 18 to 29 January and 19 to 30 July. Its report, unanimously adopted on 30 July, was transmitted to the Assembly in September by the Secretary-General.

The report consisted of five chapters, on the dynamics of the arms race, resources and the arms race, military outlays and socio-economic development, international consequences of the arms race, and conclusions and recommendations.

The Group observed that, in the four years between the first (1978) and second (1982) special sessions of the Assembly devoted to disarmament, world military expenditures had exceeded $1,600 billion—equivalent to $1 million per minute during 1981—and the international weapons trade, between 1977 and 1981, had amounted to over $120-140 billion, two thirds of it with the tension-ridden developing countries which had closely witnessed or experienced practically all the more than 130 armed conflicts since the Second World War. Annual world military expenditure (p. 115) in 1981 was $550-600 billion, as compared to $350 billion in 1977: roughly one fifth of the total military outlays were estimated to be absorbed into growing stockpiles of nuclear weapons, which already contained over 1 million times the explosive force of the Hiroshima bomb.

Four interrelated and major international consequences of the arms race discussed by the experts were: aggravated threats to international security, a worsening of the international political climate, a distortion of international economic relations and their combined effect on social values. The Group noted that the social and political implications of the arms race had become more serious as economic burdens carried the seeds of social discontent and political tensions within and among nations. Further, the conjunction of external and domestic confrontation, both of them temporarily stabilized through military build-up but ultimately exacerbated by it, could give rise to a particularly precarious situation, and escalations in the arms race, resulting in a larger resource consumption for military purposes, added to the gravity of existing resource-related conflicts which could provoke larger military outlays and further spiralling of the arms race.

In the experts' view, the current stagnation of disarmament negotiations, combined with the failure of the Assembly to adopt a comprehensive programme of disarmament, underlined the need for the United Nations to ensure the resolute pursuit of such negotiations, strengthen and adjust its mechanisms for peaceful settlement of disputes, mobilize world public opinion in sup: port of disarmament through such activities as the World Disarmament Campaign, take measures against the militarization of outer space, improve its statistical data base regarding military budgets, achieve a better understanding of the economic and technological feasibility of conversion among countries at different levels of development, and organize an international co-operative endeavour to reveal the adverse implications of military research and development on civilian sectors of industry and on economic performance in general.

General Assembly consideration (June/July). One of the uncontested paragraphs proposed for inclusion in the chapter on disarmament and development of the draft comprehensive programme of disarmament, considered by the General Assembly at its second special session devoted to disarmament, stated that the Secretary-General, assisted by experts, should periodically update the study on the economic and social consequences of the arms race and of military expenditures.[2]

In the general debate at the special session, a number of speakers referred to the pernicious effects of large military expenditures on world and national economies and on society.

Cyprus said the large military expenditures depleted natural resources and aggravated economic problems, causing political and social instability which in turn contributed to international unrest and the exacerbation of an already dangerous situation. Guinea asserted that the arms race absorbed at least one third of the GNP of the countries afflicted with serious economic and social problems. Italy also spoke of the intolerable economic and social burden of maintaining conventional arsenals (p. 110) which diverted resources essential to development. Malta said that, according to econometric studies, each extra dollar spent on arms reduced domestic investment by roughly 25 cents and agricultural output by 20 cents.

Only a few analysts, said Nigeria, appreciated the link between increasing arms expenditures and decreases in resources available for stimulating the economy, and hardly any of the world's political leaders were courageous enough to implement corrective policies. Romania said military expenditures created difficulties and distortions in the economic and social development of all countries,

particularly the developing countries. Sierra Leone viewed the waste of resources on arms as a major contributor to the current economic crisis. Sweden considered it an expression of misdirected priorities when the super-Powers and other economically advanced countries vied for acquisition of weapons while their own citizens were not provided with work and tolerable economic and social existence.

Somalia, the Sudan and Zimbabwe were among those pointing to a relationship between disarmament and the democratic restructuring of the international economic order, and the Libyan Arab Jamahiriya said the arms race had prevented the establishment of the new order. Ecuador added that disarmament consisted in eliminating economic aggression, such as blockades, tariff barriers, unfair terms of trade and the arbitrary appropriation of the oceans for purposes of war or for plundering the marine resources within the maritime jurisdiction of coastal States.

Angola, responding to the argument that it was impossible to dismantle the arms industry without causing great economic disruption, said the post-war period had already shown that such a transition could take place successfully. Bhutan urged Governments to ensure that restrictions were applied to their armaments industries, lest they discover that without such production their economy would be in serious difficulty.

Many States spoke of international trade in conventional weapons and its effects on economic development.

General Assembly action (December). Welcoming with satisfaction the updated report on the economic and social consequences of the arms race and of military expenditures, the General Assembly, by a resolution adopted without vote on 9 December,[3] recommended that the conclusions of the report be taken into account in future United Nations action on disarmament. The Secretary-General was requested to reproduce the report as a United Nations publication and to publicize it in the framework of the World Disarmament Campaign, taking also into account Member States' views on the report. The Assembly recommended that all Governments ensure the widest distribution of the report, including, where appropriate, its translation into national languages. It decided to include this item in the provisional agenda of its 1985 session.

The First Committee had approved this resolution on 24 November, also without vote, on a 24-nation text introduced by Romania and orally revised by the sponsors.

Publication. [1]*Economic and Social Consequences of the Arms Race and of Military Expenditures* (A/37/386), Sales No. E.83.IX.2.
Report. [2]*Ad Hoc* Committee, A/S-12/32.
Resolution (1982). [3]GA: 37/70, 9 Dec., text following.
Resolution (prior). [4]GA: 35/141, 12 Dec. 1980 (YUN 1980, p. 117).

Yearbook reference. [5]1977, p. 57.
Meeting records. GA: plenary, A/S-12/PV.2-26, 28, 29 (8 June–10 July), A/37/PV.98 (9 Dec.); 1st Committee, A/C.1/37/PV.3-10, 12-28, *32*, 37, *42* (18 Oct.–24 Nov.).

General Assembly resolution 37/70

9 December 1982   Meeting 98   Adopted without vote

Approved by First Committee (A/37/651 and Corr.1) without vote, 24 November (meeting 42); 24-nation draft (A/C.1/37/L.16), orally revised; agenda item 39.

Sponsors: Bahamas, Bangladesh, Colombia, Congo, Czechoslovakia, Ecuador, Egypt, Indonesia, Ireland, Jordan, Liberia, Madagascar, Mali, Malta, Mexico, Peru, Romania, Rwanda, Sweden, United Republic of Cameroon, Uruguay, Venezuela, Yugoslavia, Zaire.

Economic and social consequences of the armaments race and its extremely harmful effects on world peace and security

The General Assembly,

Having considered the item entitled "Economic and social consequences of the armaments race and its extremely harmful effects on world peace and security",

Recalling its resolutions 2667(XXV) of 7 December 1970, 2831(XXVI) of 16 December 1971, 3075(XXVIII) of 6 December 1973, 32/75 of 12 December 1977 and 35/141 of 12 December 1980,

Deeply concerned that the arms race, particularly in nuclear armaments, and military expenditures continue to increase at an alarming speed, constituting a grave danger for world peace and security,

Recalling also the conclusion of the General Assembly at its twelfth special session, the second special session devoted to disarmament, that the vastly increased military budgets have also contributed to current economic problems in certain States and that existing and planned military programmes constitute a colossal waste of precious resources which might otherwise be used to elevate the living standards of all peoples and solve the problems confronting developing countries in achieving economic and social development,

Reaffirming the need for all Governments and peoples to be informed about and understand the situation prevailing in the field of the arms race and disarmament,

Having in mind the objectives of the World Disarmament Campaign, solemnly launched by the General Assembly at its twelfth special session, which is intended to promote public interest in, and support for, reaching agreements on measures of arms limitation and disarmament,

Recalling further paragraph 93 *(c)* of the Final Document of the Tenth Special Session of the General Assembly, the first special session devoted to disarmament, in which it is provided that the Secretary-General shall periodically submit reports to the Assembly on the economic and social consequences of the armaments race and its extremely harmful effects on world peace and security,

Considering that the elaboration of such reports should be viewed as a measure aimed at building confidence among States,

1. *Welcomes with satisfaction* the updated report of the Secretary-General on the economic and social consequences of the arms race and of military expenditures;

2. *Expresses its thanks* to the Secretary-General and to the Group of Consultant Experts on the Economic and Social Consequences of the Arms Race and of Military Expenditures, as well as to the Governments and international organizations that have rendered assistance in updating the report;

3. *Recommends* that the conclusions of the updated report should be brought to the attention of public opinion and also taken into account in future action by the United Nations in the field of disarmament;

4. *Requests* the Secretary-General to make the necessary arrangements for the reproduction of the report as a United Nations publication and to give it publicity in the framework of the World Disarmament Campaign, taking also into account the views expressed on the report by Member States not later than 1 March 1983;

5. *Recommends* that all Governments should ensure the widest possible distribution of the report, including, where appropriate, its translation into the respective national languages;

6. *Invites* the specialized agencies as well as intergovernmental, national and non-governmental organizations to use their facilities to make the report widely known;

7. *Reaffirms* its decision to keep the item entitled "Economic and social consequences of the armaments race and its extremely harmful effects on world peace and security" under constant review, and decides to include it in the provisional agenda of its fortieth session.

Arms race and human rights

On 19 February 1982, the Commission on Human Rights, in a resolution dealing with the relationship between human rights and peace (see ECONOMIC AND SOCIAL QUESTIONS, Chapter XVIII), requested its Sub-Commission on Prevention of Discrimination and Protection of Minorities to carry out a study on the negative consequences of the arms race for the implementation of economic, social, cultural, civil and political rights, the establishment of the new international economic order and, above all, of the inherent right to life.[2] This resolution was forwarded to the General Assembly in June, at its second special session on disarmament, by a note by the Secretary-General.[1]

In a resolution of 18 December on the same topic,[3] the Assembly stressed the urgent need for efforts by the international community to strengthen peace, remove the threat of war, halt the arms race, achieve general and complete disarmament under effective international control, and prevent violations of the principles of the Charter of the United Nations regarding the sovereignty and territorial integrity of States and self-determination of peoples, thus contributing to assuring the right to life.

Note. [1]S-G, A/S-12/AC.1/2.
Resolutions (1982). [2]Commission on Human Rights (report, E/1982/12): 1982/7, paras. 2 & 5, 19 Feb. [3]GA: 37/189 A, para. 2, 18 Dec.

Peaceful uses of science and technology

Action by the Commission on Human Rights. On 19 February 1982, the Commission on Human Rights, in two resolutions on human rights and scientific and technological developments, called on States to use scientific and technological achievements for peaceful economic, social and cultural development and to improve the well-being of peoples,[1] and to ensure that the results of scientific and technological progress were used exclusively in the interests of international peace and for the benefit of mankind.[2]

General Assembly consideration (June/July). In the general debate at the General Assembly's 1982 special session on disarmament, Egypt called for an agreement on measures to halt the use of new technology for non-peaceful purposes, so as to prevent the discovery or development of hitherto unknown weapons or the sudden improvement of existing weapons. India suggested that the Secretary-General be requested to undertake an expert study on the possibility of devising legally binding restrictions on types of scientific and technological research for purposes inconsistent with humanitarian laws and principles.

Nicaragua called on the Assembly to affirm that technological and scientific progress must be in the service of humanity. Portugal saw a need for measures to limit military innovations. In a similar vein, Sweden stated that, in view of the increasingly uncontrolled exploitation of science and technology for military purposes, the introduction of new weapons into new environments should be prohibited, and existing treaties in those fields—covering Antarctica, the sea-bed and outer space—should be made more comprehensive and the loopholes removed. Yemen appealed to the two super-Powers and the international community for action to halt the development of military technology.

Austria considered that the realization of what it called a "technology of peace"—the development of purely defensive electronic warning, detection and protection systems—would enable States to guarantee their security at a fraction of the cost of arms technology. Romania urged that scientists be enabled to participate in United Nations debates on all problems relating to disarmament and peace.

General Assembly action (December). On 9 December, the General Assembly, stating that the time had come to consider ways to solve the problem of renunciation of the use of new discoveries and scientific and technological achievements for military purposes, called on States to ensure that, ultimately, scientific and technological achievements were used solely for peaceful purposes.[4]

The resolution was adopted by a recorded vote of 114 to 10, with 17 abstentions. On 26 November, the First Committee had approved the 13-nation text, introduced by the Byelorussian SSR and revised by the sponsors, by a recorded vote of 89 to 10, with 18 abstentions.

The Assembly mentioned the peaceful uses of scientific and technological achievements in the preamble of another 9 December resolution, calling on militarily significant States to declare that they would refuse to create new types of weapons of mass destruction,[3] as well as in a resolution of 18 December, calling on States to use the achievements of science and technology to promote peaceful social, economic and cultural development.[6]

The Netherlands voted against the 13-nation resolution on the ground that it was too vague and sweeping, asking States to renounce the use of scientific and technological achievements even in exercise of the sovereign right of self-defence. The United Kingdom, concurring, did not believe that such Utopian declarations served to promote serious disarmament measures. Also voting against, Belgium considered more appropriate another text, calling for a study on military research and development.[5] Indonesia, abstaining in the Committee vote but voting in favour in the Assembly, explained that it was a sponsor of the text

referred to by Belgium, which it described as similar to the 13-nation resolution.

Resolutions (1982). Commission on Human Rights (report, E/1982/12), 19 Feb.: [1]1982/4, para. 2; [2]1982/7, para. 3. GA: [3]37/77 A, 9 Dec.; [4]37/77 B, 9 Dec., text following; [5]37/99 J, 13 Dec.; [6]37/189 B, 18 Dec.
Meeting records. GA: 1st Committee, A/C.1/37/PV.3-10, 12-28, 36, 44 (18 Oct.–26 Nov.); plenary, A/37/PV.98 (9 Dec.).

General Assembly resolution 37/77 B

9 December 1982   Meeting 98   114-10-17 (recorded vote)

Approved by First Committee (A/37/659) by recorded vote (89-10-18), 26 November (meeting 44); 13-nation draft (A/C.1/37/L.46/Rev.1); agenda item 47.

Sponsors: Bulgaria, Byelorussian SSR, Cuba, Czechoslovakia, German Democratic Republic, Hungary, Lao People's Democratic Republic, Mali, Mongolia, Poland, Romania, Ukrainian SSR, Viet Nam.

Renunciation of the use of new discoveries and scientific and technological achievements for military purposes

The General Assembly,

Bearing in mind the provisions of paragraph 39 of the Final Document of the Tenth Special Session of the General Assembly, according to which qualitative and quantitative disarmament measures are both important for halting the arms race and efforts to that end must include negotiations on the limitation and cessation of the qualitative improvement of armaments, especially weapons of mass destruction, and the development of new means of warfare, so that, ultimately, scientific and technological achievements may be used solely for peaceful purposes,

Recalling its Declaration on the Use of Scientific and Technological Progress in the Interests of Peace and for the Benefit of Mankind,

Noting that scientific and technological progress has become one of the most important factors in the development of mankind,

Noting with concern that new discoveries and scientific and technological achievements can be used to intensify dangerously the arms race,

Recognizing the necessity to ensure that scientific and technological progress is used exclusively to serve the peaceful aspirations of humanity,

Aware that the time has come to consider ways to solve the problem of renunciation of the use of new discoveries and scientific and technological achievements for military purposes,

Calls upon all States to undertake efforts to ensure that ultimately scientific and technological achievements may be used solely for peaceful purposes.

Recorded vote in Assembly as follows:

In favour: Afghanistan, Algeria, Angola, Antigua and Barbuda, Argentina, Austria, Bahamas, Bahrain, Bangladesh, Barbados, Belize, Benin, Bhutan, Bolivia, Botswana, Brazil, Bulgaria, Burma, Burundi, Byelorussian SSR, Cape Verde, Central African Republic, Chad, Chile, Congo, Cuba, Cyprus, Czechoslovakia, Democratic Yemen, Dominican Republic, Ecuador, Egypt, El Salvador, Ethiopia, Fiji, Finland, Gabon, Gambia, German Democratic Republic, Ghana, Grenada, Guinea, Guinea-Bissau, Guyana, Haiti, Hungary, India, Indonesia, Iran, Iraq, Ireland, Ivory Coast, Jamaica, Jordan, Kenya, Kuwait, Lao People's Democratic Republic, Libyan Arab Jamahiriya, Madagascar, Malaysia, Maldives, Mali, Malta, Mauritania, Mauritius, Mexico, Mongolia, Morocco, Mozambique, Nepal, Nicaragua, Niger, Nigeria, Oman, Pakistan, Panama, Papua New Guinea, Peru, Philippines, Poland, Qatar, Romania, Rwanda, Saint Lucia, Sao Tome and Principe, Sierra Leone, Singapore, Solomon Islands, Somalia, Sri Lanka, Sudan, Suriname, Swaziland, Sweden, Syrian Arab Republic, Thailand, Togo, Trinidad and Tobago, Tunisia, Uganda, Ukrainian SSR, USSR, United Arab Emirates, United Republic of Cameroon, United Republic of Tanzania, Upper Volta, Uruguay, Vanuatu, Venezuela, Viet Nam, Yemen, Yugoslavia, Zaire, Zambia.

Against: Belgium, France, Germany, Federal Republic of, Italy, Luxembourg, Netherlands, Portugal, Turkey, United Kingdom, United States.

Abstaining: Australia, Canada, Colombia, Denmark, Greece, Guatemala, Iceland, Israel, Japan, Lebanon, Liberia, Malawi, New Zealand, Norway, Paraguay, Saudi Arabia, Spain.

Parties to and signatories of multilateral disarmament agreements

In November 1982, the Secretary-General submitted to the General Assembly a report on the status of multilateral disarmament agreements,[2] prepared at the Assembly's December 1981 request[7] on the basis of information received from the States depositaries of those agreements. The report, listing the parties to and signatories of agreements as at 31 July 1982, also contained similar information on the Convention on the Prohibition of Military or Any Other Hostile Use of Environmental Modification Techniques, of which the Secretary-General was the depositary.

As at 31 December 1982, the following numbers of States had become parties to the multilateral disarmament agreements covered in this report (listed in chronological order, with the years in which they were initially signed or opened for signature in parentheses):[1]

(Geneva) Protocol for the Prohibition of the Use in War of Asphyxiating, Poisonous or Other Gases, and of Bacteriological Methods of Warfare (1925): 104 parties
The Antarctic Treaty (1959): 26 parties
Treaty Banning Nuclear Weapon Tests in the Atmosphere, in Outer Space and Under Water (1963): 111 parties
Treaty on Principles Governing the Activities of States in the Exploration and Use of Outer Space, including the Moon and Other Celestial Bodies (1967):[3] 83 parties
Treaty for the Prohibition of Nuclear Weapons in Latin America (1967): 30 parties
Treaty on the Non-Proliferation of Nuclear Weapons (1968):[4] 119 parties
Treaty on the Prohibition of the Emplacement of Nuclear Weapons and Other Weapons of Mass Destruction on the Sea-Bed and the Ocean Floor and in the Subsoil Thereof (1971):[5] 72 parties
Convention on the Prohibition of the Development, Production and Stockpiling of Bacteriological (Biological) and Toxin Weapons and on Their Destruction (1972): 95 parties
Convention on the Prohibition of Military or Any Other Hostile Use of Environmental Modification Techniques (1977):[6] 38 parties

The Convention on Prohibitions or Restrictions on the Use of Certain Conventional Weapons Which May Be Deemed to Be Excessively Injurious or to Have Indiscriminate Effects, approved in 1980 and opened for signature in 1981, was the subject of a separate report to the Assembly (p. 113).

Publication. [1]*Status of Multilateral Arms Regulation and Disarmament Agreements*, second edition, *1982*, Sales No. E.83.IX.5 & corr.
Report. [2]S-G, A/37/560 & Corr.1.
Resolutions. GA: [3]2222(XXI), annex, 19 Dec. 1966 (YUN 1966, p. 41); [4]2373(XXII), annex, 12 June 1968 (YUN 1968, p. 17); [5]2660(XXV), annex, 7 Dec. 1970 (YUN 1970, p. 18); [6]31/72, annex, 10 Dec. 1976 (YUN 1976, p. 45); [7]36/92 H, 9 Dec. 1981 (YUN 1981, p. 109).

Institutional arrangements

General Assembly consideration (June/July). United Nations machinery for dealing with disarmament—through intergovernmental negotiating and deliberative bodies, expert study groups, and Secretariat research, training and co-ordination activities—was the topic of comment by most speakers during the general debate at the General Assembly's second special session devoted to disarmament. It was also the subject of a chapter on machinery and procedures in the draft comprehensive programme of disarmament considered at that session, but consensus was not reached on most provisions.[5]

In response to a December 1981 request of the Assembly,[8] the Secretary-General submitted to it at its special session a report[6] containing the comments received from 27 States on the 1981 study by the Group of Governmental Experts to Study the Institutional Arrangements relating to the Process of Disarmament.[9]

An agenda item on enhancement of the effectiveness of disarmament machinery and strengthening of the United Nations role was discussed in preliminary fashion on 2 and 3 July by the *Ad Hoc* Committee of the Twelfth Special Session. In addition, a contact group headed by the Committee Chairman held an exchange of views on 1 July on some aspects of the machinery question, centring on deliberative bodies, the negotiating body and secretariat support. No recommendations emerged from this discussion.

In the general debate, many countries spoke in favour of strengthening the role and responsibility of the United Nations in disarmament. Gabon, while commending the resumption of negotiations between the USSR and the United States, said they should not replace or impede the multilateral negotiations to be undertaken within the United Nations framework. Peru urged that the United Nations be given the administrative apparatus, standing and material means it needed to provide information and guidance. Uruguay believed that, although delicate political requirements called for restricted meetings to lay the first foundations of trust and understanding, all disarmament efforts should ultimately come within the United Nations framework, giving them world-wide scope and permitting each State to exercise its legitimate right to participate in the regulation of armaments. Others urging a strengthened role for the Organization in this area included Bhutan, Kuwait, Luxembourg, Maldives, Romania, Spain and Tunisia. There were also calls for strengthening United Nations information dissemination machinery on disarmament (p. 31) and for giving the Organization functions in verifying compliance with disarmament agreements (p. 136).

Several suggestions were made for strengthening the effectiveness of the United Nations in preserving international security as a means of encouraging conditions for disarmament. Chile favoured action to enable the Security Council to forestall conflicts. Along with the Congo, which said the Council should have greater capacity for action, Cyprus favoured giving it means of enforcement action for the maintenance of peace and security, including a United Nations force under Article 43 of the Charter of the United Nations. Japan advocated strengthening the Organization's fact-finding functions in international disputes and said it would co-operate in strengthening United Nations peace-keeping operations. Yugoslavia favoured the institution within the United Nations of a mandatory system for dispute settlement.

Several others, however, saw no need for institutional change. Bulgaria and Hungary considered the existing disarmament machinery capable of meeting the requirements, as did the Byelorussian SSR and Mongolia, which said that institutional restructuring would not compensate for the lack of political will, and would only divert attention and efforts from solving urgent problems. In a similar vein, Argentina attributed lack of positive achievements in disarmament to factors other than deficient machinery.

Australia asserted that there were no short-cuts to disarmament and that it did not help to make political point-scoring a first priority or to forgo partial measures in the hope that general and complete disarmament was at hand; the principle of consensus as a basis for disarmament needed to be reaffirmed, and voting, which highlighted division, should be condemned as harmful.

At the conclusion of the session, Belgium, speaking for the European Community (EC) members, reaffirmed the importance they attached to the multilateral disarmament process and expressed regret that the important agenda item relating to improving the effectiveness of disarmament machinery had not been taken up substantively at the special session. Sweden regretted that most of the leading Powers had again shown themselves unprepared to make use of the United Nations as an instrument for genuine disarmament efforts. Australia, Bangladesh, Egypt and Yugoslavia were among those urging a strengthened role for the United Nations in disarmament. Yugoslavia linked this to a call for further democratization of disarmament negotiating mechanisms—a point endorsed by Ghana, which said ways must be found to give all countries a share in nuclear-weapons negotiations, since all were victims of the nuclear monster.

General Assembly action (December). On 13 December, the General Assembly adopted without vote a five-part resolution on institutional arrangements relating to disarmament.[7] By this resolution, the Assembly requested the Committee on Disarmament to report in 1983 on a review of its membership, suggested to that Committee that it consider designating itself as a conference, requested that the United Nations Centre for Disarmament be transformed into a Department for Disarmament Affairs, took decisions on the functioning of the United Nations Institute for Disarmament Research (UNIDIR) and requested that the Advisory Board on Disarmament Studies be revived.

The First Committee had approved the draft on 26 November, also without vote. Norway introduced the 42-nation text as a combination of three draft resolutions—on the review of the membership of the Committee on Disarmament,[1] the future status of UNIDIR[2] and the establishment of a Department[3]—and a draft decision concerning the Advisory Board,[4] all of which had previously been introduced in the Committee.

Draft resolutions and decision superseded.

Draft resolutions. [1]Austria, Bahamas, Bangladesh, Bolivia, Chile, Costa Rica, Ecuador, France, Germany, Federal Republic of, Ghana, Greece, Guatemala, Hungary, Ireland, Jamaica, Kenya, Liberia, Mali, Netherlands, New Zealand, Nigeria, Norway, Panama, Philippines, Portugal, Senegal, Sierra Leone, Spain, Sri Lanka, Sudan, Sweden, Togo, Tunisia, United Republic of Cameroon, Viet Nam, A/C.1/37/L.9; [2]Argentina, Australia, Austria, Bahamas, Bangladesh, Belgium, Bolivia, Canada, Costa Rica, Cyprus, Djibouti, Ecuador, Egypt, Finland, France, Ghana, Greece, Iceland, India, Indonesia, Jamaica, Liberia, Madagascar, Mali, Malta, Mauritania, Mauritius, Mexico, Nigeria, Norway, Oman, Pakistan, Peru, Portugal, Qatar, Romania, Rwanda, Sierra Leone, Sri Lanka, Sudan, Sweden, Tunisia, Turkey, United Republic of Cameroon, Uruguay, A/C.1/37/L.23; [3]Bahamas, Colombia, Cyprus, Ecuador, Egypt, France, Ghana, Indonesia, Ireland, Lebanon, Liberia, Mexico, Nigeria, Oman, Pakistan, Peru, Romania, Sierra Leone, Singapore, Sri Lanka, Sudan, Sweden, United Republic of Cameroon, Uruguay, A/C.1/37/L.60.

Draft decision. [4]Ecuador, Norway, A/C.1/37/L.36.

Reports. [5]*Ad Hoc* Committee, A/S-12/32; [6]S-G, A/S-12/12 & Add.1-3.

Resolution (1982). [7]GA: 37/99 K, 13 Dec., text following.

Resolution (prior). [8]GA: 36/97 D, 9 Dec. 1981 (YUN 1981, p. 106).

Yearbook reference. [9]1981, p. 105.

Financial implications. ACABQ report, A/37/7/Add.16; 5th Committee report, A/37/734; S-G statements, A/C.1/37/L.68, A/C.5/37/74.

Meeting records. GA: plenary, A/S-12/PV.2-26, 28, 29 (8 June–10 July), A/37/PV.101 (13 Dec.); *Ad Hoc* Committee, A/S-12/AC.1/PV.10, 11 (29, 30 June); 1st Committee, A/C.1/37/PV.3-10, 12-28, *29*, 32, *34, 38, 40, 44*, 45 (18 Oct.–26 Nov.); 5th Committee, A/C.5/37/SR.62 (10 Dec.).

General Assembly resolution 37/99 K

13 December 1982   Meeting 101   Adopted without vote

Approved by First Committee (A/37/667) without vote, 26 November (meeting 44); 42-nation draft (A/C.1/37/L.67 and Corr.1); agenda item 55 *(c)*.

Sponsors: Algeria, Argentina, Austria, Bahamas, Bangladesh, Bolivia, Canada, Chile, Colombia, Costa Rica, Cyprus, Ecuador, France, Germany, Federal Republic of, Greece, Guatemala, Iceland, Indonesia, Ireland, Kenya, Lebanon, Liberia, Madagascar, Mali, Malta, Mauritania, Mexico, Nigeria, Norway, Oman, Panama, Portugal, Romania, Rwanda, Sierra Leone, Singapore, Spain, Sudan, Sweden, Tunisia, United Republic of Cameroon, Uruguay.

Institutional arrangements relating to the process of disarmament

The General Assembly,

Recalling its resolution 31/90 of 14 December 1976, by which it decided to keep the strengthening of the role of the United Nations in the field of disarmament under continued review,

Recalling also its resolution 34/87 E of 11 December 1979, in which it, *inter alia:*

(a) Reaffirmed that the United Nations had a central role and primary responsibility in the field of disarmament,

(b) Noted that the growing disarmament agenda and the complexity of the issues involved, as well as the more active participation of a large number of Member States, created increasing demands on United Nations management of disarmament affairs for purposes such as the promotion, substantive preparation, implementation and control of the process of disarmament,

Reaffirming the importance of the Committee on Disarmament as the single multilateral disarmament negotiating forum, in conformity with paragraph 120 of the Final Document of the Tenth Special Session of the General Assembly, the first special session devoted to disarmament,

Recognizing the growing importance attached to disarmament questions since the tenth special session, as evidenced by the increasing workload placed on the Centre for Disarmament of the Secretariat and on the Committee on Disarmament,

Bearing in mind the close relationship between matters concerning international security and disarmament and the interest in close co-operation between the units in the Secretariat dealing with them,

Noting the proposals submitted to the General Assembly at its twelfth special session, the second special session devoted to disarmament, with a view to taking certain action to strengthen the United Nations disarmament machinery,

Noting also that the General Assembly, at its twelfth special session, placed increasing duties on the Centre for Disarmament in requesting it to provide the central guidance in co-ordinating the World Disarmament Campaign activities within the United Nations system,

I

Having considered the relevant parts of section II F of the report of the Committee on Disarmament,

Reaffirming paragraph 28 of the Final Document of the Tenth Special Session of the General Assembly,

Noting that it was not possible to complete the first review of the membership of the Committee on Disarmament during the twelfth special session of the General Assembly in conformity with paragraph 120 of the Final Document of the Tenth Special Session and with Assembly resolution 36/97 J of 9 December 1981,

Noting also that the consultations in the Committee on Disarmament on the basis of paragraphs 55 and 62 of the Concluding Document of the Twelfth Special Session of the General Assembly have not been completed,

Requests the Committee on Disarmament to report to the General Assembly at its thirty-eighth session on the review of the membership of the Committee, taking into account paragraph 120 of the Final Document of the Tenth Special Session and paragraphs 55 and 62 of the Concluding Document of the Twelfth Special Session;

II

Bearing in mind the suggestion that the single multilateral disarmament negotiating forum should have the designation of a conference,

Reaffirming the validity of the provisions contained in paragraph 120 of the Final Document of the Tenth Special Session of the General Assembly,

Commends to the Committee on Disarmament that it consider designating itself as a conference without prejudice to paragraph 120 of the Final Document;

III

Recalling paragraph 124 of the Final Document of the Tenth Special Session of the General Assembly,

Requests the Secretary-General to revive the Advisory Board on Disarmament Studies in line with his note of 26 October 1982 and to entrust it with the functions listed therein, taking into account the provisions of section IV of the present resolution and further relevant decisions of the General Assembly in this regard;

IV

Aware of the need of the international community to be provided with more diversified and complete data on problems relating to international security, the armaments race and disarmament so as to facilitate progress, through negotiations, towards greater security for all States,

Convinced that negotiations on disarmament and continuing efforts to secure greater security at a lower level of armaments would benefit from objective and factual studies and analyses,

Reaffirming the importance of ensuring that disarmament studies should be conducted in accordance with the criteria of scientific independence,

Conscious that sustained research and study activity by the United Nations in the field of disarmament would promote informed participation by all States in disarmament efforts,

Stressing the need to undertake more in-depth, forward-looking and long-term research on disarmament within the United Nations,

Recalling its resolution 34/83 M of 11 December 1979,

1. *Expresses its gratitude* to the Board of Trustees of the United Nations Institute for Training and Research for its contribution to the establishment and development of the United Nations Institute for Disarmament Research;

2. *Notes with satisfaction* the activities carried out by the United Nations Institute for Disarmament Research since its establishment;

3. *Decides* that:

(a) The United Nations Institute for Disarmament Research shall:

(i) Function as an autonomous institution working in close relationship with the Department for Disarmament Affairs;

(ii) Be organized in a manner to ensure participation on an equitable political and geographical basis;

(iii) Continue to undertake independent research on disarmament and related security issues;

(iv) Duly take into account the recommendations of the General Assembly;

(b) The Secretary-General's Advisory Board on Disarmament Studies shall function as the Board of Trustees of the Institute;

(c) The headquarters of the Institute shall be at Geneva;

(d) Activities of the Institute shall be funded by voluntary contributions from States and public and private organizations;

4. *Invites* Governments to consider making contributions to the United Nations Institute for Disarmament Research;

5. *Requests* the Secretary-General to give administrative and other support to the United Nations Institute for Disarmament Research;

6. *Requests* the Board of Trustees to draft the statute of the United Nations Institute for Disarmament Research on the basis of the present mandate of the Institute, to be submitted to the General Assembly at its thirty-eighth session;

7. *Invites* the Director of the United Nations Institute for Disarmament Research to report to the General Assembly at its thirty-eighth session on the implementation of the present resolution and on the activities carried out by the Institute;

V

1. *Requests* the Secretary-General to transform the Centre for Disarmament of the Secretariat, appropriately strengthened with the existing overall resources of the United Nations, into a Department for Disarmament Affairs, headed by an Under-Secretary-General and so organized as to reflect fully the principle of equitable geographical distribution;

2. *Requests* the Secretary-General to report to the General Assembly at its thirty-eighth session on the practical implementation of the present resolution.

Committee on Disarmament

Review of membership

Consideration by the Committee on Disarmament. In 1982, the Committee on Disarmament, in addition to its substantive work, continued at informal meetings to review matters pertaining to its membership, including a possible expansion, as well as related organizational questions.

The 40-member Committee reported to the General Assembly at its special session on disarmament[6] that, during the first part of the Committee's 1982 session (February-April), it had taken into account provisions of the Final Document.of the Tenth Special Session of the Assembly (1978)—its first session devoted to disarmament—to the effect that the Committee, for the sake of convenience, should have a relatively small membership and that all States had the right to participate in disarmament negotiations.[9] The Committee had also taken account of a December 1981 request of the Assembly that the initial review of the Committee's membership be completed following consultations among United Nations Member States during the second special session on disarmament.[10]

While no objection in principle was raised to a limited expansion of the membership, a variety of views were expressed. Many members considered that the Committee was adequately representative of the world community for effective negotiations, others favoured a small increase in membership and still others proposed the possibility of rotating membership within regions or groups. While some felt that non-aligned and developing or neutral countries were inadequately represented, others believed that the Committee membership had been and should continue to be based on the principles of political balance and equitable geographical distribution.

In its annual report to the Assembly for 1982,[7] the Committee stated that it would continue in 1983 to consider membership, organizational and procedural matters; meanwhile, it appreciated the participation of interested non-members and would endeavour to facilitate their fuller participation in its work and that of its subsidiary bodies. The report noted that formal membership applications had been received from Austria, Bangladesh, Finland, Ireland, Norway, Senegal, Spain, Tunisia, Turkey and Viet Nam.

General Assembly consideration (June/July). During the second special session of the General Assembly devoted to disarmament, Norway, in a letter dated 24 June to the Chairman of the *Ad Hoc* Committee of the Twelfth Special Session,[3] suggested that the membership of the Committee on Disarmament be expanded—compatible with the requirements of its role as a negotiating forum—to allow countries with special interest to become members. By a note verbale of 24 June,[4] Turkey proposed that the Committee's membership be reasonably expanded during the special session fol-

lowing consultations among interested States. Bangladesh, in a note verbale of 22 June,[2] expressed the hope that its wish to become a member would be given sympathetic consideration.

An exchange of views on disarmament machinery, which took place in the *Ad Hoc* Committee of the session and in a contact group headed by the Committee Chairman, focused on enhancement of the effectiveness of the Committee on Disarmament. According to the *Ad Hoc* Committee's report,[5] adopted by the Assembly on 10 July as the Concluding Document of the Twelfth Special Session (p. 12), suggestions to expand the membership of the Committee on Disarmament in a limited and balanced manner, consistent with the need to enhance its effectiveness, received wide support. Other suggestions related to organization of the Committee's work (see below).

In the general debate at the special session, Belgium, on behalf of the EC members, said they were prepared to review the Committee's membership, and France added that expansion of the membership by a reasonable number could only strengthen its authority, without detriment to its function. Portugal said the membership, which currently excluded most countries from negotiations, should be made more representative so as to make the Committee more effective. Romania also expressed support for enlarging the Committee and giving other States access to its proceedings.

The Bahamas believed that the political balance in the Committee should be reinterpreted as a balance, within the framework of equitable geographical distribution, between "militarily significant" and "non-militarily-significant" States.

Candidacy for full membership in the Committee was announced during the special session by Bangladesh, Finland, Norway, Spain and Turkey.

At the conclusion of the session, Turkey, which had hoped for the membership review to be completed at the special session, was joined by Norway in expressing confidence that the Committee would be able to recommend by the next Assembly session the modalities of its expansion.

General Assembly action (December). In its 13 December resolution on institutional arrangements for disarmament,[8] the General Assembly requested the Committee on Disarmament to report in 1983 on the review of its membership, taking into account the provisions of the 1978 Final Document and of the Concluding Document of the Twelfth Special Session. This text, in the form of a separate draft resolution, was originally introduced by Norway on behalf of 35 countries[1] before it was incorporated as section I of the final resolution.

Draft resolution superseded. [1]Austria, Bahamas, Bangladesh, Bolivia, Chile, Costa Rica, Ecuador, France, Germany,

Federal Republic of, Ghana, Greece, Guatemala, Hungary, Ireland, Jamaica, Kenya, Liberia, Mali, Netherlands, New Zealand, Nigeria, Norway, Panama, Philippines, Portugal, Senegal, Sierra Leone, Spain, Sri Lanka, Sudan, Sweden, Togo, Tunisia, United Republic of Cameroon, Viet Nam, A/C.1/37/L.9.

Letter (l) and notes verbales. [2]Bangladesh, 22 June, A/S-12/AC.1/62; [3]Norway, 24 June, A/S-12/AC.1/32 *(l)*; [4]Turkey, 24 June, A/S-12/AC.1/33.

Reports. [5]*Ad Hoc* Committee, A/S-12/32; Committee on Disarmament, [6]A/S-12/2, [7]A/37/27.

Resolution (1982). [8]GA: 37/99 K, sect. I, 13 Dec.

Resolutions (prior). GA: [9]S-10/2, 30 June 1978 (YUN 1978, p. 39); [10]36/97 J, 9 Dec. 1981 (YUN 1981, p. 34).

Proposed change of name

Bearing in mind the suggestion that the single multilateral disarmament negotiating forum should have the designation of a conference, the General Assembly, by section II of its resolution of 13 December 1982 on institutional arrangements for disarmament,[2] commended to the Committee on Disarmament the idea that it consider designating itself as a conference. The Assembly added that this should be without prejudice to the paragraph on the Committee's composition and work methods contained in the Final Document of the Tenth Special Session (1978).[3]

A suggestion that the Committee be renamed "Standing Conference on Disarmament" had been made in the *Ad Hoc* Committee of the 1982 special session on disarmament, during its discussion of disarmament machinery.[1]

Report. [1]*Ad Hoc* Committee, A/S-12/32.
Resolution (1982). [2]GA: 37/99 K, sect. II, 13 Dec.
Resolution (prior). [3]GA: S-10/2, 30 June 1978 (YUN 1978, p. 39).

Organization of work

During the second special session of the General Assembly devoted to disarmament, the Netherlands, by a note verbale dated 24 June 1982 to the Chairman of the *Ad Hoc* Committee,[1] submitted a proposal on the structure of the Committee on Disarmament, recommending that the Committee consider the possibility of being in session all year round, enable its working groups to work more efficiently and independently, and make fuller use of expertise.

This was one of the proposals on the organization of work of the Committee on Disarmament considered by the *Ad Hoc* Committee and in a contact group, headed by the Committee Chairman, concerned with various aspects of United Nations disarmament machinery and focusing on enhancement of the effectiveness of the Committee on Disarmament.[2] Another suggestion was that the Committee's practice of taking decisions by consensus should not be used to obstruct adjustments to its structure, particularly the establishment of *ad hoc* working groups.

The Committee on Disarmament stated in its report to the Assembly at the special session[3] that it was continuing to examine ways of enhancing its effectiveness by streamlining the organization of its work and procedures, by increasing the activities of its subsidiary bodies and by holding more informal meetings and consultations with the participation of experts. In its annual report for 1982,[4] it noted that several proposals were under study, on such matters as procedure, organization, duration of sessions, representation, rationalization of work programmes, fuller participation of non-member States and strengthening of the secretariat. One of these proposals, submitted in September by the Group of 21 (p. 22), was to amend the Committee's rules of procedure to specify that the consensus rule would not be used to prevent the establishment of subsidiary bodies.

Note verbale. [1]Netherlands, 24 June, A/S-12/AC.1/35.
Reports. [2]*Ad Hoc* Committee, A/S-12/32; Committee on Disarmament, [3]A/S-12/2, [4]A/37/27.

Establishment of the Department for Disarmament Affairs

General Assembly consideration (June/July). At the second special session of the General Assembly devoted to disarmament, France, by a note verbale dated 23 June 1982,[1] proposed a change in status of the United Nations Centre for Disarmament to that of a Secretariat department headed by an Under-Secretary-General, commensurate with the Organization's central role and prime responsibility in disarmament. Turkey, by a note verbale to the Secretary-General dated 28 June,[2] called for the provision of additional staff and financial means to an upgraded Centre so as to enable it to act as the focal point of all disarmament efforts among United Nations institutions.

Matters relating to the Centre were discussed by the *Ad Hoc* Committee of the special session in its consideration of various aspects of United Nations disarmament machinery (see above). According to the Committee's report to the Assembly,[3] the need for strengthening the Centre was recognized and views were expressed for enhancing its status. The report added that other views had also been expressed in that connection. Paragraphs relating to the Centre and to its possible replacement by a Department were proposed for inclusion in the chapter on machinery and procedures in the draft comprehensive programme of disarmament, but consensus was not reached on them during the session.

Support for the Centre was expressed by several speakers in the special session's general debate. Bangladesh, Morocco and Romania thought the Centre should be strengthened, the Upper Volta said it deserved a wider mandate, and Egypt called for its expansion. Sierra Leone believed the Centre should receive all necessary support, and

Somalia called for augmenting the resources available to it.

Along with Spain, Belgium, on behalf of the European Community (EC) members, advised adjusting the Centre's status for better discharge of its responsibilities. France considered the Centre's current situation unsatisfactory from the standpoint of both organizational level and political arrangements. In the view of Turkey, the Centre deserved a higher status and greater financial resources to fulfil additional responsibilities in coming years, including the monitoring of compliance with disarmament conventions. Nepal supported a gradual expansion in the structure and function of the Centre. France thought the activities of the proposed satellite monitoring agency (p. 137) could be considered in the context of a restructured Centre. Greece also favoured upgrading the Centre and expanding its information activities.

General Assembly action (December). By section V of its 13 December resolution on institutional arrangements for disarmament,[4] the General Assembly requested the Secretary-General to transform the Centre for Disarmament, appropriately strengthened within the existing overall resources of the United Nations, into a Department for Disarmament Affairs, headed by an Under-Secretary-General and so organized as to reflect fully the principle of equitable geographical distribution of staff.

Notes verbales. [1]France, 23 June, A/S-12/AC.1/25; [2]Turkey, 28 June, A/S-12/AC.1/54.
Report. [3]*Ad Hoc* Committee, A/S-12/32.
Resolution (1982). [4]GA: 37/99 K, sect. V, 13 Dec.

Research and studies

A study of the economic and social consequences of the arms race, prepared by an expert group appointed by the Secretary-General at the request of the General Assembly, was submitted in 1982 as the latest in a series of disarmament studies commissioned by the Assembly. Another report by an expert group concerned an investigation into the alleged use of chemical weapons. In addition, the Assembly commended to the Disarmament Commission a 1982 report by the privately organized Independent Commission on Disarmament and Security Issues. The Assembly also took action based on two studies submitted in 1981, on the implications of establishing an international satellite monitoring agency for verification of compliance with disarmament agreements and on the relationship between disarmament and development.

The Disarmament Commission approved guidelines for a study on conventional-weapon disarmament, on the basis of which an expert group began work in 1982 with a view to its completion in 1983. In December 1982, the Assembly commissioned two new studies, on nuclear-weapon-free zones and on military research and development, both due in 1984.

Some speakers during the general debate at the Assembly's special session on disarmament in June and July cited the value of United Nations disarmament studies. Zaire said the studies merited attention as they helped the gap between developed and developing countries concerning the definition of such concepts as development, security and confidence-building measures. Agreeing that the studies deserved careful consideration and hoping they would lead to tangible results, Belgium, for the EC members, regretted that such important agenda items as studies and new initiatives had not been taken up substantively at the special session.

Bangladesh called for studies by the Secretary-General on new weapons systems and their delivery, on military research and development and its impact on the arms race, on the concept of zones of peace, and on principles and guidelines for conventional disarmament.

UN Institute for Disarmament Research

The General Assembly decided in December 1982 to give autonomous status to the United Nations Institute for Disarmament Research (UNIDIR), established in 1980 within the framework of the United Nations Institute for Training and Research (UNITAR).[5]

Activities of the Institute. UNIDIR published the results of two major research projects completed in 1982: a repertory of disarmament research, containing a comprehensive bibliography, and a book on the risks of unintentional nuclear war, analysing the circumstances in which such an event could occur and proposing steps to reduce the danger. Another UNIDIR publication in 1982 was a preliminary study on the establishment of a data base on disarmament.

A number of new projects were begun in 1982, including studies on the security of States and the lowering of the levels of armaments, disarmament as a vehicle for achieving a new international security order, and science and technology for disarmament. In addition, work commenced on a comparative analysis of various multilateral negotiations on global issues and on a study of a proposed disarmament fund for development (p. 141).

The Institute's Advisory Council was unable to meet in 1982, as the mandate of five of its members, who had belonged to the Advisory Board on Disarmament Studies (see below), had expired at the end of 1981. In September 1982, the UNITAR

Board of Trustees took note of a report by the Director of UNIDIR, but decided not to act on a future programme since the status of the Institute was to be reviewed by the Assembly later in 1982.

General Assembly consideration (June/July). During the second special session of the General Assembly devoted to disarmament, Norway, by a letter dated 24 June 1982 to the Chairman of the *Ad Hoc* Committee,[2] proposed that the Assembly make UNIDIR an autonomous body within the United Nations framework and entrust it with independent research on disarmament and security. As with other proposals submitted during the session, the Assembly took no action on it but transmitted it to the regular session beginning in September.

Proposals relating to UNIDIR and other disarmament research activities were included in the draft comprehensive programme of disarmament considered at the special session. However, consensus was not reached on the relevant paragraphs, intended for the chapters on principles and on disarmament measures.[3]

Support for UNIDIR was expressed by some in the course of the session's general debate. France urged the Assembly to decide on the final status of the Institute which, it said, had the capacity for considerable expansion in the field of research and in services to negotiators. Belgium, on behalf of the EC members, believed UNIDIR should play an important role in independent research, particularly on long-term problems, and Nepal called on it to play a more active role. Romania supported strengthening UNIDIR, and Mauritius said it should be provided with the means necessary for fulfilling its task, especially for research on long-term problems. In addition, Mauritius believed UNIDIR could study further the United Nations reporting procedures on military expenditures and budgets and sponsor the conference on that subject proposed by the United States (p. 115).

General Assembly action (December). On 13 December, the General Assembly, by section IV of its resolution on institutional arrangements for disarmament,[4] decided that UNIDIR should function as a Geneva-based autonomous institution, funded by voluntary contributions and working closely with the United Nations Department for Disarmament Affairs. The Assembly further stipulated that UNIDIR should be so organized as to ensure equitable participation politically and geographically, that it take into account the Assembly's recommendations, and that it continue to undertake independent research on disarmament and related security issues. It also decided that the Secretary-General's Advisory Board on Disarmament Studies should serve as the Board

of Trustees of UNIDIR, and requested the Board to submit a draft statute for UNIDIR to the Assembly in 1983.

The text of section IV, in the form of a separate draft resolution, was originally introduced by Norway on behalf of 45 countries,[1] and was subsequently incorporated into the final resolution.

Draft resolution superseded. [1]Argentina, Australia, Austria, Bahamas, Bangladesh, Belgium, Bolivia, Canada, Costa Rica, Cyprus, Djibouti, Ecuador, Egypt, Finland, France, Ghana, Greece, Iceland, India, Indonesia, Jamaica, Liberia, Madagascar, Mali, Malta, Mauritania, Mauritius, Mexico, Nigeria, Norway, Oman, Pakistan, Peru, Portugal, Qatar, Romania, Rwanda, Sierra Leone, Sri Lanka, Sudan, Sweden, Tunisia, Turkey, United Republic of Cameroon, Uruguay, A/C.1/37/L.23.
Letter. [2]Norway, 24 June, A/S-12/AC.1/32.
Report. [3]*Ad Hoc* Committee, A/S-12/32.
Resolution (1982). [4]GA: 37/99 K, sect. IV, 13 Dec.
Yearbook reference. [5]1980, p. 113.

Advisory Board on Disarmament Studies

On 13 December 1982, the General Assembly, by section III of its resolution on institutional arrangements for disarmament,[5] requested the Secretary-General to revive the Advisory Board on Disarmament Studies and to entrust it with the functions listed in a note he had circulated to the Assembly in October.[4]

The text of section III was almost identical to an earlier draft decision submitted by Norway and co-sponsored by Ecuador,[1] which was subsequently incorporated into the final resolution.

The Secretary-General recalled in his October note that the Board had met seven times between its inception in 1978[7] and the autumn of 1981, and that when the members' term of appointment expired at the end of 1981 the Board continued to exist in principle without members, pending a decision that the Assembly had been expected to take at its 1982 special session on disarmament. The Board's function, as specified by the Assembly in 1978, at its first special session on disarmament,[6] had been to advise the Secretary-General on various aspects of United Nations studies on disarmament and arms limitation.

The Secretary-General's note listed the following possible future activities for the Board: to serve as the Advisory Council of UNIDIR, and to advise him on disarmament studies and research within the United Nations system, on the implementation of the World Disarmament Campaign and, at his specific invitation, on other disarmament and arms-limitation matters. The Board's composition would depend on its tasks and should take account of the needs for effectiveness and financial restraint.

During the Assembly's second special session devoted to disarmament, Norway had proposed, in a letter dated 24 June to the Chairman of the

Ad Hoc Committee,[2] that a geographically balanced Advisory Board on Disarmament Research and Information should meet once or twice annually to: advise the Secretary-General on the establishment of studies and research in the United Nations system, and on any disarmament-related matter at his specific request; serve as a scientific board for UNIDIR, reviewing and approving its annual programme; and assess World Disarmament Campaign activities. A similar proposal was made by Turkey in a note verbale to the Secretary-General of 28 June,[3] suggesting that the Advisory Board serve as a governing council of UNIDIR, elaborate general guidelines for a programme of studies on the basis of the proposed comprehensive programme of disarmament, and advise the Secretary-General at his request on the conduct of the World Disarmament Campaign.

Draft decision superseded. [1]Ecuador, Norway, A/C.1/37/L.36.
Letter (l) and note verbale. [2]Norway, 24 June, A/S-12/AC.1/32 (l); [3]Turkey, 28 June, A/S-12/AC.1/54.
Note. [4]S-G, A/37/550.
Resolution (1982). [5]GA: 37/99 K, sect. III, 13 Dec.
Resolution (prior). [6]GA: S-10/2, 30 June 1978 (YUN 1978, p. 39).
Yearbook reference. [7]1978, p. 109.

Fellowships

General Assembly consideration (June/July). The General Assembly decided in July 1982, at its special session on disarmament, to increase from 20 to 25 the number of fellowships awarded annually by the United Nations programme of fellowships on disarmament.

Annexed to the Concluding Document of the Twelfth Special Session of the General Assembly, approved on 10 July, was a text agreed on by Working Group III of the *Ad Hoc* Committee of the Twelfth Special Session,[2] deciding to authorize the increase beginning in 1983. Appreciation was expressed to the German Democratic Republic, the Federal Republic of Germany, Hungary and Sweden for inviting fellows to their countries to study selected disarmament activities. Japan's offer to enable participants to visit Hiroshima and Nagasaki (see below) was welcomed and other Member States were encouraged to extend similar support.

The Assembly endorsed an assessment report submitted by the Secretary-General in April 1982,[3] covering the programme since its inception in 1979.[6] In that report he considered the programme to have clearly justified the hopes that had inspired it. Begun with the aim of promoting expertise in disarmament in more Member States, the programme, in its three years of operation, had provided 59 national public officials, from developing countries in particular, with training for effective participation in international deliberative and negotiating forums and for providing expertise at the national level.

The annual training course, not exceeding six months in duration, consisted of lectures, seminars, research and study visits, observation of the Committee on Disarmament at Geneva and the General Assembly's First Committee in New York, and a one-week course at the International Atomic Energy Agency at Vienna, Austria. Twenty fellows from as many countries participated in the 1982 programme, which included study visits in the German Democratic Republic, the Federal Republic of Germany, Sweden and the United States, at the invitation of those countries.

By a note verbale to the Secretary-General dated 25 June,[1] Japan submitted a working paper inviting the 1983 programme participants for a visit of about one week to Hiroshima and Nagasaki to observe the consequences of nuclear explosions and to exchange views with Japanese experts.

During the general debate at the special session, Nigeria recalled having proposed the programme in 1978[5] and suggested an increase in the number of fellowships.

General Assembly action (December). Acting without vote, the General Assembly, on 13 December 1982,[4] requested the Secretary-General to arrange for the disarmament fellowship programme for 1983 and to provide adequate staffing for the increased activities and expanded structure of the programme, bearing in mind savings that could be made within existing budgetary appropriations.

The First Committee had approved the text on 26 November by a recorded vote of 124 to none, as revised by its 33 sponsors and introduced by Nigeria.

Note verbale. [1]Japan, 25 June, A/S-12/AC.1/42.
Reports. [2]*Ad Hoc* Committee, A/S-12/32; [3]S-G, A/S-12/8 & Corr.1.
Resolution (1982). [4]GA: 37/100 G, 13 Dec., text following.
Yearbook references. [5]1978, p. 110; [6]1979, p. 98.
Financial implications. 5th Committee report, A/37/735; S-G statements, A/C.1/37/L.69, A/C.5/37/79.
Meeting records. GA: plenary, A/S-12/PV.2-26, 28, 29 (8 June-10 July), A/37/PV.101 (13 Dec.); 1st Committee, A/C.1/37/PV.3-10, 12-28, *29*, 32, *44*, 45 (18 Oct.-26 Nov.); 5th Committee, A/C.5/37/SR.62 (10 Dec.).

General Assembly resolution 37/100 G

13 December 1982   Meeting 101   Adopted without vote

Approved by First Committee (A/37/670) by recorded vote (124-0), 26 November (meeting 44); 33-nation draft (A/C.1/37/L.10/Rev.1); agenda item 133 (c).

Sponsors: Algeria, Bahamas, Bangladesh, Colombia, Congo, Cuba, Ecuador, Egypt, Ethiopia, Ghana, Greece, India, Indonesia, Jamaica, Kenya, Liberia, Mali, Nigeria, Pakistan, Panama, Philippines, Senegal, Sierra Leone, Sri Lanka, Sweden, Tunisia, Turkey, United Republic of Cameroon, Venezuela, Viet Nam, Yugoslavia, Zaire, Zambia.

United Nations programme of fellowships on disarmament
The General Assembly,

Recalling its decision, contained in paragraph 108 of the Final Document of the Tenth Special Session of the General Assembly, to establish a United Nations programme of fellowships on disarmament, as well as its subsequent resolutions 33/71 E of 14 December 1978,

34/83 D of 11 December 1979, 35/152 A of 12 December 1980 and 36/92 A of 9 December 1981, in which it, *inter alia*, decided to continue the programme,

Recalling also its decisions, contained in annex IV to the Concluding Document of the Twelfth Special Session of the General Assembly, to continue the programme, to increase the number of fellowships from twenty to twenty-five as from 1983 and to request the Secretary-General to submit the financial implications of awarding twenty-five fellowships, taking into account the necessary staffing requirements to meet the level of activities and structure of the programme and bearing in mind the savings that could be made within existing budgetary appropriations,

Bearing in mind that the level of activities, including the elements of the programme as outlined by the Secretary-General in his report, has increased since the inception of the programme of fellowships in 1979,

1. *Requests* the Secretary-General to make the necessary arrangements for the implementation of the programme for 1983, in accordance with the guidelines established for it, and to submit a progress report thereon to the General Assembly at its thirty-eighth session;

2. *Also requests* the Secretary-General to provide adequate staffing at the appropriate level to meet the requirements of the increased activities and the expanded structure of the programme, bearing in mind the savings that can be made within existing budgetary appropriations;

3. *Commends* the Secretary-General for the diligence with which the programme has continued to be carried out.

Proposed international organization

At the General Assembly's 1982 special session on disarmament, the Netherlands, by a note verbale to the Secretary-General dated 19 May,[1] suggested the establishment of an international disarmament organization, with United Nations affiliation, to oversee the implementation of international disarmament agreements; it proposed, as a first step, that the Secretary-General seek the views of Governments on the idea. When no action was taken in July, the Netherlands, by a note verbale of 21 October,[2] submitted an updated text of the proposal, suggesting that the Assembly, on the basis of responses by Governments, might set up a negotiating committee on the structure and functions of the proposed organization, and that the organization itself might be established at the next special session on disarmament.

Sweden proposed, in a working paper transmitted by a letter of 27 June,[3] that the Assembly decide in principle to establish a United Nations disarmament agency and request the Secretary-General to submit to the Assembly in 1983 a concrete proposal on implementation.

Neither country put its proposal in the form of a draft resolution for action by the Assembly.

Proposals on the establishment of an international disarmament organization were also presented for inclusion in the machinery and procedures chapter of the draft comprehensive programme of disarmament, but they remained among the provisions on which consensus was not reached at the special session.[4]

In the general debate at that session, the Netherlands said a body such as it had proposed, in addition to verifying the implementation of arms-control and disarmament treaties and handling complaints, could be instrumental in preparing and organizing review conferences already provided for in several existing disarmament treaties and could serve as a clearing-house for disarmament information. Zimbabwe expressed support for the establishment of a United Nations disarmament agency, to assist in disarmament deliberations, negotiations and verification.

Letter (l) and notes verbales. Netherlands: [1]19 May, A/S-12/22; [2]21 Oct., A/C.1/37/6. [3]Sweden: 27 June, A/S-12/AC.1/39 (l).

Report. [4]*Ad Hoc* Committee, A/S-12/32.

Proposed World Disarmament Conference

Activities of the *Ad Hoc* Committee. The *Ad Hoc* Committee on the World Disarmament Conference held two sessions in New York in 1982, consisting of three meetings between 5 and 8 April and three others between 23 and 27 August. No change was reported in the divergent opinions of the five nuclear-weapon States with regard to the idea of holding a conference, first endorsed by the General Assembly in 1965.[4] The Committee had been considering the idea since it first met in 1974.[5]

In a report to the Assembly at the special session on disarmament, adopted on 8 April 1982 and covering its work since 1978,[1] the Committee stated that, through its Chairman, it had maintained close contact with representatives of the nuclear-weapon States so as to remain currently informed of their attitudes.

According to the report, the USSR believed the Assembly at its special session should set a date and decide on means of preparing for a world disarmament conference; it rejected attempts by some nuclear-weapon States to justify their unconstructive attitudes to the question by allusions to the deteriorating international situation.

The four other nuclear-weapon States maintained their reservations on the practicability or value of such a conference. China's position remained unchanged: since the super-Powers had not shown sincerity towards disarmament and had refused to withdraw their troops from abroad, it was doubtful whether convening a conference would have any practical significance. France stated that the international situation was not conducive to the pursuit of such an undertaking. The United Kingdom maintained that, in the current international climate, consideration of the matter was not useful; it also doubted the usefulness of further meetings of the Committee. The United States continued to believe it premature to set a date and begin preparations for a conference; insufficient political agreement on the issues would probably hinder rather than assist efforts to reach concrete and verifiable arms-control measures.

The Committee reiterated the conclusions it had reached in 1981:[6] that the idea of a world disarmament conference had wide support among

United Nations Members, though with varying degrees of emphasis and differences regarding conditions and aspects relevant to its convening, including the deteriorating international situation; that no consensus on the convening of a conference under current conditions had been reached among the nuclear-weapon States, whose participation was widely deemed essential; and that the Assembly might decide to hold the conference after its special session on disarmament as soon as consensus had been reached.

In its annual report to the Assembly, adopted on 27 August,[2] the Committee reiterated its views on the conference and suggested the renewal of its mandate. It noted that the views of the nuclear-weapon States remained fundamentally unchanged. In the restatement of those views as contained in the report, there were additional remarks by China that the super-Powers lacked good faith for disarmament and persisted in policies of aggression and expansion, and by the United States that an unsuccessful or inconclusive conference could create impediments to future efforts towards concrete and verifiable measures.

General Assembly consideration (June/July). In the general debate at the special session of the General Assembly devoted to disarmament, Democratic Yemen, Hungary, Kenya, Sierra Leone and Zimbabwe expressed support for the convening of a world disarmament conference, as did Viet Nam, which called for universal participation. Believing such a conference to be the most effective means of dealing comprehensively with disarmament, Afghanistan expected the special session, and Angola expected the talks between the USSR and the United States, to pave the way for its convening.

General Assembly action (December). In a resolution on the World Disarmament Conference[3] adopted without vote on 13 December, the General Assembly renewed the mandate of the *Ad Hoc* Committee, requested it to maintain close contact with nuclear and all other States in order to remain informed of their attitudes, and asked it to report to the Assembly in 1983.

The text, introduced by Sri Lanka also on behalf of Burundi, Mali, Mongolia, Peru, Poland, Qatar and Spain, had been approved by the First Committee on 26 November by a recorded vote of 125 to none.

Reports. Ad Hoc Committee on World Disarmament Conference, [1]A/S-12/4, [2]A/37/28.
Resolution (1982). [3]GA: 37/97, 13 Dec., text following.
Resolution (prior). [4]GA: 2030(XX), 29 Nov. 1965 (YUN 1965, p. 62).
Yearbook references. [5]1974, p. 52; [6]1981, p. 26.
Financial implications. 5th Committee report, A/37/732; S-G statements, A/C.1/37/L.71, A/C.5/37/80.
Meeting records. GA: plenary, A/S-12/PV.2-26, 28, 29 (8 June-10 July), A/37/PV.101 (13 Dec.); *Ad Hoc* Committee, A/S-12/AC.1/PV.10, 11 (29, 30 June); 1st Committee,

A/C.1/37/PV.3-10, 12-28, *38*, *45* (18 Oct.–26 Nov.); 5th Committee, A/C.5/37/SR.62 (10 Dec.).

General Assembly resolution 37/97

13 December 1982   Meeting 101   Adopted without vote

Approved by First Committee (A/37/661) by recorded vote (125-0), 26 November (meeting 45); 8-nation draft (A/C.1/37/L.28); agenda item 49.

Sponsors: Burundi, Mali, Mongolia, Peru, Poland, Qatar, Spain, Sri Lanka.

World Disarmament Conference

The General Assembly,

Recalling its resolutions 2833(XXVI) of 16 December 1971, 2930(XXVII) of 29 November 1972, 3183(XXVIII) of 18 December 1973, 3260(XXIX) of 9 December 1974, 3469(XXX) of 11 December 1975, 31/190 of 21 December 1976, 32/89 of 12 December 1977, 33/69 of 14 December 1978, 34/81 of 11 December 1979, 35/151 of 12 December 1980 and 36/91 of 9 December 1981,

Reiterating its conviction that all the peoples of the world have a vital interest in the success of disarmament negotiations and that all States should be in a position to contribute to the adoption of measures for the achievement of this goal,

Stressing anew its conviction that a world disarmament conference, adequately prepared and convened at an appropriate time, could provide the realization of such an aim and that the co-operation of all nuclear-weapon Powers would considerably facilitate its attainment,

Taking note of the report of the *Ad Hoc* Committee on the World Disarmament Conference,

Recalling that, in paragraph 122 of the Final Document of the Tenth Special Session of the General Assembly, the first special session devoted to disarmament, it decided that, at the earliest appropriate time, a world disarmament conference should be convened with universal participation and with adequate preparation,

Recalling also that, in paragraph 23 of the Declaration of the 1980s as the Second Disarmament Decade, contained in the annex to its resolution 35/46 of 3 December 1980, the General Assembly considered it pertinent also to recall that in paragraph 122 of the Final Document of its Tenth Special Session it had stated that at the earliest appropriate time a world disarmament conference should be convened, with universal participation and with adequate preparation,

Recalling further that although the General Assembly, at its twelfth special session, the second special session devoted to disarmament, did not make any recommendations on the question of a world disarmament conference, in its report to the General Assembly, the *Ad Hoc* Committee of the Twelfth Special Session recommended that the items on the agenda on which the Assembly had not reached decisions should be taken up at its thirty-seventh session for further consideration,

1. *Notes with satisfaction* that in its report to the General Assembly the *Ad Hoc* Committee on the World Disarmament Conference stated, *inter alia*, the following:

"Having regard for the important requirements of a world disarmament conference to be convened at the earliest appropriate time, with universal participation and with adequate preparation, the General Assembly, in accordance with paragraph 64 of the report of the *Ad Hoc* Committee of the Twelfth Special Session, should take up the question at its thirty-seventh regular session for its further consideration, bearing in mind the relevant provisions of resolution 36/91, adopted by consensus, in particular paragraph 1 of the said resolution";

2. *Renews* the mandate of the *Ad Hoc* Committee;

3. *Requests* the *Ad Hoc* Committee to maintain close contact with the representatives of the States possessing nuclear weapons, in order to remain currently informed of their attitudes, as well as with all other States, and to consider any possible relevant proposals and observations which might be made to the Committee, especially having in mind paragraph 122 of the Final Document of the Tenth Special Session of the General Assembly;

4. *Requests* the *Ad Hoc* Committee to report to the General Assembly at its thirty-eighth session;

5. *Decides* to include in the provisional agenda of its thirty-eighth session the item entitled "World Disarmament Conference".

Co-ordination in the UN system

The third *Ad Hoc* Inter-agency Meeting on Co-ordination of Disarmament-related Activities within the United Nations System,[1] attended by representatives of 12 agencies and other organizations, offices and institutes, was held at Geneva on 15 April 1982. The participants exchanged information on their organizations' disarmament-related activities and reviewed plans in connection with the General Assembly's second special session devoted to disarmament, in June/July.

Report. [1]Inter-agency Meeting on Co-ordination of Disarmament-related Activities, ACC/1982/21.

Chapter II

Peaceful uses of outer space

Contents

Related topic:

Disarmament: Prevention of an arms race in outer space and prohibition of anti-satellite systems.

For resolutions and decisions of major organs mentioned but not reproduced, refer to INDEX OF RESOLUTIONS AND DECISIONS.

General aspects

The General Assembly, in the first of four resolutions on outer space adopted on 10 December 1982, noted the successful conclusion of the Second United Nations Conference on the Exploration and Peaceful Uses of Outer Space (UNISPACE-82), held at Vienna, Austria, in August. It endorsed the report of the Committee on the Peaceful Uses of Outer Space on its twenty-fifth session, held at United Nations Headquarters from 22 March to 1 April, and asked international organizations to continue their co-operation with the Committee and provide it with progress reports on their outer space work. It requested the Committee to continue its work, to consider new projects and to report to the Assembly in 1983 with its views on future subjects for study. The Assembly decided on the 1983 work programmes of the

Scientific and Technical Sub-Committee and the Legal Sub-Committee. It endorsed the United Nations Programme on Space Applications proposed for 1983 (p. 165) and invited States to consider adhering to outer space treaties.

The resolution[1] was adopted without vote, following similar approval by the Special Political Committee on 19 November. The 37-nation text was introduced by Austria.

Resolution (1982). [1]GA: 37/89, 10 Dec., text following.
Meeting records. GA: SPC, A/SPC/37/SR.15-20, 23, *25, 33* (1-19 Nov.); plenary, A/37/PV.100 (10 Dec.).
Publication. Outer Space: A Selective Bibliography, Sales No. E/F.82.I.12 (ST/LIB/SER.B/33).

General Assembly resolution 37/89

10 December 1982   Meeting 100   Adopted without vote

Approved by SPC (A/37/646) without vote, 19 November (meeting 33); 37-nation draft (A/SPC/37/L.6); agenda item 62.

Sponsors: Argentina, Australia, Austria, Bangladesh, Belgium, Bolivia, Brazil, Bulgaria, Byelorussian SSR, Canada, Chile, Czechoslovakia, Egypt, France, German Democratic Republic, Germany, Federal Republic of, Greece, Hungary, India, Italy, Japan, Mongolia, Netherlands, Nigeria, Pakistan, Philippines, Poland,

Romania, Sweden, Turkey, Ukrainian SSR, USSR, United Kingdom, United States, Uruguay, Venezuela, Yugoslavia.

International co-operation in the peaceful uses of outer space

The General Assembly,

Recalling its resolution 36/35 of 18 November 1981,

Bearing in mind the fact that twenty-five years have passed since the beginning of international co-operation in the peaceful uses of outer space in the United Nations,

Deeply convinced of the common interest of mankind in promoting the exploration and use of outer space for peaceful purposes and in continuing efforts to extend to all States the benefits derived therefrom, and of the importance of international co-operation in this field, for which the United Nations should continue to provide a focal point,

Reaffirming the importance of international co-operation in developing the rule of law for the advancement and preservation of the exploration and peaceful uses of outer space,

Taking note with satisfaction of the progress achieved in the further development of peaceful space exploration and application as well as in various national and co-operative space projects, which contribute to international co-operation in this field,

Having considered the report of the Committee on the Peaceful Uses of Outer Space on the work of its twenty-fifth session,

1. *Endorses* the report of the Committee on the Peaceful Uses of Outer Space;

2. *Invites* States that have not yet become parties to the international treaties governing the use of outer space* to give consideration to ratifying or acceding to those treaties;

3. *Takes note with appreciation* of the successful conclusion of the Second United Nations Conference on the Exploration and Peaceful Uses of Outer Space;

4. *Notes* that the Legal Sub-Committee of the Committee on the Peaceful Uses of Outer Space at its twenty-first session:

(a) Continued its efforts to formulate draft principles relating to the legal implications of remote sensing of the earth from space;

(b) Considered the possibility of supplementing the norms of international law relevant to the use of nuclear power sources in outer space through its working group;

(c) Continued its discussion of matters relating to the definition and/or delimitation of outer space and outer space activities, bearing in mind, *inter alia*, questions relating to the geostationary orbit;

5. *Decides* that the Legal Sub-Committee at its twenty-second session should:

(a) Continue on a priority basis its detailed consideration of the legal implications of remote sensing of the earth from space, with the aim of formulating draft principles relating to remote sensing;

(b) Continue its consideration of:

(i) The possibility of supplementing the norms of international law relevant to the use of nuclear power sources in outer space through its working group;

(ii) Matters relating to the definition and/or delimitation of outer space and outer space activities, bearing in mind, *inter alia*, questions relating to the geostationary orbit, and devote adequate time for a deeper consideration of this question;

6. *Notes* that the Scientific and Technical Sub-Committee of the Committee on the Peaceful Uses of Outer Space at its nineteenth session continued:

(a) Its consideration of questions relating to remote sensing of the earth by satellites;

(b) Its consideration of the United Nations Programme on Space Applications and the co-ordination of space activities within the United Nations system;

(c) Its examination of the physical nature and technical attributes of the geostationary orbit;

(d) Its consideration of technical aspects of and safety measures relating to the use of nuclear power sources in outer space;

(e) Its consideration of questions relating to space transportation systems and their implications for future activities in space;

(f) Preparations for the Second United Nations Conference on the Exploration and Peaceful Uses of Outer Space in its capacity as Advisory Committee to the Preparatory Committee;

7. *Endorses* the recommendation of the Committee on the Peaceful Uses of Outer Space that the Scientific and Technical Sub-Committee at its twentieth session should:

(a) Consider the following items on a priority basis:

(i) Consideration of the United Nations Programme on Space Applications and the co-ordination of outer space activities within the United Nations system;

(ii) Questions relating to remote sensing of the earth by satellites;

(iii) Use of nuclear power sources in outer space;

(b) Consider the following items:

(i) Questions relating to space transportation systems and their implications for future activities in space;

(ii) Examination of the physical nature and technical attributes of the geostationary orbit;

8. *Endorses* the United Nations Programme on Space Applications for 1983, as proposed to the Committee on the Peaceful Uses of Outer Space by the Expert on Space Applications, and the recommendations by the Second United Nations Conference on the Exploration and Peaceful Uses of Outer Space relating to the Programme;

9. *Requests* the Committee on the Peaceful Uses of Outer Space, with the benefit of possible advice of both its Sub-Committees in their next sessions, to consider the implementation of the recommendations of the Second United Nations Conference on the Exploration and Peaceful Uses of Outer Space, in particular the order of priorities and the carrying out of the studies recommended by the Conference;

10. *Expresses its appreciation* to all Governments as well as specialized agencies and other international organizations which acted as hosts to, offered fellowships for, or otherwise assisted in the holding of, international training seminars and workshops on space applications, particularly for the benefit of developing countries;

11. *Requests* the specialized agencies and other international organizations to continue and, where appropriate, enhance their co-operation with the Committee on the Peaceful Uses of Outer Space and to provide it with progress reports on their work relating to the peaceful uses of outer space;

12. *Requests* the Committee on the Peaceful Uses of Outer Space to continue its work, in accordance with the present resolution and previous resolutions of the General Assembly, to consider, as appropriate, new projects in outer space activities and to submit a report to the Assembly at its thirty-eighth session, including its views on which subjects should be studied in the future.

---

*Treaty on Principles Governing the Activities of States in the Exploration and Use of Outer Space, including the Moon and Other Celestial Bodies (resolution 2222(XXI), annex); Agreement on the Rescue of Astronauts, the Return of Astronauts and the Return of Objects Launched into Outer Space (resolution 2345(XXII), annex); Convention on International Liability for Damage Caused by Space Objects (resolution 2777(XXVI), annex); Convention on Registration of Objects Launched into Outer Space (resolution 3235(XXIX), annex); Agreement Governing the Activities of States on the Moon and Other Celestial Bodies (resolution 34/68, annex).

Scientific and technical aspects

UNISPACE-82, in August 1982, made recommendations on a wide range of scientific and technical questions relating to outer space (p. 162).

Prior to the Conference, the Scientific and Technical Sub-Committee of the Committee on outer space held its nineteenth session from 11 to 22 January at United Nations Headquarters. It concluded preparations for UNISPACE-82 (p. 162), considered the Programme on Space Applications and co-ordination of space activities in the United Nations system, and discussed remote sensing of the earth by satellites. It also examined nuclear power sources in outer space, space transportation systems and questions relating to the geostationary orbit. The Sub-Committee's report was examined in March/April by its parent Committee, which expressed its views on the matters considered by the Sub-Committee.[1]

On 10 December, the General Assembly, in its resolution on the peaceful uses of outer space,[2] endorsed the Committee's recommendation that the Sub-Committee consider on a priority basis in 1983 the Programme on Space Applications, co-ordination of space activities in the United Nations system, remote sensing and nuclear power sources in outer space. Other topics listed by the Assembly for the Sub-Committee were space transportation systems and their implications for future space activities, and the physical nature and technical attributes of the geostationary orbit.

Report. [1]COPUOS, A/37/20.
Resolution (1982). [2]GA: 37/89, para. 7, 10 Dec.

Conference on outer space

The Second United Nations Conference on the Exploration and Peaceful Uses of Outer Space (UNISPACE-82), convened by decision of the General Assembly in 1978,[2] met at Vienna, Austria, from 9 to 21 August 1982. Its report[1] contained a number of recommendations which the Assembly endorsed in December.

Report. [1]Conference on outer space, A/CONF.101/10 & Corr.1,2.
Resolution. [2]GA: 33/16, 10 Nov. 1978 (YUN 1978, p. 141).

Preparations for the Conference

Arrangements for the Conference were worked out by the Preparatory Committee for UNISPACE-82 and by its Advisory Committee, both made up of the same members as the Committee on the Peaceful Uses of Outer Space. The Scientific and Technical Sub-Committee, acting as the Advisory Committee, met at United Nations Headquarters for its third session during the Sub-Committee's 1982 session (11-22 January), and considered the draft final report and national and background papers of the Conference, officers and other arrangements, regional seminars and public information activities.[2]

The Advisory Committee's recommendations were endorsed by the Preparatory Committee, which, like the Advisory Committee, had first met in 1979.[4] The Preparatory Committee held its fourth and final session at United Nations Headquarters during the 1982 session of the Committee on outer space (22 March–1 April) and on 6 April.[3] The Preparatory Committee further revised the draft final report of the Conference, requesting that it be circulated to States, with square brackets indicating paragraphs on which agreement had not been reached and accompanied by a statement of financial implications. The Committee expressed the hope that all States would be represented at the highest possible level.

Six seminars on remote sensing applications and satellite communication for education and de-velopment were held as part of Conference preparations under the United Nations Programme on Space Applications. Four of these were in 1981: Addis Ababa, Ethiopia (for Africa); Buenos Aires, Argentina (for Latin America); Toulouse, France (for developing countries from various regions); and Jakarta, Indonesia (for Asia and the Pacific).[5] In 1982, similar seminars were held at Quito, Ecuador (for Latin America), and Addis Ababa (for Africa and Western Asia). Each seminar made recommendations for national and regional action which were summarized in a paper for the Conference.[1]

Fifty-eight national papers were submitted to the Conference by States, and 39 background papers were prepared by the Conference secretariat and intergovernmental and non-governmental organizations. Most dealt with aspects of space technology or the role of organizations in utilizing it.

Background paper. [1]Seminar recommendations, A/CONF.101/BP/13.
Reports. [2]Advisory Committee, A/CONF.101/PC/6; [3]Preparatory Committee, A/37/46.
Yearbook references. [4]1979, p. 117; [5]1981, p. 115.

Work of the Conference

UNISPACE-82 considered the state and applications of space science and technology, as well as international co-operation and the United Nations role in space matters.

The Conference, in its report,[2] made a number of recommendations on space technology applications, with emphasis on the development of satellite remote sensing for the detection and analysis of earth resources, and urged international agreement on legal principles to govern remote sensing. It suggested lines along which communication satellites should be developed and the need for them assessed. The development of meteorological satellites was considered, along with ways to facilitate access to information gathered by them. The Conference called for studies on the establishment of an international system of navigational and geodetic satellites, and a satellite system for search and rescue operations at sea (p. 169).

Regarding the space environment, the Conference advocated action to guard against depletion of the ozone layer and measures to eliminate debris in space (p. 170). It urged the co-ordination of space transportation efforts and study of the long-term consequences of increasing numbers of launchings. The establishment of international co-operation on space solar power systems was considered advisable, as was the continued evolution of criteria for the use of the geostationary orbit. Support for space science should be increased, the Conference recommended. It added that extension of the arms race into outer space must be prevented (see POLITICAL AND SECURITY QUESTIONS, Chapter I).

The Conference recommended measures to strengthen international co-operation on outer space, particularly through the United Nations Programme on Space Applications, a proposed International Space Information Service and a strengthened Outer Space Affairs Division in the United Nations Secretariat. It also recommended that the United Nations, in association with specialized agencies, organize studies on the technical, social, economic, environmental and legal implications of space developments, especially for developing countries. It added that primary responsibility for arranging or conducting the studies should remain with the Committee on outer space.

The original draft of the decisions and recommendations in the Conference's report was prepared by its Secretary-General, based on national and background papers, the recommendations of regional seminars, and discussions in the Conference's Preparatory Committee and the General Assembly. This draft was reviewed in January by the Advisory Committee to the Preparatory Committee[1] and revised by the Preparatory Committee at its March/April session,[3] taking into account comments of the Advisory Committee and specialized agencies. The entire report, with amendments, was adopted by the Conference on 21 August.

The Conference had three main committees. The First Committee was concerned with the state of space science and technology, the Second Committee with applications of space science and technology, and the Third Committee with international co-operation and the United Nations role. Each of these committees contributed to the Conference's report. There was also a Credentials Committee. (For participants and officers, see APPENDIX III.)

Public information activities organized before or during the Conference included demonstrations of space applications, technical presentations, lectures, essay and poster contests, exhibitions, seminars and meetings. Among the meetings were a forum sponsored by the Committee on Space Research of the International Council of Scientific Unions and by the International Astronautical Federation (Vienna, Austria, 4-6 August), and an international round table on "Alternative space futures and the human condition" organized by the Conference secretariat (New York, March).

Reports. [1]Advisory Committee, A/CONF.101/PC/6; [2]Conference on outer space, A/CONF.101/10 & Corr.1,2; [3]Preparatory Committee, A/37/46.

Implementation of Conference recommendations

The General Assembly, in a resolution adopted without vote on 10 December 1982,[3] endorsed the recommendations of UNISPACE-82 on international co-operation in the exploration and peaceful uses of outer space,[1] and invited Governments and intergovernmental organizations to implement them. Deciding that all new or expanded activities provided for in the resolution would be funded mainly through voluntary contributions and the rearrangement of budgetary priorities, the Assembly appealed to Governments to make voluntary financial and other contributions towards that end. It noted the Conference's recommendations on study projects and invited intergovernmental organizations to contribute to space studies. It emphasized the importance of co-operation between United Nations bodies engaging in space or space-related activities and with international funding agencies. The Secretary-General was requested to report to the Assembly in 1983 on implementation of the resolution.

The resolution also included provisions on prevention of an arms race in outer space (see above), regional co-operation mechanisms and their promotion and creation through the United Nations system (p. 165), the objectives of the United Nations Programme on Space Applications, the establishment of an International Space Information Service and strengthening the Secretariat's Outer Space Affairs Division.

The Special Political Committee approved the resolution without vote on 19 November, as sponsored by Austria. The United States orally proposed an amendment to the effect that in no case would financial obligations incurred under the resolution exceed the level of resources approved in the United Nations budget for 1982-1983. The Committee rejected the amendment by a recorded vote of 61 to 18, with 29 abstentions.

The Assembly, in its 10 December resolution on international co-operation in the peaceful uses of outer space,[2] noted the successful conclusion of UNISPACE-82 and requested the Committee on outer space to consider the implementation of the Conference recommendations, in particular their order of priority and the preparation of studies.

Report. [1]Conference on outer space, A/CONF.101/10.
Resolutions (1982). GA: [2]37/89, paras. 3 & 9, 10 Dec.; [3]37/90, 10 Dec., text following.
Financial implications. 5th Committee report, A/37/726; S-G statements, A/SPC/37/L.9, A/C.5/37/77.
Meeting records. GA: SPC, A/SPC/37/SR.15-20, 23, 25, 31, 33 (1-19 Nov.); 5th Committee, A/C.5/37/SR.61, 62 (9, 10 Dec.); plenary, A/37/PV.100 (10 Dec.).

General Assembly resolution 37/90

10 December 1982	Meeting 100	Adopted without vote

Approved by SPC (A/37/646) without vote, 19 November (meeting 33); draft by Austria (A/SPC/37/L.7); agenda item 62 (*b*).

Second United Nations Conference on the Exploration and Peaceful Uses of Outer Space

The General Assembly,

Recalling its resolutions 33/16 of 10 November 1978, 34/67 of 5 December 1979, 35/15 of 3 November 1980 and 36/36 of 18 November 1981 concerning the convening as well as the preparation of the

Second United Nations Conference on the Exploration and Peaceful Uses of Outer Space, held at Vienna from 9 to 21 August 1982,

Reaffirming the importance of international co-operation in the exploration and peaceful uses of outer space,

Reaffirming the importance of international co-operation in developing the rule of law for the advancement and preservation of the exploration and peaceful uses of outer space,

Gravely concerned at the extension of an arms race into outer space,

Aware of the need to increase the benefits of space technology and its applications and to contribute to an orderly growth of space activities favourable to the socio-economic advancement of mankind, in particular the peoples of developing countries,

Taking into account new developments in space science and technology which are being projected and envisaged in the coming decade as well as the new applications emerging therefrom and their potential benefits and possible implications for national development and international co-operation,

Conscious of the need further to increase the awareness of the general public with regard to space technology and its applications,

Desiring to enhance the effectiveness of the co-ordinating role of the United Nations, which is eminently suited to bring about increased international co-operation and assistance to the developing countries in the field of exploration and peaceful uses of outer space,

Expressing its satisfaction with the successful preparation of the Conference through the Committee on the Peaceful Uses of Outer Space in its capacity as Preparatory Committee for the Conference, and its Scientific and Technical Sub-Committee in its capacity as Advisory Committee, as well as through the Conference secretariat,

Taking note of the report of the Second United Nations Conference on the Exploration and Peaceful Uses of Outer Space,

1. *Expresses its appreciation and thanks* to the Government and people of Austria for the excellent facilities and generous hospitality provided for the Second United Nations Conference on the Exploration and Peaceful Uses of Outer Space;

2. *Endorses* the recommendations pertaining to international co-operation in the exploration and peaceful uses of outer space, as contained in the report of the Conference;

3. *Invites* all Governments to take effective action for the implementation of the recommendations of the Conference;

4. *Invites* all Member States, in particular those with major space capabilities, to contribute actively to the goal of preventing an arms race in outer space, as an essential condition for the promotion of international co-operation in the exploration and uses of outer space for peaceful purposes;

5. *Requests* all organs, organizations and bodies of the United Nations system and other intergovernmental organizations which are working in the field of outer space or space-related matters to co-operate in the implementation of the recommendations of the Conference;

6. *Takes note* of the recommendations of the Conference regarding study projects and invites all specialized agencies and other intergovernmental organizations concerned to contribute within their field of competence to the elaboration of those studies;

7. *Decides*, upon the recommendations of the Conference, that the United Nations Programme on Space Applications should be directed towards the following objectives:

(a) Promotion of greater exchange of actual experiences with specific applications;

(b) Promotion of greater co-operation in space science and technology between developed and developing countries as well as among developing countries;

(c) Development of a fellowship programme for in-depth training of space technologists and applications specialists, with the help of Member States and relevant international organizations and establishment and regular updating of lists containing available fellowships in all States and relevant international organizations;

(d) Organization of regular seminars on advanced space applications and new system developments for managers and leaders of space application and technology development activities as well as seminars for users in specific applications for durations, as appropriate;

(e) Stimulation of the growth of indigenous nuclei and an autonomous technological base, to the extent possible, in space technology in developing countries with the co-operation of other United Nations organizations and/or States Members of the United Nations or members of the specialized agencies;

(f) Dissemination, through panel meetings and seminars, of information on new and advanced technology and applications, with emphasis on their relevance and implications for developing countries;

(g) Provision or arrangements for provision of technical advisory services on space applications projects, upon request by Member States or any of the specialized agencies;

8. *Decides* to establish an International Space Information Service, initially consisting of a directory of sources of information and data services to provide direction upon request to accessible data banks and information sources;

9. *Requests* the Secretary-General to strengthen the Outer Space Affairs Division of the Secretariat with an appropriate augmentation of technical personnel and decides, upon the recommendation of the Conference, that all new or expanded activities contained in the present resolution are to be funded mainly through voluntary contributions of States in money or in kind, as well as through the rearrangement of priorities within the next regular budget of the United Nations;

10. *Appeals* to all Governments to make voluntary contributions, either in money or in kind, towards carrying out the recommendations of the Conference;

11. *Approves* the recommendations of the Conference regarding the establishment and strengthening of regional mechanisms of co-operation and their promotion and creation through the United Nations system;

12. *Emphasizes* the need for close co-operation between all United Nations bodies engaging in space or space-related activities, as well as the desirability of close co-operation with international funding agencies and subsidiary bodies, such as the United Nations Development Programme;

13. *Requests* the Secretary-General to assure the availability and appropriate dissemination of the report of the Conference;

14. *Further requests* the Secretary-General to report to the General Assembly at its thirty-eighth session on the implementation of the present resolution.

Space technology applications

In its report adopted in August 1982,[1] UNISPACE-82 concluded[1] that all countries should be encouraged to participate in space applications so as to benefit from space technology. Before choosing an application, they should study costs and benefits. Decisions to use space technology should be based on an assessment of needs, conditions and alternatives and, if possible, be preceded by a pilot or demonstration project. In implementing applications, countries should exploit mutually beneficial co-operation by undertaking complementary efforts. Compatibility and complementarity between systems was desirable, but should not inhibit advances in technology or self-reliance. Systems must be need-based and user-oriented, evolve within the framework of international regulations, and not result in higher costs or excessive dependence on one State by many others.

Access to knowledge of space technology should be facilitated and arrangements for technology transfer considered, the Conference stated. Countries should not place undue restrictions on the sale of components, sub-systems or systems required for space applications. Developed countries, the United Nations and international financing agencies should consider assisting developing countries in establishing indigenous centres for absorption, adaptation and development of technologies; at the same time, developing countries should decrease their dependence on foreign expertise. A means to that end would be for developing countries to identify and organize existing nuclei of their own experts, and create institutions and conditions for expanding them rapidly. Countries should modify their educational systems to place more emphasis on science and technology, and encourage postgraduate, interdisciplinary work on space technology and applications.

With regard to the acquisition of equipment, developing countries should first seek equipment from other developing countries or, alternatively, adapt off-the-shelf developed country equipment. Developed countries should be willing to provide individual elements rather than complete systems, so that system design, engineering and integration would be in accordance with the developing countries' needs and conditions. Indigenous fabrication of equipment should be encouraged.

The Conference considered that developing countries should be encouraged to negotiate with launching States for the trial use of their spacecraft for experimentation or demonstration. Developed countries should continue to provide such services on equitable terms wherever feasible, and international financial agencies should support demonstration projects of developing countries.

Report. [1]Conference on outer space, A/CONF.101/10 & Corr.2.

International co-operation

UNISPACE-82 made a number of recommendations[1] for international co-operation on outer space matters, including additional activities under the United Nations Programme on Space Applications, the establishment of an International Space Information Service, a strengthened Outer Space Affairs Division in the United Nations Secretariat and improved co-ordination in the United Nations system, as well as individual and collective actions by States. The Conference's recommendations on international co-operation, made in August 1982, were endorsed by the General Assembly in its 10 December resolution on the Conference.[2]

The Conference suggested a strengthening of national and regional data banks as well as those of the United Nations Remote Sensing Unit and the Remote Sensing Centre in the Food and Agriculture Organization of the United Nations (FAO). The United Nations should collect, collate and disseminate information on the mechanisms designed by countries having experience in space applications.

The Conference noted that, while there was a wide range of bilateral co-operation on space matters, there had been little or no such co-operation between developing countries. Accordingly, it suggested various steps in this area. Developing countries, it said, should exchange experts and promote information exchange among scientists, technologists and decision makers. With the help of international agencies, those countries might organize regional stores for critical and expensive spare parts for such facilities as satellite communication earth stations. The United Nations system, including its regional commissions, might support initiatives to establish regional space agencies by groups of developing countries, as well as other regional mechanisms.

Also along these lines, the Conference suggested that developing countries carry out regional, bilateral and multilateral co-operative programmes ranging from regional receiving stations for remote sensing data to ownership of complete systems. The United Nations and its agencies should be enabled to fund expert missions to define programmes between groups of developing countries. Developing countries with space applications programmes should provide on-the-job experience or training opportunities to persons from other developing countries, with fellowship assistance from the United Nations and its agencies.

Pointing to the importance of broad membership in non-governmental scientific organizations, the Conference said it was desirable that countries support the participation of their scientists and institutions in such bodies.

The Conference said it was understood that proposals for expanded United Nations activities, including those for personnel costs, were to be funded mainly through voluntary contributions of States. It recommended, however, that the General Assembly rearrange priorities within the following United Nations regular budget so that the increase in personnel costs could be absorbed within available resources.

The Conference also made recommendations on international co-operation in regard to specific space applications (p. 168).

Report. [1]Conference on outer space, A/CONF.101/10. *Resolution (1982).* [2]GA: 37/90, para. 2, 10 Dec.

UN activities

UN Programme on Space Applications

In preparation for UNISPACE-82, the United Nations Programme on Space Applications[3] held seminars in 1982 at Quito, Ecuador (19-23 April),[7] and Addis Ababa, Ethiopia (14-18 June),[6] the first for member States of the Economic Commission for Latin America and the second for those of the Economic Commissions for Africa and Western Asia. These were the last of six seminars held in preparation for the Conference. An international symposium on the role and impact of space research in developing countries was held at Ottawa, Canada (20-22 May), under the co-sponsorship of the Committee on Space Research of the International Council of Scientific Unions, the Committee on Science and Technology in Developing Countries and the United Nations.

Twenty-two participants from 21 countries attended the seventh United Nations training course on applications of satellite remote sensing to thematic mapping, with special reference to land use (Rome, Italy, 30 August–17 September), held in co-operation with FAO and the Government of Italy.[8]

The Programme for 1983, as endorsed by the Committee on the Peaceful Uses of Outer Space and approved by the General Assembly in December 1982, included three regional/interregional seminars, for Latin America, Asia and the Pacific, and Africa and Western Asia, focusing on implementation of the recommendations of UNISPACE-82, and two training courses on remote sensing applications to agro-meteorology in semi-arid countries and to water resources.

In January 1982,[5] the Scientific and Technical Sub-Committee of the Committee on outer space noted the satisfactory work of the Programme on Space Applications and reiterated that it should be expanded; some members indicated that this should be done within existing United Nations resources.

The Sub-Committee noted that Austria had renewed its offer of training fellowships in microwave technology for communication satellite systems for developing countries, and Italy its fellowships for the United Nations training course on remote sensing for thematic mapping. It expressed gratitude to the Netherlands and Sweden for their grants of $25,000 each for the regional seminars organized in preparation for UNISPACE-82 and hoped that more fellowships would be forthcoming. It stressed the need for providing more financial assistance to developing countries so that they could gain advanced knowledge of space applications. It welcomed Australia's offer to consider providing scholarships to the Programme and noted that the USSR had reiterated its readiness to continue holding United Nations training seminars on remote sensing.

The Committee on outer space[2] noted the progress achieved in implementing the Programme and endorsed the Programme proposed for 1983. It expressed appreciation to the USSR for its offer on training seminars, and to the European Association of Remote Sensing Laboratories (EARSeL) for its willingness to collaborate with the United Nations on the Programme. It recommended that the United Nations Expert on Space Applications, the official responsible for directing the Programme, explore United Nations co-

operation with EARSeL and report to the Sub-Committee in 1983. The Committee expressed appreciation for the support given by Austria, Italy, the Netherlands and Sweden, and welcomed Australia's offer.

A Consultative Meeting on the Implementation of the Future Activities of the United Nations Space Applications Programme, with Emphasis on Information Systems and Education and Training in Remote Sensing Technology (Enschede, Netherlands, 23 and 24 August 1982),[4] brought together representatives of EARSeL and other international scientific organizations. The participants suggested that Governments and agencies develop long-range space applications programmes making use of the persons trained under the United Nations Programme, and that communication between the United Nations and its Members be supplemented by direct communication with technologists, scientists and professional institutions.

Also in August, UNISPACE-82 suggested several areas for United Nations activities under the Programme.[1] These included the organization of a programme of at least 100 fellowships a year for graduates and post-graduates from developing countries, support for the development of regional training centres, the conduct of three- to five-week seminars for high-level personnel concerned with space technology and applications, and the collection and dissemination of information on co-ordination mechanisms devised by countries with experience in space applications.

The Conference outlined seven objectives for the Programme: to promote exchange of experiences with specific space applications; to promote co-operation in space science and technology; to develop a fellowship programme for technologists and applications specialists, with the help of Member States and international organizations, and to establish and update lists of fellowships in all States and in international organizations; to organize regular seminars on advanced space applications and new system developments for managers and leaders of space application and technology development activities, as well as for users in specific applications; to stimulate growth of indigenous nuclei and autonomous technological bases in space technology in developing countries; to disseminate information on new and advanced technology and applications, with emphasis on their implications for developing countries; and to provide or arrange for technical advisory services on request.

In its 10 December resolution on international co-operation in the peaceful uses of outer space,[9] the General Assembly listed the Programme on Space Applications as a priority item for the Scientific and Technical Sub-Committee in 1983. It endorsed UNISPACE-82 recommendations on the Programme, as well as the Programme proposed for 1983, and expressed appreciation to Governments and international organizations for assisting with seminars and workshops on space applications, particularly for the benefit of developing countries. The Assembly decided on the same date, in its resolution on the Conference,[10] to endorse the UNISPACE-82 recommendations on the Programme's seven objectives.

Reports. [1]Conference on outer space, A/CONF.101/10. [2]COPUOS, A/37/20. [3]Expert on Space Applications, A/AC.105/310. [4]Meeting on Programme on Space Applications, A/AC.105/311. [5]Scientific and Technical Sub-Committee, A/AC.105/304. Seminars: [6]Addis Ababa, A/AC.105/306; [7]Quito, A/AC.105/307. [8]Training course on remote sensing and thematic mapping, A/AC.105/312.
Resolutions (1982). GA: [9]37/89, 10 Dec.; [10]37/90, para. 7, 10 Dec.

Establishment of the International Space Information Service

On 10 December 1982, in its resolution on implementation of the recommendations of UNISPACE-82,[2] the General Assembly decided to establish an International Space Information Service. Initially, the Assembly said, the Service should consist of a directory of sources of information and data services.

The proposal for the Service had been made in August by UNISPACE-82,[1] which said it should initially be used to direct States and specialized agencies to data banks and information sources. At a later stage, the Conference added, the Committee on outer space could consider expanding the Service, bearing in mind the financial implications.

Report. [1]Conference on outer space, A/CONF.101/10. Resolution (1982) [2]GA: 37/90, para. 8, 10 Dec.

Strengthening the Outer Space Affairs Division

On 10 December 1982, in its resolution on implementation of the recommendations of UNISPACE-82,[2] the General Assembly requested the Secretary-General to strengthen the Outer Space Affairs Division of the United Nations Secretariat by increasing its technical personnel. It also decided that all new or expanded activities it approved on the recommendation of the Conference should be funded primarily through voluntary contributions of States in money or in kind, as well as through a rearrangement of priorities within the following United Nations budget.

In recommending this strengthening, UNISPACE-82 noted[1] that the work of the Division and of units of the United Nations regional commissions dealing with space matters was expected to increase. Their additional tasks would include servicing the Committee on outer space in implementing Conference recommendations, undertaking studies at the Committee's request,

implementing the expanded United Nations Programme on Space Applications, and organizing and operating the International Space Information Service. The Conference suggested that the Assembly consider integrating outer space activities into a Centre for Outer Space or providing additional personnel and resources to the existing Division.

Report. [1]Conference on outer space, A/CONF.101/10. Resolution (1982). [2]GA: 37/90, para. 9, 10 Dec.

Co-ordination in the UN system

Following consideration by the Scientific and Technical Sub-Committee in January 1982 of arrangements to co-ordinate work on outer space matters within the United Nations system,[3] the Committee on outer space, at its March/April session,[2] noted the participation of United Nations bodies, specialized agencies and other international organizations in its work, including their submission of reports. It viewed this as important in enabling the Committee and its subsidiary bodies to act as a focal point for international co-operation, especially with respect to the application of space science and technology in developing countries.

UNISPACE-82 noted in August[1] that a number of units of the United Nations system, in addition to the Outer Space Affairs Division, were involved in space-related activities and emphasized the need for co-ordination and avoidance of duplication in their programmes. It suggested that the *Ad Hoc* Sub-Committee on Outer Space Activities, a body of the inter-agency Administrative Committee on Co-ordination, continue to meet annually to consider co-ordination between agencies and the greater interchange of expertise through joint programmes. The Sub-Committee should also discuss and co-ordinate space-related agency programmes before their finalization. The Outer Space Affairs Division should co-operate with the technical and funding agencies of the system to ensure proper project co-ordination. United Nations regional commissions should be given adequate resources so that they could participate effectively in executing Conference recommendations.

On 10 December, in its resolution on international co-operation in the peaceful uses of outer space, the General Assembly listed the co-ordination of outer space activities in the United Nations system among the priority topics for the Scientific and Technical Sub-Committee in 1983.[4]

Reports. [1]Conference on outer space, A/CONF.101/10; [2]COPUOS, A/37/20; [3]Scientific and Technical Sub-Committee, A/AC.105/304.
Resolution (1982). [4]GA: 37/89, para. 7 (a) (i), 10 Dec.

Remote sensing

The use of satellites for remote sensing of data on natural resources and earth sciences, and for telecommunication of those data back to earth, was the main topic of meetings organized in 1982 by the United Nations Programme on Space Applications and figured prominently in the recommendations of UNISPACE-82.

Prior to the Conference, the Scientific and Technical Sub-Committee of the Committee on outer space considered remote sensing in January.[3] In February, a working group established by the Committee's Legal Sub-Committee continued consideration of draft principles governing remote sensing.

The Scientific and Technical Sub-Committee noted that Indonesia was willing to host a remote sensing centre under United Nations auspices to assist developing countries to establish their own programmes. It reiterated its view that remote sensing should be carried out with all possible international co-operation and with assistance provided to developing countries. It also recommended that the United Nations list of remote sensing applications continue to be updated, that more Members provide information for the list and that it be available to all interested nations.

The Committee on outer space, at its March/April session,[2] endorsed the views of its Sub-Committee on the list of remote sensing applications and noted with satisfaction Indonesia's offer on a regional centre.

In August, UNISPACE-82[1] noted the importance of remote sensing and its potential contribution to economic development. It cited the need to develop an indigenous capability to operate ground receiving and transmission facilities, and mentioned the desire of many users to be assured by countries operating the space segment of a remote sensing system that services providing direct and unrestricted access to data on their territories at reasonable prices would continue. A number of operators of space segments believed, however, that the prices users paid must reflect the high cost of the systems. By the end of the decade, it was likely that six or more remote sensing systems would be operated by national or regional agencies. This would allow the user to select the most suitable system, although prices for data were likely to rise to cover development and operating costs.

The Conference noted that space photography was a low-cost approach to data analysis and attractive to developing countries unable to afford large investments in ground hardware. It emphasized that simple, inexpensive equipment and appropriate techniques were often suitable for data processing and analysis, and that countries should devote special effort to such activities as the systematic collection of "ground truth" in order

properly to interpret remote sensing data. Because most countries might not be able to afford the sophisticated sensor equipment required, a co-operative network between national agencies and regional facilities might be considered, possibly in conjunction with a system of distributing processed data to simple, low-cost user terminals.

Before embarking on large-scale remote sensing applications and investments, the Conference added, each country should make cost-benefit assessments and decisions. The United Nations system should encourage discussion of user needs and ways of assessing remote sensing systems, and should study the need for and feasibility of a world-wide remote sensing system. Emphasis should be placed, where practical, on compatibility between systems and on equipment standardization. Given the investments already made on the ground by many countries, continuity of data availability in a form compatible with existing systems was essential.

The Conference recommended that the Remote Sensing Centre in the Food and Agriculture Organization of the United Nations, as well as regional remote sensing centres, should continue to assist countries in developing remote sensing of renewable natural resources.

On 10 December, the General Assembly, in its resolution on international co-operation in the peaceful uses of outer space,[4] endorsed the recommendation of the Committee on outer space that remote sensing should be among the priority questions for the Scientific and Technical Sub-Committee in 1983.

Reports. [1]Conference on outer space, A/CONF.101/10; [2]COPUOS, A/37/20; [3]Scientific and Technical Sub-Committee, A/AC.105/304.
Resolution (1982). [4]GA: 37/89, para. 7 *(a)* (ii), 10 Dec.

Satellite communication

UNISPACE-82, meeting in August 1982, noted the rapid technological advances made in satellite telecommunications since they became operational in 1965. However, as satellites became more versatile and powerful, the total cost of systems had increased substantially, particularly for the ground segment. Countries and international organizations, the Conference felt, should support efforts to reduce the cost of ground segment hardware.

The Conference noted that a variety of advanced technological concepts had been envisioned for the future, including the launching and the fabrication in space of large structures having sufficient power to allow for communication with small terminals. However, the introduction of such technologies created technical and legal complications. Thus, studies should be made to determine the optimal use of innovations and, in particular, their impact on the geostationary orbit.

Developing countries could benefit by joining together in setting up systems using shared or common satellites, the Conference pointed out. Countries should undertake studies, if necessary with the assistance of United Nations organizations, to determine the best approach to their communications needs. Funding institutions should recognize communications as an essential infrastructure for development and provide adequate funding for national and regional systems.

The Conference suggested further investigation of several particular types of space communication systems. Thus, it encouraged the early implementation of a satellite system to replace existing aeronautical communication systems, and suggested that developing countries be assisted to undertake the basic scientific pursuits required for conventional satellite communication applications such as video conferencing, data communication and electronic mail. The United Nations and other organizations should study the economic aspects of low-orbit satellites for use by developing countries in point-to-point communication. Countries and agencies planning mobile communication systems using satellites should be encouraged to study the feasibility of using the same system for rural communication in developing countries. United Nations agencies should assist in assessing requirements for maritime communication. They should also examine the implications of advanced communications developments, especially for the developing countries.

Satellite broadcasting

UNISPACE-82 noted in August 1982 that the development of powerful satellites, making possible the direct broadcast of radio and television programmes to home receivers, could be an important means of spreading education and disseminating information, especially in developing countries. However, this development could also have negative repercussions and could affect the sovereign rights of States.

In December, the General Assembly adopted Principles Governing the Use by States of Artificial Earth Satellites for International Direct Television Broadcasting (p. 173).

Educational broadcasting

UNISPACE-82 recommended in August 1982 that countries examine the use of direct broadcast satellites to foster education. They could explore sharing the space segment of a direct broadcast satellite system and study the feasibility of an international or regional satellite space segment for providing direct broadcast television service. The development of low-cost community receivers for direct broadcast satellites and low-cost, preferably renewable, power sources to operate the system in unelectrified locations should be encouraged and, if necessary, supported with financial and technical assistance. Efforts to develop more powerful broadcasting satellites should also be continued.

The United Nations system should encourage and provide assistance for these applications, the Conference recommended, and organizations such as the International Telecommunications Satellite Organization might develop broadcasting satellite systems which could be used for educational purposes. The United Nations, in co-operation with the specialized agencies, should study the educational opportunities emanating from satellite and related telecommunication technologies, and support studies and programmes on satellite systems for technical training and education, particularly in the developing countries. It should also assist countries to develop system configurations for using space technology for education.

Meteorological satellites

UNISPACE-82 recommended in August 1982 that encouragement be given to developing remote sensing technologies for monitoring air and water pollution and slowly changing atmospheric variables in order to assess long-term weather patterns. Experimental techniques involving microwave radiometers and radar altimeters for measuring such factors as precipitation and ocean-surface temperatures should be further developed and scientific studies on them intensified. Efforts should be made to maintain continuity in meteorological satellite programmes, particularly with regard to their financing or required modification, and countries should continue to have free access to meteorological data.

The work of the World Meteorological Organization (WMO) in establishing regional and international centres for meteorological satellite data reception should be encouraged, the Conference recommended. WMO should be encouraged to ensure optimal use of space techniques, particularly facilities for data reception and processing, data analysis and dissemination. It might also study the establishment of an international structure providing continuous availability of and access to satellite meteorological data, and should continue to encourage compatibility and complementarity among satellite systems.

Navigational and geodetic satellites

UNISPACE-82 suggested in August 1982 that there be world-wide access to navigational satellites and that computation techniques, equipment and information on their use be widely disseminated. Observing that the picture with regard to compatibility and co-operation in this area was not as positive as in others, it urged that a feasibility study be conducted on the establishment of an international system with the participation of all States. Efforts should also be made to evolve a world-wide search and rescue system.

With regard to geodetic satellites, used to measure dimensions and positions on the earth's surface, the Conference suggested that progress in interpreting the findings could be greatly accelerated by international co-operation involving a pooling of data and knowledge. Deployment of fixed and mobile ground-based laser ranging stations, used with satellites to determine positions accurate to within 1 or 2 centimetres, was desirable so that internationally co-ordinated measuring campaigns could help develop a better scientific understanding of the earth and its crustal movements.

Space environment

Addressing the impact of human activities on the space environment, UNISPACE-82 recommended in August 1982 that the international community agree on measures for eliminating debris from space, including the removal of inactive satellites from orbit. The United Nations, and in particular the United Nations Environment Programme (UNEP), should encourage studies by independent experts on the deleterious effects of releasing gaseous or other material in space for scientific studies and should recommend limits on such releases. In addition, they should study the global environmental effects of rocket launchings and the use of ion engines for propulsion.

To guard against depletion of the earth's protective atmospheric ozone layer, UNISPACE-82 recommended that an integrated global ozone observing system be created under the aegis of the World Meteorological Organization (WMO) and UNEP. National research on the ozone layer, with the asssistance of WMO and UNEP, should be encouraged. UNEP should co-ordinate world-wide monitoring of the earth's environment from space and necessary remedial action within the framework of its Global Environmental Monitoring System. All countries should provide UNEP with data required for such monitoring.

The Conference also urged support for research in the micro-gravity environment of outer space (p. 171).

UNEP continued its work on the elaboration of a draft convention on the ozone layer and the WMO Global Atmospheric Research Programme its study of environmental factors affecting climate (See ECONOMIC AND SOCIAL QUESTIONS, Chapter XVI).

Use of nuclear power sources in outer space

The Scientific and Technical Sub-Committee of the Committee on the Peaceful Uses of Outer Space[2] took note in January 1982 of the conclusion reaffirmed in February 1981 by its Working Group on the Use of Nuclear Power Sources in Outer Space[4] that nuclear power sources could be used safely in space provided that all necessary safety requirements were met. The Sub-Committee noted that the Working Group's report had been a consensus document and provided the technical basis for future work by the Legal Sub-Committee on the issue.

A working group of the Legal Sub-Committee met in February 1982 to continue considering the possibility of supplementing international legal norms relevant to the use of nuclear power sources in outer space.

A recommendation by the Scientific and Technical Sub-Committee that the technical aspects and safety measures of nuclear power sources in space be kept on its agenda on a priority basis was endorsed in March/April by the Committee on outer space[1] and approved by the General Assembly on 10 December in its resolution on international co-operation in the peaceful uses of outer space.[3]

Reports. [1]COPUOS, A/37/20; [2]Scientific and Technical Sub-Committee, A/AC.105/304.
Resolution (1982). [3]GA: 37/89, para. 7 *(a)* (iii), 10 Dec.
Yearbook reference. [4]1981, p. 117.

Space transportation

The Scientific and Technical Sub-Committee, in January 1982,[3] recognized that progress in space transportation systems was providing the international community with greater possibilities for the launching of payloads. Noting activities by China, India, Japan, the USSR, the United States and the European Space Agency, the Sub-Committee also noted that the Secretariat had updated its 1979 study on the international implications of new space transportation systems.[4]

The Sub-Committee decided to continue its consideration of space transportation systems in 1983. This decision was endorsed in April 1982 by the Committee on outer space[2] and was approved on 10 December by the General Assembly in its resolution on international co-operation in the peaceful uses of outer space.[5]

In August, UNISPACE-82 recommended[1] that launching services for peaceful purposes be provided to all countries through bilateral or multilateral arrangements on equitable terms. It encouraged the development of more economical space transportation systems, as well as study of the long-term consequences of the increasing number of launchings and, if necessary, the institution of corrective measures. Increased numbers of launchings might require co-ordination, it stated, and regulations to minimize the environmental effects of exhaust gases or of the re-entry of burned-out lower stages might have to be formulated. The development of large-scale space transportation systems, such as assembly of large multi-mission space platforms or operation of permanent space stations, carried implications for international co-operation that should be studied.

> *Reports.* [1]Conference on outer space, A/CONF.101/10; [2]COPUOS, A/37/20; [3]Scientific and Technical Sub-Committee, A/AC.105/304; [4]Secretariat, A/AC.105/244/Add.1.
> *Resolution (1982).* [5]GA: 37/89, para. 7 *(b)* (i), 10 Dec.

Solar power transmission from satellites

UNISPACE-82 noted in August 1982[1] that space solar power systems—designed to generate power from sunlight on large orbiting space stations and transmit it to earth—would be an important project for co-operative international effort. Such systems, although unlikely to be developed before the end of the century, had wide implications because of growing energy needs and dwindling conventional resources. At the same time, their potentially negative impact on the environment would require a concerted research and technology effort. It was advisable, therefore, to initiate a mechanism for international participation and co-operation.

> *Report.* [1]Conference on outer space, A/CONF.101/10.

Technical aspects of the geostationary orbit

The Scientific and Technical Sub-Committee of the Committee on the Peaceful Uses of Outer Space continued in January 1982[4] its examination of the physical nature and technical attributes of the geostationary orbit, used to enable satellites to maintain a position above a selected location on the earth's surface. It considered a Secretariat study prepared with the International Astronautical Federation as a background paper for UNISPACE-82.[1] The Sub-Committee requested that study of the topic be updated as required.

In February, the Legal Sub-Committee discussed the definition and/or delimitation of outer space and outer space activities, including questions relating to the geostationary orbit.

The Committee on outer space, at its March/April session,[3] endorsed the recommendations of the Scientific and Technical Sub-Committee. It also noted studies by the International Telecommunication Union (ITU), prepared for the World Administrative Radio Conference scheduled for 1985 and 1987, to consider the use of the geostationary orbit and the planning of services utilizing it.

In August 1982, UNISPACE-82[2] addressed problems created by what it described as the explosive growth in the use of the geostationary orbit and the fact that it was becoming increasingly crowded with objects that had lost their utility. Noting that the orbit was occupied largely by developed countries' satellites and international systems, it stated that arrangements concerning the orbit should accommodate future needs of the developing countries.

The Conference recommended that ITU consider making owners responsible for removing their satellites from the geostationary orbit when they were no longer usable. ITU should also continue evolving criteria for the best use of the orbit as well as for the radio frequency spectrum assigned to satellites using it, and develop planning methods and arrangements based on the particular needs of each country. Solutions for the use of the orbit should be equitable and flexible, and take into account economic, technical and legal considerations.

On 10 December, in its resolution on international co-operation in the peaceful uses of outer space,[5] the General Assembly endorsed the recommendation of the Committee on outer space that the Scientific and Technical Sub-Committee should again consider, at its 1983 session, the physical nature and technical attributes of the geostationary orbit.

> *Background paper.* [1]A/CONF.101/BP/7.
> *Reports.* [2]Conference on outer space, A/CONF.101/10 & Corr.2; [3]COPUOS, A/37/20; [4]Scientific and Technical Sub-Committee, A/AC.105/304.
> *Resolution (1982).* [5]GA: 37/89, para. 7 *(b)* (ii), 10 Dec.

Extraterrestrial feature names

The Fourth United Nations Conference on the Standardization of Geographical Names recommended on 14 September 1982[1] that the Working Group on Extraterrestrial Features of the United Nations Group of Experts on Geographical Names be dissolved, in view of the fact that naming extraterrestrial features was being satisfactorily done by the Working Group for Planetary System Nomenclature of the International Astronomical Union. It recommended continued liaison between the two groups.

> *Resolution (1982).* [1]Conference on geographical names (report, E/CONF.74/3, Sales No. E.83.I.7): 13, 14 Sep.

Space science

In August 1982, the Second United Nations Conference on the Exploration and Peaceful Uses of Outer Space recommended[1] that support for space science should be substantially increased and co-operative experiments by scientists of various countries continued. It noted that the encouragement of space science and space astronomy in universities and institutions of developing countries could contribute significantly to the development of practical applications of space technology.

The Conference recommended that research in the micro-gravity environment of outer space be supported and carried out in a co-operative and co-ordinated manner. Information gathered in materials science experiments should be globally disseminated, and the benefits of developments concerning the production of new engineering and industrial materials in space should be available on reasonable terms to all nations. Scientists of all countries should have access to facilities for experiments relating to space biology and medicine, including life processes such as conditioning of the cardiovascular system during prolonged exposure to weightlessness.

Report. [1]Conference on outer space, A/CONF.101/10.

Legal aspects

On 10 December 1982, as a follow-up to work done by the Legal Sub-Committee of the Committee on the Peaceful Uses of Outer Space, the General Assembly adopted Principles Governing the Use by States of Artificial Earth Satellites for International Direct Television Broadcasting. In addition, it invited States to consider adhering to the Convention on International Liability for Damage Caused by Space Objects.

The Legal Sub-Committee, at its twenty-first session, held at Geneva from 1 to 19 February,[2] continued work on draft principles relating to remote sensing of the earth from space. It also considered the possibility of supplementing the norms of international law relevant to the use of nuclear power sources in outer space, and continued its study of matters relating to the definition and/or delimitation of outer space and outer space activities, bearing in mind questions relating to the geostationary orbit. The Sub-Committee's report was examined in March/April by its parent Committee, which expressed its views on the matters considered by the Sub-Committee.[1]

The Assembly, in its resolution of 10 December on international co-operation in the peaceful uses of outer space,[3] endorsed the recommendation of the Committee on outer space that the Sub-Committee continue consideration of draft principles on remote sensing on a priority basis in 1983. It should also continue consideration of the other topics studied in 1982.

Reports. [1]COPUOS, A/37/20; [2]Legal Sub-Committee, A/AC.105/305.
Resolution (1982). [3]GA: 37/89, para. 5, 10 Dec.

Principles on direct broadcast satellites

The General Assembly, on 10 December 1982,[2] by a recorded vote of 107 to 13, with 13 abstentions, adopted a set of 15 Principles Governing the Use by States of Artificial Earth Satellites for International Direct Television Broadcasting. It expressed the belief that the operation of such satellites—used for television broadcasting directly

into the home or to community receivers, without going through ground stations—would have significant political, economic, social and cultural implications and that the establishment of principles would strengthen international co-operation.

The principles stipulated that direct television broadcasting should be compatible with the sovereign rights of States, including the principle of non-intervention, as well as with the right of everyone to seek, receive and impart information. International disputes arising from such broadcasting should be settled through established procedures for the peaceful settlement of disputes. States and intergovernmental bodies should bear international responsibility for broadcasting carried out by them or under their jurisdiction, and should be responsible for conformity of such activities with the principles. States intending to establish or authorize a broadcasting service would have to consult the proposed receiving States at their request, and the service could be established only on the basis of agreement. The principles also provided for co-operation to protect copyright and neighbouring rights, non-discriminatory access to technology, and the international dissemination, through the Secretary-General, of information on national activities.

Adoption of the principles was recommended by the Special Political Committee (SPC) on 22 November by a recorded vote of 88 to 15, with 11 abstentions. The draft resolution and annexed principles were introduced by Brazil on behalf of 20 States and were revised by the sponsors prior to approval.

Work on the principles was initially carried out in working groups of the Committee on outer space and its Legal Sub-Committee, which had been considering the subject since 1973[5] following a 1972 initiative by the USSR in the General Assembly.[4] As decided by the Assembly in November 1981,[3] the Committee on outer space, at its March/April 1982 session, sought agreement on a text through an informal working group, but the Committee reported to the Assembly that agreement was not reached.[1]

Introducing the text in SPC, Brazil emphasized the need for regulations for direct television broadcasting to promote peaceful coexistence and harmonious relations among States, and regretted that consensus on the text had not been possible. Brazil added that the principles safeguarded the sovereign rights of all States without prejudice to the free flow of information, and they stressed international co-operation, State responsibility and the need for prior consultations between States willing to establish a broadcasting service.

A number of delegations which voted against the principles, including the Federal Republic of Germany, Italy, the Netherlands, the United

Kingdom and the United States, said the text did not sufficiently respect the right to seek, receive and impart information and ideas regardless of frontiers because it required the prior consent of States before establishing direct television broadcasting. Iceland said it would have supported the text without the provisions on prior consultation and consent. In the view of Italy and others, the principles did not strike a balance between the free flow of information and State sovereignty. The United States objected to giving countries a veto over this form of broadcasting.

Some delegations, including Italy, the Netherlands, Sweden (which abstained) and the United States, also objected to provisions establishing State responsibility for the content of programmes. The media should not be required to act as organs of the State and the State should not be required to exercise full control over the media, said the Netherlands.

The Federal Republic of Germany, Iceland, Italy, Japan, the United Kingdom and the United States, which voted against, and Austria, Canada, France, Ireland, New Zealand and Sweden, which abstained, regretted that the resolution had been brought to a vote before consensus could be reached. A number of them believed that the principles, to be valid, must have the support of all United Nations Members, particularly the technologically advanced States. Principles that did not take account of the legitimate interests of all members of the international community would not have a fair chance of becoming generally accepted, the Federal Republic of Germany said. The United Kingdom remarked that a majority vote in the Assembly might have a limited political value but international law could not be affected.

France, which voted against in SPC and abstained in the Assembly, said it could have accepted the principles with reservations on those concerning State responsibility. Ireland, abstaining, said it firmly supported the free flow of information but appreciated the widely expressed concern about the social and cultural implications of direct television broadcasting.

Among those voting in favour, Chile said the principles had not established an adequate balance between the free flow of information and State responsibility, nor had they clearly established the principle of prior consent; States should go on to draft a more balanced international convention on the subject. Colombia said that the export of culture through direct television broadcasting implied a great danger, that technological development should be regulated by legal principles and that the practice of consensus should not become an instrument of veto. Ecuador and Mexico said the principle of prior consultation was necessary in broadcasting by satellite; Ecuador added that a captive audience subject to satellite-transmitted programmes would not have the freedom of choice implicit in freedom of information.

Also voting in favour, the German Democratic Republic stated that the text reflected the principle of respect for the sovereign rights of States and non-interference in their internal affairs, and met the interests of most States. Turkey voted in favour with the understanding that application of the principles must be consistent with freedom of information.

Costa Rica, which did not vote, regretted the lack of consensus and the attitude of countries which seemed to believe they could impose their ideological products on the rest of mankind.

Report. [1]COPUOS, A/37/20.
Resolution (1982). [2]GA: 37/92, 10 Dec., text following.
Resolution (prior). [3]GA: 36/35, 18 Nov. 1981 (YUN 1981, p. 113).
Yearbook references. [4]1972, p. 43; [5]1973, p. 51.
Meeting records. GA: SPC, A/SPC/37/SR.15-20, 23, 25, *33, 34* (1-22 Nov.); plenary, A/37/PV.100 (10 Dec.).

General Assembly resolution 37/92

10 December 1982   Meeting 100   107-13-13 (recorded vote)

Approved by SPC (A/37/646) by recorded vote (88-15-11), 22 November (meeting 34); 20-nation draft (A/SPC/37/L.5/Rev.1); agenda item 63.

Sponsors: Argentina, Bolivia, Brazil, Chile, Colombia, Ecuador, Egypt, India, Indonesia, Iraq, Kenya, Mexico, Niger, Nigeria, Pakistan, Peru, Philippines, Romania, Uruguay, Venezuela.

Principles Governing the Use by States of Artificial Earth Satellites for International Direct Television Broadcasting

The General Assembly,

Recalling its resolution 2916(XXVII) of 9 November 1972, in which it stressed the necessity of elaborating principles governing the use by States of artificial earth satellites for international direct television broadcasting, and mindful of the importance of concluding an international agreement or agreements,

Recalling further its resolutions 3182(XXVIII) of 18 December 1973, 3234(XXIX) of 12 November 1974, 3388(XXX) of 18 November 1975, 31/8 of 8 November 1976, 32/196 of 20 December 1977, 33/16 of 10 November 1978, 34/66 of 5 December 1979 and 35/14 of 3 November 1980, and its resolution 36/35 of 18 November 1981 in which it decided to consider at its thirty-seventh session the adoption of a draft set of principles governing the use by States of artificial earth satellites for international direct television broadcasting,

Noting with appreciation the efforts made in the Committee on the Peaceful Uses of Outer Space and its Legal Sub-Committee to comply with the directives issued in the above-mentioned resolutions,

Considering that several experiments of direct broadcasting by satellite have been carried out and a number of direct broadcasting satellite systems are operational in some countries and may be commercialized in the very near future,

Taking into consideration that the operation of international direct broadcasting satellites will have significant international political, economic, social and cultural implications,

Believing that the establishment of principles for international direct television broadcasting will contribute to the strengthening of international co-operation in this field and further the purposes and principles of the Charter of the United Nations,

Adopts the Principles Governing the Use by States of Artificial Earth Satellites for International Direct Television Broadcasting set forth in the annex to the present resolution.

ANNEX
Principles Governing the Use by States of Artificial Earth Satellites for International Direct Television Broadcasting

A.   Purposes and objectives

1.   Activities in the field of international direct television broadcasting by satellite should be carried out in a manner compatible with the sovereign rights of States, including the principle of non-intervention, as well as with the right of everyone to seek, receive and impart information and ideas as enshrined in the relevant United Nations instruments.

2.   Such activities should promote the free dissemination and mutual exchange of information and knowledge in cultural and scientific fields, assist in educational, social and economic development, particularly in the developing countries, enhance the qualities of life of all peoples and provide recreation with due respect to the political and cultural integrity of States.

3.   These activities should accordingly be carried out in a manner compatible with the development of mutual understanding and the strengthening of friendly relations and co-operation among all States and peoples in the interest of maintaining international peace and security.

B.   Applicability of international law

4.   Activities in the field of international direct television broadcasting by satellite should be conducted in accordance with international law, including the Charter of the United Nations, the Treaty on Principles Governing the Activities of States in the Exploration and Use of Outer Space, including the Moon and Other Celestial Bodies, of 27 January 1967, the relevant provisions of the International Telecommunication Convention and its Radio Regulations and of international instruments relating to friendly relations and co-operation among States and to human rights.

C.   Rights and benefits

5.   Every State has an equal right to conduct activities in the field of international direct television broadcasting by satellite and to authorize such activities by persons and entities under its jurisdiction. All States and peoples are entitled to and should enjoy the benefits from such activities. Access to the technology in this field should be available to all States without discrimination on terms mutually agreed by all concerned.

D.   International co-operation

6.   Activities in the field of international direct television broadcasting by satellite should be based upon and encourage international co-operation. Such co-operation should be the subject of appropriate arrangements. Special consideration should be given to the needs of the developing countries in the use of international direct television broadcasting by satellite for the purpose of accelerating their national development.

E.   Peaceful settlement of disputes

7.   Any international dispute that may arise from activities covered by these principles should be settled through established procedures for the peaceful settlement of disputes agreed upon by the parties to the dispute in accordance with the provisions of the Charter of the United Nations.

F.   State responsibility

8.   States should bear international responsibility for activities in the field of international direct television broadcasting by satellite carried out by them or under their jurisdiction and for the conformity of any such activities with the principles set forth in this document.

9.   When international direct television broadcasting by satellite is carried out by an international intergovernmental organization, the responsibility referred to in paragraph 8 above should be borne both by that organization and by the States participating in it.

G.   Duty and right to consult

10.   Any broadcasting or receiving State within an international direct television broadcasting satellite service established between them requested to do so by any other broadcasting or receiving State within the same service should promptly enter into consultations with the requesting State regarding its activities in the field of international direct television broadcasting by satellite, without prejudice to other consultations which these States may undertake with any other State on that subject.

H.   Copyright and neighbouring rights

11.   Without prejudice to the relevant provisions of international law, States should co-operate on a bilateral and multilateral basis for protection of copyright and neighbouring rights by means of appropriate agreements between the interested States or the competent legal entities acting under their jurisdiction. In such co-operation they should give special consideration to the interests of developing countries in the use of direct television broadcasting for the purpose of accelerating their national development.

I.   Notification to the United Nations

12.   In order to promote international co-operation in the peaceful exploration and use of outer space, States conducting or authorizing activities in the field of international direct television broadcasting by satellite should inform the Secretary-General of the United Nations, to the greatest extent possible, of the nature of such activities. On receiving this information, the Secretary-General should disseminate it immediately and effectively to the relevant specialized agencies, as well as to the public and the international scientific community.

J.   Consultations and agreements between States

13.   A State which intends to establish or authorize the establishment of an international direct television broadcasting satellite service shall without delay notify the proposed receiving State or States of such intention and shall promptly enter into consultation with any of those States which so requests.

14.   An international direct television broadcasting satellite service shall only be established after the conditions set forth in paragraph 13 above have been met and on the basis of agreements and/or arrangements in conformity with the relevant instruments of the International Telecommunication Union and in accordance with these principles.

15.   With respect to the unavoidable overspill of the radiation of the satellite signal, the relevant instruments of the International Telecommunication Union shall be exclusively applicable.

Recorded vote in Assembly as follows:

In favour: Afghanistan, Algeria, Argentina, Bahrain, Bangladesh, Barbados, Benin, Bhutan, Bolivia, Botswana, Brazil, Bulgaria, Burma, Burundi, Byelorussian SSR, Central African Republic, Chad, Chile, China, Colombia, Comoros, Congo, Cuba, Cyprus, Czechoslovakia, Democratic Kampuchea, Democratic Yemen, Djibouti, Dominican Republic, Ecuador, Egypt, El Salvador, Ethiopia, Fiji, Gabon, Gambia, German Democratic Republic, Ghana, Guyana, Haiti, Honduras, Hungary, India, Indonesia, Iran, Iraq, Jamaica, Jordan, Kenya, Kuwait, Lao People's Democratic Republic, Liberia, Libyan Arab Jamahiriya, Madagascar, Malaysia, Maldives, Mali, Malta, Mauritania, Mauritius, Mexico, Mongolia, Mozambique, Nepal, Nicaragua, Niger, Nigeria, Oman, Pakistan, Panama, Papua New Guinea, Peru, Philippines, Poland, Qatar, Romania, Rwanda, Sao Tome and Principe, Saudi Arabia, Senegal, Sierra Leone, Singapore, Solomon Islands, Somalia, Sri Lanka, Sudan, Suriname, Syrian Arab Republic, Thailand, Togo, Trinidad and Tobago, Tunisia, Turkey, Uganda, Ukrainian SSR, USSR, United Arab Emirates, United Republic of Cameroon, United Republic of Tanzania, Upper Volta, Uruguay, Venezuela, Viet Nam, Yemen, Yugoslavia, Zaire, Zambia.

Against: Belgium, Denmark, Germany, Federal Republic of, Iceland, Israel, Italy, Japan, Luxembourg, Netherlands, Norway, Spain, United Kingdom, United States.

Abstaining: Australia, Austria, Canada, Finland, France, Greece, Ireland, Lebanon, Malawi, Morocco, New Zealand, Portugal, Sweden.

Implementation of the Convention on liability for damage by space objects

The General Assembly, in a resolution of 10 December 1982[2] adopted without vote, reaffirmed the importance of the Convention on International Liability for Damage Caused by Space Objects, approved by the Assembly in 1971.[3] Noting that 72 States had signed and 62 States had ratified the Convention, the Assembly invited States to give urgent consideration to ratifying or acceding.

This action was recommended by SPC without vote on 19 November 1982. The draft resolution was introduced by Austria on behalf of 22 States.

The question had been placed on the Assembly's agenda at the request of the Secretary-

General. In a note dated 25 March annexing an explanatory memorandum,[1] he pointed out that article XXVI of the Convention provided that the question of reviewing the Convention should be placed on the Assembly's agenda 10 years after its entry into force to consider whether, in the light of its application, it required revision. The Convention entered into force on 1 September 1972.

Note. [1]S-G, A/37/141.
Resolution (1982). [2]GA: 37/91, 10 Dec., text following.
Resolution (prior). [3]GA: 2777(XXVI), annex, 29 Nov. 1971 (YUN 1971, p. 52).
Meeting records. GA: SPC, A/SPC/37/SR.15-20, 23, *25, 33* (1-19 Nov.); plenary, A/37/PV.100 (10 Dec.).

General Assembly resolution 37/91

10 December 1982   Meeting 100   Adopted without vote

Approved by SPC (A/37/646) without vote, 19 November (meeting 33); 22-nation draft (A/SPC/37/L.8); agenda item 131.

Sponsors: Australia, Austria, Belgium, Brazil, Bulgaria, Byelorussian SSR, Chile, Czechoslovakia, German Democratic Republic, Germany, Federal Republic of, Hungary, India, Mongolia, Netherlands, Pakistan, Poland, Romania, Sweden, Ukrainian SSR, USSR, United Kingdom, United States.

Question of the review of the Convention on International Liability for Damage Caused by Space Objects

The General Assembly,

Reaffirming the importance of international co-operation in the field of the exploration and peaceful uses of outer space, including the moon and other celestial bodies, and of promoting the law in this field of human endeavour,

Taking note with appreciation of the work accomplished by the Committee on the Peaceful Uses of Outer Space, in particular that of its Legal Sub-Committee,

Recognizing that, in view of the considerable increase of activities in outer space, effective international rules and procedures concerning liability for damage caused by space objects continue to be of great importance,

Having reviewed the Convention on International Liability for Damage Caused by Space Objects,

Noting with satisfaction that to date seventy-two States have signed and sixty-two States have ratified the Convention,

1. *Reaffirms* the importance of the Convention on International Liability for Damage Caused by Space Objects;

2. *Invites* all States that have not yet done so to give urgent consideration to ratifying or acceding to the Convention.

Draft principles on the legal aspects of remote sensing

From 2 to 9 February 1982, a working group re-established on 1 February by the Legal Sub-Committee of the Committee on the Peaceful Uses of Outer Space continued considering draft principles governing the remote sensing of earth from space. It reviewed the 17 draft principles as they had appeared at the conclusion of the Sub-Committee's 1981 session, with the exception of 9 principles on which tentative agreement had been reached and another which was not discussed.

In its review, the group did not reach consensus on any of the remaining principles, and therefore did not modify or elaborate the draft. It paid particular attention to principles XII and XV. As stated in principle XII, the group agreed in principle that sensing States should provide a sensed

State with timely and non-discriminatory access, on reasonable terms, to primary data concerning its territory. Agreement was not reached, however, on matters discussed at previous sessions—the time element and the necessity of agreement between sensing and sensed States on terms of access. Some delegations favoured the deletion and some the retention of principle XV, which would require approval by sensed States before information on their natural resources could be disseminated.

Scientific and technical aspects of remote sensing were discussed in January by the Scientific and Technical Sub-Committee.

The work of the working group on remote sensing, as described in its Chairman's report annexed to the report of the Legal Sub-Committee,[3] was noted by the Committee on outer space at its March/April session.[2] The Committee noted that a number of issues remained to be agreed upon before the draft principles could be finalized.

In August, the Second United Nations Conference on the Exploration and Peaceful Uses of Outer Space (p. 162) recommended[1] that the Committee on outer space continue to seek agreement on the principles as a matter of priority. It referred to the concern expressed by some countries that data not available to a sensed State might be available for commercial or other exploitation by another country. It noted that the lack of trained manpower and the high costs of processing and analysis facilities prevented some countries from benefiting more from remote sensing technology.

On 10 December, the General Assembly, in its resolution on international co-operation in the peaceful uses of outer space,[4] decided that the Legal Sub-Committee should continue considering the legal implications of remote sensing in 1983 on a priority basis, with the aim of formulating draft principles.

Reports. [1]Conference on outer space, A/CONF.101/10; [2]COPUOS, A/37/20; [3]Legal Sub-Committee, A/AC.105/305.
Resolution (1982). [4]GA: 37/89, para. 5 *(a)*, 10 Dec.

Legal aspects of the use of nuclear power sources in outer space

The working group to consider the possibility of supplementing the norms of international law relevant to the use of nuclear power sources in outer space, initially established in March 1981 by the Legal Sub-Committee of the Committee on outer space,[4] was re-established on 1 February 1982 and met until 18 February.

The group discussed assistance to States affected by accidental re-entry of a space object with a nuclear power source on board. It took into account five new working papers on this and other aspects, submitted respectively by Argentina and

Chile, by Brazil, by Canada, by Nigeria and by Sweden. The Canadian paper on assistance was submitted to the Sub-Committee taking into account the group's discussions and with a view to facilitating further deliberations.

According to the report of the group's Chairman, annexed to the report of the Sub-Committee,[2] it was generally agreed that, apart from the special responsibilities of the launching State and in the context of international humanitarianism, all States should be prepared to offer assistance to the affected State to the extent of their capabilities. Among the matters discussed were the need for a special legal régime for State responsibility and liability, as suggested in the papers by Argentina and Chile and by Brazil; the need to define the "necessary assistance" to be rendered by the launching State to the receiving State; and the need to cover both direct and indirect damage caused by a space object.

The group noted that the Scientific and Technical Sub-Committee's Working Group on the Use of Nuclear Power Sources in Outer Space had again concluded in 1981 that such power sources could be used safely provided that all necessary safety requirements were met.

Following a review of the group's work by the Committee on outer space at its March/April 1982 session,[1] the General Assembly, in its 10 December resolution on international co-operation in the peaceful uses of outer space,[3] decided that the Legal Sub-Committee should continue to consider the item through its working group.

Reports. [1]COPUOS, A/37/20; [2]Legal Sub-Committee, A/AC.105/305.
Resolution (1982). [3]GA: 37/89, para. 5 *(b)* (i), 10 Dec.
Yearbook reference. [4]1981, p. 122.

Definition of outer space and legal aspects of the geostationary orbit

The definition and/or delimitation of outer space and outer space activities, including questions relating to the geostationary orbit, were discussed by the Legal Sub-Committee in February 1982, with delegations continuing to express divergent views. According to the Sub-Committee's report,[2] some delegations believed that such a definition should be established without further delay, specifying a certain altitude between airspace and outer space, while others felt the establishment of an arbitrary boundary might prove disadvantageous. Delegations also differed on whether to establish a working group to deal with the topic.

With regard to the geostationary orbit, used by satellites to maintain a fixed position relative to some point on the earth's surface near the equator, two opposing positions continued to be voiced in the Sub-Committee: that a special legal régime should be established for the orbit, taking into account the rights and interests of equatorial States and the needs of developing countries; and that, while access to the orbit should be assured to all States on an equitable and efficient basis, the orbit derived its special attributes from the earth as a whole and regulations governing it should not give equatorial States a special position.

The physical nature and technical aspects of the geostationary orbit were discussed by the Scientific and Technical Sub-Committee in January.

The Committee on outer space[1] noted the work of the Legal Sub-Committee on this topic, with delegations expressing similar views. On 10 December, the General Assembly, in its resolution on international co-operation in the peaceful uses of outer space,[3] decided that the Legal Sub-Committee should continue to consider the topic and devote adequate time for deeper consideration.

Reports. [1]COPUOS, A/37/20; [2]Legal Sub-Committee, A/AC.105/305.
Resolution (1982). [3]GA: 37/89, para. 5 *(b)* (ii), 10 Dec.

Register of launchings of space objects

In 1982, United Nations Member States and an intergovernmental organization launching objects into orbit around the earth or farther into space continued to supply to the United Nations information on their launchings, in accordance with a 1961 General Assembly resolution[6] and the Convention on Registration of Objects Launched into Outer Space.[7]

Eighteen notifications were received in 1982 and distributed as United Nations documents. They covered launchings during the latter part of 1981 as well as in 1982.

India[1] and Japan[2] each submitted information on two launchings and the European Space Agency[5] did so with respect to one. The USSR[3] reported on 132 launchings and the United States[4] on 14. (Some of the launchings involved multiple space objects sent aloft by a single carrier rocket.)

The Convention on registration, which came into force on 15 September 1976, had 31 States parties as at 31 December 1982, including India, which acceded during 1982. The parties were as follows:

Austria, Belgium, Bulgaria, Byelorussian SSR, Canada, Chile, Cuba, Cyprus, Czechoslovakia, Denmark, France, German Democratic Republic, Germany, Federal Republic of, Hungary, India, Mexico, Netherlands, Niger, Peru, Poland, Republic of Korea, Seychelles, Spain, Sweden, Switzerland, Ukrainian

SSR, USSR, United Kingdom, United States, Uruguay, Yugoslavia.

Letters (l) and notes verbales. [1]India: 5 Jan., A/AC.105/INF.390 *(l)*; 17 May, ST/SG/SER.E/79 *(l)* (replaced A/AC.105/INF.391). [2]Japan: 5 Jan., A/AC.105/INF.389; 14 Dec., A/AC.105/INF.392. [3]USSR: 29 Jan., ST/SG/SER.E/60; 24 Feb., ST/SG/SER.E/62; 11 May, ST/SG/SER.E/64; 31 May, ST/SG/SER.E/65; 17 Aug., ST/SG/SER.E/66; 27 Sep., ST/SG/SER.E/69; 26 Nov., ST/SG/SER.E/71; 14 Dec., ST/SG/SER.E/72; 28 Dec., ST/SG/SER.E/74. [4]United States: 13 Apr., ST/SG/SER.E/63; 20 Aug., ST/SG/SER.E/67 & Corr.1; 26 Aug., ST/SG/SER.E/68; 7 Oct., ST/SG/SER.E/70. [5]European Space Agency: 25 Jan., ST/SG/SER.E/61 *(l)*.

Resolutions. GA: [6]1721 B (XVI), 20 Dec. 1961 (YUN 1961, p. 35); [7]3235(XXIX), annex, 12 Nov. 1974 (YUN 1974, p. 63).

Chapter III

Law of the sea

Contents

For resolutions and decisions of major organs mentioned but not reproduced, refer to INDEX OF RESOLUTIONS AND DECISIONS.

General aspects

The Third United Nations Conference on the Law of the Sea concluded in 1982 with the adoption in April and signature in December of the United Nations Convention on the Law of the Sea. Completed after more than 14 years of work, including annual sessions of the Conference since it was given its mandate by the General Assembly in 1973,[5] the Convention set out a legal code for most human uses of the oceans—for navigation, resource exploitation, environmental protection and scientific research.

The Convention, together with four resolutions on preparations for its entry into force and other

matters,[3] was adopted on 30 April by a recorded vote of 130 to 4, with 17 abstentions. This action was taken at the close of the first part of the Conference's eleventh session, held at United Nations Headquarters from 8 March to 30 April. After a resumed eleventh session in New York from 22 to 24 September, held to complete drafting work, the Conference reconvened at Montego Bay, Jamaica, from 6 to 10 December for the final part of its eleventh session. The Convention was opened for signature on 10 December, when it was signed by 119 delegations and ratified by one (Fiji). The Final Act of the Conference, setting out the formal account of its work, was signed on the same day by 149 delegations.

In one of the four resolutions adopted together with the Convention, the Conference decided to establish a Preparatory Commission to make arrangements for the two main organs to be set up under the Convention—the International Sea-Bed Authority and the International Tribunal for the Law of the Sea.

General Assembly action. On 3 December, the General Assembly adopted a resolution[4] by which it welcomed the adoption by the Conference of the Convention and the related resolutions, and appealed to Governments to refrain from action aimed at undermining the Convention or defeating its object and purpose. The Assembly called on States to consider signing and ratifying the Convention as soon as possible so as to allow the new régime for the uses of the sea and its resources to enter into force. It also approved the Secretary-General's assumption of the responsibilities entrusted to him under the Convention and related resolutions, as well as the stationing of an adequate number of staff in Jamaica to service the Preparatory Commission. It authorized him to convene the Commission, approved its financing from the United Nations regular budget and asked him to report in 1983 on implementation of the resolution. The Assembly accepted with appreciation Jamaica's invitation to have the Final Act signed and the Convention opened for signature at Montego Bay from 6 to 10 December 1982.

The resolution, sponsored by 49 States, was adopted by a recorded vote of 135 to 2, with 8 abstentions, following the rejection of an amendment to have the Preparatory Commission financed by the States parties to the Convention, and the adoption by separate recorded votes of the three paragraphs on signature and ratification, financing of the Commission and action to undermine the Convention. The paragraph containing the appeal to Governments to refrain from action to undermine the Convention or defeat its purpose was approved by 134 votes to 5, with 5 abstentions.

By letters dated 7 September[1] and 8 October,[2] the President of the Conference had informed the President of the Assembly of the decisions taken by the Conference at the March/April and September parts of its 1982 session. In the first letter, he said the successful outcome of the Conference proved that the United Nations could be an effective forum for important multilateral negotiations on vital issues. He recalled a statement he had made to the Conference on 30 April, after it approved the Convention, that the participants should promote public understanding of the importance of the Convention so that Governments and parliaments would be convinced to sign and ratify it in a timely manner. He had also expressed hope that delegations which had voted against or abstained in the final vote would, after reflection, find it possible to support the Convention.

Introducing the resolution in the Assembly, Singapore observed that a few States either had a negative attitude towards the Convention or were undecided. It appealed to them to re-examine their position in the light of their specific law of the sea interests and their general support for the rule of law in inter-State relations.

A number of the States which did not support the resolution cited objections to two provisions: the call on States to consider signing and ratifying the Convention (paragraph 2) and the appeal that they refrain from action to undermine it or defeat its object and purpose (paragraph 3).

Turkey and the United States, explaining their votes against the resolution, cited their objections to the Convention and to the provision for financing the Preparatory Commission from the United Nations budget. Turkey added that paragraph 3 was a violation of the principle of international law that only the States signatory to a treaty were bound to refrain from action against it. The United States restated its objections to the sea-bed provisions.

Albania, which did not take part in the vote on the resolution, said it could not support the paragraphs welcoming the Convention and calling on States to consider signing and ratifying it. Argentina said it would not participate in the vote on the resolution and would not sign the Convention or the Final Act because of its objections to the provisions in Conference resolution III on disputed territories.

Among those which abstained in the vote on the resolution, Belgium said it could not support paragraphs 2 and 3, since time would be needed for a thorough evaluation of the Convention. Israel said those paragraphs went beyond the requirements of international law providing that treaties had to be ratified before they imposed legal obligations; Israel also objected to the provision for financing the Preparatory Commission from the United Nations budget. Reservations to these provisions were also expressed by the Federal Republic of Germany, Italy, Spain and the United Kingdom. The Federal Republic of Germany said it had not decided whether to sign the Convention and could not agree to any Assembly decision prejudicial to its position. Italy believed that, as it had not concurred in the vote on adoption of the Convention, it would be premature to accept a call to sign and ratify it; moreover, the appeal in paragraph 3, not normally included in Assembly resolutions endorsing conventions, seemed out of place for a convention that had not been adopted by consensus.

Spain voted against paragraph 3, explaining that it transplanted a provision of the law of treaties with the aim of extending it for purposes other than those originally intended. The United Kingdom, announcing that it had decided against early signature of the Convention, said the provisions on sea-bed mining were unacceptable and needed to be improved; it had voted against paragraph 3 because it would set a bad precedent.

Supporting the resolution, France announced that it would sign the Convention but had reservations about the wording of paragraphs 2 and 3 and about secretariat and other arrangements. The Netherlands said it would decide later on ratification of the Convention, when there was more clarity about the régime for exploration and exploitation of sea-bed resources, the financial obligations arising therefrom and the decisions of other countries on whether to become parties. The Syrian Arab Republic stated that the agreement on sea-bed resources recently signed by France, the Federal Republic of Germany, the United Kingdom and the United States was an attempt to create a *fait accompli* contrary to the Convention. The USSR believed that the Convention would make a substantial contribution to the strengthening of peace and co-operation; any unilateral action to circumvent it would be a gross violation of international law and a challenge to the United Nations.

Comments on arrangements for the establishment of the Preparatory Commission and for the functions of the Secretary-General under the Convention were made by Belgium, France, the Federal Republic of Germany, Italy, Spain, the USSR and the United Kingdom.

Letters. Conference President: [1]7 Sep., A/37/441; [2]8 Oct., A/37/441/Add.1.
Publication. [3]*United Nations Convention on the Law of the Sea, with Index and Final Act of the Third United Nations Conference on the Law of the Sea* (A/CONF.62/122 & Corr.3,8), Sales No. E.83.V.5.
Resolution (1982). [4]GA: 37/66, 3 Dec., text following.
Resolution (prior). [5]GA: 3067(XXVIII), 16 Nov. 1973 (YUN 1973, p. 43).
Financial implications. ACABQ report, A/37/7/Add.10; 5th Committee report, A/37/687; S-G statement, A/C.5/37/58/Rev.1.
Meeting records. GA: 5th Committee, A/C.5/37/SR.52, 53 (2 Dec.); plenary, A/37/PV.91 (3 Dec.).
Other publications. Third United Nations Conference on the Law of the Sea. Official Records, vol. XVI: *Summary Records of Meetings, Eleventh Session, New York, 8 March–30 April 1982* (Plenary meetings 156-182; First Committee, meetings 55 and 56; Second Committee, meeting 59) and *Documents,* Sales No. E.84.V.2; vol. XVII: *Resumed Eleventh Session, New York, 22 and 24 September 1982; Final Part of Eleventh Session and Conclusion of Conference, Montego Bay, Jamaica, 6-10 December 1982* (Plenary meetings 183-193) and *Documents,* Sales No. E.84.V.3.

General Assembly resolution 37/66

3 December 1982				Meeting 91				135-2-8 (recorded vote)

49-nation draft (A/37/L.13/Rev.1 and Rev.1Add.1); agenda item 28.

Sponsors: Algeria, Antigua and Barbuda, Australia, Austria, Bahamas, Barbados, Belize, Canada, Colombia, Comoros, Costa Rica, Denmark, Dominica, Egypt, Ethiopia, Finland, Gambia, Ghana, Greece, Grenada, Guyana, Haiti, Iceland, India, Ireland, Jamaica, Kenya, Kuwait, Liberia, Mauritania, Mauritius, Mozambique, New Zealand, Nigeria, Norway, Oman, Saint Lucia, Saint Vincent and the Grenadines, Sierra Leone, Singapore, Sri Lanka, Sudan, Sweden, Togo, Trinidad and Tobago, Uganda, United Republic of Cameroon, United Republic of Tanzania, Zambia.

Third United Nations Conference on the Law of the Sea

The General Assembly,

Recalling its resolutions 3067(XXVIII) of 16 November 1973, 3334(XXIX) of 17 December 1974, 3483(XXX) of 12 December 1975, 31/63 of 10 December 1976, 32/194 of 20 December 1977, 33/17 of 10 November 1978, 34/20 of 9 November 1979, 35/116 of 10 December 1980 and 36/79 of 9 December 1981,

Taking note of the adoption, on 30 April 1982, of the United Nations Convention on the Law of the Sea and the related resolutions by an overwhelming majority of States and of the decision of the Third United Nations Conference on the Law of the Sea, on 24 September 1982, to accept with appreciation the invitation extended by the Government of Jamaica for the purpose of adopting and signing the Final Act and opening the Convention for signature at Montego Bay from 6 to 10 December 1982,

Taking special note of the fact that the Conference decided to establish a Preparatory Commission for the International Sea-Bed Authority and for the International Tribunal for the Law of the Sea and that the Commission shall meet at the seat of the Authority if facilities are available and as often as necessary for the expeditious exercise of its functions,

Taking note of the extensive functions entrusted to the Preparatory Commission, including the administration of the scheme governing preparatory investment in pioneer activities relating to polymetallic nodules,

Recalling that the Convention provides that the seat of the International Sea-Bed Authority shall be in Jamaica,

Taking further note of the timely measures being taken at considerable expense by the Government of Jamaica to construct an adequate administrative building and conference complex for housing the secretariat of the Preparatory Commission and providing meeting facilities for the purpose of enabling the Commission to function from Jamaica,

Recognizing the urgent need for the Preparatory Commission to be assured of adequate resources to enable it to discharge its functions efficiently and expeditiously,

Recalling also that in General Assembly resolution 35/116 the Secretary-General was requested to prepare and submit to the Conference, for such consideration as it deemed appropriate, a study identifying his future functions under the proposed Convention and that such a study was submitted on 18 August 1981,

Noting that, in a letter dated 7 September 1982 to the President of the General Assembly, the President of the Conference drew attention to the responsibilities which the Secretary-General was called upon to carry out under the Convention and the related resolutions and to the need for the Assembly to take the appropriate action to approve the assumption of these responsibilities by the Secretary-General,

Recognizing that, in accordance with the third preambular paragraph of the Convention, the problems of ocean space are closely interrelated and need to be considered as a whole,

Recognizing the need for the Secretary-General to be authorized to assume his functions under the Convention and the related resolutions, including in particular the provision of the secretariat services required by the Preparatory Commission for its effective and expeditious functioning,

1.		*Welcomes* the adoption of the United Nations Convention on the Law of the Sea and the related resolutions;

2.		*Calls upon* all States to consider signing and ratifying the Convention at the earliest possible date to allow the effective entry into force of the new legal régime for the uses of the sea and its resources;

3.		*Appeals* to the Governments of all States to refrain from taking any action directed at undermining the Convention or defeating its object and purpose;

4.		*Accepts with appreciation* the invitation extended by the Government of Jamaica for the purpose of adopting and signing the Final Act and opening the Convention for signature at Montego Bay from 6 to 10 December 1982;

5. *Authorizes* the Secretary-General to enter into the necessary agreement in this regard with the Government of Jamaica;

6. *Reiterates its gratitude* to the Government of Venezuela for the hospitality extended to the Third United Nations Conference on the Law of the Sea at its first substantive session, held at Caracas in 1974;

7. *Approves* the assumption by the Secretary-General of the responsibilities entrusted to him under the Convention and the related resolutions and also approves the stationing of an adequate number of secretariat staff in Jamaica for the purpose of servicing the Preparatory Commission for the International Sea-Bed Authority and for the International Tribunal for the Law of the Sea, as required by its functions and programme of work;

8. *Authorizes* the Secretary-General to convene the Preparatory Commission as provided in Conference resolution I, of 30 April 1982, by which the Commission was established, and to provide the Commission with the services required to enable it to perform its functions efficiently and expeditiously;

9. *Approves* the financing of the expenses of the Preparatory Commission from the regular budget of the United Nations;

10. *Requests* the Secretary-General to report to the General Assembly at its thirty-eighth session on the implementation of the present resolution.

Recorded vote in Assembly as follows:

In favour: Algeria, Angola, Australia, Austria, Bahamas, Bahrain, Bangladesh, Barbados, Belize, Benin, Bhutan, Botswana, Brazil, Bulgaria, Burma, Burundi, Byelorussian SSR, Canada, Cape Verde, Chad, Chile, China, Colombia, Comoros, Congo, Costa Rica, Cuba, Cyprus, Czechoslovakia, Democratic Kampuchea, Democratic Yemen, Denmark, Djibouti, Dominica, Dominican Republic, Egypt, El Salvador, Equatorial Guinea, Ethiopia, Fiji, Finland, France, Gabon, Gambia, German Democratic Republic, Ghana, Greece, Grenada, Guatemala, Guinea, Guinea-Bissau, Guyana, Hungary, Iceland, India, Indonesia, Iran, Iraq, Ireland, Ivory Coast, Jamaica, Japan, Jordan, Kenya, Kuwait, Lao People's Democratic Republic, Lebanon, Lesotho, Liberia, Libyan Arab Jamahiriya, Madagascar, Malawi, Malaysia, Maldives, Mali, Malta, Mauritania, Mauritius, Mexico, Mongolia, Morocco, Mozambique, Nepal, Netherlands, New Zealand, Nicaragua, Niger, Nigeria, Norway, Oman, Pakistan, Panama, Papua New Guinea, Paraguay, Peru, Philippines, Poland, Portugal, Qatar, Romania, Rwanda, Saint Lucia, Saint Vincent and the Grenadines, Samoa, Sao Tome and Principe, Saudi Arabia, Senegal, Sierra Leone, Singapore, Solomon Islands, Somalia, Sri Lanka, Sudan, Suriname, Swaziland, Sweden, Syrian Arab Republic, Thailand, Togo, Trinidad and Tobago, Tunisia, Uganda, Ukrainian SSR, USSR, United Arab Emirates, United Republic of Cameroon, United Republic of Tanzania, Upper Volta, Uruguay, Vanuatu, Viet Nam, Yugoslavia, Zaire, Zambia, Zimbabwe.

Against: Turkey, United States.

Abstaining: Belgium, Ecuador, Germany, Federal Republic of, Israel, Italy, Luxembourg, Spain, United Kingdom.

Convention on the Law of the Sea

The United Nations Convention on the Law of the Sea, approved on 30 April 1982 by the Conference on the Law of the Sea and opened for signature on 10 December, consisted of a preamble and 445 articles, divided into 17 parts (320 articles) and 9 annexes (125 articles).

Convention highlights. The preamble stated that the problems of ocean space were closely interrelated and needed to be considered as a whole. The aim of the Convention was defined as establishing, with due regard for the sovereignty of States, a legal order for the seas which would facilitate international communication and promote the peaceful uses of the seas, the equitable and efficient utilization of their resources, the conservation of their living resources, and the study, protection and preservation of the marine environment. The preamble referred to the need to take into account the interests and needs of mankind as a whole and, in particular, the special interests and needs of developing countries, coastal and land-locked.

Part I of the Convention, containing a single article, defined some terms used in the Convention: "Area" (the sea-bed beyond national jurisdiction), "Authority" (the International Sea-Bed Authority), "activities in the Area" (including resource exploration and exploitation), "pollution of the marine environment" (the introduction of deleterious substances or energy), "dumping" (deliberate disposal of wastes or other matter) and "States parties" (those States and other entities which had consented to be bound by the Convention and for which it was in force).

Part II (32 articles) defined the limits and legal status of a 12–nautical mile territorial sea, internal waters, and a contiguous zone extending a further 12 miles. It also included rules governing innocent passage in the territorial sea by various types of ships.

Part III (12 articles) dealt with straits used for international navigation, including transit passage and innocent passage through such straits.

Part IV (9 articles) related to archipelagic States—those consisting of islands—and the special rules used for delimiting their maritime boundaries and for passage of ships through their waters.

Part V (21 articles) specified the rules governing a 200-mile exclusive economic zone off the shores of coastal States and the delimitation of that zone between States with opposite or adjacent coasts. It defined the rights, jurisdiction and duties of different groups of States (coastal, fishing, land-locked, geographically disadvantaged and other) in the zone, regulated offshore structures and dealt with the conservation and utilization of its living resources.

Part VI (10 articles) defined the continental shelf and its delimitation, the rights of coastal States there, and the rights and freedoms of other States.

Part VII (35 articles) referred to the legal status of the high seas and various aspects of the utilization of that area beyond national jurisdiction, including conservation and management of living resources.

Part VIII (1 article) concerned the rules for the maritime space around islands.

Part IX (2 articles) defined enclosed or semi-enclosed seas and included provisions on co-operation among bordering States.

Part X (9 articles) laid down rules for exercise of the right of access of land-locked States to and from the sea and for freedom of transit across the territory of adjacent coastal States.

Part XI (59 articles) governed exploration for and exploitation of sea-bed resources beyond the area of national jurisdiction, including arrangements for the International Sea-Bed Authority.

Part XII (46 articles) set out rules for the protection and preservation of the marine environment, including provisions for their enforcement.

Part XIII (28 articles) dealt with the conduct and promotion of marine scientific research.

Part XIV (13 articles) related to various aspects of international co-operation for the development and transfer of marine technology.

Part XV (21 articles) contained provisions for settlement of disputes with regard to the interpretation or application of the Convention.

Part XVI (5 articles) included general provisions on the application or interpretation of the Convention as a whole or relating to matters going beyond the scope of other parts.

Part XVII (16 articles) contained the final provisions of the Convention concerning participation by States and other entities through signature and ratification, entry into force, reservations, amendments and other matters.

The nine annexes to the Convention concerned the following subjects: annex I, a list of highly migratory species of marine fish and mammals; annex II (9 articles), Commission on the Limits of the Continental Shelf; annex III (22 articles), basic conditions of sea-bed prospecting, exploration and exploitation; annex IV (13 articles), Statute of the Authority's Enterprise (mining organ); annex V (14 articles), conciliation procedures; annex VI (41 articles), Statute of the International Tribunal for the Law of the Sea; annex VII (13 articles), arbitration; annex VIII (5 articles), special arbitration procedure for certain types of disputes; and annex IX (8 articles), participation in the Convention by international organizations.

Four resolutions were adopted at the same time as the Convention. They related to the establishment of the Preparatory Commission, preparatory investment in pioneer activities relating to polymetallic nodules on the sea-bed, application of the Convention to non-independent territories and authorization for national liberation movements to sign the Final Act of the Conference as observers.

Course of 1982 session. The final text of the Convention was based on negotiating texts progressively refined during previous years by the Conference's collegium—consisting of the President and the Chairmen of the three main committees, working as a team with which the Chairman of the Drafting Committee and the Rapporteur-General of the Conference were associated. Those successive texts reflected the results of negotiations among delegations.

A draft Convention issued in August 1981[10] was the basis for the final round of negotiations in March/April 1982. On 26 March, the President issued a report[6] proposing new or revised texts on participation in the Convention by intergovernmental organizations, territories and national liberation movements—a matter that the Conference had not been able to resolve in 1981.[11] The Chairmen of the Conference's First, Second and Third Committees also presented reports on the conclusion of their work.

On 30 March and 1 April, the Conference heard delegations present their views on the proposals contained in these reports. Then, on 2 April, the collegium issued a memorandum[4] and proposals[1] setting out five substantive changes in the draft Convention and associated documents which they regarded as having received widespread and substantial support and therefore as offering a substantially improved prospect of consensus. The changes were: new draft articles, a draft annex IX, a draft decision and a draft resolution on participation of entities other than States, along the lines of the proposals the President had made on 26 March; a draft resolution on the Preparatory Commission; a draft resolution on pioneer investors; a sentence on the membership of land-based mineral-producing countries in the Economic Planning Commission of the Council of the Sea-Bed Authority; and a revised sentence on the removal of offshore structures in the exclusive economic zone.

On 13 April, while informal negotiations were still in progress, delegations submitted a total of 31 amendments or sets of amendments to various parts of the draft Convention and associated resolutions. These concerned innocent passage through the territorial sea, straits used for international navigation, the exclusive economic zone, the continental shelf, islands, semi-enclosed seas, access of land-locked States to the sea, sea-bed mining, the Sea-Bed Authority, sea-bed disputes, protection of the marine environment, participation in the Convention by entities other than States, reservations and the Preparatory Commission. Eighty-seven delegations made statements on these amendments between 15 and 17 April.

Voting on these amendments was deferred for eight days, as provided in the rules of procedure, while the President and other officers pursued efforts to reach general agreement. On 22 April, the President reported on the results of these efforts,[7] recommending the incorporation of several of them, some in revised form, into the draft Convention and associated resolutions.

With respect to the sea-bed part of the Convention, on which a number of amendments had been submitted, the President said he felt able to recommend only three changes that met the criterion of offering a substantially improved prospect of general agreement. They related to general resource development policy, decision-making at a future review conference and guaranteed membership in the Council of the Authority for the largest consumer of sea-bed minerals. He also recommended two other modifications on sea-bed matters: a revised draft resolution on pioneer investors, and provisions for a compensation fund and a special commission of the Preparatory Commission on the problems of developing country land-based mineral producers.

Two additional changes were proposed on other subjects: a revised draft resolution by Iraq to replace the draft decision proposed by the collegium on 2 April concerning the signature of the Final Act by national liberation movements, and deletion from annex IX, on participation in the Convention by intergovernmental organizations, of a paragraph restricting the mutual granting by members of an intergovernmental organization of special treatment on certain law of the sea matters (amendment by Belgium).

The Conference determined on 23 April that all efforts at reaching general agreement had been exhausted—a determination required by rule 37 of the rules of procedure before amendments could be put to a vote. On 26 April, the day fixed for voting, all but two sets of amendments were withdrawn by their sponsors, and the remaining two failed to receive the majority required for adoption. They were amendments by Spain on transit passage through straits used for international navigation and by Turkey to delete the article prohibiting States from entering reservations to Convention provisions. The Conference adopted by consensus a compromise proposal of the President authorizing the participation of Namibia, represented by the United Nations Council for Namibia, in the Preparatory Commission.

The Conference, on 28 and 29 April, heard the views of 53 delegations on the changes proposed by the President on 22 April. Following this discussion, the President, in a further report dated 29 April,[8] proposed four final changes in the draft Convention. These modifications added a paragraph on unfair economic practices in regard to sea-bed exploration and exploitation, inserted sentences on rules for the exploitation of sea-bed minerals other than those in nodules, changed from two thirds to three fourths the majority required for entry into force of future amendments on sea-bed matters and redrafted a paragraph on

work plans of sea-bed mining applicants. The President proposed one further change in the draft resolution on pioneer investors: to authorize the Enterprise to have production authority for two mine sites rather than one during the period before the Convention entered into force.

On 30 April, the Conference agreed to incorporate in the draft Convention and associated resolutions all four sets of proposals made by the President and the collegium on 26 March and 2, 22 and 29 April, as well as the amendment on participation of Namibia in the Preparatory Commission approved on 26 April. It did so after rejecting a proposal by Israel to act separately on the draft resolution authorizing national liberation movements to sign the Final Act. It then adopted the Convention and four resolutions as a whole by a recorded vote, requested by the United States, of 130 to 4, with 17 abstentions, as follows:

In favour: Afghanistan, Algeria, Angola, Argentina, Australia, Austria, Bahamas, Bahrain, Bangladesh, Barbados, Benin, Bhutan, Bolivia, Botswana, Brazil, Burma, Burundi, Canada, Cape Verde, Central African Republic, Chad, Chile, China, Colombia, Congo, Costa Rica, Cuba, Cyprus, Democratic Kampuchea, Democratic People's Republic of Korea, Democratic Yemen, Denmark, Djibouti, Dominican Republic, Egypt, El Salvador, Ethiopia, Fiji, Finland, France, Gabon, Ghana, Greece, Grenada, Guatemala, Guinea, Guinea-Bissau, Guyana, Haiti, Honduras, Iceland, India, Indonesia, Iran, Iraq, Ireland, Ivory Coast, Jamaica, Japan, Jordan, Kenya, Kuwait, Lao People's Democratic Republic, Lebanon, Lesotho, Libyan Arab Jamahiriya, Liechtenstein, Madagascar, Malawi, Malaysia, Mali, Malta, Mauritania, Mauritius, Mexico, Monaco, Morocco, Mozambique, Namibia, Nepal, New Zealand, Nicaragua, Niger, Nigeria, Norway, Oman, Pakistan, Panama, Papua New Guinea, Paraguay, Peru, Philippines, Portugal, Qatar, Republic of Korea, Romania, Rwanda, Saint Lucia, Saint Vincent and the Grenadines, Samoa, San Marino, Sao Tome and Principe, Saudi Arabia, Senegal, Seychelles, Sierra Leone, Singapore, Somalia, Sri Lanka, Sudan, Suriname, Swaziland, Sweden, Switzerland, Syrian Arab Republic, Togo, Trinidad and Tobago, Tunisia, Uganda, United Arab Emirates, United Republic of Cameroon, United Republic of Tanzania, Upper Volta, Uruguay, Viet Nam, Yemen, Yugoslavia, Zaire, Zambia, Zimbabwe.

Against: Israel, Turkey, United States, Venezuela.

Abstaining: Belgium, Bulgaria, Byelorussian SSR, Czechoslovakia, German Democratic Republic, Germany, Federal Republic of, Hungary, Italy, Luxembourg, Mongolia, Netherlands, Poland, Spain, Thailand, Ukrainian SSR, USSR, United Kingdom.

Final drafting of the Convention was completed at the Conference's resumed session from 22 to 24 September.

Explanations of vote (April). A number of specific points relating to the Convention were raised by delegations on 30 April in explanation of their vote on the Convention package (see following sections of this chapter for details).

Israel cited, in particular, objections to the resolution on observer status for national liberation movements. Turkey objected to the provision disallowing reservations and said it had voted negatively to show its determination to safeguard vital interests. The United States said that, although other provisions were basically acceptable, the Convention did not fully satisfy any of the objectives of the United States with regard to the sea-bed; although modest improvements had been made, there had been an unyielding refusal by some delegations to engage in real negotiations on most of the major concerns reflected in amendments submitted by the United States and others. Venezuela said that, since the Convention did not allow reservations, it could not accept the provisions on delimitation of maritime boundaries, the exclusive economic zone and the continental shelf between States with opposite or adjacent coasts.

(Israel and Venezuela submitted details of their objections to the Conference President in letters of 13 April[2] and 24 April[3], respectively.).

Among those which did not participate in the vote, Albania cited objections to the provisions on the territorial sea, innocent passage and the sea-bed. Ecuador expressed concern about the clauses on the territorial sea and archipelagic States. The Holy See regretted that the Conference had been obliged to take a vote, since consensus was the best way of adopting a decision on administration of the common heritage of mankind; it hoped that, once the text was implemented, the need for a legal instrument to create a world of respect for the rights and obligations of States, of justice for the distressed and of universal enjoyment of resources would become obvious.

Explaining why it had abstained, Belgium, referring to the sea-bed provisions, said due regard had not been paid to the interests of the industrialized States, although they had made major concessions to the developing countries. The Federal Republic of Germany said negotiations should have been pursued in order to achieve a better balanced result, particularly in respect of the sea-bed. Italy voiced a similar reason for its abstention and the United Kingdom said it had been obliged to abstain because its aim of adopting the Convention by consensus had not been achieved. The Netherlands, noting the lack of consensus on the sea-bed provisions, remarked that a convention to which the major countries did not adhere would not provide an adequate solution to the world's problems.

Bulgaria, the German Democratic Republic, Hungary, Mongolia, Poland and the USSR explained that they had abstained because the resolution on pioneer investors contained provisions that discriminated against the socialist countries. Nevertheless, Bulgaria, Hungary and Poland emphasized their support for the other parts of the Convention, while the German Democratic Republic considered that it took account of the rights and interests of all States and peoples. Mongolia spoke of the enormous economic, political and other benefits offered by the Convention. The USSR said that, although the Convention did not take into account the interests of all States, it did not harm any of them and represented a balanced and satisfactory compromise.

Spain said it had abstained because its amendments concerning passage through straits used for international navigation had not been adopted; moreover, it objected to the resolution on the relation of the Convention to disputed territories. Thailand, citing problems with regard to provisions on fishing in the exclusive economic zone, said it had abstained pending a closer scrutiny of the text, but without precluding the possibility that it might later decide to become a party.

Among those which voted in favour, Argentina said the overwhelming vote for the Convention should lead the Governments which had not supported it to think the matter over and encourage them to sign; however, it regretted that an earlier provision on the participation of territories in the Convention had not been retained. Brazil said its affirmative vote, cast in conformity with the position of the Group of 77, was without prejudice to Brazil's decision on signing the Convention. Chile stressed the importance of the Convention's recognition of coastal States' rights within the 200-mile limit and described the Convention as a milestone in international law with regard to dispute settlement. Colombia made a similar point in regard to the 200-mile limit and said adoption of the Convention was a historic act of the highest importance. Honduras welcomed the contribution the Conference had made to the establishment of a just and peaceful order for the seas.

For Peru, the Convention reconciled to the greatest extent possible the basic interests of the international community regarding the utilization of the oceans; however, the provisions on the territorial sea and the exclusive economic zone affected Peru's Constitution and laws, and its support for the Convention was on condition that that conflict could be resolved in accordance with the provisions of its Constitution. Uruguay viewed the recognition of the right of sovereignty of the coastal State over its exclusive economic zone and continental shelf for all economic purposes, and its exclusive jurisdiction over scientific research, preservation of the marine environment and the establishment of offshore structures, as strengthening the validity of those institutions.

Bangladesh said its favourable vote should be read in the light of its special position with regard to the drawing of coastal base lines from which areas of maritime jurisdiction were measured. China said the Convention was only the first step towards a new international legal order for the sea, because there were still imperfections and serious defects on such matters as pioneer sea-bed investors and the passage of warships through the territorial sea. Iran said it had voted for the Convention in a spirit of compromise and co-operation with the international community, but with reservations on the provisions concerning innocent passage of warships through the territorial sea, islands, right of access of land-locked States to the sea and pioneer investors. Japan cited difficulties with some of the changes introduced by the President in the sea-bed provisions but said that if no convention was adopted there would be increasing disorder and anarchy with regard to problems relating to the sea.

Canada, describing the Convention as one of the greatest achievements of the United Nations, expressed hope that those with reservations would understand that it was of decisive importance for their interests and would carefully examine not only the sea-bed provisions but the Convention as a whole. France said it had voted in favour because of such positive elements as the rules to protect pioneer investors and the constructive contribution of the Convention to the North-South dialogue; however, the sea-bed provisions had serious drawbacks which France hoped would be reviewed. Portugal disagreed with the provision on membership of the Council of the Authority and the lack of legal protection for sea-bed workers. In spite of its reservations on Council membership and the sea-bed technology transfer provisions, Switzerland supported the Convention as a reflection of the fact that the majority wanted order, not anarchy, on the oceans.

Romania said the Convention's provisions on boundary delimitation constituted a general framework that would have to be applied on the basis of international law, legal precedents and State practice, giving consideration to such factors as the need to ensure that small and unpopulated islands with no economic life of their own should not affect the maritime space of coastal States; it also made reservations or observations on provisions relating to passage of warships through the territorial sea, boundary delimitation, access to fisheries, exploitation of sea-bed resources and reservations to the Convention.

Egypt said it had wanted the question of reservations to be governed by the Vienna Convention on the Law of Treaties (which permitted certain kinds of reservations to multilateral treaties).[9] The Libyan Arab Jamahiriya said the Convention contained many positive elements which offset the difficulties caused by some other provisions; however, it felt that the exploitation of sea-bed resources should benefit all States, irrespective of their geographical position, and it rejected the idea that a small group of States should enjoy special benefits in regard to the sea-bed. Mali said the Convention had defined the political and legal elements of a promising future, which might well point the way to a fundamental change in the thinking that had brought about an unjust and deeply unbalanced world.

Sierra Leone appealed to all States to join in the new international legal order represented by the Convention, but voiced reservations on the breadth of the territorial sea, the pioneer investor arrangements and the veto principle in the decision-making process of the Sea-Bed Authority. Zaire regretted that power relationships characterized by the defence of narrow interests by certain States had made consensus impossible. Zambia voiced concern that the Convention would leave the vast bulk of ocean resources to coastal States rather than to the common heritage, and expressed dissatisfaction about some provisions on protection of land-based producers from the adverse effects of sea-bed mining and on access of land-locked States to the sea; however, it had voted for the Convention as an alternative to lawlessness on the seas.

Malaysia said it had voted in favour even though the Convention did not fully meet the requirements of all parties owing to the need for concessions; it read out a statement of understanding on the application of the Convention to the Straits of Malacca and Singapore. Pakistan reiterated its interpretation of the provision on passage of warships through the territorial sea and its objection to giving land-locked States a right of access to the sea through coastal States. The Republic of Korea said that, even though some articles did not fully correspond to its interests, it had voted for the Convention, taking into account the aspirations of most delegations including those of the Group of 77. Yemen recalled the reaffirmation of the rights of coastal States made by the sponsors of one of the amendments concerning the passage of warships through the territorial sea.

Final statements (December). At its concluding meetings at Montego Bay in December, the Conference heard general statements by delegations on various issues covered by the Convention and the related resolutions. Highlights of the general comments on the Convention follow (for comments on specific topics, see later sections of this chapter).

The Prime Minister of Jamaica, Edward Seaga, contrasted the achievements of the Conference with the gaps and failures of previous efforts on this subject, beginning in 1958: the Convention was an attempt to arrive at a compromise protecting the legitimate concerns of all interest groups, including the developing countries; it was a single text covering all ocean uses, in place of the previous four separate conventions; it was the first to succeed in establishing an outer limit for the territorial sea; and it dealt with some vital issues ignored by earlier conferences, such as the rights and interests of archipelagic, land-locked and geographically disadvantaged States.

Many speakers stressed the Convention's significance in the codification and development of international law. Australia described it as a renegotiation of the rules giving title to all the resources of the sea and sea-bed and the rules governing most of the important uses of the sea, such as navigation, research and pollution control. Without a convention, said Barbados, a small country like itself could not hope to promote and protect its interests or to share in the benefits from sea-bed exploitation. China viewed the Convention as bringing about a change in a situation in which the law of the sea had served only the interests of a few big Powers. Old concepts which served the interests of the few had been revised or replaced, said Fiji, and new concepts had been introduced so that international law could respond more adequately to the aspirations of all nations.

The Ivory Coast saw significance in the fact that the Convention incorporated all aspects and dimensions of 71 per cent of the globe's surface, that it challenged four centuries of unfair maritime legal practices and opposed the hegemony of the strongest, that it involved the entire international community and that it established a new morality. It would be a serious mistake, said Malta, to think that the Convention would have less of an influence on the behaviour of States simply because some of them, however important, found objection to one part of it. Norway regarded it as the greatest legislative effort by the United Nations and probably the greatest ever undertaken in the annals of international law.

Senegal saw the Convention as an invaluable supplement to the Charter of the United Nations. Its comprehensive range of provisions on every aspect of the peaceful uses of the seas, together with more highly developed provisions on dispute settlement than had been thought possible, said Sri Lanka, gave the Convention the highest potential of any instrument in history to serve as the foundation for peace, justice and order in the oceans. The United Republic of Cameroon stressed that the Convention did not codify existing law, which the African States could not have accepted; for the first time it represented a universal law of the seas, and any State which did not accept it would divorce its case from any legal foundation. The United Republic of Tanzania thought historians would rank the signing of the Convention with the signing of the United Nations Charter in terms of political and historical magnitude.

Other benefits to be derived from the Convention were also mentioned. Costa Rica saw the opportunity to put technology currently available to a few into the hands of all, so that as many as possible could be in a position to take advantage of the sea's wealth; it also praised the Convention for stressing the importance of conservation and sound management of ocean resources. Grenada thought one of the greatest benefits of the Convention lay in its clarification of conflicting claims among neighbouring States, thereby helping to enhance the cause of peace. Guyana believed it would serve to inhibit States from going outside international law and placing their perceived national interests above those of the international community.

Austria, Chad, China, Cuba, the Democratic People's Republic of Korea, France, the Gambia, Grenada, the Libyan Arab Jamahiriya, Mauritius, Mongolia, the Niger, Norway, Sri Lanka, the Upper Volta, Viet Nam and Zaire viewed the Convention as a step towards a new international economic order. Denmark saw it as a major progressive step in the development of North-South relations. Sierra Leone, while acknowledging that the Convention incorporated elements of the new international economic order, did not see it as representing the establishment of such an order through the back door, as it contained many features that did not benefit African States.

The United Arab Emirates stressed the need to have educational and information institutions point out the significance of the Convention.

Many speakers made the point that, as a product of compromise, the Convention did not completely satisfy any State or group. Several added that it was nevertheless the best instrument that could have been achieved under the circumstances. Bahrain expressed this view, though adding that it was not convinced about the way in which the Convention dealt with the interests of developing States in general and of geographically disadvantaged States in particular. In the words of Cyprus, although there were ambiguities in place of clarity, complexities instead of streamlining and exceptions where there should have been a general rule, that was the price that had to be paid to reach an overall agreement by consensus.

Many developing States believed that the Convention would have a generally favourable impact on the third world. Bangladesh thought the Convention offered developing States the opportunity to participate in various organs and provided for the distribution of the oceans' wealth between developed and developing nations. Benin saw a more equitable distribution among all countries—

coastal, geographically disadvantaged or land-locked—and among all peoples, oppressed or sovereign. Haiti saw a chance for the rich to become richer and the poor less poor. Viet Nam thought the Convention met the interests of all countries, especially the developing ones.

France believed the Convention had achieved a compromise between the rights of coastal States and the interests of maritime countries, and between the use of the seas for resource exploitation and for communication. New Zealand also welcomed the balance achieved by the Convention when compared to existing law, which it saw as unduly weighted in favour of a small number of major maritime Powers. Switzerland said it favoured the Convention despite its shortcomings, because its many reciprocal compromises reflected the desire to see order and not anarchy reign over the seas; Switzerland would sign when the support of other States reflected a generally shared will to make the Convention the basis for the new law of the sea.

Several speakers welcomed the fact that developing States had had the opportunity of participating in the establishment of major rules of international law. Algeria said the Conference had implemented the principle of the democratization of international relations, which it would like to see implemented in other bodies, especially those used for the North-South dialogue. Unlike the past, when rules of international law were dictated by the great Powers, the Philippines and Uganda said, the Convention was a product of the combined will of the great majority of States. For the first time, said Togo, a large number of developing States, particularly African countries, had decided on rules that would govern their relations with other States in the realm of maritime communications and the exploitation of undersea and fishery resources.

Members of the group of socialist (Eastern European and other) States viewed the Convention as a balanced document that met the needs and legitimate interests of all groups of States. These States also regarded it as a welcome replacement of existing law which, as Czechoslovakia put it, would have allowed the riches of the seas to be monopolized by a few. Mongolia felt the Convention could erect a safe barrier against the unilateral claims of the imperialist Powers and their monopolies to the expanses and resources of the oceans. The Ukrainian SSR regarded it as an extremely important political document aimed at strengthening peace, security and co-operation among States with different social and economic systems. The USSR thought it could present a serious obstacle for those who would try to carry out a policy of arbitrary control and diktat on the oceans and would have great significance in the struggle to es-

tablish international relations based on equality and mutual respect.

Egypt said the Convention would help prevent unfair competition between States in exploiting marine resources and in navigation, thus making it a means of supporting international peace; but it must not become a breeding-ground for wide-ranging interpretations that would transform its provisions into problems. Indonesia, viewing with concern the increasing exploitation of marine resources along its coast by distant countries having advanced technology, thought it appropriate that the Convention would make the use of those resources more equitable. Mexico affirmed that the legitimate rights of coastal States, especially the developing countries and those wishing to administer and conserve their maritime resources for the benefit of their nationals, formed part of the permanent effort to secure full sovereignty over their natural resources. Saint Lucia was pleased that the Convention placed specific responsibility on all States for the preservation of marine resources, thus helping to ensure that adequate living resources would be available for the continued survival of mankind.

Bulgaria remarked that the Convention strengthened freedom of navigation, notwithstanding the establishment of the exclusive economic zone and a certain expansion of coastal State jurisdiction. Czechoslovakia, Finland, Hungary and India also stressed that the Convention ensured freedom of navigation.

Japan thought the Convention would serve the long-term interests of the world community and those of Japan; though it had not had time to complete a review of the text in time for signature in 1982, Japan's basic position was that the Convention merited its support and signature. Sweden expressed the view that the Convention did not affect the rights and duties of a neutral State in case of war; it believed also that the rules of armed conflict at sea were in need of revision.

Some States, though supporting the Convention as a whole, were critical of what they regarded as an excessive allocation of jurisdiction to coastal States, to the detriment of mankind as a whole. Thus, Austria said that in some ways the Convention, especially those parts concerned with areas of national jurisdiction, increased inequality among States and tended to serve the interests of the richer nations, though other parts were clearly designed with the needs of the poorer nations in mind. Hungary saw the land-locked countries as among the chief losers, due to maritime boundary provisions which reduced the area for the common heritage of mankind and heavily favoured States with broad continental shelves. Iraq said the Convention did not meet all of its needs as a geographically disadvantaged State.

Mauritius believed that the benefits to developed countries from exploiting the exclusive economic zone and the continental shelf were likely to exceed by far those gained by developing countries. Sierra Leone argued that the African States would obtain little from the Convention in return for the rights they had granted the maritime countries; in partitioning the oceans among countries with the longest coastlines, it did not provide for an equitable distribution of resources. Singapore said the provisions on the exclusive economic zone and the continental shelf gave too much to some and little or nothing to others. Uganda thought the developing countries, especially those which were land-locked and geographically disadvantaged, had received the short end of the stick in the negotiations.

The Niger, on the other hand, said the Convention opened up possibilities that could place a country such as itself in a better position to deal with the constraints of its geographically disadvantaged location.

Peru announced that it would not sign the Convention in 1982, since the constitutional and other issues it raised were still under study. Turkey, also stating that it would not sign, said the Convention failed to achieve a balance between different groups of interests stemming from different geographical situations; it added that the Convention's provisions on maritime boundaries could in no way be applied against Turkey. The United States, while regarding the Convention's sea-bed provisions as unacceptable, believed that most other provisions served the interests of the international community and reflected prevailing international practice.

Many States which announced their intention of signing the Convention urged others which had voiced objections, particularly the United States, to reassess their position and join with the majority in the interests of universality. United States participation in the Convention, said Malaysia, would enhance its national interests, while its non-participation and thus its isolation might turn out to be costly. No State could do without the Convention, said the Sudan, if it respected international legitimacy and international law.

A number of speakers, including Burundi, the Byelorussian SSR, Canada, Cape Verde, Colombia, Cuba, Czechoslovakia, Fiji, Pakistan, Romania, Saint Vincent and the Grenadines, the USSR, the United Republic of Cameroon and Zambia, said States must not arbitrarily select some of the rights and responsibilities laid down in the Convention to the exclusion of others.

Partial application was precluded, said Colombia, because that would destroy the Convention's balance between the interests of the community and those of States; moreover, once the Conven-

tion was in force it would not be possible to invoke custom against it. Any attempt by a State or small group of States to circumvent the Convention, stated the Libyan Arab Jamahiriya, would run counter to the will of the overwhelming majority of the international community and have no legal validity capable of commanding international recognition. The Convention, Zaire said, could not be viewed as merely a general guideline for helping countries to harmonize their national policies and legislation; the intention of the international community was to make it an indivisible whole, the acceptability or unacceptability of which could not be subject to any partial agreement.

Finland stated that the Convention constituted in many fields a progressive development of international law, the benefits of which could be enjoyed only by those States that adhered to it. Similarly, the German Democratic Republic and the Ukrainian SSR expressed the view that no State refusing to become a party could claim rights or privileges which the Convention granted to those that were also prepared to assume the obligations it imposed.

Speaking of the relationship between the Convention and existing international law, the Federal Republic of Germany said States were not subject to obligations under the Convention until it had been ratified and had entered into force for them; pending that time, States could rely on and were bound by all rules developed by the generally recognized practice of States or contained in conventions already in force. Addressing the legal situation which would arise if the Convention entered into force without enjoying general acceptance, the United Kingdom said the situation would be the same for both parties and non-parties with regard to provisions in which the Convention codified or clarified existing law; with regard to provisions that sought to make new law, the parties would assume among themselves a new contractual relationship without depriving others of existing rights such as those deriving from the freedom of the high seas.

On the other hand, the Dominican Republic, while acknowledging that the Convention could have legal force only among its parties, said that, given the nature of the negotiations that had led to it and the scope of its objectives, the presumption was that its norms and principles would also serve as guidelines for non-parties. In the view of Greece, all provisions of the Convention other than those pertaining to the international sea-bed area could be considered as already part of customary international law, since almost all States which had abstained on the Convention, and even those which had voted against, had indicated their acceptance of those parts.

The Conference President, in his closing statement on 10 December, described the Convention as a monumental achievement of the international community, second only to the adoption in 1945 of the Charter of the United Nations. The provisions of the Convention were closely interrelated and formed an integral package, he added. Therefore, it was not permissible to claim rights under the Convention without being willing to shoulder the corresponding obligations. Any attempt to mine deep sea-bed resources outside the Convention would earn universal condemnation and incur grave political and legal consequences.

In addition to statements made at the plenary meetings in December, 19 States submitted written statements during the year detailing their position on the Convention or specific provisions, 5 States and a number of organizations submitted supplementary written statements in connection with the December meetings, and 10 States submitted statements in exercise of the right of reply to comments made at those meetings. All these statements were included in the official records of the Conference.[5]

Draft resolutions and decision. [1]Conference collegium, A/CONF.62/L.94.
Letters. [2]Israel, 13 Apr., A/CONF.62/L.129; [3]Venezuela, 24 Apr., A/CONF.62/L.134.
Memorandum. [4]Conference collegium, A/CONF.62/L.93 & Corr.1.
Publications. [5]Third United Nations Conference on the Law of the Sea. Official Records, vol. XVI: Summary Records of Meetings, Eleventh Session, New York, 8 March–30 April 1982 (Plenary meetings 156-182; First Committee, meetings 55 and 56; Second Committee, meeting 59) and Documents, Sales No. F.84.V.2; vol. XVII: Resumed Eleventh Session, New York, 22 and 24 September 1982; Final Part of Eleventh Session and Conclusion of Conference, Montego Bay, Jamaica, 6-10 December 1982 (Plenary meetings 183-193) and Documents, Sales No. E.84.V.3.
Reports. Conference President, [6]A/CONF.62/L.86, [7]A/CONF.62/L.132 & Corr.1 & Add.1 & Add.1/Corr.1, [8]A/CONF.62/L.141 & Add.1 & Add.1/Corr.1.
Yearbook references. [9]1969, p. 734; 1981, [10]p. 131, [11]p. 134.

Territorial sea

According to part II of the Convention on the Law of the Sea, the sovereignty of a coastal State extended, beyond its land territory and internal waters or archipelagic waters, to an adjacent belt of territorial sea, to the airspace over it, and to its bed and subsoil (article 2). The Convention set out rules for determining the limits of this belt (see below) and for innocent passage by foreign ships through it.

Limits

Convention provisions. Under the Convention on the Law of the Sea, every State had the right to establish the breadth of its territorial sea up to a limit of 12 nautical miles from coastal baselines (article 3). The outer limit of this zone was defined as the line every point of which was at a distance

from the nearest point of the baseline equal to the breadth of the territorial sea (article 4). The normal baseline was the low-water line along the coast as marked on official charts (article 5). In the case of island atolls or islands with fringing reefs, the baseline was the seaward low-water line of the reef (article 6). The Convention set conditions for drawing straight baselines in localities where the coastline was deeply indented, had a fringe of coastal islands, or was unstable due to the presence of a delta or other natural conditions (article 7).

Waters on the landward side of the territorial sea baseline, except for archipelagic States, were defined as the State's internal waters (article 8).

Dealing with the effect of some particular geographical features on the placement of baselines, the Convention provided that, in the case of rivers flowing directly into the sea, the baseline was a straight line across the river mouth between points on the low-water line of its banks (article 9). Rules were provided for drawing baselines across the mouths of bays whose coasts belonged to a single State (article 10). For ports, the outermost permanent harbour works forming an integral part of the harbour system, excluding offshore installations and artificial islands, would be regarded as part of the coast (article 11). Roadsteads normally used for the loading, unloading and anchoring of ships, and which would otherwise be situated wholly or partly outside the territorial sea, were included in that sea (article 12). Low-tide elevations—above water at low tide but submerged at high tide—could be used as the baseline only if they were no farther from shore than the breadth of the territorial sea; otherwise, they had no territorial sea of their own (article 13).

The coastal State could determine baselines by any of the foregoing methods to suit different conditions (article 14). Where the coasts of two States were opposite or adjacent to each other, neither could extend its territorial sea beyond the median line between them, unless they agreed otherwise or where it was necessary by reason of historic title or other special circumstances to delimit the area differently (article 15). Coastal States would be required to publicize, and deposit with the Secretary-General, charts or lists of geographical coordinates specifying the baselines and limits of the territorial sea (article 16).

Conference consideration. Among the States which did not participate in the vote on the Convention and which explained their positions at the meeting on 30 April 1982 at which the Conference adopted it, Albania said it had established a 15-mile territorial sea and reaffirmed that every State could determine the breadth of its territorial sea in accordance with its defence requirements, taking account of the region's geographical, biological and oceanographic conditions and without prejudice to the interests of international navigation and neighbouring States. Ecuador said that, throughout the negotiations, it had defended its rights in its 200-mile territorial sea.

Bangladesh said its vote for the Convention should be understood in the light of the special position of Bangladesh with regard to the drawing of baselines from which areas of maritime jurisdiction were measured. Sierra Leone reiterated its advocacy of a 200-mile territorial sea.

During the final week of the Conference in December, Canada described the agreement on a 12-mile territorial sea—incorporated into the laws of more than 80 coastal States—as an outstanding accomplishment, since such agreement had eluded the international community for decades and even centuries. Cyprus noted with satisfaction that delimitation of the territorial sea between States with opposite or adjacent coasts was based as in the past on equidistance. Greece thought the 12-mile limit could be regarded as part of customary international law, since it was already being applied by a majority of United Nations Members. Agreement on the breadth of the territorial sea, said the United Republic of Tanzania, would reduce conflicts of jurisdiction and competence; however, the limits agreed upon would cause serious adjustment problems for many States.

The Philippines said it had problems with the 12-mile limit because under historic and legal title it claimed a territorial sea of unique configuration, ranging in breadth from less than 3 to more than 200 miles; however, the economic rights to be gained from the even larger exclusive economic zone almost compensated for the territorial sea problem. Somalia stated that it had had a 200-mile territorial sea since adopting a decree to that effect in 1972 but, to the greatest extent possible, it would harmonize that law with its obligations under the Convention. Turkey reiterated its objection to the extension of the territorial sea to 12 miles, stating that in the narrow seas around its coasts such a rule would create inequitable results and constitute an abuse of rights; further, in delimiting the territorial sea between States with opposite or adjacent coasts, the median line could be applied only if it produced an equitable delimitation.

Communication. In a letter of 30 November to the Secretary-General,[1] Viet Nam transmitted a government statement of 12 November defining its territorial sea and declaring that all differences with countries relating to sea areas and the continental shelf would be settled through negotiations on the basis of mutual respect for each other's independence and sovereignty.

Letter. [1]Viet Nam, 30 Nov., A/37/697.

Innocent passage

Convention provisions. The Convention on the Law of the Sea affirmed the right of innocent passage through the territorial sea for ships of all States (article 17). It defined "passage" as navigation through the territorial sea whether or not the purpose was to enter internal waters or call at a roadstead or port outside those waters; in either case, passage must be continuous and expeditious, and ships could stop and anchor only for purposes of ordinary navigation or for reasons of *force majeure* or to help others in distress (article 18). Passage was innocent so long as it did not prejudice the peace, good order or security of the coastal State; that excluded such activities as threat or use of force against the coastal State, weapons practice, information gathering or propaganda acts prejudicial to the coastal State's defence or security, the launching or taking on board of aircraft or military devices, the loading or unloading of items or persons contrary to the coastal State's customs and other laws and regulations, wilful and serious pollution, fishing, research and surveying, interference with a coastal State's communications systems or other facilities, and any other activity not directly bearing on passage (article 19).

In the territorial sea, submarines were required to navigate on the surface and to show their flag (article 20).

The Convention listed subjects on which the coastal State could adopt laws and regulations relating to innocent passage and with which foreign ships in its territorial sea must comply, including safety of navigation and the regulation of maritime traffic, protection of navigational aids and facilities and other facilities or installations, protection of cables and pipelines, conservation of the living resources of the sea, prevention of infringement of the coastal State's fisheries laws and regulations, preservation of that State's environment and prevention and control of pollution thereof, marine scientific research and hydrographic surveys, and prevention of infringement of the coastal State's customs, fiscal, immigration or sanitary laws and regulations; but such laws and regulations could not apply to the design, construction, manning or equipment of foreign ships, except to give effect to generally accepted rules or standards (article 21).

The coastal State, having regard to safety of navigation, could require foreign ships to use designated sea lanes and traffic separation schemes (article 22). Foreign nuclear-powered ships and ships carrying nuclear or other inherently dangerous or noxious substances must carry documents and observe special precautionary measures established by international agreements (article 23).

The coastal State must not hamper innocent passage except in accordance with the Convention;

in particular, it must not impose requirements having the practical effect of denying or impairing the right of innocent passage, or discriminate against the ships of any State or against ships carrying cargoes to, from or on behalf of any State (article 24). However, the coastal State could act to prevent passage that was not innocent, could prevent any breach of the conditions to which admission to internal waters or to a port was subject and, after due notice, could temporarily suspend innocent passage in specified areas when that was essential to protect its security, including weapons exercises (article 25). No charge could be levied on foreign ships for their passage, but non-discriminatory charges could be levied for specific services to the ship (article 26).

The Convention provided different sets of rules applicable to ships operated for commercial and non-commercial purposes while passing through the territorial sea. With regard to merchant ships and government ships operated for commercial purposes, it limited the circumstances under which the coastal State's criminal jurisdiction could be exercised on board a foreign ship and required prior notification to a diplomatic or consular officer of the ship's flag State (article 27). It also limited civil jurisdiction, providing that a foreign ship could not be stopped or diverted to enable a coastal State to exercise such jurisdiction in regard to a person on board, and that the coastal State could not levy execution against or arrest a ship for purposes of civil proceedings except in respect of the ship's own obligations or liabilities in connection with its passage through that State's waters (article 28).

With regard to warships and other government ships operated for non-commercial purposes, the Convention defined "warship" as a ship belonging to a State's armed forces, bearing distinguishing marks, commanded by a government-commissioned officer and manned by a crew under regular armed forces discipline (article 29). The coastal State could require any warship to leave its territorial sea immediately in the case of non-compliance with its laws and regulations (article 30). The Convention established international responsibility of the flag State for damage caused by such a ship resulting from non-compliance with coastal State laws and regulations on passage or with rules of international law (article 31). However, except as specified in the Convention, nothing in the Convention would affect the immunities of such ships (article 32).

Conference consideration. Three amendments on innocent passage were presented to the Conference on the Law of the Sea in April 1982, but none was pressed to a vote. Two of them concerned the laws and regulations of coastal States relating to innocent passage (article 21). The first of these,

by Gabon, would have empowered a coastal State to adopt laws and regulations relating to the innocent passage of warships, including the right to require prior authorization and notification for passage through the territorial sea.[2] The other amendment on this topic, by 28 States, would have authorized a coastal State to adopt laws and regulations in respect of security.[1]

An amendment by Greece on the meaning of innocent passage (article 19) would have defined such passage as prejudicial to the peace, good order or security of the coastal State if the ship was engaged in any of the activities listed in the original text or in any "similar" (rather than any "other") activity.[3]

With respect to the two amendments on laws and regulations of the coastal State for innocent passage, the President reported on 22 April[4] that the Chairman of the Second Committee had convened a representative group of delegations but had been unable to find a generally acceptable solution. At a plenary meeting on 26 April, the President read out a statement to the effect that the sponsors of the 28-nation amendment had agreed not to press for a vote, without prejudice to the rights of coastal States to adopt measures to safeguard their security interests in accordance with the Convention.

During the Conference's discussion of amendments, support for the position that the national security interests of coastal States obliged them to enact legislation requiring warships passing through their territorial sea to notify them in advance of such passage and/or to receive prior authorization for passage was voiced by Albania, Algeria, Angola, Argentina, Bahrain, Barbados, Brazil, Cape Verde, China, the Congo, the Democratic People's Republic of Korea, Djibouti, Ecuador, Egypt, Gabon, Guyana, India, Iran, the Libyan Arab Jamahiriya, Malta, Morocco, Nigeria, Oman, Pakistan, Papua New Guinea, the Philippines, Qatar, the Republic of Korea, Romania, Sao Tome and Principe, Sierra Leone, Somalia, the Sudan, Suriname, Trinidad and Tobago, the United Arab Emirates, the United Republic of Cameroon, Uruguay and Zaire.

A contrary view, that the provision should be left unchanged since it already protected the security interests of coastal States and that prior authorization or notification would impose intolerable limits on freedom of navigation, was supported by Australia, the Bahamas, Bulgaria, Canada, France, the Federal Republic of Germany, Iraq, New Zealand, Spain, Sweden, the Ukrainian SSR, the USSR and the United Kingdom. Many other States, without specifically mentioning the issue of innocent passage, stated that the provisions in this part of the Convention represented a delicate balance and should not be altered.

Albania, explaining on 30 April its non-participation in the vote on the Convention, said foreign warships had no right to pass through the territorial sea without the coastal State's prior consent; thus, in its view, the Convention violated the sovereign rights of coastal States.

China and Pakistan, which voted for the Convention, expressed the view that its provisions on innocent passage did not prejudice the right of the coastal State to require prior authorization or notification for the passage of foreign warships through the territorial sea in accordance with its laws and regulations. Romania said the agreement reached with the sponsors of the 28-nation amendment should be understood as not prejudicing the right of coastal States to adopt measures to safeguard their security. Iran also voiced reservations about this provision.

During the closing week of the Conference in December, Cape Verde, the Democratic People's Republic of Korea, Iran, Malta, Romania, Somalia and the Sudan reiterated their view that the Convention recognized the right of coastal States to enact legislation to safeguard their security interests in regard to innocent passage through the territorial sea. Saint Lucia found the provision on innocent passage vague and said it could be interpreted to mean that passage through the territorial sea by foreign warships was deemed not innocent unless proven to be so. Finland stated that the Convention's enumeration of instances in which the coastal State could make laws and regulations relating to innocent passage was extremely important for a coastal State like Finland. Sweden said the régime for passage of warships and other non-commercial government-owned ships through the Swedish territorial sea was consistent with the Convention and could be maintained.

Barbados expressed concern that the Conference had not adopted a provision requiring foreign warships to seek permission from the coastal State to pass through its territorial waters, especially as Barbados legislation contained such a provision. Papua New Guinea reiterated its misgivings over the free movement of warships through the territorial sea under the guise of freedom of navigation. The United Republic of Tanzania did not regard these provisions as satisfactory in that they did not adequately protect coastal State interests. Taking a similar stand, Yemen said the passage of foreign warships and nuclear-powered vessels through the territorial waters of small developing States could hardly be described as innocent, and it would be difficult to argue that such passage did not infringe those States' sovereignty. Vanuatu regretted that the right of innocent passage probably made it impossible to attain the ideal of securing a nuclear-free Pacific zone by excluding from territorial waters vessels carrying nuclear weapons and materials.

The United Kingdom remarked that the provision stating that innocent passage was not subject to prior notification or authorization by the coastal State was a restatement or codification of existing international law.

Amendments not pressed. (1)Algeria, Bahrain, Benin, Cape Verde, China, Congo, Democratic People's Republic of Korea, Democratic Yemen, Djibouti, Egypt, Guinea-Bissau, Iran, Libyan Arab Jamahiriya, Malta, Morocco, Oman, Pakistan, Papua New Guinea, Philippines, Romania, Sao Tome and Principe, Sierra Leone, Somalia, Sudan, Suriname, Syrian Arab Republic, Uruguay, Yemen, A/CONF.62/L.117 & Corr.1; (2)Gabon, A/CONF.62/L.97; (3)Greece, A/CONF.62/L.123.

Report. (4)Conference President, A/CONF.62/L.132.

Contiguous zone

The Convention on the Law of the Sea provided that, in a contiguous zone extending not more than 24 nautical miles from the coastal baselines, a coastal State could exercise the control necessary to prevent and punish infringement of its customs, fiscal, immigration or sanitary laws and regulations committed within its territory or territorial sea (article 33).

In general statements made during the closing week of the Conference on the Law of the Sea in December 1982, Morocco remarked that the contiguous zone had been retained because it still had a function in view of the different kinds of jurisdictions exercised in the territorial sea and the exclusive economic zone. Turkey, however, considered the contiguous zone to have become obsolete in view of the establishment of the exclusive economic zone; it added that delimitation of the contiguous zone between opposite or adjacent States should be governed by the delimitation principles applied to the exclusive economic zone and the continental shelf.

Straits used for international navigation

Convention provisions. Legal rules governing straits used for international navigation, including the passage of foreign ships through such straits, made up part III of the Convention on the Law of the Sea.

These provisions began with a statement that the régime of passage through straits did not in other respects affect the legal status of the waters in those straits or the exercise by the States bordering them of their sovereignty or jurisdiction over such waters and their airspace, bed and subsoil (article 34). Nor did the provisions on straits affect internal waters within a strait, the legal status of the waters beyond the territorial sea of a bordering State or the legal régime in straits where passage was governed by long-standing international conventions (article 35). Further, this part of the Convention did not apply to straits through which ships could pass on a convenient route without leaving an exclusive economic zone or the high seas (article 36).

The Convention went on to define the right of transit passage through straits used for international navigation between different parts of an exclusive economic zone or the high seas (article 37). It provided that all ships and aircraft were to enjoy the right of transit passage, which it defined as the exercise of freedom of navigation and overflight solely for the purpose of continuous and expeditious transit from one part of the seas to another, without precluding passage for the purpose of entering, leaving or returning from a State bordering the strait (article 38).

Ships and aircraft in transit passage must proceed without delay through or over the strait, refraining from any threat or use of force against the bordering State and any activities other than those incident to their normal modes of continuous and expeditious transit, save in cases of *force majeure* or distress; ships must comply with generally accepted international regulations, procedures and practices for safety at sea and for the prevention and control of pollution from ships, and aircraft must observe the Rules of the Air set by the International Civil Aviation Organization (ICAO) and monitor the assigned air traffic control radio frequency (article 39). Ships could not carry out any research or survey activities without the bordering State's prior authorization (article 40).

States bordering straits could designate sea lanes and prescribe traffic separation schemes for navigation where necessary to promote safe passage, but such arrangements must conform to generally accepted international regulations and be approved by the competent international organization (article 41). Bordering States could also adopt non-discriminatory laws and regulations governing the safety of navigation and regulation of maritime traffic, prevention and control of pollution by giving effect to international regulations regarding the discharge of noxious substances, prevention of fishing, and the loading or unloading of any item or person in contravention of the customs, fiscal, immigration or sanitary laws of the bordering State (article 42). User and bordering States should cooperate in the establishment and maintenance of navigational and safety aids or other navigational improvements, and for the prevention, reduction and control of pollution from ships (article 43). Bordering States must not hamper transit passage and must publicize any known danger to navigation or overflight (article 44).

The régime of innocent passage, as defined elsewhere in the Convention, was to apply in straits excluded from application of the rules for transit passage, including those used for passage between a part of the high seas or an exclusive economic zone and the territorial sea of a foreign State; and innocent passage through such straits could not be suspended (article 45).

A provision on straits (article 233) in the part of the Convention concerned with protection of the marine environment allowed bordering States to take appropriate enforcement measures against a foreign commercial vessel whose violation of national laws on safety of navigation or pollution control caused or threatened major damage to the marine environment of the straits.

Conference consideration. Two of the three amendments voted on by the Conference on the Law of the Sea in April 1982 were proposals by Spain on issues relating to transit passage through straits used for international navigation.[2] Neither was approved.

One of these amendments, to the article on duties of ships and aircraft during transit passage (article 39), would have deleted the word "normally" from the provision that State aircraft in transit passage would normally comply with the ICAO Rules of the Air. This was rejected by a recorded vote of 21 to 55, with 60 abstentions.

Under the second amendment, affecting laws and regulations of States bordering straits relating to transit passage (article 42), bordering States would have been entitled to give effect to "generally accepted" (rather than "applicable") international regulations on the discharge of oil, oily wastes and other noxious substances in straits. This amendment failed to receive a simple majority (79) of the 157 delegations participating in the session—the vote having been 60 to 29, with 51 abstentions.

Spain did not press for a vote on another part of its amendment affecting the same provision, which would have broadened the reference to "wastes" by deleting "oily".

Three amendments by Greece on the transit passage of aircraft over straits were not pressed to a vote.[1] One, on the duties of ships and aircraft during such passage (article 39), would have added a clause specifying that the width of a strait, particularly for the purpose of passage by aircraft, should be at least equal to the width of an international airway. The second, affecting the provisions on sea lanes and traffic separation schemes (article 41), would have added a paragraph requiring bordering States to designate predetermined air routes and prescribe air traffic procedures for the purpose of promoting the safe and efficient passage of aircraft over straits. The third amendment, concerning the laws and regulations of bordering States relating to transit passage (article 42), would have authorized States to enact laws and regulations on air traffic safety and the rules, regulations and procedures of ICAO.

During the Conference's discussion, Bulgaria, Hungary, Mongolia, Singapore, the Ukrainian SSR and the USSR opposed amendments to change the articles on straits, on the ground that they would erode freedom of navigation or that the articles were part of a negotiated package. Malaysia supported the Spanish amendment to delete "normally" from the provision on compliance with the Rules of the Air but the United Kingdom opposed it while supporting the other two Spanish amendments. Denmark and Sweden said they could accept the proposed rules regarding passage through straits, which maintained (in article 35) the existing régime in straits where passage was regulated in whole or in part by long-standing international conventions—a situation applicable to the strait between them.

Spain, explaining on 30 April why it had abstained in the vote on the Convention, cited the fact that the Conference had not accepted its amendments on transit passage through straits; it added that Spain did not regard the Convention's provisions on that matter as constituting a codification of customary law.

During the closing week of the Conference in December, Canada spoke of the new provisions on transit passage through straits used for international navigation as offering a major inducement to maritime States to sign the Convention. Iraq said the application in good faith of the régime of navigation in straits, and its extension to access to straits and their islands, could make of such straits a channel of co-operation and peace.

On the other hand, Israel, citing its special interest in freedom of navigation and overflight through the Strait of Tiran and the Gulf of Aqaba as governed by its peace treaty with Egypt, said the Convention contained regressive elements caused by distortions introduced in the interests of political opportunism; those distortions caused great difficulty for Israel, except to the extent that broader rights were accorded to the users of some straits through particular stipulations and understandings. The United Republic of Tanzania viewed the provisions on straits as having little to do with the peaceful uses of the seas, since their main purpose was military.

Greece said it intended to submit an interpretive declaration to facilitate the just and effective application of the provisions concerning transit passage through straits used for international navigation.

Amendments. [1]Greece, A/CONF.62/L.123 (not pressed); [2]Spain, A/CONF.62/L.109 & Corr.2 (para. 1, rejected; para. 2, not adopted).

Archipelagic States

Convention provisions. The Convention on the Law of the Sea, in part IV, defined archipelagic States as those constituted wholly by one or more archipelagos, which it further defined as groups of islands, interconnecting waters and other natural features so closely interrelated as to form

an intrinsic geographical, economic and political entity, or which historically had been regarded as such (article 46).

For the purpose of defining their maritime zones, archipelagic States could draw straight archipelagic baselines up to 100 nautical miles long joining the outermost points of their outermost islands and drying reefs, so long as the ratio of water to land area within those lines did not exceed 9 to 1 and provided that the resulting area did not cut another State off from the high seas or the exclusive economic zone (article 47). The breadth of the territorial sea, the contiguous zone, the exclusive economic zone and the continental shelf would be measured from those baselines (article 48). The sovereignty of an archipelagic State extended to the waters enclosed by those baselines as well as to the airspace above and the bed and subsoil below (article 49). The rules for delimiting internal waters were the same as those for the territorial sea of continental States (article 50).

Traditional fishing rights of neighbouring States were to be respected by the archipelagic State, along with existing agreements with and existing submarine cables laid by other States; the terms and conditions for the exercise of rights and activities, including the areas to which they applied, were to be regulated by bilateral agreements at the request of any of the States concerned (article 51).

Ships of all States enjoyed the right of innocent passage through archipelagic waters, though such passage could be temporarily suspended in specified areas by the archipelagic State if that was essential to protect its security (article 52). The archipelagic State could designate sea lanes and air routes for passage through or over those waters by ships and aircraft travelling from one part of the high seas or an exclusive economic zone to another (article 53). Archipelagic sea lanes passage was to be governed, *mutatis mutandis*, by the same rules as transit passage through straits used for international navigation in respect of the duties of ships and aircraft during passage, research and survey activities, and duties and laws and regulations of the bordering State (article 54).

Conference consideration. Greece proposed in April 1982 but later withdrew an amendment that would have added a new article applying to archipelagos forming part of a State's territory the same rules for measuring maritime zones that applied to States consisting entirely of an archipelago.[1]

Canada, speaking after the adoption of the Convention in April, described the concept of archipelagic States as an important innovation that had solved one of the Conference's most delicate problems.

Speaking during the Conference's final week in December, several archipelagic States welcomed the Convention's clauses on this topic. The Bahamas saw them as balanced between the legitimate interests of archipelagos to be regarded as a single entity and the interest of the international community in free and unobstructed movement of legitimate maritime traffic. Cape Verde hailed these provisions as a major achievement for the protection of its legitimate interests in preserving the unity and integrity of its territory. Fiji said it had already incorporated the concept into its legislation.

Indonesia observed that it had promulgated the archipelagic State concept in 1957, enacted it into law in 1960 and was gratified to see it incorporated into the Convention. Malaysia, noting that it had concluded in February 1982 a treaty with Indonesia which provided for the continuance of Malaysia's legitimate rights and interests, said the Convention respected such rights and interests in cases where the archipelagic waters of one State lay between two parts of an adjacent State. The Netherlands Antilles, also welcoming the Convention's provisions on this topic, said it had taken them as a point of departure in negotiations with Venezuela on maritime boundaries which had resulted in a treaty.

Papua New Guinea, while welcoming the new régime, said freedom of navigation through archipelagic waters must always be weighed against security risks to the archipelagic State; it voiced misgivings over what it referred to as the newly created right (under article 53) of submarines to remain below the surface when passing through archipelagic sea lanes. The Philippines said the fact that the Convention recognized the sovereignty of the archipelagic State over archipelagic waters, and the airspace above and sea-bed below them, was the weightiest consideration leading it to sign the Convention; in exercise of that sovereignty, the archipelagic State could designate sea-lanes for the passage of foreign ships and enact legislation to ensure that they complied with Convention obligations, including the duty to refrain from force against the archipelagic State.

India reiterated its view that a group of islands which was an integral part of a State's territory should be entitled to the status of an archipelago. Spain thought it unfair that the Convention excluded such archipelagos from the archipelagic régime.

Amendment withdrawn. [1]Greece, A/CONF.62/L.123.

Exclusive economic zone

Convention provisions. Part V of the Convention on the Law of the Sea defined a legal régime for the maritime area beyond and adjacent to the territorial sea known as the exclusive economic zone, where the rights and jurisdiction of the coastal State and the rights and freedoms of other States were governed by the Convention (article 55). In that zone, the coastal State had sovereign rights over natural resources and economic activities, such as production of energy from water and wind, as well as jurisdiction over offshore structures, marine scientific research, and protection and preservation of the marine environment (article 56). The breadth of the zone must not extend beyond 200 nautical miles from the baselines used to measure the breadth of the territorial sea (article 57).

With regard to the rights and duties of other States in this zone, the Convention affirmed that they enjoyed the freedoms of navigation and overflight and of the laying of submarine cables and pipelines, and related lawful uses such as the operation of ships, aircraft and submarine cables and pipelines (article 58).

Conflicts between States over rights and jurisdiction in this zone should be resolved on the basis of equity and in the light of all relevant circumstances, taking into account the respective importance of the interests involved to the parties as well as to the international community as a whole (article 59).

Delimitation of the exclusive economic zone between States with opposite or adjacent coasts was to be effected by agreement on the basis of international law in order to achieve an equitable solution; failing agreement within a reasonable time, States were to resort to the dispute settlement procedures provided for in the Convention (article 74). States were required to give due publicity to charts showing the outer limits of their zone or, where appropriate, lists of geographical coordinates, and to deposit copies with the Secretary-General (article 75).

This part of the Convention also dealt with artificial islands, installations and structures in the zone and with the conservation and utilization of its living marine resources.

Conference consideration. Lesotho proposed in April 1982 but did not press to a vote an amendment (to article 56) that would have required each coastal State, particularly the developed ones, to contribute in cash or kind to a Common Heritage Fund from their proceeds from exploitation of the non-living resources of the exclusive economic zone.[1] Contribution rates, as a percentage of production volume or net revenue, would be determined by the International Sea-Bed Authority, which would divide the revenue among parties to the Convention on the basis of equitable sharing criteria, using some of it to protect the marine environment, to foster marine technology transfer and to help finance the Authority's Enterprise.

Zaire proposed, but did not press, a new article (75 *bis*) permitting States to apply to competent international bodies for the determination of technical norms related to the zone and requiring them to utilize a conciliation commission to settle disputes regarding the Convention's provisions on the zone.[2]

Support for a Common Heritage Fund was voiced by Algeria, Nepal and Singapore. Though expressing sympathy for the idea, Trinidad and Tobago reserved its position on the amendment proposed by Lesotho. Yugoslavia also favoured the concept but opposed any change in the pertinent article. The United Kingdom opposed the proposal.

Explaining their positions on the Convention following its adoption on 30 April, Chile, Colombia, Ecuador and Peru, the members of the Permanent Commission of the South Pacific, reiterated the Commission's position, stated in a 28 April letter to the Conference President,[3] that the universal recognition of the coastal State's rights of sovereignty and jurisdiction within the 200-mile limit, provided for in the Convention, was a fundamental achievement of the Commission's members. Canada viewed the zone as one of the Conference's greatest compromises, in which reciprocal concessions had been made to accommodate various interests.

During the Conference's final week in December, Brazil expressed its understanding that the Convention did not authorize other States to carry out military exercises or manoeuvres within the zone, particularly those involving weapons or explosives, or to operate any installation or structure there, without the prior consent of the coastal State. Cape Verde observed that the zone was a compromise concept that prejudiced the national interests of States such as Cape Verde which had proclaimed a broader territorial sea. Chile, observing that it had been the first country to declare such a zone—in 1947—described the zone as the essential legal concept of the Convention.

The Cook Islands, stressing the importance of the exclusive economic zone to a country such as itself with a land area of 244 square kilometres that claimed a zone of 1,360,000 square kilometres in the centre of the Pacific Ocean, was willing to negotiate on resource exploitation with other States having much greater technological capabilities. Nauru and Vanuatu also pointed out the significance of the zone for countries like themselves with few land resources. New Zealand observed that, as small Pacific island countries lacked the ability to enforce their resource jurisdiction, they would obtain the full benefit of such zones only if more powerful States respected their international obligations.

Fiji said the South Pacific countries had been the first to establish a regional fisheries organization—the South Pacific Forum Fisheries Agency—based solely on the exclusive economic zone concept.

India said the Convention protected the legitimate interests of coastal States in the seas around them, including exploitation of their living and non-living resources. Mexico pointed to the exclusive economic zone concept as one of the most important achievements of the Convention and recalled that it had pioneered in establishing such a zone as far back as 1976. Morocco mentioned its national legislation, dating back to 1973, establishing a 70-mile exclusive fishing limit, and said the establishment of that zone had not precluded the application of principles of international co-operation there.

Ireland and Italy believed that the provisions on the exclusive economic zone reconciled the interests of coastal States and others. The United Republic of Tanzania said the introduction of the zone distributed resources fairly between coastal States and the international community, and instituted a more rational system of management; however, coastal States should have been given more responsibilities and power in regard to marine scientific research and preservation of the marine environment.

Somalia opposed efforts to internationalize the exclusive economic zone, which it said was not part of either the territorial sea or the high seas. Uruguay, observing that the Convention's provisions on maritime areas adjacent to coasts were compatible with the principles underlying its own legislation, said the zone was a *sui generis* area of national jurisdiction that was not part of the high seas, where the coastal State had rights and a residual competence and where non-peaceful uses by third States were excluded, as were their installations and structures.

Iraq found the exclusive economic zone unacceptable but believed its shortcomings could be redressed with good faith on the part of the countries of each region, which could conclude additional conventions on fisheries, pollution and joint scientific research. Sweden said it had suffered as a result of the extension of the fishery zones of other States; the land-locked and geographically disadvantaged States were the losers in the hard competition for the sea's riches.

The United Kingdom said it did not agree with statements made in the Conference which purported to modify the effect of the Convention's provisions on the zone.

Delimitation. During the March/April Conference debates, some States, including Turkey, the United Arab Emirates and Venezuela, felt that the solution to the delimitation of the exclusive economic zone and the continental shelf was not clear enough and needed redrafting; Turkey sought to have delimitation through agreement between the parties based on equity, while the United Arab Emirates favoured the median line principle (drawing the boundary midway between the two coastlines).

Another group of States—including the Bahamas, Cape Verde, Cyprus, Finland, Guyana and Iraq—argued that the articles on delimitation, though not satisfactory in all respects, represented a balance resulting from arduous negotiations, and therefore opposed reopening the debate on them. A number of other States, though not specifically mentioning the delimitation provisions, believed that the parts of the Convention pertaining to the various maritime zones under national jurisdiction should be left unamended.

Venezuela based its vote against the Convention on its position that, since the Convention did not allow reservations, it could not accept the provisions on delimitation of maritime boundaries and the continental shelf between States with opposite or adjacent coasts. Thailand also cited difficulties with the delimitation provisions when explaining on 30 April why it had abstained in the vote.

During the December discussion, Bulgaria said it viewed the delimitation provisions positively in that they provided for agreement between States in accordance with international law and took account of geographic features and special circumstances with a view to achieving a just solution. In the view of Colombia, the delimitation provisions stressed the predominant role of the Convention and placed customary law in second place; conciliation was the Convention's key contribution to the settlement of maritime disputes. Guyana warned against attempts to insinuate into bilateral relations, under the guise of maritime delimitation, disputes inspired by ambitions rooted in territorial aggrandizement.

Somalia understood the delimitation provisions to mean that an equitable solution was the goal. Turkey also stressed the goal of an equitable solution as the primary factor in resolving delimitation disputes and said the article's reference to international law did not lead to a presumption that equidistance was preferred over other methods; it added that delimitation in semi-enclosed seas could be settled only through agreement reached directly between the parties on the basis of equity.

Some States reiterated their preference for the median line as the normal guide for drawing boundaries in delimitation disputes. The Bahamas was of this view, though adding that it could accept the Convention's provisions. Cyprus would have preferred a more clear-cut formulation and reiterated its view that the overall objective in delimitation should be an equitable result in accordance with international law through application of the median line where appropriate. Democratic Yemen said it would be bound by the median line principle in regard to delimitation of all maritime boundaries with its neighbours. The United Arab Emirates reiterated its belief that the median line should be employed.

Amendments not pressed. [1]Lesotho, A/CONF.62/L.115; [2]Zaire, A/CONF.62/L.107.
Letter. [3]Chile, Colombia, Ecuador, Peru, 28 Apr., A/CONF/62/L.143.

Offshore structures

The Convention on the Law of the Sea gave the coastal State the exclusive right to construct and to authorize and regulate the construction, operation and use of artificial islands, installations and structures in the exclusive economic zone, and it set up safety and other conditions for their operation and removal (article 60).

The 1981 text of this article had stipulated that any such offshore structures which were abandoned or disused must be entirely removed. The final version, taking account of factors such as cost and safety which might make complete removal impractical, provided for removal to ensure safety of navigation, taking account of generally accepted international standards and with due regard to fishing, protection of the marine environment, and the rights and duties of other States; it added that the depth, position and dimensions of structures not entirely removed must be publicized.

This change came about through the incorporation into the draft Convention of an informal United Kingdom amendment originally made in 1981[4] and reiterated at an informal meeting of the Second Committee on 16 March 1982. This was done by the Conference collegium in its memorandum of 2 April 1982[2], after the Second Committee Chairman, in a report of 26 March[3], had found the proposal to be the only one at that stage that had broad enough support for inclusion in the Convention.

A proposal by France that would have set precise limits on the height of unremoved portions of disused structures[1] was not pressed to a vote.

The United Kingdom amendment was supported during the Conference's March/April debates by Australia, Barbados, Brazil, Chile, Colombia, the Federal Republic of Germany, Guyana, Iceland, India, Ireland, Japan, Madagascar, Malaysia, the Netherlands, Nigeria, Norway, Oman, Portugal, Sierra Leone, Singapore, Sweden, and Trinidad and Tobago. Several of them felt that it provided an equitable balance between the interests of coastal States and those of other users of the sea, ensuring the safety of navigation and protection of the marine environment without interfering with fishing or shipping. The Ivory Coast preferred the text as it stood, saying that the amendment, by requiring only partial removal of offshore structures, could create obstacles to shipping and endanger fishing nets.

France, supported by the Ivory Coast, Madagascar and Yugoslavia, said in favour of its amendment that it was necessary to add specifics regarding the maximum height of any parts of installations that were not to be removed, in order to limit the danger to navigation and the risk of damage to fishing equipment. Malaysia, Trinidad and Tobago, and the United Kingdom could not support the French amendment.

Amendment not pressed. [1]France, A/CONF.62/L.106.
Memorandum. [2]Conference collegium, A/CONF.62/L.93.
Report. [3]2nd Committee Chairman, A/CONF.62/L.87.
Yearbook reference. [4]1981, p. 136.

Living resources of the zone

Convention provisions. Various rules for the protection and utilization of the fisheries resources of the exclusive economic zone, and for the rights and duties of coastal and other States in relation to those resources, were included in the Convention on the Law of the Sea.

The basic rule in regard to conservation was that the coastal State was to determine the allowable catch in the zone and, taking into account the best scientific evidence available, to ensure through proper conservation and management that the resources were not endangered by over-exploitation (article 61). Opportunities to share in those resources were offered under a provision requiring a coastal State which did not have the capacity to harvest the entire allowable catch to give other States access to the surplus; at the same time, the fishermen of other States must comply with the conservation measures and other fisheries rules established by the coastal State (article 62).

The Convention called for international agreement on conservation in the two types of cases when stocks occurred beyond a single State's exclusive economic zone ("straddling stocks"): when the stocks ranged between the zones of two or more coastal States, those States were to seek agreement; and when the stocks ranged beyond the zone into an adjacent high seas area, the coastal States and those fishing in the adjacent area were to seek agreement on conservation in that area (article 63).

With regard to highly migratory species, States whose nationals fished for them were to co-operate with coastal States on conservation and optimum utilization measures throughout the region, both within and beyond the exclusive economic zone (article 64). Such species, including tuna, mackerel, marlins, swordfish, oceanic sharks, dolphins and cetaceans (porpoises and whales), were listed in annex I to the Convention. Coastal States and international organizations could prohibit, limit or regulate the exploitation of marine mammals more strictly than required by the Convention (article 65).

The Convention provided separately for the conservation of anadromous stocks, such as salmon and shad, which ascend rivers from the sea at certain seasons for breeding, and catadromous species, such as eels, which live in fresh water but go to the sea to spawn. States in whose rivers anadromous stocks originated were given primary responsibility for such stocks and, as a rule, fisheries would be limited to waters landward of the outer limits of the exclusive economic zone (article 66). Responsibility for management of catadromous species was placed on the coastal State in whose waters they spent the greater part of their life cycle, and harvesting would be limited to waters landward of the outer limits of the exclusive economic zone (article 67). Sedentary species in the zone were excluded from the application of all fisheries rules contained in this part of the Convention (article 68); they were among the resources covered by the coastal State's sovereign rights over its continental shelf (article 77).

The Convention set out the right of land-locked States (article 69) and of geographically disadvantaged States (article 70) to participate, on an equitable basis and in agreement with the States concerned, in exploitation of an appropriate part of the surplus of the living resources of the exclusive economic zones of coastal States in the same region or subregion, taking into account the economic and geographical circumstances of all States concerned. "Geographically disadvantaged States" were defined as coastal States whose geographical situation made them dependent for adequate fish supplies on the living resources of the zones of other States in the region or subregion, and coastal States with no exclusive economic zone. These provisions for access by other States would not apply, however, in the case of a coastal State whose economy was overwhelmingly dependent on fisheries in its zone (article 71). Nor could these rights of access be transferred to others by lease or licence, joint ventures or otherwise, unless agreed by the States concerned (article 72).

The Convention gave coastal States the right to enforce their fisheries laws and regulations in the zone, but required prompt notification to the flag State when its vessel was arrested and release of vessels and crews on the posting of reasonable bond or other security; it also forbade imprisonment or other corporal punishment as a penalty for violation (article 73).

Conference consideration. Several amendments on living resources in the exclusive economic zone were presented to the Conference on the Law of the Sea in April 1982, but were not pressed to a vote.

A proposal by Romania (to article 70) on the rights of States with special geographical characteristics[3] would have had the effect of a similar amendment by Romania and Yugoslavia (to article 62) on utilization of the zone's living resources[4]—namely, to increase the access of developing States to fisheries in zones outside their own region or subregion. An amendment by Lesotho (to article 62) would have added a provision allowing developing land-locked States to participate in exploiting the allowable catch of the living resources of the zones in the same region or subregion.[2]

Zaire proposed amendments to amplify the concept of "surplus" (in article 62) by replacing it with a phrase giving other States, by agreement, access to the part of the entire allowable catch not effectively harvested by the coastal State.[5] It also proposed to delete what it called a superfluous provision stating that the provisions for access by other States did not apply in the case of a coastal State whose economy was overwhelmingly dependent on fisheries in its zone (article 71).

Eight States—Australia, Canada, Cape Verde, Iceland, the Philippines, Sao Tome and Principe, Senegal and Sierra Leone—proposed a new paragraph (in article 63) to strengthen conservation measures for "straddling stocks" in areas adjacent to the exclusive economic zone.[1] It would have made the adoption of such measures mandatory and empowered an international tribunal to establish definitive or provisional measures for such areas if the coastal and fishing States concerned could not agree.

During the Conference's March/April debate, Austria, the German Democratic Republic, Hungary, Iraq, Romania and Zimbabwe said the provisions on the exclusive economic zone should offer more just and adequate solutions to the problems of States fishing in distant waters and to those of the land-locked and geographically disadvantaged States. Canada, Cape Verde, Guyana, Iceland, Madagascar, New Zealand, Sao Tome and Principe, Somalia, Suriname, Uruguay and Yugoslavia sought a further refinement of the provision (article 63) on conservation of "straddling stocks" in areas beyond and adjacent to the exclusive economic zone in order to enlarge the scope of the coastal State's rights over the resources in its zone, as provided in the proposal by the eight States and in an informal proposal submitted by Argentina in 1980.[6] Japan, the Ukrainian SSR and the USSR opposed a change in this provision, stating that arrangements for the conservation of such stocks should be based on voluntary agreement (Japan) and that the amendment would curtail freedom to fish on the high seas (USSR).

Thailand, explaining on 30 April why it had abstained in the vote on the Convention, said its fishing industry would be adversely affected by the exclusive economic zone provisions, to the detriment of a large sector of the population.

Romania, though voting for the Convention, said the provisions on the right of access to the fishery resources of economic zones did not take sufficiently into account the situation of countries like Romania which were in regions or subregions poor in fishery resources and therefore needed access to fisheries elsewhere; Romania hoped its situation would be taken into account in bilateral fishing agreements and the arrangements of international agencies. Zambia recalled its advocacy of regional economic zones and continental shelves that would not operate to the exclusion of land-locked States.

Bulgaria said in December that it accepted the establishment of the exclusive economic zone as an essential concession to coastal States but thought there should be no unjustifiable limitation of the reasonable utilization of living resources and access by other interested countries, especially the geographically disadvantaged or those with limited fisheries of their own, whose economy depended on fishing and which had made considerable investments in long-distance fishing. The German Democratic Republic remarked that, in the interest of world-wide co-operation, especially for the benefit of developing countries, it had accepted compromises entailing substantial economic losses, as its population depended on distant-water fishing, especially in the North Atlantic, and it had had to shoulder considerable additional burdens since the introduction of economic zones. Yugoslavia said the priority attached to exploiting surpluses within a region or subregion did not preclude bilateral co-operation between developing coastal States of different regions and subregions.

Canada remarked that, after the so-called fish wars prior to 1973, the Conference had rightly recognized the need to assign to coastal States control over all living resources within a 200-mile zone. Iceland particularly welcomed the provisions on the exclusive economic zone, observing that their policy guidelines had been incorporated into Icelandic law in 1948.

Chad viewed the provision on access to the exclusive economic zones of States in the same region as a safeguard, although minimal, for the land-locked States. Mauritius said it was gratified to see the Convention reflect the basically African idea of permitting land-locked States access to the surplus of living resources. Morocco said it had long advocated the right of all States in a region to have access to the sea and, if possible, to use its living resources to meet the needs of all neighbouring States. Trinidad and Tobago believed the Convention did not properly accommodate the position of land-locked and geographically disadvantaged States in respect of access to the living resources of the exclusive economic zones of States in the same region or subregion; an accommodation should have been made for States which had traditionally fished in such areas prior to the declaration of the zones.

India said it was intensively developing its fishing capability to meet its protein needs and would base its computations of allowable catches on the ultimate level of that capability. In the view of Iran, the rights of geographically disadvantaged States were without prejudice to the exclusive right of coastal States on enclosed and semi-enclosed seas, such as the Persian Gulf and the Sea of Oman, with large populations predominantly dependent on relatively poor fishery stocks. Mauritania emphasized that land-locked and geographically disadvantaged countries could have access to another State's exclusive economic zone only on the basis of bilateral, subregional or regional agreements.

Cape Verde remarked that the Convention obliged States fishing for straddling stocks in an area adjacent to the exclusive economic zone to enter into agreement with the coastal State on the measures necessary to conserve such stocks and associated species. Costa Rica said its national law requiring foreign vessels to pay for permits to fish in its exclusive economic zone applied also to highly migratory species such as tuna, in conformity with the Convention. Noting that highly migratory species were the major living resource of the exclusive economic zones of many small Pacific island countries, New Zealand said such countries were developing co-operation with distant-water-fishing nations that were prepared to respect their sovereign rights over such resources, including tuna.

Amendments not pressed. [1]Australia, Canada, Cape Verde, Iceland, Philippines, Sao Tome and Principe, Senegal, Sierra Leone, A/CONF.62/L.114 & Corr.1; [2]Lesotho, A/CONF.62/L.99; [3]Romania, A/CONF.62/L.96; [4]Romania, Yugoslavia, A/CONF.62/L.112; [5]Zaire, A/CONF.62/L.107.
Yearbook reference. [6]1980, p. 151.

Continental shelf

Convention provisions. Rules relating to the continental shelf were set out in part VI of the Convention on the Law of the Sea.

The shelf was defined (article 76) as comprising the sea-bed and subsoil of the submarine areas that extended beyond the territorial sea to the outer edge of the continental margin—the submerged prolongation of a coastal State's land mass, short of the deep ocean floor—or, where the outer edge of the continental margin did not extend that far, to a distance of 200 nautical miles from the baselines from which the territorial sea was measured (in the latter case it would have the same outer limits as the exclusive economic zone). A State would have two options for establishing the outer edge of its continental margin: one based on the thickness of sedimentary rocks beyond the foot of the continental slope and the other defined by a line not more than 60 miles beyond the foot of the slope. Two alternative outer limits would be fixed for States whose shelf extended beyond 200 miles: 350 miles from the coastal baselines or 100 miles beyond where the ocean depth reached 2,500 metres.

A Commission on the Limits of the Continental Shelf, composed of 21 experts elected by the States parties to the Convention and set up under annex II of the Convention on the basis of equitable geographical representation, would make recommendations to coastal States on matters related to the establishment of the shelf's outer limits. Such recommendations would require the approval of two thirds of the Commission members present and voting. The limits established by the coastal State on the basis of those recommendations would be final and binding.

The coastal State would have sovereign rights to explore the shelf and exploit its natural resources, consisting of non-living resources and sedentary living species; no one could undertake such activities without its consent (article 77). However, those rights would not affect the legal status of the water or airspace above the shelf and there must be no unjustifiable interference with navigation and other rights and freedoms of others (article 78).

With regard to specific activities on the shelf, all States were entitled to lay submarine cables and pipelines there, though the coastal State could specify conditions and the course of pipelines would be subject to its consent (article 79). The rules for artificial islands, installations and structures in the exclusive economic zone would also apply to those on the shelf (article 80). The coastal State would have the exclusive right to authorize and regulate drilling on the shelf (article 81).

The Convention would require coastal States to contribute to the International Sea-Bed Authority, in cash or kind, a portion of the value or volume of production from any exploitation of the outer shelf beyond 200 miles from the coastal baselines, at a rate that would rise from zero during the first five years of exploitation at any given site to 1 per cent in the sixth year and then to a maximum of 7 per cent in the twelfth year and thereafter; the proceeds would be distributed to States parties to the Convention on the basis of equitable sharing criteria, taking account of the needs of developing countries and particularly the least developed and land-locked (article 82).

The Convention's rules for delimiting the shelf between States with opposite or adjacent coasts were similar to those governing delimitation of the exclusive economic zone—calling for agreement on the basis of international law and, failing agreement, resort to dispute settlement procedures (article 83). The requirements for charts and lists of geographical co-ordinates to define the shelf's outer limits (article 84) were also similar to those for the exclusive economic zone.

The Convention confirmed the right of coastal States to exploit the subsoil of their shelf by means of tunnelling (article 85).

A statement of understanding annexed to the Conference's Final Act[3] set out a special method for establishing the outer edge of the continental margin in the southern part of the Bay of Bengal (affecting Sri Lanka in particular).

Conference consideration. Two amendments relating to the continental shelf were submitted to the Conference on the Law of the Sea in April 1982 but neither was pressed to a vote. A United Kingdom amendment would have required States to fix the outer limits of their shelf (under article 76) after "taking into account" (rather than "on the basis of") recommendations by the Commission on the Limits of the Continental Shelf.[2] Lesotho proposed that the payments from the proceeds of exploiting the outer shelf (article 82) be made to the proposed Common Heritage Fund.[1]

Canada, speaking in December, stated that the Conference had achieved a balance between coastal States with broad and narrow continental shelves. Ireland believed the acknowledgement of the coastal State's basic jurisdiction throughout its geographical continental margin was balanced by the adoption of criteria and methods for defining the outer boundary that cut off parts of the margin from national jurisdiction, and also by the coastal State's obligation to share revenue from the outer shelf areas with the international community.

Algeria, on the other hand, thought that the extension of the continental shelf of certain coastal States beyond the limits of the exclusive economic zone was a distortion of equity. Paraguay regarded such an extension as a serious erosion of the common heritage principle and hoped the formula governing the international sharing of some of the revenues from the outer shelf would be revised in the future so as to provide a new and important source of revenue for development. The United Arab Emirates reiterated its view that the shelf should not extend beyond 200 miles. Yugoslavia added that it had accepted the Convention's compromise on this point with reluctance.

Other developments. The International Court of Justice had two cases before it in 1982 concerned with the delimitation of the continental shelf in the Mediterranean Sea: between the Libyan Arab Jamahiriya and Malta and between the Libyan Arab Jamahiriya and Tunisia (see LEGAL QUESTIONS, Chapter I).

Amendments not pressed. [1]Lesotho, A/CONF.62/L.115;
[2]United Kingdom, A/CONF.62/L.126.
Final Act. [3]A/CONF.62/121.

High seas

Convention provisions. Part VII of the Convention on the Law of the Sea pertained to all parts of the sea not included in the exclusive economic zone, the territorial sea or internal waters, or in archipelagic waters (article 86).

The high seas were open to all States, and freedom of the high seas included freedom of navigation and overflight, freedom to lay submarine cables and pipelines and to construct artificial islands and similar installations, and freedom of fishing and scientific research (article 87). The area was reserved for peaceful purposes (article 88) and no State could claim sovereignty over any part of it (article 89).

The Convention affirmed the right of every State to sail ships flying its flag on the high seas (article 90). Every State must fix the conditions for granting to ships its nationality and the right to fly its flag; a genuine link must exist between the State and the ship (article 91). Ships could sail under the flag of one State only and, save in exceptional cases, were subject to its exclusive jurisdiction on the high seas (article 92). These provisions did not prejudice the question of ships employed on the official service of the United Nations, its specialized agencies or the International Atomic Energy Agency, flying the flag of the organization (article 93).

In respect of the duties of the flag State, the Convention required every State to exercise effectively its jurisdiction and control in administrative, technical and social matters over ships flying its flag, and to take, in conformity with generally accepted regulations, procedures and practices, such measures for those ships as were necessary to ensure safety at sea (article 94). Complete immunity from the jurisdiction of any State other than the flag State was accorded to warships (article 95) and ships owned and operated by a State and used only on government non-commercial service (article 96), while on the high seas. The Convention regulated penal jurisdiction in the event of a collision or any other navigation incident, stating in particular that no arrest or detention of a ship, even for investigation, could be ordered by any authorities other than those of the flag State (article 97).

The Convention spelt out the duty of every State to require the master of a ship flying its flag, in so far as he could do so without serious danger to the ship, crew or passengers, to assist any person found at sea in danger of being lost, to proceed with all possible speed to the rescue of persons in distress and, after a collision, to assist the other ship, its crew and its passengers (article 98).

The transport of slaves was prohibited (article 99).

The Convention established the duty of all States to co-operate in the repression of piracy on the high seas or anywhere outside the jurisdiction of any State (article 100). Piracy was defined as any illegal acts of violence, detention or depredation committed for private ends by the crew or passengers of a private ship or aircraft, directed on the high seas against another ship or aircraft or against persons or property on board, or the participation in or incitement to such acts (article 101). Acts of piracy committed by a warship or government ship or aircraft whose crew had mutinied and taken control were assimilated to acts committed by a private ship or aircraft (article 102). A pirate ship or aircraft was one that was intended by those in control to be used for such acts, or one that had already been used to that end and remained under the control of the guilty persons (article 103). Such a ship or aircraft could retain its nationality, depending on the law of the State from which that nationality had been derived (article 104).

The Convention allowed every State to seize on the high seas, or anywhere outside the jurisdiction of any State, a pirate ship or aircraft, or a ship or aircraft taken by piracy and under the control of pirates, and to arrest the persons and seize the property on board (article 105). In cases where seizure had been effected without adequate grounds, however, the State making the seizure was liable to the flag State for damages (article 106). Seizure on account of piracy could be carried out only by warships or military aircraft, or others clearly marked and identifiable as being on government service and authorized to that effect (article 107).

States were required to co-operate in the suppression of illicit traffic in narcotic drugs and psychotropic substances engaged in by ships on the high seas contrary to international conventions (article 108). They must also co-operate in the suppression of unauthorized broadcasting from the high seas, defined as sound or television transmission intended for public reception contrary to international regulations (article 109).

Except where provided by treaty, a warship could not board a ship on the high seas unless there was reasonable ground for suspecting that it was engaged in piracy, the slave trade or unauthorized broadcasting, or was without nationality or, though flying a foreign flag or refusing to show its flag, had in reality the same nationality as the warship (article 110). Hot pursuit of a foreign ship could be undertaken by a military or government craft of a coastal State when that State's authorities had good reason to believe that the foreign ship had violated that State's laws or regulations; hot pursuit could be commenced in the coastal State's waters only after a signal to stop had been issued at a distance which enabled it to be seen or heard by the foreign ship (article 111).

All States were entitled to lay submarine cables and pipelines on the bed of the high seas beyond the continental shelf, having due regard to those already in position (article 112). Wilful or negligent breaking or injury of a submarine cable or pipeline was a punishable offence (article 113). Submarine cable or pipeline owners who injured another cable or pipeline while laying or repairing their own must bear the cost of repairs (article 114). Shipowners who could prove that they had sacrificed an anchor, a net or other fishing gear in order to avoid injuring a submarine cable or pipeline were to be indemnified by the cable or pipeline owner, provided that the shipowner had taken all reasonable precautions beforehand (article 115).

Conference consideration. In the general statements made during the Conference's final week in December 1982, Bulgaria and Mongolia welcomed the fact that the Convention confirmed the freedom of the high seas, including freedom of navigation and overflight, the laying of submarine cables and pipelines, the construction of artificial islands and installations, fishing, the conduct of scientific research and other recognized uses.

The United Republic of Tanzania said it was unfortunate that the high seas were not included in the common heritage of mankind.

Living resources of the high seas

The Convention on the Law of the Sea provided for the right of all States to fish on the high seas (article 116). It also established their duty to take, or to co-operate with other States in taking, measures for their nationals needed for the conservation of the area's living resources (article 117). States whose nationals exploited identical living resources, or different ones in the same area, must negotiate on conservation measures and, as appropriate, establish subregional or regional fisheries organizations to that end (article 118).

In determining the allowable catch and other conservation measures, States were to take measures designed, on the best scientific evidence available, to maintain or restore populations of harvested species at levels which could produce maximum sustainable yields, taking into consideration the effects on associated or dependent species and without discriminating against the fishermen of any State (article 119). The rule for conservation and management of marine mammals in the exclusive economic zone—that their exploitation could be prohibited, limited or regulated more strictly than provided for in the Convention—applied also to the high seas (article 120).

Islands

The Convention on the Law of the Sea, in part VIII, defined an island as a naturally formed land area surrounded by water and above water at high tide; it gave islands the same territorial sea, contiguous zone, exclusive economic zone and continental shelf as other land areas, except that rocks which could not sustain human habitation or economic life had no exclusive economic zone or continental shelf (article 121).

In April 1982, Romania proposed to the Conference on the Law of the Sea a new paragraph stating that uninhabited islets should not have any effect on the maritime spaces belonging to the main coasts of States,[1] and the United Kingdom proposed deletion of the provision on rocks.[2] Neither amendment was pressed to a vote.

Introducing its amendment, Romania said it was aimed at preventing any State from encroaching on the maritime zones of another State by invoking the existence of uninhabited islets in the delimitation area. The amendment was supported by Algeria and Mozambique, but was opposed by the Byelorussian SSR, Ecuador, the German Democratic Republic, Japan, Malta, Portugal, Trinidad and Tobago, the Ukrainian SSR, the USSR, the United Kingdom and Uruguay.

The United Kingdom, introducing its amendment, said there was no reason to discriminate between different forms of territory for the purposes of delimiting maritime zones. This amendment was opposed by Algeria, Bulgaria, the Byelorussian SSR, Colombia, Denmark, the German Democratic Republic, Mongolia, Pakistan, Trinidad and Tobago, the USSR, Uruguay and Yugoslavia, on the ground that there was no justification for an uninhabited rock to have a 200-mile exclusive economic zone. It was supported by Brazil, Ecuador, Iran, Japan and Portugal.

During the general statements on the Convention made in December, Cyprus said the principle that islands were entitled to the same maritime zones as continental territories was an example of the way the Convention incorporated rules of law that had stood the test of time; Cyprus had argued strenuously against discrimination against islands by attempting to create artificial distinctions based on size, population or location. The Netherlands Antilles also welcomed this aspect of the Convention. Turkey was of the view that the article on islands was not applicable to those located in maritime areas subject to delimitation between two States.

Colombia said the rule that rocks were entitled only to a territorial sea since they could not sustain human habitation was the logical result of the economic concept that the continental shelf and the exclusive economic zone had been granted to benefit the inhabitants. Romania reiterated its view that small and uninhabited islands lacking their own economic life could not influence the delimitation of maritime space.

On the other hand, Iran expressed the view that islets in enclosed and semi-enclosed seas which potentially could sustain human habitation or an economic life of their own, but which had not been developed for climatic or other reasons, had full effect in maritime boundary delimitation. Venezuela cited the provision on rocks as one of the reasons why it did not sign the Convention.

Some States were of the view that groups of islands forming part of a State's territory should be given the same legal treatment as archipelagic States.

Amendments not pressed. [1]Romania, A/CONF.62/L.118; [2]United Kingdom, A/CONF.62/L.126.

Semi-enclosed seas

Under part IX of the Convention on the Law of the Sea, an "enclosed or semi-enclosed sea" meant a gulf, basin or sea surrounded by two or more States and connected to another sea or the ocean by a narrow outlet, or one that consisted entirely or primarily of the territorial seas and exclusive economic zones of two or more coastal States (article 122). States bordering such seas should co-operate with each other, directly or through a regional organization, in regard to their rights and duties under the Convention regarding such matters as management and conservation of the sea's living resources, protection and preservation of the marine environment, and scientific research (article 123).

At the Conference on the Law of the Sea in April 1982, Iraq proposed but did not press a new paragraph (in article 123) providing that freedom of navigation through waterways within semi-enclosed seas must be maintained.[1]

Speaking in December, Bulgaria said it would begin to apply the provisions on semi-enclosed seas in co-operation with its Black Sea neighbours. Cyprus said it was satisfied with those provisions, as it had consistently favoured co-operation between States bordering such seas, but it opposed attempts to create particular rules for such seas in derogation of the Convention's universal rules. Malta looked forward to a regional approach in delimiting boundaries and governing other uses of the seas in the Mediterranean. The Republic of Korea stressed its readiness to co-operate and consult with its neighbour on the Yellow Sea in regard to environmental protection as well as delimitation of the continental shelf and the exclusive economic zone. Viet Nam expressed similar willingness to co-operate with its neighbours on the South China Sea, particularly in the settlement of maritime boundary disputes.

Israel said it was not satisfied that some of the Convention's major concepts were fully applicable in the narrow, semi-enclosed seas on which its two coasts lay.

Amendment not pressed. [1]Iraq, A/CONF.62/L.110.

Access of land-locked States to the sea

Convention provisions. Part X of the Convention on the Law of the Sea was concerned with the right of access of land-locked States to and from the sea and freedom of transit.

It dealt with "traffic in transit", defined as transit of persons, baggage, goods and "means of transport" (transport vehicles and, if the States so agreed, pipelines and gas lines) across the territory of a "transit State" (one lying between the land-locked State and the sea) as part of a longer journey which began or terminated within the "land-locked State" (State with no sea-coast) (article 124). The Convention assured land-locked States such right of access and freedom of transit, under terms and modalities for transit agreed upon between the States concerned, and allowing transit States to ensure that their legitimate interests were not infringed (article 125). States were not required to extend to other States, under the most-favoured-nation clause of treaties, the rights and facilities established by the Convention or special agreements on account of the special geographical position of land-locked States (article 126).

Traffic in transit must not be subject to customs duties, taxes or other charges except charges for specific services; means of transport and other facilities used by land-locked States must not be subject to taxes or charges higher than those levied for the means of transport of the transit State (article 127). Free zones or other customs facilities could be provided for such traffic at the transit State's ports of entry and exit, by agreement between the States concerned (article 128). Transit and land-locked States could co-operate in constructing or improving means of transport used for that traffic (article 129). Transit States must take all appropriate measures to avoid delays or other technical difficulties affecting that traffic (article 130). Ships flying the flag of land-locked States were entitled to treatment equal to that accorded to other foreign ships in maritime ports (article 131). The Convention did not entail the withdrawal of transit facilities greater than those it provided for, nor did it preclude the grant of greater facilities in the future (article 132).

The rights of land-locked and geographically disadvantaged States to participate in exploiting the living resources of exclusive economic zones of States in the same region or subregion were recognized in the part of the Convention dealing with that zone.

Conference consideration. Lesotho proposed to the Conference on the Law of the Sea in April 1982, but did not press, an amendment (to article 124) adding "aircraft" to the means of transport covered by this part of the Convention.[1]

Although voting in favour of the Convention, Pakistan said on 30 April that a right of access to the sea by land-locked States and freedom of transit would impinge on the sovereignty of coastal States and was therefore unacceptable; such freedom of transit would continue to be governed by bilateral agreements. Zambia expressed concern that the Convention's provisions on access of land-locked States to the sea might be interpreted by some as dependent on the negotiation of bilateral agreements. Hungary found those provisions acceptable.

During the Conference's concluding round of statements in December, Angola said the right of transit and access to the sea were matters for negotiation between the States involved; Angola would consider them on the basis of solidarity, co-operation and friendship, not as another State's inherent right under any convention. Iran expressed a similar view.

Burundi was grateful that the Convention recognized the rights of the land-locked countries, if only symbolically. Czechoslovakia remarked that, though the granting of the right of access to the sea by land-locked States was largely symbolic, it was the end result of 50 years of efforts to codify that rule in a universal convention, and was thus of great significance to those States. Although far from perfect, said Hungary, the provisions on land-locked States ensured certain basic rights without which the Convention would be meaningless for those States. Poland thought the Convention would be beneficial for the development of transit traffic through transit and land-locked States, based on the principle of reciprocity.

Several land-locked and geographically disadvantaged States were critical of the Convention's provisions designed to accommodate their interests. Bhutan thought the land-locked countries had had to be satisfied with very little. Mongolia said some provisions did not fully protect their rights and interests, and gave only limited rights of access to the exclusive economic zone. Nepal was not satisfied with the provisions on the transit rights of land-locked countries. Paraguay, while pleased with the provisions aimed at ensuring the participation of land-locked countries in the exploitation of the high seas, the international sea-bed area and the exclusive economic zone, said it was not as satisfied with the way in which the Convention dealt with the fundamental right of such States to access to the sea and freedom of transit.

Amendment not pressed. [1]Lesotho, A/CONF.62/L.99.

Sea-bed

Convention provisions. The legal régime governing the deep sea-bed area beyond national jurisdiction, including the constitutional provisions for the International Sea-Bed Authority, was set out in part XI of the Convention on the Law of the Sea and in two annexes: annex III, on basic conditions of prospecting, exploration and exploitation, and annex IV, containing the Statute of the Enterprise, the Authority's sea-bed mining organ. In addition, resolution I of the Conference on the Law of the Sea provided for the establishment of a Preparatory Commission to exercise certain interim authority until the Convention entered into force, and resolution II governed preparatory investment in pioneer activities relating to polymetallic nodules on the deep sea-bed. The resolutions were adopted by the Conference on 30 April 1982 as part of a package with the Convention.

The Convention and associated resolutions provided in detail for arrangements regarding sea-bed mining, the structure and functions of the Authority and special dispute settlement machinery. They also contained a number of general provisions and principles relating to what the Convention referred to as the Area—defined in part I as the sea-bed and ocean floor and subsoil thereof beyond the limits of national jurisdiction—and to activities in the Area, defined in part I as resource exploration and exploitation.

The Convention defined the resources it covered to include all solid, liquid or gaseous mineral resources in the Area at or beneath the sea-bed, including polymetallic nodules (mineral masses yielding mainly copper, nickel, cobalt and manganese) (article 133). Part XI of the Convention applied to the Area (article 134) and had no effect on the legal status of the waters or airspace above (article 135).

The section defining the principles governing the Area began with the statement that the Area and its resources were the common heritage of mankind (article 136). No State could claim or exercise sovereignty or sovereign rights over any part of the Area or its resources, nor could any State, person or entity appropriate any part thereof; all rights in the Area's resources were vested in mankind as a whole, on whose behalf the Authority was to act (article 137).

The general conduct of States in relation to the Area was to be in accordance with this part of the Convention, the principles of the Charter of the United Nations and other rules of international law, in the interests of maintaining peace and security and promoting international co-operation and mutual understanding (article 138). The Convention made States parties and international organizations responsible for ensuring that activities in the Area carried out by them or by persons under their control conformed to the Convention, and also made them liable for damage caused by failure to carry out that responsibility (article 139).

Activities in the Area were to be carried out for the benefit of mankind as a whole, taking into particular consideration the interests and needs of developing States and of peoples who had not attained full independence or self-government; the Authority was to provide for the equitable and non-discriminatory sharing of financial and other economic benefits derived from the Area (article 140). The Area was open for use exclusively for peaceful purposes by all States without discrimination (article 141). Activities in the Area with respect to resource deposits lying across limits of national jurisdiction must be conducted with due regard to the rights and legitimate interests of the coastal State concerned, including consultations with that State and a system of prior notification; the coastal State retained the right to protect its coastline from grave and imminent danger due to pollution or other hazards resulting from activities in the Area (article 142).

Marine scientific research in the Area must be carried out exclusively for peaceful purposes and for the benefit of mankind as a whole; both the Authority and States parties could conduct such research, and the latter were obliged to promote international co-operation by participating in international programmes, ensuring that programmes were developed to strengthen the research capabilities and train the personnel of developing States, and disseminating research results (article 143). Technology transfer was to be promoted (article 144).

Measures were to be taken to ensure effective protection of the marine environment from harmful effects arising from activities in the Area; these were to include the adoption by the Authority of rules, regulations and procedures (referred to below as rules) for the control of pollution and other environmental hazards resulting in particular from such activities as drilling, dredging, excavation, waste disposal, and construction and operation or maintenance of installations, pipelines and other devices (article 145). Measures to ensure protection of human life were to include the adoption by the Authority of rules to supplement existing international law (article 146). The Convention set out conditions for installations used to carry out activities in the Area, including due notice of emplacement and removal, non-interference with navigation and fishing, safety zones, and use exclusively for peaceful purposes; such installations would not have the status of islands (article 147).

The Convention called for promoting the participation of developing States in activities in the Area, with particular regard for the special need of land-locked and geographically disadvantaged States to overcome obstacles arising from their disadvantaged location and remoteness from the Area (article 148). It also provided that archaeological and historical objects found in the Area must be preserved or disposed of for the benefit of mankind as a whole, with particular regard to the preferential rights of the country of origin (article 149).

Conference consideration. The sea-bed provisions of the Convention and associated resolutions were the most controversial matters before the Conference on the Law of the Sea in its final year, and negotiations on several aspects continued until 30 April, the day on which the "Convention package" was adopted. In particular, the resolution spelling out the rules for pioneer investors, covering the period before entry into force of the Convention, was largely worked out during the first part of the 1982 session, in March/April.

On 29 March, the Chairman of the First Committee, which dealt with sea-bed issues, submitted a report[6] in which, among other things, he discussed the effects of the United States return to the negotiations, following a period in 1981 while it was reassessing the progress of the Conference.[7] Speaking of the United States President's announcement on 29 January 1982 that the United States was returning to the Conference to seek an acceptable treaty, the Chairman said it could have been interpreted either as an ultimatum, setting out inflexible terms which the Conference had to satisfy as the price of United States participation, or as an appeal for understanding, suggesting adjustments to the draft Convention within the parameters of existing packages.

Referring to informal consultations in New York in February which had preceded the opening of the Conference's March/April meetings, he noted that the United States had circulated, on 24 February, a document on approaches to major problems in the sea-bed provisions of the draft Convention. The document had addressed eight problems: decision-making, the review conference, mining access, technology transfer, production limitations and policies, the Enterprise, national liberation movements and "grandfather rights" (for pioneer investors).

After consultations, the Chairman went on, the United States had informally presented a so-called "green book" containing a multiplicity of sweeping amendments. Apart from some industrialized countries, all interest groups, including many Western countries, had expressed the view that the paper could not possibly provide a good basis for negotiations.

The Co-ordinators (the Conference President and the First Committee Chairman) of the Working Group of 21 on sea-bed issues had sought in vain to find some basis for negotiating the United States concerns, the Chairman continued, but the inflexibility in the United States position had provoked inflexibility elsewhere.

In the resulting hiatus, he said, a group of delegation heads from Western developed countries, known as the "group of 11" (Australia, Austria, Canada, Denmark, Finland, Iceland, Ireland, New Zealand, Norway, Sweden, Switzerland) and acting in their personal capacities, had developed proposals to bridge the gap between the United States and other potential Western sea-bed mining countries on the one hand and the Group of 77 developing countries on the other. However, although those proposals had addressed the broad critical aspects of the United States concerns, the United States and four other industrialized countries (France, Federal Republic of Germany, Japan, United Kingdom) could not accept them as a basis for negotiations on the ground that they had not treated all subjects. Moreover, the Group of 77 had rejected the proposals, feeling that the issues raised by the United States but not addressed by the group of 11 were not negotiable. The Chairman believed the proposals offered a prospect of securing agreement and that negotiations based on them would substantially meet the United States concerns, especially bearing in mind proposals by the Co-ordinators of the Working Group of 21 on pioneer investors and the Preparatory Commission.

The first set of changes in the sea-bed provisions resulted from negotiations during the first three weeks of the session. These were made in a memorandum of 2 April[3] in which the President and other collegium members proposed a draft resolution on pioneer investors and a sentence on the membership of land-based mineral-producing countries in the Economic Planning Commission of the Authority's Council.

When the Conference decided in April to receive amendments, the sea-bed proposals of two groups of Western industrialized States—the group of 11[1] and a seven-nation group (Belgium, France, Federal Republic of Germany, Italy, Japan, United Kingdom, United States)[2]—were placed before it in two documents covering a wide range of related issues. A number of other amendments addressed specific aspects of the sea-bed provisions. None of these amendments was pressed to a vote.

When the President reported on 22 April on the results of his negotiations on these amendments,[4] he said he felt able to recommend only three changes that met the criterion of offering a substantially improved prospect of general agreement. They related to general resource development policy, decision-making at a future review conference and guaranteed membership in the Council of the Authority for the largest consumer of sea-bed minerals. He also recommended two other modifications on sea-bed matters: the inclusion of changes proposed by Peru on behalf of the Group of 77 to provide for a compensation fund and a special commission of the Preparatory Commission on the problems of developing country land-based mineral producers, and a revised draft resolution on pioneer investors, based on consultations with various regional groups.

In his final report to the Conference on 29 April,[5] the President disclosed one last set of changes which he said would enhance the prospects of signature and ratification of the Convention by the United States and the other major industrialized countries without hurting the interests of the developing countries or the Eastern European socialist States. These modifications added a paragraph on unfair economic practices in regard to sea-bed exploration and exploitation, inserted sentences requiring the Council to establish rules for the exploitation of sea-bed minerals other than those in nodules when a State requested such action, raised from two thirds to three fourths the majority required for the entry into force of future amendments on sea-bed matters, and redrafted a paragraph to oblige the Authority to approve work plans submitted by sea-bed mining applicants as long as they complied with non-discriminatory requirements. The President proposed one further change in the draft resolution on pioneer investors: to authorize the Enterprise to have two mine sites rather than one during the period before the Convention entered into force.

In proposing these changes, the President said he believed the Conference was willing to pay a price in order to obtain United States support for the Convention, but that price was not an unlimited one. It must not hurt the interests of other countries, including the developing ones.

All of the changes proposed by the President and the collegium were incorporated into the draft Convention before it was adopted on 30 April.

The formal amendments proposed by delegations in April included three pertaining to the articles on principles governing the Area, all of them proposed by the group of seven Western States.

The first of these would have deleted a sentence from the provision on the legal status of the sea-bed and its resources (article 137) stating that minerals recovered from the Area could be alienated only in accordance with the Convention and the Authority's rules; this change would have been complemented by another amendment (to annex III, article 1) providing that title to recovered minerals would pass to the operator. The second amendment would have added a paragraph to the provision on the general conduct of States in relation to the Area (article 138) binding Convention signatories to enforce internationally recognized labour standards on working conditions and maritime safety. The third amendment would have deleted a phrase according to which the interests and needs of peoples not fully in-

dependent or self-governing would be taken into particular consideration; this would have been removed from the provision requiring activities in the Area to be carried out for the benefit of mankind (article 140).

During the Conference debate, developing countries voiced regret at attempts by the United States to introduce radical changes. Pakistan, as Chairman of the Group of 77, stated on 8 March that they would have the effect of scuttling the whole sea-bed régime and sending the negotiations back to the early 1970s; the Group rejected any piecemeal negotiation on issues which had already been agreed to and included in the draft Convention as a package.

The socialist States of Eastern Europe largely shared the views of the developing countries with regard to the changes proposed by the United States. They said it was not too late for the United States and the small group of countries which supported it to give up their destructive attitude, adopt a constructive and realistic approach and join with the overwhelming majority so as to make consensus possible.

Amendments not pressed. [1]Australia, Austria, Canada, Denmark, Finland, Iceland, Ireland, New Zealand, Norway, Sweden, Switzerland, A/CONF.62/L.104 & Add.1; [2]Belgium, France, Germany, Federal Republic of, Italy, Japan, United Kingdom, United States, A/CONF.62/-L.121.
Memorandum. [3]Conference collegium, A/CONF.62/L.93 & Corr.1 (related proposals, A/CONF.62/L.94).
Reports. Conference President, [4]A/CONF.62/L.132 & Corr.1 & Add.1 & Add.1/Corr.1, [5]A/CONF.62/L.141 & Add.1 & Add.1/Corr.1; [6]1st Committee Chairman, A/CONF.62/L.91.
Yearbook reference. [7]1981, p. 132.

Sea-bed mining

Convention provisions. With respect to the development of resources of the sea-bed area beyond national jurisdiction, the Convention laid down several broad objectives for activities in the Area, including: the development and orderly, safe and rational management of resources; expansion and enhancement of opportunities for participation by all States parties, and prevention of monopolization; participation in revenues by the Authority and technology transfer to the Enterprise and developing States; increased availability of sea-bed minerals as needed in conjunction with minerals from other sources; promotion of just and stable prices remunerative to producers and fair to consumers, and promotion of long-term equilibrium between supply and demand; protection of developing countries from adverse economic effects on mineral prices or exports caused by sea-bed activities; development of the common heritage to benefit mankind as a whole; and conditions of access to mineral markets that were no more favourable to sea-bed minerals than to those from other sources (article 150).

A "parallel system" for exploring and exploiting the deep sea-bed was to be established (article 153). Under this system, activities in the Area would be organized, carried out and controlled by the Authority, which would be authorized to conduct its own mining operations through its Enterprise. At the same time, the Authority would contract with States or State enterprises or private ventures to give them mining rights, including security of tenure. The Authority was required to avoid discrimination in the exercise of its powers and functions, though special consideration was permitted for developing States, particularly the land-locked and geographically disadvantaged (article 152).

The whole range of sea-bed activities, as well as other aspects of the system's operation, were to be governed by rules to be established by the Authority in accordance with basic conditions of prospecting, exploration and exploitation set out in the 22 articles of annex III to the Convention.

Prospecting could be conducted only after the Authority received a satisfactory written undertaking that the proposed prospector would comply with the Convention and the Authority's rules; no further authorization would be required (annex III, article 2). Exploration and exploitation, however, would require approval by the Authority of a plan of work, in the form of a contract, conferring on the operator the exclusive right to explore for and exploit specified categories of resources in a specified geographical area (article 3). A contract applicant would have to meet certain financial and technical qualifications and would have to be sponsored by its Government, a State party to the Convention (article 4).

Each application would have to cover an area large enough and of sufficient commercial value to allow two mining operations; the Authority would reserve one of them for its future use and assign the other to the applicant (article 8). The reserved area would then be available to the Enterprise, which could decide whether it intended to carry out activities there, either by itself or in a joint venture with another entity; an area where the Enterprise did not elect to work would be available to an applicant from a developing State (article 9).

Once an applicant was found qualified and a site was assigned, the mining contractor would need two more approvals before it could operate in the international area: a plan of work, authorizing it to develop the minesite (article 6), and a production authorization, permitting it to produce up to a specified quantity of minerals from that site (article 7). The Authority would be required by the Convention to approve plans of work and production authorizations which met the specified requirements—including anti-monopoly provisions designed to prevent any country from obtaining access to an excessive share of the Area—except that there would be a selection system for production authorizations to keep them within an overall production limitation. An operator which had an approved plan of work for exploration would be given preference over other applicants for a plan of work covering exploitation of the same area and resources (article 10).

With respect to the financial terms of contracts, the annex outlined a schedule of payments to the Authority, including a $500,000 fee for approval of a plan of work, a $1 million annual fee payable once the contract entered into force and, once production started, a production charge—actually, a tax scheme—based on a percentage of the market value of the processed metals produced; if the operator chose, it could pay a combination of production charge and a share of net proceeds (article 13).

In addition to the aforementioned obligations, the operator would be required to transfer to the Authority whatever data it needed to exercise its powers and functions in the area covered by the plan of work (article 14), and to transfer technology to the Enterprise.

In return for these contractual obligations, the Authority would accord to the operator the exclusive right to explore and exploit the area covered by the plan of work, and ensure that no other entity operated in the same area for a different category of resources in a manner that might interfere with the contractor's operations (article 16). The operator's rights under the contract could be suspended or terminated, or monetary penalties imposed, only in cases in which its activities had resulted in serious, persistent and wilful violations of the contract's fundamental terms, the Convention or the Authority's rules (article 18). The contractor and the Authority would be responsible or liable for any damage arising out of wrongful acts in the conduct of their operations, liability being for the actual amount of damage (article 22).

Where either party believed that a contract had become inequitable or that its objectives could no longer be achieved because of changed circumstances, the parties would enter into negotiations on its revision (article 19). Rights and obligations under the contract could be transferred only with the Authority's consent (article 20). The applicable law for judging rights and obligations under the contract would be the terms of the contract itself, the Authority's rules, the sea-bed provisions of the Convention and other compatible rules of international law (article 21).

The Convention and annex III also provided for a system of production control, technology transfer from contractors to the Enterprise and developing countries, principles for the operation of the Enterprise and future reviews of the operation of the entire sea-bed mining system. For the period pending entry into force of the Convention, a Conference resolution established a scheme for regulating pioneer investors.

Conference consideration. A number of amendments were offered to these sea-bed mining provisions, though none was pressed to a vote. As noted above, the most extensive were two sets of amendments by Western States: one by seven potential sea-bed mining States—Belgium, France, the Federal Republic of Germany, Italy, Japan, the United Kingdom and the United States[3]—and the other by 11 medium-sized Western industrialized States, introduced by Norway.[1]

With regard to policies relating to activities in the Area (article 150), the group of seven proposed to delete a phrase according to which minerals produced from other sources would be taken into account in supply and pricing policies for the sea-bed.

The group of seven also proposed a new article (150 *bis*) specifying development of the sea-bed resources as an objective by which the Authority must at all times be guided. The group of 11 proposed, as an alternative, the addition of a subparagraph placing development of the resources of the Area at the head of the list of objectives in the article on sea-bed policies. This alternative was incorporated into the Convention on the proposal of the Conference President, in his report of 22 April.[6]

A new paragraph to this article obliging States parties to the Convention to avoid unfair economic practices was proposed by Australia and Canada.[2] Though the amendment was not pressed, a provision on the topic was added to the article on production control.

The seven Western States sought to limit the clause making special provision for developing States (in article 152), by restricting it to clauses in the Convention specifically authorizing such treatment. In the provision defining the parallel system of exploration and exploitation (article 153), they proposed to delete a clause specifying that all sea-bed activities must be carried out in association with the Authority, and to add a clause requiring the Authority to rely in the first instance on measures by States parties to ensure that sea-bed activities carried out by entities which they sponsored complied with the Convention and the Authority's rules.

A number of amendments were proposed to annex III, seeking to change various elements in the basic conditions of prospecting, exploration and exploitation. The first of these, by both groups of Western States (to article 1), would have added a phrase specifying that title to sea-bed minerals would pass to the operator on their recovery from the ocean floor.

After defining "operator" as an entity for which the Authority had approved a plan of work for sea-bed activities, the seven-nation amendments would have limited an applicant's undertakings in the plan of work (article 3) so that it would have to accept only those rules of the Authority which were in force at the time the plan of work was approved and only those decisions directed to the operator. The 11-nation amendments to this article were essentially similar, except for the reference to the Authority's decisions: the applicant would have had to undertake to accept decisions in force at the time the plan of work was approved. Under annex III as approved by the Conference, these undertakings must be made as part of the prospective operator's application rather than at the later stage of contract approval; moreover, they would extend to acceptance of all of the Authority's rules and decisions.

The seven-nation amendments would have written into the annex (article 4) the qualifications required of applicants rather than leaving them to be spelt out in the Authority's rules; to qualify, an applicant would have to have the financial capacity to meet minimum-expenditure rules established by the Authority, to provide a financial guarantee of performance and to certify that no previous contract with the Authority had been terminated by way of penalty. The 11-nation amendments were similar in regard to minimum-expenditure rules and a financial guarantee, but they would also have authorized the Authority to establish additional technical and financial standards. As approved by the Conference, the article provided simply that the qualification standards were to relate to the applicant's financial and technical capabilities and its performance under previous contracts; the actual standards would be set out in the Authority's rules.

Under the seven-nation amendments, a new article (4 *bis*) would have placed on States sponsoring an applicant the responsibility for certifying to the Authority that it was in full compliance with the qualification standards and the Authority's rules. The 11-nation amendments were essentially similar, except that the certification would have been limited to compliance with the qualifications and the Authority's rules relating to such standards.

The seven Western States proposed to replace the provision on approval of plans of work (article 6) with a system offering greater assurances of approval to applicants certified by their States as qualified. This scheme would have called for a presumption that applicants certified by States had met the requirements unless the Council's Legal and Technical Commission decided otherwise by a three-fourths vote. The 11-nation amendments contained an essentially similar proposal, but without a 120-day time-limit for action by the Commission as proposed by the seven.

Although these amendments were not pressed, the Conference approved a change to this article proposed by the President on 29 April[7] which omitted a clause in the earlier text providing for an investigation by the Authority into whether the plans of work complied with the Convention and the Authority's rules. This was the only change to annex III approved by the Conference in 1982. As adopted, the article on approval of plans of work obliged the Authority to approve such plans provided that they met the uniform and non-discriminatory requirements of the Authority's rules, unless they covered areas overlapping with others on which action was pending or were in certain environmentally protected areas or violated the anti-monopoly provisions.

France and the USSR each proposed an amendment to the paragraph in this article intended to prevent monopolization of the sea-bed by individual States or their companies. France would have made the clause applicable to all sea-bed areas, including those reserved for the Enterprise and developing States, instead of only to non-reserved sites.[4] The USSR would have limited the maximum sea-bed area that could be allotted to any one State or its nationals to 1 per cent rather than 2 per cent of the total sea-bed area available for exploitation by States and private entities.[5]

The seven Western States proposed to revise the system for determining which of two mine sites in each sea-bed area would be exploited by an applicant for a mining contract and which would be reserved for the Authority (article 8). Under their amendments, the choice would be made by agreement between the applicant and the Enterprise or, failing that, by random allocation by the Legal and Technical Commission; after the contract was signed, the operator would submit all the data it had on the reserved site. As approved by the Conference, the applicant would turn over such data in advance, after which the Authority would designate the area it wanted to reserve.

With regard to activities in areas reserved for exploitation by the Authority or developing States (article 9), the seven Western States proposed an arrangement according to which areas remaining unexploited for 10 years would be made available to other entities, first through a joint venture with a developing State or States, then to the entity which had originally applied for the area that included the site in question, and finally to any other qualified entity.

The seven Western States proposed to add a subparagraph by which exploration for and exploitation of sea-bed resources other than polymetallic nodules would have been added to the list of matters to be covered by the Authority's future rules (article 17), and to limit the matters covered by the rules to those listed in this article, eliminating the phrase "*inter alia*" from the text. Although these amendments were not pressed, the Conference accepted an amendment (to article 162 of the Convention on the powers and functions of the Council) requiring the Council to adopt such rules within three years after any member of the Authority requested it to do so.

Explaining on 30 June its vote against the Convention, the United States presented five objections, all relating to the sea-bed: the sea-bed provisions would deter the development of deep-sea mineral resources by denying the play of basic market forces; access by existing miners to those resources was not assured, while the Enterprise would benefit from a system of privileges that would discriminate against private and national miners; the decision-making process for the sea-bed régime did not give a proportionate voice to the countries most affected by the decisions and would thus not effectively reflect and protect their interests; the Convention would allow amendments to come into force for a State without its consent, which was incompatible with United States treaty processes; and the provisions on mandatory technology transfer, potential distribution of benefits to national liberation movements and production limitation created inappropriate precedents. Repeating these objections in the General Assembly on 3 December, the United States added that it continued to enjoy the right to carry out deep sea-bed mining, which it called a lawful use of the high seas.

Explaining its non-participation in the vote on the Convention, Albania said the sea-bed provisions would allow the two super-Powers and a small group of capitalist industrial States, together with a handful of transnational corporations, to monopolize sea-bed resources to the detriment of mankind as a whole.

Among the States which abstained in the vote, Belgium said the proposed sea-bed régime might discourage investments for exploitation in the interests of both developing and industrialized countries; it also failed to meet Belgium's concerns for equitable representation on the organs of the Authority, for a decision-making process that took account of the interests of all groups of States, for a review procedure which did not call into question the basis of the system established by the Convention, and for realistic provisions on technology transfer. The Federal Republic of Germany, which also abstained, said it was particularly disappointed at the treatment accorded to the sea-bed proposals submitted by the major Western industrialized States. Italy said it had had to abstain because the Conference had not agreed to its request to continue negotiations on the sea-bed provisions. The Netherlands said that, without the participation of major countries, the elaborate system for exploitation of sea-bed resources would not function as envisaged; it would have preferred to continue the search for generally acceptable solutions.

France, which voted for the Convention, said the sea-bed provisions had serious drawbacks which it hoped would be reviewed in order to reach wider agreement and to give the Authority real prospects of success. The Libyan Arab Jamahiriya rejected the idea that a small group of States should enjoy special benefits in regard to the sea-bed and opposed any parallel system for the area. Romania considered it essential that implementation of the sea-bed provisions and the resolution on pioneer investors should not impair the common heritage and should ensure its exploitation for the benefit of all countries.

Austria, addressing the Conference in December, said the Convention provided a unique opportunity to create new forms of scientific-industrial co-operation between North and South, but if not applied in the foreseeable future it would run the risk of being overtaken by scientific and technological changes. Canada stated that the Convention provided a mechanism for the management of sea-bed resources without infringing State interests. Cape Verde thought the interests of all countries in the exploitation of these resources had been properly accommodated. Czechoslovakia said the Convention offered the less developed countries the hope of obtaining a just share of the riches of the sea-bed through membership in a new international organization. Finland believed that the sea-bed régime represented the best possible balance that could be achieved.

The Ivory Coast said the aim of the new régime was to banish the idea of the sea as an area of conflict and as private property for the exclusive profit of some maritime Powers, and open the way to the concept of sharing and developing the sea for the benefit of all. Mongolia stressed the importance of the anti-monopoly and anti-discrimination provisions. Morocco believed that, in translating this new legal régime into concrete terms, the Conference had reached the greatest possible degree of consensus without sacrificing the greatest benefit for the largest number and without compromising any acquired right. Nigeria thought the developed States ought to be pleased to see the developing States have a chance to move away from poverty by sharing in the management and wealth of the sea's resources.

The Republic of Korea said its policy was to encourage its private companies to participate in deep sea-bed mining and a modest number of them were preparing to participate actively. Under the Convention, said Tunisia, developing countries had the same right to profits from the sea-bed as developed countries with the money and technology to exploit those resources.

Algeria stated that the developing countries had gone far to meet the position of their negotiating partners with regard to the sea-bed, granting advantages to developed States that were far removed from the principles and objectives of the new international economic order. Similarly, Brazil described the sea-bed provisions as a complex of concessions made by the great majority of nations to the few that aspired to reap greater and more immediate benefits. The Bahamas thought that, in accepting those provisions as a compromise, the developing countries had barred ideological differences and concentrated on obtaining the best possible formula, which should have been acceptable to all. Iraq would have preferred a régime immune from exploitation by monopolies belonging to a handful of States. Mauritius and Yugoslavia shared the position of the Group of 77 that the sea-bed provisions represented the upper limit of concessions; to go further would render the common heritage principle meaningless.

Pakistan thought the Convention did not adequately reflect the concept of the sea-bed as a common heritage; it believed that a few industrialized countries would be the major beneficiaries. Trinidad and Tobago said it would have preferred a unitary system of exploitation rather than the parallel system provided for in the Convention, for it believed that only one limb of the parallel system, the private entity, would work. Also expressing preference for a system in which all sea-bed activities would be undertaken jointly by all States, the United Republic of Tanzania said that, under the Convention, private companies would have almost automatic access to the sea-bed, while the ability of the Enterprise to explore and exploit would be hindered by loopholes that would impede its access to capital and technology.

Several industrialized States reiterated their concern about the workability of the sea-bed régime to be established under the Convention. Belgium believed that the spirit of compromise seen in other parts of the Convention had not been maintained to the same degree with respect to the sea-bed provisions, which Belgium would have to study more closely. The Federal Republic of Germany, recalling its past criticism of the sea-bed régime, said it was especially concerned over the provisions on technology transfer, production limitation and the review conference, as well as over financial burdens resulting from the system.

Italy believed that the proposed new institutions, by their number and complexity, would be able only with great difficulty to ensure a viable system; the establishment of organs which might not guarantee profitable exploitation could become a heavy burden for the international community, including the developing countries. The United Kingdom said the sea-bed provisions, including technology transfer, were unacceptable and it wished to explore prospects for significantly improving them.

Several States viewed the Preparatory Commission's task of writing sea-bed mining rules as affording an opportunity to remedy what they or others regarded as defects in the Convention. Denmark said the future mining code must ensure that decisions would be based on objective rules and on fairness, equity and normal business practices, taking account of the interests of those that had already signed the Convention and of those that might do so later. France said some of the sea-bed provisions, such as those on mandatory technology transfer and the financing of the Authority, had serious defects which had to be corrected by the rules to be worked out by the Preparatory Commission.

Ireland believed that any shortcomings in the scheme could be met in the short term by adaptation and ultimately be remedied by the review conference. The Netherlands said it would continue efforts to implement the sea-bed provisions during the preparatory stage in such a way as to remove objections by the industrialized States which made it uncertain that the new régime would function effectively enough to enable companies to operate in the Area.

The Ukrainian SSR said it regretted the refusal of the United States to uphold agreements about the sea-bed which had been reached with its active participation.

Australia said it had long been acknowledged that the doctrine of freedom of the high seas did not provide a basis for the grant of exclusive title to mine the deep sea-bed; any attempt to exploit those resources outside the Convention would be highly divisive and the country concerned would incur the hostility of the bulk of the world. Bahrain, Brazil, Bulgaria, Chile, the Democratic People's Republic of Korea, Democratic Yemen, the German Democratic Republic, Indonesia, Iraq, Lesotho, Mauritius, Papua New Guinea, Romania, Tunisia and Yugoslavia also expressed the view that exploration and exploitation of deep sea-bed resources could legally be undertaken only under the régime established by the Convention.

For States to opt out of the Convention and pursue bilateral arrangements would be to affect the integrity of the new régime, said Barbados, and that could threaten international order, peace and security.

Amendments not pressed. [1]Australia, Austria, Canada, Denmark, Finland, Iceland, Ireland, New Zealand, Norway, Sweden, Switzerland, A/CONF.62/L.104 & Add.1; [2]Australia, Canada, A/CONF.62/L.98; [3]Belgium, France, Germany, Federal Republic of, Italy, Japan, United Kingdom, United States, A/CONF.62/L.121; [4]France, A/CONF.62/L.106; [5]USSR, A/CONF.62/L.124.
Reports. Conference President, [6]A/CONF.62/L.132 & Corr.1 & Add.1 & Add.1/Corr.1; [7]A/CONF.62/L.141/Add.1.

Production control

The Convention on the Law of the Sea set out a sea-bed production policy whose basic aim would be to encourage sea-bed production at prices remunerative to producers and fair to consumers, with the least possible harm to land-based producers of the same minerals (article 151). This policy would be enforced through the issuance by the Authority of production authorizations to approved sea-bed operators, specifying an annual production rate for each. An annual sea-bed production ceiling would be fixed, based on the trend of nickel consumption, calculated in such a way as to allow sea-bed producers a share of any increase in such consumption and leaving the rest to land-based producers. Under the pioneer investors' scheme provided for in Conference resolution II, such investors would have certain guarantees in regard to production authorizations.

To the extent that economic hardship for land-based producers could not be avoided, a compensation scheme would be set up for their benefit. Initial steps in respect of this scheme would be taken by the Preparatory Commission for the International Sea-Bed Authority and for the International Tribunal for the Law of the Sea, which would establish a special commission on the subject.[14] Once the Authority became operational, its Assembly would be empowered to establish, on the recommendation of the Council based on advice from its Economic Planning Commission, a compensation system or other economic adjustment assistance measures (article 160).

The Authority would be obliged to issue production authorizations if all of those applied for could be approved without exceeding the overall production limitation or contravening the Authority's obligations under a commodity agreement (annex III, article 7). If a selection had to be made among applicants in order to remain within the overall limit, the Authority would apply objective and non-discriminatory standards to be specified in its rules, giving priority to applicants which provided better assurance of performance or earlier financial benefits, had already invested the most or had not been selected in earlier periods.

The likely effects of the production control system on land-based producers were the subject of extensive discussion during 1982, as in previous years, in the Conference on the Law of the Sea. As requested by the Conference's First Committee in August 1981,[15] the Secretary-General presented in March 1982 a report on the possible impact of the Convention, with special reference to production policies, on developing countries which produced and exported minerals of the kind to be extracted from the sea-bed.[13] The report contained no quantitative conclusions, in view of the fact that the Committee had not given any specific guidance on the assumptions to be used for economic projections. Rather, it outlined a plan for further investigations which could take the form of a full-scale study. Annexes to the report outlined the existing production patterns of the four major sea-bed minerals—copper, nickel, cobalt and manganese—and described the role of the mineral industries in three countries deemed most likely to be affected—Gabon, Zaire and Zambia.

As requested by Zambia and endorsed by the Committee on 9 March, the Secretary-General submitted an addendum to the report showing possible production ceiling tonnages under certain assumptions about land-based production, market growth rates and start-up time for sea-bed production.

To meet some of the concerns of the land-based producers, the First Committee Chairman, in his 29 March report to the Conference[12], made two proposals: to give the Preparatory Commission the power to undertake studies on those concerns, and to approve a proposal by the Group of 77 that would guarantee membership of at least two representatives of developing land-based producer countries in the Economic Planning Commission of the Authority's Council. The first of these proposals was incorporated in revised draft resolution I, on the Preparatory Commission, submitted by the Conference collegium on 2 April.[8] The second was included in the collegium's memorandum of the same date on changes in the draft Convention, where it was revised to state that the Economic Planning Commission's membership would include at least two members from developing countries whose exports of the types of minerals found on the sea-bed had a substantial bearing on their economies.[9]

When presenting his proposals on 2 April, the First Committee Chairman indicated that Gabon, Zaire, Zambia and Zimbabwe had not considered them sufficient. They would have been happier with a provision to have the Authority set up a compensation fund on the recommendation of the Preparatory Commission.

In line with this idea, Peru, on behalf of the Group of 77, submitted two formal amendments: to add to the list of the Authority's funds (article 171) a mention of the compensation fund, whose sources would be recommended by the Economic Planning Commission, and to require the Preparatory Commission to establish a special commission on the problems of developing land-based producers likely to be seriously affected by sea-bed production.[5] These proposals were incorporated in the draft Convention and in draft resolution I, respectively, after the President announced, in his 22 April report, that he had determined in consultations that the amendments had widespread support.[10]

Gabon proposed but did not press amendments that would have included among the functions of the Authority's Assembly the establishment of a compensation fund for the exclusive benefit of land-based producers whose export receipts or economies would be affected by sea-bed exploitation (article 160), and would have guaranteed seats for two such States on the Council's Legal and Technical Commission (article 165).[4] Also not pressed was an amendment by Zaire that would have authorized the Authority to limit the production of sea-bed copper, cobalt and manganese to amounts less than the maximum that could be produced under the limits applying to nickel.[7]

Two further changes in the production control article were introduced into the Convention at the instance of the President in his final report of 29 April.[11] First, a paragraph was added stating that rights and obligations relating to unfair economic practices under multilateral trade agreements would apply to sea-bed exploration and exploitation, and that parties to such agreements could have recourse to the dispute settlement procedures contained therein. In this connection, Australia and Canada did not press an amendment (to article 150, on policies relating to activities in the Area) that would have applied the prohibition of unfair economic practices to all parties to the Convention by obliging them, in the production, processing, transport and marketing of sea-bed minerals and commodities derived therefrom, to avoid unfair economic practices which caused, or threatened to cause, material injury to the interests of another State party.[1] The second change in the Convention authorized the Authority to adopt regulations limiting the production of sea-bed minerals other than those from nodules.

Proposed changes relating to production control were included in the package of sea-bed amendments submitted by five Western European States, Japan and the United States.[2] They would have: limited the Authority's participation in commodity agreements to the production of the Enterprise rather than to all sea-bed production; added a sentence giving sea-bed production a gradually increasing share of the world nickel market, rising from 60 per cent of the annual increase in world nickel consumption (the limit in the Convention) to a maximum of 80 per cent; deleted a reference to a compensation scheme for land-based producers; and added a paragraph to ensure that all pioneer sea-bed investors would receive authorization to produce minerals even if this created a temporary excess over the allowable ceiling in a given year or years.

With regard to the approval of production authorizations (annex III, article 7), the seven Western States proposed to spell out in greater detail the entitlements of the authorized operators. Under their scheme, the Authority would have been required to issue authorizations in the order of application, the operator would have been able to commence production at any time within five years after approval, the period could be extended by the Authority if production was delayed for reasons beyond the operator's control, and once mining began at that site the operator would have been entitled to engage in commercial production according to its stated requirements.

France and the USSR did not press amendments that would have given priority for a production authorization to a State or its nationals which did not have any over a State which already had one (USSR[6]) or two or more (France[3]).

Zambia, though voting for the Convention, observed on 30 April that its past proposals to mitigate the adverse effects of sea-bed mining on its economy had not been approved and that the establishment of the compensation fund it had proposed had been postponed; Zambia hoped the weak provision for that much-needed fund would none the less result in its establishment.

In December, Indonesia, expressing concern at prospects of competition between sea-bed minerals and those produced in developing countries, said it was essential that the Authority regulate the development of sea-bed resources. Gabon and Papua New Guinea, other mineral exporters, voiced a similar concern about the production control features.

Sierra Leone envisaged a situation in which several African mineral-producing States would find themselves competing with sea-bed mines and might even go out of business, while the industrialized countries became self-sufficient in such resources. Zaire regarded the production control mechanism as one of the Convention's flagrant weaknesses, one which would result in the eviction of land-based mineral producers from the market; it hoped the Authority would close the gap between that mechanism and the principle of equity expressed in the Convention (article 150), that developing countries should be protected from the adverse effects resulting from a reduction of price or volume of a mineral export.

The Republic of Korea, voicing the interests of a mineral-consuming country, stressed the importance of secure supplies at a reasonable price.

Amendments not pressed. [1]Australia, Canada, A/CONF.62/L.98; [2]Belgium, France, Germany, Federal Republic of, Italy, Japan, United Kingdom, United States, A/CONF.62/L.121; [3]France, A/CONF.62/L.106; [4]Gabon, A/CONF.62/L.97 & Corr.1; [5]Peru, for Group of 77, A/CONF.62/L.116; [6]USSR, A/CONF.62/L.124; [7]Zaire, A/CONF.62/L.107.
Draft resolution. [8]Conference collegium, A/CONF.62/L.94.
Memorandum. [9]Conference collegium, A/CONF.62/L.93.
Reports. Conference President, [10]A/CONF.62/L.132 & Add.1, [11]A/CONF.62/L.141/Add.1; [12]1st Committee Chairman, A/CONF.62/L.91; [13]S-G, A/CONF.62/L.84 & Add.1.
Resolution (1982). [14]Conference (Final Act, A/CONF.62/121 & Corr.3): I, paras. 5 (i) & 9, 30 Apr.
Yearbook reference. [15]1981, p. 132.

Technology transfer

The Convention on the Law of the Sea contained general rules empowering the Authority to acquire for the Enterprise technology and scientific knowledge relating to sea-bed activities and to promote and encourage their transfer to developing States (article 144). Specific provisions were laid down in annex III (article 5), obliging contractors to make available to the Enterprise, on commercial terms, the technology they employed in their sea-bed mining ventures. That obligation extended to technology owned by the contractor or which he was otherwise entitled to transfer to others, as well as to so-called "third-party" technology; in the latter instance, the contractor would be obliged to acquire from the owner the right to transfer the technology to the Enterprise if that could be done without substantial cost. Disputes over these undertakings would be subject to compulsory settlement. If the Enterprise was unable to obtain the technology it needed, a group of States parties with access to such technology would be convened to take measures to ensure that it was made available to the Enterprise on fair and reasonable terms and conditions.

In order to ensure that the Enterprise was able to operate in the Area before the Convention entered into force in such a manner as to keep pace with States and other entities, Conference resolution II established the same technology transfer obligations for every registered pioneer investor.[7]

In addition, the part of the Convention concerned with marine technology development and transfer contained a set of objectives to be followed by the Authority in helping developing States to obtain such technology.

Responding to United States concerns in this sphere, the First Committee Chairman, in his report of 29 March summing up the results of the Committee's work in 1982, suggested three changes in the technology transfer provisions: a new clause requiring a contractor to undertake a general obligation to co-operate with the Authority in its efforts to acquire technology on fair and reasonable terms and conditions; adjustments to make the technology transfer obligations less stringent by including an element of consent; and a revision to make more precise the obligations of all States, especially States sponsoring sea-bed ventures, with regard to ensuring the commercial viability of the Enterprise.[6]

The Conference did not approve either of two similar sets of changes, aimed at limiting the obligations of contractors to transfer technology and removing most of the mandatory features, proposed separately by five Western European States together with Japan and the United States,[2] and by 11 medium-sized industrialized Western States (known as the group of 11).[1]

Both sets of amendments would have limited the transfer obligation to technology which the contractor had made available or was willing to make available to third parties. They would have eliminated clauses providing that the contractor could use a particular technology only if he obtained written assurance from the owner that he could make it available to the Authority, and that, when a contractor exercised effective control over the owner of technology, his failure to acquire the right to transfer that technology would be taken into account whenever he applied for any subsequent plan of work. The contractor's obligation to help the Enterprise acquire technology on the open market, not spelt out in the Convention, would have been limited to identifying possible sources and advising on how to obtain the best terms and conditions. References to penalties would have been removed from the paragraph on dispute settlement.

Both sets of amendments would also have removed the provision for convening a meeting of States to ensure that the Enterprise could obtain technology on fair and reasonable terms. They would have replaced it with a clause requiring States parties to take effective measures to ensure that the provisions on contractors' obligations were brought into effect and to take measures consistent with national law to prevent persons under their jurisdiction from engaging in a concerted refusal to supply technology to the Enterprise on commercial terms and conditions. The seven-nation amendments would have added a sentence requiring the Authority to rely on States to enforce the technology transfer obligations.

Norway, which described the technology transfer provisions as crucial for obtaining a universal convention, explained in introducing the amendments of the group of 11 that, while they sought to reduce the burden of a mandatory transfer, the mandatory feature would still apply whenever the owner of technology placed it on the open market; moreover, the contractor would still be under an obligation to secure for the Enterprise technology he did not own, but only if he could do so without substantial cost.

In the Conference's debate on amendments, these proposals were opposed by Sierra Leone (on behalf of the African Group), Trinidad and Tobago, and the United Republic of Tanzania on the ground that they removed the mandatory aspect of technology transfer, thereby eroding the guarantees essential to the Enterprise.

In the only formal amendment to the technology transfer clause of resolution II, Peru, on behalf of the Group of 77, proposed[3] that the Conference collegium's version of 2 April,[4] which had provided that pioneer investors should "be prepared" to perform their transfer obligations prior to the entry into force of the Convention, should be changed to require them to "perform" those obligations. As redrafted by the President on 22 April[5] and approved by the Conference, pioneer investors must "undertake" to perform those obligations.

Japan, Switzerland and the United States expressed misgivings about the technology transfer provisions when explaining their votes on the Convention on 30 April. Japan said it was greatly disappointed that the provisions on mandatory transfer of technology owned by a third party had not been improved. Switzerland said the provisions could not be considered a precedent in the ongoing negotiations on the subject in other bodies.

Canada, addressing the Conference in December, said the temporary and unique nature of the technology transfer provisions could not make them precedents for other international negotiations. The Netherlands said those provisions were subject to objections.

The United Republic of Cameroon stressed the importance of training nationals of developing countries in mineral exploitation of the deep sea-bed so that the Authority's technicians would not be drawn almost exclusively from industrialized countries.

Amendments not pressed. [1]Australia, Austria, Canada, Denmark, Finland, Iceland, Ireland, New Zealand, Norway, Sweden, Switzerland, A/CONF.62/L.104 & Add.1; [2]Belgium, France, Germany, Federal Republic of, Italy, Japan, United Kingdom, United States, A/CONF.62/- L.121; [3]Peru, for Group of 77, A/CONF.62/- L.116.
Draft resolution. [4]Conference collegium, A/CONF.62/L.94.
Reports. [5]Conference President, A/CONF.62/L.132 & Corr.1 & Add.1 & Add.1/Corr.1; [6]1st Committee Chairman, A/CONF.62/L.91.
Resolution (1982). [7]Conference (Final Act, A/CONF.62/121): II, para. 12 *(a)* (iii), 30 Apr.

Review

The Convention on the Law of the Sea provided for a review of the operation of the sea-bed mining system every five years by the Assembly of the Authority (article 154) and 15 years after the start of commercial production by a Review Conference (article 155). The Review Conference would consider whether the system had achieved its aims, reserved areas had been effectively exploited, sea-bed development had fostered a healthy world economy and balanced growth of international trade, monopolization had been prevented, the production policies had been fulfilled and benefits had been equitably shared. It could, by a three-fourths majority vote, introduce amendments to the system that would take effect for all parties after ratification or accession by three fourths of them. Prior to the Review Conference, amendments not prejudicing the exploitation system could be made with the approval of both the Council and the Assembly, subject to the same ratification procedure.

In April 1982, the two groups of Western States proposed amendments to have the Review Conference take its decisions according to the rules used by the Conference on the Law of the Sea, avoiding voting until all efforts at consensus had been exhausted. Moreover, under the proposals by five Western European States, Japan and the United States,[2] amendments to the Convention approved by the Review Conference would not take effect until all States parties had adhered, following which sea-bed activities would be governed by the Convention as amended. Under the proposals by the group of 11,[1] introduced by Norway, adherence by two thirds of the States parties would suffice to bring the amendments into force but, while sea-bed activities would thereafter be governed by the amended Convention, a State which had not ratified the amendments would continue to enjoy the rights and perform the obligations of the Convention's other provisions.

Although these two sets of amendments were not pressed by their sponsors, the final text of the Convention incorporated, at the President's suggestion, provisions to have the Review Conference follow the procedure of avoiding voting until all efforts at achieving consensus had been exhausted[3] and to require a three-fourths majority, instead of the two-thirds majority specified in the 1981 draft Convention, for adoption of amendments by the Conference and for their entry into force.[4]

The United States, when explaining in April its objections to the sea-bed provisions, said with respect to the review and amendment procedure that the clause allowing amendments to come into force for a State without its consent was clearly incompatible with United States processes for incurring treaty obligations.

Welcoming the provisions for review, Kenya said in December that future technological advances and other economic and social changes might require taking another look at the sea-bed provisions to see whether they had worked satisfactorily and to initiate adjustments.

Amendments not pressed. [1]Australia, Austria, Canada, Denmark, Finland, Iceland, Ireland, New Zealand, Norway, Sweden, Switzerland, A/CONF.62/L.104 & Add.1; [2]Belgium, France, Germany, Federal Republic of, Italy, Japan, United Kingdom, United States, A/CONF.62/L.121.
Reports. Conference President, [3]A/CONF.62/L.132/Add.1, [4]A/CONF.62/L.141/Add.1.

Pioneer investors

The scheme devised by the Conference on the Law of the Sea to protect investments made by States and private consortia before the Convention entered into force was set out in resolution II,[16] adopted along with the Convention. In addition, under resolution I, the Preparatory Commission for the International Sea-Bed Authority and for the International Tribunal for the Law of the Sea was to exercise powers and functions in relation to those investments.[15]

The scheme would enable States and private investors to qualify for registration by the Commission as pioneer investors. This would entitle them to explore—but not commercially exploit—a selected area of the sea-bed beyond national jurisdiction until the Convention entered into force. It would also guarantee them priority over all others—except for the Authority's Enterprise—once the Authority permitted commercial production from the sea-bed.

Pioneer investors were defined by the resolution, which placed them in three groups: (1) France, India, Japan and the USSR, and their State enterprises and corporations; (2) four entities made up of firms having the nationality of or controlled by Belgium, Canada, the Federal Republic of Germany, Italy, Japan, the Netherlands, the United Kingdom or the United States, or any combination of those States; and (3) any developing State or group of such States, or any State enterprise or corporation from such State. To qualify for pioneer status, the State concerned must have signed the Convention and the applicant would have had to have spent at least $30 million on sea-bed activities by 1 January 1983 (1 January 1985 in the case of the developing States other than India), not less than 10 per cent of which must have been spent on investigation of a specific portion of the sea-bed.

Pioneer investors would be confined during the pre-Convention period to exploration and prospecting for polymetallic nodules in an allocated area; commercial exploitation would be excluded before the Convention entered into force. Each applicant would receive only one site, not to exceed 150,000 square kilometres. The resolution specified that nothing in it derogated from the anti-monopoly provisions of the Convention.

In order to obtain pioneer investor status, the prospective pioneer, certified by a signatory State, would have to apply to the Preparatory Commission for registration. Certifying States would have to ensure, before applications were submitted, that claims for particular areas did not overlap.

Sites would be allocated in a manner similar to that provided for in the Convention: The applicant would have to present an area large enough for two commercial mining operations, whereupon the Commission would allocate one part to the pioneer investor and reserve a commercially equivalent part for development by the Enterprise. Within the area allocated to it, the pioneer investor would have exclusive exploration rights. However, it would have to relinquish progressively half of the pioneer area over an eight-year period, freeing those portions for future allocation.

Each pioneer investor would pay to the Commission a $250,000 registration fee, plus another $250,000 to the Authority—instead of the $500,000 provided for in the Convention—when it applied for a plan of work (mining contract). There would be an additional fee of $1 million a year from the time the pioneer area was allocated, payable to the Authority when the investor's plan of work was approved. Investors would have to spend a minimum amount on their site, as determined by the Commission in relation to the size of the area and the expenditures expected of an operator that intended to mine the site commercially within a reasonable time.

Pioneer investors would be guaranteed entry into sea-bed mining under the Convention once it entered into force. This would be accomplished by a provision requiring the Authority to approve their contract application as long as they met the requirements applicable to all, but only if their certifying State was a party to the Convention. In addition to a contract, they would be entitled to a production authorization permitting them to produce from at least one mine site each, while the Enterprise would be guaranteed production authorizations for two sites.

The resolution spelt out three commitments which pioneer investors would have to undertake in order to ensure that the Enterprise was able to carry out sea-bed activities in such a manner as to keep pace with States and other entities: at the Commission's request, to explore the area reserved for the Enterprise, for which their costs would be reimbursed; to provide training for personnel designated by the Commission; and to undertake to perform the technology transfer obligations prescribed in the Convention. To the same purpose, every certifying State would en-

sure that the necessary funds were available to the Enterprise once the Convention entered into force and would report to the Commission on its sea-bed activities and those carried out by entities under its jurisdiction.

Resolution II was initially negotiated in the First Committee's Working Group of 21 during the first three weeks of the March/April 1982 session. Its Co-ordinators—the Conference President and the First Committee Chairman—reported to the Committee on 29 March on the results of the negotiations and presented the first formal draft of the resolution.[14]

Explaining some of the rationale of the scheme, the Co-ordinators noted that six consortia and one State had been investing in the development of sea-bed mining technology and equipment, and the industrialized countries concerned had been demanding that the Conference and the Convention recognize those preparatory investments. The Co-ordinators felt that to be a legitimate request provided that those investments were brought within the framework of the Convention and that the interim arrangement was transitory.

The First Committee Chairman, in his 29 March report to the Conference, commended the draft resolution as providing a sufficient basis for widespread support and possible consensus.[13]

Following debate in the Conference on all aspects of the Convention and associated documents, the Conference collegium, in its memorandum of 2 April[9] and related texts,[7] decided to incorporate this draft resolution, with a few changes, into the draft Final Act. There were two main changes: the paragraph on the relationship between the pioneer investor scheme and the Authority, which originally would simply have required the Authority and its organs to be governed by the terms of the resolution, was revised to provide that the Authority and its organs must act in accordance with the resolution and the Preparatory Commission decisions taken pursuant to it; and a paragraph which would have terminated the scheme after five years was replaced by one which kept it in effect until the Convention entered into force. In addition, the collegium added a paragraph to the Convention (article 308) requiring the Authority to act in accordance with the resolution and with Commission decisions pursuant to it.

When the Conference decided to receive formal amendments, six proposals or sets of proposals were submitted relating to resolution II. After the Conference heard delegations' views on these amendments, the President and the First Committee Chairman consulted with their sponsors and with all regional groups. On the basis of those consultations, the President, in his report of 22 April,[11] presented an extensively revised draft which he considered to enjoy widespread and substantial support and to offer a substantially improved prospect of achieving general agreement. All of the President's changes, as well as one more made on 29 April, were later incorporated in the final text. Following is a summary of the amendments, their relation to the collegium's draft of 2 April and the subsequent changes introduced by the President on 22 April.

The President's text revised the definition of "pioneer investor" by limiting such investors to eight nationalities—France, India, Japan and the USSR in the first group, and four entities from seven Western States and Japan (see above) in a second group—plus an unspecified number from developing States.

Four of the amendments related to the qualifying criteria for pioneer investors. With regard to the minimum figure for prior investments, the collegium's text specified $30 million but would have allowed the Preparatory Commission to set a lower amount for developing States. Gabon[3] and Japan[4] proposed that the $30-million figure be applied to all investors. Gabon also proposed to remove the requirement that pioneers spend no less than 10 per cent of their total sea-bed investment on a specific site. The President's text retained the $30-million minimum for all investors and the 10 per cent requirement for a specific site.

Under the collegium's text the $30-million expenditure would have had to have been made by 1 January 1983 for any investor to qualify as a pioneer. Japan and Peru—the latter on behalf of the Group of 77[5]—proposed that investors in developing States be given up to 1 January 1985 to qualify, whereas France[2] proposed 1 January 1982 for all investors. The President adopted the formula proposed by Japan and Peru.

France proposed a sentence to prevent a component of a group qualifying as a pioneer investor to claim that status for itself. To similar effect, Japan would have prohibited pioneer investors from dividing into two or more entities in the eight months prior to 1 January 1983—the proposed cut-off date for pioneer status. The President's text did not deal with this issue except to add a sentence stating that the rights of a pioneer investor could devolve upon its successor.

Gabon proposed to extend the definition of "pioneer activities" to cover exploration for all sea-bed resources, not just polymetallic nodules. The definition in the President's text was unchanged.

Japan would have limited to 60,000 square kilometres rather than 150,000 the exploratory area allotted to each pioneer. Peru also proposed 60,000 square kilometres but sought to add a clause enabling the Preparatory Commission to fix another size. Gabon proposed to delete any reference to the size of the area. The President's

text retained the 150,000–square kilometre area but added a provision requiring the pioneer to relinquish half of the area in stages over eight years.

In regard to the application and allocation procedure, Belgium, the Federal Republic of Germany, Italy, the United Kingdom and the United States[1] proposed to add clauses requiring that information on mine sites and nodules submitted by applicants for pioneer status be kept confidential. Also, the part of each sea-bed area reserved for future exploitation by the Enterprise would be chosen by random selection. The President added a confidentiality-of-data clause as well as a provision requiring the Preparatory Commission to make within 45 days its allocation of areas between the applicant and the reserved area, without the possibility of deferral by a further 45 days permitted in the earlier draft.

A Peruvian amendment would have required applicants to submit details of the amounts they had invested in sea-bed activities, for the Commission's verification. No such provision was included in the President's text.

To a clause in the earlier draft stating that no investor could have more than one area, the President added a phrase to the effect that none of the components of a consortium could apply for a site in its own right or in association with a developing country.

The five Western States sought to add to the resolution a procedure for resolving conflicting claims before applications were made to the Commission. Conflicts that could not be resolved voluntarily by the claimants would be submitted to binding arbitration, with the outcome to be based on such factors as when the claimants had first presented their claims to their own Governments, how extensively they had worked in the disputed area, when they had begun working there and how much they had spent. They also proposed to allow commercial production after 1 January 1988 if the Convention had not entered into force by then. The President's text added a conflict resolution procedure substantially similar to that proposed by the Western States.

Referring to the $500,000 registration fee in the collegium's draft, the five Western States proposed that if the application cost less to process the Commission would refund the difference. Peru, on the other hand, would have required each pioneer investor to pay the Commission an annual fixed fee of $1 million in addition to the registration fee. The President's text provided for a $250,000 registration fee for the Commission plus $250,000 to the Authority when the pioneer applied for a plan of work. A $1-million annual fee was added, but it was to be payable to the Authority when the investor's plan of work was approved.

Peru would also have required each pioneer to spend not less than $10 million a year on its allotted sea-bed area, rather than the $1-million minimum in the collegium's text. The five Western States proposed that the minimum be reduced to $500,000. The President's text said that the minimum expenditure would be determined by the Commission in relation to the size of the area and the expenditures expected of an operator that intended to mine the site commercially within a reasonable time.

Under the President's text, pioneer investors would have up to six months from the time the Convention entered into force to apply to the Authority for approval of a plan of work; the collegium's draft had had no time-limit. The President's text added that the plan must comply with and be governed by the Convention as well as the Authority's rules, including operational and financial requirements and undertakings regarding technology transfer. With regard to the second group of investors—from Japan and countries of North America and Western Europe other than France—the draft added the requirement that all the States whose firms comprised the pioneer investor must have ratified the Convention before it could receive a contract from the Authority.

To a paragraph in the collegium's draft giving pioneer investors priority over all others except the Enterprise in obtaining production authorizations from the Authority, Peru proposed to specify that such authorization be granted in the order in which applicants applied for it. Peru also proposed that a pioneer lose its priority if it did not apply for production authorization within five years of the time the Authority approved a plan of work for the investor's sea-bed activities. The five Western States proposed that production authorizations be issued first to entities which had registered claims for specific sites with their own Governments prior to the date of signing of the Final Act. This would have replaced a provision in the collegium's draft stating that competition between pioneer investors for production authorization would be resolved by the Convention's provisions for selection among applicants unless they agreed to another arrangement.

The President's text contained expanded provisions relating to production authorizations to be granted by the Authority to pioneer investors. It retained priority for such investors but contained more elaborate rules to deal with situations in which the production limit would be exceeded if all investors were allowed to produce whatever quantities they wished. In such a case, the investors could agree either to apportion the allowable tonnage among themselves or to let one or more of them begin exploitation ahead of the others, within the overall ceiling. If they chose apportionment, they would be allowed to produce up to the full amount requested as soon as the overall production ceiling permitted. But whichever choice they made, no other applicant would receive a production authorization until all the pioneers were permitted to produce as much as they wished.

The production authorization paragraph in the President's text contained two other new elements. First, after each pioneer investor had obtained production authorization for its first site, the Enterprise would have priority as long as it was exploiting fewer sites than private and State entities. Second, production authorizations would be issued within 30 days of the date on which the pioneer investor notified the Authority that it would commence mining within five years, with a possibility of extension for up to five years more.

Peru proposed that an investor lose its pioneer status if its sponsoring State failed to ratify the Convention within six months after application to the Authority for approval of a plan of work. Another Peruvian amendment would allow a pioneer to alter its nationality and sponsorship—as would the collegium's text—but only if it selected a State party to the Convention which had effective control over it. The President's text incorporated both concepts.

The five Western States proposed changes in the paragraph setting out what should be done to ensure that the Enterprise was able to carry out sea-bed activities in step with States and others. Whereas the collegium's text would place obligations directly on pioneer investors for exploration of the Authority's area, training of personnel, technology transfer and ensuring funds for the Enterprise, the five States sought to place those obligations on the States which certified pioneer investors, in co-operation with the investors. Exploratory work in the Authority's area would be carried out on a "reimbursable basis in accordance with normal commercial practice" (rather than on a "cost-reimbursable basis").

A Peruvian amendment affecting the technology transfer provision was taken into account in the President's revision. That revision made three other changes in the paragraph spelling out the responsibilities of pioneer investors and their States towards the Enterprise: (1) As in the earlier draft, the pioneers might be required to explore a sea-bed area for the Enterprise, on a cost-reimbursable basis; but the revised text specified reimbursement of costs plus interest at the rate of 10 per cent a year. (2) Certifying States, rather than investors, would ensure that funds were made available to the Enterprise in a timely manner. (3) Certifying States would report periodically to the Preparatory Commission on their activities or those of their sea-bed entities, an obligation not mentioned in the collegium's draft.

In place of the clause in the collegium's draft requiring the Authority and its organs to act in accordance with the provisions of resolution II, the President's text would require them to recognize and honour the rights and obligations arising from the resolution.

Gabon proposed to restore the provision in the earlier text by the Co-ordinators of the Working Group of 21 terminating the pioneer investor scheme and all rights granted thereunder if the Convention had not entered into force within five years. The President's text made no change in this regard.

The USSR proposed a new paragraph stating that nothing in the resolution derogated from the anti-monopoly and non-discrimination provisions of the Convention.[6] This idea was incorporated in the President's text.

Finally, Peru proposed a new paragraph to the effect that no activity in respect of resources other than polymetallic nodules was authorized by the resolution and that all activities relating to such resources could take place only under the Convention.

In his report of 29 April,[12] the President presented one final change, giving the Enterprise production authorization for two mine sites rather than one during the early years of the Convention.

The President reported that this change had been made in informal consultations at the suggestion of the Group of 77, which had also proposed two other changes: to reduce the size of the pioneer area and accelerate the timetable by which the pioneer investor would be required to relinquish parts of it, and to obtain the assistance of the industrialized States in financing the exploration and exploitation of the Enterprise's second mine site. The latter demand had been opposed by the USSR and others, which argued that it was an unacceptable attempt to reopen negotiations on financial matters that had been settled. The outcome had been that the Group of 77 did not insist on changes in the size of the pioneer area and the industrialized States had agreed to letting the Enterprise have two mine sites.

The President also reported on an objection by the USSR that the definition of a pioneer investor discriminated against the States in the first (France, India, Japan, USSR) and third (developing States) investor groups by requiring them to sign the Convention before they or their State enterprises could obtain pioneer status, whereas consortia from North America and Western Europe (excluding France) could receive such status if only one certifying State from that group signed. The President observed that this provision had been agreed to by the Group of 77 in return for the even greater concession that no plan of work for exploration and exploitation could be obtained by a Western consortium unless all the States to which

its constituent members belonged became parties to the Convention. He also remarked that the USSR was guaranteed one mine site whereas seven Western States had to share four sites.

The USSR, at meetings of the Conference and in a letter to the President dated 22 April,[8] also objected that the Conference did not have the competence to grant the status of pioneer investor to private companies. The United Nations Legal Counsel, in memoranda of 21 April (annexed to the USSR letter) and 27 April, expressed the opinion that such an action would be legally permissible,[10] and the President, in his report of 29 April, said he concurred with that opinion.

Bulgaria, the German Democratic Republic, Hungary, Mongolia, Poland and the USSR, explaining on 30 April why they had abstained in the vote on the Convention and associated resolutions, said the provision in resolution II on pioneer investors, requiring States to sign the Convention before they could acquire pioneer status whereas private consortia could qualify even if some of their States had not signed, discriminated against socialist countries and had been drafted in response to the demand of various Western States which wanted to accommodate the interests of a number of transnational corporations. They said they would have voted against the resolution, had there been a separate vote. Several of these States, along with the Ukrainian SSR and Viet Nam, repeated this objection during the closing week of the Conference, at which time Hungary expressed hope that the Preparatory Commission would ensure that no State circumvented the Convention by taking advantage of legal loopholes.

Among those voting for the Convention, China thought the resolution on pioneer investors had accommodated too many of the demands of a few industrialized Powers, and insisted that its implementation be in accordance with the provisions of the Convention. France, explaining its favourable position on the Convention and associated resolutions, cited the régime for the protection of preparatory investment as one of the positive elements. Japan said one of the changes introduced by the President on 22 April (on the granting of production authorizations to pioneer investors) would add to the already congested list of authorization applicants.

Reservations on resolution II were also expressed by Iran and Sierra Leone, the latter adding in December that the scheme would reduce the Authority to a licensing organ and authorize the Enterprise to mine only two sites while States and international consortia could have up to eight.

Chile said the Preparatory Commission must give priority consideration to the adoption of rules for exploration and exploitation of sea-bed resources other than polymetallic nodules.

The Conference President and a number of developing countries and Eastern European States commented on reports of an agreement by France, the Federal Republic of Germany, the United Kingdom and the United States to establish a reciprocating States' régime, referred to by many as a "mini-treaty", governing exploration of the deep sea-bed. Mexico and Peru (speaking for the Group of 77) urged them not to take this step, which they regarded as illegal and contrary to the universal régime established under the Convention. Others expressing this view included Bulgaria, the Byelorussian SSR, China, Grenada, Iran, Pakistan, Somalia, Suriname, Uganda, the USSR, Vanuatu, Viet Nam and Zambia.

Grenada thought such a step would put the interests of transnational corporations above those of the world's peoples, and would widen the socio-economic and technological gap between nations. Suriname endorsed a statement made by the President at a press conference in May that the General Assembly would be requested to ask for an advisory opinion from the International Court of Justice on the legality of mining outside the Convention if the mining companies proceeded to mine under unilateral legislation or a limited multilateral agreement.

Many countries, such as China, and Trinidad and Tobago, also expressed the view that national legislation to allow deep-sea mining would be null and void. The activities of no State, however powerful or technically advanced, said Bangladesh, should acquire legitimacy through unilateral exploration and exploitation of the common heritage of mankind.

Addressing the Conference in December, Canada said its position as a sea-bed mining State had been secured under resolution II; it had initiated negotiations to resolve overlapping mining claims in a manner compatible with the resolution and the Convention. India said it had already spent the minimum sum qualifying it as a pioneer investor and had obtained useful data and samples from surveys of the Central Indian Basin of the Indian Ocean. Romania stressed that implementation of the pioneer investor scheme must in no way violate the principle that the resources of the Area should be exploited for the benefit of all mankind.

A number of States—including Canada, Finland and Norway—made the point that the decisions of several States on whether to ratify the Convention, and therefore the future of the new legal régime, would depend on whether the Preparatory Commission was able to find satisfactory solutions to the problems of regulating sea-bed mining.

Amendments not pressed. [1]Belgium, Germany, Federal Republic of, Italy, United Kingdom, United States, A/CONF.62/L.122; [2]France, A/CONF.62/L.106; [3]Gabon, A/CONF.62/L.97; [4]Japan, A/CONF.62/L.105; [5]Peru, for Group of 77, A/CONF.62/L.116; [6]USSR, A/CONF.62/L.125.
Draft resolution. [7]Conference collegium, A/CONF.62/L.94.
Letter. [8]USSR, 22 Apr., A/CONF.62/L.133.
Memoranda. [9]Conference collegium, A/CONF.62/L.93; [10]Legal Counsel, A/CONF.62/L.139 & Corr.1,2.
Reports. Conference President, [11]A/CONF.62/L.132 & Corr.1 & Add.1 & Add.1/Corr.1, [12]A/CONF.62/L.141 & Add.1; [13]1st Committee Chairman, A/CONF.62/L.91; [14]Working Group Co-ordinators, A/CONF.62/C.1/L.30.
Resolutions (1982). Conference (Final Act, A/CONF.62/121 & Corr.3), 30 Apr.: [15]I, para. 5 *(h)*; [16]II.
Meeting records. Conference: 1st Committee, A/CONF.62/-C.1/SR.56 (29 Mar.); plenary, A/CONF.62/SR.158-166, 168-179, 182 (30 Mar.–30 Apr.), A/CONF.62/PV.185-192 (6-9 Dec.).

Sea-Bed Authority

The Convention on the Law of the Sea provided for the establishment of the International Sea-Bed Authority, with all States parties to the Convention as members and with its seat in Jamaica (article 156). The Authority was described as the organization through which States parties would organize and control activities in the international sea-bed area in accordance with the Convention (article 157). Its principal organs would be an Assembly, a Council and a Secretariat; there would also be an Enterprise for mining operations. Advance arrangements for the Authority were to be made by the Preparatory Commission.

As part of their April 1982 package of amendments to sea-bed provisions of the Convention, two groups of Western States—Belgium, France, the Federal Republic of Germany, Italy, Japan, the United Kingdom and the United States constituting one group[2] and 11 medium-sized industrialized States (known as the group of 11) the other[1]—proposed but did not press to reword a sentence (in article 158) obligating each principal organ to "avoid taking" action which might derogate from or impede the exercise of the powers and functions of other organs, so that it would read, "No organ shall take any action that derogates from or impedes" the exercise of another's powers and functions.

Amendments not pressed. [1]Australia, Austria, Canada, Denmark, Finland, Iceland, Ireland, New Zealand, Norway, Sweden, Switzerland, A/CONF.62/L.104 & Add.1; [2]Belgium, France, Germany, Federal Republic of, Italy, Japan, United Kingdom, United States, A/CONF.62/L.121.

Assembly

The Assembly, composed of all members of the Authority, would take decisions on all matters of substance by a two-thirds majority of those present and voting (article 159). It was described by the Convention as the supreme organ of the Authority, with the power to establish general policies on any question within the Authority's competence, and specifically authorized to elect the members of the Council and the Governing Board of the Enterprise, assess budgetary contributions and approve the Authority's annual budget, approve rules for sea-bed mining and the Authority's financial management and administration, decide on the equitable sharing of benefits from sea-bed activities, examine reports from the Council and the Enterprise, initiate studies and make recommendations to promote international co-operation on sea-bed activities, establish a compensation system or other economic adjustment measures for affected land-based producers, and suspend the rights and privileges of members (article 160).

The Assembly would meet on the date the Convention entered into force, at which time it would elect the Council (article 308).

As part of their April 1982 package of amendments relating to the sea-bed provisions of the Convention, Belgium, France, the Federal Republic of Germany, Italy, Japan, the United Kingdom and the United States proposed to add to the paragraph characterizing the Assembly as the supreme organ (article 160) a sentence stating that this did not derogate from the provision (in article 158) on the division of powers among organs.[2] The same amendment was also put forward by the group of 11 medium-sized Western industrialized States.[1] The seven also proposed to add a sentence requiring the Assembly, if it did not approve the proposed budget, to return it to the Council for reconsideration and resubmission. These amendments were not pressed.

Discussing the motivation of the first of these amendments, the Chairman of the Conference's First Committee, reporting to the Conference on 29 March,[4] said it was designed to allay the apprehension, especially by the United States, that the unqualified supremacy of the Assembly might interfere at times with the efficient management of the Authority's operations.

Gabon proposed to add to the Assembly's functions the establishment of a compensation fund to benefit developing States that were land producers of the same minerals as those extracted from polymetallic nodules and whose export receipts or economies would be affected by sea-bed exploitation.[3] Although this amendment was not pressed, the Convention was revised to include mention of a compensation fund in one of its financial provisions.

Amendments not pressed. [1]Australia, Austria, Canada, Denmark, Finland, Iceland, Ireland, New Zealand, Norway, Sweden, Switzerland, A/CONF.62/L.104 & Add.1; [2]Belgium, France, Germany, Federal Republic of, Italy, Japan, United Kingdom, United States, A/CONF.62/L.121; [3]Gabon, A/CONF.62/L.97.
Report. [4]1st Committee Chairman, A/CONF.62/L.91.

Council

Several aspects of the membership, voting procedures, functions and subsidiary bodies of the executive organ of the Authority—the Council—were spelt out in the Convention on the Law of the Sea. All of these aspects were under consideration in 1982 during the final negotiating and amendment stages of the Conference on the Law of the Sea.

Membership. The Convention provided for a Council of 36 members, each elected by the Assembly for a four-year term at elections to be held every second year (article 161). Half of them would come from one of four major interest groups, while the rest would be elected in such a way as to ensure equitable geographical representation in the Council as a whole. The four groups were: the major consumers or importers of the minerals found on the sea-bed (four States), major land-based exporters of the same minerals (four States), the largest investors in sea-bed mining (four States), and developing countries representing "special interests" (six States). The "special interests" category included developing States with large populations, the land-locked or geographically disadvantaged, major mineral importers, potential producers of the minerals in question and the least developed.

The First Committee Chairman, in his report of 29 March to the Conference,[9] noted that Austria, Finland, Greece, Portugal, Spain, Sweden, Switzerland and Turkey had presented an informal proposal calling for the addition of one developed and one developing State to the Council's membership, so as to give more adequate representation to the countries concerned and still maintain a fair geographical distribution overall. However, the Chairman was unable to report consensus on that issue, which had to be considered in the light of the balance of the Council's membership and the consequences for its voting system (see below). He thought the next alternative would be to increase the size of the Council to 48 members, but added that that idea had been condemned because of its effect on efficiency.

Several amendments were presented in April relating to the Council's membership.

Five States—Austria, Greece, Spain, Switzerland and Turkey—which favoured increased representation for medium-sized industrialized States proposed an amendment to that effect.[2] It would have enlarged the Council from 36 to 38 members: 19 (instead of 18) representing special interests, the additional seat to be available for a developing State, and 19 (instead of 18) elected to ensure overall geographical balance. This proposal would enable each regional group to have at least two members from the geographical category, except for Eastern Europe which was already guaranteed two seats among the special interest categories.

Austria, Lesotho, Swaziland, Switzerland and the Upper Volta proposed to increase the representation of land-locked and geographically disadvantaged States to a degree reasonably proportionate to their representation in the Assembly.[3]

Proposals on Council membership were included in the packages of sea-bed amendments presented by two groups of Western States—one by Belgium, France, the Federal Republic of Germany, Italy, Japan, the United Kingdom and the United States[4] and the other by the group of 11, introduced by Norway.[1] Both groups proposed that the largest consumer of sea-bed minerals be entitled to a seat. The seven-nation amendments also provided that all four of the sea-bed investors' group and two of the large-consumers' group be chosen from among the eight States parties to the Convention which were the largest contributors to the United Nations regular budget. The 11-nation amendments would also have specified the overall regional composition of the Council as nine from Western European and other States, three from Eastern European (socialist) States, and 24 from Africa, Asia and Latin America.

Canada proposed, but later withdrew, an amendment that, without altering the size of the Council, would have guaranteed a seat to the State contributing the largest share of financing.[5]

None of these amendments was pressed to a vote. Following the Conference's debate on amendments, the Conference approved only one change affecting the Council's membership, as proposed by the President on 22 April.[7] It was to guarantee a seat in the Council for the largest consumer of sea-bed minerals, which the First Committee Chairman had identified as the United States.

Portugal and Switzerland, which voted for the Convention, expressed reservations on the Council membership clause, which Switzerland said would deny a seat to many medium-sized industrialized States.

Canada said in December that, as a major land-based producer of the minerals found on the sea-bed, a potential mining State and a major financial contributor, it expected to be a member of the Council. Sweden expressed regret that provisions discriminating against small and medium-sized industrialized States in regard to Council membership remained in the Convention.

Voting procedures and functions. The Convention provided for an elaborate scheme of decision-making majorities in which the Council was to decide the most important questions by consensus rather than voting (article 161). Consensus—defined as the absence of a formal objection—would be required for adoption of the rules, regulations and procedures (referred to below as rules)

for all sea-bed activities, pending approval by the Assembly, and rules for the Authority's administration and financial management, as well as measures to protect land-based producing countries from adverse economic effects of sea-bed mining, recommendations to the Assembly on economic adjustment assistance for such countries and adoption of amendments to the sea-bed provisions of the Convention. Other substantive matters would be resolved by voting majorities of three fourths or two thirds, depending on the nature of the issue. The Council was to have the power to establish, in conformity with the Convention and the general policies established by the Assembly, the specific policies to be pursued by the Authority (article 162).

The seven Western industrialized States proposed amendments affecting voting majorities and the definition of functions of the Council. With regard to voting (article 161), they proposed that decisions on a number of substantive matters, which under the existing text would require majorities of two thirds or three fourths, be taken by a three-fourths majority which must include a majority of each of the four special interest categories on the Council (investors, consumers, land-based producers and developing States with special interests) and of each geographical region. Also, all decisions on specific policies to be pursued by the Authority would have had to be taken by consensus, as would recommendations on a compensation system or other economic assistance for land-based producers. With regard to the Council's powers and functions (article 162), they proposed a number of limitations and other alterations, one of which would have replaced the function of exercising control over sea-bed activities with that of investigating the adequacy of enforcement practices by States parties.

The group of 11 proposed only one change in the voting arrangements: that Council decisions on the Authority's budget require a majority of three fourths plus one, rather than simply three fourths, of the members present and voting.

The Conference approved one change in the list of the Council's powers and functions, adding a provision that, in adopting rules for sea-bed activities, the Council was to give priority to those covering polymetallic nodules, and that rules governing other resources would have to be adopted within three years after a member of the Authority requested that this be done. This addition was proposed by the Conference President in his report of 29 April.[8]

The United States, explaining on 30 April its vote against the Convention, cited as one of the reasons its view that the decision-making process did not give a proportionate voice to the countries most affected by the decisions and would thus not fairly reflect and effectively protect their interests.

During the final week of the Conference in December, the United Republic of Tanzania criticized the composition and decision-making procedures of important organs of the Authority, stating that they were plainly undemocratic in accommodating such notions as permanent members and veto powers masquerading under the euphemisms of "special interests" and "consensus".

Subsidiary bodies. The Convention established, as organs of the Council, an Economic Planning Commission and a Legal and Technical Commission, each to have 15 members elected by the Council with due regard for equitable geographical distribution, or more if the Council decided to expand their membership having due regard to economy and efficiency (article 163). The Economic Planning Commission—which would include at least two members from developing States whose exports of minerals also found on the sea-bed had a substantial bearing on their economies—was to review supply, demand and prices of sea-bed materials; make recommendations to the Council on likely adverse effects of sea-bed mining on land-based producing countries, and propose a compensation system or other economic adjustment measures for such countries (article 164). The Legal and Technical Commission was to make recommendations on plans of work for sea-bed activities, supervise activities in the international area, recommend environmental protection measures, formulate and submit to the Council the rules governing the sea-bed mining system, calculate the production ceiling and recommend production authorizations for individual contractors (article 165).

The seven Western industrialized States proposed that each of the four special interest groups represented in the Council elect three members to each of its two commissions. They would have deleted the references to geographical balance and to possible enlargement of the commissions. They also proposed an additional subparagraph stating that the Legal and Technical Commission would utilize the Secretariat's legal staff to the maximum extent possible but that its decisions and recommendations would be its own.

Gabon proposed to revise the phrase defining the category of land-based producers on the Economic Planning Commission to cover those whose export receipts and economies would be affected by sea-bed exploitation, and to provide that two such States be represented also on the Legal and Technical Commission.[6]

Amendments not pressed. [1]Australia, Austria, Canada, Denmark, Finland, Iceland, Ireland, New Zealand, Norway, Sweden, Switzerland, A/CONF.62/L.104 & Add.1;

[2]Austria, Greece, Spain, Switzerland, Turkey, A/CONF.62/L.100; [3]Austria, Lesotho, Swaziland, Switzerland, Upper Volta, A/CONF.62/L.103; [4]Belgium, France, Germany, Federal Republic of, Italy, Japan, United Kingdom, United States, A/CONF.62/L.121; [5]Canada, A/CONF.62/L.113 (withdrawn); [6]Gabon, A/CONF.62/L.97.

Reports. Conference President, [7]A/CONF.62/L.132/Add.1, [8]A/CONF.62/L.141/Add.1; [9]1st Committee Chairman, A/CONF.62/L.91.

Enterprise

The Convention on the Law of the Sea provided that the Authority's Enterprise was to carry out sea-bed activities directly, as well as the transport, processing and marketing of recovered minerals (article 170). Specific provisions were set out in a 13-article Statute which constituted annex IV to the Convention.

As stated in this annex, the Enterprise was to operate in accordance with sound commercial principles (article 1). It was to enjoy autonomy in the conduct of its operations, while acting in accordance with the general policies of the Authority's Assembly and the directives of the Authority's Council (article 2). A Governing Board of 15 members elected by the Assembly was to decide all matters by simple majority vote (article 5). The Board was to direct the operations of the Enterprise, including preparation of plans of work and production authorizations for approval by the Council, authorization of negotiations for the acquisition of technology, approval of the results of negotiations with other entities for joint ventures and other joint arrangements, and borrowing of funds (article 6). A Director-General, nominated by the Board and elected by the Assembly on the Council's recommendation, was to be chief executive, responsible for the staff (article 7). The principal office of the Enterprise was to be at the seat of the Authority (article 8).

The Enterprise was to submit financial reports to the Council on a regular basis (article 9). It was to make the same payments to the Authority as any commercial producer, except during an initial grace period of not more than 10 years, intended to enable it to become self-supporting; aside from a share to be retained as reserves, it was to transfer its net income to the Authority (article 10). Its funds were to include amounts from the Authority, voluntary contributions by States parties to the Convention, borrowings and income from operations; half of the funds received from the Authority were to come from long-term interest-free loans which each State party must provide according to its share of the United Nations regular budget, and the other half from Enterprise borrowings guaranteed by those States (article 11).

The Enterprise was to sell its products on a non-discriminatory basis, and only commercial considerations were to be relevant to its decisions (article 12). Its property and assets were to be immune from seizure and discriminatory restrictions, and it was to negotiate tax exemptions in States where its offices were located (article 13).

The Enterprise's sea-bed activities were to be governed by the Authority's rules and decisions (annex III, article 12). A special commission for the Enterprise was to be established by the Preparatory Commission.[2] As part of the scheme for pioneer investors, and to ensure that the Enterprise would be able to keep pace with States and other entities engaged in sea-bed activities, those investors, prior to the entry into force of the Convention, were to be required to explore areas reserved for the Enterprise on a cost-plus-interest basis, train personnel and undertake to transfer technology as provided in the Convention; in addition, the States certifying those investors were to ensure that funds were made available to the Enterprise for its first two mining operations.[3]

The role of the Enterprise in the parallel system of sea-bed mining to be established under the Convention was spelt out in annex III, on basic conditions for prospecting, exploration and exploitation.

Amendments relating to the Enterprise were included by the United States and six other Western States in their April 1982 package of amendments on sea-bed provisions of the Convention.[1] With regard to activities by the Enterprise (annex III, article 12), they proposed to replace the provision that such activities would be governed by the Convention and the Authority's rules and decisions by a sentence stating that the Convention and the Authority's rules and decisions would apply to the Enterprise in the same manner as to any other sea-bed operator except where the Convention expressly provided otherwise. They also proposed that the Governing Board include members from States to which it owed at least half of its outstanding debts (annex IV, article 5). With regard to financing (annex IV, article 11), they proposed that no more than a third of the total of loans and guarantees which each State would be required to make to finance the Enterprise's first mining operation would be payable in any given year, and that the Authority's rules must specify procedures to be followed in the event of default by the Enterprise.

In separate amendments to Conference resolution II on pioneer investors, Belgium, the Federal Republic of Germany, Italy, the United Kingdom and the United States proposed changes in the paragraph on what would be done to ensure that the Enterprise could carry out sea-bed activities in step with States.

One of the reasons cited by the United States in explaining on 30 April its vote against the Convention was its view that the system of privileges established for the Enterprise would discriminate against private and national miners.

On the other hand, Mauritius, speaking in December, questioned whether the industrialized countries had fulfilled their commitment to provide the means to make the Enterprise viable. Trinidad and Tobago expressed the view that the Enterprise had not been given adequate guarantees to receive mining technology and engage in mining on an equal footing with private entities. Yugoslavia regarded the provisions on technology transfer to the Enterprise and on its initial financing as the essence of the parallel system.

The Byelorussian SSR said the secretariat of the Enterprise should be enabled to choose personnel at all levels in conformity with equitable geographical distribution.

Amendments not pressed. [1]Belgium, France, Germany, Federal Republic of, Italy, Japan, United Kingdom, United States, A/CONF.62/L.121.
Resolutions (1982). Conference (Final Act, A/CONF.62/121 & Corr.3), 30 Apr.: [2]I, para. 8; [3]II, para. 12.

Financing

According to the Convention on the Law of the Sea (article 171), the International Sea-Bed Authority was to be financed from six sources: assessed contributions from its member States on a scale based on that used by the United Nations for its regular budget, receipts from the taxes (fees and charges) collected from sea-bed operators, part of the Enterprise's net income, possible borrowings, voluntary contributions, and payments to a compensation fund for affected land-based producing States. The Authority's annual budget would be subject to approval by the Assembly after consideration by the Council (article 172). Any funds not needed for administrative expenses could be shared with member States, transferred to the Enterprise or used to compensate developing States that suffered economic harm from sea-bed production (article 173).

The Authority would be empowered to borrow funds within limits imposed by the Assembly and with specifics to be decided by the Council (article 174). The financial statements and accounts would be audited annually by an independent auditor appointed by the Assembly (article 175).

Resolution I of the Conference on the Law of the Sea, on preparations for the Authority, provided that the budget for the Authority's first financial period was to be recommended by the Preparatory Commission.[1]

The Convention made separate arrangements for the financing of the Enterprise, initially through loans and loan guarantees arranged through the Authority and eventually from the proceeds of its mining activities. Resolution II, on pioneer investors, provided that States certifying such investors (sea-bed mining States) were to ensure that funds were made available to the Enterprise for its initial mining operations.[2]

During the Conference's final week in December 1982, Sierra Leone questioned whether African States would gain much from a scheme which required them to pay approximately $1 million each to join the Authority with no guarantee that their investment would yield dividends.

Resolutions (1982). Conference (Final Act, A/CONF.62/121 & Corr.3,7,8), 30 Apr.: [1]I, para. 5 *(c)*; [2]II, para. 12.

Other aspects

The Convention on the Law of the Sea provided for the establishment of a Secretariat of the Authority, headed by a Secretary-General elected by the Assembly for a four-year, renewable term from candidates proposed by the Council (article 166). As in the case of the United Nations Secretariat, the paramount consideration in staff recruitment would be efficiency, competence and integrity, with due regard to recruitment on as wide a geographical basis as possible (article 167). Staff members would be prohibited, even after the termination of their functions, from disclosing industrial secrets or other confidential information they had learned by reason of their employment with the Authority (article 168). The Secretary-General was empowered to make arrangements for consultation and co-operation with international and non-governmental organizations (article 169).

The Authority was to have the legal capacity needed for the exercise of its functions (article 176). This was to include certain privileges and immunities (article 177), including immunity from legal process (article 178) and from search and seizure of its property and assets (article 179), and exemption from restrictions, regulations, controls and moratoria (article 180). Its archives were to be inviolable and its official communications were to be accorded treatment no less favourable than that given to other international organizations (article 181).

Representatives of States parties attending meetings, as well as the Secretary-General and staff, were to be immune from legal process with respect to their official acts, and were to be accorded the same exemptions from immigration restrictions and alien registration requirements, and the same treatment with regard to currency exchange restrictions and travel facilities, as officials and employees of comparable rank of other States parties (article 182). The Authority was to be exempt from direct taxes and customs duties on its property and official transactions, and the staff were to be exempt from paying income tax to any State other than that of which they were nationals (article 183).

A State party that fell two years or more in arrears in respect of its financial contributions to the Authority would have its voting rights suspended, unless the Assembly decided that failure to pay was due to conditions beyond the member's control (article 184). Gross and persistent violations of the sea-bed provisions, as determined by the Sea-Bed Disputes Chamber, could lead to a decision by the Assembly, on the Council's recommendation, to suspend the rights and privileges of membership (article 185).

One of the amendments submitted in April 1982 by Belgium, France, the Federal Republic of Germany, Italy, Japan, the United Kingdom and the United States would have lifted the Authority's legal immunity against the enforcement of judgements by the Sea-Bed Disputes Chamber.[1]

Amendment not pressed. [1]Belgium, France, Germany, Federal Republic of, Italy, Japan, United Kingdom, United States, A/CONF.62/L.121.

Sea-bed disputes

The establishment of a Sea-Bed Disputes Chamber as an organ of the International Tribunal for the Law of the Sea was provided for in the Convention on the Law of the Sea (article 186). This Chamber would handle disputes between States parties to the Convention on the interpretation or application of the sea-bed provisions, as well as disputes involving the Authority and contractors (article 187). States could also submit their disputes to a special chamber of the Tribunal or an *ad hoc* chamber of the Sea-Bed Disputes Chamber; contract disputes could be submitted to a commercial arbitral tribunal for binding arbitration (article 188). The Sea-Bed Disputes Chamber could not decide questions involving the discretionary powers of the Authority or the validity of its rules, regulations and procedures (referred to below as rules) (article 189). A State sponsoring a corporation involved in a dispute would be entitled to take part in the proceedings (article 190). The Assembly or the Council could obtain advisory opinions from the Chamber on legal questions (article 191).

Further details regarding this Chamber were set out in the Tribunal's Statute (annex VI to the Convention). The Chamber would be composed of 11 members of the Tribunal, selected by a majority of the Tribunal's members to serve a three-year term (article 35). The Chamber would form an *ad hoc* chamber to deal with a particular dispute, composed with the approval of the parties (article 36). The Chamber would be open to the States parties to the Convention, the Authority and other entities (article 37). It would apply the rules of the Authority and the terms of contracts governing sea-bed activities (article 38). Its decisions would be enforceable in the territories of States parties in the same manner as judgements of the State's highest court (article 39). The other provisions of the Tribunal's Statute not incompatible with those specifically relating to the Chamber applied to the Chamber (article 40).

Belgium, France, the Federal Republic of Germany, Italy, Japan, the United Kingdom and the United States, in their April 1982 package of amendments to the sea-bed provisions of the Convention,[1] sought two changes to enlarge the scope of the dispute settlement machinery: to extend the jurisdiction of special or *ad hoc* chambers to disputes between a State and the Authority, rather than limiting it to disputes between States (article 188); and to authorize the Sea-Bed Disputes Chamber to determine whether the application of the Authority's rules in individual cases would conflict with the rights and obligations of the parties and determine claims concerning lack of competence or misuse of power (article 189).

Amendments not pressed. [1]Belgium, France, Germany, Federal Republic of, Italy, Japan, United Kingdom, United States, A/CONF.62/L.121.

Protection of the marine environment

Convention provisions. Part XII of the Convention on the Law of the Sea placed on States parties the obligation to protect and preserve the marine environment (article 192). The right of States to exploit their natural resources was made contingent on that duty (article 193).

Following several general provisions explaining these obligations, the Convention outlined types of global and regional co-operation which were to be undertaken to fulfil them. It then dealt with more specific activities—technical assistance, monitoring and environmental assessment, and international rules and national legislation—to prevent, reduce and control marine pollution. Various kinds of enforcement measures were authorized, balanced by safeguards against the misuse of enforcement powers. The special status of ice-covered areas was recognized. Finally, this part of the Convention dealt with responsibility and liability for environmental damage, sovereign immunity for warships or government vessels, and the relationship of the provisions of part XII with obligations under other conventions for protection of the marine environment.

The general provisions obliged States parties to take all necessary measures consistent with the Convention to prevent, reduce and control pollution of the marine environment from any source, while refraining from unjustifiable interference with the activities of other States; they were also obliged to ensure that activities under their control or jurisdiction did not cause damage by pollution to other States or their environment (article 194). In taking such measures, States would have the duty not to transfer damage or hazards to another area or transform one type of pollution

into another (article 195). Pollution control measures would have to be taken when new technologies were used or when alien or new species that could cause harmful environmental changes were introduced (article 196).

States were required to co-operate globally and, as appropriate, regionally—directly or through international organizations—in formulating international rules, standards, and recommended practices and procedures (referred to below as rules) to protect and preserve the marine environment, taking regional features into account (article 197). When a State became aware of threatened or actual environmental damage, it would have to notify other States likely to be affected, as well as the competent international organizations (article 198). In such cases, States in the area and organizations would have to co-operate in eliminating the effects of pollution and preventing or minimizing damage, and develop contingency plans to respond to pollution incidents (article 199). States would co-operate to promote studies, undertake research programmes, encourage information exchange and participate in regional and global pollution assessment programmes (article 200). In the light of such information, they would co-operate in establishing scientific criteria for pollution control rules (article 201).

States would commit themselves to promote scientific and technical assistance to developing States on this subject, to assist other States to minimize the effects of major environmental incidents and to help with environmental assessments (article 202). Developing States would be entitled to preference by international organizations in the allocation of funds and technical assistance and the utilization of specialized services (article 203).

The Convention required States to monitor the risks or effects of marine pollution (article 204) and publish reports of the results or provide reports to international organizations for dissemination (article 205). They must also assess the potential effects of planned activities under their jurisdiction or control whenever they had reasonable grounds for believing that substantial pollution or other significant harmful environmental changes might result (article 206).

The obligation to formulate international rules and national legislation for pollution control, and to harmonize national policies, was spelt out in reference to several kinds of pollution sources.

With regard to land-based sources—including rivers, estuaries and pipelines—the obligation would fall largely on national laws and regulations, taking internationally agreed rules into account (article 207). To control pollution from sea-bed activities subject to national jurisdiction, coastal States would be required to adopt laws and regulations no less effective than international rules (article 208). For pollution from activities in the international sea-bed area, international rules would be established and national legislation no less effective would be adopted by States for operations by vessels and installations under their authority (article 209). Pollution by dumping would be governed under both national law and global and regional rules—the national to be no less effective than the global—and no dumping could be carried out without permission by State authorities (article 210).

Pollution from vessels would be controlled by: international rules and routeing systems designed to minimize the threat of accidents; flag States, through laws and regulations for vessels under their authority having at least the same effect as that of generally accepted international rules; coastal States, for vessels calling at their ports or offshore terminals, entering their internal waters or passing through their territorial sea or exclusive economic zone, except that in respect of the zone the legislation could not go beyond generally accepted international rules; and international standards for special, environmentally sensitive areas in an exclusive economic zone, to be enacted by the coastal State (article 211). Pollution from or through the atmosphere would be dealt with by national legislation applying to a State's airspace and to vessels or aircraft registered with that State, taking international rules into account (article 212).

The Convention next specified the authorities responsible for enforcing anti-pollution measures.

In the case of land-based sources, enforcement of national laws and regulations and international rules would be in the hands of States (article 213). The same was true with respect to pollution from sea-bed activities and offshore structures under their jurisdiction (article 214). Enforcement of international rules for the international sea-bed area (article 215) would be governed by the sea-bed part of the Convention (which made the International Sea-Bed Authority responsible for drawing up such rules and made the Authority and States jointly responsible for securing compliance). Regulations on pollution from dumping would be enforced by the coastal State, the flag State, or any State in whose territory waste or other matter was loaded by a vessel (article 216).

With regard to pollution from vessels, the flag State would be responsible for enforcement of both national and international regulations with respect to vessels flying its flag, wherever a violation occurred; it would be required to inspect and certify such vessels, prohibit them from sailing if they did not comply, investigate alleged violations and institute proceedings where necessary, and provide for penalties severe enough to discourage violations (article 217).

A port State (one at whose port or offshore terminal a vessel was berthed) could investigate a discharge from any vessel which occurred outside its waters; it could institute proceedings if requested to do so by the flag State, a State in whose waters an alleged violation occurred or a State affected by the discharge violation (article 218). A port State would also be required to take steps to prevent a vessel from leaving its port, except to proceed to the nearest repair yard, if it ascertained that the vessel was in violation of international seaworthiness standards and thereby threatened environmental damage (article 219).

While a vessel was within a coastal State's port or at an offshore terminal, that State could institute proceedings in respect of a violation which had occurred within its territorial sea or exclusive economic zone; it could inspect and detain a vessel located in its territorial sea for a violation occurring there; it could inspect a vessel in its exclusive economic zone under similar circumstances but could bring proceedings against and detain it only if there was clear objective evidence that the vessel was responsible for a substantial discharge causing or threatening major damage to the coastline or resources (article 220). States would retain the right to take measures beyond their territorial sea in the event of a collision or other maritime casualty that could reasonably be expected to result in major harmful consequences, but the action would have to be proportionate to the actual or threatened damage to the coastline or fishing interests (article 221).

With respect to pollution from or through the atmosphere, States would be responsible for enforcement within their airspace and with regard to vessels or aircraft of their registry, in conformity with international rules on the safety of air navigation (article 222).

The Convention contained various kinds of safeguards. Thus, in proceedings against accused violators, States would be obliged to facilitate the hearing of witnesses and the admission of evidence submitted by another State, as well as the attendance of representatives of the competent international organization, the flag State and any State affected by the pollution arising from the violation (article 223).

Enforcement powers against foreign vessels could be exercised only by authorized officials or by warships, military aircraft, or other ships or aircraft clearly marked as being on government service (article 224). In exercising those powers, a State could not endanger the safety of navigation or otherwise create a hazard to a vessel, or expose the marine environment to an unreasonable risk (article 225). The Convention laid down specific rules relating to the investigation of foreign vessels, requiring in particular that States must not delay them longer than was essential for an investigation, must not conduct a physical investigation unless an inspection of documents proved unsatisfactory and must release a detained vessel subject to the posting of a bond or other financial security (article 226). Discrimination against vessels of another State was prohibited (article 227).

Legal proceedings to impose penalties for a violation occurring beyond the territorial sea of the State instituting those proceedings would have to be suspended if the flag State brought corresponding charges against the alleged offender within six months, except in the case of major damage to the coastal State or if the flag State had repeatedly disregarded its obligation to enforce international rules against its vessels; no State could institute proceedings against a foreign vessel if another State had already done so, and any proceedings would have to be instituted within three years of the violation (article 228). The Convention would not affect civil proceedings in respect of any claim for loss or damage (article 229).

The Convention provided for the imposition of monetary penalties with respect to violations of national laws and international rules committed by foreign vessels, and required the observance in such cases of recognized rights of the accused (article 230). It also required that the flag State and any other State concerned be promptly notified of any enforcement measures against foreign vessels (article 231). States would be liable for damage or loss attributable to them arising from enforcement measures that were unlawful or exceeded those reasonably required in the light of available information (article 232).

According to the Convention (article 233), nothing in the sections on regulations against marine environmental pollution, enforcement measures and safeguards would affect the legal régime of straits used for international navigation, except that the safeguards would have to be respected whenever States bordering such straits took enforcement measures permitted by the rules of transit passage.

Coastal States would have the right to adopt and enforce laws and regulations to prevent or control pollution in ice-covered areas within their exclusive economic zone where the ice obstructed navigation for most of the year and pollution could cause major harm to or irreversible disturbance of the ecological balance (article 234).

The Convention made States responsible and liable for fulfilling their obligations to protect and preserve the marine environment, and required them to ensure that recourse was available for prompt and adequate compensation or other relief in respect of damage caused by persons or corporations under their jurisdiction (article 235).

Warships and other State vessels or aircraft used for non-commercial service would not be bound by the environmental protection provisions of the Convention, but the State concerned would have to ensure, by taking measures that did not impair the operations or operational capabilities of such craft, that they acted in a manner consistent with the Convention so far as reasonable and practical (article 236). The environmental protection measures of the Convention were without prejudice to States' obligations under previous and future conventions on the subject (article 237).

Conference consideration. The only alterations in the environmental protection provisions made during 1982 by the Conference on the Law of the Sea were drafting changes proposed in a letter of 26 March by the Chairman of the Third Committee,[6] which prepared this part of the Convention, and in his report to the Conference dated 30 March.[8] He noted in his report that this part of the Convention used the term "vessel" to apply to ships and other floating structures.

In April, France and Spain each proposed amendments to this part of the Convention but did not press for a vote on them. France proposed that the penalties provision (article 230) be strengthened by permitting penalties going beyond fines in cases of a wilful or serious act of pollution committed by foreign vessels beyond the territorial sea.[1]

Spain proposed two amendments:[2] first, to delete the phrase "beyond the territorial sea" from the provision on marine casualties (article 221), permitting States to take measures beyond the territorial sea to protect themselves against major pollution from such incidents; and second, to replace the phrase "legal régime of straits" by the phrase "régime of passage through straits" in the clause (in article 233) stating that nothing in the sections dealing with regulations against marine environmental pollution, enforcement and safeguards affected the legal régime of straits used for international navigation.

On 22 April, the President reported to the Conference that, during consultations undertaken by the Third Committee Chairman, it had been impossible to find a generally acceptable solution in regard to these amendments.[7]

By a letter to the Conference President dated 28 April, Malaysia transmitted a statement of understanding regarding the provision on environmental safeguards in straits used for international navigation (article 233) and its application to the Straits of Malacca and Singapore.[5] By letters of 29 April, the two other States bordering those Straits, Indonesia and Singapore, and States which were the major users of them—Australia, France, the Federal Republic of Germany, Japan, the United Kingdom and the United States—confirmed that understanding.[4]

Speaking after the Conference adopted the Convention on 30 April, Canada described the handling of the problem of ice-covered areas as an example of great-Power agreement with the small countries in the interest of mankind.

During the Conference's final meetings in December, several States remarked that the environmental protection provisions of the Convention struck a balance between the various interests involved, especially coastal and maritime States. Finland voiced this conclusion, adding that the true value of the environmental provisions could be realized only through further national and international regulation. Ireland expressed the view that the powers given to the coastal State to protect the marine environment were adequate while avoiding unreasonable interference with navigation and other rights of other States. France and Trinidad and Tobago also believed that the provisions on the marine environment reflected a just balance of differing interests.

Barbados stressed the importance of the marine pollution provisions for a country like itself, located in the major sea lane of the Caribbean where supertankers plied their trade, posing a constant threat to marine life and the environment. Sweden, on the other hand, regretted that the environment provisions were not as far-reaching as it would have liked; coastal States should have been given the right to take more effective measures to protect their marine environment.

UNEP action. On 31 May, the Governing Council of the United Nations Environment Programme (UNEP) recorded its satisfaction with the results of the Conference specifically in respect of the protection and preservation of the marine environment, as an essential contribution to the progressive development and codification of international law in the field of the environment.[3] This decision was adopted by a roll-call vote of 45 to 1 (United States), with 5 abstentions.

UNEP was also involved in other activities relating to protection of the marine environment.

Amendments not pressed. [1]France, A/CONF.62/L.106; [2]Spain, A/CONF.62/L.109.
Decision (1982). [3]UNEP Council (report, A/37/25): 10/23, 31 May.
Letters. [4]Australia, France, Germany, Federal Republic of, Indonesia, Japan, Singapore, United Kingdom, United States, 29 Apr., A/CONF.62/L.145/Add.1-8; [5]Malaysia, 28 Apr., A/CONF.62/L.145; [6]3rd Committee Chairman, 26 Mar., A/CONF.62/L.88 & Corr.1.
Reports. [7]Conference President, A/CONF.62/L.132; [8]3rd Committee Chairman, A/CONF.62/L.92.

Marine scientific research

Convention provisions. Part XIII of the Convention on the Law of the Sea was concerned with the conduct and promotion of marine scientific research. Following several general provisions, it dealt with international co-operation in this field and went on to lay down rules to be followed by research and coastal States, particularly with regard to research in the exclusive economic zone and on the continental shelf. Other provisions dealt with scientific research installations and equipment, responsibility and liability, and dispute settlement and interim measures.

According to this part of the Convention, all States and competent international organizations had the right to conduct marine scientific research subject to the rights and duties of other States (article 238). States and organizations were to promote and facilitate the development and conduct of such research (article 239). Four general principles were established: research must be exclusively for peaceful purposes, it must be conducted with scientific methods and means compatible with the Convention, it could not unjustifiably interfere with other legitimate uses of the sea and must be duly respected in the course of such uses, and it must abide by all relevant regulations including those for protection and preservation of the marine environment (article 240). Research activities could not constitute the legal basis for any claim to any part of the marine environment or its resources (article 241).

States and organizations were obligated to promote international co-operation in marine scientific research for peaceful purposes and to enable other States to obtain information necessary to prevent and control damage to the health and safety of persons and to the marine environment (article 242). They were to co-operate, through bilateral and multilateral agreements, in creating favourable conditions for the conduct of research and in integrating the efforts of scientists (article 243). They were to publish and disseminate information on proposed major programmes and their results (article 244).

The Convention established specific régimes for marine scientific research in different parts of the sea. In the territorial sea, coastal States had the exclusive right to regulate, authorize and conduct research, which could be carried out only with their consent (article 245).

In the exclusive economic zone and on the continental shelf (article 246), research was subject to the consent of the coastal State, but that State was obliged under normal circumstances to grant consent to a foreign State or international organization—even in the absence of diplomatic relations between two States—when the research was for peaceful purposes and was intended to increase scientific knowledge for the benefit of all. A coastal State could withhold consent for research that was directly concerned with natural resources and their exploitation, or involved drilling into the continental shelf, the use of explosives, the introduction of harmful substances, or the construction or use of offshore structures, but consent could not be denied for research on the continental shelf beyond 200 nautical miles from shore, except in areas reserved by the coastal State for exploitation.

A marine scientific research project undertaken by or under the auspices of an international organization would be deemed to have been authorized by the coastal State if that State approved the project when the organization decided to go ahead with it, or was willing to participate in it, and had not objected within four months of receiving notice about the project from the organization (article 247).

Those intending to undertake a project would be required to provide the coastal State with a full description at least six months before commencing it (article 248). They would have to comply with certain other conditions: ensuring the coastal State's right to participate or have representatives aboard the research vessel or installation, providing it with preliminary reports and final results, giving it access to data and samples, providing it on request with an assessment of the data and research results or helping it to interpret them, ensuring that the results were made available internationally, informing it of any major change in the programme, and removing installations and equipment upon completion of the research (article 249).

A research project could proceed six months after the detailed description was provided to the coastal State unless consent was withheld, the information did not conform to evident facts or had to be supplemented, or the researcher had outstanding obligations with regard to a previous project (article 252). A coastal State could require suspension of research activities if they were not conducted in accordance with the information provided to it and on which its consent was based, or if the researcher failed to observe the coastal State's rights; it could require cessation if such a situation was not corrected within a reasonable time or in the event of a major change in the project or activities (article 253).

Neighbouring land-locked and geographically disadvantaged States would receive notice of all such research projects and, at their request and when appropriate, would be given the detailed prospectus; they would be entitled to send experts not objected to by the coastal State to participate in the project whenever feasible, and at their request they would be given an assessment of the data or results (article 254).

In addition to these provisions on research in the exclusive economic zone or on the continental shelf, the Convention included provisions pertaining to marine scientific research in general.

Communications about research projects would be made through official channels unless otherwise agreed (article 250). States would seek to promote through international organizations the establishment of general criteria and guidelines to assist States in ascertaining the nature and implications of such research (article 251). States would endeavour to adopt reasonable rules, regulations and procedures to facilitate marine scientific research beyond their territorial sea, and to facilitate access to their harbours and promote assistance for research vessels (article 255).

All States and international organizations would have the right to conduct marine scientific research in the international sea-bed area (article 256) and in the water beyond the exclusive economic zone (article 257).

With regard to scientific research installations and equipment in the marine environment, the Convention would subject their deployment and use to the same conditions as were prescribed for marine scientific research (article 258). It specified that they did not possess the status of islands, had no territorial sea of their own and did not affect maritime boundary delimitation (article 259). They could be surrounded by safety zones extending up to 500 metres (article 260). They were to be deployed and used without obstructing international shipping routes (article 261). They were to bear identifying markings indicating their State of registry or the international organization to which they belonged, and must have internationally agreed warning signals to ensure safety at sea and the safety of air navigation (article 262).

States and organizations would be responsible for ensuring that marine scientific research undertaken by them or on their behalf was conducted in accordance with the Convention; they would be responsible for damage resulting from measures that contravened the Convention and damage caused by marine pollution arising from their research activities (article 263).

Disputes over the application of the Convention's provisions on marine scientific research would be settled in accordance with its clauses on compulsory dispute settlement procedures involving binding decisions (article 264), except that certain types of disputes would be exempt from such procedures and certain others would be dealt with through conciliation. Pending a settlement, the research State or organization would not allow research activities to commence or continue without the coastal State's consent (article 265).

Conference consideration. No changes were made or amendments proposed during 1982 to the provisions on marine scientific research.

During the final meetings of the Conference on the Law of the Sea in December, Ireland remarked that the Convention safeguarded the coastal State's rights to control marine scientific research in its jurisdictional area while ensuring that research would not be unreasonably prevented or hampered there. France and Trinidad and Tobago said the provisions on marine scientific research reflected a just balance of conflicting interests. Sweden, however, thought coastal States had been given too extensive rights to control research; it would have wished the Convention to put stronger emphasis on freedom of research.

Marine technology development and transfer

Convention provisions. Part XIV of the Convention on the Law of the Sea was concerned with the development and transfer of marine technology. It contained general provisions followed by sections on international co-operation, national and regional marine scientific and technological centres, and co-operation among international organizations.

In its general provisions on this topic, the Convention obliged States to co-operate in promoting the development and transfer of marine science and technology on fair and reasonable terms and conditions, to promote the development of the marine scientific and technological capacity of States which needed and requested technical assistance, and to foster conditions for the transfer of marine technology on an equitable basis (article 266). In promoting such co-operation, States were to have due regard for all legitimate interests, including the rights and duties of holders, suppliers and recipients of marine technology (article 267).

The basic objectives to be promoted were: acquisition, evaluation and dissemination of marine technological knowledge, and access to it; development of appropriate marine technology, of a technological infrastructure to facilitate marine technology transfer and of human resources through training and education; and international co-operation at all levels (article 268). To achieve those objectives, States committed themselves to endeavour to establish technical co-operation programmes, promote conditions for the conclusion of agreements and other arrangements under equitable and reasonable conditions, hold meetings on policies and methods for marine technology transfer and on other scientific and technological subjects, promote the exchange of scientists and other experts, and undertake projects and promote joint ventures and other forms of bilateral and multilateral co-operation (article 269).

International co-operation for the development and transfer of marine technology was to be carried out through existing, expanded and new programmes, including international funding for ocean research and development (article 270). Guidelines, criteria and standards for marine technology transfer were to be established bilaterally or through international organizations (article 271). International programmes were to be co-ordinated, taking account of the interests and needs of developing States, particularly the landlocked and geographically disadvantaged (article 272).

In addition to the more specific technology transfer provisions contained in the sea-bed part of the Convention, the marine technology part obliged States to co-operate with international organizations and the International Sea-Bed Authority to encourage and facilitate the transfer to developing States and the Enterprise of skills and marine technology relating to sea-bed activities (article 273). The Authority was to ensure that nationals of developing States were taken on for training as members of its managerial, research and technical staff; that technical documentation on equipment, machinery, devices and processes was made available to all States, particularly developing ones; that adequate provision was made to facilitate the acquisition of technical assistance by States needing and requesting it, and of skills, know-how and professional training by their nationals; and that requesting States were helped to acquire equipment, processes, plant and know-how through financial arrangements provided for in the Convention (article 274).

States were to promote the establishment, particularly in developing coastal States, of national marine scientific and technological research centres and the strengthening of existing ones, with the aim of stimulating research, enhancing national capabilities to utilize and preserve marine resources for their economic benefit, and providing advanced training facilities, equipment, skills and know-how (article 275). The establishment of similar centres on a regional basis was also to be promoted (article 276). The functions of regional centres were to include training and education, management studies, environmental protection study programmes, organization of meetings, acquisition and processing of information, prompt dissemination of research results in readily available publications, publicizing and comparative study of national marine technology transfer policies, compilation and systematization of information on the marketing of technology and on patent arrangements, and technical co-operation with States of the region (article 277).

International organizations were to take measures to ensure, either directly or in close co-operation among themselves, the effective discharge of their functions and responsibilities in regard to marine technology transfer and development (article 278).

Conference consideration. The Conference on the Law of the Sea received no amendments and made no changes in 1982 to part XIV of the

Convention, on marine technology transfer and development. However, it adopted on 30 April a resolution on the subject, urging industrialized countries to assist developing countries with their marine science, technology and ocean service development programmes, and recommending that United Nations organizations expand their assistance to developing countries in this field (see ECONOMIC AND SOCIAL QUESTIONS, Chapter XII). The resolution was transmitted by the Secretary-General to the General Assembly.[1]

Israel, speaking to the Conference in December, said it wished to take advantage of the new arrangements for the diffusion of marine technology and scientific research, and would be happy to make its expertise available to others. Liberia called on the international community to help the developing countries, particularly those in Africa, through training of personnel and technology transfer. Sri Lanka mentioned that it had set up a National Aquatic Resources Agency to carry out, co-ordinate and promote research and development activities concerning marine and freshwater resources, and through which Sri Lanka intended to receive and eventually extend assistance and co-operation in marine science and technology.

Resolution (1982). [1]Conference: 30 Apr., transmitted by S-G note, A/37/566 & Corr.1.

Dispute settlement

Convention provisions. Part XV of the Convention on the Law of the Sea contained a set of procedures for the settlement of disputes concerning the interpretation or application of the Convention. Under this scheme, if the parties could not agree on a means of settlement, they would have to submit most types of disputes to a compulsory procedure entailing decisions binding on all parties. They would have four options: an International Tribunal for the Law of the Sea, established under the Convention; the existing International Court of Justice; and arbitration or special arbitration procedures (annexes VII and VIII). Certain disputes would be submitted to conciliation (annex V), a procedure whose outcome would not bind the parties.

States parties would commit themselves to settle their disputes by peaceful means (article 279). The Convention would not impair their right to agree at any time to settle a dispute by any peaceful means of their choice (article 280). In that event, the Convention's dispute settlement procedures would apply only where no settlement had been reached through such means (article 281). If the parties to a dispute had agreed, through a general, regional or bilateral agreement, to submit such disputes to a procedure entailing a binding decision, that procedure would apply in lieu of the Convention's procedures unless the parties agreed otherwise (article 282). States would be obliged to exchange views on the means of settlement of any dispute arising between them in relation to the Convention, and on the manner of implementing a settlement once it was reached (article 283).

Conciliation. One of the procedures to which the parties could agree was conciliation (article 284). The details of a voluntary conciliation procedure were supplied in annex V (section 1) to the Convention.

This specified that the procedure was to be initiated by written notification from one party to the other (article 1). The United Nations Secretary-General was to maintain a list of conciliators nominated by the States parties to the Convention (article 2). The conciliation commission was to have five members: two chosen by each party, preferably from the list, and the fifth chosen from the list by the other four; the Secretary-General could appoint any conciliators required to make up the five if this procedure failed (article 3). Decisions on procedural matters, the report and recommendations were to be made by majority vote (article 4).

The commission could draw the parties' attention to any measures which might facilitate an amicable settlement (article 5). It would hear the parties, examine their claims and objections, and make proposals with a view to reaching an amicable settlement (article 6). It would submit within 12 months a report whose conclusions or recommendations would not be binding on the parties (article 7). Conciliation would terminate when a settlement had been reached, when the parties had accepted or one party had rejected the recommendations, or when three months had elapsed after transmission of the report to the parties (article 8).

The fees and expenses of the commission would be borne by the parties to the dispute (article 9). The parties could, by agreement applicable solely to their dispute, modify any provision of annex V (article 10).

Compulsory settlement. Where no settlement had been reached by recourse to procedures agreed to by the parties, any party could take the dispute to a court or tribunal whose decision would be binding on the parties, unless the dispute concerned a topic exempted by the Convention from compulsory settlement (article 286). Each State, when signing or adhering to the Convention or at any other time, could opt for one or more of four dispute settlement bodies—the Tribunal, the International Court, an arbitral tribunal or a special arbitral tribunal; then, when a dispute arose, the procedure employed would be one of those accepted by both sides or, in the absence of a common procedure, arbitration (article 287).

The court or tribunal would have jurisdiction over any dispute submitted to it under this procedure (article 288). It would apply the Convention and other rules of international law not incompatible with it (article 293). It could select two or more scientific or technical experts to sit with it without the right to vote (article 289). In preliminary proceedings, it could determine whether a claim represented an abuse of legal process or whether *prima facie* it was well founded (article 294). It could prescribe provisional measures to preserve the rights of the parties or to prevent serious harm to the marine environment; in urgent cases and before the constitution of an arbitral tribunal to which a case was being submitted, provisional measures could be prescribed by another tribunal agreed to by the parties or, failing agreement, by the Tribunal for the Law of the Sea (article 290).

A flag State of a detained vessel could apply for its release to an agreed court or tribunal or, failing agreement, to the Tribunal for the Law of the Sea; the question of release would have to be dealt with without delay and without prejudice to the merits of the case against the vessel, and the detaining State would have to comply promptly with any decision upon the posting of the bond or other financial security determined by the court or tribunal (article 292).

All dispute settlement procedures specified in this part of the Convention would be open to States parties; other entities would have access to such procedures only as specifically provided for in the Convention (article 291). Disputes could be submitted to settlement under the Convention only after local remedies had been exhausted where that was required by international law (article 295).

Any decision by a court or tribunal would be final and binding, and all parties would have to comply with it; it would have no binding force except between the parties and in respect of that particular dispute (article 296).

Arbitration. Annexes VII and VIII to the Convention spelt out the details of two arbitration procedures.

Arbitration under annex VII, instituted by the submission of a written notification by one party to the other stating the claim and its grounds (article 1), would rely by preference on selection from a list of arbitrators nominated by States parties to the Convention (article 2). The arbitral tribunal for each case would have five members, one chosen by each of the parties to the dispute and the other three, who would be nationals of third States unless otherwise agreed, selected by agreement between the parties; the President or a senior member of the Tribunal for the Law of the Sea would make any appointments on which the parties could not agree (article 3). The arbitral tribunal would determine its own procedure unless the parties agreed otherwise (article 5).

The parties would be required to facilitate the tribunal's work by providing documents, facilities and information, and by enabling it to call witnesses or experts and visit relevant localities (article 6). Unless the tribunal decided otherwise because of particular circumstances, the expenses of the tribunal would be shared equally by the parties (article 7). Decisions would be taken by majority vote, with the President having a casting vote in the event of a tie (article 8). Absence of a party or failure of a party to defend its case would not constitute a bar to the proceedings (article 9).

The tribunal's award would be confined to the subject of the case and state the reasons on which it was based (article 10). The award would be final and without appeal, unless the parties had agreed in advance to an appellate procedure (article 11). Any controversy over interpretation or implementation of the award could be submitted by either party to the same tribunal or, by agreement of the parties, to another court or tribunal (article 12).

These arbitration provisions would also apply to a dispute involving entities other than States (article 13).

Special arbitration, detailed in annex VIII, would apply to disputes relating to fisheries, protection and preservation of the marine environment, marine scientific research or navigation (article 1). Lists of experts in each of these fields would be drawn up on the basis of nominations by States parties to the Convention (article 2). A special arbitral tribunal would consist of five members, of whom two would be chosen by each party, preferably from the appropriate list of experts, while the fifth, normally a national of a third State, who would be the President, would be chosen by the parties or, failing agreement, by the United Nations Secretary-General (article 3).

The procedures established for regular arbitration would apply to special arbitral proceedings (article 4). The parties could request a special arbitral tribunal to carry out an inquiry and establish the facts giving rise to their dispute, and its findings would be conclusive unless the parties agreed otherwise; at their request, it could also make recommendations which, without having the force of a decision, would constitute the basis for a review by the parties of the questions giving rise to the dispute (article 5).

Limitations and exceptions. The Convention exempted certain categories of disputes from compulsory settlement procedures and gave States the option of excluding others.

Excluded outright were the following (article 297):

—Disputes over the exercise by a coastal State of its sovereign rights or jurisdiction, except that compulsory settlement would apply in regard to three types of alleged contraventions: by a coastal State, contravention of the freedoms and rights of navigation, overflight, or the laying of submarine cables or pipelines, or in regard to certain other lawful uses of the sea in the exclusive economic zone (article 58); by a State exercising those freedoms and rights, contravention of a coastal State's laws and regulations; and by a coastal State, contravention of international rules and standards for the protection and preservation of the marine environment.

—Disputes over a coastal State's exercise of a right or discretion to withhold consent for marine scientific research in its exclusive economic zone or on its continental shelf (article 246), or its decision to order suspension or cessation of a research project (article 253), except that allegations that a coastal State had not acted in a manner compatible with the Convention in respect to a specific project would be subject to compulsory conciliation (see below).

—Disputes over a coastal State's sovereign rights over the living resources of its exclusive economic zone, including its discretionary power to determine the allowable catch, its harvesting capacity, the allocation of surpluses to other States, and terms and conditions in its conservation and management laws and regulations, except that compulsory conciliation would apply to disputes over the coastal State's alleged failure to comply with its obligation to prevent serious harm to the living resources in its zone, over its alleged arbitrary refusal to determine the allowable catch of a stock which another State was interested in fishing, and over its alleged arbitrary refusal to allocate the surplus to any State.

A State party could at any time declare in writing its non-acceptance of compulsory settlement in regard to any or all of the following types of disputes (article 298): disputes over sea boundary delimitation or those involving historic bays or titles, which would be subject to compulsory conciliation in the event that no agreement was reached within a reasonable time; disputes over military activities, and over law enforcement activities in regard to the exercise of sovereign rights or jurisdiction over marine scientific research and fisheries; and disputes before the Security Council, unless the Council called on the parties to settle the dispute by means provided for in the Convention.

Any of these excluded or excepted types of disputes could be submitted to compulsory settlement only by agreement of the parties, but they would retain the right to agree to some other procedure or to reach an amicable settlement (article 299).

Compulsory conciliation. Annex V (section 2) obliged States to submit to conciliation proceedings in regard to the three specific types of disputes (see above) identified in the clauses excluding and exempting certain matters from compulsory proce-

dures entailing binding decisions (article 11). The failure of a party to submit to such proceedings would not constitute a bar to the proceedings (article 12). A disagreement as to whether a conciliation commission had competence in a given case would be decided by the commission (article 13). Otherwise, the rules applicable to conciliation in general (see above) would apply to these proceedings (article 14). Thus, only the submission to conciliation would be compulsory; the conclusions and recommendations of the commission would not be binding on the parties.

Conference consideration. No changes were proposed or made to the dispute settlement provisions of the Convention by the Conference on the Law of the Sea in 1982.

Chile, explaining on 30 April its vote for the Convention, described these provisions as a milestone of international law which should be considered an important part of the Convention closely linked to its substantive provisions.

During the closing week of the Conference in December, several speakers welcomed the dispute settlement features, although some expressed regret that not more of them were compulsory.

Barbados said that, although it was not happy with provisions of a less binding nature, it accepted them in a spirit of compromise. Cyprus welcomed the provisions as one of the Conference's important accomplishments but observed that its support for a system of binding decisions had been met only to a certain extent under the Convention's labyrinthine formula of exceptions for disputes affecting national sovereignty; it remained to be seen whether the compulsory conciliation procedure for resolving sea boundary disputes would serve the same purpose. The Federal Republic of Germany welcomed the provisions for compulsory settlement.

Ireland described the dispute settlement procedures as adequate and, along with Austria, welcomed the assurance that the Convention would eliminate a significant area of potential conflict from the world scene. Italy thought the provisions were a step forward in comparison with other codification conventions and an important guarantee for all States.

Some States commented on the choice of procedures provided for in the Convention. Bulgaria, stressing the Convention's provisions on dispute settlement by means chosen by the parties, reserved the right to make use of the provision allowing it to declare its non-recognition of obligatory procedures and those entailing binding decisions. The Byelorussian SSR and the Ukrainian SSR chose arbitration as the main means of dispute settlement and said they would not accept binding procedures for the types of disputes listed in article 298. The USSR made a similar statement with respect to that article. Sweden said its choice among the options for dispute settlement would be made in the light of its traditional view that strong compulsory machinery for third-party settlement was a desirable element in international agreements.

International Tribunal for the Law of the Sea

Annex VI to the Convention on the Law of the Sea contained the Statute of the International Tribunal for the Law of the Sea, with provisions on its organization, competence and procedure, and on its Sea-Bed Disputes Chamber. The Tribunal would have its seat at Hamburg, Federal Republic of Germany (article 1).

The Tribunal would be composed of 21 independent members (article 2), including at least three from each major geographical group (article 3). They would be elected by a special meeting of States parties to the Convention from among persons nominated by those States (article 4) and would serve for a nine-year, renewable term (article 5). Vacancies would be filled by the same procedure (article 6).

No member could exercise any political or administrative function, or associate with or be financially interested in any enterprise concerned with commercial use of the sea or sea-bed (article 7). No member could participate in the decision of any case in which he or she had previously taken part in any capacity (article 8). If the other members of the Tribunal unanimously found that a member had ceased to fulfil the required conditions, the President could declare the seat vacant (article 9). The members would enjoy diplomatic privileges and immunities when engaged on the Tribunal's business (article 10). Before taking up their duties, they would have to make a solemn declaration that they would exercise their powers impartially and conscientiously (article 11).

The Tribunal would elect its President and Vice-President for a renewable three-year term (article 12). The required quorum would be 11 elected members (article 13). The Tribunal would frame rules for carrying out its functions, including rules of procedure (article 16).

In addition to the Sea-Bed Disputes Chamber, the Tribunal could form special chambers of three or more elected members to deal with particular categories of disputes and, at the request of the parties, to deal with a particular dispute; a judgement by any such chamber would be considered as rendered by the Tribunal (article 15).

Each party to a dispute before the Tribunal could choose someone to participate as a Tribunal member, with the right to participate in the decision on terms of complete equality, if a person of the party's nationality was not already a member (article 17). The members would receive non-taxable remuneration in the form of an annual allowance and a special allowance for each day on which they exercised their functions (article 18). The expenses of the Tribunal would be borne by the States parties and the International Sea-Bed Authority on terms to be decided at meetings of the States parties (article 19).

With respect to the Tribunal's competence, its Statute specified that it was open to States parties and, in the case of sea-bed disputes, to other entities (article 20). Its jurisdiction would comprise all disputes and applications submitted to it in accordance with the Convention and all matters provided for in any other agreement conferring jurisdiction on it (article 21). By agreement of the parties, disputes over the interpretation or application of any other treaty on law of the sea matters could be submitted to the Tribunal (article 22). The Tribunal (article 23) would decide all disputes and applications in accordance with the applicable law specified for any court or tribunal having jurisdiction under the Convention's provisions on compulsory dispute settlement (article 293)—namely, the Convention and other rules of international law not incompatible with it.

As to the Tribunal's procedure, disputes would be submitted either by notification of a special agreement or by written application (article 24). The Tribunal could prescribe provisional measures to preserve the rights of the parties or prevent serious harm to the marine environment (article 25). Its hearing of a case would be public unless the Tribunal decided or the parties demanded otherwise (article 26). The Tribunal would make orders for the conduct of the case, decide how and when each party must conclude its arguments, and arrange for the taking of evidence (article 27). Absence of a party or its failure to defend its case would not constitute a bar to the proceedings (article 28).

All questions would be decided by a majority of the members present, with the President or other presiding officer having a casting vote in the event of a tie (article 29). The judgement would state the reasons on which it was based, and any member would be entitled to deliver a separate opinion (article 30).

The Tribunal could decide on a request by another State party to the Convention to be permitted to intervene in a case in which it had a legal interest; in such case, the Tribunal's decision would be binding on that State in regard to matters on which it had intervened (article 31). Every State party to the Convention or to an international agreement would have the right to intervene whenever the Tribunal dealt with the interpretation or application of the Convention or agreement; in such case, the Tribunal's interpretation would be binding on that State (article 32). The

Tribunal's decision would be final and all parties to the dispute would have to comply with it; however, it would bind only those parties and only in respect of that dispute (article 33). Unless the Tribunal decided otherwise, each party would bear its own costs (article 34).

Amendments to the Tribunal's Statute (article 41) could be made in accordance with the "simplified procedure" for amending the Convention (article 313) or by consensus at a review conference, except that amendments to the section on the Sea-Bed Disputes Chamber (articles 35-40) would have to follow the procedure for amending the sea-bed provisions of the Convention (article 314); the Tribunal could propose amendments.

Practical arrangements for the establishment of the Tribunal were to be submitted by the Preparatory Commission to the first meeting of States parties for the election of the Tribunal, according to Conference resolution I[(1)] on the Preparatory Commission.

Resolution (1982). [(1)]Conference (Final Act, A/CONF.62/121 & Corr.3): I, para. 10, 30 Apr.

General provisions

Part XVI of the Convention on the Law of the Sea, entitled "General provisions", contained five articles on topics going beyond the scope of individual parts of the Convention devoted to a particular area or use of the sea.

Under these provisions, States parties were to fulfil in good faith their obligations under the Convention and to exercise their rights, jurisdiction and freedoms in a manner which would not constitute an abuse of right (article 300). They were to refrain from any threat or use of force against the territorial integrity or political independence of any State, or in any other manner inconsistent with the international law principles in the Charter of the United Nations (article 301). Without prejudice to the Convention's dispute settlement procedures, nothing in the Convention would require a State party, in fulfilling its Convention obligations, to supply information whose disclosure was contrary to its essential security interests (article 302).

Archaeological and historical objects found at sea were to be protected, and coastal States would be entitled to prohibit their removal from the seabed up to the limit of the 24-mile contiguous zone (article 303). The Convention's provisions on responsibility and liability for damage would not prejudice the application of existing rules and the development of new ones in that regard (article 304).

Final clauses

The final provisions of the Convention on the Law of the Sea, set out in part XVII, dealt with various matters concerning its entry into force and application. They defined the ways in which States and other entities could participate in the Convention, prohibited reservations and specified how the Convention could be amended after it was in force.

The United Nations Secretary-General was to serve as depositary of the Convention and amendments—recording signatures and receiving instruments of ratification and accession deposited by States—and was also authorized to report on general issues arising with respect to the Convention, convene meetings of States parties and perform certain notification functions (article 319). The authentic texts of the Convention were in Arabic, Chinese, English, French, Russian and Spanish (article 320). The nine annexes formed an integral part of the Convention (article 318).

Participation in the Convention

The Convention on the Law of the Sea was open for signature (article 305), ratification (article 306) and accession (article 307) by all States and by Namibia, represented by the United Nations Council for Namibia. It was also open to self-governing associated States and non-independent territories having legal competence over the matters governed by the Convention, and to intergovernmental organizations meeting certain criteria, except that, for organizations, the procedure of formal confirmation was to replace that of ratification. Under a resolution adopted by the Conference on 30 April 1982, national liberation movements were authorized to sign the Final Act of the Conference in their capacity as observers. Another resolution adopted on that date was aimed at protecting the rights and interests of peoples in non-self-governing and disputed territories.

The Convention was to remain open for signature until 9 December 1984, after which a State or other competent entity could adhere by accession (a procedure which does not require prior signature). The Convention provided for its entry into force 12 months after the date of deposit of the sixtieth instrument of ratification or accession, at which time the Assembly of the International Sea-Bed Authority would meet to elect the Council (article 308).

Several issues pertaining to participation were resolved during the final negotiating phase of the Conference in March and April 1982. After three weeks of informal meetings and consultations on the subject, the President submitted on 26 March a report suggesting a series of articles on participation by intergovernmental organizations, and compromises on participation by national liberation movements, States, territories not fully independent and Namibia, and on the peoples of non-self-governing territories.[2] These proposals were incorporated in the draft Convention and draft Final Act through the memorandum issued on 2 April by the Conference collegium (p. 182).[1]

Memorandum. [1]Conference collegium, A/CONF.62/L.93 & Corr.1.
Report. [2]Conference President, A/CONF.62/L.86 & Corr.1.

Participation by intergovernmental organizations

The signature, ratification and accession articles of the Convention on the Law of the Sea permitted certain types of intergovernmental organizations to become party to the Convention. The conditions were specified in annex IX of the Convention, applying to organizations to which their member States had transferred competence over matters governed by the Convention, including the competence to enter into treaties in respect of those matters (article 1).

Such an organization could sign the Convention (article 2) or become a party (article 3) only if a majority of its members had done so. It could adhere by depositing an instrument of formal confirmation or of accession (equivalent to ratification or accession by a State).

Where legal competence over certain matters had been transferred to such an organization by its members, it would exercise the rights and be bound by the obligations that would otherwise be required of its members in regard to those matters, but without giving those members an additional decision-making voice in the machinery established under the Convention, and without conferring rights on those of its members which were not parties to the Convention (article 4). When adhering to the Convention, and at any time thereafter if a specific question arose, the organization would have to specify the areas of its competence; its member States would be presumed to have competence over all other matters governed by the Convention (article 5). The competent party, whether the organization or its members, would bear responsibility for any violation of the Convention (article 6).

The Convention's dispute settlement provisions would apply to organizations which adhered to the Convention (article 7). An organization's adherence would not be counted among the 60 ratifications or accessions needed to bring the Convention into force but, if it adhered to an amendment over whose entire subject-matter it had competence, that would count as adherence by each of its members which were parties to the Convention (article 8).

These provisions on intergovernmental organizations were formulated by the Conference President in his memorandum of 26 March,[2] based on a series of informal meetings and consultations.

They modified an informal text which he had proposed in 1981.[4] The March text was further modified when the President, in a report of 22 April 1982,[3] accepted an amendment by Belgium[1] for which he found widespread and substantial support. This deleted a paragraph (in annex IX, article 4) that would have restricted arrangements under which the members of an intergovernmental organization could grant special treatment to one another with regard to matters governed by the Convention.

During the concluding statements at the Conference in December, Denmark, speaking for the European Economic Community (EEC), said the complex set of rules on participation of intergovernmental organizations in the Convention was acceptable, even though it fell short of what EEC had proposed.

Amendment adopted. [1]Belgium, A/CONF.62/L.119.
Reports. Conference President, [2]A/CONF.62/L.86 & Corr.1, [3]A/CONF.62/L.132.
Yearbook reference. [4]1981, p. 134.

Participation by associated States and territories

Self-governing associated States which had retained certain links with the former administering Power, and internally self-governing territories which had not attained full independence, were entitled to sign and ratify or accede to the Convention on the Law of the Sea provided that they had legal competence over the matters governed by it, including the competence to enter into treaties on such matters (articles 305-307). Namibia, represented by the United Nations Council for Namibia, was also authorized to sign and ratify or accede.

For territories not fully independent or self-governing, and those under colonial domination, Conference resolution III,[8] adopted along with the Convention on 30 April 1982, stated that provisions concerning rights and interests under the Convention were to be implemented for the benefit of the people of the territory with a view to promoting their well-being and development. Where a territory was the object of a dispute over its sovereignty, and the United Nations had recommended specific means of settlement, the parties to the dispute would consult on the exercise of rights dealt with in the Convention. In such consultations, the interests of the territory's people would be a fundamental consideration. Any exercise of those rights would take account of United Nations resolutions and be without prejudice to the parties' positions. The States concerned should try to make provisional arrangements without jeopardizing a final settlement.

The Convention's provisions on adherence to it by self-governing associated States and territories were added to the text on the proposal of the President in his 26 March report on the participation of various entities.[6] There was no doubt, he stated, that they possessed the requisite qualifications.

The resolution, and particularly its provisions on disputed territories, aroused more controversy, however. The text was proposed by the President in his March report to replace a "transitional provision" in the 1981 draft Convention according to which rights over a non-self-governing territory's ocean resources were to have been vested in the inhabitants and exercised for their benefit and in accordance with their needs, while rights over the resources of a disputed territory were not to be exercised without the consent of the parties to the dispute. In suggesting his resolution, the President said there seemed to be no controversy over the basic principle that the peoples of the territory concerned should be the beneficiaries of the resources, but the language used to express that principle, and its placement with regard to the Convention, seemed to be a problem.

The Conference collegium, in its 2 April memorandum,[5] decided to include the draft resolution[4] in the Conference's draft Final Act.

Spain proposed, but did not press, an amendment that would have restored the pre-1982 text on disputed territories in place of the President's text.[3] In explaining its abstention in the vote on the Convention and associated resolutions, Spain said in April that it could not accept resolution III and objected particularly to the paragraph on disputed territories. Reiterating this reservation in December, it stated that the question of the part of Spanish territory under colonial domination was subject only to the relevant resolutions of the General Assembly.

Argentina, though voting for the Convention on 30 April, expressed regret that the transitional provision in the earlier negotiating texts had not been retained, as its aim had been to prevent the Powers which controlled colonial or occupied territories from exercising rights that might consolidate such unlawful situations. Argentina informed the General Assembly on 3 December that it could not sign the Convention or the Final Act because it objected to the provision on disputed territories in resolution III; it added that the provision did not affect the Malvinas Islands question.

With respect to participation by Namibia, the Conference approved by consensus on 26 April amendments proposed by the President[1] to enable that Territory, represented by the Council for Namibia, to sign the Convention and, by virtue of a change in Conference resolution I on the Preparatory Commission,[7] to become a member of that Commission.

This text replaced an amendment submitted by the Council according to which the phrase "including Namibia, represented by the United Na-

tions Council for Namibia", would have been added to a subparagraph (of article 305) stating that the Convention could be signed by all States.[2] Under the approved text, the provision on Namibia was in a separate subparagraph.

On 10 December, the Council, on behalf of Namibia, signed the Convention and the Final Act. These actions were noted by the General Assembly on 20 December, in a resolution on the Council's work programme.[9]

Speaking at the closing meetings of the Conference in December, the Council condemned South Africa's attempts to extend in its own name Namibia's territorial sea and to proclaim an exclusive economic zone for Namibia, and declared those acts null and void.

Commenting in December on the provision permitting associated States to adhere to the Convention, New Zealand said it was particularly appropriate that the Cook Islands and Niue would have the right to participate on the same basis as their Pacific island neighbours. The Netherlands Antilles believed that resolution III safeguarded its rights to and interests in ocean resources. Vanuatu said that, unless the colonized countries in the Pacific became independent, their sea and air would continue to be exploited by the colonizing nations, using the Convention as a convenient tool.

The Trust Territory of the Pacific Islands stated that the governments of its three separate entities—the Republics of Palau and the Marshall Islands and the Federated States of Micronesia— had since 1977 declared and regulated their own 200-mile zone and had concluded international treaties relating to the law of the sea, and they expected to become party to the Convention. The USSR and other Eastern European States said that any change in the status of the Trusteeship Agreement brought about by the Trust Territory's participation in the Convention would have to be sanctioned by the Security Council.

Amendments. [1]Conference President, A/CONF.62/L.137 (adopted); [2]Council for Namibia, A/CONF.62/L.102 (superseded); [3]Spain, A/CONF.62/L.109 (not pressed).
Draft resolution. [4]Conference collegium, A/CONF.62/L.94.
Memorandum. [5]Conference collegium, A/CONF.62/L.93.
Report. [6]Conference President, A/CONF.62/L.86 & Corr.1.
Resolutions (1982). Conference (Final Act, A/CONF.62/121), 30 Apr.: [7]I, para. 2; [8]III. [9]GA: 37/233 C, para. 13, 20 Dec.

Participation by national liberation movements

Under resolution IV, adopted by the Conference on the Law of the Sea on 30 April 1982, national liberation movements which had been participating in the Conference (as observers) were authorized to sign the Final Act in their observer capacity.[6] Under the Convention, they were also entitled to attend, as observers, the Assembly of the International Sea-Bed Authority (article 156) and any meetings of States parties, and to receive reports and notifications sent by the Secretary-General to States parties containing information about ratifications, proposed amendments and other matters relating to the Convention (article 319).

The provisions on liberation movements originated in proposals by the President in his 26 March report on various aspects of participation in the Convention.[4] The President commented that their observer status would enable them to present the views of the peoples they represented and request the adoption of measures to protect those peoples' interests until they attained autonomy or independence. These proposals were incorporated into the draft Convention by the Conference collegium in its memorandum[3] and proposals[2] of 2 April.

The arrangements for liberation movements were approved as proposed in amendments by Iraq,[1] which placed the authorization to sign the Final Act in a resolution, rather than a decision as the President had proposed, and which made other changes in the form of the President's proposals.

The Iraqi amendments were inserted into the draft Convention and associated texts as part of several changes in the drafts which the Conference agreed to on 30 April, as recommended by the President in his report of 22 April.[5] Before it did so, Israel asked for a separate vote on the draft resolution. When the President ruled that no separate vote was permissible, Israel appealed his ruling. The appeal was rejected by a recorded vote of 143 to 1, with 2 abstentions.

In explanation of its vote against the Convention and associated resolutions, Israel said, in reference to resolution IV, that it could not accept any provision that gave any standing to the Palestine Liberation Organization (PLO); it added in December that its signature of the Final Act implied no recognition of PLO or of any of the rights conferred on it by the documents attached to the Final Act.

Also speaking in December, Democratic Yemen, Iraq, Somalia and Viet Nam said they would have preferred to see the Convention confer on such movements the status of full-fledged parties. The Byelorussian SSR, the Ukrainian SSR and the USSR also said the Convention should be open to full participation by such movements; the Ukrainian SSR added that the notion of the common heritage of mankind would be deprived of some of its meaning if the peoples struggling for national liberation could not enjoy their rightful share of that heritage. Egypt welcomed the representation of national liberation movements as a major victory, making the Conference a unique example of universality.

Amendments adopted. [1]Iraq, A/CONF.62/L.101.
Draft decision. [2]Conference collegium, A/CONF.62/L.94.

Memorandum. [3]Conference collegium, A/CONF.62/-L.93/Corr.1.
Reports. Conference President, [4]A/CONF.62/L.86, [5]A/CONF.62/L.132.
Resolution (1982). [6]Conference (Final Act, A/CONF.62/121): IV, 30 Apr.
Meeting records. Conference: A/CONF.62/SR.158-166, 168-179, 182 (30 Mar.–30 Apr.), A/CONF.62/PV.85-192 (6-9 Dec.).

Reservations

The Convention on the Law of the Sea stated that no reservations or exceptions could be made to it unless expressly permitted by a provision in the text (article 309). But this would not preclude a State, when signing, ratifying or acceding, from making declarations or statements with a view to harmonizing its laws and regulations with the Convention's provisions, provided that it did not purport to modify the legal effect of those provisions in their application to that State (article 310). Two or more States parties could conclude agreements modifying or suspending the operation of Convention provisions, applicable solely to relations between them, provided that the agreements did not relate to a provision derogation from which was incompatible with the Convention's purpose, and that they did not affect the application of the Convention's basic principles or the rights and obligations of other States parties (article 311).

Three amendments to limit or delete the prohibition of reservations were presented to the Conference. The first, by Venezuela, would have permitted reservations with regard to delimitation of the territorial sea, the exclusive economic zone and the continental shelf between States with opposite or adjacent coasts, and to the clause providing that uninhabitable rocks had no exclusive economic zone or continental shelf.[3] The second, by Romania, would have deleted the provision prohibiting declarations or statements that purported to exclude or modify the legal effect of any article in its application to a State.[1] The third amendment, by Turkey, called for deletion of the article prohibiting reservations.[2]

The President, reporting on 22 April on his consultations concerning amendments, said he had concluded that there were no prospects of achieving a generally acceptable solution to those relating to reservations.[4]

The first two of these amendments were not pressed to a vote. On 26 April, the Conference rejected the Turkish amendment by a recorded vote of 100 to 18, with 26 abstentions. Those voting for the amendment were: Albania, Bolivia, China, Democratic Kampuchea, Democratic People's Republic of Korea, Ecuador, Egypt, El Salvador, Guatemala, Oman, Philippines, Romania, Saudi Arabia, Somalia, Turkey, Upper Volta, Venezuela, Yemen.

Turkey and Venezuela cited the reservations clause when explaining on 30 April why they had voted against the Convention; Turkey added that it had proposed the deletion of that article to accommodate those countries which wanted to adhere to the Convention while at the same time safeguarding their specific vital interests.

Albania also mentioned this clause as one of the reasons why it had not participated in the vote on the Convention; it said the provision depriving States which might wish to adhere to the Convention of the right to enter reservations was unjust.

Egypt, which voted for the Convention, said it had wanted the reservations clause to be governed by the Vienna Convention on the Law of Treaties[5] (which permitted certain types of reservations to multilateral treaties); however, it noted that (under article 310) States were allowed to make statements in relation to their national legislation. Romania said a State retained the right to enter reservations when it became a party to a multilateral treaty.

During the final week of the Conference in December, Chad, Czechoslovakia and Singapore appealed to States not to take advantage of article 310 in order to make declarations that contradicted the spirit and objectives of the Convention. Similarly, the German Democratic Republic believed States should refrain from making declarations designed to alter substantive provisions of the Convention in a one-sided manner. The Byelorussian SSR said it would refrain from such declarations if others did likewise. The Ukrainian SSR and the USSR also said they would refrain, adding that such declarations would provoke responses from other States with a different viewpoint and might complicate the situation.

Speaking of the prohibition of reservations, Colombia said it existed because every part of the Convention affected every other part; reservations would be incompatible with the unity and interrelationship of its rules.

Liberia stated that it reserved the right under article 310 to review certain articles of the Convention.

Amendments. [1]Romania, A/CONF.62/L.111 (not pressed); [2]Turkey, A/CONF.62/L.120 (rejected); [3]Venezuela, A/CONF.62/L.108 & Corr.1 (not pressed).
Report. [4]Conference President, A/CONF.62/L.132.
Yearbook reference. [5]1969, p. 734.

Amendments

Three different procedures were provided for amending the Convention on the Law of the Sea once it entered into force.

Amendments on matters other than the sea-bed could not be proposed during the first 10 years after entry into force, and would be subject to approval by an amendment conference which would resort to voting only after all efforts at consensus had been exhausted; if that happened, it would follow the rules of the Conference on the Law of the Sea (requiring a two-thirds majority for substantive decisions) unless it decided otherwise (article 312). However, a simplified procedure would permit an amendment to be adopted if no State objected to it within 12 months of the date on which it was proposed (article 313). An amendment relating to the international sea-bed area would require approval by the Council and the Assembly of the International Sea-Bed Authority, which would have to ensure that it did not prejudice the resource exploitation system pending the Review Conference to be called 15 years after the start of commercial production (article 314).

Once adopted, an amendment would be open for signature for 12 months (article 315). It would enter into force 30 days after ratification or accession by 60 States parties to the Convention or, if there were more than 90 parties, by two thirds of them, and it would be in effect only for those States which accepted it; sea-bed amendments would enter into force for all States parties one year after ratification or accession by three fourths of them (article 316).

Sri Lanka, speaking during the final week of the Conference in December, noted that the Convention had built-in machinery for orderly change through amendment, review and revision procedures, and said those who had fashioned the Convention must be vigilant in detecting obsolescence and remedying it.

Signatures and ratification

As at 31 December 1982, the following had signed the Convention:

Algeria, Angola, Australia, Austria, Bahamas, Bahrain, Bangladesh, Barbados, Belize, Bhutan, Brazil, Bulgaria, Burma, Burundi, Byelorussian SSR, Canada, Cape Verde, Chad, Chile, China, Colombia, Congo, Cook Islands, Costa Rica, Cuba, Cyprus, Czechoslovakia, Democratic People's Republic of Korea, Democratic Yemen, Denmark, Djibouti, Dominican Republic, Egypt, Ethiopia, Fiji, Finland, France, Gabon, Gambia, German Democratic Republic, Ghana, Greece, Grenada, Guinea-Bissau, Guyana, Haiti, Honduras, Hungary, Iceland, India, Indonesia, Iran, Iraq, Ireland, Ivory Coast, Jamaica, Kenya, Kuwait, Lao People's Democratic Republic, Lesotho, Liberia, Malaysia, Maldives, Malta, Mauritania, Mauritius, Mexico, Monaco, Mongolia, Morocco, Mozambique, Namibia (United Nations Council for Namibia), Nauru, Nepal, Netherlands, New Zealand, Niger, Nigeria, Norway, Pakistan, Panama, Papua New Guinea, Paraguay, Philippines, Poland, Portugal, Romania, Rwanda, Saint Lucia, Saint Vincent and the Grenadines, Senegal, Seychelles, Sierra Leone, Singapore, Solomon Islands, Somalia, Sri Lanka, Sudan, Suriname, Sweden, Thailand, Togo, Trinidad and Tobago, Tunisia, Tuvalu, Uganda, Ukrainian SSR, USSR, United Arab Emirates, United Republic of Cameroon, United Republic of Tanzania, Upper Volta, Uruguay, Vanuatu, Viet Nam, Yemen, Yugoslavia, Zambia, Zimbabwe.

All 119 signatures were affixed to the Convention at Montego Bay, Jamaica, on 10 December, the day it was opened for signature. It was to remain open for two years.

Fiji was the first State to ratify it, also on 10 December, and the only one in 1982.

In its 3 December resolution on the Conference, the General Assembly called on all States to consider signing and ratifying the Convention at the earliest possible date to allow the new legal régime for the sea to enter into force.[1] This paragraph was adopted by a recorded vote of 134 to 3, with 7 abstentions.

Objections to this paragraph were voiced by Turkey and the United States, which voted against the resolution; Israel, which cast a negative vote on the paragraph while abstaining on the resolution as a whole; Albania, which did not take part in the vote; and Belgium, the Federal Republic of Germany, Italy and the United Kingdom, which abstained on the resolution. The United Kingdom added that it was inappropriate for the Assembly to call for early signature and ratification.

Resolution (1982). [1]GA: 37/66, para. 2, 3 Dec.

Preparatory Commission

Resolution I of the Conference on the Law of the Sea, adopted on 30 April 1982, provided for the establishment of the Preparatory Commission for the International Sea-Bed Authority and for the International Tribunal for the Law of the Sea, the two major organs to be established upon the entry into force of the Convention on the Law of the Sea.[8]

According to this resolution, only States which signed or acceded to the Convention could be members of the Commission. Others could participate as observers if they signed only the Final Act of the Conference but they could not take part in decision-making. The Conference's rules of procedure would apply with respect to the adoption of the Commission's rules.

The Commission was to be convened by the United Nations Secretary-General between 60 and 90 days after 50 States signed the Convention. It was to be financed from the United Nations regular budget, subject to General Assembly approval, and serviced by the United Nations Secretariat. It would remain in existence until the conclusion of the first session of the Assembly of the Authority.

The Commission was to prepare draft rules, regulations and procedures necessary to enable the Authority to commence its functions, as well as perform the traditional preparatory functions of drafting agenda and a budget. It was also to exercise the powers and functions assigned to it in the resolution on pioneer investors and undertake studies on the problems of developing land-based

mineral-producing States likely to be seriously affected by sea-bed production.

The resolution provided for the establishment of two special commissions of the Preparatory Commission: one on the Enterprise and the other on the problems of developing land-based producer States. The Commission was also empowered to establish other subsidiary bodies as required and to make use of outside experts. It was to recommend arrangements for the establishment of the Tribunal and submit them to the first meeting of States parties for the election of the Tribunal, to be convened once the Convention entered into force.

Arrangements for the Preparatory Commission were considered in March by the First Committee's Working Group of 21 during the first three weeks of the 1982 session. Discussion was based on an informal draft submitted in August 1981 by the Working Group's Co-ordinators—the Conference President and the Chairman of the First Committee.[9] In a report to the First Committee on 29 March,[7] the Co-ordinators proposed the draft resolution on this subject that was to form the basis for the Conference's final action and described some of the issues that had emerged in the informal discussions.

On the issue of participation in the Commission, the report said, some industrialized States had continued to press their idea that signature of the Final Act should qualify a State for membership. However, there had been widespread support for maintaining the existing provision (requiring signature of the Convention), on the argument that the extent of a State's commitment to the Convention should determine the level of its participation in the Commission.

As to decision-making, the Co-ordinators noted that various views had been expressed on the majorities to be required, ranging from simple majority to consensus. They had therefore proposed to let the Commission determine its own rules on this point, with the Conference's rules to govern the initial determination.

The Co-ordinators added to their 1981 draft the provisions empowering the Commission to perform functions assigned to it by the resolution on pioneer investors and requiring it to prepare studies on the problems of developing land-based producers. Regarding financing, the Co-ordinators said there was inadequate support for any change in the provision to have the Commission financed from the United Nations regular budget, although the industrialized States had linked that issue to the requirement for membership.

The Conference collegium decided to include the Co-ordinators' draft resolution in the draft Final Act,[4] as reported in their memorandum of 2 April.[5]

Three documents containing amendments on the subject were proposed in April. One of these, presented by Peru on behalf of the Group of 77,[2] was accepted by the Conference after the President, in his report of 22 April,[6] concluded that it had widespread and substantial support; it added the provision for a special commission on the problems of developing land-based producers.

The other amendments were not pressed. One, by the USSR, would have applied the consensus rule to the Commission's approval of the Authority's draft rules, regulations and procedures.[3]

The other amendments, by seven Western States (Belgium, France, Federal Republic of Germany, Italy, Japan, United Kingdom, United States),[1] concerned both membership and decision-making. They would have opened the Commission to all States that had signed the Final Act. They also proposed that the Commission's decisions on matters of substance be taken by a two-thirds majority of 36 States elected by the Conference according to the pattern laid down for the composition of the Authority's Council, as specified in other amendments by the same delegations. However, decisions on the draft rules, regulations and procedures governing sea-bed mining, and on the operation of the pioneer investor scheme, would require consensus among the 36 States or, if consensus was not reached within 18 months of the resolution's adoption, by a majority of the Convention signatories whose nationals were involved in pioneer sea-bed activities. Such rules, regulations and procedures would extend to all sea-bed resources.

During the final week of the Conference in December, a number of States stressed the importance of the Preparatory Commission's work for inducing additional States to adhere to the Convention. Australia said the Commission's members, when working out the details of access to the sea-bed, should take account of the interests of those which might accede to the Convention in future. A similar point was made by New Zealand. Canada cited the need for a realistic and pragmatic attitude. Chile and others stressed the need to maintain a spirit of consensus in the Commission. The operation of the Commission, said Colombia, should pave the way for universality, not hamper it. Denmark said the Commission should lay the foundations for a structure large enough to hold all nations and sufficiently attractive to convince everyone that living with the Convention was worth while.

France, stating that the Commission should correct defects in the sea-bed provisions of the Convention, believed the Commission should act by consensus in order to preserve the interests of everyone involved. The Federal Republic of Germany also said the Commission might have an important role to play in respect of the adjustments and improvements needed to make the Convention effective. Whether States experiencing difficulties with the Convention would eventually become parties would depend largely on the work of the Commission, said Mauritius.

Norway saw the Commission as the only viable instrument to achieve a universal Convention and stressed the need for all States which signed the Conference's Final Act to participate in the Commission as observers. The United Kingdom believed that, starting with the Commission, States should try to build on generally agreed points in the Convention and seek co-operation between those having different views of its provisions. Uruguay believed the Commission, through the wise and balanced exercise of its discretionary powers, could play an important role in removing the difficulties experienced by some States. A similar point was made by Austria and Italy.

The United Republic of Cameroon warned, however, that it would be undesirable to attempt to make the Commission a forum for renegotiating any part of the Convention, though it could employ its expertise to remove uncertainties about the application of the Convention's broad rules. Mexico said that, in participating in the Commission, it would oppose special interests which sought to misdirect the Commission's mandate to the detriment of the will of the majority.

Amendments. [1]Belgium, France, Germany, Federal Republic of, Italy, Japan, United Kingdom, United States, A/CONF.62/L.121 (not pressed); [2]Peru, for Group of 77, A/CONF.62/L.116; [3]USSR, A/CONF.62/L.125 (not pressed).
Draft resolution. [4]Conference collegium, A/CONF.62/L.94.
Memorandum. [5]Conference collegium, A/CONF.62/L.93.
Reports. [6]Conference President, A/CONF.62/L.132 & Add.1; [7]Working Group Co ordinators, A/CONF.62/* C.1/L.30.
Resolution (1982). [8]Conference (Final Act, A/CONF.62/121 & Corr.3): I, 30 Apr.
Yearbook reference. [9]1981, p. 137.
Meeting records. Conference: A/CONF.62/SR.158-166, 168-179, 182 (30 Mar.–30 Apr.), A/CONF.62/PV.185-192 (6-9 Dec.).

Establishment of the Commission

The General Assembly, in its resolution of 3 December 1982 on the Conference on the Law of the Sea,[3] authorized the Secretary-General to convene the Preparatory Commission as provided in the Conference's establishing resolution and to provide it with services. It approved the financing of the Commission from the United Nations regular budget—as proposed by the Conference[2]—and the stationing of an adequate number of staff in Jamaica to service the Commission.

An amendment by Turkey and the United States to have the Commission's expenses met by the States signing the Convention[1] was rejected by a recorded vote of 134 to 3 (the sponsors and Israel), with 7 abstentions. The Assembly then adopted paragraph 9 of the resolution, providing for meeting the expenses from the United Nations budget, by a recorded vote of 134 to 3, with 7 abstentions.

Introducing the amendment, the United States said it was wrong to ask the United Nations to pay for a preparatory body of a separate treaty organization to which United Nations Members could not belong unless they signed the treaty, and it was doubly wrong to ask it to pay for an extensive meeting away from Headquarters. Turkey, the amendment's other sponsor, reserved the right, if it was not adopted, to refuse to contribute for expenses arising from implementation of the Convention. Israel supported the amendment, stating that it saw no reason not to follow the normal practice whereby the expenses would be met by the States that had expressed their consent to be bound by the Convention.

Abstaining in the vote on the amendment and on the resolution as a whole, the United Kingdom said that, while it would play a full part in the Commission, it regarded it as normal that the costs of administering a multilateral treaty be borne by the parties; alternatively, the Commission might have been financed by a loan from the United Nations.

Opposing the amendment, Singapore said it was not consistent with the agreement reached at the Conference and embodied in resolution I, which represented a trade-off that provided for defraying the Commission's expenses from the regular budget and allowing States that signed the Final Act but not the Convention to participate as observers in the Commission.

When introducing the Assembly resolution, Singapore said it had been agreed in consultations that the Commission would meet at Kingston, Jamaica, for four weeks in February or March 1983, with the option of extending its session or holding a further two-week session. It could establish up to four working groups that could meet for a maximum of four weeks in 1983, at Kingston or in New York.

With the signature of the Convention on 10 December 1982 by more than the required number of 50 States, the Secretary-General announced at the closing meeting of the Conference that the Preparatory Commission would be convened at Kingston on 15 March 1983.

Amendment. (1)Turkey, United States, A/37/L.15/Rev.1.
Resolutions (1982). (2)Conference (Final Act, A/CONF.62/121 & Corr.3): I, para. 14, 30 Apr. (3)GA: 37/66, paras. 7-9, 3 Dec.

Functions of the Secretary-General

In its 3 December 1982 resolution on the Conference on the Law of the Sea, the General Assembly approved the assumption by the Secretary-General of the responsibilities entrusted to him under the Convention on the Law of the Sea and the related resolutions.(5)

Those responsibilities were outlined in a November note by the Secretary-General to the Assembly(1) in which he observed that, while some were the usual functions of a treaty depositary and others were not unusual for him to discharge, some were new and unprecedented. In the latter category he mentioned reporting functions under the Convention and duties with regard to charts and lists of geographical co-ordinates relating to maritime boundaries. The Convention's requirement (article 319) that he report on issues of a general nature arising with respect to the Convention made it necessary to ensure continuity in the collection and analysis of information. Moreover, Governments would also be interested in issues arising before the Convention entered into force, since they could influence the treaty's acceptance.

The Secretary-General also had a continuing duty, under past Assembly resolutions, to provide countries with information, advice and assistance under the new legal régime, the note pointed out. Future information activities included the provision of a law of the sea information service, establishment of a reference collection based on the special library set up for the Conference, and development of information exchange arrangements among those involved in dispute settlement procedures. There would also be promotion, education and training activities, and a need to harmonize activities within the Secretariat and among United Nations organizations.

Regarding the organizational framework to perform those activities within the Secretariat, the Secretary-General said the most desirable arrangement would be to establish the existing Office of the Special Representative of the Secretary-General for the Law of the Sea as the Office for Law of the Sea Affairs. In addition to the functions described above, the office would also service the Preparatory Commission.

The Secretary-General proposed to the Assembly's Fifth (Administrative and Budgetary) Committee that the suggested Office have a staff of 64 (including 28 Professionals), divided equally between substantive and administrative personnel, and that $2,724,900 be appropriated to cover its 1983 activities.(4) The Advisory Committee on Administrative and Budgetary Questions (ACABQ), after reviewing this request, recommended that the Assembly put off until 1983 a decision on whether to establish a new office and that in the mean time the staffing level should be 55 posts (including 24 Professionals), at a 1983 cost of $324,600 less than the Secretary-General had estimated; this would maintain the current level of 30 substantive posts and provide 25 administrative posts for the Preparatory Commission's Jamaica office.[2]

The Fifth Committee, reporting to the Assembly on the financial implications of the law of the sea resolution, approved an amount of $2,728,500 for 1983.[3] This consisted of the sum recommended by ACABQ for the law of the sea secretariat plus $328,200 for costs related to the Jamaica session of the Commission in 1983, also recommended by ACABQ.

Singapore, when introducing the resolution adopted by the Assembly, described certain understandings on administrative arrangements that had been reached in consultations: that the law of the sea secretariat would be kept to the current number of 18 Professional substantive officers for 1983, in the interest of economy and in order not to create any disincentive for States to sign and ratify the Convention; that expenses would be kept within the existing level to the extent possible; that the secretariat would have duty stations at Kingston and in New York, each initially having 9 Professionals; and that the secretariat would continue to depend on other United Nations and specialized agency units for experts.

Objections to the financial arrangements for both the Preparatory Commission and the Law of the Sea secretariat were voiced in the Assembly by Israel, Turkey and the United States. Among the countries abstaining on the financial implications in the Fifth Committee, Belgium speaking in the Assembly, wondered whether sizeable expenditures were justified at a time of austerity, and regarded the division of the secretariat between Jamaica and New York as a facile and onerous solution. France said the importance of the Secretary-General's functions under the Convention clearly justified the presence of permanent secretariat services at Headquarters; France also hoped the Preparatory Commission's working groups would meet in New York. The Federal Republic of Germany, Italy and Spain urged that expenses be kept to a minimum; Italy observed that meetings of the Commission and its groups in New York would be less costly. Also urging economy, the USSR said it regretted that, in violation of an agreement reached in consultations, the Secretariat had sought an unwarranted increase for staff expenses.

A call for financial restraint and for minimizing bureaucracy in the operation of the Commission was also voiced by Australia during the closing week of the Conference in December.

Note. [1]S-G, A/37/561.
Reports. [2]ACABQ, A/37/7/Add.10; [3]5th Committee, A/37/687; [4]S-G, A/C.5/37/58/Rev.1.
Resolution (1982). [5]GA: 37/66, para. 7, 3 Dec.

Organization of the Conference

Final Act

At the closing meeting of the Conference on the Law of the Sea, on 10 December 1982, representatives of 141 States, Namibia represented by the United Nations Council for Namibia, a self-governing associated State, a territory, an intergovernmental organization and 4 national liberation movements signed the Final Act of the Conference,[1] a formal record of its actions since its start in 1973.

The signatories were all those which had signed the Convention (p. 241) plus the following:

States: Belgium, Benin, Botswana, Ecuador, Equatorial Guinea, Germany, Federal Republic of, Holy See, Israel, Italy, Japan, Jordan, Libyan Arab Jamahiriya, Luxembourg, Oman, Peru, Republic of Korea, Samoa, Spain, Switzerland, United Kingdom, United States, Venezuela, Zaire.

States and territories with observer status: Netherlands Antilles, Trust Territory of the Pacific Islands.

Intergovernmental organization: European Economic Community.

National liberation movements: African National Congress of South Africa, Palestine Liberation Organization, Pan Africanist Congress of Azania, South West Africa People's Organization.

The Final Act was approved without vote on 24 September 1982 after the Conference, by a recorded vote of 102 to 1 (Israel), with 1 abstention (Argentina), upheld a ruling by the President that no vote be taken on individual paragraphs. Israel had sought a vote on a paragraph mentioning the Conference's 1974 decision[3] to permit national liberation movements to participate in the Conference as observers.

Annexed to the Final Act were the four resolutions contained in the "Convention package" (p. 182), two tributes adopted on historic anniversaries, a tribute to Venezuela as host Government of the Conference's first substantive session,[2] a statement of understanding on a specific method for establishing the outer edge of the continental margin (p. 201), and the 1982 resolution on development of national marine science, technology and ocean service infrastructures (p. 233).

Turkey, speaking in December prior to the signing of the Final Act, said it could not sign because a statement in that document to the effect that all decisions had been taken by consensus throughout the Conference (until the voting on amendments in April 1982) failed to reflect the fact that Turkey had expressly raised objections to a number of articles and had never given its consent to those which did not accommodate Turkish views.

Final Act. [1]A/CONF.62/121 & Corr.3,7,8.
Yearbook references. 1974, [2]p. 71, [3]p. 73.
Meeting records. Conference: A/CONF.62/SR.184 (24 Sep.), A/CONF.62/PV.193 & Add.1 (10 Dec.).

Plenary meetings

As the three main committees of the Conference on the Law of the Sea had completed most of their work on the Convention in previous years, the formal business of the Conference in 1982 was conducted largely in 38 plenary meetings.

Following the opening meeting of the eleventh session on 8 March, the next plenary meeting, on 29 March, heard reports by the Chairman of each committee on the results of the informal negotiations that had taken place during the first three weeks of the session, and proposing some changes in the draft Convention and associated resolutions. From 30 March to 1 April (nine meetings), representatives expressed views as to whether those changes and others should be introduced. As agreed on 7 April, the next round of discussion, 15 to 17 April (six meetings), was devoted to comments on the formal amendments which States had submitted to the Convention.

On 23 April, the Conference entered its decision-making stage by determining that all efforts at reaching general agreement had been exhausted. On 26 April (two meetings) voting took place on amendments, and on 28 and 29 April (four meetings) the Conference heard comments by delegations on new proposals by the President. The first part of the session ended on 30 April (two meetings), with the adoption of the Convention by vote.

The Conference reconvened on 22 and 24 September (two meetings) to approve a final set of changes recommended by its Drafting Committee and to approve the Final Act. It also, on 24 September, agreed that the title of the Convention would be United Nations Convention on the Law of the Sea.

By a letter of 20 September, Venezuela transmitted to the Secretary-General a note from its Minister for Foreign Affairs stating that, as Venezuela could not associate itself with the Convention for reasons of national interest, it was withdrawing its offer of several years' standing to serve as host for the signing ceremony.[1] The Conference, on 24 September, accepted an invitation from Jamaica to serve as host. On 3 December, in its resolution on the Conference,[2] the General Assembly also accepted the invitation and reiterated its gratitude to Venezuela for having hosted the first substantive session of the Conference at Caracas in 1974.[3]

Accordingly, between 6 and 10 December the Conference held eight plenary meetings at Montego Bay, Jamaica, at which it heard statements by delegations on the Convention and related resolutions. It then concluded its work at its 193rd plenary meeting with the signature of the Convention and the Final Act.

Letter. [1]Venezuela, 20 Sep., A/CONF.62/L.153.
Resolution (1982). [2]GA: 37/66, paras. 4-6, 3 Dec.
Yearbook reference. [3]1974, p. 71.

Meeting records. Conference: A/CONF.62/SR.156, 157, 158 & Corr.1, 159-182 (8 Mar.–30 Apr.), A/CONF.62/SR.183, 184 (22, 24 Sep.), A/CONF.62/PV.185-192, 193 & Add.1 (6-10 Dec.).

Drafting Committee

A textual review of the Convention on the Law of the Sea in the six official languages of the Convention was completed by the Drafting Committee of the Conference at three series of meetings in 1982. They were held at United Nations Headquarters from 18 January to 26 February,[1] before the Conference began its eleventh session, and during the first part of that session, 8 to 26 March[2] and 29 March to 30 April;[4] and at Geneva from 12 July to 25 August.[6]

The New York meetings were devoted mainly to the sea-bed provisions of the Convention and related resolutions, as well as to the amended texts introduced by the Conference collegium. The Geneva meetings dealt with all the remaining parts of the Convention on which the Committee had not previously completed work. The convening of the inter-sessional meetings at Geneva was approved by the Conference on 30 April.

The work of the Drafting Committee in 1982 was carried out at 859 meetings of the language groups open to all delegations, 80 meetings of the language group co-ordinators under the direction of the Committee Chairman and 23 meetings of the Committee as a whole. Most of the meetings were informal, except for a few plenary meetings of the Committee. This marked the completion of three years of textual harmonization and review by the Committee.

The Conference held six informal plenary meetings—two in March,[3] one in April[5] and three in September[7]—to consider and approve the Committee's recommendations. The Conference formally approved the changes on 30 April, when it adopted the Convention as a whole subject to the final set of drafting changes which it approved on 24 September.

Reports. Drafting Committee Chairman: [1]A/CONF.62/L.85 & Add.1 & Add.1/Corr.1, Add.2 & Add.2/Corr.1, Add.3 & Add.3/Corr.1, Add.4 & Add.4/Corr.1, Add.5 & Add.5/Corr.1, Add.6 & Add.6/Corr.1, Add.7,8 & Add.8/Corr.1 & Add.9; [2]A/CONF.62/L.89; [3]A/CONF.62/L.90; [4]A/CONF.62/L.142/Rev.1 & Add.1; [5]A/CONF.62/L.147; [6]A/CONF.62/L.152 & Add.1-27; [7]A/CONF.62/L.160.
Meeting records. Conference: A/CONF.62/SR.182, 184 (30 Apr., 24 Sep.).

First Committee

The First Committee of the Conference on the Law of the Sea held two formal meetings, on 9 and 29 March 1982, at which it completed its work on the sea-bed and related provisions of the Convention on the Law of the Sea. At the first of these meetings, it considered the possible impact of the

Convention, with special reference to its sea-bed production control mechanism, on developing countries which produced and exported minerals of the kind to be extracted from the sea-bed. At the second meeting, it heard the report of the Co-ordinators of its Working Group of 21. An account of the Committee's work during the session was given to the Conference by its Chairman in a report of 29 March.[1] The Committee held a total of 56 formal meetings since the Conference began.

The Working Group of 21, which met informally during the first three weeks of the session, dealt with arrangements for the Preparatory Commission for the International Sea-Bed Authority and for the International Tribunal for the Law of the Sea and with the pioneer investors scheme for sea-bed exploration. A report on this work was presented to the First Committee on 29 March by the Group's Co-ordinators—the Conference President and the First Committee Chairman.[2] This report contained the texts of the draft resolutions on these two topics which, with subsequent alterations, were adopted by the Conference on 30 April along with the Convention.

Reports. [1]1st Committee Chairman, A/CONF.62/L.91; [2]Working Group Co-ordinators, A/CONF.62/C.1/L.30.
Meeting records. Conference: 1st Committee, A/CONF.62/C.1/SR.55, 56 (9, 29 Mar.); plenary, A/CONF.62/SR.157-166 (29 Mar.–1 Apr.).

Second Committee

The Second Committee of the Conference on the Law of the Sea held three informal meetings in March 1982, followed by a formal meeting on 29 April at which it wound up its work. During the 59 formal and many more informal meetings it held since the start of the Conference, the Committee dealt with the parts of the Convention on the Law of the Sea concerned with particular maritime zones, other than the international sea-bed area, including the exclusive economic zone, the continental shelf and the high seas.

As stated in the Chairman's final report to the Conference,[1] presented on 29 March, the informal meetings between 18 and 24 March enabled delegations to raise any issue within the Committee's competence and make informal suggestions for amendments to the draft Convention. After hearing 105 statements and receiving 10 informal suggestions for changes in the text, the Chairman reported that only one, presented by the United Kingdom on offshore structures in the exclusive economic zone, had broad enough support for inclusion in the Convention.

The Chairman also reported that he had convened two consultation meetings on innocent passage of warships through the territorial sea, but no formula had been produced for an acceptable change in the existing text. With regard to the overall texts within the Committee's competence, he concluded that the discussions had revealed a consensus on the need to preserve their fundamental elements, without excluding the possibility of changes that could facilitate adoption of the Convention.

Report. [1]2nd Committee Chairman, A/CONF.62/L.87.
Meeting records. Conference: plenary, A/CONF.62/SR.157-166 (29 Mar–1 Apr.); 2nd Committee, A/CONF.62/C.2/SR.59 (29 Apr.).

Third Committee

The Third Committee of the Conference on the Law of the Sea did not hold any formal meetings in 1982, having previously completed its substantive work on the three parts of the draft Convention with which it was concerned—protection and preservation of the marine environment, marine scientific research, and development and transfer of marine technology. The Committee had held 46 formal meetings, the last in 1980.[3]

In his final report to the Conference, dated 30 March 1982,[2] the Committee Chairman suggested a number of drafting changes for these parts of the text, some originating in the Drafting Committee and some proposed by himself after consultations. These suggestions, and others spelt out in a letter from the Chairman dated 26 March,[1] were processed by the Drafting Committee before being acted on by the Conference.

Letter. [1]3rd Committee Chairman, 26 Mar., A/CONF.62/L.88 & Corr.1.
Report. [2]3rd Committee Chairman, A/CONF.62/L.92.
Yearbook reference. [3]1980, p. 139.

Chapter IV

International peace and security

Contents

Related topics:
Legal aspects of international political relations: Manila Declaration on dispute settlement; Non-use of force in international relations; Draft code of offences against peace and security; Draft convention against mercenaries.

Implementation of the Declaration on strengthening international security

Following its annual review of the implementation of its 1970 Declaration on the Strengthening of International Security,[10] the General Assembly, in December 1982, called for several steps by States and the Security Council to improve the international security situation.

Communications. Letters and statements reflecting the concerns of Member States about prevailing world and regional security situations were circulated at their request during 1982 as documents of the General Assembly in connection with its agenda item on implementation of the Declaration on strengthening international security. A number of these dealt with disarmament or with the following specific disputes or situations: Angola and South Africa, Ethiopia and Somalia, the Kampuchea situation, the Kampuchea-Thailand border, China and Viet Nam, the Afghanistan situation, peace and security in Central America and the Caribbean area, the Libyan Arab Jamahiriya and the United States, the neutrality of Malta and the status of the Falkland Islands (Malvinas) (For page references, refer to SUBJECT INDEX). Other communications, addressed to the Secretary-General and concerned with general aspects of international security, are summarized below.

Transmitted by both parties in an annex to a letter of 14 June were excerpts from a joint declaration adopted during a visit by an Afghanistan delegation to the German Democratic Republic from 19 to 21 May.[2] The German Democratic Republic and Grenada issued a joint declaration during a visit by a Grenadian delegation from 8 to 10 June; excerpts from the text were annexed to a letter by both parties on 28 June.[3] The parties in both declarations condemned United States arms policies, denounced interference in Poland's affairs, urged progress in negotiations on strategic arms limitation and on nuclear arms limitation in Europe, and denounced United States policies in Latin America.

By a letter of 13 August, the Lao People's Democratic Republic transmitted a telegram of 18 June from the Minister for Foreign Affairs of the People's Republic of Kampuchea addressed to the President of the General Assembly's special session on disarmament condemning United States arms policies and Chinese-American collusion and supporting USSR proposals for reducing tension and safeguarding peace.[4]

Annexed to a letter of 30 December from Romania was an extract of a 16 December report by the Secretary-General of the Romanian Communist Party and President of Romania to the National Party Conference, describing the objectives of Romania's foreign policy and the international activity of the party and State, with emphasis on measures to ensure peace and friendship.[5]

An appeal for peace on the occasion of the sixtieth anniversary of the formation of the USSR, adopted on 22 December by the Supreme Soviet of the USSR and the Central Committee of the Communist Party of the Soviet Union and addressed to the parliaments, Governments, political parties and peoples of the world, was annexed to a letter of 24 December from the USSR.[8]

To a letter dated 22 September, Turkey annexed a description of an incident at Ankara airport on 7 August, stating that 9 persons had been killed and 72 wounded when two Armenian terrorists fired machine-guns at passengers in a terminal area, and statements on the incident by the Turkish Head of State and the Prime Minister.[6]

By a letter of 27 October, the USSR transmitted a communiqué adopted at a meeting of the Committee of Ministers for Foreign Affairs of the State Parties to the 1955 Warsaw Treaty of Friendship, Co-operation and Mutual Assistance (Moscow, 21 and 22 October), setting out their positions on strengthening peace and security in Europe, the reduction of nuclear weapons and other forces there, and the Middle East situation.[7]

Afghanistan annexed to a letter of 12 November a declaration adopted at the International Conference on Socio-Economic Development and the Dangers of War (Kabul, 12-15 November), supporting efforts towards a new international economic order and stating that nuclear armament and interventionism by imperialist forces, particularly the United States, threatened mankind's survival.[1]

General Assembly action. On 16 December, the General Assembly adopted, by a recorded vote of 116 to none, with 19 abstentions, a resolution on implementation of the Declaration on strengthening international security.[9] The Assembly urged States to refrain from force and intervention in violation of the sovereignty and security of other States, and invited them to refrain from pressures and threats, including military activities and manoeuvres. It urged the Security Council to report on steps to implement provisions of a 1980 Assembly resolution on the Council's effectiveness,[11] and requested that the Council examine and propose mechanisms to enhance its authority and enforcement capacity. The Assembly also reiterated the need for the Council to ensure implementation of its decisions. The legitimacy of the struggle of peoples under colonial domination was reaffirmed. Participants in the Conference on Security and Co-operation in Europe, at Madrid, Spain, were called on to ensure substantial results.

Other provisions of the resolution called for steps to promote collective security, halt the arms race and achieve general and complete disarmament under effective international control, and to prevent further deterioration of the international situation through dispute settlement, disarmament negotiations and finding solutions to international economic problems. The Assembly considered that respect for human rights and the strengthening of international security were mutually reinforcing. It also urged measures to avert a nuclear danger from South Africa, expressed hope that the Conference on the Indian Ocean would be held, and decided to include in its provisional agenda for 1983 an item on strengthening security and co-operation in the Mediterranean region.

The 22-nation text, recommended by the First Committee, was introduced by Yugoslavia and approved in Committee on 9 December, as orally revised by the sponsors, by a roll-call vote of 90 to none, with 18 abstentions.

Letters. [1]Afghanistan: 12 Nov., A/37/635-S/15497. [2]Afghanistan, German Democratic Republic: 14 June, A/37/297. [3]German Democratic Republic, Grenada: 28 June, A/37/359. [4]Lao People's Democratic Republic: 13 Aug., A/37/388. [5]Romania: 30 Dec., A/38/57. [6]Turkey: 22 Sep., A/37/498 S/15437. USSR: [7]27 Oct., A/C.1/37/7; [8]24 Dec., A/38/59.
Resolution (1982). [9]GA: 37/118, 16 Dec., text following.
Resolutions (prior). GA: [10]2734(XXV), 16 Dec. 1970 (YUN 1970, p. 105); [11]35/158, 12 Dec. 1980 (YUN 1980, p. 171).
Meeting records. GA: 1st Committee, A/C.1/37/PV.46, 49-56, 59 (29 Nov.–9 Dec.); plenary, A/37/PV.108 (16 Dec.).

General Assembly resolution 37/118

16 December 1982   Meeting 108   116-0-19 (recorded vote)

Approved by First Committee (A/37/743) by roll-call vote (90-0-18), 9 December (meeting 59); 22-nation draft (A/C.1/37/L.78), orally revised; agenda item 59.

Sponsors: Algeria, Bahamas, Bangladesh, Benin, Congo, Ecuador, Egypt, Guyana, India, Indonesia, Madagascar, Mali, Malta, Nigeria, Panama, Peru, Romania, Senegal, Sri Lanka, Togo, Yugoslavia, Zambia.

Review of the implementation of the Declaration on the Strengthening of International Security

The General Assembly,

Having considered the item entitled "Review of the implementation of the Declaration on the Strengthening of International Security",

Noting with concern that the provisions of the Declaration on the Strengthening of International Security have not been fully implemented,

Profoundly disturbed by the continued escalation of tension in the world, the ever more frequent recourse to the threat or use of force, intervention, interference, aggression and foreign occupation, the continued stalemate in the solution of crises in different regions and their aggravation, the continuous escalation of the arms race and military build-up by major Powers, the pursuance of the policy of rivalry, confrontation and continued attempts to divide the world into spheres of influence and domination, the persistence of colonialism, racism and *apartheid*, attempts to distort the nature of national liberation struggles and the lack of solution of the economic problems of developing countries, all of which endanger international peace and security,

Deeply concerned that the exacerbation of international tension has reached a point of deep crisis owing to the lack of progress in the settlement of international problems and conflicts and to the lack of progress in disarmament,

Alarmed by the intensification, the expansion in scope and the frequency of manoeuvres and other military activities, which are assuming dangerous proportions, which are conceived within the context of big-Power confrontation and which are used as an instrument of pressure against and as a threat to the independence of States and the liberation of peoples struggling against alien and colonial domination, leading to a destabilization of international relations,

Noting with concern that the United Nations system of collective security has not been used effectively,

Aware that international peace and security can be maintained and strengthened only on the basis of freedom, independence, sovereignty, territorial integrity, and equality of States, as well as of the self-determination of peoples under colonial and foreign domination, respect for fundamental human rights and the development of friendly relations among States,

Stressing the need for the main organs of the United Nations responsible for the maintenance of peace and security, particularly the Security Council, to contribute more effectively to the promotion of international peace and security by seeking solutions to the unresolved problems and crises in the world,

Emphasizing that the Movement of Non-Aligned Countries has contributed significantly to the struggle for national liberation and to the efforts of the United Nations for the promotion of international peace and security, the democratization of international relations, the development of international co-operation and the establishment of a system of international relations based on justice, sovereign equality and security for all States and peoples, in accordance with the purposes and principles of the Charter of the United Nations and the principles and policy of non-alignment,

Taking note of the report of the Secretary-General, which incorporates the views of Member States on the question of the strengthening of security and co-operation in the region of the Mediterranean, and recalling the provisions of the chapter on the Mediterranean in the Final Act of the Conference on Security and Co-operation in Europe, signed at Helsinki on 1 August 1975, the recommendations of the Movement of Non-Aligned Countries, as well as official declarations on and contributions to peace and security in that region made by individual countries,

1. *Reaffirms once more* the universal and unconditional validity of the purposes and principles of the Charter of the United Nations as the firm basis of relations among all States, irrespective of size, geographic location, level of development or political, economic, social or ideological systems;

2. *Urges* all States to abide strictly, in their international relations, by their commitment to the Charter and, to that end:

(a) To refrain from the use or threat of use of force, intervention, interference, aggression, foreign occupation and colonial domination or measures of political and economic coercion which violate the sovereignty, territorial integrity, independence and security of other States or their right freely to dispose of their natural resources;

(b) To refrain from supporting or encouraging any such act for any reason whatsoever;

(c) To reject and refuse recognition of situations brought about by any such act;

3. *Calls upon* all States to contribute effectively to the implementation of the Declaration on the Strengthening of International Security;

4. *Also calls upon* all States, in particular nuclear-weapon States and other militarily significant States, to take immediate steps aimed at promoting the system of collective security as envisaged in the Charter together with measures for the effective halting of the arms race and for the achievement of general and complete disarmament under effective international control;

5. *Invites* all States, in particular the major military Powers and States members of military alliances, to refrain, especially in critical situations and in crisis areas, from actions, including military activities and manoeuvres, which constitute pressure on and a threat to other States and regions;

6. *Urges* all States, in particular the permanent members of the Security Council, to take all necessary measures to prevent the further deterioration of the international situation and, to this end:

(a) To seek the peaceful settlement of disputes and the elimination of the focal points of crisis and tension;

(b) To start serious, meaningful and effective negotiations with a view to implementing the recommendations and decisions contained in the Final Document of the Tenth Special Session of the General Assembly, the first special session devoted to disarmament, and to fulfilling the priority tasks listed in its Programme of Action and set forth in section III of the Final Document, which were solemnly reaffirmed in the Concluding Document of the Twelfth Special Session of the General Assembly, the second special session devoted to disarmament;

(c) To contribute to the urgent solution of international economic problems and the establishment of the new international economic order;

(d) To accelerate the economic development of developing countries, particularly the least developed ones;

(e) To proceed without any delay to a global consideration of ways and means for a revival of the world economy and for the restructuring of international economic relations within the framework of the global negotiations;

7. *Takes note* of the fact that the Security Council has again failed to report to the General Assembly on steps taken to implement the provisions of paragraphs 13 and 15 of Assembly resolution 35/158 of 12 December 1980 and urges the Council to do so without delay;

8. *Requests once again* the Security Council to consider ways and means to ensure the implementation of the relevant provisions of paragraphs 4 and 6 above as well as to examine all existing mechanisms and to propose new ones aimed at enhancing the authority and enforcement capacity of the Council in accordance with the Charter, and to explore also the possibility of holding periodic meetings of the Council, in conformity with Article 28 of the Charter, at the ministerial or higher level in specific cases, so as to enable it to play a more active role in preventing potential conflicts, and to present the Council's conclusions to the General Assembly at its thirty-eighth session;

9. *Reiterates* the need for the Security Council, in particular its permanent members, to ensure the effective implementation of its decisions in compliance with the relevant provisions of the Charter;

10. *Considers* that respect for and promotion of human rights and fundamental freedoms in their civil, political, economic, social and cultural aspects, on the one hand, and the strengthening of international peace and security, on the other, mutually reinforce each other;

11. *Reaffirms* the legitimacy of the struggle of peoples under colonial domination, foreign occupation or racist régimes and their inalienable right to self-determination and independence, and urges Member States to increase their support for and solidarity with them and their national liberation movements and to take urgent and effective measures for the speedy completion of the implementation of the Declaration on the Granting of Independence to Colonial Countries and Peoples and for the final elimination of colonialism, racism and *apartheid*;

12. *Calls upon* the Security Council to take appropriate effective measures to promote the fulfilment of the objective of the denuclearization of Africa in order to avert the serious danger which the nuclear capability of South Africa constitutes to the African States, in particular the front-line States, as well as to international peace and security;

13. *Reiterates* its support for the Declaration of the Indian Ocean as a Zone of Peace and expresses the hope that the Conference on the Indian Ocean, which is an important stage in the realization of the objectives of that Declaration, will be held not later than in the first half of 1984, and, to this end, calls upon all States to contribute effectively to the success of that Conference;

14. *Calls upon* all States participating in the Conference on Security and Co-operation in Europe, at Madrid, to take all possible measures and exert every effort in order to ensure substantial and balanced results of that meeting in the implementation of the principles and goals established by the Final Act of the Conference signed at Helsinki on 1 August 1975, as well as the continuity of the multilateral process initiated by the Conference, which has great significance for the strengthening of peace and security in Europe and in the world;

15. *Considers* that the security of the Mediterranean and the security of the adjacent regions are interdependent and that further efforts are necessary for the creation of conditions of security and fruitful co-operation in all fields for all countries and peoples of the Mediterranean, on the basis of the principles of sovereignty, independence, territorial integrity, security, non-intervention and non-interference, non-violation of international frontiers, non-use of force, the inadmissibility of the acquisition of territory by force, peaceful settlement of disputes and just and viable solutions of the existing problems and crises in the area on the basis of the provisions of the Charter and of relevant resolutions of the United Nations, the withdrawal of foreign forces of occupation, respect for sovereignty over natural resources and the right of peoples under colonial or foreign domination to self-determination and independence;

16. *Calls upon* all Governments that have not done so to submit before the thirty-eighth session of the General Assembly their views on the question of the strengthening of security and co-operation in the region of the Mediterranean and requests the Secretary-General to submit, on the basis of all replies received, an analytical report on this question to the Assembly at its thirty-eighth session;

17. *Decides* to include in the provisional agenda of its thirty-eighth session an item entitled "Strengthening of security and co-operation in the Mediterranean region";

18. *Decides* to include in the provisional agenda of its thirty-eighth session the item entitled "Review of the implementation of the Declaration on the Strengthening of International Security".

Recorded vote in Assembly as follows:

In favour: Afghanistan, Algeria, Angola, Argentina, Austria, Bahamas, Bahrain, Bangladesh, Barbados, Belize, Benin, Bhutan, Bolivia, Brazil, Bulgaria, Burma, Burundi, Byelorussian SSR, Central African Republic, Chad, Chile, China, Colombia, Comoros, Congo, Cuba, Cyprus, Czechoslovakia, Democratic Kampuchea, Democratic Yemen, Djibouti, Dominican Republic, Ecuador, Egypt, El Salvador, Ethiopia, Fiji, Finland, Gabon, Gambia, German Democratic Republic, Ghana, Greece, Grenada, Guinea, Guinea-Bissau, Guyana, Honduras, Hungary, India, Indonesia, Iran, Iraq, Ireland, Ivory Coast, Jamaica, Jordan, Kenya, Kuwait, Lao People's Democratic Republic, Lebanon, Liberia, Libyan Arab Jamahiriya, Madagascar, Malawi, Malaysia, Maldives, Mali, Malta, Mauritania, Mauritius, Mexico, Mongolia, Morocco, Mozambique, Nepal, Nicaragua, Nigeria, Oman, Pakistan, Panama, Papua New Guinea, Philippines, Poland, Qatar, Romania, Rwanda, Samoa, Sao Tome and Principe, Saudi Arabia, Senegal, Sierra Leone, Singapore, Somalia, Sudan, Suriname, Sweden, Syrian Arab Republic, Thailand, Togo, Trinidad and Tobago, Tunisia, Ukrainian SSR, USSR, United Arab Emirates, United Republic of Cameroon, United Republic of Tanzania, Upper Volta, Uruguay, Vanuatu, Venezuela, Viet Nam, Yemen, Yugoslavia, Zaire, Zambia.

Against: None.

Abstaining: Australia, Belgium, Canada, Denmark, France, Germany, Federal Republic of, Iceland, Israel, Italy, Japan, Luxembourg, Netherlands, New Zealand, Norway, Portugal, Spain, Turkey, United Kingdom, United States.

Good-neighbourliness between States

In October 1982, the Secretary-General submitted to the General Assembly a report analysing views and suggestions on the development and strengthening of good-neighbourliness between States.[1] The report was based on written comments received in 1981 from 27 States and 14 specialized agencies and other United Nations bodies, and in 1982 from 14 States and 15 agencies, as well as on statements by 21 States in the First Committee's 1981 debate on the topic.[5] The report had been requested by the Assembly in December 1981.[1]

The Secretary-General concluded in the report that great importance was attached to the development and strengthening of good-neighbourly relations and that most responding States attributed to good-neighbourliness primarily a political content, considering it one of the objectives of their foreign policy. Also stressed was the responsibility of States to establish and maintain good-neighbourly relations with all States regardless of their political or social systems or foreign policy orientation. Among recommendations for Assembly action were: elaborating and identifying the essential elements of good-neighbourliness; agreeing on a set of rules aimed at regulating the behaviour of all nations towards their neighbours; establishment of a committee to draft a treaty that would strengthen and develop the principle and define ways of implementing it; having the Assembly's Sixth (Legal) Committee examine the legal and practical aspects of good-neighbourliness; and asking the Secretariat's Office of Legal Affairs

to prepare a study of treaties related to good-neighbourliness.

On 16 December,[2] the Assembly, without vote, adopted a resolution by which it reaffirmed that good-neighbourliness was founded on strict observance of the principles of the United Nations Charter and of the Assembly's 1970 Declaration on Principles of International Law concerning Friendly Relations and Co-operation among States in accordance with the Charter of the United Nations.[3] The Assembly called on States to develop good-neighbourly relations, reaffirmed that generalization of the long practice of good-neighbourliness and the principles and rules pertaining to it was likely to strengthen friendly relations, and deemed it appropriate to clarify the elements of good-neighbourliness as part of the elaboration, when appropriate, of an international document on the subject. Governments and international organizations that had not commented on the question were invited to do so.

The 30-nation draft, introduced by Romania, was recommended to the Assembly by the First Committee, which approved it without vote on 9 December.

Report. [1]S-G, A/37/476.
Resolution (1982). [2]GA: 37/117, 16 Dec., text following.
Resolutions (prior). GA: [3]2625(XXV), annex, 24 Oct. 1970 (YUN 1970, p. 789); [4]36/101, 9 Dec. 1981 (YUN 1981, p. 152).
Yearbook reference. [5]1981, p. 151.
Meeting records. GA: 1st Committee, A/C.1/37/PV.46, 49-53, 54, 55, 56, 58, 59 (29 Nov.–9 Dec.); plenary, A/37/PV.108 (16 Dec.).

General Assembly resolution 37/117

16 December 1982   Meeting 108   Adopted without vote

Approved by First Committee (A/37/742) without vote, 9 December (meeting 59); 30-nation draft (A/C.1/37/L.77); agenda item 50.

Sponsors: Bangladesh, Burundi, Colombia, Congo, France, Guinea, Guyana, Indonesia, Liberia, Madagascar, Mali, Mauritania, Niger, Nigeria, Panama, Peru, Philippines, Portugal, Romania, Rwanda, Senegal, Sierra Leone, Singapore, Spain, Sri Lanka, Sudan, Turkey, United Republic of Cameroon, Uruguay, Yugoslavia.

Development and strengthening of good-neighbourliness between States

The General Assembly,

Bearing in mind the determination of the peoples of the United Nations, as expressed in the Charter, to practise tolerance and live together in peace with one another as good neighbours,

Recalling its resolutions 1236(XII) of 14 December 1957, 1301(XIII) of 10 December 1958, 2129(XX) of 21 December 1965, 34/99 of 14 December 1979 and 36/101 of 9 December 1981,

Bearing in mind that, owing to geographic proximity, there are particularly favourable opportunities for co-operation and mutual advantage between neighbouring countries in many fields and various forms and that the development of such co-operation may have a positive influence on international relations as a whole,

Considering that the great changes of a political, economic and social nature, as well as the scientific and technological progress which have taken place in the world and led to unprecedented interdependence of nations, have given new dimensions to good-neighbourliness in the conduct of States and increased the need to develop and strengthen it,

Recalling its opinion that it is necessary to continue to examine the question of good-neighbourliness in order to strengthen and develop its content, as well as ways and modalities to enhance its effectiveness, and that the results of this examination could be included, at an appropriate time, in a suitable international document,

1.   *Reaffirms* that good-neighbourliness fully conforms with the purposes of the United Nations and is founded upon the strict observance of the principles of the Charter of the United Nations and of the Declaration on Principles of International Law concerning Friendly Relations and Co-operation among States in accordance with the Charter of the United Nations, as well as upon the rejection of any acts seeking to establish zones of influence or domination;

2.   *Calls once again upon* all States, in the interest of the maintenance of international peace and security, to develop good-neighbourly relations, acting on the basis of these principles;

3.   *Reaffirms* that the generalization of the long practice of good-neighbourliness and of principles and rules pertaining to it is likely to strengthen friendly relations and co-operation among States in accordance with the Charter;

4.   *Deems it appropriate*, taking into account the report of the Secretary-General concerning good-neighbourliness together with other ideas and proposals which may be submitted subsequently by Member States, to clarify the elements of good-neighbourliness as part of a process of elaborating, at an appropriate time, a suitable international document on the subject;

5.   *Invites once again* the Governments and the international organizations that have not communicated to the Secretary-General their views and suggestions on good-neighbourliness, in accordance with General Assembly resolutions 34/99 and 36/101, to do so as soon as possible, and the Governments that have already communicated such views and suggestions to supplement them if they deem it necessary;

6.   *Decides* to include in the provisional agenda of its thirty-eighth session the item entitled "Development and strengthening of good-neighbourliness between States".

Implementation of the security provisions of the UN Charter

In a resolution of 16 December 1982[2] adopted without vote, the General Assembly requested the Security Council to study, as a high priority, the implementation of the collective security provisions of the United Nations Charter, with a view to strengthening international peace and security, and to report on the question at the Assembly's 1983 session. In the resolution's preamble, the Assembly expressed grave concern over the growing tendency of States to use force in international relations and also voiced concern that the Council had not been able to take decisive action to maintain peace and resolve problems. It expressed regret that the collective security measures in the Charter had not been fully implemented.

The resolution, revised by its 36 sponsors twice in writing and once orally, was recommended without vote by the First Committee on 8 December.

The draft was introduced by Sierra Leone, which had requested, in a letter of 30 August to the Secretary-General,[1] that the item be included in the Assembly's agenda. Despite numerous breaches of peace, the letter stated, no successful effort had been made since the inception of the United Nations to implement the collective security provisions of the Charter, which laid down a framework for prohibitive and remedial action to

maintain or restore peace. The Organization's inability to enforce those provisions had resulted in the undermining of its authority and, if continued, would affect its capacity to act as an instrument of world peace. As a first step, Member States could declare that they would make available to the Council armed forces, assistance and facilities needed to maintain peace and security. Further, the Assembly should recommend ways of implementing the Charter's collective security provisions, particularly Article 43 (providing for agreements between the Council and Member States on the provision of armed forces, assistance and facilities).

Letter. [1]Sierra Leone, 30 Aug., A/37/241.
Resolution (1982). [2]GA: 37/119, 16 Dec., text following.
Meeting records. GA: General Committee, A/BUR/37/SR.2 (22 Sep.); 1st Committee, A/C.1/37/PV.16, *46*, 49-56, *58* (28 Oct. & 29 Nov.–8 Dec.); plenary, A/37/PV.108 (16 Dec.).

General Assembly resolution 37/119

16 December 1982   Meeting 108   Adopted without vote

Approved by First Committee (A/37/744) without vote, 8 December (meeting 58); 36-nation draft (A/C.1/37/L.73/Rev.2), orally revised; agenda item 137.

Sponsors: Algeria, Angola, Bahamas, Benin, Cape Verde, Colombia, Congo, Cyprus, Ecuador, Egypt, Gambia, Ghana, Jamaica, Kenya, Liberia, Madagascar, Mali, Malta, Nicaragua, Niger, Nigeria, Panama, Peru, Qatar, Rwanda, Sierra Leone, Singapore, Somalia, Sri Lanka, Sudan, Togo, Trinidad and Tobago, Uganda, Yugoslavia, Zambia, Zimbabwe.

Implementation of the collective security provisions of the Charter of the United Nations for the maintenance of international peace and security

The General Assembly,

Reaffirming that the primary function of the United Nations is the maintenance of international peace and security,

Reaffirming also the fundamental principle of the Charter of the United Nations that all States have the duty not to threaten or use force against the sovereignty, political independence or territorial integrity of other States,

Noting the primary responsibility of the Security Council for the maintenance of international peace and security,

Stressing that the purposes and principles of the United Nations can be achieved only under conditions in which States enjoy sovereign equality and comply fully with the requirements of these purposes and principles in their international relations,

Gravely concerned over the growing tendency by States to resort to the use of force in international relations, thus ignoring the Charter and the Declaration on Principles of International Law concerning Friendly Relations and Co-operation among States in accordance with the Charter of the United Nations,

Further concerned that the Security Council has not been able to take decisive action for the maintenance of international peace and for resolving international problems,

Recognizing that fundamental approaches to genuine security include, *inter alia*, the strengthening of the Charter system of collective security, the establishment of the new international economic order and the promotion of general and complete disarmament under effective international control, in conformity with the principles and priorities agreed upon in the Final Document of the Tenth Special Session of the General Assembly, the first special session devoted to disarmament, and reaffirmed in the Concluding Document of the Twelfth Special Session, the second special session devoted to disarmament,

Conscious of the important role that collective security measures can play in enhancing the role of the Security Council in carrying out its responsibility to promote and maintain international peace and security in accordance with the Charter,

Regretting that the provisions of the Charter concerning collective security measures have not been fully implemented,

Taking into account, in this connection, the report of the Secretary-General on the work of the Organization,

Having considered the item entitled "Implementation of the collective security provisions of the Charter of the United Nations for the maintenance of international peace and security",

Convinced that a study on collective security is timely and necessary,

1. *Requests* the Security Council as a matter of high priority to study the question of implementation of the collective security provisions of the Charter of the United Nations, with a view to strengthening international peace and security, and to report to the General Assembly at its thirty-eighth session;

2. *Decides* to include in the provisional agenda of its thirty-eighth session the item entitled "Implementation of the collective security provisions of the Charter of the United Nations for the maintenance of international peace and security".

Review of peace-keeping operations

The General Assembly, on 10 December 1982, adopted without vote a resolution by which it reaffirmed the mandate of its Special Committee on Peace-keeping Operations and decided—as in previous years—to include in the provisional agenda of its 1983 session an item on review of the whole question of peace-keeping operations in all their aspects.[2]

The resolution was recommended without vote by the Special Political Committee on 30 November 1982. The draft was presented by that Committee's Chairman on the basis of informal consultations. The Committee on Peace-keeping Operations, established by the Assembly in 1965,[3] did not meet in 1982.

A working paper by Japan on strengthening and expanding United Nations peace-keeping functions for the promotion of disarmament, annexed to a note verbale of 25 June to the Secretary-General,[1] was presented at the Assembly's second special session on disarmament. Japan proposed that a group of experts be established to undertake technical studies on this question and to submit recommendations for enhancing United Nations functions in order to realize concrete progress in disarmament.

Note verbale. [1]Japan, 25 June, A/S-12/AC.1/45.
Resolution (1982). [2]GA: 37/93, 10 Dec., text following.
Resolution (prior). [3]GA: 2006(XIX), 18 Feb. 1965 (YUN 1964, p. 59).
Meeting records. GA: SPC, A/SPC/37/SR.33-35, 39 (19-30 Nov.); plenary, A/37/PV.100 (10 Dec.).

General Assembly resolution 37/93

10 December 1982   Meeting 100   Adopted without vote

Approved by SPC (A/37/686) without vote, 30 November (meeting 39); draft by Chairman (A/SPC/37/L.17 and Corr.1); agenda item 64.

Comprehensive review of the whole question of peace-keeping operations in all their aspects

The General Assembly,

Recalling its resolutions 2006(XIX) of 18 February 1965, 2053 A (XX) of 15 December 1965, 2249(S-V) of 23 May 1967, 2308(XXII) of 13 December 1967, 2451(XXIII) of 19 December 1968, 2670(XXV) of 8 December 1970, 2835(XXVI) of 17 December 1971, 2965(XXVII) of 13 December 1972, 3091(XXVIII) of 7 December 1973, 3239(XXIX) of 29 November 1974, 3457(XXX) of 10 December 1975, 31/105 of 15 December 1976, 32/106 of 15 December 1977, 33/114 of 18 December 1978, 34/53 of 23 November 1979, 35/121 of 11 December 1980 and 36/37 of 18 November 1981,

Awaiting the issuance of the report of the Special Committee on Peace-keeping Operations to the General Assembly at its thirty-eighth session,

1. *Reaffirms* the mandate given to the Special Committee on Peace-keeping Operations by relevant resolutions of the General Assembly;

2. *Decides* to include in the provisional agenda of its thirty-eighth session the item entitled "Comprehensive review of the whole question of peace-keeping operations in all their aspects".

International Year and Day of Peace

International Year of Peace (1986)

On the recommendation of the Economic and Social Council, the General Assembly, in November 1982, declared 1986 to be the International Year of Peace.

Economic and Social Council action. The recommendation by the Economic and Social Council was contained in a resolution adopted without vote on 4 May 1982.[3] The revised 20-nation text was introduced by Costa Rica. The Council recommended that the General Assembly: establish 1986 as the International Year of Peace, to be proclaimed on 24 October 1985, the fortieth anniversary of the United Nations, and with the activities of the Year to begin on 1 January 1986; invite Member States and organizations to submit to the Secretary-General suggestions for the observance; and request the Secretary-General to propose a draft programme and budget for the Year.

In a note to the Council in April,[2] the Secretary-General recalled that the Assembly, in November 1981,[5] had invited the Council to consider the possibility of declaring such a year. Under the guidelines for international years and anniversaries adopted by the Assembly in 1980,[1] which provided for a two-year interval between such observances, he noted that the first available year would be 1989. However, the Assembly might wish to set an earlier time in view of the special nature of the observance. Annexed was a note indicating what it might cost to finance sessions of an advisory committee for the Year.

General Assembly action. On 16 November 1982,[4] the General Assembly, without vote, accepted the Council's proposal and declared 1986 to be the International Year of Peace, to be proclaimed on 24 October 1985. In the resolution, sponsored by 31 nations and introduced by Costa Rica, the Assembly invited all States, United Nations organizations and interested non-governmental organizations to exert all efforts for the preparation and observance of the Year and to contribute generously to attain its objectives. The Secretary-General was asked to prepare a draft programme for the Year in accordance with proposals by Member States and in consultation with organizations and academic institutions.

Decision. [1]GA: 35/424, 5 Dec. 1980 (YUN 1980, p. 1031).
Note. [2]S-G, E/1982/45/Rev.1.
Resolutions (1982). [3]ESC: 1982/15, 4 May, text following.
[4]GA: 37/16, 16 Nov., text following.
Resolution (prior). [5]GA: 36/67, 30 Nov. 1981 (YUN 1981, p. 155).
Meeting records. ESC: E/1982/SR.8, 20, 22 (15 Apr.–4 May). GA: A/37/PV.69 (16 Nov.).

Economic and Social Council resolution 1982/15

| 4 May 1982 | Meeting 22 | Adopted without vote |

20-nation draft (E/1982/L.30/Rev.1); agenda item 5.

Sponsors: Bahamas, Bangladesh, Bolivia, Chile, Colombia, Costa Rica, Ecuador, Malawi, Nepal, Nicaragua, Nigeria, Pakistan, Peru, Saint Lucia, Senegal, Sudan, Swaziland, Venezuela, Yugoslavia, Zaire.

International Year of Peace and International Day of Peace

The Economic and Social Council,

Recalling that in the Preamble to the Charter of the United Nations the peoples of the United Nations proclaim their determination to save succeeding generations from the scourge of war and, for that end, to practise tolerance and live together in peace with one another as good neighbours and to unite their strength to maintain international peace and security,

Recognizing that, in spite of resolute efforts of the United Nations, peace continues to be a goal the attainment of which is only precarious and is not a living and permanent awareness of all human beings and peoples,

In pursuance of General Assembly resolution 36/67 of 30 November 1981, in which the Assembly invited the Economic and Social Council to consider the possibility of declaring an International Year of Peace at the first practicable opportunity, taking into account the urgency and special nature of such an observance as well as the guidelines for international years and anniversaries adopted by the General Assembly in its decision 35/424 of 5 December 1980,

Conscious of the validity of the guidelines for international years and anniversaries adopted by the General Assembly in that decision and taking into account that the special urgency and importance which the Assembly attached to this Year seems exceptionally, in this instance, to justify some derogation from the guidelines,

Considering that, since the promotion of peace in accordance with the principles of the Charter is a fundamental purpose of the United Nations, the proclamation and subsequent observance of the International Year of Peace could be linked to the fortieth anniversary of the Organization, on 24 October 1985,

1. *Recommends* to the General Assembly that, at its thirty-seventh session, it should:

(a) Establish 1986 as the International Year of Peace;

(b) Solemnly proclaim the International Year of Peace on 24 October 1985, the date of the observance of the fortieth anniversary of the United Nations, on the understanding that the activities of the Year will begin on 1 January 1986;

(c) Invite Member States and observers, relevant organs and organizations of the United Nations system and non-governmental organizations concerned to submit to the Secretary-General suggestions for the observance of the International Year of Peace;

2. *Further recommends* to the General Assembly that, at its thirty-seventh session, it should request the Secretary-General, taking into account the suggestions referred to in paragraph 1 (c) above, to propose at its thirty-eighth session a draft programme and budget for the observance of the International Year of Peace, on the understanding that its financing will conform to the guidelines laid down by Assembly decision 35/424.

General Assembly resolution 37/16

| 16 November 1982 | Meeting 69 | Adopted without vote |

31-nation draft (A/37/L.24 and Add.1); agenda item 12.

Sponsors: Bahamas, Barbados, Bolivia, Chile, China, Colombia, Costa Rica, Cyprus, Dominican Republic, Ecuador, Egypt, El Salvador, Ghana, Guatemala, Honduras, India, Jamaica, Liberia, Malta, Nepal, Nicaragua, Pakistan, Panama, Philippines, Romania, Samoa, Senegal, Singapore, Uruguay, Venezuela, Zaire.

International Year of Peace

The General Assembly,

Recalling its resolution 36/67 of 30 November 1981, in which it invited the Economic and Social Council to consider the possibility of declaring an International Year of Peace at the first practicable opportunity, taking into account the urgency and special nature of such an observance,

Recalling Economic and Social Council resolution 1982/15 of 4 May 1982, in which the Council recommended to the General Assembly that, at its thirty-seventh session, it should establish 1986 as the International Year of Peace,

Recalling that the Preamble to the Charter of the United Nations proclaims that the peoples of the United Nations are determined to save succeeding generations from the scourge of war and for this end to practise tolerance and live together in peace with one another as good neighbours, and to unite their strength to maintain international peace and security,

Considering that the promotion of peace is the basic objective of the United Nations,

Recognizing that peace continues to be a goal instead of an achievement, in spite of the resolute efforts of the United Nations,

Taking into account the need to devote a specific time to concentrate the efforts of the United Nations and its Member States to promote the ideals of peace and give evidence of their commitment to peace in all viable ways,

Taking note of the recommendation by the Economic and Social Council that the International Year of Peace could be linked to the fortieth anniversary of the United Nations and be proclaimed on 24 October 1985,

Taking into account the guidelines for international years and anniversaries adopted by the General Assembly in its decision 35/424 of 5 December 1980,

1. *Accepts* the proposal made by the Economic and Social Council in its resolution 1982/15 and declares 1986 to be the International Year of Peace, which will be solemnly proclaimed on 24 October 1985;

2. *Invites* all States, all organizations within the United Nations system and interested non-governmental organizations to exert all possible efforts for the preparation and observance of the International Year of Peace, and to respond generously with contributions to attain the objectives of the Year;

3. *Requests* the Secretary-General to prepare, in accordance with proposals made by Member States and in consultation with interested organizations and academic institutions, a draft programme and to submit a report to the General Assembly at its thirty-eighth session.

International Day of Peace

The first annual observance of the International Day of Peace, proclaimed by the General Assembly on 30 November 1981[2] to fall on the third Tuesday of September—the opening day of regular sessions of the Assembly—took place on 21 September 1982. A note verbale of 22 September from Austria to the Secretary-General[1] annexed a declaration for this observance by the Federal President of Austria, expressing Austria's permanent commitment to understanding, negotiation and dialogue, and stressing the need for tolerance and justice.

Note verbale. [1]Austria, 22 Sep., A/37/503.
Resolution. [2]GA: 36/67, 30 Nov. 1981 (YUN 1981, p. 155).

Chapter V

Africa

Contents

Related topics:

Mediterranean area: Questions involving the Libyan Arab
Jamahiriya. Regional economic and social activities: Africa.
Human rights violations: South Africa and Namibia. Namibia.
Other colonial questions: Western Sahara question.

For resolutions and decisions of major organs mentioned but not reproduced, refer to INDEX OF RESOLUTIONS AND DECISIONS.

South Africa and *apartheid*

The year 1982 marked 30 years since the General Assembly began considering the question of race conflict in South Africa resulting from the policies of *apartheid* of the Government of South Africa.[2] Those policies, based on racial separation, had been enforced by the white minority since 1948. Despite the efforts of the United Nations during those 30 years, the Special Committee against *Apartheid* stated in its 1982 report to the Assembly,[1] oppression had increased, more than 3 million black people had been uprooted from their homes, about 13 million had been arrested under the "pass laws" which restricted movement outside reserved areas, and the Government had sought to deprive 7 million persons of citizenship through its policy of establishing bantustans, or homelands confining blacks to certain "independent" areas.

Proclaimed by the Assembly as the International Year of Mobilization for Sanctions against South Africa, 1982 also marked the seventieth anniversary of the establishment of the South African Native National Congress—later renamed African National Congress of South Africa (ANC). Special activities for the Year were co-ordinated or organized by the Committee against *Apartheid*, which carried out most of the United Nations efforts to bring an end to *apartheid*, especially by mobilizing international campaigns to exert pressure on South Africa.

Several United Nations bodies continued to consider in 1982 the *apartheid* situation in South Africa and ways to end it. The Assembly, repeatedly calling for an end to *apartheid* and condemning South Africa for its policies, adopted 10 resolutions on the issue on 9 December. By the first, an omnibus resolution on the situation in South Africa, the Assembly reiterated its call for comprehensive and mandatory sanctions against South Africa, called for an end to collaboration with that country, condemned its aggression against neighbouring States, reaffirmed the legitimacy of the struggle by the oppressed people and their national liberation movement by all available means to eliminate the *apartheid* régime, and appealed for assistance to the oppressed people.

The call for sanctions was repeated in another resolution by which the Assembly again requested the Security Council to consider action under Chapter VII of the Charter of the United Nations (on action with respect to threats to the peace, breaches of the peace and acts of aggression) (p. 265). By other resolutions, the Assem-bly called for specific action against South Africa, such as the total cessation of military and nuclear co-operation, an end of all new foreign investments in and loans to South Africa and the study of various measures to impose an oil embargo. It demanded that Israel terminate all forms of collaboration with the régime.

In addition, the Assembly called for concerted international action by States, organizations and individuals for the elimination of *apartheid*, and it approved the work programme of its Committee against *Apartheid* to promote international mobilization against *apartheid*. It appealed for contributions to the United Nations Trust Fund for South Africa, providing humanitarian and legal assistance to victims of that system, and authorized further work on the drafting of an international convention against *apartheid* in sports.

Having learned of South Africa's application for credit from the International Monetary Fund (IMF), the Assembly called in October for action to prevent the granting of the request. However, the credit was approved in November.

Both the Assembly and the Security Council adopted two resolutions each in 1982 appealing for clemency in favour of South African members of ANC who had been sentenced to death (p. 293). The Council took such action in April and December, and the Assembly took similar steps in October and December.

An International Conference on Women and *Apartheid*, held at Brussels, Belgium, in May, emphasized the need for the widest publicity about the plight of women in South Africa and Namibia and their resistance against *apartheid*, as well as for greatly increased international assistance to alleviate their hardships and enable them to participate further in the liberation struggle. The Economic and Social Council also appealed in May for assistance to women and children affected by *apartheid*.

In another action in May, the Council expressed the expectation that non-governmental organizations in consultative status with it would take account in their activities of resolutions by the Council and the Assembly condemning *apartheid* (p. 303). In October, it called on home countries of transnational corporations doing business with South Africa to take steps to terminate that collaboration (p. 284).

Steps needed to improve trade union rights for black workers in South Africa were the subject of a special report by the Committee against *Apartheid*. In addition, various meetings, missions and observances were undertaken in order to promote international mobilization for the elimination of *apartheid*.

Report. [1]Committee against *Apartheid*, A/37/22.
Yearbook reference. [2]1952, p. 297.

General aspects

Activities of the Committee against *Apartheid*. Throughout 1982 the General Assembly's Special Committee against *Apartheid* continued its work of facilitating action by the United Nations and mobilizing international support to bring about the abandonment of South Africa's racial discrimination policies. Its annual report to the Assembly,[5] adopted unanimously on 17 September, contained an account of its activities during the year as well as its conclusions and recommendations; an annex contained a review of developments in South Africa since October 1981.

The Committee said in its report that the Security Council had been paralysed because of the misuse of the veto by one or more Western Powers, in the face of aggression by South Africa against Namibia and the front-line States bordering that country. The Committee deplored the policies of the Western Powers concerned which had undermined the Council's authority. It expressed particular distress at the policies of the United States Government, stating that it bore a great responsibility as a permanent member of the Security Council, a major trading partner of South Africa and a Power which could play a crucial role in facilitating United Nations objectives in South Africa. The Committee believed that because of the selfish and short-sighted attitudes of a small minority of States, particularly the major Western Powers, the authority of the United Nations had been eroded.

The Committee emphasized the extremely grave situation in southern Africa resulting from the policies and actions of the South African régime—its aggressive posture, military build-up, nuclear plans, and links with certain Western countries and with Israel and others. It called for intensified international action, commensurate with the growing danger and reflecting a determination to achieve United Nations objectives.

The Committee, confident that the United Nations had the power to take decisive action to eradicate *apartheid*, said that Governments and organizations committed to that objective could persuade the few recalcitrant Powers and selfish interests to cease their support of *apartheid*. In view of the efforts of South Africa's main trading partners to hinder Council action, the General Assembly was obliged to intensify action and help promote action by Member States and world public opinion.

The Committee also submitted special reports on developments concerning relations between Israel and South Africa and on trade union action against *apartheid* (p. 300).

Action by the Commission on Human Rights. On 25 February, the Commission on Human Rights, in a resolution on the right of peoples to self-determination (See ECONOMIC AND SOCIAL QUESTIONS, Chapter XVIII), reaffirmed the legitimacy of the struggle of the South African people and their national liberation movements by all available means, including armed struggle, for the elimination of *apartheid* and the exercise of the right of self-determination.[9]

Communications. South Africa, in a letter of 21 January to the Secretary-General,[4] transmitted a letter of the same date from its Minister for Foreign Affairs and Information which dealt with *apartheid* as well as the Namibia question (See TRUSTEESHIP AND DECOLONIZATION, Chapter III). The Minister said there were many initiatives and developments in the economic, social, labour, education and other fields demonstrating South Africa's determination to resolve its own problems. The Government was sincerely working towards the establishment of a confederation of States in southern Africa with a view to creating a region of stability, through efforts that had been brushed aside by the majority in the General Assembly. Noting a drift towards confrontation, he appealed to the Secretary-General to encourage reconciliation and progress in southern Africa rather than to abet disharmony by supporting demands which aggravated the region's problems, and to demonstrate impartiality on the Namibia question.

In a letter of 21 July to the Secretary-General,[3] Cuba transmitted a press communiqué of the Co-ordinating Bureau of Non-Aligned Countries issued on that date, condemning the recent shooting and dismissal of gold mine workers in South Africa, referring to a widening disparity between the wages of black and white workers, stating that publicized "reforms" were designed merely to placate international opinion while control over black trade unions had been tightened, and reaffirming a call for mandatory sanctions against South Africa including an oil embargo and severance of sports and other cultural ties.

General Assembly action. In the first of 10 resolutions on *apartheid* adopted on 9 December,[11] the General Assembly condemned South Africa for its repression (p. 292). Also condemning certain States for increasing their collaboration with South Africa, it urged the Security Council to impose comprehensive and mandatory sanctions and urged States to take similar measures pending Council action. It called on the United Kingdom to stop the oil supply from Brunei to South Africa (p. 276), and requested IMF to terminate credits to South Africa and the International Atomic Energy Agency (IAEA) to refrain from aiding the régime's nuclear plans (p. 282). Condemning South African aggression against African States (p. 310), it demanded the withdrawal of South African troops from Angola (p. 312). The Assembly appealed for assistance to the South African people and their national liberation movement. It demanded prisoner-of-war treatment for captured freedom fighters (p. 296), invited assistance for conscientious objectors to South African military service, and appealed for accessions to the International Convention on the Suppression and Punishment of the Crime of *Apartheid* (See ECONOMIC AND SOICAL QUESTIONS, Chapter XVIII).

The Assembly called on States and organizations to refrain from recognition of or co-operation with the so-called "independent" bantustans. It reaffirmed the legitimacy of the struggle of the oppressed people of South Africa and their national liberation movement by all available means, including armed struggle, for the seizure of power by the people, the elimination of the *apartheid* régime and the exercise of self-determination. The Assembly reaffirmed the United Nations commitment to the eradication of *apartheid* and the establishment of a democratic society.

The resolution, sponsored by 36 States, was adopted by a recorded vote of 118 to 14, with 11 abstentions. Separate votes were taken on the twenty-first preambular paragraph, expressing concern at United States policies and actions, and operative paragraph 4, condemning the policies of certain Western States (p. 262).

In a resolution of 3 December on self-determination of peoples,[10] the Assembly condemned the "bantustanization" policy and reiterated its support for the oppressed people of South Africa in their just and legitimate struggle against the racist minority régime.

Introducing the 9 December resolution in the Assembly, the Libyan Arab Jamahiriya said that text and five others dealing with *apartheid* and South Africa were based on the recommendations of the Committee against *Apartheid*. Much more needed to be done, and with a sense of urgency, to avert the danger of wider conflict in southern Africa and to secure a just and lasting solution.

In explanation of vote, a number of countries—Australia, Austria, Bangladesh, Canada, Chile, Costa Rica, the Dominican Republic, Fiji, the Federal Republic of Germany, Guyana, Ireland, Jamaica, Lesotho, the Netherlands, Oman, Peru, Portugal, Solomon Islands, Sri Lanka, Suriname, Swaziland, Sweden (on behalf of the five Nordic States), Thailand, Turkey, the United Kingdom and Uruguay—said they condemned the *apartheid* policies of South Africa but disapproved of those paragraphs which condemned by name individual States or groups of States. Denmark, on behalf of the European Community (EC) members, rejected all arbitrary and unjustified attacks on Member States.

Several countries—Austria, Canada, Denmark (for the EC members), Fiji, Ireland, Japan, the Netherlands, Peru, Portugal, Swaziland, Sweden (on behalf of the Nordic States) and the United States—opposed the endorsement of armed struggle and several of them said they would have preferred a text emphasizing a peaceful solution to the *apartheid* problem. Swaziland stated that it did not support the use of force, by either Governments or movements. Uruguay expressed its understanding that none of the *apartheid* resolutions endorsed armed struggle. Vanuatu said that, although it abhorred armed conflict and would prefer an immediate and peaceful end to *apartheid*, South Africa had made that impossible and regrettably, by its actions, had decreed armed struggle to be the only way to freedom.

Opposing the resolution, the Federal Republic of Germany said it failed to understand the unfounded criticism in the text directed against Western countries, suggesting that they were encouraging South Africa to undertake criminal acts against neighbouring States. Japan noted particular paragraphs it could not support, including those relating to sanctions and to the legitimacy of armed struggle. The Netherlands said it could not support a policy of total isolation of South Africa because it believed that course would not lead to the desired goal. Portugal said the total isolation of South Africa would only hamper the initiatives of those fighting inside the country for fundamental reforms.

The United Kingdom, which also voted against, regretted that most of the resolutions on *apartheid* before the Assembly would provoke division, were not realistic and would not help to end *apartheid*, and several contained misleading references to Western States. Explaining its negative vote on all the 1982 resolutions on *apartheid* except the one on the United Nations Trust Fund for South Africa,[12] the United States, while reiterating its opposition to *apartheid*, said its policy of constructive engagement was more likely to bring about positive changes in South Africa than would confrontation, punishment and isolation, which was the philosophical basis of the resolutions; it denied implications in the texts that the United States supported racism or that it encouraged South Africa in aggression against its neighbours.

Among those abstaining in the vote on the resolution, Australia regretted that its language was more extreme than in the corresponding resolution of 1981.[13] Greece supported the general principles in the resolution but objected to the language of certain paragraphs. Ireland said that, in deciding to abstain, it had weighed the positive elements in the draft—United Nations commitment to the total eradication of *apartheid* and the establishment of a democratic society in South Africa—against other formulations which it considered inappropriate, in particular the endorsement of armed struggle, the call for comprehensive and mandatory sanctions, and the somewhat arbitrary naming and condemnation of the policies of particular States.

Of those explaining their votes in favour of the resolution, the Bahamas said that, while it supported all the resolutions condemning *apartheid*, it had serious reservations with regard to the language and content of a number of paragraphs embodying matters which defied compromise and thus alienated many States, including those which had the influence to persuade South Africa to abandon *apartheid*. Brazil, which voted for all 10 resolutions on *apartheid* and South Africa adopted on 9 December, said it had doubts about the usefulness of the language used in some. Costa Rica voiced reservations on the paragraphs which referred to collaboration between particular States and South Africa, and considered it advisable to search for other ways of achieving a practical solution to the problem, instead of repeating every year the same unilateral condemnations.

Fiji said its support for the resolutions was tempered by the introduction of divisive elements that it felt stood in the way of the unified front that the United Nations could effectively present towards a common goal. Guyana preferred an approach that did not single out individual countries for condemnation but said it supported the more fundamental question—namely, the political statement that the resolution sought to make.

Its positive vote, Lesotho said, should not be taken as an endorsement of those provisions with which it did not agree; it was particularly concerned about paragraphs 4, 5 and 6, by which the Assembly condemned the policies of certain States and their businesses that had increased collaboration with South Africa, reaffirmed its support for sanctions and urged the Security Council to impose them. Malta said it supported the general thrust of all the resolutions and believed in the aim of encouraging a peaceful solution, but that did not mean it agreed with every provision. Morocco and Tunisia also voted in favour but said they did not agree with the language of some paragraphs.

Several delegations expressed regret that sufficient efforts had not been made to secure the adoption of the anti-*apartheid* resolutions by consensus.

Botswana, Guyana, Japan, Suriname and a number of other countries made comments or reservations on the paragraphs in this resolution favouring sanctions and condemning specific States for collaboration with South Africa. Objections or reservations were also voiced on the paragraphs concerning the oil supply from Brunei (Botswana, Thailand, United Kingdom), South Africa's relations with IAEA (Japan) and IMF (Australia, Swaziland, Uruguay), and support for the national liberation movement (Japan, Netherlands, Sweden, United States, Uruguay).

During the Assembly's debate on *apartheid*, all speakers condemned the *apartheid* system of South Africa and most of them criticized its policies towards neighbouring States.

A number of countries—including Algeria, Botswana, the Byelorussian SSR, Czechoslovakia, Democratic Kampuchea, Egypt, Finland, the Gambia, Hungary, Japan, Madagascar, Mongolia, Norway, Romania, Somalia, Swaziland, Sweden and Uganda—criticized the proposals made earlier in the year by the South African Government to change the Constitution so that Coloureds (persons of mixed race) and Asians, but not blacks, would be able, through separate voters' rolls for each group, to elect representatives to their own chamber of Parliament. These countries believed the proposals had been made for cosmetic reasons only, to deceive world public opinion, and would do little to change the situation and nothing at all for the black majority. The new plan, Botswana said, offered the blacks nothing but more racism; the Asians and Coloureds were not the problem in South Africa. In the view of Swaziland, the so-called reforms were unacceptable because they deliberately turned a blind eye to the aspirations of the majority. Zambia and others saw the plan as intended to create conflict between the blacks on one side and the Coloured and Asian communities on the other.

Denmark, speaking for the EC members, said that mere modifications of the *apartheid* system were unsatisfactory; all international efforts should be directed towards the elimination of the system and the establishment of a government based on a purely representative democracy. New Zealand could see no sign that *apartheid* was being abandoned or even seriously modified, despite statements that some restrictions on social contact between people of different races were being relaxed. Norway agreed that the changes introduced by the South African Government did not represent a substantial change of policy; therefore it believed that *apartheid* could not be reformed but must be abolished—a view shared by Argentina and a number of others. It was saddening and shocking, said Poland, that some Governments regarded recent changes in South Africa as constructive and suggested that such gradual improvements should be encouraged as the effective way of bringing about non-violent change.

Among those condemning South Africa's policy of bantustanization, which restricted the black population to certain "homelands", were Afghanistan, the Byelorussian SSR, the Central African Republic, China, Cyprus, Democratic Kampuchea, Denmark (speaking for the EC members), Djibouti, Egypt, Gabon, the Gambia, Hungary,

India, Kenya, Kuwait, the Lao People's Democratic Republic, Mongolia, the Netherlands, Nicaragua, Romania, Somalia, Swaziland, the Syrian Arab Republic, Togo, Trinidad and Tobago, the USSR and the United States. Several of these countries considered that the policy was aimed at depriving blacks of citizenship and other human rights, at upholding *apartheid*, or at dividing the people. Afghanistan said that, in an effort to divide the non-white majority, the South African Government had adopted regulations giving the Coloured population a separate title to distinguish it from black Africans, an attempt that had been rejected by both black and Coloured sectors. Somalia called on the Assembly to condemn the proposed South African legislation euphemistically entitled "The Orderly Movement and Settlement of Black Persons", which sought to reverse a court decision on liberalization of pass laws affecting separation of families.

A number of countries, including Australia, the Byelorussian SSR, Djibouti, the Gambia, Hungary, Kuwait, the Lao People's Democratic Republic and Suriname, mentioned the economic advantages for the white minority in preserving *apartheid*, thereby guaranteeing a pool of cheap labour. The Syrian Arab Republic viewed South Africa as a military, political and economic base to serve the interests of the imperialist system at the expense of the exploited peoples. The USSR said superprofits were in the final analysis what determined the State policy of South Africa, which was based on colonialism and racism. Zambia said that exploitative economic returns were the rationale on which the *apartheid* system, with its essential ingredient—plentiful, cheap and enslaved labour—was built.

Brazil, the Gambia, Ireland, Kenya, Madagascar, New Zealand, Singapore, Sweden, Togo and Tunisia warned that if the situation did not change, violence and possibly a conflagration would break out—which, some said, would endanger peace and security in the region and beyond. Brazil added that the South African leaders should be prevailed upon by those that might exert some influence over them to realize that, unless they changed their policies, racial confrontation in South Africa would continue to increase.

Albania agreed that *apartheid* threatened peace and stability in southern Africa and added that the two imperialist super-Powers—the USSR and the United States—as well as China, did everything possible to penetrate into the African continent, to establish military bases there and to secure markets and zones of influence. Tunisia said that neither the strengthening of its military capacity nor the creation of more bantustans could serve to restore to South Africa its balance, stability and security; only the recognition of equal-

ity, freedom and respect for the rights of all could guarantee its continued existence in a continent willing to forget the past.

Among those calling for international action to combat *apartheid*, Algeria said that action under United Nations auspices would bring about political and social changes which the *apartheid* régime would never be able to initiate on its own. Austria believed it necessary to continue the annual debate because the priority assigned to *apartheid* by the United Nations had led to a world-wide consensus and a fuller awareness of the problem, and the debate lent moral support to those resisting the system. In the view of Democratic Kampuchea, it was the duty of the United Nations to continue to put pressure on the régime. Having witnessed *apartheid* in operation at close range, Swaziland said, it could testify to the need for stronger and sustained international pressure on South Africa to opt for a peaceful change. Venezuela stated that common action by all United Nations Members was needed in order to achieve change in South Africa's attitude; without actions by certain States having close relations with South Africa, Assembly decisions would be ineffective.

Some countries emphasized that change in South Africa could be brought about by peaceful means. Australia, convinced that there was an alternative to bloodshed in the region, said South Africa had forfeited its place in the international community and the community would readmit that country only when deep and abiding changes took place there. Japan felt it crucial that the international community continue to exert, through peaceful means, maximum pressure on South Africa and encourage enlightened movements within South Africa to take more effective action. The Netherlands said it was encouraging peaceful change in South African society through the continuation of dialogue with the South African authorities and the exertion of pressure on them; in addition, it was urging its companies to implement the guidelines set out in the code of conduct for European companies with interests in South Africa, which provided for freedom of association, increases in minimum pay and equal pay for equal work.

Suriname called on all responsible States, in particular the major Western States, to co-operate in order to facilitate a peaceful transition to power sharing in South Africa. Sweden said that, for a peaceful political solution, the Security Council and the leading Western Powers had a decisive role to play through measures that could defuse the situation. The United States, stressing that the objective must be to devise means by which the international community could encourage genuine change, said it did not believe such change would come about by increasing South Africa's political, economic and cultural isolation; the United States continued to encourage and support efforts by the American private sector operating in South Africa as a positive instrument of social and economic change through measures such as fair employment practices.

Egypt, on the other hand, believed that the policy of "constructive engagement" adopted by certain States towards South Africa had not borne fruit and that it was clear there would be no positive response to that policy from South Africa. The Libyan Arab Jamahiriya expressed support for armed struggle by South Africans and Namibians to obtain freedom and dignity within a society of justice and equality.

Among the countries remarking that South Africa had increased its repressive measures, Gabon said the intensification of repression and the development of racist laws were signs that the black majority must organize its resistance in the face of a régime that could maintain itself only through violence. The Gambia said popular resistance to *apartheid* had crystallized considerably during the past year despite the reinforcement of repressive legislation, and the vanguard of resistance was the black labour movement. According to Togo, South Africa had escalated internal repression, employing a policy that contained in itself the seeds of violence and hatred. Uganda stated that, despite its attempt to project an image of change and relaxation of the *apartheid* system, the minority régime was relying more and more on barbaric forms of repression in a futile attempt to halt the liberation struggle.

Ireland and Singapore said that pressure from the outside could help bring change in South Africa, but the people of South Africa would determine how the struggle was waged. Ireland added that it was for white South Africa to decide how it would face the growing militancy of those who had already endured so much—by relatively peaceful means or at the end of a drawn-out and possibly bloody process. Singapore said the international community could assist their struggle in several ways: by disseminating information, increasing international pressure, isolating South Africa by reducing or eliminating collaboration, supporting the activities of the Committee against *Apartheid*, and assisting the victims of *apartheid* and South African movements opposed to it.

Some countries mentioned the continued resistance of the South African Government to the demands of the international community. The Central African Republic said that, by refusing to meet United Nations demands and by deliberately violating the principles and purposes of its Charter, South Africa had withdrawn from the great family of nations. Finland remarked that South Africa

had reacted to international pressure with defiance and resistance and by turning increasingly inwards. According to Madagascar, the actions and statements of South African authorities showed no signs that they were ready to abandon *apartheid*, and the continued process of bantustanization indicated the contrary.

In accordance with a 24 September decision of the General Assembly,[1] on the recommendation of its General Committee,[6] that organizations and individuals having a special interest in *apartheid* would be permitted to be heard by the Special Political Committee (SPC), that Committee approved 30 requests for hearing, 27 of which were in writing.[8] On 5 and 8 November, SPC heard statements by the following 26 persons:

Michael Myerson, United States Peace Council; Beatrice von Roemer, International Confederation of Free Trade Unions; Jim Morrell, Centre for International Policy; Willis Logan and Alan Boesack, National Council of Churches of Christ in the United States of America; Abdul Samad Minty, British Anti-*Apartheid* Movement and World Campaign against Military and Nuclear Collaboration with South Africa; David Lampel, Inner City Broadcasting, Inc.; Wilfrid Grenville-Grey, International Defence and Aid Fund for Southern Africa; Gail Hovey, American Committee on Africa; Mohamed Said Ahmed, Afro-Asian Peoples' Solidarity Organization; Albert Louis Sachs; John Dommisse, American Co-ordinating Committee for Equality in Sport and Society; Philip Oke, Christian Peace Conference; Ellen Chrisman, World Assembly of Youth; Audrey C. Smock, South Africa Taskforce of the Interfaith Center on Corporate Responsibility; Romesh Chandra, World Peace Council; Jeanne Woods, on behalf of R. H. Stevenson, National Anti-Imperialist Movement in Solidarity with African Liberation; Luis Prado, International Oil Working Group; Deborah A. Jackson, National Conference of Black Lawyers; William H. Schaap, Center for Constitutional Rights; Elombe Brath, Patrice Lumumba Coalition; Jerry Herman, American Friends Service Committee; Abdul Ahmed, Phelps-Stokes Fund; Chief Abraham Ordia, Supreme Council for Sports in Africa; R. Ian Butterfield, National Heritage Foundation; and Edwin A. Locke, Jr., National Strategy Information Center.

The Assembly, by a decision adopted without vote on 9 November,[2] orally proposed by its President, took note of the SPC report on the hearings.[7]

Decisions (1982). GA: [1]37/401, 24 Sep.; [2]37/406, 9 Nov., text following.

Letters. [3]Cuba, 21 July, A/37/354-S/15306; [4]South Africa, 21 Jan., A/37/74-S/14843.

Reports. [5]Committee against *Apartheid,* A/37/22; [6]General Committee, A/37/250; [7]SPC, A/37/598.

Requests for hearing. [8]A/SPC/37/L.4 & Add.1-3 & Add.3/Corr.1, Add.4-9 & Add.9/Corr.1 & Add.10-26.

Resolutions (1982). [9]Commission on Human Rights (report, E/1982/12): 1982/16, para. 3, 25 Feb. GA: [10]37/43, para. 6, 3 Dec.; [11]37/69 A, 9 Dec., text following; [12]37/69 I, 9 Dec..

Resolution (prior). [13]GA: 36/172 A, 17 Dec. 1981 (YUN 1981, p. 161).
Financial implications. 5th Committee report, A/37/713; S-G statement, A/C.5/37/70.
Meeting records. GA: SPC, A/SPC/37/SR.7, 11, 13, 15-18 (25 Oct.–4 Nov.), A/SPC/37/PV.21-23, 26 (5-10 Nov.); plenary, A/37/PV.59-62, 65-68, 97, 98 (9 Nov.–9 Dec.); 5th Committee, A/C.5/37/SR.59 (8 Dec.).

General Assembly decision 37/406

Adopted without vote

Oral proposal by President; agenda item 33.

Policies of *apartheid* of the Government of South Africa
At its 59th plenary meeting, on 9 November 1982, the General Assembly took note of the report of the Special Political Committee.

General Assembly resolution 37/69 A

9 December 1982   Meeting 97   118-14-11 (recorded vote)

36-nation draft (A/37/L.17 and Corr.1 and Add.1); agenda item 33.

Sponsors: Afghanistan, Algeria, Angola, Benin, Bulgaria, Byelorussian SSR, Chad, Congo, Cuba, Czechoslovakia, Democratic Yemen, Ethiopia, German Democratic Republic, Ghana, Grenada, Guinea, Guyana, Hungary, Iraq, Kenya, Lao People's Democratic Republic, Libyan Arab Jamahiriya, Madagascar, Malaysia, Mauritania, Mozambique, Nigeria, Sao Tome and Principe, Syrian Arab Republic, Togo, Uganda, Ukrainian SSR, United Republic of Tanzania, Viet Nam, Zambia, Zimbabwe.

Situation in South Africa
The General Assembly,
Recalling and reaffirming its resolutions on this question, particularly resolution 36/172 of 17 December 1981,
Having considered the reports of the Special Committee against Apartheid,
Reaffirming that *apartheid* is a crime against humanity and a threat to international peace and security,
Bearing in mind that it proclaimed 1982 International Year of Mobilization for Sanctions against South Africa,
Conscious of the responsibility of the United Nations and the international community towards the oppressed people of South Africa and their national liberation movement, as proclaimed, in particular, in General Assembly resolution 3411 C (XXX) of 28 November 1975,
Convinced that it is incumbent on the international community to provide all necessary assistance to the oppressed people of South Africa and their national liberation movement in their legitimate struggle for the establishment of a democratic society pursuant to their inalienable rights, in conformity with the principles contained in the Charter of the United Nations and the Universal Declaration of Human Rights,
Commending the oppressed people of South Africa and their liberation movements, particularly the African National Congress, for intensifying the armed struggle against the racist régime,
Reaffirming that the *apartheid* régime is totally responsible for precipitating violent conflict through its policy of *apartheid* and inhuman repression,
Gravely concerned at the intensification of repression in South Africa, the growing number of deaths in detention and the imposition of death sentences on freedom fighters of the African National Congress,
Reaffirming that freedom fighters of South Africa should be treated as prisoners of war in accordance with Additional Protocol I to the Geneva Conventions of 12 August 1949,
Commending the courageous struggle of the black workers of South Africa for their inalienable rights,
Condemning the policy of "bantustanization" designed to dispossess further the African majority of its inalienable rights and to deprive it of citizenship, as well as the continuing forced removals of black people, as an international crime,
Gravely concerned at the growing number of displaced and missing persons resulting from the criminal policies of the racist régime of South Africa,
Reaffirming that *apartheid* cannot be reformed but must be totally eliminated,
Denouncing the manœuvres of the racist régime of South Africa to divide the oppressed people through so-called constitutional dispensations and other means, and commending the oppressed people of South Africa for rejecting those manœuvres,

Recognizing that comprehensive and mandatory sanctions by the Security Council under Chapter VII of the Charter of the United Nations are essential to avert the grave threat to international peace and security resulting from the policies and actions of the *apartheid* régime of South Africa,
Considering that political, economic, military and any other collaboration with the *apartheid* régime of South Africa encourages its persistent intransigence and defiance of the international community and its escalating acts of repression and aggression,
Reaffirming that the policies and actions of the *apartheid* régime, the strengthening of its military forces and its escalating acts of aggression, subversion and terrorism against independent African States have resulted in frequent breaches of the peace and constitute a grave threat to international peace and security,
Deploring the attitude of those Western permanent members of the Security Council that have so far prevented the Council from adopting comprehensive sanctions against that régime under Chapter VII of the Charter,
Condemning all military, nuclear and other collaboration by certain Western States and Israel with South Africa,
Gravely concerned at the pronouncements, policies and actions of the Government of the United States of America which have provided comfort and encouragement to the racist régime of South Africa,
Concerned that some Western States and Israel continue military and nuclear co-operation with South Africa, in gross violation of the provisions of Security Council resolution 418(1977), of 4 November 1977, and have failed to prevent corporations, institutions and individuals within their jurisdiction from carrying out such co-operation,
Gravely concerned that the racist régime of South Africa has continued to obtain military equipment and ammunition, as well as technology and know-how, to develop its armaments industry and to acquire nuclear-weapon capability,
Recognizing that any nuclear-weapon capability of the racist régime of South Africa constitutes a threat to international peace and security and a grave menace to Africa and the world,
Commending all States that have provided assistance to Angola and other front-line States in accordance with the relevant resolutions of the United Nations,
Condemning any encouragement to the *apartheid* régime in its acts of aggression, direct or indirect, as hostile to the interests of peace and freedom,
Strongly condemning the activities of those transnational corporations that continue to collaborate with the *apartheid* régime, especially in the military, nuclear, petroleum and other fields, and of those financial institutions that have continued to provide loans and credits to South Africa,
Emphasizing the conclusion of the Paris Declaration on Sanctions against South Africa that the continuing political, economic and military collaboration of certain Western States and their transnational corporations with the racist régime of South Africa encourages its persistent intransigence and defiance of the international community and constitutes a major obstacle to the elimination of the inhuman and criminal system of *apartheid* in South Africa and the attainment of self-determination, freedom and national independence by the people of Namibia,
Recalling and reaffirming the Declaration on South Africa contained in its resolution 34/93 O of 12 December 1979,
Commending the efforts of trade unions, religious institutions, student organizations and anti-*apartheid* movements in their campaigns against transnational corporations and financial institutions collaborating with the racist régime of South Africa,
   1.   *Strongly condemns* the *apartheid* régime of South Africa for its brutal repression and indiscriminate torture and killings of workers, schoolchildren and other opponents of *apartheid*, and the imposition of death sentences on freedom fighters;
   2.   *Vehemently condemns* the *apartheid* régime for its repeated acts of aggression, subversion and terrorism against independent African States, designed to destabilize the whole of southern Africa;
   3.   *Reiterates its firm conviction* that the *apartheid* régime has been encouraged to undertake these criminal acts by the protection afforded by major Western Powers against international sanctions;
   4.   *Condemns* the policies of certain Western States, especially the United States of America, and of Israel, and of their transnational corporations and financial institutions that have increased political,

economic and military collaboration with the racist régime of South Africa despite repeated appeals by the General Assembly;

5. *Reaffirms* its conviction that comprehensive and mandatory sanctions imposed by the Security Council under Chapter VII of the Charter of the United Nations, universally applied, are the most appropriate and effective means by which the international community can assist the legitimate struggle of the oppressed people of South Africa and discharge its responsibilities for the maintenance of international peace and security;

6. *Again urges* the Security Council to determine that the situation in South Africa and in southern Africa as a whole, resulting from the policies and actions of the *apartheid* régime of South Africa, constitutes a grave and growing threat to international peace and security, and to impose comprehensive and mandatory sanctions against the régime under Chapter VII of the Charter;

7. *Demands* the immediate and unconditional withdrawal of all troops of the *apartheid* régime of South Africa from Angola and demands that South Africa respect fully the independence, sovereignty and territorial integrity of Angola and other independent African States;

8. *Further demands* that the racist régime of South Africa pay full compensation to Angola and other independent African States for the damage to life and property caused by its acts of aggression;

9. *Urges* all States that have not yet done so to adopt separate and collective measures for comprehensive sanctions against South Africa, pending action by the Security Council;

10. *Calls upon* the Government of the United Kingdom of Great Britain and Northern Ireland to take the necessary measures to stop the supply of oil from Brunei to South Africa;

11. *Requests* all intergovernmental organizations to exclude the racist régime of South Africa and to terminate all co-operation with it;

12. *Expresses serious concern* over the continued granting of credits by the International Monetary Fund to the racist régime of South Africa and requests it to terminate such credits forthwith;

13. *Requests* the International Atomic Energy Agency to refrain from extending to South Africa any facilities which may assist it in its nuclear plans and, in particular, to exclude South Africa from all its technical working groups;

14. *Again calls upon* all States and organizations to refrain from any recognition of or co-operation with the so-called "independent" bantustans;

15. *Appeals* to all States that have not yet done so to accede to the International Convention on the Suppression and Punishment of the Crime of *Apartheid;*

16. *Reaffirms* the legitimacy of the struggle of the oppressed people of South Africa and their national liberation movement by all available means, including armed struggle, for the seizure of power by the people, the elimination of the *apartheid* régime and the exercise of the right of self-determination by the people of South Africa as a whole;

17. *Demands* that the *apartheid* régime treat captured freedom fighters as prisoners of war under the Geneva Conventions of 12 August 1949 and Additional Protocol I thereto;

18. *Again proclaims* its full support of the national liberation movement of South Africa as the authentic representative of the people of South Africa in their just struggle for liberation;

19. *Appeals* to all States to provide all necessary humanitarian, educational, financial and other necessary assistance to the oppressed people of South Africa and their national liberation movement in their legitimate struggle;

20. *Urges* the United Nations Development Programme and other agencies of the United Nations system to expand their assistance to the oppressed people of South Africa and to the South African liberation movements recognized by the Organization of African Unity, namely, the African National Congress and the Pan Africanist Congress of Azania, in consultation with the Special Committee against *Apartheid;*

21. *Decides* to continue the authorization of adequate financial provision in the budget of the United Nations to enable those liberation movements to maintain offices in New York in order to participate effectively in the deliberations of the Special Committee and other appropriate bodies;

22. *Invites* all Governments and organizations to assist, in consultation with the national liberation movements of South Africa and Namibia, persons compelled to leave South Africa because of their objection, on the ground of conscience, to serving in the military or police forces of the *apartheid* régime;

23. *Reaffirms* the commitment of the United Nations to the total eradication of *apartheid* and the establishment of a democratic society in which all the people of South Africa as a whole, irrespective of race, colour, sex or creed, will enjoy equal and full human rights and fundamental freedoms and participate freely in the determination of their destiny.

Recorded vote in Assembly as follows:

In favour: Afghanistan, Albania, Algeria, Angola, Antigua and Barbuda, Argentina, Bahamas, Bahrain, Bangladesh, Barbados, Benin, Bhutan, Bolivia, Botswana, Brazil, Bulgaria, Burma, Burundi, Byelorussian SSR, Cape Verde, Central African Republic, Chad, China, Colombia, Comoros, Congo, Costa Rica, Cuba, Cyprus, Czechoslovakia, Democratic Kampuchea, Democratic Yemen, Djibouti, Dominican Republic, Ecuador, Egypt, Equatorial Guinea, Ethiopia, Fiji, Gabon, Gambia, German Democratic Republic, Ghana, Grenada, Guinea, Guinea-Bissau, Guyana, Haiti, Hungary, India, Indonesia, Iran, Iraq, Jamaica, Jordan, Kenya, Kuwait, Lao People's Democratic Republic, Lesotho, Liberia, Libyan Arab Jamahiriya, Madagascar, Malaysia, Maldives, Mali, Malta, Mauritania, Mauritius, Mexico, Mongolia, Morocco, Mozambique, Nepal, Nicaragua, Niger, Nigeria, Oman, Pakistan, Panama, Papua New Guinea, Peru, Philippines, Poland, Qatar, Romania, Rwanda, Sao Tome and Principe, Saudi Arabia, Senegal, Sierra Leone, Solomon Islands, Somalia, Sri Lanka, Sudan, Suriname, Swaziland, Syrian Arab Republic, Thailand, Togo, Trinidad and Tobago, Tunisia, Turkey, Uganda, Ukrainian SSR, USSR, United Arab Emirates, United Republic of Cameroon, United Republic of Tanzania, Upper Volta, Uruguay, Vanuatu, Venezuela, Viet Nam, Yemen, Yugoslavia, Zaire, Zambia, Zimbabwe.

Against: Belgium, Canada, Denmark, France, Germany, Federal Republic of, Iceland, Italy, Luxembourg, Netherlands, New Zealand, Norway, Portugal, United Kingdom, United States.

Abstaining: Australia, Austria, Finland, Greece, Ireland, Ivory Coast, Japan,[a] Malawi, Singapore, Spain, Sweden.

[a]Later advised the Secretariat it had intended to vote against.

International mobilization
for the elimination of *apartheid*

By a resolution of 9 December 1982,[2] the General Assembly appealed to States and organizations to co-operate in international action to eliminate *apartheid*, promote the establishment of a democratic society in South Africa and secure peace in the region. It renewed its appeal that they deny assistance to the South African régime and assist the oppressed people of South Africa and their national liberation movements. The Assembly also appealed to the Western permanent members of the Security Council to co-operate in and facilitate effective Council action, and invited the Council to take such action (p. 264). It encouraged trade union action in solidarity with the oppressed workers of South Africa, and appealed to writers, artists, sportsmen and others to participate in the international campaign against *apartheid* in co-operation with the United Nations. The Assembly endorsed the campaign for the release of South African political prisoners and appealed for assistance to the front-line States (p. 310).

The Assembly adopted the resolution by a recorded vote of 135 to 3, with 8 abstentions. Sponsored by 65 nations, the text was introduced by the Libyan Arab Jamahiriya, which noted that it was based on the recommendations of the Special Committee against *Apartheid.* [1]

In another resolution of 9 December, on the work programme of that Committee, the Assembly encouraged it to promote the widest international mobilization against *apartheid* and allocated $400,000 from the United Nations budget for special projects to that end in 1983.[3]

Among those voting against the resolution on international mobilization for the elimination of *apartheid*, the United Kingdom expressed the view that references to Western States were unfounded allegations and the text did not accord with a realistic policy on international action to end *apartheid*. Portugal, which abstained, said it objected to verbal violence and certain discriminatory references in this and other anti-*apartheid* resolutions.

Having voted for the resolution, the Netherlands said the text rightly pointed to the contribution by various social groups to the elimination of *apartheid*, but the wording also led the Netherlands to call anew for respect for the division of competences between various United Nations organs.

Comments and reservations were voiced by Botswana, France and the Netherlands on the paragraph appealing to the Western permanent members of the Security Council to facilitate effective Council action.

Report. [1]Committee against *Apartheid*, A/37/22.
Resolutions (1982). GA, 9 Dec.: [2]37/69 B, text following; [3]37/69 E, paras. 3 & 7.
Financial implications. 5th Committee report, A/37/713; S-G statement, A/C.5/37/70.
Meeting records. GA: plenary, A/37/PV.59-62, 65-68, *97, 98* (9 Nov.–9 Dec.); 5th Committee, A/C.5/37/SR.59 (8 Dec.).

General Assembly resolution 37/69 B

9 December 1982   Meeting 97   135-3-8 (recorded vote)

65-nation draft (A/37/L.18 and Add.1); agenda item 33.

Sponsors: Afghanistan, Algeria, Angola, Benin, Bulgaria, Burundi, Byelorussian SSR, Cape Verde, Central African Republic, Chad, Comoros, Congo, Cuba, Cyprus, Czechoslovakia, Democratic Yemen, Djibouti, Egypt, Ethiopia, Gabon, Gambia, German Democratic Republic, Ghana, Grenada, Guinea, Guinea-Bissau, Guyana, Haiti, Hungary, India, Indonesia, Iraq, Jamaica, Kenya, Lao People's Democratic Republic, Liberia, Libyan Arab Jamahiriya, Madagascar, Malaysia, Maldives, Mali, Mauritania, Morocco, Mozambique, Nicaragua, Nigeria, Pakistan, Qatar, Romania, Rwanda, Sao Tome and Principe, Senegal, Somalia, Sudan, Syrian Arab Republic, Togo, Trinidad and Tobago, Uganda, Ukrainian SSR, United Republic of Tanzania, Vanuatu, Viet Nam, Zaire, Zambia, Zimbabwe.

Concerted international action for the elimination of *apartheid*

The General Assembly,

Meeting thirty years after it began consideration of the item entitled "Question of race conflict in South Africa resulting from the policies of *apartheid* of the Government of the Republic of South Africa",

Gravely concerned over the situation in South Africa, in particular the efforts of the racist régime of South Africa to perpetuate *apartheid*, its deportations of African people, its deprivation of the African people of their inalienable rights through the establishment of so-called "independent" bantustans and its ruthless repression against all opponents of the criminal policy of *apartheid*,

Considering that the policies and actions of the racist régime of South Africa, in particular its acts of aggression, terrorism and destabilization against independent African States, constitute a grave threat to international peace and security,

Recognizing that the racist régime of South Africa, in its persistent defiance of the United Nations, is responsible for the growing threat to the peace in southern Africa and for the repeated breaches of the peace,

Considering that the military build-up and nuclear plans of the racist régime of South Africa constitute a serious menace to international peace and security,

Recognizing further that the total elimination of *apartheid* and the establishment of a democratic State in South Africa are essential for peace, security and stability in the region,

Recalling the long struggle of the African and other people of South Africa for the elimination of racial discrimination and the establishment

of a society in which all the people of the country as a whole—irrespective of race, colour or creed—will enjoy human rights and fundamental freedoms on the basis of equality,

Reaffirming its recognition of the contribution of that struggle to the purposes of the United Nations,

Paying tribute to all those who have sacrificed their lives in the struggle for freedom and human dignity in South Africa,

Expressing its solidarity with all those imprisoned, restricted or otherwise persecuted for participation in that legitimate struggle,

Anxious that all States should co-operate in effective international action to achieve the purposes indicated in unanimous declarations and resolutions of the General Assembly and the Security Council, in particular the elimination of *apartheid*, an end to repression in South Africa and an end to all violations of the sovereignty and territorial integrity of independent African States,

Mindful of the responsibility of the United Nations and the international community to secure peace in southern Africa and to promote freedom and equality,

1. *Appeals* to all States and organizations to co-operate fully in effective international action to eliminate *apartheid* in South Africa, to promote the establishment of a democratic society in which all the people of that country will enjoy human and political rights and to secure peace in the region;

2. *Renews its appeal* to all States and organizations to deny any assistance, direct or indirect, to the racist régime of South Africa and provide all necessary assistance to the oppressed people of South Africa and their national liberation movements in this crucial period;

3. *Appeals* to the Western permanent members of the Security Council to co-operate in and facilitate effective action by the Council under Chapter VII of the Charter of the United Nations;

4. *Endorses* the campaign for the release of Nelson Mandela and all other South African political prisoners as an indispensable prerequisite for a peaceful and just solution in South Africa;

5. *Encourages* action by trade union organizations all over the world in solidarity with the oppressed workers of South Africa;

6. *Appeals* to writers, artists, sportsmen and others to participate actively in the international campaign against *apartheid* in co-operation with the United Nations;

7. *Commends* the front-line States and other States neighbouring South Africa for their sacrifices in support of freedom in South Africa;

8. *Appeals* to all States and organizations to lend all necessary moral and material assistance to those States;

9. *Warns* the racist régime of South Africa against any acts of aggression, terrorism and destabilization against independent African States, and any support to mercenaries;

10. *Requests* the Special Committee against *Apartheid* to continue:

(a) To publicize all acts of aggression, terrorism and destabilization by the racist régime of South Africa against independent African States;

(b) To promote assistance to the front-line States;

11. *Invites* the Security Council urgently to give thorough consideration to the ever-growing threat to the peace in southern Africa and to take effective measures under the Charter.

Recorded vote in Assembly as follows:

In favour: Afghanistan, Albania, Algeria, Angola, Antigua and Barbuda, Argentina, Australia, Austria, Bahamas, Bahrain, Bangladesh, Barbados, Benin, Bhutan, Bolivia, Botswana, Brazil, Bulgaria, Burma, Burundi, Byelorussian SSR, Cape Verde, Central African Republic, Chad, Chile, China, Colombia, Comoros, Congo, Costa Rica, Cuba, Cyprus, Czechoslovakia, Democratic Kampuchea, Democratic Yemen, Denmark, Djibouti, Dominican Republic, Ecuador, Egypt, Equatorial Guinea, Ethiopia, Fiji, Finland, Gabon, Gambia, German Democratic Republic, Ghana, Greece, Grenada, Guatemala, Guinea, Guinea-Bissau, Guyana, Haiti, Honduras, Hungary, Iceland, India, Indonesia, Iran, Iraq, Ireland, Italy, Ivory Coast, Jamaica, Jordan, Kenya, Kuwait, Lao People's Democratic Republic, Lesotho, Liberia, Libyan Arab Jamahiriya, Madagascar, Malaysia, Maldives, Mali, Malta, Mauritania, Mauritius, Mexico, Mongolia, Morocco, Mozambique, Nepal, Netherlands, Nicaragua, Niger, Nigeria, Norway, Oman, Pakistan, Panama, Papua New Guinea, Peru, Philippines, Poland, Qatar, Romania, Rwanda, Sao Tome and Principe, Saudi Arabia, Senegal, Sierra Leone, Singapore, Solomon Islands, Somalia, Spain, Sri Lanka, Sudan, Suriname, Swaziland, Sweden, Syrian Arab Republic, Togo, Trinidad and Tobago, Tunisia, Turkey, Uganda, Ukrainian SSR, USSR, United Arab Emirates, United Republic of Cameroon, United Republic of Tanzania, Upper Volta, Uruguay, Vanuatu, Venezuela, Viet Nam, Yemen, Yugoslavia, Zaire, Zambia, Zimbabwe.

Against: New Zealand, United Kingdom, United States.

Abstaining: Belgium, Canada, France, Germany, Federal Republic of, Japan, Luxembourg, Malawi, Portugal.

Sanctions against South Africa

The year 1982 was observed as the International Year of Mobilization for Sanctions against South Africa, proclaimed by the General Assembly to promote government actions to end all forms of collaboration with the *apartheid* régime and to encourage public action against *apartheid*.

The Assembly and its Special Committee against *Apartheid* reiterated calls for comprehensive and mandatory sanctions against South Africa, and the Assembly requested the Security Council to consider specific sanctions under Chapter VII of the Charter of the United Nations (on action with respect to threats to the peace, breaches of the peace and acts of aggression). In particular, the Assembly requested that the Council consider strengthening the arms embargo against South Africa (p. 274) and called for study of national and international arrangements for implementing oil embargoes (p. 276). In addition, it requested States to cease all collaboration with South Africa. Regarding the arms embargo, the Security Council considered the report of its Committee on ways of making the embargo more effective, but it took no action on that report in 1982.

Activities of the Committee against *Apartheid*. In its report to the Assembly adopted on 17 September,[3] the Committee against *Apartheid* stated that international commitment and action to eliminate *apartheid* had registered great advances. Many Governments—especially the African, non-aligned and socialist States—had imposed comprehensive sanctions against South Africa, at great sacrifice to some of them, especially developing countries.

Meanwhile, the report said, the principle of sanctions against South Africa had come to be supported by a majority, even among the Western States which had initially opposed sanctions when the Assembly recommended them in 1962.[24] The Western permanent members of the Security Council, however, had frustrated repeated appeals by the Assembly and other organs that the Council take mandatory measures against the racist régime under Chapter VII of the Charter. Reiterating that comprehensive and mandatory sanctions by the Council were the most effective and peaceful measures the international community could take to eliminate *apartheid*, the Committee added that the oppressed people of South Africa had declared they were prepared for the necessary sacrifices to achieve that goal. The report described the Committee's efforts in connection with the observance of 1982 as the International Year of Mobilization for Sanctions against South Africa (p. 273).

Urging action to stop continued acts of aggression and terrorism by the South African régime in order to restore peace in southern Africa and the Indian Ocean islands, the Committee recommended that the Assembly and the Council warn South Africa against any such acts, demand that it pay damages for them, especially to Angola (p. 312) and Seychelles (p. 321), and call on all States to assist States in that region in their defence and reconstruction.

The Committee, in a supplementary report issued in November on trade union action against *apartheid* in South Africa,[4] recommended that the Assembly authorize it to organize and make financial provision for an International Conference of Trade Unions on Sanctions and Other Actions against the *Apartheid* Régime in South Africa, to be held in 1983. The Committee also appealed to Governments and organizations to support the black trade union movement there.

The Chairman of the Committee, in a letter to the Secretary-General dated 1 December,[2] transmitted to the Assembly and the Security Council the text of the Declaration adopted by the Conference of West European Parliamentarians on Sanctions against South Africa, held at The Hague, Netherlands, on 26 and 27 November. Convened at the initiative of a group of Netherlands parliamentarians in co-operation with the Committee, the Conference declared that Western European Governments and peoples had a duty to co-operate with African States in order to secure peace and freedom in South Africa. The Conference recommended action to implement the mandatory arms embargo against South Africa, an oil embargo, an end to investments in and loans to South Africa, a halt to uranium and coal imports, and a boycott of *apartheid* sports. The Conference report was issued as a Committee document.[6]

An International Sanctions Workshop in observance of the International Year of Mobilization for Sanctions against South Africa was held by the Nigerian National Committee against *Apartheid* at Jos, Nigeria, on 10 and 11 December. The Workshop issued a declaration[1] which included a recommended programme of action for the Nigerian Government and organizations. Welcoming Nigeria's support of South African liberation, the Workshop recommended that the Government monitor collaboration with the *apartheid* régime by Governments and corporations, refuse facilities to collaborating corporations, deny visas to sportsmen, musicians and others who visited South Africa, and make strong representations to major Western Powers to secure the release of political prisoners. It considered informal and concerted action by all Africans a precondition for the success of sanctions against South Africa and therefore suggested that the Committee against *Apartheid*, in collaboration with the Liberation Committee of the Organization of African Unity (OAU), organize a similar workshop involving all African countries.

Action by the Commission on Human Rights.
In three resolutions adopted in February and
March, the Commission on Human Rights took
action regarding sanctions against South Africa
and foreign support of the régime (See ECONOMIC
AND SOCIAL QUESTIONS, Chapter XVIII).

On 25 February,[10] the Commission reiterated
its request that States end all forms of collaboration and assistance, including the provision of military and nuclear supplies and equipment, to the
racist régime which used such assistance to repress
the people and commit aggression against neighbouring States. In another resolution of 25 February,[11] the Commission strongly condemned and
called for the cessation of all collaboration with the
South African Government—particularly nuclear,
military and economic forms—and condemned
the actions of States, especially South Africa's
major trading partners, which had increased their
political, economic and military collaboration with
the régime. A third resolution, of 10 March,[12] included a provision by which the Commission endorsed the call for mandatory economic sanctions
against South Africa and appealed to Security
Council members to support such proposals.

Activities of the Council for Namibia. The
United Nations Council for Namibia, as the legal
Administering Authority for Namibia until independence, adopted the Arusha Declaration and
Programme of Action on Namibia[7] at the conclusion of its extraordinary meetings held at Arusha,
United Republic of Tanzania, from 10 to 14 May
(See TRUSTEESHIP AND DECOLONIZATION, Chapter III). In the Declaration, the Council said it considered that the situation in and around Namibia
constituted a breach of international peace and
security as defined in the United Nations Charter,
and reiterated its recommendation that the Security Council adopt comprehensive mandatory
sanctions in order to compel South Africa to comply with General Assembly and Security Council
resolutions. Pending the imposition of such sanctions by the Security Council, the Council for
Namibia called on all Governments to impose
voluntary comprehensive sanctions against South
Africa, including an arms embargo, an oil embargo and economic sanctions.

Reports of the Secretary-General. The
Secretary-General, in response to a December 1981
request by the General Assembly calling for action by Member States in support of Namibia,[28]
submitted to the Assembly in May 1982[8] a summary of information received from four States on
action taken or envisaged. The replies included information on economic and other action against
South Africa taken by the responding
Governments.

The Secretary-General reported to the Assembly in October[9] on an exchange of correspondence with the World Bank and the International
Monetary Fund (IMF) in regard to the Assembly's
request of December 1981[29] that he consult with
them to persuade them to respect United Nations
resolutions on collaboration with South Africa.

He stated that, in letters of 16 February to the
IMF Managing Director and the World Bank
President, he had requested their appointment of
representatives to start the consultations. The
World Bank, in a reply of 8 March, said its legal
position, made known in previous years, had not
changed, but it reiterated its desire to continue to
co-operate with the United Nations. Also looking
forward to further co-operation, IMF, in a letter
of 29 April, said that the status, rights and obligations of IMF members were governed by its Articles of Agreement, which required that members
be granted uniform treatment and excluded considerations that did not derive from the Articles.

General Assembly action. In several 1982 resolutions, the General Assembly reiterated its request that the Security Council impose comprehensive and mandatory sanctions against South
Africa under Chapter VII of the United Nations
Charter, and asked States that had been co-
operating with South Africa to cease doing so.

By the main resolution dealing with this subject, adopted on 9 December,[20] the Assembly
again requested the Council to consider action
towards comprehensive and mandatory sanctions
and, in particular, to reinforce the arms embargo,
impose an oil embargo, prohibit military and
nuclear co-operation and ban loans and new investments. The Assembly requested States, especially Western States concerned and Israel, to cease
all collaboration with the régime. It requested
States to act against corporations that violated the
arms embargo or were involved in the oil supply
to South Africa from States that had imposed an
oil embargo. The Assembly authorized the Committee against *Apartheid* to intensify activities for
the total isolation of the régime and for promoting sanctions. It urged members of the Universal
Postal Union (UPU) to resist the campaign to reinstate South Africa's membership in the Union, and
invited Governments, parliaments, non-
governmental organizations and other groups to
promote sanctions.

The resolution was adopted by a recorded vote
of 114 to 10, with 19 abstentions. A recorded vote
was taken on the seventh and ninth preambular
paragraphs together, and another on operative
paragraph 6. By the preambular paragraphs the
Assembly deplored the attitude of States, in particular the United States and Israel, that had continued political, economic and other collaboration
with South Africa, and expressed concern over increased investments and loans from the United
Kingdom, the United States, the Federal Repub-

lic of Germany and Switzerland. The vote on these paragraphs was 74 to 21, with 32 abstentions. The vote on operative paragraph 6, on South Africa and UPU, was 103 to 21, with 12 abstentions.

Sponsored by 41 nations, the draft resolution was introduced in the Assembly by the Libyan Arab Jamahiriya, which said that text and five others based on the recommendations of the Committee against *Apartheid* were designed to meet the grave situation in South Africa caused by the escalation of repression and aggression by the *apartheid* régime.

The Assembly, in its resolution on the South Africa situation adopted on 9 December,[18] reiterated that the régime had been encouraged to undertake criminal acts against African States by the protection afforded by major Western Powers against international sanctions. It condemned the policies of certain Western States, especially the United States, and of Israel, and of their transnational corporations (TNCs) and financial institutions that had increased collaboration with the régime. Reaffirming its conviction that Security Council sanctions were the most appropriate and effective means to assist the struggle of the South African people, the Assembly urged the Council to determine that the situation in southern Africa resulting from South African policies constituted a threat to international peace and security, and to impose comprehensive and mandatory sanctions. The Assembly urged States that had not done so to adopt separate and collective sanctions, pending Council action. It requested intergovernmental organizations to exclude South Africa and cease co-operating with it.

The twenty-first preambular paragraph, by which the Assembly expressed concern at United States pronouncements, policies and actions that had provided comfort and encouragement to South Africa, was adopted by a recorded vote, requested by the United States, of 73 to 26, with 31 abstentions. Operative paragraph 4, condemning the policies of certain Western States and Israel, and of their corporations that had increased collaboration with South Africa, was adopted by a recorded vote of 68 to 26, with 36 abstentions.

In its 9 December resolution on concerted international action to eliminate *apartheid*,[19] the Assembly appealed to the Western permanent members of the Security Council to co-operate in and facilitate effective Council action under Chapter VII.

In a resolution on the work programme of the Committee against *Apartheid*, also adopted on 9 December,[21] the Assembly commended the Committee for giving special attention to certain aspects of *apartheid*, including comprehensive and mandatory sanctions against South Africa. Another resolution of 9 December[22] contained a call for studies of the oil embargo against South Africa and steps to make it mandatory.

The Assembly, in a resolution of 23 November on foreign interests in colonial countries,[13] condemned Western and all other States, as well as TNCs, which continued to invest in South Africa and supply it with armaments, oil and nuclear technology. It called on all States, in particular certain Western States, to terminate political, diplomatic, economic, trade, military and nuclear collaboration, and to refrain from entering into other relations with the régime in violation of United Nations and OAU resolutions. It called on all States to terminate investments in Namibia or loans to South Africa and to refrain from measures promoting economic relations. The Assembly appealed to non-governmental organizations to continue to mobilize international public opinion for the enforcement of economic and other sanctions against the Pretoria régime.

The Assembly adopted these provisions in its 23 November resolution after the Special Committee on the Situation with regard to the Implementation of the Declaration on the Granting of Independence to Colonial Countries and Peoples[5] had taken similar action in a resolution of 20 August on foreign interests in colonial countries (See TRUSTEESHIP AND DECOLONIZATION, Chapter I).

The Assembly, in a resolution of 3 December on human rights consequences of foreign support for South Africa,[14] again condemned the collaboration of certain Western States, Israel and other States as well as TNCs and other organizations which maintained or increased collaboration with South Africa, especially in the political, economic, military and nuclear fields, thus encouraging that régime to persist in its inhuman and criminal policy of brutal oppression of the peoples of southern Africa and denial of their human rights. It requested the Security Council urgently to consider complete and mandatory sanctions, in particular the prohibition of collaboration in the manufacture of military supplies and in the nuclear field, an embargo on petroleum and other strategic goods, the cessation of trade, and the prohibition of loans and investments.

In a resolution on action against racial discrimination, also adopted on 3 December,[15] the Assembly again requested the Security Council urgently to consider the imposition of full mandatory sanctions and the strengthening of the arms embargo, with a view to ending all military and nuclear collaboration. It vigorously condemned the collaboration of certain Western States, Israel and other States and of TNCs and other organizations which maintained or increased collaboration with South Africa, particularly in the political, economic, military and nuclear fields, thereby encouraging it to persist in brutal oppression and denial of human rights.

In a third resolution of 3 December, on the self-determination of peoples,[16] the Assembly strongly condemned the policies of those Western and other countries whose political, economic, military, nuclear, strategic, cultural and sports relations with the South African régime encouraged it to persist in suppression of the aspirations of peoples to self-determination and independence. The Assembly took note with satisfaction of actions taken in May 1981 by the International Conference on Sanctions against South Africa.[30]

The Assembly, also on 3 December, in a resolution[17] on the International Convention on the Suppression and Punishment of the Crime of *Apartheid*,[25] included a request that the Commission on Human Rights take into account a 1978[26] and a 1980[27] Assembly resolution as well as documents of the Commission and its subsidiary organs reaffirming that States giving assistance to the South African régime became accomplices in the inhuman practices of racial discrimination and *apartheid*.

In a resolution of 20 December 1982 on the Namibia question,[23] the Assembly deplored increased assistance by certain Western States to South Africa and demanded its immediate termination. It requested States to take measures to isolate South Africa politically, economically, militarily and culturally, and asked the Council for Namibia to follow the implementation of such measures. It also requested the Council to continue to monitor the boycott of South Africa and to report in 1983 on all contacts between States and South Africa, with an analysis of the relations with South Africa of States and their economic and other interest groups and of measures by States to terminate dealings with the régime. The Assembly declared that South Africa's defiance of the United Nations, illegal occupation of Namibia, repression against the Namibian people, acts of aggression from Namibia against African States, *apartheid* policies and development of nuclear weapons constituted a serious threat to international peace and security. In the light of that threat, it urged the Security Council to impose comprehensive mandatory sanctions against South Africa.

Among those voting against the main resolution on sanctions, Canada said it found unacceptable the calls to terminate cultural and other relations with South Africa and the commendation of UPU for an unconstitutional decision to expel South Africa; Canada believed in the principle of universality in multilateral organizations. The latter point was also made by Denmark on behalf of the European Community (EC) members and by Sweden on behalf of the five Nordic States. Denmark added that the EC members—some of which

voted against the resolution while others abstained—did not support demands to cut off all relations with South Africa, believing that existing channels of communication should be used to permit free expression of views on all matters of concern to the South Africans. Explaining its negative vote, Japan said it did not believe sanctions would constitute an effective and expeditious means of achieving a peaceful solution; in addition, the resolution would pre-empt decisions of the Security Council, which alone had the authority to impose mandatory sanctions.

The Netherlands, explaining its negative vote, said the application of comprehensive sanctions was not the most effective way to assist the South African people but rather would exacerbate tensions; the Netherlands favoured selective sanctions, such as a strengthening of the arms embargo. Sweden, on behalf of the Nordic States, all of which abstained on the resolution, said that, because of their strict adherence to the Charter, they reserved their position on formulations which failed to take into account that only the Council could adopt decisions binding on Member States; however, they believed that increased pressure should be brought to bear on South Africa through peaceful means in order to end *apartheid*. Portugal voted against the text because it believed that the total isolation of South Africa would only hamper the initiatives of those fighting inside the country for fundamental reforms. The United Kingdom raised the objection that there were misleading references to Western States. The United States said it was attacked for increasing economic collaboration with South Africa but no mention was made that over 40 African countries carried on active trade with South Africa, as did Eastern European countries and Sweden.

Explaining its abstention in the vote, Australia said it was disappointed, given the almost universal condemnation of *apartheid*, that the authors of the resolution had not endeavoured to attract the broadest possible support by avoiding extreme and divisive language. Greece said it abstained because, while supporting the general principles, it objected to the language of certain paragraphs. Ireland said it supported the application of selected sanctions by the Security Council and would have been able to support some of the specific measures listed in the text, but it believed the right policy was one of steady and graduated pressure for change through selected sanctions which would be properly implemented by all; in addition, Ireland opposed the call to deny South Africa membership in UPU, as did the United States.

Lesotho said it abstained because it was constrained by circumstances emanating from the practical realities of economic survival, compounded by its geopolitical position; it was particularly concerned about the call for comprehensive and mandatory sanctions. Maldives said it supported comprehensive and mandatory sanctions but, because of certain references in the resolution, it had to abstain. Pointing out that some of the proposed measures would impose severe economic difficulties on it, Swaziland expressed reservations about the paragraphs in this and other resolutions requesting the Council to consider sanctions and measures to monitor and reinforce the mandatory arms embargo.

Chile, which did not vote on the sanctions resolution, said it had reservations about the application of extreme measures which, rather than encourage a Government to co-operate, contributed to its isolation and a resultant intensification of its policies; moreover, only the Security Council could decide on such measures.

Bangladesh, Bhutan, Costa Rica, the Dominican Republic, Fiji, Guyana, Jamaica, Oman, Peru, Solomon Islands, Sri Lanka, Suriname, Thailand, Turkey and Uruguay, which voted in favour of the resolution, Australia, Lesotho and Swaziland, which abstained, and Canada, which voted against, opposed the singling out of specific countries for criticism with regard to their policies towards South Africa. Costa Rica expressed a preference for a search for other ways of achieving a practical, concrete solution, instead of repeating the same unilateral condemnations.

Some countries—including Austria, Canada, Denmark (on behalf of the EC members) and Uruguay—expressed reservations about the Assembly's competence to recommend action on sanctions which only the Security Council could impose. Austria remarked that it would not support any prejudging of the Council's prerogatives and decisions.

Among those voting in favour, Morocco agreed with the text in principle but not with the language of some paragraphs.

Explaining its vote against the 3 December resolution on the human rights consequences of foreign support for South Africa, Israel said it totally rejected *apartheid* and flatly denied the repeated fabricated accusations regarding its relations with South Africa. Sweden, speaking also for Denmark, Finland and Norway, said they had abstained on this resolution because they could not accept paragraphs containing unjust accusations or recommendations which did not respect the division of competences between different United Nations organs. Norway cited similar reasons in explaining why the Nordic States had voted against the resolution on racial discrimination.

Voting for the resolution on foreign support for South Africa, Chile, Costa Rica, Turkey and Uruguay expressed reservations on the paragraph condemning the collaboration of certain States; Chile

described it as excessive and Turkey as unnecessary, while Costa Rica said it deprived the resolution of balance, moral authority and seriousness. Uruguay also reserved its position on the sanctions provision. The Dominican Republic said it would vote for that resolution and the one of the same date on racial discrimination because it had always condemned *apartheid;* however, the paragraphs referring to specific States detracted from the resolutions' objectivity. Ireland, which abstained on the resolution, described these paragraphs as difficult to accept.

Chile and Uruguay also voted for the resolutions on racial discrimination and on self-determination with reservations on the paragraphs concerning mandatory sanctions and the policies of specific States; Uruguay remarked that sanctions were a matter for the Security Council. Turkey took the same stand with regard to the paragraphs mentioning specific States.

Denmark, explaining why the EC members could not support the resolution on self-determination, said they did not accept the idea that maintaining relations with a State was equivalent to approving or encouraging its Government's policies. Greece abstained on this resolution because of the wording of this provision. The Federal Republic of Germany and the Netherlands made a similar point in explaining their vote against the resolution on foreign support for South Africa; the Netherlands added that, although complete and mandatory sanctions might lead to the eradication of *apartheid*, it could not support some of the other sanctions listed in this resolution. Voting against the self-determination resolution, Australia objected that it condemned some countries without mentioning others which maintained ties with South Africa.

The United States, voting against the three human rights resolutions adopted on 3 December, said the decision to impose sanctions was within the exclusive competence of the Security Council; it added that, if some countries were to be mentioned for trading with South Africa, all those engaging in such trade should be mentioned. Abstaining on the three resolutions, Portugal also voiced objections to the provisions on sanctions and collaboration by specific countries, remarking that to break all links with South Africa would not solve that country's problems.

The USSR, which voted for all three resolutions, said it consistently upheld the strict observance by all States of United Nations decisions aimed at the complete international isolation and boycotting of the *apartheid* régime.

Explaining its opposition to the resolution on the South Africa situation, Japan said it could not support paragraphs 4, 9 and 11, by which the Assembly condemned the policies of certain States and their businesses for collaboration with South Africa, urged States to adopt comprehensive sanctions, and requested intergovernmental organizations to end co-operation with South Africa. Speaking of the preambular paragraph in this resolution expressing concern at United States policies and actions that had encouraged South Africa, Guyana said it had voted in favour of the paragraph because that provision did not denounce the United States for such action, as the United States had suggested, but merely expressed grave concern at its policies. Voting in favour of the resolution, Suriname said it did so with reservations on paragraph 4 (condemning the policies of certain States that had increased collaboration with South Africa).

Also voting in favour of the resolution, Botswana reserved its position in respect of the paragraphs favouring sanctions.

France, which abstained in the vote on the resolution on concerted international action to eliminate *apartheid*, said it did so because of unacceptable language in the paragraph by which the Assembly appealed to the Western permanent members of the Security Council to co-operate in and facilitate effective Council action under Chapter VII. Having voted in favour, Botswana reserved its position in respect of this paragraph. The Netherlands, although it also voted for this resolution, believed an appeal should have been made to the Council and not to selected members.

With regard to the resolution on the Namibia situation, Norway, explaining the abstentions of the Nordic States, deplored the inappropriate and arbitrary singling out of certain countries and reiterated their position about wording which failed to take into account that only the Security Council could adopt decisions binding on Member States. Similar reservations were voiced by Austria in regard to both points, and by Chile, Denmark (for the EC members), Japan, the Netherlands and Portugal with respect to the mention of certain States. Japan also doubted the effectiveness of comprehensive and mandatory sanctions for achieving the desired aims. Though voting in favour, Burma, Fiji, the Gambia, Greece, Ireland, Peru, Samoa, Sri Lanka, Thailand, Turkey and Uruguay also voiced reservations about the selective singling out of countries, and Botswana and Uruguay reserved their position on the sanctions provisions.

During the Assembly's debate on *apartheid*, many States expressed the view that collaboration between certain States and South Africa was instrumental in prolonging *apartheid*. Some added that without such support it would be impossible for the régime to maintain its *apartheid* policies. Despite the argument of South Africa's friends that States had to remain on friendly terms in order to influence it, Zambia remarked, decades of open economic relations with certain Western countries had seen the escalation, not the abatement, of South Africa's repressive policies.

Of the countries criticizing collaboration, some mentioned specific States which supported the régime in that way. Bulgaria, the Byelorussian SSR, Czechoslovakia, Hungary, the Lao People's Democratic Republic, the Libyan Arab Jamahiriya, Nicaragua, Poland, the Syrian Arab Republic, the Ukrainian SSR and the USSR said that collaboration was provided mainly by Western countries, and especially by the United States. Iraq, Kenya, Kuwait, Uganda and Zambia mentioned Western countries, and Afghanistan, Djibouti, Guyana, Kuwait, the Lao People's Democratic Republic and Mongolia added Israel to that group. Mongolia supported the proposal to condemn those Western Powers which refused to implement United Nations decisions to end political, economic, military and nuclear co-operation with South Africa. India, Nepal, Somalia, the Sudan and Togo criticized collaboration and assistance in general.

Several speakers pointed to economic and strategic advantages which they said were sought by the countries maintaining relations with South Africa.

Afghanistan said that the United States, in the guise of "constructive engagement", had increased its co-operation with South Africa to an extent that left no doubt about its criminal partnership in the suppression of South Africans and in the acts of aggression against neighbouring countries. According to Albania, the super-Powers and other imperialist States, especially the United States, gave economic, political and military assistance to South Africa. The Byelorussian SSR said that support by the United States, including recently reduced trade restrictions and a flexible policy on the sale of nuclear equipment, was a result of its new regional strategy in southern Africa, based on the doctrine of recolonization. Cuba expressed the view that the United States, Israel and other Western Powers, which shared responsibility for the continuation of the *apartheid* régime, continued to provide South Africa with political, economic, military and nuclear support. In the German Democratic Republic's view, direct assistance from imperialist forces permitted the régime to pursue external and internal terrorism. Guyana said economic considerations frequently prevailed with the States having the greatest leverage on South Africa, and those considerations were allowed to thwart global action designed to end *apartheid;* condemnation of the system by those States rang hollow because their investment and trading links and TNCs buttressed the *apartheid* economy.

China said that, by their support for South Africa, certain Western forces not only had placed themselves in opposition to African countries but had provided an opportunity for outside forces to meddle in the region's affairs. Iraq believed that political, economic, military and commercial interests, the influence of TNCs and sympathy with the racist minority led a number of Western countries to enunciate contradictory positions with regard to *apartheid*. According to Kenya, any Government that continued to do business with South Africa should realize not only that it was committing a crime against Africa as a whole but that it stood condemned by the entire human race. Madagascar said the thesis of those supporting co-operation with the régime was based on the unacceptable premise that some, if not all, manifestations of *apartheid* should be tolerated for a while until the racists were willing to put an end to it; those who prevented the United Nations from adopting measures to break down South African resistance bore responsibility for the persistence of the system.

According to Nepal, the *apartheid* system had persisted largely because of external support extended to it overtly or covertly, a situation which undermined United Nations authority. Qatar said *apartheid* should be condemned, but many countries refused to do anything but make verbal statements, with the result that many United Nations resolutions were without force, thus affecting the Organization's credibility. The Ukrainian SSR said all-round collaboration by the Western imperialist States, primarily the United States, with South Africa had entered into a qualitatively new stage and was the main obstacle to the elimination of *apartheid*. South Africa, said the USSR, could not have ignored the United Nations without the support of Western States, above all the United States, which acted at complete variance with United Nations resolutions and were attempting to maintain South Africa as an outpost for their fight against the national liberation movements in Africa. Viet Nam denounced collaboration by the United States and other reactionary forces, saying that this helped to bolster South Africa's military, economic and nuclear potential.

Support for the imposition by the Security Council of sanctions against South Africa under Chapter VII of the Charter was expressed by many countries, including Algeria, Barbados, Bulgaria, the Byelorussian SSR, China, Czechoslovakia, Djibouti, Egypt, Gabon, the German Democratic Republic, Indonesia, Kenya, Kuwait, the Libyan Arab Jamahiriya, Madagascar, Mongolia, Nepal, New Zealand, Norway, Poland, Qatar, Romania, the Syrian Arab Republic, Togo, Trinidad and Tobago, Turkey, Uganda, the Ukrainian SSR, the USSR, Venezuela and Yugoslavia. Mauritania and others advocated the breaking of all forms of relations with South Africa. Indonesia mentioned

that the Asian Regional Conference on Action against *Apartheid* (Manila, Philippines, 24-26 May) had adopted a declaration calling for full implementation of existing embargoes against South Africa, cessation of loans to and investments in that country, and the implementation of sports, cultural and other boycotts. Yugoslavia said that the non-aligned countries, as part of their effort to end *apartheid*, were ready to initiate and support action for the implementation of sanctions.

Some countries mentioned steps they had taken to curtail economic and other ties with South Africa. Japan said it maintained no diplomatic relations with that country, it refused to recognize the independence of bantustans, it issued no visas to South Africans for cultural, educational or sports exchanges, it did not permit direct investment by Japanese in South Africa, and it had called on its banks to refrain from extending loans. Malaysia said it would continue its policy of complete boycott and sanctions against South Africa until the voice of the international community was heeded.

Bulgaria, Cuba and Kuwait were among those which noted that sanctions had been blocked by the Western permanent members of the Security Council. Kuwait added that, despite their argument that political dialogue was the best solution to the problem, Western countries made use of economic sanctions in other circumstances when their own interests were not jeopardized. According to Suriname, the Council had failed to discharge its responsibilities properly because some members with the veto power had prevented it from imposing comprehensive and mandatory sanctions. The Lao People's Democratic Republic said that the vetoes by the Western permanent members of the Council of proposals on sanctions had only served to encourage the régime to harden its *apartheid* policies. Pakistan agreed that the attitude of some Western nations in opposing sanctions and their restrictive interpretation of the arms embargo had encouraged South Africa to persist in its defiance of the international community.

Egypt and Indonesia appealed to the Western permanent members to respond to the wishes of the international community and not impede sanctions. Calling for further measures against South Africa, Bhutan and Malaysia urged the co-operation of Member States that had ties with South Africa.

Ireland and the Netherlands expressed support for graduated or selective sanctions. The Netherlands said it would view favourably the adoption by the Council of selective economic measures under Chapter VII of the Charter or a voluntary embargo by enough countries capable of using their economic influence in a significant way. New Zealand reiterated its willingness to carry out any economic sanctions imposed on South Africa by the Council.

Egypt suggested that, pending the imposition by the Council of mandatory sanctions, certain action should be taken: the countries that cooperated with South Africa should sever all political, economic, cultural, trade and sports relations with it; they should adopt measures in respect of their nationals and the corporations subject to their authority that owned or managed companies in South Africa; all States should strive to keep Africa a nuclear-weapon-free zone by denying material and technological assistance to South Africa in the nuclear sphere; and all possible material aid should be extended to the front-line States in their defence against South Africa's aggressive acts.

Argentina said South Africa's intransigence and the danger to peace and security demanded increased international pressure on Pretoria as a matter of urgency and in concrete form, through the effective measures repeatedly reaffirmed by the Assembly. Austria said there was no doubt that the consideration of further measures in accordance with the Charter would be pursued by the international community with a view to bringing about the long overdue change in South African policy. Cyprus said the failure of the Council to impose comprehensive sanctions had allowed the South African régime to continue its brutal repression internally and destabilization externally; the régime should be isolated politically and economically so that it was forced to heed the will of the international community.

Djibouti believed that if all Governments applied sanctions a new era of reassessment of the rights and privileges of man would dawn in that part of Africa. Gabon believed that only when the vital interests of South Africa were affected and the exploiting minority began to pay the price of its iniquity would the international community be able to compel the racist leaders to consider abandoning *apartheid*.

In Norway's opinion, the absence of a Security Council decision on sanctions could not serve as a pretext for countries not to act; for its part, Norway had taken steps to halt collaboration and exchanges with South Africa. Sweden said that only the introduction of different kinds of international sanctions could contribute to urgently needed change in South Africa's policies; but, in order to. be effective, sanctions had to be decided upon by the Security Council. The most peaceful political choice for a solution, Togo said, would be to apply sanctions—a form of specific and realistic assistance which the United Nations could provide to the struggle of the black majority. Turkey believed that the alternative to the application of such measures was the escalation of violence and conflict in southern Africa.

Declaration. [1]International Sanctions Workshop, A/AC.115/L.588.

Letter. [2]Committee against *Apartheid* Chairman, 1 Dec., A/37/691-S/15508.
Reports. Committee against *Apartheid*, [3]A/37/22, [4]A/37/22/Add.2-S/15383/Add.2; [5]Committee on colonial countries, A/37/23/Rev.1; [6]Conference of West European Parliamentarians on Sanctions against South Africa, A/AC.115/L.587; [7]Council for Namibia, A/37/24; S-G, [8]A/37/203/Rev.1, [9]A/37/474 & Corr.1.
Resolutions (1982). Commission on Human Rights (report, E/1982/12): [10]1982/12, para. 4, 25 Feb.; [11]1982/16, paras. 6 & 10, 25 Feb.; [12]1982/20, para. 5, 10 Mar. GA: [13]37/31, 23 Nov.; [14]37/39, paras. 3 & 5, 3 Dec.; [15]37/40, paras. 8 & 10, 3 Dec.; [16]37/43, paras. 13 & 15, 3 Dec.; [17]37/47, para. 9, 3 Dec.; [18]37/69 A, 9 Dec.; [19]37/69 B, para. 3, 9 Dec.; [20]37/69 C, 9 Dec., text following; [21]37/69 E, para. 4 *(a)*, 9 Dec.; [22]37/69 J, 9 Dec.; [23]37/233 A, 20 Dec.
Resolutions (prior). GA: [24]1761(XVII), 6 Nov. 1962 (YUN 1962, p. 99); [25]3068(XXVIII), annex, 30 Nov. 1973 (YUN 1973, p. 103); [26]33/23, 29 Nov. 1978 (YUN 1978, p. 683); [27]35/32, 14 Nov. 1980 (YUN 1980, p. 812); [28]36/121 B, 10 Dec. 1981 (YUN 1981, p. 1157); [29]36/172 D, 17 Dec. 1981 (*ibid.*, p. 171).
Yearbook reference. [30]1981, p. 165.
Financial implications. 5th Committee report, A/37/713; S-G statement, A/C.5/37/70.
Meeting records. GA: plenary, A/37/PV.*56*, 59-62, 65-68, *97*, *98* (5 Nov.–9 Dec.); 5th Committee, A/C.5/37/SR.59 (8 Dec.).

General Assembly resolution 37/69 C

9 December 1982   Meeting 97   114-10-19 (recorded vote)

41-nation draft (A/37/L.19 and Add.1); agenda item 33.

Sponsors: Afghanistan, Algeria, Angola, Benin, Bulgaria, Byelorussian SSR, Chad, Congo, Cuba, Czechoslovakia, Democratic Yemen, Ethiopia, Gabon, German Democratic Republic, Ghana, Grenada, Guinea, Guinea-Bissau, Guyana, Hungary, Iraq, Kenya, Lao People's Democratic Republic, Liberia, Libyan Arab Jamahiriya, Madagascar, Malaysia, Mauritania, Mozambique, Nigeria, Rwanda, Sao Tome and Principe, Somalia, Syrian Arab Republic, Togo, Uganda, Ukrainian SSR, United Republic of Tanzania, Viet Nam, Yugoslavia, Zimbabwe.

Comprehensive and mandatory sanctions against South Africa

The General Assembly,

Recalling its resolution 36/172 B of 17 December 1981, the Paris Declaration on Sanctions against South Africa and the programme for the International Year of Mobilization for Sanctions against South Africa,

Having considered the report of the Special Committee against *Apartheid,*

Considering that the policies and actions of the racist régime of South Africa, its military build-up and its nuclear plans constitute a grave threat to international peace and security,

Reaffirming its conviction that comprehensive and mandatory sanctions imposed by the Security Council under Chapter VII of the Charter of the United Nations, universally applied, are the most appropriate and effective means by which the international community can assist the legitimate struggle of the oppressed people of South Africa and discharge its responsibilities for the maintenance of international peace and security,

Recognizing the urgent need for the termination of military, nuclear, economic and technological collaboration with the racist régime of South Africa, as well as the cessation of sports, cultural and other relations with South Africa,

Deploring the attitude of those Western permanent members of the Security Council that have so far prevented the Council from adopting comprehensive sanctions against South Africa under Chapter VII of the Charter,

Deploring also the attitude of those States, in particular the United States of America and Israel, which have continued and increased their political, economic and other collaboration with South Africa,

Gravely concerned over the activities of those transnational corporations that continue to collaborate with the *apartheid* régime, especially in the petroleum and other fields, and of those financial institutions that have continued to provide loans and credits to South Africa, and over the failure of the States concerned to take effective action to prevent such collaboration,

Expressing serious concern over the greatly increased investments in and loans to South Africa from the United Kingdom of Great Britain and Northern Ireland, the United States of America, the Federal Republic of Germany and Switzerland,

Commending all States that have taken effective measures, in accordance with relevant resolutions, for the elimination of *apartheid* in South Africa,

Expressing great appreciation to intergovernmental and non-governmental organizations, in particular anti-*apartheid* and solidarity movements, trade unions and religious bodies, as well as city and other local authorities, that have taken action to isolate the racist régime of South Africa and to promote support for comprehensive sanctions against that régime,

Commending the decision taken by the Universal Postal Union at its eighteenth Congress, held at Rio de Janeiro from 12 September to 26 October 1979, to expel South Africa from the Union,

Having learned of the current moves to reverse the foregoing decision taken at the eighteenth Congress of the Universal Postal Union,

Recognizing the important role of the mass media in promoting isolation of the racist régime of South Africa and comprehensive sanctions against South Africa,

Commending the Special Committee against *Apartheid* for its activities, with the assistance of the Centre against *Apartheid* of the Secretariat and the co-operation of Governments and organizations, in promoting the widest possible support for sanctions against South Africa,

1. *Requests* all Governments and organizations to continue activities in implementation of the programme for the International Year of Mobilization for Sanctions against South Africa beyond 1982;

2. *Requests* all States, especially Western States concerned and Israel, to cease all collaboration with the racist régime of South Africa and to implement the relevant resolutions of the United Nations;

3. *Requests* all States concerned to take action against corporations and other interests that violate the mandatory arms embargo against South Africa or that are involved in the illicit supply to South Africa of oil from States that have imposed an embargo against South Africa;

4. *Again requests* the Security Council to consider action under Chapter VII of the Charter of the United Nations towards comprehensive and mandatory sanctions against South Africa and, in particular, to take measures:

   (a) To monitor effectively and to reinforce the mandatory arms embargo against South Africa;

   (b) To prohibit all co-operation with South Africa in the military and nuclear fields;

   (c) To prohibit imports of any military equipment or components from South Africa;

   (d) To prevent any co-operation or association with South Africa by any military alliances;

   (e) To impose an effective embargo on the supply of oil and oil products to South Africa;

   (f) To prohibit financial loans to and new investments in South Africa, as well as all promotion of trade with South Africa;

5. *Requests and authorizes* the Special Committee against *Apartheid* to intensify its activities for the total isolation of the racist régime of South Africa and for promoting comprehensive and mandatory sanctions against South Africa;

6. *Urges* all States members of the Universal Postal Union to resist the strong campaign being launched for the purpose of reinstating South Africa's membership in the Union;

7. *Invites* all Governments, parliaments, non-governmental organizations, anti-*apartheid* and solidarity movements, trade unions, religious bodies and other groups to intensify and concert efforts to promote comprehensive sanctions against South Africa in co-operation with the Special Committee against *Apartheid*.

Recorded vote in Assembly as follows:

In favour: Afghanistan, Albania, Algeria, Angola, Antigua and Barbuda, Argentina, Bahamas, Bahrain, Bangladesh, Barbados, Benin, Bhutan, Bolivia, Brazil, Bulgaria, Burma, Burundi, Byelorussian SSR, Cape Verde, Central African Republic, Chad, China, Colombia, Comoros, Congo, Costa Rica, Cuba, Cyprus, Czecho-slovakia, Democratic Kampuchea, Democratic Yemen, Djibouti, Dominican Republic, Ecuador, Egypt, Equatorial Guinea, Ethiopia, Fiji, Gabon, Gambia, German Democratic Republic, Ghana, Grenada, Guinea, Guinea-Bissau, Guyana, Haiti, Hungary, India, Indonesia, Iran, Iraq, Jamaica, Jordan, Kenya, Kuwait, Lao People's Democratic Republic, Liberia, Libyan Arab Jamahiriya, Madagascar, Malaysia, Mali, Malta, Mauritania, Mauritius, Mexico, Mongolia, Morocco, Mozambique, Nepal, Nicaragua, Niger, Nigeria, Oman, Pakistan, Panama, Papua New Guinea, Peru, Philippines, Poland, Qatar, Romania, Rwanda, Sao Tome and Principe, Saudi Arabia, Senegal, Sierra Leone, Solomon Islands, Somalia, Sri Lanka, Sudan, Suriname, Syrian Arab Republic, Thailand, Togo, Trinidad and Tobago, Tunisia, Turkey, Uganda, Ukrainian SSR, USSR, United Arab Emirates, United Republic of Cameroon, United Republic of Tanzania, Upper Volta, Uruguay, Vanuatu, Venezuela, Viet Nam, Yemen, Yugoslavia, Zaire, Zambia, Zimbabwe.

Against: Belgium, Canada, France, Germany, Federal Republic of, Japan, Luxembourg, Netherlands, Portugal, United Kingdom, United States.

Abstaining: Australia, Austria, Botswana, Denmark, Finland, Greece, Iceland, Ireland, Italy, Ivory Coast, Lesotho, Malawi, Maldives, New Zealand, Norway, Singapore, Spain, Swaziland, Sweden.

International Year for sanctions against South Africa (1982)

Throughout 1982, the Special Committee against *Apartheid* planned and promoted the observance of the International Year of Mobilization for Sanctions against South Africa through various activities, missions and consultations. In 1981, the General Assembly had proclaimed 1982 as the International Year in order to promote concrete actions by Governments and organizations to end collaboration with the *apartheid* régime, and to encourage wider public action against *apartheid* through such activities as a consumer boycott, a sports boycott, cultural and academic boycotts, and divestment from TNCs and financial institutions operating in South Africa.[4] The Committee described its activities in its 1982 report to the Assembly.[1]

After a special meeting on 11 January to launch the Year, the Committee Chairman, on 17 February, addressed letters to all permanent representatives to the United Nations, drawing attention to the programme approved by the Committee in October 1981[6] and inviting them to participate in the observance. To the same end, he sent letters to United Nations specialized agencies and other intergovernmental organizations. In another letter of 17 February, he requested the Secretary-General to instruct Secretariat units and United Nations offices to give high priority to promoting the Year, to encourage the specialized agencies to observe the Year and to co-ordinate the plans of United Nations organizations.

On 5 November, the Assembly held a special meeting devoted to the International Year, 20 years after it had first called for economic and other measures against South Africa.[3]

The Chairman of the Committee against *Apartheid*, on the Committee's behalf, presented awards at the meeting to the following seven persons for their outstanding contribution to the international movement for sanctions in solidarity with the national liberation movement of South Africa: the late President Houari Boumediène of Algeria; Romesh Chandra, President of the World Peace Council and Chairman of the Non-Governmental

Organizations Sub-Committee on Racism, Racial Discrimination, Decolonization and *Apartheid;* Jeanne Martin-Cissé, President of the International Committee of Solidarity with the Struggle of the Women of South Africa and Namibia; Archbishop Trevor Huddleston, President of the British Anti-*Apartheid* Movement; the late Reverend Martin Luther King, Jr., leader of the civil rights movement in the United States; Chief Abraham Ordia, President of the Supreme Council for Sports in Africa; and Jan Nico Scholten, member of the Netherlands Parliament and an organizer of the January 1981 Conference of West European Parliamentarians on an Oil Embargo against South Africa.[5]

Addressing the special meeting, the Assembly President said that, despite the lack of success of United Nations resolutions, the Assembly continued to call for sanctions because universally applied sanctions were the only peaceful means available to the world community to end *apartheid.* The Secretary-General said the United Nations must continue to impress upon the upholders of *apartheid* that it was they who were isolated and that their policies were inherently self-defeating. The Chairman of the Committee against *Apartheid* said sanctions were an expression of solidarity with the national liberation movement of South Africa and its leaders, who had struggled heroically for universal human principles.

In addition to the award recipients, the President of the African National Congress of South Africa, Oliver Tambo, and the President of the Pan Africanist Congress of Azania, Nyati John Pokela, spoke at the special meeting. Mr. Tambo said the central message of the International Year was that the allies of South Africa must not be allowed to go unchallenged by the international community. Mr. Pokela said the use of the sanctions weapon could be effective only if it was applied collectively and comprehensively, but the obstacles came mainly from the imperialist Western Powers.

As recommended by the Committee against *Apartheid,* the General Assembly, in its 9 December resolution on sanctions against South Africa, requested Governments and organizations to continue beyond 1982 their activities in implementation of the programme for the Year.[2]

Report. [1]Committee against *Apartheid,* A/37/22.
Resolution (1982). [2]GA: 37/69 C, para. 1, 9 Dec.
Resolutions (prior). GA: [3]1761(XVII), 6 Nov. 1962 (YUN 1962, p. 99); [4]36/172 B, 17 Dec. 1981 (YUN 1981, p. 178).
Yearbook references. 1981, [5]p. 175, [6]p. 177.

Arms embargo

The Special Committee against *Apartheid* reported in September 1982 that violations of the Security Council's arms embargo against South Africa continued to occur. The Security Council, also in September, considered the report of its Committee on ways of making the embargo more effective, but took no action on the document in 1982. The General Assembly, on the other hand, called in December for measures to reinforce the arms embargo, mandated by the Council in 1977.[11] It also called for Council action to halt all military and nuclear co-operation with South Africa.

Communications. By a letter to the Secretary-General dated 6 January 1982,[3] Jordan, denying a report in *The New York Times* of 14 December 1981 that South Africa had purchased 41 Centurion tanks and the Tiger Cat missile system from Jordan, stated that Jordan did not maintain any military or commercial relations with that régime. Denmark, in a note verbale of 5 May 1982 to the Secretary-General,[2] said that a Danish Royal Decree had been amended with effect from 20 April in order to widen the nation's compliance with the arms embargo.

Activities of the Committee against *Apartheid.* Following reports that the United States had relaxed its arms embargo against South Africa, the Chairman of the Special Committee against *Apartheid* issued a statement on 1 March in which he said this step, under the guise of allowing the sale of so-called non-military supplies to the South African military establishment, could only encourage the régime in its crimes. He expressed hope that the United States would be persuaded to reconsider its decision.

The Committee, in its annual report to the General Assembly submitted in September,[4] said that, since the Security Council had imposed the arms embargo, several anti-*apartheid* movements, trade unions, journalists and others had uncovered violations of its letter and spirit. Yet, although the Assembly had endorsed the Committee's recommendations by overwhelming majorities, the major Western Powers had resisted any strengthening or effective monitoring of the embargo.

Further, the Committee on the question of South Africa, requested by the Security Council to reinforce the arms embargo and make it more comprehensive, had made recommendations on which the Council had failed to act. That Committee had become paralysed, so that there was hardly any monitoring of the arms embargo by the Council. Meanwhile, South Africa had been able to expand its military apparatus and escalate aggression against neighbouring States. The Committee against *Apartheid* found it particularly alarming that the new United States Administration had deliberately relaxed its embargo.

Security Council consideration. On 20 and 23 September, the Security Council considered but did not act on the report of its Committee established by resolution 421(1977)[12] concerning the question of South Africa, on ways of making the mandatory arms embargo against South Africa more effective. At their request, Algeria, Cuba and Ghana were invited by the Council to participate without vote in the discussion. In addition, the Council extended invitations under rule 39 of its provisional rules of procedure[a] to Mexico, in its capacity as Chairman for 1981 of the Council Committee, and to the Chairman of the Committee against *Apartheid* (Nigeria).

Addressing the Council, the Chairman of its Committee recalled the conclusion of its most recent report to the Council, submitted in 1980,[13] that illicit transfers of arms and related *matériel* to South Africa continued to take place. Since then, he stated, the Committee had been brought to a standstill. Despite its efforts to compile information on embargo violations, the inadequacy of its investigatory resources and the lack of genuine co-operation on the part of some States had limited its possibilities for action. In the Chairman's view, the recommendations made in the 1980 report, intended to close loopholes in the embargo and prevent shipment of prohibited items through third countries, should serve as a basis for further Council action. He regretted that for various reasons the Committee's mandate had not been renewed.

The Chairman of the Committee against *Apartheid*, stressing that the international community must find ways to expose and stop all military and nuclear collaboration with South Africa, said that some States had made sanctions meaningless by allowing the supply of "dual-purpose" (civilian/military) equipment; some had refused to prohibit the supply of technology that could be used for military purposes or to ban the provision of capital and technical personnel for the arms industry, or to require TNCs to stop their South African subordinates or affiliates from supplying the South African military establishment; and some States had utilized weaknesses in the sanctions resolution to continue nuclear collaboration.

Most States addressing the Council on the report of its Committee supported the implementation of its recommendations to close loopholes in the arms embargo. Ghana, speaking as Chairman of the African Group at the United Nations, called for their adoption by the Council, as did Cuba and Jordan, while China said that the report contained a number of concrete recommendations which the Council should consider favourably. Algeria, Cuba, Jordan and Togo remarked in particular on the need to give the Committee the means to monitor the arms embargo with the aid of a permanent secretariat.

Two speakers believed the ineffectiveness of the arms embargo was the result of the policy of certain States. China said that, in order to protect their vested interests, certain Western countries, especially a super-Power, had supported South Africa and directly or indirectly provided it with military equipment, *matériel* and technology. Cuba stated that the Movement of Non-Aligned Countries, at the most recent Ministerial Meeting of its Co-ordinating Bureau (Havana, Cuba, 31 May–5 June),[1] had noted with regret that the Council had been unable to act in accordance with its basic responsibility for maintaining international peace and security, largely because of the policy of the United States, which had impeded implementation of sanctions against South Africa.

Ghana, for the African Group, urged several steps to strengthen the embargo, including the termination of all nuclear collaboration with South Africa, preparation of a list of prohibited items, a ban on the supply of dual purpose items that had both civilian and military applications, extension of the embargo to petroleum, establishment of a monitoring authority to bring violations to the attention of the Council for enforcement, and the imposition of severe penalties for violations. While agreeing with Ghana's proposal that petroleum should be included in the embargo, Jordan stressed that current oil sales to South Africa were made by multinational corporations and not by oil-producing countries.

General Assembly action. In five 1982 resolutions, the General Assembly called for measures regarding the arms embargo against South Africa. In other actions it called for a ban on military and nuclear relations with that Government.

The Assembly, in a resolution of 3 December on the human rights consequences of foreign support for South Africa,[5] included prohibition of technological assistance or collaboration in the manufacture of arms and military supplies in South Africa on a list of mandatory sanctions which it requested the Security Council to consider.

In another resolution of that date, concerned with racial discrimination,[6] the Assembly reaffirmed its 1981 decision[10] approving the April 1981 Declaration of the International Seminar on the Implementation and Reinforcement of the Arms Embargo against South Africa.[14]

In a third resolution of 3 December, on the self-determination of peoples,[7] the Assembly demanded the immediate application of the Security Council's arms embargo against South Africa

---

[a]Rule 39 of the Council's provisional rules of procedure states: "The Security Council may invite members of the Secretariat or other persons, whom it considers competent for the purpose, to supply it with information or to give other assistance in examining matters within its competence."

by all countries, particularly those that maintained military and nuclear co-operation with the racist régime and continued to supply it with related *matériel*.

The Assembly, in its 9 December resolution on sanctions against South Africa,[8] requested the Council to take measures to monitor effectively and to reinforce the mandatory arms embargo.

The Assembly also requested the Council to conclude expeditiously its consideration of the report of its Committee on the question of South Africa, with a view to blocking loopholes in the arms embargo, rendering it more effective and prohibiting in particular all forms of nuclear co-operation and collaboration with the South African régime. This request was made on 9 December in a resolution on the denuclearization of Africa.[9]

During the Assembly's debate on *apartheid*, Algeria, China, Ireland, the Netherlands, Sri Lanka and Yugoslavia were among those calling for the strict observance or strengthening of the existing arms embargo. Sri Lanka believed that, if the United Nations could not agree on new sanctions, it should at least ask for observance of obligations under the arms embargo resolutions. Barbados expressed support for any resolution calling for an absolute arms embargo against South Africa.

Algeria said the arms embargo had had little effect in preventing the supply of military equipment; Israel, for instance, had supplied large quantities of sophisticated equipment and major Western Powers had supplied so-called dual-purpose equipment, allowing South Africa to develop and manufacture new military equipment.

The mandatory arms embargo against South Africa was gradually losing its effectiveness, according to Suriname, owing to the restrictive interpretation by the major Western Powers of the 1977 Council resolution which had instituted the embargo. Uganda said the arms embargo had proven ineffective because of the military and economic co-operation between South Africa and its Western allies.

The United States reaffirmed its commitment to the effective implementation of the arms embargo and added that its restrictions on sales to the South African military and police went well beyond the requirements of the current embargo and were at least as rigorous as those of other nations.

Letters and note verbale (nv). [1]Cuba, 22 June, transmitting documents of Movement of Non-Aligned Countries, A/37/333-S/15278; [2]Denmark, 5 May, S/15062 (nv); [3]Jordan, 6 Jan., A/37/61-S/14830.
Report. [4]Committee against *Apartheid*, A/37/22.
Resolutions (1982). GA: [5]37/39, para. 5 (a), 3 Dec.; [6]37/40, para. 9, 3 Dec.; [7]37/43, para. 14, 3 Dec.; [8]37/69 C, para. 4 (a), 9 Dec.; [9]37/74 A, para. 5, 9 Dec.

Resolutions (prior). [10]GA: 36/8, 28 Oct. 1981 (YUN 1981, p. 867). SC: [11]418(1977), 4 Nov. 1977 (YUN 1977, p. 161); [12]421(1977), 9 Dec. 1977 (*ibid.*, p. 162).
Yearbook references. [13]1980, p. 200; [14]1981, p. 173.
Meeting records. SC: S/PV.2397, 2398 (20, 23 Sep.).

Oil embargo

Activities of the Committee against *Apartheid*. At the request of the General Assembly in December 1981,[8] the Special Committee against *Apartheid* devoted particular attention in 1982 to consultations on promoting an effective embargo against the supply of petroleum and petroleum products to South Africa. As the Committee noted in its 1982 report to the Assembly,[1] the Chairman consulted with many oil-exporting and oil-transporting countries during missions to the Middle East and Western Europe in April and at Headquarters. One subject of the consultations was the authorization given the Committee by the Assembly in 1981 to organize if necessary a conference of oil-exporting countries which had imposed an oil embargo against South Africa, to consider national and international arrangements for the effective implementation of their oil embargo.

The Committee emphasized that, while efforts for concerted action by oil-exporting and -transporting countries were pursued, individual States should take national measures to prevent their oil being supplied directly or indirectly to South Africa. They should enact legislation and regulations and punish corporations or others that violated the embargoes of oil-exporting States.

The Committee emphasized the need for the Security Council to impose a mandatory embargo on the supply of petroleum and petroleum products to South Africa, a measure it believed was an essential complement to the arms embargo and important for the maintenance of international peace and security in southern Africa. It recommended that the United Kingdom be called upon to stop the supply of oil from Brunei to South Africa. The Committee would continue, with the co-operation of all organizations concerned, to encourage support by parliaments, trade unions and other bodies for an oil embargo against South Africa. It also intended to publicize information on tankers and corporations involved in the oil supply to South Africa so that Governments and public opinion could take action.

General Assembly action. By a resolution of 9 December,[7] the General Assembly authorized the Committee against *Apartheid* to appoint a Group of Experts on the Supply of Oil and Oil Products to South Africa, nominated by Governments, to prepare a study on all aspects of the question as a basis for national and international measures to implement embargoes imposed or policies declared by oil-producing and oil-exporting countries with regard to the oil supply to South Africa. It requested the Secretary-General to organize meetings of such countries committed to an oil embargo: to consider the Group's report, to consult on arrangements for implementing embargoes, to decide on arrangements for an international conference and to consider the participation of other countries committed to the oil embargo. The Assembly also asked him, in consultation with the Committee, to organize the International Conference on an Oil Embargo against South Africa for the purpose of considering arrangements on implementing embargoes or policies declared by oil-producing and -exporting countries.

The Assembly adopted the resolution by a recorded vote of 125 to 6, with 13 abstentions. Introducing the text on behalf of the 35 sponsors, Algeria said that the measure would contribute to checking the war machine of the South African régime and to weakening its repressive arsenal.

In a resolution of 23 November on foreign interests in colonial countries,[3] the Assembly called on oil-producing and -exporting countries that had not done so to take effective measures against the oil companies concerned so as to terminate the supply of crude oil and petroleum products to the South African régime. This measure had also been included in a resolution on foreign interests in colonial countries (See TRUSTEESHIP AND DECOLONIZATION, Chapter I) adopted on 20 August by the Special Committee on the Situation with regard to the Implementation of the Declaration on the Granting of Independence to Colonial Countries and Peoples.[2]

An embargo on the supply of petroleum, petroleum products and other strategic goods to South Africa was among the items included in a list of mandatory sanctions which the Assembly requested the Security Council urgently to consider. This provision was included in a 3 December resolution on the human rights consequences of foreign support for South Africa.[4]

In its resolution of 9 December on the South Africa situation,[5] the Assembly called on the United Kingdom to take measures to stop the oil supply from Brunei to South Africa. The Assembly's resolution of the same date on sanctions against South Africa[6] included a request that the Security Council impose an effective embargo on oil and oil products.

In explanation of its negative vote on the oil embargo resolution, the United Kingdom said it considered the proposed embargo as ill-advised and thought it inappropriate for the Assembly to duplicate or circumvent the functions of the Council. Among those abstaining in the vote, Canada said it had not supported restrictions on trade in peaceful goods with South Africa and was concerned that the effect of the resolution might go beyond its stated intention by establishing a *de facto*

embargo, when the Council had not taken such a decision. Greece said it objected to the language of certain paragraphs although it supported the general principles expressed in the resolution. Lesotho said it supported the elimination of *apartheid* but it was constrained by the practical realities of economic survival and its geopolitical position in relation to South Africa. Swaziland indicated that oil sanctions against South Africa would impose economic difficulties on Swaziland.

Ireland, which voted for the resolution, said it continued to believe that the Council should consider imposing a mandatory oil embargo against South Africa, since a decision by that body would be the most effective means of imposing an embargo. The Netherlands, which believed that selective measures against South Africa were an effective means of achieving the elimination of *apartheid*, supported the resolution on an oil embargo and said it was considering participation in the existing voluntary oil embargo.

Speaking of the provision on the oil supply from Brunei contained in the 9 December resolution on the South Africa situation, the United Kingdom said the external trade of Brunei was a matter for its Government, not that of the United Kingdom. In explanation of their positive votes on that resolution, Botswana and Thailand expressed reservations about that provision. Botswana also reserved its position on the oil embargo provision in the resolution on the human rights consequences of foreign support for South Africa, though it voted for the resolution as a whole.

During the Assembly's debate on *apartheid*, Algeria, Ireland and Viet Nam were among those expressing support for a mandatory oil embargo to be imposed by the Security Council. Algeria remarked that, while embargoes by some oil-exporting States had forced South Africa to resort to the spot market and seek secret deals at a heavy price, it had been able to circumvent the embargoes to some extent because of the collaboration of a number of corporations and oil interests.

Indonesia welcomed the proposal to hold an international conference of States committed to the oil embargo against South Africa with a view to ensuring the most effective implementation of United Nations resolutions. Mexico, also welcoming this initiative, stated that it would not sell petroleum or its products to South Africa. Togo believed that an oil embargo should be implemented in order to increase economic pressure on South Africa by cutting off the lifeline of its factories. Venezuela, which said it did not sell petroleum to South Africa in accordance with a long-term practice, welcomed the preparation by the oil-producing and -exporting countries of a draft resolution aimed at the application of an oil embargo against South Africa.

Reports. [1]Committee against *Apartheid*, A/37/22;
[2]Committee on colonial countries, A/37/23/Rev.1.

Resolutions (1982). GA: [3]37/31, para. 14, 23 Nov.; [4]37/39,
para. 5 *(d)*, 3 Dec.; [5]37/69 A, para. 10, 9 Dec.;
[6]37/69 C, para. 4 *(e)*, 9 Dec.; [7]37/69 J, 9 Dec., text following.

Resolution (prior). [8]GA: 36/172 G, 17 Dec. 1981 (YUN 1981,
p. 177).

Financial implications. 5th Committee report, A/37/713; S-G
statement, A/C.5/37/70.

Meeting records. GA: plenary, A/37/PV.59-62, 65-68, *97, 98*
(9 Nov.–9 Dec.); 5th Committee, A/C.5/37/SR.59 (8 Dec.).

General Assembly resolution 37/69 J

9 December 1982   Meeting 97   125-6-13 (recorded vote)

35-nation draft (A/37/L.28 and Add.1); agenda item 33.

Sponsors: Afghanistan, Algeria, Angola, Bahrain, Congo, Ecuador, Egypt, Gabon, Haiti, India, Indonesia, Iran, Iraq, Kuwait, Liberia, Libyan Arab Jamahiriya, Madagascar, Mali, Mexico, Nicaragua, Nigeria, Norway, Oman, Qatar, Romania, Rwanda, Saudi Arabia, Syrian Arab Republic, Togo, Trinidad and Tobago, Tunisia, USSR, United Arab Emirates, Venezuela, Viet Nam.

Oil embargo against South Africa

The General Assembly,

Recalling its resolution 36/172 G of 17 December 1981,

Recalling further the Paris Declaration on Sanctions against South Africa,

Taking note of the report of the Special Committee against *Apartheid,*

Convinced of the need to ensure the effective implementation of embargoes imposed or policies declared by most oil-producing and oil-exporting countries with regard to the supply of oil and oil products to South Africa, and to promote a mandatory oil embargo against South Africa under Chapter VII of the Charter of the United Nations,

Reiterating its requests to the Security Council to consider a mandatory embargo on the supply of petroleum and petroleum products to South Africa under Chapter VII of the Charter,

1. *Authorizes* the Special Committee against *Apartheid* to appoint a Group of Experts on the Supply of Oil and Oil Products to South Africa, nominated by Governments, to prepare a thorough study and report as soon as possible on all aspects of the question as a basis for the consideration of national and international measures to ensure the effective implementation of the embargoes imposed or policies declared by oil-producing and oil-exporting countries with regard to the supply of oil and oil products to South Africa;

2. *Requests* the Secretary-General to organize, in consultation with the Special Committee, meetings of permanent representatives to the United Nations of the oil-producing and oil-exporting countries committed to the oil embargo against South Africa:

(a) To consider the report of the Group of Experts on the Supply of Oil and Oil Products to South Africa;

(b) To consult on national and international arrangements to ensure the effective implementation of the embargoes in the light of the report;

(c) To decide on all arrangements for an international conference;

(d) To consider, on the basis of the report of the Group of Experts, participation of countries concerned in addition to oil-producing and oil-exporting countries committed to the oil embargo against South Africa;

3. *Requests and authorizes* the Secretary-General, in consultation with the Special Committee and in the light of the recommendations made at the meetings of permanent representatives of the countries concerned, to organize the International Conference on an Oil Embargo against South Africa for the purpose of considering national and international arrangements to ensure the implementation of embargoes imposed or policies declared by oil-producing and oil-exporting countries with regard to the supply of oil and oil products to South Africa.

Recorded vote in Assembly as follows:

In favour: Afghanistan, Albania, Algeria, Angola, Antigua and Barbuda, Argentina, Bahamas, Bahrain, Bangladesh, Barbados, Benin, Bhutan, Bolivia, Brazil, Bulgaria, Burma, Burundi, Byelorussian SSR, Cape Verde, Central African Republic, Chad, China, Colombia, Comoros, Congo, Costa Rica, Cuba, Cyprus, Czechoslovakia, Democratic Kampuchea, Democratic Yemen, Denmark, Djibouti, Dominican Republic, Ecuador, Egypt, Equatorial Guinea, Ethiopia, Fiji, Finland, Gabon, Gambia, German Democratic Republic, Ghana, Grenada, Guatemala, Guinea, Guinea-Bissau, Guyana, Haiti, Hungary, Iceland, India, Indonesia, Iran,

Iraq, Ireland, Jamaica, Jordan, Kenya, Kuwait, Lao People's Democratic Republic, Liberia, Libyan Arab Jamahiriya, Madagascar, Malaysia, Maldives, Mali, Malta, Mauritania, Mauritius, Mexico, Mongolia, Morocco, Mozambique, Nepal, Netherlands, Nicaragua, Niger, Nigeria, Norway, Oman, Pakistan, Panama, Papua New Guinea, Peru, Philippines, Poland, Qatar, Romania, Rwanda, Sao Tome and Principe, Saudi Arabia, Senegal, Sierra Leone, Singapore, Solomon Islands, Somalia, Spain, Sri Lanka, Sudan, Suriname, Sweden, Syrian Arab Republic, Thailand, Togo, Trinidad and Tobago, Tunisia, Turkey, Uganda, Ukrainian SSR, USSR, United Arab Emirates, United Republic of Cameroon, United Republic of Tanzania, Upper Volta, Uruguay, Vanuatu, Venezuela, Viet Nam, Yemen, Yugoslavia, Zaire, Zambia, Zimbabwe.

Against: Belgium, France, Germany, Federal Republic of, Luxembourg, United Kingdom, United States.

Abstaining: Australia, Austria, Botswana, Canada, Greece, Italy, Ivory Coast, Japan, Lesotho, Malawi, New Zealand, Portugal, Swaziland.

Relations with South Africa

The General Assembly continued in 1982 to seek an end to virtually all relations between South Africa and the rest of the world as a means of isolating it and exerting pressure on the régime to abandon *apartheid*. Several United Nations bodies called for an end to relations in the military and nuclear fields, economic relations such as bank loans, foreign investments and collaboration of transnational corporations (TNCs), and relations between Israel and South Africa. In addition, the Assembly requested the International Monetary Fund to refrain from granting credit to South Africa.

Military and nuclear relations

In addition to their calls for a strengthening of the arms embargo against South Africa, the General Assembly and the Special Committee against *Apartheid* continued in 1982 to call for an end to foreign assistance and collaboration which enabled that régime to build up its military forces and nuclear capability.

Activities of the Committee against *Apartheid*. The Committee against *Apartheid* held a hearing on 14 June at which several individuals and experts discussed the topic "Threat to peace in southern Africa and the implementation of United Nations resolutions for an end to military, nuclear and other collaboration with South Africa". At the conclusion of the hearing, the Committee adopted a statement which was transmitted by a letter of 15 June from its Acting Chairman for the attention of the second special session of the General Assembly on disarmament (See POLITICAL AND SECURITY QUESTIONS, Chapter I) and the Security Council.[1]

Drawing attention to continuous acts of aggression by the South African régime against African States and brutal oppression of the South African people, the Committee, in its statement, said the recent expansion of the South African military and the régime's efforts to acquire nuclear capability threatened peace in Africa, the Indian Ocean, the South Atlantic and the entire world. The Committee noted with concern the military and nuclear collaboration by a number of Governments, corporations and institutions with South Africa in contravention of United Nations resolutions, and particularly relaxing the arms and nuclear embargo by the United States. It urged military, nuclear and other sanctions, and the mobilization of world public opinion towards that end.

In its 1982 report to the Assembly,[2] the Committee reiterated its view that any assistance to South Africa's military build-up was a hostile act against the oppressed people of that country and independent African States, and it expressed alarm at the continued military and nuclear collaboration with South Africa by certain States and TNCs. After the Committee received reports of a new United States policy allowing the export of dual-use (civilian/military) nuclear commodities to South Africa, the Acting Chairman issued a statement on 21 May expressing the Committee's indignation at United States attempts to strengthen its collaboration with the régime in those fields and calling on peace-loving forces to ensure that that régime was prevented from continuing its military adventures and nuclear build-up.

On 8 June, the Acting Chairman sent a message to the International Seminar on the Military Situation in and relating to Namibia (See TRUSTEESHIP AND DECOLONIZATION, Chapter III). He said South Africa had continued to obtain military equipment and technology to develop its armaments industry and to acquire nuclear weapons capability, particularly through the co-operation of Israel and Taiwan. He added that the Council must secure the immediate cessation of military and nuclear collaboration with South Africa.

The Committee reported that a number of countries continued to exchange military attachés with South Africa, despite appeals to end such relations, and the United States had increased the number of its military attachés there. Emphasizing that the resulting situation constituted an undermining of United Nations authority, the Committee recommended that the Assembly authorize it to monitor implementation of its recommendations on military and nuclear collaboration, to publicize relevant information and, in co-operation with interested groups, to mobilize public opinion against such collaboration.

Action by the Committee on colonial countries. The Special Committee on the Situation with regard to the Implementation of the Declaration on the Granting of Independence to Colonial Countries and Peoples,[3] in a decision of 20 August on military activities in colonial countries (See TRUSTEESHIP AND DECOLONIZATION, Chapter I), condemned continued military collaboration and support which certain Western countries and other States rendered to South Africa. The Committee called on all States to cease such collaboration, particularly the sale of weapons, which increased South Africa's capacity to wage wars against neighbouring States. In particular, the Committee called for compliance with Security Council sanctions. It also condemned continued nuclear co-operation by certain Western countries and others with South Africa, calling on the States concerned to end such co-operation and to halt the supply of equipment, technology, nuclear materials and training, which increased South Africa's nuclear capability.

General Assembly action. By a resolution of 9 December,[9] the General Assembly urged the Security Council to take mandatory decisions to ensure the cessation of all military and nuclear co-operation with the racist régime of South Africa by Governments, corporations, institutions and individuals. It deplored the actions of several Western States and Israel which had provided South Africa with military equipment and technology, as well as assistance in its nuclear plans, and which had allowed their corporations to invest in the armaments industry in South Africa. It condemned any manœuvres to create military pacts or arrangements with the participation of South Africa. The Assembly invited Governments and organizations, in consultation with the national liberation movements of South Africa and Namibia, to assist persons compelled to leave South Africa because of their objection, on the ground of conscience, to serving in the military or police force of the *apartheid* régime.

The resolution was adopted by a recorded vote of 120 to 8, with 16 abstentions. Sponsored by 47 nations, the text was introduced by the Libyan Arab Jamahiriya, which noted that the draft was one of six based on the recommendations of the Committee against *Apartheid*.

A recorded vote was first taken on the seventh preambular paragraph, expressing concern over South Africa's stepped-up arms build-up and war preparations, and condemning the growing violation of the arms embargo and the continued nuclear collaboration by the United States and some other Western States and Israel with the *apartheid* régime. The paragraph was adopted by 81 votes to 22, with 29 abstentions.

Several other 1982 Assembly resolutions contained provisions on military and nuclear relations with South Africa.

In a resolution of 23 November on foreign interests in colonial countries,[4] the Assembly strongly condemned the collusion of the Governments of certain Western and other States with South Africa in the nuclear field, and called on them and all other Governments to refrain from supplying that régime, directly or indirectly, with installations that might enable it to produce uranium, plutonium and other nuclear materials, reactors or military equipment.

The Assembly, in a resolution of 23 November on decolonization,[5] strongly condemned all collaboration with the South African Government, particularly in the nuclear and military fields, and called on the States concerned to cease forthwith.

In a resolution of 3 December on the human rights consequences of foreign support for South Africa,[6] the Assembly requested the Security Council urgently to consider complete and mandatory sanctions against the South African régime, including the prohibition of all technological assistance or collaboration in the manufacture of arms and military supplies in South Africa and the cessation of all nuclear collaboration.

The Assembly requested the International Atomic Energy Agency (IAEA) to refrain from extending to South Africa any facilities which might assist it in its nuclear plans and, in particular, to exclude South Africa from all its technical working groups. This request was made in the 9 December resolution on the situation in South Africa.[7]

In another resolution of that date, on sanctions against South Africa,[8] the Assembly requested the Council to prohibit all military and nuclear co-operation with South Africa, to prohibit imports of military equipment or components from South Africa and to prevent co-operation or association with South Africa by any military alliances.

Also on 9 December, the Assembly adopted a resolution on relations between Israel and South Africa[10] by which it condemned the increasing collaboration of the two countries, especially in the military and nuclear fields, and demanded its termination.

In its 9 December resolution on the denuclearization of Africa,[11] the Assembly called on States, corporations, institutions and individuals to terminate military and nuclear collaboration with South Africa, including the provision of such dual-purpose materials as computers, electronic equipment and related technology. It requested the Council, for the purposes of disarmament, to take enforcement measures, through adherence by all States to its decisions, to prevent any racist régimes from acquiring any arms or arms technology. Similar provisions were included in another resolution of the same date, on the nuclear capability of South Africa.[12]

In a resolution of 20 December on the Namibia question,[13] the Assembly strongly condemned the collusion by the Governments of certain Western and other States, particularly those of the United States and Israel, with the South African régime in the nuclear field, and called on France and all other States to refrain from supplying that régime, directly or indirectly, with installations that might enable it to produce uranium, plutonium or other nuclear materials, reactors or military equipment.

Among those which opposed the main resolution on military and nuclear collaboration, the United States, in explanation of its vote, denied that it was assisting South Africa in its nuclear plans and said it was committed to a nuclear policy intended to prevent the development or acquisition of nuclear explosive devices by any non-nuclear-weapon State. Portugal said it objected to verbal violence and certain discriminatory references in the resolution.

The Federal Republic of Germany said it had abstained in the vote because, although fully agreeing with the main thrust of the resolution, it believed the criticism of Western countries was unfounded. Greece explained that it had abstained because, while supporting the general principles and positions incorporated in the resolution, it objected to the language of certain paragraphs.

Ireland said it would have favoured a resolution calling for an end to military and nuclear collaboration with South Africa but it had to abstain because of certain formulations, including the unfair singling out of a number of States in a selective and arbitrary manner, which it felt was unlikely to lead to the total cessation of military and nuclear co-operation. Also abstaining, the Netherlands objected to the call for cessation of all nuclear co-operation with South Africa because it believed South Africa should accede to the Treaty on the Non-Proliferation of Nuclear Weapons[14] or accept full-scope safeguards on its nuclear activities; nor could it subscribe to a blanket condemnation of countries mentioned by name for their alleged military and nuclear co-operation with South Africa.

Among those voting for the resolution, Costa Rica said it none the less favoured a search for other ways of achieving a practical, concrete solution to the problem, instead of repeating the same unilateral condemnations. Morocco agreed in principle with the text but not with the language of some paragraphs. Speaking in explanation of its vote on several resolutions concerning *apartheid*, Oman said that, while it condemned South Africa's policies, its affirmative vote did not denote approval of paragraphs by which the Assembly condemned by name some States or groups of States with which Oman had friendly relations. Solomon Islands could not support the preambular paragraph singling out certain countries for criticism, which it believed to be divisive and inhibiting the effectiveness of the United Nations. Suriname also had reservations on that paragraph.

In explanation of their votes for the resolution on decolonization, the Netherlands and Portugal expressed reservations about the paragraph on collaboration with South Africa. Also in favour of the resolution, Iraq said the absence from that paragraph of a specific reference to Israel, which maintained nuclear and military links with South Africa, did not help to further the cause of the eradication of colonialism from Namibia and from all Arab territories.

Explaining its opposition to the resolution on the South Africa situation, Japan mentioned the paragraph on IAEA relations with South Africa among those provisions it could not support.

During the Assembly's debate on *apartheid* and South Africa, many States, including Bulgaria, Djibouti, the Lao People's Democratic Republic, the Libyan Arab Jamahiriya, Malaysia, Pakistan and Romania, said that South Africa was continuing to increase its military capability. Furthermore, Bulgaria, the Lao People's Democratic Republic, Malaysia, Mongolia and Pakistan regarded the military build-up as a threat to international peace and security.

Several countries—including Algeria, Bulgaria, Madagascar, Malaysia, the Netherlands, Pakistan, Romania, Turkey and the Ukrainian SSR—expressed concern over South Africa's plans for nuclear development or its nuclear potential that could lead to nuclear-weapon production. Algeria and Djibouti said the régime had acquired nuclear-weapon capability. Madagascar remarked that the South African authorities were scrambling to prepare for a final confrontation, as borne out by their efforts to acquire a military nuclear capability and the increases in the South African military budget. Expressing the hope that Africa would remain free of nuclear weapons, the Netherlands called on South Africa to undertake non-proliferation commitments and thereby dispel any doubts about its nuclear policy.

Uganda said that, by acquiring nuclear capability, the régime could blackmail anti-*apartheid* forces, perpetuate racism in South Africa and remain an aggressor in southern Africa. By circumventing the international system of safeguards, the USSR said, South Africa had created its own nuclear potential which placed it on the verge of manufacturing its own nuclear weapons.

Czechoslovakia, the Lao People's Democratic Republic, the Syrian Arab Republic and the USSR were among those stating that Western countries continued to provide arms to South Africa. Czechoslovakia and the Syrian Arab Republic added that Israel had also supplied arms. In addition, the Lao People's Democratic Republic said that imperialist circles were attempting to turn South Africa into a centre for a new military pact in the South Atlantic which would play the same role in that area as the North Atlantic Treaty Organization (NATO) in the north. Czechoslovakia said NATO members were relying in their strategic plans on a militarily strong South Africa. In Viet Nam's view, the strategic alliance between South Africa and the United States had manifested itself in the realm of nuclear arms and in the concept of a new South Atlantic alliance modelled on NATO.

Among other countries commenting on arms supplies to South Africa, Hungary noted press reports that said the United States had delivered arms to the South African police in violation of United Nations resolutions. The Libyan Arab Jamahiriya said that aid from Western countries and Israel, in the form of investment—directly and through TNCs—and technical assistance, had enabled the régime to have access to the technology needed for its military industries and to strengthen its military capability. Suriname said the sophisticated equipment and technology supplied to South Africa were employed for military use, thus enabling the régime to develop a sophisticated arms industry and a highly trained army. The Syrian Arab Republic said the countries providing the régime with a military and technological arsenal had helped it to draw up its nuclear programmes and allowed companies under their jurisdiction to invest in South Africa and to manufacture weapons there.

According to Togo, military co-operation with South Africa had enabled it to become a world military Power, a major producer of arms and military equipment and a nuclear Power. In the view of Trinidad and Tobago, the recently reported relaxation by the United States on exports to South African Government entities, including the military and police, might be interpreted by the régime as tacit support of South Africa's suppression of the black population.

Japan noted that it had prohibited the supply of arms and related equipment to South Africa by Japanese nationals or organizations and had not exported nuclear reactors or related materials to South Africa or given it technical assistance in that field. The United States said its restrictions on the sale of nuclear materials and any other items that could be used in developing South Africa's capacity to produce nuclear weapons were consistent with its policy of vigorously discouraging the proliferation of nuclear weapons anywhere in the world; the United States had not permitted and would not permit the sale of fuel or sensitive nuclear materials except to nations that signed the Treaty on the Non-Proliferation of Nuclear Weapons and accepted full-scope safeguards on all their nuclear facilities.

Concern was expressed by Hungary and others that Western countries and Israel had increased their assistance to South Africa in the nuclear field. The German Democratic Republic said military and nuclear collaboration had assumed dangerous dimensions, and it was alarming to see the leading imperialist State provide South Africa with the technologies and installations required to obtain nuclear weapons. In Qatar's view, countries which condemned racial discrimination had continued to provide South Africa with weapons, violating Security Council resolutions by giving technical assistance to South Africa and providing it with fissionable materials, which had enabled it to implement its nuclear programmes in collaboration with Israel.

Letter. (1)Committee against *Apartheid* Acting Chairman, 15 June, S/15247 (A/S-12/AC.1/21).
Reports. (2)Committee against *Apartheid*, A/37/22; (3)Committee on colonial countries, A/37/23/Rev.1.
Resolutions (1982). GA: (4)37/31, para. 6, 23 Nov.; (5)37/35, para. 8, 23 Nov.; (6)37/39, para. 5 *(a)* & *(b)*, 3 Dec.; (7)37/69 A, para. 13, 9 Dec.; (8)37/69 C, para. 4 *(b)-(d)*, 9 Dec.; (9)37/69 D, 9 Dec., text following; (10)37/69 F, paras. 1 & 2, 9 Dec.; (11)37/74 A, paras. 3 & 4, 9 Dec.; (12)37/74 B, paras. 4 & 5, 9 Dec.; (13)37/233 A, para. 26, 20 Dec.
Resolution (prior). (14)GA: 2373(XXII), annex, 12 June 1968 (YUN 1968, p. 17).
Meeting records. GA: A/37/PV.59-62, 65-68, *97, 98* (9 Nov.–9 Dec.).

General Assembly resolution 37/69 D

9 December 1982   Meeting 97   120-8-16 (recorded vote)

47-nation draft (A/37/L.20 and Add.1); agenda item 33.

Sponsors: Afghanistan, Algeria, Angola, Benin, Bulgaria, Burundi, Byelorussian SSR, Cape Verde, Chad, Congo, Cuba, Czechoslovakia, Democratic Yemen, Ethiopia, Gabon, Gambia, German Democratic Republic, Ghana, Grenada, Guinea, Guinea-Bissau, Guyana, Hungary, Iraq, Kenya, Lao People's Democratic Republic, Liberia, Libyan Arab Jamahiriya, Madagascar, Malaysia, Mauritania, Mozambique, Nigeria, Rwanda, Sao Tome and Principe, Senegal, Somalia, Sudan, Syrian Arab Republic, Togo, Uganda, Ukrainian SSR, United Republic of Tanzania, Viet Nam, Yugoslavia, Zambia, Zimbabwe.

Military and nuclear collaboration with South Africa

The General Assembly,

Reaffirming its resolutions on military and nuclear collaboration with South Africa, in particular its resolution 36/172 E of 17 December 1981,

Recalling its resolutions concerning the denuclearization of the continent of Africa,

Recalling also Security Council resolutions 418(1977) of 4 November 1977, 421(1977) of 9 December 1977 and 473(1980) of 13 June 1980,

Having considered the reports of the Special Committee against *Apartheid* and of the International Conference on Sanctions against South Africa, held in Paris from 20 to 27 May 1981,

Gravely concerned that the racist régime of South Africa has continued to obtain military equipment and ammunition, as well as technology and know-how, to develop its armaments industry and to acquire nuclear-weapon capability,

Recognizing that any nuclear-weapon capability of the racist régime of South Africa constitutes a threat to international peace and security,

Expressing deep concern over the stepped-up arms build-up and war preparations by the racist régime of South Africa and strongly condemning the growing violation of the arms embargo as well as the continued nuclear collaboration by the United States of America and some other Western States and Israel with the *apartheid* régime,

Condemning the actions of those transnational corporations that continue, through their collaboration with the racist régime of South Africa, to enhance its military and nuclear capabilities,

Recalling that the Security Council had determined in resolution 418(1977), under Chapter VII of the Charter of the United Nations, that the acquisition by South Africa of arms and related *matériel* constituted a threat to the maintenance of international peace and security,

Considering the urgent need for mandatory decisions by the Security Council, under Chapter VII of the Charter, to prohibit any military and nuclear collaboration with the racist régime of South Africa,

1. *Urges* the Security Council to take mandatory decisions, under Chapter VII of the Charter of the United Nations, to ensure the total cessation of all co-operation with the racist régime of South Africa in

military and nuclear fields by Governments, corporations, institutions and individuals;

2. *Deplores* the actions of several Western States and Israel which have provided the racist régime of South Africa with an enormous arsenal of military equipment and technology, as well as assistance in its nuclear plans, and which have allowed corporations under their jurisdiction to invest in the armaments industry in South Africa;

3. *Condemns* any manoeuvres to create military pacts or arrangements with the participation of the racist régime of South Africa;

4. *Invites* all Governments and organizations to assist, in consultation with the national liberation movements of South Africa and Namibia, persons compelled to leave South Africa because of their objection, on the ground of conscience, to serving in the military or police force of the *apartheid* régime.

Recorded vote in Assembly as follows:

In favour: Afghanistan, Albania, Algeria, Angola, Antigua and Barbuda, Argentina, Bahamas, Bahrain, Bangladesh, Barbados, Benin, Bhutan, Bolivia, Botswana, Brazil, Bulgaria, Burma, Burundi, Byelorussian SSR, Cape Verde, Central African Republic, Chad, Chile, China, Colombia, Comoros, Congo, Costa Rica, Cuba, Cyprus, Czechoslovakia, Democratic Kampuchea, Democratic Yemen, Djibouti, Dominican Republic, Ecuador, Egypt, Equatorial Guinea, Ethiopia, Fiji, Gabon, Gambia, German Democratic Republic, Ghana, Grenada, Guinea, Guinea-Bissau, Guyana, Haiti, Hungary, India, Indonesia, Iran, Iraq, Jamaica, Jordan, Kenya, Kuwait, Lao People's Democratic Republic, Lesotho, Liberia, Libyan Arab Jamahiriya, Madagascar, Malaysia, Maldives, Mali, Malta, Mauritania, Mauritius, Mexico, Mongolia, Morocco, Mozambique, Nepal, Nicaragua, Niger, Nigeria, Oman, Pakistan, Panama, Papua New Guinea, Peru, Philippines, Poland, Qatar, Romania, Rwanda, Sao Tome and Principe, Saudi Arabia, Senegal, Sierra Leone, Singapore, Solomon Islands, Somalia, Sri Lanka, Sudan, Suriname, Swaziland, Syrian Arab Republic, Thailand, Togo, Trinidad and Tobago, Tunisia, Turkey, Uganda, Ukrainian SSR, USSR, United Arab Emirates, United Republic of Cameroon, United Republic of Tanzania, Upper Volta, Uruguay, Vanuatu, Venezuela, Viet Nam, Yemen, Yugoslavia, Zaire, Zambia, Zimbabwe.

Against: Belgium, Canada, France, Luxembourg, New Zealand, Portugal, United Kingdom, United States.

Abstaining: Australia, Austria, Denmark, Finland, Germany, Federal Republic of, Greece, Iceland, Ireland, Italy, Ivory Coast, Japan, Malawi, Netherlands, Norway, Spain, Sweden.

Bank loans and foreign investments

The General Assembly, in December 1982, reiterated that ceasing new foreign investments in and loans to South Africa would be an important step towards the elimination of *apartheid*. A halt to foreign investments in Namibia was also called for by the Assembly and other bodies (See TRUSTEESHIP AND DECOLONIZATION, Chapter III).

Activities of the Committee against *Apartheid*. In its 1982 report, submitted to the General Assembly in September,[1] the Special Committee against *Apartheid*, recalling that the Assembly had repeatedly favoured a halt to new foreign investment in and loans to South Africa as an important step in international action for the elimination of *apartheid*, urged the Security Council urgently to consider taking steps to that end.

The Committee said South Africa had obtained large loans from foreign financial institutions and was reported to be seeking even larger ones. There had been a substantial increase in foreign investment in South Africa, especially by a number of large TNCs. Some countries had even invested in the bantustans, in flagrant defiance of unanimous Assembly resolutions. The Committee particularly emphasized the importance of withdrawing all foreign investment in South African undertakings supplying the Defence Force of South Africa, as well as investments in strategic industries.

General Assembly action. By a resolution of 9 December,[4] the General Assembly stated that a cessation of all new foreign investments in and loans to South Africa would constitute an important step in international action for the elimination of *apartheid*, as such activities abetted and encouraged *apartheid*. It again urged the Security Council to consider, at an early date, taking effective steps to achieve the cessation of further investments and loans.

The Assembly adopted the resolution by a recorded vote of 134 to 1, with 9 abstentions. Sweden introduced the draft in the Assembly on behalf of the 56 sponsors. It said that a diminishing flow of investment capital into South Africa would put pressure on that régime to change its racial and aggressive policies and make it more difficult for that country to continue the costly build-up of its military and nuclear capacity and energy reserves.

In a resolution of 3 December on the human rights consequences of foreign support for South Africa,[2] the Assembly requested the Council urgently to consider the prohibition of loans and investments as part of a package of complete and mandatory sanctions against South Africa. The Assembly also urgently requested all specialized agencies, particularly the International Monetary Fund and the World Bank, to refrain from granting loans of any type to the South African régime.

The Assembly, in its main resolution on sanctions against South Africa, adopted on 9 December, again included a prohibition of loans to and new investments in South Africa among a series of comprehensive and mandatory sanctions which it requested the Council to consider.[3]

In explanation of its vote on the resolution on loans and investments, Swaziland said it had abstained because sanctions against South Africa would impose severe economic difficulties on Swaziland.

Among those voting for the resolution, Greece said the text provided important practical means of pressure on the South African Government. The Netherlands said that selective measures against South Africa were an effective means of combating *apartheid;* furthermore, the Netherlands was considering its own measures restricting investments there.

The Federal Republic of Germany, which voted against the resolution on the human rights consequences of foreign support for South Africa, said the provision on specialized agencies seriously affected the integrity of the financial institutions mentioned, whose independence and effectiveness the Federal Republic had consistently defended as indispensable for the world economy. Botswana, Chile and Uruguay, though voting for the resolution, and Ireland and Portugal, which abstained,

also voiced reservations on this paragraph; Uruguay remarked that it was firmly opposed to politicizing economic agencies.

During the Assembly's debate on *apartheid* and South Africa, Finland, a sponsor of the resolution on investment in South Africa, said the measures it called for were particularly relevant in the context of the substantial increases in South Africa's military budget; the Security Council should, as a first step, take decisions aimed at preventing new foreign investments there. Ireland and Togo expressed support for a call by the Assembly to the Council for a ban on new investments and loans. Japan said it had called on its foreign exchange banks and their branches abroad to refrain from extending loans to South Africa, as a result of which no such loans had been made.

Certain States had encouraged their companies to invest in South Africa, the Libyan Arab Jamahiriya said, and the highest rate of increase in investments in South Africa was that of companies from the countries of the Western contact group on Namibia—the United States, the United Kingdom, the Federal Republic of Germany, France and Canada, in that order.

Report. [1]Committee against *Apartheid*, A/37/22.
Resolutions (1982). GA: [2]37/39, paras. 5 *(c)* & 12, 3 Dec.; [3]37/69 C, para. 4 *(f)*, 9 Dec.; [4]37/69 H, 9 Dec., text following.
Meeting records. GA: A/37/PV.59-62, 65-68, *97, 98* (9 Nov.–9 Dec.).

General Assembly resolution 37/69 H

| 9 December 1982 | Meeting 97 | 134-1-9 (recorded vote) |

56-nation draft (A/37/L.26 and Add.1); agenda item 33.

Sponsors: Afghanistan, Algeria, Angola, Bangladesh, Barbados, Bhutan, Burundi, Cape Verde, Congo, Cuba, Cyprus, Denmark, Egypt, Fiji, Finland, Guinea, Guinea-Bissau, Guyana, Haiti, Iceland, India, Indonesia, Iraq, Ireland, Kenya, Kuwait, Liberia, Libyan Arab Jamahiriya, Madagascar, Malaysia, Mali, Mozambique, Nepal, Netherlands, New Zealand, Nicaragua, Nigeria, Norway, Pakistan, Philippines, Qatar, Romania, Rwanda, Sao Tome and Principe, Sweden, Syrian Arab Republic, Togo, Trinidad and Tobago, Tunisia, Turkey, Uganda, United Republic of Tanzania, Viet Nam, Yugoslavia, Zambia, Zimbabwe.

Investments in South Africa

The General Assembly,

Recalling its resolution 36/172 O of 17 December 1981,

Taking note of the report of the Special Committee against *Apartheid,*

Convinced that a cessation of all new foreign investments in, and financial loans to, South Africa would constitute an important step in international action for the elimination of *apartheid*, as such investments and loans abet and encourage the *apartheid* policies of that country,

Welcoming the actions of those Governments that have taken legislative and other measures towards that end,

Noting with regret that the Security Council has not yet taken steps towards that end, as requested by the General Assembly in its resolutions 31/6 K of 9 November 1976, 32/105 O of 16 December 1977, 33/183 O of 24 January 1979, 34/93 Q of 12 December 1979, 35/206 Q of 16 December 1980 and 36/172 O of 17 December 1981,

Again urges the Security Council to consider the matter at an early date with a view to taking effective steps to achieve the cessation of further foreign investments in, and financial loans to, South Africa.

Recorded vote in Assembly as follows:

In favour: Afghanistan, Albania, Algeria, Angola, Antigua and Barbuda, Argentina, Australia, Austria, Bahamas, Bahrain, Bangladesh, Barbados, Belgium, Benin, Bhutan, Bolivia, Brazil, Bulgaria, Burma, Burundi, Byelorussian SSR, Cape Verde, Central African Republic, Chad, Chile, China, Colombia, Comoros, Congo,

Costa Rica, Cuba, Cyprus, Czechoslovakia, Democratic Kampuchea, Democratic Yemen, Denmark, Djibouti, Dominican Republic, Ecuador, Egypt, Equatorial Guinea, Ethiopia, Fiji, Finland, Gabon, Gambia, German Democratic Republic, Ghana, Greece, Grenada, Guinea, Guinea-Bissau, Guyana, Haiti, Hungary, Iceland, India, Indonesia, Iran, Iraq, Ireland, Jamaica, Japan, Jordan, Kenya, Kuwait, Lao People's Democratic Republic, Lesotho, Liberia, Libyan Arab Jamahiriya, Luxembourg, Madagascar, Malaysia, Maldives, Mali, Malta, Mauritania, Mauritius, Mexico, Mongolia, Morocco, Mozambique, Nepal, Netherlands, New Zealand, Nicaragua, Niger, Nigeria, Norway, Oman, Pakistan, Panama, Papua New Guinea, Peru, Philippines, Poland, Portugal, Qatar, Romania, Rwanda, Sao Tome and Principe, Saudi Arabia, Senegal, Sierra Leone, Singapore, Solomon Islands, Somalia, Spain, Sri Lanka, Sudan, Suriname, Sweden, Syrian Arab Republic, Thailand, Togo, Trinidad and Tobago, Tunisia, Turkey, Uganda, Ukrainian SSR, USSR, United Arab Emirates, United Republic of Cameroon, United Republic of Tanzania, Upper Volta, Uruguay, Vanuatu, Venezuela, Viet Nam, Yemen, Yugoslavia, Zaire, Zambia, Zimbabwe.

Against: United States.

Abstaining: Botswana, Canada, France, Germany, Federal Republic of, Italy, Ivory Coast, Malawi, Swaziland, United Kingdom.

TNC activities

The Economic and Social Council, in October 1982, recommended actions by Governments and organizations to have TNCs end their collaboration with South Africa. In addition, it established an *ad hoc* committee to prepare guidelines for public hearings in 1984 on TNC activities in South Africa and Namibia. The activities and effects of TNCs in southern Africa also engaged the attention of other United Nations bodies during the year.

The Commission on Human Rights, by a resolution of 25 February[5] on the human rights consequences of foreign support for South Africa (See ECONOMIC AND SOCIAL QUESTIONS, Chapter XVIII), requested an examination of whether TNC actions in South Africa came under the definition of the crime of *apartheid*, and whether legal action could be taken under the International Convention on the Suppression and Punishment of the Crime of *Apartheid*.[10]

A report listing several hundred banks, insurance companies and other firms, including TNCs, assisting the South African régime was issued in June as a document of the Sub-Commission on Prevention of Discrimination and Protection of Minorities.[3] Prepared by a Special Rapporteur of the Sub-Commission, Ahmed Mohamed Khalifa (Egypt), the list supplemented similar information in the Special Rapporteur's report of July 1981.[12]

In a resolution of 7 September on foreign support of South Africa,[8] the Sub-Commission called for continued annual updating of the list (see above). The General Assembly, in a resolution of 3 December on the same topic,[7] called on the countries where the banks, TNCs and other organizations listed in the revised report were based to stop their trading, manufacturing and investing activities in South Africa and Namibia.

The Federal Republic of Germany, voting against the Assembly resolution, expressed the view that compilation of a list of enterprises maintaining links with southern Africa was incompatible with basic legal principles. Also voting against, the United Kingdom said the Special Rapporteur's report had fundamental defects and should be eliminated, while the Netherlands stated that it could not support the assumption, on which it said the report was based, that the activities of Western enterprises in South Africa were detrimental to human rights there. Australia, which abstained, thought the report was incorrect and based on false premises. Brazil, though voting for this resolution, objected that the Special Rapporteur's report had wrongly identified as Brazilian two companies with investments in South Africa; the Central Bank of Brazil, which controlled all Brazilian investments abroad, had issued no certificates authorizing investment in that country.

As requested by the Economic and Social Council in November 1981,[9] the Secretariat submitted to the Commission on TNCs in June 1982 a report[2] which provided information on the Secretariat's work in collecting and disseminating information on TNC activities in Namibia and South Africa, described preparations for public hearings on the topic and reported on measures taken to disseminate the Council's 1981 resolution calling for measures to end TNC activities in southern Africa.

The Intergovernmental Working Group on a Code of Conduct, engaged in drafting a code to supplement and serve as a model for national legislation on the activities of TNCs and their relations with Governments (See ECONOMIC AND SOCIAL QUESTIONS, Chapter, VII), was unable to agree during 1982 on provisions relating to TNCs in southern Africa which had been provisionally included in the Group's draft in 1981.[11] Most delegations maintained that the code should explicitly require TNCs to reduce progressively their business activities in South Africa and to cease immediately all activities in Namibia. Others, however, considered eliminating *apartheid* to be a political question more appropriately treated by other United Nations bodies and believed that an evolutionary development would serve the aims of the international community better than ceasing economic activities.

The Sub-Committee on Implementation of United Nations Resolutions and Collaboration with South Africa, of the Special Committee against *Apartheid*, issued a report in September on TNCs with major investments in South Africa.[4] The report, prepared by a consultant as part of continuing research on TNC activities in South Africa, contained information on 47 corporations which were deemed strategic to the economic viability of that country.

Economic and Social Council action. By a resolution of 27 October,[6] the Economic and Social Council welcomed the policies of some Governments to end activities of their TNCs in southern Africa, and urged TNCs to discontinue collaboration with South Africa and terminate all further investments there and in Namibia. It called on home countries of TNCs to take measures to terminate such collaboration, to prevent new investments and to bring about an immediate withdrawal of all existing investments. The Council called on organizations that held shares in TNCs operating there to contribute to eradicating *apartheid* by withdrawing their shareholdings. It requested the Secretary-General: to intensify the Secretariat's work in collecting and disseminating information on TNC activities in southern Africa; to organize public hearings on TNC activities there, to be conducted by the Commission on TNCs; and to report on the policies and practices of TNCs regarding their activities in South Africa and Namibia, including a list of TNCs which operated in strategic sectors.

The Council adopted this resolution by 31 votes to 2, with 12 abstentions. The text had been recommended on 10 September by the Commission on TNCs.

The United States, which voted against the resolution, said it believed the proposed measures constituted sanctions, thus falling exclusively within the competence of the Security Council, and they would not be effective in altering *apartheid;* furthermore, it believed that TNCs could, through adherence to fair employment practices, contribute to a peaceful evolution away from the *apartheid* system.

Denmark, explaining the abstention of the members of the European Community which were members of the Economic and Social Council, said they had been unable to vote in favour of the resolution because it contained references they found unacceptable and beyond the Council's competence. Japan also said it had abstained because it considered that the Commission on TNCs was not competent to deal with the matter.

Among those voting for the resolution, Nigeria said the vote showed that the vast majority of the international community believed that TNC activities in southern Africa were a legitimate sphere of interest of the Commission. Expressing a similar view, Liberia added that TNCs contributed directly or indirectly to the maintenance of *apartheid*. Saint Lucia observed that TNC activities, while promoting South Africa's development, hindered its political evolution. The USSR voted for the resolution with reservations on its financial implications.

Communication. South Africa, in a letter of 1 December to the Secretary-General,[1] cited a newspaper report to the effect that Secretariat organizers of a seminar on the role of TNCs in southern Africa, planned for Geneva in June, had withdrawn background papers commissioned from two academics when the organizers found that the papers contradicted United Nations positions; the incident, South Africa said, damaged the integrity of the United Nations by showing that its officials paid scant attention to the need for impartiality. A note by the Secretariat, appended to the document containing this letter, stated that the studies in question, which South Africa asked to be circulated as a General Assembly document along with its letter, had been found by the Secretariat to be unsatisfactory and were not utilized as documents of the seminar.

Letter. [1]South Africa, 1 Dec., A/37/719.
Reports. [2]Secretariat, E/C.10/1982/11; [3]Special Rapporteur, E/CN.4/Sub.2/1982/10; [4]Sub-Committee on Implementation of UN Resolutions and Collaboration with South Africa, A/AC.115/L.574.
Resolutions (1982). [5]Commission on Human Rights (report, E/1982/12): 1982/12, para. 8, 25 Feb. [6]ESC: 1982/69, 27 Oct., text following. [7]GA: 37/39, para. 10, 3 Dec. [8]SCPDPM (report, E/CN.4/1983/4): 1982/16, 7 Sep.
Resolutions (prior). [9]ESC: 1981/86, 2 Nov. 1981 (YUN 1981, p. 190). [10]GA: 3068(XXVIII), annex, 30 Nov. 1973 (YUN 1973, p. 103).
Yearbook references. 1981, [11]p. 600, [12]p. 946.
Meeting records. ESC: E/1982/SR.52, 54 (25, 27 Oct.).
Publication. Transnational Corporations in Southern Africa. Update on Financial Activities and Employment Practices (E/C.10/83/Rev.1), Sales No. E.82.II.A.12.

Economic and Social Council resolution 1982/69

27 October 1982	Meeting 54	31-2-12

Draft by Commission on TNCs (E/1982/18); agenda item 25.

Activities of transnational corporations in southern Africa and their collaboration with the racist minority régime in that area

The Economic and Social Council,

Recalling General Assembly resolutions 3201(S-VI) and 3202(S-VI) of 1 May 1974, containing the Declaration and the Programme of Action on the Establishment of a New International Economic Order, 3281(XXIX) of 12 December 1974, containing the Charter of Economic Rights and Duties of States, and 3362(S-VII) of 16 September 1975 on development and international economic co-operation,

Recalling also General Assembly resolutions 35/206 F of 16 December 1980 on the role of transnational corporations in South Africa, 35/227 A of 6 March 1981 on the situation in Namibia resulting from the illegal occupation of the Territory by South Africa, 35/227 B of 6 March 1981 on the intensification and co-ordination of United Nations action in support of Namibia, 36/172 B of 17 December 1981, in which it proclaimed the year 1982 International Year of Mobilization for Sanctions against South Africa, and 36/172 O of 17 December 1981 on investments in South Africa,

Reaffirming previous Council resolutions on the activities of transnational corporations in southern Africa and their collaboration with the racist minority régime in that area,

Having considered the report of the Secretariat on the measures taken pursuant to Economic and Social Council resolution 1981/86 of 2 November 1981,

Considering that the persistent operation of transnational corporations in Namibia, in contravention of various United Nations resolutions, continues to reinforce the illegal occupation of Namibia by South Africa and to pose a serious threat to the future political and economic independence of Namibia,

Considering also that the role of transnational corporations and transnational banks in the industrial and technological development of South Africa contributes to sustaining the racist minority régime of South Africa and its illegal occupation of Namibia,

Affirming the need for action at the international level by intergovernmental as well as non-governmental organizations in order to complement national measures,

1. *Takes note with satisfaction* of the report of the Secretariat on the measures taken pursuant to Economic and Social Council resolution 1981/86;

2. *Expresses its appreciation* to the Secretariat for its efforts to publicize Council resolution 1981/86 and for its elaborate recommendations as to the modalities for organizing the hearings on the activities of transnational corporations in South Africa and Namibia;

3. *Commends* those non-governmental organizations that have made efforts to combat *apartheid* and, in particular, to terminate bank loans and capital transfers to South Africa, and calls upon such organizations to intensify their useful efforts in these areas;

4. *Welcomes* as a positive step the policies of some Governments to bring an end to the activities of their transnational corporations in southern Africa;

5. *Condemns* the racist minority régime of South Africa for its perpetuation of the inhuman system of *apartheid* and its illegal occupation of Namibia;

6. *Condemns* those transnational corporations that collaborate with the racist minority régime of South Africa, and calls upon all transnational corporations to respect the various resolutions of the United Nations concerning southern Africa;

7. *Calls upon* all home countries of transnational corporations to take effective measures to terminate the collaboration of the transnational corporations with the racist minority régime of South Africa, to prevent further new investments and reinvestments and to bring about an immediate withdrawal of all existing investments in South Africa and Namibia;

8. *Calls upon* all countries concerned to re-examine their relations with the transnational corporations operating in their territories which collaborate with the racist minority régime of South Africa;

9. *Calls upon* all anti-*apartheid* movements, religious institutions and bodies, trade unions, universities and other institutions that are shareholders of transnational corporations operating in South Africa and Namibia to contribute to the efforts of the international community to eradicate *apartheid* by withdrawing their shareholdings in such transnational corporations;

10. *Urges* all transnational corporations to comply fully with the relevant resolutions of the United Nations by terminating all further investments in South Africa and Namibia and by ending their collaboration with the racist minority régime;

11. *Further calls upon* all States Members of the United Nations and all transnational corporations operating in South Africa and Namibia to co-operate with the Secretary-General and the Commission on Transnational Corporations in organizing public hearings on the activities of transnational corporations in South Africa and Namibia;

12. *Reaffirms* Security Council resolution 301(1971) of 20 October 1971, in which that Council called upon States to abstain from entering into economic relations with South Africa in respect of Namibia and declared that rights, titles or contracts granted to individuals or corporations by South Africa after the termination of the mandate are not subject to protection or espousal by their home States against the claims of a future lawful government of Namibia;

13. *Reaffirms* that the code of conduct on transnational corporations should include effective measures against the collaboration of transnational corporations with the racist minority régime in southern Africa;

14. *Requests* the Secretary-General:

(a) To intensify the useful work of the Secretariat in the collection and dissemination of information on the activities of transnational corporations in southern Africa;

(b) To make arrangements for the organization of public hearings, to be conducted by the Commission on Transnational Corporations, with the assistance of the United Nations Centre on Transnational Corporations, on the activities of transnational corporations in South Africa and Namibia, in accordance with the modalities and procedures to be prescribed by the Commission at its ninth session;

(c) To report to the Commission on Transnational Corporations at its ninth session on the measures taken in pursuance of the present resolution;

(d) To prepare a report on the policies and practices of transnational corporations regarding their activities in South Africa and Namibia for the consideration of the Commission on Transnational Corporations at its ninth session and to include, as an annex to that report, a list of transnational corporations which continue to operate in strategic sec-

tors, including military and nuclear sectors, of the southern African economy in violation of United Nations resolutions, as well as those transnational corporations that have taken measures to terminate their activities in such sectors.

Establishment of an *ad hoc* committee on guidelines for hearings

By a resolution of 27 October 1982,[1] the Economic and Social Council decided that the public hearings on TNC activities in South Africa and Namibia which the Council had called for in 1981[2] would be conducted by the Commission on TNCs at its tenth (1984) session. They would deal with TNC operations there with a view to identifying measures by Governments and organizations to bring about the eradication of *apartheid*. The hearings would review the extent to which those TNCs sustained *apartheid* and the occupation of Namibia, TNC employment practices and their socio-cultural impact, and the implications of TNC activities in South Africa's nuclear and military sectors. The Council established an *ad hoc* committee of five States to submit to the Commission in 1983 guidelines on procedures for the hearings, persons and organizations to be invited, documentation and other matters. United Nations bodies and agencies that had worked in this area were invited to submit documents.

The draft resolution had been recommended on 10 September by the Commission on TNCs. The Council adopted it by 34 votes to 2, with 12 abstentions.

The United States, which opposed the resolution, said it would be unfortunate for the Commission to serve as the forum for the hearings because they would inevitably become politicized and were unlikely to yield any new insights; furthermore, it felt the United Nations budget should not be increased to pay for any of the new bodies or additional meetings recommended by the Commission.

Canada said it had abstained because it had doubts about the usefulness of holding official public hearings, given the political nature of the question; it would have preferred to have an *ad hoc* group meet and report to the Commission.

Resolution (1982). [1]ESC: 1982/70, 27 Oct., text following.
Resolution (prior). [2]ESC: 1981/86, 2 Nov. 1981 (YUN 1981, p. 190).
Meeting records. ESC: E/1982/SR.52, *54* (25, 27 Oct.).

Economic and Social Council resolution 1982/70

27 October 1982   Meeting 54   34-2-12

Draft by Commission on TNCs (report, E/1982/18); agenda item 25.

Public hearings on the activities of transnational corporations in South Africa and Namibia

The Economic and Social Council,

Recalling its resolutions on the activities of transnational corporations in southern Africa, in particular resolution 1981/86 of 2 November 1981, in which it called for the organization of public hearings on the activities of transnational corporations in South Africa and Namibia,

Taking note with appreciation of the report of the Secretariat on the measures taken pursuant to Economic and Social Council resolution 1981/86,

1. *Decides* that the public hearings on the activities of transnational corporations in South Africa and Namibia called for in Economic and Social Council resolution 1981/86 shall be conducted by the Commission on Transnational Corporations at its tenth session, which shall, if necessary, be extended for a period of one week for that purpose;

2. *Decides also* that the public hearings shall deal with the operations of transnational corporations in South Africa and Namibia, with a view to identifying concrete measures that could be taken by Governments and by intergovernmental and non-governmental bodies to bring about the eradication of the system of *apartheid*, in particular:

 (a) The extent to which such transnational corporations sustain the system of *apartheid* and the continued illegal occupation of Namibia by the racist minority régime of South Africa;

 (b) The employment practices of transnational corporations and their socio-cultural impact;

 (c) The implications of the activities of transnational corporations in the nuclear and military sectors of the South African economy;

3. *Decides further* to establish an *ad hoc* committee composed of five States, to be assisted by the United Nations Centre on Transnational Corporations, which would prepare and submit for adoption by the Commission on Transnational Corporations at its ninth session guidelines regarding:

 (a) Procedures for the hearings;

 (b) Persons and organizations to be invited to the hearings;

 (c) Documentation for the hearings;

 (d) Such other matters as may be pertinent to the modalities for the public hearings;

4. *Requests* the *ad hoc* committee of five States to hold one or two meetings before the ninth session of the Commission on Transnational Corporations in order to prepare the guidelines referred to in paragraph 3 above;

5. *Invites* the relevant United Nations bodies and specialized agencies that have done work on the matters referred to in paragraph 2 above to submit documentation to the Commission on Transnational Corporations at its tenth session in connection with the public hearings to be held by the Commission.

IMF and South Africa

Despite a request by the General Assembly in October 1982 that the International Monetary Fund (IMF) refrain from approving a credit requested by South Africa, the IMF Executive Board, in November, voted to grant the credit, amounting to 1 billion special drawing rights (SDR).

Activities of the Committee against *Apartheid*. The Chairman of the Special Committee against *Apartheid*, in a letter to the Secretary-General dated 10 February 1982, referred to press reports that South Africa had arranged to borrow more than $250 million from IMF. Recalling that in December 1981 the General Assembly had requested the Secretary-General to try to persuade IMF to respect United Nations resolutions on collaboration with South Africa,[12] the Chairman requested him to take appropriate action.

In its 1982 report to the Assembly,[4] submitted in September, the Committee noted with serious concern that IMF continued to provide large-scale assistance to South Africa. It recommended an urgent review of the co-operation Agreement between the United Nations and IMF if the latter did not cease such assistance forthwith.

Action by the Committee on colonial countries. The Special Committee on the Situation with regard to the Implementation of the Declaration on the Granting of Independence to Colonial Countries and Peoples[5] considered IMF loans to South Africa in the context of activities by international organizations relating to decolonization (See TRUSTEESHIP AND DECOLONIZATION, Chapter I). Its Sub-Committee on Petitions, Information and Assistance, in a report on this broader topic introduced to the Committee on 13 August, deplored the continued collaboration between IMF and South Africa in disregard of Assembly resolutions. It viewed South Africa's membership in IMF and its ability to borrow money as enabling it to borrow more and on better terms in private financial markets, thereby helping to buttress the régime.

The Sub-Committee made two recommendations which were later included in a resolution adopted by the Committee on 20 August and a similar resolution adopted by the Assembly on 23 November on the Committee's recommendation (see below): that the IMF Board of Governors consider the relationship between IMF and South Africa, and that a high-level United Nations mission be sent to IMF in 1983.

The Sub-Committee also recommended the updating of a 1981 study on IMF relations with South Africa, prepared by a consultant (David Gisselquist, Assistant Professor of Economics at the University of Maryland, Baltimore County, United States). The 1981 study was circulated as an Assembly document in response to a request by the United Nations Council for Namibia, made on 13 October 1982 and communicated to the Secretary-General by a letter of that date from the Council President.[2] The report concluded that, without South Africa's future potential borrowing from IMF (currently $5.2 billion), private foreign lending to South Africa would be seriously inhibited, and that, despite Assembly resolutions on IMF loans, the Agreement between the United Nations and IMF gave the United Nations no explicit authority over IMF actions.

Report of the Secretary-General (October). The position of IMF on this matter was restated in a letter of 29 April to the Secretary-General, reproduced in his October report to the General Assembly[6] on the action he had taken in response to the Assembly's 1981 request[12] for consultations with IMF and the World Bank. The Special Representative of IMF to the United Nations stated in this letter that the Fund's Articles of Agreement (its constitutional instrument) required uniform treatment for its members, excluding considerations that did not derive from the Articles. He added that, under the 1947 Agreement between the United Nations and IMF, the Fund was, and was required to function as, an independent international organization.

Communication. The Chairman of the Committee on colonial countries, a Vice-Chairman of the Committee against *Apartheid* and the President of the Council for Namibia, by a letter to the Secretary-General dated 18 October 1982,[1] transmitted a joint statement of 12 October calling on IMF to reject South Africa's application for credit. They said that, since the régime required such funds for military and repressive purposes, the credits violated the spirit of the mandatory arms embargo against South Africa. In their view, IMF, as a United Nations specialized agency, should be guided by Assembly resolutions adopted by overwhelming majorities.

General Assembly action (October). By a resolution of 21 October,[8] the General Assembly, having learned of South Africa's application to IMF for a credit of SDR 1 billion, again requested IMF to refrain from granting any credits or other assistance to that country. It urged IMF member States to take action towards that end and urged the Security Council to consider the matter as soon as possible with a view to taking action. The Assembly requested the Secretary-General to undertake urgent consultations with IMF and to report as soon as possible.

The resolution was adopted by a recorded vote of 121 to 3, with 23 abstentions. It was sponsored by Guinea which, introducing it on behalf of the African Group, described it as a moderate text that could be adopted by consensus. It was taken up by the Assembly at the urgent request of that Group, conveyed in a letter of 19 October to the Assembly President and signed by Guinea as Group Chairman.[3] The letter said the Group had received information that the IMF Executive Board would consider South Africa's credit application at the beginning of November. Any offer of credit by IMF to South Africa, it added, would be in disregard of United Nations resolutions.

In explanation of its vote against the resolution, the Federal Republic of Germany said it regarded the independence of IMF as indispensable to the world economy and in the interest of each country; IMF decisions must respect the rights accorded to each of its members. The United Kingdom said it supported effective international action to bring about peaceful change in South Africa, but it found that the purpose of the resolution, to exert political pressure on IMF, was inappropriate. Also opposing the resolution, the United States, which objected to politicizing IMF, said that, in seeking improperly to influence the Fund regarding a member country's request to draw on IMF resources, the Assembly would contribute not to an easing of *apartheid* but to damaging international financial institutions and the fabric of international organizations; the resolution apparently proceeded from the incorrect premise that drawing rights for IMF members were a privilege rather than an entitlement by virtue of their membership.

Among those abstaining in the vote, several countries, including Canada, France, Honduras, Iceland (on behalf of the five Nordic States), Ireland, Italy and the Netherlands, reiterated their opposition to *apartheid* but said the independent decision-making process of IMF should be respected.

Belgium said it understood the motivation of the African Group's initiative but it respected the statutes of specialized agencies and had reservations on a procedure designed to politicize them; the resolution could have adverse consequences for the observance of international law. Canada said that decisions by specialized agencies should be based on their technical and functional mandates, not on political considerations. Similarly, France said the Assembly should not intervene in the decision-making processes of specialized agencies which were, juridically speaking, entirely autonomous. Honduras believed IMF should not be affected by or involved in political issues before the Assembly.

Iceland, explaining the abstentions of the Nordic States, said they supported the cessation of further foreign investment in and loans to South Africa but they believed the resolution overlooked the practical and constitutional difficulties which would face IMF in carrying out Assembly requests; they reserved their opinion with regard to formulations which failed to take into account that only the Security Council could adopt decisions binding on Member States. Ireland said the resolution raised matters of political concern and constitutional issues between the Assembly and IMF; under the Fund's rules, its members acquired certain rights in virtue of their membership. In Italy's view, it was within the exclusive competence of IMF, in applying its own rules and principles, to judge credit requests by its members. The Netherlands opposed any attempt to politicize specialized agencies. Also abstaining, Uruguay said it was opposed in principle to having the international machinery for economic co-operation base its actions on political criteria.

Among those voting for the resolution, Algeria and Nigeria believed the IMF credit would be used in a further build-up of South Africa's military machine. Algeria added that IMF must see to it that its actions were in keeping with major decisions of the Assembly and the Security Council. According to Nigeria, the central issue was the racist policy of South Africa and not IMF policy; to regard the matter as a neutral banking transaction ignored the consequences for the South African blacks.

In explanation of its positive vote, Saint Lucia said the resolution underscored the willingness of States to take concrete measures against *apartheid* rather than engaging in mere rhetoric, and it was a first step to finding an effective means of applying sanctions against States which continued to violate international law. Sierra Leone said the IMF credit to South Africa must be resisted since it undermined the purposes and principles of the Charter of the United Nations; the action would make IMF a *de facto* partner in South Africa's *apartheid* policies and indirectly support that country's military and political capability to promote *apartheid*. The Syrian Arab Republic believed that international organizations should desist from supporting practices that violated the Charter, and that specialized agencies, financial or other, should respect Assembly resolutions asking them not to co-operate with racist régimes.

Report of the Secretary-General (November). Responding to the Assembly's request, the Secretary-General addressed a telegram to the IMF Managing Director, asking that the resolution be brought to the attention of the IMF Executive Board before a decision was taken on the South African application. He reported to the Assembly on 10 November[7] that he had consulted personally with the Managing Director on 1 November.

In a letter dated 8 November, reproduced in the report, the Managing Director informed the Secretary-General that on 3 November the Executive Board had approved South Africa's request to purchase SDR 636 million under the IMF compensatory financing facility and for a stand-by arrangement in an amount equivalent to SDR 364 million, or a total of SDR 1 billion. Approval was on the basis that the request met the requirements of the Fund's articles and policies.

General Assembly action (November-December). In a resolution of 23 November on activities of international organizations relating to decolonization[9]—based on a text recommended in August by the Committee on colonial countries (see above)—the General Assembly deeply deplored the persistent collaboration between IMF and South Africa, in disregard of repeated Assembly resolutions, and called on IMF to put an end to it. The Assembly reiterated its proposal for the urgent consideration by the IMF Board of Governors of the relationship between the Fund and South Africa, with the participation of relevant United Nations organs in Board meetings when the subject was discussed. The Assembly recommended sending in 1983 a mission to IMF, to be composed of the Chairman of the Committee on colonial countries, the President of the Council for Namibia and the Chairman of the Committee against *Apartheid*.

In a resolution of 9 December on the South Africa situation,[10] the Assembly expressed serious concern over the continued granting of credits by IMF to the racist régime of South Africa and requested IMF to terminate such credits forthwith.

The Assembly, in a resolution on the Namibia question adopted on 20 December,[11] deeply deplored the continued collaboration of IMF with South Africa, as exemplified by the grant of a credit of SDR 1 billion in disregard of the Assembly resolution of 21 October, and called on IMF to end such collaboration.

Explaining its abstention on the resolution on the South Africa situation, Australia said it supported the independence and integrity of the international financial institutions and considered it inappropriate for the Assembly to undermine that independence. Swaziland, though voting for the resolution, expressed reservations over several provisions, including this one. Uruguay, which also voted for the resolution, said the conduct of international economic co-operation organizations should be free from political considerations.

Botswana and Uruguay, though voting for the resolution on the Namibia question, reserved their positions in regard to the provision on IMF.

During the Assembly's debate on *apartheid* and South Africa, Afghanistan described the IMF action as a manifestation of the attitudes of the imperialist Powers which controlled that institution. Czechoslovakia, the Libyan Arab Jamahiriya and the Ukrainian SSR said the credit had been granted due to the weighted voting system of IMF, and they noted in particular the voting power of the United States. Egypt, Madagascar, Uganda and Zambia predicted that the credit would be used by South Africa to increase its military strength.

Egypt said it could not be claimed that IMF was a technical agency that could isolate itself from political problems, because there had been many precedents for political considerations playing an important role in the Fund's decisions; in order to avoid an argument on areas of competence in relation to the approval of credit to South Africa, Egypt called for an immediate review of the Agreement between the United Nations and IMF. Ireland said that, although it had abstained in the Assembly resolution on this topic in view of the respective competences of the Assembly and IMF, it had made clear within IMF that it would not have endorsed the credit request. The Libyan Arab Jamahiriya thought the status of IMF as a specialized agency should be reconsidered and its voting system reviewed so that it would not be able to defy United Nations resolutions. Mexico regarded the decision to flout an Assembly recommendation as having fundamental significance for the survival of the United Nations system. Nepal found it disturbing that IMF continued to provide South Africa with large-scale monetary assistance despite the Assembly resolution.

The German Democratic Republic and Mongolia viewed the IMF credit as an act of defiance of the United Nations, while Kenya saw it as another example of United Nations decisions being disregarded.

In Indonesia's view, the IMF loan would have a great negative impact on the strengthening of sanctions and would thus prolong the suffering of the South African people. Sri Lanka observed that even IMF members had to terminate contractual obligations to advance a greater good, and increasing numbers of whites in South Africa were realizing that the dismantling of *apartheid* would be a greater good. Trinidad and Tobago said the IMF credit would enable South Africa to continue its oppression, strengthen its hold on Namibia, continue attacks on the front-line States and expand the scope of its mercenary activities.

According to Somalia, the credit reflected the power of the interests vested in South Africa, which were indifferent to the fact that the funds would be used to entrench *apartheid* further. Also referring to the IMF approval of the loan, Togo said that selfish interests had made a large contribution to attempts to annihilate the black majority. In Viet Nam's view, it was significant that the United States and certain other Western Powers had opposed the resolution on the credit, for those countries reaped enormous profits from their investments in South Africa.

Letters. [1]Committee on colonial countries Chairman, Committee against *Apartheid* Vice-Chairman, Council for Namibia President, 18 Oct., A/37/554; [2]Council for Namibia President, 13 Oct., A/37/568; [3]Guinea, 19 Oct., A/37/552.
Reports. [4]Committee against *Apartheid*, A/37/22; [5]Committee on colonial countries, A/37/23/Rev.1; S-G, [6]A/37/474, [7]A/37/607.
Resolutions (1982). GA: [8]37/2, 21 Oct., text following; [9]37/32, 23 Nov.; [10]37/69 A, para. 12, 9 Dec.; [11]37/233 A, para. 31, 20 Dec.
Resolution (prior). [12]GA: 36/172 D, 17 Dec. 1981 (YUN 1981, p. 171).
Meeting records. GA: A/37/PV.*38, 40* (20, 21 Oct.).

General Assembly resolution 37/2

21 October 1982   Meeting 40   121-3-23 (recorded vote)

Draft by Guinea, for African Group (A/37/L.5); agenda item 33.

South Africa's application for credit from the International Monetary Fund

The General Assembly,

Having learned of the application by South Africa to the International Monetary Fund for a credit of one billion special drawing rights,

Recalling its resolutions on the policies of *apartheid* of the Government of South Africa, particularly its repeated requests to the International Monetary Fund for the termination of loans and credits to South Africa, and its resolution 36/172 O of 17 December 1981 on investments in South Africa,

1. *Again requests* the International Monetary Fund to refrain from granting any credits or other assistance to South Africa;

2. *Urges* States members of the International Monetary Fund to take appropriate action towards that end;

3. *Urges* the Security Council to consider the matter as soon as possible with a view to taking appropriate action;

4. *Requests* the Secretary-General to undertake urgent consultations with the International Monetary Fund and to report to the General Assembly as soon as possible on the implementation of the present resolution.

Recorded vote in Assembly as follows:

In favour: Afghanistan, Albania, Algeria, Angola, Antigua and Barbuda, Argentina, Bahamas, Bahrain, Bangladesh, Barbados, Belize, Benin, Bhutan, Bolivia, Brazil, Bulgaria, Burma, Burundi, Byelorussian SSR, Cape Verde, Central African Republic, Chad, China, Colombia, Comoros, Congo, Costa Rica, Cuba, Cyprus, Czechoslovakia, Democratic Kampuchea, Democratic Yemen, Djibouti, Dominica, Dominican Republic, Ecuador, Egypt, El Salvador, Ethiopia, Fiji, Gabon, Gambia, German Democratic Republic, Ghana, Greece, Grenada, Guinea, Guinea-Bissau, Guyana, Haiti, Hungary, India, Indonesia, Iraq, Ivory Coast, Jamaica, Jordan, Kenya, Kuwait, Lao People's Democratic Republic, Lebanon, Liberia, Libyan Arab Jamahiriya, Madagascar, Malaysia, Maldives, Mali, Malta, Mauritania, Mauritius, Mexico, Mongolia, Morocco, Mozambique, Nepal, Nicaragua, Niger, Nigeria, Oman, Pakistan, Panama, Papua New Guinea, Peru, Philippines, Poland, Qatar, Romania, Rwanda, Saint Lucia, Sao Tome and Principe, Saudi Arabia, Senegal, Seychelles, Sierra Leone, Singapore, Solomon Islands, Somalia, Sri Lanka, Sudan, Suriname, Syrian Arab Republic, Thailand, Togo, Trinidad and Tobago, Tunisia, Turkey, Uganda, Ukrainian SSR, USSR, United Arab Emirates, United Republic of Cameroon, United Republic of Tanzania, Upper Volta, Vanuatu, Venezuela, Viet Nam, Yemen, Yugoslavia, Zaire, Zambia, Zimbabwe.

Against: Germany, Federal Republic of, United Kingdom, United States.

Abstaining: Australia, Austria, Belgium, Botswana, Canada, Denmark, Finland, France, Honduras, Iceland, Ireland, Italy, Japan, Lesotho, Luxembourg, Malawi, Netherlands, New Zealand, Norway, Portugal, Spain, Sweden, Uruguay.

Israel and South Africa

Report of the Committee against *Apartheid*. In its annual report to the General Assembly, adopted in September 1982,[1] the Special Committee against *Apartheid* stated that collaboration between Israel and South Africa had greatly increased in all fields—including military, nuclear and political—since the visit of the Prime Minister of South Africa to Israel in 1976. With contempt for United Nations decisions, Israel had become a major supplier of military equipment to South Africa, providing patrol boats and missiles. The Committee proposed to take more active steps to publicize the collaboration in order to end it.

The relationship between South Africa and Israel, the Committee said, was part of South Africa's effort to build an alliance of those defiant of world public opinion as a second line of defence for *apartheid*. In the context of that alliance, the acquisition of nuclear capability by South Africa posed a particularly grave menace. The Committee hoped that States which had opposed condemnation of Israel's actions would reassess their positions and persuade it to disengage from racist oppression.

In pursuance of a December 1981 Assembly resolution,[4] the Committee submitted in September to the Assembly and the Security Council a special report on developments during the preceding year concerning military, nuclear, political, economic and other relations between Israel and South Africa.[2]

According to press reports cited in the document, Israel was planning to increase its arms exports to South Africa, which would require the approval of the United States since many Israeli weapons had United States–made components. The South African Navy was reported to have obtained seven Israeli-built fast-attack craft armed with Israeli missiles. In December 1981, the Israeli Defence Minister had visited "operational areas" in Namibia during large-scale aggression by South Africa against Angola and was reported to have made an appeal for South Africa to be supplied with sophisticated arms. According to an official South African defence periodical of February 1982, South Africa might build or purchase six Israeli frigates, equipped with missiles, torpedoes and a helicopter. A press report in May said that Israel and South Africa were developing a cruise missile with a range of 1,500 miles, a neutron bomb and various nuclear delivery systems.

As for economic collaboration, the Committee reported that Israel's trade with South Africa had decreased in 1980 as a result of Israeli financial policies but, according to the Director of the Israel Export Institute, the rate of advance of Israel's exports to South Africa was relatively greater than that of Israel's sales to other countries, and the rate of growth of imports of South African goods to Israel was greater than that from other sources. Israel, he said, bought about 1 per cent of South Africa's exports and provided South Africa with about 0.5 per cent of its imports, excluding arms, petroleum, diamonds and gold. It was reported that the Israeli Government had set up a $100-million fund in co-operation with banks and the Israeli diamond industry as an inducement to South Africa's diamond industry.

There was increasing collaboration by Israel with bantustans, the report stated, citing a December 1981 report that Israel had reached an agreement to participate in the agricultural development of Bophuthatswana. Reports of new cultural, scientific and sports contacts between Israel and South Africa were also mentioned.

General Assembly action. By a 9 December resolution on relations between Israel and South Africa,[3] the General Assembly again strongly condemned their continuing and increasing collaboration, especially in the military and nuclear fields. It demanded that Israel terminate all forms of collaboration with South Africa forthwith, particularly in those fields. The Assembly called on all Governments and organizations to exert their influence to persuade Israel to desist from such collaboration. It requested the Committee against *Apartheid* to publicize information on relations between the two countries, to keep the matter under constant review and to report to the Assembly and the Security Council as appropriate.

The Assembly took this action by a recorded vote of 113 to 18, with 10 abstentions. The draft, sponsored by 55 nations, was introduced by the Libyan Arab Jamahiriya, which noted that the text was one of six based on the Committee's recommendations.

Israel said the sponsors of the resolution had ignored the official Israeli position—that it rejected racism in any form—and had relied instead on tendentious and unsupported claims, contained in speculative press reports, to divert attention from the real problems of *apartheid;* because it had been singled out as the only country for specific condemnation based on falsehoods, Israel would not participate in the vote.

In explanation of its negative vote, Ireland said the text inappropriately singled out one State for selective condemnation. Sweden, on behalf of the five Nordic States, which also voted against the resolution, deplored the fact that it had been introduced again, as it detracted from the main thrust underlying the other resolutions on *apartheid*. Costa Rica said it would be unable to participate in the vote because the resolution was both unnecessary and discriminatory.

Having abstained in the vote, Portugal said it objected to certain discriminatory references in the text. Solomon Islands objected to naming certain countries for criticism on the ground that such measures inhibited the effectiveness of the United Nations by their divisiveness. Uruguay said its decision to abstain took into account that the intent of the resolution was covered in general terms in the resolution on military and nuclear collaboration with South Africa, without the need to single out any State.

Among those voting in favour, Ecuador said it had done so only because of the anti-discrimination proposals in the text; however, it did not share the idea that some countries and not others should be referred to when the circumstances were similar.

During the Assembly's debate on *apartheid*, Israel said the report of the Committee against *Apartheid*, which alleged that Israel had "special" relations with South Africa, was based on sources of dubious value or authenticity. The report made clear, however, that Israel accounted for less than 1 per cent of South Africa's trade, while IMF statistics indicated that Africa accounted for as much as 8.6 per cent of South Africa's exports in 1981, up by more than 3 per cent over 1980. Further, the section of the report on alleged military and nuclear collaboration between Israel and South Africa contained no verified information, indicating a lack of real evidence for its accusations. Condemning racism and *apartheid*, Israel found it discouraging that so much of the effort dealing with *apartheid* was diverted to useless documents and diatribes against Israel.

Djibouti, Iraq, Kuwait and the Sudan were among those stating that Israel continued to collaborate with South Africa in the military and nuclear fields as well as in political, economic and cultural activities. Iraq said the most dangerous aspects of the arms relationship between Israel and South Africa were their nuclear co-operation and the conduct of a nuclear test in the South Atlantic; in addition, South Africa depended on Israel to defeat the resolutions on boycotts by exporting products to Israel which Israel processed and exported to international markets.

Kuwait and the Libyan Arab Jamahiriya said the racist policies of South Africa and Israel had led them to strengthen political, economic, military and nuclear co-operation. The Syrian Arab Republic said co-operation between the two States was not illogical because they were both colonialists and imperialists serving Western interests, to the detriment of the national interests of the peoples.

The Lao People's Democratic Republic said the military and nuclear collaboration of South Africa and Israel was a source of deep international concern. In Somalia's view, the immorality and opportunism of Israel's military and nuclear co-operation with South Africa could not be too strongly condemned.

> *Reports*. Committee against *Apartheid*, [1]A/37/22, [2]A/37/22/Add.1-S/15383/Add.1.
> *Resolution (1982)*. [3]GA: 37/69 F, 9 Dec., text following.
> *Resolution (prior)*. [4]GA: 36/172 M, 17 Dec. 1981 (YUN 1981, p. 193).
> *Financial implications*. 5th Committee report, A/37/713; S-G statement, A/C.5/37/70.
> *Meeting records*. GA: plenary, A/37/PV.59-62, 65-68, *97, 98* (9 Nov.–9 Dec.); 5th Committee, A/C.5/37/SR.59 (8 Dec.).

General Assembly resolution 37/69 F

9 December 1982   Meeting 97   113-18-10 (recorded vote)

55-nation draft (A/37/L.22 and Add.1); agenda item 33.

Sponsors: Afghanistan, Algeria, Angola, Benin, Bulgaria, Burundi, Byelorussian SSR, Cape Verde, Chad, Comoros, Congo, Cuba, Czechoslovakia, Democratic Yemen, Djibouti, Ethiopia, Gambia, German Democratic Republic, Ghana, Grenada, Guinea, Guinea-Bissau, Guyana, Hungary, India, Indonesia, Iraq, Kenya, Lao People's Democratic Republic, Liberia, Libyan Arab Jamahiriya, Madagascar, Malaysia, Maldives, Mali, Mauritania, Morocco, Mozambique, Nicaragua, Nigeria, Pakistan, Qatar, Sao Tome and Principe, Senegal, Somalia, Sudan, Syrian Arab Republic, Togo, Uganda, Ukrainian SSR, United Republic of Tanzania, Vanuatu, Viet Nam, Zambia, Zimbabwe.

Relations between Israel and South Africa

The General Assembly,

Reaffirming its resolutions on relations between Israel and South Africa,

Having considered the special report of the Special Committee against *Apartheid* on recent developments concerning relations between Israel and South Africa,

Alarmed at the increasing collaboration by Israel with the racist régime of South Africa, especially in the military and nuclear fields, in defiance of resolutions of the General Assembly and the Security Council,

Considering that such collaboration is a serious hindrance to international action for the eradication of *apartheid*, an encouragement to the racist régime of South Africa to persist in its criminal policy of *apartheid* and a hostile act against the oppressed people of South Africa and the entire African continent, and constitutes a threat to international peace and security,

1. *Again strongly condemns* the continuing and increasing collaboration of Israel with the racist régime of South Africa, especially in the military and nuclear fields;

2. *Demands* that Israel desist from and terminate all forms of collaboration with South Africa forthwith, particularly in the military and nuclear fields, and abide scrupulously by the relevant resolutions of the General Assembly and the Security Council;

3. *Calls upon* all Governments and organizations to exert their influence to persuade Israel to desist from such collaboration and abide by the resolutions of the General Assembly;

4. *Requests* the Special Committee against *Apartheid* to publicize, as widely as possible, information on the relations between Israel and South Africa;

5. *Further requests* the Special Committee to keep the matter under constant review and to report to the General Assembly and the Security Council as appropriate.

Recorded vote in Assembly as follows:

In favour: Afghanistan, Albania, Algeria, Angola, Antigua and Barbuda, Argentina, Bahamas, Bahrain, Bangladesh, Barbados, Benin, Bhutan, Bolivia, Botswana, Brazil, Bulgaria, Burundi, Byelorussian SSR, Cape Verde, Central African Republic, Chad, China, Colombia, Comoros, Congo, Cuba, Cyprus, Czechoslovakia, Democratic Kampuchea, Democratic Yemen, Djibouti, Dominican Republic, Ecuador, Egypt, Ethiopia, Gabon, Gambia, German Democratic Republic, Ghana, Greece, Grenada, Guinea, Guinea-Bissau, Guyana, Haiti, Hungary, India, Indonesia, Iran, Iraq, Jamaica, Jordan, Kenya, Kuwait, Lao People's Democratic Republic, Lesotho, Liberia, Libyan Arab Jamahiriya, Madagascar, Malaysia, Maldives, Mali, Malta, Mauritania, Mauritius, Mexico, Mongolia, Morocco, Mozambique, Nepal, Nicaragua, Niger, Nigeria, Oman, Pakistan, Panama, Papua New Guinea, Peru, Philippines, Poland, Qatar, Romania, Rwanda, Sao Tome and Principe, Saudi Arabia, Senegal, Sierra Leone, Somalia, Spain, Sri Lanka, Sudan, Suriname, Syrian Arab Republic, Thailand, Togo, Trinidad and Tobago, Tunisia, Turkey, Uganda, Ukrainian SSR, USSR, United Arab Emirates, United Republic of Cameroon, United Republic of Tanzania, Upper Volta, Vanuatu, Venezuela, Viet Nam, Yemen, Yugoslavia, Zaire, Zambia, Zimbabwe.

Against: Australia, Austria, Belgium, Canada, Denmark, Finland, France, Germany, Federal Republic of, Iceland, Ireland, Italy, Luxembourg, Netherlands, New Zealand, Norway, Sweden, United Kingdom, United States.

Abstaining: Burma, Chile, Fiji, Ivory Coast, Japan, Malawi, Portugal, Singapore, Solomon Islands, Uruguay.

Situation in South Africa

The Special Committee against *Apartheid*, in its 1982 report to the General Assembly adopted on 17 September,[1] described the situation inside South Africa during the previous year as characterized by: further organized resistance by all segments of the population; increased repression by the racist régime, not only of blacks but also of whites who had participated in the resistance; the propagation by the régime of so-called political "reforms" to divide the oppressed people; and the rejection of those "reforms" by the blacks.

The Committee reported a growth of the black trade-union movement, which had spread to the mining industry. Strikes by tens of thousands of workers had occurred in several industries for better wages, working conditions, trade union rights and freedom of movement for workers. A series of strikes had obliged the régime to withdraw the Preservation of Pensions Interest Bill, which sought to prevent black workers from withdrawing their pension contributions until retirement age.

In addition to demonstrations of defiance of the régime, armed attacks by the military wing of the African National Congress of South Africa (ANC) had increased, often resulting in extensive damage to strategic or economic installations. The armed attacks had been co-ordinated with political events such as discussion of the constitutional proposals by the President's Council. Those proposals envisaged a limited form of subordinate political representation for Coloureds (the South African term for those of mixed race) and Asians, and excluded the Africans.

Moves by the régime for "reforms" were designed to maintain white minority domination and exploitation, according to a review of developments in South Africa since October 1981 annexed to the Committee's report. In what it called "limited power sharing", the régime had proposed having Coloured and Asian representation, but no representation of blacks, in separate chambers of the Parliament on a proportional basis that would guarantee the whites a majority.

The review mentioned the meting out of new death sentences in South Africa, as well as the death of two political detainees and torture of others. There had been large-scale arrests, detentions, bannings and political trials based on arbitrary security laws. Legislation had been proposed to restrict further the press and the right of assembly, and urban blacks continued to be forcibly removed from areas the Government reserved for whites.

The Commission on Human Rights took action on human rights in South Africa and Namibia on 25 February (See ECONOMIC AND SOCIAL QUESTIONS, Chapter XVIII). By a resolution on human rights violations in southern Africa,[7] it condemned or expressed profound indignation at the granting of "independence" to bantustans, child labour, torture and murder of political prisoners, and violation of international standards for trade union rights. The Commission, in a resolution on the self-determination of peoples,[3] and the Assembly, in its 9 December resolution on the South Africa situation,[4] strongly condemned the *apartheid* régime for its repression and indiscriminate torture and killings of workers, schoolchildren and other opponents of *apartheid*, and the imposition of death sentences on freedom fighters.

Report. [1]Committee against *Apartheid*, A/37/22.
Resolutions (1982). Commission on Human Rights (report, E/1982/12), 25 Feb.: [2]1982/8; [3]1982/16, para. 4. [4]GA: 37/69 A, para. 1, 9 Dec.

Sentencing of ANC members

In 1982, both the Security Council and the General Assembly called on the South African authorities to commute the death sentences imposed on nine members of the African National Congress of South Africa (ANC). The Council took such action in April regarding three ANC members, whose sentences were commuted in June to life imprisonment. In October, the Assembly called on the South African authorities not to proceed with the death sentences of three more ANC members sentenced in August, and the Council issued a statement three days later urging South Africa to commute the sentences. Again in December the Assembly called on South Africa not to proceed with the executions and recommended that the Council make an appeal for clemency for the three sentenced in August 1982 and three other freedom fighters sentenced to death in August 1981 whose appeal against their sentences had been denied in November 1982. The Council acted the same day, calling on the authorities to commute the six sentences.

Security Council action (April). By a resolution adopted unanimously on 9 April,[15] the Security Council called on the South African authorities to commute the death sentences of three ANC members—Ncimbithi Johnson Lubisi, Naphtali Manana and Petrus Tsepo Mashigo. It urged all States and organizations to use their influence and to take urgent measures in conformity with the Charter of the United Nations, Council resolutions and relevant international instruments to save them.

The three men had been sentenced in 1980 on charges of treason and attempted murder in connection with attacks that year on a bank at Silverton (a suburb of Pretoria) and a police station in northern Transvaal.[17] Their death sentences were confirmed by the South African Court of Appeal on 7 April 1982.

The Council took up the matter in April 1982 at the request of Uganda, which by a letter of 8 April[8] requested an urgent meeting to examine the situation following the confirmation of the death sentences. By another letter of that date to the Council President,[7] Uganda transmitted an 8 April letter from the Chief Representative of ANC to the United Nations by which he requested the Council to demand that the sentences be commuted and the prisoners released.

The resolution adopted by the Council was sponsored by Togo, Uganda and Zaire. Introducing the draft when the Council met on 9 April, Uganda emphasized that the text focused on a purely humanitarian concern.

After the vote of 15 in favour to none against, four delegations made statements. The United States, affirming its concern for the preservation of human rights, said its association with the resolution was based on the same concern it felt for the people of Poland, Afghanistan and Kampuchea who were being deprived of human rights, and for four persons in Moscow, currently on a hunger strike, who were seeking permission to join their spouses in other countries. Poland regretted that the United States had seen fit to deviate from the grave subject on the agenda and to make an unfounded reference to Poland, which Poland rejected. The USSR said the United States had failed in an attempt to have the Council consider the threat to the three patriots' lives in the context of human rights violations rather than in the context of *apartheid*, a policy incompatible with human rights and dignity.

Zaire said the legitimacy of the liberation struggle had been acknowledged by the entire international community and it was therefore unacceptable for South Africa to continue treating freedom fighters as common-law criminals.

Communications. The German Democratic Republic, in a letter of 14 April to the Secretary-General,[(3)] conveyed the text of a telegram from its Minister for Foreign Affairs welcoming the Council's unanimous call to commute the three death sentences and expressing his Government's demand that the illegal death sentences be rescinded. Cuba, in a letter of 26 April to the Secretary-General,[(2)] transmitted for circulation to the General Assembly and the Council a press release issued by the Co-ordinating Bureau of the Movement of Non-Aligned Countries in which it appealed for international pressure to have South Africa refrain from further executions for acts arising from opposition to *apartheid*.

Under national and international pressure, the three sentences were commuted to life imprisonment on 3 June, according to the review of developments in South Africa annexed to the annual report of the Committee against *Apartheid*.[(11)]

General Assembly action (October). The Chairman of the Committee against *Apartheid*, in a letter to the Secretary-General dated 16 September,[(1)] drew attention to death sentences imposed on 6 August on three other ANC members—Thelle Simon Mogoerane, Jerry Semano Mosololi and Marcus Thabo Motaung—on the charge of high treason. (They were convicted for attacks on police stations.) On behalf of the Committee, the Chairman requested the Secretary-General to bring the matter to the attention of the Security Council and the General Assembly to save the lives of the three young men.

On 1 October, the Assembly adopted a resolution[(12)] by which it called on the South African authorities not to proceed with the execution of the three freedom fighters and to commute the death sentences as soon as possible. It recommended that the Council direct an appeal for clemency to those authorities not to proceed with the execution, and requested the Secretary-General immediately to transmit the resolution to them and to report back by 15 October.

The Assembly took this action, on a text sponsored and orally revised by Cuba on behalf of the Movement of Non-Aligned Countries, by a recorded vote, requested by the United States, of 136 to none, with 1 abstention.

The United States, explaining its vote, said its decision to abstain was due to its objection to the haste with which the sponsors had demanded action, contrary to the practice of judicious deliberation.

Among those voting in favour of the resolution, Belgium said its positive vote was made for strictly humanitarian reasons and could in no way be interpreted as a judgement on the substance of the judicial procedure followed in that specific case; it regretted that the procedure followed in submitting the draft had not allowed sufficient time to study the text. Bolivia said it had voted for the resolution because, apart from humanitarian needs, it was in keeping with the Bolivian stand against *apartheid*. The Federal Republic of Germany and the United Kingdom also supported the resolution for humanitarian reasons but expressed regret over the procedure used for its approval, said they could not endorse all the language of the text, and declared that their vote did not imply any comment on the substance of the judicial proceedings. Uruguay said it would have voted favourably had it been present, because of the humanitarian content and Uruguay's condemnation of *apartheid*.

In a resolution of 3 December on self-determination of peoples,[(13)] the Assembly recommended that the Security Council make urgent appeals for clemency to the South African authorities in order that the lives of the three ANC freedom fighters sentenced to death on 6 August might be saved in accordance with the Assembly resolution of 1 October.

Security Council action (October). Following consultations with Security Council members, the President issued a statement on their behalf on 4 October which read as follows:[(10)]

"The members of the Security Council have entrusted me to express, on their behalf, their grave concern at the death sentences passed on 6 August 1982 in South Africa on Mr. Thelle Simon Mogoerane, Mr. Jerry Semano Mosololi and Mr. Marcus Thabo Motaung, three members of the African National Congress of South Africa.

The members of the Security Council strongly urge the Government of South Africa, in order to avoid further aggravating the situation in South Africa, to commute the death sentences."

South Africa responded to the statement in a letter to the Council President dated 19 October.[(6)] It said that the Council had intervened, without attempting to obtain the facts, in a matter which fell entirely within the domestic jurisdiction of the South African Government and therefore had contravened the United Nations Charter. The cases involved murder, attempted murder and robbery, and the presiding justice had found that there had been an intent to kill. The accused had a right to appeal, and death sentences were reviewed by the South African President, acting on the advice of the Executive Council.

General Assembly action (December). On 26 November 1982, the Appellate Division of the Supreme Court of South Africa confirmed the death sentences imposed on three other ANC members, convicted in 1981—David Moise, Johannes Shabangu and Anthony Tsotsobe. The rejection of their appeal was brought to the attention of the General Assembly President by a letter dated 3 December from the Libyan Arab Jama-hiriya on behalf of the African Group of States, asking for urgent Assembly action to save the lives of the six men under sentence of death.[5]

In a further appeal for clemency, the Assembly, by a resolution of 7 December,[14] called on the South African authorities not to proceed with the execution of the six freedom fighters and to commute the death sentences. It recommended that the Council direct an appeal for clemency to those authorities not to proceed with the executions and requested the Secretary-General to transmit the resolution to them immediately and to report back by 15 December.

The Assembly adopted the resolution by a recorded vote of 127 to none, with 1 abstention. The text was sponsored by the Libyan Arab Jama-hiriya, which introduced it in the Assembly on behalf of the African Group. The Libyan Arab Jama-hiriya said the text, dealing with a purely humanitarian matter, was a matter of urgency because the death sentences had been confirmed; its purpose was to save the lives of innocent militants whose only crime was to oppose *apartheid*.

In explanation of its abstention, the United States said it supported the humanitarian purpose of the text and would have wished to join in a consensus for that reason, but the authors of the resolution had chosen to state the appeal in contentious, politically motivated language, tending to cast doubt on the humanitarian intent.

Among those voting for the resolution, Ecuador said that, as reflected in its Constitution, it condemned all forms of colonialism and racial discrimination, recognized the right of peoples to free themselves from oppressive systems and opposed the death sentence. The United Kingdom said the motive of its positive vote was entirely humanitarian, but it had serious doubts that the language of the text was best calculated to achieve its objective; the United Kingdom's vote did not imply any comment on the merits of the court proceedings, nor did it prejudge the British position in any Security Council proceedings. Uruguay voted for the resolution taking into account its humanitarian nature, Uruguay's opposition to the death penalty and its condemnation of *apartheid*.

Security Council action (December). By a resolution of 7 December,[16] the Security Council called on the South African authorities to commute the death sentences imposed on the six ANC members. It urged all States and organizations to use their influence and to take urgent measures, in conformity with the United Nations Charter, Council resolutions and relevant international instruments, to save the lives of the six men.

The resolution, sponsored by Guyana, Jordan, Panama, Togo, Uganda and Zaire, was adopted unanimously and without discussion.

Communication (December). In a letter of 16 December to the Secretary-General, Viet Nam forwarded a message of 13 December from its Minister for Foreign Affairs referring to the death sentences as a criminal act by the South African authorities against the self-determination and human rights of the South African people, and demanding that the Council take more appropriate measures to compel South Africa to nullify the sentences.[9] Indonesia, in a letter to the Secretary-General dated 30 December, forwarded a statement of 18 December by its Department of Foreign Affairs in which the Government endorsed the Council resolution of 7 December and demanded that South Africa immediately revoke the death sentences.[4]

Letters. [1]Committee against *Apartheid* Chairman, 16 Sep., A/37/459-S/15405; [2]Cuba, 26 Apr., A/37/208-S/15004; [3]German Democratic Republic, 14 Apr., A/37/179-S/14980; [4]Indonesia, 30 Dec., S/15546; [5]Libyan Arab Jamahiriya, 3 Dec., A/37/695; [6]South Africa, 19 Oct., S/15461; Uganda, 8 Apr., [7]S/14958, [8]S/14959; [9]Viet Nam, 16 Dec., A/37/778.
Note. [10]SC President, S/15444.
Report. [11]Committee against *Apartheid*, A/37/22.
Resolutions (1982) GA: [12]37/1, 1 Oct., text following; [13]37/43, para. 25, 3 Dec.; [14]37/68, 7 Dec., text following. SC: [15]503(1982), 9 Apr., text following; [16]525(1982), 7 Dec., text following.
Yearbook reference. [17]1981, p. 195.
Meeting records. SC: S/PV.2351, 2404 (9 Apr., 7 Dec.). GA: A/37/PV.13, *14*, 59-62, 65-68, 92, *93* (1 Oct.–7 Dec.).

Security Council resolution 503(1982)

9 April 1982	Meeting 2351	Adopted unanimously

3-nation draft (S/14960).

Sponsors: Togo, Uganda, Zaire.

The Security Council,

Recalling its resolution 473(1980) and its statement of 5 February 1981 regarding the death sentences passed by the Transvaal Division of the Supreme Court at Pretoria on Ncimbithi Johnson Lubisi, Petrus Tsepo Mashigo and Naphtali Manana, three members of the African National Congress of South Africa,

Gravely concerned at the confirmation of the death sentences by the South African Court of Appeal on 7 April 1982,

Deeply concerned that the carrying out of the death sentences would further aggravate the situation in South Africa,

1. *Calls upon* the South African authorities to commute the death sentences;

2. *Urges* all States and organizations to use their influence and to take urgent measures in conformity with the Charter of the United Nations, the resolutions of the Security Council and relevant international instruments to save the lives of the three men.

General Assembly resolution 37/1

1 October 1982	Meeting 14	136-0-1 (recorded vote)

Draft by Cuba (A/37/L.2/Rev.1), orally revised; agenda item 33.

Appeal for clemency in favour of South African freedom fighters
The General Assembly,

Having been informed of the death sentence imposed on 6 August 1982 on three members of the African National Congress of South Africa, Thelle Simon Mogoerane, Jerry Semano Mosololi and Marcus Thabo Motaung,

Considering the numerous appeals for clemency already addressed to the South African régime,

1. *Calls upon* the South African authorities not to proceed with the execution of the three above-mentioned freedom fighters and to commute the death sentences as soon as possible;

2. *Recommends* that the Security Council should direct an appeal for clemency to the South African authorities not to proceed with the execution of the three above-mentioned members of the African National Congress of South Africa;

3. *Requests* the Secretary-General to transmit the present resolution to the South African authorities immediately and to report on the matter to the General Assembly not later than 15 October 1982.

Recorded vote in Assembly as follows:

In favour: Afghanistan, Albania, Algeria, Angola, Argentina, Australia, Austria, Bahamas, Bahrain, Bangladesh, Barbados, Belgium, Benin, Bhutan, Bolivia, Botswana, Brazil, Bulgaria, Burma, Burundi, Byelorussian SSR, Canada, Cape Verde, China, Colombia, Comoros, Congo, Costa Rica, Cuba, Cyprus, Czechoslovakia, Democratic Kampuchea, Democratic Yemen, Denmark, Djibouti, Dominican Republic, Ecuador, Egypt, El Salvador, Equatorial Guinea, Ethiopia, Fiji, Finland, France, Gabon, Gambia, German Democratic Republic, Germany, Federal Republic of, Ghana, Greece, Guinea, Guinea-Bissau, Guyana, Hungary, Iceland, India, Indonesia, Iran, Iraq, Ireland, Italy, Ivory Coast, Jamaica, Japan, Jordan, Kenya, Kuwait, Lao People's Democratic Républic, Lesotho, Liberia, Libyan Arab Jamahiriya, Luxembourg, Madagascar, Malaysia, Maldives, Mali, Malta, Mauritania, Mauritius, Mexico, Mongolia, Morocco, Mozambique, Nepal, Netherlands, New Zealand, Nicaragua, Niger, Nigeria, Norway, Oman, Pakistan, Panama, Papua New Guinea, Peru, Philippines, Poland, Portugal, Qatar, Romania, Rwanda, Saint Lucia, Samoa, Sao Tome and Principe, Saudi Arabia, Senegal, Sierra Leone, Singapore, Solomon Islands, Somalia, Spain, Sri Lanka, Sudan, Suriname, Swaziland, Sweden, Syrian Arab Republic, Thailand, Togo, Trinidad and Tobago, Tunisia, Turkey, Uganda, Ukrainian SSR, USSR, United Kingdom, United Republic of Cameroon, United Republic of Tanzania, Upper Volta, Venezuela, Viet Nam, Yemen, Yugoslavia, Zaire, Zambia, Zimbabwe.

Against: None.

Abstaining: United States.

General Assembly resolution 37/68

7 December 1982   Meeting 93   127-0-1 (recorded vote)

Draft by Libyan Arab Jamahiriya, for African Group (A/37/L.46/Rev.1); agenda item 33.

Further appeal for clemency in favour of South African freedom fighters

The General Assembly,

Having been informed that the appeal against the death sentences imposed on 19 August 1981 on Mr. Anthony Tsotsobe, Mr. Johannes Shabangu and Mr. David Moise, members of the African National Congress of South Africa, has been rejected by the Appellate Division,

Recalling its resolution 36/172 J of 17 December 1981, in particular its demand that the racist régime of South Africa refrain from the execution of persons sentenced under arbitrary repressive laws for acts arising from opposition to *apartheid,*

Deeply concerned that the South African authorities have not yet heeded the General Assembly's appeal for clemency contained in its resolution 37/1 of 1 October 1982 in favour of three other South African freedom fighters, namely Mr. Simon Mogoerane, Mr. Jerry Mosololi and Mr. Marcus Motaung,

Considering that the continued repression against and executions of opponents of *apartheid* are bound to have grave repercussions,

1. *Calls upon* the South African authorities not to proceed with the execution of the six above-mentioned freedom fighters and to commute the death sentences as soon as possible;

2. *Recommends* that the Security Council should direct an appeal for clemency to the South African authorities not to proceed with the execution of the six above-mentioned members of the African National Congress of South Africa;

3. *Requests* the Secretary-General to transmit the present resolution to the South African authorities immediately and to report on the matter to the General Assembly not later than 15 December 1982.

Recorded vote in Assembly as follows:

In favour: Afghanistan, Albania, Algeria, Angola, Argentina, Australia, Austria, Bahrain, Bangladesh, Barbados, Belgium, Belize, Benin, Bhutan, Bolivia, Botswana, Brazil, Bulgaria, Burma, Burundi, Byelorussian SSR, Canada, Chad, Chile, China, Colombia, Comoros, Congo, Costa Rica, Cuba, Cyprus, Czechoslovakia, Democratic Kampuchea, Democratic Yemen, Denmark, Djibouti, Dominican Republic, Ecuador, Egypt, El Salvador, Equatorial Guinea, Ethiopia, Finland, France, Gabon, Gambia, German Democratic Republic, Germany, Federal Republic of, Ghana, Greece, Grenada, Guinea, Guyana, Hungary, Iceland, India, Indonesia, Iran, Iraq, Ireland, Italy, Ivory Coast, Jamaica, Japan, Kenya, Lao People's Democratic Republic, Liberia, Libyan Arab Jamahiriya, Luxembourg, Madagascar, Malawi, Malaysia, Maldives, Mali, Malta, Mauritania, Mexico, Morocco, Mozambique, Nepal, Netherlands, New Zealand, Nicaragua, Nigeria, Norway, Oman, Pakistan, Peru, Philippines, Poland, Portugal, Qatar, Romania, Rwanda, Samoa, Sao Tome and Principe, Saudi Arabia, Senegal, Sierra Leone, Singapore, Solomon Islands, Somalia, Spain, Sri Lanka, Sudan, Swaziland, Sweden, Syrian Arab Republic, Thailand, Togo, Trinidad and Tobago, Tunisia, Turkey, Uganda, Ukrainian SSR, USSR, United Arab Emirates, United Kingdom, United Republic of Cameroon, United Republic of Tanzania, Uruguay, Venezuela, Viet Nam, Yemen, Yugoslavia, Zaire, Zambia.

Against: None.

Abstaining: United States.

Security Council resolution 525(1982)

7 December 1982   Meeting 2404   Adopted unanimously

6-nation draft (S/15511).

Sponsors: Guyana, Jordan, Panama, Togo, Uganda, Zaire.

The Security Council,

Having considered the question of the death sentences passed on 19 August 1981 in South Africa on Mr. Anthony Tsotsobe, Mr. Johannes Shabangu and Mr. David Moise,

Recalling its statement of 4 October 1982 regarding the death sentences passed on 6 August 1982 in South Africa on Mr. Thelle Simon Mogoerane, Mr. Jerry Semano Mosololi and Mr. Marcus Thabo Motaung, members of the African National Congress of South Africa, and reiterating its urgent appeal for executive clemency in this case,

Gravely concerned at the confirmation by the Appellate Division of the Supreme Court of South Africa on 26 November 1982 of the death sentences imposed on Mr. Anthony Tsotsobe, Mr. Johannes Shabangu and Mr. David Moise,

Conscious that the carrying out of the death sentences will further aggravate the situation in South Africa,

1. *Calls upon* the South African authorities to commute the death sentences imposed on the six men;

2. *Urges* all States and organizations to use their influence and to take urgent measures, in conformity with the Charter of the United Nations, the resolutions of the Security Council and relevant international instruments, to save the lives of the six men.

Political prisoners

The Commission on Human Rights, in a resolution of 25 February 1982 on human rights violations in southern Africa (See ECONOMIC AND SOCIAL QUESTIONS, Chapter XVIII), expressed profound indignation that the torture and murder of political prisoners in detention continued unabated in South Africa.[2] In another resolution of that date, on the self-determination of peoples, the Commission demanded that South Africa immediately release all people detained or imprisoned as a result of their struggle for self-determination and independence and observe the rule that no one shall be subjected to torture or to cruel, inhuman or degrading treatment.[3]

The Special Committee against *Apartheid* acted throughout the year to promote the campaign for the release of South African political prisoners, which it described in its annual report to the Assembly, adopted in September.[1] The Committee suggested that Governments support the campaign by such activities as declarations, radio and television programmes, and postage stamps devoted to South African political prisoners.

In a statement on 8 February, the Committee Chairman expressed shock at the death in detention (on 5 February) of Neil Aggett, Secretary of the African Food and Canning Workers Union in the Transvaal. Also expressing the Committee's concern for the safety of the many persons held in detention, the Chairman urged Governments, trade unions and other organizations to demand the unconditional release of all those imprisoned or restricted for their opposition to *apartheid*. On 23 December, the Chairman expressed shock at the decision of a South African magistrate exonerating police officers involved in Mr. Aggett's death.

On 21 March, the Committee published a declaration, signed by about 1,500 mayors from cities around the world, appealing to South Africa to release all prisoners detained under the *apartheid* laws for their political views, and mentioning in particular Nelson Mandela, an ANC leader who had been serving a life sentence since 1964. In a statement of 4 August marking the twentieth anniversary of Mr. Mandela's arrest, the Chairman announced that the Committee would launch a world-wide campaign for his release and that of all other South African political prisoners.

That campaign was launched on 11 October, the Day of Solidarity with South African Political Prisoners, to promote publicity for their release. In observance of the Day, the Committee held a solemn meeting at United Nations Headquarters, which was addressed by the President of the General Assembly, the Secretary-General, the President of the Security Council, the presiding officers of other United Nations bodies and the leaders of the national liberation movements of South Africa and Namibia, as well as representatives of Member States. At that meeting, the Chairman said the Committee was convinced that the release of political prisoners was a prerequisite for a peaceful solution in South Africa, to be negotiated between the leaders of the white minority and those of the national liberation movement.

Concern about the imposition of death sentences on political prisoners and the conditions under which such prisoners were held was expressed in October by the Committee of Trustees of the United Nations Trust Fund for South Africa, which continued to finance assistance to *apartheid* victims.

General Assembly action. In its resolution of 9 December on the South Africa situation,[4] the General Assembly demanded that the *apartheid* régime treat captured freedom fighters as prisoners of war under the 1949 Geneva Conventions and Additional Protocol I thereto. In its resolution of the same date on concerted international action for the elimination of *apartheid*,[5] it endorsed the campaign for the release of Mr. Mandela and all other South African political prisoners as an indispensable prerequisiste for a peaceful and just solution in South Africa. In another resolution of 9 December, on the work programme of the Committee against *Apartheid*,[6] the Assembly commended the Committee for giving special attention to that campaign.

In explanation of its affirmative vote on the resolution on international action against *apartheid*, the Netherlands said the immediate and unconditional release of all political prisoners would constitute an important first step towards realization of the elimination of *apartheid;* however, it maintained its reservations on the provision in the other resolution favouring prisoner-of-war status for freedom fighters.

During the Assembly's debate on *apartheid*, Bhutan, China, Denmark (for the European Community (EC) members), Kenya, Nicaragua, Trinidad and Tobago, Venezuela and Yugoslavia called for the immediate and unconditional release of political prisoners held by South African authorities. Of those countries, Bhutan, China, Nicaragua, Trinidad and Tobago, and Venezuela mentioned Mr. Mandela in particular. Besides calling for the release of those prisoners, Denmark, for the EC members, urged South Africa to permit open debate among all South Africans on all social, economic and political matters.

Regarding the release of political prisoners, Austria said it had joined the international campaign to liberate Mr. Mandela through direct bilateral intervention with the South African Government and had also been active on behalf of other political prisoners. Cuba said world public opinion called for the release of those prisoners. Mauritania urged an intensified international campaign for the release of Mr. Mandela and all other political prisoners. Stressing humanitarian considerations, Norway requested the South African authorities to listen to the appeals of the international community concerning the death penalties imposed on *apartheid* opponents and to spare their lives. Yugoslavia remarked that certain champions of human rights in the United Nations should be even more sensitive to a situation in which thousands of political detainees had been condemned to gaol.

Nicaragua and Viet Nam urged the granting of prisoner-of-war status to combatants of ANC and the South West Africa People's Organization captured by South Africa, in keeping with the 1977 Additional Protocols to the 1949 Geneva Convention regarding the protection of war victims.

The Netherlands said it had extended aid to political prisoners in South Africa and other victims of *apartheid* through such means as contributions to the United Nations Trust Fund for South Africa and the International Defence and Aid Fund for Southern Africa and support for South African anti-*apartheid* groups.

Report. [1]Committee against *Apartheid*, A/37/22.
Resolutions (1982). Commission on Human Rights (report, E/1982/12), 25 Feb.: [2]1982/8, para. 5 *(e)*; [3]1982/16, para. 8. GA, 9 Dec.: [4]37/69 A, para. 17; [5]37/69 B, para. 4; [6]37/69 E, para. 4 *(b)* .

Women and children under *apartheid*

Report of the Working Group of the Commission on Human Rights. The *Ad Hoc* Working Group of Experts of the Commission on Human Rights, concerned with human rights in southern Africa (See ECONOMIC AND SOCIAL QUESTIONS, Chapter XVIII), approved on 8 January 1982 a study on the effects of *apartheid* on black women and children in South Africa.[2] This study, requested by the Commission in February 1981,[7] focused on the situation of black women in the family, as workers, as political prisoners and as citizens, in the context of the race, class and sex oppression embodied in the *apartheid* system. With regard to black children, the report discussed the special rights of children, such as adequate nutrition and medical care, free education, full opportunity for play and recreation, the right to be brought up in a spirit of peace and universal brotherhood, and the right to learn to be a useful member of society and develop individual abilities. The report described the harmful effects of the denial of these basic human rights for black women and children in South Africa.

The Commission, in a resolution of 25 February on human rights violations in southern Africa,[3] expressed its profound indignation at the fact that child labour was practised in South Africa on a wide scale and that black women and children were subjected to various forms of oppression and denied the security, protection and comfort of family life.

Economic and Social Council action. By a resolution of 4 May,[4] the Economic and Social Council, reaffirming the United Nations commitment to the eradication of *apartheid* and the promotion of a democratic society in South Africa, appealed to Governments and organizations to contribute to projects of national liberation movements and front-line States for assistance to refugee women and children from South Africa and Namibia, as well as to trust funds for southern Africa. The Council invited women's organizations to intensify their solidarity with the liberation struggle in South Africa and Namibia, and to consider greater co-ordination of their efforts in co-operation with the Special Committee against *Apartheid*. Governments and organizations were invited to observe 9 August annually as the International Day of Solidarity with the Struggle of Women in South Africa and Namibia (first observed in 1981[6]). The Council welcomed the decision of the Committee against *Apartheid* to organize an international conference on women and *apartheid* in May.

The Council, acting on the recommendation of its Commission on the Status of Women, adopted the text by 35 votes to 1, with 6 abstentions. The draft was first approved by the Council's Second (Social) Committee on 26 April by a recorded vote of 38 to 1 (United States), with 7 abstentions. The Commission had approved it on 4 March.

Explaining its vote, the United States said it regretted having to oppose the resolution since it sympathized with the situation of women who lived under *apartheid;* however, the intemperate language of the draft did not advance their cause and could have the reverse effect.

Activities of the Committee against *Apartheid*. In its 1982 report to the General Assembly,[1] the Special Committee against *Apartheid* announced that, in co-operation with the International Committee of Solidarity with the Struggle of Women in South Africa and Namibia, it proposed to send high-level delegations of women leaders to various capitals to publicize the situation of women under *apartheid* and promote assistance. The Committee recommended that the Assembly endorse its proposal and invite Governments and organizations to co-operate with the delegations. In addition, the Committee suggested that United Nations programmes, including the Voluntary Fund for the United Nations Decade for Women (See ECONOMIC AND SOCIAL QUESTIONS, Chapter XIX) consider increased assistance to the oppressed women of South Africa and Namibia.

The Assembly, in a resolution of 9 December approving the Committee's work programme, commended the Committee for giving special attention to women and children under *apartheid*.[5]

Reports. [1]Committee against *Apartheid*, A/37/22; [2]Working Group of Experts, E/CN.4/1497.
Resolutions (1982). [3]Commission on Human Rights (report, E/1982/12): 1982/8, para. 5 (a) & (c), 25 Feb. [4]ESC: 1982/24, 4 May, text following. [5]GA: 37/69 E, para. 4 (c), 9 Dec.
Yearbook references. 1981, [6]p. 199, [7]p. 945.
Meeting record. ESC: E/1982/SR.23 (4 May).

Economic and Social Council resolution 1982/24

| 4 May 1982 | Meeting 23 | 35-1-6 |

Approved by Second Committee (E/1982/57) by recorded vote (38-1-7), 26 April (meeting 8); draft by Commission on women (E/1982/14); agenda item 10.

Women and children under *apartheid*
The Economic and Social Council,

Recalling General Assembly resolution 35/206 N of 16 December 1980 on women and children under *apartheid*,

Recalling also resolution 45 adopted by the World Conference of the United Nations Decade for Women,

Reaffirming that *apartheid* is a crime against humanity,

Noting with admiration the great sacrifices of the women and children in South Africa and Namibia in the struggle for their inalienable rights and their national liberation,

Recognizing that the so-called constitutional and other reforms by the racist minority régimes are no more than mere adjustments within the framework of *apartheid*,

Affirming its full solidarity with the women of South Africa and Namibia in the struggle for liberation under the leadership of their national liberation movements,

Considering that international efforts should be greatly intensified to publicize the plight of women and children in South Africa and Namibia and to promote greater solidarity with and assistance to them in the context of their heroic struggle for the liberation of South Africa and Namibia,

Appreciating the valuable contribution made by the various United Nations voluntary funds for southern Africa, including the United Nations Educational and Training Programme for Southern Africa,

Gravely concerned about the inhuman oppression of millions of women and children under *apartheid*, which manifests itself in the killing, detention and torture of schoolchildren protesting against discrimination, the enforced separation of women from their husbands and mass starvation in the reserves,

Commending the Special Committee against *Apartheid* and its Task Force on Women and Children for giving special attention to the plight of women and children under *apartheid*,

Noting with appreciation the establishment of the International Committee of Solidarity with the Struggle of Women in South Africa and Namibia,

1. *Reaffirms* the commitment of the United Nations to the total eradication of *apartheid* and the promotion of the establishment of a democratic society in which all the people of South Africa as a whole, irrespective of race, colour, sex or creed, will enjoy equal and full human rights and fundamental freedoms and will participate freely in the determination of their destiny;

2. *Invites* all Governments and organizations to observe 9 August annually as the International Day of Solidarity with the Struggle of Women in South Africa and Namibia;

3. *Appeals* to all Governments and organizations to provide generous contributions to the projects of the national liberation movements and front-line States for assistance to refugee women and children from South Africa and Namibia;

4. *Further appeals* to all Governments to make generous contributions to the various trust funds for southern Africa, including the United Nations Educational and Training Programme for Southern Africa;

5. *Welcomes* the decision of the Special Committee against *Apartheid* to organize, in co-operation with the International Committee of Solidarity with the Struggle of Women in South Africa and Namibia, an international conference on women and *apartheid*, to be held at Brussels from 17 to 19 May 1982;

6. *Invites* women's organizations all over the world to intensify their action in solidarity with the struggle for liberation in South Africa and Namibia and to consider a greater co-ordination of their efforts in co-operation with the Special Committee against *Apartheid*.

International Conference on Women and Apartheid

The International Conference on Women and *Apartheid* was held at Brussels, Belgium, from 17 to 19 May 1982, under the auspices of the Special Committee against *Apartheid* and the International Committee of Solidarity with the Struggle of Women in South Africa and Namibia. The Conference emphasized the need for the widest possible publicity about the plight of women in South Africa and Namibia and their resistance against *apartheid*, as well as for greatly increased international assistance to alleviate their hardships and enable them to participate further in the struggle for liberation.

Preparations for the Conference

The Committee against *Apartheid*, which had decided in 1981 to hold a conference on women and *apartheid*,[4] sent a mission (20 March–3 April 1982) for consultations with the Governments of the front-line States of Angola, Zambia and the United Republic of Tanzania, and the leaders of the African National Congress of South Africa, the Pan Africanist Congress of Azania and the South West Africa People's Organization. The discussions covered the situation created by South African aggression against Angola (p. 312) and other front-line States, as well as the projects being operated by the national liberation movements of South Africa and Namibia with a view to assessing their needs and to enable the Conference to promote international assistance for this cause. Among the recommendations in its report,[2] the mission suggested that the Committee make a concerted effort to persuade the Western press to pay more attention to the explosive situation in southern Africa and, in particular, to the plight of the women, children and elderly who had taken shelter in the front-line States.

The Economic and Social Council, in its resolution of 4 May on women and children under *apartheid*,[3] welcomed the decision of the Committee to organize the conference in co-operation with the International Committee of Solidarity with the Struggle of Women in South Africa and Namibia.

Also on 4 May,[1] the Council, acting without vote, designated the Chairman of the Commission on the Status of Women at its February/March 1982 session to represent the Commission as an observer at the Conference. This action had been recommended by the Commission on 4 March and was approved without vote on 23 April by the Council's Second (Social) Committee.

Decision (1982). [1]ESC: 1982/121, 4 May, text following.
Report. [2]Mission to Angola, Zambia and United Republic of Tanzania, A/AC.115/L.569.
Resolution (1982). [3]ESC: 1982/24, para. 5, 4 May.
Yearbook reference. [4]1981, p. 198.
Meeting record. ESC: E/1982/SR.23 (4 May).

Economic and Social Council decision 1982/121

Adopted without vote

Approved by Second Committee (E/1982/57) without vote, 23 April (meeting 7); draft by Commission on Women (E/1982/14), agenda item 10.

International Conference on Women and *Apartheid*

At its 23rd plenary meeting, on 4 May 1982, the Council decided to designate the Chairman of the Commission on the Status of Women at its twenty-ninth session to represent the Commission, in the capacity of observer, at the International Conference on Women and *Apartheid* to be held at Brussels from 17 to 19 May 1982.

Results of the Conference

The International Conference on Women and *Apartheid*[3] considered measures to promote assistance to women in South Africa and Namibia and action to publicize their plight and to demonstrate solidarity with them. It reviewed the general situation in southern Africa and considered the effects of *apartheid* on working women in rural and urban areas and their participation in trade unions, on women in the bantustans and on children. At the conclusion of three days of meetings, the Conference adopted a declaration that was transmitted to the General Assembly and the Security Council by the Chairman of the Special Committee against *Apartheid* in a letter to the Secretary-General of 24 May.[2]

The Conference declared that *apartheid*, especially as it affected women and children, was an international crime and an intolerable affront to the conscience of mankind. It stated that the Pretoria régime had killed, imprisoned, restricted and tortured numerous women and children for opposing *apartheid*, and had attacked refugee camps in neighbouring States, killing women and children. It deplored the actions of Governments, transnational corporations and interests which continued to collaborate with the *apartheid* régime, and called on those countries to end such collaboration. The Conference called for the implementation of United Nations decisions on military, nuclear and oil embargoes against South Africa.

The Conference emphasized the need for the widest publicity on the plight of women in South Africa and Namibia, as well as greatly increased international assistance to alleviate their hardships and enable them to participate further in the liberation struggle. It appealed, in particular, for assistance by Governments, organizations and individuals for projects of the national liberation movements and front-line States. It encouraged the Committee against *Apartheid* and the International Committee of Solidarity with the Struggle of Women in South Africa and Namibia to redouble efforts to promote publicity and assistance in co-operation with the national liberation movements and front-line States. The Conference appealed to Governments and organizations to co-operate fully with the two committees.

The Conference was attended by 300 persons, including members of the Committee against *Apartheid*, representatives of United Nations organs and other intergovernmental organizations, front-line States, member States of the European Communities and other States invited by the Committee, national liberation movements recognized by the United Nations, non-governmental organizations, anti-*apartheid* movements and trade unions.

By a letter of 24 May to the Secretary-General,[1] the Chairman of the Committee against *Apartheid* transmitted an appeal adopted by the Conference on 19 May, addressed to the 1982 special session of the General Assembly devoted to disarmament (See POLITICAL AND SECURITY QUESTIONS, Chapter I). The Conference urged the Assembly to take urgent measures for the immediate imposition of sanctions against the Pretoria régime, including action in the economic, nuclear and military fields.

Letters. Committee against *Apartheid* Chairman, 24 May: [1]A/S-12/24, [2]A/37/261-S/15150.
Report. [3]Conference on Women and *Apartheid*, A/AC.115/L.571 & Corr.1.

Observance of the Day of Solidarity with women in South Africa and Namibia

On 9 August 1982, the Committee against *Apartheid* held a special meeting in observance of the International Day of Solidarity with the Struggle of Women in South Africa and Namibia. Ten speakers addressed the meeting and the participants observed a minute of silence in tribute to the women who had sacrificed their lives for the freedom of their country.

Trade union rights

The Commission on Human Rights, in a resolution of 25 February 1982 on human rights violations in southern Africa (See ECONOMIC AND SOCIAL QUESTIONS, Chapter XVIII), expressed profound indignation at the violation in South Africa of international standards concerning trade union rights for black workers.[2]

The Special Committee against *Apartheid* issued a special report in November on trade union action against *apartheid* in South Africa.[1] It referred to the growing strength and resistance of the black trade-union movement, the brutal repression against trade union leaders, activities by the *apartheid* régime and the crucial role of trade unions throughout the world in the international campaign for the elimination of *apartheid*.

In its report, the Committee said the international community should demand full recognition of black trade unions and union rights for the entire population of South Africa, immediate release of imprisoned trade unionists, abrogation of orders prohibiting fund-raising by black and truly multiracial trade unions, penalties against transnational corporations which violated trade union rights, and abrogation of legislation restricting the freedom of movement, residence and employment of African workers.

Following consultations with trade union federations, the Committee proposed that an International Conference of Trade Unions on Sanctions and Other Actions against the *Apartheid* Régime of South Africa be held in 1983. The Conference—originally authorized by the General Assembly in December 1981[4]—was to be organized at Geneva by the Committee and the Workers' Group of the International Labour Organisation's Governing Body, in co-operation with the United Nations Council for Namibia, the Organization of African Unity and the Organization of African Trade Union Unity. Its purpose would be to promote sanctions against South Africa, world-wide solidarity with and assistance to the black trade-union movement there, and international action for the elimination of *apartheid* and for the establishment of a democratic society. The Committee recommended that the Assembly authorize it to organize the Conference.

The Assembly, in its resolution of 9 December on the Committee's work programme, authorized the Committee to organize the Conference in accordance with the Committee's recommendations.[3]

Explaining its positive vote on this resolution, Japan expressed reservations on the paragraph relating to the Conference.

During the Assembly's debate on *apartheid* and South Africa, Somalia remarked that South Africa's well-publicized decision to allow the establishment of black trade unions had been followed by the systematic persecution of active leaders of those organizations and by the death of many others, including Neil Aggett, who had lost his life while under detention (p. 296). Madagascar said black trade unions were subject to irksome surveillance, and their leaders to harassment, so as to nip in the bud any idea South African workers might have of organizing to defend their interests. The United States said its exchange programmes with South Africa included visits by American trade unionists, who lent support and encouragement to the black trade-union movement in South Africa, a movement that promised to become a significant force for democratization.

Report. [1]Committee against *Apartheid*, A/37/22/Add.2-S/15383/Add.2.

Resolutions (1982). [2]Commission on Human Rights (report, E/1982/12): 1982/8, para. 5 *(d)*, 25 Feb. [3]GA: 37/69 E, para. 2, 9 Dec.

Resolution (prior). [4]GA: 36/172 H, 17 Dec. 1981 (YUN 1981, p. 180).

Apartheid in sports

The Special Committee against *Apartheid* continued to take action in 1982 to discourage co-operation with South Africa in sports.

On 1 March and 2 November 1982, the Committee published registers of sports contacts with South Africa, covering the periods from 1 April to 31 December 1981 and 1 January to 30 June 1982, respectively. The registers contained lists of sports exchanges with South Africa and of sportsmen and sportswomen who participated in South African events. Copies were sent to organizations active in the struggle against *apartheid*. The Committee observed, in its 1982 report to the General Assembly adopted in September,[1] that fewer athletes had competed in South Africa after the publication of the first register in May 1981.[2]

The Chairman appealed to the United States on 10 February to stop deportation proceedings against Dennis Brutus, a professor of African literature at Northwestern University, Illinois, and a leader of non-racial sports movements in South Africa for 20 years. On 3 March, the Chairman issued a statement condemning a tour of South Africa by United Kingdom cricketers as an affront to the oppressed people of South Africa. In a

letter of 1 April, the Chairman expressed satisfaction to Denmark for denying visas to South African tennis players who had intended to participate in the 1982 Danish Indoor Championship. When the Committee learned that the Harlem Globetrotters basketball team of the United States was planning to visit South Africa, the Chairman, in a cable of 11 May, urged it to cancel the visit, which it did three days later.

On 11 May the Committee held a hearing on sports and *apartheid,* at which athletes and sports administrators spoke. In a statement, the Committee Chairman said the sports boycott must be intensified and continued until *apartheid* was totally abolished.

On 28 October, the Chairman of the Sub-Committee on the Implementation of United Nations Resolutions and Collaboration with South Africa expressed satisfaction that the Board of Control for Cricket in Sri Lanka had taken action against 14 cricketers who had toured South Africa in defiance of United Nations resolutions, the Gleneagles Agreement of the Commonwealth and the policy of Sri Lanka (see below). In a statement of 16 November, he expressed shock that the International Tennis Council had fined the organizers of the Swedish Grand Prix Tennis Tournament for excluding South African players.

The Committee, in its 1982 report to the Assembly, reiterated the importance of sports and cultural boycotts of South Africa. It noted with satisfaction that many sportsmen, sportswomen and entertainers had rejected offers of exorbitant payments to go to South Africa, and several events had been cancelled due to international opposition. A significant development had been action by the oppressed people there in organizing boycotts of such events despite intimidation. The Committee intended to intensify publicity for boycotts, to publicize the names of athletes, entertainers and others visiting South Africa, and to promote appropriate international action. It considered that the United Nations should recognize and express appreciation to those sports and cultural personalities who had boycotted South Africa and made sacrifices in demonstration of their opposition to *apartheid*.

During the General Assembly's debate on *apartheid* and South Africa, Barbados and Trinidad and Tobago said they would oppose all official sports contacts with South Africa; the latter welcomed a recent decision by the Commonwealth Sporting Authorities to ban from participation in the Commonwealth Games countries engaging in such contacts. Denmark, speaking on behalf of the European Community (EC) members, said they would continue to discourage any sports contacts which would have the effect of perpetuating racial discrimination. Togo supported an embargo on sports and cultural co-operation with South Africa.

Kenya said a few misguided countries had gone ahead with sports links with South Africa despite world-wide condemnation; it called on those countries to recognize that they had nothing to gain and everything to lose by continuing such contacts. The Netherlands said the pending introduction of visa requirements for South Africans who wished to visit the Netherlands would enable Netherlands authorities to restrict South African participation in sporting events there. New Zealand said it would continue to seek to prevent sports contacts with South Africa by persuasion, but it recognized the right of sports bodies to decide on such contacts for themselves. Sri Lanka, which supported the sports ban against South Africa, recounted the recent action by its Board of Control for Cricket to suspend for 25 years 14 Sri Lankans who had played cricket in South Africa.

Report. [1]Committee against *Apartheid,* A/37/22.
Yearbook reference. [2]1981, p. 201.

Draft convention

Activities of the Committee on a convention against *apartheid* in sports. The *Ad Hoc* Committee on the Drafting of an International Convention against *Apartheid* in Sports, established by the General Assembly in 1976,[3] continued efforts in 1982 to iron out remaining differences over one article of the draft convention. The text was designed to strengthen national action for the isolation of *apartheid* in sports and for its exclusion from international sports competitions. It provided for preventive and punitive measures by States to deter their nationals from participation in *apartheid* sports through such means as withholding assistance, denial of the use of public facilities, denial of visas and action to expel *apartheid* sports bodies from international associations.

In its 1982 report to the Assembly,[1] adopted on 27 August, the Committee said that positions had not changed regarding article 10, on measures to ensure compliance with the convention. It considered three versions of that article but was unable to reach agreement. Under the first version, States parties would act to ensure that their nationals refrained from participating in sports events which included individuals or teams from a country practising *apartheid.* Under the second alternative, States parties would act to ensure that their nationals refrained from participating in sports events with or which included individuals or teams from a country practising *apartheid* or from a country which included individuals or teams that engaged in sports activities with teams and individuals from a country practising *apartheid.* A third alternative was proposed by Sam Ramsammy, Chairman of the South African Non-

Racial Olympic Committee; it would require States parties to act to prevent individuals and teams that engaged in sports activities in a country practising *apartheid* or with individuals or teams representing a country practising *apartheid* from entering their respective countries to participate in sports events.

The Committee also considered substantive amendments to the draft suggested by three States. It revised the preamble taking into account suggestions by Italy and Tunisia. Regarding a proposal by Pakistan on extending recognition of the rights of *apartheid* victims in the field of sports through the International Olympic Committee, the *Ad Hoc* Committee felt the matter might better be pursued by the Olympic Committee.

The *Ad Hoc* Committee concluded that further consultations were required to overcome some of the differences, and it therefore recommended that its mandate be extended in order to continue its work with a view to submitting a draft convention to the Assembly in 1983.

General Assembly action. By a resolution of 9 December,[2] the General Assembly requested the *Ad Hoc* Committee to continue its work with a view to submitting a draft convention as soon as possible. It authorized the Committee to continue consultations with representatives of Governments and organizations and with experts on *apartheid* in sports.

The resolution, sponsored by 64 nations, was adopted by a recorded vote of 138 to 1, with 7 abstentions. Introducing the text in the Assembly, Barbados noted that article 10 of the draft convention was the only article outstanding and said the Committee members believed that with further consultations it would be possible to arrive at a suitable conclusion.

Speaking in explanation of vote, Denmark, on behalf of the EC members, which either abstained or voted for the resolution, said they rejected any form of *apartheid* in sports but pointed out that sports were privately organized in their countries; they would, however, continue to discourage sports contacts involving racial discrimination. The Netherlands, which abstained in the vote, said that, while its authorities would be able to restrict South African participation in sporting events in the Netherlands under a new visa requirement for visiting South Africans that was to come into force shortly, it could not accept an infringement of certain traditional freedoms in the Netherlands, such as the right of its nationals to travel abroad, and the proposed convention was incompatible with that tradition.

Among those voting for the resolution, Canada said its policy largely accorded with the principle underlying the attempt to draft a convention but legal and constitutional obstacles might preclude it from becoming a party. France, while reserving its position on some possible provisions of the future draft convention, said it supported the text to indicate its rejection of any discrimination in sports. Ireland, which also voted in favour, said it would have to study the draft convention when it was completed to see whether it would give rise to legal or constitutional problems.

Report. [1]Committee on convention against *apartheid* in sports, A/37/36.
Resolution (1982). [2]GA: 37/69 G, 9 Dec., text following.
Resolution (prior). [3]31/6 F, 9 Nov. 1976 (YUN 1976, p. 136).
Financial implications. 5th Committee report, A/37/713; S-G statement, A/C.5/37/70.
Meeting records. GA: plenary, A/37/PV.59-62, 65-68, *97, 98* (9 Nov.–9 Dec.); 5th Committee, A/C.5/37/SR.59 (8 Dec.).

General Assembly resolution 37/69 G

9 December 1982   Meeting 97   138-1-7 (recorded vote)

64-nation draft (A/37/L.23 and Add.1); agenda item 33.

Sponsors: Afghanistan, Algeria, Angola, Barbados, Benin, Burundi, Cape Verde, Central African Republic, Chad, Comoros, Congo, Cuba, Democratic Yemen, Djibouti, Egypt, Ethiopia, Gabon, Gambia, German Democratic Republic, Ghana, Grenada, Guinea, Guinea-Bissau, Guyana, Haiti, Hungary, India, Indonesia, Iraq, Jamaica, Kenya, Lao People's Democratic Republic, Liberia, Libyan Arab Jamahiriya, Madagascar, Maldives, Mali, Mauritania, Morocco, Mozambique, Nepal, Nicaragua, Nigeria, Pakistan, Qatar, Romania, Rwanda, Sao Tome and Principe, Senegal, Somalia, Sudan, Syrian Arab Republic, Togo, Trinidad and Tobago, Uganda, Ukrainian SSR, United Republic of Tanzania, Vanuatu, Viet Nam, Yugoslavia, Zaire, Zambia, Zimbabwe.

Apartheid in sports

The General Assembly,

Having considered the report of the *Ad Hoc* Committee on the Drafting of an International Convention against *Apartheid* in Sports,

1. *Requests* the *Ad Hoc* Committee on the Drafting of an International Convention against *Apartheid* in Sports to continue its work with a view to submitting a draft convention as soon as possible;

2. *Authorizes* the *Ad Hoc* Committee to continue consultations, as required, with representatives of Governments and organizations concerned and experts on *apartheid* in sports.

Recorded vote in Assembly as follows:

In favour: Afghanistan, Albania, Algeria, Angola, Antigua and Barbuda, Argentina, Australia, Austria, Bahamas, Bahrain, Bangladesh, Barbados, Belgium, Benin, Bhutan, Bolivia, Botswana, Brazil, Bulgaria, Burma, Burundi, Byelorussian SSR, Canada, Cape Verde, Central African Republic, Chad, Chile, China, Colombia, Comoros, Congo, Costa Rica, Cuba, Cyprus, Czechoslovakia, Democratic Kampuchea, Democratic Yemen, Djibouti, Dominican Republic, Ecuador, Egypt, Equatorial Guinea, Ethiopia, Fiji, Finland, France, Gabon, Gambia, German Democratic Republic, Ghana, Greece, Grenada, Guatemala, Guinea, Guinea-Bissau, Guyana, Haiti, Honduras, Hungary, India, Indonesia, Iran, Iraq, Ireland, Italy, Ivory Coast, Jamaica, Japan, Jordan, Kenya, Kuwait, Lao People's Democratic Republic, Lesotho, Liberia, Libyan Arab Jamahiriya, Madagascar, Malawi, Malaysia, Maldives, Mali, Malta, Mauritania, Mauritius, Mexico, Mongolia, Morocco, Mozambique, Nepal, Nicaragua, Niger, Nigeria, Norway, Oman, Pakistan, Panama, Papua New Guinea, Peru, Philippines, Poland, Portugal, Qatar, Romania, Rwanda, Sao Tome and Principe, Saudi Arabia, Senegal, Sierra Leone, Singapore, Solomon Islands, Somalia, Spain, Sri Lanka, Sudan, Suriname, Swaziland, Sweden, Syrian Arab Republic, Thailand, Togo, Trinidad and Tobago, Tunisia, Turkey, Uganda, Ukrainian SSR, USSR, United Arab Emirates, United Republic of Cameroon, United Republic of Tanzania, Upper Volta, Uruguay, Vanuatu, Venezuela, Viet Nam, Yemen, Yugoslavia, Zaire, Zambia, Zimbabwe.

Against: United States.

Abstaining: Denmark, Germany, Federal Republic of, Iceland, Luxembourg, Netherlands, New Zealand, United Kingdom.

Other activities

The Special Committee against *Apartheid* and other United Nations bodies pursued during 1982 the campaign to eliminate South Africa's policies of racial discrimination by working with non-governmental organizations (NGOs) (see below)

and through a programme of missions, meetings and observances designed to bring the problem to the attention of broader groups of the public.

NGO activities

Economic and Social Council action. By a resolution of 4 May 1982,[3] the Economic and Social Council, acting without vote, expressed its expectation that NGOs in consultative status with the Council (See ECONOMIC AND SOCIAL QUESTIONS, Chapter XXIV) would take due account in their activities of Council and General Assembly resolutions condemning *apartheid* as practised by South Africa. The Council requested its Committee on NGOs to include an examination of this question in the review of current practice of consultation with NGOs which it was to undertake in 1983.

This resolution was based on a draft introduced by India and also sponsored by Bangladesh, Ghana, Kenya, Liberia, Nigeria, Pakistan and Zaire.

The Council acted after receiving a letter dated 19 April from the Chairman of the Committee on NGOs,[1] who said he had been asked by the Committee to advise the Council President that the matter of NGO activities in relation to South Africa had been raised during the Committee's meetings in April. The item, however, had not been on its agenda. In the context of the Council's agenda item on the Decade for Action to Combat Racism and Racial Discrimination (1973-1983) (See ECONOMIC AND SOCIAL QUESTIONS, Chapter XVIII), the Chairman brought the matter to the Council's attention for any action it might wish to take, including a reminder to NGOs about the relevant United Nations resolutions.

The Council, in a resolution of 27 October 1982 on activities of transnational corporations in southern Africa,[4] commended those NGOs that had made efforts to combat *apartheid* and, in particular, to terminate bank loans and capital transfers to South Africa. It called on them to intensify their useful efforts in those areas.

Action by the Committee against *Apartheid.* On 6 April, the Committee against *Apartheid* held a meeting for consultations with representatives of NGOs, particularly anti-*apartheid* organizations. They informed the Committee about actions taken or planned for the 1982 International Year of Mobilization for Sanctions against South Africa.

In its 1982 report to the General Assembly,[2] the Committee said it benefited from close relations with anti-*apartheid* and solidarity movements and other NGOs committed to freedom in South Africa, and it intended to prepare and communicate a list of NGOs so that all United Nations offices and agencies could co-operate with them in activities in support of South African freedom.

Observing that a few NGOs continued to collaborate with South Africa and even hold conferences there, the Committee recommended that United Nations organizations suspend co-operation with them.

Letter. [1]Committee on NGOs Chairman, 19 Apr., E/1982/54.
Report. [2]Committee against *Apartheid*, A/37/22.
Resolutions (1982). ESC: [3]1982/16, 4 May, text following; [4]1982/69, para. 3, 27 Oct.
Meeting records. ESC: E/1982/SR.10-14, 22 (19 Apr.–4 May).

Economic and Social Council resolution 1982/16

4 May 1982   Meeting 22   Adopted without vote

8-nation draft (E/1982/L.31); agenda item 2.
Sponsors: Bangladesh, Ghana, India, Kenya, Liberia, Nigeria, Pakistan, Zaire.

Activities of non-governmental organizations

The Economic and Social Council,

Taking note of the letter dated 19 April 1982 from the Chairman of the Committee on Non-Governmental Organizations to the President of the Economic and Social Council regarding the question of the activities of non-governmental organizations in relation to South Africa,

Taking note with appreciation of the work done by some non-governmental organizations with a view to the eradication of the policy of *apartheid*, as practised by the Government of South Africa,

1. *Expresses its expectation* that non-governmental organizations in consultative status with the Economic and Social Council will take due account in their activities of relevant resolutions of the Council and the General Assembly condemning the policy of *apartheid* as practised by the Government of South Africa, in accordance with Council resolution 1296(XLIV) of 23 May 1968;

2. *Requests* the Committee on Non-Governmental Organizations to include an examination of this question in the review of current practice related to the implementation of Council resolution 1296(XLIV) which it is to undertake at its next session, in 1983.

Meetings, missions and observances

The Special Committee against *Apartheid* organized or co-sponsored several meetings, sent missions and held observances in 1982 to promote activities against *apartheid.*[4]

The Conference on "Southern Africa: The Time to Choose", held in London from 11 to 13 March, was co-sponsored by the Committee and the Anti-*Apartheid* Movement of the United Kingdom. It adopted a declaration[1] in which it expressed alarm over the recent relaxation by the United States of the arms embargo against South Africa, stated that the contradiction between the Western countries' professed opposition to *apartheid* and their continued collaboration with the régime must be ended, and called for effective arms, nuclear, oil, financial, sports and cultural sanctions.

The International Seminar on the History of Resistance against Occupation, Oppression and *Apartheid* in South Africa, organized by the Committee in co-operation with the United Nations Educational, Scientific and Cultural Organization, was held in Paris from 29 March to 2 April.[6] The Seminar adopted on 2 April a Paris Declaration on the History of Resistance in South Africa in which it emphasized that the struggle in South Africa and Namibia was a genuine struggle for national liberation and not an extension of the East-West conflict, that the aggressive policies of the illegitimate régime constituted the main destabilizing factor in southern Africa, and that the national liberation movement of South Africa deserved credit for its efforts to unify the resistance forces in South Africa and for its conduct of the legitimate armed struggle with a minimum loss of civilian life. The Seminar called on historians, experts and the academic community at large to observe the academic and cultural boycotts against South Africa advocated by the General Assembly.

The Asian Regional Conference for Action against *Apartheid*, held at Manila, Philippines, from 24 to 26 May,[3] adopted on its closing day a Manila Declaration for Action against *Apartheid* in which it called for intensified assistance to the oppressed people of South Africa who, it said, had no choice but to resort to armed struggle. It condemned Israel and Taiwan for collaboration with the régime and said South Africa's efforts to become integrated in the Western defence system in the southern oceans, if successful, would present grave dangers for the peace and security of the South Atlantic and Indian Ocean areas. It also supported the economic sanctions recommended by the General Assembly. By a letter of 26 May, the Committee Chairman transmitted the text of the Declaration to the Secretary-General for circulation as a document of the Assembly and the Security Council.[2]

The Committee also co-sponsored the International Conference on Women and *Apartheid*, held at Brussels, Belgium, from 17 to 19 May.

Besides organizing meetings, the Committee sent five missions during 1982 to consult with Governments and organizations on various aspects of the anti-*apartheid* campaign.

A four-member mission held consultations from 20 March to 3 April in the front-line States of Angola, Zambia and the United Republic of Tanzania to determine what assistance could be provided for oppressed people under the *apartheid* system.[5] It examined in particular projects for assistance to the women of South Africa and Namibia and the consequences of South African armed attacks against neighbouring States, notably Angola (p. 312).

The Committee sent a mission to France, Turkey and the United Kingdom from 1 to 15 March. In France, the mission, led by the Chairman, was informed that the Government would strictly implement the arms embargo against South Africa and that, while the Government had inherited a contract with South Africa in the nuclear field, it would sign no more such contracts. During his visit to Turkey, the Chairman conveyed the Committee's appreciation for Turkey's strong support of anti-*apartheid* action. The delegation visited the

United Kingdom primarily to participate in the Conference on "Southern Africa: The Time to Choose" (see above), and it also met with government and Commonwealth officials.

The Chairman undertook a mission between 5 and 24 April to Kuwait, the United Arab Emirates, Saudi Arabia, the Netherlands, Denmark, Sweden, Norway and Finland. During the Extraordinary Ministerial Meeting of the Co-ordinating Bureau of the Non-Aligned Countries (Kuwait, 5-8 April), which dealt with the Palestine question, he informed the Meeting of the Committee's serious concern at the growing collaboration between Israel and South Africa and discussed the implementation of an oil embargo against South Africa with officials of several Governments. Discussions in the Netherlands concerned all aspects of the campaign against *apartheid*. In the Nordic countries he discussed means to ensure implementation of the arms and oil embargoes.

The Committee sent a delegation to participate in the World Conference on the Indian Ocean as a Zone of Peace (New Delhi, India, 23-25 April) (See POLITICAL AND SECURITY QUESTIONS, Chapter I). Another mission went to the Philippines, Indonesia and India from 24 May to 1 June to attend the Asian Regional Conference for Action against *Apartheid* (see above) and meet with government leaders.

Observances in which the Committee participated by holding special meetings included: the seventieth anniversary of the foundation of the African National Congress of South Africa (8 January, meeting on 12 January); International Day for the Elimination of Racial Discrimination (See ECONOMIC AND SOCIAL QUESTIONS, Chapter XVIII) (21 March, meetings on 22 March); Africa Liberation Day (25 May, meeting during the Asian Regional Conference for Action against *Apartheid*); International Day of Solidarity with the Struggling People of South Africa (16 June); International Day of Solidarity with the Struggle of Women in South Africa and Namibia (9 August); and Day of Solidarity with South African Political Prisoners (11 October).

Declaration. [1]Conference "Southern Africa: The Time to Choose", A/AC.115/L.568.
Letter. [2]Committee against *Apartheid* Chairman, annexing Declaration of Asian Conference against *apartheid*, 26 May, A/37/265-S/15157.
Reports. [3]Asian Conference against *apartheid*, A/AC.115/L.573; [4]Committee against *Apartheid*, A/37/22; [5]Mission to Angola, Zambia and United Republic of Tanzania, A/AC.115/L.569; [6]Seminar on History of Resistance against Occupation, Oppression and *Apartheid* in South Africa, A/AC.115/L.576.

International assistance

The United Nations continued in 1982 to provide assistance to South Africans outside the country and to victims of *apartheid*, as well as to the two organizations recognized by the Organization of African Unity (OAU) and identifed by the General Assembly as national liberation movements—the African National Congress of South Africa (ANC) and the Pan Africanist Congress of Azania (PAC) (see below). Reiterating its support for the national liberation movement of South Africa as the authentic representative of the people, the Assembly called on States and United Nations organizations to provide assistance to the oppressed people and their movement. It also appealed for increased contributions to United Nations funds—notably the United Nations Trust Fund for South Africa—which provided legal and humanitarian assistance for the oppressed, relief for southern African student refugees as well as other refugees from South Africa in the neighbouring front-line States, and scholarships to South Africans outside their country (p. 308).

Assistance to the national liberation movement

The President of the Economic and Social Council, in a July 1982 report to the Council,[2] described his consultations with the Acting Chairman of the Special Committee against *Apartheid* on assistance by agencies and institutions within the United Nations system to the oppressed people of South Africa and their national liberation movement. During these consultations, held annually, the two officials stressed that all United Nations organizations should provide moral and material assistance to the oppressed people of southern Africa and their national liberation movement as well as contribute to the campaign for the total isolation of the racist régime. They agreed that the Council, the Committee and the Special Committee on the Situation with regard to the Implementation of the Declaration on the Granting of Independence to Colonial Countries and Peoples should maintain close co-operation in order to maximize international support for those under colonial and racist domination.

The Council, in a resolution of 27 July on assistance by United Nations organizations for colonial countries and the South African people,[4] took note of its President's report and endorsed the observations and suggestions contained therein. It requested the specialized agencies and other United Nations organizations to intensify support for the oppressed people of South Africa and to take such measures as would isolate the *apartheid* régime and mobilize world public opinion against *apartheid*.

France, explaining its abstention in the vote on the resolution, said that, although it contributed to United Nations programmes to aid *apartheid* victims and disadvantaged South Africans, it did not consider that the specialized agencies had a mission to assist national liberation movements. The

United States said that, although it could not support the resolution, it rejected *apartheid* and sought to help solve the problem by various means, including education, through its contributions to the United Nations Educational and Training Programme for Southern Africa and through an $8-million educational assistance programme it was about to launch. Several other countries explained their abstentions along similar lines (See TRUSTEESHIP AND DECOLONIZATION, Chapter I).

The Committee against *Apartheid* also emphasized the need for increased assistance to the oppressed people of South Africa and their national liberation movement. In its 1982 report to the General Assembly,[1] it stated its intention to pay special attention to providing assistance and publicizing the liberation struggle. It stressed the need to denounce moves by collaborators with *apartheid* to slander the liberation movement as a means to justify their collaboration.

The Committee recommended that the Assembly continue authorizing United Nations budget funds to enable ANC and PAC to maintain their New York offices. Noting that several institutions had in the past year honoured South African leaders of the liberation struggle, the Committee recommended that the lives and contributions of opponents of *apartheid* be made more widely known and that such honours be encouraged.

The Commission on Human Settlements, by a resolution of 7 May,[3] condemned the South African régime for its repression, occupation of Namibia and acts of aggression against neighbouring States. It commended the Executive Director of the United Nations Centre for Human Settlements (Habitat) for efforts to comply with the Commission's May 1981 request to intensify human settlements training assistance for the OAU-recognized national liberation movements and to assist countries where human settlements had been disrupted by South Africa.[7] It urged him to continue those efforts and asked him to report in 1983. The Commission also requested him to bring to the Secretary-General's attention its request that steps be taken to enable ANC and PAC to be represented by more than one person at future Commission sessions so that they could participate effectively.

UNDP action. The United Nations Development Programme (UNDP) continued in 1982 to provide assistance to ANC and PAC, consisting of (a) education and training with a view to preparing individuals for administrative, technical and managerial responsibilities in their countries, and (b) promotion of self-reliance in countries of asylum.

ANC received assistance for five projects costed at $586,551 for the year, all but one of them educa-

tional projects that provided higher training at universities and similar institutions overseas (30 students), strengthening of a primary and secondary education facility in the United Republic of Tanzania (431 students), and training and upgrading of personnel in curriculum development and educational administration (37 trainees); the fifth project was for consultancy advice on human settlements to an ANC settlement in the United Republic of Tanzania. The assistance received by PAC was exclusively for education, enabling 37 students to pursue secondary-level and university studies at a cost of $249,060 for the year, in two projects. In addition, eight joint projects—including four in education and one in health—benefited either or both of these movements together with the South West Africa People's Organization (See TRUSTEESHIP AND DECOLONIZATION, Chapter III), at a total cost of $1,292,042.

As agreed at a December 1981 meeting involving UNDP, the liberation movements, OAU and United Nations agencies,[6] all ongoing projects were halted at the end of June 1982 and new ones, or new phases of old projects, started in July. The aim was to reduce broad project objectives and activities to specific ones so that projects could be properly monitored and the results assessed. The new and continuing projects were based on requests by the liberation movements.

General Assembly action. In its resolution of 9 December on the South Africa situation,[5] the General Assembly proclaimed full support of the national liberation movement of South Africa as the authentic representative of the people of South Africa in their just struggle for liberation. It appealed to States to provide humanitarian, educational, financial and other assistance to the oppressed people of South Africa and their national liberation movement. It urged United Nations agencies to expand their assistance to the oppressed people and to ANC and PAC, in consultation with the Committee against *Apartheid*. The Assembly decided to continue the authorization of adequate funding through the United Nations budget to enable those movements to maintain offices in New York in order to participate in the deliberations of the Committee and other bodies.

Explaining its opposition to this ·resolution, Japan said it could not support certain paragraphs, including the one on support for the national liberation movement. Having voted against the resolution, the Netherlands said it supported the efforts of ANC and PAC as anti-*apartheid* movements but did not recognize them as liberation movements, since it did not believe the situation in South Africa to be a colonial one. The United States, which also opposed the resolution, warned that if United Nations aid to ANC and PAC continued, it might withhold its share of funds from

United Nations programmes assisting those organizations.

Sweden, speaking on behalf of the five Nordic States—some of which voted against the resolution while others abstained—said they considered that only a free democratic process based on universal suffrage could determine who could represent the South African people. Similarly, Uruguay, which voted in favour, said each people had to decide on its representation through the exercise of self-determination.

During the Assembly's debate on *apartheid* and South Africa, many States voiced support for the national liberation movement of South Africa and called for international assistance to that movement and to victims of *apartheid*. Algeria said solidarity with the campaign against *apartheid* should be further strengthened, particularly through such assistance. Djibouti praised the front-line States neighbouring South Africa for their role in extending moral and material support to the freedom fighters struggling against *apartheid*. Gabon welcomed the fact that the internal resistance was finding international support from governmental and non governmental organizations. Norway supported assistance to refugees from South Africa, to victims of *apartheid* and to the front-line States. Swaziland said it would continue to offer humanitarian assistance to South African refugees and would co-operate with other countries and international organizations in providing such assistance. Viet Nam expressed the view that the United Nations had a duty to mobilize support and effective assistance for the national liberation movements and for the front-line States that supported them directly.

Report. [1]Committee against *Apartheid*, A/37/22; [2]ESC President, E/1982/77.
Resolutions (1982). [3]Commission on Human Settlements (report, A/37/8): 5/19, 7 May. [4]ESC: 1982/47, paras. 1 & 6, 27 July. [5]GA: 37/69 A, paras. 18-21, 9 Dec.
Yearbook references. 1981, [6]p. 209, [7]p. 858.

UN Trust Fund for South Africa

Activities of the Fund. The United Nations Trust Fund for South Africa made seven new grants in 1982, totalling $1,870,000. The Fund, established by the General Assembly in 1965[3] to provide legal and other assistance to those persecuted under discriminatory legislation in South Africa (subsequently extended to Namibia) and relief for refugees from South Africa, receives its money from voluntary contributions.

The Fund's Committee of Trustees issued an appeal in February 1982 drawing the attention of all States to the need for increased contributions. In a report annexed to the Secretary-General's annual report to the Assembly on the Fund, issued in October,[1] the Committee noted the arrests of

large numbers of trade unionists, students and community leaders in November 1981 and the deaths of three political detainees, and expressed concern over the imposition of death sentences on opponents of *apartheid* and over the worsening conditions under which political prisoners and detainees were held.

Thirty-six States contributed a total of $2,029,396 to the Fund during 1982 (see table below).

CONTRIBUTIONS TO THE UN TRUST FUND FOR SOUTH AFRICA, 1982
(as at 31 December 1982; in US dollar equivalent)

Country	1982 payments
Austria	34,500
Brazil	10,000
Canada	16,529
China	20,000
Cyprus	225
Denmark	312,689
Finland	88,086
France	108,333
Germany, Federal Republic of	72,340
Greece	4,500
Haiti	1,000
Hungary	2,500
Iceland	4,900
Indonesia	2,500
Ireland	19,385
Italy	647
Japan	20,000
Liberia	1,000
Malaysia	1,000
Morocco	8,000
Netherlands	268,169
New Zealand	5,913
Norway	300,000
Pakistan	3,000
Philippines	5,000
Saudi Arabia	10,000
Senegal	2,165
Singapore	500
Suriname	1,000
Sweden	434,783
Syrian Arab Republic	1,000
Togo	61
Turkey	995
United States	257,000
Zambia	6,176
Zimbabwe	5,500
Total	2,029,396

SOURCE: Interim United Nations financial statements for the 12-month period ended 31 December 1982—Individual trust funds (unpublished).

General Assembly action. By a resolution of 9 December,[2] the General Assembly commended the Secretary-General and the Trust Fund's Committee of Trustees for efforts to promote humanitarian and legal assistance to persons persecuted under repressive and discriminatory legislation in South Africa and Namibia, as well as assistance to their families and to refugees from South Africa. It expressed appreciation to contributing Governments, organizations and individuals and to the voluntary agencies assisting victims of *apartheid* and racial discrimination. The Assembly appealed for generous and increased contributions to the Fund and for direct contributions to those voluntary agencies.

The resolution, sponsored by 52 nations, was adopted without vote. Iceland, which introduced the text, observed that the fight against *apartheid* was one of the few issues on which the international community stood united. The community had responded to the growing need for assistance by the Fund, but larger contributions were needed since the situation of the opponents of *apartheid* had become increasingly difficult.

Explaining their positions, Greece and Ireland said they supported the resolution because humanitarian, economic and legal assistance to *apartheid* victims contributed to the alleviation of their suffering. Speaking on behalf of the five Nordic States, Sweden said humanitarian assistance to refugees and victims of *apartheid* formed an important part of the measures by those countries in accordance with the Joint Nordic Programme of Action against South Africa. The United States said it was pleased to join the consensus on this resolution, the only one of the 10 resolutions on *apartheid* adopted on 9 December which it did not oppose, and added that it would continue to contribute to the Fund and other assistance programmes for black South Africans.

During the Assembly's debate on *apartheid*, Austria said assistance through United Nations trust funds to victims of *apartheid* must be stepped up, as well as assistance to countries which suffered from the impact of that policy, and it pledged to continue to contribute regularly.

Report. [1]S-G, annexing Committee of Trustees report, A/37/484.
Resolution (1982). [2]GA: 37/69 I, 9 Dec., text following.
Resolution (prior). [3]GA: 2054 B (XX), 15 Dec. 1965 (YUN 1965, p. 119).
Meeting records. GA: A/37/PV.59-62, 65-68, *97, 98* (9 Nov.–9 Dec.).

General Assembly resolution 37/69 I

9 December 1982   Meeting 97   Adopted without vote

52-nation draft (A/37/L.27 and Add.1); agenda item 33.

Sponsors: Afghanistan, Angola, Australia, Austria, Benin, Canada, Central African Republic, Congo, Cyprus, Denmark, Djibouti, Egypt, Finland, France, Greece, Guinea, Guinea-Bissau, Guyana, Haiti, Iceland, India, Indonesia, Ireland, Japan, Liberia, Mali, Malta, Morocco, Mozambique, Nepal, Netherlands, Nicaragua, Nigeria, Norway, Pakistan, Philippines, Rwanda, Sierra Leone, Spain, Sudan, Sweden, Syrian Arab Republic, Trinidad and Tobago, Tunisia, Turkey, Uganda, United Republic of Tanzania, Venezuela, Viet Nam, Yugoslavia, Zaire, Zambia.

United Nations Trust Fund for South Africa

The General Assembly,

Having considered the report of the Secretary-General on the United Nations Trust Fund for South Africa, to which is annexed the report of the Committee of Trustees of the United Nations Trust Fund for South Africa,

Gravely concerned at the continued and increased repression against opponents of *apartheid* and racial discrimination in South Africa, and the institution of numerous trials under arbitrary security legislation, as well as continued repression in Namibia,

Reaffirming that increased humanitarian assistance by the international community to those persecuted under repressive and discriminatory legislation in South Africa and Namibia is appropriate and essential,

Recognizing that increased contributions to the Trust Fund and to the voluntary agencies concerned are necessary to enable them to meet the increased needs for humanitarian and legal assistance,

1.   *Commends* the Secretary-General and the Committee of Trustees of the United Nations Trust Fund for South Africa for their efforts to promote humanitarian and legal assistance to persons persecuted under repressive and discriminatory legislation in South Africa and Namibia, as well as assistance to their families and to refugees from South Africa;

2.   *Expresses its appreciation* to the Governments, organizations and individuals that have contributed to the Trust Fund and to the voluntary agencies engaged in rendering humanitarian and legal assistance to the victims of *apartheid* and racial discrimination;

3.   *Appeals* for generous and increased contributions to the Trust Fund;

4.   *Also appeals* for direct contributions to the voluntary agencies engaged in assistance to the victims of *apartheid* and racial discrimination in South Africa and Namibia.

Other UN assistance

Between 1 October 1981 and 30 September 1982, the United Nations Educational and Training Programme for Southern Africa made 205 new scholarship grants to South Africans for the 1982/83 academic year and extended 408, bringing to 613 the number of scholarship holders under this programme for the 1982/83 year. According to the Secretary-General's annual report on the Programme, issued in September 1982,[1] 926 applications from South Africans were received during this period. Of the 408 recipients, 196 were placed in Africa, 127 in North America, 55 in Asia and 30 in Europe.

The General Assembly, on 23 November, noted that, in real terms, contributions to the Programme had declined in 1982, and it appealed for greater support in order to ensure the Programme's continuation and expansion.[4]

The Secretary-General, in co-operation with the United Nations High Commissioner for Refugees (UNHCR), continued to provide educational and other assistance for student refugees from South Africa and Namibia who had taken asylum in Botswana, Lesotho, Swaziland and Zambia (See ECONOMIC AND SOCIAL QUESTIONS, Chapter XXI). In October,[2] the Secretary-General described UNHCR activities in each of those countries to provide education and training, requisites for attaining self-reliance and preparation for refugees to become constructive citizens on their return home. UNHCR projects included such activities as providing scholarships, housing, books and educational materials, monthly stipends, agricultural training and equipment, and medical treatment. As at 15 July 1982, the cost of UNHCR projects for these groups totalled $17.5 million.

The Assembly, on 17 December, requested the continuation of this programme and urged States to continue contributing generously.[7]

The Economic and Social Council, in a resolution of 4 May on women and children under *apartheid*,[3] appealed to Governments to make contributions to the various trust funds for southern Africa, including the Educational and Training Programme.

In resolutions of 9 December on the South Africa situation[5] and on military and nuclear collaboration with South Africa,[6] the Assembly invited Governments and organizations to assist, in consultation with the national liberation movements of South Africa and Namibia, persons compelled to leave South Africa because of their objection, on the ground of conscience, to serving in the military or police forces of the *apartheid* régime.

Reports. S-G, [1]A/37/436, [2]A/37/495.
Resolutions (1982). [3]ESC: 1982/24, para. 4, 4 May. GA: [4]37/33, 23 Nov.; [5]37/69 A, para. 22, 9 Dec.; [6]37/69 D, para. 4, 9 Dec.; [7]37/177, 17 Dec.

Work programme of the Committee against *Apartheid*

The General Assembly, by a resolution of 9 December 1982,[2] endorsed the annual report of the Special Committee against *Apartheid*[1] and, in particular, recommendations on the Committee's work programme and on Secretariat services. It authorized the Committee to organize in 1983 an International Conference of Trade Unions on Sanctions and other Actions against the *Apartheid* Régime of South Africa (p. 300). Encouraging the Committee, with the assistance of the Secretariat's Centre against *Apartheid*, to promote the widest international mobilization against *apartheid*, it requested the Secretary-General to strengthen the Centre and to ensure co-operation by other Secretariat units in the international campaign. The Assembly allocated $400,000 to the Committee for 1983 from the United Nations budget for special projects to promote the campaign. It requested Governments and organizations to co-operate and to contribute to a trust fund for those projects. It authorized the Committee, in view of its mandate to follow the South Africa situation, to meet during Assembly sessions.

The Assembly adopted the resolution, which was sponsored by 60 nations, by a recorded vote of 142 to 1, with 3 abstentions. The Libyan Arab Jamahiriya introduced the draft resolution, one of six based on the Committee's recommendations.

Describing its intended work programme, the Committee stated in its report that it proposed in 1983 to intensify its efforts to promote campaigns for the total isolation of the racist régime, for full support to the liberation struggle, for the unconditional release of all South African political prisoners, for solidarity with the black trade-union movement, for academic, cultural and sports boycotts and an end to tourism to South Africa, and for other Assembly-approved objectives. The Committee intended to send missions to Governments and organizations, organize conferences and seminars, organize or promote art exhibits and other anti-*apartheid* projects, and ensure the expansion of information activity.

Explaining its abstention in the vote, New Zealand said the Committee's report contained a statement by the Chairman which misrepresented the New Zealand Government's attitude to the 1981 tour of New Zealand by a South African rugby team.[4] Also abstaining, the United Kingdom said it had reservations about the budgetary aspects of the Committee's work programme.

Among those voting for the resolution, Canada, France, the Federal Republic of Germany, Ireland, Japan and Portugal also expressed reservations about the allocation or about the financial implications in general. France said it did not approve of the entire work programme but, in its desire to give concrete form to its excellent relations with the Committee, it had voted for the resolution on the work programme for the first time. Ireland felt that a more selective approach to the Committee's activities could have involved a more modest budget allocation without seriously impeding its objectives. Japan could not accept a 33 per cent increase over the $300,000 allocation for 1982 (approved in December 1981[3]) when serious efforts were being made regarding United Nations budget allocations as a whole.

Botswana, which voted in favour of the resolution, reserved its position in respect of the provision commending the Committee for giving special attention to comprehensive and mandatory sanctions against South Africa. Japan reserved its position on the authorization of a Conference of trade unions on sanctions.

Report. [1]Committee against *Apartheid*, A/37/22.
Resolution (1982). [2]GA: 37/69 E, 9 Dec., text following.
Resolution (prior). [3]GA: 36/172 N, 17 Dec. 1981 (YUN 1981, p. 213).
Yearbook reference. [4]1981, p. 200.
Financial implications. 5th Committee report, A/37/713; S-G statement, A/C.5/37/70.
Meeting records. GA: plenary, A/37/PV.59-62, 65-68, *97, 98* (9 Nov.–9 Dec.); 5th Committee, A/C.5/37/SR.59 (8 Dec.).

General Assembly resolution 37/69 E

9 December 1982   Meeting 97   142-1-3 (recorded vote)

60-nation draft (A/37/L.21 and Add.1); agenda item 33.

Sponsors: Afghanistan, Algeria, Angola, Benin, Burundi, Cape Verde, Central African Republic, Chad, Comoros, Congo, Cuba, Cyprus, Democratic Yemen, Djibouti, Egypt, Ethiopia, Gabon, Gambia, German Democratic Republic, Ghana, Grenada, Guinea, Guinea-Bissau, Guyana, Haiti, Hungary, India, Indonesia, Kenya, Liberia, Libyan Arab Jamahiriya, Madagascar, Malaysia, Maldives, Mali, Mauritania, Morocco, Mozambique, Nepal, Nicaragua, Nigeria, Pakistan, Philippines, Qatar, Romania, Rwanda, Sao Tome and Principe, Senegal, Somalia, Sudan, Syrian Arab Republic, Togo, Trinidad and Tobago, Uganda, Ukrainian SSR, United Republic of Tanzania, Vanuatu, Viet Nam, Zambia, Zimbabwe.

Programme of work of the Special Committee against *Apartheid*

The General Assembly,

Having considered the reports of the Special Committee against *Apartheid,*

Reaffirming its resolution 36/172 N of 17 December 1981,

Commending the Special Committee for its activities in the discharge of the mandate given to it by the General Assembly,

Noting with appreciation the work of the Centre against *Apartheid* of the Secretariat in assisting the Special Committee,

Recognizing the urgent need for greater international efforts to eliminate *apartheid* and enable the South African people to establish a democratic society,

Considering that the implementation of the programme of the International Year of Mobilization for Sanctions against South Africa should be continued beyond the end of the year 1982,

1. *Endorses* the report of the Special Committee against *Apartheid*, in particular the recommendations contained in paragraphs 466 to 489 on the programme of work of the Special Committee and on the services of the Centre against *Apartheid* and other units of the Secretariat;

2. *Authorizes* the Special Committee to organize in 1983 an International Conference of Trade Unions on Sanctions and other Actions against the *Apartheid* Régime of South Africa, in accordance with the recommendation in its second special report;

3. *Encourages* the Special Committee, with the assistance of the Centre against *Apartheid*, to promote the widest possible international mobilization against *apartheid* in pursuance of the resolutions of the General Assembly and the programme of work of the Special Committee for 1983;

4. *Commends* the Special Committee for giving special attention to the following:

(a) Comprehensive and mandatory sanctions against South Africa;

(b) Campaign for the release of Nelson Mandela and all other South African political prisoners;

(c) Women and children under *apartheid*;

(d) Action by the trade union movement for the elimination of *apartheid*;

(e) Sports and cultural boycott against South Africa;

(f) Participation by writers, artists, sportsmen, religious leaders and others in the international campaign against *apartheid*;

(g) Implementation of United Nations resolutions for the elimination of *apartheid*;

(h) Publicizing of the struggle for liberation in South Africa;

5. *Requests* the Special Committee to participate effectively in the Second World Conference to Combat Racism and Racial Discrimination;

6. *Requests* the Secretary-General to strengthen the Centre against *Apartheid*, in consultation with the Special Committee, and to take measures to ensure effective co-operation by all relevant units of the Secretariat in the international campaign against *apartheid*, as indicated in paragraphs 484 to 489 of the report of the Committee;

7. *Decides* to make a special allocation of $400,000 to the Special Committee for 1983 from the regular budget of the United Nations for the cost of special projects to be decided on by the Committee in order to promote the international campaign against *apartheid*;

8. *Requests* Governments and organizations to make voluntary contributions or provide other assistance for the special projects of the Special Committee;

9. *Requests* the Secretary-General to establish a trust fund for such voluntary contributions to be used in accordance with the decisions of the Special Committee;

10. *Authorizes* the Special Committee, in view of its mandate to follow the situation with regard to South Africa constantly and to promote international mobilization against *apartheid*, to meet during sessions of the General Assembly as necessary;

11. *Requests* all States, specialized agencies and other intergovernmental and non-governmental organizations to co-operate with the Special Committee in the international campaign against *apartheid*.

Recorded vote in Assembly as follows:

In favour: Afghanistan, Albania, Algeria, Angola, Antigua and Barbuda, Argentina, Australia, Austria, Bahamas, Bahrain, Bangladesh, Barbados, Belgium, Benin, Bhutan, Bolivia, Botswana, Brazil, Bulgaria, Burma, Burundi, Byelorussian SSR, Canada, Cape Verde, Central African Republic, Chad, Chile, China, Colombia, Comoros, Congo, Costa Rica, Cuba, Cyprus, Czechoslovakia, Democratic Kampuchea, Democratic Yemen, Denmark, Djibouti, Dominican Republic, Ecuador, Egypt, Equatorial Guinea, Ethiopia, Fiji, Finland, France, Gabon, Gambia, German Democratic Republic, Germany, Federal Republic of, Ghana, Greece, Grenada, Guatemala, Guinea, Guinea-Bissau, Guyana, Haiti, Honduras, Hungary, Iceland, India, Indonesia, Iran, Iraq, Ireland, Italy, Ivory Coast, Jamaica, Japan, Jordan, Kenya, Kuwait, Lao People's Democratic Republic,

Lesotho, Liberia, Libyan Arab Jamahiriya, Luxembourg, Madagascar, Malaysia, Maldives, Mali, Malta, Mauritania, Mauritius, Mexico, Mongolia, Morocco, Mozambique, Nepal, Netherlands, Nicaragua, Niger, Nigeria, Norway, Oman, Pakistan, Panama, Papua New Guinea, Peru, Philippines, Poland, Portugal, Qatar, Romania, Rwanda, Sao Tome and Principe, Saudi Arabia, Senegal, Sierra Leone, Singapore, Solomon Islands, Somalia, Spain, Sri Lanka, Sudan, Suriname, Swaziland, Sweden, Syrian Arab Republic, Thailand, Togo, Trinidad and Tobago, Tunisia, Turkey, Uganda, Ukrainian SSR, USSR, United Arab Emirates, United Republic of Cameroon, United Republic of Tanzania, Upper Volta, Uruguay, Vanuatu, Venezuela, Viet Nam, Yemen, Yugoslavia, Zaire, Zambia, Zimbabwe.

Against: United States.

Abstaining: Malawi, New Zealand, United Kingdom.

Summary records of the Committee

The General Assembly, in a resolution of 16 November 1982 on reducing meeting records of subsidiary organs,[3] decided that for three years no subsidiary organ of the Assembly, except for seven bodies, would be entitled to summary records of its proceedings. The Special Committee against *Apartheid* was one of those exceptions. It was added to the list of exceptions by a 23-nation amendment submitted by Nigeria to the Assembly's Fifth (Administrative and Budgetary) Committee and adopted by 92 votes to 1, with 11 abstentions.[1]

The amendment, to a draft resolution proposed by the Committee on Conferences, was submitted after the Chairman of the Special Committee, in a letter of 14 October to the Assembly President which the latter transmitted to the Fifth Committee Chairman,[2] said that summary records of the Special Committee were important because its work was followed by many non-governmental organizations and anti-*apartheid* movements and served as guidance in their activities for effective international mobilization for sanctions against South Africa. Accordingly, he requested that the Assembly authorize summary records for the Special Committee.

Amendment. [1]Nigeria, A/C.5/37/L.11 (to draft by Committee on Conferences, A/37/32).

Letter. [2]Committee against *Apartheid* Chairman, 14 Oct., transmitted by GA President, A/C.5/37/L.8.

Resolution (1982). [3]GA: 37/14 C, para. 3 *(e)*, 16 Nov.

Other questions involving South Africa

The Special Committee against *Apartheid*, in its 1982 report to the General Assembly adopted on 17 September,[2] commented that internal repression in South Africa had been accompanied by aggression abroad. Throughout the previous year, it said, the Pretoria régime had been engaged in almost continual and large-scale aggression against Angola. It had also continued attempts at destabilization in Zimbabwe, Mozambique and Lesotho. Acts of terrorism against members of the national liberation movements had been committed in all the States neighbouring South Africa. The November 1981 attempt by mercenaries to invade Seychelles and overthrow the Government (p. 321) had been shown to have been planned and mounted from South Africa, in collusion with the highest authorities, underlining the Committee's opinion that the South African Government was a terrorist régime whose *apartheid* policies had resulted in a threat to the security of the Indian Ocean territories.

Emphasizing the grave situation resulting from South Africa's aggression and terrorism, the Committee demanded firmer international action to isolate that régime, to defend the front-line States and to mobilize support for the national liberation movement of South Africa.

In a letter of 19 May to the President of the Security Council,[1] South Africa transmitted a statement by its Minister for Foreign Affairs and Information made to its House of Assembly on 6 May, repeating past government statements on South Africa's policy towards neighbouring States to the effect that it followed a non-interference policy and regarded the conclusion of non-aggression agreements to be in the interest of all countries in southern Africa.

General Assembly action. South Africa's relations with the neighbouring front-line States were dealt with in several General Assembly resolutions in December 1982.

In a resolution of 3 December on racial discrimination,[3] the Assembly condemned the repeated acts of aggression committed by South Africa against the States of the region, particularly Angola, Botswana, Mozambique, Seychelles and Zambia. It expressed its profound solidarity with the front-line States that were victims of the racist aggression and destabilization attempts of the Pretoria régime.

In another resolution of the same date, on the self-determination of peoples,[4] the Assembly condemned South Africa for its armed attacks on the front-line States with the aim of destabilizing their Governments, and for its establishment and use of armed terrorist groups with a view to pitting them against the national liberation movements and destabilizing the legitimate Governments in southern Africa. The Assembly reaffirmed its solidarity with the countries and movements which were victims of those actions.

In a resolution of 9 December on the South Africa situation,[5] the Assembly condemned the *apartheid* régime for its repeated acts of aggression, subversion and terrorism against independent African States, designed to destabilize the whole of southern Africa.

The Assembly, in a second resolution of 9 December, on concerted international action for the elimination of *apartheid*,[6] commended the front-line States and other States neighbouring South Africa for their sacrifices in support of freedom in South Africa. It appealed to all States and organizations to lend moral and material assistance to those States, and warned the South African régime against any acts of aggression, terrorism and destabilization against African States, and any support to mercenaries. It requested the Special Committee against *Apartheid* to continue to publicize such acts by South Africa against African States and to promote assistance to the front-line States.

On 20 December, the Assembly adopted a resolution on the Namibia question[7] in which it called on the international community urgently to extend full support and assistance, including military assistance, to the front-line States in order to enable them to defend their sovereignty and territorial integrity against South African aggression. It requested the Secretary-General to continue to develop, in consultation with the United Nations Development Programme, a comprehensive programme of assistance to States neighbouring South Africa and Namibia, both to overcome short-term difficulties and to enable those States to move towards complete self-reliance. The Assembly requested the Secretary-General to report in 1983 on the development of that programme.

During the Assembly's debate on *apartheid*, almost all speakers who mentioned South Africa's relations with neighbouring States said that the régime had continued or increased acts of aggression in the region. Many of them—including Afghanistan, Austria, Bulgaria, the Byelorussian SSR, the Central African Republic, Cyprus, Czechoslovakia, Djibouti, Kuwait, Mongolia, Nicaragua, Pakistan, Romania, Togo, Uganda and Venezuela—believed that the aggression had resulted in the destabilization of Governments or was intended to have such an effect. In Gabon's view, South Africa was employing violence against neighbouring States in an attempt to perpetuate racist domination in southern Africa.

The Gambia said South Africa's aggression had recently taken the form of both covert operations, as in Botswana, Mozambique, Seychelles and Zimbabwe, and open invasion, as in Angola and Namibia. Mongolia said the régime had systematically perpetrated acts of aggression, terrorism and provocation against neighbouring independent States and continued to occupy Angolan territory in order to destabilize the political, social and economic situation in those countries.

Suriname said that South Africa, in its military actions against neighbouring States, had killed innocent citizens and destroyed villages and property indiscriminately, and the violation of the territorial integrity of those States proceeded unpunished because of the veto power of some Security Council members. In Sweden's view, South Africa's aggressive policies indicated its wish to create a _cordon sanitaire_ against its neighbours on territory outside its borders. Uganda said South Africa's destabilization campaign was part of a strategy designed to transform southern Africa into an East-West battleground.

Several States—including Algeria, Czechoslovakia, Djibouti, Kenya, Mongolia and Togo—remarked that South African aggression included acts of terrorism. Czechoslovakia, for example, said South Africa's acts of destabilization, diversion and terrorism had resulted in an explosive pocket of tension in that area.

Argentina, the Central African Republic, China, Cyprus, Egypt, the Gambia, Somalia, Sweden and Venezuela remarked that South Africa's continued aggression against the front-line States threatened peace and security in the region. Poland and Venezuela said the régime was a constant source of tension and instability in southern Africa. In Romania's view, the aggression, subversion and destabilization were intended to hinder the efforts of the African peoples to consolidate their political and economic independence. Trinidad and Tobago said the aggression was a violation of the territorial integrity of neighbouring countries and aggravated the volatile situation in the region.

According to the Lao People's Democratic Republic, the aggression was intended to force front-line countries to stop assistance to national liberation movements. The Libyan Arab Jamahiriya said South Africa had launched repeated military attacks against the front-line States, carried out subversive operations there and murdered innocent civilians under the pretext of pursuing combatants of the South West Africa People's Organization (SWAPO), the national liberation movement of Namibia.

The Central African Republic and Djibouti called for international action to restrain South Africa. Djibouti added that the front-line States had a legitimate right to protection against the aggression.

Austria said the continuing military incursions into Angola, Mozambique, Zambia and Zimbabwe had a devastating impact on those countries' economic and social development efforts. Because it believed South Africa's aggressive behaviour towards the front-line States compounded the hardships their peoples were facing, the Netherlands said it would assist the member countries of the Southern Africa Development Co-ordinating Conference to reduce their economic dependence on South Africa. The Sudan said the front-line States which were supporting liberation movements needed all forms of aid from the international community in order to safeguard their independence and territorial integrity and to

compensate them for their losses as a result of South African attacks.

Letter. [1]South Africa, 19 May, S/15096.
Report. [2]Committee against _Apartheid_, A/37/22.
Resolutions (1982). GA: [3]37/40, paras. 5 & 6, 3 Dec.; [4]37/43, paras. 7-9, 3 Dec.; [5]37/69 A, para. 2, 9 Dec.; [6]37/69 B, paras. 7-10, 9 Dec.; [7]37/233 A, paras. 20 & 21, 20 Dec.

Angola and South Africa

Angola complained to the President of the Security Council in March 1982 and again in July that South Africa had invaded its territory. South Africa responded that its operations were necessary to counteract terrorist activities. Characterizing South Africa's activities as aggression, the General Assembly demanded in December the withdrawal of its troops from Angola.

Communications. In its first letter to the Council President, dated 24 March,[1] Angola said that continued invasions into its territory and other destabilization efforts by South Africa were linked to a plan, executed by South Africa but not limited to that country, which included the illegal creation of a buffer zone in southern Angola to be controlled by the racist régime. South Africa, in a letter to the President dated 31 March,[4] said its forces would take all necessary steps to protect the people of the Territory (Namibia) against attacks by SWAPO terrorists operating from bases in Angola; it added that on 10 March SWAPO forces had attacked villages near the town of Oshakati, killing 11 persons.

Viet Nam, in a letter to the Secretary-General dated 25 May,[8] transmitted a statement of 20 May by the spokesman for its Foreign Ministry condemning the South African authorities' aggressive actions against Angola during that month, which it said were part of the United States scheme to destabilize southern Africa and check the front-line countries' support for the Namibian people.

In another letter to the Council President, Angola protested on 15 July[2] against violations of its territorial integrity and sovereignty by South Africa and the continued military occupation of Cunene province, where civilians were being massacred, women raped and children brutalized; those terrorist acts were taking place while Angola was engaged in negotiations for peace in southern Africa. South Africa, in a 20 July letter to the Secretary-General[5] rejecting Angola's allegations, said its forces were trying to curb the violence and aggression by SWAPO terrorists and would immediately suspend operations if SWAPO were to cease those activities; South Africa called on the Secretary-General to use his good offices to urge SWAPO to abandon its designs to expand its armed activities in the region.

Addressing the Council President in a letter of 29 July,[3] Angola said it possessed military intelligence which led to the conclusion that South

African armed forces were ready to attack Angola again; the latest attacks had occurred on 21 and 26 July when South African aircraft had bombed targets up to 150 kilometres inside Angolan territory, killing more than 24 Angolans. Again rejecting Angola's allegations and reaffirming the need to defend the people of Namibia from SWAPO violence, South Africa, in a letter of 3 August to the Council President,[6] said it had documents illustrating that SWAPO openly espoused violence; if SWAPO were not harboured in Angola and were not assisted in its violence in Namibia, there would be no reason for South African security forces to seek it out.

In a letter of 8 October to the General Assembly President,[7] South Africa forwarded a letter of the same date from its Minister for Foreign Affairs and Information responding to an Angolan address in the Assembly on 4 October; the Minister called for the removal of all foreign forces from southern Africa and for a decisive commitment by the international community to a settlement of the Namibia question (See TRUSTEESHIP AND DECOLONIZATION, Chapter III), and repeated South Africa's request that the Angolan Government not allow its territory to be used by SWAPO to launch its terrorist onslaught against Namibian civilians.

Other activities. The Special Committee against *Apartheid* sent a mission for consultations with the Governments of Angola, Zambia and the United Republic of Tanzania, and with national liberation movement leaders, on the situation created by the aggression against Angola and on projects being run by those movements in host countries of refugees from South Africa and Namibia (p. 304). In Angola from 20 to 23 March, the mission reported that it had visited places in southern Angola which had been bombed by South African forces and a camp of displaced persons from Cunene province. According to the mission's report to the Committee,[10] the Angolan Minister of External Relations told it that South Africa's aggression against Angola under the so-called "right of hot pursuit" against SWAPO bases was aimed at weakening those bases and at destabilizing the country; at the same time, South Africa was arming and supporting counter-revolutionary groups in Angola.

The mission remarked that it had had an opportunity to witness the suffering and intolerable conditions under which thousands of women, children and the elderly lived in camps in Angola as a result of the invasion and repeated aggression by the South African régime. It concluded that there was an increasing need to mobilize public opinion through anti-*apartheid* movements, church groups, trade unions and youth organizations on the plight of the refugees from South Africa and Namibia as well as the Angolan displaced persons.

The United Nations Council for Namibia,[9] in the Arusha (United Republic of Tanzania) Declaration and Programme of Action on Namibia adopted on 14 May (See TRUSTEESHIP AND DECOLONIZATION, Chapter III), condemned South Africa's unprovoked acts of aggression, invasion and occupation of parts of southern Angola as a breach of international peace and security, and demanded the immediate and unconditional withdrawal of its forces from Angola. The Council expressed support for the Government and people of Angola and commended them for their sacrifice and heavy burden in support of the Namibian liberation struggle.

General Assembly action. In a resolution of 3 December on the self-determination of peoples,[11] the General Assembly again strongly condemned the invasion and occupation of part of Angolan territory by troops of the racist Pretoria régime and demanded their immediate withdrawal.

The Assembly, in a resolution of 9 December on the South Africa situation,[12] demanded the immediate and unconditional withdrawal of all troops of the *apartheid* régime from Angola and demanded that South Africa respect fully the independence, sovereignty and territorial integrity of Angola and other independent African States. It further demanded that South Africa pay full compensation to Angola and other African States for the damage to life and property it had caused.

In a resolution on the Namibia question adopted on 20 December,[13] the Assembly strongly condemned South Africa for its persistent acts of subversion and aggression against Angola, including the occupation of a part of its territory, and called on South Africa to cease all acts of aggression against and withdraw all its troops from that country.

During the Assembly's debate on *apartheid*, Nicaragua called for the unconditional and total withdrawal of all South African troops occupying Angolan territory. The USSR said that the United States, in vetoing (in August 1981) a Security Council draft resolution condemning South Africa's aggression against Angola,[14] had shown that it was an accomplice of the aggressors.

Letters. Angola: [1]24 Mar., S/14925; [2]15 July, S/15295 & Corr.1; [3]29 July, S/15321. South Africa: [4]31 Mar., S/14937; [5]20 July, S/15303; [6]3 Aug., S/15338; [7]8 Oct., A/37/532. [8]Viet Nam: 25 May, A/37/255.
Reports. [9]Council for Namibia, A/37/24; [10]Mission to Angola, Zambia and United Republic of Tanzania, A/AC.115/L.569.
Resolutions (1982). GA: [11]37/43, para. 10, 3 Dec.; [12]37/69 A, paras. 7 & 8, 9 Dec.; [13]37/233 A, para. 19, 20 Dec.
Yearbook reference. [14]1981, p. 218.

Lesotho and South Africa

Following an attack on 9 December 1982 by South African forces on its capital city of Maseru,

Lesotho called for a Security Council meeting. Condemning the attack, the General Assembly urged the Council to deter South Africa from repeating its acts of aggression. The Council acted on 15 December by condemning South Africa for the act, demanding that it pay compensation to Lesotho for the resulting damage to life and property, and requesting Member States to extend economic assistance so that Lesotho could receive and maintain South African refugees.

Lesotho continued to benefit from a special economic assistance programme organized by the United Nations, while the Office of the United Nations High Commissioner for Refugees (UNHCR) helped the refugees living there (See ECONOMIC AND SOCIAL QUESTIONS, Chapter III, XXI).

Communications. Regarding an earlier incident, Lesotho, in a letter of 11 March to the President of the Security Council,[4] said that on that day a mortar attack had been launched from the South African side of the border on the headquarters of the Lesotho Paramilitary Force at Maseru; it added that South Africa could not escape responsibility for acts of violence emanating from its territory and the consequences deriving from them.

By a letter of 9 December,[5] Lesotho transmitted a telegram from its Foreign Minister to the Council President, stating that the South African Defence Force, led and guided by members of the so-called Lesotho Liberation Army, had that morning launched a commando-type attack, using military aircraft and helicopters, against Lesotho citizens, South African refugees, government apartments and flats leased to South African refugees in the capital city of Maseru. About 31 innocent people had been killed, including women and children. Lesotho called for an urgent Council meeting on the issue.

General Assembly action. By a resolution of 14 December,[11] the General Assembly condemned South Africa for its unprovoked invasion of Lesotho, resulting in the loss of innocent lives and the destruction of property. It commended Lesotho for its opposition to South Africa's *apartheid* policy and for the sanctuary it was giving to South African refugees. The Assembly urged the Security Council to take immediate steps to deter South Africa from repeating its acts of aggression against and destabilization of Lesotho and other neighbouring African States.

The resolution was adopted without vote the day it was introduced to the Assembly. Introducing the draft, the Libyan Arab Jamahiriya, on behalf of the African Group, said it dealt with matters involving a threat to peace and security, not only in southern Africa but in all of Africa. It added that South Africa would not continue such acts of aggression were it not for the support it received from some Western countries, es-

pecially the United States and the racist régime in occupied Palestine.

Explaining its support for the resolution, France, while condemning the action against Lesotho, said that under the Charter of the United Nations the primary responsibility for the maintenance of international peace and security was conferred on the Security Council and Lesotho had already placed the matter before that body. The United Kingdom condemned the flagrant violation of Lesotho's sovereignty and the loss of life as a result of South Africa's attack, but it had reservations about some of the language used in the text and about those parts which went beyond the immediate issue; it wondered whether any purpose was served by adopting an Assembly resolution when the matter had already been put before the Council. The United States, not participating in the action on the resolution, said it would state its views in the Council.

Security Council action. By a resolution of 15 December,[12] the Security Council strongly condemned South Africa for its premeditated aggressive act against Lesotho which constituted a flagrant violation of Lesotho's sovereignty and territorial integrity. It demanded that South Africa pay full compensation to Lesotho for the resulting damage to life and property. Reaffirming Lesotho's right to give sanctuary to *apartheid* victims, the Council requested the Secretary-General to consult immediately with Lesotho and United Nations agencies to ensure the welfare of refugees there in a manner consistent with their security, and requested Member States to extend economic assistance to strengthen Lesotho's capacity to receive and maintain South African refugees. It called on South Africa to declare that it would comply with the United Nations Charter and not commit aggressive acts against Lesotho either directly or through proxies. The Council requested the Secretary-General to monitor implementation of the resolution and to report regularly to the Council as the situation demanded.

The resolution, prepared in the course of the Council's consultations, was adopted unanimously.

During the Council's consideration of Lesotho's complaint against South Africa, it invited Algeria, Angola, Benin, Botswana, Egypt, Grenada, Guinea, India, Kenya, Lesotho, the Libyan Arab Jamahiriya, Nicaragua, Seychelles, Sierra Leone, South Africa, Swaziland, the United Republic of Tanzania, Yemen, Yugoslavia, Zambia and Zimbabwe, at their request, to participate in the discussion without vote. At the request of Togo, Uganda and Zaire, contained in two letters of 16 December, the Council also extended an invitation under rule 39 of its provisional rules of procedure[b] to Ike M. Mafole of the Pan

bSee footnote a, p. 275.

Africanist Congress of Azania (PAC)[9] and John-stone F. Makatini of the African National Congress of South Africa (ANC).[8]

Addressing the Council when it opened debate on Lesotho's complaint on 14 December, the Secretary-General expressed his shock on learning of the attack and described it as a violation of the United Nations Charter and the territorial integrity of a sovereign Member State. He said UNHCR had dispatched a special mission to consult with Lesotho on the situation, to ascertain the condition of survivors and to offer assistance to the families of those killed. Of the 42 victims accounted for, 19 had been registered refugees and four others had been in the process of registration. There were 11,500 refugees in Lesotho, of whom about 1,000 were formally registered. Lesotho had followed the practice of granting asylum to refugees and facilitating their integration into its society. The Secretary-General hoped that the international community would continue to assist Lesotho to strengthen the country's capacity to provide for asylum seekers.

King Motlotlehi Moshoeshoe II of Lesotho, addressing the Council, said that, during the attack of 9 December, South African forces had killed at least 42 men, women and children, including 12 Lesotho citizens, and had razed houses. Acts of sabotage allegedly committed in South Africa by refugees residing in Lesotho had occurred in towns far from the Lesotho border. Despite Lesotho's policy of peaceful coexistence and non-interference in South Africa's internal affairs, Pretoria wanted to intimidate Lesotho into dissociating itself from the world-wide condemnation of *apartheid* and from offering moral support to the oppressed people of South Africa. Lesotho was not prepared to comply with South Africa's wish that it hand over ANC freedom fighters retreating into Lesotho. The King recommended that those Council members that had influence over South African leaders be called on to exert pressure on that Government to desist from its policies of destruction and terrorism. He appealed to United Nations Members to expose and condemn covert support for South Africa's policy.

Speaking after the adoption of the resolution, South Africa said it would not tolerate the granting of sanctuary to terrorists who planned and executed sabotage and violence against it. United Nations action in endorsing resort to violence against a Member State was in direct contravention of its Charter. The resolution was one-sided in making no mention of ANC terrorist activities which had led to South Africa's action or of the fact that Lesotho allowed its territory to be used as a springboard for attacks. The targets of South Africa's action had served as planning headquarters and bases for attacks against South Africa, Transkei and Ciskei. South Africa regretted that civilians had died or suffered as a consequence of the ANC tactic of deliberately situating its bases in residential areas. The sole purpose of the South African pre-emptive strike was to prevent an escalation of terrorism. South Africa remained ready to enter into non-aggression agreements with its neighbours, but it would take any steps necessary to defend its territory and citizens.

During the Council's three further meetings on the issue, on 15 and 16 December, all other speakers condemned South Africa's aggression against Lesotho. Most of them—China, Egypt, Grenada, Guinea, Guyana, Ireland, Japan, the Libyan Arab Jamahiriya (speaking for the African Group), Panama, Poland, Swaziland, Togo, the United Kingdom, Yugoslavia, Zaire and Zimbabwe—described that action as a violation of the Charter. Some of these States and others—Algeria, China, Egypt, France, Guyana, Ireland, Japan, Poland, Sierra Leone, Spain, Swaziland, Zambia and Zimbabwe—said it was a violation of another State's sovereignty and territorial integrity. By its action, South Africa had posed a threat to international peace and security, according to Japan, the Libyan Arab Jamahiriya, Poland, Sierra Leone, Swaziland, the USSR, the United Republic of Tanzania and Zimbabwe.

Some countries expressed their belief that the States which collaborated with South Africa had hindered efforts to halt the régime's actions against neighbouring States or had given it the impression it could act without fear of any effective international reprisal. Angola, Benin, Guinea, Kenya, the Libyan Arab Jamahiriya (speaking for the African Group), Nicaragua, Poland, Togo, the USSR and the United Republic of Tanzania made such comments, and most of them mentioned either great Powers, imperialist countries or Western countries as having influence in that regard. China said that the Power which had shielded and connnived with South Africa was duty-bound to exert pressure on it in order to stop it from continuing its atrocities. Guyana said some countries had bolstered South Africa's defiance and were shielding it against action demanded by the overwhelming majority of the international community. The USSR said South Africa would never have acted so boldly if it had not been able to rely on the direct and indirect military, economic and diplomatic support of Western countries, primarily the United States.

A number of States—Algeria, China, Guinea, the Libyan Arab Jamahiriya (speaking for the African Group), Nicaragua, Sierra Leone, the USSR, the United Republic of Tanzania and Yemen—suggested that the Council should adopt mandatory sanctions against South Africa or take action under Chapter VII of the Charter (on action with respect to threats to the peace, breaches of the peace and acts of aggression) as a means of preventing the recurrence of South African aggression. Kenya urged those permanent members of the Council that were friends of South Africa to declare that South Africa posed a threat to international peace and security. Panama wondered how many more acts of aggression South Africa must perpetrate before the Council decided to take effective measures against it, including comprehensive mandatory sanctions. Poland believed that condemnation alone was insufficient and said it must not be forgotten whose veto had blocked the adoption of such sanctions. Appealing for comprehensive sanctions, the United Republic of Tanzania called in particular on the Western permanent members of the Council to reconsider their policy towards South Africa so that the Council could fulfil its responsibility regarding the future of southern Africa. Zaire thought the Council should take measures to deter South Africa from continuing or resuming acts of aggression and destabilization against Lesotho and other neighbouring States.

Japan said the Council should demand that South Africa redress the wrongs it had perpetrated against its neighbour and insist that it refrain from the use of force and settle the dispute peacefully. In Spain's view, the authorities in South Africa must realize that the patience of the international community was not boundless and that they must refrain from further attacks against States of the region.

Three speakers emphasized that the best solution to the situation was through peaceful change. Although it preferred peaceful change to violence, Ireland added that it was difficult to sustain that argument when white South African forces had carried out a brutal attack which amounted to an act of terrorism by a Government. The United Kingdom said it had always deplored violence from any quarter in southern Africa and had repeatedly appealed for restraint on all sides. The United States viewed peaceful negotiation and conciliation as the only appropriate means for solving the region's problems; it added that violence from whatever quarter must be condemned.

Jordan, Togo, the United Kingdom, Yugoslavia, Zaire, Zambia and Zimbabwe affirmed that Lesotho was entitled to compensation for damage and loss of life caused by South Africa's attack. Due to the current circumstances, Algeria, Botswana and Yugoslavia felt Lesotho should be provided with special assistance. Egypt said it would continue to extend economic assistance to Lesotho. Kenya stated that it would continue to give assistance to ANC, which had the full support of the Organization of African Unity (OAU) in its legitimate struggle. Sierra Leone believed that the Council should help Lesotho maintain its security

by dispatching substantial forces if it again fell victim to South African attack.

Regarding the refugee situation in Lesotho, Togo said the presence of ANC freedom fighters in Lesotho was a matter within the exclusive sovereignty of that country, which had the right to shelter on its territory anyone it wished. Zaire believed that the Council should reaffirm Lesotho's right to harbour refugees.

Botswana and others denied South Africa's allegation that Lesotho and other neighbouring States harboured ANC guerrillas who committed acts of sabotage on South African territory.

Several countries offered opinions on the cause or motivation of South Africa's aggression against Lesotho. Botswana and the Libyan Arab Jamahiriya, the latter speaking for the African Group, said it sought to prevent neighbouring countries from giving refuge to South African refugees. The Libyan Arab Jamahiriya added that the main purpose was to sway the front-line States from their solid stand against *apartheid* and the occupation of Namibia. Egypt and Nicaragua said it was a destabilizing tactic, which the former said included an effort to install South African agents in Governments of neighbouring States, and the latter believed was intended to suppress the liberation struggle being waged by the people of Namibia. Yugoslavia said South Africa, by applying terrorist means, sought to destabilize the whole region in order to advance its expansionist designs and strengthen its inhuman régime.

According to Benin, the action was part of a premeditated plan by South Africa to subjugate the people of the region for the benefit of international imperialism. Similarly, Grenada believed that the action must be situated in the context of a wider imperialist conspiracy to frustrate the legitimate aspirations of oppressed peoples and to derail progressive Governments. In Uganda's view, the real reason for the aggression was the fact that South Africa was feeling the pressure of the political and armed resistance within South Africa from the liberation movements.

The attack was part of South Africa's plans for permanent hegemony over southern Africa, Angola said. France believed that the cause was the *apartheid* system, which led to repression that was inevitably followed by external aggression. According to Guyana, the action was part of a pattern designed to frighten neighbouring States into submission and an external expression of the policies of fear by which the régime sought to ensure its survival. South Africa had invaded Lesotho, Zambia said, because Lesotho was making a monumental contribution to the international effort to eliminate *apartheid*.

Algeria remarked that the number of United Nations resolutions on Pretoria's aggression showed the hopeless limitations of its actions; the international community should adapt its responses to the escalation and intensity of the challenges. Describing South Africa's aggression as an act of State terrorism against a sovereign State, Jordan said it would have supported a stronger resolution in order to deter that kind of development, which had also occurred in its own region.

The Libyan Arab Jamahiriya, speaking for the African Group, said the South African action against front-line States had hindered their economic and social development. In spite of efforts by neighbouring States to create an atmosphere conducive to peaceful contacts, Swaziland said, a false picture of those States as launching bases for subversive attacks was being developed so as to justify State terrorism.

Mr. Makatini, of ANC, denied that his organization was using Lesotho for terrorist activities in South Africa; rather, it was infiltrating people into South Africa and establishing cells there as part of the liberation struggle. Thanking Lesotho for its support and protection, Mr. Mafole, of PAC, said his organization was committed to armed struggle because it was the only way to bring peace and security to southern Africa, by overthrowing and destroying *apartheid* colonialism and imperialism.

Further communications. Democratic Kampuchea, in a letter to the Secretary-General dated 13 December,[1] transmitted a Ministry of Foreign Affairs statement of 10 December condemning South African aggression against Lesotho, reiterating its support for the just struggle of the South African people for the end of *apartheid*, and expressing solidarity with Lesotho in its defence of national sovereignty and territorial integrity.

In a letter of 14 December to the Secretary-General,[3] Jamaica forwarded a statement by its Deputy Prime Minister and Minister for Foreign Affairs, condemning South Africa for its illegal violation of Lesotho's territorial integrity and calling for the strongest sanctions against South Africa for its continuing acts of aggression against its neighbours.

In a note verbale of 15 December to the President of the Security Council,[2] Guinea transmitted a 14 December message from its President appealing to the Council to adopt energetic enforcement measures against South Africa in conformity with Chapter VII of the Charter, adding that an evasive attitude on the part of certain permanent members of the Council would only encourage the South African authorities in their policy of aggression, domination and oppression.

Pakistan, in a letter of 17 December to the Secretary-General,[7] forwarded a statement by its Foreign Office issued on 13 December, condemning South Africa's raid into Lesotho as a demonstration of the régime's disregard for the norms of international conduct and stating that, by persisting with policies of *apartheid* and armed attacks, it damaged the prospects of peace and racial harmony.

By a letter of 20 December to the Secretary-General,[6] Madagascar transmitted a telegram from its President in which he said that the impunity enjoyed by South Africa was based on the active complicity of its friends; he requested the Secretary-General to call on the international community for intensified action to end the situation in southern Africa through such means as increasing political, economic and military assistance to Lesotho.

By a letter of 22 December to the Council President,[10] Uganda forwarded a telegram of 9 December from the OAU Secretary-General to the United Nations Secretary-General condemning the aggression against Lesotho and calling on the international community to take energetic measures to induce the South African régime to desist from such acts.

Letters and note verbale (nv). [1]Democratic Kampuchea: 13 Dec., A/37/754-S/15522. [2]Guinea: 15 Dec., S/15525 *(nv)*. [3]Jamaica: 14 Dec., A/37/785-S/15529. Lesotho: [4]11 Mar., S/14904; [5]9 Dec., S/15515. [6]Madagascar: 20 Dec., A/37/788-S/15534. [7]Pakistan: 17 Dec., A/37/786-S/15530. Togo, Uganda, Zaire, 16 Dec.: [8]S/15526; [9]S/15527. [10]Uganda: 22 Dec., S/15543.
Resolutions (1982). [11]GA: 37/101, 14 Dec., text following. [12]SC: 527(1982), 15 Dec., text following.
Meeting records. GA: A/37/PV.101, 103 (13, 14 Dec.). SC: S/PV.2406-2409 (14-16 Dec.).

General Assembly resolution 37/101

14 December 1982   Meeting 103   Adopted without vote

Draft by Libyan Arab Jamahiriya, for African Group (A/37/L.54); agenda item 33.

Invasion of Lesotho by South Africa

The General Assembly,

Having learned of the invasion of Lesotho by South Africa on 9 December 1982, resulting in the loss of innocent lives and the destruction of property,

Noting with deep concern the continued acts of aggression by South Africa against Lesotho and other neighbouring independent African States in complete disregard of resolutions of the General Assembly and the Security Council,

Grieved at the tragic loss of human life and concerned about the damage and destruction of property resulting from the invasion of Lesotho by South Africa,

Convinced that international solidarity with Lesotho, as a neighbouring State of South Africa, is essential to counteract effectively South Africa's policy of coercing its neighbours into not opposing its policy of *apartheid* and not giving sanctuary to South African refugees,

1. *Condemns* South Africa for its unprovoked invasion of Lesotho, resulting in the loss of innocent lives and the destruction of property;

2. *Commends* the Government of Lesotho for its opposition to the *apartheid* policy of the racist régime of South Africa and for the sanctuary it is giving to South African refugees;

3. *Urges* the Security Council to take immediate steps to deter South Africa from repeating its acts of aggression against and destabilization of Lesotho and other neighbouring independent African States.

Security Council resolution 527(1982)

15 December 1982   Meeting 2407   Adopted unanimously

Draft prepared in consultations among Council members (S/15524).

The Security Council,

Taking note of the letter dated 9 December 1982 from the Chargé d'affaires a.i. of the Permanent Mission of the Kingdom of Lesotho to the United Nations addressed to the President of the Security Council,

Having heard the statement by His Majesty King Moshoeshoe II of the Kingdom of Lesotho,

Bearing in mind that all Member States must refrain in their international relations from the threat or use of force against the territorial integrity or political independence of any State, or in any other manner inconsistent with the purposes of the United Nations,

Gravely concerned at the recent premeditated aggressive act by South Africa, in violation of the sovereignty, airspace and territorial integrity of the Kingdom of Lesotho, and its consequences for peace and security in southern Africa,

Gravely concerned that this wanton aggressive act by South Africa is aimed at weakening the humanitarian support given by Lesotho to South African refugees,

Deeply concerned about the gravity of the aggressive acts of South Africa against Lesotho,

Grieved at the tragic loss in human life and concerned about the damage and destruction of property resulting from the aggressive act by South Africa against the Kingdom of Lesotho,

1. ·*Strongly condemns* the *apartheid* régime of South Africa for its premeditated aggressive act against the Kingdom of Lesotho which constitutes a flagrant violation of the sovereignty and territorial integrity of that country;

2. *Demands* the payment by South Africa of full and adequate compensation to the Kingdom of Lesotho for the damage to life and property resulting from this aggressive act;

3. *Reaffirms* the right of Lesotho to receive and give sanctuary to the victims of *apartheid* in accordance with its traditional practice, humanitarian principles and its international obligations;

4. *Requests* the Secretary-General to enter into immediate consultations with the Government of Lesotho and agencies of the United Nations to ensure the welfare of the refugees in Lesotho in a manner consistent with their security;

5. *Requests* Member States urgently to extend all necessary economic assistance to Lesotho in order to strengthen its capacity to receive and maintain South African refugees;

6. *Declares* that there are peaceful means to resolve international problems and that, in accordance with the Charter of the United Nations, only these should be employed;

7. *Calls upon* South Africa to declare publicly that it will, in the future, comply with provisions of the Charter and that it will not commit aggressive acts against Lesotho either directly or through its proxies;

8. *Requests* the Secretary-General to monitor the implementation of the present resolution and to report regularly to the Security Council as the situation demands;

9. *Decides* to remain seized of the matter.

Mozambique and South Africa

Between August and December 1982, the Secretary-General received four letters from Mozambique and South Africa concerning relations between them. In a letter of 27 August,[1] Mozambique enclosed a communication from its Ministry of Foreign Affairs, stating that on 22 August a group of about 50 South African commandos had entered Mozambican territory near Namaacha, killed three people, kidnapped three others and destroyed property; the letter conveyed Mozambique's hope that the Secretary-General and the international community would do everything possible to prevent South Africa from repeating such actions.

Mozambique transmitted a further statement by the Ministry in a letter dated 24 November,[2] in which it warned of a threatened South African military aggression against it as evidenced by the massing of troops and military equipment along the border and a propaganda charge that Mozambique residents, on 11 November, had undertaken

an armed attack against a South African military headquarters at Komatipoort, near the border. South Africa, referring to this communication in a letter of 2 December,[4] enclosed a message to the Mozambique Government from the South African Director-General of Foreign Affairs and Information, saying South Africa had learned that acts of violence in South Africa had been planned by ANC in Mozambique and emphasizing that such acts might lead to follow-up operations with serious implications for peace.

In a letter of 9 December,[3] Mozambique said that on 6 December, a South African force had entered nine kilometres into Mozambican territory, wounding 16 men, women and children and destroying three tractors.

Letters. Mozambique: [1]27 Aug., A/37/414-S/15380; [2]24 Nov., A/37/644-S/15501; [3]9 Dec., A/38/65. [4]South Africa: 2 Dec., A/37/689-S/15506 & Corr.1.

Chad situation

The Security Council, by a resolution of 30 April 1982 adopted by consensus,[3] took note of the decision taken in June 1981 by the Organization of African Unity (OAU) to establish, in agreement with Chad, a peace-keeping force for the maintenance of peace and security in that country. The Council requested the Secretary-General to establish a fund for voluntary contributions to assist that force and to take measures to ensure the fund's management in liaison with OAU.

The resolution, which had been prepared during consultations among Council members, was adopted without discussion.

The Council's action was based on a request by OAU. The President of Kenya and OAU Chairman, in a letter to the Council President dated 2 December 1981 circulated as a Council document on 29 April 1982,[1] recalled that OAU, at the eighteenth ordinary session of its Assembly of Heads of State and Government in June 1981, had adopted a resolution calling for the establishment of a pan-African peace-keeping force for Chad. The force, drawn from Benin, Guinea, Nigeria, Senegal, Togo and Zaire, was to be joined by an observer group from Algeria, the Congo, Gabon, Guinea-Bissau, Kenya and Zambia. As OAU Chairman, he requested the Council to assist OAU financially, materially and technically in the deployment, maintenance and operation of the force.

In a further letter to the Council President, the OAU Chairman transmitted on 31 March 1982[2] an 18 March letter from President Goukouni Weddeye of Chad supporting the steps taken by the Chairman so that the United Nations could respond favourably to the OAU request regarding its commitment to Chad.

The United Nations was also engaged in a special economic assistance programme to Chad (See ECONOMIC AND SOCIAL QUESTIONS, Chapter III) and in refugee assistance there.

Letters. Kenya: [1]2 Dec. 1981, S/15011; [2]31 Mar. 1982, S/15012.
Resolution (1982). [3]SC: 504(1982), 30 Apr., text following.
Meeting record. SC: S/PV.2358 (30 Apr.).

Security Council resolution 504(1982)

30 April 1982   Meeting 2358   Adopted by consensus

Draft prepared in consultations among Council members (S/15013).

The Security Council,
Having taken note of the letters of President Arap Moi of Kenya, current Chairman of the Organization of African Unity, dated 2 December 1981 and 31 March 1982, and of the letter of President Goukouni Weddeye of Chad dated 18 March 1982,
Bearing in mind the relevant resolutions of the General Assembly on co-operation between the United Nations and the Organization of African Unity,
1. *Takes note* of the decision of the Organization of African Unity to establish, in agreement with the Government of the Republic of Chad, a peace-keeping force for the maintenance of peace and security in Chad;
2. *Requests* the Secretary-General to establish a fund for assistance to the peace-keeping force of the Organization of African Unity in Chad, to be supplied by voluntary contributions;
3. *Requests* the Secretary-General to take the necessary measures to ensure the management of the fund in liaison with the Organization of African Unity.

Status of the Comorian island of Mayotte

The General Assembly, by a resolution of 3 December 1982,[3] reaffirmed the sovereignty of the Comoros over the island of Mayotte and invited France to honour the commitments entered into prior to the 1974 referendum on the self-determination of the Comoro Archipelago (its pre-independence name) concerning respect for the unity and territorial integrity of that Indian Ocean country. The Assembly called for the translation into practice of the wish expressed by the President of France to see a just solution to the question of Mayotte adopted as soon as possible. It invited France to pursue negotiations with the Comoros with a view to ensuring the prompt return of Mayotte to the Comoros. The United Nations Secretary-General was requested to follow developments, in conjunction with the OAU Secretary-General, and to report in 1983.

The text, introduced by the Comoros and sponsored by 19 nations, was adopted by a recorded vote of 112 to 1, with 22 abstentions.

In another resolution of 3 December, on the self-determination of peoples,[2] the Assembly took note of contacts between the Governments of the Comoros and France in the search for a just solution to the integration of Mayotte into the Comoros in accordance with past OAU and United Nations resolutions.

In a report requested by the Assembly in December 1981[5] and submitted in November 1982,[1] the Secretary-General conveyed the responses he had received from OAU, the Comoros and France to his request for information pertaining to negotiations for a settlement.

OAU forwarded a report of its *Ad Hoc* Committee of Seven on the Comorian Island of Mayotte. It included recommendations adopted by the Committee in November 1981 that contacts be established between France and OAU to consider the modalities for the return of Mayotte, that OAU member States and others provide financial and technical assistance to enable the Comoros to face its difficult situation, and that the African Group at the United Nations undertake action there to expedite the return of the island. The Committee called on France to pursue negotiations with the Comoros on that objective and rejected any attempt to resort to a referendum or other form of consultation in Mayotte, which the Committee would consider null and void.

The Comoros reported to the Secretary-General on 11 October that since the 1981 Assembly session no real progress had been made. Noting that the OAU Committee of Seven had decided to send a delegation to Paris in an effort to find a solution, it said that this had not been possible because of difficulties within OAU. For its part, the Comoros had maintained bilateral negotiations with France, including a discussion between President Ahmed Abdallah Abderemane and President François Mitterrand. The latter had said that his Government wanted a satisfactory solution but, the Comoros stated, there had been no official action to translate that intention into reality.

In its response of 13 September, also incorporated in the Secretary-General's report, France said it had embarked on a constructive dialogue with the Comoros with a view to finding a solution acceptable to all parties and the dialogue was continuing.

Speaking to the Assembly in December before it adopted the 1982 resolution, the Comoros said that, despite the fact that the Assembly had been discussing the question annually for five years, no solution was in sight. Recalling that it had been admitted to the United Nations (in 1975[4]) as a State composed of four islands, including Mayotte, the Comoros said Mayotte was part of a homogeneous culture, sharing a common language and religion with the other islands. The Comoros had chosen to negotiate and had rejected any resort to violence. In 1981 it had resumed negotiations with the new French Administration with great hopes because of the position previously expressed by the French Socialist Party on the issue. President Mitterrand had expressed to President Ahmed Abdallah his readiness to reach a satisfactory solution, and the Comoros hoped his goodwill would facilitate the search for a solution to the problem, whose persistence disturbed peace and tranquillity in the region.

France regretted that the item on Mayotte had again been proposed for the Assembly's agenda because its consideration was prejudicial to Article 2, paragraph 7, of the Charter of the United Nations, prohibiting the Organization from intervening in matters within a State's domestic jurisdiction. Furthermore, Assembly debate was unlikely to bring a just and lasting solution any closer. Such a solution must meet the wishes of the inhabitants of all the islands of the archipelago. France had embarked on a constructive dialogue with the Comoros and had just appointed a high-level envoy to study the practical problems posed for the populations concerned in developing relations between Mayotte and the archipelago's other islands. Cautioning against a hasty solution that could engender lasting conflict, France said it opposed the resolution but would continue its dialogue with the Comoros.

Gabon, one of the sponsors of the resolution adopted by the Assembly, remarked that the maintenance of Mayotte outside the national community, which could not be justified on the grounds of either geography or history, would be contrary to law because it was contrary to the will of the Comorian people. Senegal, another sponsor, believed that the two countries had undertaken to resolve the question in a spirit of mutual understanding; Senegal's Head of State, Abdou Diouf, had been working with the parties for a just and lasting solution. Also sponsoring the resolution and underlining the importance of negotiations between the parties, Zambia regretted that, despite the positive attitude displayed by the new French Government, no tangible progress had been made; the Comoros could count on Zambia's full support in efforts to find a peaceful solution and to ensure full respect for its independence, sovereignty, unity and territorial integrity.

Among those which voted in favour of the resolution, Egypt invited the parties to continue their negotiations with a view to the return of Mayotte as soon as possible, and it welcomed the measures by France to promote friendly relations and permit the movement of persons between Mayotte and the other Comorian islands. Pakistan welcomed the willingness expressed by the President of France to seek a solution and thought adoption of the resolution would help expedite negotiations.

Report. [1]S-G, A/37/147.
Resolutions (1982). GA: [2]37/43, para. 5, 3 Dec.; [3]37/65, 3 Dec., text following.

Resolutions (prior). GA: [4]3385(XXX), 12 Nov. 1975 (YUN 1975, p. 309); [5]36/105, 10 Dec. 1981 (YUN 1981, p. 224).
Meeting records. GA: General Committee, A/BUR/37/SR.1 (22 Sep.); plenary, A/37/PV.91 (3 Dec.).

General Assembly resolution 37/65

3 December 1982   Meeting 91   112-1-22 (recorded vote)

19-nation draft (A/37/L.41 and Add.1); agenda item 30.

Sponsors: Benin, Botswana, Cape Verde, Chad, Comoros, Cuba, Gabon, Gambia, Guinea-Bissau, Guyana, Lesotho, Morocco, Oman, Qatar, Senegal, Somalia, Swaziland, United Arab Emirates, Zambia.

Question of the Comorian island of Mayotte

The General Assembly,

Recalling its resolutions 1514(XV) of 14 December 1960, containing the Declaration on the Granting of Independence to Colonial Countries and Peoples, and 2621(XXV) of 12 October 1970, containing the programme of action for the full implementation of the Declaration,

Recalling also its previous resolutions, in particular resolutions 3161(XXVIII) of 14 December 1973, 3291(XXIX) of 13 December 1974, 31/4 of 21 October 1976, 32/7 of 1 November 1977, 34/69 of 6 December 1979, 35/43 of 28 November 1980 and 36/105 of 10 December 1981, in which it, *inter alia,* affirmed the unity and territorial integrity of the Comoros,

Recalling, in particular, its resolution 3385(XXX) of 12 November 1975 on the admission of the Comoros to membership in the United Nations, in which it reaffirmed the necessity of respecting the unity and territorial integrity of the Comoro Archipelago, composed of the islands of Anjouan, Grande-Comore, Mayotte and Mohéli,

Recalling further that, in accordance with the agreements signed on 15 June 1973 between the Comoros and France concerning the accession of the Comoros to independence, the results of the referendum of 22 December 1974 were to be considered on a global basis and not island by island,

Convinced that a just and lasting solution to the question of Mayotte is to be found in respect for the sovereignty, unity and territorial integrity of the Comoro Archipelago,

Bearing in mind the wish expressed by the President of the French Republic to seek actively a just solution to that problem,

Taking note of the talks opened between the Government of the Islamic Federal Republic of the Comoros and the Government of the French Republic,

Taking note of the report of the Secretary-General,

Bearing in mind the decisions of the Organization of African Unity, the Movement of Non-Aligned Countries and the Organization of the Islamic Conference concerning this question,

1. *Reaffirms* the sovereignty of the Islamic Federal Republic of the Comoros over the island of Mayotte;

2. *Invites* the Government of France to honour the commitments entered into prior to the referendum on the self-determination of the Comoro Archipelago of 22 December 1974 concerning respect for the unity and territorial integrity of the Comoros;

3. *Calls* for the translation into practice of the wish expressed by the President of the French Republic to see a just solution to the question of Mayotte adopted as soon as possible;

4. *Also invites* the Government of France to pursue actively the negotiations with the Government of the Comoros with a view to ensuring the effective and prompt return of the island of Mayotte to the Comoros;

5. *Requests* the Secretary-General of the United Nations to follow developments concerning this question, in conjunction with the Secretary-General of the Organization of African Unity, and to report thereon to the General Assembly at its thirty-eighth session;

6. *Decides* to include in the provisional agenda of its thirty-eighth session the item entitled "Question of the Comorian island of Mayotte".

Recorded vote in Assembly as follows:

In favour: Albania, Algeria, Angola, Argentina, Bahamas, Bahrain, Bangladesh, Barbados, Belize, Benin, Bhutan, Brazil, Bulgaria, Burma, Burundi, Byelorussian SSR, Cape Verde, Chad, Chile, China, Colombia, Comoros, Congo, Costa Rica, Cuba, Czechoslovakia, Democratic Kampuchea, Democratic Yemen, Djibouti, Dominican Republic, Ecuador, Egypt, El Salvador, Equatorial Guinea, Ethiopia, Fiji, Finland, Gabon, Gambia, German Democratic Republic, Ghana, Grenada, Guatemala, Guinea, Guinea-Bissau, Guyana, Haiti, Hungary, India, Indonesia, Iran, Iraq, Ivory Coast, Jamaica, Kenya, Kuwait, Lesotho, Liberia, Libyan Arab

Jamahiriya, Madagascar, Malawi, Malaysia, Maldives, Mali, Malta, Mauritania, Mexico, Mongolia, Morocco, Mozambique, Nepal, Nicaragua, Nigeria, Oman, Pakistan, Panama, Papua New Guinea, Paraguay, Peru, Philippines, Poland, Qatar, Romania, Rwanda, Sao Tome and Principe, Saudi Arabia, Senegal, Sierra Leone, Singapore, Somalia, Sri Lanka, Sudan, Suriname, Sweden, Syrian Arab Republic, Thailand, Togo, Tunisia, Turkey, Uganda, Ukrainian SSR, USSR, United Arab Emirates, United Republic of Cameroon, United Republic of Tanzania, Upper Volta, Uruguay, Vanuatu, Venezuela, Viet Nam, Yugoslavia, Zambia.

Against: France.

Abstaining: Australia, Austria, Belgium, Canada, Denmark, Germany, Federal Republic of, Greece, Iceland, Ireland, Israel, Italy, Japan, Lebanon, Luxembourg, Netherlands, New Zealand, Norway, Portugal, Spain, United Kingdom, United States, Zaire.[a]

[a]Later advised the Secretariat it had intended to vote in favour.

Ethiopia and Somalia

Somalia, in a letter to the Secretary-General dated 18 January 1982,[2] said that on the previous day Ethiopian forces had attacked the town of Buuhodle and a village in Somalia, killing at least two persons, looting and causing heavy damage in what was likely to be a prelude to a wide-scale attack supported by foreign Powers. Responding in a letter of 21 January to the Secretary-General,[1] Ethiopia denied the charges, which it described as a ploy designed with an eye to the Somali President's planned visit to the United States in March, where he would seek military hardware; Ethiopia reaffirmed its desire to live in peace with its neighbours.

Letters. [1]Ethiopia, 21 Jan., A/37/73 & Corr.1; [2]Somalia, 18 Jan., A/37/69.

Status of Malagasy islands in the Indian Ocean

On 10 December 1982,[1] the General Assembly, acting without vote on the recommendation of its Special Political Committee (SPC), decided to include in the provisional agenda of its 1983 session the question of the Malagasy islands of Glorieuses, Juan de Nova, Europa and Bassas da India.

This question, pertaining to the status of four Indian Ocean islands located to the west and north of Madagascar, had been on the Assembly's agenda each year since 1979, when the Assembly invited France to negotiate with Madagascar on the reintegration of the islands with Madagascar.[2] However, the item was not discussed in 1981[3] or 1982. On 7 December 1982, the SPC Chairman announced that, following consultations with the interested parties, in particular France and Madagascar, it had been requested that consideration of the item be deferred until 1983. SPC approved the draft decision to that effect without vote.

Decision (1982). [1]GA: 37/424, 10 Dec., text following.
Resolution (prior). [2]GA: 34/91, 12 Dec. 1979 (YUN 1979, p. 270).
Yearbook reference. [3]1981, p. 225.
Meeting records. GA: General Committee, A/BUR/37/SR.2 (22 Sep.); SPC, A/SPC/37/SR.46 (7 Dec.); plenary, A/37/PV.100 (10 Dec.).

General Assembly decision 37/424

Adopted without vote

Approved by SPC (A/37/709) without vote, 7 December (meeting 46); oral proposal by Chairman; agenda item 69.

Question of the Malagasy islands of Glorieuses, Juan de Nova, Europa and Bassas da India

At its 100th plenary meeting, on 10 December 1982, the General Assembly, on the recommendation of the Special Political Committee, decided to include in the provisional agenda of its thirty-eighth session the item entitled "Question of the Malagasy islands of Glorieuses, Juan de Nova, Europa and Bassas da India".

Armed attack against Seychelles

The Commission of Inquiry established by the Security Council on 15 December 1981[15] to investigate the mercenary aggression of 25 November 1981 against the Republic of Seychelles[17] submitted reports to the Council in March and November 1982. In both reports, the Commission said it was unable to determine precisely the origin of the aggression, but it concluded that the attack was aimed at overthrowing the Government and that South African intelligence and army personnel had been involved in preparatory discussions. After receiving the first report, the Council adopted a resolution on 28 May condemning the aggression and the use of mercenaries to overthrow Governments. It appealed for assistance to Seychelles.

Report of the Commission of Inquiry (March). The Commission, composed of Ireland, Japan and Panama, first reported to the Council on 15 March,[11] following visits to Seychelles (24-30 January), Swaziland (30 January–3 February) and South Africa (3-6 February). While in Seychelles, on 27 January, it interviewed individually the seven mercenaries being held in custody following the attack.

In its findings and conclusions, the Commission said it did not have full knowledge of the origin and background of the aggression, as it had not been able to interview the mercenaries who had returned to South Africa, particularly their leader, Michael Hoare. Nevertheless, it was able to draw conclusions, assess the damage and make recommendations.

It determined that the object of the aggression had been to overthrow the Seychelles Government and, it appeared, to install James Mancham as Head of State. The leader of the mercenaries, numbering over 50, had led earlier mercenary operations in Africa. He had been in contact with Seychelles exiles in South Africa and in London, and had recruited the participants and planned the attempt in South Africa. A number of Seychellois living in exile had intended to charter an aircraft to fly immediately to Seychelles from Kenya if the mercenaries succeeded in taking over the islands.

Given the tight control exercised by security forces in South Africa, the Commission found it difficult to believe that the South African authorities did not at least have knowledge of the preparations for the attack, despite statements by the South African Prime Minister to the contrary. On the basis of information available to it at the time of the report, however, the Commission could not reach a definitive conclusion on the extent or level of South African knowledge or responsibility. It believed that the mercenaries had used Swaziland merely as a means of transit to Seychelles and that the Government of Swaziland had had no knowledge of the aggression until afterwards. As regards statements that armed personnel were ready to fly from Kenya to Seychelles if the coup had been successful, the Commission said Kenya had denied any involvement in the attempt.

The Government of Seychelles had estimated that it would cost about $1.28 million to repair or replace damaged installations or equipment at Seychelles International Airport, where the attack took place. The most severe impact on the economy was likely to be caused by a fall in income from tourism, which normally provided about 70 per cent of the country's foreign exchange earnings. Assuming an 18 per cent decline in the number of tourists, the Government anticipated a total loss of about $16.7 million. However, the Commission thought it difficult to make a definitive assessment of long-term economic damage.

The Commission made the following recommendations:

"1. The Commission endorses the view of the Government of Seychelles that the reconstruction of the airport would constitute a serious burden on the economy. This is at a time when there has been a serious diminution of earnings from the tourism sector. The Commission recommends that financial, technical and material assistance should be provided urgently by Member States and international organizations to enable the country to deal with the difficulties it is facing because of the mercenary aggression. Such contributions could be channelled through an appropriate fund. Without wishing to prejudge any decision in this regard, the Commission notes that there is a special account for Seychelles in the United Nations Trust Fund for Special Economic Assistance Programmes which is already in existence and through which, should donors wish, assistance could be channelled.

2. As the possibility of aggression by mercenaries remains a grave threat to the sovereignty and independence of States, particularly small developing countries, the Commission recommends that the work at present under way on an international convention

against the recruitment, use, financing and training of mercenaries be brought to a speedy conclusion so that the convention may be opened for signature as soon as possible.

3. The Commission also wishes to recommend that States, and the international community as a whole, should make every effort to prevent mercenary operations, having regard to the grave threat which these operations pose particularly to small island States with limited resources, such as the Republic of Seychelles.

4. In this effort and in co-operating towards the prevention of mercenary activities, Governments and Member States having information related to mercenary activities should, without delay, communicate such information directly or through the Secretary-General of the United Nations to Governments concerned.

5. It is also the view of the Commission that ICAO [International Civil Aviation Organization] should, in the light of the apparent ease with which weapons can be transported in checked baggage on commercial airlines, give further consideration to preventive measures, while taking into account the wish of Governments to facilitate tourism.

6. Should the Security Council so desire, the Commission might be authorized to furnish a supplementary report in due course containing any further information relative to its mandate."

Various documents were annexed to the Commission's report, including reports of the Seychelles Police Commissioner and the Seychelles Acting Director of Civil Aviation, Seychelles Government papers on economic damage, a list of the mercenaries' names, a transcript of the Commission's hearings of the captured mercenaries and a list of captured weapons and ammunition.

The Commission was to have submitted its report by 31 January, according to the resolution establishing it. However, the date was extended to early March at the request of its Chairman, who cited the delay caused by the complexity of preparatory work prior to its departure for the area. The extension was announced in a note of 27 January by the Council President,[8] who said that Council members had been consulted informally and that none had any objection.

Communications (May). By a letter of 6 May to the Secretary-General,[2] Seychelles forwarded an article published in *The New York Times* of 4 May which said that Colonel Hoare had testified that the South African Government had approved the attempted coup and supplied weapons for it. Seychelles later forwarded, in a letter to the Secretary-General of 10 May,[3] an article of that date from the same newspaper describing the mercenary leader's further testimony during his trial on charges of hijacking the Air India jetliner used in the November 1981 attack.

Romania, in a letter and annexed note of 14 May 1982 to the Council President,[1] stated that press agency statements purporting to establish that mercenaries employed by South Africa had obtained Romanian-made weapons were contrary to its policy of strict observance of the arms embargo against South Africa.

In a letter to the Council President dated 28 May,[7] Swaziland transmitted a statement by the Chairman of the Board of Directors of the Royal Swazi National Airline, Sishayi Nxumalo, at a meeting of the African Airline Association (Addis Ababa, Ethiopia, 5-8 April), and a resolution adopted by the Association. After Mr. Nxumalo described how the mercenaries had flown to Seychelles on a regularly scheduled Royal Swazi flight by posing as tourists, the Association resolved to urge African Governments to ratify international aircraft security conventions and to call on competent authorities to prevent such occurrences.

Security Council action. By a resolution adopted unanimously on 28 May,[13] the Security Council strongly condemned the mercenary aggression against Seychelles and the illegal acts against the security and safety of civil aviation committed there. Reaffirming a 1967 resolution on mercenaries[14] (adopted on a complaint by the Democratic Republic of the Congo, now Zaire), it condemned all external interference in the internal affairs of Member States, including the use of mercenaries to destabilize States and/or to violate their territorial integrity, sovereignty and independence. The Council called on States to provide it with information on the aggression, in particular transcripts of court proceedings. It mandated its Commission of Inquiry to examine further developments and present by 15 August a supplementary report with recommendations, taking into account the evidence and testimony presented at trials of any member of the invading force. In addition, the Council called for economic and technical assistance for Seychelles (See ECONOMIC AND SOCIAL QUESTIONS, Chapter III).

The resolution, sponsored by Guyana, Jordan, Panama, Togo, Uganda and Zaire, was adopted after discussion of the Commission's report at five meetings. Togo, introducing the text, said it had been drafted and co-sponsored by all the non-aligned members of the Council and had taken into account 11 of the 12 amendments offered by other members.

During the discussion, held from 20 to 28 May, the Council invited the following countries, at their request, to participate without the right to vote: Afghanistan, Algeria, Angola, Argentina, Bangladesh, Barbados, Benin, Botswana, Bulgaria, Cuba, Czechoslovakia, Egypt, German Democratic Republic, Grenada, Honduras, Hungary, India, Kenya, Lao People's Democratic Republic, Libyan Arab Jamahiriya, Madagasar, Maldives, Mali, Malta, Mauritius, Mongolia, Mozambique, Nicaragua, Nigeria, Pakistan, Sao Tome and Principe, Seychelles, Sri Lanka, Swaziland, Syrian Arab Republic, United Republic of Tanzania, Viet Nam, Yugoslavia, Zambia.

Panama, which introduced the report as Commission Chairman, said that the work of the Commission had not been concluded and that further significant information had become available since the report was issued, in particular statements during the trial of Mr. Hoare. If the Council saw fit to authorize a supplementary report, the Commission would be prepared to make one.

The Minister for Foreign Affairs of Seychelles said Seychelles could not be fully satisfied with the Commission's report until the origin, background and financing of the aggression, which could have been planned only with the complicity of foreign authorities, had been established. Mr. Hoare's statement to the South African court had implicated the régime at the highest levels, and the complete transcript of the trial should enable the Commission to prepare a supplementary report. The trial of the seven mercenaries in custody in Seychelles would begin on 16 June and a full transcript would be sent to the Commission. Remarking that the losses suffered by the Seychelles economy would seriously affect its development, he expressed the hope that the Council would: appeal to States to provide assistance to Seychelles to enable it to deal with problems arising from the aggression, call for the speedy drafting of an international convention on mercenaries and extend the Commission's mandate to enable it to complete its inquiry upon completion of the trials in South Africa and Seychelles.

During the Council's debate, most speakers reiterated their condemnation of the mercenary attack and praised the Commission for its work. Several States—Barbados, Benin, Egypt (speaking on behalf of the African Group), Guyana, Mongolia, Mozambique, Nicaragua, Spain, Sri Lanka, the United Kingdom, Zaire and Zambia—specifically endorsed the Commission's recommendations, and others mentioned particular proposals they supported. Poland said it understood the Commission's cautious and dispassionate approach to sensitive issues, but Poland would have wished it to be less circumspect in some of its findings and conclusions.

Most speakers believed that, according to the evidence, South Africa was responsible for or at least involved in the aggression against Seychelles. This was the view of Afghanistan, Algeria, Angola, Bangladesh, Benin, Bulgaria, China, Cuba, Czechoslovakia, Egypt (for the African Group), the German Democratic Republic, Guyana, Hungary, India, Jordan, Kenya, the Lao People's Democratic Republic, the Libyan Arab Jamahiriya, Madagascar, Malta, Mongolia, Nicaragua, Nigeria, Pakistan, Poland, Sao Tome and Principe, the Syrian Arab Republic, Togo, Uganda, the USSR, the United Republic of Tanzania, Viet Nam, Yugoslavia and Zambia.

The Minister for Foreign Affairs of Botswana, speaking as Chairman of the Council of Ministers of the Organization of African Unity (OAU), said that the holding of regular planning meetings of the mercenaries in South Africa, the assembling of exotic military hardware, the issuance of passports under false names, the use of a firing range to test weapons, and the ease with which such a large body of men passed through customs, immigration and security without being searched inspired incredulity about South Africa's protestation that it had not initiated, approved or known about the attempted coup.

Speaking for the African Group, Egypt cited six elements which led it to the same conclusion: the refusal of South Africa to permit the Commission to interview the mercenaries who had returned there, the fact that planning and recruitment for the attack had taken place in South Africa, the presence of a South African intelligence officer among the mercenaries, the testimony of Mr. Hoare that the South African intelligence service had known about the plan and that the South African Defence Force had supplied men for it, the refusal of the Speaker of South Africa's Parliament to allow a special debate on the issue, and South Africa's release of 39 of the mercenaries.

Several countries, including Algeria, Angola, Bangladesh, Benin, Cuba, Czechoslovakia, Hungary, Pakistan, Uganda, the United Republic of Tanzania and Zambia, held that the attack was part of a pattern of activities aimed at destabilizing the Governments of the region.

Thus, China mentioned reports that South Africa had been motivated by the need for a strategic outpost in the Indian Ocean to facilitate its aggression and expansion. Jordan remarked that the attack, intended to undermine the independence of Seychelles, by a powerful country against a small one, constituted a dangerous and ominous precedent. In Uganda's view, the objectives of South Africa were to weaken the economies of neighbouring countries so as to make them dependent on South Africa, and to intimidate African Governments with a view to undermining their support for liberation movements.

Others, including Afghanistan, Bulgaria, the German Democratic Republic, the Libyan Arab Jamahiriya, Mongolia, Mozambique, Sao Tome and Principe, and Viet Nam, described the mercenary attack as part of a wider scheme by imperialists, colonialists or reactionaries with that intention. Afghanistan added that the statements by Mr. Hoare had erased any doubt about the direct United States and South African involvement. In Bulgaria's view, aggression against Seychelles could not be dissociated from the intensification of the military presence in the Indian Ocean of certain imperialist Powers.

Mozambique said the attempt to overthrow the Seychelles Government was part of the strategic plans of the United States and some of its allies to extend the seige of the Indian Ocean countries and to secure certain shipping routes for themselves. The Syrian Arab Republic believed the aggression should be considered in the wider strategic context, for it coincided with the activation of the United States rapid deployment forces in the area from South Africa to the Middle East. The USSR described the aggression as another manifestation of the policy of international terrorism directed by imperialist circles against States that had embarked on the road of independent national development.

China, Nicaragua and the United Republic of Tanzania believed the Council should condemn South Africa for its role in the invasion. According to Angola, the Council should take a strong position on action intended to destabilize Governments which opposed *apartheid*. The Lao People's Democratic Republic said failure by the Council to condemn South Africa would only encourage it and its accomplices to commit similar acts in the future. Madagascar said it was not opposed to having the Council declare that South Africa was involved in the planning and execution of the invasion, that the régime bore responsibility and that it should be condemned for its aggression against Seychelles. In Yugoslavia's view, the Council should react to the two crimes—the aggression and the hijacking—and make South Africa obey the norms of international behaviour.

Bangladesh, Bulgaria, China, Czechoslovakia, Grenada, Mozambique, Nicaragua, Pakistan, Poland, the Syrian Arab Republic, Togo, the USSR and Yugoslavia condemned the aggression as a violation of the Charter of the United Nations, as contrary to international law or as a threat to international peace and security.

Most speakers condemned the threat posed by mercenaries to the independence and stability of States, especially small ones. France stated that, under international law, States must refrain from financing, encouraging or tolerating armed subversive activities aimed at changing by violence the régime of another State; a State failing to do so would be required to redress the consequences of unlawful action it had committed or incited. Nigeria considered mercenaries to pose a serious threat to the sovereignty and integrity of African States, and said they should be collectively condemned by all Members of the United Nations. The United Republic of Tanzania thought nations should denounce the concept of mercenarism as a crime against humanity, while Zaire and others regarded it as a crime against the peace and security of mankind.

Among the proposals that received wide support from countries addressing the Council was the recommendation for the early conclusion of an international convention against the recruitment, use, financing and training of mercenaries (See LEGAL QUESTIONS, Chapter II). Afghanistan, Algeria, Bangladesh, Barbados, Benin, Botswana (for the OAU Council of Ministers), Bulgaria, China, Czechoslovakia, France, the German Democratic Republic, Grenada, Guyana, India, Ireland, Jordan, Kenya, the Libyan Arab Jamahiriya, Malta, Mauritius, Mongolia, Nicaragua, Nigeria, Pakistan, Poland, Sao Tome and Principe, Spain, the Syrian Arab Republic, Togo, Uganda, the USSR, the United States, Viet Nam, Yugoslavia, Zaire and Zambia mentioned the need for such a convention.

Grenada called for harsh measures for those involved with mercenaries, and it urged the United Nations to make an inventory of individuals and groups that supported, equipped, hired, trained or encouraged mercenarism. Malta believed the Council should study recommendations to guard against a repetition of such actions, and it suggested that States take steps to prevent mercenary operations and alert both the Council and the Governments concerned if any such preparations were suspected or discovered. Similarly, Sao Tome and Principe suggested that data on mercenaries be centralized and disseminated.

Argentina said the Council must make every effort to avoid the repetition of such events which, with a view to financial profit, combined two acts condemned by the United Nations—intervention in the internal affairs of States and an attempt to re-establish colonial situations. Stressing the vulnerability of small States to mercenary attacks, Barbados said it was aware that some delegations would prefer that a convention not be concluded, and it appealed to all countries to safeguard the principle of sovereign equality by taking action to eliminate mercenary activity by their nationals and from within their borders. Benin likened the incident in Seychelles to a mercenary attack in 1977 against Cotonou, Benin.[16] Ireland observed that, if the international community could not give small States some assurance of security and deal with the causes of insecurity, they would have to divert to military defence purposes scarce resources needed for development.

Maldives warned of a dire threat to the international community if it failed to take appropriate action to curb mercenary activities. In addition to co-operating in drafting an international convention on mercenaries, Spain said, the international community should adopt measures of all kinds so that mercenary forces could not continue

to disrupt the peaceful development of nations. Sri Lanka believed that the international community should safeguard the right of small independent countries to exist without fear of being subjugated by ambitious nations and should eradicate the threat posed by mercenaries to such States.

Most speakers—Algeria, Angola, Bangladesh, Benin, Botswana (for the OAU Council of Ministers), China, Egypt (for the African Group), France, Grenada, Guyana, India, Ireland, Jordan, Kenya, the Lao People's Democratic Republic, the Libyan Arab Jamahiriya, Madagascar, Maldives, Malta, Mauritius, Mozambique, Nicaragua, Pakistan, Spain, Swaziland, Togo, Uganda, the United Republic of Tanzania, the United States, Viet Nam, Yugoslavia, Zaire and Zambia—supported the idea of special assistance for Seychelles to help it recover from damage suffered during the attack. Algeria, Bangladesh, Czechoslovakia, the German Democratic Republic, Hungary, Mongolia and Yugoslavia, which held South Africa responsible for the attack, believed that it should pay for the damage it had caused.

In addition to supporting the establishment of a voluntary fund for this purpose, France said it would be willing to play a special role in this regard. Nicaragua and Nigeria expressed readiness to assist Seychelles economically. The United Kingdom said it had decided to provide 1.5 million pounds of financial assistance and the United Republic of Tanzania said it was ready to make a modest contribution.

Another proposal of the Commission that received wide support was the call to have it prepare a supplementary report with further information on the origin and background of the aggression. Afghanistan, Algeria, Angola, Bangladesh, Benin, Botswana (for the OAU Council of Ministers), Bulgaria, Egypt (for the African Group), Guyana, Hungary, India, Jordan, Kenya, the Lao People's Democratic Republic, the Libyan Arab Jamahiriya, Madagascar, Malta, Mauritius, Mongolia, Nicaragua, Pakistan, Poland, Sao Tome and Principe, Spain, Swaziland, the Syrian Arab Republic, Togo, Uganda, the USSR, the United Kingdom, the United Republic of Tanzania, the United States, Zaire and Zambia concurred with the proposal that the Commission issue a supplementary report which would include information revealed during the trials of the mercenaries held in Seychelles and South Africa.

Angola, Bangladesh, Bulgaria, Czechoslovakia, Guyana, Hungary, India, Kenya, the Lao People's Democratic Republic, Maldives, Mauritius, Mongolia, Pakistan, the Syrian Arab Republic, Uganda and Viet Nam remarked that the initial report was incomplete; many of them said this was due to the failure of the South African authorities to co-operate with the Commission by allowing it to interview the mercenaries being held there. Botswana (for the OAU Council of Ministers), the Libyan Arab Jamahiriya and Zaire suggested that the Council seek South Africa's co-operation in the Commission's inquiry by making trial testimony available and permitting the Commission to interview the detained mercenaries.

Algeria stated that the continuation of the Commission's activities would enable the Council to place international responsibility on those who were the source of the aggression. Having served as a member of the Commission, Japan said that, in view of Mr. Hoare's recent testimony during his trial in South Africa (see above), the Commission's reservations had been fully vindicated; it added that information made available since the report was issued should be closely examined and ambiguities regarding the financing of the attack clarified. The United States, while not opposing an extension of the Commission's mandate for a fixed period, expressed doubts that a further report would prove any more conclusive than the first one because the Commission lacked the powers and competence of a court of law.

Referring to the hijacking of an Air India aircraft by the mercenaries following the failure of their Seychelles raid, India said the incident demonstrated the vulnerability of innocent civilians to terrorism and added that it would continue to work towards a convention against terrorism. Swaziland estimated that it had suffered a $2.5-million loss as a result of the disabling of the Air Swazi aircraft on which the mercenaries had flown in to carry out their abortive coup; it noted the Commission's finding that the Swaziland Government had had no foreknowledge of the attack. Togo suggested that, pending the conclusion of a convention against mercenary activities, the Council should constrain South Africa to hand over the mercenaries who had taken refuge in South Africa to the Seychelles authorities, who had promised to try them under international safeguards.

Speaking after the resolution was adopted, the United States said it shared the concern generally expressed in the Council, and it believed that the proceedings had served an important purpose in signalling that the international community would neither tolerate nor condone any form of external interference, including the use of mercenaries, in the internal affairs of sovereign States.

Communications (June-November). Seychelles, by a letter to the Secretary-General of 17 June,[4] forwarded an article published in *The New York Times* that day, in which it was reported that the South African judge trying 43 mercenaries accused of hijacking an airliner after the coup attempt in Seychelles had agreed to a request by

South Africa's Defence Minister that some evidence should not be heard because it could prejudice state security.

By a letter of 24 June to the Security Council President,[6] South Africa forwarded an article published in the Johannesburg *Rand Daily Mail* two days earlier, which said that, in sworn affidavits, mercenaries awaiting trial for treason in Seychelles had alleged they were maltreated while in custody.

Addressing the Council President in a letter dated 2 November,[5] Seychelles said that, if external attempts to destabilize economically and to overthrow its Government continued, it reserved the right to request an immediate convening of the Council.

Further work of the Commission of Inquiry. The Commission of Inquiry on the aggression against Seychelles submitted its supplementary report to the Council on 17 November.[12]

The report was based largely on court records of trials of mercenaries in Seychelles and South Africa, which those Governments had made available in response to the Commission's request. The trial in the Supreme Court of Seychelles (16 June–5 July), on charges of treason, resulted in guilty verdicts for five defendants and death sentences for four of them; the case against two others was not pursued. The trial in the Supreme Court of South Africa, Natal Provincial Division, Pietermaritzburg, at which 45 men were charged with hijacking and other interference with a civil aircraft, concluded on 27 July with a judgement of guilty against 42 of the defendants and acquittal of one; charges against two others had been withdrawn after they turned State's witness. Prison sentences ranged from 5 years (of which all but 6 months were suspended) to 20 years (10 years suspended).

The Commission, in its findings and conclusions, noted three limitations on the value of the trials as a source of information: in the South African trial, on hijacking charges, information relevant to the Commission's mandate had emerged only incidentally; some witnesses in that trial had been restricted in their testimony by the courts for security reasons; and a considerable amount of the additional information relevant to the Commission's mandate derived from Mr. Hoare's testimony, much of which had not been corroborated by other witnesses. Furthermore, the Commission had not had the opportunity of questioning any of the mercenaries in South Africa, in particular Mr. Hoare.

The Commission said it still did not have full knowledge of the background of the mercenary aggression, but it had reason to believe there had been contacts between three mercenaries and Seychelles exiles since 1977 with a view to overthrowing the Government. It made five findings regarding South African involvement which it considered clearly established: *(a)* The arms, ammunition and other equipment had been supplied by South African Defence Force personnel; *(b)* An army officer had participated in the preliminary discussions; *(c)* The Government had been generally aware of attempts by Seychelles exiles seeking support to overthrow the Government; *(d)* The South African National Intelligence Service had been aware of the plans from their inception; and *(e)* Members of the Second Reconnaissance Commando, an élite unit, had taken part in the operation. The Commission added that, given the nature of intelligence and military operations and the Commission's lack of information, it was not in a position to determine the full extent and responsibility of South African officials.

The report said Seychelles exiles had financed the operation. It estimated that the expenses would have amounted to $750,000 if the operation had been successful, but the actual expenditure of which it had knowledge did not exceed $200,000.

Referring to a statement on 29 July by the Prime Minister of South Africa that neither the South African Government, the Cabinet nor the State Security Council had been aware of the attempted coup, the Commission concluded that, if responsible ministers had not been at least aware of what was going on, that indicated both a remarkable lack of control by the Government over its own agencies and a lack of awareness that was hard to reconcile with the tight control exercised by the security authorities in South Africa.

Concerning allegations of involvement by other Governments, the Commission said it did not have enough evidence to come to any conclusions.

Reaffirming the recommendations of its March report, the Commission again stressed the need to bring to a speedy conclusion the work under way on an international convention against the recruitment, use, financing and training of mercenaries. It stressed as well that States should make every effort to prevent mercenary operations, in particular by communicating to Governments concerned any information they might have regarding possible mercenary activities. The Commission considered that South Africa had a particular obligation to take all necessary steps to ensure that mercenary operations were not launched from its territory. Noting the continuing adverse effects of the mercenary aggression against Seychelles, the Commission called attention to the appeal for contributions made by the *Ad Hoc* Committee established by the Council to administer the Special Fund for Seychelles.

The submission date of the Commission's supplementary report, set by the Council at 15 August, was twice extended by the Council at the Commission's request so that it could receive and study the record of evidence and testimony at the two trials. The first extension, to 31 October, was approved on 13 August,[9] and the second, to mid-November, on 31 October.[10] In both cases the decision was made in informal consultations, with no Council member objecting, and was announced in notes by the President.

Letters. [1]Romania: 14 May, S/15080. Seychelles: [2]6 May, S/15056; [3]10 May, S/15065; [4]17 June, S/15236; [5]2 Nov., S/15477. [6]South Africa: 24 June, S/15257. [7]Swaziland: 28 May, S/15135.
Notes. SC President, [8]S/14850, [9]S/15359, [10]S/15473.
Reports. Commission of Inquiry, [11]S/14905/Rev.1, [12]S/15492/Rev.1.
Resolution (1982). [13]SC: 507(1982), 28 May, text following.
Resolutions (prior). SC: [14]239(1967), 10 July 1967 (YUN 1967, p. 130); [15]496(1981), 15 Dec. 1981 (YUN 1981, p. 227).
Yearbook references. [16]1977, p. 207; [17]1981, p. 226.
Meeting records. SC: S/PV.2359 & Corr.1, 2361, 2365, 2367 & Corr.1, 2370 (20-28 May).

Security Council resolution 507(1982)

28 May 1982   Meeting 2370   Adopted unanimously

6-nation draft (S/15127).

Sponsors: Guyana, Jordan, Panama, Togo, Uganda, Zaire.

The Security Council,
Having examined the report of the Security Council Commission of Inquiry established under resolution 496(1981),
Gravely concerned at the violation of the territorial integrity, independence and sovereignty of the Republic of Seychelles,
Deeply grieved at the loss of life and substantial damage to property caused by the mercenary invading force during its attack on the Republic of Seychelles on 25 November 1981,
Gravely concerned at the mercenary aggression against the Republic of Seychelles, prepared in and executed from South Africa,
Deeply concerned at the danger which mercenaries represent for all States, particularly the small and weak ones, and for the stability and independence of African States,
Concerned at the long-term effects of the mercenary aggression of 25 November 1981 on the economy of the Republic of Seychelles,
Reiterating resolution 496(1981), in which it affirms that the territorial integrity and political independence of the Republic of Seychelles must be respected,
1. *Takes note* of the report of the Security Council Commission of Inquiry established under resolution 496(1981) and expresses its appreciation for the work accomplished;
2. *Strongly condemns* the mercenary aggression against the Republic of Seychelles;
3. *Commends* the Republic of Seychelles for successfully repulsing the mercenary aggression and defending its territorial integrity and independence;
4. *Reaffirms* its resolution 239(1967) by which, *inter alia,* it condemns any State which persists in permitting or tolerating the recruitment of mercenaries and the provision of facilities to them, with the objective of overthrowing the Governments of Member States;
5. *Condemns* all forms of external interference in the internal affairs of Member States, including the use of mercenaries to destabilize States and/or to violate the territorial integrity, sovereignty and independence of States;
6. *Further condemns* the illegal acts against the security and safety of civil aviation committed in the Republic of Seychelles on 25 November 1981;
7. *Calls upon* all States to provide the Security Council with any information they might have in connection with the mercenary aggression of 25 November 1981 likely to throw further light on the agression, in particular transcripts of court proceedings and testimony in any trial of any member of the invading mercenary force;
8. *Appeals* to all States and international organizations, including the specialized agencies of the United Nations, to assist the Republic of Seychelles to repair the damage caused by the act of mercenary aggression;

9. *Decides* to establish, by 5 June 1982, a special fund for the Republic of Seychelles, to be supplied by voluntary contributions, through which assistance should be channelled for economic reconstruction;

10. *Decides* to establish an *ad hoc* committee, before the end of May 1982, composed of four members of the Security Council, to be chaired by France, to co-ordinate and mobilize resources for the Special Fund established under paragraph 9 of the present resolution, for immediate disbursement to the Republic of Seychelles;

11. *Requests* the Secretary-General to provide all necessary assistance to the *Ad Hoc* Committee for the implementation, in particular, of paragraphs 8, 9 and 10 of the present resolution;

12. *Decides* to mandate the Commission of Inquiry to examine all further developments and present by 15 August 1982 a supplementary report, with appropriate recommendations, which should take into account, *inter alia*, the evidence and testimony presented at any trial of any member of the invading mercenary force;

13. *Requests* the Secretary-General to provide all necessary assistance for the implementation of the present resolution and paragraph 12 above;

14. *Decides* to remain seized of the question.

UN Educational and Training Programme for Southern Africa

A total of 1,042 persons held scholarships under the United Nations Educational and Training Programme for Southern Africa during the year ended 30 September 1982, according to a report by the Secretary-General to the General Assembly.[1] The largest number, 613, were from South Africa (p. 308). Another 271 were from Zimbabwe, and 135 were from Namibia (See TRUSTEESHIP AND DECOLONIZATION, Chapter III). The remainder of the recipients were from countries which had been under Portuguese administration prior to independence: 16 from Guinea-Bissau, 4 from Sao Tome and Principe, 2 from Cape Verde and 1 from Mozambique. The studies covered a wide variety of professional, cultural, technical and linguistic disciplines, particularly in the areas of development and international co-operation.

The number of new scholarship awards made under the Programme during the 12-month period totalled 229, of which 205 went to South Africans and 24 to Namibians. Of the latter, 14 were financed by the United Nations Fund for Namibia (see above). While the Programme continued previously granted scholarships to persons from newly independent countries, new awards were being made only to Namibians and South Africans.

Of the 827 award-holders from years prior to the 1982/83 academic year, and including the 14 financed for that year by the Fund for Namibia, 394 of the scholarships were for study in African institutions (Algeria, Botswana, Congo, Egypt, Ethiopia, Ghana, Kenya, Lesotho, Liberia, Mauritius, Mozambique, Nigeria, Senegal, Sierra Leone, Swaziland, Uganda, United Republic of Tanzania, Zambia, Zimbabwe). Of the rest, 261 were for North America (Canada, Grenada, Mexico, Montserrat, United States), 98 for Europe (Cyprus, France, Ireland, Norway, Portugal, Spain, Sweden, Switzerland,

United Kingdom) and 74 for Asia (India, Pakistan).

Thirty-one States contributed a total of $3,235,612 to the Programme in 1982 (see table below). This was less than the $3,593,954 received in 1981,[3] a decrease accentuated by inflation and rising scholarship costs. In addition, 22 States offered scholarships for training in their institutions. To ensure financial stability for the Programme, its 13-member Advisory Committee, suggested that the Programme's reserve fund be strengthened so as to cushion it against a decline in contributions and a sudden increase in scholarship costs.

CONTRIBUTIONS TO THE UN EDUCATIONAL AND TRAINING
PROGRAMME FOR SOUTHERN AFRICA, 1982
(as at 31 December 1982; in US dollars)

Country	1982 payments
Argentina	4,093
Austria	34,500
Bahamas	500
Brazil	5,000
Burma	1,000
Canada	289,256
Cyprus	225
Denmark	379,747
Finland	88,086
France	95,000
Germany, Federal Republic of	72,340
Greece	9,000
Indonesia	3,000
Iraq	10,000
Ireland	19,385
Italy	1,942
Japan	180,000
Malaysia	1,000
Mali	309
Netherlands	178,779
New Zealand	11,826
Norway	711,864
Philippines	2,000
Spain	40,000
Suriname	1,000
Sweden	313,043
Thailand	1,000
Togo	31
United Kingdom	11,098
United States	750,000
Zambia	20,588
Total	3,235,612

SOURCE: Interim United Nations financial statements for the 12-month period ended 31 December 1982—Individual trust funds (unpublished).

General Assembly action. Acting on the recommendation of its Fourth Committee, the General Assembly adopted a resolution on 23 November 1982[2] in which it endorsed the Secretary-General's report on the Programme, commended him and the Advisory Committee for their efforts to promote contributions, and expressed appreciation to those that had supported the Programme by providing contributions, scholarships or places in their educational institutions. The Assembly noted with concern that, owing to inflation and rising scholarship costs, contributions and pledges had declined in real terms. It appealed to States, institutions, organizations and individuals to offer greater financial and other support to the Programme in order to ensure its continuation and expansion.

The Assembly adopted the text without vote after its Fourth Committee approved the 39-nation draft, introduced by Canada, in the same manner on 16 November.

Report.[1]S-G,A/37/436.
Resolution (1982). [2]GA: 37/33, 23 Nov., text following.
Yearbook reference. [3]1981, p. 1117.
Meeting records. GA: 4th Committee, A/C.4/37/SR.9-11, *13,* 14, 18-23, *24* (26 Oct.–16 Nov.); plenary, A/37/PV.77 (23 Nov.).

General Assembly resolution 37/33

23 November 1982   Meeting 77   Adopted without vote

Approved by Fourth Committee (A/37/626) without vote, 16 November (meeting 24); 39-nation draft (A/C.4/37/L.7); agenda item 100.

Sponsors: Australia, Austria, Bangladesh, Barbados, Botswana, Byelorussian SSR, Canada, Cyprus, Denmark, Egypt, Finland, France, Germany, Federal Republic of, Greece, Guinea, Guyana, Haiti, India, Indonesia, Ireland, Japan, Lesotho, Liberia, Mali, Netherlands, Nigeria, Norway, Senegal, Sudan, Sweden, Syrian Arab Republic, Trinidad and Tobago, Tunisia, Turkey, United Republic of Tanzania, Venezuela, Zaire, Zambia, Zimbabwe.

United Nations Educational and Training Programme for Southern Africa

The General Assembly,

Recalling its resolutions on the United Nations Educational and Training Programme for Southern Africa, in particular resolution 36/53 of 24 November 1981,

Having considered the report of the Secretary-General, containing an account of the work of the Advisory Committee on the United Nations Educational and Training Programme for Southern Africa and the operation of the Programme for the period from 1 October 1981 to 30 September 1982,

Recognizing the valuable assistance rendered by the Programme to the peoples of South Africa and Namibia,

Strongly convinced that the continuation and expansion of the Programme is essential in order to meet the increasing demand for educational and training opportunities by the peoples of South Africa and Namibia,

Fully recognizing the need to provide educational opportunities and counselling to student refugees in a wide variety of professional, cultural, technical and linguistic disciplines, particularly in the areas of development and international co-operation,

1. *Endorses* the report of the Secretary-General on the United Nations Educational and Training Programme for Southern Africa;

2. *Commends* the Secretary-General and the Advisory Committee on the United Nations Educational and Training Programme for Southern Africa for their continued efforts to promote generous contributions to the Programme;

3. *Expresses its appreciation* to all those that have supported the Programme by providing contributions, scholarships or places in their educational institutions;

4. *Notes with concern* that, owing to inflation and rising scholarship costs, contributions and pledges have declined, in real terms, in 1982 from the corresponding figure in 1981;

5. *Appeals* to all States, institutions, organizations and individuals to offer greater financial and other support to the Programme in order to ensure its continuation and expansion.

Co-operation between the United Nations and the Organization of African Unity

In 1982, co-operation continued in a number of political and economic areas between the United Nations and the Organization of African Unity (OAU), and the General Assembly again called for a strengthening of co-operative activities between the two organizations.

Report of the Secretary-General. The Secretary-General, in reports to the Assembly in August and September,[9] reviewed co-operation in five areas: a Meeting between representatives of the OAU General Secretariat and the secretariats of the United Nations system, consultations and information exchange, the situation in southern Africa, economic and social development, and information and publicity. The second report also gave highlights of assistance rendered to African countries by the United Nations system.

The Meeting between the OAU General Secretariat and the secretariats of 31 organizations or major units in the United Nations system, one of an annual series, was held from 6 to 8 April at Geneva. The participants made recommendations on activities in connection with the Lagos Plan of Action for the Implementation of the Monrovia Strategy for the Economic Development of Africa, adopted by OAU at Lagos, Nigeria, in 1980 as the major framework for the continent's development plans (See ECONOMIC AND SOCIAL QUESTIONS, Chapter VIII). Other topics of recommendations were the newly established Pan-African Documentation and Information System, desertification control, the regional seas programme of the United Nations Environment Programme, the critical food situation in Africa and assistance to refugees in Africa.

The Secretary-General's September report described the work of 19 United Nations organizations and programmes and Secretariat units co-operating with OAU in regard to the southern Africa situation, including such activities as publicizing work on human rights, contacts with national liberation movements on development projects and other matters, legal assistance, the anti-*apartheid* campaign for the imposition of mandatory sanctions against South Africa, humanitarian assistance to refugees and agricultural assistance. A mission from the United Nations Industrial Development Organization visited the OAU Committee on National Liberation Movements at Dar es Salaam, United Republic of Tanzania, in March to brief it on proposals for technical assistance projects to the movements, formulated in consultation with them.

Co-operation on economic and social development included such activities as: strengthening links between the information services of OAU and the Economic Commission for Africa; research and planning in geology, cartography, energy, agriculture and industry; assistance in environment programmes, housing and infrastructure, child health care and education; and assistance to African refugees. The United Nations Conference on Trade and Development (UNCTAD) consulted with OAU in January 1982 to integrate the latter's views into the work programme of an upcoming UNCTAD-implemented project to provide assistance in foreign trade policy and planning to African least developed countries.

The United Nations Department of Public Information provided audio-visual coverage for OAU activities undertaken within the United Nations framework and the United Nations radio programmes dealth with the efforts of the two organizations to eliminate colonialism, racial discrimination and *apartheid* in southern Africa.

In another development, the Security Council, on 30 April, requested the Secretary-General to establish a voluntary fund, through which United Nations Members could give financial assistance to the OAU peace-keeping force in Chad, and to ensure its management in liaison with OAU.[12]

Communications. The Secretary-General received several communications during the year in which it was requested that they be issued as Assembly documents under the item on co-operation between the United Nations and OAU.

By a letter dated 29 March,[2] Djibouti, current Chairman of the African Group, transmitted the text of the 20 resolutions adopted at the thirty-eighth ordinary session of the OAU Council of Ministers, held at Addis Ababa, Ethiopia, from 22 to 28 February.

Three communications from two African States referred to that session and the decision taken there affecting the Western Sahara question (See TRUSTEESHIP AND DECOLONIZATION, Chapter IV).

Morocco, in a letter of 23 February,[6] transmitted messages of that date from King Hassan II to the OAU Chairman and the OAU Secretary-General, and a letter from the Moroccan Minister of State for Foreign Affairs to the Chairman of the OAU Council of Ministers, protesting the OAU decision to allow the "Saharan Arab Democratic Republic" to participate as an OAU member. In a letter of 3 March,[7] Morocco enclosed a message addressed to the Chairman of the OAU Council of Ministers by the 19 States that had withdrawn from the Council's February session (Central African Republic, Comoros, Djibouti, Equatorial Guinea, Gabon, Gambia, Guinea, Ivory Coast, Liberia, Mauritius, Morocco, Niger, Senegal, Somalia, Sudan, Tunisia, United Republic of Cameroon, Upper Volta, Zaire), declaring the decisions of that Council null and void due to the absence of a quorum. The United Republic of Cameroon, by a note verbale of 1 April to the Secretariat,[8] transmitted a statement that it had suspended its participation in the session in protest of the invitation to the POLISARIO Front (Frente Popular para la Liberación de Saguia el-Hamra y de Río de Oro) to take part as a representative of a member State (Saharan Arab Democratic Republic).

The Libyan Arab Jamahiriya, in a letter of 9 September,[5] forwarded the Tripoli Declaration of a meeting of African Heads of State and Government held from 5 to 8 August, attended by Algeria, Angola, Benin, Botswana, Burundi, Cape Verde, the Central African Republic, the Congo, Ethiopia, Ghana, Guinea-Bissau, Lesotho, the Libyan Arab Jamahiriya, Madagascar, Malawi, Mali, Mauritania, Mauritius, Mozambique, Rwanda, the Saharan Arab Democratic Republic, Sao Tome and Principe, Seychelles, Swaziland, Uganda, the United Republic of Tanzania, Zambia and Zimbabwe; the Declaration concerned southern Africa, Western Sahara, the Palestine question, Israel and Lebanon, and Chad. Referring to that document in a letter of 30 September,[4] Egypt, Gabon, Guinea, the Ivory Coast, Morocco, Senegal, the Upper Volta and Zaire said that OAU had been unable to hold a meeting at Tripoli due to the absence of a quorum, and the documents adopted at the August meeting had no legal validity and could not be considered as OAU documents.

By a note verbale of 25 May,[3] Egypt transmitted the text of a message of the same date from its President on the occasion of Africa Day, the nineteenth anniversary of the signature of the OAU Charter.

General Assembly action. In a resolution of 16 November,[10] the General Assembly commended OAU efforts to promote multilateral co-operation among African States and to find solutions to African problems of importance to the international community. The Assembly approved the decisions, recommendations, proposals and arrangements of the Geneva inter-secretariat Meeting and called on United Nations organizations to consider them with the objective of enhancing co-operation. The Assembly requested the United Nations Secretary-General, in consultation with OAU, to arrange the next meeting, and asked that adequate facilities be made available for technical assistance to the OAU General Secretariat. It further requested him to take measures to strengthen co-operation, particularly on assistance to victims of colonialism and *apartheid* in southern Africa. It urged United Nations organizations to expand co-operation with OAU and, through it, their assistance to the liberation movements recognized by that organization.

The Assembly also called for further work by the two organizations towards the establishment of the new international economic order, taking into account the Lagos Plan of Action, participation in programmes of special economic assistance to African States (See ECONOMIC AND SOCIAL QUESTIONS, Chapter VIII, III), support for African refugee programmes and equitable representation of Africans on the staffs of United Nations organizations (See ADMINISTRATIVE AND BUDGETARY QUESTIONS, Chapter III).

The Assembly adopted the resolution without vote, after rejecting an amendment by the United States on the financial implications. Kenya introduced the draft resolution to the Assembly on behalf of the 50 sponsors, all the members of OAU.

The United States amendment[1] would have had the Assembly authorize the Secretary-General to implement the activities approved under the resolution only to the extent that they could be financed without exceeding the level of resources approved in the 1982-1983 United Nations budget. The Assembly rejected the amendment by a recorded vote of 117 to 1, with 22 abstentions. The Assembly's Fifth (Administrative and Budgetary) Committee had reported that adoption of the resolution would require an additional appropriation of $14,500 for 1982-1983, excluding conference-servicing costs valued at $76,200.

On 17 December, in a resolution on regional arrangements for the promotion and protection of human rights, the Assembly commended OAU for its continuing efforts to promote respect for human rights guarantees and norms, and noted with interest the African Charter on Human and Peoples' Rights (adopted by OAU in 1981) and the efforts to obtain its early entry into force.[11]

Amendment rejected. [1]United States, A/37/L.30.

Letters and notes verbales (nv). [2]Djibouti, annexing OAU resolutions: 29 Mar., A/37/161. [3]Egypt: 25 May, A/37/256 *(nv).* [4]Egypt, Gabon, Guinea, Ivory Coast, Morocco, Senegal, Upper Volta, Zaire: 30 Sep., A/37/506 & Add.1. [5]Libyan Arab Jamahiriya: 9 Sep., A/37/437. Morocco: [6]23 Feb., A/37/99; [7]3 Mar., A/37/107. [8]United Republic of Cameroon: 1 Apr., A/37/167 *(nv).*

Report. [9]S-G, A/37/335 & Add.1.

Resolutions (1982). GA: [10]37/15, 16 Nov., text following; [11]37/172, para. 2, 17 Dec. [12]SC: 504(1982), 30 Apr.

Financial implications. 5th Committee report, A/37/616; S-G statement, A/C.5/37/35.

Meeting records. GA: 5th Committee, A/C.5/37/SR.34 (15 Nov.); plenary, A/37/PV.69 (16 Nov.).

General Assembly resolution 37/15

16 November 1982   Meeting 69   Adopted without vote

50-nation draft (A/37/L.14 and Add.1); agenda item 29.

Sponsors: Algeria, Angola, Benin, Botswana, Burundi, Cape Verde, Central African Republic, Chad, Comoros, Congo, Djibouti, Egypt, Equatorial Guinea, Ethiopia, Gabon, Gambia, Ghana, Guinea, Guinea-Bissau, Ivory Coast, Kenya, Lesotho, Liberia, Libyan Arab Jamahiriya, Madagascar, Malawi, Mali, Mauritania, Mauritius, Morocco, Mozambique, Niger, Nigeria, Rwanda, Sao Tome and Principe, Senegal, Seychelles, Sierra Leone, Somalia, Sudan, Swaziland, Togo, Tunisia, Uganda, United Republic of Cameroon, United Republic of Tanzania, Upper Volta, Zaire, Zambia, Zimbabwe.

Co-operation between the United Nations and the Organization of African Unity

The General Assembly,

Having considered the report of the Secretary-General on co-operation between the United Nations and the Organization of African Unity,

Recalling its previous resolutions on the promotion of co-operation between the United Nations and the Organization of African Unity and the practical measures taken for their implementation, in particular resolution 36/80 of 9 December 1981,

Taking note of the previous resolutions, decisions and declarations adopted by the Organization of African Unity on the promotion of co-operation between the United Nations and the Organization of African Unity,

Noting with satisfaction the continued co-operation between the United Nations and the Organization of African Unity in areas of common interest,

Deeply conscious of the special needs of the newly independent African States, particularly with regard to the consolidation of their national independence, their endeavours towards social and economic betterment and the adverse impact on their economies of the current international economic situation,

Gravely concerned about the adverse effect on African economies of the current international economic situation,

Recalling in this connection the Lagos Plan of Action for the Implementation of the Monrovia Strategy for the Economic Development of Africa, adopted by the Assembly of Heads of State and Government of the Organization of African Unity at its second extraordinary session, held at Lagos on 28 and 29 April 1980,

Recognizing the need for closer co-operation between the Organization of African Unity and all specialized organs, organizations and bodies of the United Nations system in realizing the goals and objectives set forth in the Lagos Plan of Action,

Deeply concerned at the gravity of the situation of refugees in Africa and their increasing needs for international assistance as well as at the heavy social and economic burden imposed on African countries of asylum,

Having considered the latest report of the Secretary-General on the International Conference on Assistance to Refugees in Africa,

Gravely concerned also at the need for special economic and emergency assistance programmes for a number of African States affected by serious economic problems, in particular problems of displaced persons, resulting from natural or other disasters, to enable them to pursue effective economic development,

Gravely concerned further at the deteriorating situation in southern Africa arising from the continued domination of the peoples of the area by the minority racist régime of South Africa and conscious of the need to provide increased assistance to the peoples of the region and to their liberation movements in their struggle against colonialism, racial discrimination and *apartheid,*

Conscious of its responsibilities to provide economic, material and humanitarian assistance to independent States in southern Africa to help them to cope with the situation caused by the acts of aggression committed against their territories by the *apartheid* régime of South Africa,

Recognizing the importance of taking effective steps to give the widest possible dissemination of information relating to the liberation struggle of the peoples of southern Africa,

Recognizing the important role which the various information units and departments of the United Nations system can play in disseminating information to bring about a greater awareness of the social and economic problems and needs of African States and their regional and subregional institutions,

Aware of the need for continuous liaison, exchange of information at the secretariat level and technical co-operation on such matters as training and research between the Organization of African Unity and the United Nations,

Having considered the report of the Secretary-General on the Meeting between representatives of the General Secretariat of the Organization of African Unity and the secretariats of the United Nations and other organizations of the United Nations system, held at Geneva from 6 to 8 April 1982,

Noting with satisfaction the useful decisions and proposals which emerged from the conclusions of the Geneva Meeting for enhancing co-operation between the United Nations and the Organization of African Unity,

1. *Takes note* of the report of the Secretary-General on co-operation between the United Nations and the Organization of African Unity and commends his efforts in strengthening such co-operation;

2. *Notes with appreciation* the increasing participation of the Organization of African Unity in the work of the United Nations and the specialized agencies and its constructive contribution to that work;

3. *Commends* the continued efforts of the Organization of African Unity to promote multilateral co-operation among African States and

to find solutions to African problems of vital importance to the international community and notes with satisfaction the increased collaboration of various United Nations agencies in support of those efforts;

4. *Reiterates* the determination of the United Nations, in cooperation with the Organization of African Unity, to intensify its efforts to eliminate colonialism, racial discrimination and *apartheid* in southern Africa;

5. *Approves* the decisions, recommendations, proposals and arrangements contained in the conclusions of the Geneva Meeting of representatives of the General Secretariat of the Organization of African Unity and the secretariats of the United Nations and other organizations of the United Nations system;

6. *Calls upon* the competent organizations and bodies of the United Nations system to give urgent consideration to the various recommendations and proposals contained in the conclusions of the Geneva Meeting, with the objective of enhancing co-operation between the United Nations system and the Organization of African Unity;

7. *Calls upon* the competent organs, specialized agencies and other organizations of the United Nations system to ensure that their personnel and recruitment policies provide for the just and equitable representation of Africa at all levels at their respective headquarters and in their regional and field operations and to give due consideration to the various suggestions and proposals in the relevant paragraphs of the conclusions and recommendations of the Geneva Meeting;

8. *Requests* the Secretary-General, in consultation with the Secretary-General of the Organization of African Unity, to arrange the date, venue and agenda for the next meeting between representatives of the General Secretariat of that organization and the secretariats of the United Nations and other organizations of the United Nations system, taking into account suggestions made at the Geneva Meeting;

9. *Recognizes* the importance of continued close association by the United Nations and the specialized agencies, where appropriate, with the efforts of the Organization of African Unity to promote social and economic development and to advance intra-African co-operation in that vital field;

10. *Reaffirms* the determination of the United Nations to work closely with the Organization of African Unity towards the establishment of the new international economic order in accordance with the resolutions adopted by the General Assembly and, in that regard, to take full account of the Lagos Plan of Action for the Implementation of the Monrovia Strategy for the Economic Development of Africa in the implementation of the International Development Strategy for the Third United Nations Development Decade;

11. *Reiterates its appreciation* to the Secretary-General for his efforts, on behalf of the international community, to organize and mobilize special programmes of economic assistance for African States experiencing grave economic difficulties, in particular for newly independent African States and the front-line States, to help them to cope with the situation caused by the acts of aggression committed against their territories by the *apartheid* régime of South Africa;

12. *Calls upon* all Member States, regional and international organizations and organizations of the United Nations system to participate actively in the implementation of those special programmes of economic assistance;

13. *Requests* the Secretary-General to keep the Organization of African Unity informed periodically of the response of the international community to those programmes and to co-ordinate efforts with all similar programmes initiated by the Organization of African Unity;

14. *Also requests* the Secretary-General and the organizations of the United Nations system to ensure that adequate facilities continue to be made available for the provision of technical assistance to the General Secretariat of the Organization of African Unity as required;

15. *Further requests* the Secretary-General to continue to take the necessary measures to strengthen co-operation at the political, economic, cultural and administrative levels between the United Nations and the Organization of African Unity in accordance with the relevant resolutions of the General Assembly, particularly with regard to the provision of assistance to the victims of colonialism and *apartheid* in southern Africa, and in this connection draws once again the attention of the international community to the need to contribute to the Assistance Fund for the Struggle against Colonialism and *Apartheid* established by the Organization of African Unity;

16. *Calls upon* all Member States and organizations of the United Nations system to increase their assistance to the African States affected by serious economic problems, in particular problems of displaced persons, resulting from natural or other disasters, by mobilizing special programmes of economic and emergency assistance;

17. *Urges* all Member States and regional and international organizations, in particular those of the United Nations system, and non-governmental organizations to continue their support of African refugee programmes and to provide material and economic assistance to help host countries to cope with the heavy burden imposed on their limited resources and weak infrastructures;

18. *Requests* the Secretary-General to draw the attention of specialized agencies and other organizations of the United Nations system to the need to give increasingly wide publicity to all matters relating to the social and economic development of Africa;

19. *Calls upon* United Nations bodies—in particular the Security Council, the Economic and Social Council, the Special Committee on the Situation with regard to the Implementation of the Declaration on the Granting of Independence to Colonial Countries and Peoples, the Special Committee against *Apartheid* and the United Nations Council for Namibia—to continue to associate closely the Organization of African Unity with all their work concerning Africa;

20. *Urges* the specialized agencies and the other organizations concerned within the United Nations system to continue and expand their co-operation with the Organization of African Unity and, through it, their assistance to the liberation movements recognized by that organization;

21. *Requests* the Secretary-General to report to the General Assembly at its thirty-eighth session on the implementation of the present resolution and on the development of co-operation between the Organization of African Unity and the organizations concerned within the United Nations system.

Chapter VI

Asia

Contents

South-East Asia

The situation in and around Kampuchea and the country's representation in the United Nations continued to occupy the attention of the Organization in 1982.

The *Ad Hoc* Committee of the International Conference on Kampuchea sent missions to five European countries and to Thailand between July and September, in pursuance of its mandate to assist in seeking a settlement of the Kampuchea situation. A Special Representative of the Secretary-General, Rafeeuddin Ahmed, visited South-East Asia in February/March to consult with Governments in the region. In October, the General Assembly restated its view of the principal components of a just and lasting solution—withdrawal of all foreign forces, restoration and preservation of the country's independence, sovereignty and territorial integrity, the people's right to determine its destiny, and a commitment by all States to non-interference and non-intervention in Kampuchea's internal affairs.

Numerous communications were received on various aspects of the situation and related issues, including the alleged use of chemical weapons (p. 334), the situation along the Kampuchea-Thailand border and general aspects of peace and security in South-East Asia. The credentials of representatives of Democratic Kampuchea to the General Assembly and other United Nations bodies were discussed in other communications, as well as in the Assembly.

Kampuchea situation

Communications. The Secretary-General received a number of communications during 1982 on the situation between Democratic Kampuchea and Viet Nam.

In a 19 March statement transmitted on 5 April,[5] the Ministry of Culture and Education of Democratic Kampuchea denounced Viet Nam's allegation that Democratic Kampuchea was responsible for the destruction and looting of antiquities, works of art and other national treasures of Kampuchea, and accused Viet Nam of perpetrating such acts, particularly at Phnom Penh and Angkor.

Assessments of the military situation in Kampuchea were given by the Military High Command of the National Army of Democratic Kampuchea in two communiqués reporting successful operations: the first, covering the dry season (October 1981–April 1982), issued on 8 May and transmitted on 7 June,[8] said that 37,372 of the enemy had been killed or wounded and attached a map of the military situation; the second, covering the rainy season (May-September), issued on 15 October and excerpts from which were transmitted on 15 November,[15] claimed an additional 22,000 casualties.

Pointing to what it considered the military and political defeats it had recently inflicted on Vietnamese invading forces, Democratic Kampuchea, in a 15 July statement transmitted on the same day,[11] labelled as propaganda Viet Nam's announcement (Ho Chi Minh City, 7 July) of an imminent partial withdrawal of its troops from Kampuchea and its proposal for an international conference on South-East Asia; it reaffirmed that the Kampuchea problem could be solved only by implementation of the General Assembly resolutions of 1979,[38] 1980[39] and 1981[40] calling for the total and unconditional withdrawal of all foreign forces from Kampuchea. The same view had been expressed earlier by a spokesman of the Ministry of Foreign Affairs of China, in a statement dated 9 July transmitted the next day.[31]

Viet Nam News Agency reports of partial troop withdrawals were transmitted by Viet Nam in July: dispatches of 17 and 18 July, transmitted by Viet Nam on 20 July,[26] described and commented on the withdrawal on 15 July of a number of units from northern Kampuchea; and another dispatch, dated 19 July and transmitted three days later,[27] described the passage through Phnom Penh of troops leaving Kampuchea. Democratic Kampuchea, on the other hand, forwarded on 27 July[12] information broadcast by the Voice of Democratic Kampuchea that fresh Vietnamese troop reinforcements had arrived in Kampuchea between 20 June and 16 July.

On 18 October,[13] Democratic Kampuchea submitted a list of crimes it said had been committed by the Vietnamese army in Kampuchea between July and September. On 9 November,[14] it submitted a telegram and extracts from a published interview ascribed to two former officials of the Vietnamese régime at Phnom Penh; their testimony showed, Democratic Kampuchea said in its transmittal letter, that that régime was a Vietnamese puppet.

Charges of chemical weapons use in the conflict between Democratic Kampuchea and Viet Nam were again submitted in 1982, and information was provided for transmittal to the Group of Experts to Investigate Reports on the Alleged Use of Chemical Weapons.

Democratic Kampuchea sent three communications on the subject. On 19 January,[2] it submitted a list of cases involving the alleged use of chemical toxins by Vietnamese forces in nine provinces during November and December 1981, mostly food and water supply poisoning, resulting in 57 known deaths. On 19 March, it transmitted a statement issued on 9 March by its Ministry of Information,[3] condemning what it described as intensified criminal use of chemical weapons by the Hanoi régime, including "yellow rain" attacks by aircraft against villages in the Pailin district of Battambang province in north-western Kampuchea on 1 and 2 March said to have resulted in 189 casualties including three deaths, and on the villages of Sala Krao and Phnom Kuy, from 26 to 28 February, killing two villagers and placing 28 in critical condition. Finally, by a letter of 19 April,[6] it annexed a list citing these and other instances of aerial

spraying of chemical toxins and firing of poison-gas shells between February and April, resulting in 66 deaths and 463 known cases of serious poisoning.

By a note verbale of 24 February,[18] the United States forwarded tabulated data, based on analyses of blood samples from victims of a reported chemical attack in Kampuchea during the autumn of 1981, which it said tended to support the hypothesis that an agent based on trichothecenes (a class of mycotoxins, or poisons produced by fungi) had been used in that attack. By another note verbale of 22 March,[19] the United States transmitted a report of the same date which its Secretary of State sent to the United States Congress, containing what it termed a comprehensive compilation and analysis of information on the use of chemical and toxin weapons by the USSR and its allies in Afghanistan, Kampuchea and the Lao People's Democratic Republic; the report's conclusion with regard to Kampuchea was that Vietnamese forces had used lethal trichothecene toxins on Democratic Kampuchean troops and Khmer villages since at least 1978, and that irritants, incapacitants and nerve agents had also been used.

Responding by a note of 5 April transmitted two days later,[16] the USSR called the United States report a collection of fabrications not based on evidence, designed to cover up traces of past United States use of poisonous substances in South-East Asia; it added that it had never used chemical weapons anywhere. A spokesman for the Ministry of Foreign Affairs of Viet Nam, in a statement of 13 April transmitted the following day,[23] similarly rejected the United States allegation of Vietnamese participation in chemical attacks on the South-East Asian countries named and added that the United States had conducted in Indo-China the biggest chemical war in history. The USSR submitted on 20 May[17] a critique prepared by Soviet scientists and other experts, evaluating the statements in the United States report and stating that its conclusions were unconvincing and contradicted objective medical and technical data.

On 20 May,[20] the United States submitted further information based on analyses of blood and other human samples taken from victims of a reported chemical attack at Tuol Chrey, Kampuchea, on 13 February, concluding that the evidence was consistent with trichothecene exposure and indicated exposure to a high concentration of T-2 toxin. On 29 November,[21] it transmitted another report from its Secretary of State to the United States Congress, dated November and updating the March report; this document concluded, with respect to Kampuchea, that Vietnamese forces had continued to use lethal and incapacitating chemical agents and toxins against resistance forces in Kampuchea at least through

June, and that trichothecene toxins had been found in the urine, blood and tissue of victims of "yellow rain" attacks there and in samples of residue collected after attacks.

Earlier, on 23 June,[30] Canada transmitted a note verbale of 21 June annexing a report to its Department of External Affairs by a member of the Toxicology Group of the University of Saskatchewan, on the alleged use of chemical weapons in South-East Asia; this study concluded that the events reported to have taken place at the time of the alleged chemical-weapon attacks could not be explained on the basis of natural phenomena and that neither mycotoxins nor diseases naturally occurring in South-East Asia could explain the reported symptoms, which were consistent with trichothecene mycotoxicosis (a pathological condition caused by fungus-produced poisons).

Other aspects of the Kampuchea situation were addressed by a number of communications.

In a 7 January speech, excerpts of which were transmitted by Viet Nam on 13 January,[22] Heng Samrin, President of the Council of State of the People's Republic of Kampuchea, reviewed the progress he said had been achieved by the People's Republic, domestically and in relations with its neighbours and allies, during the more than three years since the Kampuchean revolution had overthrown the Pol Pot régime. A Viet Nam News Agency dispatch of 17 April, transmitted three days later,[24] gave highlights of a speech by the President at a 17 April meeting at Phnom Penh to mark the seventh anniversary of the victory of the Kampuchean revolution over the Lon Nol régime.

A communiqué of 10 March by the Ministry of Information of Democratic Kampuchea, transmitted on 24 March,[4] described talks held on 21 and 23 February in Beijing, China, between Prime Minister Khieu Samphan and Samdech Norodom Sihanouk aimed at the formation of a tripartite national union against the Vietnamese occupation forces, which included arrangements for an early meeting with Son Sann, the third party to the proposed union; it summed up four principles agreed upon as the basis for the union—tripartism, equality, consensus for important decisions and preservation of the legality of the State of Democratic Kampuchea.

The Council of Ministers of Democratic Kampuchea, in a statement at the close of a two-day meeting on 21 April and transmitted on 6 May,[7] assessed the military, political and diplomatic situation; referring to efforts to form a national union, it appealed to all who opposed expansionism to support the legitimate State of Democratic Kampuchea and put an end to the unjust war.

The Declaration of the Formation of the Coalition Government of Democratic Kampuchea, signed on 22 June at Kuala Lumpur, Malaysia, by Samdech Sihanouk, Khieu Samphan, and Son Sann—who under the coalition became President, Vice-President in charge of Foreign Affairs and Prime Minister, respectively—was transmitted on 23 June.[9] It was followed by a proclamation on the formation of the new Government, issued by the President on 9 July and transmitted on 13 July.[10] The documents defined the objectives, operating principles and composition of the Coalition Government and its co-ordination committees.

An editorial in the 22 June issue of the Vietnamese daily *Nhan Dan*, extracts of which were forwarded on 28 June by Viet Nam,[25] called the Coalition Government a farce that had been in production by China and the United States for over a year, and it regretted support of that farce by the Association of South-East Asian Nations (ASEAN).

By a letter of 22 September,[32] the Lao People's Democratic Republic forwarded a transcript of an interview granted to the SPK (Samporamean Kampuchea) news agency on 18 September by the Vice-President of the Council of Ministers and Minister for Foreign Affairs of the People's Republic of Kampuchea, favourably assessing the military and food production situations, confirming the partial withdrawal of Vietnamese troops from Kampuchea and dismissing the Coalition Government as a mask designed to seduce Kampucheans into restoring the genocidal Pol Pot régime.

On 6 October,[28] Viet Nam transmitted a 2 October dispatch by its News Agency on a press conference held the day before at Phnom Penh by the Ministry of Culture and Information of the People's Republic of Kampuchea, describing documentary information that 110 foreigners had been murdered at Phnom Penh's Toul Sleng prison by the former régime between April 1975 and November 1978.

Activities of the Committee of the Conference on Kampuchea. In pursuance of the mandate given it at the first session of the Conference in July 1981,[41] which had been convened by the General Assembly, the *Ad Hoc* Committee of the International Conference on Kampuchea reported in September 1982[33] on its activities since its establishment. The 10-member Committee (enlarged from 7 members; see APPENDIX III) held an organizational meeting on 28 October 1981 and seven other meetings between 11 January and 21 September 1982. It sent missions to France, Belgium and the Federal Republic of Germany (4-10 July), to Thailand (27-30 July), and to Sweden and Austria (29 August–2 September).

The report noted that the missions had held extensive discussions with Governments to explore prospects for a political settlement of the Kampuchea situation. They had made known the Committee's objective of promoting a dialogue among all parties and had stressed the principles basic to such a settlement as identified by the Conference.

The mission to Paris, Brussels and Bonn focused on the newly formed Coalition Government of Democratic Kampuchea (see above) and on the proposals agreed upon at the sixth conference of the Foreign Ministers of the Lao People's Democratic Republic, Viet Nam and the People's Republic of Kampuchea (Ho Chi Minh City, Viet Nam, 6 and 7 July) (p. 346). At Bangkok, discussions centred on relations between ASEAN countries and Viet Nam. The Minister for Foreign Affairs of Thailand, as Chairman of the ASEAN Standing Committee, briefed the mission on the visits in July of the Minister for Foreign Affairs of Viet Nam to Burma, Malaysia and Singapore, and on a 29 July meeting between the Foreign Ministers of Thailand and Viet Nam. He stated that those exchanges had made no substantive progress towards a narrowing of differences but that the ASEAN countries were nevertheless willing to hold further consultations with Viet Nam.

The mission to Vienna reported on the Committee's activities to the Foreign Minister of Austria, in his capacity as President of the International Conference on Kampuchea, and he in turn briefed the mission on his consultations with the parties and other interested Governments.

In conclusion, the report noted the Committee's determination to continue its efforts and, in particular, to seek to develop further consultations in order to initiate the desired negotiating process.

Report of the Secretary-General. In a report to the General Assembly in October 1982,[34] submitted pursuant to the Assembly resolution of October 1981 on the Kampuchea situation,[40] the Secretary-General stated that, on assuming office in January 1982, he had consulted with the States most directly concerned with the Kampuchea situation, in exercise of his good offices. His Special Representative, Rafeeuddin Ahmed, had visited South-East Asia in February/March to consult with Governments. Thereafter the Secretary-General had continued his contacts with government leaders while visiting Beijing, Moscow, Paris and other capitals. More recently, in New York, he had talked with the Presidents of the Philippines and Democratic Kampuchea, the Prime Minister of Malaysia, and the Foreign Ministers of the Lao People's Democratic Republic, Thailand, Viet Nam and other interested Governments.

The Secretary-General regretted that, although consultations among the countries of the region and with other States had acquired new impetus, they had not achieved any substantial progress towards a resolution of the problem. However, they constituted a positive development in so far as they had led to a better perception of the different positions and had encouraged dialogue. Communications addressed to him during the year and circulated as United Nations documents had demonstrated that, despite efforts and initiatives at various levels, wide differences of position remained, both on the nature of the problem and on the modalities for a peaceful solution.

The Secretary-General said it had become increasingly clear that the region's problems could not be solved by military means. Only a comprehensive political solution, reached through genuine negotiations, would allow the countries of the region to reconstruct their economies and look to a future of peace, stability and co-operation. He hoped that the recent trend towards sustained dialogue stemmed from a shared conviction that there was no alternative to a negotiated settlement.

The report also noted that the Secretary-General continued to implement the humanitarian assistance programme for Kampuchea (See ECONOMIC AND SOCIAL QUESTIONS, Chapter III).

General Assembly action. On 28 October, the General Assembly adopted a resolution on the Kampuchea situation[37] by a recorded vote of 105 to 23, with 20 abstentions.

By this resolution, the Assembly reiterated its conviction that withdrawal of all foreign forces from Kampuchea, restoration and preservation of its independence, sovereignty and territorial integrity, the right of the people to determine their own destiny, and commitment by all States to non-interference and non-intervention in the internal affairs of Kampuchea were the principal components of a just and lasting solution. It requested the *Ad Hoc* Committee of the Conference on Kampuchea to continue work, reaffirmed its decision to reconvene the Conference when appropriate and requested the Secretary-General to continue exercising his good offices towards a comprehensive settlement. It also urged continuation of humanitarian relief. The Assembly urged the South-East Asian countries, after a comprehensive political solution, to establish a zone of peace and reiterated the hope that an intergovernmental committee would be established to assist in the reconstruction of Kampuchea and the development of the region.

Introducing the 49-nation draft resolution, which was revised by the sponsors before adoption, the Philippines noted its similarity to the 1981 Assembly resolution on the item[40] and said the increased number of sponsors reflected the international community's growing concern over the flagrant violation of Kampuchea by Viet Nam.

Explaining their votes against the resolution, the Congo, the Lao People's Democratic Republic and

Nicaragua stated that it constituted unacceptable interference in the internal affairs of a sovereign State—the People's Republic of Kampuchea—aimed at re-establishing the genocidal Pol Pot régime. Nicaragua, while supporting the aim of transforming South-East Asia and every other region into a zone of peace, added that its vote signified rejection of any attempt to re-establish the Pol Pot régime.

In addition, the Lao People's Democratic Republic, protesting inscription of the item on the Kampuchea situation on the Assembly's agenda, called attention to a 22 October message to the Secretary-General, transmitted by Viet Nam on 26 October.[29] By this message, the Vice-President of the Council of Ministers and Minister for Foreign Affairs of the People's Republic of Kampuchea stated that that régime was the only authentic and legal representative of the Kampucheans; protested United Nations discussion and all other discussions of the so-called situation in Kampuchea as gross and inadmissible interference in Kampuchea's internal affairs; and considered illegal, null and void all decisions relating to Kampuchea adopted without the participation and consent of the People's Republic.

Albania, which announced that it was not participating in the vote, said it did not share the view that the resolution contained new, positive and promising elements; the text lacked language necessary to create conditions for a just solution and prevent the super-Powers from taking advantage of the Kampucheans' difficulties.

Vanuatu, although endorsing the humanitarian provisions, abstained in the vote because it considered the text one-sided and lacking in clarity; it did not believe that a country which had suffered so much at the hands of outsiders and which shared with Kampuchea similar social and economic problems merited so strong a condemnation.

Brazil, though voting in favour, expressed reservations on the fourth preambular paragraph (mentioning the coalition), which it felt prejudged the question of which was the legitimate Government of Kampuchea. Ireland said its positive vote did not imply any change in its position on Kampuchean representation. Sweden supported the general thrust of the resolution as a reaffirmation of principles for a just settlement and the request to the Secretary-General to continue to exercise his good offices, but said its positive vote did not mean any change in Sweden's position.

In the Assembly debate, Samdech Norodom Sihanouk of Democratic Kampuchea observed that, while talk of a political solution abounded, the solution had already been identified in Assembly resolutions and the Declaration of the Conference on Kampuchea,[41] which called for unconditional withdrawal of all foreign troops, recognition of the people's sovereignty and right to self-determination, and the holding of United Nations–supervised elections. However, Viet Nam continued to maintain a massive occupation army in Kampuchea and was resettling depopulated areas in order to create a so-called Indo-Chinese federation, with Viet Nam as master and Kampuchea and the Lao People's Democratic Republic as satellites. Democratic Kampuchea could not accept such a federation; it would continue to struggle for national liberation until all Vietnamese forces were completely withdrawn and its right to self-determination restored. It would then be ready to sign a treaty of peace and non-aggression with Viet Nam, to include mutual respect for the territorial integrity of both nations.

A number of States, among them Australia, Austria, Fiji, Malaysia, Senegal, Thailand, Togo and the United States, saw the Kampuchea situation as arising from a failure to observe fundamental principles of the Charter of the United Nations—non-interference in the internal affairs of States, respect for their national independence, sovereignty and territorial integrity, inadmissibility of the threat or use of force to settle disputes and the right of States to determine their own destiny. Japan, Mauritania, Nepal and Paraguay viewed the situation as a threat to peace and security in South-East Asia, and the Central African Republic, to international peace and security.

Fiji saw the situation as an example of the dangerous logic, which appeared to be developing elsewhere as well, that instability in sovereign States was sufficient justification for foreign invasion. For the Sudan, the Kampuchean issue reflected the danger of intervention in the internal affairs of States—a danger which compelled the smaller nations, especially the non-aligned, to devote their limited resources to military forces rather than development. Any solution, said Sweden, must involve the right of the Kampuchean people to self-determination, and that right could not be exercised in the presence of foreign military forces. Yugoslavia said the attempt to change the political map by foreign intervention in Democratic Kampuchea had been a hard blow to the stability of South-East Asia and had had negative consequences for international peace and security.

Canada observed that the number of encouraging initiatives taken on this issue by the United Nations had been seriously compromised by the intransigence of certain Members; the root cause of the problem was Viet Nam's continued occupation of Kampuchea and rejection of all United Nations efforts to bring about a solution.

Singapore stated that the ASEAN countries unequivocally opposed Viet Nam's occupation of Kampuchea as a violation of the Charter and because Viet Nam, after digesting its conquest of Kampuchea and its domination over the Lao People's Democratic Republic, might cast its avaricious eye on other South-East Asian States. Denmark (for the European Community (EC) members), Fiji, Norway, Pakistan, Paraguay and Tunisia added that that record could not justify the invasion and continued occupation of Kampuchea by a foreign Power. Australia, Malaysia and Nepal, among others, regarded the immediate withdrawal of Viet Nam's forces from Kampuchea as an essential first step towards a comprehensive solution. Mauritania appealed for the total withdrawal of all foreign troops from Kampuchea.

The Central African Republic, also calling on Viet Nam to withdraw, said its well-armed troops were fighting an unequal battle against a handful of patriots who were sacrificing their lives for their country's independence and territorial integrity. The United States said the Kampuchean dictator had been installed and was being maintained only by the presence of some 180,000 troops sent by Viet Nam, which in turn was heavily dependent on USSR supplies and some 10,000 military advisers in Viet Nam.

Australia, Austria, China, Indonesia, Japan, Malaysia, Nepal, New Zealand, Pakistan, Papua New Guinea, the Philippines, Senegal, Singapore (for the ASEAN States), the Sudan, Thailand, Togo, Tunisia and Yugoslavia reaffirmed their support for the Declaration of the Conference on Kampuchea as a reasonable, balanced and proper framework for a just and comprehensive settlement.

Japan appealed to Viet Nam to respond to the will of the overwhelming majority as reflected in the Declaration and Assembly resolutions, and to negotiate in accordance with them. Indonesia, Singapore and the United States appealed to Viet Nam to participate in good faith in future efforts of the Conference. Willingness by Viet Nam to accept the United Nations initiative and to seek a political settlement in co-operation with the ASEAN countries, said Pakistan, would help bring peace to South-East Asia and have a salutary impact on the international situation as a whole.

The formation of the Coalition Government of Democratic Kampuchea was welcomed by Australia, Canada, China, Egypt, Indonesia, Japan, Malaysia, Mauritania, Nepal, Norway, Pakistan, Papua New Guinea, the Philippines, Senegal, the Sudan, Thailand, Togo, Tunisia, the United States and Yugoslavia. The Central African Republic said it reflected the will of the Kampucheans. Malaysia viewed the coalition as an important step towards a comprehensive political solution and urged Viet Nam to negotiate seriously with it. Indonesia and New Zealand welcomed the coalition's

broad representation. The Philippines regarded the event as signalling Kampuchean unity in the common effort to liberate the country from foreign invaders, disproving the myth that the Heng Samrin régime was in complete control of Kampuchea; it put Viet Nam on notice that, while Democratic Kampuchea preferred a peaceful solution, it was prepared to defend its sovereign rights as long as necessary.

Australia said it would recognize no Government in Kampuchea until an act of self-determination had taken place; none the less Australia welcomed the re-emergence through the coalition of Samdech Sihanouk and Son Sann. The United States took the participation of these two leaders in the coalition as giving substance to hopes that popular, democratic, nationalist Kampuchean movements would provide the Kampucheans with an alternative to the grim choice between the Khmer Rouge and a Vietnamese-dominated régime. Canada, noting the inclusion of Khmer Rouge elements in the coalition, said it would steadfastly oppose the return of the Pol Pot régime. Paraguay, though welcoming the coalition's establishment, also said it had serious reservations about the participation of Khmer Rouge elements.

Referring to Viet Nam's announcement of a partial withdrawal of its troops from Kampuchea, Senegal considered it a positive though inadequate development. However, Australia called it no more than seasonal troop rotation, as did China, which added that it was designed to offset the coalition's impact and head off another Assembly resolution calling for the unconditional and total withdrawal of Viet Nam's forces. Thailand and the United States also viewed the action as simply a trade of troop units, reinforcing the army of occupation. Tunisia, however, believed that the announcement of a partial withdrawal could, if put into effect, constitute an encouraging point of departure for the peace process.

Several speakers commented on the proposal by Viet Nam and others for an international conference on South-East Asia. Australia, while acknowledging that any willingness by Viet Nam to negotiate must be welcomed, described the proposal as ambiguous since it left unspecified the central issue for negotiation and the matter of participation. China termed it a rehash of the regional conference previously promoted by Viet Nam, a ruse to forestall application of United Nations resolutions and to remove the item from the Assembly's agenda. Calling the proposal deliberately vague, Malaysia, Thailand and the United States said it ignored the central issue of the continued presence of foreign forces in Kampuchea, a presence that such a conference would legitimize and entrench; Thailand added that it would undermine the negotiating framework established by the United Nations.

Commenting on Viet Nam's proposal for a demilitarized zone along the Thai-Kampuchean border, Thailand said it appeared to be an attempt to enlist Thai support against the legitimate struggle of the Kampuchean patriots; such a zone should more properly be established along the Vietnamese-Kampuchean border after Viet Nam withdrew its troops.

China, declaring that it did not wish to control Kampuchea, said that after Viet Nam withdrew its troops from that country China was willing to join others in an international guarantee that no State would occupy Kampuchea and use it to violate the independence and sovereignty of any other State or interfere in Kampuchea's internal affairs. Denmark said the EC members would support any initiative to establish a representative government in a neutral and independent Kampuchea, maintaining friendly relations with all States of the region.

Sweden said it did not consider the Coalition Government a true government, since it was not in control of the territory of the nation it purported to represent; a more positive development, in Sweden's view, was the ministerial contacts of the Governments most directly involved.

India, which abstained in the vote on the resolution, restated its opposition to the presence of foreign troops or bases in any country and its conviction that a peaceful political solution must be based on non-use of force and non-interference; at the same time, it considered unproductive any attempt to reverse the normalization under way through the commendable efforts of the People's Republic, thought it inconceivable that the Kampucheans would allow restoration of the *status quo ante* under any guise and recommended that the countries in the region strive for a comprehensive political solution.

Those speaking against the resolution protested the inscription of the item on the Kampuchea situation on the Assembly's agenda. The USSR considered it completely illegal; Afghanistan, Bulgaria, the Byelorussian SSR, the German Democratic Republic, the Lao People's Democratic Republic, Mongolia, Poland and Viet Nam said it constituted interference in the affairs of an independent, sovereign State—the People's Republic of Kampuchea—in gross violation of the United Nations Charter and, Czechoslovakia added, of international law. The USSR asserted that attempts by China, the United States and certain ASEAN countries to use the United Nations to interfere in the affairs of Kampuchea had complicated normalization of the situation in South-East Asia.

Once again, Bulgaria remarked, the United Nations was engaged in a sterile discussion without the participation of the only legitimate representa-

tative of the Kampucheans. Viet Nam added that the debate militated against the legitimate aspirations and undermined the efforts of a people who, having survived genocide, were in the process of reconstructing their country amid innumerable difficulties.

The States holding this view pointed to the general elections of May 1981, the improving food situation and other developments as evidence of the irreversible consolidation of the People's Republic of Kampuchea. They called for recognizing the People's Republic as the legitimate representative of the Kampucheans and giving it its rightful place in the United Nations. That Government, said the German Democratic Republic, exercised effective power and control in the country. The Lao People's Democratic Republic remarked that the People's Republic had for three years devoted itself to the development of its country and sought to live on good terms with its neighbours. For Viet Nam, the international community had the choice of either declaring itself in favour of the irreversible rebirth of the Kampuchean people brought about by the People's Republic of Kampuchea or promoting restoration of the genocidal Pol Pot régime in the guise of the Government of Democratic Kampuchea.

Strongly opposed to the Coalition Government were Afghanistan, Albania, Bulgaria, the Byelorussian SSR, Cuba, Czechoslovakia, the German Democratic Republic, Hungary, Mongolia, Poland, the Ukrainian SSR and the USSR; most of them saw it as a coalition of the forces that had been totally discredited as criminally responsible for the massacre of 3 million Kampucheans. The remnants of the Pol Pot régime, India said, were the driving force behind the coalition; it was ironic therefore that, while the legitimate Government of the People's Republic enjoyed the esteem and affection of its people, a delegation with neither a capital nor a country should have gained support for remaining in the Assembly. The label of "coalition", said the Ukrainian SSR, was used to make it possible for the followers of Pol Pot to receive assistance not only from China but from other sources as well.

Viet Nam contended that, while China called for the withdrawal of Vietnamese troops, it prevented Viet Nam from withdrawing because China, by increasing assistance to the Pol Pot rabble operating from their Thailand sanctuary, maintained a continual state of tension on the Kampuchea-Thailand border; once that threat was removed, Viet Nam's troops would be withdrawn. Hungary observed that the military presence of Viet Nam in Kampuchea was based on a treaty concluded between them and was thus a matter of concern only to those two States. The Byelorussian SSR viewed the partial withdrawal that had taken place as a manifestation of the good will of the People's Republic and Viet Nam.

A reliable basis for the settlement of the region's problems, the USSR said, was the constructive and flexible proposals put forward by the Indo-Chinese countries in a 15 September letter from the Lao People's Democratic Republic to the Foreign Ministers of ASEAN (p. 346). Also endorsing those proposals were Afghanistan, Bulgaria, the Byelorussian SSR, Czechoslovakia, the German Democratic Republic, Mongolia and Poland. Afghanistan believed that only a negotiated settlement with the participation of all countries of the region, including the People's Republic, could eliminate obstacles in the way of normalized relations and co-operation. Cuba viewed dialogue as the only sensible step towards a region of peace, stability and co-operation.

In the view of Albania, Kampuchea and all of Indo-China continued to be the arena of hegemonistic and expansionist rivalry among China, the USSR and the United States; it urged an end to such actions so as to allow Kampuchea to decide its own fate.

Other action. Action relating to Kampuchea was taken by other United Nations bodies during the year. The Commission on Human Rights, in a resolution of 25 February on self-determination in relation to Kampuchea, reaffirmed that the primary violation of human rights in Kampuchea was the persistence of foreign occupation, which prevented its people from exercising their right to self-determination.[35] The Economic and Social Council, on 7 May, endorsed this action and the call for the withdrawal of all foreign forces so as to allow the Kampucheans to exercise their fundamental freedoms and human rights.[1] On 4 May, the Council called on the international community to assist Kampuchean refugees and displaced persons, and expressed grave concern at the plight of women and children.[36]

The United Nations continued to organize emergency relief for Kampucheans and to assist refugees in neighbouring countries, mainly Thailand. (See ECONOMIC AND SOCIAL QUESTIONS, Chapter III and Chapter XXI).

Decision 1982: [1]ESC: 1982/143, 7 May.
Letters and notes verbales (nv).

Democratic Kampuchea: [2]19 Jan., A/37/72; [3]19 Mar., A/37/152-S/14915; [4]24 Mar., A/37/158-S/14926; [5]5 Apr., A/37/171-S/14955; [6]19 Apr., A/37/202-S/14986; [7]6 May, A/37/221-S/15054; [8]7 June, A/37/268-S/15179; [9]23 June, A/37/307-S/15252 & Corr.1; [10]13 July, A/37/340-S/15291; [11]15 July, A/37/344-S/15298; [12]27 July, A/37/363-S/15314; [13]18 Oct., A/37/551-S/15460; [14]9 Nov., A/37/609-S/15486; [15]15 Nov., A/37/628-S/15491.

USSR: [16]7 Apr., A/37/173; [17]20 May, A/37/233.

United States: [18]24 Feb., A/37/102 *(nv)*; [19]22 Mar., A/37/157 *(nv)*; [20]20 May, A/37/234 & Corr.1 *(nv)*; [21]29 Nov., A/C.1/37/10 *(nv)*.

Viet Nam: [22]13 Jan., A/37/64; [23]14 Apr., A/37/180; [24]20 Apr., A/37/204; [25]28 June, A/37/315; [26]20 July, A/37/350; [27]22 July, A/37/356; [28]6 Oct., A/37/523; [29]26 Oct., A/37/575.

Others: [30]Canada: 23 June, A/37/308. [31]China: 10 July, A/37/337-S/15286. [32]Lao People's Democratic Republic: 22 Sep., A/37/477.
Reports. [33]Committee of Conference on Kampuchea, A/CONF.109/6; [34]S-G, A/37/496.
Resolutions (1982). [35]Commission on Human Rights (report, E/1982/12): 1982/13, 25 Feb. [36]ESC: 1982/25, 4 May. [37]GA: 37/6, 28 Oct., text following.
Resolutions (prior). GA: [38]34/22, 14 Nov. 1979 (YUN 1979, p. 306); [39]35/6, 22 Oct. 1980 (YUN 1980, p. 334); [40]36/5, 21 Oct. 1981 (YUN 1981, p. 246).
Yearbook reference. [41]1981, p. 242.
Financial implications. 5th Committee report, A/37/577; S-G statement, A/C.5/37/21.
Meeting records. GA: General Committee, A/BUR/37/SR.1 (22 Sep.); plenary, A/37/PV.44-48 (26-28 Oct.); 5th Committee, A/C.5/37/SR.21 (28 Oct.).

General Assembly resolution 37/6

28 October 1982   Meeting 48   105-23-20 (recorded vote)

49-nation draft (A/37/L.1/Rev.1 and Rev.1|Add.1); agenda item 20.

Sponsors: Antigua and Barbuda, Australia, Bangladesh, Belgium, Botswana, Canada, Central African Republic, Chad, Chile, Colombia, Comoros, Costa Rica, Dominican Republic, Equatorial Guinea, Fiji, Gambia, Germany, Federal Republic of, Haiti, Honduras, Indonesia, Italy, Japan, Liberia, Luxembourg, Malaysia, Mauritania, Nepal, Netherlands, New Zealand, Niger, Nigeria, Oman, Pakistan, Papua New Guinea, Paraguay, Philippines, Saint Lucia, Saint Vincent and the Grenadines, Samoa, Senegal, Singapore, Solomon Islands, Somalia, Swaziland, Thailand, United Kingdom, Upper Volta, Uruguay, Zaire.

The situation in Kampuchea

The General Assembly,

Recalling its resolutions 34/22 of 14 November 1979, 35/6 of 22 October 1980 and 36/5 of 21 October 1981,

Recalling further the Declaration on Kampuchea and resolution 1(I) adopted by the International Conference on Kampuchea, which offer the negotiating framework for a comprehensive political settlement of the Kampuchean problem,

Taking note of the report of the Secretary-General, submitted in pursuance of General Assembly resolution 36/5,

Noting the recent developments resulting in the coalition with Samdech Norodom Sihanouk as President of Democratic Kampuchea,

Deploring that foreign armed intervention and occupation continue and that foreign forces have not been withdrawn from Kampuchea, thus causing continuing hostilities in that country and seriously threatening international peace and security,

Greatly concerned that the continuing deployment of foreign forces in Kampuchea near the Thai-Kampuchean border has maintained tension in the region,

Gravely disturbed that the continued fighting and instability in Kampuchea have forced Kampucheans to flee to the Thai-Kampuchean border in search of food and safety,

Recognizing that the assistance extended by the international community has continued to reduce the food shortages and health problems of the Kampuchean people,

Emphasizing that it is the inalienable right of the Kampuchean people who have sought refuge in neighbouring countries to return safely to their homeland,

Emphasizing further that no effective solution to the humanitarian problems can be achieved without a comprehensive political settlement of the Kampuchean conflict,

Convinced that, to bring about durable peace in South-East Asia, there is an urgent need for a comprehensive political solution to the Kampuchean problem which will provide for the withdrawal of all foreign forces and ensure respect for the sovereignty, independence, territorial integrity and neutral and non-aligned status of Kampuchea, as well as the right of the Kampuchean people to self-determination free from outside interference,

Convinced further that, after the comprehensive political settlement of the Kampuchean question through peaceful means, the countries of the South-East Asian region can pursue efforts to establish a zone of peace, freedom and neutrality in South-East Asia so as to lessen international tensions and to achieve lasting peace in the region,

Reaffirming the need for all States to adhere strictly to the principles of the Charter of the United Nations, which call for respect for the national independence, sovereignty and territorial integrity of all States, non-intervention and non-interference in the internal affairs of States, non-recourse to the threat or use of force, and peaceful settlement of disputes,

1. *Reaffirms* its resolutions 34/22, 35/6 and 36/5 and calls for their full implementation;

2. *Reiterates its conviction* that the withdrawal of all foreign forces from Kampuchea, the restoration and preservation of its independence, sovereignty and territorial integrity, the right of the Kampuchean people to determine their own destiny and the commitment by all States to non-interference and non-intervention in the internal affairs of Kampuchea are the principal components of any just and lasting resolution to the Kampuchean problem;

3. *Takes note with appreciation* of the report of the *Ad Hoc* Committee of the International Conference on Kampuchea and requests that the Committee continue its work, pending the reconvening of the Conference;

4. *Authorizes* the *Ad Hoc* Committee to convene when necessary and to carry out the tasks entrusted to it in its mandate;

5. *Reaffirms* its decision to reconvene the Conference at an appropriate time in accordance with Conference resolution 1(I);

6. *Renews its appeal* to all States of South-East Asia and others concerned to attend future sessions of the Conference;

7. *Requests* the Conference to report to the General Assembly on its future sessions;

8. *Requests* the Secretary-General to continue to consult with and assist the Conference and the *Ad Hoc* Committee and to provide them on a regular basis with the necessary facilities to carry out their functions;

9. *Expresses its appreciation once again* to the Secretary-General for taking appropriate steps in following the situation closely and requests him to continue to do so and to exercise his good offices in order to contribute to a comprehensive political settlement;

10. *Expresses its deep appreciation once again* to donor countries, the United Nations and its agencies and other national and international humanitarian organizations which have rendered relief assistance to the Kampuchean people, and appeals to them to continue existing arrangements to assist those Kampucheans who are still in need, especially along the Thai-Kampuchean border and in the holding centres in Thailand;

11. *Reiterates its deep appreciation* to the Secretary-General for his efforts in co-ordinating humanitarian relief assistance and in monitoring its distribution, and requests him to continue such efforts as are necessary;

12. *Urges* the countries of South-East Asia, once a comprehensive political solution to the Kampuchean conflict is achieved, to exert renewed efforts to establish a zone of peace, freedom and neutrality in South-East Asia;

13. *Reiterates the hope* that, following a comprehensive political solution, an intergovernmental committee will be established to consider a programme of assistance to Kampuchea for the reconstruction of its economy and for the economic and social development of all States in the region;

14. *Requests* the Secretary-General to report to the General Assembly at its thirty-eighth session on the implementation of the present resolution;

15. *Decides* to include in the provisional agenda of its thirty-eighth session the item entitled "The situation in Kampuchea".

Recorded vote in Assembly as follows:

In favour: Antigua and Barbuda, Argentina, Australia, Austria, Bahamas, Bahrain, Bangladesh, Barbados, Belgium, Belize, Bhutan, Botswana, Brazil, Burma, Burundi, Canada, Central African Republic, Chad, Chile, China, Colombia, Comoros, Costa Rica, Democratic Kampuchea, Denmark, Djibouti, Dominica, Dominican Republic, Ecuador, Egypt, El Salvador, Equatorial Guinea, Fiji, France, Gabon, Gambia, Germany, Federal Republic of, Ghana, Greece, Guatemala, Guinea, Haiti, Honduras, Iceland, Indonesia, Ireland, Israel, Italy, Ivory Coast, Jamaica, Japan, Kenya, Kuwait, Lesotho, Liberia, Luxembourg, Malaysia, Maldives, Mali, Malta, Mauritania, Mauritius, Morocco, Nepal, Netherlands, New Zealand, Niger, Nigeria, Norway, Oman, Pakistan, Papua New Guinea, Paraguay, Peru, Philippines, Portugal, Qatar, Rwanda, Saint Lucia, Saint Vincent and the Grenadines, Samoa, Saudi Arabia, Senegal, Singapore, Solomon Islands, Somalia, Spain, Sri Lanka, Sudan, Swaziland, Sweden, Thailand, Togo, Tunisia, Turkey, United Kingdom, United Republic of Cameroon, United States, Upper Volta, Uruguay, Venezuela, Yugoslavia, Zaire, Zambia, Zimbabwe.

Against: Afghanistan, Angola, Bulgaria, Byelorussian SSR, Congo, Cuba, Czechoslovakia, Democratic Yemen, Ethiopia, German Democratic Republic,

Grenada, Hungary, Lao People's Democratic Republic, Libyan Arab Jamahiriya, Mongolia, Mozambique, Nicaragua, Poland, Seychelles, Syrian Arab Republic, Ukrainian SSR, USSR, Viet Nam.

Abstaining: Algeria, Benin, Cape Verde, Finland, Guinea-Bissau, Guyana, India, Lebanon, Madagascar, Malawi, Mexico, Panama, Sao Tome and Principe, Sierra Leone, Suriname, Trinidad and Tobago, Uganda, United Arab Emirates, United Republic of Tanzania, Vanuatu.

Credentials of Democratic Kampuchea

The credentials of the representatives of Democratic Kampuchea were discussed and accepted at two 1982 General Assembly sessions (twelfth special, July; thirty-seventh regular, October) together with those submitted on behalf of other United Nations Member States. In October, the Assembly rejected by vote a proposal not to approve those credentials. Several communications on the subject were also received.

By a letter of 12 February,[5] the Lao People's Democratic Republic transmitted a telegram to the Secretary-General from the Vice-President of the Council of Ministers and Minister for Foreign Affairs of the People's Republic of Kampuchea, stating that it was the sole Government empowered to represent Kampuchea, as so-called Democratic Kampuchea had been overthrown by the Kampucheans in January 1979.

A telegram of 17 September to the Assembly President and the Secretary-General from the Foreign Minister of the People's Republic of Kampuchea, forwarded by Viet Nam on 23 September,[8] demanded the expulsion of Coalition Government representatives at the Assembly's thirty-seventh session and asked that Kampuchea's seat in the United Nations be restored to the People's Republic as the sole authentic and legitimate representative of Kampuchea; he added that all resolutions adopted in the absence of the People's Republic would be considered null and void. Responding by a letter of 28 September,[4] Democratic Kampuchea requested an emergency meeting of the Assembly's Credentials Committee to rule on the credentials question and report its findings without delay.

The question of Democratic Kampuchea's credentials was raised in the Credentials Committee on 6 October when it met to consider the credentials of representatives to the thirty-seventh session. At that meeting the Committee accepted the credentials of all States that had submitted them, which included Democratic Kampuchea. On 26 October, the Assembly adopted a resolution[14] approving the report of its Credentials Committee[13] after rejecting the day before, by a recorded vote of 90 to 29, with 26 abstentions, an 11-nation amendment, introduced by the Lao People's Democratic Republic, to have the report approved except with regard to the credentials of Democratic Kampuchea.[1] Voting in favour of the amendment were: Afghanistan, Albania, Algeria, Angola, Benin, Bulgaria, Byelorussian SSR,

Congo, Cuba, Czechoslovakia, Democratic Yemen, Ethiopia, German Democratic Republic, Grenada, Guyana, Hungary, India, Lao People's Democratic Republic, Libyan Arab Jamahiriya, Mongolia, Mozambique, Nicaragua, Poland, Sao Tome and Principe, Seychelles, Syrian Arab Republic, Ukrainian SSR, USSR, Viet Nam.

The Assembly's decision in favour of Democratic Kampuchea was categorically rejected by the Foreign Ministry of the People's Republic of Kampuchea in a 25 October statement, transmitted by Viet Nam on 29 October,[10] which reiterated that the right to authentic and legal representation of Kampuchea belonged solely to the People's Republic.

Similar Assembly decisions in 1979,[15] 1980[16] and 1981[17] were earlier challenged in a 15 September memorandum issued at Brussels, Belgium, by the International Association of Democratic Lawyers, and transmitted by Viet Nam on 14 October.[9] Stating that the overriding criterion was the objective one of a Government's effectiveness rather than the subjective one of legitimacy, the memorandum argued that the Assembly's decisions with respect to Kampuchean credentials violated its rules of procedure and consistent practice.

Three communications were also sent to the Chairman of the Commission on Human Rights. A protest against the presence of Democratic Kampuchean representatives at the Commission's February/March session was lodged by the Vice-President of the Council of Ministers and Minister for Foreign Affairs of the People's Republic of Kampuchea in a 27 January message reported by the SPK news agency on 28 January and transmitted by Viet Nam on 6 February.[7] The text of this protest in a telegram was transmitted to the Secretary-General on 30 April by the Lao People's Democratic Republic.[6]

On 4 February, 14 Eastern European and other States protested Democratic Kampuchea's representation at the Commission's session as illegal, claiming that the only existing Kampuchean State was the People's Republic.[12] Replying to this letter on 10 February,[2] Democratic Kampuchea accused Viet Nam and its supporters of impugning the Assembly resolutions recognizing it as the legitimate representative of Kampuchea, and of trying to exploit the Commission as a platform to force acceptance of Viet Nam's *fait accompli* in Kampuchea.

Two letters, one dated 12 July[11] and the other 16 July,[3] were addressed to the President of the Economic and Social Council. By the first, 15 Eastern European and other States said they considered the presence of Democratic Kampuchea's delegation at the July session of the Council to be illegal, since the only existing Kampuchean State was the People's Republic of Kampuchea. By the

second letter, Democratic Kampuchea transmitted the 9 July proclamation on the formation of the Coalition Government of Democratic Kampuchea (p. 335).

Amendment rejected. [1]Angola, Congo, Cuba, Democratic Yemen, Ethiopia, Grenada, Guyana, India, Lao People's Democratic Republic, Libyan Arab Jamahiriya, Viet Nam, A/37/L.8 & Add.1.

Letters.
　　Democratic Kampuchea: [2]10 Feb., E/CN.4/1982/12; [3]16 July, E/1982/108; [4]28 Sep., A/37/492.
　　Lao People's Democratic Republic: [5]12 Feb., A/37/87-S/14871; [6]30 Apr., E/1982/63.
　　Viet Nam: [7]6 Feb., E/CN.4/1982/11; [8]23 Sep., A/37/481; [9]14 Oct., A/37/549; [10]29 Oct., A/37/588.
　　Others: [11]Bulgaria, Byelorussian SSR, Cuba, Czechoslovakia, Democratic Yemen, Ethiopia, German Democratic Republic, Hungary, Mongolia, Nicaragua, Poland, Syrian Arab Republic, Ukrainian SSR, USSR, Viet Nam: 12 July, E/1982/107. [12]Bulgaria, Byelorussian SSR, Cuba, Czechoslovakia, Democratic Yemen, Ethiopia, German Democratic Republic, Hungary, Mongolia, Nicaragua, Poland, Ukrainian SSR, USSR, Viet Nam: 4 Feb., E/CN.4/1982/9.

Report. [13]Credentials Committee, A/37/543.
Resolution (1982). [14]GA: 37/5 A, 26 Oct.
Yearbook references. [15]1979, p. 291; [16]1980, p. 331; [17]1981, p. 248.

Kampuchea-Thailand border

During 1982, the Secretary-General received a number of letters concerning the situation on the Kampuchea-Thailand border, conveying complaints against Thailand submitted by the Lao People's Democratic Republic and Viet Nam, and complaints by Thailand against Viet Nam.

A statement by the spokesman for the Ministry of Foreign Affairs of the People's Republic of Kampuchea, as reported on 2 January by the SPK news agency and transmitted on 12 January by Viet Nam,[16] demanded the return of a Kampuchean patrol boat and five crew members, captured in Kampuchean territorial waters by three Thai navy vessels. The full text of the Ministry's statement, giving the date of the incident as 28 December 1981, was transmitted by the Lao People's Democratic Republic on 14 January 1982.[1]

Two further statements by the Foreign Ministry spokesman were transmitted. One, dated 19 February and transmitted on 28 April by the Lao People's Democratic Republic,[2] protested Thai shelling with toxic chemicals of Phnom Melai in Battambang province on 12 and 14 February, said to have injured 20 civilians. Another statement, dated 13 May and transmitted on 25 May by Viet Nam,[19] protested Thailand's intensified airspace violations in early May, the most serious on 9 May when two Thai jet fighters had fired rockets at a helicopter on a mission over the Anlung Weng region, 14 kilometres inside Kampuchea. Earlier reports, of 19 and 28 April, by the SPK news agency, transmitted by Viet Nam on 12 May,[18] listed Thai incursions between 7 and 20 April into

Kampuchean territorial airspace (over 10 reconnaissance flights between 16 and 20 April) and waters (186 violations by armed vessels cited in the first report and 134 in the second), as well as some 190 incidents of shelling, killing a civilian and wounding two others in an attack in the Preah Vihear region.

The Viet Nam News Agency, in a statement of 25 September transmitted four days later,[23] rejected an allegation by the Supreme Command of Thailand, as broadcast by Radio Beijing, that Vietnamese armed forces operating from Kampuchea had recently killed more than 100 Khmers at a village in Preyveng province, Thailand.

Focusing on what it called Thai provocations against the People's Republic of Kampuchea and a propaganda campaign against Viet Nam, a report of an interview granted to the SPK news agency on 30 September by the Vice-Chairman of the Council of Ministers and Minister of Defence of the People's Republic, transmitted on 11 October by Viet Nam,[24] accused Thailand of collaborating with Khmer reactionaries by allowing them to use its territory to conduct armed attacks on Kampuchea and of rejecting the repeated proposal for a demilitarized or security zone along the border.

A 26 November statement by the spokesman of the Foreign Ministry of the People's Republic, transmitted on 2 December by the Lao People's Democratic Republic,[3] alleged that, according to Western sources, Singapore had secretly supplied the Son Sann forces with some 2,640 automatic rifles transported across Thailand and had promised a similar supply for the Samdech Norodom Sihanouk forces.

For its part, Thailand complained of numerous incursions into its territory and violations of its airspace and waters by Vietnamese forces operating from Kampuchea. In most instances, Thailand condemned these violations as unprovoked acts of aggression and reaffirmed its right to take steps to defend its territorial integrity and protect the life and property of its nationals.

Viet Nam, in several letters, rejected the Thai allegations as groundless and slanderous, stating that they served only to promote China's scheme to foment tension along the Kampuchea-Thailand border, incite hostility between Thailand and the Indo-Chinese countries, and undermine the developing dialogue between those countries and the Association of South-East Asian Nations.

By a letter of 22 January,[4] Thailand reported that, after having been fired upon by an armed trawler in Thai territorial waters near Kut Island on 28 December 1981, Thai naval patrol ships had sunk the trawler and rescued 7 of its 13-member crew, 2 of whom had later died; the survivors had stated that the trawler was an illegally seized Thai fishing vessel and that, at the time of the sinking, 6 of its crew had been Vietnamese.

By a 29 January letter,[5] Thailand cited three incidents on 16 December 1981 and 18 January 1982 involving bombardment of Thai territory by Vietnamese aircraft, and shelling and intrusion by Vietnamese forces. Further incidents of shelling and an armed attack between 31 January and 9 February, mainly on villages in Prachinburi province, resulting in 5 deaths, injury to 8 including a Thai soldier and damage to property, were detailed in letters of 10 February[6] and 16 February.[7] A 22 February letter[8] reported that, on 17 February, 40 Vietnamese soldiers had attacked a 15-man Thai border patrol unit inside Thai territory in Chanthaburi province, leaving 5 of the border patrol dead and a civilian injured. Also on 22 February,[17] a letter from Viet Nam annexed two statements by the Viet Nam News Agency, dated 6 and 19 February, rejecting a Thai newspaper report of shellings of Thai territory by Vietnamese troops and the reported Vietnamese attack on Thai border guards.

According to a 30 April letter from Thailand,[9] areas of Prachinburi and Trat provinces had been shelled between 2 and 7 April in fighting between Democratic Kampuchea and the Vietnamese–Heng Samrin forces; casualties included 2 dead and 10 injured, among them 5 border police.

A 16 August letter,[10] covering May and June, reported more than 30 incursions into Thailand, 20 shelling incidents resulting in loss of life and property, 3 airspace violations, and intrusions into territorial waters during which 3 Thai fishing boats had been captured. Shelling attacks between 9 and 29 August on Chanthaburi, Prachinburi, Si Sa Ket and Trat provinces, resulting in damage to houses and to a village school, were detailed in a letter of 7 September.[11] Rocket attacks between 1 and 12 September on Prachinburi and Surin provinces were described in a 5 October letter,[12] in which Thailand charged that the conflict in Kampuchea and the continued presence in that country of 200,000 Vietnamese troops threatened the security of its eastern border. By letters of 23 August[20] and 24 August,[21] Viet Nam denied the May and June violations enumerated by Thailand and, on 15 September[22] and 19 October,[25] the alleged violations in August and September.

A press release by the Ministry of Foreign Affairs of Thailand, forwarded on 7 October,[13] reported the return to Viet Nam, as attested by documents signed by the two countries on 1 October, of a Vietnamese military aircraft that had crash-landed in Thailand on 11 February; 12 of its crew had been repatriated on 21 May, along with the remains of one who had died of injuries from the crash. A press release by the Permanent

Mission of Viet Nam to the United Nations, forwarded by a letter of 29 October,[26] asserted that the Vietnamese aircraft had strayed into Thailand due to bad weather and technical trouble.

On 8 December,[14] Thailand reported 5 shelling incidents during the second half of September and, throughout October, at least 6 incursions into Thai territory and regular barrages of artillery and mortar fire, killing a Thai soldier, injuring more than 6 others, damaging property and killing livestock. On 16 December,[27] Viet Nam forwarded a Viet Nam News Agency statement of the same day denying the Thai charges.

A 21 December letter from Thailand[15] reported that, following 20 serious violations since 1 November, resulting in 3 civilian deaths, another incursion had occurred on 1 December in which Vietnamese troops fired at a bus with a rocket-propelled grenade, killing 2 passengers, injuring 11 others and destroying the bus; and, on 10 December, a shelling incident had killed a woman, injured several other civilians and damaged houses.

Letters.

> Lao People's Democratic Republic: [1]14 Jan., A/37/66-S/14837; [2]28 Apr., A/37/212; [3]2 Dec., A/37/690-S/15507.
> Thailand: [4]22 Jan., A/37/76-S/14846; [5]29 Jan., A/37/78-S/14853; [6]10 Feb., A/37/86-S/14868; [7]16 Feb., A/37/88-S/14872; [8]22 Feb., A/37/98-S/14882; [9]30 Apr., A/37/216-S/15035; [10]16 Aug., A/37/391-S/15366; [11]7 Sep., A/37/429-S/15388; [12]5 Oct., A/37/524-S/15450; [13]7 Oct., A/37/529-S/15453; [14]8 Dec., A/37/729-S/15517; [15]21 Dec., A/38/56-S/15542.
> Viet Nam: [16]12 Jan., A/37/63-S/14833; [17]22 Feb., A/37/97-S/14881; [18]12 May, A/37/224-S/15075; [19]25 May, A/37/254; [20]23 Aug., A/37/400; [21]24 Aug., A/37/403; [22]15 Sep., A/37/451-S/15395; [23]29 Sep., A/37/504; [24]11 Oct., A/37/537; [25]19 Oct., A/37/559; [26]29 Oct., A/37/589; [27]16 Dec., A/37/781.

China and Viet Nam

Between January and November 1982, the Secretary-General received communications from China and Viet Nam, each continuing to charge the other with aggressive acts along their common border. The communications also contained an exchange of views on cease-fire proposals. Relations between the two countries were also discussed during the General Assembly's discussion in November on peace and security in South-East Asia.

On 14 January,[10] Viet Nam transmitted a statement of the same date by the spokesman for its Ministry of Foreign Affairs stating that, as an expression of good will, Viet Nam would unilaterally act on its 28 December 1981 proposal to China for a cessation of hostilities along their common border on the occasion of Têt (20-29 January 1982), the Lunar New Year festival. China had earlier rejected the proposal as hypocritical, in a 4 January memorandum by its Ministry of Foreign Affairs, transmitted on 22 January,[1] reiter-

ating that tension along the border was due to Viet Nam's anti-China policies and regional hegemonism; as long as Viet Nam refrained from military provocations and incursions into Chinese territory, China would not counter-attack.

A proposal for an immediate end to armed conflict in the border area and for the start of a third round of China–Viet Nam talks, to take place during the first half of the year at either Beijing or Hanoi, was made in a note of 30 January from the Vietnamese to the Chinese Foreign Ministry, transmitted on 10 February.[12] In a telegram forwarded on 15 March by the Lao People's Democratic Republic,[9] the Chairman of the Committee for the Defence of Peace in Kampuchea, speaking of a recent improvement in Viet Nam–China relations, welcomed Viet Nam's initiative as well as its earlier proposal for a suspension of hostilities along the border.

By letters of 15 February[2] and 8 March,[3] China transmitted two notes from its Foreign Ministry to the Embassy of Viet Nam in China, strongly protesting Viet Nam's intensified armed provocations and incursions across China's border. The first note, dated 11 February, said there had been 416 incidents between 21 December 1981 and 29 January 1982, resulting in 6 people dead, 11 injured and property damage; the second, dated 8 March, charged that on 3 March Vietnamese naval vessels had attacked 11 Chinese fishing boats on the high seas, leaving 18 people missing, 6 others wounded, a boat blown up and another seized with its crew. Viet Nam rejected this charge as groundless by a letter of 17 March,[13] to which were annexed: a note of 5 March from its Foreign Ministry to the Chinese Embassy, countercharging that on 2 and 3 March 40 Chinese armed boats had intruded into Viet Nam's territorial waters some 4 to nautical 10 miles off its coast in an act of espionage and provocation; and a Viet Nam News Agency dispatch of 10 March stating that the captain of the boat captured on 3 March in Vietnamese territorial waters had confessed to operating an armed boat that had intruded into Viet Nam's territorial waters on orders from higher authorities.

A note of 25 May from the Vietnamese to the Chinese Foreign Ministry, transmitted on 27 May,[14] protested numerous armed incursions by China into Viet Nam's territory since the beginning of the year, charging that they had been designed to destroy Thoong Khoang dam near Ngoc Khe in Cao Bang province, as part of a plan to sabotage Viet Nam's economy and perpetuate border tension.

0n 27 June,[4] China transmitted a 26 June note from its Foreign Ministry to the Vietnamese Embassy, alleging that, on 16 June, armed Vietnamese vessels had attacked and seized a Chinese fishing vessel in its territorial waters; it demanded the return of all vessels seized, together with their crew, and compensation for resulting losses.

In a statement of 25 August, transmitted the following day,[15] Viet Nam's Foreign Ministry reported that on 14 August it had proposed another cessation of hostilities along the China–Viet Nam border from 27 August to 7 October, to allow National Day celebrations on both sides; it added that, despite China's lack of response, Viet Nam, in a spirit of friendship with the Chinese people, had ordered its forces to observe a cease-fire during that period.

On 30 August,[5] 13 September[6] and 14 October,[7] China transmitted three notes from its Foreign Ministry to the Vietnamese Embassy. The first note, dated 25 August and responding to Viet Nam's proposal of 14 August, charged that tension on the China–Viet Nam border was due solely to Viet Nam's repeated acts of provocation in pursuit of its anti-China policies. The second, dated 12 September, protested the intrusion into China's airspace on 10 September by two MIG-21 jet fighter aircraft on a reconnaissance mission. The third, dated 13 October, protested 102 incidents of firing into Chinese territory, 3 of shelling, 2 airspace intrusions and 2 incursions by armed Vietnamese, resulting in 3 deaths and injury to 11 persons; observing that these acts had taken place during the period of National Day celebrations, the note concluded that Viet Nam's latest call for a cessation of hostilities and its announcement of a unilateral cease-fire were sheer hypocrisy designed to cover up intensified efforts to increase tension.

A Viet Nam News Agency statement of 12 September, transmitted on 20 September,[16] denied the allegation that Vietnamese MIG jet fighters had intruded into China's airspace. A 10 October note from the Vietnamese to the Chinese Foreign Ministry, transmitted on 19 October,[18] expressed regret at China's rejection and distortion of Viet Nam's cease-fire proposals and rejected as slanderous fabrications the incidents listed in China's 13 October note.

With regard to the maritime boundary between China and Viet Nam, a white paper published by the Foreign Ministry of Viet Nam was forwarded on 4 February,[11] presenting historical evidence of its claim to sovereignty over Hoang Sa (Paracels) and Truong Sa (Spratly) archipelagos in the South China Sea (called by the Vietnamese the East Sea), and refuting China's claim over them. A statement by the Viet Nam News Agency, dated 25 September and transmitted on 29 September,[17] protested contracts which, according to foreign sources, had been entered into by China and foreign petroleum companies for the exploration of oil and gas around the two archipelagos, and

declared that Viet Nam would not tolerate encroachment on resources within its territorial waters and continental shelf.

A government statement of 12 November, transmitted on 30 November,[19] defined the coastal baseline from which Viet Nam measured its territorial sea and other maritime zones in the Gulf of Bac Bo (Tonkin) between China and Viet Nam, and added that the lines around the Hoang Sa and Truong Sa archipelagos would be determined in a future instrument. The spokesman of the Ministry of Foreign Affairs of China, in a statement of 28 November transmitted the next day,[8] declared null and void the maritime boundaries in the Beibu (Tonkin) Gulf as described by Viet Nam and reiterated that the islands claimed by Viet Nam—which the Chinese called Xisha and Nansha—were an inalienable part of China's territory.

Letters. China: [1]22 Jan., A/37/77-S/14847; [2]15 Feb., A/37/90-S/14874; [3]8 Mar., A/37/110-S/14898; [4]27 June, A/37/318-S/15264; [5]30 Aug., A/37/417-S/15381; [6]13 Sep., A/37/440-S/15390; [7]14 Oct., A/37/546-S/15457; [8]29 Nov., A/37/682-S/15505. [9]Lao People's Democratic Republic: 15 Mar., A/37/117-S/14907. Viet Nam: [10]14 Jan., A/37/67-S/14839; [11]4 Feb., A/37/83-S/14861; [12]10 Feb., A/37/85-S/14865; [13]17 Mar., A/37/120-S/14911; [14]27 May, A/37/258-S/15133; [15]26 Aug., A/37/410-S/15375; [16]20 Sep., A/37/475-S/15425; [17]29 Sep., A/37/507-S/15441; [18]19 Oct., A/37/558; [19]30 Nov., A/37/697.

Peace and security of South-East Asia

A number of letters addressed to the Secretary-General during 1982 concerned general aspects of relations among the nations of South-East Asia. Most were circulated as documents under the General Assembly's agenda item on the "Question of peace, stability and co-operation in South-East Asia"—an item on which the Assembly held a two-day debate in November.

Communications. On 19 February,[3] the Lao People's Democratic Republic transmitted a communiqué issued by its Minister for Foreign Affairs and those of Viet Nam and the People's Republic of Kampuchea at a conference held at the Lao capital of Vientiane on 16 and 17 February. The communiqué affirmed their readiness to discuss with Thailand questions of common concern and also with the members of the Association of South-East Asian Nations (ASEAN), if they were still not ready for a regional conference as proposed in January 1981,[23] to discuss questions of peace and stability in South-East Asia; such contacts could be direct or indirect, bilateral or multilateral, but in no way, the communiqué stressed, could they be linked to the question of mutual *de facto* or *de jure* recognition (of the People's Republic of Kampuchea). These proposals were denounced in an 18 February statement by the spokesman of the Ministry of Foreign Affairs of Democratic Kampuchea, transmitted on 22 February,[2] which said they were attempts to gain acceptance for the *fait accompli* brought about by Viet Nam's invasion of Kampuchea.

Referring to the General Assembly's December 1981 request for suggestions on the development and strengthening of good-neighbourliness between States,[22] the Deputy Foreign Minister of Viet Nam, in a 4 June message to the Secretary-General transmitted on 7 June,[12] said Viet Nam had expressed its good will to resolve disputed problems with the other Indo-Chinese countries, with ASEAN members in general and with Thailand in particular, and it hoped that China would resume talks with Viet Nam in order to solve mutual problems.

By a joint communiqué issued on 16 June at the conclusion of a three-day meeting in Singapore, excerpts of which were transmitted by Thailand on 30 June,[6] the ASEAN Foreign Ministers reiterated their commitment to General Assembly resolutions calling for the immediate and total withdrawal of Viet Nam's forces from Kampuchea, reaffirmed that a comprehensive political settlement of the conflict could be achieved only within the framework established by those resolutions, and stated that such a settlement was essential to the establishment of a zone of peace, freedom and neutrality in South-East Asia.

On 25 June,[14] Viet Nam forwarded the transcript of an interview given on 18 June by its Foreign Minister to the Viet Nam News Agency on his scheduled visits to Burma, Indonesia, Malaysia, the Philippines and Singapore, which, he said, were intended to increase mutual understanding and trust and to discuss bilateral problems and questions of peace and stability in South-East Asia. Visits to three of the countries (Singapore, 18-20 July; Burma; Malaysia, 25-28 July) were characterized as frank and useful exchanges of views in Viet Nam News Agency interviews with the Foreign Minister and other dispatches of 22 July, transmitted by Viet Nam on 29 July,[16] and 28 July (three dispatches), transmitted on 3 August.[18] While each side retained its viewpoint, the Foreign Minister stated, there was agreement that dialogue should continue; to that end invitations to visit Viet Nam had been accepted.

A press statement issued by the ASEAN Foreign Ministers at the conclusion of a meeting at Bangkok, Thailand, on 7 August, transmitted on 10 August,[7] concluded that Viet Nam's policy on Kampuchea remained unchanged. Making the same point, an information paper issued by ASEAN and transmitted by Thailand on 20 September[8] stated that the proposals by the visiting Vietnamese Foreign Minister evaded the central issue of total withdrawal of foreign forces, ignored the basic question of the Kampucheans' right to self-determination and rejected the United Nations framework for a negotiated solution.

On 8 July,[5] the Lao People's Democratic Republic and Viet Nam transmitted a communiqué issued by their Foreign Ministers and that of the People's Republic of Kampuchea on 7 July at the end of a two-day conference held at Ho Chi Minh City, Viet Nam. The Ministers called anew on China to respond positively to past proposals for a bilateral or multilateral treaty of peaceful coexistence and supported Viet Nam's proposal to resume the China–Viet Nam talks; reaffirmed their readiness to negotiate with Thailand and consider a further partial withdrawal of Vietnamese troops if Thailand denied asylum and support to the forces intent on sabotaging Kampuchea's revival; reiterated their proposal for a demilitarized zone along the Kampuchea-Thailand border but, failing that, proposed a safety zone where only the armed forces of the People's Republic and of Thailand would be stationed, on their respective side of the border; reiterated their readiness to engage in dialogue with ASEAN; proposed an international conference on South-East Asia, with the participation of the Indo-Chinese countries, ASEAN and Burma, as well as of China, France, India, the USSR, the United Kingdom, the United States and the Secretary-General; and demanded the expulsion of representatives of Democratic Kampuchea from the General Assembly, leaving Kampuchea's seat vacant.

Elaborating on these proposals, a letter of 15 September from the Deputy Prime Minister and Minister for Foreign Affairs of the Lao People's Democratic Republic to the ASEAN Foreign Ministers, transmitted on 22 September,[4] added that disagreements between the Indo-Chinese and ASEAN countries could be settled by negotiation through dialogue based on mutual respect for each other's legitimate interests and on equality and mutual agreement, free from imposition and outside interference.

Replying by a memorandum forwarded on 21 October by Thailand,[9] ASEAN observed that the Indo-Chinese proposals appeared to have been designed to further Viet Nam's objective of bringing about a *fait accompli* in Kampuchea; it insisted on total withdrawal of all foreign forces from Kampuchea and the right of the Kampucheans to determine their own destiny.

Several letters from Viet Nam complained of United States activities against Viet Nam and against peace and stability in South-East Asia.

A 5 January statement by the spokesman for Viet Nam's Foreign Ministry, transmitted on 8 January,[10] stated that the peace and security of the region was being seriously jeopardized by Thailand's reported authorization to the United

States Seventh Fleet to reuse its U Taphao air base for a joint training programme, marking a United States attempt to re-establish itself militarily in South-East Asia with Thailand's collaboration. The same statement, as further reported by the SPK (Samporamean Kampuchea) news agency on 11 January, was transmitted by Viet Nam the next day.[11]

A statement of 24 June by the Viet Nam News Agency, transmitted a day later,[13] rejected a United States allegation that a group of its destroyers had been attacked by Vietnamese fishing boats south of Con Son Island, Viet Nam, on 20 June. Two dispatches from the same source, one on a press conference held on 13 July by Viet Nam's Vice-Minister of Culture in charge of information, transmitted on 15 July,[15] and the other a Hanoi dispatch of 24 July, transmitted on 29 July,[17] detailed the confessions of an alleged agent of the United States Central Intelligence Agency, according to which China and the United States, with Thailand's assistance, were organizing reactionary forces of Lao, Kampuchean and Vietnamese exiles to infiltrate their former countries for sabotage. By a letter of 6 August,[19] Viet Nam circulated the second part of a dossier on chemical warfare waged by the United States against Viet Nam and the other Indo-Chinese countries from 1969 to 1971 and its long-term effects on population, ecology, soil and climate.

General Assembly action. The question of peace, stability and co-operation in South-East Asia was discussed by the General Assembly on 5 and 8 November.

A number of speakers expressed the view that the policy of intervention and aggression pursued by China and the United States, with the aid of certain circles in ASEAN, were responsible for the tension in South-East Asia. To resolve this situation, they supported the July proposals by the Lao People's Democratic Republic on behalf of the Indo-Chinese countries, as clarified in September (see above), in particular the proposal for an international conference, which they considered as offering a viable prospect for normalization. Among the countries taking this position, Bulgaria said the complications and dangers in South-East Asia stemmed from the long-term strategy of those who sought to maintain a permanent hotbed of tension in the region, to hamper the establishment of good-neighbourly relations and to interfere in the internal affairs of various countries in order to establish their superiority in that part of the world.

Events in Kampuchea, Afghanistan maintained, were internal developments which could not negatively affect the situation in the region and which presented a major obstacle to China's hegemonic ambitions. In the context of continuing threats

from hegemonism and imperialism, Czechoslovakia said, the presence of Vietnamese troops in Kampuchea had been made imperative by the real need to strengthen security there. In Hungary's view, reducing the region's multifarious problems to issues exclusively related to Kampuchea was the strategy of forces which would not allow tension in the region to ease and prospects for a settlement to materialize.

Mongolia stated that foreign forces were acquiring military bases in some countries, maintaining enormous troop concentrations on frontiers of States whose legitimate Governments they were subverting, pulling others into their orbit and transforming their territories into bridgeheads for armed action against neighbouring States. Those forces, the USSR added, were trying to present the root cause of tension in the region as the presence of Vietnamese troops in Kampuchea when in reality it was their attempts to hinder the irreversible process of Kampuchea's national rebirth and to pit the Indo-Chinese countries against the ASEAN States. The USSR added that the United States was seeking to strengthen its strategic position in the region—a point also made by the Byelorussian SSR, Poland and the Ukrainian SSR—and said Australia was pandering to the United States by following its line of aggression and hostility against the Indo-Chinese peoples. Viet Nam stated that, without interference by China and the United States, the Indo-Chinese countries and ASEAN, inspired by good will, were perfectly capable of settling their problems themselves; those who called for the total withdrawal of Viet Nam's troops from Kampuchea were silent about the serious threat from 400,000 Chinese troops massed on the China–Viet Nam border.

Viet Nam said it was encouraging that all delegations, except China, had clearly spoken in favour of the need to pursue dialogue and negotiations for a solution acceptable to the parties; the choice was either to accept the unilateral solution a number of countries would impose or to seek a solution in the spirit of the February 1981 declaration by the Conference of Ministers for Foreign Affairs of the Non-Aligned Countries, which urged dialogue among all States of the region.[24] The Lao People's Democratic Republic emphasized that the Indo-Chinese countries, in proposing a conference on South-East Asia, had taken into account not only the principles and objectives of the Movement of Non-Aligned Countries but also the practice followed by regional intergovernmental bodies, which had always insisted that regional problems be settled primarily by the States of the region. Bulgaria, Cuba and the German Democratic Republic, among those supporting the conference, considered it a viable prospect for normalizing the situation in the region.

Afghanistan supported the proposal and observed that, by assigning a major role to the United Nations in the conference, the Indo-Chinese countries had accepted an important condition put forward by ASEAN. The Byelorussian SSR made a similar observation and, with Hungary and Mongolia, added that the United Nations was prevented from playing a fully positive role towards normalization of the region so long as Democratic Kampuchea continued to usurp the seat that rightfully belonged to the People's Republic of Kampuchea.

Hungary attached great importance to the proposals made by Viet Nam for normalizing its relations with China and considered equally noteworthy Viet Nam's recent gestures in the direction of the United States, since improved relations between them could prove a keystone of peace and stability in South-East Asia. The Byelorussian SSR, Poland, the Ukrainian SSR and the USSR urged the United Nations to support and encourage dialogue. Viet Nam said it was encouraging to note that throughout the year a climate of dialogue and détente had begun to emerge in relations between the countries of Indo-China and those of ASEAN.

In the view of Albania, the complicated situation in the region was a direct consequence of the policy of spoliation, expansionism and hegemonism of the USSR, China and the United States, showing that their rivalry for hegemony and spheres of influence was on the increase; the peoples of the region must not fall into the trap set by the super-Powers.

The ASEAN States, along with Australia, China and Democratic Kampuchea, maintained that Viet Nam's invasion and continued occupation of Kampuchea was the main cause of regional tension. Until Viet Nam faced up to that fact, Australia said, there could be little scope for moving seriously on the principles which the Lao People's Democratic Republic and Viet Nam maintained should govern inter-State relations in the region. It remained the ASEAN view, Thailand said, as well as that of the great majority of United Nations Members which had voted for the Assembly resolution of 28 October on the Kampuchea situation,[20] that a comprehensive political settlement of the Kampuchea problem must first be found within the framework of Assembly resolutions in order to pave the way for renewed efforts to establish a zone of peace, freedom and neutrality in the region. A similar view was expressed by the Philippines.

Democratic Kampuchea observed that for the third year the Assembly had to sit through sterile and futile debate on an item on which no resolution had ever been adopted; that was a diversionary tactic by Viet Nam to distract attention from its invasion and occupation of Kampuchea and to disguise its expansionist plans in South-East Asia.

Japan believed the item should be taken up only after a comprehensive political settlement of the Kampuchea problem had been achieved.

Malaysia said the Movement of Non-Aligned Countries, whose 1981 declaration had been quoted selectively, had urged the States of the region to undertake a dialogue, but had also referred to the withdrawal of forces from Kampuchea and the right of the Kampucheans to self-determination; Malaysia regarded the proposal for a regional conference as vague and impractical, for it ignored the source of tension and was therefore nothing more than propaganda to confuse the Kampuchean issue with a host of others.

China said it posed no obstacles to the improvement of relations with Viet Nam, which could be realized in no time if Viet Nam renounced its policies of aggression and expansion, withdrew its troops from Kampuchea and abandoned its hostility towards China; China also endorsed the ASEAN proposal for the establishment of a zone of peace, freedom and neutrality in South-East Asia.

At the conclusion of the debate on 8 November, the Assembly decided without vote[1] to include this item in the provisional agenda of its 1983 session. This action was taken on an oral proposal of the President, who said it had been proposed by the sponsors of the item.

Previously, on 28 October, in its resolution on the Kampuchea situation, the Assembly urged the South-East Asian countries, once a comprehensive political solution to the Kampuchean conflict was achieved, to exert renewed efforts to establish a zone of peace, freedom and neutrality in South-East Asia.[21]

Decision (1982). [1]GA: 37/405, 8 Nov., text following.
Letters. [2]Democratic Kampuchea: 22 Feb., A/37/96. Lao People's Democratic Republic: [3]19 Feb., A/37/93-S/14877; [4]22 Sep., A/37/477. [5]Lao People's Democratic Republic, Viet Nam: 8 July, A/37/334-S/15281. Thailand: [6]30 June, A/37/324-S/15268; [7]10 Aug., A/37/387-S/15364; [8]20 Sep., A/37/466-S/15414; [9]21 Oct., A/37/562-S/15462. Viet Nam: [10]8 Jan., A/37/62-S/14831; [11]12 Jan., A/37/63-S/14833; [12]7 June, A/37/267; [13]25 June, A/37/311; [14]25 June, A/37/319; [15]15 July, A/37/342; [16]29 July, A/37/367; [17]29 July, A/37/368; [18]3 Aug., A/37/371; [19]6 Aug., A/37/377.
Resolution (1982). [20]GA: 37/6, 28 Oct.; [21]ibid., para. 12.
Resolution (prior). [22]GA: 36/101, 9 Dec. 1981 (YUN 1981, p. 152).
Yearbook references. 1981, [23]p. 250, [24]p. 251.
Meeting records. GA: A/37/PV.57, 58 (5, 8 Nov.).

General Assembly decision 37/405

Adopted without vote

Oral proposal by President; agenda item 35.

Question of peace, stability and co-operation in South-East Asia

At its 58th plenary meeting, on 8 November 1982, the General Assembly decided to include in the provisional agenda of its thirty-eighth session the item entitled "Question of peace, stability and co-operation in South-East Asia".

Western Asia

Afghanistan situation

As it had decided in November 1981,[16] the General Assembly took up again in November 1982 the situation in Afghanistan and its implications for international peace and security. It called anew for immediate foreign troop withdrawal, reaffirmed the Afghan people's right to determine their own form of government, and requested continued efforts by the Secretary-General for a political solution. Meanwhile, the Foreign Ministers of Afghanistan and Pakistan, meeting at Geneva in June through the intermediary of the Secretary-General's Personal Representative on the Afghanistan situation, identified areas of agreement and developed ideas on the structure and contents of a comprehensive settlement.

Afghanistan, the socialist countries of Eastern Europe and others opposed the Assembly resolution and called for a negotiated political solution guaranteeing non-intervention in the country's internal affairs; they stated that Afghanistan continued to be threatened by counter-revolutionaries based in neighbouring Pakistan who sought to overthrow the Government established following the revolution of April 1978. Most of those supporting the resolution continued to call for withdrawal of USSR troops sent to Afghanistan in 1979 and the establishment of conditions that would permit the Afghan people to exercise self-determination.

Also during 1982, the Office of the United Nations High Commissioner for Refugees (UNHCR) continued to assist Afghan refugees in Pakistan (p. 354).

Communications. The Secretary-General received a number of communications on the Afghanistan situation during 1982.

By a letter of 8 February,[1] Afghanistan denied allegations by Pakistan in a 29 December 1981 letter[20] of violations of its territory by Afghan gunships and armed men, and stated that armed incursions into Afghanistan continued to be staged from Pakistan with increasing frequency and that Pakistan had been blocking the return of Afghan refugees and subjecting them to anti-Afghanistan propaganda; none the less, since contacts with Pakistan through the good offices of the Secretary-General had proved useful, Afghanistan would continue those contacts, possibly also with Iran.

By letters of 11 March,[5] 31 March[6] and 2 August 1982,[7] Pakistan complained of a series of violations of its airspace and territory by Afghanistan between 20 December 1981 and 23 February 1982, on 15 March, and between April and June; these involved some 31 instances of airspace violations, a machine-gun attack, several shelling incidents and an intrusion into Pakistan territory, resulting in injury to five civilians and loss of livestock.

On 29 June,[2] Afghanistan transmitted an open letter to the Secretary-General signed by 1.2 million Afghan youths, protesting foreign intervention in Afghanistan's internal affairs and acts of terrorism against it by bands trained in Pakistan, and praising assistance rendered by the USSR. Replying on 3 September[8] to the allegation against it and to those in Afghanistan's February letter, Pakistan called them baseless, adding that it had consistently followed a policy of strict non-interference in its neighbours' affairs and had expended much of its own resources to help Afghan refugees in Pakistan, whose return to Afghanistan it would welcome.

The President of Afghanistan, in a 27 September 1982 broadcast message transmitted two days later,[3] noted that its June 1981 decree granting amnesty to all returning counter-revolutionary Afghan nationals was still in force. A call to the United Nations, the peoples of western Asia and of the world at large to support Afghanistan's proposals of May 1980[17] and August 1981[18] for the resolution of the Afghanistan situation was transmitted on 19 November 1982,[4] as adopted by the International Conference on Socio-Economic Development and the Dangers of War (Kabul, 12-15 November).

By a note verbale of 22 March,[10] the United States transmitted a report of that date by its Secretary of State to the United States Congress, on what it termed the use of chemical and toxin weapons by the USSR and its allies in Afghanistan, Kampuchea and the Lao People's Democratic Republic; the report's conclusion with regard to Afghanistan was that USSR forces there had used a variety of lethal and non-lethal chemical agents on resistance forces and Afghan villages since 1979, including nerve agents, phosgene oxime, and various incapacitants and irritants.

The USSR submitted on 20 May[9] a critique prepared by Soviet scientists and other experts, evaluating the statements in the United States report and declaring that its conclusions were unconvincing and contradicted objective medical and technical data; it stated with respect to Afghanistan that there was not a single chemical battalion among USSR troops there, although chemical defence units were an integral part of the army structure and were justified by the use of United States–manufactured chemical weapons by insurgents.

An updated United States Department of State report to the Congress in November, transmitted by a note verbale of 29 November,[11] stated with respect to Afghanistan that reports from February through October indicated that USSR forces continued their selective use of chemicals and toxins against the Afghan resistance, and that physical samples provided new evidence of mycotoxin use.

Report of the Secretary-General. In pursuance of a November 1981 General Assembly request,[16] the Secretary-General submitted to the Assembly and the Security Council on 27 September 1982 a report on activities he had undertaken with respect to the Afghanistan situation.[12]

The report stated that, since assuming office on 1 January, the newly elected Secretary-General had consulted with representatives of Afghanistan, Iran, Pakistan and other Governments in efforts to facilitate negotiations for a political settlement. Diego Cordovez, Under-Secretary-General for Special Political Affairs, appointed in February as the Secretary-General's Personal Representative, had visited those countries (11-19 April), where he had held detailed exchanges of views on the purposes of the diplomatic process and the steps required to carry it forward. In Afghanistan he had met with President Babrak Karmal, Prime Minister Sultan Ali Kishtmand and Minister for Foreign Affairs Shah Mohammad Dost; in Iran, with Foreign Minister Ali Akbar Velayati and other senior officials; and in Pakistan, with President Zia-ul-Haq, Foreign Minister Sahabzada Yaqub-Khan and other senior officials.

As a result of those exchanges, it had been possible to define the contents and scope of the issues to be considered: withdrawal of foreign troops, non-interference in the internal affairs of States, international guarantees of non-interference and voluntary return of refugees. It had been agreed that, as the issues were interrelated, discussions would aim at a comprehensive settlement.

In accordance with agreed procedures, discussions had been held at Geneva (16-24 June) through the intermediary of the Secretary-General's Personal Representative, in which the Foreign Ministers of Afghanistan and Pakistan had taken part. The discussions, of which Iran had been kept informed, had made possible a more detailed definition of the interlocutors' positions, identification of areas of agreement, and development of ideas on the structure and contents of a comprehensive settlement. It had been agreed that the Personal Representative would remain in close contact with the interlocutors and visit the region again towards the end of the year.

The Secretary-General had also taken the opportunity, during a September visit to the USSR, to discuss the situation with the President and the Foreign Minister. He reported that the Soviet Government had affirmed its support for a continuation of his efforts to facilitate negotiations.

In conclusion, the report stated that, while the most critical stage of the diplomatic process lay ahead, the initial one had brought about some tentative progress and indicated a strong disposition towards a negotiated comprehensive settlement. Moreover, there appeared to have emerged a common understanding of the principles underlying a settlement, of the interrelationships among its elements and of measures to ensure its effective implementation. The Secretary-General would not cease to exert efforts towards securing an opportunity for the Afghans to build their future in peace.

General Assembly action. On 29 November, the General Assembly adopted a resolution on the Afghanistan situation[13] by a recorded vote of 114 to 21, with 13 abstentions.

By this resolution, the Assembly once again called for immediate foreign troop withdrawal from Afghanistan; reiterated that preservation of the country's sovereignty, territorial integrity, political independence and non-aligned character was essential for a peaceful solution; and reaffirmed the Afghan people's right to determine their own form of government free from outside intervention. It called for the creation of conditions necessary for the voluntary return of Afghan refugees and renewed its appeal for aid to them. Supporting the Secretary-General's efforts in the search for a solution, the Assembly requested him to continue efforts to promote a political solution and explore ways to guarantee non-use or threat of use of force against all neighbouring States on the basis of strict non-interference in each other's internal affairs. It asked him to report at the earliest appropriate opportunity.

Introducing the 46-nation text, Pakistan observed that it was devoid of polemics and reaffirmed the principles embodied in the Assembly resolutions of January[14] and November[15] 1980 and November 1981.[16]

Afghanistan, explaining its vote against the resolution, said it constituted outright interference in Afghanistan's internal affairs and a gross violation of the Charter of the United Nations. As to its reference to withdrawal of foreign troops, Afghanistan reiterated that the limited number of USSR troops had been invited by the lawful Government of Afghanistan to help combat armed aggression from abroad; they would be withdrawn only when all interference in its affairs ceased and its non-resumption had been guaranteed. Afghanistan stressed that the resolution would in no way be binding on it, adding that no realistic and acceptable solution could come from one-sided resolutions in the Assembly or in any other forum.

Emphasizing respect for the free will of the Afghan people and asserting that the Afghanistan situation was being exploited by colonial States for their own purposes, the Libyan Arab Jamahiriya, also explaining its vote against, said the resolution neither satisfied all parties nor contributed to a final settlement.

Among those abstaining, India expressed disappointment that the text, only marginally different from the 1981 resolution, emphasized only one element of a comprehensive solution; that selective approach made it unacceptable to some of the parties and hardly strengthened the Secretary-General's hand in the exercise of his good offices. Nicaragua, remarking that one permanent Security Council member had selectively invoked the principle of non-use or threat of use of force in the case of Afghanistan while not admitting its validity for Central America, said the Assembly resolutions on Afghanistan had had no significant impact and the current text did not reflect the flexibility and moderation essential to dialogue and political settlement.

Among those voting for the resolution, Iran said the exercise of self-determination by the Afghan people required withdrawal of all foreign troops and the return of the Afghan *mujahideen* (freedom fighters); therefore, Iran rejected any efforts, including negotiations, in which the true representatives of the Afghan people took no active part. Kenya said the obstinate attitude of the USSR in refusing to withdraw its unwelcome troops, despite international efforts to create conditions that would permit it to extricate itself from an ugly situation of its own making, did not befit a super-Power whose goodwill and intentions were heavily counted upon for the solution of international problems.

In the debate preceding adoption of the resolution, Pakistan said the foreign military presence in Afghanistan remained entrenched and the national resistance to it continued unabated, making the region a new focal point of conflict, damaging détente, darkening prospects for peace in the region and heightening global tensions; the United Nations should continue to express concern over the situation so as to exert maximum pressure for a just political settlement.

Most of the delegations speaking in the Assembly viewed the situation in Afghanistan with profound concern because of what they saw as its far-reaching implications for peace and stability in the region and the world at large; it had heightened tensions throughout South-West Asia, deepened mistrust and suspicion between the two super-Powers, eroded the basis for détente, adversely affected the vital area of arms control and damaged the general climate of international relations. They urged a political settlement based on the principles embodied in past Assembly resolutions and in the text under consideration, including immediate foreign troop withdrawal, self-determination, restoration of Afghanistan's independence and non-aligned status, and creation of conditions for the return of Afghan refugees in peace and honour. They supported the Secretary-General's efforts to achieve dialogue.

Many speakers deplored what they called the refusal of the USSR to heed the Assembly's repeated calls for withdrawal from Afghanistan, and several viewed USSR actions in Afghanistan as a signal of the aggressive expansion of its political and territorial ambitions. Democratic Kampuchea recounted information it said had come from the *mujahideen* that, in three years of occupation, the USSR army had killed almost 2 million Afghans by the use of the most sophisticated conventional and chemical weapons, tortured and murdered 70,000 political prisoners and caused the disappearance of 30,000 others, destroyed several dozen villages, and driven one fifth (3 million) of the population from their villages to become refugees in their own country, another fifth into Pakistan and a million into Iran.

For nearly three years, said the United Kingdom, the Afghans had been fighting a liberation campaign, which had won the world's admiration, against the might of USSR armed forces. Instead of withdrawing, the United States said, the USSR had increased its troop strength there to some 105,000 and during the year had conducted its most systematic and ruthless offensive of the war; according to eyewitness reports, attacks against resistance strongholds had been marked by indiscriminate bombardment, rape, plunder, group executions, the use of civilians as sandbags during street fighting, and the use of chemical weapons, booby-trapped objects and mines.

The high price which the Afghan people continued to pay for freedom, the Central African Republic stated, was proof of their refusal to accept Soviet domination; hence, to say that the USSR had intervened at their request was grotesque deception. Egypt saw it as a dangerous precedent for States to arrogate to themselves the right to interfere in the affairs of others whose régimes they viewed with disfavour. Saudi Arabia said that arguments to justify USSR actions—that its forces were in Afghanistan at that country's request to protect it against foreign interference and that its continued presence was required because of a foreign plot against Afghanistan's security—were incompatible with the exodus of 2 million refugees and the existence of thousands of resistance fighters in Afghanistan.

In Australia's view, the new USSR leadership might offer a unique opportunity for the return to a less acrimonious chapter in international relations if it was prepared to settle for a neutral and non-aligned Afghanistan. Also appealing to the new Soviet leaders, Canada urged them to take stock not only of the suffering the occupation was inflicting on Afghanistan but also of its impact on the international community. Norway said it was difficult to see how continued occupation of Afghanistan could be in the long-term interests of the USSR.

Australia, Thailand and the United States felt that to allow a small, relatively defenceless country like Afghanistan to be invaded, brutalized and subjugated would make it difficult for other similarly vulnerable countries to preserve their security and independence. Tunisia, which shared this view, believed their economic and social development programmes would also be compromised.

Costa Rica identified the cause of the Afghan people with that of the third world; militarily weak countries were firmly opposed to the peace that the strong would impose on them and rejected attempts by any Power to set itself up as a judge to decide on the legitimacy of its violence against another. To the Federal Republic of Germany, Afghanistan had become a test case of USSR respect for the independence and national integrity of third world countries and of its recognition of genuine non-alignment; the longer the USSR refused to respect Afghan rights and aspirations, the greater was the suspicion that it would not hesitate to pursue a strategy of expansion and domination wherever that was possible without major risk. Similarly, New Zealand said the military occupation of a non-aligned country had revived and vindicated long-standing concern about the intentions of the USSR.

Seeing no justification for armed intervention anywhere, Nepal said the Afghanistan situation could not be an exception. Saying it found no acceptable excuse for intervention or interference, whether in Africa, Asia, Europe or Latin America, Yugoslavia pointed out that independence and sovereignty, among the principles that had given strength to the policy of non-alignment, were considered by the non-aligned countries to be the only possible basis for developing new and more just international relations. Mauritania and the Sudan voiced similar views.

France feared that the murderous clashes between the occupation forces and the resistance fighters might spill beyond Afghan frontiers and engulf the entire region in war. Kuwait's apprehension, shared by India, was that the USSR presence in Afghanistan might serve as a pretext to force the region into participating in super-Power strategic formulae and plans; India added that it could also lead to attrition of the region's economic resources, which none of the countries could afford. Qatar viewed the news of the installation of a USSR airbase in south-east Afghanistan as a threat to the Middle East, in particular to the Gulf region, for it felt that the United States would redress the resulting imbalance of forces by establishing similar installations, thus increasing tension in the region.

Malaysia and others likened the USSR involvement with Afghanistan to the United States involvement with Viet Nam in the 1970s, saying that both were examples of a super-Power caught in a political quagmire. Singapore remarked that the Afghanistan situation was not a bilateral dispute between Afghanistan and Pakistan; its cause was the invasion and occupation of Afghanistan by the USSR, and if there was a dispute it was between the USSR and the Afghan people.

Underscoring the special responsibility vested in the permanent members of the Security Council to uphold Charter principles with regard to the maintenance of international peace and security, Sweden said that flagrant disregard of those principles by such a member damaged the foundation of international law; such behaviour had been a major factor contributing to the trend which the Secretary-General (in his annual report on the work of the Organization, p. 3 above) called a new international anarchy. Colombia believed that if the great Powers could disregard the United Nations mandate, the Organization would soon be so damaged that it could not accomplish its task. Chile also contrasted the position of the USSR on the Security Council with its actions in Afghanistan.

China stated that the USSR, while claiming to desire a political settlement, continued to insist that it be based on the August 1981 proposal by the Babrak Karmal régime, according to which foreign aggression in Afghanistan was an internal matter that could not be discussed and foreign troop withdrawal would be exclusively for the USSR and that régime to decide; thus, the proposed settlement was based on the *fait accompli* brought about by foreign invasion, which it was designed to legitimize.

Egypt called for USSR withdrawal from Afghanistan within a timetable to be established by the United Nations and also called for the *mujahideen* to take part in all efforts towards a settlement.

Denmark said that the 10 members of the European Community (EC) could not accept the attempt to impose a régime by force on the Afghan people; they reiterated the EC proposal of June 1981[19] for a comprehensive settlement through an international conference on Afghanistan and their readiness to enter into discussions about it. Thailand and Turkey also expressed support for those initiatives. Japan, stressing the importance of repeated calls by the international community for a settlement, welcomed the EC initiative in declaring 21 March 1982 as Afghanistan Day in order to call greater attention to the problem.

What was urgently needed, India said, was the evolution, through dialogue among the parties, of a political solution based on elements identified by the Movement of Non-Aligned Countries: cessation of interference and intervention in the internal affairs of States, opposition to the presence of foreign troops and reliable guarantees against interference. Austria, Bangladesh, India, the Philippines, Senegal and others urged that the modest success of the June round of talks at Geneva, as reported by the Secretary-General, be built upon. While supporting that process, Italy expressed concern at what it saw as the lack of response shown by the USSR and the consequent absence of real progress towards a solution.

Albania saw the invasion of Afghanistan and the barbarous attack on its people as a deliberate act carried out in accordance with USSR neo-colonialist, hegemonic and expansionist aims in Asia, particularly in the Gulf region; the tragedy of the Afghan people was also a result of rivalry and intrigues among the imperialist super-Powers—China, the USSR and the United States—for zones of influence in Asia.

Afghanistan declared that the United States, China and other reactionary forces were instigating an anti-Afghan campaign to serve their imperialist and hegemonic aspirations. Since the 1978 overthrow of the former feudal régime, a revolutionary transformation of Afghanistan had been under way through economic, social and political reforms, including a projected system of popular participation through village and provincial *jirgahs* (assemblies). Attempts to reverse that trend were being made through an undeclared war by gangs of bandits supported, organized and trained in Pakistan by instructors from China, Pakistan and the United States; they had caused the destruction of 230 *lycées* and secondary schools, 1,479 elementary schools, 30 major hospitals and 106 medical centres. None the less, Afghanistan reaffirmed its readiness to establish normal relations with all countries and its continued co-operation in the talks under way with the Secretary-General's Personal Representative.

Those speaking in support of Afghanistan's position—the socialist States of Eastern Europe, Cuba, Democratic Yemen, the Lao People's Democratic Republic, Mongolia and Viet Nam—insisted that the question fell exclusively within the purview of Afghanistan. The Assembly debate, they felt, worsened the atmosphere between Afghanistan and its neighbours, impeded a just political settlement and sought to divert attention from pressing issues. Tension around Afghanistan and in the region was due to aggression and intervention by hegemonists and counter-revolutionaries attempting to use Afghanistan and the region for their own purposes. Only through the cessation of such intervention could the situation in South-West Asia be normalized. They endorsed the May 1980 and August 1981 proposals

by Afghanistan as a realistic basis for negotiations with its neighbours. They also welcomed the talks begun in June 1982 between the Ministers for Foreign Affairs of Afghanistan and Pakistan through the intermediary of the Personal Representative of the Secretary-General and believed that the major aim of the United Nations should be to encourage and support that dialogue.

The Byelorussian SSR, Cuba, the Ukrainian SSR, the USSR and Viet Nam attributed the destabilization in South-West Asia mainly to the United States, which was using events in and around Afghanistan as a pretext to acquire military bases in Pakistan and on the island of Diego Garcia, and to strengthen its naval contingents in the Gulf and rapid deployment forces in the Sinai. The Lao People's Democratic Republic and the USSR further accused the United States of expanding armed intervention in Afghanistan through insurgents so as to turn that country into a military stronghold against the USSR, as it had done with Iran under the Shah.

Mongolia, the USSR and Viet Nam pointed to the publicly announced military assistance to the Afghan counter-revolution by the United States—for which, the USSR said, the United States had already allocated some $217 million and, at the prompting of the United States, the United Kingdom had contributed 17.5 million pounds. It had been in this context, said Democratic Yemen, the Lao People's Democratic Republic and Viet Nam, that the Afghan people had appealed to the USSR for help so that Afghanistan could face the undeclared war imposed from outside.

Despite the hostile activities, Bulgaria said, a new, independent and non-aligned Afghanistan was proceeding firmly along the path of social progress; it was therefore in the interest of all States in the region to put an end to interference in its internal affairs and to armed activities against it, and create conditions that would prevent their recurrence.

Endorsing Afghanistan's proposals for a settlement, the Byelorussian SSR, Czechoslovakia and the USSR stressed that only the international aspects of the problem could be negotiated, not Afghanistan's domestic affairs. They agreed, along with the German Democratic Republic, Poland and the Ukrainian SSR, that an integral part of any political settlement must be firm guarantees—to be provided by the USSR, the United States and other countries acceptable to the parties—against recurrence of armed or any other form of intervention in Afghan affairs. The USSR added that a political settlement would create conditions for a stage-by-stage withdrawal of its troops from Afghanistan to be agreed upon between the two countries.

Letters and notes verbales (nv). Afghanistan: [1]8 Feb., A/37/84-S/14863; [2]29 June, A/37/329; [3]29 Sep., A/37/505; [4]19

Nov., A/37/639-S/15498. Pakistan: [5]11 Mar., A/37/115-
S/14903; [6]31 Mar., A/37/164-S/14945; [7]2 Aug., A/37/370-
S/15339; [8]3 Sep., A/37/431-S/15389. [9]USSR: 20 May,
A/37/233. United States: [10]22 Mar., A/37/157 *(nv)*; [11]29
Nov., A/C.1/37/10 *(nv)*.

Report. [12]S-G, A/37/482-S/15429.

Resolution (1982). [13]GA: 37/37, 29 Nov., text following.

Resolutions (prior). GA: [14]ES-6/2, 14 Jan. 1980 (YUN 1980,
p. 307); [15]35/37, 20 Nov. 1980 *(ibid.*, p. 308); [16]36/34,
18 Nov. 1981 (YUN 1981, p. 237).

Yearbook references. [17]1980, p. 303; 1981, [18]p. 232, [19]p. 235,
[20]p. 236.

Financial implications. 5th Committee report, A/37/647; S-G
statement, A/C.5/37/57.

Meeting records. GA: General Committee, A/BUR/37/SR.1 (22
Sep.); plenary, A/37/PV.4, 78-82 (24 Sep. & 24-29 Nov.);
5th Committee, A/C.5/37/SR.45 (26 Nov.).

General Assembly resolution 37/37

29 November 1982   Meeting 82   114-21-13 (recorded vote)

46-nation draft (A/37/L.38 and Add.1); agenda item 25.

Sponsors: Antigua and Barbuda, Bahrain, Bangladesh, Botswana, Chile, Colombia, Comoros, Costa Rica, Djibouti, Egypt, Fiji, Gambia, Guatemala, Guinea, Haiti, Honduras, Jamaica, Jordan, Kuwait, Liberia, Malaysia, Maldives, Mauritania, Morocco, Nepal, Niger, Oman, Pakistan, Papua New Guinea, Paraguay, Philippines, Qatar, Saint Lucia, Saint Vincent and the Grenadines, Samoa, Saudi Arabia, Senegal, Singapore, Solomon Islands, Somalia, Sudan, Thailand, Tunisia, Turkey, United Arab Emirates, Uruguay.

**The situation in Afghanistan and its implications
for international peace and security**

The General Assembly,

Having considered the item entitled "The situation in Afghanistan
and its implications for international peace and security",

Recalling its resolutions ES-6/2 of 14 January 1980, 35/37 of 20 November
1980 and 36/34 of 18 November 1981, adopted at the sixth emergency
special session, the thirty-fifth session and the thirty-sixth session respectively,

Reaffirming the purposes and principles of the Charter of the United
Nations and the obligation of all States to refrain in their international
relations from the threat or use of force against the sovereignty, territorial
integrity and political independence of any State,

Reaffirming further the inalienable right of all peoples to determine
their own form of government and to choose their own economic, political and social system free from outside intervention, subversion, coercion
or constraint of any kind whatsoever,

Gravely concerned at the continuing foreign armed intervention in
Afghanistan, in contravention of the above principles, and its serious
implications for international peace and security,

Noting the increasing concern of the international community over
the continued and serious sufferings of the Afghan people and over
the magnitude of social and economic problems posed to Pakistan and
Iran by the presence on their soil of millions of Afghan refugees, and
the continuing increase in their numbers,

Deeply conscious of the urgent need for a political solution of the
grave situation in respect of Afghanistan,

Taking note of the report of the Secretary-General,

Recognizing the importance of the initiatives of the Organization of
the Islamic Conference and the efforts of the Movement of Non-Aligned
Countries for a political solution of the situation in respect of Afghanistan,

1. *Reiterates* that the preservation of the sovereignty, territorial integrity, political independence and non-aligned character of Afghanistan
is essential for a peaceful solution of the problem;

2. *Reaffirms* the right of the Afghan people to determine their own
form of government and to choose their economic, political and social
system free from outside intervention, subversion, coercion or constraint
of any kind whatsoever;

3. *Calls* for the immediate withdrawal of the foreign troops from
Afghanistan;

4. *Calls upon* all parties concerned to work for the urgent achievement of a political solution, in accordance with the provisions of the
present resolution, and the creation of the necessary conditions which
would enable the Afghan refugees to return voluntarily to their homes
in safety and honour;

5. *Renews its appeal* to all States and national and international
organizations to continue to extend humanitarian relief assistance, with
a view to alleviating the hardship of the Afghan refugees, in co-
ordination with the United Nations High Commissioner for Refugees;

6. *Expresses its appreciation and support* for the efforts and constructive steps taken by the Secretary-General in the search for a solution to the problem;

7. *Requests* the Secretary-General to continue those efforts with
a view to promoting a political solution, in accordance with the provisions of the present resolution, and the exploration of securing appropriate guarantees for non-use of force, or threat of use of force, against
the political independence, sovereignty, territorial integrity and security of all neighbouring States, on the basis of mutual guarantees and
strict non-interference in each other's internal affairs and with full regard
for the principles of the Charter of the United Nations;

8. *Requests* the Secretary-General to keep Member States and the
Security Council concurrently informed of the progress towards the
implementation of the present resolution and to report to Member
States on the situation at the earliest appropriate opportunity;

9. *Decides* to include in the provisional agenda of its thirty-eighth
session the item entitled "The situation in Afghanistan and its implications for international peace and security".

Recorded vote in Assembly as follows:

In favour: Albania, Antigua and Barbuda, Argentina, Australia, Austria, Bahamas, Bahrain, Bangladesh, Barbados, Belgium, Botswana, Brazil, Burma, Burundi, Canada, Central African Republic, Chad, Chile, China, Colombia, Comoros, Costa Rica, Democratic Kampuchea, Denmark, Djibouti, Dominica, Dominican Republic, Ecuador, Egypt, El Salvador, Fiji, France, Gabon, Gambia, Germany, Federal Republic of, Ghana, Greece, Guatemala, Guinea, Guyana, Haiti, Honduras, Iceland, Indonesia, Iran, Iraq, Ireland, Israel, Italy, Ivory Coast, Jamaica, Japan, Jordan, Kenya, Kuwait, Lebanon, Lesotho, Liberia, Luxembourg, Malawi, Malaysia, Maldives, Malta, Mauritania, Mexico, Morocco, Nepal, Netherlands, New Zealand, Niger, Nigeria, Norway, Oman, Pakistan, Panama, Papua New Guinea, Paraguay, Peru, Philippines, Portugal, Qatar, Rwanda, Saint Lucia, Saint Vincent and the Grenadines, Samoa, Saudi Arabia, Senegal, Sierra Leone, Singapore, Solomon Islands, Somalia, Spain, Sri Lanka, Sudan, Suriname, Swaziland, Sweden, Thailand, Togo, Trinidad and Tobago, Tunisia, Turkey, United Arab Emirates, United Kingdom, United Republic of Cameroon, United Republic of Tanzania, United States, Upper Volta, Uruguay, Venezuela, Yugoslavia, Zaire, Zambia, Zimbabwe.

Against: Afghanistan, Angola, Bulgaria, Byelorussian SSR, Cuba, Czechoslovakia, Democratic Yemen, Ethiopia, German Democratic Republic, Grenada, Hungary, Lao People's Democratic Republic, Libyan Arab Jamahiriya, Madagascar, Mongolia, Mozambique, Poland, Syrian Arab Republic, Ukrainian SSR, USSR, Viet Nam.

Abstaining: Algeria, Benin, Cape Verde, Congo, Cyprus, Equatorial Guinea, Finland, Guinea-Bissau, India, Mali, Nicaragua, Uganda, Yemen.

Afghan refugees

UNHCR continued in 1982 its assistance
programme for 2.2 million Afghan refugees in
Pakistan, to whom it provided basic relief items
and health, education and other services. Food aid,
in the form of wheat, edible oils and fats, and dried
skim milk, was provided by the World Food
Programme. The refugee situation was also
touched upon in the Commission on Human
Rights and the General Assembly during their
consideration of broader aspects of the Afghanistan situation.

On 25 February, in a resolution on the right of
peoples to self-determination as it applied to Afghanistan, the Commission affirmed the right of
the Afghan refugees to return to their homes in
safety and honour, and appealed to all States and
national and international organizations to extend
humanitarian relief assistance to them in co-
ordination with UNHCR.[2]

In a broadcast message of 24 August addressed
to Afghan nationals living abroad, transmitted to
the Secretary-General by a letter from Afghanistan

dated 10 September,[1] President Babrak Karmal appealed to them to return home under the amnesty proclaimed in June 1981 and assured them that the Government would ensure conditions for engaging in useful work and leading a fitting life.

In its 29 November resolution on the Afghanistan situation, the General Assembly noted the magnitude of social and economic problems posed to Pakistan and Iran by the presence of millions of Afghan refugees in increasing numbers. It appealed for the continuation of humanitarian assistance in co-ordination with UNHCR.[3]

In the Assembly debate on the Afghanistan situation, most speakers supporting the resolution adopted by the Assembly called attention to the increasing number of Afghans who had gone to neighbouring States.

Pakistan, the neighbour most directly affected, said 3 million persons had taken refuge in the country and the influx was continuing. They were placing an enormous financial burden on its limited resources. Moreover, the presence of refugees in the border areas had been used as an excuse for baseless allegations that subversive activity against Afghanistan was being mounted from Pakistan. Terrorism and cruel repression inside Afghanistan had created the refugee problem; the camps had been subject to regular inspection by officials of UNHCR and other international humanitarian organizations, who had been satisfied that activities there were entirely humanitarian.

The United Kingdom said hundreds of thousands more Afghans had fled to Iran, India, Turkey and Western Europe, while the United States remarked that hundreds of thousands of internal refugees had fled rural areas where the fighting between USSR forces and resistance fighters had been most intense. Turkey called the Afghan refugee problem one of the most tragic dimensions of the Afghanistan situation, saying the presence of millions of refugees in Pakistan strained that country's economy and society and adversely affected its relations with Afghanistan.

Observing that the Afghan refugees constituted the largest refugee group in the world, many speakers endorsed the call for continued international assistance. Citing specific co-operation in this effort were: Canada, which said it would contribute more than $18.5 million in food and other forms of humanitarian assistance during the current fiscal year; the Federal Republic of Germany, which said that it had made available in fiscal year 1981 some 60 million deutsche mark in relief assistance and an additional $28 million to EC for emergency aid; and Norway, which mentioned having provided more than 50 million kroner in humanitarian assistance during the previous two years and which promised increased assistance. On behalf of EC members, Denmark pledged continued assistance.

The Federal Republic of Germany shared with Tunisia and others the view that a solution to the refugee problem lay not in the international community's charity but in the framework of a comprehensive political settlement.

Afghanistan stated that the number of *bona fide* refugees was far less than had been claimed. The numbers had been exaggerated to include seasonal migrations of nomads, tribal members residing on the other side of the frontier, returnees whose names remained on refugee rolls, and non-existent refugee families fraudulently registered to obtain funds and material assistance. Since enactment of the amnesty decree in June 1981, tens of thousands of refugees had returned and many more would have done so had they not been prevented by counter-revolutionaries with Pakistan's aid.

Letter. [1]Afghanistan, 10 Sep., A/37/438.
Resolutions (1982). [2]Commission on Human Rights (report, E/1982/12): 1982/14, paras. 4 & 7, 25 Feb. [3]GA: 37/37, para. 5, 29 Nov.

Iran and Iraq

In July and again in October 1982, the Security Council called unanimously for a cease-fire in the armed conflict between Iran and Iraq, an immediate end to all military operations and the withdrawal of forces to internationally recognized boundaries. It also decided in July to dispatch a team of United Nations observers to supervise the cease-fire and withdrawal, and urged continued mediation efforts, co-ordinated through the Secretary-General. In October it welcomed the fact that one of the parties had expressed readiness to co-operate in implementing the July resolution and called on the other to do likewise.

The Secretary-General informed the Council in October that deployment of United Nations observers—which he had not been able to implement—was contingent on a cease-fire and on the concurrence and co-operation of the parties. He also reported that Iraq had indicated its readiness to co-operate in implementing the Council resolutions but that Iran had dissociated itself from all Council actions on the conflict and considered them as non-binding on Iran. He noted that his Special Representative, Olof Palme, who had visited the area five times since the outbreak of hostilities in 1980,[38] had agreed to continue in this role.

The Special Representative's fifth mission, in response to a request by the newly elected Secretary-General for a resumption of contacts with the two Governments, took place from 24 to 28 February 1982, during which he held extensive discussions at Baghdad, Iraq, and Teheran, Iran.

The General Assembly discussed the conflict for the first time in 1982, the item having been included in the Assembly's agenda at Iraq's request. The Assembly affirmed the necessity of an immediate cease-fire and troop withdrawal as a preliminary step, called on other States to abstain from actions which could contribute to continuation of the conflict, and requested continued efforts by the Secretary-General towards a settlement. Iran opposed the resolution as unbalanced, stating that it took no note of who began the war and of Iraq's two-year occupation of Iranian territories. Iraq and other supporters of the resolution appealed to the parties to replace confrontation with dialogue.

A number of communications on the conflict, mostly by Iran and Iraq, were addressed to the Secretary-General throughout the year for circulation as documents of the Security Council or the General Assembly, or both.

Communications (January-July). By a note verbale of 18 January 1982,[3] Iran transmitted an 11 January communiqué from its Ministry of Foreign Affairs asserting that allegations by Iraq in a letter of 17 December 1981[39] that Iran had executed Iraqi war prisoners had been made to divert attention from Iraq's own daily criminal acts against Iranian civilians, to deceive the Iraqi public into believing that the large number of Iraqi combat deaths were due to the alleged executions and to deter its soldiers from deserting to Iran; on the contrary, the communiqué stated, Iraqi prisoners in Iran were receiving more than fair treatment, as confirmed by the International Committee of the Red Cross (ICRC).

Iraq, by a letter of 16 February 1982,[13] rejected these assertions, along with charges of Iraqi air and rocket attacks on Iranian civilian centres between 9 and 11 December 1981,[39] and countercharged that Iran conducted daily attacks on civilian centres and economic installations at Al Basrah; it further accused Iran of blowing up the Embassy of Iraq at Beirut, Lebanon, in collaboration with the Syrian Arab Republic. On 23 March 1982,[30] the Syrian Arab Republic denounced the accusation against it as baseless, saying it condemned such terrorist acts.

Commenting on a Radio Teheran account on 29 March of a meeting between the President of Iran and a number of what the broadcast described as Iraqi religious dignitaries, the Minister for Foreign Affairs of Iraq, in a letter of 3 April transmitted two days later, referred to those Iraqis as terrorists who were being exhorted to set up an Islamic government in Iraq similar to the one in Iran and under its tutelage; this, he said, was evidence of Iran's policy of regarding Iraq and the Gulf region as within Iran's sphere of influence.[14]

The Revolutionary Command Council of Iraq issued an order on 3 May, transmitted four days later, by which it decided to release to ICRC a number of Iranian children who had been captured in recent battles, without demanding reciprocal release of Iraqi prisoners of war.[15]

In a communiqué transmitted by a note verbale of 25 May, Iran blamed the Iraqi army for the in-discriminate destruction of civilian installations in the recaptured town of Hoveyzeh in Khuzestan province, citing among those demolished the central mosque and other historical and religious monuments, government buildings, a hospital, schools, shops, a water reservoir and irrigation network, and other public utilities.[4]

By a note verbale of 8 June, Iraq rejected Iran's allegation in a 15 March note that it had expelled 1,500 Iraqi Moslems to Iran, thereby creating a refugee problem; the action, Iraq asserted, was a deportation of Iranians who had illegally acquired Iraqi citizenship.[16]

On 10 June,[17] Iraq transmitted a government statement of the same date by which it indicated its readiness to observe an immediate cease-fire and to withdraw its forces from all Iranian territories within two weeks, in response to an appeal by the peace committee of the Organization of the Islamic Conference (established by a resolution of the extraordinary meeting of the Ministers for Foreign Affairs of Islamic Countries, New York, 26 September 1980); should a settlement with Iran not be reached through existing mediating bodies, Iraq would submit to binding arbitration by the Organization of the Islamic Conference, the Movement of Non-Aligned Countries or the Security Council. By a note verbale of 22 June,[18] Iraq conveyed a decision taken two days earlier by its Revolutionary Command Council to begin troop withdrawal from all occupied Iranian territories, to be completed in 10 days; it stated that this would do away with Iran's excuse for continuing the war and expose its true intentions, but it added that it expected Iran to continue its aggression.

On 11 June[1] and 30 June,[2] Belgium conveyed two statements: one, issued on 24 May by the EC Foreign Ministers, expressing concern at the continued conflict, calling for a peaceful solution, and offering to participate in peace efforts and to consider, following cessation of hostilities, the possibility of co-operating in the reconstruction of the two countries; and the other, issued by the EC heads of State and Government on 29 June at the conclusion of a two-day meeting held at Brussels, Belgium, reiterating the 24 May statement, calling for an intensification of ongoing peace efforts and declaring themselves ready to assist in those efforts.

Referring to a 24 June press release and a 29 June statement by Iran alleging that Iraq had not abided by its announced cease-fire, Iraq, by a letter of 1 July, said that, as had been confirmed by a spokesman for its Foreign Ministry on 30 June, the withdrawal of its forces had been completed and was open to verification; it reiterated its demand that a fact-finding commission be set up to determine responsibility for the hostilities and called for a cease-fire guarantee by a force drawn from the United Nations, the Movement of Non-Aligned Countries, the Organization of the Islamic Conference or from all three organizations.[19]

Also on 1 July, Iran charged that Iraq's forces still occupied parts of Iranian territory, having withdrawn only from indefensible positions; that they had completely demolished the towns of Qasr-e-Shirin and Mehran and destroyed roads, bridges and other public and civilian facilities; and that Iraq continued its daily artillery attacks that had left 8 dead and 29 wounded in Abadan and Khorramshahr on the day before.[5] Iraq denied these charges on 8 July[20] and proposed verification of its troop withdrawal by appropriate United Nations machinery.

Security Council action (July). On 12 July, the Security Council, in a unanimous resolution drawn up in the course of consultations among its members,[34] called for a cease-fire and an immediate end to all military operations, as well as a withdrawal of forces to internationally recognized boundaries; decided to dispatch a team of United Nations observers to supervise the cease-fire and withdrawal, and requested the Secretary-General to report on arrangements; urged continuation of mediation efforts co-ordinated through the Secretary-General to achieve a comprehensive, just and honourable settlement based on the principles of the Charter of the United Nations, including respect for sovereignty, independence, territorial integrity and non-interference in the internal affairs of States; requested all other States to abstain from actions that could contribute to continuation of the conflict; and asked the Secretary-General to report within three months on implementation of the resolution.

The Council had been convened at Jordan's request, in a letter of 30 May,[28] which stated that the conflict between Iran and Iraq was widening and posing imminent danger to regional and world peace and security. At its request, Iraq was invited to participate without vote in the discussion.

Iraq welcomed the resolution as a timely and constructive step towards generating a new momentum for peace and an enhancement of the Council's image as the organ primarily responsible for the maintenance of international peace and security. It recalled its own efforts at ending the conflict—including its 10 June initiatives and withdrawal of its forces from Iranian territories completed on 30 June (see above)—all of which Iran had rejected. It none the less reaffirmed its faith in the principles of the Charter and in the dispute-settlement role of the United Nations, and expressed hope that Iran would respond favourably and end its policy of prolonging the war.

In the Council discussion, China, France, the USSR and the United Kingdom expressed concern that the prolonged conflict between Iran and Iraq, a cause of instability in the Gulf area and the Middle East, had taken thousands of lives and caused the exodus of large numbers of refugees, widespread suffering and destruction in both countries. China believed that no fundamental conflict of interest existed among third world countries and, therefore, that conflicts between them should be settled peacefully through consultation or negotiations; it hoped Iran and Iraq would exercise restraint and seek an early cease-fire. France welcomed the efforts of the Organization of the Islamic Conference and the Movement of Non-Aligned Countries to negotiate a settlement, the political foundations for which were laid down by the Council resolution. Along with the United States, France stressed the imperative of a solution which preserved the parties' sovereignty, independence and territorial integrity; France also stressed that any negotiations should respect the frontier between the two countries as set by the 1975 Algiers (Algeria) agreement.[38]

The USSR said the long-term interests of the parties would be served by an end to the conflict, which had diverted both countries' attention from solving vital economic and social development problems and from confronting Israeli aggression and imperialist plans for domination; it opposed imperialist attempts to exploit the conflict, favoured a prompt end to the conflict through negotiation, and supported the mediation efforts of the Secretary-General's Special Representative and other international efforts towards a settlement, whose specific aspects should be agreed upon by the parties. The United Kingdom appealed to the parties to implement the resolution in order to bring the conflict to an end through negotiation; however, it expressed doubt as to the efficacy of the resolution since, despite efforts by the Council President to obtain co-operation, one of the parties remained reluctant to accept it.

Pursuant to the Council's request, the Secretary-General submitted a report dated 15 July,[31] stating that he considered it necessary, as a first step and with the agreement of the parties, to send a small team of senior United Nations military officers who would ascertain the situation on the ground and assess arrangements for the dispatch of an observer team as called for by the Council. The report noted that, in acknowledging the text of the resolution transmitted to them, Iraq, on 13 July, had communicated its readiness to co-operate in its implementation, while Iran, in a statement transmitted on 14 July (see below), had dissociated itself from all Security Council actions with regard to Iraq's war of aggression against it. The Secretary-General would continue intensive efforts to end the fighting and achieve a settlement.

Iran maintained, in a statement of its Government's position transmitted by a letter of 14

July,[6] that Iraq was in violation of specific Articles of the Charter by resorting to armed aggression and occupation and that the Council, in its resolution of July as in that of 1980,[36] had deliberately failed to recognize that armed aggression and occupation had taken place, to condemn the aggressor, to demand restoration of previous conditions and to recognize Iran's right to punish the war criminals responsible for the destruction and misery caused by Iraqi aggression. The Council had thus disqualified itself by its disguised support of the aggressor. Though dissociating itself from past Council actions on the conflict, Iran nevertheless affirmed its readiness to co-operate with the Council when the latter took its responsibilities seriously by dealing with the realities of the conflict.

Also on 14 July, Iraq informed the Council President that Iranian forces had launched an attack the day before on Al Basrah, shelling that city, the seaport of Al Faw and Abu al Khasib township, in an attempt to cross into Iraq; it called on the Council to condemn the aggression and take appropriate action.[21]

On 15 July, the Council President issued the following statement:[37]

"The Security Council met in informal consultations this morning, 15 July 1982, to consider the recent developments in the situation between Iran and Iraq.

The members of the Security Council expressed concern at the serious situation existing between Iran and Iraq and at the fact that resolution 514(1982) has not yet been implemented. The Council remains actively seized of this question. The President will remain in contact with the two sides concerned, with a view to exploring all possible means of advancing the efforts to achieve an end to the fighting and to secure a settlement of the underlying issues."

Communications (July-October). On 19 July, Iraq drew the Security Council's attention to the deteriorating situation due to heavy fighting on its border with Iran and called on the Council to take measures to put an end to Iran's aggression.[22] On 3 September, Iraq reported that Iran had launched five large-scale armed attacks east of Al Basrah between 13 and 29 July and that Iraq had repelled them, inflicting heavy losses on the Iranians including 28,100 dead, the destruction of 300 tanks and 107 armoured personnel carriers, and the downing of four fighter aircraft and one helicopter.[25]

Iraq further informed the Council on 3 September that a large number of Iranian troops were massed along the border, poised to invade Iraq; it stressed that, while it would continue its peace efforts, it would not hesitate to exercise its right to defend itself against aggression.[24] It addressed an identical letter on 8 September to the Secretary-General for circulation to the General Assembly.

On 1 October Iraq, reporting that Iran had mounted another major armed attack that day in the Sumar sector in an attempt to cross the international frontier near the town of Mandali, urgently requested a meeting of the Security Council.[26]

Security Council action (October). On 4 October, the Security Council unanimously adopted a resolution prepared during the Council's consultations,[35] by which it urgently renewed its call for an immediate cease-fire, an end to all military operations and the withdrawal of forces to internationally recognized boundaries. It welcomed the fact that one of the parties had expressed readiness to co-operate in implementing its July resolution and called on the other to do likewise, affirmed the necessity of dispatching United Nations observers to verify and supervise the cease-fire and withdrawal, reaffirmed the urgency of continuing current mediation efforts and its request to all other States to abstain from actions which could contribute to continuation of the conflict, and requested the Secretary-General to report within 72 hours on implementation of the resolution.

The 4 October meeting at which the Council took this action had been convened at Iraq's request in a letter of 1 October (see above). Iraq and Morocco were invited, at their request, to participate without vote in the discussion.

The Secretary-General informed the Council at this meeting that the dispatch of United Nations observers as called for by the resolution was contingent on the concurrence and co-operation of the parties and on the existence of a cease-fire. To deploy unarmed United Nations observers without first meeting those prerequisites would not be consistent with United Nations peace-keeping practices. Arrangements could be made for the observers to be in the area some 48 hours after he received the concurrence and co-operation of the parties, with whom he would be in touch.

Iraq told the Council that Iran's aggression and prolongation of the war stemmed from a long-standing policy that considered Iraq and the Gulf region as falling within Iran's sphere of influence and domination. Thus, Iran under the Shah had assumed the role of the region's policeman and, under Ayatollah Khomeini, of exporter of the Islamic revolution, whose objective was to bring about Islamic unity in one Islamic State. Iran's response to Iraq's position of peaceful coexistence had been constant hostility, culminating in total war. Iran's rejection of Iraq's peace initiatives and of Council resolutions, as well as its insistence that Iraqi troops still occupied Iranian territories, were pretexts for continuing the fighting. Iraq nevertheless continued to seek a just and honourable settlement, to achieve which it pledged full co-operation with the Council. To prevent further deterioration of peace and security, the Council must take effective measures against the party that rejected peace.

Morocco, speaking on behalf of the Arab Group, paid tribute to the Secretary-General, his Special Representative, the Movement of Non-Aligned Countries and the peace committee of the Organization of the Islamic Conference for their mediation efforts, and reaffirmed the Group's desire to see both parties respond to those efforts with determination and good faith; it welcomed Iraq's readiness to initiate a peace process and believed the Council should remind Iran of its duty to co-operate with the Council in restoring peace.

In a statement of 4 October, transmitted to the Secretary-General by a note verbale of the same date,[7] Iran stated that the Iranian attack about which the Council had been convened had taken place inside Iran for the purpose of liberating Iranian territory from Iraqi occupation. The Council had been silent about such occupation and hasty in adopting a resolution on which Egypt and Jordan had been allowed to vote despite their military participation in the war that Iraq had imposed on Iran. Not only did the Council meeting constitute a challenge to Iran's right to self-defence; it was also a conspiracy by Iraq and Jordan, together with their imperialist masters, to gain international recognition for the discredited régime of Saddam Hussein Al-Takriti. If Iran's confidence in the Council was to be restored, the Council would have to condemn Iraq's occupation of Iranian territories and indiscriminate bombardment of civilian targets, and demand that Iraq pay for war damages and repatriate the Iraqis it had exiled. Without such action, Iran would not participate in the Council's meetings and would continue to regard its resolutions as non-binding on Iran.

Report of the Secretary-General. Pursuant to requests in the Security Council resolutions of July and October, the Secretary-General submitted a report, dated 7 October,[32] on his efforts to implement the resolutions.

The report noted that, in acknowledging the October resolution, Iraq, by a letter of 5 October, had indicated that it would co-operate in good faith with the Council in its implementation. Iran, through its Permanent Representative to the United Nations, had informed the Secretary-General on the same date of its desire for peace, reiterating, however, that it had consistently indicated the steps necessary to settle the conflict. The Permanent Representative had handed over a 4 October statement by his Government (see above) declaring that Iran considered the Council resolutions on the situation as not binding on Iran.

In conclusion, the report stated that the Secretary-General, who had been engaged in intensive efforts to facilitate achievement of a just and honourable settlement, would continue those efforts; and Olof Palme, his Special Representative who had visited the area five times since the outbreak of hostilities in 1980, had recently agreed to continue his role.

General Assembly action. On 22 October, the General Assembly adopted a resolution on the consequences of the prolongation of the armed conflict between Iran and Iraq by a recorded vote of 119 to 1, with 15 abstentions.[33] The text, sponsored by 14 nations including the Gulf Arab States, had been revised by its sponsors before adoption.

By this resolution, the Assembly considered that the conflict between Iran and Iraq and its prolongation and recent escalation endangered international peace and security. The Assembly affirmed the necessity of an immediate cease-fire and withdrawal of forces to internationally recognized boundaries as a preliminary step towards peaceful settlement, called on all other States to abstain from actions which could contribute to continuation of the conflict and to facilitate implementation of the resolution, and requested the Secretary-General to continue his efforts towards a settlement and to keep Member States informed.

Inclusion of the item in the Assembly's agenda had been requested by Iraq in a letter of 5 August.[23] An enclosed explanatory memorandum stated that, whereas Iraq had approved the July and October Security Council resolutions and had co-operated with efforts of the Secretary-General's Special Representative and others, the conflict continued because of Iran's policy of prolonging and expanding it. The situation, which threatened the security and stability of one of the most sensitive regions and weakened the roles of the Organization of the Islamic Conference, the Movement of Non-Aligned Countries and the United Nations, was one on which the Assembly should express its views.

Iran, the only country to vote against the Assembly resolution, said the text was unbalanced in that it took no note of who began the war and of the two-year Iraqi occupation of Iranian territories, openly deprived Iran of the right to self-defence and called for troop withdrawal to internationally recognized boundaries when such boundaries had not in fact been determined. Iran considered the resolution destructive to the cause of peace.

Earlier, on 19 October,[8] Iran had transmitted to the Secretary-General the text of what it described as a model resolution reflecting the realities of the situation. By that resolution, the Assembly, reaffirming the inadmissibility of the threat or use of force in international relations and the right of States to self-defence, would condemn Iraq for initiating armed aggression to solve its dispute with Iran, deplore Iraqi occupation of

Iranian territories and its attempt to use that occupation to extract political concessions, and further condemn Iraq for concentrating its war efforts primarily on civilian populations. It would affirm Iran's right to war reparations and demand that Iraq assist in the restoration of all civilian installations it had deliberately destroyed; call on both parties to end all military operations and resolve their dispute peacefully; and invite continuation of the Secretary-General's mediation efforts.

Among those abstaining in the Assembly vote were Cuba, India and Zambia. Speaking on their behalf as members of the ministerial good offices committee established by the Conference of Ministers for Foreign Affairs of the Non-Aligned Countries (New Delhi, India, 9-13 February 1981) to assist in the search for a settlement of the conflict, Cuba said they had decided to abstain because of their position and their inability to achieve a text acceptable to both parties. Bangladesh and Malaysia, as members of the peace committee of the Organization of the Islamic Conference, acted likewise. Bhutan said its expectations for revisions in the text that would have contributed to an end to the conflict had not been met. Bolivia felt that, as third world and non-aligned countries, Iran and Iraq should resolve their conflict by direct negotiations. Nicaragua, which preferred a more balanced wording, wanted to show its impartiality by its abstention.

Albania, while supporting all the principles in the resolution, did not participate in the vote because it considered the text incomplete: it dealt with neither the causes nor the consequences of the conflict and made reference to certain Security Council resolutions of which Albania held a different view. Sweden, expressing full support for the efforts of the Secretary-General and those of his Special Representative, said that since the Special Representative was a former Swedish Prime Minister, it had chosen not to participate in the vote or in the debate.

Some of those voting for the resolution expressed reservations about what they regarded as a lack of balance. Argentina believed the text could facilitate the achievement of agreement but it would have preferred a more balanced wording. Indonesia also said a better balance would have been preferable but added that the immediate need for initiating negotiations led it to vote affirmatively. Mexico said it would prefer any appeal for negotiation to maintain a balanced approach between the parties, as the Security Council had done in 1980. Singapore said it would have preferred paragraph 2 to have included an appeal for an immediate cease-fire. Sri Lanka said that despite the shortcomings of the text, including a lack of balance, it supported the resolution solely in the interest of advancing the Secretary-General's efforts.

Several countries mentioned particular features of the resolution that had led them to vote for it. Ecuador cited the provision for a cease-fire and withdrawal of forces. The Philippines mentioned the call for a peaceful settlement and for continued efforts by the Secretary-General. Romania emphasized its support for negotiation between the parties in explaining its affirmative vote, while Austria stressed both mediation and negotiation. Senegal based its support on the fact that the text contained a peace appeal to both parties and a call to other States not to exacerbate the conflict. Jamaica wanted it understood that nothing in the text proposed removal of the issue from the Security Council.

Panama stated that its vote in favour was not to be construed as taking sides and passing judgement on the conflict. The Lao People's Democratic Republic expressed a similar view, as did Uruguay, Venezuela and Zaire, which added that their affirmative votes were to be regarded as their modest contribution to peace.

In the Assembly debate, Iraq restated what it had told the Security Council—that, since the outbreak of hostilities in September 1980, it had never ceased to pursue a just and honourable settlement, seeking only to regain its legitimate rights to its own land and waters. However, its initiatives and proposals for ending hostilities had been consistently rebuffed by Iran, which had moreover chosen to boycott the Council and reject its unanimous resolutions. Iran's arguments—that the resolutions failed to recognize that armed aggression and occupation had taken place, to condemn the aggressor and to demand restoration of conditions prevailing before the aggression—were pretexts for continuing the war, a policy indicative of its aspiration to invade Iraq and set up a new régime in the country. In the face of Iran's defiance of the collective international judgement, Iraq urged the Assembly to employ every means at its disposal to gain Iran's respect for United Nations decisions.

Most of the speakers saw the conflict between Iran and Iraq as futile and self-defeating, having already exacted a heavy toll in human lives and suffering, and caused incalculable damage to property and wasteful diversion of energies and resources from direly needed development efforts. Many also saw it as a grave threat to the peace and stability of a strategically important region, making it vulnerable to intervention by foreign forces which could exploit the conflict for their own objectives, with far-reaching consequences not only for the Gulf region but for the Middle East and the world. They appealed to the parties to end the war and replace confrontation with dialogue. They also expressed full support for the Secretary-General's good offices and the mediation efforts of his Special Representative, the Organization of the Islamic Conference, the Movement of Non-Aligned Countries and individual countries.

China reiterated that no conflict of fundamental interests among third world countries existed and that therefore the differences between Iran and Iraq could be resolved through peaceful negotiations.

Bangladesh said that, as a member of the peace committee of the Organization of the Islamic Conference, it was committed to undertaking every possible effort to bring about a peaceful and early settlement. Cuba mentioned its contacts with the parties in 1981, when it was Chairman of the Movement of Non-Aligned Countries, aimed at promoting a peaceful settlement. Denmark, speaking for the EC members, said they were ready to contribute at any time and in any way to the restoration of peace between the parties, and to consider, once hostilities had ceased, the possibility of co-operating in the reconstruction of the two countries. Malaysia urged closer co-ordination among the various settlement efforts.

India considered it significant that Iran and Iraq had acknowledged, at the February 1981 Conference of Ministers for Foreign Affairs of the Non-Aligned Countries, that their conflict posed a threat to the Movement of Non-Aligned Countries, and that they had accepted, as the basis for ending the conflict, the principles of non-recourse to force to acquire or occupy territories, the return of territories so acquired, non-aggression, respect for the territorial integrity and sovereignty of States, non-interference in the affairs of another State, and peaceful settlement of disputes. Yugoslavia and Zambia endorsed the same principles, the latter adding that nothing could replace peaceful settlement.

Kuwait applauded Iraq's initiative in withdrawing its forces to internationally recognized boundaries and hoped Iran would take a step towards peace and accept the Council resolutions as Iraq had done. Bahrain, Egypt, Jordan, Morocco, Oman, Qatar, the Sudan, Tunisia, the United Arab Emirates and Yemen voiced similar sentiments. The Sudan regretted that Iran maintained its insistence on continuing the war despite the tremendous losses and ominous dangers it had brought.

Egypt reiterated its opposition to the use of force to settle disputes, especially between two States with more reasons for co-operation than for conflict, but at the same time affirmed its determination, in keeping with its contractual commitment, to assist Iraq in the event that Iraq's territorial integrity and internal security were endangered. Jordan said that, abiding by the joint defence agreement of the League of Arab States, it had supported Iraq in the war. Yemen also pledged assistance to Iraq in accordance with that agreement.

In Saudi Arabia's view, what caused more pain than the continuing war in the Gulf region—from which only arms suppliers benefited—was the Secretary-General's expressed concern (in his annual report on the work of the Organization, p. 3 above) over the increasing inability of the United Nations to fulfil its mandate; such inability, Saudi Arabia said, could lead to the loss of the Organization's prestige, and in turn to a great loss to the international community, in particular to small nations.

Pakistan, observing that the time was ripe for re-establishing communications between the parties, said the United Nations had an important role to play in generating the momentum necessary for realizing that objective. Uganda said the Security Council and the Assembly must help Iran and Iraq in the search for a quick solution. In the opinion of the USSR, the Assembly could promote a *rapprochement* between the parties and help steer the conflict towards a mutually acceptable solution.

For Turkey it was imperative that the parties, on their own and through means acceptable to them, agree on a settlement ensuring respect for each other's territorial integrity, independence and sovereignty; the international community should help bring the parties together but not impose a solution.

Indonesia said the conflict had diverted attention from the pressing task of achieving a just solution to the Middle East question, an observation shared by Zambia; for the USSR it diverted from the task of combating Israel's continuing aggression and plans by imperialists to establish their rule over the region.

In Qatar's view, shared by the Lao People's Democratic Republic, the Iran-Iraq war, coupled with the Arab-Israeli conflict, had turned the region into one of the most serious hotbeds of tension, threatening a confrontation between the two super-Powers because of the region's economic and strategic importance. That the super-Powers were attempting to draw the region into the arena of their struggle made it necessary to end the war, the United Arab Emirates said. Viet Nam warned that those who lived by a "divide-and-rule" policy and who fished in troubled waters could make use of the conflict for their selfish interests.

In the view of Albania, the war had been incited by the two imperialist super-Powers and primarily the United States, which had sought to destroy the Iranian revolution and prevent it from becoming an example to other Moslem peoples; the United Nations had not done its duty in this case and certain Security Council actions had not really been serious.

Iran contended that Iraq, having unilaterally abrogated the peace treaty between them when Iran became the Islamic Republic, had begun an aggressive war on the pretext of defending its territorial waters. That move, supported by the United States, was an expansionist and opportunistic act to destroy the Islamic revolution, considered by the United States as the greatest threat to its interests in the region. Because of its recent defeats, however, Iraq had been desperately seeking a peaceful settlement, which it should have sought initially instead of waging war. Its so-called tactical and unilateral troop withdrawals were in fact withdrawals from liberated Iranian territories or indefensible positions. Iran rejected a humiliating cease-fire, wanting only total victory. It would negotiate only on condition that Iraq withdrew to pre-war positions, repatriated Iraqi nationals expelled from Iraq for their opposition to the war or as a result of Iraq's racist policies, and paid war reparations, and that those guilty of war crimes were prosecuted.

Communications (October-December). A progress report on the activities since June of the Non-Aligned Ministerial Committee on the Iran-Iraq conflict, submitted to the Meeting of Ministers for Foreign Affairs and Heads of Delegation of Non-Aligned Countries held in New York from 4 to 9 October, was included together with the final communiqué of the Meeting submitted by Cuba on 11 October.[27] The Committee, composed of Cuba, India, Zambia and the Head of the Political Department of the Palestine Liberation Organization, gave an account of meetings with various Iranian and Iraqi officials and concluded that, although the positions of the parties were still wide apart, efforts towards an early settlement must continue.

By letters of 28 October[9] and 1 November,[10] Iran reported that on 26 October, escalating the conflict and violating the General Assembly resolution, Iraqi war-planes had bombarded a densely populated, residential area in the southern city of Dezful, Khuzestan, killing at least 24 civilians, injuring 107 others and destroying more than 100 houses; four days later, Iraq had fired long-range artillery at residential areas in Abadan, destroying several houses.

In a statement transmitted by a 3 November note verbale, the Foreign Ministry of Iran said that, on 1 November, Iran's armed forces had liberated a number of localities inside Iran—the border posts of Bayat, Nahranbar, Chamsari and Raboot as well as the Bayat oilfields and four strategic hilltops of the Hamiran Mountains—which had been under Iraqi occupation since the early days of the war and from which Iraq claimed to have withdrawn some time previously.[11]

On 3 December, Morocco transmitted the final declaration of the Twelfth Arab Summit Conference (Fez, Morocco, 25 November 1981 and 6-9 September 1982), stating, among other things, the Arab position on the Iran-Iraq war: it noted with regret the continuation of the war despite attempts to reach a cease-fire and offers of mediation and good offices, expressed appreciation for Iraq's initiative in withdrawing its forces, proclaimed its commitment to the defence of all Arab territories and to consider any aggression against any Arab country as aggression against all Arab countries, called on the parties to comply with the Security Council resolutions and asked all other States to refrain from taking any measure likely to encourage continuation of the war.[29]

On 21 December, Iran reported that two days earlier the residential areas of Dezful had been attacked again, with long-range, surface-to-surface missiles, resulting in 62 dead, 287 wounded, and 120 houses and 380 shops destroyed or damaged.[12]

Letters and notes verbales (nv).
   Belgium: [1]11 June, A/37/285-S/15219; [2]30 June, A/37/321-S/15266.
   Iran: [3]18 Jan., A/37/70-S/14841 *(nv)*; [4]25 May, S/15121 *(nv)*; [5]1 July, S/15270; [6]14 July, S/15292; [7]4 Oct., S/15448 *(nv)*; [8]19 Oct., A/37/555; [9]28 Oct., A/37/584-S/15471; [10]1 Nov., A/37/596-S/15479; [11]3 Nov., S/15478 *(nv)*; [12]21 Dec., S/15539.
   Iraq: [13]16 Feb., A/37/89-S/14873; [14]5 Apr., A/37/172-S/14957; [15]7 May, A/37/222 *(nv)*; [16]8 June, A/37/271-S/15184 *(nv)*; [17]10 June, A/37/279-S/15196 *(nv)*; [18]22 June, A/37/305 *(nv)*; [19]1 July, A/37/323; [20]8 July, S/15279; [21]14 July, S/15289; [22]19 July, S/15301; [23]5 Aug., A/37/191; [24]3 Sep., S/15385 (A/37/430, 8 Sep.); [25]3 Sep., A/37/428-S/15387; [26]1 Oct., S/15443.
   Others: [27]Cuba, for non-aligned countries: 11 Oct., A/37/540-S/15454. [28]Jordan: 30 May, S/15141. [29]Morocco: 3 Dec., A/37/696-S/15510. [30]Syrian Arab Republic: 23 Mar., A/37/156-S/14922 *(nv)*.
Reports. S-G, [31]S/15293, [32]S/15449.
Resolutions (1982). [33]GA: 37/3, 22 Oct., text following. SC: [34]514(1982), 12 July, text following; [35]522(1982), 4 Oct., text following.
Resolution (prior). [36]SC: 479(1980), 28 Sep. 1980 (YUN 1980, p. 318).
Statement. [37]SC President, S/15296.
Yearbook references. [38]1980, p. 312; [39]1981, p. 239.
Meeting records. SC: S/PV.2383, 2399 & Corr.1 (12 July, 4 Oct.). GA: General Committee, A/BUR/37/SR.2 (22 Sep.); plenary, A/37/PV.38-41 (20-22 Oct.).

Security Council resolution 514(1982)

12 July 1982   Meeting 2383   Adopted unanimously

Draft prepared in consultations among Council members (S/15285).

The Security Council,
   Having considered again the question entitled "The situation between Iran and Iraq",
   Deeply concerned about the prolongation of the conflict between the two countries, resulting in heavy losses of human lives and considerable material damage and endangering peace and security,
   Recalling the provisions of Article 2 of the Charter of the United Nations, and that the establishment of peace and security in the region requires strict adherence to these provisions,
   Recalling that by virtue of Article 24 of the Charter the Security Council has the primary responsibility for maintenance of international peace and security,
   Recalling its resolution 479(1980), adopted unanimously on 28 September 1980, as well as the statement of the President of the Security Council of 5 November 1980,

Taking note of the efforts of mediation pursued notably by the Secretary-General and his representative, as well as by the Movement of Non-Aligned Countries and the Organization of the Islamic Conference,

1. *Calls* for a cease-fire and an immediate end to all military operations;

2. *Calls further* for a withdrawal of forces to internationally recognized boundaries;

3. *Decides* to dispatch a team of United Nations observers to verify, confirm and supervise the cease-fire and withdrawal, and requests the Secretary-General to submit to the Security Council a report on the arrangements required for that purpose;

4. *Urges* that the mediation efforts be continued in a co-ordinated manner through the Secretary-General with a view to achieving a comprehensive, just and honourable settlement, acceptable to both sides, of all the outstanding issues, on the basis of the principles of the Charter of the United Nations, including respect for sovereignty, independence, territorial integrity and non-interference in the internal affairs of States;

5. *Requests* all other States to abstain from all actions that could contribute to the continuation of the conflict and to facilitate the implementation of the present resolution;

6. *Requests* the Secretary-General to report to the Security Council within three months on the implementation of the present resolution.

Security Council resolution 522(1982)

4 October 1982   Meeting 2399   Adopted unanimously

Draft prepared in consultations among Council members (S/15446).

The Security Council,

Having considered again the question entitled "The situation between Iran and Iraq",

Deploring the prolongation and the escalation of the conflict between the two countries, resulting in heavy losses of human lives and considerable material damage and endangering peace and security,

Reaffirming that the restoration of peace and security in the region requires all Member States strictly to comply with their obligations under the Charter of the United Nations,

Recalling its resolution 479(1980), adopted unanimously on 28 September 1980, as well as the statement of the President of the Security Council of 5 November 1980,

Further recalling its resolution 514(1982), adopted unanimously on 12 July 1982, and the statement of the President of the Security Council on 15 July 1982,

Taking note of the report of the Secretary-General of 15 July 1982,

1. *Urgently calls again* for an immediate cease-fire and an end to all military operations;

2. *Reaffirms* its call for a withdrawal of forces to internationally recognized boundaries;

3. *Welcomes* the fact that one of the parties has already expressed its readiness to co-operate in the implementation of resolution 514(1982) and calls upon the other to do likewise;

4. *Affirms* the necessity of implementing without further delay its decision to dispatch United Nations observers to verify, confirm and supervise the cease-fire and withdrawal;

5. *Reaffirms* the urgency of the continuation of the current mediation efforts;

6. *Reaffirms* its request to all other States to abstain from all actions which could contribute to the continuation of the conflict and to facilitate the implementation of the present resolution;

7. *Further requests* the Secretary-General to report to the Security Council on the implementation of the present resolution within seventy-two hours.

General Assembly resolution 37/3

22 October 1982   Meeting 41   119-1-15 (recorded vote)

14-nation draft (A/37/L.7/Rev.1); agenda item 134.

Sponsors: Antigua and Barbuda, Bahrain, Djibouti, Guyana, Jordan, Kuwait, Morocco, Oman, Qatar, Saudi Arabia, Somalia, Sudan, United Arab Emirates, Yemen.

Consequences of the prolongation of the armed conflict between Iran and Iraq

The General Assembly,

Having considered the item entitled "Consequences of the prolongation of the armed conflict between Iran and Iraq",

Noting the Preamble of the Charter of the United Nations, in which all States expressed their determination to live together in peace with one another as good neighbours,

Reaffirming the principles that no State should acquire or occupy territories by the use of force, that whatever territories had been acquired in this way should be returned, that no act of aggression should be committed against any State, that the territorial integrity and the sovereignty of all States should be respected, that no State should try to interfere or intervene in the internal affairs of other States and that all differences or claims which may exist between States should be settled by peaceful means in order that peaceful relations should prevail among Member States,

Recalling resolutions 479(1980) of 28 September 1980, 514(1982) of 12 July 1982 and 522(1982) of 4 October 1982 on the question entitled "The situation between Iran and Iraq", unanimously adopted by the Security Council,

Further recalling the statements made by the President of the Security Council on 5 November 1980 and 15 July 1982,

Taking note of the report of the Secretary-General of 7 October 1982,

Considering that the Security Council has already called for an immediate cease-fire and an end to all military operations,

Considering further that the prolongation of the conflict constitutes a violation of the obligations of Member States under the Charter,

1. *Considers* that the conflict between Iran and Iraq and its prolongation and recent escalation, resulting in heavy losses in human lives and considerable material damage in a politically and economically strategic region, endanger international peace and security;

2. *Affirms* the necessity of achieving an immediate cease-fire and withdrawal of forces to internationally recognized boundaries as a preliminary step towards the settlement of the dispute by peaceful means in conformity with the principles of justice and international law;

3. *Calls upon* all other States to abstain from all actions which could contribute to the continuation of the conflict and to facilitate the implementation of the present resolution;

4. *Requests* the Secretary-General to continue his efforts, in consultation with the parties concerned, with a view to achieving a peaceful settlement;

5. *Further requests* the Secretary-General to keep Member States informed on the implementation of the present resolution.

Recorded vote in Assembly as follows:

In favour: Afghanistan, Antigua and Barbuda, Argentina, Australia, Austria, Bahrain, Barbados, Belgium, Belize, Botswana, Brazil, Bulgaria, Burma, Burundi, Byelorussian SSR, Canada, Cape Verde, Central African Republic, Chad, Chile, China, Colombia, Comoros, Congo, Costa Rica, Cyprus, Czechoslovakia, Democratic Kampuchea, Denmark, Djibouti, Dominican Republic, Ecuador, Egypt, El Salvador, Equatorial Guinea, Ethiopia, Fiji, Finland, France, Gabon, Gambia, German Democratic Republic, Germany, Federal Republic of, Ghana, Greece, Guatemala, Guinea-Bissau, Guyana, Haiti, Honduras, Hungary, Iceland, Indonesia, Iraq, Ireland, Italy, Ivory Coast, Jamaica, Japan, Jordan, Kenya, Kuwait, Lao People's Democratic Republic, Lebanon, Lesotho, Liberia, Luxembourg, Maldives, Mali, Mauritania, Mexico, Mongolia, Morocco, Mozambique, Nepal, Netherlands, Niger, Norway, Oman, Panama, Papua New Guinea, Paraguay, Peru, Philippines, Poland, Portugal, Qatar, Romania, Saint Lucia, Samoa, Sao Tome and Principe, Saudi Arabia, Senegal, Seychelles, Singapore, Solomon Islands, Somalia, Spain, Sri Lanka, Sudan, Swaziland, Togo, Trinidad and Tobago, Tunisia, Uganda, Ukrainian SSR, USSR, United Arab Emirates, United Kingdom, United Republic of Cameroon, United Republic of Tanzania, United States, Upper Volta, Uruguay, Venezuela, Viet Nam, Yemen, Yugoslavia, Zaire.

Against: Iran.

Abstaining: Bangladesh, Bhutan, Bolivia, Cuba, Grenada, India, Malaysia, New Zealand, Nicaragua, Pakistan, Syrian Arab Republic, Thailand, Turkey, Zambia, Zimbabwe.

Chapter VII

Americas

Contents

Related topics:
Regional economic and social activities: Latin America.
Human rights violations: Latin America. Other colonial territo-
ries: Status of the Falkland Islands (Malvinas).

Peace and security in Central America and the Caribbean area

United Nations consideration in 1982 of peace and security matters in the Americas focused on tensions involving several States in Central America and the Caribbean. Letters from those States to the Security Council and the Secretary-General described situations primarily affecting Costa Rica, Honduras, Nicaragua and the United States. At the request of Nicaragua, the Security Council convened in March/April to discuss a complaint against the United States, but because of a negative vote by the United States it did not adopt a resolution.

Communications. Nicaragua transmitted to the Secretary-General on 8 February the text of a note of 7 February by its Minister for Foreign Affairs questioning the motives behind the establishment of the Central American Democratic Community, comprising Costa Rica, El Salvador and Honduras, which Nicaragua said was aimed at isolating other countries in the region.[4] In a letter of 24 February, Nicaragua transmitted to the Secretary-General a peace proposal for the Central American area presented on 21 February by the Co-ordinator of the Governing Junta of National Reconstruction of Nicaragua, stressing the need for non-alignment, non-aggression and mutual security agreements with Nicaragua's neighbours, delimitation and joint patrolling of its frontiers, and talks with the United States for the negotiated settlement of disputes and the development of regional economic co-operation; given cir-

cumstances under which it was not compelled to take strict measures for defence and survival, the document stated, Nicaragua would hold elections not later than 1985.[5]

Honduras transmitted, in a letter of 23 March to the Secretary-General, the main part of a statement made that day by its Minister of External Relations before the Permanent Council of the Organization of American States (OAS), containing a six-point plan that called for agreements on general disarmament in the region, reduction in the number of foreign military and other advisers, international supervision and monitoring mechanisms to verify compliance with international commitments, measures to halt arms traffic, respect for delimited and demarcated borders, and the framework for a permanent multilateral dialogue to create an internal climate that would strengthen democracy and respect for freedom.[3]

Referring to what it described as the worsening tension in Central America and the increasing danger of large-scale military intervention by the United States, Nicaragua requested an urgent meeting of the Security Council. The request was contained in a letter of 18 March from the Co-ordinator of Nicaragua's Governing Junta annexed to a 19 March letter to the Secretary-General; the Co-ordinator reported the blowing-up of two bridges on 15 March by terrorists operating from Honduras, attacks by Honduran and Salvadorian vessels on 15 and 17 March against two Nicaraguan boats in Nicaraguan waters, and a 9 March press conference at which United States officials displayed aerial photographs of an alleged arms build-up in Nicaragua—shown, the Co-ordinator said, with the goal of convincing the public that Nicaragua was threatening the peace.[6]

In a letter of 25 March to the Council President, El Salvador contended that the international problems and disputes in Latin America, and particularly in Central America, should be solved through recourse to the inter-American system and that Nicaragua should follow El Salvador's example in upholding the principle of non-interference in the internal affairs of States.[2] In a letter of 30 March to the Council President, Nicaragua cited articles of the Charter of the United Nations to support its position that it had the right to bring its complaint before the Security Council, which was a means of protection for all Member States threatened by imminent attack; the choice between the Council and a regional agency, it said, was an inalienable right of any Member State.[7]

Security Council consideration. The Security Council met eight times between 25 March and 2 April to consider Nicaragua's complaint. On 2 April, because of the negative vote of a permanent member, the Council failed to adopt a draft resolution sponsored by Guyana and Panama.[1] The vote was 12 to 1, with 2 abstentions, as follows:

In favour: China, France, Guyana, Ireland, Japan, Jordan, Panama, Poland, Spain, Togo, Uganda, USSR.
Against: United States.
Abstaining: United Kingdom, Zaire.

By this draft, the Council, reminding Member States of their obligations under the United Nations Charter, would have appealed to them to refrain from the direct, indirect, overt or covert use of force against any Central American or Caribbean country. It would have appealed to all parties to pursue dialogue and negotiation and called on all Members to support the search for a peaceful solution to that region's problems. The Secretary-General would have been requested to keep the Council informed of the development of the situation in the region.

Guyana, introducing the draft resolution, said it did not seek to blame any party for the crisis; it merely sought to crystallize the call made by many delegations in the Council—to bring all parties to the negotiating table.

Explaining its negative vote, the United States said it did not feel that the draft resolution supported the United Nations, the Security Council or the inter-American system for resolving disputes among member States, and did not identify key elements of the problem of Central and South America created by Nicaragua's intervention in the affairs of neighbouring States.

The United Kingdom said it could not support the draft resolution because of references to General Assembly resolutions of 1965 on non-intervention[8] and 1966 on non-use of force in international relations;[9] it regarded those resolutions as inconsistent with international law and the Charter, and added that their subjects were covered in the 1970 Declaration on Principles of International Law concerning Friendly Relations and Co-operation among States in accordance with the Charter of the United Nations.[10] Zaire said the draft resolution seemed to reject the approach to settling disputes, outlined in the Charter, that parties should first seek solutions by negotiation and through regional agencies or arrangements.

The Security Council invited the representatives of Algeria, Angola, Argentina, Benin, Chile, Colombia, the Congo, Costa Rica, Cuba, El Salvador, the German Democratic Republic, Grenada, Honduras, India, Iran, Iraq, the Lao People's Democratic Republic, the Libyan Arab Jamahiriya, Madagascar, Mauritius, Mexico, Mozambique, Nicaragua, Nigeria, Seychelles, Sri Lanka, the Syrian Arab Republic, the United Republic of Tanzania, Viet Nam, Yugoslavia, Zambia and Zimbabwe, at their request, to participate without vote in the discussion.

Debate on the item focused on Nicaragua's complaint against the United States and on the latter's response, the effect of tensions on the Central American and Caribbean region and the general situation there. Most States emphasized the need for peaceful solutions based on negotiation and respect for the principles of non-intervention and the territorial integrity of States. Several States, including Honduras, Mexico, Nicaragua, Panama and the United States, offered peace proposals.

All speakers referred to the tensions between Nicaragua and the United States.

The Co-ordinator of the Governing Junta of National Reconstruction of Nicaragua, Daniel Ortega Saavedra, citing what he called a history of United States backing of anti-popular Governments in his country, said the United States had recently been training and arming counter-revolutionary forces in the United States and Honduras and had sent aircraft to conduct espionage in Nicaraguan airspace, and its Central Intelligence Agency had participated in covert actions against Nicaragua such as the recent demolition of bridges. Calling for a halt to such acts, he stated that Nicaragua was willing to improve relations with the United States on the basis of mutual respect and unconditional recognition of its right to self-determination, and was also willing immediately to begin talks with the United States Government to reach concrete results, but it would reject any United States attempt to impose humiliating restrictions on its inviolable and sovereign prerogatives regarding national defence.

The United States said the Nicaraguan charges reflected behaviour of which Nicaragua was guilty—large-scale intervention in the internal affairs of neighbouring States and efforts to overthrow their Governments by force. The United States had no intention of invading Nicaragua. If Nicaragua were genuinely interested in alleviating tensions, it would not continue to pour arms into El Salvador, declare a state of seige on its own people to eliminate the opposition, or displace 25,000 Indians from their homes on the pretext of securing them from Honduras. The United States offered a five-point proposal involving a high-level mutual reassertion of engagements to non-intervention and non-aggression, a United States political commitment concerning the activities of Nicaraguan exiles in the United States and enforcement of the Neutrality Act, a regional undertaking not to import heavy offensive weapons and to reduce the number of foreign military and security advisers to a reasonably low level, a proposal to the United States Congress for renewed aid to Nicaragua and actions by Nicaragua to get out of El Salvador.

Nicaragua responded that the United States proposal failed to take into account the fact that the fundamental problem in Central America did not lie in the never-proven allegation that arms were reaching the Salvadorian revolutionaries via Nicaragua, while the United States was supplying the Salvadorian army.

Commenting on the dispute, Angola stated that a threat to Nicaragua was a threat to the principles of non-alignment, and attacks on its sovereignty were attacks on all countries which had a common past of colonialist domination and a similar present of neo-colonialist adventurism; Nicaragua had proposed negotiating points which, if accepted by the United States, could have brought an end to instability and wars in the area. The Congo said there was no established proof of the danger which Nicaragua supposedly constituted in Central America, used by the United States to justify its conduct; Nicaragua must be allowed freely to exercise the attributes of sovereignty without fear of outside intervention.

Mozambique thought the United States should end threats against Nicaragua and other countries in Central America, and should accept the goodwill of Nicaragua and Mexico and engage in serious talks. The United Republic of Tanzania hoped the United States would demonstrate a desire for peace in the area by refraining from acts contrary to the principles of the United Nations Charter and by reciprocating the offer for a genuine settlement. Zimbabwe said that evidence had been produced of the training of counter-revolutionaries and that serious acts of sabotage had recently been carried out in Nicaragua; at the same time, evidence cited with regard to Nicaragua's involvement in the civil war in El Salvador and its interference in the internal affairs of its neighbours had not been proved.

Iran requested all Council members to take whatever steps were necessary to end United States intimidation and intervention in Nicaragua. The aggressive and interventionist policy of the United States against Nicaragua was part of its policy of increasing international tension and escalating threats against independent States, Iraq asserted. The Libyan Arab Jamahiriya said the evidence testified to the aggressive intentions of the United States to destabilize Nicaragua and topple its Government, and indicated that American military intervention in Central America was imminent.

The Syrian Arab Republic stated that the threat to Nicaragua could not be portrayed as an East-West competition for areas of influence but was an attempt by the United States to strengthen its grip and hegemony in an area it viewed as its private domain. Viet Nam said that for some time the world had been witnessing hostile actions against Nicaragua and the countries of the Caribbean, especially Cuba and Grenada, perpetrated by the United States on the pretext that Nicaragua had helped in the struggle against the dictatorial Salvadorian régime.

The German Democratic Republic called Nicaragua a special target of the United States policy of intervention. The USSR said the evidence presented by Nicaragua attested to the presence of a direct threat by the United States to Nicaragua's sovereignty and independence, and added that the United States made no attempt to rebut the facts indicating broad and overt intervention in Nicaragua's affairs.

States participating in the debate were unanimous in calling for non-military solutions to the situation and most urged dialogue and negotiation. Jordan hoped the United States and Nicaragua would negotiate as they had expressed the willingness to do; a super-Power, it added, could afford to seek dialogue.

Negotiation was the way to halt the deterioration of relations between Nicaragua and the United States, said Ireland; on both sides there were proposals and a will to negotiate. Japan suggested that, to make the dialogue meaningful and fruitful, the United States and Nicaragua should undertake frank discussions on all issues of mutual concern. Mexico considered it feasible and desirable to create a system of mutual non-aggression pacts between Nicaragua and the United States and between Nicaragua and its neighbours, and called on the two countries to agree to an effective truce in words and fact to permit the creation of a propitious climate for understanding; it urged the United States to rule out any threat or use of force against Nicaragua. Panama remarked that negotiated political solutions for the differences between Nicaragua and the United States entailed no risks for national security or the fundamental interests of the United States, whereas pursuing a policy of force entailed serious risks. The United Kingdom believed that only in direct talks between the United States and Nicaragua could the necessary atmosphere of trust be established.

Nicaragua's demands contained nothing that could be considered unreasonable and were accompanied by an offer of negotiation, Madagascar observed; it would be a grievous error not to take up that offer and to continue acts of intimidation and destabilization against Nicaragua while accusing its leaders of being part of an international machination against the region's stability.

Nigeria said Nicaragua must enjoy the freedom to develop along the lines and in the direction it had chosen for itself; there must be no attempt to secure a settlement through threats of force or an invasion. Seychelles was apprehensive about the possibility of foreign military intervention in Nicaragua, not excluding recourse to the use of mercenaries.

France said it understood the anxiety Nicaragua might have regarding national independence and territorial integrity. The United Kingdom remarked that the increases planned for the Nicaraguan armed forces seemed to go well beyond its defence needs.

Costa Rica expressed satisfaction at the guarantees offered by the United States to respect Nicaragua's security and independence; it added that it would go to Nicaragua's defence in the case of aggression or intervention.

Argentina denied statements by Nicaragua citing broadcast information implicating Argentine military men in the training of Nicaraguan counter-revolutionaries in Honduras; Argentina added that there was no limitation on relations between the armed forces of States other than respect for non-intervention.

Many States, including the Libyan Arab Jamahiriya, Mexico, Mozambique, the Syrian Arab Republic and the United Republic of Tanzania, expressed solidarity with Nicaragua. Others taking this position, including Angola, Benin, the Lao People' Democratic Republic and Uganda, cited their own experiences as States struggling for independence or which had undergone revolutions.

China said the struggle of Nicaragua to overthrow dictatorial rule had won the sympathy of the Chinese people. Guyana expressed support for the Government and people of Nicaragua in their efforts to consolidate and defend their revolution. Poland voiced admiration for Nicaragua's determined effort to rid itself of the legacy of an op-

pressive dictatorship and of economic underdevelopment. Yugoslavia saw the revolutionary changes in Nicaragua as the direct outcome of its people's struggle to overcome past injustices and create a society in which all strata of the population would live in freedom. Zambia said it shared Nicaragua's desire for peace, adding that socialism in the world, including Central America, was not a threat to anyone, especially if it came about through a popular movement or democratic elections.

Ireland thought it understandable that those who had successfully challenged despotic rule at home should sympathize with those of like mind facing similar opponents in neighbouring countries but, if sympathy and moral support became active intervention, there would be a serious danger of hostilities.

Proposals announced by the President of Mexico at Managua, Nicaragua, on 21 February, including a plan for negotiations in Mexico between the United States and Nicaragua, were widely commented upon during the Council's debate. Mexico favoured a systematic dialogue among the parties and a genuine readiness to grant mutual concessions without abandoning essential principles or legitimate interests.

The Mexican proposals were welcomed by both Nicaragua and the United States, as well as by Algeria, Benin, China, Cuba, France, Grenada, Guyana, Madagascar, Mozambique, Panama, Poland, Uganda, the USSR, the United Republic of Tanzania, Viet Nam, Yugoslavia and Zaire. Ireland, Japan and Nigeria commended Mexico's efforts, and the Lao People's Democratic Republic and the United Republic of Tanzania urged the United States to respond positively.

Madagascar thought the Council should support the Mexican initiative. Panama said the initiative offered a valuable starting point, the further development of which would permit movement towards solutions.

In other comments on the situation in the region as a whole, Grenada called for Latin American and Caribbean support for action to declare the Caribbean a zone of peace and prohibit the introduction of nuclear weapons, stop all aggressive military manoeuvres, dismantle all foreign military bases and establish machinery to deal with all forms of aggression, including assassination, propaganda intervention, diplomatic and economic aggression, and mercenary invasion; the Security Council should also make a definitive pronouncement on the use of mercenaries.

Honduras reiterated the regional peace plan it had proposed to the OAS Permanent Council on 23 March and communicated in a letter to the Secretary-General (p. 364), calling for disarmament, fewer foreign advisers, verification measures, a halt to arms traffic, respect for borders and a framework for dialogue. Panama offered to serve as host to a conference on Central American peace, security and co-operation, attended by all Heads of State and Government of Central America and the heads of Central American armies, and culminating in a multilateral system of détente, neutrality, peace, co-operation and development.

Benin, Cuba (on behalf of the Movement of Non-Aligned Countries), the German Democratic Republic, Guyana, Poland and the United Republic of Tanzania were among those which viewed tensions in the region as a threat to international peace and security.

Many States stressed the need to enforce the principles of non-intervention, non-use of force, self-determination, and the inviolability of national sovereignty and territorial integrity with respect to Nicaragua and Central America in general.

Algeria said the turn of events in Central America and the dangers inherent in the risk of possible foreign intervention there were a serious violation of the sacred principle of the Movement of Non-Aligned Countries—to determine one's own destiny. Nigeria suggested a multilateral commitment by all States of the region to the basic policy of non-interference in one another's internal affairs.

Asserting that relations between States should be based on respect for independence, sovereignty and territorial integrity, Togo joined in the call for a negotiated solution in Central America. Uganda said no attempt should be made to impose a particular social system or political preference on the Central American nations. The United Republic of Tanzania said the parties should refrain from any acts amounting to aggression and interference in internal affairs. Zimbabwe observed that respect for such principles implied the right of nations to exist in accordance with their beliefs, aspirations and forms of government, which in turn demanded that other nations respect such choices.

China considered that the independence, sovereignty and territorial integrity of all Central American countries should be respected and questions concerning the region should be settled by its peoples, free from outside interference. India counselled restraint and encouraged a serious effort to defuse tensions in Central America; it stated that the broadening of controversy by involving extraregional and global forces could only complicate an already difficult situation. Japan felt that the instability prevailing in Central America should be resolved by the people of each State; outside intervention could aggravate the situation and hamper the healthy development of each nation. Jordan noted that the Charter specifically mandated non-interference in the internal affairs of States, either overtly or covertly.

Argentina trusted that it was still possible to adopt moderate, rational and just positions based on strict and realistic application of the essential principles of non-intervention and non-interference. Chile and Colombia, among others, expressed their complete rejection of intervention in the internal affairs of States, regardless of its form; Colombia added that any country which suffered direct, indirect or covert intervention by another State or group of States was entitled to defend its sovereignty in any way it saw fit. Guyana said the only solutions could be those which emerged from the subregion itself and respected the peoples' right to self-determination and political independence. Panama remarked that negotiated political solutions for the differences between Nicaragua and the United States entailed no risks for national security or the fundamental interests of the United States, whereas pursuing a policy of force entailed serious risks; it voiced concern about reports of the alleged use of bases in the Panama Canal region to support, execute and co-ordinate actions against other countries of the region.

France considered that tension could be reduced by negotiation, refraining from the use of force and the reduction of military build-ups in the area, as well as by external economic assistance and structural reforms. Ireland said it would like to see détente involving all countries of the region—including those hitherto excluded—which could come about through a major negotiation covering political and economic issues and providing for the reduction of armaments, restraint, regional co-operation, and respect for human rights and pluralism. Spain hoped it would be possible to reach common ground for a negotiated solution that would eliminate the basic causes of destabilization—social imbalances, injustice and repression; it opposed any type of intervention or interference in the internal affairs of States.

Several States stressed that the changes taking place in Central America were internal and not the result of outside influences. Making this point, Guyana said that any external attempt to dictate, influence or frustrate the nature of that change would abridge the right of self-determination of peoples and distort the domestic impulses for change. Costa Rica said the real inequity being committed against the peoples of Central America was turning them into chips on the table of the ideological and political interests of other regions. In Grenada's view, there would be no peace if it were believed that the revolutionary processes unfolding in Central America and the Caribbean had been parboiled somewhere else.

Mexico observed that the social revolutions of the day could not be encompassed within the framework of East-West rivalries. Nicaragua remarked that the peoples of Central America were determined to free themselves in the face of resistance by privileged minorities who sought to halt the changes which, sooner or later, must come to those unjust societies. Panama considered it artificial and facile to ascribe the social and political crisis in Central America to foreign influences or infiltration in an effort to disregard or conceal the dramatic imbalances, documented injustices, poverty and oppression endured by the peoples of Central America.

Poland disagreed with the tendency to see events in Central America as a result of imaginary Cuban, Nicaraguan or other influences; it believed the nations of Central America should be allowed to enjoy their sovereign right to determine their political, economic and social system without external interference. Yugoslavia regarded the situation in Central America and the Caribbean as an anachronism in an era when the aspiration of peoples to emancipation and the right to decide their destiny freely had become predominant.

A number of States cited the economic and social situation in Central America as a major factor in the region's problems. Algeria saw the crisis as basically the result of many decades of social injustice, tyranny and poverty. Cuba said the causes of political and social upheaval in Central America lay in illiteracy, unemployment, infant mortality and poverty. Jordan commented that there could never be a military solution to socio-economic issues. Mexico said the distinctive feature of the region was the struggle to change centuries-old conditions of poverty and exploitation. Poland said the causes of civil war in El Salvador and the tensions and upheavals in other countries of the region were deeply rooted in internal issues such as economic backwardness and extreme social inequalities.

According to Ireland, since many problems of Central America derived from long-established economic and social conditions which required reform, economic assistance, including the Caribbean Basin Initiative announced by the United States, should be part of any overall settlement. Japan welcomed that initiative and other forms of international co-operation to assist national efforts for economic development and social justice, which it regarded as essential to the fundamental solution of instability in Central America.

Cuba remarked that the United States squandered on naval exercises many more millions than the sum it offered the countries of the region allegedly for development within the framework of its Caribbean Basin Initiative. Nicaragua stated that Canada, Mexico and Venezuela had proposed a joint non-discriminatory economic programme but, instead of taking up the initiative, the United States had pursued a unilateral policy that excluded Cuba, Grenada and Nicaragua and weakened the efforts of other Governments, making it impossible to respond to the urgent request of the Central American countries for a minimum of $20 billion in financing and credits needed for survival. The United States said that, during its first 18 months, the current Nicaraguan Government had received more economic assistance from the United States than from any other Government; however, support from the United States had not changed the Nicaraguan leaders' image of it as the Yankee enemy of mankind.

Regarding United States involvement in Central America, Cuba asked whether the United States was willing to recognize the vital need for far-reaching changes in the economic and social structures of Latin America and the right of peoples to choose and rule freely over their own destinies. The German Democratic Republic said the United States and reactionary forces in the region constantly violated the sovereignty and territorial integrity of the Central American States, interfering massively in their internal affairs under the guise of the struggle against so-called international terrorism and totalitarianism. Iraq held the United States aggressive and interventionist policy responsible for endangering peace in Central America. The Lao People's Democratic Republic said the United States had actively bent its efforts to destabilizing and replacing the Governments of Central America. The Libyan Arab Jamahiriya said the United States was not aware of the necessity for change in some countries of the region and had demonstrated no encouraging response to the efforts by some, especially Mexico, to seek a political solution to the problem of El Salvador and relations between the countries of the region.

Mexico felt that a new intervention by the United States in Central America would represent a gigantic historical error leading back to the bitter days of continental relations. The USSR hoped the United States would realize that a reliable way to develop relations between States was not through stepping up tension but by respecting sovereignty and removing discord by peaceful means. Viet Nam believed that the situation was the result of United States policies which had deliberately ignored the far-reaching social, economic and political changes in the region; the United States must put an end to intervention and aggression and respect the right of peoples to self-determination.

The United States expressed solidarity with all those who hoped for change, democracy and the development of Central America, and hoped that change would be as peaceable as possible.

Discussion of the United Nations role in relation to the situation in Central America focused on two issues: whether the Security Council should have taken up Nicaragua's complaint and what the Council should do in view of the increasing tension in the region.

Regarding the role of the Council in the area, Nicaragua urged it to issue a pronouncement regarding the obligation to seek a peaceful means of solving the region's problems, to reject any acts of force or threats and to repudiate any direct, indirect or covert intervention in Central America. Nicaragua's appeal was supported by Iraq, Mozambique and the USSR. A number of States, including Algeria, Benin, Guyana, the Lao People's Democratic Republic, Mauritius, Poland, Uganda, Zaire and Zambia, called on the Council to reaffirm the principles of the United Nations Charter relating to non-intervention, the maintenance of international security and friendly relations among States.

The Council was also called upon by many States to help bring the parties to negotiation or other peaceful settlement. Among them were the Congo, Ireland, Mexico, Panama, Seychelles, Togo, Uganda, the United Republic of Tanzania, Viet Nam, Yugoslavia and Zaire.

Algeria observed that the Council had, for once, been called upon not to consider a *de facto* breach of peace but to exercise its authority to prevent a crisis, putting it in a position to fulfil its primary responsibility for maintaining international peace and security. India believed the Council debate would have been in vain if it inflamed passions, deepened mistrust and ended in mutual recrimination; it urged constructive consideration by the Council, directed towards dialogue. In Ireland's view, the Council should try to ease tensions between Nicaragua and the United States, reduce the danger of conflict and restore the previous friendly relationship between the two. The Lao People's Democratic Republic said the Council should take steps to remove the threats of direct or indirect aggression and to safeguard Nicaragua's sovereignty, independence and territorial integrity. The Libyan Arab Jamahiriya called on the Council to adopt all necessary measures to help Nicaragua maintain independence, sovereignty and territorial integrity.

Speaking for the Movement of Non-Aligned Countries, Cuba said the Council must unequivocally state its opposition to the threat or use of force against Nicaragua and other peoples of the region, and must call on all States to refrain from taking such steps and to respect the right of peoples to determine their destiny. Cuba, speaking on its own behalf, said the Council must urge the United States to rule out the use of force against Central America and the Caribbean and to restrict itself to negotiation.

France suggested that the Council call on the Secretary-General to follow developments in the area, investigate charges by Nicaragua and the United States and report within two or three weeks. Zaire also suggested that the Council ask him to follow the situation and report on it.

Differing views were expressed as to whether the Security Council or OAS should deal with the Nicaraguan complaint.

Guyana, the Lao People' Democratic Republic and Yugolsavia were among those arguing that it was proper for the Council to address the situation, in the discharge of its primary responsibility for the maintenance of peace and security.

It was up to the United Nations, rather than a regional organization which had ostracized certain States in that part of the world, to make an effective contribution to settling problems in Central America and the Caribbean by peaceful means, Benin said. Cuba believed that no regional organization or pact lay above the Council or could be invoked to the detriment of its supreme authority for the maintenance of international peace and security—even less so when the regional organization lacked universality, excluding some and denying entry to others while admitting a Power that had nothing to do with Latin America. France believed that the situation was so disquieting that it fully warranted Council consideration. The German Democratic Republic said that interventionist activities had assumed such proportions that Nicaragua had felt compelled to call for the urgent convening of the Council in full accordance with the United Nations Charter.

Mauritius stated that the Council could not lock its door against those who preferred to take their case directly to it. Mexico made the point that every Member State had a right to bring before the Council any matter which threatened international peace and security; parties to a regional agreement were not obligated to refer problems to that machinery before submitting them to the Council. Whatever other arrangements there might be for dispute settlement, Sri Lanka said, no Member State could be expected to forgo its right of recourse to the Council.

Togo pointed out that the United Nations Charter opened the way for recourse to regional agencies, but it also authorized the Council to investigate any dispute brought to it; the Council thus had two options. Uganda felt that the Council had a positive role to play in the situation to ease tension and prevent conflicts. Zaire thought it only natural for the situation in the historically sensitive area of Central America to be of concern to the Council, since it was difficult to detach the many hotbeds of local or regional tension from the context of cold war, distrust and a crisis of confidence in international relations.

On the other hand, Chile said the Council meetings ran the risk of drawing Nicaragua and the

United States farther from the chance of achieving understanding; no one could deny the Council's competence to deal with problems, but it would have been legally fitting to take the matter to the regional organization first. Colombia accepted the right of Governments to present their problems to the Council but believed that taking that as a first step weakened the regional system, to which the problem before the Council should have been brought. Costa Rica, expressing concern that Nicaragua had bypassed the more efficient inter-American system, said the Council debate had become a sad display of political rhetoric, where a series of delegations had come to parade their ignorance of the situation in Central America. El Salvador said the problems of international relations in the inter-American sphere should be solved through the organs created by the regional system. Honduras also believed that such matters should have been taken to OAS.

Japan believed that efforts to resolve the issues should be made first through bilateral talks or discussions among countries in the region or in such regional organizations as OAS. The United Kingdom questioned whether the airing of issues in the Council would help promote peaceful solutions, when it was negotiations that were needed; moreover, it was not for the Council to determine how negotiations should be handled. The United States said that, while any Member State had the right to bring before the Council an issue which seriously threatened international peace and security, it was equally clear that the Charter encouraged the resolution of disputes through regional arrangements.

The situation in El Salvador was referred to by several speakers. El Salvador said it did not constitute an international threat or source of friction for anyone, nor had it ever violated the principle of non-intervention in Central America, but it had been the victim of acts of intervention and aggressive behaviour which, if continued, would compel it to use its right to bring into operation the machinery of the inter-American regional system in order to preserve its sovereignty and national dignity.

Cuba denied that it was sending weapons to the Salvadorian revolutionaries, though it did have the right to help in the liberation of a brother people since the United States arrogated to itself the right to arm counter-revolutionary gangs in Angola and finance the destabilization of various revolutionary countries. Guyana believed that a just and lasting settlement of the problems facing El Salvador must be worked out by its people, without any outside pressure or interference.

Mexico remarked that the overwhelming majority of the international community favoured a negotiated political solution to the Salvadorian conflict. Nicaragua stated that, through sacrifice and great effort, the people of El Salvador were continuing a struggle begun many decades ago—one that had been repressed and suppressed on different occasions but which had always been just. Poland abhorred the suffering and massacres of innocent people in El Salvador and believed that a just solution must be found by the people themselves through negotiations with the patriotic forces and without outside interference. Viet Nam was convinced that the just struggle of the people of El Salvador for democracy, freedom and self-determination would triumph.

Regarding relations between Nicaragua and El Salvador, Nicaragua stated that aggressive actions by naval units of El Salvador and Honduras against Nicaraguan fishing vessels had taken place as a result of the campaign of false accusations about purported traffic in weapons from Nicaragua to El Salvador. Seychelles said the people of El Salvador were rising against oppression on their own and that no country, including Nicaragua, which had its own projects and development plans, was fostering a revolution or insurrection there. The United States, on the other hand, said Nicaragua sought to subvert and overthrow neighbouring Governments and El Salvador was the principal target; arms and ammunition for Salvadorian insurgents, reached Nicaragua by ship, and occasionally by direct flights from Cuba to Nicaragua.

Commenting on United States policy towards El Salvador, Cuba said the United States sent weapons there while raising a hypocritical outcry about the so-called arms build-up of Cuba and Nicaragua. The Lao People' Democratic Republic said the United States was trying to stifle the legitimate aspirations of the Salvadorian people to independence, freedom and dignity. The Libyan Arab Jamahiriya said that, despite its defeat in Viet Nam, the United States was still contemplating the possibility of direct military intervention in El Salvador and continued to support the régime against the will of the people and their right to adopt political, economic and social systems of their choice. Nicaragua stated that Salvadorian patriots had authorized Nicaragua to convey their willingness to begin immediate negotiations without pre-conditions.

Statements were made by several States regarding elections in El Salvador on 28 March, at the time of the Council debate. El Salvador said the voting, for a constituent assembly that would have the power to draft a constitution and lay new foundations for government, had been held in the face of threats by extreme leftists wishing to boycott the process; for the first time in 50 years there had been genuinely free elections, with a massive voter turn-out. The elections were welcomed by Costa

Rica as evidence of the massive participation of El Salvador's people, even in defiance of death. The United States called the elections a tribute to the Salvadorian people and the vitality of the democratic idea, and said that, despite the possibility of massive violence at the polling places and threats of retaliation by guerrilla forces against voters, they had voted in unprecedented numbers.

In Cuba's view, the El Salvador elections seemed to be only elections on paper; it was over-optimistic to think that, in a country shaken by a deep civil war, where human rights were not respected, there could be the minimum guarantees for holding elections.

Speaking of relations between Cuba and the United States, Cuba said a criminal economic blockade and a policy of harassment, aggression and intolerance had been maintained against it by six United States administrations. Mexico commented that the solution of the Central American problem required a substantial improvement in relations between Cuba and the United States; the Cuban revolution was an irreversible fact and keeping Cuba out of regional decision-making was a mistake.

The United States said Cuba maintained 1,800 to 2,000 security and military personnel in Nicaragua, and was attempting to export aggression, subvert established Governments and intervene persistently and massively in the internal affairs of more than one Central American nation. Cuba responded that the presence of 3,000 Cuban technicians in Nicaragua, including a small number of military personnel, represented normal practice and was based on agreements between independent and sovereign Governments; it denied that the origin of the Central American crisis lay in an alleged surge of subversion controlled from Cuba and Nicaragua.

Draft resolution not adopted. [1]Guyana, Panama, S/14941.
Letters. [2]El Salvador: 25 Mar., S/14927. [3]Honduras: 23 Mar., S/14919. Nicaragua: [4]8 Feb., A/37/104; [5]24 Feb., S/14891; [6]19 Mar., S/14913; [7]30 Mar., S/14936.
Resolutions. GA: [8]2131(XX), 21 Dec. 1965 (YUN 1965, p. 94); [9]2160(XXI), 30 Nov. 1966 (YUN 1966, p. 67); [10]2625(XXV), annex, 24 Oct. 1970 (YUN 1970, p. 789).
Meeting records. SC: S/PV.2335-2337, 2339, 2341-2343, 2347 (25 Mar.–2 Apr.).

Other questions involving Nicaragua

Costa Rica and Nicaragua

In a letter of 24 May 1982 to the President of the Security Council, Nicaragua transmitted a communiqué issued on 21 May by its Ministry of External Relations denying reports attributed to government sources in Costa Rica that troops of the Sandinista People's Army had infiltrated Costa Rican territory, and stating that alien interests were determined to create tension between the two countries with the aim of justifying foreign military aggression.[1]

Letter. [1]Nicaragua, 24 May, S/15113.

Honduras, Nicaragua and the United States

Between March and July 1982, Nicaragua addressed a number of letters to the Secretary-General and the President of the Security Council protesting what it described as acts of aggression against it by the United States. A series of letters on relations between Honduras and Nicaragua, complaining of armed attacks in the frontier areas of both sides, was sent by the two countries between July and December.

In a letter of 16 March, Nicaragua conveyed the text of a communiqué issued on 9 March by its Ministry of External Relations protesting the violation of Nicaraguan airspace by United States spy planes, as disclosed on that date by the Deputy Director of the United States Defense Intelligence Agency in connection with charges of a Nicaraguan arms build-up.[15] In a letter of the same date, Nicaragua transmitted the text of a decree it had issued on 15 March declaring a 30-day suspension of certain rights and guarantees in response to what the decree referred to as acts of aggression against Nicaragua, including the blowing-up of two bridges on 14 March.[16]

In a letter of 15 April, Nicaragua described 23 further acts between 14 March and 12 April, including 11 ground incidents involving attacks on frontier posts and other armed assaults from Costa Rican and Honduran territory; annexed was a letter of 15 April from the Minister for External Relations to the United States Secretary of State demanding the immediate withdrawal of a United States destroyer and other warships which had entered Nicaraguan waters on 12 April.[17] A letter to the Security Council President on 19 April stated Nicaragua's belief that negotiations with the United States, with Mexico as a participant, must begin immediately in view of violations of Nicaragua's waters by United States warships.[18] The Council President was told in a 16 June letter from Nicaragua of its intention to continue to strive for a peaceful solution despite repeated violations and acts of intimidation by the United States, notably the presence of a United States warship in Nicaraguan waters between 7 and 10 June.[19]

A number of letters by Honduras and Nicaragua were addressed to the Security Council President between July and December.

In a letter of 28 July, Nicaragua said it had been the target of attacks by counter-revolutionaries, resulting in 114 deaths, launched from Honduran territory between 19 and 27 July; the attacks, it said, had been promoted by the United States in order to provoke a war between Nicaragua and Honduras and justify more direct intervention against Nicaragua and El Salvador.[20]

In response to what it called a campaign in the mass media to make it appear that Honduran armed forces were intervening in the internal problems of neighbouring countries, Honduras sent a letter on 30 July reaffirming its commitment to non-intervention, reiterating its desire for peace as demonstrated by the peace proposals it had presented in March (p. 364) and repeating its proposal for an international mechanism to monitor frontier areas.[1]

In a message of 2 August from the Honduran Minister for Foreign Affairs to the Security Council President, transmitted on 4 August, Honduras charged Nicaragua with attacks against Honduran property and territory during July, including a border penetration by a Nicaraguan army patrol and an artillery attack that had wounded five peasants; the Minister stated that Nicaragua was making a serious mistake in using any problems it might have with its people as a pretext to justify such acts of aggression.[2] These charges were called unfounded in a 16 August letter by Nicaragua, which also said that it regarded as positive the peace initiatives by Honduras and that it was ready to set up machinery for monitoring of the frontier areas by United Nations observers.[21]

The Foreign Minister of Honduras annexed to a letter of 23 August a document summarizing 34 incidents between 30 January and 20 August involving alleged violations of Honduran territory, territorial waters and airspace by Nicaragua and attacks on its citizens resulting in two deaths and a number of abductions; Honduras reiterated its willingness to begin a serious dialogue towards peace.[3] Nicaragua, in a letter of 21 September,[22] responded that consolidation of social tranquillity, economic reconstruction and defence of its frontiers were priorities that did not allow it to divert its limited resources by launching campaigns against its neighbours; annexed were a letter of 6 August to the President of Honduras from the Co-ordinator of Nicaragua's Governing Junta of National Reconstruction, inviting him to a meeting at Managua on the problems between the two countries, and a communiqué of 2 September by Nicaragua's Ministry of External Relations listing actions against Nicaragua by the United States and offers by Nicaragua to improve relations with its neighbours and with the United States.

On 21 September, Honduras transmitted a protest which its Acting Minister for Foreign Affairs sent to Nicaragua on 18 September concerning an exchange of fire in Honduran territorial waters, said to have been initiated by a patrol boat of the Nicaraguan Navy against a Honduran patrol boat; a press release by Honduras describing the incident was annexed.[4] A letter of 22 September by Honduras contained the text of its response to Nicaraguan claims regarding the incident, acknowledging that there was no legally defined boundary in the Atlantic between the two countries but asserting that there was a tacit agreement on a dividing line from which Nicaragua had deviated.[5]

On 23 September, Nicaragua transmitted the text of a note it had addressed to Honduras protesting an incident on 22 September in which a Honduran Army unit was said to have fired on a Nicaraguan observation post at La Ceiba, and appealing to Honduras to end such challenges.[23] A letter of 24 September by Nicaragua transmitted the text of its note to Honduras concerning a second frontier incident on 22 September in which, Nicaragua said, two vehicles of its Ministry of Agricultural Development and Agrarian Reform had been ambushed by counter-revolutionaries from Honduran territory and two Nicaraguans had been killed; Nicaragua held Honduras indirectly responsible for such acts as long as it tolerated the use of its territory by counter-revolutionaries and stressed the need for dialogue between the two countries.[24]

Nicaragua transmitted, by a letter of 5 November, a message from its Foreign Minister to the Security Council President expressing concern that military aggression against Nicaragua was no longer a matter of isolated and sporadic actions by small groups but had become, with United States backing, a gradual, silent invasion combining Nicaraguan dissidents, the Honduran Army, and joint military manœuvres organized by Honduras and the United States; annexed were copies of articles from *The New York Times* and *The Washington Post*, which the Foreign Minister said proved the existence of a plan to destabilize the Nicaraguan Government.[25]

Nicaragua transmitted on 10 November the text of a protest note sent on the previous day to Honduras regarding the abduction on 8 November of 42 peasants from Nicaraguan territory by counter-revolutionaries from Honduran territory; the note also stated that the Honduran Foreign Minister had not gone to Nicaragua during the first week in November as he had agreed to do in a conversation with the Nicaraguan Foreign Minister held in the office of the United Nations Secretary-General.[26] By a letter of 11 November, Honduras transmitted a note of the same date from its Foreign Minister, stating that the Nicaraguan Foreign Minister had been unable to meet with him on several dates on which he was prepared to visit Managua.[6] On 19 November, Honduras transmitted a 17 November letter from its Foreign Minister affirming that Honduras would not allow acts of aggression against Nicaragua to be carried out from its territory and that its willingness to contribute to the relaxation of tensions was shown by the Foreign Minister's official visit to Nicaragua on 12 November.[7]

Four letters from Honduras in December included the texts of protest notes to Nicaragua regarding attacks against Honduran territory. A letter of 9 December conveyed a note of 22 November stating that a Nicaraguan Air Force plane had on 5 November bombed a frontier area west of Ahuasbila, Honduras, and adding that Honduras remained ready to reach agreements to avoid similar incidents.[8] On 10 December, Honduras transmitted a letter of 8 December protesting attacks on 30 November and 2 and 3 December against Honduran soldiers and civilians near the frontier.[9] Two further letters of 10 December transmitted notes of 9 December requesting the return of the body of a Honduran farmer killed by Nicaraguan soldiers on that date[10] and protesting an incident of the same date involving hostile fire by Nicaraguan troops against the Honduran frontier village of El Coyol, wounding three children.[11]

By a letter of 13 December, Nicaragua transmitted a letter of 2 December to Honduras rejecting two earlier protest notes, and saying that it was up to Honduras to respond to the many protests by Nicaragua concerning frontier attacks and to dismantle the counter-revolutionary camps on Honduran territory.[27] Aggression by counter-revolutionary military units operating from Honduran territory, with the economic and military support of the United States, was denounced by Nicaragua in a 13 December letter to the Secretary-General, annexed to which was a communiqué describing an incident of 9 December in which 75 children and 9 adults being transported away from the frontier in a Nicaraguan helicopter had been killed.[28]

Two letters of 21 December were sent to the Security Council President by Honduras. One conveyed a 20 December note from the Foreign Minister to the Council President charging that Nicaragua had intensifed its campaign of verbal and material aggression against Honduras and that its Army had made frequent incursions into Honduran territory.[12] The second transmitted a note of 17 December from the Honduran Foreign Minister to the Nicaraguan Foreign Minister rejecting charges that insurgent forces were operating from Honduran territory and stating that the fighting between such forces and the Nicaraguan Army was occurring in Nicaraguan territory.[13] A letter of 30 December from Honduras to the Council President transmitted a 29 December note to Nicaragua recalling three incidents during

which Nicaraguan attacks on Honduran territory had been answered by Honduran fire and reiterating Honduras' neutrality in Nicaragua's domestic dispute.[14]

Letters. Honduras: [1]30 July, S/15331; [2]4 Aug., S/15344; [3]23 Aug., S/15384; [4]21 Sep., S/15417; [5]22 Sep., S/15423; [6]11 Nov., S/15487; [7]19 Nov., S/15495; [8]9 Dec., S/15516; [9]10 Dec., S/15518; [10]10 Dec., S/15519; [11]10 Dec., S/15520; [12]21 Dec., S/15536; [13]21 Dec., S/15537; [14]30 Dec., S/15545. Nicaragua: [15]16 Mar., S/14908; [16]16 Mar., S/14909; [17]15 Apr., S/14992; [18]19 Apr., S/14993; [19]16 June, S/15245; [20]28 July, S/15319; [21]16 Aug., S/15365; [22]21 Sep., S/15422; [23]23 Sep., S/15431; [24]24 Sep., S/15432; [25]5 Nov., S/15484; [26]10 Nov., S/15489; [27]13 Dec., S/15521; [28]13 Dec., A/37/758.

Guyana and Venezuela

The Security Council President received four letters from Guyana and Venezuela between May and September 1982 relating to the territorial dispute between the two States over the Essequibo (Guyana Esequiba) area.

In a letter of 11 May, Guyana reported that Venezuelan troops had crossed onto the Guyana mainland on 10 May in an incident which, in Guyana's view, constituted a violation of its sovereignty and of two bilateral agreements—the Geneva Agreement of 1966 and the Port of Spain (Trinidad) Protocol of 1970—containing commitments to seek a solution by peaceful means.[1] Annexed to a 1 June letter from Venezuela was a reply by its Ministry of External Relations stating that Guyana's charges were untrue, that Venezuela desired a peaceful solution and that, instead of imagining warlike intentions, Guyana should negotiate a solution to the frontier dispute inherited from colonialism.[3]

On 14 September, Guyana again protested attempted incursions, on 3 and 5 September, by Venezuelan military personnel into Guyanese territory, stating that they had occurred at a time when Guyana was seeking to reach an agreement with Venezuela on the choice of a method for peaceful settlement.[2] In a letter of 30 September and an annex on the status of the controversy, Venezuela indicated that it had rejected on 30 August Guyana's proposal of 20 August to place the matter before the International Court of Justice, and maintained its insistence on direct negotiations; as the time-limit under the Geneva Agreement for agreeing on a means of settlement had expired on 18 September, it was necessary to apply the other provisions of the Agreement, by which the decision on means was to be referred to an international organ agreed upon by both countries or to the Secretary-General.[4]

Letters. Guyana: [1]11 May, S/15072; [2]14 Sep., S/15398. Venezuela: [3]1 June, S/15208; [4]30 Sep., S/15439.

Anniversary observances

Five hundredth anniversary of the discovery of America

The General Assembly decided in December 1982 to consider in 1983 an item on the observance of the quincentenary of the discovery of America.

A request to include the item in the agenda of the Assembly's 1982 session was forwarded to the Secretary-General in a letter of 12 October by 30 States, mainly from North and South America and the Caribbean.[3] The signatories of the letter stated that the arrival in 1492 of three ships under the command of Christopher Columbus had opened up opportunities for contact and understanding between the world's civilizations and peoples, culminating in the ideals of universality reaffirmed in the era of the United Nations. They considered that the anniversary should be observed by the United Nations and that the intervening decade should be used for organizing activities equal to the occasion.

In November, 36 States submitted a draft resolution[2] to have the Assembly declare 1992 as the Year of the Fifth Centennial of the Discovery of America and request the Secretary-General to prepare appropriate observances so that the United Nations and those Member States most directly concerned could co-operate in commemorating the event. The draft—sponsored by most of the countries of the western hemisphere as well as Equatorial Guinea, Italy, the Philippines, Portugal and Spain—also called for the submission of annual reports by the Secretary-General and the inclusion of the item in the provisional agenda of the 1983 Assembly session.

Ecuador introduced the draft resolution in the Assembly, noting that the initiative for the proposal had come from the Dominican Republic. Other sponsors—the Dominican Republic, Italy, the Philippines, Spain and the United States—urged support for the proposal to commemorate the arrival at San Salvador, Bahamas, on 12 October 1492 of three Spanish caravels under the command of Columbus. Iceland and Ireland questioned whether commemorating that event as the discovery of America would ignore earlier explorations by Vikings and possibly Irish monks; Ireland also thought the request for an annual report by the Secretary-General over the following 10 years might be excessive. Spain responded that the intention was not to deny earlier explorations but to commemorate the fact that those who had begun arriving in 1492 had left settlements and brought about the merging of races.

After the President announced that the sponsors of the draft resolution had requested deferral to the 1983 session to allow for further consultations among regional groups, the Assembly decided without vote on 21 December, on his oral proposal, to include the item in its provisional agenda for the following year.[1]

Decision (1982). [1]GA: 37/451, 21 Dec., text following.
Draft resolution not pressed. [2]Antigua and Barbuda, Argentina, Bahamas, Barbados, Bolivia, Brazil, Canada, Chile, Colombia, Costa Rica, Cuba, Dominican Republic, Ecuador, El Salvador, Equatorial Guinea, Grenada, Guatemala, Guyana, Haiti, Honduras, Italy, Jamaica, Mexico, Nicaragua, Panama, Paraguay, Peru, Philippines, Portugal, Saint Vincent and the Grenadines, Spain, Suriname, Trinidad and Tobago, United States, Uruguay, Venezuela, A/37/L.36.
Letter. [3]Argentina, Bahamas, Bolivia, Brazil, Canada, Chile, Colombia, Costa Rica, Cuba, Dominican Republic, Ecuador, El Salvador, Equatorial Guinea, Grenada, Guatemala, Haiti, Honduras, Mexico, Nicaragua, Panama, Paraguay, Peru, Philippines, Portugal, Spain, Suriname, Trinidad and Tobago, United States, Uruguay, Venezuela, 12 Oct., A/37/244.
Meeting records. GA: General Committee, A/BUR/37/SR.4 (11 Nov.); plenary, A/37/PV.65, 83, 115 (12 Nov.–21 Dec.).

General Assembly decision 37/451

Adopted without vote

Oral proposal by President; agenda item 140.

Observance of the quincentenary of the discovery of America
At its 115th plenary meeting, on 21 December 1982, the General Assembly decided to include in the provisional agenda of its thirty-eighth session the item entitled "Observance of the quincentenary of the discovery of America".

Two hundredth anniversary of the birth of Simón Bolívar

On 20 December 1982, on an oral proposal of its President, the General Assembly decided without vote to take note of the decision of the Latin American Group to take measures to commemorate the two hundredth anniversary of the birth of Simón Bolívar on 24 July 1783.[1]

An item on this observance was placed on the Assembly's agenda at the initiative of 22 Latin American and Caribbean States and the United States, which requested its inclusion in a letter of 26 November.[2] The letter stated that the political thought and inspired vision of Bolívar, the Liberator, had stamped him as a precursor of the United Nations and the League of Nations.

Decision (1982). [1]GA: 37/443, 20 Dec., text following.
Letter. [2]Argentina, Bolivia, Brazil, Chile, Colombia, Costa Rica, Dominican Republic, Ecuador, El Salvador, Grenada, Guatemala, Haiti, Honduras, Nicaragua, Panama, Paraguay, Peru, Saint Vincent and the Grenadines, Suriname, Trinidad and Tobago, United States, Uruguay, Venezuela, 26 Nov., A/37/246.
Meeting records. GA: General Committee, A/BUR/37/SR.5 (1 Dec.); plenary, A/37/PV.88, 113 (2, 20 Dec.).

General Assembly decision 37/443

Adopted without vote

Oral proposal by President; agenda item 142.

Observance of the two hundredth anniversary of the birth of Simón Bolívar, the Liberator
At its 113th plenary meeting, on 20 December 1982, the General Assembly took note of the decision of the Latin American Group to take measures to commemorate in an appropriate manner the two hundredth anniversary of the birth of Simón Bolívar, the Liberator.

Chapter VIII

Mediterranean area

Contents

	Page			Page

For resolutions and decisions of major organs mentioned but not reproduced, refer to INDEX OF RESOLUTIONS AND DECISIONS.

Cyprus question

Representatives of the Greek Cypriot and Turkish Cypriot communities continued to meet during 1982, under the auspices of the Secretary-General as requested by the Security Council, in the search for an intercommunal settlement on Cyprus. On the Secretary-General's recommendation, the Security Council in 1982 twice extended for six months the stationing of the United Nations Peace-keeping Force in Cyprus (UN-FICYP), so that it could continue monitoring the cease-fire lines drawn in 1974[39] between the Cyprus National Guard in the south and the Turkish and Turkish Cypriot forces in the north. On both occasions, the Council requested the Secretary-General to continue his good offices mission.

Although the Cyprus question was on the agenda of the General Assembly in 1982, the item was not discussed during the year. However, under another item, the Assembly adopted a resolution on missing persons in Cyprus, requesting a working group of the Commission on Human Rights to make recommendations on overcoming procedural difficulties encountered by the Committee on Missing Persons in Cyprus.

On 11 March,[1] the Commission on Human Rights decided to postpone debate on the question of human rights in Cyprus.

Cyprus and Turkey addressed a number of communications to the Secretary-General on the Cyprus question during 1982. Those from Turkey transmitted letters from representatives of the Turkish Cypriot community and were signed by Rauf R. Denktas as "President of the Turkish Federated State of Kibris" (Kibris being the Turkish-language name for Cyprus), by Kenan Atakol as "Minister for Foreign Affairs and Defence of the Turkish Federated State of Kibris" or by Nail Atalay as "representative of the Turkish Federated State of Kibris".

Communications (January-July). In a series of six letters, Cyprus and Mr. Atalay dealt with issues concerning aircraft flights over Cyprus.

On 13 January[4] and 19 March,[6] Cyprus said Turkish jet fighters had violated Cypriot airspace on 12 January and 15 March, carrying out dives as part of military exercises and, on 12 January, strafing ground targets. Mr. Atalay responded in letters transmitted by Turkey on 22 January[19] and 29 March,[21] stating that those military exercises in what he referred to as the "Turkish Federated State of Kibris" had been routine and had been carried out after notification to UNFICYP.

Cyprus, on 8 February,[5] protested that on 3 February Turkish military forces had fired at an Indian aircraft on its way to the Cypriot airport at Larnaca. By a letter transmitted by Turkey on 11 February,[20] Mr. Atalay sent the text of a statement by the "Ministry of Interior, Foreign Affairs and Defence of the Turkish Federated State of Kibris", saying that Turkish Cypriot soldiers had fired warning shots at an unidentified aircraft which was flying low over military positions and violating Turkish Cypriot airspace as a result of the Greek Cypriots' having deliberately given wrong instructions to the aircraft.

Cyprus and Mr. Denktas, in another series of letters, disputed actions by the Cyprus Government to declare access to certain northern ports illegal. Mr. Denktas, in letters of 7 May and 4 and 16 June, transmitted through Mr. Atalay by Turkey on 10 May,[22] 9 June[26] and 17 June,[28] said the Greek Cypriot administration was continuing an economic blockade against the Turkish Cypriot community by prosecuting, sentencing or imprisoning three foreign ship captains for having violated the embargoed port of Famagusta in northern Cyprus. He said these actions undermined the ongoing intercommunal talks and violated point 6 of the 19 May 1979 agreement. (This was a reference to a 10-point agreement that outlined the basis, content and priorities for the resumption of talks between representatives of the two Cypriot communities; point 6 committed the parties to abstain from any action which might jeopardize the outcome of the talks.[40])

Responding in letters dated 26 May[8] and 24 June,[10] Cyprus said it had an obligation to all its citizens to protect their property rights and, on that legal basis, it had declared as illegal ports of entry those under the occupation of Turkish forces, but it denied that it had imposed an economic embargo on the Turkish Cypriot community. The latter communication added that the socio-economic difficulties experienced by that community were the result of the Turkish occupation.

A letter from Turkey of 14 May[23] forwarded, through Mr. Atalay, a letter of 12 May from Mr. Atakol stating that the Greek Cypriot administration had no legal or constitutional authority to adhere, on behalf of the Republic of Cyprus, to the 1948 Convention on the Prevention and Punishment of the Crime of Genocide,[38] as it had done on 29 March 1982. Replying on 23 June,[9] Cyprus said the acceptance by the United Nations Office of Legal Affairs of its instrument of accession to the Convention was the proper response to Mr. Atakol's argument.

Cyprus, by a letter of 18 May,[7] forwarded a statement of the previous day by its Minister for Foreign Affairs, Nicos Rolandis, protesting Turkey's announcement that its Prime Minister, Bülend Ulusu, would visit the occupied part of Cyprus, an action Cyprus believed was aimed at legalizing what Turkey had established by occupation. In a letter from Turkey dated 4 June,[24] Mr. Atalay transmitted a letter of 31 May from Mr. Denktas stating that Mr. Ulusu had made an official three-day visit at his invitation, during which the Prime Minister, in speeches and statements, had unreservedly supported the efforts to resolve the conflict through the intercommunal talks.

In a letter of 9 June,[25] Turkey forwarded a communication from Mr. Atalay enclosing a letter of the same date from Mr. Atakol protesting the representation of Cyprus at the June/July special session of the General Assembly devoted to disarmament in the absence of a central authority in Cyprus. Referring to the 11 June statement of President Spyrus Kyprianou at the special session, containing remarks about a proposed demilitarization of Cyprus, Mr. Atakol, in a letter of 16 June[27] forwarded in the same manner, stated that, as this question was to be taken up during the intercommunal talks, Mr. Kyprianou could not speak for the bicommunal State of Cyprus as a whole. Responding to these two letters, Cyprus, in a letter of 10 July,[11] said the General Assembly had repeatedly confirmed the legality and representative capacity of the Cyprus delegation, and it was futile to dispute the legality of a Government which had been recognized by the United Nations and all international organizations.

Report of the Secretary-General (June). The Secretary-General, in a report of 1 June 1982 to the Security Council on the United Nations operation in Cyprus from 1 December 1981 to 31 May 1982,[34] described the progress of the intercommunal talks and also discussed UNFICYP operations and the situation regarding missing persons.

He said the intercommunal talks at Nicosia, Cyprus, which had resumed in August 1980[41] under the auspices of his Special Representative, Hugo J. Gobbi, had entered a new phase. The two interlocutors had embarked on 7 January on a systematic review of the main elements of the constitutional aspect of a future federal government of Cyprus. They had begun by discussing "points of coincidence" (areas where the positions of the parties largely coincided) and by the time they finished with this topic on 10 March they had arrived at common formulations of those points in a number of cases. Then, from 17 March until 18 May, the talks had dealt with "points of equidistance", on which substantial differences remained to be bridged, with special reference to freedom of movement, freedom of settlement and the right of property. On 25 May the interlocutors had begun discussing the organs of the federal government. The method of discussion and framework followed for the talks had been set out in the "evaluation" paper submitted to the parties by the Special Representative in November 1981.[42]

According to the Secretary-General's report, there had been a significant narrowing of differences on many of the general provisions of the constitution, as well as of the articles concerning fundamental rights and liberties and certain organs of the federal government. The atmosphere had been co-operative and constructive throughout. Beginning in April, the talks had been accelerated to two meetings a week.

The major substantive elements of the Cyprus problem were being systematically reconsidered, reformulated and reduced, though that did not mean they were about to be resolved, the Secretary-General said. Solutions still had to be devised for the major constitutional and territorial issues.

The Secretary-General recommended that the Council extend the mandate of UNFICYP for another six months. On 14 June, in an addendum to his report, he informed the Council that the parties had agreed to the proposed extension.

Security Council action (June). By a resolution prepared in the course of consultations by the Security Council and adopted unanimously on 15 June,[36] the Council, noting the concurrence of the parties and the Cypriot Government's view that it was necessary to keep United Nations troops there beyond 15 June, extended the stationing in Cyprus of UNFICYP for a further six months, until 15 December. The Council noted with satisfaction that the parties had resumed the intercommunal talks within the framework of the 10-point agreement of 1979 (p. 377) and urged them to pursue the talks in a sustained and result-oriented manner. In addition, the Council requested the Secretary-General to continue his mission of good offices and to submit a report on the implementation of the resolution by 30 November.

Before adopting the resolution, the Council invited Cyprus, Greece and Turkey, at their request, to participate in the discussion without the right to vote. Mr. Atalay was also invited to participate, under rule 39 of the Council's provisional rules of procedure.[a]

Cyprus said that, although the intercommunal talks had not made any progress on matters of substance because of Turkish intransigence, Cyprus intended to proceed in good faith in the search for a solution. It commended Greece's offer to withdraw its contingent from Cyprus provided that the Turkish troops were also withdrawn and a United Nations police force was stationed in Cyprus.

Greece also believed there had been no progress on the substance of the problem; it proposed a solution whereby both the Turkish troops and the Greek contingent would withdraw from Cyprus, to be followed by the establishment of an enlarged United Nations peace-keeping force, intercommunal talks to draft a constitution including safeguards for minorities, and a demilitarization of Cyprus.

Turkey said the constructive atmosphere at the talks justified hopes for the future, and it shared the Secretary-General's evaluation of the progress made; it would continue to support them actively

and encourage the Turkish Cypriot community in its search for an independent, sovereign, bicommunal, federal and bizonal—and, if it desired, non-aligned—Republic of Cyprus.

Mr. Atalay, also stating that the intercommunal talks were making progress, said the Turkish Cypriot side believed in their continuation but that the obstructive conduct of the new Prime Minister of Greece, Andreas Papandreou, including statements to the effect that Cyprus was part of Greece's territory, had seriously harmed prospects for their success and even their continuation.

Communications (August-September). In a letter of 10 August,[12] Cyprus protested statements by Mr. Denktas, as reported in Turkish Cypriot newspapers, claiming the right of separate independence for the Turkish Cypriots. Mr. Atalay replied in a letter forwarded by Turkey on 22 September[30] that the statements posed the alternative to the continued efforts by the Greek Cypriot side to impose Greek Cypriot rule on the Turkish people.

Cyprus, in a letter dated 13 August,[13] said Turkish jet fighters had violated Cypriot airspace on 11 August during military exercises which included infantry movements.

In a letter transmitted by Turkey on 20 September[29] through Mr. Atalay, Mr. Denktas, in connection with the representation of Cyprus at the 1982 regular session of the General Assembly, reiterated opposition to what he called the Greek Cypriot administration's continued attempts at representing Cyprus as a whole in international forums and said the acts of its delegation would not be binding on the Turkish Cypriot community.

General Assembly consideration (September). On 20 September 1982, at the closing meeting of its thirty-sixth session, which had begun in September 1981, the General Assembly decided to include the question of Cyprus in the draft agenda of its next regular session, opening the following day. The decision[2] was adopted without vote on an oral proposal by the President, who said he understood from consultations with all concerned that it would be desirable to defer consideration of the item. The Assembly did not discuss the item during its thirty-sixth session.

Communications (November). In a letter of 4 November 1982,[14] Cyprus rejected a statement by Mr. Denktas, as reported in a Turkish newspaper on 22 October, that the Greek Cypriots were importing arms in preparation for an attack on the

---

[a]Rule 39 of the Council's provisional rules of procedure states: "The Security Council may invite members of the Secretariat or other persons, whom it considers competent for the purpose, to supply it with information or to give other assistance in examining matters within its competence."

Turkish Cypriots and that the latter should prepare accordingly.

Cyprus, in a letter of 18 November,[15] noted the reported decision by the Denktas régime to replace the Cyprus pound with the Turkish lira as the legal tender in the area occupied by Turkish forces, and said the action made it obvious that the Turkish leadership was striving for the speedy incorporation of the occupied area into the Turkish State. Responding on 22 November, Mr. Atalay, in a letter transmitted by Turkey the next day,[31] said efforts of the Turkish Federated State of Kibris to establish a central bank and the decision to use the Turkish lira were part of its policy to develop the economy and improve the standard of living of its people; although the Cyprus pound was still legal tender, it was not available because the Bank of Cyprus had confiscated the deposits of the Turkish banks and deprived the Turkish community of its use.

Cyprus reported further violations of its airspace and territorial waters by Turkish forces in a letter dated 23 November,[16] stating that on 19 November jet fighter aircraft had hit targets with rockets and machine-guns, and that four Turkish warships had carried out exercises nine miles off the coast. (For the response, see p. 380.)

Report of the Secretary-General (December). The Secretary-General updated his account of UNFICYP activities and of the intercommunal talks in a report of 1 December covering developments from 1 June to 30 November.[35]

Concerning the talks, he said they were continuing at a steady pace. The interlocutors, meeting regularly, were still using the 1981 "evaluation" paper submitted by his Special Representative as the method of discussion, and the atmosphere remained co-operative and constructive. During the reporting period they had discussed the organs of the future federal government, the provincial governments and transitional provisions, after which they had re-examined the general constitutional provisions. Having completed discussion of almost all the constitutional aspects, they had begun on 25 November to consider the territorial aspect.

This would mark the completion of the first round of the current phase, which would have achieved most of its objectives of identifying more precisely the negotiating positions of both sides, widening the areas of coincidence and systematizing the framework for tackling the unresolved key issues. That task, the Secretary-General said, would involve a major effort to develop a "package deal" and could be accomplished with the necessary political will. He added, however, that time appeared to be eroding "the window of opportunity" to resolve the Cyprus problem and that it was the responsibility of all concerned not to let that window be closed.

As part of his efforts in 1982 to encourage negotiations, the Secretary-General met in April, June and October for separate talks with President Kyprianou and Mr. Denktas.

The Secretary-General, in his report, expressed profound concern that the Committee on Missing Persons in Cyprus had been unable so far to overcome the procedural difficulties which had prevented it from embarking on its mission.

He concluded that the continued presence of UNFICYP remained necessary and recommended that the Security Council extend its mandate for another six months. In an addendum of 13 December, he indicated that the parties had signified their concurrence.

Security Council action (December). On 14 December, the Security Council unanimously adopted a resolution[37] by which it extended once more the stationing in Cyprus of UNFICYP, this time through 15 June 1983. Again the Council noted with satisfaction that the parties had resumed the intercommunal talks and urged them to pursue those talks in a result-oriented manner. It requested the Secretary-General to continue his good offices mission and to report by 31 May 1983 on implementation of the resolution. The text of the resolution was prepared during consultations by the Council.

Before adopting the resolution, the Council invited Cyprus, Greece and Turkey, at their request, to participate without vote in the discussion. Mr. Atalay was also invited to participate, under rule 39 of the Council's provisional rules of procedure.[b]

Cyprus said the previous six months had seen additional actions demonstrating Turkey's determination to consolidate the fruits of its aggression, including the Turkish Prime Minister's visit in May to the occupied areas, the decision to establish a central bank and to introduce the Turkish lira as legal tender, and the planned issuance of title deeds to the usurpers of Greek Cypriot properties. It was thus no surprise that the intercommunal talks had failed to yield results on their crucial aspects.

Greece added to its earlier suggestions by proposing that the Cyprus problem be re-examined on a new basis by a special United Nations committee or by an international conference and welcomed any initiatives by leading international personalities; it said that at the current talks, the interlocutors were dealing mainly with minor issues and had addressed the territorial problem, a crucial aspect, only superficially because the Turkish side avoided going into the matter.

Turkey said it was essential to safeguard the intercommunal negotiations—which were the only realistic way of resolving the problem on a lasting basis—especially at a time when they were suffering a set-back; Turkey was aware that international forces had never been able to ensure the full security of populations and that was why its armed forces would remain at the request of the Turkish Feder-

[b]See footnote a on p. 378.

ated State of Cyprus until a final agreement had been concluded by all parties.

Mr. Atalay, stating that the intended annexation of Cyprus to Greece lay behind the artificial creation of the Cyprus problem, denied that northern Cyprus was being settled by Turks brought from Turkey; referring to the preparation of laws to give title deeds to Turkish Cypriots in the north, he said this was aimed at finding a solution to the social and economic problems experienced by the Turkish Cypriots who had come from the south as refugees.

General Assembly consideration (December). The Cyprus question was not taken up by the General Assembly during the 1982 part of its thirty-seventh session. Instead, the item was listed among four to be considered at a resumed session in 1983. This action was taken on 21 December 1982 when the Assembly decided to resume its current session at a date to be announced.[3]

The Assembly adopted a resolution on missing persons in Cyprus under its agenda item concerned with the work of the Economic and Social Council on human rights and other topics.

Communications (December). During December, Cyprus and Mr. Atalay each sent two more letters about the situation in Cyprus.

In a letter forwarded by Turkey on 1 December,[32] Mr. Atalay, referring to the letter from Cyprus of 23 November (p. 379), said the military exercises of 19 November in the territory of what he referred to as the "Turkish Federated State of Kibris" had been routine exercises of the Turkish Peace Force, carried out after notification to UNFICYP. In a letter forwarded in the same manner on 16 December[33] in response to the 4 November letter from Cyprus (p. 378), Mr. Atalay said the Greek Cypriot administration had vainly attempted to deny the massive arms build-up in southern Cyprus, where missiles, tanks, heavy machine-guns, armoured vehicles, and light and heavy artillery had been amassed in quantities far beyond defence requirements.

Cyprus, in a letter dated 15 December,[17] protested that on 3 December two Turkish warships carrying war material had sailed to the port of Kokkina, in violation of the 12-mile territorial sea of Cyprus. By a letter of 29 December.[18] Cyprus cited Turkish Cypriot press reports of 21 December that the Turkish occupation authorities had begun to issue "definitive possession certificates" for persons whom they deemed were eligible to receive illegally expropriated and confiscated properties of Cypriots expelled from occupied parts of Cyprus: Cyprus viewed this as another action that showed a determination not to allow the indigenous inhabitants to return home.

Decisions (1982). [1] Commission on Human Rights (report, E/1982/12): 1982/102, 11 Mar. GA: [2] 36/463, 20 Sep., text following; [3] 37/452, *item 37*, 21 Dec.

Letters.
    Cyprus: [4] 13 Jan., A/36/856-S/14835; [5] 8 Feb., A/36/858-S/14864; [6] 19 Mar., A/36/869-S/14918; [7] 18 May, A/36/875-S/15095; [8] 26 May, A/36/876-S/15130; [9] 23 June, A/36/883-S/15250; [10] 24 June, A/36/884-S/15256; [11] 10 July, A/36/885-S/15283; [12] 10 Aug., A/36/886-S/15360; [13] 13 Aug., A/36/887-S/15363; [14] 4 Nov., A/37/606-S/15485; [15] 18 Nov., A/37/634-S/15494; [16] 23 Nov., A/37/642-S/15499; [17] 15 Dec., A/37/777-S/15528; [18] 29 Dec., A/37/791-S/15544.
    Turkey: [19] 22 Jan., A/36/857-S/14845; [20] 11 Feb., A/36/859-S/14870; [21] 29 Mar., A/36/871-S/14935; [22] 10 May, A/36/873-S/15067; [23] 14 May, A/36/874-S/15086; [24] 4 June, A/36/877-S/15175; [25] 9 June, A/36/878-S/15191; [26] 9 June, A/36/879-S/15193; [27] 16 June, A/36/881-S/15227; [28] 17 June, A/36/882-S/15242; [29] 20 Sep., A/37/467-S/15415; [30] 22 Sep., A/37/478-S/15426; [31] 23 Nov., A/37/643-S/15500; [32] 1 Dec., A/37/694-S/15509; [33] 16 Dec., A/37/787-S/15533.
Reports. S-G, [34] S/15149 & Corr.1 & Add.1, [35] S/15502 & Corr.1 & Add.1.
Resolutions (1982). SC: [36] 510(1982), 15 June, text following; [37] 526(1982), 14 Dec., text following.
Resolution (prior). [38] GA: 260 A (III), annex, 9 Dec. 1948 (YUN 1948-49, p. 959).
Yearbook references. [39] 1974, p. 275; [40] 1979, p. 421; [41] 1980, p. 453; [42] 1981, p. 342.
Meeting records. SC: S/PV.2378, 2405 (15 June, 14 Dec.). GA: A/36/PV.111 (20 Sep.).

Security Council resolution 510(1982)

15 June 1982   Meeting 2378   Adopted unanimously

Draft prepared in consultations among Council members (S/15216).

The Security Council,

Taking note of the report of the Secretary-General on the United Nations operation in Cyprus of 1 June,

Noting the concurrence of the parties concerned in the recommendation by the Secretary-General that the Security Council should extend the stationing of the United Nations Peace-keeping Force in Cyprus for a further period of six months,

Noting also that the Government of Cyprus has agreed that in view of the prevailing conditions in the island it is necessary to keep the Force in Cyprus beyond 15 June 1982,

Reaffirming the provisions of its resolution 186(1964) and other relevant resolutions,

Reiterating its support of the ten-point agreement for the resumption of the intercommunal talks which was worked out at the high-level meeting on 18 and 19 May 1979 at Nicosia under the auspices of the Secretary-General,

1. *Extends once more* the stationing in Cyprus of the United Nations Peace-keeping Force established under resolution 186(1964) for a further period, ending on 15 December 1982;

2. *Notes with satisfaction* that the parties have resumed the intercommunal talks within the framework of the ten-point agreement and urges them to pursue these talks in a continuing, sustained and result-oriented manner, avoiding any delay;

3. *Requests* the Secretary-General to continue his mission of good offices, to keep the Security Council informed of the progress made and to submit a report on the implementation of the present resolution by 30 November 1982.

General Assembly decision 36/463

Adopted without vote

Oral proposal by President; agenda item 35.

Question of Cyprus

At its 111th plenary meeting, on 20 September 1982, the General Assembly decided to include in the draft agenda of its thirty-seventh session the item entitled "Question of Cyprus".

Security Council resolution 526(1982)

14 December 1982   Meeting 2405   Adopted unanimously

Draft prepared in consultations among Council members (S/15523).

Taking note of the report of the Secretary-General on the United Nations operation in Cyprus of 1 December 1982,

Noting the concurrence of the parties concerned in the recommendation by the Secretary-General that the Security Council should extend the stationing of the United Nations Peace-keeping Force in Cyprus for a further period of six months,

Noting also that the Government of Cyprus has agreed that in view of the prevailing conditions in the island it is necessary to keep the Force in Cyprus beyond 15 December 1982,

Reaffirming the provisions of its resolution 186(1964) and other relevant resolutions,

Reiterating its support of the ten-point agreement for the resumption of the intercommunal talks which was worked out at the high-level meeting on 18 and 19 May 1979 at Nicosia under the auspices of the Secretary-General,

1. *Extends once more* the stationing in Cyprus of the United Nations Peace-keeping Force established under resolution 186(1964) for a further period, ending on 15 June 1983;

2. *Notes with satisfaction* that the parties have resumed the intercommunal talks within the framework of the ten-point agreement and urges them to pursue these talks in a continuing, sustained and result-oriented manner, avoiding any delay;

3. *Requests* the Secretary-General to continue his mission of good offices, to keep the Security Council informed of the progress made and to submit a report on the implementation of the present resolution by 31 May 1983.

UN Peace-keeping Force in Cyprus

Activities of UNFICYP

The United Nations Peace-keeping Force in Cyprus (UNFICYP), established by the Security Council in 1964,[3] continued throughout 1982 to monitor, patrol and supervise the cease-fire lines of the Cyprus National Guard and of the Turkish and Turkish Cypriot forces. It also provided security for civilians in the area between the lines; used its best efforts to discharge its functions with regard to the security, welfare and well-being of the Greek Cypriots living in northern Cyprus; continued regular visits to Turkish Cypriots residing in the south; and supported United Nations relief operations.

The Secretary-General reported to the Security Council that liaison and co-operation between UNFICYP and the military and civilian authorities of both sides remained satisfactory and were undertaken on a regular basis. Since December 1979, when the Turkish Cypriot authorities had issued new guidelines on movement of United Nations troops, transit of UNFICYP vehicles in the north remained restricted, but UNFICYP reported some progress in efforts to negotiate changes. There were incidents involving restrictions on UNFICYP freedom of movement imposed by both the National Guard and the Turkish and Turkish Cypriot forces.

UNFICYP monitored the buffer zone between the 180-kilometre-long cease-fire lines through a system of 137 observation posts, 66 of them permanently manned (as at 30 November). During 1982, the frequency of shooting incidents remained unchanged, while violations involving movements forward of the lines diminished slightly. At Nicosia, which remained a sensitive area because of the proximity of the two cease-fire lines, UNFICYP strengthened its presence between the lines and made a proposal to both sides for the mutual unmanning of various positions along the "Green Line". The number of overflights of the buffer zone by both the Turkish forces from the north and the National Guard from the south diminished during the year. Disputes over the delineation of the cease-fire lines continued but there were no reports of forces of either side crossing the lines. While no injuries due to land-mines were reported, the hazard remained serious because of the many unmarked or poorly marked minefields.

In the discharge of its humanitarian responsibilities, UNFICYP monitored permanent transfers of Greek Cypriots from north to south to ensure that such movement was voluntary; 109 transfers were reported during the 12 months ended 30 November 1982. The number of Greek Cypriots residing in the north fell to 952 by the end of November. Twelve Turkish Cypriots transferred from south to north during the same period. Other humanitarian assistance provided by UNFICYP included assistance to farmers, ensuring the operation of the water supply system, supervision of anti-mosquito spraying and help in replacing uninhabitable homes in villages in the buffer zone.

With UNFICYP support, the United Nations Development Programme, the United Nations High Commissioner for Refugees (UNHCR), the United Nations Centre for Human Settlements (Habitat), the Food and Agriculture Organization of the United Nations, the International Labour Organisation and the World Health Organization also assisted projects in Cyprus. The 1982 programme for displaced and needy persons provided $10 million to finance 18 projects co-ordinated by the Cyprus Red Cross Society, in such areas as construction of temporary housing and a general hospital, procurement of equipment and supplies for health, education and agriculture, and professional training. UNHCR continued to serve as Co-ordinator of United Nations Humanitarian Assistance for Cyprus.

Relief supplies were distributed or delivered by UNFICYP. During the 12 months ended 30 November 1982, this amounted to 1,401 tons of food, clothing, gas and diesel oil, of which 954 tons went to Greek Cypriots and Maronites and 447 tons to Turkish Cypriots, all in the north. The World Food Programme was a major contributor of food.

The UNFICYP Civilian Police (UNCIVPOL) continued to support UNFICYP military units and operated in liaison with both the Cyprus and the Turkish Cypriot police, contributing to the maintenance of law and order between the cease-fire lines and to the protection of civilians, particularly in areas where intercommunal problems existed. It also assisted in the control of civilian movement between the lines.

This information on UNFICYP activities was provided in two 1982 reports by the Secretary-General, covering the periods 1 December 1981 to 31 May 1982[1] and 1 June to 30 November 1982.[2]

In both reports, the Secretary-General concluded that the presence of the Force was necessary to help maintain calm and create conditions for pursuing a peaceful solution. Acting on his recommendations, the Security Council twice in 1982 extended the UNFICYP mandate for a six-month period, first until 15 December 1982 and then until 15 June 1983.

Reports. S-G, [1]S/15149 & Corr.1 & Add.1, [2]S/15502 & Corr.1 & Add.1.
Resolution. [3]SC: 186(1964), 4 Mar. 1964 (YUN 1964, p. 165).

Composition of UNFICYP

As at 30 November 1982, UNFICYP had a strength of 2,348, including 34 civilian police, and was composed of contingents from eight States (see table below). The Force decreased by 26 since 30 November 1981.[1]

During the year ended 30 November 1982, four members of the Force died, bringing the total number of fatal casualties to 125 since the inception of UNFICYP in 1964.

CONTINGENTS OF UNFICYP
(by country of origin, as at 30 November 1982)

Military personnel

Austria	301
Canada	515
Denmark	341
Finland	10
Ireland	8
Sweden	378
United Kingdom	761
Total	**2,314**

Civilian police

Australia	20
Sweden	14
Total	**34**
Grand total	**2,348**

SOURCE: S-G report, S/15502.

Yearbook reference. [1]1981, p. 344.

Financing of UNFICYP

UNFICYP continued to be financed by voluntary contributions and by troop-contributing Governments. Contributions received in 1982 from 24 Governments totalled $23,998,621 (see table below), and estimated costs totalled $26,100,000. The expenditures figure included the direct cost to the United Nations of maintaining the Force as well as reimbursement by the United Nations of some of the extra costs of Governments providing contingents. The full 12-month cost of the Force was estimated at approximately $102

million—excluding regular troops' pay and allowances and normal *matériel* costs—but much of this was borne by the troop contributors.

As at 15 December 1982, the accumulated deficit of the Force since its inception in 1964 stood at $100.6 million. Because of the deficit, payments to troop-contributing Governments as at that date had met claims only up to December 1976.

Expressing his concern over this situation, the Secretary-General, in his reports of June[3] and December[4] 1982 on the United Nations operation in Cyprus, appealed to Governments for voluntary financial contributions and to Member States that had not contributed in the past to review their positions. In this connection, he hoped the Government of Cyprus would make a further effort to devise arrangements for absorbing a fair share of the costs incurred by the Force, including the cost of utilities.

He repeated the appeals in letters of 29 June[1] and 22 December,[2] sent following each renewal of the UNFICYP mandate to all States Members of the United Nations or members of the specialized agencies. In both letters, he explained that the rate of accumulation of the deficit had been growing, with voluntary contributions for the previous five years averaging $9 million per six-month period while expenses during that time had increased from $11 million to $15 million for a six-month period.

CONTRIBUTIONS RECEIVED IN 1982 FOR UNFICYP
(as at 31 December 1982; in US dollars)

Country	Amount
Australia	92,387
Austria	110,000
Bahamas	2,000
Barbados	500
Belgium	209,517
Cyprus	400,000
Denmark	120,000
Finland	37,500
Germany, Federal Republic of	1,023,793
Greece	877,344
Iceland	10,000
Italy	400,000
Jamaica	1,000
Japan	700,000
Luxembourg	7,132
Norway	610,000
Pakistan	3,000
Sweden	200,000
Switzerland	360,849
United Arab Emirates	10,000
United Kingdom	5,316,599
United States	13,500,000
Venezuela	5,000
Zimbabwe	2,000
Total	**23,998,621**

SOURCE: Interim United Nations financial statements for the 12-month period ended 31 December 1982 (unpublished).

Letters. SG: [1]29 June, S/15275; [2]22 Dec., S/15555.
Reports. S-G, [3]S/15149, [4]S/15502.

Missing persons

The Committee on Missing Persons in Cyprus, which had begun work in July 1981 under terms of reference agreed to between the parties but immediately encountered procedural difficulties,[5] remained unable in 1982 to embark on its substantive work of tracing and accounting for persons of both communities reported missing in intercommunal fighting and other hostilities since 1974. The Committee was composed of one member from each Cypriot community and a third member selected by the International Committee of the Red Cross with the agreement of both sides and appointed by the Secretary-General.

The Secretary-General informed the Security Council in June 1982, in his report on the United Nations operation in Cyprus, that he had asked his Special Representative to consult with both sides to help resolve the procedural problems blocking the Committee's work.[2] However, he reported similarly in December that that approach had not resulted in any substantive progress.[3] He added that the Chairman of the Working Group on Enforced or Involuntary Disappearances (See ECONOMIC AND SOCIAL QUESTIONS, Chapter XVIII), along with a member of that body of the Commission on Human Rights, had visited Cyprus in July on the Group's behalf, conversing with members of both communities and others. The Secretary-General expressed profound concern that the Committee had not overcome its procedural difficulties, but he did not believe it inherently impossible to dispose of the problem, provided both sides co-operated.

In the Security Council discussion of the Cyprus situation on 15 June, Cyprus said that, as a result of Turkish intransigence and hostility, not a single case of a missing person had been investigated in the eight years since the Turkish invasion of Cyprus. Nail Atalay, representing the Turkish Cypriot community, stated that the Greek Cypriot side had boycotted the Committee after insisting on the attendance of Greek Cypriot observers whose presence was irrelevant to its work.

General Assembly action. Expressing concern about the lack of progress by the Committee on Missing Persons in Cyprus, the General Assembly, by a resolution of 17 December,[4] invited the Working Group on Enforced or Involuntary Disappearances to follow developments, to make recommendations to the parties for overcoming the procedural difficulties and to facilitate the Committee's investigative work on the basis of existing agreements. It called on all parties to facilitate the Committee's investigation and requested the Secretary-General to continue to provide his good offices with a view to facilitating the Committee's work.

The Assembly adopted the resolution, without vote, on the recommendation of its Third (Social, Humanitarian and Cultural) Committee. The draft, introduced by Cyprus on behalf of 13 sponsors, had been approved by that Committee on 9 December by a recorded vote of 99 to 5 (Bangladesh, Indonesia, Malaysia, Pakistan, Turkey), with 18 abstentions.

The text incorporated oral amendments by Yugoslavia that were accepted by the sponsors. As a result, a paragraph of the original version, by which the Assembly would have requested the Commission on Human Rights to consider the question of missing persons in Cyprus in 1983 and to establish effective machinery for the investigation of such cases, was replaced by one inviting the Working Group on disappearances to recommend ways to overcome the procedural problems; and a request in the original version that the Secretary-General follow up the implementation of the resolution was replaced by a request that he continue to provide his good offices in helping the Committee on Missing Persons.

On the same day, before approving the draft resolution, the Third Committee rejected Turkey's request, conveyed in a letter of 3 December,[1] that a representative of the Turkish Cypriot community who was a member of the Committee on Missing Persons be permitted to speak on the subject. The decision was taken by a recorded vote of 59 to 34, with 28 abstentions.

During discussion of the Cyprus situation in the Security Council on 14 December, Cyprus expressed hope that the Turkish side would co-operate in implementing the Assembly resolution, which could lead to the speedy tracing of missing persons in Cyprus. For the Turkish Cypriot community, Mr. Atalay said it was ready to work in accounting for the missing persons, but only within the Committee on Missing Persons; decisions by any organization on the initiative of the Greek Cypriot leadership and without the equal participation of the Turkish Federated State of Kibris were null and void.

Letter. [1]Turkey, 3 Dec., A/C.3/37/10.
Reports. S-G, [2]S/15149, [3]S/15502.
Resolution (1982). [4]GA: 37/181, 17 Dec., text following.
Yearbook reference. [5]1981, p. 345.
Meeting records. GA: 3rd Committee, A/C.3/37/SR.62, 63, *64,* 65, 66, *67,* 68-71, *72, 74* (3-10 Dec.); plenary, A/37/PV.110 (17 Dec.).

General Assembly resolution 37/181

17 December 1982   Meeting 110   Adopted without vote

Approved by Third Committee (A/37/745) by recorded vote (99-5-18), 9 December (meeting 72); 13-nation draft (A/C.3/37/L.58/Rev.1); agenda item 12.

Sponsors: Bahamas, Costa Rica, Cyprus, Democratic Yemen, Ecuador, Greece, Grenada, Malta, Nicaragua, Panama, Seychelles, Sierra Leone, Syrian Arab Republic.

Missing persons in Cyprus

The General Assembly,
Recalling its previous resolutions on the question of missing persons in Cyprus,
Reaffirming the basic need of families to be informed, without further delay, about the fate of their missing relatives,
Expressing concern that the Committee on Missing Persons in Cyprus, the establishment of which was announced on 22 April 1981, has failed to overcome procedural difficulties and has achieved no progress towards the commencement of its investigative work,
Emphasizing the need for a speedy resolution of this humanitarian problem,

1. *Invites* the Working Group on Enforced or Involuntary Disappearances of the Commission on Human Rights to follow developments and to recommend to the parties concerned ways and means of overcoming the pending procedural difficulties of the Committee on Missing Persons in Cyprus and, in co-operation with the Committee, to facilitate the effective implementation of its investigative work on the basis of the existing relevant agreements;

2. *Calls upon* all parties concerned to facilitate such investigation in a spirit of co-operation and good will;

3. *Requests* the Secretary-General to continue to provide his good offices with a view to facilitating the work of the Committee on Missing Persons in Cyprus.

Other questions concerning the Mediterranean area

Security in the Mediterranean area

The General Assembly, on 16 December 1982, adopted a resolution on the strengthening of international security which included three paragraphs pertaining to security in the Mediterranean area.[3] Stating that the security of the Mediterranean and that of adjacent regions were interdependent and that further efforts were necessary to create conditions of security and co-operation in all fields for countries and peoples of the area, the Assembly called on Governments to submit before its 1983 session their views on the strengthening of security and co-operation in that region and requested the Secretary-General to submit an analytical report based on the replies. The Assembly decided to include in the provisional agenda of its 1983 session—for the first time—an item on "Strengthening of security and co-operation in the Mediterranean region".

The Assembly took note of a report by the Secretary-General[2] containing replies from 21 Governments to the Assembly's initial request for views on the question, made in December 1981.[4]

Yugoslavia, in a note verbale dated 5 July 1982,[1] presented to the Assembly's special session on disarmament a working paper favouring the strengthening of security and co-operation in the Mediterranean by making it a zone of peace (See POLITICAL AND SECURITY QUESTIONS, Chapter I).

Note verbale. [1]Yugoslavia, 5 July, A/S-12/AC.1/64.
Report. [2]S-G, A/37/355 & Add.1-5.
Resolution (1982). [3]GA: 37/118, paras. 15-17, 16 Dec.
Resolution (prior). [4]GA: 36/102, 9 Dec. 1981 (YUN 1981, p. 144).

Questions involving the Libyan Arab Jamahiriya

Continental shelf delimitation between the Libyan Arab Jamahiriya and Malta

The Libyan Arab Jamahiriya and Malta placed before the International Court of Justice in July 1982 the question of delimitation of their continental shelf areas (See LEGAL QUESTIONS, Chapter I). In a report of 29 July,[1] the Secretary-General informed the Security Council that he had been notified by the Court Registrar that the two Governments had filed with the Court on 26 July a joint notification of the 1976 special agreement, whereby the two parties had agreed to submit the question to the Court.

The Secretary-General recalled that the matter had been brought to the Council (by Malta) in 1980[2] and that he and his Special Representative on the matter, Under-Secretary-General Diego Cordovez, had sought since then to help overcome difficulties that had arisen concerning the exchange of instruments of ratification of the special agreement and the joint notification to the Court.[3] The Secretary-General had been informed by the Libyan Arab Jamahiriya that the two countries had completed on 20 March 1982 the exchange of instruments of ratification and that the special agreement had entered into force on that date. Malta had later advised him that the agreement had been jointly registered with the United Nations Secretariat on 19 April. Both parties had expressed appreciation for the efforts of the Secretary-General and his Special Representative.

Report. [1]S-G, S/15323.
Yearbook references. [2]1980, p. 465; [3]1981, p. 358.

Libyan Arab Jamahiriya and the United States

In a letter to the Secretary-General dated 3 February 1982,[1] the Libyan Arab Jamahiriya transmitted a letter from the Secretary of the People's Committee of the People's Bureau for Foreign Liaison, in which he said two United States jet fighter aircraft had committed an act of aggression by intercepting on 31 January a Libyan Arab Airlines commercial flight and following it for 7 miles in international airspace, carrying out provocative acrobatic manœuvres in violation of international conventions.

The United States, responding in a letter dated 5 March to the Secretary-General,[2] rejected the claim and said that on 31 January F-14 planes from an American aircraft carrier in the central Mediterranean had visually identified five commercial aircraft in the carrier's operating area, in accordance with standard operating procedure, but had approached none of them closely enough to identify any as Libyan.

Letters. [1]Libyan Arab Jamahiriya, 3 Feb., A/37/82-S/14860; [2]United States, 5 Mar., A/37/114-S/14902.

Neutrality of Malta

France, in a note verbale dated 1 March 1982 to the Secretary-General,[1] transmitted a declaration of 18 December 1981 in which it undertook to respect the neutrality of Malta, proclaimed by that country in May 1981,[2] and called on all other States to recognize and respect that status.

Note verbale. [1]France, 1 Mar., A/37/105-S/14892.
Yearbook reference. [2]1981, p. 141.

Chapter IX

Middle East

Contents

Related topics:

Organizational questions: Relations between the United Nations and the League of Arab States. Regional economic and social activities: Western Asia. Human rights violations: Middle East.

For resolutions and decisions of major organs mentioned but not reproduced, refer to INDEX OF RESOLUTIONS AND DECISIONS.

Middle East situation

The situation in the Middle East was again considered in 1982 as an item on the agenda of the General Assembly's regular session. By a resolution of 20 December, the Assembly condemned Israeli aggression and declared that peace in the Middle East must be based on a solution under United Nations auspices that would enable the Palestinians to exercise their rights; it also called on States to end the flow to Israel of military, economic and financial aid and human resources aimed at encouraging it to pursue its aggressive policies.

Israel reported to the Secretary-General and the President of the Security Council a series of attacks against its citizens, as well as Jews and Jewish institutions outside Israel, allegedly carried out by the Palestine Liberation Organization (PLO). Three other communications dealt with the Israeli withdrawal from the Sinai peninsula on 25 April, in accordance with the 1978 Camp David agreements between Egypt and Israel (formally called A Framework for Peace in the Middle East, Agreed at Camp David [United States], and Framework for the Conclusion of a Peace Treaty between Egypt and Israel).

In October, the Secretary-General reported on the situation in the region and on proposals for a peaceful settlement made in September by the USSR, the United States and the Arab States.

Also in October, the Assembly decided not to act on a proposal to reject the credentials of representatives of Israel to the Assembly.

Other items relating to the Middle East situation but dealt with separately by the Assembly during 1982 concerned the Palestine question, the June 1981 aerial attack by Israel against Iraqi nuclear installations, the financing of United Nations peace-keeping forces in Lebanon and on the Golan Heights between the forces of Israel and the Syrian Arab Republic, the situation in the territories occupied by Israel, the Mediterranean–Dead Sea canal project and Palestine refugees.

The Security Council also dealt during 1982 with several topics under its agenda item on "The situation in the Middle East": the situation between Israel and Lebanon, which the Assembly considered under its item on the Palestine question; continuation of the United Nations Disengagement Observer Force in the Golan Heights; annexation by Israel of the Golan Heights, and other aspects of the situation in the occupied territories, including the Al-Aqsa mosque and Israeli settlements.

Communications. By 13 letters addressed to the Secretary-General and/or the Security Council President during the first six months of 1982, Israel reported a series of attacks against its citizens, as well as against Jews and Jewish institutions outside Israel, which, it alleged, were carried out by PLO.

These attacks included: bombings at the El Al Israel Airlines office at Istanbul, Turkey, on

9 January (letter of 14 January[2]), and at a Jewish-owned restaurant in West Berlin on 15 January (letter of 19 January[3]); the infiltration of armed elements with a view to laying land-mines and attacking villages (letters of 2 February,[4] 12 April,[10] 13 April[11]); the planting of explosive devices in public places in towns and villages of Israel (letters of 15 March,[5] 10 May,[12] 24 May[13]); attacks against two members of West Bank village associations (letters of 17 March[6] and 31 March[7]); the machine-gunning of the Israel Trade Mission building in Paris on 31 March (letter of the same date[8]); the murder of an Israeli diplomat in Paris on 3 April (letter of the same date[9]); and the wounding of the Israeli Ambassador in London on 3 June (letter of 4 June[14]).

Following the completion on 25 April of Israeli withdrawal from the Sinai, three letters were sent to the Secretary-General. On 28 April,[15] the USSR transmitted a statement dated 26 April from its news agency TASS, stating that the return of the Sinai to Egypt, like other consequences of the Camp David agreements, bore no relation to the task of establishing a just and stable peace in the Middle East, particularly as United States troops were to replace the Israeli occupation, giving that country a beach-head for intervention in the affairs of the States of the Middle East and contiguous areas.

Egypt replied on 5 May[18] that Israel's withdrawal from Egyptian territories was the first direct implementation of the principle of the inadmissibility of the acquisition of territory by war, as embodied in the 1967 Security Council resolution on principles for a Middle East peace.[30]

On 3 May 1982,[17] Belgium transmitted a statement of the Ministers for Foreign Affairs of the European Community (EC) member States, meeting at the Council of Europe at Luxembourg on 26 and 27 April, welcoming the complete Israeli withdrawal from the Sinai and expressing hope that the event would be followed by further negotiations conducive to a just and lasting peace on the basis of two principles: the right of all States in the region to existence and security, and justice for all peoples, which required recognition of the legitimate rights of the Palestinians including the right to self-determination.

Report of the Secretary-General. On 12 October 1982, the Secretary-General submitted to the General Assembly and the Security Council a report on the Middle East situation,[20] as called for by the Assembly in December 1981.[29]

After giving an account of developments on various aspects of the situation since his previous report in November 1981,[32] the Secretary-General observed that the Palestinian problem and the Israel-Arab conflict had been a major concern of the United Nations for 35 years and had prob-ably claimed more of its time and attention than any other international problem. In the absence of a resolution of the underlying political and security issues, the situation remained unstable, and over the years a succession of cease-fires had been marred by numerous incidents and five full-fledged wars. With the development of increasingly sophisticated weapons, each war had become more destructive and each new round of fighting had added to the complexity of the conflict. The recent tragic events in Lebanon had forcefully highlighted the urgent need for a peaceful settlement.

While noting that recent initiatives towards such a settlement contained provisions that, for the time being at least, were unacceptable to one party or another, the Secretary-General stated that they deserved careful study and that every opportunity should be seized to overcome the current impasse and shift the conflict from military confrontation to peaceful negotiation.

He concluded that, in order to reconcile the basic aspirations and vital interests of all parties, a settlement must meet the following conditions: Israeli withdrawal from the occupied territories, including those in Lebanon; respect for and acknowledgement of the sovereignty, territorial integrity and political independence of all States in the area and their right to live in peace within secure and recognized boundaries free from the threat or acts of force; and a just settlement of the Palestinian problem, based on recognition of the legitimate rights of the Palestinians, including self-determination. In that context, he added, the question of Jerusalem remained of primary importance.

The United Nations, especially the Security Council, should and could play a constructive role, both in the peace-making process and the peace-keeping efforts essential to prevent a renewal of hostilities and to promote an atmosphere conducive to negotiations.

The report described four proposals for a peaceful Middle East settlement: principles contained in a draft resolution by Egypt and France submitted to the Security Council in July (see below, under ISRAEL AND LEBANON); proposals by the President of the United States in a statement of 1 September; principles adopted on 9 September in the Final Declaration of the Twelfth Arab Summit Conference at Fez, Morocco (transmitted to the Secretary-General on 3 December[19]); and principles set out in a statement of 15 September by the President of the Presidium of the Supreme Soviet of the USSR (transmitted to the Secretary-General on 17 September[16]).

The main points of the United States proposal were: reconciliation of Israel's legitimate security concerns with the rights of the Palestinians, on the basis of the Camp David accords; an immediate freeze on Israeli settlements in the occupied territories; Israeli withdrawal from all fronts, including the West Bank and Gaza; self-government by the Palestinians of the West Bank and Gaza in association with Jordan, following a five-year transition period in which they would have full autonomy; an undivided Jerusalem whose status would be decided by negotiations; and no threats to the security of Israel.

The principles adopted at the Arab Summit Conference were: Israeli withdrawal from all territories occupied since 1967, including Jerusalem; dismantling of Israeli settlements there; guaranteeing freedom of worship in the Holy Places; reaffirmation of Palestinian rights to self-determination and to the exercise of national rights, under PLO leadership; placing the West Bank and Gaza under United Nations control for a transitional period of a few months; establishment of an independent Palestinian State with Jerusalem as its capital; peace guarantees by the Security Council for all States of the region, including the Palestinian State, and a Council guarantee of the implementation of those principles.

The USSR proposal called for: return of all Israeli-occupied territories to the Arabs, with the borders between Israel and its Arab neighbours declared inviolable; guarantee of the Palestinians' rights to self-determination and the establishment of their own State, and the right of refugees to return home or receive compensation for properties left behind; return of East Jerusalem to the Arabs as an integral part of a Palestinian State, with freedom of access to the Holy Places throughout Jerusalem; completely reciprocal guarantees of security, independent existence and development for all States in the region; and international guarantees for the peace settlement, with the permanent members of the Security Council or the entire Council as guarantors.

General Assembly action. By a resolution of 20 December 1982,[27] the General Assembly reaffirmed that the Palestine question was the core of the Middle East conflict and that a settlement could not be achieved without the participation of all parties, including PLO. It declared that Middle East peace was indivisible and must be based on a comprehensive, just and lasting solution under United Nations auspices, ensuring Israel's complete withdrawal from the occupied territories and enabling the Palestinians to exercise their rights, including the right to an independent State. It rejected all agreements and arrangements that violated Palestinian rights and contradicted the principles of just and comprehensive solutions, and considered that the November 1981 strategic co-operation agreements between the United States and Israel encouraged Israel to pursue expansionist policies. States were called upon to put an end to military, economic and financial aid, as well

as human resources, aimed at encouraging Israel to pursue aggressive policies.

The Assembly also condemned Israel's occupation of Palestinian and other Arab territories and demanded its immediate and total withdrawal; declared null and void Israel's decision to make Jerusalem its capital; and condemned Israel's aggressive and repressive practices against Palestinians in and outside the occupied territories and its annexationist policies in the Syrian Golan Heights.

The resolution, orally revised by its sponsors, was adopted by a recorded vote of 113 to 17, with 15 abstentions. An amendment by Egypt,[1] reaffirming the principles and provisions of the 1967[30] and 1973[31] Security Council resolutions which set out the principles for a Middle East settlement, was not pressed to a vote.

In a resolution of 16 December 1982 on Israel's annexation of the Golan Heights,[22] the Assembly deplored any political, economic, financial, military and technological support to Israel that encouraged it to commit aggression and consolidate and perpetuate its occupation and annexation of Arab territories. It determined that Israel's actions confirmed that it was not a peace-loving State, had persistently violated the Charter of the United Nations and had failed to carry out its obligations under the Charter and under the 1949 Assembly resolution admitting it to United Nations membership.[28] The Assembly called on Member States to apply the following measures with respect to Israel: refrain from supplying or acquiring weapons and related equipment, and suspend military assistance; suspend economic, financial and technological assistance and co-operation; sever diplomatic, trade and cultural relations; and cease all dealings in order totally to isolate Israel in all fields. United Nations organizations were called upon to conform their relations with Israel to the resolution.

Similar provisions were included in a resolution adopted by the Assembly on 5 February at its emergency special session on the Golan Heights, except that it did not contain the determination that Israel had persistently violated Charter principles.[21]

The Assembly adopted six resolutions under its agenda item on the Middle East situation—five on 16 December dealing with specific aspects and the most general one of 20 December (summarized above). By the first five resolutions, the Assembly emphasized its demand that Israel rescind its December 1981 decision on the Syrian Golan Heights,[33] resulting in its effective annexation of that territory;[22] called on Israel to restore Palestinian cultural property seized during its occupation of Beirut, Lebanon;[23] deplored the transfer by some States of their diplomatic missions to Jerusalem;[24] condemned the massacre of Palestinian civilians in the Sabra and Shatila refugee camps near Beirut;[25] and called for strict respect of Lebanon's territorial integrity, sovereignty, unity and independence.[26]

Introducing the 20 December resolution on behalf of 12 nations, Cuba said it contained the basic principles for a comprehensive, just and lasting Middle East solution which had been established earlier by the Assembly, the Security Council and the Movement of Non-Aligned Countries.

Explaining its opposition to the resolution, Israel said it contradicted the 1967 Security Council resolution, the only agreed basis for a Middle East settlement; the so-called Arab peace plan adopted at Fez, which was welcomed in the resolution, was a step towards Israel's destruction. Denmark, speaking for the EC members, said they had important reservations on resolutions not in accordance with those States' common position on principles for an Arab-Israeli settlement.

In the opinion of the United States, the resolution was a step backwards and a reiteration of the inevitability of conflict, as it lacked balance and failed to take appropriate account of the building-blocks of the peace process—the 1967 and 1973 Council resolutions, the Camp David accords and the Egypt-Israel peace treaty.

Inclusion of a reference to those resolutions, as proposed by Egypt in the amendment it did not press to a vote, would have been preferred also by the EC members (as stated by Denmark); Finland, which abstained, and Chile, Colombia and Peru, which voted in favour.

Voting against the resolution, Portugal dissociated itself from any appeal or act that might be prejudicial to efforts aimed at a negotiated, comprehensive and just Middle East solution, in particular from paragraphs 9 and 10.

Finland and Sweden, which also abstained, took exception to the same paragraphs, Sweden particularly objecting that the call to end the flow of human resources was a curtailment of the right of individuals to move to a country willing to receive them. Chile, El Salvador, Equatorial Guinea, Paraguay, Samoa and Spain, though voting in favour, also voiced reservations on them. The Dominican Republic abstained, saying that it disagreed with some of the paragraphs; it trusted that agreements between the parties would only supplement United Nations activities.

Reservations on paragraph 9 were expressed also by other supporters of the text, such as Ecuador, Jamaica, Mexico, Peru, Singapore, Thailand and Turkey; Jamaica said it did not share the view that the agreements on strategic co-operation between Israel and the United States necessarily had an adverse effect on peace efforts or threatened the region's security, while Thailand and Turkey said

such agreements were within the prerogative of States.

Peru said it understood that neither that paragraph nor paragraph 5 disregarded peace efforts in the region. Reservations on paragraph 5 were voiced also by Ecuador, Mexico and Paraguay; Ecuador remarked that it could not oppose agreements freely entered into which had led to the restitution of some territories, giving expression to the obligation to settle disputes peacefully.

Democratic Yemen, the Libyan Arab Jamahiriya and the Syrian Arab Republic, on the other hand, emphasized that, in their understanding, the rejection of all agreements and arrangements violating Palestinian rights included the Camp David agreements.

Other supporters of the resolution expressed reservations about parts of it in more general terms. In Bolivia's opinion, the resolution contained terms that ran counter to international courtesy and distorted its underlying principles; the United Nations, in compliance with its role of preserving peace and promoting understanding, should act with impartiality. Colombia said although the resolution contained valuable elements for the achievement of peace, some of its paragraphs had been drafted in a way that might hamper a rapid and final solution. Venezuela thought that the call for an end of aid to Israel, as well as other provisions, did not contribute to peace efforts and to a recognition of Palestinian rights.

Spain would have liked the resolution to contain an explicit mention of the right of all States in the region, including Israel, to live in peace within secure and recognized borders.

Iran, on the other hand, voiced reservations on references which, in its view, implicitly or explicitly suggested recognition of or negotiation with the Zionist usurpers, and in particular: it would have liked to delete from the preamble the mention of the Fez peace plan; it objected that paragraph 3 suggested that the Palestinians recognized the Zionist usurper; and, as it did not differentiate between occupation before and after 1967, it would rather have seen the phrase "occupied since 1967" deleted from paragraph 4.

Explaining that it could not accept certain provisions, especially those welcoming the Fez peace plan, Albania did not participate in the vote. The Libyan Arab Jamahiriya also expressed reservations about the preambular paragraph welcoming the Fez peace plan.

During the Assembly debates on the Middle East situation (6-8 December) and the Palestine question (30 November–2 December), as well as during the 20-28 April and 24 September meetings of the emergency special session on the Palestine question, the view was widely voiced that, due to Israel's aggressive policy, tension in the region had heightened and was threatening international peace and security. Among those holding this position were Albania, Bahrain, Bangladesh, Bulgaria, the Byelorussian SSR, China, Cuba, Cyprus, Czechoslovakia, Democratic Yemen, Egypt, the German Democratic Republic, Greece, Guyana, Hungary, Indonesia, Malaysia, Mauritania, Nicaragua, Poland, Qatar, Romania, Tunisia, Turkey, Uganda, the Ukrainian SSR, the USSR, Viet Nam and Yugoslavia.

Algeria said Israeli leaders had an insatiable appetite for further territorial conquest in the hope of achieving a greater Israel from the Nile to the Euphrates. Although Israel had invoked the need to defend itself and guarantee its security, Bahrain stated, the international community realized that it had been the first to introduce violence, massacre and terrorism into the region. Botswana believed Israel would be dangerously deceiving itself if it depended on pre-emptive strikes against its neighbours and on the facility with which it could wreak havoc on them; the wars fought in the Middle East since 1948 had made Israel less secure and more beleaguered, because they had not addressed the root causes of the conflict. Israel had defied the authority of the only universal Organization established for the maintenance of international peace and security, ignoring the fact that it had been created by that Organization, said Finland. In the view of the German Democratic Republic, the escalation of Israel's policy of aggression and oppression was only the prelude to yet another large-scale act of international piracy. Guyana held that Israel had set itself above the law and arrogated to itself the right to attack any State in the region in the name of what it called its security interests. In that regard, Kenya commented that no State must be allowed to occupy another State in order to have what could be claimed as secure borders.

Indonesia remarked that the Assembly had been forced to put out the fires of new Israeli acts of aggression rather than beginning to build lasting peace. Turkey stated that Israel must stop treading a dangerous and destructive path, if only for the sake of its own interests.

In Egypt's view, Israel, encouraged by massive military and financial aid, had recently been relying on a long-arm policy to achieve hegemony in the Middle East. Guyana observed that Israel was occupying parts of four neighbouring States. The United Arab Emirates said the situation was deteriorating daily because the peoples of the Middle East found themselves obliged to defend themselves and resist Zionist aggression. Among others holding Israel responsible for the deterioration of the Middle East situation were Bangladesh and Nigeria.

Iran believed that peace would be restored to the Middle East only when Israel was eliminated and the State of Palestine was restored in the occupied land; concessionary negotiations would only exacerbate the situation.

Israel, for its part, maintained that the Arab-Israel conflict was but one focus of the many Middle East tensions and was far from being the most crucial; 12 armed conflicts were currently raging in the region, which was being destabilized by repression, the flagrant abuse of social groups and exploitation by undemocratically established régimes, notably in Iraq, the Libyan Arab Jamahiriya and the Syrian Arab Republic. At the root of the Arab-Israel conflict was the Arabs' refusal to recognize Israel's right to exist.

A number of speakers argued that Israel would not have been able to commit aggression and continue its occupation of Arab territories without the material and moral support of the United States. This view was expressed by Bulgaria, the Byelorussian SSR, China, Cuba, Czechoslovakia, Democratic Yemen, the German Democratic Republic, Guyana, Hungary, Mongolia, Nicaragua, Poland, the Syrian Arab Republic, the Ukrainian SSR, the USSR and Viet Nam.

The German Democratic Republic said the United States aim was to increase its military presence in the Middle East. The United States taxpayer, said Iraq, was underwriting the expenses of Israel's acts of aggression and its settlements in the occupied territories. The Libyan Arab Jamahiriya believed the American people would soon lose patience with the immoral United States policy of supporting aggression and oppression in the Middle East and question the viability of continued United States aid to Israel. The Lao People's Democratic Republic, among others, criticized the November 1981 agreements on strategic co-operation between Israel and the United States as displaying in concrete form the hegemonic and expansionist aims of the two countries in the region. The Ukrainian SSR referred to Israel as the United States gendarme in the Middle East. The United States intended to raise the non-reimbursable portion of military assistance to Israel up to one half of the total amount of $2 billion, as a reward for its aggression, according to the USSR.

In the view of Albania, both the USSR and the United States were working to the detriment of Arab countries, the latter by aiding Israel and the former by seeking to use Arab antagonism to American imperialism as an aid to its own imperialist penetration and domination.

Denmark said the EC members considered Israel's withdrawal from the Sinai on 25 April an important stage in the development of peaceful relations between Israel and Egypt, as well as the initiation of the peace process in the Middle East. Many other countries held negotiations more necessary than ever to settle the Middle East conflict peacefully. Japan felt that positive developments, such as progress in the normalization of relations between Israel and Egypt, had occurred; on the other hand, a solution to a more and more complex problem was becoming increasingly elusive.

Opposition to the consequences of the Camp David agreements continued to be voiced by some, including Bulgaria, the Byelorussian SSR, Czechoslovakia and the Ukrainian SSR. The so-called Camp David peace process had, in the opinion of Bulgaria and Hungary, among others, only helped heighten tension and the arms race in the region and had culminated in Israel's aggression against Lebanon. The German Democratic Republic saw so-called autonomy talks for the West Bank inhabitants and attempts to revive the bankrupt concept of separate deals as aimed at permanently denying Palestinian rights. In the view of the Syrian Arab Republic, the Camp David agreements were an invitation to war and an attempt to isolate Egypt. After Camp David, said the USSR, Israel's aggressive, anti-Arab policy had become even more starkly evident.

The Camp David process offered the only practical way towards a comprehensive solution, including the question of the Palestinians, Israel said. Egypt declared that any peaceful, comprehensive settlement should take into consideration the right of Israel to existence, recognition and security, on the basis of equality and reciprocity.

Austria stressed negotiation among all parties, including PLO, as the sole path to a Middle East solution, and rejected the use of force and all acts of terrorism; it repeated a previous suggestion that Israel and PLO enter into exploratory talks without pre-conditions. Bhutan called for the establishment of a State of Palestine and added that all States of the region had the right to live peacefully within internationally recognized boundaries. As the most significant representative of Palestinian aspirations, said Finland, PLO had the right to participate in negotiations on their future.

For Japan, a Middle East peace should contain four elements: it should be just, lasting and comprehensive; it should be achieved through implementation of the Security Council peace settlement resolutions of 1967 and 1973 and respect for legitimate Palestinian rights, including self-determination; consideration should be given to the legitimate security requirements of the countries of the region and to the aspirations of all peoples including the Palestinians; and Israel and PLO, representing the Palestinians, must participate in the peace process. Spain also identified four elements: Israeli withdrawal from all Arab territories occupied since 1967; the unacceptability of Israel's settlements policy and its attempts to alter the nature and status of Jerusalem; the right of all States in the area to live in peace within secure and recognized borders; and implementation of the national rights of the Palestinian people, including the right to self-determination in their homeland.

King Hassan II of Morocco, addressing the Assembly as President of the Twelfth Arab Summit Conference, observed that the peace proposals adopted at Fez on 9 September (see above) had been unanimously adopted by all Arab leaders at the highest levels.

The Fez peace plan was welcomed by a number of speakers, including Austria, Bangladesh, Bhutan, China, Egypt, the German Democratic Republic, Guyana, Hungary, India, Indonesia, Iraq, Japan, Nepal, Pakistan, Poland, Tunisia, Turkey, Uganda, the Ukrainian SSR and Zambia. Many viewed it as an historic decision and, as Iraq referred to it, a demonstration of the Arab States' unanimous and sincere desire for peace.

Denmark, for the EC members, viewed the Fez proposals as an expression of the unanimous will of the participants, including PLO, to work for a just Middle East peace encompassing all States, including Israel. In Jordan's view, the Fez Conference had been one of the most incisive and in-depth dialogues on Palestinian issues and had explored all options. In Djibouti's view, the plan included all the principles which could lead to a peaceful Middle East settlement. India considered the plan foremost among the proposals for a solution and one which could lead to a lasting and just peace.

Morocco said the plan was realistic and had led to a relaunching of efforts to resolve the Middle East crisis. In Turkey's view, the plan might establish an important threshold in the search for peace. At Fez, Egypt stated, the Arab States had proved that they could go beyond differences to adopt a common pragmatic position. The Syrian Arab Republic said the Fez plan was based on the same principles it had proclaimed. Qatar believed that the Fez resolutions restored to the United Nations its legitimate role in solving the Middle East problem, together with the other principal parties to the conflict, including PLO. Kuwait said the Fez plan should be regarded as a basis for a just solution that ensured justice for the Palestinians, the principal victims in the Middle East conflict.

In Uganda's opinion, the Fez plan took into account Israel's fears. Iran, however, felt that the decisions of the Fez Summit had given Israel more encouragement in its aggression. Saudi Arabia said Israel's reaction to the Fez plan had been the same as in the past: it would respond to any initiative aimed at settling the Palestinian problem by establishing more settlements, plundering more Arab territory, and resorting to more repressive measures and terrorist acts.

The United Arab Emirates hoped that the Security Council would bear in mind the historic significance of the development at Fez.

A number of delegations expressed their views on the proposal put forward on 1 September by the President of the United States. Turkey thought the proposal contained elements that could contribute significantly to the elaboration of a framework for negotiations. Similarly, Austria, Denmark (for the EC members) and Morocco found in the proposal many constructive elements for compromise and reconciliation, Morocco adding that it hoped the Palestinians would eventually be given their due place.

Bulgaria, Nicaragua, the Ukrainian SSR and others, however, cautioned that this so-called peace initiative was no more than an element in the political and military strategy of the United States designed to give priority to Israel's security, and an attempt to revive the Camp David agreements. Bulgaria, the Byelorussian SSR and Czechoslovakia said the United States plan contradicted the position of the Arab countries in that it did not recognize the Palestinians' right to establish an independent State, and the requirement that Israel relinquish all occupied Arab lands and recognize PLO as the sole legitimate representative of the Arab people of Palestine. Czechoslovakia said the world was coming to realize the anti-Arab and anti-Palestinian nature of the plan. Hungary remarked that proposals which did not even mention PLO as a party to the proposed settlement and completely avoided the issue of Israeli withdrawal from the occupied territories could lead nowhere. The purpose of the United States initiative was, in the view of the USSR, to divide the Arab countries, weaken their struggle against American and Israeli expansion, and impose on them decisions advantageous to the United States and Israel alone.

In the opinion of Democratic Yemen, neither the United States proposal nor the Fez plan served the Arab cause, interests or rights. Iraq believed that the United States proposal would share the fate of former plans which had been rejected by Israel.

Any proposal that discriminated in favour only of Israel, Ghana said, begged the crux of the problem.

Democratic Yemen, Mauritania, Yemen and others opposed all partial agreements which did not provide for the participation of all parties in a settlement, including PLO.

Albania believed that both the USSR and the United States proposals were directed against the vital interests of the Arabs, whom the two super-

Powers were trying to persuade had no choice but to accept their protective umbrella.

The USSR reiterated its position in favour of a fundamental comprehensive settlement based on United Nations decisions, and recalled to that effect its proposals put forward on 15 September (see above). A constructive step in the search for a negotiated comprehensive solution would be, according to Cuba and others, the convening of an international conference under the aegis of the United Nations, with the participation of all parties on an equal footing, including PLO. Bulgaria held such a conference to be the only way of bringing about a comprehensive settlement, which could not be achieved through mediation missions or by appeasing the aggressor by increasing concessions.

Bangladesh, Madagascar, Nigeria, Pakistan, Poland, Romania, Sri Lanka and Tunisia expressed support for the holding of such a conference. The German Democratic Republic and Viet Nam, among others, favoured its convening without delay, as proposed by the USSR. Romania called for a redoubling of political and diplomatic activities to that end.

Bulgaria, the Byelorussian SSR, Czechoslovakia, Hungary, the Lao People's Democratic Republic, Mongolia and the Ukrainian SSR believed that the USSR proposal met all the requirements of a comprehensive settlement and coincided with the principles adopted at Fez. Czechoslovakia noted that the Fez plan was not at variance with what the socialist States had been advocating for many years. The Byelorussian SSR held that it proceeded from the need for strict observance of the principle of the inadmissibility of the acquisition of territory by force; the recognition and implementation of Palestinian rights; and the recognition of the right of all States in the area to a secure existence and to development under international guarantees. The plan was also endorsed by the German Democratic Republic and Poland.

Finland said all three recent proposals contained a number of similar elements and had a common denominator: the achievement of peace through negotiations. Egypt felt that all the proposals offered tremendous challenges—the challenges of peace. The peace proposals were welcomed also by Romania, Sweden and Tunisia; Romania thought they created conditions for intensifying political and diplomatic activity towards a just and lasting settlement, while Sweden hoped Israel would respond to offers of negotiations based on explicit recognition by all parties of its right to exist within secure and recognized borders. India saw in those efforts a starting-point for negotiations within a United Nations framework. Malta, Rapporteur of the Committee on the Exercise of the

Inalienable Rights of the Palestinian People, found a wide area of convergence in the different proposals, which Bangladesh felt should be studied as a possible basis for negotiations.

Denmark, speaking for the EC members, called for a similar expression of a will for peace on Israel's part. Jordan considered most important the will of all parties to press ahead with the implementation of the various peace initiatives. Mali stated that Israel must be forced to agree to peace.

Bahrain, Nepal, Norway, Portugal and Uganda welcomed the United States initiative along with the Fez plan, while Japan expressed appreciation of them. Brazil saw in both a useful basis for discussion and negotiation, and Portugal felt they should not be considered separately.

Egypt welcomed the positive aspects of the United States plan but said that, without a sustained effort to implement it, the initiative would lose momentum; a constructive dialogue between the United States and PLO should start as soon as possible. In Greece's opinion, the United States initiative could be a first step and the Fez plan could lead to a settlement acceptable to the Palestinians. In Jordan's opinion, the United States initiative contained very positive elements that could evolve into a reconciliation with the Fez plan. Kuwait appealed to the United States to recognize PLO and start a dialogue with it; by excluding the basic solution of a Palestinian State, Kuwait added, the United States remained under the illusion that it could freeze the Palestine question through a patchwork solution.

Other diplomatic initiatives discussed included the proposal to the Security Council by Egypt and France on 1 July, in which Austria, Denmark (for the EC members) and Nigeria, in particular, found positive elements. Egypt said the proposal, which still stood, was based on the idea that the logical overture towards a peaceful settlement was mutual recognition of the rights of both parties by Palestinians and Israelis.

Israel said a solution was offered within the Camp David framework and there was no need for alternative plans. Though having not yet achieved its goal, the Camp David process was the greatest concrete step towards peace, the United States said.

Many speakers, including Afghanistan, Algeria, Czechoslovakia, Democratic Yemen and Pakistan, considered sanctions or measures under Chapter VII of the Charter necessary in view of Israel's aggressive policy. Bahrain felt that condemnations did not suffice and that strict measures were needed to compel Israel to respect international law. Nicaragua said the United Nations and the non-aligned countries had on innumerable occasions urged that no military agreement be concluded which would strengthen Israel's military ca-

pacity and enable it to develop its aggressive and expansionist policies. The Syrian Arab Republic favoured a resolution asking Member States to break relations with Israel, calling on the United States to end all its assistance to that country, rescinding the admission of Israel to the United Nations and asking that aid be given to the Arab States so that they could face up to aggression.

Nigeria said it had severed all political and economic links with Israel since 1967 as a demonstration of its displeasure with Israeli policies. Malaysia regretted that the United Nations had on several occasions been prevented from playing a more effective role; it believed that the unified determination of the international community to compel Israel to comply with United Nations decisions and international norms, complemented by the efforts of the countries of the region, had become more imperative. Cuba, Democratic Yemen, Nicaragua and others deplored the fact that the Security Council had been prevented by the United States veto from adopting enforcement measures against Israel. Failure to secure Israel's compliance with the collective demands of the United Nations membership, Pakistan cautioned, could lead to incalculable consequences.

Amendment not pressed. [1]Egypt, A/37/L.55.
Letters.
    Israel: [2]14 Jan., A/37/65-S/14836; [3]19 Jan., A/37/71-S/14842; [4]2 Feb., A/37/79-S/14856; [5]15 Mar., A/37/116-S/14906; [6]17 Mar., A/37/118-S/14910 & Corr.1; [7]31 Mar., S/14938 (1 Apr., A/37/165); [8]31 Mar., S/14939 (1 Apr., A/37/166); [9]3 Apr., S/14951; [10]12 Apr., A/37/175 (S/14965); [11]13 Apr., S/14972 (16 Apr., A/37/190); [12]10 May, A/37/223 (S/15066); [13]24 May, S/15107 (25 May, A/37/253); [14]4 June, A/37/266 (S/15158).
    USSR: [15]28 Apr., A/37/213-S/15015; [16]17 Sep., A/37/457-S/15403.
    Others. [17]Belgium: 3 May, A/37/218-S/15039. [18]Egypt: 5 May, A/37/220-S/15051. [19]Morocco, 3 Dec., transmitting Arab Summit Conference Declaration, A/37/696-S/15510.
Report. [20]S-G, A/37/525-S/15451.
Resolutions (1982). GA: [21]ES-9/1, 5 Feb.; [22]37/123 A, 16 Dec; [23]37/123 B, 16 Dec.; [24]37/123 C, 16 Dec.; [25]37/123 D, 16 Dec.; [26]37/123 E, 16 Dec.; [27]37/123 F, 20 Dec., text following.
Resolutions (prior). GA: [28]273(III), 11 May 1949 (YUN 1948-49, p. 405); [29]36/226 A, 17 Dec. 1981 (YUN 1981, p. 262). SC: [30]242(1967), 22 Nov. 1967 (YUN 1967, p. 257); [31]338(1973), 22 Oct. 1973 (YUN 1973, p. 213).
Yearbook references. 1981, [32]p. 258, [33]p. 309.
Meeting records. GA: A/37/PV.44, 92-96, 108, 112 (26 Oct. & 6-20 Dec.).

General Assembly resolution 37/123 F

20 December 1982   Meeting 112   113-17-15 (recorded vote)

12-nation draft (A/37/L.48 and Corr.1 and Add.1), orally revised; agenda item 34.
Sponsors: Bangladesh, Cuba, Guyana, India, Lao People's Democratic Republic, Malaysia, Mongolia, Nigeria, Pakistan, Sri Lanka, Viet Nam, Yugoslavia.

The General Assembly,
Having discussed the item entitled "The situation in the Middle East",
Reaffirming its resolutions 36/226 A and B of 17 December 1981 and ES-9/1 of 5 February 1982,
Recalling Security Council resolutions 425(1978) of 19 March 1978, 497(1981) of 17 December 1981, 508(1982) of 5 June 1982, 509(1982)

of 6 June 1982, 511(1982) of 18 June 1982, 512(1982) of 19 June 1982, 513(1982) of 4 July 1982, 515(1982) of 29 July 1982, 516(1982) of 1 August 1982, 517(1982) of 4 August 1982, 518(1982) of 12 August 1982, 519(1982) of 17 August 1982, 520(1982) of 17 September 1982 and 521(1982) of 19 September 1982,

Taking note of the report of the Secretary-General of 12 October 1982,

Welcoming the world-wide support extended to the just cause of the Palestinian people and the other Arab countries in their struggle against Israeli aggression and occupation in order to achieve a comprehensive, just and lasting peace in the Middle East and the full exercise by the Palestinian people of its inalienable national rights, as affirmed by previous resolutions of the General Assembly relating to the question of Palestine and the situation in the Middle East,

Gravely concerned that the Arab and Palestinian territories occupied since 1967, including Jerusalem, still remain under Israeli occupation, that the relevant resolutions of the United Nations have not been implemented and that the Palestinian people is still denied the restoration of its land and the exercise of its inalienable national rights in conformity with international law, as reaffirmed by resolutions of the United Nations,

Reaffirming the applicability of the Geneva Convention relative to the Protection of Civilian Persons in Time of War, of 12 August 1949, to all the occupied Palestinian and other Arab territories, including Jerusalem,

Reiterating all relevant United Nations resolutions which emphasize that the acquisition of territory by force is inadmissible under the Charter of the United Nations and the principles of international law and that Israel must withdraw unconditionally from all the Palestinian and other Arab territories occupied by Israel since 1967, including Jerusalem,

Reaffirming further the imperative necessity of establishing a comprehensive, just and lasting peace in the region, based on full respect for the Charter and the principles of international law,

Gravely concerned also at recent Israeli actions involving the escalation and expansion of the conflict in the region, which further violate the principles of international law and endanger international peace and security,

Welcoming the Arab peace plan adopted unanimously at the Twelfth Arab Summit Conference, held at Fez, Morocco, on 25 November 1981 and 9 September 1982,

Bearing in mind the address made, on 26 October 1982, by His Majesty King Hassan II of Morocco, in his capacity as President of the Twelfth Arab Summit Conference,

1. *Condemns* Israel's continued occupation of the Palestinian and other Arab territories, including Jerusalem, in violation of the Charter of the United Nations, the principles of international law and the relevant resolutions of the United Nations, and demands the immediate, unconditional and total withdrawal of Israel from all these occupied territories;

2. *Reaffirms its conviction* that the question of Palestine is the core of the conflict in the Middle East and that no comprehensive, just and lasting peace in the region will be achieved without the full exercise by the Palestinian people of its inalienable national rights and the immediate, unconditional and total withdrawal of Israel from all the Palestinian and other occupied territories;

3. *Reaffirms further* that a just and comprehensive settlement of the situation in the Middle East cannot be achieved without the participation on an equal footing of all the parties to the conflict, including the Palestine Liberation Organization, the representative of the Palestinian people;

4. *Declares once more* that peace in the Middle East is indivisible and must be based on a comprehensive, just and lasting solution of the Middle East problem, under the auspices of the United Nations, which ensures the complete and unconditional withdrawal of Israel from the Palestinian and other Arab territories occupied since 1967, including Jerusalem, and which enables the Palestinian people, under the leadership of the Palestine Liberation Organization, to exercise its inalienable rights, including the right to return and the right to self-determination, national independence and the establishment of its independent sovereign State in Palestine, in accordance with the resolutions of the United Nations relevant to the question of Palestine, in particular General Assembly resolutions ES-7/2 of 29 July 1980, 36/120 A to F of 10 December 1981, 37/86 A to D of 10 December 1982 and 37/86 E of 20 December 1982;

5. *Rejects* all agreements and arrangements in so far as they violate the recognized rights of the Palestinian people and contradict the principles of just and comprehensive solutions to the Middle East problem to ensure the establishment of a just peace in the area;

6. *Deplores* Israel's failure to comply with Security Council resolutions 476(1980) of 30 June 1980 and 478(1980) of 20 August 1980 and General Assembly resolutions 35/207 of 16 December 1980 and 36/226 A and B of 17 December 1981, determines that Israel's decision to annex Jerusalem and to declare it as its "capital" as well as the measures to alter its physical character, demographic composition, institutional structure and status are null and void and demands that they be rescinded immediately, and calls upon all Member States, the specialized agencies and all other international organizations to abide by the present resolution and all other relevant resolutions, including Assembly resolutions 37/86 A to E;

7. *Condemns* Israel's aggression and practices against the Palestinian people in the occupied Palestinian territories and outside these territories, particularly Palestinians in Lebanon, including the expropriation and annexation of territory, the establishment of settlements, assassination attempts and other terrorist, aggressive and repressive measures, which are in violation of the Charter and the principles of international law and the relevant international conventions;

8. *Strongly condemns* the imposition by Israel of its laws, jurisdiction and administration on the occupied Syrian Golan Heights, its annexationist policies and practices, the establishment of settlements, the confiscation of lands, the diversion of water resources and the imposition of Israeli citizenship on Syrian nationals, and declares that all these measures are null and void and constitute a violation of the rules and principles of international law relevant to belligerent occupation, in particular the Geneva Convention relative to the Protection of Civilian Persons in Time of War, of 12 August 1949;

9. *Considers* that the agreements on strategic co-operation between the United States of America and Israel signed on 30 November 1981 would encourage Israel to pursue its aggressive and expansionist policies and practices in the Palestinian and other Arab territories occupied since 1967, including Jerusalem, would have adverse effects on efforts for the establishment of a comprehensive, just and lasting peace in the Middle East and would threaten the security of the region;

10. *Calls upon* all States to put an end to the flow to Israel of any military, economic and financial aid, as well as human resources, aimed at encouraging it to pursue its aggressive policies against the Arab countries and the Palestinian people;

11. *Requests* the Secretary-General to report to the Security Council periodically on the development of the situation and to submit to the General Assembly at its thirty-eighth session a comprehensive report covering the developments in the Middle East in all their aspects.

Recorded vote in Assembly as follows:

In favour: Afghanistan, Algeria, Angola, Argentina, Bahrain, Bangladesh, Benin, Bhutan, Bolivia, Botswana, Brazil, Bulgaria, Burundi, Byelorussian SSR, Cape Verde, Central African Republic, Chad, Chile, China, Colombia, Comoros, Congo, Cuba, Cyprus, Czechoslovakia, Democratic Kampuchea, Democratic Yemen, Djibouti, Ecuador, Egypt, El Salvador, Equatorial Guinea, Ethiopia, Gabon, Gambia, German Democratic Republic, Ghana, Greece, Grenada, Guinea, Guinea-Bissau, Guyana, Hungary, India, Indonesia, Iran, Iraq, Jamaica, Jordan, Kenya, Kuwait, Lao People's Democratic Republic, Lebanon, Lesotho, Liberia, Libyan Arab Jamahiriya, Madagascar, Malaysia, Maldives, Mali, Malta, Mauritania, Mauritius, Mexico, Mongolia, Morocco, Mozambique, Nepal, Nicaragua, Niger, Nigeria, Oman, Pakistan, Panama, Papua New Guinea, Paraguay, Peru, Philippines, Poland, Qatar, Romania, Rwanda, Samoa, Sao Tome and Principe, Saudi Arabia, Senegal, Seychelles, Sierra Leone, Singapore, Somalia, Spain, Sri Lanka, Sudan, Suriname, Syrian Arab Republic, Thailand, Togo, Trinidad and Tobago, Tunisia, Turkey, Uganda, Ukrainian SSR, USSR, United Arab Emirates, United Republic of Cameroon, United Republic of Tanzania, Upper Volta, Venezuela, Viet Nam, Yemen, Yugoslavia, Zambia, Zimbabwe.

Against: Australia, Belgium, Canada, Denmark, France, Germany, Federal Republic of, Iceland, Ireland, Israel, Italy, Luxembourg, Netherlands, New Zealand, Norway, Portugal, United Kingdom, United States.

Abstaining: Antigua and Barbuda, Austria, Bahamas, Barbados, Burma, Dominican Republic, Fiji, Finland, Haiti, Ivory Coast, Japan, Malawi, Sweden, Uruguay, Zaire.

Credentials of Israel in the General Assembly

By a letter of 22 October 1982 to the General Assembly President,[2] 49 States conveyed their reservations to the credentials of Israel to the Assembly's regular session, citing the following reasons: Israel had flagrantly and persistently violated international law and the United Nations Charter, and had consistently defied United Nations resolutions; the Assembly had declared on 5 February that Israel was not a peace-loving State;[5] Israel had refused to implement United Nations resolutions on Jerusalem, which it had illegally annexed and claimed as its capital, and had refused to implement resolutions demanding that it rescind its December 1981 decision which had resulted in the effective annexation of the Syrian Golan Heights; its credentials, issued in Jerusalem, implicitly alleged that the delegation represented the inhabitants of Jerusalem and the Golan Heights; it had consistently refused to implement United Nations resolutions on Palestinian rights and on its withdrawal from occupied territories; and it had invaded Lebanon and committed genocide against the Palestinians there.

On 25 October,[3] Israel responded that the completely unfounded attack on its credentials was an attempt to abuse the credentials procedure and was one more manifestation of the obsessive hatred of States bent on Israel's destruction, in violation of international law and the Charter, particularly the provisions prohibiting the use or threat of force against the territorial integrity or political independence of any State and enjoining all Members to settle their international disputes peacefully; the approach in the letter of 22 October was liable to affect adversely the ability of the United Nations to perform its primary functions for the maintenance of international peace and security.

On 26 October, the Assembly adopted, by a recorded vote of 74 to 9, with 32 abstentions, a motion submitted by Finland also on behalf of Denmark, Iceland, Norway and Sweden,[4] by which it decided not to act on an amendment by Iran[1] to add the phrase "except with regard to the credentials of Israel" to a draft resolution by the Credentials Committee proposing that the Assembly approve its report accepting all credentials for the regular session received to date. Following the vote on the motion, the Assembly adopted the credentials resolution[6] unamended and without vote.

Presenting its amendment, Iran said the time had come to act against Israel's credentials, because by the following year the Assembly was likely to have moved further away from consensus on the issue and Israel's recognition by a group of Arab States would be only a matter of time; if the United States carried out its threat to withdraw from the Assembly because of such an action, Iran was ready to pay more than its share to make up the resulting financial deficit.

Putting forward the motion, Finland said the Nordic States were motivated by their dedication to uphold the capacity and authority of the United Nations to maintain international peace and security.

Israel stated that unjustified aspersions, such as Iran's, cast on credentials that were in due form and had been accepted by the Credentials Committee, were in clear violation of the Charter and of the Assembly's rules of procedure.

Explanations of vote in support of the Nordic States' motion were made by Chad and Greece.

During the November/December Assembly debate on the Palestine question, the Libyan Arab Jamahiriya called again for the expulsion of Israel from the United Nations and its specialized agencies, adding that the signing by 49 States of a document expressing reservations on Israel's credentials was a step in the right direction.

Portugal, on the other hand, believed that a peaceful solution could be reached only through constant dialogue between all the parties; for this reason, it condemned any attempt to prevent a Member State from participating in the Assembly.

Speaking in April at the resumed seventh emergency special session, Jordan said if Israel was allowed to persist in its aggression, the Assembly would find itself with no alternative but to declare Israel a non-peace-loving State and to review its United Nations status and credentials. Saudi Arabia believed that Israel had forfeited its eligibility for United Nations membership many years ago.

In view of the Security Council's failure to shoulder its responsibilities for safeguarding international peace and security, the Syrian Arab Republic stated, the Assembly had no choice but to revoke Israel's membership on the grounds that it had not fulfilled its obligations as a Member State.

In addition to Israel's expulsion, Iran requested that States withdraw their recognition of Israel as a decisive step towards the restoration of justice to the Palestinians.

Norway, Sweden, the United States and others opposed any effort aimed at excluding Israel from the United Nations. The United States said the attempts to expel Israel and to assert that it was not a peace-loving State were not consistent with the Charter purposes. Sweden considered such efforts to be extremely harmful to the Organization's universality and authority, and Norway said such attempts would damage not only the possibilities for the United Nations to help the Middle East peace process, but the United Nations itself.

Following Israel's invasion of Lebanon in June, Cuba stated that Israel had committed enough criminal acts against the Charter and had adopted so hostile an attitude towards the United Nations that whether it deserved to belong to the Organization should urgently be considered. In Jordan's opinion, Israel had proved once more that it was a non-peace-loving nation and should therefore not continue to enjoy the respectability the United Nations conferred. PLO considered it incumbent on the international community to impose sanctions on Israel or to expel it or suspend its membership, treating it as an outlaw. The United Arab Emirates said the Assembly was obliged to implement the Charter and expel Israel as it did not respect United Nations resolutions or the United Nations observers to be deployed in the Beirut area. In the view of the Libyan Arab Jamahiriya, Israel must be expelled as it did not respect the Charter, or must at least be castigated by declaring its illegitimacy. The Syrian Arab Republic held it imperative to deprive Israel of United Nations membership or at least exclude it from participating in the work of the Assembly.

Amendment not acted upon. [(1)]Iran, A/37/L.9.
Letters. [(2)]Afghanistan, Algeria, Bahrain, Bangladesh, Benin, Bulgaria, Byelorussian SSR, China, Comoros, Cuba, Czechoslovakia, Democratic Yemen, Djibouti, Gambia, German Democratic Republic, Guinea, Hungary, Indonesia, Iran, Iraq, Jordan, Kuwait, Lao People's Democratic Republic, Libyan Arab Jamahiriya, Madagascar, Malaysia, Maldives, Mali, Mauritania, Mongolia, Morocco, Nicaragua, Niger, Oman, Pakistan, Poland, Qatar, Saudi Arabia, Senegal, Somalia, Sudan, Syrian Arab Republic, Tunisia, Turkey, Ukrainian SSR, USSR, United Arab Emirates, Viet Nam, Yemen, 22 Oct., A/37/563 & Add.1; [(3)]Israel, 25 Oct., A/37/565.
Motion adopted. [(4)]Denmark, Finland, Iceland, Norway, Sweden, A/37/L.11.
Resolutions (1982). GA: [(5)]ES-9/1, 5 Feb.; [(6)]37/5 A, 26 Oct.
Meeting record. GA: A/37/PV.45 (26 Oct.).

Palestine question

In 1982, the General Assembly dealt on several occasions with the Palestine question. The seventh emergency special session, originally convened in 1980,[(37)] resumed in April, June, August and September 1982.

Of the seven resolutions adopted at the 1982 emergency special session, one, adopted in April, concerned the credentials of representatives to the session, and two, adopted in June and September, dealt mainly with Israel and Lebanon. By two others, in August 1982, the Assembly set dates in 1983 for the International Conference on the Question of Palestine and decided on the annual commemoration of the International Day of Innocent Children Victims of Aggression.

Five resolutions adopted in December of the regular Assembly session included two on broad aspects of the question and one each on the work programme of the Committee on the Exercise of the Inalienable Rights of the Palestinian People, the work of the Secretariat's Division for Palestinian Rights and the 1983 Conference.

Action by the Commission on Human Rights and its Sub-Commission. On 11 February 1982,[(9)] the Commission on Human Rights, in a resolution on self-determination for the Palestin-

ians, reaffirmed the inalienable rights of the Palestinian people to establish a fully independent and sovereign State of Palestine and to return to their homes and property; it expressed strong opposition to all partial agreements and treaties violating Palestinian rights, and rejected negotiations on "autonomy" for the Palestinians within the Camp David framework.

The Sub-Commission on Prevention of Discrimination and Protection of Minorities called on 8 September[(26)] for the full exercise of those rights, and urged the implementation of all United Nations resolutions on the Palestine question and other occupied Arab territories in order to establish a just and lasting peace in the Middle East.

General Assembly action (April). The seventh emergency special session was reconvened on 20 April at the request of the Movement of Non-Aligned Countries, following a decision of the Extraordinary Ministerial Meeting of the Coordinating Bureau of the Non-Aligned Countries, held in Kuwait from 5 to 8 April. At that meeting, according to its final communiqué transmitted to the Secretary-General by Kuwait on 20 April,[(5)] the Ministers approved a programme of action which, in addition to calling for resumption of the Assembly session, called for an intensified campaign for political and economic sanctions against Israel and for the application by the Security Council of comprehensive and mandatory sanctions, called on the Council to compel Israel to rescind the annexation of the Golan Heights, and called on the Secretary-General to initiate contacts with the parties to the Arab-Israeli conflict in search of concrete ways to achieve a just and lasting solution.

Israel, by a letter of 21 April,[(3)] and the United States, by a letter of 19 April,[(6)] opposed the resumption so long after the session had been temporarily adjourned, saying that the action undermined the Assembly's rules of procedure; Israel considered the emergency to be contrived and any resolutions adopted at the session illegal, while the United States said the session was being reconvened without regard to the views of the majority. By a letter of 20 April to the United States,[(1)] the Assembly President responded that the 1980 resolution by which the emergency special session had been temporarily adjourned[(32)] permitted such resumption, on the request of Member States, even after several Assembly sessions had intervened.

By a resolution of 28 April 1982,[(10)] the Assembly reaffirmed the inadmissibility of the acquisition of territory by force; rejected plans to resettle Palestinians outside their homeland; and condemned policies which frustrated the exercise of the Palestinians' inalienable rights, including encouragement of the flow of human resources to

Israel, enabling it to proceed with colonization and settlement in the occupied territories, as well as the provision of military, economic and political assistance and the misuse of the veto in the Security Council, enabling Israel to continue its aggression and occupation. The Assembly declared that Israel's actions confirmed that it was not a peace-loving State and had not carried out its obligations under the United Nations Charter. It urged the Security Council to recognize Palestinian rights and called on the Secretary-General to initiate contacts with all parties, including PLO, in search of a just and lasting solution.

The Assembly also reaffirmed the applicability of conventions on the protection of civilians in wartime to all territories occupied by Israel since 1967, demanded that Israel comply with United Nations resolutions on Jerusalem and condemned it for various actions in the occupied territories.

The 26-nation draft was adopted by a roll-call vote, requested by Israel, of 86 to 20, with 36 abstentions.

Introducing the text, Senegal said it recalled facts and advocated peaceful means in the spirit of the Charter to solve the Palestine question; its scrupulous implementation would contribute towards strengthening the credibility of the United Nations and restoring peace, mutual understanding and co-operation among all States and peoples of the region.

In Israel's view, the resolution regurgitated the main components of the many anti-Israel resolutions that had been steamrolled through the Assembly in recent years by the Committee on Palestinian rights as a tool of PLO. The text did not mention the 1967 Security Council resolution[33] which had served as the basis for the Camp David accords and the Israel-Egypt peace treaty and which remained the only agreed framework for a negotiated settlement. Paragraph 7 contained a series of blatant lies that had failed of adoption in the Security Council and maintained that Israel had failed to fulfil its alleged obligations under the Geneva Convention relative to the Protection of Civilian Persons in Time of War, of 12 August 1949, yet in the same breath chided Israel for dismissing certain mayors and disbanding a municipal council, acts that were explicitly authorized under the Convention. The libel in paragraph 11 that Israel was not a peace-loving State was an abomination.

The United States rejected the draft as ill-inspired and offensive, saying it violated the spirit of reason and peace, debased the Charter, reinforced an attitude of cynicism towards the United Nations, and not only rejected the framework for peace established by the Council in 1967[33] and 1973,[34] but condemned the United States for exercising its constitutional prerogative under the Charter to vote against resolutions which aggravated international situations and harmed the cause of peace.

Norway opposed the resolution on the grounds that it was one-sided and unbalanced, lacked any reference to Israel's right to exist, appeared to move towards Israel's exclusion or suspension from the United Nations, prejudged the outcome of a comprehensive settlement and reaffirmed earlier resolutions which Norway had voted against.

Sweden explained that the overriding reason for its negative vote was the inclusion of elements aiming at Israel's exclusion from the United Nations; its vote should be interpreted as a vote for a strong United Nations and should in no way be construed as support for various elements of Israel's policy.

Speaking also on behalf of Denmark, France, the Federal Republic of Germany, Italy, Luxembourg, the Netherlands and the United Kingdom, Belgium said the resolution did not reflect the principles they regarded as fundamental. They opposed in particular paragraph 11, saying it might lead to a questioning of Israel's membership status in the United Nations, a negative process for the chances of achieving peace. The measures in paragraphs 8 and 9 sought to isolate Israel and could not contribute to the quest for a peaceful solution; the eight European States also could not associate themselves with the criticism of the exercise of a right a Council member possessed under the Charter. They disagreed in particular with the language in paragraph 10, saying its substance ran counter to the fundamental freedoms contained in the 1948 Universal Declaration of Human Rights.[29] In addition, they regretted that paragraph 15 tied the Secretary-General's action to the implementation of controversial proposals. In their view, the resolution did not respond to the challenge of the Palestine question in all its complexity and seriously departed from the 1967 and 1973 Council resolutions.

Associating itself with Belgium's statement, Ireland said that, despite elements with which it agreed, the resolution would not advance but could hinder a comprehensive settlement.

Portugal said it was prevented from voting in favour by references to third States, and in particular by the unacceptable implications of the language used, which gave the text a scope that might cause acute apprehension against the spirit of universality of the United Nations.

France declared its opposition to any action prejudicial to the principle of universality and deemed it illogical to wish to exclude one of the parties essential to the search for a settlement. Also, the text did not take account of the relevant Charter provisions which laid down the respective competencies and responsibilities of the Security Council and the Assembly.

Canada and Finland said the resolution contained many elements they could not support, particularly paragraph 11 which might be employed to limit Israel's participation in the Assembly and ran counter to the principle of universality. Though Canada felt that the call on the Secretary-General to initiate contacts moved in a positive direction, it could not support the paragraph fully as it attempted to set pre-conditions which were unacceptable to one of the parties and therefore undermined the prospects of success; the basic guidelines for any efforts should continue to be those in the 1967 and 1973 Council resolutions. Finland regretted that the text fell short of its expectations—to recognize Palestinian rights and achieve peace on the basis of the 1967 Council resolution.

Though expressing agreement with a number of elements of the resolution, Austria voted against, saying it neglected Israel's right to exist within safe boundaries and lacked the balance on which any constructive steps towards peace would have to be based. Referring specifically to paragraphs 8 and 10, Austria felt it was clearly beyond Assembly prerogatives to condemn the exercise of the veto of permanent Council members or to attempt to curtail the basic human rights of emigration and choice of residence. Austria also rejected the attempt to put into question Israel's status in the United Nations as a possible interpretation of paragraph 11.

Reservations on the same paragraphs were voiced by Japan which abstained. Also abstaining, Argentina, Bolivia, Ecuador and Thailand did not accept the attempt to expel Israel. Bolivia considered that within an Organization devoted basically to preserving peace, no accusatory or cutting terms should be used against Member States. In Ecuador's opinion, the attempt to disqualify Israel as a Member would dislocate the structure of the Organization and run counter to Article 6 of the Charter (stating that a Member which had persistently violated the Charter principles might be expelled on the recommendation of the Security Council); it would also frustrate the purposes sought in paragraphs 14 and 15.

Thailand believed that for the United Nations to continue to provide the framework for a settlement, the principle of universality must be upheld; also, it was convinced that a settlement acceptable to all parties could be based only on the 1967 Council resolution and other relevant resolutions. Japan had reservations also on the second preambular paragraph—noting with regret and concern that the Council, on 2 and 20 April 1982, at meetings on the Israeli-occupied territories and on the attack against the Islamic Holy Places in Jerusalem, respectively, had failed to take a decision as a result of the negative votes of the United

States—and expressed doubts whether the resolution would contribute to the search for a just solution.

Costa Rica felt that the imbalance of and certain expressions in the text seriously hindered a solution. It especially could not accept paragraphs 8 and 11. With regard to the former, Costa Rica remarked that if the right of veto did not exist, the very existence of the United Nations would be at stake, and no United Nations organ could legitimately even discuss the exercise of that right. As to paragraph 11, Costa Rica considered it an unjust and dangerous anachronism at a time when universality was an accepted principle.

Panama and Peru also had reservations on the language and meaning of some paragraphs. Peru disagreed in particular with the second and eighth preambular paragraphs and operative paragraphs 8 and 11. In its opinion, the resolution did not reflect fundamental elements for a Middle East peace and an impartial approach to a complex situation, and prejudged and indiscriminately condemned the powers of a permanent Council member. Even though some points condemned the Israeli acts in the occupied territories in a broader context, they were none-the-less incompatible with the efforts that should be undertaken on the basis of the 1967 and 1973 Council resolutions.

Chile abstained on the grounds that the resolution was unbalanced and did not contribute to harmonizing the positions of the interested parties. In particular, it had serious reservations on paragraphs 8 to 11 and on the second, third and eighth preambular paragraphs.

Emphasizing its attachment to the use of procedures governing international law and its opposition to the use or threat of force to resolve conflicts, Colombia said it would have liked a more balanced text which took into account not only the negative aspects but also the positive advances, such as the return of the Sinai to Egypt. It felt that there should have been positive elements which would provide the Secretary-General with a basis for acting successfully in bringing about a settlement.

Zaire said that, while accepting most of the stipulations, it could not vote in favour because paragraph 11 created a fundamental imbalance and went far beyond the framework of the discussion; also, it might create a serious precedent and might backfire against one or the other Member State.

Fiji and Spain felt obliged to abstain because of the inclusion of certain critical or negative aspects; Spain did not agree in particular with certain interpretations of the Charter.

Brazil explained that its abstention reflected a divergence on the proceedings that could take place on the basis of the resolution; such proceedings would have to be considered without the necessary legislative authority and their very implementation might fall short of the results the resolution purported to achieve, which would lead to a further deterioration of negotiation possibilities.

Egypt said a resolution that resorted to threat and intimidation was a slow-acting sedative which might calm extreme feelings but would not redress the situation, restore rights and bring peace in the Middle East closer. The text omitted indispensable principles and bases for a solution, such as the 1967 Security Council resolution.

Though voting in favour, Nepal dissociated itself from paragraph 11 and reiterated its view that certain measures called for were the exclusive prerogative of the Council. It would have preferred a different formulation of certain elements in paragraphs 7 and 8. Suriname reserved its position on paragraphs 11 and 4 (the latter demanding that Israel comply with a 1980 Council resolution on Israel's settlements policy[35]); however, it was pleased with the call on the Secretary-General to initiate negotiations with all parties, including PLO.

Greece and Turkey had reservations on paragraph 8. Greece regarded it as not proper to single out one specific case of the exercise of the veto, and Turkey said such condemnations were not likely to bring useful elements to the search for a solution. Turkey also had doubts on the meaning and legal implications of paragraph 11, and could not support the references in the preamble to the negative vote of the United States in the Council.

Togo stressed that its vote in favour should not be interpreted as the taking of any stand on the suspension or possible exclusion of Israel from the United Nations. In addition, it reserved its position on paragraph 11 which, it said, was taken from a resolution on the situation in the occupied territories, adopted in February at the Assembly's ninth emergency special session;[16] Togo believed the situation had evolved a great deal since then, particularly with the return of the Sinai to Egypt on 25 April. It also felt that paragraph 10 prejudged the right of any individual to move freely; with regard to paragraph 7 *(d)*, Togo would have liked a distinction between the act of an individual and the act of a State.

Though supporting the text, Trinidad and Tobago declared that it had difficulties with certain elements. The United Republic of Cameroon regretted that the text did not take note of the 1967 and 1973 Council resolutions outside which there could be no solution. Sierra Leone voted for the resolution in view of Israel's policies and increased military repression in the occupied territories, and the launching of a military attack against Lebanese territory.

Jordan felt that the resolution did not go far enough and would neither alleviate the plight of the Palestinians nor change the irreversible course of Israeli aggression.

Iraq voted in favour, though it believed that the resolution merely reaffirmed previous resolutions which Israel had refused to implement; Iraq would have liked to see measures likely to put an end to the Israeli acts of aggression. It believed that the United States should have been condemned not only because of its veto, but also because of its pursuit of a policy hostile to Palestinians and Arabs and its military and material support to the aggressor. Also, paragraph 15 was not compatible with Iraq's position.

The Syrian Arab Republic believed that the resolution should have explicitly condemned the United States for its support to Israel and should have imposed sanctions against both countries. Also, paragraph 5 was not clear, and those of ill will—Egypt, Israel and the United States—could interpret it outside its true context, namely, the rights of the Palestinians.

The Libyan Arab Jamahiriya felt that, although representing collective support for the Palestinians, the resolution did not meet the demands of the majority of States which had condemned Israel's aggressive actions and crimes; no action had been taken to punish the aggressor and expel it from the United Nations, even though its very existence was no more legitimate than had been the existence of the Smith régime in Zimbabwe. The Libyan Arab Jamahiriya stressed that paragraph 15 should not be understood to imply recognition of the legitimacy of Israeli occupation or of the Nazi Zionist entity.

Democratic Yemen reserved its position on paragraphs 1 and 15, on the grounds that they contained an indirect reference to the 1967 Council resolution.

Referring to reservations by several States, PLO said the exercise of the veto was nowhere challenged, only its misuse condemned. With regard to the 1967 and 1973 Council resolutions, PLO asked how they could provide for peace when the right to self-determination of the Palestinians was not taken into consideration. Concerning the initiation of contacts by the Secretary-General, PLO believed that he did not need the support and concurrence of the Security Council for his endeavours. PLO regretted that the Assembly failed to discharge its task and to honour its first purpose, namely, the suppression of acts of aggression.

During the debate, Senegal, speaking as Chairman of the Committee on Palestinian rights, pointed to the need to defuse a dangerous situation by seeing to it that the Palestinians achieved their inalienable rights, in particular in view of Israel's seeming to step up its annexation process.

In the view of PLO, the emergency special session would not have been necessary had the United

States not prevented the Security Council from punishing Israel for pursuing its war against the Palestinians and its occupation of Arab territories. The Palestinians, however, would fight for their right to exist on their land until complete Israeli withdrawal. In this context, PLO appealed to the Council to take measures for the protection of the Palestinians and their land.

As a result of Israel's persistence in a policy of aggression, expansion and oppression, China stated, tension in the Middle East had been aggravated, making a resumption of the session necessary. A similar position was held by others, among them Albania, Algeria, Argentina, Bangladesh, Burundi, Cyprus, Czechoslovakia, Djibouti, the German Democratic Republic, Ghana, Hungary, India, Iraq, Jordan, Malaysia, Mali, Malta, Mongolia, Poland, Saudi Arabia, the Sudan, the Syrian Arab Republic, Togo, the USSR, the United Arab Emirates, the United Republic of Cameroon, Venezuela and Yugoslavia. In view of the deteriorating situation, Japan and the Philippines held the discussion of the Palestine question most timely.

Democratic Yemen said it was not surprised that both Israel and the United States had strong reservations about the resumption of the session, as obviously the United States would prefer to have the Palestine and Middle East questions dealt with exclusively in the Security Council, where it used its veto power to block even the most reasonable resolutions.

Speaking for the European Community (EC) members, Belgium stated that any solution to the Palestine question implied the reconciliation of two realities, the State of Israel and the Palestinians. Sweden said PLO must recognize Israel's right to exist within secure and recognized borders, just as Israel must recognize the rights of the Palestinians, including the right to establish an independent State. A similar position was held by Bangladesh, Czechoslovakia, Fiji, Finland, Hungary, India, Japan, Nicaragua, Poland, Tunisia, Turkey and others.

Mutual recognition, the Philippines stated, would enable the parties to resolve their differences and learn to live in peaceful coexistence.

New Zealand saw little chance for real progress towards a settlement until Israel was prepared to respect the rights and interests of the other States and peoples of the region and until it came to terms with the concept of an independent Arab Palestinian State; at the same time, there was no prospect of worthwhile negotiations unless all parties were prepared formally to recognize Israel's right to exist.

Israel said the fact that two States had been established on the territory of the former Palestine Mandate, the Palestinian Arab State Jordan and the Palestinian Jewish State Israel, was central to any discussion of the Arab-Israeli conflict; the cause of the conflict was the Arabs' refusal to recognize Israel's right to exist.

The Philippines felt that Israel's intransigence was a direct effect of its concern over its safety and its right to exist within secure and recognized boundaries.

Romania supported the call of the non-aligned countries in Kuwait in April that the Secretary-General should undertake contacts with the parties towards a settlement, and Togo considered it even a turning-point. Zambia commended the efforts of the non-aligned countries, and Indonesia urged the Assembly to endorse the programme of action adopted at that meeting.

In the opinion of the United Republic of Cameroon, the fate of the Palestinians, reduced to stateless refugees, was the very heart of the Middle East problem, a view shared by Fiji and others. Angola, Djibouti, Finland, Ghana, Madagascar, Mali, Mexico, New Zealand, Norway, the United Republic of Cameroon and many others believed that no viable peace could be achieved without the restoration of Palestinian rights. Mexico declared its strong support for any decisions aimed at guaranteeing the full exercise of those rights.

The absence of progress in a Palestinian solution could lead only to an increasingly dangerous situation in the region and throughout the world, Romania believed. A similar view was expressed by Djibouti, Madagascar and Mali. The failure to find a solution, Ghana thought, would be to acquiesce directly in the further violation of Palestinian and Arab rights.

Failure to recognize Palestinian rights, Nepal said, had led to violence and human tragedy on a great scale, and in Yugoslavia's opinion, the Palestine question was reaching a turning-point.

A basic corollary of the restoration of Palestinian rights, Nigeria said, was the recognition of PLO as representative of the Palestinians, a view shared by many other speakers, among them Afghanistan, Argentina, Bangladesh, Djibouti, Madagascar, Malaysia, Pakistan, Uganda and Zambia. Sri Lanka considered Israel's refusal to recognize PLO as the truest manifestation of the authenticity of PLO. In the opinion of the United Republic of Cameroon, the recent events in the West Bank and Gaza demonstrated that it was futile to attempt to separate the Palestinians from their sole authentic representative.

New Zealand believed that major obstacles to a solution would remain until PLO was acknowledged by all principal parties, and Yemen said if the United States truly desired to establish peace in the Middle East, it behoved it first to recognize PLO.

Participation of PLO in any peace negotiations was also advocated by Belgium (for the EC members).

Afghanistan, Argentina, Austria, Bhutan, Brazil, Bulgaria, the Byelorussian SSR, Czechoslovakia, Fiji, Finland, Hungary, India, Japan, Mali, Mongolia, Nigeria, the Philippines, Romania, Togo, the Ukrainian SSR, the USSR, Venezuela and others stated that a comprehensive, just and lasting Middle East settlement required unconditional Israeli withdrawal from the occupied territories; implementation of Palestinian rights, including the right to establish their own State; and the guarantee of the security and sovereignty of all States of the region, including Israel. Israeli withdrawal and recognition of Palestinian rights was considered a prerequisite for a settlement by most other countries, including Bangladesh, Jordan, Malaysia, Mauritius, Nepal, the Sudan, the Syrian Arab Republic, Turkey, Uganda, the United Republic of Cameroon, Viet Nam and Yugoslavia.

While Afghanistan, Albania, Algeria, Bulgaria, Czechoslovakia, the Libyan Arab Jamahiriya, Seychelles, the Ukrainian SSR, the USSR and others believed that the Camp David accords, ignoring the question of self-determination of the Palestinians, had created new obstacles to a Middle East settlement, the United States regarded them as the greatest concrete step towards peace in the history of the Arab-Israeli conflict; however, it added, a great distance remained to be travelled towards real peace in accordance with the 1967 and 1973 Security Council resolutions.

Reiterating its commitment to the Camp David accords and the establishment of a comprehensive peace based on the recognition of Palestinian rights, as well as rejecting Israel's policies in the occupied territories, Egypt saw the Israeli withdrawal from the Sinai as a significant step forward in the peace process and as a new incentive to continue the march towards justice and sovereignty of all countries and peoples in the area.

The Egypt-Israel peace treaty and Israel's withdrawal from the Sinai were welcomed by a number of speakers, among them Austria, Japan, Mauritius, New Zealand, Norway, the Philippines and Sweden. For the first time, Sweden stated, there existed a recognized international border between Israel and one of its neighbours. For the first time in nearly two decades, Malta said, Israeli-occupied territory had been returned, a restitution that was overdue and did not generate the right to compensation by expansion in other illegally occupied territory.

While the Philippines saw the return of the Sinai to Egypt as a point of departure for possible peaceful agreements in other areas of the region, Austria expressed regret that Israel showed no intention of taking similar steps with regard to other occupied territories, and Japan pointed out that the Palestinian autonomy talks had not achieved the hoped-for progress. Finland said a comprehensive Middle East peace seemed as remote as ever.

Democratic Yemen, on the other hand, considered the withdrawal the dead end of the Camp David path, with Israeli forces terminating their occupation but leaving behind American soldiers and a neutralized Egypt. Iraq said there was every indication that the Camp David accords had died with Israel's withdrawal from the Sinai and with the failure of the capitulationist policy which had brought Egypt isolation and weakness against Israel. Yemen maintained that the peace between Egypt and Israel was about to collapse any day because it ignored the Palestine problem and Palestinian rights. A similar position was held by several others, including Seychelles. Jordan said Israel's withdrawal from the Sinai had been made conditional on giving Israeli aggression a more or less free hand in obliterating the existence of the Palestinians, and the Byelorussian SSR considered Israel's aggressive actions a direct outcome of the policies of separate deals.

The United States wondered if it would have been too much to expect the Assembly to welcome the signing of the peace treaty and Israel's withdrawal as a momentous step towards a Middle East peace; the peace treaty had been achieved according to the 1967 Security Council resolution, a process which stood in stark contrast to the approach that insisted on Israeli withdrawal in the absence of peace.

Primarily due to United States support, Cuba stated, Israel had been able to disregard United Nations resolutions and to continue its aggressive and expansionist policy, a view shared by Afghanistan, Bahrain, Burundi, the Byelorussian SSR, Czechoslovakia, the German Democratic Republic, Iran, Iraq, Kuwait, Mongolia, Nicaragua, Nigeria, Qatar, Saudi Arabia, the United Arab Emirates and Viet Nam, among others. The stepped-up involvement of external forces in the region, India said, could hardly be conducive to a relaxation of tension; in Albania's view, Israel benefited from the difficulties created for the Arabs because of the Middle East rivalry and bargaining between the two imperialist super-Powers.

The United States sheltering of Israel from international censure of its policies, Pakistan and others believed, only served to aggravate the already explosive Middle East situation. The misuse of one of the Security Council's primary powers was far more dangerous than missiles, Mauritius said. The Libyan Arab Jamahiriya said amendment of the Charter and abolition of the veto must be considered.

Due to the United States veto, the Lao People's Democratic Republic stated, the Council had been unable to carry out its mandate and had failed to take a decision on Palestinian rights. The United States veto demonstrated Washington's direct participation in Israel's anti-Arab aggression, the USSR said. Indonesia and Nicaragua saw in the veto an encouragement of the escalation of Israeli violence and oppression. In Burundi's opinion, a Palestine solution had been delayed because of the interests pursued by the imperialist Powers.

Turkey called on Israel's friends to exercise their influence to impel it to stop its aggression, and Nicaragua believed that the United States must seriously review its policy towards Israel.

In view of Israel's refusal to implement United Nations resolutions and its continued occupation of Arab territories, China called for enforcement measures, including sanctions, a call supported by Afghanistan, the Byelorussian SSR, Cuba, Djibouti, the German Democratic Republic, Ghana, India, Iraq, the Lao People's Democratic Republic, Mongolia, Morocco, Pakistan, the Sudan, the Syrian Arab Republic, Tunisia, the United Arab Emirates, Viet Nam and Yugoslavia. In addition, India called for individual action by States to isolate Israel in all fields. Enforcement measures were also called for by Saudi Arabia, Seychelles and Tunisia. If Israel persisted in its lawlessness, Pakistan believed, the Security Council must act firmly in view of its primary responsibility for the maintenance of international peace and security. Mali said the provisions of Chapter VII of the Charter should be applicable to any Member State that imperilled peace. Malaysia held it imperative that the international community did its utmost to obliterate the injustice against the Palestinians.

Holding the Security Council fully responsible for all that happened on Palestinian land, PLO appealed to it to take the necessary measures for the protection of the Palestinians and their land, and to ensure Israel's full withdrawal.

Many speakers, among them Cyprus, Malaysia and Pakistan, saw in the 1976 recommendations of the Committee on Palestinian rights[36] a firm basis for a solution to the Palestine problem. The German Democratic Republic, Turkey, Yugoslavia and Zambia called for endorsement of these recommendations by the Security Council as a concrete step towards a just and durable settlement. Malta considered such endorsement a positive step towards ending the cycle of violence; the process recommended by the Committee advocated a role for the Council where all parties to the Middle East conflict were represented.

In Angola's opinion, an international mechanism was needed to oversee the delivery of justice to the Palestinians. Romania reiterated its suggestion that a committee of Member States undertake efforts to achieve a Middle East settlement.

Brazil felt that the only alternative to the use of force was to resort fully to United Nations mechanisms. Argentina said the United Nations had a fundamental role to play and could not shirk its responsibilities, a view shared by Ghana. Bangladesh, Fiji, Finland, Japan and others saw the framework for a comprehensive settlement in various United Nations resolutions. In Jordan's view, the only legally binding decisions on the future of Palestine were the 1947 plan for the partition of Palestine[27] and the 1948 resolution establishing the Conciliation Commission for Palestine,[28] which provided for a Palestinian Arab State and a Jewish State and for the right of the Palestinians to return; Israel's admittance to United Nations membership in 1949[30] had been conditional on its acceptance of those resolutions. Iran, however, felt that the partition resolution was a conspiracy and without validity from the very beginning and that its reference to the maintenance of peace had been a deception to manipulate the United Nations.

A settlement could best be achieved through an international conference under United Nations auspices with the participation of all interested parties, including PLO, Czechoslovakia and Hungary believed. As a first step towards a settlement, Austria thought, direct talks without any pre-condition should be initiated between Israel and PLO. Negotiations between the parties concerned were also advocated by the Philippines and Sweden.

Romania supported the call of the non-aligned countries at the Kuwait meeting that the Secretary-General undertake contacts with the parties towards a settlement. That approach, Togo believed, was likely to be a decisive turning-point. Zambia commended the programme of action adopted at the Kuwait meeting and Indonesia urged the Assembly to endorse it.

General Assembly action (June). At the request of the Movement of Non-Aligned Countries, conveyed by Cuba as its current Chairman, the General Assembly again resumed its seventh emergency special session on 25 and 26 June, mainly to consider the situation resulting from Israel's invasion of Lebanon.

Reaffirming its conviction that the Palestine question was the core of the Arab-Israeli conflict and that no comprehensive, just and lasting peace settlement would be achieved without the full exercise by the Palestinians of their inalienable rights and without PLO participation, the Assembly, by a resolution of 26 June,[11] supported the Security Council demands that Israel withdraw from Lebanon and that all military activities cease within Lebanon and across the Lebanese-Israeli border. It again decided to adjourn the session temporarily and authorized its President to resume its meetings upon request.

During the debate, PLO charged that the aim of Israel's acts of aggression, particularly in Lebanon, was the elimination of the Palestinians and PLO, a view shared by many others. Yugoslavia said the only way out of the vicious circle and towards a peaceful settlement was the recognition for the Palestinians of the rights which all peoples enjoyed. Indonesia believed that a Middle East solution could never be achieved until the Palestinians regained their rights.

General Assembly action (August). In view of the situation in Lebanon, the General Assembly again resumed its emergency special session on 16 August and adopted three resolutions on 19 August. The request to reconvene the session by the end of August had been made by an Extraordinary Ministerial Meeting of the Co-ordinating Bureau of the Non-Aligned Countries on the Palestine question (Nicosia, Cyprus, 15-17 July), and was contained in a final communiqué and programme of action transmitted to the Secretary-General by Cyprus on 29 July.[2]

By the first resolution,[12] the Assembly called for the free exercise in Palestine of the rights of the Palestinians to self-determination and national independence—a paragraph adopted by 107 votes to 5, with 26 abstentions. It reaffirmed its rejection of policies and plans to resettle the Palestinians outside their homeland and called again on the Secretary-General to initiate contacts with all parties to the Arab-Israeli conflict, including PLO, with a view to convening an international conference on ways of achieving a just and lasting solution.

By other provisions, the Assembly demanded that Israel carry out United Nations resolutions on the occupied territories and the Security Council resolutions on the Israel-Lebanon situation, and urged the Council, in the event of Israel's continued failure to comply, to consider the application of relevant Charter provisions. The Secretary-General was urged to take measures to guarantee the security of Palestinian and Lebanese civilians in South Lebanon, and to investigate Israel's application of international instruments in the case of detained persons.

By the second resolution,[13] the Assembly decided to convene an International Conference on the Question of Palestine in Paris in August 1983. By the third,[14] it decided to commemorate 4 June of each year as the International Day of Innocent Children Victims of Aggression.

Israel rejected the first resolution as another attempt to undermine the peace process and its only agreed basis, the 1967[33] and 1973[34] Security Council resolutions.

Haiti felt obliged to abstain in view of the imminent ending of the Lebanese crisis.

Also abstaining, Sweden regretted that the resolution did not address itself directly to the situation in Lebanon and did not reaffirm the inviolability of Lebanon's sovereignty and territorial integrity. Some provisions were unacceptable to it, in particular paragraph 2 as it could be interpreted that Israel as a State should be eliminated, and paragraph 4 which reaffirmed a number of resolutions which Sweden had been unable to support.

Canada could not accept the assertion that the Palestine question was the core of the Arab-Israeli dispute; it did not agree that the Assembly was the appropriate body to determine the existence of a threat to peace, breach of peace or act of aggression, and could not endorse the implied status regarding PLO as the only representative of the Palestinians. Concerning paragraphs 2 (on which it cast a negative vote) and 11, Canada did not want to advocate specific options regarding the nature of the homeland, which would have to be settled through negotiations, and it did not believe that an international conference would currently promote a comprehensive settlement.

New Zealand felt that the resolution ignored many elements of the interrelated fates of the Lebanese and Palestinians; it had particular difficulties with paragraphs 2, 4, 6, 9 and 11.

Norway had reservations about the wording of certain paragraphs and felt that the resolution did not strike the balance between the interests of the parties needed for progress towards a just and lasting solution and tended to prejudice the outcome of future negotiations.

For the EC members, Denmark expressed agreement with the general thrust of the text but considered that it did not reflect the necessary balance on which a just and lasting settlement must be based.

Ireland added that it abstained with some regret; however, it felt that it could not vote in favour of a text asserting the Palestinians' right to self-determination, including the right to an independent State, without reference to the principle of the right of all States, including Israel, to live in peace.

France deemed the resolution not timely under current conditions; it also believed that several formulations impinged on the Security Council's competence.

Australia was unable to support a number of aspects of the resolution, particularly paragraphs 2 (on which it cast a negative vote) and 4, and considered that no account had been taken of the stage reached in the negotiations for a settlement in Lebanon.

Though voting in favour of the text as a whole, Fiji abstained on paragraph 2; it believed that any settlement arising out of the exercise by the Palestinians of their right to self-determination should recognize the right of all States, including Israel, to exist within secure boundaries. Honduras, on the other hand, expressed the opinion that the free exercise of the Palestinian right to self-determination did not imply ignoring Israel's right to exist within its own clearly defined frontiers.

Also voting in favour but abstaining on paragraph 2, Austria regretted that the resolution did not take into account the most recent development, especially the efforts of the United States, and contained a number of formulations that lacked clarity or might have legal or political implications that could complicate future efforts.

Burma stressed reservations on the wording and formulation of operative paragraph 11 and the second and tenth preambular paragraphs. To be consistent with its past stand on specific aspects, Burma had found it necessary to abstain in the vote on paragraph 2.

Declaring that its affirmative vote did not affect its position on the Palestine question, Japan stated difficulties with the wording and content of paragraphs 2 and 11 in particular. In connection with paragraph 2, on which it abstained, Japan felt that reference should have been made to the principles for a Middle East peace, adopted by the Council in 1967[33] and 1973.[34]

Singapore also expressed support for these principles and stressed that, in its understanding, paragraph 2 referred to the Israeli-occupied West Bank and Gaza, and that one element of lasting peace would be the recognition of the right of all States, including Israel, to existence and security.

Uruguay reserved its position on the Assembly resolutions on the occupied territories mentioned in paragraph 4, saying it had not supported them at the time of their adoption; in addition, it emphasized that the Assembly could not encroach on the Council's competence by adopting measures exclusively in the latter's purview.

Paraguay regretted that the text did not fully answer the need for measures to alleviate the suffering of the people of Lebanon as well as to guarantee its territorial integrity and independence.

Spain felt that the resolution was moderate and realistic and put forward a number of praiseworthy ideas, in both political and humanitarian terms. Panama said the text coincided with its own position. Ecuador felt that the machinery for the peaceful settlement of disputes needed to be strengthened and considered it unacceptable that repeated United Nations decisions continued to be ignored.

Turkey stressed that its vote in favour should be understood in the light of its established Middle East policy, particularly given the fact that there existed certain elements in the text which lacked clarity in terms of their implications and consequences.

Colombia voted for the resolution as it held necessary the quest for a just solution through talks involving all parties and it thought that account should be taken of the interests and obligations of the parties, together with respect for Israel's existence and rights. Though stating reservations on certain formulations and abstaining on paragraph 2, Finland saw the resolution as an expression of universal indignation at Israel's military actions in Lebanon and as a serious effort to call for a new and decisive United Nations effort to reach an agreement on the entire Middle East problem, not only a just solution of the Palestine question.

Chile also supported the text saying it was consistent with its basic approach of not accepting the use of force in settling international disputes. However, it had reservations on certain preambular and operative paragraphs which did not include all Palestinians, implied excessive condemnation and called for actions impinging prerogatives within the exclusive competence of the Security Council, and it believed that the inclusion of a reference to the 1967 and 1973 Council resolutions would have been a very positive step.

Iran felt that the resolution could have been much stronger and more constructive by punishing the Zionist usurpers and by including the right to payment of war reparations and the right of the Syrian supporters.

The Syrian Arab Republic would have wished a firm condemnation of Israel and the reaffirmation that it was not a peace-loving State, as well as a call on Israel to be a good neighbour and a reiteration that numerous States had broken off their relations with Israel as a last resort.

Reservations on the paragraph calling for contacts with a view to convening a conference were expressed by Albania, Democratic Yemen and the Libyan Arab Jamahiriya. Democratic Yemen emphasized that its affirmative vote was based on the understanding that the reference to "relevant resolutions" did not include the 1967 Security Council resolution. Albania declared its opposition to plans by the imperialist super-Powers to convene meetings and conferences on the Middle East situation and the Palestine problem. The Libyan Arab Jamahiriya said its attitute towards an international conference was well known.

In addition, Albania voiced reservations to references in the text to certain Council resolutions which it deemed harmful to the just struggle of the Palestinians, in particular provisions that tended to put on an equal footing the aggressor and its victim. In the view of the Libyan Arab Jamahiriya, the text was a strict minimum and did not reflect in detail the ideas expressed during the session; the Assembly ought to have taken effective action against Israel by expelling it and ought to have condemned United States policy designed to encourage Israel.

During the debate, China, Cuba, the Libyan Arab Jamahiriya, Nicaragua, Nigeria, Viet Nam and others expressed the conviction that the heroic struggle of the Palestinians would eventually triumph. Turkey said Israel's policies of aggression, suppression and annexation could not weaken the Palestinians' determination to exercise their rights, a view shared by Democratic Yemen, Mauritania and others. Indonesia said PLO remained the soul and conscience of the Palestinians. In Cuba's view, any agreement or initiative that did not take PLO into account was treachery.

General Assembly action (September). At a one-meeting resumption of the seventh emergency special session on 24 September, the General Assembly adopted a resolution[15] urging the Security Council to investigate the circumstances and extent of the massacre of Palestinians and other civilians in Beirut on 17 September, demanded respect for Lebanon's sovereignty and independence, supported Council demands for Israel's withdrawal and cessation of military activities in Lebanon, and urged the Council to consider practical ways and means in accordance with the Charter in the event of Israel's continued failure to comply with those demands. The Assembly resolved that the Palestine refugees should be enabled to return to their homes and property, and called for humanitarian aid to the victims of the Israeli invasion. The session was again adjourned temporarily and the Assembly President was authorized to resume meetings upon request from Member States.

Though voting in favour, Chile, Guatemala and Uruguay expressed reservations on the call for practical means in the case of Israel's non-compliance, saying it infringed on the Council's prerogatives. Uruguay had similar reservations on the seventh preambular paragraph.

Canada, Denmark (also speaking for Belgium, France, the Federal Republic of Germany, Italy, Luxembourg, the Netherlands and the United Kingdom), Ireland and Norway had reservations on a mention in the preamble of the PLO statement during the debate.

Costa Rica said that, as long as the Palestinians did not have a State in which they could live in peace, there would be no definitive solution to the Palestine question. Canada, Denmark (again also for the seven Western European States), Haiti, Ireland, New Zealand and Norway voiced reservations on the paragraph stating that the Palestine refugees should be enabled to return to their homes and property.

Democratic Yemen would have liked the resolution to contain a clear condemnation of Israel and the United States. Iran deemed the resolu-

tion to be very reticent; it expected a stronger and more explicit statement that the Zionist base of imperialism must be destroyed, and said there was no Palestine problem, rather the problem of the Zionist régime. Iraq said its favourable vote should not be construed as a change in its position on settlement of the Palestinian question. The Libyan Arab Jamahiriya believed that the resolution was not an appropriate response to Israel's crimes; the United Nations must impose comprehensive sanctions and expel Israel so that the Palestinians could return to their territory and create their own independent State.

By a letter of 22 September to the Assembly President,[4] Israel stated that there was no basis for holding an emergency special session simultaneously with the regular session, particularly as the item to be dealt with was on the agenda of the regular session.

Activities of the Committee on Palestinian rights. The Committee on the Exercise of the Inalienable Rights of the Palestinian People continued throughout 1982 to follow developments in the territories occupied by Israel and actions by Israel which the Committee regarded as violations of international law or of United Nations resolutions.

In a number of letters to the Secretary-General and the President of the Security Council, the Committee Chairman drew attention to Israeli plans to evacuate Palestinian Bedouins from the Negev Desert, requested decisive steps to protect the rights of the Palestinians in the West Bank and Gaza, drew attention to Israeli actions against Palestinian demonstrators and expressed concern at the Israeli decision to dissolve the elected municipal council of two West Bank towns. He called for action to end Israel's invasion of Lebanon, expressed extreme concern at the massacre of Palestinians in the Shatila and Sabra refugee camps near Beirut, called attention to Israeli plans to establish new settlements in the West Bank and expressed concern at the closing of Bir Zeit University.

In its September report to the General Assembly,[8] the Committee again expressed its conviction that positive action by the Security Council on the Committee's recommendations, which constituted the basic principles for a solution to the Palestine problem, would advance prospects for a just and lasting peace. It therefore unanimously decided to reiterate the validity of the recommendations it had first made in 1976[36] and which had been repeatedly endorsed by the Assembly. (These called, among other things, for the establishment by the Council of a timetable for Israeli withdrawal, a United Nations take-over of the evacuated territories, handing them over to PLO as representative of the Palestinians, and the establishment of an independent Palestinian entity.) The Committee expressed its conviction that the repression of Palestinians in the occupied territories, as well as the tragic events in Lebanon, could have been avoided if the Council had taken timely and positive action on those recommendations.

The Committee met at United Nations Headquarters on 29 November in observance of the International Day of Solidarity with the Palestinian People. The New York meeting and a similar one at Geneva were addressed by a number of United Nations officials and government representatives.

With the Committee's participation, three seminars on the Palestine question were organized in 1982 by the United Nations Secretariat's Special Unit on Palestinian Rights (redesignated in August as the Division for Palestinian Rights).

The first North American seminar (New York, 15-19 March) included in its report a suggestion that a better organized campaign be made on behalf of the Palestinian aspect at various levels, particularly through non-governmental organizations, since only an elementary awareness of the question had been reached in North America. The second seminar (Valletta, Malta, 12-16 April) adopted a programme of action and an appeal to Western European Governments for justice in Palestine, and the Western European participants addressed an appeal for a Western European initiative in the Near East. The third seminar (Dakar, Senegal, 9-13 August) addressed several recommendations to the Committee, including one that it consider the utility and viability of convening a war crimes tribunal to assess Israel's conduct of hostilities. The reports of the seminars were annexed to the Committee's report to the Assembly.

Presenting the Committee's report to the Assembly, the Rapporteur said that against Israeli repression and violence which had run riot in the occupied territories, the Security Council had remained immobilized and it did not take Israel too long to go even further and launch a massive military incursion against Palestinians and civilians in Lebanon. As a last resort, the Committee recommended holding an international conference on the Palestine question in 1983, earlier than originially planned.

General Assembly action (December). In December, at its 1982 regular session, the General Assembly adopted five resolutions on the Palestine question.

By one of these,[22] of 10 December, the Assembly again reaffirmed that a comprehensive, just and lasting Middle East peace could not be established without unconditional Israeli withdrawal from the occupied territories, including Jerusalem, and without the exercise and attainment of Palestinian rights. The Assembly requested the Secu-

rity Council to discharge its responsibilities under the United Nations Charter and to recognize those rights, including the rights to self-determination and the establishment of an independent Arab State in Palestine. The Assembly reiterated its request that the Council take measures to implement the plan recommending the establishment of such a State.

This resolution was adopted by a recorded vote of 113 to 4, with 23 abstentions. It was sponsored by 22 nations and introduced by Malta, as Rapporteur of the Committee on Palestinian rights.

Palestinian rights were reaffirmed by the Assembly in another resolution, adopted on 20 December.[23] Stating that the internationally accepted principles relevant to the Palestine question—including the right of all States in the region to exist within internationally recognized boundaries, and justice and security for all peoples—required the recognition and attainment of the Palestinians' rights, the Assembly demanded Israel's complete and unconditional withdrawal from the occupied territories, to be followed by a short transitional period of United Nations supervision during which the Palestinians would exercise self-determination. It urgently called for a comprehensive, just and lasting peace, based on resolutions of the United Nations and under its auspices, with the participation of all parties, including PLO, on an equal footing. It recommended that the Security Council take early action to promote a just and comprehensive solution. The Assembly declared Israeli policies and practices aimed at annexing the occupied territories to be in violation of international law.

This resolution was adopted by a recorded vote of 123 to 2, with 19 abstentions. It was sponsored and revised by 25 States, including 18 of the 23 members of the Committee on Palestinian rights, and was introduced by Senegal, Chairman of the Committee.

By the three other resolutions on the Palestine question, adopted on 10 December, the Assembly again endorsed the 1976 recommendations of the Committee and requested it to keep the situation under review;[19] requested the Secretary-General to ensure that the Secretariat's Division for Palestinian Rights continued to discharge its tasks;[20] and endorsed recommendations on preparations for the 1983 International Conference on the Question of Palestine.[21] In the last resolution, the Assembly also called on Member States to contribute to the achievement of Palestinian rights and to support modalities for their implementation.

Aspects of the Palestine question were dealt with in four other resolutions adopted by the Assembly in December 1982.

In a resolution of 3 December on the self-determination of peoples,[17] the Assembly strongly condemned Israel's expansionist activities and the continual bombing of Palestinians, and urged States and organizations to support the Palestinians through PLO, as their sole and legitimate representative, in their struggle for self-determination and independence.

In another resolution of the same date,[18] the Assembly expressed grave concern at Israel's policy of defiance of basic principles and objectives of the International Convention on the Elimination of All Forms of Racial Discrimination,[31] and called for the respect and preservation of the national and cultural identity of the Palestinian people. This paragraph was adopted in the Third (Social, Humanitarian and Cultural) Committee by a recorded vote of 98 to 16, with 20 abstentions.

In a resolution of 10 December on United Nations public information activities,[24] the Assembly requested the preparation by the Secretariat of a documented summary account of world media coverage of developments affecting the Palestinians from June to December.

Finally, by a 20 December resolution on the Middle East situation,[25] the Assembly reaffirmed that the Palestine question was the core of the Middle East conflict and that no comprehensive, just and lasting peace would be achieved without the full exercise by the Palestinians of their inalienable national rights and Israel's immediate, unconditional and total withdrawal from the occupied territories.

Introducing the 22-nation draft, Malta said it took into account the developments in the area as well as the recently reiterated PLO declaration that it would pursue its role in a solution to the Palestine question on the basis of the attainment in Palestine of the inalienable rights of the Palestinian people in accordance with United Nations resolutions.

Israel opposed the resolution, saying it attempted to set back the clock of history 35 years. The Arabs could not ask for what they had destroyed by armed force in 1947 and 1948, and the spurned proposals of the 1947 partition resolution[27] could not now be resurrected into reality.

Also casting a negative vote, Canada found the reference in the preamble to the 1947 partition plan inappropriate and could not accept the reaffirmations of certain political objectives; the nature of the Palestinian homeland and its relations to its neighbours should not be prejudged, but should be decided by the parties through negotiations. Costa Rica voted against because it thought that the call for unconditional withdrawal interfered with the work of the Security Council and was not in line with the search for a constructive solution within the framework of the Council resolutions of 1967[33] and 1973[34] setting out the principles for a Middle East peace.

In the opinion of the United States, the resolution sought to define in advance the nature of a solution, when this could come only through negotiations by the parties and could not be dictated by the Council; it spoke of the need for unconditional Israeli withdrawal, when withdrawal would be part of a comprehensive peace to be worked out by the parties; and it lacked balance, making demands on and ascribing sinister motives to one party while affirming alleged rights of another, and failing to call on any other party to make the concessions necessary for negotiations to commence.

Abstaining, Australia considered it inappropriate to prejudge the outcome of negotiations on a settlement and believed that some wording in the resolution would not assist in constructive efforts. Japan abstained because the text did not refer to the 1967 and 1973 Council resolutions, specify the geographical area of the proposed State or refer to Israel's right to exist. In New Zealand's view, the resolution did not adequately reflect the balance of principles in the 1967 resolution.

Explaining the abstentions of the EC members, Denmark said they had important reservations on those elements which were not in accordance with their common position on principles for a comprehensive settlement and considered that the approach to a solution should have been more balanced. Greece did not like the wording of the paragraph requesting implementation of the plan for an Arab State in Palestine; while it supported the establishment of an independent State, it maintained also that Israel should live sovereign and secure within the boundaries shaped before 1967.

Norway believed that the resolution, like the others presented on the Palestine question, did not reflect the balance between the interests of the parties necessary to achieve a just and lasting peace; Norway supported the right of the Palestinians to self-determination but thought that principle must be transformed into reality through negotiation. Finland also found the resolutions unbalanced. Portugal abstained owing to procedural and conceptual reservations on the requests to the Security Council. Sweden considered that the resolution ignored the need to resolve the conflict through negotiations.

Though voting in favour, Albania observed that it disagreed with or had reservations on some past resolutions on the Palestine question and the Middle East situation, and said it consequently had reservations on the unspecific mention of such texts in paragraphs 1 and 5. Iran said the establishment of justice and lasting peace simply implied elimination of the result of the original aggression, namely, the illicit creation of the Zionist base in the area. The Libyan Arab Jamahiriya opposed the references in the preamble to the 1947 partition resolution[27] and the 1948 resolution establishing a conciliation Commission for Palestine,[28] as well as any other reference which might be construed to imply recognition of the Zionist entity.

Austria voted for the resolution on the ground that it incorporated essential elements on which there was wide international agreement, relating to secure boundaries, Palestinian self-determination and Israeli withdrawal. Spain, though voting in favour, would have preferred recommendations instead of requests to the Council, as only the Council could adopt measures in cases jeopardizing international peace and security; it would have abstained on those paragraphs if there had been a separate vote. Speaking of the same paragraphs, Uruguay felt they safeguarded the Council's competence in accordance with the Charter. Jamaica stated that its vote in favour was in accord with its policy, which consistently advocated Israeli withdrawal and recognition of Palestinian rights to statehood as well as of the right of every State in the area to live in peace and security within internationally recognized boundaries.

Singapore supported both the 22- and 25-nation texts on the understanding that the request to implement the plan for an independent Arab State in Palestine referred to the Israeli-occupied West Bank and Gaza Strip.

The 25-nation draft resolution was revised by its sponsors to have the Assembly call for the achievement of peace based on United Nations resolutions and under its auspices, instead of having it call for negotiations aimed at a comprehensive, just and lasting peace based on United Nations resolutions.

Introducing the revised text, Senegal said it had been changed in the light of the views expressed during consultations with various parties and particularly in the light of the primary objective, the restoration of peace, for which certain preconditions had to be met, such as: participation of all interested parties in negotiations, respect for international law and conventions with regard to occupation, Israeli withdrawal from all the occupied territories, and the role of the Security Council in the process of Israeli withdrawal.

Israel rejected the resolution as an attempt at political warfare and as detrimental to the idea of conciliation, undermining the peace process and degrading the principles of the United Nations. The text tampered with and sought to isolate in a selective and deliberately distorted manner elements of the 1967 Security Council resolution which, together with the 1973 Council resolution, constituted the only agreed framework for a peaceful settlement. The resolution deliberately ignored the inalienable rights of Israel and the Jewish people, and the sole purpose of some ostensibly non-

controversial provisions was to mislead certain well-intentioned, if not naïve, observers of the Middle East scene.

The United States opposed the text because of its selective approach; however, it applauded the fact that the resolution explicitly recalled the right of all States to exist within recognized borders, even as it also recognized the need to meet the rights and requirements of the Palestinians.

Albania did not participate in the vote because of what it regarded as certain inaccurate and complicated elements, such as the recalling of numerous past resolutions and documents, some of which it disapproved of or had reservations on.

Among those abstaining, Canada, though welcoming the mention of the right of all States in the region to existence and security, thought the call for complete and unconditional Israeli withdrawal did not reflect the spirit or letter of the Security Council's 1973 resolution and would not promote a negotiated settlement.

Speaking on behalf of the EC members, Denmark said that, while they welcomed the efforts to introduce new elements reflecting a more balanced approach, they abstained because of important reservations on elements not in accordance with their position on principles for a comprehensive settlement; specifically, the reference in the preamble to the right of all States in the region to exist within internationally recognized boundaries should have stated that this included Israel, and an explicit reference to negotiations should have been retained in the paragraph calling for a comprehensive peace.

Japan said the resolution was not well-balanced in that it did not clearly acknowledge Israel's right to exist or refer to the 1967 and 1973 Council resolutions which called for a negotiated settlement.

Although abstaining, Portugal stressed the importance of the preamble in reference to the two principles which it considered fundamental: the right of all States in the region, including Israel, to live in peace and security within internationally recognized boundaries, and recognition of the Palestinians' right freely to determine their future.

Though voting in favour, Austria said that, while the resolution incorporated essential elements on which there was wide international agreement, it would have preferred a more affirmative recognition in the operative part to the right of all States in the region, including Israel, to exist within secure boundaries; and it would have preferred the call for complete and unconditional Israeli withdrawal from all occupied territories to be less sweeping, as territorial aspects formed part of peace negotiations. Voting in favour as an expression of its support for the Palestinians' right to self-determination, Finland emphasized that it continued to conceive the realization of those rights within the framework of a comprehensive Middle East settlement on the basis of the 1967 and 1973 Council resolutions.

Sweden had reservations on the demand for complete and unconditional Israeli withdrawal from all occupied territories, believed that some elements of the resolution would prejudge the outcome of negotiations, would have preferred the explicit reference to negotiations contained in the original version of paragraph 6, and stressed that a settlement must be based on the 1967 and 1973 Council resolutions as well as on recognition of the legitimate national rights of the Palestinians.

The Dominican Republic said its positive vote was on the understanding that the 1967 and 1973 Council resolutions would be respected. Uruguay voted in favour on the understanding that the resolution implied recognition of Israel's right to exist within secure boundaries; it added that the representation of the Palestinians should be decided by them in exercise of their right to self-determination.

New Zealand did not consider the order of the elements in the resolution as prejudging the outcome of the negotiations called for in paragraph 6; it particularly welcomed the mention in the fourth preambular paragraph of the right of all States in the region to existence within internationally recognized boundaries but would have preferred reaffirmation of that right in the operative part. However, five States voting for the resolution criticized that paragraph and its specific provisions.

Algeria stressed that the paragraph could be interpreted only in the context of the principles adopted on 9 September in the Final Declaration of the Twelfth Arab Summit Conference at Fez, Morocco; total and unconditional Israeli withdrawal from the occupied territories must be among the principles of a just and lasting solution. Democratic Yemen said its positive vote did not imply recognition of Israel. Iraq considered that the reference did not apply to the Zionist entity, which had officially rejected the boundaries delineated and recognized by the United Nations, and beyond which it could not acquire sovereignty. The Syrian Arab Republic criticized the fact that the principle of complete Israeli withdrawal was not included and said the text paved the way for recognition of the Zionist entity which occupied Palestine. The United Arab Emirates said it would have voted against the paragraph because the indirect reference to recognition of Israel went beyond the statement of the Fez Conference.

Iran maintained its reservations on the phrase "all parties" or other phrases which presumed a status for the Zionist usurping elements equal to that of the Palestinians or which implied any legality or legitimacy for the Zionist entity.

The Libyan Arab Jamahiriya explained that it had not participated in the vote as it felt that the rights of the Palestinians to regain their usurped land and to self-determination were not ensured; it also objected to the 1947 partition resolution and to the indirect recognition of the Zionist entity in the preamble.

Several States explained their votes in the Assembly's Third Committee on the paragraph of the resolution on racial discrimination expressing concern at Israel's defiance of the Convention against racial discrimination, as reflected in the 1982 report of the Committee on the Elimination of Racial Discrimination (CERD).[7]

Those voting against this paragraph or abstaining on it gave the following reasons: It was improper for the Assembly, whose membership included many States not parties to the Convention, to judge the policies of a State party with reference to the Convention (Australia, Canada, against) or to single out a particular State party (Federal Republic of Germany, against; Italy, abstaining). The paragraph dealt with a political issue outside the scope of the Convention (Costa Rica, France, Netherlands, Portugal, abstaining). The CERD report had been used in a distorted or misleading fashion (Australia, Belgium, Federal Republic of Germany, against), since CERD had expressed no views on the subject (Finland, New Zealand, United Kingdom, against). In addition, Finland said the Nordic States could not agree that Israel's policy was in defiance of the Convention.

Also in the Third Committee, explaining its negative vote on the resolution on self-determination of peoples, the United States gave as one of its reasons its objection to the treatment of the Arab-Israeli conflict. Ireland, which abstained in the vote, said that although the resolution recognized the right of the Palestinians to self-determination, it did not recognize Israel's right to exist within secure frontiers. Uruguay, which voted in favour, said it would have preferred a wording on the Middle East reflecting all the reasons for friction there. Austria, however, though abstaining, said it condemned Israel's policy in relation to the problems addressed in the resolution.

Regarding the provision urging support for the Palestinians through PLO in their self-determination struggle, Uruguay said the Palestinians would select their legitimate representative through exercise of their right to self-determination. Portugal, which abstained, said it had reservations on this provision. Greece, also abstaining, said it agreed with the right of the Palestinians to self-determination and the establishment of their own independent State under PLO leadership.

During the debates on the Palestine question and on the Middle East situation at the Assembly's regular session, as well as at the seventh emergency special session, most speakers agreed that the Palestine question was the core of the Middle East conflict, while Israel stated that it was clearly not the central problem.

Declaring their support for Palestinian rights, Austria, Denmark (for the EC members), Finland, Greece, India, Nepal, Norway, Singapore, Turkey and others also emphasized that every State in the region had the right to live within secure and recognized boundaries. Portugal and others held both principles fundamental for a peaceful solution. Israel's existence and security and that of its neighbours were two sides of one coin, Guyana stated, a view shared by several others. The secure existence and development of all States in the region under international guarantees was advocated by a number of States.

Speaking for the EC members, Denmark mentioned a 20 September statement by those countries at Brussels, Belgium, declaring that a Middle East settlement should be based on the principles of security for all States in the region, recognition of Israel's right to exist, self-determination for the Palestinians and mutual recognition by all parties.

Declaring its commitment to Israel's existence within internationally recognized boundaries, Brazil said that while Israel had expanded and thrived, that had not been the case with the Arab Palestinian State for whose existence the United Nations, under the 1947 partition plan, was just as responsible. Bahrain held that the Palestinians did not reject the idea of coexistence with the Jews in Palestine on a basis of equality and without Zionist domination. In the opinion of Botswana, the denial of Israel's right to exist could only complicate the situation; Israel should be deprived of the excuse to persist in its expansionist course.

Israel reiterated its view that the core and cause of the Arab-Israeli conflict stemmed from the unwillingness of the Arabs to accept and coexist with a sovereign Jewish State and their refusal to recognize Israel's right to exist, with everything else a pretext or subterfuge.

Saudi Arabia stated that Israel had pretended to seek peace and coexistence with the Palestinians, provided the security of its borders was guaranteed; Palestinians who had lived side by side with Jews in Palestine, however, knew that that was a deceitful claim and that the Zionist movement's real purpose was to seize the whole of Palestine and transform it into a Jewish State, cleared of its Arab inhabitants.

Jordan said over most of the past 35 years, the real issue had been the denial of rights of the Palestinians, of whom 2 million were refugees, more than half a million displaced and 1.3 million under occupation. India said the non-aligned countries viewed Israeli policies as racist since they were based on an exclusionary doctrine that divided people into arbitrary categories. Kenya stated that Israeli policies towards the Palestinians hinged on the false assumption that the Palestinians did not exist as a people and therefore had no right to a homeland of their own.

The PLO observer challenged the view that Israel had ever offered the Palestinians any alternative other than displacement, annexation, confiscation of land, imprisonment, concentration camps and persistent denial of their national identity and inalienable rights. In Algeria's opinion, the repeated acts of Israeli aggression were part of a deliberate policy to side-step the Palestine question as the central element of the Middle East conflict. The Ukrainian SSR said any diplomatic or military manoeuvres to side-step or eliminate the Palestinian problem were doomed to failure. In the view of Cyprus and others, the Palestine question gave rise to one of the most dangerous hotbeds of tension in the world, primarily as a result of Israel's aggressive and expansionist policy manifested by the denial of Palestinian rights.

Viet Nam considered the struggle of the Palestinians for their rights to be an integral part of the joint struggle of the Arab peoples to safeguard their independence, national sovereignty and territorial integrity.

Attempts to give a distorted image of the just struggle of the Palestinians and to place it in the context of bloc rivalry, Yugoslavia felt, were reminiscent of the cold war. Albania said that, during recent years, a whole series of events dangerous and harmful to the Palestinian cause had occurred in the Middle East because of the direct intervention and plotting of the two super-Powers. For the non-aligned countries, India stated, the Palestine question had always been more than a colonial question or a refugee problem; it had affected the relationship between the major Powers, especially because of the possibility of the region's becoming an arena for their confrontation.

Backed and supported by the main imperialist Power, the German Democratic Republic stated, Israel was trying to solve the Palestine question by committing genocide against the Palestinians. Turkey said Israel appeared intent on liquidating the Palestinian problem by physically and morally decimating the Palestinians. A similar view was expressed by Iraq, among others. Botswana felt that the major cause of the perpetual conflict was the brutalization of the Palestinians by Israel, a reality which Israel could ignore only at the risk of endangering its own right to exist as a permanent reality. Morocco blamed the cycle of violence on two factors: Israeli underestimation of the Palestinians' capacity for resistance, and the indifference and complicity of many major Powers in abandoning the Palestinians to their fate. Malaysia was confident that the Palestinians would emerge the ultimate victors in their struggle to regain their freedom and rights.

Denmark (for the EC members), the Gambia, Japan, Pakistan, the United Arab Emirates and many others believed that no viable peace could be achieved without the restoration of Palestinian rights. Yugoslavia maintained that peace in the Middle East could not be based on the denial of the existence of a whole people. Instead of restoring Palestinian rights, Uganda said, emphasis had been put on the consequences of the problem, namely, the refugees and the Arab-Israeli conflict.

Unless the Palestine question was solved, Pakistan warned, not only would the region be confronted with explosions of increasing intensity but serious conflicts might erupt even beyond. This view was shared by Botswana, Romania and others.

Romania considered it high time for an intensification of political and diplomatic efforts to bring about a settlement. Unless the new possibilities for substantive negotiations were grasped, Sweden feared that the conflict and frustration of Palestinian national aspirations might continue beyond the foreseeable future.

Many speakers expressed the view that a just and lasting Middle East peace could be achieved only by a comprehensive settlement that ensured Israeli withdrawal from the territories occupied since 1967 and that would enable the Palestinians to exercise their rights, including the rights to return to their homes and land, to self-determination and national independence and to establish their own sovereign State in Palestine. Those taking this position included Algeria, Austria, Bahrain, Bangladesh, Bhutan, Botswana, Brazil, Bulgaria, the Byelorussian SSR, China, Cuba, Cyprus, Czechoslovakia, Democratic Yemen, Djibouti, Egypt, the German Democratic Republic, Greece, Guyana, India, Indonesia, Jordan, Kenya, Kuwait, the Lao People's Democratic Republic, Malaysia, Mauritania, Mexico, Mongolia, Morocco, Nepal, Poland, Romania, Sri Lanka, the Sudan, Sweden, Thailand, Tunisia, Turkey, Uganda, the USSR, Viet Nam, Yugoslavia and Zambia.

India observed that recognition of the Palestinians' right to national independence was premised on the consciousness of their distinct territorial and national identity and not merely a response to Israel's occupation of their lands. Madagascar suggested that the Security Council amend its resolutions on a Middle East peace to recognize Palestinian rights.

Stating that the United States President's proposals of 1 September had shown some progress in the American position, the PLO observer said they nevertheless lacked the basic components needed for a just settlement—recognition of PLO as the sole legitimate representative of the Palestinians, recognition of their right to self-determination and to establish their own independent State, and complete and unconditional Israeli withdrawal from the occupied territories, including Jerusalem. Iraq stated that although the United States initiative recognized Palestinian rights, it made it very clear that the right to self-determination was not included. In Egypt's view, the common approach in the different peace proposals, despite their different manifestations, had led them to confirm the legitimacy of the wishes and aspirations of the Palestinians; the proposals had emphasized that the Palestine question was a question of people and of a State, not a matter of refugees.

Iraq said Israel persistently rejected or sabotaged every initiative that even remotely tried to secure acceptance of Palestinian rights or Israeli withdrawal. Israel's refusal to heed and implement United Nations decisions was deplored by many others.

Bahrain believed that the creation of a Palestinian State would facilitate the establishment of a society in which there would be coexistence between the different races, religions and cultures, as there had been before the creation of Israel. Romania said there was room in the Middle East for both an independent Palestinian State and the State of Israel.

Israel said it was well known that Jordan was the State in which the national identity and aspirations of the Palestinians had already found full expression; the terms "Palestinian Arabs" and "Jordanians" were virtually interchangeable and the Palestinians had achieved self-determination and national independence on more than three quarters of the area of the former Palestine Mandate, while the Jewish community in Palestine had achieved its national rights on considerably less than one fifth of that area. The only practical way towards a solution of the question of the Palestinian Arabs was the Camp David process, which invited the Palestinian residents of Judaea, Samaria and Gaza to play a far more active role than in their past experience in shaping their own future, by calling on them to participate in negotiations to determine the final status of the areas they lived in, as well as in the eventual negotiations on a peace treaty between Israel and Jordan in which the delimitation of boundaries between the two countries would be agreed.

Austria called on Israel and PLO to enter into exploratory talks without any pre-conditions. Kuwait said the countries which bore the major responsibility for creating the Palestine issue had the duty to recognize PLO and address the real party through its legitimate representative; Kuwait deplored the United States stand that it would not even engage in dialogue with PLO unless that organization recognized Israel's right to exist, particularly in view of Israel's position that it would never negotiate with PLO even if it recognized Israel. The Lao People's Democratic Republic said that, because of the constant United States obstruction in the Security Council, ways of eliminating obstacles to the exercise of Palestinian rights had not been found. The United Arab Emirates asked the United States to regard the Palestinians as the equal of all other peoples aspiring to freedom and self-determination.

The participation of PLO in any peace negotiations was advocated also by many others, including Austria, Bangladesh, Bhutan, Brazil, China, the Congo, Cuba, Cyprus, Democratic Yemen, Denmark (for the EC members), Djibouti, Finland, Greece, Guyana, Hungary, India, Indonesia, Japan, the Lao People's Democratic Republic, Mauritania, Mongolia, Nepal, Pakistan, Poland, Romania, Singapore, the Sudan, Thailand, Turkey, Uganda, the Ukrainian SSR, the USSR, Viet Nam, Yugoslavia and Zambia. The PLO observer said that, without its full participation, as repeatedly affirmed by the Assembly, a solution to the Palestinian and Middle East problems could not be achieved.

In Nicaragua's opinion, any negotiations or agreement that did not include PLO on an equal footing would be unacceptable and legally invalid. Norway felt that the Palestinians could not be expected to accept the responsibilities inherent in any peace solution unless they had a voice in the negotiations. Sweden said Israel must realize that there could be no negotiations or agreements involving the Palestinians unless PLO was accepted as a party on an equal footing.

In Djibouti's view, PLO was the vanguard of the Palestinians' struggle. Qatar remarked that the support of the international community for Palestinian rights had not been confined to the adoption of resolutions, but had extended to increased recognition of PLO. Tunisia said that if there were some who still questioned that PLO represented the Palestinians, it was because they disregarded history and facts, which included the massive demonstrations and repeated strikes in the West Bank and Jerusalem in support of it. The USSR believed that the international prestige and authority of PLO had increased.

Denmark, for the EC members, said they wished to see the Palestinians in a position to pursue their demands by political means and by negotiation, and they believed PLO must be associated with the negotiations. Egypt called on PLO to weigh things from the standpoint of its national goals and aspirations, and to take calculated, well-considered and courageous practical steps; it also called on all Palestinians to close ranks. Japan

held it essential that Israel and PLO recognize each other's position.

Israel said that, as stated in its charter, PLO aspired to the whole territory between the River Jordan and the Mediterranean Sea as the future Arab State of Palestine and openly sought the destruction of Israel; there was growing awareness among the Palestinians that PLO leadership was incapable of guiding them towards any realistic solution.

Viet Nam believed that the Assembly must take more forceful steps, on the basis of the recommendations of the Committee on Palestinian rights, to create favourable conditions for the implementation of Palestinian rights, including a demand that the United States give up its policy of intervention in the Middle East and support of Israel. The Libyan Arab Jamahiriya considered the recommendations an important step towards righting the wrong the Assembly had done to the Palestinians when it accepted the partition of Palestine and the establishment of Israel. Malaysia and others regretted that none of the recommendations, reaffirmed by the United Nations on so many occasions, had been implemented so far.

By adopting the recommendations, Senegal felt, the Security Council would greatly increase the chances of a Middle East settlement. Action in the spirit of those recommendations was called for by Hungary, while Guyana called for their widest possible acceptance.

Kuwait said a solution could only be reached by implementing United Nations resolutions, which, however, required means the United Nations lacked.

To force Israel to implement United Nations resolutions on the Palestine question, the German Democratic Republic said it supported the demand by many States that the Security Council apply sanctions.

India considered it clearer than ever that a solution to the Palestine question could only be found if Israel's compliance with United Nations resolution was enforced by methods available in the Charter. The Libyan Arab Jamahiriya called for a political, military and economic boycott of Israel, its expulsion from the United Nations, and condemnation of United States aid to Israel.

Mongolia held further efforts by the international community necessary to compel Israel to put into effect the repeated United Nations decisions and to prompt a Middle East settlement. Qatar appealed to the Council to assume its responsibilities fully, not only to restore Palestinian rights but also United Nations authority. The Syrian Arab Republic thought it time to deal with the matter not by statements but by action to force Israel to grant the Palestinians their rights. The United Arab Emirates said the Council was the only organ capable of giving tangible expression to the will of the international community by applying the provisions of Chapter VII of the Charter. Sanctions under Chapter VII should be considered if Israel refused to abide by the Assembly's resolutions, said Viet Nam. In Zambia's opinion, what was required was the political will, particularly of the permanent Council members, to find a solution within the United Nations framework. The Council's failure to apply sanctions was regretted by several others, among them Djibouti.

Summing up the debate, the United States said it repeated language that was clearly unacceptable to one or more of the parties, instead of bringing them together in the search for peace.

Letters. [1]GA President: 20 Apr., A/ES-7/17. [2]Cyprus: 29 July, transmitting communiqué of non-aligned countries, A/37/366-S/15327. Israel: [3]21 Apr., A/ES-7/18 (A/37/217, annex II, 3 May); [4]22 Sep., A/ES-7/20. [5]Kuwait: 20 Apr., transmitting communiqué of non-aligned countries, A/37/205-S/14990. [6]United States: 19 Apr., A/ES-7/16.
Reports. [7]CERD, A/37/18; [8]Committee on Palestinian rights, A/37/35 & Corr.1.
Resolutions (1982). [9]Commission on Human Rights (report, E/1982/12): 1982/3, 11 Feb. GA: [10]ES-7/4, 28 Apr., text following; [11]ES-7/5, 26 June; [12]ES-7/6, 19 Aug.; [13]ES-7/7, 19 Aug.; [14]ES-7/8, 19 Aug.; [15]ES-7/9, 24 Sep.; [16]ES-9/1, para. 11, 5 Feb.; [17]37/43, paras. 21 & 23, 3 Dec.; [18]37/46, para. 7, 3 Dec.; [19]37/86 A, 10 Dec.; [20]37/86 B, 10 Dec.; [21]37/86 C, 10 Dec.; [22]37/86 D, 10 Dec., text following; [23]37/86 E, 20 Dec., text following; [24]37/94 B, para. 15, 10 Dec.; [25]37/123 F, para. 2, 20 Dec. [26]SCPDPM (report, E/CN.4/1983/4): 1982/18, para. 1 (*g*) & (*h*), 8 Sep.
Resolutions (prior). GA: [27]181 A (II), 29 Nov. 1947 (YUN 1947-48, p. 247); [28]194(III), 11 Dec. 1948 (YUN 1948-49, p. 174); [29]217 A (III), 10 Dec. 1948 (*ibid.*, p. 535); [30]273(III), 11 May 1949 (*ibid.*, p. 405); [31]2106 A (XX), annex, 21 Dec. 1965 (YUN 1965, p. 440); [32]ES-7/2, 29 July 1980 (YUN 1980, p. 391). SC: [33]242(1967), 22 Nov. 1967 (YUN 1967, p. 257); [34]338(1973), 22 Oct. 1973 (YUN 1973, p. 213); [35]465(1980), 1 Mar. 1980 (YUN 1980, p. 427).
Yearbook references. [36]1976, p. 235 (text, 1980, p. 394); [37]1980, p. 382.
Meeting records. GA: A/ES-7/PV.12-19, *20, 21* (20-28 Apr.), A/37/PV.84-89, 99, 112 (30 Nov.–20 Dec.).

General Assembly resolution ES-7/4

28 April 1982   Meeting 20   86-20-36 (roll-call vote)

26-nation draft (A/ES-7/L.3 and Add.1); agenda item 5.
Sponsors: Afghanistan, Bangladesh, Chad, Congo, Cuba, Gambia, German Democratic Republic, Guinea, Guyana, Hungary, India, Indonesia, Lao People's Democratic Republic, Madagascar, Malaysia, Mali, Malta, Niger, Nigeria, Pakistan, Senegal, Sierra Leone, Tunisia, Ukrainian SSR, Viet Nam, Yugoslavia.

Question of Palestine

The General Assembly,

Having considered the question of Palestine at its resumed seventh emergency special session,

Noting with regret and concern that the Security Council, at its 2348th meeting, on 2 April 1982, and at its 2357th meeting, on 20 April 1982, failed to take a decision as a result of the negative votes of the United States of America,

Having heard the statement by the Head of the Political Department of the Palestine Liberation Organization, the representative of the Palestinian people,

Convinced that the worsening situation in the Middle East and the failure to find a solution to this question pose a grave threat to international peace and security,

Deploring the repressive measures taken by the Israeli authorities in the illegally occupied Palestinian Arab territories, including Jerusalem,

Recalling the relevant United Nations resolutions pertaining to the status and unique character of the Holy City of Jerusalem, in particular Security Council resolutions 465(1980) of 1 March 1980, 476(1980) of 30 June 1980 and 478(1980) of 20 August 1980,

Affirming once more that the Geneva Convention relative to the Protection of Civilian Persons in Time of War, of 12 August 1949, is applicable to all territories occupied by Israel since 1967, including Jerusalem,

Noting with regret that, owing to the negative vote of one of its permanent members, the Security Council has, so far, failed to take a decision on the recommendations of the Committee on the Exercise of the Inalienable Rights of the Palestinian People endorsed by the General Assembly in its resolutions 31/20 of 24 November 1976, 32/40 A of 2 December 1977, 33/28 A of 7 December 1978, 34/65 A of 29 November 1979, 35/169 A of 15 December 1980 and 36/120 D of 10 December 1981,

1. *Reaffirms* its resolutions ES-7/2 of 29 July 1980 and 3236(XXIX) and 3237(XXIX) of 22 November 1974 and all other relevant United Nations resolutions pertinent to the question of Palestine;

2. *Reaffirms* the fundamental principle of the inadmissibility of the acquisition of territory by force;

3. *Reaffirms* that all the provisions of the Hague Conventions of 1907 and the Geneva Convention relative to the Protection of Civilian Persons in Time of War, of 12 August 1949, apply to all territories occupied by Israel since 1967, including Jerusalem, and calls upon all parties to these instruments to respect and ensure respect of their obligations in all circumstances;

4. *Demands* that Israel should comply with the provisions of Security Council resolution 465(1980);

5. *Further demands* that Israel should comply with all United Nations resolutions relevant to the status and unique character of the Holy City of Jerusalem, in particular with Security Council resolutions 476(1980) and 478(1980);

6. *Expresses its rejection* of all policies and plans aiming at the resettlement of the Palestinians outside their homeland;

7. *Condemns* Israel, the occupying Power, for its:

(a) Failure to fulfil its obligations under the provisions of the Geneva Convention relative to the Protection of Civilian Persons in Time of War;

(b) Disbanding of the elected municipal council of El-Bireh;

(c) Dismissal of the elected mayors of Ramallah and Nablus;

(d) Violation of the sanctity of the Holy Places, particularly of Al-Haram Al-Shareef in Jerusalem;

(e) Shooting and killing and wounding of worshippers in the precincts of Al-Haram Al-Shareef by members of the Israeli army on 11 April 1982;

(f) Repressive measures, including shooting at the unarmed civilian population in the occupied Palestinian territory and in the occupied Syrian Golan Heights, resulting in death and injury;

(g) Attacks against and interference with the functions of various civic and religious institutions in the occupied Palestinian territory, including Jerusalem, in particular educational institutions;

8. *Condemns* all policies which frustrate the exercise of the inalienable rights of the Palestinian people, in particular providing Israel with military, economic and political assistance and the misuse of the veto by a permanent member of the Security Council, thus enabling Israel to continue its aggression, occupation and unwillingness to carry out its obligations under the Charter and the relevant resolutions of the United Nations;

9. *Urges* all Governments which have not yet done so:

(a) To recognize the inalienable rights of the Palestinian people;

(b) To renounce the policy of providing Israel with military, economic and political assistance, thus discouraging Israel from continuing its aggression, occupation and disregard of its obligations under the Charter and the relevant resolutions of the United Nations;

(c) To act accordingly in all the organs of the United Nations;

10. *Condemns* the policies which encourage the flow of human resources to Israel, enabling it to implement and to proceed with its colonization and settlement policies in the occupied Arab territories;

11. *Declares once again* that Israel's record and actions confirm that it is not a peace-loving Member State and that it has carried out neither its obligations under the Charter nor its commitment under General Assembly resolution 273(III) of 11 May 1949;

12. *Calls again upon* Israel, the occupying Power, to observe and apply scrupulously the provisions of the Geneva Convention relative to the Protection of Civilian Persons in Time of War and the principles of international law governing military occupation in all the occupied Palestinian and other Arab territories, including Jerusalem;

13. *Demands* that Israel, the occupying Power, should permit entry into the occupied territories of the Special Committee to Investigate Israeli Practices Affecting the Human Rights of the Population of the Occupied Territories and of the Commission established by Security Council resolution 446(1979), in order to facilitate the fulfilment of the mandates entrusted to them by the General Assembly and by the Council, respectively;

14. *Urges* the Security Council to recognize the inalienable rights of the Palestinian people as defined in General Assembly resolution ES-7/2 and to endorse the recommendations of the Committee on the Exercise of the Inalienable Rights of the Palestinian People, as endorsed by the Assembly in its resolution 31/20 and in subsequent resolutions;

15. *Calls upon* the Secretary-General, in concurrence with the Security Council and in consultation as appropriate with the Committee on the Exercise of the Inalienable Rights of the Palestinian People, to initiate contacts with all parties to the Arab-Israeli conflict in the Middle East, including the Palestine Liberation Organization, the representative of the Palestinian people, with a view to finding concrete ways and means to achieve a comprehensive, just and lasting solution, conducive to peace, in conformity with the principles of the Charter and relevant resolutions and based on the implementation of the recommendations of the Committee as endorsed by the General Assembly at its thirty-first session;

16. *Requests* the Secretary-General to follow up the implementation of the present resolution and to report thereon at appropriate intervals to Member States as well as to the Security Council and to submit a comprehensive report to the General Assembly at its thirty-seventh session under the item entitled "Question of Palestine";

17. *Decides* to adjourn the seventh emergency special session temporarily and to authorize the President of the latest regular session of the General Assembly to resume its meetings upon request from Member States.

Roll-call vote in Assembly as follows:

In favour: Afghanistan, Albania, Algeria, Angola, Bahrain, Bangladesh, Benin, Bhutan, Botswana, Bulgaria, Burundi, Byelorussian SSR, Cape Verde, Chad, China, Congo, Cuba, Cyprus, Czechoslovakia, Democratic Yemen, Djibouti, Ethiopia, Gambia, German Democratic Republic, Ghana, Greece, Grenada, Guinea, Guinea-Bissau, Guyana, Hungary, India, Indonesia, Iran, Iraq, Jordan, Kenya, Kuwait, Lao People's Democratic Republic, Lebanon, Libyan Arab Jamahiriya, Madagascar, Malaysia, Maldives, Mali, Malta, Mauritania, Mongolia, Morocco, Mozambique, Nepal, Nicaragua, Niger, Nigeria, Oman, Pakistan, Poland, Qatar, Romania, Rwanda, Sao Tome and Principe, Saudi Arabia, Senegal, Sierra Leone, Somalia, Sri Lanka, Sudan, Suriname, Syrian Arab Republic, Togo, Trinidad and Tobago, Tunisia, Turkey, Uganda, Ukrainian SSR, USSR, United Arab Emirates, United Republic of Cameroon, United Republic of Tanzania, Upper Volta, Viet Nam, Yemen, Yugoslavia, Zambia, Zimbabwe.

Against: Australia, Austria, Belgium, Canada, Denmark, Finland, France, Germany, Federal Republic of, Iceland, Ireland, Israel, Italy, Luxembourg, Netherlands, New Zealand, Norway, Portugal, Sweden, United Kingdom, United States.

Abstaining: Argentina, Bahamas, Barbados, Bolivia, Brazil, Burma, Chile, Colombia, Costa Rica, Dominican Republic, Ecuador, Egypt, El Salvador, Fiji, Guatemala, Haiti, Honduras, Ivory Coast, Jamaica, Liberia, Malawi, Mexico, Panama, Papua New Guinea, Paraguay, Peru, Philippines, Samoa, Singapore, Spain, Swaziland, Thailand, Uruguay, Venezuela, Zaire.

General Assembly resolution 37/86 D

10 December 1982   Meeting 99   113-4-23 (recorded vote)

22-nation draft (A/37/L.47 and Add.1); agenda item 31.

Sponsors: Afghanistan, Bangladesh, Cuba, Cyprus, Gambia, Guinea, Guyana, India, Indonesia, Lao People's Democratic Republic, Madagascar, Mali, Malta, Mongolia, Pakistan, Sao Tome and Principe, Senegal, Sri Lanka, Tunisia, Viet Nam, Yemen, Yugoslavia.

The General Assembly,

Recalling its resolutions relevant to the question of Palestine, in particular resolutions 181(II) of 29 November 1947, 194(III) of 11 December 1948, 3210(XXIX) of 14 October 1974, 3236(XXIX) of 22 November 1974 and ES-7/2 of 29 July 1980,

Recalling the resolutions of the Security Council relevant to Palestine,

Having heard the statement of the representative of the Palestine Liberation Organization,

1. *Takes note* of the declaration of the Palestine Liberation Organization of 19 April 1981 of its intention to pursue its role in the solution of the question of Palestine on the basis of the attainment by the Palestinian people of its inalienable rights in Palestine, in accordance with the relevant resolutions of the United Nations;

2. *Reaffirms* the principle of the inadmissibility of the acquisition of territory by force;

3. *Reaffirms once again* that a comprehensive, just and lasting peace in the Middle East cannot be established without the unconditional withdrawal of Israel from the Palestinian and the other Arab territories occupied since 1967, including Jerusalem, and without the exercise and attainment by the Palestinian people of its inalienable rights in Palestine, in accordance with the principles of the Charter and the relevant resolutions of the United Nations;

4. *Requests* the Security Council to discharge its responsibilities under the Charter and recognize the inalienable rights of the Palestinian Arab people, including the right to self-determination and the right to establish its independent Arab State in Palestine;

5. *Reiterates* its request that the Security Council take the necessary measures, in execution of the relevant United Nations resolutions, to implement the plan which, *inter alia*, recommends that an independent Arab State shall come into existence in Palestine;

6. *Requests* the Secretary-General to report on the progress made in implementing the present resolution as soon as possible.

Recorded vote in Assembly as follows:

In favour: Afghanistan, Albania, Algeria, Angola, Antigua and Barbuda, Argentina, Austria, Bahrain, Bangladesh, Belize, Benin, Bhutan, Brazil, Bulgaria, Burma, Burundi, Byelorussian SSR, Cape Verde, Central African Republic, Chad, Chile, China, Colombia, Comoros, Congo, Cuba, Cyprus, Czechoslovakia, Democratic Kampuchea, Democratic Yemen, Djibouti, Ecuador, Egypt, El Salvador, Equatorial Guinea, Ethiopia, Fiji, Gabon, Gambia, German Democratic Republic, Ghana, Guinea, Guyana, Honduras, Hungary, India, Indonesia, Iran, Iraq, Jamaica, Jordan, Kenya, Kuwait, Lao People's Democratic Republic, Lebanon, Liberia, Libyan Arab Jamahiriya, Madagascar, Malawi, Malaysia, Maldives, Mali, Malta, Mauritania, Mauritius, Mexico, Mongolia, Morocco, Mozambique, Nepal, Nicaragua, Niger, Nigeria, Oman, Pakistan, Panama, Papua New Guinea, Peru, Philippines, Poland, Qatar, Romania, Rwanda, Sao Tome and Principe, Saudi Arabia, Senegal, Sierra Leone, Singapore, Somalia, Spain, Sri Lanka, Sudan, Suriname, Syrian Arab Republic, Thailand, Togo, Tunisia, Turkey, Uganda, Ukrainian SSR, USSR, United Arab Emirates, United Republic of Cameroon, United Republic of Tanzania, Upper Volta, Uruguay, Vanuatu, Viet Nam, Yemen, Yugoslavia, Zaire, Zambia, Zimbabwe.

Against: Canada, Costa Rica, Israel, United States.

Abstaining: Australia, Bahamas, Barbados, Belgium, Denmark, Dominican Republic, Finland, France, Germany, Federal Republic of, Greece, Guinea-Bissau, Haiti, Iceland, Ireland, Italy, Japan, Luxembourg, Netherlands, New Zealand, Norway, Portugal, Sweden, United Kingdom.

General Assembly resolution 37/86 E

20 December 1982   Meeting 112   123-2-19 (recorded vote)

25-nation draft (A/37/L.45/Rev.1); agenda item 31.

Sponsors: Afghanistan, Bangladesh, Comoros, Cuba, Cyprus, Czechoslovakia, Gambia, German Democratic Republic, Guinea, Hungary, India, Indonesia, Lao People's Democratic Republic, Madagascar, Malaysia, Mali, Malta, Mongolia, Nigeria, Pakistan, Sao Tome and Principe, Senegal, Ukrainian SSR, Viet Nam, Yugoslavia.

The General Assembly,

Having considered the report of the Committee on the Exercise of the Inalienable Rights of the Palestinian People,

Expressing its extreme concern that no just solution to the problem of Palestine has been achieved and that this problem therefore continues to aggravate the Middle East conflict, of which it is the core, and to endanger international peace and security,

Recalling its previous relevant resolutions, particularly resolutions 181(II) of 29 November 1947, 194(III) of 11 December 1948, 3236(XXIX) of 22 November 1974, ES-7/2 of 29 July 1980, 36/120 D of 10 December 1981 and ES-7/9 of 24 September 1982,

Recalling, in particular, the principles relevant to the question of Palestine that have been accepted by the international community, including the right of all States in the region to existence within internationally recognized boundaries, and justice and security for all the peoples, which requires recognition and attainment of the legitimate rights of the Palestinian people,

Recognizing the necessity of participation by all parties concerned in any efforts aimed at the attainment of a just and lasting solution,

1. *Reaffirms* the inalienable legitimate rights of the Palestinian people, including the right to self-determination and the right to establish, once it so wishes, its independent State in Palestine;

2. *Declares* all Israeli policies and practices of, or aimed at, annexation of the occupied Palestinian and other Arab territories, including Jerusalem, to be in violation of international law and of the relevant United Nations resolutions;

3. *Demands*, in conformity with the fundamental principle of the inadmissibility of the acquisition of territory by force, that Israel should withdraw completely and unconditionally from all the Palestinian and other Arab territories occupied since June 1967, including Jerusalem, with all property and services intact;

4. *Urges* the Security Council to facilitate the process of Israeli withdrawal;

5. *Recommends* that, following the withdrawal of Israel from the occupied Palestinian territories, those territories should be subjected to a short transitional period under the supervision of the United Nations, during which period the Palestinian people would exercise its right to self-determination;

6. *Urgently calls* for the achievement of a comprehensive, just and lasting peace, based on the resolutions of the United Nations and under its auspices, in which all parties concerned, including the Palestine Liberation Organization, the representative of the Palestinian people, participate on an equal footing;

7. *Recommends* that the Security Council should take early action to promote a just and comprehensive solution to the question of Palestine;

8. *Requests* the Secretary-General to report to the General Assembly at its thirty-eighth session on the progress made in implementing the present resolution.

Recorded vote in Assembly as follows:

In favour: Afghanistan, Algeria, Angola, Argentina, Austria, Bahamas, Bahrain, Bangladesh, Barbados, Benin, Bhutan, Bolivia, Botswana, Brazil, Bulgaria, Burundi, Byelorussian SSR, Cape Verde, Central African Republic, Chad, Chile, China, Colombia, Comoros, Congo, Cuba, Cyprus, Czechoslovakia, Democratic Kampuchea, Democratic Yemen, Djibouti, Dominican Republic, Ecuador, Egypt, El Salvador, Equatorial Guinea, Ethiopia, Fiji, Finland, Gabon, German Democratic Republic, Ghana, Greece, Grenada, Guinea, Guinea-Bissau, Guyana, Hungary, India, Indonesia, Iran, Iraq, Ivory Coast, Jamaica, Jordan, Kenya, Kuwait, Lao People's Democratic Republic, Lebanon, Lesotho, Liberia, Madagascar, Malaysia, Maldives, Mali, Malta, Mauritania, Mauritius, Mexico, Mongolia, Morocco, Mozambique, Nepal, New Zealand, Nicaragua, Niger, Nigeria, Oman, Pakistan, Panama, Papua New Guinea, Paraguay, Peru, Philippines, Poland, Qatar, Romania, Rwanda, Saint Lucia, Samoa, Sao Tome and Principe, Saudi Arabia, Senegal, Seychelles, Sierra Leone, Singapore, Somalia, Spain, Sri Lanka, Sudan, Suriname, Sweden, Syrian Arab Republic, Thailand, Togo, Trinidad and Tobago, Tunisia, Turkey, Uganda, Ukrainian SSR, USSR, United Arab Emirates, United Republic of Cameroon, United Republic of Tanzania, Upper Volta, Uruguay, Venezuela, Viet Nam, Yemen, Yugoslavia, Zaire, Zambia, Zimbabwe.

Against: Israel, United States.

Abstaining: Australia, Belgium, Burma, Canada, Denmark, France, Germany, Federal Republic of, Guatemala, Haiti, Iceland, Ireland, Italy, Japan, Luxembourg, Malawi, Netherlands, Norway, Portugal, United Kingdom.

Work programme of the Committee on Palestinian rights

By a resolution of 10 December 1982,[6] adopted by a recorded vote of 119 to 2, with 21 abstentions, the General Assembly endorsed the 1982 recommendations of the Committee on the Exercise of the Inalienable Rights of the Palestinian People[4] and drew the attention of the Security Council to the fact that action on the recommendations it had made in 1976 was long overdue. The Assembly requested the Committee to keep under review the situation relating to the Palestine question and to report and make suggestions to the Assembly or the Council as appropriate, and authorized it to continue efforts to promote implementation of its recommendations. The United Nations Conciliation Commission for Palestine and other United Nations bodies asso-

ciated with the Palestine question were requested to co-operate fully with the Committee.

In other actions relating to the Committee's work, the Assembly, on 16 November, included it among seven bodies exempted from the general rule that subsidiary bodies of the Assembly would not be entitled to have summary records of their meetings during a three-year experimental period;[5] and on 24 September, authorized several of its subsidiary bodies, including the Committee, to hold meetings during the regular 1982 Assembly session.[2]

The original draft of the resolution on summary records, submitted by the Committee on Conferences, did not include the Committee on Palestinian rights among the bodies to be entitled to that service. However, the Committee Chairman, in a letter of 20 October to the Assembly President, requested that summary records continue to be provided in recognition of the political importance of the Committee's work.[3] On 25 October, the Assembly's Fifth (Administrative and Budgetary) Committee adopted, by 86 votes to 2, with 16 abstentions, an amendment, introduced by the Syrian Arab Republic and also sponsored by 13 other States, adding the Committee on Palestinian rights to the list of exceptions.[1]

The 10 December resolution on the Committee's work was introduced by Senegal, as Chairman of the Committee, on behalf of 21 nations, most of them Committee members. Senegal said it reflected the consensus arrived at in Committee discussions and its adoption could only contribute to progress on the Palestine question.

Israel rejected the text, saying that the Committee's work was utterly biased and irresponsible. The United States voted against the resolution on the ground that the Committee was a partisan and therefore unhelpful body—as confirmed by its report—whose functions appeared to contribute not to solutions but to a solution-inhibiting acrimony.

Abstaining, Canada could not support all of the Committee's recommendations. On behalf of the EC members, Denmark said they had important reservations on elements in the recommendations which were not in accordance with their common position on principles for a peace settlement. New Zealand felt that the recommendations did not adequately reflect the 1967 Security Council principles on a Middle East peace.[8]

Costa Rica abstained because it could not approve the Committee's work. Finland abstained on the grounds that the resolution did not represent the balance which it considered to be a prerequisite for a negotiated settlement. A similar opinion was expressed by Norway.

Though voting in favour, the Libyan Arab Jamahiriya did not accept the reference to the 1948

Assembly resolution establishing the United Nations Conciliation Commission for Palestine,[7] or any other reference which might be construed to imply recognition of the Zionist entity. In Iran's view, the establishment of justice and lasting peace in the Middle East implied the elimination of the illicit creation of the Zionist base in the area.

Reservations on some paragraphs and provisions were expressed by Albania.

Spain said its positive vote was in line with its firmly established policy of support for the Palestinian cause. Jamaica, Portugal and Thailand gave similar explanations. Singapore regarded the resolution as a positive contribution to the search for a solution.

> *Amendment adopted.* [1]Benin, Egypt, Ethiopia, Guinea, Lebanon, Mali, Niger, Senegal, Sierra Leone, Somalia, Sri Lanka, Syrian Arab Republic, Togo, Tunisia, A/C.5/37/L.15 (to draft by Committee on Conferences, A/37/32).
> *Decision.* [2]GA: 37/403, para. *(d)*, 24 Sep.
> *Letter.* [3]Committee on Palestinian rights Chairman, 20 Oct., A/C.5/37/L.17.
> *Report.* [4]Committee on Palestinian rights, A/37/35 & Corr.1.
> *Resolutions (1982).* GA: [5]37/14 C, para. 3 *(b)*, 16 Nov.; [6]37/86 A, 10 Dec., text following.
> *Resolutions (prior).* [7]GA: 194(III), 11 Dec. 1948 (YUN 1948-49, p. 174). [8]SC: 242(1967), 22 Nov. 1967 (YUN 1967, p. 257).
> *Meeting records.* GA: A/37/PV.84-89, *99* (30 Nov.–10 Dec.).

General Assembly resolution 37/86 A

10 December 1982   Meeting 99   119-2-21 (recorded vote)

21-nation draft (A/37/L.42 and Add.1); agenda item 31.
Sponsors: Afghanistan, Bangladesh, Comoros, Cuba, Cyprus, Gambia, German Democratic Republic, Guinea, Hungary, India, Indonesia, Lao People's Democratic Republic, Madagascar, Mali, Malta, Mongolia, Pakistan, Senegal, Ukrainian SSR, Viet Nam, Yugoslavia.

The General Assembly,

Recalling its resolutions 3376(XXX) of 10 November 1975, 31/20 of 24 November 1976, 32/40 of 2 December 1977, 33/28 of 7 December 1978, 34/65 of 29 November and 12 December 1979, ES-7/2 of 29 July 1980, 35/169 of 15 December 1980, 36/120 of 10 December 1981, ES-7/4 of 28 April 1982, ES-7/5 of 26 June 1982 and ES-7/9 of 24 September 1982,

Having considered the report of the Committee on the Exercise of the Inalienable Rights of the Palestinian People,

1. *Expresses its appreciation* to the Committee on the Exercise of the Inalienable Rights of the Palestinian People for its efforts in performing the tasks assigned to it by the General Assembly;

2. *Endorses* the recommendations of the Committee contained in paragraphs 114 to 119 of its report and draws the attention of the Security Council to the fact that action on the Committee's recommendations, as endorsed by the General Assembly in its resolution 31/20, is long overdue;

3. *Requests* the Committee to keep the situation relating to the question of Palestine under review and to report and make suggestions to the General Assembly or the Security Council, as appropriate;

4. *Authorizes* the Committee to continue to exert all efforts to promote the implementation of its recommendations, to send delegations or representatives to international conferences where such representation would be considered by it to be appropriate, and to report thereon to the General Assembly at its thirty-eighth session and thereafter;

5. *Requests* the United Nations Conciliation Commission for Palestine, established under General Assembly resolution 194(III) of 11 December 1948, as well as other United Nations bodies associated with the question of Palestine, to co-operate fully with the Committee and to make available to it, at its request, the relevant information and documentation which they have at their disposal;

6. *Decides* to circulate the report of the Committee to all the competent bodies of the United Nations and urges them to take the necessary action, as appropriate, in accordance with the Committee's programme of implementation;

7. *Requests* the Secretary-General to continue to provide the Committee with all the necessary facilities for the performance of its tasks.

Recorded vote in Assembly as follows:
In favour: Afghanistan, Albania, Algeria, Angola, Antigua and Barbuda, Argentina, Bahamas, Bahrain, Bangladesh, Barbados, Belize, Benin, Bhutan, Brazil, Bulgaria, Burundi, Byelorussian SSR, Cape Verde, Central African Republic, Chad, Chile, China, Colombia, Comoros, Congo, Cuba, Cyprus, Czechoslovakia, Democratic Kampuchea, Democratic Yemen, Djibouti, Dominican Republic, Ecuador, Egypt, El Salvador, Equatorial Guinea, Ethiopia, Gabon, Gambia, German Democratic Republic, Ghana, Greece, Guinea, Guinea-Bissau, Guyana, Haiti, Honduras, Hungary, India, Indonesia, Iran, Iraq, Ivory Coast, Jamaica, Jordan, Kenya, Kuwait, Lao People's Democratic Republic, Lebanon, Liberia, Libyan Arab Jamahiriya, Madagascar, Malawi, Malaysia, Maldives, Mali, Malta, Mauritania, Mauritius, Mexico, Mongolia, Morocco, Mozambique, Nepal, Nicaragua, Niger, Nigeria, Oman, Pakistan, Panama, Papua New Guinea, Peru, Philippines, Poland, Portugal, Qatar, Romania, Rwanda, Sao Tome and Principe, Saudi Arabia, Senegal, Sierra Leone, Singapore, Somalia, Spain, Sri Lanka, Sudan, Suriname, Syrian Arab Republic, Thailand, Togo, Tunisia, Turkey, Uganda, Ukrainian SSR, USSR, United Arab Emirates, United Republic of Cameroon, United Republic of Tanzania, Upper Volta, Uruguay, Vanuatu, Venezuela, Viet Nam, Yemen, Yugoslavia, Zaire, Zambia, Zimbabwe.
Against: Israel, United States.
Abstaining: Australia, Austria, Belgium, Burma, Canada, Costa Rica, Denmark, Fiji, Finland, France, Germany, Federal Republic of, Iceland, Ireland, Italy, Japan, Luxembourg, Netherlands, New Zealand, Norway, Sweden, United Kingdom.

Work programme of the Division for Palestinian Rights

Acting on a 1979 General Assembly request,[2] repeated in December 1981,[3] the Secretary-General, on 11 August 1982, redesignated the United Nations Secretariat's Special Unit on Palestinian Rights as the Division for Palestinian Rights in keeping with its expanded work programme.

By a resolution of 10 December,[1] adopted by a recorded vote of 121 to 3, with 18 abstentions, the Assembly requested the Secretary-General: to ensure that the Division continued to discharge its tasks, in consultation with and under the guidance of the Committee on Palestinian rights; to provide the necessary resources for that purpose; and to ensure the continued co-operation of the Department of Public Information and other Secretariat units. Governments and organizations were also invited to co-operate. The Assembly noted with appreciation the action taken by Member States to observe annually on 29 November the International Day of Solidarity with the Palestinian People and their issuance of special postage stamps for that occasion.

Introducing the draft on behalf of 21 nations, most of them members of the Committee on Palestinian rights, Senegal, as the Committee Chairman, said it would make the Division's work easier.

Casting a negative vote, Canada had reservations with regard to the usefulness and appropriateness of the Division's activities. The United States saw no apparent merit in promoting the Unit to a division and regretted that it had been perpetuated at all, as its sole function in the past had been to generate acrimonious and irrelevant rhetoric. Israel said the unjustified upgrading of an illegitimate Secretariat unit into a division would be a heavy drain on United Nations resources and severely compromised the Secretariat's standing and integrity.

Reservations particularly about the escalating cost of the Division were also expressed by New Zealand, which abstained. Costa Rica did not approve of the Division's work. Norway abstained on the grounds that the resolution did not reflect a balance between the interests of the parties which was necessary for a just and lasting peace. Finland gave a similar explanation.

Portugal, Spain and Thailand voted in favour out of support for the Palestinian cause.

Replying to statements that the Division would be a drain on United Nations resources, PLO said it wondered whether people were thinking of the hundreds of millions of dollars the United Nations was paying for a peace-keeping force as a result of Israel's aggression, violations and acts of genocide.

Resolution (1982). [1]GA: 37/86 B, 10 Dec., text following.
Resolutions (prior). GA: [2]34/65 D, 12 Dec. 1979 (YUN 1979, p. 379); [3]36/120 B, 10 Dec. 1981 (YUN 1981, p. 273).
Meeting records. GA: A/37/PV.84-89, *99* (30 Nov.–10 Dec.).

General Assembly resolution 37/86 B

10 December 1982   Meeting 99   121-3-18 (recorded vote)

21-nation draft (A/37/L.43 and Add.1); agenda item 31.
Sponsors: Afghanistan, Bangladesh, Comoros, Cuba, Cyprus, Gambia, German Democratic Republic, Guinea, Hungary, India, Indonesia, Lao People's Democratic Republic, Madagascar, Mali, Malta, Mongolia, Pakistan, Senegal, Ukrainian SSR, Viet Nam, Yugoslavia.

The General Assembly,

Having considered the report of the Committee on the Exercise of the Inalienable Rights of the Palestinian People,

Noting, in particular, the information contained in paragraphs 103 to 111 of that report,

Recalling its resolutions 32/40 B of 2 December 1977, 33/28 C of 7 December 1978, 34/65 D of 12 December 1979, 35/169 D of 15 December 1980 and 36/120 B of 10 December 1981,

1. *Takes note with appreciation* of the action taken by the Secretary-General in compliance with General Assembly resolution 36/120 B;

2. *Requests* the Secretary-General to ensure that the Division for Palestinian Rights of the Secretariat continues to discharge the tasks detailed in paragraph 1 of General Assembly resolution 32/40 B, paragraph 2 *(b)* of resolution 34/65 D and paragraph 3 of resolution 36/120 B, in consultation with the Committee on the Exercise of the Inalienable Rights of the Palestinian People and under its guidance;

3. *Also requests* the Secretary-General to provide the Division for Palestinian Rights with the necessary resources to carry out its tasks as urged in paragraph 109 of the Committee's report;

4. *Further requests* the Secretary-General to ensure the continued co-operation of the Department of Public Information and other units of the Secretariat in enabling the Division for Palestinian Rights to perform its tasks and in covering adequately the various aspects of the question of Palestine;

5. *Invites* all Governments and organizations to lend their co-operation to the Committee and the Division for Palestinian Rights in the performance of their tasks;

6. *Takes note with appreciation* of the action taken by Member States to observe annually on 29 November the International Day of Solidarity with the Palestinian People and the issuance by them of special postage stamps for the occasion.

Recorded vote in Assembly as follows:
In favour: Afghanistan, Albania, Algeria, Angola, Antigua and Barbuda, Argentina, Bahamas, Bahrain, Bangladesh, Barbados, Belize, Benin, Bhutan, Brazil, Bulgaria, Burma, Burundi, Byelorussian SSR, Cape Verde, Central African Republic, Chad, Chile, China, Colombia, Comoros, Congo, Cuba, Cyprus, Czechoslovakia, Democratic Kampuchea, Democratic Yemen, Djibouti, Dominican Republic, Ecuador, Egypt, El Salvador, Equatorial Guinea, Ethiopia, Fiji, Gabon, Gambia, German Democratic Republic, Ghana, Greece, Guinea, Guinea-Bissau, Guyana, Haiti, Honduras, Hungary, India, Indonesia, Iran, Iraq, Ivory Coast, Jamaica, Jordan, Kenya, Kuwait, Lao People's Democratic Republic, Lebanon, Liberia, Libyan Arab Jamahiriya, Madagascar, Malawi, Malaysia, Maldives, Mali, Malta, Mauritania, Mauritius, Mexico, Mongolia, Morocco, Mozambique, Nepal, Nicaragua, Niger, Nigeria, Oman, Pakistan, Panama, Papua New Guinea, Peru, Philippines, Poland, Portugal, Qatar, Romania, Rwanda, Sao Tome and Principe, Saudi Arabia, Senegal, Sierra Leone, Singapore, Somalia, Spain, Sri Lanka, Sudan, Suriname, Syrian Arab Republic, Thailand, Togo, Tunisia, Turkey, Uganda, Ukrainian SSR, USSR, United Arab Emirates, United Republic of Cameroon, United Republic of Tanzania, Upper Volta, Uruguay, Vanuatu, Venezuela, Viet Nam, Yemen, Yugoslavia, Zaire, Zambia, Zimbabwe.
Against: Canada, Israel, United States.
Abstaining: Australia, Austria, Belgium, Costa Rica, Denmark, Finland, France, Germany, Federal Republic of, Iceland, Ireland, Italy, Japan, Luxembourg, Netherlands, New Zealand, Norway, Sweden, United Kingdom.

Status of Jerusalem

Communications and report. By a letter of 27 January 1982,[4] Jordan protested the transfer of the Israeli Ministry of Housing to East Jerusalem on 30 December 1981, an action which, it said, violated Security Council and General Assembly resolutions on the status of the city and aggravated an already explosive situation; annexed was a letter of 12 January from the Minister for Occupied Territories Affairs to the Minister for Foreign Affairs of Jordan informing the latter that other government buildings had also been erected in the district, including the premises for the Israeli Prime Minister's office and for the Office of Public Works and the Ministry of Agriculture.

By a letter of 17 May,[1] Costa Rica stated that on 9 May, in exercise of its national sovereignty, it had announced its decision to transfer its diplomatic seat from Tel Aviv to the western sector of Jerusalem after having sought and received assurances from Israel that the Holy Places of Christianity and Islam would be protected at all times; it regretted that it could not comply with the 1980 Security Council call on States to withdraw their diplomatic missions from Jerusalem.[14]

Protests against Costa Rica's decision were conveyed by Jordan in a letter of 18 May;[6] by the Secretary-General of the League of Arab States, whose statement was transmitted by Jordan also on 18 May;[5] and by Iraq as Chairman of the Organization of the Islamic Conference, in a note verbale of 21 May transmitting a communiqué issued by that organization following a 19 May emergency meeting on the matter.[3] They considered it an act of provocation and a violation of United Nations resolutions and of Article 25 of the Charter of the United Nations, by which Member States agreed to accept and carry out Security Council decisions. The two organizations urged Costa Rica to reconsider its decision.

On 1 June,[2] Costa Rica transmitted a communiqué from its Foreign Minister, dated 14 May, reiterating that the transfer of its diplomatic seat to Jerusalem should not be interpreted as an unfriendly act towards the Arab States and was based on the law applicable to relations between two sovereign States and on the respect for the decision of any State to establish the seat of its Government wherever it chose.

Reference to these letters was made in a June report of the Secretary-General to the General Assembly[7] on implementation of a December 1981 resolution[12] calling on Israel to rescind its 1978 proclamation of Jerusalem as the country's capital as well as other Israeli actions seeking to alter the Holy City's character and status. The Secretary-General also reported that, on 24 May 1982, in response to his request for information on action taken in regard to that resolution, Israel had stated in a note verbale (reproduced in the report) that, as it had told the Assembly in December 1981, Jerusalem remained the eternal capital of Israel and the Jewish people, and that Israel had given ample evidence of its profound regard for the city's religious and cultural legacy.

Action by the Commission on Human Rights. On 11 February 1982, in a resolution on human rights in the territories occupied by Israel, the Commission on Human Rights firmly rejected, and reiterated its condemnation of, Israel's decision to annex Jerusalem and alter its physical character, demographic composition, institutional structure and status, and considered all those measures and their consequences to be null and void.[8]

General Assembly action. In a resolution of 28 April,[9] adopted at its emergency special session on the Palestine question, the General Assembly demanded that Israel comply with all United Nations resolutions on Jerusalem, in particular the two 1980 Security Council resolutions reconfirming that Israel's actions to alter the character and status of Jerusalem had no legal validity[13] and determining that all such actions must be rescinded.[14]

By a resolution of 16 December 1982,[10] the Assembly deplored the transfer by some States of their diplomatic missions to Jerusalem, in violation of the latter Council resolution, and called on them to abide by the relevant United Nations resolutions, in conformity with the United Nations Charter.

In a resolution of 20 December on the Middle East situation,[11] the Assembly deplored Israel's failure to comply with United Nations resolutions on Jerusalem; determined that Israel's decision to annex the city and declare it as its capital, as well as measures to alter its physical character, demographic composition, institutional structure and status, were null and void; demanded that those actions be rescinded immediately; and called on Member States and international organizations to abide by the relevant resolutions.

The 16 December resolution orally revised by its sponsors, was adopted by a recorded vote of 137

to 1, with 4 abstentions. Cuba introduced the text on behalf of 15 nations.

Rejecting the text, Israel stressed that only the Jewish people had always regarded Jerusalem as the centre of their national and spiritual life. Reunited since 1967, the city enjoyed unprecedented freedom, which guaranteed access and right of worship to the adherents of all faiths. Israel would continue to further the peace and well-being of Jerusalem and its people, as well as preserve it as a special place for people of diverse faiths around the globe.

Abstaining, the United States expressed the view that the Council's call for the withdrawal of diplomatic missions from Jerusalem was not binding and had been an attempt to dictate to Member States; the city's ultimate character and status would emerge in peace negotiations.

Support for the resolution was expressed by a number of countries, among them Albania, Argentina, Malta, Peru, Portugal, Singapore, Spain, Sweden, and Trinidad and Tobago. Denmark, speaking for the European Community (EC) members, recalled the importance they attached to the 1980 Council resolution calling for the withdrawal of diplomatic missions from Jerusalem.[14] Venezuela stated that it had been the first country to withdraw its Embassy from Jerusalem, one month before the adoption of that resolution. Ecuador said it voted in favour because of its principles in the field of international relations and its respect for human rights.

A number of speakers during the Assembly debates on the Middle East situation and the Palestine question, among them Denmark (for the EC members) and Malaysia, regarded Israel's decision as contrary to international law and invalid. Cyprus thought that Israel's attempt to gain international acceptance of the transfer of its capital to Jerusalem could not be seen as contributing to peace. Morocco considered the unilateral proclamation of Jerusalem as Israel's unified and eternal capital the most significant example of illegal Israeli acts in the occupied territories, and one which had wounded the most intimate feelings of hundreds of millions of Moslems and Christians. Thailand did not recognize Israel's annexation of Jerusalem or the claim for it to become Israel's capital.

A number of States charged that Israel was trying to alter the character of the Holy City as a place common to several major religions. Bahrain said the international community had a responsibility to safeguard the spiritual heritage of Jerusalem, which had to be saved from Judaization. Malaysia added that Israel had tried to alter the character and identity of Jerusalem, and said the city's restoration to the Arabs was an essential element for a political settlement. Turkey regarded the preservation of the unique and historical character of Jerusalem and respect for its special status as an essential ingredient of a peace settlement. The Syrian Arab Republic charged that, in order to annex the city, approximately 90,000 Jews had been transported there.

At the seventh emergency special session, Belgium said the EC members rejected any initiative that would change the status of the city; any agreement on Jerusalem should guarantee the protection of and free access by all to the Holy Places.

Argentina expressed the view that the status of Jerusalem could not be defined in terms of strategic or military interests, but must take into account the values of the communities of Christianity, Judaism and Islam.

Norway maintained that the final status of Jerusalem could not be settled through unilateral acts but only through a comprehensive peace settlement which guaranteed free access to the Holy Places for Jews, Christians and Moslems alike.

Letters and note verbale (nv). Costa Rica: [1]17 May, S/15109; [2]1 June, A/37/262. [3]Iraq: 21 May, transmitting Organization of Islamic Conference communiqué, A/37/239-S/15114 (nv). Jordan: [4]27 Jan., A/37/80-S/14858, [5]18 May, S/15091; [6]18 May, A/37/231-S/15093.
Report. [7]S-G, A/37/275.
Resolutions (1982). [8]Commission on Human Rights (report, E/1982/12): 1982/1 A, para. 4, 11 Feb. GA: [9]ES-7/4, para. 5, 28 Apr.; [10]37/123 C, 16 Dec., text following; [11]37/123 F, para. 6, 20 Dec.
Resolutions (prior). GA: [12]36/120 E, 10 Dec. 1981 (YUN 1981, p. 270). SC: [13]476(1980), 30 June 1980 (YUN 1980, p. 425); [14]478(1980), 20 Aug. 1980 (*ibid.*, p. 426).
Meeting records. GA: A/37/PV.92-96, *108* (6-16 Dec.).

General Assembly resolution 37/123 C

16 December 1982   Meeting 108   137-1-4 (recorded vote)

15-nation draft (A/37/L.51 and Add.1), orally revised; agenda item 34.
Sponsors: Bangladesh, Comoros, Cuba, Guyana, India, Indonesia, Lao People's Democratic Republic, Madagascar, Malaysia, Mali, Nigeria, Pakistan, Viet Nam, Yemen, Yugoslavia.

The General Assembly,
Recalling its resolution 36/120 E of 10 December 1981, in which it determined that all legislative and administrative measures and actions taken by Israel, the occupying Power, which had altered or purported to alter the character and status of the Holy City of Jerusalem, in particular the so-called "Basic Law" on Jerusalem and the proclamation of Jerusalem as the capital of Israel, were null and void and must be rescinded forthwith,
Recalling Security Council resolution 478(1980) of 20 August 1980, in which the Council, *inter alia*, decided not to recognize the "Basic Law" and called upon those States that had established diplomatic missions at Jerusalem to withdraw such missions from the Holy City,
1. *Deplores* the transfer by some States of their diplomatic missions to Jerusalem in violation of Security Council resolution 478(1980);
2. *Calls upon* those States to abide by the provisions of the relevant United Nations resolutions, in conformity with the Charter of the United Nations.

Recorded vote in Assembly as follows:

In favour: Afghanistan, Albania, Algeria, Angola, Argentina, Australia, Austria, Bahamas, Bahrain, Bangladesh, Barbados, Belgium, Benin, Bhutan, Bolivia, Botswana, Brazil, Bulgaria, Burma, Burundi, Byelorussian SSR, Canada, Cape Verde, Central African Republic, Chad, Chile, China, Colombia, Comoros, Congo, Cuba, Cyprus, Czechoslovakia, Democratic Kampuchea, Democratic Yemen, Denmark, Djibouti, Ecuador, Egypt, El Salvador, Ethiopia, Finland, France, Gabon, Gambia, German Democratic Republic, Germany, Federal Republic of, Ghana, Greece, Grenada, Guinea, Guinea-Bissau, Guyana, Honduras, Hungary, Iceland, India, Indonesia, Iran, Iraq, Ireland, Italy, Ivory Coast, Jamaica, Japan, Jordan, Kenya, Kuwait, Lao People's Democratic Republic, Lebanon, Lesotho, Liberia, Libyan Arab Jamahiriya, Luxembourg, Madagascar, Malaysia, Maldives, Mali, Malta, Mauritania, Mauritius, Mexico, Mongolia, Morocco, Mozambique, Nepal, Netherlands, New Zealand, Nicaragua, Nigeria, Norway, Oman, Pakistan, Panama, Paraguay, Peru, Philippines, Poland, Portugal, Qatar, Romania, Rwanda, Samoa, Sao Tome and Principe, Saudi Arabia, Senegal, Seychelles, Sierra Leone, Singapore, Somalia, Spain, Sri Lanka, Sudan, Suriname, Sweden, Syrian Arab Republic, Thailand, Togo, Trinidad and Tobago, Tunisia, Turkey, Uganda, Ukrainian SSR, USSR, United Arab Emirates, United Kingdom, United Republic of Cameroon, United Republic of Tanzania, Upper Volta, Uruguay, Vanuatu, Venezuela, Viet Nam, Yemen, Yugoslavia, Zaire, Zambia.
Against: Israel.
Abstaining: Dominican Republic, Guatemala, Malawi, United States.

Conference on the Palestine question (1983)

Convening of the Conference

The General Assembly, by a resolution adopted on 19 August 1982 at its resumed seventh emergency special session on the Palestine question,[3] decided to convene an International Conference on the Question of Palestine in Paris from 16 to 27 August 1983. States were invited to establish national focal points to co-ordinate preparations.

The resolution, sponsored by 39 nations, was adopted by a roll-call vote, requested by Israel, of 123 to 2, with 18 abstentions.

The initial decision to hold the Conference, not later than 1984, had been taken by the Assembly in December 1981.[4]

The recommendation to advance the date to 1983 was made by the Committee on Palestinian rights, acting as the Preparatory Committee for the Conference. After initially recommending on 27 May that the Conference be held in the first half of 1984, the Committee, according to its report to the Assembly,[2] reconsidered the matter in July in the light of the political and military situation in Lebanon and of a recommendation by the Extraordinary Ministerial Meeting of the Co-ordinating Bureau of the Non-Aligned Countries (Nicosia, Cyprus, 15-17 July) to review the decision with a view to advancing the date.[1]

Israel, explaining its position in the Assembly, rejected the holding of the Conference as another narcissistic excess.

Abstaining, Ireland said the Conference would have to involve all parties, including Israel and the recognized representatives of the Palestinians, and would have to address itself to all aspects of the Palestine problem; however, as envisaged, it did not meet those requirements. Sweden expressed a similar view, adding that, for any likelihood of positive results, the parties must agree on negotiations and on the procedure for them. France held the convening of a conference premature and said the elements of a settlement must be found through discussion among all States and political forces in the region, including the Palestine Liberation Organization (PLO). Though doubting whether the Conference would contribute towards a Middle East settlement, Canada nevertheless hoped it would make a serious effort to reach balanced conclusions and perhaps explore new directions. Denmark, speaking for the EC members, expressed reservations in particular on the proposed basis of and preparations for the Conference.

Several countries, among them Chile, stated their support for the holding of the Conference. Honduras considered it a further means of bringing about the desired objective of a durable peace. Austria felt that the Conference could emphasize the urgency of achieving a peaceful solution to the Palestine question. Haiti believed that the Conference might prove useful in view of the turn of the events and hoped that it might produce at least a possible outline for a comprehensive solution. Fiji said the calling for an international conference was consistent with the policy of exploring all peaceful avenues to resolve the Middle East conflict. In Ecuador's opinion, there was a pressing need to strengthen United Nations machinery for a peaceful settlement. Singapore voted in favour in view of Israel's invasion of Lebanon and because it believed that a settlement could not be achieved without PLO participation.

Spain felt that the resolution was moderate and realistic and put forward a number of praiseworthy ideas. Panama said the substance of the text essentially coincided with its own position on the Palestine question.

Though voting in favour, Burma had some reservations on the establishment of national focal points. In Iran's opinion, the resolution could have been much stronger and more constructive.

PLO expressed satisfaction that there was agreement that it was the responsibility of the United Nations to convene a conference, which should be held on the basis of the principles of the United Nations Charter and of Assembly resolutions.

Speaking during the debate, Madagascar felt that it was time to convene such a conference, as the Middle East could not be left to piecemeal impulsive ventures or moves. The German Democratic Republic said such a conference could decide on measures which would help the Palestinians in the struggle for their rights and would relieve their suffering.

Among the supporters for the holding of a conference were Argentina, Bulgaria, the Byelorussian SSR, Czechoslovakia, the German Democratic Republic, Hungary, the Lao People's Democratic Republic, Madagascar, Malta, Romania, Togo, Turkey, the Ukrainian SSR and Yemen.

Also during the Assembly debates on the Middle East situation and on the Palestine question at the regular session, several speakers, including Bahrain, Bangladesh, the Gambia, the Libyan Arab Jamahiriya, Mongolia, Pakistan, Poland, Qatar, Sri Lanka and Tunisia, expressed support for the Conference. The German Democratic

Republic and Viet Nam, among others, favoured its convening without delay, as proposed by the USSR. Romania called for a redoubling of political and diplomatic activities to that end.

Speaking as Rapporteur of the Committee on Palestinian rights and the Preparatory Committee for the Conference, Malta said the Conference could establish and define the broad parameters for a peaceful Middle East solution, and so set the seal of universal approval on the different peace proposals. Speaking as Chairman of the Committee on Palestinian rights, Senegal said the Conference should give the international community an exceptional opportunity to guide the development of the Middle East situation. Nigeria regarded the Conference as the best way to resolve all outstanding issues, and Qatar believed that its successful outcome would be of great value in restoring stability in the region.

The Ukrainian SSR hoped that all States would take part in the Conference and that its decisions would contribute to the restoration of Palestinian rights. Democratic Yemen, the Gambia and Yugoslavia had similar expectations, and Indonesia was convinced that a conference with the widest possible participation could lead to a breakthrough in the search for effective measures to enable the Palestinians to attain and exercise their rights. A breakthrough was also hoped for by Jordan.

Letter. [1]Cyprus, 29 July, transmitting communiqué of non-aligned countries, A/37/366-S/15327.
Report. [2]Preparatory Committee, A/37/49 & Corr.1.
Resolution (1982). [3]GA: ES-7/7, 19 Aug., text following.
Resolution (prior) [4]GA: 36/120 C, 10 Dec. 1981 (YUN 1981, p. 271).
Financial implications. ACABQ report, A/37/7/Add.2; S-G statements, A/ES-7/19, A/C.5/37/4.
Meeting records. GA: A/ES-7/PV.12-19 (20-26 Apr.), 22 (25 June), 25-28, *29-31* (16-19 Aug.).

General Assembly resolution ES-7/7

19 August 1982   Meeting 31   123-2-18 (roll-call vote)

39-nation draft (A/ES-7/L.6 and Add.1); agenda item 5.
Sponsors: Afghanistan, Bangladesh, Benin, Cape Verde, Chad, Congo, Cuba, Cyprus, Czechoslovakia, Gambia, German Democratic Republic, Grenada, Guinea, Guinea-Bissau, Guyana, Hungary, India, Indonesia, Jamaica, Lao People's Democratic Republic, Madagascar, Malaysia, Maldives, Mali, Malta, Niger, Nigeria, Pakistan, Romania, Sao Tome and Principe, Senegal, Sri Lanka, Sudan, Tunisia, Uganda, Ukrainian SSR, Viet Nam, Yemen, Yugoslavia.

International Conference on the Question of Palestine

The General Assembly,

Recalling its resolution 36/120 C of 10 December 1981, by which it decided to convene an International Conference on the Question of Palestine, not later than 1984, for a comprehensive effort to seek effective ways and means to enable the Palestinian people to attain and exercise its rights,

Deeply alarmed at the explosive situation in the Middle East resulting from the Israeli aggression against the sovereign State of Lebanon and the Palestinian people, which poses a threat to international peace and security,

Deeply aware of the responsibility of the United Nations under its Charter for the maintenance of international peace,

Gravely concerned that no just solution to the problem of Palestine has been achieved and that this problem therefore continues to aggravate the Middle East conflict, of which it is the core, and to endanger international peace and security,

Taking note of the final communiqué of the Extraordinary Ministerial Meeting of the Co-ordinating Bureau of the Non-Aligned Countries on the Question of Palestine, held at Nicosia from 15 to 17 July 1982,

Recognizing the need to intensify all efforts by the international community to enable the Palestinian people to attain and exercise its inalienable rights as defined and reaffirmed in United Nations resolutions,

Stressing the importance of the work of the Preparatory Committee for the International Conference on the Question of Palestine and the need for securing the broadest possible involvement of Member States in the preparatory processes leading up to the Conference, and in the Conference itself,

1. *Decides* to convene the International Conference on the Question of Palestine at the headquarters of the United Nations Educational, Scientific and Cultural Organization, in Paris, from 16 to 27 August 1983;

2. *Requests* the Secretary-General to ensure that adequate resources from the regular budget of the United Nations are provided urgently in order to enable the successful holding of the Conference and to carry out the necessary preparations for and follow-up activities to the Conference;

3. *Calls upon* all States to co-operate with the Preparatory Committee for the International Conference on the Question of Palestine in the implementation of the present resolution and invites them to establish national focal points for effective co-ordination of preparations at the national level.

Roll-call vote in Assembly as follows:

In favour: Afghanistan, Albania, Algeria, Angola, Argentina, Austria, Bahamas, Bahrain, Bangladesh, Barbados, Benin, Bhutan, Bolivia, Botswana, Brazil, Bulgaria, Burma, Burundi, Byelorussian SSR, Cape Verde, Chad, Chile, China, Colombia, Congo, Costa Rica, Cuba, Cyprus, Czechoslovakia, Democratic Kampuchea, Democratic Yemen, Djibouti, Dominican Republic, Ecuador, Egypt, El Salvador, Ethiopia, Fiji, Gabon, Gambia, German Democratic Republic, Ghana, Greece, Grenada, Guinea, Guinea-Bissau, Guyana, Haiti, Honduras, Hungary, India, Indonesia, Iran, Iraq, Ivory Coast, Jamaica, Jordan, Kenya, Kuwait, Lao People's Democratic Republic, Lebanon, Lesotho, Liberia, Libyan Arab Jamahiriya, Madagascar, Malawi, Malaysia, Maldives, Mali, Malta, Mauritania, Mauritius, Mexico, Mongolia, Morocco, Mozambique, Nepal, Nicaragua, Niger, Nigeria, Oman, Pakistan, Panama, Paraguay, Peru, Philippines, Poland, Qatar, Romania, Rwanda, Samoa, Sao Tome and Principe, Saudi Arabia, Senegal, Seychelles, Sierra Leone, Singapore, Somalia, Spain, Sri Lanka, Sudan, Swaziland, Syrian Arab Republic, Thailand, Togo, Trinidad and Tobago, Tunisia, Turkey, Uganda, Ukrainian SSR, USSR, United Arab Emirates, United Republic of Cameroon, United Republic of Tanzania, Upper Volta, Uruguay, Venezuela, Viet Nam, Yemen, Yugoslavia, Zaire, Zambia, Zimbabwe.

Against: Israel, United States.

Abstaining: Australia, Belgium, Canada, Denmark, Finland, France, Germany, Federal Republic of, Iceland, Ireland, Italy, Japan, Luxembourg, Netherlands, New Zealand, Norway, Portugal, Sweden, United Kingdom.

Conference preparations

Preparatory Committee activities. As authorized by the General Assembly in December 1981,[4] the Committee on the Exercise of the Inalienable Rights of the Palestinian People started acting in 1982 as the Preparatory Committee for the International Conference on the Question of Palestine. To that end, the Preparatory Committee held its first session, consisting of seven meetings, in New York from 31 March to 22 October. The Secretary-General appointed Lucille M. Mair as Secretary-General of the Conference as from 1 May.

In its report to the Assembly,[1] the Committee recommended that the Conference focus on two main objectives: to increase international awareness of the facts of the Palestine question, and to attain governmental and non-governmental support for effective ways to enable the Palestinians to exercise their rights in Palestine on the basis of United Nations resolutions. The Conference was to ensure a universal commitment by States to the achievement of Palestinian rights and the estab-

lishment of a Palestinian State within the framework adopted by the Assembly in 1976[3] (when it endorsed a plan by the Committee on Palestinian rights for a solution based on Israeli withdrawal from the occupied territories and the establishment of an independent Palestinian entity) and to set in motion agreed modalities for the implementation of agreed decisions.

The Committee made recommendations on the Conference's agenda, preparatory activities, organization of work, documentation, participation and rules of procedure.

General Assembly action. The General Assembly, on 10 December 1982,[2] endorsed the Preparatory Committee's recommendations and called for the fullest support by United Nations organizations to the Conference and its preparation. The Assembly urged Member States to promote awareness of the Conference's importance, intensify national and regional preparations, participate in the Conference and in regional preparatory meetings, contribute to the achievement of Palestinian rights and support modalities for their implementation.

The resolution was adopted by a recorded vote of 123 to 2, with 17 abstentions. Introducing it on behalf of 22 nations, Senegal, Chairman of the Committee on Palestinian rights, stated that the Conference would provide a unique opportunity to heighten awareness of the underlying causes of the Palestine question and to contribute to a comprehensive, just and lasting solution. Senegal stressed the importance of the participation of all Member States.

Opposing the text, Israel said it provided for another narcissistic excess, blowing away $5.7 million on sightseeing excursions by PLO propagandists and their fellow travellers. The United States regretted that the Assembly had again endorsed a propaganda exercise that could foster only continuing animosity and confrontation.

The EC members abstained on the ground, as stated by Denmark on their behalf, that such a conference would be worth while only if it were likely to assist progress towards a just, lasting and comprehensive peace settlement; they had serious doubts about Preparatory Committee recommendations which were not in accordance with a balanced and constructive approach. Australia regretted that the resolution would not aid in the endeavour to achieve a settlement, to be negotiated directly by the principal parties. Norway believed the right to self-determination of the Palestinians must be transformed into reality through negotiations between the parties. In Finland's opinion, the resolution failed to provide the balance which was a prerequisite for a negotiated settlement.

Canada could not support the objectives of the Conference as recommended by the Preparatory

Committee. Though it had originally voted to convene the Conference, Costa Rica abstained on the 1982 resolution after remarking that the work of the Preparatory Committee had not only failed to contribute to peace in the region but had tended to exacerbate tension. In spite of continued reservations, Sweden voted in favour in the hope that the Conference would indeed realize the other objective stated by the Committee, namely, to heighten awareness of the underlying causes of the Palestine question.

Casting an affirmative vote, Thailand expressed the view that a solution to the Palestine question must be found through a peaceful negotiated settlement with the participation of all parties, including PLO, and on the basis of United Nations resolutions. Portugal supported the text on the basis of the principles of its foreign policy, such as respect for human rights, implementation of the right to self-determination and condemnation of all armed intervention. Jamaica and Spain voted affirmatively in line with their support for the just cause of the Palestinians.

In the understanding of the Syrian Arab Republic, the establishment of a comprehensive, just and lasting peace in the Middle East, as referred to in the third preambular and first operative paragraphs, must be based on two fundamental and inseparable principles: the Palestinians must be allowed to exercise their rights to self-determination, to return and to establish a national State in Palestine; and Israel must be compelled to withdraw completely and unconditionally from all occupied territories, including Jerusalem.

Speaking on behalf of the Committee on Palestinian rights during the Assembly debate on the Palestine question, Senegal held it a good idea that the Assembly once again called on all States to take an active part in the preparatory and actual work of the Conference.

Endorsing the Committee recommendations, Viet Nam said they would undoubtedly help mobilize even wider international support for the Palestinian cause and would contribute to a Middle East solution. The recommendations were endorsed also by others, including Bangladesh and the Ukrainian SSR. Hungary hoped and Guyana and India believed the Conference would help enhance the Palestinians' cause, Indonesia believed it could lead to a breakthrough in the search for measures to enable them to attain their rights peacefully, Pakistan that it would help mobilize international support for the struggle for their rights, and Poland that it would play an important role in making possible the attainment of those rights. Sri Lanka called the Conference a laudable attempt to demonstrate concern. The Conference was also welcomed by Afghanistan, Bahrain,

Czechoslovakia, the Gambia, the Libyan Arab Jamahiriya, Madagascar, Qatar and Tunisia.

The United Arab Emirates declared that it was prepared to host a meeting of the Economic Commission for Western Asia (ECWA) in April 1983 to discuss Conference-related questions.

Report. [1]Preparatory Committee, A/37/49 & Corr.1.
Resolution (1982). [2]GA: 37/86 C, 10 Dec., text following.
Resolutions (prior). GA: [3]31/20, 24 Nov. 1976 (YUN 1976, p. 245); [4]36/120 C, 10 Dec. 1981 (YUN 1981, p. 271).
Meeting records. GA: A/37/PV.84-88, 89, 99 (30 Nov.–10 Dec.).

General Assembly resolution 37/86 C

10 December 1982   Meeting 99   123-2-17 (recorded vote)

22-nation draft (A/37/L.44 and Add.1); agenda item 31.
Sponsors: Afghanistan, Bangladesh, Comoros, Cuba, Cyprus, Gambia, German Democratic Republic, Guinea, Hungary, India, Indonesia, Lao People's Democratic Republic, Madagascar, Mali, Malta, Mongolia, Pakistan, Romania, Senegal, Ukrainian SSR, Viet Nam, Yugoslavia.

The General Assembly,

Recalling its resolutions 3236(XXIX) and 3237(XXIX) of 22 November 1974 and all other United Nations resolutions, including resolution ES-7/2 of 29 July 1980, pertinent to the question of Palestine,

Recalling also its resolutions 36/120 C of 10 December 1981, in which it decided to convene an International Conference on the Question of Palestine for a comprehensive effort to seek effective ways and means to enable the Palestinian people to attain and to exercise their rights, and ES-7/7 of 19 August 1982, in which it decided to convene the Conference at the headquarters of the United Nations Educational, Scientific and Cultural Organization, in Paris, from 16 to 27 August 1983,

Convinced that a comprehensive, just and lasting peace in the Middle East can be established, in accordance with the Charter and relevant resolutions of the United Nations, through a just solution to the problem of Palestine on the basis of the attainment of the legitimate rights of the Palestinian people,

Convinced that the Conference will provide a unique opportunity to heighten awareness of the underlying causes of the question of Palestine and to contribute actively and constructively to a solution of the question on the basis of relevant United Nations resolutions,

Stressing the need to assure the participation of all Member States in the Conference and their support for its preparation,

Taking note with appreciation of the report of the Preparatory Committee for the International Conference on the Question of Palestine,

1. *Reiterates* the responsibility of the United Nations to strive for a lasting peace in the Middle East through a just solution of the problem of Palestine;

2. *Endorses* the recommendations of the Preparatory Committee for the International Conference on the Question of Palestine, contained in paragraph 32 of its report, concerning the preparatory activities for the Conference, the objectives, the documentation, the draft provisional agenda and the draft provisional rules of procedure of the Conference, the participation in the Conference and the organization of work of the Preparatory Committee;

3. *Calls upon* all organizations of the United Nations system to continue to extend their fullest support to the Conference and to its preparation;

4. *Urges* all Member States to promote heightened awareness of the importance of the Conference and to intensify preparations at the national, subregional and regional levels in order to ensure its success;

5. *Calls upon* all Member States to contribute to the achievement of Palestinian rights and to support modalities for their implementation, and to participate in the Conference and the regional preparatory meetings preceding it;

6. *Decides* to consider the results of the Conference at its thirty-eighth session.

Recorded vote in Assembly as follows:

In favour: Afghanistan, Albania, Algeria, Angola, Antigua and Barbuda, Argentina, Austria, Bahamas, Bahrain, Bangladesh, Barbados, Belize, Benin, Bhutan, Brazil, Bulgaria, Burma, Burundi, Byelorussian SSR, Cape Verde, Central African Republic, Chad, Chile, China, Colombia, Comoros, Congo, Cuba, Cyprus, Czechoslovakia, Democratic Kampuchea, Democratic Yemen, Djibouti, Dominican Republic, Ecuador, Egypt, El Salvador, Equatorial Guinea, Ethiopia, Fiji,

Gabon, Gambia, German Democratic Republic, Ghana, Greece, Guinea, Guinea-Bissau, Guyana, Haiti, Honduras, Hungary, India, Indonesia, Iran, Iraq, Ivory Coast, Jamaica, Jordan, Kenya, Kuwait, Lao People's Democratic Republic, Lebanon, Liberia, Libyan Arab Jamahiriya, Madagascar, Malawi, Malaysia, Maldives, Mali, Malta, Mauritania, Mauritius, Mexico, Mongolia, Morocco, Mozambique, Nepal, Nicaragua, Niger, Nigeria, Oman, Pakistan, Panama, Papua New Guinea, Peru, Philippines, Poland, Portugal, Qatar, Romania, Rwanda, Sao Tome and Principe, Saudi Arabia, Senegal, Sierra Leone, Singapore, Somalia, Spain, Sri Lanka, Sudan, Suriname, Sweden, Syrian Arab Republic, Thailand, Togo, Tunisia, Turkey, Uganda, Ukrainian SSR, USSR, United Arab Emirates, United Republic of Cameroon, United Republic of Tanzania, Upper Volta, Uruguay, Vanuatu, Venezuela, Viet Nam, Yemen, Yugoslavia, Zaire, Zambia, Zimbabwe.

Against: Israel, United States.

Abstaining: Australia, Belgium, Canada, Costa Rica, Denmark, Finland, France, Germany, Federal Republic of, Iceland, Ireland, Italy, Japan, Luxembourg, Netherlands, New Zealand, Norway, United Kingdom.

Assistance to Palestinians

During 1982, United Nations assistance—particularly education and training—continued to be provided to Palestinians in the West Bank, the Gaza Strip and neighbouring Arab States. This was in addition to aid supplied by the United Nations Relief and Works Agency for Palestine Refugees in the Near East (UNRWA).

Much of this assistance continued to be financed by the United Nations Development Programme (UNDP). By the end of 1982, the initial $3.5 million allocated by the UNDP Governing Council in 1979[8] had been fully committed for projects to assist Palestinians in various sectors, including pre-primary education, technical and vocational training, health manpower development, housing, industrial development, and children's and youth institutions. Except for a project in the Syrian Arab Republic, executed by the Food and Agriculture Organization of the United Nations, all operations were in the West Bank and the Gaza Strip.

In consultations held by UNDP with the Governments directly concerned and representatives of the Palestinians, new project proposals for future years were developed in 1982, characterized by a greater involvement of private institutions. These included assistance to community centres, specialized training for the glass and ceramics industry, and assistance to private medical institutions.

In an April report to the Governing Council,[4] the UNDP Administrator made a number of suggestions concerning the future direction of the assistance programme. He informed the Council that an agreement had been worked out with all directly interested parties on an *ad hoc* project implementation system which took into account the special conditions of the West Bank and Gaza. Under these arrangements, all projects were to be implemented directly by UNDP rather than another executing agency, the transfer of UNDP funds to any Government or organization as an intermediary in project implementation would be prohibited, visits by UNDP personnel to the West Bank and Gaza and meetings there with organizations and individuals would be subject to advance approval by the authorities concerned, and the Adminis-

trator would be personally involved in all aspects of project design and implementation.

The cost of the programme for the remainder of the third programming cycle ending in 1986 was estimated at about $12 million, involving average annual expenditures of $2.7 million (as compared with the previous rate of about $1 million annually).

The Governing Council, on 18 June 1982,[1] endorsed the Administrator's approach and authorized him to draw up to $4 million from UNDP Special Programme Resources for the rest of the third programming cycle. It appealed to Governments and intergovernmental organizations to provide at least an additional $8 million for that period to supplement those resources.

In addition to this direct assistance, Palestinian trainees and scholars took part in UNDP-financed training programmes for the Arab States, including such institutions as the Arab Maritime Academy and the Arab Organization for Administrative Sciences, as well as in organizations aided by UNDP, such as the Regional Institute for Training and Research in Statistics (Baghdad, Iraq) and the Arab Planning Institute (Kuwait).

The Industrial Development Board of the United Nations Industrial Development Organization (UNIDO), on 28 May,[5] took note with appreciation of the participation of Palestinian trainees in UNIDO-organized training programmes and sought the expansion of such activities. It noted with regret that other approved technical projects of assistance to Palestinians had not been implemented and condemned the Israeli occupation authorities for blocking UNIDO efforts. The Board urged the UNIDO secretariat to take all possible measures to implement the projects and increase technical assistance to Palestinians in consultation with PLO. The Board's conclusion was adopted by a roll-call vote of 30 to 1 (United States), with 11 abstentions.

An amount of $56,000 was allocated from the United Nations Industrial Development Fund for a survey of manufacturing in the West Bank and the Gaza Strip, to be carried out as part of the development survey of Palestine to be prepared by the United Nations Conference on Trade and Development (UNCTAD). Funds for the UNCTAD survey, authorized by the Trade and Development Board in October 1981,[9] had not been found by the end of 1982.

The United Nations Children's Fund (UNICEF) spent $263,612 on assistance to Palestinian children and mothers in Jordan, Lebanon, the Syrian Arab Republic, the West Bank and Gaza. Much of this was provided through UNRWA centres. In addition, throughout the hostilities in Lebanon, UNICEF undertook relief operations for women and children in Lebanon, as well as Lebanese and Palestinian women and children temporarily sheltered in the Syrian Arab Republic. The World Food Programme supplied 340 tons of food to those refugees between July and October, enough for basic rations for 7,000 persons for 90 days.

Also during the hostilities in Lebanon, special measures were taken, at the request of the Security Council and the General Assembly, to arrange for the protection of Palestine refugees and civilians in Lebanon.

On 11 May,[6] ECWA requested its Executive Secretary, when receiving requests from PLO for assistance, to be guided by the scale on which ECWA provided assistance to the region's least developed countries. It also acted to advance work on a census of the Palestinian population.

In May 1982 (and in a later addendum),[2] the Secretary-General reported to the Assembly on assistance to Palestinians provided or planned by 21 United Nations organizations and agencies with a view to establishing and implementing projects, many of them at the request of or in co-operation with PLO, to improve the social and economic conditions of the Palestinians. A similar report, mainly covering 1982 activities, was submitted to the Economic and Social Council in May 1983.[3]

General Assembly action. By a resolution of 17 December 1982,[7] the General Assembly requested intensification of United Nations efforts, in co-operation with PLO, to provide economic and social assistance to the Palestinians, and requested that such assistance in the Arab host countries be rendered in co-operation with PLO and with the host Government's consent. The Assembly also condemned Israel for its invasion of Lebanon, inflicting severe damage on civilian Palestinians, and called for assistance to the victims.

The text was adopted by a recorded vote of 143 to 2, following its approval by the Second (Economic and Financial) Committee on 19 November by a recorded vote, requested by the United Arab Emirates, of 126 to 2, with 2 abstentions.

Introducing the 22-nation draft, Pakistan said that, when the entire Palestinian nation was fighting for survival, the international community had a moral obligation to offer assistance, and a massive emergency assistance programme would be required.

Voting against the resolution, Israel said it would try to prevent the adoption of resolutions which merely hampered future assistance efforts to the Palestinians in Lebanon and elsewhere. The United States cast a negative vote on the ground that the resolution had nothing to do with practical assistance to the Palestinians but rather aimed at strengthening the PLO claim to be their representative.

Lebanon declared its understanding that all assistance to Palestinians in Lebanon would be chan-nelled through UNRWA under Lebanese supervision.

Though voting in favour on humanitarian grounds, Chile said it did not share some of the views in the text and thought political ideas alien to the issue should have been omitted. Japan voiced reservations on assistance through the United Nations system to national liberation movements. Speaking for the EC members, Denmark said they would continue to contribute humanitarian assistance directly, through the Community and through United Nations institutions, each of which should determine for itself how and through what channels it could assist the Lebanese and Palestinians. Norway cast an affirmative vote in support of United Nations humanitarian assistance to the Palestinians but added that its position towards PLO remained unchanged.

Also voting affirmatively, Benin urged increased United Nations assistance to the Palestinians. The USSR said it supported the resolution in accordance with its desire for a just solution to Middle East problems.

Speaking during the Assembly's resumed seventh emergency special session, Bangladesh said the Palestinian refugee problem was political in origin and no humanitarian measures would eliminate the problem unless a just and lasting solution was found to the Palestine question. The Palestinians must be settled in their own homeland from where they had been uprooted; meanwhile, the United Nations and its specialized agencies should provide the economic and technical assistance necessary for the consolidation of the Palestinian entity.

Decision (1982). [1]UNDP Council (report, E/1982/16/Rev.1), 82/13, 18 June.
Reports. S-G, [2]A/37/214 & Add.1, [3]E/1983/72; [4]UNDP Administrator, DP/1982/18 & Corr.1; [5]IDB, A/37/16.
Resolutions (1982). [6]ECWA (report, E/1982/22): 108(IX), 11 May. [7]GA: 37/134, 17 Dec., text following.
Yearbook references. [8]1979, p. 372; [9]1981, p. 322.
Meeting records. GA: 2nd Committee, A/C.2/37/SR.3-12, 32, 36, 40-42 (28 Sep.–19 Nov.); plenary, A/37/PV.109 (17 Dec.).

General Assembly resolution 37/134

17 December 1982   Meeting 109   143-2 (recorded vote)

Approved by Second Committee (A/37/679) by recorded vote (126-2-2), 19 November (meeting 41); 22-nation draft (A/C.2/37/L.39); agenda item 12.

Sponsors: Afghanistan, Algeria, Bangladesh, China, Congo, Cuba, German Democratic Republic, Guinea, India, Kuwait, Malaysia, Morocco, Nicaragua, Oman, Pakistan, Saudi Arabia, Senegal, Sudan, Tunisia, United Arab Emirates, Viet Nam, Yugoslavia.

Assistance to the Palestinian people
The General Assembly,

Recalling its resolution ES-7/5 of 26 June 1982,

Recalling also Security Council resolution 512(1982) of 19 June 1982,

Recalling further Economic and Social Council resolution 1982/48 of 27 July 1982,

Expressing its deep alarm at the Israeli invasion of Lebanon, which claimed the lives of a very large number of civilian Palestinians,

Horrified by the Sabra and Shatila massacre,

Noting with deep concern the dire need of the Palestinian victims of the Israeli invasion for urgent humanitarian assistance,

Noting the need to provide economic and social assistance to the Palestinian people,

1. *Condemns* Israel for its invasion of Lebanon, which inflicted severe damage on civilian Palestinians, including heavy loss of human life, intolerable suffering and massive material destruction;

2. *Endorses* Economic and Social Council resolution 1982/48;

3. *Calls upon* Governments and relevant United Nations bodies to provide humanitarian assistance to the Palestinian victims of the Israeli invasion of Lebanon;

4. *Requests* the relevant programmes, agencies, organs and organizations of the United Nations system to intensify their efforts, in co-operation with the Palestine Liberation Organization, to provide economic and social assistance to the Palestinian people;

5. *Also requests* that United Nations assistance to the Palestinians in the Arab host countries should be rendered in co-operation with the Palestine Liberation Organization and with the consent of the Arab host Government concerned;

6. *Requests* the Secretary-General to report to the General Assembly at its thirty-eighth session, through the Economic and Social Council, on the progress made in the implementation of the present resolution.

Recorded vote in Assembly as follows:

In favour: Afghanistan, Albania, Algeria, Angola, Argentina, Australia, Austria, Bahamas, Bahrain, Bangladesh, Barbados, Belgium, Benin, Bhutan, Botswana, Brazil, Bulgaria, Burma, Burundi, Byelorussian SSR, Canada, Cape Verde, Central African Republic, Chad, Chile, China, Colombia, Comoros, Congo, Costa Rica, Cuba, Cyprus, Czechoslovakia, Democratic Kampuchea, Democratic Yemen, Denmark, Djibouti, Dominica, Dominican Republic, Ecuador, Egypt, El Salvador, Ethiopia, Fiji, Finland, France, Gabon, Gambia, German Democratic Republic, Germany, Federal Republic of, Ghana, Greece, Grenada, Guinea, Guinea-Bissau, Guyana, Honduras, Hungary, Iceland, India, Indonesia, Iran, Iraq, Ireland, Italy, Ivory Coast, Jamaica, Japan, Jordan, Kenya, Kuwait, Lao People's Democratic Republic, Lebanon, Lesotho, Liberia, Libyan Arab Jamahiriya, Luxembourg, Madagascar, Malawi, Malaysia, Maldives, Mali, Malta, Mauritania, Mauritius, Mexico, Mongolia, Morocco, Mozambique, Nepal, Netherlands, New Zealand, Nicaragua, Niger, Nigeria, Norway, Oman, Pakistan, Panama, Papua New Guinea, Paraguay, Peru, Philippines, Poland, Portugal, Qatar, Romania, Rwanda, Samoa, Sao Tome and Principe, Saudi Arabia, Senegal, Sierra Leone, Singapore, Solomon Islands, Somalia, Spain, Sri Lanka, Suriname, Swaziland, Sweden, Thailand, Togo, Trinidad and Tobago, Tunisia, Turkey, Uganda, Ukrainian SSR, USSR, United Arab Emirates, United Kingdom, United Republic of Cameroon, United Republic of Tanzania, Upper Volta, Uruguay, Vanuatu, Venezuela, Viet Nam, Yemen, Yugoslavia, Zaire, Zambia, Zimbabwe.

Against: Israel, United States.

Situation between individual Arab States and Israel

Israel's invasion of Lebanon in June 1982, and its aftermath when hostilities ended in August, was a major focus of attention in the Security Council and the General Assembly. The Assembly also dealt with the situation between Iraq and Israel resulting from Israel's aerial attack against an Iraqi nuclear reactor in June 1981, and between Israel and the Syrian Arab Republic. In the Assembly debates on the Middle East situation and the Palestine question, several speakers referred to Israel's withdrawal from the Sinai peninsula and its return to Egypt (see above, under MIDDLE EAST SITUATION).

Iraq and Israel

Communications. By a letter of 6 January[1] 1982 to the Security Council President and one of 13 January[2] to the Secretary-General, Iraq charged Israeli war-planes with violation of Iraqi airspace on 31 December 1981 and 4 January 1982.

Action by the Commission on Human Rights. Expressing its conviction that the Israeli aggression against the Iraqi nuclear installation in June 1981[9] constituted a violation of the right of States to scientific and technological progress for social and economic development, the Commission on Human Rights, on 19 February 1982,[4] strongly condemned Israel for its premeditated act and called on States to cease any moral, material or human assistance which would enable Israel to pursue its policies of aggression, expansion and human rights violations.

Report of the Secretary-General. In July 1982 and in an October addendum,[3] the Secretary-General transmitted to the General Assembly and the Security Council replies received from 19 Governments to his request of 12 April for information on action taken by them in response to a November 1981 Assembly resolution calling on States to cease providing arms and related material to Israel which enabled it to commit aggression.[7] The 19 Governments either stated that they did not supply weapons of any kind to Israel or condemned the 1981 Israeli attack.

The Secretary-General also reported that on 6 April 1982 he had requested information from Israel with regard to the Assembly's demand in the same resolution that it compensate promptly and adequately for the material damage and loss of life resulting from its 1981 attack. On 9 June, Israel responded that it did not consider itself bound by the resolution but that, out of humanitarian considerations, it had made an *ex gratia* payment to the family of a French citizen who had lost his life in the wake of Israel's action; the nature of Iraq's relations with Israel, however, did not require or permit consideration by Israel of Iraqi claims.

General Assembly action. By a resolution of 16 November 1982,[5] the General Assembly condemned Israel for its refusal to implement the June 1981 Security Council resolution[8] on the attack against Iraq's nuclear research centre (calling on Israel to place its nuclear facilities under International Atomic Energy Agency (IAEA) safeguards, and stating that Iraq was entitled to redress), as well as for its threats to repeat such attacks and for its escalation of aggression in the region. Considering the Israeli act to be a violation and a denial of human rights as well as of the right of a State to scientific and technological progress for social and economic development, the Assembly requested the Council to consider measures to deter Israel from repeating such an attack. It called for the continued consideration of international legal measures to prohibit armed attacks against nuclear facilities and threats thereof, and requested the Secretary-General to prepare in 1983, with the aid of a group of experts, a study on the consequences of the Israeli attack.

The twice-revised 32-nation draft was adopted by a recorded vote of 119 to 2, with 13 abstentions.

Introducing the text, Tunisia said it reflected the international concern at the grave precedent which seriously violated international law and confirmed Israel's selfish designs in the Middle East and its determination to thwart the legitimate aspirations of the Arab peoples to scientific and technological progress.

Rejecting the resolution, Israel said it was one-sided, contained unwarranted and unacceptable demands, and would require the expenditure of funds on a group of experts at a time when the United Nations could not find even lesser sums for constructive projects. Iraq had been in a state of war with Israel for over 30 years, had consistently violated prohibitions against the threat or use of force and had openly rejected Security Council resolutions on a Middle East peace. The best way to prevent the spread of nuclear weapons in the region would be the creation of a nuclear-weapon-free zone.

The United States, which also voted against, believed that the resolution served only to reopen old wounds; the Security Council had acted promptly at the time of the attack, and intemperate and futile debate in the Assembly, resulting in unenforceable resolutions, would do nothing to serve peace.

Abstaining, Chile stated that a number of paragraphs went beyond the topic and condemned alleged intentions without providing sufficient evidence; in addition, it was up to the Council to determine whether further action was warranted. Canada abstained on the ground that the Council had the sole responsibility for determining the existence of a threat to peace, breach of peace or act of aggression; it also reserved its position on paragraph 5, which could be interpreted as meaning that States had human rights, as well as on the efficacy and cost of the proposed study. The Ivory Coast, although recalling its condemnation of Israel's aggression at the time, stressed the importance of avoiding measures that would adversely affect the quest for peace.

Though voting for the resolution, Belgium, Denmark, the Netherlands and the United Kingdom expressed the view that it would serve no useful purpose for the issue to become a permanent agenda item. Belgium also believed that the preamble raised extraneous matters, and Denmark voiced reservations on operative paragraphs 2 and 3. The Netherlands, pointing out that the Council was already seized of the matter by virtue of its 1981 resolution, said its primary responsibility for the maintenance of international peace and security must be respected. France and the United Kingdom voiced reservations on paragraph 7.

The Federal Republic of Germany believed that other United Nations forums would be more appropriate for discussions of the attack and its consequences; it did not believe that repeated condemnations of Israel were likely to promote conditions for solving the problems resulting from the attack, and it would not support future resolutions which perpetuated those elements. Though regarding the text as a considerable improvement over the 1981 resolution on the subject,[7] Italy objected to the use in an Assembly resolution of certain terms having specific legal implications according to the Charter of the United Nations. Norway questioned the usefulness of studies and reports on the consequences of the Israeli attack, and had strong reservations on the inclusion of the item in the 1983 Assembly agenda. Sweden could not fully support all the proposals in the text, or the general and sweeping character of some formulations.

India stated that its support of the resolution was without prejudice to its views on issues such as the Treaty on the Non-Proliferation of Nuclear Weapons[6] (NPT) and related safeguards, as well as on the understanding that nothing in the text, in particular the proposed study, would be interpreted or used in any manner to strengthen the Treaty or the safeguards régime.

During the debate, Iraq stated that the Assembly had to look into the implications and consequences of Israel's act of aggression, which had attacked the principle of international security and had established a precedent that had brought the world closer to a nuclear holocaust. Pointing to reports indicating the possession of atomic weapons by Israel, Iraq said the real motive behind Israel's acquisition of such weapons was to impose a solution to the Arab-Israeli conflict on its own terms. In addition to depriving the Arabs of their lands and national rights, Israel was seeking to deprive them of scientific and technological progress. Meanwhile, Israel still refused to place its nuclear facilities under IAEA safeguards and to entertain any consideration of redress for the damage its aggression had caused.

Most speakers in the debate recalled the condemnation of the Israeli raid voiced by the Assembly and the Council in 1981 and deplored Israel's failure to comply with those resolutions. Taking this position were Albania, Algeria, Bahrain, Bulgaria, the Byelorussian SSR, China, Cuba, Cyprus, Czechoslovakia, the German Democratic Republic, India, Indonesia, Jordan, the Libyan Arab Jamahiriya, Malaysia, Mauritania, Pakistan, Qatar, Tunisia, Turkey, the USSR, the United Arab Emirates, Yemen and Yugoslavia. Most of them viewed the action as a continuation of an aggressive policy that had manifested itself again in Israel's invasion of Lebanon.

Denmark, for the European Community (EC) members, repeated their call on Israel to comply fully with the Council's 1981 resolution.

Cuba and India rejected the doctrine of preventive attack. The United Arab Emirates said Israel did not have the right to decide on its own that its action was in self-defence, and Yugoslavia stated that arbitrary interpretations of the right of self-defence could not be accepted. Given Israel's refusal to renounce its proclaimed pre-emptive right to attack the peaceful nuclear installations of other countries, said Indonesia, no country with a peaceful nuclear programme under IAEA safeguards could feel secure.

Many States expressed concern that Israel had not relinquished the threat to repeat such attacks. Bahrain and the United Arab Emirates mentioned statements by the Israeli Prime Minister to the effect that Israel would destroy any nuclear installation in any Arab country. That policy, said Algeria, constituted a serious threat to peace. India said the Assembly should demand a commitment from Israel that it would not resort to such actions in future. Pakistan remarked that Israel, having developed a nuclear capacity itself, had declared its intention to deprive other States in the region of the possibility of developing even peaceful nuclear energy programmes. A similar point was made by Jordan and other Arab States.

Bulgaria warned of the hazards that could be created by military attacks against nuclear reactors, notably the spread of deadly radiation among civilians. The German Democratic Republic urged that the intentional destruction of peaceful nuclear facilities be outlawed. Indonesia and Pakistan suggested that measures be considered to prohibit attacks on such installations.

Turkey remarked that Israel's presumably increased sense of security after the destruction of the Iraqi nuclear installation and the invasion of Lebanon was deceptive and ephemeral, as real security for Israel could come only with a just and durable Middle East settlement.

Albania, Bulgaria, the Byelorussian SSR, Cuba, Czechoslovakia, the German Democratic Republic, the Libyan Arab Jamahiriya, the USSR and the United Arab Emirates deplored the support given to Israel's position by the United States, especially through the supply of arms. They urged all States to cease providing such support.

Bahrain and the Libyan Arab Jamahiriya urged the application of sanctions against Israel, while the Byelorussian SSR and Tunisia were among those favouring effective measures by the Security Council to restrain the aggressor. Had enforcement measures been taken after the attack against Iraq, said Indonesia, subsequent Israeli aggression could have been mitigated. Algeria thought the Assembly should demand the dismantling of the Israeli nuclear arsenal.

Several speakers mentioned the decision by the IAEA General Conference on 24 September 1982 not to accept the credentials of Israel. The United Arab Emirates regarded what it called Israel's suspension from IAEA as the first step to putting an end to that country's resort to the law of the jungle.

China, Cuba, Cyprus, Denmark (for the EC members), India, Indonesia, Kuwait, Malaysia, Turkey, the United Arab Emirates, Yemen and Yugoslavia reaffirmed the right of all States to use nuclear energy for peaceful purposes. India and others added that there was no evidence to support Israel's contention that Iraq had been on the verge of producing nuclear weapons. All of Iraq's nuclear activities had been carried out in the light of day and under IAEA safeguards, said Qatar, while Israel based its nuclear activity on clandestine operations.

Noting that Iraq was a party to NPT, Kuwait and Turkey urged that IAEA safeguards be applied to Israeli nuclear activities. Unless that happened, said Qatar, Israel would persist in its nuclear blackmail against the Arab countries. The USSR said the June 1981 attack had placed into sharp relief the danger inherent in Israel's refusal to adhere to NPT.

Letters. Iraq: [1]6 Jan., S/14826; [2]13 Jan., A/37/68.
Report. [3]S-G, A/37/365-S/15320 & Add.1.
Resolutions (1982). [4]Commission on Human Rights (report, E/1982/12): 1982/5, 19 Feb. [5]GA: 37/18, 16 Nov., text following.
Resolutions (prior). GA: [6]2373(XXII), annex, 12 June 1968 (YUN 1968, p. 17); [7]36/27, 13 Nov. 1981 (YUN 1981, p. 282). [8]SC: 487(1981), 19 June 1981 (*ibid.*, p. 282).
Yearbook reference. [9]1981, p. 275.
Financial implications. 5th Committee report, A/37/615; S-G statement, A/C.5/37/36.
Meeting records. GA: plenary, A/37/PV.49, 50, 70 (29 Oct.–16 Nov.); 5th Committee, A/C.5/37/SR.34 (15 Nov.).

General Assembly resolution 37/18

16 November 1982   Meeting 70   119-2-13 (recorded vote)

32-nation draft (A/37/L.12/Rev.2 and Rev.2/Corr.1 and Rev.2/Add.1); agenda item 24.
Sponsors: Algeria, Bahrain, Comoros, Cuba, Cyprus, Democratic Yemen, Djibouti, Grenada, Indonesia, Iraq, Jordan, Kuwait, Lao People's Democratic Republic, Libyan Arab Jamahiriya, Madagascar, Malaysia, Maldives, Mali, Mauritania, Morocco, Nicaragua, Oman, Pakistan, Qatar, Saudi Arabia, Sudan, Syrian Arab Republic, Tunisia, United Arab Emirates, Viet Nam, Yemen, Yugoslavia.

Armed Israeli aggression against the Iraqi nuclear installations and its grave consequences for the established international system concerning the peaceful uses of nuclear energy, the non-proliferation of nuclear weapons and international peace and security

The General Assembly,

Having considered the item entitled "Armed Israeli aggression against the Iraqi nuclear installations and its grave consequences for the established international system concerning the peaceful uses of nuclear energy, the non-proliferation of nuclear weapons and international peace and security",

Recalling the relevant resolutions of the Security Council and the General Assembly,

Taking note of the report of the Secretary-General,

Taking note also of the relevant resolution of the International Atomic Energy Agency and the Commission on Human Rights,

Viewing with deep concern Israel's refusal to comply with those resolutions, particularly Security Council resolution 487(1981) of 19 June 1981,

Gravely alarmed by the dangerous escalation of Israel's acts of aggression in the region,

Gravely concerned that Israel continues to maintain its threats to repeat such attacks against nuclear installations,

Reiterating its alarm over the information and evidence regarding the acquisition and development of nuclear weapons by Israel,

Recalling the Declaration and the Programme of Action on the Establishment of a New International Economic Order, the Charter of Economic Rights and Duties of States and the Declaration on the Use of Scientific and Technological Progress in the Interests of Peace and for the Benefit of Mankind,

Affirming the need to ensure against the repetition of such an attack on nuclear facilities by Israel or any other State,

1. *Condemns* Israel's refusal to implement resolution 487(1981), unanimously adopted by the Security Council;

2. *Strongly condemns* Israel for the escalation of its acts of aggression in the region;

3. *Condemns* Israel's threats to repeat such attacks, which would gravely endanger international peace and security;

4. *Demands* that Israel withdraw forthwith its officially declared threat to repeat its armed attack against nuclear facilities;

5. *Considers* the Israeli act of aggression to be a violation and a denial of the inalienable sovereign right of States to scientific and technological progress for achieving social and economic development and raising the standards of peoples and the dignity of the human person, as well as a violation and a denial of inalienable human rights and the sovereign right of States to scientific and technological development;

6. *Requests* the Security Council to consider the necessary measures to deter Israel from repeating such an attack on nuclear facilities;

7. *Calls* for the continuation of the consideration, at the international level, of legal measures to prohibit armed attacks against nuclear facilities, and threats thereof as a contribution to promoting and ensuring the safe development of nuclear energy for peaceful purposes;

8. *Requests* the Secretary-General to prepare, with the assistance of a group of experts,* a comprehensive study on the consequences of the Israeli armed attack against the Iraqi nuclear installations devoted to peaceful purposes, and to submit that study to the General Assembly at its thirty-eighth session;

9. *Further requests* the Secretary-General to report to the General Assembly at its thirty-eighth session on the implementation of the present resolution;

10. *Decides* to include in the provisional agenda of its thirty-eighth session the item entitled "Armed Israeli aggression against the Iraqi nuclear installations and its grave consequences for the established international system concerning the peaceful uses of nuclear energy, the non-proliferation of nuclear weapons and international peace and security".

---

*Subsequently named Group of Experts on the Consequences of the Israeli Armed Attack against the Iraqi Nuclear Installation.

Recorded vote in Assembly as follows:

In favour: Albania, Algeria, Angola, Argentina, Austria, Bahrain, Bangladesh, Barbados, Belgium, Benin, Bhutan, Brazil, Bulgaria, Burundi, Byelorussian SSR, Cape Verde, Central African Republic, Chad, China, Comoros, Congo, Cuba, Cyprus, Czechoslovakia, Democratic Kampuchea, Democratic Yemen, Denmark, Djibouti, Ecuador, Egypt, El Salvador, Equatorial Guinea, Ethiopia, Finland, France, Gabon, Gambia, German Democratic Republic, Germany, Federal Republic of, Ghana, Greece, Grenada, Guinea, Guyana, Honduras, Hungary, Iceland, India, Indonesia, Iraq, Ireland, Italy, Japan, Jordan, Kenya, Kuwait, Lao People's Democratic Republic, Liberia, Libyan Arab Jamahiriya, Luxembourg, Madagascar, Malaysia, Maldives, Mali, Malta, Mauritania, Mauritius, Mexico, Mongolia, Morocco, Mozambique, Nepal, Netherlands, New Zealand, Nicaragua, Niger, Nigeria, Norway, Oman, Pakistan, Panama, Papua New Guinea, Peru, Philippines, Poland, Portugal, Qatar, Romania, Sao Tome and Principe, Saudi Arabia, Senegal, Seychelles, Singapore, Somalia, Spain, Sri Lanka, Sudan, Suriname, Swaziland, Sweden, Syrian Arab Republic, Thailand, Togo, Trinidad and Tobago, Tunisia, Turkey, Uganda, Ukrainian SSR, USSR, United Kingdom, United Republic of Cameroon, United Republic of Tanzania, Upper Volta, Uruguay, Venezuela, Viet Nam, Yemen, Yugoslavia, Zambia.

Against: Israel, United States.

Abstaining: Australia, Bahamas, Canada, Chile, Colombia, Dominican Republic, Fiji, Guatemala, Haiti, Ivory Coast, Jamaica, Malawi, Paraguay.

Israel and Lebanon

During the first half of 1982, the cease-fire in the Israel-Lebanon sector which had come into effect in July 1981[24] generally held, although there were serious breaches on 21 April and 9 May and tension remained at a high level (see below). Intensive efforts were made both in the field and at United Nations Headquarters to maintain the cease-fire and to restore it after hostile acts occurred. In February, the Security Council approved an increase in strength of the United Nations Interim Force in Lebanon (UNIFIL)—stationed in the southern part of the country north of the border with Israel—from 6,000 to approximately 7,000 troops.

The situation changed radically in early June, when Israeli aircraft attacked targets in the Beirut area and Israeli forces moved into Lebanese territory in strength. They pushed through the UNIFIL area of operation and, by late June, reached the Beirut area.

The Security Council in June twice demanded an immediate cessation of all hostilities throughout Lebanon and unconditional Israeli withdrawal to the internationally recognized boundaries. It also extended the mandate of UNIFIL for two months and authorized it on an interim basis to protect and assist the civilians in the area. A call for a cease-fire and troop withdrawal was also made in June by the General Assembly, recalled into emergency special session. As fighting continued into July the Council demanded that Israel lift its blockade of Beirut so that supplies could be sent to the civilian population.

In August, following several aborted attempts to stop the fighting and after the Council authorized the deployment of United Nations observers to monitor the situation in and around Beirut, a general cease-fire was achieved. The Council again extended the UNIFIL mandate, initially for two months and then, in October, for a further three months. Meeting again in August, the Assembly condemned Israel for non-compliance with Council resolutions. Israeli incursions into Beirut in violation of the cease-fire were condemned in September by the Council, which also authorized an increase in the number of United Nations observers in the area, from 10 to 50. With the end of hostilities but with Israeli troops remaining in southern Lebanon, the Assembly, in September and again in December, called for strict respect for the sovereignty, territorial integrity, unity and political independence of Lebanon.

Throughout the period of hostilities and afterwards, the Council and the Assembly called repeatedly for measures to protect Palestine refugees and civilians in Lebanon. On the scene, several United Nations organizations were involved in emergency relief and rehabilitation efforts (see ECONOMIC AND SOCIAL QUESTIONS, Chapter III). A massacre of Palestinian and other civilians in two refugee camps near Beirut on 17 September was condemned by the Assembly as an act of genocide. In related action, the Assembly called in August for the annual observance on 4 June of an International Day of Innocent Children Victims of Aggression and called on Israel in December to restore Palestinian cultural property seized by Israeli forces.

Throughout this period, the Secretary-General kept the Council informed of developments in Lebanon through a series of reports, and both the Council and the Assembly received a large number of communications from Governments, particularly concerning the situation of civilians in the area.

Report and communications (February). In a special report of 16 February 1982 on UNIFIL,[18] the Secretary-General informed the Security Council that, since the adoption of its December 1981 resolution reaffirming the UNIFIL mandate until 19 June 1982,[22] the cease-fire in southern Lebanon had been maintained. The basic underlying tensions in the area had persisted, however, and the situation had remained extremely volatile. The Force had continued to face attempts at infiltration by armed elements (mainly the Palestine Liberation Organization (PLO) and the Lebanese National Movement) and encroachments established in the UNIFIL area of deployment by the *de facto* forces (Christian and associated militias) had not been removed.

The Secretary-General noted that, while impediments remained to the further deployment of UNIFIL in its entire area of operation up to the international border, the Lebanese Government had strongly reiterated its view that a phased programme should be set in motion to achieve an increased military and civilian presence of the Government in the south, along with consolidation of the UNIFIL area of deployment and its further deployment in accordance with its mandate. He supported the strong recommendation of the Commander and the wish of the Lebanese Government that the ceiling for UNIFIL troops (currently 6,000) be increased by no less than 1,000 to reinforce operations and make further deployment possible. He also stressed the importance of the full co-operation of the parties and remarked that the precarious cease-fire had never been intended as a substitute for fulfilment of the UNIFIL mandate.

By a letter of 16 February to the Council,[9] Lebanon confirmed the requests of its Government concerning UNIFIL, as presented in a memorandum to the Secretary-General on 14 December 1981.[25] On 23 February 1982,[10] Lebanon transmitted a memorandum of 16 February, prepared by a Lebanese parliamentary delegation prior to a meeting with the Secretary-General on 18 February, calling for full implementation of the UNIFIL mandate through the complete withdrawal of Israeli troops from Lebanon and the return of the Lebanese Government's effective authority in the area.

By a letter of 19 February,[3] Cuba, as Chairman of the Movement of Non-Aligned Countries and on behalf of its Co-ordinating Bureau, expressed concern over the concentration of Israeli war resources and troops at the border with Lebanon, and called on the Security Council President and the Secretary-General to bring an end to those Israeli actions.

Security Council action (February). The Security Council met on 23 and 25 February 1982 in accordance with its December 1981 decision, at the time of its most recent renewal of the UNIFIL mandate, to review within two months the situation in southern Lebanon.

By a resolution of 25 February,[20] the Council reaffirmed its 1978 resolution calling on Israel to cease its military action against Lebanese territorial integrity and establishing UNIFIL,[21] and approved an immediate increase in the strength of the Force from 6,000 to approximately 7,000 troops. The Council re-emphasized the terms of reference and general guidelines of UNIFIL, and called on the Secretary-General to renew his efforts to reactivate the 1949 General Armistice Agreement[23] and, in particular, to convene an early meeting of the Israel-Lebanon Mixed Armistice Commission (ILMAC). The Secretary-General was also requested to continue discussions with the Lebanese Government and the parties, with a view to submitting a report by 10 June 1982 on the requirements for further progress in a phased programme of activities with the Government of Lebanon. He was also asked for a progress report on the situation as a whole within two months.

The resolution, prepared in the course of consultations, was adopted by 13 votes to none, with 2 abstentions. Before its adoption, Israel, Lebanon and the Syrian Arab Republic were invited, at their request, to participate without vote in the discussion.

At the request of Jordan in a letter of 23 February,[7] the Council decided on the same day that an invitation should be accorded to PLO to participate in the debate and that the invitation would confer on it the same rights of participation as those conferred on a Member State invited to participate under rule 37 of the Council's provisional rules of procedure.[a] The Council took this decision by a vote, requested by the United States, of 11 to 1 (United States), with 3 abstentions (France, Japan, United Kingdom).

---

[a] Rule 37 of the Council's provisional rules of procedure states: "Any Member of the United Nations which is not a member of the Security Council may be invited, as the result of a decision of the Security Council, to participate, without vote, in the discussion of any question brought before the Security Council when the Security Council considers that the interests of that Member are specially affected, or when a Member brings a matter to the attention of the Security Council in accordance with Article 35 (1) of the Charter."

The Council acted without vote to extend an invitation under rule 39[b] to the Permanent Observer of the League of Arab States, as requested by Jordan in a letter of the same date.[(8)]

Poland and the USSR abstained in the vote on the resolution because of their positions of principle on UNIFIL. The USSR said, however, that it did not object to the increase in the Force's strength, primarily to ensure its possible further deployment in accordance with its mandate; in the light of the extremely tense and explosive situation in southern Lebanon, the Council must be enabled to monitor the situation and keep abreast of all matters connected with the strength of the Force and its deployment.

France and the United States supported the increase. France also favoured redeployment of the strengthened Force to effect a continuous link between its two current emplacements, endorsed its right to defend itself and return fire, and held it necessary to reaffirm Israel's obligation to withdraw from the enclave of the *de facto* forces and to resume the activities of ILMAC. The United States said the dangerous cycle of violence should be addressed in all its aspects and complexities, and hoped that a reinforced UNIFIL would be able to deal more effectively with incursions and violence of all kinds and from all sources; it regretted that some elements had been added that seemed extraneous to the basic purpose of the resolution.

Opening the debate, Lebanon said the Council had the power to reverse what otherwise appeared to be an irreversible process towards war, by reinforcing the existing conflict-control mechanisms and acting to prevent a frail and volatile cease-fire from becoming another prelude to death and destruction. To that end, Lebanon proposed the following Council action: an injunction to ensure Israel's withdrawal so that the 1949 General Armistice Agreement might be reinstated; a qualitative and quantitative enhancement of UNIFIL capabilities; and strict and forceful implementation of a joint phased programme of action, agreed upon between the Lebanese Government and the Secretary-General, to ensure the gradual transition of the responsibilities for peace and security from UNIFIL to the Lebanese Army, thereby restoring Lebanese sovereignty and territorial integrity. Lebanon reaffirmed its strong conviction that if UNIFIL was not given a new lease on life, it would remain a helpless hostage caught in an ever-expanding cycle of turmoil and violence.

Jordan stated that Israel's so-called *de facto* enclave, intended for use as a springboard for the seizure and annexation of southern Lebanon to steal the waters of the Litani River, had prevented UNIFIL and the Lebanese Army from carrying out their task of restoring the Lebanese Government's authority. The League of Arab States observer,

supporting Lebanon's plea to recover its full authority in the south, said Israel, with its long-planned threat of invasion, intended to destroy the Palestinians' political and social presence everywhere, in all their places of temporary or permanent abode, as it had done in Palestine.

The Syrian Arab Republic charged Israel with plans for establishing a "Greater Israel" through occupation and annexation.

Israel stated that Lebanon's problems far transcended the issue of the UNIFIL area of operation; the erosion of Lebanon's sovereignty had begun in the early 1970s with the arrival of large numbers of armed PLO terrorists, who over recent years had turned southern Lebanon into a staging-post for murderous incursions into Israel. As long as non-Lebanese elements, including an occupying army of upwards of 25,000 Syrian troops, were allowed to operate within and from Lebanon, there would be no real progress towards the return of the Lebanese Government's effective authority. With regard to the 1949 General Armistice Agreement, Israel said it had been brought to an end by Lebanon in June 1967; after that, Lebanon had repeatedly demonstrated that it no longer considered the Agreement in force by concluding a series of agreements with PLO that were totally incompatible with its obligations under the Agreement. Israel continued to support the political independence, sovereignty, territorial integrity and unity of Lebanon.

The PLO observer warned that Israel's statement and the concentration of its troops along the Lebanese border were a prelude to another invasion of southern Lebanon, aimed at eliminating the Palestinians and occupying Lebanese territory.

Ireland stated that the Council, in addition to approving the request to strengthen UNIFIL, should insist on full respect for the Force, maintain pressure on all concerned to co-operate with it and allow it to deploy fully; UNIFIL was not a substitute for continuing peace efforts.

The United States expressed its commitment to the restoration of Lebanon's sovereignty and territorial integrity; believed that the cycle of violence afflicting the area was profoundly dangerous to the security, peace and well-being of the region and should be addressed in all its aspects and complexities. It expected that the reinforced UNIFIL troops would be able to deal more effectively with the incursions and violations of all kinds and from all sources.

The USSR shared the concern of the Lebanese Government over the abnormal situation in

---

[b] Rule 39 of the Council's provisional rules of procedure states: "The Security Council may invite members of the Secretariat or other persons, whom it considers competent for the purpose, to supply it with information or to give it other assistance in examining matters within its competence."

southern Lebanon and the failure of UNIFIL to implement its mandate, and charged that there were preparations for a new stage of Israeli aggression and the existence of a threat to Lebanon.

Communications (March). By a letter of 1 March,[2] the Secretary-General informed the Security Council President of his intention, in the light of the Council's resolution of 25 February, to request France to provide an infantry battalion to UNIFIL, to request other troop-contributing countries whose contingents needed to be strengthened to do so, and to request additions to the existing logistic and maintenance units of the Force.

The President responded on 11 March[1] that the Council members, in informal consultations, had agreed with the Secretary-General's proposals (see below, under UN INTERIM FORCE IN LEBANON).

Security Council action (April). By a letter of 10 April,[1] Lebanon complained to the Security Council President about massive Israeli troop concentrations on the Lebanese-Israeli border and Israeli threats against its territorial integrity. On 21 April,[12] it further charged that the Israeli Air Force had launched three extensive attacks on the coastal area south of Beirut and north-east of Sidon, causing heavy casualties and severe damage to civilian property, and requested urgent consultations of the Council on measures to avoid further escalation and deterioration of the situation.

On 22 April, following consultations, the President issued the following statement on behalf of the Council members:[17]

> "The President of the Security Council and the members of the Council, having taken note of the letter dated 21 April 1982 from the Permanent Representative of Lebanon to the United Nations, the oral report of the Secretary-General and his appeal of 21 April 1982, which reads as follows:
> 'The Secretary-General has learned with deep concern of the Israeli air strikes today in Lebanon.
> 'He urgently appeals for an immediate cessation of all hostile acts and urges all parties to exercise the maximum restraint so that the cease-fire, which has generally held since July 1981, can be fully restored and maintained.',
> 1. Urgently demand an end to all armed attacks and violations which jeopardize the cease-fire which has been in effect since 24 July 1981 and warn against any recurrence of violations of the cease-fire, in accordance with Security Council resolution 490(1981) of 21 July 1981;
> 2. Enjoin all the parties to fulfil their responsibilities with respect to peace and invite them to work for consolidation of the cease-fire."

Report of the Secretary-General (April). On 25 April 1982,[19] in pursuance of the Council resolution of 25 February (see above), the Secretary-General submitted a special report on UNIFIL, in which he stressed that the situation in southern Lebanon had remained extremely volatile. While the cease-fire had generally held, unresolved tensions had led to the real danger of widespread hostilities. He referred to the Israeli air strikes into Lebanon on 21 April and to the appeal he had made that day for an immediate cessation of all hostile acts and for maximum restraint by all parties. Yet the cease-fire, however important, was no substitute for fulfilment of the UNIFIL mandate, and there had been little progress in that direction.

The Secretary-General informed the Council that Ghana, Ireland, Nepal and Norway had agreed to increase their UNIFIL contingents, and that France had agreed in principle to his request for a battalion of approximately 600 men. Further, he had instructed the Chief of Staff of the United Nations Truce Supervision Organization (UNTSO) to contact the Israeli and Lebanese Governments with a view to reactivating the 1949 General Armistice Agreement and convening an early meeting of ILMAC.

With regard to implementation of the phased programme of activities with the Government of Lebanon, the Secretary-General reported that the UNIFIL Commander had initiated meetings aimed at enlisting support for certain early steps that would demonstrate the parties' desire to co-operate with UNIFIL and contribute to a reduction of tension. He expressed the conviction that the unimpeded implementation of the UNIFIL mandate was in the best interest of all parties and that the Force was a critical factor for restraint and stability in a continuously dangerous situation.

Other communications (April-May). In connection with Israeli air strikes against Lebanon, a number of communications were addressed to the Secretary-General, including a letter from Japan, of 22 April, transmitting a statement of that date by the Director-General of the Public Information and Cultural Affairs Bureau of its Ministry of Foreign Affairs;[6] a letter of 26 April from the USSR transmitting a TASS statement of 22 April;[16] and a letter of 3 May from Mongolia conveying a statement of 24 April by its Ministry of Foreign Affairs.[15] All three deplored the bombardments, which the Japanese statement called an infringement on Lebanon's sovereignty and territorial integrity, and which the others said were partly a United States responsibility because of its support for the aggressor.

On 10 May,[13] Lebanon complained to the Security Council President of further Israeli air raids against its territory on 9 May, which had resulted, according to preliminary reports, in the death of at least 11 persons, the wounding of 37 others and extensive property damage.

By a letter of the same date to the Secretary-General and the Council President,[4] Israel charged that PLO, operating from Lebanese territory against civilians in Israel, had been responsible for a number of terrorist attacks, including a bomb explosion on a passenger bus in Jerusalem and an explosion at a high school in Ashkelon, both on 9 May; Israel added that it was duty-bound to take all necessary measures to protect its citizens.

In a response of 17 May,[14] Lebanon stated that it could not be held accountable in that context and was not a party to the cease-fire of July 1981, which according to Israeli and United States statements was between Israel and PLO; the only agreement governing Lebanese-Israeli relations was the 1949 General Armistice Agreement.

Israel took exception to the Lebanese position in a letter of 27 May, stating that Lebanon's duty to prevent its territory from being used for terrorist attacks against other States was based on international law.[5]

General Assembly consideration (April). During the General Assembly's resumed seventh emergency special session in April, called to consider the Palestine question, a number of speakers, among them China, Sweden, Uganda, the United Kingdom and Venezuela, condemned Israel's aggression against Lebanon. Concern at the renewed fighting was expressed by Japan, Norway and others. Once again, Malta remarked, Lebanon had become a synonym for senseless destruction and bloodshed.

Several countries expressed the fear that Israel was preparing for an invasion. In Iraq's view, Israel was preparing to strike at the Palestinian resistance in southern Lebanon; in preparation for its aggression, Israel had spread a huge wave of terror across the occupied territories. Qatar said 14,000 heavily armed Israeli soldiers had already been massed at the border.

The German Democratic Republic, Madagascar, the Philippines and others were concerned that the events in Lebanon were leading to the deterioration of an already explosive situation and towards war.

Austria also believed that the recent Israeli attacks on Lebanese territory had escalated the risk of confrontation. While Belgium (speaking for the EC members) said the recent development in Lebanon emphasized the need for peace efforts, Romania believed that Israel's air raids made it more difficult to begin a genuine peace process. Far from reflecting a desire for peace, Pakistan stated, Israel's bellicose behaviour betrayed its insatiable avarice for expansion and its attempt to terrorize its Arab neighbours into accepting its occupation of Arab and Palestinian territories. In Djibouti's opinion, the attack on southern Lebanon revealed that Israel's policy was aimed at intimidating the Palestinians and weakening their determination to exercise their right to establish an independent State in Palestine. Togo felt that the bombing of Beirut on 21 April was pouring oil on the flames at a time when the Secretary-General had been requested to undertake new efforts to persuade all the parties to sit down at the negotiating table.

Sweden and Romania urged restraint by all parties, and Finland called for respect of Lebanon's territorial integrity and sovereignty. Norway strongly appealed to the parties to help UNIFIL fulfil its mandate.

Letters. [1]SC President: 11 Mar., S/14900. [2]S-G: 1 Mar., S/14899. [3]Cuba: 19 Feb., A/37/95-S/14880. Israel: [4]10 May, A/37/223 (S/15066); [5]27 May, A/37/257-S/15132. [6]Japan: 22 Apr., S/14994. Jordan, 23 Feb.: [7]S/14878; [8]S/14883. Lebanon: [9]16 Feb., S/14875; [10]23 Feb., S/14888; [11]10 Apr., S/14962; [12]21 Apr., S/14989; [13]10 May, S/15064 & Corr.1; [14]17 May, A/37/228 (S/15087). [15]Mongolia: 3 May, S/15034. [16]USSR: 26 Apr., S/15005. *Note.* [17]SC President, S/14995. *Reports.* S-G, [18]S/14869, [19]S/14996 & Corr.1. *Resolution (1982).* SC: [20]501(1982), 25 Feb., text following. *Resolutions (prior).* SC: [21]425(1978), 19 Mar. 1978 (YUN 1978, p. 312); [22]498(1981), 18 Dec. 1981 (YUN 1981, p. 292). *Yearbook references.* [23]1948-49, p. 185; 1981, [24]p. 289, [25]p. 290. *Meeting records.* SC: S/PV.2331, 2332 (23, 25 Feb.).

Security Council resolution 501(1982)

25 February 1982   Meeting 2332   13-0-2

Draft prepared in consultations among Council members (S/14890).

The Security Council,

Recalling its resolutions 425(1978), 426(1978), 427(1978), 434(1978), 444(1979), 450(1979), 459(1979), 467(1980), 474(1980), 483(1980), 488(1981), 490(1981) and 498(1981),

Acting in accordance with its resolution 498(1981), and in particular with paragraph 10 of that resolution in which it decided to review the situation as a whole,

Having studied the special report of the Secretary-General on the United Nations Interim Force in Lebanon,

Taking note of the letter of the Permanent Representative of Lebanon to the President of the Security Council,

Having reviewed the situation as a whole in the light of the report of the Secretary-General and of the letter of the Permanent Representative of Lebanon,

Noting from the report of the Secretary-General that it is the strong recommendation of the Commander of the United Nations Interim Force in Lebanon, and also the wish of the Government of Lebanon, that the ceiling for troops of the Force should be increased, and that the Secretary-General fully supports the recommendation for an increase by one thousand of the troop strength of the Force,

1. *Reaffirms* its resolution 425(1978) which reads:

"*The Security Council,*

"*Taking note* of the letters from the Permanent Representative of Lebanon and from the Permanent Representative of Israel,

"*Having heard* the statements of the Permanent Representatives of Lebanon and Israel,

"*Gravely concerned* at the deterioration of the situation in the Middle East and its consequences to the maintenance of international peace,

"*Convinced* that the present situation impedes the achievement of a just peace in the Middle East,

"1. *Calls* for strict respect for the territorial integrity, sovereignty and political independence of Lebanon within its internationally recognized boundaries;

"2. *Calls upon* Israel immediately to cease its military action against Lebanese territorial integrity and withdraw forthwith its forces from all Lebanese territory;

"3. *Decides*, in the light of the request of the Government of Lebanon, to establish immediately under its authority a United Nations interim force for southern Lebanon for the purpose of confirming the withdrawal of Israeli forces, restoring international peace and security and assisting the Government of Lebanon in ensuring the return of its effective authority in the area, the force to be composed of personnel drawn from Member States;

"4. *Requests* the Secretary-General to report to the Council within twenty-four hours on the implementation of the present resolution."

2. *Decides* to approve the immediate increase in the strength of the United Nations Interim Force in Lebanon recommended by the Secretary-General in paragraph 6 of his report, from six thousand to approximately seven thousand troops, to reinforce present operations as well as to make further deployment possible on the lines of resolution 425(1978);

3. *Re-emphasizes* the terms of reference and general guidelines of the Force as stated in the report of the Secretary-General of 19 March 1978 confirmed by resolution 426(1978), and particularly:

(a) That the Force "must be able to function as an integrated and efficient military unit";

(b) That the Force "must enjoy the freedom of movement and communication and other facilities that are necessary to the performance of its tasks";

(c) That the Force "will not use force except in self-defence";

(d) That "self-defence would include resistance to attempts by forceful means to prevent it from discharging its duties under the mandate of the Security Council";

4. *Calls upon* the Secretary-General to renew his efforts to reactivate the General Armistice Agreement between Lebanon and Israel of 23 March 1949 and, in particular, to convene an early meeting of the Mixed Armistice Commission;

5. *Requests* the Secretary-General to continue his discussions with the Government of Lebanon and the parties concerned with a view to submitting a report by 10 June 1982 on the necessary requirements for achieving further progress in a phased programme of activities with the Government of Lebanon;

6. *Decides* to remain seized of the question and invites the Secretary-General to report to the Security Council on the situation as a whole within two months.

Vote in Council as follows:

In favour: China, France, Guyana, Ireland, Japan, Jordan, Panama, Spain, Togo, Uganda, United Kingdom, United States, Zaire.
Against: None.
Abstaining: Poland, USSR.

Armed conflict

Following further Israeli air raids in the Beirut area on 4 June and intense exchanges of fire on the ground in southern Lebanon, Israeli forces moved into Lebanon in strength on 6 June. At 10 meetings throughout June and July, the Security Council considered the situation, calling on 5 and 6 June for a cessation of all military activities, adherence to the cease-fire that had been in effect since July 1981, and unconditional Israeli withdrawal. The Council was kept informed of the events in Lebanon by the Secretary-General, who received information from UNIFIL and United Nations officials in various parts of Lebanon.

The Council's demands were supported by the General Assembly in a resolution adopted on 26 June at its seventh emergency special session on the Palestine question.

As recommended by the Secretary-General, the Council renewed on 18 June the mandate of UNIFIL for an interim period of two months and authorized the Force to carry out humanitarian assistance. On 19 June, the Council called on the combatants to refrain from violence against civilians and appealed to them to facilitate relief efforts. On 4 July, the Council called for a restoration of vital facilities such as water supply, electricity, food and medicines, particularly to the Beirut population. Further, on 29 July, the Council demanded that Israel lift its blockade of Beirut to permit the dispatch of supplies and distribution of aid.

Not adopted because of negative votes by a permanent member of the Council—the United States—were a draft resolution by Spain (8 June) and one by France (26 June). A proposal by Egypt and France was not pressed to a vote (29 July).

Security Council action (4 June). By a letter of 4 June,[36] Lebanon complained that Israeli military aircraft had conducted nine successive bombing raids on the city of Beirut that afternoon, hitting civilian targets in densely populated areas. Further, Israeli forces supported by seacraft had begun to shell the area north of Nabatiych in southern Lebanon, causing an undetermined number of casualties. By the same letter, and by another of the same date,[37] Lebanon called for urgent consideration of the situation by the Security Council.

Also on 4 June, Jordan transmitted a letter of the same date from the PLO Deputy Permanent Observer at the United Nations charging Israel with bombing attacks against Beirut and southern Lebanon lasting two hours, hitting the Palestine refugee camps at Sabra and Shatila, and leaving at least 35 dead and 150 seriously wounded by incomplete count.[24]

On the same day, following consultations, the Council members authorized the President to make the following statement on their behalf:[89]

"The President and the members of the Council have learned with concern of the serious events which occurred today in Lebanon and of the loss of human life and the destruction caused by those events. The President and the members of the Council make an urgent appeal to all the parties to adhere strictly to the cease-fire that had been in effect since 24 July 1981 and to refrain immediately from any hostile act likely to provoke an aggravation of the situation."

Security Council action (5 June). On 5 June,[11] Cuba transmitted to the Security Council President a message of the same date from the Chairman of the Co-ordinating Bureau of the Non-Aligned Countries, then in session at Havana, Cuba, requesting an immediate Council meeting to put an end to Israel's continued aggression and to adopt appropriate measures in accordance with the Charter of the United Nations.

The Council, meeting on 5 June in response to Lebanon's request of the previous day, unanimously adopted a resolution[79] by which it called on all parties to cease immediately and simultaneously all military activities within Lebanon and across the Lebanese-Israeli border by 0600 hours local time on 6 June. The Council requested Member States in a position to do so to bring their influence to bear on those concerned so that the cessation of hostilities declared by the Council in July 1981[87] could be respected. The Secretary-General was requested to report within 48 hours on implementation of and compliance with the resolution.

Submitting the text, Japan warned that the use of force could escalate further.

Before the adoption of the resolution, the Council invited Israel and Lebanon, at their request, to participate in the discussion without vote.

At Jordan's request, conveyed by a letter of 5 June,[25] the Council also decided that an invitation should be accorded to a PLO representative and that the invitation would confer on it the same rights of participation as those conferred on a Member State invited under rule 37 of its provisional rules of procedure.[c] The decision was taken by a vote, requested by the United States, of 11 to 1 (United States), with 3 abstentions (France, Japan, United Kingdom).

Also at the request of Jordan,[26] the Council extended an invitation under rule 39[d] to the Permanent Observer of the League of Arab States to the United Nations.

Addressing the Council, the Secretary-General gave an overview of developments in Beirut and southern Lebanon, based on information from UNIFIL and UNTSO. He reported that Israeli air strikes around Beirut had lasted about an hour on 4 June. Targets had included a Palestinian camp, the sports stadium area next to Sabra camp and the western perimeter of Beirut airport. Initial casualty estimates included some 40 dead, but the number could be higher. In the south, heavy exchanges of fire had commenced between positions of the armed elements (mainly PLO and the Lebanese National Movement) on one side and the Israel Defence Forces (IDF) and the *de facto* forces (Christian and associated militia) on the other. As of 5 June, firing was still in progress, and Israeli air strikes had taken place in southern Lebanon and around Beirut and Damour. In view of the continuing hostilities, the build-up of forces south of the border and the danger of further escalation, he had remained in close touch with the parties, urging them to restore and maintain the cease-fire and to cease hostilities simultaneously by 0600 hours on 6 June.

Lebanon considered the resolution adopted by the Council a practical measure to stop a catastrophe, adding that not only the fate of Lebanon was at stake, but also peace and security in the Middle East. Air raids and artillery shelling from land and sea were continuing, not against mili-

tary positions but against civilians. Thousands of refugees were flooding Beirut from the south, seeking shelter despite the air raids against the city itself. To penalize Lebanon for everyone's crimes was simply murderous.

Israel said that if Lebanon was unwilling or unable to prevent the harbouring, training and financing of PLO terrorists openly operating from Lebanese territory with a view to harassing Israel, Israelis and Jews world-wide, it must be prepared to face the risk of Israeli countermeasures. Since July 1981 about 150 terrorist acts had been instigated by PLO against Israelis and Jews in Israel and elsewhere, most recently the wounding of the Israeli Ambassador in London (on 3 June). PLO deliberately established bases in civilian neighbourhoods and thus bore responsibility for losses of civilian lives in such places.

The PLO observer stated that his organization had no connection with the attempt to assassinate the Ambassador and was opposed to any act of violence outside the occupied land or involving an innocent party; however, Israel, which had expelled the Palestinians from their homes, had pursued them into their places of refuge, killing and destroying indiscriminately.

Ireland and the United Kingdom believed that the assassination attempt did not justify the massive Israeli attacks on Lebanese cities and towns, and called for a halt to the conflict and restoration of the cease-fire. France, condemning the Israeli air raids, said force would not guarantee Israel's right to live within secure and recognized boundaries, the right of the Palestinians to their own land and Lebanon's right to live in peace.

The USSR believed that in adopting the resolution the Council had not met all its responsibilities; the text did not reflect clearly enough the condemnation Israel deserved and the Council should use all means available in accordance with the United Nations Charter to halt Israeli aggression.

The observer of the League of Arab States said the Council's resolution should be a deterrent to the further escalation of aggression and the invasion of Lebanon which Israel had been planning.

Report of the Secretary-General (6 June). Submitting on 6 June the report[74] requested by the Council on 5 June, the Secretary-General stated that, following the adoption of the Council resolution, PLO had reaffirmed its commitment to stop all military operations across the Lebanese border, while reserving its right to respond to any Israeli aggression. Israel had informed him that, while it had been acting in exercise of its right to self-defence, the Council resolution would be brought before the Cabinet. The Secretary-

[c]See footnote a on p. 429.
[d]See footnote b on p. 430.

General also had instructed the UNIFIL Commander to use every possibility to follow up on his appeal to the parties and on the Council resolution.

Despite all efforts throughout the night, however, it had not been possible to effect a cease-fire. Rather, the hostilities had escalated dangerously and Israeli ground forces, estimated at more than two mechanized divisions with full air and naval support, had moved into southern Lebanon. This movement, including a large number of tanks and armoured personnel carriers in the coastal, central and eastern sectors, had begun at around 0930 hours (GMT) (11.30 a.m. local time) on 6 June, following intensive air attacks.

As Israeli forces moved into southern Lebanon, the report stated, the UNIFIL Commander had ordered standard operational procedures to be put into effect by all units, including measures to block advancing forces and also defence measures. However, the overwhelming strength and weight of the Israeli forces had precluded the possibility of stopping them, and UNIFIL positions in the line of the invasion had been overrun or bypassed. One Norwegian soldier of the Force had been killed by shrapnel.

Security Council action (6 June). By a resolution of 6 June,[80] the Council demanded that Israel withdraw all its military forces forthwith and unconditionally to the internationally recognized boundaries of Lebanon, and that all parties strictly observe its 5 June call for immediate and simultaneous cessation of all military activities within Lebanon and across the Lebanese-Israeli border. All parties were called upon to communicate to the Secretary-General their acceptance of the resolution within 24 hours.

The resolution was adopted unanimously. Introducing it, Ireland said that, in view of the massive invasion, the Council had to demand an end to all hostilities and the strictest respect for Lebanon's territorial integrity, sovereignty and political independence.

In addition to Israel, Lebanon, PLO and the League of Arab States, invited by the Council on 5 June, Egypt was invited, at its request, to participate without vote in the discussion.

Speaking in the Council, Israel reaffirmed its right to self-defence to stop the attacks across its northern border from PLO bases in southern Lebanon, to deter continued terrorism against its citizens and to ensure their safety. Of the 15,000 armed PLO terrorists in Lebanon, operating under complete Syrian control, over 2,000 were positioned south of the Litani River, including around 700 within the UNIFIL area of operation. However, the Council had not evinced the slightest interest in the warfare, violence and terrorism committed by Arabs against Israel. The Israeli Cabinet had decided on 6 June to instruct the IDF, in an oper-

ation called "Peace for Galilee", to place all the civilian population of Galilee (in northern Israel) beyond the range of the terrorists' fire from Lebanon. During that operation, the Syrian army would not be attacked unless it attacked Israeli forces. Israel continued to aspire to signing a peace treaty with Lebanon, its territorial integrity preserved, the Cabinet had added.

Lebanon stated that the aggressor, having sent its armies, air force and navy to kill and destroy, was pretending to be the victim of aggression. According to Israel's interpretation of international law, the United Nations should be disbanded and Israel should be entrusted with implementation of the Charter and preservation of the rights of nations. However, Israel could not live peacefully by endlessly killing and destroying. While Lebanon would have preferred a different resolution, it considered the text adopted an important step towards peace and the guarantee of everybody's rights.

The PLO observer said that, as long as Palestinian children slept in refugee camps, Israel could expect no peace in Palestine; in the face of Israel's brutal attacks aimed at extermination of the Palestinians, the latter were simply exercising their right to self-defence.

Declaring firm support for the Lebanese struggle against aggression, China said the Council should adopt a resolution which explicitly condemned Israeli aggression, demanded its cessation and called on Israel to withdraw its troops immediately, totally and unconditionally.

Egypt, condemning the invasion, said the Council had to prevent a return to concepts and doctrines which should have been abandoned after the initiation of the Middle East peace process.

Guyana stated that the unfortunate attack on the Israeli Ambassador in London did not justify the widespread destruction, human suffering and illegal invasion that had taken place; to accept such justification would be to usher in a system of inter-State relations based on vengeance and violence.

In Poland's opinion, there were good reasons to believe that Israel's attack was only the first stage of a larger military and political design; something more forceful than remonstrations had to be applied in order to deter the aggressor. Though holding that the resolution did not fully respond to the extremely serious and steadily worsening situation and did not reflect the need to condemn Israel for its acts of aggression, the USSR supported the text, taking into consideration the demand for full and unconditional Israeli withdrawal; it saw Israel's action as an attempt to annihilate the Palestinian resistance fighters, frighten the Palestinian people and break their resolve to struggle for freedom and independence.

The United States said the two interrelated objectives of the resolution—cessation of hostilities by all parties and Israeli withdrawal from Lebanon—had to be implemented simultaneously.

The Permanent Observer of the League of Arab States, interpreted the resolution as transitional and aimed at rectifying a fundamental transgression of Lebanese sovereignty; in the case of Israel's non-compliance, the Council must see to it that there was a contingency plan.

By a letter of 6 June,[44] Oman, on behalf of the members of the League of Arab States at the United Nations, urged the Council to take immediately all necessary measures to ensure the credibility and effectiveness of its resolutions and to help restore Lebanon's territorial integrity, and called for condemnation of Israel's defiance of the Council's unanimous will.

The Secretary-General informed the Council, in a report of 7 June,[75] of the responses received that day to its resolution of 6 June. While it would have preferred a resolution clearly based on the 1949 General Armistice Agreement and calling on Israel to abide by it, Lebanon pledged its full support for the Council's efforts to restore peace and security. Israel declared that any withdrawal of its military forces prior to the conclusion of concrete arrangements which would permanently and reliably preclude hostile action against its citizens was inconceivable. The PLO reply was that its Lebanese Palestinian Joint Command agreed with the Secretary-General's message transmitting the resolution.

Security Council consideration (8 June). Stating that the Council's urgent appeal had been totally ignored by Israel, Spain introduced on 8 June a draft resolution[3] condemning Israel's non-compliance with the Council resolutions of 5 and 6 June, and urging the parties to comply strictly with the regulations attached to the Hague Convention of 1907 (on the conduct of warfare). The Council was asked to reiterate the demand for withdrawal of all Israeli military forces and strict observance of the call for immediate and simultaneous cessation of all military activities, and to demand that all hostilities be stopped within six hours. In the event of non-compliance, the Council would have met again to consider practical ways and means in accordance with the United Nations Charter.

The resolution received 14 votes to 1 (United States) and was not adopted owing to the negative vote of a permanent Council member.

Introducing the draft, Spain said it was difficult for Israel to convince the Council by citing a long list of acts of violence, when the most serious violence was that of depriving a people of the right to its homeland, its territory and to a free life; it was tragic that Israel should point an accusing finger and attempt to undermine the prestige and prerogatives of the Council at the very time when

it was launching an armed invasion against a sovereign State, ignoring both the calls of the Council and the requests and appeals for peace made by numerous heads of State.

Explaining its opposition, the United States said the text was not sufficiently balanced to end the cycle of violence in Lebanon; the United States would continue its own efforts to bring the violence to an end.

Expressing deep regret at the non-adoption of the text, Ireland said it had voted in favour because it wanted an end to the bloodshed, was concerned about the dangers of the conflict spreading and feared the damage to the concept of United Nations peace-keeping; the total of lives lost and casualties suffered in all attacks on Israeli citizens over recent years must have been less than the deaths and injuries caused by the Israeli air raids on Beirut, which were merely one aspect of the larger attack.

Describing the United States vote as disgraceful, the USSR said the attack on Lebanon, undertaken with Washington's agreement and support, was a direct consequence of American-Israeli strategic co-operation. The Council should immediately take measures to ensure that the aggression ceased, to force Israel to respect the Charter and United Nations resolutions, and to protect Lebanon's sovereignty and territorial integrity and legitimate Arab rights and interests.

France, stating that it fully supported the draft resolution, said it had no hesitation in condemning Israel's intervention just as it had had none in condemning the other interventions in Lebanon carried out against the country's legitimate rulers.

Lebanon trusted that the Council would take note of the fact that there was also a serious United States commitment to immediate and unconditional Israeli withdrawal, and that the United States would continue its efforts in response to the Council's appeal.

The PLO observer stated that the veto of a resolution that would have helped to maintain international peace and security meant that the United States was determined to maintain war, aggression and bloodshed; it had not tried to stop the invasion and it had had a part in what was happening. The Permanent Observer of the League of Arab States, remarked that the perception of the United States being in collusion with Israel could have been corrected, had the United States not exercised its veto.

At a meeting of 8 June preceding the one at which the vote was taken, the Secretary-General reported that information received from the area indicated that extensive hostilities were still in progress. On the coast, the inhabitants had left the town of Tyre and UNIFIL was trying to get food, water and medical supplies to the area. Intensive military activity had continued north of the Litani River, including air strikes. Positions of UNIFIL continued to be overrun despite their efforts to place obstacles in the way of advancing Israeli tank columns. Force headquarters at Naquora had been cut off from all UNIFIL battalions since the start of the operation. The continuing spread and escalation of the hostilities was a matter of most profound concern.

Lebanon appealed to the Council to enforce its resolutions of 5 and 6 June and to take all measures in its power and under the Charter to stop the war immediately and to prevent a Member State from being murdered. Israel was not only violating Lebanon's integrity, but also human rights and the 1949 Geneva Convention relative to the Protection of Civilian Persons in Time of War. The Lebanese Red Cross had stated that its ambulances, automobiles and volunteers had been attacked by Israelis and prevented from fulfilling their duty to evacuate the wounded and to transport medical supplies and food.

Israel said the Council had convened in order to save a terrorist organization from well-deserved and long-overdue retribution, after having treated with indifference Israeli complaints with regard to PLO barbarism originating from Lebanon. It was Israel's right and duty to protect the lives of its citizens and ensure their safety. Israel had no territorial ambitions in Lebanon, but was entitled to demand arrangements to ensure that Lebanon would no longer serve as a staging ground for terrorist attacks against Israeli civilians. Israel fully supported restoration of Lebanon's sovereignty but insisted that Lebanon equally acknowledge Israel's right to live in peace and security without the threat of harassment and attacks.

Expressing concern that the stability of the entire Middle East might be seriously jeopardized if Israel's massive invasion was prolonged and the counter-attacks continued, Japan demanded that all parties cease hostilities at once and that Israel withdraw immediately and unconditionally.

Security Council action (18 June). As the mandate of UNIFIL was due to expire on 19 June 1982, the Secretary-General submitted on 10 June (with later addenda) a report on the activities of the Force from the period just prior to the most recent renewal of its mandate in December 1981[88] until 13 June when the large-scale movement of Israeli forces into Lebanon was still in progress.[76]

In the main part of this report, covering the period 11 December 1981 to 3 June 1982, the Secretary-General noted continued activities by armed elements, the Lebanese Shi'ite armed organization AMAL, the *de facto* forces and IDF within and near the UNIFIL area of operation, along with attempts by armed elements to establish positions in the UNIFIL area. The presence of Israeli personnel and equipment inside the enclave of the *de facto* forces (a zone on the Lebanese side of the Israel-Lebanon border within which UNIFIL could not fully exercise its functions) remained at a high level, and further work had been undertaken by IDF to strengthen observation posts and gun positions. During 17 reported incidents, UNIFIL positions and personnel had come under close fire by IDF. Force personnel had observed numerous violations by Israel of Lebanese airspace and waters. Both at United Nations Headquarters and in the field, intense efforts had been made to restore the cease-fire, especially after the Israeli air attacks on 21 April and 9 May.

In two addenda to his report, dated 11 and 14 June, the Secretary-General referred to events between 4 and 10 June and between 11 and 13 June, respectively, during which time Israeli forces moved into Lebanon in strength (see above). By 7 June, Israeli forces had reached positions north of the UNIFIL area, and subsequent events, including intense fighting reported from numerous areas of Lebanon, occurred outside its area of operation. Despite the fundamentally altered situation and restrictions of movement, UNIFIL troops continued to man their positions and were endeavouring, to the extent possible, to extend protection and humanitarian assistance to the population in the area, as instructed by the Secretary-General.

There were reported agreements on a cease-fire on 11 and 12 June but the fighting had continued. On both occasions, PLO had informed the United Nations of its acceptance of the Council's cease-fire resolutions.

The Secretary-General believed that UNIFIL could usefully contribute to the objectives prescribed by the Council. However, for the Force to function effectively, there would need to be a clear definition by the Council of its terms of reference in the current situation, as well as full cooperation from the parties. Lebanon had expressed the view that UNIFIL should continue to be stationed in the area pending further consideration of the situation in the light of the 6 June Council resolution.

By a resolution of 18 June,[81] the Council decided, as an interim measure, to renew the UNIFIL mandate for two months, until 19 August. The Council also authorized the Force during that period to carry out certain interim tasks described in the Secretary-General's report, concerned with extending protection and humanitarian assistance to the population. It called on all parties to cooperate fully with the Force.

The resolution, drawn up in consultations among the Council members, was adopted by 13 votes to none, with 2 abstentions (Poland, USSR).

Prior to the vote, the Council invited Israel, Lebanon, the Netherlands, Sweden and the Syrian Arab Republic, at their request, to participate without vote in the discussion. At Jordan's request,[27] the Council also decided that an invitation should be accorded to a PLO representative under rule 37 of its provisional rules of procedure. The Council took this decision by a vote, requested by the United States, of 11 to 1 (United States), with 3 abstentions (France, Japan, United Kingdom).

Also at Jordan's request,[28] the Council invited under rule 39 the Permanent Observer of the League of Arab States.

The USSR emphasized that the decision to extend the mandate was an interim measure. Poland stated that its previous reservations concerning certain political and financial aspects of UNIFIL remained valid.

The United States said it had voted in favour of extending the UNIFIL mandate without any extension of responsibilities, functions or territorial scope in the belief that that course would contribute most directly to the restoration of peace and of Lebanon's sovereignty.

Ireland noted that the events of the past two weeks had brought a major change in the situation and said contempt had been shown for a United Nations peace-keeping force, which had been brushed aside by a vastly superior military force; in the circumstances, prolongation of the mandate was no more than a holding operation, after which larger decisions and new dispositions must be made.

The United Kingdom felt that it was still too early to know whether there was a role for UNIFIL in the new and radically altered circumstances, but believed that the option for such a role should be preserved; it called on Israel to show full respect for the Force.

China said it had voted for extending the mandate in view of the need created by the development of the situation and the request of the Lebanese Government.

France was in favour of the interim renewal of the Force's mandate, since the Lebanese authorities so desired; in its opinion, the decision must be followed by a thorough review of the situation so as to define the modalities of the UNIFIL mission and enable it fully to discharge its duties.

Zaire, deploring the lack of co-operation by the parties in UNIFIL efforts fully to discharge its mandate, said the Council must immediately call on all the parties to refrain from activities incompatible with the objectives of the Force.

In Israel's understanding, the resolution was not intended to change the existing UNIFIL mandate. Israel would reject any attempt to make a *de facto* change in that mandate.

Appealing to Israel to respect UNIFIL fully, to withdraw its units from UNIFIL sectors and to allow humanitarian assistance without hindrance, the Netherlands believed that in the future the Force should serve the interests of all parties concerned, should be ensured of their full co-operation in the implementation of a durable mandate, and should operate in an uninterrupted and clearly defined area.

Sweden expressed the view that Israel's invasion violated not only the independence of Lebanon but also the political authority of UNIFIL and of the Council; that UNIFIL should provide relief to the population in as wide an area as possible, not confined to what had been its area of operations; and that a continued UNIFIL operation would not be construed as confirming the advancement of positions which Israel had obtained through its aggression against Lebanon.

Paying tribute to UNIFIL, Lebanon said the Council had taken a risk by asking the Force to stay, to maintain positions, to ensure freedom of movement and perform a humanitarian task.

The Permanent Observer of the League of Arab States described the Council's action as an expression of international insistence on the continued legitimacy of a United Nations presence in Lebanon, in the face of Israel's contempt for United Nations resolutions and its attempt to remove the international authority from the scene so that it could pursue its objectives of destroying Lebanon and dispersing the country's Lebanese and Palestinian population.

Most speakers also commented on the situation in Lebanon resulting from the continuing hostilities, including what Ireland described as Israel's occupation of the whole of southern Lebanon up to the suburbs of Beirut, which was under siege. Most repeated the call for a cessation of fighting and for the withdrawal of Israeli forces back to the Israel-Lebanon boundary.

Israel repeated that it did not want to stay in any part of Lebanon and that it supported Lebanese sovereignty, eroded over the past 10 years by PLO and then by the Syrian occupation army.

China expressed support for the Lebanese, Palestinian and Syrian armed forces and peoples in their struggle to resist Israeli aggression and safeguard their national rights.

Deploring and condemning the Israeli invasion, Ireland said its fruits could be a source of deep bitterness for which Israel and the world might pay heavily in years to come. The recent display of force, stated the Netherlands, could not be justified under international law and created the danger of further escalation rather than conditions for a durable settlement. Sweden said Israel could not secure its right to live within secure and recognized boundaries by military means; only through negotiations could a lasting peaceful solution be attained. Noting that there had been fighting between Israeli and Syrian forces, the United Kingdom expressed concern about the risks of spreading the conflagration and said it could not accept that Israel's action amounted to self-defence.

Poland read out a 9 June statement by its Ministry of Foreign Affairs charging that the aim of the invasion was the physical liquidation of Palestine refugees in Lebanon, the destruction of their political and military organizations, terrorizing the Arab nations and imposing separatist solutions that negated Palestinian rights. The USSR mentioned a 14 June statement by its Government warning Israel that events in the Middle East could not but affect the interests of the Soviet Union. Both countries again accused the United States of seeking advantages from Israel's actions in Lebanon.

The Syrian Arab Republic held the view that the Council could no longer delay the application of mandatory sanctions against Israel.

Most speakers also expressed sympathy for the suffering of civilians in Lebanon and several announced contributions to international relief efforts. Israel said it had authorized representatives of the International Committee of the Red Cross (ICRC) to assess the situation of the Lebanese civilians and had sent a team of 70 doctors to study immediate problems; IDF had distributed bread, milk powder and tents within 48 hours of entry into Lebanese towns and villages, and was repairing water, electricity and communications systems.

The immediate dispatch of a special commission to investigate the Israeli crimes and the situation in Lebanon was requested by PLO in a letter of 16 June to the Secretary-General, transmitted on the same date by Oman; the letter cited what it called preliminary casualty figures of 30,000 killed or wounded, 10,000 missing and 800,000 displaced.[45]

Security Council action (19 June). By a resolution of 19 June in which it expressed deep concern at the sufferings of the Lebanese and Palestinian civilian populations,[82] the Security Council called on all parties to respect the rights of civilians, to refrain from acts of violence against them and to take measures to alleviate their suffering, particularly by facilitating the dispatch and distribution of United Nations and non-governmental aid. It appealed to Member States to continue to provide the most extensive humanitarian aid possible, stressed the humanitarian responsibilities of the United Nations and called on the parties not to hamper the exercise of those responsibilities and to assist in humanitarian efforts.

The resolution was adopted unanimously. Introducing it, France said urgent action was required, many obstacles remained to be overcome, and the Council must see to it that aid was dispatched and distributed effectively.

Speaking after the vote, Japan urged that all the parties, in particular the Israeli occupying forces, fully co-operate with the international organizations engaged in humanitarian relief activities. Expressing its commitment to serving the human needs of the people of Lebanon, the United States hoped that no party and no Government would exploit fundamental humanitarian concerns for narrow political purposes.

Israel welcomed co-operation with the Secretary-General in promoting genuine humanitarian efforts but asked what humanitarian resolutions the Council had adopted over the previous seven years when 100,000 or so Lebanese had been killed and more than 1 million displaced in Lebanon; it rejected the innuendo in the paragraph calling on all the parties not to hamper the exercise of United Nations responsibilities and to assist in humanitarian efforts.

The USSR remarked that the United States had originally objected to the humanitarian resolution, agreeing to it only out of fear of finding itself completely isolated. Replying, the United States said the improvements it had suggested in informal consultations had been intended to make the text a well-designed and finely targeted resolution.

Expressing appreciation for the prompt Council reaction, Lebanon stated that its future depended a great deal on the United Nations response.

In accordance with the resolution, the Secretary-General submitted on 30 June an interim report[77] on humanitarian assistance to Lebanon (see ECONOMIC AND SOCIAL QUESTIONS, Chapter III). It said that UNIFIL had provided food and medical supplies from its own stocks, and its hygiene and medical teams and engineers had aided civilians. The United Nations Relief and Works Agency for Palestine Refugees in the Near East (UNRWA) was providing food, blankets and other household supplies to over 12,000 displaced Palestine refugees in west Beirut, 7,000 in the Bekaa Valley and over 12,000 at Sidon. The United Nations Children's Fund had launched a $5-million relief programme to assist severely affected children and mothers and had delivered four plane-loads of medicines, blankets and other necessities. Other co-operating United Nations organizations were the Food and Agriculture Organization of the United Nations, the World Food Programme, the United Nations High Commissioner for Refugees, the World Health Organization and the United Nations Disaster Relief Coordinator.

As at 30 June, 25 Governments and one intergovernmental organization had made or pledged contributions to relief agencies. ICRC and a number of national and international non-governmental organizations were also providing relief supplies. To obtain precise estimates on relief and rehabilitation needs, the Secretary-General had appointed on 25 June an inter-agency survey mission.

Security Council consideration (26 June). As fighting extended closer to the centre of Beirut, France proposed on 24 June that west Beirut be neutralized under the supervision of United Nations observers and that the Lebanese Army, possibly with the backing of a United Nations force, be allowed to interpose itself between the Israeli and Palestinian combatants. This proposal was initially made in a statement by the President of France, transmitted to the Secretary-General on 24 June.[60] It was then incorporated into a draft resolution, which France revised twice before introducing it at a Security Council meeting on 26 June.[2]

Under the resolution, the Council would demand that all parties observe an immediate cessation of hostilities and that, as a first step towards complete Israeli withdrawal from Lebanon, the Israeli forces around Beirut immediately withdraw to 10 kilometres from the city's periphery, with the Palestinian armed forces simultaneously withdrawing to existing camps. All armed elements in the Beirut area would be called upon to respect the exclusive authority of the Lebanese Government, which would receive the Council's support in its efforts to ensure its sovereignty throughout the territory. Also with Council support, the Government would install its armed forces within Beirut and interpose themselves on its periphery. As an immediate measure, United Nations military observers would supervise the cease-fire and disengagement in and around Beirut. Further, the Secretary-General would be requested to study any request by Lebanon for the installation of a United Nations force to take up positions beside the Lebanese interposition forces, or for the use of the forces available to the United Nations in the region.

Introducing this draft, France stated that disengagement and neutralization were needed to protect innocent civilians and spare the city from destruction. Neutralization of west Beirut was a prerequisite for the early opening of negotiations and could not be considered as a lasting political solution.

The draft resolution received 14 votes to 1 (United States) and was not adopted owing to the negative vote of a permanent Council member.

Though expressing support for many elements of the text, including the call for an immediate cease-fire and simultaneous withdrawal of Israeli and Palestinian forces and monitoring of the cease-fire by United Nations observers, the United States said the draft failed to call for the essential requisite for the restoration of the Lebanese Government's authority, namely, the elimination from Beirut and elsewhere of armed Palestinian elements which did not respect the Government's authority.

Lebanon regretted that the draft had not been adopted.

Israel said that, following the completion of its mission, IDF had been instructed to cease fire on all fronts in Lebanon, and the cease-fire had been holding for the past 13 hours.

General Assembly action (June). The General Assembly, which resumed on 25 June its seventh emergency special session on the Palestine question, adopted on 26 June a resolution[78] by which it fully supported the Security Council resolutions of 5 and 6 June, condemned Israel for non-compliance and demanded that it comply. Calling on the Council to authorize practical steps to implement its resolutions, the Assembly urged the Council, in the event of Israel's continued non-compliance, to consider practical means in accordance with the United Nations Charter. Reaffirming the principle of the inadmissibility of the acquisition of territory by force, the Assembly demanded that all Member States and other parties observe strict respect for Lebanon's sovereignty, territorial integrity, unity and political independence. It called for the continuation of humanitarian aid, and requested the Secretary-General to delegate a high-level commission to report on the extent of loss of human life and material damage.

The resolution, sponsored by 64 nations, was adopted by a recorded vote of 127 to 2.

The introducer of the text, Senegal, speaking also as Chairman of the Committee on Palestinian rights, said the resolution contained all the elements likely to lead to a restoration of peace and tranquillity in Lebanon, and the Assembly must do everything within its means to ensure speedy and full implementation.

Voting against, Israel said the resolution was inimical to the goal of restoring sovereignty to the Lebanese people. For the past decade and more, Lebanese territory had been the launching-pad for hundreds of attacks on Israeli civilians; operation "Peace for Galilee" had been prompted solely by self-preservation and self-defence. Immense quantities of arms and ammunition, placed by various quarters at the terrorists' disposal, had been found in Lebanon in recent weeks. Israel was entitled to demand concrete arrangements that would permanently and reliably preclude hostile action against Israel from Lebanese soil. Contrary to grossly exaggerated casualty figures mentioned in the debate, the number of civilian lives lost in the cities of Tyre, Sidon and Nabatiyeh was 460, and the best estimate of homeless persons was 20,000. The responsibility for the suffering must be borne by PLO, which had placed its camps and depots in civilian areas.

Also explaining its negative vote, the United States said that, though recognizing that the resolution reflected everyone's profound anguish at the continuing loss of life and human suffering, it could not be party to an unbalanced statement which might heighten animosities and increase the danger of a wider conflict; a just and lasting settlement could not be achieved by issuing declarations and ultimatums motivated sometimes by vindictiveness and even by hatred.

Lebanon stated that its support of the resolution did not mean that it was renouncing its right to call for an emergency special session of the Assembly should the Council fail to act. Referring to the suffering undergone by the Lebanese in recent weeks, it expressed confidence in a strengthened ability to meet the challenges, overcome the dangers and confront the threats, and voiced determination to preserve the country's national unity, territorial integrity and independence.

Voting in favour, Belgium, the Federal Republic of Germany, Ireland, Italy, the Netherlands and the United Kingdom voiced reservations on the second and eleventh preambular paragraphs (referring to the PLO statement during the debate, and reaffirming that a just and comprehensive Middle East settlement could not be achieved without PLO participation). Australia, Canada, Chile, Colombia, Denmark and France voiced reservations on the latter provision, Canada stating that it implied a status for PLO which Canada had not endorsed. Uruguay pointed out that the role of PLO as a spokesman was provisional.

Canada, Denmark, the Netherlands and the United Kingdom also reserved their position on the tenth preambular paragraph (reaffirming that the Palestine question was the core of the Arab-Israeli conflict); Canada said there were other central issues, including Israel's existence and its right to secure and recognized boundaries. Ireland stated that its positive vote did not imply a change of its position on issues such as the Palestine question, Palestinian rights and PLO as the representative of the Palestinians.

Regretting the lack of a direct warning to the armed groups that were using Lebanese territory as a base for warlike activities against other States, Bolivia considered that the imposition of sanctions was within the purview of the Council and not of the Assembly. Chile said that, when interpreting in particular the paragraph urging the Council to consider practical means in accordance with the Charter in the event of Israel's non-compliance, it must be borne in mind that there was a need

to uphold the Charter provisions on the powers and functions of every United Nations organ, as well as to preserve the principle of universality of the United Nations; also, the mention of the Council's most recent resolutions did not mean that its earlier resolutions on a Middle East peace had been superseded.

With regard to the reference to Israel's acts of aggression in the third preambular paragraph, Canada noted that it was the sole responsibility of the Council to determine the existence of any threat to or breach of peace or act of aggression. Finland pointed out that it was the Council which had the primary responsibility for the maintenance of international peace and security. Sweden stressed that some formulations with regard to the respective responsibilities of the Assembly and the Council did not fully correspond with its view—a point made also by France.

Ecuador explained that it had voted in favour to reaffirm the principle of the inadmissibility of the acquisition of territory by force and because Lebanon's sovereignty and territorial integrity had to be respected; it hoped Israeli troops and all other foreign troops would be withdrawn.

Though supporting the resolution, the Libyan Arab Jamahiriya was convinced that it would accomplish nothing; in its view, Israel must be condemned and expelled because it did not respect the Charter.

At the start of the Assembly debate preceding adoption of the resolution, Cuba said the non-aligned countries had requested the resumption of the session so that the international community could prevent the consummation of genocide against the Palestinians in Lebanon and assure PLO of support.

The PLO observer stated that the aim of Israel's aggression was to eliminate the Palestinians and PLO, which had honoured its commitment under the July 1981 cease-fire while Israel had violated Lebanese territory, airspace and waters almost 4,000 times.

The invasion was denounced by the majority of countries. China voiced strong condemnation and Canada expressed profound sadness and dismay. France said the gravity and urgency of the situation required the immediate expression of the gravest concern by the international community.

Israel's invasion, China, Yugoslavia and others believed, was a premeditated aggression. Indonesia stated that for many months Israel had massed its troops on the border with Lebanon and had threatened punitive actions against Lebanese territory.

By its efforts to annihilate the PLO forces in Lebanon, China said, Israel was attempting to write off the struggle of the Palestinians for their right to self-determination and to perpetuate its armed occupation of the West Bank and the Gaza Strip. Egypt urged all States to prevent the attainment of Israel's objectives—to eliminate the social and political basis of the Palestinians and their leadership, and to disrupt and fragment Lebanon into weak puppets of Israel. In Malaysia's opinion, one objective of the invasion was to dismember Lebanon.

The elimination of PLO was seen as an objective of the Israeli invasion also by the German Democratic Republic and a number of others. Indonesia and Iraq charged Israel with trying in addition to annihiliate the Palestinian people. Bangladesh, Bulgaria, Hungary, Lebanon, Malaysia, the Syrian Arab Republic, Tunisia, Yemen and others spoke of holocaust, genocide and attempts to create a "final solution" to the Palestine question. Qatar characterized Israel's attempt to exterminate an entire people, using internationally prohibited weapons of mass destruction such as cluster and fragmentation bombs, napalm and other weapons in the American arsenal, as an atrocity.

Czechoslovakia and others saw the invasion not as an isolated act but as a link in a long chain of Israel's expansion and aggression against the Arabs.

Canada could not accept Israel's proposition that its military activities in Lebanon were justified or that they would provide long-term security. Israel's arguments that security measures were involved had convinced no one, Egypt said. New Zealand said that whatever provocation Israel might have considered itself to be acting under, its response had been frighteningly disproportionate.

Iraq said Israel's aggression against Lebanon had revealed the falseness of its allegations that it was the victim of aggression and acted only in self-defence. Pakistan said the pretext used by Israel for its aggression, as well as the professed aim of creating a buffer zone on the border with Lebanon, was eyewash; Israel's ambition was nothing less than to impose its hegemony over Lebanon's destiny. Poland considered the invocation by Israel of its right to self-defence as a cynical affront. Israel's claim to have acted in self-defence was also rejected by others, among them Belgium (for the EC members), Indonesia and Zaire.

Other speakers stressed the severity of the military operation. Finland described the situation as full-scale war waged with the most modern means of destruction and Indonesia characterized it as all-out war; Indonesia cited figures of at least 10,000 civilians dead, 16,000 wounded and over 600,000 homeless as confirming that Israel's strategy was to attack and annihilate civilian as well as military targets. In Egypt's opinion, Israel's aggression against southern Lebanon, Beirut and

the Palestinians was unprecedented since the Second World War; the crimes and massacres by the invasion forces placed Israel on an equal footing with nazism. Iraq said the Lebanese and Palestinians were being subjected to the most wide-scale massacre of the century, while the USSR said the mass terror and violence were reminiscent of the fascist period.

Virtually every speaker called for a cessation of hostilities, Israeli withdrawal, and restoration of Lebanon's territorial integrity, sovereignty and independence. Those making these points included Belgium (for the EC members), Bulgaria, Canada, China, Cyprus, Czechoslovakia, Ecuador, Ethiopia, Finland, France, the German Democratic Republic, Indonesia, Japan, New Zealand, Norway, Pakistan, Poland, Romania, Tunisia, Turkey, the USSR, Viet Nam, Yugoslavia and Zaire. Ecuador and Zaire urged the withdrawal of all foreign troops from the country.

The Byelorussian SSR, Czechoslovakia, India, Indonesia, Mexico, Poland, Romania, the USSR, Viet Nam and others said the situation created by the invasion was a danger not only to peace and stability in the region but to world peace. Cyprus said the sad impotence of the United Nations to enforce its decisions and maintain international peace and security had been further demonstrated. Malaysia viewed Israel's actions as a challenge to the fundamentals of peaceful conduct among States and the resolution of conflict through peaceful means. In Turkey's view, the invasion had brought tension in the Middle East to a new high, and the danger of further escalation was frighteningly imminent. Yugoslavia said the invasion threatened to cause a war of the widest dimensions.

In the view of Turkey, Zaire and others, the events in Lebanon once again proved that the Palestine question remained at the heart of the Arab-Israeli conflict and that without a Palestine solution there could be no just and lasting Middle East settlement. A similar position was held by Senegal.

The Palestinian cause could not be defeated by force or violence, Madagascar believed. Repressive acts could only increase Palestinian resistance and provoke new explosions of violence, Romania warned.

Efforts to restore peace and security to Lebanon, Belgium stated on behalf of the EC members, must be accompanied by an attempt to restore Palestinian rights. Turkey, however, felt that the restoration of Lebanon's sovereignty and territorial integrity could not be made conditional on a settlement of the Palestine question and vice versa.

In Indonesia's opinion, it was a delusion for Israel to think that by its attempt to decimate PLO it could destroy the aspirations of the Palestinians.

Ethiopia believed such action would in the long run contribute only to strengthening the resolve of Palestinians everywhere in their just quest for a homeland in Palestine. Malta said Israel had neither the right nor the authority to impose conditions on Lebanon or to destroy the Palestinians because they engaged in protest against Israeli policies and aggression in the occupied territories.

The United States was charged by a number of speakers with having co-operated in or at least known about Israel's plans. China said the United States had actively supported Israel in attaining its strategic objectives in Lebanon and should be condemned by the international community for the Israeli aggression. American assistance and support were also condemned by Albania and Kuwait, the latter adding that there was a gap between United States public opinion and the actions of the Government, as well as a gap between that country's obligations as a permanent member of the Security Council and its actions in support of Israel. In Iraq's opinion, United States support for Israel would intensify the feeling among the Arabs that their principal enemy was the United States and that Israel was nothing but its tool.

The Syrian Arab Republic held the United States responsible, whether through collusion or incitement. Everything was proceeding as though Israel's genocidal operation against the people of Palestine had United States support, said Tunisia. Yemen said history would attest to the participation of the United States in the acts of genocide against Lebanon. The PLO observer asserted that the United States had known about the planned aggression for more than a year; the fact that it was supplying more than $1 billion worth of arms to Israel proved its complicity.

Bulgaria, Hungary and Poland believed that Israel would never have dared undertake its aggression against Lebanon without United States agreement and support. In the opinion of the USSR, Israel's attack on Lebanon was one more in a long chain of criminal anti-Arab actions with the consent and support of Washington, and was a direct consequence of the Camp David deal and the American-Israeli strategic alliance. A similar position was taken by the Byelorussian SSR, the German Democratic Republic and Viet Nam.

A number of countries deplored not only United States military and economic assistance, but also its political and diplomatic support of Israel. Several speakers, among them Indonesia, Iraq, the Libyan Arab Jamahiriya and Qatar, maintained that the United States veto of Security Council measures against Israel encouraged the latter in its aggression. Hungary said the veto placed on the United States an even heavier responsibility than in the past. Without the political, economic and military support of the United States, said

Nicaragua, Israel would not act with such impunity and could not rely on the veto in the Council, which licensed its excesses by preventing that body from acting. Pakistan regretted that the Council had failed to adopt the proposal by Spain on 8 June, supported by 14 of its members, to set a time-limit for compliance with its resolutions; that result, it felt, had provided further encouragement to Israel.

Egypt urged the United States to condemn the aggression against Lebanon and the Palestinians, which was also against United States interests and endangering its good relations in the region. Yugoslavia called especially on the big countries to meet their responsibility to check the war and protect its victims.

In the United States opinion, the humanitarian task of aiding the victims of the conflict was no less urgent than the goal of bringing the conflict to an end. France attached highest priority to humanitarian tasks. Above all else, New Zealand stated, there must be concern for the welfare of the people caught up in the fighting.

To alleviate the suffering of the civilian population, many countries, including Austria, Senegal, Tunisia, Turkey and Uruguay, urged the provision of humanitarian assistance and expressed support for the Security Council's call on the parties to facilitate relief work. Australia, Belgium (for the EC members), Cyprus, Finland, India, Malaysia, Malta, Norway, Pakistan and the United States said they were providing such assistance.

Sweden stressed Israel's duty to facilitate humanitarian efforts and to comply with the humanitarian obligations in the 1949 Geneva Conventions on the protection of civilians. By initially refusing access to UNIFIL, ICRC and other organizations, Indonesia charged, Israel had attempted to hide from the world the cost of its indiscriminate attacks. Japan urged that all concerned, especially the Israeli occupying forces in Lebanon, co-operate with relief organizations.

Israel said it was already contributing its share, bringing relief for the civilians under its control to the point where, according to international relief organizations, there no longer existed any problems of food shortages or medical aid in those areas.

Belgium said Israel had not given a satisfactory answer to a request by the EC members for assurances that it would: admit international humanitarian aid organizations into the Israeli-occupied territory and facilitate their work; admit press representatives and give them the usual facilities; comply with the Geneva Conventions, particularly with regard to prisoners; recognize Lebanese sovereignty and the international borders; not seek to annex or occupy any part of Lebanon or intervene in its domestic affairs; co-operate fully with the Secretary-General in all areas; have no hostile intentions towards the Palestinians or any intention of attacking neighbouring countries, including the Syrian Arab Republic; and observe the cease-fire.

A number of States, among them the Byelorussian SSR, Iraq, Ireland, Malaysia and Mexico, called for the demands of the Security Council to be implemented. Malta called for an immediate stop to the carnage as a first step, after which all should join efforts to bring about peace in the Middle East. Qatar said that if the international community did not act quickly and firmly, history would judge it an accomplice in the crime. Nothing must be done that would lead to direct or indirect acceptance of the consequences of Israel's latest aggression, said Yugoslavia.

Indonesia believed that the Assembly had been obliged to resume its session, particularly in the light of the Council's inability to enforce its decisions. A similar opinion was held by several other countries, including Ethiopia. India believed the emergency special session should achieve what the Council had failed to do, namely, to bring about a total cessation of hostilities and to force Israel to withdraw.

In the event of Israel's continued disregard of the Council's demands, Austria appealed to the Council to decide on measures under Article 41 of the United Nations Charter (sanctions not involving the use of armed force) and it considered action to impede the flow of military equipment to be of special urgency. Should Israel continue to refuse to implement the Council's resolutions, Belgium stated, EC would consider the possibilities of future action; the signing of a financial protocol with Israel had already been postponed *sine die*.

Cuba stated that, if Israel did not comply with an order to withdraw its troops from Lebanon without delay and without conditions, United Nations Members would have an inescapable duty to apply sanctions against it. Agreeing, Indonesia declared itself ready to support the strongest possible measures the Assembly might adopt to force Israel to cease its policy of destruction and to withdraw unconditionally from Lebanon.

The USSR called on the Council to take immediate measures to halt the killing and destruction, and to ensure Lebanon's sovereignty and territorial integrity, the exercise by the Arabs and Palestinians of their rights and the protection of their interests. In Bulgaria's view, it was the Council's duty to take decisive measures to stop the aggression and prevent further massacres. The call for measures by the Council was supported by several others, including Czechoslovakia and the German Democratic Republic.

Measures to compel Israel to comply with the Council's demands were also called for by a number of other States, among them Iraq and Nicaragua. Kuwait asked what more Israel must do before those who opposed any punishment or restraint on Israel realized the need for such action. If the United Nations could not expel Israel because of United States protection, Yemen said, the Member States should at least, individually or collectively, sever their diplomatic, consular and economic relations with Israel so as to isolate it.

France reiterated its proposal to the Council for a neutralization of the combat zone in Beirut as a pre-condition for the early opening of negotiations; to preserve the city from total destruction, it added, there should be a reciprocal disengagement of forces. Zaire suggested that the permanent Council members be asked to guarantee jointly the security of the Palestinians, Israel and its neighbouring Arab States, and that negotiations for a Middle East solution be resumed.

Canada said Lebanon's territorial integrity, sovereignty and unity could only be ensured in the framework of a comprehensive Middle East settlement which guaranteed peace and security for all States in the region, including Israel, and the legitimate rights of the Palestinians.

Other communications (June). During June, a number of communications were addressed to the Secretary-General and to the Presidents of the General Assembly and the Security Council with regard to the situation between Israel and Lebanon. Several of them conveyed the views of regional and other intergovernmental organizations, and others the positions of individual States.

On 7 June,[70] Saudi Arabia transmitted to the Secretary-General a letter from King Khaled Bin Abdul Aziz as President of the Third Islamic Summit Conference of the Organization of the Islamic Conference, appealing for all measures stipulated in the United Nations Charter to guarantee immediate cessation of the genocidal war against the Lebanese and Palestinians and to effect immediate Israeli withdrawal. By a note verbale of 14 June,[62] Iraq transmitted a communiqué issued on 11 June after an emergency meeting in New York of the members of the Organization of the Islamic Conference at the United Nations, condemning Israel's non-compliance with the Council demands of 5 and 6 June and urging the Council to take measures to halt Israeli aggression and to ensure the cessation of hostilities and unconditional Israeli withdrawal beyond Lebanon's borders.

On 10 June,[6] Belgium transmitted a statement by the Ministers for Foreign Affairs of the EC members (Bonn, Federal Republic of Germany, 9 June) vigorously condemning Israel's invasion and reaffirming that Lebanon's independence, sovereignty, territorial integrity and national unity were indispensable for Middle East peace; they urgently called on the parties, in particular Israel, to act in accordance with the Security Council demands, and stated that in the event of Israel's non-compliance they would examine the possibilities for future action. On 30 June,[7] Belgium transmitted a statement by a meeting of heads of State and Government of EC members (Brussels, Belgium, 28 and 29 June) calling for Israeli withdrawal from positions around Beirut simultaneously with withdrawal of Palestinian forces in west Beirut, the separation of forces during a short transitional period to be controlled by Lebanese forces and United Nations observers or forces; negotiations on a Middle East peace should follow, based on security and justice for all States and peoples.

On 11 June,[12] Cuba transmitted to the Secretary-General a communiqué issued on that date in New York by the Co-ordinating Bureau of the Non-Aligned Countries, urging Council action to ensure the cessation of hostilities and immediate, total and unconditional Israeli withdrawal from Lebanon. On 18 June, Cuba transmitted messages from its President, in his capacity as Chairman of the Movement of Non-Aligned Countries, to the Secretary-General[14] and the Presidents of the Assembly[15] and of the Security Council,[13] urging them to ensure that the United Nations took firm, decisive and immediate action to secure Israel's withdrawal.

Also on 11 June,[73] Singapore transmitted a statement of the same date by the Foreign Ministers of the States members of the Association of South-East Asian Nations strongly condemning Israel's aggression and declaring full support of the Council's call for a cease-fire and unconditional Israeli withdrawal.

On 7 June,[57] Egypt transmitted a statement by its Presidency calling on Israel to cease all military operations and withdraw from Lebanese territory, and calling on all peace-loving peoples to ensure the security of all peoples against the military occupation by Israel and to adopt resolutions that would ensure respect for legality and the rule of law.

By a letter of 8 June,[51] Viet Nam transmitted to the Secretary-General a statement of its Ministry of Foreign Affairs condemning Israel's aggressive acts against Palestinians and Lebanese. On 17 June,[52] it transmitted a message of 11 June from its President to the PLO Chairman, reiterating Viet Nam's support for the Palestinians under PLO leadership.

Israel's aggression was also condemned by the German Democratic Republic and the USSR. The former transmitted on 8 June a statement of the Central Committee of the Socialist Unity Party of Germany, the Council of State and the Council of Ministers, declaring full solidarity with the steps taken by the Lebanese and Palestinians.[22] On 25 June,[23] it conveyed a telegram from its For-

eign Minister declaring his support for the Security Council demands for an immediate cease-fire and unconditional Israeli withdrawal, and announcing humanitarian assistance. By a letter of 9 June,[48] the USSR transmitted a TASS statement of 7 June calling for immediate steps by the Council to halt the aggression and force Israel to comply with the Charter and decisions of the United Nations. On 15 June,[49] the USSR transmitted a government statement of 14 June warning Israel that events in the Middle East were bound to affect USSR interests, and demanding that Israel withdraw and that its aggression be stopped.

By a letter of 8 June,[4] the Chairman of the Committee on Palestinian rights appealed to the Secretary-General to request that decisive steps be taken by the Council to ensure that the explosive situation brought about by Israel's invasion of southern Lebanon was brought to an immediate end. On 15 June,[5] the Chairman stated that the Committee was gravely concerned at the loss of Lebanese, Palestinian and other lives and at Israel's declared aim of eliminating PLO, and felt strongly that Israel should withdraw its forces immediately and unconditionally in accordance with the Council resolutions of 5 and 6 June.

On 10 June, Fiji[59] and Sierra Leone[72] conveyed statements of 8 June by their respective Governments calling for complete and unconditional Israeli withdrawal. Also on 10 June,[69] the Niger transmitted to the Secretary-General a press communiqué of 8 June expressing the support of its Supreme Military Council and its Government for Lebanon's sovereignty, and reaffirming its conviction that any lasting Middle East settlement must involve recognition of the right of the Palestinians to establish their own State under PLO leadership.

On 10 June,[67] Mongolia conveyed a statement of 9 June by its Ministry of Foreign Affairs, condemning Israel's actions and calling for their immediate cessation and Israeli withdrawal, and declaring that the responsibility for the crimes must be shared by the United States, under whose protection Israel's hostile actions were being perpetrated.

By a letter of 11 June,[56] Czechoslovakia conveyed a statement of its Foreign Ministry demanding that Israel halt its aggression and withdraw its troops from Lebanon immediately, and expressing the expectation that the Security Council would adopt effective measures to safeguard Lebanese sovereignty and territorial integrity and to restore Palestinian rights.

On 15 June,[46] Pakistan forwarded a statement of 8 June from its Foreign Office spokesman declaring full support of the Council demand for an immediate cease-fire and unconditional Israeli withdrawal, and urging all countries to condemn the brutal use of force by Israel and to take all possible measures to frustrate its aggressive and expansionist designs.

By a letter of 15 June,[18] Cyprus forwarded a resolution adopted on 10 June by its House of Representatives condemning Israel's aggression, declaring its support of all resolutions on the Middle East problem adopted by the United Nations and other intergovernmental organizations, and inviting the Government to consider interrupting diplomatic relations with Israel.

Also on 15 June,[8] China transmitted a government statement of the same date declaring its firm support for the Lebanese, Palestinian and Syrian armed forces and peoples in their struggle to resist Israeli aggression, condemning the United States veto in the Security Council, and calling for Israel's compliance with the Council's calls for a halt to hostilities and its unconditional withdrawal.

By a letter dated 21 June,[64] the Lao People's Democratic Republic conveyed a statement of 10 June by its Foreign Ministry strongly condemning Israel's aggression and demanding its immediate and unconditional withdrawal.

Also on 21 June,[68] Mozambique transmitted a declaration by its Foreign Ministry condemning the invasion and its imperialist accomplices, demanding Israel's withdrawal, and appealing for intensified international efforts to stop Israel's massacre of Palestinians and Lebanese.

On 22 June,[29] Jordan transmitted a message of 13 June from King Hussein to the five permanent Security Council members, appealing to them to take the strongest possible action to prevent further bloodshed and to dissociate themselves from any tolerance or acquiescence of the blood-bath created by Israel.

By a letter of 23 June,[61] Hungary transmitted a government statement of 18 June demanding an end to Israel's genocidal war, and calling for Israel's withdrawal, restoration of Lebanese sovereignty, and reimbursement by Israel for the loss of life and property; Hungary expected action by the United States and the other members of the North Atlantic Treaty Organization maintaining good relations with Israel to halt Israeli aggression.

On 25 June,[65] Madagascar conveyed a telegram of 8 June from its President calling on the Secretary-General to draw the attention of United Nations Members to the necessity of taking specific measures against Israel and its accomplices to prevent the recurrence of Israeli acts of aggression.

Mauritania, by a letter of 28 June,[66] transmitted a telegram of that date by its President calling on the Secretary-General to use all his influence to demand an end to the massacre of Palestinians and Lebanese and total and unconditional Israeli withdrawal.

On the same date,[38] Lebanon conveyed an appeal of 27 June by its President to all heads of State seeking their assistance in saving Beirut from certain and imminent disaster as a result of the Israeli invasion. On 2 July,[55] Brazil transmitted a letter of 28 June from its President to the Lebanese President, stating his repudiation of Israel's aggression and offering humanitarian aid.

In a letter of 2 July to the Security Council President,[63] Israel stated that the communications addressed to the Secretary-General and the Council President during June contained insinuations, distortions and sheer fabrications; its operation in Lebanon was directed solely against PLO, which had deliberately used the civilian population as a shield, while the Israeli forces had attempted to minimize civilian casualties.

Security Council action (4 July). By a letter of 4 July,[30] Jordan requested an immediate Security Council meeting to examine what it called the grave and deteriorating situation in Lebanon resulting from Israel's genocidal campaign against Lebanese and Palestinian civilians, including its decision to strangulate the civilians in west Beirut and prohibit the transfer of medical supplies.

Meeting that day, the Council unanimously adopted a resolution,[83] prepared in the course of consultations, calling for respect for the rights of the civilian populations and repudiating all acts of violence against them. Expressing alarm at the continued sufferings of Lebanese and Palestinian civilians in southern Lebanon and west Beirut, the Council called for the restoration of the normal supply of vital facilities such as water, electricity, food and medical provisions, particularly in Beirut. It commended and requested the continuation of efforts by the Secretary-General and international agencies to alleviate civilian suffering.

Addressing the Council, the PLO observer stated that the Israeli forces had displayed vindictiveness and malice, and expressed concern about the fate of some 6,000 Palestinians detained by the occupation force.

Lebanon said that, while the resolution had been adopted on humanitarian grounds, it hoped that Israel would listen to the message it contained and would facilitate the negotiations that should lead to full implementation of previous Council resolutions.

Communications (July). On 5 July[16] and 29 July,[17] Cuba transmitted messages from its President, in his capacity as Chairman of the Movement of Non-Aligned Countries. In the first message, dated 3 July and addressed to the other heads of State or Government of the Movement, he cited the appeal of 27 June from the Lebanese President concerning the plight of Beirut (see above) and called on them to support the Lebanese and Palestinian peoples and to condemn the Israeli aggressor. In the second message, dated 28 July and addressed to the Security Council President, the Chairman called for quick Council action to order the termination of the siege and bombardment of Beirut; enclosed was a message to him from the PLO Chairman asking support for efforts to have the Council discuss the situation despite efforts by certain permanent members to postpone its meetings.

By a letter of 8 July,[71] Seychelles conveyed a message of 10 June from its President to the Lebanese President, condemning Israel's aggression and expressing solidarity with the people and Government of Lebanon.

On 10 July,[9] China transmitted a letter of 8 July from the Premier of its State Council to the PLO Chairman condemning Israel's aggression and expressing support for the struggle of the Palestinians and Arabs. By a letter of 15 July,[10] China transmitted a message of 12 July from its Minister for Foreign Affairs to the Extraordinary Ministerial Meeting of the Co-ordinating Bureau of the Non-Aligned Countries at Nicosia, Cyprus, appealing for urgent action to stop Israeli aggression, support the just cause of the Palestinians and Arabs, and maintain peace in the Middle East.

On 12 July,[47] Pakistan transmitted a letter from its President to the heads of State or Government of the permanent Security Council members, calling on them to use their power and influence to stop Israel from pursuing its genocidal war to the bitter end.

By a letter of 20 July,[58] Ethiopia transmitted a statement of 10 July by its Foreign Ministry condemning Israel's aggression and demanding its prompt and unconditional withdrawal and full respect for Lebanon's sovereignty and territorial integrity.

On 23 July,[50] the USSR transmitted replies, published in the Soviet press on 21 July, by the General Secretary of the Central Committee of the Communist Party and President of the Presidium of the Supreme Soviet to questions on the Israeli invasion; he stated that, to end the Israeli siege of Beirut, the USSR would not oppose the use of a United Nations force to separate the forces defending west Beirut and the Israeli forces, but it would firmly oppose the stationing of United States troops in Lebanon.

Viet Nam, by a letter of 30 July,[53] transmitted a government statement of 26 July condemning the actions of Israel and the United States in Lebanon and demanding a halt to the invasion and the unconditional withdrawal of Israeli troops.

By a letter of 27 July,[54] Afghanistan forwarded a statement by the Presidium of the Peace, Solidarity and Friendship Organization of the Democratic Republic of Afghanistan, expressing support for the establishment of an international commission to assess Israeli crimes in Lebanon.

On 29 July,[19] Cyprus transmitted the final communiqué of the Extraordinary Ministerial Meeting of the Co-ordinating Bureau of the Non-Aligned Countries on the question of Palestine (Nicosia, 15-17 July). The Ministers demanded that Israel lift the blockade of Beirut, observe a cease-fire and withdraw immediately and unconditionally from Lebanon. They called on the Security Council to establish a United Nations interim peace-keeping force in Lebanon, and requested the resumption by the end of August of the General Assembly's seventh emergency special session on the Palestine question.

On 30 July,[34] Jordan conveyed an urgent appeal of 29 July by six international non-governmental organizations, asking Security Council members to condemn the war in Lebanon and demand its immediate cessation.

Security Council action (29 July). In the two weeks prior to its 29 July meeting on the Israel-Lebanon situation—when it demanded that Israel lift the blockade of Beirut to let civilian supplies through—the Security Council received several letters on developments in the area from Lebanon and Jordan, the latter transmitting communications from PLO. Most of the letters concerned the effects of the fighting in and around Beirut, which had been encircled by Israeli forces. In addition, the Council received and briefly discussed a proposal by Egypt and France to put a stop to the fighting through a disengagement of forces and also to lay down principles for a future negotiated settlement of the Middle East problem.

By a letter of 16 July,[31] Jordan transmitted a 14 July letter from PLO reporting a bombing on 13 July outside the Palestine Research Centre in Beirut after a cease-fire and cessation of hostilities had been declared effective 11 July; it said the Centre had been severely damaged and a number of civilians injured.

Also by a letter of 16 July,[39] Lebanon conveyed a communiqué of 14 July by its Council of Ministers indicating that negotiations were under way to obtain the withdrawal of all non-Lebanese forces from Lebanon and to seek the assistance of a multinational force to make possible the Palestinian withdrawal from Beirut; the communiqué added that the Council supported principles adopted to secure the withdrawal of all non-Lebanese armed forces from Lebanese territory.

On 26 July,[40] Lebanon protested that Israel was violating international law in its occupation of southern Lebanon by establishing parallel local administrations and ignoring the legitimate Lebanese local authorities; Lebanon requested the Secretary-General to help redress the situation and suggested that UNIFIL be instructed to assist the Lebanese authorities in discharging their duties.

By a letter of the same date,[41] Lebanon charged that Israel had been using the intermittent cease-fires to conduct a war of attrition; since 22 July it had launched incessant air, sea and land attacks on west Beirut and its suburbs, killing at least 100 civilians, and had conducted air raids in the Bekaa Valley, causing 182 casualties.

On 26 July,[32] Jordan transmitted letters to the Council President of 22 and 23 July from the PLO observer, reporting shelling and air raids by Israeli forces in the Bekaa Valley on 22 July and air raids against west Beirut on both days, causing hundreds of civilian casualties and violating the cease-fire. Continued daily attacks until 26 July were reported in a further letter of that date from the PLO observer, transmitted by Jordan on 28 July.[33]

On 29 July,[42] Lebanon conveyed an appeal by its Ministers of National Economy and of Industry and Petroleum, on behalf of the Government, stating that the siege of west Beirut imposed by Israel had created hardship for the population; they appealed to all those in a position to help urgently to exert their utmost influence to lift the blockade and allow food supplies and basic necessities to enter west Beirut.

By letters of 2 July[20] and 28 July,[21] Egypt and France requested a Council meeting to take up a draft resolution they were submitting.[1]

This draft would have had the Council demand an immediate cease-fire throughout Lebanon and simultaneous withdrawal of Israeli and Palestinian forces from west Beirut—the Israelis to an agreed distance as a first step towards their complete withdrawal from Lebanon, and the Palestinians, with their light weapons, to camps, preferably outside Beirut, through modalities to be agreed, thus putting an end to their military activities. The Palestinian forces and the Lebanese Government were to conclude an agreement on the destination and destiny of their other weapons. The Council would have called for the departure of all non-Lebanese forces, except those authorized by the legitimate and representative authorities of Lebanon. It would have supported the Government in its efforts to regain exclusive control of Beirut and to ensure Lebanese sovereignty throughout the territory. Lebanese armed forces were to take up positions in Beirut and interpose themselves on its periphery.

The Secretary-General would have been requested to station United Nations military observers to supervise the disengagement in and around Beirut. He would also have been asked to prepare a report on the prospects for having a United Nations peace-keeping force take up positions beside the Lebanese interposition forces.

The draft would have had the Council state that the settlement of the Lebanese problem should contribute to the initiation of a durable restoration of peace and security in the region within the framework of negotiations based on the principles of security for all States and justice for all peoples. Such a settlement was to reaffirm the right of all States in the region to existence and security; reaffirm the legitimate national rights of the Palestinian people, including the right to self-determination with all its implications, on the understanding that the Palestinians would be represented in the negotiations and PLO would be associated therein; and call for the mutual and simultaneous recognition of the parties.

The Council discussed the draft resolution at two meetings on 29 July but did not act on it, after its sponsors indicated that they were not pressing for an immediate vote and that the text was open to amendment. Introducing the draft, France said that, with the threat of an attack continuing to hang over west Beirut, Council members must be aware of the essential relationship between the search for a solution to the immediate problem of Beirut and the search for direction on the fundamental problems that had led to the current crisis; it was the Council's task to define the principles of a settlement.

In Egypt's view, the situation in Lebanon had arisen from the continued Israeli denial of Palestinian rights and Israeli aggression against Lebanese sovereignty; on 25 July the PLO position towards Israel had taken a new turn when the PLO Chairman signed a document accepting United Nations resolutions on the Palestine question, and in the light of that positive initiative the simultaneous mutual recognition of the rights of both Israel and the Palestinians should be energetically promoted.

Jordan said it supported the basic spirit and thrust of the proposal and would be ready to endorse it with such peripheral amendments as Council members might propose. Lebanon expressed support for the initiative and stated that it was nothing less than a charter for mutual recognition of every nation's and people's right to exist; peace in Lebanon could not wait for a comprehensive Middle East settlement. The Franco-Egyptian proposal was also welcomed by Pakistan which added that the primary responsibility for stopping Israel from pursuing its genocidal war rested with the permanent Council members.

Support in principle for the draft was also expressed by Ireland and Spain. Ireland stressed the need to open a political dialogue and then negotiations, which, in addition to the principles enunciated by the Council in 1967[85] and 1973,[86] would have to be based on recognition of the right of the Palestinians to self-determination within the framework of a peace settlement. The United Kingdom emphasized the direct connection between the events in Lebanon and the Palestine problem, and considered that the Egyptian-French proposal set out constructive and equitable principles for a comprehensive solution.

The Egyptian-French initiative was welcomed by the PLO observer, who hoped that constructive elements mentioned by Egypt, including statehood for the Palestinians in the West Bank and Gaza and PLO participation in the future negotiations, would find their way into the draft resolution.

Israel reiterated that the 1967 Council resolution on principles for a Middle East peace was the only agreed basis for a settlement and that the terrorist PLO would not be a partner to any negotiations, let alone to any international arrangement concerning the Arab-Israeli conflict.

Also on 29 July, the Council adopted, by 14 votes to none, with the United States not participating in the vote, a resolution[84] demanding that Israel lift immediately the blockade of Beirut in order to permit the dispatch of supplies and the distribution of aid. The Secretary-General was requested to keep the Council informed of the implementation of this demand. Introducing the draft, Spain stated that it was merely humanitarian and requested that it be given priority to put an end to the siege of Beirut.

Before adoption of the resolution, the Council invited Pakistan, at its request, to participate without vote in the discussion.

The United States remarked that the resolution called only on Israel and did not ask that PLO abandon its occupation of Beirut or desist from military activities, yet everyone understood that Israel sought to affect supplies to the PLO forces and not to the civilians; such a one-sided appeal suggested purposes that were political as well as humanitarian.

A United States motion to adjourn the meeting for two hours to allow for consultations with Governments was rejected by 6 votes to 6, with 3 abstentions, after Jordan and Panama spoke in opposition to adjournment.

Lebanon expressed its gratitude for the adoption of the resolution.

Supporting the Council's demand that Israel lift its blockade, the USSR said Israel's action in cutting off food and electricity supplies to Beirut was anti-humanitarian, and the yardstick used by the United States must be monstrous and strange if it failed to support an elementary humanitarian resolution. Poland stated that when people were suffering and dying it could not be argued that some political balancing should take place at the expense of a humanitarian proposal.

Israel said its forces had strict instructions to facilitate the passage of ICRC convoys to west Beirut and it fully supported any genuine humanitarian concern designed to alleviate human suffering. However, it rejected any attempt to abuse such concern for political objectives. Israel read out a United Nations press release containing a 27 July dispatch from UNRWA headquarters at Vienna, Austria, stating that the movement of UNRWA supplies to 30,000 displaced Palestine refugees in west Beirut and to homeless families in south Lebanon had been stopped by PLO since 19 July.

The PLO observer replied that the Beirut inhabitants refused to have food and supplies taken out of the city; he wondered what city under siege would permit the contents of its warehouses to leave the city, especially in a case where there was no guarantee that the Palestine refugees who were supposed to receive the UNRWA rations would eventually get them.

Ireland, observing that the siege of Beirut had been under way for 40 days and that the Council's call for a cease-fire and immediate Israeli withdrawal had gone unimplemented for nearly two months, said the negotiations to end the fighting, conducted by United States Ambassador Philip Habib and others, deserved encouragement and support. The United Kingdom, noting that efforts had been under way outside the Council to prevent an all-out assault on west Beirut, said its Government wished to leave Israel in no doubt of the total unacceptability of such an assault.

Jordan said that massive Israeli bombardments by air, sea and land had spared hardly a single building, and civilian losses were staggering; but the few thousand heroic Lebanese and Palestinian resistance fighters were determined to turn an invaded Beirut into a vast cemetery for the invaders. Pakistan, stating that the Council's failure to act firmly in the face of Israeli defiance of its resolutions had resulted in ever-widening Israeli aggression, remarked that the destruction and siege of Beirut would be remembered as a most tragic chapter in the history of the Middle East.

The Permanent Observer of the League of Arab States informed the Council of an announcement by the League on 29 July that PLO had decided to move its armed forces from Beirut, and that safeguards and guarantees for the move, as well as for the safety of refugee camps, would be determined in an agreement between the Lebanese Government and PLO. The text of this announcement, in the form of a declaration by the Committee of Six of the League Council (Jeddah, Saudi Arabia, 28 and 29 July), was annexed to a letter of 30 July from the observer of the League to the Security Council President, transmitted by Jordan on the same date.[35]

By a letter of 30 July,[43] Lebanon transmitted an appeal by the Deputy Speaker of its Parliament to the speakers of Parliament of nine European countries, Canada and the United States, asking them to demand that Israel lift its genocidal siege of west Beirut, which was causing increasing suffering to the 700,000 inhabitants.

Draft resolutions. [1]Egypt, France, S/15317 (not pressed); [2]France, S/15255/Rev.2 (not adopted); [3]Spain, S/15185 (not adopted).

Letters and notes verbales (nv).

Committee on Palestinian rights Chairman: [4]8 June, A/37/274-S/15188; [5]15 June, A/37/288-S/15222.

Belgium, transmitting EC statements: [6]10 June, A/37/277-S/15195; [7]30 June, A/37/320-S/15265.

China: [8]15 June, A/37/293-S/15224; [9]10 July, A/37/336-S/15284; [10]15 July, A/37/343-S/15297.

Cuba: [11]5 June, transmitting non-aligned countries' message, S/15165; [12]11 June, A/37/281-S/15200; [13]18 June, S/15233; [14]18 June, A/37/299-S/15243; [15]18 June, A/37/300; [16]5 July, A/37/332 (S/15274); [17]29 July, S/15322.

Cyprus: [18]15 June, A/37/294-S/15225; [19]29 July, A/37/366-S/15327.

Egypt, France: [20]2 July, S/15315; [21]28 July, S/15316.

German Democratic Republic: [22]8 June, A/37/272-S/15186; [23]25 June, A/37/313-S/15262.

Jordan: [24]4 June, S/15164; [25]5 June, S/15166; [26]5 June, S/15167; [27]18 June, S/15238; [28]18 June, S/15239; [29]22 June, A/37/304-S/15248; [30]4 July, S/15272; [31]16 July, A/37/345-S/15299; [32]26 July, S/15308; [33]28 July, S/15318; [34]30 July, S/15328; [35]30 July, transmitting League of Arab States declaration, S/15329.

Lebanon: [36]4 June, S/15161; [37]4 June, S/15162; [38]28 June, A/37/316 (S/15261); [39]16 July, A/37/346-S/15300; [40]26 July, A/37/360 (S/15309); [41]26 July, S/15310; [42]29 July, S/15324; [43]30 July, S/15326.

Oman: [44]6 June, for Arab States, S/15170; [45]16 June, A/37/295-S/15226.

Pakistan: [46]15 June, A/37/287-S/15221; [47]12 July, S/15288.

USSR: [48]9 June, S/15187; [49]15 June, A/37/289-S/15223; [50]23 July, A/37/361-S/15312.

Viet Nam: [51]8 June, A/37/273; [52]17 June, A/37/298; [53]30 July, A/37/369.

Others: [54]Afghanistan: 27 July, A/37/364. [55]Brazil: 2 July, A/37/331-S/15276. [56]Czechoslovakia: 11 June, A/37/284-S/15211. [57]Egypt: 7 June, A/37/270-S/15183 *(nv).* [58]Ethiopia: 20 July, S/15302. [59]Fiji: 10 June, A/37/276-S/15190 *(nv).* [60]France: 24 June, A/37/309 (S/15254). [61]Hungary: 23 June, A/37/306-S/15251. [62]Iraq: 14 June, annexing communiqué of Organization of Islamic Conference, A/37/286-S/15220 *(nv).* [63]Israel: 2 July, A/37/327 (S/15271). [64]Lao People's Democratic Republic: 21 June, A/37/303. [65]Madagascar: 25 June, A/37/312-S/15259. [66]Mauritania: 28 June, A/37/314-S/15263. [67]Mongolia: 10 June, A/37/280-S/15197. [68]Mozambique: 21 June, A/37/302. [69]Niger: 10 June, A/37/282-S/15209. [70]Saudi Arabia: 7 June, A/37/269-S/15180. [71]Seychelles: 8 July, A/37/341-S/15294. [72]Sierra Leone: 10 June, A/37/278. [73]Singapore: 11 June, transmitting ASEAN statement, A/37/283-S/15210.

Reports. S-G, [74]S/15174, [75]S/15178, [76]S/15194 & Add.1,2, [77]S/15267 & Corr.1.

Resolutions (1982). [78]GA: ES-7/5, 26 June, text following. SC, texts following: [79]508(1982), 5 June; [80]509(1982), 6 June; [81]511(1982), 18 June; [82]512(1982), 19 June; [83]513(1982), 4 July; [84]515(1982), 29 July.

Resolutions (prior). SC: [85]242(1967), 22 Nov. 1967 (YUN 1967, p. 257); [86]338(1973), 22 Oct. 1973 (YUN 1973, p. 213); [87]490(1981), 21 July 1981 (YUN 1981, p. 292); [88]498(1981), 18 Dec. 1981 *(ibid.).*

Statement. [89]SC President, S/15163.

Meeting records. GA: A/ES-7/PV.12-19, *22-24* (20-26 Apr. & 25, 26 June). SC: S/PV.2374-2377, 2379, 2380, 2381 & Corr.1, 2382, 2384, 2385 (5 June–29 July).

Security Council resolution 508(1982)

5 June 1982   Meeting 2374   Adopted unanimously

Draft by Japan (S/15168).

The Security Council,

Recalling its resolutions 425(1978), 426(1978) and its ensuing resolutions and, more particularly, resolution 501(1982),

Taking note of the letters of the Permanent Representative of Lebanon dated 4 June 1982,

Deeply concerned at the deterioration of the present situation in Lebanon and in the Lebanese-Israeli border area, and its consequences for peace and security in the region,

Gravely concerned at the violation of the territorial integrity, independence and sovereignty of Lebanon,

Reaffirming and supporting the statement made by the President and the members of the Security Council on 4 June 1982, as well as the urgent appeal issued by the Secretary-General on 4 June 1982,

Taking note of the report of the Secretary-General,

1. *Calls upon* all the parties to the conflict to cease immediately and simultaneously all military activities within Lebanon and across the Lebanese-Israeli border and not later than 0600 hours, local time, on Sunday, 6 June 1982;

2. *Requests* all Member States which are in a position to do so to bring their influence to bear upon those concerned so that the cessation of hostilities declared by Security Council resolution 490(1981) can be respected;

3. *Requests* the Secretary-General to undertake all possible efforts to ensure the implementation of and compliance with the present resolution and to report to the Security Council as early as possible and not later than forty-eight hours after the adoption of the present resolution.

Security Council resolution 509(1982)

6 June 1982   Meeting 2375   Adopted unanimously

Draft by Ireland (S/15171).

The Security Council,

Recalling its resolutions 425(1978) and 508(1982),

Gravely concerned at the situation as described by the Secretary-General in his report to the Council,

Reaffirming the need for strict respect for the territorial integrity, sovereignty and political independence of Lebanon within its internationally recognized boundaries,

1. *Demands* that Israel withdraw all its military forces forthwith and unconditionally to the internationally recognized boundaries of Lebanon;

2. *Demands* that all parties observe strictly the terms of paragraph 1 of resolution 508(1982) which called on them to cease immediately and simultaneously all military activities within Lebanon and across the Lebanese-Israeli border,

3. *Calls* on all parties to communicate to the Secretary-General their acceptance of the present resolution within twenty-four hours;

4. *Decides* to remain seized of the question.

Security Council resolution 511(1982)

18 June 1982   Meeting 2379   13-0-2

Draft prepared in consultations among Council members (S/15235).

The Security Council,

Recalling its resolutions 425(1978), 426(1978), 427(1978), 434(1978), 444(1979), 450(1979), 459(1979), 467(1980), 483(1980), 488(1981), 490(1981), 498(1981) and 501(1982),

Reaffirming its resolutions 508(1982) and 509(1982),

Having studied the report of the Secretary-General on the United Nations Interim Force in Lebanon and taking note of the conclusions and recommendations expressed therein,

Bearing in mind the need to avoid any developments which could further aggravate the situation and the need, pending an examination of the situation by the Security Council in all its aspects, to preserve in place the capacity of the United Nations to assist in the restoration of the peace,

1. *Decides,* as an interim measure, to extend the present mandate of the United Nations Interim Force in Lebanon for a period of two months, that is, until 19 August 1982;

2. *Authorizes* the Force during that period to carry out, in addition, the interim tasks referred to in paragraph 17 of the report of the Secretary-General on the Force;

3. *Calls on* all concerned to extend full co-operation to the Force in the discharge of its tasks;

4. *Requests* the Secretary-General to keep the Security Council regularly informed of the implementation of resolutions 508(1982) and 509(1982) and the present resolution.

Vote in Council as follows:

In favour: China, France, Guyana, Ireland, Japan, Jordan, Panama, Spain, Togo, Uganda, United Kingdom, United States, Zaire.
Against: None.
Abstaining: Poland, USSR.

Security Council resolution 512(1982)

| 19 June 1982 | Meeting 2380 | Adopted unanimously |

Draft by France (S/15240).

The Security Council,

Deeply concerned at the sufferings of the Lebanese and Palestinian civilian populations,

Referring to the humanitarian principles of the Geneva Conventions of 1949 and to the obligations arising from the regulations annexed to The Hague Convention of 1907,

Reaffirming its resolutions 508(1982) and 509(1982),

1. *Calls upon* all the parties to the conflict to respect the rights of the civilian populations, to refrain from all acts of violence against those populations and to take all appropriate measures to alleviate the suffering caused by the conflict, in particular, by facilitating the dispatch and distribution of aid provided by United Nations agencies and by non-governmental organizations, in particular, the International Committee of the Red Cross;

2. *Appeals* to Member States to continue to provide the most extensive humanitarian aid possible;

3. *Stresses* the particular humanitarian responsibilities of the United Nations and its agencies, including the United Nations Relief and Works Agency for Palestine Refugees in the Near East, towards civilian populations and calls upon all the parties to the conflict not to hamper the exercise of those responsibilities and to assist in humanitarian efforts;

4. *Takes note* of the measures taken by the Secretary-General to co-ordinate the activities of the international agencies in this field and requests him to make every effort to ensure the implementation of and compliance with the present resolution and to report on these efforts to the Security Council as soon as possible.

General Assembly resolution ES-7/5

| 26 June 1982 | Meeting 24 | 127-2 (recorded vote) |

64-nation draft (A/ES-7/L.4 and Add.1); agenda item 5.

Sponsors: Afghanistan, Algeria, Angola, Bahrain, Bangladesh, Benin, Bulgaria, Chad, Congo, Cuba, Cyprus, Czechoslovakia, Democratic Yemen, Djibouti, Ethiopia, Gambia, German Democratic Republic, Ghana, Greece, Guinea-Bissau, Guyana, Hungary, India, Indonesia, Iran, Iraq, Jordan, Kenya, Kuwait, Lao People's Democratic Republic, Libyan Arab Jamahiriya, Madagascar, Malaysia, Maldives, Mali, Malta, Mauritania, Morocco, Mozambique, Nicaragua, Niger, Nigeria, Oman, Pakistan, Qatar, Sao Tome and Principe, Saudi Arabia, Senegal, Seychelles, Somalia, Sri Lanka, Sudan, Syrian Arab Republic, Togo, Tunisia, Turkey, Ukrainian SSR, United Arab Emirates, United Republic of Cameroon, United Republic of Tanzania, Viet Nam, Yemen, Yugoslavia, Zambia.

Question of Palestine

The General Assembly,

Having considered the question of Palestine at its resumed seventh emergency special session,

Having heard the statement of the Palestine Liberation Organization, the representative of the Palestinian people,

Alarmed by the worsening situation in the Middle East resulting from Israel's acts of aggression against the sovereignty of Lebanon and the Palestinian people in Lebanon,

Recalling Security Council resolutions 508(1982) of 5 June 1982, 509(1982) of 6 June 1982 and 512(1982) of 19 June 1982,

Taking note of the reports of the Secretary-General relevant to this situation, particularly his report of 7 June 1982,

Taking note of the two positive replies to the Secretary-General by the Government of Lebanon and the Palestine Liberation Organization,

Noting with regret that the Security Council has, so far, failed to take effective and practical measures, in accordance with the Charter of the United Nations, to ensure implementation of its resolutions 508(1982) and 509(1982),

Referring to the humanitarian principles of the Geneva Convention relative to the Protection of Civilian Persons in Time of War, of 12 August 1949, and to the obligations arising from the regulations annexed to the Hague Conventions of 1907,

Deeply concerned at the sufferings of the Palestinian and Lebanese civilian populations,

Reaffirming once again its conviction that the question of Palestine is the core of the Arab-Israeli conflict and that no comprehensive, just and lasting peace in the region will be achieved without the full exercise by the Palestinian people of its inalienable national rights,

Reaffirming further that a just and comprehensive settlement of the situation in the Middle East cannot be achieved without the participation on an equal footing of all the parties to the conflict, including the Palestine Liberation Organization as the representative of the Palestinian people,

1. *Reaffirms* the fundamental principle of the inadmissibility of the acquisition of territory by force;

2. *Demands* that all Member States and other parties observe strict respect for Lebanon's sovereignty, territorial integrity, unity and political independence within its internationally recognized boundaries;

3. *Decides* to support fully the provisions of Security Council resolutions 508(1982) and 509(1982) in which the Council, *inter alia*, demanded that:

(a) Israel withdraw all its military forces forthwith and unconditionally to the internationally recognized boundaries of Lebanon;

(b) All parties to the conflict cease immediately and simultaneously all military activities within Lebanon and across the Lebanese-Israeli border;

4. *Condemns* Israel for its non-compliance with resolutions 508(1982) and 509(1982);

5. *Demands* that Israel comply with all the above provisions no later than 0600 hours (Beirut time) on Sunday, 27 June 1982;

6. *Calls upon* the Security Council to authorize the Secretary-General to undertake necessary endeavours and practical steps to implement the provisions of resolutions 508(1982), 509(1982) and 512(1982);

7. *Urges* the Security Council, in the event of continued failure by Israel to comply with the demands contained in resolutions 508(1982) and 509(1982), to meet in order to consider practical ways and means in accordance with the Charter of the United Nations;

8. *Calls upon* all States and international agencies and organizations to continue to provide the most extensive humanitarian aid possible to the victims of the Israeli invasion of Lebanon;

9. *Requests* the Secretary-General to delegate a high-level commission to investigate and assess the extent of loss of human life and material damage and to report, as soon as possible, on the result of this investigation to the General Assembly and the Security Council;

10. *Decides* to adjourn the seventh emergency special session temporarily and to authorize the President of the latest regular session of the General Assembly to resume its meetings upon request from Member States.

Recorded vote in Assembly as follows:

In favour: Afghanistan, Albania, Algeria, Angola, Argentina, Australia, Austria, Bahamas, Bahrain, Bangladesh, Barbados, Belgium, Benin, Bhutan, Bolivia, Botswana, Brazil, Bulgaria, Burma, Burundi, Byelorussian SSR, Canada, Cape Verde, Chile, China, Colombia, Congo, Costa Rica, Cuba, Cyprus, Czechoslovakia, Democratic Kampuchea, Democratic Yemen, Denmark, Djibouti, Ecuador, Egypt, Fiji, Finland, France, Gabon, Gambia, German Democratic Republic, Germany, Federal Republic of, Ghana, Greece, Guinea-Bissau, Guyana, Hungary, Iceland, India, Indonesia, Iran, Iraq, Ireland, Italy, Jamaica, Japan, Jordan, Kenya, Kuwait, Lao People's Democratic Republic, Lebanon, Lesotho, Liberia, Libyan Arab Jamahiriya, Luxembourg, Madagascar, Malaysia, Maldives, Mali, Malta, Mauritania, Mauritius, Mexico, Mongolia, Morocco, Mozambique, Nepal, Netherlands, New Zealand, Nicaragua, Niger, Norway, Oman, Pakistan, Panama, Paraguay, Peru, Philippines, Poland, Portugal, Qatar, Romania, Sao Tome and Principe, Saudi Arabia, Senegal, Seychelles, Sierra Leone, Singapore, Somalia, Spain, Sri Lanka, Sudan, Suriname, Sweden, Syrian Arab Republic, Thailand, Togo, Trinidad and Tobago, Tunisia, Turkey, Uganda, Ukrainian SSR, USSR, United Arab Emirates, United Kingdom, United Republic of Cameroon, United Republic of Tanzania, Upper Volta, Uruguay, Venezuela, Viet Nam, Yemen, Yugoslavia, Zaire, Zambia.
Against: Israel, United States.

Security Council resolution 513(1982)

4 July 1982   Meeting 2382   Adopted unanimously

Draft prepared in consultations among Council members (S/15273).

The Security Council,
Alarmed by the continued sufferings of the Lebanese and Palestinian civilian poulations in southern Lebanon and in west Beirut,
Referring to the humanitarian principles of the Geneva Conventions of 1949 and to the obligations arising from the regulations annexed to The Hague Convention of 1907,
Reaffirming its resolutions 508(1982), 509(1982) and 512(1982),
1. *Calls* for respect for the rights of the civilian populations without any discrimination and repudiates all acts of violence against those populations;
2. *Calls further* for the restoration of the normal supply of vital facilities such as water, electricity, food and medical provisions, particularly in Beirut;
3. *Commends* the efforts of the Secretary-General and the action of international agencies to alleviate the sufferings of the civilian population and requests them to continue their efforts to ensure their success.

Security Council resolution 515(1982)

29 July 1982   Meeting 2385   14-0

Draft by Spain (S/15325).

The Security Council,
Deeply concerned at the situation of the civilian population of Beirut,
Referring to the humanitarian principles of the Geneva Conventions of 1949 and to the obligations arising from the regulations annexed to The Hague Convention of 1907,
Recalling its resolutions 512(1982) and 513(1982),
1. *Demands* that the Government of Israel lift immediately the blockade of the city of Beirut in order to permit the dispatch of supplies to meet the urgent needs of the civilian population and allow the distribution of aid provided by United Nations agencies and by non-governmental organizations, particularly the International Committee of the Red Cross;
2. *Requests* the Secretary-General to transmit the text of the present resolution to the Government of Israel and to keep the Security Council informed of its implementation.

Vote in Council as follows:
In favour: China, France, Guyana, Ireland, Japan, Jordan, Panama, Poland, Spain, Togo, Uganda, USSR, United Kingdom, Zaire.
Against: None.
The United States did not participate in the vote.

Cease-fire

Amidst continued fighting in and around Beirut, the Security Council, on 1 August 1982, authorized the dispatch of United Nations observers to the area. At the same time, and again on 4 and 12 August, the Council repeated its call for a cessation of military activities. On 6 August, a USSR draft resolution condemning Israel for non-implementation of the Council's demands and calling on States to refrain from supplying weapons and military aid to Israel was not adopted owing to the negative vote of a permanent member (United States).

A cease-fire in the Beirut area finally took effect from 12 August. Thereafter, on 17 August and again on 18 October, the Council extended the mandate of UNIFIL in southern Lebanon—on the second occasion until 19 January 1983. The General Assembly, in a resolution of 19 August 1982, urged measures to guarantee the safety of civilians pending Israel's withdrawal from Lebanon.

The United Nations Observer Group Beirut reported on the temporary deployment in Beirut of a three-nation force (France, Italy, United States) and the concurrent evacuation of Palestinian armed elements (21 August–1 September). Then, a period of calm, during which Lebanese forces took positions in west Beirut, was shattered by the killing on 14 September of the President-elect of Lebanon, followed the next day by an advance of Israeli positions into west Beirut. These events drew condemnation from the Council on 17 September and a call for an Israeli pull-back. On 18 September, hundreds of Palestine refugees were found murdered at the Sabra and Shatila camps on the outskirts of Beirut (see below), an act to which the Council responded on 19 September with a condemnation and by authorizing an increase in the number of United Nations observers in the Beirut area from 10 to 50, with a mandate to do what they could to ensure protection for civilians.

With Israeli troops remaining in southern Lebanon, the Assembly, on 24 September, again declared its support for the Council's original call in June for the unconditional withdrawal of Israeli forces to the Lebanese boundaries. At that time, and again on 16 December, the Assembly called for strict respect for Lebanon's sovereignty, territorial integrity, unity and independence.

During August and September, the Secretary-General submitted to the Security Council several reports on developments in and around Beirut. A number of communications were addressed by States to the Secretary-General and the Security Council President.

Security Council action (1 August). On 1 August,[6] Jordan transmitted a letter of the same date from the PLO observer to the Security Council President charging that the situation in Lebanon had escalated to extremely serious proportions due to renewed and intensified air, land and sea bombardments of Beirut by Israeli forces, particularly as part of a battle begun by the Israelis that morning for control of the international airport.

Meeting that day at the urgent request of Lebanon in view of the new outbreak of fighting in and around Beirut, the Security Council adopted unanimously a resolution,[53] prepared during consultations, demanding an immediate cease-fire and cessation of all military activities within Lebanon and across the Lebanese-Israeli border. The Secretary-General was authorized to deploy immediately United Nations observers to monitor the situation in and around Beirut, and was requested to report on compliance with the resolution within four hours.

Following this action, Lebanon read out a statement issued earlier that day by its Prime Minister, saying that a ferocious Israeli attack had taken place from land, sea and air just as Lebanon was getting ready to start implementing the arrangements announced on 29 July at Jeddah for the withdrawal of armed forces from west Beirut (see below). The Prime Minister appealed to the Council, the Secretary-General and United Nations Members to go to Lebanon's rescue and save its people besieged in its own capital and devoured by the Israeli war machine.

Israel said it had repeatedly indicated its readiness to maintain and observe the cease-fire, provided that it was observed by all. However, the terrorists had repeatedly and consistently violated the cease-fires in recent weeks, around Beirut and elsewhere in Lebanon. Following heavy shelling that morning of the area held by Israeli troops, IDF had been instructed to respond firmly. However, there was no intention to move into west Beirut. A new cease-fire had gone into effect two hours earlier.

Egypt condemned Israel's renewed aggression against west Beirut and PLO, which, it observed, was taking place after the PLO leadership had announced its readiness to co-operate towards solving the situation there. Zaire, remarking that proclamations of cease-fires had been alternating with their breach, welcomed the authorization of United Nations observers and hoped that would be a positive step towards ending the cycle of violence in and around Beirut.

The USSR, stating that the Israeli forces had broken the eighth cease-fire agreement, called on the Council to ensure implementation of the resolution and of earlier decisions by making use of the means available under Chapter VII of the United Nations Charter (on action with respect to threats to the peace, breaches of the peace and acts of aggression). It read out a TASS statement of 2 August—later transmitted to the Secretary-General by a USSR letter of 4 August[34]—calling for a stop to Israeli aggression through coercive measures by the Council.

The need for complete and unconditional Israeli withdrawal from Lebanon, not only from Beirut, was stressed by PLO.

Following the adoption of the Council resolution, Lebanon, by a letter dated 1 August,[15] requested the stationing of United Nations observers in Beirut to ensure full observance of the cease-fire.

Report of the Secretary-General (1 August). In accordance with the Council resolution of 1 August, the Secretary-General reported on the same date[37] that he had instructed the Chief of Staff of UNTSO, Lieutenant-General Emmanuel Alexander Erskine, to arrange for the immediate deployment of United Nations observers in and around Beirut. The Israeli authorities had informed the Chief of Staff that the matter would be brought before the Israeli Cabinet. The Com-

mander of the Lebanese Army had assured him that the Army was ready to provide all facilities and to assist the observers. The Secretary-General had been informed by the PLO Chairman that PLO accepted the resolution and would do its utmost to co-operate with the observers. According to preliminary observations, the cease-fire appeared to be holding.

In an addendum of 3 August, the Secretary-General stated that intensive efforts had continued for the speedy implementation of the Council resolution. The Israeli authorities had informed the UNTSO Chief of Staff that the Israeli Cabinet would discuss the subject on 5 August and that, pending a government decision, no co-operation would be extended to UNTSO personnel in the execution of the resolution. A group of 28 observers assigned to temporary offices at Yarze, near Lebanese Army headquarters, had been turned back by Israeli forces seven kilometres away.

Noting that every effort was being made to stress to the Israeli authorities the importance and urgency of the matter, the Secretary-General said that although a detailed plan for deployment of the observers had been ready since 1 August, it could not be put into full effect until the reply from the Israeli Government was received. As a temporary measure, he had instructed the UNTSO Chief of Staff to take immediate steps to set up observation machinery in the territory controlled by the Lebanese Government, in close consultation and co-operation with the Lebanese Army. United Nations observers assigned to the Israel-Lebanon Mixed Armistice Commission (ILMAC) and currently in the Beirut area had been constituted as the Observer Group Beirut, with the Chairman of ILMAC, Lieutenant-Colonel Pierre Letourneur, appointed as Officer-in-Charge.

Communications (2 and 3 August). By a letter of 2 August to the Security Council President, transmitted by Jordan on the same date,[7] the PLO observer reiterated his organization's commitment to the cease-fire and stated that, in spite of that commitment, Israel was trying to advance and its aggression continued. Also annexed was a telegram of the same date from the PLO Chairman to the observer, stating that no one on behalf of the UNTSO Chief of Staff had contacted PLO in spite of the latter's attempt to contact him. By a letter of 3 August, transmitted by Jordan on the same date,[8] the PLO observer gave details of continued shelling on that date from Israeli positions.

Also on 3 August,[2] Israel protested that, in violation of the understanding reached on 1 August by the UNTSO Chief of Staff and Israel that no attempt would be made to deploy United Nations observers before obtaining the consent and co-operation of all parties, a group of UNTSO members had attempted on 2 August to make their way to Beirut without prior consultation or consent and had been turned back by IDF; Israel insisted on full United Nations compliance with the agreed principle of consultation.

Security Council action (3 August). On 3 August, the President of the Security Council made the following statement:[63]

"Following consultations with the members of the Security Council, I have been authorized to make the following statement on their behalf in connection with the present grave situation in Lebanon:

'1. The members of the Security Council are seriously concerned at the prevailing high state of tension and at reports of military movements and continued outbreaks of firing and shelling in and around Beirut, contrary to the demand in resolution 516(1982), which was adopted at 1325 hours, New York time, on 1 August 1982, for an immediate cease-fire and cessation of all military activities within Lebanon and across the Lebanese-Israeli border. They consider it vital that these provisions be fully implemented.

2. The members of the Security Council have taken note of the Secretary-General's reports submitted pursuant to resolution 516(1982). They express full support for his efforts and for the steps he has taken, following the request of the Government of Lebanon, to secure the immediate deployment of United Nations observers to monitor the situation in and around Beirut. They note with satisfaction from the Secretary-General's report that some of the parties have already assured General Erskine of their full co-operation for the deployment of United Nations observers and they call urgently on all of the parties to co-operate fully in the effort to secure effective deployment of the observers and to ensure their safety.

3. They insist that all parties must observe strictly the terms of resolution 516(1982). They call further for the immediate lifting of all obstacles to the dispatch of supplies and the distribution of aid to meet the urgent needs of the civilian population in accordance with previous resolutions of the Council. The members of the Security Council will keep the situation under close review.' "

The USSR said the statement was not as strong as it should have been because the United States was protecting the aggressor; while Council members were discussing the text, the Israeli war machine had again undertaken a massive attack against west Beirut, yet the United States was acting behind the scenes to help Israel block the sending of observers. Poland read out a news dispatch stating that Israeli tanks had entered west Beirut and had advanced into the heart of the PLO stronghold.

Israel denied the USSR and Polish statements, stating that its forces had not been moving into west Beirut. The United States also rejected the USSR statement, asserting that it was deeply involved in the search for a peaceful solution to the crisis in Lebanon.

The PLO observer also regretted that the Council had not taken stronger action, at least by calling for a prompt return to the cease-fire positions of 1 August when the Council had adopted its latest resolution.

Security Council action (4 August). At a meeting on 4 August, requested by the USSR, the Security Council adopted a resolution[54] expressing deep shock and alarm at the deplorable consequences of the Israeli invasion of Beirut on 3 August and confirming the demand for an immediate cease-fire and Israeli withdrawal from Lebanon. The Council censured Israel for its failure to comply with its previous resolutions and called for the prompt return of Israeli troops to the lines of 1 August. As an immediate step, the Secretary-General was authorized to increase the number of United Nations observers in and around Beirut. The Council decided, in case of failure to comply by any of the parties, to consider adopting effective ways in accordance with the United Nations Charter.

The resolution, sponsored by Jordan and Spain, was adopted by 14 votes to none, with 1 abstention, after the original draft was modified twice (in writing and orally) to delete a reference in the preamble to atrocities by the Israeli forces and a mention in operative paragraph 8 of Chapter VII of the Charter. The revised version also had the Council censure rather than condemn Israel and included a reference to the PLO decision to move the Palestinian armed forces from Beirut.

Before adoption of the text, the Council invited Cuba and India, at their request, to participate without vote in the discussion.

Introducing the draft, Jordan urged the Council to take the most determined measures to let Israel know it could not continue to defy Council decisions; the Israeli onslaught on west Beirut was continuing, despite the assurance to the contrary given the Council on 3 August, with the apparent aim of aborting any chance of a peaceful solution that might emerge from current discussions among United States Ambassador Habib, PLO and the Lebanese Government. Spain concurred and said the Council must put an end to Israel's arrogance.

Abstaining in the vote, the United States said the resolution lacked balance since it did not explicitly call for the withdrawal of PLO from Lebanon.

Israel reiterated that the charge of a massive invasion of Beirut was untrue. Its objective was that all foreign forces be removed from Lebanon and it insisted that the Palestinian fighters leave west Beirut without further delay. The PLO terrorists, who had hijacked the population of Beirut, were in no position to lay down conditions and the Israeli offer to let them go was made only in order to spare as many lives as possible.

Lebanon stated that the call for Israel's return to the lines of 1 August should in no way mean that the objective of total and unconditional Israeli withdrawal was relinquished. Also, by taking note of the decision of PLO to move its forces from Beirut, Lebanon was not underwriting a policy confined to that very limited move; Lebanon's objectives were the withdrawal of all non-Lebanese forces and the deployment of its Army and security forces on all of Lebanon's territory.

France said it had voted for the resolution as a warning and an appeal to Israel for reason and respect for law. Casting an affirmative vote, Japan strongly condemned Israel's thrust into west Beirut as a serious challenge to the international community and urged it to withdraw its forces unconditionally. Supporting the deployment of United Nations observers as an important step in helping to maintain a cease-fire, the United Kingdom said it was appalled by the further attacks, which amounted to the piecemeal destruction of a large part of one of the great cities of the Middle East.

The USSR stated that in view of the extremely serious situation, it was most urgent for the Council to take all possible measures against the aggressor as provided for in Chapter VII of the Charter. Poland called for prompt and decisive Council action, and China said the Council should consider severe sanctions. China added that the United States behaviour in shielding the aggressors should be severely condemned.

Welcoming the resolution, Egypt expressed the view that the exit of the Palestinians from Beirut should be a step in a package towards a comprehensive and just solution and should take place together with security guarantees for the Palestinians, simultaneous withdrawal of Israeli troops from the Beirut area as a step towards their total withdrawal from Lebanon, and a clear and concrete step towards recognizing the right of the Palestinians to self-determination.

The PLO observer stated that two IDF divisions were engaged in the current attack on Beirut, and shells and internationally banned arms such as phosphorus, fragmentation and cluster bombs were being directed from land and sea against residential areas. He viewed the resolution as a serious attempt to have the Council meet its responsibilities and take immediate action; the Council should see to it that all powers vested in it by the Charter were invoked in order to deal with the aggressor.

Report of the Secretary-General (5 August). In pursuance of the Security Council resolution of 4 August, the Secretary-General reported on 5 August[38] that the Lebanese Government had given assurance of its readiness to co-operate fully in the implementation of the resolution and that the PLO Chairman had reaffirmed the commitment of PLO to the cease-fire. As soon as transit arrangements were completed, additional observers would be dispatched from UNTSO to the Beirut area. The Officer-in-Charge of Observer Group Beirut had reported the situation in that area as generally calm.

On 4 August, the Secretary-General had appealed to the Israeli Prime Minister to adhere to the cease-fire and to co-operate in the deployment of United Nations observers, and had expressed his readiness to go immediately to Israel and Lebanon to discuss the matter. The Prime Minister had informed him that Israel would welcome his visit if there were not a parallel visit to the PLO Chairman. The Secretary-General had not found that position acceptable and had reiterated his appeal for co-operation.

Following a Cabinet meeting on 5 August, Israel had responded that it had acceded to the previous 10 cease-fires on the condition that they be mutual and absolute. However, they had been violated by the terrorist organizations, whose activities could in no feasible way be monitored by United Nations observers; on the contrary, the presence of observers would signal to the terrorists that they were under no obligation to leave Beirut and Lebanon. Following the departure of the terrorist organizations operating in Beirut, the Cabinet statement added, arrangements for the deployment of Israeli forces would be determined by the principle that all foreign forces would leave Lebanon.

Security Council consideration (6 August). Again at the request of the USSR, the Security Council held two meetings on 6 August to consider the Secretary-General's report.

A draft resolution by the USSR, strongly condemning Israel for not complying with the Council's demands for a cease-fire, demanding that it implement those resolutions fully, and deciding that all United Nations Member States should refrain from supplying weapons and military aid to Israel until it fully withdrew its forces from Lebanon,[1] received 11 votes to 1 (United States), with 3 abstentions (Togo, United Kingdom, Zaire). It was not adopted owing to the negative vote of a permanent Council member.

The original draft had been revised by its sponsor to add the words "until the full withdrawal of Israeli forces from all Lebanese territory" to the paragraph calling for a suspension of the supply of weapons and military aid. Introducing the initial version, the USSR said the Israeli aggressors would have been unable to make their attempts to storm Beirut if they had not been sure of the economic, political and military assistance of their overseas protector. Israel must not be allowed to add the name of Beirut to the sinister list of European cities mercilessly destroyed by Hitler's Fascists during the Second World War.

Voting against the resolution, the United States said it was unbalanced and would not contribute to the goal of a peaceful settlement, towards which the United States was working; it regretted that one member had tried to polarize the situation in the Council.

Abstaining, the United Kingdom said it had announced at the end of June that it would issue no further licences for the supply of military equipment to Israel until further notice; nevertheless, the draft resolution would make no positive contribution to peace in the Middle East and a veto might send the wrong signal to Jerusalem.

Of those voting in favour, China felt that the text was a minimum, falling short of what was required for immediately halting Israel's aggression. In Egypt's view, the adoption of the resolution would have constituted one of the steps needed to check, even to a limited extent, Israeli policies and measures in Lebanon. Jordan viewed the resolution as a first step which should be followed by sterner measures.

France considered the measures envisaged to be justified until full Israeli withdrawal from Lebanon. Ireland said it did not feel the Council could simply accept that its decisions taken over a two-month period remained unimplemented while fighting, destruction and loss of life continued; it was right for the Council to signal the seriousness of its intentions by calling on States to be prepared to apply certain measures until its authority was upheld.

Lebanon said its main concern was that the Council preserve unanimity and a measure of consensus in order to continue to influence events in a positive manner and not give Israel further licence to resume hostilities.

Israel stated that it would not be bullied by the USSR, the foremost violator of international law in contemporary life.

The Permanent Observer of the League of Arab States called on the Council, despite the veto just cast, to remain seized of the priorities, namely, an effective cease-fire, the lifting of the blockade of Beirut and the beginning of an honourable solution.

The PLO observer stated that on 6 August, while the Council was deliberating and Israel was gaining encouragement from its failure to act, an Israeli air raid on a building in west Beirut had killed or wounded an estimated 250 people.

Commenting on the response of the parties to the Council's call for the stationing of observers and the withdrawal of Israeli forces, Lebanon feared that Israel's demand for symmetrical withdrawal might be conducive to symmetrical presence or even symmetrical occupation; Israel's withdrawal must not be made contingent on the withdrawal of other non-Lebanese forces. Jordan stated that Israel had rejected the call because it wanted to carry on with its barbaric aggression and

invasion; Jordan saw it as ominous that the Israeli reply had spoken not of withdrawal but of deployment of its forces. Jordan read out a 5 August communication from PLO—transmitted to the Council President on the same date[9]—calling for the prompt arrival of United Nations observers in view of the continued Israeli military build-up.

Communications (9 and 12 August). On 9 August, Jordan transmitted a letter of the same date to the Security Council President from the PLO observer, stating that since the previous night Israel had been escalating its bombardment of Beirut from land, air and sea.[10] On 12 August, Jordan transmitted a letter of the same date from the PLO observer protesting nine continuous hours of Israeli air attacks that day on west Beirut, said to have caused an estimated 300 civilian casualties in residential areas and refugee camps.[11]

By a letter also dated 12 August, Lebanon charged that Israeli armed forces, taking advantage of the intensive negotiations being conducted on the fate of west Beirut, had undertaken military advances in areas north of Beirut.[16]

Security Council action (12 August). On 12 August, the Security Council held a further meeting at the urgent request of the USSR to deal with what it called the worsening situation in Lebanon in connection with Israel's continued aggression.

The Council unanimously adopted a resolution[55] demanding that Israel and all parties to the conflict observe strictly the terms of previous Council resolutions on the immediate cessation of military activities in Lebanon, particularly in and around Beirut. The Council demanded that all restrictions on Beirut be lifted in order to permit the free entry of supplies to meet urgent civilian needs and that Israel co-operate fully in the effective deployment of United Nations observers. The Council requested the observers in and around Beirut to report on the situation.

The original draft resolution had been revised to have the Secretary-General report to the Council as soon as possible, instead of within three hours, and to alter the provision demanding Israeli co-operation in the deployment of observers by adding that this was at the request of Lebanon. In the revised preamble, the Council recalled its previous resolutions on the cessation of hostilities, rather than reaffirming them, and expressed most serious concern about continued military activities, without referring specifically to Israeli activities.

Introducing the text also on behalf of Guyana, Panama, Togo, Uganda and Zaire, Jordan charged that, after having destroyed southern Lebanon, Israel was systematically and ruthlessly devastating Beirut, and its advances indicated that it planned to either take over or encircle the Bekaa Valley, the bread-basket of the whole of Lebanon.

Lebanon thought that, as a step towards a peaceful settlement, the resolution should have reflected more comprehensively its Government's policy that Lebanese sovereignty must be restored over all of Lebanon and therefore that all non-Lebanese forces should withdraw.

Expressing the hope that the cease-fire would be maintained, the United States emphasized that the Council should avoid any action that could upset the negotiations under way. France and the United Kingdom held it most urgent to put an end to the fighting and suffering in Beirut; if the negotiations were successful, the United Kingdom added, the Palestinian armed forces would leave Beirut and go elsewhere, but the Palestinian problem would not thereby go away.

China said the Council was duty-bound to take further action to ensure the effective deployment and functioning of United Nations observers in order to put an end to the bombing of west Beirut and Israeli aggression against Lebanon.

Ireland found it difficult to understand why Israel refused to accept the observers; in its opinion, the resolution was a minimum measure. Japan hoped the Council's call would be heeded and a peaceful settlement of the crisis in and around Beirut would be secured, thereby opening the way towards restoration of peace throughout Lebanon.

Egypt stated that any reluctance to act decisively and put an immediate end to the atrocities committed by Israel could not be tolerated; Israel clearly was buying time to accomplish a final solution by killing as many Palestinians and Lebanese as possible. Uganda said the numerous cease-fires were better known for their violations than for their observance by Israel, which had ignored all previous Council resolutions; a continuation of the situation was unacceptable and it was the Council's responsibility to continue efforts to bring Israel to order and end the genocide in Lebanon.

The USSR stated that, in view of the worsening situation in Lebanon and Israel's continuing violation of the cease-fire, the Council should undertake immediate action to put an end to Israeli aggression.

Immediate and firm Council action was also called for by the PLO observer, who read out a communication from the PLO Chairman in Beirut stating that, following the announcement by United States Ambassador Habib of a cease-fire as at 5 p.m. local time, aerial bombing had stopped but shelling had not. The Permanent Observer of the League of Arab States stated that every time Israel broke the United States–negotiated cease-fires, it introduced greater fire-power and more destruction; meanwhile, the Council had been expected to remain paralysed so as not to disturb

Israel and the diplomatic process being conducted by the United States.

Israel, on the other hand, charged that the Palestinian terrorists had systematically broken every cease-fire, causing scores of casualties among the Israeli forces and the civilian population of east Beirut. Israeli forces had been instructed to cease fire as at 5.30 p.m.—the eleventh cease-fire in recent weeks—and would continue to do so unless there was a violation by the terrorists.

Further communications. In letters to the Secretary-General and the Security Council President, several States expressed their views on the developments in the Israel-Lebanon situation.

On 9 August,[32] Nicaragua conveyed a communiqué of 5 August from its Ministry of External Relations expressing concern at the genocide of Palestinians and Lebanese and announcing the breaking off of relations with Israel.

On 10 August,[36] Viet Nam transmitted a telegram of 4 August to the Director-General of the United Nations Educational, Scientific and Cultural Organization (UNESCO) from the Chairman of the Vietnamese National Commission for UNESCO, condemning the fierce bombing of Beirut, the destruction of historical and cultural monuments, and the genocide against Lebanese and Palestinians, and requesting the Director-General to use his authority and the competence of UNESCO to halt Israeli aggression and to include the subject on the agenda of the next Executive Board session.

By a letter of 11 August,[28] the German Democratic Republic transmitted a message of 6 August to the PLO Chairman from the General Secretary of the Central Committee of the Socialist Unity Party and President of the Council of State, condemning the Israeli war of extermination against Lebanese and Palestinians and assuring PLO of the support of the German Democratic Republic.

By a letter of 12 August,[24] Australia transmitted a statement of 9 August by its Prime Minister declaring that, despite the provocations Israel had received, its persistence in using its formidable military strength in Beirut, long after achieving its initially declared objective, was short-sighted and foolish; the belief that military victory alone could achieve solutions was making it difficult for Israel's traditional friends to sustain their support.

Report of the Secretary-General (13 August). In pursuance of the Security Council resolution of 12 August demanding a cessation of all military activities, the Secretary-General reported to the Council on 13 August[40] on the response of the parties. Israel had informed him that: its forces strictly observed the cease-fire throughout Lebanon on the axiomatic condition that it was mutual and absolute; Israel did not fight the civilian population but the terrorists hiding behind them while establishing their positions; and Israel's position with regard to the deployment of United Nations observers had been set out in its letter of 5 August (see above). The Lebanese Government and PLO had accepted the resolution.

The Secretary-General reported that there were 10 United Nations observers in the Beirut area but they had not been able to establish adequate observation facilities near the parties' forward positions. Efforts were continuing to move additional observers there and enable them to function effectively. According to information from the observers, after 6.10 p.m on 12 August the situation was generally calm except for occasional and light small-arms fire.

Stating that he had been following with deep anxiety the deterioration of the situation affecting the civilian population in west Beirut, the Secretary-General informed the Council that he had asked the Chairman of the United Nations inter-agency survey mission appointed on 25 June (see above) to return to Lebanon on 10 August to reassess immediate needs, and that he was continuing efforts to secure the free entry of supplies into Beirut.

Security Council action (17 August). As the mandate of UNIFIL was due to expire on 19 August, the Secretary-General submitted on 13 August a report[39] on developments relating to the Force since the last renewal of its mandate on 18 June.[52]

He stated that during the period, the Force, despite the difficulties it had faced, had been deeply engaged in extending protection and humanitarian assistance to the civilian population in its area, and its presence had provided an important stabilizing and moderating influence in southern Lebanon. Conditions in Lebanon had complicated the logistic support of the Force and further difficulties had been created by restrictions on freedom of movement imposed by the Israeli forces. Incidents involving Israeli forces in the UNIFIL area of deployment in the days immediately following the Israeli invasion—including forced entry into UNIFIL installations, destruction of its check-points, firing close to its positions and blocking of roads—had been strongly protested to the Israeli authorities.

The Force had taken action to contain the activities of a new armed group, which had appeared in parts of the UNIFIL area at the end of June and which was equipped and controlled by the Israeli forces, and it had continued to resist attempts by the *de facto* forces to operate in the UNIFIL area of deployment, although in some instances they had been able to enter that area with Israeli assistance. During the latter part of the reporting period, however, the UNIFIL area had been generally quiet and no armed clashes had been observed.

The Secretary-General reported further that, until 16 June, UNIFIL humanitarian teams had been able to assist the population of Tyre through the distribution of food and water and the dispensing of medical aid, but those efforts had been halted by the Israeli authorities. In the second half of June, UNIFIL had co-operated with various United Nations agencies and ICRC by providing transport, storage facilities and procurement support.

Describing the situation in southern Lebanon as uncertain and fraught with danger, the Secretary-General stated that the Lebanese Government had indicated that UNIFIL should continue to be stationed in the area for an additional interim period of two months, pending further consideration of the situation. Taking all factors into account and bearing in mind that position, the Secretary-General recommended that the Security Council extend the UNIFIL mandate for a further interim period.

Following that recommendation, the Council, on 17 August, extended the UNIFIL mandate for another two months, until 19 October.[56] It authorized the Force to continue to carry out the interim humanitarian and administrative tasks assigned to it on the previous renewal of its mandate, and called on all concerned to extend full co-operation to UNIFIL. The Council decided to consider the situation in all its aspects before 19 October.

The resolution, prepared during consultations, was adopted without discussion by a vote of 13 to none, with 2 abstentions (Poland, USSR).

General Assembly action (August). For the second time since the armed conflict in Lebanon began in June, the General Assembly resumed on 16 August its seventh emergency special session, originally convened to deal with the Palestine question.

By a resolution adopted on 19 August,[46] the Assembly demanded that Israel carry out the provisions of the Security Council resolutions on the Israel-Lebanon situation adopted since the miliary action began in June. The Assembly condemned Israel for its non-compliance with those resolutions and urged the Council to consider practical ways and means in the event of Israel's failure to comply.

Under other provisions, the Assembly called for the free exercise in Palestine of the Palestinians' right to self-determination—in paragraph 2 adopted by a separate vote—and reaffirmed its rejection of policies to resettle them outside their homeland; demanded that Israel carry out previous Assembly resolutions on the occupied territories; urged the Secretary-General to take measures to guarantee the safety of Palestinian and Lebanese civilians in south Lebanon and to investigate Israel's application of international instruments in the case of detained persons; and requested him to delegate a high-level commission to assess the extent of loss of human life and material damage in Lebanon.

The resolution, sponsored by 35 States, was adopted by a roll-call vote, requested by Israel, of 120 to 2, with 20 abstentions.

Israel rejected the text saying it presented yet another attempt to undermine the Middle East peace process and its only agreed basis, the 1967[61] and 1973[62] Security Council resolutions.

Abstaining, New Zealand said there were many elements of the currently interrelated fates of Lebanese and Palestinians that the resolution ignored, and some paragraphs made ambiguous proposals; New Zealand had difficulties particularly with paragraphs 2, 4, 6, 9 and 11.

Speaking for the EC members, Denmark said they agreed with the general thrust, but held that the text did not reflect the necessary balance on which a just and lasting Middle East peace settlement must be based.

Expressing a similar view, Norway said the resolution also tended to prejudice the outcome of future negotiations and contained certain wording on which Norway had reservations.

France could not accept several formulations which, in its opinion, tended to impinge on the Security Council's competence; the essential point, it added, was to restore peace to Lebanon and particularly Beirut, and priority must be given to the efforts currently under way to promote a solution, with the humanitarian problem to be solved in the immediate future.

Sweden regretted that the resolution did not address itself directly to the situation in Lebanon and did not reaffirm the inviolability of Lebanon's sovereignty and territorial integrity.

Canada said it had hoped the emergency special session would have had something new to offer to the parties in dealings with the broader issues relating to the Arab-Israeli dispute which had given rise to the tragedy in Lebanon; the resolution, however, did not break new ground and did not contribute to a solution of the essential problem of bringing the parties together to negotiate a settlement.

Haiti abstained saying the outcome of the Lebanese crisis seemed already to be discernible.

Though voting in favour, Austria said the text contained a number of formulations which lacked clarity or might have legal or political implications that could further complicate, rather than facilitate, future efforts.

Finland saw the resolution as an expression of the universal indignation at Israel's military action in Lebanon, which was but the latest manifestation of the absence of peace in the Middle East; the challenge to the authority of the United Nations and its capacity to act as a main instrument of peace did not absolve it from its responsibility as spelled out in the 1967 and 1973 Security Council resolutions.

Chile cast an affirmative vote on the grounds that the use of force as a legitimate means of settling international disputes was inadmissible; it was urgent for the international community to end the violence and seek means to ensure respect for Lebanon's territorial integrity for which a stop to all outside interference was an essential prerequisite. Lebanon's tragic experience, Chile added, should encourage a sensible and realistic search for a way to resolve the Middle East problem once and for all.

Paraguay regretted that the resolution did not fully provide for the need to adopt measures effectively to alleviate the suffering of the Lebanese, as well to ensure Lebanon's unity and territorial integrity and independence.

Honduras expressed concern at Israel's failure to fulfil United Nations decisions and said it joined the demand of the overwhelming international majority that Israel unconditionally withdraw from Lebanon.

Uruguay supported the references to implementation of the Council resolutions relating to the question of Lebanon; at the same time, it emphasized that the Assembly could not encroach on the competence of the Council by adopting measures that fell exclusively within the latter's purview. It also expressed its support of measures aimed at bringing about the withdrawal of all foreign contingents and believed that the resolution should not involve any delay in achieving those objectives. With regard to the Assembly resolutions mentioned in paragraph 4, Uruguay reserved its position on those it had not supported at the time of their adoption.

Panama considered that the tragedy suffered by Lebanon and the Palestinians must induce the international community to deal decisively with the Middle East problem on the basis of United Nations resolutions; the substance of the adopted text essentially coincided with its own position.

Colombia voted in favour on the ground that the quest for a Middle East solution was necessary, as were talks which would involve all parties and take account of their interests and obligations, including respect for Israel's right to exist.

Ecuador felt a pressing need to strengthen the machinery for the peaceful settlement of disputes and the role of United Nations observers and peace-keeping forces, particularly in Lebanon, where the key to stability and understanding lay in the elimination of the injustice to and mistreatment of the Palestinians.

Spain believed that, regardless of a possible settlement of the Lebanon crisis, no just or lasting Middle East peace could be achieved without the exercise of Palestinian rights; the resolution was moderate and realistic and put forward a number of praiseworthy political and humanitarian ideas.

The Syrian Arab Republic would have wished a firm condemnation of Israel for its invasion and barbaric acts, as well as inclusion of a provision reiterating that Israel was not a peace-loving State and had not fulfilled its commitments in keeping with the United Nations Charter and the 1949 resolution admitting it to United Nations membership.[60]

In the view of the Libyan Arab Jamahiriya, the resolution adopted was a strict minimum; the Assembly ought to have expelled Israel for having ignored United Nations decisions and for its acts of aggression. The Libyan Arab Jamahiriya emphasized its view that the 1967 Security Council resolution was incompatible with the rights of the Palestinians.

Portugal welcomed the resumption of the session as a reflection of the profound concern at the situation in Lebanon, as did Benin, Hungary, Indonesia and the Libyan Arab Jamahiriya. Czechoslovakia felt that the session was reconvened at a critical time for the fate of the Palestinians and, in Mexico's opinion, the resumption would prove timely provided the international community took the opportunity clearly and vigorously to express its views. The Syrian Arab Republic said it placed great hope in the session, convened not only to affirm Palestinian rights but also to stand up to the imperialist Zionist plot aimed at liquidating the Palestinians and PLO.

Israel termed the emergency special session illegal and a contrived exercise; the alleged emergency and its precise timing had been predetermined many weeks past. During the eight years of slaughter of Lebanese by PLO and Syrians, there had been no emergency special session, and there had never been such a session to discuss the PLO terror régime in areas that had fallen victim to its tyranny; the real reason for reconvening the session was that the rhetorical barrage was intended to deaden the sounds of reality with regard to the Arabs' true position towards PLO.

During the debate, many speakers, among them Cuba (for the non-aligned countries) and the USSR, denounced the continued aggression in Lebanon, especially the attacks on Beirut. In the view of Malaysia, Mongolia and others, the devastation, brutality and vandalism had few parallels in recent history. Not even the Jews had experienced at the hand of the Nazis what the Lebanese and Palestinians experienced at the hands of the Israelis, Iraq stated; reportedly more than 200,000 bombs had been dropped on Beirut and, for three months, thousands of innocent people had been subjected to the worst aggression—denying them water and electricity, and the shelling of hospitals,

schools and nursing homes. Speaking for the EC members, Denmark stressed the total unacceptability of further attacks, especially in view of the fact that PLO had left Beirut.

The United Arab Emirates requested the establishment of an inquiry commission or a special tribunal to judge Israeli Prime Minister Menachem Begin and his henchmen for their crimes of war, a request supported by Qatar and Saudi Arabia.

The view expressed during the debate in June, that the aim of Israel's aggression in Lebanon was to eliminate the Palestinians and PLO, was reiterated by many speakers, among them Bulgaria, China, Cyprus, Democratic Yemen, Egypt, the German Democratic Republic, India, Indonesia, Iran, Malta, Mexico, Mongolia, Pakistan, the Ukrainian SSR, the United Arab Emirates, Yemen and Yugoslavia. Nepal said Israel had wreaked havoc on the Palestinians and, in Benin's opinion, the invasion of Lebanon was the most cynical form of Israel's terrorism and its campaign to annihilate the Palestinians.

Afghanistan, Albania, Algeria, Bangladesh, the Byelorussian SSR, Cuba, Czechoslovakia, Iraq, Jordan, the Lao People's Democratic Republic, the Libyan Arab Jamahiriya, Mali, Morocco, Nicaragua, Nigeria, Poland, Qatar, Saudi Arabia, Senegal, Somalia, Sri Lanka, Togo, Uganda, the USSR and Viet Nam spoke of holocaust, genocide and a "final solution".

Pakistan believed that the Palestinians' survival was at stake. Afghanistan said Israel did not need gas chambers to eradicate the Palestinians since it had turned the whole of Beirut into an inferno.

As a result of the war waged by Israel, PLO said, several Lebanese cities and more than 30 villages and 14 Palestinian refugee camps had been destroyed; more than 30,000 Lebanese and Palestinians had been killed or wounded, and 1 million had been displaced. In addition, thousands had been detained. Israel's alleged objective had been to push Palestinian resistance back 45 kilometres, a pretext which had survived for only a few days.

Israel, on the other hand, charged that, true to its well-known tactic, PLO had hijacked the Lebanese capital and taken its population hostage. PLO had used the months since the cease-fire in July 1981 to build up an extraordinary arsenal of weapons.

Israel's claim to have acted in self-defence was again rejected by several speakers, among them Mexico, Mongolia, Senegal and Uganda. In Nigeria's view, there could be no greater prescription for international anarchy than Israel's doctrine that, in exercise of its right to self-defence, it could invade its neighbours' territory at will. In Finland's opinion, the fact that Israel's integrity had not at all times been respected did not legitimize its actions. Egypt said there was no justification for calling the Palestinians terrorists when their oppressors were destroying Lebanon and murdering thousands of civilians.

Bangladesh, Hungary, Mali and others saw the invasion not as an isolated act but as another link in the long chain of Israel's expansion policy and aggression against the Arabs. In Pakistan's view, the invasion marked yet another stage in Israel's scheme to occupy and annex Arab and Palestinian territories and to drive their inhabitants into permanent exile. Cuba said the invasion of Lebanon and the siege and bombing of Beirut were part of a strategic plan to quash the struggle of the Palestinians and to make the occupation and annexation of the West Bank, Gaza, the Golan Heights and Jerusalem irreversible.

Albania believed that it was Israel's intention to repeat the aggression, using the same pretext and methods, in order to realize the dream of creating Greater Israel. Afghanistan said the aggression in Lebanon was a warning to other countries that the quest for land and aggrandizement under absurd pretexts would sooner or later endanger their own sovereignty and territorial integrity.

The Syrian Arab Republic found it obvious that Israel's military movements towards the north of Beirut were but an attempt to expand the scope of its aggression. PLO charged that Israel's aggression was designed to isolate Lebanon from its Arab context so that it could be annexed in the future.

Apart from undermining Lebanon's unity, sovereignty and independence, Democratic Yemen said, the invasion was aimed at bringing pressure on the Syrian Arab Republic and weakening its role for the purpose of imposing the Zionist-American settlement plan. In Iraq's opinion, Israel was pursuing two goals: to internationalize Lebanon and find an opening for United States influence, and to establish buffer zones bordering on Israeli settlements in upper Galilee, in order geographically to neutralize the Arab territories bordering on occupied Palestine.

Israel's logic, Senegal believed, was that the military destruction of PLO would make it possible to impose on the inhabitants of the occupied territories an "autonomy" which would not conflict with its designs of annexation. By evacuating the Palestinian fighters to another Arab country, Yemen stated, Israel could occupy also that country under the pretext of retribution and could thus impose its unjust conditions on one Arab State after another. In Mexico's view, Lebanon was the victim of armed blackmail designed to impose on it conditions in exchange for peace; this was a grave threat to the survival of medium-sized and small countries exposed to the aggression of those who were stronger.

Albania, Argentina, Bangladesh, Bulgaria, China, Cuba (for the non-aligned countries), Cyprus, Hungary, the Lao People's Democratic Republic, Mali, Nigeria, Qatar, Senegal, Somalia and others believed that the situation created by the invasion was a danger not only to peace in the region but to world peace.

The majority of countries, among them Afghanistan, Albania, Austria, Bhutan, Bulgaria, the Byelorussian SSR, Cuba, Democratic Yemen, Denmark (also on behalf of the EC members), Egypt, Greece, Hungary, India, Indonesia, Kuwait, Madagascar, Malaysia, Maldives, Mauritania, Mexico, Morocco, Nepal, Nigeria, Pakistan, Portugal, Senegal (as Chairman of the Committee on Palestinian rights), Somalia, Sweden, Thailand, Turkey and Uganda, called for a cessation of hostilities, Israeli withdrawal, and restoration of Lebanon's territorial integrity, sovereignty and independence.

In that context, a number of States, including Denmark (for the EC members) and Poland, reiterated their support for the demands of the Security Council.

Israel reiterated that it did not want to stay in Lebanon, but was entitled to demand that proper arrangements be made to preclude permanently and reliably hostile action against Israel and its citizens from Lebanese soil; no one in the Middle East was more eager than Israel to see Lebanese sovereignty restored, its internal strife resolved, the Syrian occupiers removed, PLO subdued, and freedom and tranquillity returned. Israel would do everything in its power to maintain peace and good-neighbourly relations with Lebanon.

For years, the United States said, Lebanon's sovereignty had been sacrificed as external parties had pursued their own interests and conflicts within its borders; Lebanon's suffering had become a source of instability for the entire region.

Based on its right to self-determination and assuming its national responsibility, the Syrian Arab Republic said, it had challenged Israel's aggression aimed at extending Israeli hegemony over Lebanon, crushing the Palestinian revolution and creating conditions for attacking the Syrian Arab Republic.

Kuwait rejected all pre-conditions by Israel as a price for its withdrawal. Egypt said Israel's withdrawal should not depend on any condition, especially since PLO had accepted to withdraw. PLO explained that it had agreed to the withdrawal of its military forces from Beirut in the interest of the remaining inhabitants, so as not to provide a pretext for Israel to refuse to withdraw and to continue its aggression. In Malaysia's view, the evacuation of the Palestinians from Beirut and Lebanon was only a temporary measure and could not in the long term contribute to a durable Middle East solution.

Saudi Arabia said Israel's statements that it did not wish to retain a single inch of Lebanese territory had been contradicted by its actions; when PLO was scrupulously observing the cease-fire despite Israeli provocations and continued bombardments, Israel had been mobilizing its forces on the Lebanese border months before the invasion.

Having given a green light to Israel to wage war against Lebanon, Iran stated, the United States had imposed a bloody peace on PLO and had assumed the role of the middleman to convince the Palestinians that they must surrender to force, recognize political forgery as a legal State, sit at the negotiating table with it and give in to its terms of the deal; such a "solution" only created a new problem. The proper course for the Assembly to follow was: strongly to condemn Israel and its supporters; to expel Israel from the United Nations; to propose strong political and economic measures against it, should it refuse to withdraw; to force the United States and Israel to compensate the Palestinians and Lebanese for all the losses and damages; and to stand for the Palestinians' right to return and to re-establish the State of Palestine.

On behalf of the EC members, Denmark urged Israel to recognize its humanitarian responsibilities. Pakistan said the Assembly must recommend measures to guarantee the safety and security of Palestinian and Lebanese civilians and must call for extensive humanitarian aid. Mali thought it was perhaps for military reasons that Israel refused to allow foodstuffs, water and medical assistance to Tyre, the refugee camps and elsewhere; it was undoubtedly for military reasons that the population of west Beirut had been deprived of water, food and medical care.

In the view of Brazil, Indonesia, Madagascar, Mauritania and Togo, the events in Lebanon again proved that the Palestine question was the core of the Arab-Israeli conflict and that, without a Palestine solution, there could be no just and lasting Middle East settlement. A similar position was held by Algeria, Bangladesh, Czechoslovakia, Denmark (for the EC members), Hungary, India, Iraq, the Lao People's Democratic Republic, Malaysia, Maldives, Nicaragua, Poland, Sri Lanka, the Ukrainian SSR and the USSR.

Senegal considered the situation in Lebanon but one of the aspects of the Palestine problem. Finland thought that the Lebanon crisis was but a consequence of the unresolved Palestine question, and Greece considered the events in Lebanon a particularly tragic repercussion of the Palestinian problem. Japan saw the Lebanon situation as the result of various attempts to settle the Palestine question by military force, and PLO said what was unfolding in Lebanon was but a new chapter in the long tragedy of the Palestinians. Nepal said the aggression against and in Lebanon had brought the Palestine question into sharp focus.

Beyond the Lebanon crisis, Sweden stated, there remained the broader problem of the Middle East, the core of which was the realization of the national rights of the Palestinians, including the right to a State of their own. Cyprus felt that the problem went beyond the Palestinian question and entered the sphere of the very usefulness and existence of the United Nations which stood aside when Israel arrogated to itself the right to decide not only the fate of Beirut and Lebanon, or the future of Palestine or PLO, but also that of mankind through a decision for world war or world peace.

PLO said one of the greatest delusions was the attempt to treat the Lebanon problem as though it were a matter of lifting the siege of Beirut and withdrawing Palestinian resistance; unless the Palestine question was solved, there would be numerous further problems which could lead to more bloodshed and jeopardize international peace and security.

Many speakers, among them Afghanistan, Algeria, Argentina, Benin, Bhutan, Brazil, Bulgaria, the Byelorussian SSR, Cuba (for the non-aligned countries), Cyprus, Denmark (for the EC members), Egypt, Finland, the German Democratic Republic, Greece, Hungary, Iran, Iraq, Japan, Jordan, Kuwait, the Lao People's Democratic Republic, Madagascar, Malaysia, Maldives, Mali, Malta, Mexico, Nepal, Poland, Portugal, Saudi Arabia, Togo, Yemen and Yugoslavia, again emphasized the necessity of the recognition and exercise of Palestinian rights, in particular the right to self-determination. Only thus, Hungary felt, could the way towards an overall settlement be paved.

A solution that ignored the Palestine question was doomed to failure in the view of several speakers, including Algeria and Cuba (for the non-aligned countries). Greece held it urgent and necessary, parallel with the restoration of peace in Lebanon, to redouble efforts towards a speedy and comprehensive Palestine solution. Malaysia felt that cognizance must be taken of the Palestinian grievances if peace in the Middle East was to be achieved. Madagascar found a peace based on the denial of Palestinian rights inconceivable. In Morocco's view, the central problem of the Lebanon crisis remained that of restoring the rights of the Palestinians to their national territory and to their own and sovereign State.

A comprehensive Middle East settlement could not be based on the elimination of PLO or annihilation of the Palestinians, Mexico said. The most pressing and urgent issue, Afghanistan stated, was the Palestinians' right to life which should be safeguarded by all means.

Romania said all efforts to solve the problem of west Beirut and Lebanon must facilitate a solution to the Palestinian problem; Israel must understand that it was not through military means that it could ensure peace on its borders, but rather through its withdrawal from all occupied territories and through recognition of the right of all peoples in the region to a free and independent existence, including the Palestinians. A similar view was expressed by Bangladesh. Concern for Israeli withdrawal from Lebanon should not divert attention from the larger issue of the restoration of Palestinian rights, Pakistan stressed; the invasion of Lebanon and the destruction of Beirut should stir the world's conscience and underline the need for more vigorous efforts to resolve the Palestinian tragedy.

Regardless of how the ordeal of Beirut and Lebanon was resolved and while Lebanon must be free, independent and sovereign, Jordan stated, a few established facts could not be ignored, such as: the rights of the Palestinians under PLO leadership must be redeemed in full in accordance with United Nations resolutions and in the context of a comprehensive peace; the usurpation of Palestine was merely a first step to taking over or imposing Israeli hegemony on adjacent States; the aggression against Lebanon was an eye-opener for all the peoples of the Middle East as to what was in store for all of them; and the genocide in Lebanon had at long last destroyed the image of Israel's being an example of human and democratic values. No less dangerous than the war in Lebanon, PLO felt, was the war against the Palestinians in the West Bank, Gaza and Jerusalem. Afghanistan said that, while international attention was focused on the situation in Beirut, Israel tightened its grip on the occupied territories.

In spite of its attempts at annihilation, annexation and containment, PLO said, Israel had failed to destroy the national identity and aspirations of the Palestinians and on the contrary had made them more determined to regain their land and rights. A similar view was expressed by Indonesia and others. Nigeria said PLO and the Palestinians might have lost a battle, but there could be no doubt about their ultimate success, and Malaysia believed that their current set-back should lead to an even firmer conviction of the inevitability of the triumph of their cause. A similar position was held by Uganda and Yemen. Somalia believed that the determination of the Palestinians to achieve nationhood in Palestine had undoubtedly been strengthened by the Lebanon crisis.

By refusing to submit to imperialist and Zionist policy, the Lao People's Democratic Republic stated, the Palestinians had demonstrated their firm determination to struggle and their will to win. The Israeli massacres in Lebanon,

Democratic Yemen believed, would create new generations of combatants whose just cause would inevitably be crowned with victory. Nicaragua said the withdrawal of the Palestinians from Beirut to prevent further massacres of civilians could be viewed as one more proof of the flexibility, maturity and high-mindedness of PLO.

Morocco was convinced that the prestige of the Palestinians and PLO would emerge greatly enhanced from the events in Lebanon. In Afghanistan's opinion, the resistance of the Palestinians and Lebanese against Israel was yet another brilliant page in their history of courage and determination. Mali said Israel's relentless hostility towards PLO and the failure of its operation in Lebanon bore witness to the fact that the use of weapons would only forge Palestinian national unity still further and stiffen its determination to regain its homeland. In Egypt's view, the Israeli invasion, the onslaught on the Palestinians and the new Palestinian displacement and exodus could achieve only one thing: Palestinian devotion to Palestine.

Supporting the 29 July initiative of Egypt and France in the Security Council (see above, under ARMED CONFLICT) which, it said, aimed at combining a solution for Lebanon with a comprehensive political approach to the Palestinian question, Austria believed that a just and lasting Middle East settlement could best be achieved by starting with the mutual recognition of the rights of Israel and of the Palestinians. Such mutual recognition was also advocated by others, among them Romania.

Speaking for the non-aligned countries, Cuba said the Extraordinary Ministerial Meeting of the Co-ordinating Bureau of the Non-Aligned Countries at Nicosia in July had established a ministerial committee of nine non-aligned countries, which was entrusted with the task of holding consultations with the Lebanese Government and PLO leadership; despite repeated efforts, however, Israeli troops had prevented the committee from travelling to Lebanon and Beirut, and the United States Government had refused to receive the committee on the grounds that Cuba and Nicaragua should not be part of the delegation.

Finland, India and others felt that the United Nations should do its utmost to contribute to a negotiated solution; beyond the immediate task of bringing the conflict in Lebanon to an end, Finland added, the international community should make full use of the various proposals aiming at a comprehensive Middle East settlement (see above, under MIDDLE EAST SITUATION). Cyprus believed that the United Nations was the appropriate forum for a solution and that UNIFIL should help monitor Israel's withdrawal, protect the Palestinian refugees and ensure the continuing flow of supplies into Beirut. Egypt urged enhancement of the United Nations role in Lebanon.

In Iraq's opinion, the United Nations bore responsibility for the tragedy in Lebanon since it had approved the establishment of the racist Israeli State on the territory of Palestine.

Failure to put an end to the tragedy of Lebanon, Senegal stated, would be tantamount to undermining United Nations authority once and for all; the Assembly must assume all its responsibilities under the Charter and induce Israel to heed the consensus of the international community.

The deployment of United Nations observers as an immediate measure was held necessary by several countries, including Pakistan and Romania. Israel's scorn for United Nations decisions, Cuba stated, had reached a new height when it did not allow United Nations observers to be present in Lebanon, especially in Beirut, and when it rejected the possibility of a tour to the area by the Secretary-General in order to appraise the situation.

Declaring its commitment to a comprehensive settlement of the Arab-Israeli conflict, the United States said a settlement in Beirut appeared imminent and there was little the United Nations could currently do to affect the outcome of the negotiations. The goal of the mission of United States Ambassador Philip Habib was to achieve a resolution of the crisis in a manner that avoided further bloodshed, secured the removal from Lebanon of all foreign forces and allowed the Lebanese Government to re-establish its full authority throughout the country. The mediation efforts proceeded on two assumptions: that the terms of a settlement could not be dictated from above or outside, but could only be determined through negotiations; and that it was necessary to deal first with the immediate problem in Beirut before tackling the broader objectives of a Lebanon solution and a comprehensive Middle East peace, with the efforts under way in Beirut being a step towards a wider peace settlement.

Japan, Nepal, Somalia and several others welcomed the United States efforts, while Algeria called them a fraud. Under the guise of so-called peace-making efforts, the Byelorussian SSR charged, the United States had enabled Israel to continue to carry out its aggression.

PLO regretted that the United States, which had not uttered a word of condemnation of Israel's massacres in Lebanon and which through its veto had prevented the Security Council from condemning the aggression, was now trying to play the role of a mediator and peacemaker in a process of flagrant hypocrisy and blackmail.

Cuba said the United States media accompanied the report about the bombing of Beirut with information about so-called negotiations for the departure of PLO from Beirut, negotiations which were nothing but part of the aggression against the right of the Palestinians to return to their homeland.

Sweden said the impression had been created that once an agreement on the evacuation of PLO from Beirut was ensured, the Lebanon crisis would essentially be resolved; much, however, remained to be done. Egypt called for the establishment of contacts between the United States and PLO; the United States could play a vital part in convincing the Palestinians and PLO that their rights could be obtained through negotiations and that they could find their place in the family of nations through a peaceful, legitimate process.

In the view of the United Arab Emirates, the United States could have stopped the massacre of Palestinians by merely stopping the supply of weapons and putting an end to its economic and political support to Israel. China and others charged the United States not only with providing military assistance to Israel but also actively supporting and defending it in the diplomatic field, while exercising pressure on PLO. The Syrian Arab Republic said it was no longer a secret that the aggression against Lebanon had Washington's blessing, and the Lao People's Democratic Republic charged that Israel's acts in Lebanon were coordinated by the United States.

Saudi Arabia said the international community could not disregard the military support Israel received from the United States, which enabled it to pursue its aggression, even to the point of adopting positions contrary to the interests of its supporting ally.

Iraq said the encouragement and support of Israel by the United States were the main reason for the United Nations failure to find a just and peaceful solution to the Palestine problem, and Nicaragua said that support was a great disservice to the United Nations. India considered it to be a matter of deep concern and regret that the constant threat of a United States veto in the Security Council had so far prevented the imposition of sanctions or suspension of arms supplies. The veto was also deplored by several other countries, among them Benin, the Byelorussian SSR, Cuba, for the non-aligned countries, Cyprus, Iraq, Madagascar, Mauritania, Nicaragua and the USSR. By preventing action to restrain the aggressor, Bulgaria stated, the United States officially endorsed genocide and destruction. After the Council's failure to take a decision, the Libyan Arab Jamahiriya said, the Assembly must take practical steps to abolish the right of veto. Saudi Arabia believed that those who drew up the Charter had not intended the right of veto to be applied in cases of flagrant aggression against a neighbouring State.

Mexico said the international community must resolutely take a stand against Israel's aggression; otherwise, similar events could be multiplied. Uganda warned that if Israel was allowed to get away with the invasion of Lebanon and the carnage in Beirut, other potential aggressors would gain encouragement for similar adventures.

Cuba said the non-aligned countries had urged the Council to apply against Israel measures under Chapter VII of the Charter for failure to comply with United Nations resolutions and for gravely endangering international peace and security.

Measures to compel Israel to comply with the Council's demands were also called for by a number of other States, among them Afghanistan, Cyprus, Hungary, India, Mongolia, Uganda, Viet Nam and Yugoslavia. Romania said the Assembly must call firmly for compliance.

PLO considered it incumbent on the international community to prevent Israel from pursuing its criminal and expansionist designs and to impose deterrent sanctions. The Syrian Arab Republic urged severe sanctions in view of Israel's violations of its commitments under the Charter. With Israel remaining adamant in its aggressive stand, China held it incumbent on the Assembly to adopt firm and effective measures, including sanctions. Pakistan said Israel must be clearly warned of punitive sanctions if it refused to withdraw and persisted in its defiance of United Nations decisions, and must be reminded that compliance with Council resolutions was a mandatory obligation for United Nations Members. Indonesia called for a concerted drive to convince Israel's friends to join with the international community in the imposition of sanctions.

Mauritania declared its support for sanctions under Chapter VII of the Charter, as proposed by the Arab League. Sanctions were also called for by Democratic Yemen, Iraq and Nicaragua. The United Arab Emirates urged an end to economic and military assistance. Iran held strong political and economic measures necessary, should Israel refuse to withdraw, while Madagascar favoured the suspension of weapons and military aid until Israel's withdrawal.

In view of its prerogatives, Benin said the Assembly should not confine itself merely to condemning Israel's aggression, but should contemplate measures designed to prevent once and for all acts which endangered peace. In Nigeria's opinion, it was time that the Assembly impressed on Israel in no uncertain terms that international peace and security were at stake. Nicaragua believed that Member States were obliged to go much further than condemning Israel or expressing solidarity with the Palestinians. Morocco believed that the United Nations should stay the criminal hand and render justice to the Palestin-

ians. Mali said the Assembly's decisions would show whether it continued to be equal to its international responsibilities. Speaking as Chairman of the Committee on Palestinian rights, Senegal expressed the hope that the international community would take measures under the Charter to ensure peace and justice for the Palestinians and Lebanese and co-operation among the States of the region.

Qatar believed that Israel would not have had the audacity to cause such a tragedy if the international community had taken effective action. In Bangladesh's opinion, the failure of the United Nations to act firmly had encouraged Israel to intensify its aggression.

Further developments. By a letter of 20 August, the Secretary-General was informed by Lebanon that the Government had requested the deployment in Beirut of a multinational force to assist the Lebanese armed forces in carrying out the departure from Lebanon of Palestinian armed personnel in the Beirut area. France, Italy and the United States had agreed to deploy troops for that force, which would consist of approximately 2,000 men and would remain in west Beirut for 30 days. Lebanon added that it had requested the force to make it possible to begin restoring the country's independence, sovereignty and territorial integrity. (The letter was summarized in the Secretary-General's October report to the General Assembly on the Middle East situation.[44])

Also on 20 August,[22] the United States conveyed a message from its President informing the Secretary-General that the United States had agreed, in response to a Lebanese request, to deploy a force of about 800 personnel to Beirut for a period not exceeding 30 days; the force would work closely with the United Nations Observer Group Beirut. France and Italy also informed the Secretary-General of their participation in the force.

The Japanese Ministry of Foreign Affairs, in a statement of 19 August transmitted on 23 August,[31] declared that Japan attached great importance to the participation of the three countries in the multinational force, welcomed that agreement that had been reached to break through the deadlock and save west Beirut from street fighting, and called on Israel to withdraw from Lebanon immediately and unconditionally so that a viable government could be established and order in Lebanon restored, following national reconciliation among the Lebanese.

Also welcoming the agreement reached, Egypt stated in a letter of 26 August[26] that no framework would be viable while Israel occupied Lebanese territory and conducted a policy aimed at settling the occupied territories; Egypt reiterated its July proposal, made jointly with France, reaffirming the right of all States in the region to existence and security, reaffirming Palestinian rights, and calling for mutual and simultaneous recognition of the parties.

Report of the Secretary-General (2 September). Reporting on 2 September to the Security Council on the situation in the Beirut area since 13 August,[41] the Secretary-General indicated that the cease-fire which had gone into effect on 12 August had generally held with no major incidents, though a Syrian reconnaissance aircraft had been shot down on 31 August. Despite persistent efforts, however, it had not been possible to increase the number of United Nations observers in Beirut beyond 10. Although since 21 August members of the Observer Group had been able to move in and around Beirut with greater ease, their freedom of movement had been on occasion curtailed by the Israeli forces. Nevertheless, through arrangements with the Lebanese authorities and with contingents of the multinational force, the observers had been able to report on major developments in and around Beirut.

Their reports indicated that: The contingents of the multinational force, which had arrived in Beirut between 21 and 26 August, numbered as at 26 August 2,285 members, from France (860), Italy (575) and the United States (850). Palestinian armed elements and members of the Arab Deterrent Force (Syrian) numbering 14,737 had departed from Beirut between 21 August and 1 September, accompanied by a total of 378 noncombatants (women and children under the age of 15). They had left by sea for Algeria, Cyprus, Democratic Yemen, Greece, Iraq, Jordan, the Sudan, the Syrian Arab Republic, Tunisia and Yemen, and overland by the Beirut-Damascus road.

In addenda, dated 15 and 17 September, the Secretary-General outlined further developments on the basis of reports from United Nations observers. He stated that the situation had remained generally calm from 2 to 13 September, during which time elements of the Lebanese armed forces and the internal security forces had moved to new positions in west and south Beirut. However, tension had greatly increased on 14 September when Bashir Gemayel, the President-elect of Lebanon, and several others, were killed by a bomb explosion at the headquarters of the Lebanese Christian Phalangist Party. On 15 September, Israeli infantry personnel and armour had moved forward from their previous positions in west Beirut, and shelling from Israeli tanks and gunboats had been observed. Small- and heavy-arms fire had continued through the evening of 16 September, after which no further shooting had been observed. The multinational force had withdrawn between 10 and 13 September.

Security Council action (17 September). Meeting on 16 and 17 September at the urgent request of Lebanon—in a letter of 16 September complaining of what it called the latest Israeli incursion into Beirut[17]—the Security Council unanimously adopted on 17 September a resolution sponsored by Jordan[57] condemning the recent Israeli incursions into Beirut in violation of the cease-fire agreements and of Council resolutions, and demanding an immediate return to the positions occupied by Israel before 15 September. The Council called again for the strict respect of Lebanon's sovereignty, territorial integrity, unity and political independence, reaffirmed its call for respect for the rights of the civilian populations, and repudiated all violence against them. The Council declared its support for the Secretary-General's efforts to deploy United Nations observers and asked him to inform it of developments within 24 hours.

Before adoption of the resolution, Kuwait and the Syrian Arab Republic were invited, at their request, to participate in the discussion without vote.

Submitting the revised text, Jordan expressed the hope that it would give some solace to the inhabitants of Beirut.

Condemning Israel's incursion as another gross violation of Lebanon's sovereignty, China said Israel must turn over a new leaf, implement the Council resolutions, abide by the norms of international law, immediately cease its aggression and withdraw all its troops from Lebanon; the presence of Palestinian and Syrian forces in Lebanon had nothing to do with Israeli withdrawal.

By its incursions into west Beirut, France said, Israel had seriously compromised the agreement drawn up in August with the co-operation of the United States, France and Italy; France expected immediate Israeli withdrawal to the positions occupied before 15 September as a first step towards subsequent withdrawal from Beirut, and called for the immediate deployment of United Nations observers in Beirut in sufficient numbers so as to evaluate the threat facing the civilian population and the extent to which the agreements had been respected.

In the view of the USSR, the resolution might be a first step towards ending Israel's aggression and ensuring its unconditional withdrawal; to ensure such a breakthrough, however, all Council members must sincerely be willing to implement it.

The United Kingdom regarded the resolution as clear, concise and constructive, and expressed support for the call for an immediate Israeli withdrawal to the positions before 15 September, adding that, instead of exercising restraint, Israeli forces had caused further conflict and destruction by moving deep into west Beirut.

Also supporting the resolution, Uganda said the Council could not stand idly and watch Israel implement with impunity its strategy for a weak and divided Lebanon; the only contribution Israel could make towards the restoration of law and order was to withdraw its troops immediately. Israel had used the assassination of the Lebanese President-elect as a pretext for occupying west Beirut, thereby aggravating the suffering of the population and shattering the fragile peace that had been emerging.

At last, the PLO observer stated, the Council had adopted a resolution demanding immediate Israeli withdrawal; the question remained, however, whether in the case of Israel's non-compliance it would invoke its powers and adopt effective means to see to it that justice was done and that the lives of civilians were guaranteed.

On 16 September, at the Council meeting prior to the introduction of the resolution, Lebanon stated that, on the day Lebanon was mourning the death of a young President, struck down at the threshold of success in his dream to unite the country, Israel had chosen to invade Beirut and occupy government buildings, houses and streets. Noting that Israel had claimed that its actions were to keep the peace, Lebanon asked what right Israel had to allot itself the mission of maintaining law and order in the capital of a sovereign country that had been destabilized for years because it had become the theatre of Israel's wars. Lebanon urged the Council to call on Israel unequivocally and immediately to withdraw its forces from Beirut, without prejudice to Lebanon's determination to seek total and unconditional evacuation of Israeli and all non-Lebanese forces from its territory.

Israel maintained that its forces had moved into west Beirut following the criminal assassination of the President-elect in order to counter designs aimed at plunging the area into renewed violence as a smoke-screen to enable PLO remnants to regain their lost positions in Beirut and to fan out from there. Although the agreement on the departure of PLO from Beirut provided that spare weapons and munitions would be turned over to the Lebanese armed forces, the terrorists had left behind in west Beirut over 2,000 of their operatives armed with large quantities of light and heavy weapons. Moreover, large numbers of terrorists had been infiltrating back into the Bekaa Valley and had opened fire at Israeli forces through the protective screen of the Syrian army, while others had slipped back to Tripoli and other locations in Lebanon. Israeli forces would give up their positions in west Beirut when the Lebanese forces were ready to assume control over those positions in coordination with IDF.

Jordan charged that Israeli agents had planted the remote-controlled high-explosive device that had killed the President-elect, with whom Israel had grown disenchanted because he could not be treated as a pliant tool, and whose term would have seen the emergence of a strong and unified central Lebanese authority that would have restored unity—an objective which Israel could not countenance.

The Syrian Arab Republic charged that Israel had planned the assassination of the President-elect in advance and wanted to terrorize, subjugate and annex Lebanon.

Stating that the Israeli invasion of Beirut had violated the agreement reached in August between Israel and Lebanon, which had led to the withdrawal of the Palestinian and Syrian forces and was guaranteed by the United States, Kuwait, as Chairman of the Arab Group, called on the latter to force Israel to withdraw; the fact that Israeli troops had occupied the whole of Beirut at a time when the Lebanese were trying to establish a strong Government cast doubts on the sincerity of Israel's claims that one of its objectives in invading Lebanon had been to assist in that attempt, as well as on Israel's credibility as a party to an agreement genuinely entered into by the other parties.

The USSR stated that Israel's seizure of Beirut was the latest move in its expansionist policy, carried out with United States arms and money in pursuit of the goals of American imperialist policy; the Council must condemn Israel's flagrant violations of Council decisions, call for immediate Israeli withdrawal from west Beirut, provide for machinery to monitor implementation of its decisions, and issue a decisive warning to Israel that, in the event of non-compliance, measures set forth in the United Nations Charter would be applied.

To the PLO observer, it was clear that Israel's aim was to continue its war of annihilation against Palestinians and Lebanese even after PLO had decided to remove its forces to spare Beirut more bloodshed; however, PLO was confident that the Council would fully assume its responsibilities as prescribed in the Charter.

The Permanent Observer of the League of Arab States also charged that Israel had used the assassination of the President-elect as a pretext for its invasion of Beirut; Israel had been foiled in its attempt to perpetuate destabilization, factionalism and conflict by the evidence of growing cohesion and political reconciliation within Lebanon, and it had realized that the Palestinian movement, in the aftermath of the withdrawal from Beirut, had re-established the PLO mandate, regained its unity and recouped its political effectiveness.

Report and communication (18 September). In accordance with the 17 September resolution, the Secretary-General informed the Council on 18 September of further developments.[(42)] He reported that, in response to his request for information on action taken, the Israeli Foreign Ministry had conveyed a message reiterating that Israeli forces in west Beirut had been instructed to evacuate their positions when the Lebanese Army was ready to assume control over them in co-ordination with the Israeli forces; discussions to that end had been proposed by Israel and accepted by Lebanon.

The report went on to detail information available to the observers on the circumstances surrounding the mass slaughter, which they had discovered on 18 September, of large numbers of civilians at the Palestine refugee camps of Sabra and Shatila, on the outskirts of Beirut (see below).

The Secretary-General reported that representatives of France, Italy and the United States had subsequently visited him to urge the immediate dispatch of United Nations observers to the sites of the greatest human suffering and losses in and around Beirut. Following that request, with which Lebanon had concurred, he had immediately instructed the UNTSO Chief of Staff to make a renewed approach to Israel to obtain its co-operation in increasing the number of observers; however, it seemed that in the current situation unarmed observers were not enough.

On 18 September,[12] Jordan transmitted a letter of the same date from the PLO observer, calling on the Council immediately to dispatch an international military force to protect the Palestinians in Beirut and other parts of Lebanon.

Security Council action (19 September). The Security Council convened on 18 September in response to a request by Jordan for an urgent meeting. A similar request had been made in an 18 September letter from Greece asking the Council to examine the critical situation created by the massacre of civilian Palestinians in Beirut and to take without delay effective measures to protect the Palestinians in Lebanon.[29]

The Council, by a resolution prepared during consultations and adopted unanimously early on 19 September,[58] condemned the massacre, reaffirmed its earlier resolutions calling for respect for the rights of the civilian populations, and authorized the Secretary-General to increase the number of United Nations observers in the Beirut area from 10 to 50. The Secretary-General was requested to initiate urgent consultations on additional steps to be taken, including the possible deployment of United Nations forces, in order to assist the Lebanese Government in ensuring full protection for civilians in and around Beirut, and to report within 48 hours. The Council insisted that all concerned must permit United Nations observers and forces to discharge their mandates, calling attention in that connection to the obligation of all Member States under Article 25 of the Charter to accept and carry out Council decisions.

Prior to the adoption of the resolution, Algeria, Democratic Yemen and Greece were invited, at their request, to participate without vote in the discussion.

The Council's discussion centred on the circumstances of the massacre at Sabra and Shatila (see below) as well as on steps that should be taken to protect the civilian population.

Lebanon said its Army was prepared to assume its responsibilities but had been thwarted in its effort to establish control over Beirut by the Israeli occupation; none the less, Lebanon would welcome the sending of international forces and supported a suggestion by Ireland that the Secretary-General engage immediately in consultations as to how the Council could best assume its responsibilities.

Israel said it had left one side of the camps open to permit access by the Lebanese Army, which had not taken control of the camps. Israel joined in the expression of revulsion and indignation at such crimes, adding that the Council had remained silent in the face of the massacre of 100,000 Lebanese over the years and of some 6,000 to 25,000 persons at Hammah in the Syrian Arab Republic.

Algeria said the situation called for the Council to apply the relevant Charter provisions and to send a force to Lebanon immediately with a view to saving the defenceless population. Democratic Yemen said no pretext should be used to stop the Council from taking the most urgent action necessary to stop the genocide. Egypt called on the Council to act immediately to guarantee the safety of the Palestinians in west Beirut and to dispatch forces or observers to prevent further massacres, and called on the countries that had participated in the multinational force to consider immediately sending it back to Beirut.

Kuwait said the Palestinians had believed and trusted in agreements, guaranteed by the United States, that had been savagely flouted by the Israeli invasion of west Beirut and by the planning and sponsoring of an extermination campaign against the Palestinians in the camps; the Council must take immediate measures to ensure the survival of Lebanese and Palestinian civilians threatened by holocaust. In the opinion of the Syrian Arab Republic, Israel saw the cease-fire as giving it and its surrogates a chance to continue the onslaught against unarmed Lebanese and Palestinian civilians; if Council resolutions were not implemented, effective action must be taken under Chapter VII of the Charter.

China held it extremely urgent to stop the hands of the aggressor and restore Lebanese sovereignty, and called for sanctions if Israel continued to defy Council resolutions.

France said that by invoking the need to ensure order and to prevent further tragedy, Israel had occupied west Beirut; it refused to co-operate with United Nations observers and rejected any United Nations intervention, but its attitude had not brought about the results it said it had sought to achieve. Greece said what was needed was a succinct resolution that would provide within the next 24 hours for effective measures to protect all Palestinian and Lebanese civilians. Ireland suggested that the number of unarmed United Nations observers be increased to 50, and that they be given full co-operation and freedom to deploy; as a second stage, the Secretary-General should immediately consult with Lebanon to see whether there were further steps the Council might consider to assist the Government in ensuring full protection for civilians.

Spain said the Council must give serious thought to measures to be taken in the face of Israel's rebellion in order to maintain Lebanon's political independence, territorial integrity and sovereignty, as well as international peace and security. The United Kingdom said the tragedy had confirmed its belief that the first step to stop the spiral of violence in Beirut must be Israel's immediate withdrawal to the positions it had occupied before 15 September.

Guyana held it imperative that the resolution be complied with as the barest minimum to ensure the safety of the Beirut civilians. Panama said the resolution contained important steps towards a solution to the crisis in Lebanon; it hoped the Council could discharge its mission with the co-operation in particular of those Council members able to bring a decisive influence to bear on Israel.

Jordan said the Council had the sacred duty under the Charter to send armed forces to protect the Palestinians from additional acts of genocide; condemnations had been rendered meaningless and irrelevant.

In Poland's opinion, there was an urgent need for decisiveness and the co-operation of all Council members to stop the bloodshed in Beirut immediately; the Council could not remain indifferent when its resolutions were ignored. The USSR called for strong and effective Council measures to halt the massacre of Palestinians and curb the Israeli aggressor; the resolution to be adopted must contain a provision to the effect that the Council warned Israel that it was obliged to abide by Council decisions.

Uganda believed the United Nations had a positive role to play in ensuring that Lebanese and Palestinians were not subjected to more massacres; it regarded the resolution as at least a first step in arresting a situation which could become even more dangerous.

The PLO observer said that sending observers and a monitoring team was not sufficient to deter the criminals; the Council should at least provide some safeguards to the civilians in Beirut and especially the Palestinians in refugee camps.

The Permanent Observer of the League of Arab States welcomed the United Nations observers to monitor Israel's crimes, but considered such a measure insufficient; the Council must take immediate action to impose penalties and deter Israel.

Report and communications (20 September–1 October). In pursuance of the Security Council resolution of 19 September, the Secretary-General reported to the Council on 20 September[43] that he had been informed that day that the Israeli Cabinet had decided to concur with the dispatch of an additional 40 United Nations observers to the Beirut area. Twenty-five observers had arrived in Beirut on 19 September, with the remaining 15 scheduled to arrive on 21 and 22 September. Observer Group Beirut had reported the situation generally calm in west Beirut, with a Lebanese battalion deploying in the Sabra and Shatila camp areas on 19 September and no major change observed in the deployment of Israeli forces.

The Secretary-General stated that he had requested the Commander of UNIFIL to comment on the possibility of sending UNIFIL units to the Beirut area. The answer was that, if required, about 2,000 men could be sent to Beirut without seriously affecting the capacity of UNIFIL to perform its interim tasks in southern Lebanon.

Also on 20 September, Lebanon had informed him that it had formally requested the reconstitution of the multinational force. On the same date, PLO had informed him that it insisted that United Nations military forces or agreed multinational forces be deployed immediately to undertake effective safeguards. The President of the United States had announced that he had decided, together with France and Italy, to send the multinational force back to Beirut for a limited period.

Annexed to the report were the letters from Israel, Lebanon and the PLO observer. The Israeli letter included a Cabinet statement of 19 September relating to the massacre (see below). The PLO letter, as addressed to the Security Council President, was also transmitted on 20 September by Jordan.[13]

By a letter of 21 September,[27] France informed the Secretary-General that it had given an affirmative response to the Lebanese Government's request for its co-operation in the deployment in and around Beirut of a multinational force to support the operations of the Lebanese armed forces in order to restore Lebanese authority and ensure protection for the civilian population; France would have wished the creation of a United Nations force but, from consultations conducted by the Secretary-General, it was apparent that lengthy negotiations would be necessary before agreement could be reached on such a force.

Italy, by a letter of 23 September,[30] informed the Security Council President that it was proceeding, in close consultation with France and the United States as well as with the Lebanese Government, to assess the legal and operational aspects of sending a multinational force to Beirut.

By a letter of 24 September,[23] the United States conveyed a message from its President informing the Secretary-General that his Government had agreed, in response to Lebanon's request, to deploy about 1,200 men, together with military personnel from France and Italy, for a limited period of time; it was his firm intention and belief that the presence of the troops would assist the Lebanese Government and that they would not be involved in hostilities, although isolated incidents of violence could not be ruled out.

In two addenda of 27 and 30 September, the Secretary-General reported that all observers had arrived in Beirut by 22 September, bringing their total strength to 50. In liaison with the Lebanese armed forces, they had formed six mobile liaison teams and had established four static observation posts. In addition, the observers had carried out varied humanitarian tasks in co-operation with ICRC, the Lebanese Red Cross, local hospitals, and United Nations agencies and programmes. On 25 September, four observers had been killed when their vehicle hit a mine east of Beirut.

Since 21 September, according to the observers' reports, Israeli forces had been withdrawing from Beirut. As at 30 September, no presence of Israeli forces had been observed north and west of the separation line, and throughout the rest of Beirut and the airport only two Israeli check-points had been observed.

On 24 September, the report stated, contingents of the multinational force had begun arriving in Beirut. As at 30 September, the strength of the force was 3,997, deployed in three sectors in and around Beirut. The Lebanese armed forces (about 3,500 as at 30 September) were maintaining static positions, establishing check-points and conducting patrols throughout Beirut. Beirut International Airport, closed to civilian traffic since early June, had been reopened on 30 September.

By a letter of 1 October,[19] Lebanon transmitted a message from its Deputy Prime Minister and Foreign Minister stating that the Government had requested deployment of the multinational force. France, Italy and the United States had agreed to participate in a force of approximately 3,500 men which would remain in Beirut for a limited time; the Government did not expect the troops to become involved in hostilities.

General Assembly action (September). Resuming again its seventh emergency special session on the Palestine question, the General Assembly, by a resolution of 24 September,[47] condemned the massacre of Palestinian and other civilians on 17 September and called for a Security Council investigation. The Assembly expressed full support for the Council demands for an immediate cease-fire and unconditional Israeli withdrawal from Lebanon, and urged the Council to consider practical means in the event of continued Israeli failure to comply with its demands. The Assembly demanded strict respect for Lebanon's sovereignty, territorial integrity, unity and political independence. It called for extensive humanitarian aid to the victims of the Israeli invasion. It also resolved that the Palestine refugees should be enabled to return to their homes and property.

The resolution, sponsored by 45 States, was adopted by a recorded vote of 147 to 2. Paragraph 2 was adopted by a recorded vote, requested by the United States, of 146 to none, and paragraph 4 by a recorded vote of 149 to none.

Senegal stated, in introducing the resolution as Chairman of the Committee on Palestinian rights, that it stemmed from its sponsors' desire to create conditions for the restoration of peace to the Middle East, particularly Lebanon.

Lebanon welcomed particularly the demand for strict respect of its sovereignty.

Voting for the two paragraphs, but rejecting the text as a whole, the United States said it contained unacceptable language in several provisions and would rather prolong and embitter the conflict than assist in its resolution.

Though voting in favour, Chile, Guatemala and Uruguay expressed reservations on paragraph 7, saying it infringed on the Council's prerogatives. Guatemala and Norway reserved their positions on paragraph 9.

Canada, New Zealand and Norway reserved their positions on paragraph 6. Haiti said refuge for the Palestinians should be found on the basis of the 1967 Security Council resolution on a Middle East peace.[61] Reservations on a reference in the preamble to the PLO statement during the debate were expressed by Canada, Denmark and Norway.

Iran felt that certain elements were missing in the resolution, such as a strong and explicit statement that the Zionist base of imperialism must be destroyed.

During the debate, most speakers again denounced what they termed Israel's aggression. Sweden particularly condemned the indiscriminate bombing and shelling of civilian targets. The PLO observer said the withdrawal of PLO from Beirut had only facilitated the disruption of law and order and of the restoration of Lebanese sovereignty and authority over Beirut.

China and Thailand, among others, called for a cessation of hostilities and Israeli withdrawal, and restoration of Lebanon's territorial integrity, sovereignty and independence. A number of States, including Sweden and Turkey, emphasized the necessity of the recognition and exercise of Palestinian rights.

The USSR said if talk was to be serious about real developments towards a Middle East settlement, first and foremost the aggressor must be forced to comply with Security Council decisions, leave Lebanon, cease provocation of the Syrian Arab Republic and refrain from its aggressive policy.

The role of the multinational force that had recently returned to Beirut was mentioned by a few speakers in the debate preceding adoption of the resolution. On behalf of the EC members, Denmark welcomed the decision to respond promptly to Lebanon's request for the force. For the African Group, however, Ghana, while appreciating the initiative, said it tended to circumvent the United Nations and undermine its role.

Other communications (September). By a letter of 3 September,[3] Israel, in response to the letter from Egypt of 26 August[26] (see above), stated that some countries paying lip-service to Lebanese sovereignty and territorial integrity had chosen to ignore the gradual and systematic subjugation of Lebanon by PLO and the Syrian Arab Republic; the only agreed basis for a peaceful settlement remained the 1967 Security Council resolution[61] and the 1978 Camp David accords.

By a letter of 16 September,[20] the Libyan Arab Jamahiriya stated that, in view of Israel's continued aggression in co-ordination with the United States, the Council must assume its responsibilities with regard to the application of Chapter VII of the United Nations Charter. On 20 September,[21] the Libyan Arab Jamahiriya transmitted a message to the Secretary-General from its head of State deploring Israel's persistent aggression against Palestinians and Lebanese and the continued inability of the United Nations to stop that aggression, mainly because of the paralysis of the Council through the repeated use of the veto by the United States in the interest of Israeli aggression.

On 17 September,[33] Tunisia transmitted a statement of the same date by its Foreign Minister, on behalf of the President, expressing deep concern over the recent developments in Lebanon and calling for international measures to stop Israel's aggression.

On 20 September,[25] Denmark transmitted a statement issued on the same date by the EC Foreign Ministers at Brussels, strongly condemning the massacre; calling for measures to ensure the safety of the civilian population, including the strengthening of the United Nations observer team and the possible deployment of United Nations or multinational forces; demanding Israel's immedi-

ate withdrawal from west Beirut; and favouring the earliest possible withdrawal of all foreign forces except those authorized by the Lebanese Government, whose authority should be fully established over all its national territory.

On 24 September,[18] Lebanon transmitted a speech by its new President, Amin Gemayel, on the occasion of his taking the constitutional oath before Parliament on 23 September, calling for restoration of Lebanon's independence, sovereignty and unity, and the withdrawal of all foreign armies from its soil.

A number of letters were received relating to the massacre near Beirut (see below).

Report of the Secretary-General (14 October). As the mandate of UNIFIL was due to expire on 19 October, the Secretary-General submitted on 14 October a report[45] on the developments relating to the Force since the renewal of its mandate by the Security Council on 17 August.[56]

The Secretary-General noted that throughout the period, the UNIFIL area had remained generally quiet, except for a few isolated incidents, and no armed clashes had been observed. The presence and activities of the Israeli forces in the UNIFIL area had significantly decreased and the activities of the *de facto* forces and the new local groups, armed and uniformed by the Israeli forces, had been effectively contained. In addition to providing protection and humanitarian assistance to the local population, UNIFIL had extended its fullest co-operation to the humanitarian efforts of various United Nations programmes and ICRC. Logistic support of the Force, however, had continued to be problematic owing to the restrictions imposed by the Israeli forces on freedom of movement, although some improvements had occurred since 11 October. The deployment of UNIFIL had been affected by the temporary release on 29 September of 482 French soldiers to the multinational force in Beirut (see below).

The increase in population in the UNIFIL area of deployment from a few thousand in 1978 to more than a quarter of a million by June 1982, with an influx of approximately 150,000 since then, also had increased the responsibility of UNIFIL for security in the area.

Despite the difficulties, UNIFIL had carried out its interim tasks with dedication and efficiency. The existing situation, however, was clearly unsatisfactory. While the original mandate of the Force remained valid, the conditions under which it was expected to carry out that mandate had radically changed. Owing to the attitude of the Israeli authorities, it had not been possible for UNIFIL to play a useful role in providing humanitarian assistance outside its area of deployment.

The Secretary-General expressed his deep conviction that the withdrawal of UNIFIL in the current circumstances would have highly undesirable consequences. Lebanese forces were not in a position to assume full control of the area and the danger of violent incidents between the various factions could not be ruled out. Accordingly, and following the request of the Lebanese Government for a three-month extension, he recommended that the Council extend the UNIFIL mandate for a further limited period. While Israel's attitude had not been in favour of continued UNIFIL activity, he hoped for its co-operation.

Security Council action (18 October). By a resolution of 18 October,[59] the Security Council extended the mandate of UNIFIL for another three months, until 19 January 1983. The Council insisted that there should be no interference with UNIFIL operations and that it should have full freedom of movement. The Council authorized the Force to carry out interim humanitarian and administrative tasks as previously authorized,[52] and to assist the Lebanese Government in ensuring the security of the inhabitants. It requested the Secretary-General to consult with the Government on ways to ensure full implementation of the Force's mandate.

The resolution, prepared during consultations, was adopted by 13 votes to none, with 2 abstentions (Poland, USSR).

Prior to its adoption, Lebanon, at its request, was invited to participate without vote in the discussion. Also, at the request of Jordan,[14] the Council decided that an invitation should be accorded to a PLO representative to participate in the debate and that the invitation would confer on it the same rights of participation as those conferred on a Member State invited under rule 37 of the Council's provisional rules of procedure.[e] The decision on PLO was taken by a vote, requested by the United States, of 11 to 1 (United States), with 3 abstentions (France, Japan, United Kingdom).

Addressing the Council, the President of Lebanon stated that although the Council's resolutions had not led to the liberation of Lebanon or put an end to the recurring invasions, they had condemned the aggression, confirmed the legitimacy of Lebanon's rights and contributed to preserving the country's unity and sovereignty. UNIFIL must be capable of restoring international peace and security in southern Lebanon and of assisting the Government in ensuring the return of its effective authority in the area; however, the extension of the mandate could not be indefinite. The current objective was withdrawal of Israeli forces, but Lebanon also awaited the withdrawal of all non-Lebanese forces on its territory. The Lebanese were determined to live together, yet alone, in an indivisible and independent Lebanon.

Communications (November-December). By a letter of 5 November to the Security Council

President,[4] Israel, in connection with the Council resolution of 18 October, reiterated its belief that, in the new circumstances surrounding the Lebanon situation, the presence of UNIFIL was no longer called for; the security arrangements deemed necessary by Israel and Lebanon should be arrived at through negotiations between them.

By another letter of the same date to the Secretary-General,[5] Israel strongly objected to the publication of what it called biased and tendentious information on the events in Lebanon by the *UN Chronicle*, a monthly magazine issued by the United Nations Department of Public Information.

The United Kingdom informed the Secretary-General on 22 December[35] that it had decided, in response to a Lebanese request, to contribute to the multinational force in Lebanon a unit of about 80 men for three months, to be drawn from the United Kingdom contingent in the United Nations Peace-keeping Force in Cyprus.

General Assembly action (December). Taking note of the decision of the Lebanese Government calling for the withdrawal of all non-Lebanese troops and forces not authorized by it, the General Assembly, by a resolution of 16 December,[49] called for strict respect of the territorial integrity, sovereignty, unity and political independence of Lebanon, and declared its support for the efforts of the Lebanese Government to restore its exclusive authority throughout Lebanese territory up to the internationally recognized boundaries.

The resolution was adopted by a recorded vote of 145 to none. An amendment by the Syrian Arab Republic, to include in the preamble reference to the Security Council resolutions of 5 June[50] and 6 June[51] calling for a cease-fire and Israeli troop withdrawal from Lebanon, was adopted by a recorded vote of 140 to 1, with 1 abstention.

In a resolution on the self-determination of peoples, adopted on 3 December, the Assembly strongly condemned Israel's aggression against Lebanon, and reiterated its support for the efforts to implement the Security Council resolutions, in particular those demanding immediate and unconditional Israeli withdrawal and respect for Lebanon's sovereignty and territorial integrity.[48]

In an address to the Assembly on 18 October, the Lebanese President said his country had been in a continuous state of war since 1975, fomented by third-party conflicts of interest, tension among States, competing Arab ideologies, the armed and uncontrolled Palestinian presence, recurring Israeli invasions and incursions, and continued violation of Lebanese sovereignty and human rights. Lebanon had had enough bloodshed, destruction, dislocation and despair. The Palestinians should live

---

[e]See footnote a on p. 429.

in peace and self-determination in their land, and the Syrian Arab Republic and Lebanon should develop strong relations in the context of independence, sovereignty and mutual respect. The President called for the immediate and unconditional withdrawal of all non-Lebanese forces from Lebanon, and for help from the world community so that Lebanon could regain its independence and rebuild its economy.

Introducing the resolution of 16 December on behalf of its 33 sponsors, Colombia said the Lebanese Government was the only legal authority that could determine which troops were to remain on its territory to guarantee peace. The continued presence of foreign troops against the express will of the Lebanese people was highly disturbing to the region's stability and constituted an obstacle to peace.

Introducing the amendment, the Syrian Arab Republic said it sought unanimous support for efforts to end the Israeli occupation of Lebanon.

Voting in favour of the resolution but abstaining on the amendment, the United States expressed the view that the Council resolutions referred to, while they had received United States support at the time, were irrelevant to the current situation and a needless intrusion into an otherwise precisely focused and vitally important affirmation.

The USSR said the foundations for a settlement to the Lebanese situation were enshrined in the Council's demand for immediate cessation of all military activities and unconditional Israeli withdrawal from all of Lebanon; the reference in paragraph 1 to international support for the efforts of the Lebanese Government did not apply to the multinational force, which undermined United Nations efforts.

Voting against the amendment but for the resolution, Israel said it supported complete restoration of Lebanese sovereignty and territorial integrity and the restoration of the Government's authority throughout the country—and thus the removal of all non-Lebanese elements without exception—it being understood that nothing in the resolution affected Israel's right to demand that any future arrangements in Lebanon permanently and reliably precluded hostile action against Israel and its citizens from Lebanese soil.

Ecuador hoped that after the withdrawal of all non-Lebanese troops, the martyrdom of the Lebanese people would come to an end and peace would be established. Malta stressed that its affirmative vote did not necessarily imply full agreement with every provision.

Albania explained that it had not participated in the voting as some of the resolution's sponsors, in particular the United States, were responsible for the serious situation in Lebanon; further, the resolution was not specific about the troops that had to leave Lebanon and did not mention the fact that it was the Israeli occupying troops which had seriously infringed Lebanon's sovereignty and integrity.

Voting against the 3 December resolution on the self-determination of peoples, Australia and Denmark, the latter speaking for the EC members, said they believed all foreign forces in Lebanon that were there without the Government's authorization should be withdrawn immediately. Uruguay, which voted in favour, also supported the Lebanese Government's insistence on the withdrawal of all foreign forces. Portugal, which abstained, said it had reservations on the provision on the Israel-Lebanon situation. Greece, on the other hand, though abstaining, supported efforts to ensure immediate Israeli withdrawal.

There were a number of comments on the situation between Israel and Lebanon during the Assembly debates on the Palestine question and on the Middle East situation in November and December.

Israel said the Arab leaders had unloaded PLO onto the back of Lebanon, which thereby became a symbol of what their intrigues could do to a democratic country with no muscle to resist them; for weeks Arab Governments had refused to accept PLO stragglers from Beirut, giving them asylum only after proof that they had been defeated.

Denmark, speaking for the EC members, called on all concerned to uphold the authority of the Lebanese Government, condemned all bloodshed in Lebanon, and called for the departure of Israeli forces and all other foreign forces except those authorized by the Lebanese Government, to take place progressively but within a fixed, short time-frame. Egypt called for the total withdrawal of Israeli forces from Lebanon in accordance with a timetable; termination of all forms of foreign intervention in its internal affairs and the withdrawal of all foreign forces; respect for the legitimate authority in Lebanon and for the rights of all the Lebanese people; support for reconstruction; preservation of mutual security through international peace-keeping forces with emphasis on the United Nations role; and the rejection of all attempts to impose conditions on Lebanon.

Cyprus said the international community had been a bystander for months while the Palestinian people had been targeted for extinction, witnessing the naked military invasion of a Member State, the tragic siege of west Beirut, indiscriminate Israeli bombing unparalleled in brutality, and the killing of thousands of Lebanese and Palestinian civilians. Jordan said Israel's long-prepared design against southern Lebanon meant the dismemberment of that country and the undermining of its independence and territorial integrity; if Israeli had more people, it would not hesitate to colonize southern Lebanon as it had the other occupied territories. The Syrian Arab Republic stated that Israel had destroyed the human, economic, social and political structures of Lebanon, depriving the population of everything the Lebanese people had acquired through the efforts of their workers, farmers and intellectuals. Israel, said the United Arab Emirates, was making its withdrawal conditional on demands that were humiliating to Lebanese dignity and sovereignty.

Indonesia, making a point also endorsed by several others, thought the invasion had been planned in advance with the purpose of achieving a final solution to the Palestine question through the indiscriminate use of military force. Iraq said the invasion had been intended to exterminate Palestinian nationalism by exterminating the military arm of PLO and thereby eliminating the determination of the Palestinians to achieve national self-determination in their homeland.

Bangladesh said it had never doubted that Israel would not succeed in eliminating PLO and was proud to find the freedom fighters emerge stronger than ever. India stated that they had emerged with their determination strengthened, their sense of nationalism sharpened and their cause universally respected. Pakistan remarked that the martyrdom and sacrifices of thousands of men, women and children in the refugee camps in Lebanon had convinced the world as never before of the justice of the Palestinian cause. Poland said PLO had won another victory and the Palestinians had emerged from the fierce battles firmer, stronger, more determined and more consolidated.

Bulgaria said Israel intended to establish a springboard in Lebanon as a bulwark of its future anti-Arab policy. In the view of the German Democratic Republic, Israel was making arrangements for a long occupation in Lebanon. Expressing a similar view, Kuwait said that, by instigating sectarian dissent among Lebanese communities and making endless demands on the Government, Israel had proved that it was planning to stay in Lebanon indefinitely.

Botswana, urging Israeli withdrawal from Lebanon, said Israel could not transform its neighbour into a puppet friend by force of arms. Finland said it had joined the rest of the international community in condemning Israel for its violence in Lebanon. Israel's invasion might have given it some temporary military gains, said Pakistan, but its outrageous actions in Lebanon had exposed it and its aggressive policies to the world. In Sweden's view, Israel's invasion of Lebanon would be seen not to have brought the fundamental problems closer to solution.

Qatar said the United States veto in the Security Council had enabled Israel to invade Lebanon, leaving the Council powerless even to condemn Israel. The Syrian Arab Republic asserted that the United States, though it had known in advance of Israel's plan to invade Lebanon, had done nothing to stop it; on the contrary, it had profited from the tragedy of the Lebanese and Palestinians. Israel had made broad use of the latest United States weapons during its invasion, the Ukrainian SSR remarked. The USSR said the United States had regarded Israel's war against the Lebanese and the Palestinians as a helpful means of radically refashioning the Middle East political map in accordance with its global ambitions; meanwhile, the announced intention by the United States to investigate Israel's use of cluster bombs against Lebanese civilians had vanished without trace, and 75 F-16 fighter aircraft promised to Israel by the United States had been delivered on schedule, despite talk of postponement at the height of the Lebanese war.

Spain said it acknowledged with bitterness and discouragement that most of the Security Council resolutions on the Israel-Lebanon situation had remained a dead letter because Israel flagrantly and stubbornly flouted United Nations decisions; if those who had the power to enforce compliance with resolutions used the measures available to them, the United Nations would stand to gain considerably.

Bhutan, Norway and Turkey urged the withdrawal of all foreign forces from Lebanon; Norway added that it supported United States diplomatic efforts to that end.

Viet Nam said that, should Israel refuse to withdraw from Lebanon and the other occupied territories, sanctions must be considered as laid down in Chapter VII of the Charter.

Several speakers urged steps to bring about national reconciliation in Lebanon. Japan hoped the people of Lebanon would unite in support of President Gemayel.

Draft resolution not adopted. [1]USSR, S/15347/Rev.1.
Letters and note verbale (nv).

Israel: [2]3 Aug., S/15341; [3]3 Sep., A/37/423-S/15386; [4]5 Nov., S/15480; [5]5 Nov., A/37/601.

Jordan: [6]1 Aug. S/15332; [7]2 Aug., S/15336; [8]3 Aug., S/15340; [9]5 Aug., S/15348; [10]9 Aug., S/15350; [11]12 Aug., S/15354; [12]18 Sep., S/15399; [13]20 Sep., S/15404; [14]18 Oct., S/15459 *(nv)*.

Lebanon: [15]1 Aug., S/15333; [16]12 Aug., S/15353; [17]16 Sep., S/15392; [18]24 Sep., A/37/491; [19]1 Oct., S/15445.

Libyan Arab Jamahiriya: [20]16 Sep., A/37/456-S/15397; [21]20 Sep., A/37/472.

United States: [22]20 Aug., A/37/393-S/15371; [23]24 Sep., S/15435.

Others: [24]Australia: 12 Aug., S/15356. [25]Denmark: 20 Sep., A/37/473-S/15421. [26]Egypt: 26 Aug., A/37/411-S/15376. [27]France: 21 Sep., S/15420. [28]German Democratic Republic: 11 Aug., A/37/383-S/15352. [29]Greece: 18 Sep., S/15401. [30]Italy: 23 Sep., S/15442. [31]Japan: 23 Aug., A/37/399-S/15372. [32]Nicaragua: 9 Aug., A/37/379 (S/15349). [33]Tunisia: 17 Sep., S/15396. [34]USSR: 4 Aug., A/37/374-S/15346. [35]United Kingdom: 22 Dec., S/15540. [36]Viet Nam: 10 Aug., A/37/385.

Reports. S-G, [37]S/15334 & Add.1, [38]S/15345 & Add.1,2, [39]S/15357, [40]S/15362, [41]S/15382 & Add.1,2, [42]S/15400, [43]S/15408 & Add.1,2, [44]A/37/525-S/15451, [45]S/15455 & Corr.1.

Resolutions (1982). GA: [46]ES-7/6, 19 Aug., text following; [47]ES-7/9, 24 Sep., text following; [48]37/43, para. 22, 3 Dec.; [49]37/123 E, 16 Dec., text following. SC: [50]508(1982), 5 June; [51]509(1982), 6 June; [52]511(1982), 18 June; [53]516(1982), 1 Aug., text following; [54]517(1982), 4 Aug., text following; [55]518(1982), 12 Aug., text following; [56]519(1982), 17 Aug., text following; [57]520(1982), 17 Sep., text following; [58]521(1982), 19 Sep., text following; [59]523(1982), 18 Oct., text following.

Resolutions (prior). [60]GA: 273(III), 11 May 1949 (YUN 1948-49, p. 405). [61]SC: 242(1967), 22 Nov. 1967 (YUN 1967, p. 257); [62]338(1973), 22 Oct. 1973 (YUN 1973, p. 213).

Statement. [63]SC President, S/15342.

Meeting records. GA: A/ES-7/PV.12-19 (20-26 Apr.), 22 (25 June), 25-28, *29-32* (16-19 Aug. & 24 Sep.); A/37/PV.*35*, 92-96, *100* (18 Oct. & 6-16 Dec.). SC: S/PV.2386-2391, 2392 & Corr.1, 2393-2396, 2400 (1 Aug.–18/19 Sep. & 18 Oct.).

Security Council resolution 516(1982)

1 August 1982 Meeting 2386 Adopted unanimously

Draft prepared in consultations among Council members (S/15330).

The Security Council,

Reaffirming its resolutions 508(1982), 509(1982), 511(1982), 512(1982) and 513(1982),

Recalling its resolution 515(1982),

Alarmed by the continuation and intensification of military activities in and around Beirut,

Taking note of the latest massive violations of the cease-fire in and around Beirut,

1. *Confirms* its previous resolutions and demands an immediate cease-fire, and a cessation of all military activities within Lebanon and across the Lebanese-Israeli border;

2. *Authorizes* the Secretary-General to deploy immediately, on the request of the Government of Lebanon, United Nations observers to monitor the situation in and around Beirut;

3. *Requests* the Secretary-General to report back to the Security Council on compliance with the present resolution as soon as possible and not later than four hours from now.

Security Council resolution 517(1982)

4 August 1982 Meeting 2389 14-0-1

2-nation draft (S/15343/Rev.1), orally revised.
Sponsors: Jordan, Spain.

The Security Council,

Deeply shocked and alarmed by the deplorable consequences of the Israeli invasion of Beirut on 3 August 1982,

1. *Reconfirms* its resolutions 508(1982), 509(1982), 512(1982), 513(1982), 515(1982) and 516(1982);

2. *Confirms once again* its demand for an immediate cease-fire and withdrawal of Israeli forces from Lebanon;

3. *Censures* Israel for its failure to comply with the above resolutions;

4. *Calls* for the prompt return of Israeli troops which have moved forward subsequent to 1325 hours, eastern daylight time, on 1 August 1982;

5. *Takes note* of the decision of the Palestine Liberation Organization to move the Palestinian armed forces from Beirut;

6. *Expresses its appreciation* for the efforts and steps taken by the Secretary-General to implement the provisions of resolution 516(1982) and authorizes him, as an immediate step, to increase the number of United Nations observers in and around Beirut;

7. *Requests* the Secretary-General to report to the Security Council on the implementation of the present resolution as soon as possible and not later than 1000 hours, eastern daylight time, on 5 August 1982;

8. *Decides* to meet at that time, if necessary, in order to consider the report of the Secretary-General and, in case of failure to comply by any of the parties to the conflict, to consider adopting effective ways

and means in accordance with the provisions of the Charter of the United Nations.

Vote in Council as follows:

In favour: China, France, Guyana, Ireland, Japan, Jordan, Panama, Poland, Spain, Togo, Uganda, USSR, United Kingdom, Zaire.
Against: None.
Abstaining: United States.

Security Council resolution 518(1982)

12 August 1982 Meeting 2392 Adopted unanimously

6-nation draft (S/15355/Rev.1).

Sponsors: Guyana, Jordan, Panama, Togo, Uganda, Zaire.

The Security Council,

Recalling its resolutions 508(1982), 509(1982), 511(1982), 512(1982), 513(1982), 515(1982), 516(1982) and 517(1982),

Expressing its most serious concern about continued military activities in Lebanon and, particularly, in and around Beirut,

1. *Demands* that Israel and all parties to the conflict observe strictly the terms of Security Council resolutions relevant to the immediate cessation of all military activities within Lebanon and, particularly, in and around Beirut;

2. *Demands* the immediate lifting of all restrictions on the city of Beirut in order to permit the free entry of supplies to meet the urgent needs of the civilian population in Beirut;

3. *Requests* the United Nations observers in, and in the vicinity of, Beirut to report on the situation;

4. *Demands* that Israel co-operate fully in the effort to secure the effective deployment of the United Nations observers, as requested by the Government of Lebanon, and in such a manner as to ensure their safety;

5. *Requests* the Secretary-General to report as soon as possible to the Security Council on the implementation of the present resolution;

6. *Decides* to meet, if necessary, in order to consider the situation upon receipt of the report of the Secretary-General.

Security Council resolution 519(1982)

17 August 1982 Meeting 2393 13-0-2

Draft prepared in consultations among Council members (S/15367).

The Security Council,

Recalling its resolutions 425(1978), 426(1978), 427(1978), 434(1978), 444(1979), 450(1979), 459(1979), 467(1980), 483(1980), 488(1981), 490(1981), 498(1981), 501(1982) and 511(1982),

Reaffirming its resolutions 508(1982) and 509(1982), as well as subsequent resolutions on the situation in Lebanon,

Having studied with grave concern the report of the Secretary-General on the United Nations Interim Force in Lebanon and noting its conclusions and recommendations and the wishes of the Government of Lebanon as set out therein,

Bearing in mind the need, pending an examination by the Security Council of the situation in all its aspects, to preserve in place the capacity of the United Nations to assist in the restoration of the peace and of the authority of the Government of Lebanon throughout Lebanon,

1. *Decides* to extend the present mandate of the United Nations Interim Force in Lebanon for a further interim period of two months, that is, until 19 October 1982;

2. *Authorizes* the Force during that period to continue to carry out, in addition, the interim tasks in the humanitarian and administrative fields assigned to it in paragraph 2 of resolution 511(1982);

3. *Calls on* all concerned, taking into account paragraphs 5, 8 and 9 of the report of the Secretary-General on the Force, to extend full co-operation to it in the discharge of its tasks;

4. *Supports* the efforts of the Secretary-General, with a view to optimum use of observers of the United Nations Truce Supervision Organization, as envisaged by relevant resolutions of the Security Council;

5. *Decides* to consider the situation fully and in all its aspects before 19 October 1982.

Vote in Council as follows:

In favour: China, France, Guyana, Ireland, Japan, Jordan, Panama, Spain, Togo, Uganda, United Kingdom, United States, Zaire.
Against: None.
Abstaining: Poland, USSR.

General Assembly resolution ES-7/6

19 August 1982   Meeting 31   120-2-20 (roll-call vote)

35-nation draft (A/ES-7/L.5 and Add.1); agenda item 5.

Sponsors: Afghanistan, Bangladesh, Benin, Cape Verde, Chad, Congo, Cuba, Cyprus, Ethiopia, Gambia, Grenada, Guinea, Guinea-Bissau, Guyana, India, Indonesia, Jordan, Lao People's Democratic Republic, Madagascar, Malaysia, Maldives, Mali, Malta, Mozambique, Nigeria, Pakistan, Qatar, Sao Tome and Principe, Senegal, Sri Lanka, Sudan, Uganda, United Arab Emirates, Yemen, Yugoslavia.

Question of Palestine

The General Assembly,

Having considered the question of Palestine at its resumed seventh emergency special session,

Having heard the statement of the Palestine Liberation Organization, the representative of the Palestinian people,

Guided by the purposes and principles of the United Nations, in particular the respect for the principle of equal rights and self-determination of peoples,

Aware of the functions of the Security Council during its meetings relevant to the situation in the Middle East, in particular since 4 June 1982,

Expressing its deep regret that the Security Council has, so far, failed to take effective and practical measures in accordance with the Charter of the United Nations to ensure implementation of its resolutions 508(1982) of 5 June 1982 and 509(1982) of 6 June 1982,

Alarmed that the situation in the Middle East has further worsened as a result of Israel's acts of aggression against the sovereignty of Lebanon and the Palestinian people in Lebanon,

Guided further by the purposes and principles of the United Nations, in particular to take effective collective measures for the prevention and removal of threats to the peace and for the suppression of acts of aggression,

Mindful of the humanitarian principles and provisions of the Geneva Conventions of 1949 and Additional Protocol I thereto and the obligations arising from the regulations annexed to the Hague Conventions of 1907,

Reaffirming its conviction that the question of Palestine is the core of the Arab-Israeli conflict and that no comprehensive, just and lasting peace in the region will be achieved without the full exercise by the Palestinian people of its inalienable rights in Palestine,

Reaffirming once again that a just and comprehensive settlement of the situation in the Middle East cannot be achieved without the participation on an equal footing of all the parties to the conflict, including the Palestine Liberation Organization as the representative of the Palestinian people,

Expressing its indignation at the continuation and intensification of military activities by Israel within Lebanon, particularly in and around Beirut,

Recalling all its resolutions relevant to the question of Palestine,

Recalling Security Council resolutions 508(1982) of 5 June 1982, 509(1982) of 6 June 1982, 511(1982) of 18 June 1982, 512(1982) of 19 June 1982, 513(1982) of 4 July 1982, 515(1982) of 29 July 1982, 516(1982) of 1 August 1982, 517(1982) of 4 August 1982 and 518(1982) of 12 August 1982,

1.   *Reiterates* its affirmation of the fundamental principle of the inadmissibility of the acquisition of territory by force;

2.   *Calls* for the free exercise in Palestine of the inalienable rights of the Palestinian people to self-determination without external interference and to national independence;

3.   *Reaffirms* its rejection of all policies and plans aiming at the resettlement of the Palestinians outside their homeland;

4.   *Demands* that Israel respect and carry out the provisions of the previous resolutions of the General Assembly relating to the occupied Palestinian and other Arab territories, including Jerusalem, as well as the provisions of Security Council resolution 465(1980) of 1 March 1980, in which the Council, *inter alia:*

(a) Determined that all measures taken by Israel to change the physical character, demographic composition, institutional structure or status of the Palestinian and other Arab territories occupied since 1967, including Jerusalem, or any part thereof, had no legal validity and that Israel's policy and practices of settling parts of its population and new immigrants in those territories constituted a flagrant violation of the Geneva Convention relative to the Protection of Civilian Persons in Time of War, of 12 August 1949, and also constituted a serious obstruction to achieving a comprehensive, just and lasting peace in the Middle East;

(b) Strongly deplored the continuation and persistence of Israel in pursuing those policies and practices and called upon the Government and people of Israel to rescind those measures, to dismantle the existing settlements and in particular to cease, on an urgent basis, the establishment, construction and planning of settlements in the Arab territories occupied since 1967, including Jerusalem;

5.   *Demands also* that Israel carry out the provisions of Security Council resolutions 509(1982), 511(1982), 512(1982), 513(1982), 515(1982), 516(1982), 517(1982) and 518(1982);

6.   *Urges* the Secretary-General, with the concurrence of the Security Council and the Government of Lebanon and pending the withdrawal of Israel from Lebanon, to undertake effective measures to guarantee the safety and security of the Palestinian and Lebanese civilian population in south Lebanon;

7.   *Condemns* Israel for its non-compliance with resolutions of the Security Council, in defiance of Article 25 of the Charter of the United Nations;

8.   *Urges once again* the Security Council, in the event of continued failure by Israel to comply with the demands contained in its resolutions 465(1980), 508(1982), 509(1982), 515(1982) and 518(1982), to meet in order to consider practical ways and means in accordance with the relevant provisions of the Charter;

9.   *Requests once again* the Secretary General to delegate a high-level commission to investigate and make an up-to-date assessment of the extent of loss of human life and material damage and to report, as soon as possible, on the result of this investigation to the General Assembly and the Security Council;

10.   *Requests* the Secretary-General and organizations of the United Nations system, in co-operation with the International Committee of the Red Cross and other non-governmental organizations, to investigate the strict application by Israel of the provisions of the Geneva Conventions of 1949 and other instruments in the case of those detained;

11.   *Calls once again upon* the Secretary-General to initiate contacts with all the parties to the Arab-Israeli conflict in the Middle East, including the Palestine Liberation Organization, the representative of the Palestinian people, with a view to convening an international conference, under the auspices of the United Nations, to find concrete ways and means of achieving a comprehensive, just and lasting solution, conducive to peace in conformity with the principles of the Charter and relevant resolutions;

12.   *Decides* to adjourn the seventh emergency special session temporarily and to authorize the President of the latest regular session of the General Assembly to resume its meetings upon request from Member States.

Roll-call vote in Assembly as follows:

In favour: Afghanistan, Albania, Algeria, Angola, Argentina, Austria, Bahamas, Bahrain, Bangladesh, Barbados, Benin, Bhutan, Bolivia, Botswana, Brazil, Bulgaria, Burma, Burundi, Byelorussian SSR, Cape Verde, Chad, Chile, China, Colombia, Congo, Cuba, Cyprus, Czechoslovakia, Democratic Kampuchea, Democratic Yemen, Djibouti, Ecuador, Egypt, El Salvador, Ethiopia, Fiji, Finland, Gabon, Gambia, German Democratic Republic, Ghana, Greece, Grenada, Guinea, Guinea-Bissau, Guyana, Honduras, Hungary, India, Indonesia, Iran, Iraq, Ivory Coast, Japan, Jordan, Kenya, Kuwait, Lao People's Democratic Republic, Lebanon, Lesotho, Liberia, Libyan Arab Jamahiriya, Madagascar, Malaysia, Maldives, Mali, Malta, Mauritania, Mauritius, Mexico, Mongolia, Morocco, Mozambique, Nepal, Nicaragua, Niger, Nigeria, Oman, Pakistan, Panama, Paraguay, Peru, Philippines, Poland, Qatar, Romania, Rwanda, Samoa, Sao Tome and Principe, Saudi Arabia, Senegal, Seychelles, Sierra Leone, Singapore, Somalia, Spain, Sri Lanka, Sudan, Swaziland, Syrian Arab Republic, Thailand, Togo, Trinidad and Tobago, Tunisia, Turkey, Uganda, Ukrainian SSR, USSR, United Arab Emirates, United Republic of Cameroon, United Republic of Tanzania, Upper Volta, Uruguay, Venezuela, Viet Nam, Yemen, Yugoslavia, Zaire, Zambia, Zimbabwe.

Against: Israel, United States.

Abstaining: Australia, Belgium, Canada, Denmark, Dominican Republic, France, Germany, Federal Republic of, Haiti, Iceland, Ireland, Italy, Jamaica, Luxembourg, Malawi, Netherlands, New Zealand, Norway, Portugal, Sweden, United Kingdom.

Security Council resolution 520(1982)

17 September 1982   Meeting 2395   Adopted unanimously

Draft by Jordan (S/15394/Rev.1).

The Security Council,

Having considered the report of the Secretary-General of 15 September 1982,

Condemning the murder of Bashir Gemayel, the constitutionally elected President-elect of Lebanon, and every effort to disrupt by violence the restoration of a strong, stable government in Lebanon,

Having listened to the statement by the Permanent Representative of Lebanon,

Taking note of the determination of Lebanon to ensure the withdrawal of all non-Lebanese forces from Lebanon,

1. *Reaffirms* its resolutions 508(1982), 509(1982) and 516(1982) in all their components;

2. *Condemns* the recent Israeli incursions into Beirut in violation of the cease-fire agreements and of Security Council resolutions;

3. *Demands* an immediate return to the positions occupied by Israel before 15 September 1982, as a first step towards the full implementation of Security Council resolutions;

4. *Calls again* for the strict respect of the sovereignty, territorial integrity, unity and political independence of Lebanon under the sole and exclusive authority of the Government of Lebanon through the Lebanese Army throughout Lebanon;

5. *Reaffirms* its resolutions 512(1982) and 513(1982), which call for respect for the rights of the civilian populations without any discrimination, and repudiates all acts of violence against those populations;

6. *Supports* the efforts of the Secretary-General to implement resolution 516(1982), concerning the deployment of United Nations observers to monitor the situation in and around Beirut, and requests all the parties concerned to co-operate fully in the application of that resolution;

7. *Decides* to remain seized of the question and asks the Secretary-General to keep the Security Council informed of developments as soon as possible and not later than within twenty-four hours.

Security Council resolution 521(1982)

19 September 1982   Meeting 2396   Adopted unanimously

Draft prepared in consultations among Council members (S/15402).

The Security Council,

Appalled at the massacre of Palestinian civilians in Beirut,

Having heard the report of the Secretary-General at its 2396th meeting,

Noting that the Government of Lebanon has agreed to the dispatch of United Nations observers to the sites of greatest human suffering and losses in and around that city,

1. *Condemns* the criminal massacre of Palestinian civilians in Beirut;

2. *Reaffirms* once again its resolutions 512(1982) and 513(1982), which call for respect for the rights of the civilian populations without any discrimination, and repudiates all acts of violence against those populations;

3. *Authorizes* the Secretary-General, as an immediate step, to increase the number of United Nations observers in and around Beirut from ten to fifty, and insists that there shall be no interference with the deployment of the observers and that they shall have full freedom of movement;

4. *Requests* the Secretary-General, in consultation with the Government of Lebanon, to ensure the rapid deployment of those observers in order that they may contribute in every way possible within their mandate to the effort to ensure full protection for the civilian populations;

5. *Requests* the Secretary-General, as a matter of urgency, to initiate appropriate consultations and, in particular, consultations with the Government of Lebanon on additional steps which the Security Council might take, including the possible deployment of United Nations forces, to assist that Government in ensuring full protection for the civilian populations in and around Beirut and requests him to report to the Council within forty-eight hours;

6. *Insists* that all concerned must permit United Nations observers and forces established by the Security Council in Lebanon to be deployed and to discharge their mandates and, in this connection, solemnly calls attention to the obligation of all Member States, under Article 25 of the Charter of the United Nations, to accept and carry out the decisions of the Council in accordance with the Charter;

7. *Requests* the Secretary-General to keep the Security Council informed on an urgent and continuing basis.

General Assembly resolution ES-7/9

24 September 1982   Meeting 32   147-2 (recorded vote)

45-nation draft (A/ES-7/L.8); agenda item 5.

Sponsors: Afghanistan, Bangladesh, Benin, Comoros, Congo, Cuba, Cyprus, Egypt, Gambia, Ghana, Greece, Grenada, Guinea, Guyana, India, Indonesia, Jordan,

Kenya, Kuwait, Lao People's Democratic Republic, Madagascar, Malaysia, Maldives, Mali, Malta, Mauritania, Nicaragua, Niger, Nigeria, Pakistan, Panama, Senegal, Sri Lanka, Sudan, Syrian Arab Republic, Turkey, Uganda, United Arab Emirates, United Republic of Tanzania, Upper Volta, Viet Nam, Yemen, Yugoslavia, Zambia, Zimbabwe.

Question of Palestine

The General Assembly,

Having considered the question of Palestine at its resumed seventh emergency special session,

Having heard the statement of the Palestine Liberation Organization, the representative of the Palestinian people,

Recalling and reaffirming, in particular, its resolution 194(III) of 11 December 1948,

Appalled at the massacre of Palestinian civilians in Beirut,

Recalling Security Council resolutions 508(1982) of 5 June 1982, 509(1982) of 6 June 1982, 513(1982) of 4 July 1982, 520(1982) of 17 September 1982 and 521(1982) of 19 September 1982,

Taking note of the reports of the Secretary-General relevant to the situation, particularly his report of 18 September 1982,

Noting with regret that the Security Council has so far not taken effective and practical measures, in accordance with the Charter of the United Nations, to ensure implementation of its resolutions 508(1982) and 509(1982),

Referring to the humanitarian principles of the Geneva Convention relative to the Protection of Civilian Persons in Time of War, of 12 August 1949, and to the obligations arising from the regulations annexed to the Hague Conventions of 1907,

Deeply concerned at the sufferings of the Palestinian and Lebanese civilian populations,

Noting the homelessness of the Palestinian people,

Reaffirming the imperative need to permit the Palestinian people to exercise their legitimate rights,

1. *Condemns* the criminal massacre of Palestinian and other civilians in Beirut on 17 September 1982;

2. *Urges* the Security Council to investigate, through the means available to it, the circumstances and extent of the massacre of Palestinian and other civilians in Beirut on 17 September 1982, and to make public the report on its findings as soon as possible;

3. *Decides* to support fully the provisions of Security Council resolutions 508(1982) and 509(1982), in which the Council, *inter alia*, demanded that:

(a) Israel withdraw all its military forces forthwith and unconditionally to the internationally recognized boundaries of Lebanon;

(b) All parties to the conflict cease immediately and simultaneously all military activities within Lebanon and across the Lebanese-Israeli border;

4. *Demands* that all Member States and other parties observe strict respect for the sovereignty, territorial integrity, unity and political independence of Lebanon within its internationally recognized boundaries;

5. *Reaffirms* the fundamental principle of the inadmissibility of the acquisition of territory by force;

6. *Resolves* that, in conformity with its resolution 194(III) and subsequent relevant resolutions, the Palestinian refugees should be enabled to return to their homes and property from which they have been uprooted and displaced, and demands that Israel comply unconditionally and immediately with the present resolution;

7. *Urges* the Security Council, in the event of continued failure by Israel to comply with the demands contained in resolutions 508(1982) and 509(1982) and the present resolution, to meet in order to consider practical ways and means in accordance with the Charter of the United Nations;

8. *Calls upon* all States and international agencies and organizations to continue to provide the most extensive humanitarian aid possible to the victims of the Israeli invasion of Lebanon;

9. *Requests* the Secretary-General to prepare a photographic exhibit of the massacre of 17 September 1982 and to display it in the United Nations visitors' hall;

10. *Decides* to adjourn the seventh emergency special session temporarily and to authorize the President of the latest regular session of the General Assembly to resume its meetings upon request from Member States.

Recorded vote in Assembly as follows:

In favour: Afghanistan, Albania, Algeria, Angola, Argentina, Australia, Austria, Bahamas, Bahrain, Bangladesh, Barbados, Belgium, Benin, Bhutan, Bolivia,

Botswana, Brazil, Bulgaria, Burma, Burundi, Byelorussian SSR, Canada, Cape Verde, Chad, Chile, China, Colombia, Comoros, Congo, Costa Rica, Cuba, Cyprus, Czechoslovakia, Democratic Kampuchea, Democratic Yemen, Denmark, Djibouti, Dominican Republic, Ecuador, Egypt, El Salvador, Ethiopia, Fiji, Finland, France, Gabon, Gambia, German Democratic Republic, Germany, Federal Republic of, Ghana, Greece, Grenada, Guatemala, Guinea, Guinea-Bissau, Guyana, Haiti, Honduras, Hungary, Iceland, India, Indonesia, Iran, Iraq, Ireland, Italy, Ivory Coast, Jamaica, Japan, Jordan, Kenya, Kuwait, Lao People's Democratic Republic, Lebanon, Lesotho, Liberia, Libyan Arab Jamahiriya, Luxembourg, Madagascar, Malaysia, Maldives, Mali, Malta, Mauritania, Mauritius, Mexico, Mongolia, Morocco, Mozambique, Nepal, Netherlands, New Zealand, Nicaragua, Niger, Nigeria, Norway, Oman, Pakistan, Panama, Papua New Guinea, Paraguay, Peru, Philippines, Poland, Portugal, Qatar, Romania, Rwanda, Saint Lucia, Samoa, Sao Tome and Principe, Saudi Arabia, Senegal, Seychelles, Sierra Leone, Singapore, Solomon Islands, Somalia, Spain, Sri Lanka, Sudan, Suriname, Swaziland, Sweden, Syrian Arab Republic, Thailand, Togo, Trinidad and Tobago, Tunisia, Turkey, Uganda, Ukrainian SSR, USSR, United Arab Emirates, United Kingdom, United Republic of Cameroon, United Republic of Tanzania, Upper Volta, Uruguay, Vanuatu, Venezuela, Viet Nam, Yemen, Yugoslavia, Zaire, Zambia, Zimbabwe.

Against: Israel, United States.

Security Council resolution 523(1982)

13-0-2   Meeting 2400   18 October 1982

Draft prepared in consultations among Council members (S/15458).

The Security Council,

Having heard the statement of the President of the Republic of Lebanon,

Recalling its resolutions 425(1978), 426(1978) and 519(1982),

Reaffirming its resolutions 508(1982) and 509(1982), as well as all subsequent resolutions on the situation in Lebanon,

Having studied the report of the Secretary-General and taking note of its conclusions and recommendations,

Responding to the request of the Government of Lebanon,

1. *Decides* to extend the present mandate of the United Nations Interim Force in Lebanon for a further interim period of three months, that is, until 19 January 1983;

2. *Insists* that there shall be no interference under any pretext with the operations of the Force and that it shall have full freedom of movement in the discharge of its mandate;

3. *Authorizes* the Force during that period to carry out, with the consent of the Government of Lebanon, interim tasks in the humanitarian and administrative fields, as indicated in resolutions 511(1982) and 519(1982), and to assist the Government of Lebanon in ensuring the security of all the inhabitants of the area without any discrimination;

4. *Requests* the Secretary-General, within the three-month period, to consult with the Government of Lebanon and to report to the Security Council on ways and means of ensuring the full implementation of the mandate of the Force as defined in resolutions 425(1978) and 426(1978), and the relevant decisions of the Council;

5. *Requests* the Secretary-General to report to the Security Council on the progress of his consultations.

Vote in Council as follows:

In favour: China, France, Guyana, Ireland, Japan, Jordan, Panama, Spain, Togo, Uganda, United Kingdom, United States, Zaire.
Against: None.
Abstaining: Poland, USSR.

General Assembly resolution 37/123 E

16 December 1982   Meeting 108   145-0 (recorded vote)

33-nation draft (A/37/L.53 & Corr.1 & Add.1), amended by Syrian Arab Republic (A/37/L.59); agenda item 34.

Sponsors: Australia, Austria, Belgium, Bolivia, Brazil, Canada, Colombia, Denmark, Ecuador, Equatorial Guinea, Finland, France, Germany, Federal Republic of, Greece, Guyana, Ireland, Italy, Jamaica, Japan, Lebanon, Luxembourg, Mali, Nepal, Netherlands, New Zealand, Norway, Peru, Portugal, Sweden, United Kingdom, United States, Uruguay, Venezuela.

The General Assembly,

Having heard the address by the President of the Lebanese Republic on 18 October 1982,

Taking note of the decision of the Government of Lebanon calling for the withdrawal from Lebanon of all non-Lebanese troops and forces which are not authorized by the Government to deploy therein,

Bearing in mind Security Council resolutions 508(1982) of 5 June 1982 and 509(1982) of 6 June 1982,

1. *Calls* for strict respect of the territorial integrity, sovereignty, unity and political independence of Lebanon and supports the efforts of the Government of Lebanon, with regional and international endorsement, to restore the exclusive authority of the Lebanese State throughout its territory up to the internationally recognized boundaries;

2. *Requests* the Secretary-General to report to the General Assembly on the implementation of the present resolution.

Recorded vote in Assembly as follows:

In favour: Afghanistan, Algeria, Angola, Argentina, Australia, Austria, Bahamas, Bahrain, Bangladesh, Barbados, Belgium, Belize, Benin, Bhutan, Bolivia, Botswana, Brazil, Bulgaria, Burma, Burundi, Byelorussian SSR, Canada, Cape Verde, Central African Republic, Chad, Chile, China, Colombia, Comoros, Congo, Costa Rica, Cuba, Cyprus, Czechoslovakia, Democratic Kampuchea, Democratic Yemen, Denmark, Djibouti, Dominican Republic, Ecuador, Egypt, El Salvador, Ethiopia, Fiji, Finland, France, Gabon, Gambia, German Democratic Republic, Germany, Federal Republic of, Ghana, Greece, Grenada, Guatemala, Guinea, Guinea-Bissau, Guyana, Honduras, Hungary, Iceland, India, Indonesia, Iran, Iraq, Ireland, Israel, Italy, Ivory Coast, Jamaica, Japan, Jordan, Kenya, Kuwait, Lao People's Democratic Republic, Lebanon, Lesotho, Liberia, Libyan Arab Jamahiriya, Luxembourg, Madagascar, Malawi, Malaysia, Maldives, Mali, Malta, Mauritania, Mauritius, Mexico, Mongolia, Morocco, Mozambique, Nepal, Netherlands, New Zealand, Nicaragua, Nigeria, Norway, Oman, Pakistan, Panama, Papua New Guinea, Paraguay, Peru, Philippines, Poland, Portugal, Qatar, Romania, Rwanda, Samoa, Sao Tome and Principe, Saudi Arabia, Senegal, Seychelles, Sierra Leone, Singapore, Somalia, Spain, Sri Lanka, Sudan, Suriname, Sweden, Syrian Arab Republic, Thailand, Togo, Trinidad and Tobago, Tunisia, Turkey, Uganda, Ukrainian SSR, USSR, United Arab Emirates, United Kingdom, United Republic of Cameroon, United Republic of Tanzania, United States, Upper Volta, Uruguay, Vanuatu, Venezuela, Viet Nam, Yemen, Yugoslavia, Zaire, Zambia.
Against: None.

Protection of Palestinian refugees and civilians in Lebanon

During and after the armed conflict in Lebanon which began in June 1982, the Security Council, the General Assembly, the Economic and Social Council and the Sub-Commission on Prevention of Discrimination and Protection of Minorities of the Commission on Human Rights called for measures to protect Palestinian refugees and civilians in the country, as well as persons detained by the Israeli forces in Lebanon. Such calls were made with particular urgency following the massacre of civilians in the Beirut area on 17/18 September. They were coupled with appeals for emergency humanitarian assistance by United Nations organizations and Governments.

To express its concern at the number of Palestinian and Lebanese children victimized by the hostilities, the Assembly decided in August to commemorate 4 June of each year as the International Day of Innocent Children Victims of Aggression. It also called in December for the restitution of Palestinian cultural property seized by Israeli forces. The World Assembly on Aging, in August, condemned aggression against civilian areas and the use of weapons of mass destruction causing indiscriminate casualties, particularly among the elderly.

Security Council action. During the 10 weeks of active hostilities in southern Lebanon (4 June–12 August) and in the unsettled period afterwards, the Security Council called frequently for urgent steps to protect Palestinian and Lebanese civilians. It made repeated reference to the humanitarian principles of the Geneva Conventions of 1949 and the obligations arising from regulations annexed to the Hague Convention of 1907, both concerned with the treatment of military and civilian persons during wartime.

The first such Council action was taken on 18 June when, after being informed by the Secretary-General that UNIFIL was endeavouring to extend protection and humanitarian assistance to the population in its area of operation in southern Lebanon, it authorized the Force to carry out those interim tasks in addition to its regular peace-keeping functions.[11] This authorization was continued when the Council extended the Force's mandate twice more, on 17 August[16] and 18 October.[19]

On 19 June, expressing deep concern at the sufferings of Lebanese and Palestinian civilians, it called on all parties to the conflict to respect the rights of civilians and refrain from violence against them.[12] Again on 4 July,[13] the Council called for respect for the rights of the civilian population in Lebanon without discrimination. By two later resolutions, dated 29 July[14] and 12 August,[15] it demanded that Israel lift immediately its blockade of Beirut to permit the dispatch of supplies to civilians.

Receiving further reports of killings after a formal cease-fire finally went into effect in August, the Council, by resolutions of 17 September[17] and 19 September,[18] repudiated all acts of violence against civilians. By the latter resolution, which closely followed news of the massacre of civilians at the Sabra and Shatila refugee camps near Beirut (see below), it also requested the Secretary-General to ensure the rapid deployment of United Nations observers to help ensure protection for civilians, and to initiate urgent consultations on additional steps to assist the Lebanese Government in that regard. The United Nations was later informed that, at Lebanon's request, France, Italy and the United States were sending contingents of a multinational force to assist the Lebanese armed forces carry out their responsibilities around Beirut. The first elements of that force began arriving on 24 September.

Economic and Social Council action. Stressing its support for the victims of the Israeli invasion, the Economic and Social Council, in a resolution of 27 July on assistance to the Palestinians in Lebanon,[6] called on Israel to release detained civilians in Lebanon, to apply fully the 1949 Geneva Convention relative to the Protection of Civilian Persons in Time of War and to apply the Geneva Conventions to imprisoned combatants.

Explaining its position on these provisions, Australia, which voted for the resolution as a whole, said it regarded the reference to the Geneva Conventions as an important humanitarian element of the resolution. Brazil noted that the Geneva Convention on the treatment of prisoners of war

applied to regular armed forces; however, because the resolution was concerned with an exceptional situation in which the Palestinians were fighting for rights recognized by the General Assembly, it had voted in favour of the resolution without prejudging its position on similar situations in the future. Canada called for the full application of the Conventions on protection of civilians and imprisoned combatants.

In its response of 27 October, transmitted to the Assembly in a report of the Secretary-General on implementation of the Council resolution,[5] Israel stated that it had applied the four Geneva Conventions since the commencement of its operations in Lebanon and was making every effort to safeguard civilians against the effects of hostilities. While the Third Geneva Convention relating to prisoners of war was being applied to Syrian soldiers, PLO members were not entitled to prisoner-of-war status in view of the fact that they had consistently violated accepted norms of civilization by choosing the unarmed and defenceless as their exclusive target and that the Convention did not apply to terrorist organizations. However, the humanitarian provisions of the Fourth Geneva Convention on protection of civilians were being applied to PLO detainees and Israel had granted ICRC officials permission to visit them.

Action by the Sub-Commission on discrimination and minorities. On 17 August,[1] the Sub-Commission on Prevention of Discrimination and Protection of Minorities approved for transmission to Israel a text voicing grave concern at the human suffering resulting from the invasion of Lebanon and the blockade and bombardment of Beirut, and expressing the urgent wish that all military operations would stop immediately and that international humanitarian norms on the protection of civilians and war prisoners would be respected (see ECONOMIC AND SOCIAL QUESTIONS, Chapter XVIII).

In a resolution of 8 September on human rights violations in Israeli-occupied Lebanon and the territories occupied by Israel,[20] the Sub-Commission recommended that the Commission on Human Rights: condemn Israel for its invasion of Lebanon and destruction of Lebanese cities and Palestine refugee camps; declare that Israel's grave breaches of the 1949 Geneva Conventions in Lebanon and the occupied territories could be assimilated to war crimes; urge Israel to grant Palestinian combatants prisoner-of-war status and to release all detained civilians; and call on Israel to comply with the Security Council resolutions asking for Israeli withdrawal from Lebanon.

General Assembly action. In its resolution of 19 August on the Israel-Lebanon situation,[7] the General Assembly urged the Secretary-General to undertake effective measures to guarantee the safety and security of Palestinian and Lebanese civilians in southern Lebanon. In addition, the Secretary-General and United Nations organizations were requested, in co-operation with ICRC and other non-governmental organizations, to investigate Israel's application of international instruments relating to detained persons.

In a resolution of 24 September,[8] the Assembly resolved that the Palestinian refugees be enabled to return to their homes and property, and demanded that Israel comply unconditionally and immediately.

An Assembly resolution of 16 December[9] on the protection of Palestine refugees was concerned largely with the situation of those refugees in Lebanon. The Assembly called on Israel to desist from preventing Palestinians registered by the United Nations Relief and Works Agency for Palestine Refugees in the Near East (UNRWA) as refugees in Lebanon from returning to their camps there, and to allow the resumption of UNRWA health, medical, educational and social services to the Palestinians in the refugee camps in southern Lebanon. It requested the UNRWA Commissioner-General to provide housing, in consultation with the Lebanese Government, to refugees whose houses had been demolished or razed by the Israeli forces, and to prepare a report on the damage caused to the Palestine refugees and their property, as well as to UNRWA facilities, as a result of Israel's aggression. The Assembly urged effective measures by the Secretary-General to guarantee the security and rights of Palestine refugees in general, and called on Israel to release all detained Palestine refugees.

This resolution was adopted by a recorded vote of 127 to 2, with 16 abstentions, following its approval by the Special Political Committee on 3 December by a recorded vote of 97 to 2, with 16 abstentions.

By its resolution of 17 December on assistance to Palestinians,[10] the Assembly called on Governments and United Nations bodies to provide humanitarian assistance to the Palestinian victims of the invasion, and endorsed the Economic and Social Council resolution of 27 July.

Introducing the resolution on protection of Palestine refugees—sponsored also by Afghanistan, Bangladesh, Cuba, Indonesia and Yugoslavia—Pakistan said that, as UNRWA had not been able to restore its services in Lebanon, it was time for the international community to do everything possible to make Israel respect its obligations under the Charter of the United Nations.

Lebanon, which voted for the resolution, said the Palestinians legally residing in Lebanon, like Lebanese nationals and other legal residents, were under the protection of Lebanese law; the problem was to obtain the withdrawal of non-Lebanese armed forces from the country so that the Government could provide protection for everyone residing there.

Canada, which abstained, questioned whether UNRWA resources should be devoted to the preparation of a report on damage in Lebanon when it was already so greatly burdened with humanitarian priorities. Finland shared these doubts.

Comments on the provision urging measures by the Secretary-General to protect Palestine refugees in the territories occupied by Israel were made by the United Nations Legal Counsel and by Austria, Canada, Denmark (for the EC members), Finland, Ireland, the Philippines, Portugal, Sweden, the United Arab Emirates, the United States, Uruguay and Venezuela (see below, under PALESTINE REFUGEES).

During the Assembly debate on the Middle East situation in December, Jordan asked that the Presidents of the Assembly and the Security Council seek information about the fate of 5,000 missing persons whom the Israelis had reportedly rounded up in Beirut for interrogation.

Communications. By a letter of 7 December,[2] Jordan transmitted the testimony of a Canadian physician who had reported witnessing Israeli crimes against the civilians of southern Lebanon and inhabitants of Palestine refugee camps there, including bombing and shelling of camps and hospitals and beatings of prisoners. By a letter of the same date,[3] Jordan transmitted the account of two Norwegians arrested by Israeli authorities, detailing alleged maltreatment of prisoners by Israeli soldiers at Saida, Lebanon.

As Chairman of the Arab Group, Yemen conveyed on the same date a letter of 3 December to the Secretary-General from the PLO observer, stating that two Palestinians had been killed and four others wounded by Israeli soldiers on 2 December at the Ansar concentration camp in southern Lebanon, where about 5,000 to 6,000 Palestinians and Lebanese were said to be detained under inhuman conditions.[4]

Decision (1982). [1]SCPDPM (report, E/CN.4/1983/4): 1982/2, 17 Aug.
Letters. Jordan, 7 Dec.: [2]A/37/704-S/15512; [3]A/37/705-S/15513. [4]Yemen, for Arab Group: 7 Dec., A/37/708.
Report. [5]S-G, A/37/571.
Resolutions (1982). [6]ESC: 1982/48, paras. 4 & 5, 27 July. GA: [7]ES-7/6, paras. 6 & 10, 19 Aug.; [8]ES-7/9, para. 6, 24 Sep.; [9]37/120 J, 16 Dec., text following; [10]37/134, paras. 2 & 3, 17 Dec. SC: [11]511(1982), para. 2, 18 June; [12]512(1982), para. 1, 19 June; [13]513(1982), para. 1, 4 July; [14]515(1982), 29 July; [15]518(1982), para. 2, 12 Aug.; [16]519(1982), para. 2, 17 Aug.; [17]520(1982), para. 5, 17 Sep.; [18]521(1982), 19 Sep.; [19]523(1982), para. 3, 18 Oct.. [20]SCPDPM: 1982/18, para. 1, 8 Sep.
Meeting records. GA: SPC, A/SPC/37/SR.24, 26-33, *42, 44, 45* (9 Nov.-6 Dec.); plenary, A/37/PV.108 (16 Dec.)

General Assembly resolution 37/120 J

16 December 1982   Meeting 108   127-2-16 (recorded vote)

Approved by SPC (A/37/723) by recorded vote (97-2-16), 3 December (meeting 44); 6-nation draft (A/SPC/37/L.24); agenda item 65.

Sponsors: Afghanistan, Bangladesh, Cuba, Indonesia, Pakistan, Yugoslavia.

Protection of Palestine refugees

The General Assembly,

Recalling Security Council resolutions 508(1982) of 5 June 1982, 509(1982) of 6 June 1982, 511(1982) of 18 June 1982, 512(1982) of 19 June 1982, 513(1982) of 4 July 1982, 515(1982) of 29 July 1982, 517(1982) of 4 August 1982, 518(1982) of 12 August 1982, 519(1982) of 17 August 1982, 520(1982) of 17 September 1982 and 523(1982) of 18 October 1982,

Recalling General Assembly resolutions ES-7/5 of 26 June 1982, ES-7/6 of 24 August 1982, ES-7/8 of 19 August 1982 and ES-7/9 of 24 September 1982,

Having considered the report of the Commissioner-General of the United Nations Relief and Works Agency for Palestine Refugees in the Near East, covering the period from 1 July 1981 to 30 June 1982, and his special report covering the period from 6 June to 31 August 1982,

Referring to the humanitarian principles of the Geneva Convention relative to the Protection of Civilian Persons in Time of War, of 12 August 1949, and to the obligations arising from the regulations annexed to the Hague Convention of 1907,

Deeply distressed at the sufferings of the Palestinians resulting from the Israeli invasion of Lebanon,

1. *Urges* the Secretary-General, in consultation with the United Nations Relief and Works Agency for Palestine Refugees in the Near East, and pending the withdrawal of Israeli forces from the Palestinian and other Arab territories occupied by Israel since 1967, including Jerusalem, to undertake effective measures to guarantee the safety and security and the legal and human rights of the Palestine refugees in the occupied territories;

2. *Calls upon* Israel, the occupying Power, to release forthwith all detained Palestine refugees, including the employees of the United Nations Relief and Works Agency for Palestine Refugees in the Near East;

3. *Also calls upon* Israel to desist forthwith from preventing those Palestinians registered by the United Nations Relief and Works Agency for Palestine Refugees in the Near East as refugees in Lebanon from returning to their camps in Lebanon;

4. *Further calls upon* Israel to allow the resumption of health, medical, educational and social services rendered by the United Nations Relief and Works Agency for Palestine Refugees in the Near East to the Palestinians in the refugee camps in southern Lebanon;

5. *Requests* the Commissioner-General of the United Nations Relief and Works Agency for Palestine Refugees in the Near East to co-ordinate his activities in rendering those services with the Government of Lebanon, the host country;

6. *Urges* the Commissioner-General to provide housing, in consultation with the Government of Lebanon, to the Palestine refugees whose houses were demolished or razed by the Israeli forces, in order to protect them from the severity of the weather;

7. *Requests* the Commissioner-General, in consultation with the Government of Lebanon, to prepare a report on the totality of the damage caused to the Palestine refugees and their property and to the Agency's facilities, as well as those of other international bodies, as a result of the Israeli aggression;

8. *Requests* the Secretary-General, in consultation with the Commissioner-General, to report to the General Assembly before the opening of its thirty-eighth session on the implementation of the present resolution.

Recorded vote in Assembly as follows:

In favour: Afghanistan, Albania, Algeria, Angola, Argentina, Austria, Bahamas, Bahrain, Bangladesh, Barbados, Belize, Benin, Bhutan, Bolivia, Botswana, Brazil, Bulgaria, Burma, Burundi, Byelorussian SSR, Cape Verde, Central African Republic, Chad, Chile, China, Colombia, Comoros, Congo, Cuba, Cyprus, Czechoslovakia, Democratic Kampuchea, Democratic Yemen, Djibouti, Dominican Republic, Ecuador, Egypt, El Salvador, Ethiopia, Fiji, Finland, France, Gabon, Gambia, German Democratic Republic, Ghana, Greece, Grenada, Guinea, Guinea-Bissau, Guyana, Honduras, Hungary, India, Indonesia, Iran, Iraq, Ivory Coast, Jamaica, Japan, Jordan, Kenya, Kuwait, Lao People's Democratic Republic, Lebanon, Lesotho, Liberia, Libyan Arab Jamahiriya, Madagascar, Malawi, Malaysia, Maldives, Mali, Malta, Mauritania, Mauritius, Mexico, Mongolia, Morocco, Mozambique, Nepal, New Zealand, Nicaragua, Nigeria, Oman, Pakistan, Panama, Papua

New Guinea, Peru, Philippines, Poland, Qatar, Romania, Rwanda, Samoa, Sao Tome and Principe, Saudi Arabia, Senegal, Seychelles, Sierra Leone, Somalia, Spain, Sri Lanka, Sudan, Suriname, Sweden, Syrian Arab Republic, Thailand, Togo, Trinidad and Tobago, Tunisia, Turkey, Uganda, Ukrainian SSR, USSR, United Arab Emirates, United Republic of Cameroon, United Republic of Tanzania, Upper Volta, Uruguay, Vanuatu, Venezuela, Viet Nam, Yemen, Yugoslavia, Zaire, Zambia.

Against: Israel, United States.

Abstaining: Australia, Belgium, Canada, Costa Rica, Denmark, Germany, Federal Republic of, Guatemala, Iceland, Ireland, Italy, Luxembourg, Netherlands, Norway, Paraguay, Portugal, United Kingdom.

Massacre in the Beirut area

On 18 September 1982, hundreds of Palestine refugees were found murdered in the refugee camps of Sabra and Shatila, on the southern outskirts of Beirut. Upon receipt of a report from the Secretary-General, the Security Council, on 19 September, condemned the massacre and requested the initiation of consultations on possible assistance to the Lebanese Government in ensuring full protection for the civilians in and around Beirut. The massacre was also condemned by the General Assembly in September and December. On the latter occasion, the Assembly resolved that the massacre was an act of genocide. A number of countries expressed horror, shock and condemnation in communications to the Secretary-General and the President of the Security Council.

Report of the Secretary-General. Initial information on the massacre was included in a report of 18 September by the Secretary-General to the Security Council.[21]

The report gave an account submitted on the same date by United Nations observers in Beirut. They reported that fighting in the Sabra camp had been in progress on 17 September and the presence of Kataeb units (the military branch of the Phalange Party) had been observed at Bir Hassan, in the hospital and the airport areas, in the vicinity of the Sabra camp. West Beirut had been reported under Israeli control, with the exception of the Sabra camp area. In the afternoon, sporadic explosions had been heard and before midnight flares had been seen over the Sabra area. In the morning of 18 September, all of west Beirut had been under Israeli control. Kataeb units had again been observed in the vicinity of the Sabra camp, as well as at least 1,000 Kataeb soldiers with tanks and vehicles in the airport area. According to the Lebanese Army, the units seen in the Bir Hassan, Sabra and airport areas had been Kataeb units mixed with Lebanese *de facto* forces from southern Lebanon.

When on the morning of 18 September the observers reached the camp, which was dominated by two Israeli positions to the west, they had found many clusters of bodies of men, women and children in civilian clothes who appeared to have been massacred in groups of 10 or 20.

The Secretary-General's report also gave an Israeli account of circumstances surrounding this event, as given in messages on 18 September from the Foreign Ministry and the representative to the United Nations. The Foreign Ministry stated that Israel's forces had been deployed west of the Fakhani, Sabra and Shatila refugee camps, and had left access from the east open in the expectation that the Lebanese Army would enter the camps and take up positions, as called for by the plan of United States Special Envoy Philip Habib on the disengagement of forces around Beirut. As that had not happened, Israeli forces, on finding out what had occurred at the camps during the night, had surrounded them on the morning of 18 September to protect the population. A message from the representative of Israel added that an arrangement had been reached between the Israeli and Lebanese forces for the latter to enter the three camps on 19 September.

Expressing shock and horror at the reports of the killings, the Secretary-General called urgently for an end to the violence. In a statement delivered to him, France, Italy and the United States had urged the immediate dispatch of United Nations observers to the sites of the greatest human suffering and losses. Lebanon had informed him that it concurred with that request.

Security Council action. On 18 September,[3] Jordan transmitted a letter from the PLO observer to the Security Council President charging that innocent Palestinian civilians in refugee camps and other parts of Beirut were being massacred by Israeli agents, whose entry had been facilitated by Israeli troops which had surrounded the camps. Holding Israel primarily responsible, PLO called on the Security Council to dispatch an international military force to provide protection to the Palestinians in Beirut and other parts of Lebanon.

Meeting at the urgent request of Jordan, followed by one from Greece,[11] the Council unanimously adopted on 19 September a resolution[26] condemning the massacre, reaffirming previous calls for respect for the rights of civilians, authorizing an increase in the number of United Nations observers in and around Beirut from 10 to 50, and requesting the Secretary-General to consult urgently on additional steps, including possible deployment of United Nations forces.

Virtually all speakers in the debate preceding adoption of the resolution—among them China, Democratic Yemen, Egypt, France, Greece, Guyana, Ireland, Israel, Jordan, Panama, Poland, the Syrian Arab Republic, Uganda, the USSR and the United Kingdom—expressed shock and indignation at the massacre.

The PLO observer said the camp had been stormed by Israeli commandos who had sought the help of some militiamen from the forces of Major Saad Haddad and who had butchered 1,500 civilians, mostly women and children. The send-

ing of observers and of a monitoring team was not sufficient; the Council should at least provide some safeguards to the civilians in Beirut and especially the Palestinians in refugee camps.

Israel was held responsible for the massacre, either directly or indirectly, by most of the speakers, including Algeria, China, Egypt, Guyana, Jordan, Poland, Spain, the Syrian Arab Republic and the USSR. Spain said the Israeli occupation had been a cover for atrocities.

Algeria said the massacre could not have taken place without Israel's collaboration and without the weakness and passivity of the international community, which had avoided using firm language with the aggressor. Guyana charged that Israel had used the opportunity of the withdrawal of the Palestinian freedom fighters to take control of west Beirut and had caused the planned and premeditated massacre to be perpetrated. Jordan alleged that under the protection of Israeli tanks, which had encircled the refugee camps and cut them off from the rest of Beirut, the Israelis and their henchmen had committed the massacres. Similarly, the USSR said Israeli troops had set up their tanks around the camps and opened the gates so that their henchmen—the Phalangist soldiers and the *de facto* forces of Major Haddad—could complete their crimes. Kuwait said the agreements guaranteed by the United States had been savagely flouted by the planning and sponsoring of an extermination campaign against the Palestinians in the camps.

In Egypt's opinion, the massacre had been calculated to exacerbate tension and undermine conciliation and restoration efforts, and to create conditions that would serve as a pretext for Israel's continued occupation of Beirut and Lebanon. The Syrian Arab Republic said the massacres were the extension of a plan to achieve three goals: to liquidate the Palestinians and PLO, to dismantle Lebanon by rekindling a civil war and to divert attention from the execution of a master-plan aiming at the final liquidation of the Palestinians in the occupied territories.

Israel rejected the allegations and reiterated the account it had given to the Secretary-General and which had been included in his report (see above).

Stating that the Kataeb party had denied any participation in the massacre, Lebanon said such information was a conspiracy aimed at preventing the Lebanese from cementing their unity and moving forward to restore national sovereignty. The Lebanese Army, which had started to assume its responsibilities and establish control over Beirut, had been thwarted in its effort by the Israeli occupation beginning on 15 September.

The Permanent Observer of the League of Arab States said that by trying to put the blame on those whom it called "extreme Phalangists", thus ascribing the crime to a mainstream political force in Lebanon which had provided the President-elect and a new presidential candidate, Israel was attempting to pre-empt the constitutional process and make the candidate controversial; no Lebanese could have reached the camps unless brought in by Israel.

As requested by the Council, the Secretary-General reported on 20, 27 and 30 September on implementation of the resolution.[22] He stated that deployment of Lebanese armed forces in the Sabra, Shatila and Burj Al-Barajneh refugee camp areas had started on 19 September, and three United Nations observer teams had also been patrolling the area. No major change in the deployment of the Israeli forces had been observed, and no Kataeb or *de facto* militia units had been observed in the general west Beirut area.

By a letter of 20 September attached to the report, Israel transmitted a Cabinet statement of 19 September, rejecting as baseless all accusations that it bore any blame for the tragedy at Shatila, adding that without intervention of its forces there would have been much greater loss of life; in a place where there was no position of the Israel Army, a Lebanese unit that had entered a refugee centre where terrorists had been hiding had caused many civilian casualties, to Israel's deep grief and regret.

Communications (September). By a letter of 20 September,[1] the Chairman of the Committee on the Exercise of the Inalienable Rights of the Palestinian People conveyed to the Secretary-General the Committee's horror and consternation at the massacre. Reiterating its conviction that such tragedies could have been avoided had the Security Council taken positive action to implement the Committee's 1976 recommendations (see above, under PALESTINE QUESTION), the Committee urged the Council to do so without further delay.

The massacre was condemned in a number of other communications of the same date, from Cuba, as Chairman of the Movement of Non-Aligned Countries;[8] Egypt, transmitting a message from the Deputy Prime Minister and Minister for Foreign Affairs;[9] France, transmitting an 18 September statement by the President and a 17 September statement by the Foreign Minister, the latter denouncing the Israeli offensive in west Beirut and calling for an immediate return to previous positions;[10] Jordan, transmitting a letter from the Foreign Minister;[4] Madagascar, transmitting a 19 September message from the President;[15] and Suriname.[18]

Horror, shock and condemnation were also voiced in letters from Austria (21 September, transmitting a letter of that date from the Foreign Minister);[6] China (22 September, transmitting statements of 19 September by the Foreign Ministry spokesman and 22 September by the Premier of the State Council);[7] Guyana (23 September, transmitting a 22 September Foreign Ministry statement);[12] Jamaica (23 September, transmitting a statement by the Deputy Prime Minister and Foreign Minister to the House of Representatives);[13] Mongolia (22 September, transmitting a government statement of that date);[16] Pakistan (23 September, transmitting a 19 September statement by the President);[17] the USSR (21 September, transmitting a 19 September TASS statement);[19] and Viet Nam (23 September, transmitting a 22 September message from the President of the Council of State to the PLO Chairman).[20]

By his letter, the Austrian Foreign Minister also suggested that the Security Council dispatch an investigation commission to Beirut. In a response of 23 September,[2] the Council President stated that Council members were giving serious consideration to the possible dispatch of such a commission and that he had been in contact with the parties, in particular the Lebanese Government.

General Assembly action (September). The massacre of Palestinian and other civilians at Beirut was condemned by the General Assembly in a resolution adopted on 24 September, dealing with several aspects of the Israel-Lebanon situation and the Palestine question.[23] A paragraph urging the Security Council to investigate the circumstances and extent of the massacre, and to make public its findings as soon as possible, was adopted by a recorded vote, requested by the United States, of 146 to none. Under another provision, the Secretary-General was requested to prepare a photographic exhibit of the massacre for display in the visitors' hall at United Nations Headquarters.

Introducing the resolution, Senegal, as Chairman of the Committee on Palestinian rights, said the carnage at Sabra and Shatila—the direct outcome of the Israeli invasion of west Beirut in violation of the evacuation agreements to which PLO had been a party—opened a new chapter in the campaign of intimidation and terrorism against the Palestinians, whom Israel sought to stifle at all costs. Concerning the provision for an exhibit, Senegal noted that a similar one had been organized on the occasion of the shooting of South Africans at Sharpeville in 1960.

Though voting in favour, Bolivia, Denmark (also for Belgium, France, the Federal Republic of Germany, Italy, Luxembourg and the United Kingdom), Guatemala, Haiti, Norway, and Trinidad and Tobago had reservations with regard to the preparation of an exhibit; Haiti felt an exhibit would not contribute to peace and might inflame antagonisms. In Costa Rica's opinion, the massacre demonstrated the urgency of a Middle East solution, which could not be found as long as the Palestinians did not have a State. New Zealand also stressed the urgency of a settlement and called for immediate Israeli withdrawal. The Libyan Arab Jamahiriya stated that the resolution did not measure up to the tragedy in that it did not indicate Israel and the United States as responsible.

During the debate, many speakers expressed outrage at the massacre and condemned it as a crime against humanity. Pakistan, speaking for the non-Arab Asian States of the Movement of Non-Aligned Countries, stated that the massacre was the direct consequence of Israel's invasion of Lebanon and had rightly exposed Israel to world condemnation.

In the opinion of the German Democratic Republic, the mass murder of defenceless Palestinians was irrefutable proof that Israel was trying to solve the Palestinian question by genocide. The crime had not been the first of its kind, the PLO observer stated, and Kuwait, speaking for the Arab Group, added that it would not be the last; all the massacres had the aim of terrorizing the Palestinians to make them abandon their claims to their rights and their lands and to pave the way for the creation of Greater Israel.

China said that, by plotting the cold-blooded massacre, the Israeli authorities owed a new debt of blood to the Palestinians. Although perhaps not committed by the Israeli forces directly, Ghana stated on behalf of the African Group, authentic accounts had revealed their involvement and assistance. Denmark, speaking for the EC members, said it was clear that the massacre had taken place at a time when Israeli forces had assumed control in the area. Sweden said the Israeli Government had admitted that its Army had made arrangements for militia forces to enter the camps; therefore, it should not be difficult for the Israeli authorities to identify the perpetrators so that they could be brought to justice. The USSR stated that Israel's attempts to absolve itself could not conceal the truth that the killing had been planned in advance and carried out under the control of the Israeli Army; responsibility for the crime, however, lay also with those who had put arms in its hands. Israel was also held responsible by others, including Romania, Turkey and Yugoslavia (for the non-aligned countries in Europe). Thailand felt that Israel could not escape at least moral responsibility, as the atrocities had followed its violation of the cease-fire.

Israel, on the other hand, said the accusations were part of the onslaught against Israel for which the United Nations had become notorious, despite the unchallenged fact that the massacre had not been perpetrated by Israelis. The United Nations had not acted on reports of massacres in

Afghanistan, Iraq, Lebanon, the Syrian Arab Republic and Uganda; instead of heeding Israel's repeated calls to look into the true causes of Lebanon's agony, it had given the terrorist PLO and the Syrian occupation army a free hand in Lebanon and the opportunity to brutalize the country.

Kuwait was convinced that the massacre had been premeditated and planned since Israel's incursion into west Beirut; it quoted from a 22 September statement of an emergency meeting of Arab Foreign Ministers at Tunis, Tunisia, declaring that the United States shared legal and moral responsibility as it had provided the Lebanese Government and PLO with guarantees that it would protect the security of civilians and refugees as well as prevent the Israeli forces from entering west Beirut. A similar view was expressed by Cuba, which said the recent events in Beirut revealed Israel's true character, cynicism and disdain for basic human values. Those who had given Israel succour despite its transgressions, stated Ghana on behalf of the African Group, bore some of the responsibility for the tragedy because of their failure to discipline the warmongering Israeli Government.

The United States was charged with heavy responsibility by the Libyan Arab Jamahiriya, on the ground that it had imposed an agreement whereby the Palestinian resistance was evacuated from Beirut to open the way for the Israeli forces and the lackeys of zionism, such as Major Haddad and other isolationist militia. In Pakistan's opinion, it was ironical that all the resources of the United States could not prevent Israel from setting in motion a process which ended inevitably in the massacre. Albania said Israel and the United States had used every means to deceive world public opinion and to dissociate themselves from the crime; Israel had also benefited from the anti-Arab policies of the USSR, which formally declared its support for the victims but took advantage of events to serve its interests as a super-Power and to create the best possibilities for itself in the course of its rivalry and dealings with the United States.

Israel announced that on 24 September its Government had requested the President of its Supreme Court to head a commission to investigate various aspects of the massacre. Lebanon said it alone had the right to conduct an on-site investigation and had started proceedings to that end.

Many speakers, including Austria, the German Democratic Republic, Ghana, Mexico, the Niger, Pakistan, Romania, Sweden, Thailand and the PLO observer, called for an international investigation.

Urging a United Nations inquiry, Ghana said Israel's decision to investigate the incident at an appropriate time in the future must be rejected, while Pakistan felt that Israel's refusal to allow an impartial investigation amounted to an admission of its complicity. The Niger noted that the Organization of the Islamic Conference, on 26 August, had decided to ask the Assembly to establish an international committee to investigate the crimes perpetrated by Israeli forces during their invasion of Lebanon in order to bring the leaders of Israel to international justice as war criminals. Thailand declared its support for any investigation, either by individual Governments or by the United Nations, carried out with the consent of the Lebanese Government and the co-operation of all parties. The United States said it was ready to join with other Security Council members in support of any inquiry that Lebanon and Council members found constructive.

Punishment of the perpetrators of the massacre was called for by Austria, China, the German Democratic Republic, Thailand and PLO. The Libyan Arab Jamahiriya called for an international tribunal to bring Israeli Prime Minister Menachem Begin and Defence Minister Ariel Sharon to trial.

In that context, several countries, among them China and the German Democratic Republic, reiterated the call for sanctions. Cuba said all were duty-bound to ensure that the Security Council fulfilled its obligations under the Charter. In Pakistan's opinion, the United Nations had to act decisively to ensure the safety of the Palestine refugees in Lebanon. Ecuador declared its support for any initiative designed to reaffirm the inadmissibility of the acquisition of territory by force, to condemn the criminal killing of Palestinians in Beirut and to ensure the implementation of United Nations resolutions, and Ghana said it would lend support to any effort that might achieve a guarantee against the repetition of such genocide. The Libyan Arab Jamahiriya held it regrettable that the Security Council had merely recommended the dispatch of observers instead of adopting measures to punish the aggressor. Yugoslavia felt that Council action was indispensable.

Bolivia, on the other hand, thought that an impartial inquiry should determine the scope of responsibility for the massacre before sanctions could be considered.

Attainment of a peace based on total Israeli withdrawal and full exercise of Palestinian rights was considered all the more urgent by several others, among them Cuba, the German Democratic Republic, Kuwait and Romania. The EC members, as stated by Denmark, considered it more than ever incumbent to work towards a Middle East settlement which would take account of all aspects of the problem, including Palestinian rights. More than ever, Ecuador believed, the possibility of further such crimes existed and there could be no peace and security in the Middle East until the Palestinian question was resolved. Ghana considered it high time for the United Nations not only to end the harassment and massacres of Palestinians but also to create a homeland for them. Malta, the Rapporteur of the Committee on Palestinian rights, was convinced that if Palestinian rights had been recognized, this and other tragedies would have been prevented.

The Niger, speaking for the Organization of the Islamic Conference, said Israel's attempts to decimate PLO and to annihilate the Palestinians had further complicated the Palestinian problem. Thailand held it imperative that the quest for peace go forward to ensure strict observance of the rights of all States and of Palestinian rights. Turkey called for a redemption through the realization of the Palestinian national cause.

The PLO observer said it was clear that the Palestinian armed presence in southern Lebanon had been a necessity, as their absence had facilitated the genocide of Palestinian civilians; the Security Council, having identified the crime by condemning it, must also identify the criminals who planned and perpetrated it and take effective measures against them.

Communications (October-December). On 22 October,[14] the Libyan Arab Jamahiriya transmitted a letter of the same date from the PLO observer annexing a petition dated 24 September from Palestinian women in the territories occupied by Israel; they called on the United Nations to put an end to the successive massacres of Palestinians, to work for Israeli withdrawal from Lebanon and to take action to grant the Palestinians their right to establish their own independent State under PLO leadership.

On 7 December,[5] Jordan transmitted what it identified as the verbatim record of an interview with two correspondents regarding the massacre at the Sabra and Shatila refugee camps on 18 September; the transcript showed, Jordan said in its covering letter, that the massacre had been planned, commanded and executed by the overall command of the Israeli regular armed forces.

General Assembly action (December). The massacre was again strongly condemned by the General Assembly on 3 December in its resolution on the self-determination of peoples[24] as well as in a resolution of 16 December.[25] By the latter, the Assembly also resolved that the massacre was an act of genocide.

The 16 December resolution was adopted by 123 votes to none, with 22 abstentions. Paragraph 1 was adopted by 145 votes to none, while paragraph 2 was adopted by 98 votes to 19, with 23 abstentions. All votes were recorded. The text was introduced by Cuba on behalf of 16 nations.

Abstaining on the resolution as a whole but voting against paragraph 2, the United States said it was a serious and reckless misuse of language to label the massacre genocide, as defined in the Convention on the Prevention and Punishment of the Crime of Genocide.[27] Sweden also found the assertion incorrect. Canada and Denmark, the latter for the EC members, questioned the Assembly's competence to determine whether the massacre had been genocide. Voting in favour of paragraph 1 and abstaining on the text as a whole, Israel opposed paragraph 2 because of irresponsible and inaccurate terminology bound to compromise United Nations credibility.

Though voting for the resolution, Finland voted against paragraph 2, voicing serious doubts on legal and factual grounds about the applicability of the term "genocide"; it regretted that, by the introduction of that element, the Assembly had been prevented from unanimously expressing outrage and condemnation.

Among those voting in favour of the resolution but abstaining on paragraph 2, the Philippines said it was not certain that the massacre was an act of genocide in accordance with the Convention. Singapore, noting that genocide was defined by the Convention to mean an act intended to destroy a national, ethnic, racial or religious group, regretted the tendency in the Assembly to use casual language when referring to issues with a precise legal definition; it thought the determination should be left to the appropriate legal body. Spain stated that, although the text might raise legal problems, it wished through its affirmative vote to reiterate its outrage and condemnation. The Assembly's competence to determine whether there had been an act of genocide was doubted by Turkey. Jamaica, which voted for the resolution but did not take part in the vote on paragraph 2, doubted the appropriateness of the language.

During the debates on the Middle East situation and the Palestine question which preceded the adoption of this resolution, Austria said it had been shocked by the atrocities because they had been committed against refugees, the most helpless of all people and most in need of protection. Bhutan said those responsible for the massacre must be brought to justice once the investigations were completed.

In the view of Malaysia, Israel had collaborated with Phalangist militias in the massacre. Qatar said the action had been conducted in the guise of Phalangist reprisals. China stated that Israel had plotted the massacre and Nigeria that it had aided and abetted the crime, while Tunisia said Israeli occupiers had organized it.

Japan urged the parties, in order to prevent the recurrence of such outrageous acts, to ensure the life and security of civilians, including Palestinians.

The massacre was condemned or deplored by most countries, among them Cyprus and Poland. The Gambia and others held Israel, as the occupying Power, largely responsible for the act.

Cuba said the act was equalled only by Nazi barbarism and far exceeded all previous Israeli crimes. A similar view was expressed by Djibouti, the USSR and others. Democratic Yemen and India said the conscience of humanity had been shaken by the massacre, while Albania charged that Governments that could have acted to stay the hands of the assassins did not even lift a finger. Iraq likened it to the 1948 massacre at Deir Yassin outside Jerusalem, stating that both had been planned to disperse Palestinians and enable the Zionists to acquire Palestinian land. Kuwait, stating that Israel had planned and perpetrated the massacre, called for treatment of the perpetrators as war criminals. Mauritania characterized the killings as an act of genocide. In Mongolia's opinion, the massacre was the culmination of genocide, which had been elevated to Israeli State policy.

The Syrian Arab Republic held that by committing its act of genocide, Israel had violated the Geneva Conventions, which had been adopted to prevent a repetition of Nazi crimes. PLO held it regrettable that months after the massacre the criminals had yet to be punished and were planning new massacres.

In Bulgaria's view, the massacre demonstrated that Israel was implementing a programme of physical extermination of the Palestinians and of a "final solution" to the Palestinian question. A similar position was held by the United Arab Emirates. Never had the racist character of zionism appeared in such undisguised inhuman form, the Ukrainian SSR said. The Congo stated that the crimes at Sabra and Shatila had truly conveyed the extent of Israel's cynicism.

Pakistan said the martyrdom of thousands of Palestinians in the camps and other refugee settlements had convinced the world as never before of the justice of the Palestinian cause. The mass murder, Djibouti said, had given the Palestinian question yet another dimension, and international support for and solidarity with the Palestinians had increased tremendously. The events since the massacre, Qatar said, had demonstrated that PLO was equal to its responsibilities and that the other side was ineffectual and unable to implement its pledge to protect the Palestinian refugees in Lebanon. In the opinion of Democratic Yemen, the Palestinians, under PLO leadership, emerged more resolved than ever to pursue the struggle for their rights.

Cuba held the United States responsible for the genocide against Palestine refugees because it had prevented the Security Council from sending United Nations forces to Beirut and acting against

Israel, and had facilitated the entry of Israeli forces into west Beirut and the refugee camps by withdrawing the multinational buffer force two weeks earlier than had been agreed.

Letters and note verbale (nv).
[1]Committee on Palestinian rights Chairman: 20 Sep., A/37/462-S/15410.
[2]SC President: 23 Sep., S/15428.
Jordan: [3]18 Sep., S/15399; [4]20 Sep., A/37/463-S/15411; [5]7 Dec., A/37/706-S/15514.
Others: [6]Austria: 21 Sep., S/15416. [7]China: 22 Sep., A/37/483-S/15430. [8]Cuba: 20 Sep., A/37/470-S/15418. [9]Egypt: 20 Sep., A/37/464-S/15412. [10]France: 20 Sep., S/15407. [11]Greece: 18 Sep., S/15401. [12]Guyana: 23 Sep., A/37/486-S/15433. [13]Jamaica: 23 Sep., A/37/487-S/15434. [14]Libyan Arab Jamahiriya: 22 Oct., A/37/572. [15]Madagascar: 20 Sep., A/37/465-S/15413. [16]Mongolia: 22 Sep., A/37/480. [17]Pakistan: 23 Sep., A/37/502-S/15438. [18]Suriname: 20 Sep., S/15406 *(nv).* [19]USSR: 21 Sep., A/37/471-S/15419. [20]Viet Nam: 23 Sep., A/37/489.
Reports. S-G, [21]S/15400, [22]S/15408 & Add.1,2.
Resolutions (1982). GA: [23]ES-7/9, 24 Sep.; [24]37/43, para. 20, 3 Dec.; [25]37/123 D, 16 Dec., text following. SC: [26]521(1982), paras. 1-5, 19 Sep.
Resolution (prior). [27]GA: 260 A (III), annex, 9 Dec. 1948 (YUN 1948-49, p. 959).
Meeting records. GA: A/37/PV.92-96, *108* (6-16 Dec.).

General Assembly resolution 37/123 D

16 December 1982   Meeting 108   123-0-22 (recorded vote)

16-nation draft (A/37/L.52 and Add.1); agenda item 34.

Sponsors: Bangladesh, Comoros, Cuba, Guyana, India, Indonesia, Lao People's Democratic Republic, Madagascar, Malaysia, Mali, Mongolia, Nigeria, Pakistan, Viet Nam, Yemen, Yugoslavia.

The General Assembly,
Recalling its resolution 95(I) of 11 December 1946,
Recalling also its resolution 96(I) of 11 December 1946, in which it, *inter alia,* affirmed that genocide is a crime under international law which the civilized world condemns, and for the commission of which principals and accomplices—whether private individuals, public officials or statesmen, and whether the crime is committed on religious, racial, political or any other grounds—are punishable,
Referring to the provisions of the Convention on the Prevention and Punishment of the Crime of Genocide, adopted by the General Assembly on 9 December 1948,
Recalling the relevant provisions of the Geneva Convention relative to the Protection of Civilian Persons in Time of War, of 12 August 1949,
Appalled at the large-scale massacre of Palestinian civilians in the Sabra and Shatila refugee camps situated at Beirut,
Recognizing the universal outrage and condemnation of that massacre,
Recalling its resolution ES-7/9 of 24 September 1982,
1.   *Condemns* in the strongest terms the large-scale massacre of Palestinian civilians in the Sabra and Shatila refugee camps;
2.   *Resolves* that the massacre was an act of genocide.

Recorded vote in Assembly as follows:

In favour: Afghanistan, Albania, Algeria, Angola, Argentina, Austria, Bahamas, Bahrain, Bangladesh, Belize, Benin, Bhutan, Bolivia, Botswana, Brazil, Bulgaria, Burma, Burundi, Byelorussian SSR, Cape Verde, Central African Republic, Chad, Chile, China, Colombia, Comoros, Congo, Costa Rica, Cuba, Cyprus, Czechoslovakia, Democratic Kampuchea, Democratic Yemen, Djibouti, Ecuador, Egypt, El Salvador, Ethiopia, Fiji, Finland, Gabon, Gambia, German Democratic Republic, Ghana, Greece, Grenada, Guatemala, Guinea, Guinea-Bissau, Guyana, Honduras, Hungary, India, Indonesia, Iran, Iraq, Jamaica, Japan, Jordan, Kenya, Kuwait, Lao People's Democratic Republic, Lesotho, Liberia, Libyan Arab Jamahiriya, Madagascar, Malawi, Malaysia, Maldives, Mali, Malta, Mauritania, Mauritius, Mexico, Mongolia, Morocco, Mozambique, Nepal, Nicaragua, Nigeria, Oman, Pakistan, Panama, Paraguay, Peru, Philippines, Poland, Qatar, Romania, Rwanda, Samoa, Sao Tome and Principe, Saudi Arabia, Senegal, Seychelles, Sierra Leone, Singapore, Somalia, Spain, Sri Lanka, Sudan, Suriname, Syrian Arab Republic, Thailand, Togo, Trinidad and Tobago, Tunisia, Turkey, Uganda, Ukrainian SSR, USSR, United Arab Emirates, United Republic of Cameroon, United Republic of Tanzania, Upper Volta, Uruguay, Vanuatu, Venezuela, Viet Nam, Yemen, Yugoslavia, Zaire, Zambia.

Against: None.
Abstaining: Australia, Barbados, Belgium, Canada, Denmark, Dominican Republic, France, Germany, Federal Republic of, Iceland, Ireland, Israel, Italy, Ivory Coast, Luxembourg, Netherlands, New Zealand, Norway, Papua New Guinea, Portugal, Sweden, United Kingdom, United States.

International Day of Innocent Children Victims of Aggression

Stating that it was appalled by the great number of innocent Palestinian and Lebanese children victims of Israel's acts of aggression, the General Assembly, by a resolution of 19 August 1982, decided to commemorate 4 June each year as the International Day of Innocent Children Victims of Aggression.[1]

The text, introduced by Kuwait on behalf of 35 nations, was adopted at the Assembly's seventh emergency special session on the Palestine question by a roll-call vote, requested by Israel, of 102 to 2, with 34 abstentions. The sponsors deleted a paragraph by which the Assembly would have requested the Secretary-General to display at United Nations Headquarters a permanent commemorative plaque dedicated to the Palestinian and Lebanese child victims.

Proposing the display of such a plaque, Cuba said a memento of that nature would be as moving and instructive to visitors as the impression caused today by a visit to Auschwitz or Buchenwald.

Israel rejected the resolution as perverted and said if its logic had been followed to its conclusion, the United Nations would be studded with plaques commemorating numerous instances around the world in which, in contradistinction to Israel's operation in Lebanon, children had been the deliberate targets of premeditated murder and genocidal policies.

Abstaining, Sweden considered the resolution to be selective by commemorating children of only certain nationalities and victims of violence inflicted by one side only. Bolivia, Canada, Colombia and Honduras abstained on similar grounds. Austria felt that the fate suffered by victims in other wars and conflicts should not be forgotten; in addition, it had doubts as to the manner in which the resolution should be implemented.

Haiti felt that such an initiative was hardly likely to serve the cause of peace. Burma cited similar reasons for its abstention. Chile did not participate in the vote as it considered that the resolution established a discriminatory precedent inconsistent with mediation efforts and the search for a peaceful settlement.

Norway did not believe that the measures provided for represented the most appropriate way to commemorate the victims of war; a better way to manifest sympathy and sorrow would be to donate funds to relief work. A similar opinion was expressed by Denmark on behalf of the EC and by Ireland. In New Zealand's opinion, the resolution ignored elements of the currently interrelated fates of Lebanese and Palestinians and had a tendency towards propaganda. Reservations were also voiced by Fiji.

Spain voted in favour because it felt that the resolution was moderate and realistic and put forward a praiseworthy idea. Support of the text was also expressed by others, including Panama, Singapore and Turkey, the last adding that it sympathized with all innocent victims—men, women and children.

Iran, on the other hand, regarded the resolution as very weak and devoid of substance.

Resolution (1982). [1]GA: ES-7/8, 19 Aug., text following.
Meeting records. GA: A/ES-7/PV.25-29, 30, 31 (16-19 Aug.).

General Assembly resolution ES-7/8

19 August 1982   Meeting 31   102-2-34 (roll-call vote)

35-nation draft (A/ES-7/L.7/Rev.1); agenda item 5.

Sponsors: Afghanistan, Algeria, Bahrain, Bangladesh, Benin, Bulgaria, Cape Verde, Cuba, Democratic Yemen, Djibouti, Gambia, Grenada, Guyana, Iraq, Jordan, Kuwait, Lao People's Democratic Republic, Libyan Arab Jamahiriya, Madagascar, Maldives, Mali, Mauritania, Morocco, Nigeria, Oman, Pakistan, Qatar, Saudi Arabia, Somalia, Sudan, Syrian Arab Republic, Tunisia, Uganda, United Arab Emirates, Yemen.

International Day of Innocent Children Victims of Aggression

The General Assembly,

Having considered the question of Palestine at its resumed seventh emergency special session,

Appalled by the great number of innocent Palestinian and Lebanese children victims of Israel's acts of aggression,

Decides to commemorate 4 June of each year as the International Day of Innocent Children Victims of Aggression.

Recorded vote in Assembly as follows:

In favour: Afghanistan, Albania, Algeria, Angola, Argentina, Bahamas, Bahrain, Bangladesh, Barbados, Benin, Bhutan, Botswana, Brazil, Bulgaria, Burundi, Byelorussian SSR, Cape Verde, Chad, China, Congo, Cuba, Cyprus, Czechoslovakia, Democratic Kampuchea, Democratic Yemen, Djibouti, Ecuador, Egypt, Ethiopia, Gabon, Gambia, German Democratic Republic, Ghana, Greece, Grenada, Guinea, Guinea-Bissau, Guyana, Hungary, India, Indonesia, Iran, Iraq, Jamaica, Jordan, Kenya, Kuwait, Lao People's Democratic Republic, Lebanon, Lesotho, Libyan Arab Jamahiriya, Madagascar, Malaysia, Maldives, Mali, Malta, Mauritania, Mauritius, Mexico, Mongolia, Morocco, Mozambique, Nepal, Nicaragua, Niger, Nigeria, Oman, Pakistan, Panama, Peru, Philippines, Poland, Qatar, Romania, Rwanda, Sao Tome and Principe, Saudi Arabia, Senegal, Seychelles, Sierra Leone, Singapore, Somalia, Spain, Sri Lanka, Sudan, Syrian Arab Republic, Thailand, Trinidad and Tobago, Tunisia, Turkey, Uganda, Ukrainian SSR, USSR, United Arab Emirates, United Republic of Cameroon, United Republic of Tanzania, Venezuela, Viet Nam, Yemen, Yugoslavia, Zambia, Zimbabwe.

Against: Israel, United States.

Abstaining: Australia, Austria, Belgium, Bolivia, Burma, Canada, Colombia, Denmark, Dominican Republic, El Salvador, Fiji, Finland, France, Germany, Federal Republic of, Haiti, Honduras, Iceland, Ireland, Italy, Japan, Liberia, Luxembourg, Malawi, Netherlands, New Zealand, Norway, Paraguay, Portugal, Samoa, Swaziland, Sweden, United Kingdom, Uruguay, Zaire.

Aging persons in Lebanon

Stating that the Israeli aggression against Lebanese and Palestinians had again brought to international attention the vulnerability of civilians and in particular the elderly, the World Assembly on Aging, on 5 August 1982,[1] condemned military aggression against civilian areas inhabited by Lebanese and Palestinian families as well as the use of mass destruction weapons such as cluster bombs which caused indiscriminate casualties among innocent victims, particularly the elderly. The Assembly urged Member States to ensure the protection of and to safeguard all civilians, in particular the elderly, during periods of tension and armed conflict, and it requested the General Assembly to declare institutions for the elderly as "immune protected areas" in armed conflict. It requested the Secretary-General to call on Israel to permit Arab refugees of 60 years and older to rejoin immediately their extended and dispersed families in the occupied Arab territories.

This resolution was adopted by a roll-call vote of 73 to 2 (Israel, United States), with 26 abstentions.

Israel rejected the resolution as unjust, based on untruth and harmful for the cause of the elderly by selecting only elderly refugees in Lebanon while discriminating against those suffering in other areas of conflict.

Resolution (1982). [1]World Assembly on Aging (report, A/CONF.113/31): 1, 5 Aug.

Protection of Palestinian cultural property

By a resolution of 16 December 1982,[1] the General Assembly condemned acts of plundering the Palestinian cultural heritage such as the seizure by the Israeli army, during the occupation of Beirut, of archives and documents on Palestinian history and culture. The Assembly called on Israel to make full restitution, through the United Nations Educational, Scientific and Cultural Organization (UNESCO), of all cultural property belonging to Palestinian institutions, including material removed from the Palestine Research Centre.

The revised text was adopted by a recorded vote of 138 to 1, with 4 abstentions. It was introduced by Cuba on behalf of 17 nations.

Opposing the resolution, Israel said the Centre had engaged not merely in the production of anti-Israel propaganda but also in the collection of operational intelligence data, including personal files of high-ranking Israeli officers, and lists of gas stations, bridges and water and electricity installations in Israel, for use by terrorist groups against Israel and Jewish civilian targets. Genuine research material would be returned to the Government of Lebanon in due course.

Abstaining, the United States considered a condemnation premature until the full facts surrounding the charges were known; however, it supported international instruments on the protection of persons and property in occupied territories.

Explaining the positive votes of the EC members, Denmark said they supported the general thrust, if not all the specific wording used; noting that UNESCO had dealt extensively with the matter and that a commission had been established to investigate, they urged Israel to return the cultural and historical material involved. Malta said its affirmative vote did not necessarily imply full agreement with every provision.

Resolution (1982). [1]GA: 37/123 B, 16 Dec., text following. *Meeting records.* GA: A/37/PV.92-96, *108* (6-16 Dec.).

General Assembly resolution 37/123 B

16 December 1982   Meeting 108   138-1-4 (recorded vote)
17-nation draft (A/37/L.50/Rev.1); agenda item 34.

Sponsors: Bangladesh, Comoros, Cuba, Guyana, India, Indonesia, Lao People's Democratic Republic, Madagascar, Malaysia, Mali, Mongolia, Nigeria, Pakistan, Sri Lanka, Viet Nam, Yemen, Yugoslavia.

The General Assembly,

Recalling the relevant provisions of the Universal Declaration of Human Rights,

Recalling also the Constitution of the United Nations Educational, Scientific and Cultural Organization and all other relevant international instruments concerning the right to cultural identity in all its forms,

Having learned that the Israeli army, during its occupation of Beirut, seized and took away the archives and documents of every kind concerning Palestinian history and culture, including cultural articles belonging to Palestinian institutions—in particular the Palestine Research Centre—archives, documents, manuscripts and materials such as film documents, literary works by major authors, paintings, *objets d'art* and works of folklore, research works and so forth, serving as a foundation for the history, culture, national awareness, unity and solidarity of the Palestinian people,

1. *Condemns* those acts of plundering the Palestinian cultural heritage;

2. *Calls upon* the Government of Israel to make full restitution, through the United Nations Educational, Scientific and Cultural Organization, of all the cultural property belonging to Palestinian institutions, including the archives and documents removed from the Palestine Research Centre and arbitrarily seized by the Israeli forces.

Recorded vote in Assembly as follows:

In favour: Afghanistan, Albania, Algeria, Angola, Argentina, Australia, Austria, Bahamas, Bahrain, Bangladesh, Barbados, Belgium, Belize, Benin, Bhutan, Bolivia, Botswana, Brazil, Bulgaria, Burma, Burundi, Byelorussian SSR, Canada, Cape Verde, Central African Republic, Chad, Chile, China, Colombia, Comoros, Congo, Costa Rica, Cuba, Cyprus, Czechoslovakia, Democratic Kampuchea, Democratic Yemen, Denmark, Djibouti, Ecuador, Egypt, Ethiopia, Fiji, Finland, France, Gabon, Gambia, German Democratic Republic, Germany, Federal Republic of, Ghana, Greece, Grenada, Guinea, Guinea-Bissau, Guyana, Honduras, Hungary, Iceland, India, Indonesia, Iran, Iraq, Ireland, Italy, Ivory Coast, Jamaica, Japan, Jordan, Kenya, Kuwait, Lao People's Democratic Republic, Lebanon, Lesotho, Liberia, Libyan Arab Jamahiriya, Luxembourg, Madagascar, Malaysia, Maldives, Mali, Malta, Mauritania, Mauritius, Mexico, Mongolia, Morocco, Mozambique, Nepal, Netherlands, New Zealand, Nicaragua, Nigeria, Norway, Oman, Pakistan, Panama, Paraguay, Peru, Philippines, Poland, Portugal, Qatar, Romania, Rwanda, Samoa, Sao Tome and Principe, Saudi Arabia, Senegal, Seychelles, Sierra Leone, Singapore, Somalia, Spain, Sri Lanka, Sudan, Suriname, Sweden, Syrian Arab Republic, Thailand, Togo, Trinidad and Tobago, Tunisia, Turkey, Uganda, Ukrainian SSR, USSR, United Arab Emirates, United Kingdom, United Republic of Cameroon, United Republic of Tanzania, Upper Volta, Uruguay, Venezuela, Viet Nam, Yemen, Yugoslavia, Zaire, Zambia.

Against: Israel.

Abstaining: Dominican Republic, Malawi, Papua New Guinea, United States.

UN Interim Force in Lebanon

In southern Lebanon north of the border with Israel, where the United Nations Interim Force in Lebanon (UNIFIL) had been stationed since 1978,[1] the first five months of 1982 saw a period of relative quiet punctuated by a number of incidents in which UNIFIL was involved with local armed forces. Intense efforts were made to maintain and restore the cease-fire in effect since July 1981.[2]

During that period, UNIFIL continued to contend with two main groupings of forces, identified in the Secretary-General's reports to the Security Council as follows: armed elements, mainly PLO and the Lebanese National Movement, whose attempts to establish positions in the UNIFIL area were resisted by the Force; and *de facto* forces,

which were Christian militias headed by Major Saad Haddad and associated militias, supported and supplied by Israel and controlling an enclave on the Lebanese side of the border. In that enclave, restrictions of movement on UNIFIL personnel continued to limit the Force's operational capability.

The situation changed radically on 4 June with Israel's military move into Lebanon (see above, under ARMED CONFLICT). Thereafter, the Force's mandate, previously renewed at six-month intervals, was extended by the Security Council in June and August for two-month periods and in October for three months. During and after the cease-fire in Lebanon, UNIFIL was also authorized, as an interim task, to extend protection and humanitarian assistance to the civilian population in its area.

As requested by Lebanon and recommended by the Secretary-General, the Council approved in February an increase in the Force's strength from 6,000 to approximately 7,000 troops. The Force, with contingents from 11 nations as of October 1982, continued to be financed by assessments on United Nations Members in an amount of $181 million for the year ended 18 December.

Yearbook references. [1]1978, p. 303; [2]1981, p. 289.

Activities

During the first five months of 1982, UNIFIL continued to supervise the cease-fire in southern Lebanon and to restore it after hostile acts occurred (see above, under ARMED CONFLICT). (According to its original mandate, set out by the Security Council in 1978,[8] UNIFIL was to confirm the withdrawal of Israeli forces from Lebanese territory, restore international peace and security, and assist the Lebanese Government in ensuring the return of its authority.)

In a special report of 16 February to the Security Council,[1] the Secretary-General stated that the cease-fire had been maintained but that the situation had remained extremely volatile. By another special report of 25 April,[2] he informed the Council that the cease-fire had generally held but that unresolved tensions had led to the danger of widespread hostilities. That situation was pointed up by Israeli air strikes into Lebanon on 21 April.

On 10 June,[3] the Secretary-General reported that on 9 May Israeli aircraft again had attacked targets in Lebanon. However, intense efforts continued to be made to maintain the cease-fire and to restore it after hostile acts. The relative quiet in the UNIFIL area and the combined efforts of the Lebanese Government, UNIFIL and other international agencies had facilitated economic and social progress. The Force had continued to hold regular meetings with the Governor of South Lebanon and the President of the Council for the

South, with a view to co-ordinating approaches to a wide range of economic, social and humanitarian matters. It had supported the implementation of projects financed by the Lebanese Council for Development and Reconstruction and by the United Nations Children's Fund by providing mainly logistical and security assistance.

In two addenda to his report, dated 11 and 14 June, the Secretary-General described increased hostilities starting on 4 June with Israeli air strikes and leading up to the massive movement of Israeli troops across the border, radically altering the circumstances in which UNIFIL functioned. Following the start of this operation, the contingents followed the Secretary-General's instructions to continue to man their positions and to provide protection and humanitarian assistance to the local population. They had attempted to prevent the entry and advance of the Israeli soldiers, but the overwhelming strength and weight of the Israeli forces had precluded the possibility of stopping them and UNIFIL positions in the line of the invasion had been thus overrun or bypassed. By 7 June, Israeli forces had reached positions north of the UNIFIL area of deployment.

At the end of June, a new armed group, locally recruited but equipped and controlled by the Israeli forces, had appeared in parts of the UNIFIL area. With a view to protecting the civilian population, UNIFIL had taken action to contain their activities. The Force also had continued to resist attempts by the *de facto* forces to operate in the UNIFIL area of deployment, although in some instances they had been able to enter that area with the assistance of the Israeli forces.

These developments were described in a report of 13 August,[4] in which the Secretary-General also stated that, despite difficulties, the Force had extended protection and humanitarian assistance to the civilians in its area, as called for by the Security Council on 18 June,[7] and had co-operated in humanitarian efforts of the United Nations and the International Committee of the Red Cross.

In a report of 14 October,[5] the Secretary-General observed that the UNIFIL area had remained generally quiet and the presence and activities of Israeli forces in the area had significantly decreased. However, UNIFIL had continued to resist attempts of the *de facto* forces to enter its area; in a few instances those forces had been able to operate within the UNIFIL area in combined patrols with, or under the escort of, Israeli forces. By June 1982, the population in the UNIFIL area of deployment had increased to more than a quarter of a million and had subsequently risen by approximately 150,000. Humanitarian assistance continued to be extended to the population in the area, including displaced persons from the north who had sought temporary refuge from the hostilities.

As reported by the Secretary-General in early 1983,[6] the presence and activities of the Israeli forces in the UNIFIL area had been generally limited during November and December 1982. Commencing on 19 October and lasting for approximately a month, a series of incidents involving the *de facto* forces had taken place in the Norwegian battalion area, including the kidnapping of a soldier for 10 hours, hijacking of vehicles, removal of equipment and firing close to UNIFIL positions. Except for those incidents, attempts of the *de facto* forces to operate in the UNIFIL area had remained limited, although on a number of occasions members of those forces had been able to enter the area together with Israeli military personnel.

Reports. S-G, [1]S/14869, [2]S/14996, [3]S/15194 & Add.1,2, [4]S/15357, [5]S/15455 & Corr.1, [6]S/15557.
Resolution (1982). [7]SC: 511(1982), 18 June.
Resolution (prior). [8]SC: 425(1978), 19 Mar. 1978 (YUN 1978, p. 312).

Composition

As at 14 October 1982, the composition of UNIFIL was as follows:

Infantry battalions	
Fiji	629
France	126
Ghana	558
Ireland	671
Nepal	462
Netherlands	810
Nigeria	696
Norway	648
Senegal	561
Headquarters camp command	
Ghana	140
Ireland	51
Logistic units	
France	775
Italy	40
Norway	189
Sweden	144
	6,500

SOURCE: S-G report, S/15455.

In addition, UNIFIL was assisted by 72 military observers of the United Nations Truce Supervision Organization. The number of observers, which had been temporarily reduced by the transfer of 25 of them to Observer Group Beirut on 20 September (see above, under CEASE FIRE), was brought back up to strength on 20 December.

By a resolution of 25 February,[7] the Security Council approved an immediate increase in the Force's strength from 6,000 to approximately 7,000 troops, as recommended by the Secretary-General in a 16 February report.[5]

By a letter of 1 March to the Council President,[3] the Secretary-General declared his intention to request France to provide an infantry battalion (approximately 600 men); to request other troop-contributors, whose contingents needed to be strengthened, to increase their numbers; and to request additions to the existing logistic and maintenance units.

The Council President responded on 11 March[1] that the Council members had considered the matter in informal consultations from 4 to 10 March and agreed with the Secretary-General's proposals. The President added that the USSR had emphasized the importance of abiding by the principle of equitable geographical representation in selecting contingents of the Force, and that the United Kingdom had emphasized the importance of the contingents being selected in consultation with the Council and with the parties concerned, bearing in mind the principle of equitable geographical representation.

In a special report of 25 April,[6] the Secretary-General informed the Council that Ghana, Ireland, Nepal and Norway had agreed to increase their contingents by 221, 70, 30 and 20 men, respectively, and that France had agreed in principle with his request for a 600-man battalion.

At France's request, 482 men of the French battalion were temporarily released on 29 September from UNIFIL and were incorporated into the French contingent of the multinational force in Beirut.

On 27 October, the Secretary-General informed the Council President that Nepal had signified its inability to continue its participation in UNIFIL (a 462-man battalion) beyond the mandate ended 19 October and that Finland had informed him that it was willing to provide a replacement contingent of equivalent strength.[4] The agreement of the Council members was expressed by the President in a letter of 28 October.[2]

The Nepalese battalion completed its withdrawal by 18 November, while the new Finnish battalion completed its deployment on 11 December.

On 2 November, Nigeria informed the Secretary-General that it would discontinue its participation in UNIFIL after expiration of the current mandate on 19 January 1983. During the Assembly debate on the Middle East situation, Nigeria explained that its decision had been made in protest against the flagrant manner in which Israeli forces had invaded Lebanon and overrun United Nations forces.

Between 11 December 1981 and 14 October 1982, 13 UNIFIL members died, including four as a result of firing and mine explosions. The number of members of the Force that had died since its establishment in 1978 was 83, of which 37 had been killed by firing or mine explosions.

Letters. SC President: [1]11 Mar., S/14900; [2]28 Oct., S/15469.
S-G: [3]1 Mar., S/14899; [4]27 Oct., S/15468.
Reports. S-G, [5]S/14869, [6]S/14996 & Corr.1.
Resolution (1982). [7]SC: 501(1982), para. 2, 25 Feb.

Continuation

In 1982, at the request of Lebanon and on the recommendation of the Secretary-General, the Security Council extended the mandate of UNIFIL twice for two months, on 18 June[3] and 17 August,[4] and on 18 October for three months, until 19 January 1983.[5]

Reporting to the Council on 13 August,[1] before the second 1982 extension of the mandate, the Secretary-General stated that the presence of the Force had provided an important stabilizing and moderating influence in southern Lebanon during the difficult weeks after the start of the Israeli military operation. In a report of 14 October,[2] prior to the third extension, he expressed the conviction that the withdrawal of UNIFIL under the current circumstances would have highly undesirable consequences and would be a serious blow to the early restoration of the effective authority of the Lebanese Government in southern Lebanon, as the Lebanese battalion and gendarmes stationed in the UNIFIL area were not in a position to assume full control.

Speaking during the Assembly debate on the Middle East situation, Finland said that, while the process towards a negotiated settlement was evolving, UNIFIL continued to have a vital role in all efforts to normalize the situation in Lebanon.

Reports. SG, [1]S/15357, [2]S/15455.
Resolutions (1982). SC: [3]511(1982), 18 June; [4]519(1982), 17 Aug.; [5]523(1982), 18 Oct..

Financing

General Assembly action (March). By a resolution of 19 March 1982,[6] the General Assembly authorized additional commitments for UNIFIL in an amount not to exceed $9,825,000 gross ($9,822,000 net of staff assessment) for the period from 25 February to 18 June, and at a monthly rate not to exceed $1,913,000 gross ($1,910,333 net) for the period from 19 June to 18 December, should the Council decide to continue the Force beyond the six months authorized in December 1981. These amounts were to finance the increase in UNIFIL strength from 6,000 to approximately 7,000 troops authorized by the Council on 25 February 1982. They were in addition to the monthly rate of $13,316,666 gross ($13,177,500 net) authorized by the Assembly in December 1981 to finance UNIFIL for the period from 19 December 1981 to 18 December 1982.[9]

The resolution authorizing the increase was adopted by a recorded vote of 90 to 12, with 3 abstentions, following its approval by the Fifth (Administrative and Budgetary) Committee on 18 March by a recorded vote of 65 to 9, with 1 abstention. The Secretary-General, in a note of 3 March,[1] had requested the Assembly to consider the matter at its resumed thirty-sixth session, held to consider a few items left unfinished at the close of 1981.

The increase amounted to $21,303,000 gross ($21,284,000 net) for the period from 25 February to 18 December 1982 (the end of the UNIFIL financial year). As detailed in a March report by the Secretary-General on the cost estimates for additional troops,[4] some $8.6 million was needed for pay and allowances for troops at the standard rate of $950 per man-month plus a supplementary $280 per man-month for a limited number of specialists. Other funds were needed for such items as construction and maintenance of premises and for purchase of transportation. and other equipment.

The total amount authorized was $1 million less than the Secretary-General had estimated. The Assembly approved the lower figure on the recommendation of the Advisory Committee on Administrative and Budgetary Questions (ACABQ), which believed that savings could be achieved particularly in regard to rental, maintenance, utilities, construction of premises, and the purchase of transportation and other equipment.[2] Accordingly, $400,000 was cut from the estimate for the period ending 18 June and $600,000 from the estimate for the period from 19 June to 18 December.

Introducing the 17-nation draft on funding for the additional troops, Sweden said Fifth Committee members were aware not only of the unique contribution of peace-keeping operations to the preservation of peace and security, but also of the budget difficulties caused in large part by the withholding of assessed contributions by certain States.

General Assembly action (December). By a resolution of 17 December 1982,[7] the Assembly appropriated a total of $181,102,992 gross ($179,413,998 net) for UNIFIL for the period 19 December 1981 to 18 December 1982. This was the sum of four separate figures approved by the Assembly, covering three of the UNIFIL mandate periods approved by the Security Council and the first part of a fourth period: $89,724,996 gross ($88,887,000 net) for 19 December 1981 to 18 June 1982, and $30,459,332 gross ($30,175,666 net) each for the periods from 19 June to 18 August 1982, 19 August to 18 October and 19 October to 18 December. For UNIFIL operation for the month from 19 December 1982 to the expiry of its then current mandate on 18 January 1983, the Secretary-General was authorized to enter into commitments in an amount not to exceed $15,229,666 gross ($15,087,833 net). For the period from 19 January to 18 December 1983, he was authorized to enter into commitments at that monthly rate, should the Council continue the Force's mandate and subject to prior ACABQ concurrence for each mandate period.

Under other provisions, the Assembly apportioned the expenses for the Force among all Mem-

ber States in accordance with the special scale used for this purpose since the establishment of the former United Nations Emergency Force in 1973.[8] Under this arrangement, the permanent members of the Security Council were assessed more than under the scale of assessments for the United Nations regular budget, while most developing countries were assessed 80 per cent less and the least developed countries 90 per cent less than under the regular scale. The Assembly decided that Antigua and Barbuda, Belize and Vanuatu, admitted to the United Nations in 1981,[10] would be placed in the category of least developed States for assessment purposes. It again invited States to make voluntary contributions.

The resolution was adopted by a recorded vote of 119 to 14, with 5 abstentions. The draft had been approved by the Fifth Committee on 2 December, together with the draft resolution on suspension of certain Financial Regulations (see below), by a recorded vote of 74 to 12, with 2 abstentions.

The financing of UNIFIL was considered by the Committee on the basis of reports by the Secretary-General and ACABQ.

In a November report to the Assembly,[5] the Secretary-General stated that, as at 30 September, he had received $448.5 million from Member States in assessed contributions for UNIFIL since inception of the Force in 1978. The balance due from Member States amounted to $192.2 million, of which only $48.4 million could be considered collectable. The shortfall of $143.8 million was mainly due to withholdings of contributions by Member States which had stated their intention not to pay. Thus, more than 22 per cent of the total amounts apportioned among Member States to finance UNIFIL since its inception would not be received, posing a very serious financial management problem.

As a result of the shortfall, payments to troop-contributing countries, which had never been made on a current and full basis in accordance with agreed rates, were falling farther behind. The troop contributors had again conveyed to the Secretary-General their serious concern over that situation, which placed a heavy burden on them. Voluntary contributions to help alleviate that burden amounted to only $18,356.

The prospects for UNIFIL beyond January 1983 still unknown, the Secretary-General held it not feasible to formulate for the Assembly in 1982 cost estimates that would accurately reflect anticipated needs. He proposed that, should the Council decide to continue the Force, he be authorized to enter into commitments for the period from 19 January to 18 December 1983 at a monthly rate not to exceed $15,229,666 gross ($15,087,833 net), the previously authorized rate for the period from 19 June to 18 December 1982. In the event that future Council decisions on the status of the Force entailed additional costs, he would seek Assembly authorization if it was in session; otherwise, he would make use of established procedures for dealing with unforeseen and extraordinary expenses.

The Secretary-General's figures were endorsed by ACABQ in a November report[3] and were incorporated by the Assembly into its financial authorization resolution.

Introducing the 17-nation draft resolution, Finland said that, despite the difficult political setting in which almost all peace-keeping forces operated, they had made a valuable contribution to the maintenance of international peace and security. Member States bore a collective responsibility to enable the United Nations to carry out its obligations. The current situation, in which not all Members were fulfilling their responsibilities and a disproportionate burden was placed on Governments that provided troops and other support, not only undermined the efficiency of peace-keeping operations but might also make it increasingly difficult to find additional States to take part in such operations.

Explaining its negative votes in both March and December, the USSR reaffirmed its position of principle that the cost of eliminating the consequences of Israeli armed aggression should be met by the aggressor; the USSR would not contribute for UNIFIL. Also voting against, Czechoslovakia, the German Democratic Republic, Hungary, Iraq, Poland and the Syrian Arab Republic stated that they would not participate in the financing of UNIFIL. For similar reasons, Benin, Democratic Yemen and the Libyan Arab Jamahiriya did not take part in the voting. Albania voted against, stating that it opposed United Nations peace-keeping forces because they did not serve the cause of peace or of the independence and freedom of peoples. Abstaining, Yemen also believed the aggressor alone should bear the consequences of its aggression.

Voting in favour and expressing concern at the growing deficit of UNIFIL, Lebanon said it had always accepted as incontrovertible the principle of collective financial responsibility for United Nations activities. The refusal of some States to pay their share was unfair both to the developing countries which contributed and to the troop contributors; if the practice continued, rich countries would soon be the only ones to contribute, which would upset the geographical balance of contributions. The problem in Lebanon was not the making of the Lebanese people, who should not have to bear the consequences.

Ireland, also stressing collective responsibility and equitable sharing of costs, said that, with only three quarters of its resources collectable, UNIFIL could not be expected to continue to function efficiently. Also casting an affirmative vote, Israel said that, as the Security Council resolutions establishing peace-keeping forces had been adopted with the concurrence of all countries concerned, the Assembly should allow the Secretary-General all the resources necessary; States withholding their contributions, including one super-Power that professed itself to be peace-loving, were doing so in clear violation of their responsibilities under the Charter of the United Nations.

The United States said its position was the same as on financing for the United Nations Disengagement Observer Force.

CONTRIBUTIONS TO UNIFIL

(as at 31 December 1982; in US dollars)

Country	Assessments in 1982	Paid in 1982	Total contributions outstanding	Country	Assessments in 1982	Paid in 1982	Total contributions outstanding
Afghanistan	1,795	—	5,331	Chad	1,795	—	6,319
Albania	3,586	—	13,376	Chile	25,105	37,616	15,287
Algeria	43,036	—	151,665	China	3,389,087	3,389,087	—
Angola	1,795	—	5,453	Colombia	39,448	—	39,448
Argentina	279,738	157,523	141,165	Comoros	1,795	—	6,319
Australia	3,281,875	2,177,922	1,103,953	Congo	3,586	—	13,376
Austria	1,273,297	1,273,297	—	Costa Rica	7,174	5,229	18,187
Bahamas	3,586	1,777	4,297	Cuba	39,448	—	147,129
Bahrain	3,586	3,586	—	Cyprus	3,586	2,184	1,402
Bangladesh	7,175	4,464	15,299	Czechoslovakia	1,488,501	—	5,575,522
Barbados	3,586	2,380	2,654	Democratic Kampuchea	3,586	—	13,376
Belgium	2,187,916	882,805	2,187,916	Democratic Yemen	1,795	—	6,319
Benin	1,795	—	6,319	Denmark	1,327,097	1,327,097	—
Bhutan	1,795	1,795	—	Djibouti	1,795	—	3,783
Bolivia	3,586	—	13,376	Dominica	1,795	302	6,611
Botswana	1,795	1,750	702	Dominican Republic	10,760	—	31,365
Brazil	455,474	371,588	451,477	Ecuador	7,174	6,467	3,621
Bulgaria	57,383	—	205,167	Egypt	25,105	12,436	42,774
Burma	3,586	2,380	1,206	El Salvador	3,586	—	12,349
Burundi	1,795	—	6,319	Equatorial Guinea	3,586	—	13,376
Byelorussian SSR	699,417	—	2,653,699	Ethiopia	1,795	—	4,440
Canada	5,882,267	5,882,267	—	Fiji	3,586	2,184	2,850
Cape Verde	1,795	—	3,105	Finland	860,820	716,035	144,785
Central African Republic	3,586	—	13,376	France	13,521,719	6,698,915	12,713,494

Country	Assessments in 1982	Paid in 1982	Total contributions outstanding	Country	Assessments in 1982	Paid in 1982	Total contributions outstanding
Gabon	7,174	3,143	19,184	Pakistan	25,105	25,664	12,669
Gambia	3,586	—	13,376	Panama	7,174	—	22,828
German Democratic Republic	2,492,787	—	9,167,410	Papua New Guinea	1,795	98	4,530
Germany, Federal Republic of	14,902,942	14,902,942	—	Paraguay	3,586	—	13,376
Ghana	10,760	19,444	—	Peru	21,519	—	73,843
Greece	125,523	97,549	27,974	Philippines	35,865	49,956	24,091
Grenada	1,795	—	5,662	Poland	2,223,785	—	8,628,699
Guatemala	7,174	9,339	3,621	Portugal	68,140	45,216	22,924
Guinea	1,795	5,715	604	Qatar	10,760	13,581	7,962
Guinea-Bissau	1,795	—	3,705	Romania	75,315	—	268,354
Guyana	3,586	3,503	83	Rwanda	1,795	889	906
Haiti	1,795	—	6,319	Saint Lucia	1,795	—	4,487
Honduras	3,586	3,225	1,809	Saint Vincent and the			
Hungary	118,351	—	441,410	Grenadines	1,795	2,654	702
Iceland	53,801	53,801	—	Samoa	1,795	791	2,726
India	215,183	—	215,183	Sao Tome and Principe	1,795	—	4,852
Indonesia	57,383	47,730	9,653	Saudi Arabia	208,000	221,969	69,969
Iran	233,118	—	715,870	Senegal	1,795	634	4,651
Iraq	43,036	—	142,822	Seychelles	1,795	1,493	302
Ireland	286,939	286,941	—	Sierra Leone	3,586	196	13,180
Israel	89,661	35,064	60,529	Singapore	28,694	23,867	4,827
Italy	6,187,139	6,602,306	2,081,288	Solomon Islands	1,795	—	6,913
Ivory Coast	10,760	—	15,102	Somalia	1,795	302	2,807
Jamaica	7,174	5,575	1,599	South Africa	753,217	—	2,810,147
Japan	17,180,525	14,503,133	9,609,575	Spain	609,690	—	1,703,402
Jordan	3,586	2,983	603	Sri Lanka	7,174	3,553	3,621
Kenya	3,586	1,206	6,129	Sudan	1,795	—	4,852
Kuwait	71,727	71,727	—	Suriname	1,795	3,783	—
Lao People's Democratic				Swaziland	3,586	—	13,376
Republic	1,795	—	6,319	Sweden	2,349,323	1,954,179	395,144
Lebanon	10,760	—	34,228	Syrian Arab Republic	10,760	—	35,707
Lesotho	1,795	—	4,657	Thailand	35,865	27,872	7,993
Liberia	3,586	—	13,376	Togo	3,586	—	5,719
Libyan Arab Jamahiriya	82,490	—	276,690	Trinidad and Tobago	10,760	8,950	1,810
Luxembourg	89,673	89,673	—	Tunisia	10,760	10,894	15,653
Madagascar	3,586	—	10,216	Turkey	107,591	180,218	60,174
Malawi	1,795	—	3,204	Uganda	1,795	—	5,840
Malaysia	32,276	29,014	27,818	Ukrainian SSR	2,618,326	—	9,923,573
Maldives	1,795	1,191	1,771	USSR	23,976,207	—	89,828,730
Mali	1,795	—	3,109	United Arab Emirates	35,865	72,355	20,059
Malta	3,586	3,586	—	United Kingdom	9,633,683	8,607,680	6,913,307
Mauritania	3,586	—	13,376	United Republic of Cameroon	3,586	—	4,867
Mauritius	3,586	1,777	3,257	United Republic of Tanzania	1,795	—	6,319
Mexico	272,568	403,164	59,276	United States	54,496,799	54,496,799	—
Mongolia	3,586	—	13,376	Upper Volta	1,795	—	6,319
Morocco	17,935	7,904	33,922	Uruguay	14,349	5,788	21,955
Mozambique	1,795	—	8,384	Venezuela	179,322	—	251,681
Nepal	1,795	400	2,648	Viet Nam	10,760	—	40,130
Netherlands	2,923,200	2,431,533	491,667	Yemen	1,795	—	6,319
New Zealand	484,208	402,767	81,441	Yugoslavia	150,629	86,976	379,538
Nicaragua	3,586	—	13,376	Zaire	7,174	—	18,728
Niger	1,795	—	4,212	Zambia	7,174	11,753	1,207
Nigeria	57,383	20,000	60,538	Zimbabwe	3,587	3,664	3,046
Norway	896,690	896,690	—				
Oman	3,586	3,586	—	Total	179,795,498	129,769,471	171,209,172

NOTE: Total contributions outstanding covers the period from the inception of UNIFIL (19 March 1978) to 18 December 1982, as at 31 December 1982.

SOURCE: Status of contributions, ST/ADM/SER.B/265.

Note. [1]S-G, A/36/860.

Reports. ACABQ, [2]A/36/868, [3]A/37/649; S-G, [4]A/36/865 & Corr.1, [5]A/37/535.

Resolutions (1982). GA: [6]36/138 C, 19 Mar., text following; [7]37/127 A, 17 Dec., text following.

Resolutions (prior). GA: [8]3101(XXVIII), 11 Dec. 1973 (YUN 1973, p. 222); [9]36/138 A, 16 Dec. 1981 (YUN 1981, p. 299).

Yearbook reference. [10]1981, p. 348.

Meeting records. GA: plenary, A/36/PV.106, 108 (16, 19 Mar.), A/37/PV.109 (17 Dec.); 5th Committee, A/C.5/36/SR.84, 85 (17, 18 Mar.), A/C.5/37/SR.51, 53 (1, 2 Dec.).

Status of contributions. ST/ADM/SER.B/265.

UNIFIL assessments. 19 June 1981–18 June 1982, ST/ADM/SER.B/257; 19 June 1982–18 Jan. 1983, ST/ADM/SER.B/263.

General Assembly resolution 36/138 C

19 March 1982	Meeting 108	90-12-3 (recorded vote)

Approved by Fifth Committee (A/36/720/Add.2) by recorded vote (65-9-1), 18 March (meeting 85); 17-nation draft (A/C.5/36/L.51); agenda item 110 *(b)*.

Sponsors: Australia, Canada, Denmark, Fiji, Finland, France, Ghana, Ireland, Italy, Lebanon, Nepal, Netherlands, Nigeria, Norway, Panama, Senegal, Sweden.

The General Assembly,

Having considered the report of the Secretary-General on the financing of the United Nations Interim Force in Lebanon and the related report of the Advisory Committee on Administrative and Budgetary Questions,

Bearing in mind Security Council resolutions 425(1978) and 426(1978) of 19 March 1978, 427(1978) of 3 May 1978, 434(1978) of 18 September 1978, 444(1979) of 19 January 1979, 450(1979) of 14 June 1979, 459(1979) of 19 December 1979, 474(1980) of 17 June 1980, 483(1980) of 17 December 1980, 488(1981) of 19 June 1981, 498(1981) of 18 December 1981 and 501(1982) of 25 February 1982,

Recalling its resolutions S-8/2 of 21 April 1978, 33/14 of 3 November 1978, 34/9 B of 17 December 1979, 35/44 of 1 December 1980, 35/115 A of 10 December 1980 and 36/138 A of 16 December 1981,

Reaffirming its previous decisions regarding the fact that, in order to meet the expenditures caused by such operations, a different procedure from the one applied to meet expenditures of the regular budget of the United Nations is required,

Taking into account the fact that the economically more developed countries are in a position to make relatively larger contributions and that the economically less developed countries have a relatively limited capacity to contribute towards peace-keeping operations involving heavy expenditures,

Bearing in mind the special responsibilities of the States permanent members of the Security Council in the financing of peace-keeping operations decided upon in accordance with the Charter of the United Nations,

1. *Authorizes* the Secretary-General to enter into commitments for the United Nations Interim Force in Lebanon in an amount not to exceed $9,825,000 gross ($9,822,000 net) for the period from 25 February to 18 June 1982 inclusive, in addition to the amounts authorized for the Force under General Assembly resolution 36/138 A, to finance the increase in the strength of the Force approved by the Security Council under its resolution 501(1982), the said amount to be apportioned among Member States in accordance with the scheme set out in Assembly resolution 33/14 and the provisions of section V, paragraph 1, of resolution 34/9 B, section VI, paragraph 1, of resolution 35/115 A and section VI, paragraph 1, of resolution 36/138 A, in the proportions determined by the scale of assessments for the years 1980, 1981 and 1982;

2. *Further authorizes* the Secretary-General to enter into commitments for the United Nations Interim Force in Lebanon, for the same purpose, at a rate not to exceed $1,913,000 gross ($1,910,333 net) per month for the period from 19 June to 18 December 1982 inclusive, in addition to the amounts authorized for the Force under General Assembly resolution 36/138 A, should the Security Council decide to continue the Force beyond the period of six months authorized under its resolution 498(1981), the said amount to be apportioned among Member State in accordance with the scheme set out in Assembly resolution 33/14 and the provisions of section V, paragraph 1, of resolution 34/9 B, section VI, paragraph 1, of resolution 35/115 A and section VI, paragraph 1, of resolution 36/138 A, in the proportions determined by the scale of assessments for the years 1980, 1981 and 1982.

Recorded vote in Assembly as follows:

In favour: Argentina, Australia, Austria, Bahamas, Bahrain, Bangladesh, Barbados, Belgium, Bhutan, Bolivia, Brazil, Burma, Canada, Chile, China, Colombia, Costa Rica, Denmark, Djibouti, Ecuador, Egypt, Ethiopia, Fiji, Finland, France, Gabon, Germany, Federal Republic of, Ghana, Greece, Iceland, India, Indonesia, Ireland, Israel, Italy, Ivory Coast, Jamaica, Japan, Jordan, Kenya, Kuwait, Lebanon, Luxembourg, Madagascar, Malawi, Malaysia, Maldives, Mali, Malta, Mauritania, Mexico, Morocco, Nepal, Netherlands, New Zealand, Niger, Norway, Oman, Pakistan, Panama, Paraguay, Peru, Philippines, Portugal, Qatar, Romania, Rwanda, Saint Lucia, Samoa, Saudi Arabia, Senegal, Sierra Leone, Singapore, Spain, Sweden, Thailand, Togo, Trinidad and Tobago, Tunisia, Turkey, United Arab Emirates, United Kingdom, United Republic of Cameroon, United Republic of Tanzania, United States, Uruguay, Venezuela, Yugoslavia, Zaire, Zambia.

Against: Albania, Byelorussian SSR, Czechoslovakia, German Democratic Republic, Hungary, Lao People's Democratic Republic, Mongolia, Poland, Syrian Arab Republic, Ukrainian SSR, USSR, Viet Nam.

Abstaining: Chad, Democratic Yemen, Guinea.

General Assembly resolution 37/127 A

17 December 1982   Meeting 109   119-14-5 (recorded vote)

Approved by Fifth Committee (A/37/681/Add.1) by recorded vote (74-12-2), 2 December (meeting 53); 17-nation draft (A/C.5/37/L.32, part A, approved together with part B (see resolution 37/127 B)); agenda item 114 *(b)*.

Sponsors: Australia, Canada, Denmark, Fiji, Finland, France, Ghana, Ireland, Italy, Lebanon, Nepal, Netherlands, New Zealand, Norway, Panama, Senegal, Sweden.

The General Assembly,

Having considered the report of the Secretary-General on the financing of the United Nations Interim Force in Lebanon and the related report of the Advisory Committee on Administrative and Budgetary Questions,

Bearing in mind Security Council resolutions 425(1978) and 426(1978) of 19 March 1978, 427(1978) of 3 May 1978, 434(1978) of 18 September 1978, 444(1979) of 19 January 1979, 450(1979) of 14 June 1979, 459(1979) of 19 December 1979, 474(1980) of 17 June 1980, 483(1980)

of 17 December 1980, 488(1981) of 19 June 1981, 498(1981) of 18 December 1981, 501(1982) of 25 February 1982, 511(1982) of 18 June 1982, 519(1982) of 17 August 1982 and 523(1982) of 18 October 1982,

Recalling its resolutions S-8/2 of 21 April 1978, 33/14 of 3 November 1978, 34/9 B of 17 December 1979, 35/44 of 1 December 1980, 35/115 A of 10 December 1980, 36/138 A of 16 December 1981 and 36/138 C of 19 March 1982,

Reaffirming its previous decisions regarding the fact that, in order to meet the expenditures caused by such operations, a different procedure from the one applied to meet expenditures of the regular budget of the United Nations is required,

Taking into account the fact that the economically more developed countries are in a position to make relatively larger contributions and that the economically less developed countries have a relatively limited capacity to contribute towards peace-keeping operations involving heavy expenditures,

Bearing in mind the special responsibilities of the States permanent members of the Security Council in the financing of peace-keeping operations decided upon in accordance with the Charter of the United Nations,

I

Decides to appropriate to the Special Account referred to in section I, paragraph 1, of General Assembly resolution S-8/2 an amount of $89,724,996 gross ($88,887,000 net), being the amount authorized and apportioned under the provisions of section III of Assembly resolution 36/138 A and paragraph 1 of resolution 36/138 C for the operation of the United Nations Interim Force in Lebanon from 19 December 1981 to 18 June 1982, inclusive;

II

Decides to appropriate to the Special Account referred to in section I, paragraph 1, of General Assembly resolution S-8/2 an amount of $30,459,332 gross ($30,175,666 net), being the amount authorized and apportioned under the provisions of section III of Assembly resolution 36/138 A and paragraph 1 of resolution 36/138 C for the operation of the United Nations Interim Force in Lebanon from 19 June to 18 August 1982, inclusive;

III

Decides to appropriate to the Special Account referred to in section I, paragraph 1, of General Assembly resolution S-8/2 an amount of $30,459,332 gross ($30,175,666 net), being the amount authorized and apportioned under the provisions of section III of Assembly resolution 36/138 A and paragraph 1 of resolution 36/138 C for the operation of the United Nations Interim Force in Lebanon from 19 August to 18 October 1982, inclusive;

IV

Decides to appropriate to the Special Account referred to in section I, paragraph 1, of General Assembly resolution S-8/2 an amount of $30,459,332 gross ($30,175,666 net), being the amount authorized and apportioned under the provisions of section III of Assembly resolution 36/138 A and paragraph 1 of resolution 36/138 C for the operation of the United Nations Interim Force in Lebanon from 19 October to 18 December 1982, inclusive;

V

Authorizes the Secretary-General to enter into commitments for the operation of the United Nations Interim Force in Lebanon from 19 December 1982 to 18 January 1983 inclusive, in an amount not to exceed $15,229,666 gross ($15,087,833 net), the said amount to be apportioned among Member States in accordance with the scheme set out in General Assembly resolution 33/14 and the provisions of section V, paragraph 1, of resolution 34/9 B, section VI, paragraph 1, of resolution 35/115 A and section VI, paragraph 1, of resolution 36/138 A; the scale of assessments for the years 1980, 1981 and 1982 shall be applied against a portion thereof, that is, $6,386,634 gross ($6,327,156 net), being the amount pertaining on a *pro rata* basis to the period from 19 to 31 December 1982 inclusive, and the scale of assessments for the years 1983, 1984 and 1985 shall be applied against the balance for the period thereafter;

VI

Authorizes the Secretary-General to enter into commitments for the operation of the United Nations Interim Force in Lebanon at a rate not to exceed $15,229,666 gross ($15,087,833 net) per month for the period from 19 January 1983 to 18 December 1983 inclusive, should the Security Council decide to continue the Force beyond the period of three months authorized under its resolution 523(1982), subject to obtaining the prior concurrence of the Advisory Committee on Administrative and Budgetary Questions for the actual level of commitments to be entered into for each mandate period that may be approved subsequent to 19 January 1983, the said amount to be apportioned among Member States in accordance with the scheme set out in General Assembly resolution 33/14 and the provisions of section V, paragraph 1, of resolution 34/9 B, section VI, paragraph 1, of resolution 35/115 A and section VI, paragraph 1, of resolution 36/138 A, in the proportions determined by the scale of assessments for the years 1983, 1984 and 1985;

VII

1. *Renews its invitation* to Member States to make voluntary contributions to the United Nations Interim Force in Lebanon both in cash and in the form of services and supplies acceptable to the Secretary-General;

2. *Invites* Member States to make voluntary contributions in cash to the Suspense Account established in accordance with its resolution 34/9 D of 17 December 1979;

VIII

Requests the Secretary-General to take all necessary action to ensure that the United Nations Interim Force in Lebanon shall be administered with a maximum of efficiency and economy;

IX

1. *Decides* that Antigua and Barbuda, Belize and Vanuatu shall be included in the group of Member States mentioned in section I, paragraph 2 *(d)*, of General Assembly resolution S-8/2 and that their contributions to the United Nations Interim Force in Lebanon shall be calculated in accordance with the provisions of paragraphs 1 and 6 of Assembly resolution 37/125 A of 17 December 1982;

2. *Decides further* that, in accordance with regulation 5.2 *(c)* of the Financial Regulations of the United Nations, the contributions to the United Nations Interim Force in Lebanon until 18 December 1982 of the Member States referred to in paragraph 1 of the present section shall be treated as miscellaneous income to be set off against the apportionments authorized in section V above.

Recorded vote in Assembly as follows:

In favour: Angola, Argentina, Australia, Austria, Bahamas, Bahrain, Bangladesh, Barbados, Belgium, Bhutan, Bolivia, Botswana, Brazil, Burma, Burundi, Canada, Cape Verde, Central African Republic, Chad, Chile, China, Colombia, Comoros, Congo, Costa Rica, Cyprus, Denmark, Djibouti, Dominica, Dominican Republic, Ecuador, Egypt, El Salvador, Fiji, Finland, France, Gabon, Gambia, Germany, Federal Republic of, Ghana, Greece, Guatemala, Guinea, Guinea-Bissau, Guyana, Honduras, Iceland, India, Indonesia, Ireland, Israel, Italy, Ivory Coast, Jamaica, Japan, Jordan, Kenya, Kuwait, Lebanon, Lesotho, Liberia, Luxembourg, Madagascar, Malawi, Malaysia, Mali, Malta, Mauritania, Mauritius, Mexico, Morocco, Nepal, Netherlands, New Zealand, Nicaragua, Niger, Norway, Oman, Pakistan, Panama, Papua New Guinea, Paraguay, Peru, Philippines, Portugal, Qatar, Romania, Rwanda, Samoa, Saudi Arabia, Senegal, Sierra Leone, Singapore, Solomon Islands, Somalia, Spain, Sri Lanka, Sudan, Suriname, Swaziland, Sweden, Thailand, Togo, Trinidad and Tobago, Tunisia, Turkey, Uganda, United Arab Emirates, United Kingdom, United Republic of Cameroon, United Republic of Tanzania, United States, Upper Volta, Uruguay, Venezuela, Yugoslavia, Zaire, Zambia, Zimbabwe.

Against: Afghanistan, Albania, Bulgaria, Byelorussian SSR, Czechoslovakia, German Democratic Republic, Hungary, Iraq, Mongolia, Poland, Syrian Arab Republic, Ukrainian SSR, USSR, Viet Nam.

Abstaining: Cuba, Grenada, Maldives, Sao Tome and Principe, Yemen.

Suspension of Financial Regulations

Continuing a practice begun in 1979,[4] the General Assembly, by a resolution of 17 December 1982,[3] decided to suspend certain provisions of the Financial Regulations of the United Nations to enable the Organization to retain the "surplus balance" of $5,939,256 in the UNIFIL account, instead of having to return these "book surpluses" to Member States as a credit against their subsequent assessments. The Assembly recognized that, because of the withholding of contributions by certain States, the surplus balance had been fully drawn upon to supplement the income received from contributions for meeting the expenses of the Force. Applying the rules, it added, would aggravate the already difficult financial situation of UNIFIL.

This resolution was adopted by a recorded vote of 118 to 14, with 6 abstentions. It had been approved by the Fifth Committee on 2 December by a recorded vote of 74 to 12, with 2 abstentions, together with the resolution on UNIFIL appropriations.[2] Both drafts were sponsored by 17 nations and introduced by Finland.

As explained by ACABQ in its November report on UNIFIL financing,[1] the surplus balance represented an excess of assumed income (some of it uncollectable due to withholding) over expenditure as at 31 December 1981, due to interest and miscellaneous credits. The Secretariat followed the practice of spending the full amount authorized by each year's appropriation, tapping interest income in the UNIFIL account to make up for the shortfall caused by the withholding of some contributions. Under the Financial Regulations, the amount of interest would have had to be credited to Member States even though it had been used to meet the expenses of the Force. The Assembly decision to suspend the Regulations in this case made the interest income available for meeting UNIFIL expenses, to supplement the income received from contributions.

Report. [1]ACABQ, A/37/649.
Resolutions (1982). GA, 17 Dec.: [2]37/127 A; [3]37/127 B, text following.
Resolution (prior). [4]GA: 34/9 E, 17 Dec. 1979 (YUN 1979, p. 353).
Meeting records. GA: 5th Committee, A/C.5/37/SR.51, 53 (1, 2 Dec.); plenary, A/37/PV.109 (17 Dec.).

General Assembly resolution 37/127 B

17 December 1982   Meeting 109   118-14-6 (recorded vote)

Approved by Fifth Committee (A/37/681/Add.1) by recorded vote (74-12-2), 2 December (meeting 53); 17-nation draft (A/C.5/37/L.32, part B, approved together with part A (see resolution 37/127 A)); agenda item 114 *(b)*.

Sponsors: Australia, Canada, Denmark, Fiji, Finland, France, Ghana, Ireland, Italy, Lebanon, Nepal, Netherlands, New Zealand, Norway, Panama, Senegal, Sweden.

The General Assembly,

Having regard to the financial position of the Special Account for the United Nations Interim Force in Lebanon, as set forth in the report of the Secretary-General, and referring to paragraph 7 of the report of the Advisory Committee on Administrative and Budgetary Questions,

Mindful of the fact that it is essential to provide the United Nations Interim Force in Lebanon with the necessary financial resources to enable it to fulfil its responsibilities under the relevant resolutions of the Security Council,

Concerned that the Secretary-General is continuing to face growing difficulties in meeting the obligations of the United Nations Interim Force in Lebanon on a current basis, particularly those due to the Governments of troop-contributing States,

Recalling its resolutions 34/9 E of 17 December 1979, 35/115 B of 10 December 1980 and 36/138 B of 16 December 1981,

Recognizing that, in consequence of the withholding of contributions by certain Member States, the surplus balances in the Special Account for the United Nations Interim Force in Lebanon have, in effect, been drawn upon to the full extent to supplement the income received from contributions for meeting expenses of the Force,

Concerned that the application of the provisions of regulations 5.2 *(b)*, 5.2 *(d)*, 4.3 and 4.4 of the Financial Regulations of the United Nations would aggravate the already difficult financial situation of the United Nations Interim Force in Lebanon,

Decides that the provisions of regulations 5.2 *(b)*, 5.2 *(d)*, 4.3 and 4.4 of the Financial Regulations of the United Nations shall be suspended in respect of the amount of $5,939,256, which otherwise would have to be surrendered pursuant to those provisions, this amount to be entered in the account referred to in the operative part of General Assembly resolution 34/9 E and held in suspense until a further decision is taken by the Assembly.

Recorded vote in Assembly as follows:

In favour: Angola, Argentina, Australia, Austria, Bahamas, Bahrain, Bangladesh, Barbados, Belgium, Bhutan, Bolivia, Botswana, Brazil, Burma, Burundi, Canada, Cape Verde, Central African Republic, Chad, Chile, China, Colombia, Comoros, Congo, Costa Rica, Cyprus, Denmark, Djibouti, Dominica, Dominican Republic, Ecuador, Egypt, El Salvador, Fiji, Finland, France, Gabon, Gambia, Germany, Federal Republic of, Ghana, Greece, Guatemala, Guinea, Guinea-Bissau, Guyana, Honduras, Iceland, India, Indonesia, Ireland, Israel, Italy, Ivory Coast, Jamaica, Japan, Jordan, Kenya, Kuwait, Lebanon, Lesotho, Liberia, Luxembourg, Madagascar, Malawi, Malaysia, Mali, Malta, Mauritania, Mauritius, Mexico, Morocco, Nepal, Netherlands, New Zealand, Nicaragua, Niger, Norway, Oman, Pakistan, Panama, Papua New Guinea, Paraguay, Peru, Philippines, Portugal, Qatar, Rwanda, Samoa, Saudi Arabia, Senegal, Sierra Leone, Singapore, Solomon Islands, Somalia, Spain, Sri Lanka, Sudan, Suriname, Swaziland, Sweden, Thailand, Togo, Trinidad and Tobago, Tunisia, Turkey, Uganda, United Arab Emirates, United Kingdom, United Republic of Cameroon, United Republic of Tanzania, United States, Upper Volta, Uruguay, Venezuela, Yugoslavia, Zaire, Zambia, Zimbabwe.

Against: Afghanistan, Albania, Bulgaria, Byelorussian SSR, Czechoslovakia, German Democratic Republic, Hungary, Iraq, Mongolia, Poland, Syrian Arab Republic, Ukrainian SSR, USSR, Viet Nam.

Abstaining: Cuba, Grenada, Maldives, Romania, Sao Tome and Principe, Yemen.

Israel and the Syrian Arab Republic

In 1982, the General Assembly as well as the Security Council dealt with the situation in the Syrian Golan Heights following Israel's December 1981 decision to impose its laws, jurisdiction and administration on the Israeli-occupied territory (see below, under ANNEXATION OF THE GOLAN HEIGHTS).

The United Nations Disengagement Observer Force (UNDOF), established by the Council in 1974,[1] continued to supervise the observance of the cease-fire between Israel and the Syrian Arab Republic in the Golan Heights area and to ensure, in accordance with its mandate, that there were no military forces in the area of separation. Its mandate was renewed by the Council twice during the year, in May and November, each time for six months. Composed of contingents from four countries and operating under a new Commander, it continued to be financed by assessments on all Member States, with costs totalling $33 million for the year ending 31 May 1983.

Resolution. [1]SC: 350(1974), 31 May 1974 (YUN 1974, p. 205).

UN Disengagement Observer Force

Activities

With the mandate of UNDOF expiring on 31 May and 30 November 1982, the Secretary-General submitted to the Security Council two reports, on 20 May and 18 November, giving an account of the activities of the Force for the two

six-month periods from 21 November 1981 to 20 May 1982[1] and 21 May to 18 November 1982,[2] respectively.

The Secretary-General stated that UNDOF had continued to perform its functions effectively and that, during the periods under review, the situation in the Israel-Syria sector had remained quiet, with no serious incidents. The cease-fire in the area of separation between Israel and the Syrian Arab Republic had been maintained, and no complaints had been lodged by either party. However, restrictions on the Force's freedom of movement still existed and efforts to correct the situation were continuing.

As at 18 November, UNDOF maintained 34 positions and 12 outposts, and conducted 33 patrols daily and 26 at irregular intervals. It continued to conduct fortnightly inspections of armaments and forces in the area of limitation, and to clear land-mines.

The Secretary-General stated in each report that, despite the prevailing quiet in the sector, the Middle East situation as a whole continued to be potentially dangerous and was likely to remain so without a comprehensive settlement. In the circumstances, he considered the continued presence of UNDOF in the area to be essential and recommended, with the assent of the Syrian Arab Republic and the agreement of Israel, that the Council extend its mandate for further periods of six months each.

Reports. S-G, [1]S/15079, [2]S/15493.

Composition

As at 18 November 1982, the composition of UNDOF was as follows:

Country	Number of troops
Austria	528
Canada	220
Finland	388
Poland	131
United Nations military observers	18
	1,285

SOURCE: S-G report, S/15493.

In addition, observers of the United Nations Truce Supervision Organization assigned to the Israel-Syria Mixed Armistice Commission assisted UNDOF as required.

Commander

By a letter of 28 April 1982,[2] the Secretary-General informed the Security Council President that the Commander of UNDOF, Major-General Erkki Raine Kaira of Finland, was resigning and that he intended, subject to consultations, to appoint Major-General Carl-Gustav Stahl of Sweden as Commander, effective 1 June. By a letter of 30 April,[1] the President replied that the Council members had considered the matter in informal consultations on 29 April and had agreed with the Secretary-General's proposal.

Major-General Kaira was repatriated on medical grounds and was replaced temporarily by the Chief of Staff, Colonel Walter Schmit (19 February–12 June), until Major-General Stahl assumed command on 13 June.

Letters. [1]SC President, 30 Apr., S/15020; [2]S-G, 28 Apr., S/15019.

Continuation

By resolutions of 26 May[3] and 29 November 1982,[4] prepared during consultations and adopted unanimously, the Security Council renewed the mandate of UNDOF for six months, until 30 November 1982 and 31 May 1983, respectively. It requested the Secretary-General to submit at the end of each period a report on developments and measures taken to implement a 1973 Council resolution calling for a cease-fire and peace negotiations.[5]

Following adoption of the resolutions, the President made the following statement on behalf of the Council:[1,2]

"In connection with the adoption of the resolution on the renewal of the mandate of the United Nations Disengagement Observer Force, I have been authorized to make the following complementary statement on behalf of the Security Council regarding the resolution just adopted:

'As is known, the report of the Secretary-General on the United Nations Disengagement Observer Force states, in paragraph 28 [27 in the November report], that "despite the present quiet in the Israel-Syria sector, the situation in the Middle East as a whole continues to be potentially dangerous and is likely to remain so unless and until a comprehensive settlement covering all aspects of the Middle East problem can be reached." This statement of the Secretary-General reflects the view of the Security Council.' "

Notes. SC President, [1]S/15124, [2]S/15504.
Resolutions (1982). SC: [3]506(1982), 26 May, text following; [4]524(1982), 29 Nov., text following.
Resolution (prior). [5]SC: 338(1973), 22 Oct. 1973 (YUN 1973, p. 213).
Meeting records. SC: S/PV.2369, 2403 (26 May, 29 Nov.).

Security Council resolution 506(1982)

26 May 1982   Meeting 2369   Adopted unanimously

Draft prepared in consultations among Council members (S/15118).

The Security Council,
Having considered the report of the Secretary-General on the United Nations Disengagement Observer Force,
Decides:
(a) To call upon the parties concerned to implement immediately Security Council resolution 338(1973);
(b) To renew the mandate of the United Nations Disengagement Observer Force for another period of six months, that is, until 30 November 1982;
(c) To request the Secretary-General to submit, at the end of this period, a report on the developments in the situation and the measures taken to implement resolution 338(1973).

Security Council resolution 524(1982)

29 November 1982   Meeting 2403   Adopted unanimously

Draft prepared in consultations among Council members (S/15503).

The Security Council,
Having considered the report of the Secretary-General on the United Nations Disengagement Observer Force,
Decides:
(a) To call upon the parties concerned to implement immediately Security Council resolution 338(1973);
(b) To renew the mandate of the United Nations Disengagement Observer Force for another period of six months, that is, until 31 May 1983;
(c) To request the Secretary-General to submit, at the end of this period, a report on the developments in the situation and the measures taken to implement resolution 338(1973).

Financing

By a resolution of 30 November 1982,[3] the General Assembly appropriated a total of $33,160,498 for UNDOF spanning the two six-month extensions of the Force's mandate approved by the Security Council in 1982—1 June to 30 November 1982 and 1 December 1982 to 31 May 1983. The amount for the first period was $15,973,998 gross ($15,784,998 net of staff assessment) and $17,186,500 gross ($16,984,000 net) for the second. Should the Council decide to continue the Force beyond 31 May 1983, the Secretary-General was authorized to enter into commitments at a rate not to exceed $2,864,416 gross ($2,830,666 net) per month for the period from 1 June to 30 November 1983. Under other provisions, the Assembly stressed the need for voluntary contributions and decided on the apportionment of expenses among Member States in a pattern similar to that for the United Nations Interim Force in Lebanon (see above).

The resolution was adopted by a recorded vote of 95 to 3, with 17 abstentions. The Fifth (Administrative and Budgetary) Committee, on 29 November, had approved the draft, which incorporated cost estimates prepared by the Secretary-General, together with a text on suspension of Financial Regulations (see below), by a recorded vote of 73 to 3, with 14 abstentions.

The financing of UNDOF was considered by the Committee on the basis of reports by the Secretary-General and the Advisory Committee on Administrative and Budgetary Questions (ACABQ).

In an October report,[2] the Secretary-General gave cost estimates for the period from 1 December 1982 to 30 November 1983 totalling $34,373,000, assuming an average strength of 1,290 troops. Among the major components of the total were $15.4 million for pay and allowances for troops, $3.2 million for salaries and related costs of staff, $3.1 million for maintenance and operation of motor transport and other equipment, $2.4 million for premises and utilities, and $2.1 million for rations.

(continued on p. 500)

CONTRIBUTIONS TO UNDOF

(as at 31 December 1982; in US dollars)

Country	Assessments in 1982	Paid in 1982	Total contributions outstanding	Country	Assessments in 1982	Paid in 1982	Total contributions outstanding
Afghanistan	317	—	2,841	Kuwait	12,623	12,623	—
Albania	630	—	20,271	Lao People's Democratic Republic	317	—	1,792
Algeria	7,574	3,582	38,193	Lebanon	1,893	—	36,220
Angola	317	—	1,255	Lesotho	317	—	958
Argentina	49,229	34,100	15,129	Liberia	630	—	13,125
Australia	577,483	577,483	—	Libyan Arab Jamahiriya	14,515	—	188,445
Austria	224,051	224,051	—	Luxembourg	15,780	15,780	—
Bahamas	630	315	1,875	Madagascar	630	—	2,067
Bahrain	630	630	—	Malawi	317	—	1,153
Bangladesh	1,260	540	3,523	Malaysia	5,678	9,584	1,002
Barbados	630	630	—	Maldives	317	317	135
Belgium	384,989	94,029	385,504	Mali	317	—	587
Benin	317	—	9,944	Malta	630	926	—
Bhutan	317	317	—	Mauritania	630	—	10,538
Bolivia	630	—	12,303	Mauritius	630	315	611
Botswana	317	452	116	Mexico	47,966	48,318	182
Brazil	80,156	—	117,752	Mongolia	630	315	8,441
Bulgaria	10,099	—	107,339	Morocco	3,153	—	6,565
Burma	630	630	—	Mozambique	317	—	6,170
Burundi	317	—	9,944	Nepal	317	—	568
Byelorussian SSR	123,070	104,944	711,234	Netherlands	514,370	514,370	—
Canada	1,035,051	1,035,051	—	New Zealand	85,203	85,203	—
Cape Verde	317	135	4,354	Nicaragua	630	—	3,577
Central African Republic	630	—	20,271	Niger	317	—	618
Chad	317	—	9,944	Nigeria	10,099	—	14,836
Chile	4,417	4,417	—	Norway	157,781	157,781	—
China	615,727	615,727	—	Oman	630	630	858
Colombia	6,943	6,943	—	Pakistan	4,417	5,129	2,147
Comoros	317	—	4,624	Panama	1,263	—	18,342
Congo	630	—	20,271	Papua New Guinea	317	—	421
Costa Rica	1,263	1,855	—	Paraguay	630	—	20,271
Cuba	6,943	1,358	5,585	Peru	3,783	—	22,375
Cyprus	630	630	—	Philippines	6,312	6,312	—
Czechoslovakia	261,918	245,707	845,353	Poland	391,298	948,662	195,655
Democratic Kampuchea	630	—	20,271	Portugal	11,991	11,955	36
Democratic Yemen	317	—	5,024	Qatar	1,893	1,845	5,343
Denmark	233,517	233,517	—	Romania	13,255	—	84,157
Djibouti	317	—	999	Rwanda	317	158	159
Dominica	317	—	999	Saint Lucia	317	—	587
Dominican Republic	1,893	—	9,554	Saint Vincent and the Grenadines	317	159	158
Ecuador	1,263	1,224	631	Samoa	317	159	969
Egypt	4,417	2,210	11,730	Sao Tome and Principe	317	—	1,074
El Salvador	630	—	5,604	Saudi Arabia	36,606	36,606	—
Equatorial Guinea	630	315	14,353	Senegal	317	1,302	158
Ethiopia	317	—	317	Seychelles	317	317	—
Fiji	630	315	315	Sierra Leone	630	296	11,412
Finland	151,472	151,472	—	Singapore	5,047	5,047	—
France	2,379,281	3,494,667	519,403	Solomon Islands	317	—	999
Gabon	1,263	552	7,227	Somalia	317	—	317
Gambia	630	2,034	—	South Africa	132,538	—	2,720,044
German Democratic Republic	438,635	300,000	1,748,715	Spain	107,294	538,688	6
Germany, Federal Republic of	2,622,341	2,622,341	—	Sri Lanka	1,263	632	1,223
Ghana	1,893	—	2,782	Sudan	317	159	6,271
Greece	22,091	22,091	—	Suriname	317	—	568
Grenada	317	159	6,589	Swaziland	630	—	20,271
Guatemala	1,263	2,313	631	Sweden	413,390	413,390	—
Guinea	317	4,614	—	Syrian Arab Republic	1,893	—	27,142
Guinea-Bissau	317	—	703	Thailand	6,312	6,312	—
Guyana	630	630	—	Togo	630	—	815
Haiti	317	—	9,280	Trinidad and Tobago	1,893	1,893	—
Honduras	630	611	315	Tunisia	1,893	947	5,977
Hungary	20,828	—	222,102	Turkey	18,936	—	19,627
Iceland	9,467	9,467	—	Uganda	317	—	7,018
India	37,869	37,869	—	Ukrainian SSR	460,724	392,865	2,657,471
Indonesia	10,099	10,099	8,725	USSR	4,218,855	3,596,598	23,667,767
Iran	41,024	—	132,511	United Arab Emirates	6,312	13,500	3,156
Iraq	7,574	—	92,014	United Kingdom	1,695,142	1,695,142	—
Ireland	50,491	50,491	—	United Republic of Cameroon	630	—	1,472
Israel	15,779	29,810	—	United Republic of Tanzania	317	—	7,148
Italy	1,088,698	1,055,025	544,598	United States	9,612,689	9,612,689	—
Ivory Coast	1,893	—	6,023	Upper Volta	317	—	2,655
Jamaica	1,263	632	631	Uruguay	2,521	1,184	3,149
Japan	3,023,106	2,929,073	1,511,596	Venezuela	31,556	—	46,356
Jordan	630	315	315				
Kenya	630	250	926				

Country	Assessments in 1982	Paid in 1982	Total contributions outstanding	Country	Assessments in 1982	Paid in 1982	Total contributions outstanding
Viet Nam	1,893	—	10,733	Zambia	1,263	2,447	—
Yemen	317	—	9,544	Zimbabwe	630	313	317
Yugoslavia	26,507	60,183	84,701				
Zaire	1,263	—	4,065	Total	31,679,813	32,116,673	37,203,032

NOTE: Total contributions outstanding includes contributions due for UNDOF from its inception on 31 May 1974 through 30 November 1982 and those due for the second United Nations Emergency Force (1973-1979); between 1974 and 1979 there was a single account for the two Forces.

SOURCE: Status of contributions, ST/ADM/SER.B/265.

The Secretary-General reported that, as at 30 September 1982, he had received $18.4 million in contributions for UNDOF for the period from 1 December 1981 to 30 November 1982. The balance due from Member States for this period amounted to $13.3 million, of which $0.1 million comprised amounts apportioned among States which had stated that they did not intend to pay.

For the period from 25 October 1979 to 30 November 1982, out of appropriations totalling $73.1 million, there had been a shortfall estimated at $3.4 million in contributions owing to non-payment by certain Member States. That situation, the Secretary-General said, placed a heavy burden on the troop contributors, as reimbursements to them had not been made in time or in accordance with agreed rates. No voluntary contributions had been received in response to a call made by the Assembly in November 1981.[5]

The Secretary-General's cost estimates for the 12 months beginning 1 December 1982 were approved by the Assembly as recommended by ACABQ in a November report.[1]

Introducing both draft resolutions, Canada, on behalf of the 10 sponsors, explained that they were based on 1980[4] and 1981[5] resolutions on the same subject. Peace-keeping operations being among the most important United Nations activities, all Member States, particularly Security Council members, had a responsibility to support UNDOF. The refusal of some States to pay and the lack of voluntary contributions had resulted in the Organization's inability to reimburse the troop contributors, which was likely to lessen the ability of developing countries to participate in peace-keeping operations. The fact that China had joined those paying their contributions[6] was an example which others would do well to follow.

Though expressing appreciation for UNDOF, the Syrian Arab Republic voted against the appropriation resolution, saying that, as the presence of the Force was a direct result of Israel's aggression and continued occupation of Arab territories in defiance of United Nations resolutions, its financing should be borne by the aggressor and those who supported it; by financing UNDOF through contributions from all Member States, no distinction was made between the aggressor and the victim of aggression.

A similar view that the aggressor should pay was expressed by Benin and Iraq, which voted against, as well as by Cuba, Democratic Yemen and Yemen, which abstained. In Benin's opinion, it was obvious that the peace-keeping operations had not produced any solution and were ineffective; international imperialism had even taken advantage of their presence by permitting Israel to continue its military operations. Cuba stated that it had not contributed to the financing of the Force in the hope that that would improve the Middle East situation.

Abstaining in the vote, the USSR said that, while it supported UNDOF in general, it could not support the increase in expenditures, for which neither the Secretary-General nor ACABQ had given any cogent reasons.

The Congo said it voted in favour in the hope that the great Powers and the United Nations would settle the Middle East question taking into account the inalienable rights of the Palestinians. Also supporting the resolutions, Israel said peace-keeping operations were by definition only temporary and could be no substitute for a peaceful settlement; as imperfect as they were in bringing about a final solution, they seemed better than any alternative in the current circumstances. Japan, stressing the valuable role of peace-keeping operations and the collective financial responsibility of all Member States, said the withholding of contributions was one of the main causes of the financial emergency of the United Nations and imposed an additional financial burden on contributing States.

Morocco remarked that the mandates of the peace-keeping forces had been renewed year after year with no thought given to the rights which had been violated, the populations displaced and the atmosphere of insecurity created by one country which continued its aggression; the United Nations must take steps to ensure security in the region. The United States said peace-keeping forces were the very essence of the principles for which the United Nations had been established and provided a means of maintaining peace while long-term solutions were negotiated; the withholding of contributions threatened the continued participation of some troop-contributing countries and the viability of the United Nations as a peacekeeping organization.

Reports. [1]ACABQ, A/37/597; [2]S-G, A/37/534 & Corr.1.
Resolution (1982). [3]GA: 37/38 A, 30 Nov., text following.
Resolutions (prior). GA: [4]35/45 A, 1 Dec. 1980 (YUN 1980,
p. 366); [5]36/66 A, 30 Nov. 1981 (YUN 1981, p. 296).
Yearbook reference. [6]1981, p. 1298.
Status of contributions. ST/ADM/SER.B/265.
Meeting records. GA: 5th Committee, A/C.5/37/SR.45, 47 (26,
29 Nov.); plenary, A/37/PV.85 (30 Nov.).

General Assembly resolution 37/38 A

30 November 1982   Meeting 85   95-3-17 (recorded vote)

Approved by Fifth Committee (A/37/681) by recorded vote (73-3-14), 29 November
(meeting 47); 10-nation draft (A/C.5/37/L.26, part A, approved together with part
B (see resolution 37/38 B)); agenda item 114 *(a)*.

Sponsors: Australia, Austria, Canada, Denmark, Finland, Ghana, Ireland, New
Zealand, Norway, Sweden.

The General Assembly,

Having considered the report of the Secretary-General on the financing of the United Nations Disengagement Observer Force, as well as
the related report of the Advisory Committee on Administrative and
Budgetary Questions,

Bearing in mind Security Council resolutions 350(1974) of 31 May
1974, 363(1974) of 29 November 1974, 369(1975) of 28 May 1975,
381(1975) of 30 November 1975, 390(1976) of 28 May 1976, 398(1976)
of 30 November 1976, 408(1977) of 20 May 1977, 420(1977) of 30
November 1977, 429(1978) of 31 May 1978, 441(1978) of 30 November
1978, 449(1979) of 30 May 1979, 456(1979) of 30 November 1979,
470(1980) of 30 May 1980, 481(1980) of 26 November 1980, 485(1981)
of 22 May 1981, 493(1981) of 23 November 1981, 506(1982) of 26 May
1982 and 524(1982) of 29 November 1982,

Recalling its resolutions 3101(XXVIII) of 11 December 1973,
3211 B (XXIX) of 29 November 1974, 3374 C (XXX) of 2 December
1975, 31/5 D of 22 December 1976, 32/4 C of 2 December 1977, 33/13 D
of 8 December 1978, 34/7 C of 3 December 1979, 35/44 of 1 December 1980, 35/45 A of 1 December 1980 and 36/66 A of 30 November
1981,

Reaffirming its previous decisions regarding the fact that, in order
to meet the expenditures caused by such operations, a different procedure is required from that applied to meet expenditures of the regular
budget of the United Nations,

Taking into account the fact that the economically more developed
countries are in a position to make relatively larger contributions and
that the economically less developed countries have a relatively limited
capacity to contribute towards peace-keeping operations involving
heavy expenditures,

Bearing in mind the special responsibilities of the States permanent
members of the Security Council in the financing of such operations,
as indicated in General Assembly resolution 1874(S-IV) of 27 June 1963
and other resolutions of the Assembly,

I

Decides to appropriate to the Special Account referred to in section
II, paragraph 1, of General Assembly resolution 3211 B (XXIX) the
amount of $15,973,998 gross ($15,784,998 net) authorized and apportioned by section III of Assembly resolution 36/66 A for the operation
of the United Nations Disengagement Observer Force for the period
from 1 June to 30 November 1982, inclusive;

II

1. *Decides* to appropriate to the Special Account an amount of
$17,186,500 for the operation of the United Nations Disengagement
Observer Force for the period from 1 December 1982 to 31 May 1983,
inclusive;

2. *Decides further*, as an *ad hoc* arrangement, without prejudice
to the positions of principle that may be taken by Member States in
any consideration by the General Assembly of arrangements for the
financing of peace-keeping operations, to apportion the amount of
$17,186,500 among Member States in accordance with the scheme
set out in Assembly resolution 3101(XXVIII) and the provisions of section II, paragraphs 2 *(b)* and 2 *(c)*, and section V, paragraph 1, of resolution 3374 C (XXX), section V, paragraph 1, of resolution 31/5 D, section V, paragraph 1, of resolution 32/4 C, section V, paragraph 1, of
resolution 33/13 D, section V, paragraph 1, of resolution 34/7 C, section V, paragraph 1, of resolution 35/45 A and section V, paragraph 1,

of resolution 36/66 A; the scale of assessments for the years 1980, 1981
and 1982 shall be applied against a portion thereof, that is $2,864,417,
being the amount pertaining on a *pro rata* basis to the month of December 1982, and the scale of assessments for the years 1983, 1984
and 1985 shall be applied against the balance for the period thereafter;

3. *Decides* that there shall be set off against the apportionment
among Member States, as provided in paragraph 2 above, their respective share in the estimated income of $10,000 other than staff assess-
ment income approved for the period from 1 December 1982 to 31
May 1983, inclusive;

4. *Decides* that, in accordance with the provisions of its resolution 973(X) of 15 December 1955, there shall be set off against the
apportionment among Member States, as provided for in paragraph
2 above, their respective share in the Tax Equalization Fund of the estimated staff assessment income of $192,500 approved for the period
from 1 December 1982 to 31 May 1983, inclusive;

III

Authorizes the Secretary-General to enter into commitments for the
United Nations Disengagement Observer Force at a rate not to exceed
$2,864,416 gross ($2,830,666 net) per month for the period from 1 June
to 30 November 1983 inclusive, should the Security Council decide
to continue the Force beyond the period of six months authorized under
its resolution 524(1982), the said amount to be apportioned among
Member States in accordance with the scheme set out in the present
resolution;

IV

1. *Stresses* the need for voluntary contributions to the United Nations Disengagement Observer Force both in cash and in the form of
services and supplies acceptable to the Secretary-General;

2. *Requests* the Secretary-General to take all necessary action to
ensure that the United Nations Disengagement Observer Force is conducted with a maximum of efficiency and economy;

V

1. *Decides* that Antigua and Barbuda, Belize and Vanuatu shall be
included in the group of Member States mentioned in paragraph 2 *(d)*
of General Assembly resolution 3101(XXVIII) and that their contributions to the United Nations Disengagement Observer Force shall be
calculated in accordance with the provisions of the resolution adopted
by the Assembly at the current session regarding the scale of assessments;

2. *Decides further* that, in accordance with regulation 5.2 *(c)* of
the Financial Regulations of the United Nations, the contributions to
the United Nations Disengagement Observer Force until 30 November 1982 of the Member States referred to in paragraph 1 of the present
section shall be treated as miscellaneous income to be set off against
the appropriations apportioned in section II above.

Recorded vote in Assembly as follows:

In favour: Argentina, Australia, Austria, Bahamas, Bahrain, Bangladesh, Barbados, Belgium, Bhutan, Brazil, Burma, Burundi, Canada, Central African Republic, Chile, China, Colombia, Comoros, Congo, Costa Rica, Cyprus, Denmark,
Ecuador, Egypt, Fiji, Finland, France, Gabon, Gambia, Germany, Federal Republic
of, Ghana, Greece, Guyana, Honduras, Iceland, India, Indonesia, Ireland, Israel,
Italy, Ivory Coast, Japan, Jordan, Kenya, Kuwait, Lesotho, Luxembourg, Malawi,
Malaysia, Mali, Malta, Mauritania, Mauritius, Mexico, Morocco, Nepal, Netherlands, New Zealand, Niger, Nigeria, Norway, Oman, Pakistan, Paraguay, Peru,
Philippines, Poland, Portugal, Qatar, Romania, Rwanda, Samoa, Senegal, Sin-
gapore, Solomon Islands, Somalia, Spain, Sri Lanka, Sudan, Sweden, Thailand,
Togo, Trinidad and Tobago, Tunisia, Turkey, United Arab Emirates, United King-
dom, United Republic of Cameroon, United Republic of Tanzania, United States,
Uruguay, Venezuela, Yugoslavia, Zaire, Zambia.

Against: Albania, Iraq, Syrian Arab Republic.

Abstaining: Algeria, Bulgaria, Byelorussian SSR, Cuba, Czechoslovakia,
Democratic Yemen, Dominican Republic, Ethiopia, German Democratic Republic,
Grenada, Hungary, Lao People's Democratic Republic,[a] Mongolia, Ukrainian SSR,
USSR, Viet Nam, Yemen.

[a]Later advised the Secretariat it had not intended to participate in the vote.

Suspension of Financial Regulations

By a resolution of 30 November 1982,[3] the
General Assembly decided to suspend certain provisions of the Financial Regulations of the United
Nations to enable the Organization to retain the
surplus balance of $7,403,489 in the UNDOF

account, instead of having to return this "book surplus" to Member States as a credit against their subsequent assessments.

The resolution was adopted by a recorded vote of 95 to 11, with 11 abstentions. The Fifth Committee, on 29 November, had approved the draft, together with the resolution on appropriations for UNDOF,[2] by a recorded vote of 73 to 3, with 14 abstentions. The drafts were sponsored by 10 nations and introduced by Canada.

According to the ACABQ report of November 1982 on UNDOF financing,[1] the surplus balance represented the interest and miscellaneous income recorded as at 31 December 1981 in the combined account of the former United Nations Emergency Force (1973-1979) and UNDOF. This amount remained on the books after the annual appropriation for UNDOF had been fully spent, although it had in fact been drawn upon to meet the Force's expenses as a supplement to income from contributions, because of the need to make up the shortfall resulting from withholding by some States.

The USSR, explaining its vote against the resolution, advocated strict compliance with the Financial Regulations to ensure economy and efficiency and the return of unspent funds to Member States.

Report. [1]ACABQ, A/37/597.
Resolutions (1982). GA, 30 Nov.: [2]37/38 A; [3]37/38 B, text following.
Meeting records. GA: 5th Committee, A/C.5/37/SR.45, 47 (26, 29 Nov.); plenary, A/37/PV.85 (30 Nov.).

General Assembly resolution 37/38 B

30 November 1982   Meeting 85   95-11-11 (recorded vote)

Approved by Fifth Committee (A/37/681) by recorded vote (73-3-14), 29 November (meeting 47); 10-nation draft (A/C.5/37/L.26, part B, approved together with part A (see resolution 37/38 A)); agenda item 114 *(a)*.

Sponsors: Australia, Austria, Canada, Denmark, Finland, Ghana, Ireland, New Zealand, Norway, Sweden.

The General Assembly,

Having regard to the financial position of the Special Account for the United Nations Emergency Force and the United Nations Disengagement Observer Force, as set forth in the report of the Secretary-General, and referring to paragraph 5 of the report of the Advisory Committee on Administrative and Budgetary Questions,

Mindful of the fact that it is essential to provide the United Nations Disengagement Observer Force with the necessary financial resources to enable it to fulfil its responsibilities under the relevant resolutions of the Security Council,

Concerned that the Secretary-General is continuing to face growing difficulties in meeting the obligations of the Forces on a current basis, particularly those due to the Governments of troop-contributing States,

Recalling its resolutions 33/13 E of 14 December 1978, 34/7 D of 17 December 1979, 35/45 B of 1 December 1980 and 36/66 B of 30 November 1981,

Recognizing that, in consequence of the withholding of contributions by certain Member States, the surplus balances in the Special Account for the United Nations Emergency Force and the United Nations Disengagement Observer Force have, in effect, been drawn upon to the full extent to supplement the income received from contributions for meeting expenses of the Forces,

Concerned that the application of the provisions of regulations 5.2 *(b)*, 5.2 *(d)*, 4.3 and 4.4 of the Financial Regulations of the United Nations would aggravate the already difficult financial situation of the Forces,

Decides that the provisions of regulations 5.2 *(b)*, 5.2 *(d)*, 4.3 and 4.4 of the Financial Regulations of the United Nations shall be suspended in respect of the amount of $7,403,489, which otherwise would have to be surrendered pursuant to those provisions, this amount to be entered in the account referred to in the operative part of General Assembly resolution 33/13 E and held in suspense until a further decision is taken by the Assembly.

Recorded vote in Assembly as follows:

In favour: Argentina, Australia, Austria, Bahamas, Bahrain, Bangladesh, Barbados, Belgium, Bhutan, Brazil, Burma, Burundi, Canada, Central African Republic, Chile, China, Colombia, Comoros, Congo, Costa Rica, Cyprus, Denmark, Ecuador, Egypt, Fiji, Finland, France, Gabon, Gambia, Germany, Federal Republic of, Ghana, Greece, Guyana, Honduras, Iceland, India, Indonesia, Ireland, Israel, Italy, Ivory Coast, Japan, Jordan, Kenya, Kuwait, Lesotho, Luxembourg, Malawi, Malaysia, Mali, Malta, Mauritania, Mauritius, Mexico, Morocco, Nepal, Netherlands, New Zealand, Niger, Nigeria, Norway, Oman, Pakistan, Paraguay, Peru, Philippines, Portugal, Qatar, Rwanda, Samoa, Senegal, Sierra Leone, Singapore, Solomon Islands, Somalia, Spain, Sri Lanka, Sudan, Swaziland, Sweden, Thailand, Togo, Trinidad and Tobago, Tunisia, Turkey, United Arab Emirates, United Kingdom, United Republic of Cameroon, United Republic of Tanzania, United States, Uruguay, Venezuela, Yugoslavia, Zaire, Zambia.

Against: Albania, Bulgaria, Byelorussian SSR, Czechoslovakia, German Democratic Republic, Hungary, Iraq, Mongolia, Syrian Arab Republic, Ukrainian SSR, USSR.

Abstaining: Algeria, Cuba, Democratic Yemen, Dominican Republic, Ethiopia, Grenada, Lao People's Democratic Republic,[a] Poland, Romania, Viet Nam, Yemen.

[a]Later advised the Secretariat it had not intended to participate in the vote.

Situation in the territories occupied by Israel

Annexation of the Golan Heights

In 1982, the Security Council, at nine meetings in January, and the General Assembly, in January/February and November/December, dealt with the situation concerning the Golan Heights following the enactment by Israel's Knesset (Parliament) on 14 December 1981 of legislation to extend Israeli laws, jurisdiction and administration to the area.[29] Since 1967 the Golan Heights, a part of the Syrian Arab Republic near the borders with Israel and Lebanon, had been occupied by Israel. On 17 December 1981, both the Council and the General Assembly had decided that the decision was null and void and called on Israel to rescind it.

In January 1982, the Council, owing to the negative vote of a permanent member (United States), failed to adopt a draft resolution by Jordan calling for a condemnation of Israel and deciding that all United Nations Members should refrain from assisting and co-operating with Israel. In view of the lack of unanimity among its permanent members, the Council called on 28 January for the holding of an emergency special session of the Assembly. Accordingly, the Assembly convened its ninth such session from 29 January to 5 February and, by a resolution of 5 February, condemned Israel for not rescinding its decision and called for the severance of relations with Israel and for its total isolation; the Assembly termed the Israeli decision an act of aggression and effective annexation.

By several resolutions adopted in December at the regular session, the Assembly reiterated its demand that Israel rescind its decision. The decision was also condemned by the Commission on Human Rights in February, and by a number of States in communications to the Secretary-General and the President of the Security Council.

The situation in the Golan Heights was also examined by the Special Committee to Investigate Israeli Practices Affecting the Human Rights of the Population of the Occupied Territories. The Committee stated in its annual report, adopted in August,[15] that the decision to annex the area had triggered an unprecedented wave of resistance.

Communications (6-15 January). On 6 January 1982,[3] Cuba transmitted a communiqué of a 5 January meeting in New York of the Movement of Non-Aligned Countries, condemning Israel's action of 14 December 1981 to impose its laws, jurisdiction and administration on the Golan Heights, and calling on the Security Council to take measures under Chapter VII of the Charter of the United Nations (on action with respect to threats to the peace, breaches of the peace and acts of aggression) to oblige Israel to restore all occupied Syrian territories to the full sovereignty of the Syrian Arab Republic.

On 8 January,[10] Jordan conveyed a letter of 7 January from the Secretary-General of the Organization of the Islamic Conference to the Security Council President, calling on the Council to adopt firmer and more effective measures against Israel in view of its annexation of the Golan Heights.

On 5 and 7 January, respectively, Mongolia[11] and Benin[2] transmitted government statements (Mongolia, Ministry of Foreign Affairs representative, 18 December 1981; Benin, Political Bureau of the Central Committee of the Parti de la Révolution Populaire du Bénin, 28 December 1981) condemning Israel's action. Similarly, Cyprus, by a note verbale of 15 January,[5] informed the Secretary-General of the adoption on 14 January by its House of Representatives of a resolution condemning the annexation.

Security Council consideration (6-20 January). At eight meetings between 6 and 20 January 1982, the Security Council resumed its consideration of the situation in the Golan Heights resulting from Israel's December 1981 decision to apply its laws, jurisdiction and administration to that territory. The meetings were held in accordance with the Council's decision, in its December 1981 resolution on the question,[27] that in the event of Israel's non-compliance with its demand to rescind the decision it would meet again urgently to consider taking appropriate measures in accordance with the Charter.

On 20 January, the Council voted on a revised draft resolution submitted by Jordan,[1] strongly condemning Israel for its failure to comply with the resolutions on the Golan Heights adopted in December 1981 by the Council[27] and the General Assembly,[24] and determining that Israel's measures in the area, culminating in its December 1981 decision, were an act of aggression under Article 39 of the Charter (the first Article of Chapter VII). The Council would have decided that all Member States should consider applying concrete measures in order to nullify the annexation and to refrain from providing any assistance to and cooperation with Israel, in all fields, in order to deter it in its policies and practices of annexation.

Acting under Article 25 (by which United Nations Members agree to accept and carry out Council decisions), the Council would have called on Member States to carry out its decision. It would also have urged non-members to act accordingly and called on United Nations bodies and agencies to conform their relations with Israel to the terms of the resolution. A committee would have been established to examine and report on implementation of the resolution.

The draft, which received 9 votes to 1 (United States), with 5 abstentions (France, Ireland, Japan, Panama, United Kingdom), was not adopted due to the negative vote of a permanent Council member.

The original version of this proposal would have had the Council decide that all Member States should refrain from supplying Israel with any weapons and related military equipment and should suspend any military as well as economic, financial and technological assistance to Israel. In addition, it would have requested that Members consider suspending diplomatic and consular relations with Israel.

Jordan, introducing the original version, said it was the unanimous draft of the Arab world represented in the League of Arab States and had the consensus support of the Movement of Non-Aligned Countries and the support of all other regions. The Arab world, facing all-out aggression, was determined to defeat and repel that aggression by all possible means provided in the Charter; nevertheless, to facilitate acceptance, the proposal was selective in its choice of measures and was truly minimal.

Opposing the draft, the United States considered it an aberration of the very purpose of the Council because, far from preventing an aggravation of the situation, it had already exacerbated the problem by dividing people, sowing suspicions and feeding hostilities; although disapproving of Israel's annexation of the Golan Heights, the United States would not be deterred from its search for constructive means to achieve peace for Israel and its neighbours.

Those abstaining in the vote nevertheless reiterated their condemnation of Israel's decision and considered it null and void. France and the United

Kingdom felt that the draft did not provide the basis for a consensus. France thought a really constructive resolution should have recalled the need for withdrawal from the territories occupied by Israel since 1967 and should have included provisions opening the way to a Middle East peace, including recognition of the rights of the Palestinians. The United Kingdom had doubts about a Council determination that Israel's action constituted an act of aggression; instead, the Council should have called on all States to refrain from any acts or dealings which would imply recognition of or lend support to Israel's decision, and should have required Member States to refrain from providing assistance that would be used in the Golan Heights, refuse to have any contact with Israeli institutions there and refrain from participation in events or activities organized there by Israel.

Ireland expressed similar views about the desirable contents of a Council resolution; it also found the call on Member States to refrain from co-operating with Israel in all fields to be too broad, adding that it would have preferred a call to refrain from aid or co-operation which would encourage Israel in its annexation policies.

Though demanding that Israel immediately rescind its decision and seeing grounds for considering some kind of punitive action, Japan questioned whether the draft would contribute to a real solution of the problem, which was rooted in the unstable Middle East situation.

The USSR felt that the draft was not enough, as it did not provide the necessary decisive measures against Israel; under the circumstances, however, its adoption would be in the interests of the Syrian Arab Republic and other victims of Israeli aggression. Zaire explained that the draft had to be seen as the outcome of intensive efforts at compromise in the group of the non-aligned countries members of the Council.

The Syrian Arab Republic stated that, by trying to absolve Israel, the United States was helping to legitimize and prolong Israeli occupation not only of the Golan Heights but also of other Arab territories; both the United States and Israel were blackmailing the Syrian Arab Republic to make it surrender its rights as well as those of the people of Palestine.

Because of permissiveness and depleted resolve, Jordan said, one or more of the major Powers was unwilling to go along with the draft, suggesting conditions and negotiations with the aggressor after he had eaten the cake. The draft was a mere first step towards implementation of Chapter VII of the Charter. The latest Israeli measures not only constituted a clear-cut act of aggression, but also a continuing threat to peace and security in the Middle East as in the whole world.

The United Arab Emirates expressed grave concern at the United States veto; had it not been for United States support, Israel would not have dared to commit acts of aggression against the Arabs and to treat the Council resolutions with defiance and contempt.

Prior to the vote, Israel and the Syrian Arab Republic, as well as Afghanistan, Algeria, Bangladesh, Bulgaria, Burundi, Cuba, Czechoslovakia, Democratic Yemen, the German Democratic Republic, Greece, Grenada, Hungary, India, Indonesia, Iraq, Kuwait, the Lao People's Democratic Republic, the Libyan Arab Jamahiriya, Mauritania, Mongolia, Morocco, Nicaragua, Oman, Pakistan, Portugal, Qatar, Saudi Arabia, Senegal, Sri Lanka, the Sudan, the Ukrainian SSR, the United Arab Emirates, Viet Nam, Yemen and Yugoslavia, were invited, at their request, to participate in the debate without the right to vote.

At Jordan's request in a letter of 5 January,[9] the Council extended an invitation under rule 39 of its provisional rules of procedure[f] to the Permanent Observer of the League of Arab States to the United Nations. The Council also decided by a vote, requested by the United States, of 11 to 1 (United States), with 3 abstentions (France, Japan, United Kingdom), to accord an invitation to a representative of the Palestine Liberation Organization (PLO) to participate in the debate and that the invitation would give PLO the same rights of participation as those conferred on a Member State when invited under rule 37.[g] The latter invitation had also been proposed by Jordan on 5 January.[8]

Starting the debate, the Syrian Arab Republic reaffirmed its view that the annexation of the Golan Heights by Israel was an act of aggression and a grave breach of international law, as well as a unilateral breach of the 1967 cease-fire.[28] By changing the status of the Golan Heights from an occupied to an annexed territory, Israel was threatening the foundations of the international political system, returning to the time when States took the law into their own hands. The Council had the duty to determine the existence of a threat to peace, breach of peace and a flagrant act of aggression. The Syrian Arab Republic also reaffirmed its right to demand that the Council impose sanctions in order to compel Israel to abrogate its annexation, withdraw unconditionally from the occupied Syrian territories and thereby protect Syrian territorial integrity. If the Council failed to discharge its responsibilities, the Syrian Arab Republic reserved its right to deal with Israel's aggression under Article 51 (on the right of self-defence).

[f]See footnote b on p. 430.
[g]See footnote a on p. 429.

Israel stated that the Syrian Arab Republic had persistently and adamantly refused to recognize or negotiate with Israel, or even to maintain tolerable neighbourly relations. Between 1948 and 1967 it had made the Golan Heights the most advanced bridgehead for aggression and harassment of Israel and its population. In disregard of the Council's affirmation in 1967 of the right of every State in the area to live in peace within secure and recognized boundaries[25] and its 1973 call for peace negotiations,[26] it had refused to go beyond agreements on a cease-fire and military disengagement. The aim of the legislation for the Golan Heights, enacted in the absence of peace or even negotiations, was to normalize the situation in the area. The rights of the local population, including property rights and the right to education and religious worship, were fully safeguarded. Israel declared itself ready to negotiate unconditionally with the Syrian Arab Republic and its other neighbours for a lasting peace in accordance with the 1967[25] and 1973[26] Council resolutions on principles for a Middle East peace.

Most of the other speakers condemned Israel's annexation of the Golan Heights, urged its withdrawal from the area and urged the Council to take strong measures in order to bring about Israel's compliance and reinforce its own authority and credibility. Most of these specifically called for the imposition of sanctions, including Afghanistan, Algeria, Bangladesh, Bulgaria, Burundi, China, Cuba (for the Movement of Non-Aligned Countries), Czechoslovakia, Democratic Yemen (as Chairman of the Arab Group), the German Democratic Republic, Grenada, Guyana, Hungary, India, Indonesia, Iraq, Kuwait, the Lao People's Democratic Republic, the Libyan Arab Jamahiriya, Mauritania, Mongolia, Morocco, Nicaragua, Oman, Pakistan, Poland, Qatar, Saudi Arabia, Sri Lanka, the Sudan, Togo, Uganda, the Ukrainian SSR, the USSR, the United Arab Emirates, Viet Nam, Yemen, Yugoslavia, the PLO observer and the Permanent Observer of the League of Arab States. Others calling for Council action to obtain Israel's compliance but not specifically urging sanctions were Greece and Senegal.

Portugal, stressing the unanimity with which the Council had acted in December 1981, asked it to ensure favourable conditions for the observance of principles agreed on by the international community; if the Council were again to act unanimously, it would increase its moral authority to which Portugal attached particular importance. Though regarding the request for sanctions as legitimate and well founded, Zaire remarked that any division in the Council on the means would complicate peace initiatives, whereas a unanimous position would have enormous moral weight, which Israel could not disregard because of its increasing isolation; Zaire suggested that the Council call on Member States to refrain from all actions that might imply recognition or support of Israel's decision to annex the Golan Heights, and that it consider having the Secretary-General or a committee undertake renewed efforts for a solution to the Middle East crisis.

In Spain's opinion, the Council could not remain inactive, because that would open the door to similar Israeli action in another territory; Spain would support measures to compel Israel to rescind its decisions and withdraw from the occupied territories.

Many speakers referred to Israel's latest action as an act of aggression. Jordan and the Syrian Arab Republic cited the Definition of Aggression adopted by the General Assembly in 1974,[23] which included "any annexation by the use of force of the territory of another State or part thereof".

In the opinion of Algeria, Guyana, Mongolia, the Sudan, the USSR, Yemen and the PLO observer, the annexation was another step towards the annexation of other occupied Arab territories. Without firm Council action, stated China, what had happened in regard to the 1,600 square kilometres of the Golan Heights occupied by Israel could recur in another Arab nation, and what had happened in the Middle East could recur elsewhere, with the result that aggressors would become even more reckless and unbridled. Democratic Yemen warned that the annexation might be a harbinger of more United States military involvement in the Middle East.

Guyana stated that, by annexing the Golan Heights, Israel was unilaterally seeking to alter the accepted basis for a Middle East settlement, which the Council must not permit. Others, among them Senegal, also felt that the issue of the Golan Heights had to be considered in the context of an overall solution to the Middle East problem. Togo said that, by increasing tension in the region, Israel's decision jeopardized efforts to bring about a negotiated settlement of the Israel-Arab conflict and the establishment of a just, lasting and comprehensive peace. In the opinion of Poland and Zaire, the Israeli decision emphasized more forcefully than ever the urgency of achieving an overall political settlement.

Yugoslavia expressed the view that the annexation had unforeseeable consequences for the Middle East situation as well as for wider international relations, and was a serious blow to all constructive efforts for a peaceful Middle East solution. Saudi Arabia considered the annexation a calculated move to undermine the Middle East peace process and to render a just, permanent and comprehensive solution an impossibility. Bulgaria said Israel's decision was a premeditated political provocation designed to heighten tension in the Middle East.

Ireland said any implication that Israel did not consider its decision as absolutely unalterable should be welcomed.

Several speakers said Israel was being shielded from the consequences of its aggressive moves by the United States veto in the Council, which prevented the Council from taking effective measures to deter Israel. Among those holding this opinion, or otherwise criticizing United States support for Israel, were Afghanistan, Bulgaria, Czechoslovakia, Democratic Yemen, the German Democratic Republic, Hungary, Iraq, Mongolia, Qatar, the Ukrainian SSR, the United Arab Emirates, Viet Nam, Yemen and the Permanent Observer of the League of Arab States.

India welcomed the fact that the United States had suspended its strategic co-operation agreement with Israel following the Golan Heights decision. However, the USSR remarked that the verbal acrobatics and pseudo-quarrels surrounding the revocation of that agreement did not alter the essence of the relationship between Washington and Tel Aviv; Israel had virtually received its mandate for the annexation from the United States, in spite of the latter's attempt to dissociate itself from the action through symbolic reprimands.

Further communication (25 January). By a note verbale of 25 January,[4] Cuba transmitted a communiqué adopted that day by a meeting in New York of the Movement of Non-Aligned Countries, expressing grave concern at the Security Council's failure to take measures against Israel under Chapter VII of the Charter and strongly urging the Council to convene an emergency special session of the General Assembly on the Israeli annexation of the Golan Heights.

Security Council action (28 January). Stating that the lack of unanimity among its permanent members had prevented it from exercising its primary responsibility for the maintenance of international peace and security, the Security Council, by a resolution of 28 January,[22] decided to call an emergency special session of the General Assembly on the Golan Heights issue.

The resolution was adopted by 13 votes to none, with 2 abstentions (United Kingdom, United States). Its sponsor, Jordan, stated in introducing it that Israel's refusal to heed the Council's December 1981[27] call to rescind its decision compelled United Nations Members to decide on measures to restore and maintain international peace and security.

The United Kingdom was not convinced that a further discussion in the Assembly would help achieve the objective of getting Israel to rescind its decision and to refrain from similar actions; it would prefer to see the Council make a further

effort to reach agreement on a resolution. The United States argued that no practical purpose would be served by holding another debate, which would be an exercise in futility that would not advance the cause of peace.

Agreeing with the convening of an emergency special session, France said it was prepared to join in measures designed to express the fact that Israel's decision was null and void; however, it could not support provisions which contravened the rules of competence applied to the Council and the Assembly as set forth in the Charter, and would oppose in particular any resolution involving sanctions.

Israel held that there was no basis for convening an emergency special session simultaneously with the regular Assembly session (then in recess), even if one were to assume that an emergency situation did exist. Israel reiterated this opinion in letters of 28 January to the Secretary-General and the Council President.[6]

General Assembly action (February). In accordance with the 28 January Security Council resolution, the General Assembly convened from 29 January to 5 February in its ninth emergency special session.

By a resolution of 5 February,[17] adopted after 10 meetings of debate, the Assembly strongly condemned Israel for its failure to comply with the Security Council's and its own call to rescind the decision to impose Israeli laws, jurisdiction and administration on the Golan Heights. Declaring that the decision constituted an act of aggression and was null and void, the Assembly determined that all actions by Israel to give effect to it were illegal and invalid, and that Israel's continued occupation and annexation of the Golan Heights were a continuing threat to international peace and security. The Assembly strongly deplored the negative vote by a permanent Council member which had prevented the adoption of measures under Chapter VII of the Charter, and deplored any political, economic, military and technological support to Israel that encouraged it to commit acts of aggression and to consolidate and perpetuate its occupation and annexation of occupied Arab territories.

The Assembly firmly emphasized its demands that Israel rescind its decision, which had resulted in the effective annexation of the Golan Heights; reaffirmed the necessity of total and unconditional Israeli withdrawal from the occupied territories; and declared that Israel's actions confirmed that it was not a peace-loving State. The Assembly called on Member States to: refrain from supplying Israel with weapons, related equipment and military assistance; refrain from acquiring weapons or military equipment from Israel; suspend economic, financial and technological assistance and co-operation; sever diplomatic, trade and cultural relations; and cease all dealings with Israel in order totally to isolate it. Nonmember States, United Nations agencies and international institutions were called upon to conform their relations with Israel to the terms of the resolution. The Secretary-General was requested to report every two months on its implementation.

The resolution was adopted by a roll-call vote of 86 to 21, with 34 abstentions. Prior to its adoption, the Assembly rejected, by a roll-call vote of 76 to 39, with 19 abstentions, a motion by France to take separate votes on several paragraphs. Opposing that proposal, Jordan requested a vote on the text as a whole, saying it was coherent, balanced and logical and there was not a word in it that did not come from the Charter or Assembly or Security Council resolutions.

Introducing the draft on behalf of 56 nations, Cuba stated that the overwhelming majority of participants in the Assembly debate agreed in their total rejection and condemnation of the annexation, and in their collective determination to prevent acceptance of Israel's expansionist action; it was unfortunate that the Council had been prevented from imposing sanctions. By turning to the United Nations, the Syrian Arab Republic had demonstrated its willingness to act in accordance with international law.

Rejecting the text as a shameless document and a monument to moral degeneration and intellectual corruption, Israel said it would neither contribute to the advancement of peace in the Middle East nor deter Israel from doing everything necessary to ensure its existence and security.

Expressing agreement with many elements of the text, New Zealand cast a negative vote on the grounds that the resolution sought to have the Assembly assume the Council's responsibilities and did not improve the prospects of negotiations for a comprehensive and durable peace; New Zealand also could not support the proposed measures against Israel and the implication that future action could be taken to limit Israel's participation in the United Nations.

Australia, Belgium (speaking also on behalf of Denmark, France, the Federal Republic of Germany, Italy, Luxembourg, the Netherlands and the United Kingdom), Canada, Fiji, Finland, Ireland, Japan and Norway expressed similar views. Sweden said a series of provisions were unacceptable from the point of view of the Charter or for their substantive content. Belgium, Ireland and Japan cautioned that their vote should not be interpreted as condoning Israel's actions, and the others reiterated their objection to the Israeli decision on the Golan Heights.

Norway also voiced reservations on the determination that Israel's decision was an act of aggression, and on the provisions deploring the United States veto in the Security Council and support to Israel. The latter two provisions also met with the disapproval of Belgium and Ireland, Belgium remarking that the criticism was groundless and unacceptable. In addition, Canada and Sweden objected to the determination that the annexation decision was a threat to international peace and security, and Canada said it could not support any provision which attempted to prejudge the outcome of negotiations, such as the one reaffirming the necessity of total Israeli withdrawal from the occupied territories. Belgium and Ireland thought the appeal for sanctions would make the prospects for negotiations more remote; they suggested that the Assembly would be better advised to call on States to refrain from acts implying recognition of or support for Israel's decision. Norway believed the call for sanctions was wrong and unproductive and that such measures would only heighten tension and bitterness. Fiji believed that any State had the right to acquire arms for its defence commensurate with its genuine security needs, that the severance of relations with another State was the prerogative of individual States and that the resolution would run counter to the universality of United Nations membership. Portugal regretted that the resolution was deprived of the undisputed authority it would have had if it had reflected an international consensus condemning Israel's action; however, certain elements made the text clearly unacceptable.

France felt that the text was aimed at ostracizing and isolating a Member State, particularly in United Nations agencies.

Though disapproving of Israel's decision, the United States found the resolution profoundly objectionable and procedurally flawed for several reasons: it assigned to the Assembly responsibilities of the Security Council; it damaged prospects of peace, distorted reality, was unreasonably punitive, and sought revenge and retribution rather than conciliation and compromise; it described the Israeli legislation as annexation, when neither the United States nor the Security Council had recognized it as such; it attacked the United States by deploring the veto cast in the Council to block action which the United States deemed profoundly ill-conceived and imprudent; and it attempted to submit questions of membership to the Assembly, thereby striking at the principle of minority rights.

Abstaining in the vote, Egypt said that, while it fully sympathized with and subscribed to the just Syrian cause, it felt that the resolution had far-reaching consequences and could not be an optimally practical or practicable avenue leading to a Middle East solution.

Chile stated that some provisions did not reduce the scope of the conflict and, on the contrary, might contribute to spreading it; Chile also expressed concern about the absence of a reference to the 1967[25] and 1973[26] Council resolutions. Zaire said some provisions would not encourage efforts to find a comprehensive, just and lasting Middle East solution, and might even lead to a more serious deterioration.

Costa Rica felt that the resolution involved questions of competence and legality incompatible with the treatment of the subject by the Assembly. El Salvador said some paragraphs were excessive and did not contribute to peace, while Spain held that some paragraphs went considerably beyond the draft resolution considered by the Security Council, and one of them raised problems with regard to the interpretation of the Charter; Spain would have preferred to have the text vetoed in the Council resubmitted to the Assembly with the required adaptations. Trinidad and Tobago said it had reservations on certain elements.

Argentina, observing that the Council alone was authorized to apply broad and binding sanctions, said it did not consider itself bound by the sanctions provisions of the resolution. Barbados, Guatemala and Venezuela said the call for sanctions would not help achieve peace, or, Barbados added, enhance the Assembly's reputation for even-handed justice. The Bahamas, Bolivia, Chile, the Dominican Republic and Honduras also disagreed with the sanctions provisions, the Bahamas objecting that such extreme measures had proved unrealistic and non-productive in other situations and Bolivia stating that they were within the exclusive purview of the Security Council. Colombia stated that those provisions were contrary to the Charter, within the competence of other organs and encroached on areas within the sovereign competence of States. Ecuador reserved its position on what it regarded as provisions of questionable legality in regard to the relations of States with Israel, remarking that the establishment or non-establishment of relations with a country was a matter within each State's jurisdiction.

Brazil believed that the prospects of attaining Israel's withdrawal from the occupied territories and the right of the Palestinians to establish their own State should not be curtailed as a result of the diplomatic isolation of one of the parties, even if that party was behaving in a manner incompatible with international law and United Nations resolutions; Israel should not be given any pretext to act with still greater contempt for the principles of mutually respectful relations. Saint Lucia's view was that, if the sanctions were ineffective because of non-compliance of a large number of States, Israel would only become more brazen; moreover, to ostracize Israel so completely would leave it aloof from the very States it must negotiate with.

Argentina, the Bahamas, Bolivia, Chile, Colombia, Costa Rica, the Dominican Republic, Ecuador, Honduras and Turkey objected to the declaration that Israel was not a peace-loving State. Argentina added that it rejected any move to suspend a Member State or to reject its credentials. Chile believed that the principle of universality of United Nations membership was essential.

Bolivia, Chile, the Dominican Republic, Honduras and Turkey disagreed with the provisions deploring the veto by a Council member; Turkey said it had consistently objected to singling out third-party Governments for condemnation. Turkey also had reservations on the call on United Nations agencies and international institutions to conform their relations with Israel to the terms of the resolution, saying that intent and ultimate purpose was not clear.

The Bahamas, Bolivia and the Dominican Republic disagreed with the provision deploring support to Israel.

Regretting the introduction of highly controversial elements with serious legal and political implications for the distribution of competences between United Nations organs, Austria expressed concern that the vote on the resolution had failed to express the unanimous rejection of the *de facto* annexation; in proper consultations, it would have been possible to arrive at a resolution that would have found the broadest support, would have been oriented towards positive action and, through a call for negotiations between the parties, would have contributed to promoting a process towards a peace settlement.

Though voting in favour, Burma, Nepal, Peru, Suriname and Togo had reservations on the provision declaring that Israel was not a peace-loving State. Togo remarked that the provision should be strictly interpreted as not going beyond an observation, which it hoped Israel would disprove. Nepal and Peru also reserved their position on the call for measures against Israel; Nepal believed such measures to be within the Security Council's prerogative, while Peru described them as extreme steps that would not contribute to a dialogue. Greece and Suriname voiced reservations on the provisions calling for suspension of assistance to Israel and of co-operation and dealings with it, and for the severance of relations; Greece said it would vote against the paragraph calling for a cessation of all dealings with Israel if there were a separate vote. Burma, Greece and Nepal reserved their position on the paragraph deploring the veto. Burma further had serious reservations on the provisions declaring Israel's action to be an act of aggression, deploring support to Israel, and calling on specialized agencies and institutions to conform their relations with Israel to the terms of the resolution.

Romania explained that it had been unable to participate in the vote since it had not been possible to achieve a resolution acceptable to the great majority of Member States; in its opinion, the Assembly would have been well advised to set up a committee of United Nations Members to try to bring about a comprehensive Middle East settlement through negotiations.

Democratic Kampuchea said that, although it supported condemnation of Israel's annexation of the Golan Heights, it had not participated in the vote because Viet Nam was among the resolution's sponsors.

Opening the debate, the Syrian Arab Republic said the usurpation of part of Syrian soil manifested Israel's aggressive and expansionist objectives, aimed at establishing a State extending from the Nile to the Euphrates. Its decision was only a chapter in a long series of aggressive, expansionist actions. Even Israel's friends were unable to justify and defend such a policy, in the face of which it was important to impose deterrent sanctions that would compel Israel to review its measures and abandon its aggression and racism. Those sanctions should include a suspension of Israel's membership in the United Nations, a halt to all military, political, economic and cultural dealings with it, and a call to the United States to desist from support to Israel.

Israel, on the other hand, charged that for over a quarter of a century the Syrian Arab Republic had been engaging in relentless hostilities against it, with the Golan Heights as the most advanced bridgehead for aggression until Israel stormed the area in 1967 and forced the Syrian army back to a point where it could no longer threaten Israeli villages. Israel could not be expected to maintain indefinitely a military administration on the Golan Heights merely to accommodate Syrian interests in persistent conflict. It was unconscionable for the Syrian Arab Republic to find fault with legislation which sought, in the absence of peace, to normalize the situation in the area and which in no way precluded or impaired the prospect of peace negotiations.

During the debate, most speakers denounced or condemned Israel's decision as a clear violation of international law, in particular the principle of the inadmissibility of the acquisition of territory by force, and an action that increased tension in the region and threatened or was likely to threaten international peace and security. The doctrine as stated by Ecuador was that armed force did not create rights and armed victory conferred no rights.

Several of those regarding the action as a violation of international law cited the 1949 Geneva Convention relative to the Protection of Civilian Persons in Time of War, especially its article 47, stating that protected persons could not be deprived of the benefits of the Convention by a purported annexation of occupied territories. A number of speakers also regarded the action as contravening the 1967[25] and 1973[26] Security Council resolutions, specifically the provisions stipulating the inadmissibility of the acquisition of territory by force and the right of States in the region to live in peace within secure and recognized boundaries.

Jordan said the annexation of the Golan Heights would perpetuate the dispersal of close to 200,000 inhabitants who had lived there before the Israeli occupation and overnight transform the remnants—a mere 13,000 whose Syrian roots went back thousands of years—from Syrian into Israeli citizens. The Niger said that, according to information addressed to the Commission on Human Rights, the inhabitants of the Golan Heights had been subjected to new harassment since 14 December 1981, including the seizure of pastureland and water resources, arbitrary arrests, expropriation and unjustified dismissals, and the first Israeli magistrate's court in the Golan Heights had been opened on 3 February 1982 by Israel's Minister of Justice—all demonstrating that Israel had no intention of complying with the Security Council's injunctions.

Speaking for the European Community (EC) members, Belgium characterized Israel's action as tantamount to annexation—a view shared by most other speakers.

The Byelorussian SSR, Czechoslovakia and Iran considered the annexation a direct consequence of the policy of separate negotiations. The USSR considered it quite instructive that the new hostile step against the Syrian Arab Republic had been decided on immediately after the signing in November 1981 of Israeli-American strategic co-operation agreements; Israel had clearly intended to punish the Syrian Arab Republic for its rejection of the Camp David accords, the USSR added. Madagascar and others also saw a connection between the strategic co-operation agreements and the Golan Heights action.

United States support of Israel was held responsible for Israel's defiance of the international community by a number of speakers, many of whom also said its use of the veto in the Security Council served to shield Israel from effective international deterrence. Among those expressing such views were Afghanistan, Albania, Bahrain, Benin, Bulgaria, the Byelorussian SSR, Cuba, Czechoslovakia, Democratic Yemen, the German Democratic Republic, Guinea, Hungary, Iran, Iraq, Jordan, Kuwait, the Lao People's Democratic Republic, the Libyan Arab Jamahiriya, Madagascar, Mauritania, Mongolia, Nicaragua, the Syrian Arab Republic, the Ukrainian SSR, the USSR, the United Arab Emirates, the United Republic of Tanzania and Viet Nam.

Afghanistan said the United States, besides giving Israel a mandate to appropriate Syrian lands, had encouraged Israeli extremists to go ahead with new territorial acquisitions. Mauritania regarded the United States veto as giving encouragement to Israel for its misdeeds and therefore dangerous encouragement to repeat them—a view shared by Malaysia. Similarly, Saudi Arabia feared that Israel would interpret the United States veto as a signal to annex other parts of the occupied territories and to pursue its expansionist policy. Viet Nam thought the Assembly should condemn the United States as the instigator and protector of the Zionist aggressors.

Sri Lanka, commenting on the view expressed in the Security Council that it was important to maintain consensus, said it was for that purpose that the draft resolution in the Council had been revised to make it non-mandatory; Sri Lanka asked whether the United Nations had no alternative but to provide through the consensus principle another display of forbearance to a State that had defied its principal organs.

Many speakers argued that no country had the right to use the defence of its own security or the existence of a state of war as a pretext for invading and annexing the territory of a neighbouring State. This point was made by, among others, China, Cyprus, Kenya, the Niger, Nigeria, Poland, Romania, Singapore, Suriname, the United Republic of Cameroon, the United Republic of Tanzania and Zaire.

In response to Israel's statement that its action was aimed at normalizing the situation in the Golan Heights, Uganda said the situation could be normalized only by restoring the territory to the Syrian Arab Republic, not by annexing it—a view shared by China, India, Madagascar, Pakistan, Singapore and Suriname. Somalia considered it a strong possibility that Israel would proceed to "normalize" in similar fashion the undoubtedly anomalous situation in other illegally occupied territories.

In the opinion of Senegal, Sweden, Turkey and others, Israel's action weakened the prospects for negotiations. Belgium, on behalf of the EC members, said the decision further complicated the search for a Middle East settlement—a view widely shared by others, including Egypt, Finland, Kenya, Malaysia, Nepal, the Philippines, Romania and Venezuela. Malta said Israel had shattered any immediate prospect of reconciliation; Uganda believed the annexation was intended to block a peaceful settlement, and the USSR thought that Israel's decision on the Golan Heights reflected its lack of interest in peaceful relations with its neighbours. Singapore believed that the annexation further encouraged extremism in the Arab world and compromised the Camp David peace process. In

order to create an atmosphere conducive to negotiations, Sweden stated, it was imperative that the parties show restraint and avoid provocative measures such as the decision taken by Israel.

New Zealand saw little chance of real progress towards a settlement until Israel was prepared to respect the rights and interests of other States and peoples in the region; at the same time, there was little prospect for worthwhile negotiations unless all parties were prepared formally to recognize Israel's right to exist.

In Japan's view, Israel's attitude would never contribute to the consolidation of its own security but would only result in deepening mistrust of Israel on the part of the Arab countries and increasing isolation in the international community. Jamaica felt that the annexation had intensified the animosities between the Arabs and Israel. Peru feared that Israel's counter-productive policy encouraged retaliation, while Benin believed that its actions, and the failure of the United Nations to respond, left the Syrian Arab Republic with no choice other than recourse to the right to self-defence—or, as Nigeria put it, redress through force.

In Senegal's opinion, Israel seemed determined to oppose a peaceful settlement, except perhaps one that would accord with conditions Israel itself had imposed by force. A similar position was held by the Congo and Madagascar. Egypt said Syrian sovereignty and territorial integrity were matters and principles not subject to negotiation and must not be the object of bargaining or blackmail. Sri Lanka questioned whether the Syrian Arab Republic could be expected to negotiate on the basis of a *fait accompli* and under duress, a position also held by Ethiopia. The United Republic of Tanzania said Israel could not call for unconditional negotiations while, through its continued occupation of Arab territories and illegal annexation of Syrian territory, it was in fact creating conditions for such negotiations. A similar point was made by Somalia. Bulgaria considered the formula of negotiations without preconditions as a pre-condition in itself; by insisting that the Arabs recognize the consequences of Israel's aggression against them, Israel attempted to camouflage its refusal to engage in genuine negotiations and sought to cover up its expansionist plans.

Israel was urged to rescind its decision by most delegations, including Austria, Belgium (on behalf of the EC members), Egypt, Finland, Gabon, Jamaica, Japan, Nepal, New Zealand, Panama, Peru, the Philippines, Romania, Singapore, Thailand, Turkey, the USSR, the United States and Yugoslavia. Panama said Israel could give concrete proof of its good will by speedily rescinding its decision.

Albania, Bhutan, Czechoslovakia, Djibouti, Grenada, Guyana, Jordan, Mali, the Sudan, Togo, Uganda and others regarded Israel's decision and its refusal to rescind its law as an act of aggression under the Charter and as defined by the Assembly in 1974.[23] Benin considered it an act of war. The German Democratic Republic charged Israel with suppressing legitimate protests of the Syrian population in the area and openly threatening war against the Syrian Arab Republic.

Many States saw the annexation of the Golan Heights as part of an Israeli design to annex or otherwise consolidate and perpetuate control over all occupied territories or even to expand beyond its original boundaries. This was the opinion of Albania, Algeria, Bahrain, Bangladesh, Bulgaria, the Byelorussian SSR, Cuba, Czechoslovakia, Democratic Yemen, the German Democratic Republic, India, Iraq, Jordan, Kenya, Kuwait, the Lao People's Democratic Republic, the Libyan Arab Jamahiriya, Madagascar, Malaysia, Mali, Malta, Mongolia, Nigeria, Pakistan, Poland, Saudi Arabia, Somalia, Sweden, Togo, Turkey, Uganda, the USSR, the United Arab Emirates, the United Republic of Cameroon, Yemen, Yugoslavia and Zambia. The Byelorussian SSR, Democratic Yemen, Guinea, India, Iran, Morocco and others said the decision marked another stage in the escalation of Israel's expansionism. Qatar considered the annexation to be another stage in a long series of Israeli violations of United Nations resolutions.

Kenya believed that the annexation was part of an overall policy which sought the extinction of the Palestinians, and Somalia and Uganda said it had to be seen in the context of creeping annexation through expropriation and establishment of Jewish settlements on occupied Arab lands.

Iran said the annexation of the Golan Heights was certainly not the last stage of Israel's expansionism; having come to an agreement with Egypt and separating it from the liberation forces of Palestine, Israel was trying to annex other Islamic lands in return for its withdrawal from the Sinai peninsula and also to increase its pressure on the Arab steadfastness front headed by the Syrian Arab Republic.

Yemen warned that Israel might in the near future annex the West Bank and Gaza, a fear also expressed by others, among them Czechoslovakia and Democratic Yemen. Bahrain, Pakistan and Somalia saw the possibility that southern Lebanon might become Israel's next target. Cuba said the annexation of the Golan Heights formed part of a chain of events which, if not broken by collective action, would continue with large-scale military aggressions against Palestinians in southern Lebanon as well as against the Syrian Arab Republic. Lebanon was convinced that the seizure of the Golan Heights would intensify the risk of an explosion of the Middle East situation and compound the complexity of the Lebanese problem. The Libyan Arab Jamahiriya said the annexation of the Golan Heights was aimed at making Damascus the target of Israeli fire.

Jordan, the Lao People's Democratic Republic and others charged that the annexation had been pursued systematically and according to premeditated plans. In Albania's opinion, Israel had acted at a time when events in the world and in the Middle East had taken a dangerous turn and because it believed that the difficulties the peoples of the Middle East were encountering in their struggle against many enemies would prevent them from dealing with Zionist expansionism. Also in Austria's view, Israel had acted unilaterally at a moment when tensions in the area had markedly increased and, on the other side, efforts were being intensified to keep the peace process from collapsing.

In Yugoslavia's opinion, Israel's action underlined the need to protect the rights of the Syrian Arab Republic and of the people in the occupied territories.

The Lao People's Democratic Republic believed that the latest turn of events had made more necessary and urgent than ever the search for a comprehensive Middle East settlement. Brazil stated that acts of aggression such as the annexation of the Golan Heights must come to an end before an accepted basis for a settlement could be found.

A large number of delegations called for strong measures, and many of them specifically mentioned sanctions, to compel Israel to rescind its decision and to put an end to its expansion and annexation policy. Among them were Afghanistan, Algeria, Bangladesh, Benin, the Byelorussian SSR, China, the Congo, Cuba, Cyprus, Czechoslovakia, Democratic Yemen, Djibouti, Ethiopia, the German Democratic Republic, Grenada, Guyana, Hungary, India, Indonesia, Iran, Iraq, Jordan, Kenya, Kuwait, the Lao People's Democratic Republic, the Libyan Arab Jamahiriya, Madagascar, Malaysia, Mauritania, Mexico, Mongolia, Morocco, Nicaragua, the Niger, Nigeria, Pakistan, Qatar, Saudi Arabia, the Sudan, the Syrian Arab Republic, Tunisia, Turkey, Uganda, the Ukrainian SSR, the USSR, the United Arab Emirates, the United Republic of Cameroon, the United Republic of Tanzania, Viet Nam, Yemen and Yugoslavia.

Suspension of Israel's United Nations membership was advocated by the Syrian Arab Republic, a demand also supported by Afghanistan, Bahrain and the Libyan Arab Jamahiriya. Nicaragua and Qatar suggested that Israel's right to membership be reconsidered. On the other hand, Ecuador said it valued the universality of the United Nations and would not agree with any step aimed at its disintegration.

In India's view, the Security Council's failure to take further action as a result of the negative vote by the United States raised strong doubts as to its ability or willingness to preserve international peace and security; the negative vote had seriously undermined confidence in the Council's special responsibility for safeguarding international law and ensuring world peace. Yugoslavia said the use of the veto even in unquestionable cases of annexation and aggression reflected a wider negative phenomenon: that collective security, built on implied agreement—above all, of the permanent Council members—on the need to maintain world peace and security could not be achieved in the existing division of the world into blocs; such a situation stressed the urgency of efforts to strengthen the role of the Council and the Assembly as the most democratic organs for the maintenance of peace and security.

In Bulgaria's view, the Assembly must adopt a resolution containing an unequivocal condemnation of the aggressor's illegal acts, demanding that its decision to annex the Golan Heights be rescinded and calling on Israel's overseas protectors to cease providing it with the massive support which was at the root of its intransigence. Zaire believed that the Assembly's response should be to call on Member States to refrain from action which could imply any recognition or support of the Israeli decision to annex the Golan Heights, and also to consider the possibility of new efforts to settle the Middle East crisis as a whole.

If a few Members failed to see the sinister nature of Israel's actions, said Pakistan, the rest of the membership could not escape the responsibility to take firm action to compel respect for the rule of law. The Council's failure to discharge its responsibilities did not relieve the Assembly of its obligations to take effective measures, the Sudan said. In Tunisia's view, the Assembly was vested with the competence and responsibilities, transferred by the Council itself, to take steps to ensure respect for justice and law. A similar view was held by Algeria, Bhutan, Guyana, Jordan, Zambia and others.

Mexico said that to fail to compel Israel to abide by international law and to continue to tolerate the flouting of United Nations decisions would be to admit that the Charter had no substance; an institution whose authority was continually questioned would become a historical remnant barely cloaking the resurgence of a policy of force. Somalia said the Assembly must use its moral authority to call on the Council to take effective measures to check Israel's continuing policies of expansion, belligerency and contempt.

Bhutan hoped that peaceful and practical measures would be taken so that the Golan Heights and all occupied territories could be restored to their pre-1967 status. Guinea felt that the seriousness of the situation required that the Assembly adopt just and constructive decisions in order to forestall any further breach of international peace and security. Jordan believed that even though an Assembly resolution was not mandatory, it could be as efficacious as mandatory sanctions if the international community had the will to make it so; the Council had entrusted the Assembly with ensuring that aggression not be allowed to prevail.

When taking a decision, Austria stated, the Assembly had to bear in mind that the significance of the unanimous Council resolution of December 1981 demanding that Israel rescind its decision should not be minimized by introducing legally or politically controversial issues which could further complicate the search for peace and security.

Finland held it imperative that the ultimate status of the occupied territories not be prejudiced before a comprehensive solution had been found. Thailand felt that unless a peaceful approach through negotiations had been totally rejected by all parties, no measures should be taken which would further diminish the prospects of such a peaceful settlement.

Yugoslavia held it imperative to prevent the annexation of the Golan Heights, as a test for the United Nations to prevent the legitimization of the practice of changing the map of the Middle East by force.

Iran felt that the struggle against the criminal Zionist acts was possible only through the unity of all Moslems and on the basis of rejection of all so-called political solutions proposed by the imperialist and Zionist circles; United Nations resolutions were not to be depended on and were to be considered at most as weak slogans.

Action by the Commission on Human Rights. By a resolution of 11 February,[16] adopted in connection with its consideration of human rights violations in the territories occupied by Israel, the Commission on Human Rights condemned and declared null and void Israel's decision annexing the Golan Heights through imposition of its laws, jurisdiction and administration, and called on Member States to apply the measures called for in the Assembly resolution of 5 February.

Communications (February-March). By letters of 18 February[12] and 2 March,[13] the Syrian Arab Republic charged that Israel had taken a series of repressive measures against Syrians in the Golan Heights, including the arrest and imprisonment of their leaders, demolition of houses and sealing of stores on the pretext that authorization for them had not been sought, confiscation of land for the establishment of Israeli settlements, travel restrictions, mass arrests, and the reduction of water supply to villagers as a means of forcing them to end their general strike in protest of the Israeli laws imposed on them. In addition, Israeli authorities were imposing new civil procedures in order to compel Syrians to accept Israeli citizenship, refusing birth and marriage certificates and automobile registrations to those who did not hold Israeli identity cards.

These charges were described by Israel as distortions in a letter of 19 March[7] which stated that no houses had been demolished or sealed, additional water supplies had been made available and agricultural production had increased since 1967, assistance to agriculture had been stepped up, certain restrictions on movement between villages had been lifted, more than 50 Golan Heights residents were studying at Syrian universities and teachers were carrying out their functions normally.

Report of the Secretary-General. By a report of 5 April 1982,[14] the Secretary-General informed the General Assembly and the Security Council that, in accordance with the Assembly's request to follow up the implementation of its 5 February resolution, he had transmitted the text on 19 February to Member States, specialized agencies and international institutions. In response, he had received replies from seven States and four agencies and institutions. In three addenda between June and December, the Secretary-General included replies from eight more States and two agencies and institutions.

General Assembly action (December). Two further resolutions on the Golan Heights were adopted by the General Assembly in December.

On 10 December,[19] the Assembly strongly condemned Israel for refusing to heed the demands to rescind its decision to impose its laws, jurisdiction and administration in the Golan Heights; for its persistence in changing the physical character, demographic composition, institutional structure and legal status of the area; and for its attempts and measures to impose Israeli citizenship and identity cards on Syrian nationals there. The Assembly determined that all Israeli measures purporting to alter the character and status of the Golan Heights were null and void and constituted a flagrant violation of international law and the 1949 Geneva Convention relative to the Protection of Civilian Persons in Time of War (see below, under OTHER ASPECTS OF THE SITUATION IN THE OCCUPIED TERRITORIES). Member States were called upon not to recognize any such measures.

The resolution was adopted by a recorded vote of 133 to 1, with 2 abstentions, following its approval by the Special Political Committee on 3 December by a recorded vote of 109 to 1, with 2 abstentions. Introducing it in the Committee on behalf of 10 nations, Bangladesh said its content had been the subject of past resolutions, which, however, had not produced substantive results.

Condemning Israel for its failure to comply with past demands to rescind its decision on the Golan Heights, the Assembly, by a resolution of 16 December,[20] again declared that the decision was an act of aggression and was null and void, and determined that all actions taken by Israel to give effect to it were illegal and invalid, and that Israel's occupation and annexation were a threat to international peace and security. As in its 5 February resolution, it strongly deplored the negative vote in the Security Council which had prevented the adoption of measures against Israel, determined that Israel was not a peace-loving State, deplored the support given it, and called for measures against Israel, including the suspension of military, economic and financial assistance and the severance of diplomatic and other relations. The Assembly declared that Israeli policies and practices aimed at annexation of the occupied territories, including Jerusalem, violated international law, and reaffirmed the necessity of total and unconditional Israeli withdrawal.

The resolution was adopted by a recorded vote of 87 to 22, with 31 abstentions. Introducing it on behalf of 15 nations, Cuba said it contained the basic principles for a Middle East solution.

Explaining its abstention in the vote on the 10 December resolution, the United States said it went further than the December 1981 Security Council resolution declaring the Israeli law to be null and void, and contained harsh, unbalanced language and references to resolutions which the United States had opposed.

Sweden voted in favour, being convinced that the Geneva Convention on the protection of civilians was fully applicable to all the territories held by Israel since 1967; however, its support did not alter its negative attitude to the February Assembly resolution recalled in the preamble.

With regard to the 16 December resolution, Israel stated that the attempts to vilify it as a non-peace-loving State were grotesque in the light of the well-known sacrifices it had made for peace. Instead of calling for negotiation and conciliation, the resolution called on States to refrain from supplying Israel, the victim of repeated Arab aggression, with the necessary means of defence, and sought to isolate it so that the Arab aggressors might be emboldened to continue their warfare across Israel's borders. The resolution not only ignored the adamant Syrian refusal to recognize and negotiate with Israel, but also ignored every hostile act committed by the Syrian Arab Republic to subvert any movement towards a peaceful settlement.

Among others voting negatively, Denmark, speaking on behalf of the EC members, stressed the need for a balanced approach towards a comprehensive settlement and said they could not accept formulations criticizing a permanent Council member for exercising its right. Portugal took a similar position; Portugal and Sweden particularly objected to the determination that Israel was not a peace-loving State and to the call for measures against Israel, Sweden adding that they could not be reconciled with the division of responsibilities between the Assembly and the Council.

Japan said it had been obliged to vote against because the text contained several paragraphs incompatible with some of Japan's fundamental beliefs: that the United Nations must be universal, that the isolation of a particular country did not necessarily contribute to a solution and that all conflicts must be resolved peacefully through negotiations. The United States said the resolution was full of reckless condemnations and demands, served only to polarize positions instead of resolving conflicts and further eroded the Assembly's credibility; its essential objective was to isolate a Member State and party to the conflict, and lay the groundwork for expelling it from the United Nations.

Abstaining, Peru did not believe that adoption of the measures proposed would be the best way to get a peace process under way; on the contrary, it would further reduce the effectiveness of the United Nations. In Argentina's view, the competence of the main bodies of the United Nations must be respected in compliance with the Charter. Chile and Spain expressed a similar opinion, adding that only the Security Council was competent to apply the sanctions recommended; in addition, Chile thought that the resolution contained excessive language and made an ineffective contribution to the search for peace, and that the call on United Nations Members to apply certain measures against Israel prejudged the destiny of assistance to one sovereign State by another. Ecuador felt similarly about the call for measures against Israel and also objected to the determination that Israel was not a peace-loving State; it said any action, however preliminary, to expel or suspend a Member State would create greater difficulties in any negotiation process.

Brazil abstained for reasons given when the Assembly adopted its February resolution on the subject (see above). Jamaica had difficulties with the paragraph deploring the negative vote by a permanent member of the Security Council as well as with the measures recommended against Israel.

Trinidad and Tobago felt that the resolution raised fundamental questions of interpretation. In Venezuela's understanding, any resolution that departed from moderation did not effectively contribute to efforts to ensure the achievement of Palestinian rights, including the right to create an independent State.

Though voting in favour, Mexico, Nepal, Suriname and Turkey reserved their position on the determination that Israel was not a peace-loving State. Mexico and Nepal also had reservations with regard to the application of measures against and isolation of Israel, while Greece and Suriname had reservations about the calls for suspension of economic, financial and technological assistance and of diplomatic, trade and cultural relations. Greece, Nepal, Togo and Turkey could not associate themselves with the paragraph deploring the United States veto in the Security Council; Nepal also disagreed with the provision deploring support to Israel. It was Nepal's view that initiation of the measures called for was the prerogative of the Council.

Malta stated that its affirmative vote did not necessarily imply full agreement with each and every provision, nor did it imply that the legal issues that might arise could be decided by the Assembly.

Iran said it had voted for the resolution in view of its friendly relations with the Syrian Arab Republic and in defence of Moslem land; however, it was not happy to see the call for Israeli withdrawal limited to the Arab territories occupied since 1967, as all Israeli acts of aggression and occupation, whether before or since 1967, remained illegal consequences of its illegal existence.

The imposition of Israeli laws, jurisdiction and administration, resulting in the effective annexation of the Golan Heights, was condemned by the Assembly also in two other resolutions, on 10 December on the territories occupied by Israel[18] and on 20 December on the Middle East situation.[21] In the latter resolution, the Assembly also condemned Israel's annexationist policies and practices, the establishment of settlements, confiscation of lands, diversion of water resources and imposition of Israeli citizenship. It declared all such measures null and void and said they violated international law relevant to belligerent occupation, in particular the 1949 Geneva Convention on protection of civilians in wartime (see below).

During the debates on the Middle East situation and on the Palestine question, several speakers, including Algeria, Bahrain, Denmark (for the EC members), Hungary, Japan, Morocco and the United Arab Emirates, reiterated their opposition to Israel's decision. Malaysia said Israeli legislation had reduced the territory to an adjunct of Israel, with a view to obliterating its Arab identity. Poland saw the act as a prelude to the aggression against Lebanon, while Cyprus remarked that the illegal effort at annexation and the brutal repression of the local population did not contribute to peace.

Draft resolution not adopted. [1]Jordan, S/14832/Rev.1.

Letters and notes verbales (nv). [2]Benin: 7 Jan., S/14827. Cuba: [3]6 Jan., A/37/60-S/14829 & Corr.1; [4]25 Jan., S/14849 *(nv)*. [5]Cyprus: 15 Jan., S/14838 & Corr.1 *(nv)*. Israel: [6]28 Jan., A/ES-9/4 (S/14852) (A/37/217, annex I); [7]19 Mar., A/37/151-S/14914. Jordan: [8]5 Jan., S/14823; [9]5 Jan., S/14824; [10]8 Jan., S/14828. [11]Mongolia: 5 Jan., S/14825. Syrian Arab Republic: [12]18 Feb., A/37/92-S/14876; [13]2 Mar., A/37/106-S/14893.

Reports. [14]S-G, A/37/169-S/14953 & Add.1-3; [15]Committee on Israeli practices in occupied territories, transmitted by S-G note, A/37/485.

Resolutions (1982). [16]Commission on Human Rights (report, E/1982/12): 1982/2, 11 Feb. GA: [17]ES-9/1, 5 Feb., text following; [18]37/88 C, para. 7 *(b)*, 10 Dec.; [19]37/88 E, 10 Dec., text following; [20]37/123 A, 16 Dec., text following; [21]37/123 F, para. 8, 20 Dec. [22]SC: 500(1982), 28 Jan., text following.

Resolutions (prior). GA: [23]3314(XXIX), annex, 14 Dec. 1974 (YUN 1974, p. 847); [24]36/226 B, 17 Dec. 1981 (YUN 1981, p. 313). SC: [25]242(1967), 22 Nov. 1967 (YUN 1967, p. 257); [26]338(1973), 22 Oct. 1973 (YUN 1973, p. 213); [27]497(1981), 17 Dec. 1981 (YUN 1981, p. 312).

Yearbook references. [28]1967, p. 183; [29]1981, p. 309.

Meeting records. SC: S/PV.2322 & Corr.1, 2323-2330 (6-28 Jan.). GA: plenary, A/ES-9/PV.2-5, 6 & Corr.1, 7-12 (29 Jan.–5 Feb.), A/37/PV.92-96, *100, 108* (6-16 Dec.); SPC, A/SPC/37/SR.35-41, *42, 44* (23 Nov.–3 Dec.).

Security Council resolution 500(1982)

28 January 1982   Meeting 2330   13-0-2

Draft by Jordan (S/14848).

The Security Council,

Having considered the item on the agenda of its 2329th meeting, as contained in document S/Agenda/2329/Rev.1,

Taking into account that the lack of unanimity of its permanent members at the 2329th meeting has prevented it from exercising its primary responsibility for the maintenance of international peace and security,

Decides to call an emergency special session of the General Assembly to examine the question contained in document S/Agenda/2329/Rev.1.

Vote in Council as follows:

In favour: China, France, Guyana, Ireland, Japan, Jordan, Panama, Poland, Spain, Togo, Uganda, USSR, Zaire.

Against: None.

Abstaining: United Kingdom, United States.

General Assembly resolution ES-9/1

5 February 1982   Meeting 12   86-21-34 (roll-call vote)

56-nation draft (A/ES-9/L.1 and Add.1); agenda item 5.

Sponsors: Afghanistan, Algeria, Angola, Bahrain, Benin, Bulgaria, Byelorussian SSR, Cape Verde, Chad, Congo, Cuba, Czechoslovakia, Democratic Yemen, Djibouti, Ethiopia, German Democratic Republic, Grenada, Guinea, Guinea-Bissau, Guyana, Hungary, India, Indonesia, Iran, Iraq, Jordan, Kuwait, Lao People's Democratic Republic, Lebanon, Libyan Arab Jamahiriya, Madagascar, Malaysia, Maldives, Mali, Malta, Mauritania, Mongolia, Morocco, Mozambique, Niger, Nigeria, Oman, Pakistan, Qatar, Saudi Arabia, Somalia, Sri Lanka, Sudan, Syrian Arab Republic, Tunisia, Ukrainian SSR, United Arab Emirates, Viet Nam, Yemen, Yugoslavia, Zimbabwe.

The situation in the occupied Arab territories

The General Assembly,

Having considered the item entitled "The situation in the occupied Arab territories" at its ninth emergency special session, in accordance with Security Council resolution 500(1982) of 28 January 1982,

Noting with regret and concern that the Security Council, at its 2329th meeting, on 20 January 1982, failed to take appropriate measures against Israel, as requested by the Council in resolution 497(1981) of 17 December 1981, as a result of the negative vote of a permanent member of the Council,

Recalling Security Council resolution 497(1981),

Recalling its resolution 35/122 E of 11 December 1980,

Reaffirming its resolution 36/226 B of 17 December 1981,

Having considered the reports of the Secretary-General of 21 December 1981 and 31 December 1981,

Recalling its resolution 3314(XXIX) of 14 December 1974, in which it defined an act of aggression as, *inter alia,* "the invasion or attack by the armed forces of a State of the territory of another State, or any military occupation, however temporary, resulting from such invasion or attack, or any annexation by the use of force of the territory of another State or part thereof", and provided that "no consideration of whatever nature, whether political, economic, military or otherwise, may serve as justification for aggression",

Stressing once again that the acquisition of territory by force is inadmissible under the Charter of the United Nations, the principles of international law and relevant United Nations resolutions,

Reaffirming once more the applicability of the Geneva Convention relative to the Protection of Civilian Persons in Time of War, of 12 August 1949, to the occupied Syrian territory,

Noting that Israel's record and actions establish conclusively that it is not a peace-loving Member State and that it has not carried out its obligations under the Charter,

Noting further that Israel has refused, in violation of Article 25 of the Charter, to accept and carry out the numerous relevant decisions of the Security Council, the latest being resolution 497(1981),

1. *Strongly condemns* Israel for its failure to comply with Security Council resolution 497(1981) and General Assembly resolution 36/226 B;

2. *Declares* that Israel's decision of 14 December 1981 to impose its laws, jurisdiction and administration on the occupied Syrian Golan Heights constitutes an act of aggression under the provisions of Article 39 of the Charter of the United Nations and General Assembly resolution 3314(XXIX);

3. *Declares once more* that Israel's decision to impose its laws, jurisdiction and administration on the occupied Syrian Golan Heights is null and void and has no legal validity and/or effect whatsoever;

4. *Determines* that all actions taken by Israel to give effect to its decision relating to the occupied Syrian Golan Heights are illegal and invalid and shall not be recognized;

5. *Reaffirms* its determination that all the provisions of the Hague Conventions of 1907 and the Geneva Convention relative to the Protection of Civilian Persons in Time of War, of 12 August 1949, continue to apply to the Syrian territory occupied by Israel since 1967, and calls upon all parties thereto to respect and ensure respect of their obligations under these instruments in all circumstances;

6. *Determines* that the continued occupation of the Syrian Golan Heights since 1967 and its effective annexation by Israel on 14 December 1981, following Israel's decision to impose its laws, jurisdiction and administration on that territory, constitute a continuing threat to international peace and security;

7. *Strongly deplores* the negative vote by a permanent member of the Security Council which prevented the Council from adopting against Israel, under Chapter VII of the Charter, the "appropriate measures" referred to in resolution 497(1981) unanimously adopted by the Council;

8. *Further deplores* any political, economic, military and technological support to Israel that encourages Israel to commit acts of aggression and to consolidate and perpetuate its occupation and annexation of occupied Arab territories;

9. *Firmly emphasizes* its demands that Israel, the occupying Power, rescind forthwith its decision of 14 December 1981 to impose its laws, jurisdiction and administration on the Syrian Golan Heights, which has resulted in the effective annexation of that territory;

10. *Reaffirms* the overriding necessity of the total and unconditional withdrawal by Israel from all Palestinian and other Arab territories occupied since 1967, including Jerusalem, which is a primary requirement for the establishment of a comprehensive and just peace in the Middle East;

11. *Declares* that Israel's record and actions confirm that it is not a peace-loving Member State and that it has carried out neither its obligations under the Charter nor its commitment under General Assembly resolution 273(III) of 11 May 1949;

12. *Calls upon* all Member States to apply the following measures:

(a) To refrain from supplying Israel with any weapons and related equipment and to suspend any military assistance which Israel receives from them;

(b) To refrain from acquiring any weapons or military equipment from Israel;

(c) To suspend economic, financial and technological assistance to and co-operation with Israel;

(d) To sever diplomatic, trade and cultural relations with Israel;

13. *Also calls upon* all Member States to cease forthwith, individually and collectively, all dealings with Israel in order totally to isolate it in all fields;

14. *Urges* non-member States to act in accordance with the provisions of the present resolution;

15. *Calls upon* all specialized agencies of the United Nations system and international institutions to conform their relations with Israel to the terms of the present resolution;

16. *Requests* the Secretary-General to follow up the implementation of the present resolution and to report thereon at intervals of two months to Member States as well as to the Security Council and to submit a comprehensive report to the General Assembly at its thirty-seventh session under the item entitled "The situation in the Middle East".

Recorded vote in Assembly as follows:

In favour: Afghanistan, Albania, Algeria, Angola, Bahrain, Bangladesh, Benin, Bhutan, Botswana, Bulgaria, Burma, Burundi, Byelorussian SSR, Cape Verde, China, Congo, Cuba, Cyprus, Czechoslovakia, Democratic Yemen, Djibouti, Ethiopia, Gambia, German Democratic Republic, Ghana, Greece, Grenada, Guinea, Guinea-Bissau, Guyana, Hungary, India, Indonesia, Iran, Iraq, Ivory Coast, Jordan, Kenya, Kuwait, Lao People's Democratic Republic, Lebanon, Lesotho, Libyan Arab Jamahiriya, Madagascar, Malaysia, Maldives, Mali, Malta, Mauritania, Mongolia, Morocco, Mozambique, Nepal, Nicaragua, Niger, Nigeria, Oman, Pakistan, Peru, Poland, Qatar, Rwanda, Sao Tome and Principe, Saudi Arabia, Senegal, Seychelles, Sierra Leone, Somalia, Sri Lanka, Sudan, Suriname, Syrian Arab Republic, Togo, Tunisia, Uganda, Ukrainian SSR, USSR, United Arab Emirates, United Republic of Cameroon, United Republic of Tanzania, Upper Volta, Viet Nam, Yemen, Yugoslavia, Zambia, Zimbabwe.

Against: Australia, Belgium, Canada, Denmark, Fiji, Finland, France, Germany, Federal Republic of, Iceland, Ireland, Israel, Italy, Japan, Luxembourg, Netherlands, New Zealand, Norway, Portugal, Sweden, United Kingdom, United States.

Abstaining: Argentina, Austria, Bahamas, Barbados, Bolivia, Brazil, Chile, Colombia, Costa Rica, Dominican Republic, Ecuador, Egypt, El Salvador, Gabon, Guatemala, Haiti, Honduras, Liberia, Malawi, Panama, Papua New Guinea, Paraguay, Saint Lucia, Saint Vincent and the Grenadines, Samoa, Singapore, Spain, Swaziland, Thailand, Trinidad and Tobago, Turkey, Uruguay, Venezuela, Zaire.

General Assembly resolution 37/88 E

10 December 1982　　　　Meeting 100　　　　133-1-2 (recorded vote)

Approved by SPC (A/37/698) by recorded vote (109-1-2), 3 December (meeting 44); 10-nation draft (A/SPC/37/L.32); agenda item 61.

Sponsors: Afghanistan, Bangladesh, Cape Verde, Cuba, India, Indonesia, Madagascar, Malaysia, Pakistan, Qatar.

The General Assembly,

Deeply concerned that the Arab territories occupied since 1967 have been under continued Israeli military occupation,

Recalling Security Council resolution 497(1981) of 17 December 1981 and General Assembly resolutions 36/226 B of 17 December 1981 and ES-9/1 of 5 February 1982,

Recalling its previous resolutions, in particular resolutions 3414(XXX) of 5 December 1975, 31/61 of 9 December 1976, 32/20 of 25 November 1977, 33/28 and 33/29 of 7 December 1978, 34/70 of 6 December 1979 and 35/122 E of 11 December 1980, in which it, *inter alia*, called upon Israel to put an end to its occupation of the Arab territories and to withdraw from all those territories,

Reaffirming once more the illegality of Israel's decision of 14 December 1981 to impose its laws, jurisdiction and administration on the occupied Syrian Golan Heights, which has resulted in the effective annexation of that territory,

Reaffirming that the acquisition of territory by force is inadmissible under the Charter of the United Nations and that all territories thus occupied by Israel must be returned,

Recalling the Geneva Convention relative to the Protection of Civilian Persons in Time of War, of 12 August 1949,

1. *Strongly condemns* Israel, the occupying Power, for its refusal to comply with the relevant resolutions of the General Assembly and the Security Council, particularly Council resolution 497(1981), in which the Council, *inter alia*, decided that the Israeli decision to impose its laws, jurisdiction and administration in the occupied Syrian Golan Heights was null and void and without international legal effect and that Israel, the occupying Power, should rescind forthwith its decision;

2. *Condemns* the persistence of Israel in changing the physical character, demographic composition, institutional structure and legal status of the occupied Syrian Arab Golan Heights;

3. *Determines* that all legislative and administrative measures and actions taken or to be taken by Israel, the occupying Power, that purport to alter the character and legal status of the Syrian Arab Golan Heights are null and void and constitute a flagrant violation of international law and of the Geneva Convention relative to the Protection of Civilian Persons in Time of War, of 12 August 1949, and have no legal effect;

4. *Strongly condemns* Israel for its attempts and measures to impose forcibly Israeli citizenship and Israeli identity cards on the Syrian citizens in the occupied Syrian Arab Golan Heights and calls upon it to desist from its repressive measures against the population of the Syrian Arab Golan Heights;

5. *Calls upon* Member States not to recognize any of the legislative or administrative measures and actions referred to above;

6. *Requests* the Secretary-General to report to the General Assembly at its thirty-eighth session on the implementation of the present resolution.

Recorded vote in Assembly as follows:

In favour: Afghanistan, Albania, Algeria, Argentina, Australia, Austria, Bahrain, Bangladesh, Barbados, Belgium, Benin, Bhutan, Bolivia, Botswana, Brazil, Bulgaria, Burma, Burundi, Byelorussian SSR, Canada, Central African Republic, Chad, Chile, China, Colombia, Comoros, Congo, Costa Rica, Cuba, Cyprus, Czechoslovakia, Democratic Kampuchea, Democratic Yemen, Denmark, Djibouti, Dominican Republic, Ecuador, Egypt, El Salvador, Ethiopia, Fiji, Finland, France, Gabon, Gambia, German Democratic Republic, Germany, Federal Republic of, Ghana, Greece, Guyana, Haiti, Honduras, Hungary, Iceland, India, Indonesia, Iran, Iraq, Ireland, Italy, Jamaica, Japan, Jordan, Kenya, Kuwait, Lao People's Democratic Republic, Lebanon, Liberia, Libyan Arab Jamahiriya, Luxembourg, Madagascar, Malaysia, Maldives, Mali, Malta, Mauritania, Mauritius, Mexico, Mongolia, Morocco, Mozambique, Nepal, Netherlands, New Zealand, Nicaragua, Niger, Nigeria, Norway, Oman, Pakistan, Panama, Papua New Guinea, Peru, Philippines, Poland, Portugal, Qatar, Romania, Rwanda, Sao Tome and Principe, Saudi Arabia, Senegal, Sierra Leone, Singapore, Solomon Islands, Somalia, Spain, Sri Lanka, Sudan, Suriname, Sweden, Syrian Arab Republic, Thailand, Togo, Trinidad and Tobago, Tunisia, Turkey, Uganda, Ukrainian SSR, USSR, United Arab Emirates, United Kingdom, United Republic of Cameroon, United Republic of Tanzania, Upper Volta, Uruguay, Vanuatu, Venezuela, Viet Nam, Yemen, Yugoslavia, Zaire, Zambia.

Against: Israel.

Abstaining: Malawi, United States.

General Assembly resolution 37/123 A

16 December 1982　　　　Meeting 108　　　　87-22-31 (recorded vote)

15-nation draft (A/37/L.49 and Add.1); agenda item 34.

Sponsors: Bangladesh, Cuba, Guyana, India, Indonesia, Lao People's Democratic Republic, Madagascar, Malaysia, Mali, Mongolia, Nigeria, Pakistan, Viet Nam, Yemen, Yugoslavia.

The General Assembly,

Having discussed the item entitled "The situation in the Middle East",

Taking note of the reports of the Secretary-General,

Recalling Security Council resolution 497(1981) of 17 December 1981,

Reaffirming its resolutions 36/226 B of 17 December 1981 and ES-9/1 of 5 February 1982,

Recalling its resolution 3314(XXIX) of 14 December 1974, in which it defined an act of aggression, *inter alia*, as "the invasion or attack by the armed forces of a State of the territory of another State, or any military occupation, however temporary, resulting from such invasion or attack, or any annexation by the use of force of the territory of another State or part thereof" and provided that "no consideration of whatever nature, whether political, economic, military or otherwise, may serve as a justification for aggression",

Reaffirming the fundamental principle of the inadmissibility of the acquisition of territory by force,

Reaffirming once more the applicability of the Geneva Convention relative to the Protection of Civilian Persons in Time of War, of 12 August 1949, to the occupied Palestinian and other Arab territories, including Jerusalem,

Noting that Israel's record and actions establish conclusively that it is not a peace-loving Member State and that it has not carried out its obligations under the Charter of the United Nations,

Noting further that Israel has refused, in violation of Article 25 of the Charter, to accept and carry out the numerous relevant decisions of the Security Council, the latest of which was resolution 497(1981), thus failing to carry out its obligations under the Charter,

1. *Strongly condemns* Israel for its failure to comply with Security Council resolution 497(1981) and General Assembly resolutions 36/226 B and ES-9/1;

2. *Declares once more* that Israel's decision of 14 December 1981 to impose its laws, jurisdiction and administration on the occupied Syrian Golan Heights constitutes an act of aggression under the provisions of Article 39 of the Charter of the United Nations and General Assembly resolution 3314(XXIX);

3. *Declares once more* that Israel's decision to impose its laws, jurisdiction and administration on the occupied Syrian Golan Heights is null and void and has no legal validity and/or effect whatsoever;

4. *Declares* all Israeli policies and practices of, or aimed at, annexation of the occupied Palestinian and other Arab territories, including Jerusalem, to be in violation of international law and of the relevant United Nations resolutions;

5. *Determines once more* that all actions taken by Israel to give effect to its decision relating to the occupied Syrian Golan Heights are illegal and invalid and shall not be recognized;

6. *Reaffirms its determination* that all the provisions of the Hague Convention of 1907 and the Geneva Convention relative to the Protection of Civilian Persons in Time of War, of 12 August 1949, continue to apply to the Syrian territory occupied by Israel since 1967, and calls upon the parties thereto to respect and ensure respect of their obligations under these instruments in all circumstances;

7. *Determines once more* that the continued occupation of the Syrian Golan Heights since 1967 and their effective annexation by Israel on 14 December 1981, following Israel's decision to impose its laws, jurisdiction and administration on that territory, constitute a continuing threat to international peace and security;

8. *Strongly deplores* the negative vote by a permanent member of the Security Council which prevented the Council from adopting, against Israel, under Chapter VII of the Charter, the "appropriate measures" referred to in resolution 497(1981) unanimously adopted by the Council;

9. *Further deplores* any political, economic, financial, military and technological support to Israel that encourages Israel to commit acts of aggression and to consolidate and perpetuate its occupation and annexation of occupied Arab territories;

10. *Firmly emphasizes once more* its demands that Israel, the occupying Power, rescind forthwith its decision of 14 December 1981 to impose its laws, jurisdiction and administration on the Syrian Golan Heights, which has resulted in the effective annexation of that territory;

11. *Reaffirms once more* the overriding necessity of the total and unconditional withdrawal by Israel from all the Palestinian and other Arab territories occupied since 1967, including Jerusalem, which is an essential prerequisite for the establishment of a comprehensive and just peace in the Middle East;

12. *Determines once more* that Israel's record and actions confirm that it is not a peace-loving Member State, that it has persistently violated the principles contained in the Charter and that it has carried out neither its obligations under the Charter nor its commitment under General Assembly resolution 273(III) of 11 May 1949;

13. *Calls once more upon* all Member States to apply the following measures:

(a) To refrain from supplying Israel with any weapons and related equipment and to suspend any military assistance that Israel receives from them;

(b) To refrain from acquiring any weapons or military equipment from Israel;

(c) To suspend economic, financial and technological assistance to and co-operation with Israel;

(d) To sever diplomatic, trade and cultural relations with Israel;

14. *Reiterates its call* to all Member States to cease forthwith, individually and collectively, all dealings with Israel in order totally to isolate it in all fields;

15. *Urges* non-member States to act in accordance with the provisions of the present resolution;

16. *Calls upon* the specialized agencies and other international organizations to conform their relations with Israel to the terms of the present resolution.

Recorded vote in Assembly as follows:

In favour: Afghanistan, Albania, Algeria, Angola, Bahrain, Bangladesh, Benin, Bhutan, Botswana, Bulgaria, Burundi, Byelorussian SSR, Cape Verde, Chad, China, Comoros, Congo, Cuba, Cyprus, Czechoslovakia, Democratic Kampuchea, Democratic Yemen, Djibouti, Ethiopia, Gambia, German Democratic Republic, Ghana, Greece, Grenada, Guinea, Guinea-Bissau, Guyana, Hungary, India, Indonesia, Iran, Iraq, Jordan, Kenya, Kuwait, Lao People's Democratic Republic, Lebanon, Lesotho, Liberia, Libyan Arab Jamahiriya, Madagascar, Malaysia, Maldives, Mali, Malta, Mauritania, Mauritius, Mexico, Mongolia, Morocco, Mozambique, Nepal, Nicaragua, Nigeria, Oman, Pakistan, Poland, Qatar, Rwanda, Sao Tome and Principe, Saudi Arabia, Senegal, Seychelles, Sierra Leone, Somalia, Sri Lanka, Sudan, Suriname, Syrian Arab Republic, Togo, Tunisia, Turkey, Uganda, Ukrainian SSR, USSR, United Arab Emirates, United Republic of Cameroon, United Republic of Tanzania, Viet Nam, Yemen, Yugoslavia, Zambia.

Against: Australia, Belgium, Canada, Costa Rica, Denmark, Finland, France, Germany, Federal Republic of, Guatemala, Iceland, Ireland, Israel, Italy, Japan, Luxembourg, Netherlands, New Zealand, Norway, Portugal, Sweden, United Kingdom, United States.

Abstaining: Argentina, Austria, Bahamas, Barbados, Brazil, Burma, Central African Republic, Chile, Colombia, Dominican Republic, Ecuador, El Salvador, Fiji, Gabon, Ivory Coast, Jamaica, Malawi, Panama, Papua New Guinea, Paraguay, Peru, Philippines, Samoa, Singapore, Spain, Thailand, Trinidad and Tobago, Upper Volta, Uruguay, Venezuela, Zaire.

Other aspects of the situation in the occupied territories

The situation in the territories occupied by Israel was considered again in 1982 by the Security Council, the General Assembly and its Special Committee to Investigate Israeli Practices Affecting the Human Rights of the Population of the Occupied Territories.

Because of the negative vote of a permanent member (United States), a draft resolution to have the Council denounce Israeli measures imposed on the Palestinians of the occupied territories was not adopted when the Council met in March and April in response to reports that Israel was using force to suppress popular protests there. However, the Assembly, on 28 April, condemned Israel for disbanding the elected municipal council of Al Bireh and dismissing the Mayors of Ramallah and Nablus, and for repressive measures including shooting at unarmed civilians.

The Council also met in April to consider the preservation of Al-Aqsa Mosque in Jerusalem and in November on the issue of Israeli settlements in the territories.

The occupied territories—those taken over by Israel in 1967 as a result of hostilities with neighbouring States—consisted of the West Bank of the Jordan River (including East Jerusalem), the Golan Heights (see above) and the Gaza Strip. The remaining Egyptian territory under Israeli military occupation on the Sinai peninsula was restored to the Egyptian Government on 25 April 1982 in accordance with the 1979 Treaty of Peace between the Arab Republic of Egypt and the State of Israel (see above, under MIDDLE EAST SITUATION).

Communications (January-March). The Acting Chairman of the Committee on Palestinian rights, by a letter of 22 January 1982,[2] expressed concern at reported plans by Israel to clear all Palestinian Bedouins out of a great swath of the Negev Desert; about 15,000 had been resettled in two large tracts of land near Beersheba, another 6,000 were to be removed from an area where a new Israeli air base was planned, and an additional 19,000 were to be resettled. By a letter of 8 March,[3] the Committee Chairman said there had been further Israeli human rights violations in the West Bank and Gaza, and asked that decisive steps be taken to protect the rights of the Palestinians there.

Israel, in a letter of 17 March,[10] stated that on 12 March the home of a village association member at Bitunia, in the Ramallah area, had been struck by a barrage of bullets in a continuing campaign of PLO harassment against Arabs in Judaea, Samaria and the Gaza district (Israel's term for the occupied territories of the West Bank and Gaza) who had indicated their desire to live in peace with Israel.

On 19 March,[12] Jordan transmitted to the Secretary-General and the Security Council President a letter of 18 March from the PLO observer to the United Nations, protesting Israeli action on that date to dissolve the elected municipal council of Al Bireh, a West Bank town north of Jerusalem, and to evict the elected Mayor, Ibrahim Al-Taweel; the letter added that a general strike had been called to protest the action. The dissolution of the council was also protested in a letter of 23 March to the Council President from the Secretary-General of the Organization of the Islamic Conference, transmitted by Jordan on 24 March.[17]

On 22 March,[13] Jordan transmitted two further PLO letters, dated 21 and 22 March, indicating that 13 West Bank inhabitants had been shot or otherwise injured by Israelis during a continuation of the general strike, which had been extended by another two days in protest against collective punishments. Additional Palestinian casualties, including one death, were reported by the PLO observer in a letter of 23 March, conveyed by Jordan on 24 March,[18] stating that there had been further clashes with Israelis, accompanied by curfews and efforts to intimidate shopkeepers participating in general strikes.

Jordan transmitted on 25 March[19] a further letter of the same date from the PLO observer, stating that the Mayor of Nablus, Basam Al-Shaka, and the Mayor of Ramallah, Karim Khalaf, had been removed from their elected offices on 25 March and replaced by Israeli civilian administrators, and that Palestinians continued to be shot and arrested in various localities.

In a letter of 31 March,[11] Israel stated that on that date a member of a village association in the Hebron area had been seriously wounded in an explosion when his car was booby-trapped by PLO terrorists—an incident which the letter described as the latest in a series of assassinations and attempted assassinations carried out by PLO against Palestinian personalities.

Action by the Commission on Human Rights and its Sub-Commission. On 11 February, the Commission on Human Rights strongly condemned, and demanded that Israel desist from, most of the policies and practices in the occupied territories condemned by the Assembly in December (see below), and also called on Israel to release all Arabs detained or imprisoned as a result of their struggle for self-determination and liberation of their territories (see ECONOMIC AND SOCIAL QUESTIONS, Chapter XVIII). As requested by the Commission, the resolution was brought to the attention of the General Assembly and the Security Council by the Secretary-General in a note of 14 July.[27]

The Sub-Commission on Prevention of Discrimination and Protection of Minorities, in a resolution of 8 September on various aspects of human rights violations involving Israel,[41] recommended that the Commission again call on Israel to withdraw from the occupied territories.

Security Council consideration (March/April). At Jordan's urgent request of 22 March,[14] transmitted in its capacity as Chairman of the Arab Group, the Security Council held five meetings between 24 March and 2 April on the situation in the occupied territories. Jordan's letter spoke of a grave situation underscored by a general strike, curfews, indiscriminate use of firearms against peaceful demonstrations, and deliberate provocations and assaults by Israeli troops and settlers. It stated that the rising violence threatened the survival of the Palestinian people, foreclosing options for a peaceful Middle East solution and thereby posing a threat to peace and security.

At the conclusion of the debate, a draft resolution sponsored by Jordan was not adopted because of the negative vote of a permanent Council member. The vote, taken on 2 April, was 13 to 1 (United States), with 1 abstention (Zaire).

Under the draft,[1] the Council would have denounced Israeli measures imposed on the Palestinians of the occupied territories, such as the dismissal of elected mayors and the violation of liberties and rights of the inhabitants of the West Bank and Gaza following Israel's December 1981 decision on the Golan Heights (see above). It would have called on Israel to rescind its decisions to disband the municipal council of Al Bireh and remove from their posts the Mayors of Nablus and Ramallah. It would have reaffirmed that the 1949 Geneva Convention relative to the Protection of Civilian Persons in Time of War continued to apply in full to all of the occupied territories and would have called on Israel to cease all measures contravening the Convention (see below).

Explaining its opposition, the United States said the draft would not have achieved the Council's primary objectives—to urge restraint on the parties so as to avoid any new outbreak of violence and to take a step on the road to a secure and lasting peace; instead of the draft's strongly denunciatory language, the United States would have preferred a text expressing in a non-condemnatory way the Council's great concern about the recent tragic events, which had resulted in injury and loss of life on both sides.

Reaffirming its support for the Palestinian cause, Zaire said it abstained as the efforts undertaken with a view to obtaining a unanimous resolution, hinging on a unanimous and constructive approach, had been thwarted and defeated by rigidity of position which was apparently not based on the desire to find an appropriate solution.

Voting in favour, Poland said the steps taken by Israel stemmed from a programme of step-by-step destruction of the Arab character of the occupied territories; one of the methods applied was the constant broadening and intensification of colonization, leading to eventual annexation.

Spain found it difficult not to see in the recent Israeli measures in the West Bank and Gaza the continuation of a deliberate and planned policy designed ultimately to perpetuate the occupation of the territories acquired by force in contravention of international law; it was impossible to believe in the sincerity of the peace intentions of those who, declaring their support for negotiations, seemed to think that repression and intimidation was the best way to prepare for dialogue.

Japan deplored Israel's latest actions as violations of Security Council resolutions and the 1949 Geneva Convention, adding that they heightened tensions in the occupied territories and throughout the Middle East, had made a solution to the Palestine problem even less attainable and obstructed international efforts for a comprehensive peace.

France and the United Kingdom denounced the disbanding of the Al Bireh municipal council and the dismissal of the Mayors of Nablus and Ramallah, as well as the violence and repression in the West Bank and Gaza, and requested respect for democratic liberties. France considered Israel's policy of *faits accomplis* in the occupied territories to be unacceptable and contrary to international law. The United Kingdom expressed disappointment that there had been no agreement on a text which could have commanded consensus; only through consensus could the Council contribute effectively to the problems relating to the Arab-Israeli dispute.

Ireland said it had worked informally with other delegations on a text it had hoped would secure a consensus on the basis of the following points: a call for restraint, addressed particularly to Israel; a request to Israel to rescind its decisions; reaffirmation of the inadmissibility of the acquisition of territory by force; and reaffirmation of the continued and full applicability of the 1949 Geneva Convention to all of the occupied territories. Support for Ireland's draft was expressed by Zaire, which said the Middle East and Palestine problems could not be solved by grabbing the occupied territories.

Israel said Jordan's draft resolution would place another obstacle in the path of peace; the text said nothing about instigation from abroad from some Arab countries which had supplied money and organized subversion, it avoided the ongoing peace process, and it did not support understanding and conciliation.

Commenting on the United States veto, Jordan said it hoped that one day the American voice would be in accord with the general will of international legality, morality and justice, and with the country's fundamental values. By vetoing the resolution, the Syrian Arab Republic said, the United States also had vetoed the obligation of States to respect universally acknowledged rights and Charter principles, particularly those relating to non-intervention and non-interference in domestic affairs, self-determination, territorial integrity and political independence, resistance to foreign occupation, and non-use or threat of use of force; the United States veto would encourage Israeli occupying authorities to escalate their inhuman practices and would contribute to a worsening of the situation in the occupied territories. In the opinion of PLO, the veto was a deliberate obstruction of the Council's constructive role and duty, an affirmation of hostile policy towards Palestinians and Arabs, an invitation to bloodshed and instability.

During its deliberations, the Council invited Algeria, Bangladesh, Cuba, Democratic Yemen, Egypt, the German Democratic Republic, India, Iran, Iraq, Israel, the Libyan Arab Jamahiriya, Morocco, Pakistan, Saudi Arabia, Senegal, the Syrian Arab Republic, Turkey, Viet Nam, Yemen and Yugoslavia, at their request, to participate without vote in the discussion. In addition, on the proposal of Jordan,[16] the Council extended an invitation under rule 39 of its provisional rules of procedure[h] to the Permanent Observer of the League of Arab States to the United Nations.

On 24 March, at the request of Jordan,[15] the Council decided that an invitation should be accorded to a PLO representative to participate in the debate and that the invitation would confer on it the same rights of participation as those conferred on a Member State invited to participate under rule 37 of the provisional rules of procedure.[i] The Council took this decision by a vote, requested by the United States, of 11 to 1 (United States), with 3 abstentions (France, Japan, United Kingdom).

Opening the debate, Jordan said the battle for the occupied territories had intensified and would

[h]See footnote b on p. 430.
[i]See footnote a on p. 429.

not end until the yoke of one of the worst occupations in history was terminated. The turmoil, triggered by the ejection of the town mayors and councillors of Al Bireh and their replacement by an Israeli colonel, had entered its sixth day and had left scores of dead and wounded. Israel's objective in instituting a reign of terror was to subdue the will to resistance as a prelude to imposing its version of administrative self-rule and emptying the territories of their lawful inhabitants as a final step in its officially declared aim of annexing the rest of the territories. The Council's inaction and complacency had created an untenable situation which would soon pose a grave threat to peace and security and which rendered meaningless any talk about a peaceful solution.

The PLO observer appealed to the Council to take prompt action; a resolution, even if adopted unanimously, might not be accepted and carried out by Israel, but at least it would strengthen faith in the United Nations.

Expressing support for the draft submitted by Jordan, India and Senegal considered it to be time that the Council put into effect the 1976 recommendations of the Committee on Palestinian rights, which had been repeatedly endorsed by the Assembly;[45] since Israel had treated those recommendations with contempt, India added, the only option available to the Council was to take punitive action as provided for in the Charter.

In the opinion of the Syrian Arab Republic, the disbanding of the Al Bireh municipal council and its replacement by Israeli military rule was an indication that Israel had embarked on the annexation of the West Bank bit by bit, and was forcing skilled Palestinian and Arab labourers to emigrate; the Assembly having declared that Israel was not a peace-loving Member, the Council had the obligation to apply mandatory sanctions and to recommend that Israel be expelled from the United Nations.

Algeria, Bangladesh, the German Democratic Republic, Iraq, the Libyan Arab Jamahiriya, Pakistan, Turkey, the USSR, Viet Nam, the Permanent Observer of the League of Arab States and others perceived the recent Israeli measures and coercive methods against the Palestinian population as further manifestations of Israel's scheme to bring the occupied territories under its permanent annexation and control.

Egypt said that Israel's policies and practices, aimed at intimidating, eliminating and liquidating the indigenous Palestinians and at depopulating the occupied territories, were undermining sincere attempts to achieve a peaceful, just and comprehensive Middle East settlement; the general strike in the West Bank was a natural expression of resistance against those iron-fist policies. The view that resistance in the form of strikes and demonstrations had been provoked by repres-

sive measures by Israeli occupying forces was also voiced by others, among them Algeria, Bangladesh, India, Iraq and Viet Nam. Bangladesh added that Israel's recent actions demonstrated its reluctance to accept the very limited autonomy of the occupied territories.

In the opinion of the German Democratic Republic and Viet Nam, the renewed stepping up of Israel's annexation policy was directly related to the so-called strategic alliance between the United States and Israel. Cuba, Iraq, the Libyan Arab Jamahiriya and others said that, without United States support, Israel would not have dared to commit its aggressive and expansionist acts.

Super-Power rivalry, Yemen stated, had played a big role in delaying a solution and had almost completely prevented the Council from taking appropriate measures in accordance with the Charter; it was high time that the Council assumed its responsibility.

Bangladesh, Pakistan, Yugoslavia and others believed that the situation posed a grave threat to international peace and security or threatened a wider conflict. India said a wider conflict could be avoided only if the Council responded to the challenge promptly and effectively.

The German Democratic Republic said the situation in the occupied territories had further deteriorated as a result of new acts of Israeli State terrorism, which further impeded a Middle East solution.

The PLO observer stated that Israeli civilian administration in the occupied territories was based on the denial of political and other rights of the population; the only way to redress the situation was by ending the illegal occupation and by guaranteeing the freedom and independence of the people and territory.

Israel, on the other hand, stated that responsibility for the recent unrest lay with PLO and must to a large extent be shared by Jordan, both of which were conspiring to eliminate any emerging and promising alternative to PLO terror. The Prime Minister of Jordan had threatened the inhabitants of Judaea and Samaria with treason charges and death penalties if they favoured peace with Israel by participating in village associations. Israel had set up a civilian administration to replace the military one, seeking to create the framework for a Palestinian Arab autonomy which would eventually take over from the civilian administration. The Council could discharge its tasks and promote peace only by supporting the promise of reconciliation rather than condoning violence and fear, even by implication; it must call on those responsible for the instigation of terror and tension to desist from their provocations.

In a subsequent statement following the dismissal of the Mayors of Nablus and Ramallah, Israel said they had been dismissed in order to root out agitation at one of its sources. The United States remarked in this connection that the Geneva Convention gave the occupying Power the unrestricted right to dismiss public officials, whether appointed or elected.

Most speakers, including Bangladesh, Egypt, Morocco, Pakistan, Turkey and the USSR, called on Israel to rescind its decision and reinstitute the municipal council and the mayors, and to end its violence and restrictive measures against the population of the occupied territories. Morocco also called on the Council to declare the recent measures null and void and to condemn any Israeli action that would make it impossible to restore peace and justice founded on restoration of Palestinian rights and unconditional Israeli withdrawal from the occupied territories. The USSR added that the Council must condemn Israel for its continuing acts of terrorism and take measures against any further creeping annexation. Turkey hoped that a resolute stand by the Council would impel Israel to come to terms with the inevitable reality of the Palestinians and their inalienable rights.

Pakistan believed that recent events in the occupied territories had demonstrated that paralysis on the part of the Council, preventing it from acting expeditiously and firmly, would aggravate the situation. Yugoslavia considered it the Council's duty to compel Israel to respect and implement the principles of international law and international relations; the Council must take measures to end Israel's policy of violence, denationalization and national obliteration of the occupied territories and reprisals against their population, and then embark energetically on the creation of conditions favourable for a Middle East solution.

Cuba called on the Council to adopt the measures necessary to put an end to the cause of the conflict; it hoped Israeli occupation and annexation of the territories of others would cease, the Palestinians would be enabled unconditionally to exercise their inalienable rights, justice would be restored, and the way would be opened to a comprehensive and lasting Middle East solution.

Bangladesh stated that the permanent Council members had a particularly heavy responsibility to enable the Council to bring peace to the Middle East.

Algeria felt that restrained condemnations and appeals to goodwill were inadequate to block Israeli designs of domination and conquest; the Council must do everything in its power to stop the violations of the human rights of the Palestinians.

The Libyan Arab Jamahiriya called on the Council to condemn Israel and fully to apply Chapter VII of the Charter.

The Permanent Observer of the League of Arab States said that, if Israel's annexationist policies remained uninterrupted by the United Nations, the havoc all were seeking to avoid would be conjured up and enforced.

Israel said the Council was being used as a forum to engender tensions and to echo the provocations inside the occupied territories; the Council must allow reason to assert itself. Israel, in any case, would not be deterred from striving for greater Israel-Arab understanding and cooperation within the framework of peaceful coexistence.

Pakistan believed that the continuing Palestinian resistance to the Israeli occupation highlighted the primary imperative of the Middle East conflict—that peace could not be attained without full restitution of Palestinian rights, including the right to self-determination and to the establishment of an independent State in Palestine. In Egypt's view, as in that of many other States, the situation in the territories was a direct corollary of Israel's rejection of the recognition or acknowledgement of the existence of an independent Palestinian national entity.

Iran said the answer to the Palestinian problem could not be found in debates and resolutions; it lay only in vigorously convincing the usurping agent that it could no longer count on the inactivity of the majority of inhabitants of the occupied territories and that it could no longer impose tranquillity on the area by means of military power.

Communications (April). On 2 April, Morocco transmitted a telegram of 23 March from King Hassan II of Morocco, in his capacity as President of the Summit Conference of Arab States, condemning what he called repressive and inhuman acts by Israel against the Palestinian population in the occupied territories.[24]

Also on 2 April, Belgium transmitted a statement of the EC heads of State and Government, made at a meeting of the European Council in Brussels, Belgium, on 29 and 30 March, denouncing measures against the Palestinians such as the dismissal of elected mayors, as well as what they called the violation of liberties and rights of the inhabitants.[9]

On 20 April, Jordan forwarded to the Security Council President, at the request of the PLO observer, a letter of 19 April from the Mayor of Gaza, appealing to the President to intervene in order to alleviate what the Mayor said were brutal attacks of the Israeli army against the civilians of the Gaza Strip and the West Bank, including a curfew at Rafah which had been in effect for five days.[20]

General Assembly action (April). At its resumed seventh emergency special session on the Palestine question, the General Assembly adopted on 28 April a resolution[28] in which it demanded that Israel comply with the 1980 Security Council resolution demanding that Israel rescind measures to change the physical character, demographic composition, institutional structure and status of the occupied territories.[44] Under other provisions, the Assembly condemned Israel for its failure to fulfil its obligations under the 1949 Geneva Convention on the protection of civilians (see below), for disbanding the elected municipal council of Al Bireh and dismissing the Mayors of Ramallah and Nablus, for repressive measures including shooting at unarmed civilians, and for attacks against and interference with the functions of civic, educational and religious institutions. It demanded that Israel permit the Committee on Israeli practices in the occupied territories to enter those territories to fulfil the mandate given it by the Assembly.

Introducing the resolution, Senegal said that, by recalling the recent events in the occupied territories, deplored and condemned by the international community, it was merely being consistent.

Democratic Yemen, Iraq, the Libyan Arab Jamahiriya, Togo, Turkey and others stated that they voted for the resolution primarily in support of the victims of Israeli occupation, annexation and colonization and of the struggle of the Palestinians. The legitimate anger of a desperate people taken to the extremes, Turkey said, had been drowned in violence and blood. Greece declared it voted in favour in support of the principles of non-use of force and inadmissibility of the acquisition or control over a territory through military invasion and occupation and in support of the right to self-determination. Suriname expressed the view that the continuing aggravation and deterioration of the situation especially in the occupied territories called for international action to take appropriate measures and implement the relevant Security Council resolutions; Suriname felt that the provisions adequately addressed the tension caused by Israel's policies.

Jordan, however, felt that the resolution would not alleviate the plight of the Palestinians, nor change the irreversible course of Israel's aggression, bringing the just Palestinian cause and Palestinian rights to the point of no return; Israel had clearly demonstrated its determination to expel by force, intimidation and strangulation the remnants of the Palestinians from their homeland. The facts described in the paragraph condemning Israel's policies were there for all to see.

Israel, on the other hand, said the paragraph contained a series of blatant lies that had failed of adoption in the Security Council.

Though casting an affirmative vote, Nepal would have preferred a different formulation of certain subparagraphs of the provision condemning Israeli practices.

Israel's policies were denounced and rejected by the majority of speakers, among them Bahrain, Bolivia, Bulgaria, Burundi, the Byelorussian SSR, China, Democratic Yemen, Egypt, the German Democratic Republic, Ghana, Hungary, India, Ireland, Jordan, Mongolia, Portugal, Romania, the Syrian Arab Republic and Yugoslavia. Concern over the repressive policy and escalating tension was expressed by Belgium (on behalf of the EC members), Canada, Sweden and others. Sierra Leone said Israel's recent policies had further threatened peace and stability and further aborted the Palestinian struggle for self-determination. Madagascar believed that Israel's policy seemed to consist in preventing any real progress towards establishing a just and lasting peace and in maintaining a constant state of tension, if not terror.

In Finland's view, Israel's policies in the occupied territories continued to breed frustration and violence and made the achievement of a comprehensive peace more difficult. Norway thought the recent disturbances in the West Bank were a sign of mounting frustration.

Support for the call for Israeli withdrawal from the occupied territories and the recognition of Palestinian rights was expressed by Austria, Brazil, Canada, Costa Rica, Ecuador, Panama, Peru, Spain, Suriname, the United Republic of Cameroon and others.

The Middle East and Palestine problem would continue, Sierra Leone stated, until Israel terminated its annexation policies and repeated predatory and military attacks against Palestinians, and until it ceased the expulsion of Palestinians from their homeland.

Recent events, Zaire and others said, had proved the need for increased efforts and new initiatives to find a negotiated, comprehensive, just and lasting solution to the Middle East and Palestine problem.

The PLO observer appealed to the Security Council to take the necessary measures for the protection of the Palestinians and their land in the West Bank and Gaza and to ensure Israel's full withdrawal, and appealed to the United Nations to dispatch immediately an international committee to inquire into Israel's crimes.

Zambia said that, in its attempts to deprive the Palestinians of their homeland and their right to self-determination, Israel had increased its repression which, in Bulgaria's opinion, was aimed at crushing Palestinian resistance. Nigeria felt that Israel was not only destroying the Palestinian nation but also the way of life of the Palestinians. In Viet Nam's view, Israel's aggressive acts were part of its systematic policy to eliminate the Palestinians.

Thailand said the continued mistreatment of the Arab population underscored the urgent need for full restoration of Palestinian rights, particularly the right to self-determination free from outside interference or coercion; Israel, however, appeared more determined to hold onto the occupied territories.

India believed that Israel's actions were designed to consolidate its stranglehold over the occupied territories and to perpetuate their occupation, as well as to intimidate its Arab neighbours. Togo was convinced that a new flare-up of violence in the region could only give Israel reasons to continue its illegal occupation. A number of countries, among them Bahrain, the Byelorussian SSR, Hungary, Indonesia, Kuwait, Pakistan, Poland, Uganda, the Ukrainian SSR, the United Republic of Cameroon and Yugoslavia, charged that Israel's policies were aimed at annexing the occupied territories. The Sudan stated that Israel wanted to build a State with no definite borders. In Morocco's view, the occupation of the Arab territories after the 1967 six-day war had been the point of departure for the implementation of the dream of Greater Israel. Jordan said Israel had already seized 40 per cent of the territories occupied in 1967 and more than 90 per cent of those occupied in 1948.

In Tunisia's opinion, Israel's aggression against the Palestinians and Arabs was designed to keep the Middle East in a permanent state of tension which served its hegemonism. Israel's practices were nothing but usurpation, Iran stated, and as long as the original mistake of the creation of an Israeli State was not rectified, any attempt at reformation or prevention of other crimes and aggression remained useless.

According to Morocco, there had been a catastrophic acceleration of Israel's colonization and expansion. Ghana considered the increase in the tempo of annexation, expropriation of Arab land and other Israeli acts in the territories a threat to international peace and security and international law.

Bangladesh, Cyprus, Djibouti, Iraq, Japan, the Philippines, Poland, Yemen, Yugoslavia and others believed that Israel's occupation policy had exacerbated the Middle East situation. Norway saw the disturbances as a sign of mounting frustration among the Palestinians. In Pakistan's view, the Palestinian protests and street demonstrations were the manifestation of the aggravation of an already explosive situation. Speaking for the EC members, Belgium said they were profoundly disturbed by the toll of killed and wounded; Israel's recent steps had only served to undermine the peace process. A similar position was held by Malaysia and the Sudan, which added that Israel's actions had the potential of drawing the region into armed confrontation.

The Ukrainian SSR said Israeli colonization of seized lands had assumed particularly large proportions since the Camp David plot, and the cruel repression of Palestinians was serving to force them to give up their rights and to agree with the so-called administrative autonomy provided for them by that anti-Arab plot. The Byelorussian SSR believed that Israel was determined to expedite the implementation of its plans for the creation of a Greater Israel by imposing on the Palestinians a Camp David–style autonomy which would deprive them of their right to self-determination and creation of their own national State. The so-called autonomy envisaged in the Camp David agreement, Democratic Yemen said, merely paved the way for total annexation. In Afghanistan's opinion, the Camp David process proved to be a process for creeping annexation and for mounting ruthless repression, and Qatar said Israel exploited the so-called autonomy talks to mask its usurpation of Arab and Palestinian territories.

Saudi Arabia said the annexation of the Golan Heights (see above) had followed the establishment of Israeli settlements in the area and Israel now followed the same course with regard to the West Bank. Also in the opinion of Hungary, Kuwait, Mongolia and Poland, Israel intended to annex the West Bank and Gaza, an intention already proved in the case of Jerusalem and the Golan Heights. Czechoslovakia regarded the new wave of repression against the Palestinians in the West Bank and Gaza, as well as Israel's unlawful measures in Jerusalem and the Golan Heights, as a prelude to a new display of Israel's wilfulness. New Zealand felt that there had been a succession of acts in defiance of the principle of non-acquisition of territory by force, including the annexation of East Jerusalem, the Israeli decision on the Golan Heights, and the seizure and settlement of large amounts of land and property in the West Bank.

The Lao People's Democratic Republic feared that the occupied territories would fall one after the other under the stroke of Israeli legislation; the annexation of the Golan Heights and Jerusalem and Israel's attacks against Lebanon were proof of its efforts to legalize for all time its occupation of Arab territories. Once Israel had put into effect its decision to annex Jerusalem and the Golan Heights, Iraq stated, it began its preparations for forging another link in its chain of expansionism; it aimed at preparing the ground not only for the annexation of the West Bank and Gaza, but also for military aggression against southern Lebanon.

Mongolia said the annexation was being carried out in stages: after repopulating the occupied territories on a broad scale, which violated the basic rights and freedoms of the indigenous population, and repressing the slightest opposition, legislation followed. Pakistan said Israel's repressive measures against the Palestinians were coupled with administrative and juridical steps aimed at changing the character, structure and status of the territories; Israel's objective was clearly to change facts on the ground and consolidate its control over the territories.

In the view of the USSR, it was Israel's expansionist policy aimed at perpetuating its occupation of Arab lands and at imposing alien domination on the Palestinians that stood in the way of a Middle East settlement and just and lasting peace. Burundi felt that Israel's practices and policies destroyed the climate needed for negotiations. Jordan held it indisputable that Israel's policies could not be allowed to continue unchecked and unchallenged.

Israel was urged by many countries to rescind its measures. Romania called on Israel to nullify immediately its unlawful actions and put an end to repression; Israel's security and independence could be ensured only if it respected the security and independence of other countries and the right of the Palestinians to live in their own independent State. By putting an end to its policies in the territories, Nepal believed, Israel would create confidence in its stated willingness to negotiate.

As a condition for a settlement, many speakers, including China and the United Republic of Cameroon, called for Israeli withdrawal from the occupied territories.

Israel said with regard to the Palestinian residents of Judaea, Samaria and Gaza, the Camp David framework saw the solution in terms of their full autonomy, for a transitional period of five years, before reaching an agreement on the final status of the area. The Camp David framework invited the Palestinians to play an active role in shaping their future and offered them greater opportunities than they had ever experienced.

In the opinion of the PLO observer, however, the Camp David plot was meant to torpedo United Nations efforts for a comprehensive peace; nowhere in the accords were the rights of the Palestinians mentioned, their rights to return, to self-determination and sovereignty. The USSR and a number of other, mainly Eastern European and Arab, States cited similar reasons for their opposition to the Camp David accords. Angola believed that a temporary or partial peace merely served to disguise the Palestine problem and sought to buy time for Israel to entrench all the more its illegal and racist policies in the occupied territories.

Finland held it imperative that the ultimate status of the territories not be prejudged before a comprehensive solution had been found.

Communications (May-July). By a letter of 24 May to the Secretary-General,[4] the Chairman of the Committee on Palestinian rights expressed grave concern over what he regarded as the dangerous deterioration in the West Bank and Gaza due to Israel's repressive policy; the letter cited press reports of the death of several Palestinians and the wounding of many others in protests against Israeli policies, including an attack by Israeli soldiers against a girls' school, causing the death of a Palestinian girl.

In a similar letter of 18 June,[5] the Chairman called attention to a press report that Israel had dissolved the elected city councils of two West Bank towns, Dura and Nablus. Reports that the Mayor of Djenin had been removed from office and that two young Palestinian demonstrators had been wounded were cited in a further letter by the Chairman dated 9 July.[6]

General Assembly action (August). In its resolution of 19 August concerned mainly with Israel and Lebanon,[29] the General Assembly again demanded that Israel carry out the provisions of previous Assembly resolutions on the occupied territories, as well as of the 1980 Security Council resolution on the subject.[44] It mentioned in particular the Council's determination that Israeli measures to change the character, demography, institutions or status of the territories had no legal validity, and that Israel's settlement policy (see below) violated the 1949 Geneva Convention on the protection of civilians and obstructed a Middle East peace; and the Council's call on Israel to rescind those measures, dismantle settlements, and cease establishing and planning new ones.

Communications (September-December). Press reports that Israeli frontier police had shot two young Arabs in the West Bank were cited in a letter of 14 September to the Secretary-General from the Chairman of the Committee on Palestinian rights.[7] By a letter of 29 October,[8] the Chairman expressed the belief that Israel had embarked on a new wave of repression in the wake of demonstrations protesting the shooting death on 27 October of a young Palestinian, reportedly killed by Israeli settlers.

On 25 October,[21] 29 October[22] and 21 December,[23] Jordan transmitted to the Security Council President letters from the PLO observer, alleging further repressive measures by Israel, including a curfew imposed on Hebron on 20 October following incidents between Israelis and Palestinians (PLO letter of 21 October); firing at and wounding of demonstrators protesting the killing of a Palestinian by Israeli settlers (two letters of 27 October); and the killing of two demonstrators and imposition of curfews (two letters of 20 December).

Activities of the Committee on Israeli practices in the occupied territories. In its annual report, approved on 27 August and transmitted to the General Assembly by the Secretary-General,[26] the Special Committee to Investigate Israeli Practices Affecting the Human Rights of the Population of the Occupied Territories, established in 1968,[42] presented information on the situation of the civilian population, on Israeli civil administration in the territories, Israel's annexation and settlement policies, and treatment of detainees. The report, with an annexed map showing Israeli settlements established, planned or under construction, covered the situation since the adoption of the Committee's previous report in September 1981.[46] As in previous years, the Committee worked without the co-operation of Israel.

During 1982, the Committee held three series of meetings. At the first, from 18 to 22 January at Geneva, the Committee reviewed its mandate and decided on the organization of its work. At the second series of meetings, from 4 to 14 May, beginning at Geneva and moving to Amman, Jordan, and Damascus, Syrian Arab Republic, the Committee heard the testimony of persons living in the occupied territories, including the Mayors of Halhul and Hebron and the President of Bir Zeit University. It also consulted with Jordanian and Syrian officials, and visited a camp for approximately 61,000 persons operated by the United Nations Relief and Works Agency for Palestine Refugees in the Near East and the King Hussein Bridge, the crossing point between Jordanian territory and the Israeli-occupied West Bank, to examine procedures and practices regarding civilians crossing to and from the occupied area. During a third series of meetings, held from 23 to 27 August at Geneva, the Committee examined communications and adopted its report.

In the conclusions of its report, the Committee stated that since September 1981, when the Israeli Minister of Defence had announced a "new policy" and the subsequent imposition of "civil administration", the situation in the occupied territories had taken a distinct turn for the worse. After declaring their opposition to the civil administration, lawfully elected municipal authorities in the West Bank and Gaza had been systematically dismissed. The situation had become yet more explosive, leading to the death of several persons at the hands of Israeli forces or settlers in the course of demonstrations by the Arab population against the dismissal of the municipal authorities. No less than 21 persons were reported to have been shot dead within two months early in 1982.

The Committee further concluded that the prolonged Israeli occupation had led to complete subjugation of the economy of the occupied territories to the Israeli economy. Agriculture, the main economic sector, was largely conditioned by the vicissitudes of Israeli agriculture. The latter, benefiting from subsidies and centralized planning, had taken control of markets that would normally constitute the outlets for agriculture in the West Bank.

Parallel to these events, the Government, in its effort to eliminate the popular base of the municipalities, had undertaken the establishment of "village leagues", including persons with doubtful reputation and standing in the Palestinian community. Those institutions had been accorded power and influence over matters such as the issuance of certain building and travel permits, so to make them indispensable in daily life. In addition, Israeli settlement policy had been intensified and there was a greater tendency to consolidate the settlements already established, particularly in areas densely populated by Palestinians (see below).

The Committee stated that the civilian population did not benefit from any means of legal protection and had been completely deprived of any remedy. Recourse to the Israeli Supreme Court and the High Court of Justice had been shown to be without any significant result. The number of detainees continued to increase and prison conditions were very unsatisfactory, due mainly to overcrowding.

The Committee concluded that the information it had received indicated that the 1949 Geneva Convention on the protection of civilians continued to be contravened (see below). It also heard testimony on the resistance of the Golan Heights population to Israel's action extending its law to the Syrian territory (see above).

In accordance with a December 1981 General Assembly resolution,[43] the Secretary-General submitted to the Assembly in October 1982 a report on the measures taken by the Secretariat to provide the facilities required by the Committee and to ensure the widest dissemination of information on its work.[25] He stated that an additional staff member had been made available to the Committee.

General Assembly action (December). On 10 December, the General Assembly adopted seven resolutions on the report of the Committee on Israeli practices, one dealing with the general situation of the territories occupied by Israel and the rest concerning specific aspects.

By the general resolution,[33] the Assembly strongly condemned a number of Israeli policies and practices and demanded that Israel desist from them. They included annexation, imposition of Israeli laws and administration on the Golan Heights, establishment and expansion of settlements, evacuation and displacement of Arabs, confiscation of Arab property, excavation and transformation of cultural and religious sites, destruction of houses, collective punishment, torture of detainees, interference with religious freedoms, family customs, education, development and freedom of movement, and illegal exploitation of natural resources. The Assembly reaffirmed that occupation itself constituted a grave violation of human rights and reiterated its call for non-recognition of changes carried out by Israel in the territories. The Assembly requested the Committee to continue its work, deplored Israel's continued refusal to allow the Committee access to the occupied territories and demanded that it grant such access.

By the other resolutions, the Assembly: demanded that Israel comply with the 1949 Geneva Convention on the protection of civilians in wartime;[31] deplored Israel's establishment of settlements in the occupied territories;[32] demanded that Israel rescind the expulsion and imprisonment of the Mayors of Hebron and Halhul and the expulsion of the Sharia (Islamic) Judge of Hebron;[34] condemned Israel's decision to impose its laws, jurisdiction and administration in the Golan Heights;[35] demanded that Israel rescind all actions against Palestinian educational institutions,[36] and expressed deep concern that Israel had failed for two years to apprehend and prosecute the perpetrators of assassination attempts against the Mayors of Nablus, Ramallah and Al Bireh.[37]

The Assembly also dealt with the occupied territories in three other resolutions adopted in December. By its resolutions of 16 December on the Golan Heights[38] and 20 December on the Palestine question,[30] the Assembly declared all Israeli policies and practices of, or aimed at, annexation of the occupied territories, including Jerusalem, to be in violation of international law and United Nations resolutions, and demanded that Israel withdraw completely and unconditionally therefrom. In the latter resolution, it urged the Security Council to facilitate Israel's withdrawal and recommended that the territories be placed under United Nations supervision for a short transitional period, during which the Palestinians would exercise their right to self-determination. Condemning the continued occupation of Arab and Palestinian territories, the Assembly demanded Israeli withdrawal in another resolution of 20 December, on the Middle East situation.[40]

In addition, by a resolution of 16 December,[39] the Assembly deplored the transfer by some States of their diplomatic missions to Jerusalem.

The 10 December resolution condemning Israeli practices in the territories was adopted by a recorded vote of 112 to 2, with 21 abstentions, following its approval on 3 December by the Special Political Committee by a recorded vote of 85 to 2, with 22 abstentions. Paragraphs 6 and 16 were adopted in Committee by recorded votes of 72 to 18, with 14 abstentions, and 83 to 17, with 7 abstentions, respectively.

The United States, rejecting the text as severely biased and polemical, particularly opposed the costs envisaged for the Special Committee's activities—estimated by the Secretary-General at $323,900 over the previously budgeted expenses for 1983.

Abstaining in the vote, Sweden said that although it supported most of the resolution's contents, and specifically the condemnation of various Israeli policies and practices, the text was not always fully justified by proven facts, went beyond the Assembly's competence and contained sweeping generalizations which Sweden could not support.

Though voting in favour, Jamaica regarded the language of the paragraph condemning the ill-treatment and torture of detainees as excessive.

Introducing the draft in Committee on behalf of 11 nations, Bangladesh noted that its content had been the subject of many previous resolutions which had not produced substantive results.

During the Assembly debates on the Middle East situation and on the Palestine question, many speakers denounced or deplored Israeli practices and policies in the occupied territories. Concern was expressed by Denmark, on behalf of the EC members, which believed that those policies and practices had led to mounting tension and continued unrest. The denial of human rights in the territories was also of concern to others, among them Nigeria, which added that Israel's continued occupation of Arab lands was a threat to international peace and security.

The Congo, the United Arab Emirates and others held that Israel's measures in the territories were arbitrary, illegal and contrary to international law; Portugal believed that they violated in particular the principle of the inadmissibility of the acquisition of territory by force. Palestinians were killed because they dared to cast a stone against the occupying Power, said the United Arab Emirates; their homes were destroyed because they had a brother or son suspected of involvement in the resistance to the occupation, their elected representatives had been eliminated or attacked because they rejected occupation, and their books were confiscated and their schools and universities closed for months because they had shown opposition or expressed opinions.

A number of States felt that the situation in the occupied territories had worsened; at no past time, Indonesia remarked, had the Palestinians been subjected to such brutal oppression. The Lao People's Democratic Republic also saw a deterioration and observed that Israel was committing acts of terrorism and repression against the territories' civilians. Cyprus said Israel had been allowed to proceed with its policies almost with impunity, and Saudi Arabia charged that Israel made use of Western money to consolidate its aggression against the occupied territories with a view to settling and annexing them and terrorizing the Palestinians to induce them to emigrate so that they would completely lose their identity and any hope of living in freedom and dignity in their native land. Madagascar saw an unprecedented increase in violence and brutality, with Israeli authorities harassing civilians who opposed the introduction of a civil administration system and the setting up of village leagues as a prelude to annexation of the territories by Israel.

The PLO observer stated that under Israeli occupation the Palestinians lived in conditions that were a travesty of law; however, they were determined to achieve their rights. In spite of Israel's repression, which was becoming more ruthless, Morocco said, the Palestinians were succeeding in asserting their existence, identity and rights. In Sri Lanka's opinion, the most tenacious defenders of their rights had been the Palestinians themselves, who had resisted and survived despite the repression and banishment of their leadership. Responsibility for the liberation of the territories, the Syrian Arab Republic declared, rested with the Arab nation.

On the pretext of ensuring the existence of its people, Nicaragua said, Israel had never hesitated to practise the most cruel, inhuman and racist methods. A similar opinion was expressed by the USSR, which added that those methods had become a daily norm of Israeli occupation policy; for 15 years, the longest period of military occupation in the twentieth century, Israel had been drawing the noose ever tighter around the Arab and Palestinian lands it had seized. Democratic Yemen stated that Israel was exercising every form of violence and intimidation, and Iraq found it obvious that it was the Palestinians and not Israel's population that had to be liberated from continuous acts of terror and aggression. The Libyan Arab Jamahiriya said Israel's actions were designed to terrorize and intimidate the Palestinians so that Israel could impose its expansionist policy and consecrate its *faits accomplis.*

Algeria believed that Israel was attempting to modify fundamentally the legal status of the territories, an attempt which in Indonesia's opinion added a new, more ominous dimension to the Middle East problem. Nepal and others felt that Israel's continued actions to change the legal status and demographic character of the territories could not be condoned.

Besides attempting to change the demographic, historical and cultural features of the territories, Pakistan stated, Israel was annexing them outright. A similar opinion was expressed by Djibouti, Greece, Hungary, Qatar, Viet Nam and Yugoslavia. The Israelis, said Guyana, had manifested a ruthless determination to hold onto and even expand their territorial acquisitions. Sweden rejected Israeli claims to supremacy over the territories as without basis in international law and could not

accept Israel's attempts to create facts with the intent of making Israeli control irreversible. Uganda said Israel's design to annex the West Bank and the Gaza Strip was betrayed by its replacement of its military authorities in the West Bank with a civilian administration and its construction of massive settlements.

Jordan charged Israel with carrying out a systematic programme of colonization and annexation, a position held by several others, including Bahrain, Bulgaria, Czechoslovakia, Guyana, Hungary, Indonesia, Saudi Arabia, the Sudan, the Ukrainian SSR and Yugoslavia. Kenya urged that Israel's supporters who had means of persuasion over it assist in reversing the annexation of Arab lands. Malta, the Rapporteur of the Committee on Palestinian rights, said Israel's policies represented a *de facto* annexation, with old maps no longer recognizable. Tunisia said Israel believed that its policy of *fait accompli* would enable it to give the dream of Greater Israel a concrete form. Israel's intentions, the Gambia thought, had been eloquently illustrated in March by the transfer to a civilian administrator of territories administered by a military governor, a move rightly condemned by Palestinian leaders as creeping annexation. The USSR said the purpose of Israel's policy was to force the Palestinians to accept Israeli occupation and to impose on them a meagre Camp David–style administrative autonomy.

Israel's land policies in the occupied territories were criticized by several speakers. The Byelorussian SSR said that in implementing its annexation policy, Israel was using both open violence to drive people out and such juridical casuistry as requiring the registration of all landholdings and then making it impossible in practice for the Palestinians to register their lands. The Syrian Arab Republic said Israel had taken 54 per cent of the land on the West Bank. In the view of the United Arab Emirates, Israel's aim was to expel all the indigenous population from Palestine so that it could seize the remaining Palestinian lands.

On the basis of a racist theory designed to preserve Israel's racist existence, thus preventing a large number of Palestinians in the occupied territories from remaining as citizens, PLO stated, Israel offered a distorted autonomy plan for the West Bank and Gaza.

Malaysia believed that Israel's aggressive policy in the territories confirmed that Israel would accept peace only on its terms. In the view of Cyprus, the increasingly brutal repression of civilians and actions to deprive Arab and Palestinian inhabitants of their land and water could not possibly be considered peace gestures. Brazil said some Israeli actions had hardly contributed to a climate of moderation. Austria believed that Israel's actions were in clear violation of international law and remained a fundamental impediment to the initiation of an effective peace process.

Many countries, including Bulgaria, Democratic Yemen, Hungary, Indonesia, Madagascar, Malaysia and Nigeria, saw Israel's unconditional withdrawal from the occupied territories as a pre-condition of any Middle East solution. The position of the EC members on this point, as stated by Denmark, was that an end must be put to the territorial occupation within the framework of a comprehensive, just and lasting settlement. In the framework of a solution, Iraq stated, first attention must be paid to the crux of the problem, namely, the fate of the inhabitants of territories. Pakistan said the United Nations had an immediate obligation to protect the human rights of the Palestinians in the occupied territories and in Lebanon and to exert pressure on Israel to prevent it from pursuing its repressive policies.

Dominating over approximately 60 per cent of the West Bank, having annexed Jerusalem and having imposed its law on the Golan Heights, Israel could not modify the historical facts and must realize that violence and terrorism could not resolve the Middle East conflict, Bahrain said. Japan urged Israel to make special efforts to protect human rights and promote the welfare of the Palestinians.

Draft resolution not adopted. [1]Jordan, S/14943.
Letters. Committee on Palestinian rights Acting Chairman *(AC)* and Chairman: [2]22 Jan., A/37/75-S/14844 *(AC)*; [3]8 Mar., A/37/109-S/14897; [4]24 May, A/37/240-S/15120; [5]18 June, A/37/301-S/15244; [6]9 July, A/37/339-S/15290; [7]14 Sep., A/37/449-S/15393; [8]29 Oct., A/37/587-S/15476. [9]Belgium: 2 Apr., A/37/170-S/14954. Israel: [10]17 Mar., A/37/118-S/14910 & Corr.1; [11]31 Mar., S/14938 (1 Apr., A/37/165). Jordan: [12]19 Mar., A/37/153 (S/14912); [13]22 Mar., A/37/155 (S/14916); [14]22 Mar., S/14917; [15]23 Mar., S/14920; [16]23 Mar., S/14921; [17]24 Mar., S/14923; [18]24 Mar., S/14924; [19]25 Mar., S/14930; [20]20 Apr., S/14991; [21]25 Oct., S/15465; [22]29 Oct., S/15470; [23]21 Dec., S/15541. [24]Morocco: 2 Apr., A/37/168-S/14952.
Reports. [25]S-G, A/37/541; [26]Committee on Israeli practices in occupied territories, transmitted by S-G note, A/37/485.
Resolutions (1982). [27]Commission on Human Rights (report, E/1982/12): 1982/1 A, 11 Feb. (transmitted by S-G note, A/37/322-S/15269). GA: [28]ES-7/4, 28 Apr.; [29]ES-7/6, 19 Aug.; [30]37/86 E, paras. 2-5, 20 Dec.; [31]37/88 A, [32]37/88 B, 10 Dec.; [33]37/88 C, 10 Dec., text following; [34]37/88 D, [35]37/88 E, [36]37/88 F, [37]37/88 G, 10 Dec.; [38]37/123 A, paras. 4 & 11, 16 Dec.; [39]37/123 C, 16 Dec.; [40]37/123 F, para. 1, 20 Dec. [41]SCPDPM (report, E/CN.4/1983/4): 1982/18, para. 1 *(c)* & *(f)*, 8 Sep.
Resolutions (prior). GA: [42]2443(XXIII), 19 Dec. 1968 (YUN 1968, p. 555); [43]36/147 C, 16 Dec. 1981 (YUN 1981, p. 305). [44]SC: 465(1980), 1 Mar. 1980 (YUN 1980, p. 427).
Yearbook references. [45]1976, p. 235 (text, 1980, p. 394); [46]1981, p. 301.
Financial implications. 5th Committee report, A/37/725; S-G statements, A/SPC/37/L.38, A/C.5/37/87.
Meeting records. SC: S/PV.2334 & Corr.1, 2338, 2340, 2344, 2348 (24 Mar.–2 Apr.). GA: SPC, A/SPC/37/SR.35-41, *42, 44* (23 Nov.–3 Dec.); 5th Committee, A/C.5/37/SR.61 (9 Dec.); plenary, A/37/PV.100 (10 Dec.).

General Assembly resolution 37/88 C

10 December 1982   Meeting 100   112-2-21 (recorded vote)

Approved by SPC (A/37/698) by recorded vote (85-2-22), 3 December (meeting 44); 11-nation draft (A/SPC/37/L.30); agenda item 61.

Sponsors: Afghanistan, Bangladesh, Cape Verde, Cuba, India, Indonesia, Madagascar, Malaysia, Pakistan, Qatar, Senegal.

The General Assembly,

Guided by the purposes and principles of the Charter of the United Nations and by the principles and provisions of the Universal Declaration of Human Rights,

Bearing in mind the provisions of the Geneva Convention relative to the Protection of Civilian Persons in Time of War, of 12 August 1949, as well as of other relevant conventions and regulations,

Recalling all its resolutions on the subject, in particular resolutions 32/91 B and C of 13 December 1977, 33/113 C of 18 December 1978, 34/90 A of 12 December 1979, 35/122 C of 11 December 1980 and 36/147 C of 16 December 1981, and also those adopted by the Security Council, the Commission on Human Rights and other United Nations organs concerned and by the specialized agencies,

Having considered the report of the Special Committee to Investigate Israeli Practices Affecting the Human Rights of the Population of the Occupied Territories, which contains, *inter alia*, public statements made by the leaders of the Government of Israel,

1. *Commends* the Special Committee to Investigate Israeli Practices Affecting the Human Rights of the Population of the Occupied Territories for its efforts in performing the tasks assigned to it by the General Assembly and for its thoroughness and impartiality;

2. *Deplores* the continued refusal by Israel to allow the Special Committee access to the occupied territories;

3. *Demands* that Israel allow the Special Committee access to the occupied territories;

4. *Reaffirms* the fact that occupation itself constitutes a grave violation of the human rights of the civilian population of the occupied Arab territories;

5. *Condemns* the continued and persistent violation by Israel of the Geneva Convention relative to the Protection of Civilian Persons in Time of War, of 12 August 1949, and other applicable international instruments, and condemns in particular those violations which that Convention designates as "grave breaches" thereof;

6. *Declares once more* that Israel's grave breaches of that Convention are war crimes and an affront to humanity;

7. *Strongly condemns* the following Israeli policies and practices:

(a) Annexation of parts of the occupied territories, including Jerusalem;

(b) Imposition of Israeli laws, jurisdiction and administration on the Syrian Golan Heights, which has resulted in the effective annexation of the Syrian Golan Heights;

(c) Establishment of new Israeli settlements and expansion of the existing settlements on private and public Arab lands, and transfer of an alien population thereto;

(d) Evacuation, deportation, expulsion, displacement and transfer of Arab inhabitants of the occupied territories and denial of their right to return;

(e) Confiscation and expropriation of private and public Arab property in the occupied territories and all other transactions for the acquisition of land involving the Israeli authorities, institutions or nationals on the one hand and the inhabitants or institutions of the occupied territories on the other;

(f) Excavations and transformations of the landscape and the historical, cultural and religious sites, especially in Jerusalem;

(g) Destruction and demolition of Arab houses;

(h) Collective punishment, mass arrests, administrative detention and ill-treatment of the Arab population;

(i) Ill-treatment and torture of persons under detention;

(j) Pillaging of archaeological and cultural property;

(k) Interference with religious freedoms and practices as well as family rights and customs;

(l) Interference with the system of education and with the social and economic development of the population in the occupied Palestinian and other Arab territories;

(m) Interference with the freedom of movement of individuals within the occupied Palestinian and other Arab territories;

(n) Illegal exploitation of the natural wealth, resources and population of the occupied territories;

8. *Reaffirms* that all measures taken by Israel to change the physical character, demographic composition, institutional structure or status of the occupied territories, or any part thereof, including Jerusalem, are null and void, and that Israel's policy of settling parts of its population and new immigrants in the occupied territories constitutes a flagrant violation of the Geneva Convention and of the relevant resolutions of the United Nations;

9. *Demands* that Israel desist forthwith from the policies and practices referred to in paragraphs 7 and 8 above;

10. *Urges* the international organizations and the specialized agencies, in particular the International Labour Organisation, to examine the conditions of Arab workers in the occupied Palestinian and other Arab territories, including Jerusalem;

11. *Reiterates its call* upon all States, in particular those States parties to the Geneva Convention, in accordance with article 1 of that Convention, and upon international organizations and the specialized agencies not to recognize any changes carried out by Israel in the occupied territories and to avoid actions, including those in the field of aid, which might be used by Israel in its pursuit of the policies of annexation and colonization or any of the other policies and practices referred to in the present resolution;

12. *Requests* the Special Committee, pending the early termination of Israeli occupation, to continue to investigate Israeli policies and practices in the Arab territories occupied by Israel since 1967, to consult, as appropriate, with the International Committee of the Red Cross in order to ensure the safeguarding of the welfare and human rights of the population of the occupied territories and to report to the Secretary-General as soon as possible and whenever the need arises thereafter;

13. *Requests* the Special Committee to continue to investigate the treatment of civilians in detention in the Arab territories occupied by Israel since 1967;

14. *Condemns* Israel's refusal to permit persons from the occupied territories to appear as witnesses before the Special Committee;

15. *Requests* the Secretary-General:

(a) To provide all necessary facilities to the Special Committee, including those required for its visits to the occupied territories, with a view to investigating the Israeli policies and practices referred to in the present resolution;

(b) To continue to make available additional staff as may be necessary to assist the Special Committee in the performance of its tasks;

(c) To ensure the widest circulation of the reports of the Special Committee, and of information regarding its activities and findings, by all means available through the Department of Public Information of the Secretariat and, where necessary, to reprint those reports of the Special Committee which are no longer available;

(d) To report to the General Assembly at its thirty-eighth session on the tasks entrusted to him in the present paragraph;

16. *Requests* the Security Council to ensure Israel's respect for and compliance with all the provisions of the Geneva Convention relative to the Protection of Civilian Persons in Time of War, of 12 August 1949, in Palestinian and other Arab territories occupied since 1967, including Jerusalem, and to initiate measures to halt Israeli policies and practices in those territories;

17. *Decides* to include in the provisional agenda of its thirty-eighth session the item entitled "Report of the Special Committee to Investigate Israeli Practices Affecting the Human Rights of the Population of the Occupied Territories".

Recorded vote in Assembly as follows:

In favour: Afghanistan, Albania, Algeria, Argentina, Bahrain, Bangladesh, Benin, Bhutan, Bolivia, Botswana, Brazil, Bulgaria, Burma, Burundi, Byelorussian SSR, Central African Republic, Chad, China, Colombia, Comoros, Congo, Cuba, Cyprus, Czechoslovakia, Democratic Kampuchea, Democratic Yemen, Djibouti, Ecuador, Egypt, El Salvador, Ethiopia, Fiji, Gabon, Gambia, German Democratic Republic, Ghana, Greece, Guyana, Haiti, Honduras, Hungary, India, Indonesia, Iran, Iraq, Jamaica, Jordan, Kenya, Kuwait, Lao People's Democratic Republic, Lebanon, Liberia, Libyan Arab Jamahiriya, Madagascar, Malawi, Malaysia, Maldives, Mali, Malta, Mauritania, Mauritius, Mexico, Mongolia, Morocco, Mozambique, Nepal, Nicaragua, Niger, Nigeria, Oman, Pakistan, Panama, Papua New Guinea, Peru, Philippines, Poland, Portugal, Qatar, Romania, Rwanda, Sao Tome and Principe, Saudi Arabia, Senegal, Sierra Leone, Singapore, Solomon Islands, Somalia, Spain, Sri Lanka, Sudan, Suriname, Syrian Arab Republic, Thailand, Togo, Trinidad and Tobago, Tunisia, Turkey, Uganda, Ukrainian SSR, USSR,

United Arab Emirates, United Republic of Cameroon, United Republic of Tanzania, Upper Volta, Uruguay, Vanuatu, Venezuela, Viet Nam, Yemen, Yugoslavia, Zaire, Zambia.

Against: Israel, United States.

Abstaining: Australia, Austria, Barbados, Belgium, Canada, Costa Rica, Denmark, Dominican Republic, Finland, France, Germany, Federal Republic of, Iceland, Ireland, Italy, Japan, Luxembourg, Netherlands, New Zealand, Norway, Sweden, United Kingdom.

Observance of the 1949 Convention on protection of civilians

Respect for and compliance, particularly by Israel, with the Geneva Convention relative to the Protection of Civilian Persons in Time of War, of 12 August 1949 (fourth Geneva Convention), was called for on several occasions in 1982—by the Commission on Human Rights and its Sub-Commission on Prevention of Discrimination and Protection of Minorities, and by the General Assembly.

In addition, the Security Council referred to the humanitarian principles of the Convention in the preambles of three resolutions adopted after the Israeli military move into Lebanon in June: a resolution of 19 June on protection of civilians in the conflict and on humanitarian assistance to the Lebanese and Palestinians,[9] a resolution of 4 July calling for respect for the rights of civilians in Lebanon[10] and a resolution of 29 July demanding that Israel lift the blockade of Beirut.[11]

Action by the Commission on Human Rights and its Sub-Commission. On 11 February, after examining alleged human rights violations in the territories occupied by Israel, the Commission on Human Rights condemned Israel's failure to acknowledge the applicability of the Convention to the occupied territories, called on Israel to respect its obligations under the Convention and urged all parties to the Convention to exert all efforts to ensure Israel's compliance.[2] Also on that date, the Commission declared that Israel's grave breaches of the Convention (a term defined in the Convention to include certain specified violations) were war crimes and an affront to humanity.[1] A similar provision was included in a resolution adopted on 8 September by the Sub-Commission on Prevention of Discrimination and Protection of Minorities.[12]

General Assembly action. Condemning Israel for its failure to fulfil its obligations under the Convention, the General Assembly, in a resolution on the Palestine question adopted on 28 April at its resumed seventh emergency special session,[3] reaffirmed that all the provisions of that Convention and of the Hague Conventions of 1907 on the law of war applied to all occupied territories, including Jerusalem, and called on all parties to those instruments to respect and ensure respect of their obligations in all circumstances. The Assembly called again on Israel to apply the Convention's provisions and the principles of international law in the occupied territories.

During the April debate, Belgium, speaking for the EC members, emphasized that the Geneva Convention as well as the Hague Convention of 18 October 1907 were applicable to all occupied territories. A similar view was expressed by several other countries, among them Austria. Norway regretted that Israel had violated the Geneva Convention on different occasions, particularly through its settlement policy and its decision to apply its civilian law to the Golan Heights. In Mali's opinion, the situation in the territories showed that Israel could not assure the security of the Palestinian population and could not carry out its obligations under the Convention.

Israel's settlement and occupation policy was regarded as a violation of the Convention also by others, such as the Philippines. Japan strongly appealed to Israel to make special efforts to protect the human rights and promote the welfare of the Palestinians, in accordance with the Convention.

In a resolution adopted on 19 August,[4] also at the seventh emergency special session, the Assembly requested the Secretary-General and United Nations organizations, in co-operation with the International Committee of the Red Cross (ICRC) and other non-governmental organizations, to investigate the application by Israel of the provisions of the Convention and other instruments in the case of detainees.

During the August debate, Denmark, on behalf of the EC members, expressed concern at the future of the thousands of Palestinian prisoners held by Israel. Voicing serious concern about the human consequences both for the prisoners of war and the civilian population, Austria urgently asked all to abide by the Convention. The PLO observer charged that Israel refused to treat the Palestinians detained in Lebanon as prisoners of war, denying them the rights provided for by the Convention and preventing ICRC from visiting them.

By a resolution of 10 December,[5] the General Assembly reaffirmed that the Convention was applicable to the occupied territories, including Jerusalem, and condemned Israel's failure to acknowledge its applicability. The Assembly strongly demanded that Israel acknowledge and comply with the Convention, and urgently called on the States parties to ensure respect for and compliance with its provisions in the occupied territories.

The resolution was adopted by a recorded vote of 134 to 1, with 1 abstention, following its approval by the Special Political Committee on 3 December by a recorded vote, requested by the United States, of 103 to 1, with 1 abstention. Paragraph 1 was adopted in Committee by a recorded vote, also requested by the United States, of 99 to 1. The draft was introduced by Pakistan on behalf of 10 nations.

Abstaining in the vote on the resolution as a whole, the United States said it was just one more ritualistic, unproductive condemnation of Israel; however, the United States voted for paragraph 1, saying that it attached importance to the Convention's application in the occupied territories. Sweden said it had voted in favour of the resolution in the firm conviction that the Convention was fully applicable to all Israeli-occupied territories.

Three other resolutions adopted on 10 December, also concerned with the occupied territories, contained calls for compliance with the Convention.

By the first of these, having particular reference to Israel's settlement policies,[6] the Assembly demanded that Israel comply strictly with its obligations in accordance with international law and the Convention, determined that all Israeli measures designed to change the legal status, geographical nature and demographic composition of the occupied territories were in violation of the Convention; and called on States parties to the Convention to exert efforts to ensure compliance with its provisions in the territories.

By its general resolution on the situation in the occupied territories,[7] the Assembly condemned Israel's continued and persistent violation of the Convention and declared the violations designated in the Convention as "grave breaches" to be war crimes and an affront to humanity. It reaffirmed that Israel's settlement policy constituted a flagrant violation of the Convention, and requested the Security Council to ensure Israel's compliance with all of the Convention's provisions. Paragraphs 6 (declaring Israel's grave breaches of the Convention as war crimes) and 16 (requesting the Council to ensure Israel's compliance) were adopted in Committee by recorded votes of 72 to 18, with 14 abstentions, and 83 to 17, with 7 abstentions, respectively.

Again reaffirming the applicability of the Convention to the occupied territories, the Assembly, in a resolution on educational institutions there,[8] condemned what it called Israel's systematic campaign of repression against Palestinian universities as in clear contravention of the Convention, and demanded that Israel comply with the Convention and rescind all measures against those institutions.

During the Assembly's debates on the Palestine question and the Middle East situation, the Byelorussian SSR said that, in implementing its annexation policy, Israel was using both open violence and juridical casuistry, in contradiction of the Convention. Denmark, on behalf of the EC members, reaffirmed their view that the Convention applied to all the occupied territories. Kenya said Israel had acted contrary to its obligations under the Convention, which prohibited the annexation of occupied territory and the forcible transfer or deportation of occupants regardless of motive. Saudi Arabia charged that Israel's actions contravened the United Nations Charter, the Geneva Convention, the Universal Declaration of Human Rights and United Nations resolutions.

By promulgating more than a thousand decrees since 1967, PLO stated, Israel had changed the laws in the occupied territories in violation of the Convention.

Resolutions (1982). Commission on Human Rights (report, E/1982/12), 11 Feb.: [1]1982/1 A, para. 3; [2]1982/1 B. GA: [3]ES-7/4, 28 Apr.; [4]ES-7/6, para. 10, 19 Aug.; [5]37/88 A, 10 Dec., text following; [6]37/88 B, [7]37/88 C, [8]37/88 F, 10 Dec. SC: [9]512(1982), 19 June; [10]513(1982), 4 July; [11]515(1982), 29 July. [12]SCPDPM (report, E/CN.4/1983/4): 1982/18, para. 1 (*c*), 8 Sep.

Meeting records. GA: SPC, A/SPC/37/SR.35-41, *42, 44* (23 Nov.–3 Dec.); plenary, A/37/PV.100 (10 Dec.).

General Assembly resolution 37/88 A

10 December 1982   Meeting 100   134-1-1 (recorded vote)

Approved by SPC (A/37/698) by recorded vote (103-1-1), 3 December (meeting 44); 10-nation draft (A/SPC/37/L.28); agenda item 61.

Sponsors: Afghanistan, Bangladesh, Cape Verde, Cuba, India, Indonesia, Madagascar, Malaysia, Pakistan, Qatar.

The General Assembly,

Recalling its resolutions 3092 A (XXVIII) of 7 December 1973, 3240 B (XXIX) of 29 November 1974, 3525 B (XXX) of 15 December 1975, 31/106 B of 16 December 1976, 32/91 A of 13 December 1977, 33/113 A of 18 December 1978, 34/90 B of 12 December 1979, 35/122 A of 11 December 1980 and 36/147 A of 16 December 1981,

Recalling also Security Council resolution 465(1980) of 1 March 1980 in which, *inter alia*, the Council affirmed that the Geneva Convention relative to the Protection of Civilian Persons in Time of War, of 12 August 1949, is applicable to the Arab territories occupied by Israel since 1967, including Jerusalem,

Considering that the promotion of respect for the obligations arising from the Charter of the United Nations and other instruments and rules of international law is among the basic purposes and principles of the United Nations,

Bearing in mind the provisions of the Geneva Convention,

Noting that Israel and those Arab States whose territories have been occupied by Israel since June 1967 are parties to that Convention,

Taking into account that States parties to that Convention undertake, in accordance with article 1 thereof, not only to respect but also to ensure respect for the Convention in all circumstances,

1. *Reaffirms* that the Geneva Convention relative to the Protection of Civilian Persons in Time of War, of 12 August 1949, is applicable to Palestinian and other Arab territories occupied by Israel since 1967, including Jerusalem;

2. *Condemns once again* the failure of Israel as the occupying Power to acknowledge the applicability of that Convention to the territories it has occupied since 1967, including Jerusalem;

3. *Strongly demands* that Israel acknowledge and comply with the provisions of that Convention in Palestinian and other Arab territories it has occupied since 1967, including Jerusalem;

4. *Urgently calls upon* all States parties to that Convention to exert all efforts in order to ensure respect for and compliance with its provisions in Palestinian and other Arab territories occupied by Israel since 1967, including Jerusalem;

Recorded vote in Assembly as follows:

In favour: Afghanistan, Albania, Algeria, Argentina, Australia, Austria, Bahrain, Bangladesh, Barbados, Belgium, Benin, Bhutan, Bolivia, Botswana, Brazil, Bulgaria, Burma, Burundi, Byelorussian SSR, Canada, Central African Republic, Chad, Chile, China, Colombia, Comoros, Congo, Costa Rica, Cuba, Cyprus, Czechoslovakia, Democratic Kampuchea, Democratic Yemen, Denmark, Djibouti, Dominican Republic, Ecuador, Egypt, El Salvador, Ethiopia, Fiji, Finland, France, Gabon, Gambia, German Democratic Republic, Germany, Federal Republic of, Ghana, Greece, Guyana, Haiti, Honduras, Hungary, Iceland, India, Indonesia, Iran, Iraq, Ireland, Italy, Jamaica, Japan, Jordan, Kenya, Kuwait, Lao People's Democratic Republic, Lebanon, Liberia, Libyan Arab Jamahiriya, Luxembourg, Madagascar, Malawi, Malaysia, Maldives, Mali, Malta, Mauritania, Mauritius,

Mexico, Mongolia, Morocco, Mozambique, Nepal, Netherlands, New Zealand, Nicaragua, Niger, Nigeria, Norway, Oman, Pakistan, Panama, Papua New Guinea, Peru, Philippines, Poland, Portugal, Qatar, Romania, Rwanda, Sao Tome and Principe, Saudi Arabia, Senegal, Sierra Leone, Singapore, Solomon Islands, Somalia, Spain, Sri Lanka, Sudan, Suriname, Sweden, Syrian Arab Republic, Thailand, Togo, Trinidad and Tobago, Tunisia, Turkey, Uganda, Ukrainian SSR, USSR, United Arab Emirates, United Kingdom, United Republic of Cameroon, United Republic of Tanzania, Upper Volta, Uruguay, Vanuatu, Venezuela, Viet Nam, Yemen, Yugoslavia, Zaire, Zambia.

Against: Israel.

Abstaining: United States.

Al-Aqsa Mosque

A shooting incident on 11 April at Al-Haram Al-Sharif—the principal Moslem Holy Place of Jerusalem, centred on Al-Aqsa Mosque and the adjacent mosque known as the Dome of the Rock—was taken up in 1982 by the Security Council and the General Assembly. As described in a message from the King of Morocco to the Council members, an Israeli soldier in uniform had opened fire with an automatic rifle in front of the Mosque, killing two men, and had then entered the Dome of the Rock, where he had wounded 22 people.

The Council met between 13 and 20 April but, because of the negative vote of a permanent member (United States), did not adopt a draft resolution deploring the destruction or profanation of the Holy Places as tending to disturb world peace. The Assembly, on 28 April, condemned Israel for the shooting.

Other incidents before and after the one of 11 April were also the subject of communications to the United Nations.

Communication. By a letter of 25 March to the Secretary-General,[3] Jordan complained of what it called a new wave of desecration of Moslem shrines by Israeli settlers and charged that on 2 March a group of 15 Jews armed with machine-guns and bayonets had stormed Al-Aqsa Mosque, wounding one of its guards.

Security Council consideration. By a letter of 12 April,[8] Morocco conveyed a request of King Hassan II, Chairman of the Al-Quds (Jerusalem) Committee of the Organization of the Islamic Conference, for an urgent meeting of the Security Council to consider events in the occupied territories, particularly the latest attack against the Islamic Holy Places in Jerusalem. A meeting was also requested by Iraq, current Chairman of that organization, in a letter of 13 April on behalf of 37 of its member States.[2]

On 15 April, Jordan transmitted a 12 April statement of the Islamic Higher Council in Jerusalem, charging that the attack within and against Al-Aqsa Mosque and the Dome of the Rock had been a planned and co-ordinated operation involving Israeli army elements, and not, as alleged by the occupation authorities, the work of a lone, deranged soldier.[6]

The Council held six meetings between 13 and 20 April to consider the situation. On 20 April, the Council acted on a draft resolution by Iraq, Jordan, Morocco and Uganda,[1] which received 14 votes to 1 and was not adopted due to the negative vote of a permanent member (United States).

By this text, the Council would have condemned in the strongest terms the appalling acts of sacrilege at Al-Haram Al-Sharif and deplored any act or encouragement of destruction or profanation of the Holy Places, religious buildings and sites in Jerusalem as tending to disturb world peace. It would have called on Israel to apply the 1949 Geneva Convention on the protection of civilians and the principles of international law governing military occupation, and to refrain from hindering the Islamic Higher Council in Jerusalem from discharging its functions.

Israel told the Council just before the vote that the person responsible for the sacrilege at the Dome of the Rock had been arraigned and would be tried by an Israeli court.

Though strongly condemning the act of violence, the United States, in voting against the draft, said it would further embitter the peoples of the region and deepen the divisions that could lead to conflict; the text implied that responsibility for the incident lay with the Israeli authorities and that Israel had hindered the efforts of the Islamic Higher Council to administer the Holy Places, whereas evidence showed that Israel had in the main carefully respected the Council's role.

France called for severe punishment of those responsible and said the Israeli authorities must take all necessary measures to prevent a repetition of such tragic events. The United Kingdom said it had voted in favour to associate itself with the condemnation of the act of sacrilege but on the understanding that the draft resolution could not prejudge the facts of the incident under investigation; though condemning Israel's practices in East Jerusalem and other occupied territories, it recognized that the Israeli authorities had in general fulfilled their obligations on access to the Holy Places.

The sense of the United States veto, the USSR stated, was that the United States did not recognize that East Jerusalem was occupied by Israel and did not intend to limit Israel in any way; having thrown overboard in the past few months its policy of apparent even-handedness between Israel and the Arabs, the United States was covering up and thereby encouraging Israel's annexationist policy. Kuwait said it was time that the United States, which provided Israel through its veto with a protective shield, reassess its position and live up to its commitment as a guardian of world peace.

In Guyana's view, the Israeli authorities could not escape blame for the violence and sacrilege committed on 11 April; Israel's deliberate policies

of State-sponsored violence against Arabs in the occupied territories, of colonization and annexation, of expulsion and repression of the Palestinians had provided encouragement for the criminal act.

Acknowledging that Israel had condemned the act, Ireland stressed that it must observe and apply fully throughout the occupied territories the 1949 Geneva Convention; in the current atmosphere of tension, grievance and alienation, any spark could strike a flame that could easily lead to a wider conflagration in the region.

Japan feared that, following the incidents, the situation in the occupied territories might deteriorate further; it hoped that Israel would fulfil its responsibilities by protecting and safeguarding the sanctity of the Holy Places and by preventing any future acts of destruction or profanation.

In Morocco's view, the results of the vote could not change the unanimous condemnation of Israel nor attenuate the seriousness of the crime committed by at least one armed Israeli soldier in uniform; Israel's responsibility was beyond doubt, as it had been constantly and openly encouraging potential or actual criminals of that kind. The Syrian Arab Republic said the United States had indicated through its veto that Jerusalem must be left apart because of some secret or overt agreements reached at Camp David; the attack had not been an isolated act but a continuation of the zionization of Palestine started in 1948.

Uganda said it did not accept Israel's explanation that the attack had been the act of a lone and mentally deranged individual; it had followed a series of legislative and administrative measures aimed at altering the status and character of Jerusalem. Zaire stated that it supported the draft resolution without necessarily linking the act of sacrilege to the Israeli Government.

Submitting the draft, Jordan said it fell far short of what would be commensurate with the crime, which was part of a continuing pattern. A mild text was being presented in order to obtain the maximum number of votes.

Prior to the vote, the Council invited Bangladesh, Djibouti, Guinea, India, Indonesia, Iran, Iraq, Israel, Kuwait, the Libyan Arab Jamahiriya, Malaysia, Morocco, the Niger, Pakistan, Saudi Arabia, Senegal, Somalia, the Sudan, the Syrian Arab Republic, Turkey and the United Arab Emirates, at their request, to participate without vote in the debate.

By a vote of 11 to 1 (United States), with 3 abstentions (France, Japan, United Kingdom), the Council also decided, at Jordan's request of 13 April,[4] that an invitation should be accorded to a PLO representative to participate in the debate with the same rights of participation as those conferred on a Member State invited under rule 37 of the Council's provisional rules of procedure.[j] Also at the request of Jordan,[(5)] the Council extended an invitation under rule 39[k] to the Permanent Observer of the League of Arab States to the United Nations.

Opening the debate, Morocco read a message from King Hassan II, as Chairman of the Al-Quds Committee, stating that Israel bore responsibility for the attack in view of what the international press had reported as its extreme passivity in regard to various Zionist terrorist movements. Jordan charged that the premeditated and well-planned assault, preceded by written threats to blow up the Moslem Holy Places, was part of Zionist efforts to incarcerate, strangulate and expel the Palestinians, and to destroy every vestige of Islamic legacy in the Holy Land; Jordan put the casualties at 100, with 12 dead, and said Israeli troops had then fired at the crowd and the mosques and had whisked the perpetrator away to safety.

Israel, on the other hand, stated that the Council had been summoned by those who sought cynically to exploit the misdeeds of one possibly deranged individual, acting on his own, who had committed a crime that had been denounced by the Israeli Government, its Chief Rabbis and the Mayor of Jerusalem; Israel's considerable efforts to protect the Holy Places were unfortunately no guarantee against such isolated acts, which, however, did not change Israel's policy of striving for tolerance, reconciliation and coexistence in Jerusalem.

Condemning the incident, the United States, in a Department of State statement of 11 April that was read to the Council, called on Middle East Governments and peoples to refrain from further violence.

Iraq interpreted the attack as a manifestation of Israel's racism and colonialism, encouraged and protected by the United States. The Syrian Arab Republic expressed a similar opinion, adding that the tragic event had only strengthened the Arabs' determination to regain their usurped rights. In the view of Saudi Arabia, the perpetrator was an integral part of a deranged society. The Permanent Observer of the League of Arab States saw a connection between the attack on the Mosque and what he described as Israel's institutionalized racism.

Israel and its policies were held responsible by others as well, among them Bangladesh, China, Djibouti, Guinea, Indonesia, Iran, Kuwait, the Libyan Arab Jamahiriya, Malaysia, the Niger, Senegal, Somalia, the Sudan, Turkey, the USSR and the United Arab Emirates.

Malaysia said the ease with which the soldier who committed the attack had passed through the Israeli security checkpoints gave strong grounds to believe that the incident was not an isolated one but part of a bigger conspiracy to terrorize and demoralize the Arab population.

In Somalia's view, the attack had been encouraged and abetted by Israel's contempt for human rights and international law.

Iran said the occupying forces had demonstrated not only that they were incapable of safeguarding the Islamic sanctuaries but that they were determined gradually to destroy them. In the opinion of the Libyan Arab Jamahiriya, the act was a violation of Islamic sanctity and a challenge to the sentiments of Moslems all over the world. A number of speakers reported that their predominantly Moslem populations had observed on 14 April a day of solidarity with the Palestinians, involving the closure of government offices and private businesses in a protest against the shootings in Jerusalem.

China believed that the incident had further revealed Israel's designs deliberately to alter the legal status, physical features and demographic composition of the occupied territories, including Jerusalem, in disregard of international law and the 1949 Geneva Convention. In Senegal's opinion, the incident resulted from the 1980 Israeli decision to annex Jerusalem by declaring it Israel's capital.

Spain said the repetition of sacrilegious acts occurred in the context of a series of legislative and administrative measures adopted by Israel to alter the status and character of Jerusalem.

By creating an atmosphere of harassment and provocations, the Niger stated, Israeli fanatics were hoping to justify and maintain a state of repeated crises in order to vindicate a policy of repression, aggression, war and domination.

In Turkey's view, the issue was not whether the soldier involved was insane and had acted alone; Israel could not be absolved of its obligations towards the Holy Places.

India said the recent events could not be divorced from the general atmosphere of hatred and anti-Arab fanaticism, which was being deliberately encouraged.

In the opinion of the USSR and the United Arab Emirates, Israel's overseas protectors—notably the United States—shared equal responsibility, since their assistance and support had permitted Israel to keep the territories under occupation.

The PLO observer accused Israel of shooting at unarmed civilians, injuring over 100, in response to the protests following the incident, which he described as the logical outcome of a system that propagated the inferiority of the Christians and Moslems in Palestine and the superiority of Jews.

The incident, or the issues it raised with regard to preservation of the Holy Places, was seen as a

[j]See footnote a on p. 429.

[k]See footnote b on p. 430.

threat to international peace and security by a number of countries, among them Bangladesh, Djibouti, Guinea and Pakistan.

China, Poland, Saudi Arabia, the USSR and others called on the Council to approve a strong condemnation of Israel's actions in Jerusalem. Bangladesh felt that the Council should condemn the sacrilege and deplore Israel's failure to protect the Holy Places. China said the Council should take effective measures to ensure the implementation of its resolutions on the occupied territories. Malaysia urged the Council to demand that Israel take adequate measures to protect the Mosque, while Poland and others believed that it should reaffirm the applicability of the 1949 Geneva Convention. Turkey also called for a condemnation of the sacrilege and said Israel should be reminded of its responsibilities and obligations as the occupying Power; anything less might invite more violence and greater tension.

Indonesia urged the Council to take steps to force Israel to cease the judaization of Jerusalem, to compel it to revoke the law purporting to make Jerusalem its capital, to discontinue archaeological diggings and other acts of desecration of the Holy Places, and to stop the terror campaign against the Arab population.

Iraq believed that condemnation and censure were no longer enough and that mandatory sanctions had to be imposed, including interruption of economic and military relations with Israel. Sanctions were favoured also by others, including the Libyan Arab Jamahiriya and the Syrian Arab Republic; the latter also favoured Israel's expulsion from the United Nations.

The Sudan said the Council must use its mandate under the United Nations Charter to bring about Israeli withdrawal from all occupied territories—a point made by a number of speakers. Somalia believed that the Council should insist on restoring to Jerusalem its international status as a *corpus separatum*. The United Arab Emirates wanted the Council to put a final end to the illegal Israeli occupation of Palestine and to enable the Palestinians to exercise their right to self-determination. A similar position was voiced by Poland.

Pakistan urged the Council to demand that Israel end its repression of the Arabs and Palestinians in the occupied territories; deplore its failure to protect the sanctity of Al-Aqsa; emphasize that any act of destruction or profanation of the Holy Places, or any encouragement or connivance at such acts, seriously endangered international peace and security; and reactivate the Commission established by the Council in 1979[10] and ask it to investigate the situation in the occupied territories and especially the safety and sanctity of the Holy Places.

Iran said that, rather than wasting efforts on trying to extract resolutions condemning Israel for its policies, the potentialities of all Moslem nations should be mobilized to establish Islamic control over the Islamic shrines and sanctuaries.

France, on the other hand, believed that only through dialogue and by working towards an agreement among the parties would it be possible to preserve the unique and universal character of Jerusalem.

General Assembly action. In a resolution adopted on 28 April 1982 at its resumed seventh emergency special session on the Palestine question,[9] the General Assembly condemned Israel for violating the sanctity of the Holy Places, particularly of Al-Haram Al-Sharif, in Jerusalem, and for the shooting, killing and wounding of worshippers by members of the Israeli army on 11 April.

The attack was denounced or condemned by many speakers during the special session as well as during the regular session in December, among them Djibouti, the Gambia, Ghana, Iran, Japan, Kuwait, the Lao People's Democratic Republic, Morocco, Nicaragua, Nigeria, Pakistan, Qatar and the United Republic of Cameroon. Norway expressed regret at the incident, and Venezuela expressed deepest rejection and sorrow.

The act was considered a sacrilege by several countries, including the Gambia, Iran, Japan and Venezuela.

Ghana said the cold-blooded assassinations were a violation of all written and unwritten laws, and a provocation of Arabs and Palestinians.

Pakistan said there was deep fear that the Islamic holy shrines were being destroyed by fanatics in their design to judaize the Holy City. In the opinion of Bahrain, the attack had clear implications concerning Israel's schemes aimed at removing all the Islamic Holy Places from Jerusalem. Through its excavation activity at Al-Haram Al-Sharif, Israel was striving to obtain any relics which had any relation with Jewish history in order to use them as a historic pretext further to damage and despoil the Holy Places; it used history as an ideological weapon to justify its occupation, to legitimize an illegal action and distort historical facts. The Gambia thought that official indulgence of vigilante groups and not mental aberration must have encouraged the perpetrator. Similarly, Morocco said the attack was neither an isolated act nor a chance occurrence; since the Israeli occupation of Jerusalem and other territories, an insistent campaign had been maintained aimed at eliminating the Arab-Islamic features of Jerusalem and bringing about the departure of the Arabs deeply rooted there and in the country for more than a millennium.

In Sri Lanka's view, the firing on worshippers at the Mosque was yet another episode in Israel's attempts to prepare the annexation of the West Bank. Viet Nam said the premeditated attack was just one more manifestation of a long process of destruction of the Arabs of the occupied territories, and Iraq believed that the attack worsened the already critical situation both inside and outside occupied Palestine. Djibouti felt that Israel's atrocities in the occupied territories had been highlighted by the shooting of worshippers and attacks against the Mosque. Nigeria saw the attack as a symptom of Israel's aggressive and expansionist policy; Iran held a similar position.

Speaking for the EC members, Belgium said the pressing need to get out of the circle of violence in the occupied territories and to find a just solution to the Palestinian problem was very clearly brought out by the intensification of the climate of confrontation resulting from the gun battle of 11 April.

PLO regarded the aggression against the Mosque as the height of Israeli crimes aimed at terrorizing the Palestinians and forcing them out of their homeland in preparation for the annexation of the West Bank and Gaza, the annexation of the Golan Heights and Jerusalem having been completed.

Pakistan, Zambia and others regretted that the Security Council had been unable to take action as a result of the United States veto; in Djibouti's opinion, the Council's failure to adopt a resolution condemning the act fell into line with Israel's intention.

Togo said the Council owed it to itself to condemn the sacrilege and to reaffirm the applicability of the 1949 Geneva Convention on the protection of civilians. Norway urged Israel to do everything in its power to ensure that such acts did not recur.

Further communication. On 28 July,[7] Jordan transmitted to the Security Council President a letter of the same date from the PLO observer, stating that on that day 150 Israelis had attempted to climb into Al-Haram Al-Sharif from two adjacent houses which they had entered by force.

Draft resolution not adopted. [1]Iraq, Jordan, Morocco, Uganda, S/14985.

Letters. [2]Iraq: 13 Apr., S/14969. Jordan: [3]25 Mar., A/37/159-S/14928; [4]13 Apr., S/14970; [5]13 Apr., S/14971; [6]15 Apr., S/14982; [7]28 July, S/15318. [8]Morocco: 12 Apr., S/14967.

Resolution (1982). [9]GA: ES-7/4, para. 7 (*d*) & (*e*), 28 Apr.

Resolution (prior). [10]SC: 446(1979), 22 Mar. 1979 (YUN 1979, p. 400).

Meeting records. SC: S/PV.2352-2357 (13-20 Apr.).

Israeli settlements

Communications. By letters of 2 February,[3] 3 March,[4] 14 April[5] and 29 April 1982,[6] Jordan gave details of what it reported as a series of land confiscations by Israeli authorities in the occupied territories along with the establishment of new settlements, which it described as a prelude to an-

nexation of the territories. By a letter of 4 May,[7] Jordan asked that the Security Council address itself to the 1980 report[19] of the Commission established by the Council in 1979 to examine the situation relating to Israeli settlements in the occupied territories;[17] Jordan also suggested that the Council reconstitute the Commission's membership.

The Chairman of the Committee on the Exercise of the Inalienable Rights of the Palestinian People, by a letter of 14 September to the Secretary-General,[1] emphasized the Committee's concern at reports that the Israeli Government had allocated $18.5 million to construct three new settlements on the West Bank and had announced that it would authorize seven others, raising to 109 the total number of Israeli settlements in the West Bank and Gaza, in violation of the 1949 Geneva Convention relative to the Protection of Civilian Persons in Time of War. By a letter of 8 November,[2] the Chairman drew attention to press reports indicating Israel's plans to establish additional settlements on the West Bank, including an official announcement on 5 November that five more were to be built.

Action by the Commission on Human Rights. In a resolution of 11 February[13] on human rights violations in the occupied territories, the Commission on Human Rights strongly condemned Israeli policies and practices, administrative and legislative measures to promote and expand the establishment of settler colonies on private and public Arab lands, the transfer of an alien population thereto, and the arming of settlers to commit acts of violence against Arab civilians, causing injury and death and wide-scale damage to Arab property.

General Assembly action (August). In a resolution adopted on 19 August during the resumed seventh emergency special session on the Palestine question,[14] the General Assembly demanded that Israel carry out the provisions of a 1980 resolution in which the Security Council determined that Israel's settlement policy constituted a serious obstruction to a comprehensive, just and lasting Middle East peace and called on Israel to dismantle the existing settlements and to cease the establishment, construction and planning of new ones.[18]

Report of the Committee on Israeli practices in the occupied territories. In its 1982 report to the General Assembly, adopted in August,[12] the Special Committee to Investigate Israeli Practices Affecting the Human Rights of the Population of the Occupied Territories stated that Israel's settlement policy had been distinctly intensified. According to a map annexed to the report, over 130 settlements had been established by July. The Committee reported a greater tendency to consolidate the settlements already established, particularly in areas densely populated by Palestinians, such as the environs of Hebron, Nablus and Ramallah. It concluded that there was no justification for the argument of security invoked in support of the annexation and settlement policy.

Security Council consideration. The Security Council met on 12 November at the request of Morocco, as Chairman of the Arab Group, and the Niger, on behalf of the Organization of the Islamic Conference, to consider what Morocco called, in a letter of 5 November,[10] Israel's perseverance in establishing settlements in the occupied territories. In its letter of 9 November,[11] the Niger stated that Israel's announcement of new settlements marked a continued policy of defiance, colonization and domination despite international disapproval and Council resolutions.

On 12 November, Jordan transmitted for distribution to Council members a map of Israeli settlements in the West Bank, Gaza and the Golan Heights, identified as having been prepared and printed in July by the Settlement Department of the Jewish Agency and the Settlement Division of the World Zionist Organization, and showing the location of 118 of the 139 settlements which Jordan said existed in the occupied territories as of September.[8]

The Council held a single meeting on this subject, at which it took no substantive action. It invited Morocco, the Niger and Senegal, at their request, to participate without vote in the discussion. Under rule 39 of its provisional rules of procedure,[l] the Council also invited the Chairman of the Committee on Palestinian rights, at his request.

At Jordan's request,[9] the Council decided, by a vote of 12 to 1 (United States), with 2 abstentions (France, United Kingdom), to invite a PLO representative to participate in the debate and that the invitation would confer on PLO the same rights of participation as those conferred on a Member State when invited under rule 37.[m]

Opening the debate, Morocco stated that the forcible transfer of Arab lands to public and private Israeli institutions had reached emergency level; the Council must condemn Israel's violations of the principles of the Charter of the United Nations and of international decisions guaranteeing the rights of individuals and peoples in the Middle East. The Niger requested the Council to express strong and unanimous disapproval of Israel's settlement policy and to consider specific measures of deterrence against that country. Jordan charged that the Israeli occupation authorities had embarked on large-scale annexation of the territories, allocating huge financial and human resources, in a frantic race against time, to foreclose any possibility of achieving a just and lasting peace.

Senegal, speaking as Chairman of the Committee on Palestinian rights, observed that the nature of settlements was changing from small agricultural co-operatives to urban centres situated near the Israeli frontier, which would make it difficult for a future Government to restore the illegally acquired territories to the Arabs; the establishment and strengthening of settlements, in defiance of international public opinion and international law, affected not only Palestinians' rights but also international peace and security.

PLO said the Council must take effective measures to end the prolonged Israeli occupation, which was responsible for exacerbating the situation in the occupied territories.

General Assembly action (December). By a resolution of 10 December,[15] the General Assembly strongly deplored Israel's persistence in the establishment of settlements in the occupied territories, including Jerusalem. It determined that all Israeli actions designed to change the legal status, geographical nature and demographic composition of the territories were a serious obstruction to peace efforts and had no legal validity, and demanded that Israel desist from taking such actions. The Assembly demanded that Israel comply strictly with its international obligations in accordance with international law and the 1949 Geneva Convention on the protection of civilians.

By another resolution of the same date,[16] the Assembly strongly condemned, among other Israeli policies and practices, the establishment of new and the expansion of existing settlements, and the transfer of an alien population thereto. It reaffirmed that all Israeli measures to change the physical character, demographic composition, institutional structure or status of the occupied territories were null and void, and that Israel's settlement policy was a flagrant violation of the Geneva Convention and United Nations resolutions.

The first of these resolutions, sponsored by 10 nations and introduced by Pakistan, was adopted by a recorded vote of 134 to 1, with 1 abstention, following its approval by the Special Political Committee on 3 December by a recorded vote of 104 to 1, with 1 abstention.

Abstaining, the United States declared its opposition to the further creation and expansion of Jewish settlements in the territories, adding that they undermined the confidence necessary for the current peace process to succeed; however, it considered it sterile to focus on whether the settlement policy was legal or illegal.

Voting in favour, Sweden said one of the most constructive steps Israel could take to improve peace prospects would be to dismantle the settlements.

---

[l]See footnote b on p. 430.
[m]See footnote a on p. 429.

A number of speakers during the November/December Assembly debates on the Middle East situation and the Palestine question, as well as during the emergency special session in April, denounced or condemned Israel's settlement policy as illegal. Among them were Algeria, Bahrain, the Byelorussian SSR, Cyprus, Czechoslovakia, Greece, India, Indonesia, Japan, Kenya, the Lao People's Democratic Republic, Malaysia, Nepal, Portugal, Romania, the Syrian Arab Republic and Turkey. New Zealand did not recognize the validity of that policy. Belgium and Denmark, both on behalf of the EC members, considered Israel's settlement policy contrary in particular to the principle of the inadmissibility of the acquisition of territory by force; they called on Israel to end the policy, which they viewed as a grave obstacle to peace, and in particular to rescind its recent decision to expand the programme. Kenya said the creation of settlements was specifically prohibited by international law and by the 1949 Geneva Convention on the protection of civilians, a view shared by the Philippines and others.

Bahrain said the military nature of Israeli settlements was reflected in the fact that the settlers were constantly armed, often attacking and killing inhabitants of the occupied territories. China said the stepping up of the establishment of settlements served to alter the physical character, demographic composition and legal status of the territories in order to perpetuate their occupation. In establishing new settlements, India stated, Israel had trampled on the rights of the local population, destroyed dissent by the use of brutal force and systematically depleted the resources of the Arab-inhabited areas. Sri Lanka said the policies which had led to the placement of 130 settlements in the West Bank and Gaza had been accurately described as colonization, with the difference that the Israeli colonizer had been more ruthless than his classical counterpart. The USSR said that, according to a recent announcement at Tel Aviv, there were plans for an abrupt increase in the number of Israeli settlers in the West Bank and Gaza: from 25,000 to 100,000 by 1986 and to 1.5 million by the year 2000.

Viet Nam charged that Israel continued to establish new settlements in order to prepare the annexation of the occupied territories, a position also held by Algeria, Bahrain, Djibouti and others. Bulgaria charged Israel with having launched by force a programme of territorial expansion, with new settlements being established at an increased rate and existing ones being strengthened and expanded. The Gambia stated that the systematic expropriation of Arab lands to make them available for Israeli settlements provided civilian cover for Israel's expansionist intentions. Malaysia

regarded the establishment of new settlements as a manifestation of Israel's expansionist policy. Malta felt that the new Jewish settlers represented a broadening constituency which regarded the area as an integral part of Israel; the point of no return, where political and physical considerations would make withdrawal elusive, might have already been reached.

Morocco stated that Israel's armed colonies in the occupied territories constituted hotbeds of future disturbances, whose consequences would become clear when the occupier had to restore the territory to its legitimate owners. In Tunisia's opinion, the stepping up of the establishment of settlements revealed Israel's true objective: to dispossess the Arabs and facilitate the annexation of the occupied territories. The Syrian Arab Republic said the Camp David plot had helped Israel intensify its settlement policy, giving it a pretext for not withdrawing from the occupied territories; Israel had repeatedly stated that negotiations with its Arab neighbours would not lead to the dismantling of its settlements.

The Philippines attributed the recent disturbances in the West Bank to a considerable extent to Israel's occupation and settlement policy. That policy, Bangladesh felt, could hardly be seen as a step towards peace. Similarly, Thailand believed that the establishment of settlements undermined prospects for a Middle East peace.

Denmark conveyed a statement of 20 September by the EC Foreign Ministers considering Israel's decision to establish eight new settlements to be illegal under international law and a serious obstacle to peace efforts. Norway urged Israel to reconsider its plans for further settlements, which it said could have negative consequences for the general political climate.

Letters. Committee on Palestinian rights Chairman: [1]14 Sep., A/37/449-S/15393; [2]8 Nov., A/37/604-S/15482. Jordan: [3]2 Feb., A/37/81-S/14859; [4]3 Mar., A/37/108-S/14895; [5]14 Apr., A/37/189-S/14983; [6]29 Apr., A/37/215-S/15029; [7]4 May, S/15038; [8]12 Nov., S/15488; [9]12 Nov., S/15490. [10]Morocco: 5 Nov., S/15481. [11]Niger: 9 Nov., S/15483.

Report. [12]Committee on Israeli practices in occupied territories, transmitted by S-G note, A/37/485.

Resolutions (1982). [13]Commission on Human Rights (report, E/1982/12): 1982/1 A, para. 5 (b) & (c), 11 Feb. GA: [14]ES-7/6, para. 4, 19 Aug.; [15]37/88 B, 10 Dec., text following; [16]37/88 C, paras. 7 (c) & 8, 10 Dec.

Resolutions (prior). SC: [17]446(1979), 22 Mar. 1979 (YUN 1979, p. 400); [18]465(1980), 1 Mar. 1980 (YUN 1980, p. 427).

Yearbook reference. [19]1980, p. 416.

Meeting records. SC: S/PV.2401 (12 Nov.). GA: SPC, A/SPC/37/SR.35-41, 42, 44 (23 Nov.–3 Dec.); plenary, A/37/PV.100 (10 Dec.).

General Assembly resolution 37/88 B

10 December 1982   Meeting 100   134-1-1 (recorded vote)

Approved by SPC (A/37/698) by recorded vote (104-1-1), 3 December (meeting 44); 10-nation draft (A/SPC/37/L.29); agenda item 61.

Sponsors: Afghanistan, Bangladesh, Cape Verde, Cuba, India, Indonesia, Madagascar, Malaysia, Pakistan, Qatar.

The General Assembly,

Recalling its resolutions 32/5 of 28 October 1977, 33/113 B of 18 December 1978, 34/90 C of 12 December 1979, 35/122 B of 11 December 1980 and 36/147 B of 16 December 1981,

Recalling also Security Council resolution 465(1980) of 1 March 1980,

Expressing grave anxiety and concern at the present serious situation in the occupied Palestinian and other Arab territories, including Jerusalem, as a result of the continued Israeli occupation and the measures and actions taken by the Government of Israel, the occupying Power, designed to change the legal status, geographical nature and demographic composition of those territories,

Considering that the Geneva Convention relative to the Protection of Civilian Persons in Time of War, of 12 August 1949, is applicable to all Arab territories occupied since 5 June 1967, including Jerusalem,

1. *Determines* that all such measures and actions taken by Israel in the Palestinian and other Arab territories occupied since 1967, including Jerusalem, are in violation of the relevant provisions of the Geneva Convention relative to the Protection of Civilian Persons in Time of War, of 12 August 1949, and constitute a serious obstruction of efforts to achieve a just and lasting peace in the Middle East and therefore have no legal validity;

2. *Strongly deplores* the persistence of Israel in carrying out such measures, in particular the establishment of settlements in the Palestinian and other occupied Arab territories, including Jerusalem;

3. *Demands* that Israel comply strictly with its international obligations in accordance with the principles of international law and the provisions of the Geneva Convention;

4. *Demands once more* that the Government of Israel, the occupying Power, desist forthwith from taking any action which would result in changing the legal status, geographical nature or demographic composition of the Palestinian and other Arab territories occupied since 1967, including Jerusalem;

5. *Urgently calls upon* all States parties to the Geneva Convention to respect and to exert all efforts in order to ensure respect for and compliance with its provisions in all Arab territories occupied by Israel since 1967, including Jerusalem.

Recorded vote in Assembly as follows:

In favour: Afghanistan, Albania, Algeria, Argentina, Australia, Austria, Bahrain, Bangladesh, Barbados, Belgium, Benin, Bhutan, Bolivia, Botswana, Brazil, Bulgaria, Burma, Burundi, Byelorussian SSR, Canada, Central African Republic, Chad, Chile, China, Colombia, Comoros, Congo, Costa Rica, Cuba, Cyprus, Czechoslovakia, Democratic Kampuchea, Democratic Yemen, Denmark, Djibouti, Dominican Republic, Ecuador, Egypt, El Salvador, Ethiopia, Fiji, Finland, France, Gabon, Gambia, German Democratic Republic, Germany, Federal Republic of, Ghana, Greece, Guyana, Haiti, Honduras, Hungary, Iceland, India, Indonesia, Iran, Iraq, Ireland, Italy, Jamaica, Japan, Jordan, Kenya, Kuwait, Lao People's Democratic Republic, Lebanon, Liberia, Libyan Arab Jamahiriya, Luxembourg, Madagascar, Malawi, Malaysia, Maldives, Mali, Malta, Mauritania, Mauritius, Mexico, Mongolia, Morocco, Mozambique, Nepal, Netherlands, New Zealand, Nicaragua, Niger, Nigeria, Norway, Oman, Pakistan, Panama, Papua New Guinea, Peru, Philippines, Poland, Portugal, Qatar, Romania, Rwanda, Sao Tome and Principe, Saudi Arabia, Senegal, Sierra Leone, Singapore, Solomon Islands, Somalia, Spain, Sri Lanka, Sudan, Suriname, Sweden, Syrian Arab Republic, Thailand, Togo, Trinidad and Tobago, Tunisia, Turkey, Uganda, Ukrainian SSR, USSR, United Arab Emirates, United Kingdom, United Republic of Cameroon, United Republic of Tanzania, Upper Volta, Uruguay, Vanuatu, Venezuela, Viet Nam, Yemen, Yugoslavia, Zaire, Zambia.

Against: Israel.

Abstaining: United States.

Expulsion of the Mayors of Hebron and Halhul and the Islamic Judge of Hebron

In December 1982, the General Assembly called on Israel to allow the return of three West Bank officials—Fahd Kawasmeh, Mayor of Hebron; Mohamed Milhem, Mayor of Halhul; and Rajab Tamimi, Kadi of Hebron—so that they could resume the functions for which they had been elected and appointed. Israel had deported the three Palestinian officials in May 1980, on the ground that they had systematically engaged in inciting the local Arab population to acts of violence and subversion, abusing their public offices.[9]

The Commission on Human Rights, on 11 February,[4] also called for the immediate return of the expelled Mayors.

Report of the Secretary-General. On 1 April 1982,[3] the Secretary-General reported to the Assembly that he had requested Israel on 18 February to inform him of any action with regard to the implementation of the December 1981 resolution[6] demanding that Israel rescind the expulsion and imprisonment of the Mayors, as well as the expulsion of the Sharia (Islamic) Judge of Hebron. On 19 March, Israel had replied that the Palestinian officials had abused their public and official positions in order to incite the Arab population to violence and subversion, and their expulsion had contributed to a general improvement in the maintenance of public order in Hebron and Halhul. The Secretary-General added that he would continue his efforts to secure the implementation of the relevant United Nations decisions.

General Assembly action. By a resolution of 10 December 1982,[5] the General Assembly, recalling the 1949 Geneva Convention relative to the Protection of Civilian Persons in Time of War which prohibited forcible transfers or deportations, demanded once more that Israel rescind the expulsion and imprisonment of the Mayors and the expulsion of the Sharia Judge, and that it facilitate their immediate return so that they could resume their functions.

The resolution was adopted by a recorded vote of 133 to 1, with 1 abstention, following its approval by the Special Political Committee on 3 December by a recorded vote of 109 to 1, with 1 abstention.

Explaining its abstention, the United States said the expulsion of the Palestinian officials had been unwise and impolitic, but not illegal as the resolution maintained; what was required was to affirm the need for them to return to their homes.

Sweden stated that its affirmative vote was based on its conviction that the Geneva Convention was fully applicable to all the occupied territories and that Israeli measures to change the status of the territories were illegal and incompatible with the 1967[7] and 1973[8] Security Council resolutions on principles for a Middle East peace, which Israel claimed to support.

Introducing the draft on behalf of 10 nations, Bangladesh noted that its content had been the subject of previous resolutions which, however, had not produced substantive results.

On 30 November, the Committee granted without objection requests made on 29 November for hearings: one by Morocco,[2] as Chairman of the Arab Group of States at the United Nations, for authorization for the two Mayors to speak, and another by Jordan,[1] for a hearing for Mr. Milhem, Mayor of Halhul.

Israel objected strongly to the granting of hearings, saying it was a transparent attempt to introduce tension into the Committee's work and to misrepresent the situation in the West Bank and Gaza.

Speaking before the Committee, Mr. Milhem stated that, in violation of Jordanian law and the 1949 Geneva Convention, the municipal elections that should have been held in the West Bank in April 1980 still had not taken place, that it was Israel's policy not to allow elections until all the mayors and municipal councils elected in 1976 had been removed from office, and that armed "village leagues" had been created in order to put further pressure on them to resign.

At the resumed seventh emergency special session in April, Democratic Yemen said the designation of a so-called civil administration in the West Bank and Gaza was a step towards annexation, an opinion shared by Sri Lanka which added that neither arrests, detentions, curfews nor wanton killings of unarmed protestors had enabled Israel to restore a semblance of order. In Morocco's view, the dissolution of the municipal councils and the dismissal of the Mayors and their replacement by Israeli civilian and military officials were a stage in restoring the occupied territories to Israeli sovereignty.

Saudi Arabia said the Geneva Convention stipulated that the occupying Power may not alter the status of public officials or judges in occupied territories, or apply sanctions or take any measures of coercion against them; the Convention allowed for the removal of public officials only if it was not intended to coerce or discriminate against officials who abstained from fulfilling their functions for reasons of conscience. In accusing the elected Mayors of complicity with PLO, Saudi Arabia said, Israel applied a peculiar logic for, until recently, Israel had alleged that PLO had no base in the occupied territories and imposed its will on the Palestinian inhabitants through terrorism.

The dismissal of the Mayors was also deplored by others, among them Sweden.

Letters. [1]Jordan, 29 Nov., A/SPC/37/L.27; [2]Morocco, 29 Nov., A/SPC/37/L.26.
Report. [3]S-G, A/37/162.
Resolutions (1982). [4]Commission on Human Rights (report, E/1982/12): 1982/1 A, para. 7, 11 Feb. [5]GA: 37/88 D, 10 Dec., text following.
Resolutions (prior). [6]GA: 36/147 D, 16 Dec. 1981 (YUN 1981, p. 314). SC: [7]242(1967), 22 Nov. 1967 (YUN 1967, p. 257); [8]338(1973), 22 Oct. 1973 (YUN 1973, p. 213).
Yearbook reference. [9]1980, p. 411.
Meeting records. GA: SPC, A/SPC/37/SR.35-38, *39*, 40, 41, *42, 44* (23 Nov.–3 Dec.); plenary, A/37/PV.100 (10 Dec.).

General Assembly resolution 37/88 D

10 December 1982	Meeting 100	133-1-1 (recorded vote)

Approved by SPC (A/37/698) by recorded vote (109-1-1), 3 December (meeting 44); 10-nation draft (A/SPC/37/L.31 and Corr.1); agenda item 61.

Sponsors: Afghanistan, Bangladesh, Cape Verde, Cuba, India, Indonesia, Madagascar, Malaysia, Pakistan, Qatar.

The General Assembly,

Recalling Security Council resolutions 468(1980) of 8 May 1980, 469(1980) of 20 May 1980 and 484(1980) of 19 December 1980 and General Assembly resolution 36/147 D of 16 December 1981,

Deeply concerned at the expulsion by the Israeli military occupation authorities of the Mayors of Hebron and Halhul and of the Sharia Judge of Hebron,

Recalling the Geneva Convention relative to the Protection of Civilian Persons in Time of War, of 12 August 1949, in particular article 1 and the first paragraph of article 49, which read as follows:

"Article 1

"The High Contracting Parties undertake to respect and to ensure respect for the present Convention in all circumstances."

"Article 49

"Individual or mass forcible transfers, as well as deportations of protected persons from occupied territory to the territory of the occupying Power or to that of any other country, occupied or not, are prohibited, regardless of their motive . . .",

Reaffirming the applicability of the Geneva Convention to the Palestinian and other Arab territories occupied by Israel since 1967, including Jerusalem,

1. *Demands once more* that the Government of Israel, the occupying Power, rescind the illegal measures taken by the Israeli military occupation authorities in expelling and imprisoning the Mayors of Hebron and Halhul and in expelling the Sharia Judge of Hebron and that it facilitate the immediate return of the expelled Palestinian leaders so that they can resume the functions for which they were elected and appointed;

2. *Requests* the Secretary-General to report to the General Assembly as soon as possible on the implementation of the present resolution.

Recorded vote in Assembly as follows:

In favour: Afghanistan, Albania, Algeria, Argentina, Australia, Austria, Bahrain, Bangladesh, Barbados, Belgium, Benin, Bhutan, Bolivia, Botswana, Brazil, Bulgaria, Burma, Burundi, Byelorussian SSR, Canada, Central African Republic, Chad, Chile, China, Comoros, Congo, Costa Rica, Cuba, Cyprus, Czechoslovakia, Democratic Kampuchea, Democratic Yemen, Denmark, Djibouti, Dominican Republic, Ecuador, Egypt, El Salvador, Ethiopia, Fiji, Finland, France, Gabon, Gambia, German Democratic Republic, Germany, Federal Republic of, Ghana, Greece, Guyana, Haiti, Honduras, Hungary, Iceland, India, Indonesia, Iran, Iraq, Ireland, Italy, Jamaica, Japan, Jordan, Kenya, Kuwait, Lao People's Democratic Republic, Lebanon, Liberia, Libyan Arab Jamahiriya, Luxembourg, Madagascar, Malawi, Malaysia, Maldives, Mali, Malta, Mauritania, Mauritius, Mexico, Mongolia, Morocco, Mozambique, Nepal, Netherlands, New Zealand, Nicaragua, Niger, Nigeria, Norway, Oman, Pakistan, Panama, Papua New Guinea, Peru, Philippines, Poland, Portugal, Qatar, Romania, Rwanda, Sao Tome and Principe, Saudi Arabia, Senegal, Sierra Leone, Singapore, Solomon Islands, Somalia, Spain, Sri Lanka, Sudan, Suriname, Sweden, Syrian Arab Republic, Thailand, Togo, Trinidad and Tobago, Tunisia, Turkey, Uganda, Ukrainian SSR, USSR, United Arab Emirates, United Kingdom, United Republic of Cameroon, United Republic of Tanzania, Upper Volta, Uruguay, Vanuatu, Venezuela, Yemen, Yugoslavia, Zaire, Zambia.

Against: Israel.

Abstaining: United States.

Attempted assassinations of the Mayor of Nablus and others

In 1982, the General Assembly again considered the assassination attempt of 2 June 1980 against Basam Al-Shaka, Mayor of Nablus; Karim Khalaf, Mayor of Ramallah; and Ibrahim Al-Taweel, Mayor of Al Bireh.[3]

Communication. On 25 March, Jordan transmitted a letter of the same date from PLO protesting further acts of brutality against the Mayors of Nablus and Ramallah, who had been arrested and removed from their legally elected offices and replaced by civilian administrators.[1]

General Assembly action. By a resolution of 10 December,[2] the Assembly expressed concern that Israel had failed for two years to apprehend and prosecute the perpetrators of the assassination attempts against the Mayors, and demanded that Israel inform the Secretary-General of the results of the investigations.

The resolution was adopted by a recorded vote of 134 to 1, with 1 abstention, following its approval by the Special Political Committee on 3 December by a recorded vote of 112 to 1, with 1 abstention.

Casting a negative vote, Israel stated that the resolution was motivated purely by the desire to vilify Israel; there were far more opportunities for justice under Israeli administration than under the 1949 Geneva Convention, and every effort was being made to arrest the culprits.

The United States abstained, saying the language was too narrow and implied without justification that Israel was not making any attempt to arrest and prosecute the culprits.

Sweden cast an affirmative vote based on its conviction that the Geneva Convention was fully applicable to the occupied territories.

Introducing the draft on behalf of 10 nations, Afghanistan said the use of violence against the population of the occupied territories was widespread and took a variety of forms; apart from the open resort to violence by the Israeli authorities, prominent Palestinians were easy targets for assassination and harassment. Israel, as the occupying Power, was responsible for prosecuting the perpetrators of such crimes.

Letter. [1]Jordan, 25 Mar., S/14930.
Resolution (1982). [2]GA: 37/88 G, 10 Dec., text following.
Yearbook reference. [3]1980, p. 413.
Meeting records. GA: SPC, A/SPC/37/SR.35-42, *43, 44* (23 Nov.–3 Dec.); plenary, A/37/PV.100 (10 Dec.).

General Assembly resolution 37/88 G

10 December 1982   Meeting 100   134-1-1 (recorded vote)

Approved by SPC (A/37/698) by recorded vote (112-1-1), 3 December (meeting 44); 10-nation draft (A/SPC/37/L.34); agenda item 61.

Sponsors: Afghanistan, Bangladesh, Cape Verde, Cuba, India, Indonesia, Madagascar, Malaysia, Pakistan, Qatar.

The General Assembly,

Recalling Security Council resolution 471(1980) of 5 June 1980, in which the Council condemned the assassination attempts against the Mayors of Nablus, Ramallah and Al Bireh and called for the immediate apprehension and prosecution of the perpetrators of those crimes,

Recalling also General Assembly resolution 36/147 G of 16 December 1981,

Recalling once again the Geneva Convention relative to the Protection of Civilian Persons in Time of War, of 12 August 1949, in particular article 27, which states, *inter alia:*

"Protected persons are entitled, in all circumstances, to respect for their persons . . . . . They shall at all times be humanely treated, and shall be protected especially against all acts of violence or threats thereof . . .",

Reaffirming the applicability of that Convention to the Arab territories occupied by Israel since 1967, including Jerusalem,

1. *Expresses deep concern* that Israel, the occupying Power, has failed for two years to apprehend and prosecute the perpetrators of the assassination attempts;

2. *Demands once more* that Israel, the occupying Power, inform the Secretary-General of the results of the investigations relevant to the assassination attempts;

3. *Requests* the Secretary-General to report to the General Assembly at its thirty-eighth session on the implementation of the present resolution.

Recorded vote in Assembly as follows:

In favour: Afghanistan, Albania, Algeria, Argentina, Australia, Austria, Bahrain, Bangladesh, Barbados, Belgium, Benin, Bhutan, Bolivia, Botswana, Brazil, Bulgaria, Burma, Burundi, Byelorussian SSR, Canada, Central African Republic, Chad, Chile, China, Colombia, Comoros, Congo, Costa Rica, Cuba, Cyprus, Czechoslovakia, Democratic Kampuchea, Democratic Yemen, Denmark, Djibouti, Dominican Republic, Ecuador, Egypt, El Salvador, Ethiopia, Fiji, Finland, France, Gabon, Gambia, German Democratic Republic, Germany, Federal Republic of, Ghana, Greece, Guyana, Haiti, Honduras, Hungary, Iceland, India, Indonesia, Iran, Iraq, Ireland, Italy, Jamaica, Japan, Jordan, Kenya, Kuwait, Lao People's Democratic Republic, Lebanon, Liberia, Libyan Arab Jamahiriya, Luxembourg, Madagascar, Malawi, Malaysia, Maldives, Mali, Malta, Mauritania, Mauritius, Mexico, Mongolia, Morocco, Mozambique, Nepal, Netherlands, New Zealand, Nicaragua, Niger, Nigeria, Norway, Oman, Pakistan, Panama, Papua New Guinea, Peru, Philippines, Poland, Portugal, Qatar, Romania, Rwanda, Sao Tome and Principe, Saudi Arabia, Senegal, Sierra Leone, Singapore, Solomon Islands, Somalia, Spain, Sri Lanka, Sudan, Suriname, Sweden, Syrian Arab Republic, Thailand, Togo, Trinidad and Tobago, Tunisia, Turkey, Uganda, Ukrainian SSR, USSR, United Arab Emirates, United Kingdom, United Republic of Cameroon, United Republic of Tanzania, Upper Volta, Uruguay, Vanuatu, Venezuela, Viet Nam, Yemen, Yugoslavia, Zaire, Zambia.

Against: Israel.

Abstaining: United States.

Economic and social conditions

Mediterranean–Dead Sea canal project

In 1982, Israel's plan of March 1981[5] to construct a 67-mile hydraulic structure to channel water from the Mediterranean Sea to the Dead Sea for electric power generation was the subject of a resolution of the General Assembly and of the Governing Council of the United Nations Environment Programme (UNEP). The effects of the project, under which part of the conduit would pass through the Gaza Strip, occupied by Israel since 1967, were studied by the Secretary-General.

UNEP Council action. By a resolution of 18 May 1982,[3] the UNEP Governing Council requested the Executive Director to prepare a study on any adverse environmental implications resulting from Israel's decision to build a canal linking the Mediterranean Sea to the Dead Sea.

Israel called for a vote on the resolution and the Libyan Arab Jamahiriya, supported by Saudi Arabia, requested that it be taken by roll-call. The resolution was adopted by a roll-call vote of 60 to 2 (Israel, United States), with 26 abstentions. Before the vote, Israel challenged the Council's competence to adopt the resolution, saying that the issue had already been discussed in the General Assembly and Israel had transmitted to the Secretary-General a report on the environmental effects of the project. By 54 votes to 2, with 28 abstentions, the Council decided that it was competent to act on the text.

Israel pointed out that no final decision had been taken to proceed with the project, which was still in the feasibility study and research stage; all its environmental implications would be studied. The project's effects on the chemical composition of the Dead Sea's waters would be negligible, if not non-existent.

Report of the Secretary-General. On 30 June 1982,[1] the Secretary-General transmitted in accordance with a December 1981 General Assembly resolution[4] an expert study on the canal and its effects on Jordan and the occupied territories. The study was prepared by three United Nations experts on the basis of their visits to Jordan (24-29 May) and Israel (30 May–1 June), which included discussions with government officials and others involved, and inspection of sites along the Dead Sea and in the Gaza Strip.

The experts reported that, as envisaged by Israel, the project consisted of a hydroelectric scheme diverting water from the Mediterranean to the Dead Sea, in order to produce peak energy; Israeli authorities had told the experts that the official decision to proceed with the project would be taken when the feasibility study under way was concluded. The completion of the project was envisaged around 1990.

The experts concluded that the rise in the Dead Sea level would be the most obvious effect of the project, which could flood or affect some surrounding infrastructure, lands earmarked for agricultural development, archaeological sites and some mining projects; the project would also affect the quality of the Dead Sea water. In the West Bank and the Gaza Strip, the effects of leakage from the conveyance of sea water were under study.

General Assembly action. By a resolution of 16 December,[2] the General Assembly emphasized that the canal, if constructed, violated the rules and principles of international law. It demanded that Israel not construct the canal and cease all actions or plans towards implementation of the project. The Assembly called on States, specialized agencies, governmental and non-governmental organizations not to assist in the project preparations and execution, and strongly urged corporations to do likewise. The Secretary-General was requested to monitor and assess on a continuing basis and through experts all aspects of the adverse effects of the project on Jordan and the occupied territories, including Jerusalem, and to report regularly to the Assembly.

The resolution was adopted by a recorded vote of 139 to 2, with 1 abstention, following its approval by the Special Political Committee on 9 December by a recorded vote, requested by Israel, of 101 to 2, with 2 abstentions. The draft was introduced by Jordan also on behalf of India, Iraq, Morocco, Pakistan, Saudi Arabia and Yemen.

The United States said it could not support the resolution because it censured a State for a decision not yet taken; the concerns expressed in the text were premature and not conducive to a peaceful settlement of the differences between Jordan and Israel.

Voting in favour, Jamaica said the Secretary-General's report clearly showed that the project would have serious economic implications and could have adverse effects on Jordan's potash production; it also would involve the construction of permanent installations in the Gaza Strip, in violation of the 1949 Geneva Convention.

Jordan said the illegitimate project sought to ensure Israeli acquisition and control of the area's waterways and water resources, which was fundamental to its programme to colonize the occupied territories and support its hegemonic policy. To settle Jewish immigrants in the new cities to be built along the canal, more Arab land would have to be expropriated, with further displacement of Arabs. Jordanian potash production, which accounted for 15 per cent of the country's yearly gross national product, would be seriously affected. In addition, four major nuclear plants were to be established on the canal, and more damage would result from the dumping of nuclear wastes.

Israel protested as unacceptable the Committee decision to circulate a technical study which Israel had transmitted to the Secretary-General as an act of courtesy; it would agree to the publication of an updated version of that paper, provided that the related document transmitted to the Secretariat by Jordan was treated similarly.

During the Assembly debate on the Middle East situation, Tunisia said the project would have harmful economic and social consequences in addition to violating international law. By changing the course of the Jordan River and trying to appropriate the territorial waters of Lebanon, Bahrain stated, Israel's canal would serve its expansionist colonization plans.

At the resumed seventh emergency special session in April, Burundi said the annexation of Arab lands as well as the canal project were only part of Israel's expansionist policy and showed that Israel had no intention of returning to its own borders.

Report. [1]S-G, A/37/328-S/15277 & Corr.1.
Resolutions (1982). [2]GA: 37/122, 16 Dec., text following. [3]UNEP Council (report, A/37/25): IV, 18 May.
Resolution (prior). [4]GA: 36/150, 16 Dec. 1981 (YUN 1981, p. 320).
Yearbook reference. [5]1981, p. 318.
Financial implications. 5th Committee report, A/37/763; S-G statements, A/SPC/37/L.42, A/C.5/37/95.
Meeting records. GA: SPC, A/SPC/37/SR.46-49 (7-9 Dec.); 5th Committee, A/C.5/37/SR.71 (15 Dec.); plenary, A/37/PV.108 (16 Dec.).

General Assembly resolution 37/122

16 December 1982   Meeting 108   139-2-1 (recorded vote)

Approved by SPC (A/37/724) by recorded vote (101-2-2), 9 December (meeting 49); 7-nation draft (A/SPC/37/L.41/Rev.1); agenda item 68.

Sponsors: India, Iraq, Jordan, Morocco, Pakistan, Saudi Arabia, Yemen.

Israel's decision to build a canal linking the Mediterranean Sea to the Dead Sea

The General Assembly,

Recalling its resolution 36/150 of 16 December 1981,

Recalling the rules and principles of international law relative to the fundamental rights and duties of States,

Bearing in mind the principles of international law relative to belligerent occupation of land, including the Geneva Convention relative to the Protection of Civilian Persons in Time of War, of 12 August 1949, and reaffirming their applicability to all Arab territories occupied since 1967, including Jerusalem,

Taking note of the report of the Secretary-General,

Recognizing that the proposed canal, to be constructed partly through the Gaza Strip, a Palestinian territory occupied in 1967, would violate the principles of international law and affect the interests of the Palestinian people,

Confident that the canal linking the Mediterranean Sea with the Dead Sea, if constructed by Israel, will cause direct, serious and irreparable damage to Jordan's rights and legitimate vital interests in the economic, agricultural, demographic and ecological fields,

Noting with regret the non-compliance by Israel with General Assembly resolution 36/150,

1. *Deplores* Israel's non-compliance with General Assembly resolution 36/150;

2. *Emphasizes* that the canal linking the Mediterranean Sea with the Dead Sea, if constructed, is a violation of the rules and principles of international law, especially those relating to the fundamental rights and duties of States and to belligerent occupation of land;

3. *Demands* that Israel not construct this canal and cease forthwith all actions and/or plans taken towards the implementation of this project;

4. *Calls upon* all States, specialized agencies, governmental and non-governmental organizations not to assist, directly or indirectly, in preparations for and execution of this project and strongly urges national, international and multinational corporations to do likewise;

5. *Requests* the Secretary-General to monitor and assess, on a continuing basis and through a competent expert organ, all aspects—juridical, political, economic, ecological and demographic—of the adverse effects on Jordan and on the Arab territories occupied since 1967, including Jerusalem, arising from the implementation of the Israeli decision to construct this canal and to forward the findings of that organ on a regular basis to the General Assembly;

6. *Requests* the Secretary-General to report to the General Assembly at its thirty-eighth session on the implementation of the present resolution;

7. *Decides* to include in the provisional agenda of its thirty-eighth session the item entitled "Israel's decision to build a canal linking the Mediterranean Sea to the Dead Sea".

Recorded vote in Assembly as follows:

In favour: Afghanistan, Albania, Algeria, Angola, Argentina, Australia, Austria, Bahamas, Bahrain, Bangladesh, Barbados, Belgium, Belize, Benin, Bhutan, Bolivia, Botswana, Brazil, Bulgaria, Burma, Burundi, Byelorussian SSR, Canada, Cape Verde, Central African Republic, Chad, Chile, China, Colombia, Comoros, Congo, Costa Rica, Cuba, Cyprus, Czechoslovakia, Democratic Kampuchea, Democratic Yemen, Denmark, Djibouti, Dominican Republic, Ecuador, Egypt, El Salvador, Ethiopia, Fiji, Finland, France, Gambia, German Democratic Republic, Germany, Federal Republic of, Ghana, Greece, Grenada, Guinea, Guinea-Bissau, Guyana, Hungary, Iceland, India, Indonesia, Iran, Iraq, Ireland, Italy, Ivory Coast, Jamaica, Japan, Jordan, Kenya, Kuwait, Lao People's Democratic Republic, Lebanon, Liberia, Libyan Arab Jamahiriya, Luxembourg, Madagascar, Malaysia, Maldives, Mali, Malta, Mauritania, Mauritius, Mexico, Mongolia, Morocco, Mozambique, Nepal, Netherlands, New Zealand, Nicaragua, Nigeria, Norway, Oman, Pakistan, Panama, Papua New Guinea, Paraguay, Peru, Philippines, Poland, Portugal, Qatar, Romania, Rwanda, Samoa, Sao Tome and Principe, Saudi Arabia, Senegal, Seychelles, Sierra Leone, Singapore, Somalia, Spain, Sri Lanka, Sudan, Suriname, Sweden, Syrian Arab Republic, Thailand, Togo, Trinidad and Tobago, Tunisia, Turkey, Uganda, Ukrainian SSR, USSR, United Kingdom, United Republic of Cameroon, United Republic of Tanzania, Upper Volta, Uruguay, Vanuatu, Venezuela, Viet Nam, Yemen, Yugoslavia, Zaire, Zambia.

Against: Israel, United States.

Abstaining: Malawi.

Educational institutions

In 1982, the General Assembly and the Commission on Human Rights condemned Israel's repression against and closing of Palestinian universities. Protest against Israeli measures with regard to the Palestinian educational institutions and their faculty was voiced in several letters to the Secretary-General and the President of the Security Council. The Secretary-General reported to the Assembly that, while progress had been achieved in terms of student enrolment and the number of schools, classes and teachers, the frequent closure of educational institutions, harassment and the restrictions on academic freedom had hindered teaching and learning. Israel, on the other hand, stated that it refrained from interfering with study programmes and curricula and that the entire educational network operated in line with standards and structures that had existed before the occupation.

Action by the Commission on Human Rights. In a resolution of 11 February,[8] the Commission on Human Rights condemned, among other Israeli policies and practices in the occupied territories, the systematic repression against Palestinian universities, restricting and impeding academic activities by subjecting selections of courses, textbooks and educational programmes, admission of students and appointment of faculty members to the control and supervision of the military occupation authorities.

Communications and report. By a letter of 18 February,[1] the Chairman of the Committee on the Exercise of the Inalienable Rights of the Palestinian People expressed profound concern over Israel's decision to close Bir Zeit University for the second time in four months.

The two-month closure of the University on 16 February and the arrest of several students and faculty members—only two weeks after it was reopened following a similar closure—was opposed also by the Palestine Liberation Organization (PLO) in a letter of 18 February, transmitted on 23 February by Jordan.[4]

By a letter of 9 July,[2] the Chairman of the Committee on Palestinian rights reiterated that body's concern over Israel's continuing repressive policy, including the reported Israeli order to again close the University for three months due to students' protests against that country's invasion of Lebanon.

Complaints about Israeli attempts to stifle university education in the West Bank by imposing conditions for the renewal of work permits for foreign faculty members were voiced in a letter of 13 September from PLO, transmitted on 15 September by Jordan.[5]

Protests against the treatment and expulsion of faculty members at the Al-Najah and Bethlehem Universities were voiced by PLO in a letter of 22 October, transmitted by Jordan on 26 October.[6]

In a government report on living conditions in Judaea-Samaria and the Gaza district (see below), transmitted on 16 July,[3] Israel stated that it refrained from interfering with study programmes and curricula. During the years of Israeli occupation since 1967, the total number of classrooms had grown by 72 per cent—from 6,148 in 1967/68 to 10,599 in 1980/81—and the total student population at institutions of higher education had reached 6,218, while before 1967 no such institutions had existed in Judaea-Samaria.

Report of the Secretary-General. In his report of 15 June 1982 on the living conditions of the Palestinians in the occupied territories,[7] the Secretary-General informed the General Assembly that, with regard to education, the number of classes, teachers and students in the territories had increased since 1968; however, the enrolment ratios of the West Bank lagged behind those of the Gaza Strip and neighbouring Arab countries. The frequent closing of schools and harassment of students had created an atmosphere of anxiety and apprehension, and the placing of all educational institutions under the absolute control of the military authorities by a Military Order of 8 July 1980, had deprived those institutions of academic freedom.

The Secretary-General reported that the education system was basically the same in all the occupied territories. The educational institutions were managed by the Government, private bodies or the United Nations Relief and Works Agency for Palestine Refugees in the Near East. As far as practicable, the schools followed the Jordanian curriculum in the West Bank and the Egyptian curriculum in the Gaza Strip; books used, however, were subject to Israeli censorship. There had been a considerable increase in the number of educational institutions since 1967 (from 1,091 to 1,366 in 1979/80, with an 80 per cent increase in the number of classrooms from 6,187 in 1967/68 to 11,187 in 1979/80); in addition, the 18 vocational training centres on the West Bank and the eight centres in Gaza had provided training for over 40,000 people, mainly for semi-skilled jobs in industry and construction and, according to information from Arab sources, were geared towards meeting the needs of the Israeli economy.

The three universities in the West Bank and an Institute of Islamic Religious Studies in Gaza, the report went on, were supported by private sources and catered for Arab students from both the occupied territories and Israel. The universities, especially Bir Zeit, appeared to have had more intensified problems with the administering authorities in the past few years, but the harassment of students extended to secondary schools as well. In 1980/81, 12 schools were shut down by the military authorities for various periods, three of them permanently.

General Assembly action. By a resolution of 10 December 1982,[9] the General Assembly condemned Israeli policies and practices against Palestinian students and faculties, especially the opening of fire on students, and its systematic campaign of repression against and closing of Palestinian universities, restricting and impeding academic activities, in contravention of the 1949 Geneva Convention on the protection of civilians. It demanded that Israel rescind all actions and measures against all educational institutions, ensure their freedom and refrain from hindering their effective operation.

The resolution was adopted by a recorded vote of 110 to 2, with 24 abstentions, following its approval by the Special Political Committee on 3 December by a recorded vote of 88 to 2, with 22 abstentions.

Israel rejected the resolution as yet another example of distortions of facts and wild accusations.

The United States voted against the resolution saying it contained harsh, unbalanced language and a wholly unacceptable attack on Israel; none the less, it agreed that recent aspects of Israeli policy towards academic institutions in the occupied territories were open to reasonable criticism.

Sharing that concern, Ireland said its abstention was largely determined by the inclusion of certain language in the paragraph condemning Israel's campaign of repression and closing of universities, which it did not feel to be entirely warranted. Though voting in favour, Jamaica also voiced reservations on the paragraph's language. Abstaining, Sweden said the text contained sweeping generalizations.

India, also on behalf of the other nine sponsors, said it had once again become necessary to introduce such a resolution because of the unabated strangulation of educational institutions in the occupied territories; infringement of the freedom of education was a heinous crime against humanity.

In a resolution of 16 December on grants and scholarships for Palestine refugees,[11] the Assembly appealed to States, specialized agencies and the United Nations University to contribute generously to the Palestinian universities in the occupied territories.

By another resolution of the same date,[10] the Assembly emphasized the need to establish the University of Jerusalem for Palestine refugees, requested the Secretary-General to continue taking measures towards that end, and called on Israel to remove the hindrances it had put in its way.

Letters. Committee on Palestinian rights Chairman: [1]18 Feb., A/37/94-S/14879; [2]9 July, A/37/339-S/15290. [3]Israel: 16 July, A/37/347 & Corr.1. Jordan: [4]23 Feb., A/37/101 (S/14884); [5]15 Sep., A/37/448-S/15391; [6]26 Oct., S/15467.
Report. [7]S-G, A/37/238.
Resolutions (1982). [8]Commission on Human Rights (report, E/1982/12): 1982/1 A, para. 5 (j), 11 Feb. GA: [9]37/88 F, 10 Dec., text following; [10]37/120 C, 16 Dec.; [11]37/120 D, para. 5, 16 Dec.
Meeting records. GA: SPC, A/SPC/37/SR.35-42, *43, 44* (23 Nov.-3 Dec.); plenary, A/37/PV.100 (10 Dec.).

General Assembly resolution 37/88 F

10 December 1982   Meeting 100   110-2-24 (recorded vote)

Approved by SPC (A/37/698) by recorded vote (88-2-22), 3 December (meeting 44); 10-nation draft (A/SPC/37/L.33); agenda item 61.

Sponsors: Afghanistan, Bangladesh, Cape Verde, Cuba, India, Indonesia, Madagascar, Malaysia, Pakistan, Qatar.

The General Assembly,

Bearing in mind the Geneva Convention relative to the Protection of Civilian Persons in Time of War, of 12 August 1949,

Deeply shocked by the most recent atrocities committed by Israel, the occupying Power, against educational institutions in the occupied Palestinian territories,

1. *Reaffirms* the applicability of the Geneva Convention relative to the Protection of Civilian Persons in Time of War, of 12 August 1949, to the Palestinian and other Arab territories occupied by Israel since 1967, including Jerusalem;

2. *Condemns* Israeli policies and practices against Palestinian students and faculties in schools, universities and other educational institutions in the occupied Palestinian territories, especially the policy of opening fire on defenceless students, causing many casualties;

3. *Condemns* the systematic Israeli campaign of repression against and closing of universities in the occupied Palestinian territories, restricting and impeding academic activities of Palestinian universities by subjecting the selection of courses, textbooks and educational programmes, the admission of students and the appointment of faculty members to the control and supervision of the military occupation authorities, in clear contravention of the Geneva Convention;

4. *Demands* that Israel, the occupying Power, comply with the provisions of that Convention, rescind all actions and measures against all educational institutions, ensure the freedom of these institutions and refrain forthwith from hindering the effective operation of the universities and other educational institutions;

5. *Requests* the Secretary-General to report on the implementation of the present resolution before the end of 1983.

Recorded vote in Assembly as follows:

In favour: Afghanistan, Albania, Algeria, Argentina, Austria, Bahrain, Bangladesh, Benin, Bhutan, Bolivia, Botswana, Brazil, Bulgaria, Burundi, Byelorussian SSR, Central African Republic, Chad, China, Colombia, Comoros, Congo, Cuba, Cyprus, Czechoslovakia, Democratic Kampuchea, Democratic Yemen, Djibouti, Dominican Republic, Ecuador, Egypt, El Salvador, Ethiopia, Fiji, Gabon, Gambia, German Democratic Republic, Ghana, Greece, Guyana, Haiti, Honduras, Hungary, India, Indonesia, Iran, Iraq, Jamaica, Jordan, Kenya, Kuwait, Lao People's Democratic Republic, Lebanon, Liberia, Libyan Arab Jamahiriya, Madagascar, Malaysia, Maldives, Mali, Malta, Mauritania, Mauritius, Mexico, Mongolia, Morocco, Mozambique, Nepal, Nicaragua, Niger, Nigeria, Oman, Pakistan, Panama, Papua New Guinea, Peru, Philippines, Poland, Portugal, Qatar, Romania, Rwanda, Sao Tome and Principe, Saudi Arabia, Senegal, Sierra Leone, Singapore, Solomon Islands, Somalia, Spain, Sri Lanka, Sudan, Suriname, Syrian Arab Republic, Thailand, Togo, Trinidad and Tobago, Tunisia, Turkey, Uganda, Ukrainian SSR, USSR, United Arab Emirates, United Republic of Cameroon, United Republic of Tanzania, Upper Volta, Vanuatu, Venezuela, Viet Nam, Yemen, Yugoslavia, Zambia.

Against: Israel, United States.

Abstaining: Australia, Barbados, Belgium, Burma, Canada, Chile, Costa Rica, Denmark, Finland, France, Germany, Federal Republic of, Iceland, Ireland, Italy, Japan, Luxembourg, Malawi, Netherlands, New Zealand, Norway, Sweden, United Kingdom, Uruguay, Zaire.

Living conditions of Palestinians

Reports. In accordance with a December 1981 General Assembly resolution,[7] the Secretary-General submitted on 15 June 1982 a report on the living conditions of the Palestinians in the occupied Palestinian territories.[5] Of the two experts engaged to prepare the report, one remained at United Nations Headquarters to research the written material, while another went on an information-gathering mission in February and March and visited Egypt, Jordan, the Syrian Arab Republic and the PLO offices at Beirut and Damascus as well as relevant United Nations agencies in Europe and the Middle East; information

had also been collected from academic and research institutions in the neighbouring Arab countries. Since Israel had not granted permission to visit the occupied territories, the experts relied on secondary sources of information, including reports of 1981 missions to the territories by the International Labour Organisation and the World Health Organization.

The experts reported that Israeli policies with regard to land and water usage (see below) were adversely affecting the living conditions and agricultural activities of the Palestinians, creating among them a sense of insecurity and frustration. The increase in housing stock since the occupation had not kept pace with the rate of dilapidation, and overcrowding remained severe. Despite certain improvements, health care had not kept pace with the population increase and the need for specialized hospital care. Education suffered from harassment of students and faculty and restrictions on academic freedom (see above). Due to declining employment opportunities, many Palestinians had been forced to migrate to Israel or the Gulf States, and their social and cultural life had been affected by the various constraints and restrictions intensified in recent years.

In a government report transmitted to the Assembly by a letter of 16 July,[3] Israel, on the other hand, stated that since 1967 economic life in Judaea-Samaria and the Gaza district had been characterized by rapid growth and a substantial rise in living standards, made possible by interaction with the Israeli economy. There had been marked improvements in housing, water supply and consumption, agricultural productivity and income, public health, civil liberties, public order and security.

Economic and Social Council action. Taking note of the Secretary-General's report, the Economic and Social Council decided on 27 July to transmit it to the General Assembly.[1]

The decision, adopted without vote following its approval by the First (Economic) Committee on 21 July in like manner, was orally proposed by the Committee Chairman.

General Assembly action. By a resolution of 20 December,[6] the General Assembly took note of the report and expressed alarm at the deterioration in the living conditions of the Palestinians. It affirmed that the exercise by the Palestinian people of their right to self-determination was a prerequisite for their social and economic development in the occupied West Bank and Gaza Strip, and that the Israeli occupation was contradictory to the basic requirements for such development. The Assembly called on the Israeli authorities to give United Nations bodies and experts access to the occupied territories, and requested the Secretary-General to submit to it in 1983 a comprehensive report.

The resolution was adopted by a recorded vote of 145 to 2, with 3 abstentions, following its approval on 19 November by the Second (Economic and Financial) Committee by a recorded vote, requested by the United Arab Emirates, of 128 to 2, with 4 abstentions.

Introducing the 17-nation draft, Saudi Arabia said the Palestinians were waging a struggle for their very survival, while the Israeli occupation authorities resorted to inhuman measures.

Israel rejected the text as having been motivated solely by political aims and as seeking to redress through rhetoric what had been ignored in practice; it demonstrated once again the disregard for the real problem that had long characterized the policy of the Arab States which, while professing deep concern for the Palestinians and despite the vast resources at their disposal, had done nothing for more than 30 years to alleviate the situation.

The United States opposed the resolution on the grounds that it did nothing to address the economic needs of the Palestinians but simply raised political questions which could be resolved only through negotiations.

Abstaining, Australia expressed deep concern about the deterioration of the living conditions of the Palestinians, but felt that paragraph 5 would prejudge the outcome of negotiations.

Though voting in favour, Chile reserved its position on the third preambular paragraph, saying it had not participated in the vote on the 1981 Assembly resolution on the same subject.[7] Sweden reserved its position on references in the preamble to the recommendations of the 1976 United Nations Conference on Human Settlements.[8]

Jordan declared its willingness to co-operate with the Secretary-General in the implementation of the resolution; however, that attitude should not be construed as any change in its position on the question of the occupied territories, and nothing in the resolution should be taken as impairing its obligations and responsibilities towards the occupied territories.

Support of the resolution was expressed by a number of speakers, among them China, Fiji and the USSR. In the opinion of the USSR, the report confirmed once again that the inhabitants of the occupied territories continued to be unable to exercise their rights. Morocco (on behalf of the Group of Arab States) said the least the United Nations could do was to remain concerned with the living conditions of the Palestinians until they achieved their legitimate rights.

PLO said the Secretary-General's report, while not complete in all aspects, indicated a pattern of continued deterioration. Most of the statistics given by Israel were manipulated and disputable.

During the Committee debate on 2 November, the Syrian Arab Republic made a personal reference to the representative of Israel. By a 3 November letter to the Committee Chairman, the United States voiced objection to that reference, stating that everything must be done to prevent such practices and to admonish those who engaged in them.[4] The Chairman responded by a letter of 5 November,[2] asserting that the rules of procedure, including those relating to his functions and responsibilities, had been strictly observed.

Decision (1982). [1]ESC: 1982/153, 27 July, text following.
Letters. [2]2nd Committee Chairman, 5 Nov., A/C.2/37/7; [3]Israel, 16 July, A/37/347 & Corr.1; [4]United States, 3 Nov., A/C.2/37/6.
Report. [5]S-G, A/37/238.
Resolution (1982). [6]GA: 37/222, 20 Dec., text following.
Resolution (prior). [7]GA: 36/73, 4 Dec. 1981 (YUN 1981, p. 322).
Yearbook reference. [8]1976, p. 443.
Financial implications. 5th Committee report, A/37/683; S-G statements, A/C.2/37/L.62, A/C.5/37/55.
Meeting records. ESC: E/1982/SR.48 (27 July). GA: 2nd Committee, A/C.2/37/SR.3, 5-8, 20-24, 25, 26, 27, 36, 41, 42 (28 Sep–19 Nov); 5th Committee, A/C.5/37/SR.49 (30 Nov.); plenary, A/37/PV.113 (20 Dec.).

Economic and Social Council decision 1982/153

Adopted without vote

Approved by First Committee (E/1982/101) without vote, 21 July (meeting 12); oral proposal by Chairman; agenda item 13.

Report of the Secretary-General on the living conditions of the Palestinian people in the occupied Palestinian territories

At its 48th plenary meeting, on 27 July 1982, the Council took note of the report of the Secretary-General on the living conditions of the Palestinian people in the occupied Palestinian territories, and decided to transmit it to the General Assembly at its thirty-seventh session for consideration.

General Assembly resolution 37/222

20 December 1982   Meeting 113   145-2-3 (recorded vote)

Approved by Second Committee (A/37/680/Add.9) by recorded vote (128-2-4), 19 November (meeting 41); 17-nation draft (A/C.2/37/L.29); agenda item 71 (j).

Sponsors: Afghanistan, Bangladesh, Cuba, German Democratic Republic, Guinea, India, Malaysia, Morocco, Nicaragua, Oman, Pakistan, Saudi Arabia, Sudan, United Arab Emirates, Viet Nam, Yemen, Yugoslavia.

Living conditions of the Palestinian people in the occupied Palestinian territories

The General Assembly,

Recalling the Vancouver Declaration on Human Settlements, 1976, and the relevant recommendations for national action adopted by Habitat: United Nations Conference on Human Settlements,

Recalling also resolution 3, entitled "Living conditions of the Palestinians in occupied territories", contained in the recommendations for international co-operation adopted by Habitat: United Nations Conference on Human Settlements,

Recalling further its resolution 36/73 of 4 December 1981,

1. *Takes note* of the report of the Secretary-General on the living conditions of the Palestinian people in the occupied Palestinian territories;

2. *Takes note* of the statement made by the observer of the Palestine Liberation Organization;

3. *Expresses its alarm* at the deterioration in the living conditions of the Palestinian people in the Palestinian territories occupied since 1967 as a result of the Israeli occupation;

4. *Affirms* that the Israeli occupation is contradictory to the basic requirements for the social and economic development of the Palestinian people in the occupied West Bank and Gaza Strip;

5. *Affirms also* that the exercise by the Palestinian people of their right to self-determination is a prerequisite for their social and economic development in the Palestinian territories occupied since 1967;

6. *Calls upon* the Israeli occupation authorities to give United Nations bodies and experts access to the Palestinian territories occupied since 1967;

7. *Recognizes* the need for a comprehensive report on the social and economic conditions of the Palestinian people in the Palestinian territories occupied since 1967;

8. *Requests* the Secretary-General to prepare and submit to the General Assembly at its thirty-eighth session, through the Economic and Social Council, a comprehensive report on the living conditions of the Palestinian people in the occupied Palestinian territories.

Recorded vote in Assembly as follows:

In favour: Afghanistan, Albania, Algeria, Angola, Antigua and Barbuda, Argentina, Austria, Bahamas, Bahrain, Bangladesh, Barbados, Belgium, Benin, Bhutan, Bolivia, Botswana, Brazil, Bulgaria, Burundi, Byelorussian SSR, Cape Verde, Central African Republic, Chad, Chile, China, Colombia, Comoros, Congo, Costa Rica, Cuba, Cyprus, Czechoslovakia, Democratic Kampuchea, Democratic Yemen, Denmark, Djibouti, Dominican Republic, Ecuador, Egypt, El Salvador, Ethiopia, Fiji, Finland, France, Gabon, Gambia, German Democratic Republic, Germany, Federal Republic of, Ghana, Greece, Grenada, Guinea, Guinea-Bissau, Guyana, Haiti, Honduras, Hungary, Iceland, India, Indonesia, Iran, Iraq, Ireland, Italy, Ivory Coast, Jamaica, Japan, Jordan, Kenya, Kuwait, Lao People's Democratic Republic, Lebanon, Lesotho, Liberia, Libyan Arab Jamahiriya, Luxembourg, Madagascar, Malawi, Malaysia, Maldives, Mali, Malta, Mauritania, Mauritius, Mexico, Mongolia, Morocco, Mozambique, Nepal, Netherlands, New Zealand, Nicaragua, Niger, Nigeria, Norway, Oman, Pakistan, Panama, Papua New Guinea, Paraguay, Peru, Philippines, Poland, Portugal, Qatar, Romania, Rwanda, Saint Lucia, Saint Vincent and the Grenadines, Samoa, Sao Tome and Principe, Saudi Arabia, Senegal, Sierra Leone, Singapore, Somalia, Spain, Sri Lanka, Sudan, Suriname, Swaziland, Sweden, Syrian Arab Republic, Thailand, Togo, Trinidad and Tobago, Tunisia, Turkey, Uganda, Ukrainian SSR, USSR, United Arab Emirates, United Kingdom, United Republic of Cameroon, United Republic of Tanzania, Upper Volta, Uruguay, Vanuatu, Venezuela, Viet Nam, Yemen, Yugoslavia, Zaire, Zambia, Zimbabwe.

Against: Israel, United States.

Abstaining: Australia, Burma, Canada.

Census of the Palestinian population

By a resolution of 11 May 1982,[1] the Economic Commission for Western Asia, recalling its 1976 decision on a census of the Palestinians,[2] urged States hosting Palestinians to allow PLO to make arrangements and take the measures necessary to carry out the census in a manner compatible with the regulations and laws in the States concerned. The Commission requested the United Nations Fund for Population Activities to continue financing the project.

Resolution (1982). [1]ECWA (report, E/1982/22): 109(IX), 11 May.

Yearbook reference. [2]1976, p. 504.

Permanent sovereignty over resources

Report of the Secretary-General. In accordance with a December 1981 General Assembly resolution,[6] the Secretary-General submitted in November 1982 a report on permanent sovereignty over national resources in the occupied territories.[1] He informed that in a note verbale he had asked Egypt, Israel, Jordan, Lebanon, the Syrian Arab Republic, PLO and United Nations agencies and organs for information. He had received replies from Israel and the Syrian Arab Republic, as well as from several agencies. In addition, publicly available data had been collected.

The Secretary-General was not in a position to complete the requested comprehensive report in 1982, due to insufficient information available; in particular, lack of access to the territories had prevented the collection of information on the ef-

fects of developments in the preceding 12 months, such as the extension of Israeli law to the Golan Heights and certain administrative measures taken in the West Bank and Gaza (see above). The Secretary-General stated that efforts would be made to prepare such a report for 1983.

Action by the Commission on Human Rights. In a resolution of 11 February 1982,[2] the Commission on Human Rights condemned, among other Israeli policies and practices, the illegal exploitation of the natural wealth, resources and population of the occupied territories.

General Assembly action. Expressing regret that the Secretary-General's comprehensive report was not submitted, the Assembly, by a resolution of 17 December 1982,[4] requested its submission in 1983. The Assembly condemned Israel for its exploitation of the national resources of the occupied territories and emphasized the right of the people living there to full and effective permanent sovereignty and control over all resources. It reaffirmed that all Israeli measures to exploit those resources were illegal, and called on Israel to desist immediately from such measures and to meet the just claims for restitution of and full compensation for the damage to and loss of resources. The Assembly called on States to support the Palestinian and other Arab peoples in the exercise of their rights to sovereignty over their resources and not to recognize any Israeli measures exploiting those resources.

In a resolution of 10 December,[3] the Assembly condemned—among other Israeli policies and practices—the illegal exploitation of the natural wealth, resources and population of the occupied territories, and demanded that Israel desist from it.

The 17 December resolution was adopted by a recorded vote of 124 to 2, with 20 abstentions, following its approval by the Second (Economic and Financial) Committee on 19 November by a recorded vote, requested by the United Arab Emirates, of 113 to 2, with 19 abstentions.

Casting a negative vote, Israel said the actual situation did not correspond to what was described in the resolution; the resources of the occupied territories had been developed, not "exploited". Israel rejected particularly the accusation of "racial domination" in the preamble, saying that such vile and slanderous phrases recalled dark events in other places and at other times.

In the opinion of the United States, the resolution did nothing to address the economic needs of the Palestinians, but simply raised political questions and made veiled calls for sanctions.

Though voting in favour, Chile did not support paragraph 1, and Portugal had reservations on paragraph 4.

Support for the resolution was expressed by a number of other speakers, among them China, Cyprus, Greece, Japan, Turkey and the USSR.

The USSR explained it voted in favour in accordance with its desire that a just solution be found to the Middle East problems and that the Palestinians be enabled to exercise their rights. Israel's goal, Morocco stated, was not to achieve peace but to annex the Arab territories and expel the population in order to exercise illegitimate sovereignty over Palestinian and Arab resources. Japan said it sympathized with the Arab peoples regarding the problem of national resources and hoped the problem would be solved by the parties in an expeditious and peaceful manner in accordance with international law; its position on permanent sovereignty over national resources in general, however, remained unchanged.

Introducing the 15-nation draft, Senegal stated that in previous years similar resolutions had been adopted in order to support the efforts of peoples under racist or foreign domination to regain control of their resources, in keeping with the Charter of Economic Rights and Duties of States.[5]

During the Assembly debate on the Palestine question, the Syrian Arab Republic stated that Israel had monopolized 94 per cent of all income from Arab property in Palestine, while the true owners were living in camps; the Israeli invasion of Lebanon was aimed at claiming its waters and its riches. Jordan said the deprivation of the Palestinians in the occupied territories of their houses, liberty, water and land violated human rights and international law, particularly the 1949 Geneva Convention on the protection of civilians.

Report. [1]S-G, A/37/600.
Resolutions (1982). [2]Commission on Human Rights (report, E/1982/12): 1982/1 A, para. 5 (*k*), 11 Feb. GA: [3]37/88 C, paras. 7 (*n*) & 9, 10 Dec.; [4]37/135, 17 Dec., text following.
Resolutions (prior). GA: [5]3281(XXIX), 12 Dec. 1974 (YUN 1974, p. 403); [6]36/173, 17 Dec. 1981 (YUN 1981, p. 324).
Meeting records. GA: 2nd Committee, A/C.2/37/SR.3-12, 32, 36, 40-42 (28 Sep.–19 Nov.); plenary, A/37/PV.109 (17 Dec.).

General Assembly resolution 37/135

17 December 1982   Meeting 109   124-2-20 (recorded vote)

Approved by Second Committee (A/37/679) by recorded vote (113-2-19), 19 November (meeting 41); 15-nation draft (A/C.2/37/L.44); agenda item 12.

Sponsors: Congo, Cuba, German Democratic Republic, Guinea, India, Malaysia, Morocco, Nicaragua, Oman, Pakistan, Senegal, Sudan, United Arab Emirates, Viet Nam, Yugoslavia.

Permanent sovereignty over national resources in the occupied Palestinian and other Arab territories

The General Assembly,

Recalling its resolutions 3175(XXVIII) of 17 December 1973, 3336(XXIX) of 17 December 1974, 3516(XXX) of 15 December 1975, 31/186 of 21 December 1976, 32/161 of 19 December 1977, 34/136 of 14 December 1979, 35/110 of 5 December 1980 and 36/173 of 17 December 1981 on permanent sovereignty over national resources in the occupied Palestinian and other Arab territories,

Recalling also its previous resolutions on permanent sovereignty over natural resources, particularly their provisions supporting resolutely the efforts of the developing countries and the peoples of territories under colonial and racial domination and foreign occupation in their struggle to regain effective control over their natural and all other resources, wealth and economic activities,

Bearing in mind the relevant principles of international law and the provisions of the international conventions and regulations, in particu-

lar Convention IV of the Hague of 1907, and the fourth Geneva Convention of 12 August 1949, concerning the obligations and responsibilities of the occupying Power,

Bearing in mind also the pertinent provisions of its resolutions 3201(S-VI) and 3202(S-VI) of 1 May 1974, containing the Declaration and the Programme of Action on the Establishment of a New International Economic Order, and 3281(XXIX) of 12 December 1974, containing the Charter of Economic Rights and Duties of States,

Regretting that the report of the Secretary-General on permanent sovereignty over national resources in the occupied Palestinian and other Arab territories, requested in General Assembly resolution 36/173, was not submitted,

1. *Condemns* Israel for its exploitation of the national resources of the occupied Palestinian and other Arab territories;

2. *Emphasizes* the right of the Palestinian and other Arab peoples whose territories are under Israeli occupation to full and effective permanent sovereignty and control over their natural and all other resources, wealth and economic activities;

3. *Reaffirms* that all measures undertaken by Israel to exploit the human, natural and all other resources, wealth and economic activities in the occupied Palestinian and other Arab territories are illegal and calls upon Israel to desist immediately from such measures;

4. *Further reaffirms* the right of the Palestinian and other Arab peoples subjected to Israeli aggression and occupation to the restitution of and full compensation for the exploitation, depletion and loss of and damage to their natural, human and all other resources, wealth and economic activities, and calls upon Israel to meet their just claims;

5. *Call upon* all States to support the Palestinian and other Arab peoples in the exercise of their above-mentioned rights;

6. *Calls upon* all States, international organizations, specialized agencies, business corporations and all other institutions not to recognize, or co-operate with or assist in any manner in, any measures undertaken by Israel to exploit the national resources of the occupied Palestinian and other Arab territories or to effect any changes in the demographic composition, the character and form of use of their natural resources or the institutional structure of those territories;

7. *Requests* the Secretary-General to prepare and submit to the General Assembly at its thirty-eighth session, through the Economic and Social Council, the two reports requested in Assembly resolution 36/173.

Recorded vote in Assembly as follows:

In favour: Afghanistan, Albania, Algeria, Angola, Argentina, Bahamas, Bahrain, Bangladesh, Barbados, Benin, Bhutan, Bolivia, Botswana, Brazil, Bulgaria, Burundi, Byelorussian SSR, Cape Verde, Central African Republic, Chad, Chile, China, Colombia, Comoros, Congo, Costa Rica, Cuba, Cyprus, Czechoslovakia, Democratic Kampuchea, Democratic Yemen, Djibouti, Dominica, Dominican Republic, Ecuador, Egypt, El Salvador, Ethiopia, Gabon, Gambia, German Democratic Republic, Ghana, Greece, Grenada, Guinea, Guinea-Bissau, Guyana, Honduras, Hungary, India, Indonesia, Iran, Iraq, Jamaica, Japan, Jordan, Kenya, Kuwait, Lao People's Democratic Republic, Lebanon, Lesotho, Liberia, Libyan Arab Jamahiriya, Madagascar, Malawi, Malaysia, Maldives, Mali, Malta, Mauritania, Mauritius, Mexico, Mongolia, Morocco, Mozambique, Nepal, Nicaragua, Niger, Nigeria, Oman, Pakistan, Panama, Papua New Guinea, Paraguay, Peru, Philippines, Poland, Portugal, Qatar, Romania, Rwanda, Samoa, Sao Tome and Principe, Saudi Arabia, Senegal, Sierra Leone, Singapore, Solomon Islands, Somalia, Spain, Sri Lanka, Suriname, Swaziland, Thailand, Togo, Trinidad and Tobago, Tunisia, Turkey, Uganda, Ukrainian SSR, USSR, United Arab Emirates, United Republic of Cameroon, United Republic of Tanzania, Upper Volta, Uruguay, Vanuatu, Venezuela, Viet Nam, Yemen, Yugoslavia, Zaire, Zambia, Zimbabwe.

Against: Israel, United States.

Abstaining: Australia, Austria, Belgium, Burma, Canada, Denmark, Fiji, Finland, France, Germany, Federal Republic of, Iceland, Ireland, Italy, Ivory Coast, Luxembourg, Netherlands, New Zealand, Norway, Sweden, United Kingdom.

Palestinian women

Expressing deep concern over the conditions of the Palestinians, particularly women and children, the Economic and Social Council, by a resolution of 4 May 1982,[1] appealed to all women of the world to proclaim their solidarity with Palestinian women and people in their drive to put an end to Israel's violation of human rights in the occupied territories, and to act in order to secure the release of thousands of persons, including women and children, held arbitrarily in the prisons of the occupying forces. The Council appealed to States and international organizations to extend moral and material assistance to Palestinian and Arab women and people in their struggle for the restoration of their right to return to their homes and property. United Nations organs and agencies, as well as national, regional and international women's organizations, were requested to extend such assistance to Palestinian women and their organizations and institutes.

The resolution was adopted by a recorded vote, requested by Jordan, of 28 to 9, with 15 abstentions, following its approval on 26 April by the Council's Second (Social) Committee by a recorded vote of 25 to 9, with 10 abstentions. The draft originated in the Commission on the Status of Women which adopted it on 4 March by a roll-call vote of 14 to 8, with 4 abstentions. The text was introduced in the Commission by Iraq, also on behalf of Cuba and Tunisia.

Casting a negative vote, the United States considered the resolution obnoxious and detrimental to the cause of peace, and found unacceptable the equation of zionism with fascism, as well as the assertion that thousands of persons, including women and children, were held arbitrarily in Israeli prisons.

The linking of fascism, racial discrimination and zionism in the preamble was also unacceptable to the States members of the European Community, as stated by Belgium.

Austria, Chile, Greece, Liberia, Mexico and Portugal abstained, and Canada voted against, on the same grounds.

Reservations on that provision were also voiced by Argentina and Zaire which voted in favour. Brazil and Romania also had reservations on the wording of parts of the preamble, and Colombia could not support part of the text.

Israel said Arab countries, most of which did not grant women equal rights or status under the law, had used the resolution as an instrument to combat Israel rather than discrimination against women; the text made no mention of the fact that tens of thousands of Palestinian Arabs had been allowed to return to join their families while hundreds of thousands of Jewish women had been forced to flee Arab lands which they had inhabited for many centuries.

Resolution (1982). [1]ESC: 1982/18, 4 May, text following. *Meeting record.* ESC: E/1982/SR.22 (4 May).

Economic and Social Council resolution 1982/18

4 May 1982   Meeting 22   28-9-15 (recorded vote)

Approved by Second Committee (E/1982/57) by recorded vote (25-9-10), 26 April (meeting 8); draft by Commission on women (E/1982/14); agenda item 10.

Situation of women and children in the occupied Arab territories

The Economic and Social Council,

Deeply concerned about the prevailing conditions of the Palestinian people, particularly the women and children,

Noting the great sacrifices of the Palestinian women and children in pursuit of their inalienable right to have their own homeland,

Considering that international co-operation and peace are threatened by colonialism, neo-colonialism, fascism, zionism, *apartheid* and foreign occupation, alien domination and racial discrimination in all its forms,

Affirming its full solidarity with the Palestinian women in their struggle for independence under the leadership of the Palestine Liberation Organization,

Expressing its grave concern that the Palestinian women and people continue to be denied their inalienable rights, in particular their right to return to their homes and property from which they have been displaced and uprooted, the right to self-determination and the right to national independence and sovereignty,

Recognizing that the mass uprooting from their homeland obstructs the participation and integration of women in efforts to achieve progress,

1. *Appeals* to all women of the world to proclaim their solidarity with and support for the Palestinian women and people in their drive to put an end to the flagrant violation by Israel of fundamental human rights in the occupied territories;

2. *Also appeals* to all States and international organizations to extend all moral and material assistance to the Palestinian and Arab women and people in their struggle for the restoration of their inalienable right to return to their homes and property from which they have been displaced and uprooted;

3. *Further appeals* to all women of the world to take the necessary measures to secure the release of thousands of persons, including women and children, fighters for the cause of self-determination, liberation and independence, held arbitrarily in the prisons of the occupying forces;

4. *Requests* the United Nations and its organs and specialized agencies, as well as all national, regional and international women's organizations, to extend their help, both moral and material, to the Palestinian women and their organizations and institutes.

Recorded vote in Council as follows:

In favour: Argentina, Bangladesh, Benin, Brazil, Bulgaria, Burundi, Byelorussian SSR, China, Ethiopia, India, Iraq, Jordan, Kenya, Libyan Arab Jamahiriya, Mali, Nepal, Nicaragua, Nigeria, Pakistan, Poland, Qatar, Romania, Sudan, Tunisia, USSR, United Republic of Cameroon, Yugoslavia, Zaire.

Against: Australia, Belgium, Canada, Denmark, Germany, Federal Republic of, Italy, Norway, United Kingdom, United States.

Abstaining: Austria, Bahamas, Chile, Colombia, Fiji, France, Greece, Japan, Liberia, Malawi, Mexico, Portugal, Saint Lucia, Thailand, Venezuela.

Palestine refugees

UN Agency for Palestine refugees

In 1982, the United Nations Relief and Works Agency for Palestine Refugees in the Near East (UNRWA) continued to provide education, health and relief services for 1.9 million Palestine refugees in Jordan, Lebanon, the Syrian Arab Republic and the Israeli-occupied territories of the West Bank and the Gaza Strip. It responded to the emergency situation in Lebanon arising from the Israeli military incursion in June, with a programme worth some $52 million, of which $41 million were contributions made or pledged in response to special appeals.

Total expenditure for assistance provided by UNRWA since 1950 had reached $2.2 billion by the end of 1982, excluding Lebanon emergency relief programmes but including the 1982 expenditure of $182.9 million.

UNRWA activities

The number of refugees registered with UNRWA rose by 38,948 during 1982, to 1,941,791 at 31 December. Of these, about 830,000 were eligible for food rations (until the programme's suspension in September) (see below), and approximately 1.5 million were eligible for health and education services.

About 35 per cent (some 680,000 persons) of the registered population lived in 61 camps.

The Agency, in co-operation with the World Health Organization, continued provision of health education and integrated family health care, with emphasis on preventive medicine, including supplementary feeding for nutritionally vulnerable groups. Despite financial constraints, specialized medicine programmes and laboratory facilities were improved. Agency health care facilities included 98 general health units, 26 laboratories, 26 dental clinics and nine maternity centres. Expenditure on health services in 1982 totalled $33.9 million.

Expenditure on relief services in 1982 was $31.3 million, mainly for hardship cases such as widows, orphans and the aged. A report on UNRWA assistance to the aged was presented to the World Assembly on Aging in July/August (see ECONOMIC AND SOCIAL QUESTIONS, Chapter XX) by the United Nations High Commissioner for Refugees who observed that Palestine refugees aged 60 years or older constituted 7.9 per cent (or 150,000) of the persons registered with UNRWA, and that 90 per cent of them were eligible for health services.[1] More than 7,000 persons over 60 years of age benefited from special hardship assistance, and some 225 aged refugees received institutional care.

After 32 years, the distribution of foodstuffs to eligible refugees was suspended in September, except for those affected by the emergency situation in Lebanon (see ECONOMIC AND SOCIAL QUESTIONS, Chapter III) and some 80,000 refugees identified as hardship cases. With the cessation of the ration programme, the Agency decided to replace family registration cards with individual cards to identify refugees eligible for UNRWA services. The Agency also distributed rations to about 230,000 displaced persons and refugee children in Jordan, at the expense of the Jordanian Government.

Spending on education increased by 6 per cent over 1981, from $104.5 million to $110.5 million. Under the programme, operated with the techni-cal assistance of the United Nations Educational, Scientific and Cultural Organization (UNESCO), over 336,000 pupils were enrolled, as at October 1982, in the 651 Agency elementary and preparatory schools. There were also more than 92,000 refugee pupils enrolled in local government and private schools. Of the 17,000 UNRWA employees, almost all Palestine refugees themselves, nearly 12,000 were working in the education field, most of them (9,816) as teachers.

Capacity at the eight UNRWA/UNESCO technical and teacher training centres increased by 202 places to a total of 5,188, which was still far from satisfying demand since four out of five applicants had to be turned away for lack of facilities. By the end of 1982, more than 35,000 trainees had graduated from these centres. The UNRWA/UNESCO Institute for Education continued to emphasize refresher courses for qualified teachers and courses in educational techniques to meet special needs and new curriculum requirements (see below). Recipients of university scholarships numbered 351 for the 1981/82 academic year.

Lebanon emergency. Immediately after the Israeli invasion of Lebanon in June 1982, UNRWA organized an emergency assistance programme for an estimated 175,000 Palestinian refugees, regardless of whether or not they were registered with the Agency, who had been affected by the hostilities; the emergency provision of water, medical supplies and sanitation services helped prevent any serious epidemic or other major health problem. In a special report of 28 September,[3] the Commissioner-General outlined UNRWA relief operations and forecast a continuing emergency relief and reconstruction programme until June 1983.

By the end of 1982, the Agency's regular programmes in Lebanon had recovered from the state of paralysis following the invasion and during subsequent fighting. Many of the estimated 73,000 refugees made homeless by the fighting were given cash contributions and/or building materials to help rebuild or repair their dwellings. Out of the 85 UNRWA schools in Lebanon, 82 were reopened before year's end to provide education to over 31,000 students, only 4,000 less than the enrolment in the previous school year.

Report of the Commissioner-General. In a report covering UNRWA activities for the period from 1 July 1981 to 30 June 1982,[2] the Commissioner-General termed the year under review as a very difficult one, with serious disruption to its services by the Israeli invasion of Lebanon in June, political tensions and unrest in the West Bank and Gaza, and fighting in the Syrian Arab Republic. The situation in Jordan, however, had remained relatively calm. The Agency's financial difficulties had been exacerbated by the cost of the emergency operations in Lebanon.

CONTRIBUTIONS TO UNRWA FOR LEBANON EMERGENCY RELIEF
(as at 31 December 1982; in US dollar equivalent)

Contributor	Payments in kind*	Payments in cash	Total
Australia	—	575,445	575,445
Austria	—	28,818	28,818
Canada	—	758,120	758,120
China	—	20,000	20,000
Denmark	—	684,658	684,658
European Economic Community	685,804	—	685,804
Finland	—	531,124	531,124
Germany, Federal Republic of	—	392,157	392,157
India	—	19,890	19,890
Italy	1,403,179	—	1,403,179
Netherlands	—	650,523	650,523
New Zealand	—	17,984	17,984
Norway	—	584,163	584,163
Saudi Arabia	—	2,915,452	2,915,452
Sweden	294,610	1,353,357	1,647,967
Switzerland	227,273	211,966	439,239
Thailand	—	1,000	1,000
United Kingdom	1,850,274	—	1,850,274
United States	—	2,000,000	2,000,000
Subtotal	4,461,140	10,744,657	15,205,797
United Nations agencies:			
WHO			6,800
UNDRO			216,148
Subtotal			222,948
Non-governmental sources			1,817,949
Total			17,246,694

*At donor's valuation.
NOTE: Contributions include only amounts for 1982 paid as at 31 December.
SOURCE: A/38/5/Add.3.

The Commissioner-General told the Special Political Committee (SPC) in November that much of the work done by UNRWA in the course of three decades had been undone in the three months following the Israeli invasion of Lebanon, and that the Agency's future was unclear.

General Assembly action. On 16 December,[4] the General Assembly thanked the UNRWA Commissioner-General and staff as well as the specialized agencies and private organizations for their assistance to refugees, and reiterated its request that the Agency headquarters should be relocated as soon as practicable to its former site at Beirut, Lebanon, from where it had been moved in 1978.[6]

The Commissioner-General told SPC on 18 November 1982 that a major factor that would affect the timing of moving the headquarters from its present location at Vienna, Austria, was the prospect of its being able efficiently to co-ordinate and supervise UNRWA operations.

In a 21 December resolution on questions relating to the programme budget for 1982-1983,[5] the Assembly approved the reclassification, from 1 January 1983, of the UNRWA Commissioner-General to the level of Under-Secretary-General.

Speaking during the Assembly's resumed seventh emergency special session on the Palestine question in April, Bangladesh called the Palestinian refugee problem political in origin, which no humanitarian measures could eliminate without a just and lasting solution to the Palestine question; the Palestinians must be returned to their own homeland, and the United Nations and its specialized agencies, in the mean time, should provide the economic and technical assistance for the consolidation of the Palestinian entity.

In September, also at the special session, Sweden said UNRWA should receive financial support from all and vigorous political backing from those Governments best placed to exert influence so that it could provide assistance in the most effective way.

Reports. [1]UNHCR, A/CONF.113/21/Add.1; UNRWA Commissioner-General, [2]A/37/13, [3]A/37/479.
Resolutions (1982). GA: [4]37/120 K, paras. 2 & 3, 16 Dec.; [5]37/237, sect. XII, para. *(a)* (ii), 21 Dec.
Yearbook reference. [6]1978, p. 358.

UNRWA finances

In 1982, the Agency's income fell $65.4 million short of the budget of $248.3 million. Actual expenditure was $182.9 million, while income was $181.9 million, resulting in an excess of expenditure over income of $1 million.

Acting on the recommendations of the Working Group on the Financing of UNRWA, which held eight meetings between 20 January and 10 March,[3] the General Assembly, by a decision of 16 March,[1] called on Governments to contribute in cash or permit UNRWA to sell their contributions for cash. The Assembly also requested the Joint Inspection Unit to review comprehensively the Agency's organization, budget and operations with a view to assisting the Commissioner-General to make the most effective and economical use of the limited funds available to UNRWA. The Assembly acted without vote, on an oral proposal by the President.

The Commissioner-General, in his report covering Agency activities for the year ended 30 June 1982,[2] reported that of the income of $191.5 million expected as at that date, only $121 million was freely disposable cash, and that the Agency's financial difficulties had been exacerbated by the cost of the emergency operations in Lebanon.

In a November report to the Assembly,[4] the Working Group reiterated the recommendations it had made earlier in the year and concluded that the continuing shortfall in income emphasized the urgent need for more stable financing and for broadening the participation in the financing of UNRWA. Despite the fact that various efforts by the Commissioner-General as well as additional cash contributions had made it possible during the year to reduce the estimated deficit for 1982 to $43.5 million, further drastic cuts in programme and management expenditure needed to be made. The Working Group viewed with concern the estimated deficit of $60.5 million for 1983.

On 16 December 1982,[5] the Assembly commended the Working Group for its efforts to assist in ensuring the Agency's financial security and requested it to continue its work for another year.

The text was adopted without vote, following its similar approval by SPC on 3 December. Introducing the 18-nation draft, the Netherlands noted the comment by the Working Group that the humanitarian services of UNRWA remained indispensable and worthy of unreserved support.

By another resolution of the same date, on assistance to Palestine refugees,[6] the Assembly directed attention to the seriousness of the Agency's financial position and noted with concern that the increased level of income was still insufficient to cover budget requirements. The Assembly called on Governments as a matter of urgency to make generous efforts to meet the Agency's anticipated needs, to contribute regularly and to consider increasing contributions. Other provisions dealt with repatriation or compensation of the refugees (see below) and relocation of UNRWA headquarters (see above).

The resolution was adopted by a recorded vote of 144 to none, with 1 abstention, following its ap-proval by SPC on 3 December by a recorded vote of 111 to none, with 1 abstention.

Introducing the text, the United States reaffirmed the need to assist Palestine refugees and reiterated its support for the voluntary principle of funding UNRWA. Canada said it particularly supported the call on Governments to meet the Agency's anticipated financial needs.

On 22 November, the *Ad Hoc* Committee of the General Assembly for the Announcement of Voluntary Contributions to UNRWA met at United Nations Headquarters.

The contributions for 1982 pledged by Governments amounted to about $202.9 million, the Lebanon Emergency Fund included. As at 31 December 1982, $58.9 million remained unpaid. In addition, the unpaid balance of prior years stood at $6.5 million. Government contributions in 1982 totalled $128.7 million for the UNRWA General Fund (see table below) and $15.2 million for the Lebanon Emergency Fund (see above).

CONTRIBUTIONS TO UNRWA GENERAL FUND, FOR THE YEAR ENDING 31 DECEMBER 1982
(in US dollar equivalent)

Contributor	Payments in kind	Payments in cash	Total	Contributor	Payments in kind	Payments in cash	Total
Argentina	—	6,700	6,700	Norway	—	5,710,463	5,710,463
Australia	—	902,045	902,045	Oman	—	25,000	25,000
Austria	—	190,250	190,250	Pakistan	—	17,086	17,086
Bahamas	—	500	500	Panama	—	1,000	1,000
Bahrain	—	15,000	15,000	Philippines	—	6,000	6,000
Barbados	—	1,000	1,000	Portugal	—	10,000	10,000
Belgium	—	391,304	391,304	Qatar	—	600,000	600,000
Benin	—	854	854	Republic of Korea	—	5,000	5,000
Brazil	—	10,000	10,000	San Marino	—	2,002	2,002
Canada	—	2,858,277	2,858,277	Saudi Arabia	—	6,200,000	6,200,000
Chile	—	4,000	4,000	Senegal	—	1,868	1,868
China	—	50,000	50,000	Seychelles	—	1,500	1,500
Cyprus	—	2,260	2,260	Singapore	—	3,000	3,000
Denmark	—	2,526,244	2,526,244	Spain	—	1,000,000	1,000,000
Egypt	—	7,299	7,299	Sri Lanka	1,000	—	1,000
European Economic Community	1,991,327*	—	1,991,327	Sweden	—	10,413,870	10,413,870
Finland	—	297,291	297,291	Switzerland	3,496,675*	807,370	4,304,045
France	362,001	832,588	1,194,589	Syrian Arab Republic	174,420	—	174,420
Gaza authorities	100,148	—	100,148	Thailand	—	15,640	15,640
Germany, Federal Republic of	1,689,244†	3,946,405	5,635,649	Tunisia	—	11,223	11,223
Greece	—	40,000	40,000	Turkey	—	20,000	20,000
Holy See	—	2,500	2,500	United Kingdom	—	7,211,000	7,211,000
Iceland	—	17,500	17,500	United Republic of Cameroon	—	1,410	1,410
Indonesia	—	8,000	8,000	United States	—	62,000,000	62,000,000
Iraq	—	500,000	500,000	Venezuela	—	10,000	10,000
Ireland	—	165,120	165,120				
Israel	336,706	—	336,706	Subtotal	8,950,512	119,774,902	128,725,414
Italy	—	1,402,069	1,402,069	*United Nations and*			
Japan	—	7,000,000	7,000,000	*specialized agencies:*			
Jordan	754,326	—	754,326	United Nations			5,664,204
Kuwait	—	2,100,000	2,100,000	UNESCO			815,279
Lebanon	44,665	14,940	59,605	WHO			398,150
Luxembourg	—	7,557	7,557				
Madagascar	—	2,650	2,650	Subtotal			6,877,633
Malaysia	—	5,000	5,000	*Organization of Petroleum*			
Maldives	—	2,000	2,000	*Exporting Countries*			51,453
Malta	—	988	988	*Non-governmental sources*			3,040,931‡
Mexico	—	5,035	5,035	*Miscellaneous income and*			
Monaco	—	822	822	*exchange adjustments*			3,287,096
Netherlands	—	2,297,077	2,297,077				
New Zealand	—	88,195	88,195	Total			141,982,527

*At donor's valuation.
†At Agency's 1982 standard price.
‡Includes $199,812 for 1982, paid in 1983.
NOTE: Contributions include only amounts for 1982 paid as at 31 December 1982, except as indicated.
SOURCE: A/38/5/Add.3 and Corr.1.

Decision (1982). (1)GA: 36/462, 16 Mar., text following.
Reports. (2)UNRWA Commissioner-General, A/37/13; Working Group on UNRWA financing, (3)A/36/866 & Corr.1, (4)A/37/591.
Resolutions (1982). GA, 16 Dec.: (5)37/120 A, text following; (6)37/120 K, text following.
Financial implications. S-G statement, A/SPC/37/L.12.
Meeting records. GA: plenary, A/36/PV.106, 110 (16 Mar., 28 Apr.), A/37/PV.108 (16 Dec.); SPC, A/SPC/37/SR.24, 26-31, *32, 42, 44, 45* (9 Nov.-6 Dec.). Committee on contributions to UNRWA: A/AC.216/SR.1 (22 Nov.).

General Assembly decision 36/462

Adopted without vote

Oral proposal by Assembly President on recommendation of Working Group on UNRWA financing (A/36/866); agenda item 60.

Financing of the United Nations Relief and Works Agency for Palestine Refugees in the Near East

At its 106th plenary meeting, on 16 March 1982, the General Assembly, having considered the recommendations of the Working Group on the Financing of the United Nations Relief and Works Agency for Palestine Refugees in the Near East:

(a) Took note of the report of the Working Group;

(b) Urged the Commissioner-General of the United Nations Relief and Works Agency for Palestine Refugees in the Near East to continue his efforts to make the most efficient use of the resources of the Agency and requested the Joint Inspection Unit to carry out a comprehensive review of the Agency's organization, budget and operations with a view to assisting the Commissioner-General to make the most effective and economical use of the limited funds available to the Agency;

(c) Called upon:

(i) Governments that had not yet contributed to the United Nations Relief and Works Agency for Palestine Refugees in the Near East to start contributing;

(ii) Governments that had hitherto only made relatively small contributions to contribute more generously;

(iii) Governments in a special position to do so to increase their contributions;

(iv) Governments that in the past had made generous contributions to continue to make generous contributions and strive whenever possible to increase their contributions;

(d) Called upon Governments and organizations making contributions in kind either to give cash instead or to allow the United Nations Relief and Works Agency for Palestine Refugees in the Near East to sell their contributions for cash;

(e) Decided to suspend temporarily the consideration of agenda item 60 (United Nations Relief and Works Agency for Palestine Refugees in the Near East).

General Assembly resolution 37/120 A

16 December 1982   Meeting 108   Adopted without vote

Approved by SPC (A/37/723) without vote, 3 December (meeting 44); 18-nation draft (A/SPC/37/L.10); agenda item 65.

Sponsors: Austria, Bangladesh, Canada, Denmark, Germany, Federal Republic of, India, Indonesia, Liberia, Mali, Netherlands, New Zealand, Nigeria, Pakistan, Philippines, Spain, Sri Lanka, Sweden, Yugoslavia.

Working Group on the Financing of the United Nations Relief and Works Agency for Palestine Refugees in the Near East

The General Assembly,   ,

Recalling its resolutions 2656(XXV) of 7 December 1970, 2728(XXV) of 15 December 1970, 2791(XXVI) of 6 December 1971, 2964(XXVII) of 13 December 1972, 3090(XXVIII) of 7 December 1973, 3330(XXIX) of 17 December 1974, 3419 D (XXX) of 8 December 1975, 31/15 C of 23 November 1976, 32/90 D of 13 December 1977, 33/112 D of 18 December 1978, 34/52 D of 23 November 1979, 35/13 D of 3 November 1980 and 36/146 E of 16 December 1981,

Recalling also its decision 36/462 of 16 March 1982, whereby the General Assembly took note of the special report of the Working Group on the Financing of the United Nations Relief and Works Agency for Palestine Refugees in the Near East and adopted the recommendations contained therein,

Having considered the report of the Working Group on the Financing of the United Nations Relief and Works Agency for Palestine Refugees in the Near East,

Taking into account the report of the Commissioner-General of the United Nations Relief and Works Agency for Palestine Refugees in the Near East, covering the period from 1 July 1981 to 30 June 1982, and his special report issued on 28 September 1982,

Gravely concerned at the critical financial situation of the United Nations Relief and Works Agency for Palestine Refugees in the Near East, which has already reduced the essential minimum services being provided to the Palestine refugees and which threatens even greater reductions in the future,

Emphasizing the urgent need for extraordinary efforts in order to maintain, at least at their present minimum level, the activities of the United Nations Relief and Works Agency for Palestine Refugees in the Near East,

1. *Commends* the Working Group on the Financing of the United Nations Relief and Works Agency for Palestine Refugees in the Near East for its efforts to assist in ensuring the Agency's financial security;

2. *Takes note with approval* of the report of the Working Group;

3. *Requests* the Working Group to continue its efforts, in co-operation with the Secretary-General and the Commissioner-General of the United Nations Relief and Works Agency for Palestine Refugees in the Near East, for the financing of the Agency for a further period of one year;

4. *Requests* the Secretary-General to provide the necessary services and assistance to the Working Group for the conduct of its work.

General Assembly resolution 37/120 K

16 December 1982   Meeting 108   144-0-1 (recorded vote)

Approved by SPC (A/37/723) by recorded vote (111-0-1), 3 December (meeting 44); draft by United States (A/SPC/37/L.25); agenda item 65.

Assistance to Palestine refugees

The General Assembly,

Recalling its resolution 36/146 F of 16 December 1981 and all previous resolutions on the question, including resolution 194(III) of 11 December 1948,

Taking note of the report of the Commissioner-General of the United Nations Relief and Works Agency for Palestine Refugees in the Near East, covering the period from 1 July 1981 to 30 June 1982,

1. *Notes with regret* that repatriation or compensation of the refugees as provided for in paragraph 11 of General Assembly resolution 194(III) has not been effected, that no substantial progress has been made in the programme endorsed by the Assembly in paragraph 2 of its resolution 513(VI) of 26 January 1952 for the reintegration of refugees either by repatriation or resettlement and that, therefore, the situation of the refugees continues to be a matter of serious concern;

2. *Expresses its thanks* to the Commissioner-General and to all the staff of the United Nations Relief and Works Agency for Palestine Refugees in the Near East, recognizing that the Agency is doing all it can within the limits of available resources, and also expresses its thanks to the specialized agencies and private organizations for their valuable work in assisting the refugees;

3. *Reiterates its request* that the headquarters of the United Nations Relief and Works Agency for Palestine Refugees in the Near East should be relocated to its former site within its area of operations as soon as practicable;

4. *Notes with regret* that the United Nations Conciliation Commission for Palestine has been unable to find a means of achieving progress in the implementation of paragraph 11 of General Assembly resolution 194(III) and requests the Commission to exert continued efforts towards the implementation of that paragraph and to report to the Assembly as appropriate, but not later than 1 October 1983;

5. *Directs attention* to the continuing seriousness of the financial position of the United Nations Relief and Works Agency for Palestine Refugees in the Near East, as outlined in the report of the Commissioner-General;

6. *Notes with concern* that, despite the commendable and successful efforts of the Commissioner-General to collect additional contributions, this increased level of income to the United Nations Relief and Works Agency for Palestine Refugees in the Near East is still insufficient to cover essential budget requirements in the present year and that, at currently foreseen levels of giving, deficits will recur each year;

7. *Calls upon* all Governments as a matter of urgency to make the most generous efforts possible to meet the anticipated needs of the United Nations Relief and Works Agency for Palestine Refugees in the Near East, particularly in the light of the budgetary deficit projected in the report of the Commissioner-General, and therefore urges non-contributing Governments to contribute regularly and contributing Governments to consider increasing their regular contributions.

Recorded vote in Assembly as follows:

In favour: Afghanistan, Algeria, Angola, Argentina, Australia, Austria, Bahamas, Bahrain, Bangladesh, Barbados, Belgium, Belize, Benin, Bhutan, Bolivia, Botswana, Brazil, Bulgaria, Burma, Burundi, Byelorussian SSR, Canada, Cape Verde, Central African Republic, Chad, Chile, China, Colombia, Comoros, Congo, Costa Rica, Cuba, Cyprus, Czechoslovakia, Democratic Kampuchea, Democratic Yemen, Denmark, Djibouti, Dominican Republic, Ecuador, Egypt, El Salvador, Ethiopia, Fiji, Finland, France, Gabon, Gambia, German Democratic Republic, Germany, Federal Republic of, Ghana, Greece, Grenada, Guatemala, Guinea, Guinea-Bissau, Guyana, Honduras, Hungary, Iceland, India, Indonesia, Iran, Iraq, Ireland, Italy, Ivory Coast, Jamaica, Japan, Jordan, Kenya, Kuwait, Lao People's Democratic Republic, Lebanon, Lesotho, Liberia, Libyan Arab Jamahiriya, Luxembourg, Madagascar, Malawi, Malaysia, Maldives, Mali, Malta, Mauritania, Mauritius, Mexico, Mongolia, Morocco, Mozambique, Nepal, Netherlands, New Zealand, Nicaragua, Nigeria, Norway, Oman, Pakistan, Panama, Papua New Guinea, Paraguay, Peru, Philippines, Poland, Portugal, Qatar, Romania, Rwanda, Samoa, Sao Tome and Principe, Saudi Arabia, Senegal, Seychelles, Sierra Leone, Singapore, Somalia, Spain, Sri Lanka, Sudan, Suriname, Sweden, Syrian Arab Republic, Thailand, Togo, Trinidad and Tobago, Tunisia, Turkey, Uganda, Ukrainian SSR, USSR, United Arab Emirates, United Kingdom, United Republic of Cameroon, United Republic of Tanzania, United States, Upper Volta, Uruguay, Vanuatu, Venezuela, Viet Nam, Yemen, Yugoslavia, Zaire, Zambia.

Against: None.

Abstaining: Israel.

Accounts for 1981

For the year ended 31 December 1981, expenditure and commitments of UNRWA amounted to $180,728,868 under its General Fund in addition to an expenditure of $170,424 under the Bayssarieh Camp Fund.[1]

The Board of Auditors noted that, while UNRWA had made significant improvement in the investment of its funds, it had not developed detailed guidelines prescribing procedures and policies relating to financial management and control over investments of temporary cash balances. It also noted that approximately $27.5 million of $171.5 million pledged by Governments for 1981 remained unpaid as at 31 December 1981. In view of the financial difficulties, the Board again recommended that UNRWA intensify its efforts to collect outstanding pledges on time.

By a resolution of 16 November 1982,[2] the General Assembly accepted the UNRWA financial report and accounts, endorsed the audit opinion of the Board and requested remedial action as required by the Board's comments and observations.

Report. [1]Board of Auditors and financial statements, A/37/5/Add.3.
Resolution (1982). [2]GA: 37/12, 16 Nov.

Arrest of UNRWA staff

Report of the Secretary-General. In November 1982, the Secretary-General informed the General Assembly that between 1 July 1981 and 30 June 1982, UNRWA had reported 28 cases of arrest and detention of its staff: 18 in the West Bank, five in the Gaza Strip, four in the Syrian Arab Republic and one in Jordan.[1] Of those, one in the Syrian Arab Republic was still in detention at the end of

June, while two in the West Bank and one in Jordan had been tried and convicted; the remaining 24 had been released without charge or trial after varying periods of detention, the longest having been one year in the Syrian Arab Republic.

Since June 1982, UNRWA had received reports of 166 cases of arrest of its staff in Lebanon by the Israeli armed forces. Of these, 37 had been released by the end of September. UNRWA had no further information on two staff members in the Syrian Arab Republic—one detained since September 1980 and the other missing since April 1980.

Report of the Commissioner-General. In his report for the year ended 30 June 1982,[2] the UNRWA Commissioner-General observed that the difficulties in obtaining adequate and timely information from the authorities concerned on the reasons for the arrest and detention prevented UNRWA from ascertaining whether the staff member's official functions were involved, and consequently hampered its giving effect to the rights and duties of the staff member and the Agency itself under the Charter of the United Nations and the 1946 Convention on the Privileges and Immunities of the United Nations.[4]

The Commissioner-General told SPC on 9 November that some of the 2,373 locally-recruited UNRWA staff in Lebanon, most of whom were Palestinian refugees themselves, had disappeared or been arrested, and 125 of them were still in detention.

General Assembly action. Drawing attention to the unprecedented character of the mass arrest of UNRWA officials by Israeli authorities in Lebanon, the General Assembly, by a resolution of 21 December,[3] called on the Secretary-General to take measures without delay to establish the whereabouts of, to find out the charges against and to arrange a meeting with the incarcerated, in order to obtain their earliest release.

The resolution was adopted by a recorded vote of 141 to 1, with 1 abstention, following its approval by the Fifth (Administrative and Budgetary) Committee on 14 December by a vote, requested by Israel, of 94 to 1, with 2 abstentions.

Introducing the draft also on behalf of Cuba, Yemen said the arrest and detention of international civil servants by Israeli authorities violated international law and the privileges and immunities of United Nations staff (see ADMINISTRATIVE AND BUDGETARY QUESTIONS, Chapter III), and set an extremely dangerous precedent.

Israel, on the other hand, stated that the only civilians detained in southern Lebanon had been those suspected of having engaged in or been connected with terrorist activities against Israel; all those not guilty of any wrongdoing had been released. Representatives of the International

Committee of the Red Cross had visited the detainees and Israel was in contact with UNRWA.

In the opinion of the USSR, the resolution raised a number of important issues and was a test case for the United Nations; the information available to the Secretary-General was unsatisfactory and the Committee had yet to receive a clear reply with regard to the possibility of arranging for access to the detained UNRWA staff.

Morocco charged that Israel did not intend to observe the principles related to privileges and immunities of United Nations officials; the detainees in question were not terrorists and had been imprisoned as a result of their attempt to ensure that international principles were observed.

Voting in favour, Canada and Honduras said it was worth remembering that the staff referred to in the resolution were not the only ones still imprisoned. Sweden, joined by the Netherlands, said the particular case of UNRWA staff need not have been singled out in a separate resolution, the wording of which they had reservations about.

Reports. [1]S-G, A/C.5/37/34; [2]UNRWA Commissioner-General, A/37/13.
Resolution (1982). [3]GA: 37/236 B, 21 Dec., text following.
Resolution (prior). [4]GA: 22 A (I), annex, 13 Feb. 1946 (YUN 1946-47, p. 100).
Meeting records. GA: 5th Committee, A/C.5/37/SR.23, 25-34, 36-38, 40, 41, 43, 47, *65, 70* (1 Nov.–14 Dec.); plenary, A/37/PV.114 (21 Dec.).

General Assembly resolution 37/236 B

21 December 1982   Meeting 114   141-1-1 (recorded vote)

Approved by Fifth Committee (A/37/764) by vote (94-1-2), 14 December (meeting 70); 2-nation draft (A/C.5/37/L.42); agenda item 111 *(b).*

Sponsors: Cuba, Yemen.

The General Assembly,

Having considered the report of the Secretary-General on respect for the privileges and immunities of officials of the United Nations and the specialized agencies and related organizations,

Drawing attention to the unprecedented character of the mass arrest by the Israeli authorities in the territory of Lebanon of a great number of the officials of the United Nations Relief and Works Agency for Palestine Refugees in the Near East, and as mentioned in paragraph 6 of the Secretary-General's report,

1. *Calls upon* the Secretary-General to take measures without delay to establish the whereabouts of, to find out the charges made against and to arrange a meeting with the officials of the United Nations Relief and Works Agency for Palestine Refugees in the Near East incarcerated by the Israeli authorities in Lebanon, in order to obtain their earliest release;

2. *Requests* the Secretary-General to inform Member States promptly about measures taken under paragraph 1 above and about their results.

Recorded vote in Assembly as follows:

In favour: Afghanistan, Algeria, Angola, Argentina, Australia, Austria, Bahamas, Bahrain, Bangladesh, Barbados, Belgium, Benin, Bhutan, Bolivia, Botswana, Brazil, Bulgaria, Burma, Burundi, Byelorussian SSR, Canada, Cape Verde, Central African Republic, Chad, Chile, China, Colombia, Comoros, Congo, Costa Rica, Cuba, Cyprus, Czechoslovakia, Democratic Kampuchea, Democratic Yemen, Denmark, Dominican Republic, Ecuador, Egypt, El Salvador, Ethiopia, Fiji, Finland, France, Gabon, Gambia, German Democratic Republic, Germany, Federal Republic of, Ghana, Greece, Grenada, Guinea, Guinea-Bissau, Guyana, Honduras, Hungary, Iceland, India, Indonesia, Iran, Iraq, Ireland, Italy, Ivory Coast, Jamaica, Japan, Jordan, Kenya, Kuwait, Lao People's Democratic Republic, Lebanon, Lesotho, Liberia, Libyan Arab Jamahiriya, Luxembourg, Madagascar, Malawi, Malaysia, Maldives, Mali, Malta, Mauritania, Mexico, Mongolia, Morocco, Mozambique, Nepal, Netherlands, New Zealand, Nicaragua, Niger, Nigeria, Nor-

way, Oman, Pakistan, Panama, Papua New Guinea, Paraguay, Peru, Philippines, Poland, Portugal, Qatar, Romania, Rwanda, Saint Lucia, Samoa, Sao Tome and Principe, Saudi Arabia, Senegal, Sierra Leone, Singapore, Solomon Islands, Somalia, Spain, Sri Lanka, Sudan, Suriname, Swaziland, Sweden, Syrian Arab Republic, Thailand, Togo, Trinidad and Tobago, Tunisia, Turkey, Uganda, Ukrainian SSR, USSR, United Arab Emirates, United Kingdom, United Republic of Cameroon, United Republic of Tanzania, Upper Volta, Uruguay, Venezuela, Viet Nam, Yemen, Yugoslavia, Zaire, Zambia.

Against: Israel.

Abstaining: United States.

Special aspects

Assistance to displaced persons

Expressing concern about the continued human suffering resulting from the hostilities in the Middle East, the General Assembly, by a resolution of 16 December 1982,[1] endorsed the efforts of the UNRWA Commissioner-General to continue to provide humanitarian assistance, on an emergency basis and as a temporary measure, to persons displaced as a result of the June 1967 and subsequent hostilities and in need of continued assistance. Governments, organizations and individuals were asked to contribute for that purpose to UNRWA and other organizations concerned.

The resolution was adopted without vote, following its approval in like manner by SPC on 3 December.

Introducing the 19-nation text, Sweden said it was similar to previous resolutions on the question, except that a reference to hostilities subsequent to those of 1967 had been added in order to take account of the new situation confronting UNRWA.

Resolution (1982). [1]GA: 37/120 B, 16 Dec., text following.
Meeting records. GA: SPC, A/SPC/37/SR.24, 26-31, *32, 33, 44, 45* (9 Nov.–6 Dec.); plenary, A/37/PV.108 (16 Dec.).

General Assembly resolution 37/120 B

16 December 1982   Meeting 108   Adopted without vote

Approved by SPC (A/37/723) without vote, 3 December (meeting 44); 19-nation draft (A/SPC/37/L.11); agenda item 65.

Sponsors: Austria, Belgium, Canada, Cyprus, Denmark, Finland, Germany, Federal Republic of, Greece, India, Indonesia, Ireland, Italy, Japan, Netherlands, Norway, Pakistan, Philippines, Sri Lanka, Sweden.

Assistance to persons displaced as a result of the June 1967 and subsequent hostilities

The General Assembly,

Recalling its resolution 36/146 D of 16 December 1981 and all previous resolutions on the question,

Taking note of the report of the Commissioner-General of the United Nations Relief and Works Agency for Palestine Refugees in the Near East, covering the period from 1 July 1981 to 30 June 1982, and his special report covering the period from 6 June to 31 August 1982,

Concerned about the continued human suffering resulting from the hostilities in the Middle East,

1. *Reaffirms* its resolution 36/146 D and all previous resolutions on the question;

2. *Endorses,* bearing in mind the objectives of those resolutions, the efforts of the Commissioner-General of the United Nations Relief and Works Agency for Palestine Refugees in the Near East to continue to provide humanitarian assistance as far as practicable, on an emergency basis and as a temporary measure, to other persons in the area who are at present displaced and in serious need of continued assistance as a result of the June 1967 and subsequent hostilities;

3. *Strongly appeals* to all Governments and to organizations and individuals to contribute generously for the above purposes to the United Nations Relief and Works Agency for Palestine Refugees in the Near East and to the other intergovernmental and non-governmental organizations concerned.

Repatriation

Action by the Commission on Human Rights. In a resolution of 11 February 1982,[3] the Commission on Human Rights called on Israel to take immediate steps for the return of the displaced Arab inhabitants to their homes and property in Palestine and the other occupied territories.

Report of the Secretary-General. By a report of 20 September 1982,[2] the Secretary-General informed the General Assembly that, in accordance with a December 1981 Assembly resolution,[7] he had requested from Israel information on steps taken for the return of all displaced inhabitants. By a note verbale of 27 August 1982, Israel had reaffirmed its position as set out in previous years, i.e., that the primary objective of the resolution on repatriation was to obstruct the ongoing peace process and to serve the aims of those Arab States with hostile and destructive intentions towards Israel. Notwithstanding the security risks involved, which inevitably resulted in some constraints on the return of displaced persons, Israel remained committed to its humanitarian approach of family reunification.

Report of the Conciliation Commission. By a report transmitted to the Assembly on 29 September,[1] the United Nations Conciliation Commission for Palestine reiterated its previous conclusion that all the ways envisaged for advancing towards repatriation and resettlement of displaced persons presupposed substantial changes in the situation. Recent events had further complicated an already very complex situation and the Commission's possibilities of action remained limited. However, the Commission expressed the hope that the situation would improve towards the achievement of a comprehensive, just and lasting Middle East peace, thus enabling it to carry out its mandate.

General Assembly action. Reaffirming the right of all displaced inhabitants to return to their homes or former places of residence in the occupied territories, the General Assembly, by a resolution of 16 December,[5] considered all agreements restricting or attaching conditions for their return as null and void. It deplored Israel's continued refusal to take steps for the return of displaced inhabitants, and called on it to take such steps and to desist from all measures obstructing the return, including those affecting the physical and demographic structure of the occupied territories.

In a resolution on assistance to Palestine refugees, adopted on the same date,[6] the Assembly noted with regret that repatriation or compensation of the refugees had not been effected and that no substantial progress had been made in the reintegration of refugees either by repatriation or resettlement. The Assembly requested the Conciliation Commission to exert continued efforts towards that goal and to report to it not later than 1 October 1983.

The repatriation concept was also included in the Assembly's resolution of 24 September on the Palestine question and the Israel-Lebanon situation,[4] adopted shortly after the massacre in the Beirut area. The Assembly resolved that, in conformity with past resolutions, Palestine refugees should be enabled to return to their homes and property from which they had been uprooted and displaced, and demanded unconditional and immediate Israeli compliance.

The resolution on displaced inhabitants of the occupied territories was adopted by a recorded vote of 126 to 2, with 19 abstentions, following its approval by SPC on 3 December by a recorded vote of 97 to 2, with 19 abstentions.

Bangladesh introduced the draft, also on behalf of Afghanistan, India, Indonesia, Pakistan and Yugoslavia, saying it was of a humanitarian nature.

Israel explained that it voted against the resolution in view of its obviously destructive intent; the text was out of touch with the facts, as over 60,000 displaced persons had been permitted to return to their homes since 1967.

The United States opposed it on the grounds that it purported to prejudge the issues of repatriation and compensation, which could only be settled through negotiations between the parties. New Zealand and Sweden abstained for similar reasons.

Canada abstained saying that paragraph 2 was an implicit criticism of the Camp David accords, which Canada supported as providing a possible basis for a negotiated settlement of the Palestinian problem.

Explaining their votes for the September resolution, Canada, Denmark (also speaking for Belgium, France, the Federal Republic of Germany, Ireland, Italy, Luxembourg, the Netherlands and the United Kingdom), Haiti, New Zealand and Norway reserved their positions on the provision concerning the right of the Palestinians to return home. Canada felt that the nature of a settlement of the refugee problem should not be prejudged but determined in negotiations; Denmark, Ireland and New Zealand believed that the rights of the Palestine refugees should be addressed in the context of a comprehensive peace settlement, and Haiti said refuge must be found for the Palestinians on the basis of the 1967 Security Council resolution on principles for a Middle East peace.[8]

Reports. [1]Conciliation Commission for Palestine, transmitted by S-G note, A/37/497; [2]S-G, A/37/426.
Resolutions (1982). [3]Commission on Human Rights (report, E/1982/12): 1982/1 A, para. 6, 11 Feb. GA: [4]ES-7/9, para. 6, 24 Sep.; [5]37/120 G, 16 Dec., text following; [6]37/120 K, paras. 1 & 4, 16 Dec.
Resolutions (prior). [7]GA: 36/146 B, 16 Dec. 1981 (YUN 1981, p. 334); [8]SC: 242(1967), 22 Nov. 1967 (YUN 1967, p. 257).
Meeting records. GA: SPC, A/SPC/37/SR.24, 26-33, *42, 44, 45* (9 Nov.–6 Dec.); plenary, A/37/PV.108 (16 Dec.).

General Assembly resolution 37/120 G

16 December 1982   Meeting 108   126-2-19 (recorded vote)

Approved by SPC (A/37/723) by recorded vote (97-2-19), 3 December (meeting 44); 6-nation draft (A/SPC/37/L.21); agenda item 65.

Sponsors: Afghanistan, Bangladesh, India, Indonesia, Pakistan, Yugoslavia.

Population and refugees displaced since 1967

The General Assembly,

Recalling Security Council resolution 237(1967) of 14 June 1967,

Recalling also General Assembly resolutions 2252(ES-V) of 4 July 1967, 2452 A (XXIII) of 19 December 1968, 2535 B (XXIV) of 10 December 1969, 2672 D (XXV) of 8 December 1970, 2792 E (XXVI) of 6 December 1971, 2963 C and D (XXVII) of 13 December 1972, 3089 C (XXVIII) of 7 December 1973, 3331 D (XXIX) of 17 December 1974, 3419 C (XXX) of 8 December 1975, 31/15 D of 23 November 1976, 32/90 E of 13 December 1977, 33/112 F of 18 December 1978, 34/52 E of 23 November 1979, ES-7/2 of 29 July 1980, 35/13 E of 3 November 1980 and 36/146 B of 16 December 1981,

Having considered the report of the Commissioner-General of the United Nations Relief and Works Agency for Palestine Refugees in the Near East, covering the period from 1 July 1981 to 30 June 1982, and the report of the Secretary-General of 20 September 1982,

1. *Reaffirms* the inalienable right of all displaced inhabitants to return to their homes or former places of residence in the territories occupied by Israel since 1967 and declares once more that any attempt to restrict, or to attach conditions to, the free exercise of the right of return by any displaced person is inconsistent with that inalienable right and inadmissible;

2. *Considers* any and all agreements embodying any restriction on or condition for the return of the displaced inhabitants as null and void;

3. *Strongly deplores* the continued refusal of the Israeli authorities to take steps for the return of the displaced inhabitants;

4. *Calls once more upon* Israel:

(a) To take immediate steps for the return of all displaced inhabitants;

(b) To desist from all measures that obstruct the return of the displaced inhabitants, including measures affecting the physical and demographic structure of the occupied territories;

5. *Requests* the Secretary-General, after consulting with the Commissioner-General of the United Nations Relief and Works Agency for Palestine Refugees in the Near East, to report to the General Assembly before the opening of its thirty-eighth session on Israel's compliance with paragraph 4 above.

Recorded vote in Assembly as follows:

In favour: Afghanistan, Albania, Algeria, Angola, Argentina, Bahamas, Bahrain, Bangladesh, Barbados, Belize, Benin, Bhutan, Bolivia, Botswana, Brazil, Bulgaria, Burma, Burundi, Byelorussian SSR, Cape Verde, Central African Republic, Chad, Chile, China, Colombia, Comoros, Congo, Costa Rica, Cuba, Cyprus, Czechoslovakia, Democratic Kampuchea, Democratic Yemen, Djibouti, Dominican Republic, Ecuador, Egypt, El Salvador, Ethiopia, Fiji, Gabon, Gambia, German Democratic Republic, Ghana, Greece, Grenada, Guinea, Guinea-Bissau, Guyana, Honduras, Hungary, India, Indonesia, Iran, Iraq, Ivory Coast, Jamaica, Japan, Jordan, Kenya, Kuwait, Lao People's Democratic Republic, Lebanon, Lesotho, Liberia, Libyan Arab Jamahiriya, Madagascar, Malaysia, Maldives, Mali, Malta, Mauritania, Mauritius, Mexico, Mongolia, Morocco, Mozambique, Nepal, Nicaragua, Nigeria, Oman, Pakistan, Panama, Papua New Guinea, Paraguay, Peru, Philippines, Poland, Portugal, Qatar, Romania, Rwanda, Samoa, Sao Tome and Principe, Saudi Arabia, Senegal, Seychelles, Sierra Leone, Singapore, Somalia, Spain, Sri Lanka, Sudan, Suriname, Syrian Arab Republic, Thailand, Togo, Trinidad and Tobago, Tunisia, Turkey, Uganda, Ukrainian SSR, USSR, United Arab Emirates, United Republic of Cameroon, United Republic of Tanzania, Upper Volta, Uruguay, Vanuatu, Venezuela, Viet Nam, Yemen, Yugoslavia, Zaire, Zambia, Zimbabwe.

Against: Israel, United States.

Abstaining: Australia, Austria, Belgium, Canada, Denmark, Finland, France, Germany, Federal Republic of, Guatemala, Iceland, Ireland, Italy, Luxembourg, Malawi, Netherlands, New Zealand, Norway, Sweden, United Kingdom.

Resettlement of refugees in the Gaza Strip

Report of the Secretary-General. In a report of 17 September 1982,[1] submitted in accordance with a December 1981 General Assembly resolution calling on Israel to desist from removing and resettling Palestine refugees in the Gaza Strip and from destroying their shelters,[3] the Secretary-

General stated that, by a note verbale of 1 March 1982, he had requested Israel to inform him of the implementation of that resolution. Replying on 27 August, Israel reiterated its previous position (stating that refugee families were being assisted in obtaining better housing outside the squalid and cramped conditions in the camps).

The report also provided information from the Commissioner-General of the United Nations Relief and Works Agency for Palestine Refugees in the Near East (UNRWA), which indicated that UNRWA had constructed replacement shelters for the refugee families whose shelters had been demolished by Israel on punitive grounds in 1981. While the Israeli Minister of Defence subsequently informed UNRWA of the plans on humanitarian grounds to resettle those families in a housing project in Gaza, the families whose shelters had been demolished in 1979 and 1980 had not been rehoused, nor had UNRWA been compensated for the demolition of the shelters.

UNRWA further reported that, in the year under review, 358 refugee families from the camps and 35 families from outside the camps had moved into homes built on land they had purchased in one or another Israeli housing project; 314 shelter rooms in the camps were demolished in compliance with the Israeli pre-condition for the acquisition of new housing. The Israeli authorities had to date allocated 2,866 plots of land in the Gaza Strip for housing projects for refugees; on 919 of these, houses had been built and were occupied by 1,143 families (6,936 persons)—including 1,077 refugee families (6,545 persons)—while houses were under construction on 736 plots. Three new housing projects in Beit, Lahia and Nazleh were under development.

With the re-establishment of the border between Egypt and the Gaza Strip following the return of the Sinai to Egypt in April 1982, 515 shelter rooms housing 173 families (1,060 persons) had been demolished in order to make way for a security zone and a border fence. The occupying authorities had paid compensation to all the families concerned, and they took advantage of the Israeli offer of plots of land in a housing project.

General Assembly action. By a resolution of 16 December 1982,[2] the General Assembly reiterated its demand that Israel desist from removing and resettling Palestine refugees in Gaza and from destroying their shelters, and requested the Secretary-General to report before its 1983 regular session on Israel's compliance.

The resolution was adopted by a recorded vote of 143 to 2, following its approval by SPC on 3 December by a recorded vote of 114 to 2. It was introduced by Pakistan, also on behalf of Afghanistan, Bangladesh, Egypt, India, Indonesia and Yugoslavia.

Israel rejected the resolution, saying that it disregarded the true needs of the refugees and that demanding Israel to cease rehousing them in better accommodation was cynical.

The United States said it opposed the text because of its biased nature, singling out for censure Israel's destruction of certain refugee shelters, while ignoring the fact that Israel had made available new and superior housing to many refugees.

While supporting the text, Denmark, speaking for the 10 States members of the European Community (EC), noted that, according to the Commissioner-General's reports, no demolition of refugees shelters on punitive grounds had occurred during the period under review; also, the resolution should not be held to interfere with the refugees' freedom to choose where they wished to live.

Report. [1]S-G, A/37/425 & Corr.1.
Resolution (1982). [2]GA: 37/120 E, 16 Dec., text following.
Resolution (prior). [3]GA: 36/146 A, 16 Dec. 1981 (YUN 1981, p. 335).
Meeting records. GA: SPC, A/SPC/37/SR.24, 26-33, 42, 44, 45 (9 Nov.–6 Dec.); plenary, A/37/PV.108 (16 Dec.).

General Assembly resolution 37/120 E

16 December 1982   Meeting 108   143-2 (recorded vote)

Approved by SPC (A/37/723) by recorded vote (114-2), 3 December (meeting 44); 7-nation draft (A/SPC/37/L.19); agenda item 65.

Sponsors: Afghanistan, Bangladesh, Egypt, India, Indonesia, Pakistan, Yugoslavia.

Palestine refugees in the Gaza Strip

The General Assembly,

Recalling Security Council resolution 237(1967) of 14 June 1967,

Recalling also its resolutions 2792 C (XXVI) of 6 December 1971, 2963 C (XXVII) of 13 December 1972, 3089 C (XXVIII) of 7 December 1973, 3331 D (XXIX) of 17 December 1974, 3419 C (XXX) of 8 December 1975, 31/15 E of 23 November 1976, 32/90 C of 13 December 1977, 33/112 E of 18 December 1978, 34/52 F of 23 November 1979, 35/13 F of 3 November 1980 and 36/146 A of 16 December 1981,

Having considered the report of the Commissioner-General of the United Nations Relief and Works Agency for Palestine Refugees in the Near East, covering the period from 1 July 1981 to 30 June 1982, and the report of the Secretary-General of 17 September 1982,

Recalling the provisions of paragraph 11 of its resolution 194(III) of 11 December 1948 and considering that measures to resettle Palestine refugees in the Gaza Strip away from the homes and property from which they were displaced constitute a violation of their inalienable right of return,

Alarmed by the reports received from the Commissioner-General that the Israeli occupying authorities persist in their policy of demolishing, on punitive grounds, shelters occupied by refugee families,

1. *Reiterates its demand* that Israel desist from the removal and resettlement of Palestine refugees in the Gaza Strip and from the destruction of their shelters;

2. *Requests* the Secretary-General, after consulting with the Commissioner-General of the United Nations Relief and Works Agency for Palestine Refugees in the Near East, to report to the General Assembly, before the opening of its thirty-eighth session, on Israel's compliance with paragraph 1 above.

Recorded vote in Assembly as follows:

In favour: Afghanistan, Albania, Algeria, Angola, Argentina, Australia, Austria, Bahamas, Bahrain, Bangladesh, Barbados, Belgium, Belize, Benin, Bhutan, Bolivia, Botswana, Brazil, Bulgaria, Burma, Burundi, Byelorussian SSR, Canada, Cape Verde, Central African Republic, Chad, Chile, China, Colombia, Comoros, Congo, Costa Rica, Cuba, Cyprus, Czechoslovakia, Democratic Kampuchea, Democratic Yemen, Denmark, Djibouti, Dominican Republic, Ecuador, Egypt, El Salvador, Ethiopia, Fiji, Finland, France, Gabon, Gambia, German Democratic Republic, Germany, Federal Republic of, Ghana, Greece, Grenada, Guinea, Guinea-Bissau, Guyana, Honduras, Hungary, Iceland, India, Indonesia, Iran, Iraq, Ireland, Italy, Ivory Coast, Jamaica, Japan, Jordan, Kenya, Kuwait, Lao People's Democratic Republic, Lebanon, Liberia, Libyan Arab Jamahiriya, Luxembourg, Madagascar, Malawi, Malaysia, Maldives, Mali, Malta, Mauritania, Mauritius, Mexico, Mongolia, Morocco, Mozambique, Nepal, Netherlands, New Zealand, Nicaragua, Nigeria, Norway, Oman, Pakistan, Panama, Papua New Guinea, Paraguay, Peru, Philippines, Poland, Portugal, Qatar, Romania, Rwanda, Samoa, Sao Tome and Principe, Saudi Arabia, Senegal, Seychelles, Sierra Leone, Singapore, Somalia, Spain, Sri Lanka, Sudan, Suriname, Sweden, Syrian Arab Republic, Thailand, Togo, Trinidad and Tobago, Tunisia, Turkey, Uganda, Ukrainian SSR, USSR, United Arab Emirates, United Kingdom, United Republic of Cameroon, United Republic of Tanzania, Upper Volta, Uruguay, Vanuatu, Venezuela, Viet Nam, Yemen, Yugoslavia, Zaire, Zambia, Zimbabwe.

Against: Israel, United States.

Protection

By a resolution of 16 December 1982,[1] the General Assembly urged the Secretary-General, in consultation with UNRWA, to undertake effective measures to guarantee the safety and security and the legal and human rights of the Palestine refugees in the occupied territories. It called on Israel to release all detained Palestine refugees, including UNRWA employees (see above), and requested the Secretary-General, in consultation with the UNRWA Commissioner-General, to report to it before its 1983 regular session. Under other provisions, the Assembly dealt mainly with protection of Palestinian refugees in Lebanon following the Israeli invasion in June.

Commenting on the text, the United Nations Legal Counsel told SPC on 3 December that the 1949 Geneva Convention relative to the Protection of Civilian Persons in Time of War, which the Assembly held applicable to the situation in the territories occupied by Israel, reiterated the general principle of international law that the occupying Power was responsible for ensuring human and other rights within such territories, and that any external attempts to assume part of that responsibility would obscure that duty of the occupying Power. Further, it was difficult to see how the Secretary-General could guarantee the safety and rights of the Palestinian refugees without exercising certain sovereign powers, including police powers, in the occupied territories or exerting authority and control over the occupying Power itself. When international organizations carried out any activity within a given territory, they must do so with the consent and co-operation of the authorities; if such conditions were not met, the Secretary-General would be unable to undertake the measures required to fulfil the objectives of the resolution.

The United Arab Emirates asserted that the Geneva Convention also provided for the possibility of entrusting an organization with the duties incumbent on the protecting Power, which was supposed to see to it that the Convention provisions were observed, especially when the occupying Power was delinquent in applying them. Israel having violated almost every provision of the Convention, the United Nations or any of its organs could act as protecting Power; it was not asking the Secretary-General to assume police powers.

Speaking for the EC members which abstained, Denmark questioned the appropriateness of calling on the Secretary-General to guarantee the safety and security as well as the legal and human rights of the Palestinian refugees; it also considered it important not to detract from the responsibility of the occupying Power to protect the civilian population. A similar opinion was expressed by Canada and Ireland.

Although voting in favour, Sweden did not believe it proper to place that responsibility on the Secretary-General, while Venezuela said the clause should be implemented with the full consent of the authorities of the country concerned and without undermining sovereign rights. Austria, Finland, Jamaica, New Zealand, Peru, the Philippines and Uruguay also voiced reservations on that provision.

Lebanon said the withdrawal of non-Lebanese forces from the country would enable it to provide the necessary protection for all those residing in its territory.

Resolution (1982). [1]GA: 37/120 J, 16 Dec.

Identification cards

By a resolution of 16 December 1982,[1] the General Assembly requested the Secretary-General, in co-operation with the UNRWA Commissioner-General, to issue identification cards to all Palestine refugees and their descendants, as well as to all displaced persons and those prevented from returning to their homes as a result of the 1967 hostilities. The Secretary-General was requested to report to the Assembly in 1983.

The resolution was adopted by a recorded vote of 106 to 16, with 20 abstentions, following its approval by SPC on 3 December by a recorded vote of 83 to 16, with 16 abstentions.

Pakistan, introducing the text also on behalf of Afghanistan, Bangladesh, Cuba, Indonesia and Yugoslavia, said it was designed to facilitate the work of UNRWA; the provision of identification cards might help not to have the Palestinian refugees regarded as terrorists and disturbers of peace.

Lebanon cast a negative vote saying the proposal, whose objectives it did not understand, required additional study and possible consultations at the level of the League of Arab States; any action which might involve a census-taking of any group in Lebanon should have Lebanon's prior approval.

The United States said the resolution had been drawn up with too little thought given to its legal and practical effects and the enormous costs of no less than $10 million for its implementation. Australia cited similar reasons for its negative vote.

In Canada's view, it was not clear under what authority the Secretary-General, in co-operation with the UNRWA Commissioner-General, would be able to issue identification cards to all Pales-

tine refugees and their descendants, irrespective of their location.

Though being sympathetic to the issuing of identification cards, the United Kingdom believed that the resolution did not give proper consideration to the far-reaching legal, administrative and financial implications. In the view of Belgium, the Federal Republic of Germany and the Netherlands, those implications required more detailed consideration. Abstaining, Ireland held a similar position.

Austria, which also abstained, doubted whether UNRWA could implement the resolution due to financial or political and legal impediments. The Philippines said it did not have a clear idea of the practical benefits or possible legal implications of special identification cards. Uruguay said the text ignored a fundamental principle of international law by failing to mention due respect for the rights and sovereignty of the States in the area. In Sweden's opinion, the resolution would place on the Secretary-General new tasks which would be extremely difficult to carry out in the current circumstances.

Poland, while voting in favour, voiced concern at what it called the unwarranted cost involved in implementing the resolution. Also voting for the resolution, Venezuela said it understood that the issuance of identification cards would be carried out with the full consent of the authorities of the country concerned and without undermining its sovereign rights.

Resolution (1982). [1]GA: 37/120 I, 16 Dec., text following.
Financial implications. 5th Committee report, A/37/747; S-G statements, A/SPC/37/L.40, A/C.5/37/88.
Meeting records. GA: SPC, A/SPC/37/SR.24, 26-33, *42, 44, 45* (9 Nov.–6 Dec.); 5th Committee, A/C.5/37/SR.66 (13 Dec.); plenary, A/37/PV.108 (16 Dec.).

General Assembly resolution 37/120 I

16 December 1982   Meeting 108   106-16-20 (recorded vote)

Approved by SPC (A/37/723) by recorded vote (83-16-16), 3 December (meeting 44); 6-nation draft (A/SPC/37/L.23); agenda item 65.

Sponsors: Afghanistan, Bangladesh, Cuba, Indonesia, Pakistan, Yugoslavia.

Special identification cards to all Palestine refugees

The General Assembly,

Recalling its resolution 36/146 F of 16 December 1981 and all previous resolutions on the question,

Recalling, in particular, its resolutions 194(III) of 11 December 1948 and 302(IV) of 8 December 1949,

Recognizing the concern of the United Nations with the problem of the Palestine refugees,

1. *Reiterates its regret* that paragraph 11 of General Assembly resolution 194(III) has not thus far been implemented;

2. *Requests* the Secretary-General, in co-operation with the Commissioner-General of the United Nations Relief and Works Agency for Palestine Refugees in the Near East, to issue identification cards to all Palestine refugees and their descendants, irrespective of whether they are recipients or not of rations and services from the Agency, as well as to all displaced persons and to those who have been prevented from returning to their homes as a result of the 1967 hostilities, and their descendants;

3. *Requests* the Secretary-General to report to the General Assembly at its thirty-eighth session on the implementation of the present resolution.

Recorded vote in Assembly as follows:

In favour: Afghanistan, Albania, Algeria, Angola, Argentina, Bahrain, Bangladesh, Benin, Bhutan, Bolivia, Botswana, Brazil, Bulgaria, Burundi, Byelorussian SSR, Cape Verde, Central African Republic, Chad, China, Colombia, Comoros, Congo, Cuba, Cyprus, Czechoslovakia, Democratic Kampuchea, Democratic Yemen, Djibouti, Dominican Republic, Ecuador, Egypt, El Salvador, Ethiopia, Gabon, Gambia, German Democratic Republic, Ghana, Greece, Grenada, Guinea, Guinea-Bissau, Guyana, Honduras, Hungary, India, Indonesia, Iran, Iraq, Ivory Coast, Jordan, Kenya, Kuwait, Lao People's Democratic Republic, Lesotho, Liberia, Libyan Arab Jamahiriya, Madagascar, Malaysia, Maldives, Mali, Malta, Mauritania, Mauritius, Mexico, Mongolia, Morocco, Mozambique, Nepal, Nicaragua, Nigeria, Oman, Pakistan, Panama, Peru, Poland, Qatar, Romania, Rwanda, Sao Tome and Principe, Saudi Arabia, Senegal, Seychelles, Sierra Leone, Somalia, Sri Lanka, Sudan, Suriname, Syrian Arab Republic, Thailand, Togo, Trinidad and Tobago, Tunisia, Turkey, Uganda, Ukrainian SSR, USSR, United Arab Emirates, United Republic of Cameroon, United Republic of Tanzania, Upper Volta, Vanuatu, Venezuela, Viet Nam, Yemen, Yugoslavia, Zambia.

Against: Australia, Belgium, Canada, Denmark, France, Germany, Federal Republic of, Iceland, Israel, Italy, Japan, Lebanon, Luxembourg, Netherlands, Norway, United Kingdom, United States.

Abstaining: Austria, Bahamas, Barbados, Chile, Costa Rica, Fiji, Finland, Guatemala, Ireland, Jamaica, Malawi, New Zealand, Papua New Guinea, Paraguay, Philippines, Portugal, Spain, Sweden, Uruguay, Zaire.

Property rights

Report of the Secretary-General. On 28 September 1982,[1] the Secretary-General reported to the General Assembly on the implementation of a December 1981 resolution on revenues derived from Palestine refugee properties.[3] He stated that he had brought that resolution to the attention of the Chairman of the United Nations Conciliation Commission for Palestine and to Israel, as well as to all other States, and had requested information on its implementation. In the absence of replies, he had again requested them for information on 12 July. Israel responded on 27 August that its position remained the same as in 1981.[4]

General Assembly action. By a resolution of 16 December 1982,[2] the General Assembly requested the Secretary-General to take all steps, in consultation with the Conciliation Commission, for the protection and administration of Arab property, assets and property rights in Israel, and to establish a fund for the receipt of income derived therefrom. The Assembly called again on the Governments concerned, especially Israel, to assist the Secretary-General in that task, and requested him to report in 1983 on the implementation of the resolution.

The text was adopted by a recorded vote of 121 to 2, with 24 abstentions, following its approval by SPC on 3 December by a recorded vote of 95 to 2, with 21 abstentions. It was introduced by Bangladesh, also on behalf of Afghanistan, India, Indonesia, Pakistan and Yugoslavia, as humanitarian in nature.

Israel rejected the resolution as yet another example of the Arab countries' misuse of the Assembly in pursuit of an anti-Israeli campaign; the subject fell entirely within Israel's sovereign jurisdiction over its internal affairs and the United Nations had no competence in the matter.

Abstaining, Austria voiced serious doubts whether the resolution could be implemented because of political and legal impediments. Speaking for the European Community members, Denmark said a solution to the problem of Palestinian property rights and return of the refugees must be sought in the framework of a just, lasting and comprehensive Middle East settlement. Canada shared that view. Though agreeing in principle that the Palestinian refugees were entitled to their property or to compensation, Sweden believed it unrealistic in the existing circumstances to expect the Secretary-General to accomplish the task.

During the Assembly debate on the Palestine question, the Byelorussian SSR said that, in order to deprive the Palestinians of their lands, Israel resorted to a law dating from the time of the Ottoman Empire requiring the registration of all landholdings, which the occupation authorities made impossible in practice by passing a legislation.

Report. [1]S-G, A/37/488 & Corr.1.
Resolution (1982). [2]GA: 37/120 H, 16 Dec., text following.
Resolution (prior). [3]GA: 36/146 C, 16 Dec. 1981 (YUN 1981, p. 336).
Yearbook reference. [4]1981, p. 336.
Meeting records. GA: SPC, A/SPC/37/SR.24, 26-33, *42, 44, 45* (9 Nov.–6 Dec.); plenary, A/37/PV.108 (16 Dec.).

General Assembly resolution 37/120 H

16 December 1982   Meeting 108   121-2-24 (recorded vote)

Approved by SPC (A/37/723) by recorded vote (95-2-21), 3 December (meeting 44); 6-nation draft (A/SPC/37/L.22 and Corr.1); agenda item 65.

Sponsors: Afghanistan, Bangladesh, India, Indonesia, Pakistan, Yugoslavia.

Revenues derived from Palestine refugee properties

The General Assembly,

Recalling its resolutions 35/13 A to F of 3 November 1980, 36/146 C of 16 December 1981 and all its previous resolutions on the question, including resolution 194(III) of 11 December 1948,

Taking note of the report of the Secretary-General of 28 September 1982,

Taking note also of the report of the United Nations Conciliation Commission for Palestine, covering the period from 1 October 1981 to 30 September 1982,

Recalling that the Universal Declaration of Human Rights and the principles of international law uphold the principle that no one shall be arbitrarily deprived of one's private property,

Considering that the Palestinian Arab refugees are entitled to their property and to the income derived from their property, in conformity with the principles of justice and equity,

Recalling, in particular, its resolution 394(V) of 14 December 1950, in which it directed the United Nations Conciliation Commission for Palestine, in consultation with the parties concerned, to prescribe measures for the protection of the rights, property and interests of the Palestinian Arab refugees,

Taking note of the completion of the programme of identification and evaluation of Arab property, as announced by the United Nations Conciliation Commission for Palestine in its twenty-second progress report, of 11 May 1964, and of the fact that the Land Office had a schedule of Arab owners and file of documents defining the location, area and other particulars of Arab property,

1. *Requests* the Secretary-General to take all appropriate steps, in consultation with the United Nations Conciliation Commission for Palestine, for the protection and administration of Arab property, assets and property rights in Israel, and to establish a fund for the receipt of income derived therefrom, on behalf of their rightful owners;

2. *Calls once again upon* the Governments concerned, especially Israel, to render all facilities and assistance to the Secretary-General in the implementation of the present resolution;

3. *Requests* the Secretary-General to report to the General Assembly at its thirty-eighth session on the implementation of the present resolution.

Recorded vote in Assembly as follows:

In favour: Afghanistan, Albania, Algeria, Angola, Argentina, Bahrain, Bangladesh, Barbados, Belize, Benin, Bhutan, Bolivia, Botswana, Brazil, Bulgaria, Burma, Burundi, Byelorussian SSR, Cape Verde, Central African Republic, Chad, Chile, China, Colombia, Comoros, Congo, Costa Rica, Cuba, Cyprus, Czechoslovakia, Democratic Kampuchea, Democratic Yemen, Djibouti, Dominican Republic, Ecuador, Egypt, El Salvador, Ethiopia, Gabon, Gambia, German Democratic Republic, Ghana, Greece, Grenada, Guinea, Guinea-Bissau, Guyana, Honduras, Hungary, India, Indonesia, Iran, Iraq, Ivory Coast, Jamaica, Jordan, Kenya, Kuwait, Lao People's Democratic Republic, Lebanon, Lesotho, Liberia, Libyan Arab Jamahiriya, Madagascar, Malawi, Malaysia, Maldives, Mali, Malta, Mauritania, Mauritius, Mexico, Mongolia, Morocco, Mozambique, Nepal, Nicaragua, Nigeria, Oman, Pakistan, Panama, Paraguay, Peru, Philippines, Poland, Portugal, Qatar, Romania, Rwanda, Sao Tome and Principe, Saudi Arabia, Senegal, Seychelles, Sierra Leone, Singapore, Somalia, Spain, Sri Lanka, Sudan, Suriname, Syrian Arab Republic, Thailand, Togo, Trinidad and Tobago, Tunisia, Turkey, Uganda, Ukrainian SSR, USSR, United Arab Emirates, United Republic of Cameroon, United Republic of Tanzania, Upper Volta, Uruguay, Vanuatu, Venezuela, Viet Nam, Yemen, Yugoslavia, Zambia, Zimbabwe.

Against: Israel, United States.

Abstaining: Australia, Austria, Bahamas, Belgium, Canada, Denmark, Fiji, Finland, France, Germany, Federal Republic of, Guatemala, Iceland, Ireland, Italy, Japan, Luxembourg, Netherlands, New Zealand, Norway, Papua New Guinea, Samoa,[a] Sweden, United Kingdom, Zaire.

[a]Later advised the Secretariat it had intended to vote in favour.

Food aid

In his annual report covering the activities of the United Nations Relief and Works Agency for Palestine Refugees in the Near East (UNRWA) from 1 July 1981 to 30 June 1982,[1] the Commissioner-General stated that approximately 827,000 persons, or less than half the number of refugees registered with the Agency, were receiving rations in 1981. The number of refugees classified as special hardship cases (including widows, orphans, the aged, the handicapped and the chronically sick), entitled to larger rations, totalled some 42,700 by the end of June 1982.

Owing to the Agency's financial difficulties and the need to divert available resources to the highest priority programmes, the general distribution of foodstuffs to eligible refugees was suspended in September, with the exception of Lebanon where, because of the emergency situation, distribution was increased in terms of the number of recipients and the quantities of foodstuffs distributed. Destitute families, however, continued to receive foodstuffs and other forms of support.

General Assembly action. By a resolution of 16 December 1982,[2] the General Assembly requested the Commissioner-General to resume on a continuing basis and as soon as possible the general ration distribution to Palestine refugees and called for regular and increased contributions to UNRWA.

The resolution was adopted by a recorded vote of 121 to 13, with 10 abstentions, following its approval by SPC on 3 December by a recorded vote of 94 to 13, with 9 abstentions.

The United States said it considered the request as an unwise intrusion into the administrative discretion of UNRWA management, which had reached a commendable decision on the matter for sound fiscal and programme reasons; if the Agency was compelled to resume the full general ration

distribution, its projected deficit could reach as high as $90 million to $110 million. Also casting a negative vote, Ireland said the request ran counter to the Commissioner-General's decision to phase out the programme in order to concentrate the Agency's limited resources on the education programme. Canada abstained for similar reasons.

Among those abstaining in the vote, Sweden believed that, without sufficient financial resources, a resumption of the general ration distribution would endanger the Agency's educational, health care and relief activities. In Norway's understanding, the request was to be implemented only when UNRWA had secured the necessary resources to resume that distribution, without prejudice to the educational programmes. Endorsing the Commissioner-General's priorities, Australia believed that contributions to UNRWA must be made in cash and not in kind.

The Philippines voted in favour on the understanding that the increase in contributions would actually take place, and Turkey supported the resumption of the general ration distribution in that context.

Introducing the resolution also on behalf of Bangladesh and Yugoslavia, Pakistan emphasized that it was not a criticism of the work of UNRWA which had had to set priorities because of its financial difficulties; however, it was important to resume the ration distribution with the co-operation of the entire international community.

Report. [1]UNRWA Commissioner-General, A/37/13.
Resolution (1982). [2]GA: 37/120 F, 16 Dec., text following.
Meeting records. GA: SPC, A/SPC/37/SR.24, 26-33, *42, 44, 45* (9 Nov.–6 Dec.); plenary, A/37/PV.108 (16 Dec.).

General Assembly resolution 37/120 F

16 December 1982   Meeting 108   121-13-10 (recorded vote)

Approved by SPC (A/37/723) by recorded vote (94-13-9), 3 December (meeting 44); 3-nation draft (A/SPC/37/L.20); agenda item 65.

Sponsors: Bangladesh, Pakistan, Yugoslavia.

Resumption of the ration distribution to Palestine refugees
The General Assembly,

Recalling its resolution 36/146 F of 16 December 1981 and all previous resolutions on the question, including resolution 302(IV) of 8 December 1949,

Having considered the report of the Commissioner-General of the United Nations Relief and Works Agency for Palestine Refugees in the Near East, covering the period from 1 July 1981 to 30 June 1982, and his special report covering the period from 6 June to 31 August 1982,

Deeply concerned at the interruption by the United Nations Relief and Works Agency for Palestine Refugees in the Near East, owing to financial difficulties, of the general ration distribution to Palestine refugees in all fields in the occupied Palestinian territories, Jordan and the Syrian Arab Republic,

1. *Calls upon* all Governments, as a matter of urgency, to make the most generous efforts possible to meet the interrupted needs of the United Nations Relief and Works Agency for Palestine Refugees in the Near East, particularly in the light of the interruption by the Agency of the general ration distribution to Palestine refugees in all fields, and therefore urges non-contributing Governments to contribute regularly and contributing Governments to consider increasing their regular contributions;

2 *Requests* the Commissioner-General of the United Nations Relief and Works Agency for Palestine Refugees in the Near East to resume

on a continuing basis and as soon as possible the interrupted general ration distribution to the Palestine refugees in all fields.

Recorded vote in Assembly as follows:

In favour: Afghanistan, Algeria, Angola, Argentina, Bahamas, Bahrain, Bangladesh, Barbados, Belize, Benin, Bhutan, Bolivia, Botswana, Brazil, Bulgaria, Burma, Burundi, Byelorussian SSR, Cape Verde, Central African Republic, Chad, Chile, China, Colombia, Comoros, Congo, Costa Rica, Cuba, Cyprus, Czechoslovakia, Democratic Kampuchea, Democratic Yemen, Djibouti, Dominican Republic, Ecuador, Egypt, El Salvador, Ethiopia, Fiji, Gabon, Gambia, German Democratic Republic, Ghana, Greece, Grenada, Guinea, Guinea-Bissau, Guyana, Honduras, Hungary, India, Indonesia, Iran, Iraq, Ivory Coast, Jamaica, Jordan, Kenya, Kuwait, Lao People's Democratic Republic, Lebanon, Liberia, Libyan Arab Jamahiriya, Madagascar, Malawi, Malaysia, Maldives, Mali, Malta, Mauritania, Mauritius, Mexico, Mongolia, Morocco, Mozambique, Nepal, Nicaragua, Nigeria, Oman, Pakistan, Panama, Papua New Guinea, Paraguay, Peru, Philippines, Poland, Qatar, Romania, Rwanda, Samoa, Sao Tome and Principe, Saudi Arabia, Senegal, Seychelles, Sierra Leone, Somalia, Sri Lanka, Sudan, Suriname, Syrian Arab Republic, Thailand, Togo, Trinidad and Tobago, Tunisia, Turkey, Uganda, Ukrainian SSR, USSR, United Arab Emirates, United Republic of Cameroon, United Republic of Tanzania, Upper Volta, Uruguay, Vanuatu, Venezuela, Viet Nam, Yemen, Yugoslavia, Zaire, Zambia, Zimbabwe.

Against: Belgium, Denmark, France, Germany, Federal Republic of, Iceland, Ireland, Israel, Italy, Japan, Luxembourg, Netherlands, United Kingdom, United States.

Abstaining: Australia, Austria, Canada, Finland, Guatemala, New Zealand, Norway, Portugal, Spain, Sweden.

Education

Report of the Secretary-General. On 20 September 1982,[1] the Secretary-General reported on the responses to the General Assembly's December 1981 appeal for special allocations, scholarships and grants for higher education for Palestine refugees.[3]

Among the respondents, Kuwait mentioned its scholarship offers made directly to the Palestine Liberation Organization (PLO) and to the Jordanian Government, and financial assistance paid through the Islamic Committee to Palestinians studying abroad. In the Federal Republic of Germany, nine Palestinians were training to be vocational education instructors. France had offered two scholarships in 1982 for UNRWA refugee teachers of French in Lebanon. Candidates were tested for five awards remaining of the six offered by Australia for tertiary studies.

Fellowships or specialized training were offered by the Food and Agriculture Organization of the United Nations, the International Labour Organisation, the United Nations Educational, Scientific and Cultural Organization (UNESCO), the World Health Organization, the World Intellectual Property Organization and the World Meteorological Organization. In addition, the Universal Postal Union indicated its willingness to consider the idea of establishing a training centre for Palestinians.

General Assembly action. Noting that fewer than one per thousand of the Palestine refugee students had the chance to continue higher education and vocational training, and that the number of UNRWA scholarships had been reduced due to the Agency's recurring budgetary difficulties, the General Assembly, by a resolution of 16 December 1982,[2] appealed for increased special allocations for grants and scholarships to Palestine refugees and for contributions to the Palestinian universities in the occupied territories and towards the establishment of vocational training centres. It requested UNRWA to act as recipient and trustee for such allocations and invited United Nations agencies to continue to expand assistance for higher education to Palestine refugees.

The resolution was adopted by a recorded vote of 143 to none, with 1 abstention, following its approval on 3 December by SPC by a recorded vote of 114 to none, with 1 abstention.

Introducing the text also on behalf of Bangladesh, Cyprus, Jordan, Kuwait, Pakistan and Yugoslavia, Egypt said that, since the existing educational system was inadequate, support must continue to be given to anything that would strengthen the educational infrastructure for the Palestinians.

Report. [1]S-G, A/37/427.
Resolution (1982). [2]GA: 37/120 D, 16 Dec., text following.
Resolution (prior). [3]GA: 36/146 H, 16 Dec. 1981 (YUN 1981, p. 338).
Meeting records GA· SPC, A/SPC/37/SR.24, 26 33, 42, 44, 45 (9 Nov.–6 Dec.); plenary, A/37/PV.108 (16 Dec.).

General Assembly resolution 37/120 D

16 December 1982   Meeting 108   143-0-1 (recorded vote)

Approved by SPC (A/37/723) by recorded vote (114-0-1), 3 December (meeting 44); 7-nation draft (A/SPC/37/L.14); agenda item 65.

Sponsors: Bangladesh, Cyprus, Egypt, Jordan, Kuwait, Pakistan, Yugoslavia.

Offers by Member States of grants and scholarships for higher education, including vocational training, for Palestine refugees

The General Assembly,

Recalling its resolution 212(III) of 19 November 1948 on assistance to Palestine refugees,

Recalling also its resolutions 35/13 B of 3 November 1980 and 36/146 H of 16 December 1981,

Cognizant of the fact that the Palestine refugees have, for the last three decades, lost their lands and means of livelihood,

Having examined with appreciation the report of the Secretary-General on offers of grants and scholarships for higher education for Palestine refugees and on the scope of the implementation of resolution 36/146 H,

Having also examined the report of the Commissioner-General of the United Nations Relief and Works Agency for Palestine Refugees in the Near East, covering the period from 1 July 1981 to 30 June 1982, dealing with this subject,

Noting that fewer than one per thousand of the Palestine refugee students have the chance to continue higher education, including vocational training,

Noting also that over the past several years the number of scholarships offered by the United Nations Relief and Works Agency for Palestine Refugees in the Near East has dwindled to half of what it was because of the Agency's recurring budgetary difficulties,

1. *Urges* all States to respond to the appeal contained in General Assembly resolution 32/90 F of 13 December 1977 in a manner commensurate with the needs of the Palestine refugees for higher education and vocational training;

2. *Strongly appeals* to all States, specialized agencies and non-governmental organizations to augment the special allocations for grants and scholarships to Palestine refugees in addition to their contributions to the regular budget of the United Nations Relief and Works Agency for Palestine Refugees in the Near East;

3. *Expresses its appreciation* to all Governments, specialized agencies and non-governmental organizations that responded favourably to General Assembly resolution 36/146 H;

4. *Invites* the relevant United Nations agencies to continue, within their respective spheres of competence, to expand assistance for higher education to Palestine refugee students;

5.   *Appeals* to all States, specialized agencies and the United Nations University to contribute generously to the Palestinian universities in the territories occupied by Israel since 1967;

6.   *Also appeals* to all States, specialized agencies and other international bodies to contribute towards the establishment of vocational training centres for Palestine refugees;

7.   *Requests* the United Nations Relief and Works Agency for Palestine Refugees in the Near East to act as recipient and trustee for such special allocations and scholarships and to award them to qualified Palestine refugee candidates;

8.   *Requests* the Secretary-General to report to the General Assembly at its thirty-eighth session on the implementation of the present resolution.

Recorded vote in Assembly as follows:

In favour: Afghanistan, Algeria, Angola, Argentina, Australia, Austria, Bahamas, Bahrain, Bangladesh, Barbados, Belgium, Belize, Benin, Bhutan, Bolivia, Botswana, Brazil, Bulgaria, Burma, Burundi, Byelorussian SSR, Canada, Central African Republic, Chad, Chile, China, Colombia, Comoros, Congo, Costa Rica, Cuba, Cyprus, Czechoslovakia, Democratic Kampuchea, Democratic Yemen, Denmark, Djibouti, Dominican Republic, Ecuador, Egypt, El Salvador, Ethiopia, Fiji, Finland, France, Gabon, Gambia, German Democratic Republic, Germany, Federal Republic of, Ghana, Greece, Grenada, Guatemala, Guinea, Guinea-Bissau, Guyana, Honduras, Hungary, Iceland, India, Indonesia, Iran, Iraq, Ireland, Italy, Ivory Coast, Jamaica, Japan, Jordan, Kenya, Kuwait, Lao People's Democratic Republic, Lebanon, Liberia, Libyan Arab Jamahiriya, Luxembourg, Madagascar, Malawi, Malaysia, Maldives, Mali, Malta, Mauritania, Mauritius, Mexico, Mongolia, Morocco, Mozambique, Nepal, Netherlands, New Zealand, Nicaragua, Nigeria, Norway, Oman, Pakistan, Panama, Papua New Guinea, Paraguay, Peru, Philippines, Poland, Portugal, Qatar, Romania, Rwanda, Samoa, Sao Tome and Principe, Saudi Arabia, Senegal, Seychelles, Sierra Leone, Singapore, Somalia, Spain, Sri Lanka, Sudan, Suriname, Sweden, Syrian Arab Republic, Thailand, Togo, Trinidad and Tobago, Tunisia, Turkey, Uganda, Ukrainian SSR, USSR, United Arab Emirates, United Kingdom, United Republic of Cameroon, United Republic of Tanzania, United States, Upper Volta, Uruguay, Vanuatu, Venezuela, Viet Nam, Yemen, Yugoslavia, Zaire, Zambia, Zimbabwe.

Against: None.

Abstaining: Israel.

Proposed university

Report of the Secretary-General. In a report of 5 November 1982 on the establishment of a university at Jerusalem for Palestine refugees,[1] submitted in response to a December 1981 General Assembly request,[3] the Secretary-General stated that Secretariat officials had consulted with representatives of Israel, Jordan and PLO, as well as with officials of the universities in the area, on the possibility of strengthening existing academic institutions in the region as an initial step towards that goal. Similar consultations were held with officials of UNESCO, UNRWA, the United Nations Development Programme and other interested organizations and bodies.

On that basis, the Secretary-General considered that, depending on the purpose and scope of the proposed university at Jerusalem, some advantage could be derived from establishing close links between the new institutions and the existing universities, with each serving some of the needs of the other while preserving its academic independence. Although special provision could be made to cater to the academic needs of Palestine refugees, the new university, as part of the system of higher education for the West Bank, Gaza and East Jerusalem, would not be exclusive in its admissions. The Secretary-General considered that the feasibility study requested by the Assembly in 1981[3] would be facilitated if undertaken by a small group of

academics and university administrators of high international standing and bearing in mind the wider context of higher educational needs in the area. A report on the group's progress would be submitted to the 1983 Assembly session.

General Assembly action. By a resolution of 16 December 1982,[2] the General Assembly commended the efforts of the Secretary-General, the UNRWA Commissioner-General, the Council of the United Nations University and UNESCO, as well as the co-operation of the educational authorities concerned, in exploring ways of establishing a Palestinian university at Jerusalem. The Assembly emphasized the need for strengthening the educational system in the occupied territories, specifically the need for the proposed university, and endorsed the steps recommended in the Secretary-General's report, including the creation of a voluntary fund to provide graduate and post-doctoral fellowships for a highly trained core faculty. The Secretary-General was requested to continue taking measures, including a feasibility study, for establishing the University of Jerusalem, and Israel was called on to co-operate and to remove hindrances.

The resolution, as orally revised by Jordan, was adopted by a recorded vote of 141 to 2, following its approval by SPC on 3 December by a recorded vote of 114 to 2.

Rejecting the text, Israel said the proposed university would discriminate among students, would isolate Palestinian refugees from the rest of the population and had nothing to do with their true educational needs. There was no precedent for United Nations sponsorship of a university for refugees anywhere in the world; Israel had established and developed several universities and advanced vocational schools in the area since 1967.

While voting in favour, Canada questioned whether the establishment of the proposed university was the most effective means to strengthen the educational system in the occupied territories. In a similar vein, Austria viewed it preferable to expand existing educational facilities to meet the increased demand.

Speaking for the European Community (EC) members, Denmark said the need for the proposed university reflected the need for better facilities for higher education generally; at the same time, EC considered that the Secretary-General's report contained constructive suggestions on how to meet the need for higher education by building on existing facilities.

Egypt, introducing the text also on behalf of Bangladesh, Cyprus, India, Jordan, Kuwait and Pakistan, said that, since the existing educational system was inadequate, support should be given to measures that would strengthen the educational infrastructure for the Palestinians.

Report. [1]S-G, A/37/599.
Resolution (1982). [2]GA: 37/120 C, 16 Dec., text following.
Resolution (prior). [3]GA: 36/146 G, 16 Dec. 1981 (YUN 1981, p. 339).
Financial implications. 5th Committee report, A/37/747; S-G statements, A/SPC/37/L.39, A/C.5/37/89.
Meeting records. GA: SPC, A/SPC/37/SR.24, 26-33, *42, 44, 45* (9 Nov.–6 Dec.); 5th Committee, A/C.5/37/SR.66 (13 Dec.); plenary, A/37/PV.108 (16 Dec.).

General Assembly resolution 37/120 C

16 December 1982   Meeting 108   141-2 (recorded vote)

Approved by SPC (A/37/723) by recorded vote (114-2), 3 December (meeting 44); 7-nation draft (A/SPC/37/L.13/Rev.2), orally revised; agenda item 65.

Sponsors: Bangladesh, Cyprus, Egypt, India, Jordan, Kuwait, Pakistan.

University of Jerusalem for Palestine refugees

The General Assembly,

Recalling its resolution 36/146 G of 16 December 1981,

Having examined with appreciation the report of the Secretary-General concerning the establishment of a university at Jerusalem in pursuance of paragraphs 5 and 6 of resolution 36/146 G,

Having also examined with appreciation the report of the Commissioner-General of the United Nations Relief and Works Agency for Palestine Refugees in the Near East, covering the period from 1 July 1981 to 30 June 1982,

1. *Commends* the constructive efforts made by the Secretary-General, the Commissioner-General of the United Nations Relief and Works Agency for Palestine Refugees in the Near East, the Council of the United Nations University and the United Nations Educational, Scientific and Cultural Organization, which worked diligently towards the implementation of General Assembly resolution 36/146 G;

2. *Further commends* the close co-operation of the competent educational authorities concerned;

3. *Emphasizes* the need for strengthening the educational system in the Arab territories occupied since 5 June 1967, including Jeru-salem, and specifically the need for the establishment of the proposed university;

4. *Endorses* the various steps recommended in the report of the Secretary-General, including the creation of a voluntary fund to be administered by the Department of Technical Co-operation for Development of the Secretariat, in order to provide graduate and post-doctoral fellowships for a highly trained core faculty of the proposed university;

5. *Requests* the Secretary-General to continue to take all necessary measures, including the conduct of a functional feasibility study, for establishing the University of Jerusalem in accordance with the recommendations contained in the report of the Secretary-General;

6. *Calls upon* Israel as the occupying Power to co-operate in the implementation of the present resolution and to remove the hindrances which it has put in the way of establishing the University of Jerusalem;

7. *Requests* the Secretary-General to report to the General Assembly at its thirty-eighth session on the progress made in the implementation of the present resolution.

Recorded vote in Assembly as follows:

In favour: Afghanistan, Albania, Algeria, Angola, Argentina, Australia, Austria, Bahamas, Bahrain, Bangladesh, Barbados, Belgium, Belize, Benin, Bhutan, Bolivia, Botswana, Brazil, Bulgaria, Burma, Burundi, Byelorussian SSR, Canada, Central African Republic, Chad, Chile, China, Colombia, Comoros, Congo, Costa Rica, Cuba, Cyprus, Czechoslovakia, Democratic Kampuchea, Democratic Yemen, Denmark, Djibouti, Dominican Republic, Ecuador, Egypt, El Salvador, Ethiopia, Fiji, Finland, France, Gabon, Gambia, German Democratic Republic, Germany, Federal Republic of, Ghana, Greece, Grenada, Guatemala, Guinea, Guinea-Bissau, Guyana, Honduras, Hungary, Iceland, India, Indonesia, Iran, Iraq, Ireland, Italy, Ivory Coast, Jamaica, Japan, Jordan, Kenya, Kuwait, Lao People's Democratic Republic, Lebanon, Liberia, Libyan Arab Jamahiriya, Luxembourg, Madagascar, Malawi, Malaysia, Maldives, Mali, Malta, Mauritania, Mauritius, Mexico, Mongolia, Morocco, Mozambique, Nepal, Netherlands, New Zealand, Nicaragua, Nigeria, Norway, Oman, Pakistan, Panama, Paraguay, Peru, Philippines, Poland, Portugal, Qatar, Romania, Rwanda, Samoa, Sao Tome and Principe, Saudi Arabia, Senegal, Seychelles, Sierra Leone, Singapore, Somalia, Spain, Sri Lanka, Sudan, Suriname, Sweden, Syrian Arab Republic, Thailand, Togo, Trinidad and Tobago, Tunisia, Turkey, Uganda, Ukrainian SSR, USSR, United Arab Emirates, United Kingdom, United Republic of Cameroon, United Republic of Tanzania, Upper Volta, Uruguay, Vanuatu, Venezuela, Viet Nam, Yemen, Yugoslavia, Zaire, Zambia.

Against: Israel, United States.

Chapter X

Other political questions

Contents

Information

The General Assembly, on 10 December 1982, adopted two resolutions on information questions. The first was concerned with the development of mass communication, particularly through programmes of the United Nations Educational, Scientific and Cultural Organization (UNESCO). The second was mainly concerned with United Nations public information activities and policies. Both resolutions called for steps to promote a new world information and communication order.

The resolutions were prepared in a working group of the Assembly's Special Political Committee (SPC), established on 26 October and open to all members of the Committee, and were introduced by Colombia as Chairman of the group and a Vice-Chairman of the Committee. They were approved by SPC on 2 December.

Both resolutions were based largely on the recommendations of the 67-member Committee on Information, established by the Assembly in 1978 as the Committee to Review United Nations Public Information Policies and Activities.[2] The Committee continued in 1982 to evaluate efforts and progress by the United Nations system in the field of information and communication, and to promote the establishment of a new world information and communication order. At its fourth substantive session, held at United Nations Head-

quarters from 21 June to 9 July, the Committee made 43 recommendations on promoting a new order and on public information activities in the United Nations system.[1] It held an organizational session on 15 March.

Report. [1]Committee on Information, A/37/21 & Corr.1.
Resolution. [2]GA: 33/115 C, 18 Dec. 1978 (YUN 1978, p. 1043).

Mass communication

The General Assembly, in the first of the two resolutions on information adopted on 10 December 1982,[3] called on Member States, the United Nations system and other organizations to publicize the issues underlying the demand for the development of communication capacities in developing countries as a step towards establishing a new world information and communication order. It called for contributions to the International Programme for the Development of Communication (IPDC), a project of UNESCO, which it regarded as a significant step towards a new world order. The Assembly considered that the proposed Global Satellite Project for Dissemination and Exchange of Information, planned by UNESCO in co-operation with other organizations, was a step towards reducing the imbalance in the global information flow. In this connection, it called on Member States to respond to a 1980 resolution of the UNESCO General Conference concerning the reduction of telecommunication tariffs for news exchanges. It invited UNESCO to report in 1983 on activities in this sphere.

This resolution was approved by SPC and adopted by the Assembly without vote.

By the other resolution on information adopted on the same date, concerned with United Nations information policies and activities,[4] the Assembly reaffirmed the mandate of its Committee on Information, including promotion of the establishment of a new world information and communication order. The Assembly requested the Committee, in its efforts in this regard, to seek the participation of all United Nations organizations, particularly UNESCO and the International Telecommunication Union (ITU), and affirmed its support for UNESCO efforts to promote this goal. In addition, the Assembly requested the Secretary-General to ensure that the United Nations Department of Public Information (DPI) organized, in co-operation with UNESCO, a round table on a new world information and communication order, bringing together major news media editors from all regions.

The Committee on Information, at its June/July session,[1] reiterated the aims of a new world information and communication order, in a formulation that was repeated in the Assembly resolution on United Nations public information. The new order, it said, should be based on the free circulation and wider and better balanced dissemination of information and free access to information and, in particular, the urgent need to change the dependent status of the developing countries in the field of information and communication, and intended also to strengthen peace and international understanding.

UNESCO report. The General Assembly noted with satisfaction a report submitted in October by the Director-General of UNESCO on implementation of IPDC and on UNESCO efforts to establish a new world information and communication order. The report was transmitted by a note from the Secretary-General to the Assembly.[2]

The Director-General reported that at the second session of the Intergovernmental Council of IPDC, held from 18 to 25 January at Acapulco, Mexico, the Chairman had said that the essential task of IPDC was to set in motion practical technical co-operation that would develop training and establish structures for communication. At that session, the Council had taken decisions on general priorities, criteria for selecting projects, financing and resources. The priorities emphasized the development of communication capabilities in developing countries, with the object of facilitating a free flow and a wider and better balanced exchange of news and cultural products by improving policies and plans, the support structure, research, training of personnel, regional co-operation and technology.

The Council had approved and decided to finance 12 regional and 2 interregional projects. The interregional projects were a feasibility study on facilities for the international dissemination and exchange of information by global satellite systems, and the application of communication technology to rural areas.

Member States of UNESCO had, by 31 July, contributed $3,363,989 to the IPDC Special Account, of which $1,184,568 had actually been paid. The Council had approved a $910,000 budget for 1982, to be met from the Special Account. Some of the approved projects would receive funding from other sources, especially the United Nations Development Programme and trust funds.

Describing other UNESCO projects in information and communication, the report mentioned efforts in collaboration with ITU to reduce telecommunication tariffs for the transmission of news and television material. Also, the UNESCO Global Satellite Project for Dissemination and Exchange of Information was preparing for an experiment in 1983 towards its goal of enabling broadcasting houses, news agencies and newspaper organizations to lease additional satellite capacity on a permanent basis from the International Telecommunications Satellite Organization (INTELSAT) and the International System and Organization of Space Communications (INTERSPUTNIK). UNESCO, in collaboration with ITU, was assisting in the development of the Pan-African News Agency and of national news agencies.

In addition, UNESCO had organized a World Congress on Books (London, 7-11 June) with the aim of devising new strategies to promote reading and the use of books. The Congress, by its London Declaration called "Towards a Reading Society", reaffirmed the right of men and women to learn, educate themselves, acquire knowledge and acquaint themselves with the wisdom and experience of other nations, cultures and previous generations.

The World Conference on Cultural Policies (Mexico City, 26 July–6 August) had considered the relationships between cultural and communication policies, and the national and local production of audio-visual programmes for the cinema, radio and television. By the Mexico City Declaration on Cultural Policies, the Conference called for the free flow and widest and most balanced dissemination of information, implying for all nations the right not only to receive but also to transmit cultural, educational, scientific and technical information.

Reports. [1]Committee on Information, A/37/21; [2]UNESCO Director-General, transmitted by S-G note, A/37/453 & Corr.1.
Resolutions (1982). GA, 10 Dec.: [3]37/94 A, text following; [4]37/94 B.
Meeting records. GA: SPC, A/SPC/37/SR.6-14, *38, 43* (22 Oct.–2 Dec.); plenary, A/37/PV.100 (10 Dec.).

General Assembly resolution 37/94 A

10 December 1982 Meeting 100 Adopted without vote

Approved by SPC (A/37/707) without vote, 2 December (meeting 43); draft by Vice-Chairman based on deliberations in working group (A/SPC/37/L.16); agenda item 67.

The General Assembly,

Recalling its resolutions 34/181 and 34/182 of 18 December 1979, 35/201 of 16 December 1980 and 36/149 A of 16 December 1981,

Recalling relevant provisions of the Mexico City Declaration on Cultural Policies, adopted by the World Conference on Cultural Policies, held at Mexico City from 26 July to 6 August 1982,

Recalling the relevant provisions of the Final Declaration of the Sixth Conference of Heads of State or Government of Non-Aligned Countries, held at Havana from 3 to 9 September 1979, which stressed that co-operation in the field of information is an integral part of the struggle for the creation of a new world information order, of the Declaration of the Conference of Ministers for Foreign Affairs of Non-Aligned Countries, held at New Delhi from 9 to 13 February 1981, and of the Fifth and Sixth Meetings of the Intergovernmental Council of Ministers of Information of Non-Aligned Countries, held at Georgetown in May 1981 and at Valletta in June 1982,

Recalling the relevant resolutions adopted by the Assembly of Heads of State and Government of the Organization of African Unity at its eighteenth ordinary session, held at Nairobi from 24 to 27 June 1981,

Recalling article 19 of the Universal Declaration of Human Rights, which provides that everyone has the right to freedom of opinion and expression and that this right includes freedom to hold opinions without interference and to seek, receive and impart information and ideas through any media and regardless of frontiers, and article 29, which stipulates that these rights and freedoms may in no case be exercised contrary to the purposes and principles of the United Nations,

Recalling the relevant provisions of the Final Act of the Conference on Security and Co-operation in Europe, signed at Helsinki on 1 August 1975,

Recalling also the relevant provisions of the Declaration on the Preparation of Societies for Life in Peace,

Recalling resolutions 4/19 and 4/21 adopted by the General Conference of the United Nations Educational, Scientific and Cultural Organization at its twenty-first session, held at Belgrade from 23 September to 28 October 1980,

Considering that the publication of the final report of the International Commission for the Study of Communication Problems is a valuable contribution to the study of information and communication problems and that its recommendations also constitute valuable encouragement for the continuing examination, analysis and study of information and communication problems,

Considering that international co-operation in the field of communication development should take place on the basis of equality, justice, mutual advantage and the principles of international law,

Conscious that the development of communication infrastructures, including national and regional capacity for indigenous message production and dissemination, is one of the important factors of genuine participation by a large majority of developing countries in international exchanges,

Recognizing the central role of the United Nations Educational, Scientific and Cultural Organization in the field of information and communications within its mandate, as well as the progress accomplished by the organization in that field,

1. *Takes note with satisfaction* of the report of the Director-General of the United Nations Educational, Scientific and Cultural Organization on the implementation of the International Programme for the Development of Communication and the Establishment of a New World Information and Communication Order;

2. *Underlines* the importance of efforts for the implementation of the principles set forth in the Declaration on Fundamental Principles concerning the Contribution of the Mass Media to Strengthening Peace and International Understanding, to the Promotion of Human Rights and to Countering Racialism, *Apartheid* and Incitement to War, adopted on 28 November 1978 by the General Conference of the United Nations Educational, Scientific and Cultural Organization;

3. *Calls upon* all Member States and all organizations of the United Nations system, international, governmental and non-governmental organizations and professional organizations in the field of communications to exert every effort to make better known through all means at their disposal the issues underlying the demand for the development of communication capacities in developing countries as a step towards the establishment of a new world information and communication order;

4. *Considers* that the International Programme for the Development of Communication represents a significant step towards the establishment of a new world information and communication order and welcomes the decisions adopted by the Intergovernmental Council of the Programme at its second session, held at Acapulco, Mexico, from 18 to 25 January 1982;

5. *Notes with satisfaction* the co-operation existing between the United Nations, the United Nations Educational, Scientific and Cultural Organization and all other organizations of the United Nations system, particularly the International Telecommunication Union, in the implementation of the Programme;

6. *Expresses its appreciation* to all Member States that have made or pledged a contribution towards the implementation of the Programme;

7. *Calls upon* Member States—developed and developing countries alike—and organizations and bodies of the United Nations system, as well as other intergovernmental organizations and concerned public and private enterprises, to respond to the appeals of the Director-General of the United Nations Educational, Scientific and Cultural Organization and make contributions to the Programme, since the availability of additional resources is essential for its implementation;

8. *Considers* that the proposed Global Satellite Project for Dissemination and Exchange of Information, planned by the United Nations Educational, Scientific and Cultural Organization in co-operation with INTELSAT and INTERSPUTNIK and supported by the Programme, is a positive step towards reducing the existing imbalance in global information flow;

9. *Calls upon* Member States to respond positively to resolution 4/22 concerning the reduction of telecommunication tariffs for news exchanges, adopted by the General Conference of the United Nations Educational, Scientific and Cultural Organization at its twenty-first session;

10. *Invites* the Director-General of the United Nations Educational, Scientific and Cultural Organization to continue his efforts in the field of information and communications and to submit to the General Assembly at its thirty-eighth session a comprehensive report on the implementation of the Programme, on the activities related to the establishment of a new world information and communication order and, in co-operation with the International Telecommunication Union, on the impact of the current technological developments and practices and their application in the information and communication sector, especially in the developing countries, bearing in mind, *inter alia*, the forthcoming relevant meetings of the United Nations Educational, Scientific and Cultural Organization on the subject.

UN public information

The General Assembly, by its resolution on United Nations public information activities adopted on 10 December 1982,[3] approved the report and recommendations of its Committee on Information[2] and reaffirmed the Committee's mandate as established in 1979.[5] The Assembly reiterated its appeal to Member States, the public and private media and non-governmental organizations to disseminate more objective and better balanced information about the United Nations, developing countries and the international community, in order to achieve a more comprehensive and realistic image of the activities and potential of the United Nations system. In addition, the Assembly called on all United Nations organizations to develop integrated public information programmes to promote understanding of and support for the activities of the system in all fields, in particular in the economic, social, development and cultural fields. The Assembly requested further reports from the Committee and the Secretary-General in 1983.

By this resolution, the Assembly also made recommendations on specific DPI activities as well as on inter-agency activities and their co-ordination. The Committee on Information was asked to continue to promote a new world information and communication order (p. 4). The Assembly asked the Secretary-General to ensure that the World Disarmament Campaign (See POLITICAL AND SECURITY QUESTIONS, Chapter I) gave full consideration to the role of mass media in promoting a climate conducive to peace and disarmament, and that DPI utilized its resources to ensure maximum effectiveness of the Campaign. Another request called for him to report on the possible acquisition of a United Nations communications satellite (See ADMINISTRATIVE AND BUDGETARY QUESTIONS, Chapter IV). The Secretariat was asked to prepare an account of world media coverage of developments affecting the Palestinian people from June to December 1982 (See POLITICAL AND SECURITY QUESTIONS, Chapter IX).

The Assembly adopted the resolution by a recorded vote of 131 to 1, with 1 abstention, following its approval on 2 December by SPC by a recorded vote of 105 to 1, with 1 abstention.

By a recorded vote of 72 to 2 (Israel, United States), with 31 abstentions, SPC rejected a United States amendment[1] that would have added a paragraph authorizing the Secretary-General to implement the activities approved in the resolution only to the extent that they could be financed by resources already approved in the United Nations programme budget for 1982-1983.[6] The Fifth (Administrative and Budgetary) Committee reported to the Assembly that implementation of the resolution would require a net addition of $640,100 to the budget for 1983 activities.

The resolution was drafted in the open-ended working group on information questions established by SPC. Ecuador, as Chairman of the Committee on Information, said the document, for which the Group of 77 developing countries had submitted the initial text, reflected the consensus already reached by that Committee. The spirit of understanding in the working group had made it possible to find common ground which respected the positions of all participants.

Explaining its negative vote, the United States objected to the additional resources required to implement the resolution; in addition, it said the resolution confused image-building with the free flow of ideas, and tended to impose on the free media

specific tasks and responsibilities which the United States found to be impermissible restraints on their freedom, independence and professionalism. Israel said it had abstained because it believed DPI was being used for purposes of adverse propaganda against a Member State.

Among those voting in favour, Algeria said the Group of 77 had made major concessions in an effort to reach a consensus; it had therefore been surprised to learn that one delegation opposed the resolution. The Congo deplored the fact that SPC had not been able to reach its customary consensus on the omnibus resolution on information questions, which it attributed to a lack of good will in the negotiations. Denmark, speaking for the European Community members, said they had supported the resolution despite the fact that the text did not entirely reflect their views; they regretted that consensus on the resolution had not been attained, because they felt the work of DPI was so important that it should be universally supported. Sweden, referring to a mention in the resolution's preamble of article 20 of the International Covenant on Civil and Political Rights,[4] recalled its reservation on the paragraph in that article requiring the prohibition of war propaganda; Sweden also commented on provisions in the resolution on geographical distribution of DPI staff and co-operation with news agencies.

Amendment rejected. [1]United States, A/SPC/37/L.18.
Report. [2]Committee on Information, A/37/21 & Corr.1.
Resolution (1982). [3]GA: 37/94 B, 10 Dec., text following.
Resolutions (prior). GA: [4]2200 A (XXI), annex, 16 Dec. 1966 (YUN 1966, p. 423); [5]34/182, 18 Dec. 1979 (YUN 1979, p. 457); [6]36/240 A, 18 Dec. 1981 (YUN 1981, p. 1278).
Financial implications. 5th Committee report, A/37/711; S-G statements, A/SPC/37/L.35, A/C.5/37/83.
Meeting records. GA: SPC, A/SPC/37/SR.6-14, *38, 43* (22 Oct.–2 Dec.); 5th Committee, A/C.5/37/SR.59 (8 Dec.); plenary, A/37/PV.100 (10 Dec.).

General Assembly resolution 37/94 B

10 December 1982	Meeting 100	131-1-1 (recorded vote)

Approved by SPC (A/37/707) by recorded vote (105-1-1), 2 December (meeting 43); draft by Vice-Chairman based on deliberations in working group (A/SPC/37/L.15); agenda item 67.

The General Assembly,

Recalling its resolutions 3535(XXX) of 17 December 1975, 31/139 of 16 December 1976, 33/115 A to C of 18 December 1978, 34/181 and 34/182 of 18 December 1979, 35/201 of 16 December 1980 and 36/149 B of 16 December 1981 on questions relating to information,

Recalling article 19 of the Universal Declaration of Human Rights, which provides that everyone has the right to freedom of opinion and expression and that this right includes freedom to hold opinions without interference and to seek, receive and impart information and ideas through any media and regardless of frontiers, and article 29, which stipulates that these rights and freedoms may in no case be exercised contrary to the purposes and principles of the United Nations,

Recalling also articles 19 and 20 of the International Covenant on Civil and Political Rights,

Recalling the relevant provisions of the Final Declaration of the Sixth Conference of Heads of State or Government of Non-Aligned Countries, held at Havana from 3 to 9 September 1979, which stressed that co-operation in the field of information is an integral part of the struggle for the creation of a new world information order, of the Declaration of the Conference of Ministers for Foreign Affairs of Non-Aligned Countries, held at New Delhi from 9 to 13 February 1981, and of the Fifth and Sixth Meetings of the Intergovernmental Council of Ministers of Information of Non-Aligned Countries, held at Georgetown in May 1981 and at Valletta in June 1982,

Recalling its resolutions 3201(S-VI) and 3202(S-VI) of 1 May 1974, containing the Declaration and the Programme of Action on the Establishment of a New International Economic Order, 3281(XXIX) of 12 December 1974, containing the Charter of Economic Rights and Duties of States, and 3362(S-VII) of 16 September 1975 on development and international economic co-operation,

Recalling the Declaration on Fundamental Principles concerning the Contribution of the Mass Media to Strengthening Peace and International Understanding, to the Promotion of Human Rights and to Countering Racialism, *Apartheid* and Incitement to War, adopted on 28 November 1978 by the General Conference of the United Nations Educational, Scientific and Cultural Organization, as well as the relevant resolutions on information and mass communications adopted by the General Conference at its nineteenth, twentieth, twenty-first and twenty-second sessions,

Recalling the relevant provisions of the Final Act of the Conference on Security and Co-operation in Europe, signed at Helsinki on 1 August 1975,

Recalling the relevant provisions of the Declaration on the Preparation of Societies for Life in Peace,

Recalling also the relevant recommendations and provisions of the Declarations adopted by the World Congress on Books, held in London from 7 to 11 June 1982, and by the World Conference on Cultural Policies, held at Mexico City from 26 July to 6 August 1982,

Conscious of the need for all to collaborate in the establishment of a new world information and communication order based, *inter alia*, on the free circulation and wider and better balanced dissemination of information, guaranteeing the diversity of the sources of information and free access to information, and, in particular, the urgent need to change the dependent status of the developing countries in the field of information and communications, and intended also to strengthen peace and international understanding,

Reaffirming that the establishment of a new world information and communication order is linked to the new international economic order and is an integral part of the international development process,

Emphasizing the important role that public information plays in promoting understanding of and support for the establishment of the new international economic order and international co-operation for development,

Emphasizing the role that public information plays in promoting support for universal disarmament and in increasing awareness of the relationship between disarmament and development among as broad a public as possible,

Reaffirming the primary role which the General Assembly is to play in elaborating, co-ordinating and harmonizing United Nations policies and activities in the field of information and recognizing the central and important role of the United Nations Educational, Scientific and Cultural Organization in the field of information and communications,

Emphasizing the complementarity of the activities in the field of information and communications and the need to strengthen co-operation and co-ordination between the organs, organizations and bodies of the United Nations system that deal with different aspects of information and communications,

Emphasizing its full support for the International Programme for the Development of Communication, which constitutes an important step in the development of the infrastructures of communications in the developing countries,

Expressing its satisfaction with the work of the Committee on Information as reflected in its report to the General Assembly at its thirty-seventh session,

Expressing its appreciation to the Joint United Nations Information Committee for its efforts towards improving co-ordination of the public information activities of the various organizations of the United Nations system,

Taking note with satisfaction of the report of the Secretary-General on questions relating to information,

Also taking note with satisfaction of the report of the Director-General of the United Nations Educational, Scientific and Cultural Organization,

1. *Approves* the report of the Committee on Information and all its recommendations and urges their full implementation;

2. *Reaffirms* the mandate given to the Committee on Information by the General Assembly in its resolution 34/182, namely:

(a) To continue to examine United Nations public information policies and activities, in the light of the evolution of international relations, particularly during the past two decades, and of the imperatives of the establishment of the new international economic order and of a new world information and communication order;

(b) To evaluate and follow up the efforts made and the progress achieved by the United Nations system in the field of information and communications;

(c) To promote the establishment of a new, more just and more effective world information and communication order, intended to strengthen peace and international understanding and based on the free circulation and wider and better balanced dissemination of information, and to make recommendations thereon to the General Assembly;

3. *Requests* the Committee on Information, keeping in mind its mandate, the essential tasks of which are to continue to examine the policies and activities of the Department of Public Information of the Secretariat, to continue to promote the establishment of a new, more just and effective world information and communication order and to continue to seek the co-operation and active participation of all organizations of the United Nations system, particularly the United Nations Educational, Scientific and Cultural Organization and the International Telecommunication Union, while avoiding any overlapping of activities on this subject;

4. *Affirms* its strong support for the United Nations Educational, Scientific and Cultural Organization and for its efforts to promote the establishment of a new world information and communication order;

5. *Reiterates again its appeal* to Member States, to the information and communication media, both public and private, as well as to non-governmental organizations, to disseminate more widely objective and better balanced information about the activities of the United Nations and, *inter alia*, about the efforts of the developing countries towards their economic, social and cultural progress and about the efforts of the international community to achieve international social justice and economic development, international peace and security and the progressive elimination of international inequities and tensions, such dissemination being aimed at achieving a more comprehensive and realistic image of the activities and potential of the United Nations system in all its purposes and endeavours;

6. *Calls upon* all organs, organizations and bodies of the United Nations system to develop, in a concerted manner, integrated and coherent public information programmes to promote understanding of and support for the activities of the system in all its fields, in particular in the economic, social, development and cultural fields;

7. *Requests* that the Joint United Nations Information Committee, as the essential instrument for inter-agency co-ordination and co-operation in the field of public information, be strengthened and made more effective and that its secretariat elaborate new methods of work and longer-term indicative planning and joint action, especially in the promotion of a new world information and communication order;

8. *Requests* the Committee on Information and the Joint United Nations Information Committee to take action in accordance with paragraphs 15 and 16 of the recommendations of the Committee on Information for its consideration at its substantive session in 1983;

9. *Reaffirms* the importance of the rapidly increasing role of United Nations public information programmes in fostering public understanding and support of United Nations activities and requests the Secretary-General to continue to review the current activities of the Department of Public Information with a view to ensuring a better and more efficient use of its available resources;

10. *Requests* the Secretary-General to ensure that future reports of the Department of Public Information to the Committee on Information and to the General Assembly should contain the information set out in paragraph 42 of the recommendations of the Committee;

11. *Reiterates* the recommendation contained in its resolution 35/201 that additional resources for the Department of Public Information should be commensurate with the increase in the activities of the United Nations which the Department is called upon to cover for the purpose of public information, and that the Secretary-General should provide such resources to the Department to this end where needed;

12. *Requests* the Secretary-General to ensure that the activities of the Department of Public Information, as the focal point of the public information tasks of the United Nations, should be strengthened, keeping in view the principles of the Charter of the United Nations and along the lines established in the relevant resolutions of the General Assembly and the recommendations of the Committee on Information, to ensure a more coherent coverage of, and a better knowledge about, the United Nations and its work, especially in its priority areas, such as those stated in section III, paragraph 1, of Assembly resolution 35/201, including international peace and security, disarmament, peace-keeping and peacemaking operations, decolonization, the promotion of human rights, the struggle against *apartheid* and racial discrimination, economic, social and development issues, the integration of women in the struggle for peace and development, the establishment of the new international economic order and of a new world information and communication order, the work of the United Nations Council for Namibia and programmes on women and youth;

13. *Requests* the Secretary-General, in view of the vital role that information plays in the development process, to ensure that the Department of Public Information co-operates more closely with the United Nations development agencies and programmes, in particular the United Nations Development Programme, both at Headquarters and in the field, in order to pool their resources, avoid duplication and foster effectively the process of development;

14. *Requests* the Secretary-General to ensure that the World Disarmament Campaign gives full consideration to the role of mass media as the most effective way to promote in world public opinion a climate of understanding, confidence and co-operation conducive to peace and disarmament and the enhancement of human rights and development and further requests the Secretary-General to ensure that, within the World Disarmament Campaign, the Department of Public Information fulfils the role assigned to it by the General Assembly by utilizing its expertise and resources in public information to ensure its maximum effectiveness;

15. *Requests* the Secretary-General to ensure that, within existing resources, the competent organs of the Secretariat prepare a documented factual summary account of the coverage by widely representative world media of developments affecting the Palestinian people from June to December 1982;

16. *Requests* the Secretary-General to ensure that the Department of Public Information organizes as soon as possible, in close co-operation with the United Nations Educational, Scientific and Cultural Organization, a round table on a new world information and communication order, with the wide participation of major news media editors and with representation from all regions;

17. *Requests* the Secretary-General to continue and intensify his efforts to redress the existing imbalance in the staff of the Department of Public Information, and, until equitable geographical distribution is achieved, to take urgent steps to increase the representation of the group of developing countries, particularly at senior and policy-making levels, by a policy of recruiting among their nationals, taking into account also the interests of other under-represented groups of countries, in accordance with Article 101, paragraph 3, of the Charter of the United Nations and General Assembly resolutions 33/143 of 20 December 1978, 35/201 and 36/149 B;

18. *Requests* the Secretary-General to take the necessary measures to implement the existing plan regarding programming in the Portuguese language and to submit to the Committee on Information at its next session specific proposals, including estimates of costs and benefits, for a separate plan to enable the African Unit in the Radio Service to undertake programming at a meaningful level in French and major languages of the region other than those already in use;

19. *Notes* that a separate Caribbean Unit has been established and has begun functioning and requests the Secretary-General to report on measures needed for its possible expansion so that it may offer effective programming in French and in the other languages of the subregion;

20. *Requests* the Secretary-General to submit to the Committee on Information at its next session a new, extensive and detailed report on the acquisition of a United Nations communications satellite, which would include the different alternatives and analyse and evaluate the current administrative costs in relation to telephone, telex, radio, video, document processing, the holding of conferences, travel by interpreters, and so on, and, while projecting seven-year operational goals, compare them with the cost to the United Nations of its own satellite, taking into account all potential uses of such a satellite by the United Nations system and also presenting feasible financing and self-maintenance alternatives, and in this regard requests that the Committee on Information should, at its next session, also take into account the basic report on communications to be produced by the Joint Inspection Unit;

21. *Requests* the Secretary-General further to strengthen co-operation by the Department of Public Information with the Pool of Non-Aligned News Agencies, as well as with the regional news agencies of developing countries, and furthermore requests that the practice of coverage by the agencies of the Pool, in co-operation with the Department of Public Information, of important conferences and events within the United Nations system should be continued and strengthened;

22. *Requests* the Secretary-General to publish the *UN Chronicle* in all the official languages of the United Nations and, within existing financial resources, to take the measures necessary to ensure that the *UN Chronicle* be further improved to present a wide and more comprehensive coverage of United Nations activities and that it be published in an attractive and appropriate format to ensure its wide, timely and effective circulation;

23. *Requests* the Secretary-General to strengthen the capacity and enhance the role of the United Nations information centres through, in particular, the implementation of the provisions of paragraph 22 of the recommendations of the Committee on Information;

24. *Requests* the Secretary-General to initiate practical efforts towards a balance in the use of all the official languages of the United Nations in the radio broadcasting programme covering United Nations conferences held away from United Nations Headquarters;

25. *Requests* the Secretary-General to proceed, without prejudice to any future plan concerning the regionalization of the Radio and Visual Services Division, to maintain and enhance the functions of the Arabic and Middle East Unit in the Radio Service as the producer of television and radio programmes for the Arabic-speaking countries and requests that he should, similarly, enlarge it through the redeployment of existing resources;

26. *Reaffirms* the importance of *Development Forum* as the only inter-agency publication of the United Nations system which concentrates on development issues, requests the Secretary-General to continue to support its publication from the regular budget of the United Nations while intensifying his efforts to secure a sound and independent financial basis for its continued publication and calls upon all the specialized agencies and other organizations of the United Nations system to contribute to this system-wide publication;

27. *Requests* the Secretary-General to report further to the Committee on Information at its next session on the viability of a world-wide United Nations short-wave network, its regional segments and its pertinent frequencies, as well as on the alternative solution of continuing to rent broadcast time on existing national short-wave transmitters;

28. *Requests* the Secretary-General to continue the co-operation between the Department of Public Information and the Union of National Radio and Television Organizations of Africa, as well as with radio stations which are members of that Union, in order to broadcast United Nations radio programmes on those radio stations, and further requests the Secretary-General to co-operate with the national radio broadcasting organizations in Africa for the establishment of a pilot project for wider broadcasting of United Nations radio programmes;

29. *Requests* the Secretary-General to report to the Committee on Information, at its substantive session in 1983, on the implementation of all the recommendations contained in the Committee's report;

30. *Requests* the Secretary-General to report to the General Assembly at its thirty-eighth session on the implementation of the present resolution, in particular on the implementation of all the recommendations contained in the report of the Committee on Information;

31. *Requests* the Committee on Information to report to the General Assembly at its thirty-eighth session;

32. *Decides* to include in the provisional agenda of its thirty-eighth session the item entitled "Questions relating to information".

Recorded vote in Assembly as follows:

In favour: Afghanistan, Algeria, Argentina, Australia, Austria, Bahrain, Bangladesh, Barbados, Belgium, Benin, Bhutan, Bolivia, Botswana, Brazil, Bulgaria,

Burma, Burundi, Byelorussian SSR, Canada, Central African Republic, Chad, Chile, China, Colombia, Comoros, Congo, Costa Rica, Cuba, Cyprus, Czechoslovakia, Democratic Kampuchea, Democratic Yemen, Denmark, Djibouti, Dominican Republic, Ecuador, Egypt, El Salvador, Ethiopia, Fiji, Finland, France, Gabon, Gambia, German Democratic Republic, Germany, Federal Republic of, Ghana, Greece, Guyana, Haiti, Honduras, Hungary, Iceland, India, Indonesia, Iran, Iraq, Ireland, Italy, Jamaica, Japan, Jordan, Kenya, Kuwait, Lao People's Democratic Republic, Lebanon, Liberia, Libyan Arab Jamahiriya, Luxembourg, Madagascar, Malawi, Malaysia, Maldives, Mali, Malta, Mauritania, Mauritius, Mexico, Mongolia, Morocco, Mozambique, Nepal, Netherlands, New Zealand, Nicaragua, Niger, Nigeria, Norway, Oman, Pakistan, Panama, Papua New Guinea, Peru, Philippines, Poland, Portugal, Qatar, Romania, Rwanda, Sao Tome and Principe, Saudi Arabia, Senegal, Sierra Leone, Singapore, Somalia, Spain, Sri Lanka, Sudan, Suriname, Sweden, Syrian Arab Republic, Thailand, Togo, Trinidad and Tobago, Tunisia, Turkey, Uganda, Ukrainian SSR, USSR, United Arab Emirates, United Kingdom, United Republic of Cameroon, United Republic of Tanzania, Upper Volta, Uruguay, Venezuela, Viet Nam, Yemen, Yugoslavia, Zaire, Zambia.

Against: United States.

Abstaining: Israel.

DPI activities

The General Assembly, in its resolution of 10 December 1982 on United Nations public information activities,[3] reaffirmed the importance of the rapidly increasing role of United Nations public information programmes in fostering public support of the Organization's activities. The Assembly reiterated that additional resources for DPI should be commensurate with the increase in United Nations activities which it was called upon to cover for public information purposes, and that the Secretary-General should provide such resources to DPI where needed. The Assembly requested the Secretary-General to strengthen DPI activities to ensure more coherent coverage of and better knowledge about the United Nations, especially in priority areas. Asking him to continue to review DPI activities to ensure a more efficient use of available resources, the Assembly also requested him to ensure that future DPI reports to the Committee on Information and to the Assembly contained additional information sought by the Committee in July.

Regarding specific activities, the Secretary-General was requested: to enhance the role of United Nations information centres; to strengthen co-operation with the Pool of Non-Aligned News Agencies and with regional news agencies of developing countries; to publish the *UN Chronicle* in all United Nations official languages; to report on the viability of a world-wide United Nations short-wave network and to expand United Nations radio broadcasting in certain areas; to redress the geographical imbalance in the DPI staff; and to continue to provide United Nations financial support to the inter-agency publication *Development Forum*. The Assembly recommended that DPI organize a round table for news media editors on a new world information and communication order.

The Assembly's request that future DPI reports contain certain information was based on a recommendation of the Committee on Information.[1] The Committee, in July, asked for information on DPI output regarding each topic in its work programme, the costs of activities in respect of each

topic, the end-use of DPI products, the Department's evaluation of its programmes, and the priority level which the Secretary-General attached to current and future DPI activities. It also requested DPI to present, at the Committee's 1983 session, a sample of DPI programmes and activities, including journals, booklets, news items, exhibits, films, and radio and television recordings, and to undertake a more thorough analysis of the Department's future planning and programming activities.

A September 1982 report on information questions,[2] prepared by the Secretary-General in response to a December 1981 request by the Assembly,[4] described steps taken to implement several Assembly recommendations made that year. The report covered the strengthening of radio and visual services, the role of United Nations information centres, *Development Forum*, co-operation with news organizations, and training of journalists and broadcasters.

Reports. [1]Committee on Information, A/37/21; [2]S-G, A/37/446.

Resolution (1982). [3]GA: 37/94 B, 10 Dec.

Resolution (prior). [4]GA: 36/149 B, 16 Dec. 1981 (YUN 1981, p. 363).

UN information centres

In its 10 December 1982 resolution on United Nations public information activities,[5] the General Assembly requested the Secretary-General to strengthen the role of the United Nations information centres—the DPI field offices—as recommended in July by the Committee on Information.[2]

The Committee recommendations referred to by the Assembly called for reallocating DPI personnel and resources to improve efficiency; having the centres disseminate information according to mandates and priorities set by the Assembly; studying ways to enhance the centres' role by increasing their flexibility so that they could assess their financial, material and personnel needs and adjust to the interests of the countries they served; reviewing the post levels of centre directors in order to upgrade them, where needed, to a level commensurate with their responsibilities; establishing a category of national information officers (to improve the career prospects of locally recruited information officers serving at centres); establishing new centres at Brazzaville, Congo, and Luanda, Angola, and ensuring that the Information Service at Vienna, Austria, gave adequate service in German for use in Austria and the Federal Republic of Germany; and strengthening the role of the External Relations Division of DPI—responsible for the centres' supervision—as needed to implement these measures.

In other recommendations, the Committee said the centres should assist the media in their respective countries and promote a new world information and communication order, and DPI should provide a summary of the reports submitted by the centres on their activities.

The network of DPI field offices numbered 63 information centres and services as at 31 December 1982 (see APPENDIX V). The newest of these, at Harare (formerly Salisbury), Zimbabwe, was established in September.

A report of the Secretary-General on measures to strengthen the capacity and enhance the role of the information centres,[3] which had been requested by the Assembly in December 1981,[6] was submitted to the Committee on Information in May 1982. In identifying such measures, the report treated separately those which could be implemented within current DPI resources and those requiring additional funds. Those in the first category—such as increasing coverage in different languages, improving administration and management, and seeking the co-operation of non-governmental organizations (NGOs) and national institutions—had been put into effect or were planned. Those requiring additional funds were: reassessment of the post levels of centre directors, establishment of a category of national information officers, improvement of communication and other equipment, establishment of Arabic-language capacity in information support for centres from Headquarters, and the strengthening of links with NGOs through NGO conferences away from headquarters.

Comments in reference to information centres were made in April 1982 by the Administrative Committee on Co-ordination (ACC)[1] in connection with a February 1981 report of the Joint Inspection Unit (JIU) on co-ordination of public information activities in the United Nations system.[7] JIU had recommended that, in cities where no United Nations organization had a headquarters or regional office, the centre should become the only distribution point for information materials from the United Nations system; in cities where there was more than one information service (serving different organizations), possibilities of pooling resources should be explored. ACC responded that it would continue to follow closely the progress of the Committee on Information, which was seized with the question of co-ordination of information activities among international organizations.

In his September report to the Assembly on various aspects of DPI work,[4] the Secretary-General cited specific measures taken or contemplated to enhance the centres' role. He planned to negotiate with the Governments concerned on the establishment of centres at Luanda and Brazzaville, as

requested by Angola and the Congo, and was pursuing the proposal to establish a category of national information officers. Remarking on the concern expressed by certain delegations regarding the adequacy of the German-language Information Service at Vienna, he said the Secretariat was reviewing, as requested by the Committee on Information, the levels of centre director posts to ensure that they were commensurate with their responsibilities. He noted that, within current resources, some Spanish-language materials were being produced at Headquarters and dispatched regularly to centres, pending the recruitment of an officer to produce information that would be telexed daily to centres in Spanish-speaking countries.

Note. [1]S-G, annexing ACC comments, A/37/174.
Reports. [2]Committee on Information, A/37/21; S-G, [3]A/AC.198/45 & Add.1, [4]A/37/446.
Resolution (1982). [5]GA: 37/94 B, para. 23, 10 Dec.
Resolution (prior). [6]GA: 36/149 B, 16 Dec. 1981 (YUN 1981, p. 363).
Yearbook reference. [7]1981, p. 370.

Co-operation with news agencies

The General Assembly, in its 10 December 1982 resolution on United Nations public information activities,[3] requested the Secretary-General to strengthen DPI co-operation with the Pool of Non-Aligned News Agencies as well as with regional news agencies of developing countries. It asked that the practice of coverage of United Nations conferences and other events by the agencies of the Pool, in co-operation with DPI, be continued and strengthened.

This had been recommended in July by the Committee on Information,[1] which had mentioned in particular the newly established Pan-African News Agency. In addition, it suggested that DPI receive the daily dispatches of the Pool in the interest of more balance in information sources used by the Department.

As requested by the Assembly in December 1981,[4] DPI continued to develop links with international and regional news organizations and encouraged more media coverage of United Nations activities. The Secretary-General described these efforts in his September 1982 report to the Assembly on United Nations information activities.[2] According to the report, DPI had increased its information supply to the Pool and regional news agencies, sending out daily press dispatches in English and French to the Tanjug Agency at Belgrade, Yugoslavia, for redistribution to more than 80 agencies belonging to the Pool. To encourage media coverage, DPI held an annual editors' round table, providing senior editors and broadcasters with briefings and discussion by United Nations officials. In addition, more correspondents from news media in developing countries had been allocated work space at Headquarters.

Sweden, when explaining its vote for the resolution on United Nations public information activities, said it understood that DPI would co-operate fully with all news agencies.

Reports. (1)Committee on Information, A/37/21; (2)S-G, A/37/446.
Resolution (1982). (3)GA: 37/94 B, para. 21, 10 Dec.
Resolution (prior). (4)GA: 36/149 B, 16 Dec. 1981 (YUN 1981, p. 363).

Publications

In its 10 December 1982 resolution on United Nations public information activities,(3) the General Assembly called for improvements in the *UN Chronicle*, the monthly magazine produced by DPI. It requested the Secretary-General to publish the *Chronicle* in all official United Nations languages and in an attractive format to ensure a wide, timely and effective circulation. He was also requested to take measures, within existing financial resources, to ensure that the *Chronicle* was further improved to present a wide and more comprehensive coverage of United Nations activities. The Assembly also called for improvement of *Development Forum*.

The effect of the Assembly recommendation on languages was to add a Chinese version of the *Chronicle* to the five language versions already produced or scheduled.

The Secretary-General, in an April report to the Committee on Information,(2) described efforts to ensure balance in the use of official languages in DPI publications and programmes. Among the publications, the *UN Chronicle* had added a monthly Arabic version in 1981 to those already issued in English, French and Spanish, and the first Russian quarterly edition covered January-March 1982. The number of non-English editions of leaflets, pamphlets and booklets had been increased. DPI was making a constant effort to achieve a reasonable balance among official languages in publications, press releases, radio and television programmes, films, posters and information sent to information centres, within budgetary appropriations and the practical considerations of production facilities, regional requirements and potential audiences. Within its resources, DPI intended to improve the balance and to expand information dissemination in other languages where appropriate and feasible.

In a letter to the Secretary-General dated 5 November,(1) Israel objected to the publication in the *UN Chronicle* of material it described as marked by declining professional standards and blatant bias on various issues regarding the Arab-Israeli conflict, as well as to the treatment of political and human rights issues in the booklet *United Nations Today— 1982 (Suggestions for Speakers)*.

Letter. (1)Israel, 5 Nov., A/37/601.
Report. (2)S-G, A/AC.198/46.
Resolution (1982). (3)GA: 37/94 B, para. 22, 10 Dec.

Radio broadcasting

In its 10 December 1982 resolution on United Nations public information activities,(7) the General Assembly called for several steps to expand the radio broadcasting programme. It requested implementation of an existing programme plan in Portuguese and the submission of a plan for more programming in French and in additional African languages. It asked for a report on possible expansion of programming for the Caribbean area in French and other languages, and requested the enlargement—by redeploying resources—of the Arabic and Middle East Unit in the DPI Radio Service, producing television and radio programmes for Arabic-speaking countries. It asked for efforts towards a balanced use of all official United Nations languages in radio programmes covering United Nations conferences held away from Headquarters. A report was requested on the viability of a world-wide United Nations short-wave network and on the alternative solution of continuing to rent broadcast time on national short-wave transmitters. The Assembly also requested continued co-operation with African broadcasters.

These provisions on strengthening radio services were based on recommendations of the Committee on Information approved in July.(2) The Committee proposed that certain languages be added to the service within existing resources: Lingala for Africa, Bengali and Indonesian for Asia, and Serbo-Croat for Yugoslavia. The Committee called for proposals on programming in Africa at a meaningful level in English and French and in major languages of the region not already in use. To the extent possible through existing resources, the Committee said, United Nations short-wave broadcasts over rented transmitters should be placed on a daily schedule and, to expand United Nations broadcasts in Africa, technical and financial aspects and audience demands should be studied as part of a pilot project. The Committee also called for a report on the acquisition of a United Nations communications satellite.

The Secretary-General, in an April report to the Committee,(4) reviewed the work of the Radio Service. He said that, as requested by the Assembly in December 1981,(9) a Caribbean Unit consisting of four staff members had been established as at 1 January 1982 and the African Unit had been expanded from four to six posts for programming in Swahili, with another post to be transferred from the European Unit during 1983. There was scope for increasing the programme output of the Arabic and Middle East Unit without enlarging its current staff of four. Programme production in additional languages by the Asian Unit—Bengali, Indonesian/Malay, Japanese and Urdu—would require additional staff.

A second report in April[5] discussed technical, financial and legal aspects of United Nations–owned and –operated short-wave broadcast facilities and frequencies as a possible alternative to the current system, under which the United Nations rented broadcast time on national short-wave transmitters. It concluded that rental of national facilities could be regarded only as a stop-gap arrangement that was less effective than a United Nations network. As a global United Nations short-wave broadcasting network would take years to construct, equip and staff, the cost could be spread out over a period of time. Regional segments of such a network could be established consecutively, starting with Latin America, for which only two languages would be needed. A further study to identify specific radio frequencies would be required. Such a study would not prejudge the broader question of whether the United Nations should engage in short-wave broadcasting with its own facilities, which had considerable policy and budgetary implications.

The Secretary-General, in another April report to the Committee,[6] described the advantages, disadvantages and cost-effectiveness of radio and visual means of transmission, including three means of transmitting United Nations radio programmes: dispatch of programmes on tape, cassette or disc by diplomatic pouch or air mail; feeds over radio line, telephone, radio circuit or satellite radio channel; and short-wave broadcasts. According to the report, considerations of timeliness and cost-effectiveness suggested that primary reliance should be placed on short-wave transmissions, supplemented by direct feeds of certain programmes to major users.

In a note to the Committee in April,[1] the Secretary-General reported on legal questions concerned with the possible introduction of United Nations frequency modulation (FM) broadcasts in the Headquarters area, which would require an agreement supplemental to the 1947 Agreement between the United Nations and the United States of America regarding the Headquarters of the United Nations.[8] While that was feasible, the report said, it was difficult to predict whether it would be possible to obtain a satisfactory agreement in view of the legal complexities.

The Committee on Information, at its June/July session, briefly discussed the impediments to establishing a United Nations FM station in New York City and the possibility of overcoming them with help from the host country, which had pointed out that the New York FM reception area was already saturated.

In his September report to the General Assembly on information questions,[3] the Secretary-General said preparations were being made to act on the Committee's recommendations on radio

and visual services in anticipation of their approval by the Assembly. The feasibility of placing short-wave broadcasts over rented transmitters on a daily basis throughout the year was being examined.

Note. [1]S-G, A/AC.198/50.
Reports. [2]Committee on Information, A/37/21; S-G, [3]A/37/446, [4]A/AC.198/48, [5]A/AC.198/49, [6]A/AC.198/54.
Resolution (1982). [7]GA: 37/94 B, 10 Dec.
Resolutions (prior). GA: [8]169(II), 31 Oct. 1947 (YUN 1947-48, p. 199); [9]36/149 B, 16 Dec. 1981 (YUN 1981, p. 363).

Television broadcasting

The Committee on Information, in its August 1982 report to the General Assembly,[1] recommended that the Assembly take note with satisfaction of the work done by DPI regarding the satellite transmission of weekly television programmes on the United Nations.

The Committee was referring to a proposal, detailed by the Secretary-General in an April report,[2] for the preparation by DPI of weekly 5-10 minute television news magazines in Arabic, French and Spanish on United Nations activities. They were to be prepared during Assembly sessions beginning in 1982, using the Atlantic satellite of the International Telecommunications Satellite Organization (INTELSAT). The plan had been endorsed by the Assembly in December 1981,[4] on the Committee's recommendation, and took into account the result of a DPI survey of potential recipient stations in Africa, Latin America and the Middle East. The cost to the United Nations of the uplink of a direct satellite transmission was estimated at about $50,000 for each Assembly session. After the first stage, the Secretary-General said, proposals regarding the transmission of such magazines throughout the year would be presented to the Committee.

In another report to the Committee in April,[3] the Secretary-General described the advantages, disadvantages and cost-effectiveness of different means of television transmission. The three means used for transmission of United Nations events—direct feed, satellite, and video-cassette or film—were speedy, effective and involved no cost to the Organization, the report said. However, the worldwide trend in television transmission was towards satellite use.

Reports. [1]Committee on Information, A/37/21; S-G, [2]A/AC.198/52, [3]A/AC.198/54.
Resolution. [4]GA: 36/149 B, 16 Dec. 1981 (YUN 1981, p. 363).

Proposed regional units in the Radio and Visual Services Division

The Committee on Information, at its June/July 1982 session,[2] recommended that the Secretary-General report to it in 1983 on all aspects of the regionalization of the Radio and Visual Services Division of DPI—as far as possible within existing resources—taking into account views expressed in the Committee and consultations with experts. The Committee would then submit a recommendation to the Assembly in 1983.

In an April note to the Committee on this topic,[1] the Secretary-General, pointing out that the Radio Service was already divided into units serving individual regions, advised a step-by-step approach to regionalization of the Visual Service. Over the previous year, that Service had established a Latin American/Iberian Unit and a Middle East/North African Unit. African and Asian Units were planned for 1983 or 1984, requiring a total of seven new posts. Further plans included the establishment of a European Unit and diversification of languages in the Asian Unit, thus completing regionalization of the Visual Service by 1984 or 1985. Other requirements for regionalization were the maintenance of central sections for promotion and distribution, library services and feature production, the development of programmes for regional audiences, and the filling of vacant or new posts with qualified nationals of developing and under-represented countries. A decision would be taken later on the feasibility of integrating the visual and radio regional units.

However, in his September 1982 report to the Assembly on information questions,[3] the Secretary-General said that, in consideration of the views expressed in the Committee on Information, plans to establish additional pilot regional units had been suspended, pending preparation of the new report requested by the Committee.

Note. [1]S-G, A/AC.198/47.
Reports. [2]Committee on Information, A/37/21; [3]S-G, A/37/446.

Staffing

In its 10 December 1982 resolution on United Nations public information activities,[3] the General Assembly requested the Secretary-General to intensify efforts to redress the existing imbalance in DPI staff and, until equitable geographical distribution was achieved, to take steps to increase the representation of developing countries, particularly at senior levels, by recruiting their nationals, taking into account the interests of other under-represented countries.

The Assembly acted on the recommendation of the Committee on Information, which, in its report to the Assembly on its June/July session,[2] mentioned in particular the imbalance in the Radio and Visual Services Division of DPI.

The Secretariat, in an April note to the Committee,[1] gave a progress report on steps taken to improve the nationality balance of DPI staff in posts subject to geographical distribution, showing the percentage of Professional-category staff from seven regional groups. According to this note,

as at 1 January 1982 the greatest gain in percentage since 1 January 1981 had been recorded for Africa (13.2 per cent) and the Middle East (9 per cent), placing them above the mid-point of their desirable ranges (See ADMINISTRATIVE AND BUDGETARY QUESTIONS, Chapter III). There had been declines in the proportion of staff from Eastern Europe (9.7 per cent), North America and the Caribbean (7.5 per cent) and Western Europe (6.4 per cent).

Sweden, explaining its favourable vote on the Assembly resolution, reiterated that the principle of equitable geographical distribution applied to the Secretariat as a whole.

Note. [1]Secretariat, A/AC.198/44.
Report. [2]Committee on Information, A/37/21.
Resolution (1982). [3]GA: 37/94 B, para. 17, 10 Dec.

Evaluation

In its July 1982 recommendations to the General Assembly,[2] the Committee on Information encouraged the Secretary-General to continue his efforts to develop a system for monitoring and evaluating the effectiveness of DPI activities. The process of continual evaluation should be complemented by evaluation carried out by the Joint Inspection Unit, it said, and observations by consumers of materials and services should be taken into account. The Committee called for a progress report in 1983 and said future DPI reports to the Committee should contain the Department's evaluation of the effectiveness of its activities.

The Secretary-General, in a note to the Committee in April,[1] outlined DPI proposals for developing systematic evaluation procedures for its activities, and described contacts with international associations for mass communication research and their potential role in evaluation. Three stages were envisaged: first, compiling data on quantifiable outputs and services rendered by DPI; next, assessing the effectiveness of information dissemination to verify that the output actually reached the intended audiences; and finally, assessing the impact of information on its audiences, possibly with the collaboration of international research organizations on communication. The first stage had been accomplished and was providing a comparative base for future analysis of DPI activities.

Note. [1]S-G, A/AC.198/53.
Report. [2]Committee on Information, A/37/21.

Other aspects of the DPI work programme

The Committee on Information, among its July 1982 recommendations to the General Assembly,[1] expressed the view that the United Nations should aim at providing all possible support to the developing countries with regard to their information needs. It referred in particular to assistance to developing countries in training journalists and technicians and in setting up educational and research facilities; the granting of favourable conditions to provide developing countries with communication technology; the creation of conditions enabling developing countries to produce their own communication technology and programme material; and assistance in establishing subregional, regional and interregional telecommunication links, free from any conditions. The Committee also suggested that Member States make voluntary contributions to the United Nations Trust Fund for Economic and Social Information.

Report. (1)Committee on Information, A/37/21.

Co-ordination in the UN system

The General Assembly, in its resolution of 10 December 1982 on United Nations public information activities,(9) recommended strengthening the inter-agency Joint United Nations Information Committee (JUNIC) and called for greater efforts to place the periodical *Development Forum* on a sound financial basis. The Assembly called on United Nations organizations to develop concerted, integrated and coherent public information programmes to promote understanding of and support for the activities of the United Nations system, particularly in the economic, social, development and cultural fields. Stressing the vital role of information in development, the Assembly requested the Secretary-General to ensure closer DPI co-operation with United Nations development agencies and programmes, in particular the United Nations Development Programme (UNDP), in order to pool resources, avoid duplication and foster development.

In a March report to the Committee for Programme and Co-ordination (CPC),(8) the Secretary-General updated a 1981 document on the mechanisms and procedures for co-ordination of public information activities within the United Nations Secretariat. The report noted that a number of information units in the Secretariat existed outside DPI, and cited two main reasons for what it called a proliferation of such units: insufficient DPI resources to handle the information needs of new programmes, and the inability of DPI to produce certain politically sensitive materials. It concluded that, in view of the inherent conflict in the United Nations system between centrist and pluralistic approaches to programmes, it would be difficult for public information to follow one approach or the other.

In May 1982, after examining this report, CPC made two recommendations on co-ordination of public information activities within the Secretariat:(3) that the DPI co-ordination function should be strengthened and that no new information units should be created within the Secretariat.

CPC decided to review the JUNIC programme in 1983 in order to improve inter-agency co-ordination in this field.

Co-ordination of information activities among members of the United Nations system was dealt with by the Administrative Committee on Co-ordination (ACC) in comments, transmitted by the Secretary-General to the Assembly in April 1982,(2) on a February 1981 report on this subject by the Joint Inspection Unit (JIU).(10) The ACC comments dealt with the cost of public information activities in the United Nations system, the functioning of JUNIC and its use in planning joint projects, the continued publication of *Development Forum*, and common facilities away from Headquarters where a pooling of resources was desirable, including the better use of United Nations information centres.

The Committee on Information called in July(4) for co-ordination between DPI and the United Nations Educational, Scientific and Cultural Organization (UNESCO) in the promotion of a new world information and communication order, and between DPI and UNDP in fostering development. It recommended the strengthening of JUNIC, organization of a round table of media editors on a new world information and communication order, the continued publication of *Development Forum* and the strengthening of the Non-Governmental Liaison Services.

JUNIC activities. At its ninth session, held at Geneva from 19 to 23 April,(6) JUNIC dealt with several aspects of co-ordination and co-operation in the field of public information within the United Nations system.

It adopted a report on public perceptions of the United Nations system(7) which stressed the importance of broad support from special groups, parliaments and the general public. The report described some of the factors influencing public perceptions, analysed the role of the information services of the United Nations system, and identified practical constraints and internal problems. It included proposals to its parent body, ACC, on initial steps towards improving public perceptions of the United Nations through monitoring and responding to media, an editorial reference service in the form of a loose-leaf fact book, a feature service, constituency contact, and expansion of professional relations with the media.

The Committee on Information recommended in July that the report on public perceptions be submitted to it for review and comments. On 3 November,(1) ACC decided to follow the outline of action recommended by JUNIC and agreed that JUNIC member organizations should pursue its recommendations. It requested JUNIC to keep the matter under review and to report to ACC.

In general comments on the need for harmonizing public information activities, included in its progress report to the Committee on Information,[5] JUNIC stated that while pooling of resources would lead to greater economy and efficiency in many areas, United Nations organizations had to sustain their separate profiles before the world community. Given the diversity within the United Nations system, perhaps few subjects lent themselves to an overall approach that could satisfy all sources; it was therefore important for JUNIC to have a clear idea of those activities which could and should be jointly undertaken, and for their audiences to be well defined.

JUNIC adopted a plan of action for 1982-1983 outlining two types of projects: joint information projects to be carried out under its auspices, including new projects in regard to *apartheid*, disarmament and the environment, and individual projects to be co-ordinated between interested organizations. JUNIC remarked that the plan should be viewed as flexible in its presentation and implementation so as to accommodate all members of the system. Joint audio-visual services, as well as information activities on 14 United Nations events and themes, were also discussed.

At the session, JUNIC also approved recommendations on development education, involving public awareness in industrialized countries about development issues, and on development support communication, concerned with the role of communication in and for development projects in developing countries (See ECONOMIC AND SOCIAL QUESTIONS, Chapter I). Based on these recommendations, ACC adopted in November a statement on development support communication.

The Committee on Information recommended in July that JUNIC continue to report to it on programmes and activities. The General Assembly, in its December resolution on United Nations public information, requested action on this recommendation and on the Committee's request to see the report on public perceptions of the United Nations system.

Decision (1982). [1]ACC, 1982/28, 3 Nov.
Note. [2]S-G, annexing ACC comments, A/37/174.
Reports. [3]CPC, A/37/38; [4]Committee on Information, A/37/21; JUNIC, [5]A/AC.198/56, [6]ACC/1982/14, [7]ACC/1982/22; [8]S-G, E/AC.51/1982/2.
Resolution (1982). [9]GA: 37/94 B, 10 Dec.
Yearbook reference. [10]1981, p. 370.

Strengthening of JUNIC

The General Assembly, in its 10 December 1982 resolution on United Nations public information activities,[3] requested that JUNIC, as the essential instrument for inter-agency co-ordination in the field of public information, be strengthened and that its secretariat elaborate new work methods, longer-term indicative planning and joint action,

especially in the promotion of a new world information and communication order.

In its April 1982 comments[1] on the JIU recommendations of February 1981 concerning co-ordination of public information activities in the United Nations system,[4] ACC stated that more joint action, and consequently larger joint expenditures, could be undertaken if the capacity of JUNIC to undertake longer-range indicative planning and proposals were enhanced. *Ad hoc* working groups and task forces of JUNIC provided an opportunity for new joint approaches to common problems and events such as international years and major conferences. More could be done if planning for special issues or events were to take place early enough to allow individual organizations to take a more active part in the identification of joint projects and to set aside funds for joint financing. Individual organizations were prepared to co-operate in joint activities provided they were clearly identified, well designed and presented in time for financial planning.

ACC agreed with JIU that JUNIC and its secretariat should be strengthened. Regarding the proposal that JUNIC should report to the Economic and Social Council through CPC, ACC observed that JUNIC already reported through ACC to the Committee on Information and Member States should decide if additional reporting was required. ACC agreed with JIU that, as far as possible, JUNIC sessions should be attended by heads of information services and should be held primarily at the headquarters of the main organizations in order to minimize costs; however, it was more important that those attending have the authority to commit their organizations, especially in the selection and implementation of joint projects. ACC disagreed with a JIU recommendation that JUNIC have its own budget, but it said most members realized the importance of joint financing of projects.

The Committee on Information, in its July recommendations to the Assembly,[2] also called for strengthening JUNIC and giving it more responsibility so as to improve co-ordination and efficiency of the public information activities of the entire United Nations system. As a means of strengthening JUNIC, the Committee proposed reinforcing its secretariat so that it could elaborate new work methods for longer-term indicative planning and joint action, especially in the promotion of a new world information and communication order. Another recommendation called for JUNIC to strengthen its activities for development education and development support communication (see above).

Note. [1]S-G, annexing ACC comments, A/37/174.
Report. [2]Committee on Information, A/37/21.
Resolution (1982). [3]GA: 37/94 B, para. 7, 10 Dec.
Yearbook reference. [4]1981, p. 370.

Costs of public information activities

In its April 1982 comments[1] on the JIU recommendations of February 1981 concerning co-ordination of public information activities in the United Nations system, ACC noted that JIU had pointed out the difficulties in estimating the cost of such activities system-wide.[2] ACC believed that any conclusions drawn from such figures should be treated with caution because methods for identification and costing of public information activities varied considerably from agency to agency. Regarding the JIU suggestion for a standardized form for reporting the amounts spent on these activities, ACC thought there was no case for treating this matter separately from the general subject, already under study, of the presentation of expenditures for all programmes.

Instead of reporting regularly to CPC and others on cost estimates for information activities, ACC proposed that it continue to respond to requests for estimates by intergovernmental bodies and to intensify efforts to pool resources. As for the proposal that public information programmes and budgets be submitted to CPC, ACC said this did not take into account the fact that JUNIC reported to, and received guidance from, ACC and the Committee on Information on all joint activities undertaken under the JUNIC plan of action.

Note. [1]S-G, annexing ACC comments, A/37/174.
Yearbook reference. [2]1981, p. 371.

Publication of Development Forum

In its 10 December 1982 resolution on United Nations public information activities,[7] the General Assembly reaffirmed the importance of the periodical *Development Forum* as the only inter-agency publication of the United Nations system which concentrated on development issues, and requested the Secretary-General to continue to support its publication from the regular United Nations budget while intensifying efforts to secure for it an independent financial basis. The Assembly called on all United Nations organizations to contribute.

Commenting in April 1982[2] on the February 1981 report by JIU on the co-ordination of public information in the United Nations system,[8] ACC agreed on the importance of *Development Forum* for mobilizing public opinion on behalf of development. Noting its precarious financial situation, ACC concurred with the JIU view that a decisive step was required to maintain the publication on a long-term basis. Regarding the recommendation to improve the geographical distribution of the Professional staff of *Development Forum*, ACC pointed out that the editorial staff numbered only four and the short duration of contracts was a deterrent to recruitment. An Editorial Advisory Board, composed of nine specialists from all parts of the world, had held its first meeting in December 1981. As for the recommendation that high-level staff of United Nations organizations contribute articles to the publication, ACC said that the aim of *Development Forum* was to be a platform for dialogue rather than a vehicle for institutional news, a role which was assumed by other United Nations publications.

In an April report to the Committee on Information,[6] the Secretary-General reviewed the financial situation of *Development Forum*, including the question of long-term financial support from United Nations organizations. Stating his view that a continuing annual subvention from the United Nations regular budget was necessary, he considered that such an allotment should not cover all costs but should be a significant contribution to its core budget. Consequently, he would continue to request such a subvention in future budgets. At the same time, he intended to persist in efforts to make financial arrangements more predictable, particularly those involving other United Nations organizations.

He noted that the $400,000 contribution from the 1982-1983 United Nations budget was the same as for 1980-1981. The estimate of 1982 income was $1,580,400, of which $514,400 came from other United Nations organizations and $736,000 from subscriptions to the business edition. This compared with a total income of $1,524,100 for 1981, with contributions from those organizations amounting to $624,000 and subscription income to $625,100.

At its April 1982 session,[4] JUNIC praised the quality and relevance of *Development Forum*. It endorsed the project of a *Development Forum* Anniversary Colloquium to be held in February 1983 to celebrate the tenth anniversary of the publication. Also noting the importance of long-term financing, JUNIC appealed for continued and increased contributions.

In July,[3] the Committee on Information joined those calling for continuation of the publication. The Committee suggested that the Secretary-General be invited to contribute to securing a sound financial basis through the United Nations regular budget, while intensifying efforts to ensure an independent financial basis for the publication.

The Secretary-General, in his September report to the General Assembly on information questions,[5] reiterated his intention to intensify efforts to obtain voluntary contributions from United Nations bodies. He noted that the traditional donor countries had indicated that, effective from 1983, they would no longer be in a position to contribute.

On 3 November, ACC noted the Secretary-General's intention to establish a working group to review the various aspects of *Development Forum* and decided to place this question on the provisional agenda of its first regular session of 1983.[1]

Decision (1982). [1]ACC, 1982/29, 3 Nov.
Note. [2]S-G, annexing ACC comments, A/37/174.
Reports. [3]Committee on Information, A/37/21; [4]JUNIC,
    A/AC.198/56; S-G, [5]A/37/446, [6]A/AC.198/55.
Resolution (1982). [7]GA: 37/94 B, para. 26, 10 Dec.
Yearbook reference. [8]1981, p. 370.
Publication. Development Forum, vol. X, Nos. 1-9 (regular edi-
    tion), Nos. 94-117 (business edition).

Non-Governmental Liaison Services

The Committee on Information recommended to the General Assembly in July 1982[2] that the Non-Governmental Liaison Services in Geneva and New York, as permanent joint projects within JUNIC promoting public support for development, should be strengthened. The Committee said that continuation of their work should be ensured by having JUNIC members reserve the necessary funds as well as by appealing to Governments for voluntary support.

The two Liaison Services continued in 1982 to assist United Nations and non-governmental organizations. In April, JUNIC urged support for the Services through longer-term commitments by organizations, and noted that the scope of their activities had enlarged in the light of new trends, notably the peace movement on both sides of the Atlantic and public concern about disarmament, the environment and development.[3] On 3 November, ACC endorsed the JUNIC recommendations on seeking financial contributions for the Services' work.[1]

Decision (1982). [1]ACC, 1982/19, 3 Nov.
Reports. [2]Committee on Information, A/37/21; [3]JUNIC,
    A/AC.198/56.

Radiation effects

UNSCEAR activities. The United Nations Scientific Committee on the Effects of Atomic Radiation (UNSCEAR) submitted in 1982 a comprehensive report entitled *Ionizing Radiation: Sources and Biological Effects.*[2] This document, the eighth substantive report prepared by UNSCEAR since its establishment by the General Assembly in 1955,[5] was finalized at the Committee's thirty-first session, held from 15 to 26 March 1982 at Vienna, Austria. It analysed information which the Committee had gathered since its last such report, in 1977.[6] The summary and main text of the 1982 report were submitted as the Committee's annual report to the Assembly;[3] 12 scientific annexes detailing the procedures and information on which its conclusions were based were published with the full report.

The report systematically reviewed all major sources of human exposure to ionizing radiation: natural sources, such as cosmic rays and naturally occurring substances in the ground, building materials, air and diet; fall-out from nuclear explosions; nuclear power reactors; occupational hazards; medical, industrial and research uses of radiation; and radiation-emitting consumer products. Exposures from various sources were compared in terms of collective effective dose equivalent rates, expressing for a given time period the radiation impact on a population group resulting from a given source or practice, weighted to take account of the fact that different organs are variously affected by given amounts of exposure.

According to the report, the major contribution to the annual average radiation dosage came from natural sources, of which the most significant was radon gas, found in the ground, building materials, tap water and natural gas. In contrast to exposures to natural sources, which varied little from year to year and involved the world population to about the same extent, exposures to man-made sources varied significantly with time and from one population group to another. The main radiation sources in this second category were medical uses, nuclear explosions and power production; other sources gave rise to much lower collective effective dose equivalent rates.

Of the man-made sources, the highest radiation exposure rate came from medical use, particularly for diagnostic purposes and therapy. The average annual effective dose equivalent from medical use throughout the world, which had not changed appreciably over 35 years, was approximately 20 per cent of the average annual exposure to natural sources. UNSCEAR believed that there was a good potential for significant dose reduction in this area, compatible with the objective of its use.

The contribution of nuclear explosions had mostly decreased since 1963—the year after most atmospheric nuclear testing ceased. The average annual dose from this source had fallen from a 1963 level corresponding to about 7 per cent of average annual exposure to natural sources, to below 1 per cent in 1982. The collective effective dose equivalent commitment resulting from all nuclear explosions that had taken place up to 1980—an estimate of past, current and future exposure from all fall-out since 1945—corresponded to about four years of natural radiation exposure. About 10 per cent of that dose had already been delivered, and the remainder would be delivered in the next 10,000 years or so.

On the other hand, the annual collective effective dose equivalent attributable to nuclear power production had been increasing continuously due to the expansion of nuclear power programmes, although its share of the total dose was substantially less than that of the other major man-made sources. The total collective effective dose equivalent commitment due to the production of electrical energy by nuclear fission, up to the time of the report, was roughly estimated to correspond to one day of average exposure to natural background. At a projected installed capacity of some 7 to 11 times the 1980 capacity by the year 2000, this rate might rise to about two days' equivalent, though technological developments and the evolution of regulatory actions could make unrealistic the assumptions on which those calculations were based.

UNSCEAR also reviewed studies on biological effects of radiation. It reported that, although they did not result in major revisions of the current thinking about genetic risks or somatic effects, they had focused on some new developments and had strengthened its belief that the mechanisms of some radiation effects were becoming reasonably well understood. That applied particularly to non-stochastic effects—arising when a large proportion of cells in a tissue are killed or inactivated by radiation, thus causing anatomical or functional tissue damage. Regarding other effects, such as those depending on neoplastic (tumorous) transformation of irradiated cells, current knowledge of mechanisms remained largely incomplete. UNSCEAR said it would continue its surveillance of radiation carcinogenesis, including the theoretical foundations and the actual risk estimates of cancer induction in humans.

With regard to hereditary effects, the report said extensive use of experimental data for genetic risk assessment—based largely on data from laboratory tests on mice and non-human primates—was considered essential in the absence of significant results from studies on hereditary effects after human exposures. Further work was needed on the extent to which recessive mutations—expressed only when an individual received the same mutated gene from both parents—led to genetic damage over many generations.

General Assembly action. By a resolution of 10 December 1982,[4] the General Assembly commended UNSCEAR for its excellent report and for its valuable contribution to wider knowledge of the levels, effects and risks of radiation. Commending its scientific authority and independence of judgement, the Assembly requested UNSCEAR to continue its work, endorsed its plans for future review and assessment activities, and requested it to report in 1983 on important radiation problems. The Assembly noted with satisfaction the growing scientific co-operation between UNSCEAR and the United Nations Environment Programme (UNEP), and requested UNEP to continue supporting UNSCEAR work and disseminating its findings. Expressing appreciation for the assistance rendered to UNSCEAR by Member States, specialized agencies, the International Atomic Energy Agency and non-governmental organizations, the Assembly invited them to increase their co-operation and to provide further data about doses, effects and risks.

The Assembly adopted the resolution without vote, acting on the recommendation of the Special Political Committee (SPC). Argentina introduced the 21-nation draft in SPC, which approved it without vote on 19 October.

Japan, in a note verbale of 25 June addressed to the Secretary-General in connection with the World Disarmament Campaign, suggested that the United Nations assemble audio-visual materials on the Japanese atomic bomb experiences in 1945 at Hiroshima and Nagasaki, and make such materials available to all peoples as as a warning of the dangers inherent in the arms race.[1]

Note verbale. [1]Japan, 25 June, A/S-12/AC.1/44 & Corr.1.
Publication. [2]*Ionizing Radiation: Sources and Biological Effects*, Sales No. E.82.IX.8.
Report. [3]UNSCEAR, A/37/45.
Resolution (1982). [4]GA: 37/87, 10 Dec., text following.
Resolution (prior). [5]GA: 913(X), 3 Dec. 1955 (YUN 1955, p. 21).
Yearbook reference. [6]1977, p. 99.
Meeting records. GA: SPC, A/SPC/37/SR.4, 5 (18, 19 Oct.); plenary, A/37/PV.100 (10 Dec.).

General Assembly resolution 37/87

10 December 1982   Meeting 100   Adopted without vote

Approved by SPC (A/37/573) without vote, 19 October (meeting 5); 21-nation draft (A/SPC/37/L.3); agenda item 60.

Sponsors: Argentina, Australia, Austria, Bangladesh, Chile, Czechoslovakia, Denmark, Egypt, France, Germany, Federal Republic of, India, Japan, Malaysia, Netherlands, New Zealand, Peru, Poland, Sweden, USSR, United States, Uruguay.

Effects of atomic radiation

The General Assembly,

Recalling its resolution 913(X) of 3 December 1955, by which it established the United Nations Scientific Committee on the Effects of Atomic Radiation, and its subsequent resolutions on the subject, including resolution 36/14 of 28 October 1981, by which it, *inter alia,* requested the Scientific Committee to continue its work,

Taking note with appreciation of the report of the United Nations Scientific Committee on the Effects of Atomic Radiation with its scientific annexes,

Reaffirming the desirability of the Scientific Committee continuing its work,

Concerned about the potentially harmful effects on present and future generations, resulting from the levels of radiation to which man is exposed,

Conscious of the continued need to examine and compile information about atomic and ionizing radiation and to analyse its effects on man and his environment,

1. *Commends* the United Nations Scientific Committee on the Effects of Atomic Radiation for its excellent substantive report and for the valuable contribution it has been making in the course of the past twenty-seven years, since its inception, to wider knowledge and understanding of the levels, effects and risks of atomic radiation and for fulfilling its original mandate with scientific authority and independence of judgement;

2. *Notes with satisfaction* the continued and growing scientific co-operation between the Scientific Committee and the United Nations Environment Programme;

3. *Requests* the Scientific Committee to continue its work, including its important co-ordinating activities, to increase knowledge of the levels, effects and risks of ionizing radiation from all sources;

4. *Welcomes and endorses* the Scientific Committee's intentions and plans for its future activities of scientific review and assessment on behalf of the General Assembly;

5. *Requests* the Scientific Committee to review at its next session the important problems in the field of radiation and to report thereon to the General Assembly at its thirty-eighth session;

6. *Requests* the United Nations Environment Programme to continue providing support for the effective conduct of the Scientific Committee's work and for the dissemination of its findings to the General Assembly, the scientific community and the public;

7. *Expresses its appreciation* for the assistance rendered to the Scientific Committee by Member States, the specialized agencies, the International Atomic Energy Agency and non-governmental organizations, and invites them to increase their co-operation in this field;

8. *Invites* Member States and the United Nations agencies and non-governmental organizations concerned to provide further relevant data about doses, effects and risks from various sources of radiation, which would greatly help in the preparation of the Scientific Committee's future reports to the General Assembly.

Chapter XI

Organizational questions

Contents

Security Council organizational questions

Agenda

The Security Council held 89 meetings during 1982—its thirty-seventh year—at which it considered a total of 13 items. It continued to follow the practice of adopting at each meeting the agenda for that meeting. (For list of agenda items, see (APPENDIX IV.)

Five of the items considered in 1982 were included in the Council's agenda for the first time. In the chronological order of their inclusion, they concerned peace and security in Central America and the Caribbean area, the status of the Falkland Islands (Malvinas) (two items relating to different phases of the situation, dealt with consecutively), the Chad situation and Arabic language services.

By a 16 November decision,[1] adopted without vote, the General Assembly, on an oral proposal of its President, took note of a note by the Secretary-General dated 22 September. In this note,[2] the Secretary-General notified the Assembly, in accor-

dance with Article 12, paragraph 2, of the Charter of the United Nations, of 13 matters relative to the maintenance of international peace and security which the Security Council had discussed since his previous annual notification.[3] In addition, he listed 88 matters of which the Council remained seized but which it had not discussed during the period.

Decision (1982). [1]GA: 37/410, 16 Nov., text following.
Notification. [2]S-G note, A/37/468.
Yearbook reference. [3]1981, p. 353.
Compilation of resolutions and decisions. SC: 37th year, S/INF/38.
Index. Index to Proceedings of the Security Council, Thirty-seventh Year, 1982 (ST/LIB/SER.B/S.19), Sales No. E.83.I.11.
Meeting record. GA: A/37/PV.70 (16 Nov.).

General Assembly decision 37/410

Adopted without vote

Oral proposal by President; agenda item 7.

Notification by the Secretary-General under Article 12, paragraph 2, of the Charter of the United Nations

At its 70th plenary meeting, on 16 November 1982, the General Assembly took note of the note by the Secretary-General dated 22 September 1982.

Arabic language services

The Security Council decided by consensus on 21 December 1982[4] to include Arabic among its official and working languages and to amend its provisional rules of procedure[3] accordingly. The resolution to this effect, making Arabic the sixth such language of the Council, was sponsored by Jordan which, in a letter of 17 December to the Council President,[2] had requested that the Council consider the matter. Jordan recalled in its letter that the General Assembly, in December 1980,[5] had requested the Council to take this step no later than 1 January 1983. Egypt, in a letter of 21 December,[1] congratulated the President and Council members for their unanimity in adopting the resolution.

Letters. [1]Egypt, 21 Dec., S/15535; [2]Jordan, 17 Dec., S/15532.
Publication. [3]*Provisional Rules of Procedure of the Security Council (December 1982)* (S/96/Rev.7), Sales No. E.83.I.4.
Resolution (1982). [4]SC: 528(1982), 21 Dec., text following.
Resolution (prior). [5]GA: 35/219 A, 17 Dec. 1980 (YUN 1980, p. 1245).
Meeting record. SC: S/PV.2410 (21 Dec.).

Security Council resolution 528(1982)

21 December 1982	Meeting 2410	Adopted by consensus

Draft by Jordan (S/15531).

The Security Council,

Having considered the question concerning the inclusion of Arabic among the official and working languages of the Security Council,

Bearing in mind General Assembly resolution 35/219 of 17 December 1980,

Bearing in mind also General Assembly resolutions 3190(XXVIII) of 18 December 1973 and 34/226 of 20 December 1979,

Taking into account that the General Assembly, in its resolution 35/219 A, after affirming that, in the interest of the full effectiveness of the work of the United Nations, Arabic should be accorded the same status as the other official and working languages, requested, *inter alia,* the Security Council to include Arabic among its official and working languages not later than 1 January 1983,

Decides to include Arabic among the official and working languages of the Security Council and to amend rules 41 and 42 of the provisional rules of procedure of the Council to read as follows:

"Rule 41

"Arabic, Chinese, English, French, Russian and Spanish shall be both the official and the working languages of the Security Council.

"Rule 42

"Speeches made in any of the six languages of the Security Council shall be interpreted into the other five languages."

Report

On 24 November 1982, the Security Council unanimously adopted its report to the General Assembly for the period 16 June 1981 to 15 June 1982.[2] The Assembly took note of this report on 17 December, acting without vote on an oral proposal by its President.[1]

The Council's activities during the remainder of 1982 were covered in its report to the Assembly for the period 16 June 1982 to 15 June 1983.[3]

Decision (1982). [1]GA: 37/435, 17 Dec., text following.
Reports. SC, [2]A/37/2, [3]A/38/2.
Communiqué. SC: S/PV.2402 (24 Nov.).
Meeting record. GA: A/37/PV.110 (17 Dec.).

General Assembly decision 37/435

Adopted without vote

Oral proposal by President; agenda item 11.

At its 110th plenary meeting, on 17 December 1982, the General Assembly took note of the report of the Security Council.

Proposed increase in membership

In 1982, the General Assembly again postponed consideration of the question of equitable representation on and increase in the membership of the Security Council, as it had done in 1981.[4] Draft resolutions on this item, proposing an increase in membership from 15 to 21, had been presented and discussed at both the 1979[2] and 1980[3] sessions, but no action had been taken.

On 21 December 1982,[1] the Assembly decided to include the item in the provisional agenda of its 1983 regular session. The decision was adopted, without vote, on an oral proposal by the President, who stated that no request for consideration of the matter had been made during the session.

Decision (1982). [1]GA: 37/450, 21 Dec., text following.
Yearbook references. [2]1979, p. 435; [3]1980, p. 461; [4]1981, p. 353.
Meeting record. GA: A/37/PV.115 (21 Dec.).

General Assembly decision 37/450

Adopted without vote

Oral proposal by President; agenda item 36.

Question of equitable representation on and increase in the membership of the Security Council

At its 115th plenary meeting, on 21 December 1982, the General Assembly decided to include in the provisional agenda of its thirty-eighth session the item entitled "Question of equitable representation on and increase in the membership of the Security Council".

Voting procedures

On 1 December 1982, the General Assembly's Sixth (Legal) Committee decided not to act on a draft resolution[1] asking for consideration of aspects of the Security Council's rule of unanimity by the Special Committee on the Charter of the United Nations and on the Strengthening of the Role of the Organization (See LEGAL QUESTIONS, Chapter IV). This decision was taken on an oral motion by Australia adopted by a recorded vote of 52 to 32, with 24 abstentions.[2] The draft was introduced by the Libyan Arab Jamahiriya and also sponsored by Benin, Iran, Mali and Mauritania.

The draft called for the Special Committee to examine and report in 1983 on the possibility of eliminating the adverse effects for international peace and security arising from the abuse of the rule of unanimity. This examination would have taken four factors into account: the need to ensure that the rule of unanimity was not resorted to on matters relating to the inalienable rights of peoples struggling for self-determination against colonialism, *apartheid*, foreign domination, intervention, aggression and occupation; the fact that the maintenance of international peace and security was a common responsibility of all Member States; proposals in the Committee to strengthen the role of the Assembly; and a study of the possibility that Assembly resolutions on maintaining international peace and security be considered binding.

Draft resolution not voted upon. [1]Benin, Iran, Libyan Arab Jamahiriya, Mali, Mauritania, A/C.6/37/L.5/Rev.1.
Report. [2]6th Committee, A/37/722.

General Assembly organizational questions

Dates of sessions

The General Assembly met in five separate sessions during 1982—concluding its thirty-sixth regular session and holding the major part of its thirty-seventh, as well as convening in its ninth emergency special session on the situation in the territories occupied by Israel, with special reference to Israel's annexation of the Golan Heights (See POLITICAL AND SECURITY QUESTIONS, Chapter IX); reconvening its seventh emergency special session on the Palestine question and related matters; and holding its twelfth special session, the second devoted to disarmament.

The thirty-sixth regular session, which had opened on 15 September 1981 and had been suspended on 18 December,[2] was resumed on 16 March 1982 and continued until 29 March. Another meeting of the resumed session took place on 28 April and the session closed on 20 September.

The ninth emergency special session was held from 29 January to 5 February to consider the situation in the occupied Arab territories.

The seventh emergency special session (second part), which was resumed from 1980 to consider the question of Palestine, met from 20 to 28 April, on 25 and 26 June, from 16 to 19 August and on 24 September.

The twelfth special session, on disarmament, was held from 7 June to 10 July.

The Assembly opened its thirty-seventh regular session on 21 September. The session continued until 21 December, when the Assembly, on an oral proposal of its President, decided without vote to suspend the session and to resume it at a date to be announced in order to complete consideration of four items remaining on its agenda.[1] From 27 September to 15 October, during the period of the Assembly's general debate, 142 statements were made by heads of State or Government and by other heads or members of delegations.

Decision (1982). [1]GA: 37/452, 21 Dec., text following.
Decision (prior). [2]GA: 36/461, 18 Dec. 1981 (YUN 1981, p. 350).
Meeting record. GA: A/37/PV.115 (21 Dec.).

General Assembly decision 37/452

Adopted without vote

Oral proposal by President; agenda item 8.

Suspension of the thirty-seventh session

At its 115th plenary meeting, on 21 December 1982, the General Assembly decided to resume its thirty-seventh session, at a date to be announced, for the sole purpose of considering the following agenda items:

Item 27: Preparation of the United Nations Conference for the Promotion of International Co-operation in the Peaceful Uses of Nuclear Energy;

Item 37: Question of Cyprus;

Item 38: Launching of global negotiations on international economic co-operation for development;

Item 141: Implementation of the resolutions of the United Nations.

Agenda

The General Assembly adopted without vote on 29 January 1982[1] a five-item agenda for its ninth emergency special session,[5] including one substantive item: the situation in the occupied Arab territories.

Seven items remained on the agenda for consideration at the resumed thirty-sixth session, as decided by the Assembly in December 1981.[4]

The agenda of the seventh emergency special session remained the same as that approved in 1980,[13] containing five items including one substantive one: the question of Palestine.

The Assembly adopted without vote on 7 June 1982[2] a 14-item agenda[6] (annotated by the Secretariat[7]) for its twelfth special session, devoted to disarmament, and allocated nine of those items for consideration in plenary meetings and five to the *Ad Hoc* Committee of the Twelfth Special Session.

A 137-item agenda for the Assembly's thirty-seventh session was adopted on 24 September, and five additional items were included on 8 October, 12 November and 2 December.[3] In addition to adopting the agenda,[8] (annotated by the Secretariat[10]), the Assembly allocated each of the 142 items for consideration by one of its Main Committees or directly in plenary meetings.[9]

These actions at the thirty-seventh session were taken on the recommendations of the General Committee. The Committee acted on 22 September on the basis of a provisional agenda of 133 items[11] and a supplementary list of 5 items[12] proposed prior to the session, and on 8 October, 11 November and 1 December it recommended approval of the additional items proposed during the session. By a roll-call vote of 11 to 7, with 8 abstentions, the Committee decided on 22 September not to recommend inclusion of the question of Puerto Rico (See TRUSTEESHIP AND DECOLONIZATION, Chapter I). On the same date, a proposal by the USSR to delete sub-item 54 *(b)* (Chemical and bacteriological (biological) weapons: Report of the Secretary-General), relating to an investigation of the alleged use of chemical weapons (See POLITICAL AND SECURITY QUESTIONS, Chapter I), was rejected by 13 votes to 4, with 5 abstentions. The Committee recommended the inclusion of all other items without vote.

The Assembly's actions on inclusion and allocation of items were also taken without vote, with two exceptions. On 24 September, it rejected, by a recorded vote of 70 to 30, with 43 abstentions, a proposal by Cuba that the question of Puerto Rico be included in the agenda. On the same date, a decision to have the question of the Falkland Islands (Malvinas) considered in plenary meeting was amended, by a recorded vote of 41 to 33, with 24 abstentions, to provide that bodies and individuals interested in the question would be heard in the Fourth Committee (See TRUSTEESHIP AND DECOLONIZATION, Chapter IV).

(For lists of agenda items, see APPENDIX IV.)

Decisions (1982). GA: [1]ES-9/21, 29 Jan., text following; [2]S-12/23, 7 June, text following; [3]37/402, 24 Sep., 8 Oct., 12 Nov. & 2 Dec. (& 10 May 1983), text following.
Decision (prior). [4]GA: 36/461, 18 Dec. 1981 (YUN 1981, p. 350).
Documents. [5]9th emergency special session: agenda, A/ES-9/5. 12th special session: [6]agenda, A/S-12/20; [7]annotated provisional agenda, A/S-12/10/Add.1. 37th session: [8]agenda, A/37/251 & Add.1-3; [9]allocation, A/37/252 & Add.1-3; [10]annotated preliminary list and agenda, A/37/100 & Add.1; [11]provisional agenda, A/37/150; [12]supplementary list, A/37/200.
Yearbook reference. [13]1980, p. 382.
Compilations of resolutions and decisions. GA: 9th emergency special session, A/ES-9/7; 7th emergency special session (2nd part), A/ES-7/14/Rev.1; 12th special session, A/S-12/6; 37th session, A/37/51.
Indexes. Index to Proceedings of the General Assembly, Ninth Emergency Special Session, Seventh Emergency Special Session (second part), Twelfth Special Session—1982 (ST/LIB/SER.B/A.35), Sales No. E.83.I.15; *Thirty-seventh session—1982/1983* (ST/LIB/SER.B/A.36), Sales No. E.83.I.23.
Meeting records. GA: A/ES-9/PV.1 (29 Jan.), A/S-12/PV.1 (7 June), A/37/PV.4, 24, 65, 88 (24 Sep.–2 Dec.).

General Assembly decision ES-9/21

Adopted without vote

Oral proposal by President; agenda item 4.

Adoption of the agenda
At its 1st plenary meeting, on 29 January 1982, the General Assembly adopted the agenda for its ninth emergency special session.

General Assembly decision S-12/23

Adopted without vote

Oral proposal by President; agenda item 7.

Adoption of the agenda and allocation of agenda items
At its 1st plenary meeting, on 7 June 1982, the General Assembly adopted the agenda for the twelfth special session.

At the same meeting, the General Assembly:

(a) Decided that items 1 to 8 and 14 would be considered directly in plenary meeting;

(b) Decided to allocate items 9 to 13 to the *Ad Hoc* Committee of the Twelfth Special Session and to entrust it with the task of considering all the proposals submitted under those items during the special session and of reporting to the General Assembly.

General Assembly decision 37/402

Adopted without vote

Approved by General Committee (A/37/250 & Add.1-3), 22 September, 8 October, 11 November and 1 December (meetings 1-5); agenda item 8 *(a)*.

Adoption of the agenda and allocation of agenda items
At its 4th, 24th, 65th, 88th and 116th plenary meetings, on 24 September, 8 October, 12 November and 2 December 1982 and 10 May 1983, the General Assembly, on the recommendations of the General Committee as set forth in its first, second, third, fourth and fifth reports, adopted the agenda and the allocation of agenda items for the thirty-seventh session.

Organization of work

On 24 September 1982,[1] the General Assembly adopted without vote provisions concerning the organization of the thirty-seventh session, similarly recommended by the General Committee on 22 September.

These organizational arrangements set a daily timetable for meetings and called for limits on the reproduction of speeches in meeting records, agreement among regional groups on the distribution of Committee chairmanships for the following session, the fixing of a 1 December deadline for submission of draft resolutions with financial implications, the establishment of deadlines for the submission of subsidiary organ reports requiring consideration by the Fifth (Administrative and Budgetary) Committee, and provision for a 48-hour period between the submission and the voting of proposals involving expenditure to permit statements of administrative and financial implications to be prepared. The Assembly urged States and subsidiary organs to exercise maximum restraint in requesting circulation of material as official documents.

The Assembly decided on 24 September, 8 and 14 October, and 2 December that 11 subsidiary organs should be authorized to hold meetings during its 1982 session, as recommended by the Committee on Conferences and the General Committee.[2]

Decisions (1982). GA: [1]37/401, 24 Sep., text following; [2]37/403, 24 Sep., 8 & 14 Oct. & 2 Dec.
Publication. Rules of Procedure of the General Assembly (embodying amendments and additions adopted by the General Assembly up to 31 December 1981) (A/520/Rev.14), Sales No. E.82.I.9.
Meeting record. GA: A/37/PV.4 (24 Sep.).

General Assembly decision 37/401

Adopted without vote

Approved by General Committee (A/37/250) without vote, 22 September (meeting 1); agenda item 8 *(a)*.

Organization of the thirty-seventh session
At its 4th plenary meeting, on 24 September 1982, the General Assembly, on the recommendations of the General Committee as set forth in its first report, adopted a number of provisions concerning the organization of the thirty-seventh session.

Credentials of representatives

At each of its 1982 sessions except the resumed regular session continued from 1981, the General Assembly approved reports of its Credentials Committee accepting the credentials submitted by Member States for representatives attending those sessions. In each case the Committee, acting without vote, adopted resolutions orally proposed by its Chairman by which it accepted the credentials concerned, and the Assembly similarly adopted resolutions submitted by the Committee to approve its reports.

The Assembly resolution at the ninth emergency special session[1] was adopted on 5 February 1982, based on a draft approved by the Committee on 3 February. The resolution at the seventh emergency special session[2] was adopted on 28 April, based on a draft the Committee had approved on 23 April. The resolution at the twelfth special session,[3] adopted on 10 July, was based on a draft approved by the Committee on 6 July.

On 26 October[4] and 17 December,[5] at its thirty-seventh regular session, the Assembly adopted two resolutions approving reports of the Credentials Committee as recommended by the Committee on 6 October and 7 December, respectively. An amendment to have the Assembly approve the Committee's first report except with regard to the credentials of Democratic Kampuchea was rejected on 25 October by a recorded vote of 90 to 29, with 26 abstentions. On 26 October, by a recorded vote of 74 to 9, with 32 abstentions, the Assembly decided not to act on an amendment by Iran to reject the credentials of Israel (See POLITICAL AND SECURITY QUESTIONS, Chapters VI, IX).

Resolutions (1982). GA: [1]ES-9/2, 5 Feb., text following; [2]ES-7/1 B, 28 Apr., text following; [3]S-12/1, 10 July, text following; [4]37/5 A, 26 Oct., text following; [5]37/5 B, 17 Dec., text following.

Meeting records. GA: A/ES-9/PV.12 (5 Feb.), A/ES-7/PV.21 (28 Apr.), A/S-12/PV.29 (10 July), A/37/PV.45, 110 (26 Oct., 17 Dec.).

General Assembly resolution ES-9/2

5 February 1982   Meeting 12   Adopted without vote

Approved by Credentials Committee (A/ES-9/6) without vote, 3 February (meeting 1); oral proposal by Chairman; agenda item 3 *(b)*.

Credentials of representatives to the ninth emergency special session of the General Assembly

The General Assembly
Approves the report of the Credentials Committee.

General Assembly resolution ES-7/1 B

28 April 1982   Meeting 21   Adopted without vote

Approved by Credentials Committee (A/ES-7/13/Add.1) without vote, 23 April (meeting 2); oral proposal by Chairman; agenda item 3.

Credentials of representatives to the seventh emergency special session of the General Assembly

The General Assembly
Approves the second report of the Credentials Committee.

General Assembly resolution S-12/1

10 July 1982   Meeting 29   Adopted without vote

Approved by Credentials Committee (A/S-12/28) without vote, 6 July (meeting 1); oral proposal by Chairman; agenda item 3 *(b)*.

Credentials of representatives to the twelfth special session of the General Assembly

The General Assembly
Approves the report of the Credentials Committee.

General Assembly resolutions 37/5 A and B

A: 26 October 1982   Meeting 45   Adopted without vote
B: 17 December 1982   Meeting 110   Adopted without vote

Approved by Credentials Committee (A/37/543 and Add.1) without vote, 6 October and 7 December (meetings 1 and 2); oral proposals by Chairman; agenda item 3 *(b)*.

Credentials of representatives to the thirty-seventh session of the General Assembly

A

The General Assembly
Approves the first report of the Credentials Committee.

B

The General Assembly
Approves the second report of the Credentials Committee.

Relations between the United Nations and other intergovernmental organizations

In 1982, the General Assembly adopted without vote six resolutions on co-operation between the United Nations and the following intergovernmental organizations: the Agency for Cultural and Technical Co-operation, the Asian-African Legal Consultative Committee, the League of Arab States, the Organization of African Unity, the Organization of the Islamic Conference and the Southern African Development Co-ordination Conference. By each resolution, the Secretary-General was requested to report to the Assembly in 1983 on measures taken to futher co-operation between the United Nations and the organization concerned.

Agency for Cultural and Technical Co-operation

The Secretary-General reported to the General Assembly through the Economic and Social Council in June 1982[3] that the United Nations and the Agency for Cultural and Technical Co-operation were considering eight areas of potential co-operation between them—new and renewable energy sources, environmental protection, science and technology for development, joint training programmes, recruitment of technical assistance personnel, regional and subregional co-operation, exchange of information and publications, and co-operation with the United Nations Development Programme. Further consultations on specific activities were envisaged.

The Council, acting without vote, took note of this report on 28 July and transmitted it to the Assembly.[1] The Council's Third (Programme and Co-ordination) Committee had recommended this action on 19 July, also without vote, as proposed by the Chairman.

On 17 December, the Assembly,[4] acting without vote, also took note of the Secretary-General's report and requested him, in collaboration with the Secretary-General of the Agency, to specify the areas of co-operation envisaged in the report, to consider the modalities of co-operation, taking duly into account the proposals of the Agency's Secretary-General, and to report to the Assembly in 1983 through the Council.

The Second (Economic and Financial) Committee had recommended this action without vote on 19 November on the basis of a draft submitted by a Vice-Chairman after informal consultations. A previous 28-nation draft introduced by Benin,[2] by which the Secretary-General would have been requested to specify areas of co-operation between the United Nations and the Agency "on the basis of proposals by the Agency" rather than "taking duly into account the proposals of the Secretary-General of the Agency", was subsequently withdrawn.

Decision (1982). [1]ESC: 1982/164, 28 July, text following.
Draft resolution withdrawn. [2]Belgium, Benin, Burundi, Canada, Central African Republic, Chad, Comoros, Congo, Djibouti, France, Gabon, Haiti, Ivory Coast, Lao People's Democratic Republic, Lebanon, Mali, Mauritania, Niger, Romania, Rwanda, Senegal, Togo, Tunisia, United Republic of Cameroon, Upper Volta, Vanuatu, Viet Nam, Zaire, A/C.2/37/L.11.
Report. [3]S-G, A/37/290.
Resolution (1982). [4]GA: 37/132, 17 Dec., text following.
Meeting records. ESC: E/1982/SR.49 (28 July). GA: 2nd Committee, A/C.2/37/SR.3-12, *26*, 32, *41* (28 Sep.-19 Nov.); plenary, A/37/PV.109 (17 Dec.).

Economic and Social Council decision 1982/164

Adopted without vote

Approved by Third Committee (E/1982/91) without vote, 19 July (meeting 11); draft by Chairman (E/1982/C.3/L.3); agenda item 20.

Report of the Secretary-General on co-operation between the United Nations and the Agency for Cultural and Technical Co-operation

At its 49th plenary meeting, on 28 July 1982, the Council took note of the report of the Secretary-General on co-operation between the United Nations and the Agency for Cultural and Technical Co-operation, and decided to transmit it to the General Assembly at its thirty-seventh session.

General Assembly resolution 37/132

17 December 1982   Meeting 109   Adopted without vote

Approved by Second Committee (A/37/679) without vote, 19 November (meeting 41); draft by Vice-Chairman (A/C.2/37/L.27), based on consultations on 28-nation draft (A/C.2/37/L.11); agenda item 12.

Co-operation between the United Nations and the Agency for Cultural and Technical Co-operation

The General Assembly,

Recalling its resolution 33/18 of 10 November 1978, by which it accorded observer status to the Agency for Cultural and Technical Co-operation,

Recalling also its resolution 36/174 of 17 December 1981, in which it recognized the necessity of strengthening co-operation between the United Nations and the Agency for Cultural and Technical Co-operation,

1. *Takes note* of the report of the Secretary-General on co-operation between the United Nations and the Agency for Cultural and Technical Co-operation;

2. *Requests* the Secretary-General, in collaboration with the Secretary-General of the Agency for Cultural and Technical Co-operation, to specify in detail the areas of co-operation envisaged in his report and to consider the modalities of this co-operation, taking duly into account the proposals of the Secretary-General of the Agency;

3. *Also requests* the Secretary-General to report on this subject to the General Assembly at its thirty-eighth session through the Economic and Social Council.

League of Arab States

Reporting to the General Assembly in October 1982 on co-operation between the United Nations and the League of Arab States,[4] the Secretary-General outlined suggestions for strengthening and expanding co-operation made separately by the United Nations system and the League. These pertained to political, industrial, technical co-operation, agricultural, labour, educational, health and other matters.

The League proposed that the United Nations system allow the League and its specialized organizations to participate actively in all activities relating to the Arab States. Periodic consultations should be carried out on topics of mutual interest and to follow up on agreements and decisions. The efficient use of the Arabic language in United Nations bodies should be ensured and Arabic should be introduced where it was not currently employed. A number of the League's specialized organizations believed that further efforts at co-operation should be embodied in formal agreements identifying areas for further co-operation and dealing with modalities for follow-up and implementation of agreed programmes.

The Secretary-General concluded that many of the proposals of the United Nations and the League could best be pursued within the framework of existing memoranda of understanding and agreements between bodies of the United Nations system and the corresponding departments of the League and its specialized organizations. Proposals of a regional nature could be examined most appropriately within the framework of arrangements between the League and the United Nations commissions for Africa and Western Asia. A number of suggestions could be studied at a joint meeting proposed by the League.

Acting without vote, the General Assembly, on 16 November,[5] took note of the report and expressed appreciation for the Secretary-General's initiatives to strengthen and expand co-operation between the United Nations and the League. It commended the League for its efforts and co-operation, and for its increased political, economic, cultural and humanitarian collaboration with the United Nations system. It recommended that the suggestions by the United Nations system and the League be considered by United Nations organizations and form the basis for new and expanded co-operation. The United Nations Secretary-General, in consultation with his counterpart in the League, was asked to determine which suggestions could be dealt with bilaterally and which multilaterally, and to arrange for them to be considered accordingly. The Assembly endorsed the proposal for a meeting between the United Nations system and the League's General Secretariat and specialized organizations, welcomed the League's invitation to hold it at the current headquarters of the League at Tunis, Tunisia, and requested that it be held by 30 June 1983.

Morocco sponsored this resolution on behalf of the Arab Group. The Assembly rejected, by a recorded vote of 104 to 1, with 23 abstentions, a United States amendment by which the Assembly would have authorized the Secretary-General to implement the activities approved under the resolution only to the extent that they could be financed without exceeding the United Nations budget for 1982-1983.[1] The Assembly's Fifth (Administrative and Budgetary) Committee reported that an additional appropriation of $22,500 would be required to implement the resolution in 1983 and that conference services valued at $101,200 would also be needed.

By a letter of 16 November 1982, Jordan transmitted to the Secretary-General the Strategy for Joint Arab Economic Development adopted at the Eleventh Arab Summit Conference (Amman, November 1980).[2] By a letter of 3 December 1982, Morocco transmitted the declaration adopted on 9 September by the Twelfth Arab Summit Conference (Fez, 25 November 1981, 6-9 September 1982) dealing with several political problems of the region.[3]

Amendment rejected. [1]United States, A/37/L.31.
Letters. [2]Jordan, 16 Nov., A/37/638; [3]Morocco, 3 Dec., annexing declaration of Twelfth Arab Summit Conference, A/37/696-S/15510.
Report. [4]S-G, A/37/536.
Resolution (1982). [5]GA: 37/17, 16 Nov., text following.
Financial implications. 5th Committee report, A/37/614; S-G statement, A/C.5/37/38.
Meeting records. GA: 5th Committee, A/C.5/37/SR.34 (15 Nov.); plenary, A/37/PV.70 (16 Nov.).

General Assembly resolution 37/17

16 November 1982   Meeting 70   Adopted without vote

Draft by Morocco (A/37/L.16); agenda item 23.

Co-operation between the United Nations and the League of Arab States

The General Assembly,

Having considered the report of the Secretary-General on co-operation between the United Nations and the League of Arab States,

Recalling the pertinent Articles of the Charter of the United Nations which encourage activities through regional arrangements for the promotion of the purposes and principles of the United Nations,

Noting with satisfaction the co-operation that has developed for more than thirty years between the United Nations and the League of Arab States and the effective participation of the League in the work of the United Nations,

Noting with appreciation the desire of the League of Arab States to consolidate and develop the existing ties with the United Nations in all areas relating to the maintenance of international peace and security, and to co-operate in every possible way with the United Nations in the implementation of United Nations resolutions relating to the question of Palestine and the situation in the Middle East,

Noting also with appreciation the commitment of the League of Arab States to the eradication of *apartheid* and all other forms of racial dis-

crimination, to the elimination of colonization and to the promotion of the right of self-determination and the safeguarding of human rights and fundamental freedoms for all,

Recalling its resolution 36/24 of 9 November 1981 in which, *inter alia*, it recognized the importance of continued close association by the United Nations and the specialized agencies, where appropriate, with the efforts of the League of Arab States in order to promote social and economic development and to advance intra-Arab as well as international co-operation in that vital field,

Noting also the signing of co-operation agreements between the organizations of the United Nations system and the League of Arab States and a number of its specialized organizations,

Convinced of the need to strengthen further the co-operation between the organizations of the United Nations system and the League of Arab States and its specialized organizations,

1. *Takes note with satisfaction* of the report of the Secretary-General;

2. *Expresses its appreciation* to the Secretary-General for the initiatives he has taken and the efforts he has made to strengthen and expand co-operation between the United Nations and the League of Arab States;

3. *Commends* the League of Arab States for its efforts and the co-operation it has extended to the United Nations in furtherance of the purposes and principles of the Charter of the United Nations and for its increased collaboration with various components of the United Nations system in the political, economic, cultural and humanitarian fields;

4. *Also expresses its appreciation* to the specialized agencies for their efforts to maintain and increase co-operation with the specialized organizations of the League of Arab States;

5. *Takes note with satisfaction* of the suggestions by the organizations of the United Nations system and the League of Arab States, contained in the report of the Secretary-General, for strengthening and expanding co-operation between the United Nations system and the League of Arab States;

6. *Recommends* that those suggestions should be given careful consideration by the competent organizations of the United Nations system and should form the basis for new and expanded areas of co-operation between the United Nations and the League of Arab States;

7. *Also recommends* that the Secretary-General, in consultation with the Secretary-General of the League of Arab States, should determine which suggestions could be dealt with more appropriately at the bilateral level and which suggestions could be dealt with more appropriately at the multilateral level and arrange for them to be considered accordingly;

8. *Endorses* the proposal that a meeting be held between representatives of organizations of the United Nations system and representatives of the General Secretariat of the League of Arab States and its specialized organizations;

9. *Welcomes* the invitation by the League of Arab States that the Meeting be held at the present headquarters of the League at Tunis and requests the Secretary-General to provide whatever assistance will be necessary to ensure the successful organization of the Meeting;

10. *Requests* the Secretary-General, in consultation with the League of Arab States, to ensure that the Meeting referred to in paragraph 9 above is held not later than 30 June 1983;

11. *Further requests* the Secretary-General to report to the General Assembly at its thirty-eighth session on the state of co-operation between the United Nations and the League of Arab States;

12. *Decides* to include in the provisional agenda of its thirty-eighth session the item entitled "Co-operation between the United Nations and the League of Arab States".

Organization of the Islamic Conference

In an August 1982 report to the General Assembly on co-operation between the United Nations and the Organization of the Islamic Conference,[3] the Secretary-General described ongoing co-operation in the political and the economic and social fields with both the United Nations and its specialized agencies, mentioned consultations between representatives of the two organizations and representation at each other's meetings, and suggested ways of strengthening co-operation.

In the political field, the report mentioned the convening of the Security Council in April at the request of the Chairman of the Al-Quds (Jerusalem) Committee of the Organization of the Islamic Conference (See POLITICAL AND SOCIAL QUESTIONS, Chapter IX), as well as examples of co-operation on disarmament, *apartheid*, outer space and decolonization. In the economic and social field, framework agreements establishing formal relations ranging from observer status to co-operation in specific activities or projects had been signed or were being negotiated between the Islamic Conference and various bodies of the United Nations system. The United Nations Industrial Development Organization had prepared five papers for a Ministerial Consultation on Industrial Co-operation among Islamic Countries (Islamabad, Pakistan, 14-17 February).

The report suggested that co-ordination machinery was needed between the United Nations system and the secretariat of the Islamic Conference, located at Jiddah, Saudi Arabia. As an initial step towards such a mechanism, United Nations bodies and organizations had been asked to designate focal points for contact and information concerning co-operation. To review progress and proposals for co-operation, meetings of the focal points could be held, preferably in conjunction with meetings of the inter-agency Administrative Committee on Co-ordination and of the executive secretaries of United Nations regional commissions. For the United Nations Secretariat, the Department of Political Affairs, Trusteeship and Decolonization was chiefly responsible for co-ordinating co-operation between the United Nations system and the Islamic Conference.

On 22 October, the General Assembly, without vote, took note of the report and endorsed its proposals.[4] It requested the United Nations and the Islamic Conference to intensify co-operation in their common search for solutions to global problems. It asked the Secretary-General to prepare guidelines based on Assembly resolutions for promoting such co-operation. It invited him, in consultation with the Secretary-General of the Islamic Conference, to organize an annual meeting, beginning in 1983, between the secretariat of the Islamic Conference and the secretariats of the United Nations and other organizations in the system to examine co-operation and make proposals for promoting it. United Nations organizations were encouraged to continue to expand their co-operation with the Islamic Conference, *inter alia* by negotiating agreements. The Assembly asked the Secretary-General to report back in 1983.

The text was introduced in the Assembly by the Niger as current Chairman of the Islamic Group in the United Nations, on behalf of the members of the Organization of the Islamic Conference.

The Thirteenth Islamic Conference of Foreign Ministers, meeting at Niamey, Niger, from 22 to 26 August, adopted a series of resolutions on political, economic, social, cultural and information matters. Their texts, reports and a final declaration were transmitted to the Secretary-General by a 21 October letter from the Niger.[1] A communiqué following the co-ordination meeting of the Ministers for Foreign Affairs of the Islamic Conference's member States, held on 12 October at United Nations Headquarters, was transmitted in a note verbale from the Niger dated 21 October.[2]

Letter and note verbale (nv). Niger, 21 Oct.: [1]A/37/567-S/15466, annexing resolutions and declaration of Islamic Conference of Foreign Ministers; [2]A/37/576 *(nv)*, annexing communiqué of Foreign Ministers meeting.
Report. [3]S-G, A/37/352.
Resolution (1982). [4]GA: 37/4, 22 Oct., text following.
Meeting record. GA: A/37/PV.41 (22 Oct.).

General Assembly resolution 37/4

22 October 1982   Meeting 41   Adopted without vote

Draft by Niger (A/37/L.6); agenda item 22.

Co-operation between the United Nations and the Organization of the Islamic Conference

The General Assembly,

Having considered the report of the Secretary-General on co-operation between the United Nations and the Organization of the Islamic Conference,

Recalling its resolution 3369(XXX) of 10 October 1975, by which it granted observer status to the Organization of the Islamic Conference,

Recalling its resolutions 35/36 of 14 November 1980 and 36/23 of 9 November 1981,

Noting with satisfaction the continued development of co-operation between the United Nations and the Organization of the Islamic Conference,

Noting the strengthening of co-operation between the specialized agencies and other organizations of the United Nations system and the Organization of the Islamic Conference,

Taking into account the desire of both organizations to co-operate more closely in their common search for solutions to global problems, such as questions relating to international peace and security, disarmament, self-determination, decolonization, fundamental human rights and the establishment of a new international economic order,

Noting also the signing of co-operation agreements between a number of specialized agencies and the Organization of the Islamic Conference,

Convinced of the need to strengthen further the co-operation between the United Nations and the Organization of the Islamic Conference,

Noting further the proposals of the Secretary-General,

1. *Takes note with satisfaction* of the report of the Secretary-General and endorses the proposals contained therein;

2. *Requests* the United Nations and the Organization of the Islamic Conference to intensify co-operation in their common search for solutions to global problems, such as questions relating to international peace and security, disarmament, self-determination, decolonization, fundamental human rights and the establishment of a new international economic order;

3. *Requests* the Secretary-General to prepare guidelines based on resolutions of the General Assembly for promoting co-operation with the Organization of the Islamic Conference;

4. *Invites* the Secretary-General, in consultation with the Secretary-General of the Organization of the Islamic Conference, to organize an annual meeting, beginning in 1983, between the secretariat of the

Organization of the Islamic Conference and the secretariats of the United Nations and other organizations concerned within the United Nations system to examine the stage reached in the development of co-operation and to put forward proposals for promoting co-operation with the Organization of the Islamic Conference;

5. *Encourages* the specialized agencies and other organizations concerned within the United Nations system to continue to expand their co-operation with the Organization of the Islamic Conference, *inter alia* by negotiating co-operation agreements;

6. *Requests* the Secretary-General to continue to take steps to strengthen the co-ordination of the activities of the United Nations system in this field with a view to intensifying co-operation between the United Nations and the United Nations system and the Organization of the Islamic Conference;

7. *Calls upon* the Secretary-General to report to the General Assembly at its thirty-eighth session on the state of co-operation between the United Nations and the Organization of the Islamic Conference;

8. *Decides* to include in the provisional agenda of its thirty-eighth session the item entitled "Co-operation between the United Nations and the Organization of the Islamic Conference".

Other intergovernmental organizations

At the request of the host Governments of several intergovernmental conferences, the main documents of those meetings were transmitted to the Secretary-General during 1982 for circulation as documents of the General Assembly, the Security Council or both, as follows:

—Final communiqué and other documents of the Ministerial Meeting of the Co-ordinating Bureau of the Non-Aligned Countries (Havana, Cuba, 31 May–5 June);[1] final communiqué and other documents of the Meeting of Ministers for Foreign Affairs and Heads of Delegation of Non-Aligned Countries (New York, 4-9 October).[2]

—Excerpts from the joint communiqué of the Foreign Ministers of the Association of South-East Asian Nations (ASEAN) issued at the conclusion of their fifteenth annual meeting (Singapore, 14-16 June);[5] press statement issued at the conclusion of the special meeting of the ASEAN Ministers for Foreign Affairs (Bangkok, Thailand, 7 August).[6]

—Resolutions of the sixty-ninth Inter-Parliamentary Conference (Rome, Italy, 12-23 September).[4]

—Final communiqué of the Third Commonwealth Heads of Government Regional Meeting (Suva, Fiji, 14-18 October).[3]

Letters. Cuba: [1]22 June, annexing communiqué and other documents of Ministerial Meeting of Co-ordinating Bureau of Non-Aligned Countries, A/37/333-S/15278; [2]11 Oct., annexing communiqué and other documents of Meeting of Foreign Ministers and Heads of Delegation of Non-Aligned Countries, A/37/540-S/15454. [3]Fiji: 25 Oct., annexing communiqué of 3rd Commonwealth Heads of Government Regional Meeting, A/37/586-S/15472. [4]Italy: 19 Oct., annexing resolutions of 69th Inter-Parliamentary Conference, A/37/578. Thailand: [5]30 June, annexing excerpts of communiqué by ASEAN Foreign Ministers, A/37/324-S/15268; [6]10 Aug., annexing press statement by ASEAN Foreign Ministers, A/37/387-S/15364.

Other organizational questions

Composition of UN organs

On 10 December 1982,[1] the General Assembly deferred consideration of the question of the composition of the relevant organs of the United Nations. On the recommendation of its Special Political Committee, the Assembly decided, without vote, to include the item in its 1983 provisional agenda. The Committee had agreed without vote on 7 December to make this recommendation, on an oral proposal by its Chairman, who noted that no member had asked to speak on the question.

The item had been deferred by the Assembly each year since 1979. No substantive proposal had been made in connection with it since 1978, when the Assembly decided to increase the number of its Vice-Presidents and thereby the size of its General Committee.[2]

Decision (1982). [1]GA: 37/425, 10 Dec., text following.
Resolution. [2]GA: 33/138, 19 Dec. 1978 (YUN 1978, p. 400).
Meeting records. GA: SPC, A/SPC/37/SR.46 (7 Dec.); plenary, A/37/PV.100 (10 Dec.).

General Assembly decision 37/425

Adopted without vote

Approved by SPC (A/37/703) without vote, 7 December (meeting 46); oral proposal by Chairman; agenda item 70.

Question of the composition of the relevant organs of the United Nations

At its 100th plenary meeting, on 10 December 1982, the General Assembly, on the recommendation of the Special Political Committee, decided to include in the provisional agenda of its thirty-eighth session the item entitled "Question of the composition of the relevant organs of the United Nations".

Economic and social questions

Development and international economic and social policy

Contents

Related topics:
International trade and finance: Trade policy; Financial policy. Regional economic and social activities—Economic and social trends, development policy and regional economic co-operation: Africa; Asia and the Pacific; Europe; Latin America; Western Asia. Social and cultural development: Social survey; Popular participation in development. Environment: Environment and development.

For resolutions and decisions of major organs mentioned but not reproduced, refer to INDEX OF RESOLUTIONS AND DECISIONS.

International economic relations

The continuing international economic crisis was again the backdrop in 1982 for attempts in United Nations bodies to find ways of reorienting international economic relations in the interests of developed and developing countries alike.

Development and economic co-operation

Several United Nations bodies, at both the expert and intergovernmental level, dealt in 1982 with broad aspects of development and international economic co-operation. The Committee for Development Planning (CDP) and the inter-agency Administrative Committee on Co-ordination (ACC), both meeting in April, commented on the subject in their reports to the Economic and Social Council, which considered the matter during its annual review of international economic developments held in July. Later in the year, the General Assembly, and particularly its Second (Economic and Financial) Committee, discussed various aspects of the subject. Several States submitted communications on the topic.

The Assembly, in December, called for the immediate adoption of special measures for the developing countries during the current economic crisis. However, no final agreement was reported on the terms for launching global negotiations on international co-operation for development, aimed at finding long-term solutions to the world's economic ills, particularly as they affected developing countries. The Assembly called for study of a proposed new international human order that would stress the moral aspects of development. It also decided to hold a tenth anniversary review, in 1984, of steps taken to implement its Charter of Economic Rights and Duties of States (see below).

CDP consideration. Expressing grave concern about the difficulties currently confronting the international economy, particularly the impact on developing countries, CDP, at its April session,[7] also saw an alarming weakening of the spirit of international co-operation to seek constructive answers to current problems. That trend, it stated, was particularly reflected in the rising tide of protectionist sentiment and the hardening attitude towards aid policies (See ECONOMIC AND SOCIAL QUESTIONS, Chapter IV).

The Committee advanced some general suggestions about policy measures needed to rectify the situation. It stated that measures to benefit all countries, rich and poor, should involve a greatly increased flow of international finance. Observing that the contracting world economy threatened world prosperity and security, with the arms race enhancing the threat to both, CDP called for a new conception of international security, based on the shared interests of all nations in survival and world development.

ACC consideration. Echoing this concern over the arms race, ACC, at its April session and in its annual report to the Economic and Social Council in May,[6] stated that a main goal of international co-operation should be to help developing countries create long-term equilibrium and reduce the severity of the crisis for those least able to bear it. Of equal concern, it said, was the erosion of multilateral co-operation and its replacement by an inward orientation of national action. In trade, aid and other areas, there was growing evidence of a return to bilateral practices, especially but not exclusively by developed countries, which threatened to erode multilateralism.

Developed countries bore special responsibility, ACC felt, to adopt monetary, budgetary, income and structural measures to achieve sustainable growth. Combating inflation was of central importance, not only for long-term growth in developed countries but also for its indirect impact on developing countries. The emphasis on internal adjustments by developed countries should not mean a lessened responsibility to assist developing countries. At the same time, developing countries must improve their economic management and establish priorities for their national development.

While prospects remained unclear for global negotiations on international economic co-operation for development, ACC stressed the need for urgent action on development assistance, balance-of-payments financing, trade, unemployment and underemployment, food, energy and population, balanced with the need to maintain a long-term perspective, including structural revisions. Concerning concessional resources for technical co-operation and other development activities (see Chapter II of this section), ACC saw a danger that the amounts made available to United Nations organizations would stagnate or decline at a time when the system was being asked to assume expanding responsibilities.

Economic and Social Council consideration. During its annual discussion of international economic and social policy, which took place in July, the Economic and Social Council heard a variety of opinions but, according to the Council's annual report to the General Assembly,[8] there was no general consensus on policy prescriptions. The Council President expressed the view that the focus by some developed countries on their own problems was threatening international economic and development co-operation, and that any subordination of the role of existing multilateral institutions to bilateral approaches would have serious negative consequences. The Secretary-General urged Member States to focus on a concerted programme for world recovery such as that recommended by CDP (see Chapter IV of this section) and remarked that the flagging spirit of international economic co-operation, as in the 1930s, was mirrored by heightened political tension.

One of the greatest concerns expressed in the discussion, according to the Council's report, was the decline in multilateral co-operation in finance as reflected in the difficulties in replenishing the International Development Association and the decline in contributions to the United Nations Development Programme. Some speakers voiced concern about the future of the major multilateral international financial institutions, while others expressed support for those bodies. With regard to official development assistance—sums made available by Governments to aid developing countries—it was noted that, even though there had been increased aid by certain countries, the total level of support furnished by the major Western donors making up the Development Assistance Committee of the Organisation for Economic Co-operation and Development had fallen from 0.38 per cent of those States' combined gross national product (GNP) in 1980 to 0.35 per cent in 1981.

While much of the discussion, as summarized in the Council's report, focused on efforts to organize global negotiations, a number of delegations expressed concern at developments in other multilateral forums concerned with specific areas of co-operation. Among the subjects mentioned were the slow progress on commodity trade, especially in regard to the establishment of the Common Fund for Commodities; the November 1982 Ministerial Meeting of the General Agreement on Tariffs and Trade and the hope that it would work to turn back protectionist pressures and resolve issues remaining from the Tokyo Round of multilateral trade negotiations; the unfinished draft code of conduct on transnational corporations; the fact that consensus had not been reached in the adoption of the United Nations Convention on the Law of the Sea, and the need to improve food production and food security. Some delegations were encouraged by progress on economic co-operation among developing countries.

General Assembly action. The General Assembly's Second Committee devoted a major part of its 1982 session to development and international economic co-operation, making recommendations on a large number of specific topics (see APPENDIX IV, agenda item 71). A list of pertinent documents was included in the first part of the Committee's report on this item.[9] The Assembly, on an oral proposal by its President adopted without vote, took note of this part of the report on 20 December.[1]

In a 16 December resolution[10] reviewing the implementation of the 1970 Declaration on the Strengthening of International Security,[11] the Assembly urged States to contribute to the urgent solution of international economic problems and the establishment of the new international economic order, to accelerate the economic development of developing countries, particularly the least developed, and to proceed without delay to a global consideration of ways for reviving the world economy and for restructuring international economic relations within the framework of global negotiations.

Communications. Several communications dealing with general aspects of international economic relations were received by the Secretary-General in 1982.

On 15 September,[2] the German Democratic Republic transmitted the communiqué of the thirty-sixth meeting of the Session of the Council for Mutual Economic Assistance (Budapest, Hungary, 8-10 June), which endorsed a programme to co-ordinate national economic plans for 1986-1990, acted to develop co-operation by member countries in specific technical areas, and stressed the importance of strengthening co-operation with socialist-oriented countries and all developing countries.

The economic relations of the USSR with developing countries were described in its letter of 12 October,[5] which valued net economic assistance from the USSR to those countries at about 30 billion roubles in the period 1976-1980, averaging 1 per cent of GNP; the USSR said it rejected the idea that it should give a fixed proportion of its GNP to developing countries on an equal footing with those responsible for plundering their former colonies, continuing their neo-colonialist exploitation, exacerbating the arms race and spreading the effects of the capitalist economic crisis. On 12 July,[4] the USSR had sent an identical text to the President of the Economic and Social Council.

The German Democratic Republic's aid to developing countries and national liberation movements was outlined in a statement by its Ministry of Foreign Affairs annexed to a 20 October letter;[3] in 1981, aid totalled 1,529.7 million marks, or 0.78 per cent of national income, while between 1970 and 1980 material assistance worth more than 285 million marks was provided to the least developed countries.

Decision (1982). [1]GA: 37/439, 20 Dec., text following.
Letters. German Democratic Republic: [2]15 Sep., A/37/447; [3]20 Oct., A/C.2/37/5. USSR: [4]12 July, E/1982/86; [5]12 Oct., A/C.2/37/4.
Reports. [6]ACC, E/1982/4; [7]CDP, E/1982/15; [8]ESC, A/37/3; [9]2nd Committee, A/37/680.
Resolution (1982). [10]GA: 37/118, para. 6 *(c)-(e)*, 16 Dec.

Resolution (prior). [11]GA: 2734(XXV), 16 Dec. 1970 (YUN 1970, p. 105).
Meeting records. ESC: E/1982/SR.31-44 (8-16 July). GA: 2nd Committee, A/C.2/37/SR.3, 5-8, 10, 13-26, 33, 40 (28 Sep.–18 Nov.); plenary, A/37/PV.113 (20 Dec.).

General Assembly decision 37/439

Adopted without vote

Oral proposal by President; agenda item 71.

Development and international economic co-operation
At its 113th plenary meeting, on 20 December 1982, the General Assembly took note of part I of the report of the Second Committee.

Special measures for developing countries

General Assembly action. On 21 December 1982, the General Assembly adopted a resolution[3] calling on the international community to act immediately in areas of critical importance to developing countries such as food, assistance in developing energy resources, balance-of-payments support, financial flows, trade and raw materials. Pointing to a need for immediate action to benefit all developing countries, the Assembly affirmed that developed countries should complement the efforts of developing countries to meet the problems resulting from the world economic crisis. The Assembly called for effective negotiations towards establishing the new international economic order (see below).

The resolution was adopted by a recorded vote of 124 to 1, with 22 abstentions. On 20 December, the Second Committee had approved the draft by a recorded vote, requested by the United States, of 94 to none, with 22 abstentions. The text, submitted and later revised by Bangladesh for the Group of 77 developing countries, was orally amended by the Committee Chairman to replace the word "a" before "new international economic order" with "the".

The critical economic situation affecting in particular the developing countries was further stressed by the Assembly in a 20 December resolution on negative trends in the world economy,[2] and all States, particularly the developed, were urged to reverse those trends.

Introducing in Committee the initial draft of the resolution on immediate measures for developing countries, Bangladesh said it contained many elements of the Declaration adopted on 8 October by the Ministers for Foreign Affairs of the Group of 77 (sixth annual meeting, New York, 6-8 October). Subsequently introducing the revised draft, Bangladesh said extensive consultations had been held in order to take account of the concerns of other delegations on certain parts of the text.

The Declaration of the Group of 77, covering a wide range of development and other economic issues, was transmitted to the Secretary-General by the Group's Chairman, Algeria, on 11 October;[1] it contained an appeal to the developed countries to respond favourably to the Group's

proposals for the launching of global negotiations and included a call for international financial institutions, such as the International Monetary Fund and the World Bank, to play a larger catalytic role in assisting the recovery of developing countries.

Explaining its negative vote in the Assembly following its abstention in Committee, the United States said it objected not to the concept that immediate measures were necessary but rather to the language of the text; it was also unhappy that the draft had been introduced late in the session without adequate discussion and negotiation and that, minutes before the Committee vote, the sponsors had introduced changes to a previously agreed text.

Several States explained their abstentions in the Committee. Australia, Austria, Canada and Denmark (for the European Economic Community) regretted that a consensus had not been achieved; they were in favour of immediate measures but felt that the text failed to distinguish between such measures and the call to restructure international economic relations. Japan spoke similarly, as did Sweden, for the Nordic countries; the latter added that they would also have liked to see a reference to the primary responsibility of the developing countries for their own development. Austria also felt that the resolution's analysis of the problems of developing countries was unbalanced and that the measures should have been spelt out more clearly.

Letter. [1]Algeria, 11 Oct., transmitting Group of 77 Declaration, A/37/544.
Resolutions (1982). GA: [2]37/203, para. 3, 20 Dec.; [3]37/252, 21 Dec., text following.
Meeting records. GA: 2nd Committee, A/C.2/37/SR.3, 5-8, 10, 13-26, 33, 40, *46, 51* (28 Sep.–20 Dec.); plenary, A/37/PV.115 (21 Dec.).

General Assembly resolution 37/252

21 December 1982   Meeting 115   124-1-22 (recorded vote)

Approved by Second Committee (A/37/680/Add.13) by recorded vote (94-0-22), 20 December (meeting 51); draft by Bangladesh, for Group of 77 (A/C.2/37/L.101/Rev.1), orally amended by Chairman; agenda item 71.

Immediate measures in favour of the developing countries

The General Assembly,

Recalling its resolutions 3201(S-VI) and 3202(S-VI) of 1 May 1974, containing the Declaration and the Programme of Action on the Establishment of a New International Economic Order, 3281(XXIX) of 12 December 1974, containing the Charter of Economic Rights and Duties of States, 3362(S-VII) of 16 September 1975 on development and international economic co-operation and 35/56 of 5 December 1980, the annex to which contains the International Development Strategy for the Third United Nations Development Decade,

Deeply concerned by the world economic crisis, which creates great economic problems for the developing countries and has a negative impact on their development process,

Convinced that the structural economic problems facing the development of the developing countries require solution through a restructuring of international economic relations within the framework of the establishment of the new international economic order,

Further convinced that immediate measures in favour of the developing countries would contribute to the lessening of their present economic problems,

Noting, in this context, that the increased deficit in the balance of payments of the developing countries, the deterioration of their terms of trade, the adverse effects of high interest rates on the servicing of their external debt and on their access to international capital markets, insufficient increase of flows of multilateral assistance on concessional terms, including technical assistance, the severity of the terms of financial assistance, the precarious nature of the food situation, the adverse effects of protectionist pressures in the international economy on the economies of the developing countries, the inequitable terms of transfer of technology, the impediments for developing countries to gain access to the international capital markets and the price fluctuations of raw materials, as well as the downward trend in the prices of commodities, constitute serious obstacles to the economic growth of the developing countries, to the servicing of their external debt, to the procurement of their essential imports of food, industrial products, energy and technology and to the earnings for their exports, and that these symptoms of deep crisis require urgent and effective measures on the part of the international community,

Calling for the immediate launching and successful conclusion of the global negotiations on international co-operation for development,

Reaffirming that resolution 34/138 of 14 December 1979 provides that global negotiations should not involve any interruption of, or have any adverse effect upon, the negotiations in other United Nations forums but should reinforce and draw upon them,

Reiterating in this context the need for urgent concurrent efforts in fields that are of critical importance for the developing countries such as food, assistance in the development of energy resources of developing countries by the World Bank and balance-of-payments support by the International Monetary Fund, financial flows, trade and raw materials at the forthcoming conferences and meetings of the United Nations system,

Noting the Declaration by the Ministers for Foreign Affairs of the Group of Seventy-seven, adopted in New York on 8 October 1982, which, *inter alia,* stressed that without prejudice to the adoption and the implementation of long-term and structural changes and the launching of the global negotiations, concrete emergency action, to benefit all developing countries, should be taken on the most pressing economic questions which present a short-term threat to the international community,

Taking note of the statement made by the Secretary-General on 17 July 1982 to the Economic and Social Council at its second regular session of 1982, in which he, *inter alia,* called for concerted and immediate international action aiming at a broad economic recovery,

1. *Agrees* that concrete immediate action to benefit all developing countries should be taken on the pressing economic problems which present a short-term threat to the world economy;

2. *Affirms* that, in order to create favourable conditions for the development of developing countries, the developed countries should, individually and collectively, take effective and concrete measures to complement the efforts of the developing countries to meet the problems resulting from the world economic crisis, which affects, in particular, the development of developing countries and severely threatens their economies;

3. *Calls upon* the international community, particularly within the framework of the United Nations, to take immediate, effective and concrete measures in the areas of critical importance to developing countries, as outlined in the eighth preambular paragraph above, in forthcoming conferences and meetings;

4. *Reaffirms* that the present world economic crisis and, in particular, the obstacles to the development of the developing countries are a result of structural malfunctioning and disequilibrium in present international economic relations and, therefore, calls upon the international community to engage in effective negotiations, within the framework of restructuring the international economic relations, towards the establishment of the new international economic order.

Recorded vote in Assembly as follows:

In favour: Afghanistan, Algeria, Angola, Argentina, Bahamas, Bahrain, Bangladesh, Barbados, Benin, Bhutan, Bolivia, Botswana, Brazil, Bulgaria, Burma, Burundi, Byelorussian SSR, Cape Verde, Central African Republic, Chad, Chile, China, Colombia, Comoros, Congo, Costa Rica, Cuba, Cyprus, Czechoslovakia, Democratic Kampuchea, Democratic Yemen, Djibouti, Dominican Republic,

Ecuador, Egypt, El Salvador, Ethiopia, Fiji, Gabon, Gambia, German Democratic Republic, Ghana, Grenada, Guinea, Guinea-Bissau, Guyana, Honduras, Hungary, India, Indonesia, Iran, Iraq, Ivory Coast, Jamaica, Jordan, Kenya, Kuwait, Lao People's Democratic Republic, Lebanon, Lesotho, Liberia, Libyan Arab Jamahiriya, Madagascar, Malawi, Malaysia, Maldives, Mali, Malta, Mauritania, Mauritius, Mexico, Mongolia, Morocco, Mozambique, Nepal, Nicaragua, Niger, Nigeria, Oman, Pakistan, Panama, Papua New Guinea, Paraguay, Peru, Philippines, Poland, Qatar, Romania, Rwanda, Saint Lucia, Samoa, Sao Tome and Principe, Saudi Arabia, Senegal, Sierra Leone, Singapore, Solomon Islands, Somalia, Sri Lanka, Sudan, Suriname, Swaziland, Syrian Arab Republic, Thailand, Togo, Trinidad and Tobago, Tunisia, Turkey, Uganda, Ukrainian SSR, USSR, United Arab Emirates, United Republic of Cameroon, United Republic of Tanzania, Upper Volta, Uruguay, Vanuatu, Venezuela, Viet Nam, Yemen, Yugoslavia, Zaire, Zambia, Zimbabwe.

Against: United States.

Abstaining: Australia, Austria, Belgium, Canada, Denmark, Finland, France, Germany, Federal Republic of, Greece, Iceland, Ireland, Israel, Italy, Japan, Luxembourg, Netherlands, New Zealand, Norway, Portugal, Spain, Sweden, United Kingdom.

Proposed global negotiations

Ground rules for the launching of global negotiations on international economic co-operation for development, originally scheduled to begin in 1980,[7] remained under discussion throughout 1982. Proposals and counter-proposals were made by the Group of 77 and a group of major Western industrialized countries, but no agreement was reported by year's end at the informal consultations conducted under the auspices of the General Assembly President. The issues related mainly to the structure of the proposed negotiations and how they would relate to the ongoing work of existing organizations of the United Nations system.

Twice during the year the Assembly heard and briefly discussed reports from its President on the progress of the informal consultations. As it had done in 1981,[8] it adopted procedural decisions keeping the question on its agenda while the consultations continued.

Developments on the topic were initially referred to by the Assembly President on 28 April, when the Assembly resumed its thirty-sixth session with seven items including global negotiations remaining from its 1981 agenda.[3] He mentioned that the Group of 77 had submitted proposals but added that there had been no progress towards agreement.

At the closing meeting of that session, on 20 September 1982, the President reported that the Group of 77 proposals, submitted by Algeria (on 31 March), had been presented as an attempt to facilitate agreement on the major issues, taking account of the views of all parties on such aspects as the competence, functions and powers of specialized forums in the process of global negotiations. The summit meeting of seven major industrialized countries, held in June at Versailles, France, had agreed that the Group's text was helpful and had concluded that there was a good prospect for the early launching and success of the global negotiations, provided that the independence of the specialized agencies was guaranteed. The industrialized countries had proposed four amendments to the text and two had been accepted by the Group of 77, which had put forward new formulations on the others. Official reaction to the latest proposals was still awaited.

Describing the proposals of the Group of 77, Algeria, speaking for the Group, said the March draft would codify the consensus rule for the negotiations and confirm the central role of the Assembly while consecrating respect for the jurisdiction and functions of the specialized agencies; the Group's subsequent counter-amendments would commit the international community to be guided by the 1979 resolution by which the Assembly had decided to launch the negotiations[7] and would make the establishment of special negotiating groups subject to consensus, thereby assuring the developed countries that their interests would be absolutely guaranteed in the substantive stages of the negotiations.

China stated that the March proposals manifested the determination and flexibility of the Group of 77; China urged the major developed countries to change their attitudes and to join the developing countries in launching a constructive dialogue.

Three Western developed countries felt considerable progress towards the launching of global negotiations had been made during the past year. Denmark, speaking for the European Community (EC) members, said EC had endorsed the Versailles proposals, whose main purpose was to avoid duplication between the global negotiations and ongoing activities in United Nations forums. Japan, a participant at Versailles, said the summit conference's proposals represented the best chance of achieving an early start to the negotiations. The United States, another participant, said the text agreed to at Versailles demonstrated the developed countries' willingness to launch the negotiations on a fair and realistic basis; the United States looked forward to the early resolution of the few outstanding issues.

The USSR said the socialist community was prepared to discuss the Group of 77 proposals and continued to advocate the speedy start of global negotiations, with the participation of all States and bearing in mind the legitimate interests of all.

After hearing the President appeal to all Member States to show political will in order to start the negotiations successfully, the Assembly agreed to his oral proposal to include the item in the draft agenda of its thirty-seventh (1982 regular) session.[1]

On 20 December, when the Assembly again took up the matter, several delegations commented on the status of informal consultations held during the session under the chairmanship of Olara Otunnu (Uganda). Bangladesh, on behalf of the Group of 77, voiced disappointment that, after seven months, there had been no response to the Group's counter-amendments; the Group was committed to global negotiations but it could not afford to wait indefinitely. China, expressing similar views, said the principal divergence of views concerned the issue of maintaining the coherent and integrated nature of global negotiations; as that was the fundamental difference between the global and the ongoing sectoral negotiations, eliminating the difference would cause the global negotiations to lose their original meaning.

Canada and Denmark, the latter speaking for the EC members, expressed support for continued consultations and reiterated their view that the March proposals of the Group of 77 and the Versailles clarifications remained a good basis for the launching of negotiations. The United States expressed the same view of the Versailles text and, along with Japan, expressed its willingness to continue to co-operate in an effort to overcome the remaining obstacles.

Bulgaria, speaking also on behalf of the other Eastern European socialist States and Mongolia, reiterated their support for the launching of global negotiations and said the backward movement on this matter was due to attempts by certain Western States to renounce previous agreements. The USSR contrasted its economic and technical assistance to developing countries with the economic practices of Western States which, it said, led to an outflow of resources from the developing world due to the activities of foreign capital, trade protectionism, an unjust monetary system, the export of inflation to developing countries and the brain drain of skilled personnel; it regarded the global negotiations as an appropriate forum to resolve such issues.

The Assembly agreed, on the proposal of its President, to keep the item open and to reconvene at short notice to consider any decision or arrangement emerging from the informal consultations which the President said he understood delegations wished to purse on an urgent basis after the session's suspension. On the following day, in suspending its session, the Assembly listed the launching of global negotiations among four items to be taken up at a resumed session in 1983.[2]

In a resolution of 16 December 1982[4] reviewing the implementation of the 1970 Declaration on the Strengthening of International Security,[6] the Assembly urged States to proceed without delay to a global consideration of ways for reviving the world economy and for restructuring international economic relations within the framework of global negotiations.

In its 21 December 1982 resolution on immediate measures for developing countries,[5] the Assembly reaffirmed that the current world economic crisis, particularly obstacles to the development of the developing countries, resulted from structural malfunctioning and disequilibrium in international economic relations. It therefore called on the international community to engage in effective negotiations, within the framework of restructuring international economic relations, towards establishing the new international economic order.

Several States explained that their abstentions in the Second Committee's vote on the latter resolution were due to its linking of immediate measures for developing countries with a call to restructure international economic relations (see above).

Decisions (1982). GA: [1]36/464, 20 Sep., text following; [2]37/452, *item 38*, 21 Dec.
Decision (prior). [3]GA: 36/461, 18 Dec. 1981 (YUN 1981, p. 350).
Resolutions (1982). GA: [4]37/118, para. 6 *(e)*, 16 Dec.; [5]37/252, para. 4, 21 Dec.
Resolutions (prior). GA: [6]2734(XXV), 16 Dec. 1970 (YUN 1970, p. 105); [7]34/138, 14 Dec. 1979 (YUN 1979, p. 468).
Yearbook reference. [8]1981, p. 378.
Meeting records. GA: A/36/PV.110, 111 (28 Apr., 20 Sep.), A/37/PV.113 (20 Dec.).

General Assembly decision 36/464

Adopted without vote

Oral proposal by President; agenda item 37

Launching of global negotiations on international economic co-operation for development
At its 111th plenary meeting, on 20 September 1982, the General Assembly decided to include in the draft agenda of its thirty-seventh session the item entitled "Launching of global negotiations on international economic co-operation for development".

Proposed new international human order

A proposal for the drafting of a declaration on a new international human order, concerned with the moral aspects of development, was taken up by the General Assembly in 1982 at the request of the Philippines and referred for further study to the Economic and Social Council.

The request for a new agenda item on this topic at the Assembly's 1982 regular session was made by the Philippines in a letter of 12 August.[2] In an explanatory memorandum accompanying the letter, the Philippines said that, although it was thought that economic development would automatically result in social amelioration, people in developed countries were not happier than those less fortunate in developing countries. Therefore, human needs should be given equal consideration in any development programme.

The topic was included in the Assembly's agenda as a sub-item of the item on development and international economic co-operation.

The Philippines introduced in the Second Committee a draft resolution[1] by which the Assembly would decide that there was an urgent need to draw on the basic moral principles of equity, justice and co-operation which dictated that developed countries and others in a position to do so had a moral responsibility to assist developing countries in the context of a new international human order

based on a moral and humanistic approach to development. The Secretary-General would be requested to prepare a draft declaration on the topic with the help of a small, voluntarily financed, geographically balanced intergovernmental group of experts, and to submit a progress report in 1983 containing the draft declaration. Governments would be requested to comment by 31 July 1983. The Assembly would take note of the Philippine offer to contribute to the cost.

On 20 December 1982, the Assembly adopted a resolution[3] by which it transmitted the Philippine draft to the Economic and Social Council for consideration at that body's 1983 second regular session, and requested Governments to comment by 30 April.

The resolution was adopted without vote. On 2 December, the draft, introduced by the Philippines and also sponsored by Indonesia, Malaysia, Sierra Leone, Singapore and Thailand, had been similarly approved by the Second Committee.

On 18 December, the Assembly requested the views of Governments on a proposed new international humanitarian order.

Draft resolution deferred. [1]Philippines, A/C.2/37/L.40.
Letter. [2]Philippines, 12 Aug., A/37/192.
Resolution (1982). [3]GA: 37/225, 20 Dec., text following.
Meeting records. GA: General Committee, A/BUR/37/SR.2 (22 Sep.); 2nd Committee, A/C.2/37/SR.3, 5-8, 20-26, 33, 37, 40, *44, 46* (28 Sep.-2 Dec.); plenary, A/37/PV.113 (20 Dec.).

General Assembly resolution 37/225

20 December 1982   Meeting 113   Adopted without vote

Approved by Second Committee (A/37/680/Add.12) without vote, 2 December (meeting 46); 6-nation draft (A/C.2/37/L.90); agenda item 71 *(p)*.

Sponsors: Indonesia, Malaysia, Philippines, Sierra Leone, Singapore, Thailand.

New international human order: moral aspects of development

The General Assembly,

Noting the proposal relating to the question of a new international human order: moral aspects of development,

Realizing the need for a further elaboration of the proposal,

1. *Decides* to transmit the draft resolution entitled "New international human order: moral aspects of development" to the Economic and Social Council, with the request that it consider the matter at its second regular session of 1983, taking into account the deliberations of the General Assembly at its thirty-seventh session;

2. *Requests* Governments to submit their comments on this question before 30 April 1983 to the Secretary-General, for transmission by him to the Economic and Social Council at that session;

3. *Decides* to take up this question at its thirty-eighth session on the basis of the report of the Economic and Social Council.

Economic rights and duties of States

In July 1982, a draft resolution on economic measures as means of political and economic coercion against developing countries was introduced in the Economic and Social Council.[1] Sponsored by Argentina, Brazil, Cuba, Nicaragua, Peru and Venezuela, the text sought to have the Council deplore the adoption by certain developed countries of economic measures to exert pressure on the political decisions of developing countries members of the Group of 77. The Council would have urged those developed countries to refrain from such measures and reaffirmed the right of States to resort to economic and other measures in their struggle against colonialism, neo-colonialism, racism, *apartheid*, foreign aggression and occupation, and alien domination. Also, the Secretary-General would have been requested to prepare a report on those measures for the General Assembly in 1983.

On a motion by Saint Lucia, adopted by a roll-call vote (requested by Venezuela) of 20 to 18, with 15 abstentions, the Council decided to take no action on the draft resolution. Voting against the motion were Argentina, Benin, Brazil, Bulgaria, the Byelorussian SSR, Chile, Colombia, Ethiopia, Iraq, the Libyan Arab Jamahiriya, Mexico, Nicaragua, Peru, Poland, Romania, Tunisia, the USSR and Venezuela.

Draft resolution not acted upon. [1]Argentina, Brazil, Cuba, Nicaragua, Peru, Venezuela, E/1982/L.51.
Meeting record. ESC: E/1982/SR.50 (29 July).

Implementation of the 1974 Charter

On 20 December 1982, the General Assembly adopted a resolution[1] by which it decided to review in 1984 the implementation of its 1974 Charter of Economic Rights and Duties of States.[4] It requested the Secretary-General to prepare a report on the Charter's implementation, based on information from Governments and intergovernmental organizations.

The resolution was adopted by a recorded vote of 144 to 1, with 4 abstentions. On 8 December, the Second (Economic and Financial) Committee had approved the draft, as revised by the sponsors, by a recorded vote, requested by the United States, of 127 to 1, with 4 abstentions.

The draft was submitted by Bangladesh on behalf of the Group of 77. Bangladesh explained that the Group attached great importance to the Charter's principles and its close relation to the Assembly's 1974 Declaration[2] and Programme of Action[3] on the Establishment of a New International Economic Order.

The United States, voting against, said it considered the Charter unbalanced because it discouraged inflows of development capital; since few Governments had provided information on their efforts to implement the Charter, there was little reason for them to do so currently.

The Federal Republic of Germany, which abstained, said it could not support the Charter's basic tenor, particularly article 34 calling for periodic review by the Assembly.

The Federal Republic of Germany, Israel, Japan and the United Kingdom, explaining their absten-

tions, and Austria, Belgium, Canada, Denmark, France, Italy, the Netherlands and Norway, explaining their positive votes, pointed out that their votes should not be interpreted as a change in the positions they had taken in 1974 at the time of the Charter's adoption.[5]

France and the Federal Republic of Germany also stated that they would participate in a review in 1984, while Denmark hoped a more comprehensive and satisfactory text would be negotiated in 1984.

Resolution (1982). [1]GA: 37/204, 20 Dec., text following.
Resolutions (prior). GA: [2]3201(S-VI), 1 May 1974 (YUN 1974, p. 324); [3]3202(S-VI), 1 May 1974 (*ibid.*, p. 326); [4]3281(XXIX), 12 Dec. 1974 (ibid., p. 403).
Yearbook reference. [5]1974, p. 391.
Meeting records. GA: 2nd Committee, A/C.2/37/SR.3, 6, 7, 10, 13-19, 33, *40*, *47* (28 Sep.–8 Dec.); plenary, A/37/PV.113 (20 Dec.).

General Assembly resolution 37/204

20 December 1982   Meeting 113   144-1-4 (recorded vote)

Approved by Second Committee (A/37/680/Add.1) by recorded vote (127-1-4), 8 December (meeting 47); draft by Bangladesh, for Group of 77 (A/C.2/37/L.26/Rev.1); agenda item 71 *(b)*.

Review of the implementation of the Charter of Economic Rights and Duties of States

The General Assembly,

Recalling its resolutions 3201(S-VI) and 3202(S-VI) of 1 May 1974, containing the Declaration and the Programme of Action on the Establishment of a New International Economic Order, 3281(XXIX) of 12 December 1974, containing the Charter of Economic Rights and Duties of States, and 3362(S-VII) of 16 September 1975 on development and international economic co-operation, which laid down the foundations of the new international economic order,

Bearing in mind article 34 of the Charter of Economic Rights and Duties of States and General Assembly resolution 3486(XXX) of 12 December 1975, relating to the review of the implementation of the Charter,

Mindful of the importance of the principles set forth in the Charter of Economic Rights and Duties of States and the close relationship between the Charter and the Declaration and the Programme of Action on the Establishment of a New International Economic Order,

Conscious that the immediate launching and the successful conclusion of the global round of negotiations on international economic co-operation for development will be an important contribution to the solution of international economic problems, within the framework of the restructuring of international economic relations, and to steady global development, in particular the development of developing countries,

1. *Decides* to conduct at its thirty-ninth session, on the occasion of the tenth anniversary of the adoption of the Charter of Economic Rights and Duties of States, a comprehensive review of its implementation, as provided for in article 34 thereof;

2. *Requests* the Secretary-General to prepare a report on the implementation of the Charter of Economic Rights and Duties of States, based on information provided by Governments as well as the intergovernmental organizations concerned, and to submit it to the General Assembly at its thirty-ninth session through the Economic and Social Council at its second regular session of 1984;

3. *Calls upon* all Member States to co-operate with the Secretary-General in the preparation of the report requested in paragraph 2 above;

4. *Invites* all Member States to participate actively in the review of the implementation of the Charter of Economic Rights and Duties of States to be undertaken in 1984;

5. *Decides* to include in the provisional agenda of its thirty-ninth session an item entitled "Review of the implementation of the Charter of Economic Rights and Duties of States".

Recorded vote in Assembly as follows:

In favour: Afghanistan, Algeria, Angola, Antigua and Barbuda, Argentina, Australia, Austria, Bahamas, Bahrain, Bangladesh, Barbados, Belgium, Benin, Bhutan, Bolivia, Botswana, Brazil, Bulgaria, Burma, Burundi, Byelorussian SSR, Canada, Cape Verde, Central African Republic, Chad, Chile, China, Colombia, Comoros, Congo, Costa Rica, Cuba, Cyprus, Czechoslovakia, Democratic Kampuchea, Democratic Yemen, Denmark, Djibouti, Dominican Republic, Ecuador, Egypt, El Salvador, Equatorial Guinea, Ethiopia, Fiji, Finland, France, Gabon, Gambia, German Democratic Republic, Ghana, Greece, Grenada, Guatemala, Guinea, Guinea-Bissau, Guyana, Haiti, Honduras, Hungary, Iceland, India, Indonesia, Iran, Iraq, Ireland, Italy, Ivory Coast, Jamaica, Jordan, Kenya, Kuwait, Lao People's Democratic Republic, Lebanon, Lesotho, Liberia, Libyan Arab Jamahiriya, Luxembourg, Madagascar, Malawi, Malaysia, Maldives, Mali, Malta, Mauritania, Mauritius, Mexico, Mongolia, Morocco, Mozambique, Nepal, Netherlands, New Zealand, Nicaragua, Niger, Nigeria, Norway, Oman, Pakistan, Panama, Papua New Guinea, Paraguay, Peru, Philippines, Poland, Portugal, Qatar, Romania, Rwanda, Samoa, Sao Tome and Principe, Saudi Arabia, Senegal, Sierra Leone, Singapore, Somalia, Spain, Sri Lanka, Sudan, Suriname, Swaziland, Sweden, Syrian Arab Republic, Thailand, Togo, Trinidad and Tobago, Tunisia, Turkey, Uganda, Ukrainian SSR, USSR, United Arab Emirates, United Republic of Cameroon, United Republic of Tanzania, Upper Volta, Uruguay, Vanuatu, Venezuela, Viet Nam, Yemen, Yugoslavia, Zaire, Zambia, Zimbabwe.

Against: United States.

Abstaining: Germany, Federal Republic of, Israel, Japan, United Kingdom.

Economic co-operation among developing countries

Throughout 1982 the United Nations continued to help in promoting economic co-operation among developing countries (ECDC), mainly through the United Nations Conference on Trade and Development (UNCTAD). In October, the Trade and Development Board decided on procedures governing future UNCTAD work in this area; the action was taken by vote after consultations carried over from 1981 failed to resolve a disagreement between developing and developed countries over the exclusion from UNCTAD meetings on ECDC of developing countries not members of the Group of 77. Meanwhile, technical co-operation among those countries received the support of the United Nations Development Programme (UNDP).

UNCTAD action. As authorized by the UNCTAD Trade and Development Board in November 1981,[11] its President at that session submitted a report to the Board on consultations he had undertaken to resolve problems underlying UNCTAD activities on ECDC.[6] The report, introduced by the 1981 President in March 1982, set out points of agreement on the role of UNCTAD in support of ECDC and identified issues on which full agreement had not been reached.

The report pointed out that, while the importance of ECDC and the role of UNCTAD were not in doubt, the question at issue was how meetings of exclusive interregional groups of UNCTAD member States within the context of the work of the Board's Committee on Economic Co-operation among Developing Countries could be reconciled with the principles of universality and sovereign equality. Specifically, some States did not believe UNCTAD was authorized to organize meetings confined to the Group of 77, thereby excluding some developing countries which were not members of that Group; others, including the President, saw

no legal contradiction between the universality principle and the holding of preparatory meetings restricted to such groups. A further issue was how to ensure that Committee members who had not participated in such meetings could be kept aware of their proceedings.

The President submitted four suggestions: (1) the Group of 77, as a recognized grouping of developing countries, had the right to be recognized as an appropriate body to put forward plans for adoption by the Committee on ECDC and met the UNCTAD guidelines for organizing meetings on the subject; (2) UNCTAD secretariat studies on ECDC and reports on meetings of developing countries should have general distribution, while documents relating to negotiations among meeting participants should be limited to them; (3) the Committee should serve as a forum for all UNCTAD members to express their views without intervening in negotiations conducted by groups of developing countries; and (4) it should also be a forum where all members were kept informed of the progress of activities by developing countries under its auspices.

On 19 March 1982,[5] the Trade and Development Board requested its former President to continue his consultations, in co-ordination with the current President, in order to reach generally acceptable solutions by the second part of the Board's session, in May.

In his second report,[7] submitted in May, the former President stated that, while differences over the issues had narrowed, they had not been completely eliminated. As a means of resolving the impasse, he suggested that a country which considered itself a developing country be enabled to participate in an ECDC project or other activity of UNCTAD covering problems common to a group of countries, provided that all countries participating in that activity concurred.

On 18 May,[5] the Board agreed to continue considering the subject later in 1982.

After further discussion in October, the Board, on 28 October, first rejected a proposal by Group B (developed market-economy countries) to continue negotiations and then adopted by vote a resolution submitted on behalf of the Group of 77 setting out procedures for the work of the Committee on ECDC.[9]

By this resolution, the Board reaffirmed the Committee's role as the main UNCTAD committee on ECDC, responsible for making recommendations to provide support and assistance in this area to developing countries or groups thereof. The Board agreed to the following modalities:

All developing countries were entitled to submit, jointly or in groups, proposals on projects and programmes for the Committee's consideration; any such country or group of them wishing to join in could do so based on agreement reached through consultation between the requesting country or group and the group of parties to the project/programme. Members of and non-voting participants in the Committee not participating in specific projects/programmes were entitled to attend related plenary meetings on a non-deliberative basis, without being entitled to participate in the negotiations. General secretariat documents and progress and final reports on project/programme negotiations would be distributed universally, but documents on direct negotiations would go only to participants. The UNCTAD Secretary-General would prepare reports for the Committee on the financial requirements of a project/programme and options for funding it, taking into account resources under the UNCTAD regular budget as well as other sources.

By this resolution, the Board also authorized UNCTAD funding and support for a 1983 meeting of developing countries participating in negotiations on a global system of trade preferences among developing countries (GSTP) (see Chapter IV of this section), and a meeting of the Committee on ECDC immediately after the sixth session of UNCTAD, scheduled for June 1983. The Committee was to review UNCTAD activities on ECDC and make recommendations to the Board on UNCTAD support for the GSTP negotiations. Preparatory work on GSTP was done by the UNCTAD Meeting of Governmental Experts of Developing Countries on ECDC (third session, Geneva, 19-28 July).

The resolution was adopted by a roll-call vote of 63 to 22 (Australia, Austria, Belgium, Canada, Denmark, Finland, France, Germany, Federal Republic of, Ireland, Israel, Italy, Japan, Luxembourg, Netherlands, New Zealand, Norway, Portugal, Spain, Sweden, Switzerland, United Kingdom, United States), with 9 abstentions (Eastern European States and Mongolia).

While discussions on procedures were under way in the Board, several ECDC activities were carried out under UNCTAD auspices during 1982.

An International Symposium of State Trading Organizations (STOs) of Developing Countries (Ljubljana, Yugoslavia, 29 March–2 April) recommended establishing a permanent institutional framework to promote STO co-operation and nominated a project steering committee.

The Working Party on Trade Expansion and Regional Economic Integration among Developing Countries, established by the Committee on ECDC in 1978,[10] held its second session at Geneva from 28 June to 2 July 1982, at which it established a programme for co-operation among economic co-operation and integration groupings of developing countries.[8] The programme provided for measures to strengthen co-operation between groupings in various sectors, a research programme on economic integration, increased technical co-operation and information exchange, procedures for participation by the groupings in interregional ECDC programmes, and institutional arrangements for implementing this programme and attracting financial and other support for it.

A Round Table on Economic Co-operation among Developing Countries—sponsored by the Mexican Centre for Economic and Social Studies of the Third World (CEESTEM), the Research Centre for Co-operation with Developing Countries, Ljubljana, and UNCTAD, with UNDP financial support—was held at CEESTEM headquarters, Mexico City, from 22 to 29 November.[3] Conclusions and recommendations were adopted on trade, money and finance, technology, industrialization and institutional matters.

Outside UNCTAD, a Joint Meeting of Governmental Experts from Africa and Latin America on Economic and Technical Co-operation (Addis Ababa, Ethiopia, 1-4 June) was organized by the United Nations economic commissions for the two regions.

CDP consideration. In studying international monetary and financial co-operation, the Committee for Development Planning (CDP), at its April 1982 session,[2] focused on needs and opportunities for closer co-operation among developing countries. It singled out as some of the more promising opportunities in that regard: strengthening and interlinking of payments arrangements; enlarging existing financial facilities; promoting investment flows; increasing participation by developing countries in regional development banks; term deposits with those banks; and export credit guarantee facilities.

General Assembly consideration. In December, in the General Assembly's Second Committee, a draft decision[1] to have the Assembly endorse the Trade and Development Board's October resolution on ECDC was put forward on behalf of the Group of 77 by Bangladesh but was later withdrawn.[4]

Under a sub-item on economic and technical co-operation among developing countries, the Assembly adopted a resolution calling for co-operation between the United Nations system and the Southern African Development Co-ordination Conference.

Draft decision withdrawn. [1]Bangladesh, for Group of 77, A/C.2/37/L.95.
Reports. [2]CDP, E/1982/15; [3]Round Table on ECDC, UNCTAD/ECDC/TA/15; [4]2nd Committee, A/37/680/Add.6; [5]TDB, A/37/15, vol. I; TDB President, [6]TD/B/892, [7]TD/B/905; [8]Working Party on Trade Expansion and Regional Economic Integration among Developing Countries, TD/B/C.7/55.
Resolution (1982). [9]TDB (report, A/37/15, vol. II): 264(XXV), sect. A, 28 Oct.
Yearbook references. [10]1978, p. 432, [11]1981, p. 383.

Meeting records. GA: 2nd Committee, A/C.2/37/SR.*45, 48* (1, 13 Dec.).
Publication. Juridical Aspects of the Establishment of Multinational Marketing Enterprises among Developing Countries (TD/B/C.7/28/Rev.1), Sales No. E.82.II.D.9.

Economic and social conditions and trends

Reports prepared in 1982 by the United Nations Secretariat continued to reflect a crisis in the world economy, limiting growth in the industrialized countries and severely restricting the development prospects of the third world. The two major reports were submitted as background documents for the annual discussion of economic and social conditions and trends in the Economic and Social Council and the Trade and Development Board. CDP, the chief United Nations expert body on economic trends and their impact on development, suggested elements of a world recovery programme and the Secretary-General elaborated on this in his annual economic address to the Council. A CDP Working Group, meeting in November, saw no immediate prospect of a strong recovery. In December, the General Assembly urged all States, particularly developed ones, to pursue concerted efforts to reduce the negative trends.

Secretariat reports. Issued in mid-1982, the *World Economic Survey 1981-1982*,[3] prepared by the United Nations Department of International Economic and Social Affairs, reported that world economic expansion continued to decelerate markedly in 1981 and estimated that 1982 would be particularly difficult. Lower growth rates of output had became more apparent in 1981, with world production only 1.2 per cent over the 1980 level, and the rate was unlikely to surpass 2 per cent in 1982.

In the developed market economies the recession had worsened in 1981, with growth rates declining in almost all countries. Their average growth rate of gross domestic product (GDP) had dropped from 1.5 per cent in 1980 to 1.2 per cent in 1981 and, although a mild recovery was possible in the second half of 1982, it was not expected to exceed 1.5 per cent for the third consecutive year. The anti-inflation policies of those countries had had a severe impact on total output. The tight monetary policies in most major countries, combined with increasing fiscal deficits resulting from the recession, had led also to sharply increased interest rates and high unemployment.

The centrally planned economies had experienced a slow-down of net material product growth to a rate of 1.7 per cent in 1981 compared to a 2.5 per cent average for the two preceding years, due partly to another year of disappointing or poor harvests and to slowness in industrial expansion. The faltering pace of investment activity had, however, permitted a sharp curtailment of imports.

By far the sharpest deceleration in economic growth in 1981 had taken place in the developing countries, where the GDP growth rate had fallen for the fourth year in a row and was estimated at only 0.6 per cent in 1981, down from 2.9 per cent in 1980. At the same time, the average growth rate for energy-importing developing countries had fallen from 4.1 to 1.4 per cent. A major factor behind the downturn had been the recession in industrialized countries, which had severely curtailed world demand for commodities and other developing country exports. The outlook for oil-exporting developing countries had worsened, since global oil consumption was likely to contract again in 1982 and new producers were bent on expanding production.

The *Survey*—which was based on information available to the Secretariat as at 1 April—concluded that world economic recovery would depend in large part on a significant lowering of interest rates and on the avoidance of protectionist barriers; otherwise, there was a distinct possibility that the world economy could be engulfed in a recession of proportions not seen since the 1930s.

A chapter in the *Survey* discussed the way in which inadequate capital movement to developing countries hindered their efforts to adjust their productive sector to sharp changes in international prices for energy and other items. A supplement to the *Survey* contained articles on recent changes in commercial policy of developed market economies and on medium-term growth and trade in the light of the socio-economic development plans of Eastern Europe and the USSR for 1981-1985.[4]

The *Trade and Development Report, 1982*[5] elaborated on the same themes as that of the previous year[15] and reported on the serious deepening of the development crisis that had occurred since then and on the further deterioration in the international economic environment. It examined aspects of the dynamic relationship between the two situations, concluding that urgent action in trade, commodities and international finance was required in support of development. It stated that the crisis was the product of the malfunctioning of the economies of developed market-economy countries and had been intensified by the growing disarray of trade and financing systems.

Assessing the economic situation of the developing countries, the *Report* said the continuing economic crisis that had begun in 1979 differed from the previous one (1974-1975) in that countries could not rely on the international capital market for support because of the heavy volume of accumulated debt and high interest rates. Increased balance-of-payments pressures and accelerated inflation had narrowed policy options, obliging many developing countries to rely more on reducing demand than on increasing supply. The result had been a marked reduction in GDP growth, with the growth performance of oil-importing developing countries in 1981 worse than at any time since the Second World War. Constraints on their growth were expected to continue throughout 1982 and growth was unlikely to exceed 5 per cent in 1983, since many were expected to use increased export earnings associated with a moderate upturn forecast in world demand to avoid increasing unduly their reliance on private capital flows.

The pace of economic activity in developed market-economy countries had not been synchronized in 1981 and the trend might continue in 1982, the *Report* said. The persistence of high interest rates in the face of sluggish growth and high unemployment in those countries had been unprecedented in the post-war period and could jeopardize the modest rebound in economic activity expected in the near term. Inflation had abated in 1981, though at a high cost in terms of output and employment. Citing the public sector deficit in the United States as a major cause of such high rates, the *Report* pointed out that the deficit was likely to increase dramatically.

Turning to trends in the Eastern European socialist countries, the *Report* said their average planned growth rate for 1981 had been set at the historically low figure of 3.2 per cent, reflecting the constraints on more rapid growth imposed by major structural adjustments in all countries of the region and the unfavourable world economy. Largely because of poor weather, agricultural output had declined for the third successive year. The new five-year plans (1981-1985) emphasized rationalization of resource allocation and increased productivity, reflecting the steadily slower growth of the labour force and the recent realignment of world energy prices.

The *Trade and Development Report* also analysed the international trade picture in 1981 and likely short-term trends therein.

CDP report. At its April 1982 session,[6] CDP recommended that Governments consider a programme of world recovery and indicated some elements which it considered essential for such a programme.

It attributed the severity of the recession to turmoil in the international economy in the 1970s and deep uncertainties resulting from accelerated inflation and volatility of exchange rates and the prices of oil and other resources. Commodity markets were also in disarray, with prices at very low levels, imposing extraordinary hardships on countries dependent on commodity exports for revenue. The weakening demand for raw materials was a principal channel for transmitting recession from developed market economies to developing countries. Protectionist measures threatened to transmit contraction throughout the world economy.

CDP noted that, in the mid-1970s recession, the growth momentum of developing countries had been maintained by the provision of finance on much more suitable terms than currently. The prevailing situation was different in that the steep rise in international interest rates, combined with large existing debt, made debt servicing a consuming preoccupation in all deficit countries and threatened to halt investment projects everywhere. It concluded that the way out of the trend to ever-worsening economic contraction must initially be through imaginative use of international financial institutions.

Economic and Social Council action. The main features of an economic recovery programme, based on the CDP recommendations, were presented to the Economic and Social Council by the Secretary-General on 7 July in a statement preceding its annual discussion of international economic and social policy and the current world economic situation. He cited five requirements: a decisive change in the direction of national and international policy towards sustained economic expansion; an open international trading system and a reversal of recent moves towards protectionism; revival and stabilization of international commodity markets; stepped-up flow of capital and technology to the developing countries; and international monetary co-operation to create conditions in which the forces for economic development could realize their full potential.

During the discussion, as summarized in the Council's report to the General Assembly,[7] virtually every speaker pointed to the difficulties imposed by the widespread slow-down of economic activity in 1981. Many pointed out that development plans had had to be cut back, investments curtailed and projects discontinued even at the risk of abandoning essential services. Several speakers pointed to an extreme drop in the international prices of goods exported by developing countries. It was also observed that the unusually high interest rates for international borrowing contributed substantially to a growing burden of external debt servicing for developing countries. Without substantial export growth, a number of those countries observed, their ability to service debts would not adequately improve.

The current crisis in the developing countries, it was widely remarked, stemmed not only from structural problems of development but was a consequence of recession and economic policies in developed market-economy countries. The high interest rates which had added to the debt-servicing burden of the developing countries were seen by a number of speakers to have resulted from a disproportionate reliance on monetary restraint as an anti-inflation policy, while government budget deficits remained excessive.

Many delegations observed that inflation continued to be a significant problem in the developed countries, that unemployment had risen to record levels and that growth had suffered. Maintenance of restrictive policies could be expected for the time being. At the same time, it was recalled that the seven major Western industrialized States which had held a summit meeting in June at Versailles, France, had agreed that a further reduction of inflation, higher employment levels and a return to steady growth must remain the principal objectives of their individual and joint efforts.

A number of speakers commented on policy issues concerned with development and international economic co-operation.

On 30 July, by a decision[1] adopted without vote on an oral proposal by its President, the Council took note of the *World Economic Survey* and other reports submitted in connection with its discussion, including those prepared on current economic conditions in Africa, Asia and the Pacific, Europe, Latin America and Western Asia, and reports on long-term trends in economic development and on restructuring the economic and social sectors of the United Nations system (see Chapter XXIV of this section).

UNCTAD consideration. The world economic situation was discussed by the UNCTAD Trade and Development Board in March and September,[8] the latter discussion focusing on the *Trade and Development Report, 1982* (see above).

At the end of each discussion, on 19 March and 14 September, the Board referred to its following session a draft resolution submitted in 1974 by 14 African developing countries on institutional aspects of the interdependence of problems of trade, development finance and the international monetary system.[13] Also on 19 March 1982, the Board called for information on the current terms for access of developing countries to capital markets.

Report of the CDP Working Group. The Working Group on Development Prospects, convened by CDP to prepare material for its 1983 session, met at Geneva from 1 to 5 November 1982 to consider development prospects in the 1980s and policies for sustained world economic recovery and development.[9] This was a follow-up to an April 1981 decision by CDP to study particular aspects of the world economic situation and prospects.[14]

Examining prospects in the 1980s, the Group agreed that the short-term outlook was bleak and that a strong and spontaneous recovery was not expected in the near future. Views were divided over the medium- and long-term outlook for developed and developing countries: it was suggested that recovery in the former would not mean a return to earlier growth rates, while another view held that rapid technological change and the likelihood of falling oil prices would lead to vigorous and cumulative recovery. However, recent experiences had raised doubts about a continued linkage between growth in developed market economies and that in the developing countries. The medium-term prospects of the centrally planned economies were also dimmed by uncertainties surrounding future conditions of trade and finance, and agricultural production; institutional and managerial change in some countries was also seen as essential to improved economic performance.

Concerning policies for sustained recovery and development, the general view was that inflation rates were currently low enough to permit a shift towards expansion. A comprehensive world recovery programme should aim at stimulating demand in the industrialized countries, since they had large unused capacity, high unemployment, significantly lowered inflation rates and expectations, and the prospect of productivity increases as output increased. This should be coupled with forceful international measures to reactivate developing economies. Expansionary policies should be concerted among key countries, implying commitment to stimulate the economy through a mix of monetary and fiscal measures. Monetary policy should be eased to cut further real interest rates. To reverse protectionist trends, an across-the-board approach on non-tariff barriers was preferable to a sector-by-sector approach. Another important element was an increased commitment to take into account the impact of domestic policies on partner countries.

Long-term projections indicated that, even under favourable conditions, developing countries were lagging behind in development. Income differentials between them were likely to widen, requiring a new focus for international attention. More effective approaches to the transfer of food, financial resources, technology, and managerial and organizational skills should be devised, the Group concluded.

The Group also made suggestions about the CDP role with regard to the 1984 review and appraisal of the International Development Strategy for the Third United Nations Development Decade.

General Assembly action. On 20 December 1982, the General Assembly adopted a resolution[11] urging States, particularly developed countries, to pursue efforts to reverse the negative trends in the world economy and to overcome the critical economic situation affecting developing countries in particular. The Assembly requested the Secretary-General, as part of the International Development Strategy's 1984 review, to analyse trends affecting international economic co-operation and endangering the Strategy's fulfilment, and to reflect the analysis in the *World Economic Survey* and other documents to be prepared for the review.

The resolution was adopted without vote. On 13 December, the revised draft had been similarly approved by the Second Committee after a minor oral revision was made to the preamble by the sponsor—Bangladesh for the Group of 77.

Concern at the serious world economic crisis was voiced by the Assembly in other 1982 resolutions. It expressed great concern over the rapidly deteriorating situation and the lack of implementation of the Strategy in a 3 December resolution on the world social situation.[10] In a 20 December resolution on preparations for the 1983 session of UNCTAD, the Assembly expressed deep concern at the serious crisis facing the world economy, particularly its grave negative impact on the development process of the developing countries.[12] This paragraph of the latter resolution, in a draft submitted in the Second Committee by a Vice-Chairman, replaced a clause in an earlier text by Bangladesh for the Group of 77,[2] subsequently withdrawn, which would have had the Assembly express deep concern at "the aggravation of" the serious crisis.

Decision (1982). [1]ESC: 1982/177, 30 July, text following.
Draft resolution withdrawn. [2]Bangladesh, for Group of 77, A/C.2/37/L.73/Rev.1.
Publications. [3]World Economic Survey 1981-1982: Current Trends in the World Economy (E/1982/46), Sales No. E.82.II.C.1; [4]Supplement to World Economic Survey 1981-1982 (ST/ESA/126), Sales No. E.82.II.C.2; [5]Trade and Development Report, 1982 (UNCTAD/TDR/2/Rev.1), Sales No. E.82.II.D.12.
Reports. [6]CDP, E/1982/15; [7]ESC, A/37/3; [8]TDB, A/37/15, vols. I, II; [9]Working Group on Development Prospects, E/AC.54/1983/L.1.
Resolutions (1982). GA: [10]37/54, paras. 1 & 2, 3 Dec.; [11]37/203, 20 Dec., text following; [12]37/208, para. 7, 20 Dec.
Yearbook references. [13]1974, p. 450; 1981, [14]p. 381, [15]p. 385.
Meeting records. ESC: E/1982/SR.*30*, 31-44, *51* (7-30 July). GA: 2nd Committee, A/C.2/37/SR.3, 6, 7, 10, 13-19, 33, 40, *45, 48* (28 Sep.–13 Dec.); plenary, A/37/PV.113 (20 Dec.).

Economic and Social Council decision 1982/177

Adopted without vote

Oral proposal by President; agenda item 3.

Reports considered by the Economic and Social Council in connection with its general discussion of international economic and social policy, including regional and sectoral developments

At its 51st plenary meeting, on 30 July 1982, the Council took note of the following documents:

(a) *World Economic Survey 1981-1982: Current Trends in the World Economy;*

(b) Report of the Committee for Development Planning on its eighteenth session;

(c) Report of the Task Force on Long-Term Development Objectives of the Administrative Committee on Co-ordination;

(d) Summary of the annual economic survey of the region of the Economic Commission for Western Asia;

(e) Summary of the survey of economic and social conditions in Africa, 1980-1981, and outlook for 1981-1982;

(f) Report entitled "Recent economic developments in the region of the Economic Commission for Europe";

(g) Summary of the economic and social survey of Asia and the Pacific, 1981;

(h) Summary of the economic survey of Latin America, 1981;

(i) Report of the Secretary-General entitled "Development and international economic co-operation—Restructuring of the economic and social sectors of the United Nations system: implementation of General Assembly resolution 35/203";

(j) Comments of the Secretary-General on the report of the Joint Inspection Unit on the relationships between the Director-General for Development and International Economic Co-operation and entities of the United Nations Secretariat.

General Assembly resolution 37/203

20 December 1982   Meeting 113   Adopted without vote

Approved by Second Committee (A/37/680/Add.1) without vote, 13 December (meeting 48); draft by Bangladesh, for Group of 77 (A/C.2/37/L.94/Rev.1), orally revised; agenda item 71 *(a)*.

Negative trends in the world economy

The General Assembly,

Recalling its resolutions 3201(S-VI) and 3202(S-VI) of 1 May 1974, containing the Declaration and the Programme of Action on the Establishment of a New International Economic Order, 3281(XXIX) of 12 December 1974, containing the Charter of Economic Rights and Duties of States, and 3362(S-VII) of 16 September 1975 on development and international economic co-operation,

Recalling also its resolution 35/56 of 5 December 1980, the annex to which contains the International Development Strategy for the Third United Nations Development Decade,

Expressing concern about the worsening of certain trends in international economic relations, which run counter to the objectives of international co-operation contained in the above-mentioned resolutions and constitute serious obstacles to the international economy, in particular to the economic growth and development prospects of the developing countries,

Concerned that the international economy remains in a state of structural disequilibrium characterized by a slowing-down of activities and of economic growth, accompanied by, *inter alia*, prolonged monetary instability, intensified protectionist pressures, structural problems and maladjustment and uncertain long-term growth prospects,

1. *Considers* that the continuation or worsening of the current situation could lead to a climate of mistrust in international economic relations, with unpredictable consequences for international economic co-operation as well as for world peace and security;

2. *Expresses its deep concern* about the grave international economic situation, in particular of the developing countries, and about the perspectives arising from the current trends in the world economy, which, if they continue, will endanger the realization of the goals and objectives of the International Development Strategy for the Third United Nations Development Decade;

3. *Urges* all States, in particular the developed countries, to pursue concerted efforts to reverse the present negative trends and to overcome the critical economic situation currently affecting in particular the developing countries;

4. *Requests* the Secretary-General, as part of the preparations for the review and appraisal of the International Development Strategy, to analyse also the current negative trends in the world economy, which affect international economic co-operation and endanger the efforts towards the fulfilment of the goals and objectives of the International Development Strategy, and to reflect such analysis appropriately in the *World Economic Survey* and other documentation to be prepared for the review and appraisal of the International Development Strategy.

Long-term trends in economic development

Report of the Secretary-General. A preliminary draft of an overall socio-economic perspective of the world economy to the year 2000, under preparation since 1980, was circulated in May 1982 for consideration by the Economic and Social Council and the General Assembly.[4] It was a revised version of an incomplete draft considered by the Council in November 1981.[10] Work on the perspective had been initiated in response to a 1979 request of the Assembly.[8]

The report, supplemented with a statistical annex containing historical data and projections, attempted to provide a perspective on the challenges and potentials of the International Development Strategy for the Third United Nations Development Decade.[9] It reviewed the past and current economic situation and analysed long-term development possibilities under two principal scenarios: low growth and the Strategy. Added to the report was a section providing regional development perspectives; other sections dealt with the social dimensions of development and some critical areas for international policy action.

The following were among the report's major conclusions: If recent economic trends continued, growth in the developed market economies in the 1980s and 1990s would fall to about half the rates experienced in the 1960s, severely limiting the growth of world trade and worsening the export prospects of many developing countries. The prospects for developing countries were sombre—as a group their economic growth would be only 4.8 per cent a year in the last two decades of the century, well below the 5.5 per cent rate of the 1960s and 1970s. For the low-income and least developed countries prospects were even more disturbing, with an annual growth rate of 3.5 per cent or less, implying an increase of less than 1 per cent in per capita GDP.

To fulfil the goals of the International Development Strategy, the report stated, future growth rates for the developing countries should be significantly higher than those implied by their recent experience or historical trends. The central question examined in the report was how the halting growth performance of recent years could be replaced by sustained high growth rates in both developed and developing countries.

Among the policy measures needed to approach the Strategy's targets, the report mentioned national action to increase domestic savings and capital productivity, encourage more capital inflows, substitute domestic products for imported ones and promote exports; and concerted international action to remove trade barriers, facilitate adjustments to the constantly changing pattern of comparative advantage in the production of goods and services, increase concessional aid to the low-income and least developed countries, and increase the availability of private capital to middle- and high-income developing countries.

Addressing the social dimension, the report noted that, even if the overall development goals of the Strategy were attained, hundreds of millions of people would still be living in unsatisfactory economic and social conditions by the turn of the century. However, the number of people living in poverty could be significantly reduced through a major improvement in income distribution and definite socio-economic policies aimed at alleviating the conditions of the neediest by such means as direct aid for increased government services to the poor, human resources development, and increased public expenditure on essential needs such as education and health.

Task Force consideration. The Task Force on Long-Term Development Objectives, a subsidiary body of the Administrative Committee on Co-ordination (ACC), held its ninth session at Geneva from 24 to 26 February 1982[5] and continued to assess the world economic situation and prospects, as had been urged by the Economic and Social Council in July 1981.[7]

The Task Force concentrated on prospects for development objectives in the light of the current world economic situation. Noting the severity of the world economic recession, it stated that poverty was increasing and that the distribution of income, services, opportunities and power was becoming more unequal as nations and social groups struggled to protect acquired rights and benefits in an atmosphere of economic stagnation and fear of the future. Rising mortality rates suggested a deterioration of the social situation in some parts of the world.

These developments were occurring at a time, the Task Force noted, when economic policies were surrounded with disagreement and uncertainty, and international economic co-operation was weakening. Policies tended to be defensive in both industrialized and developing countries, and they were disjointed as regards their international impact. Influential economic policies, with their inward-looking preoccupation and concern with the short term, tended to export domestic problems to weaker partners.

To overcome this situation, the Task Force advocated anti-inflationary and adjustment policies that would restore economic dynamism, changes in economic management to scrutinize unproductive expenditures including the surge of military budgets, social innovation through such approaches as primary health care, and greater popular participation in society's decision-making.

The Task Force also gave preliminary consideration to approaches to the issue of changes in styles of development, and made suggestions on the 1984 review and appraisal of the implementation of the International Development Strategy.

Economic and Social Council action. On 29 July,[1] the Economic and Social Council decided to transmit to the General Assembly a draft resolution submitted by Algeria for the Group of 77.[3] The draft, annexed to the decision, would have had the Assembly decide that the socio-economic perspective of the world economy to the year 2000 should be reviewed and updated triennially. The Assembly would have requested the Secretary-General to prepare the next report on the perspective in 1985, assisted by CDP and in consultation with United Nations organizations, for submission that year to the Assembly through the Council. CDP would also have been invited to take the content of the perspective into account in its future work.

The decision, orally proposed by the Council President, was adopted without vote.

Also, in a 30 July decision covering various economic reports,[2] the Council took note of the ACC Task Force report.

General Assembly action. On 21 December, the General Assembly adopted a resolution[6] based on the text forwarded by the Council. However, rather than a triennial reviewing and updating of the perspective, the Assembly decided that it should be revised and updated to serve as background material for the review and appraisal of the International Development Strategy. It further decided that in 1985 a decision would be taken on the advisability and periodicity of future reports.

The resolution was adopted without vote. On 8 December, the Second Committee had approved the draft similarly. The text was submitted by a Committee Vice-Chairman after informal consultations on the Council draft.

Decisions (1982). ESC: [1]1982/172, 29 July, text following; [2]1982/177, para. *(c),* 30 July.
Draft resolution transmitted. [3]Algeria, for Group of 77, E/1982/L.47 (transmitted to GA by Secretariat note, A/C.2/37/L.8).
Reports. [4]S-G, A/37/211 & Corr.1,2,4 & Add.1; [5]Task Force on Long-Term Development Objectives, E/1982/74.
Resolution (1982). [6]GA: 37/249, 21 Dec., text following.
Resolutions (prior). [7]ESC: 1981/64, 23 July 1981 (YUN 1981, p. 381). GA: [8]34/57, 29 Nov. 1979 (YUN 1979, p. 743); [9]35/56, annex, 5 Dec. 1980 (YUN 1980, p. 503).
Yearbook reference. [10]1981, p. 389.
Meeting records. ESC: E/1982/SR.31-44, *48, 50* (8-29 July). GA: 2nd Committee, A/C.2/37/SR.3, 6, 7, 10, 13-19, 33, 40, *47* (28 Sep.–8 Dec.); plenary, A/37/PV.115 (21 Dec.).

Economic and Social Council decision 1982/172

Adopted without vote

Oral proposal by President; agenda item 3.

Long-term trends in world economic and social development
At its 50th plenary meeting, on 29 July 1982, the Council decided to transmit the draft resolution annexed hereto to the General Assembly at its thirty-seventh session, for consideration and appropriate action.

ANNEX

Long-term trends in world economic and social development

The General Assembly,
Recalling its resolution 3508(XXX) of 15 December 1975, in which it initiated within the United Nations system analytical work relating to the examination of long-term trends in world economic and social development,
Recalling the Declaration and the Programme of Action on the Establishment of a New International Economic Order, contained in its resolutions 3201(S-VI) and 3202(S-VI) of 1 May 1974, which laid the foundations for the new international economic order, the Charter of Economic

Rights and Duties of States, contained in its resolution 3281(XXIX) of 12 December 1974, General Assembly resolution 3362(S-VII) of 16 September 1975 on development and international economic co-operation, and the International Development Strategy for the Third United Nations Development Decade, contained in Assembly resolution 35/56 of 5 December 1980,
Recalling also that its resolution 34/57 of 29 November 1979, its decision 36/423 of 4 December 1981 and Economic and Social Council decision 1981/200 of 2 November 1981 call for a review of the progress made in the implementation of resolution 34/57 at the thirty-seventh session of the Assembly, and taking note of Council decision 1982/172 of 29 July 1982,
Drawing attention to the need to strengthen and expand international co-operation for development, made most urgent by the long-term implications of prevailing economic and social conditions and trends in the world economy and in the economies of the developing countries in particular,
Reaffirming the relevance of long-term perspectives for providing impetus to policies and decision-making processes in relation to development strategies and economic co-operation on a national, regional and global scale,
Bearing in mind the views expressed by the Committee for Development Planning at its sixteenth session, particularly the view that long-term perspectives should serve as a coherent framework for concerted policy action with a focus on facilitating the implementation of the policy measures specified in the International Development Strategy for the Third United Nations Development Decade,
1. *Takes note* of the report of the Secretary-General on an overall socio-economic perspective of the world economy to the year 2000, and of the progress made in the implementation of General Assembly resolution 34/57;
2. *Welcomes* the contributions of Member States and of the United Nations organizations, organs and bodies concerned to the implementation of the relevant provisions of General Assembly resolution 34/57 and of Economic and Social Council decision 1981/200;
3. *Decides* that the overall socio-economic perspective of the world economy to the year 2000 shall be reviewed and updated on a triennial basis, and requests the Secretary-General to prepare the next comprehensive report on the socio-economic perspective in 1985, with the assistance of the Committee for Development Planning and in consultation with the competent organizations of the United Nations system, and to submit it to the General Assembly at its fortieth session through the Economic and Social Council at its second regular session of 1985;
4. *Invites* the Committee for Development Planning to take fully into account in the regular conduct of its future work the content of the report on an overall socio-economic perspective of the world economy to the year 2000;
5. *Decides* to include in the provisional agenda of its fortieth session an item entitled "Long-term trends in economic development";
6. *Calls upon* all States, as well as the United Nations organizations, organs and bodies concerned, to contribute in their respective areas of competence to the implementation of the present resolution.

General Assembly resolution 37/249

21 December 1982   Meeting 115   Adopted without vote

Approved by Second Committee (A/37/680/Add.10) without vote, 8 December (meeting 47); draft by Vice-Chairman (A/C.2/37/L.116), based on informal consultations on draft transmitted by Economic and Social Council decision 1982/172; agenda item 71 *(I).*

Long-term trends in economic development

The General Assembly,
Recalling its resolution 3508(XXX) of 15 December 1975, in which it recommended the initiation within the United Nations system of analytical work relating to the examination of long-term trends in world economic and social development,
Recalling the Declaration and the Programme of Action on the Establishment of a New International Economic Order, contained in its resolutions 3201(S-VI) and 3202(S-VI) of 1 May 1974, which laid the foundations for the new international economic order, the Charter of Economic Rights and Duties of States, contained in its resolution 3281(XXIX) of 12 December 1974, resolution 3362(S-VII) of 16 September 1975 on development and international economic co-operation and the International Development Strategy for the Third United Nations Development

Decade, contained in the annex to its resolution 35/56 of 5 December 1980,

Recalling also that its resolution 34/57 of 29 November 1979, its decision 36/423 of 4 December 1981 and Economic and Social Council decision 1981/200 of 2 November 1981 called for a review by the General Assembly of the progress made in the implementation of resolution 34/57, and taking note of Council decision 1982/172 of 29 July 1982,

Drawing attention to the need to strengthen and expand international co-operation for development, made most urgent by the long-term implications of prevailing economic and social conditions and trends in the world economy and in the economies of the developing countries in particular,

Reaffirming the relevance of long-term perspectives for providing impetus to policies and decision-making processes in relation to development strategies and economic co-operation on a national, regional and global scale,

Bearing in mind the views expressed by the Committee for Development Planning at its sixteenth session, particularly the view that long-term perspectives should serve as a coherent framework for concerted policy action with a focus on facilitating the implementation of the policy measures specified in the International Development Strategy for the Third United Nations Development Decade,

Conscious of the importance of protecting international economic relations from the negative consequences of political tensions and of strengthening confidence among nations in their economic co-operation by placing this co-operation on a long-term stable basis,

1. *Takes note* of the report of the Secretary-General on the overall socio-economic perspective of the world economy to the year 2000 and of the progress made in the implementation of General Assembly resolution 34/57;

2. *Welcomes* the contributions of Member States and of the United Nations organizations, organs and bodies concerned to the implementation of the relevant provisions of General Assembly resolution 34/57 and of Economic and Social Council decision 1981/200;

3. *Requests* the Secretary-General to prepare the next comprehensive report on the socio-economic perspective in 1985, with the assistance of the Committee for Development Planning and in consultation with the competent organizations of the United Nations system, and to submit it to the General Assembly at its fortieth session through the Economic and Social Council at its second regular session of 1985;

4. *Decides* that the overall socio-economic perspective of the world economy to the year 2000 should be revised and updated so that it can serve as background material in the process of the review and appraisal of the International Development Strategy for the Third United Nations Development Decade;

5. *Invites* the Committee for Development Planning to take fully into account in the regular conduct of its future work the content of the report on the overall socio-economic perspective of the world economy to the year 2000;

6. *Decides* to include in the provisional agenda of its fortieth session the item entitled "Long-term trends in economic development" and to take a decision at that session regarding the advisability and periodicity of the submission of future comprehensive reports;

7. *Calls upon* all States, as well as the United Nations organizations, organs and bodies concerned, to contribute in their respective areas of competence to the implementation of the present resolution.

Inflation and development

A report on world inflation and the development process,[2] aimed at helping Governments to identify national and international policy measures to control inflation while safeguarding development in developing countries, was submitted in 1982 by the Secretary-General of the United Nations Conference on Trade and Development (UNCTAD). The report, discussed in September 1982 by the UNCTAD Trade and Development Board, had been requested by the General Assembly in 1979[3] for consideration in 1981, but its submission had been postponed because the UNCTAD Secretary-General

felt that a comprehensive review was needed in view of economic and policy shifts since the Assembly's original request.[4] The report was transmitted to the Assembly in October 1982 through a note by the United Nations Secretary-General.

The report stated that whereas excess aggregate demand had stimulated inflation in the 1960s and early 1970s, cost-push factors appeared to have provided the primary impetus from the late 1970s to date. While inflation was generally accompanied by monetary expansion, in most cases such expansion appeared to accommodate an inflation whose causes lay elsewhere.

Developing countries had been seriously affected in the 1970s by the transmission of inflation to their economies, with higher prices for imports and exports directly affecting domestic price levels, the report stated. Inflation had widened their current-account deficits, increased pressure on public finances and worsened income distribution. Further, many had also suffered from restrictive monetarist policies followed by developed market-economy countries to combat inflation.

The report concluded that, while no unique formula would successfully combat inflation in every economy, success was predicated on basic agreement among economic groups in each society on rules for income distribution, including the way wage bargaining was carried out. At the same time, Governments should co-ordinate the broad thrust of domestic economic policies so as to take account of their impact on the rest of the international community. Recourse to a mix of anti-inflation policies, rather than sole reliance on control of the money supply, could minimize adverse external repercussions without weakening their domestic effectiveness. Restrictive monetary and fiscal policies alone were unlikely to control inflation without excessive cost in unemployment and idle resources.

On 15 September, the Trade and Development Board decided that comments made on the report would be incorporated in the Board's report to the General Assembly.[1]

Reports. [1]TDB, A/37/15, vol. II; [2]UNCTAD S-G, TD/B/914 & Corr.1 (annexed to S-G note, A/37/518).
Resolution. [3]GA: 34/197, 19 Dec. 1979 (YUN 1979, p. 580).
Yearbook reference. [4]1981, p. 393.

Review of implementation of the Strategy for the Third UN Development Decade

General Assembly action. On 20 December 1982, the General Assembly adopted a resolution[4] by which it decided to establish a Committee on the Review and Appraisal of the Implementation of the International Development Strategy for the Third United Nations Development Decade. This Committee of universal membership was to meet in 1983 to organize its work and was to report through the Economic and Social Council to the Assembly in 1984, at which time the Secretary-General was also to report to assist in the review and appraisal. Bodies of the United Nations system were called on to report on the results achieved in their respective sectors and regions in applying the Strategy. The Assembly invited Governments to reflect the Strategy's goals, objectives and policy measures in their policy formulation and developed countries to transmit reports of their development assistance. The agreed results were to be incorporated by the Assembly into the Strategy as appropriate.

Provision for a review in 1984 had been made in the text of the Strategy as adopted by the Assembly in 1980.[7]

The resolution was adopted without vote. On 8 December 1982, the draft had been similarly approved by the Second (Economic and Financial) Committee after oral revisions—agreed upon in informal consultations held by a Vice-Chairman—had been made in a text submitted by Bangladesh for the Group of 77. These revisions added the word "especially" in the eighth preambular paragraph, in a reference to the adverse effects of the international economic crisis especially on the economies of the developing countries, and deleted the words "process of" in paragraph 8 from a phrase that would have had the Committee for Development Planning (CDP) submit observations and recommendations on the process of review and appraisal.

The Assembly took two further actions in 1982 relating to the review and appraisal. On 20 December, it requested the Secretary-General, as part of preparations for this exercise, to analyse current negative trends in the world economy affecting international economic co-operation and endangering efforts to fulfil the goals of the Strategy.[5] On 21 December, it decided that the United Nations Secretariat's socio-economic perspective of the world economy to the year 2000 should be revised and updated to serve as background material for the review and appraisal.[6]

Reports. In its annual report to the Economic and Social Council, issued following its April 1982 session,[1] the Administrative Committee on Coordination, acknowledging that little progress had been made in achieving the goals of the International Development Strategy, said it was important for Member States to adopt decisions with regard to the 1984 review exercise so that the United Nations system could make a useful contribution. In addition, CDP, reporting on its April session,[2] noted that the Strategy's objectives appeared to be vitiated in current economic circumstances and stressed that the major part of its 1984 session would have to be devoted to the mid-Decade appraisal.

The CDP Working Group on Development Prospects (see above) suggested in November[3] that its parent body might bear in mind that the review

should concentrate not merely on quantitative targets but also on policy instruments used to implement the Strategy. Also, CDP might present a single, condensed analytical document containing a synthesis of contributions from the various agencies and suggestions as to what should be done in the remainder of the Decade.

Reports. [1]ACC, E/1982/4; [2]CDP, E/1982/15; [3]Working Group on Development Prospects, E/AC.54/1983/L.1.
Resolutions (1982). GA: [4]37/202, 20 Dec., text following; [5]37/203, para. 4, 20 Dec.; [6]37/249, para. 4, 21 Dec.
Resolution (prior). [7]GA: 35/56, annex, 5 Dec. 1980 (YUN 1980, p. 503).
Financial implications. 5th Committee report, A/37/762; S-G statements, A/C.2/37/L.109, A/C.5/37/96.
Meeting records. GA: 2nd Committee, A/C.2/37/SR.3, 6, 7, 10, 13-19, 33, 40, *45, 47* (28 Sep.–8 Dec.); 5th Committee, A/C.5/37/SR.71 (15 Dec.); plenary, A/37/PV.113 (20 Dec.).

General Assembly resolution 37/202

20 December 1982   Meeting 113   Adopted without vote

Approved by Second Committee (A/37/680/Add.1) without vote, 8 December (meeting 47); draft by Bangladesh, for Group of 77 (A/C.2/37/L.91), orally revised in informal consultations; agenda item 71 *(a)*.

Review and appraisal of the implementation of the International Development Strategy for the Third United Nations Development Decade

The General Assembly,

Recalling its resolutions 3201(S-VI) and 3202(S-VI) of 1 May 1974, containing the Declaration and the Programme of Action on the Establishment of a New International Economic Order, 3281(XXIX) of 12 December 1974, containing the Charter of Economic Rights and Duties of States, and 3362(S-VII) of 16 September 1975 on development and international economic co-operation,

Recalling also its resolution 35/56 of 5 December 1980, the annex to which contains the International Development Strategy for the Third United Nations Development Decade,

Aware of its responsibility to carry out in 1984 the first overall review and appraisal of the implementation of the International Development Strategy,

Recalling also that the process of review and appraisal forms an integral part of the International Development Strategy and provides an opportunity to strengthen it as an instrument of policy for the attainment of the goals and objectives set out therein,

Recalling further that the process of review and appraisal should, within the context of an overall review of the international economic situation, scrutinize the state of the implementation of the International Development Strategy and identify the factors responsible for the shortfalls,

Stressing that such a review and appraisal should be undertaken within the United Nations system at the regional, sectoral and global levels, and by the respective Governments at the national level,

Noting with deep regret that global negotiations relating to international economic co-operation for development, which are intended to be one of the principal instruments for facilitating the implementation of the International Development Strategy, have not been launched,

Conscious that the adverse effects of the continuing international economic crisis, especially on the economies of the developing countries, make particularly necessary the task of carrying out such a review and appraisal with a view to considering the adjustment, intensification or reformulation of the policy measures required in the light of evolving needs and developments, in order to achieve the goals and objectives of the International Development Strategy,

1. *Reaffirms* the decision to carry out in 1984, at the global level, the first overall review and appraisal of the state of implementation of the policy measures, as well as the realization of the goals and objectives of the International Development Strategy for the Third United Nations Development Decade;

2. *Stresses* that the process of review and appraisal at the global level shall take into account the results achieved at the sectoral, regional and national levels;

3. *Emphasizes* that the review and appraisal shall, at all levels, take into account the results of various United Nations conferences as well as the results of relevant regional and interregional meetings, and that the agreed results will be incorporated in the International Development Strategy by the General Assembly when and as appropriate, with a view to contributing to its effective implementation;

4. *Emphasizes further* that the review and appraisal, based on an assessment provided for in General Assembly resolutions 33/201 of 29 January 1979, 35/81 of 5 December 1980 and 36/199 of 17 December 1981, should ensure that the operational activities of the United Nations system contribute effectively to the implementation of the International Development Strategy;

5. *Decides* to establish a committee of universal membership to carry out in 1984 a review and appraisal of the implementation of the International Development Strategy, and further decides that the Committee on the Review and Appraisal of the Implementation of the International Development Strategy for the Third United Nations Development Decade, which will meet in a brief organizational session during the thirty-eighth session of the General Assembly, will report to the Assembly at its thirty-ninth session through the Economic and Social Council at its second regular session of 1984;

6. *Calls upon* the relevant organs, organizations and bodies of the United Nations system to report, for consideration, to the Committee on the Review and Appraisal of the Implementation of the International Development Strategy for the Third United Nations Development Decade on the results achieved in their respective sectors in applying the International Development Strategy as the policy framework in the formulation and implementation of their programmes of work and medium-term plans;

7. *Requests* the regional commissions to carry out in 1984, as part of their regular activity of preparing economic surveys of the regions, a review of the implementation of the International Development Strategy in their respective regions;

8. *Invites* the Committee for Development Planning to submit its observations and recommendations regarding the review and appraisal to the General Assembly at its thirty-ninth session, through the Committee on the Review and Appraisal of the Implementation of the International Development Strategy for the Third United Nations Development Decade and the Economic and Social Council at its second regular session of 1984;

9. *Requests* the Secretary-General to prepare and submit to the General Assembly at its thirty-ninth session, through the Committee on the Review and Appraisal of the Implementation of the International Development Strategy for the Third United Nations Development Decade and the Economic and Social Council, a comprehensive report and other appropriate documentation in order to assist in the review and appraisal;

10. *Invites* Governments to reflect appropriately, at the national level, in accordance with their national priorities and plans, the goals and objectives and the policy measures of the International Development Strategy in their policy formulation;

11. *Invites* developed countries, individually or through their relevant organizations, to transmit reports of their development assistance efforts in the light of the commitments undertaken by them under the International Development Strategy and in relevant international forums;

12. *Decides* to consider, at its thirty-eighth session, other arrangements necessary for fulfilling its task in connection with the review and appraisal of the International Development Strategy.

Development planning and information

Development planning

The Committee for Development Planning (CDP) held its eighteenth session at United Nations Headquarters from 19 to 28 April 1982.[1]

The Committee—composed of 24 experts appointed by the Economic and Social Council—

analysed the current international economic situation, advanced ideas to attain world economic recovery (see above), and suggested immediate monetary and financial measures to restore non-inflationary world growth, including specific areas for monetary and financial co-operation among developing countries, ideas for reform of the international monetary system and improvements in development assistance policies. It also recommended five African countries for inclusion in the list of least developed countries.

The CDP Working Group on Development Prospects met in November to consider prospects of the world economy to the year 1990, in preparation for a study of the subject by the Committee in 1983. The Committee planned to devote the major part of its 1984 session to its contribution to the review and appraisal of the International Development Strategy for the Third United Nations Development Decade.

Report. [1]CDP, E/1982/15 & Corr.1,2.
Publication. World Economic Recovery: The Priority of International Monetary and Financial Co-operation (ST/ESA/127), Sales No. E.82.II.C.3.

Technical co-operation

During 1982, the United Nations Department of Technical Co-operation for Development implemented some 80 projects in more than 60 countries on various aspects of development planning. These projects were aimed at helping countries expand their capacity to control the socio-economic situation, manage their economies and development programmes through monitoring and forecasting, and improve their negotiating position in the world economy.

Projects in national planning were initiated in Malawi, Saudi Arabia and Zambia, and in regional planning in two states of Malaysia. New phases were begun in projects to assist the multinational Gambia and Senegal river basin development schemes, regional (subnational) planning in Nigeria and Senegal, and project evaluation in Rwanda. One continuing activity, financed by Japan, involved training and research in regional planning at the United Nations Centre for Regional Development (Nagoya, Japan).

Development information

Mass communication

In a September 1982 report[2] to the Administrative Committee on Co-ordination (ACC), the Joint United Nations Information Committee (JUNIC) examined development support communication—the role of communication in development programmes. After examining the issues, making a number of findings and outlining its future work plan, JUNIC recommended that heads of United Nations organizations incorporate development support communication policies and procedures in their programme guidelines, include briefings on the topic in their staff orientation and training programmes, and determine what resources were available and needed for functions in this area.

On 3 November,[1] ACC endorsed the JUNIC recommendations and work plan, and adopted a statement on how the United Nations system could help developing countries in development support communication planning, services and activities, and on steps United Nations organizations and JUNIC might take to improve their assistance. In this statement, ACC recognized that communication media and techniques were particularly effective in reaching millions of people in the developing world and eliciting information from them as a basis for planning development activities. Listed among the areas of possible assistance by the United Nations system were the identification of communication needs in development programmes, the drawing up of national strategies, the establishment of communication systems and services using audio-visual and printed media, and the training of national personnel.

Decision. [1]ACC: 1982/20, 3 Nov.
Report. [2]JUNIC, ACC/1982/27.

Information Systems Unit

In response to a December 1981 General Assembly resolution,[3] the Secretary-General submitted in February 1982 a report[2] to the Committee for Programme and Co-ordination (CPC) on the Information Systems Unit (ISU) in the United Nations Department of International Economic and Social Affairs. The report gave information on the computerized Development Information System maintained by ISU, the information systems of the regional commissions which used the same indexing tool—the *Macrothesaurus for Information Processing in the Field of Economic and Social Development*, maintained by ISU—and initiatives to strengthen compatibility among systems. The report also outlined the mechanisms being used to manage the *Macrothesaurus* and to exchange information among the regions, pointing out that the merged file of ISU and regional data bases, to be ready in 1982, would make some 11,000 references to unpublished reports on United Nations development activities available in New York for on-line searching.

During the CPC discussion in April, doubts expressed by some members about the usefulness of ISU led the Committee to request that a more detailed final report be presented to it in 1983.[1]

Reports. [1]CPC, A/37/38; [2]S-G, E/AC.51/1982/3.
Resolution. [3]GA: 36/237, 18 Dec. 1981 (YUN 1981, p. 398).

Other developments

Computerized information systems continued to be maintained by United Nations bodies on such topics as industrial development. In July the Economic and Social Council called for continued co-operation in regard to the Second Intergovernmental Conference on Strategies and Policies for Informatics, to be held in 1983. In November the Council urged further steps to co-ordinate information systems in the United Nations system through a central mechanism under the Administrative Committee on Co-ordination.

Public administration

UN programme

In 1982 the United Nations Department of Technical Co-operation for Development (DTCD) carried out a $12.7 million programme of assistance to Governments in public administration and finance. This covered institution-building, administrative reform and improvement, financial management, and personnel administration and training. The United Nations Development Programme (UNDP) was the main source of funds for the programme, providing $10.8 million.

Projects in administrative reform and improvement were carried out in many countries, some to adjust administrative structures to major changes and others to eliminate obsolete structures and practices. Manpower development and in-service training, fellowships and seminars continued as major elements, with emphasis on the training of senior public managers, including scientists and technical personnel. Curriculum design and training of management trainers also received special attention. The growth in the public sector in developing countries was responsible for an increased number of projects in the management of public enterprises. Improvement in public budgeting and financial management was another continuing concern, and new auditing projects were begun in three countries.

Advisory services and programme support continued to be given to the International Center for Public Enterprises in Developing Countries, at Ljubljana, Yugoslavia, and to regional and subregional institutions, including the African Training and Research Centre in Administration for Development and the Central American Institute for Public Administration. Advisory services were provided in financial management, administrative reform, computer use and public enterprise management. Manuals were prepared on the role of public accounting and auditing for management of development, and on strategies for dealing with problems in institution-building.

The Sixth Meeting of Experts on the United Nations Programme in Public Administration and Finance was held at Geneva from 10 to 19 March to review issues and priorities in public administration and finance for developing countries, national measures required to promote development administration, and the existing and proposed United Nations work programme in this field for the 1980s.[2]

The 21 experts from different regions concluded that many developing countries needed to strengthen their administrative and managerial capabilities and that this would call for far-reaching national measures with international support. Developing countries were urged to plan and implement a coherent set of administrative and financial reforms, and the least developed countries (LDCs) were asked to formulate an integrated national programme for technical co-operation. At the international level, the experts stressed three main areas for action: an analysis of challenges and constraints of public administration and finance, formulation of policies and mechanisms to augment technical co-operation among developing countries, and promotion of managerial capability in LDCs, including identification of their administrative and institutional needs.

Regarding the United Nations programme for 1982-1983 and the proposed medium-term plan for 1984-1989, the Meeting noted that the main thrust of the latter was on problems of LDCs and on promoting co-operation among developing countries. Making suggestions on specific projects and activities, the Meeting attached special importance to continued work towards the establishment of a network of public administration and finance institutions, which would serve as a mechanism through which the United Nations could collaborate with other organizations in this field. It suggested several subjects for further investigation and analysis, including administrative aspects of the environmental dimensions of development and analysis of measures by various countries to fight corruption in the national administration.

In an April report to the Economic and Social Council,[3] the Secretary-General requested the Council to commend the report of the Sixth Meeting to Governments for review and action. Regarding its recommendations for international action, he believed they were consistent with the developmental concerns of the 1980s. He would take into account the experts' suggestions on the United Nations work programme for 1982-1983 and requested that their observations on 1984-1989 be considered by the appropriate bodies when the proposed medium-term plan for that period was reviewed.

Economic and Social Council action. On 27 July, in a resolution adopted without vote,[4] the Economic and Social Council requested the Secretary-General to provide, within existing resources, the technical assistance developing countries might need to promote public administration and finance for development, and invited UNDP, in formulating its regional and interregional programmes, to bear in mind the need for improving the administrative and managerial capabilities of developing countries, particularly LDCs. The Council also noted the recommendations of the Meeting of Experts and requested the Secretary-General to prepare for the next meeting, in 1984.

The resolution had been recommended by the Council's First (Economic) Committee without vote on 16 July. It was submitted by a Vice-Chairman on the basis of informal consultations held on a 12-nation draft presented to the Committee by Yugoslavia,[1] later withdrawn. The adopted text was nearly identical to the initial one, except that its preamble included mention of a 1980 General Assembly resolution on the role of qualified national personnel in the social and economic development of developing countries.[5]

Draft resolution withdrawn. [1]Bangladesh, India, Iraq, Kenya, Mexico, Nepal, Qatar, Sudan, Tunisia, Venezuela, Yugoslavia, Zaire, E/1982/C.1/L.4.
Reports. [2]Meeting of Experts on UN Programme, E/1982/52/Add.1; [3]S-G, E/1982/52.
Resolution (1982). [4]ESC: 1982/44, 27 July, text following.
Resolution (prior). [5]GA: 35/80, 5 Dec. 1980 (YUN 1980, p. 595).
Meeting record. ESC: E/1982/SR.48 (27 July).
Publication. Elements of Institution-building for Institutes of Public Administration and Management (ST/ESA/SER.E/25), Sales No. E.82.II.H.2.

Economic and Social Council resolution 1982/44

27 July 1982	Meeting 48	Adopted without vote

Approved by First Committee (E/1982/97) without vote, 16 July (meeting 8); draft by Vice-Chairman (E/1982/C.1/L.7), based on informal consultations on 12-nation draft (E/1982/C.1/L.4); agenda item 10.

Public administration and finance for development

The Economic and Social Council,

Recalling General Assembly resolutions 35/56 of 5 December 1980, containing the International Development Strategy for the Third United Nations Development Decade, 36/194 of 17 December 1981 on the United Nations Conference on the Least Developed Countries, particularly paragraph 3 thereof, 34/137 of 14 December 1979 on the role of the public sector in promoting the economic development of developing countries and 35/80 of 5 December 1980 on the role of qualified national personnel in the social and economic development of developing countries,

Recalling also Council resolutions 1978/6 of 4 May 1978, 1978/75 of 8 November 1978 and 1980/12 of 28 April 1980, concerning public administration and finance for development in the 1980s, and 1981/45 of 20 July 1981 on the role of the public sector in promoting the economic development of developing countries,

Reiterating the importance of developing and strengthening the public administration and finance capabilities of developing countries, including training and institution-building, in the formulation and carrying out of policies for the economic and social development of those countries,

1. *Takes note* of the report of the Sixth Meeting of Experts on the United Nations Programme in Public Administration and Finance, held at Geneva from 10 to 19 March 1982, and the report of the Secretary-General thereon;

2. *Takes note also* of the major recommendations made by the Sixth Meeting of Experts and requests the Secretary-General to transmit them

to the States Members of the United Nations for their review and appropriate action at the national level;

3. *Requests* the Secretary-General to provide, within existing resources and at the request of Governments of developing countries, the technical assistance they may need for promoting public administration and finance for development;

4. *Invites* the United Nations Development Programme, in formulating its regional and interregional programmes, to bear in mind the need for improving the administrative and managerial capabilities of developing countries, in particular the least developed ones, in the field of public administration and finance;

5. *Notes* the recommendation of the Sixth Meeting of Experts that its next meeting should be convened in 1984, and requests the Secretary-General to make the necessary preparations for that meeting, which, in reviewing, in accordance with its mandate, the United Nations Programme in Public Administration and Finance, should also deal in particular with:

(a) Challenges and constraints in public administration and finance in the developing countries in the 1980s;

(b) The specific needs of developing countries, in particular the least developed ones, especially in the field of training and institution-building;

(c) Support and assistance by the United Nations system for technical co-operation among developing countries in the development of public administration and finance.

Activities of the UN system

Public administration and finance activities throughout the United Nations system were considered by the Committee for Programme Co-ordination (CPC) in April/May 1982 when it reviewed a cross-organizational programme analysis on the subject, prepared by the Secretary-General.[2] That report, issued in February, concluded that, while there was an appropriate division of labour on the topic between organizations concerned with general administrative matters and those concerned with sectoral administration, there had been continuing jurisdictional problems in some areas between the International Labour Organisation and DTCD, particularly on management training and management of public enterprises. The Secretary-General suggested that CPC might recommend either that such questions be resolved case by case, as had already been tried, or that the division of labour be more precisely defined through a common conceptual approach.

The analysis also found that, while the key issues identified by the Meetings of Experts on the United Nations Programme in Public Administration and Finance were adequately covered by the United Nations system, a number of Governments felt that the volume of country-level activities was insufficient. Co-ordination between organizations could be enhanced if programme issues in public administration received more frequent review by the Administrative Committee on Co-ordination (ACC) and if the Meetings of Experts covered system-wide aspects more adequately. Programme harmonization could be improved through prior consultations on programme-planning and budget documents. Co-ordination among regional and national training and research institutions also needed improve-

ment. Better co-ordination at the country level could be achieved through ensuring an effective relationship between sectoral administration activities and assistance to general administration activities.

After reviewing this report, CPC recommended[1] that: ACC should try to propose a clear working definition of public administration and finance; it should ensure a more coherent approach to United Nations system activities on this topic, and the definition of relative responsibilities should be clarified with the assistance of a future Meeting of Experts as a basis for resolving outstanding problems; existing ACC mechanisms for inter-agency consultation and co-operation should be used more effectively to develop co-ordinated approaches to the formulation and implementation of programme activities; United Nations organizations should apply more rigorously the existing ACC guidelines for resolving jurisdictional problems case by case; joint planning and implementation of technical assistance projects should be ensured when two or more agencies had a significant contribution to make; and co-ordination between national and regional training and research institutions should be improved.

Reports. [1]CPC, A/37/38; [2]S-G, E/AC.51/1982/4.

Rural and urban development

Rural development

The inter-agency Task Force on Rural Development, a body of ACC, held its tenth meeting at Rome, Italy, from 15 to 17 March 1982.[1] The Task Force endorsed inter-agency missions launched by the Food and Agriculture Organization of the United Nations, as lead agency for action by the United Nations system in this field, to countries requesting assistance on agrarian reform and rural development policies. It urged organizations to continue monitoring their own efforts to alleviate rural poverty and approved the preparation of guidelines on operational procedures for monitoring and evaluation. It also approved a 1982-1983 work programme providing for regional inter-agency meetings and additional missions to individual countries.

Report. [1]Task Force, ACC/1982/13.

Satellite communication

The Second United Nations Conference on the Exploration and Peaceful Uses of Outer Space (Vienna, Austria, 9-21 August 1982)[1] suggested that countries and agencies planning mobile communications systems using satellites should be encouraged to look at the feasibility of using the same system for rural communication in developing countries. This was one of several recommendations made by the Conference on satellite communication systems.

Report. [1]Conference on outer space, A/CONF.101/10.

Urban development

As part of its research into problems of urbanization, the United Nations Centre for Regional Development convened an Expert Group Meeting on the Role of Small- and Intermediate-Sized Cities in National Development (Nagoya, Japan, 26 January–1 February 1982). Its task was to make a preliminary assessment of the role of such cities in developing countries, in preparation for research on selected cities. The Group made a number of general observations and conclusions about that role, suggested ways of assessing the cities' development performance, discussed policies for promoting them and identified areas for further research. Working groups of the Expert Group drew up guidelines for case studies.

Special measures for the least developed and other developing countries

Least developed countries

Implementation of the Programme of Action for the 1980s

During 1982, the United Nations system began monitoring the implementation of the Substantial New Programme of Action for the 1980s for the Least Developed Countries, adopted in September 1981 by the United Nations Conference on the Least Developed Countries[10] and endorsed by the General Assembly in a December 1981 resolution.[9]

Responding to that resolution, the Secretary-General submitted to the Assembly in October 1982 a report, with later addenda,[6] containing information received from 43 States, 15 specialized agencies and related organizations, 14 intergovernmental organizations and 13 other United Nations bodies, on the first year of implementation of the Substantial New Programme of Action (SNPA).

Some progress had been made, the report stated. National focal points had been established by a number of least developed countries (LDCs) and most were preparing for country review meetings, at which progress would be assessed and further aid sought. Similarly, donor countries, United Nations agencies and other international organizations had also begun their support. United Nations agencies were making use of focal points for implementation and follow-up, and the regional

commissions had strengthened the relevant sections within their secretariats. The United Nations Conference on Trade and Development (UNCTAD) had the focal role in elaborating global-level arrangements for implementation and monitoring, while the Director-General for Development and International Economic Co-operation was responsible for mobilization and co-ordination within the United Nations system.

However, the report continued, resource flows to LDCs had been far from the "substantial increase" called for by the Assembly. Improvements in aid practices and management were considered necessary, and States, the United Nations system and others were urged to participate at a high level in the review meetings and provide full financial and technical assistance to implement country programmes. Attention was also drawn to the decrease in resources available from the United Nations Development Programme (UNDP) and insufficient amounts pledged for 1982 to the UNDP Special Measures Fund for LDCs ($17 million) and to the United Nations Capital Development Fund (UNCDF) ($25 million).

Also in accordance with the Assembly's 1981 resolution as well as an October 1981 decision by the Administrative Committee on Co-ordination,[11] the first inter-agency consultation on SNPA follow-up was held at Geneva on 25 and 26 May 1982.[4] The consultation dealt with ways of assisting LDCs in preparing country review meetings and of enhancing the global monitoring of implementation.

In further follow-up action, the Second Meeting of Multilateral and Bilateral Financial and Technical Assistance Institutions with Representatives of LDCs, convened by UNCTAD, was held at Geneva from 11 to 20 October.[5] It reviewed the requirements and progress of LDCs and problems arising for donors and recipients in co-ordinating and implementing assistance programmes.

In its agreed conclusions, the Meeting expressed a preference for certain terms of aid, including grants and concessional loans, untying of aid from expenditure restrictions requiring purchases to be made in the donor country, debt cancellation, provision for the effects of inflation and greater predictability of external assistance. It suggested criteria for assistance to meet longer-term social needs, including minimum levels of consumption, human welfare and public services. It outlined the advantages and disadvantages, economic impact and conditions for effective use of various types of aid, including non-project aid such as balance-of-payments support and commodity aid, disaster relief, sectoral aid, and aid for maintenance of capital stock and capacity utilization.

The Meeting stressed the need for donors to finance the local costs of investment programmes and projects as well as recurrent costs following their completion, and it suggested the use for this purpose of counterpart funds in local currencies, generated from the sale of donor-financed commodity imports or from balance-of-payments support. The Meeting urged improvements in the administration and management of aid programmes, including the management of regular financial resources and human resources, by improving the development administration and management of recipient Governments, speeding disbursements, managing human resources more effectively, strengthening co-ordination and taking other steps to make technical co-operation more effective.

Many LDCs were also the object of special economic assistance programmes organized at the behest of the General Assembly.

UNDP activities. Together with the World Bank, UNDP served as lead agency in organizing country review meetings, whose aim was to enable individual LDCs to consult with their aid partners on the recipient country's economic situation, on progress in SNPA implementation, on aid conditions and on needs for additional assistance. Twenty-seven LDCs requested UNDP assistance in organizing their review meetings. Round tables for this purpose were held during 1982 for four African countries—Cape Verde (June), Equatorial Guinea (April), Mali and Rwanda (December)— and, in November, an international donors' conference for Chad was held under the aegis of the Secretary-General with UNDP assistance.

Funds for this assistance, and for other activities benefiting LDCs, were provided by the UNDP Special Measures Fund for LDCs, which spent $13,808,240 on programmes in 1982. Five Governments paid a total of $16,429,641 in contributions to the Fund during 1982 and nine Governments pledged a total of $13,878,983 for 1983. Expenditures on round table conferences from the Fund were limited to $100,000 for each LDC.

From its overall resources, UNDP budgeted some $215 million during 1982 for the 31 countries designated by the General Assembly as least developed. (For indicative planning figures and UNDP project expenditures relating to individual countries, see Chapter II of this section.) In addition, UNCDF, whose mandate was to assist LDCs first and foremost, concluded basic agreements with 24 of those countries in 1982; its new project commitments in LDCs totalled over $90 million since the September 1981 Conference.

To help implement SNPA, the UNDP Governing Council, on 18 June,[1] urged States and financial institutions to make substantial contributions to the Special Measures Fund and UNCDF, and through other channels for LDCs. The Council requested the UNDP Administrator to support SNPA implementation and to act as lead agency, when requested by Governments, in support of national consultation mechanisms.

UNIDO activities. The value of projects for LDCs approved in 1982 under the regular technical co-operation programme of the United Nations Industrial Development Organization (UNIDO) doubled in comparison to 1981 and quadrupled under the Special Industrial Services (SIS) programme, while remaining at about the same level under the United Nations Industrial Development Fund. About 33 per cent of the regular programme and 30 per cent of the SIS programme was allocated in 1982 to LDCs. UNIDO also provided financial support for the participation of LDCs at the industrial consultation meetings it organized in 1982.

The progress of industrialization in LDCs was considered by the UNIDO Industrial Development Board in May. The Board requested the UNIDO Executive Director, in consultation with LDCs, to consider specific proposals to implement SNPA and to continue helping in project identification and feasibility studies to facilitate investment.[3]

General Assembly action. On 20 December, the General Assembly adopted a resolution[8] calling on Member States and organizations to accelerate SNPA implementation and on donor countries and financial institutions to help LDCs overcome the adverse effects of global recession. It urged donors to implement their commitments under SNPA so as to achieve a substantial increase of resources for the development of those countries. It recommended that the first round of country review meetings be completed by 1983, requested donors and multilateral institutions to participate in those meetings at a high level, and called for improvement in the quality and effectiveness of official development assistance. Donors were also urged to make special allocations to the Special Measures Fund and to UNCDF or through other channels. The Assembly decided that regular monitoring of progress should be undertaken, requesting the UNCTAD Secretary-General to report to the sixth (1983) session of UNCTAD and the United Nations Secretary-General to report to the Assembly in 1983.

The resolution was adopted without vote. On 13 December 1982, the Second (Economic and Financial) Committee had approved the draft in like manner. It had been submitted by a Committee Vice-Chairman after informal consultations on a text put forward by Bangladesh for the Group of 77 and subsequently withdrawn.[2]

In addition to drafting changes, the approved resolution added a paragraph by which the Assembly reaffirmed that LDCs had primary responsibility for their own development and that their domestic policies would be critical for the success of their development efforts. Also, in calling for improved development assistance, the approved text added that this should increase responsiveness to the requirements of LDCs.

The need to implement the socio-economic objectives of SNPA was further reaffirmed by the Assembly in its 3 December resolution on the world social situation.[7]

Decision (1982). [1]UNDP Council (report, E/1982/16/Rev.1): 82/11, 18 June.
Draft resolution withdrawn. [2]Bangladesh, for Group of 77, A/C.2/37/L.78.
Reports. [3]IDB, A/37/16; [4]Inter-agency consultation on follow-up of SNPA, ACC/1982/19; [5]Meeting of financial and technical assistance institutions with LDCs, TD/B/933; [6]S-G, A/37/197 & Corr.1,2 & Add.1,2.
Resolutions (1982). GA: [7]37/54, para. 6, 3 Dec.; [8]37/224, 20 Dec., text following.
Resolution (prior). [9]GA: 36/194, 17 Dec. 1981 (YUN 1981, p. 410).
Yearbook references. 1981, [10]p. 406, [11]p. 408.
Meeting records. GA: 2nd Committee, A/C.2/37/SR.3, 5-8, 20-26, 33, 40, *43, 48* (28 Sep.–13 Dec.); plenary, A/37/PV.113 (20 Dec.).

General Assembly resolution 37/224

20 December 1982   Meeting 113   Adopted without vote

Approved by Second Committee (A/37/680/Add.12) without vote, 13 December (meeting 48); draft by Vice-Chairman (A/C.2/37/L.121), based on informal consultations on draft by Bangladesh, for Group of 77 (A/C.2/37/L.78); agenda item 71 (o).

Implementation of the Substantial New Programme of Action for the 1980s for the Least Developed Countries

The General Assembly,

Recalling its resolutions 3201(S-VI) and 3202(S-VI) of 1 May 1974, containing the Declaration and the Programme of Action on the Establishment of a New International Economic Order, 3281(XXIX) of 12 December 1974, containing the Charter of Economic Rights and Duties of States, and 3362(S-VII) of 16 September 1975 on development and international economic co-operation,

Reaffirming that in the International Development Strategy for the Third United Nations Development Decade it was stated, *inter alia*, that, as an essential priority within the Strategy, the least developed countries—the economically weakest and poorest countries with the most formidable structural problems—require a special programme of sufficient size and intensity consistent with their national plans and priorities to make a decisive break from their past and present situation and their bleak prospects,

Recalling resolution 122(V) of 3 June 1979 of the United Nations Conference on Trade and Development, which was endorsed by the General Assembly in its resolution 34/210 of 19 December 1979,

Reaffirming the Substantial New Programme of Action for the 1980s for the Least Developed Countries, adopted unanimously by the United Nations Conference on the Least Developed Countries and endorsed by the General Assembly in its resolution 36/194 of 17 December 1981,

Reaffirming also that the main objectives of the Substantial New Programme of Action are to transform the economies of the least developed countries towards self-sustaining development, to promote the structural changes necessary to overcome the extreme economic difficulties of the least developed countries, to provide fully adequate and internationally accepted minimum standards of nutrition, health, transport and communications, housing and education as well as job opportunities to all their citizens, to identify and support major investment opportunities and priorities, and to mitigate the adverse effects of natural disasters,

Stressing the immediate need for greatly expanded support measures, including a major increase in the transfer of additional resources from all developed countries, developing countries in a position to do so, multilateral development and financial institutions and other sources, for the realization of the objectives of the Substantial New Programme of Action,

Emphasizing the need for improvements in aid modalities and practices and their responsiveness to the requirements of the least developed countries,

Expressing its deepest concern at the continued deterioration of the economic and social situation of the least developed countries and their dismal development, even after adoption of the Substantial New Programme of Action,

Noting with concern that the present external resource flows to the least developed countries are not in line with the substantial increases envisaged in the Substantial New Programme of Action, thus contributing to the slow implementation of the Programme,

Noting with appreciation the progress made by some of the donor countries towards the implementation of their commitments, as contained in paragraphs 61 to 69 of the Substantial New Programme of Action,

Taking note of the report of the Secretary-General on the implementation of the Substantial New Programme of Action for the 1980s for the Least Developed Countries,

1. *Emphasizes* that, in view of their desperate socio-economic plight, the least developed countries need the urgent and special attention and the large-scale support on a continuous basis of the international community to enable them to progress towards self-reliant development, consistent with the plans and programmes of each least developed country;

2. *Calls upon* all Member States, as well as multilateral development and financial institutions, the organs, organizations and bodies of the United Nations system and all others concerned to take immediate, concrete and fully adequate measures and steps to accelerate the implementation of the Substantial New Programme of Action for the 1980s for the Least Developed Countries;

3. *Strongly urges* all donor countries to implement their commitments, as stated in paragraphs 61 to 69 of the Substantial New Programme of Action, so as to achieve, in that regard, a substantial increase of resources for the development of the least developed countries;

4. *Reaffirms* that the least developed countries have primary responsibility for their overall development and that, although international support measures are vitally important, the domestic policies that those countries pursue will be of critical importance for the success of their development efforts;

5. *Calls upon* all Member States, as well as multilateral development and financial institutions, the organs, organizations and bodies of the United Nations system and all others concerned to consider favourably giving their full support to aid consultative groups or other arrangements to be established at the initiative of the least developed countries in accordance with paragraphs 110 to 116 of the Substantial New Programme of Action;

6. *Recommends strongly* that the first round of review meetings at the country level on the implementation of the Substantial New Programme of Action in accordance with paragraphs 110 to 116 of the Programme should be completed by 1983;

7. *Requests* all donors and multilateral development, financial and technical assistance institutions to participate in these review meetings at an appropriately high level with a view to providing support for the implementation of the plans and programmes of the individual countries;

8. *Calls upon* donor countries and institutions urgently to improve further the quality and effectiveness of official development assistance in order to increase its responsiveness to the requirements of the least developed countries, as called for in paragraph 70 of the Substantial New Programme of Action;

9. *Urges* all donor countries and multilateral development and financial institutions to take immediate concrete measures and steps in accordance with the Substantial New Programme of Action to help the least developed countries to overcome the adverse effects of global recession;

10. *Also urges* all donor countries to make adequate special allocations to the Special Measures Fund for the Least Developed Countries of the United Nations Development Programme and to the United Nations Capital Development Fund or through other suitable channels for the least developed countries and, for that purpose, invites the Administrator of the United Nations Development Programme to continue his efforts to mobilize additional resources for the activities under his administration;

11. *Decides* that regular review and monitoring of the progress in the implementation of the Substantial New Programme of Action at the national, regional and global levels should be undertaken, as envisaged in the Programme, to maintain the momentum of commitments made by the international community and to promote the implementation of the plans and programmes of the least developed countries with a view to achieving accelerated growth rates and structural transformation of their economies;

12. *Renews its invitation* to the governing bodies of appropriate organs, organizations and bodies of the United Nations system to take the necessary and appropriate measures for effective implementation and follow-up of the Substantial New Programme of Action within their respective spheres of competence and mandate;

13. *Requests* the Administrator of the United Nations Development Programme to continue supporting and making arrangements for the round-table meetings for the least developed countries, including the Round-Table Meeting for the Least Developed Countries in the Asia and Pacific Region, to be held from 9 to 18 May 1983 at the United Nations Office at Geneva;

14. *Requests* the Secretary-General of the United Nations Conference on Trade and Development to report to the Conference at its sixth session on the progress made in the implementation of the Substantial New Programme of Action and on measures for ensuring its full and expeditious implementation;

15. *Requests* the Director-General for Development and International Economic Co-operation to continue, in close collaboration with the Secretary-General of the United Nations Conference on Trade and Development, the executive secretaries of the regional commissions and lead agencies for the aid consultative groups, to ensure at the Secretariat level the full mobilization and co-ordination of the United Nations system for the purpose of implementing and following up the Substantial New Programme of Action;

16. *Requests* the Secretary-General to report to the General Assembly at its thirty-eighth session, in the light of the outcome of the sixth session of the United Nations Conference on Trade and Development and other developments, on the implementation of the present resolution.

Identification of LDCs

The number of LDCs on the United Nations list was raised to 36 in 1982 with the addition of Djibouti, Equatorial Guinea, Sao Tome and Principe, Sierra Leone and Togo. The decision to add these countries was taken in December by the General Assembly in accordance with a July recommendation by the Economic and Social Council. The Council, in turn, acted on a recommendation made in April by its Committee for Development Planning (CDP), which applied standard criteria relating to per capita gross domestic product (GDP), share of manufacturing output in GDP and adult literacy rate.

The others on the list were Afghanistan, Bangladesh, Benin, Bhutan, Botswana, Burundi, Cape Verde, the Central African Republic, Chad, the Comoros, Democratic Yemen, Ethiopia, the Gambia, Guinea, Guinea-Bissau, Haiti, the Lao People's Democratic Republic, Lesotho, Malawi, Maldives, Mali, Nepal, the Niger, Rwanda, Samoa, Somalia, the Sudan, Uganda, the United Republic of Tanzania, the Upper Volta and Yemen.

Economic and Social Council action (February). On 4 February, the Economic and Social Council requested CDP to consider the eligibility of Djibouti, Equatorial Guinea, Liberia, Sao Tome and Principe, and Sierra Leone for inclusion in the LDC list. The Council mentioned the requests

for such consideration made by the General Assembly in December 1981 with regard to four of these States,[7] and referred to the critical economic situation of the fifth, Sierra Leone.

This action was taken by a decision,[1] adopted without vote, submitted by the Council President and based on informal consultations. An earlier text by Burundi, Ethiopia, Saint Lucia, Sierra Leone, the Sudan, Swaziland, the United Republic of Cameroon, and Zaire, which called for such action only with respect to Sierra Leone, was withdrawn.[2]

CDP action. In April 1982, CDP considered the Council's request together with a similar one of July 1981 concerning the inclusion of Togo.[6] Reporting to the Council,[3] CDP stated that, whereas Liberia did not meet the criteria for identification as an LDC, the other five countries did; therefore it recommended that they be added to the list.

The Committee reiterated that the criteria used for identifying LDCs deserved to be reappraised to allow meaningful consideration of cases on the margin. It also recalled the broader question of the usefulness of the numerous and overlapping groupings of disadvantaged developing countries, particularly the possibility of their future integration and simplification. Observing that the concept of LDCs had initially been formulated as a guide to the allocation of technical co-operation, it said the original purpose would be distorted by too general an application to all forms of development assistance.

Economic and Social Council action (July). On 27 July, the Economic and Social Council adopted without vote a resolution[4] approving the CDP recommendation and recommending that the General Assembly approve inclusion of the five countries in the list. The draft was submitted by Algeria for the Group of 77.

General Assembly action. On 17 December, the General Assembly decided to include Djibouti, Equatorial Guinea, Sao Tome and Principe, Sierra Leone and Togo in the list of LDCs.[5] The resolution to that effect was adopted without vote. On 2 November, the Second Committee had similarly approved the draft, proposed by a Vice-Chairman following informal consultations.

Decision (1982). [1]ESC: 1982/106, 4 Feb., text following.
Draft decision withdrawn. [2]Burundi, Ethiopia, Saint Lucia, Sierra Leone, Sudan, Swaziland, United Republic of Cameroon, Zaire, E/1982/L.10.
Report. [3]CDP, E/1982/15.
Resolutions (1982). [4]ESC: 1982/41, 27 July, text following. [5]GA: 37/133, 17 Dec., text following.
Resolution (prior). [6]ESC: 1981/47, 20 July 1981 (YUN 1981, p. 413).
Yearbook reference. [7]1981, p. 412.
Meeting records. ESC: E/1982/SR.2, 31-44, *48* (4 Feb. & 8-27 July). GA: 2nd Committee, A/C.2/37/SR.3-12, *27* (28 Sep.–2 Nov.); plenary, A/37/PV.109 (17 Dec.).

Economic and Social Council decision 1982/106

Adopted without vote

Draft by President (E/1982/L.13), based on informal consultations and incorporating 8-nation draft (E/1982/L.10); agenda item 2.

Request for the inclusion of Djibouti, Equatorial Guinea, Liberia, Sao Tome and Principe and Sierra Leone in the list of the least developed countries

At its 2nd plenary meeting, on 4 February 1982, the Council, having considered the requests made by the General Assembly in resolutions 36/204, 36/207, 36/209 and 36/216 of 17 December 1981 regarding the inclusion of Equatorial Guinea, Liberia, Sao Tome and Principe and Djibouti in the list of the least developed countries, and taking into account the critical economic situation of Sierra Leone, decided to request the Committee for Development Planning, in the light of new data and information provided by the Governments of Djibouti, Equatorial Guinea, Liberia, Sao Tome and Principe and Sierra Leone, to consider, on the basis of existing criteria, the eligibility of Djibouti, Equatorial Guinea, Liberia, Sao Tome and Principe and Sierra Leone for inclusion in the list of the least developed countries.

Economic and Social Council resolution 1982/41

27 July 1982   Meeting 48   Adopted without vote

Draft by Algeria, for Group of 77 (E/1982/L.45); agenda item 3.

Identification of the least developed among the developing countries

The Economic and Social Council,

Recalling General Assembly resolutions 2768(XXVI) of 18 November 1971, 3487(XXX) of 12 December 1975, and 32/92 and 32/99 of 13 December 1977, and Council resolution 1981/34 of 8 May 1981, establishing the current list of the least developed countries,

Recalling also Council resolution 1981/47 of 20 July 1981 and decision 1982/106 of 4 February 1982, on the basis of which the Committee for Development Planning undertook to consider whether certain countries met the existing criteria for inclusion in the list of the least developed countries in the light of new data and information provided by the Governments of those countries,

1. *Approves* the recommendation made by the Committee for Development Planning at its eighteenth session regarding the inclusion of new countries in the list of the least developed countries;

2. *Recommends* that the General Assembly at its thirty-seventh session should approve the inclusion of Djibouti, Equatorial Guinea, Sao Tome and Principe, Sierra Leone and Togo in the list of the least developed countries.

General Assembly resolution 37/133

17 December 1982   Meeting 109   Adopted without vote

Approved by Second Committee (A/37/679), without vote, 2 November (meeting 27); draft by Vice-Chairman (A/C.2/37/L.17) based on informal consultations; agenda item 12.

Identification of the least developed among the developing countries

The General Assembly,

Recalling its resolutions 2768(XXVI) of 18 November 1971, 3487(XXX) of 12 December 1975 and 32/92 and 32/99 of 13 December 1977 and Economic and Social Council resolution 1981/34 of 8 May 1981, on the basis of which the current list of the least developed countries was established,

Recalling also its resolutions 36/204, 36/209 and 36/216 of 17 December 1981 and Economic and Social Council decision 1982/106 of 4 February 1982 and resolution 1982/41 of 27 July 1982,

Decides to include Djibouti, Equatorial Guinea, Sao Tome and Principe, Sierra Leone and Togo in the list of the least developed countries, in accordance with the recommendation made by the Committee for Development Planning at its eighteenth session.

Bolivia

The Committee of the Whole of the Economic Commission for Latin America (ECLA), meeting in New York on 2 and 3 December 1982, recom-mended that, until the situation returned to normal, Bolivia be treated as an LDC, although not officially designated as such.[1] Citing the serious economic crisis in Bolivia and the marked deterioration in its situation over the previous few years, the Committee requested the Secretary-General to invite the United Nations specialized agencies to allocate all possible resources to Bolivia and, to the extent possible, to expand their programmes for the country. It requested the ECLA secretariat, the Latin American Institute for Economic and Social Planning and the Latin American Demographic Centre to extend the fullest co-operation to the Bolivian Government on any requests it might make.

Resolution (1982). [1]ECLA Committee of Whole (report, E/CEPAL/G.1239): 450(PLEN.16), 3 Dec.

Special measures for land-locked developing countries

The special needs and problems of land-locked developing countries were the subject in 1982 of a progress report by the secretariat of the United Nations Conference on Trade and Development (UNC-TAD) and a proposal to the General Assembly made by a group of those countries and others, which the Assembly referred to its 1983 session.

The UNCTAD report, of which the Trade and Development Board took note on 14 September 1982,[3] was prepared in response to a request by UNC-TAD at its 1979 session[6] for a review of the special economic problems deriving from the geographical situation of those countries. Submitted in July 1982, with later addenda,[4] the report contained information from 28 Governments, 19 United Nations bodies (including specialized and related agencies) and 9 other intergovernmental organizations.

The progress report concluded that the international community's response to the urgent assistance needs of land-locked developing countries had been diverse. Several major donors providing assistance did not have particular development aid policies in favour of those countries, although it was generally recognized that they faced problems because of their geographical location. Also, the assistance programmes of several donors and institutions were not always directly linked to solving transit-transport bottle-necks. Although most land-locked developing countries were also least developed, and thus urgently in need of overall development aid, additional direct, specific measures to ease transit-transport constraints should be undertaken. Despite international efforts, the general economic performance of those countries continued to be extremely poor, the report stated.

General Assembly consideration. In the General Assembly's Second (Economic and Financial) Committee in November, a 22-nation draft resolution, sponsored by a number of land-locked and other States, was introduced by Nepal.[2] The text largely reiterated the provisions of a December 1981 Assembly resolution[5] reaffirming the land-locked developing countries' rights to access to the sea and to freedom of transit, urging provision of aid for transport and transit facilities, and inviting transit States to co-operate with those countries in transport planning and in promoting joint transport ventures. In addition, the draft would have had the Assembly recommend that UNCTAD take further specific actions at its 1983 session on the particular needs and problems of land-locked developing countries, and request the United Nations Secretary-General to submit to the Assembly in 1983 a report on progress made in implementing the resolution.

Following informal consultations on the 22-nation draft, the General Assembly decided without vote[1] on 20 December 1982 to refer the draft to its 1983 session. This action was taken on the Second Committee's recommendation, approved without vote on 8 December on an oral proposal by the Chairman.

The right of access of land-locked States to and from the sea and freedom of transit was further elaborated in the United Nations Convention on the Law of the Sea, which was opened for signature in December 1982.

Decision (1982). [1]GA: 37/440, 20 Dec., text following.
Draft resolution deferred. [2]Afghanistan, Bangladesh, Bhutan, Bolivia, Botswana, Burundi, Central African Republic, Chad, Lao People's Democratic Republic, Lesotho, Malawi, Mali, Mongolia, Nepal, Nigeria, Paraguay, Rwanda, Swaziland, Uganda, Upper Volta, Zambia, Zimbabwe, A/C.2/37/L.41.
Reports. [3]TDB, A/37/15, vol. II; [4]UNCTAD secretariat, TD/B/916 & Corr.1,2 & Add.1 & Add.1/Corr.1 & Add.2.
Resolution. [5]GA: 36/175, 17 Dec. 1981 (YUN 1981, p. 414).
Yearbook reference. [6]1979, p. 570.
Meeting records. GA: 2nd Committee, A/C.2/37/SR.3, 5-8, 20-26, 33, *37*, 40, *47* (28 Sep.–8 Dec.); plenary, A/37/PV.113 (20 Dec.).

General Assembly decision 37/440

Adopted without vote

Approved by Second Committee (A/37/680/Add.2) without vote, 8 December (meeting 47); draft orally proposed by Chairman following informal consultations on 22-nation draft (A/C.2/37/L.41); agenda item 71 *(c)*.

Specific action related to the particular needs and problems of land-locked developing countries

At its 113th plenary meeting, on 20 December 1982, the General Assembly, on the recommendation of the Second Committee, decided to refer to its thirty-eighth session for consideration the draft resolution entitled "Specific action related to the particular needs and problems of land-locked developing countries".

UN Special Fund for Land-locked Developing Countries

Three new projects costing a total of $57,871 were approved in 1982 for financing under the United Nations Special Fund for Land-locked Developing Countries: in the Lao People's Democratic Republic, for strengthening transit vehicle maintenance facilities ($12,100); in Paraguay,

for assistance in hydrography for the Paraguay River ($23,171); and in Swaziland, for a consultancy in aircraft selection ($22,600).[2] This brought the number of projects approved over the Fund's six years of operation to 15, in 12 countries. Expenditures on individual projects during the year amounted to $23,000 in Paraguay, $22,000 in Swaziland and $1,000 in Mali. Commitments since the start of the Fund totalled $749,662 as at 31 December 1982, of which $72,382 represented support costs paid to agencies for executing projects financed by the Fund. Uncommitted resources totalled $508,587.

The decision to establish the Fund was taken in 1975[4] and its statute was approved in 1976[5] with the aim of helping land-locked developing countries overcome transport and communications problems. In 1982, the Fund continued to be managed on an interim basis by the Administrator of the United Nations Development Programme (UNDP) in collaboration with the UNCTAD Secretary-General.

In his report to the UNDP Governing Council on 1982 activities,[1] the Administrator pointed out that the previous low level of contributions to the Fund had continued in 1982. During the year, $48,682 was received from six States while for 1983 a total of $66,654 was pledged by 13 States as at 31 December 1982 (see table below). Most of these States were themselves land-locked.

CONTRIBUTIONS TO THE UN SPECIAL FUND FOR LAND-LOCKED DEVELOPING COUNTRIES, 1982 AND 1983
(as at 31 December 1982; in US dollar equivalent)

Country	1982 payment	1983 pledge
Afghanistan	5,000	5,000
Bolivia	—	500
Botswana	—	1,376
Brazil	—	10,000
Burundi	—	1,117
Lao People's Democratic Republic	1,000	1,000
Lesotho	—	1,500
Malawi	—	1,722
Senegal	—	2,500
Thailand	1,000	1,000
Tunisia	1,996	1,926
Zambia	37,686	32,503
Zimbabwe	2,000	6,510
Total	48,682	66,654

SOURCE: 1982 UNDP accounts, A/38/5/Add.1.

General Assembly action. On 20 December, the General Assembly adopted a resolution[3] urging Member States to give due consideration to the special constraints affecting the development of land-locked developing countries and appealing to donor countries to review their position with respect to the Fund, with a view to giving it greater support. The Assembly also appealed to Member States, particularly developed countries, and financing institutions to contribute generously in order to implement measures for the land-locked developing countries provided for in the International Development Strategy for the Third United Nations Development Decade.[6] The UNDP Administrator was requested, in consultation with the UNCTAD Secretary-General and the heads of other bodies, to continue pursuing action in favour of those countries. The Secretary-General was asked to report in 1983 on implementation of the resolution.

The resolution was adopted by a recorded vote of 129 to none, with 21 abstentions. On 8 December, the Second Committee had approved the draft by a recorded vote, requested by the United States, of 112 to none, with 21 abstentions. The text was submitted by Bangladesh on behalf of the Group of 77.

Reports. UNDP Administrator, [1]DP/1983/6/Add.3, [2]DP/1983/42 & Corr.1.
Resolution (1982). [3]GA: 37/230, 20 Dec., text following.
Resolutions (prior). GA: [4]3504(XXX), 15 Dec. 1975 (YUN 1975, p. 387), [5]31/177, annex, 21 Dec. 1976 (YUN 1976, p. 356); [6]35/56, annex, 5 Dec. 1980 (YUN 1980, p. 503).
Meeting records. GA: 2nd Committee, A/C.2/37/SR.4, 6, 7, 32-40, *43, 47* (30 Sep.-8 Dec.); plenary, A/37/PV.113 (20 Dec.).

General Assembly resolution 37/230

20 December 1982   Meeting 113   129-0-21 (recorded vote)

Approved by Second Committee (A/37/774) by recorded vote (112-0-21), 8 December (meeting 47); draft by Bangladesh, for Group of 77 (A/C.2/37/L.77); agenda item 72 *(g)*.

**United Nations Special Fund for
Land-locked Developing Countries**

The General Assembly,

Recalling its resolution 31/177 of 21 December 1976, by which it approved the statute of the United Nations Special Fund for Land-locked Developing Countries,

Recalling also its resolutions 32/113 of 15 December 1977, 33/85 of 15 December 1978, 34/209 of 19 December 1979, 35/82 of 5 December 1980 and 36/195 of 17 December 1981,

Bearing in mind resolution 123(V) of 3 June 1979 of the United Nations Conference on Trade and Development and decisions 80/21 of 26 June 1980 and 81/3 of 19 June 1981 of the Governing Council of the United Nations Development Programme,

Recalling the relevant provisions of the International Development Strategy for the Third United Nations Development Decade,

Recalling further the relevant paragraphs of the Substantial New Programme of Action for the 1980s for the Least Developed Countries, adopted by the United Nations Conference on the Least Developed Countries,

Convinced that access to world markets at the least possible cost is an integral part of meaningful economic development of land-locked developing countries,

Bearing in mind that a large number of countries classified as least developed are land-locked developing countries,

Expressing deep concern at the consistently very low level of contributions that have been pledged to the Fund since its establishment,

Noting that, according to the report of the Secretary-General prepared in response to General Assembly resolution 34/207 of 19 December 1979, contributions to the Fund must increase significantly if it is to be effective in meeting the large requirements for reducing the real costs of transit for land-locked developing countries,

Noting further that the demands for assistance from the Fund are additional to, and generally different from, the types of activities financed from other sources of the United Nations system,

1. *Urges* all Member States to give due consideration to the special constraints affecting the economic and social development of land-locked developing countries;

2. *Appeals* to all donor countries to review their position with respect to the United Nations Special Fund for Land-locked Developing Countries, with a view to extending their greater support to it;

3. *Also appeals* to all Member States, in particular developed countries, and to multilateral and bilateral financing institutions to contribute significantly and generously to the Fund in order to implement the measures relating to land-locked developing countries provided for in the International Development Strategy for the Third United Nations Development Decade;

4. *Requests* the Administrator of the United Nations Development Programme, in consultation with the Secretary-General of the United Nations Conference on Trade and Development and the executive heads of other related bodies, to continue to pursue action in favour of land-locked developing countries within the framework of the interim arrangements, bearing in mind that each country concerned should receive appropriate technical and financial assistance;

5. *Requests* the Secretary-General to report to the General Assembly at its thirty-eighth session on the implementation of the present resolution.

Recorded vote in Assembly as follows:

In favour: Afghanistan, Algeria, Angola, Antigua and Barbuda, Argentina, Austria, Bahamas, Bahrain, Bangladesh, Barbados, Benin, Bhutan, Bolivia, Botswana, Brazil, Bulgaria, Burma, Burundi, Byelorussian SSR, Cape Verde, Central African Republic, Chad, Chile, China, Colombia, Comoros, Congo, Costa Rica, Cuba, Cyprus, Czechoslovakia, Democratic Kampuchea, Democratic Yemen, Djibouti, Dominican Republic, Ecuador, Egypt, El Salvador, Ethiopia, Fiji, Gabon, Gambia, German Democratic Republic, Ghana, Grenada, Guatemala, Guinea, Guinea-Bissau, Guyana, Haiti, Honduras, Hungary, India, Indonesia, Iran, Iraq, Israel, Ivory Coast, Jamaica, Jordan, Kenya, Kuwait, Lao People's Democratic Republic, Lebanon, Lesotho, Liberia, Libyan Arab Jamahiriya, Madagascar, Malawi, Malaysia, Maldives, Mali, Malta, Mauritania, Mauritius, Mexico, Mongolia, Morocco, Mozambique, Nepal, Nicaragua, Niger, Nigeria, Oman, Pakistan, Panama, Papua New Guinea, Paraguay, Peru, Philippines, Poland, Qatar, Romania, Rwanda, Saint Lucia, Saint Vincent and the Grenadines, Samoa, Sao Tome and Principe, Saudi Arabia, Senegal, Sierra Leone, Singapore, Somalia, Sri Lanka, Sudan, Suriname, Swaziland, Syrian Arab Republic, Thailand, Togo, Trinidad and Tobago, Tunisia, Turkey, Uganda, Ukrainian SSR, USSR, United Arab Emirates, United Republic of Cameroon, United Republic of Tanzania, Upper Volta, Uruguay, Vanuatu, Venezuela, Viet Nam, Yemen, Yugoslavia, Zaire, Zambia, Zimbabwe.

Against: None.

Abstaining: Australia, Belgium, Canada, Denmark, Finland, France, Germany, Federal Republic of, Greece, Iceland, Ireland, Italy, Japan, Luxembourg, Netherlands, New Zealand, Norway, Portugal, Spain, Sweden, United Kingdom, United States.

Appointment of an Executive Director

On 20 December 1982,[1] the General Assembly took note of information contained in a note by the Secretary-General[2] to the effect that he was not submitting for the Assembly's confirmation an appointment for the post of Executive Director of the Special Fund for Land-locked Developing Countries. The Secretary-General recounted the circumstances of the Fund, including the interim arrangements for its management by the UNDP Administrator and the amount pledged for its 1983 operations (see above).

The decision was adopted without vote, as orally proposed by the Assembly President.

Decision (1982). [1]GA: 37/323, 20 Dec., text following.
Note. [2]S-G, A/37/773.
Meeting record. GA: A/37/PV.113 (20 Dec.).

General Assembly decision 37/323

Adopted without vote

Oral proposal by President; agenda item 17 *(l)*.

**Confirmation of the appointment of the Executive
Director of the United Nations Special Fund
for Land-locked Developing Countries**

At its 113th plenary meeting, on 20 December 1982, the General Assembly took note of the information contained in the note by the Secretary-General.

Special measures for island developing countries

The problems of island developing countries were examined in 1982 by the Trade and Development Board of the United Nations Conference on Trade and Development (UNCTAD) and by the General Assembly.

On 19 March,[1] the Trade and Development Board requested the UNCTAD Secretary-General to ensure that documentation was available to allow UNCTAD, at its sixth (1983) session, to address effectively the problems of island developing countries. The Board reiterated the specific action programme in favour of such countries envisaged by the Conference in 1976[6] and 1979.[7]

As it had decided in 1980,[5] the General Assembly reviewed, in 1982, measures taken by the international community for these countries.

To assist in this review, the Secretary-General submitted in October a report,[3] prepared by the UNCTAD secretariat, containing information provided by Governments and international organizations. The report noted that several States did not recognize island developing countries as a special group. Characteristics such as smallness and remoteness were emphasized, as were other special problem areas such as transport and communications, insufficient diplomatic staff, fragile economies lacking the potential to maintain even a minimum standard of living, energy, development of marine resources especially in exclusive economic zones, and natural disasters.

General Assembly action. On 20 December, the General Assembly adopted a resolution[4] calling on States, international organizations and financial institutions to intensify efforts to implement the specific actions in favour of island developing countries envisaged by UNCTAD. The Assembly requested United Nations organizations to enhance their ability to respond positively to those countries' needs during the Third United Nations Development Decade (the 1980s), and asked UNCTAD at its 1983 session to review progress and to consider measures needed to facilitate implementation of the resolutions adopted in favour of island developing countries. The United Nations Secretary-General was requested to report in 1984 on international measures to respond to the special needs of those countries and to recommend further actions to permit the Assembly to review the matter comprehensively in 1984.

The resolution was adopted without vote. On 8 December the Second (Economic and Financial) Committee had approved the draft in like manner. It had been submitted by a Committee Vice-Chairman after informal consultations on a text put forward by Bangladesh for the Group of 77, and subsequently withdrawn.[2]

In addition to drafting differences, the Group's text would have had the Assembly request that UNCTAD agree in 1983 on further specific actions and programmes (rather than consider measures needed to implement past resolutions).

Decision (1982). [1]TDB (report, A/37/15, vol. I): 247(XXIV), 19 Mar.
Draft resolution withdrawn. [2]Bangladesh, for Group of 77, A/C.2/37/L.93.
Report. [3]S-G, A/37/196 & Corr.1.
Resolution (1982). [4]GA: 37/206, 20 Dec., text following.
Resolution (prior). [5]GA: 35/61, 5 Dec. 1980 (YUN 1980, p. 560).
Yearbook references. [6]1976, p. 398; [7]1979, p. 569.
Meeting records. GA: 2nd Committee, A/C.2/37/SR.20-26, 45, 47 (25 Oct.–8 Dec.); plenary, A/37/PV.113 (20 Dec.).

General Assembly resolution 37/206

20 December 1982   Meeting 113   Adopted without vote

Approved by Second Committee (A/37/680/Add.2) without vote, 8 December (meeting 47); draft by Vice-Chairman (A/C.2/37/L.111), based on informal consultations on draft by Bangladesh, for Group of 77 (A/C.2/37/L.93); agenda item 71 (c).

Action programme in favour of island developing countries

The General Assembly,

Recalling its resolutions 3201(S-VI) and 3202(S-VI) of 1 May 1974, containing the Declaration and the Programme of Action on the Establishment of a New International Economic Order, 3281(XXIX) of 12 December 1974, containing the Charter of Economic Rights and Duties of States, and 3362(S-VII) of 16 September 1975 on development and international economic co-operation,

Recalling also its resolution 35/56 of 5 December 1980, the annex to which contains the International Development Strategy for the Third United Nations Development Decade,

Recalling further its resolutions 31/156 of 21 December 1976, 32/185 of 19 December 1977, 34/205 of 19 December 1979 and 35/61 of 5 December 1980 and other relevant resolutions of the United Nations relating to the special needs and problems of island developing countries,

Reiterating the programme of specific action in favour of island developing countries envisaged in resolutions 98(IV) of 31 May 1976 and 111(V) of 3 June 1979 of the United Nations Conference on Trade and Development,

Welcoming Trade and Development Board decision 247(XXIV) of 19 March 1982, in which the Secretary-General of the United Nations Conference on Trade and Development was requested to submit a report on the problems of island developing countries for consideration by the Conference at its sixth session,

Mindful of the fact that additional efforts are needed to implement the specific measures required to assist island developing countries—in particular those which suffer handicaps owing especially to smallness, remoteness, frequent natural disasters, discontinuity and scattering of territory, constraints in transport and communications, great distances from market centres, limited internal markets, lack of marketing expertise, low resource endowment, lack of natural resources, heavy dependence on a few commodities for their foreign exchange earnings, shortage of administrative expertise and heavy debt burdens—in offsetting the major handicaps which retard their development process,

Welcoming the analysis of the problems facing smaller island countries undertaken at the meeting on the special problems of those countries, held at Alofi, Niue, from 9 to 12 February 1982,

Recognizing that appropriate industrial development can be vital to the economic development of small island countries,

1. *Takes note* of the report of the Secretary-General on the progress made in the implementation of specific action in favour of island developing countries;

2. *Takes note* of the analysis contained in section III of the report of the Secretary-General on the difficulties encountered by island developing countries;

3. *Expresses its appreciation* to all States and organizations that have facilitated the implementation of resolutions in favour of island developing countries;

4. *Calls upon* all States, international organizations and financial institutions to intensify efforts to implement specific actions in favour of island developing countries as envisaged in resolutions 98(IV) and 111(V) of the United Nations Conference on Trade and Development as well as in other relevant resolutions;

5. *Requests* the competent organizations of the United Nations system, in particular the United Nations Conference on Trade and Development, the United Nations Development Programme, the United Nations Industrial Development Organization and the United Nations Capital Development Fund, to take adequate measures to enhance their ability to respond positively to the particular needs of island developing countries during the Third United Nations Development Decade;

6. *Requests* the United Nations Conference on Trade and Development, at its sixth session, to review the progress made in this area and to consider the measures needed to facilitate the implementation of the resolutions adopted so far in favour of island developing countries;

7. *Requests* the Secretary-General to report to the General Assembly at its thirty-ninth session on the measures taken by the international community to respond to the specific needs of island developing countries, as called for in the relevant United Nations resolutions, and to recommend further appropriate actions to permit the Assembly to undertake a comprehensive review of the problems and needs of the island developing countries at that session.

Chapter II

Development assistance

Contents

Related topics:
Development and international economic and social policy: Special measures for the least developed and other developing countries. Economic assistance, disasters and emergency relief. Food.

For resolutions and decisions of major organs mentioned but not reproduced, refer to INDEX OF RESOLUTIONS AND DECISIONS.

General aspects of operational activities for development

In 1982, operational activities for development comprised the programmes of the United Nations Development Programme (UNDP), the United Nations Children's Fund, the United Nations Fund for Population Activities and other funds and programmes covered by the annual United Nations Pledging Conference for Development Activities; the technical co-operation and related operational activities of the specialized agencies and other United Nations organizations; and the food aid provided by the World Food Programme

(WFP). Some 40 per cent of operational activities took place in the least developed countries (compared to 20 per cent of bilateral assistance). Nearly 50 per cent was allocated to three sectors—agriculture, health and population. About 20 per cent was allocated to regional, interregional and global programmes. Activities were increasingly concentrated in regions with a large number of low-income countries.

Total operational development assistance by the United Nations system—comprising expenditures and disbursements from all organizations, including the International Development Association (IDA), the International Fund for Agricultural Development (IFAD), the refugee, humanitarian and related activities and the programmes of the Environment Fund of the United Nations Environment Programme—to developing countries amounted to $4.5 billion in 1982 (excluding cost-sharing and self-supporting contributions to organizations, and the programme expenditures financed therefrom, and expenditures on administrative and programme support costs), or about 13 per cent of the total assistance they received.

Review of operational activities

Report of the Director-General. The second annual report of the Director-General for Development and International Economic Co-operation on United Nations operational activities for development, submitted to the General Assembly by the Secretary-General by a note of 28 September 1982,[4] warned of a financial crisis at hand, with sharp curtailments and possibly even greater cutbacks in development activities of the United Nations system, coinciding with greater needs than ever before in the developing countries.

The report, responding to 1980[7] and 1981[8] requests by the Assembly for information and recommendations, concentrated on two issues: mobilization of resources in a financial environment adversely affected by such factors as exchange-rate fluctuations and the hardening attitude of some donors with regard to providing official development assistance through either bilateral or multilateral channels; and measures to reduce administrative and other support costs and to improve the efficiency and effectiveness of operational activities for development.

The report noted that major efforts had been made by the Secretary-General, the United Nations Secretariat, agencies, programmes and funds to alert Governments to the seriousness of the situation, particularly that of UNDP, which was having widespread repercussions on many operational activities. The report suggested methods to mobilize more predictable resources and to place the organizations engaged in operational activities on a more secure financial basis.

To reduce costs, rationalize and simplify procedures, and enhance efficiency in programme/project execution, the report stressed that further efforts were needed to promote the integration of United Nations operational activities with national programmes, to strengthen the capacities and institutions of developing countries in the interest of self-reliance, and to enhance the flexibility and diversity of the system to better its response to the varying circumstances of those countries, particularly the needs of the least developed.

The report explored ways to promote system-wide collaboration through greater uniformity of, and improvements in, the programming, management and implementation procedures of operational activities. It discussed the role of evaluation as a means of improving programme effectiveness and suggested measures to apply evaluation findings to planning, programming and budgeting.

General Assembly action. By a resolution[6] adopted without vote on 20 December 1982, the General Assembly took note with appreciation of the report and reaffirmed the important contribution of the United Nations system to the development of developing countries within the framework of the International Development Strategy for the Third United Nations Development Decade[9]. It welcomed the Director-General's recommendations and invited United Nations bodies to make greater use of the capacities of developing countries in local procurement, training and services.

The Assembly reiterated the need for increased resources, and asked that the usefulness of contribution targets be examined, as well as the practice of conditioned contributions. Progress towards attaining the WFP contribution target was welcomed.

It urged continued efforts to minimize support costs without affecting field programmes and to harmonize procedures for operational activities, and requested a report of the inter-agency Administrative Committee on Co-ordination (ACC) in 1984. In other provisions, the Assembly dealt with co-operation between UNDP and the World Bank; information on support cost payments; procurement of supplies; government execution of projects; co-ordination of field-level development assistance; resource mobilization; and the replenishment of IDA and IFAD resources.

In a resolution of 3 December on the world social situation,[5] the Assembly emphasized that rapid socio-economic progress of developing countries required enhanced financial and technological contributions to national development efforts.

The Assembly's Second (Economic and Financial) Committee approved the resolution on operational activities on 13 December, also without vote. The text was submitted by a Committee Vice-Chairman following informal consultations on a draft introduced by Bangladesh on behalf of the Group of 77 developing countries and later withdrawn.[2]

The main differences between the original draft and the adopted resolution were in the following paragraphs: 3, 4, and 6 (originally paragraph 7) on contributions; paragraph 11 (originally 13) welcoming (instead of endorsing) the Director-General's recommendations designed to enhance the responsiveness of operational activities to the needs of developing countries; 14 (originally 15) welcoming the UNDP decision on government execution of projects, and the real savings that could result therefrom (instead of merely welcoming the decision); paragraph 16, on integration of United Nations operational activities with national programmes; paragraph 22 (originally 20) on co-ordination of those activities at the field level; and 23 (originally 21) on the role of resident co-ordinators and a register on development activities.

The resolution did not include a provision urging the UNDP Intersessional Committee of the Whole to formulate measures to help Governments increase contributions, but added a paragraph on co-operation between UNDP and the World Bank (see below, under UNDP ACTIVITIES), as well as requests for information on support cost payments and on the relationship between programme delivery and administrative costs, and a decision on guidelines for procurement activities.

Other action. The deteriorating situation facing all United Nations organizations regarding the declining level of resources available in real terms for international technical co-operation and other development activities was also considered by ACC at its November 1982 session. Being conscious of the increasing constraints on available development resources in the current world economic situation, of the overriding interests of developing countries and of the need for concerted United Nations action to assist in reversing the adverse trends in resources for development, ACC decided on 3 November[1] to reinforce system-wide measures with specific objectives and to request several measures to improve such action and to mobilize additional funds. These included asking the Joint United Nations Information Committee for a feasibility study for a system-wide public information campaign, and requests to the ACC Consultative Committee on Substantive Questions (Operational Activities) (CCSQ(OPS)) to recommend ways to improve complementarity of country-level action within the United Nations system and between the system and other organizations, to formulate guidelines for more effective use of the United Nations development system's experience to influence bilateral aid flow, and to make proposals for supporting actions within the system to enhance its effectiveness in support of development efforts.

Commenting on the Advisory Committee's suggestions, the Committee for Programme and Co-ordination (CPC) recommended[3] that CCAQ(OPS) should include, in its exercise on the issue of increasing support for multilateral co-operation activities, a study of the question of improved co-operation and more systematic evaluation procedures and explore new forms of co-operation with bilateral and other aid institutions.

Decision (1982). [1]ACC: 1982/27, 3 Nov.
Draft resolution withdrawn. [2]Bangladesh, for Group of 77, A/C.2/37/L.92.
Reports. [3]CPC, A/37/38; [4]Director-General for DIEC, transmitted by S-G note, A/37/445 & Add.1.
Resolutions (1982). GA: [5]37/54, para. 9, 3 Dec.; [6]37/226, 20 Dec., text following.
Resolutions (prior). GA: [7]35/81, 5 Dec. 1980 (YUN 1980, p.612); [8]36/199, 17 Dec. 1981 (YUN 1981, p. 429); [9]35/56, annex, 5 Dec. 1980 (YUN 1980, p. 503).
Meeting records. GA: 2nd Committee, A/C.2/37/SR. 4, 6, 7, 32-40, *45, 48* (30 Sep.–3 Dec.); plenary, A/37/PV.113 (20 Dec.).

General Assembly resolution 37/226

20 December 1982   Meeting 113   Adopted without vote

Approved by Second Committee (A/37/774) without vote, 13 December (meeting 48); draft by Vice-Chairman (A/C.2/37/L.123), based on informal consultations on draft by Bangladesh, for Group of 77 (A/C.2/37/L.92); agenda item 72 *(a)*.

**Operational activities for development
of the United Nations system**

The General Assembly,

Recalling its resolutions 3201(S-VI) and 3202(S-VI) of 1 May 1974, containing the Declaration and the Programme of Action on the Establishment of a New International Economic Order, 3281 (XXIX) of 12 December 1974, containing the Charter of Economic Rights and Duties of States, and 3362(S-VII) of 16 September 1975 on development and international economic co-operation,

Recalling also its resolution 35/56 of 5 December 1980, the annex to which contains the International Development Strategy for the Third United Nations Development Decade,

Recalling further its resolutions 32/197 of 20 December 1977, 33/201 of 29 January 1979 and 35/81 of 5 December 1980 on a comprehensive policy review of operational activities for development and 36/199 of 17 December 1981 on operational activities for development,

Recalling also its resolutions 2688 (XXV) of 11 December 1970 on the capacity of the United Nations development system and 3405 (XXX) of 28 November 1975 on new dimensions in technical co-operation,

Noting that co-ordination of national action with regard to operational activities by Governments makes it possible for concerted policies to be pursued in the United Nations and other organizations of the United Nations system,

Noting with deep concern the outcome of the 1982 United Nations Pledging Conference for Development Activities, held on 8 and 9 November 1982,

Having examined the annual report for 1982 of the Director-General for Development and International Economic Co-operation on operational activities for development of the United Nations system,

Reiterating that a substantial part of world resources, material as well as human, continues to be diverted to armaments, with detrimental effect on international security and on efforts to achieve the new international economic order, including the operational activities for development of the United Nations system, and calling upon all Governments to take effective measures in the field of real disarmament that would increase the possibilities of allocation of resources now being used for military purposes to economic and social development, especially the development of developing countries,

1. *Takes note with appreciation* of the annual report of the Director-General for Development and International Economic Co-operation;

2. *Reaffirms* the important contribution that operational activities of the United Nations system make to the development of developing countries within the framework of the International Development Strategy for the Third United Nations Development Decade;

3. *Expresses its deep concern* that overall voluntary contributions from Governments and other sources to the funds and programmes announced during the 1982 United Nations Pledging Conference for Development Activities were highly unsatisfactory, falling short, in many cases, of targets that have been set by the relevant intergovernmental bodies, with serious consequences for the organizations concerned with respect to their capacity to maintain the level of their operational programmes in support of the growing needs of developing countries for multilateral concessional assistance through the United Nations system;

4. *Strongly reiterates* the need for a substantial and real increase in the flow of resources for operational activities on an increasingly predictable, continuous and assured basis, so as to enable the organizations of the system to maintain and, where possible, increase the level of their operational programmes and, in that context, strongly urges all countries, particularly developed countries, whose overall performance is not commensurate with their capacities, to increase rapidly and substantially their voluntary contributions for operational activities for development, taking into account the targets that have been set by relevant intergovernmental bodies;

5. *Decides* to conduct its regular review and appraisal of the mobilization of resources for operational activities in the light of each of the four objectives for the restructuring of operational activities contained in paragraph 28 of the annex to resolution 32/197, and requests the Director-General for Development and International Economic Co-operation to include the necessary information for this purpose in his annual reports, as well as information on the resource situation and prospects of the International Development Association, the International Fund for Agricultural Development and the World Food Programme;

6. *Requests* the Director-General for Development and International Economic Co-operation to examine, in the comprehensive policy review of operational activities to be submitted, together with his recommendations, to the General Assembly at its thirty-eighth session, taking into account the relevant paragraphs of his report and all other pertinent considerations, the feasibility and usefulness of establishing targets for voluntary contributions, including annual growth rate targets, for those funds and programmes for development activities covered by the United Nations pledging conferences where such targets do not exist, and the strengthening of the review and appraisal procedures, and to comment on the existing system of pledging conferences and make specific proposals aimed at establishing more effective procedures for the mobilization of resources;

7. *Invites* the organs, organizations and bodies of the United Nations system dealing with the flows of concessional resources to developing countries to pay greater attention, in their reviews of these issues, to the funding needs of the United Nations funds and programmes;

8. *Urges* all Governments concerned to release as early as possible their third instalment of the sixth replenishment of the International Development Association, and to continue negotiations regarding the seventh replenishment of the Association with a view to ensuring an appropriately substantial increase in resources;

9. *Welcomes* the agreement on the establishment of the first replenishment of the International Fund for Agricultural Development and urges all Governments concerned to deposit their instruments of contribution as early as possible and to release their contributions according to agreed schedules in order to enable the Fund to maintain its lending programme;

10. *Welcomes* the progress towards the attainment of the 1983-1984 target for voluntary contributions to the World Food Programme and urges Governments to make every effort to ensure the full attainment of the target;

11. *Welcomes* the recommendations made in section III of the report of the Director-General for Development and International Economic Co-operation designed to enhance the responsiveness of operational activities to the needs and requirements of developing countries in accordance with their objectives and priorities and their efforts to promote greater economic and technical co-operation among themselves, and requests the executive heads of the organizations concerned to take appropriate action in this regard in the programming and implementation of operational activities;

12. *Invites* all organs, organizations and bodies of the United Nations system engaged in operational activities for development to adopt appropriate measures leading to a greater use of the capacities of developing countries in local or regional procurement of material and equipment, in training and in services, in facilitating the increased use of local contractors, and in the recruitment of training, technical and managerial personnel, bearing in mind decision 81/28 of 30 June 1981 of the Governing Council of the United Nations Development Programme;

13. *Decides* that the guidelines on procurement to be issued pursuant to paragraph 7 of decision 81/28 and section II, paragraph 2, of decision 82/34 of 18 June 1982 of the Governing Council of the United Nations Development Programme should, in due course, govern the procurement activities of organs and bodies under the authority of the General Assembly in their execution of projects financed by the Programme;

14. *Welcomes* decision 82/8 of 18 June 1982 of the Governing Council of the United Nations Development Programme, designed to promote government execution of projects assisted by the Programme, and the real savings that could result therefrom;

15. *Invites* the Administrator of the United Nations Development Programme and the President of the World Bank to examine the possibilities of further co-operation between the Programme and the World Bank regarding utilization of facilities available to the two organizations, and requests the Administrator to report thereon to the Governing Council of the United Nations Development Programme;

16. *Reaffirms* the exclusive responsibility of the Government of the recipient country regarding formulation of its national development plan or priorities and objectives, as set out in the consensus set forth in the annex to General Assembly resolution 2688 (XXV) of 11 December 1970, and emphasizes that the integration of the operational activities of the United Nations system with national programmes would enhance the impact and relevance of these activities;

17. *Requests* the Director-General for Development and International Economic Co-operation to include in his 1983 comprehensive policy review an examination of the extent and implications of the growing practice of contributions being provided to organizations with conditions attached to their use;

18. *Takes note* of the measures being pursued to reduce costs and to improve efficiency described in the report of the Director-General for Development and International Economic Co-operation, and urges the Secretary-General and the executive heads of organs, organizations and bodies of the United Nations system to seek to minimize administrative and other support costs without affecting the field programmes and the network of United Nations Development Programme offices in developing countries and bearing in mind the need to maintain an appropriate level of support functions, with a view to increasing the proportion of resources available to improve the programme delivery to developing countries;

19. *Requests* the organs and bodies of the United Nations system receiving resources of an extrabudgetary nature, such as support cost payments, to include information on these resources and their utilization in the reports to their governing bodies, and invites the governing bodies of the organizations of the United Nations system receiving support cost payments from Governments and voluntary funds to examine information thereon;

20. *Requests* the Director-General for Development and International Economic Co-operation to report on the implementation of paragraphs 18 and 19 of the present resolution and to include in his comprehensive policy overview a comparative analysis of the relationship between programme delivery and administrative costs pertaining to operational activities for development executed by organs, organizations and bodies of the United Nations system;

21. *Urges* all organs, organizations and bodies of the United Nations system, in the light of the recommendations contained in section III of the report of the Director-General for Development and International Economic Co-operation, to take the necessary steps to ensure the harmonization of administrative, financial, personnel, planning and procurement procedures, and requests the Administrative Committee on Co-ordination to report, in its annual overview report of 1984, on specific action taken;

22. *Reiterates* the importance of co-ordination of multilateral development assistance at the field level and requests the Director-General for Development and International Economic Co-operation to pay particular attention, in the comprehensive policy review of operational activities of 1983, to the need for improved coherence of action and effective integration at the country level in accordance with section V of the annex to resolution 32/197 and paragraph 11 of resolution 35/81, including a report on measures taken to date in this regard, together with his recommendations thereon, with specific reference to the role of resident co-ordinators in the co-ordination of operational activities of the United Nations system;

23. *Invites* the Administrative Committee on Co-ordination to report to the Economic and Social Council at its second regular session of 1983 and to the General Assembly at its thirty-eighth session on the outcome of the review of the arrangements for the exercise of the functions of resident co-ordinators in accordance with General Assembly resolutions 2688 (XXV) of 11 December 1970, 32/197 of 20 December 1977 and 34/213 of 19 December 1979, and also requests the Committee to develop, within a year, the register on development activities in conformity with Economic and Social Council resolution 1982/71 of 10 November 1982.

Financing of operational activities

Contributions to the funds and programmes of the United Nations, the operational activities of the specialized agencies and other organizations financed from regular and extrabudgetary contributions and to WFP increased to $2.5 billion in 1982, up from $2.4 billion in 1981. This represented a growth in nominal dollars, but could mean stagnation in real terms if adjustments were made for increases in price levels.

Flows of concessional and non-concessional resources for United Nations operational activities amounted to $6.6 billion in 1982, grant-financed expenditures were $2.1 billion, and expenditures from cost-sharing and other similar contributions increased to $140 million.

By far the largest share of operational activities, about 93 per cent, went directly to developing countries in support of national development programmes. The balance was directed towards operational activities carried out on a regional, interregional and global basis. The share of total concessional resources (grants and concessional loans) amounted to 56 per cent of the total net transfer of resources through the system, compared to 64 per cent in 1981.

Total gross disbursements by the World Bank group (including IDA and the International Finance Corporation (IFC)) amounted to $8.9 billion in 1982, net disbursements to $6.8 billion and net transfers to $4.4 billion. Unilateral or self-supporting expenditures of the specialized agencies appeared to be concentrated in such sectors as transport and communications (34 per cent) and culture (22 per cent).

Information on 1982 expenditures and contributions for operational activities for development of the United Nations system was provided in a 1983 report of the Director-General for Development and International Economic Co-operation[1] and in a 1983 report of the UNDP Administrator on technical co-operation expenditures in 1982.[2]

Reports. Director-General for DIEC, transmitted by S-G note, [1]A/38/258/Add.1-E/1983/82/Add.1; [2]UNDP Administrator, DP/1983/57.

Expenditures

Flows of concessional and non-concessional resources (on a net transfer basis) for operational activities for development, including technical co-operation, commodity and capital assistance by United Nations organizations amounted to $6,637.9 million in 1982, compared to $6,024.5 million in 1981.

Grant-financed expenditures—those undertaken by the organizations of the system other than the World Bank group and the International Fund for Agricultural Development (IFAD)—totalled $2,096 million in 1982, compared to $2,159 million in 1981, a decline of about 3 per cent in nominal dollar terms. The main reason for the overall decline in the dollar value of expenditures was the drop in UNDP main programme expenditures by $80 million, to $590 million. The World Food Programme (WFP) was able to increase its programme expenditures by about 10 per cent in 1982, to reach $594 million. Almost all other organizations experienced little or no increase. Technical co-operation expenditures financed from regular budgets declined in 1982, as did overall per capita expenditures on operational activities, after years of sustained increases.

Countries with a per capita gross national product (GNP) of less than $500 accounted for 70 per cent of grant-financed operational activities. Of these activities, 42.5 per cent took place in Africa; 38.8 per cent in Asia and the Pacific; 10.5 per cent in Latin America; 6.2 per cent in Western Asia, and 2 per cent in Europe. There was a fairly even distribution of resource flows among the developing regions of the world on a per capita basis.

Total system-wide expenditures on technical co-operation were $2.2 billion in 1982, compared to $2.0 million in 1981, including the technical co-operation embodied in World Bank lending operations. Nearly 46 per cent of the system's technical co-operation activities (i.e. all grant-financed activities other than those financed by the United Nations Children's Fund and WFP, including cost-sharing and similar expenditures but exclusive of World Bank operations) were financed by UNDP, compared to 50 per cent in 1981.

Nearly two fifths of system-wide expenditures on technical co-operation in 1982 took place in two sectors: health (19.5 per cent) and agriculture, forestry and fisheries (18.0 per cent). Another two thirds took place in four sectors: natural resources (9.8 per cent); transport and communications (9.0 per cent); general development, planning and statistics (8.4 per cent); and population (7.7 per cent) (see table below).

1982 EXPENDITURES BY THE UN SYSTEM ON OPERATIONAL ACTIVITIES FOR DEVELOPMENT
(in millions of US dollars)

CONCESSIONAL ASSISTANCE

A. *Grants*

1.	Financed from regular budgets	198.9
2.	Financed by UNDP*	589.8
3.	Financed from funds administered by UNDP	61.4
4.	Financed by UNFPA	106.3
5.	Financed by UNICEF	213.4
6.	Financed by specialized agencies and other organizations from extrabudgetary resources†	332.9
7.	Financed by WFP	593.8
	Subtotal (1-7)	2,096.2

B. *Loans*

8.	Disbursed by IDA	
	(a) Gross disbursements	1,679.3
	(b) Net disbursements	1,611.4
	(c) Net transfer	1,507.7
9.	Disbursed by IFAD‡	109.1
	Subtotal (8 (c) and 9)	1,616.8
	Total (1-7, 8 (c) and 9)	3,713.0

NON-CONCESSIONAL ASSISTANCE

10.	Disbursed by World Bank	
	(a) Gross disbursements	6,835.3
	(b) Net disbursements	4,935.8
	(c) Net transfer	2,634.3
11.	Disbursed by IFC	
	(a) Gross disbursements	387.6
	(b) Net disbursements	290.6
	(c) Net transfer (10 (c) and 11 (b))	2,924.9
	Total (1-7, 8 (c), 9, 10 (c) and 11 (b))	6,637.9

Other expenditures:

Expenditure financed from cost-sharing contributions to UNDP	62.2
Expenditure financed from Government cash counterpart contributions to UNDP	8.6
Expenditure financed from self-financing contributions to specialized agencies and other organizations	77.4
World Bank/IDA technical co-operation	730.7
Refugee, humanitarian and disaster relief activities	621.3

*Main UNDP programme; excludes expenditures financed from cost-sharing and from cash counterpart contributions.

†From funds not elsewhere specified in the table.

‡Includes a small amount of grants.

NOTE: Totals may differ from sum of figures because of rounding.

SOURCE: A/38/258/Add.1-E/1983/82/Add.1.

UN TECHNICAL CO-OPERATION EXPENDITURES IN 1982, BY SECTOR
(in thousands of US dollars)

Sector	Non-UNDP	UNDP	Total
Political affairs	4,837	300	5,137
General development	35,535	84,600	120,135
Natural resources	60,267	79,900	140,167
Agriculture, forestry and fisheries	100,262	159,100	259,362
Industry	28,624	78,500	107,124
Transport and communications	42,825	86,400	129,225
International trade and development finance	17,911	14,700	32,611
Population	115,102	2,700	117,802
Human settlements	5,423	11,700	17,123
Health	250,759	29,300	280,059
Education	23,539	35,600	59,139
Employment	33,242	38,200	71,442
Humanitarian aid and relief	107	1,800	1,907
Social conditions and equity	6,573	5,700	12,273
Culture	24,253	5,700	29,953
Science and technology	34,694	26,400	61,094
Unspecified	36	—	36
Total	783,989	660,600	1,444,589

NOTE: Figures for UNDP are provisional data covering indicative planning figures, Special Programme Resources, Special Measures Fund for the Least Developed Countries, Special Industrial Services and cost-sharing.

SOURCE: DP/1983/57.

UN SYSTEM TECHNICAL CO-OPERATION EXPENDITURES IN 1982, BY EXECUTING AGENCY
(in thousands of US dollars)

Executing agency	Non-UNDP	UNDP	Total
UNIDO	23,328	67,600	90,928
UNCTAD	1,580	14,500	16,080
UN Centre on Transnational Corporations	955	—	955
ECA	6,624	8,700	15,324
ECE	48	800	848
ECLA	5,856	1,800	7,656
ECWA	1,535	400	1,935
ESCAP	9,162	4,900	14,062
UNHCR	19	—	19
UNCHS	3,836	12,700	16,536
Other UN	46,080	85,100	131,180
Subtotal UN	99,023	196,500	295,523
IAEA	19,377	4,300	23,677
ILO	51,519	51,100	102,619
FAO	135,041	141,100	276,141
UNESCO	64,364	44,500	108,864
WHO	257,415*	20,000	277,415
World Bank and IDA†	2,007	39,200	41,207
ICAO	23,197	35,300	58,497
UPU	972	2,000	2,972
ITU	6,146	25,100	31,246
WMO	10,283	11,800	22,083
IMO	3,657	6,800	10,457
WIPO	1,676	700	2,376
ITC	11,350	—	11,350
UNDP	27,665	51,900	79,565
UNICEF	5,548	—	5,548
UNFPA	15,419	—	15,419
WFP	12	—	12
Subtotal other UN system	635,648	433,800	1,069,448
World Tourism Organization	5	800	805
Asian Development Bank	—	4,100	4,100
Arab Fund for Economic and Social Development	—	200	200
Governments	39,427	25,200‡	64,627
Non-governmental organizations	9,886	—	9,886
Subtotal non-UN system	49,318	30,300	79,618
Total	783,989	660,600	1,444,589

*Including support costs.

†Excluding $730,726 million financed by World Bank loans, IDA credits and the EEC.

‡Including government cash counterpart expenditures of $8,600,000.

NOTE: Figures for UNDP are provisional data covering indicative planning figures, Special Programme Resources, Special Measures Fund for the Least Developed Countries, Special Industrial Services and cost-sharing; UNDP-administered funds outside the Programme's central resources are included in the "non-UNDP" column.

SOURCE: DP/1983/57.

Extrabudgetary resources contributed directly for technical co-operation activities were an important source of funding, amounting to 29 per cent in 1982. Two organizations—the Food and Agriculture Organization of the United Nations (FAO) and the World Health Organization (WHO)—accounted for nearly 38 per cent of total expenditures on technical co-operation, followed by the Department of Technical Co-operation for Development (DTCD) of the United Nations Secretariat, the International Labour Organisation (ILO), the United Nations Industrial Development Organization (UNIDO), the United Nations Educational, Scientific and Cultural Organization (UNESCO) and the Office for Projects Execution of UNDP (see table above).

Expenditures of the system financed mainly by developing countries themselves from cost-sharing contributions to UNDP and similar self-supporting

(continued on p. 632)

1982 EXPENDITURES BY THE UN SYSTEM ON OPERATIONAL ACTIVITIES FOR DEVELOPMENT AND NON-DEVELOPMENT ASSISTANCE, BY RECIPIENT COUNTRY AND REGION
(in thousands of US dollars)

RECIPIENT	Development assistance*	Other assistance†	RECIPIENT	Development assistance*	Other assistance†	RECIPIENT	Development assistance*	Other assistance†
Developing Member States			Indonesia	456,314	9,180	Sudan	111,529	26,858
			Iran	(83,211)	—	Suriname	1,470	—
Afghanistan	8,141	—	Iraq	(7,671)	—	Swaziland	11,011	2,641
Albania	630	—	Ivory Coast	181,085	—	Syrian Arab Republic	4,577	—
Algeria	(12,779)	1,814	Jamaica	99,001	—	Thailand	283,190	39,919
Angola	14,295	4,745	Jordan	28,472	—	Togo	14,655	—
Antigua and Barbuda	605	—	Kenya	81,446	2,350	Trinidad and Tobago	(5,881)	—
Argentina	(2,099)	2,450	Kuwait	213	—	Tunisia	46,983	30
Bahamas	4,294	—	Lao People's			Turkey	293,815	841
Bahrain	1,215	—	Democratic			Uganda	59,638	1,647
Bangladesh	143,966	—	Republic	9,971	1,307	United Arab Emirates	356	—
Barbados	8,626	—	Lebanon	27,038	3,829	United Republic of		
Belize	774	—	Lesotho	17,653	788	Cameroon	35,741	4,717
Benin	14,836	20	Liberia	11,841	—	United Republic of		
Bhutan	8,320	—	Libyan Arab			Tanzania	67,106	7,145
Bolivia	12,751	20	Jamahiriya	7,420	—	Upper Volta	29,358	—
Botswana	12,320	1,023	Madagascar	37,089	5	Uruguay	11,814	—
Brazil	345,069	—	Malawi	46,896	—	Vanuatu	1,058	—
Bulgaria	1,530	—	Malaysia	41,467	9,265	Venezuela	(25,093)	—
Burma	53,889	—	Maldives	2,003	—	Viet Nam	24,504	4,138
Burundi	28,489	1,729	Mali	31,250	—	Yemen	34,072	60
Cape Verde	7,014	—	Malta	705	—	Yugoslavia	127,599	1,565
Central African			Mauritania	31,330	—	Zaire	30,125	16,395
Republic	6,287	—	Mauritius	4,024	—	Zambia	854	3,527
Chad	9,974	30	Mexico	99,194	—	Zimbabwe	24,524	540
Chile	6,092	—	Mongolia	2,850	—			
China	52,470	11,269	Morocco	78,712	—	Subtotal	5,886,535	336,896
Colombia	99,696	—	Mozambique	25,653	—			
Comoros	6,854	10	Nepal	57,593	—	Developing non-member States		
Congo	11,535	—	Nicaragua	17,174	30			
Costa Rica	(5,761)	3,354	Niger	27,492	20	Bermuda	61	—
Cuba	15,075	30	Nigeria	77,253	1,096	Democratic People's		
Cyprus	8,777	9,759	Oman	(962)	—	Republic of Korea	4,525	—
Czechoslovakia	538	—	Pakistan	204,078	93,978	Hong Kong	144	5,556
Democratic			Panama	18,254	—	Namibia	3,042	—
Kampuchea	28,547	—	Papua New Guinea	5,446	—	Republic of Korea	422,632	—
Democratic Yemen	43,117	—	Paraguay	33,874	—	Tonga	1,805	—
Djibouti	5,068	4,071	Peru	43,007	889	Other countries	(22,631)	45,652
Dominica	1,474	—	Philippines	114,000	11,026			
Dominican Republic	17,969	—	Poland	1,149	—	Subtotal	409,578	51,208
Ecuador	16,369	20	Portugal	57,427	1,073			
Egypt	198,569	3,222	Qatar	304	—	Total	6,296,113	388,104
El Salvador	10,154	30	Romania	255,684	—			
Equatorial Guinea	4,475	—	Rwanda	20,822	5,897	Developed countries	(115,015)	5,870
Ethiopia	65,246	5,374	Saint Lucia	949	—			
Fiji	10,620	10	Saint Vincent and			TOTAL (all countries)	6,181,098	393,974
Gabon	(1,469)	—	the Grenadines	664	—			
Gambia	12,163	—	Samoa	2,666	—	Intercountry		
Ghana	21,246	—	Sao Tome and			Regional Africa	83,423	110
Greece	(570)	1,003	Principe	1,344	—	Regional Americas	53,575	—
Grenada	556	—	Saudi Arabia	12,888	—	Regional Arab States	24,138	848
Guatemala	4,893	30	Senegal	31,201	1,174	Regional Asia	68,626	—
Guinea	10,055	—	Seychelles	1,061	—	Regional Europe	11,875	—
Guinea-Bissau	9,319	—	Sierra Leone	8,992	—	Interregional	129,960	—
Guyana	12,991	—	Singapore	(16,620)	—	Global	85,271	25,850
Haiti	26,313	—	Solomon Islands	965	—			
Honduras	35,349	30	Somalia	56,100	32,430	Total	456,868	26,808
Hungary	965	—	Spain	(50,714)	2,493	Not elsewhere classified	—	200,522
India	1,029,349	—	Sri Lanka	64,503	—	GRAND TOTAL	6,637,966	621,304

*Represents the sum of operational activities financed under regular United Nations and agency budgets ($198,941 million), the UNDP main programme ($589,753 million), UNDP-administered funds ($61,248 million), UNFPA ($106,292 million), UNICEF ($213,091 million), other extrabudgetary funds ($332,938 million) and WFP ($593,835 million), plus net transfers from the World Bank ($2,634,292 million), IDA ($1,507,657 million) and IFC ($290,600 million) and net IFAD disbursements ($109,139 million).

†Represents expenditure financed by UNHCR ($420.2 million), UNRWA ($200.5 million), UNDRO ($0.6 million) and the Trust Fund for Special Economic Assistance Programmes ($12,262).

NOTE: Figures in parentheses are negative.

SOURCE: A/38/258/Add.1-E/1982/82/Add.1.

1982 CONTRIBUTIONS TO THE UN SYSTEM FOR OPERATIONAL ACTIVITIES FOR DEVELOPMENT AND FOR OTHER ECONOMIC AND SOCIAL ACTIVITIES, BY DONOR COUNTRY
(contributions in thousands of US dollars)

CONTRIBUTOR	1982 Contributions to operational activities for development	1982 Contributions to other economic and social activities*	1981-1982 Annual average	1981-1982 Dollars per capita	1981-1982 Percentage of total
Member States					
Afghanistan	105	—	104	0.01	0.002
Albania	25	—	25	0.01	—
Algeria	47,957	60	26,258	1.34	0.421
Angola	73	—	47	0.01	0.001
Antigua and Barbuda	—	—	10	0.13	
Argentina	6,390	126	5,965	0.21	0.096
Australia	277,159	16,480	199,138	13.34	3.196
Austria	65,786	626	61,215	8.10	0.983
Bahamas	29	9	73	0.34	0.001
Bahrain	1,670	15	903	2.49	0.014
Bangladesh	1,340	3	960	0.01	0.015
Barbados	1,271	3	656	2.61	0.011
Belgium	95,589	3,451	98,315	9.97	1.578
Belize	442	—	229	1.53	0.004
Benin	58	6	110	0.03	0.002
Bhutan	5	—	59	0.06	0.001
Bolivia	37	—	137	0.02	0.002
Botswana	373	56	238	0.26	0.004
Brazil	62,586	25	34,764	0.29	0.558
Bulgaria	1,342	12	1,293	0.15	0.021
Burma	2,007	10	1,552	0.05	0.025
Burundi	25	2	37	0.01	0.001
Byelorussian SSR	959	18	992	0.10	0.016
Canada	443,604	23,322	369,618	15.25	5.933
Cape Verde	19	—	24	0.08	—
Central African Republic	47	—	35	0.01	0.001
Chad	20	—	21	—	—
Chile	2,546	29	2,469	0.22	0.040
China	108,492	410	57,452	0.06	0.922
Colombia	1,375	72	2,081	0.08	0.033
Comoros	19	—	20	0.06	—
Congo	138	11	266	0.16	0.004
Costa Rica	438	—	295	0.13	0.005
Cuba	2,267	—	2,335	0.24	0.037
Cyprus	303	18	263	0.42	0.004
Czechoslovakia	2,607	—	2,676	0.17	0.043
Democratic Kampuchea	20	—	21	—	—
Democratic Yemen	1,193	—	623	0.32	0.010
Denmark	146,786	16,817	151,512	29.58	2.432
Djibouti	30	—	27	0.07	—
Dominica	66	—	41	0.55	0.001
Dominican Republic	1,468	—	1,466	0.26	0.024
Ecuador	874	—	961	0.11	0.015
Egypt	1,905	57	2,001	0.05	0.032
El Salvador	73	—	60	0.01	0.001
Equatorial Guinea	18	—	19	0.05	—
Ethiopia	365	—	226	0.01	0.004
Fiji	288	—	185	0.29	0.003
Finland	51,197	3,043	52,960	11.03	0.850
France	274,421	3,636	242,484	4.49	3.892
Gabon	699	12	419	0.63	0.007
Gambia	417	—	224	0.38	0.004
German Democratic Republic	3,621	159	3,796	0.23	0.061
Germany, Federal Republic of	448,385	24,125	439,614	7.13	7.056
Ghana	274	—	513	0.04	0.008
Greece	2,591	278	2,291	0.24	0.037
Grenada	44	—	39	0.35	0.001
Guatemala	335	—	495	0.07	0.008
Guinea	198	—	114	0.02	0.002

| CONTRIBUTOR | 1982 | | 1981-1982 PERFORMANCE INDICATORS FOR CONTRIBUTIONS TO OPERATIONAL ACTIVITIES FOR DEVELOPMENT | | |
	Contributions to operational activities for development	Contributions to other economic and social activities*	Annual average	Dollars per capita	Percentage of total
Member States (cont.)					
Guinea-Bissau	20	2	21	0.03	—
Guyana	2,155	—	1,232	1.55	0.020
Haiti	97	—	105	0.02	0.002
Honduras	153	—	143	0.04	0.002
Hungary	26,768	21	14,029	1.31	0.225
Iceland	963	106	749	3.24	0.012
India	21,026	200	68,699	0.10	1.103
Indonesia	5,308	28	4,948	0.03	0.079
Iran	1,465	30	1,725	0.04	0.028
Iraq	1,593	500	1,559	0.12	0.025
Ireland	16,317	401	10,921	3.17	0.175
Israel	666	352	859	0.22	0.014
Italy	214,535	9,197	248,584	4.42	3.990
Ivory Coast	3,400	10	1,916	0.23	0.031
Jamaica	354	4	351	0.16	0.006
Japan	293,585	61,761	443,407	3.77	7.117
Jordan	1,841	764	1,293	0.38	0.021
Kenya	1,315	33	929	0.05	0.015
Kuwait	149,821	2,430	110,378	75.40	1.772
Lao People's Democratic Republic	59	10	43	0.01	0.001
Lebanon	9,434	70	9,240	3.40	0.148
Lesotho	91	2	444	0.32	0.007
Liberia	43	12	73	0.04	0.001
Libyan Arab Jamahiriya	2,531	2,242	4,343	1.41	0.070
Luxembourg	2,142	93	2,352	6.46	0.038
Madagascar	131	5	224	0.02	0.004
Malawi	73	4	106	0.02	0.002
Malaysia	3,239	25	2,516	0.18	0.040
Maldives	24	2	26	0.17	—
Mali	65	—	48	0.01	0.001
Malta	103	4	106	0.29	0.002
Mauritania	20	—	172	0.11	0.003
Mauritius	159	3	139	0.14	0.002
Mexico	7,937	205	13,693	0.19	0.220
Mongolia	212	1	215	0.13	0.003
Morocco	10,958	69	6,132	0.29	0.098
Mozambique	162	—	94	0.01	0.002
Nepal	1,339	—	736	0.05	0.012
Netherlands	431,714	11,452	342,934	24.07	5.504
New Zealand	11,401	339	10,539	3.19	0.169
Nicaragua	77	1	68	0.02	0.001
Niger	35	—	41	0.01	0.001
Nigeria	14,696	50	20,699	0.24	0.332
Norway	169,647	17,436	175,269	42.75	2.813
Oman	1,590	41	1,455	1.58	0.023
Pakistan	4,350	31	4,158	0.05	0.067
Panama	711	6	849	0.45	0.014
Papua New Guinea	980	—	784	0.26	0.013
Paraguay	620	—	513	0.17	0.008
Peru	1,474	—	2,266	0.13	0.036
Philippines	16,638	72	10,135	0.20	0.163
Poland	3,328	—	3,748	0.10	0.060
Portugal	673	113	806	0.08	0.013
Qatar	15,026	725	8,252	34.97	0.132
Romania	5,761	5	3,562	0.16	0.057
Rwanda	1,371	—	1,638	0.31	0.026
Saint Lucia	32	—	20	0.16	—
Saint Vincent and the Grenadines	114	—	70	0.64	0.001
Samoa	17	—	21	0.14	—
Sao Tome and Principe	19	—	20	0.17	—
Saudi Arabia	247,991	10,125	197,233	21.20	3.166
Senegal	54	10	165	0.03	0.003
Seychelles	21	2	27	0.42	—
Sierra Leone	43	—	162	0.05	0.003
Singapore	382	14	394	0.16	0.006
Solomon Islands	104	—	73	0.30	0.001

CONTRIBUTOR	1982		1981-1982 PERFORMANCE INDICATORS FOR CONTRIBUTIONS TO OPERATIONAL ACTIVITIES FOR DEVELOPMENT		
	Contributions to operational activities for development	Contributions to other economic and social activities*	Annual average	Dollars per capita	Percentage of total
Member States (cont.)					
Somalia	38	1	44	0.01	0.001
South Africa	4,026	—	4,698	0.16	0.075
Spain	36,028	2,518	21,068	0.55	0.338
Sri Lanka	3,023	3	2,124	0.14	0.034
Sudan	57	8	64	—	0.001
Suriname	23	—	66	0.19	0.001
Swaziland	1,253	2	650	1.01	0.010
Sweden	377,829	29,258	325,876	39.21	5.230
Syrian Arab Republic	4,525	180	2,597	0.28	0.042
Thailand	14,826	37	9,047	0.19	0.145
Togo	241	1	363	0.14	0.006
Trinidad and Tobago	1,841	5	1,446	1.22	0.023
Tunisia	1,593	22	1,237	0.19	0.020
Turkey	16,889	142	12,731	0.28	0.204
Uganda	645	12	347	0.03	0.006
Ukrainian SSR	3,236	45	3,359	0.07	0.054
USSR	25,306	3,677	26,436	0.10	0.424
United Arab Emirates	28,474	800	16,370	15.00	0.263
United Kingdom	382,541	19,009	406,177	7.25	6.519
United Republic of Cameroon	239	14	399	0.05	0.006
United Republic of Tanzania	188	4	386	0.02	0.006
United States	2,190,774	214,458	1,574,705	6.85	25.275
Upper Volta	100	3	102	0.02	0.002
Uruguay	90	—	422	0.14	0.007
Vanuatu	300	—	363	3.00	0.006
Venezuela	3,818	10	3,995	0.26	0.064
Viet Nam	93	6	86	—	0.001
Yemen	65	2	197	0.03	0.003
Yugoslavia	7,370	113	7,890	0.35	0.127
Zaire	457	20	598	0.02	0.010
Zambia	908	29	821	0.14	0.013
Zimbabwe	88	—	56	0.01	0.001
Total	6,878,231	482,279	5,933,897	1.33	95.240
Non-member States					
Bermuda	14	10	15	0.25	—
Democratic People's Republic of Korea	292	—	303	0.02	0.005
Kiribati	19	—	18	0.30	—
Republic of Korea	14,032	25	7,908	0.20	0.127
Switzerland	51,024	10,685	48,650	7.52	0.781
Tonga	15	—	16	0.16	—
Other	413	36	433	0.06	0.007
Total	65,808	10,757	57,343	0.80	0.920
TOTAL (all countries)	6,944,039	493,036	5,991,240	1.32	96.160
Inter/non-governmental					
Arab Gulf Programme for UN Development Organizations	30,792	—	26,396	—	0.424
European Communities	61,655	91,382	74,653	—	1.198
Other intergovernmental	107,737	10,011	91,746	—	1.473
Non-governmental	63,604	17,709	55,223	—	0.886
Total	263,787	119,102	248,017	—	3.981
GRAND TOTAL	7,207,827	612,138	6,239,257	1.38	100.000

*Includes contributions from Governments and other sources to UNHCR, UNRWA, UNDRO and Trust Fund for Special Economic Assistance Programmes.

NOTE: Totals may differ from sum of figures because of rounding.

SOURCE: A/38/258/Add.1-E/1983/82/Add.1.

contributions to the agencies amounted to $140 million in 1982, up from $109 million in 1981. UNDP cost-sharing expenditures tended to correspond broadly to the sectoral distribution of country programmes. Two thirds of expenditures financed from cost-sharing and similar contributions took place in countries with a per capita income greater than $2,500.

General Assembly action. In its resolution of 20 December 1982[2] on operational activities for development, the General Assembly requested the Director-General to include in his 1983 policy overview report a comparative analysis of the relationship between programme delivery and administrative costs pertaining to operational activities for development executed by United Nations organs, organizations and bodies. This request was added to the original draft submitted to the Assembly's Second Committee by Bangladesh on behalf of the Group of 77.[1]

Draft resolution withdrawn. [1]Bangladesh, for Group of 77, A/C.2/37/L.92.
Resolution. [2]GA: 37/226, para. 20, 20 Dec.

Contributions

Total contributions by Governments and other official and non-official sources to the development activities of the United Nations system totalled $7.2 billion in 1982, compared to $5.3 billion in 1981 (see table above). Covered in these totals were all United Nations funds and programmes, the operational activities of the specialized agencies and WFP. Contributions to those funds, programmes and agencies and WFP were $2,367.4 million. Contributions to the World Bank group and IFAD reached $4,840.6 million in 1982, compared to $3,020.3 million in 1981, the result of the effect of the timing of payments for the sixth replenishment of the International Development Association (IDA), for the partial replenishment of IFAD and for capital subscriptions to the World Bank and to the International Finance Corporation (IFC).

Extrabudgetary contributions placed directly at the disposal of specialized agencies and other organizations for their operational activities continued to increase, although at a declining rate, to nearly $300 million in 1982. Over 80 per cent of total contributions were received by four agencies: FAO, WHO, ILO and UNESCO.

Contributions to WFP, including those for the International Emergency Food Reserve, had grown by 31 per cent since 1979 to reach over $745 million in 1982. By the end of the year, 99 donors had pledged $838 million for the regular resources of WFP for 1981-1982, 84 per cent of the $1 billion target set for that period.

Cost-sharing contributions to UNDP and self-supporting contributions to other organizations amounted to $180.3 million, a doubling since 1979. Cost-sharing and other similar contributions from middle- and higher-income developing countries continued to grow in 1982.

Contributions for refugee, humanitarian, special economic assistance programmes and disaster relief activities amounted to $574 million in 1982, a slight drop from $625 million in 1981.

The Director-General for Development and International Economic Co-operation gave the figures on contributions to United Nations development activities in a September 1983 addendum to his June 1983 report to the General Assembly.[4]

UN Pledging Conference for Development Activities. The 1982 United Nations Pledging Conference for Development Activities was held at United Nations Headquarters on 8 and 9 November to receive government pledges for 1983 to United Nations funds and programmes concerned with development and related assistance.

Contributions to the funds and programmes participating in the Pledging Conference grew in 1982 by 7.8 per cent, very largely the result of an increase of 34 per cent to $321 million in contributions to the supplementary funds of the United Nations Children's Fund (UNICEF). Most other funds and programmes experienced stagnation, or at best a slight marginal increase in the dollar value of contributions. Contributions to the main programme of UNDP, which represented over 55 per cent of total contributions, stagnated for the third consecutive year at around $700 million. The United Nations Fund for Population Activities (UNFPA) experienced similar stagnation at around $129 million.

Total pledges for UNDP (including the Special Measures Fund for the Least Developed Countries and the Energy Account) were $677.8 million plus some $344.9 million for other funds. As at 30 June 1983, pledges and payments to all the development funds by individual Governments totalled $1,022,673,000, down from $1,073,059,000 in payments received for 1982 (see table on next page).

General Assembly action. In its resolution[5] of 20 December 1982 on operational activities for development, the General Assembly expressed concern that overall voluntary contributions announced during the 1982 Pledging Conference were unsatisfactory. It reiterated the need for a substantial and real increase in the flow of resources on a predictable, continuous and assured basis so as to enable United Nations organizations to maintain and increase their programme activities. The Assembly strongly urged all countries, particularly developed countries, to increase rapidly and substantially their contributions, taking into account the targets set by intergovernmental bodies.

CONTRIBUTIONS TO FUNDS AND PROGRAMMES INCLUDED IN THE
UN PLEDGING CONFERENCE FOR DEVELOPMENT ACTIVITIES, 1982 AND 1983
(1982, as at 31 December 1982; 1983, as at 30 June 1983;
in thousands of US dollars)

FUND OR PROGRAMME	1982 PAYMENT		1983 PLEDGE	
	Amount	Number of donor countries	Amount	Number of donor countries
UN Development Programme	679,664	130	660,069	129
Special Measures Fund for the Least Developed Countries	16,430	5	16,303	9
Energy Account	2,798	5	1,419	5
UN Children's Fund	167,350	132	160,062	102
UN Fund for Population Activities	129,029	67	130,075	81
UN Capital Development Fund	27,941	35	24,859	41
UN Industrial Development Fund	14,143	83	12,986	84
UN Financing System for Science and Technology for Development	8,034	28	318	20
UN Fund for Drug Abuse Control	6,762	43	4,318	40
UN Revolving Fund for Natural Resources Exploration	4,539	5	2,118	6
Trust Fund for the UN Centre on Transnational Corporations	3,059	4	694	5
Voluntary Fund for the UN Decade for Women	2,812	34	1,771	34
UN Trust Fund for African Development Activities	2,692	NA	1,764	26
Special Voluntary Fund for the UN Volunteers	2,210	18	446	17
UN Institute for Training and Research	1,733	39	1,236	35
UN Habitat and Human Settlements Foundation	1,576 *	37	2,427	42
UN Trust Fund for Sudano-Sahelian Activities	1,131	6	595	7
UN Trust Fund for Social Defence	621	7	586	10
UN Trust Fund for the International Research and Training Institute for the Advancement of Women	409	13	506	14
UN Trust Fund for the Transport and Communications Decade in Africa	77	NA	61	3
UN Special Fund for Land-locked Developing Countries	49	6	61	14
Total	1,073,059		1,022,673	

*Amount pledged for 1982, as at 30 June 1982.

NA = Not available.

SOURCES: For 1982, A/38/5/Adds.1, 4; Interim United Nations financial statements for the 12-month period ended 31 December 1982 and individual trust funds (unpublished); A/CONF.110/2; E/C.10/1984/16. For 1983, A/CONF.115/2.

The Assembly asked the Director-General for Development and International Economic Co-operation to include in his annual reports information on the resource situation and mobilization, and prospects of IDA, IFAD and WFP; that he examine the feasibility and usefulness of establishing targets for contributions; comment on the existing system of pledging conferences; make proposals for more effective procedures for mobilizing resources; and examine the growing practice of conditional contributions. United Nations bodies dealing with concessional resource flows were invited to pay greater attention to programme funding.

The original draft[2] of this resolution, submitted by Bangladesh on behalf of the Group of 77 and later withdrawn, would have had the Assembly express deep concern at the alarming results of the Pledging Conference and the unfavourable prospects of realizing the targets established, resulting in the disruption of United Nations development activities. The Assembly also would have affirmed that the efforts of developed countries should be greater, the lower their relative performance. It would have requested the Director-General to examine the feasibility of establishing an annual growth-rate target for contributions,

and ways of enabling such conferences to be a more effective mechanism for mobilizing resources (instead the text adopted in paragraph 6).

The adopted text also did not include a provision contained in the original strongly urging the UNDP Intersessional Committee of the Whole to formulate measures to enable Governments to increase their contributions to UNDP, and reiterating appeals to place United Nations organizations engaged in operational activities on a more secure, predictable and stable financial basis.

Other action. Concern about declining resources in real terms for international technical co-operation and development activities and its impact on developing countries was also expressed by the Administrative Committee on Co-ordination (ACC) in its annual overview for 1981/82.[3] On 3 November 1982,[1] ACC decided that, based on the periodic assessment of the situation by ACC and its subsidiary bodies, the Secretary-General and the executive heads of United Nations organs and specialized agencies would reinforce concerted measures with the specific objectives of: stressing the need for commitment of additional resources to support development activities within the framework of the objectives of the International Development

Strategy for the Third United Nations Development Decade[6] and legislative decisions of United Nations governing bodies; and mobilizing additional funds for United Nations operational activities for development.

Decision. [1]ACC: 1982/27, para. *(a),* 3 Nov.
Draft resolution withdrawn. [2]Bangladesh, for Group of 77, A/C.2/37/L.92.
Reports. [3]ACC, E/1982/4; [4]Director-General for DIEC, transmitted by S-G note, A/38/258/Add.1-E/1983/82/Add.1.
Resolution (1982). [5]GA: 37/226, 20 Dec.
Resolution (prior). [6]GA: 35/56, annex, 5 Dec. 1980 (YUN 1980, p. 503).
Meeting records. Pledging Conference for Development Activities: A/CONF.115/SR.1-3 (8, 9 Nov.).

Co-ordination in the UN system

Report of ACC. In its annual overview report for 1981/82 on co-ordination of operational activities for development within the United Nations system,[3] submitted in May 1982 to the Economic and Social Council, ACC reiterated its grave concern about the difficulties confronting the international economy and their impact on developing countries which, it said, threatened the whole development process and had serious social and political implications. The Committee noted general agreement among its members that the United Nations system was facing a major challenge, unpredictability and erosion of resources making rational forward-planning virtually impossible.

With regard to co-ordination within the United Nations system, ACC concluded that if efforts to provide support to Member States for promoting their economic and social development were to succeed, States must make full use of the system's potential and provide direction to guide the work of ACC and its subsidiary bodies. In addition, the international community must provide the resources to carry out any wider responsibilities and new activities it asked the system to undertake.

The Committee noted that inter-agency collaboration to improve overall efficiency in executing operational programmes and projects had continued. Its Consultative Committee on Substantive Questions (Operational Activities) (CCSQ (OPS)) was reviewing the challenges and constraints facing United Nations operational activities in the 1980s in the light of decreasing resources. ACC expressed serious concern about a trend towards bilateral solutions rather than multilateral approaches to international economic and social issues.

Referring to the system of resident co-ordinators of United Nations operational activities for development, established in accordance with General Assembly resolutions of 1977[7] and 1979[8] on restructuring of economic and social sectors of the United Nations system, ACC reported that as of May 1982, 93 resident co-ordinators were in place.

They were consulting with Governments and organizations of the system to assess how they might best be able to exercise their functions; the results would be brought to the attention of ACC in the context of a review of co-ordinators' functions it was to undertake in 1983.

Economic and Social Council action. Following a similar action taken by the UNDP Governing Council on 18 June 1982,[1] the Economic and Social Council, by a resolution of 29 July,[5] invited recipient countries and urged all United Nations organizations to facilitate the role of the resident co-ordinator in strengthening the co-ordination of technical assistance activities.

General Assembly action. In his September 1982 report[4] on United Nations operational activities for development, the Director-General for Development and International Economic Co-operation informed the General Assembly that the system of resident co-ordinators had been operating for 18 months. Under the new arrangements for field representation of the United Nations system as a whole, overall responsibility for, and co-ordination of, operational activities for development was entrusted to a single official who functioned in support of, and in conformity with, the criteria and priorities of the competent national authorities and who exercised team leadership and was responsible for evolving a multidisciplinary dimension in sectoral country-level development assistance programmes. The Director-General said that United Nations intergovernmental bodies had expressed appreciation of the new arrangements, which were seen as contributing to improved coherence of action. However, time would be needed to develop the arrangements so that they could respond effectively to each country's particular circumstances.

As requested by the Assembly in December 1981,[9] the Director-General reported that consultations had taken place with over 90 Governments, on the basis of which ACC would review the arrangements under which co-ordinators exercised their functions. Information on this review would be included in his 1983 report on policy issues related to operational activities.

The Assembly, in its 20 December 1982 resolution[6] on operational activities for development, reiterated the importance of co-ordinating multilateral development assistance at the field level (a provision not included in the original draft submitted by Bangladesh for the Group of 77[2]). The Assembly requested the Director-General to pay (in the original, it would have decided to pay) particular attention in the 1983 policy review of operational activities, to the need for improved coherence of action (here the words "and effective integration" were added) at the country level, including a report on measures and recommendations on the role of resident co-ordinators (the request for the report was not included in the original draft). The Assembly also invited ACC to report in 1983 on the outcome of its review of arrangements for the exercise of the resident co-ordinators' functions, and requested ACC to develop within a year a register on development activities (a request also not included in the original draft).

Decision. [1]UNDP Council (report, E/1982/16/Rev.1): 82/5, sect. III, para. 2, 18 June.
Draft resolution withdrawn. [2]Bangladesh, for Group of 77, A/C.2/37/L.92.
Reports. [3]ACC, E/1982/4; [4]Director-General for DIEC, A/37/445.
Resolutions (1982). [5]ESC: 1982/53, para. 9, 29 July; [6]GA: 37/226, paras. 22 & 23, 20 Dec.
Resolutions (prior). GA: [7]32/197, annex, 20 Dec. 1977 (YUN 1977, p. 439); [8]34/213, 19 Dec. 1979 (YUN 1979, p. 528); [9]36/199, 17 Dec. 1981 (YUN 1981, p. 129).

Inter-Agency Task Force

The UNDP Inter-Agency Task Force, established in 1977[2] to assist in defining United Nations operational policies for development and in translating these into more effective action, was placed by ACC, on 6 April 1982, on a continuing basis with fixed-term membership. By the same decision,[1] ACC requested the UNDP Inter-Agency Consultative Meeting to review the Task Force's terms of reference in respect of its functions as substantive secretariat for the ACC Consultative Committee on Substantive Questions (Operational Activities) (CCSQ (OPS)).

At its 13-15 December session, the Inter-Agency Consultative Meeting endorsed a UNDP statement on the objectives and formal terms of reference of the Task Force. It decided that the Task Force should consist of permanent members designated by their respective organizations to work full time on the Task Force and the substantive secretariat of the Consultative Committee, and associate *ad hoc* or part-time members designated by UNDP or the agencies. The Task Force would continue to be chaired by the UNDP Deputy Administrator, and as the substantive secretariat of CCSQ (OPS) by the chairperson designated by ACC.

During 1982, UNDP consulted the Task Force on a series of subjects, particularly: direct and government execution; reimbursement for services provided by UNDP field offices to other United Nations bodies; and a policy review paper on the future role of UNDP, concerning its structure and new, specific ways of mobilizing resources on an increasingly predictable, continuous and assured basis. In addition, the Task Force prepared documentation for two CCSQ (OPS) sessions in 1982, including a paper on the evolution of oper-

ational activities for development in the 1980s, submitted to ACC.

Decision (1982). [1]ACC: 1982/6, 6 Apr.
Resolution. [2]GA: 32/197, annex, 20 Dec. 1977 (YUN 1977, p. 439).

Technical co-operation through UNDP

For the United Nations, the major tool used to respond to requests for assistance in the field of operational activities was technical co-operation. To assist developing countries to attain self-reliance, particularly by enhancing their capacity for autonomous decision-making, technical co-operation encompassed all spheres of development activities, such as developing human resources, strengthening of institutional capabilities, examining the feasibility of investment, exploring natural resources, improving data bases, facilitating the transfer and adaptation of indigenous technologies, and supporting inter-country co-operation. Objectives were realized by thousands of projects, based on government priorities and carried out in partnership with Governments and United Nations agencies and organizations. Within the United Nations system, the United Nations Development Programme (UNDP) continued to have a central funding and co-ordinating role in technical co-operation.

UNDP activities

In 1982, UNDP, like the developing countries it served, struggled against adverse international economic trends, such as the combined effects of world-wide recession, declining world trade, reduced official development assistance flows, lower or negative growth rates, depressed commodity prices and severe debt funding requirements. The least developed countries, were particularly affected during the year. The UNDP Administrator described these trends and their effects on UNDP in his 1982 annual report.[5]

Compared to target expenditures for technical co-operation, known as indicative planning figures (IPFs), amounting to $750 million, UNDP had available in 1982 only $568 million, a reduction of $90 million compared to IPF field expenditures in 1981. Reduced development assistance flows to multilateral institutions accounted for almost all of the UNDP decline, in which exchange-rate fluctuations were a major factor. The effectiveness of UNDP was severely threatened by shortfalls in resource levels which required cutbacks in planned expenditures for technical co-operation, affecting the 154 developing countries and self-governing territories served by the Programme, its partnership arrangements with executing United Nations agencies and its network of 116 field offices.

Concerned about the dichotomy between the expressed wishes of Governments and the Programme's resources, the UNDP Governing Council in 1982 established an Intersessional Committee of the Whole to study options for the longer-term financing of UNDP, together with recommendations for strengthening the effectiveness of the Governing Council itself.

In light of the World Bank's growing technical assistance operations and the world-wide, on-the-spot UNDP field presence, UNDP strengthened its collaboration with the Bank, already strong through a close working relationship in areas such as energy, water and sanitation, health and agricultural research, and in holding roundtable conferences for least developed countries. On a case-by-case basis, UNDP also managed, in agreement with the developing countries concerned, technical assistance funds provided by the Bank, particularly where such funds were not associated with a capital project. Along similar lines, UNDP provided management services for bilaterally financed activities.

UNDP also sought ways to expand co-ordination with non-governmental organizations (NGOs) in technical co-operation efforts.

Because of lower estimated UNDP resource levels, programming levels were reduced to 80 per cent of approved IPFs at the time of the Governing Council's session in June 1982. In November, after the 1982 United Nations Pledging Conference for Development Activities, programming levels were further reduced to 55 per cent of IPFs. Developing countries themselves took further steps to reduce project personnel costs, and savings were also achieved at both UNDP headquarters and in the field offices.

In 1982, 860 new projects were approved under the main Programme, with a total value of more than half a billion dollars. Of the $513.9 million in project approvals, $58.6 million was being provided under cost-sharing arrangements. The largest number of newly approved projects, 163, came in the sector of agriculture, forestry and fisheries followed by 137 projects in the development policy and planning sector, 127 in industry, 99 in transport and communications, 87 in natural resources, and 53 in education. On a regional basis, 288 projects in Africa, valued at $179.9 million were approved; 250 in Asia and the Pacific, valued at $149.4 million; 177 in Latin America, valued at $88.4 million; 72 in the Arab States, valued at $47.3 million; 47 in Europe, valued at $11.3 million; and 26 new global and interregional projects, valued at $37.3 million. As at 30 September 1982, 4,642 UNDP-financed projects were under way.

During the year, UNDP continued its special activities on behalf of the least developed countries (LDCs), as requested by the 1981 United Nations Conference on Least Developed Countries at Paris.[9] Twenty-five of the countries designated as least developed requested UNDP assistance in organizing round-table review meetings to assess national progress under the Substantial New Programme of Action for the 1980s for the Least Developed Countries, adopted at the Conference, and reviews with interested donors and representatives of LDCs were scheduled through 1983.

During 1982, UNDP resident representatives continued their pre-disaster planning and disaster relief and rehabilitation functions as field representatives of the Office of the United Nations Disaster Relief Co-ordinator. The role of the resident co-ordinator in this respect had been expanded by the General Assembly in December 1981.[8] Important relief and rehabilitation activities by field offices in 1982 included disaster relief in Chad and Yemen.

Governing Council activities. The Governing Council of UNDP held its twenty-ninth regular session at Geneva from 1 to 18 June 1982. It also convened for an organizational meeting at United Nations Headquarters on 25 February, and held a special meeting on country and intercountry programmes and projects at Geneva from 24 to 28 May, which was continued on 4 and 18 June in New York, during the Council's regular session. The Council submitted its report on the 1982 meetings to the Economic and Social Council.[6] Among decisions adopted at the special meeting on 18 June were decisions on UNDP involvement in establishing a World Maritime University and support for Multinational Programming and Operational Centres.

By a decision of 18 June,[1] the Council took note with appreciation of the report of the UNDP Administrator for 1981,[4] and of several reports by the Joint Inspection Unit (JIU) on co-ordination of United Nations activities related to development assistance and other matters of interest to UNDP. The Council welcomed the Administrator's intention, indicated in a note of 11 May 1982,[3] to update the data base for annual reports better to reflect qualitative output.

Also on 18 June, the Council adopted four decisions on United Nations operational activities: on technical co-operation programmes on the United Nations Volunteers programme; on technical co-operation among developing countries; and on the Capital Development Fund.

Development activities in 14 other decisions adopted on the same date, dealt with: assistance to Palestinians; follow-up action on the 1981 Conference on LDCs; assistance to Uganda and Lebanon; plan of action and institutional support for combating desertification of the Sudano-Sahelian region and its rehabilitation programme; the United Nations Revolving Fund for Natural Resources Exploration; energy development programmes; the United Nations Fund for Population Activities; and integrating women in development.

General Assembly action. In its resolution of 20 December on operational activities for development,[7] the General Assembly invited the UNDP Administrator and the President of the World Bank to examine further co-operation between their organizations regarding utilization of facilities, and requested the Administrator to report thereon to the UNDP Governing Council. This paragraph was not included in the original draft submitted by Bangladesh on behalf of the Group of 77.[2]

Decision (1982). [1]UNDP Council (report, E/1982/16/Rev.1): 82/6, 18 June.
Draft resolution withdrawn. [2]Bangladesh, for Group of 77, A/C.2/37/L.92.
Note. [3]UNDP Administrator, DP/1982/7.
Reports. UNDP Administrator: [4]DP/1982/6 & Add.1 & Add.1/Annex & Add.2 & Add.2/Corr.1 & Add.3,4; [5]DP/1983/6 & Add.1,2. [6]UNDP Council: E/1982/16/Rev.1.
Resolution (1982). [7]GA: 37/226, para. 15. 20 Dec.
Resolution (prior). [8]GA: 36/225, para. 8 (YUN 1981, p. 481).
Yearbook reference. [9]1981, p. 406.

Country and intercountry programmes

Through country programming, UNDP sought to ensure the equitable distribution of resources among developing countries and to allocate funds to sectors reflecting host Government objectives. With the agreement of the Government concerned, country programming could also provide a framework for the programming of resources from elsewhere in the United Nations system.

At its organizational meeting on 25 February 1982,[1] the Governing Council approved the provisional agenda for its special meeting on country and intercountry programmes and projects, to be held from 24 to 28 May.

The special meeting was continued during the Council's regular 1982 session, on 4 and 18 June. The Council approved all the programmes and projects separately by region and consolidated all its actions on country, intercountry and global programmes and projects, approval-authority decisions, and other action taken during the special meeting in an omnibus decision.

In implementing the programmes, the Administrator was requested to take into account the views of Governments. By the same decision of 18 June,[2] the Council authorized him to proceed with approval of requests for country and regional assistance, keeping expenditures in reasonable conformity with IPFs and Government contributions, but within available resources.

Total UNDP project expenditures in 1982 amounted to $651 million, excluding some $8.6 million which recipient Governments made available for projects in their own country through cash counterpart contributions (see table below). This was a reduction of some 10 per cent below the 1981 level. Responsible for the execution of these projects were: UNDP itself, through its Office for Projects Execution; 12 United Nations specialized agencies; the International Atomic Energy Agency; a number of United Nations units and bodies; Governments; and non-governmental and three other organizations outside the United Nations system (see table on p. 627). The largest project sectors, by order of expenditure, were: agriculture, forestry and fisheries; transport and communications; general development; natural resources; and industry (see table on p. 627).

Decisions (1982). UNDP Council (report, E/1982/16/Rev.1): [1]82/1, 25 Feb.; [2]82/4, sect. VI & IX, 18 June.

Country programmes

By a decision of 18 June 1982,[1] the UNDP Governing Council approved programmes and projects in the following countries:

Africa: Angola, Botswana, Burundi, Comoros, Gabon, Guinea, Guinea-Bissau, Lesotho, Madagascar, Malawi, Mozambique, Seychelles, Somalia, United Republic of Tanzania, Zaire, Zambia, Zimbabwe.

Arab States: Bahrain, Democratic Yemen, Djibouti, Iraq, Jordan, Libyan Arab Jamahiriya, Morocco, Oman, Tunisia, United Arab Emirates.

Asia and the Pacific: Burma, China, Cook Islands, Fiji, Malaysia, Pakistan, Samoa, Singapore, Solomon Islands, Thailand.

Europe: Albania, Czechoslovakia, Hungary, Malta, Portugal, Romania, Turkey, Yugoslavia.

Latin America: Antigua and Barbuda, Argentina, Bahamas, Barbados, Bermuda, Brazil, British Virgin Islands, Caribbean multi-island programme, Cayman Islands, Chile, Dominica, Dominican Republic, Ecuador, Grenada, Guyana, Haiti, Honduras, Jamaica, Mexico, Montserrat, Netherlands Antilles, Panama, Paraguay, Peru, Saint Kitts–Nevis, Saint Lucia, Saint Vincent and the Grenadines, Turks and Caicos Islands, Venezuela.

The Council also approved the extension of the country programmes for India until March 1985, and took note of one-year extensions approved for 17 African (Cape Verde, Central African Republic, Chad, Gambia, Ghana, Ivory Coast, Liberia, Mali, Mauritania, Niger, Sao Tome and Principe, Senegal, Sierra Leone, Swaziland, Togo, United Republic of Cameroon, Upper Volta), five Latin American (Bolivia, Colombia, Costa Rica, Suriname, Trinidad and Tobago), three Arab (Saudi Arabia, Syrian Arab Republic, Yemen), three Asia and Pacific (Mongolia, Papua New Guinea, Republic of Korea) countries and one European country (Greece).

UNDP INDICATIVE PLANNING FIGURES AND EXPENDITURES, 1982
(in thousands of US dollars)

Africa

	IPFs 1982-1986	Project expenditures
Angola	41,500	4,604
Benin	33,500	3,806
Botswana	8,500	1,569
Burundi	48,500	6,621
Cape Verde	11,250	1,153
Central African Republic	29,500	2,863
Chad	52,000	3,082
Comoros	12,000	2,358
Congo	11,000	2,790
Equatorial Guinea	11,750	1,590
Ethiopia	112,000	13,929
Gabon	6,000	1,849
Gambia	14,250	1,889
Ghana	40,000	3,627
Guinea	44,500	6,457
Guinea-Bissau	21,750	2,621
Ivory Coast	16,500	2,244
Kenya	52,000	7,072
Lesotho	22,250	2,988
Liberia	13,500	2,313
Madagascar	49,000	5,519
Malawi	53,000	6,667
Mali	65,000	7,698
Mauritania	24,500	2,647
Mauritius	7,000	694
Mozambique	74,000	9,418
Namibia	7,750	606
Niger	45,000	5,214
Nigeria	55,000	10,311
Rwanda	45,000	5,387
Sao Tome and Principe	2,000	288
Senegal	33,000	4,074
Seychelles	1,600	217
Sierra Leone	32,500	4,417
Somalia	48,000	5,797
Swaziland	5,750	1,078
Togo	21,750	2,651
Uganda	59,500	7,852
United Republic of Cameroon	27,500	4,935
United Republic of Tanzania	72,000	11,106
Upper Volta	55,000	6,988
Zaire	79,000	9,189
Zambia	21,250	3,517
Zimbabwe	24,250	3,200
Subtotal	1,510,600	194,895

Asia and the Pacific

	IPFs 1982-1986	Project expenditures
Afghanistan	71,500	6,240
Bangladesh	201,000	20,911
Bhutan	36,500	3,600
Brunei	200	—
Burma	102,000	11,076
China	134,900	17,350
Cook Islands	1,400	468
Democratic Kampuchea	25,500	471
Democratic People's Republic of Korea	24,750	3,662
Fiji	5,000	1,309
Hong Kong	500	66
India	252,000	30,224
Indonesia	106,000	17,556
Iran	20,000	198
Kiribati	1,300	178

Asia and the Pacific (cont.)

	IPFs 1982-1986	Project expenditures
Lao People's Democratic Republic	52,500	4,656
Malaysia	15,000	2,423
Maldives	7,000	821
Mongolia	10,000	1,528
Nauru	60	—
Nepal	98,000	11,878
Niue	1,000	186
Pakistan	118,000	12,428
Papua New Guinea	13,500	1,598
Philippines	46,000	7,854
Republic of Korea	18,000	1,791
Samoa	5,250	761
Singapore	7,500	1,503
Solomon Islands	4,000	609
South Pacific islands	—	216
Sri Lanka	76,000	7,630
Thailand	43,000	5,762
Tokelau	950	80
Tonga	2,500	668
Trust Territory of the Pacific Islands	1,000	161
Tuvalu	1,140	240
Vanuatu	2,000	507
Viet Nam	118,000	6,207
Subtotal	1,622,950	182,816

Arab States

	IPFs 1982-1986	Project expenditures
Algeria	20,000	4,141
Bahrain	2,500	1,412
Democratic Yemen	22,250	4,304
Djibouti	5,250	1,085
Egypt	56,000	9,342
Iraq	15,000	2,207
Jordan	15,000	2,800
Kuwait	—	2,162
Lebanon	10,000	3,087
Libyan Arab Jamahiriya	5,000	2,748
Morocco	27,000	3,803
Oman	4,000	1,464
Qatar	—	307
Saudi Arabia	10,000	7,153
Sudan	58,500	8,807
Syrian Arab Republic	15,000	2,445
Tunisia	15,000	2,638
United Arab Emirates	1,000	2,242
Yemen	30,000	10,538
Other*	—	954
Subtotal	311,500	73,639

Europe

	IPFs 1982-1986	Project expenditures
Albania	10,250	454
Bulgaria	6,000	1,180
Cyprus	5,000	1,028
Czechoslovakia	2,500	368
Greece	6,000	632
Hungary	3,500	479
Malta	2,500	375
Poland	6,000	740
Portugal	4,000	717
Romania	7,500	567
Turkey	20,000	4,464
Yugoslavia	7,500	876
Subtotal	80,750	11,880

Latin America

	IPFs 1982-1986	Project expenditures
Antigua and Barbuda	1,765	415
Argentina	20,000	3,167
Bahamas	2,400	590
Barbados	2,500	380
Belize	1,650	526
Bermuda	550	63
Bolivia	19,500	2,724
Brazil	30,000	8,407
British Virgin Islands	300	159
Cayman Islands	560	122
Chile	20,000	3,097
Colombia	22,000	4,811
Costa Rica	5,000	525
Cuba	20,500	3,300
Dominica	2,300	458
Dominican Republic	12,000	1,648
Ecuador	15,000	3,396
El Salvador	15,250	2,277
Grenada	2,100	301
Guatemala	13,000	2,283
Guyana	8,500	1,391
Haiti	38,000	4,980
Honduras	16,000	4,352
Jamaica	7,500	1,340
Mexico	20,000	2,323
Montserrat	700	65
Netherlands Antilles	1,500	1,127
Nicaragua	9,500	2,258
Panama	7,500	1,515
Paraguay	9,750	1,511
Peru	25,000	4,257
St. Kitts–Nevis–Anguilla	1,300	159
Saint Lucia	2,100	383
Saint Vincent and the Grenadines	3,250	548
Suriname	3,500	298
Trinidad and Tobago	5,000	2,545
Turks and Caicos Islands	850	61
Uruguay	10,000	2,282
Venezuela	10,000	3,779
Subtotal	386,325	73,823
Total	3,912,125	537,053

INTERCOUNTRY

	IPFs 1982-1986	Project expenditures
Global	114,800	16,119
Interregional	73,500	12,579

Regional

	IPFs 1982-1986	Project expenditures
Africa	283,400	...
Asia and the Pacific	296,100	...
Arab States	57,800	...
Europe	16,200	...
Latin America	76,500	...
Total	730,000	83,248

OTHER

	IPFs 1982-1986	Project expenditures
Multi-island country projects	4,516	663
National liberation movements	15,000	1,441
GRAND TOTAL	4,849,941	651,103

*Expenditure for Palestinian people.

NOTES:

Indicative planning figures: Figures are illustrative; actual figures may vary from those in the table, depending on the total financial resources available to UNDP. Amounts are given as of April 1983.

Programme expenditures: Data cover expenditures financed under IPFs, Special Programme Resources, Special Measures Fund for Least Developed Countries, Special Industrial Services and government cost-sharing. Not covered is $8.6 million in government cash counterpart.

Three dots (. . .) indicate that data are not available or are not separately reported.

Regional classification provided by UNDP.

SOURCES: DP/1983/6/Add.4 and DP/1984/5/Add.3

In addition, the Council authorized assistance to projects submitted by 21 Governments which had never had a country programme or for which the date of submission of the next country programme could not be determined: Belize, Brunei, Cyprus, Democratic People's Republic of Korea, Equatorial Guinea, Hong Kong, Iran, Kiribati, Lebanon, Nauru, Nicaragua, Nigeria, Qatar, Sudan, Swaziland, Tokelau, Tonga, Trust Territory of the Pacific Islands, Tuvalu, Uganda and Vanuatu.

The Council also approved preparatory action for a diesel-locomotive maintenance project for Viet Nam.

Highlights of the new country programmes follow. (Key: LDC—least developed country; IDC—island developing country; MSA—most seriously affected LDC.)

AFRICA

Angola. Agricultural, educational and social-sector support, improvement of living standards.

Botswana (LDC). Expertise, advisory services and training in major sectors.

Burundi (MSA). Addressing lack of personnel and agricultural energy and mineral resources, soil erosion, rapid population increase, traditional rural sector.

Comoros (LDC, IDC). Food production, socio-economic development policy.

Gabon. Agriculture.

Guinea (MSA). Rural development, transport and communications, industry, water and energy resources, planning; training; pre-investment.

Guinea-Bissau (LDC). Agriculture, education, health.

Lesotho (MSA). Co-operation to meet plan requirements and enhance self-reliance; pre-investment, e.g. in natural resource exploitation.

Madagascar (MSA, IDC). Agricultural production, industrial development.

Malawi (LDC). Rural development, particularly to benefit small land-holders; land, water resources, planning.

Mozambique (MSA). Agriculture, natural resources, industry, education; training, institution-building and planning.

Seychelles (IDC). Food production; educational, housing and health facilities; increase income; development and efficient utilization of human resources.

Somalia (MSA). Priority sectors in national plan; technical assistance and co-operation; national project management and greater participation of women.

United Republic of Tanzania (MSA). Economic survival plan, particularly improving food and consumer goods production, balance of trade, transport.

Zaire. Rural development (previous programme with emphasis on urban areas).

Zambia. Agriculture, industry; women's participation in projects.

Zimbabwe. Institutional support, short-term expertise and training; planning, social services, Government execution.

ARAB STATES

Bahrain (IDC). Middle- and higher-level education, social services and strengthening services sector.

Democratic Yemen (MSA). Agricultural production, fisheries and industry; transport and communications; human resources development.

Djibouti (LDC). Training, particularly in planning and statistics, employment, social security, industry.

Iraq. Consolidation of ongoing projects: assistance to long-term projects; technical expertise, training.

Jordan. Agriculture, human resources, government infrastructure, natural resources, education.

Libyan Arab Jamahiriya. Industry, planning and human resources development.

Morocco. Training in agriculture, water, mining and energy, industry, infrastructure.

Oman. Development of national capabilities, economic diversification, infrastructure; consolidation and expansion of successful projects.

Tunisia. Agriculture, pre-investment activities, in-service training of nationals.

United Arab Emirates. Institutional support, planning and research in infrastructure, human resources development, planning and administration.

ASIA AND THE PACIFIC

Burma (MSA). Agriculture; health.

China. Agricultural production; consumer goods and services; energy development and conservation; human resources for development; infrastructure.

Cook Islands (IDC). Agriculture, marine resources and tourism, rationalizing transport services and infrastructure, technical training.

Fiji (IDC). Industry, primary production; training and social development.

Malaysia. Agriculture, manufacturing; services and studies for plan implementation; policy planning, research and human resources development.

Pakistan. Agriculture, natural and human resources development.

Samoa (LDC, IDC). Agriculture; development administration.

Solomon Islands (IDC). Training, infrastructure development, pre-investment and support to investment in natural resources, social services.

Singapore. Upgrading technology in industries, developing human resources in education, training and public administration.

Thailand. Development management; rural development and poverty alleviation; economic diversification; energy.

EUROPE

Albania. Application of modern science and technology, higher education to sustain industrial development; research for development; management; telecommunications technology.

Czechoslovakia. Assistance to one major and a few smaller projects.

Hungary. Energy, science and technology, particularly acquisition of advanced technology and training.

Malta. Ship repairing and ship building, transport; water resources development, irrigation; postal service development.

Portugal. Water resources development, environment improvement, agriculture.

Romania. Energy, natural resources, transportation, communications and industry; training.

Turkey. Improving industrial and agricultural exports; development of human resources, particularly in technology, vocational skills, literacy, health, and domestic energy resources.

Yugoslavia. High-technology development in industry, agriculture and natural resources, particularly for energy, pollution problems and use of indigenous materials.

LATIN AMERICA AND THE CARIBBEAN
Antigua and Barbuda (IDC). Investment-support; resources pooled for subregional activities.

Argentina. Technological development; transport and communication services; strengthening national institutions, assisting productivity; planning of human resources and improvement of living conditions.

Bahamas (IDC). Transport, water resources development and fisheries.

Barbados (IDC). Export promotion, including establishment of institutional framework; energy; public sector investment.

Brazil. Strengthening national science and technology potential.

British Virgin Islands (IDC). Two projects in fisheries and planning.

Chile. Scientific and technological research, especially basic sciences; agricultural export products, particularly fruits, vegetables and livestock; foreign investment promotion.

Cayman Islands (IDC). Training.

Dominica (IDC). Institution-building and planning rehabilitation.

Dominican Republic (IDC). Agriculture and renewable natural resources; social sectors, especially education, housing and health; strengthening public administration, planning, statistics and national budgeting; food production and rural income; agrarian reform.

Ecuador. Transport and communications, agriculture; institutional development and training of human resources.

Grenada. Food and export crops; alternative sources of energy; agro-industries based on local raw materials; education; rural health services.

Guyana (MSA). Institutional planning and execution of externally supported projects; mineral exploration; public enterprises; planning and project preparation; veterinary services; application of science and technology to industry and natural resource development; participation of women in development.

Haiti (MSA, IDC). Pre-investment activities; agricultural extension services; co-operatives and livestock production; water resources and mining; human resources development; telecommunications; civil aviation.

Honduras (MSA). Training and employment; education; income-earning employment of women; agrarian reform and co-operative development; strengthening national institutions in infrastructure, agriculture and industry; better utilization of resources.

Jamaica (IDC). Infrastructure, construction and agriculture.

Mexico. Rural development, science and technology, industrial development, food production and nutrition, employment, social development.

Montserrat (IDC). Agriculture and agro-industries; exploitation of raw materials.

Netherlands Antilles (IDC). Employment and industry.

Panama. Development of human resources; productivity in agriculture, industries and exports.

Paraguay. Improvement of human resources; study and utilization of natural resources; research in science and technology, and energy development; development of administrative, planning and financial institutions; export development.

St. Kitts–Nevis (IDC). Agricultural planning, industry, civil aviation; pre-investment, increase in productivity, improvement of skills.

Saint Lucia (IDC). Reconstruction of post-hurricane economy, housing, education and industry; developing alternative energy sources; diversifying agriculture; light industry; tourism.

Saint Vincent and the Grenadines (IDC). Socio-economic planning, project preparation and implementation; diversification of agriculture, development of alternative energy sources, improvement of transport and education facilities.

Turks and Caicos Islands (IDC). Training.

Venezuela. Improvement of national planning, especially in agriculture, transport and communications; higher education; promotion of non-traditional exports; human resources development, with training in economic, social and urban planning, production engineering, civil aviation, and science and technology.

These trends in country programmes and projects were shown in the annex to a May 1982 report of the Administrator to the Governing Council.[3]

General Assembly action. In its resolution of 20 December 1982 on operational activities for development,[4] the General Assembly reaffirmed the exclusive responsibility of the recipient country in formulating its national development plan or priorities and objectives. The original draft,[2] submitted by Bangladesh for the Group of 77, had reaffirmed the country's responsibility to define the terms of reference for elaborating and executing programmes and projects of operational activities for development within the framework of its plan, priorities and objectives. The Assembly also emphasized that integrating United Nations operational activities with national programmes would enhance the impact and relevance of these activities—a provision not in the original draft.

Decision (1982). [1]UNDP Council (report, E/1982/16/Rev.1): 82/4, sect. A, 18 June.
Draft resolution withdrawn. [2]Bangladesh, for Group of 77, A/C.2/37/L.92.
Report. [3]UNDP Administrator, DP/1982/4 & Add.1.
Resolution (1982). [4]GA: 37/226, para. 16, 20 Dec.

Regional programmes

On 18 June 1982,[1] the UNDP Governing Council took note of the second regional programme for Africa[2] and the first regional programme for Europe[3] for the 1982-1986 programming cycle, presented by the UNDP Administrator, and of the general arrangements for their implementation. Under other provisions of that decision, it requested him to continue UNDP support to the five Multinational Programming and Operational Centres in Africa.

Programme for Africa. The Governing Council had originally approved an indicative planning figure (IPF) of $283.4 million for Africa for 1982-1986, later revised to $226.72 million. As the first regional programme (1977-1981) had "borrowed" $20.7 million from the 1982-1986 cycle, the net IPF available was $206.02 million, with 68.9 per cent of the programmed resources to be used for continuing projects and 57 per cent to be devoted to three priority sectors: transport and communications (21.1 per cent), regional and subregional co-operation (18.7 per cent) and food self-sufficiency (17.2 per cent).

Programme for Europe. For the first regional programme for Europe, the Governing Council, in 1980, had set the illustrative IPF for 1982-1986 at $16.2 million. The actual amount available for programming was $14.36 million, i.e. 80 per cent of the IPF plus a carry-over of $1.4 million from the 1977-1981 programming cycle.

The UNDP Administrator proposed an emphasis that differed from the more traditional type of regional programme, because of national capabilities being generally above those in other recipient regions, project components being of actual or potential benefit to developing countries, and the type of projects being determined by the modest size of the IPF.

The sectoral distribution of resources, as proposed by the Administrator, was: energy, and transport and communications (24 per cent each), environment (22 per cent), science and technology (20 per cent), and others (10 per cent), including olive production, migration and exchange of educational materials. He suggested the following types of projects: networks, i.e. co-operation among national institutions dealing with problems common to several countries; joint endeavours, i.e. projects that could only be undertaken jointly by two or more Governments; projects benefiting developing countries in other regions; cost-sharing projects; projects in which non-IPF countries participated.

Decision (1982). [1]UNDP Council (report, E/1982/16/Rev.1): 82/4, sect. A III, 18 June.
Regional programmes. [2]Africa, DP/RAF/2; [3]Europe, DP/RER/1 & Corr.1.

Global projects

The UNDP Governing Council approved nine global projects on 18 June 1982 and authorized the Administrator to arrange for their execution.[1] The projects were in the following areas: vaccine and drug development for diarrhoeal disease control (phase II); tropical wheat improvement; iden-

tification of world marine fish resources; rice testing and improvement; food systems and policies; fertilizer technology and utilization (phase II); technology transfer on root and tuber crops (phase II); research and training in sorghum and millet (phase III) (International Crops Research Institute for Semi-Arid Tropics); and research and training in animal trypanosomiasis (phase II) (International Laboratory for Research on Animal Diseases).

Expenditures for global projects in 1982 totalled $16.1 million.

Decision (1982). [1]UNDP Council (report, E/1982/16/Rev.1): 82/4, sect. A VII, 18 June.

Fisheries vessels pool

In March 1982,[2] the UNDP Administrator reported to the Governing Council on the continued need to develop the fisheries vessels pool, consisting of 16 fisheries research and training vessels used for UNDP projects throughout the world and managed by the Food and Agriculture Organization of the United Nations (FAO). Since its formal establishment in May 1974, the pool had provided vessel services to 40 countries.

The Administrator stated that while the need for large-scale national fisheries surveys would diminish, establishing exclusive economic zones by the Convention on the Law of the Sea would increase the need for: monitoring stocks to avoid overfishing; identifying exploitable species within the new limits; and developing efficient techniques for catching, processing and marketing new species.

Acting on the Administrator's proposals, the Council, in a decision of 18 June 1982,[1] authorized him to refit, at a cost of approximately $1.8 million, five UNDP-owned vessels. The sale of some vessels would finance refitting others and the balance of UNDP costs were to be recovered from vessel-service fees within approximately seven years of refitting.

In June,[3] the UNDP Budgetary and Finance Committee informed the Council of the intention of UNDP and FAO to study development of a co-operative use programme with countries whose survey and research vessels were under-utilized.

Decision (1982). [1]UNDP Council (report, E/1982/16/Rev.1): 82/39, 18 June.
Note. [2]UNDP Administrator, DP/1982/62.
Report. [3]UNDP Budgetary and Finance Committee, DP/1982/95.

Pre-investment activities

In a March 1982 report on UNDP pre-investment activities,[2] the UNDP Administrator summarized progress achieved since June 1981 in stimulating such activities, and discussed the need to find an alternative source for funding investment feasibility studies for which financing might not be available under a country's indicative planning figure. Those studies would be designed to meet least developed countries' unforeseen needs for follow-up investment from identified sources and assist investors in reaching immediate decisions on government-designated priority projects.

As proposed by the Administrator, the Governing Council, by a decision of 18 June,[1] approved the establishment of a special account of $1 million from the UNDP Special Programme Resources for the 1982-1986 programming cycle, to set up a facility to help countries finance the studies. Noting measures taken to develop a closer relationship with the World Bank and regional development banks for follow-up investment, the Council requested the Administrator to broaden co-operation with other sources of finance. The Council also took note of the joint efforts of the Administrator and the World Bank President to promote further investment development through special training of UNDP and agency staff, and requested the Administrator to evaluate the training in a 1983 report.

For 1982, investment commitments related to UNDP-assisted pre-investment projects amounted to $3.2 billion, an increase of 28 per cent over 1981. The ratio of the UNDP cost for pre-investment projects to the amount of reported investment commitments resulting from them was 1:45.

During the year, UNDP strengthened its relationships with development finance institutions, in particular with the World Bank, regional development banks and the International Fund for Agricultural Development. Funding for the 31 UNDP-assisted projects for which the World Bank was executing agency in 1982 amounted to some $28 million, of which about $8.5 million was cost-sharing. The Asian Development Bank was designated as executing agency for 20 UNDP-assisted projects between 1980 and 1982, of which nine, at an estimated cost to UNDP of about $3.4 million, were to implement studies of investment projects.

The training of UNDP field-office personnel in investment development was given particular emphasis. Between 1980, when an arrangement was concluded with the World Bank, and the end of 1982, such training was provided to 74 UNDP staff members and 14 persons from United Nations agencies.

Projects carried out under co-operative arrangements included reviews of the vocational training system in the Sudan (in co-operation with the International Labour Organisation (ILO)), and of designs for a sewerage and marine waste disposal system in the Cook Islands and updating a pre-feasibility study on sewerage, waste disposal and storm-water drainage for Libreville, Gabon, in co-operation with the World Health Organization (WHO).

Many projects reflected the growing impact of the investment-oriented work. For example, from the $1.5 million UNDP/Department of Technical Co-operation for Development (DTCD) feasibility studies on the exploration and development of geothermal power in Kenya, follow-up investments totalling $118 million had been committed by three bilateral sources, the Government of Kenya and the World Bank. Based on the success of the project, Kenya requested UNDP support for a second round of geothermal exploration under the 1982-1986 country programme, with $2.5 million already allocated. In Burma, pre-investment activities had generated some $320 million in investment follow-up. A UNDP/United Nations Industrial Development Organization (UNIDO) project for the industrial development of capital goods in Mexico helped generate $1.2 billion in follow-up investments, and UNDP-supported efforts in the United Republic of Tanzania has been important in oil and gas exploration, helping build national capacity.

Decision (1982). [1]UNDP Council (report, E/1982/16/Rev.1): 82/9, 18 June.
Report. [2]UNDP Administrator, DP/1982/12 & Add.1.

Programme planning and execution

IPFs for the 1982-1986 programme cycle

In 1982, the UNDP Governing Council approved certain changes in individual country illustrative indicative planning figures (IPFs) for the 1977-1981 and 1982-1986 programming cycles, as recommended by the UNDP Administrator in a note of 5 April 1982.[2]

For Antigua and Barbuda, as well as Belize, which became independent in 1981, a bonus for newly independent status was awarded; accordingly, the 1982-1986 IPFs were increased for Antigua and Barbuda from $1.1 million to $1.765 million, and for Belize from $1.4 million to $1.65 million. The Administrator recommended that the resulting deficit of $816,000 created in the IPFs be charged to the Programme Reserve.

The Administrator also submitted revised IPFs for the Central African Republic (from $25.5 million to $29.5 million) and Democratic Yemen (from $17.25 million to $22.25 million), based on revisions approved by the World Bank in the basic data used in calculating its IPFs—a larger than previously estimated population in the former country and a new estimate of the per capita gross national product (GNP) of the latter. For Iran, the Administrator recommended an IPF of $20 million. The $9,915,000 needed for these increases could be met from the $162,374,000 available at the end of the Council's 1981 session for the 1982-1986 unallocated IPFs, reducing that amount to $152,459,000. The Administrator, in an addendum of 27 May to his note, recommended approval of an IPF for Equatorial Guinea for 1982-1986 of $11.75 million, based on World Bank data.

Given a 1980 Council decision calling for flat across-the-board reductions of IPFs if resources fell short of the 14 per cent annual growth target, the Administrator said that Special Programme Resources (formerly the Programme Reserve) should be commensurate with IPF expenditures, and he concluded that, in view of the resource outlook, it would be unwise to plan for an expenditure of more than 60 per cent of the IPFs for 1982-1986. Applying a pro rata reduction to the Special Programme Resources, the $83.4 million for that cycle would be reduced to $50.04 million.

The Governing Council, taking note of the Administrator's action to apply a flat across-the-board reduction of IPFs, approved on 18 June 1982[1] the revised country IPFs and recommended sources of financing.

Decision (1982). [1]UNDP Council (report, E/1982/16/Rev.1): 82/17, 18 June.
Note. [2]UNDP Administrator, DP/1982/21 & Add.2.

Government execution of projects

By a decision of 18 June,[1] the UNDP Governing Council approved arrangements recommended by the Administrator, for an experimental period, designed to encourage and facilitate government execution of projects, in order to enhance participation and self-reliance of the developing countries in operational activities. UNDP field offices were playing an increasing role in assisting Governments to undertake the responsibility for project execution. While most UNDP projects continued to be executed by intergovernmental organizations, expenditures on projects directly executed by Governments and funded by UNDP central resources increased by 61 per cent in 1982 over the 1981 level, to $16.6 million. After the Governing Council approved the Administrator's recommendations, more flexible guidelines on government execution of projects were issued by UNDP in December under which the Administrator's prior approval for such execution was no longer required.

In March, the Administrator reported[3] to the Governing Council on the factors affecting government execution of projects, as requested by the Council in June 1981.[7] In his report, he reviewed the performance of government-executed projects until the end of 1981, the reasons for progress or lack of it, the adequacy of financial and administrative arrangements for government execution, compensation to Governments for additional costs, and the involvement of UNDP field offices. The review confirmed the validity of government execution as an additional modality for implementing UNDP assistance and of the guidelines issued in 1979, which stressed that the multilateral character of technical co-operation through UNDP should be preserved and that the technical experience and knowledge of United Nations organizations should be brought to bear on government execution.

Overall experience with government execution had been positive with progress in both the number of projects approved and the resources dedicated to them. Activities were concentrated in four sectors: natural resources (including land, water and energy); development planning; agriculture, forestry and fisheries; and employment. They included small- and large-scale projects and reflected a preference for those with large subcontracting and equipment components.

To improve and facilitate government execution, the Administrator recommended: that UNDP support-cost resources remaining unutilized due to government execution be credited annually, as an add-on to the country or intercountry IPF; that additional staff needed because of an increase in government execution be met by the Government concerned; and that he be authorized to approve the use of IPF resources available to the country to finance such additional administrative support.

The Governing Council, by the 18 June decision, approved the Administrator's recommendations for an experimental period from 1 January 1983 to 30 June 1985, following which he was to report to the Council on government execution, taking into account the countries, number and types of projects, assistance requested and including the following factors which the add-on to the IPFs (not to exceed 13 per cent) were expected to meet: payment of support costs to co-operating agencies; assistance to Governments in meeting additional administrative costs; training of government staff; increases in field office staff; and executing agency services (advice or support other than that provided as co-operating agency) for project formulation and similar activities. The report should also take into account alternative methods of encouraging and assisting Governments in execution, and analyse real savings resulting from it.

In his annual report for 1982,[4] the Administrator reported that revised guidelines were issued in December, updating procedures and financial arrangements in accordance with the Council's decisions. By other changes, the resident representative was designated as the focal point within UNDP for the financial monitoring of government-executed projects, through whom co-operating agencies were to report their expenditures to the Government. Detailed financial guidelines for use by field offices and Governments were also in preparation.

The Governing Council's decision of 18 June was welcomed by the Economic and Social Council in a resolution of 29 July[5] and by the General Assembly in its 20 December resolution on operational activities for development.[6] The Assembly also welcomed the savings that could result from that decision, a provision not included in the original draft submitted by Bangladesh for the Group of 77 and later withdrawn.[2]

Decision (1982). [1]UNDP Council (report, E/1982/16/Rev.1): 82/8, 18 June.
Draft resolution withdrawn. [2]Bangladesh, for Group of 77, A/C.2/37/L.92.
Reports. UNDP Administrator, [3]DP/1982/11 & Add.1, [4]DP/1983/6/Add.1.
Resolutions (1982). [5]ESC: 1982/53, para. 8, 29 July. [6]GA: 37/226, para. 14, 20 Dec.
Yearbook reference. [7]1981, p. 446.

Programme evaluation

By a note of 19 March 1982,[2] the UNDP Administrator informed the Governing Council of two 1981 reports of the Joint Inspection Unit (JIU) evaluating United Nations programmes, which were also relevant to UNDP.[5] The first, on the status of internal evaluation in the United Nations system, contained information on UNDP thematic and project evaluation efforts. The second recommended an improvement of the UNDP evaluation system and procedures, on which UNDP had already planned action towards enhancing the quality of technical co-operation.

The Council, by a decision of 18 June 1982,[1] welcomed the Administrator's initiative to study further improvement, including the possible establishment of an independent evaluation unit, and invited him to submit proposals in 1983.

In his annual report for 1982,[4] the Administrator said that new criteria had been issued to improve project implementation and tighten monitoring and evaluation procedures. He suggested that evaluations must be built into the original project document for projects exceeding $1 million in cost to UNDP, as well as into country programme management plans.

During the year, reviews were conducted on formulating and implementing planning projects in: Niger, Sierra Leone, Upper Volta, Zaire and Zimbabwe. They stressed the need for greater use of national expertise, for formal and informal training, for more precise responsibility for trained planners; and for a shift from macro- towards micro-planning to achieve improved short-term results.

Reports on UNDP activities in key sectors, prepared for publication in 1982, covered rural co-operatives, innovation and reform in education, and export promotion. Work progressed on four other evaluation studies: industrial training; national agricultural research centres; manufacturing industries; and human resources development in primary health care.

In his September report to the General Assembly on operational activities for development,[3] the Director-General for Development and International Economic Co-operation reviewed evaluation. He found that evaluation was currently more widely conducted in the United Nations system, partly as a result of successive JIU studies. Activities subject to evaluation had increased, and the concept as an integral part of overall planning, programming and budgetary processes had been accepted in principle but not fully applied. The report also mentioned factors inhibiting progress in introducing more effective evaluation, including the fact that evaluating technical co-operation was methodologically less well developed than evaluating capital projects.

Decision (1982). [1]UNDP Council (report, E/1982/16/Rev.1): 82/15, 18 June.
Note. [2]UNDP Administrator, DP/1982/8.
Reports. [3]Director-General for DIEC, transmitted by S-G note, A/37/445 & Add.1; [4]UNDP Administrator, DP/1983/6/Add.1.
Yearbook reference. [5]1981, p. 1310.

UNDP finances

Financial situation

During 1982, the resource situation of UNDP suffered from the global recession and from exchange-rate fluctuations. At the November 1982 United Nations Pledging Conference for Development Activities, however, there were indications of an improvement in the resource outlook. Some 21 countries—mostly developing countries—exceeded the 14 per cent target in their pledges for 1983. Later, Canada, Norway and Sweden announced additional pledges and the largest single donor, the United States, pledged a significantly higher contribution. For 1982 as a whole, cost-sharing contributions by both government and third-party donors rose to a record peak of $75.3 million, a 20 per cent increase over the $62.7 million in 1981. The downward trend in financing had come to a halt, and an increase in resources of $15 million (about 2 per cent) for 1983 seemed assured.

Total income in 1982 amounted to $792.7 million ($31.1 million lower than forecast) and total expenditure, $859.1 million ($13.9 million higher than forecast). This resulted in an excess of expenditure over income of $66.4 million, as a result of which the revenue reserve of UNDP went down to $5.6 million as at 31 December 1982, from $71.1 million at 31 December 1981.

In an April 1982 report,[7] the UNDP Administrator provided a comprehensive review of the activities financed from the UNDP Account—i.e. UNDP central resources—during 1981 and a forecast of activities in 1982 and 1983. The report dealt with the unfavourable developments in the UNDP financial situation, including: a shortfall in voluntary contributions; the curtailment of programme expenditure in 1982 and 1983; and the projected

UNDP liquidity situation, including the timing of payments of contributions. The report also dealt with the status of investments, the utilization and balances of accumulating non-convertible currencies, and the status of the Operational Reserve.

Governing Council action. In an April 1982 report on the future role and structure of UNDP,[5] the Administrator presented to the Governing Council an analysis of the UNDP resources situation over the past decade, in the context of the increasing importance of multilateral technical co-operation for development. A main feature of this growth, however, was a proliferation of funding sources, mainly outside UNDP, with a consequent sharp diminution of the central role of UNDP in United Nations technical co-operation funding.

The Administrator suggested that UNDP programming and co-ordination activities be expanded by: a more vigorous role for field offices in programming; assistance to least developed countries in establishing consultative aid groups; extended use of UNDP structure for administering global special funds; servicing of non-UNDP funded assistance; and facilitating private or mixed investment when requested.

In another report submitted in April,[6] the Administrator indicated ways for mobilizing increased resources on a more predictable, continuous and assured basis, with particular emphasis on the replenishment method—which generated reasonably assured resources over a defined multiyear period on the basis of explicit and equitable cost sharing by Governments—practised by a number of multilateral funds for development assistance; and examined alternative ways of financing and providing development assistance through UNDP and UNDP-administered funds (see below).

The Governing Council, in a decision of 18 June,[1] took note of the Administrator's reports and invited the General Assembly to consider the financial situation of UNDP and the need to sustain technical assistance to developing countries through UNDP in the light of the outcome of the 1982 Pledging Conference.

The Council also established an Intersessional Committee of the Whole to study the longer-term financing of UNDP, and removed the ceilings on cost-sharing activities financed by recipient countries (see below).

In another decision of the same date,[2] the Council endorsed the steps taken to ensure that programme delivery was consistent with resource availability.

In his 1982 annual report,[8] the Administrator stated that adequate assured funding remained his foremost concern. Implicit in this concern was the need for a strong, impartial and objective central funding mechanism and a strong field organization.

Economic and Social Council action. By a resolution of 29 July,[9] the Economic and Social Council expressed serious concern at the alarming decline in the rate of growth of UNDP resources, threatening its effectiveness and the full implementation of the Substantial New Programme of Action for the 1980s for the Least Developed Countries.[11] The Council appealed for increased contributions, especially to benefit the least developed countries, and endorsed the Governing Council's invitation to the General Assembly to consider the UNDP financial situation and the need to sustain technical assistance through it.

Under other provisions, the Council welcomed the Governing Council's 1982 decision on establishing an Intersessional Committee of the Whole, sought facilitation of the role of the resident co-ordinator, and reaffirmed the need to reduce overall support costs.

The resolution was adopted without vote, following similar approval by the Third (Programme and Co-ordination) Committee on 28 July. The text was submitted by a Committee Vice-Chairman following informal consultations on a draft introduced by Tunisia on behalf of 19 nations and subsequently withdrawn.[3]

The adopted text added references to the Substantial New Programme of Action, as well as paragraphs: urging all States, particularly donor countries and financial institutions, to make all possible efforts to contribute to the UNDP Special Measures Fund for the Least Developed Countries (LDCs) and Capital Development Fund, and through other channels to benefit LDCs; and welcoming the UNDP decision to promote government execution of projects. Other changes included taking note (rather than endorsing, as in the original text) of the Governing Council's earlier decisions on indicative planning figures, assumed overall growth rate of contributions and the resource level for the 1982-1986 programming cycle; as well as appealing for (rather than urging) increases in contributions.

General Assembly action. The Economic and Social Council resolution of 29 July 1982 (see above) was endorsed by the General Assembly in a resolution of 20 December[10] on the critical financial situation of UNDP. Under other provisions, the Assembly noted with deep concern the result of the 1982 Pledging Conference and its serious consequences for UNDP programme delivery, and expressed appreciation to Governments which had announced contributions or their intention to contribute in amounts at or above an average annual increase of 14 per cent. All other Governments were urged to renew their efforts to provide UNDP with the resources necessary to establish a sound financial basis for its 1982-1986 programming cycle, which, for the purpose of forward planning, would assume a 14 per cent annual growth rate of resources. The Assembly expressed appreciation to the UNDP Administrator for his efforts to obtain the necessary level of resources.

The resolution was adopted without vote, following similar approval by the Second (Economic and Financial) Committee on 13 December. The text was submitted and orally revised by a Vice-Chairman of the Committee following informal consultations on a draft submitted by Bangladesh, for the Group of 77, and subsequently withdrawn.[4]

The adopted text differed from the original draft in the addition of phrases welcoming the establishment of the Intersessional Committee of the Whole, expressing appreciation to Governments which had maintained high-level contributions, and encouraging the Administrator to continue trying to obtain resources, taking into account the need to restrain administrative expenditures in order to maximize programme delivery. Reference to the "negative impact" of the results of the 1982 Pledging Conference on programme delivery was changed to "serious consequences", and a phrase urging Governments to contribute "as early as possible", was removed.

Decisions (1982). UNDP Council (report, E/1982/16/Rev.1), 18 June: [1]82/5, sect. I; [2]82/29, para. 5.
Draft resolutions withdrawn. [3]Algeria, Bahamas, Benin, Canada, China, India, Kenya, Malawi, Mali, Nepal, Nigeria, Norway, Peru, Romania, Saint Lucia, Trinidad and Tobago, Tunisia, Turkey, Yugoslavia, E/1982/C.3/L.8; [4]Bangladesh, for Group of 77, A/C.2/37/L.75.
Reports. UNDP Administrator, [5]DP/1982/5, [6]DP/1982/15, [7]DP/1982/49, [8]DP/1983/6.
Resolutions (1982). [9]ESC: 1982/53, 29 July, text following. [10]GA: 37/227, 20 Dec., text following.
Yearbook reference. [11]1981, p. 406.
Meeting records. ESC: E/1982/SR.50 (29 July). GA: 2nd Committee, A/C.2/37/SR.4, 6, 7, 32-40, *43, 48* (30 Sep.–13 Dec.); plenary, A/37/PV.113 (20 Dec.).

Economic and Social Council resolution 1982/53

29 July 1982   Meeting 50   Adopted without vote

Approved by Third Committee (E/1982/90/Add.1), without vote, 28 July (meeting 17); draft by Vice-Chairman (E/1982/C.3/L.12), based on informal consultations on 19-nation draft, E/1982/C.3/L.8; agenda item 19.

Report of the Governing Council of the United Nations Development Programme

The Economic and Social Council,

Reaffirming the importance of technical co-operation in the United Nations system and the central role of the United Nations Development Programme in its funding and co-ordination,

Reaffirming the basic principles of universality and of the voluntary nature of the Programme, as stated, in particular, in General Assembly resolutions 1240(XIII) of 14 October 1958, 2688(XXV) of 11 December 1970 and 3405(XXX) of 28 November 1975,

Taking note of decision 82/11 of 18 June 1982 of the Governing Council of the United Nations Development Programme on the United Nations Conference on the Least Developed Countries,

Having considered the report of the Governing Council of the United Nations Development Programme for the year 1982,

1. *Takes note* of the report of the Governing Council of the United Nations Development Programme for the year 1982, and of decisions contained in annex I thereto;

2. *Expresses its serious concern* at the alarming decline in the rate of growth of the resources of the United Nations Development

Programme, which threatens its effectiveness with respect to the third programming cycle, 1982-1986, as well as the full implementation of the Substantial New Programme of Action for the 1980s for the Least Developed Countries;

3. *Takes note* of decision 82/5 of 18 June 1982 of the Governing Council of the United Nations Development Programme, by which the Governing Council reaffirmed its decisions 80/30 of 26 June 1980 and 81/16 of 27 June 1981, including, in particular, those provisions relating to the indicative planning figures, the assumed overall average annual rate of growth of voluntary contributions and the level of resources envisaged for the third programming cycle for the purposes of forward planning;

4. *Welcomes* the establishment of an intersessional committee of the whole to study options and recommendations for the longer-term financing of the United Nations Development Programme and for strengthening the effectiveness of the work of the Governing Council;

5. *Appeals* to all Governments, in particular those whose previous contributions may have been below their capacity to pledge, to increase their voluntary contributions, starting with the 1982 United Nations Pledging Conference for Development Activities, so as to achieve an overall average annual rate of growth of 14 per cent for the third programming cycle, as envisaged by the Governing Council in its decision 80/30;

6. *Urges* all States, particularly donor countries, international financial institutions in a position to do so and other multilateral financial institutions to make all possible efforts with a view to contributing substantially and effectively to the Special Measures Fund for the Least Developed Countries of the United Nations Development Programme and to the United Nations Capital Development Fund, as well as through other suitable channels for the benefit of the least developed countries, in order to assist in ensuring the timely and full implementation of the Substantial New Programme of Action;

7. *Endorses* the invitation of the Governing Council of the United Nations Development Programme to the General Assembly to consider, during its thirty-seventh session, the financial situation of the Programme and the need to sustain technical assistance to developing countries through the Programme in the light of the outcome of the 1982 United Nations Pledging Conference for Development Activities;

8. *Welcomes* decision 82/8 of 18 June 1982 of the Governing Council of the United Nations Development Programme, designed to promote government execution of projects assisted by the Programme;

9. *Invites* Governments of recipient countries and urges all organizations of the United Nations system to facilitate the role of the resident co-ordinator in strengthening the co-ordination of all United Nations technical assistance activities in accordance with the consensus of 1970 and in carrying out the tasks assigned to him or her by the General Assembly in its resolutions 32/197 of 20 December 1977, 33/202 of 29 January 1979 and 34/213 of 19 December 1979;

10. *Reaffirms* the need for the United Nations Development Programme and its executing agencies to review their operational support systems, working methods, arrangements and staffing, with a view to bringing about significant reductions in overall support costs, in order to make more resources available to meet the assistance requirements of developing countries.

General Assembly resolution 37/227

20 December 1982   Meeting 113   Adopted without vote

Approved by Second Committee (A/37/774) without vote, 13 December (meeting 48); draft by Vice-Chairman (A/C.2/37/L.124), based on informal consultations on draft by Bangladesh, for Group of 77 (A/C.2/37/L.75); orally revised; agenda item 72 *(b)*.

Critical situation of financial resources of the United Nations Development Programme

The General Assembly,

Recalling its resolutions 3201(S-VI) and 3202(S-VI) of 1 May 1974, containing the Declaration and the Programme of Action on the Establishment of a New International Economic Order, 3281(XXIX) of 12 December 1974, containing the Charter of Economic Rights and Duties of States, and 3362(S-VII) of 16 September 1975 on development and international economic co-operation,

Recalling also its resolution 35/56 of 5 December 1980, the annex to which contains the International Development Strategy for the Third United Nations Development Decade,

Stressing the urgent need to strengthen multilateral co-operation for development, particularly through a substantial increase in the flow of multilateral official development assistance,

Emphasizing the importance of multilateral technical co-operation in the process of economic and social development of developing countries and the urgent need to provide the necessary level of financial resources on an increasingly predictable, continuous and assured basis to enable the United Nations Development Programme to continue its unique and important role in that process,

Reaffirming the validity of the consensus as set forth in the annex to its resolution 2688(XXV) of 11 December 1970,

Having considered the report of the Governing Council of the United Nations Development Programme for the year 1982 and Economic and Social Council resolution 1982/53 of 29 July 1982 on the report of the Governing Council,

Having also considered the critical financial situation of the United Nations Development Programme in the light of the outcome of the 1982 United Nations Pledging Conference for Development Activities and its serious impact on the level of technical assistance to developing countries through the Programme,

Aware that, together with efforts to obtain additional voluntary contributions, steps are being taken to increase further the quality, efficiency and effectiveness of the United Nations Development Programme,

Aware also that the Intersessional Committee of the Whole of the Governing Council of the United Nations Development Programme has undertaken to study, *inter alia*, options and recommendations for strengthening the work of the Governing Council,

1. *Takes note* of the report of the Governing Council of the United Nations Development Programme for the year 1982 and the decisions contained therein;

2. *Endorses* Economic and Social Council resolution 1982/53 of 29 July 1982, in which the Council, *inter alia*, took note of decision 82/5 of 18 June 1982 of the Governing Council of the United Nations Development Programme, by which the Governing Council reaffirmed its decisions 80/30 of 26 June 1980 and 81/16 of 27 June 1981, including, in particular, those provisions relating to the indicative planning figures, the assumed overall average annual rate of growth of voluntary contributions and the level of resources envisaged for the third programming cycle, 1982-1986, for the purposes of forward planning, and welcomes the establishment of an Intersessional Committee of the Whole to study options and recommendations for the longer-term financing of the Programme and for strengthening the effectiveness of the work of the Governing Council;

3. *Notes with deep concern* the result of the 1982 United Nations Pledging Conference for Development Activities and the serious consequences it would have on the proposed programme delivery for the third programming cycle, 1982-1986, of the United Nations Development Programme;

4. *Expresses its appreciation* to all Governments, of both developed and developing countries, which, at the 1982 Pledging Conference, announced contributions or their intention to contribute to the United Nations Development Programme for 1983 in amounts approaching, equalling or exceeding an average annual increase of 14 per cent in their contributions, and to those Governments which have consistently maintained their contributions at a high level;

5. *Urges* all other Governments, especially those whose voluntary contributions may not reflect their capacity to contribute, to renew their efforts to provide the United Nations Development Programme with the resources necessary to establish a sound financial basis for the implementation of its planned activities for the third programming cycle, 1982-1986, which, for the purpose of forward planning, would assume an overall average annual growth of resources of at least 14 per cent;

6. *Expresses its appreciation* to the Administrator of the United Nations Development Programme for his tireless efforts to obtain the necessary level of resources envisaged for the third programming cycle, 1982-1986, in order to secure the financial viability of the Programme and to improve further the quality, efficiency and effectiveness, and encourages the Administrator to continue those efforts, taking into account, *inter alia*, the need to restrain administrative expenditures in order to maximize programme delivery in accordance with paragraph 4 of Governing Council decision 81/16;

7. *Expresses its hope* that the Intersessional Committee of the Whole of the Governing Council of the United Nations Development Programme, in accordance with its mandate as set out in decision 82/5, will succeed in identifying measures, in accordance with the principles and objectives as reflected in the consensus, as set forth in the annex to General Assembly resolution 2688(XXV), that would enable the implementation of the Programme's planned activities for the third programming cycle, 1982-1986, and beyond.

Expenditures

Expenditures of UNDP for 1982 reflected resource constraints. Total main field-programme expenditures amounted to $660.6 million (see table below), a 10 per cent reduction compared to the $731.6 million expended on projects and programmes in 1981. Of the 1982 total, indicative planning figure (IPF) expenditures were $567.8 million (exclusive of cost sharing), of which $463.4 million was expended on country programmes, $79.1 million on regional programmes, $9.3 million on interregional programmes and $16.1 million on the global programme. Expenditures were down in virtually every project-cost category except cost sharing.

Total UNDP expenditures for the year, including overhead costs, were $859.1 million, compared with $973.5 million in 1981. Excess of expenditure over income was $66.4 million, resulting in a balance of the UNDP revenue reserve of $5.6 million as at 31 December 1982 (down from $71.1 million a year earlier). The expenditure of $13.9 million more than forecast occurred mostly in expenditures related to main field programme and cost sharing.

The number of project personnel recruited by Governments and agencies for service on UNDP-supported projects declined from 9,863 in 1981 to 9,081 in 1982. The value of equipment ordered for projects fell from $141.2 million to $138 million, while the value of subcontracts awarded rose slightly from $81.7 million to $84.2 million. A total of 10,765 developing-country nationals received training abroad under UNDP-financed projects, compared with 11,443 in 1981.

From the provisional 1982-1983 budget, 323 posts were eliminated. Agency support costs (14 per cent of project costs during 1972-1981) were reduced to 13 per cent. New partnership arrangements with the World Bank and other key executing agencies helped enhance Programme efficiency, and closer co-ordination with non-governmental organizations and UNDP had their impact.

Other measures to cut costs included elimination of overlapping functions, simplified audit and field office procedures, and administrative management reform with emphasis in 1982 on personnel and staff security arrangements.

Information on the financial situation of UNDP in 1982 was provided to the UNDP Governing Council in the annual report of the Administrator for 1982[1] and in his annual financial review.[2]

UNDP EXPENDITURES, 1982
(in US dollars)

UNDP Account:

Programme expenditure:

Project costs:

Indicative planning figures	567,830,918
From government cost-sharing contributions	62,204,691
Special Measures Fund for the Least Developed Countries	13,808,240
From government cash-counterpart contributions	8,623,224
Special Programme Resources	5,033,574
Special Industrial Services	3,081,000
Subtotal project costs	660,581,647
Reimbursement of programme support costs to participating and executing agencies	85,057,407
UNDP sectoral support	5,539,250
Expert hiatus financing and extended sick leave	1,832,144
Adjustments to 1981 programme expenditure and programme support costs (net)	(980,911)
Subtotal programme expenditure	91,447,890
UNDP biennial budget expenditure	104,093,465
UNDP extrabudgetary expenditure	2,970,323
Total UNDP Account	859,093,325

Trust funds:

UN Capital Development Fund	36,152,934
UN Financing System for Science and Technology for Development*	13,460,249
UN Trust Fund for Sudano-Sahelian Activities	11,017,302
UN Revolving Fund for Natural Resources Exploration	7,594,498
UNDP Energy Account	1,897,187
UN Volunteers	1,820,693
UNDP Trust Fund for the Nationhood Programme for Namibia	1,685,841
UNDP Trust Fund for Projects financed by the Voluntary Fund for the UN Decade for Women	1,565,836
UN Trust Fund for Operational Programme in Lesotho	688,958
Trust Fund for Technical Assistance to World Bank Project in Jamaica	176,257
Trust Fund for the Training in the USSR of Specialists from Developing Countries	150,711
UN Trust Fund for Provision of Operational Personnel in Swaziland	107,158
UN Special Fund for Land-locked Developing Countries	49,033
Trust Fund for Assistance to Colonial Countries and Peoples	33,115
UN Korean Reconstruction Agency (residual assets)	3,165
Trust Fund for Children's Famine Relief in Uganda	670
Total trust funds	76,403,607
Junior Professional Officers' Programme	7,405,303
GRAND TOTAL	942,902,235

*Includes two sub-trust funds established by the Administrator: Special Purpose Contribution Agreements with Federal Republic of Germany ($2,064,300) and Goodwill Mission ($51,901).
SOURCE: A/38/5/Add.1.

Reports. UNDP Administrator, [1]DP/1983/6/Add.1, [2]DP/1983/43.

Administrative budgets

Programme support and administrative services costs constitute the UNDP administrative budget, adopted biennially.

Budget for 1980-1981

On 18 June 1982,[1] the UNDP Governing Council took note of the report[2] of the Administrator on programme support and administrative service expenditures 1980-1981. That report, submitted in April 1982, listed the expenditures as $196.2 million (net) against approved appropriations of $199.4 million. The main reasons for the $3.2 million under-expenditure were currency movements, lower inflationary increases, and a higher staff vacancy rate than that forecast in the budget estimates, offset by a shortfall in income caused by the change to a cash basis in the accounting for Government contributions towards local office costs.

Decision (1982). [1]UNDP Council (report, E/1982/16/Rev.1): 82/43, para. *(i)*, 18 June.
Report. [2]UNDP Administrator, DP/1982/51.

Revised budget for 1982-1983

On 18 June 1982,[1] the UNDP Governing Council approved revised appropriations covering the administrative costs of the main Programme and of five other activities managed by UNDP: the United Nations Volunteers, the United Nations Capital Development Fund (UNCDF), the United Nations Revolving Fund for Natural Resources Exploration (UNRFNRE), the United Nations Sudano-Sahelian Office (UNSO) and the joint venture organized by UNSO, UNDP and the United Nations Environment Programme (see Chapter XVI of this section).

The Council approved revised net appropriations of $252,544,000, $10,115,100 less than it had originally approved in June 1981.[3] Included in the main Programme allocation of $241,854,200 was $2.5 million authorized for use during the biennium for measures related to staff separation costs. The Administrator was asked to report on his use of this authority, and was authorized to exceed the approved appropriations for the Office for Project Execution (OPE)—the unit responsible for executing projects carried out directly by UNDP—to be offset by increased support-cost income, but OPE expenditures were limited to 13 per cent of its total project delivery.

The figures were based on revised budget estimates presented by the Administrator in April 1982,[2] which had been calculated on the assumption that UNDP would have 323 fewer posts effective 1 January 1982.

Expenditures under this budget in 1982 came to $107.1 million.

Decision. [1]UNDP Council (report, E/1982/16/Rev.1): 82/31, 18 June.
Report. [2]UNDP Administrator, DP/1982/53.
Yearbook reference. [3]1981, p. 448.

Support costs

Agency support costs reimbursed by UNDP in 1982 decreased by $9.1 million to $85.1 million, down from $94.2 million in 1981.

From 1982 onward, revised support-cost flexibility arrangements—to permit higher reimbursement rates to agencies executing a relatively small volume of UNDP projects—applied, as approved by the UNDP Governing Council in June 1981.[13] These arrangements consisted of sliding maximum rates from 22 per cent to 14 per cent established at particular levels of delivery up to a level of

UNDP ADMINISTRATIVE BUDGET, 1982-1983
(in US dollars; as adopted on 18 June 1982)

PROGRAMME	Gross appropriations	Estimated income	Net appropriations
Resources of UNDP			
UNDP core activities	287,791,400	54,430,500	233,360,900
Transitory measures	2,500,000	–	2,500,000
OPE and Inter-Agency Procurement Services Unit	14,401,800	14,401,800*	–
UN Volunteers	5,925,900	858,100	5,067,800
UNSO-UNDP/UNEP joint venture (institutional support)	2,395,300	1,469,800†	925,500
Subtotal UNDP	313,014,400	71,160,200	241,854,200
Resources of UNCDF	4,990,200	540,900	4,449,300
Resources of UNRFNRE	3,514,400	309,100	3,205,300
Resources of UNSO	3,447,300	412,100	3,035,200
Total	324,966,300	72,422,300	252,544,000

*Includes *(i)* reimbursement of $1.6 million for the Inter-Agency Procurement Services Unit from the agency support-costs provision within the general resources of UNDP, and *(ii)* estimated support-cost reimbursements to OPE of $7.7 million in respect of UNDP-funded activities; $1.7 million in respect of UNCDF-funded activities and $1.9 million in respect of UNSO-funded activities. The balance of income of $1.5 million relates to staff assessment.

†Includes UNEP half-share of the cost of the joint venture institutional support
SOURCE: E/1982/16/Rev.1.

$15 million. Guidelines on arrangements were issued in January 1982.

On the basis of detailed support-cost forecasts submitted by the agencies for 1982, the UNDP Administrator initially authorized the amounts requested by five agencies—the International Atomic Energy Agency (IAEA), the International Maritime Organization (IMO), the Universal Postal Union (UPU), the World Intellectual Property Organization (WIPO) and the World Meteorological Organization (WMO)—for support-cost flexibility, subject to calculation of final costs. Total actual delivery was, however, 1.3 per cent below the agencies' delivery forecasts, down from $26,050,000 to $25,709,000. Reimbursements under the standard 13 per cent rate decreased accordingly from $3,386,500 to $3,375,300.

Governing Council action. On 18 June 1982, the Governing Council decided[3] that only agencies providing reasonably documented evidence of support costs incurred in respect of the UNDP-financed programme were to benefit from the flexibility arrangements. The Council agreed with a proposal by the Administrator to study provision of more precise calculations of support costs for the United Nations Sudano-Sahelian Office (UNSO), and requested him to continue consulting the agencies with a view to reaching an agreed level of support-cost reimbursements for activities financed by UNSO and the United Nations Capital Development Fund (UNCDF), and to report thereon in 1983.

By another decision of the same date,[2] the Council reaffirmed that the support-cost reimbursement arrangements, which it had decided on in 1980,[12] should also apply to technical co-operation activities financed from all other extrabudgetary resources, including trust funds or similar funds.

The Council's decisions were based on three reports submitted by the Administrator in April 1982. The first[7] contained the results of a UNDP study to determine support-cost rates associated with delivery by OPE of capital assistance and technical co-operation projects financed from UNCDF, UNSO and indicative planning figure (IPF) resources, and other UNDP main resources. The Administrator concluded that the study of OPE support costs indicated that support cost rates for IPF- and UNCDF-funded projects were approximately 11 and 5 per cent, respectively. In view of substantial disagreement between UNDP and agencies on the results of the study, however, the Administrator stated that he would prefer to undertake a further study to confirm the validity of his findings. The Governing Council, on 18 June,[3] agreed to this proposal. With regard to UNSO-financed projects, the Administrator requested an appropriation from UNSO resources, which was the estimated cost of OPE support relating to execution of UNSO-financed projects in 1982-1983. For other agencies executing UNSO- and UNCDF-financed projects, he proposed to continue the current support-cost arrangements pending a definite conclusion on the rates to be applied.

In a second report,[9] the Administrator drew attention to reimbursements made in 1980 and 1981 under the support-cost flexibility arrangements which had gone into effect in January 1982, annexing revised guidelines to be used in reviewing agencies' requests for flexibility.

The third report[8] informed the Council of action taken and the progress made on a common format for *ex post facto* reports on agency support costs, developed in consultations between UNDP and executing agencies and reviewed by the Consultative Committee on Administrative Questions of the Administrative Committee on Co-ordination in March 1982. The Administrator recommended that the Council take note of the consultations, approve the agreed format and endorse the proposal that agencies with annual budgets submit their first report to the Council in June 1983, and those with biennial budgets, in 1984.

On 18 June,[3] the Council welcomed the arrangements between UNDP and the executing agencies for the submission of *ex post facto* reports on support costs.

Economic and Social Council action. By a resolution of 29 July,[10] the Economic and Social Council reaffirmed the need for UNDP and its executing agencies to review their operational support systems, working methods, arrangements and staffing, with a view to significantly reducing overall support costs, in order to make more resources available for assistance to developing countries. The last half of this provision was changed after the original draft submitted in the Council's Third (Programme and Co-ordination) Committee by

19 sponsors[5] was amended and withdrawn in favour of a text produced in consultations.[6] The original draft had said "with a view to increasing the proportion of resources available to meet the assistance requirements of developing countries".

General Assembly action. In its resolution of 20 December on operational activities for development,[11] the General Assembly requested United Nations organs and bodies receiving extrabudgetary resources, such as support-cost payments, to include information on these resources and their utilization in the reports to their governing bodies, and invited them to examine that information. This provision was not included in the original draft submitted by Bangladesh for the Group of 77.[4]

Other action. The Commission on Human Settlements, by a decision,[1] noted that the United Nations Centre for Human Settlements (Habitat), being considered part of the United Nations for reimbursement of agency overheads, was not eligible for the support-cost flexibility arrangement of UNDP, under which the Centre, based on its delivery volume, would have been entitled to the reimbursement of actual support costs or a minimum of 16 per cent of agency overheads, instead of the 13 per cent received.

Decisions (1982). [1]Commission on Human Settlements (report, A/37/8): 5/23, 7 May. UNDP Council (report, E/1982/16/Rev.1), 18 June: [2]82/5, sect. IV, para. 2; [3]82/36.
Draft resolutions withdrawn. [4]Bangladesh, for Group of 77, A/C.2/37/L.92; [5]E/1982/C.3/L.8; [6]E/1982/C.3/L.12.
Reports. UNDP Administrator, [7]DP/1982/58, [8]DP/1982/59, [9]DP/1982/93.
Resolutions. [10]ESC: 1982/53, para. 10, 29 July; [11]GA: 37/226, para. 19, 20 Dec.
Yearbook references. [12]1980, p. 592; [13]1981, p. 449.

Reimbursement for support services by field offices

In April, the UNDP Administrator reported[2] that an average 33.8 per cent of UNDP field office staff time was spent on activities on behalf of other United Nations organizations; of this percentage, nearly a third was devoted to activities unrelated to projects financed or administered by UNDP. Where possible, UNDP had negotiated with executing agencies and host Governments to obtain payment for such services.

By a decision of 18 June,[1] the Governing Council authorized the Administrator to continue providing, at the current levels, services which were in accordance with UNDP aims and responsibilities and were currently provided without charge. It also authorized him to make arrangements to meet agencies' needs where they required field offices to perform additional tasks or to assume significantly increased workloads requiring further resources.

Decision (1982). [1]UNDP Council (report, E/1982/16/Rev.1): 82/33, 18 June.
Report. [2]UNDP Administrator, DP/1982/52.

Sectoral support activities

In 1982, UNDP allocated $2.042 million to 12 executing agencies for sectoral support activities—principally regional advisers and short-term missions of experts—designed to complement similar activities by the agencies from their own resources. This was in addition to $3.852 million for the largest programme of this type, Senior Industrial Development Field Advisers (SIDFAs), managed by the United Nations Industrial Development Organization (UNIDO). The original tentative allocation approved by the UNDP Governing Council was $37.5 million for the third (1982-1986) programming cycle, and $15 million for the 1982-1983 biennium.

In accordance with its 1980 decision to apply a flat across-the-board reduction if resources fell short of target, the Governing Council in June 1981[3] reduced the $15 million to 80 per cent, i.e. $12 million.

In an April 1982 report,[2] the UNDP Administrator stated that the resource outlook necessitated a further reduction, to $10,297,000, of which $7,105,000 would be available for the SIDFA programme and $3,192,000 for sectoral support for agencies other than UNIDO. Of the latter amount, $2,042,000 was for 1982 activities and the remainder for 1983. As sectoral support was intended primarily for the smaller agencies, the International Labour Organisation (ILO) and the United Nations Educational, Scientific and Cultural Organization (UNESCO) were apprised that, starting in 1983, such costs would have to be met entirely from their own resources; for 1982, they were allocated small amounts.

By a decision of 18 June 1982,[1] the Governing Council endorsed the Administrator's proposed allocation for 1982, decided to provide sectoral support financing in the future primarily to the smaller agencies, reaffirmed that the sectoral support programme should be subject to the same across-the-board percentage reductions as those in the indicative planning figures of all countries, and requested the Administrator to maintain the programme within UNDP overall finances. The Council decided to review progress in the matter in 1983.

Other provisions of the decision dealt with the SIDFA services (see Chapter VI of this section).

Decision (1982). [1]UNDP Council (report, E/1982/16/Rev.1): 82/38, paras. 1-4 & 8, 18 June.
Note. [2]UNDP Administrator, DP/1982/61.
Yearbook reference. [3]1981, p. 450.

Contributions

Total income of UNDP for 1982 amounted to $792.7 million. Income from voluntary contributions totalled $679.7 million compared with $688.7 million in 1981, a 1 per cent decline. Income from

(continued on p. 654)

CONTRIBUTIONS TO UNDP, 1982 AND 1983
(as at 31 December 1982; in US dollar equivalent)

CONTRIBUTOR	1982 PAYMENT						1983 PLEDGE		
	UNDP Account*	Fund for LDCs	Government cost-sharing	Government cash counterpart	Assessed programme costs	Total	UNDP Account	Fund for LDCs	Total
Afghanistan	33,000	—	—	—	—	33,000	33,000	—	33,000
Albania	5,000	—	—	—	—	5,000	5,000	—	5,000
Algeria	694,622	—	3,704,297	470,159	—	4,869,078	834,000	—	834,000
Angola	33,761	—	—	—	—	33,761	—	—	—
Argentina	2,023,305	—	270,591	—	—	2,293,896	—	—	—
Australia	14,631,685	—	404,370	—	—	15,036,055	—	—	—
Austria	6,000,000	—	—	—	—	6,000,000	6,800,000	—	6,800,000
Bahamas	—	—	435,587	—	—	435,587	—	—	—
Bahrain	56,000	—	1,841,569	—	—	1,897,569	56,000	—	56,000
Bangladesh	179,335	—	—	—	—	179,335	183,900	—	183,900
Barbados	36,838	—	—	2,047	—	38,885	25,781	—	25,781
Belgium	—	—	—	—	—	—	12,244,898	—	12,244,898
Belize	16,000	—	1,263	4,074	—	21,337	30,303	—	30,303
Benin	—	—	—	—	—	—	5,000	2,000	7,000
Bermuda	14,320	—	50,000	—	—	64,320	—	—	—
Bhutan	—	—	—	—	—	—	2,920	1,200	4,120
Bolivia	—	—	695,541	139,026	—	834,567	20,000	—	20,000
Botswana	17,283	—	1,539,010	—	—	1,556,293	17,156	—	17,156
Brazil	1,784,318	—	4,780,905	221,172	—	6,786,395	2,503,394	—	2,503,394
British Virgin Islands	33,800	—	60,000	—	—	93,800	7,000	—	7,000
Bulgaria	850,939	—	—	—	—	850,939	892,018	—	892,018
Burma	761,129	—	—	—	—	761,129	114,650	—	114,650
Burundi	—	—	—	—	—	—	11,167	3,350	14,517
Byelorussian SSR	189,341	—	—	—	—	189,341	184,426	—	184,426
Canada	41,819,526	—	848,849	—	—	42,668,375	—	—	—
Cayman Islands	8,640	—	66,540	—	—	75,180	—	—	—
Chile	820,000	—	263,612	15,739	—	1,099,351	820,000	—	820,000
China	1,500,000	—	—	—	—	1,500,000	1,650,000	—	1,650,000
Colombia	575,009	—	1,801,139	244,317	—	2,620,465	1,331,916	—	1,331,916
Congo	—	—	1,166,415	—	—	1,166,415	8,000	—	8,000
Cook Islands	1,473	—	48,613	—	—	50,086	—	—	—
Costa Rica	38,607	—	6,491	—	—	45,098	—	—	—
Cuba	686,599	—	—	—	—	686,599	736,145	—	736,145
Cyprus	127,500	—	—	—	—	127,500	149,500	—	149,500
Czechoslovakia	602,503	—	59,900	—	—	662,403	587,621	—	587,621
Democratic People's Republic of Korea	198,020	—	—	—	—	198,020	185,185	—	185,185
Democratic Yemen	7,606	—	—	—	—	7,606	8,987	—	8,987
Denmark	39,284,946	1,744,186	—	—	—	41,029,132	37,485,714	—	37,485,714
Djibouti	2,000	—	100,000	9,650	—	111,650	2,000	—	2,000
Dominica	55,440	—	—	—	—	55,440	37,037	—	37,037
Dominican Republic	—	—	125,976	18,000	—	143,976	—	—	—
Ecuador	333,169	—	1,004,875	62,240	—	1,400,284	686,997	—	686,997
Egypt	605,850	—	592,015	959,284	—	2,157,149	691,979	21,166	713,145
El Salvador	52,350	—	164,295	—	—	216,645	305,000	—	305,000
Ethiopia	290,949	—	—	—	—	290,949	144,928	—	144,928
Fiji	50,000	—	—	—	—	50,000	50,000	—	50,000
Finland	7,663,237	—	100,850	—	—	7,764,087	7,945,455	545,455	8,490,910
France	25,696,078	—	—	—	—	25,696,078	27,635,037	1,459,854	29,094,891
Gabon	262,570	—	2,084,527	—	—	2,347,097	—	—	—
Gambia	14,614	—	—	—	—	14,614	—	—	—
German Democratic Republic	851,486	—	—	—	—	851,486	400,000	—	400,000
Germany, Federal Republic of	46,380,785	—	490,226	—	—	46,871,011	—	—	—
Ghana	200,000	—	—	97,000	—	297,000	—	—	—
Greece	943,954	—	5,160	—	—	949,114	910,000	—	910,000
Grenada	23,918	—	—	—	—	23,918	—	—	—
Guatemala	189,000	—	776,491	66,000	—	1,031,491	189,000	—	189,000

	1982 PAYMENT						1983 PLEDGE		
CONTRIBUTOR	UNDP Account*	Fund for LDCs	Government cost-sharing	Government cash counterpart	Assessed programme costs	Total	UNDP Account	Fund for LDCs	Total
Guinea	6,519	—	114,000	—	—	120,519	—	—	—
Guyana	264,840	—	—	—	—	264,840	200,000	—	200,000
Haiti	—	—	187,950	—	—	187,950	—	—	—
Holy See	2,000	—	—	—	—	2,000	2,000	—	2,000
Honduras	56,955	—	1,926,328	150,000	—	2,133,283	43,500	—	43,500
Hong Kong	25,414	—	—	—	—	25,414	25,000	—	25,000
Hungary	714,163	—	—	—	—	714,163	696,809	—	696,809
Iceland	455,696	—	—	—	—	455,696	—	—	—
India	7,650,273	—	756,200	24,331	—	8,430,804	7,399,577	—	7,399,577
Indonesia	1,000,000	—	1,802,000	20,000	—	2,822,000	1,100,000	—	1,100,000
Iraq	—	—	33,744	—	—	33,744	—	—	—
Ireland	951,165	—	—	—	—	951,165	—	—	—
Israel	—	—	—	—	—	—	69,009	—	69,009
Italy	23,239,437	—	1,308,231	—	—	24,547,668	25,665,529	—	25,665,529
Ivory Coast	68,182	—	83,948	—	—	152,130	—	—	—
Jamaica	77,742	—	176,998	4,064	—	258,804	88,626	—	88,626
Japan	47,308,000	—	200,000	—	—	47,508,000	—	—	—
Jordan	240,000	—	140,056	—	—	380,056	—	—	—
Kenya	171,443	—	186,916	280,374	—	638,733	59,524	—	59,524
Kiribati	16,860	—	—	—	—	16,860	—	—	—
Kuwait	570,000	—	5,500,738	—	—	6,070,738	—	—	—
Lao People's Democratic Republic	24,340	—	—	800	—	25,140	19,600	—	19,600
Lebanon	—	—	206,815	46,236	—	253,051	360,000	—	360,000
Lesotho	38,916	—	—	—	—	38,916	45,000	—	45,000
Liberia	—	—	—	27,500	—	27,500	—	—	—
Libyan Arab Jamahiriya	—	—	3,308,002	—	—	3,308,002	—	—	—
Luxembourg	86,860	—	—	—	—	86,860	76,224	—	76,224
Madagascar	71,974	—	—	—	—	71,974	—	—	—
Malawi	21,534	1,743	—	—	—	23,277	33,338	—	33,338
Malaysia	385,000	—	—	—	—	385,000	385,000	—	385,000
Maldives	1,800	—	—	—	—	1,800	1,800	—	1,800
Malta	67,257	—	—	—	—	67,257	—	—	—
Mauritius	61,186	—	—	—	—	61,186	—	—	—
Mexico	1,815,135	—	405,382	—	—	2,220,517	2,008,572	—	2,008,572
Monaco	3,795	—	—	—	—	3,795	3,796	—	3,796
Mongolia	185,733	—	—	—	—	185,733	179,205	—	179,205
Montserrat	10,741	—	—	—	—	10,741	—	—	—
Morocco	265,833	—	188,744	328,125	—	782,702	249,219	—	249,219
Mozambique	45,074	—	—	—	—	45,074	50,000	—	50,000
Nepal	46,000	—	—	—	—	46,000	—	—	—
Netherlands	67,874,631	—	1,922,915	—	—	69,797,546	6,363,636	—	6,363,636
Netherlands Antilles	—	—	862,495	—	—	862,495	—	—	—
New Zealand	1,074,074	—	—	—	—	1,074,074	1,074,074	—	1,074,074
Nicaragua	20,400	—	53,558	—	—	73,958	—	—	—
Nigeria	36,186	—	999,223	—	—	1,035,409	—	—	—
Niue	—	—	—	—	—	—	5,000	—	5,000
Norway	55,061,935	4,833,108	36,000	—	—	59,931,043	51,408,451	2,816,901	54,225,352
Oman	75,000	—	2,155,346	—	—	2,230,346	75,000	—	75,000
Pakistan	1,957,751	—	—	2,290,504	—	4,248,255	1,936,000	—	1,936,000
Panama	620,000	—	1,178,559	50,568	—	1,849,127	389,040	—	389,040
Papua New Guinea	151,918	—	83,390	204,714	—	440,022	59,868	—	59,868
Paraguay	—	—	255,091	(29,585)	—	225,506	30,000	—	30,000
Peru	947,484	—	896,487	—	—	1,843,971	725,647	—	725,647
Philippines	918,439	—	—	10,000	—	928,439	700,000	—	700,000
Poland	518,792	—	—	—	—	518,792	566,465	—	566,465
Portugal	173,333	—	383,017	10,000	—	566,350	95,000	—	95,000
Qatar	200,000	—	663,611	—	—	863,611	200,000	—	200,000
Republic of Korea	893,000	—	17,500	76,822	—	987,322	893,000	—	893,000
Romania	673,560	—	—	—	—	673,560	640,909	—	640,909
Rwanda	—	—	1,292	—	—	1,292	10,000	—	10,000
St. Kitts–Nevis–Anguilla	18,460	—	—	6,096	—	24,556	—	—	—

	1982 PAYMENT						1983 PLEDGE		
CONTRIBUTOR	UNDP Account*	Fund for LDCs	Government cost-sharing	Government cash counterpart	Assessed programme costs	Total	UNDP Account	Fund for LDCs	Total
St. Lucia	9,231	—	—	—	—	9,231	1,000	—	1,000
Saint Vincent and the Grenadines	13,680	—	—	—	—	13,680	15,595	—	15,595
Samoa	—	—	—	—	—	—	7,937	—	7,937
Saudi Arabia	2,500,000	—	3,033,876	439,799	—	5,973,675	2,500,000	—	2,500,000
Senegal	(2,165)	—	—	—	—	(2,165)	100,000	—	100,000
Sierra Leone	4,059	—	—	—	—	4,059	79,365	—	79,365
Singapore	220,000	—	—	—	—	220,000	220,000	—	220,000
Solomon Islands	1,000	—	—	—	—	1,000	—	—	—
Somalia	2,326	—	—	312,815	—	315,141	—	—	—
Spain	1,611,740	—	—	—	—	1,611,740	1,417,864	—	1,417,864
Sri Lanka	563,981	—	—	3,778	—	567,759	752,400	—	752,400
Sudan	—	—	274,190	—	—	274,190	200,000	—	200,000
Suriname	—	—	157,000	—	—	157,000	82,500	—	82,500
Swaziland	22,704	—	299,943	—	—	322,647	—	—	—
Sweden	53,143,594	7,485,013	—	—	—	60,628,607	48,648,649	6,756,757	55,405,406
Switzerland	17,688,172	2,365,591	381,417	—	—	20,435,180	16,995,305	2,272,300	19,267,605
Syrian Arab Republic	—	—	—	300,000	—	300,000	—	—	—
Thailand	1,001,030	—	—	5,009	—	1,006,039	1,001,030	—	1,001,030
Togo	151,572	—	39,652	86,135	—	277,359	297,959	—	297,959
Tokelau	16,093	—	—	—	—	16,093	4,000	—	4,000
Trinidad and Tobago	166,667	—	1,727,725	—	—	1,894,392	166,667	—	166,667
Tunisia	218,612	—	310,873	3,323	277,008	809,816	426,164	—	426,164
Turkey	1,095,761	—	945,564	47,073	—	2,088,398	1,150,765	—	1,150,765
Turks and Caicos Islands	17,400	—	—	—	—	17,400	—	—	—
Uganda	—	—	259,649	—	—	259,649	12,097	—	12,097
Ukrainian SSR	473,352	—	—	—	—	473,352	461,066	—	461,066
USSR	2,103,787	—	—	—	—	2,103,787	3,688,525	—	3,688,525
United Arab Emirates	—	—	3,513,808	—	—	3,513,808	—	—	—
United Kingdom	32,587,383	—	—	—	—	32,587,383	—	—	—
United Republic of Cameroon	—	—	659,497	3,030	—	662,527	270,633	—	270,633
United Republic of Tanzania	104,603	—	1,803,223	—	—	1,907,826	104,603	—	104,603
United States	147,102,278	—	1,311,292	—	—	148,413,570	—	—	—
Upper Volta	—	—	—	91,794	—	91,794	—	—	—
Uruguay	—	—	1,020,920	171,295	—	1,192,215	—	—	—
Vanuatu	—	—	11,860	—	—	11,860	—	—	—
Venezuela	2,200,000	—	2,421,932	—	—	4,621,932	—	—	—
Viet Nam	10,000	—	—	—	—	10,000	10,000	—	10,000
Yemen	10,000	—	2,743,641	859,411	—	3,613,052	11,500	—	11,500
Yugoslavia	2,138,405	—	—	—	—	2,138,405	—	—	—
Zambia	627,515	—	—	—	—	627,515	260,022	—	260,022
Zimbabwe	50,000	—	—	—	—	50,000	97,614	—	97,614
Arab Gulf Programme for United Nations Development and Organizations	—	—	1,847,965	—	—	1,847,965	—	—	—
Caribbean Development Bank	—	—	58,000	—	—	58,000	—	—	—
Central African Development Bank	—	—	249,041	—	—	249,041	—	—	—
Inter-American Development Bank	—	—	400,000	—	—	400,000	—	—	—
Latin American Association for Integration	—	—	126,500	—	—	126,500	—	—	—
OPEC Special Fund	—	—	2,101,865	—	—	2,101,865	—	—	—
United Nations Centre for Human Settlements (HABITAT)	—	—	83,950	—	—	83,950	—	—	—
United Nations Environment Programme	—	—	14,204	—	—	14,204	—	—	—
West African Development Bank	—	—	(206,586)	—	—	(206,586)	—	—	—
World Bank	—	—	216,000	—	—	216,000	—	—	—
Total	679,664,115	16,429,641	75,330,644	8,132,719	277,008	779,834,127	288,847,792	13,878,983	302,726,775

*Includes only those pledges made at the 1982 UN Pledging Conference for Development Activities.

SOURCE: A/38/5/Add.1.

assessed programme costs was $277,000; from cost sharing, $75.3 million; from miscellaneous sources, including interest earned, $12.1 million; and from other contributions, $25.3 million, of which $16.4 million represented contributions to the UNDP Special Measures Fund for Least Developed Countries (see table above).

By a decision of 18 June 1982,[2] the UNDP Governing Council called on Governments to increase their contributions, taking into consideration the need for a more equitable distribution of contributions. Expressing deep concern at the lagging pace of payment, the Council strongly reiterated its call for payment as early as possible during the year, and called on Governments to provide a proposed payment plan and to pay without delay all amounts due.

In another decision of the same date,[1] the Council appealed particularly to countries whose contributions might have been below their capacity, to step them up starting with the 1982 United Nations Pledging Conference for Development Activities, so as to achieve an overall annual growth rate of 14 per cent for the 1982-1986 programming cycle.

Reiterating the Governing Council's appeal, the Economic and Social Council, in a resolution of 29 July 1982,[4] added a new provision to the text following consultations in Committee, by which it urged donor countries and financial institutions to contribute substantially to the Special Measures Fund and other channels for the benefit of the least developed countries.

A draft resolution on United Nations development activities submitted by Bangladesh for the Group of 77 to the General Assembly's Second (Economic and Financial) Committee[3] and later withdrawn, would have had the Assembly strongly urge the UNDP Intersessional Committee of the Whole (see below) to formulate measures to enable Governments to increase their contributions to UNDP (a provision not included in the resolution adopted by the Assembly[5]).

Decisions (1982). UNDP Council (report, E/1982/16/Rev.1), 18 June: [1]82/5, sect. I, para. 3; [2]82/29, paras. 1-4.
Draft resolution withdrawn. [3]Bangladesh, for Group of 77, A/C.2/37/L.92.
Resolutions (1982). [4]ESC: 1982/53, paras. 5 & 6, 29 July; [5]GA: 37/226, 20 Dec.

Contributions by the host country to field offices

In view of declining host government contributions for local costs of UNDP field offices (from 20.2 per cent of total UNDP field office costs in 1977 to 10.5 per cent by the end of 1981), the UNDP Administrator, in an April 1982 report to the UNDP Governing Council,[2] outlined elements relevant to formulating practical guidelines, on the basis of which he could undertake consultations with host Governments in order to obtain increased contributions. His approach called for a clearer identification of the nature and genesis of field office costs, a review of the level of host government contributions to these costs, and identification of priorities.

Taking note that, notwithstanding the Administrator's appeals, the majority of Governments had not contributed as agreed on, the Council, by a decision of 18 June,[1] authorized the Administrator to negotiate further with Governments to agree on the amounts and modalities of their contributions, and to waive in part the contribution towards local office costs when the economic conditions of the countries concerned warranted.

Decision (1982). [1]UNDP Council (report, E/1982/16/Rev.1): 82/18, 18 June.
Report. [2]UNDP Administrator, DP/1982/21/Add.1,3.

Cost sharing

In his 1982 annual report,[4] the UNDP Administrator indicated a significant increase in the level of cost-sharing activities, particularly in view of the decrease of UNDP resources from voluntary contributions. First introduced in 1973, cost-sharing contributions were a means of expanding the financial resources that could be made available to developing countries through UNDP. They were mainly made by recipient countries to their own specific projects or to the totality of their country programme, but also by third parties.

From 1981 to 1982, cost-sharing expenditures rose by almost 23 per cent. By the end of 1982, main field programme expenditures under government and third-party cost-sharing arrangements had advanced to $62.2 million (exclusive of support costs), or 9.4 per cent of all field expenditures. Of the 1982 total, developing countries themselves provided $44.4 million to projects, and $9.6 million to general programme support activities. Third-party donors provided $8.2 million of the total.

Of the $513.9 million in project approvals in 1982, $58.6 million was being provided under cost-sharing arrangements.

Income from cost-sharing contributions increased to $75.3 million in 1982, up from $62.7 million in 1981. Of the 1982 total, $50.9 million was contributed as project cost sharing, $12.5 million as programme cost sharing and $11.9 million as third-party cost sharing.

In an April report on new ways of financing and providing development assistance through UNDP,[3] the Administrator said that current cost-sharing procedures required that all contributions be paid annually in advance of project implementation and that payment delays were covered by the indicative planning figure (IPF) concerned. The greater the extent of cost-sharing activities, the more difficult it might be for IPFs to absorb such costs, and the more important it was to observe payment requirements strictly. Where such activities exceeded 50 per cent of the IPF, he suggested that UNDP require financial guarantees that projects be funded on a timely basis.

The Governing Council decided[1] on 18 June 1982 to remove the ceilings on cost sharing for activities financed by recipient countries, and, for third-party cost sharing, to maintain the ceiling at 150 per cent of the IPF or $15 million, whichever was larger. By another decision of the same date,[2] the Council took note of the Administrator's intention to make available to cost-sharing programmes the interest earned on cost-sharing balances to finance non-core support costs relating to those programmes.

Decision (1982). UNDP Council (report, E/1982/16/Rev.1), 18 June: [1]82/5, sect. IV, para. 1; [2]82/18, para. 3.
Reports. UNDP Administrator, [3]DP/1982/35 & Corr.1, [4]DP/1983/6/Add.1.

Trust funds

During 1982, the Administrator established five trust funds, three on behalf of UNDP, one for the United Nations Capital Development Fund (UNCDF) and one on behalf of the United Nations Financing System for Science and Technology for Development; none was conditioned on procurement from the donor countries. The value of the five trust funds was about $6.5 million, donated by several Governments and non-governmental organizations. The authority to accept trust funds for specific purposes had been given to the Administrator in revised financial regulations adopted in 1981,[9] as another way of channelling resources through UNDP. (Information on the trust funds established in 1982 was contained in an April 1983 report of the Administrator.[6])

In a report of April 1982 on new ways of financing and providing development assistance through UNDP,[4] the Administrator stated that the channelling of trust fund monies through UNDP allowed UNDP to co-ordinate the funded projects with the country programme and other United Nations activities, although central resources financed by voluntary contributions must remain the basis for UNDP activities. He suggested that the Governing Council set a ceiling on trust funds supplementing UNDP programmes, the Special Measures Fund for the Least Developed Countries and UNCDF. Other programmes, such as the United Nations Sudano-Sahelian Office (UNSO) or the Financing System for Science and Technology, operated with different financing mechanisms.

In another April 1982 report,[5] the Administrator informed the Council of action he had taken since June 1981 regarding trust funds. Annexed to the report were the financial regulations for UNDP-administered trust funds, adopted by the General Assembly in December 1981,[8] and information on the five trust funds established since June 1981, each from the same donor Government (the Federal Republic of Germany) and on behalf of the United Nations Financing System for Science and Technology for Development, with a total value of approximately $2.8 million. The Administrator also set guidelines for establishing such trust funds, specifying that: the purposes should be clearly defined and consistent with UNDP policies; an agreement should be signed by the Administrator, donor and recipient; normal UNDP procedures for project execution should be applied; the Governing Council should approve trust funds involving a financial liability for UNDP; trust funds should normally be fully funded; expenditures should not exceed their budget; and the Administrator could reduce or terminate the project if adequate financing were not received.

The Governing Council, by a decision of 18 June 1982,[2] expressed satisfaction with the guidelines, subject to a modification of one permitting non-acceptance of non-convertible and other currencies, so that it would not appear to be discriminatory to any one currency.

By another decision of the same date,[1] the Council authorized the Administrator to accept trust funds conditioned on procurement from donor countries in respect of the operations of UNSO, UNCDF and the United Nations Financing System for Science and Technology for Development. This authorization would be automatically terminated after one year, unless the Council expressly authorized otherwise. The Council reaffirmed that arrangements for support-cost reimbursements should also apply to technical co-operation activities financed from trust funds, and authorized the Administrator to lower the support-cost reimbursement rate for projects so financed when the executing agency had indicated its willingness to accept a lower rate for the same project. The Administrator was to report on this authority in his next annual review.

In its comments on the 1981 UNDP accounts,[3] submitted to the General Assembly's Fifth (Administrative and Budgetary) Committee in 1982, the United Nations Board of Auditors, noting that in the case of two trust funds, allocations had exceeded resources, recommended that efforts be made to avoid allocations in anticipation of resources.

In its resolution of 20 December 1982 on operational activities for development,[7] the Assembly requested the Director-General for Development and International Economic Co-operation to examine the extent and implications of the growing practice of contributions with conditions attached to their use (such as, among other types, contributions to special purpose funds).

Decisions (1982). UNDP Council (report, E/1982/16/Rev.1), 18 June: [1]82/5, sect. IV, paras. 3-6; [2]82/34, sect. III.
Reports. [3]Board of Auditors, and financial statements, A/37/5/Add.1. UNDP Administrator, [4]DP/1982/35 & Corr.1, [5]DP/1982/57, [6]DP/1983/49.
Resolution (1982). [7]GA: 37/226, para. 17, 20 Dec.
Resolution (prior). [8]GA: 36/227, 18 Dec. 1981 (YUN 1981, p. 451).
Yearbook reference. [9]1981, p. 451.

Accounts

Accounts of executing agencies for 1980

The audited accounts of the participating and executing agencies, relating to funds allocated to them by UNDP as at 31 December 1980, together with the reports of the external auditors thereon, were submitted to the UNDP Governing Council in March 1982.[2] (The accounts, together with the observations and comments by the General Assembly's Advisory Committee on Administrative and Budgetary Questions (ACABQ), had been presented to the Assembly in 1981.[3]) The Administrator's March 1982 report included a summary of action taken by UNDP in response to Governing Council requests for comments on the auditors' observations and for consultations with agencies that used commercial external auditors on the possibility of their including such observations in future audit reports.

The Council, by a decision of 18 June 1982,[1] requested the Administrator to reiterate to the executing agencies the importance it attached to the matter and to consult with them again with a view to obtaining audit reports which would satisfy its concern. He was requested to provide in 1983 estimates of the costs involved in providing such reports.

Decision (1982). [1]UNDP Council (report, E/1982/16/Rev.1): 82/37, 18 June.
Report. [2]UNDP Administrator, DP/1982/60.
Yearbook reference. [3]1981, p. 450.

UNDP accounts for 1981

By a resolution[3] of 16 November 1982 on the 1981 accounts of various United Nations programmes and funds, the General Assembly accepted the UNDP accounts for the year ended 31 December 1981,[2] concurred with the observations and comments of ACABQ,[1] requested the Secretary-General to strengthen financial discipline further and to remove the shortcomings referred to by the Board of Auditors and ACABQ, and requested remedial action.

The Board had urged UNDP to intensify utilization of non-convertible currencies, which stood at approximately $40.1 million as at 31 December 1981; recommended that cash management and project expenditures at field offices be more closely monitored; and that the internal audit system be improved. Further recommendations related to accounting procedures, trust funds and procurement. The Board stated that its opinion on the financial statements was subject to the utilization or realization of the accumulated non-convertible currencies and unpaid contributions of about $2.2 million pledged for 1978 and prior years.

The UNDP administration responded in its financial statements and in the Assembly's Fifth (Administrative and Budgetary) Committee. It informed ACABQ that of the $74.5 million in government contributions outstanding as at 31 December 1981, $43.5 million had been collected by 31 May 1982; that of the $1,210,424 in unidentified deposits in UNDP accounts—mostly government contributions for which inadequate information had been provided as to the purpose of payment—only $429,150 remained unidentified by May; and that steps had been taken to recover salary advances and to increase internal audit coverage of headquarters activities during 1982-1983.

Reports. [1]ACABQ, A/37/443 and Corr.1; [2]Board of Auditors, and financial statements, A/37/5/Add.1 and Corr.1.
Resolution (1982). [3]GA: 37/12, 16 Nov.

Revision of financial regulations

On 18 June 1982,[1] the UNDP Governing Council decided that in the absence of a consensus on certain proposed revisions to the financial regulations dealing with the currencies of contributions, the existing financial regulations should remain in effect until a decision was reached in 1983. Under other provisions, the Council requested the Administrator to pursue his efforts to prepare guidelines for the procurement of equipment, supplies and services, and expressed satisfaction with the proposed guidelines for the establishment of trust funds by the Administrator.

Also on 18 June 1982,[2] the Council decided that its Budgetary and Finance Committee would consider the question of financial regulations again at its 1983 session.

Decisions (1982). UNDP Council (report, E/1982/16/Rev.1), 18 June: [1]82/34, sect. I; [2]82/35.

Management and staffing of UNDP

Field personnel

As in other years, the 116 UNDP field offices devoted about one third of staff time in 1982 to activities not directly related to a UNDP funding source, including advisory and representational services on behalf of United Nations organizations, albeit with a 7.5 per cent reduction in staff. The central service function of UNDP field offices expanded and strengthened the country programme framework, generated complementary funds for UNDP-supported projects and eased the administrative burdens of Governments *vis-à-vis* external assistance.

An attempt to measure the extent and value of such functions was made in 1982. The 82 offices that responded to a request for data had provided administrative or programming support in 1982 to more than 1,200 projects funded by bilateral or multilateral organizations other than UNDP or its funds, with an estimated expenditure of almost $250 million. Roughly 73 per cent of the value of the projects assisted received major support, including staff, from field offices; on a regional basis, UNDP supported more such non-Programme-funded projects in Arab States than elsewhere ($110 million in 1982), followed by Africa ($90 million).

Data on the UNDP field office survey were provided by the Administrator in his 1982 annual report.[1]

Report. [1] UNDP Administrator, DP/1983/6/Add.1.

Recruitment of professional staff and consultants

The expanded use of national experts and consultants for UNDP-supported projects, first introduced on a significant level in 1978, continued in 1982. Efforts concentrated on improvement of guidelines first issued in 1979.[4] Based on its experience, UNDP was working with its agency partners to ensure, among other principles, that host Governments assumed a major responsibility in determining remuneration. As stated before an informal meeting of agency representatives in 1982 by the Deputy Administrator and reported by the Administrator in his 1982 annual report,[3] UNDP was promoting the utilization of national experts as another approach to obtaining the best qualified expertise and to making full use of all available national human resources.

In March 1982,[2] the UNDP Administrator submitted, as requested by the UNDP Governing Council in June 1981,[5] information on rules and practices for updating rosters of project professional staff and for circulating vacancy announcements. Based on information from the executing agencies, with whom the responsibility for recruitment of experts and consultants rested, the Administrator formulated recommendations to improve recruitment methods and procedures.

The Governing Council, in a decision of 18 June 1982,[1] endorsed several of these recommendations. It urged the agencies to make better use of national recruitment services, and invited them: to improve the forecasting of project personnel requirements; to ensure timely circulation of vacancy announcements; to reduce recruitment time; and to achieve earlier contacts between project-design staff and recruitment personnel. The Council welcomed the recommendations to be made by recipient Governments to identify

project candidates and requested the Administrator to prepare guidelines for the executing agencies and to submit periodic progress reports.

The Administrator was to keep recruitment measures under review to ensure that the most suitable experts were being recruited world-wide, to continue to co-operate with developing countries in establishing and strengthening national recruitment services, and to submit in 1983 proposals on reducing the cost of international experts' and consultants' services.

For 1982, the Administrator noted important progress in regularizing the category of local professional staff in field offices. By the end of the year, 85 such National Officers were serving in 41 countries.

Decision (1982). [1]UNDP Council (report, E/1982/16/Rev.1): 82/7, 18 June.
Reports. UNDP Administrator, [2]DP/1982/10 & Add.1 & Add.1/Corr.1, [3]DP/1983/6/Add.1.
Yearbook reference. [4]1979, p. 543; [5]1981, p. 458.

Field post levels

In his annual report for 1982,[2] the UNDP Administrator stated that as a result of the findings of a UNDP headquarters and field staffing survey, he had recommended a reduction of 323 posts compared with the provisional 1982-1983 budget.

Noting that it was unlikely that any posts would need to be reinstated for 1982-1983, but that the Administrator might need the flexibility to do so, the Governing Council, by a decision of 18 June 1982,[1] authorized him to propose, if necessary, additional field posts in 1983, should resources permit programming for 1983 of the indicative planning figures at the 80 per cent level or above (see above). He was requested to review the operational implications of the Governing Council's June 1981 decision[3] that supplementary budget estimates should be limited to unavoidable increases.

Decision (1982). [1]UNDP Council (report, E/1982/16/Rev.1): 82/32, 18 June.
Report. [2]UNDP Administrator, DP/1983/6/Add.1.
Yearbook reference. [3]1981, p. 448.

Housing

In April 1982,[2] the UNDP Administrator provided the Governing Council with an analysis of the field personnel's difficulties in securing adequate housing and office accommodation, and enumerated the measures UNDP was taking to alleviate the problem. Apart from the granting of construction loans to Governments from a $25 million reserve established by the Council in 1979, these measures included leasing, financing from project funds, advances for repairs and maintenance and, exceptionally, purchase.

The Administrator reported that altogether over 250 housing units had been obtained through loans to Governments. Loans under consideration or negotiation concerned over 300 housing units in 19 countries, and office facilities in eight countries. If all the requests for loans under consideration were approved, he added, they would exceed the $25 million loan reserve.

With regard to field office accommodation, the least developed countries had been unable in many cases to fulfil their obligations to provide adequate premises. The Administrator believed that UNDP should finance the construction of such premises when the host Government was unable to do so and when the commercial market did not offer an alternative solution.

On the Administrator's recommendation, the Governing Council, by a decision of 18 June,[1] approved the current arrangements for the provision of housing and office accommodation to field personnel. It authorized the use of up to 20 per cent (instead of 25 per cent, or $6.25 million, as recommended by the Administrator) of the Reserve for Construction Loans to Governments for field office accommodations. The Administrator was authorized to use in a selective and prudent manner UNDP funds to purchase housing units and was requested to report on such use in his annual financial review.

Decision (1982). [1]UNDP Council (report, E/1982/16/Rev.1): 82/30, 18 June.
Report. [2]UNDP Administrator, DP/1982/50.

Study programme

In March 1982,[2] the UNDP Administrator reported to the Governing Council on action taken to implement a June 1981 Council decision[4] establishing a UNDP development study programme, financed by voluntary contributions, to organize seminars for high-level policy makers and secretariat officials to promote greater understanding of development problems and to generate new resources and ideas.

The Administrator observed that because of financial constraints, the programme's activities were currently restricted to those that did not involve additional expenditure. He said that the Council might wish to consider allocating a small amount from UNDP resources.

Commending the Administrator for the action taken to launch the programme, the Council, by a decision of 18 June 1982,[1] invited financial contributions to the UNDP Development Study Programme, and endorsed his proposals to convene an Honorary Advisory Committee to chart future activities and funding and to organize a seminar for parliamentarians attending General Assembly sessions in order to familiarize them with technical assistance activities.

In his annual report for 1982,[3] the Administrator noted that during the year, five events had been organized under the study programme: two workshops,

jointly sponsored with universities in the United States, drew a total of 170 participants; and some 500 persons attended three lectures, featuring discussions on the general theme of future issues in multilateral development and technical co-operation.

At the November 1982 United Nations Pledging Conference for Development Activities, several Governments pledged financial resources or assistance in kind for study programme seminars in their countries during 1983 and 1984.

Decision (1982). [1]UNDP Council (report, E/1982/16/Rev.1): 82/10, 18 June.
Reports. UNDP Administrator, [2]DP/1982/13, [3]DP/1983/6/Add.1.
Yearbook reference. [4]1981, p. 458.

Procurement of project equipment and supplies

During 1972-1981, expenditure on equipment ranged from 21.7 per cent of total technical assistance (in the industrial sector) to 29.9 per cent (in the humanitarian aid and disaster relief sector). The proportion of resources devoted to equipment had increased and there were indications that this trend might continue, particularly in the areas of industry, human settlements, culture, transport and communications.

In a March 1982 report to the UNDP Governing Council,[6] the Administrator summarized the findings of an in-depth study, undertaken in collaboration with the executing agencies, on the use of programme resources for equipment and supplies. The results suggested that the issuance of supplementary instructions on such use would facilitate compliance with the existing legislation. The Administrator recommended inclusion in project documents of detailed evidence of equipment needs, as well as an evaluation of the use of equipment in the post-project period.

In April 1982,[7] the Administrator described his actions to prepare guidelines, in response to a June 1981 Governing Council request made in the context of approving a new financial regulation,[10] and in collaboration with the agencies, for the procurement of equipment, supplies and services, and the reasons why he was unable to submit such guidelines at the current stage. In the light of the advice received from the United Nations Office of Legal Affairs and the inability to reach an understanding with the agencies, he proposed to carry out a detailed review of existing procurement procedures, to formulate guidelines based on the results, and to identify necessary modifications.

By a decision of 18 June 1982,[2] the Council requested the Administrator to pursue his efforts to prepare guidelines in consultation with the executing agencies, and to report in 1983. By another decision of the same date,[1] the Council requested him to pursue action along the lines of the recommendations in his March report.

In his September 1982 report on operational activities for development,[5] the Director-General for Development and International Economic Co-operation described the role and function of the Inter-Agency Procurement Services Unit of UNDP, established in 1978, and various measures taken or under consideration in the area of system-wide procurement. These measures included: developing a list of common-user items of certain major categories of equipment, increasing procurement from developing countries, and applying a preferential margin for locally manufactured products consistent with existing regulations. Though considering the establishment of a common procurement system as likely to be difficult, the Director-General recognized the need to simplify and improve the quality of procurement methods and to formulate an inter-agency code for those operations. In this connection, he noted UNDP efforts to develop procurement guidelines in consultation with the executing agencies, and suggested a possible need for a further review of the adequacy of existing inter-agency arrangements and of basic policy principles and practices.

The General Assembly, in its resolution of 20 December 1982 on operational activities for development,[9] decided that the new guidelines should in due course govern the procurement activities of organs and bodies under the authority of the Assembly in their execution of UNDP-financed projects. This paragraph had not been included in the original draft, submitted by Bangladesh for the Group of 77.[3]

In its comments on the 1981 UNDP accounts,[4] submitted to the 1982 Assembly session, the Board of Auditors recommended a standard format for submission of procurement-contract proposals, and noted that the UNDP administration had agreed to take action to ensure adherence to the prescribed rules in respect of procurement by field offices, as suggested by the Board.

In his annual report for 1982,[8] the Administrator estimated that the annual average dollar volume for common-user items (such as vehicles, office and laboratory equipment, electronic data-processing supplies, audio-visual equipment, construction equipment, hand tools) by all United Nations organizations was some $200 million, specialized equipment not included.

Decisions (1982). UNDP Council (report, E/1982/16/Rev.1), 18 June: [1]82/4, sect. B; [2]82/34, sect. II.
Draft resolution withdrawn. [3]Bangladesh, for Group of 77, A/C.2/37/L.92.
Reports. [4]Board of Auditors, and financial statements, A/37/5/Add.1; [5]Director-General for DIEC, transmitted by S-G note, A/37/445; UNDP Administrator, [6]DP/1982/3, [7]DP/1982/56, [8]DP/1983/6/Add.3.
Resolution (1982). [9]GA: 37/226, para. 13, 20 Dec.
Yearbook reference. [10]1981, p. 451.

JIU reports

By a decision of 18 June 1982,[1] the UNDP Governing Council took note of eight reports of the Joint Inspection Unit relevant to UNDP (seven issued in 1981 and one in 1982), and requested the Administrator to take into account the Inspectors' recommendations on improving UNDP-supported programmes and projects.

The 1981 reports dealt with: co-ordination in public information among members of the United Nations system,[4] management services,[8] internal evaluation in United Nations organizations (two reports),[7] application by the United Nations system of the 1977 Mar del Plata Action Plan[3] on water development and administration,[5] relationships between the Director-General for Development and International Economic Co-operation and entities of the United Nations Secretariat,[6] and the United Nations University (see Chapter XV of this section). The 1982 report was on the Economic Commission for Africa (see Chapter VII of this section).

A brief account of UNDP involvement in these reports was given to the Governing Council in a note of March 1982 by the Administrator.[2] With regard to the UNDP comments on the report on relationships between the Director-General and Secretariat entities, the Administrator observed that UNDP had emphasized its close co-operation with the Director-General's Office. In providing information for the report on the Economic Commission for Africa, UNDP had commented especially on priority setting in intercountry programming. With regard to programme evaluation, UNDP referred to its planned action towards improving its evaluation system and procedures, and towards enhancing the quality of technical co-operation.

Decision (1982). [1]UNDP Council (report, E/1982/16/Rev.1): 82/6, paras. 2 & 3, 18 June.
Note. [2]UNDP Administrator, DP/1982/8.
Yearbook references. [3]1977, p. 555; 1981, [4]p. 370, [5]p. 686, [6]p. 1093, [7]p. 1310, [8]p. 1378.

Organizational questions

Governing Council

Establishment of the Intersessional Committee

By a decision of 18 June 1982,[1] the UNDP Governing Council established an Intersessional Committee of the Whole to study, in consultation with the UNDP Administrator, options and recommendations for the long-term financing of UNDP. Options included voluntary contributions, replenishment, multi-year pledging, assessed contributions and various combinations of measures of a voluntary and assessed nature. The Committee was also requested to study other matters that might facilitate longer-term financing, in particular ways of strengthening the work of the

Council itself. The Council President was requested to convene the Committee at the earliest possible date.

The Committee held its first session in New York from 13 to 15 September.[5] Its agenda included: a review of the financial resource situation, prospects and needs of UNDP for the 1982-1986 programming cycle; options for longer-term financing; other matters which would facilitate resource mobilization and strengthen the effectiveness of the Governing Council's work (such as strengthening the role of the Council and participating Governments in programme planning and review, evaluation arrangements and measures to promote a better understanding of the role of UNDP, its activities and resource needs); and the Committee's work programme for consideration of questions that required further study.

The Committee decided to invite to its plenary meetings observers of States members of the Governing Council and representatives of the executing agencies and organizations. It was generally agreed that, in light of the seriousness of the resource situation, it should also examine shorter-term measures which might alleviate the constraints experienced in 1982 and expected in 1983. With regard to the options for longer-term financing, the Committee agreed that it would not consider any measures based on assessed contributions.[4]

Consideration of the Committee's work programme was postponed until the Committee's second session.

In his annual report for 1982,[6] the Administrator stated that the Committee was a key factor in focusing intergovernmental attention on the Programme's inadequate funding levels.

The establishment of the Committee was welcomed by the Economic and Social Council in a resolution of 29 July.[7] The original 19-nation draft[3] was withdrawn in the Council's Third (Programme and Co-ordination) Committee in favour of a consultation-produced text incorporating amendments, one of which was to add mention of the Committee's mandate for strengthening the effectiveness of the Governing Council's work while studying options proposed for study.

The General Assembly, in its resolution of 20 December on the critical situation of the financial resources of UNDP,[9] expressed its hope that the Committee would succeed in identifying measures that would enable the implementation of the planned UNDP activities for 1982-1986.

In a draft submitted to the Assembly's Second (Economic and Financial) Committee by Bangladesh for the Group of 77,[2] which was later withdrawn in favour of a resolution presented by the Vice-Chairman,[8] the Assembly would have strongly urged the Intersessional Committee to formulate measures to enable Governments to increase their contributions to UNDP.

Decision (1982). [1]UNDP Council (report, E/1982/16/Rev.1): 82/5, sect. II, 18 June.
Draft resolutions withdrawn. [2]Bangladesh, for Group of 77, A/C.2/37/L.92, [3]Algeria, Bahamas, Benin, Canada, China, India, Kenya, Malawi, Mali, Nepal, Nigeria, Norway, Peru, Romania, Saint Lucia, Trinidad and Tobago, Tunisia, Turkey, Yugoslavia, E/1982/C.3/L.8.
Record of decisions. [4]Intersessional Committee of Whole, DP/1982/ICW/6.
Reports. [5]Inter-sessional Committee of Whole, DP/1983/5; [6]UNDP Administrator, DP/1983/6/Add.1.
Resolutions. [7]ESC: 1982/53, para. 4, 29 July. GA, 20 Dec.: [8]37/226; [9]37/227, para. 7.

Arabic language services

By a decision taken at its organizational meeting on 25 February 1982,[1] the UNDP Governing Council amended its rules of procedure to include Arabic as one of its official languages. The proposed amendments were contained in a January note[2] prepared by the United Nations Secretariat in response to a 1980 General Assembly request that the Economic and Social Council include Arabic among the official languages.[3]

Decision (1982). [1]UNDP Council (report, E/1982/16/Rev.1): 82/3, 25 Feb.
Note. [2]UN Secretariat, DP/1982/L.3.
Resolution. [3]GA: 35/219 A, 17 Dec. 1980 (YUN 1980, p. 1245).
Publication. Rules of Procedure of the Governing Council of the United Nations Development Programme (April 1982) (DP/1/Rev.4), Sales No. E.82.I.11.

Relations with intergovernmental organizations

At its organizational meeting on 25 February 1982,[1] the UNDP Governing Council granted observer status to the Gulf Arab Programme for United Nations Development Organizations, following the Programme's request.

Decision (1982). [1]UNDP Council (report, E/1982/16/Rev.1): 82/2, 25 Feb.

Relations with NGOs

In 1982, UNDP sought ways of expanding co-ordination of technical co-operation with non-governmental organizations (NGOs). Operational relations with NGOs at the country level were pursued with the consent of the Governments. New, more elaborate guidelines to enhance collaboration between UNDP and NGOs were issued in 1982, aimed at attracting additional resources, services and expertise, and at making UNDP a channel of communication between developing countries and NGOs, with a minimum of centralized co-ordination.

The guidelines, originally approved by the Council in 1979 for a three-year trial period, were reaffirmed at its 1982 session, by a decision of 18 June.[1] In future the Council was to be informed, in the Administrator's annual report, of activities carried out under the guidelines.

At the end of the trial period, 15 organizations had officially been recognized as co-operating in development activities with UNDP on the basis of the guidelines. In an April report to the Governing Council,[2] the Administrator stated that the guidelines provided a useful policy framework and at the current level of activities did not require further formalization and institutionalization.

The Administrator, in his 1982 annual report,[3] also reported that during 1982, UNDP had sponsored consultations in Bangladesh, India, Nepal and Sri Lanka—involving about 20 NGOs in each country—to determine how they could support national plans for the International Drinking Water Supply and Sanitation Decade (1981-1990), proclaimed in 1980.[4] At UNDP headquarters, an extensive review was undertaken with NGO participation to try to ensure a more effective association of NGO activities with those assisted by UNDP. The Administrator decided that UNDP should pursue a flexible, country-by-country approach, sponsoring workshops and leading to a direct project-level collaboration.

Decision (1982). [1]UNDP Council (report, E/1982/16/Rev.1): 82/40, 18 June.
Reports. UNDP Administrator, [2]DP/1982/65, [3]DP/1983/6/Add.1.
Resolution. [4]GA: 35/18, 10 Nov. 1980 (YUN 1980, p. 712).

Other technical co-operation activities

UN technical co-operation programmes

In 1982, the United Nations continued its work to further the economic and social progress of the developing countries by supplying experts and advisory services, awarding fellowships and organizing workshops and study tours. These activities covered a broad range of subjects, including development planning and administration, rural and social development, international trade, industrial development, transnational corporations, mineral resources, energy, ocean economics, environment, science and technology, population, women, human rights and statistics.

Responsibility for the management and substantive support for the system's technical co-operation activities rested with the United Nations Department of Technical Co-operation for Development (DTCD), a separate organizational entity of the Secretariat. During 1982, DTCD faced severe constraints in discharging its responsibility, mainly as a result of shrinking resources of its main funding partners—the United Nations Development Programme (UNDP) and the United Nations Fund for Population Activities (UNFPA). Technical co-operation activities were also carried out under the United Nations regular programme of technical co-operation.

DTCD activities. The United Nations delivered a technical co-operation programme totalling around $303 million in 1982, a 2 per cent increase in project expenditures over 1981 (see table below). Out of

the 1982 total, DTCD executed a programme valued at $126.9 million (compared to $136.6 million in 1981) comprising more than 1,400 projects.

Of the DTCD programme delivery, $85,469,000 came from UNDP, $19,361,000 from UNFPA (a decline of $6 million in comparison with 1981), $15,633,000 from trust funds and $6,388,000 from the United Nations regular programme of technical co-operation. The distribution of DTCD expenditures reflected the severe reduction in funds from UNFPA, which was only partly offset by an increase in trust funds. While the share of programmes funded by UNDP decreased by $7 million, expenditures for UNDP-funded projects still represented 67 per cent of total delivery. UNFPA funding accounted for 15 per cent of all projects (19 per cent in 1981), while trust funds contributed 13 per cent to total delivery and 5 per cent was financed from the regular programme.

In the face of a 13 per cent ($22.6 million) decrease (to $150.5 million) in approved budgets, the reduction in project expenditures of only 7 per cent ($9.7 million) was due to the Department's higher implementation rate of 84 per cent, up from 82 per cent in 1981. In spite of that delivery rate, the value of DTCD field activities declined in 1982, reversing for the first time the pattern of continuous growth.

While the level of indicative planning figures (IPFs) and cost-sharing expenditures by UNDP, which financed the larger part of the Department's field operations, fell by about 10 per cent, the drop in expenditures by DTCD for UNDP-funded projects amounted to less than 7 per cent. The decline in UNFPA resources, however, was reflected in a drop of 25 per cent in DTCD expenditures, due to the change in UNFPA policies regarding allocation of resources (with reduced emphasis on population policies, demography, censuses, etc.).

UNITED NATIONS TECHNICAL CO-OPERATION PROJECT EXPENDITURES
IN 1982, BY ORGANIZATIONAL ENTITY
(in thousands of US dollars)

	Regular programme	UNDP	UNFPA	Trust funds	Total
DTCD	6,388	85,469	19,361	15,633	126,851
Other United Nations	298*	—	—	11,551†	11,849
ECA	1,342	8,711	2,719	3,096	15,868
ECE	—	798	10	36	844
ECLA	523	1,811	2,099	3,031	7,464
ECWA	672	331	248	480	1,731
ESCAP	851	5,091	983	6,716	13,641
UNCHS	538	12,680	—	2,113	15,331
UNCTAD	260	14,430	—	1,603	16,293
UNIDO	3,121	68,107	—	22,252	93,480
Total	13,993	197,428	25,420	66,511	303,352

*Human rights advisory services under the regular programme.

†Comprises technical co-operation expenditure incurred against the following trust funds: United Nations Fund for Drug Abuse Control $7,609,928, United Nations Nationhood Programme for Namibia $902,652, Voluntary Fund for the United Nations Decade for Women $2,032,790, Trust Fund for the United Nations Centre on Transnational Corporations Technical Co-operation Programme $866,316, and Trust Fund to Provide Advisory Services to Developing Countries in Matters of Policy, Laws, Regulations and Contracts relating to Transnational Corporations $139,771.
SOURCE: DP/1983/18/Add.2.

Despite a reduction in administrative costs (financed largely out of programme support-cost earnings) and other corrective measures, DTCD faced an operating deficit of $3.6 million at the end of 1982.

To counteract the effects of the cutbacks and to maintain the most critically needed programmes, DTCD intensified its efforts to secure funding from various multilateral aid organizations, such as the Arab Gulf Fund. A number of countries, including Italy, Japan and Sweden, made special funds available, particularly in new and emerging technological fields such as mini-hydropower and geothermal energy development, where possible channelling these funds through UNDP by cost-sharing arrangements rather than as funds-in-trust.

Reported investment commitments relating to DTCD projects totalled $479 million in 1982, a substantial increase over 1981. External investors included the World Bank, France, the German Democratic Republic, the Federal Republic of Germany, Japan, Kuwait, the Netherlands, Nigeria, Sweden, Switzerland and the USSR. Special efforts were made to improve working relationships and establish closer contacts with major financial institutions, particularly the Arab development funds and the Inter-American and Asian Development Banks. The Department also provided investment advisory services to assess particular resources and help prepare projects for presentation to investors. In 1982, the ratio of pre-investment project cost to investment was 1 to 42.

Cutbacks in resources were translated into reduced programmes for all geographic regions, with the exception of the Americas where the level of expenditures increased slightly from $20 million in 1981 to $21 million (16 per cent), due to increased government cost sharing. The programme for Africa remained the largest, accounting for $51 million (40 per cent). Expenditures in Asia were $30 million (25 per cent), while those in the Middle East and Europe, including interregional and global projects, totalled $24 million (19 per cent).

The reduction in project funding was also reflected in a corresponding reduction in DTCD programme support income, amounting to $16.7 million, broken down as follows: $11.8 million from UNDP, $2.7 million from UNFPA, $1.4 million from trust funds and 0.8 million in other income. The Department received no compensation for activities financed through special arrangements such as the United Nations Educational and Training Programme for Southern Africa (UNETPSA), fellowships under the General Account of the United Nations Fund for Namibia and similar programmes.

The Department's expenditures against programme support-cost resources amounted to $20.2 million, which included costs incurred by units outside DTCD in support of technical co-operation activities. The expenditures comprise $18.5 million for staff costs and $1.7 million for non-staff costs. The $3.6 million operating deficit would have been higher had DTCD not introduced certain measures to reduce costs before the end of 1981, including: a freeze on recruitment resulting in a cutback of 65 posts, a new travel-expenditures control system, improvement of procedures and increased delegation of functions to the field, an improved computerized system for contracting and procurement, and an expanded programme-monitoring system.

The sectoral breakdown, reflecting government priorities, changed only slightly, with the exception of projects in statistics, which decreased from $30 million (22 per cent of the programme) to $23 million (18 per cent). Natural resources and energy projects remained 37 per cent of the programme ($47 million), while development planning projects increased from 20 to 21 per cent ($27 million). Projects in public administration increased from 9 to 10 per cent ($13 million), and those in population went up slightly to 6 per cent ($7 million). Social development projects represented 3 per cent or $3 million. Fellowships under UNETPSA and programmes in other sectors accounted for the remaining 5 per cent ($7 million) of expenditures.

There were also some variations in other components. The emphasis placed on human resources development was reflected in the reversal of the previous decline in the training component, which increased from 13 to 16 per cent of the programme ($20 million in expenditures). Experts and consultants accounted for 54 per cent ($69 million), in comparison with 56 per cent in 1981, while equipment and subcontracts dropped to 26 per cent ($33 million) due mainly to a decrease in the cost of subcontracts placed. Miscellaneous components remained at a fixed cost of $5 million or 4 per cent of the total.

In these fields, the Department provided: special assistance to Governments in identifying their needs for external aid on the basis of national and regional development priorities; support for donors' round-table conferences; strengthening government co-ordinating machinery in the least developed countries (LDCs); and advisory services, including 25 interregional advisory missions, missions in mineral and energy assessments, and other sectoral and development planning missions in 33 of the 36 LDCs.

DTCD efforts in public administration and finance included: institution building; administrative reform and improvement; financial management; and personnel administration and training, with in-service training, seminars and fellowships in public service.

DTCD implemented some 80 development planning projects in more than 60 countries in 1982, and interregional advisers and other staff undertook missions to an equal number of countries, particular attention being given to LDCs, with supporting efforts to: expand their capacity to control the socio-economic situation, manage their economies and development programmes through monitoring and forecasting, and improve their negotiating position in the world economy. Extensive use was made of technical co-operation among developing countries, by: employing developing country nationals as experts, applying experience gained in one country to similar problems elsewhere, and organizing international workshops.

Continued emphasis was placed on assisting developing countries in preparing their UNDP country programmes (including Ghana, Nigeria and Uganda in 1982), and in helping countries (eight in 1982) assess needs for and review special assistance programmes, including an emergency mission to Lebanon. Projects in national planning were initiated in Malawi, Saudi Arabia and Zambia, and in subnational planning in two states of Malaysia. New phases were begun in projects to assist the multinational Gambia and Senegal river basin development schemes, subnational planning in Nigeria and Senegal, and project evaluation in Rwanda. Substantive evaluations of ongoing projects were undertaken in co-operation with UNDP, leading to reorientation of projects in nine countries.

The Department's programme in natural resources and energy, which maintained a prominent position, included field projects, assessment missions, advisory services, several symposia and technical publications; institution building, exploration and development, and training were emphasized. In 1982, DTCD carried out 14 country missions to estimate financial requirements for exploration and location of mineral and energy resources, and supported 58 mineral projects in 43 countries, including exploration and investigation projects in nine countries. Ninety-one missions by interregional advisers and others were undertaken in 50 countries.

Requests for assistance in the conventional energy field increased to 24 in 1982. Technical advisory or programming missions on petroleum were undertaken in nine countries, on petroleum legislation in four, and on coal in six. A workshop on geophysical methods in petroleum exploration with participants from 31 developing countries was organized in co-operation with Norway, and a meeting on oilfield development techniques, funded by the regular programme in co-operation with China, included participants from 22 countries. Energy planning and management projects were active in 20 countries and short-term missions were carried out in 12. In co-operation with France and funded by the regular programme, a symposium was convened on energy supply management.

Management and development of electric power was supported in 26 projects. A symposium on coal for electricity generation was organized under the regular programme in co-operation with Australia.

Geothermal energy projects were implemented in eight countries. Country projects in solar and wind energy, energy conservation, and rural energy supplies were implemented in eight more, as well as interregional and other projects in Asia and Latin America. Assistance was requested by many other countries in these areas, and projects were formulated. The Department also provided advisory services for resources assessment in 19 countries. Jointly funded by Japan, Sweden and the regular programme, DTCD executed a programme of mini-hydropower surveys eventually to encompass 42 countries with particular emphasis on the LDCs. By year's end, 20 countries had been surveyed.

Other project activities covered development and management of ground- and surface-water resources, including river basin development, drilling, supply and demand management, exploration and assessment. An important area of work was rural water supply, especially in West Africa. At a workshop on the use of sub-surface space for water storage through artificial recharge, convened in co-operation with Sweden, the need was stressed for the United Nations to act as a clearing-house and co-ordinating agency for information.

With regard to remote sensing (see POLITICAL AND SECURITY QUESTIONS, Chapter II), DTCD assisted in formulating projects in Argentina and Kenya, and in identifying needs in Egypt and the Sudan. With funds from the Financing System for Science and Technology for Development, China was helped to establish a national remote sensing centre.

In the area of population and statistics, emphasis was placed on censuses and the strengthening of institutions and capacities for compiling data. Of 151 country projects, 67 were in Africa, 34 in Asia and the Pacific, 27 in Latin America and the Caribbean, and 23 in the Middle East and Western Asia. Censuses were conducted in 12 countries, including China. More than 100 UNFPA-supported demographic projects were active in 1982 in 75 countries. In addition, DTCD participated in a number of UNFPA-sponsored missions for population needs assessment, project formulation and tripartite reviews.

Through the Task Force on Rural Development of the Administrative Committee on Coordination, DTCD collaborated with other agencies, focusing on participatory activities and the monitoring and evaluation of projects, exchanges of experiences, and joint ventures. Projects included the establishment of village development committees, rural training centres and self-help income-generating activities.

Among DTCD activities in social aspects of development were crime prevention and criminal justice work, including support to United Nations–affiliated regional institutes, strengthened relations with regional commissions and advisory missions.

On behalf of the United Nations, as a co-parent with the Food and Agriculture Organization of the United Nations (FAO) of the World Food Programme (WFP), DTCD was closely involved in strengthening the technical inputs of WFP activities. WFP requested United Nations scrutiny of 47 project requests and 32 project summaries in 1982.

The Department also provided support services to United Nations agencies and programmes and to the regional commissions in the areas of recruitment, administration, contracts and procurement, training, project evaluation and report formulation.

In a report on United Nations technical co-operation activities in 1982,[3] with statistical information in an addendum,[4] the Secretary-General provided an overview of the activities of the Department, the regular programme of technical co-operation (see below) and all other organizational entities of the United Nations that also had responsibilities for technical co-operation programmes. He reported on funding and the use of resources, and gave an account of the major programme areas and of action taken in response to resolutions of the General Assembly and various governing bodies.

The Secretary-General reported that DTCD had under consideration new approaches for the management of technical co-operation projects, including guidelines and procedures in providing administrative and technical backstopping to the increasing number of projects which differed in scope and content from the traditional types of multilateral development assistance. Being without separate field representation, DTCD relied heavily on UNDP resident representatives for communication with recipient Governments and intensified its efforts to maintain close links with the field through such means as regular briefings and special meetings. During 1982, DTCD made particular efforts to increase Government participation in projects and reliance on available national capabilities, including recruitment of national experts, selection of local subcontractors, and the use of national or regional training facilities. Monitoring and evaluation was improved and introduced more systematically in field projects.

Regular programme of technical co-operation. The United Nations regular programme of technical co-operation, financed as part of the United Nations regular budget, included: sectoral advisory services implemented by DTCD (see below), the Centre for Human Rights, the United Nations Centre for Human Settlements (HABITAT) and the United Nations Conference on Trade and Development (UNCTAD); regional and subregional advisory services provided by the regional commissions (except the Economic Commission for Europe); and industrial development activities by the United Nations Industrial Development Organization (UNIDO).

The portion of the regular programme administered by DTCD had several important characteristics: it provided for interregional advisory services and for missions in response to government requests in diverse specialized fields; it adhered strictly to types of assistance with multiplier and catalytic effects; it was devoted to activities complementary to other technical co-operation efforts; and although modest in level, it played a crucial role in responding quickly to priority development needs. In addition to the interregional advisory services, activities included pilot projects, seminars and training programmes. Assistance to LDCs and to island and land-locked developing countries continued to receive high priority.

Governing Council action. Taking note of the Secretary-General's report on 1981 United Nations technical co-operation activities, submitted in April 1982,[2] the UNDP Governing Council, by a decision of 18 June,[1] endorsed the continuing efforts of DTCD to streamline operational processes and procedures, to improve project design and format, and to strengthen co-operation with Governments and UNDP field offices. The Council commended the use by DTCD of its technical expertise for the follow-up activities of the September 1981 United Nations Conference on the Least Developed Countries[6] and the August 1981 United Nations Conference on New and Renewable Sources of Energy,[7] and its increased delivery to developing countries in 1981, and invited the UNDP Administrator to take into account the Department's special competence and capability when designating executing agencies. The Council urged that the restructuring of the economic and social sectors of the United Nations system be completed, in order that DTCD might achieve greater flexibility in administrative, personnel and financial matters related to technical co-operation projects.

General Assembly action. Endorsing the Governing Council's decision, the General Assembly, by a resolution of 20 December 1982,[5] requested the Secretary-General to make future annual reports on United Nations technical co-operation activities available to the Assembly, through the Economic and Social Council, and recommended that, with reference to DTCD, the report be expanded to contain a qualitative and quantitative analysis of the relationship between programme delivery and administrative costs, the level and use of programme support cost earnings, and expenditures by sources of funds and by components, with an indication of the origin of inputs. He was also requested to include in his annual report a succinct evaluation of the results achieved during the preceding year, with regard to completed projects.

The 21-nation text, introduced by Belgium on behalf of the sponsors, was adopted without vote, following similar approval by the Second (Economic and Financial) Committee on 2 December.

Decision (1982). [1]UNDP Council (report, E/1982/16/Rev.1): 82/19, 18 June.
Reports. S-G, [2]DP/1982/22 & Add.1, [3]DP/1983/18 & Add.1, [4]DP/1983/18/Add.2.
Resolution (1982). [5]GA: 37/232, 20 Dec., text following.
Yearbook references. 1981: [6]p. 406; [7]p. 689.
Meeting records. GA: 2nd Committee, A/C.2/37/SR.1, *6*, 7, 32-40, *44*, *46* (30 Sep.–2 Dec.); plenary, A/37/PV.113 (20 Dec.).

General Assembly resolution 37/232

20 December 1982   Meeting 113   Adopted without vote

Approved by Second Committee (A/37/774) without vote, 2 December (meeting 46); 21-nation draft (A/C.2/37/L.89); agenda item 72 *(j).*

Sponsors: Argentina, Australia, Belgium, Canada, China, Denmark, Ecuador, Egypt, Finland, Germany, Federal Republic of, Jamaica, Japan, Morocco, Netherlands, New Zealand, Norway, Sudan, Sweden, United Kingdom, United States, Yugoslavia.

United Nations technical co-operation activities

The General Assembly,

Recalling its resolution 2029(XX) of 22 November 1965, by which it established the Governing Council of the United Nations Development Programme to provide general policy guidance and direction for the United Nations Development Programme as a whole, as well as for the United Nations regular programmes of technical assistance,

Recalling also its resolution 2688(XXV) of 11 December 1970, in particular paragraph 43 of the annex thereto regarding the accountability of the executing agents to the Administrator of the United Nations Development Programme for the implementation of projects funded by the Programme,

Recalling further its resolution 32/197 of 20 December 1977, in the annex to which were set out the functions of a separate organizational Secretariat entity for, *inter alia,* the management of technical co-operation activities carried out by the United Nations, and the need for that resolution to be fully implemented in order to accomplish economies of scale,

Bearing in mind the goals and objectives of the International Development Strategy for the Third United Nations Development Decade set out in the annex to its resolution 35/56 of 5 December 1980,

Taking into account Economic and Social Council resolution 1982/71 of 10 November 1982 concerning a register of development activities to be developed by the Administrative Committee on Co-ordination within a year,

Convinced that greater transparency in activities of technical co-operation will support the mobilization of financial resources for accelerated development,

Mindful that the Department of Technical Co-operation for Development of the Secretariat is the second largest executing agency of projects financed by the United Nations Development Programme,

Noting with appreciation in this respect the statement made on 5 October 1982 by the Under-Secretary-General for Technical Co-operation for Development,

1. *Endorses* decision 82/19 of 18 June 1982 of the Governing Council of the United Nations Development Programme, in which the Council

took note, *inter alia,* of the annual report of the Secretary-General on technical co-operation activities of the United Nations;

2. *Requests* the Secretary-General to make his annual report on technical co-operation activities of the United Nations also available in the future, through the Economic and Social Council, to the General Assembly, and recommends that, with reference to the Department of Technical Co-operation for Development, the report should be expanded in order to contain a qualitative and quantitative analysis of the relationship between programme delivery and administrative costs, the level and use of programme support cost earnings, and expenditures by sources of funds and by components, with an indication of the origin of inputs;

3. *Requests* the Secretary-General also to include in his annual report a succinct evaluation of the results achieved, during the preceding year, with regard to completed projects.

United Nations Volunteers

UNV activities. During 1982, the United Nations Volunteers (UNV) programme continued to respond to the need for operational, middle-level expertise, with orientation towards assistance to the least developed countries (LDCs) and towards carrying out technical co-operation among developing countries. The UNV activities were described by the UNDP Administrator in two annual reports for 1982—one on the volunteers programme[6] and the other, containing a briefer summary, on UNDP special funds and activities.[5]

In collaboration with UNDP, UNV organized from 7 to 13 March at Sana'a, Yemen, a symposium on the role and potential of volunteerism in international development, with high-level participants from Governments, UNDP and other United Nations organizations, and from bilateral co-operating organizations.

The Sana'a Declaration (annexed to the April report of the UNDP Administrator on UNV operational policy matters[3]), which was adopted by consensus, confirmed and underlined the vital dimensions brought to international development co-operation by volunteer service in general and UNV in particular, and recommended a series of actions to broaden the programme role of UNV and enhance its effectiveness.

Various new UNV programme activities were initiated in 1982, among them a project for assistance to regional and sub-regional intergovernmental institutions and programmes in Africa, participation in an interregional project in the context of the International Drinking Water Supply and Sanitation Decade (1981-1990), increased involvement in technical co-operation among developing countries, more co-operation with the 36 least developed countries in the context of the Substantial New Programme of Action for the 1980s, launched by the United Nations Conference on Trade and Development in 1979,[8] and increased participation in refugee assistance (especially in Africa and Asia) and emergency assistance (such as in Lebanon). UNV participated in country missions and country programme reviews, project design and review meetings, and donor conferences.

The programme expanded its co-operation with United Nations agencies and organizations by introducing seminar-type consultations with individual agencies and organizations.

Youth and domestic development service (DDS) activities continued to grow in importance within the overall UNV programme, in accordance with recommendations in the Sana'a Declaration. The aim of these activities was to strengthen grassroots DDS by sending experienced development workers for two years to share their expertise with people engaged in similar work in another country. A three-year extension of the regional Asia and Pacific DDS project was approved, with UNDP contributing $1.5 million, as was a new DDS project for Africa. By year's end, the number of countries participating in the Asia and Pacific DDS project was close to 50.

Among other activities during 1982 were preparatory activities for the International Youth Year (IYY) (1985). The regional Latin American youth project, "Promotion of Youth Participation in Socio-Economic Development", which assisted in the establishment of youth policies, programmes and projects, was successfully concluded.

By the end of 1982, almost 1,000 volunteers were serving in 90 developing countries, with 81 per cent coming from 53 developing countries themselves. At the end of 1982, 500 volunteers were assigned in LDCs, with 180 additional volunteers under recruitment. About 56 per cent of the volunteers served under UNV-executed sectoral or multisectoral projects; the other 44 per cent were directly attached to projects executed by various United Nations agencies. In accordance with the recommendations of the Sana'a Declaration, efforts were being made to increase the number of women volunteers.

Governing Council action. Having considered the UNDP Administrator's April 1982 reports on 1981 UNV activities[4] and on UNV operational policy matters,[3] the UNDP Governing Council, by a decision of 18 June 1982,[2] requested the Administrator to take appropriate follow-up action to the Sana'a Declaration. The Executive Co-ordinator of UNV was requested to continue his efforts to recruit more women, and to promote the concept of volunteer service in international co-operation with a view to enhancing the utilization and integration of UNV within technical co-operation activities under United Nations auspices. The Council also strongly appealed for contributions to the Special Voluntary Fund.

Economic and Social Council action. The Economic and Social Council, on 28 July,[1] took note of the Governing Council's decision and of the Administrator's report on 1981 UNV activities.

The Council adopted the decision without vote, following similar approval by its Third

(Programme and Co-ordination) Committee on 23 July, on a text proposed by the Committee Chairman.

General Assembly action. The General Assembly, by a resolution of 20 December 1982,[7] noted with satisfaction the continued contribution of the UNV programme as a cost-effective instrument of international development co-operation, as well as its activities in support of youth and domestic development services. It noted the successful outcome and the recommendations of the Sana'a High-Level Symposium on International Volunteer Service and Development; stressed the importance of UNV activities in support of IYY, particularly to operational and pilot activities to increase the participation of youth in development; and expressed the hope that United Nations and other international organizations would fully utilize the programme in development activities, as well as in IYY field activities. The Assembly also renewed its appeal for increased contributions.

The resolution was adopted without vote, following similar approval by the Second (Economic and Financial) Committee on 8 December. The 36-nation draft was introduced by Yemen.

Decisions (1982). [1]ESC: 1982/157, 28 July, text following. [2]UNDP Council (report, E/1982/16/Rev.1): 82/21, 18 June.
Reports. UNDP Administrator, [3]DP/1982/34, [4]DP/1982/37, [5]DP/1983/6/Add.3, [6]DP/1983/31 & Corr.1.
Resolution (1982). [7]GA: 37/229, 20 Dec., text following.
Yearbook reference. [8]1979, p. 568.
Meeting records. ESC: E/1982/SR.49 (28 July). GA: 2nd Committee, A/C.2/37/SR.4, 6, 7, 32-40, *43, 47* (30 Sep.–8 Dec.); plenary, A/37/PV.113 (20 Dec.).

Economic and Social Council decision 1982/157

Adopted without vote

Approved by Third Committee (E/1982/90) without vote, 23 July (meeting 16); draft by Chairman (E/1982/C.3/L.10); agenda item 19.

Report of the Administrator of the United Nations Development Programme on the United Nations Volunteers programme
At its 49th plenary meeting, on 28 July 1982, the Council took note of the annual report of the Administrator of the United Nations Development Programme on the United Nations Volunteers programme and of decision 82/21, adopted on 18 June 1982 by the Governing Council of the United Nations Development Programme.

General Assembly resolution 37/229
20 December 1982   Meeting 113   Adopted without vote

Approved by Second Committee (A/37/774) without vote, 8 December (meeting 47); 36-nation draft (A/C.2/37/L.70); agenda item 72 (f).

Sponsors: Algeria, Austria, Bangladesh, Belgium, Bhutan, China, Costa Rica, Democratic Yemen, Denmark, Djibouti, Egypt, Germany, Federal Republic of, Guinea-Bissau, India, Italy, Jordan, Kenya, Kuwait, Lebanon, Lesotho, Maldives, Nepal, Netherlands, Oman, Philippines, Somalia, Sri Lanka, Sudan, Suriname, Syrian Arab Republic, United Arab Emirates, United States, Upper Volta, Venezuela, Yemen, Yugoslavia.

United Nations Volunteers programme
The General Assembly,
Recalling its resolution 2659(XXV) of 7 December 1970 and subsequent related resolutions, including resolution 36/198 of 17 December 1981,
Having considered the report of the Governing Council of the United Nations Development Programme on its twenty-ninth session and Governing Council decision 82/21 of 18 June 1982 on the United Nations Volunteers programme,

1. *Notes with satisfaction* the continued contribution of the United Nations Volunteers programme as a relevant and cost-effective instrument of international development co-operation, as well as the programme's activities in support of youth and domestic development services;

2. *Further notes* the successful outcome of the first High-level Symposium on International Volunteer Service and Development, held at Sana'a, Yemen, in March 1982, and the ensuing recommendations contained in the Sana'a Declaration and endorsed by the Governing Council of the United Nations Development Programme in its decision 82/21 for follow-up action;

3. *Stresses the importance* of the contribution and activities of the United Nations Volunteers programme in support of the International Youth Year, particularly to operational and pilot activities to increase the participation of youth in development;

4. *Expresses the hope* that the organizations of the United Nations system and other international organizations involved in development activities will fully utilize the potential of the United Nations Volunteers programme in the execution of operational development activities, as well as in the implementation of field activities in the context of the International Youth Year;

5. *Renews its appeal* to Governments, organizations and individuals to contribute or to increase their contributions to the Special Voluntary Fund for the United Nations Volunteers, and notes with appreciation that a substantial contribution has been made to the programme this year by one individual.

Contributions and expenditures

Total income of the UNV programme from the Special Voluntary Fund in 1982 amounted to $3.2 million, including $2.2 million in voluntary contributions from 18 Governments (see table below). Expenditures amounted to $1.8 million, and the balance of funds as at 31 December 1982 was $3.3 million.

The UNDP annual allocation to the Fund was discontinued for the first time in 1982, as directed by the Governing Council in 1977.[5] Noting that $500,000 had been received from a private donor, the UNDP Administrator stated in his report for 1982 on special funds and activities[2] that the overall resource situation nevertheless continued to be unpromising and UNV could not long maintain the programme at its current growth rate.

The costs of volunteers included in projects executed by various United Nations agencies amounted to approximately $5.2 million, or 44 per cent of the overall UNV programme. Eighty-five per cent of the UNV-executed sectoral or multisectoral projects were funded by country indicative planning figures (IPFs) and other UNDP sources representing about $4.8 million in expenditures; the remaining 15 per cent was financed from sources such as government and third-party cost sharing and trust funds representing approximately $860,000.

UNV expenditures by country were shown in a statistical annex to the Administrator's report for 1982.[3] The Special Voluntary Fund continued to finance in-country costs for UNV programme assistants in least developed countries (eight were serving in December), and external costs of volunteers from developing countries for whom no co-sponsorship was available.

Expressing concern about the deteriorating financial situation, the UNDP Governing Council, by a decision of 18 June 1982,[1] strongly appealed to Governments, organizations and individuals to increase their contributions so that additional charges would not have to be made to recipient countries' IPFs. The Council noted with appreciation the donation by an individual and encouraged the Executive Co-ordinator to continue efforts to attract similar contributions. It postponed its review of support-cost reimbursement until 1983.

The appeal for increased contributions and expression of appreciation for the individual contribution were reiterated by the General Assembly in a resolution of 20 December 1982.[4]

CONTRIBUTIONS TO THE SPECIAL VOLUNTARY FUND
FOR THE UN VOLUNTEERS, 1982 AND 1983
(as at 31 December 1982; in US dollar equivalent)

Country	1982 payment	1983 pledge
Austria	7,700	7,700
Bangladesh	1,029	1,000
Belgium	202,532	—
Bhutan	—	690
Botswana	462	459
Brazil	—	10,000
China	—	20,000
Denmark	—	57,143
Germany, Federal Republic of	113,636	120,000
India	5,000	5,000
Indonesia	1,000	—
Italy	346,166	136,519
Lesotho	200	1,000
Liberia	1,600	—
Morocco	5,000	5,000
Netherlands	177,481	—
Norway	366,436	70,423
Solomon Islands	500	—
Sri Lanka	3,000	3,000
Switzerland	126,289	—
Thailand	1,500	1,500
Tunisia	—	4,061
United States	850,000	—
Total	2,209,531	443,495

SOURCE: A/38/5/Add.1.

Decision. [1]UNDP Council (report), E/1982/16/Rev.1): 82/21, paras. 4-6, 18 June.
Reports. UNDP Administrator, [2]DP/1983/6/Add.3, [3]DP/1983/6/Add.4/Corr.1.
Resolution. [4]GA: 37/229, para. 5, 20 Dec.
Yearbook reference. [5]1977, p. 455.

Technical co-operation among developing countries

In 1982, the United Nations Development Programme (UNDP), in concert with the organizations of the United Nations system, continued to carry out its special responsibility for technical co-operation among developing countries (TCDC)—a major effort by developing countries to promote their collective self-reliance. These activities paralleled action in favour of economic co-operation among developing countries, taken by the United Nations Conference on Trade and Development (UNCTAD) and others.

United Nations–supported TCDC activities were, for the most part, either operational or promotional. Operational activities involved sharing or exchange of technical resources, skills and capabilities between developing countries, with participating developing countries themselves largely responsible for their initiation, management and financing. Promotional activities took the form of surveys and studies, workshops, seminars and study tours, expansion of information systems, institution-building in training and research, and training.

The main sources of support for promotional activities were global, interregional, regional and national indicative planning figures (IPFs), the regular budgets of United Nations agencies and regional commissions and UNDP special programme resources. Current procedures, approved by the UNDP Governing Council in June 1981,[7] permitted the use of country IPFs for the support of TCDC projects.

For 1980-1982, the country IPFs used by 20 countries for TCDC involving 51 projects amounted to $9.2 million. Most of the TCDC activities supported by country IPFs concerned training, but others facilitated participation of officials in meetings or assignments of experts from developing countries. In most countries with no previous IPF expenditures on TCDC, significant amounts of IPF resources were being programmed for TCDC activities in 1982-1986, although some Governments were not prepared to use country IPF resources for TCDC activities, as such funds were already insufficient for their development programmes through traditional technical co-operation. A few other Governments made cost-sharing arrangements with UNDP in which all in-country costs were met by contributions of the host Government.

Some additional support for TCDC activities was available from special development funds set up by some agencies, such as the development programme of the World Health Organization and the technical co-operation programme of the Food and Agriculture Organization of the United Nations. Bilateral sources, agencies' funds-in-trust, regional development banks and multilateral funds set up by Governments represented important potential sources of finance for operational TCDC programmes.

In 1982, UNDP continued to implement the June 1981 decisions of the High-level Committee on the Review of Technical Co-operation among Developing Countries[6] and the UNDP Governing Council aimed at promoting TCDC in general and in specific areas. A review of intercountry projects financed from the regional, interregional and global IPFs and having TCDC potential was completed.

The Special Unit for TCDC, established by the UNDP Governing Council in 1974 to assist Governments in TCDC activities and to develop new concepts for promoting TCDC,[5] continued to develop the multisectoral Information Referral System under which it was compiling information on the capacities of, initially, 8,000 institutions of developing countries offering training, research, expertise and consultancy services to other developing countries. The Special Unit also made preparations for, and participated in, a number of meetings and conferences on TCDC, among them the first Meeting of Heads of National Technical Co-operation Agencies of Developing Countries (Tunis, Tunisia, 25-29 October) and the Solidarity Ministerial Meeting on the Industrial Development of Nepal (Kathmandu, November). Together with the UNDP regional bureaux, the Unit reviewed project proposals with a view to strengthening their TCDC aspects.

The regional programme for Africa for the 1982-1986 programming cycle involved 179 projects in 10 sectors; of these, 119, with a total allocation of $132.6 million, were ongoing from the 1977-1981 cycle. In terms of IPF resources earmarked for new projects in 1982-1986, African Governments put priority on self-sufficiency in food, regional co-operation, human resources development, energy, and transport and communications, with a total allocation of $59.6 million. The Second Conference of African Governmental Experts on Technical Co-operation among African Countries on Human Resources Development and Utilization was held from 2 to 11 August 1982 at Libreville, Gabon.

In developing the 1982-1986 regional programme for Asia and the Pacific, the regional bureau convened the first intergovernmental meeting of development assistance co-ordinators for the region. Of the 150 projects for Asia and the Pacific, 43, or 30 per cent (about $50.2 million), were operational and four, or 3 per cent (about $4.7 million) were promotional. The expected cost of the 118 projects for which allocations had been determined was $147 million. Among the 1982-1986 projects, 23 were ongoing, while 24 were new.

Several projects in 1982-1986 were intended to provide continuing support to intergovernmental activities initiated by Governments themselves, with a shift in emphasis from institutional to actual programme support. The South China Sea Fisheries Development and Co-ordinating Programme was an example; it was currently under the direction of the co-operating countries' six-nation management committee. Assistance during 1982-1986 was likely to be $1.2 million (compared to $3.2 million during 1977-1981), the tapering off of the UNDP contribution reflecting the gradual takeover of activities by the Governments themselves. Most regional projects initiated by regional and subregional groupings were under the umbrella of their own permanent committees, intended eventually to take over all functions. Jointly with India and in co-operation with the Economic and Social Commission for Asia and the Pacific, UNDP convened a seminar on TCDC for senior government officials of the Asia and the Pacific region (New Delhi, India, April/May). Representatives from Indonesia, Malaysia, Singapore and Thailand attended the first meeting of the Association of South-East Asian Nations (ASEAN) on TCDC, hosted by the Philippines on 23 and 24 September.

In Latin America, there were 68 IPF-financed ongoing projects in 1982, at a total cost of some $10.9 million. About 80 per cent were promotional, 5 per cent operational, and the remainder mostly pre-operational institution- or framework-building activities. For 1982-1986, $61.2 million was available to the regional programme and 176 new project proposals had been received from Governments and institutions.

The 1982-1986 regional programme for Europe, with an IPF of $16.2 million, planned to support network projects (co-operation among institutions dealing with problems a number of countries had in common), joint endeavours by two or more Governments, and projects of benefit to other regions.

The regional programme for the Arab States for 1982-1986 was being prepared and was to include more TCDC modalities in projects supported by the regional IPF.

Nine new global agricultural research projects were planned for 1982-1986, involving an IPF contribution of $34.7 million. Their training components amounted to $11 million.

The interregional IPF promoted TCDC activities in human resources development by encouraging institutional co-operation among public enterprises in developing countries. It also supported projects for development in telecommunications and training in maritime transport.

Information on 1982 TCDC activities was provided in March[4] and April 1983[3] reports by the UNDP Administrator.

Report of the Administrator. In an April 1982 report on the use of funds from the Special Programme Resources during 1982-1983 for promotional TCDC activities,[2] the UNDP Administrator reported that the $1 million allocated by the UNDP Governing Council in 1981 for TCDC promotional purposes was reduced to $600,000, since resources fell short of the target. The Special Unit for TCDC would use the balance of this amount—$245,000, after deduction for commitments such as the TCDC training programme, consultancy services and *TCDC News*—for supporting promotional TCDC activities during 1982 and 1983. With a view to exploring the possibility of transforming some UNDP intercountry projects into TCDC activities or enhancing their TCDC elements, a review of ongoing regional projects had been initiated in collaboration with the regional UNDP bureaux. Identification of national research and training centres with multinational scope and development of their mutual co-operation, as well as collaboration with United Nations agencies, intergovernmental and non-governmental organizations to promote TCDC, were among continuing activities.

The Administrator also provided information on the use of regional, interregional and global IPFs. He concluded that regional projects involving TCDC had been increasing; he felt, however, that project design should include more basic elements of TCDC, such as developing countries' own capabilities in initiative, management, financing and inputs. He saw a need to continue reviewing the TCDC elements and potential in projects, especially through regional and country programming exercises. In the programmes for 1982-1986, the regional, interregional and global IPFs would be more consciously used for promoting and supporting TCDC activities.

Many potential sources existed for financing TCDC both within and outside the United Nations system, he stated, including several funds managed by United Nations agencies, bilateral aid and investment institutions, development banks and government funds.

Governing Council action. Taking note of the Administrator's report, the UNDP Governing Council, on 18 June 1982,[1] requested him to consult with the High-level Committee on TCDC at its 1983 session on measures to facilitate TCDC, including the streamlining of existing procedures, and on the activities of the Special Unit for TCDC, with a view to promoting further TCDC.

Decision. [1]UNDP Council (report, E/1982/16/Rev.1): 82/24, 18 June.
Reports. UNDP Administrator, [2]DP/1982/42 & Add.1, [3]DP/1983/6/Add.3, [4]TCDC/3/2.
Resolution (prior). [5]GA: 3251(XXIX), 4 Dec. 1974 (YUN 1974, p. 419).
Yearbook references. 1981: [6]p. 463; [7]p. 467.

UN Capital Development Fund

By the end of 1982, the eighth year of its operations, the United Nations Capital Development Fund's (UNCDF) cumulative project commitments totalled $277 million for financing 219 projects in 42 countries, while cumulative expenditures totalled $132 million.

The Fund assisted developing countries, first and foremost the least developed, in the development of their economies by supplementing existing sources of capital assistance through grants and loans, particularly long-term loans free of interest or at low interest rates, credit and guarantee schemes, and revolving funds. The Fund provided concessional capital assistance for projects smaller than those usually considered by other multilateral financing institutions. It offered a variety of contribution modalities for donors, such as cost-sharing and trust fund arrangements, including trust funds conditioned on procurement in the donor country, and contributions in kind. The Fund's assistance was not confined to any particular sector of activity; it provided not only for development of new infrastructure but also for overcoming bottlenecks and strengthening national capacity by the expansion, equipment, and rehabilitation of existing infrastructure and industrial plants.

Management and administration of the Fund were provided by the United Nations Development Programme (UNDP). The complementarity between the UNDP technical co-operation activities and UNCDF capital assistance enabled beneficiary Governments to follow through on technical assistance activities carried out under IPF funding.

Taking note of the increase in the volume of the Fund's activities and endorsing their orientation, including the emphasis on small-scale development projects, the UNDP Governing Council, by a decision of 18 June,[1] requested the UNDP Administrator to strengthen the complementarity between the Fund's capital assistance and other UNDP-administered assistance, and to ensure that the Fund would be fully associated with UNDP follow-up to the 1981 United Nations Conference on the Least Developed Countries,[3] including round-table meetings for that purpose.

Consideration of the Fund's operations by the Council was based on a report by the Administrator submitted in April 1982.[2]

In line with the Council's request, the Fund gave particular emphasis in 1982 to co-ordinating its activities and participated in follow-up round-table meetings organized by Cape Verde, Mali and Rwanda. Of the 34 projects approved by UNCDF in 1982, 22 were co-financed with UNDP through indicative planning figure (IPF) resources, the Special Measures Fund for the Least Developed Countries and the United Nations Sudano-Sahelian Office, and four were co-financed with bilateral organizations. At the field operations level, the UNDP Office for Projects Execution assisted a number of Governments in implementing UNCDF-financed projects. Several other United Nations specialized agencies, including the United Nations Children's Fund, the United Nations Industrial Development Organization, and the World Food Programme, as well as the United

Nations Department of Technical Co-operation for Development, co-operated with UNCDF. At the end of 1982, 28 UNCDF-assisted projects were benefiting from joint financing provided by bilateral agencies and multilateral financing institutions.

The Fund continued negotiations, initiated in 1981, for a basic agreement with each beneficiary Government towards establishing a legal framework governing the general terms and conditions of partnership under which UNCDF provided assistance. In 1982, 24 Governments signed the agreement, bringing the total to 36.

The largest portion (30.6 per cent) of the Fund's assistance in 1982 continued to be directed to the agricultural sector, including development of water resources for agricultural purposes. Assistance was also provided for primary health care, safe drinking-water supply, low-cost housing, primary education and employment-generating activities; and to develop the productive sectors and economic infrastructure, particularly in agriculture, transportation, energy and small-scale industries. The percentage distribution of UNCDF project commitments by main sector of activity was: agriculture, 20.8 per cent; potable water supply and sanitation, 20.4 per cent; transport and communications, 17.2 per cent; industries, 10 per cent; development of water resources for agricultural purposes, 9.8 per cent; health, 6.4 per cent; education and training, 6 per cent; energy and shelter, 4.7 per cent each.

UNCDF assistance was provided to 43 countries, including the 36 designated least developed countries, and seven countries which the General Assembly had directed be given special consideration.

During the year, the Fund fielded 10 planning and programming missions to review ongoing UNCDF-funded projects and to consider project proposals. As a follow-up to such efforts, it dispatched 48 project formulation missions in 22 countries.

Decision (1982). UNDP Council (report, E/1982/16/Rev.1): [1]82/22, 18 June.
Report. [2]UNDP Administrator, DP/1982/38.
Yearbook reference. [3]1981, p. 406.

UNCDF finances

Payments in 1982 to the Fund's general resources amounted to $27,940,550 in voluntary contributions by 35 Governments (see table below), augmented by interest and other adjustments which raised total income to $41,843,197.

By the end of 1982, total cumulative voluntary contributions to the Fund's general resources amounted to $178 million. In addition, the Fund received $1.8 million under cost-sharing arrangements and $1.5 million under trust fund arrangements, for a total of $181.3 million. For 1983, voluntary contributions pledged to the Fund by 34 Governments amounted to $16.5 million as at 31 December 1982.

By its 18 June 1982 decision on UNCDF,[3] the Governing Council urged Governments, non-governmental and other donor agencies to contribute to the Fund's resources, and decided that the Fund should continue its operations under the partial funding system.

In another decision of the same date,[1] the Council authorized acceptance, for an experimental period of one year, of trust funds for UNCDF conditioned on procurement from donor countries. By the end of 1982, negotiations were under way for such conditioned trust-fund agreements for four projects costing approximately $8 million.

In a third decision adopted on 18 June,[2] on the Conference on Least Developed Countries (LDCs), the Governing Council, emphasizing the Fund's role in providing additional resources to LDCs, urged substantial contributions to UNCDF.

New project commitments approved in 1982 amounted to $59.9 million for 34 projects in 22 countries, with nearly $21 million to be expended directly by government executing agencies and more than $39 million by co-operating United Nations agencies. Actual project expenditures of $27.7 million—$10.5 million by government executing agencies and $17.2 million by United Nations agencies—were lower than expected, mainly because of the rescheduling of procurement, delays in project implementation and savings resulting from favourable exchange rates. At year's end, the Fund had 185 ongoing projects with a total cost of $251.4 million. Against this amount, $129.3 million had been expended. In addition, 34 projects with a total cost of $25.8 million were completed by the end of 1982.

The total administrative costs for 1982 met from the Fund's general resources were $2.149 million. The total disbursements for programme support services (introduced in 1981) amounted to $1.263 million.

For 1982, UNCDF resources increased by $8.9 million, thus bringing the Fund's total available resources to $95.5 million at the end of the year, inclusive of the fully funded operational reserve of $29.6 million (compared to $23.3 million at the end of 1981). These resources represented 64.5 per cent of the Fund's total outstanding project commitments of $148 million.

Information on the Fund's activities and finances were provided in the annual report of the UNDP Administrator for 1982,[4] with a statistical annex,[5] and in a report on 1982 UNCDF activities.[6]

CONTRIBUTIONS TO UNCDF, 1982 AND 1983
(as at 31 December 1982; in US dollar equivalent)

Country	1982 payment	1983 pledge
Afghanistan	2,000	2,000
Algeria	30,566	37,000
Argentina	23,646	—
Australia	523,150	528,846
Austria	—	16,949
Bangladesh	3,847	3,289
Benin	—	2,000
Bhutan	—	1,380
Botswana	4,621	4,587
China	119,565	111,111
Cuba	23,923	23,641
Cyprus	500	500
Democratic Yemen	1,456	1,602
Denmark	1,675,978	2,285,714
Egypt	21,166	—
Finland	545,455	636,364
Greece	5,000	10,000
Italy	3,403,128	2,047,782
Jamaica	—	3,000
Japan	2,000,000	—
Lao People's Democratic Republic	6,000	1,500
Lesotho	1,000	1,500
Malawi	6,535	7,028
Maldives	000	600
Mauritius	1,267	—
Morocco	8,333	7,813
Nepal	1,000	—
Netherlands	5,424,825	—
Norway	4,794,521	4,225,352
Pakistan	85,076	—
Senegal	—	30,410
Sweden	4,790,409	4,324,324
Switzerland	—	1,988,263
Tunisia	3,411	3,050
Turkey	163,833	153,153
United Republic of Cameroon	—	962
United Republic of Tanzania	2,092	2,092
United States	4,000,000	—
Viet Nam	1,000	1,000
Yemen	2,300	3,000
Yugoslavia	242,888	—
Zambia	21,459	10,834
Zimbabwe	—	6,510
Total	27,940,550	16,483,156

SOURCE: A/38/5/Add.1.

Decisions (1982). UNDP Council (report, E/1982/16/Rev.1): [1]82/5, sect. IV, paras. 4 & 5; [2]82/11, para. 1; [3]82/22, 18 June.
Reports. UNDP Administrator, [4]DP/1983/6/Add.3, [5]DP/1983/6/Add.4/Corr.1, [6]DP/1983/33.

Partial funding system

In a decision of 18 June 1982,[1] the UNDP Governing Council, as recommended by the UNDP Administrator in an April report on UNCDF,[3] authorized UNCDF to continue its operations under the partial funding system, which it had originally approved in 1979 for an experimental period of two years,[4] and had extended in June 1981 for another year.[5] Partial funding enabled UNCDF to increase the level of project disbursements and to absorb accumulated liquidity resulting from the former full funding policy, and permitted it to plan projects on a cash-flow basis beyond resources actually pledged, while maintaining an operational reserve at 20 per cent of outstanding project commitments. During the period that the system had been in effect until the end of 1982, compared to the full funding system in 1975-1978, the Fund had been able to quadruple its expenditures, nearly triple its project commitments and increase the country coverage from 26 to 42.

Under its 18 June 1982 decision, the Council also requested the Administrator to include in his annual report a chapter on the operation of the partial funding system.

During the year, the partial funding system enabled the Fund to approve new project commitments in the amount of $60 million ($11.2 million less than the 1981 approval level), instead of $30 million, which would have been the approval ceiling for the full year had the Fund been required to revert to a full funding system in June 1982.

The difference between outstanding project commitments and available resources was $52.5 million at the end of the year. In accordance with the financial control formula under the partial funding system, this amount was expected to be covered by pledges for 1983 and contributions for 1984.

In his report on the Fund's operations in 1982,[2] the UNDP Administrator considered the partial funding system to be an efficient instrument for maximizing the utilization of resources and increasing assistance to beneficiary countries.

Decision (1982). [1]UNDP Council (report, E/1982/16/Rev.1): 82/22, para. 3, 18 June.
Reports. UNDP Administrator, [2]DP/1983/33, [3]DP/1982/39.
Yearbook references. [4]1979, p. 604; [5]1981, p. 470.

Chapter III

Economic assistance, disasters and emergency relief

Contents

Related topics:

Development and international economic and social policy: Special measures for the least developed and other developing countries. Development assistance: General aspects of operational activities for development. Environment: Desertification control. Refugees and displaced persons.

For resolutions and decisions of major organs mentioned but not reproduced, refer to INDEX OF RESOLUTIONS AND DECISIONS.

General aspects

Assistance rendered by the United Nations through special economic, humanitarian and disaster relief assistance to countries in several parts of the world, notably in Africa, was reviewed in 1982 by the Economic and Social Council and the General Assembly. The Council decided without vote on 5 February 1982 that, beginning in 1983, it would normally consider this topic at its second regular session in the middle of each year, unless circumstances warranted earlier consideration.[1] It took this action on a proposal by its President, submitted on the basis of informal consultations.

At its second session of 1982, in July, the Council heard oral reports by the Joint Co-ordinator for Special Economic Assistance Programmes on the situation in 17 African countries; by the United Nations Disaster Relief Co-ordinator on measures taken following floods in Democratic Yemen and Madagascar; and by the United Nations High Commissioner for Refugees on several refugee situations in Africa. It also received a report by the Secretary-General on assistance to drought-stricken areas in East Africa. On 27 July, acting without vote on a proposal by the President, it took note of these reports and appealed to Member States and organizations to continue providing assistance.[2]

Reports on special economic and disaster relief assistance were also considered by the Assembly's Second (Economic and Financial) Committee. On the Committee's recommendation, approved without vote on 2 December on an oral proposal of the Chairman, the Assembly took note of written reports by the Secretary-General on the countries receiving special economic assistance and an oral report by the Disaster Relief Co-ordinator on measures following the floods in Madagascar.[4] The first part of the Committee's report on the item,[5] listing the documents before it, was noted by the Assembly in a decision orally proposed by the President.[3] Both decisions were adopted without vote on 17 December.

Decisions (1982). ESC: [1]1982/101, 5 Feb., text following; [2]1982/151, 27 July, text following. GA: [3]37/432, 17 Dec., text following; [4]37/434, 17 Dec., text following.
Report. [5]GA, 2nd Committee, A/37/702.
Meeting records. ESC: E/1982/SR.3, 46-48 (5 Feb. & 19-27 July). GA: 2nd Committee, A/C.2/37/SR.6, 31, 38, 40, 42, 44, 46 (5 Oct.–2 Dec.); plenary, A/37/PV.109 (17 Dec.).

Economic and Social Council decision 1982/101

Adopted without vote

Draft by President (E/1982/L.14), based on informal consultations; agenda item 3.

Special economic, humanitarian and disaster relief assistance
At its 3rd plenary meeting, on 5 February 1982, the Council decided that, beginning in 1983, the item entitled "Special economic, humanitarian and disaster relief assistance" should normally be considered at its second regular session, unless circumstances warranted earlier con-

sideration of the matter.

Economic and Social Council decision 1982/151

Adopted without vote

Draft by President (E/1982/L.49); agenda item 4.

Special economic, humanitarian and disaster relief assistance
At its 48th plenary meeting, on 27 July 1982, the Council:
(a) Took note of:
(i) The oral report made by the Joint Co-ordinator for Special Economic Assistance Programmes, on behalf of the Secretary-General, on the situation in Benin, Botswana, Cape Verde, the Central African Republic, Chad, the Comoros, Djibouti, Equatorial Guinea, the Gambia, Guinea-Bissau, Lesotho, Liberia, Mozambique, Sao Tome and Principe, Uganda, Zambia and Zimbabwe;
(ii) The oral report made by the United Nations Disaster Relief Co-ordinator, on behalf of the Secretary-General, on the measures taken following the heavy floods that have affected Democratic Yemen and the cyclones and floods in Madagascar;
(iii) The oral report made by the United Nations High Commissioner for Refugees, on behalf of the Secretary-General, on assistance to student refugees in southern Africa, on assistance to the refugees in Somalia, and on the report of the Secretary-General on the International Conference on Assistance to Refugees in Africa;
(b) Took note also of the report of the Secretary-General on assistance to the drought-stricken areas in Djibouti, Ethiopia, Kenya, Somalia, the Sudan and Uganda, and decided to transmit it to the General Assembly at its thirty-seventh session;
(c) Took note further of the statements made by delegations during the discussion of the item entitled "Special economic, humanitarian and disaster relief assistance" at the second regular session of 1982 of the Council;
(d) Decided to appeal to all Member States, organs and organizations of the United Nations system, and to other intergovernmental and non-governmental organizations, to continue their efforts in providing the necessary assistance, pursuant to the relevant resolutions of the General Assembly and the Economic and Social Council.

General Assembly decision 37/432

Adopted without vote

Oral proposal by President; agenda item 74.

Special economic and disaster relief assistance
At its 109th plenary meeting, on 17 December 1982, the General Assembly took note of part I of the report of the Second Committee.

General Assembly decision 37/434

Adopted without vote

Approved by Second Committee (A/37/702/Add.2) without vote, 2 December (meeting 46); draft orally proposed by Chairman; agenda item 74 *(b)*.

Reports on special economic and disaster relief assistance
At its 109th plenary meeting, on 17 December 1982, the General Assembly, on the recommendation of the Second Committee, took note of the following reports:
(a) Report of the Secretary-General on assistance to Equatorial Guinea;
(b) Report of the Secretary-General on assistance to Zambia;
(c) Report of the Secretary-General on assistance to Zimbabwe;
(d) Report of the Secretary-General on assistance to Benin, Botswana, Cape Verde, the Central African Republic, Chad, the Comoros, Djibouti, Equatorial Guinea, the Gambia, Guinea-Bissau, Lesotho, Liberia, Mozambique, Sao Tome and Principe, Uganda, Zambia and Zimbabwe;
(e) Oral report made on behalf of the Secretary-General by the United Nations Disaster Relief Co-ordinator on measures taken following the cyclones and floods in Madagascar.

Economic assistance

The United Nations continued in 1982 to mobilize special economic assistance programmes for countries identified by the General Assembly as facing particularly onerous economic difficulties. Under mandates from the Assembly, the United Nations Secretariat's Unit for Special Economic Assistance Programmes helped to co-ordinate activities by the United Nations system and monitored other assistance efforts by Governments.

For most of the affected countries, multiagency missions in previous years had drawn up assistance programmes and identified individual projects, as guidance for multilateral and bilateral assistance. During 1982, similar missions, organized by the United Nations, again visited most of the countries to assess the situation and update the assistance programmes. Missions were sent for the first time to the Gambia, Liberia and Uganda. In their reports, the various missions described ongoing projects and, in many cases, identified new projects proposed by the Government. The estimated cost of projects was given, for the information of potential donors. The missions' reports were annexed to a series of reports by the Secretary-General to the Assembly, which had requested this information in December 1981.[3]

The Secretary-General also submitted to the Assembly in October a report containing replies by 24 United Nations bodies and specialized agencies, describing their assistance to the countries concerned.[2] The Assembly took note of this report on 17 December.[1]

After receiving these reports, the Assembly, on 17 December, adopted resolutions on most of the countries, endorsing the missions' assessments and recommendations, appealing to United Nations Member States and intergovernmental bodies to give aid, and requesting United Nations organizations and programmes to increase their assistance, co-operate with the Secretary-General in organizing a programme for each country, and report to him periodically on what they had done and spent for that purpose. The Secretary-General was asked to continue mobilizing resources, to maintain contact with States and organizations, and to arrange for a further review of each country's economic situation and of progress in organizing and implementing the programmes. He was to apprise the Economic and Social Council in 1983 of the status of the programmes and report to the Assembly later in 1983—or, in a few cases, in 1984.

Information on the status of the programmes was given to the Economic and Social Council on 19 July by the Joint Co-ordinator for Special Economic Assistance Programmes, Gordon K. Goundrey, and to the Assembly's Second Committee on 5 October by the Under-Secretary-General for Special Political Questions and Co-ordinator of Special Economic Assistance Prgrammes, Abdulrahim Abby Farah.

Of the 23 countries which were the object of special economic assistance programmes and related activities, 19 were in Africa. Two were in Latin America, and the others were Democratic Yemen (a new programme) and Tonga. Unlike the case of the other countries, special assistance for Seychelles was arranged on the initiative of the Security Council. Sierra Leone was added in 1982 to the list of countries benefiting from special economic assistance programmes. An emergency assistance programme was also under way in Lebanon. Most of the affected countries were also classified as least developed countries, for which a new programme of special measures was under way (see Chapter I of this section).

Most financing for the projects identified in these programmes was provided bilaterally or through the assistance programmes of multilateral agencies. Five Governments contributed a total of $490,977 in 1982 to the United Nations Trust Fund for Special Economic Assistance Programmes and to similar special accounts for Botswana and Mozambique: Cyprus, $8,000 ($1,500 for Zambia; $1,000 for Chad; $500 each for Benin, Botswana, Cape Verde, Comoros, Djibouti, Equatorial Guinea, Grenada, Guinea-Bissau, Mozambique, Nicaragua, Sao Tome and Principe); the Philippines, $6,000 ($1,000 each for Benin and Liberia; $500 each for Central African Republic, Chad, Djibouti, Equatorial Guinea, Gambia, Grenada, Zambia, Zimbabwe); the United Kingdom, $466,606 (for Uganda); the United Republic of Cameroon, $8,371 ($5,596 for Benin; $2,775 for Grenada); and Viet Nam, $500 (for Seychelles). Also included in the total were $500 from Cyprus and $1,000 from the Philippines to an account for St. Kitts–Nevis, Anguilla, Saint Lucia, and Saint Vincent and the Grenadines.

Including interest, these and related accounts received a total of $725,822 in income during 1982, as follows: Angola, $100; Benin, $8,527; Botswana, $1,274; Cape Verde, $5,486; Central African Republic, $579; Chad, $1,838; Comoros, $1,015; Djibouti, $11,707; Equatorial Guinea, $3,053; Gambia, $579; Grenada, $4,373; Guinea-Bissau, $998; Liberia, $1,159; Mozambique, $57,319; Nicaragua, $634; St. Kitts–Nevis, Anguilla, Saint Lucia, and Saint Vincent and the Grenadines, $1,847; Sao Tome and Principe, $904; Seychelles, $1,009; Sudan, $62,142; Tonga, $2,996; Uganda, $554,498; Yugoslavia, $189; Zambia, $2,827; Zimbabwe, $769. The only expenditure during the year was $12,262 from the special account for the Sudan.

A separate Special Fund for the Republic of Seychelles was established during 1982.

Decision (1982). [1]GA: 37/434, para. *(d)*, 17 Dec.
Report. [2]S-G, A/37/140.
Yearbook reference. [3]1981, p. 496.
Meeting records. ESC: E/1982/SR.46 (19 July). GA: 2nd Committee, A/C.2/37/SR.6 (5 Oct.).

Africa

All 19 of the African States for which special economic assistance programmes or similar activities were under way by the end of 1982 were south of the Sahara, and 10 of them were on the General Assembly's list of least developed countries (see Chapter I of this section)—all but Djibouti, Equatorial Guinea, Liberia, Mozambique, Sao Tome and Principe, Seychelles, Sierra Leone, Zambia and Zimbabwe. The beneficiaries were: in Central Africa, the Central African Republic, Chad, Equatorial Guinea and Sao Tome and Principe; in East Africa, Djibouti and Uganda; in the Indian Ocean off the East African coast, the Comoros and Seychelles; in southern Africa, Botswana, Lesotho, Mozambique, Zambia and Zimbabwe; and in West Africa, Benin, Cape Verde, the Gambia, Guinea-Bissau, Liberia and Sierra Leone.

These programmes were in addition to assistance rendered to the drought-stricken areas of Africa.

The Assembly, in a resolution of 16 November on co-operation between the United Nations and the Organization of African Unity (OAU),[1] reiterated its appreciation for the Secretary-General's efforts to organize and mobilize special economic assistance programmes for African States with grave economic difficulties, in particular for newly independent and front-line States, to help them cope with the situation caused by South African acts of aggression. It called on Member States, regional and international organizations and the United Nations system to participate in implementing the programmes. It requested the Secretary-General to keep OAU informed of the international response to the programmes and to co-ordinate efforts with similar OAU programmes. It called on Member States and the United Nations system to increase assistance to the African States affected by serious economic problems, in particular problems of displaced persons, resulting from natural or other disasters, by mobilizing special programmes of economic and emergency assistance.

Resolution (1982). [1]GA: 37/15, paras. 11-13 & 16, 16 Nov.

Benin

An inter-agency review mission sent from 12 to 17 July 1982 to study Benin's economic situation[1] in pursuance of a December 1981 request by the General Assembly[3] noted the country's growing external trade deficit, poor harvests resulting from drought, and serious coastal flooding in June and July 1982. Positive developments included the implementation of major cement, maize, sugar and offshore petroleum exploitation projects, a modest government budget surplus,

the restructuring of state and parastatal organizations, and the promulgation on 20 May of a new investment code.

The mission reported on 51 projects in the country's $212-million assistance programme directed to strengthen Benin's physical and social infrastructure and its modest but growing industries. Among the largest of urgent programmes were a national seed-multiplication plan, potable water supply for villages, urban water development, five university departments and polytechnical colleges. While most of the projects were for economic development, some $41 million of them were designed to meet urgent food and health needs. The mission reported that foreign contributions of about $81 million had been provided or firmly pledged by 17 July, permitting a number of projects to commence or be completed.

Benin informed the General Assembly's Second (Economic and Financial) Committee in November that, in addition to adopting a new investment code aimed at attracting foreign capital, it was preparing a 1983-1987 plan for integrated development of rural areas, industry, energy, transportation, education and health, for which it needed large sums of money.

The Assembly, on 17 December,[2] endorsed the mission's recommendations and urged Member States and organizations to respond generously at a donors' conference to be held in Benin in 1983. It also urged them to provide food, medicines, and equipment for hospitals and schools. This action was taken by a resolution adopted without vote, following similar approval by the Second Committee on 2 December.

The text was introduced by Algeria on behalf of 46 nations and was approved with oral revisions resulting from informal consultations. As a result of these revisions, the Assembly endorsed the mission's recommendations "fully" rather than "without reservation", and it requested of the Secretary-General a 1984 report rather than a 1983 review of the progress made in Benin's economic situation and the special economic assistance programme.

Report. [1]S-G, annexing mission report, A/37/134 & Corr.1.
Resolution (1982). [2]GA: 37/151, 17 Dec., text following.
Resolution (prior). [3]GA: 36/208, 17 Dec. 1981 (YUN 1981, p. 498).
Meeting records. ESC: E/1982/SR.46 (19 July). GA: 2nd Committee, A/C.2/37/SR.27-30, *31, 33, 38, 46* (2 Nov.–2 Dec.); plenary, A/37/PV.109 (17 Dec.).

General Assembly resolution 37/151

17 December 1982   Meeting 109   Adopted without vote

Approved by Second Committee (A/37/702Add.2) without vote, 2 December (meeting 46); 46-nation draft (A/C.2/37/L.50), orally revised in informal consultations; agenda item 74 *(b).*

Sponsors: Afghanistan, Algeria, Angola, Barbados, Benin, Botswana, Burundi, Cape Verde, Central African Republic, Chad, China, Cuba, Djibouti, Dominican Republic, Ethiopia, France, Gambia, Guinea-Bissau, Guyana, India, Kenya, Libyan Arab

Jamahiriya, Madagascar, Mali, Mauritania, Mongolia, Mozambique, Nicaragua, Niger, Nigeria, Pakistan, Romania, Sao Tome and Principe, Senegal, Sierra Leone, Sudan, Swaziland, Thailand, Togo, Tunisia, Uganda, United Republic of Cameroon, Upper Volta, Viet Nam, Yugoslavia, Zambia.

Special economic assistance to Benin

The General Assembly,

Recalling its resolutions 35/88 of 5 December 1980 and 36/208 of 17 December 1981, in which it appealed to the international community to provide effective and continuous financial, material and technical assistance to Benin so as to help that country overcome its financial and economic difficulties,

Recalling also Security Council resolution 419(1977) of 24 November 1977, in which the Council appealed to all States and all appropriate international organizations, including the United Nations and the specialized agencies, to assist Benin,

Having heard the statement made by the representative of Benin before the Second Committee on 4 November 1982 describing his country's serious economic and financial situation and the measures adopted by his Government to tackle those difficulties,

Having considered the report of the Secretary-General to which is annexed the report of the review mission which he dispatched to Benin in July 1982,

Noting from the report that there has been an encouraging development in Benin as a result of the measures adopted by the Government and the appeal of the Secretary-General,

Deeply concerned, however, by the fact that Benin continues to experience serious economic and financial difficulties, characterized by a severe balance-of-payments disequilibrium, heavy burdens of external debt and a lack of resources to implement its planned economic and social development programme,

Noting further that unfavourable climatic conditions in Benin have entailed losses in agricultural and livestock production and that serious floods have led the Government to introduce emergency measures to assist the stricken populations,

Taking note of the recommendation concerning the programme of assistance to Benin as referred to in the report of the Secretary-General,

Noting further Benin's urgent need for international assistance in its health programmes, as well as for food aid,

Aware of the desire of the Government of Benin to organize in January 1983, with the assistance of the United Nations Development Programme, a round-table conference of partners in development to discuss the country's development needs and to consider ways and means of helping the Government in its efforts to meet those needs,

Bearing in mind that Benin is classified as one of the least developed countries,

1. *Expresses its appreciation* to the Secretary-General for the measures he has taken to organize an international programme of economic assistance for Benin;

2. *Endorses fully* the assessment and recommendations of the mission contained in the annex to the report of the Secretary-General;

3. *Expresses its appreciation* for the assistance already given or pledged to Benin by Member States, organizations of the United Nations system and regional, interregional and intergovernmental organizations;

4. *Takes note with appreciation* of the various measures adopted by the Government of Benin to strengthen the country's economy, and of the fruitful implementation of a number of economic initiatives of prime importance;

5. *Expresses its concern* at the fact that, in spite of those favourable developments, the Government of Benin continues to encounter serious economic and financial difficulties and that those problems have been aggravated by losses in agricultural and livestock production as a result of the floods in the south of the country and the drought in the north;

6. *Draws attention* to the needs of Benin for supplementary external assistance in order to implement fully the recommended special programme of economic assistance;

7. *Urgently reiterates the appeal* it has addressed to all Member States to provide substantial and appropriate assistance bilaterally and multilaterally, if possible in the form of grants-in-aid or loans granted on favourable terms, in order to enable Benin to carry out fully the recommended special programme of economic assistance;

8. *Urges* Member States, organizations and programmes of the United Nations, regional and interregional organizations, financing and development institutions and intergovernmental and non-governmental organizations to respond generously to the needs of Benin at the round-table conference, scheduled to be held at Cotonou in January 1983;

9. *Requests* the appropriate bodies and programmes of the United Nations—in particular the United Nations Development Programme, the Food and Agriculture Organization of the United Nations, the International Fund for Agricultural Development and the United Nations Children's Fund—to maintain and expand their programmes of assistance to Benin, to co-operate closely with the Secretary-General in organizing an effective international programme of assistance and to report periodically to him on the measures they have taken and the resources they have made available to help that country;

10. *Calls upon* regional and interregional organizations and other intergovernmental bodies and non-governmental organizations, as well as international development and financial institutions, to give urgent consideration to the establishment of a programme of assistance to Benin or, where one is already in existence, to the expansion of that programme;

11. *Urges* Member States and appropriate United Nations agencies—in particular the United Nations Development Programme, the World Food Programme and the United Nations Fund for Population Activities—to provide all possible assistance to help the Government of Benin to meet the critical humanitarian needs of the population, and to provide to that Government, as appropriate, food, medicines and equipment for hospitals and schools;

12. *Invites* the United Nations Development Programme, the United Nations Children's Fund, the World Food Programme, the World Health Organization, the Food and Agriculture Organization of the United Nations, the World Bank and the International Fund for Agricultural Development to bring to the attention of their governing bodies, for their consideration, the special needs of Benin and to report the decisions of those bodies to the Secretary-General by 15 July 1983;

13. *Requests* the Secretary-General:

(a) To continue his efforts to mobilize the necessary resources for an effective programme of financial, technical and material assistance to Benin;

(b) To ensure that the necessary financial and budgetary arrangements are made to continue the organization of the international programme of assistance to Benin and the mobilization of that assistance;

(c) To keep the situation in Benin under constant review, to maintain close contact with Member States, the specialized agencies, regional and other intergovernmental organizations and the international financial institutions concerned, and to apprise the Economic and Social Council, at its second regular session of 1983, of the status of the special programme of economic assistance for Benin;

(d) To report on the progress made in the economic situation of Benin and in the organization and implementation of the special programme of economic assistance for that country in time for the matter to be considered by the General Assembly not later than at its thirty-ninth session.

Botswana

Four of the original 16 projects in the special economic assistance programme begun in 1977[4] to meet the emergency and strategic needs of Botswana remained to be completed, according to an inter-agency mission sent there in 1982 to review the economic situation.[1] The mission, dispatched in pursuance of a December 1981 request by the General Assembly,[3] visited Botswana from 24 to 30 June 1982. The projects remaining to be completed were: take-over of the rail system and fleet from Zimbabwe Railways; filling of petroleum storage tanks; the Botswana-Zambia road; and construction of a new national airport at Gaborone and improvement of terminals and runways at other airports. The mission also reviewed and updated five rehabilitation and development projects related to forest-fire control, tourism, and strengthening of transport and communications links with Zimbabwe, and reported the successful implementation of a foot-and-mouth disease control programme.

The mission reported that no real growth in Botswana's gross domestic product was expected in 1981/82, principally as a result of a fall in diamond exports. To expand job creation, the Government had set up a fund to meet part of the labour costs of new or expanding small businesses. In April the President had declared the country to be drought-stricken as a consequence of inadequate rainfall in 1981/82. As a result, special feeding measures were needed for some 200,000 people and international assistance was urgently required.

The General Assembly, by a resolution of 17 December 1982,[2] endorsed the revised programme of assistance to Botswana contained in the mission's report and drew particular attention to the transport and communications projects as well as those for rehabilitation of border areas. It appealed to Member States and organizations to expand their assistance.

The Assembly adopted this text without vote, following its approval in like manner by the Second Committee on 2 December. The draft, which was introduced by Kenya and sponsored by 23 nations, incorporated minor oral revisions agreed upon in informal consultations.

Report. [1]S-G, annexing mission report, A/37/132-S/15311.
Resolution (1982). [2]GA: 37/148, 17 Dec., text following.
Resolution (prior). [3]GA: 36/222, 17 Dec. 1981 (YUN 1981, p. 499).
Yearbook reference. [4]1977, p. 219.
Meeting records. ESC: E/1982/SR.46 (19 July). GA: 2nd Committee, A/C.2/37/SR.27-31, 33, *40, 46* (2 Nov.–2 Dec.); plenary, A/37/PV.109 (17 Dec.).

General Assembly resolution 37/148

17 December 1982   Meeting 109   Adopted without vote

Approved by Second Committee (A/37/702/Add.2) without vote, 2 December (meeting 46); 23-nation draft (A/C.2/37/L.37), orally revised in informal consultations and further orally revised; agenda item 74 *(b)*.

Sponsors: Afghanistan, Botswana, Cape Verde, Central African Republic, Djibouti, Ethiopia, Gambia, Guinea-Bissau, Kenya, Lesotho, Madagascar, Malawi, Mozambique, Niger, Nigeria, Sierra Leone, Sudan, Swaziland, Sweden, Thailand, United Republic of Cameroon, United Republic of Tanzania, Zimbabwe.

Assistance to Botswana

The General Assembly,

Recalling Security Council resolutions 403(1977) of 14 January 1977 and 406(1977) of 25 May 1977, which concerned the complaint by the Government of Botswana regarding acts of aggression committed against its territory by the illegal régime in Southern Rhodesia,

Recalling also Security Council resolution 460(1979) of 21 December 1979, in which all Member States and specialized agencies were called upon to provide urgent assistance to Zimbabwe and the frontline States,

Recalling its resolutions 32/97 of 13 December 1977, 33/130 of 19 December 1978 and 34/125 of 14 December 1979, in which the General Assembly, *inter alia,* recognized the special economic hardship confronting Botswana as a result of diverting funds from development projects to effective arrangements for security against attacks and threats by Southern Rhodesia, and endorsed the assessments and

recommendations contained in the notes of the Secretary-General dated 28 March 1977 and 26 October 1977 and in his reports of 7 July 1978 and 28 August 1979,

Having examined the report of the Secretary-General of 16 August 1982, to which was annexed the report of the mission which he sent to Botswana in response to General Assembly resolution 36/222 of 17 December 1981,

Taking into account the fact that Botswana's economic situation has been further aggravated by a serious drought and a sharp fall in export earnings,

Noting the need of the Government of Botswana to rehabilitate and develop effective road, rail and air communications, both internally and with the rest of the world, in view of the uncertain political situation in the region, Botswana's vulnerability as a land-locked country and its dependence on externally controlled railway systems for the transport of its principal exports and imports,

Noting with appreciation Botswana's desire to establish its own railway system,

Noting also the urgent need to complete speedily the projects that have been identified in the annex to the report of the Secretary-General,

1. *Notes with satisfaction* the efforts of Botswana in implementing its development projects;

2. *Endorses fully* the revised programme of assistance contained in the annex to the report of the Secretary-General and calls the attention of the international community to the outstanding needs for assistance identified therein;

3. *Notes* that, while the response from some Member States and international organizations to the appeals of the Secretary-General has been encouraging, there is an urgent need to maintain the flow of contributions to carry out the remainder of the emergency programme, the implementation of parts of which remains a critical necessity;

4. *Draws the attention* of States and international and intergovernmental organizations particularly to the projects in the field of transport and communications, as well as to the priority requirements to rehabilitate the border areas most adversely affected by the war, in accordance with the recommendations contained in the annex to the report of the Secretary-General;

5. *Reiterates its appeal* to all States and intergovernmental organizations to provide generous assistance to enable Botswana to carry out the remainder of its planned development projects, as well as those made necessary by the current political and economic situation;

6. *Appeals* to all Member States, regional and interregional organizations and other intergovernmental bodies to provide financial, material and technical assistance to Botswana to enable it to carry out its planned development programme without interruption;

7. *Urges* Member States and organizations which are already implementing or are negotiating assistance programmes for Botswana to expand them, wherever possible;

8. *Invites* the United Nations Development Programme, the United Nations Children's Fund, the World Food Programme, the World Health Organization, the United Nations Industrial Development Organization, the World Bank and the International Fund for Agricultural Development to bring to the attention of their governing bodies, for their consideration, the assistance they are rendering to Botswana, for which the General Assembly has requested the Secretary-General to implement a special economic assistance programme, and to report on the results of that assistance and on their decisions to the Secretary-General in time for consideration by the Assembly at its thirty-eighth session;

9. *Appeals* to the international community to contribute to the special account established by the Secretary-General for the purpose of facilitating the channelling of contributions to Botswana;

10. *Requests* the appropriate specialized agencies and other organizations of the United Nations system to co-operate closely with the Secretary-General for the purpose of facilitating the channelling of contributions to Botswana;

11. *Requests* the Secretary-General:

(a) To continue his efforts to mobilize the necessary resources for an effective programme of financial, technical and material assistance to Botswana;

(b) To keep the situation in Botswana under constant review, to maintain close contact with Member States, regional and other intergovernmental organizations, the specialized agencies and the international financial institutions concerned, and to apprise the Economic and Social Council, at its second regular session of 1983, of the cur-

rent status of the special programme of economic assistance for Botswana;

(c) To report on the progress made in the economic situation of Botswana and in organizing and implementing the special economic assistance programme for that country in time for the matter to be considered by the General Assembly at its thirty-eighth session.

Cape Verde

Food production in Cape Verde fell dramatically in 1981, one of the driest years of a drought which had continued virtually without interruption since 1968. According to the economic review mission which visited the country from 19 to 23 April 1982[1] as a follow-up to a December 1981 General Assembly resolution,[3] the estimated food deficit for 1982 exceeded 40,000 tonnes. Export earnings covered only a fraction of the cost of imports, but the growing trade deficit was almost completely offset by heavy inflows of foreign assistance and remittances from abroad. The Government was finalizing its first national development plan, for 1982-1985, to deal with such areas as land reform, desertification control, livestock production, agricultural diversification, fisheries, stabilization of local industries, energy and desalination, transport, tourism, education, health, housing, urban growth, sanitation, trade, employment and human resource development.

The mission reviewed 61 projects included in the special economic assistance programme and found that 14 had been fully funded, partial funding had been secured for 18, no international support had been forthcoming for 25 and the Government had withdrawn 4; 27 projects had been modified or elaborated. Among projects in the programme were those to develop river basins ($8.5 million), artisanal fisheries ($8 million) and sanitation measures ($12 million).

The United Nations Development Programme helped to organize a round table (Praia, Cape Verde, 21-24 June) at which potential donors reviewed the Government's economic and social priorities and the resources needed for its development plan.

The General Assembly, by a resolution of 17 December[2] adopted without vote, reiterated its appeal for international assistance for Cape Verde, called attention to the projects identified by the mission, and invited donors to support the country's development plan and to contribute food and fodder.

The text was introduced in the Second Committee by Kenya on behalf of the African Group and was sponsored by 53 nations. Following informal consultations, oral revisions were incorporated in the text, which was approved without vote on 2 December. The main change was to request that the Secretary-General report to the Assembly in 1984 rather than 1983 on implementation of the special economic assistance programme.

Report. [1]S-G, annexing mission report, A/37/124.
Resolution (1982). [2]GA: 37/152, 17 Dec., text following.
Resolution (prior). [3]GA: 36/211, 17 Dec. 1981 (YUN 1981, p. 501).
Meeting records. ESC: E/1982/SR.46 (19 July). GA: 2nd Committee, A/C.2/37/SR.27-31, 33, 40, 46 (2 Nov.–2 Dec.); plenary, A/37/PV.109 (17 Dec.).

General Assembly resolution 37/152

17 December 1982   Meeting 109   Adopted without vote

Approved by Second Committee (A/37/702/Add.2) without vote, 2 December (meeting 46); 53-nation draft (A/C.2/37/L.51), orally revised in informal consultations; agenda item 74 (b).

Sponsors: Afghanistan, Algeria, Angola, Benin, Botswana, Brazil, Burundi, Canada, Cape Verde, Central African Republic, Chad, China, Comoros, Congo, Cuba, Democratic Yemen, Djibouti, Egypt, Ethiopia, France, Gambia, Guinea, Guinea-Bissau, Guyana, India, Italy, Japan, Kenya, Lesotho, Liberia, Madagascar, Mali, Mozambique, Nepal, Nicaragua, Niger, Nigeria, Pakistan, Portugal, Romania, Rwanda, Sao Tome and Principe, Senegal, Sierra Leone, Sweden, Tunisia, Uganda, United Republic of Cameroon, United Republic of Tanzania, United States, Viet Nam, Zambia, Zimbabwe.

Assistance to Cape Verde

The General Assembly,

Recalling its resolution 36/211 of 17 December 1981, in which the International community was called upon to take adequate measures to support the realization of the Five-Year Plan of Cape Verde,

Recalling also its resolutions 32/99 of 13 December 1977, 33/127 of 19 December 1978, 34/119 of 14 December 1979 and 35/104 of 5 December 1980, in which the international community was requested to provide an appropriate level of resources for the implementation of the programme of assistance to Cape Verde as envisaged in the reports of the Secretary-General,

Recalling further its resolution 36/194 of 17 December 1981, endorsing the Substantial New Programme of Action for the 1980s for the Least Developed Countries,

Acknowledging the difficulties inherent in the fragile economy of Cape Verde, aggravated by a permanent and severe drought situation,

Noting that Cape Verde is a least developed country, a small archipelago and a member of the Permanent Inter-State Committee on Drought Control in the Sahel,

Recognizing that increased substantial and continuous assistance from the international community, both in the short term and in the long term, will contribute to the effective development of Cape Verde,

Taking into account that a round table of Cape Verde's partners in development was organized jointly by Cape Verde and the United Nations Development Programme at Praia, Cape Verde, from 21 to 24 June 1982, which undertook a concrete and detailed analysis of the priorities of Cape Verde and the level of resources needed for the implementation of the Five-Year Plan,

Gravely concerned that the expected harvest for 1983 has been lost as a result of the failure of the seasonal rains and the recurrence of drought,

Noting that, according to a joint report of the Food and Agriculture Organization of the United Nations and the World Food Programme of January 1982, the food situation of Cape Verde will remain very critical in the short term and the medium term,

Recognizing the strenuous efforts deployed by the Government and the people of Cape Verde in the process of the socio-economic development of the country, despite existing constraints,

Having examined the report of the Secretary-General of 14 June 1982 on assistance to Cape Verde,

1. *Expresses its appreciation* to the Secretary-General for the efforts deployed in the process of mobilizing resources for the implementation of the programme of assistance to Cape Verde;

2. *Expresses its gratitude* to States, and to international, regional and interregional organizations and other intergovernmental organizations for their contribution to the programme of assistance to Cape Verde;

3. *Expresses its appreciation* to those Governments and international organizations and non-governmental organizations which participated in the round table of Cape Verde's partners in development, and urges them to take appropriate measures to implement the conclusions of that meeting;

4. *Calls the attention* of the international community to table 6 of the annex to the report of the Secretary-General, which enumerates the projects to which the Government attaches priority;

5. *Urges* Governments and international, regional and interregional organizations and other intergovernmental organizations to extend and intensify substantially their assistance with a view to implementing the programme of assistance to Cape Verde as soon as possible;

6. *Invites* the international community, in particular donor countries, to take appropriate and urgent measures to support the realization of the Five-Year Plan of Cape Verde, in accordance with the Substantial New Programme of Action for the 1980s for the Least Developed Countries;

7. *Requests* the organizations, organs and bodies of the United Nations system to continue and to increase their assistance to Cape Verde, to co-operate with the Secretary-General in his efforts to mobilize resources for the implementation of the programme of assistance and to report periodically to him on the measures they have taken and the resources they have made available to help that country;

8. *Calls upon* the international community to continue to contribute generously to all appeals for food and fodder assistance, made by the Government of Cape Verde or on its behalf by the specialized agencies and other competent organizations of the United Nations system to help it cope with the critical situation in the country;

9. *Draws once again the attention* of the international community to the special account which was established at United Nations Headquarters by the Secretary-General, in accordance with General Assembly resolution 32/99, for the purpose of facilitating the channelling of contributions to Cape Verde;

10. *Invites* the United Nations Conference on Trade and Development, the United Nations Children's Fund, the World Food Programme, the World Health Organization, the United Nations Industrial Development Organization, the Food and Agriculture Organization of the United Nations, the World Bank and the International Fund for Agricultural Development to continue to consider, through their governing bodies, the special needs of Cape Verde and to report the decisions of those bodies to the Secretary-General by 15 July 1983;

11. *Requests* the Secretary-General:

(a) To continue his efforts to mobilize the necessary resources for implementing the programme of development assistance to Cape Verde;

(b) To keep the situation in Cape Verde under constant review and to apprise the Economic and Social Council, at its second regular session of 1983, on the progress made in the implementation of the present resolution, and to report thereon to the General Assembly at its thirty-eighth session;

(c) To arrange for a review of the economic situation in Cape Verde and to make a substantive report on further progress in organizing and implementing the special programme of economic assistance for that country in time for the matter to be considered by the General Assembly at its thirty-ninth session.

Central African Republic

The gross domestic product (GDP) of the Central African Republic (at constant prices) decreased by 1.8 per cent in 1981 and the rate of inflation was 14.3 per cent. A United Nations mission,[1] which visited the country from 13 to 17 June 1982 in response to a request made by the General Assembly in December 1981,[3] reported that, while coffee production had increased by 20 per cent, cotton and mine production, including diamonds and gold, had fallen by an estimated 20 per cent. Moreover, the textile industry had virtually ceased to function. The balance of payments during the past three years had been characterized by large deficits, and public and publicly guaranteed external debt at the end of 1981 totalled $213.1 million, representing approximately 32 per cent of GDP.

Of the 33 projects in the country's special economic assistance programme, 14 had received full funding and 6 had been partially funded. Two projects had been withdrawn and 11 required financing. Among the fully funded projects were two roads ($41.3 million), a telephone network at Bangui ($28.8 million), development programmes for coffee ($22.6 million) and cattle-raising ($11.8 million), and a school rehabilitation project ($10 million). Partially funded projects included programmes to provide medical supplies and primary health care to rural areas, electricity to regional centres, and assistance for community development. Funds were being sought for several schemes, including $48.8 million for an integrated programme in food crops in primarily cotton-growing areas.

The Central African Republic stated in the General Assembly's Second Committee in November that the country would require increased external financial and technical assistance for its three-year (1982-1985) programme to revive the economy and restore financial equilibrium; priority would be given to increasing agricultural and livestock production in order to achieve national self-sufficiency in food and the subsistence of the mostly rural population.

The Assembly, by a resolution of 17 December adopted without vote,[2] drew attention to those projects in the Central African Republic for which financing was partially assured and to those awaiting funds, and called on States and organizations to expand assistance, particularly to meet critical needs for food, medicines, and hospital and school equipment, and for the emergency needs of people in drought-stricken areas. The Secretary-General was requested to continue to organize a special emergency assistance programme with regard to food and health.

The text was introduced in the Second Committee by Kenya for the African Group and had 52 sponsors. It was approved without vote on 2 December after having been orally revised following informal consultations, to request that the Secretary-General report in 1983 on the economic situation in the country and on its special economic assistance programme rather than arrange for a review of those matters in 1983.

Report. [1]S-G, annexing mission report, A/37/131.
Resolution (1982). [2]GA: 37/145, 17 Dec., text following.
Resolution (prior). [3]GA: 36/206, 17 Dec. 1981 (YUN 1981, p. 503).
Meeting records. ESC: E/1982/SR.46 (19 July). GA: 2nd Committee, A/C.2/37/SR.27-30, *31*, 33, *40*, 46 (2 Nov.–2 Dec.); plenary, A/37/PV.29, 109 (13 Oct., 17 Dec.).

General Assembly resolution 37/145

17 December 1982   Meeting 109   Adopted without vote

Approved by Second Committee (A/37/702/Add.2) without vote, 2 December (meeting 46); 52-nation draft (A/C.2/37/L.33), orally revised in informal consultations and further orally revised; agenda item 74 *(b)*.

Sponsors: Afghanistan, Algeria, Argentina, Benin, Botswana, Cape Verde, Central African Republic, Chad, Chile, China, Comoros, Congo, Czechoslovakia, Democratic Kampuchea, Djibouti, Egypt, Ethiopia, France, Gabon, Gambia, Guinea, Guinea-Bissau, Indonesia, Ivory Coast, Japan, Kenya, Lesotho, Liberia, Madagascar, Mali, Mauritania, Mozambique, Nicaragua, Niger, Nigeria, Pakistan, Saint Lucia, Sao Tome and Principe, Senegal, Sierra Leone, Somalia, Sudan, Swaziland, Thailand, Togo, Tunisia, Uganda, United Republic of Cameroon, Upper Volta, Yugoslavia, Zambia, Zimbabwe.

Assistance for the reconstruction, rehabilitation and development of the Central African Republic

The General Assembly,

Recalling its resolutions 35/87 of 5 December 1980 and 36/206 of 17 December 1981, in which it affirmed the urgent need for international action to assist the Government of the Central African Republic in its reconstruction, rehabilitation and development efforts and invited the international community to provide sufficient resources to carry out the programme of assistance to the Central African Republic,

Noting the statement made by the Minister for Foreign Affairs and International Co-operation of the Central African Republic before the General Assembly on 13 October 1982, in which he described the serious economic and financial problems of the country and observed that the situation had not improved, owing to the insufficiency of financial resources, and that external assistance continued to be essential,

Noting also the statement made by the representative of the Central African Republic before the Second Committee on 4 November 1982, according to which the response of the international community to the urgent appeal of the General Assembly had not been adequate to meet the needs of the situation,

Bearing in mind that the Central African Republic is land-locked and is classified as one of the least developed countries,

Recalling the Substantial New Programme of Action for the 1980s for the Least Developed Countries, which called for increased aid to these countries,

Particularly concerned that the Government of the Central African Republic is unable to provide the population with adequate health, educational and other essential social and public services because of an acute shortage of financial and material resources,

Noting with satisfaction the considerable efforts exerted by the Government and people of the Central African Republic for national reconstruction, rehabilitation and development despite the limitations confronting them,

Having examined the report of the Secretary-General, to which is annexed the report of the mission which was present in the Central African Republic during the period from 13 to 17 June 1982 to carry out a study of the economic situation and the progress being made in organizing and carrying out the special economic assistance programme for that country, in accordance with General Assembly resolution 36/206,

Noting that, according to that report, the budgetary situation of the Central African Republic continues to make it impossible for the Government to undertake a programme of reconstruction, rehabilitation and development, owing to inadequate external financial assistance,

1. *Expresses its gratification* to the Secretary-General for the efforts he has made to mobilize resources for carrying out the programme of assistance to the Central African Republic;

2. *Expresses its appreciation* to the States, the international, regional and interregional organizations and other intergovernmental organizations for their contribution to the programme of assistance to the Central African Republic;

3. *Notes with concern,* however, that the assistance provided under this heading continues to fall far short of the country's urgent needs;

4. *Urgently draws the attention* of the international community to table 6 of the annex to the Secretary-General's report, which indicates the projects for which financing is partially assured and those for which no financing has been forthcoming;

5. *Reiterates its appeal* to all States to contribute generously, through bilateral or multilateral channels, to the reconstruction, rehabilitation and development of the Central African Republic;

6. *Requests* the appropriate organizations and programmes of the United Nations system—in particular the United Nations Development Programme, the World Bank, the International Monetary Fund, the Food and Agriculture Organization of the United Nations, the International Fund for Agricultural Development, the World Food Programme, the World Health Organization, the United Nations Children's Fund and the United Nations Industrial Development Organization—to maintain their programmes of assistance to the Central African Republic, to co-operate closely with the Secretary-General in his efforts to organize an effective international programme of assistance and to report periodically to him on the steps they have taken and the resources they have made available to help that country;

7. *Calls upon* regional and interregional organizations and other intergovernmental bodies and non-governmental organizations—in particular the European Economic Community, the European Development Fund, the African Development Bank, the Arab Bank for Economic Development in Africa, the Organization of Petroleum Exporting Countries Fund for International Development, the International Fund for Agricultural Development, the Kuwaiti Fund and the Abu Dhabi Fund—to give urgent consideration to the establishment of a programme of assistance to the Central African Republic or, where one is already in existence, to the expansion and considerable strengthening of that programme with a view to its implementation as soon as possible;

8. *Urges* all States and relevant United Nations bodies—in particular the United Nations Development Programme, the World Food Programme, the United Nations Children's Fund, the World Health Organization, the United Nations Fund for Population Activities and the United Nations Industrial Development Organization—to provide all possible assistance to help the Government of the Central African Republic to cope with the critical humanitarian needs of the population and to provide, as appropriate, food, medicines and essential equipment for schools and hospitals, as well as to meet the emergency needs of the population in the drought-stricken areas of the country;

9. *Invites* the United Nations Development Programme, the United Nations Children's Fund, the World Food Programme, the World Health Organization, the United Nations Industrial Development Organization, the Food and Agriculture Organization of the United Nations, the World Bank and the International Fund for Agricultural Development to bring to the attention of their governing bodies, for their consideration, the special needs of the Central African Republic and to report the decisions of those bodies to the Secretary-General by 15 July 1983;

10. *Again draws the attention* of the international community to the special account opened by the Secretary-General at United Nations Headquarters in accordance with General Assembly resolution 35/87 for the purpose of facilitating the channelling of contributions to the Central African Republic;

11. *Requests* the Secretary-General:

(a) To continue his efforts to organize a special emergency assistance programme with regard to food and health, especially medicaments, vaccines, hospital equipment, generating sets for field hospitals, water pumps and food products in order to help the vulnerable populations, whose steadily deteriorating situation is becoming a matter of increasingly serious concern;

(b) To continue also his efforts to mobilize necessary resources for an effective programme of financial, technical and material assistance to the Central African Republic;

(c) To ensure that the necessary financial and budgetary arrangements are made to continue the organization of the international programme of assistance to the Central African Republic and the mobilization of that assistance;

(d) To keep the situation in the Central African Republic under constant review, to maintain close contact with Member States, the specialized agencies, regional and other intergovernmental organizations and the international financial institutions concerned and to apprise the Economic and Social Council, at its second regular session of 1983, of the status of the special programme of economic assistance for the Central African Republic;

(e) To report on the progress made in the economic situation of the Central African Republic and in organizing and implementing the special programme of economic assistance for that country in time for the matter to be considered by the General Assembly at its thirty-eighth session.

Chad

An International Conference on Assistance to Chad, called for by the General Assembly in December 1981,[(3)] was a highlight of United Nations efforts in 1982 to mobilize aid for that country, affected by some 17 years of civil strife. Postponed from March 1982 because of the unsettled political conditions in the country, the Conference was held on 29 and 30 November at Geneva. Commitments made there totalled about $185 million, covering approximately half of Chad's medium-term needs, estimated at $370 million by a study financed by the United Nations Development Programme (UNDP). The Government's priority programme for 1983-1984 was aimed mainly at satisfying basic food, health and educational needs, rehabilitation of private and public property, and the achievement of strong economic growth. One of the most pressing needs was for the supply of 50,000 tons of food by February 1983 and another 142,000 tons by June 1983.

Contributions to ongoing projects and new programmes were announced at the Conference by Belgium, Egypt, France, the Federal Republic of Germany, Indonesia, Saudi Arabia, Switzerland and the United States, as well as by a number of organizations. Twenty-nine States, 24 United Nations bodies and organizations, and 31 other intergovernmental and non-governmental organizations participated in the Conference, the initial results of which were conveyed to the Assembly in a report by the Secretary-General.[1]

The report also noted that the United Nations emergency assistance programme, established to help the country meet urgent humanitarian needs, had organized a meeting at Geneva on 5 and 6 April 1982, with the participation of 37 countries, 9 United Nations organizations, and 15 intergovernmental and non-governmental organizations. The Office of the United Nations Disaster Relief Co-ordinator (UNDRO)—designated by the Secretary-General in November 1981 as lead agency to co-ordinate emergency relief for Chad[4]—had presented a $6.8-million programme, to which several participants had announced contributions. The programme covered seeds, educational material, medicines and medical supplies, as well as part of the requirements for food and transportation. In September, five chartered aircraft flew 1,500 tons of food supplied by the World Food Programme to previously inaccessible famine-stricken areas in the north and north-east, and another 1,500 tons was sent by road.

A Resident Co-ordinator for United Nations activities in the country was appointed and designated the Secretary-General's Special Representative for Reconstruction, Rehabilitation, Development and Emergency Relief Operations in Chad. UNDRO was designated to co-ordinate efforts to mobilize international relief.

During 1982, UNDP oversaw relief, reconstruction and development activities, including the rehabilitation of the country's telecommunication network, the central mechanical workshop, the N'Djamena electricity and water supply, and the international airport. It assisted with the emergency vaccination of 3.5 million cattle against rinderpest, with financing by the Food and Agriculture Organization of the United Nations and other donors. Other programmes dealt with desertification control, tree planting, secondary roads, and agro- and hydro-meteorological services—with help from the United Nations Sudano-Sahelian Office. More than $550,000 in emergency food aid was distributed for 40,000 people returning from Nigeria, some of whom were brought to transit and resettlement areas in trucks of United Nations organizations diverted for that purpose.

In the General Assembly's Second Committee in November, Chad announced that the fratricidal battles in that country had ended and that a new Government had been installed under Hissène Habré (whose forces had seized control of N'Djamena, the capital, on 7 June). The most important task was to respond to urgent problems, such as feeding and giving medical care to women, children and aged persons suffering from famine, resettling refugees and displaced persons who were returning by the thousands to homes destroyed by the war, providing school buildings, rehabilitating the administrative structure, paying public and private employees, and clearing wells to obtain water for people and livestock.

The Assembly, by a resolution of 17 December[2] adopted without vote, renewed its appeal for international assistance for the rehabilitation and reconstruction of Chad. Noting with satisfaction the International Conference, it invited the States and agencies which had participated to honour as soon as possible the commitments made there.

The resolution, introduced by Kenya on behalf of the African Group and sponsored by 50 nations, was orally revised in the Second Committee following informal consultations and was approved without vote on 2 December. The main change replaced an appeal to "Member States" by one to "all States". The final text included an amendment presented in the Assembly by nine of the original sponsors (Central African Republic, Chad, Egypt, France, Ivory Coast, Morocco, Sudan, Togo, United States) adding the paragraph on the International Conference; this was adopted without vote.

On 30 April 1982, the Security Council requested the establishment of a United Nations fund for voluntary contributions to the peace-keeping force in Chad established in June 1981 by the Organization of African Unity. The United Nations High Commissioner for Refugees continued to assist refugees in Chad.

Report. [1]S-G, A/37/125 & Add.1.
Resolution (1982). [2]GA: 37/155, 17 Dec., text following.

Resolution (prior). [3]GA: 36/210, 17 Dec. 1981 (YUN 1981, p. 505).
Yearbook reference. [4]1981, p. 483.
Meeting records. ESC: E/1982/SR.46 (19 July). GA: 2nd Committee, A/C.2/37/SR.27, 28-31, 33, 40, 46 (2 Nov.–2 Dec.); plenary, A/37/PV.109 (17 Dec.).

General Assembly resolution 37/155

17 December 1982   Meeting 109   Adopted without vote

Approved by Second Committee (A/37/702/Add.2) without vote, 2 December (meeting 46); 50-nation draft (A/C.2/37/L.54), orally revised in informal consultations; amended in Assembly by 9 nations (A/37/L.62); agenda item 74 *(b)*.

Sponsors of draft resolution: Afghanistan, Algeria, Angola, Belgium, Benin, Botswana, Burundi, Cape Verde, Central African Republic, Chad, Chile, China, Comoros, Djibouti, Egypt, Ethiopia, France, Gabon, Gambia, Guinea, Guinea-Bissau, India, Indonesia, Ivory Coast, Kenya, Lesotho, Liberia, Madagascar, Mali, Mauritania, Morocco, Nepal, Nicaragua, Niger, Nigeria, Rwanda, Senegal, Sierra Leone, Somalia, Sudan, Swaziland, Thailand, Togo, Tunisia, Uganda, United Republic of Cameroon, United States, Zaire, Zambia, Zimbabwe.

Sponsors of amendment: Central African Republic, Chad, Egypt, France, Ivory Coast, Morocco, Sudan, Togo, United States.

Special economic assistance to Chad

The General Assembly,

Recalling its resolution 36/210 of 17 December 1981 and its previous resolutions on the reconstruction, rehabilitation and development of Chad and emergency humanitarian assistance to that country,

Taking note of the reports of the Secretary-General on assistance to Chad and on the work of the Office of the United Nations Disaster Relief Co-ordinator in this regard, as well as of the Co-ordinator's statement,

Noting with satisfaction that the stability of the situation in Chad has enabled the Secretary-General to organize an international conference on assistance to Chad in late November 1982 at Geneva, in close co-operation with the Organization of African Unity and the Government of Chad,

Aware that serious destruction of property and extensive damage to the economic and social infrastructure of Chad over more than fifteen years, together with the effects of natural disasters, have placed the country in a situation of dire need,

1. *Expresses its satisfaction* to the Secretary-General on the steps he has taken to mobilize assistance for Chad;

2. *Expresses its gratitude* to all States, international organizations and other agencies that have provided assistance to Chad;

3. *Renews its appeal* to all States, the appropriate organs, organizations and programmes of the United Nations, regional and international organizations and other intergovernmental and non-governmental organizations, and the international financial institutions to contribute to the rehabilitation and reconstruction of Chad through bilateral or multilateral channels, as appropriate;

4 *Notes with satisfaction* that the International Conference on Assistance to Chad was held at Geneva on 29 and 30 November 1982 and invites the States and agencies which participated to honour as soon as possible the commitments they entered into at that Conference;

5. *Notes* that the Government of Chad has expressed its appreciation of the activities undertaken by the United Nations Disaster Relief Co-ordinator in Chad and requests the Co-ordinator to continue his emergency relief activities in Chad;

6. *Requests* the Secretary-General:

(a) To continue his efforts to mobilize the necessary resources for an effective programme of financial, technical and material assistance to Chad;

(b) To keep the situation in Chad under constant review and to report to the Economic and Social Council at its second regular session of 1983 on the status of the assistance provided for the rehabilitation and reconstruction of Chad;

(c) To arrange for a review of the economic situation of Chad and the progress made in organizing and executing the special programme of economic assistance for that country in time for the matter to be considered by the General Assembly at its thirty-eighth session.

Comoros

As many as 200,000 persons were affected in the Comoros by a drought in 1981, and crop produc-

tion, also hampered by cyclones, amounted to about half the annual average, according to the review mission which visited the country from 27 May to 2 June 1982[1] in pursuance of a December 1981 request by the General Assembly.[3] The year 1981 had seen a favourable performance in price and production levels of vanilla and cloves which, together with copra and ylang-ylang essence, accounted for 99 per cent of Comorian exports. However, the marked increase in imports of such items as food and petroleum products had resulted in a trade deficit of over $15 million, virtually the equivalent of export earnings. The current account deficit had reached an unprecedented $8.1 million, a 49 per cent increase over the preceding year, despite a significant increase in official transfers and grants.

The development plans of the Comoros Government included 19 projects to develop self-sufficiency in food ($10.6 million), improve transport and communications ($22.5 million), and develop energy production and water supply ($10.2 million), health programmes ($3 million) and training ($5.4 million). The total estimated cost of the programme was $51.7 million. This would form part of an interim development plan for 1983-1985 which the Government intended to submit to a donors' conference to be held in the Comoros early in 1983.

The General Assembly, by a resolution of 17 December 1982[2] adopted without vote, noted with concern that assistance had fallen short of the urgent requirements of the Comoros, reiterated its appeal for international assistance, and appealed to States and organizations invited to the donors' conference to respond generously to the Government's assistance programme.

This resolution had been approved without vote by the Second Committee on 2 December. It was introduced by Kenya for the African Group and was sponsored by 41 nations. The sponsors accepted an oral suggestion by Denmark on behalf of the members of the European Economic Community (EEC) to have the Secretary-General report in 1983 on the progress made in the Comoros economic situation rather than to arrange for a review of the situation in 1983.

Report. [1]S-G, annexing mission report, A/37/128.
Resolution (1982). [2]GA: 37/154, 17 Dec., text following.
Resolution (prior). [3]GA: 36/212, 17 Dec. 1981 (YUN 1981, p. 507).
Meeting records. ESC: E/1982/SR.46 (19 July). GA: 2nd Committee, A/C.2/37/SR.27-31, 33, 40, 46 (2 Nov.–2 Dec.); plenary, A/37/PV.109 (17 Dec.).

General Assembly resolution 37/154

17 December 1982   Meeting 109   Adopted without vote

Approved by Second Committee (A/37/702/Add.2) without vote, 2 December (meeting 46); 41-nation draft (A/C.2/37/L.53), orally amended by Denmark, for EEC members; agenda item 74 *(b)*.

Sponsors: Afghanistan, Algeria, Argentina, Benin, Botswana, Burundi, Cape Verde, Central African Republic, Chad, China, Djibouti, Egypt, Ethiopia, France, Gambia, Guinea, Guinea-Bissau, Guyana, Indonesia, Kenya, Lesotho, Madagascar, Malawi, Mali, Mauritania, Morocco, Niger, Nigeria, Rwanda, Senegal, Sierra Leone,

Somalia, Sudan, Thailand, Togo, Tunisia, Uganda, United Republic of Cameroon, United Republic of Tanzania, Upper Volta, Zambia.

Assistance to the Comoros

The General Assembly,

Recalling its resolution 36/212 of 17 December 1981 and its previous resolutions on assistance to the Comoros in which it appealed to the international community to provide effective and continuous financial, material and technical assistance to the Comoros in order to help that country overcome its financial and economic difficulties,

Taking note of the special problems confronting the Comoros as a developing island country and as one of the least developed countries,

Noting the priority which the Government of the Comoros has assigned to the questions of infrastructure, transport and telecommunications,

Noting also the economic difficulties arising from the country's scarcity of natural resources, compounded by recent drought and cyclones,

Noting further the grave budgetary and balance-of-payments problems facing the Comoros,

Aware of the intention of the Government of the Comoros to convene a donors' conference in the first quarter of 1983,

Having examined the report of the Secretary-General, to which was annexed the report of the review mission which he sent to the Comoros in May 1982,

1. *Expresses its appreciation* to the Secretary-General for the steps he has taken to mobilize assistance to the Comoros;

2. *Notes with satisfaction* the response by Member States, organizations of the United Nations system and other organizations to its appeals and those of the Secretary-General for assistance to the Comoros;

3. *Notes with concern,* however, that the assistance thus far provided continues to fall short of the country's urgent requirements and that assistance is still urgently required to carry out the projects identified in the annex to the report of the Secretary-General;

4. *Appeals* to those States and organizations invited to the donors' conference to be held in the Comoros early in 1983 to respond generously to the programme of assistance that will be presented by the Government of the Comoros at that time;

5. *Renews its appeal* to Member States, the appropriate organs, organizations and programmes of the United Nations system, regional and international organizations and other intergovernmental bodies and non-governmental organizations, as well as international financial institutions, to provide the Comoros with assistance to enable it to cope with its difficult economic situation and pursue its development goals;

6. *Requests* the appropriate organizations and programmes of the United Nations system to increase their current programmes of assistance to the Comoros, to co-operate closely with the Secretary-General in organizing an effective international programme of assistance and to report periodically to him on the steps they have taken and the resources they have made available to help that country;

7. *Requests* the Secretary-General:

(a) To continue his efforts to mobilize the necessary resources for an effective programme of financial, technical and material assistance to the Comoros;

(b) To keep the situation in the Comoros under constant review, to maintain close contact with Member States, the specialized agencies, regional and other intergovernmental organizations and the international financial institutions concerned, and to apprise the Economic and Social Council, at its second regular session of 1983, of the current status of the special programme of economic assistance for the Comoros;

(c) To report on the progress made in the economic situation of the Comoros and in organizing and implementing the special programme of economic assistance for that country in time for the matter to be considered by the General Assembly at its thirty-eighth session.

Djibouti

Djibouti was characterized as having few natural resources, little industrial activity, recurrent drought and a large refugee population by an economic review mission which visited the country from 28 August to 3 September 1982[1] in pursuance of a December 1981 General Assembly request.[3] Much of the population lived in the service-oriented port city of Djibouti and practically all consumer goods and food products, other than the livestock-derived staples of the nomadic population, were imported. About 76 per cent of Djibouti's gross domestic product (GDP) was generated by the service sector, including transport and communications, commerce, banking, real estate, insurance and public administration. In general, the economy was heavily dependent on foreign demand for services and on external budgetary and financial assistance.

The mission's report listed 68 projects in the special economic assistance programme for Djibouti for which funding had been fully or partially arranged, and described another 29 projects for which assistance was being sought. Among the latter were projects to improve Djibouti port, the service economy and transport links, and to help the poor through better facilities and services, as well as pilot projects, studies and surveys. The report also listed 83 projects costing some $319 million which the Government intended to submit to a donors' conference in 1983.

Djibouti pointed out in the General Assembly's Second Committee in November that the country required international assistance in order to combat urban and rural poverty, reduce the country's dependence on food and energy imports, develop industry and make the city of Djibouti a major international maritime centre.

By a resolution of 17 December 1982[2] adopted without vote, the Assembly endorsed the recommendations of the review mission, renewed its appeal to Member States, organizations and international financial institutions to assist Djibouti, and appealed to States and organizations invited to the 1983 donors' conference to respond generously to the assistance programme which Djibouti would present there.

The 37-nation draft was introduced by Kenya in the Second Committee on behalf of the African Group. It was orally amended by Denmark for the EEC members, to have the Secretary-General report in 1983 on the progress made in the economic situation of Djibouti rather than to arrange for a review of the situation in 1983. The draft was approved on 2 December without vote.

Report. [1]S-G, annexing mission report, A/37/136.
Resolution (1982). [2]GA: 37/153, 17 Dec., text following.
Resolution (prior). [3]GA: 36/216, 17 Dec. 1981 (YUN 1981, p. 508).
Meeting records. ESC: E/1982/SR.46 (19 July). GA: 2nd Committee, A/C.2/37/SR.27-30, *31,* 33, *40, 46* (2 Nov.–2 Dec.); plenary, A/37/PV.109 (17 Dec.).

General Assembly resolution 37/153

17 December 1982   Meeting 109   Adopted without vote

Approved by Second Committee (A/37/702/Add.2) without vote, 2 December (meeting 46); 37-nation draft (A/C.2/37/L.52), orally amended by Denmark, for EEC members; agenda item 74 *(b).*

Sponsors: Afghanistan, Algeria, Bangladesh, Benin, Botswana, Cape Verde, Central African Republic, Chad, Comoros, Democratic Yemen, Egypt, Ethiopia, France, Gambia, Guinea, Guinea-Bissau, Kenya, Madagascar, Malawi, Nepal, Nigeria, Oman, Pakistan, Rwanda, Senegal, Sierra Leone, Somalia, Sudan, Swaziland,

Togo, Tunisia, Uganda, United Republic of Cameroon, United Republic of Tanzania, Upper Volta, Zaire, Zambia.

Assistance to Djibouti

The General Assembly,

Recalling its resolution 36/216 of 17 December 1981 and its previous resolutions on the same subject in which it drew the attention of the international community to the critical economic situation confronting Djibouti and to the country's urgent need for assistance,

Recalling also its resolution 36/156 of 16 December 1981 in which it called upon the international community to continue to support the efforts made by the Government of Djibouti to cope with the needs of the refugee population,

Recalling further its resolution 36/221 of 17 December 1981 in which it appealed to the international community to contribute generously towards the projects and programmes to help the drought-affected populations,

Aware of Economic and Social Council resolution 1982/41 of 27 July 1982 in which the Council recommended the inclusion of Djibouti in the list of least developed countries,

Having examined the report of the Secretary-General, to which was annexed the report of the review mission which he sent to Djibouti in 1982,

Taking note of the critical economic situation of Djibouti and the list of urgent and priority projects, formulated by the Government, that require international assistance,

Noting further that the Government of Djibouti will convene a donors' conference early in 1983 in order to seek international support for the country's economic and social development,

1. *Expresses its appreciation* to the Secretary-General for the steps he has taken to organize an international programme of economic assistance for Djibouti;

2. *Endorses fully* the assessment and recommendations contained in the annex to the report of the Secretary-General;

3. *Notes with appreciation* the assistance already provided or pledged to Djibouti by Member States, organizations of the United Nations system and other organizations;

4. *Again draws the attention* of the international community to the difficult economic situation confronting Djibouti and to the severe structural constraints to its development;

5. *Renews its appeal* to Member States, the appropriate organs, organizations and programmes of the United Nations system, regional and international organizations and other intergovernmental bodies and non-governmental organizations, as well as international financial institutions, to provide assistance bilaterally and multilaterally, as appropriate, to Djibouti in order to enable it to cope with its difficult economic situation and to implement its development strategies;

6. *Requests* the appropriate specialized agencies and other organizations of the United Nations system to maintain and increase their current and future programmes of assistance to Djibouti, to co-operate closely with the Secretary-General in organizing an effective international programme of assistance and to report periodically to him on the steps they have taken and the resources they have made available to help that country;

7. *Appeals* to those States and organizations invited to the donors' conference to be held in Djibouti early in 1983 to respond generously to the programme of assistance that will be presented by the Government of Djibouti at that time;

8. *Requests* the Secretary-General:

(a) To continue his efforts to mobilize the necessary resources for an effective programme of financial, technical and material assistance to Djibouti;

(b) To continue to ensure that adequate financial and budgetary arrangements are made to mobilize resources and to co-ordinate international assistance to Djibouti;

(c) To keep the situation in Djibouti under constant review, to maintain close contact with Member States, the specialized agencies, regional and other intergovernmental organizations and the international financial institutions concerned, and to apprise the Economic and Social Council, at its second regular session of 1983, of the current status of the special programme of economic assistance for Djibouti;

(d) To report on the progress made in the economic situation of Djibouti and in organizing and implementing the special programme of economic assistance for that country in time for the matter to be considered by the General Assembly at its thirty-eighth session.

Equatorial Guinea

Improvements were reported in Equatorial Guinea during 1981 in the production of cocoa, coffee and timber, the country's main exports. However, according to an economic review mission which visited the country from 7 to 12 June 1982[2] in pursuance of a December 1981 General Assembly request,[3] an increase in imports had resulted in a trade deficit of $23.7 million in 1981, and the account deficit for the year represented 45 per cent of GDP. Because exports could not be expected to recover in the short term, the Government's development efforts were likely to increase the balance-of-payments deficit unless more international assistance was provided. The country's external public debt, which had reached $57.2 million at the end of 1981, represented 93 per cent of GDP. The growth of debt-servicing payments could restrict the future use of foreign exchange for financing imports and for promoting export-oriented investments.

Of 51 projects in the country's special economic assistance programme, 10 had been fully funded and 12 had been partially funded. Most of the 29 projects remaining to be financed had been reformulated and presented at a donors' conference held at Geneva in April 1982. The country's development objectives included unification of all parts of the national territory, elimination of the remaining vestiges of colonization in order to achieve autonomous development, establishment of an effective and dynamic public administration, development of popular participation, and integration of the country internationally, especially with other African countries.

The General Assembly, on 17 December,[1] took note of the economic review mission's report along with several other reports on special economic and disaster relief assistance.

Decision (1982). [1]GA: 37/434, para. *(a)*, 17 Dec.
Report. [2]S-G, annexing mission report, A/37/130.
Resolution. [3]GA: 36/204, 17 Dec. 1981 (YUN 1981, p. 510).

Gambia

Rural and urban incomes, government revenue and foreign exchange earnings had declined substantially in the Gambia in recent years and a serious unemployment situation had developed, according to an inter-agency economic review mission which visited the country from 18 to 22 March and from 19 to 24 July 1982[1] in pursuance of a December 1981 request of the General Assembly.[3] The mission—the first of its kind to visit the country—said this situation was due in part to a drastic, drought-caused reduction in the output of ground-nuts, the principal agricultural export, and a substantial reduction in earnings from tourism because of adverse economic conditions in Europe. A large portion of counterpart (local cost) funding for development projects had had to be borrowed, and the Government had had to approach the International Monetary Fund for balance-of-payments support.

Eight days of riots and disturbances beginning on 30 July 1981 had caused considerable loss of life and property, the mission reported. Economic losses included damage of $1.5 million to public assets and $20 million to business property. In addition, agricultural production and tourism had been disrupted.

The report gave details of three projects formulated after the disturbances, for which the Government sought external assistance of $7.8 million: for rice irrigation development ($4.9 million), rehabilitation of Radio Gambia ($1.3 million) and a national youth programme ($1.6 million). After publication of the mission's report, the Government requested that the country's special economic assistance programme be expanded to include three additional projects: a five-year tourism marketing plan ($4.9 million), maintenance of urban roads ($4.6 million) and the repair of a major road bridge ($1.2 million); these were described in an addendum to the Secretary-General's report on the Gambia.

The General Assembly, in a resolution adopted without vote on 17 December 1982,[2] endorsed the mission's report, renewed its appeal to Member States and organizations to contribute to the country's reconstruction and rehabilitation, and urged them to respond generously to the needs of the Gambia at the round-table conference to be held there in 1983.

The text, submitted by Kenya on behalf of the African Group, was sponsored by 37 nations in the Second (Economic and Financial) Committee, where it was approved without vote on 2 December after having been orally revised following informal consultations. As a result of these changes, the Assembly endorsed the recommendations in the report rather than endorsing "fully" its assessments and recommendations; urged rather than "strongly" urged Member States and organizations to respond generously at the donors' conference; and requested the Secretary-General to report in 1983 on progress in the Gambia's economic situation rather than to arrange for a review of that situation.

Report. [1]S-G, annexing mission report, A/37/138 & Add.1.
Resolution (1982). [2]GA: 37/159, 17 Dec., text following.
Resolution (prior). [3]GA: 36/220, 17 Dec. 1981 (YUN 1981, p. 511).
Meeting records. ESC: E/1982/SR.46 (19 July). GA: 2nd Committee, A/C.2/37/SR.27-31, 33, *40, 46* (2 Nov.–2 Dec.); plenary, A/37/PV.109 (17 Dec.).

General Assembly resolution 37/159

17 December 1982   Meeting 109   Adopted without vote

Approved by Second Committee (A/37/702/Add.2) without vote, 2 December (meeting 46); 37-nation draft (A/C.2/37/L.58), orally revised in informal consultations; agenda item 74 *(b)*.

Sponsors: Afghanistan, Algeria, Bangladesh, Benin, Botswana, Cape Verde, Central African Republic, Djibouti, Ethiopia, France, Guinea, Guinea-Bissau, India, Indonesia, Ivory Coast, Kenya, Lesotho, Liberia, Madagascar, Mali, Mauritania, Mauritius, Morocco, Nepal, Niger, Nigeria, Pakistan, Qatar, Senegal, Sierra Leone, Somalia, Sudan, Thailand, United Kingdom, United Republic of Cameroon, United States, Yugoslavia.

Assistance to the Gambia

The General Assembly,

Recalling its resolution 36/220 of 17 December 1981 in which it, *inter alia,* expressed its deep concern about the extensive destruction of life and property as well as the severe damage to infrastructure which were inflicted on the Gambia as the result of the events of 30 July 1981,

Noting that the Gambia is a least developed country with acute economic and social problems arising from its weak economic infrastructure and that it also suffers from many of the serious problems common to countries of the Sahelian region, notably drought,

Having considered the report of the Secretary-General on assistance for the rehabilitation and reconstruction of the Gambia,

Noting that the economy of the Gambia is vulnerable to several factors that are entirely beyond the Government's control, such as the fall in prices and in the volume of its exports,

Noting also that declining revenues and rising costs have caused serious budgetary difficulties for the Government of the Gambia and that budget deficits continue to persist,

Aware of the intention of the Government of the Gambia to organize, with the assistance of the United Nations Development Programme, a round-table conference of donors early in 1983 to discuss the country's development needs and to consider ways and means of helping the Government in its efforts to meet those needs,

1. *Expresses its appreciation* to the Secretary-General for the steps he has taken to mobilize assistance for the Gambia;

2. *Endorses* the recommendations contained in the report of the Secretary-General and draws the attention of the international community to the requirements of assistance for the projects and programmes identified therein;

3. *Expresses its appreciation* to those States and organizations which have provided assistance to the Gambia;

4. *Renews its urgent appeal* to all Member States, the specialized agencies and other organizations of the United Nations system, as well as international development and financial institutions, to contribute generously, through bilateral or multilateral channels, to the rehabilitation and reconstruction of the Gambia;

5. *Calls upon* regional and interregional organizations and other intergovernmental bodies and non-governmental organizations, as well as international development and financial institutions, to provide financial, technical and material assistance for the implementation of the projects and programmes recommended in the annex to the report of the Secretary-General;

6. *Urges* Member States, organizations and programmes of the United Nations system, regional and interregional bodies, financial and development institutions and intergovernmental and non-governmental organizations to respond generously to the needs of the Gambia at the round-table conference to be held at Banjul early in 1983;

7. *Requests* the appropriate organizations and programmes of the United Nations system — in particular the United Nations Development Programme, the United Nations Children's Fund, the World Food Programme, the World Health Organization, the United Nations Industrial Development Organization, the Food and Agriculture Organization of the United Nations and the International Fund for Agricultural Development — to increase their current and future programmes of assistance to the Gambia, to co-operate closely with the Secretary-General in organizing an effective international programme of assistance and to report periodically to him on the steps they have taken and the resources they have made available to help that country;

8. *Invites* the United Nations Development Programme, the United Nations Children's Fund, the World Food Programme, the World Health Organization, the United Nations Industrial Development Organization, the Food and Agriculture Organization of the United Nations, the World Bank and the International Fund for Agricultural Development to bring to the attention of their governing bodies, for their consideration, the special needs of the Gambia and to report the decisions of those bodies to the Secretary-General in time for the consideration of the question by the General Assembly at its thirty-eighth session;

9. *Requests* the Secretary-General:

(a) To continue his efforts to mobilize the necessary resources for an effective programme of financial, technical and material assistance to the Gambia;

(b) To keep the situation in the Gambia under constant review, to maintain close contact with Member States, the specialized agencies, regional and other intergovernmental organizations and the international financial institutions concerned and to apprise the Economic and Social Council, at its second regular session of 1983, on the status of the special programme of economic assistance for the Gambia;

(c) To report on the progress made in the economic situation of the Gambia and in organizing and implementing the special programme of economic assistance for that country in time for the matter to be considered by the General Assembly at its thirty-eighth session.

Guinea-Bissau

The medium- and long-term external debt of Guinea-Bissau, among the 20 poorest nations in the world, reached a total of $169 million at the end of the first half of 1982, a value comparable to the country's gross domestic product (GDP), according to an economic review mission which visited there from 19 to 27 August 1982[1] in pursuance of a December 1981 General Assembly request.[3] Servicing of the public debt amounted to $10.1 million in 1981, or 72 per cent of the value of exports. The budget deficit, which was 15.5 per cent of GDP in 1980, was expected to increase in 1982, after a slight reduction in 1981. The national development strategy placed renewed emphasis on rural and agricultural development. Estimated requirements for imported food in 1982 were approximately 64,000 tonnes, of which 40,000 tonnes had been delivered or pledged. The chronic food deficit was expected to persist in 1983, and the Government had decided to establish food security stocks of 15,000 tonnes of basic food items.

The special economic assistance programme for Guinea-Bissau consisted of 129 projects, of which 69 had been fully funded, 18 partially funded and 42, including new projects, remained to be financed. The Government was seeking $119 million to meet these costs. Among the fully funded projects were those to develop the Cumaré agro-industrial complex ($18 million), improve rice production in the Geba River area ($4.5 million), construct small reservoirs ($7.5 million) and provide electricity to rural centres ($6.3 million). Funds were sought for projects to create rural brigades for rural engineering ($7.9 million), build a dam ($7 million), produce palm-oil and coconuts ($5.6 million), train agricultural extension workers ($3.4 million), reorganize shipyard facilities ($3.4 million) and combat tuberculosis ($6 million).

In the General Assembly's Second Committee in November, Guinea-Bissau stated that, although its economic and financial situation was fragile, it had many resources whose exploitation could break the vicious circle of poverty, including the fisheries above its continental shelf, cultivable lands, extensive forests, and major reserves of bauxite, phosphate, petroleum and other minerals.

The Assembly, by a resolution of 17 December 1982[2] adopted without vote, endorsed the review mission's report, appealed to Member States and organizations to continue providing assistance to Guinea-Bissau, and requested the Secretary-General to review the results of a round table of donors scheduled for the first half of 1983.

This resolution had been approved without vote on 2 December by the Second Committee, where it was introduced by Kenya on behalf of the African Group and sponsored by 50 nations. Denmark, on behalf of the European Economic Community members, withdrew an amendment which would have deleted the request to the Secretary-General that he review the results of the round table.

Report. [1]S-G, annexing mission report, A/37/137.
Resolution (1982). [2]GA: 37/156, 17 Dec., text following.
Resolution (prior). [3]GA: 36/217, 17 Dec. 1981 (YUN 1981, p. 512).
Meeting records. ESC: E/1982/SR.46 (19 July). GA: 2nd Committee, A/C.2/37/SR.27, 28, 29, 30, 31, 33, 40, 46 (2 Nov.–2 Dec.); plenary, A/37/PV.109 (17 Dec.).

General Assembly resolution 37/156

17 December 1982   Meeting 109   Adopted without vote

Approved by Second Committee (A/37/702/Add.2) without vote, 2 December (meeting 46); 50-nation draft (A/C.2/37/L.55); agenda item 74 *(b)*.

Sponsors: Afghanistan, Algeria, Angola, Benin, Botswana, Brazil, Cape Verde, Central African Republic, Chad, China, Comoros, Congo, Djibouti, Egypt, Ethiopia, France, Gambia, Guinea, Guinea-Bissau, Guyana, Japan, Kenya, Lesotho, Liberia, Libyan Arab Jamahiriya, Madagascar, Mali, Mauritania, Mauritius, Morocco, Mozambique, Nicaragua, Niger, Nigeria, Pakistan, Portugal, Sao Tome and Principe, Senegal, Sierra Leone, Somalia, Sudan, Swaziland, Sweden, Tunisia, Uganda, United Republic of Cameroon, Vanuatu, Viet Nam, Zaire, Zambia.

Special economic assistance to Guinea-Bissau

The General Assembly,

Recalling its resolution 35/95 of 5 December 1980, in which it reiterated its appeal to the international community to provide continuous financial, material and technical assistance to Guinea-Bissau to help it overcome its financial and economic difficulties and to permit the implementation of the projects and programmes recommended by the Secretary-General in his report of 21 August 1980 submitted in response to General Assembly resolution 34/121 of 14 December 1979,

Recalling also its resolution 36/217 of 17 December 1981,

Recalling further its resolution 3339(XXIX) of 17 December 1974, in which it invited Member States to provide economic assistance to the then newly independent State of Guinea-Bissau, and its resolutions 32/100 of 13 December 1977 and 33/124 of 19 December 1978, in which it, *inter alia*, expressed deep concern at the serious economic situation in Guinea-Bissau and appealed to the international community to provide financial and economic assistance to that country,

Having examined the report of the Secretary-General of 15 October 1982, to which was annexed the report of the mission which he sent to Guinea-Bissau in response to General Assembly resolution 36/217,

Recalling that Guinea-Bissau is one of the least developed countries,

Noting with concern that Guinea-Bissau continues to be beset by a wide range of economic and financial difficulties,

Noting that Guinea-Bissau will continue to be dependent in the years to come, for its public capital expenditure, on external sources of financing,

Also noting with concern the chronic deficit in the balance of payments of Guinea-Bissau, the substantial increase in its loans and the inordinately low level of its foreign-exchange reserves,

Noting that Guinea-Bissau is experiencing difficulties, aggravated by irregular rainfall, in its agricultural production and that it needs emergency food aid,

Noting that the Government of Guinea-Bissau, in view of the seriousness of the economic situation, decided to implement an economic and financial stabilization programme, the main purpose of which is to remedy the economic situation,

Noting further that the Government of Guinea-Bissau is preparing a first four-year development plan 1983/1986 and proposes to hold a round table of donors during the first half of 1983,

Bearing in mind the results of the United Nations Conference on the Least Developed Countries, particularly the Substantial New Programme of Action for the 1980s for the Least Developed Countries,

1. *Expresses its appreciation* to the Secretary-General for the steps he has taken to mobilize assistance to Guinea-Bissau;

2. *Endorses fully* the assessment and recommendations contained in the annex to the report of the Secretary-General and draws the attention of the international community to the requirements for assistance for the projects and programmes identified therein;

3. *Expresses its appreciation* to those States and organizations that have provided assistance to Guinea-Bissau in response to appeals by the General Assembly and the Secretary-General;

4. *Calls upon* Member States and the international organizations concerned to be generous in granting Guinea-Bissau the food aid it needs;

5. *Renews its urgent appeal* to Member States, regional and interregional organizations and other intergovernmental bodies to continue providing financial, material and technical assistance to Guinea-Bissau to help it overcome its economic and financial difficulties and to permit the implementation of the projects and programmes identified in the annex to the report of the Secretary-General;

6. *Appeals* to the international community to contribute to the special account established at United Nations Headquarters by the Secretary-General, in accordance with General Assembly resolution 32/100, for the purpose of facilitating the channelling of contributions to Guinea-Bissau;

7. *Invites* the United Nations Development Programme, the United Nations Children's Fund, the World Food Programme, the World Health Organization, the Food and Agriculture Organization of the United Nations, the World Bank and the International Fund for Agricultural Development to bring to the attention of their governing bodies, for their consideration, the special needs of Guinea-Bissau and to report the decisions of those bodies to the Secretary-General by 15 July 1983;

8. *Requests* the appropriate specialized agencies and other bodies of the United Nations system to report periodically to the Secretary-General on the steps they have taken and the resources they have made available to assist Guinea-Bissau;

9. *Requests* the Secretary-General:

(a) To continue his efforts to mobilize the necessary resources for an effective programme of financial, technical and material assistance to Guinea-Bissau;

(b) To keep the situation in Guinea-Bissau under constant review, to maintain close contact with Member States, the specialized agencies, regional and other intergovernmental organizations and the international financial institutions concerned, and to apprise the Economic and Social Council, at its second regular session of 1983, of the status of the special programme of economic assistance for Guinea-Bissau;

(c) To arrange for a review of the results of the round table of donors scheduled to be held during the first half of 1983, and of the progress made in organizing and implementing the special programme of economic assistance for Guinea-Bissau in time for the matter to be considered by the General Assembly at its thirty-eighth session.

Lesotho

Adverse economic and climatic factors had seriously affected production in various sectors of Lesotho's economy during 1981 and early 1982, according to an economic review mission which visited the country from 2 to 5 June 1982[2] in pursuance of a December 1981 General Assembly request.[4] Because of drought and early frost, the 1981/82 crop harvest was some 90,000 tonnes less than had been anticipated, and the total grain shortfall was 214,000 tonnes, to be met by commercial imports or food donations. Diamond exports, which accounted for 60 per cent of Lesotho's total exports in 1980, were expected to decline

sharply as a result of the depressed world diamond markets. Activity in the construction industry had slackened, and a refugee population, estimated at more than 26,000 in early 1981, had placed a considerable burden on the economy.

The review mission reported that 14 projects in Lesotho's special economic assistance programme had been completed, with the aid of $27 million in international assistance. Another $124 million had been pledged for ongoing projects which were fully funded, as well as $47 million for projects only partially financed. Among the fully funded projects were those for a new international airport ($51.5 million) and a major road ($34 million). Those for which funding was required included projects to construct maize storage silos ($10.2 million) and to train medical personnel ($8.3 million).

A Solidarity Ministerial Meeting for Co-operation in the Industrial Development of the Kingdom of Lesotho, attended by nine developing countries, was held at Maseru, Lesotho, from 7 to 11 June 1982.[1] It was organized by the United Nations Industrial Development Organization as one of a series of meetings to explore ways in which the participating States could co-operate in promoting the industrial development of individual countries (see Chapter VI of this section). Offers of assistance included a grant from Yugoslavia to construct 20 to 25 hammer mills, $200,000 from Algeria for the establishment of rural leather tanning units, and a pledge of $52,300 from India for consultancy and training.

Lesotho informed the General Assembly's Second Committee in November that international assistance provided during the past year had already shown results in the form of a doubling of the maize harvest in the 1981/82 season and a start on the project to build a new international airport at the capital, Maseru, scheduled for completion in 1985; but, despite an aggressive government campaign to create jobs by promoting investment in labour-intensive and export-oriented industries, some of the available capital was being attracted by South African subsidies for investment in its bantustans.

The Assembly, by a resolution of 17 December 1982,[3] endorsed the assessment of the economic review mission, and noted Lesotho's requirements to carry out the rest of its development programme, implement projects necessitated by the political situation in the region and lessen its dependence on South Africa. Reiterating its appeal for international assistance for unfunded projects, the Assembly called on Member States and organizations to assist Lesotho in achieving greater self-sufficiency in food, ensuring a regular petroleum supply, and developing road and air transport. The Secretary-General was requested to consult with the Government on the help it needed for its efforts to integrate women more fully into development and to report on the type of assistance required to establish labour-intensive projects so that migrant workers returning from South Africa could be absorbed into the Lesotho economy.

This resolution was adopted without vote, following similar approval by the Second Committee on 2 December. The text, sponsored by 28 nations, was introduced by Kenya and was orally revised following informal consultations. The revision replaced a request to the Secretary-General to arrange for a review of Lesotho's economic situation by a request that he report on the progress made in its economic situation.

On 15 December, following an attack by South African forces on Lesotho's capital, the Security Council condemned South Africa and requested Member States to extend economic assistance so that Lesotho could receive and maintain South African refugees.

Reports. [1]Meeting on industrial development co-operation for Lesotho, UNIDO/PC.43; [2]S-G, annexing mission report, A/37/126-S/15280.
Resolution (1982). [3]GA: 37/160, 17 Dec., text following.
Resolution (prior). [4]GA: 36/219, 17 Dec. 1981 (YUN 1981, p. 514).
Meeting records. ESC: E/1982/SR.46 (19 July). GA: 2nd Committee, A/C.2/37/SR.27-30, *31*, 33, *40*, *46* (2 Nov.–2 Dec.); plenary, A/37/PV.109 (17 Dec.).

General Assembly resolution 37/160

17 December 1982   Meeting 109   Adopted without vote

Approved by Second Committee (A/37/702/Add.2) without vote, 2 December (meeting 46); 28-nation draft (A/C.2/37/L.59), orally revised in informal consultations; agenda item 74 *(b)*.

Sponsors: Afghanistan, Algeria, Botswana, Canada, Cape Verde, Central African Republic, Denmark, Ethiopia, France, Gambia, Guinea-Bissau, India, Ireland, Japan, Kenya, Lesotho, Madagascar, Malawi, Mauritania, Mozambique, Nepal, Niger, Nigeria, Sudan, Swaziland, Sweden, Uganda, United Republic of Cameroon.

Assistance to Lesotho

The General Assembly,

Recalling Security Council resolution 402(1976) of 22 December 1976, in which the Council, *inter alia*, expressed concern at the serious situation created by South Africa's closure of certain border posts between South Africa and Lesotho aimed at coercing Lesotho into according recognition to the bantustan of the Transkei,

Commending the decision of the Government of Lesotho not to recognize the Transkei, in compliance with United Nations decisions, particularly General Assembly resolution 31/6 A of 26 October 1976,

Fully aware that the decision of the Government of Lesotho not to recognize the Transkei has imposed a special economic burden upon its people,

Strongly endorsing the appeals made in Security Council resolutions 402(1976) of 22 December 1976 and 407(1977) of 25 May 1977, in General Assembly resolutions 32/98 of 13 December 1977, 33/128 of 19 December 1978, 34/130 of 14 December 1979, 35/96 of 5 December 1980 and 36/219 of 17 December 1981, and by the Secretary-General, calling upon all States, regional and intergovernmental organizations and the appropriate agencies of the United Nations system to contribute generously to the international programme of assistance to enable Lesotho to carry out its economic development and enhance its capacity to implement fully resolutions of the United Nations,

Having examined the report of the Secretary-General, to which was annexed the report of the mission which he sent to Lesotho, in response to General Assembly resolution 36/219, to review the economic situation as well as the progress made in the implementation of the special programme of economic assistance for Lesotho,

Noting the priority which the Government of Lesotho accords to raising levels of food production through increased productivity, thus lessening the country's dependency on South Africa for food imports,

Aware that the high prices paid by Lesotho for its imports of petroleum products as a result of the oil embargo on South Africa have become a serious impediment to the development of the country,

Recognizing, in connection with such embargoes, the obligation of the international community to help countries such as Lesotho that act in support of the Charter of the United Nations and in compliance with General Assembly resolutions,

Recalling its resolutions 32/160 of 19 December 1977 and 33/197 of 29 January 1979 concerning the Transport and Communications Decade in Africa and, in this regard, noting Lesotho's geopolitical situation, which necessitates the urgent development of air and telecommunication links with neighbouring countries of Africa and the rest of the world,

Taking account of Lesotho's need for a national network of roads, both for its planned social and economic development and to lessen its dependence on the South African network, to reach various regions of the country affected by the imposition of travel restrictions by South Africa,

Taking note of Lesotho's special problems associated with the employment of large numbers of its able-bodied men in South Africa,

Taking note also of the priority which the Government of Lesotho has accorded to the problem of absorbing into the economy the young generation, as well as migrant workers returning from South Africa,

Welcoming the action taken by the Government of Lesotho to make more effective use of women in the development process by promoting their participation in the economic, social and cultural life of the country,

Taking account also of the fact that Lesotho is not only land-locked but also one of the least developed and most seriously affected countries,

Recalling its resolution 32/98, in which it, *inter alia*, recognized that the continuing influx of refugees from South Africa imposed an additional burden on Lesotho,

1. *Expresses its concern* at the difficulties that confront the Government of Lesotho as a result of its decision not to recognize the so-called independent Transkei;

2. *Endorses fully* the assessment of the situation contained in the annex to the report of the Secretary-General;

3. *Takes note* of the requirements of Lesotho, as described in the report of the Secretary-General, to carry out the remainder of its development programme, implement projects necessitated by the present political situation in the region and lessen its dependence on South Africa;

4. *Expresses its appreciation* to the Secretary-General for the measures he has taken to organize an international economic assistance programme for Lesotho;

5. *Notes with appreciation* the response made thus far by the international community to the special programme of economic assistance for Lesotho, which has enabled it to proceed with the implementation of parts of the recommended programme;

6. *Reiterates its appeal* to Member States, regional and interregional organizations and other intergovernmental bodies to provide financial, material and technical assistance to Lesotho for the implementation of several projects and programmes which are still unfunded, as identified in the report of the Secretary-General;

7. *Calls upon* Member States and the appropriate agencies, organizations and financial institutions to provide assistance to Lesotho so as to enable it to achieve a greater degree of self-sufficiency in food production;

8. *Also calls upon* Member States to give all possible assistance to Lesotho to ensure an adequate and regular supply of oil to meet its national requirements;

9. *Further calls upon* Member States to assist Lesotho in developing its internal road and air systems and its air communication with the rest of the world;

10. *Commends* the efforts of the Government of Lesotho to integrate women more fully into development efforts, and requests the Secretary-General to consult with the Government on the type and amount of assistance it will require to achieve this objective;

11. *Draws the attention* of the international community to the meeting of donors held in Lesotho from 5 to 9 November 1979, as well as

the agricultural sector conference held in Lesotho from 20 to 24 October 1980, and urges Member States and the appropriate agencies and organizations to provide assistance to Lesotho in accordance with the outcome of those meetings;

12. *Further draws the attention* of the international community to the special account which was established at United Nations Headquarters by the Secretary-General, in accordance with Security Council resolution 407(1977), for the purpose of facilitating the channelling of contributions to Lesotho;

13. *Invites* the United Nations Development Programme, the United Nations Children's Fund, the World Health Organization, the United Nations Industrial Development Organization, the Food and Agriculture Organization of the United Nations and the International Fund for Agricultural Development to bring further to the attention of their governing bodies the special needs of Lesotho and to report to the Secretary-General by 15 August 1983 on the steps they have taken;

14. *Requests* the appropriate specialized agencies and other organizations of the United Nations system to co-operate closely with the Secretary-General in organizing an effective international programme of assistance to Lesotho and to report periodically to him on the steps they have taken and the resources they have made available to help that country;

15. *Requests* the Secretary-General:

(a) To continue his efforts to mobilize the necessary resources for an effective programme of financial, technical and material assistance to Lesotho;

(b) To consult with the Government of Lesotho on the question of migrant workers returning from South Africa and to report on the type of assistance which the Government requires in order to establish labour-intensive projects to deal with their absorption into the economy;

(c) To ensure that adequate financial and budgetary arrangements are made to continue the organization of the international programme of assistance to Lesotho and the mobilization of that assistance;

(d) To keep the situation in Lesotho under constant review, to maintain close contact with Member States, the specialized agencies, regional and other intergovernmental organizations, and the international financial institutions concerned, and to apprise the Economic and Social Council, at its second regular session of 1983, of the current status of the special programme of economic assistance for Lesotho;

(e) To report on the progress made in the economic situation of Lesotho and in organizing and implementing the special programme of economic assistance for that country in time for the matter to be considered by the General Assembly at its thirty-eighth session.

Liberia

Liberia was experiencing grave economic and financial difficulties, according to an inter-agency mission which visited the country from 8 to 17 March 1982[1] in pursuance of a December 1981 General Assembly request[3] that the Government be consulted on its reconstruction, rehabilitation and development needs. The mission, the first of its kind to be sent there, reported a 4.4 per cent decline in gross domestic product in 1980 and a further drop in 1981. There were substantial budget and balance-of-payments deficits and a severe shortage of foreign exchange. Agricultural productivity was low, and skilled personnel and the required technical and social infrastructure were lacking. The productive base was limited to a few export commodities, including iron ore, rubber, diamonds and timber, and the country was heavily dependent on imports, especially petroleum products. The internal market was limited by the small population, of which 60 to 70 per cent depended on subsistence crops.

The Government's four-year public investment programme (1981/82-1984/85) amounted to $768 million at 1982 prices. Although foreign donors had been secured for most of the ongoing public investment projects, $140 million was required for the Liberian counterpart contribution which, in the absence of budgetary and foreign exchange resources, the Government could not meet. Agriculture and rural development accounted for about 57 per cent of the total value of the Liberian contribution to ongoing projects and a road programme for a further 14 per cent. Total funding required for new projects was $227 million at 1982 prices, with emphasis on roads ($70 million), ports ($28 million), agriculture and rural development ($24 million), and health and social welfare ($20 million).

Liberia stated in the General Assembly's Second Committee in November that the Government had adopted stringent economic measures, including policies to control public-sector expenditure, increase revenue collection and make the economic management of the public sector more effective; it had requested the World Bank to assist in making the necessary structural adjustments in the economy.

By a resolution of 17 December,[2] the Assembly endorsed the inter-agency mission's recommendations and urgently reiterated its appeal for international assistance for the reconstruction, rehabilitation and development of Liberia, including a generous response at a round-table conference of donors planned for 1983. It urged Member States and United Nations organizations to provide food, medicines, and hospital and school equipment, and to meet emergency needs in the region recently hit by landslides and floods. In view of the critical economic situation, Member States were called on to accord Liberia special measures and give special consideration to including it in their development assistance programmes.

The resolution was adopted without vote, following similar approval by the Second Committee on 2 December. It was introduced by Kenya on behalf of 35 nations, and orally revised after informal consultations. By one of the changes, the Assembly called on Member States to accord Liberia "special measures" rather than "privileges and benefits similar to those accorded the least developed countries". Also, the Secretary-General was requested to keep under review the situation regarding "assistance to" Liberia rather than the "situation in" Liberia, and to report in 1983 on the progress made in Liberia's economic situation rather than to arrange for a review of that situation in 1983.

Report. [1]S-G, annexing mission report, A/37/123.
Resolution (1982). [2]GA: 37/149, 17 Dec., text following.
Resolution (prior). [3]GA: 36/207, 17 Dec. 1981 (YUN 1981, p. 516).

Meeting records. ESC: E/1982/SR.46 (19 July). GA: 2nd Committee, A/C.2/37/SR.27-29, *30,* 31, 33, *40, 46* (2 Nov.–2 Dec.); plenary, A/37/PV.109 (17 Dec.).

General Assembly resolution 37/149

17 December 1982   Meeting 109   Adopted without vote

Approved by Second Committee (A/37/702/Add.2) without vote, 2 December (meeting 46); 35-nation draft (A/C.2/37/L.38), orally revised in informal consultations; agenda item 74 *(b).*

Sponsors: Algeria, Burundi, Cape Verde, Central African Republic, China, Egypt, Ethiopia, France, Gambia, Guinea, Guinea-Bissau, Guyana, Indonesia, Kenya, Liberia, Madagascar, Malawi, Mali, Nicaragua, Niger, Nigeria, Pakistan, Saint Lucia, Senegal, Sierra Leone, Singapore, Sudan, Swaziland, Thailand, Tunisia, Uganda, United Republic of Cameroon, United States, Yugoslavia, Zambia.

Assistance for the development of Liberia

The General Assembly,

Recalling its resolution 36/207 of 17 December 1981, in which it appealed to all Member States, the specialized agencies and other organizations of the United Nations system and international financial and development institutions to provide all possible assistance for the reconstruction, rehabilitation and development of Liberia,

Noting the statement made by the representative of Liberia before the Second Committee on 4 November 1982, describing his country's serious economic and financial situation,

Having examined the report of the Secretary-General, to which was annexed the report of the inter-agency mission he dispatched to Liberia in March 1982 to consult with the Government on the additional assistance needed for the reconstruction, rehabilitation and development of the country,

Noting from the report the serious economic and financial problems that confront Liberia, which arise primarily from the weak and underdeveloped state of the economic and social infrastructure,

Noting also that the budgetary situation in Liberia, according to the report, makes it impossible for the Government to embark on a development programme without sufficient external financial aid,

Particularly concerned that the Government of Liberia is unable to provide the population with adequate health, educational and other essential social and public services because of an acute shortage of financial and material resources, especially so in the wake of the recent national disaster arising from the landslide and floods which caused the loss of lives,

Taking note of the recommended programme of assistance to Liberia, drawn up by the inter-agency mission in consultation with the Government,

Aware of the intention of the Government of Liberia to organize, with the assistance of the United Nations Development Programme, a round-table conference of donors in 1983 to discuss the country's development needs and to consider ways and means of helping the Government in its efforts to meet those needs,

Noting that the Government of Liberia, with the assistance of the United Nations Secretariat, has prepared and submitted to the Committee for Development Planning, for consideration at its nineteenth session, in 1983, a report containing additional and up-to-date information relating to the economic situation of Liberia,

1. *Notes with satisfaction* the efforts exerted by the Government and people of Liberia for national reconstruction, rehabilitation and development;

2. *Expresses its appreciation* to the Secretary-General for his report on the economic situation of Liberia and the additional assistance required by that country for its reconstruction, rehabilitation and development;

3. *Endorses fully* the assessment and recommendations of the inter-agency mission, contained in the annex to the report of the Secretary-General;

4. *Urgently reiterates its appeal* to all Member States to contribute generously, through bilateral or multilateral channels, to the reconstruction, rehabilitation and development of Liberia;

5. *Urges* Member States, organizations and programmes of the United Nations system, regional and interregional governmental bodies, development and financial institutions and non-governmental organizations to support fully the efforts of the Government of Liberia to mobilize funds for its special economic assistance programme and,

to this end, to respond generously to the needs of Liberia at the forthcoming round-table conference;

6. *Requests* the appropriate organizations and programmes of the United Nations system—in particular the United Nations Development Programme, the World Bank, the Food and Agriculture Organization of the United Nations, the International Fund for Agricultural Development, the World Food Programme, the World Health Organization, the United Nations Children's Fund and the United Nations Industrial Development Organization—to maintain and expand their programmes of assistance to Liberia, to co-operate closely with the Secretary-General in his efforts to organize an effective international programme of assistance and to report periodically to him on the steps they have taken and the resources they have made available to help that country;

7. *Calls upon* regional and interregional organizations and other intergovernmental bodies and non-governmental organizations, as well as international financial institutions—in particular the European Economic Community, the European Development Fund, the African Development Bank, the Arab Bank for Economic Development in Africa, the Organization of Petroleum Exporting Countries Fund for International Development and the International Fund for Agricultural Development—to give urgent consideration to the establishment of a programme of assistance for Liberia or, where one is already in existence, to the expansion of that programme;

8. *Calls upon* Member States, pending consideration by the Committee for Development Planning at its nineteenth session of the report submitted to it and in view of the critical economic situation of Liberia, to accord Liberia special measures and, as a matter of priority, to give special consideration to the early inclusion of Liberia in their programme of development assistance;

9. *Urges* Member States and the appropriate United Nations bodies—in particular the United Nations Development Programme, the World Food Programme, the United Nations Children's Fund, the World Health Organization, the United Nations Fund for Population Activities and the United Nations Industrial Development Organization—to provide all possible assistance to help the Government of Liberia to cope with the critical humanitarian needs of the population and to provide, as appropriate, food, medicine and essential equipment for schools and hospitals, as well as to meet the emergency needs of the population in the region hit by the recent landslide and floods;

10. *Invites* the United Nations Development Programme, the United Nations Children's Fund, the World Food Programme, the World Health Organization, the Food and Agriculture Organization of the United Nations, the World Bank and the International Fund for Agricultural Development to bring to the attention of their governing bodies, for their consideration, the special needs of Liberia and to report the decisions of those bodies to the Secretary-General by 15 July 1983;

11. *Requests* the Administrator of the United Nations Development Programme and the World Bank to provide all possible assistance to the Government of Liberia in organizing the round-table conference of donors;

12. *Requests* the Secretary-General:

(a) To continue his efforts to mobilize the necessary resources for an effective programme of financial, technical and material assistance to Liberia;

(b) To ensure that adequate financial and budgetary arrangements are made to continue the organization of the international programme of assistance for Liberia and the mobilization of assistance;

(c) To keep the situation regarding assistance to Liberia under constant review, to maintain close contact with Member States, regional and other intergovernmental organizations, the specialized agencies and the international financial institutions concerned, and to apprise the Economic and Social Council, at its second regular session of 1983, of the current status of the special programme of economic assistance for Liberia;

(d) To report on the progress made in the economic situation of Liberia and in organizing and implementing the programme of assistance for that country in time for the matter to be considered by the General Assembly at its thirty-eighth session.

Mozambique

Numerous armed attacks on economic targets in central and southern Mozambique, which the Government said were sponsored by South Africa, had resulted in significant economic costs and disruption in 1981/82. This was reported by a United Nations economic mission which visited Mozambique from 10 to 17 June 1982[1] in pursuance of a December 1981 General Assembly request.[3] Moreover, the country had suffered from drought since 1978, and the Government estimated that 1.4 million people were affected by March 1982; in mid-1982 the southern provinces of Gaza and Maputo had been hit and food shortages had obliged people to consume about half of the cashewnut crop, normally destined for export. A foreign exchange shortage, reflected by a balance-of-payments deficit of $175 million to $200 million a year since 1976, had restricted commercial food imports, and the situation was likely to become critical by September 1982, with the deficit expected to mount to 303,000 tonnes for all of 1982.

In describing Mozambique's economic assistance needs, the mission concentrated on transport and communications reconstruction and rehabilitation projects. Of 16 projects identified by a United Nations mission that had visited Mozambique in June 1981,[4] substantial progress had been made in securing funding for 7, including rehabilitation of a major road and four railway lines, improvement of airport lighting and construction of a container terminal at Nacala port. Some progress had been made on funding for 6 projects, while 3 had not attracted concrete donor interest. Some $70 million had been pledged towards the $100 million needed for the first phase of a national microwave system, with connections to neighbouring countries. In addition, funds were urgently required to complete telecommunication installations and connections at Maputo. All these projects were being co-ordinated by the Southern Africa Development Co-ordination Conference.

Speaking to the General Assembly's Second Committee in November, Mozambique said the undeclared war waged by South Africa against Mozambique since the end of the conflict in Zimbabwe (1980), involving armed incursions by regular troops and by bandits in South Africa's pay, was preventing Mozambique from turning its full attention to reconstruction and development; the country still needed food donations and large investments for transport and communications, especially to develop rural and trunk roads and coastal shipping.

The Assembly, by a resolution of 17 December 1982,[2] endorsed the mission's recommendations and appealed for food and other relief assistance relating to the continued drought. Expressing regret that assistance had fallen far short of needs, the Assembly urged Member States and organizations to strengthen their aid programmes and provide assistance in the form of grants wherever possible.

This resolution was adopted without vote, following similar approval by the Second Committee on 2 December. The text, introduced by Kenya on behalf of 39 States, was orally revised following informal consultations. The main revision had the Assembly request the Secretary-General to report in 1983 on the development of Mozambique's economic situation rather than requesting him to arrange for a review of that situation.

Report. [1]S-G, annexing mission report, A/37/129-S/15304.
Resolution (1982). [2]GA: 37/161, 17 Dec., text following.
Resolution (prior). [3]GA: 36/215, 17 Dec. 1981 (YUN 1981, p. 517).
Yearbook reference. [4]1981, p. 516.
Meeting records. ESC: E/1982/SR.46 (19 July). GA: 2nd Committee, A/C.2/37/SR.*27, 28-31, 33, 40, 46* (2 Nov.–2 Dec.); plenary, A/37/PV.109 (17 Dec.).

General Assembly resolution 37/161

17 December 1982   Meeting 109   Adopted without vote

Approved by Second Committee (A/37/702/Add.2) without vote, 2 December (meeting 46); 39-nation draft (A/C.2/37/L.60), orally revised in informal consultations; agenda item 74 *(b)*.

Sponsors: Afghanistan, Algeria, Angola, Benin, Botswana, Brazil, Cape Verde, Central African Republic, China, Cuba, Ethiopia, France, German Democratic Republic, Guinea-Bissau, India, Italy, Kenya, Lesotho, Madagascar, Malawi, Mali, Mauritania, Mongolia, Mozambique, Nicaragua, Niger, Nigeria, Portugal, Romania, Rwanda, Sao Tome and Principe, Sudan, Sweden, Tunisia, United Republic of Cameroon, United Republic of Tanzania, Viet Nam, Yugoslavia, Zimbabwe.

Assistance to Mozambique

The General Assembly,

Recalling the decision of the Government of Mozambique to implement mandatory sanctions against the illegal régime in Southern Rhodesia in accordance with Security Council resolution 253(1968) of 29 May 1968,

Recognizing the substantial economic sacrifices, with lasting adverse effects on its economy, made by Mozambique in the implementation of its decision to enforce United Nations sanctions and to close its borders with Southern Rhodesia,

Recalling Security Council resolution 386(1976) of 17 March 1976, in which the Council appealed to all States to provide, and requested the Secretary-General, in collaboration with the appropriate organizations of the United Nations system, to organize, with immediate effect, financial, technical and material assistance to enable Mozambique to carry out its economic development programme,

Noting with deep concern the loss of life and the destruction of essential infrastructures such as roads, railways, bridges, petroleum facilities, electricity supply, schools and hospitals identified in the annex to the report of the Secretary-General of 16 August 1979,

Recalling further its resolutions 31/43 of 1 December 1976, 32/95 of 13 December 1977, 33/126 of 19 December 1978, 34/129 of 14 December 1979, 35/99 of 5 December 1980 and 36/215 of 17 December 1981, in which it urged the international community to respond effectively and generously with assistance to Mozambique,

Taking into account the food deficit of over 300,000 tonnes for 1982 and the other serious effects of the continued drought on the economy of the country,

Having considered the report of the Secretary-General on assistance to Mozambique and noting with concern that the economic and financial position of that country remains grave and beset by budgetary and balance-of-payments deficits,

Recognizing that substantial international assistance is required for the implementation of a number of reconstruction and development projects,

1. *Strongly endorses* the appeals made by the Security Council and the Secretary-General for international assistance to Mozambique;

2. *Expresses its appreciation* to the Secretary-General for the measures he has taken to organize an international economic assistance programme for Mozambique;

3. *Also expresses its appreciation* for the assistance provided to Mozambique by various States and regional and international organizations;

4. *Regrets,* however, that the total assistance provided to date falls far short of Mozambique's pressing needs;

5. *Endorses fully* the assessment and recommendations contained in the annex to the report of the Secretary-General on assistance to Mozambique;

6. *Draws the attention* of the international community to the additional financial, economic and material assistance identified in the annex to the report of the Secretary-General as urgently required by Mozambique;

7. *Calls upon* Member States, regional and interregional organizations and other governmental, intergovernmental and non-governmental organizations to provide financial, material and technical assistance to Mozambique, wherever possible in the form of grants, and urges them to give special consideration to the early inclusion of Mozambique in their programmes of development assistance, if it is not already included;

8. *Urges* Member States and organizations which are already implementing or are negotiating assistance programmes for Mozambique to strengthen them, wherever possible;

9. *Appeals* to the international community to provide financial and material assistance to Mozambique to meet its food and other relief requirements arising out of the continued drought;

10. *Also appeals* to the international community to contribute to the special account for Mozambique established by the Secretary-General for the purpose of facilitating the channelling of contributions to Mozambique;

11. *Invites* the United Nations Development Programme, the United Nations Children's Fund, the World Food Programme, the World Health Organization, the United Nations Industrial Development Organization, the Food and Agriculture Organization of the United Nations, the International Fund for Agricultural Development and the International Labour Organisation to bring to the attention of their governing bodies, for their consideration, the special needs of Mozambique and to report the decisions of those bodies to the Secretary-General in time for consideration by the General Assembly at its thirty-eighth session;

12. *Requests* the appropriate organizations and programmes of the United Nations system—in particular, the United Nations Development Programme, the Food and Agriculture Organization of the United Nations, the International Fund for Agricultural Development, the World Food Programme, the World Health Organization and the United Nations Children's Fund—to maintain and increase their current and future programmes of assistance to Mozambique, to co-operate closely with the Secretary-General in organizing an effective international programme of assistance and to report periodically to him on the steps they have taken and the resources they have made available to help that country;

13. *Requests* the Secretary-General:

(a) To continue his efforts to mobilize the necessary resources for an effective programme of financial, technical and material assistance to Mozambique;

(b) To keep the situation in Mozambique under constant review, to maintain close contact with Member States, regional and other intergovernmental organizations, including the specialized agencies and international financial institutions, and other bodies concerned and to apprise the Economic and Social Council, at its second regular session of 1983, of the current status of the special programme of economic assistance for Mozambique;

(c) To prepare, on the basis of sustained consultations with the Government of Mozambique, a report on the development of the economic situation and the implementation of the special programme of economic assistance for that country in time for the matter to be considered by the General Assembly at its thirty-eighth session.

Sao Tome and Principe

The demand for cocoa, a crop which averaged over 90 per cent of Sao Tome and Principe's exports, declined in 1981 and international prices fell sharply. According to an economic mission which visited the country from 27 April to 1 May 1982[1]

in pursuance of a December 1981 General Assembly request,[3] Sao Tome and Principe was unable to market all its production, and exports fell from 7,335 tonnes in 1980 to 5,279 tonnes in 1981. Copra, palm-oil and coffee exports had reached $2.5 million in 1979, but fell to $1.1 million in 1981. As a result, there were continuing shortages of food and other essential imports, whose prices continued to rise. Persistent drought and an erratic pattern of rainfall had also proven detrimental to the economy.

The mission reported that fewer than half of the 52 projects in the country's special economic assistance programme had attracted international support during the past four years. The Government was therefore seeking bilateral support to implement a number of them and had identified 18 priority projects for which it continued to seek international assistance. Among these were the construction of a national library, a port at Santo Antonio, health infrastructure construction and facilities for schools.

Sao Tome and Principe stated in the General Assembly's Second Committee in November that the volume of international economic assistance the country had received had not covered its requirements; its export earnings had declined sharply despite efforts to diversify crops in order to reduce the huge food-import bill.

The Assembly, by a resolution of 17 December 1982,[2] endorsed the mission's recommendations and renewed its appeal for international assistance to help develop the country.

This resolution was adopted without vote, following similar approval in the Second Committee on 2 December. The text, introduced by Kenya on behalf of 25 nations, was orally revised after informal consultations. As a result of the revision, the Secretary-General was requested to report in 1984 on progress in the country's economic situation rather than to arrange for a review of the situation by then.

Report. [1]S-G, annexing mission report, A/37/127.
Resolution (1982). [2]GA: 37/146, 17 Dec., text following.
Resolution (prior). [3]GA: 36/209, 17 Dec. 1981 (YUN 1981, p. 519).
Meeting records. ESC: E/1982/SR.46 (19 July). GA: 2nd Committee, A/C.2/37/SR.27, *28,* 29-31, 33, *40, 46* (2 Nov.–2 Dec.); plenary, A/37/PV.109 (17 Dec.).

General Assembly resolution 37/146

17 December 1982   Meeting 109   Adopted without vote

Approved by Second Committee (A/37/702/Add.2) without vote, 2 December (meeting 46); 25-nation draft (A/C.2/37/L.35), orally revised in informal consultations; agenda item 74 *(b).*

Sponsors: Afghanistan, Algeria, Angola, Benin, Brazil, Cape Verde, Central African Republic, Congo, Ethiopia, France, Guinea-Bissau, Kenya, Madagascar, Mozambique, Nicaragua, Niger, Nigeria, Portugal, Rwanda, Sao Tome and Principe, Sierra Leone, Sudan, United Republic of Cameroon, Viet Nam, Zaire.

Assistance to Sao Tome and Principe

The General Assembly,

Recalling its resolutions 32/96 of 13 December 1977, 33/125 of 19 December 1978, 34/131 of 14 December 1979, 35/93 of 5 December 1980 and 36/209 of 17 December 1981, in which it reiterated its appeal to the international community to provide financial, material and technical assistance to Sao Tome and Principe to enable it to establish the necessary social and economic infrastructure for development,

Aware that the economic and social development of Sao Tome and Principe has been seriously hindered by inadequate health, educational and housing facilities, as well as by inadequate infrastructure, and that urgent improvement in these sectors is a prerequisite for the country's future progress,

Having examined the report of the Secretary-General, to which was annexed the report of the review mission sent to Sao Tome and Principe,

1. *Expresses its appreciation* to the Secretary-General for the steps he has taken to mobilize assistance to Sao Tome and Principe;

2. *Endorses fully* the assessment and recommendations contained in the annex to the report of the Secretary-General;

3. *Expresses its appreciation* to those Member States and international organizations which have contributed assistance to Sao Tome and Principe;

4. *Renews its appeal* to Member States, the appropriate organs, organizations and programmes of the United Nations system, regional and interregional organizations and other intergovernmental bodies and non-governmental organizations, as well as international financial institutions, to assist in the development of Sao Tome and Principe through bilateral and multilateral channels, as appropriate;

5. *Requests* the Secretary-General:

(a) To keep the situation in Sao Tome and Principe under constant review and to apprise the Economic and Social Council, at its second regular session of 1984, of the current status of the special economic assistance for Sao Tome and Principe;

(b) To report on the progress made in the economic situation of Sao Tome and Principe and in organizing and implementing the special programme of economic assistance for that country in time for the matter to be considered by the General Assembly at its thirty-ninth session.

Seychelles

The Government of Seychelles had to spend $100,000 for urgent repairs to reopen its international airport as a result of a November 1981 attack on it by foreign mercenaries.[6] It estimated that permanent repairs to damaged installations and replacing equipment would cost $1.28 million, according to a Commission of Inquiry which the Security Council had established in December 1981.[5]

The Commission reported in March 1982[3] that the tourism industry, which normally provided 70 per cent of the foreign exchange earnings of Seychelles, had been seriously affected as a result of the attack, and that the Government anticipated an economic loss of about $16.7 million, assuming an 18 per cent drop in the number of tourist arrivals. While it was too soon to make a definitive evaluation of damage, it was clear that the aggression would result in a significant adverse impact on the Seychelles economy. Accordingly, the Commission recommended that financial, technical and material assistance be provided urgently by Member States and international organizations to enable the country to deal with the difficulties it was facing because of the aggression, and noted the existence of the special account for Seychelles in the United Nations Trust Fund for Special Economic Assistance Programmes.

The Security Council, in a resolution of 28 May on the armed attack against Seychelles,[4] appealed to all States and international organiza-

tions, including United Nations specialized agencies, to assist Seychelles to repair the damage caused by the mercenary aggression. It decided to establish, by 5 June, a special fund for voluntary contributions, through which assistance should be channelled for economic reconstruction. It also decided to establish, before the end of May, an *ad hoc* committee composed of four Council members, and chaired by France, to co-ordinate and mobilize resources for the Special Fund for immediate disbursement to Seychelles.

During the Council's discussion of the Commission's report (See POLITICAL AND SECURITY QUESTIONS, Chapter V), Seychelles stated that an $18-million loss represented a considerable amount to a small island State with few natural resources and would seriously affect the country's economic and social development unless prompt financial and technical assistance was forthcoming.

The Council President announced on 28 May[1] that, following consultations with Council members, agreement had been reached that, in addition to France, the other members of the *Ad Hoc* Committee would be Guyana, Jordan and Uganda.

By a note verbale of 7 October, India informed the Secretary-General of its pledge of $25,000 to the Special Fund.[2] By 31 December, the Fund had received $1,000 from Sri Lanka and $500 each from Maldives and Nicaragua.

Note. [1]SC President, S/15138.
Note verbale. [2]India, 7 Oct., S/15456.
Report. [3]Commission of Inquiry, S/14905/Rev.1.
Resolution (1982). [4]SC: 507(1982), paras. 8-11, 28 May.
Resolution (prior). [5]SC: 496(1981), 15 Dec. 1981 (YUN 1981, p. 227).
Yearbook reference. [6]1981, p. 226.

Sierra Leone

The General Assembly, by a resolution of 17 December 1982,[1] strongly recommended urgent international action to assist the Government of Sierra Leone to strengthen the country's infrastructure, develop its natural and human resources, and accelerate economic growth and social advancement. It urged States and United Nations bodies to help the Government meet critical humanitarian needs and to provide food, medicines, and essential equipment for hospitals and schools. It requested the Secretary-General to organize an international programme of financial, technical and material assistance and to dispatch a multi-agency mission to consult with the Government on additional development assistance.

The resolution was adopted without vote, following similar approval in the Second (Economic and Financial) Committee on 2 December. It was introduced by Kenya, on behalf of 47 nations, and was orally revised following informal consultations. Among the revisions were one which had the Assembly address its appeal for contributions for Sierra Leone's development to all States rather than all Member States; another which added the United Nations Educational, Scientific and Cultural Organization to the list of United Nations organizations urged to assist; a third which added the African Development Bank to the list of organizations invited to report the decisions of their governing bodies to the Secretary-General; and a fourth which had the Assembly request the Secretary-General to keep under review the situation regarding assistance to Sierra Leone rather than the situation in Sierra Leone.

The Assembly took this action following a statement to it in September by the Minister for Foreign Affairs of Sierra Leone who reported that the country's economic situation had worsened, the purchasing power of its exports had progressively diminished, and the terms of trade and balance of trade had turned against it, causing the Economic and Social Council to recommend (in July) that Sierra Leone be classified as a least developed country.

Resolution (1982). [1]GA: 37/158, 17 Dec., text following.
Meeting records. GA: 2nd Committee, A/C.2/37/SR.27-31, 33, 40, 46 (2 Nov.–2 Dec.); plenary, A/37/PV.10, 109 (29 Sep., 17 Dec.).

General Assembly resolution 37/158

17 December 1982	Meeting 109	Adopted without vote

Approved by Second Committee (A/37/702/Add.2) without vote, 2 December (meeting 46); 47-nation draft (A/C.2/37/L.57), orally revised in informal consultations; agenda item 74 *(b)*.

Sponsors: Afghanistan, Algeria, Bangladesh, Barbados, Benin, Botswana, Cape Verde, Central African Republic, Chad, China, Comoros, Cuba, Djibouti, Egypt, Ethiopia, Gambia, Guinea, Guinea-Bissau, Guyana, Ivory Coast, Jamaica, Japan, Kenya, Liberia, Madagascar, Mauritania, Niger, Nigeria, Pakistan, Philippines, Romania, Saint Lucia, Sao Tome and Principe, Senegal, Sierra Leone, Singapore, Somalia, Sudan, Swaziland, Thailand, Trinidad and Tobago, Tunisia, Uganda, United Republic of Cameroon, Uruguay, Yugoslavia, Zaire.

Assistance for the development of Sierra Leone

The General Assembly,

Having heard the statement made by the Minister for Foreign Affairs of Sierra Leone before the General Assembly on 29 September 1982, in which he described the serious economic situation facing Sierra Leone,

Deeply concerned about the weak and underdeveloped state of the economic and social infrastructure of Sierra Leone and the lack of capital resources, which constitute serious obstacles to the economic and social development of the country and to the raising of the living standards of the population,

Also concerned about the weak growth rate experienced by the economy during the five-year period of the first National Development Plan and the decline in real terms of per capita gross domestic product during that period,

Noting that the country's mining industry has encountered serious difficulties and that the manufacturing industries are highly dependent on foreign exchange for the import of almost all of the materials consumed,

Further concerned about the critical unemployment problem which prevails in Sierra Leone,

Taking note of the recommendation made by the Committee for Development Planning at its eighteenth session that Sierra Leone should be included in the list of the least developed countries and of the endorsement of that recommendation by the Economic and Social Council in its resolution 1982/41 of 27 July 1982,

Bearing in mind its resolution 37/133 of 17 December 1982, in which it decided to include Sierra Leone in the list of least developed countries,

1. *Strongly recommends* urgent international action to assist the Government of Sierra Leone in its efforts to strengthen the country's infrastructure, to develop more fully the country's natural and human resources and to accelerate economic growth and the social advancement of its people;

2. *Urgently appeals* to all States and international development and financial institutions to contribute generously, through bilateral or multilateral channels, to the economic and social development of Sierra Leone;

3. *Requests* the Secretary-General to organize an international programme of financial, technical and material assistance to Sierra Leone to enable the Government to overcome the severe obstacles which stand in the way of the country's economic and social development;

4. *Requests* the appropriate organizations and programmes of the United Nations system—in particular the United Nations Development Programme, the United Nations Fund for Population Activities, the Food and Agriculture Organization of the United Nations, the International Fund for Agricultural Development, the World Food Programme, the World Health Organization, the United Nations Industrial Development Organization and the United Nations Children's Fund—to expand their programmes of assistance to Sierra Leone, to co-operate closely with the Secretary-General in organizing an effective international programme of assistance and to report periodically to him on the steps they have taken and the resources they have made available to help that country;

5. *Calls upon* regional and interregional organizations and other intergovernmental bodies and non-governmental organizations, as well as the international development and financial institutions, to give urgent consideration to the establishment of a programme of assistance to Sierra Leone or, where one is already in existence, to the expansion of that programme;

6. *Urges* all States and relevant United Nations bodies—in particular the United Nations Development Programme, the World Food Programme, the United Nations Industrial Development Organization, the United Nations Children's Fund, the World Health Organization, the United Nations Educational, Scientific and Cultural Organization and the United Nations Fund for Population Activities—to provide all possible assistance to help the Government of Sierra Leone meet the critical humanitarian needs of the population and to provide, as appropriate, food, medicines and essential equipment for hospitals and schools;

7. *Invites* the United Nations Development Programme, the United Nations Children's Fund, the World Food Programme, the World Health Organization, the United Nations Industrial Development Organization, the Food and Agriculture Organization of the United Nations, the World Bank, the African Development Bank and the International Fund for Agricultural Development to bring to the attention of their governing bodies, for their consideration, the special needs of Sierra Leone and to report the decisions of those bodies to the Secretary-General by 15 July 1983;

8. *Requests* the Secretary-General:

(a) To dispatch a multi-agency mission to Sierra Leone with a view to holding consultations with the Government on the additional assistance which it needs for the economic and social development of the country and to communicate the report of the mission to the international community, the Economic and Social Council and the General Assembly;

(b) To ensure that adequate financial arrangements are made for the organization of an effective international programme of assistance to Sierra Leone and for the mobilization of international assistance;

(c) To inform the Economic and Social Council, at its second regular session of 1983, of the assistance granted to Sierra Leone;

(d) To keep the situation regarding assistance to Sierra Leone under review and to report to the General Assembly at its thirty-eighth session on the implementation of the present resolution.

Uganda

A large volume of external assistance to Uganda was urgently required to rehabilitate production units and infrastructure, and to reverse nearly a decade of administrative, social and economic deterioration under the régime that had been in power between 1971 and 1979. This was one of the main recommendations of an inter-agency economic review mission which visited Uganda from 17 to 27 January 1982[2] in pursuance of a 1980 General Assembly request.[4] The mission reported that some 150,000 people still required emergency food relief in the north in the aftermath of a severe food shortage in 1979 and 1980 and civil disturbances in 1981. The total external debt of Uganda was around $737 million in mid-1981, and an additonal $220 million of unverified, largely unguaranteed, short-term debt also existed.

The report described 161 projects at a two-year cost of $1,760 million which the Government had identified for its Recovery Programme (1982-1984), the most urgent of which it had presented to international donors at the Consultative Group on Uganda convened by the World Bank in Paris in May 1982. Among the largest projects were those to meet urgent equipment and supply needs for agriculture and agro-industry ($166.6 million), rehabilitate the Uganda Bata Shoe Company factory ($40 million), repair and regravel roads ($220.5 million), drill boreholes for rural water supplies ($23.1 million), build a new hydroelectric scheme at Ayago ($14 million), and rehabilitate sub-dispensaries and health posts ($23 million). The principal need was for foreign exchange so that Uganda could raise imports by 10 to 15 per cent above the 1981 level in order to increase petroleum supplies; this would not, however, be sufficient to replace worn-out and damaged industrial plant.

On 18 June 1982,[1] the Governing Council of the United Nations Development Programme (UNDP) requested the UNDP Administrator to continue to co-operate closely with and to assist the Ugandan Government in its rehabilitation, reconstruction and development efforts. It also asked him to co-operate with the World Bank in assisting the country to mobilize international support for its programme.

Uganda informed the General Assembly's Second Committee in November that available assistance fell far short of the country's urgent needs in the following few years; Uganda hoped the international community would provide the support needed during the crucial implementation period of its Recovery Programme.

The Assembly, by a resolution of 17 December,[3] endorsed the mission's recommendations, urgently renewed its appeal for international assistance for the reconstruction, rehabilitation and development of Uganda, and invited donor countries and organizations to make resources available for its Recovery Programme and other needs identified by the mission. The Assembly also re-

quested the United Nations High Commissioner for Refugees to continue his humanitarian programmes (see Chapter XXI of this section).

This resolution was adopted without vote, following similar approval by the Second Committee on 2 December. It was introduced by Kenya for the African Group and sponsored by 21 nations. It was orally revised following informal consultations to have the Assembly request the Secretary-General to report in 1983 on the progress made in Uganda's economic situation rather than to arrange for a review of it.

Decision (1982). [1]UNDP Council (report, E/1982/16/Rev.1): 82/14, 18 June.
Report. [2]S-G, annexing mission report, A/37/121.
Resolution (1982). [3]GA: 37/162, 17 Dec., text following.
Resolution (prior). [4]GA: 35/103, 5 Dec. 1980 (YUN 1980, p. 290).
Meeting records. ESC: E/1982/SR.46 (19 July). GA: 2nd Committee, A/C.2/37/SR.27, *28,* 29-31, 33, *40, 46* (2 Nov.–2 Dec.); plenary, A/37/PV.109 (17 Dec.).

General Assembly resolution 37/162

17 December 1982   Meeting 109   Adopted without vote

Approved by Second Committee (A/37/702/Add.2) without vote, 2 December (meeting 46); 21-nation draft (A/C.2/37/L.61), orally revised; agenda item 74 *(b).*

Sponsors: Afghanistan, Algeria, Benin, Burundi, Cape Verde, Central African Republic, Djibouti, Ethiopia, Kenya, Lesotho, Madagascar, Mauritania, Nepal, Niger, Nigeria, Rwanda, Sierra Leone, Sudan, Tunisia, Uganda, United Republic of Cameroon.

Assistance to Uganda

The General Assembly,

Recalling its resolutions 35/103 of 5 December 1980 and 36/218 of 17 December 1981 on assistance to Uganda,

Bearing in mind the enormous economic and social set-backs suffered by Uganda and the resultant precipitous decline in the well-being of its people,

Taking into account the Recovery Programme (1982-1984) presented by the Government of Uganda to the meeting of the Consultative Group on Uganda held in Paris in May 1982 under the auspices of the World Bank,

Recognizing that Uganda is not only land-locked but also one of the least developed and most seriously affected countries,

Noting the appeals of the Secretary-General for assistance to Uganda,

Taking note of the report of the Secretary-General, submitted in response to General Assembly resolution 36/218, to which was annexed the report on Uganda's needs for assistance,

Aware that in its Recovery Programme (1982-1984) the Government of Uganda identified a priority list of projects from among the projects described in the annex to the report of the Secretary-General,

Reaffirming the urgent need for further international action to assist the Government of Uganda in its continuing efforts for national reconstruction, rehabilitation and development,

1. *Expresses its appreciation* to the Secretary-General for the steps he has taken to mobilize assistance for Uganda;

2. *Also expresses its appreciation* to those States and organizations which have provided assistance to that country;

3. *Endorses fully* the assessment and recommendations contained in the annex to the report of the Secretary-General;

4. *Regrets* that the international assistance provided to Uganda to date falls far short of even its most urgent needs;

5. *Requests* the Secretary-General to ensure that adequate financial and budgetary arrangements are made for the organization of an effective international programme of assistance to Uganda and for the mobilization of that assistance;

6. *Invites* the international community, in particular the United Nations system and donor countries and organizations, to make available

the necessary resources to implement the country's Recovery Programme (1982-1984) and meet the remaining needs described in the annex to the report of the Secretary-General;

7. *Urgently renews its appeal* to all Member States, specialized agencies and other organizations of the United Nations system and international economic and financial institutions to contribute generously, through bilateral and multilateral channels, to the reconstruction, rehabilitation and development needs of Uganda and to its emergency requirements;

8. *Renews its appeal* to the international community to contribute to the special account which was established at United Nations Headquarters for the purpose of facilitating the channelling of contributions to Uganda;

9. *Requests* the appropriate organizations and programmes of the United Nations system to maintain and increase their current and future programmes of assistance to Uganda and to report periodically to the Secretary-General on the steps they have taken and the resources they have made available to help that country;

10. *Invites* the United Nations Conference on Trade and Development, the United Nations Industrial Development Organization, the United Nations Children's Fund, the United Nations Development Programme, the World Food Programme, the International Fund for Agricultural Development, the International Labour Organisation, the Food and Agriculture Organization of the United Nations, the United Nations Educational, Scientific and Cultural Organization, the World Health Organization and the World Bank to bring to the attention of their governing bodies, for their consideration, the special needs of Uganda and to report the decisions of those bodies to the Secretary-General by 15 July 1983;

11. *Requests* the United Nations High Commissioner for Refugees to continue his humanitarian assistance programmes in Uganda;

12. *Requests* the Secretary-General:

(a) To continue his efforts to mobilize the necessary resources for an effective programme of financial, technical and material assistance to Uganda;

(b) To keep the situation in Uganda under constant review, to maintain close contact with Member States, regional and other intergovernmental organizations, the specialized agencies and international financial institutions concerned, and to apprise the Economic and Social Council, at its second regular session of 1983, of the current status of the special programme of economic assistance for Uganda;

(c) To report on the progress made in the economic situation in Uganda and in organizing international assistance for that country in time for the matter to be considered by the General Assembly at its thirty-eighth session.

Zambia

The gross domestic product (GDP) of Zambia fell by 1.8 per cent in 1981 after having shown a modest growth of 3.1 per cent in 1980, according to the report of a mission which visited there from 18 to 24 June 1982[2] in pursuance of a December 1981 General Assembly request.[3] In 1981 the average price of copper, which accounted for 87 per cent of total export earnings for that year, had fallen by 10 per cent compared to 1980. In the first six months of 1982 the price had dropped further, to about 12 per cent below the 1981 average. The foreign exchange shortage had become a crippling burden. There had been a partial drought in 1981 and famine relief operations had been conducted in the Western Province in the latter part of the year. During 1982 the anticipated grain deficit— maize, wheat and rice—was estimated at over 350,000 tonnes. A number of the 42,000 refugees in Zambia were affected by the drought and required emergency assistance.

Railway, road, air transport and telecommuni-cations projects were among the urgent reconstruction and rehabilitation needs identified in the mission's report. Other projects in this category concerned water catchment and supply and animal disease control in border areas. Among the most urgent long-term development projects for which funding was required were those for trypanosomiasis and tsetse fly control ($24.5 million), water supply ($19.4 million) and the building of a pulp and paper mill ($125 million). There were also projects for grain and legume research and development ($1 million), civil aviation training and airport development ($1.1 millon), and improvement of science and mathematics teaching ($1.4 million). New projects requiring international assistance called for the construction or reconstruction of five roads, the development of a local pharmaceutical industry, and the funding of the Zambia Agricultural Development Bank and of a financial institution for small-scale industries.

The General Assembly took note on 17 December of this and several other reports on special economic and disaster relief assistance.[1]

Decision (1982). [1]GA: 37/434, para. *(b),* 17 Dec.
Report. [2]S-G, annexing mission report, A/37/133-S/15337.
Resolution. [3]GA: 36/214, 17 Dec. 1981 (YUN 1981, p. 523).

Zimbabwe

Although the GDP of Zimbabwe grew by 12 per cent in 1981, the shortage of foreign exchange in that year emerged as a major constraint on growth, according to an economic review mission which visited the country from 22 to 27 August 1982[2] in pursuance of a December 1981 General Assembly request.[3] External public debt had risen from $385 million at the end of 1981 to $509 million in mid-1982. Over a third of the country had been affected by drought at the end of 1981 and agricultural output for the 1981/82 season was expected to fall by 10 to 15 per cent. The drought had also depleted grazing for 1.4 million head of cattle, or over half of the cattle in the communal sector. However, Zimbabwe had a surplus of 850,000 tonnes of maize available for export and the mission suggested that donors consider its purchase for food aid to other African countries.

Participants in the March 1981 Zimbabwe Conference on Reconstruction and Development[4] were providing $1.3 billion in assistance. Some $60 million had been spent in 1981 and, as of mid-1982, a total of $432 million had either been spent or was firmly committed to specific projects. A total investment of $4.6 billion was planned for the country's three-year transitional development plan (1982/83-1984/85) for agricultural and rural development, transport and communications, social services and housing, energy and water development, and administrative services including defence.

The General Assembly, on 17 December 1982, [1] took note of the mission's report on Zimbabwe along with several other reports on special economic and disaster relief assistance.

Decision (1982). [1]GA: 37/434, para. *(c),* 17 Dec.
Report. [2]S-G, annexing mission report, A/37/139.
Resolution. [3]GA: 36/223, 17 Dec. 1981 (YUN 1981, p. 524).
Yearbook reference. [4]1981, p. 524.

Other regions

Democratic Yemen

Following extensive damage in Democratic Yemen caused by heavy flooding in March 1982 (see below), the General Assembly, on 17 December,[1] requested the Secretary-General to continue to mobilize resources for a comprehensive programme of financial, technical and material assistance to the country. It called for assistance to meet Democratic Yemen's reconstruction and development needs from Member States, the United Nations system, and intergovernmental and non-governmental bodies.

This action was taken without vote, following similar approval by the Second (Economic and Financial) Committee on 2 December. The text was introduced by Bangladesh on behalf of 33 States.

Appealing to the Committee in November for increased international assistance, Democratic Yemen said the floods had inflicted $1 billion in damage, had destroyed the country's economic infrastructure, and had had an extremely adverse effect on agricultural output, the environment and the development projects undertaken in the 15 years since independence.

Resolution (1982). [1]GA: 37/150, 17 Dec., text following.
Meeting records. GA: 2nd Committee, A/C.2/37/SR.*27, 28,* 29-31, 33, *40, 46* (2 Nov.–2 Dec.); plenary, A/37/PV.109 (17 Dec.).

General Assembly resolution 37/150

17 December 1982   Meeting 109   Adopted without vote

Approved by Second Committee (A/37/702/Add.2) without vote, 2 December (meeting 46); 33-nation draft (A/C.2/37/L.43); agenda item 74 *(b).*

Sponsors: Afghanistan, Algeria, Argentina, Bangladesh, Cape Verde, Cuba, Democratic Yemen, Djibouti, Ethiopia, France, Guyana, India, Jordan, Kuwait, Lebanon, Libyan Arab Jamahiriya, Madagascar, Mongolia, Mozambique, Nepal, Nicaragua, Nigeria, Oman, Pakistan, Qatar, Saudi Arabia, Sudan, Syrian Arab Republic, United Arab Emirates, United Republic of Cameroon, Viet Nam, Yemen, Yugoslavia.

Assistance to Democratic Yemen

The General Assembly,

Recalling Economic and Social Council resolution 1982/6 of 28 April 1982 concerning the extensive devastation caused by the heavy floods in Democratic Yemen,

Recalling also resolution 107(IX) of 11 May 1982 of the Economic Commission for Western Asia, in which the Commission called for the urgent establishment of a programme for the rehabilitation and reconstruction of the flood-stricken areas of Democratic Yemen,

Recalling further Economic and Social Council resolution 1982/59 of 30 July 1982,

Having considered the report prepared by the Office of the United Nations Disaster Relief Co-ordinator on the extent and nature of the damage caused by the floods,

Taking note of the oral report presented by the United Nations Disaster Relief Co-ordinator in response to Economic and Social Council resolution 1982/59,

Recognizing that Democratic Yemen, being one of the least developed countries, is unable to bear the mounting burden of rehabilitation and reconstruction of the affected areas,

Recognizing also the efforts made by Democratic Yemen to alleviate the sufferings of the victims of the floods,

1. *Expresses its appreciation* to the Secretary-General for the steps he has taken regarding assistance to Democratic Yemen;

2. *Expresses its gratitude* to States, international, regional and intergovernmental organizations which have provided assistance to Democratic Yemen;

3. *Requests* the Secretary-General to continue to mobilize the necessary resources for an effective comprehensive programme of financial, technical and material assistance to Democratic Yemen in order to help mitigate the damage inflicted on it and implement its rehabilitation and reconstruction plans;

4. *Appeals* to Member States to contribute generously through bilateral and/or multilateral channels to the reconstruction and development process in Democratic Yemen;

5. *Requests* the appropriate organizations and programmes of the United Nations system—in particular the United Nations Development Programme, the World Bank, the World Food Programme, the Food and Agriculture Organization of the United Nations, the International Fund for Agricultural Development, the World Health Organization, the United Nations Fund for Population Activities, the United Nations Children's Fund and the United Nations Industrial Development Organization—to maintain and expand their programmes of assistance to Democratic Yemen and to co-operate closely with the Secretary-General in organizing an effective programme of assistance to that country;

6. *Calls upon* regional and interregional organizations and other intergovernmental bodies and non-governmental organizations to give urgent consideration to the needs and development requirements of Democratic Yemen;

7. *Requests* the Secretary-General to keep the situation in Democratic Yemen under review and to report to the General Assembly at its thirty-eighth session on the progress made in the implementation of the present resolution.

Nicaragua

International assistance from bilateral and multilateral sources for the reconstruction and development of Nicaragua totalled $263 million between July 1979 and February 1982, according to an October 1982 report of the Secretary-General which conveyed figures received from the Nicaraguan Government's Fondo Internacional para Reconstrucción.[1] A further $75 million had been pledged but not received during that period. Of the assistance received, the United Nations system had provided $63 million, or 24 per cent of the total from all sources. In addition, between July 1979 and March 1982 Nicaragua had entered into loan agreements amounting to $1,232 million, many on relatively soft terms. Of these, $677 million had been disbursed by March 1982.

The Secretary-General's report detailed assistance provided by nine donor countries—Austria, Finland, the German Democratic Republic, the Federal Republic of Germany, Japan, Mexico, Norway, the Republic of Korea and Spain—as well as that by the United Nations system and the Fund for International Development of the Organization of Petroleum Exporting Countries.

As a result of rains and hurricanes which struck the country at the end of May 1982, 70,000 people had had to take refuge in emergency centres, the report stated. According to the Office of the Resident Co-ordinator of the United Nations System for Operational Activities for Development at Managua, emergency assistance to Nicaragua reported by the international community had totalled $7.6 million at the end of August. On 29 July, the Economic and Social Council endorsed a July resolution of the Committee of the Whole of the Economic Commission for Latin America recommending international support for the country's relief and rehabilitation following the floods (see below).

On 17 December,[2] the General Assembly renewed with urgency its call for continued and increased international assistance to Nicaragua. It recommended that Nicaragua continue to receive treatment appropriate to its special needs.

This action was taken without vote, following similar approval by the Second Committee on 2 December. The text was introduced by Mexico on behalf of 74 States and was orally revised following informal consultations to address the call for increased assistance to all States rather than Member States.

Report. [1]S-G, A/37/135.
Resolution (1982). [2]GA: 37/157, 17 Dec., text following.
Meeting records. GA: 2nd Committee, A/C.2/37/SR.27-31, 33, 40, 46 (2 Nov.-2 Dec.); plenary, A/37/PV.109 (17 Dec.).

General Assembly resolution 37/157

17 December 1982　　　Meeting 109　　　Adopted without vote

Approved by Second Committee (A/37/702/Add.2) without vote, 2 December (meeting 46); 74-nation draft (A/C.2/37/L.56), orally revised in informal consultations; agenda item 74 (b).

Sponsors: Afghanistan, Algeria, Angola, Argentina, Austria, Bangladesh, Barbados, Belize, Benin, Bolivia, Botswana, Brazil, Bulgaria, Burundi, Cape Verde, Central African Republic, Chad, China, Colombia, Comoros, Congo, Costa Rica, Cuba, Cyprus, Czechoslovakia, Democratic Yemen, Dominican Republic, Ecuador, Egypt, Equatorial Guinea, Ethiopia, France, German Democratic Republic, Greece, Grenada, Guinea-Bissau, Guyana, India, Iran, Liberia, Libyan Arab Jamahiriya, Madagascar, Malawi, Mali, Mauritania, Mexico, Mongolia, Mozambique, Nicaragua, Nigeria, Panama, Papua New Guinea, Peru, Romania, Saint Lucia, Sao Tome and Principe, Seychelles, Spain, Sudan, Suriname, Sweden, Syrian Arab Republic, Thailand, Trinidad and Tobago, Tunisia, United Republic of Cameroon, United Republic of Tanzania, Uruguay, Vanuatu, Venezuela, Viet Nam, Yugoslavia, Zambia, Zimbabwe.

Assistance to Nicaragua

The General Assembly,

Recalling its resolutions 34/8 of 25 October 1979, 35/84 of 5 December 1980 and 36/213 of 17 December 1981 concerning assistance for the reconstruction of Nicaragua,

Taking note of the report of the Secretary-General on assistance to Nicaragua,

Bearing in mind that the floods of May 1982 caused grave damage to the infrastructure of Nicaragua, reducing its productive capacity and worsening the situation existing before that date, as reflected in the report of the Economic Commission for Latin America entitled "Nicaragua: the May 1982 floods and their repercussions on the economic and social development of the country",

Also bearing in mind that Nicaragua suffered, from June to September 1982, an intense drought which seriously affected the agricultural and livestock sectors, the country's most important economic activities,

Considering Economic and Social Council decision 1982/168 of 29 July 1982, in which the Council decided to endorse resolution 419(PLEN.15) on international assistance to alleviate the economic and social problems faced by Nicaragua as a result of the May 1982 floods,

which was adopted by the Committee of the Whole of the Economic Commission for Latin America at its fifteenth special session, held in New York on 22 and 23 July 1982, and to recommend that the General Assembly at its thirty-seventh session also endorse the resolution,

Considering also resolution 982 adopted by the Seventeenth Regional Conference for Latin America of the Food and Agriculture Organization of the United Nations, held at Managua from 30 August to 10 September 1982, in which the Conference recommended to the World Food Programme and to the Food and Agriculture Organization of the United Nations that special measures of assistance to Nicaragua should be adopted,

Considering further that, despite the efforts of the Government and people of Nicaragua, the economic situation of Nicaragua has not become normalized, and requires the assistance of the international community,

1. *Endorses* Economic and Social Council decision 1982/168;
2. *Expresses its appreciation* to the Secretary-General for his efforts regarding assistance to Nicaragua;
3. *Expresses its appreciation* to those States and organizations which have provided assistance to Nicaragua;
4. *Renews with urgency its call* to all States and the bodies of the United Nations system to continue and to increase their assistance to Nicaragua;
5. *Recommends* that Nicaragua should continue to receive treatment that will be appropriate to the special needs of the country;
6. *Requests* the Secretary-General to report to the General Assembly at its thirty-eighth session on the progress made in the implementation of the present resolution.

Tonga

The production of coconut, accounting for two thirds of the total exports of Tonga, was severely curtailed by hurricane "Isaac", which struck the South Pacific island country in March 1982. According to a mission which visited there from 12 to 21 October[1] in response to a 1979 General Assembly request,[3] direct losses to agriculture from the storm—which also destroyed 90 per cent of producing banana plants, much of the vegetable harvest and the total bread-fruit crop—totalled $6.4 million. During 1981 the external payments situation in Tonga was characterized by an increasingly large trade deficit, with only a quarter of imports covered by export earnings. As a result, the Government lacked the funds to contribute significantly to the 1981/82 development budget. The hurricane had aggravated structural and regional imbalances in Tonga's economy, which was handicapped by remoteness from major economic centres and widely dispersed islands.

The Government presented the mission with 48 projects for which assistance was urgently needed, at a total cost of $58.1 million. The proposed activities addressed basic development needs as well as post-hurricane reconstruction, and included projects to revitalize the coconut industry ($3.2 million), develop commercial fisheries ($2.5 million), improve the main international airport on Tongatapu ($8.2 million), construct foreshore protection to guard Tongatapu from winds and storms ($10.3 million), and reconstruct damaged schools ($3.6 million).

The General Assembly endorsed the mission's recommendations by a resolution adopted on 17

December.[2] It renewed its appeal to States and organizations for financial, material and technical assistance so that Tonga could overcome its serious development constraints and establish the necessary social and economic infrastructure, and requested the Secretary-General to continue to mobilize resources for assistance to the country.

This action was taken without vote, following similar approval in the Second Committee on 2 December. The text, introduced by Fiji on behalf of 17 States, was orally revised following informal consultations to have the Assembly request the Secretary-General to report in 1984 on the progress in Tonga's economic situation rather than to arrange for a review of that situation.

Report. [1]S-G, annexing mission report, A/37/583.
Resolution (1982). [2]GA: 37/164, 17 Dec., text following.
Resolution (prior). [3]GA: 34/132, 14 Dec. 1979 (YUN 1979, p. 514).
Meeting records. GA: 2nd Committee, A/C.2/37/SR.27-31, 33, 40, 44, 46 (2 Nov.–2 Dec.); plenary, A/37/PV.109 (17 Dec.).

General Assembly resolution 37/164

17 December 1982　　　　Meeting 109　　　　Adopted without vote

Approved by Second Committee (A/37/702/Add.2) without vote, 2 December (meeting 46); 17-nation draft (A/C.2/37/L.88), orally revised in informal consultations and further orally revised; agenda item 74 *(b)*.

Sponsors: Australia, Bangladesh, Ethiopia, Fiji, France, India, New Zealand, Pakistan, Papua New Guinea, Saint Lucia, Samoa, Singapore, Solomon Islands, United Kingdom, United Republic of Cameroon, United States, Vanuatu.

Assistance to Tonga

The General Assembly,

Recalling its resolution 34/132 of 14 December 1979, in which it drew the attention of the international community to the special problems confronting Tonga as a developing island country with a small population and appealed to Member States, regional and interregional organizations and other intergovernmental bodies to provide financial, material and technical assistance to Tonga to enable it to establish the social and economic infrastructure that is essential for the well-being of its people,

Recalling also its resolutions 31/156 of 21 December 1976 and 32/185 of 19 December 1977 in which, respectively, it urged all Governments, in particular those of the developed countries, to lend their support, in the context of their assistance programmes, for the implementation of the specific action envisaged in favour of developing island countries, and urged all organizations of the United Nations system to implement, within their respective spheres of competence, appropriate specific action in favour of developing island countries,

Concerned at the severe constraints on the economic development of Tonga, particularly those arising from its geographical isolation and dispersion, small size, heavy dependence on a limited range of economic activities, and from its economy's susceptibility to factors beyond national control,

Distressed at the devastation, economic loss and suffering wrought by hurricane "Isaac" in March 1982,

Having examined the report of the Secretary-General, prepared in response to General Assembly resolution 34/132, to which was annexed the report of the mission to Tonga which was organized by the Secretary-General and which consulted with the Government of Tonga on its most urgent needs,

1. *Expresses its appreciation* to the Secretary-General for the steps he has taken to mobilize assistance for Tonga;

2. *Endorses fully* the assessment and recommendations contained in the annex to the report of the Secretary-General;

3. *Also expresses its appreciation* to those States, United Nations organizations and other organizations which have provided assistance to Tonga for the purpose of development and for hurricane relief;

4. *Renews its appeal* to all States, the appropriate organs, organizations and programmes of the United Nations system, regional and international organizations and other intergovernmental bodies and non-governmental organizations, as well as international financial institutions, to provide financial, material and technical assistance to Tonga to enable it to overcome its serious development constraints and to establish the social and economic infrastructure that is essential for the well-being of its people;

5. *Requests* the appropriate organizations and programmes of the United Nations system to maintain and increase their current and future programmes of assistance to Tonga, to co-operate closely with the Secretary-General in organizing an effective international programme of assistance and to report periodically to the Secretary-General on the steps they have taken and the resources they have made available;

6. *Invites* the Economic and Social Commission for Asia and the Pacific, the United Nations Conference on Trade and Development, the United Nations Industrial Development Organization, the United Nations Children's Fund, the United Nations Development Programme, the World Food Programme, the International Labour Organisation, the Food and Agriculture Organization of the United Nations, the International Civil Aviation Organization, the World Health Organization, the World Bank, the International Telecommunication Union, the World Meteorological Organization, the International Maritime Organization and the International Fund for Agricultural Development to bring to the attention of their governing bodies, for their consideration, the special needs of Tonga and to report their decisions to the Secretary-General by 15 July 1983;

7. *Requests* the Secretary-General:

(a) To continue his efforts to mobilize the necessary resources for an effective programme of financial, technical and material assistance to Tonga;

(b) To continue to ensure that adequate financial and budgetary arrangements are made to mobilize resources and to continue the organization of international assistance to Tonga;

(c) To study and apprise the Economic and Social Council, at its second regular session of 1983, of the current status of the special programme of economic assistance for Tonga;

(d) To report on the progress made in the economic situation of Tonga and in organizing and implementing the special programme of economic assistance for that country so that the matter may be considered by the General Assembly at its thirty-ninth session.

Disasters

Following action by the General Assembly in December 1981 laying down guidelines for the United Nations system to follow in response to major disasters,[1] the inter-agency Administrative Committee on Co-ordination (ACC), in April 1982, filled in additional details of the standard procedures to apply in the face of complex emergency situations. Meanwhile, the Office of the United Nations Disaster Relief Co-ordinator (UNDRO), designated by the Assembly as the focal point for disaster relief co-ordination in the United Nations system, stepped up its response to the devastating storms, floods and other natural and man-made disasters occurring in a number of developing countries in 1982, and the Assembly, in December, approved several additional steps to strengthen its capacity to help nations cope with disasters.

Among the major disasters dealt with by UNDRO and other United Nations organizations during the year—and also the subject of resolutions by the Economic and Social Council, the General Assembly or both—were drought in the

Sudano-Sahelian region of West and Central Africa and in East Africa, civil strife in Chad, floods in Democratic Yemen and in Honduras and Nicaragua, cyclones and floods in Madagascar and an earthquake in Yemen. There were also major emergency relief operations under way for the Kampucheans and for Lebanon, both affected by military operations.

Resolution. [1]GA: 36/225, 17 Dec. 1981 (YUN 1981, p. 480).

Disaster relief

At the request of the Governments concerned, UNDRO responded during 1982 to 35 disasters, including flood and drought emergencies, cyclones, earthquakes, volcanic eruptions, military operations, civil strife, and situations involving displaced persons and large numbers of persons returning to countries from abroad.

During the year, UNDRO issued 217 situation reports (up from 88 in 1981) to inform the international community of relief needs in particular disasters. It helped organize inter-agency missions which visited disaster sites and communicated their assessment of damage and relief needs to UNDRO headquarters at Geneva, taking into account data supplied by the Government of the affected country. In major emergencies, it worked with other United Nations organizations to develop concerted relief programmes, convening meetings which often involved voluntary relief agencies. Information meetings were organized periodically to brief government representatives and other organizations about the work of UNDRO.

UNDRO convened a meeting of heads of special units set up by Governments and intergovernmental and non-governmental organizations (27-29 April) to exchange information about disaster relief operations and help improve co-operation in the field. The participants agreed on recommendations to strengthen the role of UNDRO in co-ordinating relief efforts and providing information.

During 1982, the United Nations Institute for Training and Research published a study on model rules for disaster relief operations, which UNDRO intended to use as a basis for consultations with Governments with a view to developing recommendations to the General Assembly.

Emergency assistance was provided by UNDRO and other United Nations organizations to Chad, Honduras and Nicaragua, Madagascar, Yemen and Lebanon. Other disaster relief operations in which UNDRO was involved during the year included the following:

—*Angola.* UNDRO operations to assist displaced persons in Angola continued into 1982. The relief programme for the southern part of the country, scheduled to end in March, was not completed because of continuing military operations in the area. A $12-million

target for the programme, which a multi-agency mission led by UNDRO had established following the Government's original request for assistance in July 1981,[5] was met. Cash contributions of $120,000 made available to UNDRO were used to purchase items such as medicines, building materials and agricultural implements, and to engage experts in hydrogeology, transport and logistics. UNDRO participated with the World Food Programme in monitoring the distribution of emergency food assistance, and collaborated with the World Health Organization in purchasing and dispatching in May 17 tons of medical supplies valued at $20,000.

—*Ecuador.* Some 100,000 persons required emergency aid as a result of flooding which began in December and affected five provinces. On 30 December, UNDRO appealed for emergency relief.

—*Indonesia.* Mt. Galunggung, in west Java, erupted more than 400 times between April and mid-December, affecting 300,000 people and causing $160 million in damage. An UNDRO co-ordination officer visited the country in May to review relief needs and another assisted the Government in organizing a national workshop on volcanic risk management (Bandung, 20-25 September). A joint mission of UNDRO and the United Nations Educational, Scientific and Cultural Organization (7 August–5 September) visited Mt. Galunggung to establish ways of measuring volcanic gas emission and to train personnel for a vulcanological survey of Indonesia. International contributions for relief assistance in cash and kind totalled $5.6 million.

—*Mozambique.* On 17 March, UNDRO appealed for assistance to drought-stricken areas in the north of the country. The situation came under control at the end of 1982 after contributions were received from a number of donors and heavy rains fell. The drought situation worsened in central and southern Mozambique, however.

—*Tonga.* A cyclone struck this Pacific island country in March, causing $21.2 million in damage to buildings, crops, port facilities, and fishing boats and equipment. UNDRO provided information on damage to the international community and sent a representative to assist the resident co-ordinator for United Nations system development assistance and the national and international relief officials in Tonga.

—*Tunisia.* On 30 and 31 October torrential rains led to flooding and, on 3 November, UNDRO appealed for assistance to the 35,000 people who required emergency aid and to repair $4.5 million of damage to roads, railways, housing, cereal crops and the urban infrastructure.

—*Viet Nam.* As a result of a typhoon which struck on 19 and 20 October, 1.9 million people required relief assistance and 150,000 tons of rice were lost. UNDRO appealed on 25 October for international relief, organized a relief assessment mission in November and provided a grant to purchase urgently needed cabbage seeds.

In addition to its disaster relief activities, UNDRO engaged in pre-disaster planning functions and co-sponsored meetings on earthquake prediction and on continental seismicity and earthquake prevention. UNDRO continued to be financed from the United Nations regular budget as well as from voluntary contributions to its Trust Fund.

To improve co-ordination in the United Nations system for dealing with complex emergency situations, ACC adopted guiding principles on the role of the lead entity and participating organizations.

The 1982 activities of UNDRO were described in reports of the Secretary-General to the Economic and Social Council and the General Assembly in June 1982[2] and June 1983.[3]

The Council, acting without vote on 28 July 1982,[1] took note of the report covering the period through 31 March and transmitted it to the General Assembly. This action was taken following similar approval on 20 July in the Third (Programme and Co-ordination) Committee, where the text had been proposed by the Chairman. The Assembly took note of the report with appreciation in its 17 December resolution on the strengthening of UNDRO.[4]

Decision (1982). [1]ESC: 1982/165, 28 July, text following.
Reports. S-G, [2]A/37/235 & Corr.1, [3]A/38/201-E/1983/69 & Corr.1.
Resolution (1982). [4]GA: 37/144, para. 1, 17 Dec.
Yearbook reference. [5]1981, p. 483.
Meeting record. ESC: E/1982/SR.49 (28 July).
Publications. Model Rules for Disaster Relief Operations, Sales No. 82.XV.PE.8; UNDRO News (issued every 2 months).

Economic and Social Council decision 1982/165

Adopted without vote

Approved by Third Committee (E/1982/91) without vote, 20 July (meeting 12); draft by Chairman (E/1982/C.3/L.6); agenda item 20.

Report of the Secretary-General on the work of the Office of the United Nations Disaster Relief Co-ordinator

At its 49th plenary meeting, on 28 July 1982, the Council took note of the report of the Secretary-General on the work of the Office of the United Nations Disaster Relief Co-ordinator and decided to transmit it to the General Assembly at its thirty-seventh session.

Strengthening of UNDRO

The General Assembly, on 17 December 1982,[2] after considering the annual report on UNDRO,[1] approved several measures intended to strengthen the capacity of the Office to respond to disasters. These included: higher priority for strengthening its financial and staff resources, preferably within available means; authority for the rapid appointment of temporary staff and procurement of supplies; maintenance of the UNDRO Trust Fund and raising from $30,000 to $50,000 the maximum assistance provided by UNDRO for any one disaster; authorization to mobilize additional voluntary resources for complex disasters and emergencies of exceptional magnitude; a request that United Nations organizations develop concerted relief programmes and co-ordinate their response to disasters; a call for an improved flow of information on relief assistance and plans; and an improved capability

to take advantage of and co-ordinate early-warning systems. The Secretary-General was requested to present a comprehensive report in 1983.

This action was taken in a resolution adopted by a recorded vote of 132 to 8, with 3 abstentions, following its approval on 8 December in the Second (Economic and Financial) Committee by a recorded vote of 119 to 8, with 2 abstentions. The text was introduced by Kenya on behalf of 53 nations.

It was revised by the sponsors in writing and orally, including the addition of a paragraph orally proposed by Turkey which the sponsors accepted in a revised form. By it the Assembly, noting that Chad and Lebanon had expressed appreciation for activities undertaken by UNDRO, requested the Co-ordinator to continue his action in response to needs as they arose. The original Turkish amendment had called for continuance of UNDRO emergency relief activities in the two countries.

The Committee rejected, by a recorded vote of 96 to 19, with 12 abstentions, an oral amendment by the United States to authorize the Secretary-General to implement the activities approved under the resolution only to the extent that they could be financed without exceeding the 1982-1983 United Nations budget.[4]

The Fifth (Administrative and Budgetary) Committee reported to the Assembly that adoption of the resolution would entail an additional appropriation of $53,900 for 1983.

Kenya, introducing the original draft, noted that the text stressed the need to strengthen and improve the capacity and effectiveness of UNDRO, and to co-ordinate humanitarian assistance and disaster relief throughout the United Nations system. When introducing the revised draft, Kenya recalled that the December 1981 Assembly resolution on the response of the United Nations system to disasters[3] had made UNDRO the lead United Nations agency for the mobilization and co-ordination of disaster and other emergency relief. With the broadened responsibilities of UNDRO provided for in that resolution and the 1982 text, especially in reference to disasters of exceptional complexity and magnitude, the Secretary-General would probably not have to take special measures to cope with such emergencies, thus making it possible to streamline the current system and redeploy resources currently devoted to such measures.

Explaining its negative vote on the resolution, the USSR said it could not accept a proposal to increase UNDRO funds and staff presented under the pretext of strengthening the capacity of the United Nations to deal with disasters. Czechoslovakia also objected to the increased expenditure. The German Democratic Republic said its negative vote was motivated by the considerations voiced by the socialist countries when the 1981 resolution had been adopted.[5] The United States thought it inopportune to request a budget increase for UNDRO without a precise explanation of how its effectiveness would be increased by such action.

Poland, abstaining in the vote, said that while it did not agree with the resolution's assessment of UNDRO or the attempt to reformulate the principles governing its operation, it recognized the valuable assistance being rendered by the Office.

Canada said it voted for the resolution to demonstrate the importance it attached to UNDRO, but it was nevertheless unconvinced that a staff increase was entirely justified. Similarly, France and the Federal Republic of Germany believed that major decisions on staff increases and financial and organizational matters should await the 1983 report on UNDRO. Also voting in favour, Argentina and Ecuador expressed the view that UNDRO should give priority to natural disasters.

Report. [1]S-G, A/37/235 & Corr.1.
Resolution (1982). [2]GA: 37/144, 17 Dec., text following.
Resolutions (prior). GA: [3]36/225, 17 Dec. 1981 (YUN 1981, p. 480); [4]36/240 A, 18 Dec. 1981 (*ibid.*, p. 1278).
Yearbook reference. [5]1981, p. 477.
Financial implications. 5th Committee report, A/37/760; S-G statements, A/C.2/37/L.107, A/C.5/37/93.
Meeting records. GA: 2nd Committee, A/C.2/37/SR.*27*, 28-31, 33, *44*, *47*, *48* (2 Nov.–13 Dec.); 5th Committee, A/C.5/37/SR.69 (14 Dec.); plenary, A/37/PV.109 (17 Dec.).

General Assembly resolution 37/144

17 December 1982　　　Meeting 109　　　132-8-3 (recorded vote)

Approved by Second Committee (A/37/702/Add.1) by recorded vote (119-8-2), 8 December (meeting 47); 53-nation draft (A/C.2/37/L.82/Rev.1), orally revised; agenda item 74 *(a)*.

Sponsors: Algeria, Angola, Benin, Botswana, Burundi, Cape Verde, Central African Republic, Chad, Comoros, Congo, Djibouti, Egypt, Equatorial Guinea, Ethiopia, Gabon, Gambia, Ghana, Guinea, Guinea-Bissau, Ivory Coast, Kenya, Kuwait, Lebanon, Lesotho, Liberia, Libyan Arab Jamahiriya, Madagascar, Malawi, Mali, Mauritania, Mauritius, Morocco, Mozambique, Niger, Nigeria, Rwanda, Sao Tome and Principe, Senegal, Seychelles, Sierra Leone, Somalia, Sudan, Swaziland, Togo, Tunisia, Turkey, Uganda, United Republic of Cameroon, United Republic of Tanzania, Upper Volta, Zaire, Zambia, Zimbabwe.

Office of the United Nations Disaster Relief Co-ordinator

The General Assembly,

Recalling its resolution 36/225 of 17 December 1981, by which it reaffirmed the mandate of the Office of the United Nations Disaster Relief Co-ordinator and called for the strengthening and improvement of the capacity and effectiveness of the Office,

Recalling also its resolution 35/107 of 5 December 1980, by which it reaffirmed the necessity of ensuring a continued sound financial basis for the Office of the United Nations Disaster Relief Co-ordinator and extended until 31 December 1983 the term of the Trust Fund established pursuant to its resolution 3243(XXIX) of 29 November 1974 and modified under its resolutions 3440(XXX) of 9 December 1975 and 3532(XXX) of 17 December 1975 and by its decision 33/429 of 19 December 1978,

Recalling further its resolution 34/55 of 29 November 1979, by which it requested an increase in emergency disaster assistance, with a normal ceiling of $30,000 per country in the case of any one disaster,

Deeply concerned about the additional economic burden placed upon the developing countries by the increasing number of natural disasters and other disaster situations, as well as the disruption caused to their development process,

Recognizing the contribution made by the United Nations system to the relief of suffering and provision of humanitarian assistance in natural disasters and other disaster situations,

Recognizing also that the primary responsibilities of administration, relief operations and disaster preparedness lie with the affected countries and that the major part of the material assistance and human effort in disaster relief comes from the Governments of those countries,

Recognizing further the importance of the contribution of the International Committee of the Red Cross, the League of Red Cross and Red Crescent Societies and appropriate voluntary organizations,

Recognizing that, in order to attain an effective co-ordination system of humanitarian and disaster relief assistance, it is essential to strengthen and improve the capacity and effectiveness of the Office of the United Nations Disaster Relief Co-ordinator and the United Nations system as a whole in order to enable the Office to respond to natural disasters and other disaster situations speedily, efficiently and effectively, thereby ensuring prompt delivery of concerted relief,

Recognizing that a major constraint on an effective response of the United Nations to natural disasters and other disaster situations has been the shortage of resources,

1. *Takes note with appreciation* of the report of the Secretary-General on the work of the Office of the United Nations Disaster Relief Co-ordinator and of the statement made by the Co-ordinator before the Second Committee on 2 November 1982;

2. *Takes note* of the progress made by the Secretary-General and the Administrative Committee on Co-ordination in initiating improvements in the management operations of the Office of the United Nations Disaster Relief Co-ordinator and in establishing modalities for the implementation of the procedures, outlined in General Assembly resolution 36/225 and decision 1982/1 of the Administrative Committee on Co-ordination, for dealing with requests for disaster relief from a disaster-stricken State and for dealing with complex disasters and emergencies of exceptional magnitude;

3. *Takes note* of the appreciation expressed by the Governments of Chad and Lebanon for the activities undertaken by the United Nations Disaster Relief Co-ordinator in those two countries, and requests him to continue his action in response to needs as they arise;

4. *Requests* the Secretary-General to facilitate, when necessary, rapid appointment of temporary staff and procurement of supplies by the United Nations Disaster Relief Co-ordinator in order to permit a timely response to requests for emergency assistance;

5. *Requests* the Secretary-General to raise the normal maximum of $30,000 to $50,000, the additional $20,000 to come from voluntary sources, to permit the United Nations Disaster Relief Co-ordinator to respond with grants to requests for emergency disaster assistance up to a total of $600,000 in any one year, with a normal ceiling of $50,000 per country in the case of any one disaster;

6. *Authorizes* the Secretary-General to permit the United Nations Disaster Relief Co-ordinator to mobilize additional voluntary resources to meet the needs presented by complex disasters and emergencies of exceptional magnitude;

7. *Decides* to maintain, as from 1 January 1984, the Trust Fund of the Office of the United Nations Disaster Relief Co-ordinator and its sub-accounts;

8. *Reiterates*, in particular, the appeals made in its resolutions 35/107 and 36/225 for increased contributions to the Trust Fund established pursuant to its resolution 3243(XXIX) and modified as indicated in the second preambular paragraph and in paragraph 7 above;

9. *Endorses* the measures taken by the Secretary-General and the Administrative Committee on Co-ordination to implement General Assembly resolution 36/225 and calls upon the Secretary-General, who will normally be represented by the United Nations Disaster Relief Co-ordinator, to consult with the concerned agencies of the United Nations system in order to develop concerted relief programmes as a basis for united appeals for funds to be launched by the Co-ordinator on behalf of the Secretary-General;

10. *Reiterates its desire* further to strengthen and improve the capability of the Office of the United Nations Disaster Relief Co-ordinator to take full advantage of information provided by existing early-warning systems and to co-ordinate, to the extent feasible and useful, all relevant early-warning systems, taking into account new technological developments in this field, including communications;

11. *Urges* all Governments and relevant organs and organizations to co-operate with the United Nations Disaster Relief Co-ordinator and to improve in particular their flow of information on relief assistance, actions and plans;

12. *Calls upon* the specialized agencies and other constituent organizations of the United Nations system, in order to eliminate wasteful duplication of resources, to co-ordinate, in accordance with the provisions of paragraph 3 of General Assembly resolution 36/225, their efforts at all stages of the response of the international community to natural disasters and other disaster situations;

13. *Reaffirms* its belief that the strengthening and reinforcing of the Office of the United Nations Disaster Relief Co-ordinator offers the most efficient and economic means of effectively co-ordinating the relief activities of the United Nations system as a whole in the interest of the survivors of disasters, and requests the Secretary-General to assign a higher priority to strengthening, preferably within the means at his disposal, the financial and manpower resources of the Office;

14. *Requests* the Secretary-General to submit a comprehensive report on the implementation of General Assembly resolution 36/225, including a report on the implementation of the present resolution, to the Assembly at its thirty-eighth session, through the Economic and Social Council at its second regular session of 1983.

Recorded vote in Assembly as follows:

In favour: Albania, Algeria, Angola, Argentina, Australia, Austria, Bahamas, Bahrain, Bangladesh, Barbados, Belgium, Benin, Bhutan, Bolivia, Botswana, Brazil, Burma, Burundi, Canada, Cape Verde, Central African Republic, Chad, Chile, China, Colombia, Comoros, Congo, Costa Rica, Cyprus, Democratic Kampuchea, Democratic Yemen, Denmark, Djibouti, Dominica, Dominican Republic, Ecuador, Egypt, El Salvador, Ethiopia, Fiji, Finland, France, Gabon, Gambia, Germany, Federal Republic of, Ghana, Greece, Grenada, Guatemala, Guinea, Guinea-Bissau, Guyana, Honduras, Iceland, India, Indonesia, Iran, Iraq, Ireland, Israel, Italy, Ivory Coast, Jamaica, Japan, Jordan, Kenya, Kuwait, Lebanon, Lesotho, Liberia, Libyan Arab Jamahiriya, Luxembourg, Madagascar, Malawi, Malaysia, Maldives, Mali, Malta, Mauritania, Mauritius, Mexico, Morocco, Mozambique, Nepal, Netherlands, New Zealand, Niger, Nigeria, Norway, Oman, Pakistan, Panama, Papua New Guinea, Paraguay, Peru, Philippines, Portugal, Qatar, Romania, Rwanda, Samoa, Sao Tome and Principe, Saudi Arabia, Senegal, Sierra Leone, Singapore, Somalia, Spain, Sri Lanka, Sudan, Suriname, Swaziland, Sweden, Thailand, Togo, Trinidad and Tobago, Tunisia, Turkey, Uganda, United Arab Emirates, United Kingdom, United Republic of Cameroon, United Republic of Tanzania, Upper Volta, Uruguay, Vanuatu, Venezuela, Yemen, Yugoslavia, Zaire, Zambia, Zimbabwe.

Against: Bulgaria, Byelorussian SSR, Czechoslovakia, German Democratic Republic, Hungary, Ukrainian SSR, USSR, United States.

Abstaining: Afghanistan, Mongolia, Poland.

UNDRO finances

The activities of UNDRO in 1982 continued to be financed partly from the United Nations budget and partly from the voluntary Trust Fund for Disaster Relief Assistance. Net budget appropriations for 1982-1983, as revised by the General Assembly on 21 December 1982,[2] totalled $4,856,200; expenditures under the Trust Fund in 1982 were $8,419,977.

Contributions paid to the Trust Fund in 1982 totalled $7,286,653, consisting of $7,060,434 from 19 Governments and the European Economic Community (see table below) and public donations of $226,219. The Fund's total income, including interest earnings, was $8,576,985, or $157,008 more than its expenditures.

The Trust Fund had three main sub-accounts, under which 1982 expenditures were as follows: emergency relief assistance, mainly in individual countries, $7,152,833 (85 per cent); strengthening of UNDRO (including $15,092 for joint projects with the United Nations Environment Programme), $678,945 (8 per cent); and disaster prevention and pre-disaster planning (including $374,113 for the UNDRO Pan-Caribbean Disaster Preparedness and Prevention Project), $588,199 (7 per cent) (see table below).

From its regular budget appropriation, UNDRO was authorized to draw up to $30,000 per country for relief assistance in the case of any one disaster.

Under this authority it made allocations on 17 occasions during 1982, as follows ($30,000 each time except as specified):

Civil strife: Chad, 1981/1982; Lebanon, June 1982.
Cyclones: Madagascar, January; Mauritius, January ($4,000).
Earthquake: Yemen, December.
Fire: Niger, March ($20,000).
Floods: Yemen, April; Honduras, May; Nicaragua, May; Benin, July ($20,000); El Salvador, September; Guatemala, September; Tunisia, November; Ecuador, December ($20,000).
Hurricane: Cuba, June.
Typhoon: Viet Nam, October.
Volcanic eruptions: Indonesia, April.

In its 17 December resolution on the strengthening of UNDRO,[1] the General Assembly requested the Secretary-General to raise the normal maximum allocation for each disaster from $30,000 to $50,000—the additional $20,000 to come from voluntary sources—up to a total of $600,000 in any one year. Reiterating past appeals for contributions, the Assembly decided to maintain the Trust Fund beyond 1 January 1984, thereby making it a permanent feature of the financial base of UNDRO.

In addition to these allocations, UNDRO used money voluntarily contributed by States to the Trust Fund for Disaster Relief Assistance and earmarked by the contributors for disaster relief in specific countries. In 1982 the sub-account for disaster relief received a total of $6,208,890 in contributions earmarked for specific countries (see table below) compared to $421,348 in 1981.[3]

TRUST FUND FOR DISASTER RELIEF ASSISTANCE
EXPENDITURES, 1982
(as at 31 December 1982; in US dollars)

ACCOUNT/PURPOSE	AMOUNT
Disaster relief assistance	
Angola	350,098
Benin	20,000
Caribbean	374,113
Chad	2,249,340
Comoros	4,000
Cuba	30,000
Democratic Yemen	30,000
El Salvador	30,000
Guatemala	48,182
Honduras	30,000
Indonesia	175,962
Lebanon	3,336,563
Madagascar	572,268
Mauritius	3,981
Mozambique	30,000
Nicaragua	39,000
Niger	20,000
Tonga	41,856
General disaster relief operations	141,583
Subtotal	7,526,946
Strengthening of UNDRO	663,853
UNDRO/UNEP projects	15,092
Disaster prevention and pre-disaster planning	214,086
Total	8,419,977

SOURCE: Interim United Nations financial statements for the 12-month period ended 31 December 1982—Individual trust funds (unpublished).

CONTRIBUTIONS TO THE TRUST FUND FOR
DISASTER RELIEF ASSISTANCE, 1982
(as at 31 December 1982; in US dollar equivalent)

PURPOSE/CONTRIBUTOR	AMOUNT PAID
Disaster relief in Angola	
Botswana	53,500
Subtotal	53,500
Disaster relief in the Caribbean	
United States	190,000
Subtotal	190,000
Disaster relief in Chad	
Canada	405,449
European Economic Community	476,132
Netherlands	3,000
Switzerland	103,093
United Kingdom	65,378
United States	1,000,000
Subtotal	2,053,052
Disaster relief in Ethiopia	
Cyprus	1,000
Subtotal	1,000
Disaster relief in Guatemala	
Switzerland	18,182
Subtotal	18,182
Disaster relief in Honduras	
Luxembourg	2,885
Subtotal	2,885
Disaster relief in Indonesia	
Australia	106,701
Canada	40,055
Italy	16,151
Luxembourg	5,943
Philippines	5,000
Singapore	10,000
Subtotal	183,850
Disaster relief in Lebanon	
Australia	111,598
European Economic Community	3,186,957
Philippines	4,000
Subtotal	3,302,555
Disaster relief in Madagascar	
Australia	42,268
Cyprus	500
Saudi Arabia	500,000
Subtotal	542,768
Disaster relief in Nicaragua	
Luxembourg	5,771
Subtotal	5,771
Disaster relief in Tonga	
Italy	34,574
Switzerland	10,753
Subtotal	45,327
General disaster relief operations	
Cyprus	500
Madagascar	883
Nigeria	50,000
Subtotal	51,383
Disaster prevention and pre-disaster planning	
Madagascar	883
Subtotal	883
Strengthening of UNDRO	
Australia	119,114
Bahamas	1,500
Iceland	10,000

Strengthening of UNDRO (cont.)	
Italy	414,472
New Zealand	15,330
Switzerland	45,455
Tunisia	3,407
Subtotal	609,278
Total	7,060,434

SOURCE: Interim United Nations financial statements for the 12-month period ended 31 December 1982—Individual trust funds (unpublished).

Resolutions (1982). GA: [1]37/144, 17 Dec.; [2]37/243 A (section 22), 21 Dec.
Yearbook reference. [3]1981, p. 484.

Co-ordination in the UN system

On 6 April 1982, the inter-agency Administrative Committee on Co-ordination (ACC) adopted guiding principles on the role of the lead entity and participating organizations of the United Nations system when confronted with complex emergency situations.[1] Action on this matter had been called for by the General Assembly in December 1981, when it approved measures to strengthen the capacity of the United Nations system to respond to disasters.[3]

Under this ACC decision, the United Nations Secretary-General or the executive head of a United Nations organization would initiate consultations to determine if a disaster requiring a system-wide response existed. The Secretary-General would then designate a lead entity to develop and co-ordinate a concerted relief programme and ensure its effective execution. At the country level, he would designate an entity to co-ordinate and/or carry out relief operations.

The lead entity would seek solutions to administrative, funding and other problems affecting United Nations organizations. It would assist the disaster-stricken country on procedures for handling relief goods and services, channels of communication with the United Nations system and logistic support. It would set up channels with organizations inside and outside the United Nations system, organize consultations among them, organize meetings with donors, prepare progress reports and a budget for the operation, recommend whether the Secretary-General should launch a united appeal and co-ordinate public information. Because complex disaster situations were so varied, the specific actions of the lead entity and participating organizations would have to be established case by case.

During 1982, UNDRO took up its newly assigned task of developing relief programmes for major emergencies, in consultation with United Nations organizations and others. These consultations were undertaken in multilateral meetings supplemented by bilateral contacts, and pertained to emergencies in Angola, Chad and Lebanon.

The General Assembly, in its 17 December resolution on UNDRO,[2] endorsed the measures taken by the Secretary-General and by ACC in its April decision, and called on the Secretary-General, normally represented by UNDRO, to consult with United Nations organizations to develop concerted relief programmes as a basis for united appeals for funds. The Assembly called on United Nations organizations to co-ordinate their efforts at all stages of the international response to disasters.

Decision (1982). [1]ACC (report, E/1982/4): 1982/1, 6 Apr.
Resolution (1982). [2]GA: 37/144, paras. 9 & 12, 17 Dec.
Resolution (prior). [3]GA: 36/225, 17 Dec. 1981 (YUN 1981, p. 480).

Satellite communication

The Second United Nations Conference on the Exploration and Peaceful Uses of Outer Space (UNISPACE-82), held at Vienna in August 1982, recommended that international organizations operating commercial components of a satellite communication system should make them available at minimal or no cost during disaster operations, as part of an international disaster communications system to be governed by an appropriate body of the United Nations system.[1]

This was one of several recommendations made by UNISPACE-82 in the area of satellite communication.

Report. [1]Conference on outer space, A/CONF.101/10.

Drought-stricken areas of Africa

Sudano-Sahelian region

The United Nations Sudano-Sahelian Office (UNSO), operating within the United Nations Development Programme (UNDP), continued in 1982 to serve as the principal unit of the United Nations system for co-ordinating efforts by United Nations agencies to help eight drought-stricken countries of the Sahel—an arid zone in West and Central Africa south of the Sahara—to implement medium- and long-term recovery and rehabilitation programmes. These programmes were aimed at mitigating the effects of future droughts, achieving self-sufficiency in food staples and accelerating socio-economic development. The countries assisted—Cape Verde, Chad, the Gambia, Mali, Mauritania, the Niger, Senegal and the Upper Volta—were the members of the Permanent Inter-State Committee on Drought Control in the Sahel (CILSS), a non-United Nations body through which the participating States co-ordinated national and regional projects.

Under a separate mandate, UNSO also assisted 19 countries in a broader area of Central, East and West Africa to control desertification through a joint venture between UNDP and the United Nations Environment Programme.

The Secretary-General, in reports to the General Assembly in 1982[3] and early 1983,[4] described the activities undertaken in 1982 under the medium- and long-term recovery programme. The number of UNSO-assisted projects reached 129 (32 regional and 97 national) at the end of 1982, at a total cost of $701 million.

In 1982, UNSO mobilized $28.1 million in international assistance to finance priority drought-related recovery and rehabilitation projects as well as desertification control projects of the States members of CILSS; $14.7 million of this amount was for recovery and rehabilitation. Sources for these funds were bilateral and multilateral, and included the United Nations Trust Fund for Sudano-Sahelian Activities. Since the inception of UNSO in 1973,[7] $431 million had become available from various sources by the end of 1982, of which more than $60 million was contributed through the Trust Fund.

Prominent among UNSO-assisted regional activities was a $203-million programme for the construction, improvement and maintenance of a region-wide, 5,000-kilometre system of all-weather feeder (secondary) roads. Approximately $123 million had been secured by the end of 1982 for the construction of some 3,000 kilometres of roads, including $82.6 million for UNSO projects, of which $12.7 million was secured in 1982. Since the programme's inception, a total of 1,300 kilometres had been constructed. A mission of road engineers and transport economists sent to the Sahel by UNSO in January to evaluate the programme produced a report giving a positive assessment of the efficiency of the road building operation and its socio-economic impact. Current and future partners of the programme, at a meeting at Geneva on 16 and 17 November, reviewed progress and decided on new projects.

A programme of strengthening agro-meteorological and hydrological services entered its second phase (1982-1986), during which it was expected to intensify applied research activities and develop collaboration with agricultural research institutions. Meetings were held to finalize a $2.1 million project for the agro-sylvo-pastoral development of the Fouta-Djallon massif in Guinea, the area where three major West African rivers rise. The United Nations Financing System for Science and Technology for Development financed a regional seminar (Bamako, Mali, 1-8 December) on the technical and socio-economic aspects of improved wood-stoves development, part of a larger programme of national and regional projects on the design, development and production of fuel-efficient cooking stoves.

A post-graduate training project in management and pasture lands conservation at Dakar,

Senegal—organized by the Institute of the Sahel with the support of UNSO, UNDP, and the United Nations Educational, Scientific and Cultural Organization—was reformulated in April to institute a training programme for middle-level technicians. The second class of senior Sahelian professionals completed training under this programme in June and another class began in September.

The UNDP Governing Council, on 18 June,[1] urged Governments to make special efforts to enable UNSO to respond to priority requirements, including voluntary contributions at the 1982 United Nations Pledging Conference for Development Activities. It requested that UNSO continue close co-operation with CILSS and its member States to hasten implementation of the recovery and rehabilitation programme. On the same date, the Council appropriated $3,447,300 (gross) for the UNSO administrative and programme support budget, including $1.9 million to reimburse the UNDP Office for Project Execution for its execution of UNSO funded projects.[2]

Economic and Social Council action. In a resolution of 28 July,[5] the Economic and Social Council urged Governments to make special efforts to increase UNSO resources through voluntary contributions so that the Office could respond more fully to the priority requirements of the CILSS Governments. It noted with satisfaction arrangements for joint undertakings by the United Nations system and UNSO to increase assistance to the Sudano-Sahelian countries for their recovery, rehabilitation and development programmes, and it requested the Secretary-General to continue to keep it informed of such undertakings.

This resolution, introduced by Mali and sponsored by 16 nations, was adopted without vote following similar approval by the Third (Programme and Co-ordination) Committee on 14 July.

General Assembly action. Another call for voluntary contributions to increase the resources of UNSO, through the Pledging Conference and bilateral channels, was made by the General Assembly in a resolution of 17 December,[6] adopted without vote. The Assembly requested Governments and the United Nations system to give special attention to the critical food situation in Cape Verde, Chad, Mali and Mauritania. It commended UNDP for the results UNSO had achieved, and invited UNSO to continue to strengthen its close co-operation with CILSS and its member States.

This resolution, introduced by Cape Verde and sponsored by 21 nations, mainly African, was approved by the Second (Economic and Financial) Committee without vote on 2 December.

Decisions (1982). UNDP Council (report, E/1982/16/Rev.1), 18 June: [1]82/27; [2]82/31, para. 4.
Reports. S-G, [3]A/37/209 & Add.1, [4]A/38/152-E/1983/38.

Resolutions (1982). [5]ESC: 1982/49, 28 July, text following. [6]GA: 37/165, 17 Dec., text following.
Yearbook reference. [7]1973, p. 454.
Meeting records. ESC: E/1982/SR.49 (28 July). GA: 2nd Committee, A/C.2/37/SR.27-31, 33, *38*, *46* (2 Nov.–2 Dec.); plenary, A/37/PV.109 (17 Dec.).

Economic and Social Council resolution 1982/49

28 July 1982	Meeting 49	Adopted without vote

Approved by Third Committee (E/1982/94) without vote, 14 July (meeting 7); 16-nation draft (E/1982/C.3/L.1); agenda item 24.

Sponsors: Algeria, China, France, India, Iraq, Libyan Arab Jamahiriya, Mali, Morocco, Portugal, Senegal, Sudan, Tunisia, United States, Venezuela, Yugoslavia, Zaire.

Implementation of the medium-term and long-term recovery and rehabilitation programme in the Sudano-Sahelian region

The Economic and Social Council,

Recalling the relevant resolutions of the General Assembly and the Economic and Social Council, particularly Assembly resolution 36/203 of 17 December 1981 and Council resolution 1981/55 of 22 July 1981,

Recalling also decision 82/27 of 18 June 1982 of the Governing Council of the United Nations Development Programme,

Having considered the report of the Secretary-General on the implementation of the medium-term and long-term recovery and rehabilitation programme in the Sudano-Sahelian region,

1. *Takes note with satisfaction* of the report of the Secretary-General on the implementation of the medium-term and long-term recovery and rehabilitation programme in the Sudano-Sahelian region;

2. *Expresses its profound gratitude* to the Governments, agencies of the United Nations system, intergovernmental organizations, private organizations and individuals that have contributed to the implementation of the recovery, rehabilitation and development programme in the Sahel;

3. *Strongly urges* all Governments to make special efforts to increase the resources of the United Nations Sudano-Sahelian Office through voluntary contributions, so as to enable the Office to respond more fully to the priority requirements of the Governments of the States members of the Permanent Inter-State Committee on Drought Control in the Sahel;

4. *Notes with satisfaction* the arrangements made for joint undertakings by several United Nations organs, agencies and programmes with the United Nations Sudano-Sahelian Office so as to increase their assistance in response to requests from the Governments of the Sudano-Sahelian countries for the implementation of their recovery, rehabilitation and development programmes;

5. *Requests* the Secretary-General, in his annual report on this question, to continue to keep the Economic and Social Council informed of the progress achieved in identifying and executing further joint undertakings to enhance the assistance of the United Nations system to the countries members of the Permanent Inter-State Committee on Drought Control in the Sahel.

General Assembly resolution 37/165

17 December 1982	Meeting 109	Adopted without vote

Approved by Second Committee (A/37/702/Add.2) without vote, 2 December (meeting 46); 21-nation draft (A/C.2/37/L.34); agenda item 74 *(c)*.

Sponsors: Afghanistan, Cape Verde, Chad, Egypt, Ethiopia, Gambia, Guinea, Guinea-Bissau, Ivory Coast, Malaysia, Mali, Mauritania, Niger, Nigeria, Senegal, Sierra Leone, Somalia, Sudan, Uganda, United Republic of Cameroon, Upper Volta.

Implementation of the medium-term and long-term recovery and rehabilitation programme in the Sudano-Sahelian region

The General Assembly,

Recalling its resolutions 2816(XXVI) of 14 December 1971, 2959(XXVII) of 12 December 1972, 3054(XXVIII) of 17 October 1973, 3253(XXIX) of 4 December 1974, 3512(XXX) of 15 December 1975, 31/180 of 21 December 1976, 32/159 of 19 December 1977, 33/133 of 19 December 1978, 34/16 of 9 November 1979, 35/69 and 35/86 of 5 December 1980 and 36/203 of 17 December 1981,

Recalling also Economic and Social Council resolutions 1918(LVIII) of 5 May 1975, 2103(LXIII) of 3 August 1977, 1978/37 of 21 July 1978,

1979/51 of 2 August 1979, 1980/51 of 23 July 1980, 1981/55 of 22 July 1981 and 1982/49 of 28 July 1982,

Taking note of decision 82/27 of 18 June 1982 of the Governing Council of the United Nations Development Programme concerning the implementation of the medium-term and long-term recovery and rehabilitation programme in the Sudano-Sahelian region,

Noting with satisfaction the decisive role played by the United Nations Sudano-Sahelian Office in helping to combat the effects of the drought and to implement the medium-term and long-term recovery and rehabilitation programme adopted by the States members of the Permanent Inter-State Committee on Drought Control in the Sahel, and in mobilizing the necessary resources to finance priority projects,

Considering that the nature and magnitude of the needs of the countries of the Sudano-Sahelian region call for the continuation and further strengthening of actions of solidarity by the international community in support of the recovery efforts and the economic development of those countries,

Bearing in mind the critical food situation which obtains this year again in some countries of the Sahel, particularly in Cape Verde, Chad, Mali and Mauritania,

Having considered the report of the Secretary-General on the implementation of the medium-term and long-term recovery and rehabilitation programme in the Sudano-Sahelian region,

1. *Takes note with satisfaction* of the report of the Secretary-General on the implementation of the medium-term and long-term recovery and rehabilitation programme in the Sudano-Sahelian region;

2. *Expresses its gratitude* to the Governments, agencies of the United Nations system, intergovernmental organizations, private organizations and individuals that have contributed to the implementation of the medium-term and long-term recovery and rehabilitation programme in the Sudano-Sahelian region;

3. *Strongly urges* all Governments to make special efforts to increase the resources of the United Nations Sudano-Sahelian Office, including voluntary contributions through the United Nations Pledging Conference for Development Activities, as well as other, including bilateral, channels, so as to enable it to respond more fully to the priority requirements of the Governments of the States members of the Permanent Inter-State Committee on Drought Control in the Sahel;

4. *Requests* all Governments, organs, agencies and programmes of the United Nations system to give special attention to the critical food situation which obtains in Cape Verde, Chad, Mali and Mauritania;

5. *Commends* the Administrator of the United Nations Development Programme for the results achieved through the United Nations Sudano-Sahelian Office in assisting the States members of the Permanent Inter-State Committee on Drought Control in the Sahel in the implementation of their medium-term and long-term recovery and rehabilitation programme;

6. *Invites* the United Nations Sudano-Sahelian Office to continue to strengthen its close co-operation with the States members of the Permanent Inter-State Committee on Drought Control in the Sahel and with the Committee, with a view to hastening the implementation of the medium-term and long-term recovery and rehabilitation programme in the Sudano-Sahelian region;

7. *Requests* the Secretary-General to continue to report to the General Assembly, through the Governing Council of the United Nations Development Programme and the Economic and Social Council, on the implementation of the medium-term and long-term recovery and rehabilitation programme in the Sudano-Sahelian region.

UN Trust Fund for Sudano-Sahelian Activities

Expenditures from the United Nations Trust Fund for Sudano-Sahelian Activities totalled $11,017,302 in 1982. Of this sum, $8,994,130 represented project costs (see table below), $1,500,853 was for administrative costs and $522,319 was paid to agencies executing UNSO projects in reimbursement for their support costs.

Eleven Governments paid a total of $7,331,607 in voluntary and cost-sharing contributions to the Trust Fund in 1982 (see table below). Total income for the year, including interest, came to

$9,487,528, or $1,529,774 less than expenditures. Pledges for 1983, from six Governments, totalled $1,202,472 as at 31 December 1982.

CONTRIBUTIONS TO THE UN TRUST FUND FOR
SUDANO-SAHELIAN ACTIVITIES, 1982
(as at 31 December 1982; in US dollar equivalent)

Country	1982 Payment	1983 Pledge
Australia	829,510	—
Chile	—	5,000
Denmark	823,599	602,971
Finland	284,270	—
Gambia	379,020	—
Germany, Federal Republic of	230,906	—
Italy	1,368,748	569,297
Netherlands	3,091,429	—
Philippines	5,000	5,000
Portugal	10,000	10,000
Sweden	303,317	—
United Republic of Cameroon	—	10,204
Yugoslavia	5,808	—
Total	7,331,607	1,202,472

SOURCE: A/38/5/Add.1.

PROGRAMME EXPENDITURES UNDER THE UN TRUST FUND
FOR SUDANO-SAHELIAN ACTIVITIES, 1982
(as at 31 December 1982; in thousands of US dollars)

Country/Region	Amount
Benin	1
Cape Verde	171
Ethiopia	71
Gambia	1,511
Guinea-Bissau	2
Mali	674
Mauritania	1,415
Niger	1,656
Senegal	1,419
Somalia	490
Sudan	437
Uganda	4
Upper Volta	700
Subtotal	8,551
Regional Africa	371
Interregional	71
Subtotal	442
Total	8,994

*Total varies from sum of individual country figures due to rounding.
SOURCE: DP/1983/6/Add.4/Corr.1.

East Africa

Six East African countries affected by drought—Djibouti, Ethiopia, Kenya, Somalia, the Sudan and Uganda—were the subject of a May 1982 report of the Secretary-General to the General Assembly,[2] requested by the Assembly in December 1981.[6] The Secretary-General stated that the countries, with the exception of Djibouti and parts of Ethiopia, had had sufficient rainfall during 1981, and their agriculture and livestock situations had improved, relieving some of the pressure on the food supply and environment. Because the response to the Secretary-General's appeal for voluntary contributions had been limited, the United Nations Development Programme (UNDP) could not implement various recommendations on rehabilitation, drought-policy development and fund-raising. Nevertheless, UNDP was prepared to co-operate with the Governments concerned in their requests for assistance.

A United Nations multi-agency mission which visited Ethiopia from 15 to 20 August 1982[3] concluded that drought was a perennial problem for the country and was likely to occur in two out of three years. Therefore, the interactions between drought mitigation, desertification control and development were constant and should be realistically reflected in government plans and operations. The most important drought mitigation measure, in the mission's view, was resettlement of population in less drought-prone areas; it urged high priority for external financing to accelerate the resettlement movement that had already begun. It pointed to the damage done by deforestation and overgrazing, and listed a number of desirable steps in agriculture and food production, irrigation, forestry, livestock control and development of the transport system, especially rural roads. It also recommended a strengthening of meteorological and hydrological services, better land-use planning, provision of a safe water supply in rural areas, and a comprehensive educational and training plan.

On 27 July,[1] the Economic and Social Council took note of the Secretary-General's report on assistance to drought-stricken areas in the six East African countries and transmitted it to the General Assembly.

By a resolution adopted without vote on 17 December,[4] the Assembly endorsed the recommendations of the multi-agency mission. It took note of the ongoing consultations of Governments on the establishment of an intergovernmental body to combat the effects of drought and other natural disasters—suggested by the Assembly in 1980[5]—and urged them to finalize arrangements. Noting that the Secretary-General had made arrangements with the UNDP Administrator, subject to the availability of funds, for a UNDP unit to assist the affected countries and to co-ordinate the recovery and rehabilitation activities of the United Nations system, it appealed to Member States to meet the costs of the unit when the intergovernmental body was established. It requested the Secretary-General, in co-ordination with the UNDP Administrator and other United Nations organizations, to assist in combating the effects of drought pending the establishment of the intergovernmental body, including the establishment or improvement of national machinery. The Secretary-General was asked to report back in 1983 on the progress made.

This resolution, introduced by Kenya in the Second (Economic and Financial) Committee on behalf of 12 nations, including the six directly affected, was approved without vote on 2 December, after oral revisions by the sponsors.

Decision (1982). [1]ESC: 1982/151, para. *(b)*, 27 July.
Reports. S-G: [2]A/37/122; [3]A/37/198, annexing mission report.
Resolution (1982). [4]GA: 37/147, 17 Dec., text following.
Resolutions (prior). GA: [5]35/90, 5 Dec. 1980 (YUN 1980, p. 978); [6]36/221, 17 Dec. 1981 (YUN 1981, p. 490).
Meeting records. GA: 2nd Committee, A/C.2/37/SR.27-30, *31, 33, 40, 46* (2 Nov.–2 Dec.); plenary, A/37/PV.109 (17 Dec.).

General Assembly resolution 37/147

17 December 1982   Meeting 109   Adopted without vote

Approved by Second Committee (A/37/702/Add.2) without vote, 2 December (meeting 46); 12-nation draft (A/C.2/37/L.36), orally revised; agenda item 74 *(b)*.

Sponsors: Afghanistan, Bangladesh, Djibouti, Ethiopia, Kenya, Niger, Nigeria, Philippines, Somalia, Sudan, Uganda, United Republic of Cameroon.

Assistance to the drought-stricken areas of Djibouti, Ethiopia, Kenya, Somalia, the Sudan and Uganda

The General Assembly,

Recalling its resolutions 35/90 and 35/91 of 5 December 1980 and 36/221 of 17 December 1981 on the question of assistance to the drought-stricken areas of Djibouti, Ethiopia, Kenya, Somalia, the Sudan and Uganda,

Concerned about the continued adverse effects of drought on the economic and social development of those countries,

Noting the reports of the Secretary-General on Djibouti, Ethiopia, Kenya, Somalia, the Sudan and Uganda,

Bearing in mind the ongoing consultations between the countries concerned to establish the intergovernmental body recommended by the General Assembly in its resolution 35/90,

1. *Reaffirms* its resolution 36/221 on assistance to the drought-stricken areas of Djibouti, Ethiopia, Kenya, Somalia, the Sudan and Uganda;

2. *Endorses* the recommendations made by the multi-agency mission to Ethiopia;

3. *Takes note* of the ongoing consultations between the Governments concerned on the establishment of the intergovernmental body to combat the effects of drought and other natural disasters and urges them to finalize, as soon as possible, the necessary arrangements for the establishment of that body;

4. *Notes* that the Secretary-General has made arrangements with the Administrator of the United Nations Development Programme, subject to the availability of funds, for a unit within the programmes administered by the Administrator to be assigned responsibility for assisting the affected countries in the region and for co-ordinating the activities of the United Nations system in support of recovery and rehabilitation in those countries;

5. *Appeals* to Member States to provide the Secretary-General with the resources required to meet the operational costs of such a unit as soon as the intergovernmental body is established;

6. *Requests* the Secretary-General, in close co-ordination with the Administrator of the United Nations Development Programme and the appropriate specialized agencies and other organizations of the United Nations system, to continue to extend all necessary assistance to those countries in their efforts to combat the effects of drought on the basis of the recommendations of various multi-agency missions, pending the establishment of the intergovernmental body;

7. *Also requests* the Secretary-General, in close co-ordination with the Administrator of the United Nations Development Programme and the appropriate specialized agencies and other organizations of the United Nations system, to assist the Governments of the region, at their request, in establishing or improving national machinery to combat the effects of drought and other natural disasters and to report to the Economic and Social Council, at its second regular session of 1983, and to the General Assembly at its thirty-eighth session on the progress achieved in the implementation of the present resolution.

Floods

Democratic Yemen

Several United Nations bodies mobilized international relief efforts following floods in Democratic Yemen caused by heavy rains on 29 and 30 March 1982.

The Resident Representative of UNDP and the Office of the United Nations Disaster Relief Co-ordinator (UNDRO) flew over some of the affected areas on 30 March; on 1 April he sent the first of a series of messages to UNDRO and UNDP head-quarters reporting on the disaster. Both organizations promptly authorized their normal cash contribution of $30,000 each for the procurement of immediate relief assistance. An UNDRO representative arrived from headquarters on 3 April and on 7 April UNDRO made an international appeal for food, medicines, tents and blankets. Situation reports distributed by UNDRO on 7 and 14 April confirmed widespread damage. In the following weeks, the World Food Programme (WFP) provided wheat flour and edible oils, the United Nations Children's Fund flew in tents and blankets, the World Health Organization shipped medicines, and the Food and Agriculture Organization of the United Nations (FAO) joined with WFP in sending a mission to prepare rehabilitation and reconstruction programmes.

In a resolution adopted without vote on 28 April,[6] the Economic and Social Council urged States to participate in relief operations and programmes for the rehabilitation and reconstruction of the areas affected by floods in Democratic Yemen. It requested international and regional organizations and voluntary agencies to support United Nations and UNDRO efforts in mobilizing relief, and to consider urgently the Government's requests for rehabilitation and reconstruction assistance. It expressed hope that UNDP, the World Bank and other financial institutions would also consider those requests, including requests for improving disaster warning and protection systems.

The draft, introduced by the Libyan Arab Jamahiriya on behalf of 23 nations, was orally revised by the sponsors before its adoption.

This item had been added to the Council's agenda at the request of Democratic Yemen, in a letter to the Secretary-General dated 19 April.[3] The letter, which included descriptions of damage from the UNDRO situation reports of 7 and 14 April, reported that at least 482 people had been killed, 50,000 were homeless and emergency food was required for 300,000 persons for a six-month period. Total damage was estimated at $975 million.

Democratic Yemen told the Council on 23 April that, besides the loss of lives, the floods had severely damaged the agricultural and communications infrastructures and had washed away fertile soil. The Government was working to alleviate the suffering of displaced families and to avert outbreaks of disease, but required urgent and large-scale assistance.

In May the Economic Commission for Western Asia (ECWA) was informed, in a preliminary report prepared by UNDRO,[4] of the details of the damage and the steps taken by United Nations organizations immediately following the disaster (see above). The report said that the extensive damage to irrigation systems was expected to result in a 50 per cent reduction in agricultural production in 1982 and that the country would continue to require urgent food assistance. The report described 11 emergency rehabilitation projects costing $14.4 million, drawn up by the FAO/WFP mission with a view to obtaining international support. Their aim was to reduce the risk of further flood damage, utilize the flood water of forthcoming seasons for irrigation, expand the crop production area by increased utilization of ground water, increase yields by greater use of fertilizer, and install a water management and flood warning system.

On 11 May,[5] ECWA requested the Economic and Social Council to adopt a resolution calling for the urgent establishment of a programme, including the creation of a special fund, for the rehabilitation and reconstruction of the flood-stricken areas of Democratic Yemen. It appealed to United Nations Member States and, in particular, to members of ECWA to expedite and facilitate the urgent establishment and implementation of the programme and to contribute generously to the proposed fund.

In a resolution of 30 July,[7] adopted without vote, the Council endorsed the ECWA request for the urgent establishment of a rehabilitation and reconstruction programme. It requested the Secretary-General to assist the Government in preparing a comprehensive programme for the rehabilitation and reconstruction of the affected areas within the framework of the Substantial New Programme of Action for the 1980s for the Least Developed Countries. It urgently appealed to Member States and organizations to contribute to and participate in the programme for Democratic Yemen. The Secretary-General was requested to report orally to the General Assembly at its regular 1982 session.

This action was taken following approval without vote by the Council's First (Economic) Committee on 28 July. The draft was introduced in Committee by a Vice-Chairman on the basis of informal consultations on an earlier draft,[2] sponsored by 17 nations and introduced by Qatar, which was later withdrawn. The approved draft differed from the initial one in specifying that the report to be submitted by the Secretary-General should go to the Assembly in 1982 rather than the Council in 1983.

On 27 July,[1] the Council took note of an oral report by the Disaster Relief Co-ordinator on measures taken following the floods in Democratic Yemen.

The Co-ordinator informed the General Assembly's Second Committee in November that, as a result of the April appeal by UNDRO, the United Nations system, the European Economic Community, 12 Governments and non-governmental organizations had sent relief supplies valued at $11 million. UNDRO was ensuring co-ordination between Democratic Yemen and Switzerland in a project to draw up plans for reconstructing bridges and roads. China was to help in building a bridge, and UNDP, the World Bank and the Arab Fund for Economic and Social Development were providing funds to rebuild the road network.

The Assembly, on 17 December,[8] requested the Secretary-General to continue to mobilize resources for a programme of assistance to Democratic Yemen to mitigate the damage inflicted on it and implement its rehabilitation and reconstruction plans.

Decision (1982). [1]ESC: 1982/151, para. *(a)* (ii), 27 July.
Draft resolution withdrawn. [2]Algeria, Bangladesh, Benin, Cuba, Ethiopia, Iraq, Jordan, Kuwait, Lebanon, Libyan Arab Jamahiriya, Nepal, Pakistan, Qatar, Sudan, Tunisia, Yemen, Zambia, E/1982/C.1/L.12.
Letter. [3]Democratic Yemen, 19 Apr., E/1982/53.
Report. [4]UNDRO, E/ECWA/156.
Resolutions (1982). [5]ECWA (report, E/1982/22): 107(IX), 11 May. ESC: [6]1982/6, 28 Apr., text following; [7]1982/59, 30 July, text following. [8]GA: 37/150, para. 3, 17 Dec.
Meeting records. ESC: E/1982/SR.13, *14, 16,* 17, *18, 51* (22-28 Apr. & 30 July).

Economic and Social Council resolution 1982/6

28 April 1982   Meeting 18   Adopted without vote

23-nation draft (E/1982/L.22), orally revised; agenda item 3.

Sponsors: Algeria, Angola, Bahrain, Bangladesh, Cuba, Democratic Yemen, Djibouti, Ethiopia, India, Iraq, Jordan, Kuwait, Lebanon, Libyan Arab Jamahiriya, Madagascar, Mauritania, Morocco, Qatar, Saudi Arabia, Syrian Arab Republic, Tunisia, United Arab Emirates, Yugoslavia.

Measures to be taken following the heavy floods which have affected Democratic Yemen

The Economic and Social Council,

Considering that Democratic Yemen has recently suffered the effects of heavy floods which have caused loss of life and considerable damage to the economy of the country,

Having heard the statement of the delegation of Democratic Yemen on the extent of the damage caused by the unprecedented heavy floods,

Recalling the resolutions of the General Assembly and its own resolutions on assistance in cases of natural disasters, in which appeals have been made to the international community to give special attention to the phenomenon of natural disasters,

Taking into account the fact that the provision of assistance to countries stricken by natural disasters is an expression of the international solidarity proclaimed in the Charter of the United Nations,

Noting with satisfaction the assistance provided by several countries, international and regional organizations and voluntary agencies,

Noting also the efforts made by the Government of Democratic Yemen to relieve the suffering of the victims of the heavy floods,

1. *Expresses its profound sympathy* with the people and Government of Democratic Yemen for the loss of life and the serious damage which the recent floods have caused to the economy of the country;

2. *Urges* all States to participate or to continue to participate in relief operations and in the implementation of programmes for the rehabilitation and reconstruction of the areas affected by the floods;

3. *Requests* international and regional organizations, including specialized agencies, and voluntary agencies, particularly those most directly concerned, to lend their support and assistance, within the framework of their respective programmes, to the efforts of the Secretary-General and the United Nations Disaster Relief Co-ordinator to mobilize relief and assistance, and also to consider urgently the requests for assistance made by the Government of Democratic Yemen during the phase of rehabilitation and reconstruction;

4. *Expresses the hope* that the United Nations Development Programme, the World Bank and all other international financial institutions concerned will give sympathetic and urgent consideration to requests for assistance which the Government of Democratic Yemen may submit under its rehabilitation, reconstruction and development programmes and with a view to improving the existing disaster warning and protection systems;

5. *Requests* the Secretary-General to report to the Economic and Social Council, at its second regular session of 1982, on the implementation of the present resolution.

Economic and Social Council resolution 1982/59

30 July 1982   Meeting 51   Adopted without vote

Approved by First Committee (E/1982/96) without vote, 28 July (meeting 15); draft by Vice-Chairman (E/1982/C.1/L.25), based on informal consultations on 17-nation draft (E/1982/C.1/L.12); agenda item 9.

International assistance to the flood-stricken areas of Democratic Yemen

The Economic and Social Council,

Recalling its resolution 1982/6 of 28 April 1982, concerning the extensive devastation caused by the recent floods in Democratic Yemen,

Noting with satisfaction the prompt relief assistance rendered by Member States and agencies of the United Nations system, as well as by regional and international organizations,

Taking note of the detailed assessment of the extent and nature of the damage caused by the floods, as contained in the report prepared by the Office of the United Nations Disaster Relief Co-ordinator,

Considering that Democratic Yemen, being one of the least developed countries, is unable to sustain the mounting burden of providing prompt and adequate food and shelter for the large number of people made homeless by the floods and of undertaking rehabilitation and reconstruction measures in the affected areas,

1. *Endorses* the request contained in resolution 107(IX) of 11 May 1982 of the Economic Commission for Western Asia for the urgent establishment of a programme for the rehabilitation and reconstruction of the flood-stricken areas of Democratic Yemen;

2. *Requests* the Secretary-General to take the necessary measures to assist the Government of Democratic Yemen in the preparation of a comprehensive programme for the rehabilitation and reconstruction of the affected areas within the framework of the Substantial New Programme of Action for the 1980s for the Least Developed Countries;

3. *Urgently appeals* to States Members of the United Nations, as well as to regional and international organizations, to contribute generously to the funding of the rehabilitation and reconstruction programme and to participate actively in its implementation;

4. *Requests* the Secretary-General to submit an oral report on the implementation of the present resolution to the General Assembly at its thirty-seventh session.

Floods in Honduras and Nicaragua

Following a tropical storm which struck Honduras and Nicaragua from 22 to 30 May 1982, the Economic and Social Council and the General Assembly approved a request for emergency assistance. Total losses in Nicaragua alone were estimated at approximately $357 million, including material losses ($220 million), soil damage ($55 million) and indirect losses ($82 million), the Secretary-General informed the Assembly in October in a report[6] on economic assistance to that country.

According to the Secretary-General's 1982/83 report to the Assembly on UNDRO,[7] the floods in

Nicaragua severely affected the central and western areas of the country. Sixty-nine people died, 60,000 individuals were reported to require emergency assistance, bridges collapsed, large numbers of houses were destroyed and agricultural damage was severe. At the Government's request, UNDRO launched an international appeal and contributions in the amount of $8,129,743 had been reported to UNDRO by mid-December.

An initial request for aid was made by a special mission of the Economic Commission for Latin America (ECLA), which recommended granting food assistance to Nicaragua until August or September and implementing an emergency reconstruction programme.[5]

On 23 July,[8] the ECLA Committee of the Whole urged Governments and organizations to expand co-operation and intensify support for the rehabilitation of Nicaragua and Honduras. It invited Governments to give bilateral support by donations or concessional loans, and appealed to international financial institutions to contribute to the countries' rehabilitation and reconstruction. It urged ECLA members to intensify their efforts for Nicaraguan reconstruction within the framework of the action committee of the Latin American Economic System. It appealed to United Nations Members to permit access to their markets by Honduran and Nicaraguan products on non-reciprocal terms so that those countries could obtain urgently required foreign exchange. The Secretary-General was requested to ask the United Nations system to expand programmes for Honduras and Nicaragua, and UNDP and ECLA bodies were requested to respond favourably to requests for assistance.

On 29 July[1] the Economic and Social Council, acting without vote on an oral proposal of its President, endorsed the ECLA resolution—which had been sent to the President by a letter of 23 July from the ECLA Committee Chairman[3]—and recommended that the General Assembly do the same.

On 17 December[2] the Assembly endorsed the ECLA resolution, which had been circulated through a note by the Secretariat.[4] This action was taken without vote, following similar approval by the Second Committee on 2 December as orally proposed by the Chairman.

Also on 17 December, the Assembly renewed with urgency its call for continued and increased international assistance to Nicaragua.[9]

Decisions (1982). [1]ESC: 1982/168, 29 July, text following.
[2]GA: 37/433, 17 Dec., text following.
Letter. [3]ECLA Committee of Whole Chairman, 23 July, annexing resolution 419(PLEN.15), E/1982/L.50.
Note. [4]Secretariat, A/C.2/37/L.9, annexing ECLA Committee of Whole resolution.
Reports. [5]ECLA secretariat, E/CEPAL/G.1206; S-G, [6]A/37/135, [7]A/38/201-E/1983/69.

Resolutions (1982). [8]ECLA Committee of Whole (report, E/CEPAL/G.1209/Rev.2): 419(PLEN.15), 23 July.
[9]GA: 37/157, para. 4, 17 Dec.
Meeting records. ESC: E/1982/SR.46-48, *49, 50* (19-29 July). GA: 2nd Committee, A/C.2/37/SR.27-31, 33, *46* (2 Nov.–2 Dec.); plenary, A/37/PV.109 (17 Dec.).

Economic and Social Council decision 1982/168

Adopted without vote

Oral proposal by President; agenda item 4.

International assistance to alleviate the economic and social problems faced by Honduras and Nicaragua as a result of the May 1982 floods

At its 50th plenary meeting, on 29 July 1982, the Council decided to endorse resolution 419(PLEN.15) on international assistance to alleviate the economic and social problems faced by Honduras and Nicaragua as a result of the May 1982 floods, adopted by the Committee of the Whole of the Economic Commission for Latin America at its fifteenth special session, held in New York on 22 and 23 July 1982, and to recommend the General Assembly at its thirty-seventh session also to endorse the resolution.

General Assembly decision 37/433

Adopted without vote

Approved by Second Committee (A/37/702/Add.2) without vote, 2 December (meeting 46); oral proposal by Chairman; agenda item 74 *(b)*.

International assistance to alleviate the economic and social problems faced by Honduras and Nicaragua as a result of the floods of May 1982

At its 109th plenary meeting, on 17 December 1982, the General Assembly, on the recommendation of the Second Committee, in pursuance of Economic and Social Council decision 1982/168 of 29 July 1982, decided to endorse resolution 419(PLEN.15) on international assistance to alleviate the economic and social problems faced by Honduras and Nicaragua as a result of the floods of May 1982, adopted by the Committee of the Whole of the Economic Commission for Latin America at its fifteenth special session.

Cyclones and floods in Madagascar

Five tropical storms hit Madagascar between December 1981 and March 1982, causing heavy flooding. According to the Secretary-General's annual report on UNDRO,[5] that Office had immediately offered to assist the Government in co-ordinating relief assistance and on 28 January had launched an international appeal for emergency aid. A staff member was sent to the country to assist UNDP in assessing damage and co-ordinating international relief. The UNDRO mission had found that, in the area of the capital, Antananarivo, 100,000 persons were homeless, there was danger of epidemics, and serious damage had been caused to roads, bridges and railways. Urgent relief requirements included food, reconstruction material, transportation of relief supplies and medical supplies. The damage was estimated at $250 million, including a crop loss of 40,000 hectares. Contributions for international assistance reported to UNDRO amounted to more than $9 million.

By a resolution of 28 April,[6] the Economic and Social Council urged States to participate or continue to participate in relief operations and rehabilitation and reconstruction programmes for areas in Madagascar affected by the cyclones and floods. It expressed hope that UNDP, the World Bank and other international financial institutions would give sympathetic and urgent consideration to Madagascar's requests for assistance under its reconstruction and development programmes, and with a view to improving disaster warning and protection systems.

The text, introduced by Zaire, sponsored by 26 nations and revised by them in writing and orally, was adopted without vote.

The item had been placed on the Council's agenda at the request of Madagascar, in a letter of 30 March[3] and an explanatory note of 14 April.[4] It reported in the note that 80 per cent of the crops in the affected areas had been lost, with losses reaching 90 per cent in the main rice-growing areas. In regard to export products, 80 per cent of the standing coffee and ylang-ylang crops had been spoiled, and there had been extensive damage to vanilla and clove plantations. Roads, bridges and dikes had been partly or totally destroyed, communications seriously affected, and airports and port facilities damaged.

On 27 July,[1] the Council took note of an oral report by the United Nations Disaster Relief Co-ordinator on further measures taken following the cyclones and floods in Madagascar.

The Co-ordinator told the General Assembly's Second Committee in November that contributions of $21 million had been made for assistance to Madagascar. Additional international aid was required, however, primarily for the restoration of transport and to offset agricultural losses.

On 17 December,[2] the Assembly took note of the Co-ordinator's oral report along with reports on several other countries receiving economic assistance or disaster aid.

Decisions (1982). [1]ESC: 1982/151, para. *(a)* (ii), 27 July. [2]GA: 37/434, para. *(e),* 17 Dec.
Letters. Madagascar: [3]30 Mar., E/1982/44; [4]14 Apr., E/1982/44/Add.1.
Report. [5]S-G, A/37/235.
Resolution (1982). [6]ESC: 1982/5, 28 Apr., text following.
Meeting records. ESC: E/1982/SR.13, 14, *16-18, 48* (22-28 Apr. & 27 July).

Economic and Social Council resolution 1982/5

28 April 1982   Meeting 18   Adopted without vote

26-nation draft (E/1982/L.21/Rev.1), orally revised; agenda item 3.

Sponsors: Algeria, Bahamas, Bangladesh, Benin, Burundi, China, Cuba, Democratic Yemen, Djibouti, Ethiopia, Kenya, Lao People's Democratic Republic, Liberia, Libyan Arab Jamahiriya, Malawi, Mali, Nicaragua, Nigeria, Pakistan, Senegal, Sierra Leone, Somalia, United Republic of Cameroon, Viet Nam, Yugoslavia, Zaire.

Measures to be taken following the cyclones and floods in Madagascar

The Economic and Social Council,

Considering that Madagascar has recently suffered the effects of several tropical cyclones and floods which have caused loss of life and considerable damage to the economy of the country,

Having heard the statement of the delegation of Madagascar on the cyclones which affect the countries situated in the south-western part of the Indian Ocean, and the statement of the representative of the Office of the United Nations Disaster Relief Co-ordinator,

Recognizing that climatic hazards create in countries subject to seasonal disasters emergency situations having medium-term and long-term economic, social and structural consequences which affect development,

Recalling the resolutions of the General Assembly and its own resolutions on assistance in cases of natural disasters, in which appeals have been made to the international community to give special attention to these phenomena,

Taking into account the fact that the provision of assistance to countries stricken by natural disasters is an expression of the international solidarity proclaimed in the Charter of the United Nations,

Noting with satisfaction the emergency assistance provided by a number of States, specialized agencies and other international and regional organizations, and by voluntary agencies,

Noting also the efforts made by the Government of Madagascar to relieve the suffering of the victims of the cyclones and floods,

1. *Expresses its profound sympathy* with the people and Government of Madagascar for the loss of life and the serious damage which the recent cyclones and floods have caused to the economy of the country;

2. *Urges* all States to participate or to continue to participate in relief operations and in the implementation of programmes for the rehabilitation and reconstruction of the areas affected by the cyclones and floods;

3. *Requests* the specialized agencies and other international and regional organizations, as well as voluntary agencies, particularly those most directly concerned, to lend their support, within the framework of their respective programmes, to the efforts of the Secretary-General and the United Nations Disaster Relief Co-ordinator to mobilize relief and assistance, and also to consider urgently the requests for assistance made by the Government of Madagascar during the phase of rehabilitation and reconstruction;

4. *Expresses the hope* that the United Nations Development Programme, the World Bank and all other international financial institutions concerned will give sympathetic and urgent consideration to requests for assistance which the Government of Madagascar may submit under its rehabilitation, reconstruction and development programmes and with a view to improving the existing disaster warning and protection systems;

5. *Requests* the Secretary-General to report to the Economic and Social Council at its second regular session of 1982 and to the General Assembly at its thirty-seventh session on the implementation of the present resolution.

Earthquake in Yemen

By a resolution of 17 December 1982,[2] adopted without vote, the General Assembly requested the Secretary-General to mobilize resources to alleviate the sufferings and mitigate the damages in Yemen caused by an earthquake which had occurred on 13 December. It appealed for international bilateral and multilateral assistance for the reconstruction of the affected areas and requested the Secretary-General to continue, through UNDRO, his efforts in mobilizing emergency assistance. It requested that the United Nations system maintain and expand assistance to the country, and co-operate with the Secretary-General in organizing an effective aid programme. It called on intergovernmental and non-governmental bodies to make urgent relief contributions.

The text was introduced by Oman on behalf of 23 nations.

In his report covering UNDRO activities in 1982/83,[1] the Secretary-General stated that the earthquake, lasting 40 seconds, had damaged or destroyed 300 villages. Deaths had been estimated at 2,500, the injured had exceeded 1,500 and there had been 400,000 homeless. An UNDRO official had been in the country between 14 and 24 December, assisting the UNDP/UNDRO Resident Representative in emergency relief co-ordination. Chartered aircraft had begun arriving the day after the earthquake with food, medicines, medical teams, mobile hospitals and blankets.

Report. [1]S-G, A/38/201-E/1983/69.
Resolution (1982). [2]GA: 37/166, 17 Dec., text following.
Meeting record. GA: A/37/PV.109 (17 Dec.).

General Assembly resolution 37/166

17 December 1982   Meeting 109   Adopted without vote

23-nation draft (A/37/L.58/Rev.1 and Rev.1Add.1); agenda item 74 *(b)*.

Sponsors: Algeria, Bahrain, Bangladesh, Democratic Yemen, Djibouti, Egypt, Iraq, Jordan, Kuwait, Lebanon, Libyan Arab Jamahiriya, Mauritania, Morocco, Oman, Qatar, Saudi Arabia, Somalia, Sudan, Syrian Arab Republic, Tunisia, United Arab Emirates, Yemen, Yugoslavia.

Assistance to Yemen

The General Assembly,

Fully aware of the extensive devastation and substantial loss of life caused by the earthquake which struck several towns and tens of villages in Yemen on 13 December 1982,

Recognizing the efforts being made by the Government of Yemen to alleviate the sufferings of the victims of the earthquake,

Recognizing also that Yemen, being one of the least developed countries, is unable to bear the mounting burden of the relief efforts, rehabilitation and reconstruction of the affected areas,

1. *Expresses its gratitude* to the States and international and regional organizations that have undertaken efforts to provide relief assistance to Yemen;

2. *Requests* the Secretary-General to mobilize the necessary material resources in order to help alleviate the sufferings and mitigate the damages inflicted on Yemen as a result of the earthquake;

3. *Appeals* to Member States to contribute generously to the relief efforts, through bilateral and/or multilateral channels, for the reconstruction of the affected areas in Yemen;

4. *Requests* the Secretary-General to continue, through the Office of the United Nations Disaster Relief Co-ordinator, his efforts in mobilizing all emergency assistance to Yemen;

5. *Requests* the appropriate organizations and programmes of the United Nations system—in particular the United Nations Development Programme, the Economic Commission for Western Asia, the World Bank, the World Food Programme, the Food and Agriculture Organization of the United Nations, the International Fund for Agricultural Development, the World Health Organization, the United Nations Fund for Population Activities, the United Nations Children's Fund and the United Nations Industrial Development Organization—to maintain and expand their programmes of assistance to Yemen and to co-operate closely with the Secretary-General in organizing an effective programme of assistance to that country;

6. *Calls upon* regional and interregional organizations and other intergovernmental bodies and non-governmental organizations to give urgent relief contributions to Yemen.

Disaster preparedness and prevention

In addition to its disaster relief activities, UNDRO continued in 1982 its pre-disaster planning functions, which involved it in promoting the study, control and prediction of natural disasters, collection and dissemination of information.

An International Seminar on Disaster Preparedness and Relief, sponsored by UNDRO and the League of Red Cross Societies, was held at Is-

lamabad, Pakistan, from 6 to 10 March. Senior government officials from seven South Asian countries, national Red Cross and Red Crescent officials, and representatives from several United Nations organizations and donor countries attended. The Seminar reviewed the state of disaster preparedness and relief in South-East Asia and discussed possibilities of strengthening regional co-operation.

UNDRO provided assistance with pre-disaster planning to Governments that requested it, as summarized below.

—*Chad.* A co-ordination and information centre for emergencies and a co-ordination centre for distribution logistics were created to centralize information on disaster needs and relief assistance for national authorities and international donors.

—*Indonesia.* An UNDRO official helped draw up a three-year project (September) for financing by UNDP, designed to strengthen counter-disaster management by reinforcing administrative mechanisms, training relief and preparedness officials, encouraging emergency planning and improving emergency communications.

—*Nepal.* An advisory mission helped finalize a national disaster plan (March) along lines developed by UNDRO.

—*Papua New Guinea.* An advisory mission on the establishment of a national disaster preparedness organization was carried out (March-May).

—*Samoa.* UNDRO assisted the Government (May-July) in reviewing disaster hazards and in formulating a national disaster preparedness plan.

—*Tonga.* An UNDRO expert assisted the Government (July/August) in strengthening the national Office for Disaster Relief and Reconstruction and in preparing a national disaster plan.

The Pan-Caribbean Disaster Preparedness and Prevention Project, with UNDRO as co-ordinating agency, provided technical assistance, vulnerability assessment and disaster management activities for 21 Caribbean countries and territories. During 1982, it promoted or co-sponsored 23 seminars, workshops and training programmes attended by 294 persons. With the assistance of North American countries, the Project put into operation an emergency telecommunication network linking the countries in the region.

Within the Typhoon Committee, composed of nine countries and one territory in Asia and the Pacific (see Chapter VIII of this section), UNDRO participated in a Typhoon Operation Experiment (1982-1983) aimed at minimizing the effects of such storms by improved forecasting and warning systems. An inter-agency disaster preparedness mission (September-November), organized in co-operation with the World Health Organization and the League of Red Cross Societies, visited six South and South-East Asian countries to discuss preparedness measures. UNDRO financed a study (April/May) on regional disaster preparedness plans for countries in the south-west Pacific and organized a meeting at Geneva (April) for heads of mobile disaster units. It helped organize the "Emergency 82" Congress in October at Geneva, where 400 participants discussed disaster preparedness.

With the Economic and Social Commission for Asia and the Pacific, UNDRO organized a seminar at Bangkok, Thailand (7-13 September), on flood vulnerability analysis. It co-ordinated a mission (November) to study flood and landslide risks in Cuzco, Peru, and was part of an inter-agency mission that assessed damage caused by flooding in Poland (26 April–3 May). Following a series of volcanic eruptions in Indonesia (see above), UNDRO arranged for the provision of equipment to monitor such eruptions and training in its use, and helped organize a national workshop to review prevention and preparedness needs.

In pursuance of a December 1981 General Assembly resolution,[6] UNDRO reviewed early-warning systems and services for responding to natural and other disasters, and took the information supplied by these systems into account in its operations. In its resolution of 17 December 1982 on strengthening UNDRO, the Assembly reiterated its desire to improve the Office's capability in this area so that it could take full advantage of information provided by such systems and could co-ordinate them to the extent feasible and useful, taking account of new technological developments including communications.[5]

UNDRO also engaged in activities related to earthquake preparedness and prevention.

Action by the Commission on Human Settlements. On 6 May,[3] the Commission on Human Settlements requested the Executive Director of the United Nations Centre for Human Settlements (UNCHS), also known as Habitat, to promote the study of a plan to link study and research centres dealing with natural disasters and their impact on human settlements.

On the same date,[4] the Commission requested him to distribute widely the conclusions of a joint UNDP/UNCHS/UNDRO project on assistance for reconstruction and flood protection in Upper (southern) Egypt, and of an UNDRO/United Nations Environment Programme project on guidelines for disaster prevention. It asked that he intensify co-operation with potential donors to mobilize resources so that developing countries could adopt measures for similar disasters. It also requested him to advise Governments on mobilizing resources for implementing the Egyptian project as a demonstration for other countries.

Also on 6 May,[1] the Commission recommended that, in developing policies, programmes and plans to minimize disaster vulnerability, governmental, non-governmental and intergovernmental agencies should emphasize techniques to reduce loss of life and property among the poor. It recommended that they accord high priority to immediate action programmes to that end, especially in the field of low-income shelter, to include research on ways to improve the performance of indigenous structures in disasters, the promotion of appropriate technology, and the preparation of educational materials and training programmes for the informal construction sector, with particular efforts on indigenous construction in slums and squatter and rural settlements. It requested the Executive Director to pay special attention to disaster-mitigation measures in UNCHS activities.

In a January report to the Commission on planning for human settlements in disaster-prone areas,[2] UNCHS recommended that countries integrate development planning with disaster prevention and mitigation planning, and that UNCHS support those efforts. To that end, UNCHS should conduct demonstration projects and develop a prototype information system and education and training projects, along with guidelines for disaster mitigation in different national contexts. International organizations should collaborate with Governments of disaster-prone countries to reduce disaster vulnerability, and UNCHS should encourage United Nations agencies to include disaster-mitigation policies in their projects and programmes.

Decision (1982). [1]Commission on Human Settlements (report, A/37/8): 5/20, 6 May.
Report. [2]UNCHS Executive Director, HS/C/5/3.
Resolutions (1982). Commission on Human Settlements, 6 May: [3]5/1, [4]5/3. [5]GA: 37/144, para. 10, 17 Dec.
Resolution (prior). [6]GA: 36/225, 17 Dec. 1981 (YUN 1981, p. 480).

Earthquakes

A seminar to examine cases of earthquake prediction which had had adverse social and economic effects was held at Geneva in October 1982 on the recommendation of the International Advisory Committee on Earthquake Risk, a body supported by UNDRO and the United Nations Educational, Scientific and Cultural Organization. Twenty-seven participants from 14 countries attended the seminar, to which 15 papers were submitted.

A Symposium on Continental Seismicity and Earthquake Prevention was co-sponsored by UNDRO in Beijing, China, in September. The meeting discussed continental seismicity and seismotectonics, precursors of continental earthquakes, and prediction and seismic hazard assessment.

On 6 May,[1] the Commission on Human Settlements requested the Executive Director of UNCHS to recommend, in collaboration with Governments, a policy for determining the action to be taken in order to predict seismic disasters and mitigate their consequences in earthquake-prone countries. It requested him to provide countries with technical assistance to understand and monitor seismic activity, prepare vulnerability maps of potentially seismic regions, establish earthquake-resistance regulations, foster exchange of information and experience, and assist in training specialists in earthquake engineering and engineering seismology. It asked that assistance be provided in drawing up relief plans, educating the population threatened by earthquakes, and developing broadcasting and communications infrastructure.

Resolution (1982). [1]Commission on Human Settlements (report, A/37/8): 5/2, 6 May.

Emergency relief and assistance

Kampucheans

The United Nations continued in 1982 to implement the voluntarily financed programme of humanitarian assistance to the people of Kampuchea, operating in Kampuchea, in Thailand and at the border between the two countries. Kampucheans seeking refuge along the border and those in holding centres of the United Nations High Commissioner for Refugees (UNHCR) in Thailand (see Chapter XXI of this section) continued to be dependent on the international community's relief assistance, the Secretary-General reported to the General Assembly in October.[2]

The programme had been in operation for three years and, as a result of substantial international assistance and the Kampucheans' own efforts, the food situation in the country was acceptable, he stated. However, agricultural conditions were frail and vulnerable.

Beginning in 1982, the World Food Programme (WFP) was designated by the Secretary-General as lead agency for the programme, under the overall supervision of the Special Representative of the Secretary-General who had been appointed in 1979 to co-ordinate the humanitarian operations. As a result, a new unit called the United Nations Border Relief Operation was established at Bangkok, Thailand, with the WFP Regional Representative directly responsible for the programme's day-to-day activities.

WFP co-ordinated the procurement and delivery of food aid to Kampuchea and relief operations along the Thai-Kampuchean border which, by the end of 1982, amounted to $314 million. It was responsible for emergency food aid to over 200,000 people along that border and helped co-ordinate international relief efforts covering health, education, water supplies and shelter. Between 1979 and December 1982 approximately 362,000 tons of food, 80 per cent of it rice, was shipped to Kampuchea. To the extent possible, with the co-operation of Kampuchean authorities, WFP officials monitored the distribution of food during field trips.

The United Nations Children's Fund (UNICEF) reported in March 1982 that its role as lead agency for activities of the United Nations system in Kampuchea had ended on 31 December 1981[4] but that it had offered to provide the legal umbrella under which activities of WFP and the Food and Agriculture Organization of the United Nations (FAO) could be maintained.[1] It also reported that the International Committee of the Red Cross (ICRC) was concentrating on tracing unaccompanied minors and children in orphanages, and was maintaining the essential airlink for communications and the transport of medical supplies and personnel from Bangkok to Phnom Penh, Democratic Kampuchea, and within Kampuchea. Assistance to returnees and to Kampucheans in holding centres continued to be provided by UNHCR.

As in previous years, periodic meetings chaired by the Secretary-General's Special Representative were held with donor Governments to keep them informed of financial needs and to provide details on implementation of the programme. Early in 1982 they were given a detailed statement on the financial situation, outlining the programme's needs for the coming year. These included approximately $49.1 million for the border and $38.4 million for Kampuchea. While a substantial part of the resources needed for the border operation was subsequently provided, the contribution for Kampuchea fell far short of estimated requirements.

On 28 October, in a resolution on the Kampuchea situation,[3] the General Assembly expressed appreciation to the international community for its relief assistance to the Kampuchean people and appealed for the continuation of arrangements to assist Kampucheans still in need, especially along the Thai-Kampuchean border and in holding centres in Thailand. It reiterated its appreciation to the Secretary-General for his efforts in co-ordinating humanitarian relief assistance and in monitoring its distribution, and requested that he continue his efforts as necessary.

Note. [1]UNICEF Executive Director, E/ICEF/L.1449.
Report. [2]S-G, A/37/496.
Resolution (1982). [3]GA: 37/6, paras. 10 & 11, 28 Oct.
Yearbook reference. [4]1981, p. 495.

Lebanon

Military actions in Lebanon in June 1982 caused large numbers of casualties and serious damage to cities and villages, creating an emergency situation requiring large-scale relief assistance. On 9 June, three days after the outbreak of hostilities, the Secretary-General asked United Nations agencies and programmes to inform him how they could provide emergency assistance to the country.[6] He requested the United Nations Co-ordinator of Assistance for the Reconstruction and Development of Lebanon to co-ordinate the United Nations system's humanitarian relief efforts and, on 11 June, appealed to Member States, through the Office of the United Nations Disaster Relief Co-ordinator (UNDRO), for assistance and resources. He instructed the United Nations Interim Force in Lebanon (UNIFIL) to provide protection and assistance to the population.

On 25 June, the Secretary-General appointed an inter-agency survey mission to assess the situation and estimate emergency requirements. After visiting Lebanon in early July, the mission estimated that 300,000 Lebanese and 83,000 Palestinians needed shelter, medical aid, food, water and sanitation services.[2] It outlined four major priority areas: repair and re-equipment of hospitals and health clinics, repair of water supply systems, repair and refurnishing of elementary schools and other community centres, and emergency shelter.

During this initial period, several United Nations organizations, particularly UNICEF and the United Nations Relief and Works Agency for Palestine Refugees in the Near East (UNRWA), assisted those sections of the population that could be reached.

UNICEF, which had been providing relief and rehabilitation assistance to Lebanon since 1975, responded to the emergency by distributing food as well as medical and other essential supplies to Palestinian and Lebanese women and children, and helping to maintain water supplies to beseiged West Beirut and to neighboring camps.[3] A UNICEF appeal on 16 June for an initial 90-day programme of intensive relief and rehabilitation assistance raised $5.84 million from Governments; UNICEF National Committees contributed $533,000 and non-governmental organizations $50,000 in addition to in-kind contributions. After the immediate emergency, UNICEF worked to restore basic services, repaired and rebuilt water supply networks, and worked on a plan to rehabilitate health, education and social services.

In addition to its emergency activities, UNICEF raised an additional $32 million for reconstruction in Beirut and southern Lebanon. Eighty-seven projects were identified for implementation over two years. Work on the programme began in October and included the reconstruction of a destroyed pumping station, which had provided water to 150 villages, and the repair of the Tyre hospi-

tal. By the end of 1982, 21 health, water and education projects had been completed at a cost of $2 million. Seventeen additional projects were being implemented and four were under procurement at a further cost of $4 million.

On 8 June, UNRWA—the other major United Nations agency with operations under way in Lebanon at the time hostilities began—ordered $1.5 million of relief supplies and food and, on 24 June, it appealed for $39 million to provide emergency aid to 175,000 Palestine refugees for six months. By the end of August, 2,750 tons of food, 116,000 blankets and $55,000 worth of medical supplies had been provided for needy refugees. The estimated cost of these and additional relief activities through the end of December was estimated at $21.5 million. The UNRWA Commissioner-General submitted a special report to the General Assembly in September on the Agency's emergency relief efforts in Lebanon.[7]

Implementation of a WFP emergency operation, approved by the Director-General of FAO on 15 June, began on 28 June with the distribution of family rations to about 55,000 displaced persons in West Beirut. WFP provided 22,319 tons of food valued at $9.44 million for 600,000 people.

A total of $660,000 for assistance to displaced and needy Lebanese in Lebanon and the Syrian Arab Republic was provided by UNHCR from June until the end of August. An initial $100,000 was used to purchase ambulances, and further allocations totalling $140,000 made it possible to distribute drugs and blankets, and to repair fishing boats. UNHCR distributed $2-million worth of clothes, kitchen utensils and blankets donated by the Spanish Government. It later contributed $215,000 for the care of displaced children, orphans and the aged. In October, UNHCR allocated an additional $1,750,000 from its Emergency Fund to be used for displaced persons in Lebanon.

A relief programme formulated by UNDRO, in which United Nations agencies and international voluntary organizations co-operated, included rubble clearance and sanitary installations in refugee camps, emergency repair of the drinking water supply system, medical assistance, emergency repair of housing and distribution of winter clothing. In October the Commission of the European Community contributed $8 million, covering half the programme's requirements. Officials of UNDRO helped to co-ordinate, supervise and execute the relief programme.

Emergency health supplies worth $100,000 were provided by the World Health Organization (WHO), together with $90,000 for financing medical staff as United Nations volunteers. A joint Lebanese Government/United Nations group headed by WHO prepared a $75-million programme for the repair of hospitals and health centres and the supply of vaccines and water purification products. The United Nations Educational, Scientific and Cultural Organization continued efforts to preserve the archaeological sites of Tyre, including the dispatch of a mission to the site in July.

In an October report to the Assembly on reconstruction and development assistance for Lebanon provided by the United Nations system,[3] the Secretary-General said that, as a result of the June 1982 Israeli invasion of Lebanon, the reconstruction and development work being carried out under the 1978 plan of the Lebanese Government Council for Development and Reconstruction had come to a halt. The programme would have to be reviewed and substantially revised, and external assistance would be required over a number of years.

In an oral report in October to the General Assembly's Second (Economic and Financial) Committee, the United Nations Co-ordinator of Assistance for the Reconstruction and Development of Lebanon, Iqbal A. Akhund, said that when the active fighting had stopped in August and emergency assistance needs had been met, attention had turned to rehabilitation of the water supply systems, power stations, schools, hospitals, roads and means of transport of Beirut and the cities of southern Lebanon, which had been extensively damaged. Public buildings and private housing had also been heavily damaged and some refugee camps had been razed. The sudden Israeli incursion into West Beirut on 15 September had inflicted fresh damage on the city, affecting some areas spared in the previous fighting. It was not known exactly how many people had been killed or wounded in the military operations throughout the country or had been evicted from their homes, but the Government had estimated that 750,000 people would need relief assistance for some time to come.

Because statistics were lacking, the Governing Council of the United Nations Development Programme (UNDP), on 18 June 1982,[1] deferred its determination of the indicative planning figure that was to have been used to project the level of UNDP assistance to Lebanon for the 1982-1986 development cycle. Referring to the country's difficult situation and its urgent need for assistance, the Council decided to consider the matter in 1983 with a view to increasing UNDP assistance.

Security Council and General Assembly action (June/July). Provisions on humanitarian assistance to Lebanon were included in several Security Council and General Assembly resolutions adopted after the outbreak of hostilities in June.

On 18 June,[15] the Security Council, referring to a report by the Secretary-General stating that UNIFIL had been endeavouring to extend protection and humanitarian assistance to the population of the area,[5] authorized the Force to carry out that interim task.

On 19 June,[16] the Council called on the parties to the conflict to take measures to alleviate suffering, in particular by facilitating the dispatch and distribution of aid. It appealed to Member States to continue to provide the most extensive humanitarian aid possible, and stressed the humanitarian responsibilities of the United Nations and its agencies, including UNRWA, towards civilian populations. It called on the parties not to hamper the exercise of those responsibilities and to assist in humanitarian efforts. It took note of the Secretary-General's measures to co-ordinate the activities of international agencies and requested that he make every effort to ensure the implementation of and compliance with the resolution and to report on those efforts to the Council as soon as possible. On 30 June, in pursuance of this resolution, the Secretary-General submitted an interim report on the humanitartian efforts of the United Nations system in Lebanon.[6]

On 26 June, in a resolution on aspects of the Palestine question and on the situation between Israel and Lebanon,[9] the General Assembly called on all States and international agencies and organizations to continue to provide the most extensive humanitarian aid possible to victims of the Israeli invasion of Lebanon. It requested the Secretary-General to delegate a high-level commission to investigate the extent of loss of human life and material damage and to report as soon as possible to the Assembly and the Council.

On 4 July,[17] the Council commended the efforts of the Secretary-General and the action of international agencies to alleviate civilian suffering and requested them to continue their efforts.

On 29 July,[18] the Council demanded that the Government of Israel lift immediately the blockade of Beirut to permit the dispatch of urgent supplies for civilians and allow the distribution of aid provided by United Nations agencies and by non-governmental organizations, particularly ICRC.

During this period, much of the debate in the Council was concerned with the plight of civilians in Lebanon. France stressed this aspect when introducing the resolution on humanitarian assistance which the Council adopted on 19 June; observing that the Council had not until then dealt with that tragic situation, France said it must ensure that civilians received large-scale and effective aid. Endorsing that concern, Japan and the United States announced specific commitments of funds to Lebanon. Israel said it welcomed co-operation with the Secretary-General in promoting genuine humanitarian efforts in Lebanon but it asked the Council to refrain from innuendoes and from attempts to abuse humanitarian concerns for political objectives.

Economic and Social Council action (July). By a resolution of 27 July,[8] the Economic and Social Council endorsed the Assembly resolution of 26 June and called on Governments to provide emergency assistance to the Palestinians in Lebanon. It urged the United Nations system to initiate and provide, in co-operation with the Palestine Liberation Organization (PLO), urgent humanitarian assistance to those Palestinians. It requested the Secretary-General to report to the Assembly at its 1982 regular session and to the Council in 1983 on implementation of the resolution. It also called on Israel to release detained civilians, to apply the Geneva Convention relative to the Protection of Civilian Persons in Time of War and to apply the Geneva Conventions to imprisoned combatants.

This action was taken by 48 votes to 1. The text was adopted with a change suggested by the Council President, specifying the sessions of the Assembly and the Council at which the Secretary-General was to report.

The Third (Programme and Co-ordination) Committee had approved the resolution on 21 July by 37 votes to 1. It was introduced by Algeria on behalf of the Group of 77, with China and the German Democratic Republic joining as sponsors.

Also on 27 July, the Council President expressed deep concern over the events in Lebanon. He appealed to the parties to the conflict to respect the rights of the civilian population and to alleviate suffering, in particular by expediting the dispatch and distribution of international humanitarian aid to West Beirut and other affected areas. He asked that essential supplies and services such as water and electricity be restored, and that all States intensify their efforts to provide humanitarian assistance.

The United States, explaining its negative vote, said the resolution dealt with political issues which were not the Council's concern, and that it disregarded parties other than Israel; also, United Nations agencies should not co-operate with PLO in providing assistance, as stipulated by the resolution, since that organization did not warrant the status of the Palestinian people's representative and the Lebanese Government was the appropriate body for channelling aid. Israel, addressing the Council as an observer, opposed the resolution, stating that it was a politically motivated text instigated by PLO, a terrorist group which had been instrumental in bringing about the devastation and disintegration of Lebanon; Israel had implemented an aid programme for the Lebanese to ensure that they had adequate housing and sufficient food, water and other basic needs.

Qatar responded that Israel, in speaking of its aid to the Lebanese people, had failed to mention the deaths and casualties its war machine had inflicted on them and on the Palestinians. The Libyan Arab Jamahiriya rejected allegations that PLO was a terrorist organization and said the real terrorists were those who had invaded Lebanon—a point also made by the Syrian Arab Republic. The PLO representative stated that the besieging Israeli army had deliberately cut off medicine, food, fuel and electricity from West Beirut, yet Israel had tried to convince the Council that its intention was to bring prosperity to Lebanon.

Australia, Austria and Norway, explaining their votes for the resolution, said they would have preferred the text to refer to all those affected, whether Palestinians or Lebanese; Australia added that there should be no formal recognition of PLO so long as it did not explicitly recognize the right of Israel to exist. Canada said the nature and extent of co-operation with PLO should be governed by the objective of providing emergency assistance to all innocent victims of the situation in Lebanon and should take account of practical requirements. Brazil explained its position on the provision concerning the application of the Geneva Conventions to captured combatants. The Byelorussian SSR expressed its support and that of the USSR for the resolution.

The report of the Secretary-General[4] submitted to the General Assembly in October as a follow-up to this resolution referred to other documents with information on the United Nations relief effort in Lebanon (see above) and also contained an Israeli statement on application of the Geneva Conventions in Lebanon.

General Assembly action (August-December). In a resolution of 19 August on the Palestine question and the situation in Lebanon,[10] the General Assembly again requested the Secretary-General to delegate a high-level commission to investigate and assess the extent of loss of human life and material damage and to report as soon as possible on the investigation to the Assembly and the Security Council.

In a resolution of 24 September following the massacre of Palestinian refugees and other civilians outside Beirut, the Assembly called on States and international organizations to continue to provide the most extensive humanitarian aid possible to the victims of the Israeli invasion of Lebanon.[11]

By a resolution of 17 December on assistance for the reconstruction and development of Lebanon,[14] the Assembly welcomed the Secretary-General's appeal for assistance to Lebanon and urged all Governments to contribute substantially. It commended the United Nations Co-ordinator of Assistance for the Reconstruction and Development of Lebanon and his staff for their efforts under the most adverse circumstances. It expressed appreciation for the humanitarian and emergency relief assistance provided by the United Nations system, ICRC, the League of Red Cross and Red Crescent Societies and other benevolent agencies. It requested the Secretary-General to continue efforts to mobilize assistance within the United Nations system to help the Government of Lebanon in its reconstruction and development efforts, and it called on the United Nations system to expand and intensify assistance programmes for Lebanon. It asked for progress reports from the Secretary-General in 1983 to the Economic and Social Council and the Assembly.

This action was taken without vote following similar approval in the Second Committee on 2 December. It was introduced by Jordan and sponsored by 43 nations.

On 16 December, in a resolution on the protection of Palestine refugees,[12] the Assembly called on Israel to allow the resumption of UNRWA health, medical, educational and social services to Palestinians in southern Lebanon refugee camps; requested UNRWA to co-ordinate those services with the Government of Lebanon; urged UNRWA to provide housing to Palestine refugees whose houses had been destroyed by the Israeli forces; and requested the UNRWA Commissioner-General, in consultation with the Government, to prepare a report on the damage to the Palestine refugees and their property and to the Agency's facilities, as well as those of other international bodies, as a result of the Israeli aggression.

In a resolution of 17 December on assistance to the Palestinians,[13] the Assembly referred to the severe damage to civilian Palestinians, including heavy loss of life, intolerable suffering and massive material destruction, resulting from the invasion of Lebanon, for which it condemned Israel. It called for humanitarian assistance from Governments and United Nations bodies to the Palestinian victims.

Voting against the 17 December resolution, Israel said the text ignored the Syrian invasion of Lebanon and the use of the civilian population by PLO as a human shield; Israel would continue to co-operate with United Nations agencies in providing aid to the civilians in Lebanon but would try to prevent the adoption of resolutions which merely hampered future assistance efforts to the Palestinians there and elsewhere.

Speaking for the European Community members, which voted in favour, Denmark said they would continue to contribute humanitarian assistance directly, through the Community and through United Nations institutions, each of which should determine for itself how and through what channels it could assist the Lebanese and Palestinians.

Lebanon declared that it would support all assistance efforts and make facilities available; however, its understanding was that all such assistance would be channelled through UNRWA under Lebanese supervision. Reaffirming its determination to rehabilitate the country, it recalled that it had been stressing since 1976 its pressing need for assistance to reconstruct the country's infrastructure and for its development programme. It was strange, Lebanon added, that at the height of the emergency assistance operations the Security Council had had to call on all parties to co-operate in facilitating the dispatch and distribution of aid, a responsibility that was normal for all parties to any armed conflict.

Decision (1982). [1]UNDP Council (report, E/1982/16/Rev.1): 82/16, 18 June.
Note. [2]UNICEF Executive Director, E/ICEF/Misc.400.
Reports. S-G, [3]A/37/508 & Add.1, [4]A/37/571, [5]S/15194/Add.2, [6]S/15267 & Corr.1; [7]UNRWA Commissioner-General, A/37/479.
Resolutions (1982). [8]ESC: 1982/48, 27 July, text following. GA: [9]ES-7/5, paras. 8 & 9, 26 June; [10]ES-7/6, para. 9, 19 Aug.; [11]ES-7/9, para. 8, 24 Sep.; [12]37/120 J, paras. 4-7, 16 Dec.; [13]37/134, 17 Dec.; [14]37/163, 17 Dec., text following. SC: [15]511(1982), para. 2, 18 June; [16]512(1982), 19 June; [17]513(1982), para. 3, 4 July; [18]515(1982), para. 1, 29 July.
Meeting records. ESC: E/1982/SR.48 (27 July). GA: 2nd Committee, A/C.2/37/SR.7, 27-30, *31*, 33, *42*, *44*, *46* (5 Oct.- 2 Dec.); plenary, A/37/PV.109 (17 Dec.).

Economic and Social Council resolution 1982/48

27 July 1982   Meeting 48   48-1

Approved by Third Committee (E/1982/93) by vote (37-1), 21 July (meeting 13); 3-nation draft (E/1982/C.3/L.7), orally amended by President in Council; agenda items 22 and 23.

Sponsors: Algeria (for Group of 77), China, German Democratic Republic.

Assistance to the Palestinian people

The Economic and Social Council,

Recalling General Assembly resolution ES-7/5 of 26 June 1982,

Recalling further Security Council resolution 512(1982) of 19 June 1982,

Expressing its deep alarm at the Israeli invasion of Lebanon, which claimed the lives of a very large number of civilian Palestinians,

Gravely concerned at the Israeli destruction in Lebanon of Palestinian camps and other areas heavily inhabited by civilian Palestinians, together with their social and economic structures,

Noting with deep concern the dire need of the Palestinians in Lebanon for urgent humanitarian assistance as a result of the Israeli invasion,

Referring to the humanitarian principles of the Geneva Convention relative to the Protection of Civilian Persons in Time of War, of 12 August 1949, and to the obligations arising from the regulations annexed to the Hague Conventions of 1907,

1. *Endorses* General Assembly resolution ES-7/5, in which the Assembly condemned Israel for its non-compliance with Security Council resolutions 508(1982) of 5 June 1982 and 509(1982) of 6 June 1982 and stressed its support for victims of the Israeli invasion of Lebanon, which inflicted severe damage on the civilian population, including the heavy loss of human lives and social and economic structures;

2. *Calls upon* all Governments to provide, as a matter of urgency, emergency assistance to the Palestinians in Lebanon;

3. *Urges* the relevant programmes, organizations, agencies and organs of the United Nations system to initiate and provide, in co-operation with the Palestine Liberation Organization, urgent humanitarian assistance to the Palestinians in Lebanon;

4.   *Calls upon* Israel to release civilians detained by the Israeli occupation army in Lebanon and to apply fully to the civilians the Geneva Convention relative to the Protection of Civilian Persons in Time of War;

5.   *Also calls upon* Israel to apply fully the Geneva Conventions to imprisoned combatants;

6.   *Requests* the Secretary-General to report to the General Assembly at its thirty-seventh session and to the Economic and Social Council at its second regular session of 1983 on the progress made in the implementation of the present resolution.

General Assembly resolution 37/163

17 December 1982   Meeting 109   Adopted without vote

Approved by Second Committee (A/37/702/Add.2) without vote, 2 December (meeting 46); 43-nation draft (A/C.2/37/L.67); agenda item 74 *(b)*.

Sponsors: Algeria, Australia, Austria, Bahrain, Bangladesh, Belgium, Brazil, Cyprus, Democratic Yemen, Ecuador, Ethiopia, France, India, Indonesia, Iraq, Ireland, Italy, Japan, Jordan, Kuwait, Liberia, Madagascar, Malaysia, Morocco, Nepal, Niger, Nigeria, Oman, Pakistan, Paraguay, Peru, Philippines, Qatar, Saudi Arabia, Senegal, Sierra Leone, Spain, Sudan, United Arab Emirates, United Republic of Cameroon, United States, Yemen, Yugoslavia.

Assistance for the reconstruction and development of Lebanon

The General Assembly,

Recalling its resolutions 33/146 of 20 December 1978, 34/135 of 14 December 1979, 35/85 of 5 December 1980 and 36/205 of 17 December 1981 on assistance for the reconstruction and development of Lebanon,

Recalling also Economic and Social Council resolution 1980/15 of 29 April 1980,

Deeply concerned about the heavy and tragic loss of life and the mass destruction of property as well as the extensive damage to the economic and social structures of Lebanon,

Taking into consideration the will and the determination of the Government of Lebanon to undertake a large-scale reconstruction and rehabilitation programme in the immediate future,

Affirming the urgent need for substantial international action to assist the Government of Lebanon in its efforts for reconstruction and development,

Taking note of the report of the Secretary-General and of the statement made by the United Nations Co-ordinator of Assistance for the Reconstruction and Development of Lebanon,

1.   *Expresses its appreciation* to the Secretary-General for his report;

2.   *Welcomes* the appeal of the Secretary-General for international assistance to Lebanon and urges all Governments to contribute substantially to this end;

3.   *Commends* the United Nations Co-ordinator of Assistance for the Reconstruction and Development of Lebanon and his staff for their valuable and relentless efforts in the discharge of their duties under the most adverse circumstances;

4.   *Expresses its appreciation* for the humanitarian and emergency relief assistance provided by the United Nations Children's Fund, the Food and Agriculture Organization of the United Nations, the World Food Programme, the Office of the United Nations Disaster Relief Co-ordinator, the United Nations High Commissioner for Refugees, the World Health Organization, the International Committee of the Red Cross, the League of Red Cross and Red Crescent Societies and other benevolent agencies, and for their prompt and effective response;

5.   *Requests* the Secretary-General to continue his intensive efforts to mobilize all possible assistance within the United Nations system to help the Government of Lebanon in its reconstruction and development efforts;

6.   *Calls upon* the organs, organizations and bodies of the United Nations system to expand and intensify programmes of assistance in response to the needs of Lebanon;

7.   *Requests* the Secretary-General to report to the Economic and Social Council at its first regular session of 1983 and to the General Assembly at its thirty-eighth session on the progress achieved in the implementation of the present resolution.

Chapter IV

International trade and finance

Contents

Related topics:

Transport. Industrial development: International trade aspects; Export-oriented industries. Regional economic and social activities—International trade and finance: Africa; Asia and the Pacific; Europe; Latin America; Western Asia. International economic law: International trade law.

For resolutions and decisions mentioned but not reproduced, refer to INDEX OF RESOLUTIONS AND DECISIONS.

Programme and finances of UNCTAD

The Trade and Development Board—the executive body of the United Nations Conference on Trade and Development (UNCTAD)—held two sessions in 1982, both at Geneva. Its twenty-fourth session was held in three parts, from 8 to 24 March, from 11 to 18 May and from 30 June to 2 July. The twenty-fifth session was held in two parts, from 6 to 23 September and from 19 to 28 October. The second and third parts of the year's first session were concerned mainly with preparations for the sixth session of UNCTAD, scheduled for 1983, while arrangements for UNCTAD activities relating to economic co-operation among developing countries (ECDC) were the sole subject of the October meetings (see Chapter I of this section).

The Board adopted three resolutions and 17 decisions during 1982. By the first of the resolutions, adopted in May, it recommended that the 1983 UNCTAD session be held in Yugoslavia. By the second, in September, it remitted to that session a proposal on trade among countries having different economic and social systems. By the third resolution, adopted in October, it agreed to procedures for UNCTAD activities on ECDC.

Two sessional committees of the Board met in March: Sessional Committee I from 8 to 18 March and Sessional Committee II from 8 to 19 March. The latter dealt solely with protectionism and structural adjustment. Two sessional committees also met from 6 to 16 September, when Sessional Committee II was concerned wholly with trade among countries having different economic and social systems.

The Board's Working Party on the Medium-term Plan and the Programme Budget held two sessions in 1982.

The Board's report for 1982[1] was considered by the General Assembly, which on 20 December adopted seven resolutions dealing with various aspects of the UNCTAD programme. In those resolutions, the Assembly called for special measures for island developing countries, endorsed arrangements for the 1983 session of UNCTAD, urged the signature and ratification of the Agreement Establishing the Common Fund for Commodities, decided to convene a conference on the registration of ships, approved the organization of a meeting on transport projects for Zaire, called for efforts to complete a code of conduct on technology transfer and approved meetings on the brain drain.

Report. [1]TDB, A/37/15, vols. I, II.
Publication. Trade and Development: An UNCTAD Review, No. 4, Winter 1982, Sales No. E.83.II.D.1.

Programme policy decisions

Programme evaluation

The Trade and Development Board's Working Party on the Medium-term Plan and the Programme Budget devoted the main part of its August/September 1982 session to a discussion of methods and procedures for evaluating the impact of UNCTAD programmes. It considered the internal evaluation systems used elsewhere in the United Nations, and heard differing views on whether it would be opportune to introduce new evaluation methods and on how such methods might be adapted to the particular circumstances and programmes of UNCTAD. Proposals by Group B (developed market economy) countries on principles and objectives of an evaluation system that would become an integral part of the UNCTAD management process were annexed to the Working Party's report.[2] The Working Party recommended on 3 September that it continue to examine this question in 1983, and requested a further report on the topic from the UNCTAD Secretary-General, bearing in mind the views expressed at the 1982 session.

The Working Party's recommendations were endorsed by the Trade and Development Board on 17 September.[1]

Reports. [1]TDB, A/37/15, vol. II; [2]Working Party on Medium-term Plan and Programme Budget, TD/B/928.

Technical co-operation

Total project expenditure incurred by UNCTAD in 1982 for technical co-operation activities amounted to $16,293,000, a decline of over $3 million from 1981[5] which corresponded to the general down-turn in technical co-operation resources of the United Nations system. Allocations from the United Nations Development Programme (UNDP), totalling $14,430,000, were the main source of funds.

The main aim of these activities was to strengthen the external sector of developing countries by: enhancing their participation in international trade negotiations; improving trade mechanisms, procedures and related supporting services; developing and strengthening institutional structures; and fostering collective self-reliance through economic co-operation among developing countries (ECDC). Support was provided for subregional integration movements, preferential trade areas, customs unions, commodity associations, the development of a global system of trade preferences among developing countries and the expansion of trade between developing countries and the socialist countries of Eastern Europe. One area receiving particular attention was a programme to develop a world-wide network of training institutions in maritime transport. The training needs of the least developed, land-locked and island developing countries were emphasized in these programmes.

In addition to these UNCTAD activities, the International Trade Centre continued to provide technical co-operation for trade promotion.

The Working Party on the Medium-term Plan and the Programme Budget, at its March session, continued a review of the technical co-operation activities of UNCTAD and their financing.[3] On 12 March, it asked for a document from UNDP outlining the procedures through which UNDP provided resources for UNCTAD technical assistance activities, and urged that a UNDP representative attend its sessions when a technical assistance–related item was scheduled for discussion. These recommendations were endorsed by the Trade and Development Board on 19 March.[1]

After hearing and discussing a statement by a representative of UNDP on its project approval procedures, the Working Party recommended on 3 September[4] that it perform its annual review of UNCTAD technical assistance activities at its 1983 session on the basis of a report to be prepared by the UNCTAD secretariat. The Trade and Development Board endorsed this recommendation on 17 September.[2]

Reports. TDB: [1]A/37/15, vol. I; [2]ibid., vol. II. Working Party on Medium-term Plan and Programme Budget: [3]TD/B/902, [4]TD/B/928.
Yearbook reference. [5]1981, p. 535.

Organizational questions

Preparations for the 1983 session of the Conference

In December 1982, on the recommendation of the Trade and Development Board, the General Assembly decided to convene the sixth session of UNCTAD at Belgrade, Yugoslavia, from 6 to 30 June 1983.

Trade and Development Board action. The recommendation to hold the session at Belgrade was made by the Trade and Development Board on 18 May 1982[7] after Gabon—citing cost and other factors—withdrew in March an offer to host the Conference which it had made in October 1981[8] and Yugoslavia extended an invitation. The Board further recommended that the session should have a selective agenda and action-oriented documents, and should be organized to ensure the attendance of ministers and other high-level policy-makers and to permit all delegations to contribute effectively to decision-making. On 30 June, the Board recommended the dates of 6 to 30 June 1983, preceded by a meeting of senior officials on 2 and 3 June.[1]

The Board convened the second and third parts of its twenty-fourth session (11-18 May and 30 June–2 July) to consider the provisional agenda for the 1983 UNCTAD session. On 18 May 1982, it authorized its President to consult on the matter between the second and third parts. It also annexed to its report to the General Assembly[5] proposals for the agenda made by the UNCTAD Secretary-General, the Group of 77 developing countries, Group B (developed market economies) and Group D (centrally planned economies).

On 2 July, following unsuccessful consultations aimed at a consensus, the Board adopted a provisional agenda for the Conference by a roll-call vote of 89 to 2 (Israel, United States).[2] Items to be covered included the world economic situation with special emphasis on development, commodity issues, issues related to international trade in goods and services, and financial and monetary issues. Also to be discussed was progress in implementing the Substantial New Programme of Action for the 1980s for the Least Developed Countries and UNCTAD activities in regard to technology, shipping, land-locked and island developing countries, trade relations among countries having different economic and social systems, ECDC, assistance to national liberation movements and institutional matters.

On 17 September, the Board approved organizational arrangements for the session and commended them to the pre-Conference meeting of senior officials and to the Conference itself, subject to further decisions by the Board in 1983.[3] These arrangements distributed the items on the provisional agenda among plenary meetings and four main committees, each open to all UNCTAD members.

General Assembly action. On 20 December 1982,[6] as recommended by the Board, the General Assembly decided without vote to convene the sixth session of UNCTAD at Belgrade from 6 to 30 June 1983, preceded by a two-day meeting of senior officials. Taking note of the Board's adoption of a provisional agenda, the Assembly endorsed its May resolution and September decision on organizational arrangements. Emphasized in the Assembly resolution was the importance of the session as an opportunity to review world development and its impact on the trade and development of developing countries, at a time when those countries in particular faced grave economic problems. Countries were urged to work for a meaningful and action-oriented outcome that would contribute to overcoming the difficulties facing the world economy, to the economic development of developing countries and to attaining a new international economic order. The Assembly also expressed deep concern at the economic crisis.

The resolution had been recommended by the Second (Economic and Financial) Committee without vote on 13 December. It was submitted by a Committee Vice-Chairman following informal consultations on a revised draft introduced by Bangladesh on behalf of the Group of 77,[4] which was withdrawn in the light of the adoption of the Vice-Chairman's draft.

Three paragraphs of the original draft were changed in the Vice-Chairman's version. In paragraph 7, the word "aggravation" was removed from an expression of concern at the aggravation of the serious crisis facing the world economy. In paragraph 8, the Conference was described as a major opportunity for a "comprehensive and interrelated" rather than an "integrated" review of world development. In paragraph 9, on the goals of the Conference, a reference to "the establishment of the new international economic order" was changed to "the attainment of a new international economic order".

Decisions (1982). TDB: [1]255(XXIV), 30 June; [2]256(XXIV), 2 July; [3]258(XXV), 17 Sep.
Draft resolution withdrawn. [4]Bangladesh, for Group of 77, A/C.2/37/L.73/Rev.1.
Report. [5]TDB, A/37/15, vols. I, II.
Resolutions (1982). [6]GA: 37/208, 20 Dec., text following. [7]TDB: 253(XXIV), 18 May.
Yearbook reference. [8]1981, p. 537.
Meeting records. GA: 2nd Committee, A/C.2/37/SR.3, 5-8, 20-26, 33, 40, *43, 48* (28 Sep.–13 Dec.); plenary, A/37/PV.113 (20 Dec.).

General Assembly resolution 37/208

20 December 1982   Meeting 113   Adopted without vote

Approved by Second Committee (A/37/680/Add.2) without vote, 13 December (meeting 48); draft by Vice-Chairman (A/C.2/37/L.126), based on informal consultations on draft by Bangladesh, for Group of 77 (A/C.2/37/L.73/Rev.1); agenda item 71 *(c)*.

Sixth session of the United Nations Conference on Trade and Development

The General Assembly,

Recalling its resolutions 1995(XIX) of 30 December 1964 on the establishment of the United Nations Conference on Trade and Development as an organ of the General Assembly, as amended, 3201(S-VI) and 3202(S-VI) of 1 May 1974, containing the Declaration and the Programme of Action on the Establishment of a New International Economic Order, 3281(XXIX) of 12 December 1974, containing the Charter of Economic Rights and Duties of States, 3362(S-VII) of 16 September 1975 on development and international economic co-operation and 35/56 of 5 December 1980, the annex to which contains the International Development Strategy for the Third United Nations Development Decade,

Recalling also its resolutions 34/196 of 19 December 1979 on the report of the United Nations Conference on Trade and Development on its fifth session and 36/142 of 16 December 1981 on the sixth session of the Conference,

Recalling further Trade and Development Board decision 237(XXIII) of 8 October 1981, by which the Board endorsed the decision taken by the Latin American countries to hold the seventh session of the Conference in one of those countries on the understanding that the final decision on the venue in Latin America would be taken at the right time and in the right place, and having noted with interest the desire of Cuba to act as host to the seventh session of the Conference,

Noting Trade and Development Board resolution 253(XXIV) of 18 May 1982 and decision 255(XXIV) of 30 June 1982, in which the Board recommended that the sixth session of the Conference should be held at Belgrade from 6 to 30 June 1983 and should be preceded by a meeting of senior officials at Belgrade on 2 and 3 June 1983,

Bearing in mind its resolution 31/140 of 17 December 1976 on the pattern of conferences,

Taking note of the report of the Trade and Development Board on its twenty-fourth session and on the first and second parts of its twenty-fifth session,

Expressing its appreciation to the Government of Gabon for its efforts to act as host to the sixth session of the United Nations Conference on Trade and Development and recognizing the reasons for which it was not in a position to do so,

1. *Welcomes with appreciation* the offer of the Government of Yugoslavia to act as host to the sixth session of the United Nations Conference on Trade and Development at Belgrade;

2. *Decides* to convene the sixth session of the United Nations Conference on Trade and Development at Belgrade from 6 to 30 June 1983, to be preceded by a two-day meeting of senior officials at Belgrade on 2 and 3 June 1983;

3. *Takes note* of the adoption by the Trade and Development Board at its twenty-fourth session of the provisional agenda for the sixth session of the United Nations Conference on Trade and Development;

4. *Endorses* Trade and Development Board resolution 253(XXIV) that the sixth session of the United Nations Conference on Trade and Development should be so organized as to ensure the attendance of ministers and other high-level policy-makers and to permit all delegations to contribute effectively to its decision-making process;

5. *Endorses* Trade and Development Board decision 258(XXV) of 17 September 1982 on the organization of the sixth session of the United Nations Conference on Trade and Development;

6. *Requests* the Secretary-General of the United Nations Conference on Trade and Development to make all necessary arrangements for the Conference, to submit to the Conference all relevant documentation as far in advance of the six weeks' rule as possible and to arrange for the necessary staff facilities and services that it will require, including the provision of summary records for plenary meetings of the Conference in accordance with General Assembly resolution 37/14 C of 16 November 1982;

7. *Expresses its deepest concern* at the serious crisis facing the world economy and, in particular, its grave negative impact on the development process of the developing countries;

8. *Emphasizes* the particular importance of the sixth session of the United Nations Conference on Trade and Development as a major opportunity to review, in a comprehensive and interrelated manner, world development and its impact on the trade and development of developing countries, at a time when the developing countries in particular continue to face grave economic problems;

9. *Urges* all countries, bearing in mind the particular contribution developed countries can make, to work towards ensuring a positive, constructive, meaningful and action-oriented outcome, at the sixth session of the United Nations Conference on Trade and Development, on the important issues concerning trade, development and related problems, taking fully into account their interrelationship, and thus contribute effectively to the overcoming of the grave difficulties facing the world economy, to the economic development of developing countries and to the attainment of a new international economic order.

Effectiveness of the Working Party on the Medium-term Plan and the Programme Budget

On 12 March 1982, the Working Party on the Medium-term Plan and the Programme Budget of the Trade and Development Board,[2] recognizing the need to formulate agreed conclusions or recommendations on items under its consideration for action by the Board, recommended that the Working Party, at its session following the sixth UNCTAD session in 1983, examine the main thrusts of the work programme decided upon at the Conference. It also recommended that discussions of the UNCTAD medium-term plan and programme budget be focused on substance rather than procedure.

The recommendations were made in response to a March 1981 request by the Board, in a resolution on ways of rationalizing UNCTAD machinery,[4] for an examination of ways of improving the Working Party's effectiveness. The Board endorsed the Working Party's recommendations on 19 March 1982.[1]

The Working Party considered two other main questions during 1982: programme evaluation and UNCTAD technical co-operation activities. The second of these was examined at both its fifth session, from 1 to 12 March, and its sixth session, from 30 August to 3 September. At both sessions, which were held at Geneva, it also discussed the frequency and duration of its meetings, deciding in September to continue consideration of the issue in 1983.[3]

Reports. [1]TDB, A/37/15, vol. I; Working Party, [2]TD/B/902, [3]TD/B/928.
Yearbook reference. [4]1981, p. 536.

Conferences and meetings

Calendar of UNCTAD meetings for 1982-1983

On 19 March 1982, the Trade and Development Board approved a calendar of meetings for the remainder of 1982 and a tentative schedule for 1983.[1]

On 18 May 1982, it made three adjustments to these lists, convening the Board for a third part of its twenty-fourth session to consider arrangements for the 1983 UNCTAD session, scheduling a further session of the Intergovernmental Preparatory Group on Conditions for Registration of Ships and postponing until 1983 a session of the Working Group on International Shipping Legislation.[2] The Board made additional changes to the 1982 calendar on 2 July, adding meetings on jute, tea, tropical timber and the draft code of conduct on technology transfer.[3] On 17 September, the Board approved a revised calendar for the remainder of 1982, including a second part of its twenty-fifth session in October to consider UNCTAD activities on economic co-operation among developing countries.[4] Finally, on 28 October, the Board approved a calendar for the remainder of 1982 and for 1983, and tentative schedules for 1984-1985.[5]

Decisions (1982). TDB (report, A/37/15, vols. I, II): [1]251(XXIV), 19 Mar.; [2]254(XXIV), 18 May; [3]257(XXIV), 2 July; [4]263(XXV), 17 Sep.; [5]266(XXV), 28 Oct.

Conference and meeting services

On 9 March 1982, the Trade and Development Board requested that the supplementary conference services provided to UNCTAD by the United Nations Office at Geneva should be continued, to the extent possible within existing resources.[1] These services were instituted in 1980 to improve the availability of in-session documentation for UNCTAD meetings, especially those held at night.

Report. [1]TDB, A/37/15, vol. I.

Report of the Trade and Development Board

In response to a General Assembly request of December 1981 that the reports of its subsidiary bodies should be no longer than 32 pages,[4] the UNCTAD Trade and Development Board, on 17 September 1982,[2] approved revised guidelines for its annual report to the Assembly, to take effect from 1983 for an experimental two-year period. According to these guidelines, the reports, prepared separately on each session, were to include an introduction, the Board's resolutions and decisions, and a possible second part containing additional material the Board might specifically decide to transmit to the Assembly. Annexes would normally include the session's agenda, statements of the financial implications of the Board's decisions, and draft resolutions. A full version of the report would be issued as part of the Board's official records. (Prior to 1983 the reports to the Assembly also contained summaries of the discussion of each item.)

On 30 July 1982,[1] the Economic and Social Council authorized the Secretary-General to transmit the Board's 1982 report[3] directly to the Assembly.

Decisions (1982). [1]ESC: 1982/178, para. *(a)*, 30 July. [2]TDB: 259(XXV), 17 Sep.
Report. [3]TDB, A/37/15, vols. I, II.
Resolution. [4]GA: 36/117 A, 10 Dec. 1981 (YUN 1981, p. 1364).

International trade

Trade policy

Developing countries at the start of the 1980s were faced with a bleak international trade environment, marked by steep falls in the prices of their exports, according to the *Trade and Development Report, 1982*[1]—the annual survey by the UNCTAD secretariat of world economic conditions and trends with particular reference to the development prospects of developing countries. Their trade position, as measured by a combined index of the prices of their non-oil primary commodities, expressed in special drawing rights and deflated by the unit value of manufactured exports from the developed market-economy countries, deteriorated at an annual rate of more than 19 per cent between October 1980 and March 1982. In March 1982 the deflated index stood at its lowest level since UNCTAD began compiling the data, and the secretariat predicted that the prices of primary commodity exports would deteriorate further relative to those of manufactured exports during 1982.

According to UNCTAD secretariat estimates in this report, total world exports declined in volume in 1981, for the first time since 1975. While this was mainly due to a steep drop in petroleum trade, a deceleration in the volume growth of manufactured exports to 2.2 per cent in 1981 from rates exceeding 5 per cent during each of the preceding three years contributed to the poor overall performance.

Publication. [1] *Trade and Development Report, 1982* (UNC-TAD/TDR/2/Rev.1), Sales No. E.82.II.D.12.
Other publication. Trends in World Production and Trade (TD/B/887/Rev.1), Sales No. E.82.II.D.13.

Protectionism and structural adjustment

The Trade and Development Board conducted in March 1982 its first annual review of protectionism and structural adjustment. With the aid of factual and analytical studies by the UNCTAD secretariat, Board members discussed various forms of trade restrictions and other actions by Governments to adjust to new patterns of production and trade. Arrangements for the annual review had been agreed upon by the Board in March 1981.[9]

The principal UNCTAD secretariat report, on protectionism and structural adjustment in the world economy,[5] pointed out that the efficient functioning of the international economy required a continuous process of structural adjustment and that the need to adjust was likely to become greater in the 1980s. However, many countries, and developed market-economy countries in particular, had attempted to limit the social costs of such change by *ad hoc* protectionist measures which did not serve the long-run interests of either importing or exporting countries. The main characteristics of current protectionism appeared to be: a weakening of the unconditional most-favoured-nation principle through the tendency to negotiate bilateral restraint arrangements outside the multilateral rules and principles for international trade, thereby involving discrimination between exporters; a preference for flexible over fixed measures; and increased government involvement in the activities of commercial enterprises, including subsidization.

The report suggested several steps to counter such trends. To make the world economy more efficient, countries should allow increasing access to markets and be willing to restructure domestic economies in line with comparative advantage as revealed by trade flows. In the interest of equity, the brunt of the protectionism inflicted by countries reluctant or unable to adjust to structural changes should not be borne by the weaker members of the international system. As an alternative to protection, countries could employ adjustment assistance measures such as subsidies to facilitate the relocation

of labour. More information should be made available about existing trade restrictions, so as to render the international trade system more transparent.

The second secretariat report described some results of UNCTAD studies on protectionism and structural adjustment in the agricultural and other commodity sectors (see below).

On 19 March 1982, following its discussion, the Trade and Development Board adopted a set of agreed conclusions on protectionism and structural adjustment, indicating which issues it should deal with in its 1983 review and providing guidance to the secretariat in the preparation of documents for that review.[2] It stated that all relevant factors should be examined, and that the reports should present up-to-date statistics and give consistent coverage to all countries, groups of countries and sectors; in-depth analyses of policies should cover agriculture and services, and not be limited to manufactures; the Board should examine steps for securing transparency regarding international trade policies as a basis for evaluating the effectiveness of such steps and suggesting ways of increasing their effectiveness; and the Board's review should also address recommendations for solutions.

The Board was unable to reach agreement on how to deal with an earlier secretariat study on protectionism in relation to air transport, an issue which it took up in March separately from the main item on protectionism.

A major part of the *Trade and Development Report, 1982*[6] was devoted to structural changes in the world economy. It reviewed the meaning and relevance of structural change, the impact of industrialization and economic growth, patterns of demand for food and raw materials, structural change in manufacturing industries, structural change and trade in manufactures, selected issues involving levels of activity and trade, and the implications of recent developments in energy.

Another warning of the dangers of increasing protectionism was voiced by the Committee for Development Planning in April.[7] It cited the Multifibre Arrangement as an example of an agreement that sharply limited the market access of producers in developing countries. It added that protectionist pressures had caused increasingly serious disputes among large industrial countries and noted that a substantial share of Japanese exports was subject to quantitative restrictions. A protectionist surge, the Committee stated, would transmit contraction and unemployment throughout the world and further obstruct the growth of developing countries' capacity to service their external debts.

General Assembly action. On 20 December 1982, the General Assembly decided without vote to take no action on a draft resolution on protectionism and structural adjustment submitted on behalf of the Group of 77,[4] and to consider the question again in 1983 in the light of the outcome of the sixth UNCTAD session.[1]

The decision was recommended by the Second (Economic and Financial) Committee without vote on 13 December, on an oral proposal by the Chairman based on a suggestion by Bangladesh, speaking for the Group of 77. The draft resolution, originally submitted in 1980[8] and revised in 1981,[10] was annexed to a December 1981 decision by which the Assembly referred the text to its 1982 session.[3] The draft resolution, addressed mainly to developed countries, would have the Assembly urge them to limit protectionist policies and facilitate measures to increase the share of developing countries in international trade. A table containing suggestions by some developed countries for changes in the draft had also been transmitted to the 1982 Assembly session.

Decisions (1982). [1]GA: 37/441, 20 Dec., text following. [2]TDB (report, A/37/15, vol. I): 250(XXIV), 19 Mar.
Decision (prior). [3]GA: 36/429, 16 Dec. 1981 (YUN 1981, p. 544).
Note. [4]Secretariat, reproducing draft resolution, A/C.2/37/L.4.
Publications. [5]Protectionism and Structural Adjustment in the World Economy (TD/B/888/Rev.1), Sales No. E.82.II.D.14; [6]Trade and Development Report, 1982 (UNCTAD/TDR/2/Rev.1), Sales No. E.82.II.D.12.
Report. [7]CDP, E/1982/15.
Yearbook references. [8]1980, p. 627; 1981, [9]p. 541, [10]p. 542.
Meeting records. GA: 2nd Committee, A/C.2/37/SR.3, 5-8, 20-26, 33, 40, 48 (28 Sep.–13 Dec.); plenary, A/37/PV.113 (20 Dec.).

General Assembly decision 37/441

Adopted without vote

Approved by Second Committee (A/37/680/Add.2) without vote, 13 December (meeting 48); oral proposal by Chairman on suggestion by Bangladesh for Group of 77; agenda item 71 (c).

Protectionism and structural adjustment

At its 113th plenary meeting, on 20 December 1982, the General Assembly, on the recommendation of the Second Committee, decided to take no action on the draft resolution on protectionism and structural adjustment and to return to the consideration of this question at its thirty-eighth session, in the light of the outcome of the sixth session of the United Nations Conference on Trade and Development.

Trade negotiations

Multilateral trade negotiations

The Trade and Development Board continued in March and September 1982 its discussion of multilateral trade negotiations, with particular reference to the implementation of agreements reached in 1979 at the Tokyo Round of negotiations conducted by the General Agreement on Tariffs and Trade (GATT).[3]

At the start of the March discussion, the Director of the Manufactures Division, addressing Sessional Committee I of the Board on behalf of the UNCTAD Secretary-General, said that, through its analysis of the results of the multilateral trade negotiations, the UNCTAD secretariat had concluded that there were serious contradictions in the current system, calling into question its efficacy as a framework for international trade relations in the 1980s and 1990s. The first step towards a more universal system could be achieved through mutually acceptable principles and practices for trade among developed market-economy countries, developing countries and centrally planned economy countries, as well as within those groups.

In September, the Director stated that international trade relations had been consistently moving in the direction of managed trade, achieved through a series of pragmatic decisions rather than under internationally agreed principles. An examination was needed to determine whether that was an irresistible move, in which case the logical next step would be to create a new and equitable framework within which trade management could take place, or whether it was possible to return to the tariff-based GATT system.

At the close of discussion at each session, on 19 March[1] and 17 September,[2] the Board took note of the statements by the Director of the Manufactures Division and decided to remit the question of multilateral trade negotiations to the following session, together with a draft resolution submitted in October 1981 on behalf of the Group of 77 calling for an annual Board review of developments in the international trading system.[4]

Decisions (1982). TDB (report, A/37/15, vols. I, II): [1]248(XXIV), 19 Mar.; [2]260(XXV), 17 Sep.
Yearbook references. [3]1979, p. 1328; [4]1981, p. 539.
Publication. Assessment of the Results of the Multilateral Trade Negotiations (TD/B/778/Rev.1), Sales No. E.82.II.D.1.

Trade preferences

The Trade and Development Board's Special Committee on Preferences, meeting at Geneva in its eleventh session from 3 to 11 May 1982,[1] conducted its seventh periodic review of the operation and effects of the generalized system of preferences (GSP), but did not reach agreement on the conclusions to be drawn. Also in connection with GSP, the Committee adopted the report of its Working Group on Rules of Origin, which contained a new text for explanatory notes on the rules. The Board took note of the Committee's report on 17 September.[2]

Arrangements for continued work on a proposed global system of trade preferences among developing countries were approved by the Board in October.

Reports. [1]Committee on Preferences, TD/B/906; [2]TDB, A/37/15, vol. II.

Generalized system of preferences

Market access for developing countries had improved through GSP and, in terms of current value, trade in products covered by the scheme had more than doubled between 1976 and 1980, according to a report on the system's implementation[2] prepared by the UNCTAD secretariat for the seventh periodic review by the Special Committee on Preferences. Imports under GSP by the members of the Organisation for Economic Co-operation and Development and two socialist preference-giving countries had been of the order of $27 billion in 1980, compared with $12 billion in 1976.

The number of preference-granting countries remained at 25, of which 20 were developed market-economy countries (the 10 members of the European Economic Community plus Australia, Austria, Canada, Finland, Japan, New Zealand, Norway, Sweden, Switzerland and the United States) and five were from Eastern Europe (Bulgaria, Czechoslovakia, Hungary, Poland and the USSR). Each national scheme under the 11-year-old GSP established preferential tariffs for selected products imported from specified beneficiaries among the developing countries.

Since the previous review in 1981,[3] several preference-giving countries had extended or improved their schemes through additional beneficiary lists, expanded coverage and deeper tariff cuts, and the least developed countries continued to receive special advantages, the report stated. However, restrictive measures applied in some schemes represented drawbacks to GSP and promoted the risk of emulation by other preference-giving countries and of spreading to other areas of international economic relations. An example was the application by the United States of graduation measures which had resulted in the exclusion from preferential treatment of some $450 million in trade from beneficiaries regarded as competitive. Such differentiation among developing countries in the context of GSP was found to penalize successful exporters that were seen as a threat to producers in preference-giving countries.

The amount of trade carried on under GSP represented only one quarter of the preference-giving countries' dutiable imports from beneficiaries, the report noted. Thus, there was considerable scope for improvement in the system through expansion of product coverage, removal of limitations and competitive need exclusions under some schemes, and simplification and harmonization of rules of origin.

The Committee considered a draft resolution on the question submitted on behalf of the Group of 77, which reflected the feelings of preference-receiving countries and called for fundamental changes in the system, including the elimination of restrictive and discriminatory features, particularly measures of graduation. The Committee reached no agreement on the draft but annexed it to its report to the Board.[1]

Reports. [1]Committee on Preferences, TD/B/906; [2]UNCTAD secretariat, TD/B/C.5/81 & Corr.1,2. *Yearbook reference.* [3]1981, p. 546.

Rules of origin

At its ninth session, held at Geneva from 28 to 30 April 1982, the Working Group on Rules of Origin of the Special Committee on Preferences continued work on harmonization and simplification of rules of origin, used to ensure that preferential tariff treatment under GSP was given only to goods originating in preference-receiving countries.[1]

To improve the explanatory notes on the back of the certificate of origin known as Form A—a customs document filled out by exporters of goods moving in international trade—the Working Group, on 30 April, adopted a revised version of the notes prepared by a Technical Group it had established on 28 April. The text, annexed to the Working Group's report, consisted of a short description of the origin requirements and instructions on how to complete the form. In addition to this text, to be printed on the back of Form A, the UNCTAD secretariat would prepare, update and distribute an information note containing a condensed version of the rules of origin, which could be printed in the language of the exporting country. The Working Group agreed that the notes should be used as soon as possible but that use of the existing Form A would be permitted until stocks were exhausted.

The Working Group's report was adopted by the Special Committee on Preferences on 6 May.

Report. [1]Working Group, TD/B/C.5/83.

Technical co-operation

Technical assistance to help developing countries make optimum use of the benefits offered under GSP continued to be provided in 1982 under a joint project of UNCTAD and the United Nations Development Programme. Advisory missions or consultations on the operations of GSP, the organization of training activities and trade matters related to various GSP schemes were sent to five preference-receiving countries—Chile, Cuba, Ecuador, Mexico and Peru. Seminars or workshops were conducted in Cuba, Ecuador, Pakistan, Peru and the Philippines. Seminars were conducted jointly with regional GSP projects for the Association of South-East Asian Nations (Manila, Philippines, 12-14 July) and for Asia and the Pacific (Bangkok, Thailand, 22-24 November). A seminar was also conducted for Costa Rica, the Dominican Republic, Haiti and Panama (San José, Costa Rica, December).

A report on technical co-operation activities in 1981 relating to GSP was submitted in February 1982 to the Special Committee on Preferences.[1]

Report. [1]UNCTAD secretariat, TD/B/C.5/82 & Corr.1.

Global system of trade preferences among developing countries

On 8 October 1982, the Ministers for Foreign Affairs of the States members of the Group of 77 adopted a Ministerial Declaration on the Global

System of Trade Preferences (GSTP) among Developing Countries. The Declaration was transmitted to the Secretary-General in a letter of 11
October from Algeria on behalf of the Group of
77.[1] In it the Ministers proclaimed their decision
to begin negotiations on GSTP and established a
negotiating committee which was to hold its opening meeting before 30 April 1983 and conclude its
first phase of negotiations by 1985. The committee would be open to developing countries members of the Group of 77 and to subregional,
regional and interregional groupings of developing countries. The UNCTAD secretariat was requested to provide support to the committee.

On 28 October,[2] the Trade and Development
Board asked the UNCTAD Secretary-General to
provide the necessary support, from within existing budgetary resources, for a meeting at UNCTAD
headquarters (Geneva) in April 1983 to enable the
developing countries participating in the GSTP
negotiations to define the scope and extent of the
support they would request from UNCTAD. The
Board also agreed to convene the third session of
the Committee on Economic Co-operation among
Developing Countries (ECDC) immediately after
the sixth UNCTAD session in June 1983 with a view
to making recommendations to the Board on the
nature, extent and terms of UNCTAD support for
the negotiations. This action was taken in a resolution on UNCTAD work in relation to ECDC (see
Chapter I of this section).

Letter. [1]Algeria, 11 Oct., annexing Declaration by Group of
    77 Foreign Ministers, A/37/544.
Resolution (1982). [2]TDB (report, A/37/15, vol. II):
    264(XXV), sect. B, 28 Oct.

Trade among countries having
different economic and social systems

The Trade and Development Board decided, on
17 September 1982,[3] to remit to the sixth UNCTAD
session in 1983 the informal text of a draft resolution calling for further expansion of East-West
trade and trade between developing countries and
the socialist countries of Eastern Europe. The
Board noted that its efforts to reach agreement on
the basis of the informal text annexed to an October 1981 Board resolution requesting continued
consideration of the question[4] had not resulted in
agreement.

The Chairman of the Board's Sessional Committee II reported that, by the Committee's closing meeting on 16 September 1982, five bilateral
consultations on questions of trade and economic
relations had taken place within UNCTAD between
one Eastern European socialist country and five
developing countries.[1]

A study by the UNCTAD secretariat[2] issued in
July 1982 and reviewed by the Board in connection with this question concluded that, in spite of

the worsening situation in world markets in 1981,
trade between countries having different economic
and social systems continued to progress. Trade
between developing countries and the socialist
countries of Eastern Europe had increased by 20.5
per cent, with exports to developing countries up
by 23.3 per cent and imports from them up by 17.3
per cent. However, imports by Poland from developing countries, which had previously
registered the highest growth rate, recorded a 33
per cent decrease in 1981. Further progress in economic co-operation between the two groups had
been generated by various agreements and
projects. Socialist countries were reported to enter
each year into about 100 intergovernmental agreements with developing countries and there were
nearly 6,400 projects shared by the two groups,
mainly in technical co-operation.

Trade between developed market-economy
countries and socialist countries (East-West trade)
had increased about 4 per cent in value, the report
said, in contrast to increases of 18 per cent in 1980
and 28 per cent in 1979. However, its share in the
overall trade turnover of the socialist countries of
Eastern Europe had diminished. The development
of that trade had been slowed by restrictive policies, adopted primarily by the United States, and
by increased application of discriminatory measures against the socialist countries. While trade
had been adversely affected by the United States
embargo on the export of various commodities and
high technology products to the socialist countries,
trade between the socialist countries and France,
Canada, Australia and some other Western countries was actively developing, and measures had
been taken by various partners in East-West trade
to expand co-operation and to strengthen the institutional basis of their economic relations.

Reports. [1]TDB, A/37/15, vol. II; [2]UNCTAD secretariat,
    TD/B/912 & Add.1 & Add.1/Corr.1.
Resolution (1982). [3]TDB: 262(XXV), 17 Sep.
Yearbook reference. [4]1981, p. 541.

Technical co-operation

The United Nations Development Programme
(UNDP)/UNCTAD Comprehensive Programme of
Technical Assistance to develop trade and economic relations between the socialist countries of
Eastern Europe and developing countries was
completed in December 1982. The Programme,
started in 1979 in response to a 1976 UNCTAD
resolution,[1] covered group training, advisory services and information dissemination. More than
250 officials and representatives of the business
sector in 78 developing countries participated in
interregional and regional training events during
the Programme, including an interregional workshop for trade representatives of developing coun-

tries accredited to the USSR (Moscow, June/July 1982) and a second regional seminar for African countries (Moscow and Sofia, Bulgaria, October). In addition, more than 350 officials from economic ministries and business organizations participated in national seminars in five developing countries, including India, Nicaragua and Peru in 1982.

UNDP, which had contributed $1.47 million to the Programme, was unable to continue financing it beyond 1982 due to financial constraints. Accordingly, the UNCTAD secretariat sought authority to continue activities in this sphere from its share of the United Nations regular budget.

Yearbook reference. [1]1976, p. 400.

Trade promotion and facilitation

Several United Nations bodies continued work in 1982 to help developing countries promote their exports and to facilitate the movement of goods in international commerce by harmonizing procedures, standardizing documents, and developing new data processing and communication methods for exports, imports and transit. The main originator of technical co-operation projects in this area was the International Trade Centre (see below). An UNCTAD group considered ways of eliminating restrictive business practices as barriers to trade flows and another studied ways of making export credit insurance more readily available. The United Nations Industrial Development Organization (UNIDO) continued its co-operative work with UNCTAD in regard to the international trade aspects of industrial co-operation and UNIDO technical co-operation activities helped promote export-oriented industries (see Chapter VI of this section).

International Trade Centre

During 1982, the International Trade Centre (ITC) at Geneva, under the joint sponsorship of UNCTAD and the General Agreement on Tariffs and Trade (GATT), continued its technical co-operation activities, serving as the focal point for United Nations assistance to developing countries in the formulation and implementation of trade promotion programmes.[1] A modest increase in activities in some regions and programmes was recorded by ITC in spite of financial constraints affecting most voluntarily financed United Nations development assistance activities. Project implementation continued to fall short of the target set in the Centre's medium-term programme for 1981-1983.

Programme implementation expanded slightly in Africa (16 country and 5 regional projects), maintained its momentum in Asia and the Pacific (23 country and 9 regional projects) and increased slightly in value in Latin America (10 country and 12 regional projects). Activities in Europe, the Mediterranean and the Middle East were adversely influenced by a scarcity of resources for some projects nearing completion, constraints hampering some programmed activities and delays in launching new projects.

Approximately 35.1 per cent of the ITC programme was devoted to export market development, 20.1 per cent to manpower development for trade promotion, 15 per cent to strengthening national trade promotion institutions, 15 per cent to specialized national trade promotion services, 5.6 per cent to multinational trade promotion, 3.9 per cent to import operations and techniques, 2.2 per cent to the special programme of technical co-operation with the least developed countries, 2 per cent to technical co-operation with national chambers of commerce and 1.1 per cent to trade promotion oriented to rural development.

Among ITC activities in 1982 for export market development were the following: A market news service for horticultural products, operational for Africa in 1981, was expanded in July 1982 to cover more regions and products. The Centre dealt with about 1,200 requests for special trade information, up 9 per cent over 1981. It added about 8,000 items to its information files by scanning periodicals and other materials, and produced nine monographs on trade channels. Consultancy services on trade statistics were provided to 14 developing countries. Thirty-five countries and 30 product groups were selected for an interregional project, financed by the United Nations Development Programme (UNDP) and begun in 1982, to collect and computerize information on importers in developing countries. A full-scale supply and demand survey project began in September with the aim of solving specific interregional trade problems between developing countries.

In the area of specialized national trade promotion services, a course was held for packaging designers from Mexico and Cuba (Mexico City, September) and a one-day workshop on export packaging took place (Macao, May). In-service training at ITC was given to 14 national trade promotion officials. The second Foundation Course on National Trade Information Services was held (Geneva, 15 March-14 May) for 20 participants.

With regard to multinational trade promotion, ITC co-operated with the International Institute for Cotton on a series of seminars in 1982, held at 20 locations in 16 countries and attended by more than 1,000 participants, to provide information on the critical role of fashion, fabric, colour and style in the export marketing of apparel.

Trade promotion activities oriented to rural development included a country workshop at Kathmandu, Nepal (April), at which recommendations were made on mechanisms for rural export promotion and several products were identified for pilot programmes. To promote trade between developing countries and the socialist countries of Eastern Europe, ITC and UNIDO co-operated with the Hungarian Chamber of Commerce to sponsor a seminar on the role of trade fairs in the trade promotion and industrialization of developing countries (Budapest, 17 September).

Total ITC expenditure in 1982 was $26.3 million. Of this amount, technical co-operation activities accounted for $16.1 million, slightly more than the $15.7 million in 1981.[6] Trust fund contributions furnished $11.3 million of the 1982 amount for technical co-operation; the remainder, $4.8 million, was provided by UNDP. The Centre's 1982 regular budget of $8.4 million, covering headquarters operations, was contributed in equal parts by the United Nations and GATT.

In November ITC had a headquarters-based staff of 77 Professionals and 117 in the General Service category. It had 489 experts assigned to projects during the year.

JAG action. The ITC contribution to the United Nations medium-term plan for 1984-1989 was endorsed by the Joint Advisory Group (JAG) on the International Trade Centre at its resumed fourteenth session, held for that purpose at Geneva on 21 January 1982.[3] The trade promotion programme, covering ITC activities, continued to be divided into nine subprogrammes (see percentage breakdown above).

On 12 March, the Trade and Development Board took note of the JAG report.[5]

At its fifteenth session, held at Geneva from 22 to 26 March, JAG made several recommendations on ITC technical co-operation activities.[4] It recommended that high priority be given to identifying the export potential of developing countries and to developing products for export, in co-operation with UNIDO, the Food and Agriculture Organization of the United Nations and the World Bank group. It also recommended that ITC try to increase assistance to the least developed countries and to Africa, that its programme on import operations and techniques concentrate on fewer countries, that more manufactured products be included in market surveys and that increased attention be given to the possibilities of technical co-operation with the Commission of the European Communities. Priority items recommended by JAG, to the extent that resources permitted, were manpower development, expansion of specialized trade promotion services, technical co-operation with the socialist countries of Eastern Europe for expanded trade with developing countries, facilitation of South-South trade and training programmes to help developing country personnel evaluate the efficiency of their trade promotion activities.

Regarding financing and organization, JAG recommended that ITC resources be strengthened by seeking increased trust fund contributions and UNDP financing. It also recommended that ITC explore securing additional resources through participation in technical co-operation programmes of donor countries and regional organizations, facilitate cross-fertilization of experiences between developing countries and hold regular workshops for senior executives of national trade promotion bodies with wide participation of ITC staff.

As a special topic, JAG discussed a consultant's evaluation report on the ITC market development services subprogramme,[2] and generally endorsed its findings and recommendations.

Regarding its own activities, JAG endorsed the recommendation of its Working Party on Future Arrangements for the Joint Advisory Group and its Technical Committee, made in June 1981,[7] that JAG hold only one meeting a year for a trial period of two years, combining the participation of officials dealing with policy matters and experts specializing in technical aspects of trade and promotion. This would replace the previous arrangement, under which JAG and its Technical Committee each met annually.

The JAG session was preceded by the eleventh session of its Technical Committee, which met at Geneva from 18 to 22 January 1982. The Committee commented on the slow growth of the ITC programme and the apparent fall in the rate of project implementation. Its report, dealing with most of the subjects also discussed by JAG, was annexed to that of JAG.

On 7 September, the Trade and Development Board took note of the JAG report.[5]

Reports. [1]ITC, ITC/AG(XVI)/86 & Add.1; [2]ITC consultant, ITC/AG(XV)/78; JAG, [3]ITC/AG(XIV)/75/Add.1 (transmitted by UNCTAD secretariat note, TD/B/890), [4]ITC/AG(XV)/81 (transmitted by UNCTAD secretariat note, TD/B/911); [5]TDB, A/37/15, vols. I, II.
Yearbook references. 1981, [6]p. 548, [7]p. 549.

Accounts for 1980-1981

Reporting in 1982 on its audit of ITC for the biennium 1980-1981,[2] the Board of Auditors suggested improvements to the financial management and control systems of the Centre. It recommended that the regular ITC budget be reimbursed for the cost of supplies used for processing and reproducing project reports, that unsatisfactory work done by consultants should not be certified as satisfactory, that an objective basis be established for determining and evaluating staff resources within the various sections of the Centre and that action be taken to ensure a more effective allocation and utilization of staff. The Board also urged immediate action to establish closer co-ordination between ITC and the United Nations and between GATT and the United Nations to improve budgetary control procedures.

The Advisory Committee on Administrative and Budgetary Questions (ACABQ), commenting on the

Board's report,[1] agreed that the costs of supplies used for producing project reports should be charged to projects and not to the regular budget.

On 16 November 1982, the General Assembly accepted the financial reports and accounts reviewed by the Board of Auditors on various United Nations programmes including that of ITC, endorsed the Board's audit opinions, requested the Secretary-General to remove the shortcomings identified in the reports of the Board and ACABQ, and asked programme heads to take remedial action as required.[3]

Reports. [1]ACABQ, A/37/443; [2]Board of Auditors, and financial statements, A/37/5, vol. II.
Resolution (1982). [3]GA: 37/12, 16 Nov.

State trading enterprises

An International Symposium of State Trading Organizations of Developing Countries, organized jointly by the United Nations Conference on Trade and Development (UNCTAD), ITC and the International Center for Public Enterprises in Developing Countries, and with financial support from the United Nations Development Programme, met at Ljubljana, Yugoslavia, from 29 March to 2 April 1982. The Symposium recommended establishing a permanent institutional framework to promote co-operation among such enterprises and nominated a steering committee of nine of them, including three members from each regional group, to organize an association.

Restrictive business practices

On 19 March 1982,[1] the UNCTAD Trade and Development Board took note of the report of the Intergovernmental Group of Experts on Restrictive Business Practices on its first session, held in November 1981.[2] The Board endorsed a resolution adopted by the Group in which it expressed concern about the persistent resort to restrictive business practices in international trade and called on countries to control them.

Report. [1]TDB, A/37/15, vol. I.
Yearbook reference. [2]1981, p. 545.

Commodities

The first special session of the UNCTAD Committee on Commodities, held at Geneva from 8 to 12 February 1982, resulted in the adoption on 12 February of a series of agreed conclusions relating to international commodity trade.[2]

Strong concern was expressed about problems created by the declining trend in the prices of many commodities of export interest to developing countries, aggravated by the rising prices of their imports. The Committee emphasized that international action on price stabilization should be complemented by other measures, including those for increasing the participation of developing coun-

tries in processing, marketing and distributing their export commodities. It urged that, within the framework of the Integrated Programme for Commodities, negotiations be intensified in cases where adequate preparations had been made for effective international agreements or arrangements and that such work be expedited where it had not been done. The intention of the UNCTAD Secretary-General to consult with producers and consumers of mineral and metal commodities so as to advance dialogue between them was noted.

The Committee noted with concern the status of work on the Common Fund for Commodities and urged States to sign and ratify the Agreement Establishing the Common Fund. The UNCTAD Secretary-General was requested to elaborate work on a proposed complementary financing facility for commodity-related shortfalls in export earnings, consult with producers and consumers of hides and skins, and expedite studies on processing and product development and on marketing and distribution of commodity exports of developing countries called for in a 1979 UNCTAD resolution.[8]

The Committee took note of the report of its Permanent Sub-Committee on its second session, held at Geneva from 1 to 8 February,[3] and agreed to its conclusion that, for the Sub-Committee to fulfil its mandate in regard to processing, marketing and distribution, a third session should be convened before the Committee's tenth session (scheduled for January/February 1983).

Discussions at the Sub-Committee's second session focused on identifying and examining problems impeding greater participation by developing countries in marketing and processing their export commodities. Agreement was reached that the UNCTAD Secretary-General should complete the commodity-by-commodity studies called for by UNCTAD in 1979, and that written comments on the studies by Governments and other bodies be synthesized together with the comments made in the Sub-Committee.

No agreement was reached in the Sub-Committee on a mandate to the UNCTAD Secretary-General for further drafting, as called for in 1979, in regard to frameworks of international co-operation for expanded processing of export commodities in developing countries and for marketing and distribution of commodity exports from developing countries. According to the Chairman's summary of the discussions and conclusions, included in the Sub-Committee's report, the Group of 77 favoured having the Secretary-General prepare a draft framework of international co-operation but Group B (developed market economies) felt that was the responsibility of the Sub-Committee.

On 19 March 1982, the Trade and Development Board[4] took note of the agreed conclusions of the

Committee on Commodities and endorsed its recommendations. On 17 September, the Board took note of the Committee's report on its 1982 session.

A February 1982 progress report by the UNC-TAD secretariat to the Board[5] assessed the effects of the 1979 Tokyo Round of multilateral trade negotiations (see above) on trade in primary and processed agricultural and mineral commodities. Among its findings were the following: Developed market-economy countries discouraged trade in processed agricultural products by applying significantly higher duties to such items than to primary products, even after the tariff cuts resulting from the Tokyo Round. Following those negotiations, developing countries appeared to have recorded relatively small gains in all developed country markets. In the fibres sector, the 1974 Arrangement regarding International Trade in Textiles (Multifibre Arrangement), negotiated under the General Agreement on Tariffs and Trade in 1973[7] and extended in December 1981,[9] preserved the trend towards increasing protectionism for textiles. Non-tariff trade measures applied to commodity trade bore disproportionately on developing countries.

Remarking on the low level of prices in commodity markets, the Committee for Development Planning, in its April 1982 assessment[1] of world economic conditions and trends, said the instability of such markets had long been recognized as one of the weakest links of the world economy. The benefits that consuming countries derived from the low prices of raw materials had to be weighed against the consequence of the contraction of their markets in developing countries.

In a review of commodity trade prepared late in 1982 for the 1983 session of the Committee on Commodities,[6] the UNCTAD secretariat reported that the situation had worsened since the Committee's February 1982 session. In terms of manufactured goods prices, the average of commodity prices had fallen to the lowest level since the end of the Second World War; by October 1982, the fall from October 1980 levels was over 35 per cent in dollar terms. The volume of commodity exports from developing countries had increased marginally in 1981 as countries tried to sustain earnings by greater volume sales.

Reports. [1]CDP, E/1982/15; [2]Committee on Commodities, TD/B/894; [3]Sub-Committee, TD/B/C.1/230 & Corr.1; [4]TDB, A/37/15, vols. I, II; UNCTAD secretariat, [5]TD/B/885, [6]TD/B/C.1/241.
Yearbook references. [7]1973, p. 969; [8]1979, p. 562; [9]1981, p. 556.

Common Fund for Commodities

Preparatory work continued in 1982 on arrangements for the Common Fund for Commodities, a mechanism intended to stabilize the commodities market by helping to finance buffer stocks of specific commodities as well as commodity development activities such as research and marketing. Additional States adhered to the 1980 Agreement Establishing the Common Fund for Commodities,[2] which was not in force by the end of 1982.

The Preparatory Commission for the Fund, established in 1980 by the United Nations Negotiating Conference on a Common Fund,[3] did not meet during 1982, but its Working Party II held its third and fourth sessions at Geneva. At the third session, from 25 to 29 January, discussion focused on rules and regulations for the Fund's second account, intended to finance commodity development measures other than stocking. A preliminary discussion took place on rules covering such aspects as lending policies and criteria, general conditions applicable to loan and guarantee agreements, procurement of goods and services, and borrowing for the account. No attempt was made to reach final conclusions on the text of draft general conditions applicable to loan and guarantee agreements, which the Working Party examined in depth, because it was felt that some of the issues required further consideration.

At its fourth session, from 22 to 26 March, the Working Party heard the views of international commodity organizations on issues relating to the first account, through which the Fund was to finance international buffer stocks and internationally co-ordinated national stocks of commodities. The Working Party agreed to take account of those views in the re-drafting of regulations for first account operations and the preparation of an outline for a model association agreement. The four organizations represented—the International Cocoa Organization, the International Natural Rubber Organization, the International Sugar Organization and the International Tin Council—stressed that the model association agreement, setting out the terms under which the organizations would be associated with the Fund, should be restricted to broad policy outlines, leaving details to be negotiated between the organizations and the Fund's management as equal partners.

On 12 February, the Committee on Commodities noted with concern the status of the Preparatory Commission's work and that of its working parties.[1]

Report. [1]Committee on Commodities, TD/B/894.
Yearbook references. 1980, [2]p. 621, [3]p. 622.

Signatures and ratifications

As at 31 December 1982, the 1980 Agreement Establishing the Common Fund for Commodities[4] had been signed by 90 States and the European Economic Community, and 39 States had formally adhered by ratifying, accepting or approving it. Of these, 15 States signed the Agreement and 20 adhered during 1982 (italicized in the lists below).

By 31 March, the date originally envisaged for the Agreement to enter into force, instruments of ratification, acceptance or approval had been received from 25 of the 90 States required. Moreover, the share subscriptions of the 25 accounted for only 23.03 per cent of the Fund's directly contributed capital, far short of the two-thirds needed before the Agreement could enter into force. Accordingly, as requested in 1980 by the Negotiating Conference which established the Agreement, the Secretary-General of the United Nations Conference on Trade and Development (UNCTAD) convened on 3 June a meeting to which the 25 States were invited. The meeting adopted a decision extending until 30 September 1983 the period for fulfilling the requirements for entry into force of the Agreement and urging States which had not ratified to do so as soon as possible. Information on this meeting was conveyed to the General Assembly by the Secretary-General in a report listing signatures and ratifications of the Agreement as at 1 September 1982.[2]

The States which had both signed and adhered to the Agreement as at 31 December were:

Algeria, Australia, Bangladesh, *Benin*, *Botswana*, *Burundi*, China, Denmark, *Ecuador*, *Egypt*, Ethiopia, Finland, *France*, Gabon, *Guinea*, Haiti, India, Indonesia, Iraq, *Ireland*, Japan, *Kenya*, Malawi, *Mali*, *Mexico*, Niger, Norway, *Papua New Guinea*, Philippines, *Republic of Korea*, *Sierra Leone*, Sri Lanka, Sweden, *Switzerland*, *Tunisia*, Uganda, United Kingdom, *United Republic of Tanzania*, *Venezuela*.

In addition, the Agreement had been signed but not adhered to by the following States:

Afghanistan, *Argentina*, Austria, Belgium, Brazil, Canada, Cape Verde, *Central African Republic*, Chad, Comoros, Congo, Costa Rica, Democratic Yemen, Gambia, Germany, Federal Republic of, *Ghana*, Greece, Guinea-Bissau, Italy, Kuwait, Lesotho, Liberia, Luxembourg, Malaysia, Morocco, *Mozambique*, Nepal, Netherlands, *New Zealand*, Nicaragua, Nigeria, *Pakistan*, Peru, Portugal, Rwanda, *Samoa*, Senegal, *Singapore*, Somalia, Spain, Sudan, *Syrian Arab Republic*, Turkey, *United Arab Emirates*, United Republic of Cameroon, United States, Upper Volta, Yemen, *Yugoslavia*, Zaire, Zambia.

Pledges of voluntary contributions to the Fund's second account, for commodity development measures other than stocking, had reached about $255 million by the end of the year, as against the target of $280 million.

On 12 February, the Committee on Commodities noted with concern the status of signatures and ratifications, and urged Governments to expedite the process.[1]

On 20 December, the General Assembly, in a resolution[3] adopted without vote, urged States to sign and ratify the Agreement without delay and reiterated that further concerted efforts were required to bring about the conclusion of negotiations on new international commodity agreements. The resolution had been recommended by the Second (Economic and Financial) Committee without vote on 13 December, on a draft submitted by a Vice-Chairman.

Reports. [1]Committee on Commodities, TD/B/894; [2]S-G, A/37/373.
Resolution (1982). [3]GA: 37/211, 20 Dec., text following.
Yearbook reference. [4]1980, p. 621.
Meeting records. GA: 2nd Committee, A/C.2/37/SR.3, 5-8, 20-26, 33, 40, *48* (28 Sep.–13 Dec.); plenary, A/37/PV.113 (20 Dec.).

General Assembly resolution 37/211

20 December 1982   Meeting 113   Adopted without vote

Approved by Second Committee (A/37/680/Add.2) without vote, 13 December (meeting 48); draft by Vice-Chairman (A/C.2/37/L.125); agenda item 71 *(c)*.

Signature and ratification of the Agreement Establishing the Common Fund for Commodities

The General Assembly,

Recalling its resolutions 3201(S-VI) and 3202(S-VI) of 1 May 1974, containing the Declaration and the Programme of Action on the Establishment of a New International Economic Order, 3281(XXIX) of 12 December 1974, containing the Charter of Economic Rights and Duties of States, and 3362(S-VII) of 16 September 1975 on development and international economic co-operation,

Recalling also its resolution 35/56 of 5 December 1980, the annex to which contains the International Development Strategy for the Third United Nations Development Decade,

Recalling further its resolution 36/143 of 16 December 1981, in which it expressed concern at the slow pace of progress in the signature and ratification of the Agreement Establishing the Common Fund for Commodities and urged States that had not yet done so to sign and ratify the Agreement without delay,

Taking note of the report of the Secretary-General on the signature and ratification of the Agreement,

Noting with concern that so far eighty-nine States have signed the Agreement and only thirty-nine States have ratified, accepted or approved it,

Reiterating its concern at the slow pace of progress in the signature and ratification of the Agreement,

Noting with interest the conclusion of the International Agreement on Jute and Jute Products, 1982,

Reaffirming the need for further progress at an early date in the negotiations on international commodity agreements,

Mindful that the importance of the early entry into force of the Agreement Establishing the Common Fund for Commodities has been emphasized by the General Assembly in its resolutions 35/60 of 5 December 1980 and 36/143 of 16 December 1981, as well as by a number of intergovernmental meetings and conferences held at the highest political levels in 1981 and 1982,

Welcoming the pledges announced for voluntary contributions to the second account of the Common Fund,

Welcoming further the generous offer made by the States members of the Organization of Petroleum Exporting Countries to pay the full capital subscriptions of the least developed countries and a number of other developing countries concerned,

Bearing in mind the objectives of the Common Fund for Commodities, as reaffirmed by the General Assembly in its resolution 36/143,

1. *Notes with regret* that the Agreement Establishing the Common Fund for Commodities did not enter into force on the date envisaged, namely 31 March 1982, and that, consequently, a new time-frame had to be set for the purpose, in accordance with article 57 of the Agreement, extending the date until 30 September 1983;

2. *Reaffirms* its strong support for the Agreement and for its early entry into force;

3. *Strongly urges* all States that have not yet done so to sign and ratify the Agreement without any further delay;

4. *Expresses the hope* that States that have signed but not yet ratified the Agreement will expedite the necessary action to that effect;

5. *Reiterates* that further concerted and constructive efforts are required in order to bring about the conclusion of negotiations on new international commodity agreements;

6. *Requests* the Secretary-General of the United Nations Conference on Trade and Development to submit a report on the progress made towards the entry into force of the Agreement to the Conference at its sixth session, to be held at Belgrade in June 1983;

7. *Decides* to consider this question at its thirty-eighth session, in the context of its consideration of the work of the sixth session of the United Nations Conference on Trade and Development and other related developments.

Individual commodities

Work in 1982 towards agreements on international trade and development of individual agricultural products and mineral commodities was highlighted by the adoption in October by a United Nations conference of an International Agreement on Jute and Jute Products.

Similar agreements were sought for a number of other commodities covered by the UNCTAD Integrated Programme for Commodities (IPC),[1] including tropical timber, on which the preparatory phase of a proposed agreement was completed. On cotton, tea, hard fibres, and hides and skins, discussions did not provide a basis for negotiating agreements. However, work continued towards agreement on non-price-stabilization measures for bananas, primarily concerning research and development. Consideration was also given to problems of international trade in aluminium and bauxite and in manganese.

Outside IPC, the Sixth International Tin Agreement, concluded by an UNCTAD conference in 1981, provisionally entered into force in July 1982. The UNCTAD Committee on Tungsten continued to monitor the market situation in that metal.

Interested countries reached or extended agreements with regard to three other commodities outside the United Nations framework. The 1976 International Coffee Agreement[4] was renegotiated by participating States in September 1982 and extended for six years from the 1983/84 coffee year. The International Natural Rubber Agreement, which entered into force provisionally on 23 October 1980,[5] came into force definitively on 15 April 1982. The International Wheat Council, in November 1982, decided to extend for the seventh time the 1971 International Wheat Agreement,[3] for the three years from 1 July 1983 to 30 June 1986 (see Chapter XI of this section).

In its resolution of 20 December 1982 urging States to sign and ratify the 1980 Agreement Establishing the Common Fund for Commodities, the General Assembly also reiterated that further concerted and constructive efforts were required to conclude negotiations on new international commodity agreements.[2]

Report. [1]UNCTAD secretariat, TD/B/C.1/241.
Resolution (1982). [2]GA: 37/211, para. 5, 20 Dec.
Yearbook references. [3]1971, p. 274; [4]1976, p. 831; [5]1980, p. 623.
Publication. International Cocoa Agreement, 1980 (TD/COCOA.6/7/Rev.1), E/S.82.II.D.6.

Agricultural products

Bananas

The Intergovernmental Group of Experts on Bananas, meeting at Geneva under UNCTAD auspices from 1 to 5 November 1982, endorsed a 12-project research and development programme costing some $30 million over a five-year period.[1] The proposals had been submitted by banana-producing countries in response to a request made at the First Preparatory Meeting on Bananas in 1980.[2] Nine of the projects were assigned priority status; the rest required technical study before a decision could be made to implement them. Two further projects, submitted by exporters just before the expert group meeting, were referred to the Second Preparatory Meeting on Bananas, scheduled for 1983.

The most important of the approved projects required $5.9 million to establish a breeding programme to develop new pest-resistant varieties of bananas. Closely related were three plant-protection projects for controlling leaf disease and insects. Another project was aimed at improving mineral nutrition programmes for bananas. Other priority projects were to improve sowing and plantation management, banana quality and conservation methods.

Report. [1]Group of Experts, TD/B/IPC/BANANAS/9.
Yearbook reference. [2]1980, p. 624.

Cotton

Efforts to negotiate an international commodity agreement on cotton were pursued in 1982 by the UNCTAD Secretary-General in consultation with interested cotton-producing and -consuming countries. The consultations, held at Geneva from 30 March to 2 April, had been called for in May 1981 by the Sixth Preparatory Meeting on Cotton[1] to ensure the success of a planned resumed Preparatory Meeting.

The UNCTAD secretariat proposed the negotiation of a comprehensive international cotton agreement under which all internationally agreed activities on the commodity would be carried out, including research and development, market promotion, marketing, economic and statistical information, reporting and analysis, and continued consideration of the stabilization of prices and supplies. The proposal also suggested a system of consultations that could be convened at the request of an agreed number of member countries, but without binding any country. The consultations failed to produce general agreement to reconvene the Sixth Preparatory Meeting on the basis of the secretariat proposal and the UNCTAD Secretary-General proposed to organize a second round of consultations later.

Yearbook reference. [1]1981, p. 552.

Hides and skins

On 12 February 1982, the UNCTAD Committee on Commodities took note of conclusions adopted in December 1981 by the Third Preparatory Meeting on Meat,[3] and asked the UNCTAD Secretary-General to hold *ad hoc* consultations with producers and consumers of hides and skins with a view to promoting a dialogue between them and to report on the results to the Trade and Development Board.[1]

In September 1982, a representative of the UNCTAD Secretary-General informed the Board[2] that it had not been possible to hold the consultations. To avoid duplication and to explore the possibilities of integrating the efforts of various agencies into an international programme on hides and skins, the secretariat was trying to arrange an inter-agency meeting of the Food and Agriculture Organization of the United Nations, the International Labour Organisation, the United Nations Industrial Development Organization, the General Agreement on Tariffs and Trade, and the International Trade Centre. After that meeting, the secretariat would circulate a paper to serve as a basis for the consultations.

Reports. [1]Committee on Commodities, TD/B/894; [2]TDB, A/37/15, vol. II.
Yearbook reference. [3]1981, p. 554.

Jute

An International Agreement on Jute and Jute Products, 1982, was concluded at the end of the third part of the 1981 United Nations Conference on Jute and Jute Products, convened by UNCTAD at Geneva from 20 September to 1 October 1982. The Agreement[2] contained no price stabilization measures but was intended to provide an international framework for efforts to improve structural conditions in the jute market and enhance the competitiveness of jute and jute products, especially in relation to synthetics. The Agreement was to come into force on 1 July 1983 if by that date it had been signed or ratified by 3 Governments representing at least 85 per cent of net world exports and 20 Governments representing at least 65 per cent of net world imports.

The Agreement established an International Jute Organization with headquarters at Dhaka, Bangladesh, and an International Jute Council. The organization was charged with collecting, collating and publishing statistics needed for the oper-

ation of the Agreement. The main operational activity of the Council would be to arrange for the drawing up and implementation of projects in research and development, market promotion and cost reduction. The projects were to be financed by the second account of the Common Fund for Commodities, regional and international institutions such as the United Nations Development Programme and the World Bank, and voluntary contributions.

A Conference resolution established a Preparatory Committee, to prepare provisional rules of procedure for the Council and an agenda for its first session.

Acting on a request by the Conference that the General Assembly authorize an advance of United Nations funds for the Preparatory Committee and the first session of the Council, the Assembly's Fifth (Administrative and Budgetary) Committee decided without objection on 29 October 1982 to approve a $150,000 advance, refundable when members of the Council contributed to the Jute Organization's administrative budget. This amount had been requested by the Secretary-General[1] as an addition to the United Nations budget for 1982-1983.

Further, as recommended by the Advisory Committee on Administrative and Budgetary Questions[3] and approved by the Fifth Committee without objection on 29 October, the Assembly decided without vote on 21 December[4] that any part of this appropriation not needed for the International Jute Council by the end of 1983 should be credited to United Nations Members in accordance with the Financial Regulations of the United Nations, without applying an Assembly resolution of December 1981[5] that allowed unspent appropriations to be retained by the United Nations in view of its financial situation.

Note. [1]S-G, A/C.5/37/14.
Publication. [2]*International Agreement on Jute and Jute Products, 1982* (TD/JUTE/11), Sales No. E.83.II.D.3.
Report. [3]ACABQ, A/37/7/Add.5.
Resolution (1982). [4]GA: 37/237, sect. IV, 21 Dec., text following.
Resolution (prior). [5]GA: 36/116 B, 10 Dec. 1981 (YUN 1981, p. 1298).
Meeting records. GA: 5th Committee, A/C.5/37/SR.22 (29 Oct.); plenary, A/37/PV.114 (21 Dec.).

General Assembly resolution 37/237, section IV

21 December 1982   Meeting 114   Adopted without vote

Approved by Fifth Committee (A/37/790) without objection, 29 October (meeting 22); oral proposal by Chairman to approve ACABQ recommendation (A/37/7/Add.5); agenda item 103.

Interim arrangements for the International Jute Council
[*The General Assembly . . .*]

Decides that, should the appropriations approved at the current session as an advance to the International Jute Council not be required in 1983 or should they be used only partially, any uncommitted balance remaining at the end of the biennium 1982-1983 should be treated in accordance with the provisions of regulations 5.2 *(d)*, 4.3 and 4.4 of the Financial Regulations of the United Nations, and that the provisions of General Assembly resolution 36/116 B of 10 December 1981 should not apply to any such balance;

...

Tea

Steps towards an international agreement on tea were decided upon at two intergovernmental meetings held under UNCTAD auspices in 1982.

The Intergovernmental Group of Experts on Tea, at its third session at Geneva from 3 to 7 May,[1] examined proposals by exporting countries placing major emphasis on price objectives and targets. They called for regular reviews and, where necessary, revision of price levels, as well as for the regulation of supply through export quotas and, if necessary, by a buffer stock. Other measures provided for raising export standards and for promoting research and development aimed at increasing productivity and reducing costs throughout the industry. Although consuming countries indicated that they would find it difficult to accept some of these proposals, it was generally agreed that an agreement based primarily on export quotas offered reasonable prospects for orderly expansion of the world tea economy.

Immediately after that meeting, the Third Preparatory Meeting on Tea, held at Geneva from 10 to 14 May,[2] agreed to advance towards an international tea agreement. It agreed on objectives for the agreement, including: orderly expansion of world trade in tea while maintaining prices at levels remunerative and just to producers and equitable to consumers; a balance between import demand and export supply, avoiding excessive price fluctuations; improved quality and market access; adequate supplies to consumers; improvements in growing, processing, marketing and distribution; and increased tea consumption. Export quotas would be adjusted according to a scheme providing for a maximum price level, upper intervention level, mid-point, lower intervention level and minimum price level. The Meeting also agreed that a study be made of the feasibility of an international tea buffer stock. Expressing reservations to these conclusions, the United States said it could not accept the view that an agreement should include measures to influence tea supplies or prices.

At a meeting of experts from tea-exporting and -consuming countries on minimum export standards (Geneva, 11-15 October), progress was made towards determining the primary elements for such standards. However, the experts felt that levels for the different parameters could not be specified until more technical data were available. Exporting countries agreed to expedite technical work on the analysis of tea and to reconvene the meeting of experts in the second half of 1983.

Reports. [1]Group of Experts, TD/B/IPC/TEA/13; [2]Preparatory Meeting, TD/B/IPC/TEA/14.

Tropical timber

The Sixth Preparatory Meeting on Tropical Timber, held at Geneva from 1 to 11 June 1982, completed the preparatory phase of a proposed international agreement on tropical timber, after nearly five years of discussion under UNCTAD auspices. It adopted texts dealing with possible elements of an agreement, namely research and development, improvement of market intelligence, increased processing in developing countries, and reforestation and forest management.[2] The Preparatory Meeting also endorsed the agreed conclusions of the November 1981 meetings of intergovernmental groups of experts on research and development and on improvement of market intelligence for tropical timber.[3]

A Meeting on Tropical Timber was held at Geneva from 29 November to 3 December 1982 to consider institutional arrangements and other questions related to the planned agreement.[1] The Meeting agreed that the agreement should establish an autonomous International Tropical Timber Organization, consisting of producing and consuming members, to administer its provisions and supervise its operation. It took note of the position of producing countries that industrial tropical timber meant non-coniferous industrial tropical wood which grew on, or was produced from, the woodlands of countries located between the Tropic of Cancer and the Tropic of Capricorn. Agreement was also reached on elements of the organization's structure and organs, the frequency of sessions, decision-making procedures including distribution of votes and voting procedures, finances and contributions, duration of the agreement, and other questions relating to a negotiating conference.

Reports. [1]Meeting, TD/TIMBER/3; [2]Preparatory Meeting, TD/B/IPC/TIMBER/39.
Yearbook reference. [3]1981, p. 555.

Minerals and metals

Discussions on international trade in several minerals and metals and their ores proceeded in 1982 under UNCTAD auspices. In addition, a major feature of the United Nations Convention on the Law of the Sea, signed in December, was a system for governing the exploitation of mineral and other resources of the international sea-bed area beyond national jurisdiction.

Aluminium and bauxite

The Permanent Sub-Committee of the UNCTAD Committee on Commodities examined in February 1982 a study by the UNCTAD secretariat on areas for international co-operation in the processing and marketing of bauxite ore and its processed derivatives, alumina and aluminium.[2] The study reviewed obstacles to increased participation by developing countries in the processing and marketing of these products. Among issues which seemed amenable to intergovernmental negotiation in an industry characterized by high concentration in a few commercial enterprises, the study cited the need for more information about markets, a possible international financial facility to help developing countries with the large capital outlay needed for new production facilities, and the lowering of tariff barriers facing developing countries in their efforts to increase exports of processed products.

A June 1982 report by the United Nations Centre on Transnational Corporations (TNCs) on the role of TNCs in the shipping sector focused on the shipping of bauxite/alumina and outlined benefits which might accrue to exporting countries through participation in joint shipping ventures.[1] The report was a product of the Centre's research into various aspects of TNCs.

A Preparatory Meeting on Bauxite, organized by UNCTAD at Geneva from 8 to 12 November, marked the first occasion on which the Governments of producing and consuming countries met to discuss international trade in this mineral. Producing countries stated their concerns in the areas of marketing, financing, technology, energy and taxation, which they considered amenable to international co-operative efforts. Consuming countries agreed that it was in the interest of all parties to continue efforts to identify and clarify areas of concern with a view to considering possible action. The Meeting requested the UNCTAD Secretary-General to invite all member Governments to present further views by 31 July 1983 and to convene a second preparatory meeting at a date to be determined.

Also during 1982, the United Nations Industrial Development Organization continued its technical co-operation activities for the development of the aluminium industry in developing countries (see Chapter VI of this section).

Reports. [1]UN Secretariat, E/C.10/1982/14; [2]UNCTAD secretariat, TD/B/C.1/PSC/19.

Manganese

The UNCTAD Intergovernmental Group of Experts on Manganese, meeting at Geneva from 13 to 17 December 1982,[1] focused on problems affecting producers in both industrialized and developing countries. These included deteriorating prices, declining consumption and reliability of ore supplies. The Group also examined problems affecting developing producing countries, including processing in developing countries, market access, research and development in respect of mining operations in developing countries, market transparency and transport. The Group took note of the views presented to it by Governments.

Report. [1]Group of Experts, TD/B/IPC/MANGANESE/10.

Tin

The Sixth International Tin Agreement entered into force provisionally on 1 July 1982. According to the Agreement, adopted in June 1981 by an UNCTAD conference,[1] it would have entered into force definitively on that date if Governments of producing countries accounting for at least 80 per cent of world production and Governments of consuming countries accounting for at least 80 per cent of total consumption had deposited instruments of ratification, acceptance, approval or accession. As those requirements had not been met by early June 1982—when the percentages were 79 for producers and 47.65 for consumers—the adhering Governments, at meetings on 10, 11 and 23 June, decided that the Agreement would provisionally enter into force among themselves. Because the demand for tin was weak, the International Tin Council decided to intensify export controls until the end of the first quarter of 1983.

As at 31 December 1982, the following five States had definitively ratified or accepted the Agreement (the names of those doing so in 1982 are italicized): *Indonesia, Japan,* Malaysia, *Norway, Sweden.*

The Agreement had been provisionally applied as at that date by the European Economic Community (in 1982) and the following 17 States: *Australia, Belgium, Canada, Denmark, Finland, France, Germany, Federal Republic of, Greece, India, Ireland, Italy, Japan, Luxembourg, Netherlands, Thailand, United Kingdom, Zaire.*

Yearbook reference. [1]1981, p. 553.

Tungsten

The UNCTAD Committee on Tungsten, meeting in its fourteenth session at Geneva from 25 to 29 October 1982, reviewed the tungsten market situation and the discussions, proposals and work done on stabilizing the market.[1] The Committee examined two UNCTAD secretariat reports, on tungsten price indicators and products. It requested the secretariat to advance and deepen its analysis of possible improvements in, or additions to, the existing range of price indicators, and to prepare a supplementary report on tungsten products for consideration by the Committee at its next (1983) session, paying particular attention to changes in the structure of the world tungsten industry, the recycling of tungsten and substitution. The Committee also asked the secretariat to take steps to improve the coverage and usefulness of the quarterly bulletin *Tungsten Statistics.*

Report. [1]Committee on Tungsten, TD/B/C.1/238.

Transnational corporations and commodity trade

On 19 March 1982, the Trade and Development Board[1] decided to remit to its September/October session consideration of a draft resolution on transnational corporations and international commodity trade, originally submitted by Group D (centrally planned economies) at the 1979 UNCTAD session. The draft resolution was again remitted by the Board on 17 September 1982 for consideration at its twenty-sixth session (April 1983).

Report. [1]TDB, A/37/15, vols. I, II.

Finance

Financial policy

The Committee for Development Planning, meeting in April 1982 (see Chapter I of this section), focused on critical issues of international monetary and financial co-operation.[1] The Committee addressed those issues in the light of the world economic crisis and the need for a programme of world recovery. It suggested some immediate monetary and financial measures to restore non-inflationary world growth (see below), including specific areas for monetary and financial co-operation among developing countries and proposals to expand the sources of development finance and investment through changes in international financial institutions. It also called attention to inadequacies in development assistance policies.

The Committee saw an immediate need to enhance the capacity of the intergovernmental financial institutions as a source of financial assistance. To alleviate the erratic growth and uneven distribution of reserves in the international monetary system, it suggested that the creation of special drawing rights (SDRs) be resumed. It noted in this connection that the proportion of SDRs in world non-gold reserves had declined from 8 per cent at the end of 1972 to less than 4 per cent by the end of 1981.

The Committee observed that the International Monetary Fund (IMF) seemed to be attaching so many conditions to its financial support operations that many members were unable to meet its rigid performance criteria. It recommended that a greater portion of IMF resources be made available with fewer conditions, that member Governments be more closely involved in the formulation of adjustment programmes, that criteria to assess performance be less rigid and reviews less frequent, and that greater attention be paid to sectoral requirements and investment programmes for expansionary adjustment. It also suggested that, in exceptional cases, third parties be associated with negotiations on IMF allocations. The Fund's resources should also be enlarged.

The Committee also recommended a return to greater co-ordination of foreign exchange rate policies. For the future it said that, if the world economy was launched on a more expansionary path,

the possibilities for constitutional changes with regard to decision-making in the international institutional framework might arrive sooner than expected.

As in previous years, the UNCTAD Trade and Development Board discussed at both of its 1982 sessions, in March and September,[2] an agenda item on an evaluation of the world trade and economic situation and consideration of measures to facilitate structural changes in the international economy with a view to establishing a new international economic order. The wide-ranging debate also dealt with the interdependence of problems of trade, development finance and the international monetary system. No substantive action was taken, except for approval of a request for a study on the current terms for access of developing countries to capital markets.

On another aspect of international finance, the Board discussed but took no action on UNCTAD secretariat reports on the worsening debt servicing situation of developing countries. With regard to domestic finance for development, a United Nations symposium drew up recommendations on the mobilization of personal savings in developing countries. In the area of trade-related finance, an UNCTAD intergovernmental group of experts suggested details of a possible export credit guarantee facility to provide export insurance for developing countries, while the Committee on Commodities asked for further work on proposals for a supplementary financing facility to compensate developing countries for shortfalls in commodity export earnings. The UNCTAD Committee on Invisibles and Financing relating to Trade devoted a series of meetings to several aspects of insurance.

Reports. [1]CDP, E/1982/15; [2]TDB, A/37/15, vols. I, II.
Publication. Report of the Ad Hoc Intergovernmental High-level Group of Experts on the Evolution of the International Monetary System (TD/B/823/Rev.1), Sales No. E.82.II.D.2.

Debt servicing

At consultations held in February 1982 between the UNCTAD Secretary-General and the executive heads of the World Bank and IMF on development prospects and the external financing of developing countries, the participants concluded that there was little prospect for relief of pressures on the external accounts of most developing countries and that, in many cases, management of those accounts could entail lower growth.

Reporting these conclusions to the Trade and Development Board in March,[3] the Secretary-General annexed an UNCTAD secretariat note on selected topics related to the international economic environment and debt-related problems of developing countries. According to the secretariat's analysis, the international economic environment facing developing countries in 1982 was expected to worsen for the third year running. The level of their medium- and long-term outstanding debt, including IMF drawings, was close to 125 per cent of their current annual export earnings. Interest payments were pre-empting about 10 per cent of export earnings, compared with 7 per cent in 1979.

The difficulty of meeting that debt, together with the concern of some creditors regarding the magnitude of their exposure to certain debtor countries, had led to a marked reduction in the growth rate of bank credit disbursements. Debt service payments were proceeding on schedule in most developing countries but in many cases that was possible only through a compression of imports and a reduction of growth below otherwise attainable rates; in some countries, servicing difficulties had become overt. UNCTAD research missions to debtor countries had helped the secretariat assist them in preparing cases for debt rescheduling.

In another note,[1] which was before the Trade and Development Board in September, the UNCTAD secretariat supplied information on what developed donor countries had done to implement a 1978 Board resolution calling for retroactive adjustment of terms of official development assistance (ODA) to relieve the debt problems of developing countries.[4] The note's findings were based on replies from developed donor countries; the substance of replies from 14 Governments was circulated in addenda to the note. As at July 1982, specific measures had been announced which had benefited or would benefit over 45 developing countries. Since 1981, when a more comprehensive report indicated a total nominal value of debt relief valued at $5.7 billion,[5] additional relief reported by three donor countries had amounted to $59.1 million.

The note stated that the public and publicly guaranteed disbursed debt of the countries categorized in the 1970s as most affected by the economic crisis had risen from $40 billion (151 per cent of their export earnings) in 1976 to $77 billion (169 per cent of export earnings) in 1981. Observing that the debt relief measures envisaged by the Board in 1978 had been modest, the secretariat suggested that it might consider a thorough re-examination of the scope of such action in the light of the current economic climate and the critical situation of the poorer developing countries.

During the Board's consideration of the question in March 1982, the UNCTAD Secretary-General noted that the medium- and long-term debt of non-oil-producing developing countries totalled about $384 billion, an increase of almost $100 billion over the preceding two years. Short-term debt had also risen sharply. There had been 20 debt reschedulings in the preceding five years in contrast to 13 in the five years before that.

The Board decided, on 19 March, to include the item in the provisional agenda of its September session.[2] Following further discussion at that time, the Board on 17 September included an item on reviewing arrangements concerning debt problems of developing countries in the provisional agenda of its twenty-sixth session (April 1983).

Note. [1]UNCTAD secretariat, TD/B/915 & Add.1,2.
Reports. [2]TDB, A/37/15, vols. I, II; [3]UNCTAD S-G, TD/B/897.
Yearbook references. [4]1978, p. 429; [5]1981, p. 559.

Development finance and investment

The Committee for Development Planning, in the review of international financial co-operation which was a feature of the report on its April 1982 session,[1] suggested several steps to strengthen the capacity of international financial institutions—notably the World Bank group—to provide development finance for developing countries.

The contribution of the World Bank and of regional development banks to world adjustment was particularly great in supporting productive investments for development and structural change, the Committee stated, and proposals to enlarge their lending capacity in ways that did not impose pressures on government budgets deserved greater attention. Such ways included raising the ratio of loans to capital, increasing the subscribed stock without paid-in capital contributions, creating an energy facility with a voluntarily subscribed equity base and accepting term deposits from capital-surplus countries.

The Committee also expressed the view that national pressures to prevent multilateral institutions from lending to public-sector enterprises or to countries which favoured a particular public-private mix were not in order.

The problem of capital movements to developing countries was discussed in a special chapter of the *World Economic Survey 1981-1982.* The *Survey*[2] found that there had not been the required increase in medium- and long-term flows which developing countries needed to adjust the structure of their economies to sharp and permanent changes in international prices. They required substantial investment to make such adjustments, which included increased domestic production of energy, more efficient industrial technology and, in energy-importing countries, the allocation of additional resources to produce tradable commodities to counteract the effects of deteriorating terms of trade and consequent balance-of-payments deficits. Lacking the needed capital inflows, these countries had been forced to reduce import growth, in conflict with the efforts under way for a number of years to adjust their productive structures. A significant increase in ODA would particularly benefit the least developed and other low-income countries.

Report. [1]CDP, E/1982/15.
Publication. [2]*World Economic Survey 1981-1982: Current Trends in the World Economy* (E/1982/46), Sales No. E.82.II.C.1.

Mobilization of savings

The Second International Symposium on the Mobilization of Personal Savings in Developing Countries was held at Kuala Lumpur, Malaysia, from 15 to 21 March 1982.[2] Like the first Symposium, held at Kingston, Jamaica, in 1980,[5] it was organized by the United Nations Secretariat as part of a programme on the subject financed by the Swedish International Development Authority. The National Savings Bank of Malaysia, the International Savings Banks Institute and the Swedish Savings Banks Association were co-organizers of the Second Symposium. The Symposium's conclusions and recommendations were included in a May 1982 report by the Secretary-General,[3] submitted to the Economic and Social Council in accordance with a November 1981 request by the General Assembly.[4]

The Second Symposium approved a number of conclusions and recommendations, including the following:

> When a country did not already have a security market, its establishment could be contemplated only where other satisfactory networks for mobilizing domestic savings existed, such as commercial, savings and investment banks and collective provident funds. Given the right conditions for them, the establishment of securities markets could modify the structure of savings in favour of productive investments, improve the allocation of savings and promote the transfer of corporation ownership from non-residents to residents, thus making development less dependent on foreigners. Provident funds and other contractual savings schemes were an appropriate source of long-term financing, and where such funds were at the Government's disposal they should be used first of all to finance development projects.
>
> Policies to encourage savings in rural areas should be the key element of any savings policy in developing countries. To provide sufficient credit to farmers and small entrepreneurs, funds mobilized from rural areas must be supplemented by diverting resources from urban areas through commercial and savings banks and the Government. In order to survive in competition with commercial banks and other financial institutions, savings banks should acquire a general-purpose character, providing a series of services to their customers.

On 27 July, the Economic and Social Council took note of the Secretary-General's report on the Symposium. It took this decision,[1] without vote, on the recommendation of its First (Economic) Committee, which had similarly approved it on 21 July on an oral proposal by the Chairman.

The role of life insurance in national development efforts was noted in December by the Committee on Invisibles and Financing related to Trade, a body of the United Nations Conference on Trade and Development (UNCTAD).

Decision 1982. [1]ESC: 1982/152, 27 July, text following.
Publication. [2]*Savings for Development. Report of the Second International Symposium on the Mobilization of Personal Savings in Developing Countries* (ST/ESA/129), Sales No. E.84.II.A.1.
Report. [3]S-G, E/1982/66.
Resolution. [4]GA: 36/42, 19 Nov. 1981 (YUN 1981, p. 559).
Yearbook reference. [5]1981, p. 558.
Meeting record. ESC: E/1982/SR.48 (27 July).
Statement. NGO, E/1982/NGO/2.

Economic and Social Council decision 1982/152

Adopted without vote

Approved by First Committee (E/1982/97) without vote, 21 July (meeting 12); oral proposal by Chairman; agenda item 10.

Report of the Secretary-General on the results of the Second International Symposium on the Mobilization of Personal Savings in Developing Countries

At its 48th plenary meeting, on 27 July 1982, the Council took note of the report of the Secretary-General on the results of the Second International Symposium on the Mobilization of Personal Savings in Developing Countries.

Capital markets

On 19 March 1982, the Trade and Development Board requested the UNCTAD Secretary-General to prepare a factual and analytical report on the terms and conditions for the access of developing countries to capital markets in the light of their balance-of-payments situation.[1] The report was to be prepared in conjunction with the documentation on the topic called for in a 1980 decision of the Board's Committee on Invisibles and Financing related to Trade.[2] The Board also requested that Committee to pay particular attention in 1983 to the terms and conditions for improved access to capital markets by developing countries.

Decision (1982). [1]TDB (report, A/37/15, vol. I): 252(XXIV), 19 Mar.
Yearbook reference. [2]1980, p. 632.

Trade-related finance

Export credit insurance

Some operational features of a proposed international financial institution to give support to the exports of developing countries were outlined by an Intergovernmental Group of Experts on an Export Credit Guarantee Facility, which met at Geneva from 11 to 22 January 1982.[2]

Convened as requested in 1980 by the UNCTAD Committee on Invisibles and Financing related to Trade,[3] the Group generally agreed that the facility's function would be to guarantee negotiable export credit paper arising from exports on credit by its developing country members. It should cover products and related services normally requiring medium- to long-term export credit in international trade. The facility might eventually provide technical assistance to developing countries on matters concerning trade financing.

The facility's guarantee should be its unconditional obligation to pay immediately the holder of the guaranteed paper the amount due if the paper had not been honoured upon maturity. The national agency of the exporting country—preferably its national export credit insurance organization—should unconditionally guarantee to reimburse the facility in such cases. The creditworthiness of individual transactions should be evaluated by both the national agency and the facility, and the latter should also evaluate the importing and exporting countries' credit-worthiness.

The facility should have an adequate capital base and be empowered to borrow short-term funds. Its income should be derived from the fees associated with providing guarantees and from its investments, and income in excess of operating costs should be used to build reserves so that it could become self-financing as soon as possible. The users would be developing countries but membership should be as wide as possible.

Further study was recommended of the possible establishment of objective technical criteria for eligibility for access to the proposed facility and of its administrative and financial feasibility.

Taking note of this report on 19 March, the Trade and Development Board[1] invited the Committee on Invisibles and Financing related to Trade to establish in 1983 a sessional committee to evaluate the operational features of an export credit guarantee facility with a view to completing consideration of the matter.

Decision 1982. [1]TDB (report, A/37/15, vol. I): 249(XXIV), 19 Mar.
Report. [2]Group of Experts, TD/B/889.
Yearbook reference. [3]1980, p. 632.

Export earnings

Expressing deep concern about the severity of the problem of export earnings shortfalls of developing countries, the UNCTAD Committee on Commodities,[1] in one of a series of agreed conclusions adopted on 12 February 1982, requested the UNCTAD Secretary-General to elaborate work on a study of a proposed complementary financing facility for commodity-related shortfalls in export earnings. He was requested to report in 1983 on the operation of the compensatory financing facility of the International Monetary Fund (IMF) and others.

On 19 March,[2] the Trade and Development Board endorsed the Committee's recommendations and decided to defer consideration of such a facility until it received the Committee's 1983 report.

In December 1982, the UNCTAD secretariat submitted a report for the 1983 session of the Committee[3] proposing that new arrangements for financing shortfalls in commodity export earnings

be established in two stages. The first stage could consist of a substantial enlargement of the IMF facility, together with its liberalization, to reduce or eliminate certain major shortcomings such as the formula used for calculating shortfalls. The socialist countries of Eastern Europe could also consider establishing a financial support programme which would make drawings available to developing countries for shortfalls in the earnings received for their commodity exports to that region.

The aim for the second stage would be to establish a facility based mainly on borrowing from the private capital market. To cope with shortfalls estimated at $60.8 billion for 1981-1985, the proposed facility might require $10 billion in subscribed capital and be authorized to borrow up to $10 billion for lending to developing countries for approved purposes. In addition, Governments could contribute an initial lump sum for use in concessional financing. Drawings from this facility were envisaged for three purposes: short-term income support for individual commodities, to ensure that production did not fall below levels consistent with medium- to longer-term trends; financing structural adjustment in cases of chronic over- or under-supply; and financing projects or activities to eradicate the causes of supply instability for specific commodities, such as crop rehabilitation and relocation, water supply and control, disease eradication, access roads, land improvement, storage, and product preparation and packaging.

Reports. [1]Committee on Commodities, TD/B/894; [2]TDB, A/37/15, vol. I; [3]UNCTAD secretariat, TD/B/C.1/234.

Insurance

The UNCTAD Committee on Invisibles and Financing related to Trade devoted the first part of its tenth session, held at Geneva from 13 to 17 December 1982, exclusively to insurance.[1] On 17 December, it approved recommendations to developing countries on life insurance, shipping insurance and motor vehicle insurance, and requested a study on captive insurance companies.

Report. [1]Committee on Invisibles, TD/B/937.

Life insurance

A study by the UNCTAD secretariat, issued in 1982 for the Committee on Invisibles, highlighted the contribution that life insurance could make to development, mainly by contributing to social stability and by mobilizing domestic savings.[2]

After considering this study the Committee, recognizing that life insurance could play an important role in promoting individual economic security as well as in national development efforts, recommended on 17 December[1] that Governments of developing countries ensure that reserves and guarantee deposits of life insurance companies were invested in the country where the premium income arose, taking into account risks, security, liquidity and income. It also recommended improved training for insurance personnel of developing countries and offered UNCTAD technical assistance for such training and for creating country and regional mortality tables. The Committee requested the UNCTAD secretariat to prepare studies on fiscal and other measures that developing countries could adopt to make life insurance more flexible for policy-holders and more competitive with other savings media.

Resolution (1982). [1]Committee on Invisibles (report, TD/B/937): 21(X), 17 Dec.
Study. [2]UNCTAD secretariat, TD/B/C.3/177 & Corr.1.

Insurance companies

An UNCTAD secretariat study of insurance developments in developing countries during 1980 and 1981,[2] issued in October 1982, called attention to the growing establishment in such countries of "captive" insurance companies, set up by large corporations in developed countries as a form of self-insurance at a lower cost than they could obtain from regular insurers. The study noted that, while developing countries might derive some benefits from such arrangements, their own insurance market might suffer from the shift of business to such overseas insurers. The Committee on Invisibles, after noting this study on 17 December,[1] requested the UNCTAD secretariat to conduct a further study on the possible impact of captive insurance companies on the operation of developing country domestic insurance markets.

Resolution (1982). [1]Committee on Invisibles (report, TD/B/937): 20(X), 17 Dec.
Study. [2]UNCTAD secretariat, TD/B/C.3/178.

Public finance

Proposed government accounting and auditing centre

A proposal to establish an international centre for public accounting and auditing, made in 1980 by the Fifth Meeting of Experts on the United Nations Programme in Public Administration and Finance,[5] received the endorsement of the Economic and Social Council in 1982. On 27 July, the Council adopted without vote a resolution[3] requesting the Secretary-General to take preparatory measures, subject to the availability of voluntary resources, towards establishing such a centre, and to consult on the matter with Governments, including those of prospective host countries. Stating that the centre should be conceived of as an interregional technical co-operation activity among Governments, the Council reiterated that it would have to be financed exclusively on a voluntary basis and urged Governments to consider con-

tributing or otherwise facilitating its functioning. The Council also requested the United Nations Development Programme and other international and regional institutions to co-operate with the centre.

The resolution had been recommended by the Council's First (Economic) Committee on 16 July, also without vote. It was submitted by a Vice-Chairman after informal consultations on a draft introduced by India on behalf of 10 nations[1] and later withdrawn. The approved text was substantially similar to the initial one, except that it added the word "exclusively" in reference to the voluntary financing of the centre.

Possible objectives and activities of such a centre, as well as its membership, structure, estimated cost and financing, were discussed in a feasibility study and project proposal presented to the Council by the Secretary-General in May,[2] pursuant to a July 1981 request by the Council.[4] After reviewing the demand for public finance information in developing countries, the state of public accounting and auditing there, international support measures, and the status of national, regional and international training programmes and facilities, the Secretary-General concluded that the proposed centre would be feasible, would not duplicate the work of other institutions and would lend itself to being considered a technical co-operation activity, to be financed by voluntary contributions.

The project proposal suggested two objectives for the centre: to provide support to the national, subregional and regional training institutes in developing countries concerned with public accounting and auditing by strengthening their technical and training capabilities; and to provide management training to the personnel in those institutes responsible for the design of training programmes. The centre's principal activities would be to collect and analyse information on public accounting and auditing standards and procedures; prepare training material, bibliographies and methodologies for evaluating training programmes; develop material on management training in public accounting and auditing; organize annual training seminars for managers of training programmes; and disseminate the centre's output to institutes. The centre might cost between $443,000 and $767,000 a year to operate, depending on its location.

Draft resolution withdrawn. [1]Austria, Bangladesh, Canada, China, India, Kenya, Nepal, Pakistan, Peru, Sri Lanka, E/1982/C.1/L.3.
Report. [2]S-G, E/1982/69.
Resolution (1982). [3]ESC: 1982/43, 27 July, text following.
Resolution (prior). [4]ESC: 1981/53, 22 July 1981 (YUN 1981, p. 563).
Yearbook reference. [5]1980, p. 565.
Meeting record. ESC: E/1982/SR.48 (27 July).
Publication. Changes and Trends in Public Administration and Finance for Development, Second Survey, 1977-1979 (ST/ESA/SER.E/27), Sales No. E.82.II.H.1.

Economic and Social Council resolution 1982/43

27 July 1982   Meeting 48   Adopted without vote

Approved by First Committee (E/1982/97) without vote, 16 July (meeting 8); draft by Vice-Chairman (E/1982/C.1/L.6), based on informal consultations on 10-nation draft (E/1982/C.1/L.3); agenda item 10.

International centre for public accounting and auditing

The Economic and Social Council,

Recalling paragraphs 30 and 47 of the annex to General Assembly resolution 35/56 of 5 December 1980, containing the International Development Strategy for the Third United Nations Development Decade, paragraph 3 of Assembly resolution 36/194 of 17 December 1981 on the United Nations Conference on the Least Developed Countries and Assembly resolution 34/137 of 14 December 1979 on the role of the public sector in promoting the economic development of developing countries,

Recalling also Council resolutions 1978/6 of 4 May 1978 and 1980/12 of 28 April 1980 on public administration and finance for development in the 1980s and 1981/45 of 20 July 1981 on the role of the public sector in promoting the economic development of developing countries,

Recalling further Council resolutions 1979/47 of 31 July 1979 on public accounting and auditing for national development and 1981/53 of 22 July 1981 on an international centre for public accounting and auditing,

Re-emphasizing the necessity and importance of the role of public accounting and auditing in the effective management of national development plans and programmes in developing countries and the urgency of the need to organize technical co-operation activities at all levels in order to support national efforts to improve the accounting and auditing systems of those countries,

1. *Takes note* of the report of the Secretary-General concerning the proposal for the establishment of an international centre for public accounting and auditing, and of the conclusions of the feasibility study and the project proposal contained therein;

2. *Believes* that the establishment of an international centre for public accounting and auditing should be conceived of as a technical co-operation activity among Governments at the interregional level;

3. *Reiterates* the guidelines set out in paragraph 3 of its resolution 1981/53 regarding the activities of the proposed centre, in particular the need for close collaboration with the regional and international institutions which have similar objectives;

4. *Reiterates further* that the proposed centre would be financed exclusively on a voluntary basis;

5. *Urges* all Governments to consider contributing financially to the international centre for public accounting and auditing or co-operating in other ways with the centre in order to facilitate its regular and effective functioning;

6. *Requests* the Secretary-General to consult with interested Governments, including Governments of prospective host countries, and, subject to the availability of voluntary resources, to take preparatory measures towards the establishment of the centre;

7. *Requests* the United Nations Development Programme, other international institutions and the appropriate regional institutions to extend their full co-operation to the centre in their respective fields of competence.

Terms of reference of the Group on international co-operation in tax matters

By a resolution adopted without vote on 27 July 1982, the Economic and Social Council set new terms of reference for the *Ad Hoc* Group of Experts on International Co-operation in Tax Matters.[4] It recommended that the Group continue its work on improving international co-operation to combat tax avoidance and evasion and urged it to make proposals in the field of taxation, including examination of the United Nations Model Double Taxation Convention between Developed and Developing Countries (adopted by a predecessor Group in 1979) and of countries' experiences in bilateral applications of that model text. The Group was requested to study possibilities of enhancing the efficiency of tax administrations and of reducing potential conflicts among tax laws of various countries.

The resolution had been recommended by the Council's First Committee, which on 21 July approved without vote a draft submitted by a Vice-Chairman. It was based on informal consultations on a text submitted by the United Kingdom, also on behalf of the Federal Republic of Germany, the Netherlands and the United States, and later withdrawn.[2] The approved version differed from the initial one in two respects. First, it omitted a phrase (in paragraph 2) to have the Group continue its work "of promoting international trade, investment and transfer of technology" by proposals in the field of taxation. Second, it omitted a proposal that a steering group composed of members from developing and developed countries be established to organize the Group's work; instead, the Council decided to consider in 1983 measures enabling the Group to carry out its future work most effectively.

The Council acted after receiving a report by the Secretary-General, issued in May 1982,[3] containing the recommendations of the Group at its first meeting, in December 1981, on the functions it might perform as a forum for developed and developing countries on tax issues.[6] Such recommendations had been requested by the Council in July 1981[1] after discussion of the possible creation of an intergovernmental tax co-operation council—an idea submitted to the Council in 1980 by the Group's predecessor body, the Group of Experts on Tax Treaties between Developed and Developing Countries.[5]

Commenting on the Group's recommendations, the Secretary-General expressed the belief that some of the suggested functions—such as those relating to application of the Model Convention—were not necessary at that time, while others—such as promoting the understanding of tax treaties, facilitating the exchange of experience about particular problems and disseminating information—could be performed more effectively in other ways. He noted that the Group had not expressed an interest in performing functions relating to the harmonization of direct taxation procedures, which had formed an important part of the proposal for a direct tax co-operation council, and he observed that the somewhat elaborate methods of operation suggested by the Group for the performance of its expanded functions would have substantial institutional and financial implications. In those circumstances, he thought the idea of enlarging the Group's functions should be set aside until it completed its work on international tax evasion and avoidance.

Decision. [1]ESC: 1981/1983, 23 July 1981 (YUN 1981, p. 564).
Draft resolution withdrawn. [2]Germany, Federal Republic of, Netherlands, United Kingdom, United States, E/1982/C.1/L.2.
Report. [3]S-G, E/1982/71.
Resolution (1982). [4]ESC: 1982/45, 27 July, text following.
Yearbook references. [5]1980, p. 531; [6]1981, p. 564.
Meeting record. ESC: E/1982/SR.48 (27 July).
Publications. Supplement No. 37 to International Tax Agreements, vol. IX, Sales No. E.82.XVI.1; *No. 38,* Sales No. E.82.XVI.2.

Economic and Social Council resolution 1982/45

27 July 1982   Meeting 48   Adopted without vote

Approved by First Committee (E/1982/97) without vote, 21 July (meeting 12); draft by Vice-Chairman (E/1982/C.1/L.10), based on informal consultations on 4-nation draft (E/1982/C.1/L.2); agenda item 10.

International co-operation in tax matters

The Economic and Social Council,

Recalling its resolution 1980/13 of 28 April 1980,

Recognizing the importance of international co-operation on a broad basis with the object of combating international tax avoidance and evasion, and of reducing as far as possible incompatibilities in tax systems in order to promote international trade, investment and the transfer of technology,

Having examined the report of the *Ad Hoc* Group of Experts on International Co-operation in Tax Matters on the work of its first meeting, and the recommendations of the Secretary-General relating thereto,

1.   *Recommends* that the *Ad Hoc* Group of Experts on International Co-operation in Tax Matters should continue its work on improving international co-operation to combat tax avoidance and evasion, and seek to develop guidelines to meet that objective;

2.   *Urges* the Group to continue its work by appropriate proposals in the field of taxation, including its examination of the United Nations Model Double Taxation Convention between Developed and Developing Countries and its consideration of the experiences of countries in bilateral applications of that Model Convention;

3.   *Requests* the Group to study possibilities of enhancing the efficiency of tax administrations and of reducing potential conflicts among the tax laws of various countries;

4.   *Recognizes* the importance of adequate preparation for its work by the Group, and decides to consider, at its second regular session of 1983, measures enabling the Group to carry out its future work in the most effective manner.

Chapter V

Transport and communications

Contents

Related topics:

International trade. Industrial development: Shipbuilding and ship repair. Regional economic and social activities— Transport and communications: Africa; Asia and the Pacific; Europe (Inland transport); Latin America; Western Asia.

Transport

Maritime transport

The United Nations Conference on Trade and Development (UNCTAD) and its subsidiary bodies continued in 1982 to deal with problems of transport, particularly shipping.

The United Nations Industrial Development Organization also undertook projects in transport, concentrating on shipbuilding and ship repair (see Chapter VI of this section).

Publication. Main Issues in Transport for Developing Countries during the Third United Nations Development Decade, 1981-1990 (ST/ESA/117), Sales No. E.82.II.A.5.

Shipping

At its tenth session, held at Geneva from 14 to 25 June 1982,[1] the Committee on Shipping of the UNCTAD Trade and Development Board reviewed world developments in maritime transport in 1980[3] and 1981.[4] It considered and took action on the specific topics of merchant fleet development; protection of shipper interests; international maritime legislation, including the Convention on a Code of Conduct for Liner Conferences, adopted in 1974[5] but not currently in force; port problems; technical assistance and training; and multimodal transport and containerization (see below).

On 17 September, during the first part of its twenty-fifth session, the Board took note of the Committee's report on its June session and of the resolutions and decision annexed to it, as well as the financial implications of the decision and two of the resolutions.[2]

Reports. [1]Committee on Shipping, TD/B/921; [2]TDB, A/37/15, vol. II; UNCTAD secretariat, [3]TD/B/C.4/222 & Corr.1, [4]TD/B/C.4/251.
Yearbook reference. [5]1974, p. 460.

Registration of ships

UNCTAD activities. On the recommendation of the Committee on Shipping and as approved by the Trade and Development Board in 1981,[6] the Intergovernmental Preparatory Group on Conditions for Registration of Ships met at Geneva from 13 to 30 April 1982 to propose a set of basic principles governing conditions under which vessels should be accepted on national shipping registers, with a view to preparing documents for the holding of a United Nations conference of plenipotentiaries to consider adopting an international agreement.[2]

At the close of the session on 30 April, the Preparatory Group approved, with minor amendments, a draft set of basic principles applicable to the manning of vessels, the role of flag countries in the management of shipowning companies and vessels, equity participation in capital, joint ventures, bareboat charters, identification and accountability, measures to protect the interests of labour-supplying countries and additional measures to ensure full jurisdiction of the flag State over vessels flying its flag. The draft texts on each aspect were agreed by the Group of 77 developing countries, by countries in Group B (developed market economies) and Group D (centrally planned economies) and by China, either singly or together with one or more of the other groups.

The Preparatory Group recommended, also on 30 April, that the Board include in the calendar of meetings for the remainder of 1982 a second session of the Group in November and recommend to the General Assembly that it provide for the convening of the plenipotentiary conference in 1983. These recommendations were endorsed by the Board on 17 September,[4] when it took note of the Group's report on its first session.

Accordingly, the Preparatory Group met again at Geneva, from 8 to 26 November.[3] At the close of the session, it approved a set of basic principles and agreed that a note reflecting the reservations expressed by Group D be inserted in the text; it also agreed that a draft composite text submitted by the Chairman, as amended, be annexed to the report on its second session. Questions concerning the time-frame for the registration of vessels, reporting procedures for review and implementation, and definitions, which were not taken up by the Preparatory Group, were to be considered by the conference.

In addition, the Group recommended that the Board, at its next session in 1983, request the UNCTAD Secretary-General to make the arrangements necessary for the proposed conference. The Group also requested him to prepare alternative draft texts for an international agreement based on the set of principles it had submitted; to circulate such texts to Governments for comment not later than six months before the conference; and to place those texts and comments before the conference, together with all relevant documentation.

General Assembly action. The General Assembly, acting without vote on 20 December 1982,[5] decided to convene early in 1984 a three-week United Nations Conference on Conditions for Registration of Ships to consider adopting an international agreement on the subject. It requested the Board to establish a Preparatory Committee for the Conference open to all States, charged with the preparation of the draft agreement based on all relevant documents and views of all parties, and to set the dates for the Conference. It also requested the UNCTAD Secretary-General to: circulate to Governments for comment the set of principles drafted by the Preparatory Group at least nine months in advance of the Committee's meeting; circulate the comments received to all Governments three months before that meeting; place all

such comments before the Committee and transmit to it and to the Conference all relevant documentation; and make the necessary arrangements for the Conference, including the Committee meetings, staff, facilities and services.

The text was recommended by the Assembly's Second (Economic and Financial) Committee, which had approved it, also without vote, on 13 December. It had been submitted by a Committee Vice-Chairman, following informal consultations on a draft resolution sponsored and introduced by Bangladesh on behalf of the Group of 77 and subsequently withdrawn.[1]

The adopted text differed from the original mainly in that it specified three weeks for the Conference period and preparation of the draft international agreement on the basis, not merely of the Preparatory Group's work, but of all relevant documentation. It also included an additional paragraph containing the requests made of the UNCTAD Secretary-General on the circulation and presentation of documentation.

Draft resolution withdrawn. [1]Bangladesh, for Group of 77, A/C.2/37/L.100.
Reports. Preparatory Group, [2]TD/B/904, [3]TD/B/935; [4]TDB, A/37/15, vol. II.
Resolution (1982). [5]GA: 37/209, 20 Dec., text following.
Yearbook reference. [6]1981, p. 566.
Financial implications. 5th Committee report, A/37/779; S-G statements, A/C.2/37/L.105, A/C.5/37/99.
Meeting records. GA: 2nd Committee, A/C.2/37/SR.3, 5-8, 20-26, 33, 40, *46, 48* (28 Sep.–13 Dec.); 5th Committee, A/C.5/37/SR.75 (17 Dec.); plenary, A/37/PV.113 (20 Dec.).

General Assembly resolution 37/209

20 December 1982	Meeting 113	Adopted without vote

Approved by Second Committee (A/37/680/Add.2) without vote, 13 December (meeting 48); draft by Vice-Chairman (A/C.2/37/L.122), based on informal consultations on draft by Bangladesh, for Group of 77 (A/C.2/37/L.100); agenda item 71 (c).

United Nations Conference on Conditions for Registration of Ships

The General Assembly,

Recalling its resolutions 3201(S-VI) and 3202(S-VI) of 1 May 1974, containing the Declaration and the Programme of Action on the Establishment of a New International Economic Order, 3281(XXIX) of 12 December 1974, containing the Charter of Economic Rights and Duties of States, and 3362(S-VII) of 16 September 1975 on development and international economic co-operation,

Recalling its resolution 35/56 of 5 December 1980, the annex to which contains the International Development Strategy for the Third United Nations Development Decade, which called, *inter alia*, in paragraph 128, for an increase in the participation by developing countries in world transport of international trade and, to this end, for appropriate structural changes to be carried out where necessary, and for the international community to continue to take the necessary steps to enable developing countries to compete more effectively and to expand their national and multinational merchant fleets so as to increase their share substantially with a view to reaching as close as possible to 20 per cent of the dead-weight tonnage of the world merchant fleet by 1990,

Recognizing the need to promote the orderly expansion of world shipping as a whole,

Taking note of the report of the Intergovernmental Preparatory Group on Conditions for Registration of Ships at its first session, held at Geneva from 13 to 30 April 1982,

Noting that the Trade and Development Board, at the first part of its twenty-fifth session, endorsed the resolution adopted by the Intergovernmental Preparatory Group on Conditions for Registration of Ships at its first session and recommended that the General Assembly should convene a plenipotentiary conference on the conditions of registration of vessels,

1. *Decides* to convene, taking into account the recommendations of the Trade and Development Board at the first part of its twenty-fifth session and the conclusions of necessary preparatory work, a plenipotentiary conference early in 1984, for a period of three weeks, in order to consider the adoption of an international agreement concerning the conditions under which vessels should be accepted on national shipping registers;

2. *Requests* the Trade and Development Board to establish a Preparatory Committee for the United Nations Conference on Conditions for Registration of Ships, open to the participation of all States;

3. *Requests* the Secretary-General of the United Nations Conference on Trade and Development:

(a) To circulate to Governments for comments, at least nine months before the holding of the meeting of the Preparatory Committee, the set of principles drafted by the Intergovernmental Preparatory Group at its second session concerning the conditions under which vessels should be accepted on national shipping registers;

(b) To circulate the comments received to all Governments at least three months in advance of the meeting of the Preparatory Committee;

(c) To place before the Preparatory Committee all comments received from Governments;

(d) To transmit all relevant documentation to the Preparatory Committee and the United Nations Conference on Conditions for Registration of Ships;

4. *Decides* that the Preparatory Committee, on the basis of the above documents, should prepare and recommend a draft international agreement on conditions of registration of ships, taking fully into account the views of all interested parties;

5. *Requests* the Trade and Development Board, taking into account the work of the Preparatory Committee, to decide on appropriate dates for the convening of the Conference;

6. *Requests* the Secretary-General of the United Nations Conference on Trade and Development to make all the necessary arrangements for holding the United Nations Conference on Conditions for Registration of Ships, including the meetings of the Preparatory Committee, and to arrange for the necessary staff, facilities and services that will be required;

7. *Decides* that the languages of the Conference shall be those used in the General Assembly, its committees and its sub-committees as official and working languages.

Bulk cargoes

On 25 June 1982, the Committee on Shipping, having noted the 1981 report of the Group of Experts on Problems Faced by the Developing Countries in the Carriage of Bulk Cargoes,[2] adopted a resolution on merchant fleet development,[1] annexing seven recommendations unanimously adopted by the Group to overcome such problems. Recommended were a clause in sales and purchase contracts to give favourable consideration to ships owned or operated by shipowners in developing countries, information dissemination to permit the matching of services with requirements, granting opportunities for participation in regular bulk transport, establishment of regional and interregional pools for better utilization of transport capacity, enactment of maritime and corporate legislation for joint ventures, long-term shipping arrangements as a means of providing collateral for long-term financing, and establishment of institutional financing houses and sovereign guarantees for ship acquisition.

The Committee called on UNCTAD members to urge commercial parties involved in the transport of bulk commodities to follow up on the recommendations on sales and purchase contracts, information dissemination, bulk trade and long-term shipping arrangements; and to consider implementing those on regional pools, maritime legislation and joint ventures, and ship financing. The Committee called on the UNCTAD secretariat to prepare surveys of developing countries' operation of dry bulk carriers and participation in the world dry bulk trades and to report to the Committee. It requested the UNCTAD Secretary-General to convene an expert group of 19 members to study the problems faced by developing countries seeking participation in international sea transport of liquid hydrocarbons in bulk and urged UNCTAD members to provide him with details of any barriers encountered for the group's consideration.

Resolution (1982). [1]Committee on Shipping (report, TD/B/921): 48(X), 25 June.
Yearbook reference. [2]1981, p. 567.

Co-operation among shipowners and shippers

On 25 June 1982, the Committee on Shipping recommended[1] that UNCTAD members invite shipping lines belonging to liner conferences to communicate the results of consultations at one end of the trade to the appropriate organization or national authority at the other end and, when requested, to provide data on conference operations to shippers' organizations. Governments were also invited to encourage shippers' organizations to maintain contact with organizations at the other end of the trade. The UNCTAD secretariat was asked to collect information from shippers' organizations and liner conferences on the effectiveness of the consultation machinery and to report to the Committee in 1984. Governments were requested to encourage shippers to form commodity groups to provide an infrastructure for shippers' organizations, with a view to ensuring a balance of interest between suppliers and users of liner conference services.

Resolution (1982). [1]Committee on Shipping: 46(X), 25 June.

International shipping legislation

By a resolution of 25 June 1982,[2] the Committee on Shipping decided to convene not later than 1983 an *ad hoc* intergovernmental group to consider means of combating maritime fraud, including piracy. To facilitate the group's work, the Committee requested from the UNCTAD secretariat a comprehensive report on the subject. It amended the work programme of the Working Group on International Shipping Legislation so that the Group would consider at each session two of the following topics together: maritime liens and mortgages;

hull and cargo marine insurance; rights registration of vessels under construction; arrest of vessels or other sanctions; and charter parties and general average, in that order. The Committee requested the UNCTAD Secretary-General to expedite work on a model code for maritime legislation to guide developing countries in formulating their national legislation.

The Committee urged its members to ratify the Convention on a Code of Conduct for Liner Conferences[3] and the United Nations Convention on the Carriage of Goods by Sea, 1978,[4] so as to bring them into force. Parties to the former Convention were asked to provide information on its implementation to the UNCTAD secretariat.

This resolution was adopted by the Committee by a roll-call vote of 51 to none, with 20 abstentions, following examination of an UNCTAD secretariat report on international maritime legislation.[1] The report reviewed the work programme of the Working Group—examining the question of maritime fraud, existing maritime conventions predominantly economic in content, and terms of shipment—and made recommendations for future action. It also reviewed UNCTAD secretariat activities to assist developing countries to modernize their maritime legislation and annexed a draft outline of a model code for such legislation.

Report. [1]UNCTAD secretariat, TD/B/C.4/244 & Corr.1.
Resolution (1982). [2]Committee on Shipping: 49(X), 25 June.
Yearbook references. [3]1974, p. 460; [4]1978, p. 956.

Ports

On 25 June 1982,[1] the Committee on Shipping requested the UNCTAD secretariat to examine the principles that should underlie port congestion measurement and determination of port congestion surcharges; to identify a trade route in which a scheme to rationalize such surcharges could be elaborated and implemented on a trial basis; and to report to the Committee at its next session. The Committee invited the UNCTAD Secretary-General to continue the study on a port data bank, limiting the study to elaborating and updating data on container terminals, and to expedite production of the monographs on port management.[2] It requested the UNCTAD secretariat to continue or extend its studies in port operation and development and its related advisory services and training activities. Financial institutions and countries were invited to contribute to the costs of such development, services and activities. The Committee recommended that UNCTAD members give attention to effective port policies and urge port authorities to provide technical assistance and advice to other port authorities on request.

Resolution (1982). [1]Committee on Shipping (report, TD/B/921): 44(X), 25 June.
Yearbook reference. [2]1980, p. 633.

Technical assistance and training

UNDP activities. In response to a 1981 request of the Governing Council of the United Nations Development Programme (UNDP),[5] the UNDP Administrator submitted a report[3] to the Council at its twenty-ninth session, held at Geneva from 1 to 18 June 1982, describing measures taken or planned by UNDP, in co-operation with the International Labour Organisation, the International Maritime Organization (IMO), UNCTAD and the regional commissions, to enhance the capabilities of maritime transport training institutions with multinational scope in developing countries, through interregional, regional and national programmes.

The report, taken note of by the Council on 18 June,[1] cited direct assistance in the form of advisers and consultants; reference documents for maritime training institutions and administrations; and intensive fellowship programmes, workshops, seminars, courses and study tours. A major interregional training programme, TRAINMAR, whose first phase (1979–March 1982) was financed by UNDP at a cost of $1.1 million and executed by UNCTAD, entered its second phase (April 1982–March 1984), with additional UNDP support of $1 million from its interregional indicative planning figure (IPF) and $200,000 from its intercountry programme for Asia and the Pacific. Under its regional programme for Africa, UNDP provided more than $25 million to the transport and communications sector for 1977-1981; a good part of the increased support in this sector for the 1982-1986 programming cycle would be for maritime training. Other regional programmes were pursued in the Caribbean, the Arab region, Asia and the Pacific, and Pacific island countries, in addition to national projects in Africa, Latin America, West Asia, and Asia and the Pacific.

UNCTAD activities. On 25 June, the UNCTAD Committee on Shipping[4] requested the Trade and Development Board to recommend increased resources during 1984-1985 for feasibility studies on ship acquisition, in order to finance part of an UNCTAD advisory service on shipping, ports and multimodal transport. It invited UNDP to maintain sectoral support advisory services in shipping, re-establishing them at the regional and interregional levels, and to allocate resources to the UNCTAD programme of technical assistance in shipping, ports, multimodal transport and personnel training. To expand such assistance and supplement UNCTAD advisory services, adequate resources were requested of countries and financial institutions, as also of UNDP for the TRAINMAR programme (see above). The UNCTAD secretariat was requested to give priority to technical assistance and training programmes in shipping and, at future Committee sessions, to present an analytical report of facilities and resources, including criteria for delivery of assistance.

The Committee requested information from donor countries and financial institutions for the UNCTAD directory SHIPASSIST,[2] which was also to cover multimodal transport, freight-forwarding operations and cargo insurance.

Decision (1982). [1]UNDP Council (report, E/1982/16/Rev.1): 82/43, para. (b), 18 June.
Publication. [2]Directory of Services for Technical Assistance in Shipping and Ports to Developing Countries (SHIPASSIST), UNCTAD/Ship/196 & Add.1.
Report. [3]UNDP Administrator, DP/1982/14.
Resolution (1982). [4]Committee on Shipping (report, TD/B/921): 45(X), 25 June.
Yearbook reference. [5]1981, p. 568.

Proposed establishment of the World Maritime University

On 18 June 1982, the UNDP Governing Council authorized the UNDP Administrator to undertake consultations with IMO and the Government of Sweden to clarify policy and technical and financial issues so that possible UNDP involvement in the establishment of a World Maritime University could be determined and action taken. The Administrator was requested to report on the consultations to the Council in 1983.[1] These actions were taken after the Council noted the IMO Secretary-General's statement on the proposed University and delegation support for it; Sweden's offer to facilitate establishment of the University, provided its contribution was matched by UNDP; and the views expressed by the Deputy Administrator at the Council's May 1982 special meeting on the level of commitments against the UNDP interregional IPF.

Subsequent consultations among IMO, UNDP and Sweden resulted in UNDP approval on 31 August of a nine-month preparatory assistance project from 1 October, to which UNDP contributed $215,750 and Sweden $100,000. UNDP and IMO, in consultation with Sweden and other interested parties, would take the steps necessary to bring the proposed University into being in 1983. Five core administrative staff, including the Rector, assumed duty in mid-October 1982, and consultants in various disciplines had been recruited. By December, agreements concerning the University premises at Malmö, Sweden, had been concluded between the IMO Secretary-General and the Municipality of Malmö, as had an agreement between IMO and Sweden on the internationalization of the University. A prospectus was in preparation and resources were being sought to cover the difference between Sweden's pledge of $1 million yearly and the estimated yearly operating costs.

Decision (1982). [1]UNDP Council (report, E/1982/16/Rev.1): 82/4 C, 18 June.

Multimodal and container transport

By a decision of 25 June 1982,[1] adopted during its tenth session, the Committee on Shipping requested the UNCTAD Secretary-General to: submit to its next session a study on national policy measures concerning multimodal transport operations and containerization; continue to give guidance and assistance, on request, to Governments of developing countries in implementing the United Nations Convention on International Multimodal Transport of Goods;[2] and convene in 1983 a group of 19 experts to recommend principles for developing model rules for multimodal container tariffs, which could be used by commercial parties in establishing the terms and conditions of carriage. The Committee requested the UNCTAD secretariat to prepare the relevant documentation and the group to submit its findings and recommendations to the Committee's next session.

Decision (1982). [1]Committee on Shipping (report, TD/B/921): 47(X), 25 June.
Yearbook reference. [2]1980, p. 1020.

Air transport

During the first part of its twenty-fourth session, held at Geneva from 8 to 24 March 1982,[1] the Trade and Development Board resumed consideration of the item on protectionism in the services sector, in connection with a report on only one industry in the sector—the effects of discriminatory and unfair civil aviation practices employed by developed countries on the growth of air transport in developing countries—which had been submitted to the Board in 1981.[2] The Group of 77 introduced in the Board's Sessional Committee I a draft decision sponsored by Jordan on the Group's behalf, requesting a study of international trade in services, on the basis of which the Board would examine ways of enhancing that trade and increasing developing countries' participation in it. In the absence of agreement as to whether UNCTAD was the proper forum for the subject, the Committee decided to remit the item and the draft decision to the contact group of the Board President. On 19 March, the President informed the Board that the draft had been withdrawn. No action was taken on the item.

Report. [1]TDB, A/37/15, vol. I.
Yearbook reference. [2]1981, p. 568.

Transport of dangerous goods

The Committee of Experts on the Transport of Dangerous Goods held its twelfth session at Geneva from 6 to 15 December 1982.[2]

Over the two-year period since its previous session in December 1980,[8] the Committee continued harmonizing codes and regulations relating to the transport of liquefied gases, radioactive materials, explosives and other hazardous substances.[6] Specifically, its work included changes in methods for classifying dangerous goods, resulting in amendments to or deletions of about 60 existing entries and adoption of 55 new ones; revisions to the special recommendations relating to explosives; adoption of a revised chapter of general recommendations on packing; addition of new criteria for defining oral and inhalation toxicity, a new section relating to desensitization of organic peroxides and a new chapter of special recommendations on self-reactive substances (commonly used as sponge-blowing agents, polymerization initiators and diazotype printing materials); and some general recommendations on the transport of specific classes of goods in limited quantities.

While noting the continuing increase in the quantity and variety of dangerous goods being transported, the Committee expressed satisfaction that its recommendations were being progressively incorporated into national and international requirements and regulations, thus contributing to co-ordination and harmonization. It hoped that future revised editions of its recommendations, as contained in *Transport of Dangerous Goods*,[1] would be produced regularly and more rapidly, to fulfil the Economic and Social Council's May 1981 request for its circulation to all concerned[7] and thereby realize the value of the work accomplished. The Committee also approved, with revisions, the recommendations made in 1981[9] and 1982 by its two subsidiary bodies—the Group of Rapporteurs and the Group of Experts on Explosives—and agreed on their work programmes.

The Group of Rapporteurs met for its twenty-eighth[4] and twenty-ninth[5] sessions at Geneva, from 8 to 12 March and from 9 to 13 August 1982. Besides recommending at those sessions a number of classification amendments, deletions and additions to the list of dangerous goods commonly carried, the Group, at the earlier session, reviewed and recommended: definitions, criteria and methods of classification relating to oral and inhalation toxicity and to determination of fluidity; special recommendations on organic peroxides and on substances with explosive properties also appropriate to other classes of substances; and an amendment relating to multimodal tank containers; it discussed but took no action on the question of gas cylinders. At the later session, the Group recommended a series of amendments relating to packing. It took note of and attached to its report a proposal for a new chapter of special recommendations concerning the transport of certain classes of dangerous goods in limited quantities, on which there had been considerable divergence of opinion.

The Group of Experts on Explosives, at its twenty-second session held at Geneva from 2 to 6 August,[3] recommended amendments to the special recommendations on the segregation of goods in different compatibility groups and on packing methods. It agreed on the preparation of a list of substances forbidden to be transported and on a comparative examination of testing methods and criteria for explosives based on the results of experimental tests being conducted. Other topics discussed included the possible reclassification of water-wetted explosive substances, proposals for loading and carriage of intermodal freight containers, and streamlining a glossary and harmonizing technical definitions.

Publication. [1] *Transport of Dangerous Goods*, second revised edition, ST/SG/AC.10/1/Rev.2.
Reports. [2] Committee of Experts, ST/SG/AC.10/8 & Corr.1 & Add.1-5; [3] Group of Experts on Explosives, ST/SG/AC.10/C.1/8; Group of Rapporteurs, [4] ST/SG/AC.10/C.2/11 & Add.1,2, [5] ST/SG/AC.10/C.2/13 & Add.1,2; [6] S-G, E/1983/25.
Resolution. [7] ESC: 1981/3, 4 May 1981 (YUN 1981, p. 570).
Yearbook references. [8] 1980, p. 1023; [9] 1981, pp. 569 & 571.

Transport planning

During its fifth session, at Nairobi, Kenya, from 26 April to 7 May 1982, the Commission on Human Settlements on 6 May[2] requested the Executive Director of the United Nations Centre for Human Settlements (Habitat) to continue work on transportation in human settlements. He was to concentrate on promoting greater consideration of transportation issues in formulating human settlements policies, strategies and plans, paying special attention to reducing transportation needs through the appropriate design of such settlements; promoting appropriate transport technologies and intermediate transportation systems, such as paratransit services and non-motorized vehicles; and communicating the experience acquired to developing countries through training and information dissemination.

This action was taken following consideration of a report by the Executive Director on transportation for urban and rural areas, with emphasis on groups with limited resources.[1] The report examined the transportation problems of those groups in the light of current transportation policies, both urban and rural, and of transportation planning for human settlements including measures to reduce transport requirements. The report noted that the ability of the poor to engage in economic activity was limited by inadequate transport facilities and services and generally hindered by transportation policies. Rural policy, oriented mainly towards providing trunk and feeder roads built to a high standard of design, should be reformulated to provide essential access facilities and appropriate vehicles for use on and off the farm. A reorientation of urban settlements development, by shifting its emphasis from formal to informal economy and from central-area to dispersed growth, might reduce the need for travel while increasing opportunities for participation in economic and social activities.

Report. [1]UNCHS Executive Director, HS/C/5/4.
Resolution (1982). [2]Commission on Human Settlements (report, A/37/8): 5/21, 6 May.

Communications

Preparations for World Communications Year (1983)

In response to a November 1981 General Assembly request,[4] the Secretary-General of the International Telecommunication Union (ITU) prepared a report on the state of preparations for World Communications Year (1983), transmitted to the Assembly, through the Economic and Social Council, by the United Nations Secretary-General.[3]

The outline of the report was agreed on by the Inter-Agency Committee for the Year when it met at Geneva on 15 April 1982 to review the programme of activities proposed by United Nations bodies. The report described those proposals, as well as action taken, in accordance with the 1982 action plan adopted in 1981,[5] towards establishment of national committees to serve as forums for the concerted review of national policies for the development of communications infrastructures. The report provided guidelines for programmes at all levels. National programmes were to include pilot projects to stimulate infrastructure development; conferences and seminars to analyse issues relating to communications policies and development; and information activities to promote public awareness of the Year's objectives through press campaigns, radio and television programmes, and distribution of documentation, posters and other material. The same programme categories at the regional and international levels would complement national programmes and provide national committees with logistic support.

In addition, the report noted the activities undertaken by the ITU Administrative Council towards achieving the Year's objectives.

Economic and Social Council action. The Economic and Social Council, acting without vote on 28 July 1982,[1] took note of the report of the ITU Secretary-General and decided to transmit it to the General Assembly at its 1982 session. The Council also decided to request the ITU Secretary-General to submit to the Assembly in 1983, through the Council, a report on the execution of the programme for the Year. The draft decision had been approved, also without vote, on 19 July by the Third (Programme and Co-ordination)

Committee, where it had been proposed by the Chairman.

General Assembly action. On 17 December 1982,[2] the General Assembly took note of the Secretary-General's note transmitting the report of the ITU Secretary-General. The decision, adopted without vote by the Assembly, had been similarly approved on 8 December by the Second (Economic and Financial) Committee, on an oral proposal of its Chairman.

Decisions (1982). [1]ESC: 1982/163, 28 July, text following. [2]GA: 37/431, 17 Dec., text following.
Report. [3]ITU S-G, transmitted by S-G note, A/37/232.
Resolution. [4]GA: 36/40, 19 Nov. 1981 (YUN 1981, p. 573). *Yearbook reference.* [5]1981, p. 573.
Meeting records. ESC: E/1982/SR.49 (28 July). GA: 2nd Committee, A/C.2/37/SR.3-12, 32, 47 (28 Sep.–8 Dec.); plenary, A/37/PV.109 (17 Dec.).

Economic and Social Council decision 1982/163

Adopted without vote

Approved by Third Committee (E/1982/01) without vote, 19 July (meeting 11), draft by Chairman (E/1982/C.3/L.3); agenda item 20.

Report of the Secretary-General of the International Telecommunication Union on the preparations for the World Communications Year: Development of Communications Infrastructures

At its 49th plenary meeting, on 28 July 1982, the Council:

(a) Took note of the report of the Secretary-General of the International Telecommunication Union on the preparations for the World Communications Year;

(b) Decided to transmit that report to the General Assembly at its thirty-seventh session;

(c) Decided also to request the Secretary-General of the International Telecommunication Union to submit to the General Assembly at its thirty-eighth session, through the Economic and Social Council at its second regular session of 1983, a report on the execution of the programme for the Year.

General Assembly decision 37/431

Adopted without vote

Approved by Second Committee (A/37/679/Add.1) without vote, 8 December (meeting 47); oral proposal by Chairman; agenda item 12.

World Communications Year

At its 109th plenary meeting, on 17 December 1982, the General Assembly, on the recommendation of the Second Committee, took note of the note of the Secretary-General transmitting the report of the Secretary-General of the International Telecommunication Union, prepared in accordance with Assembly resolution 36/40 of 19 November 1981.

Rural communications

The Second United Nations Conference on the Exploration and Peaceful Uses of Outer Space, meeting in August 1982,[1] dealt with space communications as one element in its review of space applications. With reference to rural communications, it noted that world-wide expansion of telephone and telex services focused on high-usage interconnections and relied increasingly on satellite transmissions, which were insensitive to earth surface distances. As a result, rural communications needs of developing countries had been ignored in favour of intercontinental and inter-city connections, making it easier to contact a distant capital than a neighbouring village. Since communications played a key role in development, the Conference drew attention to the desirability of studies to be undertaken by developing countries and appropriate United Nations agencies, especially ITU and the United Nations Educational,

Scientific and Cultural Organization, aimed at establishing rural communications infrastructures, to be strengthened with support from funding institutions.

Report. [1]Conference on outer space, A/CONF.100/10.

Chapter VI

Industrial development

Contents

Related topics:

Regional economic and social activities—Industrial development: Africa; Asia and the Pacific; Europe; Latin America; Western Asia. Energy: Industrial uses. Science and technology: Technology transfer. Environment and industry. Women in development.

For resolutions and decisions of major organs mentioned but not reproduced, refer to INDEX OF RESOLUTIONS AND DECISIONS.

Programme and finances of UNIDO

Programme policy

The United Nations Industrial Development Organization (UNIDO) continued in 1982 its efforts to help developing countries raise their share of world industrial production to the target of 25 per cent by the year 2000. Its activities were geared to implementation of the instrument containing this goal—the Lima Declaration and Plan of Action on Industrial Development and Co-operation,[9] adopted in 1975 at the Second General Conference of UNIDO (Lima, Peru). The activities of UNIDO in 1982 were described in a report by its Executive Director[5] to the Industrial Development Board.

The 45-nation Board held its sixteenth session at UNIDO headquarters, Vienna, Austria, from 11 to 28 May. At the closing of the session, the Board adopted its report and a resolution on the Industrial Development Decade for Africa. The Board's Permanent Committee met twice at Vienna, for its seventeenth (10, 11 and 14 May)[3] and eighteenth (15-19 November)[4] sessions.

The work of UNIDO was reviewed at meetings in May and December by UNIDO senior officers under the chairmanship of the Executive Director, and by the Economic and Social Council and the General Assembly, each of which adopted a resolution on various aspects of UNIDO operations—the Council in July and the Assembly in December.

Economic and Social Council action. By a resolution on industrial development co-operation adopted on 30 July 1982,[7] the Economic and Social Council took note of the report of the Industrial Development Board on its May session.[2] It endorsed the Board's 1981 conclusions,[10] reaffirming that activities in the areas of energy-related and other industrial technology, industrial production, human resources development, special measures for the least developed countries and the System of Consultations should be accorded priority, and recommended that these activities be given continued priority for 1983-1985.

Referring to specific UNIDO activities, the Council supported strengthening the System of Consultations; requested the Secretary-General to organize consultations on the entry into force of the UNIDO Constitution; recommended that the General Assembly arrange for funds to cover the increased UNIDO share of the cost of the Senior Industrial Development Field Advisers (SIDFAs) Programme; urged contributions to the United Nations Industrial Development Fund; took note

of the Board's decision on a proposed international bank for industrial development (see below); reiterated the importance of restructuring world industrial production and redeployment of industrial capacities; recognized the importance of financial flows to industrial development in developing countries; and recommended for Assembly approval the draft agenda for the Fourth (1984) General Conference of UNIDO and approved establishment of an open-ended preparatory working group.

The Council adopted the resolution, sponsored by Algeria, on behalf of the Group of 77 developing countries, and Austria, by 42 votes to none, with 4 abstentions, having first adopted paragraph 5 (on funds for the SIDFA Programme) by 42 votes to 4. The text, orally amended by a Vice-Chairman, had been approved by the First (Economic) Committee on 29 July, by 40 votes to none, with 4 abstentions, following a vote, taken at the request of the USSR, on paragraph 5 that resulted in its retention by 39 votes to 4. The text was based on informal consultations on a draft resolution submitted by Algeria, also for the Group of 77,[1] and subsequently withdrawn.

The oral amendments included deletion of a paragraph on the need for increased participation in the System of Consultations.

Reservations and statements of position were made after adoption of the resolution in the Council in regard to the provisions on the System of Consultations (Eastern European States, United States), the financing of the SIDFA Programme (Eastern European States), the consultations envisaged on the entry into force of the UNIDO Constitution (European Community (EC) members, United States), the establishment of an international bank for industrial development (EC members), and the restructuring of world industrial production and redeployment of industrial capacities (United States).

The UNIDO draft programme of work for 1984-1985[6] reflected the priorities recommended by the Council, grouping programme activities into three categories: policy co-ordination, industrial studies and research, and industrial operations. It was prepared and submitted by the UNIDO Executive Director for review in November by the Board's Permanent Committee, which requested him to submit a revised programme reflecting delegation views and comments.

General Assembly action. By a resolution of 20 December 1982 on industrial development co-operation,[8] the General Assembly took note of the report of the Industrial Development Board; commended the Executive Director for his efforts to enhance the role of UNIDO in promoting industrialization of developing countries; and reaffirmed the Council's July resolution reaffirming the priority areas for industrial development activities and recommending the same priorities for 1983-1985.

As recommended by the Council, the Assembly decided that resources be provided in the 1983 UNIDO budget for additional SIDFA posts, inviting the Board to examine in 1983 the SIDFA Programme's financing; approved the draft provisional agenda for the Fourth General Conference, as well as establishment of a preparatory working group, and decided that resources be provided for the preparatory activities; and took note of the Board's decision on the proposed international bank for industrial development.

These actions were contained in section I of the resolution; section II concerned the Industrial Development Decade for Africa (1980-1990).

Sponsored by Bangladesh on behalf of the Group of 77, the resolution as a whole was adopted by a recorded vote of 129 to 10, with 12 abstentions, following adoption of paragraphs 4 and 7 together by a recorded vote, taken at Denmark's request, of 118 to 20, with 11 abstentions. The text, which had been revised, was approved on 13 December by the Second (Economic and Financial) Committee by a recorded vote of 101 to 9, with 12 abstentions, preceded by the approval of paragraphs 4 and 7 together by a vote, taken at the request of Denmark on behalf of the EC members, of 91 to 19, with 11 abstentions.

Before and following Committee approval of the text, comments or reservations similar to those voiced in the Council were expressed regarding the expansion of the System of Consultations (Eastern European States), the financing of additional SIDFA posts in 1983 and budgetary support for the SIDFA Programme during 1984-1985 (Eastern European States, EC members), the resources for the Fourth General Conference, including preparatory work (Eastern European States, EC members, Japan, United States), and the establishment of an industrial development bank (United States).

Draft resolution withdrawn. [1]Algeria, for Group of 77, E/1982/C.1/L.22.
Reports. [2]IDB, A/37/16; Permanent Committee, [3]ID/B/288 & Corr.1, [4]ID/B/290; UNIDO Executive Director, [5]ID/B/300, [6]ID/B/C.3/116.
Resolutions (1982). [7]ESC: 1982/66 A, 30 July, text following. [8]GA: 37/212, 20 Dec., text following.
Yearbook references. [9]1975, p. 473; [10]1981, p. 576.
Financial implications. 5th Committee report, A/37/780; S-G statements, A/C.2/37/L.106, A/C.5/37/101, E/1982/C.1/L.36.
Meeting records. ESC: E/1982/SR.51 (30 July). GA: 2nd Committee, A/C.2/37/SR.3, 6, 7, 10, 13-19, 33, 40, *43, 48* (28 Sep.–13 Dec.); 5th Committee, A/C.5/37/SR.75 (17 Dec.); plenary, A/37/PV.113 (20 Dec.).

Economic and Social Council resolution 1982/66 A

30 July 1982	Meeting 51	42-0-4

Approved by First Committee (E/1982/104) by vote (40-0-4), 29 July (meeting 16); 2-nation draft (E/1982/C.1/L.35, part A), based on informal consultations on draft by Algeria, for Group of 77 (E/1982/C.1/C.22), as orally amended by Vice-Chairman; agenda item 16.

Sponsors: Algeria (for Group of 77), Austria.

Report of the Industrial Development Board

The Economic and Social Council,

Recalling General Assembly resolutions 3201(S-VI) and 3202(S-VI) of 1 May 1974, containing the Declaration and the Programme of Action on the Establishment of a New International Economic Order, 3281(XXIX) of 12 December 1974, containing the Charter of Economic Rights and Duties of States, and 3362(S-VII) of 16 September 1975 on development and international economic co-operation,

Recalling also the Lima Declaration and Plan of Action on Industrial Development and Co-operation, adopted at the Second General Conference of the United Nations Industrial Development Organization, which laid down the main measures and principles for industrial development and co-operation within the framework of the establishment of the new international economic order, and the New Delhi Declaration and Plan of Action on Industrialization of Developing Countries and International Co-operation for their Industrial Development, adopted at the Third General Conference of the United Nations Industrial Development Organization, which spelt out a strategy for the further industrialization of developing countries for the 1980s and beyond, as well as a plan of action for the restructuring of world industry,

Stressing the importance and urgency of the industrialization of developing countries in the implementation of the International Development Strategy for the Third United Nations Development Decade,

Reiterating the need for increased flows of financial resources to developing countries for their accelerated industrialization,

Endorsing General Assembly resolution 36/182 of 17 December 1981 on industrial development co-operation, in which the Assembly, *inter alia*, decided to ensure that adequate resources were made available to the United Nations Industrial Development Organization for agreed priority activities,

Noting decision 82/30 of 18 June 1982 of the Governing Council of the United Nations Development Programme, in which the Governing Council invited the attention of the General Assembly to the urgent need for the United Nations Industrial Development Organization to bear an increased share of the cost of the Senior Industrial Development Field Advisers Programme,

Bearing in mind the necessity of maintaining the momentum of technical assistance delivery achieved by the United Nations Industrial Development Organization in recent years,

Conscious of the role of the United Nations Industrial Development Organization as the central co-ordinating organ within the United Nations system for the promotion of industrial development co-operation and for the fulfilment of the agreed measures and the attainment of the agreed targets in both the Lima Declaration and Plan of Action and the New Delhi Declaration and Plan of Action,

Having considered the report of the Industrial Development Board on its sixteenth session and the progress report submitted jointly by the Executive Director of the United Nations Industrial Development Organization and the Executive Secretary of the Economic Commission for Africa concerning action taken with regard to the Industrial Development Decade for Africa,

1. *Takes note* of the report of the Industrial Development Board on its sixteenth session;

2. *Endorses* the conclusions reached by the Industrial Development Board at its fifteenth session, reaffirming that activities in the areas of industrial technology, energy-related industrial technology, industrial production, the development of human resources, special measures for the least developed countries, and the System of Consultations should be accorded priority, and recommends that these activities should be given continued priority for 1983-1985, as established by the Board at its fourteenth session;

3. *Strongly supports* the strengthening of the System of Consultations, particular attention being given to measures that could increase the industrial capacities of developing countries in accordance with the principles, objectives and characteristics contained in the rules of procedure of the System;

4. *Requests* the Secretary-General to organize consultations among representatives of all Member States that have ratified the Constitution of the United Nations Industrial Development Organization, and all other interested Member States, with a view to the entry into force of the Constitution, and to report to the General Assembly at its thirty-seventh session;

5. *Recommends* to the General Assembly that it should arrange for adequate funds to be provided from sources to be determined by

the Assembly, so that senior industrial development field advisers may be appointed in the countries that need them, in particular all the least developed countries, especially those in Africa, in accordance with the terms of decision 82/38 of the Governing Council of the United Nations Development Programme, in which the Governing Council stressed the urgent need for the United Nations Industrial Development Organization to bear an increased share of the cost of the Senior Industrial Development Field Advisers Programme;

6. *Urges* all countries in a position to do so, in particular the developed countries, to contribute or increase their contributions to the United Nations Industrial Development Fund at the 1982 United Nations Pledging Conference for Development Activities, so that the agreed desirable funding level of $50 million annually may be reached in 1982;

7. *Takes note* of the decision taken by the Industrial Development Board at its sixteenth session, concerning the proposal of the Executive Director of the United Nations Industrial Development Organization for an international bank for industrial development, as reflected in paragraphs 66 to 71 of the report of the Board, and also notes that consideration of the proposal will revert to the Board at its seventeenth session;

8. *Reiterates* the importance of facilitating the restructuring of world industrial production through, *inter alia*, the implementation of General Assembly resolution 35/66 of 5 December 1980 and resolution 131(V) of 3 June 1979 of the United Nations Conference on Trade and Development;

9. *Recognizes* the importance of financial flows to industrial development in developing countries;

10. *Reiterates* the importance of the redeployment of industrial capacities, as described in paragraph 73 of the International Development Strategy for the Third United Nations Development Decade, and supports the efforts of the United Nations Industrial Development Organization in further improving and developing its programme of industrial redeployment, as outlined in paragraphs 127 to 131 of the report of the Board;

11. *Takes note* of the draft provisional agenda for the Fourth General Conference of the United Nations Industrial Development Organization, as generally endorsed by the Industrial Development Board, recommends it for approval by the General Assembly and approves the establishment of an open-ended working group of the Board to meet periodically with the secretariat of the United Nations Industrial Development Organization to exchange information and views on the preparations for the Conference, including its timing.

General Assembly resolution 37/212

20 December 1982   Meeting 113   129-10-12 (recorded vote)

Approved by Second Committee (A/37/680/Add.3) by recorded vote (101-9-12), 13 December (meeting 48); draft by Bangladesh, for Group of 77 (A/C.2/37/L.76/Rev.1); agenda item 71 *(d)*.

Industrial development co-operation

The General Assembly,

Recalling its resolutions 3201(S-VI) and 3202(S-VI) of 1 May 1974, containing the Declaration and the Programme of Action on the Establishment of a New International Economic Order, 3281(XXIX) of 12 December 1974, containing the Charter of Economic Rights and Duties of States, and 3362(S-VII) of 16 September 1975 on development and international economic co-operation,

Recalling also the Lima Declaration and Plan of Action on Industrial Development and Co-operation, adopted at the Second General Conference of the United Nations Industrial Development Organization, in which were laid down the main measures and principles for industrial development and co-operation within the framework of the establishment of the new international economic order,

Recalling further the New Delhi Declaration and Plan of Action on Industrialization of Developing Countries and International Co-operation for their Industrial Development, adopted at the Third General Conference of the United Nations Industrial Development Organization, in which a strategy was spelt out for the further industrialization of developing countries for the 1980s and beyond, as well as a plan of action for the restructuring of world industry,

Endorsing the consensus reached at the fourteenth session of the Industrial Development Board on the follow-up to the Third General Conference of the United Nations Industrial Development Organization,

Bearing in mind that, within the framework of the new international economic order, far-reaching changes in the structure of the world economy involve the restructuring of world industry, taking fully into account the capacities and potential of the developing countries,

Conscious of the role of the United Nations Industrial Development Organization as the central co-ordinating organ having primary responsibility within the United Nations system for the promotion of industrial development co-operation and for facilitating the transfer of industrial technology,

Recalling its resolution 35/56 of 5 December 1980, the annex to which contains the International Development Strategy for the Third United Nations Development Decade, in which, *inter alia*, the importance of industrialization in the development of developing countries was stressed,

Expressing its concern at the negative impact of the worsening world economic situation on the industrialization of the developing countries and reiterating the need for a substantially increased transfer of financial and technical resources to developing countries for their accelerated industrialization,

Recalling its resolutions 35/66 of 5 December 1980 and 36/182 of 17 December 1981 on industrial development co-operation,

Bearing in mind the central role of the United Nations Industrial Development Organization for increased technical assistance delivery,

Noting decision 82/38 of 18 June 1982 of the Governing Council of the United Nations Development Programme,

I

Report of the Industrial Development Board on its sixteenth session

1. *Takes note* of the report of the Industrial Development Board on its sixteenth session;

2. *Commends* the Executive Director of the United Nations Industrial Development Organization for his efforts to enhance the role of the Organization in promoting the industrialization of developing countries as described in his report for 1981 presented to the Industrial Development Board at its sixteenth session;

3. *Reaffirms* Economic and Social Council resolution 1982/66 of 30 July 1982 on industrial development co-operation, in which the Council reaffirmed that activities in the areas of industrial technology, energy-related industrial technology, industrial production, the development of human resources, special measures for the least developed countries, and the System of Consultations should be accorded priority, and recommended that those activities should be given continued priority for 1983-1985;

4. *Decides* that adequate resources should be provided in the budget of the United Nations Industrial Development Organization for 1983 to finance up to 10 additional posts in order that senior industrial development field advisers may be appointed, in particular in the least developed countries, especially those in Africa, and in order that in future these advisers might be appointed in all developing countries that need them, as mentioned in Economic and Social Council resolution 1982/66;

5. *Invites* the Industrial Development Board to examine the question of financing the posts of senior industrial development field advisers in the developing countries at its seventeenth session and decides to consider at its thirty-eighth session, on the basis of the recommendations of the Industrial Development Board, the question of appropriate budgetary support for the biennium 1984-1985 with a view to maintaining and, if necessary, increasing the Senior Industrial Development Field Advisers Programme;

6. *Approves* the draft provisional agenda for the Fourth General Conference of the United Nations Industrial Development Organization, as recommended by the Industrial Development Board in paragraph 167 of its report, and also approves the establishment of an open-ended working group of the Board to meet periodically and together with the secretariat of the United Nations Industrial Development Organization during the period of preparation for the Conference to exchange information and views, on an informal basis, on the progress, direction and contents of the preparations;

7. *Decides* that adequate resources should be provided to cover the costs of the preparatory work and documentation to be undertaken during 1983 for the Fourth General Conference of the United Nations Industrial Development Organization, as decided by the Industrial Development Board in paragraphs 166 to 170 of its report, including five expert group meetings on major topics of the Conference and meetings of the working group referred to in paragraph 6 above, and

decides to consider the question of providing adequate and necessary resources for the holding of the Fourth General Conference at the time of the consideration of the proposed programme budget for the biennium 1984-1985 at its thirty-eighth session;

8. *Takes note* of the decision taken by the Industrial Development Board concerning the proposal of the Executive Director of the United Nations Industrial Development Organization for an international bank for industrial development, as reflected in paragraphs 66 to 71 of the report of the Board, and also notes that consideration of the proposal will revert to the Board at its seventeenth session;

II

Industrial Development Decade for Africa

Bearing in mind the Lagos Plan of Action for the Implementation of the Monrovia Strategy for the Economic Development of Africa,

Having considered the note by the Secretary-General on the implementation of the Industrial Development Decade for Africa,

Also bearing in mind that the Sixth Conference of African Ministers of Industry, held at Addis Ababa from 23 to 25 November 1981, adopted proposals for the formulation and implementation of a programme for the Industrial Development Decade for Africa,

Recalling Industrial Development Board resolutions 54(XV) of 30 May 1981 and 55(XVI) of 28 May 1982, in which the Board, *inter alia*, declared the Industrial Development Decade for Africa to be one of the most important programmes of the United Nations Industrial Development Organization,

Noting the endorsement of the programme for the Industrial Development Decade for Africa by the Conference of Ministers of the Economic Commission for Africa in its resolution 442(XVII) of 30 April 1982,

Taking note of the report submitted jointly by the Executive Director of the United Nations Industrial Development Organization and the Executive Secretary of the Economic Commission for Africa on action taken with regard to the Industrial Development Decade for Africa,

1. *Takes note* of the progress report submitted jointly by the Executive Director of the United Nations Industrial Development Organization and the Executive Secretary of the Economc Commission for Africa regarding the Industrial Development Decade for Africa;

2. *Requests* the Secretary-General to allocate adequate staff and financial resources so as to ensure the effective co-ordination and implementation of the activities of the United Nations Industrial Development Organization and the Economic Commission for Africa related to the Industrial Development Decade for Africa;

3. *Requests* the Executive Director of the United Nations Industrial Development Organization to report through the Industrial Development Board at its seventeenth session to the Economic and Social Council at its second regular session of 1983 on the contacts made and the responses of the United Nations system to the proposals for implementation of the programme for the Industrial Development Decade for Africa;

4. *Appeals* to all countries to contribute generously to the Industrial Development Fund in order to support activities related to the Industrial Development Decade for Africa.

Recorded vote in Assembly as follows:

In favour: Afghanistan, Algeria, Angola, Antigua and Barbuda, Argentina, Australia, Austria, Bahamas, Bahrain, Bangladesh, Barbados, Benin, Bhutan, Bolivia, Botswana, Brazil, Burma, Burundi, Cape Verde, Central African Republic, Chad, Chile, China, Colombia, Comoros, Congo, Costa Rica, Cuba, Cyprus, Democratic Kampuchea, Democratic Yemen, Denmark, Djibouti, Dominican Republic, Ecuador, Egypt, El Salvador, Equatorial Guinea, Ethiopia, Fiji, Finland, Gabon, Gambia, Ghana, Greece, Grenada, Guatemala, Guinea, Guinea-Bissau, Guyana, Haiti, Honduras, Iceland, India, Indonesia, Iran, Iraq, Ivory Coast, Jamaica, Jordan, Kenya, Kuwait, Lao People's Democratic Republic, Lebanon, Lesotho, Liberia, Libyan Arab Jamahiriya, Madagascar, Malawi, Malaysia, Maldives, Mali, Malta, Mauritania, Mauritius, Mexico, Morocco, Mozambique, Nepal, Nicaragua, Niger, Nigeria, Norway, Oman, Pakistan, Panama, Papua New Guinea, Paraguay, Peru, Philippines, Portugal, Qatar, Romania, Rwanda, Saint Lucia, Saint Vincent and the Grenadines, Samoa, Sao Tome and Principe, Saudi Arabia, Senegal, Sierra Leone, Singapore, Somalia, Spain, Sri Lanka, Sudan, Suriname, Swaziland, Sweden, Syrian Arab Republic, Thailand, Togo, Trinidad and Tobago, Tunisia, Turkey, Uganda, United Arab Emirates, United Republic of Cameroon, United Republic of Tanzania, Upper Volta, Uruguay, Vanuatu, Venezuela, Viet Nam, Yemen, Yugoslavia, Zaire, Zambia, Zimbabwe.

Against: Bulgaria, Byelorussian SSR, Czechoslovakia, German Democratic Republic, Hungary, Mongolia, Poland, Ukrainian SSR, USSR, United States.

Abstaining: Belgium, Canada, France, Germany, Federal Republic of, Ireland, Israel, Italy, Japan, Luxembourg, Netherlands, New Zealand, United Kingdom.

Evaluation

In 1982, as in previous years, the principal mechanism for reviewing the work of UNIDO as a whole remained the biannual implementation review meeting of senior officers under the chairmanship of the Executive Director. The first meeting, convened in May, reviewed implementation during 1981 against targets for that year and in the light of which it established 1982 implementation targets; the second, in December, conducted a similar review for 1982 and set 1983 targets. In addition, UNIDO headquarters staff participated in 48 tripartite reviews, undertaken jointly by the Government involved, the executing agency and the United Nations Development Programme (UNDP)—this tripartite review being the principal tool for monitoring field projects. Also undertaken were 52 evaluation missions.

The first and second phases of a special joint United Nations/UNDP/UNIDO evaluation of UNDP-financed and UNIDO-executed technical assistance field projects on manufactures, initiated in 1981,[4] were completed in 1982. The second phase comprised in-country studies and missions to Argentina, Egypt, India, Indonesia, Kenya, Peru and Yugoslavia, followed by a synthesis workshop in November. The third and final phase, comprising preparation and review of the staff evaluation and draft reports to the Committee for Programme and Co-ordination, was begun in December.

Two progress reports on evaluation were submitted to the Permanent Committee of the Industrial Development Board at its May session.[1] One described the design work leading to the installation of a comprehensive internal evaluation system for field projects, which became operational in May.[2] The other described the activities, accomplishments and plans for a programme evaluation system, including joint exercises with the United Nations and UNDP.[3]

Following review of these reports, the Committee, on 14 May, recommended that the Board request the Executive Director to submit to the Committee at its 1983 spring session a report on the first year's operation of the new system, including evaluation results and the use made of them by UNIDO management. An inventory of such evaluations by country and region, distinguishing between large- (over $400,000) and small-scale projects, was also to be included. Account was to be taken of the Committee's and the Board's previous decisions on the subject; of the views expressed at the Committee's May 1982 session, especially on the role of recipient and participating States in the evaluation process; and of those portions of the system that might benefit from simplification. The Committee also recommended that the next report on evaluation and related exercises be consolidated in one document to include estimated financial implications, particularly of the internal evaluation system.

The Committee further took note of the progress of evaluation in other areas, including that covering manufactures (see above), and of UNIDO staff participation in in-depth evaluations.

Reports. (1)Permanent Committee, ID/B/288 & Corr.1; UNIDO secretariat, (2)ID/B/C.3/112, (3)ID/B/C.3/113. *Yearbook reference.* (4)1981, p. 580.

Organizational questions

Proposed consultative meetings on the 1979 Constitution to convert UNIDO into a specialized agency

The Constitution to establish UNIDO as a specialized agency, adopted by a United Nations Conference in 1979,[3] had been signed by 131 States and ratified, accepted or approved by 87 of them as at 31 December 1982.

The States that had adhered to the Constitution (the 21 in italics acted during 1982) were:

Afghanistan, Algeria, Argentina, *Australia*, Austria, Bangladesh, Barbados, Belgium, Bolivia, Brazil, *Burundi*, *Central African Republic*, Chile, China, Colombia, Cuba, Democratic People's Republic of Korea, *Democratic Yemen*, Denmark, *Dominica*, *Ecuador*, Egypt, Ethiopia, Fiji, Finland, *France*, *Gabon*, *Ghana*, Guinea, *Haiti*, India, Indonesia, Iraq, Ivory Coast, *Jamaica*, Japan, *Jordan*, Kenya, *Kuwait*, Lao People's Democratic Republic, Lesotho, Libyan Arab Jamahiriya, Madagascar, Malawi, Malaysia, Mali, *Malta*, Mauritania, Mauritius, Mexico, Netherlands, Nicaragua, Niger, Nigeria, Norway, Oman, Pakistan, Panama, Paraguay, *Peru*, Philippines, Republic of Korea, Romania, *Saint Lucia*, *Seychelles*, Somalia, Spain, Sri Lanka, Sudan, Suriname, Swaziland, Sweden, Switzerland, *Syrian Arab Republic*, Thailand, Togo, Trinidad and Tobago, Tunisia, *Turkey*, United Arab Emirates, United Republic of Cameroon, United Republic of Tanzania, *Upper Volta*, Uruguay, Yugoslavia, *Zaire*, Zambia.

The following 44 States had signed but not formally adhered to the Constitution as at 31 December (the 6 in italics acted during 1982):

Angola, *Antigua and Barbuda*, Benin, Bulgaria, Byelorussian SSR, *Canada*, *Chad*, Comoros, Congo, Cyprus, Czechoslovakia, Djibouti, Dominican Republic, El Salvador, German Democratic Republic, Germany, Federal Republic of, Greece, Guatemala, Guinea-Bissau, Honduras, Hungary, Iran, Ireland, *Israel*, Italy, Lebanon, Liberia, Luxembourg, Mongolia, Morocco, *Mozambique*, Poland, Portugal, Rwanda, Senegal, Sierra Leone, Uganda, Ukrainian SSR, USSR, United Kingdom, United States, Venezuela, Viet Nam, Yemen.

Under its article 25, the Constitution was to take effect after at least 80 States which had deposited instruments of ratification, acceptance, approval or accession agreed, after consultations among

themselves, that it would enter into force. The minimum number of ratifications having been attained by 12 July, the stage for such consultations was set.

Economic and Social Council action. The Economic and Social Council, in its resolution of 30 July on industrial development co-operation,[1] requested the Secretary-General to organize consultations among all Member States that had ratified the Constitution and all other interested Members, with a view to the Constitution's entry into force, and to report to the General Assembly at its 1982 session.

During the explanations of vote in the Council, Denmark, speaking on behalf of the European Community (EC) members, stated that, while they had voted for the resolution, they disagreed with the Secretary-General's interpretation, as contained in his statement of the resolution's programme budget implications, that the consultations requested by the Council would not include those referred to in article 25 of the Constitution. Denmark recalled that, during informal discussions on the draft resolution, there had been a clear understanding that the consultations in question would consist of a single session; the United States said it had the same understanding.

General Assembly action. On 20 December, the General Assembly adopted without vote a resolution on the conversion of UNIDO into a specialized agency.[2] The Assembly recommended that consultations among States that had ratified, accepted or approved the UNIDO Constitution and other interested States, to determine the date of entry into force of that Constitution, should be organized in three stages, as follows: a one-day procedural meeting in New York in January 1983; a series of consultations at Vienna, Austria, leading to a formal meeting not to exceed one week, to discuss substantive questions; and a one-day closing meeting in New York to receive the conclusions of the substantive meeting and to execute individual notifications to the Secretary-General of agreement for the Constitution's entry into force.

The text, sponsored and revised by the Chairman of the Second (Economic and Financial) Committee, was approved, also without vote, by the Committee on 13 December 1982.

Resolutions (1982). (1)ESC: 1982/66 A, para. 4, 30 July. (2)GA: 37/213, 20 Dec., text following.
Yearbook reference. (3)1979, p. 618.
Financial implications. 5th Committee report, A/37/780; S-G statements, A/C.2/37/L.119/Rev.1, A/C.5/37/100, E/1982/C.1/L.36.
Meeting records. GA: 2nd Committee, A/C.2/37/SR.3, 6, 7, 10, 13-19, 33, 40, *48* (28 Sep.–13 Dec.); 5th Committee, A/C.5/37/SR.75 (17 Dec.); plenary, A/37/PV.113 (20 Dec.).

General Assembly resolution 37/213

20 December 1982   Meeting 113   Adopted without vote

Approved by Second Committee (A/37/680/Add.3) without vote, 13 December (meeting 48); draft by Chairman (A/C.2/37/L.118/Rev.1); agenda item 71 *(d)*.

Conversion of the United Nations Industrial Development Organization into a specialized agency

The General Assembly,

Bearing in mind the Constitution of the United Nations Industrial Development Organization,

Noting that the Constitution has been ratified, accepted or approved by more than the minimum number of States whose agreement is required for its entry into force,

Recalling paragraph 4 of Economic and Social Council resolution 1982/66 A of 30 July 1982, concerning arrangements for consultations leading to the notifications foreseen in paragraph 1 of article 25 of the Constitution,

Appreciating the efforts of the Secretary-General and the Director-General for Development and International Economic Co-operation in organizing informal preliminary consultations,

1. *Recommends* that consultations to determine the date of entry into force of the Constitution of the United Nations Industrial Development Organization should be organized in three stages among States that have ratified, accepted or approved that Constitution and other interested States, as follows:

(a) A one-day procedural meeting in New York in January 1983 to determine the date of substantive meetings and to give interested delegations an opportunity for a preliminary discussion of the agenda and other organizational matters relating thereto;

(b) A series of consultations at Vienna, leading to a formal meeting not exceeding one week, if possible immediately following the seventeenth session of the Industrial Development Board, during the first half of 1983, to discuss all relevant substantive questions;

(c) A one-day closing meeting in New York to receive the conclusions of the substantive meetings and to execute individual notifications to the Secretary-General of agreement for the entry into force of the Constitution of the United Nations Industrial Development Organization;

2. *Requests* the Secretary-General to provide the necessary conference services for the meetings in New York and Vienna, and resources from voluntary contributions, to the extent possible, and extrabudgetary resources, as appropriate, to cover the travel costs of one representative of each of the least developed countries participating in the meetings at Vienna.

Preparations for the 1984 General Conference

Pursuant to a December 1981 General Assembly request,[5] the Industrial Development Board, acting as the Preparatory Committee for the Fourth (1984) General Conference of UNIDO, agreed at its May 1982 session[1] to recommend to the Assembly a draft provisional agenda for the Conference to include: organization of the Conference; a review of progress in the implementation of the 1975 Lima Declaration and Plan of Action on Industrial Development and Co-operation,[6] the 1980 New Delhi Declaration and Plan of Action on Industrialization of Developing Countries and International Co-operation for their Industrial Development,[7] and the Industrial Development Decade for Africa (1980-1990); the contribution of UNIDO in the critical areas of industrial development for 1985-2000 and its role in co-ordinating industrial development activities in the United Nations system; and conclusions and recommendations.

At the same time, the Board established an open-ended working group to meet periodically with the secretariat during the preparatory period.

It also decided that Conference preparations be included in the agenda of the Permanent Committee's November 1982 session and requested the Executive Director to report orally on them to the Committee.

Accordingly, bearing in mind the possibility that UNIDO might become a specialized agency before the Conference, the Permanent Committee in November considered the question of Conference preparations,[2] together with the financial implications. Many delegations expressed disappointment that in his oral report the Executive Director could not give details on preparation costs. He was therefore requested by the Committee to provide such information to the Board's open-ended working group and to ensure that Conference documentation gave appropriate attention to alternative industrial development experiences for use by developing countries at their discretion.

As recommended by the Economic and Social Council in its 30 July resolution on industrial development co-operation,[3] the Assembly, in its 20 December resolution on the same topic,[4] approved the draft provisional agenda for the Conference and, like the Council, approved the establishment of the Board's open-ended working group. It decided that adequate resources be provided to cover costs of pre-Conference activities, including work and documentation to be undertaken and five expert group meetings to be held on major topics in 1983, and to consider the question of providing resources necessary for the Conference itself when the Assembly examined the proposed programme budget for 1984-1985 at its 1983 session. Paragraph 7 on resources for the Conference was adopted—together with paragraph 4 on financing additional senior industrial development field advisers—by 18 votes to 20, with 11 abstentions, following approval by the Second Committee by 91 votes to 19, with 11 abstentions.

Explaining the socialist countries' negative vote, as a whole, Bulgaria said they believed the Conference should be funded from regular budget appropriations and that the proposed expert group meetings, involving financial implications of $684,000 for the regular budget, were unjustified. Denmark said the EC members felt that no decision should be taken at the 1982 Assembly session that would prejudge discussions to be held by the competent bodies at Vienna on technical and political preparations for the Conference. Japan was convinced that neither the five expert group meetings nor the additional financial requirements for Conference preparations were necessary—the reason for its vote against paragraph 7 and among the reasons for its abstention in the vote on the resolution as a whole; it regretted that a draft resolution with extensive programme and financial implications should have been adopted by a vote.

The United States voiced its inability to accept the financial implications of the resolution, a substantial portion of which (estimated by the Secretary-General at $1,082,900) related to the Conference, which might not take place under Assembly auspices since UNIDO might become a specialized agency before the Conference.

Reports. [1]IDB, A/37/16; [2]Permanent Committee, ID/B/290.
Resolutions (1982). [3]ESC: 1982/66 A, para. 11, 30 July. [4]GA: 37/212, sect. I, paras. 6 & 7, 20 Dec.
Resolution (prior). [5]GA: 36/182, sect. I, 17 Dec. 1981 (YUN 1981, p. 579).
Yearbook references. [6]1975, p. 473; [7]1980, p. 648.

Co-ordination in the UN system

At its November 1982 session, the Permanent Committee of the Industrial Development Board reviewed a report on the co-ordination of industrial development activities in the United Nations system for the period November 1981 to October 1982,[2] with emphasis on co-operation in the System of Consultations, technology, energy, industrial manpower training, the Industrial Development Decade for Africa, preparations for the UNIDO Fourth General Conference and operational activities.

On 16 November, following review of the report, the Committee requested the UNIDO secretariat to continue its efforts, taking into account the comments made at the November session, and to include in future reports information on the benefits and costs of the secretariat's co-ordination activities as well as problems encountered, and greater detail of its co-ordination efforts with United Nations organizations with which it had the most contact. It endorsed the Executive Director's efforts to keep staffing and finances for co-ordination activities at a minimum and requested further reductions.[1]

Reports. [1]Permanent Committee, ID/B/290; [2]UNIDO secretariat, ID/B/C.3/117.

Appointment of the Executive Director

By a decision of 20 December 1982, adopted without vote, the General Assembly, on an oral proposal by its President, confirmed the appointment by the Secretary-General of Abd-El Rahman Khane as Executive Director of UNIDO for a further two-year term ending on 31 December 1984, or until UNIDO became a specialized agency, whichever date came first.[1] The appointment was proposed by the Secretary-General in a note of 16 December 1982.[2]

Decision (1982). [1]GA: 37/321, 20 Dec., text following.
Note. [2]S-G, A/37/770.
Meeting record. GA: A/37/PV.113 (20 Dec.).

General Assembly decision 37/321

Adopted without vote

Oral proposal by President; agenda item 17 (i).

Confirmation of the appointment of the Executive Director of the United Nations Industrial Development Organization
At its 113th plenary meeting, on 20 December 1982, the General Assembly confirmed the appointment by the Secretary-General of Mr. Abd-El Rahman Khane as Executive Director of the United Nations Industrial Development Organization for a further two-year term ending on 31 December 1984, or until the United Nations Industrial Development Organization becomes a specialized agency, whichever date comes first.

Financial questions

UN Industrial Development Fund

During 1982, the UNIDO secretariat continued to strengthen activities on programme development and project preparation and to improve the overall quality of the projects financed under the United Nations Industrial Development Fund (UNIDF), promoting those innovative in nature. Dialogue with recipient and donor countries was intensified and efforts were made to ensure familiarity with the priority criteria of donor countries.

Approved were 134 projects with a total value of $15.5 million, including overheads. Of these, 69 projects were financed from the Fund's general-purpose convertible component, with a value of $3.4 million; 36 from the special-purpose convertible component valued at $9 million; and 29 from the non-convertible component valued at $3.1 million, complemented by additional inputs from the general-purpose component.

While the nine priority criteria endorsed by the Industrial Development Board continued to be applied, certain programmes of special concern were sponsored, notably those relating to the least developed countries (LDCs), the Industrial Development Decade for Africa), energy and environment.

Several countries increased their special-purpose contributions to the Fund. Projects financed from this component covered new and renewable sources of energy and utilization of agricultural waste. Several projects for pre-investment studies were under consideration.

A total of $14,142,593 was paid by 83 countries in voluntary contributions to UNIDF in 1982, and 72 countries pledged a total of $11,881,591 for 1983, as at 31 December 1982 (see table on next page).

A report by the Executive Director on the Fund's 1981 activities[2] was considered on 24 and 28 May 1982 by the Board,[1] which approved the proposed programme for 1983 and delegated authority to the Executive Director to approve projects for financing during that year. Noting with concern the constraints and difficulties under which UNIDF continued to operate and recalling the December 1981 General Assembly appeal,[4] the Board urged all States, particularly the developed countries, to contribute or raise their contribution with a view to reaching the desirable annual funding level of $50 million.

This appeal for increased funding, so that the $50-million target might be reached in 1982, was repeated by the Economic and Social Council on 30 July in its resolution on industrial development co-operation.[3]

Reports. [1]IDB, A/37/16; [2]UNIDO Executive Director, ID/B/279.
Resolution (1982). [3]ESC: 1982/66 A, para. 6, 30 July.
Resolution (prior). [4]GA: 36/182, sect. I, 17 Dec. 1981 (YUN 1981, p. 579).

Industrial development activities

Technical co-operation

In 1982, a total of 1,510 projects were completed or being implemented under the programme of technical co-operation of UNIDO,[5] its traditional substantive function. Of these, 127 were of more than $1 million in value, 415 of more than $150,000 and 968 below that value. Approved were 717 new projects with a value of $99.3 million, compared to 687 the previous year with a value of $70.9 million. UNIDO maintained its position as the third largest executing agency for projects financed by

CONTRIBUTIONS TO THE UN INDUSTRIAL DEVELOPMENT FUND, 1982 AND 1983
(as at 31 December 1982; in US dollar equivalent)

Country	1982 payment	1983 pledge	Country	1982 payment	1983 pledge
Afghanistan	—	1,500	Lesotho	2,000	2,000
Algeria	83,596	40,000	Luxembourg	7,733	5,918
Angola	20,000	—	Madagascar	7,067	—
Argentina	82,710	—	Malawi	2,700	2,196
Australia	402,200	303,208	Malaysia	20,000	20,000
Austria	438,462	677,967	Malta	7,500	—
Bahrain	5,000	5,000	Mauritius	980	903
Bangladesh	6,000	2,000	Mexico	14,831	—
Barbados	—	2,000	Mongolia	2,222	2,141
Belgium	375,523		Mozambique	—	5,026
Benin	—	2,000	Nepal	700	—
Botswana	4,130	—	Nicaragua	1,000	—
Brazil	15,000	15,000	Norway	(39,612) *	—
Bulgaria	88,028	117,371	Oman	—	12,000
Burma	1,000	1,000	Pakistan	109,947	48,000
Burundi	2,223	—	Panama	1,000	1,000
Chile	10,000	10,000	Philippines	19,211	22,500
China	359,017	354,974	Poland	192,018	147,727
Colombia	5,971	—	Portugal	15,000	15,000
Congo	14,253	10,000	Qatar	30,000	30,000
Cuba	30,311	24,823	Republic of Korea	30,000	30,000
Cyprus	3,090	1,016	Romania	36,364	—
Czechoslovakia	171,821	162,075	Rwanda	1,600	4,000
Democratic Yemen	3,306	3,637	Saudi Arabia	1,000,000	1,000,000
Djibouti	4,000	—	Senegal	—	1,000
Dominica	—	1,000	Seychelles	1,000	—
Ecuador	2,000	5,000	Sri Lanka	3,000	3,000
Egypt	63,589	63,589	Sudan	—	15,000
Fiji	1,100	1,000	Suriname	2,000	2,000
Finland	224,656	109,313	Swaziland	5,347	1,773
France	826,460	979,021	Sweden	324,068	—
German Democratic Republic	139,130	519,685	Switzerland	532,815	—
Germany, Federal Republic of	2,274,207	2,440,945	Syrian Arab Republic	83,523	—
Greece	32,000	30,000	Thailand	23,144	23,144
Guatemala	5,000	5,000	Togo	3,535	2,801
Guinea-Bissau	395	—	Trinidad and Tobago	—	20,000
Guyana	—	1,183	Tunisia	23,000	22,231
Hungary	65,714	64,643	Turkey	204,521	141,243
India	1,010,286	1,000,000	USSR	701,262	671,141
Indonesia	50,000	50,000	United Kingdom	723,357	—
Iran	85,000	—	United Republic of Tanzania	2,424	2,092
Italy	1,400,686	2,076,125	Venezuela	21,000	21,000
Ivory Coast	10,000	—	Viet Nam	3,000	1,000
Jamaica	—	4,000	Yugoslavia	165,363	—
Japan	1,427,969	407,977	Zambia	23,731	13,001
Jordan	6,086	6,000	Zimbabwe	5,000	13,020
Kenya	2,724	18,182			
Kuwait	75,000	—			
Lao People's Democratic Republic	1,500	1,500	Total	14,142,593	11,881,591
Lebanon	—	2,000			

*Adjustment.

SOURCE: Interim United Nations financial statements for the 12-month period ended 31 December 1982 (unpublished).

the United Nations Development Programme (UNDP) (see Chapter II of this section).

Programme expenditures for the year reached $91.9 million, a 3.8 per cent increase over the $88.5 million recorded for 1981.[7] The main programme components were: chemical industries, $18.9 million; engineering industries, $14 million; agro-industries, $12.2 million; institutional infrastructure, $11.9 million; metallurgical industries $9.2 million; training, $6.7 million; feasibility studies, $4.8 million; industrial planning, $4.4 million; factory establishment, $3.7 million; and $6.1 million for other related activities.

Asia and the Pacific accounted for $33.7 million (36.6 per cent); Africa, $31 million (33.7 per cent); the Americas, $10.7 million (11.7 per cent); the Arab States (excluding those in Africa), $5.1 million (5.6 per cent); Europe, $3.7 million (4 per cent); and global and interregional, $7.7 million (8.4 per cent).

By project component, personnel accounted for $44.3 million (48.2 per cent); equipment $24.4 million (26.6 per cent); fellowships and training, $12 million (13 per cent); sub-contracts, $9.2 million (10.1 per cent); and miscellaneous expenditures, $2 million (2.1 per cent). In this connection, of 1,005 experts appointed, 242 (24.1 per cent) came from developing countries.

In Africa, activities focused on the development of industrial institutional infrastructure and on the improvement of skilled human resources for operating existing industries and establishing new ones. In the Americas, as in Africa, programmes for integrated agro-industrial development, aimed at encouraging food processing in rural areas, were given priority, in addition to human resources development. In the Arab States, emphasis was on strengthening industrial institutional infrastructure and establishing new industries; technical assistance covered such areas as packaging, industrial management, the iron and steel industry and industrial advisory services. In Asia and the Pacific, activities ranged from pre-investment studies to electronics, precision engineering and quality control. In Europe, they related mostly to development of sophisticated technologies and training in electronics, automation, data-processing, energy and robotics.

The major areas of activity under the UNIDO regular programme of technical co-operation were: personnel training in various industrial fields through individual fellowships, group training programmes and assistance in establishing and strengthening training facilities; special measures for LDCs, such as industrial planning, development of industrial infrastructure and manpower, promotion of small- and medium-scale industries and transfer of technology; advisory services undertaken jointly with the regional commissions to identify specific needs, priority areas and trends, and those provided by interregional advisers in specific technologies and industries; co-operation among developing countries; and programme consultations with Governments.

Approximately 77.6 per cent of UNIDO technical co-operation was financed by UNDP including UNDP-administered trust funds; 19 per cent from UNIDF, various trust funds and other sources; and 3.4 per cent from the United Nations regular budget.

United Nations financing amounted to $3.1 million. A little over a third went for personnel training and assistance for the establishment and strengthening of training facilities in developing countries, including large-scale group training and industrial information in the iron and steel industries. A little less than a third of the resources was taken up by special assistance to LDCs.

A report by the Executive Director revising the proposed financial allocations of the regular programme for 1982-1983[6] was considered by the Permanent Committee of the Industrial Development Board at its May 1982 session.[3] Concerned over the continuing decline in real terms of the value of the allocations, the Committee, in recommending Board approval of the revisions ($6,695,400, instead of the $6,746,400 originally proposed), proposed that the Board maintain the real value of the programme and that it invite the Executive Director, when preparing future allocations, to take account of the comments during the Committee debate, particularly those on strengthening economic co-operation among developing countries and among the least developed of them. By adopting the Committee report as a whole on 17 May, the Board approved the revised allocations.[2]

The Secretary-General submitted an interim report[4] on a joint United Nations/UNDP/UNIDO in-depth evaluation of UNIDO technical co-operation activities in manufactures, undertaken in response to a 1980 recommendation of the Committee for Programme and Co-ordination (CPC). The report, considered by CPC on 20 and 21 April 1982, described the scope, purpose and design of the study, as well as the roles of the three organizational entities. It indicated progress made as at February and summarized the work programme to be completed in 1983. The final report was to be submitted to CPC that year.

CPC endorsed the design of the study and recommended that the Secretariat ensure that selection of country projects was not biased towards those known to be successful and that subjects for future evaluation be chosen on the basis of activities already well defined, readily identifiable and specific.[1]

UNIDO TECHNICAL CO-OPERATION AND SUPPORT EXPENDITURES
BY PROGRAMME COMPONENT, 1982
(as at 31 December 1982; in thousands of US dollars)

Programme component	Technical co-operation	Support
Policy-making organs	—	871
Executive direction and management*	39	1,491
Policy co-ordination	832	—
Economic co-operation among developing countries	—	484
Field reports monitoring	—	526
Inter-agency programme co-ordination	—	500
Least developed countries	—	463
Negotiations	—	2,019
New York Liaison Office	—	400
Non-governmental organizations	—	309
Programme development and evaluation	—	1,462
Programme formulation and direction	—	666
Subtotal	**832**	**6,829**
Industrial operations		
Agro-industries	12,181	1,003
Chemical industries	18,909	1,575
Engineering industries	13,963	899
Factory establishment and management	3,728	796
Feasibility studies	4,012	540
Industrial planning	4,438	742
Institutional infrastructure	11,912	1,088
Investment co-operative programme	2,517	1,401
Metallurgical industries	9,241	624
Programme formulation and direction	724	1,135
Project personnel recruitment†	—	1,498
Purchase and contract	—	1,107
Training	6,715	1,121
Subtotal	**89,140**	**13,537**
Industrial studies		
Development and transfer of technology	585	1,106
Global and conceptual studies	47	1,130
Industrial and Technological Information Bank	—	387
Industrial information and information services	181	535
Programme formulation and direction	373	1,382
Regional and country studies	428	1,444
Sectoral studies	14	1,185
Technological advisory services	11	290
Subtotal	**1,639**	**7,459**
Conference services, public information and external relations	126	—
Conference service	—	5,837
Governments and intergovernmental organizations relations	—	324
IDB secretariat	—	280
Programme formulation and direction	—	256
Public information	—	597
Subtotal	**126**	**7,294**
Administrative and common services		
Electronic data processing	—	1,117
Financial service	—	2,266
General services	—	1,674
Personnel service	—	2,019
Programme direction	—	842
Subtotal	**—**	**7,918**
Unspecified	103	—
Total	**91,879**	**45,399**

*Includes UNIDO representation at Geneva.
†Includes Technical Assistance Recruitment Service at Geneva and New York.

SOURCE: ID/B/300.

Reports. [1]CPC, A/37/38; [2]IDB, A/37/16; [3]Permanent Committee, ID/B/288; [4]S-G, E/AC.51/1982/6; UNIDO Executive Director, [5]ID/B/300, [6]ID/B/C.3/114.
Yearbook reference. [7]1981, p. 585.

Training of personnel

Expenditures for the fellowship and training components of all technical co-operation projects implemented by UNIDO in 1982 amounted to $12 million, against $9.9 million in 1981.[3] Of the 1982 figure, fellowships and study tours accounted for $6.9 million, and group training programmes and meetings for $5.1 million.

The number of individual training programmes (fellowships) started in 1982, which totalled 1,246, was 8.6 per cent higher than in 1981, while the number of placement arrangements by host countries decreased by 7.1 per cent (1,800 as compared to 1,972). Of these, 349 were arranged in developing countries, 191 of the trainees came from LDCs and 143 were women. The ratio between fellowships and study tours was 33 to 67, indicating the continuing trend towards study tours for high-level industrial personnel.

Under the System of Consultations, the First Consultation on the Training of Industrial Manpower, authorized by the Industrial Development Board in May 1981,[3] was held in 1982 (Stuttgart, Federal Republic of Germany, 22-26 November).[1]

Based on agreement reached at a Global Preparatory Meeting (Innsbruck, Austria, 25-27 January),[2] the Consultation focused on the problem of matching demand for industrial training in developing countries with supply and on co-operative arrangements for technology acquisition. The Consultation recommended that UNIDO, in collaboration with the International Labour Organisation and the United Nations Educational, Scientific and Cultural Organization, should: continue to develop methodologies for the determination of training needs in relation to levels of technological complexity, on the basis of which strategies for the mastery of the industrialization process might be formulated; and draw up a check-list to assist in the preparation of multilateral, bilateral and/or commercial training contracts. Co-ordinating mechanisms for information dissemination on training needs and opportunities were to be strengthened or created, and financial institutions and agencies were to include a training component in all capital projects.

Reports. [1]Consultation on Training of Industrial Manpower, ID/294; [2]Global Preparatory Meeting for Consultation on Training of Industrial Manpower, ID/WG.354/2/Rev.1.
Yearbook reference. [3]1981, p. 588.

Strengthening the SIDFA Programme

Efforts of the Senior Industrial Development Field Advisers (SIDFAs) Programme in 1982 were directed mainly towards programming and implementation of field projects on the transfer of technology, energy, training and investment promotion. As focal points of UNIDO activities in the countries of their assignment, SIDFAs also assisted in securing wider participation of Governments in the System of Consultations and in evolving a continuous system of project evaluation. SIDFA regional meetings were convened in Asia (Bangkok, Thailand, 15-20 February), Latin America (Caracas, Venezuela, September) and Africa (Dakar, Senegal, November).

By an 18 June decision on sectoral support, the Governing Council of the United Nations Development Programme (UNDP) authorized its Administrator to finance the maximum number of SIDFAs possible within existing resources; decided that countries which had agreed to pay up to a quarter of the cost of SIDFA services be given priority, taking into account the particular situation of LDCs; and invited the attention of the Economic and Social Council and the General Assembly to the urgent need for UNIDO to bear an increased share of the cost of the SIDFA Programme.[1]

The decision, taken in view of the UNDP Administrator's proposed reduction across the board of 36 per cent in sectoral support owing to lower contribution pledges to UNDP in 1982, would reduce to 24 the 45 SIDFA posts recommended to be established for 1982-1983.[2] Of the reduced number, at least 8 would be assigned to LDCs because of their priority status, 5 to countries with large programmes and 11 to over 100 developing countries.

The Economic and Social Council, in paragraph 5 of its 30 July resolution on industrial development co-operation,[3] recommended that the Assembly arrange for the provision of adequate funds for the appointment of SIDFAs in countries needing them, in particular in LDCs, especially those in Africa, in accordance with the terms of the UNDP Governing Council decision.

The paragraph had been approved in the First (Economic) Committee by a vote, requested by the USSR, of 39 to 4. The Council adopted it by 42 votes to 4.

Bulgaria, speaking in the Council also on behalf of the Byelorussian SSR, Poland and the USSR, said they had voted against paragraph 5 because of their opposition to the proposed financing of SIDFA work from the United Nations regular budget—among their reasons for their vote against the resolution as a whole.

By paragraph 4 of its 20 December resolution on industrial development co-operation,[4] the Assembly decided that adequate resources be provided in the 1983 UNIDO budget to finance up to 10 additional SIDFA posts. By paragraph 5, the Assembly invited the Industrial Development Board to examine in 1983 the financing of SIDFA posts and, based on the Board's recommendations, decided to consider at its 1983 session the question of appropriate budgetary support for

1984-1985 with a view to maintaining and, if necessary, increasing the SIDFA Programme.

Paragraph 4 had been adopted together with paragraph 7 (see above) by the Assembly by a recorded vote, taken at Denmark's request, of 118 to 20, with 11 abstentions. The paragraphs had likewise been approved together in the Second (Economic and Financial) Committee by a vote, also requested by Denmark on behalf of the European Community (EC) members, of 91 to 19, with 11 abstentions.

During the debate in Committee, Denmark, speaking for the EC members, said the proposed SIDFA appointments should be financed from voluntary contributions. Japan, which had voted against paragraph 4, was of the same view, saying that SIDFA activities were operational. Bulgaria stated on behalf of the socialist countries that among their reasons for voting against the resolution was their inability to agree to the financing of SIDFA posts from the regular United Nations budget.

Pursuant to the Assembly's decision, the Fifth (Administrative and Budgetary) Committee in the revised estimates for the 1982-1983 budget included an allocation of $943,400 for the financing of 10 additional SIDFA posts in 1983.

Decision (1982). [1]UNDP Council (report, E/1982/16/Rev.1): 82/38, paras. 5-7, 18 June.
Note. [2]UNDP Administrator, DP/1982/61.
Resolutions (1982). [3]ESC: 1982/66 A, para. 5, 30 July. [4]GA: 37/212, sect. I, paras. 4 & 5, 20 Dec.

Special Industrial Services

The Special Industrial Services (SIS) programme, a source of funding created to permit action in areas not covered by existing methods of financing, was designed primarily to enable UNIDO to meet priority requirements of an urgent nature through the rapid provision of experts to developing countries.

During 1982, 196 requests were received from 95 countries and, by the end of December, 148 projects were approved with a value of $5.4 million. Of these, 37 pertained to LDCs with a project value of $1,468,292. The bulk of the requests came from Africa (36.2 per cent) and the Americas (35.3 per cent). Technical co-operation delivery under the programme covered mainly chemical, metallurgical, agro- and engineering industries; feasibility studies; and factory establishment and management.

The UNDP Governing Council in 1981 had authorized an increase in SIS allocations for the 1977-1981 programming cycle from $17.5 million to $18.2 million, in order to accommodate an anticipated delivery in excess of the original authorization.[3] However, 1981 expenditure for SIS amounted to $1.6 million and cumulative expenditure for 1977-1981 to $17.1 million. The Governing Council, on 18 June 1982,[1] decided to restore the level of SIS allocations for that period to $17.5 million and to carry the difference of $0.4 million forward and add it to the SIS allocation for 1982-1986, as recommended by the Administrator.[2] However, a 60 per cent ceiling imposed by UNDP on the forward planning value for all programmes limited the 1982 technical assistance delivery under SIS to $3 million, compared to the previous yearly allocation of $3.5 million. This reduction of more than 14 per cent, as well as inflationary factors restricting the 1982 expenditure level to 318 work-months of experts' services at a pro forma monthly cost of $6,700, impaired the programme.

Decision (1982). [1]UNDP Council (report, E/1982/16/Rev.1): 82/29, para. 6, 18 June.
Report. [2]UNDP Administrator, DP/1982/49 & Corr.1.
Yearbook reference. [3]1981, p. 587.

Industrial co-operation

System of Consultations

On 17 May 1982, the Industrial Development Board, in adopting the Permanent Committee's report on the work of its November 1981 session,[7] endorsed the rules of procedure according to which the System of Consultations—established by the Board on a permanent basis in May 1980,[6]—was to operate, including its principles, objectives and characteristics, as approved by the Committee.

On 28 May 1982,[2] following a review of the UNIDO Executive Director's report on the System for 1976-1981,[3] the Board decided to strengthen the System in the light of the experience gained and requested the secretariat to take account of delegation views, particularly the concern over focusing on practical and well-defined issues directly related to advancing the industrialization of developing countries. The Board requested the Executive Director for more detailed information on operating costs at its 1983 session. It noted preparations for consultations in 1982-1983 and for those envisaged for 1984-1985, including possible consultations on building materials, energy-related industrial technology and non-ferrous metals, and requested the Executive Director to examine the possibility of including a consultation on the fisheries industry. It also noted a renewed proposal for the creation of a committee on consultations, as a subsidiary organ of the Board.

The Economic and Social Council, in paragraph 3 of its 30 July 1982 resolution on industrial development co-operation,[4] strongly supported strengthening the System of Consultations, with particular attention to measures that could increase the industrial capacities of developing countries.

The resolution had been orally amended by a Vice-Chairman of the Council's First (Economic) Committee to delete an operative paragraph that would have stressed the need for increased participation of all parties in the individual sectoral consultations within the System's framework. The text on which the resolution was based and which was later withdrawn would have strongly supported the strengthening and expansion of the System, using it to monitor trends in world industry.[1]

Bulgaria, speaking also on behalf of the Byelorussian SSR, Poland and the USSR in explanation of their votes against the resolution, said they were opposed to the System's expansion, as provided for in paragraph 3, because it would lead to foreign investment under United Nations auspices in developing countries without solving their overall industrial problems—among the provisions which they viewed as an attempt to maintain within UNIDO tendencies contrary to the industrialization interests of developing countries and to international co-operation. The United States stated that, as the System would be reviewed by the Board in 1983, neither the Council nor the General Assembly should take any action that might prejudice the outcome of the Board's deliberations.

In 1982, UNIDO organized the first global consultations not concerned with specific industrial sectors, on industrial financing and on training of industrial manpower; and the first regional sectoral consultation, on the agricultural machinery industry in Africa (see below). Another sectoral consultation, on the iron and steel industry (third), was also organized, bringing to 18 the number of consultation meetings since 1977.[5] Preparatory and follow-up work continued in sectors not the subject of 1982 consultations: fertilizers, petrochemicals, pharmaceuticals, capital goods, food processing, leather and wood, in addition to the new sectors of building materials, non-ferrous metals, fisheries and energy-related technology and equipment.

Draft resolution withdrawn. [1]Algeria, for Group of 77, E/1982/C.1/L.22.
Reports. [2]IDB, A/37/16; [3]UNIDO Executive Director, ID/B/284.
Resolution (1982). [4]ESC: 1982/66 A, para. 3, 30 July.
Yearbook references. [5]1977, p. 493; [6]1980, p. 656; [7]1981, p. 589.

Co-operation among developing countries

During 1982, UNIDO efforts to promote its programme of economic and technical co-operation among developing countries focused on organizing solidarity meetings at the ministerial level in least developed countries—in Mauritania (Nouakchott, 18-20 January), in Lesotho (Maseru, 7-11 June), and Nepal (Kathmandu, 29 November–3 December)—to bring together developing countries interested in promoting industrialization; preparing for future meetings; following up and participating in implementation of agreements reached at previous meetings; and promoting joint programmes for the development of specific industrial subsectors.

At the Mauritania meeting, attended by six Arab States, five Arab financial institutions and international organizations, Algeria offered a $400,000 grant for a market survey of foundry projects, a feasibility study and training for tannery projects. The Lesotho meeting, attended by 11 States, resulted in offers of assistance, including a grant for the construction of 25 hammer mills (Yugoslavia), securing short-term loans for such construction (Turkey), the setting up of rural training units equivalent to $200,000 (Algeria), and a pledge of $52,300 for consultancy and training (India). The Nepal meeting, attended by 18 developing countries and 6 international organizations, considered 57 project proposals. Pledged were a grant for the construction of an industrial glove and apron manufacturing plant (China), assistance of $1 million for co-operation projects (India), $200,000 for technical assistance (Algeria), 3 million dinars for equipment (Yugoslavia), and a range of training opportunities, partly or totally cost free (Egypt, Malaysia, Philippines, Turkey, Venezuela).

Follow-up activities covered agreements reached at previous solidarity meetings in Haiti and the United Republic of Tanzania (1979), Bangladesh (1980), and the Sudan and the Upper Volta (1981), as well as recommendations of the first High-level Meeting on Co-operation among Developing Countries in the Field of Cement, Lime and Related Industries held in Turkey (1981).[1] Joint programmes were promoted in the following industrial subsectors: agro-industries, non-metallic minerals in relation to the construction industry, machine tool industry, and small-scale shipbuilding and ship repair (see below).

Yearbook reference. [1]1981, p. 599.

International trade aspects

The subject of trade and trade-related aspects of industrial collaboration arrangements continued in 1982 to be of concern to the United Nations Conference on Trade and Development (UNCTAD) and UNIDO. The report on the second session of an *Ad Hoc* UNCTAD/UNIDO Group of Experts,[3] first convened on the subject in 1979,[4] had been considered in October 1981 by the Trade and Development Board of UNCTAD,[5] whose decisions were then submitted to the Industrial Development Board of UNIDO.

The Group found that, in essence, enterprise-to-enterprise arrangements, including those within the framework of intergovernmental agreements, were not only increasing but also becoming more complex and wider in scope, covering equipment delivery and organization of production and marketing.

On 28 May 1982,[2] the Industrial Development Board welcomed the collaboration between UNCTAD and UNIDO, and considered the work of the *Ad Hoc* Group completed; it recommended further in-depth examination of the Group's report by the UNCTAD and UNIDO secretariats for submission to their respective Boards.

On 17 September,[1] the Trade and Development Board decided that the Group's work was completed and that its report, together with the UNCTAD study on the subject, be examined by the Committee on Manufactures at its tenth (1983) session.

The UNCTAD study, well under way, was to analyse the existing types of industrial collaboration arrangements at the enterprise-to-enterprise level, between developed and developing countries, classifying the arrangements and identifying the characteristics of each category. Attention was to be given to the role of Governments in the conclusion and implementation of the arrangements. UNIDO was to organize its activities in the context of co-operation arrangements in various sectors covered by consultations.

Decision (1982). [1]TDB (report, A/37/15, vol. II): 261(XXV), 17 Sep.
Reports. [2]IDB, A/37/16; [3]UNCTAD/UNIDO Group of Experts on Trade and Trade-related Aspects of Industrial Collaboration Arrangements on Its Second Session, ID/B/287 & Add.1.
Yearbook references. [4]1979, p. 588; [5]1981, p. 590.
Publication. Changing Patterns of Trade in World Industry: An Empirical Study on Revealed Comparative Advantage (ID/281), Sales No. 82.II.B.1.

Co-operation among countries having different economic and social systems

By a letter of 8 October 1982 to the Secretary-General,[1] Bulgaria transmitted a communiqué issued by the Symposium on Industrial Co-operation between Partners from the East and the West (Varna, Bulgaria, 11-13 May), recommending ways of strengthening and broadening economic co-operation between East and West, especially in the industrial sector, by such means as long-term trade agreements, joint ventures including research and development programmes, licensing agreements, innovative financing and improved communication among partners.

Letter. [1]Bulgaria, 8 Oct., A/C.2/37/2.

Industrial co-operation contracts

UNCITRAL activities. At its third session, held in New York from 12 to 23 July 1982, the Working Group on the New International Economic Order of the United Nations Commission on International Trade Law (UNCITRAL) concluded its consideration, begun in 1981,[4] of various types of clauses commonly occurring in contracts on large industrial works.[2]

The clauses dealt with drawings and descriptive documents, supply, erection, passing of risk, transfer of property, applicable law, feasibility studies, contract formation, variation and interpretation, contract assignment or transfer, subcontracting, co-ordination and liaison agents, role of the engineer, third-party liabilities, training and acquisition of skills, maintenance and spare parts, price, price revision, payment conditions, performance guarantees, insurance, customs duties and taxes, bankruptcy, notification, and dispute settlement. Discussion of these issues was based on a series of studies by the Secretary-General.

The Working Group agreed that the Secretariat should begin drafting a legal guide to drawing up contracts and accordingly requested the Secretariat to submit, to the Group's 1983 session, a few sample chapters and an outline of the guide. It was suggested that the guide should include the topic of scheduling and not quote clauses from existing forms and models. The Group requested UNCITRAL to decide that the Group's session be held at Vienna, Austria, in the week immediately preceding the Commission's 1983 session, so as to ensure adequate representation of developing countries.

At its July/August 1982 session,[1] UNCITRAL approved the Working Group's report and suggested that the legal guide should moreover deal with problems arising out of a Government's withdrawal of a licence or failure to grant one, whether import or export, or of government restrictions making performance of a party's contractual obligations impossible; and it should include a model clause clarifying the importance of the choice of law applicable by the parties in such instances, and, in cost-reimbursable contracts, a preliminary estimate of costs.

The General Assembly, in its 16 December resolution on the report of UNCITRAL,[3] noted the completion of the examination of studies related to clauses in contracts for the supply and construction of large industrial works, preparatory to the drafting of a legal guide identifying the issues involved in such contracts and suggesting possible solutions to assist parties, in particular those from developing countries, in their negotiations.

Reports. [1]UNCITRAL, A/37/17; [2]Working Group on New International Economic Order, A/CN.9/217.
Resolution (1982). [3]GA: 37/106, para. 4, 16 Dec.
Yearbook reference. [4]1981, p. 1260.

Redeployment of industrial production to developing countries

Pursuant to a 1976 General Assembly request,[4] the Executive Director of the United Na-

tions Industrial Development Organization (UNIDO) continued to carry out studies on the redeployment of industrial production from developed to developing countries. Based on such studies, he submitted to the Industrial Development Board in 1982 a report providing an overview of past and existing redeployment strategies and policies, as well as an extensive analysis of possible future redeployment and the difficulties in predicting trends for the coming decade, drawing attention to the need for action to counteract negative trends.[2]

On 28 May,[1] the Board took note of the Executive Director's report; stressed the importance of redeployment and recognized the continuing need for UNIDO to examine the restructuring process and assist developing countries to obtain insights into international developments in this area; reaffirmed that redeployment should be in accordance with national priorities, in particular of developing countries, and lead to viable industrial development and to an ecologically safe industrial environment in those countries; agreed that future secretariat studies should be action-oriented; and requested the Executive Director to continue to strengthen co-operation with regional commissions, and to report to the Board at its 1983 session on the results of redeployment activities and on how UNIDO could further improve and strengthen its role.

The Economic and Social Council, in its 30 July resolution on industrial development co-operation,[3] reiterated the importance of: facilitating the restructuring of world industrial production by, *inter alia*, implementation of the 1980 Assembly resolution on the Third General Conference of UNIDO[6] (emphasizing the need to restructure such production) and the 1979 United Nations Conference on Trade and Development resolution containing a programme of action in the areas of protectionism and structural adjustment in international trade;[7] and redeployment of industrial capacities as described in paragraph 73 of the International Development Strategy for the Third United Nations Development Decade, adopted by the Assembly in 1980.[5] The Council also supported UNIDO efforts in further improving and developing its redeployment programme, as outlined in the Board's report.

The United States, explaining its position following adoption of the resolution, said it viewed restructuring and structural adjustment in the industrial sector as phenomena occurring continuously on a global scale, primarily in response to market forces. International redeployment of industries was the result of the evolution of economies rather than of international negotiation.

Reports. [1]IDB, A/37/16; [2]UNIDO Executive Director, ID/B/282.

Resolution (1982). [3]ESC: 1982/66 A, paras. 8 & 10, 30 July.
Resolutions (prior). GA: [4]31/163, 21 Dec. 1976, (YUN 1976, p. 426); [5]35/56, annex, 5 Dec. 1980 (YUN 1980, p. 503); [6]35/66 A, 5 Dec. 1980 (*ibid.* p. 660).
Yearbook reference. [7]1979, p. 560.

Industrial financing

The First Consultation on Industrial Financing, authorized by the Industrial Development Board in May 1981,[2] was held in 1982 (Madrid, Spain, 18-22 October),[1] with 180 participants from 65 countries and 16 international organizations attending. An informal meeting on the same topic had been held earlier in the year (Vienna, Austria, 18 and 19 January).

The Consultation considered three questions, namely, whether a quantitative and qualitative gap in external financial flows for industrial investment in developing countries existed, how and to what extent existing mechanisms and institutions could provide additional industrial financing, and whether a financing gap could be overcome by innovative concepts leading to acceptance of new mechanisms and/or institutions. The Consultation recommended that UNIDO continue to examine obstacles to the flow of industrial finance. It also requested an analysis of the benefits to developing countries of the extended use of co-financing arrangements and how these might be improved, as well as promotion of foreign investment and industrial financing, particularly in relation to small- and medium-scale enterprises, by dissemination of information on industrial investment opportunities by such means as periodic meetings on investment promotion.

Report. [1]Consultation on Industrial Financing, ID/293 & Corr.1.
Yearbook reference. [2]1981, p. 588.

Proposed international bank for industrial development

The Industrial Development Board at its May 1982 session[1] continued consideration of the UNIDO Executive Director's proposal for the establishment of an international bank for industrial development, begun in 1981.[5]

In a follow-up report of March 1982,[2] the Executive Director described the decisions and recommendations of intergovernmental bodies on the proposed bank; outlined the economic problems and prospects of industrialized and non-energy-producing developing countries in the ongoing recession, whose impact on international and financial flows he also analysed; and illustrated the features of the bank and the role it could play in offsetting the reduced financing capabilities of existing international finance institutions. Accompanying the report were the draft articles of agreement, covering the purpose, functions and membership of the bank; its capital; operations; borrowing power and other powers; currencies; organization and management; withdrawal and suspension; status, immunities, exemptions and privileges; amendments, interpretation and arbitration; and final provisions.

As the Board was unable to reach a decision, the proposal was to revert to the Board at its 1983 session. Nevertheless, reaffirming its recognition of the importance of financial flows to industrial development in developing countries, the Board requested the Executive Director to submit to that session a brief report indicating any developments. It noted the suggestion by several delegations that large sums of money could be made available if part of the funds spent on armaments was used for developing countries' economic development.

The Economic and Social Council, in its 30 July 1982 resolution on industrial development co-operation,[3] noted the Board's decision and that consideration of the proposal would revert to the Board at its 1983 session—a similar action taken by the General Assembly in its resolution of 20 December 1982 on the same topic[4]—and also recognized the importance of financial flows to industrial development in developing countries.

Following adoption of the Council's resolution, Denmark, speaking on behalf of the European Community members, said it wanted to record their negative position on the proposed international bank. In the Assembly's Second (Economic and Financial) Committee, the United States said it felt strongly that, with respect to financing mechanisms, the World Bank and regional development banks were the competent organizations.

Reports. [1]IDB, A/37/16; [2]UNIDO Executive Director, ID/B/275 & Add.1.
Resolutions (1982). [3]ESC: 1982/66 A, paras. 7 & 9, 30 July.
[4]GA: 37/212, sect. I, para. 8, 20 Dec.
Yearbook reference. [5]1981, p. 591.

Investment promotion

In 1982, under the Investment Co-operative Programme (ICP) of UNIDO, the seven Investment Promotion Services—at Brussels, Belgium; Cologne, Federal Republic of Germany; New York; Paris; Tokyo; Vienna, Austria; and Zurich, Switzerland—in operation (the number in 1982 remained at seven) continued to promote the flow of external financial and other resources to developing countries by identifying foreign partners, providing information on the host country and assisting in the preparation of the financial package. Those in Paris, Tokyo and Vienna were extended for two years. Poland had expressed its intention to open a Service in Warsaw, while negotiations continued for the establishment of Services in selected developing countries, including India and one of the Gulf States. During the year, the Services promoted 43 industrial investment projects in 23 developing countries, with a total investment value of some $300 million.

Because the world economic situation in 1982 had dampened promotion of industrial investment, the Services concentrated on informational activities, organizing 33 country presentation meetings for 13 countries—Chile, China, Colombia, Egypt, Indonesia, Kenya, Lesotho, Malaysia, Peru, Saint Lucia, Saint Vincent and the Grenadines, Senegal and Sri Lanka—as a result of which 237 industrial investment projects were generated. Thirty-six officials from 16 developing countries undertook investment promotion activities for their countries while attached to the Services.

National investment promotion meetings in Bangladesh (February), Chile (October) and China (June), and a subregional meeting for 16 African countries in Senegal (November) were also organized. More than 40 industrial investment proposals with a total value of $800 million were discussed at the Bangladesh investors' forum, resulting in 12 letters of intent signed by local sponsors and foreign partners. The Chile forum, attended by 165 participants from 17 countries, discussed some 87 projects. The China meeting, the largest of its kind ever organized by UNIDO, attracted some 400 investors representing 260 public and private companies from 24 countries—mainly European, and Japan and the United States—and about 800 Chinese nationals; 77 letters of intent were signed for projects assessed at $559 million, agreed mostly on the basis of compensatory or buy-back trade, with equity participation. At the Senegal forum, some 130 projects were identified for promotion.

In April, a video teleconference via satellite, sponsored by the United Nations Development Programme (UNDP), UNIDO and the United States Overseas Private Investment Corporation, allowed over 600 United States industrialists, bankers and businessmen to learn about Egyptian foreign investment policies on various industrial subsectors.

Continued use was made of promotional tools, among them the List of Industrial Investment Project Proposals (in 1982, 445 proposals were received from 27 developing countries bringing the ICP portfolio by year's end to 947 proposals located in 60 developing countries), supplemented by 84 country industrial investment profiles; the directory, *Financial Resources for Industrial Projects in Developing Countries*,[1] revised and expanded in 1982 to include 340 banks and institutions; the roster of resources, of over 4,000 private and public enterprises; and the series of about 100 plant profiles titled "How to Start Manufacturing Industries—Technological and Investment Perspectives".

Publication. [1]*Financial Resources for Industrial Projects in Developing Countries*, second edition, PI/61/Rev.1.

Pre-investment studies

In 1982, expenditures for the UNIDO technical co-operation programme on feasibility studies amounted to $4.8 million, with some 82 per cent financed from UNDP resources. Of that total, Africa accounted for 49 per cent; the Americas, 4; the Arab States (excluding those in Africa), 18; Asia and the Pacific, 26; Europe, 1; and inter-regional and global, 2. In all, 58 projects were completed or being implemented, 7 of them greater than $1 million in value, 25 greater than $150,000 and 26 below that value.

Despite the unfavourable economic climate, the programme continued to expand, particularly through establishment of industrial advisory units, each consisting of a team of experts to assist Governments, for periods of three to five years, in establishing or strengthening national capabilities in pre-investment work. Such units were in operation in 16 countries, with a new one set up in the United Arab Emirates in 1982.

Development of the UNIDO Computer Model for Feasibility Analysis and Reporting was completed. Aimed at facilitating accurate and efficient processing of pre-investment studies, the model, together with a software package, would be available in 1983 to all countries requesting it.

In 1982, standardization of feasibility and pre-investment studies continued. Invitations to lecture on standardization were received from consulting firms, banks and enterprises in Austria, Czechslovakia, the German Democratic Republic, the Federal Republic of Germany and Poland. Efforts were made to widen the scope and objectives of workshops on industrial project preparation, evaluation and financing held in the Philippines—where a regional workshop on the same subject was also held—Poland and Qatar.

Industrial management

In 1982, UNIDO technical co-operation expenditures for factory establishment and management amounted to $3.7 million, with 93 per cent of total implementation financed from UNDP resources. Of that amount, Africa accounted for 59 per cent; the Americas, 15; the Arab States (excluding those in Africa), 12; and Asia and the Pacific, 14. Completed or under implementation were 50 projects, 6 of them greater than $1 million in value, 24 greater than $150,000 and 20 less than that value. During the year, more effort was directed towards industrial energy management and application of management information systems.

Large-scale reorientation projects to improve production through new management practices in Guyana, Somalia and the Sudan were undertaken. The project in Guyana was aimed at improving profitability of enterprises, with the aid of the Caribbean Project Development Facility. In Somalia, management reporting systems were introduced and enterprises assisted in setting up production engineering and financial management systems. In the Sudan, a sectoral approach was introduced to enhance competitiveness of public and private enterprises and eventually provide extension services for different types of enterprises. Projects in Benin, Uruguay, Zaire and Zambia introduced improved management systems and financial practices in government departments, development corporations and development banks.

A regional project in the application of mini-computers to improve management efficiency, at the Asian Institute of Technology at Bangkok, Thailand, was completed, resulting in the training of 34 specialists from several Asian countries.

Industrial consulting

In industrial management consultancy, a regional project in Asia was assisted in 1982 under the United Nations Industrial Development Fund. In co-operation with the Economic Commission for Africa and the Organization of African Unity, UNIDO continued to improve mechanisms for strengthening co-operation between countries for the development of industrial consulting in the African region. A project was being developed for co-operation with the Southern African Development Co-ordination Conference, to upgrade management skills and provide management consultancy to southern African countries through the Eastern and Southern African Management Institute at Arusha, United Republic of Tanzania. To strengthen the consultancy capacities of the University of Aleppo in the Syrian Arab Republic, its computer was being linked to international data bases to permit direct utilization of technical information from international computer networks.

Training of personnel

UNIDO technical co-operation activities to upgrade managerial skills through on-the-job training continued in 1982 in connection with most projects, particularly in El Salvador, Ethiopia, Malawi, Mauritius and Uruguay. Under the Special Industrial Services programme, direct management assistance was provided to factories in Ethiopia, the Gambia, Ghana, Somalia, Togo and Uganda. In Somalia and Zambia, improved organizational, production, maintenance and financial systems were introduced and put into operation, thus creating greater awareness of the essential role of industrial management and consultancy in overall performance and productivity. In Zaire, two projects continued to provide accountancy systems for public as well as for small- and medium-scale enterprises.

Industrial planning

In 1982, expenditures for UNIDO technical co-operation in industrial planning amounted to $4.4 million, with about 83 per cent financed from United Nations Development Programme (UNDP) resources. Of that amount, Africa accounted for 46 per cent; the Americas, 26; the Arab States (excluding those in Africa), 2; Asia and the Pacific, 20; and Europe, 6. Completed or under implementation were 61 projects, 11 of them greater than $1 million in value, 23 greater than $150,000 and 27 less than that value. Efforts were directed mainly towards industrial energy management and application of management information systems.

Assistance in industrial planning, provided on a continuous basis through multidisciplinary projects, concentrated on strengthening or restructuring national planning institutions, establishment of planning methodology and formulating national industrial plans. Among the recipients of such assistance were Bolivia, the Ivory Coast, Nicaragua, Pakistan, Sierra Leone and Sri Lanka. Haiti and Honduras were assisted in formulating plans for the industrial segments of their overall national development programmes. A project for the preparation of a master plan for the industrialization of the United Republic of Cameroon was approved by the Government of that country, UNDP and UNIDO.

A regional seminar for the integration of women in the process of industrial planning in the Sahelian zone (Ouagadougou, Upper Volta, 20-25 September), attended by 23 participants from Mali, Mauritania, the Niger, Senegal and the Upper Volta, dealt with planning and management of enterprises, village industries and co-operatives. An expert group meeting on industrial planning (Vienna, Austria, 1-5 November) reviewed planning practices in developing countries and recommended procedures, mechanisms and institutions for formulating, monitoring and evaluating industrial development plans; it also identified areas of concentration during the Third United Nations Development Decade (the 1980s), with special attention to the least developed countries.

Industrial studies

UNIDO global and conceptual studies focused on industrial restructuring, production and technology. In 1982, work was completed on an overview of the international industrial restructuring process and on studies of the long-term effects of technological innovation on restructuring, of the impact of electronics and of global restructuring in the automotive industry. Other studies completed included 10 for a research seminar on structural changes in industry in the centrally planned economies of Eastern Europe (Budapest, Hungary,

22-26 March); 5 in respect of developed countries and 2 of developing countries; 7 related to specific industrial sectors; and 1 on patterns and prospects for East-South trade in the 1980s. Several scenarios were developed for the 1990s examining four different perspectives for the world economy: trend extrapolation, South-South co-operation, de-linking (i.e. confrontation) and North-South plus South-South co-operation.

Regional and subregional surveys and analyses, aimed at enhancing industrial co-operation among developing countries, covered the countries of the Association of South-East Asian Nations, the Andean Group and the Gulf and South Pacific regions. In a series of country industrial development profiles, studies were issued in respect of the Central African Republic, Chad, the Democratic People's Republic of Korea, the Libyan Arab Jamahiriya, Mongolia, the Niger, Senegal, the Upper Volta and Zimbabwe. Also issued were in-depth studies of four least developed African countries—Botswana, Burundi, Mali and the United Republic of Tanzania—and a specific study on six least developed Arab countries—Democratic Yemen, Djibouti, Mauritania, Somalia, the Sudan and Yemen.

Under the World Bank/UNIDO Co-operative Programme, involved mainly in mission work for the preparation of industrial sectoral and subsectoral studies, eight operational missions were carried out and support was provided for six organized by the World Bank; in all, 14 developing countries were covered. A study was prepared on opportunities for small- and medium-scale industry in Djibouti. Missions focusing on industrial policy and planning were undertaken in the Comoros, the Lao People's Democratic Republic, Trinidad and Tobago, Zambia and some Andean Group countries. Other missions covered textiles (Turkey), geothermal power applications (Philippines), export processing zones (Indonesia), building materials (Nigeria) and agro-industrial opportunities (Fiji).

Industrial technology

The UNIDO industrial technology programme, to assist developing countries to establish and/or strengthen their technological capabilities in the selection, acquisition and development of technology, was in its third year of operation in 1982.

Policy formulation in technology through country-level activities geared to the development of a conceptual framework for national action was promoted and negotiating capacities were strengthened through *ad hoc* specialized advisory services and a system that periodically brought together staff from technology transfer registries of developing countries. Also promoted were selection and development through a co-operative programme on appropriate industrial technology, complemented by information provided by the Industrial and Technological Information Bank.

UNIDO also continued to play an important role in the exchange of industrial and technological information (see below); the promotion of technology transfer; industrial research; and standardization, quality control and testing of industrial products.

Information systems

In the area of industrial information, six countries—Angola, Mauritania, Mongolia, Nepal, Nigeria and Uruguay—and two regional intergovernmental organizations—the Arab International Development Organization (AIDO) and the Latin American Network of Technological Information—received assistance in 1982 to set up or develop documentation and information services for the collection, processing and dissemination of technical information on industry. Significant progress was achieved in the implementation of the third phase of a project, begun in 1981, to assist AIDO in the development of an industrial information network for the Arab States.

UNIDO organized a meeting of selected industrial development finance institutions from developing countries (Bridgetown, Barbados, 26-28 January) to consider the feasibility of establishing, under UNIDO auspices, a technological information exchange network to provide such institutions with information on the terms and conditions of those portions of the projects they financed or co-financed.

The UNIDO Technological Information Exchange System (TIES) continued to expand activities in the exchange of information among technology transfer registries. A coding manual was prepared and operations began for information exchange on service agreements. UNIDO also provided TIES member countries with guidelines for an approach to software licensing agreements, issued a number of publications on specific technological issues, and assisted in the seventh meeting of the heads of technology transfer registries (New Delhi, India, 7-10 December).

Industrial and Technological Information Bank

The Industrial and Technological Information Bank (INTIB), in its third year of operation in 1982, concentrated on increasing and updating sources of information and meeting end-user requirements.

More than 150 data bases related to all aspects of technology became accessible through the Vienna International Centre library, compared to over 100 in 1981.[7] In addition to the compilation of external information sources for inclusion in the publication series *UNIDO Guides to Information Sources*,[3] mobilization of in-house information continued through the *Industrial Development Abstracts* (IDA) and On-Line Information Key (LINK) data bases. The IDA data base, containing 12,000 references and abstracts of UNIDO documents, included three volumes published in 1982.[5] The LINK data base, containing information on institutions, inquiries received by INTIB, subject files and technology suppliers, was expanded by the addition of a file on building materials.

A volume on metal production development units for the series on development and transfer of technology[4] was published. Revision of the *Thesaurus of Industrial Development Terms*, used worldwide in classifying industrial development documents, was completed. The "Industrial opportunities" and "Publications" columns of the *UNIDO Newsletter*[6] drew more than 11,000 requests for some 110,000 documents during the year, almost double the number sent out in 1981.

A total of 1,363 substantive inquiries were received by the Industrial Inquiry Service, an increase of more than one third over the previous year. The major users continued to be industrial enterprises, research and development institutes, development banks, and productivity and development centres in developing countries. Requests for information packages totalled 689.

Having considered the UNIDO Executive Director's report on development and transfer of technology, including INTIB,[2] the Industrial Development Board, on 19 May,[1] stressed the increasing importance of INTIB and requested the Executive Director to prepare a report on its activities for the Board's 1983 session to include data on volume, sources of requests for information by country and by institutional categories, and links with other information centres.

Reports. [1]IDB, A/37/16; [2]UNIDO Executive Director, ID/B/281.

Publications. [3]*UNIDO Guides to Information Sources*, No. 8 (revised edition): *Information Sources on the Agricultural Implements and Machinery Industry*, ID/270 (UNIDO/LIB/SER.D/8/Rev.1); No. 10 (revised edition): *Information Sources on the Pesticides Industry*, ID/280 (UNIDO/LIB/SER.D/10/Rev.1); No. 40: *Information Sources on Grain Processing and Storage*, ID/283 (UNIDO/LIB/SER.D/40). [4]*Development and Transfer of Technology Series*, No. 16: *Metal Production Development Units*, ID/271. [5]*Industrial Development Abstracts: UNIDO Industrial Information System (INDIS)*, 10701-10900, ID/279 (UNIDO/LIB/SER.D/45); *10901-11200*, ID/286 (UNIDO/LIB/SER.D/46); *11201-11500*, ID/292 (UNIDO/LIB/SER.D/47). [6]*UNIDO Newsletter*, Nos. 165-176 (monthly).

Yearbook reference. [7]1981, p. 593.

Research and development

In 1982, UNIDO initiated or continued activities to establish multi-purpose, multidisciplinary research and development institutions in 16 countries: Bhutan, Burma, Chile, China, Dominican Republic, Guyana, Indonesia, Lebanon, Libyan Arab Jamahiriya, Mexico, Philippines, Syrian Arab Republic, United Republic of Cameroon, United Republic of Tanzania, Zaire, Zambia.

Assistance was provided to research and development institutions in Brazil dealing with enzymatic hydrolysis of cellulosic materials for the production of ethanol, and in Bhutan, Burma, China, Indonesia and the Philippines for the design of appropriate technologies and corresponding equipment; to the National Council for Science and Technology in Mexico, a large-scale project which covered a broad spectrum of activities, such as technology policy organization and methodology applied to technological programming and project implementation, technical information, industrial liaison, shared-risk financing of research and development, metal-working, agro-industries and chemical industry; and to Iraq's Specialized Institute for Engineering Industries.

The second phase of a large-scale project, to strengthen the Industrial Testing, Research and Development Centre in the Syrian Arab Republic, was completed. The total value of technical assistance provided under this project exceeded $1.5 million. Co-operation between the Centre and the Institute for Instrument Design at Sofia, Bulgaria, was also developed.

Standardization, quality control and product testing

Recognizing the importance of product reliability, performance and safety for the improvement of export possibilities, UNIDO continued in 1982 to help improve the capabilities of institutions for standardization as well as establish infrastructure for the introduction of national standards, quality control and certification marking systems in developing countries, and promoted linkages between institutes and industries for quality improvement of manufactured goods.

Specifically, UNIDO supplied or strengthened physical and technological requirements, such as laboratory facilities and testing equipment, for the definition of product characteristics and establishment of specifications against which to check and certify products in compliance with national or international standards. Such assistance was provided to 19 developing countries: Bangladesh, Ethiopia, Greece, Honduras, India, Iraq, Lebanon, Mauritius, Nepal, Nigeria, Pakistan, Peru, Philippines, Saudi Arabia, Syrian Arab Republic, Thailand, Turkey, Viet Nam, Zaire.

National institutions which received assistance included the Ethiopian Standards Institution, for setting up equipment and putting into operation laboratories in mechanical and building materials, chemicals, textiles, leather, and electrical, agricultural and food products; the Federal Institute of Industrial Research in Nigeria, to expand facilities and establish a laboratory for the testing and quality control of textiles and related materials; and the Hellenic Organization for Standardization and the National Council of Standardization in Greece, for the establishment of a national certification marking system.

In Honduras, assistance was provided for the establishment of an infrastructure for standardization, quality control and metrology; in Brazil, a project on standardization, quality control and certification of iron and steel products was completed; and in Iraq, a large-scale project contributed substantially to the improvement of the national economy through the wide application of standardization principles and techniques to industry, among other sectors. A project to create a regional network of non-destructive nuclear testing institutions was initiated in Latin America, while in China, a medium scale project provided five engineers from the Shanghai Research Institute of Building Materials an opportunity to visit non-destructive testing facilities in Japan and the United States, and furnished equipment and documents not available in China.

Technological innovations

In 1982, ideas for inter-agency co-operation in micro-electronics, marine technologies, genetic engineering and biotechnology, and technologies for energy, remote sensing and new materials were discussed at three meetings held at Vienna, Austria, by a working group of the Task Force on Science and Technology for Development of the Administrative Committee on Co-ordination. Among the projects proposed was one on the implications of micro-electronics for developing countries, to be executed jointly by the United Nations Centre on Transnational Corporations, the International Labour Organisation and UNIDO.

An Expert Meeting Preparatory to the International Forum on Technological Advances and Development (1983) was held under UNIDO auspices in 1982 (Moscow, 29 November–3 December) to define the issues to be brought before that forum.[1] The meeting, in drawing attention to specific, new technologies, concluded that application of such technologies by developing countries was feasible and recommended that they establish appropriate mechanisms to monitor and assess technological advances in terms of their social and economic development, formulate policy to maximize benefits, and promote co-operation among themselves so as to harmonize policies and strategies. The meeting also recommended that UNIDO continue to expand its programme on technological advances to assist developing countries in these efforts.

Report. [1]Expert Meeting Preparatory to International Forum on Technological Advances and Development, ID/WG.384/16.

Development of specific industries

Many of the technical co-operation activities, studies and meetings carried out by UNIDO in 1982—including two meetings under the System of Consultations—related to specific industrial sectors or industries. The major sectors were agro-industries (see below), chemical industries, engineering industries, and metallurgical and mineral industries.

Agro-industries

In 1982, UNIDO technical co-operation expenditures for activities in the agro-industries amounted to $12.2 million. Of that amount, Africa accounted for 33 per cent; the Americas, 13; the Arab States (excluding those in Africa), 2; Asia and the Pacific, 48; and interregional and global, 4. A total of 187 projects were involved, 16 of them greater than $1 million in value, 59 greater than $150,000 and 112 below that value.

About 79 per cent of the total implementation was financed from United Nations Development Programme resources, mostly for activities covering such light industries as textiles and wearing apparel, leather and leather products, and packaging. Financing by the United Nations Industrial Development Fund played an important role in the wood and food industries.

In co-operation with the Government of Iraq, UNIDO organized a ministerial meeting (Baghdad, 15-19 February) that adopted a series of recommendations for promoting co-operation among developing countries in agro-industries. Activities to promote such co-operation were jointly undertaken by UNIDO and Yugoslavia at an international agricultural fair (Novi Sad, May), as a result of which a number of projects were selected for bilateral and multilateral follow-up action.

Clothing and textile industry

As in the previous year, UNIDO continued in 1982 to move from directly assisting individual mills and factories of the textile and garment industry towards strengthening and establishing institutions serving the industry. In addition to five ongoing large-scale projects in Bangladesh (two), Egypt, India and the United Republic of Tanzania, new ones were initiated in Bangladesh, India, Sri Lanka and Viet Nam. Assignments to Turkey were undertaken for the World Bank, to assist in evaluating the effectiveness of a local textile consulting service.

Food industry

UNIDO activities. Projects in the food industry gave increased attention to the utilization of the industry's by-products and to animal feed manufacture.

In Latin America, UNIDO assisted the Governments of Brazil, Colombia, the Dominican Republic, El Salvador, Guatemala, Panama, Paraguay, Peru, Uruguay and Venezuela in planning programmes for integrated agro-industrial complexes, linking agricultural production, industrial processing and commercial distribution of processed foods. To tackle some specific aspects of such programmes at the national and subregional levels, UNIDO organized a third Latin American seminar on the science and technology of food processing (São Paulo, Brazil, 21-25 November). In Guatemala, a project was implemented to incorporate medium-sized farms into the industrial economy; in Argentina, direct support was provided for food processing plants; and in Haiti, a project was initiated, in co-operation with the Government of Brazil, to produce composite flour as a substitute for wheat.

Under its Coconut Technology Consultancy Service, established in 1981,[2] UNIDO carried out an evaluation of coconut-cream products and of the production methods involved, in order to identify quality criteria and technical parameters for a more efficient processing of coconut. It also undertook: development of an integrated cassava processing technology for better use of the cassava resources of many developing countries; a study on the industrial utilization of the fruit of *Balanites aegyptiaca*, a tree widely found in the Sahelian zone, for the production of high-quality edible oil, a variety of food items and animal feed, and of the derivatives saponin and sapogenin for the pharmaceutical industry; and preparation of a study on the utilization of sugar industry by-products. Other projects included improving the operation of bakeries and of biscuit-making and meat/bacon processing plants, maintenance of sugar mills in Cuba, trouble-shooting in a sugar plant in the Dominican Republic, and a fish-meal study in Sao Tome and Principe.

UNCTAD activities. A Meeting of Governmental Experts on the Transfer, Application and Development of Technology in the Food Processing Sector was convened (Geneva, 1-10 June 1982),[1] in response to a 1981 resolution[3] of the Trade and Development Board of the United Nations Conference on Trade and Development. The conclusions and recommendations of the experts, endorsed by the Committee on Transfer of Technology, invited the developing countries to adopt an integrated approach to the technological development of their food processing industries consistent with broad economic and social objectives and long-term national development strategies. To that end a food policy framework was necessary that took into account interrelationships among agriculture, storage, transport, processing, distribution, marketing and finance, as well as sectoral and regional priorities. The experts suggested specific ways of strengthening co-operative links among developing countries so as to maximize benefits and proposed supporting measures for consideration by developed countries.

Report. [1]Meeting of Governmental Experts on Transfer, Application and Development of Technology in Food Processing Sector, TD/B/C.6/78.
Yearbook references. 1981, [2]p. 596, [3]p. 754.

Leather industry

At its sixth session (Vienna, Austria, 29 November–1 December 1982),[1] the UNIDO Leather and Leather Products Industry Panel approved a check-list for the tanning industry, indicating the components of contractual agreements between enterprises interested in international co-operation. It was to be circulated together with a similar check-list for the footwear industry, approved in November 1981. The Panel also concluded that it was not yet possible to formulate a globally acceptable set of ground rules for the rationalization of world production, marketing and trade in the leather and leather products industry. A regional approach could identify areas and problems for co-operation and negotiation.

Report. [1]Sixth Session of Leather and Leather Products Industry Panel, ID/WG.386/5.

Packaging

By the end of 1982, UNIDO projects for the establishment or strengthening of research and information centres on packaging were either completed or nearing completion in India, Mexico, Morocco and the Republic of Korea, while national projects of a similar type were initiated in Brazil and Cuba.

Other projects involved assistance on specific aspects of package use or manufacture (Cuba, Mali), a general appraisal of packaging demands and constraints (Guinea-Bissau), advisory services on national requirements for packaging and on technical assistance services that could be rendered by national packaging institutions (Jordan, Turkey), a large-scale project on food processing and packaging technology (Mexico), development of research and experimental facilities for packaging materials suited to the diversified demands of the agro-processing industry and to the requirements of modern transport and storage techniques (Poland), strengthening the National Centre for

Packaging laboratory (Portugal), and drawing up the framework for the establishment of the Arab Regional Packaging Centre. The organizational phase of a regional project to promote technical co-operation in packaging among Latin American countries was completed.

Wood-using industry

Technical assistance to the wood and wood products industry continued in 1982 to concentrate on relatively small-scale but high-impact projects. Notable initiatives in construction were the increased use of coconut wood for low-cost housing in Asia and the Pacific, and the development of roof trusses and glue-laminated beams of rubber wood and coconut wood in Sri Lanka. With the use of the UNIDO low-cost modular prefabricated wooden bridge system, bridges were erected in the Central African Republic, Honduras and Madagascar; in addition, in Honduras, a large-scale project to rebuild 10 bridges was initiated.

Special-purpose contributions from Finland and Italy enabled UNIDO to repeat in 1982 two specialized training courses for managers and entrepreneurs: a technical course on criteria for the selection of woodworking machinery (Milan, Italy, 10-26 May) and a seminar on the furniture and joinery industries (Lahti, Finland, 9-28 August). A manual was prepared on processing technology for rattan furniture.

Regional meetings in preparation for the proposed First (1983) Consultation on the Wood and Wood Products Industry were convened for Asia (Manila, Philippines, 22-26 March),[2] Africa (Vienna, Austria, 21-25 June)[1] and Latin America (São Paulo, Brazil, 4-8 October)[3] to discuss the status of the industry in each of those regions; identify constraints to the further development of primary and secondary processing; draw up proposals to improve international co-operation; and identify specific issues for further elaboration at a global preparatory meeting.

Reports. Regional Meeting in Preparation of Consultation on Wood and Wood Products Industry for: [1]Africa, ID/WG.373/12; [2]Asia, ID/WG.371/16; [3]Latin America, ID/WG.380/13.

Chemical industries

In 1982, UNIDO technical co-operation expenditures for activities in the chemical industries amounted to $18.9 million, with about 72 per cent financed from United Nations Development Programme resources. Of that amount, Africa accounted for 36 per cent; the Americas, 11; the Arab States (excluding those in Africa), 3; Asia and the Pacific, 42; Europe, 4; and interregional and global, 4. Completed or under implementation were 307 projects, 27 of them greater than $1 million in value, 84 greater than $150,000 and 196 less than that value.

Biomass processing

In the area of bioscience and engineering, involving microbiological processes for the production of fuels and chemicals from biomass, UNIDO assistance was provided in 1982 to strengthen the research and development capabilities of institutions: in the use of cellulosic materials for the production of microbial biomass animal feed and glucose, and ethanol from glucose (Brazil, and National Chemical Laboratory, Poona, India); and in the production from local carbohydrate raw materials, including by-products and wastes of the cane sugar industry, of selected chemicals—dextran, fructose, simple organic chemicals, complex organic acids—and single-cell proteins (National Science and Technology Authority (Philippines) and the affiliated organizations of the National Institute of Science and Technology and the University of the Philippines at Los Baños).

Building materials

In 1982, the increased use of local natural resources, such as clay, limestone and sand, was among the objectives of most technical co-operation projects in building materials. A large-scale project in Indonesia helped develop technologies for lime and brick production. Another project, to assist the construction industry in the Oran region of Algeria, particularly in prefabrication, was completed. In Malaysia, in co-operation with the Rubber Research and Development Board and in consultation with the International Society for Seismic Isolation, UNIDO organized a consultation on the protection of buildings from earthquake damage, attended by 14 developing countries.

In addition to an interregional cement technology forum (Benghazi, Libyan Arab Jamahiriya, 13-20 April), two workshops focusing on building materials for the construction industry were organized: one, financed from a special-purpose contribution to the United Nations Industrial Development Fund by Australia, dealt with the development of industries for timber, concrete, masonry, asbestos, cement, iron and gypsum for housing and other low-rise buildings (Sydney, Australia, 19-30 April); and another, organized in co-operation with the United Nations Development Programme and the Government of Yugoslavia, dealt with research, utilization and processing of non-metallic minerals for the construction industry (Belgrade, Yugoslavia, 10-16 May).

As noted by the Industrial Development Board at its May session,[1] UNIDO undertook a survey of building materials and of the construction industry, as well as a preliminary study of building techniques, in preparation for the inclusion of the building materials industry in the consultations programme for 1984-1985. The findings were reviewed by an *ad hoc* expert group meeting

(Vienna, Austria, 15-17 December) so that priority areas for further consideration might be proposed and issues identified for possible discussion.

Report. [1]IDB, A/37/16.

Fertilizer industry

Assistance to the fertilizer industry in 1982 included direct support to fertilizer plants and factories and the establishment of industry-oriented training and information centres on fertilizer production and application. Bangladesh and India were the recipients of such assistance.

In preparation for the Fourth (1984) Consultation on the Fertilizer Industry, a composite study was undertaken of capital cost analyses of fertilizer plants and of the benefits and potential offered by small-scale fertilizer plants in developing countries.

The international group of experts on the UNIDO model forms of turnkey lump sum and cost reimbursable contracts met to finalize the guidelines to the articles of a model contract for the construction of fertilizer plants (Vienna, 17-19 February). A Technical Conference on Ammonia Fertilizer Technology for Promotion of Economic Co-operation among Developing Countries was held (Beijing, China, 13-28 March),[1] as was a seminar, to assess the possibility of establishing mini–fertilizer plants in developing countries (Lahore, Pakistan, 15-20 November), at which was presented a basic engineering design for an ammonia plant with a production capacity of 100 metric tons per day.

To promote greater co-operation among developing countries in the fertilizer industry, a directory of their technical capabilities in the industry was in preparation, to include information on plants and projects, engineering services, equipment and raw materials.

Report. [1]Technical Conference on Ammonia Fertilizer Technology for Promotion of Economic Co-operation among Developing Countries, ID/WG.364/38.

Glass industry

In co-operation with the Intermediate Technology Industrial Service of the United Kingdom, UNIDO had developed a technology for the semi-automatic production of high quality glass containers, with an output of up to 5,000 tons a year. Preparatory work was begun in 1982 on the application of this technology in a factory in Malawi for the production of bottles, jars and other utility-ware.

Petrochemical industry

In the petrochemical sector, a project to provide technical support services to the petrochemical complex at Bahía Blanca, Argentina, was completed in 1982, with a total United Nations Development Programme input of $1.8 million.

About 200 technical personnel were trained by UNIDO, and modern facilities were established, including a polymer laboratory and a catalysis laboratory equipped to internationally competitive standards to provide technical and long-range research services to the petrochemical industry. Computer services were set up to carry out computer-aided modelling for the plants at the complex and a training simulator for operators and engineers was supplied.

A study for presentation to the Third (1983) Consultation on the Petrochemical Industry was begun. To contain data on consumption, production and trade in petrochemicals, as well as a description of the means of monitoring trends in technology development, the study was to provide regional and global projections for the medium and long term. Another study begun, in co-operation with the Arab Industrial Development Organization, was on world demand for petrochemical products and the petrochemical industry in the Arab region. A second draft of a model licensing agreement relating to the petrochemical industry was completed and circulated for review by experts.

An exchange of information on the status of the petrochemical and polymer industries in nine countries of Latin America and the Caribbean—Argentina, Bolivia, Colombia, Costa Rica, Ecuador, Honduras, Peru, Trinidad and Tobago and Uruguay—took place at a regional petrochemical and polymer consultation week (Porto Alegre, Brazil, 17-21 May).

Pesticide industry

Large-scale projects in China, India (two) and Egypt dealt in 1982 with the establishment of new research and development facilities for pesticide formulation or with the modernization of existing ones. Development continued of flexible multipurpose production units for local manufacture where the market for individual pesticides was small; in this connection, companies from industrialized countries showed considerable interest in co-operating with UNIDO.

Pharmaceutical industry

In 1982, UNIDO technical co-operation expenditures for activities in the pharmaceutical industry amounted to some $2.6 million, with the programme of assistance grouped in three categories. The first concerned the use of local natural resources for the production of medicines to supplement imported chemicals, projects for which were under implementation in Nepal, Rwanda, the United Republic of Cameroon and the Upper Volta; prefeasibility studies were completed on the establishment of pilot plants for such production in Mongolia and Viet Nam. The second category dealt with formulation and packaging of pharmaceuticals, projects for which were being carried out in Nepal, jointly with the World Health Organization, and in Zanzibar, United Republic of Tanzania. The third category concerned establishment of facilities for basic manufacture from chemical raw materials; Cuba and India received such assistance.

Several technical meetings were organized: a consultation on the production of drugs in a multipurpose plant (Visegrad, Hungary, 1-12 March), a seminar for developing countries on national self-reliance in blood and blood fractions (Stockholm, Sweden, 27 September-1 October) and a workshop to promote co-operation in the pharmaceutical industry among developing countries (Beijing, China, 1-14 November).

As a follow-up to the First (1980) Consultation on the Pharmaceutical Industry,[2] a study was begun on the production of immunizing agents and diagnostic antigens in developing countries, especially in the least developed countries of Africa. The Committee of Experts on Pharmaceuticals met (Paris, 11-13 October) to discuss the technical and economic aspects of the availability of bulk drugs and their intermediates, particularly those with limited sources of supply. The first draft of a directory of supply sources of essential bulk drugs was prepared. Also drafted and presented to the First Meeting of the *Ad Hoc* Panel of Experts on Contractual Arrangements in the Pharmaceutical Industry (Vienna, Austria, 15-17 December)[1] were a licensing agreement for the formulation of dosage forms, another for the manufacture of intermediates, and a model contract for the construction of a pharmaceutical plant for the formulation and production of the active ingredients of a drug.

Report. [1]First Meeting of Panel of Experts on Contractual Arrangements in Pharmaceutical Industry, ID/WG.385/4. *Yearbook reference.* [2]1980, p. 656.

Plastics industry

In 1982, the in-plant group training programmes in plastics technology and group training on synthetic fibres, regularly sponsored by Austria, were attended by 32 trainees. In addition, a new research programme in polymer technology was organized for specialized engineers.

The first phase of two large-scale projects on the uses of plastics in agriculture, one in Egypt and the other in Mexico, was completed and the second phase begun on the expansion of such uses in arid and semi-arid zones. In Bombay, India, a demonstration plant for the production of polyester and polyamide synthetic fibres was set up and the processing equipment installed at the Silk and Art Silk Mill Industries Research Association; also set up was a fully equipped laboratory for testing and analysing synthetic fibres, a project jointly undertaken by the Indian Research Association, the Agency for Technical Co-operation of the Federal Republic of Germany and UNIDO.

The situation of the synthetic fibre industry in each of seven countries—Bangladesh, China, Colombia, Indonesia, Peru, Thailand and Turkey—was presented at a conference on man-made fibres (Bombay, 29 March-2 April); that of the polymer industry in nine countries of Latin America and the Caribbean was presented at a regional consultation week (see above).

Pulp and paper industry

Technical assistance in the pulp and paper industry was provided in 1982 to straw-pulping mills (Yugoslavia), for the maintenance of paper-board coating instruments and for kaolin production (Turkey), and for the construction of a paper mill (Bolivia) and a bagasse-pulping line (Uganda). A paper pilot plant in Burma, in operation since mid-1981, was equipped with a pulp plant at the end of 1982. A fibre fractionation demonstration plant for waste paper in Egypt underwent testing. In India, a bamboo fibre fractionation plant was under construction, as was a modern cellulose chemistry unit in the Sudan for the conversion of agricultural waste materials into pulp and paper, besides animal fodder, fuel and fertilizers.

Engineering industries

UNIDO activities. In 1982, technical co-operation expenditures for activities in the engineering industries amounted to $14 million, with some 94 per cent financed from United Nations Development Programme resources. Of that amount, Africa accounted for 12 per cent; the Americas, 9; the Arab States (excluding those in Africa), 4; Asia and the Pacific, 71; and Europe, 4. A total of 154 projects were completed or under implementation, 22 of them greater than $1 million in value, 49 greater than $150,000 and 83 below that value.

Activities fell into two categories, namely, those contributing to overall economic development in a broad spectrum of sectors and those to technological development in specific industrial subsectors. Under the first, activities gave priority to energy-related and other industrial technology, industrial production, human resources development and special measures for the least developed countries. Under the second, they continued to be in the design, manufacture and maintenance of engineering products in five industrial product groups: agricultural machinery and implements, metalworking and machine tools, land-based and water-borne transport equipment, electronic and electrical machinery and equipment, and computers and computer-related equipment.

Formulated and proposed were some 50 projects, valued at about $48 million, for some 32 countries located in all geographical regions. These were undertaken in response to developing countries' preferences for assistance in three areas: development of agricultural machinery industries, expansion of electronics industries and increased use of computers in industry.

With respect to the application of advanced technologies in developing countries with suitable infrastructures, the Numerical Control (NC) Centre at Bangalore, India, received assistance in developing the capability to design and implement computer-aided manufacture (CAM) equipment and systems; and the NC/CAM Centre in Bulgaria, in the introduction of minicomputers, personal computers and calculators. In Czechoslovakia, a complete turnkey CAM system was installed. Large-scale manufacturing projects in China and the Republic of Korea were provided with computer-aided design (CAD) and CAM expertise. Other projects begun included: CAD projects with emphasis on power distribution networks, construction, finite element analysis and printed circuit boards (Bulgaria, India), introduction of robotics (Bulgaria) and appropriate automation and agro-electronics (India). As a result of programming missions to Argentina, Brazil, Cuba, India, Mexico and Turkey, projects were formulated covering fibre optics, CAD/CAM, manufacturing engineering computer applications, microcomputer systems, applications and software engineering.

In line with the recommendations of the First Consultation on the Capital Goods Industry in September 1981,[2] work was begun in assisting developing countries plan for the development of the capital goods industry, using a scheme classifying the main groups of machines and equipment into six levels of technological complexity, thereby providing a clear view of the conditions required to engage in the sector and move from one level to another; and a preliminary study on the improvement of existing training programmes was presented to the First Consultation on the Training of Industrial Manpower. As to the exchange of information on capital goods technology and engineering services, compilation was begun of a comprehensive list of technology suppliers for selected capital goods.

UNCTAD activities. In response to a March 1981 resolution of the Trade and Development Board of the United Nations Conference on Trade and Development,[3] a Meeting of Governmental Experts on the Transfer, Application and Development of Technology in the Capital Goods and Industrial Machinery Sector was convened (Geneva, 7-16 July 1982).[1] The conclusions and recommendations of the experts, endorsed by the Committee on Transfer of Technology, invited the developing countries to adopt strategies and take measures to ensure the efficient technological modernization of their capital goods industries, selectively strengthening those branches and technologies for which need and potential existed. The experts also suggested specific ways to strengthen co-operative links among developing countries so as to maximize benefits and proposed supporting measures for consideration by the developed countries.

Report. [1]Meeting of Governmental Experts on Transfer, Application and Development of Technology in Capital Goods and Industrial Machinery Sector, TD/B/C.6/82 & Corr.1. *Yearbook references.* 1981, [2]p. 598, [3]p. 754.

Electrical and electronics industry

In 1982, technical co-operation activities of UNIDO in the electrical and electronics industries were in the areas of institutional development, establishment of pilot manufacturing plants, factory-level assistance, component manufacture and systems development, precision engineering and quality control, and training.

In response to developing countries' demands for institutional development projects and pilot plants, activities were initiated for the establishment of a process control computer centre for electrical machinery and equipment (Bulgaria), a reliability and environmental test centre (Republic of Korea), a system of laboratories for the electrical industry (Mexico), an electronic and optical maintenance and repair centre (Viet Nam), and a project to strengthen the National Institute of Electronics (Pakistan).

At the factory level, assistance was provided to the electronics industry in general (Albania) and to a postal administration and communications equipment factory in particular (Turkey).

In component manufacture and systems development, a project was devised for micromechanics and micro-electronic interfaces (Brazil) and another begun for the design of microprocessor-based dairy instruments (India); a project on integrated circuit technology progressed as scheduled (Romania).

Projects in precision engineering and quality control included electrostatic precipitator testing and development (China), increasing manometer accuracy (Bulgaria) and laboratory studies in automatic information systems (Albania). Project implementation modalities were developed for a qualification laboratory for electronic products (China), the start-up of an evaluation and product process centre (India), and design, development and marketing of advanced technology products (Greece). Assistance was provided to Hong Kong in the development of interference detection and assessment of test facilities, as well as in microprocessor technology and industrial application of computers.

Projects with emphasis on training covered development of microprecision system application (China) and training centres for the repair and maintenance of biomedical equipment (Hungary) and for microprocessor application (Romania).

A 1981 meeting of experts at Vienna, Austria, on the implications of technological advances in micro-electronics for developing countries was followed up at the national, regional and international levels. A national meeting on co-operation between scientific and industrial sectors in micro-electronics (Mexico City, 14 and 15 June 1982) brought together government representatives, research institutions and industry to review the national situation and recommend approriate action. An expert group meeting—organized jointly by UNIDO and the Economic Commission for Latin America (ECLA)— on the implications of micro-electronics for the ECLA region (Mexico City, 7-11 June)[1] recommended elaboration of a Latin American programme of co-operation in micro-electronics. An expert mission visited Egypt, India, Mexico and Thailand to promote selective applications of micro-electronics and software development.

> *Report.* [1]UNIDO/ECLA Expert Group Meeting on Implications of Micro-electronics for ECLA Region, ID/WG.372/17.
> *Publication. Microelectronics Monitor*, Nos. 1-3 (1982).

Genetic engineering

As a result of keen interest expressed by many Governments, a High-level Meeting on the Establishment of an International Centre for Genetic Engineering and Biotechnology was convened (Belgrade, Yugoslavia, 13-17 December 1982).[1] The Meeting considered, in addition to a report on the physical facilities required for the proposed centre, a five-year plan of work outlining activities in the areas of: selective application of advanced biotechnology for developing countries, application of genetic engineering for energy and fertilizer production from biomass, hydrocarbon microbiology relative to tertiary oil recovery from petroleum wells, application of genetic engineering and biotechnology for the production of improved human and animal vaccines especially for tropical diseases, improved agricultural and food products through genetic engineering and biotechnology, and bio-informatics.

While some delegations thought the proposed centre too ambitious, preferring a modest mechanism in the form of an international network, many emphasized that only a centre on the scale envisaged could provide the critical mass of expertise required for co-operative efforts to be effective. Concluding that there was an urgent need for more effective international co-operation in genetic engineering and biotechnology, to be promoted primarily for the benefit of developing countries,

the Meeting recommended prompt establishment of the centre, in a developing country, with affiliated national and regional centres, each specializing in a specific subject area. A committee was to be set up to select the host country and complete formalities for the installation and functioning of the centre. A two-part ministerial meeting to resolve outstanding issues and agree and subscribe to the final act of establishing the centre was to be held in 1983.

Follow-up meetings of high-level policy makers and industrial representatives and technologists were held in India and Kuwait.

> *Report.* [1]High-level Meeting on Establishment of International Centre for Genetic Engineering and Biotechnology, ID/WG.382/7 & Corr.1.
> *Publication. Genetic Engineering and Biotechnology Monitor*, Nos. 1-3 (1982).

Machinery industry

Technical co-operation activities in 1982 in the metalworking and machine-tool industries covered: engineering institutional development; pilot manufacturing plants; components and products manufacture; engineering product efficiency and reliability; repair, maintenance and training; rural engineering; energy-related equipment and technologies; and new sources of energy.

Assistance to the Rangoon Institute of Technology, Burma, was completed in 1982; the Institute, in co-operation with manufacturing units, built a lathe and a drill press prototype. In India, the preparatory phase of a project to assist the Automotive Research Association Institute at Poona in setting up a fatigue laboratory was completed and two projects were begun: one for a national bicycle research and development centre to assist small-scale bicycle manufacturers in product improvement, quality control and rationalization of component manufacture; and another to strengthen industrial design services at the National Institute of Design. A project to assist the engine parts and allied components industry in Yugoslavia was developed. In addition to providing assistance to the general machine-building industry in China, UNIDO helped equip the Tropicalization Centre in Viet Nam with environmental testing equipment for the development of new materials designed to withstand climatic conditions.

In February, UNIDO sponsored a four-week visit to India of senior design and technology staff of the machine-tool industry in Beijing, China, in an effort to promote co-operation between the two countries.

Agricultural machinery

In the framework of the programme for the Industrial Development Decade for Africa, the First Regional Consultation Meeting on the

Agricultural Machinery Industry (Addis Ababa, Ethiopia, 5-9 April 1982),[1] attended by 116 participants from 49 countries and 9 international organizations, dealt with the status of the agricultural machinery industry and strategies for its development, in the context of the 1980 Lagos Plan of Action for the Implementation of the Monrovia Strategy for the Economic Development of Africa.[2] The Meeting discussed measures for promoting production capabilities and adopted a tentative proposal for the formulation of an African development plan for agricultural machinery and equipment. As a follow-up, a workshop on design and development of agricultural equipment in Africa (Cairo, Egypt, 17-28 October) made specific recommendations for national, subregional and regional actions and programmes.

Projects approved and implemented in the agricultural machinery sector included: machinery testing and industrial extension (China); design and industrial extension (Pakistan); expansion of implements production (Democratic Yemen); development of magnetic resonance spectrometers for oil-seed characterization (India); assistance to the Agricultural Machinery Agency (Somalia); technical evaluation of low-powered tractors (Kenya); maintenance of tractors (Upper Volta) and of irrigation equipment (subregions of Africa); and assistance to the Sahel Institute in the development of a subregional programme on agricultural machinery.

UNIDO reached agreement with the United Nations Capital Development Fund on a joint project in Uganda on the local manufacture of simple, low-cost agricultural tools and implements, and, with the Food and Agriculture Organization of the United Nations, on the joint implementation of a United Nations Development Programme–Government cost-sharing project in Algeria to assist in the establishment of a techno-economic programme network for agricultural machinery, based on local infrastructure.

Report. [1]Regional Consultation Meeting on Agricultural Machinery Industry, ID/285.
Yearbook reference. [2]1980, p. 548.

Metalworking industry

Projects initiated by UNIDO in 1982 in the metalworking industry covered work on a pump repair section of a mechanical workshop (Somalia); development of rural engineering processing techniques for selected artisanal products (Ecuador), as well as of prototype wood-burning stoves, based on technologies adapted to local socio-economic conditions, for batch-level production in small-scale rural production units (Fiji); upgrading rural blacksmith workshops (Nepal); and development of motorized cycle rickshaws (India).

Transport engineering and equipment

UNIDO projects in transport concentrated in 1982 on shipbuilding and ship repair (see below), and on automotive and railway engineering (Angola, Costa Rica, Romania, Viet Nam, Yugoslavia), in the light of the increased importance attached to these activities by developing countries. Under the programme for the United Nations Transport and Communications Decade for Africa (1978-1988), activities continued for the establishment and strengthening of appropriate production units, the application of new technologies and manufacture of spare parts.

Shipbuilding and ship repair

Projects in marine engineering industries assisted by UNIDO in 1982 included rehabilitation of ship-repair facilities (Yugoslavia), development of welding technology (Malta), formulation of a policy for shipbuilding and ship-repair industries (Syrian Arab Republic) and establishment of a scrap-metal workshop and construction of boats (Cuba). A large-scale project funded by the United Nations Industrial Development Fund was under implementation for the establishment of a boat-building and maintenance yard in Seychelles.

An Expert Group Meeting on Small-Scale Shipbuilding and Ship-Repair Development for Latin American and Caribbean Countries (Havana, Cuba, 9-12 November)[1] recommended that a Latin American programme of co-operation in small-scale shipbuilding and ship repair be set up, particularly for fishing boats, with support from regional and international organizations. To that end, the Meeting requested that a detailed programme proposal be presented to a 1983 meeting of ministers of fisheries of the Latin American Programme of Fishing Development.

Preparations for a similar meeting for Asia and the Pacific were under way.

A report to the Governing Council of the United Nations Development Programme (UNDP) described assistance by the United Nations system to maritime transport training institutions in developing countries (see previous chapter).

Report. [1]Expert Group Meeting on Small-Scale Shipbuilding and Ship-Repair Development for Latin American and Caribbean Countries, ID/WG.375/43.

Metallurgical and mineral industries

In 1982, UNIDO technical co-operation expenditures for activities in metallurgical industries amounted to $9.2 million, with about 76 per cent financed from UNDP resources. Of that amount, Africa accounted for 27 per cent; the Americas, 16; the Arab States (excluding those in Africa), 5; Asia and the Pacific, 45; and Europe, 7. Completed or under implementation were 104 projects,

12 of them greater than $1 million in value, 38 greater than $150,000 and 54 less than that value.

As in previous years, efforts concentrated on the development, transfer, application and adaptation of metallurgical technology within the following broad subsectors: light (aluminium, titanium) and heavy (copper, lead, zinc, rare metals) non-ferrous metals; iron and steel industry (conventional routes and direct reduction); ferrous and non-ferrous foundries; metal transformation processes (rolling, forging, extruding, heat treating); and processing of metallurgical minerals (concentration, beneficiation).

In metallurgical technology, assistance in research and development was provided, within the framework of the Central Metallurgical Research and Development Institute at Jos (Nigeria), in mineral beneficiation, alloy heat treatment and production technology, and mechanical metallurgy; to the National Welding Research Institute at Tiruchirapalli (India), in its second phase of implementation, in sophisticated welding technology of high-pressure boilers, super-alloys and alloy steels; and to the Mineral and Metallurgical Research Centre in Santiago (Chile), in the separation of arsenic from copper concentrates through froth flotation. Implementation of a new large-scale project was started to strengthen an iron and steel research and development centre in Argentina.

Aluminium industry

Owing to the significant increase in the alumina production capacity of developing countries in the past 15 years and to an even greater increase in aluminium metal production, the greatest proportion of UNIDO assistance in 1982, with respect to the non-ferrous metal subsector, was again provided to the aluminium industry. The Zheng Zhou Light Metal Research Institute of China was supplied with laboratory equipment for bauxite research and development, and the Jamaica Bauxite Institute received assistance to upgrade its scientific and technological capabilities.

Several studies carried out in 1982 included one on the development of the aluminium industry in Mozambique and another on its fluorite deposits; and a design study for a demonstration plant in China for the manufacture of door and window frames from aluminium alloy. A project report was prepared for the establishment of an aluminium research development and design institute in India. A similar institute to be attached to the aluminium plant at Titograd, Yugoslavia, was at the planning stage. UNIDO also assisted in establishing contacts between India and Mozambique for possible co-operation in the smelting of aluminium, using alumina from India's significant bauxite deposits and Mozambique's vast hydro-electric resources generated by its Cabora Bassa dam.

Iron and steel industry

The Third Consultation on the Iron and Steel Industry (Caracas, Venezuela, 13-17 September 1982),[1] attended by 185 participants from 45 countries and 11 international organizations, recognized manpower training to be an important requisite for the industry, and considered new financing arrangements for training activities and social and physical infrastructure. Noting that projects in 32 countries involving a total capacity of 4.5 million tons up to 1990 had been identified, the Consultation recommended that newcomers to the industry be assisted with experts' services and information on the mini-steel plant, considered the most desirable route for newcomers.

The Second Working Group Meeting on Scenarios of the Iron and Steel Industry's Development (Estoril, Portugal, 3-5 February 1982)[2] submitted to the Consultation updated scenarios of future trends, papers on specific issues and suggestions for their practical resolution.

In Latin America, a net importer of 5 million tons of steel per year, a new large-scale UNIDO project was started to strengthen an iron and steel research and development centre in Argentina, while a large-scale project was completed on standardization, quality control and certification of iron and steel in Brazil. The Chimbote steel plant in Peru received further assistance in electrical and utility services distribution systems, as did the Companhia Industrial de Fundação e Laminagem plant in Mozambique, for upgrading the merchant steel rolling mill. Three projects were started in India, involving standardization of melting technology of sponge iron, design development of a concurrent top and bottom blow reactor for steel making, and design development of an experimental blast furnace. Preparatory work was undertaken for a preliminary programme of development of the iron and steel industry in Uganda and for mini–steel plants in Democratic Yemen and Yemen. A techno-economic evaluation together with laboratory investigations of raw materials for the establishment of the iron and steel industry was being implemented in the United Republic of Tanzania.

Reports. [1]Consultation on Iron and Steel Industry, ID/291; [2]Working Group Meeting on Scenarios of Iron and Steel Industry's Development, ID/WG.363/4.

Foundries

To promote development of the foundry industry, particularly in least developed countries, a number of comprehensive guidelines and documents on the establishment of various standard foundry shops were prepared by UNIDO in 1982 with the assistance of the Foundry Research Institute at Cracow, Poland.

The bulk of technical assistance to African countries in the field of metallurgical industries continued to be provided to foundries. The Foundry and

Mechanical Workshop in Somalia was aided through a sub-contract with the Egyptian Iron and Steel Company in the form of training and advisory services for improved productivity and equipment installation. At a Swaziland foundry, assistance related to upgrading production and assessing demand for the plant's products with a view to possible co-operation with Mozambique. A techno-economic evaluation was undertaken of the foundry industry in Angola in order to upgrade it to meet local demand for castings. Construction of a pilot and demonstration foundry in Nepal was completed and equipment delivered to the site. Advisory services were provided to Ethiopia for a study on a projected pilot foundry with an integrated forge shop, and to Malta, regarding establishment of a grey cast-iron foundry. In Paraguay, a large-scale project to strengthen metallurgical industries was initiated, with particular emphasis on foundry industries.

Other industrial categories

Export-oriented industries

Technical co-operation in the development of competitive products for export was pursued by UNIDO in 1982 in the following areas: product adaptation for export, sub-contracting exchanges and investment promotion.

More than 20 developing countries accorded priority to export development projects. Four projects on product adaptation—covering such products as silk fabrics, fishing rods, jigs and fixtures, press tools and dies—were completed (India (two), Kenya, Republic of Korea). Projects in sub-contracting exchanges were carried out (Costa Rica, Philippines) and the possibility of setting up such an exchange was examined under a Special Industrial Services project (Malaysia). To strengthen investment promotion institutions, assistance was provided to Nigeria and Tonga.

These UNIDO activities were in addition to the trade promotion and facilitation work of the International Trade Centre.

Public enterprises

A large-scale UNIDO project provided assistance in 1982 to the Government of Guyana in introducing new management procedures and in improving productivity in public sector industries. In Uruguay, government and parastatal bodies continued to receive technical assistance to strengthen national management capacities and introduce measures for improved productivity.

A series of studies on the role of the public sector in the industrialization of eight developing countries—Bangladesh, Brazil, India, Mexico, Nigeria, Pakistan, Sri Lanka and the United Republic of Tanzania—was completed, while six studies evaluating the performance of public industrial en-

terprises were incorporated in the journal *Industry and Development*.[1]

Publication. [1]*Industry and Development*, No. 7 (ID/SER.M/7), Sales No. E.82.II.B.4.

Small-scale industry

In small-scale industry development, assistance was provided by UNIDO in 1982 to 39 countries to establish and strengthen institutions for the provision of, among other things, common services facilities, assistance in the choice of appropriate technology, factory accommodation and extension services. Among the recipient countries were Burundi, Honduras, Indonesia and Nigeria, where large-scale projects to strengthen national agencies covered activities such as establishing central offices for project opportunities and management services, consolidating common service facilities and directly assisting small-scale industrial entrepreneurs through consultancy.

Assistance was also provided for the promotion of industrial co-operatives for self-reliance (United Republic of Tanzania), strengthening industrial estates (Iraq, Panama, Thailand), and entrepreneurship development through mechanical production workshops (Fiji, Guinea, Upper Volta). Projects on industrial extension were also supported (Liberia, Togo, Turkey).

Eighteen proposals were being finalized for the transfer of technology between small-scale metal-working and light engineering plants in Sweden to similar plants in Egypt, India, Kenya and Sri Lanka; field surveys were under way on possible co-operation in the food processing industry between the Netherlands and Thailand, as well as China, Mexico and the Sudan. A project involving co-operation between selected Indian and Nepalese enterprises was completed and resulted in concrete proposals for co-operation and training programmes. In Samoa, a project involving co-operation among developing countries in the coir industry and its by-products was under way.

Rural industries

In 1982, UNIDO explored new approaches for industrialization of rural areas to improve living conditions and reduce migration to urban centres, particularly in Africa. At the beginning of the year, a project was launched to rehabilitate existing rural industries and create new ones in Zaire.

Projects carried out in Nigeria, Zaire, Zambia and Zimbabwe were geared to support rural and village industries, while those in Argentina and the Philippines called for the transfer of more sophisticated technologies and industrial processes to provincial areas. In Botswana, Ethiopia, Jamaica and the Upper Volta, large-scale projects were aimed at upgrading traditional artisan and craft-based industries to industrial levels.

Chapter VII

Transnational corporations

Contents

Draft code of conduct

The Intergovernmental Working Group on a Code of Conduct finalized in 1982 its work on a draft international code relating to the activities of transnational corporations (TNCs) and submitted it to the Commission on Transnational Corporations at its August/September session without having agreed on all provisions. On the Commission's recommendation, the Economic and Social Council authorized the Commission to hold a special session in 1983 to consider the draft code.

Working Group activities. As authorized by the Economic and Social Council in November 1981,[1] the Working Group met three more times in 1982, in New York, for its fifteenth, sixteenth and seventeenth sessions, from 4 to 15 January, from 1 to 12 March and from 10 to 21 May.

At those sessions, the Group concluded consideration of provisions relating to: implementation; definitions and scope of application; adherence to the economic goals and development objectives, policies and priorities of the countries in which TNCs operate; conformity with their intergovernmental co-operative arrangements; contract renegotiation; limitations on government action on behalf of TNCs; abstention from corrupt practices; conformity with laws and regulations of the countries in which TNCs operate in relation to the balance of payments of those countries, and with laws and regulations governing the transfer of technology; treatment of TNCs and their entities; nationalization and compensation; jurisdiction over TNCs; and the clarification of the code's provisions in the light of actual situations.

The text of the draft code of conduct constituted the main body of the Group's final report.[4]

Formulations completed were for five of the six main parts of the draft code. The first part, for which no formulations were drafted, was to be the code's preamble and statement of objectives. The second part consisted of a set of provisions on definitions and scope of application. The third contained provisions addressed to TNCs, specifying the kinds of conduct deemed permissible and proper: one set of paragraphs dealt with general and political issues; another set with specific economic, financial and social issues; and still another with TNC disclosure of information. The fourth part covered the treatment TNCs were to receive from Governments of the countries in which they operate, including the questions of nationalization and compensation, and jurisdiction. The fifth part addressed intergovernmental co-operation for the application of the code. The sixth dealt with action needed at the national and international levels for implementation of the code.

Of the draft code's 71 provisions, two thirds were fully agreed and contained definitive language acceptable to all delegations. These included provisions on adherence to socio-cultural objectives and values, ownership and control, balance of payments and financing, taxation, consumer protection, environmental protection, information disclosure, intergovernmental co-operation and implementation. Alternative formulations or wordings were bracketed, as were compromise texts on which agreement was not achieved. More than half of these could be removed without great effort, but five or six areas presented considerable difficulty, according to an assessment by the Working Group Chairman made at the 1982 session of the Commission.[2]

The major issues outstanding were: the legal nature of the code—whether it should be mandatory and legally binding, or voluntary and thus not legally enforceable; the preamble and objectives, which remained to be drafted and for which the Group had endorsed certain items; the definition of "transnational corporation" and the precise scope of the code's application; key norms to regulate TNC activities—whether the provision requiring TNCs to respect national sovereignty should extend to the State's right to exercise permanent sovereignty over its natural resources, wealth and economic activities, the feasibility of requiring TNCs to contribute to the economic goals and development objectives of host countries, norms prohibiting TNC activities that would adversely affect the balance of payments of those countries and the precise nature of "non-interference" in internal political affairs; and substantive provisions on TNCs operating in southern Africa.

Also outstanding were a number of provisions on the treatment of TNCs which hinged on the fundamental questions of whether there were universally recognized principles of international law prescribing minimum standards for the treatment of TNCs to which national law should adhere, and whether the concept of national sovereignty dictated that all aspects of such treatment were to be governed by national law, subject to international obligations freely subscribed to by the State concerned. The main provisions in question concerned the treatment of TNCs relative to that of domestic enterprises; safeguards on confidential business information; compensation in the case of nationalization; and the exact relationship between national jurisdiction and other methods of settlement of disputes between States and TNCs, the choice of law and forum in private law contracts, and conflicts of jurisdiction between States in multi-party disputes.

Following consideration of the Working Group's report, the Commission on 9 September 1982[3] recommended that the Economic and Social Council authorize a special session for the Commission of up to four weeks' duration, in early 1983, to complete formulation of the code, giving priority to the preamble and objectives, definitions

and scope of application, TNC activities including those in southern Africa, and treatment of TNCs.

Economic and Social Council action. Acting without vote on 27 October[5] on the Commission's recommendation, the Council took note of the work done by the Commission and the Working Group. Reaffirming that it attached the highest priority to the code's completion, it decided that the Commission hold in 1983 a special session, open to all States, to pursue work on those parts of the code where no provisions had been finalized, as specified by the Commission (see above). To facilitate that work, the Council called on all States to be represented at the appropriate level. It requested the United Nations Centre on Transnational Corporations to provide the necessary documentation and the Commission to submit to the Council the full and final draft code of conduct for transmittal to the General Assembly at its 1983 session.

By a further resolution of the same date, on TNC activities in southern Africa, the Council reaffirmed that the code should include effective measures against TNC collaboration with the racist minority régime in that region.[6]

Decision. [1]ESC: 1981/198, 2 Nov. 1981 (YUN 1981, p. 605).
Note. [2]Secretariat, E/C.10/1983/S/2.
Reports. [3]Commission on TNCs, E/1982/18; [4]Working Group, E/C.10/1982/6.
Resolutions (1982). ESC, 27 Oct.: [5]1982/68, text following; [6]1982/69, para. 13.
Meeting records. ESC: E/1982/SR.52, _54_ (25, 27 Oct.).

Economic and Social Council resolution 1982/68

27 October 1982   Meeting 54   Adopted without vote

Draft by Commission on TNCs (E/1982/18); agenda item 25.

Arrangements for completing the formulation of a draft code of conduct on transnational corporations

The Economic and Social Council,

Recalling General Assembly resolutions 3201(S-VI) and 3202(S-VI) of 1 May 1974, containing the Declaration and the Programme of Action on the Establishment of a New International Economic Order, 3281(XXIX) of 12 December 1974, containing the Charter of Economic Rights and Duties of States, and 3362(S-VII) of 16 September 1975 on development and international economic co-operation,

Reaffirming its resolutions 1908(LVII) of 2 August 1974 and 1913(LVII) of 5 December 1974, by which it established the Commission on Transnational Corporations and the United Nations Centre on Transnational Corporations and identified the principal tasks assigned to the Commission,

Reaffirming also its resolution 1980/60 of 24 July 1980, entitled "Progress made towards the establishment of the new international economic order and obstacles that impede it: the role of transnational corporations",

1. _Reaffirms_ that it attaches the highest priority to the expeditious conclusion of a comprehensive and integrated code of conduct on transnational corporations that will be effective, generally accepted and universally adopted;

2. _Takes note with appreciation_ of the work done by the Commission on Transnational Corporations and the Intergovernmental Working Group on a Code of Conduct and, in particular, of the results of that work as embodied in the report of the Intergovernmental Working Group on its fifteenth, sixteenth and seventeenth sessions;

3. _Decides_ that the Commission on Transnational Corporations shall hold a special session, of up to four weeks' duration, early in 1983 for the purpose of continuing and completing the formulation of the code of conduct;

4. _Decides also_ that such work shall be based on the work done thus far by the Commission on Transnational Corporations and the

Intergovernmental Working Group on a Code of Conduct as reflected in the report of the Intergovernmental Working Group, on the understanding that the work of the Commission in special session will be pursued in those areas where no provisions have been finalized by the Intergovernmental Working Group, priority to be given to the sections entitled "Preamble and objectives", "Definitions and scope of application", "Activities of transnational corporations", including the question of southern Africa, and "Treatment of transnational corporations";

5. *Decides further* that the special session of the Commission on Transnational Corporations shall be open to the participation of all States;

6. *Calls upon* all States to be represented at the special session at the appropriate level in order to facilitate the finalization of the code of conduct;

7. *Requests* the United Nations Centre on Transnational Corporations to take steps to ensure that all States are provided with the necessary documentation in order to facilitate their participation in the special session;

8. *Requests* the Secretary-General to ensure that all necessary conference and other supporting facilities are made available for the special session of the Commission on Transnational Corporations;

9. *Requests* the Commission on Transnational Corporations to submit to it the full and final draft code of conduct for its consideration and transmission to the General Assembly at its thirty-eighth session for consideration and appropriate action.

Definition of TNC

On 9 September 1982, when the Commission on TNCs considered the work related to the definition of the term "transnational corporation",[1] delegation views differed over whether the definition should encompass privately owned, as well as publicly owned and mixed, enterprises. The Commission decided that those views be taken into account when the issue came before its special session in 1983.

Report. [1]Commission on TNCs, E/1982/18.

Standards of accounting and reporting

As authorized by the Economic and Social Council in November 1981,[1] the *Ad Hoc* Intergovernmental Working Group of Experts on International Standards of Accounting and Reporting met twice more in 1982, in New York, for its fifth and sixth sessions, from 18 to 29 January and from 29 March to 9 April. The Group, which began work in 1980,[5] submitted its final report and recommendations[2] to the Commission on TNCs at its 1982 session.

The report stated that in pursuance of its mandate—to promote adoption of accounting and reporting standards to improve the availability and comparability of information on TNC operations, taking into account an expert group report of 1977[4] on the subject—the Group examined various issues of particular concern to information users, reporting entities and standard-setting bodies for a better understanding, analysis and evaluation of the performance of TNCs. It reached agreement on a number of items for inclusion in minimum lists of financial and non-financial information for general-purpose reporting by an enterprise as a whole and by individual member enterprises. Other items

not on the lists but material enough to user evaluations and decisions should also be included in corporate reports. If a code of conduct failed to be adopted within a reasonable time, the Group recommended Commission action to make information disclosure by TNCs possible, using the agreed minimum items. The Group also recommended that the United Nations orient its development efforts towards the national and regional levels, where the long, complex process of standard-setting primarily occurred.

The Group agreed on the importance of achieving greater comparability with regard to disclosure by TNCs through appropriate United Nations action. Accordingly, it recommended that an intergovernmental working group of experts on international standards of accounting be established to serve as an international body for the consideration of accounting and reporting issues falling within the scope of the Commission's work; to review developments in this field, including the work of standard-setting bodies; and to concentrate on establishing priorities, taking into account the needs of home and host countries, particularly developing countries. Among the issues meriting further study by the proposed working group were: the identification of areas for special-purpose reporting; an understanding of what TNCs could reasonably be expected to disclose within the context of their need to maintain confidentiality in sensitive business areas to protect their competitive position; and a cost-benefit analysis of implementing recommended reporting requirements.

The United Nations Centre on TNCs, which had been requested to provide the necessary services for the *Ad Hoc* Group's work, had prepared a number of studies focusing on regional and international efforts to harmonize corporate accounting and reporting.[3]

Decision. [1]ESC: 1981/198, 2 Nov. 1981 (YUN 1981, p. 605). *Publications.* [2]*International Standards of Accounting and Reporting: Report of the* Ad Hoc *Intergovernmental Working Group of Experts on International Standards of Accounting and Reporting* (E/C.10/1982/8/Rev.1), Sales No. E.84.II.A.2; [3]*Towards International Standardization of Corporate Accounting and Reporting* (ST/CTC/30), Sales No. E.82.II.A.3. *Yearbook references.* [4]1977, p. 532; [5]1980, p. 669.

Establishment of an Intergovernmental Group

By a resolution of 27 October 1982,[1] the Economic and Social Council approved the *Ad Hoc* Group's report (see above) and commended it for its work. It decided to establish an Intergovernmental Working Group of Experts on International Standards of Accounting and Reporting to act as an international body for the consideration of issues of accounting and reporting in order to improve the availability and comparability of information disclosed by TNCs, to review developments in this field, including the work of standard-setting bodies, and to establish priorities. The Group was to meet not more than once yearly and report to the Commission on TNCs on further steps to be taken in pursuit of the long-term objective of the international harmonization of accounting and reporting within the scope of the Commission's work, particularly with regard to the comprehensive information system and the code of conduct on TNCs currently being formulated. The Council fixed the Group's membership at 34 and determined the distribution of seats among the five regional groups.

The draft text, adopted without vote by the Council, was recommended by the Commission.

Resolution (1982). [1]ESC: 1982/67, 27 Oct., text following.
Meeting records. ESC: E/1982/SR.52, *54* (25, 27 Oct.).

Economic and Social Council resolution 1982/67

27 October 1982   Meeting 54   Adopted without vote

Draft by Commission on TNCs (E/1982/18); agenda item 25.

Establishment of an Intergovernmental Working Group of Experts on International Standards of Accounting and Reporting

The Economic and Social Council,

Recalling its resolution 1979/44 of 11 May 1979,

Having considered the report of the *Ad Hoc* Intergovernmental Working Group of Experts on International Standards of Accounting and Reporting,

Acting upon the recommendation made by the Commission on Transnational Corporations at its eighth session concerning the establishment of an Intergovernmental Working Group of Experts on International Standards of Accounting and Reporting,

1. *Recognizes* that the process of setting standards for accounting and reporting is complex, that it takes place primarily at the national and sometimes regional levels, and that the efforts of the United Nations should be oriented towards making a positive contribution to developments at those levels;

2. *Agrees* on the importance and desirability of achieving greater comparability with regard to disclosure by transnational corporations through, *inter alia*, appropriate action within the United Nations;

3. *Approves* the report of the *Ad Hoc* Intergovernmental Working Group of Experts on International Standards of Accounting and Reporting and commends the Group for its work;

4. *Decides:*

(a) To establish an Intergovernmental Working Group of Experts on International Standards of Accounting and Reporting composed of thirty-four members;

(b) That, taking into account the different existing systems of accounting and reporting and without prejudice to the principle of equitable geographical distribution, the Group should be composed as follows:

Nine members from African States;
Seven members from Asian States;
Three members from Eastern European States;
Six members from Latin American States;
Nine members from Western European and other States;

(c) That the members of the Group shall be elected by the Council at its resumed second regular session of 1982 and that each State so elected shall appoint an expert with appropriate experience in the field of accounting and reporting;

(d) That the members shall be elected for a period of three years, beginning on 1 January following their election, except that, for one half of the members elected at the first eletion, the term of membership shall be two years; members shall be eligible for re-election;

(e) That the Group should serve as an international body for the consideration of issues of accounting and reporting falling within the scope of the work of the Commission on Transnational Corporations, in order to improve the availability and comparability of information disclosed by transnational corporations; should review developments in this field, including the work of standard-setting bodies; and should concentrate on establishing priorities, taking into account the needs of home and host countries, particularly those of developing countries;

(f) That the Group should take into account the work of the *Ad Hoc* Intergovernmental Working Group of Experts on International Standards of Accounting and Reporting as well as other relevant activities in the field; should consult the international bodies which it deems appropriate on matters pertaining to the development of international standards of accounting and reporting and should elicit views of other interested parties on specific issues on an *ad hoc* basis;

(g) That the Group should meet for a period of two weeks not more than once a year and should report to the Commission on Transnational Corporations on further steps to be taken in pursuit of the long-term objective of the international harmonization of accounting and reporting within the scope of the work of the Commission, particularly with regard to the comprehensive information system and the code of conduct on transnational corporations currently being formulated, on the understanding that duplication of work should be avoided;

(h) That the Commission on Transnational Corporations, at its annual session, shall keep under review the work of the Group; in particular, it shall review the mandate, terms of reference and achievements of the Group after three years, with a view to deciding on the advisability of its continuation;

(i) That, as directed by the Group, the United Nations Centre on Transnational Corporations, through appropriate arrangements, should provide the necessary preparations and services for the Group's work;

(j) To request the Secretary-General to facilitate, when necessary, the effective participation of members of the Group through payment of their travel and subsistence expenses from extrabudgetary resources.

Centre on TNCs

During 1982, the United Nations Centre on Transnational Corporations, the main Secretariat unit for matters relating to TNCs, continued to develop a comprehensive information system, carried out research and conducted and supervised technical co-operation activities. It assisted the working groups engaged in the formulation of a code of conduct and of international standards of accounting and reporting. It co-operated with other organizations and units inside and outside the United Nations system, in particular with the joint units operated by the Centre and the United Nations regional commissions.

Taking note of the Secretary-General's report summarizing the Centre's activities since mid-1981,[3] together with a report on the financial implications of its 1982 work programme,[2] the Commission on TNCs, on 1 September 1982,[1] requested the Centre to take account of the comments made during the discussion of its activities.

Reports. [1]Commission on TNCs, E/1982/18; [2]Secretariat, E/C.10/1982/5; [3]S-G, E/C.10/1982/3.

Information system

In 1982, the Centre on TNCs continued development of its comprehensive information system on TNCs and responded to a wide variety of requests for information, particularly from developing countries. As in the past, special emphasis was given to those elements accorded priority by the Commission on TNCs: legal information (national policies, laws and regulations, contracts and agreements), macro-economic information, industry studies of special importance to host developing countries, and corporate profiles of selected individual corporations. The work accomplished was detailed by the Secretariat in a progress report[7] to the 1982 session of the Commission, which also described co-ordination with information systems of other United Nations bodies, data verification, information dissemination and the Centre's resources.

According to that report and a subsequent one covering the remainder of 1982,[8] the Centre completed analyses of national legislation and regulations of 12 additional countries: Australia, Bolivia, Botswana, Canada, Italy, Kuwait, Liberia, Libyan Arab Jamahiriya, Peru, Portugal, Thailand, Venezuela. The issues reviewed included principal investment legislation; screening and monitoring procedures; ownership control and divestment; regulations relating to foreign exchange control, technology transfer and restrictive business practices; fiscal incentives and taxation; export processing zones; regulation of corporate conduct; and investment guarantees and other assurances to investors on substantive and procedural matters. The Centre also updated its 1981 survey[12] of national legislation relating to TNCs, adding another 20 countries to the survey.[3] It issued technical papers on equipment leasing contracts[5] and on contractual arrangements in the uranium industry.[4]

Macro-economic data were updated in respect of inflows of foreign direct investment to developing countries and to outflows of income payments to TNCs from such investment and for technology transfer and services. Contacts with institutional sources of such data were also expanded.

A technical paper analysing investment trends in the 1970s was completed,[2] as were two studies on TNCs in the international automotive[1] and semiconductor industries.[9]

The computer system on TNCs currently included 13 data bases. The general corporate data system, providing details on relationships between various companies and on parent corporations and their subsidiaries and affiliates, was expanded to cover all major geographic regions and to include information on new items such as exports, assets, earnings, employment, research and development. In-depth corporate profiles, selected largely on the basis of size and sectors in which Governments showed interest, continued to include composite indicators of transnationality, notably the number of foreign subsidiaries and affiliates, the magnitude of world-wide resources controlled by the corporation and the level of employment in host countries. By the end of 1982, 100 profiles had been completed, bringing the total to 380. These profiles continued to be verified routinely.

In co-operation with other United Nations bodies and specialized agencies, the Centre continued to develop its programme for the improvement of information exchange on toxic or hazardous chemicals and pharmaceuticals. Information on TNC involvement in the manufacture and distribution of these products would be collected and verified, as called for by the General Assembly in December 1981.[11] Responding to another Assembly request of November 1981,[10] the Centre also submitted a report reflecting the progress made in the preparation of a register of 2,099 TNC affiliates operating in colonial Territories, including data on sales and profits, activities in major sectors of each Territory and parent companies.

Taking note of the Secretariat report on 3 September,[6] the Commission reiterated that the objectives of the information system be those it had defined at earlier sessions and that special attention be given to national legislation and regulations, contracts and agreements, macro-economic information, periodic studies on trends, flows and payments in respect of foreign direct investment and technology, TNC activities in sectors of special significance to developing countries, and profiles on individual corporations. The Commission again emphasized the importance for developing countries of the development of national information systems on TNCs. It urged the Centre to continue its efforts to ensure the accuracy and regular updating of the system's data.

Publications. [1]*Transnational Corporations in the International Auto Industry* (ST/CTC/38), Sales No. E.83.II.A.6; [2]*Salient Features and Trends in Foreign Direct Investment* (ST/CTC/14), Sales No. E.83.II.A.8; [3]*National Legislation and Regulations Relating to Transnational Corporations: A Technical Paper* (ST/CTC/35), Sales No. E.83.II.A.15; [4]*Transnational Corporations and Contractual Relations in the World Uranium Industry: A Technical Paper* (ST/CTC/37), Sales No. E.83.II.A.17; [5]*Analysis of Equipment Leasing Contracts: A Technical Paper* (ST/CTC/36), Sales No. E.84.III.A.4.
Reports. [6]Commission on TNCs, E/1982/18; Secretariat, [7]E/C.10/1982/7, [8]E/C.10/1983/7, [9]ST/CTC/39.
Resolutions. GA: [10]36/51, 24 Nov. 1981 (YUN 1981, p. 1108); [11]36/166, 16 Dec. 1981 (*ibid.*, p. 825).
Yearbook reference. [12]1981, p. 602.

Joint units with regional commissions

Joint units established between the Centre on TNCs and the United Nations regional commissions in developing areas continued to operate during 1982 in Africa, Asia and the Pacific, Europe, Latin America and Western Asia. Each unit's work programme, tailored to the region's specific needs and to complement the work of the Centre, included research on the economic, social and institutional issues of TNCs mainly through case studies; information dissemination; and training and advisory services.

Despite major constraints resulting from limited resources, the units continued to make contributions in the areas of their expertise to the Centre's activities. This evaluation was contained in the first of two Secretariat reports, one describing the work of the units from May 1981 to May 1982,[2] submitted to the Commission at its 1982 session, and another covering May 1982 to April 1983,[3] prepared for its 1983 session.

A number of studies were updated or completed and new ones initiated on primary export commodities of particular interest to the region or as part of an ongoing interregional project (Africa, Asia and the Pacific, Latin America), financed by the United Nations Development Programme, on the production, processing and marketing of nine such commodities. Sectoral surveys were conducted of contracts and long-term co-operative agreements involving TNCs in such key areas as the automotive, chemical, electronic and power-engineering industries. Other research concentrated on TNC operations in non-conventional energy, agro-industry, banking, technology transfer and transfer pricing.

Information activities included preparation of lists of TNCs operating or based in the region; collection and analysis of data on TNC subsidiaries and affiliates and on government policies on the treatment of TNCs; and direct mailing of publications and bibliographic lists. Advisory and training services consisted in providing technical and administrative support to the Centre in the organization of workshops and seminars, and in identifying consultants and resource persons for technical assistance projects for these services. In addition, the units continued to perform liaison functions for the Centre.

On 1 September,[1] taking note of the 1981/82 Secretariat report, the Commission requested the Centre to take into account the comments made—some delegations emphasized the need for more effective co-ordination arrangements between the Centre and the units and a few mentioned the possible enhancement of the units' work by limiting the number of studies undertaken.

Reports. [1]Commission on TNCs, E/1982/18; Secretariat, [2]E/C.10/1982/4, [3]E/C.10/1983/4.

Research

Six reports prepared by the research programme of the Centre on TNCs, concerned with the economic, political, social and legal effects of TNCs in home and host countries, were presented to the Commission on TNCs in 1982 on the following subjects: the current position of TNCs in the world economy;[10] the Latin American experience in utilizing joint industrial ventures as a means of enhancing negotiating capacity with TNCs;[8] the TNC role in the shipping of bauxite and alumina;[13] effective host government policies towards transnational banks;[12] TNCs and transborder data flows;[11] and the Centre's ongoing and future research.[14] Two technical papers on transborder data flows were also completed: one with respect

to Brazil[7] and the other to access to the international on-line data-base market.[6] In addition, four studies completed previously—on transborder data flows,[1] measures to strengthen regional negotiating capacity with TNCs,[2] TNCs in international tourism,[3] and alternative arrangements for petroleum development[5]—were issued as publications.

The Centre continued work on a comprehensive integrated study on TNCs in world development, the centre-piece of its research activities in 1982 as in the previous year, for presentation to the Commission in 1983. Other research activities related to TNCs in southern Africa, the TNC role in certain international industries, national legislation relating to TNCs, contractual arrangements with them, and corporate profiles. A pilot study on TNCs in the armaments industry was begun, as were a number of country case studies on operations of international banks. The relationships between TNCs and State-owned enterprises were also under review. A series of workshops and seminars were organized, a bibliography of research was in preparation and a list of company directories was being updated.

On 1 and 9 September 1982,[9] the Commission took note of the reports presented to it. In so doing, it decided to retain as regular items on its agenda the topics on: recent developments related to TNCs and international economic relations, under which it discussed the report on the position of TNCs in the world economy; and the role of TNCs in transborder data flows. In requesting the Centre to continue its research work, the Commission reiterated that the research should be action-oriented and should contribute to the formulation of the code of conduct on TNCs and to strengthening the negotiating capacity of host countries, particularly the developing ones. The Commission encouraged the Centre to strengthen its co-operative arrangements with the regional commissions through the joint units and commended the Centre for *The CTC Reporter*[4] as a valuable means for disseminating information.

Publications. [1]*Transnational Corporations and Transborder Data Flows—A Technical Paper* (ST/CTC/23), Sales No. E.82.II.A.4. [2]*Measures Strengthening the Negotiating Capacity of Governments in Their Relations with Transnational Corporations: Regional Integration cum/versus Corporate Integration—A Technical Paper* (ST/CTC/10), Sales No. E.82.II.A.6. [3]*Transnational Corporations in International Tourism* (ST/CTC/18), Sales No. E.82.II.A.9. [4]*The CTC Reporter*, No. 11, Sales No. E.82.II.A.15; No. 12, Sales No. E.82.II.A.14; No. 13, Sales No. E.82.II.A.16. [5]*Alternative Arrangements for Petroleum Development* (ST/CTC/43), Sales No. E.82.II.A.22. [6]*Transborder Data Flows: Access to the International On-Line Data-Base Market—A Technical Paper* (ST/CTC/41), Sales No. E.83.II.A.1. [7]*Transborder Data Flows and Brazil: The Role of Transnational Corporations, Impacts of Transborder Data Flows, and Effects of National Policies* (ST/CTC/40), Sales No. E.83.II.A.3. [8]*Measures Strength-*

ening the Negotiating Capacity of Governments in Their Relations with Transnational Corporations: Joint Ventures Among Firms in Latin America—A Technical Paper (E/C.10/1982/15, ST/CTC/47), Sales No. E.83.II.A.19.

Reports. [9]Commission on TNCs, E/1982/18; Secretariat, [10]E/C.10/1982/2, [11]E/C.10/1982/12 & Corr.1, [12]E/C.10/1982/13, [13]E/C.10/1982/14, [14]E/C.10/1982/16.

Technical co-operation

According to two reports—one for the period May 1981–June 1982[2] and the other for July 1982–March 1983[3]—the programme of technical co-operation in advisory and training services of the Centre on TNCs continued to expand in quantity and scope in 1982. The Centre completed or initiated advisory projects in response to 109 requests for advisory assistance from 50 developing countries and conducted 22 training workshops for over 700 officials from 75 developing countries. These figures compared to 95 advisory requests and 19 workshops in 1981.

The advisory assistance delivered was largely for countries in Africa, Asia and the Pacific, and Latin America, with only a small part for Europe and the west Asian subregion. Almost one third of the projects related to overall policies, laws and regulations on foreign investment or to screening and monitoring procedures; to legislation and institutional arrangements in the petroleum, mining and other natural resource-based industries (forestry, fisheries, alumina/aluminium, petrochemicals); and to such issues as bilateral investment agreements, export processing zones, taxation and transfer pricing. The other two thirds of the projects dealt with specific arrangements with TNCs in petroleum exploration and mining (bauxite, coal, copper, diamonds, gold, magnesite, uranium); and in a variety of resource-processing, manufacturing and service industries (alumina, cement, dairy, fisheries and timber products; garments and pharmaceuticals; and airlines, hotels and transnational banks).

Of the 22 training workshops conducted, 13 were national, 8 were regional or subregional, and 1 was interregional. They dealt with general legal and negotiating issues arising from relationships between host countries and TNCs on a cross-sectoral basis, as well as with issues in such specific sectors as banking, fisheries, minerals, mining, petrochemicals, petroleum, tourism and technology acquisition. The national workshops were for Bolivia, Cuba (two), Grenada, India (two), Pakistan, Sri Lanka (two), Suriname, Trinidad and Tobago (two) and the United Republic of Cameroon. There were regional and subregional exercises for Asia (two); east and southern, and west and central, Africa; central America; the Pacific islands (two); and the Association of South-East Asian Nations.

On 7 September,[1] the Commission took note of the report on the Centre's activities for the period ended June 1982. It took note also of the statement by the Centre's Executive Director on the need for increased voluntary contributions if response to the growing demand for advisory and training services was to continue, urged Governments to make such contributions and expressed appreciation to Norway, Sweden and Switzerland for having done so. The Commission requested the Centre to submit in 1983 specific proposals for enlarging the scope of extrabudgetary financial arrangements and for increased expense-sharing by requesting Governments. It also requested the Centre, in reporting on its technical co-operation programme, to include the cost of completed, ongoing and planned projects, experts engaged and workshop content and documentation, as well as an evaluation of services already provided.

Reports. [1]Commission on TNCs, E/1982/18; Secretariat, [2]E/C.10/1982/9, [3]E/C.10/1983/9.

Trust Fund

In 1982, funds available from the Trust Fund for the United Nations Centre on Transnational Corporations, the main source of funding for implementation of the Centre's technical co-operation programme, totalled $2,545,038. Of that amount, $305,852 was contributed by four Governments: Finland, $33,078; Greece, $30,000; the Netherlands, $72,952; and Norway, $169,822.[1] Expenditures came to $1,605,633, of which the share of the United Nations Development Programme was approximately 30 per cent ($479,533),[2] compared to 31 per cent in 1981.[3] Pledged in 1982 for 1983 were $27,660 and $209,292 by Finland and Norway.

Reports. Secretariat, [1]E/C.10/1983/9, [2]E/C.10/1984/16. *Yearbook reference.* [3]1981, p. 604.

Commission on TNCs

Report on the 1982 session

By a decision taken without vote on 27 October 1982,[1] the Economic and Social Council, on an oral proposal of its President, took note of the report of the Commission on TNCs on its eighth session, held at Manila, Philippines, from 30 August to 10 September.[2]

Decision (1982). [1]ESC: 1982/185, 27 Oct., text following.
Report. [2]Commission on TNCs, E/1982/18 & Add.1 & Add.1/Corr.1.
Meeting records. ESC: E/1982/SR.*52, 54* (25, 27 Oct.).

Economic and Social Council decision 1982/185

Adopted without vote

Oral proposal by President; agenda item 25.

Report of the Commission on Transnational Corporations on its eighth session

At its 54th plenary meeting, on 27 October 1982, the Council took note of the report of the Commission on Transnational Corporations on its eighth session.

1983 regular session

Agenda

Acting without vote on the recommendation of the Commission on TNCs, the Economic and Social Council, on 27 October 1982, approved the provisional agenda and documentation for the Commission's ninth (1983) session.[1]

Decision (1982). [1]ESC: 1982/184, 27 Oct., text following.
Meeting records. ESC: E/1982/SR.52, *54* (25, 27 Oct.).

Economic and Social Council decision 1982/184

Adopted without vote

Draft by Commission on TNCs (E/1982/18); agenda item 25.

Provisional agenda and documentation for the ninth session of the Commission on Transnational Corporations

At its 54th plenary meeting, on 27 October 1982, the Council decided to approve the provisional agenda and documentation for the ninth session of the Commission on Transnational Corporations set out below.

1. *Recent developments related to transnational corporations and international economic relations*
   Documentation:
   Third integrated study on transnational corporations in world development
2. *Activities of the United Nations Centre on Transnational Corporations:*
   (a) *Reports on the activities of the United Nations Centre on Transnational Corporations*
   Documentation:
   Report of the Secretary-General on the activities of the United Nations Centre on Transnational Corporations
   Report on the activities of the joint units with the regional commissions
   (b) *Allocation of resources among the programme elements of the United Nations Centre on Transnational Corporations*
   Documentation:
   Note on the allocation of resources among the programme elements of the United Nations Centre on Transnational Corporations
3. *Work related to the formulation of a code of conduct on transnational corporations*
   Documentation:
   Report on the status of discussions at the special session of the Commission
4. *Comprehensive information system on transnational corporations*
   Documentation:
   Report on the comprehensive information system on transnational corporations
5. *International standards of accounting and reporting*
   Documentation:
   Report of the Intergovernmental Working Group of Experts on International Standards of Accounting and Reporting
6. *Technical co-operation*
   Documentation:
   Report on the programme of technical co-operation
   Report on the evaluation of completed technical co-operation projects

7. *Studies on the effects of the operations and practices of transnational corporations:*
   (a) *Activities of transnational corporations in southern Africa and their collaboration with the racist minority régime in that area*
   Documentation:
   Report on the policies and practices of transnational corporations regarding their activities in South Africa and Namibia
   Report on the modalities for public hearings on the activities of the transnational corporations in southern Africa
   (b) *The role of transnational corporations in transborder data flows and their impact on home and host countries, particularly developing countries*
   Documentation:
   Progress report on transnational corporations and transborder data flows
   (c) *Ongoing and future research*
   Documentation:
   Report on ongoing and future research
8. *Work related to the definition of transnational corporations*
   Documentation:
   Report of the Secretariat

Dates and place

On 27 October 1982, the Economic and Social Council decided that the ninth session of the Commission on TNCs be held at United Nations Headquarters from 20 to 29 June 1983.[1] The text, recommended by the Commission, was adopted without vote following an oral amendment by the President, on behalf of the Bureau of the Council, to specify the exact dates of the Commission's session.

The amendment was made, the President stated, in the light of a provision of a 28 July resolution of the Council on its revitalization,[2] which sought to end the practice of holding resumed sessions. That provision contained a Council request that the meetings of its subsidiary bodies end at least eight weeks before the regular Council session at which their reports were to be considered.

Decision (1982). [1]ESC: 1982/183, 27 Oct., text following.
Resolution (1982). [2]ESC: 1982/50, 28 July.
Meeting records. ESC: E/1982/SR.52, 54 (25, 27 Oct.).

Economic and Social Council decision 1982/183

Adopted without vote

Draft by Commission on TNCs (E/1982/18), orally amended by Bureau; agenda item 25.

Date of the ninth session of the Commission on Transnational Corporations

At its 54th plenary meeting, on 27 October 1982, the Council decided that the ninth session of the Commission on Transnational Corporations would be held at United Nations Headquarters from 20 to 29 June 1983.

Chapter VIII

Regional economic and social activities

Contents

Related topics:

Economic assistance and disasters: Africa; Assistance to drought-stricken areas of Africa. Environment: Co-operation with regional commissions; Marine ecosystems—Regional programmes.

Regional co-operation

The role of United Nations regional commissions in promoting new forms of co-operation between developed and developing countries and in following up action programmes designed by United Nations conferences was discussed during 1982 at two meetings of the executive secretaries of the five regional commissions (New York, 8-9 February; Geneva, 12 July). Reporting on those meetings in July to the Economic and Social Council,[5] the Secretary-General said the commissions were well placed to provide an infrastructure for global negotiations on development and international economic co-operation (see Chapter I of this section) by their work in promoting subregional, regional and interregional economic and technical co-operation among developing countries as well as co-operation between countries having different economic and social systems.

The Secretary-General also observed that implementation of recommendations of global conferences through the commissions would permit sectoral decisions to be balanced according to the priorities of each region. In this connection the executive secretaries commented on issues raised at two such conferences held in 1981, on the least developed countries[7] and on new and renewable energy sources.[8] Regarding energy, they thought the United Nations should devote special attention to promoting research into new energy sources in the tropics, where most developing countries were located; that consultative groups should be organized to help mobilize resources for new and renewable energy sources; and that the United Nations system, faced with limited resources, might have to reorient its priorities to give appropriate emphasis to this area. Regarding assistance to the least developed countries, the executive secretaries suggested that the regional commissions be consulted on and participate in the round-table meetings being planned to consider development assistance for individual countries (see Chapter I of this section).

On other programme questions, the Secretary-General, noting a 1982 decision of the Governing Council of the United Nations Environment Programme (UNEP) to strengthen the UNEP regional presence, suggested that the environment co-ordination units within regional commission secretariats in developing regions should be expanded to give them executing functions with regard to projects of the United Nations Development Programme (UNDP). The executive secretaries also thought it indispensable for the commissions to play an active role in a global information system on science and technology. Strengthened co-operation was urged between the commissions and the United Nations Centre for Social Development and Humanitarian Affairs, particularly on aging persons, the disabled, women and youth. Also, it was felt that the commissions needed more resources to give proper attention to population and to participate fully in preparations for the 1984 International Conference on Population.

Another suggestion, arising from a preliminary discussion at the executive secretaries' July meeting, was that UNDP consider raising its reimbursement to the commissions for their overhead costs in executing UNDP projects (see Chapter II of this section), since the current rate of 13 per cent of project costs was inadequate.

On 30 July 1982[1] the Economic and Social Council took note of the Secretary-General's report on the executive secretaries' meetings and of his annual report submitted in June, summarizing major economic and social developments in the regions and giving highlights of the regional commissions' work.[4] This decision was taken without vote after having been similarly recommended on 28 July by the Council's First (Economic) Committee, where it had been orally proposed by the Chairman.

Summaries of the annual surveys of current economic conditions in each region, prepared by the secretariats of each regional commission, were examined by the Council in July during its annual discussion of the world economic situation (see Chapter I in this section). The surveys covered Africa, Asia and the Pacific, Europe, Latin America and Western Asia. The Council took note on 30 July of these and other reports on economic conditions and trends.[2]

A Joint Meeting of Governmental Experts from Africa and Latin America on Economic and Technical Co-operation, organized by the secretariats of the two regional commissions directly concerned, was held at Addis Ababa, Ethiopia, from 1 to 4 June 1982.[3] The meeting proposed a number of specific co-operative activities in trade and finance, science and technology, and human resources.

Among issues of concern to the regional commissions considered by the General Assembly in 1982 were funding arrangements for regional population projects threatened with loss of financial support from the United Nations Fund for Population Activities. The Assembly, on 17 December, requested the Secretary-General to consider making budget proposals for continuing such activities.[6]

Decisions (1982). ESC, 30 July: [1]1982/175, text following; [2]1982/177, paras. (d)-(h).
Reports. [3]Meeting on economic and technical co-operation, E/CEPAL/G.1212-ECO/ETC/I/5; S-G, [4]E/1982/88, [5]E/1982/88/Add.1.
Resolution (1982). [6]GA: 37/136, 17 Dec.
Yearbook references. 1981, [7]p. 406, [8]p. 689.
Meeting record. ESC: E/1982/SR.51 (30 July).

Economic and Social Council decision 1982/175

Adopted without vote

Approved by First Committee (E/1982/96) without vote, 28 July (meeting 15); oral proposal by Chairman; agenda item 9.

Reports of the Secretary-General on regional co-operation and on the meetings of the executive secretaries of the regional commissions

At its 51st plenary meeting, on 30 July 1982, the Council took note of:
(a) The report of the Secretary-General on regional co-operation;
(b) The report of the Secretary-General on the meetings of the executive secretaries of the regional commissions.

Strengthening of regional commissions

On 20 December 1982, the General Assembly called on the Secretary-General to investigate new approaches to regional and subregional programming and management of intercountry projects of the United Nations system. He was asked to initiate immediately an examination of progress made in decentralizing United Nations activities, and to report to the Committee for Programme and Co-ordination and the Economic and Social Council with a view to determining the specific authorities, responsibilities and resources to be decentralized and the timing of such decentralization. He was asked to strengthen liaison between United Nations Headquarters and the regional commissions, bearing in mind the role of the Regional Commissions Liaison Office in New York. The executive secretaries

of the regional commissions were urged to make their staff exchange programmes more effective so as to foster interregional co-operation.

These requests, affecting the regional commissions in general, were included in a resolution on restructuring issues concerning the Economic Commission for Africa (ECA).[5] The resolution was adopted following Assembly consideration of a January report by the Joint Inspection Unit (JIU) on regional programming, operations, restructuring and decentralization issues affecting ECA,[3] and comments thereon in August by the Secretary-General.[4]

The original draft,[2] sponsored by Kenya for the African Group and withdrawn in favour of one proposed by a Vice-Chairman of the Assembly's Second (Economic and Financial) Committee, differed from the adopted text in that it would have had the Assembly call on the Secretary-General to strengthen the status and functions of the Regional Commissions Liaison Office so that it could better carry out its representation responsibilities, and urge the executive secretaries to increase their staff exchanges. The two other general recommendations in the Kenya draft were retained in the adopted version.

These four requests in the proposal by Kenya were based on recommendations in the JIU report. In making them, JIU stressed the need for extending the concept of self-reliance to regional activities, and said new approaches were needed to enable Governments to assume responsibility for executing regional and subregional projects supported by the United Nations system. The JIU report also called for simplifying and possibly decentralizing recruitment of technical co-operation experts.

Commenting on these JIU recommendations, the Secretary-General agreed on the need to investigate approaches to regional and subregional authority for intercountry projects, and said he intended actively to pursue decentralization. He also shared the view that staff exchanges between the commissions should be increased, and said arrangements would be formulated to strengthen liaison between Headquarters and the commissions. Regarding recruitment of experts, he said practices would be kept under review but he pointed out that the commissions already had authority to recruit regional advisers and project personnel other than those living outside the region and those above the P-5 level, whose recruitment remained the responsibility of the Technical Assistance Recruitment Service at Headquarters.

The JIU recommendations were fully endorsed by ECA, which recommended on 30 April that the Council call for decentralizing technical assistance recruitment and urge a strengthening of the Regional Commissions Liaison Office.

Another JIU recommendation called for the annual consideration by the Council of regional co-ordination problems and needs. In line with this idea, ECA recommended, also on 30 April, that the Council resolve to consider devoting a regular agenda item to regional co-ordination problems of the United Nations system.

The Council responded on 30 July[1] by deciding to identify each year a subject relating to interregional co-operation, of common interest to all regions, for detailed consideration under its agenda item on regional co-operation. The executive secretaries were requested to submit joint recommendations in that regard each year at the Council's organizational session. This decision was taken without vote after having been similarly recommended on 28 July by the Council's First Committee, where it had been orally proposed by the Chairman.

At the third meeting of executive secretaries in 1982 (New York, 5 November), it was agreed that the secretariat of the Economic Commission for Latin America would act as a focal point for consultations on the proposed topic on interregional co-operation and on preparation in 1983 of a joint paper on the commissions' involvement in the promotion of interregional economic and technical co-operation between developing countries.

Decision (1982). [1]ESC: 1982/174, 30 July, text following.
Draft resolution withdrawn. [2]Kenya, for African Group, A/C.2/37/L.84.
Report. [3]JIU, transmitted by S-G note, A/37/119, and [4]S-G comments, Add.1.
Resolution (1982). [5]GA: 37/214, paras. 3 *(a)-(c)* and 5, 20 Dec.

Economic and Social Council decision 1982/174

Adopted without vote

Approved by First Committee (E/1982/96) without vote, 28 July (meeting 15); oral proposal by Chairman; agenda item 9.

Rationalization of the work of the Economic and Social Council
At its 51st plenary meeting, on 30 July 1982, the Council decided:
(a) To identify, at its annual organizational session, a subject relating to interregional co-operation, of common interest to all regions, for detailed consideration under the agenda item on regional co-operation;
(b) To request the executive secretaries of the regional commissions to submit their joint recommendations in this regard to the Council at its annual organizational session.

Africa

ECA activities. The Economic Commission for Africa (ECA) held its seventeenth session, which was also the eighth meeting of its Conference of Ministers, at Tripoli, Libyan Arab Jamahiriya, from 27 to 30 April 1982. The session, at which 31 resolutions were adopted on the final day, was preceded from 19 to 24 April, also at Tripoli, by the third meeting of the Technical Preparatory Committee of the Whole,[3] whose recommendations were approved by the Conference. Annual reports to the Economic and Social Council on the Commission's activities and those of its subsidi-

ary bodies and secretariat covered the years ended 30 April 1982[1] and beginning 1 May.[2]

ECA and its secretariat, with headquarters at Addis Ababa, Ethiopia, continued to concentrate on implementation of the 1980 Lagos Plan of Action for the Implementation of the Monrovia Strategy for the Economic Development of Africa (see below). In a Declaration of Tripoli the Conference reaffirmed the goals of the Plan, and in a resolution urged African countries to work to achieve those goals. In December the General Assembly urged donor countries to provide substantial and sustained resources to that end. The Conference also appealed for contributions to the United Nations Trust Fund for African Development.

The Joint Conference of African Planners, Statisticians and Demographers (Addis Ababa, March) gave guidance for continued secretariat studies on economic planning and statistics. The Conference of Ministers acted to strengthen the financing of the African Institute for Economic Development and Planning. It called for expanded aid to the continent's least developed countries (LDCs), on the basis of recommendations by the Conference of Ministers of African LDCs (Tripoli, April). It urged continued support for the Pan-African Documentation and Information System, which began to establish several data banks for economic and social information. It resolved to set up an African Institute for Future Studies as soon as sufficient funds could be found.

The Conference of Ministers endorsed the regional programme of technical co-operation to be provided in 1982-1986 by the United Nations Development Programme.

The Conference of African Ministers of Trade (Addis Ababa, February) proposed steps to implement the Lagos Plan, including monitoring by its newly renamed Ministerial Follow-up Committee on Trade and Finance for African Development in the Framework of the Lagos Plan of Action. The ECA Conference of Ministers requested its secretariat to intensify work on intra-African trade and to organize a meeting on Africa's external debt. In response to the international trade and transport problems of Zaire, the secretariat continued to provide technical assistance and received approval from the Council and the General Assembly for the organization of a donors' meeting to mobilize resources.

ECA helped to organize three donors' meetings seeking funds for African transport development within the framework of the Transport and Communications Decade in Africa (1976-1988), while further work on the two-phase programme for the Decade was authorized by the Assembly on the Council's recommendation. An Inter-Agency Co-ordinating Committee on Satellite Communications, to harmonize studies for an African satellite communication system, held its first session (Addis Ababa, August). The secretariat began implementing a Council request to help evaluate studies on a proposed transport link across the Strait of Gibraltar. The Conference of Ministers sought funds for proposed seminars on African multimodal transport.

In another priority area, ECA continued to co-operate with other United Nations bodies in the preparatory phase of the Industrial Development Decade for Africa (1980-1990), and the Conference of Ministers asked its members to identify projects and set up national co-ordinating committees.

The African Regional Centre for Solar Energy was established and its Council held an inaugural meeting (Addis Ababa, May). Several United Nations bodies including ECA worked to alleviate Africa's food and agricultural problems, prodded by the Assembly's call for national and international efforts to stimulate the region's food production. Calling for strengthened science and technology machinery within African Governments, the Conference of Ministers stressed the importance of relating national programmes to agricultural and industrial production.

Concern expressed by ECA over a decision to reduce funding for certain demographic data collection and analysis activities in Africa led the Assembly to request consideration of ways in which regional commmissions could continue such activities. The Assembly approved new statutes of the two ECA-affiliated African population institutes—the Regional Institute for Population Studies and the Institut de formation et de recherche démographiques. The Conference of Ministers urged the States served by the latter institute to help meet its urgent need for funds.

The first Conference of Vice-Chancellors, Presidents and Rectors of Higher Learning in Africa (Addis Ababa, January) recommended steps to popularize the objectives and strategy of the Lagos Plan. In other action to develop Africa's human resources, the ECA Conference of Ministers sought international funding for a new set of proposals for planning, education and training, and urged African Governments to accord special priority to industrial and technological manpower development.

The Joint Intergovernmental Regional Committee on Human Settlements and Environment held its first session (Addis Ababa, June/July), calling for strengthened national machinery to cope with the environmental consequences of rapid industrialization and for a pilot project to demonstrate the advantages of integrating physical planning with socio-economic planning. The Conference of Ministers urged the affected States to form a regional intergovernmental committee to combat desertification in Africa.

The Conference of Ministers decided to hold in 1984 the third Regional Conference on the Integration of Women in Development. It sought funds for surveys of African households to collect demographic, social and economic statistics.

On organizational matters, recommendations by the Conference of Ministers to restructure aspects of ECA functioning so that it could be more responsive to African development needs were acted upon by the Economic and Social Council and the Assembly. The Assembly also agreed to an ECA request that the United Nations budget take over from the United Nations Development Programme responsibility for financing the core staff of the ECA subregional offices, known as Multinational Programming and Operational Centres. Acting on an ECA plea for expanded conference facilities, the Assembly authorized an architectural and engineering study for future construction at Commission headquarters.

Reports. ECA, [1]E/1982/21, [2]E/1983/44; [3]Technical Preparatory Committee, E/ECA/CM.8/31 & Corr.1.

Economic and social trends

The developing countries of Africa suffered in 1981, as in 1980, from chronic food deficits, drought, high prices of imported oil, adverse terms of trade and a continuing external debt burden, according to a summary,[2] issued in May 1982, of the ECA survey of economic and social conditions in Africa, 1980-1981. Gross domestic product (GDP) grew by an estimated 4.1 per cent in 1981, less than in 1979 and 1980. This was due in large measure to poor economic performance by the major oil-exporting countries, whose estimated growth averaged only 4.3 per cent as compared to 5.6 per cent in 1980. The balance of payments showed a record deficit of $16.5 billion in 1981, after a $4.2 billion surplus in 1980. Agricultural production was likely to have grown by only 1.7 per cent in 1981, leaving an import gap estimated at 6 to 7 million tons, including 2 million tons in food aid. An upturn linked to an improved world market situation was foreseen for 1982, when GDP was forecast to rise by 5.7 per cent, with manufacturing accounting for the largest part of the expansion.

The summary was noted by the Economic and Social Council on 30 July.[1]

Decision (1982). [1]ESC: 1982/177, para. *(e)*, 30 July. *Survey.* [2]Summary, E/1982/61.

Development policy and regional economic co-operation

Implementation of the 1980 Lagos Plan of Action for economic development of Africa

ECA activities. Virtually all of the work of ECA in 1982 continued to revolve around action to implement the Lagos Plan of Action for the Implementation of the Monrovia Strategy for the Economic Development of Africa, adopted in 1980 at Lagos, Nigeria, by the Assembly of African Heads of State and Government, an annual conference of the Organization of African Unity (OAU).[15] Most of these activities were in specific sectors, with emphasis on transport and communications and industrial development, which were the subject of special decade-long programmes. Recommendations on Plan implementation were made by several sectoral bodies, including the Conference of African Ministers of Trade and a conference of senior officials of higher educational institutions in Africa. Much of the work was carried out in co-operation between the secretariats of ECA and OAU.

From 1 to 4 March 1982, the Conference of Directors of Social Research Institutes and Policy Makers, sponsored by ECA and the Council for the Development of Economic and Social Research in Africa, met at ECA headquarters to assess the Lagos Plan and the growth patterns implicit in it, and to consider the role of researchers and research institutes in implementing the Plan. According to a note by the ECA secretariat,[2] the Conference concluded that mobilization of human resources was an important ingredient in the Plan and that there was a need to reorient African educational systems to eliminate inadequacies in training and employment and to improve the use of the region's resources. The Conference suggested that subregional economic groups should revise their treaties where necessary to reflect the Plan's objectives and set up institutions to implement the Plan and monitor progress. It suggested that a systematic diagnosis be undertaken in each country to determine the causes of poor performance in agriculture and industry.

On 30 April[8] the ECA Conference of Ministers urged all African countries to intensify their efforts, create a spirit of co-operation and work towards achieving the goals of integrated development of African countries, in accordance with the Lagos Plan. Affirming the sovereignty of African countries over their natural resources and their right to use them to benefit their peoples, the Conference condemned economic and social pressures by imperialist Powers and their transnational corporations which exploited African resources to the detriment of the people's interests.

Also at the ECA Conference of Ministers, the African ministers responsible for economic development and planning agreed on 30 April on a Declaration of Tripoli in which they took issue with the economic strategy outlined in a World Bank report entitled, "Accelerated development in sub-Saharan Africa: An agenda for action". The ministers said the report adopted approaches, concepts and objectives divergent from those of the Lagos Plan in that it emphasized export orientation in general and primary-commodity exports in particular, regarded industrialization and economic co-operation and integration as longer-term issues, and completely disregarded external factors as major constraints on African development. Reaffirming the goals of the Plan and endorsing the objectives of self-reliant and self-sustaining development, they stressed the need to reduce Africa's extreme dependence on primary-commodity exports and on the import of almost everything required for development, and stated that externally oriented strategies could not be expected to help Africa.

At a joint meeting of the secretariats of ECA and other United Nations organizations and the OAU General Secretariat (Geneva, 6-8 April) (see POLITICAL AND SECURITY QUESTIONS, Chapter V), consensus was reached on a number of proposals relating to implementation of the Lagos Plan.[6] It was agreed that OAU should play a role in identifying specific activities, programmes or projects in major sectors of the Plan through joint programming sessions with ECA and other United Nations organizations. It was further agreed that those organizations should keep OAU informed of their programmes related to the Plan and that the United Nations system should increase its assistance to help strengthen the capacity of the OAU General Secretariat to monitor Plan implementation. An institutional framework of co-operation should be established between OAU and each relevant United Nations organization to ensure co-ordination of their activities in Plan implementation.

A first progress report on implementation of the Lagos Plan, describing activities by the two organizations in each major economic sector since 1980, was prepared by the OAU Secretary-General and the ECA Executive Secretary.[3] Pointing to some problems encountered, they said a number of projects and programmes had had to be cut back for lack of funds, staff recruitment difficulties had been compounded by the requirement to adhere to equitable geographical distribution, and a more reliable mechanism, perhaps through the establishment of national committees, was needed for the efficient supply of information from States. To make the participation of States in the secretariats' activities more effective, they suggested that: States maintain continuity in their representation, particularly at technical meetings; meetings concerned with particular subregions be held within those subregions at the invitation of Governments; States should reflect their collective decisions in their national development plans; and States should avoid duplicating requests to different institutions, especially requests to non-African institutions for studies.

In a report to the General Assembly in October,[7] the United Nations Secretary-General indicated that, since the OAU session at which the progress report was to have been discussed had not taken place, it was not being submitted to the Assembly in 1982 as called for by the Assembly in December 1981.[14]

General Assembly action. Expressing regret that the progress report had not been made available, the General Assembly, by a resolution of 17 December 1982 on special measures for the social and economic development of Africa in the 1980s,[12] urged donor countries to provide substantial and sustained resources for the accelerated development of African countries and implementation of the Lagos Plan. It invited international financial institutions, particularly the World Bank, the International Development Association and the International Fund for Agricultural Development, to continue actively to consider increasing substantially their development assistance to Africa. The Secretary-General was requested to submit a full progress report in 1983. The Assembly also took note of a report on non-governmental organization contributions to the Plan's implementation, renewed a call for study of ways to increase resources for the Industrial Development Decade for Africa and requested the continued allocation of resources to ECA.

This resolution was adopted without vote after having been similarly recommended by the Assembly's Second (Economic and Financial) Committee on 8 December. Sponsored by Bangladesh on behalf of the Group of 77 developing countries, the text was approved with revisions submitted orally by the Chairman as agreed in informal consultations conducted by a Vice-Chairman. These changes affected the provision on measures to increase resources for the Decade (deleting "concrete" before "measures") and the paragraph urging substantial and sustained contributions for African development (replacing "rising" by "sustained").

In a resolution of 16 November on co-operation between the United Nations and OAU, the Assembly requested the Secretary-General to draw the attention of United Nations organizations to the need for wider publicity for all matters relating to African social and economic development.[11]

JIU report. As recommended in a January report by the Joint Inspection Unit (JIU) on restructuring issues related to ECA,[4] the ECA Conference of Ministers, the Economic and Social Council and the General Assembly requested United Nations organizations to assist African Governments in incorporating the goals of the Lagos Plan into their development assistance country programmes and adapting them to regional and subregional priorities. In line with a JIU suggestion that resident co-ordinators in Africa of the United Nations development system should assist in achieving such conformity, the Council stressed the co-ordinators' role in this respect. Picking up another JIU recommendation, the ECA Conference and the Assembly called on the ECA Executive Secretary to institute subject-oriented and high-level regional inter-agency meetings to develop guidelines for co-ordinated action towards attaining the Plan's objectives.

These decisions, taken in resolutions on ECA restructuring issues, were adopted by the ECA Conference on 30 April,[9] the Council on 30 July[10] and the Assembly on 20 December.[13] The recommendations of JIU had been endorsed by the Secretary-General, who, in commenting on its report in August, observed that special efforts would be required to relate country programming more closely to regional programming and that ECA was well placed to promote such efforts through closer regional and subregional co-ordination among agencies.[5]

In related recommendations, JIU said that organizations should report periodically to the Council and to their governing bodies on their contributions to the Plan's implementation and consider seconding staff to ECA to assist in specific tasks related to the Plan. On the latter point, the Secretary-General referred to the financial and organizational problems entailed for smaller organizations and said any proposals for temporary staff exchanges would be based on full consultations among all concerned.

The mention of the role of resident co-ordinators was added to the Council resolution as a result of informal consultations conducted by a Vice-Chairman of the First (Economic) Committee on an original draft by Algeria for the Group of 77,[1] later withdrawn in favour of the Vice-Chairman's draft.

Draft resolution withdrawn. [1]Algeria, for Group of 77, E/1982/C.1/L.21.
Note. [2]ECA secretariat, E/ECA/CM.8/30.
Reports. [3]ECA/OAU, E/ECA/CM.9/1 & Summary; [4]JIU, transmitted by S-G note, A/37/119, and [5]S-G comments, Add.1; S-G, [6]A/37/335, [7]A/37/526.
Resolutions (1982). ECA (report, E/1982/21), 30 Apr.: [8]439(XVII); [9]449(XVII), paras. 8 & 11. [10]ESC: 1982/63, para. 4, 30 July. GA: [11]37/15, para. 18, 16 Nov.; [12]37/139, 17 Dec., text following; [13]37/214, para. 6, 20 Dec.
Resolution (prior). [14]GA: 36/180, 17 Dec. 1981 (YUN 1981, p. 612).
Yearbook reference. [15]1980, p. 548.
Meeting records. GA: 2nd Committee, A/C.2/37/SR.3-12, 32, 33, 47 (28 Sep.-8 Dec.); plenary, A/37/PV.109 (17 Dec.).

General Assembly resolution 37/139

17 December 1982   Meeting 109   Adopted without vote

Approved by Second Committee (A/37/679/Add.1) without vote, 8 December (meeting 47); draft by Bangladesh, for Group of 77 (A/C.2/37/L.20), orally revised in informal consultations; agenda item 12.

Special measures for the social and economic development of Africa in the 1980s

The General Assembly,

Recalling its resolutions 3201(S-VI) and 3202(S-VI) of 1 May 1974, containing the Declaration and the Programme of Action on the Establishment of a New International Economic Order, 3281(XXIX) of

12 December 1974, containing the Charter of Economic Rights and Duties of States, and 3362(S-VII) of 16 September 1975 on development and international economic co-operation,

Recalling also its resolution 35/56 of 5 December 1980, the annex to which contains the International Development Strategy for the Third United Nations Development Decade,

Recalling also its resolutions 35/64 of 5 December 1980 and 36/180 of 17 December 1981 concerning the adoption of a wide range of special measures for the social and economic development of Africa in the 1980s,

Recalling further its resolutions 35/66 B of 5 December 1980 and 36/182, section II, of 17 December 1981 on the Industrial Development Decade for Africa, 36/177 of 17 December 1981 on the Transport and Communications Decade in Africa and 36/186 of 17 December 1981 on the situation of food and agriculture in Africa,

Deeply concerned at the continuing low level of economic activities in Africa and the devastating effects of the current world economic crisis on the particularly vulnerable economies of the countries in the region that has the largest number of the least developed countries,

Fully aware that the Lagos Plan of Action for the Implementation of the Monrovia Strategy for the Economic Development of Africa provides a framework of priority actions for achieving the rapid overall economic and social development of Africa, as reiterated in the Declaration of Tripoli adopted by the Conference of Ministers of the Economic Commission for Africa on 30 April 1982,

Recognizing the primary responsibility of the African countries for their development and the importance of the mobilization of their national resources for their socio-economic development,

Convinced of the need for increased and sustained external resources in order to achieve the aims and objectives of the Lagos Plan of Action for the Implementation of the Monrovia Strategy for the Economic Development of Africa,

Recalling also the interim report of the Secretary-General submitted to the General Assembly at its thirty-sixth session, concerning special measures for the social and economic development of Africa in the 1980s, in which were indicated the contributions planned by organs, organizations and bodies of the United Nations system to the implementation of the Lagos Plan of Action for the Implementation of the Monrovia Strategy for the Economic Development of Africa,

Noting the report of the Secretary-General submitted to the Economic and Social Council at its second regular session of 1982,

1. *Takes note with appreciation* of the report of the Secretary-General indicating the actions proposed by non-governmental organizations for promoting the realization of the objectives of the Lagos Plan of Action for the Implementation of the Monrovia Strategy for the Economic Development of Africa;

2. *Expresses regret*, however, that no comprehensive report on the progress made in the implementation of General Assembly resolution 36/180 has been made available for the current session as requested in the aforementioned resolution;

3. *Renews its call* upon the organs, organizations and bodies of the United Nations system to examine measures to increase the resources for the execution of the programmes for the Industrial Development Decade for Africa and to apply the special measures in a comprehensive and co-ordinated manner;

4. *Urges* donor countries to provide substantial and sustained levels of resources for promoting the accelerated development of African countries and effective implementation of the Lagos Plan of Action, and to contribute generously to the United Nations Trust Fund for African Development;

5. *Invites* all international financial institutions, particularly the World Bank, the International Development Association and the International Fund for Agricultural Development, to continue actively to consider increasing substantially their development assistance to Africa during the Decade;

6. *Requests* the Secretary-General to continue to allocate the necessary resources to the Economic Commission for Africa, taking into account its role as the main economic and social development centre within the United Nations system for the African region, in accordance with General Assembly resolutions 32/197 of 20 December 1977 and 33/202 of 29 January 1979;

7. *Further requests* the Secretary-General to submit to the General Assembly at its thirty-eighth session, through the Economic and Social Council at its second regular session of 1983, a full report on the progress made in the implementation of the present resolution.

UN Trust Fund for African Development

On 30 April 1982, the ECA Conference of Ministers appealed to States to participate in the United Nations Trust Fund for African Development, called on them to pay pledges promptly, and appealed to African and non-African States and to financial institutions to pledge generously at the 1983 Pledging Conference for the Fund.[1]

Resolution (1982). [1]ECA (report, E/1982/21): 453(XVII), 30 Apr.

Role of NGOs

Information from 12 non-governmental organizations on the contributions they intended to make in implementation of the Lagos Plan of Action was communicated to the Economic and Social Council in a June 1982 report of the Secretary-General.[2] Their activities were in agriculture, air transport, population, monetary studies, the environment and wildlife.

The report also included information on the contributions of regional and subregional institutions sponsored by ECA.

The Council took note of the report on 29 July, in a decision[1] adopted without vote on the recommendation of its First (Economic) Committee, which had similarly approved it on 28 July on an oral proposal by its Chairman. The General Assembly also took note of the report on 17 December, in its resolution on special measures for Africa's social and economic development in the 1980s.[3]

Decision (1982). [1]ESC: 1982/171, 29 July, text following.
Report. [2]S-G, E/1982/80.
Resolution (1982). [3]GA: 37/139, para. 1, 17 Dec.
Meeting record. ESC: E/1982/SR.50 (29 July).

Economic and Social Council decision 1982/171

Adopted without vote

Approved by First Committee (E/1982/99) without vote, 28 July (meeting 15); oral proposal by Chairman; agenda item 12.

Report of the Secretary-General containing suggestions by non-governmental organizations regarding the implementation of the Lagos Plan of Action

At its 50th plenary meeting, on 29 July 1982, the Council took note of the report of the Secretary-General containing suggestions by non-governmental organizations regarding possible contributions to the implementation of the Lagos Plan of Action for the Implementation of the Monrovia Strategy for the Economic Development of Africa.

Development planning

The Joint Conference of African Planners, Statisticians and Demographers (second session, Addis Ababa, 8-17 March 1982)[1] reviewed studies and other work by the ECA secretariat in development planning, and gave guidance for future activities. After reviewing a study on sectoral projections, it recommended that such work be extended and deepened by the inclusion of more socio-economic variables. It also recommended continued work on a project to explore socio-economic indicators best suited to African conditions and needs, and suggested that a seminar be convened to make recommendations to African Governments on indicator systems. Further co-operation between the ECA secretariat and that of the Organization of African Unity was recommended on research into the impact of tariff and non-tariff protection on industrialization in Africa, also the subject of a study presented to the Conference.

Report. [1]Joint Conference of African Planners, Statisticians and Demographers, E/ECA/CM.8/22 & Corr.1,2.

African Institute for Economic Development and Planning

As the African Institute for Economic Development and Planning continued in 1982 its research and training activities and advisory services to African Governments, the ECA Conference of Ministers took steps to strengthen its financial base by applying an indexation formula to the financial contributions of those Governments to the Institute. The Joint Conference of African Planners, Statisticians and Demographers, which proposed this step in March, estimated that it would raise their contribution from its current level of $1 million a year to $1.6 million. At the same time, the Conference of Ministers, on 30 April,[1] urged the United Nations Development Programme (UNDP) to continue its support at least at the current level of $1.3 million a year. To tap other sources of financing, it requested ECA members to supply fellowships for training at the Institute financed from their UNDP country programme or elsewhere.

Resolution (1982). [1]ECA (report, E/1982/21): 433(XVII), 30 Apr.

Least developed countries

The ECA Conference of Ministers took action on 30 April 1982 to ensure follow-up in Africa to the Substantial New Programme of Action for the 1980s for the Least Developed Countries (LDCs), adopted in September 1981 by the United Nations Conference on the Least Developed Countries.[6] It called on African LDCs to establish national mechanisms for implementation and monitoring of the Programme, and recommended that they submit annual progress reports to the ECA Conference of Ministers of African Least Developed Countries. It recommended that ECA be closely associated in preparing for and organizing meetings between individual LDCs and their aid partners, and appealed to UNDP to help ECA in carrying out its Programme-related responsibilities.[3]

In line with principles of self-reliance, the Conference of Ministers[4] called on LDCs to identify investment opportunities, maximize the use of in-digenous production factors and inputs, and promote indigenous research and development capabilities as well as national, subregional and regional markets. It authorized ECA assistance for planning and programming studies at the request of individual LDCs, and requested the United Nations Conference on Trade and Development to help in evaluating their international trade potentials. Land-locked LDCs and coastal African States were called upon to co-operate in transport and communications, and the ECA Executive Secretary was invited to help island and continental African States identify ways of exploiting the resources of adjacent seas.

Expressing concern that financial constraints had led UNDP to decrease by 20 per cent its planned programmes for developing countries including the least developed, the Conference of Ministers appealed to the international community to provide sufficient resources to enable UNDP to achieve its financial objectives and urgently requested States to contribute to the UNDP Special Measures Fund for LDCs (see Chapter I of this section).[5]

These recommendations were based on texts drafted by the ECA Conference of Ministers of African LDCs (second meeting, Tripoli, Libyan Arab Jamahiriya, 26-28 April).[2] The ministerial Conference was preceded by a meeting of the Intergovernmental Committee of Experts of African Least Developed Countries (Tripoli, 17 and 18 April).[1]

Reports. [1]Committee of Experts, E/ECA/LDCs.2/6; [2]Conference of Ministers, E/ECA/CM.8/28.
Resolutions (1982). ECA (report, E/1982/21), 30 Apr.: [3]456(XVII), [4]457(XVII), [5]458(XVII).
Yearbook reference. [6]1981, p. 406.

Economic integration

A ministerial meeting of Central African States (Libreville, Gabon, March 1982) adopted a timetable for and guidelines on activities towards the establishment of an economic community for that subregion. A draft treaty and protocols were prepared for consideration by a meeting of governmental experts. The proposed community was to encompass the members of the Customs and Economic Union of Central Africa and the Economic Community of Great Lakes Countries. In a resolution on intraregional trade, adopted on 30 April, the ECA Conference of Ministers wished the States concerned full success in the conduct of negotiations for the creation of the Community.[2]

Appeals for additional signatures to the treaty for a Preferential Trade Area encompassing some 18 countries in Eastern and Southern Africa, signed in December 1981 by 11 States,[4] were made in February 1982 by the Conference of African Ministers of Trade and on 30 April by the ECA Conference of Ministers. The Conference of

Ministers of Trade requested ECA to assist the new institution,[1] and the ECA Conference of Ministers requested UNDP to earmark funds to promote intercountry trade within the area.[3]

Report. [1]Conference of African Ministers of Trade, E/ECA/CM.8/13.
Resolution (1982). ECA (report, E/1982/21): [2]441(XVII), para. 1, 30 Apr.; [3]*ibid.*, paras. 3 & 4.
Yearbook reference. [4]1981, p. 612.

Pan-African Documentation and Information System

Following the establishment in 1981 of a Central Co-ordination Office at Addis Ababa,[3] the Pan-African Documentation and Information System (PADIS), designed to gather and disseminate a wide range of economic and social data on African countries, moved in 1982 into its second phase. The primary objectives of this phase were to assist ECA members to strengthen their information handling capabilities, establish links among national centres participating in the PADIS network and with international data bases, and expand the services of the Central Co-ordination Office and subregional centres.

At the Central Office, an information referral system for technical co-operation among developing countries in Africa was established to gather and disseminate data on available expertise, research and development projects, and institutions and training facilities. PADIS co-operated with the ECA Statistics Division towards the installation of a statistical data base consisting of country profiles and time-series statistics structured for random needs. Work began on data bases on food and agriculture (in collaboration with the Food and Agriculture Organization of the United Nations), population (in collaboration with the ECA Population Division), and science and technology (in collaboration with the African Regional Centre for Technology). Plans moved ahead towards the establishment of the first national and subregional participating centres.

Arrangements for co-operation with information systems operated by several United Nations organizations were discussed at the 1982 joint meeting of the secretariats of ECA and other United Nations organizations and the General Secretariat of the Organization of African Unity (Geneva, 6-8 April).[1]

On 30 April[2] the ECA Conference of Ministers urged its member States to take prompt action on national and subregional centres and requested the ECA Executive Secretary to identify and approach new funding sources for them. He was also asked to pursue the feasibility study on telecommunication links for the network, including satellite communications. Industrialized countries were asked to assist PADIS by providing computer software for data base management, and United Nations and other international organizations were requested to furnish information useful for African development. UNDP, the International Development Research Centre and the African Development Bank were asked to continue their financial support.

Report. [1]S-G, A/37/335.
Resolution (1982). [2]ECA (report, E/1982/21): 438(XVII), 30 Apr.
Yearbook reference. [3]1981, p. 612.

Proposed institute for future studies

Citing the lack of African institutions to study, analyse and evaluate strategic issues as a prerequisite to economic policy-making, the ECA Conference of Ministers resolved on 30 April 1982[2] that an African institute for future studies be speedily established. It appealed to African countries, enterprises and individuals, as well as regional and national development and financial institutions and UNDP, to contribute towards an endowment fund for the institute, and it invited ECA members to set up institutions and programmes for future studies.

The Conference endorsed the conclusions and recommendations of an expert group meeting (Addis Ababa, 20-29 January) on the establishment, objectives and functions of the institute.[1] The meeting proposed that the institute undertake analyses and studies of policies and issues that could help African decision makers evolve self-reliant strategies on the continent's major economic, social and cultural issues. The institute would harness the potential of African higher educational and research institutions, provide an early warning forum where analyses of global issues could be prepared from an African perspective, offer training in future-studies methodology, and help build a network of similar institutions in Africa.

Report. [1]ECA secretariat, E/ECA/TPCW.3/2.
Resolution (1982). [2]ECA (report, E/1982/21): 434(XVII), 30 Apr.

Development assistance

Technical co-operation

A $15.9 million programme of technical co-operation activities was carried out by ECA in 1982.

Of this amount, UNDP contributed $8.7 million to support projects in intra-African trade, statistics, national accounts, transport and communications, and technical support to least developed countries. Support was also given to the following regional training institutions and research centres: the African Institute for Economic Development and Planning, the African Institute for Higher Technical Training and Research, the African

Regional Centre for Engineering Design and Manufacturing, the African Regional Centre for Technology, and the Eastern and Southern African Mineral Resources Development Centre.

An amount of $1.3 million was provided from the United Nations regular programme of technical co-operation (see Chapter II of this section) to finance regional and subregional advisory services in economic integration, energy, public finance, budgeting and management, social welfare, statistics, transport and communications, and administrative and programme support to the ECA Multinational Programming and Operational Centres (MULPOCs).

The United Nations Fund for Population Activities provided $2.7 million for technical co-operation, and the Voluntary Fund for the United Nations Decade for Women, $350,000. The United Nations Environment Programme provided $179,500 for the ECA Environment Co-ordination Unit.

ECA also received direct grants of $3 million from donor Governments and organizations to cover expert services under non-reimbursable loan arrangements and bilateral technical co-operation programmes.

In accordance with UNDP procedures providing for co-operation with regional commissions in the preparation and approval of its regional technical co-operation programmes, the ECA Conference of Ministers, on 30 April,[1] endorsed the UNDP regional programme for Africa for 1982-1986 (see Chapter II of this section). It appealed to UNDP to release unprogrammed funds as soon as possible, and further appealed for continued UNDP financing of MULPOCs.

Resolution (1982). [1]ECA (report, E/1982/21): 452(XVII), 30 Apr.

International trade and finance

The Conference of African Ministers of Trade (seventh session, Addis Ababa, 1-3 February 1982),[1] sponsored jointly by ECA and the Organization of African Unity (OAU), recommended a series of measures by African Governments to implement the Lagos Plan of Action for the economic development of Africa. It suggested that Governments assess their domestic and international trade policies in the light of the Plan, consider designating government units to monitor implementation, and place an item on Plan implementation on the agenda of meetings of each subregional MULPOC.

On other matters, the Conference urged African countries to establish national chambers of commerce for trade promotion, requested a study by the ECA and OAU secretariats on the possibility of obtaining United Nations aid in financing preparations for the next all-Africa trade fair, and requested the ECA secretariat to continue to help African

Governments take full advantage of trade potentials with Eastern Europe. It also made recommendations on two new subregional economic communities being planned for Central Africa and Eastern and Southern Africa, on intraregional trade and on Africa's external debt problems.

The Conference session was preceded by a meeting of its Ministerial Follow-up Committee on International Trade and Finance for African Development (second session, Addis Ababa, 25-28 January), which reviewed global, regional and subregional developments in these areas.[2] The Committee's report was reviewed by the Conference, which decided to change its name to Ministerial Follow-up Committee on Trade and Finance for African Development in the Framework of the Lagos Plan of Action. The Committee was given new terms of reference, calling for it to monitor implementation of African strategy in trade and finance, co-ordinate an African position on international issues in these fields, and review progress under multilateral agreements between African countries and those of other regions.

As part of its technical co-operation activities, ECA co-operated with the International Trade Centre in a seminar on import management for officials from French-speaking African countries (Douala, United Republic of Cameroon, April).

Reports. [1]Conference of African Ministers of Trade, E/ECA/CM.8/13; [2]Follow-up Committee, ST/ECA/WP.1/17.

Intraregional trade

The ECA Conference of Ministers, on 30 April 1982,[2] requested the ECA Executive Secretary to intensify his assistance and advisory activities for promoting intra-African trade, both within and between subregions. Expressing gratitude to the United Nations Development Programme (UNDP) for its funding of a 1979-1981 project on intra-African trade and monetary and financial co-operation, the Conference appealed for continued financing for the scheme during 1982-1986. It also urged States to sign the 1981 treaty on a Preferential Trade Area in Eastern and Southern Africa.

In one of several recommendations made to encourage all-Africa trade fairs, the Conference of African Ministers of Trade decided that "Buy African goods" campaigns should be organized in connection with future fairs.[1]

An intergovernmental group of experts from African central banks and ministries of finance (Addis Ababa, October) examined draft terms of reference and guidelines for the establishment of an African monetary fund, prepared by ECA in collaboration with the African Centre for Monetary Studies, the African Development Bank (ADB), the West African Clearing House and other African institutions.

Report. [1]Conference of African Ministers of Trade, E/ECA/CM.8/13.
Resolution (1982). [2]ECA (report, E/1982/21): 441(XVII), 30 Apr.

External debt

The ECA Conference of Ministers, on 30 April 1982, called on the ECA secretariat, in collaboration with the Organization of African Unity and ADB, to organize a meeting of government economic and finance ministries on Africa's external debt.[2] This problem had also been addressed in February by the Conference of African Ministers of Trade, which appealed to donor and lending countries and institutions to leave political considerations aside in extending financial assistance to Africa, urged creditor countries to implement a 1978 resolution of the United Nations Conference on Trade and Development (UNCTAD)[3] by cancelling or rescheduling the debts of developing countries in economic difficulty, and urged African countries to rely more on their domestic savings to finance investment projects.[1]

Reports. [1]Conference of African Ministers of Trade, E/ECA/CM.8/13.
Resolution (1982). [2]ECA (report, E/1982/21): 440(XVII), 30 Apr.
Yearbook reference. [3]1978, p. 429.

International trade and transport of Zaire

ECA activities. The ECA secretariat continued during 1982 to provide advice and other technical assistance to help the semi-land-locked State of Zaire with its international trade and transit problems, in response to several past requests by the Economic and Social Council and the General Assembly. Reporting on these activities in June,[3] the ECA Executive Secretary said that an ECA mission which visited the country from 29 March to 3 April had drawn up a programme to implement the recommendations of missions sent in 1978[6] and 1981.[7] It was agreed between Zaire and ECA that the ECA secretariat would provide further assistance in two railway-line feasibility studies and a study on dredging of the Zaire River estuary, in preparation for a 1983 round-table meeting of donor countries and institutions to mobilize resources in support of Zaire's transport and communications needs, and for the proposed establishment of a commission on the development of the Zaire River, to consist of the Central African Republic, the Congo and Zaire.

The terms of reference of a pre-feasibility study for one of the proposed railway lines (Ilébo-Kinshasa), and of the river-dredging project, to be jointly undertaken by Angola and Zaire, were drawn up by a September 1982 mission sent by ECA and UNCTAD. ECA officials visited Zaire in November and December to gather information for both studies.

Economic and Social Council action. Taking note of the ECA report on 30 July 1982, the Economic and Social Council adopted without vote a resolution[4] by which it approved the proposal for a 1983 round-table meeting with donor countries and financing agencies for Zaire's transport and transit projects, and appealed for positive participation in that meeting. It requested that ECA be given funds, within existing resources, to organize a round-table technical consultative meeting with donors and to accelerate implementation of resolutions on this subject. The ECA Executive Secretary was asked to report again in 1983.

The resolution had been approved without vote on 28 July 1982 by the Council's First (Economic) Committee, on a draft by a Vice-Chairman resulting from informal consultations on an earlier text by 10 African States, Nepal and Yugoslavia,[2] which was introduced by Zaire and later withdrawn. The 12-nation draft would have had the Council recommend the organization of the 1983 round-table meeting, rather than approve the ECA proposal for such a meeting. Further, the approved text added the phrase "within existing financial resources" to the request for assistance in organizing a technical consultative meeting and other activities.

General Assembly action. A similar resolution was adopted by the General Assembly, also without vote, on 20 December 1982.[5] As the Council had done, the Assembly approved the organization of a round-table meeting, appealed to donor countries and financing agencies to participate positively, requested that, within existing resources, ECA be given the funds required to organize a technical consultative meeting and to accelerate implementation of past resolutions, and asked the ECA Executive Secretary to report to the Assembly through the Council in 1983.

The resolution had been approved without vote on 29 November 1982 by the Assembly's Second (Economic and Financial) Committee, based on a text by a Vice-Chairman resulting from informal consultations on a draft resolution introduced by Zaire and sponsored by 13 African States, Belgium and France,[1] but later withdrawn. The approved version differed from the original in adding the phrase "within existing resources" to the request that ECA be given the resources required for the technical consultative meeting and other activities, and in asking for a single report from the Secretary-General rather than one from him and another from the ECA Executive Secretary.

Zaire said in introducing the original draft that the studies of its transport and transit problems which ECA was required to carry out in accordance with past Assembly resolutions were still unimplemented, despite the fact that the $200,000 needed for them had become available. Zaire welcomed the recent agreement with ECA and asked that the roundtable, costing an estimated $63,000, be financed from the available funds.

> *Draft resolutions withdrawn.* [1]Belgium, Central African Republic, Congo, Djibouti, France, Guinea, Liberia, Nigeria, Rwanda, Sao Tome and Principe, Sierra Leone, Togo, United Republic of Cameroon, Zaire, Zambia, A/C.2/37/L.22; [2]Benin, Egypt, Ethiopia, Kenya, Liberia, Mali, Morocco, Nepal, Nigeria, United Republic of Cameroon, Yugoslavia, Zaire, E/1982/C.1/L.13.
> *Report.* [3]ECA Executive Secretary, E/1982/78.
> *Resolutions (1982).* [4]ESC: 1982/61, 30 July, text following. [5]GA: 37/205, 20 Dec., text following.
> *Yearbook reference.* [6]1980, p. 618; [7]1981, p. 620.
> *Financial implications.* S-G statements, A/C.2/37/L.32, E/1982/C.1/L.18.
> *Meeting records.* ESC: E/1982/SR.51 (30 July). GA: 2nd Committee, A/C.2/37/SR.3, 5-8, 20-26, 33, *40, 44* (28 Sep.-29 Nov.); plenary, A/37/PV.113 (20 Dec.).

Economic and Social Council resolution 1982/61

30 July 1982   Meeting 51   Adopted without vote

Approved by First Committee (E/1982/96) without vote, 28 July (meeting 15); draft by Vice-Chairman (E/1982/C.1/L.32), based on informal consultations on 12-nation draft (E/1982/C.1/L.13); agenda item 9.

Particular problems facing Zaire with regard to transport, transit and access to foreign markets

The Economic and Social Council,

Referring to General Assembly resolution 32/160 of 19 December 1977, in which the Assembly recalled Council resolution 2097(LXIII) of 29 July 1977 and proclaimed the period 1978-1988 as the Transport and Communications Decade in Africa,

Referring also to General Assembly resolutions 34/193 of 19 December 1979, 35/59 of 5 December 1980 and 36/139 of 16 December 1981 on particular problems facing Zaire with regard to transport, transit and access to foreign markets,

Recalling resolution 110(V) of 3 June 1979, adopted by the United Nations Conference on Trade and Development at its fifth session, held at Manila from 7 May to 3 June 1979,

Recalling also Council decision 249(LXIII) of 25 July 1977 and Council resolution 1981/68 of 24 July 1981, as well as resolution 293(XIII) of 26 February 1977 of the Conference of Ministers of the Economic Commission for Africa,

Aware of the fact that, until a durable solution is found to the particular problems facing Zaire with regard to transport and transit, its external trade and its economy will continue to be seriously affected,

1. *Takes note* of the report of the Executive Secretary of the Economic Commission for Africa on particular problems facing Zaire with regard to transport, transit and access to foreign markets and of activities carried out to date concerning the search for solutions to the transport and transit problems facing Zaire, particularly measures taken by the Commission regarding the timetable for the activities to be undertaken;

2. *Approves* the proposal of the Commission to organize a round-table meeting in 1983 with donor countries and financing agencies for Zaire's transport and transit projects;

3. *Appeals* to donor countries and financing agencies to participate in a positive manner in the round-table meeting;

4. *Requests* the Secretary-General, within existing financial resources, to make available to the Economic Commission for Africa the resources required to organize a round-table technical consultative meeting with donor countries and to accelerate the implementation of the relevant resolutions of the Council and the General Assembly;

5. *Also requests* the Executive Secretary of the Economic Commission for Africa to submit a report on particular problems facing Zaire with regard to transport, transit and access to foreign markets to the Council at its second regular session of 1983.

General Assembly resolution 37/205

20 December 1982   Meeting 113   Adopted without vote

Approved by Second Committee (A/37/680/Add.2) without vote, 29 November (meeting 44); draft by Vice-Chairman (A/C.2/37/L.85), based on informal consultations on 15-nation draft (A/C.2/37/L.22); agenda item 71 *(c)*.

Particular problems facing Zaire with regard to transport, transit and access to foreign markets

The General Assembly,

Recalling its resolution 32/160 of 19 December 1977, in which it recalled Economic and Social Council resolution 2097(LXIII) of 29 July 1977 and proclaimed the period 1978-1988 the Transport and Communications Decade in Africa,

Recalling also its resolutions 34/193 of 19 December 1979, 35/59 of 5 December 1980 and 36/139 of 16 December 1981 on particular problems facing Zaire with regard to transport, transit and access to foreign markets,

Recalling resolution 110(V) of 3 June 1979 adopted by the United Nations Conference on Trade and Development at its fifth session, held at Manila from 7 May to 3 June 1979,

Recalling also Economic and Social Council decision 249(LXIII) of 25 July 1977 and resolution 1981/68 of 24 July 1981, as well as resolution 293(XIII) of 26 February 1977 adopted by the Conference of Ministers of the Economic Commission for Africa,

Taking note of Economic and Social Council resolution 1982/61 of 30 July 1982,

Aware of the fact that, until a durable solution is found to the particular problems facing Zaire with regard to transport, transit and access to foreign markets, its external trade and economy will continue to be seriously affected,

1. *Takes note* of the report of the Executive Secretary of the Economic Commission for Africa on particular problems facing Zaire with regard to transport, transit and access to foreign markets and of activities carried out to date concerning the search for solutions to the transport and transit problems facing Zaire, particularly measures taken by the Commission regarding the timetable for the activities to be undertaken;

2. *Approves* the organization in 1983 of a round-table meeting with donor countries and financing agencies for Zaire's transport and transit projects;

3. *Appeals* to donor countries and financing agencies to participate in a positive manner in the round-table meeting;

4. *Requests* the Secretary-General to provide, within existing resources, the Economic Commission for Africa with the resources required to organize a round-table technical consultative meeting with donor countries and to accelerate the implementation of the relevant resolutions of the Economic and Social Council and the General Assembly;

5. *Requests* the Secretary-General, in consultation with the Executive Secretary of the Economic Commission for Africa, to submit to the General Assembly at its thirty-eighth session, through the Economic and Social Council, a report on the particular problems facing Zaire with regard to transport, transit and access to foreign markets and on the implementation of the present resolution.

Transport and communications

Transport and Communications Decade in Africa (1978-1988)

Three consultative meetings between African countries and potential donors, seeking funds for the development of Africa's railways, roads, water transport and ports, were held in 1982 under the Transport and Communications Decade in Africa, and another meeting was authorized for 1983. Organized with the help of ECA, the 1982 meetings identified $742 million in potential new financing. The ECA secretariat prepared a revised draft programme for the first phase of the Decade (1980-1983), adding more than 300 projects to the original list of 771[7] and raising the cost from $9 billion to well over $15 billion. In June 1982, ECA reported that financing—largely domestic—had been arranged for 360 projects, some completed and others under way. A $31 billion draft programme was prepared by ECA for the Decade's second phase (1984-1988), including many projects for which financing was not expected to be found during the first phase.

Also in connection with the Decade, plans were being drawn up for a satellite communications network, studies were under way on a possible bridge or tunnel from Africa to Europe across the Strait of Gibraltar and ECA sought funds for a series of seminars on multimodal transport.

In a resolution of 30 April 1982 on assistance to the least developed countries (LDCs), the ECA Conference of Ministers called on both land-locked LDCs and coastal African States to intensify efforts to develop transport and communication infrastructures in the framework of the Decade.[3]

The Secretary-General reported in June to the General Assembly and the Economic and Social Council on activities relating to the Decade.[2] Both bodies adopted resolutions encouraging further efforts to develop the programme and secure financing, and pointing out that the resources mobilized so far were well below the amount required to finance the first-phase programme.

The Decade, spanning 1978-1988, was proclaimed by the Assembly in 1977.[6] The role of ECA, the lead United Nations body for this programme, was largely to help African States draw up a programme of feasible projects and to help arrange financing from public and private international sources of capital. The Council, in July 1982, and the Assembly, in December, requested that ECA continue to be provided with resources for these activities.

Economic and Social Council action. On 29 July, by a resolution on the Decade adopted without vote,[4] the Economic and Social Council requested the Assembly to provide ECA with financial and other resources, using extrabudgetary funds and existing resources to the maximum, so that it could hold a further consultative meeting in 1983, complete the plan for the second phase and fulfil its role as lead agency for the Decade. It appealed for increased financial support from donor countries and financial institutions, noted the encouraging results of the consultative meetings already held and appealed to donors for positive participation in the 1983 meeting, noted progress made in the first phase, requested a report from ECA in 1983 on preparations for the second phase, and requested continued assistance by ECA in the study on a regional satellite communication system for Africa.

The resolution had been recommended without vote on 28 July 1982 by the Council's First (Economic) Committee. The text, submitted by a Vice-Chairman, emerged from informal consultations

on a draft submitted by Algeria for the Group of 77 developing countries and later withdrawn.[1] The only substantive difference was the addition to the approved version of a phrase specifying that, in providing ECA with resources for its activities relating to the Decade, extrabudgetary funds and existing resources should be used to the maximum.

General Assembly action. A similar resolution on the Decade was adopted by the General Assembly on 17 December 1982 by a recorded vote of 145 to 1.[5] Like the Council, the Assembly requested the Secretary-General to provide ECA with financial and other resources, using extrabudgetary funds and existing resources to the maximum, so that it could hold the 1983 consultative technical meeting and complete preparation of the second-phase plan. The Assembly requested the ECA Executive Secretary to continue to submit progress reports and the Secretary-General to report to the Assembly in 1983 on progress achieved. It appealed to donor countries and financial institutions to increase their financial support, requested ECA to organize the 1983 consultative meeting and to follow up on the results of all such meetings, requested a report from ECA on second-phase preparations and asked it to continue assisting in the satellite communication project.

The resolution had been approved on 8 December 1982 by the Assembly's Second (Economic and Financial) Committee, by a recorded vote, requested by the United States, of 130 to 1. The draft had been submitted by Bangladesh on behalf of the Group of 77 developing countries. The text incorporated an additional phrase, agreed upon in informal consultations conducted by a Vice-Chairman, specifying that extrabudgetary funds and existing resources, *inter alia*, were to be used to the maximum extent possible in financing ECA activities relating to the Decade. The resolution was approved after the Committee rejected an oral amendment by the United States to delete "*inter alia*" and "to the maximum extent possible".

Introducing the draft resolution, Bangladesh said that while the consultative meetings had produced encouraging results, sustained efforts would be necessary to mobilize further resources and thus guarantee the complete execution of the programme for the Decade.

Draft resolution withdrawn. [1]Algeria, for Group of 77, E/1982/C.1/L.19.
Report. [2]S-G, A/37/296.
Resolutions (1982). [3]ECA (report, E/1982/21): 457(XVII), para. 6, 30 Apr. [4]ESC: 1982/54, 29 July, text following. [5]GA: 37/140, 17 Dec., text following.
Resolution (prior). [6]GA: 32/160, 19 Dec. 1977 (YUN 1977, p. 603).
Yearbook reference. [7]1980, p. 761.
Financial implications. S-G statement, A/C.2/37/L.31.
Meeting records. ESC: E/1982/SR.50 (29 July). GA: 2nd Committee, A/C.2/37/SR.3-12, 32, *33, 47* (28 Sep.-8 Dec.); plenary, A/37/PV.109 (17 Dec.).

Economic and Social Council resolution 1982/54

29 July 1982   Meeting 50   Adopted without vote

Approved by First Committee (E/1982/98) without vote, 28 July (meeting 15); draft by Vice-Chairman (E/1982/C.1/L.29), based on informal consultations on draft by Algeria, for Group of 77 (E/1982/C.1/L.19); agenda item 11.

Transport and Communications Decade in Africa

The Economic and Social Council,

Recalling its resolutions 1979/61 of 3 August 1979, 1980/46 of 23 July 1980 and 1981/67 of 24 July 1981 on the Transport and Communications Decade in Africa,

Noting the decision by which the Conference of African Ministers of Transport, Communications and Planning, at its first session, held at Addis Ababa from 9 to 12 May 1979, adopted the global strategy for the implementation of the programme for the Transport and Communications Decade in Africa, and the programme of action for the first phase (1980-1983) of the Decade,

Noting further resolution CM/Res.889(XXXVII) on the Transport and Communications Decade in Africa, adopted by the Council of Ministers of the Organization of African Unity at its thirty-seventh ordinary session, held at Nairobi from 15 to 26 June 1981,

Recalling the decision by which the Conference of African Ministers of Transport, Communications and Planning, at its second session, held at Addis Ababa from 16 to 18 March 1981, authorized the Executive Secretary of the Economic Commission for Africa to organize four consultative technical meetings between member States, interested African intergovernmental organizations and donors,

Recalling also General Assembly resolutions 35/108 of 5 December 1980 and 36/177 of 17 December 1981 concerning the organization of consultative technical meetings with a view to mobilizing additional financial resources for the financing of the programme for the Decade,

Referring to resolution 422(XVI) of 10 April 1981 of the Conference of Ministers of the Economic Commission for Africa, in which the Conference in the main requested the Commission to continue to monitor the progress in the implementation of the programme for the first phase of the Decade, to update the programme, to organize four consultative technical meetings and to undertake the preparation of the plan of action for the second phase (1984-1988) of the Decade,

Referring also to resolution 435(XVII) of 30 April 1982 of the Conference of Ministers of the Economic Commission for Africa, in which the Conference requested the Executive Secretary to monitor the follow-up to the first four consultative technical meetings and recommended that a fifth meeting should be organized for the countries of North Africa, East Africa and the islands of the Indian Ocean,

Considering that sustained efforts should be made to mobilize additional resources, in order to ensure the implementation of the programme for the Decade,

Conscious of the role which the Economic Commission for Africa plays as the lead agency in the implementation of the programme for the Decade,

1. *Takes note* of the report of the Secretary-General on the Transport and Communications Decade in Africa;

2. *Notes with satisfaction* the progress thus far made concerning the implementation of the first phase (1980-1983) of the Decade and the encouraging results of the four consultative technical meetings, held at Lomé from 8 to 11 June 1981, Ouagadougou from 20 to 23 January 1982, Yaoundé from 15 to 17 March 1982 and Abidjan from 3 to 5 May 1982;

3. *Further notes with appreciation* the contribution made by certain countries towards the implementation of the programme for the Decade;

4. *Appeals* to donor countries, financing organs and various financial institutions to increase their financial support to the programme for the Decade, in view of the fact that the total volume of the resources thus far mobilized is well below the amount required to finance the whole of the programme for the first phase;

5. *Requests* the Executive Secretary of the Economic Commission for Africa to organize, during the second half of 1983, a fifth consultative technical meeting on roads, maritime transport and ports for the countries of North Africa, East Africa and the islands of the Indian Ocean;

6. *Appeals once again* to donor countries and financing institutions to participate fully and positively in the fifth consultative technical meeting;

7. *Requests* the Executive Secretary of the Economic Commission for Africa to maintain good co-ordination between the financing sources and the African countries, in order to monitor the follow-up to the four consultative technical meetings by closely assisting the countries in their contacts with donors and in formulating and presenting their requests for financing;

8. *Notes* the measures taken by the Executive Secretary of the Commission with regard to the preparation of the plan of action for the second phase (1984-1988) of the Decade and requests him to submit a report on its preparation to the Economic and Social Council at its second regular session of 1983;

9. *Further notes* the establishment of the Inter-Agency Co-ordinating Committee, comprising the African Development Bank, the African Postal and Telecommunications Union, the Economic Commission for Africa, the International Telecommunication Union, the Organization of African Unity, the Pan-African Telecommunications Union, the Union of National Radio and Television Organizations of Africa and the United Nations Educational, Scientific and Cultural Organization, with a view to harmonizing and co-ordinating studies for the prompt implementation of the project on a regional satellite communication system for Africa;

10. *Reiterates* its request to the Executive Secretary of the Economic Commission for Africa to continue to intensify his efforts with a view to assisting the Inter-Agency Co-ordinating Committee in the study on the regional satellite communication system for Africa, and to give assistance to African States in the full implementation of the programme for the first phase of the Decade;

11. *Requests* the General Assembly at its thirty-seventh session to provide the Economic Commission for Africa with financial and other resources, using, *inter alia*, extra-budgetary funds and existing resources to the maximum extent possible, to enable it to hold the fifth consultative technical meeting scheduled for 1983, to complete the preparation of the plan of action for the second phase of the Decade and to fulfil efficiently its role as the lead agency for the implementation of the programme for the Decade.

General Assembly resolution 37/140

17 December 1982   Meeting 109   145-1   (recorded vote)

Approved by Second Committee (A/37/679/Add.1) by recorded vote (130-1), 8 December (meeting 47); draft by Bangladesh, for Group of 77 (A/C.2/37/L.21), orally revised in informal consultations; agenda item 12.

Transport and Communications Decade in Africa

The General Assembly,

Recalling its resolutions 32/160 of 19 December 1977, 33/197 of 29 January 1979 and 34/15 of 9 November 1979 on the Transport and Communications Decade in Africa and, in particular, its resolutions 35/108 of 5 December 1980 and 36/177 of 17 December 1981, by which it approved the organization of consultative technical meetings for the various African subregions,

Recalling Economic and Social Council resolutions 1979/61 of 3 August 1979, 1980/46 of 23 July 1980 and 1981/67 of 24 July 1981 on the Transport and Communications Decade in Africa and Council resolution 1982/54 of 29 July 1982, in which the Council requested the organization of a fifth consultative technical meeting for the countries of North Africa, East Africa and the islands of the Indian Ocean,

Recalling also resolution 341(XIV) adopted on 27 March 1979 by the Conference of Ministers of the Economic Commission for Africa, in which the Conference urged Member States to give high priority to the development of transport and communications in the region,

Noting resolution CM/Res.889(XXXVII) on the Transport and Communications Decade in Africa, adopted by the Council of Ministers of the Organization of African Unity at its thirty-seventh ordinary session, held at Nairobi from 15 to 26 June 1981,

Referring to resolution 422(XVI) adopted on 10 April 1981 by the Conference of Ministers of the Economic Commission for Africa, in which the Conference, *inter alia*, requested the Executive Secretary of the Commission to continue to monitor the progress in the implementation of the programme for the first phase (1980-1983) of the Decade, to update the programme, to organize four consultative technical meetings and to undertake the preparation of the plan of action for the second phase (1984-1988) of the Decade,

Referring also to resolution 435(XVII) adopted on 30 April 1982 by the Conference of Ministers of the Economic Commission for Africa, in which the Conference requested the Executive Secretary of the Commission to monitor the follow-up to the first four consultative technical meetings and recommended that a fifth meeting should be organized for the countries of North Africa, East Africa and the islands of the Indian Ocean,

Considering that sustained efforts should be made to mobilize additional resources in order to ensure the implementation of the programme for the Decade,

Aware of the role which the Economic Commission for Africa plays as the lead agency in the implementation of the programme for the Decade,

1. *Takes note* of the report of the Secretary-General on the Transport and Communications Decade in Africa;

2. *Notes with satisfaction* that a measure of progress has been made concerning the implementation of the first phase (1980-1983) of the Decade, including the encouraging results of the four consultative technical meetings, held at Lomé from 8 to 11 June 1981, Ouagadougou from 20 to 23 January 1982, Yaoundé from 15 to 17 March 1982 and Abidjan from 3 to 5 May 1982;

3. *Notes with appreciation* the contribution made by certain countries and financial institutions towards the implementation of the programme for the Decade;

4. *Appeals* to donor countries, financing organs and various financial institutions to increase their financial support to the programme for the Decade in view of the fact that the total volume of the resources thus far mobilized is well below the amount required to finance the whole of the programme for the first phase;

5. *Requests* the Executive Secretary of the Economic Commission for Africa to organize, during the second half of 1983, a fifth consultative technical meeting on roads, maritime transport and ports for the countries of North Africa, East Africa and the islands of the Indian Ocean;

6. *Appeals once again* to donor countries and financing institutions to participate fully and positively in the fifth consultative technical meeting;

7. *Requests* the Executive Secretary of the Economic Commission for Africa to maintain good co-ordination between the financing sources and the African countries in order to monitor the follow-up to the four consultative technical meetings by closely assisting the countries in their contacts with donors and in formulating and presenting their requests for financing;

8. *Notes* the measures taken by the Executive Secretary of the Economic Commission for Africa with regard to the preparation of the plan of action for the second phase (1984-1988) of the Decade and requests him to submit a report on its preparation, through the Economic and Social Council at its second regular session of 1983, to the General Assembly at its thirty-eighth session;

9. *Further notes* the establishment of the Inter-Agency Co-ordinating Committee, comprising the Organization of African Unity, the African Development Bank, the African Postal and Telecommunications Union, the Economic Commission for Africa, the International Telecommunication Union, the Pan-African Telecommunications Union, the Union of National Radio and Television Organizations of Africa and the United Nations Educational, Scientific and Cultural Organization, with a view to harmonizing and co-ordinating studies for the prompt implementation of the project on a regional satellite communication system for Africa;

10. *Reiterates* its request to the Executive Secretary of the Economic Commission for Africa to continue to intensify his efforts with a view to assisting the Inter-Agency Co-ordinating Committee in the study on the regional satellite communication system for Africa, and to give assistance to African States in the full implementation of the programme for the first phase of the Decade;

11. *Requests* the Secretary-General to provide the Economic Commission for Africa, as the lead agency for the implementation of the Decade, with the financial and other resources using, *inter alia*, extrabudgetary funds and existing resources to the maximum extent possible, to enable it to hold the fifth consultative technical meeting, scheduled to be held in 1983, and to complete the preparation of the plan of action for the second phase of the Decade;

12. *Requests* the Executive Secretary of the Economic Commission for Africa to continue to submit progress reports on the implementation of the programme for the Transport and Communications Decade in Africa;

13. *Requests* the Secretary-General to report to the General Assembly at its thirty-eighth session on the progress achieved in the implementation of the present resolution.

Recorded vote in Assembly as follows:

In favour: Afghanistan, Algeria, Angola, Argentina, Australia, Austria, Bahamas, Bahrain, Bangladesh, Barbados, Belgium, Benin, Bhutan, Bolivia, Botswana, Brazil, Bulgaria, Burma, Burundi, Byelorussian SSR, Canada, Cape Verde, Central African Republic, Chad, Chile, China, Colombia, Comoros, Congo, Costa Rica, Cuba, Cyprus, Czechoslovakia, Democratic Kampuchea, Democratic Yemen, Denmark, Djibouti, Dominica, Dominican Republic, Ecuador, Egypt, El Salvador, Ethiopia, Fiji, Finland, France, Gabon, Gambia, German Democratic Republic, Germany, Federal Republic of, Ghana, Greece, Grenada, Guatemala, Guinea, Guinea-Bissau, Guyana, Honduras, Hungary, Iceland, India, Indonesia, Iran, Iraq, Ireland, Israel, Italy, Ivory Coast, Jamaica, Japan, Jordan, Kenya, Kuwait, Lao People's Democratic Republic, Lebanon, Lesotho, Liberia, Libyan Arab Jamahiriya, Luxembourg, Madagascar, Malawi, Malaysia, Maldives, Mali, Malta, Mauritania, Mauritius, Mexico, Mongolia, Morocco, Mozambique, Nepal, Netherlands, New Zealand, Nicaragua, Niger, Nigeria, Norway, Oman, Pakistan, Panama, Papua New Guinea, Paraguay, Peru, Philippines, Poland, Portugal, Qatar, Romania, Rwanda, Samoa, Sao Tome and Principe, Saudi Arabia, Senegal, Sierra Leone, Singapore, Solomon Islands, Somalia, Spain, Sri Lanka, Suriname, Swaziland, Sweden, Thailand, Togo, Trinidad and Tobago, Tunisia, Turkey, Uganda, Ukrainian SSR, USSR, United Arab Emirates, United Kingdom, United Republic of Cameroon, United Republic of Tanzania, Upper Volta, Uruguay, Vanuatu, Venezuela, Viet Nam, Yemen, Yugoslavia, Zaire, Zambia, Zimbabwe.

Against: United States.

Financing the programme for the Decade

Some 360 African transport and communications projects, representing over a third of the number included in the revised first-phase programme for the Decade, were being implemented, were completed, or had found financing or serious prospects of financing, according to the Secretary-General's June 1982 report to the Economic and Social Council on the progress of the Decade's programme.[3] Roads and railways had attracted the most funds. A relatively large number of air transport projects had obtained financing, but the costs were rather low since they related mainly to fellowships and other training and technical assistance. African countries had supplied 65 per cent of the financing.

Regional and subregional projects had attracted little external financing, except for that provided by the United Nations Development Programme (UNDP), the report stated. It suggested that, in addition to seeking funds through consultative meetings, ECA, the Organization of African Unity (OAU) and United Nations specialized agencies, after consulting with potential donors on specific projects, should help countries to formulate and present their requests and in negotiations on financing. Such assistance should be limited to promoting regional and subregional projects and, exceptionally, national projects with a subregional impact.

Under its regional programme for Africa for 1982-1986, UNDP approved $8.5 million for Decade activities, including specific regional and subregional pre-investment and technical assistance projects to be executed by ECA either alone or in collaboration with the specialized agencies and OAU. However, because of overall financial constraints, this amount was reprogrammed to $6.5 million.

The Council, in its 29 July 1982 resolution on the Decade,[4] appealed to donor countries, financing organs and financial institutions to increase their financial support to the Decade's programmes, in view of the fact that the resources mobilized thus far were well below the amount required to finance the whole first-phase programme. A similar appeal was made by the General Assembly in its 17 December resolution.[6]

The cost to the United Nations for first- and second-phase preparatory activities during 1980-1983 was estimated at over $3.4 million, according to a report to the Assembly in November 1982 by the Advisory Committee on Administrative and Budgetary Questions.[2] The first-phase cost of $1.3 million was borne entirely by UNDP, which was expected to give $1 million for the second phase, leaving $963,100 to be provided from the United Nations regular budget and $147,600 from bilateral arrangements. The regular budget component included $480,000 for the consultative meetings and $483,100 added to the 1982-1983 budget on a 10 November recommendation of the Assembly's Fifth (Administrative and Budgetary) Committee; the sum was $59,300 less than the Secretary-General had requested.

The additional $483,100 was provided in accordance with an Assembly request, included in its December resolution on the Decade,[7] that ECA be given financial resources to enable it to hold the 1983 consultative meeting and complete preparation of the second-phase plan of action. The Secretary-General was instructed to use, *inter alia*, extrabudgetary funds and existing resources to the maximum extent possible. A request to the Assembly to take this action had been made in the Council's July resolution on the Decade,[5] where the request to use extrabudgetary funds and existing resources to the maximum had been added as a result of consultations in which the original draft, by Algeria for the Group of 77,[1] was replaced by a text submitted by a Vice-Chairman of the Council's First Committee.

The reference to the maximum use of extrabudgetary funds and existing resources was also added in the Assembly's Second Committee to the original draft resolution as a result of consultations conducted by a Vice-Chairman. The Committee rejected, by 110 votes to 8, with 11 abstentions, a United States oral amendment to delete the phrases "*inter alia*" and "to the maximum extent possible". Explaining its subsequent vote against the resolution, the United States voiced support for the Decade but deplored the budget increase to finance second-phase activities.

Draft resolution withdrawn. [1]Algeria, for Group of 77, E/1982/C.1/L.19.
Reports. [2]ACABQ, A/37/7/Add.7; [3]S-G, A/37/296.

Resolutions (1982). [4]ESC: 1982/54, paras. 3 & 4, 29 July; [5]*ibid.*, para. 11. [6]GA: 37/140, paras. 3 & 4, 17 Dec.; [7]*ibid.*, para. 11.

Consultative meetings

During 1982, three consultative technical meetings, designed to bring together African countries and potential sources of finance for specific lists of transport and communications projects, were organized by ECA, as follows:

—Railways throughout Africa (Ouagadougou, Upper Volta, 20-23 January). The meeting examined 65 projects costing an estimated $3.9 billion. It uncovered financing or opened new prospects of financing amounting to some $253 million. Attendance included 19 African countries and 12 donor countries and international financial institutions.

—Roads and inland waterways in the 10 Central African countries (Yaoundé, United Republic of Cameroon, 15-17 March). A $1.8 billion programme of 44 road projects and 22 inland waterway projects was examined by seven African countries and 13 donor countries and financial institutions. Financing was obtained or prospects of financing opened up in the amount of $342 million.

—Maritime transport and ports in the 25 countries members of the Ministerial Conference of West and Central African States on Maritime Transport (Abidjan, Ivory Coast, 3-5 May). Consideration was given to 39 maritime transport projects and 30 port projects, at a total cost of $1.3 billion. Participants included 21 African countries and 18 potential donors (Governments and intergovernmental organizations). Some $147 million was mobilized over the financing previously secured.

The three meetings, along with a June 1981 meeting at Lomé, Togo, on roads, air transport, telecommunications and postal services in West African countries,[5] uncovered some $940 million in financing or prospective financing, according to the Secretary-General's report on the Decade submitted to the General Assembly in June 1982.[1] The report concluded that the meetings had been highly successful in relation to the $400,000 cost of organizing them. However, as few firm commitments had been made at the meetings, countries were advised to approach donors that had shown interest in specific projects. The decision to hold the four meetings had been taken in March 1981 by the ECA Conference of Ministers of Transport, Communications and Planning.[5]

Expressing appreciation to the donors that had attended these meetings, the ECA Conference of Ministers, on 30 April 1982,[2] requested the ECA Executive Secretary to monitor the follow-up by assisting countries in their contacts with donors and in formulating and presenting their requests for financing projects with a potential subregional or regional impact. It recommended that a fifth such meeting be organized in 1983 on roads, maritime transport and ports for the countries of North Africa, East Africa and the Indian Ocean islands.

The Economic and Social Council, in its July 1982 resolution on the Decade, requested the ECA Executive Secretary to maintain good co-ordination between financing sources and African countries in order to monitor the follow-up to the previous meetings, and asked him to organize the 1983 meeting proposed by the Conference of Ministers.[3] Noting with satisfaction the encouraging results of the four meetings, the General Assembly, in its December resolution on the Decade, made similar requests to ECA to follow up on previous meetings and to organize a fifth one in 1983.[4]

Report. [1]S-G, A/37/296.
Resolutions (1982). [2]ECA (report, E/1982/21): 435(XVII), paras. 1-7, 30 Apr. [3]ESC: 1982/54, paras. 5-7, 29 July. [4]GA: 37/140, paras. 2 & 5-7, 17 Dec..
Yearbook reference. [5]1981, p. 617.

Implementation of the Phase I programme (1980-1983)

In addition to organizing consultative meetings on project financing, the ECA secretariat carried out in 1982 a number of activities related to implementation of the first phase (1980-1983) of the Transport and Communications Decade in Africa. They were described in reports to the General Assembly on the Decade, by the Secretary-General covering 1981/1982[2] and by the ECA Executive Secretary covering 1982/1983.[1]

The major task was to update the programme, which had originally included 771 projects costing nearly $9 billion.[6] On the basis of proposals by individual African countries, the ECA secretariat worked out in the second half of 1982 a draft revised programme which initially contained more than 1,000 projects at a total estimated cost of over $15 billion, subject to review in 1983 by the Conference of African Ministers of Transport, Communications and Planning. This draft was first reviewed by an inter-agency working group of representatives of United Nations agencies and African intergovernmental and regional and subregional organizations (30 August–11 September 1982), and then by the Inter-agency Co-ordinating Committee (Dakar, Senegal, 18-20 October), the highest technical body responsible for co-ordination and preparation of activities for the Decade. Missions sent in October to six countries not previously visited collected information on the status of first-phase projects.

In other activities, the African Highway Maintenance Conference (third session, Addis Ababa, 20-24 September) was organized by ECA with financial and technical assistance from France, the Federal Republic of Germany and the United Kingdom. The ECA secretariat provided eight reports for, and participated in, a meeting of the Working Group of Intergovernmental Experts on Transport and Communications Development of the Eastern and Southern African Preferential Trade Area (Lusaka, Zambia, 1-5 November).

A Port Operations Seminar (Odessa, USSR, 9-23 August), organized by ECA in collaboration with the United Nations Conference on Trade and Development, was attended by 35 senior-level managers from 23 African countries. A training course on railway management and operations, providing top-level African railway personnel with information on modern railway management and operations techniques, was organized by ECA in co-operation with the Union of African Railways and France (Addis Ababa, 22-26 November). A seminar on the development of air services in Africa, to formulate proposals and solutions, was organized by ECA in co-operation with the African Civil Aviation Commission and the African Airlines Association (Addis Ababa, 29 November–3 December).

Regarding specific projects, the United Nations Development Programme (UNDP), Austria and Italy agreed in January to co-operate in a feasibility study on railway links between Burundi and Rwanda. In April, ECA requested the European Development Fund to finance a study—for which it had prepared terms of reference—on the establishment of a multinational shipping company involving six East African and Indian Ocean island countries.

In its 30 April resolution dealing mainly with consultative meetings, the ECA Conference of Ministers reiterated an earlier request to the Executive Secretary to continue to intensify efforts to assist ECA members in the full implementation of the first-phase programme.[3] Progress made in implementing the first phase was noted by the Economic and Social Council and the Assembly in their July[4] and December[5] resolutions on the Decade.

Reports. [1]ECA, transmitted by S-G note, A/38/259-E/1983/79; [2]S-G, A/37/296.
Resolutions (1982). [3]ECA (report, E/1982/21): 435(XVII), para. 8, 30 Apr. [4]ESC: 1982/54, para. 2, 29 July. [5]GA: 37/140, para. 2, 17 Dec.
Yearbook reference. [6]1980, p. 761.

Preparations for the Phase II programme (1984-1988)

Preparation of a $31 billion programme for the second phase (1984-1988) of the Transport and Communications Decade in Africa was completed by the ECA secretariat in December 1982. It consisted of 1,322 projects, 452 of them carried forward from the first phase and 870 of them new. The transport sector (721 projects, $26.6 billion) represented 86 per cent of the total cost, and communications (591 projects, $4.3 billion) the remaining 14 per cent.

This programme was based on provisional lists of projects submitted by States and intergovernmental organizations. These lists were initially classified and considered sector by sector in February by working groups in which experts from United Nations specialized agencies and the Organization of African Unity (OAU) participated. Then, consultants were recruited and sent on project identification and preparation missions to individual countries. Thirty experts were involved in preparing the draft programme, which was reviewed at meetings of the working groups and the Inter-agency Co-ordinating Committee on the Decade that also examined the revised first-phase programme. Like that programme, the one for the second phase was to be reviewed in 1983 by the Conference of African Ministers of Transport, Communications and Planning.

The measures taken by ECA to prepare the second-phase programme were noted by the Economic and Social Council in its July 1982 resolution on the Decade, in which the Executive Secretary was requested to report again in 1983 on the preparations.[2] They were also noted by the General Assembly in its December resolution on the same subject, requesting the Executive Secretary to report to the Assembly in 1983 through the Council.[3]

The Advisory Committee on Administrative and Budgetary Questions reported to the Assembly in November 1982 that the cost of preparations for the second phase was estimated at $1,690,000, of which UNDP was expected to provide $1 million, with most of the rest coming from the United Nations budget.[1] This total included an additional appropriation of $483,100 for 1982-1983, approved by the Assembly's Fifth (Administrative and Budgetary) Committee on 10 November, largely for second-phase preparations.

Report. [1]ACABQ, A/37/7/Add.7.
Resolutions (1982). [2]ESC: 1982/54, para. 8, 29 July. [3]GA: 37/140, para. 8, 17 Dec.

Satellite communication

An Inter-Agency Co-ordinating Committee on Satellite Communications (IACC) was established in 1982 to harmonize and co-ordinate studies for a proposed regional satellite communication system for Africa. Its members were the African Development Bank, the African Postal and Telecommunications Union, ECA, the International Telecommunication Union, OAU, the Pan-African Telecommunications Union, the Union of National Radio and Television Organizations of Africa, and the United Nations Educational, Scientific and Cultural Organization. The Committee held its first session at Addis Ababa from 25 to 27 August.

The decision to establish the Committee was taken on 30 April by the ECA Conference of Ministers,[2] which endorsed a recommendation to that effect made by an intergovernmental experts meeting (Addis Ababa, 22-26 March) convened by several organizations including ECA to serve as the inter-agency steering committee for a project to develop modern telecommunication technology for integrated rural development. This project was one of three concerned with African satellite communication, to be co-ordinated by IACC in a detailed feasibility study on appropriate telecommunication for the development of Africa.

In a related action, the ECA Conference of Ministers requested the Executive Secretary, in collaboration with the OAU Secretary-General, to ensure the speedy realization of the feasibility study, and urged him, in collaboration with the Committee, to explore sources of finance.[3]

In his June report to the General Assembly on the Transport and Communications Decade in Africa,[1] the Secretary-General explained that the feasibility study would cover various communications services, including telecommunication for inter-urban and intra-African rural connections and radio and television broadcasting. It was understood, he added, that the European Economic Community and several of its members were ready to consider financing a single study if African Governments were interested in the project.

At its first session in August, IACC agreed to deal with the harmonization and integration of the existing studies, both at its own meetings and at a special meeting of the co-operating agencies, where the terms of reference for the studies could be compared and amended if necessary. In addition, IACC would give preliminary consideration to its mandate to implement the feasibility phase of the integrated study and to mobilize funds for it.

The Economic and Social Council and the Assembly, in their July[4] and December[5] resolutions on the Decade, reiterated their request to the ECA Executive Secretary to continue to intensify his efforts to assist IACC in the study on a regional satellite communication system for Africa.

Report. [1]S-G, A/37/296.
Resolutions (1982). ECA (report, E/1982/21), 30 Apr.: [2]436(XVII); [3]438(XVII), paras. 6-9. [4]ESC: 1982/54, paras. 9 & 10, 29 July. [5]GA: 37/140, paras. 9 & 10, 17 Dec.

Strait of Gibraltar

The Economic and Social Council, by a resolution of 30 July 1982,[2] requested the Executive Secretaries of ECA and the Economic Commission for Europe to prepare a synthesis and evaluation of studies and reports on a proposed permanent transport link connecting Africa and Europe across the Strait of Gibraltar, and on similar links throughout the world. They were also asked to identify the problems related to ensuring a permanent link between the road networks of the two continents, with a view to submitting proposals and recommendations to the two commissions and to Governments for possible further action. They were requested to report to the Council in 1983.

The resolution was adopted without vote following similar approval by the Council's First (Economic) Committee on 28 July 1982. The draft was submitted by a Vice-Chairman on the basis of informal consultations on a text introduced by Tunisia and sponsored also by Gabon, Liberia, Mali, Morocco, Senegal, the Sudan and Zaire.[1] The original draft would have had the Council note progress made on preliminary studies by the Co-ordinating Committee on the Permanent Link through the Strait of Gibraltar, recommend that the Secretary-General give strong support to the project and funds to ECA so that studies on the link could be completed without delay, and invite the ECA Executive Secretary to ensure full implementation of the resolution and submit the conclusions of the studies to the Council in 1983.

In follow-up to this resolution, the ECA secretariat participated in a colloquium on the feasibility of the link (Madrid, Spain, 9-13 November 1982), which reviewed progress made in efforts to build a permanent fixed structure across the Strait. The secretariat presented progress reports on sections of the trans-African highways leading to Tangiers, Morocco, and on the development of other corridors leading to the proposed link.

Draft resolution withdrawn. [1]Gabon, Liberia, Mali, Morocco, Senegal, Sudan, Tunisia, Zaire, E/1982/C.1/L.8.
Resolution (1982). [2]ESC: 1982/57, 30 July, text following.
Financial implications. S-G statement, E/1982/C.1/L.17.
Meeting record. ESC: E/1982/SR.51 (30 July).

Economic and Social Council resolution 1982/57

30 July 1982	Meeting 51	Adopted without vote

Approved by First Committee (E/1982/96) without vote, 28 July (meeting 15); draft by Vice-Chairman (E/1982/C.1/L.23), based on informal consultations on 8-nation draft (E/1982/C.1/L.8); agenda item 9.

Europe-Africa permanent link through the Strait of Gibraltar

The Economic and Social Council,

Recalling its resolution 2097(LXIII) of 29 July 1977 and General Assembly resolution 32/160 of 19 December 1977, proclaiming the Transport and Communications Decade in Africa during the years 1978-1988,

Bearing in mind the decision by which the Conference of African Ministers of Transport, Communications and Planning, at its first session, held at Addis Ababa from 9 to 12 May 1979, adopted the global strategy for the implementation of the programme for the Transport and Communications Decade in Africa, and the programme of action for the first phase (1980-1983) of the Decade,

Also bearing in mind the decision adopted by the Conference of African Ministers of Transport, Communications and Planning at its second session, held at Addis Ababa from 16 to 18 March 1981, with regard to the updating of the programme for the first phase and the preparation of the plan of action for the second phase (1984-1988) of the Decade,

Noting that the Conference of African Ministers of Transport, Communications and Planning, at its second session, retained the feasibility study on the crossing of the Strait of Gibraltar,

Conscious of the role of the Economic Commission for Africa in the implementation of the programme for the Decade,

Taking into account the favourable decisions on the permanent link through the Strait of Gibraltar taken respectively by the Third Conference on African Roads, held at Abidjan in October 1976, the Thirteenth Permanent Transport Conference of Arab Countries, held at Cairo in February 1977, and the Fourth Conference on African Roads, held at Nairobi in January 1980,

Convinced of the importance of the permanent link through the Strait of Gibraltar for the political, cultural, economic and social relations between Africa and Europe,

Taking note of the existence of a co-ordinating committee for the monitoring of the construction of the permanent link project,

Noting further that the Economic Commission for Europe is following with interest the work regarding the establishment of a permanent link between Europe and Africa and that it has not yet taken a final decision on the matter,

1. *Requests* the Executive Secretaries of the Economic Commission for Africa and the Economic Commission for Europe:

(a) To prepare a synthesis and an evaluation of the various studies and reports currently available throughout the world regarding such links, particularly studies on the proposed link through the Strait of Gibraltar;

(b) To identify, on that basis, the problems related to ensuring a permanent link between the European road network and that of the region of the Economic Commission for Africa, with a view to submitting proposals and recommendations to the regional commissions and Governments concerned for possible further action, and to report to the Economic and Social Council at its second regular session of 1983;

2. *Requests* the Secretary-General, within existing resources, to support the Economic Commission for Africa and the Economic Commission for Europe in the most appropriate manner in the implementation of this task.

Proposed seminars on multimodal transport

The ECA Conference of Ministers, on 30 April 1982,[1] requested the United Nations Development Programme to provide funds for the organization of seminars on multimodal transport operations in Africa. The regional seminars were scheduled for 1982 and 1983 under a joint project of ECA, the Organization of African Unity and the United Nations Conference on Trade and Development. They were to examine the economic, legal, commercial and other implications of the 1980 United Nations Convention on the Multimodal Transport of Goods,[2] and its impact on African economies.

Resolution (1982). [1]ECA (report, E/1982/21): 437(XVII), 30 Apr.
Yearbook reference. [2]1980, p. 1020.

Technical co-operation for highways

The Commission on Human Settlements, on 6 May 1982,[1] requested the Executive Director of the United Nations Centre for Human Settlements (Habitat) to intensify contact and co-operate with ECA with a view to providing technical assistance for the development of trans-African highways. The Commission mentioned in particular the East-West Trans-African Highway (Mombasa, Kenya–Accra, Ghana), the North-South Highway (Cairo, Egypt–Gaborone, Botswana) and the African Unity Road (Algiers, Algeria–Lagos, Nigeria).

Resolution (1982). [1]Commission on Human Settlements (report, A/37/8): 5/4, 6 May.

Implementation of the programme for the Industrial Development Decade for Africa (1980-1990)

The year 1982 was the start of a three-year preparation period leading to the implementation phase of the Industrial Development Decade for Africa (1980-1990), according to a programme for the Decade approved in November 1981,[17] refined in further consultations and published in October 1982.[2] The undertaking was a joint effort of ECA, the United Nations Industrial Development Organization (UNIDO) and the Organization of African Unity (OAU), the Decade having been proclaimed by the General Assembly in 1980.[16]

A Joint Committee of the OAU, ECA and UNIDO secretariats held its first meeting (Vienna, Austria, 11-14 January 1982) to co-ordinate activities during the preparatory phase. It agreed that all such activities should contribute to the basic objectives of collective self-reliance and self-sustaining development, to make Africa less dependent on external assistance and inputs.

The Committee agreed on a series of measures to assess industrial potentials and needs and to popularize the Decade. To assist Governments in such assessments so that they could propose measures to develop and rationalize individual industrial sectors, the three co-operating organizations would gather and analyse industrial data, draw up guidelines for national assessments and help Governments analyse the findings for incorporation into national development plans. In addition, the three organizations would analyse possibilities for intra-African industrial co-operation and work with regional and subregional organizations to generate project ideas and mechanisms for implementing them, including African multinational corporations.

To secure financing for industrial development, the Committee agreed that a general paper would be prepared on mobilizing financial resources and a project document drafted on the use of the $3 million earmarked by the United Nations Development Programme (UNDP) for assistance to Decade activities during 1982-1986. Other project documents would be directed towards securing additional financing from the United Nations Industrial Development Fund and other specific sources.

An expert group meeting convened by the three organizations (Addis Ababa, September) made proposals for a clearer identification of action to be taken by Governments and subregional organizations during the preparatory phase. Terms of reference were prepared for experts to assist Governments in establishing national co-ordinating committees and focal points which would monitor and report on developments during the Decade.

An expert group meeting on popularization of the Decade (Addis Ababa, September), recognizing the role of the national press in reminding decision makers of their commitments to the Decade, recommended steps to ensure that the media, including major newspapers and broadcasting organizations in developed countries, received information about the Decade, preferably from a single source to be designated by the three co-operating organizations.[5]

Secretariat objectives with regard to the Decade—covering such activities as workshops, project identification and monitoring of progress—were incorporated in the proposed United Nations medium-term plan for 1984-1989, as recommended by the Committee for Programme and Co-ordination at its April/May session.[3]

Apart from the planning effort for the Decade, a number of activities were under way to assist in the development of specific industrial subsectors and the mobilization of industrial institutions, manpower and finance.

The First Regional Consultation on the Agricultural Machinery Industry in Africa (Addis Ababa, 5-9 April) adopted a tentative proposal for the formulation of an African development plan for agricultural machinery and equipment (1982-1990), comprising a collective action programme for national decision makers and a series of subregional programmes.[6] The meeting was organized by ECA, UNIDO, OAU and the Food and Agriculture Organization of the United Nations as part of the UNIDO System of Consultations (see Chapter VI of this section). During the Consultation, a number of bilateral arrangements relating to the development of the agricultural machinery industry were concluded. At a follow-up Workshop on Design and Development of Agricultural Equipment in Africa (Cairo, Egypt, October 1982), organized by UNIDO, experts from 17 countries exchanged views on the design and development of simple equipment.

The first meetings of the Eastern and Southern African Steel Development Committee and the Intergovernmental Committee of Experts on Engineering Industries in Eastern and Southern Africa (Redcliff, Zimbabwe, 8-11 November) made recommendations for the development of those industrial sectors.[4] The Steel Development Committee, pointing to the low level of steel consumption in the subregion and the high cost of integrated steel complexes, recommended that countries develop plants for specialized products. Along those lines, it suggested that they work out arrangements to purchase from Zimbabwe such semi-finished products as pig-iron and billets, for further processing in their own factories. The Committee on Engineering Industries recommended measures to promote trade in engineering products within the subregion through trade fairs, the establishment of an information clearing house, preferential tariff treatment, technical study tours, studies of supply and demand, subcontracting, joint field testing of equipment, and the use of consultants from the subregion.

An ECA mission in January to Botswana, Lesotho and Zimbabwe provided advice to companies and governmental institutions concerned with the engineering industry. In preparation for expert meetings planned for 1983 on metals and the engineering industry in West Africa, ECA sent missions in July 1982 to four countries in that subregion.

A training programme in the pharmaceutical industry, covering formulation, packaging and quality control, was conducted by UNIDO for participants from French-speaking Africa (Paris, June). A second meeting of the Intergovernmental Committee of Experts on Chemicals for the Eastern and Southern African Countries was organized by ECA (Lusaka, Zambia, November), as was a regional workshop on the potential for the industrial processing of millet in the baking and allied industries in Africa (Dakar, Senegal, December).

Two national training workshops on the policies and problems of procurement and supply management were organized earlier by ECA in Burundi (February).

National seminars were organized by UNIDO in Senegal (June) on industrial technology and in Egypt (December) on advanced technologies.

For the promotion of industrial investment in Africa, a regional meeting was held among 16 member States of the Economic Community of West African States (Senegal, November). A teleconference, involving satellite transmission, was organized between entrepreneurs in the United States and senior Egyptian Government officials (April).

The Committee on Industrial Co-operation held its first meeting (Lusaka, Zambia, 25-29 October), at which it considered a draft charter on multinational industrial enterprises and reviewed ongoing projects in Eastern and Southern Africa.

Activities in support of the Decade were reported to the Industrial Development Board, the Economic and Social Council and the Assembly by the UNIDO Executive Director and the ECA Executive Secretary in May 1982[7] and May 1983.[8]

ECA action. The ECA Conference of Ministers, on 30 April 1982,[9] called on its member countries to take steps, including the establishment of national co-ordinating committees and focal points, to adjust their development plans with a view to incorporating the principles and objectives of the programme for the Decade into their national economic perspectives and development plans. They were called on to identify national and multina-

tional projects that could accelerate industrial development, and urged to assess their capacities and capabilities for project preparation and implementation, contract negotiation, procurement, research and development, training, production, marketing and distribution. The Conference recommended a multinational approach for the development of strategic industries such as the metallurgical, chemical and engineering industries. It called on member countries to strengthen consultations with a view to the eventual establishment of an African mechanism for industrial consultations, negotiations and arbitration.

The ECA Executive Secretary was called on to take vigorous steps to promote intra-African trade in industrial raw materials and products. Together with the heads of UNIDO, OAU and other organizations, he was asked to adjust work programmes so as to provide greater support to Governments in such areas as realigning development plans, organizing workshops, assessing and developing natural resources and national capacities and capabilities, and identifying projects. UNDP was urged to increase fund allocations for the industrial sector in its national and regional programme for Africa. The Secretary-General was requested to make resources available to strengthen the ECA and UNIDO secretariats in this area.

In another action on 30 April,[10] the Conference of Ministers requested the ECA Executive Secretary to initiate, in collaboration with other organizations, a training and fellowship programme for industrial and technological manpower development within the Decade's framework.

UNIDO action. On 28 May the Industrial Development Board of UNIDO,[15] after noting the Executive Director's progress report on the Industrial Development Decade for Africa,[7] requested that the UNIDO work programme be adjusted to take account of the Decade's requirements. It appealed to donor countries and institutions for increased contributions to African industrial development so as to meet the target set by African Governments for a 1.4 per cent share for Africa in world industrial production during the Decade. The Board requested UNDP to increase its support to the Decade by allocating adequate funds, and United Nations agencies to adjust their programmes to the same end. The Assembly was requested to allocate adequate staff and funds so as to ensure effective co-ordination and implementation of Decade-related activities by UNIDO and ECA.

Economic and Social Council action. On 30 July the Economic and Social Council [12] similarly requested the Assembly to allocate adequate staff and financial resources so as to ensure co-ordination and implementation of Decade-related activities by UNIDO and ECA. It renewed its request to the UNIDO Executive Director to intensify contacts with other United Nations organizations to ascertain their proposed contributions and asked UNIDO and ECA for a further report in 1983, identifying any constraints encountered in fully implementing the Board's May 1982 resolution on the Decade. United Nations agencies were requested to adjust their programmes so as to contribute to the Decade.

This resolution, together with one on global industrial development co-operation,[11] was adopted by the Council by a vote of 42 to none, with 4 abstentions. Paragraph 2, requesting adequate staff and financial resources, was approved by 44 votes to 4.

The resolution had been recommended by the Council's First (Economic) Committee, which had approved it on 29 July by 40 votes to none, with 4 abstentions, after approving paragraph 2 by 39 votes to 4.

The original draft on which this resolution was based had been submitted by Algeria for the Group of 77 developing countries.[1] It was withdrawn in favour of a text submitted, with oral revisions, by a Committee Vice-Chairman following consultations based on the original. However, when the USSR announced its difficulties with the text, the Vice-Chairman withdrew it, to be later reintroduced by Austria, joined by Algeria on behalf of the Group of 77.

The original draft would have had the Council strongly urge the Assembly to provide the required resources to UNIDO and ECA (rather than request it to allocate adequate staff and financial resources to them for the Decade) and endorse and transmit the progress report to the Assembly for approval and adoption (rather than note and transmit it for consideration).

General Assembly action. In a 20 December resolution on industrial development co-operation,[14] the General Assembly, responding to requests by the Industrial Development Board and the Council, asked the Secretary-General to allocate adequate staff and financial resources so as to ensure co-ordination and implementation of Decade-related activities by UNIDO and ECA. As the Council had done, the Assembly requested the UNIDO Executive Director to report through the Board to the Council in 1983 on the responses of the United Nations system to proposals for implementing the programme for the Decade. It appealed to all countries to contribute generously to the Industrial Development Fund in support of Decade-related activities.

In a 17 December resolution on special measures for the social and economic development of Africa in the 1980s,[13] the Assembly renewed its call on United Nations organizations to examine

measures to increase resources for execution of the Decade's programmes. The draft text specified "concrete measures" in this paragraph, but "concrete" was removed when a Vice-Chairman of the Assembly's Second (Economic and Financial) Committee announced revisions agreed upon in informal consultations.

Draft resolution withdrawn. [1]Algeria, for Group of 77, E/1982/C.1/L.22.
Publication. [2]*A Programme for the Industrial Development Decade for Africa,* ID/287.
Reports. [3]CPC, A/37/38, para. 340(e); [4]Eastern and Southern African Steel Development Committee and Committee on engineering industries, E/ECA/INR/2; [5]Expert group meeting on popularization of Decade, ECA/FCIA.7/INR/WP/2/Add.1; [6]Regional Consultation on Agricultural Machinery Industry, ID/285; UNIDO Executive Director and ECA Executive Secretary: [7]ID/B/274, transmitted by S-G note, A/37/291; [8]ID/B/297, transmitted by UNIDO Executive Director note, E/1983/104.
Resolutions (1982). ECA, 30 Apr. (report, E/1982/21): [9]442(XVII); [10]443(XVII), para. 6. ESC, 30 July: [11]1982/66 A; [12]1982/66 B, text following. GA: [13]37/139, para. 3, 17 Dec.; [14]37/212, sect. II, 20 Dec.. [15]IDB (report, A/37/16): 55(XVI), 28 May.
Resolution (prior). [16]GA: 35/66 B, 5 Dec. 1980 (YUN 1980, p. 662).
Yearbook reference. [17]1981, p. 621.
Meeting record. ESC: E/1982/SR.51 (30 July).

Economic and Social Council resolution 1982/66 B

30 July 1982	Meeting 51	42-0-4

Approved by First Committee (E/1982/104) by vote (40-0-4), 29 July (meeting 16); 2-nation draft (E/1982/C.1/L.35, part B), based on informal consultations on draft by Algeria, for Group of 77 (E/1982/C.1/L.22); agenda item 16.

Sponsors: Algeria (for Group of 77), Austria.

Industrial Development Decade for Africa

The Economic and Social Council,

Bearing in mind the Lagos Plan of Action for the Implementation of the Monrovia Strategy for the Economic Development of Africa,

Having considered the note by the Secretary-General on the implementation of the Industrial Development Decade for Africa,

Bearing in mind that the Sixth Conference of African Ministers of Industry adopted proposals for the formulation and implementation of a programme for the Industrial Development Decade for Africa,

Declaring the Industrial Development Decade for Africa to be one of the most important programmes of the United Nations Industrial Development Organization in the proposed medium-term plan for the period 1984-1989,

Having considered the progress report on the Industrial Development Decade for Africa submitted jointly by the Executive Director of the United Nations Industrial Development Organization and the Executive Secretary of the Economic Commission for Africa, and having noted Industrial Development Board resolution 55(XVI) of 28 May 1982 on the Industrial Development Decade for Africa,

Expressing its appreciation to the secretariats of the United Nations Industrial Development Organization and the Economic Commission for Africa for the formulation of a programme of work for the Industrial Development Decade for Africa, in collaboration with the Organization of African Unity,

1. *Takes note* of the progress report on the Industrial Development Decade for Africa submitted jointly by the Executive Secretary of the Economic Commission for Africa and the Executive Director of the United Nations Industrial Development Organization, and transmits it, for consideration, to the General Assembly at its thirty-seventh session;

2. *Requests* the General Assembly to allocate adequate staff and financial resources, so as to ensure the effective co-ordination and implementation of the activities of the United Nations Industrial Development Organization and the Economic Commission for Africa related to the Industrial Development Decade for Africa;

3. *Renews* its request to the Executive Director of the United Nations Industrial Development Organization to intensify contacts with the organs, organizations and bodies of the United Nations system, with a view to ascertaining the contributions they propose to make towards the implementation of the Industrial Development Decade for Africa;

4. *Requests* the secretariats of the United Nations Industrial Development Organization and the Economic Commission for Africa to report to the Economic and Social Council at its second regular session of 1983, through the Industrial Development Board at its seventeenth session, on the implementation of Industrial Development Board resolution 55(XVI), and to identify any constraints on its full implementation which may be encountered;

5. *Further requests* the appropriate United Nations agencies to make any necessary adjustments in their programmes, with a view to contributing effectively to the implementation of the Industrial Development Decade for Africa, as called for by the General Assembly in its resolution 35/66 B of 5 December 1980.

Natural resources

The ECA secretariat stepped up its assistance in 1982 to the Eastern and Southern African Mineral Resources Development Centre, based in Dodoma, United Republic of Tanzania. The Centre continued to assist countries in the subregion through activities such as workshops and seminars. Preparations were under way for the establishment of a similar centre at Brazzaville, Congo, for Central African countries.

A group of African mineral specialists went on a study tour to Latin America to examine the organization, financing and management of mineral development activities. Their experience was incorporated into a study on the possibility of establishing similar African institutions.

During the year, ECA distributed to its member States a series of geological, mineral resources, oil and gas maps of Africa. It also carried out land and water resources surveys in Botswana, Mozambique, Somalia and the United Republic of Tanzania to assess potential irrigation schemes.

On 30 April, the ECA Conference of Ministers affirmed the right of African countries to exercise sovereignty over their natural resources and to utilize them for the benefit of their peoples.[1]

Resolution. [1]ECA (report, E/1982/21), 439(XVII), para. 1, 30 Apr.

Energy

In 1982, the African Regional Centre for Solar Energy was established. Its Council held an inaugural meeting (Addis Ababa, 12-14 May),[1] at which it approved the general principles and policies governing the Centre, elected the Executive Board, approved the work programme and budget for the first two phases from June to December and decided to hold an extraordinary meeting in 1983 to select the host country for the Centre. A permanent demonstration centre for solar energy became operational at ECA headquarters, Addis Ababa.

A seminar on fuelwood and energy (Ethiopia, July/August) was organized by the Forest Indus-

tries Advisory Group for Africa, jointly operated by the Food and Agriculture Organization of the United Nations (FAO), the United Nations Industrial Development Organization (UNIDO) and ECA. A workshop on biogas technology (Arusha, United Republic of Tanzania, February) was organized by UNIDO in co-operation with the United Nations Educational, Scientific and Cultural Organization. An *ad hoc* committee (Abidjan, Ivory Coast, 1-5 June) organized by ECA discussed personnel training in power production and distribution.

Report. [1]Council of Centre for Solar Energy, ST/ECA/NRD/E/9.

Food and agriculture

A shortfall in Africa's food production, together with high levels of post-harvest losses and periodic severe shortages arising from natural and man-made disasters had led to rapidly increasing dependence on food imports, according to a September 1982 report to the General Assembly by the Secretary-General.[4] The result had been a drain on foreign exchange resources, creating serious constraints on financing economic development. Africa supplied only about 90 per cent of its food, and the ratio had decreased by about 1.1 per cent in 1980 and 0.5 per cent in 1981.

The report identified a number of obstacles to the attainment of the goal of African food self-sufficiency. At the national level, these included a lack of funds and trained manpower, particularly acute at a time when most African countries faced serious economic situations largely beyond the control of most Governments; inadequate and ineffective research; poor transportation; and low prices and incentives for producers. At the subregional and regional levels, interregional transport links were poor and inefficient, and transport rules and regulations and vehicle insurance requirements were often cumbersome. Internationally, the level of external aid for agriculture and food production had diminished in real terms, due to insufficient allocations by organizations to that sector, the economic crisis in donor countries and the fact that most external assistance had been piecemeal and insufficient to allow many African countries to make desired structural changes in agriculture.

The report found that several African countries had substantially increased their investment for food and agriculture through both national budgets and national investment banks, the latter providing long-term credit and subsidized imports for food development. However, total domestic investment, roughly estimated at about $1 billion in 1981, fell short by $800 million, or 44 per cent, of the annual target envisaged for 1980-1985 by the 1980 Lagos Plan of Action for Africa's economic development.[9] External assistance for this sector totalled an estimated $1.5 billion, or some $335 million short of the $1.8 billion target. To meet this target by 1985, Africa's share of official development assistance would have to rise from 50 to 60 per cent of the total.

To improve the food situation in Africa, the report concluded, a greatly increased volume of resources would have to be channeled to agriculture and social systems reoriented to induce small farmers to achieve higher productivity. The objective for 1982-1985 should be to bring about an immediate improvement in the food situation and lay the foundations for achieving self-sufficiency in cereals, livestock and fish products. The priority should be to secure a substantial reduction in food wastage, attain a markedly higher degree of food security, and bring about a large and sustained increase in food production, especially of tropical cereals. Since the increased flow of domestic resources to agriculture had proved inadequate, African Governments must make a co-ordinated effort to call on international bodies for increased assistance.

Assistance rendered by the United Nations system—mainly FAO, the World Food Programme (WFP) and ECA—included the following:

—*Food security.* FAO supported the Sudano-Sahelian countries (see Chapter III of this section) in preparing a programme for a grain reserve system in the Sahel, considered at a meeting with donors in Rome, Italy, in 1982. WFP continued emergency food aid to countries in need.

—*Post-harvest losses and food processing.* An inter-agency meeting convened by ECA (Addis Ababa, 6 and 7 April) recommended stepped-up activities by participating agencies through information exchange on projects and programmes, co-operation in project formulation and execution, intensified efforts to mobilize resources, regular evaluation of projects to identify successful ones that could be replicated, and co-operation with subregional organizations in monitoring, information dissemination and promotion of joint activities. A subregional consultation on post-harvest food losses in Eastern and Southern Africa (Lusaka, Zambia, 26-28 October) adopted recommendations for strengthened training of farmers through extension services and of agriculture faculties.

—*Agronomic research and inputs for increased food output.* Work continued to support research organizations and services through improved seed projects, the development of industries producing agricultural inputs such as fertilizers and machinery, expanded fertilizer use, livestock productivity improvement, and the control of African animal trypanosomiasis and tick-borne diseases.

—*Transport infrastructure for food self-sufficiency.* Greater attention was being placed on the development of farm-to-market transport infrastructures and facilities in Phase II (1984-1988) of the Transport and Communications Decade in Africa.

—*Food trade and marketing organizations.* Studies were being carried out by FAO and ECA on the operations and environmental conditions of markets in several countries, problems and prospects of intra-African trade in food products and the improvement of agricultural marketing institutions, and aid was being channelled through the recently established African Regional Association for Agricultural Credit, composed of agricultural credit institutions of 30 African countries.

—*Manpower development.* An ECA study of African intergovernmental organizations concerned with food development showed that effective implementation had been severely constrained by overlap and duplication, lack of trained staff and facilities, and inadequate co-ordination and resources. The ECA-sponsored African Training and Research Centre for Women began a three-year pilot project in 1982 to train women farmers in new production and crop-storage techniques. An ECA study on manpower aspects of agro- and forest-based food industries in Botswana, Ethiopia, Kenya, Mauritius and the United Republic of Tanzania recommended training and manpower development in those sectors.

Several suggestions to improve the quality of international assistance to Africa on food and agricultural matters were made by the joint meeting of secretariats of the United Nations system and of OAU held at Geneva from 6 to 8 April.[3] They called for communicating information to Governments about the nature and extent of development and emergency assistance they were eligible to receive from United Nations organizations and establishment of an inter-agency co-ordination committee whose agenda would include the African food situation as a permanent item.

World Food Council action. The Ministers for Food and Agriculture of African States members of the World Food Council (WFC) met at Nairobi, Kenya, on 16 and 17 March in a Regional Consultation for Africa to review the African food problem and other pressing global food issues.

In their conclusions and recommendations, annexed to the annual report of WFC,[5] the Ministers observed that the deteriorating food trends in Africa required critically urgent measures, among them disengagement from the colonial legacies of urban-biased development, deeply embedded trade dependence and unrealistic terms of exchange; better co-ordination of agency and donor efforts; development of staple food crops, for which research and support services had historically been weak in Africa, as the basis for attaining increased food self-sufficiency; expanded credit and technology for small land-holders, small credit programmes for the landless, and production-oriented public works programmes for marginal farmers and the landless poor; and a contingency arrangement under which developing countries could build adequate national food reserves by utilizing existing financial and aid channels.

The Ministers specifically called for an urgent programme to develop technical manpower through training in food-policy planning and project preparation and management; to strengthen storage, transport and marketing facilities, and to encourage adaptive research and better delivery systems, with emphasis on low-cost, quick-yielding technical improvements. They also concluded that, while African Governments and peoples were the ultimate arbiters of their drive for increased food self-sufficiency, they would continue to need, in the foreseeable future, substantially increased external support.

General Assembly action. By a resolution of 21 December 1982 on the food and agriculture situation in Africa,[7] the General Assembly urged African countries to implement measures to increase substantially their food and agricultural production, and urged the international community to increase its support for policy adjustments by African Governments to alleviate food deficits, taking account of the conclusions and recommendations adopted by the African Ministers in March. Continued international support was urged for African efforts to increase food production, through additional financial and technical assistance by the United Nations system and agricultural lending by the World Bank. Existing and new donor countries were requested to increase resources for African food aid and agricultural development. The Secretary-General was asked to provide ECA with resources for a survey of food and agriculture technology in Africa, to be submitted in 1983. United Nations organizations were urged to expand training programmes for agricultural project preparation and execution.

This resolution was adopted without vote, following similar approval on 8 December 1982 by the Assembly's Second (Economic and Financial) Committee. The text, submitted by a Committee Vice-Chairman, was based on consultations on a draft resolution by Bangladesh on behalf of the Group of 77 developing countries, later withdrawn.[2]

The approved text had three additional preambular paragraphs, recognizing Africa's commitment to devoting its limited resources to agricultural development, the primary responsibility of developing countries for such development, and the role of food-sector strategies as a means for

adopting an integrated approach to increasing production and consumption while attracting additional international resources. Also added was paragraph 3, urging measures by African countries to increase food and agricultural production. The call for international assistance to support policy adjustments by African Governments, within the framework of the Lagos Plan of Action to alleviate food deficits (paragraph 4) replaced a paragraph in the original draft calling for a renewed and effective international commitment to assist in implementing the Lagos Plan. Added to the original request for a survey of food and agriculture technology in Africa (paragraph 8) were provisos that it be carried out within existing resources and that FAO and other organizations dealing with food and agriculture and inter-governmental institutions based in Africa be consulted; a provision to convene an expert group for the purpose was omitted.

By a further resolution of 21 December on world food problems,[8] the Assembly urged increased international assistance to support policy adjustments by African Governments to alleviate food deficits. Referring to the conclusions and recommendations of the African Ministers in March, it called in particular for: speeding national food strategy implementation and financing, with emphasis on improving producer incentives and raising the standard of living of the rural population; stepped-up training in food-policy planning and investment preparation and management; substantially increased technical and resource support for adaptive research, technology and related services to farmers, emphasizing early low-cost improvement in cultivation practices; and improved food-security infrastructure, including transport, storage and marketing.

The references to producer incentives, raising the rural standard of living and early low-cost improvement in cultivation practices were added in a draft submitted by a Second Committee Vice-Chairman, as a result of informal consultations on a draft originally submitted by Algeria on behalf of the Group of 77 in the First (Economic) Committee of the Economic and Social Council, and transmitted by the Council to the Assembly.[1]

In a 17 December resolution on recovery and rehabilitation in the Sudano-Sahelian region, the Assembly requested Governments and United Nations organizations to give special attention to the critical food situation in Cape Verde, Chad, Mali and Mauritania.[6]

Decision (1982). [1]ESC: 1982/176, annex, para. 13, 30 July.
Draft resolution withdrawn. [2]Bangladesh, for Group of 77, A/C.2/37/L.18.
Reports. S-G, [3]A/37/335, [4]A/37/390; [5]WFC, A/37/19.
Resolutions (1982). GA: [6]37/165, para. 4, 17 Dec.; [7]37/245, 21 Dec., text following; [8]37/247, para. 17, 21 Dec.
Yearbook reference. [9]1980, p. 548.

Financial implications. S-G statement, A/C.2/37/L.79.
Meeting records. GA: 2nd Committee, A/C.2/37/SR.3, 6, 7, 10, 13-19, *33, 47* (28 Sep.–8 Dec.); plenary, A/37/PV.115 (21 Dec.).

General Assembly resolution 37/245

21 December 1982   Meeting 115   Adopted without vote

Approved by Second Committee (A/37/680/Add.5) without vote, 8 December (meeting 47); draft by Vice-Chairman (A/C.2/37/L.117), based on informal consultations on draft by Bangladesh, for Group of 77 (A/C.2/37/L.18); agenda item 71 *(f)*.

Situation of food and agriculture in Africa

The General Assembly,

Recalling its resolutions 3201(S-VI) and 3202(S-VI) of 1 May 1974, containing the Declaration and the Programme of Action on the Establishment of a New International Economic Order, 3281(XXIX) of 12 December 1974, containing the Charter of Economic Rights and Duties of States, and 3362(S-VII) of 16 September 1975 on development and international economic co-operation,

Noting with grave concern that, over the past two decades, the situation of food and agriculture in Africa has drastically deteriorated, resulting in a decline in food production per capita with detrimental effects on dietary standards, which are already well below the minimum requirements, as well as in an alarming increase in the number of people exposed to malnutrition, hunger and starvation,

Recognizing the high priority attached to food and agriculture in the Lagos Plan of Action for the Implementation of the Monrovia Strategy for the Economic Development of Africa,

Recognizing the commitment and determination of Africa to devoting its limited resources on a priority basis to agricultural development, in accordance with the Lagos Plan of Action,

Recognizing that the responsibility for the development of food and agricultural production lies primarily with the developing countries themselves and that there is an increasing effort and growing commitment by the developing countries to accelerate the development of their food and agricultural sectors,

Recognizing the role of food-sector strategies, which emerged from the World Food Council as a means for interested developing countries to adopt an integrated approach for increasing food production, improving consumption and attracting the necessary additional international resources,

Welcoming the priority assigned to food and agricultural development in the deliberations of heads of State and Government held in 1981 and 1982,

Noting with interest the conclusions of the African Ministers for Food and Agriculture at the World Food Council Regional Consultation for Africa, held at Nairobi on 16 and 17 March 1982, as well as the special attention devoted to food and agriculture by the Ministerial Conference of the Food and Agriculture Organization of the United Nations, held in Rome in November 1981, and by the World Food Council at its eighth ministerial session, held at Acapulco from 21 to 24 June 1982,

Convinced that increased international support to combat drought, desertification, African animal trypanosomiasis, African migratory locust and post-harvest losses, among other problems, is crucial to the attainment of food self-sufficiency in Africa,

Further convinced that collective action at the global level can reinforce the efforts of the African countries to resolve the technological, managerial and financial resource gaps impeding food and agricultural production in Africa,

1. *Takes note with satisfaction* of the report of the Secretary-General on the situation of food and agriculture in Africa;

2. *Reaffirms* its resolutions 35/69 of 5 December 1980 and 36/186 of 17 December 1981 and calls for their early and full implementation;

3. *Urges* all the countries of Africa to implement, in accordance with their national development programmes and priorities, measures to increase substantially their food and agricultural production;

4. *Urges* the international community to provide increased assistance in support of essential policy adjustments by African Governments, within the framework of the Lagos Plan of Action for the Implementation of the Monrovia Strategy for the Economic Development of Africa, to alleviate food deficits in Africa, taking into account the conclusions and recommendations adopted by the African Ministers for Food and Agriculture at the World Food Council Regional Consul-

tation for Africa and endorsed by the Council at its eighth ministerial session;

5. *Calls upon* the international community to continue to support efforts undertaken by African countries at the national, subregional and regional levels to increase food production through, *inter alia*, the provision, on a priority and long-term basis, of additional financial and technical assistance to Africa by organizations of the United Nations system, such as the International Fund for Agricultural Development, the United Nations Development Programme and other organizations involved in the financing of agricultural development, and through an increase in lending by the World Bank to the agricultural sector in Africa;

6. *Also calls* for the adoption by multilateral and governmental institutions, when providing financing for agricultural development in the form of grants and loans on concessional terms, of a positive and flexible approach which would take into account, *inter alia*, the recurrent expenditure arising from investment and the cost of factors of production;

7. *Recognizes* the role of the international community, the Food and Agriculture Organization of the United Nations, the World Food Programme, the World Food Council and the International Fund for Agricultural Development in mobilizing food aid and agricultural assistance in Africa, and requests existing and new donor countries to increase the resources required to meet African needs for food aid and agricultural development;

8. *Requests* the Secretary-General to provide, within existing resources, the Economic Commission for Africa with the necessary resources to undertake, in consultation with relevant organizations, such as the Food and Agriculture Organization of the United Nations and other organizations dealing with food and agriculture and intergovernmental institutions based in Africa, a survey of existing food and agriculture technology in Africa, taking into account the existing and ongoing studies thereon, and to make an assessment of the gap, detailing what exists and what is required to enable the countries in the region to begin to make an effective impact on the resolution of the food and agriculture problem, and to submit a report, through the Economic and Social Council at its second regular session of 1983, to the General Assembly at its thirty-eighth session;

9. *Urges* all relevant organs, organizations and bodies of the United Nations system to expand their training programmes in the building up of national capabilities for the preparation, execution, monitoring and evaluation of agricultural development projects in Africa;

10. *Requests* the Secretary-General, in consultation with the Organization of African Unity and relevant organs, organizations and bodies of the United Nations system, to submit to the General Assembly, at its thirty-eighth session, a progress report on the situation of food and agriculture in Africa and on the implementation of the present resolution.

Proposed international year

On 21 December 1982, the General Assembly adopted without vote a resolution[(2)] by which it expressed the view that an international year devoted to the mobilization of financial and technological resources for food and agriculture in Africa could focus international attention on the problem and stimulate a process that would significantly improve the situation. It requested the Secretary-General, after consulting Governments and other organizations, to report in 1983, through the Economic and Social Council, on the implications of declaring such a year, in accordance with criteria for holding international years approved by the Council in 1980.[(3)]

This resolution was adopted without vote following similar approval on 8 December by the Assembly's Second Committee. It was submitted by a Vice-Chairman after informal consultations on a draft by Kenya on behalf of the African Group, later withdrawn.[(1)] In the final version, a preambular paragraph recognizing that all African countries should implement measures to increase substantially their national food and agriculture programmes through such means as economic and technical co-operation among developing countries, replaced a paragraph in the original recognizing the primary responsibility of the developing countries for the development of food and agricultural production and the increasing effort to that end by those countries. Added to the request for a report was a clause specifying that the declaration of a year should be in accordance with approved criteria for holding such years.

Draft resolution withdrawn. [1]Kenya, for African Group, A/C.2/37/L.81.
Resolution (1982). [2]GA: 37/246, 21 Dec., text following.
Resolution (prior). [3]ESC: 1980/67, 25 July 1980 (YUN 1980, p. 1029).
Meeting records. GA: 2nd Committee, A/C.2/37/SR.3, 6, 7, 10, 13-19, *46, 47* (28 Sep.-8 Dec.); plenary, A/37/PV.115 (21 Dec.).

General Assembly resolution 37/246

21 December 1982   Meeting 115   Adopted without vote

Approved by Second Committee (A/37/680/Add.5) without vote, 8 December (meeting 47); draft by Vice-Chairman (A/C.2/37/L.113), based on informal consultations on draft by Kenya, for African Group (A/C.2/37/L.81); agenda item 71 *(f)*.

International year for the mobilization of financial and technological resources for food and agriculture in Africa
The General Assembly,

Noting with grave concern that, over the past two decades, the situation of food and agriculture in Africa has drastically deteriorated, resulting in a decline in food production per capita and a reduction of average dietary standards below essential requirements,

Recalling its resolutions 3201(S-VI) and 3202(S-VI) of 1 May 1974, containing the Declaration and the Programme of Action on the Establishment of a New International Economic Order, 3281(XXIX) of 12 December 1974, containing the Charter of Economic Rights and Duties of States, and 3362(S-VII) of 16 September 1975 on development and international economic co-operation,

Recalling its resolutions 35/69 of 5 December 1980 and 36/186 of 17 December 1981 on the critical situation of food and agriculture in Africa,

Recalling also the relevant decisions and recommendations of the World Food Conference,

Recalling further Economic and Social Council resolution 1980/67 of 25 July 1980, the annex to which contains the guidelines for international years,

Recalling, in particular, Economic and Social Council resolution 1980/58 of 24 July 1980 relating to the report of the World Food Council on the work of its sixth ministerial session,

Taking into account the deep concern reflected in the decisions on the food situation and agriculture outlook in Africa adopted by the Conference of the Food and Agriculture Organization of the United Nations at its twentieth session,

Recognizing that all countries of Africa should implement, in accordance with their national development programmes and priorities, measures to increase substantially their national food and agriculture programmes through, *inter alia,* national, subregional and regional measures, including economic and technical co-operation among developing countries,

Recognizing the commitment and determination of Africa to devoting its limited resources on a priority basis to food and agricultural development in accordance with the Lagos Plan of Action for the Implementation of the Monrovia Strategy for the Economic Development of Africa,

Stressing that the current shortages demonstrate the continued vulnerability of many countries in the region to food crises owing to, *inter alia,* crop failures, drought, soil erosion, desertification and the high level of post-harvest losses,

Recognizing the role of food-sector strategies, which emerged from the World Food Council as a means for interested developing countries to adopt an integrated approach for increasing food production, improving consumption and attracting the necessary additional international resources,

Regretting that food aid has not been adequate to cope with the emergency food shortages in many African countries,

Deeply concerned at the unabated encroachment of the desert in many countries of Africa, which has continued to accentuate the food problem on that continent,

Deeply concerned at the critical food shortages currently affecting many countries in the African region, which necessitate a distressingly large allocation of the scarce foreign exchange of those countries for the import of foodstuffs, to the detriment of their overall development,

Convinced that substantial and sustained international efforts by Governments, organs, organizations and bodies of the United Nations system, intergovernmental bodies, non-governmental organizations and other bodies could significantly augment domestic efforts to resolve the crisis of hunger and malnutrition in Africa,

Encouraged by the priority given to food and agriculture by the heads of State and Government at the summit conferences held in 1981 and 1982,

1. *Expresses the view* that an international year devoted to the mobilization of financial and technological resources for food and agriculture in Africa could be an appropriate occasion to focus the attention of the international community on this problem and would stimulate a process that would lead to a significant improvement in the situation in the region;

2. *Requests* the Secretary-General, after appropriate consultations with Governments, the Organization of African Unity, the Economic Commission for Africa, the Food and Agriculture Organization of the United Nations, the World Food Council, the International Fund for Agricultural Development and the United Nations Development Programme, to submit an interim report, through the Economic and Social Council at its second regular session of 1983, to the General Assembly at its thirty-eighth session on the implications of declaring an international year which would be committed to mobilizing financial and technological resources for food and agriculture in Africa, in accordance with the criteria for holding international years set out in the annex to Economic and Social Council resolution 1980/67.

Science and technology

Endorsing recommendations made in November 1981 by the ECA Intergovernmental Committee of Experts on Science and Technology Development,[2] the ECA Conference of Ministers, on 30 April 1982, urged African States to: create or strengthen central co-ordinating machinery for science and technology policy-making and implementation; ensure that national programmes were directly related to agricultural and industrial production and that effective links were forged between research and development institutions on the one hand and final users on the other; and ensure that Africa received at least 40 per cent of the fund allocations of the United Nations Financing System for Science and Technology for Development.[1]

Resolution (1982). [1]ECA (report, E/1982/21): 445(XVII), 30 Apr.
Yearbook reference. [2]1981, p. 627.

Population

Demographic research and statistics

Concern expressed by ECA intergovernmental bodies in 1982 about a decision to reduce funding for certain demographic data collection and analysis activities in Africa led the General Assembly, in December, to request consideration of ways in which the regional commissions could continue such activities.

The problem was called to the attention of the ECA Conference of Ministers by the Joint Conference of African Planners, Statisticians and Demographers (second session, Addis Ababa, 8-17 March).[1] The Conference expressed concern about what it called action by the United Nations Fund for Population Activities (UNFPA) to scale down dramatically its contribution to country and regional population programmes in Africa, especially in the area of data collection and analysis. This concern was conveyed to the Economic and Social Council by the ECA Conference of Ministers, which on 30 April drew attention to the priority Africa accorded to that area, requested measures to alleviate the reduction in resources, appealed for additional posts in the ECA secretariat so that it could meet its increased responsibilities in the field of population, appealed for support to UNFPA so that it could increase its assistance in those areas, and requested consideration of ways to sustain the recent improvement in demographic knowledge.[2]

The Council, by a resolution of 30 July,[3] transmitted to the Assembly a draft resolution by which the Assembly would request the Secretary-General and the UNFPA Executive Director to alleviate the current reduction in resources for the regional population programme. The Assembly would also decide to allocate posts to the ECA secretariat to enable it to meet its increased responsibilities in the field of population.

The Council adopted the resolution without vote after similar approval on 28 July by its First (Economic) Committee, on the basis of a draft by a Vice-Chairman following informal consultations.

In the Assembly's Second Committee, informal consultations on the Council's draft resolution resulted in a substitute text adopted by the Assembly on 17 December.[4] By that resolution, the Assembly took note of a June decision by the Governing Council of the United Nations Development Programme to discontinue UNFPA support for the infrastructure (including staff) of its project-executing agencies including the regional commissions, and requested the Secretary-General, in consultation with the commissions' executive secretaries, to consider including in the draft United Nations programme budget for 1984-1985 proposals on modalities for continuing regional population activities.

In 1982, UNFPA made available some $2.7 million for regional and subregional population activities in Africa. In addition to maintaining the ECA infrastructure in this field, the funds were used for regional advisory services in demographic statistics, information and clearing-house activi-

ties, national workshops in population and development, the Regional Institute for Population Studies, the Demographic Research and Development Institute, and the Regional Centre for Population Studies of the Central African Customs Union.

One such activity was a feedback seminar in April on the results of the joint ECA/Zambia survey on interrelationships of infant and childhood mortality and fertility. Experts from Zambia and neighbouring countries reviewed the survey's findings and recommended action to combat problems related to high fertility and mortality and women's role in economic and social development.

Report. [1]Conference of African Planners, Statisticians and Demographers, E/ECA/CM.8/22.
Resolutions (1982). [2]ECA (report, E/1982/21): 431(XVII), 30 Apr. [3]ESC: 1982/65 B, 30 July, text following. [4]GA: 37/136, 17 Dec.
Meeting record. ESC: E/1982/SR.51 (30 July).

Economic and Social Council resolution 1982/65 B
30 July 1982   Meeting 51   Adopted without vote

Approved by First Committee (E/1982/96) without vote, 28 July (meeting 15); draft by Vice-Chairman (E/1982/C.1/L.34, part B), based on informal consultations; agenda item 9.

Demographic data collection and analysis

The Economic and Social Council,

Recalling its resolutions 1279(XLIII) of 4 August 1967, 1672(LII) of 2 June 1972 and 1763(LIV) of 18 May 1973,

Taking note of the report of the Joint Conference of African Planners, Statisticians and Demographers on its second session and, in particular, of the decreasing shares of assistance being made available by the United Nations Fund for Population Activities and other multilateral and bilateral donor agencies to States members of the Economic Commission for Africa and to the Commission itself for demographic data collection, processing, evaluation, analysis and dissemination,

Having considered the draft resolution recommended by the Economic Commission for Africa on demographic data collection and analysis,

Decides to transmit the following text to the General Assembly for consideration:

The General Assembly

1. *Requests* the Secretary-General of the United Nations and the Executive Director of the United Nations Fund for Population Activities to take the necessary measures to alleviate the current reduction in resources for the regional population programme;

2. *Decides* to allocate the necessary infrastructure posts to the Economic Commission for Africa to enable it to meet its increased responsibilities in the field of population.

Training and research institutes

Statutes of the Regional Institute for Population Studies and the Institut de formation et de recherche démographiques

In December 1982 the General Assembly approved new statutes of the two ECA-affiliated regional population institutes in Africa—the Regional Institute for Population Studies at Accra, Ghana, serving English-speaking Africa, and the Institut de formation et de recherche démographiques at Yaoundé, United Republic of Cameroon, for French-speaking Africa. The statutes, initially endorsed by ECA in 1980,[9] were intended to involve the countries served by each institute in its financing and management, following an initial phase, since their establishment in 1972, when they were managed from United Nations Headquarters.

The 1980 statutes had been referred back to the Commission by the Assembly in December 1981[3] and by the Economic and Social Council on 4 February 1982,[1] after the Assembly's Advisory Committee on Administrative and Budgetary Questions (ACABQ) had recommended changes to bring them into line with United Nations rules and procedures.[10] The Council's action was taken without vote on a text submitted by the President on the basis of informal consultations. The statutes were then revised by ECA, endorsed in March by the Joint Conference of African Planners, Statisticians and Demographers,[6] and on 30 April the ECA Conference of Ministers recommended their submission for Assembly approval.[7]

Economic and Social Council action (July). On 30 July[8] the Economic and Social Council recommended that the Assembly consider approval of the revised statutes as resubmitted by ECA and annexed to a note by the Secretary-General.[4] This resolution was adopted without vote on the recommendation of the Council's First Committee, which had similarly approved the text on 28 July on a draft submitted by a Vice-Chairman on the basis of informal consultations.

General Assembly action. On 21 December[2] the General Assembly approved the two proposed statutes and endorsed the ACABQ observations and understandings on them. This decision, taken without vote, had been similarly recommended on 23 November by the Assembly's Fifth (Administrative and Budgetary) Committee, on an oral proposal by the Chairman.

In summary, the ACABQ observations and understandings, communicated in a November report to the Assembly,[5] provided that the directors and staff of the institutes were assumed to be United Nations officials within the meaning of the Charter of the United Nations and of agreements and resolutions defining the status of such officials. Letters of appointment should specify that staff members were specifically recruited for the institutes and limited to such service. Work programmes and budgets should be based on firm income estimates, taking into account only pledges of contributions that had been confirmed in writing. The institutes must reimburse the United Nations for the cost of services provided to them by the ECA secretariat.

Decisions (1982). [1]ESC: 1982/107, 4 Feb., text following.
[2]GA: 37/444, 21 Dec., text following.
Decision (prior). [3]GA: 36/450, 16 Dec. 1981 (YUN 1981, p. 628).
Note. [4]S-G, A/37/236.
Reports. [5]ACABQ, A/37/613; [6]Conference of African Planners, Statisticians and Demographers, E/ECA/CM.8/22.

Resolutions (1982). [7]ECA (report, E/1982/21): 429(XVII), 30 Apr. [8]ESC: 1982/65/A, 30 July, text following.
Yearbook references. [9]1980, p. 758; [10]1981, p. 628.
Meeting records. ESC: E/1982/SR.2, 51 (4 Feb., 30 July). GA: 5th Committee, A/C.5/37/SR.42 (23 Nov.); plenary, A/37/PV.114 (21 Dec.).

Economic and Social Council decision 1982/107

Adopted without vote

Draft by President (E/1982/L.13), based on informal consultations; agenda item 2.

Economic Commission for Africa: regional institutes for population studies

At its 2nd plenary meeting, on 4 February 1982, the Council, recalling its decision 1981/189 of 24 July 1981 and pursuant to General Assembly decision 36/450 of 18 December 1981, decided to invite the Conference of Ministers of the Economic Commission for Africa to take up once again, at its session in 1982, the proposed statutes for the regional institutes for population studies at Accra and Yaoundé, in the light of the points raised by the Advisory Committee on Administrative and Budgetary Questions in its report and such suggestions as might be made by the Secretary-General thereon.

Economic and Social Council resolution 1982/65 A

30 July 1982   Meeting 51   Adopted without vote

Approved by First Committee (E/1982/96) without vote, 28 July (meeting 15); draft by Vice-Chairman (E/1982/C.1/L.34, part A), based on informal consultations; agenda item 9.

New statutes of the Regional Institute for Population Studies at Accra and the Institut de formation et de recherche démographiques at Yaoundé

The Economic and Social Council,

Recalling resolution 393(XV) of 12 April 1980 of the Conference of Ministers of the Economic Commission for Africa, by which the Conference endorsed the new statutes of the Regional Institute for Population Studies at Accra and the Institut de formation et de recherche démographiques at Yaoundé and recommended that the statutes should be submitted, through the Council, for approval by the General Assembly,

Recalling also resolution 426(XVI) of 10 April 1981 of the Conference of Ministers of the Economic Commission for Africa, by which the Conference submitted the new statutes to the General Assembly, through the Council,

Recalling further Council decision 1981/189 of 24 July 1981, by which the Council endorsed the new statutes of the two institutes and recommended that the General Assembly should approve those statutes at its thirty-sixth session, in order to enable the institutes to become operational as soon as possible,

Noting General Assembly decision 36/450 of 18 December 1981, in which the Conference of Ministers of the Commission was requested to revise the draft statutes so that they would comply with United Nations rules and procedures,

Recommends that the General Assembly should consider approval of the revised statutes of the Regional Institute for Population Studies at Accra and the Institut de formation et de recherche démographiques at Yaoundé at its thirty-seventh session.

General Assembly decision 37/444

Adopted without vote

Approved by Fifth Committee (A/37/783) without objection, 23 November (meeting 42); oral proposal by Chairman; agenda item 12.

Statutes of the regional institutes for population studies at Accra and Yaoundé

At its 114th plenary meeting, on 21 December 1982, the General Assembly, on the recommendation of the Fifth Committee, approved the proposed statutes of the Regional Institute for Population Studies at Accra and of the Institut de formation et de recherche démographiques at Yaoundé and endorsed the observations and understandings reflected in the report of the Advisory Committee on Administrative and Budgetary Questions.

Financing the Institut de formation et de recherche démographiques

On 30 April 1982, the ECA Conference of Ministers, referring to the urgent need to obtain funds so that the Institut de formation et de recherche démographiques could continue functioning beyond 30 June, urged the Governments of States served by the Institute to pay as soon as practicable a $10,000 advance from their 1982 contributions.[1]

The Institute's new Governing Council, meeting at Yaoundé on 28 and 29 June, approved a provisional budget of 50 million Central African francs for the remainder of 1982 and CFAF 125 million for 1983. As an interim measure, it decided that each member State would pay CFAF 7 million for 1982 and 1983, including the $10,000 advance. In the meantime, the United Republic of Cameroon, the host Government, agreed to continue to bear all of the Institute's local expenses through June 1982.

Resolution (1982). [1]ECA (report, E/1982/21): 432(XVII), 30 Apr.

Human resources development

The first Conference of Vice-Chancellors, Presidents and Rectors of Institutions of Higher Learning in Africa (Addis Ababa, 25-29 January 1982) brought together 150 representatives of 63 institutions of higher learning in 26 African States.[1] Its main purpose was to review the institutions' role in implementing the 1980 Lagos Plan of Action for the economic development of Africa.[5] It produced recommendations for popularizing the objectives and strategy of the Plan, preparing textbooks and instructional materials, producing educational equipment and tools, maximizing the use of educational resources, developing curricula and courses, expanding rural development programmes, using local talent for consultancy services for the Government and the private sector, and monitoring and follow-up.

On 30 April,[4] the ECA Conference of Ministers accepted a number of project proposals as a basis for national action and technical cooperation in human resources development and utilization, and appealed for international support to finance such programmes on a regional basis. The proposed programmes covered manpower and employment planning, reorientation of education to facilitate the development of African resources, training and employee career planning capacity, administrative and financial management, and an effort to induce skilled African emigrés to return to their home countries. Interim terms of reference were approved to include as a regular part of ECA machinery, subject to review in 1984, the Conference of African Ministers Responsible for Human Resources Planning, Development and

Utilization, which met for the first time in October 1981.[6]

To deal with what it described as Africa's chronic shortage of technical manpower, the ECA Conference of Ministers, on 30 April 1982,[3] urged African countries to accord special priority to industrial and technological manpower development and to lend full support to regional institutions active in that area. It appealed for expanded technical and financial assistance, and requested the ECA Executive Secretary to initiate, in collaboration with other organizations, a training and fellowship programme for industrial and technological manpower development within the framework of the Industrial Development Decade for Africa (1980-1990).

In a further resolution of 30 April 1982 on the African Institute for Economic Development and Planning, the ECA Conference of Ministers requested African States to utilize fully the Institute's training capacity by insisting whenever possible that the manpower training components of capital projects be undertaken at the Institute.[2]

Consultative missions were sent to several East African countries to assess what they had done to develop national machinery for manpower planning and policy formulation, and to review progress in other training areas. Country studies were undertaken on employment planning and creation, labour productivity enhancement, and resource utilization in African institutions of higher learning. The first of a series of national workshops on various human resources development topics was held in Lesotho in November.

Report. [1]Conference of institutes of higher learning, E/ECA/TPCW.3/7.
Resolutions (1982). ECA (report, E/1982/21), 30 Apr.: [2]433(XVII), para. 6 *(b)*; [3]443(XVII); [4]444(XVII).
Yearbook reference. [5]1980, p. 548; [6]1981, p. 629.

Human settlements and environment

The ECA Joint Intergovernmental Regional Committee on Human Settlements and Environment, replacing a commmittee that had dealt with human settlements only,[2] held its first session in 1982 (Addis Ababa, 28 June–2 July).[1]

Report. [1]Committee on human settlements and environment, E/ECA/HUS/ENV/1.
Yearbook reference. [2]1981, p. 630.

Environment

The Governing Council of the United Nations Environment Programme (UNEP), on 31 May 1982,[1] authorized continued support for environmental educational and training activities in Africa, with a view to advising on the incorporation of environmental components into curricula at all levels, identifying and promoting institutions active in this area, supporting training programmes for decision makers and others, and strengthening the UNEP Regional Office for Africa for work in that field. It also authorized a meeting of governmental and scientific experts to develop a programme for African environmental education and training.

The ECA Joint Intergovernmental Regional Committee on Human Settlements and Environment, in July,[2] called on Governments to strengthen their national environmental machineries to cope with natural resources exploitation and pollution control problems involved in the rapid industrialization being planned under the Industrial Development Decade for Africa (1980-1990). It requested the ECA Executive Secretary to examine modalities and costs involved in creating an environmental training institution. He was also asked to strengthen the ECA Environment Coordination Unit and to consult with the UNEP Executive Director on ways to enhance ECA environmental activities.

Decision (1982). [1]UNEP Council (report, A/37/25): 10/25/A, 31 May.
Report. [2]Committee on human settlements and environment, E/ECA/HUS/ENV/1.

Desertification control

The ECA Conference of Ministers, on 30 April 1982,[1] urged African States affected or threatened by desertification—in the northern Sahara, the Sudano-Sahelian region including the Horn of Africa, and the Kalahari Desert—to concert efforts by establishing a regional intergovernmental committee to combat desertification in Africa. The ECA Environment Co-ordination Office would serve as the committee's secretariat. The main functions of the proposed body would be to enable its members to examine successful projects with a view to mounting demonstration activities elsewhere, promote co-operation in training local experts and technicians, facilitate development of environmental educational materials from research and field work, and reassess periodically the methodologies, strategies and programmes for combating desertification. The Conference also recommended establishment by the General Assembly of machinery to combat drought and desertification in Eastern and Southern Africa.

The United Nations Sudano-Sahelian Office continued to co-operate with UNEP in a series of measures to combat desertification and provide emergency assistance in that African region.

Resolution (1982). [1]ECA (report, E/1982/21): 446(XVII), 30 Apr.

Human settlements

On 6 May 1982 the Commission for Human Settlements, noting that the African Development Bank was in the process of establishing Shelter Afrique to contribute to the improvement of human settlements in Africa, decided to encourage close co-operation, especially for information exchange, between the United Nations Centre for Human Settlements (Habitat) and the Bank.[2]

To demonstrate the advantages of integrating physical (spatial) planning with socio-economic planning, the ECA Joint Intergovernmental Regional Committee on Human Settlements and Environment, in July,[1] requested the ECA secretariat to undertake a pilot project that could serve as a model to African countries and to convene in 1983 an *ad hoc* group of experts that would recommend the best techniques and machinery to employ for this purpose at the national level. The secretariat was also asked to organize the compilation of data on African countries' experiences in locating sources of housing finance—ranging from pension fund investments to lotteries—and to help one or two of them with technical assistance in organizing finance schemes. The Committee requested the ECA secretariat to consult with other organizations on an action plan for assisting Governments in the building materials and construction industries, with emphasis on using local materials and skills.

Report. [1]Committee on human settlements and environment, E/ECA/HUS/ENV/1.
Resolution (1982). [2]Commission on Human Settlements (report, A/37/8): 5/6, 6 May.

Women

The Africa Regional Co-ordinating Committee for the Integration of Women in Development (third meeting, Douala, United Republic of Cameroon, 15-17 March 1982),[1] adopted five resolutions proposing action by ECA and its member States.

The Committee called for the establishment of an information network on African activities and programmes to promote women's participation in development, allocation of additional funds by ECA and Governments for activities relating to women, and a study of ways to accelerate programme implementation by decentralizing activities to the subregional Multinational Programming and Operational Centres. With regard to specific sectors, the Committee called for the inclusion of special programmes for women as part of the Industrial Development Decade for Africa (1980-1990) and recommended steps to give women a role in alleviating the African food crisis, to help women refugees and displaced persons become self-supporting, to eliminate *de facto* and *de jure* discrimination against women and to emphasize vocational training for them, including those no longer in school.

As recommended by the Committee, the ECA Conference of Ministers, on 30 April 1982,[2] decided to hold in 1984 the third Regional Conference on the Integration of Women in Development. Conceived as part of the preparations for the 1985 World Conference of the United Nations Decade for Women, the Regional Conference was to consider the issues covered in the Committee's 1982 recommendations, including the setting up of national machinery and the utilization of research. The Conference urged the United Nations Development Programme to provide the North African programme for women with resources similar to those available to the other African subregions.

The Voluntary Fund for the Decade for Women provided $350,000 through ECA in 1982 for various activities to enhance the role of women in Africa, including the strengthening of national machinery, information, training, equipment, and support to the African Training and Research Centre for Women.

Report. [1]Committee on women in development, E/ECA/CM.8/23.
Resolution (1982). [2]ECA (report, E/1982/21): 447(XVII), 30 Apr.

Statistics

The ECA Joint Conference of African Planners, Statisticians and Demographers[1] (second session, Addis Ababa, 8-17 March 1982) approved guidelines and priorities for a self-reliant effort to develop African price statistics. It also adopted conclusions and recommendations on the planning, co-ordination and direction of national census operations within the framework of the 1983 World Programme of Industrial Statistics (see Chapter XXIII of this section). Emphasizing the importance of national accounts statistics for purposes of planning and economic policy formulation, the Conference approved a draft document prepared by the ECA secretariat on a National Accounts Capability Programme for African countries, examined the functions of the ECA Statistical Data Base and its uses in socio-economic analysis, and discussed the design and applicability of socio-economic indicators in Africa and the innovations being introduced into statistical computing by the use of micro-computers.

The Conference expressed concern at the decreasing share of assistance being made available for demographic data collection and analysis and called attention to the importance of the African Household Survey Capability Programme.

During 1982, the ECA secretariat undertook some advisory work in industrial statistics. A workshop on this topic was organized at ECA headquarters in January by the Munich Centre for Advanced Training in Applied Statistics, in collaboration with the United Nations Industrial Development Organization and ECA.

Report. [1]Joint Conference of African Planners, Statisticians and Demographers, E/ECA/CM.8/22.

Household surveys

The importance of the African Household Survey Capability Programme, aimed at enabling African countries to collect, process and analyse demographic, social and economic data on households and household members, was reaffirmed on 30 April 1982 by the ECA Conference of Ministers.[1] On the recommendation of the Joint Conference of African Planners, Statisticians and Demographers, the Conference of Ministers drew the attention of African States to the need to provide adequate funds for their national household survey programme, and requested that funds to continue the regional programme beyond 1982 be sought from the United Nations Development Programme and other aid agencies.

Resolution (1982). [1]ECA (report, E/1982/21): 430(XVII), 30 Apr.

Programme, organizational and administrative questions concerning ECA

Restructuring

The General Assembly, in December 1982, called for action on a number of proposals to strengthen the programming and management functions of the ECA secretariat. This was one of several aspects dealt with in a report by the Joint Inspection Unit (JIU) on ways of strengthening ECA and United Nations regional commissions generally, so that they could carry out their functions as development centres for their region, as defined by the Assembly in earlier resolutions on restructuring the economic and social sectors of the United Nations system to make them more responsive to the needs of development and international economic co-operation. Another main focus of the report was on ways in which ECA and the United Nations system in general could help implement the 1980 Lagos Plan of Action for the economic development of Africa.[11] Both the Assembly and the Economic and Social Council, in July, approved comments by the Secretary-General on steps that could be taken in the areas specified by JIU.

JIU report. Several measures to improve the capacity of the ECA secretariat to programme and manage its activities were recommended in a January report by JIU, transmitted to the Assembly in March.[5] The report covered regional programming, operations, restructuring and decentralization issues facing ECA.

The JIU report, prepared by Inspectors Alfred Nathaniel Forde and Miljenko Vukovic, called attention to the need for strengthened and more systematic programming, monitoring and evaluation to ensure that the work of ECA was well co-ordinated and that its broader responsibilities for joint programming with Governments and other organizations and as a development centre for Africa were effectively carried out. The report suggested that this be accomplished by such measures as establishing a new top-level (D-2) ECA post with responsibility for supervising all programming functions, strengthening the capabilities of the Policy and Programme Co-ordination Office, establishing a unit to develop a monitoring and evaluation system, training or assigning programme assistants in the secretariat's various divisions, and reporting annually to the Commission on joint programming with other organizations and with Governments.

The report also observed a "management gap" brought about by the fact that management posts and resources had not expanded to match the rapid growth in programmes and responsibilities. To overcome that problem, it was recommended that, as an urgent priority, a management services unit be provisionally established, subject to review by the end of three years. The unit would analyse ECA management and administration to identify performance responsibilities, highlight serious problems and develop a streamlined system.

The JIU report also dealt with several matters concerned with the strengthening of United Nations regional commissions in general, implementation of the Lagos Plan and the financing of the ECA subregional units known as Multinational Programming and Operational Centres (MULPOCs).

Commenting on these recommendations in August,[6] the Secretary-General said he would consider the idea of a new high-level post for programming when preparing the 1984-1985 programme budget. While agreeing that ECA should ensure continuing attention to effective management, he did not concur in the establishment of a separate unit, remarking that such responsibilities belonged to the Secretariat's Administrative Management Service. He planned consultations to determine the best way of introducing management improvements.

ECA action. The ECA Conference of Ministers, on 30 April 1982,[7] fully endorsed the JIU recommendations and recommended a number of steps to ensure that they would be carried out. The Conference urged the ECA Executive Secretary to make the organizational and administrative arrangements recommended by JIU to ensure optimum efficiency and effectiveness of programming and management.

Economic and Social Council action. By a resolution of 30 July,[8] the Economic and Social Council took note of the recommendations, approved the Secretary-General's comments and requested him to take appropriate measures on the JIU recommendations, particularly those requir-

ing priority. The Council decided to examine further the restructuring and decentralization issues, and requested the Assembly to consider ways of ensuring implementation of the measures to be taken by the Secretary-General. The latter was asked to submit a progress report in 1984 through the Council to the Assembly. On another matter arising from the JIU recommendations, the Council appealed to United Nations organizations to assist African Governments in incorporating the goals of the Lagos Plan into their development assistance programmes and in adapting them to subregional priorities.

This resolution was adopted without vote following similar approval on 28 July 1982 by the Council's First (Economic) Committee. It was submitted by a Vice-Chairman based on informal consultations on an earlier draft by Algeria on behalf of the Group of 77 developing countries, later withdrawn.[3] The earlier draft would have had the Council endorse the JIU recommendations (rather than the Secretary-General's comments). Instead of requesting the Secretary-General to implement in particular those recommendations which were urgent and required priority, it would have singled out for implementation those concerning MULPOCs, regional and subregional programming and management of United Nations intercountry projects, the pace of decentralization of authority and responsibility from Headquarters to ECA, the development of effective management capabilities, and strengthening of the Regional Commission Liaison Office at Headquarters. Finally, a request in the earlier draft that the Assembly provide resources to implement the recommendations was replaced in the final text by a request that it consider measures to ensure implementation.

General Assembly action. By a resolution of 20 December[10] on the matters raised by JIU, the General Assembly endorsed the Council resolution, welcomed the JIU recommendations and approved the Secretary-General's comments. It called on him to ensure that the measures he had proposed to implement the recommendations on programming and management in ECA were undertaken, particularly in regard to the speedy development of management services for optimum efficiency and effectiveness, and to report in 1983 on progress. The Secretary-General was also called upon to act on other JIU recommendations to strengthen the regional commissions through programming and management of intercountry projects, decentralization and improved liaison with Headquarters; and the commissions' executive secretaries were urged to make their staff exchanges more effective. Also called for was action to implement the Lagos Plan.

This resolution was adopted without vote following similar approval on 8 December 1982 by the Assembly's Second (Economic and Financial) Committee of the text submitted by a Vice-Chairman. That text emerged from informal consultations on an earlier draft by Kenya on behalf of the African Group, later withdrawn.[4] The earlier draft would have had the Assembly take note of (rather than endorse) the Council resolution and endorse (rather than welcome) the JIU recommendations, and it omitted the approval of the Secretary-General's comments contained in the adopted version. The provision on implementation of the JIU recommendations on programming and management improvements would have called for taking measures (instead of taking those proposed by the Secretary-General) to implement the recommendations. A subparagraph in the earlier draft on resources for MULPOCs was dropped in the final text, and provisions on the regional commissions' liaison with Headquarters and on staff exchanges between commissions were altered.

The Assembly repeated its endorsement of the July Council resolution in a decision of 20 December on restructuring the economic and social sectors of the United Nations system.[1] The original version of this proposal, submitted by Jamaica on behalf of 13 sponsors,[2] would have had the Assembly take note of the resolution, but the wording was changed in informal consultations.

In its 17 December resolution on special measures for the social and economic development of Africa in the 1980s, the Assembly requested the Secretary-General to continue to allocate the necessary resources to ECA, taking into account its role as the main economic and social development centre in the United Nations system for Africa.[9]

Decision (1982). [1]GA: 37/442, sect. III, 20 Dec.
Draft decision and resolutions withdrawn. Draft dec.: [2]Algeria, Argentina, Belgium, Canada, Denmark, Jamaica, Nigeria, Philippines, Sudan, Sweden, Trinidad and Tobago, Uganda, Yugoslavia, A/C.2/37/L.72. *Draft res.:* [3]Algeria, for Group of 77, E/1982/C.1/L.21; [4]Kenya, for African Group, A/C.2/37/L.84.
Report. [5]JIU, transmitted by S-G note, A/37/119, and [6]S-G comments, Add.1.
Resolutions (1982). [7]ECA (report, E/1982/21): 449(XVII), 30 Apr. [8]ESC: 1982/63, 30 July, text following. GA: [9]37/139, 17 Dec., para. 6; [10]37/214, 20 Dec., text following.
Yearbook reference. [11]1980, p. 548.
Financial implications. S-G statement, A/C.2/37/L.108.
Meeting records. ESC: E/1982/SR.51 (30 July). GA: 2nd Committee, A/C.2/37/SR.3, 5-8, 20-26, 33, 40, *44, 47* (28 Sep.–8 Dec.); plenary, A/37/PV.113 (20 Dec.).

Economic and Social Council resolution 1982/63

30 July 1982   Meeting 51   Adopted without vote

Approved by First Committee (E/1982/96) without vote, 28 July (meeting 15); draft by Vice-Chairman (E/1982/C.1/L.30), based on informal consultations on draft by Algeria, for Group of 77 (E/1982/C.1/L.21); agenda item 9.

Regional programming, operations, restructuring and decentralization issues with respect to the Economic Commission for Africa

The Economic and Social Council,

Recalling General Assembly resolution 3362(S-VII) of 16 September 1975, by which, *inter alia,* the Ad Hoc Committee on the Restructur-

ing of the Economic and Social Sectors of the United Nations System was established,

Recalling further General Assembly resolutions 32/197 of 20 December 1977, 33/202 of 29 January 1979 and 34/206 of 19 December 1979 on the restructuring of the economic and social sectors of the United Nations system,

Mindful of the terms of reference of the Economic Commission for Africa, in which it is stated, *inter alia,* that the Commission shall participate in measures for facilitating concerted action for the economic development of Africa, including its social aspects, with a view to raising the level of economic activity and levels of living in Africa, and shall assist in the formulation and development of co-ordinated policies as a basis for practical action in promoting economic and technological development in the region,

Having considered the report of the Joint Inspection Unit entitled "Economic Commission for Africa: regional programming, operations, restructuring and decentralization issues", which is one of a number of studies on progress in the implementation of General Assembly resolution 32/197, and the comments of the Secretary-General thereon,

1. *Takes note* of the recommendations contained in the report of the Joint Inspection Unit;

2. *Approves* the comments of the Secretary-General on the report of the Joint Inspection Unit;

3. *Decides* to examine further the restructuring and decentralization issues, taking into account the comments of the Secretary-General;

4. *Appeals* to organizations of the United Nations system, in the context of the present resolution, to assist Governments of African States, within the framework of their country programming process, in incorporating the goals and objectives of the Lagos Plan of Action for the Implementation of the Monrovia Strategy for the Economic Development of Africa in their sectoral country programmes and projects, and in adapting them to subregional and regional priorities, and stresses the role of the resident co-ordinators in Africa in this respect;

5. *Requests* the Secretary-General to take appropriate measures with regard to the recommendations contained in the report of the Joint Inspection Unit, in particular those which are urgent and require priority, and to report thereon to the Economic and Social Council at its second regular session of 1983;

6. *Requests* the General Assembly to consider appropriate measures to ensure the effective and efficient implementation of the abovementioned measures, and requests the Secretary-General to submit a progress report on the implementation of the present resolution through the Economic and Social Council at its second regular session of 1984 to the General Assembly at its thirty-ninth session.

General Assembly resolution 37/214

20 December 1982   Meeting 113   Adopted without vote

Approved by Second Committee (A/37/680/Add.7) without vote, 8 December (meeting 47); draft by Vice-Chairman (A/C.2/37/L.114), based on informal consultations on draft by Kenya, for African Group (A/C.2/37/L.84); agenda item 71 *(h).*

Economic Commission for Africa: regional programming, operations, restructuring and decentralization issues

The General Assembly,

Recalling its resolutions 3201(S-VI) and 3202(S-VI) of 1 May 1974, containing the Declaration and the Programme of Action on the Establishment of a New International Economic Order, and 3281(XXIX) of 12 December 1974, containing the Charter of Economic Rights and Duties of States,

Recalling also its resolution 3362(S-VII) of 16 September 1975, by which, *inter alia,* the Ad Hoc Committee on the Restructuring of the Economic and Social Sectors of the United Nations System was established for the purpose of preparing detailed action proposals with a view to initiating the process of restructuring the United Nations system so as to make it more fully capable of dealing with problems of international economic co-operation and development in a comprehensive and effective manner, and to make it more responsive to the objectives of the provisions of the Declaration and the Programme of Action on the Establishment of a New International Economic Order, as well as those of the Charter of Economic Rights and Duties of States,

Recalling further its resolutions 32/197 of 20 December 1977, 33/202 of 29 January 1979 and 34/206 of 19 December 1979 on the restructuring of the economic and social sectors of the United Nations system, which process was affirmed as an integral part of the efforts for ensuring the equitable, full and effective participation of the developing countries in the formulation and application of all decisions within the United Nations system in the field of development and international economic co-operation and by which process specific, additional tasks were assigned to the regional commissions, including the task of being the main general economic and social development centres for their respective regions, providing team leadership and responsibility for co-ordination and co-operation at the regional level and acting as executing agencies,

Mindful of the terms of reference of the Economic Commission for Africa, in which it is stated, *inter alia*, that the Commission shall participate in measures for facilitating concerted action for the economic development of Africa, including its social aspects, with a view to raising the level of economic activity and levels of living in Africa, and shall assist in the formulation and development of co-ordinated policies as a basis for practical action in promoting economic and technological development in the region,

Mindful, in particular, of the importance attached by the Economic Commission for Africa to economic co-operation among member States, particularly at the subregional level, and to the various resolutions adopted by the Assembly of Heads of State and Government of the Organization of African Unity in this regard, culminating in the Lagos Plan of Action for the Implementation of the Monrovia Strategy for the Economic Development of Africa and the Final Act of Lagos,

Having considered the report of the Joint Inspection Unit entitled "Economic Commission for Africa: regional programming, operations, restructuring and decentralization issues", the comments of the Secretary-General thereon and the views of the Economic and Social Council at its second regular session of 1982,

1. *Endorses* Economic and Social Council resolution 1982/63 of 30 July 1982 on regional programming, operations, restructuring and decentralization issues with respect to the Economic Commission for Africa;

2. *Welcomes* the recommendations made by the Joint Inspection Unit in its report and approves the comments of the Secretary-General thereon;

3. *Calls upon* the Secretary-General:

(a) To investigate new approaches to regional and subregional programming and management of the intercountry projects of the United Nations system, working closely with the organizations of the system;

(b) To initiate immediately, in consultation with all concerned United Nations organizations, an examination of the progress made thus far in the decentralization of United Nations activities and to report thereon to the Committee for Programme and Co-ordination and the Economic and Social Council, with a view to determining the specific authorities, responsibilities and resources that should be decentralized and the timing of such decentralization;

(c) To take practical measures aimed at strengthening liaison functions between the United Nations Headquarters and the regional commissions, bearing in mind the role of the Regional Commissions Liaison Office;

(d) To ensure that the necessary measures proposed by the Secretary-General are undertaken to implement recommendations 6 to 8 of the Joint Inspection Unit, in particular the speedy development of management services, in order to ensure that the Economic Commission for Africa functions at optimum efficiency and effectiveness bearing in mind the ongoing consultations;

4. *Calls upon* the Executive Secretary of the Economic Commission for Africa to institute, under the aegis of the Commission, regional subject-oriented and high-level inter-agency meetings to discuss common issues aimed at the development of firm guidelines for co-ordinated action towards attainment of the objectives of the Lagos Plan of Action for the Implementation of the Monrovia Strategy for the Economic Development of Africa;

5. *Urges* the executive secretaries of the regional commissions to increase the effectiveness of the programme of their exchanges of staff in order to foster the broader scheme of interregional co-operation;

6. *Requests* organizations of the United Nations system to assist African Governments, within the framework of the country programming process, in incorporating the goals and objectives of the Lagos Plan of Action into their sectoral country programmes and projects and adapting them to subregional and regional priorities;

7. *Invites* the Secretary-General to report on the progress made in the implementation of the present resolution to the General Assembly at its thirty-eighth session.

Financing of MULPOCs

As requested by ECA in April 1982 and proposed by the Secretary-General in June, the General Assembly decided in December to finance from the United Nations regular budget—at a continuing cost of about $1 million a year—the core staff of the five Multinational Programming and Operational Centres (MULPOCs), the subregional bodies of the Commission. The United Nations Development Programme (UNDP), which had been financing the infrastructure of MULPOCs, discontinued that support at the end of 1982 after agreeing in June to continue support for their operational activities, including specific technical co-operation activities.

Established in 1977 and 1978 as the operational arms of ECA in African subregions, MULPOCs were responsible for promoting economic integration schemes and overseeing United Nations technical co-operation projects. They were located at Gisenyi, Rwanda, for the Economic Community of the Great Lakes Countries (Burundi, Rwanda, Zaire); Lusaka, Zambia, for Eastern and Southern Africa (18 countries); Niamey, Niger, for West Africa (16 countries); Tangier, Morocco, for North Africa (6 countries); and Yaoundé, United Republic of Cameroon, for Central Africa (7 countries).

JIU report. In its January 1982 report on ECA, transmitted to the Assembly in March,[4] JIU found that MULPOCs had considerable potential for African development but that their resources, primarily supplied by UNDP, were neither adequate nor stable, and various programming and operational problems existed. Without a firm foundation and basic core staff, their future would be in jeopardy.

Consequently, JIU recommended that each MULPOC have a small core group of programme and administrative professionals financed by the United Nations regular budget. As a first step, the five MULPOC liaison-officer posts at ECA headquarters should be redeployed to the centres. Translation arrangements should be made for the centres in bilingual subregions (Niamey, English/French; Lusaka, English/Portuguese). Better co-ordination should be developed with UNDP field offices. Backstopping of MULPOCs by ECA should allow for direct contacts between MULPOC experts and substantive divisions at ECA headquarters. MULPOC directors should meet at least annually and assess their common experiences to improve programming and administration.

Commenting in August on these recommendations,[5] the Secretary-General recognized that MULPOCs were the principal ECA mechanisms for economic and technical co-operation in the subregions, and supported the Inspectors' view that they should be adequately funded, as indicated in his report to the Economic and Social

Council on their financing (see below). Regarding the more specific recommendations, he favoured particular attention to the language requirements of MULPOCs, and he concurred in the view that relations with UNDP and other United Nations field offices should be improved through greater support and information exchange, and that due provision should be made for substantive backstopping of MULPOC programmes from ECA headquarters in the context of available resources.

ECA action. On 30 April,[9] the ECA Conference of Ministers endorsed recommendations on the financing of MULPOCs which the Secretary-General had prepared for the Council (see below). To implement them, the Conference recommended that the Assembly provide budget resources for the centres' basic functions, including programme direction and management, preparation of studies, information collection and dissemination, and development research. At the same time, UNDP was requested to finance the operational activities approved by each centre's legislative organ. African Governments were invited to contribute to MULPOCs through the United Nations Trust Fund for African Development, and the ECA Executive Secretary was called upon to intensify efforts to secure funding from other sources, multilateral and bilateral.

Another call for resources to be provided to MULPOCs through the United Nations regular budget was contained in an ECA resolution of April on restructuring issues.[8]

Report of the Secretary-General. The recommendations by the Secretary-General which ECA endorsed in April were submitted to the Council in June 1982 in a report[7] which the Assembly had requested in December 1981.[13] After citing the importance ECA members attached to economic co-operation, the report described the evolution of institutional arrangements for decentralizing ECA activities, first through subregional offices (1962-1975), then through United Nations Multinational Interdisciplinary Development Advisory Teams (1969-1977) and finally, beginning in 1977, through MULPOCs. In view of expanded ECA responsibilities under the restructuring of the economic and social sectors of the United Nations system, the report said of the role of MULPOCs that they brought ECA much nearer to the grass roots, thus enabling it to work out solutions for problems peculiar to each subregion.

The report categorized MULPOC work programmes into three broad areas: decision-making and substantive studies, broad technical co-operation functions and implementation of technical co-operation projects. It noted that the infrastructural support (including payment of staff salaries) which UNDP had provided since 1977,

programmed in the amount of $2 million for 1982, was to be discontinued at the end of the year, leaving some 60 posts without funding; but that UNDP had agreed to support specific activities such as feasibility studies.

As African Governments were in no position to support these activities directly, and since funding was not likely to be available from either UNDP or other United Nations organizations, the Secretary-General recommended that at least $2 million per biennium be provided from the United Nations regular budget to finance 19 posts in the four MULPOCs of sub-Saharan Africa, along with travel costs, communications, furniture and supplies. At the same time, financial support from UNDP should be maintained and if possible stepped up, but redirected to support operational activities. Other possible sources of extrabudgetary support should be explored. These were the recommendations endorsed by ECA in April (see above).

UNDP action. On 18 June 1982, the UNDP Governing Council, in a decision on country and intercountry programmes and projects[1] (see Chapter II of this section), authorized continued UNDP support for MULPOCs throughout the third UNDP programming cycle (1982-1986). This would be done by financing operational activities identified by the centres' legislative organs, and allocating funds to ensure continuation of MULPOC activities at least at their current levels and within resources available for African regional programmes. Appropriate priority was to be given to the MULPOC for North Africa.

Economic and Social Council action. On 30 July, in a resolution on the financing of MULPOCs,[10] the Economic and Social Council took note of the Secretary-General's report, expressed appreciation for the June decision by the UNDP Governing Council to provide support through 1986, renewed its call for support by other United Nations organizations, called on the Secretary-General to explore other sources including bilateral donors, urged African States to increase their financial support where possible, and invited the Assembly to examine the Secretary-General's proposals to make use of the United Nations regular budget.

This resolution was adopted without vote after similar approval by the Council's First Committee on 28 July 1982 of the text, submitted and orally revised by a Vice-Chairman. That text was the outcome of informal consultations held on an earlier proposal by Algeria for the Group of 77, later withdrawn.[2] The proposal would have had the Council endorse the Secretary-General's recommendation for support from the United Nations budget and recommend that the Assembly provide such resources to ensure continuing implementation of the centres' basic functions relating to programme direction, studies, information dissemination and development research.

A proposal to have the Secretary-General ensure implementation of the JIU recommendations on MULPOCs was included in a draft resolution submitted by Algeria on behalf of the Group of 77[3] in connection with the JIU report (see above). However, as a result of informal consultations, a Vice-Chairman of the Council's Second (Social) Committee submitted an alternative text, which the Council adopted on 30 July,[11] requesting the Secretary-General to take appropriate measures regarding the JIU recommendations; no specific topics were singled out.

General Assembly action. By a resolution of 17 December on the financing of MULPOCs,[12] the General Assembly endorsed the Secretary-General's recommendations calling for the provision of the required funds on an established basis from the United Nations regular budget. It also welcomed the UNDP decision, renewed its call for financial and other support by other United Nations organizations, called on the Secretary-General to explore other sources including bilateral ones, and urged African Governments, where possible, to increase their contributions through the Trust Fund for African Development and host country facilities.

This resolution was adopted by a recorded vote of 113 to 14, with 16 abstentions. It had been recommended by the Assembly's Second Committee on 8 December by a recorded vote of 98 to 14, with 16 abstentions, on a draft sponsored by Bangladesh on behalf of the Group of 77. In introducing this draft, Bangladesh said that the Group of 77 regarded MULPOCs as a vital part of ECA and as its machinery for promoting subregional economic and technical co-operation.

The Assembly acted on a revised version of the Secretary-General's report, submitted in October,[6] which indicated that, if his proposal to finance 19 posts from the regular budget was approved, the MULPOCs would have a total of 35 posts, distributed as follows: Gisenyi, 4; Lusaka, 12; Niamey, 9; Tangier, 6, and Yaoundé, 4.

The Fifth (Administrative and Budgetary) Committee decided on 14 December 1982, by a recorded vote of 68 to 20, with 9 abstentions, to inform the Assembly that the proposal would require an additional appropriation of $813,700 (net) for 1982-1983 to meet MULPOC costs in 1983.

Explaining its negative vote, France said it did not question the value of MULPOCs but thought they should be funded by voluntary contributions rather than from an additional appropriation under the regular budget. Japan expressed the view that proposals with substantial financial and programme implications should always be adopted by consensus. The United States said it could not agree to the use of regular budget funds for bodies that were originally to have been financed from extrabudgetary resources; if that course continued, the United Nations budget would soon rise to such proportions that certain countries might reconsider their support for the Organization and thus endanger its viability.

Among those abstaining in the vote, Canada said it could agree to modest resources provided from the regular budget, but only for a one-year trial period; voluntary contributions should be sought as far as possible. The Netherlands said it would have voted against the provision to make use of the regular budget had there been a separate vote on that paragraph.

Brazil explained that, although voting for the resolution in the Second Committee, it had not participated in the Assembly vote because some of the sponsors had followed in the Fifth Committee a course not previously agreed by all of them.

Decision (1982). [1]UNDP Council (report, E/1982/16/Rev.1): 82/4 A, sect. IV, 18 June.
Draft resolutions withdrawn. Algeria, for Group of 77: [2]E/1982/C.1/L.20, [3]E/1982/C.1/L.21.
Reports. [4]JIU, transmitted by S-G note, A/37/119, and [5]S-G comments, Add.1; S-G, [6]A/37/520, [7]E/1982/70 & Corr.1.
Resolutions (1982). ECA (report, E/1982/21), 30 Apr.: [8]449(XVII), para. 5; [9]450(XVII). [10]ESC, 30 July: 1982/62, text following; [11]1982/63, para. 5. [12]GA: 37/138, 17 Dec., text following.
Resolution (prior). [13]GA 36/178, 17 Dec. 1981 (YUN 1981, p. 632).
Financial implications. 5th Committee report, A/37/759; S-G statements, A/C.2/37/L.66, A/C.5/37/92.
Meeting records. ESC: E/1982/SR.51 (30 July). GA: 2nd Committee, A/C.2/37/SR.3-12, 32, 33, 47 (28 Sep.-8 Dec.); 5th Committee, A/C.5/37/SR.69 (14 Dec.); plenary, A/37/PV.109 (17 Dec.).

Economic and Social Council resolution 1982/62

30 July 1982	Meeting 51	Adopted without vote

Approved by First Committee (E/1982/96) without vote, 28 July (meeting 15); draft by Vice-Chairman (E/1982/C.1/L.31), based on informal consultations on draft by Algeria, for Group of 77 (E/1982/C.1/L.20), orally revised; agenda item 9.

Financing of the Multinational Programming and Operational Centres of the Economic Commission for Africa on an established basis

The Economic and Social Council,

Recalling General Assembly resolutions 32/197 of 20 December 1977 and 33/202 of 29 January 1979 on the restructuring of the economic and social sectors of the United Nations system, in particular the designation therein of the regional commissions as, *inter alia,* the main general economic and social development centres within the United Nations system for their respective regions, having responsibility for the promotion of subregional and regional co-operation,

Bearing in mind resolution 3II (XIII) of 1 March 1977 of the Conference of Ministers of the Economic Commission for Africa, by which the Conference established the Multinational Programming and Operational Centres to foster sectoral and subregional integration,

Recognizing the prominent role given to subregional and regional economic integration in the Lagos Plan of Action for the Implementation of the Monrovia Strategy for the Economic Development of Africa, as a means towards achieving the establishment of an African economic community by the year 2000,

Recognizing also that the Multinational Programming and Operational Centres constitute an integral part of the Economic Commission for Africa, through which the Commission effectively carries out certain parts of the mandate set forth in its terms of reference, and that they serve as the principal mechanism of the Commission for fostering economic and technical co-operation at the subregional level in Africa,

Recalling General Assembly resolution 35/64 of 5 December 1980 on special measures for the social and economic development of Africa in the 1980s,

Recalling also General Assembly resolution 36/178 of 17 December 1981, in which the Assembly called for a report by the Secretary-General on the financing of Multinational Programming and Operational Centres on an established basis,

Taking into account the views, expressed by the Conference of Ministers of the Economic Commission for Africa in its resolution 450(XVII) of 30 April 1982, concerning the need to correct the present situation regarding the inadequacy of the human and financial resources available to the Centres, as a result of which their very existence is threatened,

Having considered the report of the Secretary-General on the financing, on an established basis, of the Multinational Programming and Operational Centres of the Economic Commission for Africa, prepared pursuant to General Assembly resolution 36/178,

1. *Takes note with interest* of the report of the Secretary-General on the financing, on an established basis, of the Multinational Programming and Operational Centres of the Economic Commission for Africa;

2. *Expresses its appreciation* to the Governing Council of the United Nations Development Programme for having requested the Administrator of the Programme to continue to provide the support of the Programme to the five Multinational Programming and Operational Centres during the whole of the third programming cycle, 1982-1986, which is in accordance with the recommendation contained in paragraph 50 of the report of the Secretary-General;

3. *Renews its call* to other organs, organizations and bodies of the United Nations system, as well as intergovernmental and non-governmental organizations, to give their fullest support to the activities of the Multinational Programming and Operational Centres of the Economic Commission for Africa;

4. *Calls upon* the Secretary-General to explore further ways and means of ensuring substantial increases in contributions from extrabudgetary sources, including bilateral donors;

5. *Takes note* of the financial support being given to the Multinational Programming and Operational Centres by States members of the Economic Commission for Africa through voluntary contributions to the United Nations Trust Fund for African Development and through facilities of the Governments of the host countries, and urges those States, where possible, to increase such contributions;

6. *Invites* the General Assembly to examine, at its thirty-seventh session, the proposals contained in paragraphs 47 to 49 of the report of the Secretary-General concerning regular budget financial resources, with a view to arriving at a decision on the funding of the Multinational Programming and Operational Centres on an established basis, bearing in mind, *inter alia*, the action taken on this question by the Executive Secretary of the Economic Commission for Africa.

General Assembly resolution 37/138

17 December 1982　　　　Meeting 109　　　　113-14-16 (recorded vote)

Approved by Second Committee (A/37/679/Add.1) by recorded vote (98-14-16), 8 December (meeting 47); draft by Bangladesh, for Group of 77 (A/C.2/37/L.19); agenda item 12.

Financing of the Multinational Programming and Operational Centres of the Economic Commission for Africa on an established basis

The General Assembly,

Recalling its resolutions 32/197 of 20 December 1977 and 33/202 of 29 January 1979 on the restructuring of the economic and social sectors of the United Nations system, in particular the designation therein of the regional commissions as, *inter alia*, the main general economic and social development centres within the United Nations system for their respective regions, having responsibility for the promotion of subregional and regional co-operation,

Bearing in mind resolution 311(XIII) adopted on 1 March 1977 by the Conference of Ministers of the Economic Commission for Africa,

by which the Conference established the Multinational Programming and Operational Centres to foster sectoral and subregional integration,

Recognizing the prominent role given to subregional and regional economic integration in the Lagos Plan of Action for the Implementation of the Monrovia Strategy for the Economic Development of Africa as a means towards achieving the establishment of an African economic community by the year 2000,

Recognizing also that the Multinational Programming and Operational Centres constitute an integral part of the Economic Commission for Africa, through which the Commission effectively carries out aspects of its mandate, as set forth in its terms of reference, and that they serve as the principal mechanism of the Commission for fostering economic and technical co-operation at the subregional level in Africa,

Recalling also its resolutions 35/64 of 5 December 1980 and 36/180 of 17 December 1981 on special measures for the social and economic development of Africa in the 1980s,

Recalling further its resolution 36/178 of 17 December 1981, in which it invited the Secretary-General to submit a report on the financing of Multinational Programming and Operational Centres on an established basis and Economic and Social Council resolution 1982/62 of 30 July 1982 on the same subject,

Taking into account the views expressed by the Conference of Ministers of the Economic Commission for Africa in its resolution 450(XVII) of 30 April 1982 on the need to correct the present situation regarding the inadequacy of the human and financial resources available to the Multinational Programming and Operational Centres for regular budget and operational activities, as a result of which their very existence is threatened,

Bearing in mind the action already taken by the Executive Secretary of the Economic Commission for Africa to improve the resource situation of the Multinational Programming and Operational Centres,

Having considered the report of the Secretary-General on the financing of the Multinational Programming and Operational Centres of the Economic Commission for Africa on an established basis, prepared pursuant to General Assembly resolution 36/178, and having examined, in particular, paragraphs 47 to 49 of that report,

1. *Takes note with appreciation* of the report of the Secretary-General on the financing of the Multinational Programming and Operational Centres of the Economic Commission for Africa on an established basis;

2. *Welcomes* the decision adopted by the Governing Council of the United Nations Development Programme at its twenty-ninth session, in which the Council requested the Administrator of the Programme to continue to provide financial support to the five Multinational Programming and Operational Centres during the whole of the third programming cycle, 1982-1986;

3. *Renews its call* upon other organs, organizations and bodies of the United Nations system, as well as intergovernmental bodies and non-governmenal organizations, to give their fullest financial and other support to the activities of the Multinational Programming and Operational Centres of the Economic Commission for Africa;

4. *Calls upon* the Secretary-General further to explore ways and means of ensuring substantial increases in contributions from extrabudgetary sources, including bilateral donors;

5. *Takes note* of the financial support being given to the Multinational Programming and Operational Centres by States members of the Economic Commission for Africa through voluntary contributions to the United Nations Trust Fund for African Development and through facilities of the host Government, and urges them, where possible, to increase such contributions;

6. *Endorses* the recommendations contained in paragraphs 47 to 49 of the report of the Secretary-General, which call for the provision of the financial resources required from the regular budget, among other sources, for funding the Multinational Programming and Operational Centres on an established basis in order to bring about their immediate and effective implementation.

Recorded vote in Assembly as follows:

In favour: Afghanistan, Algeria, Angola, Argentina, Bahamas, Bahrain, Bangladesh, Barbados, Benin, Bhutan, Bolivia, Botswana, Burma, Burundi, Cape Verde, Central African Republic, Chad, Chile, China, Colombia, Comoros, Congo, Costa Rica, Cuba, Cyprus, Democratic Kampuchea, Democratic Yemen, Djibouti, Dominica, Dominican Republic, Ecuador, Egypt, El Salvador, Ethiopia, Gabon, Gambia, Ghana, Greece, Grenada, Guatemala, Guinea, Guinea-Bissau, Guyana, Honduras, India, Indonesia, Iran, Iraq, Ivory Coast, Jamaica, Jordan, Kenya, Kuwait, Lao People's Democratic Republic, Lebanon, Lesotho, Liberia, Libyan

Arab Jamahiriya, Madagascar, Malawi, Malaysia, Maldives, Mali, Malta, Mauritania, Mauritius, Mexico, Morocco, Mozambique, Nepal, Nicaragua, Niger, Nigeria, Oman, Pakistan, Panama, Papua New Guinea, Paraguay, Peru, Philippines, Qatar, Romania, Rwanda, Samoa, Sao Tome and Principe, Saudi Arabia, Senegal, Sierra Leone, Singapore, Solomon Islands, Somalia, Sri Lanka, Suriname, Swaziland, Thailand, Togo, Trinidad and Tobago, Tunisia, Turkey, Uganda, United Arab Emirates, United Republic of Cameroon, United Republic of Tanzania, Upper Volta, Uruguay, Vanuatu, Venezuela, Viet Nam, Yemen, Yugoslavia, Zaire, Zambia, Zimbabwe.

Against: Belgium, Bulgaria, Byelorussian SSR, Czechoslovakia, France, Germany, Federal Republic of, Hungary, Japan, Luxembourg, Poland, Ukrainian SSR, USSR, United Kingdom, United States.

Abstaining: Australia, Austria, Canada, Denmark, Finland, German Democratic Republic, Iceland, Ireland, Israel, Italy, Netherlands, New Zealand, Norway, Portugal, Spain, Sweden.

Expansion of Addis Ababa conference facilities

After receiving complaints from the ECA Conference of Ministers and reports from the Secretary-General indicating that conference facilities at ECA headquarters in Addis Ababa were inadequate for the Commission's expanded membership, the General Assembly, in December 1982, authorized an architectural and engineering study for the construction of new facilities. The Secretary-General's reports noted that, although additional office space had been completed in 1976, there had been no additions to the original conference building since its construction in 1961. That building and an adjoining eight-storey office building, forming the nucleus of the ECA complex, were known as Africa Hall.

ECA action. On 30 April 1982[7] the ECA Conference of Ministers, citing a need for adequate facilities at its headquarters to service meetings with an increasing number of participants from the Commission's enlarged membership, requested the ECA Executive Secretary to arrange for an architectural and engineering design study, with cost estimates, of required new conference facilities and allied services. It asked that this be done in time for the Assembly to approve the project so that construction could begin in 1983.

In a preliminary report to the Economic and Social Council in July,[5] the Secretary-General said there was not enough time to prepare the design study and costing for the Council's consideration. However, programme recommendations would be presented at the 1982 session of the Assembly.

Economic and Social Council action. By a resolution adopted without vote on 30 July,[8] the Economic and Social Council requested the Secretary-General to submit as a matter of urgency his final report on expansion of ECA conference facilities, and invited the Assembly to take appropriate action on that report at its 1982 session.

This resolution had been recommended without vote on 28 July by the Council's First Committee, on a revised draft submitted by a Vice-Chairman following informal consultations on an earlier text sponsored by 15 African States and introduced by Nigeria.[2] That text, later withdrawn, would have had the Council decide to take measures to ensure that the Assembly made a final decision in 1982 on expansion of ECA conference facilities so that implementation of the project could commence in 1983.

Reporting to the Council in October 1982,[6] the Secretary-General again said there had not been sufficient time for a full-scale architectural and engineering study, which normally took up to 10 months. However, inadequacies of existing facilities had been identified and feasibility studies had pointed to possible solutions. The facilities were considered inadequate because the 84 seats at table in Africa Hall (the main meeting room) were insufficient for normal ECA meetings, the small committee rooms were inadequate for subcommittees and should be converted to office space, and large meetings had sometimes had to be accommodated in a converted lounge in the cafeteria building.

Design studies had examined two possible solutions: enlarging Africa Hall and adding dependent buildings, or erecting a new building. The only way to commence construction in 1983 would be by altering the existing building, but that could lead to design and construction problems which could prevent the start of work in 1983. A complete remodelling of Africa Hall could increase seating capacity at table by about 75 per cent, but such alteration work might make it necessary to suspend or seriously reduce the conference schedule for up to two years. Moreover, any additions to the building would present architectural and aesthetic problems, as the structure was considered a historic building and the surroundings left little room for additions. A new building could be erected at the rear of the existing site on land that would be given to the United Nations by the Ethiopian Government.

On 27 October 1982, acting on an oral proposal by its President, the Council decided without vote to take note of the Secretary-General's report and transmit it to the Assembly.[1]

General Assembly action. As requested by the General Assembly in December 1981,[10] the Secretary-General presented to the Assembly's Fifth Committee in December 1982 a report on the adequacy of conference facilities at ECA headquarters.[4] The report stated his conclusion that the construction of additional facilities was required and that the need had become acute because of the substantial increase in the number and size of ECA meetings. At least one large, two medium-sized and four small conference rooms were needed, the large one designed for 200 delegates at table and 200 advisers behind. The existing Africa Hall could be remodeled to serve as one of the medium-sized rooms. He suggested that architects study possible variations to this scheme allowing the construction of up to nine conference rooms. Conference-servicing and documentation facilities should also be relocated for greater efficiency.

The Secretary-General requested authorization for an architectural and engineering study for the proposed new construction and modifications to existing buildings, to be submitted in 1983 at an approximate cost of $500,000. In addition, to alleviate overcrowding for the five years or so before new facilities became available, he proposed the temporary conversion of some existing areas into meeting rooms and the purchase of three sets of portable electronic equipment for simultaneous interpretation, at a cost of some $335,000.

Reporting on these proposals,[3] the Advisory Committee on Administrative and Budgetary Questions (ACABQ) recommended approval of the architectural and engineering study but at a cost of $400,000. It also endorsed the purchase of two rather than three sets of portable interpretation equipment which, with elimination of $15,000 requested for new furniture, would reduce the cost of the interim measures to $235,000.

By a recorded vote of 132 to 1, with 11 abstentions, the Assembly, on 21 December 1982, took note of the reports by the Secretary-General and ACABQ.[9] This action had been recommended on 11 December by the Fifth Committee on an oral proposal by its Chairman. At the same time the Committee approved the additional appropriation of $635,000 recommended by ACABQ. Both actions were taken by 62 votes to 1, with 10 abstentions.

Decision (1982). [1]ESC: 1982/182, 27 Oct., text following.
Draft resolution withdrawn. [2]Algeria, Benin, Egypt, Ethiopia, Kenya, Liberia, Malawi, Mali, Morocco, Nigeria, Sudan, Swaziland, Tunisia, United Republic of Tanzania, Zaire, E/1982/C.1/L.16.
Reports. [3]ACABQ, A/37/7/Add.18; S-G, [4]A/C.5/37/67, [5]E/1982/83, [6]E/1982/111.
Resolutions (1982). [7]ECA (report, E/1982/21): 454(XVII), 30 Apr. [8]ESC: 1982/60, 30 July, text following. [9]GA: 37/237, sect. XI, 21 Dec., text following.
Resolution (prior). [10]GA: 36/176, 17 Dec. 1981 (YUN 1981, p. 635).
Meeting records. ESC: E/1982/SR.51, 54 (30 July, 27 Oct.). GA: 5th Committee, A/C.5/37/SR.64 (11 Dec.); plenary, A/37/PV.114 (21 Dec.).

Economic and Social Council resolution 1982/60

30 July 1982   Meeting 51   Adopted without vote

Approved by First Committee (E/1982/96) without vote, 28 July (meeting 15); draft by Vice-Chairman (E/1982/C.1/L.26/Rev.1), based on informal consultations on 15-nation draft (E/1982/C.1/L.16); agenda item 9.

Expansion of the conference facilities of the Economic Commission for Africa at Addis Ababa

The Economic and Social Council,

Recalling General Assembly resolutions 2616(XXIV) of 17 December 1969 and 2745(XXV) of 17 December 1970, in which the inadequacy of the conference facilities at the headquarters of the Economic Commission for Africa and the responsibility of States Members of the United Nations for the solution of that problem were recognized,

Recalling also Council resolution 1981/65 of 24 July 1981, in which the Council recommended that the General Assembly should request the Secretary-General to study the adequacy of existing conference facilities at the headquarters of the Economic Commission for Africa

to meet the demands thereon as a result of its enlarged membership and increased activities,

Recalling further General Assembly resolution 36/176 of 17 December 1981, in which the Assembly requested the Secretary-General to report the findings of the study, together with his suggestions, through the Economic and Social Council at its second regular session of 1982, to the General Assembly at its thirty-seventh session,

Taking note of resolution 454(XVII) of 30 April 1982 of the Conference of Ministers of the Economic Commission for Africa, in which the Conference recommended that the Economic and Social Council, at its second regular session of 1982, should take all necessary measures to ensure that the General Assembly, at its thirty-seventh session, would approve the project and make the necessary provision so that construction work could begin in 1983,

1. *Takes note* of the preliminary report of the Secretary-General on the expansion of the conference facilities of the Economic Commission for Africa at Addis Ababa;

2. *Requests* the Secretary-General to submit, as a matter of urgency, his final report to the Economic and Social Council at its resumed second regular session of 1982;

3. *Invites* the General Assembly to consider at its thirty-seventh session the final report of the Secretary-General and the comments formulated thereon by the Economic and Social Council during its resumed second regular session of 1982, and to take all appropriate action.

Economic and Social Council decision 1982/182

Adopted without vote

Oral proposal by President; agenda item 9.

Expansion of the conference facilities of the Economic Commission for Africa at Addis Ababa

At its 54th plenary meeting, on 27 October 1982, the Council took note of the report of the Secretary-General on the adequacy of the conference facilities of the Economic Commission for Africa at Addis Ababa, prepared in pursuance of its resolution 1982/60 of 30 July 1982, and decided to transmit it, together with the views expressed by delegations during the resumed second regular session of 1982 of the Council, to the General Assembly for consideration at its thirty-seventh session.

General Assembly resolution 37/237, section XI

21 December 1982   Meeting 114   132-1-11 (recorded vote)

Approved by Fifth Committee (A/37/790) by vote (62-1-10), 11 December (meeting 64); oral proposal by Chairman; agenda item 103.

Adequacy of the conference facilities of the Economic Commission for Africa at Addis Ababa

[*The General Assembly . . .*]

Takes note of the report of the Secretary-General on the adequacy of the conference facilities of the Economic Commission for Africa at Addis Ababa and of the related report of the Advisory Committee on Administrative and Budgetary Questions;

. . .

Recorded vote in Assembly as follows:

In favour: Afghanistan, Algeria, Angola, Argentina, Austria, Bahamas, Bahrain, Bangladesh, Barbados, Benin, Bhutan, Bolivia, Botswana, Brazil, Bulgaria, Burma, Burundi, Byelorussian SSR, Cape Verde, Central African Republic, Chad, Chile, China, Colombia, Comoros, Congo, Costa Rica, Cuba, Cyprus, Czechoslovakia, Democratic Kampuchea, Democratic Yemen, Denmark, Dominican Republic, Ecuador, Egypt, Ethiopia, Fiji, Finland, Gabon, Gambia, German Democratic Republic, Ghana, Greece, Grenada, Guatemala, Guinea, Guinea-Bissau, Guyana, Honduras, Hungary, Iceland, India, Indonesia, Iran, Iraq, Ireland, Israel, Ivory Coast, Jamaica, Jordan, Kenya, Kuwait, Lao People's Democratic Republic, Lebanon, Lesotho, Liberia, Libyan Arab Jamahiriya, Madagascar, Malawi, Malaysia, Maldives, Mali, Malta, Mauritania, Mexico, Mongolia, Morocco, Mozambique, Nepal, Nicaragua, Niger, Nigeria, Norway, Oman, Pakistan, Panama, Papua New Guinea, Paraguay, Peru, Philippines, Poland, Portugal, Qatar, Romania, Rwanda, Saint Lucia, Samoa, Sao Tome and Principe, Saudi Arabia, Senegal, Sierra Leone, Singapore, Solomon Islands, Somalia, Spain, Sri Lanka, Sudan, Suriname, Swaziland, Sweden, Syrian Arab Republic, Thailand, Togo, Trinidad and Tobago, Tunisia, Turkey, Uganda, Ukrainian SSR, USSR, United Arab Emirates, United Republic of Cameroon, United Republic of Tanzania, Upper Volta, Uruguay, Venezuela, Viet Nam, Yemen, Yugoslavia, Zaire, Zambia, Zimbabwe.

Against: United States.

Abstaining: Australia, Belgium, Canada, France, Germany, Federal Republic of, Italy, Japan, Luxembourg, Netherlands, New Zealand, United Kingdom.

Regional institutions

The establishment of a buffer fund to help ECA-sponsored regional and subregional institutions through temporary periods of financial need was noted with satisfaction on 30 April 1982 by the ECA Conference of Ministers.[3] The Conference appealed to African States to join the various institutions and asked those in arrears to pay up.

The Conference of Chief Executives of ECA-sponsored Regional and Subregional Institutions, which had established the buffer fund in 1981, held its third meeting in 1982 (Addis Ababa, 29 November–2 December).[1] It set up a committee to draw up rules for the fund's operation and management, and decided that each institution contribute no less than $10,000 for each of the years 1983 and 1984. The Conference also decided to inaugurate in 1983 a bulletin on the activities of the institutions.

The Secretary-General presented to the Economic and Social Council in June 1982 a report[2] describing work done by non-governmental organizations and by some of the ECA-sponsored institutions in implementing the 1980 Lagos Plan of Action for the economic development of Africa.[4] It said there were 24 such institutions, active in regard to financial and banking services (4), earth resources services (5), industrial development (6), social and economic development planning and management (6), and trade and transport (3). They were financed by African Governments, the United Nations Development Programme, the United Nations Fund for Population Activities and bilateral donors.

Developments affecting individual institutions in 1982 included action to strengthen the financial base of the African-Institute for Economic Development and Planning, and General Assembly approval of new statutes for the Regional Institute for Population Studies and the Institut de formation et de recherche démographiques. A decision in principle was taken to establish an African institute for future studies.

Reports. [1]Conference of chief executives of ECA-sponsored institutions, E/ECA/CM.9/14 (summary); [2]S-G, E/1982/80.
Resolution (1982). [3]ECA (report, E/1982/21): 451(XVII), 30 Apr.
Yearbook reference. [4]1980, p. 548.

Twenty-fifth anniversary observance

Proclaiming 1983 as the Silver Jubilee Anniversary of the establishment of ECA by the Economic and Social Council in 1958,[2] the ECA Conference of Ministers, on 30 April 1982,[1] called on its members to join in the commemoration by issuing postage stamps and souvenirs, organizing local celebrations, participating in exhibitions and other social and cultural events at ECA headquarters, and donating prizes for competitions.

Resolution (1982). [1]ECA (report, E/1982/21): 455(XVII), 30 Apr.
Resolution (prior). [2]ESC: 617 A (XXV), 29 Apr. 1958 (YUN 1958, p. 194).

Co-operation between the Southern African Development Co-ordination Conference and the United Nations

By a resolution of 21 December 1982,[1] the General Assembly recognized the Southern African Development Co-ordination Conference as a subregional organization whose work was consistent with the objectives and principles of the Charter of the United Nations. Recognizing also that the Conference had been mandated by its members to co-ordinate projects and programmes, the Assembly requested the Secretary-General to promote co-operation between United Nations bodies and organizations and the Conference. United Nations organizations were requested, in formulating their programmes, to take into account the need to enhance their co-operation with the Conference. The Secretary-General was asked to report in 1983 on implementation of the resolution.

The resolution was adopted without vote, following similar approval on 29 November by the Assembly's Second (Economic and Financial) Committee. The draft was sponsored by 17 African States, Australia and Sweden, and was introduced by Botswana. It was approved with one change agreed upon in informal consultations and announced orally by a Committee Vice-Chairman: in the last preambular paragraph, which had stated that the attainment of economic self-reliance by members of the Conference would contribute to the struggle against *apartheid* in South Africa, the words "attainment of" were replaced by the word "increased".

Resolution (1982). [1]GA: 37/248, 21 Dec., text following.
Meeting records. GA: 2nd Committee, A/C.2/37/SR.3, 5-8, 20-26, 33, 40, *43, 44* (25 Oct.-29 Nov.); plenary, A/37/PV.115 (21 Dec.).

General Assembly resolution 37/248

21 December 1982   Meeting 115   Adopted without vote

Approved by Second Committee (A/37/680/Add.6) without vote, 29 November (meeting 44); 19-nation draft (A/C.2/37/L.42), orally revised in informal consultations; agenda item 71 *(g).*

Sponsors: Angola, Australia, Botswana, Burundi, Cape Verde, Egypt, Guinea-Bissau, Lesotho, Liberia, Malawi, Mali, Mozambique, Sao Tome and Principe, Sierra Leone, Swaziland, Sweden, United Republic of Tanzania, Zambia, Zimbabwe.

Co-operation between the United Nations and the Southern African Development Co-ordination Conference

The General Assembly,

Having heard the statement made on behalf of the States members of the Southern African Development Co-ordination Conference (Angola, Botswana, Lesotho, Malawi, Mozambique, Swaziland, United Republic of Tanzania, Zambia and Zimbabwe) by the representative of Botswana as Chairman of the Conference,

Noting that the aims of the States members of the Southern African Development Co-ordination Conference are to strengthen their economies, to reduce their economic dependence, in particular but not only on South Africa, to forge links between member States in order to create genuine and equitable regional integration, to mobilize resources for the implementation of national, inter-State and regional policies and to harmonize action to secure international co-operation within the framework of the strategy for economic liberation,

Recalling its resolutions 3201(S-VI) and 3202(S-VI) of 1 May 1974, containing the Declaration and the Programme of Action on the Establishment of a New International Economic Order, 3281(XXIX) of 12 December 1974, containing the Charter of Economic Rights and Duties of States, 3362(S-VII) of 16 September 1975 on development and international economic co-operation and 35/56 of 5 December 1980, the annex to which contains the International Development Strategy for the Third United Nations Development Decade,

Recalling also its resolutions 35/66 B of 5 December 1980 and section II of resolution 36/182 of 17 December 1981 on the Industrial Development Decade for Africa, resolutions 36/180 of 17 December 1981 on special measures for the social and economic development of Africa in the 1980s, 36/177 of 17 December 1981 on the Transport and Communications Decade in Africa, 35/58 of 5 December 1980 on the specific action related to the particular needs and problems of land-locked developing countries and 36/194 of 17 December 1981, in which it endorsed the Substantial New Programme of Action for the 1980s for the Least Developed Countries,

Recalling further paragraph 26 of its resolution 36/121 B of 10 December 1981, in which it requested the Secretary-General to prepare, in consultation with the United Nations Development Programme, a comprehensive programme of assistance to States which are neighbours of South Africa and Namibia, with a view to enabling those States to move towards complete self-reliance,

Recognizing that primary responsibility for their development rests with those States and that there is an increasing commitment by the States members of the Southern African Development Co-ordination Conference to deploy domestic resources towards the implementation of its programmes,

Welcoming the initiative taken by the States members of the Southern African Development Co-ordination Conference, some of which are least developed and land-locked developing countries, to implement an integrated and co-ordinated regional economic strategy aimed at collective self-reliance and autonomous development in harmony with the Lagos Plan of Action for the Implementation of the Monrovia Strategy for the Economic Development of Africa,

Noting with appreciation the assistance which has been rendered and the pledges made by the international community for projects falling within the framework of the Southern African Development Co-ordination Conference,

Convinced that the increased economic self-reliance by the States members of the Southern African Development Co-ordination Conference would contribute to the struggle against the *apartheid* policies of South Africa,

1. *Recognizes* the Southern African Development Co-ordination Conference as a subregional organization whose work is consistent with the objectives and principles enshrined in the Charter of the United Nations;

2. *Recognizes* that the Southern African Development Co-ordination Conference has been mandated by the member States concerned to co-ordinate projects and programmes falling within its competence;

3. *Requests* the Secretary-General to take appropriate measures to promote co-operation between the organs, organizations and bodies of the United Nations system and the Southern African Development Co-ordination Conference;

4. *Requests* the organs, organizations and bodies of the United Nations system, in formulating their programmes, to take into account the need to further enhance their co-operation with the Southern African Development Co-ordination Conference;

5. *Further requests* the Secretary-General to report to the General Assembly at its thirty-eighth session on the implementation of the present resolution.

Asia and the Pacific

ESCAP activities. The Economic and Social Commission for Asia and the Pacific (ESCAP) held its thirty-eighth session at its headquarters at Bangkok, Thailand, from 23 March to 2 April 1982.[1] Food supply and distribution was the session's main theme, and ESCAP discussed ways to increase regional food security, including the possibility of creating an Asia-Pacific food bank. The Commission initiated a study of subregional and regional food security arrangements, a possible trade information and management network of food and agricultural inputs, and means of increasing financial resources for food and agriculture.

Eight ESCAP committees met in 1982. The Committee on Development Planning (November) reviewed proposed activities to assist least developed, land-locked and island developing countries, as well as possible studies on Pacific basin co-operation. The Committee on Trade (November) reiterated the importance of expanding intraregional trade and strengthening regional co-operation. The Committee on Shipping, and Transport and Communications (December) discussed developments and activities in shipping, ports and inland waterways. The Committee on Industry, Technology, Human Settlements and the Environment (September) recommended that ESCAP develop small- and medium-scale industries, expand advisory services for technology and technology transfer, and strengthen promotion of environmental awareness; it also emphasized the importance of settlement planning.

The Committee on Natural Resources (October) made recommendations on mineral and water resources and energy, and suggested that ESCAP prepare guidelines to assist developing countries to implement the United Nations Convention on the Law of the Sea. The Committee on Agricultural Development (January) recommended further consideration of a proposed regional food trade information and management network, and urged efforts to strengthen national farm broadcasting systems. The Committee on Social Development (November) reviewed programmes to integrate women and youth in development, and initiated a programme on health and development. The Typhoon Committee (November) noted the successful completion of the first Typhoon Operational Experiment, improving typhoon forecasting techniques.

The Third Asian and Pacific Population Conference (September) adopted the Asia-Pacific Call for Action on Population and Development, which encouraged an integrated approach to population, resources and development, and co-operation among ESCAP members.

With regard to two regional centres established in 1981, ESCAP approved the charter of the Asian and Pacific Development Centre, and the statute of the Regional Co-ordination Centre for Research and Development of Coarse Grains, Pulses, Roots and Tuber Crops.

Increased attention was given to the Pacific member countries, facilitated by a new ESCAP/Pacific Liaison Office in Nauru. ESCAP expanded its co-operation with the South Pacific Commission and the South Pacific Bureau for Economic Co-operation, and continued its industrial survey of the South Pacific, undertaken in conjunction with the Asian Development Bank and the South Pacific Bureau for Economic Co-operation. The Pacific island countries requested an expansion of ESCAP activities in the subregion.

The Meeting on Reassessment of Programme Priorities of the Commission (September) established criteria for the ESCAP 1984-1985 work programme. In one of the 11 resolutions adopted at its 1982 session, ESCAP decided on terms of reference for its legislative committees to enhance co-ordination of activities.

Report. [1]ESCAP, E/1982/20.
Publications. Economic Bulletin for Asia and the Pacific, vol. XXXIII, No. 1 (ST/ESCAP/242), Sales No. E.84.II.F.2; No. 2 (ST/ESCAP/272), Sales No. E.84.II.F.16.

Economic and social trends

Problems relating to food supplies, to the availability of energy resources and to the capacity to finance imports continued to be major constraints on the economic growth of ESCAP member countries in 1982, according to the *Economic and Social Survey of Asia and the Pacific 1981*,[2] a summary of which was noted by the Economic and Social Council on 30 July 1982.[1] Although food accounted for more than four fifths of agricultural production in the region and most countries made good recovery in 1981 from bad harvests, many remained net grain importers. The energy crisis related more to a growing scarcity of traditional fuels than to high prices for commercial energy; oil prices in real terms had fallen by about 7 per cent by the end of 1981, with a further decrease of one tenth expected in 1982. Terms of trade for non-oil developing countries, which had deteriorated by almost one fifth in 1980, did not improve in 1981, as prices for primary commodities fell by 14 per cent. The combined trade deficit of non-oil developing countries in Asia (including China) was $18 billion in the first half of 1981.

Decision (1982). [1]ESC: 1982/177, para. (g), 30 July.
Surveys. [2]*Economic and Social Survey of Asia and the Pacific 1981* (ST/ESA/187), Sales No. E.82.II.F.1 (summary, E/1982/64); *1982* (ST/ESCAP/217), Sales No. E.83.II.F.1 (summary, E/1983/51).
Publication. Economic Bulletin for Asia and the Pacific, vol. XXXIII, No. 2 (ST/ESCAP/272), Sales No. E.84.II.F.16.

Development policy and regional economic co-operation

The ESCAP Committee on Development Planning (Bangkok, 23-26 November 1982)[3] considered project proposals for 1983 to assist least developed, land-locked and island developing countries. The Committee advised the ESCAP secretariat to conduct activities in accordance with the priorities of the Substantial New Programme of Action for the 1980s for the Least Developed Countries (LDCs), adopted in August 1981 by the United Nations Conference on Least Developed Countries,[9] and to act in close co-ordination with Governments of LDCs. Regarding possible studies on the implications of Pacific basin co-operation for the region's developing countries, the Committee recommended that ESCAP work in clearly delineated technical areas, bearing in mind the goals of the International Development Strategy for the Third United Nations Development Decade (1981-1990).[8] It supported ESCAP activities on the analysis and provision of assistance on special aspects of public administration, and suggested further studies on transnational corporations.

The Expert Group Meeting on Domestic Stabilization of International Trade Instability in the South Pacific (Pattaya, Thailand, 4-6 August)[5] recommended several policy and planning options, including increased economic co-operation among South Pacific island countries, diversification of export markets and import sources, integrated planning for stabilization and improved commodity stabilization designs and arrangements. The Group also recommended that ESCAP undertake further analytical studies and provide technical assistance to the subregion in this regard.

The Expert Group Meeting on Integration of Tax Planning into Development Planning in the ESCAP Region (Bangkok, 21-24 September)[2] found an urgent need for the region's developing countries to incorporate tax planning into development planning in an operationally useful manner. Recommended were national studies to improve tax planning and the establishment or strengthening of national tax research institutions, with ESCAP assistance, to ensure consistency between tax policies and development objectives. Analytical studies on six countries, completed in February and presented at the Meeting, were the result of the first phase of a project begun in 1981 to examine the integration of tax planning into development planning.

The Expert Group on the Association of South-East Asian Nations (ASEAN) and Pacific Economic Co-operation (Bangkok, 1 and 2 June)[1] recommended a series of tripartite (government, private sector and academia) consultative meetings to discuss possible regional co-operation in manufactures, agricultural products, minerals, investment and technology. It also recommended that ESCAP provide technical assistance to further Pacific basin co-operation.

The Expert Group on Development Issues and Policies (Bangkok, 10-12 November)[4] suggested drafting improvements to the chapter on major constraints on regional progress for the *Economic and Social Survey of Asia and the Pacific 1982* and advised the secretariat on topics and organization of future surveys.

The Regional Seminar on an Interlinked Country Model System (Bangkok, 8-10 November) reviewed the econometric modelling work carried out by the participants and discussed how the secretariat might further assist member countries in developing short-term planning and projection models to aid in management of their economies. Also discussed was the ongoing ESCAP work to develop a linkage system based on trade flows among the region's countries and between them and the rest of the world, as part of a global link system of econometric projections.

A regional workshop on the role of mini-computers and micro-computers as tools for economic and social development (Bangkok, 8-16 November)[6] suggested the establishment of a high-level national body in each country to make better use of modern technology by co-ordinating government information systems and by monitoring and promoting new information products and services.

On 1 April,[7] ESCAP urged Governments to renew efforts for the early launching of global negotiations on international economic co-operation for development and requested the Secretary-General to convey to the international community the concern of the Asian and Pacific countries for such negotiations.

The ESCAP Development Planning Division offered a course on problems of development in Asia and the Pacific at Chulalongkorn University (Bangkok, November 1981–February 1982).

Publications. [1]*ASEAN and Pacific Economic Co-operation: Report of the Expert Group Meeting* (ST/ESCAP/228), Sales No. E.83.II.F.17; [2]*Integration of Tax Planning into Development Planning in the ESCAP Region: Report of the Expert Group Meeting* (ST/ESCAP/231), Sales No. E.84.II.F.3.
Reports. [3]Committee on Development Planning, E/ESCAP/290; [4]Expert Group on Development Issues and Policies, DP/EGDIP/1; [5]Expert Group Meeting on Domestic Stabilization of International Trade Instability, E/ESCAP/DP.4/2; [6]Workshop on mini-computers and micro-computers and development, E/ESCAP/STAT.5/241.
Resolution (1982). [7]ESCAP (report, E/1982/20): 227(XXXVIII), 1 Apr.
Resolution (prior). [8]GA: 35/36, annex, 5 Dec. 1980 (YUN 1980, p. 503).
Yearbook reference. [9]1981, p. 406.

Asian and Pacific Development Centre

On 1 April 1982,[2] ESCAP adopted the Charter of the Asian and Pacific Development Centre, which had been established in August 1981 at Kuala Lumpur, Malaysia,[3] and requested the Executive Secretary to open it for signature. The Centre's General Council and Management Board were urged to ensure that the representative of Malaysia—the host country—be Chairman of the

Board for the first three years. The Charter, opened for signature at ESCAP headquarters on 9 September, was signed by Malaysia and 11 other countries.

By the Charter's provisions, the Centre had been established as an intergovernmental institution for policy research and training relating to Asian and Pacific development. The Centre's functions were to conduct research on its own and encourage research among regional institutions; to conduct programmes for the exchange of development experience; to facilitate training, utilizing networks of national, regional and subregional research and training institutions; to serve as a clearing-house for information; and to provide consultancy services. In addition to a General Council, to be composed of all Centre members, a Management Board was to be established to ensure proper implementation of the Centre's work programme and accountability of expenditures. A Director was to be appointed to administer the Centre with the aim of making it an institution of high academic standing.

The Board met in February and November to monitor programme progress.[1] Transitional research projects were completed on rural employment strategies, rural migration policies and development, access planning for target groups and strategies for integrating women in national planning processes. Long-term research work was begun in energy planning and management, food security, human resources mobilization and integration of women in development. Six training seminars were organized in collaboration with national institutes, as were four major workshops, in collaboration with United Nations agencies and national institutions. A development information clearing-house and referral system programme was initiated.

Jointly with the Ministry of Science, Technology and Environment of Malaysia, the Centre conducted a regional symposium (11-15 January) to integrate environmental and economic assessment of development projects and to improve the methodology and analytical techniques for such a unified assessment.

Report. [1]Asian and Pacific Development Centre Management Board, E/ESCAP/329.
Resolution (1982). [2]ESCAP (report, E/1982/20): 225(XXXVIII), 1 Apr.
Yearbook reference. [3]1981, p. 636.

Mekong River basin development

The Interim Committee for Co-ordination of Investigations of the Lower Mekong Basin (thirteenth, fourteenth and fifteenth sessions: Hanoi, Viet Nam, 14-19 January; Bangkok, 23-31 March and 6-11 September) reviewed implementation of its 1982 work programme and adopted one for

1983. Activities fell under six main areas: hydrology and meteorology; basin planning; land and water resources development; navigation improvement; agriculture and fisheries; and power, industry and minerals. As noted by the Committee's annual report to ESCAP,[1] continuing institutional support for these activities by the United Nations Development Programme (UNDP), the main funding agency, was confirmed by a new project document, signed with UNDP, for the period April 1982 to March 1985.

During 1982, the network of hydrologic and meteorologic stations was expanded, including installation of hydrologic stations in the upper Nam Ngum reaches (Lao People's Democratic Republic). Equipment, including a river tugboat, was delivered to the Huong My water control project designed to control salinity intrusion and to supply irrigation water (Viet Nam). A technical seminar on tidal hydraulics and salinity intrusion was held to improve technical knowledge of riparian engineers and awareness of latest developments (Ho Chi Minh City, Viet Nam, 21-27 October).

Surveys and mapping were completed for six pump stations for the Mekong pump irrigation project (Lao People's Democratic Republic). Under a project to improve agricultural production in northeast Thailand, 26 electrical pump units were installed at 18 stations along the Mun and Chi rivers, and construction work on the distribution systems at 16 stations was completed. Construction continued on a flood protection and swamp reclamation project on the Vientiane plain (Lao People's Democratic Republic), and work began on a flood control and irrigation project on the Huai Mong River (Thailand). Improvement of the main ferry channels of the Nong Khai/Thanaleng river-crossing was carried out by a joint Lao/Thai team from January to April.

Additional contributions (including pledges) for projects in the Committee's work programme totalled some $30 million in 1982, raising to $509 million the total resources contributed to the programme from its inception to 31 December 1982.

Report. [1]Committee on Mekong basin, MKG/104, transmitted by ESCAP secretariat note, E/ESCAP/323.

Unified approach to development planning

On 1 April 1982,[1] ESCAP called on its Executive Secretary to continue efforts to pay appropriate attention to a unified approach to economic and social development and planning. It invited him to collect, on request, information from member countries on the application of such an approach to development planning—in particular, to plan formulation, monitoring and implementation—and to synthesize the information for distribution.

Resolution (1982). [1]ESCAP (report, E/1982/20): 229(XXXVIII), 1 Apr.

Technical co-operation

Expenditures on ESCAP technical co-operation activities[1] in 1982 totalled $13.6 million. While some $6.7 came from trust funds, the largest single source was the United Nations Development Programme (UNDP), which supplied $5.1 million for projects on agricultural machinery, industrial development, manpower training and development, maritime transport, natural resources and energy, public administration, remote sensing, science and technology, development of national statistical capabilities and trade promotion.

The United Nations Fund for Population Activities provided institutional support to the ESCAP Population Division and some $983,000 for: advisory services on demography, population censuses and surveys, and vital statistics; training in demography and population statistics; studies on fertility levels and trends; and fellowships for demographers.

Under the United Nations regular programme of technical co-operation, ESCAP responded to 35 government requests for advisory services by sending 27 missions which stressed the needs of the least developed and island developing countries. In all, expenditures under this programme amounted to $851,000.

The United Nations Development Advisory Team for the South Pacific, financed by ESCAP donor countries and UNDP, sent 37 short-term consultancy missions to the island developing countries.

A Regional Seminar on Technical Co-operation among Developing Countries (TCDC) for Senior Government Officials of Asia and the Pacific Region (New Delhi, India, 23 April–1 May) discussed ways of identifying TCDC capacities and needs; the institutional framework, and legal and financial arrangements for TCDC; and the role of developing and developed countries, the United Nations system and intergovernmental and non-governmental organizations in supporting TCDC.

Report. [1]S-G, DP/1983/18/Add.1, 2.

International trade

The ESCAP Committee on Trade (twenty-fourth session, Bangkok, 2-8 November 1982),[1] drew attention to the adverse economic conditions that were straining international trade relations, with severe consequences for the poorest countries. Cited were proliferating protectionist measures; declining export earnings due to reduced demand for primary commodities; the high cost of fuel, capital goods and technology; declining aid flows; and high interest rates and rapidly swelling debts. Agreeing that a ministerial conference should consider these issues in relation to trade co-operation in the region, the Committee asked the secretariat to make proposals to the next ESCAP session for such a conference, its agenda, a date and venue.

The Committee observed that its Trade Co-operation Group should concentrate on activities yielding practical results. It reiterated the desirability of a regional export refinancing scheme and urged increased assistance to national focal points of trade information including personnel training. It endorsed the secretariat's work in promoting regional co-operative arrangements on selected commodities and urged technical assistance to commodity-producing and -exporting countries to help them prepare for international commodity agreements and form producers' associations. Financial support was requested for expert group meetings to consider setting up a multinational export credit insurance scheme, as well as for a proposed meeting to review a draft agreement to combat customs fraud and smuggling in the light of comments from Governments.

The Trade Co-operation Group (fourth session, Bangkok, 14 and 15 January)[5] reviewed progress in intraregional trade co-operation and expansion based on the reports of its subgroups. The Subgroup for a Network of Trade Promotion Centres (fourth and fifth sessions, Bangkok: 12 and 13 January; 18 and 19 October)[3] completed the design and operational procedures for a regional trade information network. It urged completion of national trade profiles for compilation and dissemination through the network. The Subgroup for Harmonization of Trade Statistics, Customs Tariff Nomenclature and Customs and Transport Facilitation Procedures and Documentation (Bangkok, 6 and 7 January) continued to give priority to the preparation of a manual on harmonizing the collection and presentation of international trade statistics and considered a study on a model constitution for a national facilitation institution with a view to setting up a regional network of such institutions. The Subgroup for Trade-creating Joint Ventures (fifth session, Bangkok, 13 and 14 October)[4] recommended that an expert group consider market access, fiscal privileges, pricing guidelines, investment guarantees and other issues so that a co-ordinated approach to policy formulation might be evolved.

An expert group meeting, sponsored by ESCAP and the United Nations Conference on Trade and Development (UNCTAD) (Kathmandu, Nepal, 26-29 January),[2] examined a draft multilateral agreement on mutual administrative assistance for the prevention, investigation and repression of customs offences. The group recommended transmittal of the draft to ESCAP members for consideration.

The *Ad Hoc* Expert Group Meeting on an Export Refinancing Scheme agreed that if the proposed refinancing facility could be operated by an existing multinational regional institution, such as the Asian Development Bank, inaugural delays

would be avoided; failing that, a similar institution could be set up for the purpose.

The Meeting of the Board of Directors of the Asian Clearing Union (tenth session, New Delhi, India, 11 and 12 February) decided that a technical committee be set up to consider ways of improving current procedures and to examine the possibility of channelling payments for petroleum products through the Union.

The Standing Committee of the Bangkok Agreement (twelfth session, Bangkok, 20-22 October), decided that, for the next round of negotiations to update the First Agreement on Trade Negotiations among Developing Member Countries of ESCAP, the region's developing countries should be invited to accede to the Agreement and join the negotiations.

Other 1982 activities included a joint ESCAP/UNCTAD/UNDP workshop on special measures in favour of least developed land-locked countries (Kathmandu, November)[2] to discuss specific aspects of the transit trade of those countries; meetings on import management, dissemination of trade information, trade with China, and the role of private trade organizations in trade promotion; and advisory services to more than 20 countries and institutions. A survey of Pacific island Governments was undertaken in October to determine their priorities in trade information.

Reports. [1]Committee on Trade, E/ESCAP/289. [2]Expert Group Meeting for action against fraud and smuggling, TRADE/MAACFS/2; [3]Subgroup for Network of Trade Promotion Centres, TRADE/TCG/SG.1/11; TRADE/TCG.5/1 (Oct.); [4]Subgroup for Trade-creating Joint Ventures, TRADE/TCG.5/1; [5]Trade Co-operation Group, E/ESCAP/TRADE.24/6-TRADE/TCG.4/4.

Publications. Foreign Trade Statistics of Asia and the Pacific, 1976-1979, vol. XII, Series B (ST/ESCAP/200), Sales No. E.82.II.F.13; *1979,* vol. XVIII, Series A (ST/ESCAP/206), Sales No. E.82.II.F.14. *Prices of Selected Asia/Pacific Products* (quarterly).

Trade expositions

On 1 April 1982,[1] ESCAP requested its Executive Secretary to consult interested member countries and international organizations on the possibilities of organizing an ESCAP trade exposition and of providing assistance for countries wishing to participate. He was requested, in the event of such an exposition, to evaluate its benefits with a view to holding such events regularly, and member countries were urged to consider the possibility of hosting them.

Resolution (1982). [1]ESCAP (report, E/1982/20): 221(XXXVIII), 1 Apr.

Commodities

The Government Consultation among Jute Producing Countries[1] (fourth session, Kathmandu, Nepal, 27-30 January; special session, Bangkok, 18-21 May; fifth session, Calcutta, India,

31 August–4 September) agreed on a plan to implement several co-operative activities such as export market strategies, supply adjustment, and improvement of productivity and quality. The Meeting of Directors of Research/Scientists and Experts on Standardization and Quality Control of Jute Goods (Calcutta, 17-20 March)[4] discussed existing standards, specifications and quality control methods adopted by the jute-producing countries of Bangladesh, China, India and Nepal for selected jute goods. The Meeting made recommendations for formulating uniform standards to help promote jute products in the international market.

On the recommendation of a Regional Working Group Meeting on Silk (Bangalore, India, 1-4 June),[5] a Regional Consultative Group on Silk was organized. At its first meeting (Pattaya, Thailand, 14 and 15 December),[2] the Consultative Group adopted its constitution and rules of procedure and elaborated the activities of a co operative programme for silk in the ESCAP region, proposed by the Working Group. Those activities included production, processing, marketing, research and development, and collection of statistics and information dissemination. An Expert Group Meeting on Research and Development of Silk followed (Pattaya, 16-20 December),[3] to identify common problems faced by the silk-producing countries and to recommend solutions.

The Intergovernmental Consultative Forum of Developing Tropical Timber-Producing/Exporting Countries (Kuala Lumpur, Malaysia, October) recommended that the Forum continue to serve as the regional institution to facilitate dialogue and co-operative efforts, and asked that the ESCAP secretariat serve as transitional co-ordinator.

Reports. [1]Consultation among Jute Producing Countries, TRADE/GCJPC/8 (Jan.), TRADE/GCJPC/13 (Aug./Sept.), TRADE/GCJPC (SS)/2 (May); [2]Consultative Group on Silk, TRADE/TCG/RCGS/4; [3]Expert Group Meeting on Research and Development of Silk, TRADE/TCG/RDS/1; [4]Meeting of Research/Scientists and Experts on Jute Goods, TRADE/MQCJG/1; [5]Working Group Meeting on Silk, TRADE/TCG/RMS/2.

Transport, communications and tourism

At its March/April 1982 session, ESCAP considered proclaiming a Transport and Communications Decade for Asia and the Pacific and gave its secretariat responsibility for servicing a regional railway co-operation group. It noted new work on postal service promotion in co-operation with the Universal Postal Union, and supported the secretariat's more active role in work on the economic aspects of air cargo transport in co-operation with the International Civil Aviation Organization.

The Regional Meeting to Promote Transport Infrastructure Development in Rural and Isolated Communities (Bangkok, 1-4 June) discussed the transport planning methodology developed by ESCAP and recommended its application by member countries with changes as appropriate.

ESCAP provided technical advice on tourism development in the Cook Islands, Palau, Samoa, the Solomon Islands and Vanuatu (August/September).

Publication. Transport and Communications Bulletin for Asia and the Pacific, No. 55 (ST/ESCAP/SER.E/55), Sales No. E.82.II.F.12.

Proposed transport and communications decade (1985-1994)

On 1 April 1982,[1] ESCAP invited the Executive Secretary to consult with member countries on the practical desirability of a proposal to proclaim 1985-1994 transport and communications decade for Asia and the Pacific and on the probability of real results from such a decade.

Resolution (1982). [1]ESCAP (report, E/1982/20): 230(XXXVIII), 1 Apr.

Maritime and inland water transport

In 1982, the ESCAP Committee on Shipping, and Transport and Communications: Shipping, Ports and Inland Waterways Wing (sixth session, Bangkok, 7-13 December)[2] made a series of recommendations on maritime and inland water transport. These called for more comprehensive studies on freight charges, continued efforts in establishing and strengthening national freight study units, an expansion of manpower training, expediting the setting up of a regional institute on multimodal transport, studies on cost-saving measures in shipping and on the development of wind-powered vessels, improving national capabilities in ship building and repair, and continued support to national and subregional shippers' organizations. Recommendations relating to ports called for seminars on port containerization, a study of port pricing, greater attention to the mechanization and automation of cargo handling, continued assistance to national port training institutions and intensified work on dredging.

Among activities carried out under the Committee's auspices, the Joint Meeting of Chief Executives of National Shippers' Organizations and Shipowners' Associations (third session, Bangkok, 27 October)[3] decided to organize, with ESCAP assistance, training courses and seminars on currency and bunker adjustment factors and on shippers' contracts, in the light of reports submitted by two working groups which had met in September to study those issues. The Meeting of Chief Executives of National Shippers' Organizations (sixth session, Bangkok, 26 and 27 October) urged co-operation between shippers and shipowners by increasing traffic between national carriers and agreed that freight forwarding should be studied independently by individual shippers' councils since conditions pertaining to freight forwarders' operations differed from country to country.

The Meeting of Chief Executives of Inland Water Transport and Inland Waterways Authorities (first session, Bangkok, 3 and 4 June)[4] reiterated the need to develop inland water transport as an integral part of the region's transport network and gave priority to development and maintenance of inland waterways, terminals and landing facilities, and fleets. A seminar-cum-study tour on inland waterways terminals and landing facilities (China, 16-28 December) stressed the importance and potential of inland waterways as a mode of transport.

The Meeting of Legal Experts on a Model Maritime Code for the ESCAP Region (second session, Bangkok, January) gave further consideration to the preparation of guidelines for drafting a maritime code with the assistance of relevant international organizations.

A Seminar on Planned Maintenance for Port Equipment (Bangkok, 27 September–2 October),[5] held to enhance self-reliance of ports, requested the ESCAP secretariat to organize other seminars on specialized topics for marine, electrical and civil engineers working in ports; to provide guidelines for standard definitions; to act as a clearing-house for performance data; and to mobilize funds for these objectives.

An expert group meeting on Port Management Information Systems (PORTMIS) (Bangkok, 15-19 February) concluded that PORTMIS be further developed by putting it to test and documenting the results for dissemination to all ports and other maritime interests in the region. The test was subsequently carried out and some 800 copies of the report on it were distributed within and outside the region, according to a secretariat note of 8 October.[1]

A seminar on ship financing for the countries of the Association of South-East Asian Nations (Bangkok, March)[6] reported on financing requirements for vessel acquisition by shipowners.

Note. [1]ESCAP secretariat, E/ESCAP/STC.6/18.
Reports. [2]Committee on Shipping, and Transport and Communications: Shipping Ports and Inland Waterways Wing, E/ESCAP/293 & Corr.1; [3]Joint Meeting of national shippers' organizations and shipowners' associations, E/ESCAP/STC.6/24; [4]Meeting on inland water transport and inland waterways, transmitted by ESCAP secretariat note, E/ESCAP/STC.6/21; [5]Seminar on port equipment maintenance, transmitted by ESCAP secretariat note, E/ESCAP/STC.6/28; [6]Seminar on ship financing, ST/ESCAP/215.

Railways

The Intergovernmental Railway Group Meeting (third session, Bangkok, 24-30 August 1982)[1]

reviewed activities related to railway modernization, technology transfer and training, the Trans-Asian railway network and Asian railway master plan, and containerization development for inland multimodal transport.

The Railway Research Co-ordination Group (ninth meeting, Bangkok, 20-23 August),[2] composed of members of research institutes in China, India, Japan and the USSR and of the International Union of Railways, identified the region's railway requirements so that research findings from the institutes might inform the practical recommendations to be made. The Group recommended a feasibility study on a proposed regional railway research centre.

The Seminar-cum-Study Tour on Railway Track Maintenance (Moscow, 22 September–5 October) exposed its participants to USSR railway planning, design, construction, management and maintenance in track technology. Two other seminar-cum-study tours for railway engineers from the ESCAP region were conducted in 1982: on railway electrification (Paris, June) and on modernization of railway signalling and telecommunication (Tokyo, October/November).

The Meeting of the Working Group of Experts on the Trans-Asian Railway Network and the Asian Railway Master Plan (Moscow, 6-9 October)[3] strongly urged ESCAP to implement the network and draw up the master plan as part of a proposed transport and communications decade for Asia and the Pacific. The master plan was to be based on the network and be freight-oriented, and a subgroup of railway experts was to assist ESCAP in following up on the two projects.

Reports. [1]Intergovernmental Railway Group Meeting, E/ESCAP/STC.7/5; [2]Railway Research Co-ordination Group, TRANS/IRGM(3)/20; [3]Working Group of Experts on Trans-Asian Railway Network and Asian Railway Master Plan, E/ESCAP/STC.7/9.

Telecommunication

A Regional Conference-cum-Seminar on Development and Mangement of Telecommunications in Asia and the Pacific (Bangkok, 19-27 January 1982), convened jointly by ESCAP and the International Telecommunication Union, proposed measures to overcome obstacles in telecommunication development and to promote training, regional co-operation, better management and equipment maintenance, the introduction of digital switching and satellite transmission, and resource mobilization.

Industrial development

The ESCAP Committee on Industry, Technology, Human Settlements and the Environment (sixth session, Bangkok, 7-13 September 1982)[1] recommended that the secretariat promote and develop small- and medium-scale industries, complete a project on the public sector's role in large-scale manufacturing industries, continue its study of industrialization trends in developing ESCAP countries, and strengthen and expand the work of the ESCAP Club for Industrial Co-operation. The Committee also made recommendations on the three other main topics of its mandate—science and technology, human settlements and the environment.

The *Ad Hoc* Intergovernmental Meeting of Industrial Planners on Financing Industrialization (Bangkok, 21-25 June)[3] recommended a second meeting to discuss integration of fiscal and financial targets in the economic and industrial plans of ESCAP member countries. The Meeting also recommended studies on ailing industries and on the role of development and finance institutions in assisting small-scale industries.

The Seminar on the Integrated Silk Processing Industry (China, 17-29 September)[4] recommended establishment of a forum for the continuous exchange of information on the development of the silk industry and of a mechanism for intercountry co-operation for other commodities. The Intergovernmental Meeting on Agro- and Allied Industries (fourth session, Bangkok, 30 November–3 December)[2] recommended re-examining export strategies to ensure optimum exploitation of export-growth possibilities in agro- and other resource-based industries.

The Technical Advisory Committee of the Regional Network for Agricultural Machinery (Tokyo, October) reviewed implementation of 1982 programme activities—strengthening of design capabilities, mutual exchange of prototypes and drawings, promotion of local manufacture of agricultural implements and machinery, and information dissemination—and made recommendations for their continued implementation in 1983. The first Regional Workshop of Agricultural Machinery Manufacturers' Associations (Lahore, Pakistan, August) recommended measures to promote local manufacture of agricultural implements and machinery and the organization of zonal or national workshops to consider follow-up action. Another workshop, of agricultural machinery manufacturers' associations, took place in the Philippines.

Under the Regional Network for Agricultural Machinery, a three-month training programme on industrial extension, from 22 August, was organized at the Zhenjiang Institute of Agricultural Machinery (Jiangsu Province, China).

Reports. [1]Committee on Industry, Technology, Human Settlements and Environment, E/ESCAP/288; [2]Intergovernmental Meeting on Agro- and Allied Industries, IHT/IMAAI(4)/16; [3]Intergovernmental Meeting on financing industrialization, E/ESCAP/IHT.6/2; [4]Seminar on Integrated Silk Processing Industry, IHT/IMAAI(4)/9.
Publication. Industrial Development News—Asia and the Pacific, No. 14 (ST/ESCAP/183), Sales No. E.82.II.F.7.

Transnational corporations

In 1982, the Joint Unit of ESCAP and the United Nations Centre on Transnational Corporations (TNCs) continued research, information dissemination, training and advisory services towards strengthening the negotiating capacity of host Governments in relation to TNCs. The Unit completed an interregional project on TNCs and primary commodity exports, and continued projects on technology transfer costs, transnational trading corporations, and on export processing zones and TNCs based in developing countries. Work began on the establishment of national information systems and of a regional information network on TNCs.

The Committee on Development Planning, at its November session, endorsed the research programmes of the Unit and recommended that it study the reasons for minimal TNC investments in the least developed, land-locked and island developing countries and suggest measures to attract more investments. The Committee supported the Unit's research on the feasibility of harmonizing tax and other incentives for TNCs and suggested that a competitive scramble for funds could be minimized through coordination among host countries. Further investigation of the use of transfer prices, aimed at redressing their misuse, was also suggested.

The Regional Workshop on Negotiating with TNCs in the Petrochemical Sector (Bangkok and Pattaya, Thailand, April/May) discussed worldwide markets, international trade, production costs and prices of selected petrochemical products, and financing of petrochemical projects.

Natural resources

The ESCAP Committee on Natural Resources (ninth session, Bangkok, 19-25 October 1982)[1] requested the secretariat to pursue establishment of a Regional Centre for Quaternary Geology in China and to seek member Governments' views on the creation of an intergovernmental consultative committee to the Regional Remote Sensing Programme. It affirmed that the preparation of regional maps should proceed according to the ESCAP work programme. Regarding the 1982 United Nations Convention on the Law of the Sea, the Committee suggested that the ESCAP secretariat consider preparing guidelines on policy framework formulation and management structures, and determine how it could assist developing countries to take advantage of the benefits and meet the obligations resulting from the Convention. The Committee also made recommendations on mineral resources and energy.

The *ESCAP Atlas of Stratigraphy III*[2] was published, with contributions from Australia, Bangladesh, Fiji, India, Indonesia, Nepal, the Solomon Islands and the USSR.

Publications. [1]*Proceedings of the Committee on Natural Resources, Ninth Session, incorporating the triennial review of mineral development activities in the ESCAP region, 1979-1981* (ST/ESCAP/265), Sales No. E.84.II.F.13; [2]*ESCAP Atlas of Stratigraphy III. Stratigraphic Correlation between Sedimentary Basins of the ESCAP Region,* vol. VIII (ST/ESCAP/137), Sales No. E.82.II.F.6.

Mineral resources

At its October 1982 session, the ESCAP Committee on Natural Resources urged donor countries of the Southeast Asia Tin Research and Development Centre to provide experts and equipment for the Centre's proposed geophysical section. It approved the legend and guidelines for an atlas of mineral resources of the ESCAP region, having decided that neither the atlas nor other thematic maps to be prepared would show political boundaries.

At the Meeting on Co-ordination in ESCAP Mineral Programmes (tenth session, Bangkok, March), current and future programmes of the Mineral Resources Section and of related regional and national projects were considered, and activities of mutual interest and co-operation were defined. The Fourth Working Group Meeting on Stratigraphic Correlation between Sedimentary Basins of the ESCAP Region considered the project's progress since the third meeting in 1978 and recommended two new subprojects.

The Committee for Co-ordination of Joint Prospecting for Mineral Resources in Asian Offshore Areas (nineteenth session, Tokyo, 29 November–10 December 1982)[2] decided to establish a working group to synthesize heat flow and geothermal gradient data and agreed that a Regional Centre for Quaternary Geology be established in China. Among a number of meetings held under Committee auspices were two workshops: on sedimentology of Quaternary sediments associated with tin deposits (Phuket, Thailand, 29 January–11 February) and on recoverable hydrocarbon resources (Jakarta, Indonesia, 22-25 February); and a seminar on hydrocarbon occurrence in carbonate rocks (Surabaya, Indonesia, 2-7 August).

The Committee for Co-ordination of Joint Prospecting for Mineral Resources in South Pacific Offshore Areas (eleventh session, Wellington, New Zealand, 9-17 November)[3] admitted Guam as a member. It convened the first session of a working group to implement research programmes on science, tectonics and resources, and recommended that the Intergovernmental Oceanographic Commission co-sponsor the group. It endorsed a preliminary proposal for a South Pacific region diploma in earth science and marine geology at the University of the South Pacific at Suva, Fiji. In co-operation with the Committee, a joint

programme on regional marine geoscientific and mineral resources research (Australia, New Zealand, United States) began in March with the arrival in the region of two United States research vessels to assess hydrocarbon potential and investigate problems of regional tectonic and structural relations.

In 1982, the Regional Mineral Resources Development Centre, at Bandung, Indonesia, carried out 27 technical advisory missions to 19 developing member countries and issued 25 technical reports, according to an ESCAP secretariat note.[1] The Centre completed the second phase of a project to investigate the magnetism and other physical properties of rocks in selected areas of the region's tin granite belt. Two workshops were held, on the importance of mining to industrial development and on biogeochemical exploration in the tropical rain-forest environment (Bandung, 1-6 November and 29 November–4 December). The Centre's Governing Council, at its fifth session, (Bangkok, 1-6 September), urged the United Nations Development Programme to reconsider its decision to terminate support of the Co-ordinator's post at the end of December and requested ESCAP members for increased contributions for the post.

Note. [1]ESCAP secretariat, E/ESCAP/326.
Reports. [2]CCOP, transmitted by ESCAP secretariat note, E/ESCAP/324; [3]CCOP/SOPAC, transmitted by ESCAP secretariat note, E/ESCAP/325.
Publication. Stratigraphic Correlation between Sedimentary Basins of the ESCAP Region, vol. IX: *Proceedings of the Fourth Working Group Meeting, 1982* (ST/ESCAP/310), Sales No. E.85.II.F.8.

Water

At its March/April 1982 session, ESCAP supported a proposal to establish a regional network for training in water resources development and to organize interdisciplinary advisory missions in water resources, as mandated by the Economic and Social Council in July 1981.[4]

The Inter-agency Task Force on Water for Asia and the Pacific (ninth and tenth sessions, Bangkok, 16 June and 7 December)[2] finalized a draft proposal to obtain funding for the accelerated manufacture of hand pumps for rural water supply and a questionnaire to determine country training requirements in connection with the proposed regional training network.

The Seminar on Catchment Management for Optimum Use of Land and Water Resources (Hamilton, New Zealand, 15-19 March)[3] recommended national measures (land resource inventories, soil erosion monitoring, application of land zoning, soil conservation programmes) and international measures (workshops and study tours to promote international co-operation, and establishment of catchment management training centres) to solve catchment management problems.

The Seminar on Flood Vulnerability Analysis (Bangkok, 7-13 September)[1] recommended that international organizations establish a pilot project to prepare flood-hazard maps in a selected regional river basin to serve as a case study in flood-loss prevention and management.

The Seminar on Water Resources Development Planning (Kiev, Ukrainian SSR, August/September) recommended that international organizations help in strengthening the institutional and legal framework for water resource development planning in ESCAP countries, organize a workshop on water legislation in the USSR, develop curricula for the transfer of modern and specialized technology, and encourage exchanges of experts between the USSR and ESCAP countries.

Advisory services were provided to the Philippines to assess activities related to the International Drinking Water Supply and Sanitation Decade (1981-1990) and to evaluate ground-water data collection and monitoring.

Publication. [1]*Proceedings of the Seminars on Flood Vulnerability Analysis and on the Principles of Floodplain Management for Flood Loss Prevention* [1982] (ST/ESCAP/SER.F/58), Sales No. E.84.II.F.12.

Reports. [2]Inter-agency Task Force on water, NR/ITFW(9)1 (June), NR/ITFW(10)/1/Corr.1 (Dec.); [3]Seminar on catchment management for land and water resources, NR/MOLWR/3.

Resolution. [4]ESC: 1981/80, 24 July 1981 (YUN 1981, p. 681).

Other publications. Proceedings of the Seminar on the Improvement of Irrigation Performance at the Project Level Held at Krasnodar, USSR, from 25 August to 3 September 1980 (ST/ESCAP/SER.F/56), Sales No. E.82.II.F.8; *Water Resources Journal* (1982), ST/ESCAP/SER.C/132-135 (quarterly).

Energy

In 1982, the Regional Expert Group Meeting on the Follow-up of the Nairobi Programme of Action on New and Renewable Sources of Energy (Colombo, Sri Lanka, 2-8 March)[1] formulated a comprehensive regional programme constituting the ESCAP contribution to the June meeting of the Interim Committee on New and Renewable Sources of Energy. The Meeting emphasized the need for regional networks in major areas of new and renewable energy sources, and urged the Executive Secretary to negotiate with member Governments for the establishment of such networks and explore financial arrangements to implement regional programmes.

In addition to endorsing the Meeting's recommendations, ESCAP established two subregional energy programmes, in Asia and the Pacific respectively, to be funded by the United Nations Development Programme and implemented with assistance from the World Bank, the Asian Development Bank, the Food and Agriculture Organization of the United Nations and other international organizations.

Work on all 28 activities of the regional programme was initiated. Sponsored or co-sponsored by the programme were an expert group meeting to create a regional network system and assess priority needs in small hydropower generation (Hangzhou, China, July); a meeting on a coal study by the Association of South-East Asian Nations (Bangkok, August); a training course in biogas technology (Chengdu, China, September/October); a workshop on domestic energy utilization (Manila, Philippines, October); an expert group meeting on training courses in energy statistics and another to assess manpower and training needs for the energy sector (Bangkok, October and December).

The ESCAP Commitee on Natural Resources, at its October session, urged continued work on an oil and natural gas map of Asia.

Report. [1]Expert Group Meeting on new and renewable energy sources, NR/PANRSE/7.

Publications. Optimization of the Utilization of Electricity Generating Plants (ST/ESCAP/177), Sales No. E.82.II.F.5; *Proceedings of the ESCAP/FAO/UNEP Expert Group Meeting on Fuelwood and Charcoal* (ST/ESCAP/190), Sales No. E.82.II.F.10; *Electric Power in Asia and the Pacific 1979 and 1980* (ST/ESCAP/197), Sales No. E.82.II.F.15; *1981 and 1982* (ST/ESCAP/294), Sales No. E.85.II.F.2.

Food and agriculture

On 1 April 1982,[2] ESCAP requested its Executive Secretary, with the assistance of a high-level expert group nominated by international organizations and member Governments, to study the feasibility of proposals for subregional and regional food security arrangements, for a trade information and management network for food and agriculture, and for increasing financial resources. He was to report on the possible timing, funding and operational modalities and organizational framework, paying due regard to a proposed Asia-Pacific food bank. The report was to be referred to the ESCAP Committee on Agricultural Development or to an intergovernmental meeting. The Executive Secretary was to seek the co-operation of international organizations in preparing the studies, to ensure a co-ordinated approach to food security in the region.

ESCAP also adopted the statute of the Regional Co-ordination Centre for Research and Development of Coarse Grains, Pulses, Roots and Tuber Crops in the Humid Tropics of Asia and the Pacific (see below).

The Committee on Agricultural Development (fourth session, Bangkok, 12-18 January),[1] having examined an interim report on a special study on regional food supply and distribution systems, recommended further consideration of a proposed regional food-trade information and management network, priority to training in agricultural planning and a study of commodity terms of trade in respect of rice prices. The Committee also recommended continuing efforts to strengthen national farm broadcasting systems and endorsed three proposed regional workshops on fertilizers.

Other 1982 activities related to agriculture included a training workshop on farm radio-programme production in the Solomon Islands (Honiara, March/April) and another for instructors of agri-pesticide distributors in the South Pacific (Koronivia, Fiji, May/June); a training course on rural broadcasting (Rabaul, Papua New Guinea, July/August); a study tour on post-harvest processing, marketing and consumption of aquaculture product in China (Beijing, Guangzhou, Shanghai and Wusi, September); and workshops on import procurement of chemical fertilizers (Bangkok, September/October), on bulk-blending and mixing of fertilizers (Penang, Malaysia, November) and on agricultural and agro-industrial residue utilization (Cha-am, Thailand, December). Advisory services were provided to Bangladesh, Burma, Fiji, Pakistan and Thailand.

Report. [1]Committee on Agricultural Development, E/ESCAP/248.
Resolution (1982). [2]ESCAP (report, E/1982/20): 226(XXXVIII), 1 Apr.
Publications. Agricultural Information Development Bulletin, vol. 4, Nos. 1-3; *News in Brief. Agro-chemicals, Fertilizers and Agro-pesticides*, vol. V, Nos. 1-4 (quarterly) & special issues (Nov., Dec.).

Centre on coarse grains, pulses, roots and tuber crops

On 1 April 1982,[1] ESCAP adopted the Statute of the Regional Co-ordination Centre for Research and Development of Coarse Grains, Pulses, Roots and Tuber (CGPRT) Crops in the Humid Tropics of Asia and the Pacific. The statute set forth the Centre's objective; namely, to provide ESCAP members with technical services and facilities for the development of production, utilization and trade of CGPRT crops in order to solve food problems, increase employment, and achieve better income distribution and diet. The statute outlined the Centre's functions to include assistance for the development of an agricultural co-operative research network, preparation of agro-economic studies, training of national research and extension workers, and collection and dissemination of information. It provided for a Governing Board, a Director and staff, and a Technical Advisory Committee. It listed the sources for the Centre's financial resources.

Established in April 1981[2] initially at ESCAP headquarters, the Centre moved to its permanent site at Bogor, Indonesia, on 25 September 1982.

Resolution (1982). [1]ESCAP (report, E/1982/20): 220(XXXVIII), 1 Apr.
Yearbook reference. [2]1981, p. 645.

Science and technology

In 1982, the ESCAP Committee on Industry, Technology, Human Settlements and the Environment, at its September session,[1] suggested expanding the secretariat's technical advisory services in technology and technology transfer and in training. The Committee stressed the need for institutional support for the Regional Centre for Technology Transfer (RCTT) to enable it to function effectively, and recommended that the Centre accelerate its activities to solve technology transfer problems, giving attention to strengthening national focal points.

RCTT continued to assist ESCAP member countries to strengthen their policies and institutions in science and technology under a regional project financed by the United Nations Interim Fund for Science and Technology for Development. An advisory mission was sent to Sri Lanka, at its request, to suggest measures to strengthen its technology transfer arrangements. Technical inquiries from Argentina, Brazil, India, Pakistan and Sri Lanka also received the Centre's attention.

The Third Meeting of National Focal Points for RCTT (Bangalore, India, 15-17 February) stressed the need for institutional support, identified priorities for the next two years, reviewed activities proposed for RCTT and projects assisted by the Interim Fund, and approved national focal points for specific RCTT technological networks.

At its March/April session,[2] ESCAP noted that the Meeting's discussions had shown the need for core activities in specific technological sectors without excessive diversification, and for RCTT collaboration with the secretariat, regional institutions and international organizations in implementing those activities.

Reports. [1]Committee on Industry, Technology, Human Settlements and Environment, E/ESCAP/288; [2]ESCAP, E/1982/20.

Social development

In 1982, the ESCAP Committee on Social Development (third session, Bangkok, 16-22 November)[1] reviewed emerging trends and perspectives and specific social issues in the context of the International Development Strategy for the Third United Nations Development Decade.[2] Among major ESCAP activities in social development, the Committee reviewed implementation of programmes to integrate women and youth in development. It endorsed the regional programme of action on aging adopted by the October 1981 Regional Intergovernmental Preparatory Meeting for the World Assembly on Aging[3] and considered follow-up activities to the 1981 International Year of Disabled Persons.[4]

The ESCAP Indonesia-Malaysia-Thailand Law and Participation Consultation (Bangkok and

Kuala Lumpur, Malaysia, 20-27 April 1982) discussed the regional relevance of legal aid, drawing on the structure and experience of the Indonesian Legal Aid Bureau to assist Malaysian and Thai legal aid programmes.

Advisory services in training and education for social development were provided to Guam, India, Indonesia, the Philippines, the Republic of Korea and Vanuatu. An advisory mission to Nepal assisted the Ministry of Labour and Social Welfare in setting up a national social development information centre.

Report. [1]Committee on Social Development, E/ESCAP/291.
Resolution. [2]GA: 35/56, annex, 5 Dec. 1980 (YUN 1980, p. 503).
Yearbook reference. 1981, [3]p. 647, [4]p. 795.
Publication. Social Development Newsletter (3 issues yearly).

Women

The ESCAP Committee on Social Development, in November 1982,[1] examined programmes relating to women and development in the region. Drawing attention to the urgency of assisting women migrants concentrated in the service and entertainment sectors in urban areas, the Committee recommended individual country assessment of the situation to serve as the basis for such preventive and protective schemes as education and vocational training, greater employment opportunities and public health services. For women engaged in family income-generating activites, support in terms of day-care services for their children, working women's hostels and employment information centres was suggested, as was further regional action to fulfil the mandates of the United Nations Decade for Women (1976-1985). The Voluntary Fund for the United Nations Decade for Women was to be used for practical projects including a data base to be set up at ESCAP for intercountry information exchange.

The Inter-agency Committee on Women in Development (first session, Bangkok, November), a standing inter-agency co-ordination mechanism for ESCAP programmes for women, considered guidelines for the development of indicators on women's situation in the region.

In other 1982 activities, a workshop was held on the role and rights of young women in the development of Asia (Manila, Philippines, August/September). Advisory missions to provide technical assistance for Voluntary Fund–supported projects for the integration of women in development were undertaken to Burma, India, Malaysia, Nepal, the Philippines and Singapore.

Report. [1]Committee on Social Development, E/ESCAP/291.

Youth

On 1 April 1982,[2] ESCAP called on member countries to: implement the Specific Programme of Measures and Activities to be undertaken prior to the 1985 International Youth Year—endorsed by the General Assembly in November 1981[3]—set up national co-ordinating committees with broad participation of youth and youth organizations, and keep the Executive Secretary informed of their activities. ESCAP requested the Executive Secretary to disseminate information on regional activities for the Year and on national experience in solving youth problems, and invited him to explore the possibility of a 1982 advisory meeting of youth experts and leaders to plan for a 1983 regional meeting.

Regarding youth unemployment and underemployment in the region, the Committee on Social Development, at its November 1982 session,[1] suggested expanding employment opportunities by involving non-governmental organizations (NGOs) and the business sector in community programmes including training. The Committee stressed the urgency for such opportunities in rural areas, to discourage urban migration. It expressed support for the ESCAP intercountry youth worker/organizer exchange programme and its role in collecting and disseminating information on youth, and suggested studies on the situation of various segments of the youth population.

An *ad hoc* meeting of agencies and NGOs concerned with youth development (Bangkok, 23-26 November), in planning the Year's activities, urged ESCAP to consider establishing a regional co-ordinating committee and to assist member Governments in developing guidelines for evaluating youth activities.

The Technical Meeting of Youth Experts on the International Youth Year (Chiang Mai, Thailand, 29 November–5 December), held in preparation for the 1983 regional intergovernmental meeting, concluded that a regional review of existing youth policies and programmes should be undertaken prior to formulating a regional plan of action.

The Eighth Asian-Pacific Youth Forum for Community Development (Suva, Fiji, 15-18 February 1982), co-sponsored by ESCAP, focused on the active participation of youth in development and regional co-operation.

Training programmes, workshops and field studies in youth development were held in 1982 to teach management skills to people working with youth, to establish a network of youth organizations and to provide opportunities for the exchange of methodologies.

Report. [1]Committee on Social Development, E/ESCAP/291.
Resolution (1982). [2]ESCAP (report, E/1982/20): 223(XXXVIII), 1 Apr.
Resolution (prior). [3]GA:36/28, 13 Nov. 1981 (YUN 1981, p. 1021).

Population

In 1982, the Third Asian and Pacific Population Conference (Colombo, Sri Lanka, 20-29 September)[2] addressed itself to the theme of an integrated approach to population and related development issues, reviewed the region's progress in implementing the 1974 World Population Plan of Action,[3] and considered future actions. It adopted the Asia-Pacific Call for Action on Population and Development, whose main objective was the improvement of the quality of life in the region through an integrated and balanced approach to population, resources and development. The specific recommendations for Government action in this context related to: population and development policy; fertility and family planning; mortality and morbidity rates; urbanization; migration; women's role; children and youth; the aged; population data, research and information; training and manpower development; community participation; the role of the private sector and NGOs; and resources for population programmes. Also recommended were ways in which regional and subregional organizations, the ESCAP secretariat, the United Nations system and donor Governments could facilitate the Call's implementation.

In collaboration with the South Pacific Commission, ESCAP convened a seminar on population problems of the region's small island countries (Noumea, New Caledonia, 15-19 February),[1] which made recommendations on collection and analysis of demographic data and on country and intercountry studies.

Also convened were a regional seminar on strategies for increasing women's participation in development to achieve population goals (Pattaya, Thailand, April/May); a regional meeting on social and cultural factors affecting family planning (Pattaya, November); and a South Asian subregional seminar on population and development planning (Bangalore, India, December). Fifteen fellowships to the International Institute for Population Studies, Bombay, India, for 1982/1983, were provided to 14 member countries.

Reports. [1]Conference Seminar on population problems of small island countries, ST/ESCAP/194; [2]Third Asian and Pacific Population Conference, E/ESCAP/301.
Yearbook reference. [3]1974, p. 552.
Publications. ADOPT (Asia and world-wide documents on population topics), vol. 4, Nos. 1-12 (monthly); *Asian-Pacific Population Programme News*, vol. 11, Nos. 1-4.

Health

On 1 April 1982,[1] ESCAP requested its Executive Secretary to convene, in consultation with the World Health Organization (WHO) and the United Nations Children's Fund (UNICEF), an intersectoral intergovernmental meeting to advise how ESCAP programmes could be strengthened to ensure a positive impact on the health of the poorest segments of the region's population. He was also asked to strengthen collaboration with WHO, UNICEF and other organizations, which were invited to assist ESCAP in pursuing its health programme. Donor countries and multilateral development institutions were urged to maintain, increase or initiate financial support.

The Fifth ESCAP/UNICEF Seminar (Regional) on Basic Community Services through Primary Health Care (PHC) (Bangkok, October/November) was held to develop planning skills in communities, to clarify basic services and PHC concepts, to analyse the implications of community mobilization for PHC and national development, and to help prepare national PHC training programmes.

Resolution (1982). [1]ESCAP (report, E/1982/20): 228(XXXVIII), 1 Apr.

Environment

On 1 April 1982,[6] ESCAP urged member Governments to reiterate their support for its environmental activities. It requested the Executive Secretary to consult with the United Nations Environment Programme (UNEP) so as to ensure continued incorporation of environmental considerations in those activities. He was also requested to ensure three regular budget posts for the ESCAP Environmental Co-ordinating Unit by redeploying existing United Nations resources or by other means.

The Committee on Industry, Technology, Human Settlements and the Environment recommended in September[2] that ESCAP intensify promotion of environmental awareness and expedite a regional project to protect the marine environment and related ecosystems. It suggested a review of ESCAP environmental activities by the *Ad Hoc* Working Group of Experts on the Environment and endorsed revised terms of reference for the Environmental Co-ordinating Unit, as drawn up by the UNEP Governing Council and modified by ESCAP.

The *Ad Hoc* Working Group (first meeting, Bangkok, 14-17 December)[5] suggested that a regional state-of-the-environment report—whose preparation had been endorsed by ESCAP at its March/April session[3] and by the Committee in September—should emphasize linkages between development and the environment, the concept of resource management and promotion of environmental awareness. It recommended a one-week ministerial-level conference on the environment, including a preparatory meeting of senior officials in 1985 before the ESCAP session; and formation of an expert working group on the environment, to meet each alternate year when environment was not the Committee's main theme.

The Expert Group Meeting on Methods and Costs of Industrial Pollution Control (Bangkok, 15-19 June 1982)[4] concluded that effluents from agro-based, agro-allied and small-scale industries posed significant environmental pollution problems. The Group made a series of general recommendations, including installation of individual and collective waste treatment systems; waste reuse and/or recycling; improved monitoring of pollution control facilities to ensure their efficient functioning; and establishment of a data bank on regional experience in industrial pollution control. Other recommendations concerned control of pollution from brewing and distilling, electroplating, fertilizer, palm oil, sugar, tapioca, tanning and fish-processing industries.

The South Pacific Regional Environment Programme—established by ESCAP, the South Pacific Commission, the South Pacific Bureau for Economic Co-operation and UNEP—organized a ministerial-level conference on the human environment in the South Pacific (Rarotonga, Cook Islands, 8-11 March), which adopted a South Pacific Declaration on Natural Resources and the Environment and an action plan for managing the subregion's natural resources and environment.

As part of its assistance to the Programme, ESCAP provided financial and technical support for a regional training course on environmental management in the Pacific, held at the University of the South Pacific (Suva, Fiji, 16-26 November). The course emphasized environmental management of the island nations' ecosystems and coastal zones.

To promote environmental awareness through mass media campaigns, ESCAP co-sponsored a media seminar on the environment and development (Bangkok, 15-20 March); a broadcasters' workshop on the same topic, with emphasis on the marine environment (Kuala Lumpur, Malaysia, 14-24 April); and a national seminar on environment reporting (Dhaka, Bangladesh, 1-5 November).

Regarding institutional and legislative aspects of environmental protection, ESCAP began work towards establishing an information network on environmental legislation. It formulated a programme to assess institutional and legislative frameworks for environmental protection and management in the region; the results were to be incorporated into the state-of-the-environment report.

On 31 May, the UNEP Governing Council, in a decision on the UNEP regional seas programme,[1] requested the the Executive Director to consult with concerned States of the South Asia Co-operative Environment Programme to ascertain their views on a similar programme for the South Asia seas.

Decision (1982). [1]UNEP Council (report, A/37/25): 10/20, para. 1, 31 May.
Reports. [2]Committee on Industry, Technology, Human Settlements and Environment, E/ESCAP/288; [3]ESCAP, E/1982/20; [4]Expert Group Meeting on industrial pollution control, ECU/MCIPC/11; [5]Working Group of Experts on Environment, E/ESCAP/IHT.7/3.
Resolution (1982). [6]ESCAP: 224(XXXVIII), 1 Apr.

Human settlements

In 1982, the Regional Congress of Local Authorities for Development of Human Settlements in Asia and the Pacific (Yokohama, Japan, June) recommended measures on development, urbanization and physical conditions in cities; policies, planning and programmes for shelter development, infrastructure and services; upgrading the quality of urban life; functional relationships among governmental authorities; management and co-ordination within and among local authorities; and public participation and access to information on human settlements.

The ESCAP Committee on Industry, Technology, Human Settlements and the Environment, at its September session,[1] emphasized the importance of settlement planning, which should aim at a balanced development to include small and intermediate cities and rural centres. The Committee urged developing countries to give priority to upgrading slum and squatter settlements as well as improving rural settlements, using indigenous building materials, and improving building technologies and manpower resources. It asked countries to follow up on the recommendations of the Regional Congress of Local Authorities for Development of Human Settlements in Asia and the Pacific (Yokohama, Japan, 9-16 June) and to assist work on the ESCAP atlas on human settlements.

The International Seminar on Urban Development Policies: Focus on Land Management (Nagoya, Japan, October) dealt with the process of land readjustment, whereby groups of landowners could develop land on a co-operative basis in collaboration with public agencies.

Outside the ESCAP framework,[2] the *Ad Hoc* Group of Experts on a Feasibility Study for an Asian Human Settlements Bank (Manila, Philippines, 7-11 December 1981; Bangkok, 7-12 January 1982) responding to a May 1981 request[4] of the Commission on Human Settlements, submitted to the Commission a preliminary report on work towards the creation of a regional human settlements financing institution, composed of a federation of national financial institutions dealing with human settlements. To complete the feasibility study, the Group recommended a study of the whole spectrum of development finance institutions in the region; consultations with national agencies to ascertain financial and technical needs; an evaluation of a regional institution's role in meeting those needs; formulation of a plan and design of an appropriate structure including functional links with national institutions and regional and international agencies; and finalization of the proposal in consultation with relevant institutions and government agencies.

On 7 May 1982,[3] the Commission requested the Executive Director of the United Nations

Centre for Human Settlements (UNCHS) to accelerate work on the feasibility study.

Accordingly, an *ad hoc* expert group was convened (Manila, 29 November–3 December) to analyse Governments' response to a questionnaire designed to elicit the information required to complete the study. Based on that analysis, the group recommended that the objectives of the proposed institution—no longer referred to as a bank—should be to provide technical and managerial services, to assist in training personnel, to mobilize capital and technical resources, and to aid in developing a regionalized secondary mortgage market. A small working group would report to the Commission in 1983 on the institution's structure; a preparatory committee, in consultation with UNCHS, would submit a final proposal to ESCAP in 1984; and liaison with the Asian Development Bank, which should be actively associated with the institution's creation, was to be established.

Reports. [1]Committee on Industry, Technology, Human Settlements and Environment, E/ESCAP/288; [2]UNCHS Executive Director, HS/C/5/8.
Resolution (1982). [3]Commission on Human Settlements (report, A/37/8): 5/12, 7 May.
Yearbook reference. [4]1981, p. 856.

Typhoons

In 1982, the First Typhoon Operational Experiment (TOPEX), in which four selected typhoons were the subject of intensive observation, was successfully completed between 1 August and 15 October. The experiment led to the improvement of typhoon forecasting techniques in the region by the exchange of ideas, methods and experiences. Plans for the experiment, begun in 1981,[2] had been completed by the Second Planning Meeting for TOPEX (Tokyo, 18-22 February).

The ESCAP Typhoon Committee (fifteenth session, Bangkok, 9-15 November)[1] evaluated progress in implementing the 1982 work programme encompassing meteorological, hydrological, disaster prevention and preparedness, training and research components. The Committee noted improvements made by member States to observation facilities and typhoon forecasting and warning services, as demonstrated during TOPEX.

In the area of training, ESCAP organized a seminar on flood vulnerability analysis (Bangkok, 7-13 September). China held two seminars on satellite picture interpretation and application (February/March) and on radar echo analysis and interpretation (August/September), and hosted a third, on typhoon forecasting (Hangzhou, 25-27 October). A training seminar/workshop on disaster preparedness was conducted in two Philippine provinces. A regional seminar was scheduled for national meteorological instructors including

Typhoon Committee members (Colombo, Sri Lanka, 15-26 November).

Report. [1]Typhoon Committee, E/ESCAP/294.
Yearbook reference. [2]1981, p. 644.

Statistics

In 1982, the Working Group on Evaluation and Utilization of Population and Housing Census Data (Bangkok, 19-25 January)[2] discussed various techniques of evaluating the quality and consistency of the 1980s round of population and housing censuses in ESCAP countries. Also discussed were the uses to which census data could be put, such as for administrative needs, economic and social planning, and the construction of a sampling frame.

The Expert Group Meeting on Training Courses in Energy Statistics (Bangkok, 25-29 October)[1] reviewed statistical information for energy planning, emphasizing statistics on traditional and non-conventional energy sources, the role of rural energy surveys, current energy statistics and their sources, the compilation of national energy accounts and balances, training needs, and institutional arrangements for collecting and disseminating energy data. It formulated a 1983 training course in energy statistics and recommended the organization of other courses, including one for the South Pacific island countries.

The Pacific Subregional Workshop on Energy Statistics (Suva, Fiji, 2-8 February)[3] focused on traditional and non-conventional energy sources for the Pacific islands, including methodologies for collecting such information.

The Statistical Institute for Asia and the Pacific conducted at its Tokyo headquarters an advanced course in modern statistical data processing with special reference to data-base methods (21 June–23 July) and another on social accounting matrices (5-30 July). The Institute also conducted training courses for trainers of personnel at the front line of statistical survey work (Bangladesh, Republic of Korea), and courses in sampling methods (China), demographic statistics (Pakistan), and agricultural statistics (Philippines).

Reports. [1]Expert Group Meeting on training courses in energy statistics, E/ESCAP/STAT.5/16; [2]Working Group on Evaluation and Utilization of census data, E/ESCAP/STAT.5/19; [3]Workshop on energy statistics, E/ESCAP/STAT.5/15.
Publications. Foreign Trade Statistics of Asia and the Pacific, 1978, vol. XVII, Series A (ST/ESCAP/180), Sales No. E.82.II.F.3; 1976-1979, vol. XII, Series B (ST/ESCAP/200), Sales No. E.82.II.F.13; 1979, vol. XVIII, Series A (ST/ESCAP/206), Sales No. E.82.II.F.14; 1979-1982, vol. XV, Series B (ST/ESCAP/310), Sales No. E.84.II.F.19; Quarterly Bulletin of Statistics for Asia and the Pacific, vol. XII, No. 1 (ST/ESCAP/192), Sales No. E.82.II.F.11; No. 2 (ST/ESCAP/201), Sales No. E.83.II.F.5; No. 3 (ST/ESCAP/214), Sales No. E.83.II.F.6; No. 4 (ST/ESCAP/221), Sales No. E.83.II.F.10. Statistical Yearbook

for Asia and the Pacific, 1982 (ST/ESCAP/235), Sales No.E.84.II.F.8. *Handbook on Agricultural Statistics for Asia and the Pacific 1982* (yearly). *Statistical Indicators for Asia and the Pacific*, vol. 12, Nos. 1-4 (quarterly); *Statistical Newsletter*, Nos. 45-48 (quarterly).

Programme, organizational and administrative questions concerning ESCAP

At its March/April 1982 session, ESCAP considered a report by its Executive Secretary on the reassessment of programme priorities and decided to take the matter up again in more detail at an intergovernmental meeting to be held for the purpose and at its 1983 session. ESCAP also approved revised terms of reference for its main subsidiary bodies.

Programme planning

The Committee for Programme and Coordination, in one of several recommendations made in May 1982[1] in connection with United Nations programme planning, strongly endorsed a recommendation that ESCAP planning and programming methodology should conform to that laid down for the United Nations as a whole.

Report. [1]CPC, A/37/38.

Work programme for 1984-1985

In 1982, the Intergovernmental Meeting on Reassessment of Programme Priorities of the Commission (Bangkok, 13-15 September)[1] adopted the revised priority-setting criteria proposed by the ESCAP secretariat and made recommendations on their application to the ESCAP 1984-1985 work programme, subject to endorsement by the Commission in 1983. The priority areas of ESCAP activities were to: deal with issues of major importance to the region's developing countries; promote economic growth and social development leading to the alleviation of poverty; assist the least developed, land-locked developing, and developing South Pacific island countries; promote regional and subregional co-operation; and receive strong and specific support from member countries. The Executive Secretary was to continue to examine sectoral priority areas and present a report to ESCAP in 1983.

Reports. [1]Meeting on reassessment of programme priorities, E/ESCAP/DP.4/14 (E/ESCAP/NR.9/27, E/ESCAP/STC.6/27).

Terms of reference of subsidiary bodies

On 1 April 1982,[1] ESCAP decided on revised terms of reference for nine of its legislative committees: Committee on Agricultural Development; Committee on Development Planning; Committee on Industry, Technology, Human Settlements and the Environment; Committee on Natural Resources; Committee on Population; Committee on Shipping, and Transport and Communications; Committee on Social Development; Committee on Statistics; and Committee on Trade. The proposed terms of reference had been formulated by the Executive Secretary, in consultation with the Advisory Committee of Permanent Representatives and Other Representatives Designated by Members of the Commission, to enhance coordination of activities and United Nations responsiveness to developing countries' needs, avoid duplication of effort at the regional level and employ similar terminology in the various terms of reference.

Resolution (1982). [1]ESCAP (report, E/1982/20): 222(XXXVIII), 1 Apr.

Europe

The Economic Commission for Europe (ECE) held its thirty-seventh session at Geneva from 23 March to 3 April 1982.[1] It examined the main economic problems facing Europe and North America, reviewed the ECE activities and approved plans for its future work.

In a resolution of 2 April on its work and future activities,[2] ECE called on its members to continue taking full advantage of its potential as an instrument for strengthening regional economic relations and mulitilateral co-operation, adding that implementation of and respect for the Final Act of the 1975 Helsinki (Finland) Conference on Security and Co-operation in Europe were essential for fostering such activities. It requested its subsidiary bodies to continue taking account of the pertinent provisions of that document, the interests of economically developing European States and the need for effective co-operation with other international organizations. The Commission approved its 1982/1983 work programme and endorsed in principle, subject to review in 1983, its long-term work programme for 1982-1986.

Report. [1]ECE, E/1982/19 & Add.1.
Resolution (1982). [2]ECE: 1(XXXVII), 2 Apr.

Economic and social trends

The 1981 economic development in Europe and North America fell short of expectations, according to the *Economic Survey of Europe in 1982*,[2] prepared by the ECE secretariat and noted by the Economic and Social Council on 30 July.[1] The economies of western Europe were still constrained by the restrictive policies adopted in the wake of the second oil-price shock of 1979; instead of recovery, total west European gross domestic product (GDP) fell for the first time since 1975, by nearly 0.5 per cent. In eastern Europe and the USSR, aggregate output increased slightly less than 2 per cent, while expansion generally fell short of the targets envisaged for 1981, due partly to the balance of payments constraints and poor harvests.

For 1982, only a slow and hesitant recovery of output, with aggregate GDP rising at just under 1.5 per cent, was anticipated for western Europe. Unemployment would continue to rise to more than 8 per cent, while the rate of inflation was likely to decline from an average rate of 11 per cent in 1981 to about 9.5 per cent in 1982. Although the year 1981 was unfavourable for most of southern Europe, official forecasts predicted a faster rate of economic growth in 1982 and, except for Portugal, a deceleration in the inflation rate.

In eastern Europe and the USSR, annual growth rates in net material product were envisaged at levels lower than those recorded in 1981. Industrial growth rates were expected to be lower as a result of constraining factors of energy, fuels and raw materials, while higher than average agricultural growth rates were planned for 1982.

The Secretary-General, in a June report to the Economic and Social Council on regional co-operation,[3] asserted that the ECE region faced problems stemming from the deteriorating political climate in East-West relations, combined with the most serious economic developments since the Second World War. Economic difficulties in the socialist and market economy countries were occurring simultaneously and influencing the course of economic co-operation within the region, and the creation of favourable trade conditions, particularly East-West trade, remained a basic task for ECE.

Decision (1982). [1]ESC: 1982/177, para. *(f)*, 30 July.
Publication. [2]*Economic Survey of Europe in 1982*, Sales No. E.83.II.E.1 (summary, E/1982/62).
Report. [3]S-G, E/1982/88.

Regional economic co-operation in Europe

The Senior Economic Advisers to ECE Governments (eighteenth session, Geneva, 15-19 February 1982),[1] discussed problems and prospects facing their respective economies and the long-term economic prospects for the ECE region, and agreed on a work programme for 1982-1983 which included consideration of major changes in the production factors for future economic growth, and analyses of labour productivity, structural changes, trends in international trade and energy activities. Economic projections would include the impact of trade relations and that of energy on future economic growth, and preliminary results of long-term overall projections to the year 2000. Preparatory work would be based on information provided by Governments concerning their future economic prospects, analysis from macro-economic projection systems, international comparisons, and findings of long-term projects undertaken by ECE subsidiary bodies and other studies prepared by the secretariat. Most delegations at the session expressed their wish that ana-

lytical work be carried out in a future-oriented way in order to continue long-term projections on a macro-economic level; those global projections would provide a starting point for sectoral studies and a background for national planning.

Report. [1]Senior Economic Advisers to ECE Governments, ECE/EC.AD/21 & Corr.1.

Co-operation among Mediterranean countries

The January 1982 report[2] of the ECE Executive Secretary on economic co-operation in the Mediterranean, submitted in response to the Commission's 1981 request,[3] contained information on recent activities including expert group meetings or seminars held in 1982 or planned in the near future on a wide range of subjects of interest to the countries in that region.

By a decision of 2 April,[1] ECE requested its Executive Secretary to continue co-operation with the secretariats of the economic commissions for Africa and Western Asia and other United Nations bodies and to pursue contacts with all Mediterranean countries not members of ECE on subjects of common interest to Mediterranean countries. It recommended that its subsidiary bodies continue efforts to identify areas of interest for economic co-operation in the region within the framework of ECE activities and its work programme.

Decision (1982). [1]ECE (report, E/1982/19): G(XXXVII), 2 Apr.
Report. [2]ECE Executive Secretary, E/ECE/1042.
Yearbook reference. [3]1981, p. 649.

Technical co-operation

Expenditures by ECE for technical co-operation activities in 1982[1] totalled $844,000, including $36,000 provided by trust funds. Funds from the United Nations Development Programme, totalling $798,000 went to regional and subregional projects in electric power, energy, transport and statistics. Funds from the United Nations Fund for Population Activities amounting to $10,000 were used for demographic research activities, and the United Nations Environment Programme financed certain environmental protection activities.

Report. [1]S-G, DP/1983/18/Add.1, 2.

International trade in Europe

In 1982, the ECE Committee on the Development of Trade (thirty-first session, Geneva, 6-10 December)[1] focused its efforts on refining the Consolidated Inventory of All Kinds of Obstacles to the Development of Trade and studying transactions favourable to the promotion and diversification of exports. Agreement was reached for special meetings of experts to be held in 1983 on obstacles to trade development and on compensation trade. Studies were undertaken on industrial co-operation including five new "country profiles" on East-West trade and on tripartite co-operation. Trade facilitation continued to form an important part of the work programme with emphasis on standards needed for automatic trade data interchange. In addition, preparations continued for the sixth East-West marketing seminar, on the marketing of construction machinery and of producers' goods for that sector.

The Group of Experts on International Contract Practices in Industry (Geneva: twentieth session, 12-14 July;[6] twenty-first session, 13-15 December[7]) adopted a *Guide for drawing up international contracts on consulting engineering, including related aspects of technical assistance*, and considered a study on the use of ECE General Conditions in international trade.

The Working Party on Facilitation of International Trade Procedures (Geneva: fifteenth session, 18 and 19 March;[8] sixteenth session, 22-24 September[9]) took note of the progress made by its two working groups, both of which held their twenty-fifth and twenty-sixth sessions in 1982 at Geneva. The Group of Experts No. 1: Data Elements and Automatic Data Interchange (16 and 17 March,[2] 21 and 22 September[3]) approved, subject to agreement on a definition, rules for registration of trade data interchange systems. The Group of Experts No. 2: Procedures and Documentation (15 and 16 March,[4] 20 September[5]) continued work on draft guidelines for the application of the United Nations Layout for Key Trade Documents,[10] an international standard with terminology adapted to data-processing vocabulary.

Reports. [1]Committee on Development of Trade, ECE/TRADE/144; Group of Experts No. 1: Data Elements and Automatic Data Interchange, [2]TRADE/WP.4/GE.1/47, [3]TRADE/WP.4/GE.1/49; Group of Experts No. 2: Procedures and Documentation, [4]TRADE/WP.4/GE.2/47, [5]TRADE/WP.4/GE.2/49; Group of Experts on International Contract Practices in Industry, [6]TRADE/GE.1/53, [7]TRADE/GE.1/55; Working Party on Facilitation of International Trade Procedures, [8]TRADE/WP.4/139, [9]TRADE/WP.4/141.

Yearbook reference. [10]1981, p. 650.

Publication. Correspondence Table between the Standard International Trade Classification of the United Nations (SITC) and the Standard Foreign Trade Classification of the Council for Mutual Economic Assistance (SFTC), Sales No. E/R.82.II.E.10.

Inland transport in Europe

The ECE Inland Transport Committee (Geneva: forty-second session, 1-5 February;[13] forty-third session, 18-21 October 1982[14]) adopted the International Convention on the Harmonization of Frontier Controls of Goods,[1] to be opened for signature on 1 April 1983, aimed at facilitating the international movement

of goods through joint control of goods and documents, co-ordination of frontier post operations, exchange of information, and the use of commonly accepted document forms. The text had been finalized by the Group of Experts on Customs Questions Affecting Transport at its forty-sixth (special) session (15-19 March).[4] At its other session in 1982 (forty-seventh session, Geneva, 20-22 November),[5] the Group discussed harmonization of conditions for exercising customs and other frontier controls and accession to customs conventions. Its subsidiary body, the Group of Rapporteurs on Customs Questions concerning Containers (twenty-seventh session, Geneva, 28 June–2 July),[12] adopted a recommendation on measures to be taken by those engaged in international trade to help the frontier control services expedite the clearance of goods.

The Administrative Committee for the TIR Convention 1975 (fifth session, Geneva, 21 and 22 October)[2] dealt with problems relating to the application of, and possible amendments to, the treaty governing permits for the transport of merchandise by motor vehicles between customs ports without customs inspection (*transport international routier*). It agreed that the permits within a regional guarantee chain could be printed in any United Nations official language, accompanied by English or French.

The Group of Experts on the Transport of Dangerous Goods (thirty-fourth session, Geneva, 11-14 May)[7] continued to develop and revise relevant regulations, including the revision of those governing the transport of inflammable liquids, toxics and corrosives. Work commenced on up-dating the regulations concerning explosives. A joint meeting of the Group and the RID (International Regulations for the Carriage of Dangerous Goods by Rail) Safety Committee (Geneva, 19-30 April)[8] adopted amendments to the European Agreement concerning the International Carriage of Dangerous Goods by Road and considered a special appendix to cover short sea crossings.

The Group of Experts on Combined Transport (fourth session, Geneva, 1-4 June)[3] focused on problems arising from the simultaneous development of different techniques in combined rail/road transport, such as piggyback and container transport, and safety questions including implementation of the International Convention for Safe Containers.

The financing of transport infrastructure investments was the main concern of the Group of Experts on Transport Economics (second session, Geneva, 11-13 October),[6] which also suggested topics for a 1984 seminar.

The Group of Experts on Transport Trends and Policy (second session, Geneva, 7-9 July)[11] studied an intermodal approach to the problem of main transport axes, in order to make the best possible contribution of transport to society as a whole.

The Group of Experts on Transport Statistics (thirty-fourth session, Geneva, 6-10 December)[10] focused on the improvement and possible extension of statistical data published regularly by ECE, the 1980 and 1985 censuses of road traffic on main international traffic arteries, and amendments to the terms and definitions appearing in the *Annual Bulletin of Transport Statistics in Europe* and in the glossary for Inland Transport.

The Group of Experts on the Transport of Perishable Foodstuffs (thirty-seventh session, Geneva, 11-14 October)[9] continued work on the implementation of the Agreement on the International Carriage of Perishable Foodstuffs and on the Special Equipment to be Used for Such Carriage, recommending changes in requirements and certificates for food transport equipment.

Convention. [1]1982 International Convention on Harmonization of Frontier Controls of Goods, ECE/TRANS/55.

Reports. [2]Administrative Committee for TIR Convention 1975, TRANS/GE.30/AC.2/10; [3]Group of Experts on Combined Transport, TRANS/GE.24/8; Group of Experts on Customs Questions Affecting Transport, [4]TRANS/GE.30/29 & Add.1, [5]TRANS/GE.30/31; [6]Group of Experts on Transport Economics, TRANS/GE.37/4; [7]Group of Experts on Transport of Dangerous Goods, TRANS/GE.15/21, and [8]Joint Meeting with RID Safety Committee, TRANS/GE.15/AC.1/12; [9]Group of Experts on Transport of Perishable Foodstuffs, TRANS/GE.11/21; [10]Group of Experts on Transport Statistics, TRANS/GE.6/12; [11]Group of Experts on Transport Trends and Policies, TRANS/GE.36/4; [12]Group of Rapporteurs on Customs Questions concerning Containers, TRANS/GE.30/GRCC/10; Inland Transport Committee, [13]ECE/TRANS/47 & Add.1,2, [14]ECE/TRANS/52.

Inland water transport

The Working Party on Inland Water Transport (twenty-sixth session, Geneva, 8-12 November 1982)[6] adopted an improved signalling system for European inland waterways, which took into account a new maritime buoyage system to facilitate river-sea traffic, and made recommendations on preventing pollution by inland navigation vessels. The final text of the signalling system had been adopted by the Group of Experts on the Standardization of Rules of the Road and Signs and Signals in Inland Navigation, which held three sessions in 1982 (nineteenth session, Geneva, 19-23 April;[1] twentieth (special) session, Finland, 14-18 June;[2] twenty-first session, Geneva, 13-17 September[3]).

The Group of Experts on the Standardization of Technical Requirements for Vessels and of Ships' Papers (Geneva: nineteenth session, 1-5 March;[4] twentieth session, 30 August–3 September[5]) considered measures to prevent inland water pollution, and made other relevant recommendations to the Working Party.

Reports. Group of Experts on Standardization of Rules of Road and Signs and Signals in Inland Navigation, [1]TRANS/SC3/GE.2/37, [2]TRANS/SC3/GE.2/38, [3]TRANS/SC3/GE.2/40; Group of Experts on Standardization of Technical Requirements for Vessels and of Ships' Papers, [4]TRANS/SC3/GE.1/36, [5]TRANS/SC3/GE.1/38; [6]Working Party on Inland Water Transport, TRANS/SC3/107 & Corr.1.

Rail transport

The Working Party on Rail Transport (thirty-sixth session, Geneva, 2-5 November 1982)[1] agreed on a plan for the development of a European railway network, to be studied further by a group of rapporteurs. It also decided on a number of subjects for a seminar on financial aspects of international transport infrastructure investments and made recommendations on the application and harmonization of summer time in Europe.

Report. [1]Working Party on Rail Transport, TRANS/SC2/156.

Road transport

The Working Party of Road Transport (Geneva: seventieth (special) session, 5-9 July;[1] seventy-first session, 15-19 November 1982[2]) continued preparation of recommendations on road transport facilitation and a plan of action for the harmonization and simplification of road transport documents and procedures. The required conditions were met for the entry into force of the European Agreement on Main International Traffic Arteries.

Reports. Working Party on Road Transport, [1]TRANS/SC1/309, [2]TRANS/SC1/311.

Motor vehicles

Several expert groups on motor vehicles reported to the ECE Inland Transport Committee in 1982 through the Working Party on Road Transport.

The Group of Experts on the Construction of Vehicles (sixty-sixth to sixty-seventh sessions, Geneva: 8-12 March,[1] 21-25 June,[2] 25-29 October[3]) worked on the elaboration of international regulations and recommendations in the construction of motor vehicles for improved safety and environmental protection. During 1982, four new regulations dealing with noise limitation, air pollution and light signals on vehicles, were annexed to the 1958 Agreement concerning the Adoption of Uniform Conditions of Approval and Reciprocal Recognition of Approval for Motor Vehicle Equipment and Parts. Amendments were adopted concerning the operation of mopeds, power-driven vehicles with handlebars, external projections of commercial vehicles, and the braking systems of agricultural vehicles. Progress was made on recommendations for the adaptation of public transport vehicles and passenger cars to the needs of disabled persons.

The Group of Rapporteurs on Brakes and Running Gear (Geneva: eleventh session, 27-30 April;[4] twelfth session, 30 November–3 December[5]) approved a regulation on electric service brakes for trailers and amendments to a draft regulation on steering equipment.

The Group of Rapporteurs on Crashworthiness (Geneva: tenth session, 18-20 January;[6] eleventh session, 24-26 August[7]) continued work on a draft regulation on the protection of the occupants of private (passenger) cars in the event of a head-on collision. The Group of Rapporteurs on General Safety Provisions (thirty-ninth session, Frankfort, Federal Republic of Germany, 11-14 May;[8] fortieth session, London, United Kingdom, 12-15 October;[9] forty-first session, Geneva, 7-10 December[10]) adopted amendments on motor cycle safety regulations and proposed a simplified procedure for the exchange of type approval documentation for vehicle manufacturers. The Group of Rapporteurs on Lighting and Light Signalling (tenth session, the Hague, the Netherlands, 28 September–1 October)[11] approved a draft regulation on the installation of such devices on agricultural or forestry tractors.

The Group of Rapporteurs on Noise (eleventh session, Rome, Italy, 11-13 October)[12] adopted changes in regulations on noise measuring methods, replacement silencing systems and audible warning devices. The Group of Rapporteurs on Pollution and Energy (Geneva: fifth session, 9-12 February;[13] sixth session, 31 August–3 September[14]) discussed energy saving, air pollution safety regulations for liquefied petroleum gases, and adopted a method of measuring fuel consumption.

Amendments to regulation on vehicle seats were adopted by the Group of Rapporteurs on Protective Devices (eleventh session, Geneva, 20-23 July),[15] which also discussed amendments to regulations on protective helmets, safety belts and child restraint systems. The Group of Rapporteurs on Safety Provisions on Motor Coaches and Buses (twenty-seventh session, Budapest, Hungary, 2-5 November)[16] adopted amendments to regulations on the strength of seats and seat mountings, and considered a number of other safety requirements, including guidelines for the carriage of disabled persons in public service vehicles.

During 1982, there were three *Ad Hoc* Meetings on Co-ordination (eighteenth to twentieth meetings, Geneva: 4 and 5 March,[17] 17 June[18] and 21 October[19]), at which decisions were taken on the organization of work of the Group of Experts on the Construction of Vehicles, and the groups of rapporteurs.

Reports. Group of Experts on Construction of Vehicles, [1]TRANS/SC1/WP29/90, [2]TRANS/SC1/WP29/93, [3]TRANS/SC1/WP29/99; Group of Rapporteurs on Brakes and Running Gear, [4]TRANS/SC1/WP29/GRRF/11, [5]TRANS/SC1/WP29/GRRF/12; Group of Rapporteurs on Crashworthiness, [6]TRANS/SC1/WP29/GRCS/10, [7]TRANS/SC1/WP29/GRCS/11; Group of Rapporteurs on General Safety Provisions, [8]TRANS/SC1/WP29/GRSG/18, [9]TRANS/SC1/WP29/GRSG/19, [10]TRANS/SC1/WP29/GRSG/20; [11]Group of Rapporteurs on Lighting and Light-signalling, TRANS/SC1/WP29/GRE/10; [12]Group of Rapporteurs on Noise, TRANS/SC1/WP29/GRB/9; Group of Rapporteurs on Pollution and Energy, [13]TRANS/SC1/WP29/GRPE/5, [14]TRANS/SC1/WP29/GRPE/6; [15]Group of Rapporteurs on Protective Devices, TRANS/SC1/WP29/GRDP/11; [16]Group of Rapporteurs on Safety Provisions on Motor Coaches and Buses, TRANS/SC1/WP29/GRSA/18; Meetings on Co-ordination of Work of Group of Experts on Construction of Vehicles, [17]TRANS/SC1/WP29/AC.2/17, [18]TRANS/SC1/WP29/AC.2/18, [19]TRANS/SC1/WP29/AC.2/19.

Other road transport questions

The *Ad Hoc* Meeting on Road Traffic Censuses (thirty-second session, Geneva, 3-5 May 1982)[3] made recommendations on implementing a 1985 census of the E-road network (main arteries) described in the European Agreement on Main International Traffic Arteries (AGR).

The Group of Experts on Road Traffic Safety (Geneva: forty-third session, 24-28 May;[1] forty-fourth session, 27 September–1 October[2]) considered amendments to update various road safety conventions and agreements, and made recommendations on special warning lights for motor vehicles.

Work continued in 1982 on the 10-nation Trans-European North-South Motorway Project (TEM). Its Steering Committee (Geneva: eighth session, 28-30 April;[4] ninth session, 14-16 December[5]) continued its assessment of environmental impact; considered standards for drainage, bridges and frontier crossings; and began studies on the international financing aspects of the motorway's construction. In addition, meetings were held during the year by the TEM Panel of Experts on follow-up of the December 1981 seminar, held in Athens, Greece, on techniques in transmission of legal and commercial information (Geneva, 16 and 17 November 1982)[6] and by the TEM Panel of Experts on Standards (Rome, Italy, 23-25 November).[7]

Reports. Group of Experts on Road Traffic Safety, [1]TRANS/SC1/GE.20/37, [2]TRANS/SC1/GE.20/39 & Corr.1; [3]Meeting on Road Traffic Censuses, TRANS/GE.6/AC.2/4; Steering Committee of Trans-European North-South Motorway Project, [4]TEM/10, [5]TEM/12; [6]Meeting of the Panel of Experts on Follow-up of Athens Seminar, TEM/TC/WP.65; [7]Panel of Experts on Standards, TEM/TC/WP.66.

Standardization of summertime

By a decision of 30 March 1982,[1] ECE noted with satisfaction that summertime had been introduced in 1981 for the same period in nearly all European continental countries, thereby eliminating difficulties caused in transport and other sectors by time differences. It recommended that all interested ECE member Governments should endeavour to standardize over a medium-term period the application of summertime in the region, and requested them to inform the Executive Secretary of any changes contemplated in the period of application, so that others could be informed. The Executive Secretary was asked to continue to approach the Governments and bodies concerned so as to harmonize the dates of application of summertime.

Efforts continued during the year to standardize the transition to summertime on the last Sunday in March and the end of summertime on the last Sunday in September.

Decision (1982). [1]ECE (report, E/1982/19): F(XXXVII), 30 Mar.

Industry in Europe

Chemical industries

In 1982, the ECE Chemical Industry Committee (fifteenth session, Geneva, 6-8 October)[1] considered the draft Annual Review of the Chemical Industry 1981, which was expected to be made available in 1983, and endorsed the plans for an abbreviated advance version of the Review, along with the report of its Group of Experts on the Periodic Survey of the Chemical Industry (tenth session, Geneva, 4 and 5 October)[2] and the Group's proposal to meet next in 1984.

The Committee welcomed the publication of the study on East-West trade in chemical products among ECE member countries, and endorsed the report of the second *Ad Hoc* Meeting for the Study on the Influence of Environmental Protection Measures on the Development of Pesticide Production and Consumption (Geneva, 9 and 10 March),[3] which had concluded its work by leaving the secretariat to finalize the study on the basis of comments made at that session.

The Committee also endorsed the reports of the first *Ad Hoc* Meeting for the Study on Trends in Feedstocks for Organics (Geneva, 11 and 12 March),[6] the first *Ad Hoc* Meeting for the Study on Non-Waste Technologies in the Production of Organics (Geneva, 1 and 2 February)[5] and the *Ad Hoc* Meeting on the Role and Place of the Chemical Industry in the Economies of ECE Member Countries (Geneva, 6 and 7 May).[4]

In the area of petrochemical raw materials, the Committee convened a Seminar on the Rational Use of Crude Oil by the Chemical Industry (Prague, Czechoslovakia, 20-24 September).[7]

Reports. [1]Chemical Industry Committee, ECE/CHEM/42; [2]Group of Experts on Periodic Survey of Chemical Industry, CHEM/GE.1/14; [3]Meeting for Study on Influence of Environmental Protection Measures on Development of Pesticide Production and Consumption, CHEM/AC.9/4; [4]Meeting for Role and Place of Chemical Industry in

Economies of ECE Member Countries, CHEM/AC.14/2; [5]Meeting for Study on Non-Waste Technologies in Production of Organics, CHEM/AC.12/2; [6]Meeting for Study on Trends in Feedstocks for Organics, CHEM/AC.13/2; [7]Seminar on Rational Use of Crude Oil by Chemical Industry, CHEM/SEM.11/3.

Publications. Market Trends for Chemical Products, 1975-1980 and Prospects to 1990, vol. I (ECE/CHEM/40/Vol.I), Sales No. E.82.II.E.13; vol. II: *Statistical Annex* (ECE/CHEM/40/Vol.II), Sales No. E.82.II.E.14. *Annual Review of the Chemical Industry 1982* (ECE/CHEM/50), Sales No. E.84.II.E.2. *Annual Bulletin of Trade in Chemical Products*, vol. IX, *1982*, Sales No. E/F/R.84.II.E.3.

Engineering industries

The ECE Working Party on Engineering Industries and Automation (second session, Geneva, 24-26 February)[7] published in 1982 an enlarged version of the Annual Review of Engineering Industries and Automation, covering 1980 and estimates for 1981. Work continued on studies on industrial robots, the international division of labour in the automotive industry, improvement of engineering equipment for more effective energy use, and engineering equipment and automation methods for preventing water pollution.

The fourth *Ad Hoc* Meeting on Questions of Statistics concerning Engineering Industries and Automation (Geneva, 10 and 11 June)[5] continued work in the methodological approach to the comparability and collection of data for production and international trade of engineering products, and agreed on a provisional agenda for the 1983 joint meeting of the Working Group with the Conference of European Statisticians.

A Seminar on Present Use and Prospects for Precision Measuring Instruments in Engineering Industries (Dresden, German Democratic Republic, 20-24 September)[6] recommended that ECE organize seminars on precision measuring equipment, that countries pay attention to educating management and workers in the gains to be made from the introduction of such equipment, and that international standardization be encouraged in order to ensure compatibility of equipment, especially electronic components. The first *Ad Hoc* Meeting for the Study on Measures for Improving Engineering Equipment with a View to More Effective Energy Use (Geneva, 8 and 9 June)[3] agreed on a draft outline and scope for a survey of the current state and trends, the share of energy-efficient engineering equipment in general engineering and an inventory of all related types of equipment.

Also meeting in 1982 were the first *Ad Hoc* Meeting for the Study on Production and Use of Industrial Robots (Geneva, 16 and 17 November)[2] and the second *Ad Hoc* Meeting for the Study of Techno-Economic Aspects of the International Division of Labour in the Automative Industry (Geneva, 18 and 19 November).[4]

By a decision of 30 March,[1] ECE approved the work programme of its Working Party on Engineering Industries and Automation, and took note of the relevant report of the Executive Secretary.

Decision (1982). [1]ECE (report, E/1982/19), I(XXXVII), 30 Mar.
Reports. [2]Meeting for Study on Production and Use of Industrial Robots, ENG.AUT/AC.5/2; [3]Meeting for Studies on Measures for Improving Engineering Equipment with a View to More Effective Energy Use, ENG.AUT/AC.4/2; [4]Meeting for Study on Techno-economic Aspects of International Division of Labour in Automotive Industry, ENG.AUT/AC.2/4; [5]Meeting on Questions of Statistics concerning Engineering Industries and Automation, ENG.AUT/AC.1/4; [6]Seminar on Present Use and Prospects for Precision Measuring Instruments in Engineering Industries, ENG.AUT/SEM.1/3; [7]Working Party on Engineering Industries and Automation, ECE/ENG.AUT/6;
Publication. Annual Review of Engineering Industries and Automation 1980 (ECE/ENG.AUT/7), Sales No. E.82.II.E.18.

Iron and steel industry

The ECE Steel Committee (fiftieth session, Geneva, 27-29 October 1982)[4] reviewed current steel market trends and decided to convene in 1983 a group of rapporteurs to assist the secretariat in the preparation of a study on the trend in 1982, and another group to continue work on the study on the strategy for energy use in the iron and steel industry.

The Committee endorsed the report of the Seminar on Changes in Quality Requirements of Steel Demand (Turin, Italy, 28 June-2 July),[3] which had concluded that the steel industry had made progress in elaborating new types of steels and that it was capable of meeting, at competitive prices, the quality requirements for conventional and special steels.

The Working Party on the Steel Market (twenty-first session, Geneva, 17 and 18 June)[5] suggested changes in the study "The Steel Market in 1981" to benefit from the latest available information, and asked the secretariat to prepare the final version.

The third *Ad Hoc* Meeting on the Evolution of the Specific Consumption of Steel (Geneva, 25 and 26 October)[1] approved the final draft questionnaire on the subject, which was intended to assist national steel industries in adapting their production to demand. The second *Ad Hoc* Meeting on Strategy for Energy Use in Iron and Steel Industry (Geneva, 17 and 18 February)[2] concluded that an evaluation of new energy-saving techniques was needed in preparing the strategy.

Reports. [1]Meeting on Evolution of Specific Consumption of Steel, STEEL/AC.6/6; [2]Meeting on Strategy for Energy Use in Iron and Steel Industry, STEEL/AC.7/4; [3]Seminar on Changes in Quality Requirements of Steel Demand, STEEL/SEM.8/3; [4]Steel Committee, ECE/STEEL/38; [5]Working Party on Steel Market, STEEL/WP.1/20 & Add.1.

Publication. The Steel Market in 1982 (E/ECE/STEEL/42), Sales No. E.83.II.E.13.

Water in Europe

The ECE Committee on Water Problems (fourteenth session, Geneva, 23-26 November 1982)[1] reviewed the implementation by Governments of the ECE Declaration of Policy on Prevention and Control of Water Pollution, including Transborder Pollution, and continued to elaborate a draft ECE declaration of policy on the rational use of water, aimed at assisting Governments in the formulation of such strategies. Work also continued on reports dealing with flood management, industrial and municipal sewage effluent purification, and reduction of industrial water pollution, as did activities in co-operation with the Conference of European Statisticians, on statistics of water use and quality.

The Group of Experts on Aspects of Water Quality and Quantity (tenth session, Geneva, 26-29 April)[2] agreed on preparatory work for a 1983 Seminar on Groundwater Protection Strategies and Practices and adopted an outline for a report on techniques and means for drought management in the region.

As a contribution to the International Drinking Water Supply and Sanitation Decade (1981-1990),[4] the Committee convened a Seminar on Drinking Water Supply and Effluent Disposal Systems (Albufeira, Portugal, 18-22 October),[3] which adopted recommendations for dealing with the relevant changes brought about by urban concentration and renewal of town centres, rising living standards in rural areas and increasing seasonal tourism.

Reports. [1]Committee on Water Problems, ECE/WATER/30; [2]Group of Experts on Aspects of Water Quality and Quantity, WATER/GE.1/20; [3]Seminar on Drinking Water Supply and Effluent Disposal Systems, WATER/SEM.9/3.
Yearbook reference. [4]1980, p. 704.

Shared water resources

By a decision of 30 March 1982,[1] ECE called on member Governments to co-operate in the elaboration of policy aims, programmes and planning regarding the development, use and conservation of shared water resources. It encouraged them to extend relevant international arrangements, speed up procedures within international river commissions and governmental bodies to cope with emergency situations and to promote international co-operation through the commissions by improving their efficiency and by establishing new ones where needed.

It decided to convene under the auspices of its Committee on Water Problems, as and if required, meetings on international river commissions in order to promote and facilitate such co-operation in the region. ECE reiterated its decision to strengthen the Committee, and requested it to elaborate a report on international co-operation in shared water resources development and to carry out projects on compatible statistical data, comparison of water quality norms, comparison of methods for analysing water composition and properties, review of emergency measures and those for assessment of socio-economic impacts due to accidental pollution and floods.

Decision (1982). [1]ECE (report, E/1982/19): D(XXXVII), 30 Mar.

Transboundary water pollution

By a decision of 30 March 1982,[1] ECE welcomed the November 1981 adoption by the Committee on Water Problems of the Terms of Reference for a Programme on Monitoring and Evaluation of Transboundary Water Pollution[3] and took note of the readiness of some ECE member countries to participate in pilot projects.

In a February report,[2] the ECE Executive Secretary noted that among the 13 countries responding to the secretariat's queries, four expressed interest in project participation, with or without comments on feasibility or conditions; one had the matter under consideration; and eight others expressed lack of interest.

Decision (1982). [1]ECE (report, E/1982/19), E(XXXVII), 30 Mar.
Report. [2]ECE Executive Secretary, E/ECE/1038.
Yearbook reference. [3]1981, p. 653.

Energy in Europe

On 2 April 1982,[1] ECE approved the 1982/1983 work programme of the Senior Advisers to ECE Governments on Energy, and invited the Executive Secretary in consultation with member Governments to convene the fifth session of the Senior Advisers and an *ad hoc* meeting on new and renewable sources of energy. The Senior Advisers were invited to consider convening an *ad hoc* meeting on energy conservation.

An *Ad Hoc* Meeting on New and Renewable Sources of Energy (Geneva, 30 November–3 December)[2] made recommendations on several projects to begin in 1983.

A Symposium on the Comparative Merits of Energy Sources in Meeting End-Use Heat Demand (Ohrid, Yugoslavia, 6-10 September)[3] noted that over 60 per cent of the energy consumed in the ECE region was in the form of heat, that this pattern was expected to prevail up to the year 2000, and that the heat demand could be met more effectively through improved economy and efficiency and through fuel substitution. The Symposium recommended that the Senior Advisors undertake an international analysis of the trends of end-use demand; develop statistics on energy end-uses by categories, sectors and fuels; compare the cost-efficiency of various energy conservation measures and technologies; and promote research and development.

Decision (1982). [1]ECE (report, E/1982/19): A(XXXVII), 2 Apr.
Reports. [2]Meeting on New and Renewable Sources of Energy, ECE/AC.8/2; [3]Symposium on Comparative Merits of Energy Sources in Meeting End-Use Heat Demand, ENERGY/SEM.2/2.
Publication. Energy Transition in the ECE Region (E/ECE/1063), Sales No. E.83.II.E.21.

Coal

In 1982, the ECE Coal Committee (seventy-eighth session, Geneva, 20-23 September)[1] completed its work on technical and economic problems connected with opencast and underground coal-mining, international co-operation in research and development, coal's future role in the energy economy of the ECE region, the preparation and utilization of solid fuels, and coal trade prospects. It decided to issue several studies completed by its subsidiary bodies and approved its 1982-1986 work programme.

The third *Ad Hoc* Meeting on the Preparation of a New ECE Classification of Coals (Geneva, 22-24 February)[6] agreed on the principles for a new classification of medium-rank coals, a grade of coal used for industry. The Group of Experts on Coal Statistics (nineteeth session, Geneva, 21-23 June)[2] considered the preliminary version of the Annual Bulletin of Coal Statistics for 1981, and accepted that coal statistics be presented in "terajoules", a measure of energy based on net calorific value, for purposes of comparison with general energy statistics.

The Group of Experts on Productivity and Management Problems in the Coal Industry (thirteenth session, Geneva, 16-18 June)[3] considered methods of eliminating firedamp and utilizing it as a source of energy, and ways of increasing productivity in mines. It initiated a joint study, with the Group of Experts on Coal Statistics, on the comparative analysis of working time at mechanized coal faces.

The Meeting of Directors of National Mining Research Institutes (sixth session, Essen, Federal Republic of Germany, 19-23 April)[5] emphasized the necessity of introducing computer technology in the control of operations as well as management.

Noting that the trends towards gasification and liquefaction of coal were no longer as pronounced as in previous years due to the high price of coal-conversion products in relation to natural gas and crude oil, the Group of Experts on the Utilization and Preparation of Solid Fuels (thirteenth session, Geneva, 14-16 June)[4] requested the secretariat to propose topics for consideration in 1983.

The Working Party on Coal Trade (twenty-third session, Geneva, 23-25 June)[7] examined country statistics for 1970-1980 as well as international coal trade in 1981, and decided to consider on a permanent basis the problem of world coal trade up to the year 2000.

> *Reports.* [1]Coal Committee, ECE/COAL/65; [2]Group of Experts on Coal Statistics, COAL/GE.2/20; [3]Group of Experts on Productivity and Management Problems in Coal Industry, COAL/GE.1/20; [4]Group of Experts on Utilization and Preparation of Solid Fuels, COAL/GE.3/20; [5]Meeting of Directors of National Mining Research Institutes, COAL/GE.4/10; [6]Meeting on Preparation of a New ECE Classification of Coals, COAL/AC.5/6; [7]Working Party on Coal Trade, COAL/WP.1/48.

Electric power

The ECE Committee on Electric Power (fortieth session, Geneva, 18-22 January 1982)[1] approved the report of the 1981 Seminar on the Medium-term and Long-term Prospects for the Electric Power Industry[7] and asked its expert groups to study the Seminar's recommendations. The Committee recommended that the Group of Experts on Problems of Planning and Operating Large Power Systems consider studying problems associated with the use of new direct-current techniques in electric power transmission installations, and the experience of the various international unions of interconnected systems which operated such installations. The Committee accepted the invitation of the Senior Advisers to ECE Governments on Science and Technology to co-operate in the preparations for the 1983 Seminar on the Integrated Utilization of Low-calorific-value Fuels.

The Group of Experts on Distribution and Rural Electrification (twenty-third session, Geneva, 24-26 May)[2] decided to circulate the secretariat report on the state of rural electrification in the ECE region 1975-1978 and discussed progress on several other reports.

The Group of Experts on Electric Power Stations (thirteenth session, Geneva, 25-27 October)[3] continued its work on various studies dealing with technical, design and operational aspects of conventional and nuclear power stations, and requested the secretariat to issue the report of the Seminar on the Extraction, Removal and Use of Ash from Coal-fire Thermal Power Stations (Geneva, 10-13 May).[6]

The Group of Experts on Problems of Planning and Operating Large Power Systems (fourteenth session, Geneva, 28-30 June)[4] expressed satisfaction with the results of the work done by the group of Balkan countries on the interconnection of their electric power transmission systems. It continued work on East-West interconnection of electric power transmission systems, energy conservation measures, and other selected technological, economic and managerial problems.

The Group of Experts on the Relationship between Electricity and the Environment (eleventh session, Geneva, 22-24 November)[5] reviewed the progress of several studies, including those methods of measuring and monitoring pollution caused by electric power stations, noise emission by thermal power stations, and problems linked with the cooling towers of large-capacity thermal and nuclear power stations.

> *Reports.* [1]Committee on Electric Power, ECE/EP/47; [2]Group of Experts on Distribution and Rural Electrification, EP/GE.1/10; [3]Group of Experts on Electric Power Stations, EP/GE.3/20; [4]Group of Experts on Problems of Planning and Operating Large Power Systems, EP/GE.2/20; [5]Group of Experts on Relationship between Electricity and Environment, EP/GE.4/20; [6]Seminar on Extraction, Removal and Use of Ash from Coal-fired Thermal Power Stations, ECE/EP/57.
> *Yearbook reference.* [7]1981, p. 655.
> *Publication. Annual Bulletin of Electric Energy for Europe 1982*, vol. XXVIII, Sales No. E/F/R/83.II.E.29.

Natural gas

The ECE Committee on Gas (twenty-eighth session, Geneva, 11-15 January 1982)[1] continued its work on natural gas resources, their exploration and exploitation, transport and storage, distribution and use, gas statistics and investments. The Committee added to its work programme a project on development and prospects of trade in gas between ECE and other regions, and agreed to study natural gas and liquefied petroleum gas (LPG) export possibilities from the Middle East and Africa to the ECE region.

An *Ad Hoc* Meeting on LPG Problems (Geneva, 1-3 November)[6] agreed on the implementation of the recommendations of the 1981 Symposium on the LPG Situation in the ECE region during 1980-1990,[7] and suggested that the Committee on Gas convene the *Ad Hoc* Meeting on LPG Problems at the earliest opportunity.

Besides its work on the Annual Bulletin of Gas Statistics for Europe, the Group of Experts on Gas Statistics and Forecasting Problems (nineteenth session, Geneva, 1 and 2 July)[2] discussed the harmonization of gas statistics questionnaires and the use of computers in forecasting gas demand, and agreed to initiate a new study on the industry's use of computers for statistical purposes.

The Group of Experts on Natural Gas Resources (seventh session, Geneva, 6-8 September)[3] continued to study a series of technical questions and continued work on the revision of the international map of natural gas fields in Europe.

The Group of Experts on the Transport and Storage of Gas (thirteenth session, 9-11 June)[4] completed a study on problems in the management of international gas pipelines. The Group of Experts on the Use and Distribution of Gas (thirteenth session, Geneva, 7-9 June)[5] agreed to initiate a study on the use of gas for the drying and storage of agricultural produce.

Reports. [1]Committee on Gas, ECE/GAS/59; [2]Group of Experts on Gas Statistics and Forecasting Problems, GAS/GE.1/16; [3]Group of Experts on Natural Gas Resources, GAS/GE.4/14; [4]Group of Experts on Transport and Storage of Gas, GAS/GE.3/20; [5]Group of Experts on Use and Distribution of Gas, GAS/GE.2/20; [6]*Ad Hoc* Meeting on Liquefied Petroleum Gases (LPG) Problems, GAS/AC.7/2.
Yearbook reference. [7]1981, p. 655.

Food and agriculture in Europe

The ECE Committee on Agricultural Problems (thirty-third session, Geneva, 8-12 March 1982)[1] elaborated and reviewed commercial quality standards for fruit, vegetables, egg products and poultry meat. A technical review was prepared on triticale (a hybrid of wheat and rye), and reports and symposia were being prepared on animal husbandry. The Committee initiated a review of new agro-technical developments and market trends for selected protein-rich feedingstuffs, of which there was a considerable deficit in Europe.

Report. [1]Committee on Agricultural Problems, ECE/AGRI/63.
Publications. Prices of Agricultural Products and Selected Inputs in Europe and North America 1981/82 (E/ECE/AGRI/69), Sales No. E.83.II.E.7; *Review of the Agricultural Situation in Europe at the End of 1982,* vol. I: *General Review, Grain, Livestock and Meat* & vol. II: *Dairy Products and Eggs* (E/ECE/AGRI/71, vols. I, II), Sales No. E.83.II.E.15, vols. I, II.

Standardization of agricultural products

The Working Party on Standardization of Perishable Produce (thirty-eighth session, Geneva, 6-9 July 1982)[8] reviewed and revised standards for fresh vegetables and fruit, and agreed that the Group of Experts on Standardization of Dry and Dried Produce should prepare a simplified revised protocol applicable to all the standards for fruits and vegetables, with two separate "Standard Layouts" for fresh and dried produce. It decided as premature, but worth pursuing, the revised proposals by the Codex Alimentarius Commission, a joint body of the Food and Agriculture Organization of the United Nations and the World Health Organization, on improving the co-ordination of work between the two bodies.

In addition to its input to the draft protocol on produce-standards, the Group of Experts on Co-ordination of Standardization of Fresh Fruit and Vegetables (twenty-seventh session, Geneva, 2-4 March)[1] considered partial revision of the UN/ECE standards for fruit and vegetables, and discussed labelling provisions.

The Group of Experts on International Trade Practices relating to Agricultural Products (twenty-fifth session, Geneva, 8-10 November)[2] dis-

cussed, and requested the secretariat to revise, a draft document on General Conditions of Sale for Milk and Milk Products.

The Group of Experts on Standardization of Cut Flowers (ninth session, Geneva, 5-7 April)[3] virtually completed its work programme after considering proposals on marking a freshness date, chemical treatment and quality codes on cut flowers and foliage; it noted, however, that the standards would need to be reviewed again in about five years.

Recommendations for the commercial standardization of pistachio nuts and dates and revised standards for dried figs were made by the Group of Experts on Standardization of Dry and Dried Produce (Fruit) (twenty-eighth session, Cesme-Izmir, Turkey, 14-17 June).[4] The Group of Experts on Standardization of Seed Potatoes (twenty-second session, Geneva, 26-28 January)[6] revised the existing standard and recommended it for adoption by the Working Party.

The Group of Experts on Standardization of Poultry Meat (second session, Geneva, 11-13 Janaury),[5] agreed on the scope and field of application, as well as on definitions and certain provisions of a revised draft standard for poultry.

The Joint ECE/Codex Alimentarius Group of Experts (fifteenth session, Rome, Italy, 8-12 February)[7] continued its work on elaboration of worldwide food standards, and added two new general standards—for fruit juices and for fruit nectars—to the work programme.

Reports. [1]Group of Experts on Co-ordination of Standardization of Fresh Fruits and Vegetables, AGRI/WP.1/GE.1/18; [2]Group of Experts on International Trade Practices relating to Agricultural Products, AGRI/WP.1/GE.7/73; [3]Group of Experts on Standardization of Cut Flowers, AGRI/WP.1/GE.9/18; [4]Group of Experts on Standardization of Dry and Dried Produce (Fruit), AGRI/WP.1/GE.2/27; [5]Group of Experts on Standardization of Poultry Meat, AGRI/WP.1/GE.10/4; [6]Group of Experts on Standardization of Seed Potatoes, AGRI/WP.1/GE.6/16; [7]Joint ECE/Codex Alimentarius Group of Experts on Standardization of Fruit Juices, AGRI/WP.1/GE.4/12; [8]Working Party on Standardization of Perishable Produce, AGRI/WP.1/31.

Other agricultural questions

The joint Food and Agriculture Organization of the United Nations (FAO)/ECE Working Party on Agrarian Structure and Farm Rationalization (fifth session, Geneva, 4-8 October 1982)[1] discussed economic and social aspects of a rational use of natural resources, alternative forms of agricultural production (use of organic fertilizers), energy and water. Technical reports were under preparation on methods of erosion control, land recultivation, soil quality improvement, and legal aspects of protecting agricultural land. An outline was prepared for national reports on economic instruments for the rational use of water in irrigation.

The FAO/ECE Working Party on Mechanization of Agriculture (twenty-eighth session, Geneva, 25-29 October)[2] reviewed recent changes in mechanization, including those relating to transport and the use of electronics and microprocessors.

ECE and FAO organized two symposia in 1982. A Symposium on Agriculture and Tourism (Mariehamn, Finland, 7-12 June)[3] dealt with interrelationships between tourism and agricultural development, and benefits and disadvantages of farm tourism (holiday on farms). A Symposium on Technological and Economic Aspects of Catering (Budapest, Hungary, 20-23 April)[4] recommended that Governments devote greater financial resources to research in the catering industry, collect statistical information and increase training opportunities.

Reports. [1]Joint FAO/ECE Working Party on Agrarian Structure and Farm Rationalization, FAO/ECE/AGRI/WP.3/10; [2]Joint FAO/ECE Working Party on Mechanization of Agriculture, FAO/ECE/AGRI/WP.2/55; [3]Symposium on Agriculture and Tourism, AGRI/SEM.17/2 & Corr.1; [4]Symposium on Technological and Economic Aspects of Catering, AGRI/SEM.16/2.

Timber

In 1982, the ECE Timber Committee (fortieth session, Geneva, 11-15 October)[6] observed the effects of the world economic depression on the forestry and forest industries sector, and concluded that the timber markets would likely retain a cautious approach until signs of economic recovery were apparent. The Committee finalized two ECE recommended standards on stress grading and on finger-jointing of coniferous sawn timber.

The Joint Committee on Forest Working Techniques and Training of Forest Workers (fourteenth session, Sandefjord, Norway, 22-25 June),[1] organized by ECE, FAO and the International Labour Organisation, reviewed the activities carried out by teams of specialists in such areas as labour productivity measurement, forest operations management, afforestation, compatibility of harvesting methods with silviculture and the environment, and wood harvesting for energy purposes.

The Seminar on the Management of Forest Working Training (Dumfries, Scotland, United Kingdom, 10-14 May)[3] agreed that, in a period characterized by technological advances and escalating costs of labour and equipment, the need to increase the skills of forest workers was greater than ever.

The Seminar on Energy Conservation and Self-Sufficiency in the Sawmilling Industry (Bonn, Federal Republic of Germany, 13-17 September)[2] formulated a number of recommendations on improving the efficiency of energy use in sawmilling. The Seminar on Reducing Biomass Losses in Logging Operations (Moscow, 6-10 December)[5] explored various such approaches and considered the environmental implications of the removal of biomass from the forest. The Seminar on the Planning and Techniques of Transport and its Relation to Forest Operation Activities (Sandefjord, Norway, 17-22 June)[4] considered ways to improve the economic accessibility of forest strands, notably those in steep terrain, through planning and lay-out of cable and road networks, centralized processing operations and transfer of experience to developing countries.

Reports. [1]Joint FAO/ECE/ILO Committee on Forest Working Techniques and Training of Forest Workers, TIM/EFC/WP.1/12; [2]Seminar on Energy Conservation and Self-Sufficiency in Sawmilling Industry, TIM/SEM.13/2; [3]Seminar on Management of Forest Worker Training, TIM/EFC/WP.1/SEM.13/2; [4]Seminar on Planning and Techniques of Transport and Its Relation to Forest Operational Activities, TIM/EFC/WP.1/SEM.14/1; [5]Seminar on Reducing Forest Biomass Losses in Logging Operations, TIM/EFC/WP.1/SEM.15/2; [6]Timber Committee, ECE/TIM/21.
Publication. Timber Bulletin for Europe, vol. XXXV, No. 2.

Science and technology in Europe

By its decision of 2 April 1982,[1] ECE invited its member Governments to submit their views on specific proposals on its follow-up contribution to the 1979 United Nations Conference on Science and Technology for Development,[4] and invited the Advisers to ECE Governments on Science and Technology to examine the utility of convening, before the 1983 ECE session, an *ad hoc* meeting on the subject. It requested the Executive Secretary to up-date and complete the document on ECE follow-up activities and the Senior Advisers to examine it at its 1982 session.

The Senior Advisers (tenth session, Geneva, 27 September–1 October)[3] considered the updated report and agreed to decide in 1983 on recommendations and the utility of convening an *ad hoc* meeting.

In 1982, the Senior Advisers undertook a study on policies relating to technological innovation and focused on international co-operation in research and development in electronics, automation, biotechnology and raw materials. In order to promote East-West co-operation in science and technology, the Advisers agreed on the preparation of a compendium of national experience in ECE member countries on the organization and management of international co-operative research, focusing on legal and administrative requirements. The Advisers endorsed the recommendations of an *Ad Hoc* Meeting concerning the Inter-Country Project on Research relating to the Utilization of Low-Calorific-Value Coals (Geneva, 28 and 29 June)[2] and invited ECE countries to contribute to the project.

Decision (1982). [1]ECE (report, E/1982/19): C(XXXVII), 2 Apr.
Reports. [2]Meeting concerning Inter-country Project on Research relating to Utilization of Low-Calorific-Value Coals, SC.TECH./AC.18/2; [3]Senior Advisers to ECE Governments on Science and Technology, ECE/SC.TECH./23.
Yearbook reference. [4]1979, p. 635.

Environment in Europe

On 2 April 1982,[1] ECE appealed for an early ratification of the Convention on Long-range Transboundary Air Pollution, adopted under its auspices in 1979,[11] while expressing satisfaction with the progress made to that end and with the work of the Interim Executive Body, entrusted with the treaty implementation. The Convention was expected to enter into force on 16 March 1983. The Commission also approved the work programme of the Senior Advisers to ECE Governments on Environmental Problems on environment impact assessment, and welcomed further co-operation within the region in the protection of flora and fauna and their habitats. Noting the activities of the Working Party on Low- and Non-waste Technology and Re-utilization and Recycling of Wastes, ECE emphasized the importance of the conservation and sustainable use of natural resources.

The Working Party on non-waste technology (third session, Geneva, 13-15 October)[10] examined the progress made in compiling the Compendium on Low- and Non-waste Technology and urged the national focal points to consider technical aspects of information computerization for effective dissemination.

The fifth meeting of the National Focal Points for the Compilation of a Compendium on Low- and Non-waste Technology (Geneva, 11 and 12 October)[5] agreed on the inclusion of 27 additional monographs on specific industrial technologies to the document.

The Senior Advisers (tenth session, Geneva, 9-12 February)[6] urged ECE Governments to increase participation in the Compendium compilation; requested its task force to develop a set of recommendations on the protection of flora, fauna and their habitats; and accepted to co-operate with the Senior Advisers to ECE Governments on Science and Technology in preparing the Seminar on the Integrated Utilization of Low-Calorific-Value Fuels.

The Group of Experts on Environmental Impact Assessment (first session, Geneva, 2-5 November)[3] decided to exchange information on national experiences of ECE countries in this field.

The Meeting on Cost-Benefit Analysis of Sulphur Emission Control (Geneva, 13-15 December)[4] elaborated a draft methodology for such an analysis of alternative programmes for sulphur pollution control. The Working Group on Effects of Sulphur Compounds on the Environment (se-

cond session, Geneva, 30 August-3 September)[9] agreed on research plans and adopted conclusions and recommendations dealing with effects of sulphur pollution on materials (including historic and cultural monuments), aquatic ecosystems, and soil, ground water and vegetation. The Working Party on Air Pollution Problems (twelfth session, Geneva, 20 and 21 September)[8] adopted conclusions on the efficiency and costs of technologies for controlling sulphur emissions, and recommended that identification of the least-cost combination of desulphurization technologies be carried out on a country-by-country basis. The Steering Body to the Co-operative Programme for Monitoring and Evaluation of Long-range Transmission of Air Pollutants in Europe (sixth session, Geneva, 1-3 December)[7] made recommendations on the intercomparison of sulphur measurement techniques in 20 countries, envisaged for 1983 and 1984.

In a decision of 31 May,[2] the Governing Council of the United Nations Environment Programme (UNEP) requested its Executive Director, in view of the need for more effective and economically sound co-operation with ECE, to consult with Governments and the Commission on the desirability of establishing a joint UNEP/ECE division.

Decisions (1982). [1]ECE (report, E/1982/19): B(XXXVII), 2 Apr.; [2]UNEP Council (report, A/37/25): 10/2, sect. V, 31 May.
Reports. [3]Group of Experts on Environmental Impact Assessment, ENV/GE.1/2; [4]Meeting on Cost-Benefit Analysis of Sulphur Emission Control, ENV/IEB/AC.1/2; [5]National Focal Points for Compilation of Compendium on Low- and Non-waste Technology, ENV/AC.7/10; [6]Senior Advisers to ECE Governments on Environmental Problems, ECE/ENV/38; [7]Steering Body to Co-operative Programme for Monitoring and Evaluation of Long-range Transmission of Air Pollutants in Europe (EMEP), ENV/WP.1/GE.1/12; [8]Working Party on Air Pollution Problems, ENV/WP.1/18; [9]Working Group on Effects of Sulphur Compounds on Environment, ENV/IEB/WG.1/4; [10]Working Party on Low- and Non-waste Technology and Re-utilization and Recycling of Wastes, ENV/WP.2/7.
Yearbook reference. [11]1979, p. 710.

Human settlements in Europe

The ECE Committee on Housing, Building and Planning (forty-third session, Geneva, 13-17 September 1982)[1] reviewed human settlements trends and policies in the region, and pursued work on various aspects of urban renewal and modernization policies.

The Working Party on Building (fourteenth session, Geneva, 9-12 November)[8] completed the first stage of the work on an ECE Compendium of Model Requirements for Building Regulations, and agreed with the 1981 Seminar on Construction in Seismic Regions[11] that the secretariat should issue a report on the subject. An *Ad Hoc* Meeting on the ECE Model for Building Regulations (Geneva, 1-3 June)[4] reported to the Working Party on the elaboration of the Model, which was intended to serve as a checklist from which countries could select appropriate national regulations. In order to stress the non-mandatory nature of the Model, the Meeting proposed that the name be changed to "ECE Guide for the Technical Content of Building Regulations".

The Working Party on Housing (eleventh session, Geneva, 26-29 October)[9] initiated preparations for a seminar on housing financing and continued work on reports on the programming and forecasting of housing. The Working Party's *Ad Hoc* Meeting on Housing Management (Geneva, 23-26 February)[5] discussed the legal framework, the cost and financing, and the social aspects of housing management.

The Working Party on Urban and Regional Planning (fourteenth session, Geneva, 19-22 April)[10] finalized preparations for a 1983 Seminar on Integrated Planning, and agreed to consider the questions of urban renewal and recreational leisure areas. The Working Party's Group of Experts on Urban and Regional Research (thirteenth session, Geneva, 13-16 April)[3] discussed long-term perspectives for human settlements development in the ECE region.

The Group of Experts on Human Settlements Problems in Southern Europe (eleventh meeting, Perugia, Italy, 24-28 May)[2] discussed problems of inland areas, which suffered from disadvantageous socio-economic, morphological and other conditions.

The second Seminar on Energy Aspects of Human Settlements Policies (Gävle and Malmö, Sweden, 7-18 June)[6] made recommendations on housing-related energy conservation policies and the impact of energy considerations on urban and regional planning. The Seminar on the Relationship between Housing and the National Economy (Prague, Czechoslovakia, 10-14 May)[7] adopted conclusions on such relationships and on the social effectiveness of housing policy, and stressed the need for better comparability of housing statistics in the ECE region.

Reports. [1]Committee on Housing, Building and Planning, ECE/HBP/42; [2]Group of Experts on Human Settlements Problems in Southern Europe, HBP/GE.2/15; [3]Group of Experts on Urban and Regional Research, HBP/WP.3/GE.1/21; [4]Meeting on ECE Model for Building Regulations, HBP/WP.2/AC.10/2; [5]Meeting on Housing Management, HBP/WP.1/AC.5/2; [6]Second Seminar on Energy Aspects of Human Settlements Policies, HBP/SEM.30/2; [7]Seminar on Relationship between Housing and National Economy, HBP/SEM.29/2; [8]Working Party on Building, HBP/WP.2/20; [9]Working Party on Housing, HBP/WP.1/16; [10]Working Party on Urban and Regional Planning, HBP/WP.3/16.
Yearbook reference. [11]1981, p. 658.

Statistics in Europe

The Conference of European Statisticians (thirtieth session Geneva, 21-25 June 1982)[1] continued work in the promotion of international comparisons of main economic aggregates among different countries of the region, and in the development and harmonization of concepts, classifications and nomenclatures. The Conference emphasized the importance of work in the use of computers for statistical purposes and design and development of statistical information systems, discussed ways to adapt statistics to users' needs, and considered possibilities of replacing exhaustive statistical inquiries, especially population and housing censuses, by using administrative registers.

The Third Joint ECE/World Health Organization (WHO) Meeting on Health Statistics (Geneva, 15-18 February)[8] recognized the need to adapt the WHO International Classification of Impairments, Disabilities and Handicaps for use in household surveys in order to allow for international comparisons. The Meeting made suggestions for the work aimed at establishing a list of indicators for countries to assess achievements of their national health strategies.

The Study Group on Food and Agricultural Statistics in Europe, convened jointly by the Food and Agriculture Organization of the United Nations (FAO), the Conference of European Statisticians and the ECE Committee on Agricultural Problems (thirteenth session, Geneva, 3-6 May)[3] referred to the close link between cost and quality of data, agreed that statistical agencies could provide short-term, but not long-term, forecasts in cooperation with other technical agencies, and expressed the view that current requirements for agricultural data might call for a modification of census approaches and/or the use of other sources such as farm registers.

The Fourth Joint ECE/United Nations Educational, Scientific and Cultural Organization Meeting on Statistics of Education (Geneva, 21-24 September)[2] considered standardization and international comparability of statistics of education, social indicators, and national reports on individual data systems in education.

The Meeting on Frameworks for Environment Statistics (Geneva, 4-6 October)[4] discussed an approach to a comparative survey of national compilations of environmental statistics, approaches used in natural resource accounting schemes, and links between environment statistics and systems of national accounts or socio-demographic statistics. The general need for arriving at international conventions concerning classifications and definitions for purposes of environment statistics was confirmed by the Meeting.

The Meeting on Human Settlements Statistics (Geneva, 15-18 March),[5] convened jointly by the

Conference of European Statisticians and the Committee on Housing, Building and Planning, decided that the United Nations illustrative guidelines for indicators in this field, which had not been reviewed since 1976, should be revised to take into account the issues raised at the 1976 United Nations Conference on Human Settlements;[10] the Meeting identified, as being of particular current interest to policy makers, household consumption of energy, expenditures for housing, transportation, access to social services and estimates of housing demands. It also recommended restructuring the Annual Bulletin of Housing and Building Statistics for Europe.

The Meeting on Statistics of Water Use and Quality (Geneva, 18-21 January)[6] agreed that the elaboration of a draft standard international classification of water use and quality should start with two general points: the overall information needs of water management at the national level and the availability of indicators chosen for inclusion in the classification.

The Working Party on National Accounts and Balances (eleventh session, Geneva, 1-4 June)[9] considered proposals for the revision and expansion of the System of National Accounts (SNA) and for short-term changes to the System. It welcomed a secretariat survey of national practices in regard to enterprise statistics in countries with centrally planned economies.

The Seminar on Integrated Statistical Information Systems and Related Matters (Bratislava, Czechoslovakia, 10-14 May)[7] studied selected topics connected with the design and development of computerized statistical information systems.

Reports. [1]Conference of European Statisticians, ECE/CES/20; [2]Fourth Joint ECE/UNESCO Meeting on Statistics of Education, CES/AC.23/32; [3]Joint FAO/ECE Study Group on Food and Agricultural Statistics in Europe, FAO/ECE/CES:ESS(82)-6; [4]Meeting on Frameworks for Environment Statistics, CES/AC.40/23; [5]Meeting on Human Settlements Statistics, CES/AC.55/7; [6]Meeting on Statistics of Water Use and Quality, CES/AC.56/16; [7]Seminar on Integrated Statistical Information Systems and Related Matters, CES/SEM.15/2; [8]Third Joint ECE/WHO Meeting on Health Statistics, CES/AC.36/25; [9]Working Party on National Accounts and Balances, CES/WP.22/73.
Yearbook reference. [10]1976, p. 444.
Publications. Annual Bulletin of Steel Statistics for Europe, vol. X, *1982,* Sales No. E/F/R.83.II.E.11; *Annual Bulletin of Coal Statistics for Europe,* vol. XVII, *1982,* Sales No. E/F/R.83.II.E.16; *Annual Bulletin of Housing and Building Statistics for Europe,* vol. XXVI, *1982,* Sales No. E/F/R.83.II.E.18; *Statistics of World Trade in Steel 1982,* Sales No. E/F/R.83.II.E.24; *Annual Bulletin of Gas Statistics for Europe 1982,* vol. XXVIII, Sales No. E/F/R/83.II.E.26; *Annual Bulletin of Transport Statistics for Europe,* vol. XXXIV, *1982,* Sales No. E/F/R.83.II.E.28; *Statistics of Road Accidents in Europe 1982,* Sales No. E/F/R.83.II.E.30; *Bulletin of Statistics on World Trade in Engineering Products 1982,* Sales No. E/F/R.84.II.E.5; *Annual Bulletin of General Energy Statistics for Europe 1982,* Sales No. E/F/R.84.II.E.6.

Standardization in Europe

By a decision of 30 March 1982,[1] ECE expressed the hope that the Seventh (1982) Meeting of Government Officials for Standardization Policies would result in further progress towards ECE four main objectives in standardization policies: the safeguard of public health and safety, the improvement of the environment, the promotion of scientific and technological co-operation, and the removal of technical barriers to international trade resulting from disparate standards and technical regulations. ECE also decided to convene two more sessions of the Group of Experts on Standardization Policies to consider such matters as might be referred to it by the Seventh Meeting of government officials.

The Seventh Meeting of Government Officials Responsible for Standardization Policies (Geneva, 26-29 April)[3] adopted a new version of the ECE Standardization List which, after further work, would be published in 1983. It approved proposals for further work in harmonization of standards, conformity certification, testing and definitions.

The Group of Experts on Standardization Policies (tenth session, Geneva, 22-24 November)[2] established an *ad hoc* informal Group to discuss the revised Standardization List before a final version was submitted for adoption by the Eighth Meeting of government officials.

Decision (1982). [1]ECE (report, E/1982/19): H(XXXVII), 30 Mar.
Reports. [2]Group of Experts on Standardization Policies, STAND/GE.1/21; [3]Seventh Meeting of Government Officials Responsible for Standardization Policies, ECE/STAND/24.
Publication. Standardized Input-Output Tables of ECE Countries for Years around 1970 (ST/CES/33 & Corr.1), Sales No. E.82.II.E.23 & Corr.1; *for Years around 1975* (ST/CES/34 & Corr.1), Sales No. E.82.II.E.24 & Corr.1.

Programme questions concerning ECE

Work programmes

By a resolution of 2 April 1982,[1] ECE approved its work programme for 1982/1983 and endorsed in principle, subject to review in 1983, its long-term work programme for 1982-1986.

ECE also called on member Governments to continue taking full advantage of the ECE potential for strengthening economic relations and multilateral co-operation in the region, and requested its subsidiary bodies to take into account the interests of member countries, as well as the possible contributions of ECE to United Nations programmes of assistance to developing countries.

Resolution (1982). [1]ECE (report, E/1982/19): 1(XXXVII), 2 Apr.

Latin America

ECLA activities. During 1982, the Economic Commission for Latin America (ECLA) acted to implement the Regional Programme of Action for Latin America in the 1980s, which it had adopted in May 1981.[5] The Programme identified economic and social development goals for Latin America, including the Caribbean area, and suggested action which the region's Governments could take to achieve them, both in their mutual relations and in their contacts outside the region. Activities relating to the Programme included numerous seminars, workshops and other meetings for government officials, technicians, international experts and others in order to seek solutions to problems in such areas as economic policy, environment, human settlements, transnational corporations, natural resources, transport, social development, international trade, technical and economic co-operation, industrial development, agriculture and statistics. The Commission, in a November report to the Economic and Social Council,[1] described its activities since May 1981, and the Secretary-General provided a brief summary of those activities in a June 1982 report[4] to that body.

Although ECLA—with headquarters at Santiago, Chile—did not meet during 1982, a number of meetings were held on specific economic and social topics, including two sessions of the Committee of the Whole.

The fifteenth special session of the Committee[2] (New York, 22-23 July) met to discuss international assistance to Nicaragua and Honduras to alleviate problems resulting from the May floods (see Chapter III of this section). The Committee urged intensified support by ECLA member Governments and appealed to international agencies and organizations to contribute to the rehabilitation and reconstruction of the two countries.

The Committee's sixteenth session[3] (New York, 2-3 December) was convened to analyse the Commission's 1984-1985 work programme and to inform member States about the implementation in 1981 of specific ECLA secretariat assignments. The Committee adopted by consensus four resolutions, by which it: urged the General Assembly to provide ECLA with sufficient resources for its expanded functions and responsibilities; approved the ECLA work programme and calendar of conferences; urged support for Bolivia to cope with its economic emergency (see Chapter III of this section); and asked that sufficient United Nations funds be provided for the ECLA Office for the Caribbean to carry out those activities in its work programme that had been assigned priority (see below).

At the Latin American Regional Preparatory Meeting for the World Assembly on Aging (San José, Costa Rica, 8-12 March), ECLA members adopted a regional plan of action, which emphasized action at the national level and the role of the family in resolving the problems arising in this field (see Chapter XX of this section).

The two major institutes of the ECLA system— the Latin American Institute for Economic and Social Planning and the Latin American Demographic Centre—continued their work of gathering information, publishing studies and advising Governments.

Reports. [1]ECLA, E/CEPAL/PLEN.16/L.3; ECLA Committee of Whole: [2]E/CEPAL/G.1209/Rev.2, [3]E/CEPAL/G.1239; [4]S-G, E/1982/88.
Yearbook reference. [5]1981, p. 660.
Publications. CEPAL Review, No. 16 (E/CEPAL/G.1195), Sales No. E.82.II.G.2; No. 17 (E/CEPAL/G.1205), Sales No. E.82.II.G.3; No. 18 (E/CEPAL/G.1221), Sales No. E.82.II.G.4.

Economic and social trends

The year 1981 was one of the worst years on record for Latin America since the Second World War, according to virtually all economic indicators described in the *Economic Survey of Latin America 1981*.[2] By a decision of 30 July 1982,[1] the Economic and Social Council noted a preliminary summary of the survey, which was prepared by the ECLA secretariat.

The survey stated that an economic growth rate of 1.2 per cent, the lowest for the region in 40 years, was a sharp decrease from 6 per cent in 1980. Inflation rose for the third year in a row, averaging 57 per cent, 4 percentage points below the 1976 peak. The current account in the balance of payments reached an unprecedented deficit of $38 billion, 34 per cent greater than in 1980. It was fully financed by capital inflows, but at a record 7 per cent interest rate, higher than any experienced since the 1930s depression. The region's gross external debt was up 15 per cent from 1980 to approximately $240 billion. The current account deficit had occurred despite an impressive 7 per cent growth in the volume of exports, reflecting domestic efforts at export promotion. Among the reasons cited in the *Survey* for the economic performance were: the slow growth of the industrial nations for the second consecutive year; the lagged response to the oil shock of 1979, followed by higher oil prices; a sharp rise in interest rates; and various internal problems. According to the *Survey*, prospects for significant improvement were not good, at least as long as the economic situation remained depressed.

Decision. [1]ESC, 1982/177, para. *(h)*, 30 July.
Publications. [2]*Economic Survey of Latin America 1981* (E/CEPAL/G.1248), Sales No. E.83.II.G.2 (summary, E/1982/75); *Economic Survey of Latin America and the Carib-*

bean 1982, vols. I, II, E/LC/G.1320 and Add.1, Sales No. E.84.II.G.1.

Other publications. CEPAL Review, No. 16 (E/CEPAL/G.1195), Sales No. E.82.II.G.2; No. 17 (E/CEPAL/G.1205), Sales No. E.82.II.G.3; No. 18 (E/CEPAL/G.1221), Sales No. E.82.II.G.4. *Energy in Latin America: The Historical Record*, E.82.II.G.14. *The Economic Relations of Latin America with Europe* (E/CEPAL/G.1116), Sales No. E.82.II.G.16.

Development policy and regional economic co-operation

The ECLA Committee of High-level Government Experts (CEGAN), at its sixth annual session in New York on 6 December 1982,[1] reviewed problems in implementing the International Development Strategy for the Third United Nations Development Decade[2] and the Regional Programme of Action for Latin America in the 1980s,[3] adopted by the Commission in 1981. CEGAN examined the region's development problems, especially in connection with the world economic crisis, and proposed action to tackle them and to promote economic and social development.

The Committee reported that Latin America's prospects in 1980 for reasonable economic growth had been suddenly changed by the 1981-1982 world recession. Indebtedness had created severe economic problems, including a decline in production, reduction of payments and deterioration of Latin American business, causing the region to adjust by adopting protectionist and recessive policies. The situation was marked by a fall in real wages and higher unemployment. CEGAN believed that the objectives of the Strategy and the Programme of Action still provided a valid approach to overcoming the difficulties, and that the Committee played an important role in reviewing the Strategy. It advised the Latin American countries to create a basis for participating in high-technology industries through such means as joint ventures in order to avoid domination of their economies, and to increase domestic savings rather than consumption. At the regional and international levels, it called for improvement of existing mechanisms for payments, and urged reconciliation of balances and reciprocal loans. It encouraged development of technology, joint investments, marketing arrangements and joint production, as well as increased regional co-operation in the sectors in which Latin America was most vulnerable—financing, trade technology, food, transport, communications, insurance and reinsurance.

To produce a positive change in international financing trends, CEGAN suggested the following measures: expansion of the resources of the International Monetary Fund (IMF), creation of institutional machinery allowing the refinancing of the external debt, greater support by industrial countries of their banking systems, consideration of a new allocation of special drawing rights to prevent a fall in world liquidity, and a revision of the terms of IMF loans.

The ECLA Committee of the Whole, at its December session (see above), agreed that in 1983 CEGAN would convene as the Latin American Regional Preparatory Meeting for the International Population Conference, planned for 1984 in Mexico.

Report. [1]Committee of High-level Government Experts, E/CEPAL/G.1260-E/CEPAL/CEGAN.6/L.3/Rev.1.
Resolution. [2]GA: 35/56, annex, 5 Dec. 1980 (YUN 1980, p. 503).
Yearbook reference. [3]1981, p. 661.

Development information

The Latin American Economic and Social Documentation Centre (CLADES) held a regional assessment meeting on the information for planning system (INFOPLAN) (Santiago, Chile, 8-10 November 1982) to evaluate project activities from 1980 to 1982, identify future activities, and evaluate strategies used to implement a decentralized information system. It also organized training seminars on the operation of INFOPLAN in Venezuela (17-21 May), Costa Rica (24-28 May), Honduras (31 May–4 June), Guatemala (7-11 June) and Panama (14-18 June).

In addition to publishing a number of studies, CLADES continued to provide advisory assistance to specific countries on their development information needs, and pursued cataloguing and indexing of ECLA and other documents.

The Caribbean Documentation Centre organized four workshops on indexing and abstracting techniques for participation in the Caribbean Information System for Economic and Social Planning (Cuba, 14-21 May; Dominican Republic, 11-15 October; Haiti, 25-29 October; Suriname, 8-13 November) and a workshop on user education techniques for special libraries (Jamaica, 19-24 July).

Development planning

In 1982, the Latin American Institute for Economic and Social Planning (ILPES) provided advisory services to Brazil, Colombia, Ecuador, Haiti, Nicaragua, Panama and Venezuela on issues related to industrialization, urban planning, agricultural planning, and economic and development planning. The Institute organized courses and seminars on projection methodologies, and collaborated with the Economic Projections Centre in organizing classes on models, styles of development and the environment.

ILPES continued to exchange information and documents with Governments, and published studies on the state of planning, economic policy and regional development. In addition, it collaborated with CLADES in implementing the INFOPLAN project (see above).

The Fifth Meeting of the Technical Sub-Committee of ILPES (San José, Costa Rica, 10 November) dealt with the proposal for a regular system of supplementary financing for the Institute and the proposed programme of activities.

Caribbean area

The ECLA Caribbean Development and Co-operation Committee (CDCC), which had met at the technical level in 1981,[5] convened at the ministerial level in New York on 3 and 4 February 1982 (sixth session)[1] to review its secretariat's work during 1980-1981 and analyse the work programme for 1982-1983. It accepted the Netherlands Antilles as an associate member[2] and called for measures to strengthen the secretariat (see below).

In regard to priorities of its work programme, CDCC mandated the secretariat to establish a Caribbean data base of national information units, urged financing for a programme on removal of language barriers in the Caribbean and support for the Caribbean Council for Science and Technology, and accepted recommendations by an experts' meeting on maritime transport facilitation (see below). CDCC restated its mandate for the formation of a Caribbean council for social and economic development and called for support for activities in education, planning, demographic analysis and tourism.

To improve co-operation in implementing its work programme, CDCC recommended consultations between its secretariat and the Caribbean Group for Co-operation in Economic Development and the Caribbean Community (CARICOM), and other related regional organizations.[4] It asked the ECLA Executive Secretary to establish a relationship with the newly formed Organization of Eastern Caribbean States,[3] and requested its secretariat to develop proposals for multinational enterprises in co-ordination with United Nations specialized agencies, concentrating initially on a fishing project and on book production.

Report. [1]CDCC, E/CEPAL/G.1202-E/CEPAL/CDCC/91 & Add.1.
Resolutions. CDCC, 4 Feb.: [2]8(VI), [3]11(VI), [4]9(VI).
Yearbook reference. [5]1981, p. 662.

Strengthening the CDCC secretariat

On 30 July 1982,[4] the Economic and Social Council, acting without vote, took note of the determination of CDCC member States to strengthen the Committee's secretariat, and of the additional resources required to carry out its 1982-1983 work programme. The Council requested the Secretary-General to consider an internal reallocation for the additional resources requested by CDCC for 1983, and to consider including additional resources as requested in the proposed United Nations 1984-1985 programme budget, within the framework of his budget policy of no real growth.

Introduced in the Council's First (Economic) Committee by the Bahamas also on behalf of Colombia, Jamaica, Saint Lucia, and Trinidad and Tobago, the original draft[1] contained a request that the Secretary-General consider including provisions in his supplementary 1983 budget proposals, rather than consider finding those resources through reallocation. Further, the Council would have asked him to include in the 1984-1985 programme budget submission the additional resources requested by CDCC, rather than to consider their inclusion within the no-growth policy. The sponsors withdrew their draft when a Vice-Chairman submitted the final version after holding informal consultations on the text. The Committee approved the draft on 28 July, also without vote.

Also in connection with the work of its secretariat, CDCC recommended[2] that each member State establish a focal point to centralize and collect information from the secretariat and ECLA, to work with the secretariat on monitoring and evaluating regional projects, and to establish channels for the timely flow of information.

On 3 December,[3] the ECLA Committee of the Whole, noting the CDCC report and resolutions, again expressed concern that resources of the ECLA Office for the Caribbean were not sufficient for its priority activities. It requested the CDCC secretariat to implement the 1982-1983 work programme, observing the CDCC priorities. The Committee requested the ECLA Executive Secretary to continue decentralizing posts and related resources to the Caribbean subregional office, and report to CDCC and ECLA. It again requested him to ensure General Assembly appropriation of funds sufficient for the Caribbean Office's work programme, and asked him to make arrangements with United Nations specialized agencies to obtain their co-operation in implementing CDCC activities.

Draft resolution withdrawn. [1]Bahamas, Colombia, Jamaica, Saint Lucia, Trinidad and Tobago, E/1982/C.1/L.9.
Resolutions. [2]CDCC (report, E/CEPAL/G.1202-E/CEPAL/CDCC/91), 10(VI), 4 Feb.; [3]ECLA Committee of Whole (report, E/CEPAL/G.1239), 451(PLEN.16), 3 Dec.; [4]ESC, 1982/58, 30 July, text following.
Meeting record. ESC, E/1982/SR.51 (30 July).

Economic and Social Council resolution 1982/58

30 July 1982   Meeting 51   Adopted without vote

Approved by First Committee (E/1982/96) without vote, 28 July (meeting 15); draft by Vice-Chairman (E/1982/C.1/L.24), based on informal consultations on 5-nation draft (E/1982/C.1/L.9); agenda item 9.

Caribbean Development and Co-operation Committee of the Economic Commission for Latin America

The Economic and Social Council,

Recalling that the Caribbean Development and Co-operation Committee was established in 1975 by the Economic Commission for Latin America to act as a co-ordinating body for activities relating to development and co-operation and as a consultative organ of the Commission,

Noting that the Committee drew up at its annual sessions a work programme, which was subsequently endorsed by the Commission at its biennial sessions, in particular its seventeenth session, held at Guatemala City from 25 April to 5 May 1977, its eighteenth session, held at La Paz from 18 to 26 April 1979, and its nineteenth session, held at Montevideo from 4 to 15 May 1981,

Considering that the Committee, at its fifth session, held at Kingston, Jamaica, from 4 to 10 June 1980, approved a series of urgent projects within the framework of that work programme,

Recalling that the Committee of the Whole of the Commission, at its fourteenth special session, held in New York on 20 November 1980, endorsed that work programme, including the supplementary resources required for 1981, and the additional resources which would be required for the biennium 1982-1983 in order to ensure its implementation,

Bearing in mind Council resolution 1980/56 of 24 July 1980, by which the Council requested the Secretary-General to make appropriate provision for the implementation of those priority projects and for the strengthening of the secretariat of the Caribbean Development and Co-operation Committee in his supplementary budget estimates for 1981 for consideration by the Advisory Committee on Administrative and Budgetary Questions and the Fifth Committee of the General Assembly in the course of the thirty-fifth session of the Assembly, bearing in mind that the implementation of such projects constituted an urgent need,

Noting with appreciation that an additional appropriation for the Caribbean Development and Co-operation Committee of $128,100 was approved by the General Assembly at its thirty-fifth session, thus providing the necessary resources to implement the work programme for the biennium 1980-1981,

Conscious of the fact that the additional resources required for the implementation of that work programme in the biennium 1982-1983 were not included in the presentation of the Secretary-General to the appropriate intergovernmental organs, as a result of the policy of zero growth of the United Nations budget for that biennium,

Noting further that the Committee, at its sixth session, held at St. George's, Grenada, from 4 to 10 November 1981 and at United Nations Headquarters on 3 and 4 February 1982, adopted resolution 10(VI), in which the Committee stressed once again the importance it attaches to the strengthening of its secretariat,

Conscious of the fact that, without supplementary appropriations for 1983, the implementation of the work programme of the Committee will be greatly delayed,

1.   *Takes note* of the determination of Governments of States members of the Caribbean Development and Co-operation Committee, expressed at its fifth and sixth sessions, to pursue activities aimed at strengthening its secretariat, including those measures recommended by the Joint Inspection Unit;

2.   *Takes note also* of the additional resources required for the biennium 1982-1983 in order to carry out the work programme of the Committee, as set out in the report on its sixth session;

3.   *Requests* the Secretary-General to consider the possibility of finding, through an internal reallocation of resources within the programme budget for the biennium 1982-1983, the additional resources required in 1983 to enable the Committee to carry out its programme of work;

4.   *Further requests* the Secretary-General to consider, within the framework of his general budget policy, which is at present one of no real growth in the regular budget, the inclusion in the proposed programme budget for the biennium 1984-1985 of the additional resources requested by the Committee at its sixth session.

Central America

The Intergovernmental Co-ordinating Committee of the Central American Economic and Social Development Co-operation Group, at its second meeting held at Tegucigalpa, Honduras, on 5 March 1982,[1] agreed to seek to establish a joint position with the Inter-American Development Bank to raise the level of external co-operation directed towards the region. The Committee, established in August 1981 by the Central American foreign ministers,[2] had met for the first time in December 1981 in Panama to analyse institutional and substantive aspects of international co-operation to assist Central American development.

In a related area, a seminar on transnational corporations and Central American development was convened at San José, Costa Rica, from 20 to 27 October.

Report. [1]Co-ordinating Committee of Central American Economic and Social Development Co-operation Group, E/CEPAL/CCE/L.412.

Yearbook reference. [2]1981, p. 662.

Technical co-operation

Expenditures in 1982 for technical co-operation activities of the Economic Commission for Latin America (ECLA) totalled $7.5 million.[1] ECLA provided a wide range of technical assistance as requested by Member States, including advisory services and regional training courses funded by specialized agencies. The Latin American Institute for Economic and Social Planning (ILPES) (see above) trained 36 fellows from 15 Latin American countries, and the Latin American Demographic Centre (CELADE) (see below) awarded 35 fellowships to participants from 13 countries. Projects were carried out in social development, including integration of women; international trade, particularly export promotion and its financial and monetary implications; water resources and energy; transport; industrial development; agriculture; and critical poverty. ECLA collaborated with the Economic Commission for Africa (ECA) to promote co-operation between the two regions in international trade, manpower development, and science and technology. A meeting of government experts, held at Addis Ababa, Ethiopia, in June, endorsed that programme as a framework for future joint activities (see below).

Report. [1]S-G, DP/1983/18/Add.1,2.

International trade

In 1982, activities to promote international trade in Latin American countries included the publication of studies on various aspects of trade and several meetings and seminars. An informal high-level seminar was held on the international economic situation and its impact on the region (Buenos Aires, Argentina, 23-25 September). Under an export promotion project carried out by ECLA and the International Trade Centre (ITC), the statutes of the Latin American Association of Export Credit Insurance agencies, drawn up in 1981,[1] were adopted at a meeting of export credit insurance bodies (Rio de Janeiro, Brazil, 17-18 August 1982). A round-table meeting was held on the obstacles preventing access of Latin American manufactured and semi-manufactured leather products to the markets of industrialized countries (Buenos Aires, 14-16 April). Other joint ECLA/ITC projects included a seminar/workshop on the study of exportable supply (Lima, Peru, 8-13 February), a seminar on export promotion (Brazil, September/October), and a course on foreign trade financing (Lima, 18-20 October). Advisory assistance missions, particularly in the field of export promotion, were carried out in Costa Rica, Guatemala, Haiti, Honduras and Paraguay.

Advisory assistance was given to banks and institutions on monetary and financial policies. Studies were initiated in 1982 on economic interdependence and national development, seeking to analyse transnationalization and its implications for Latin America. Regarding economic co-operation between the countries of Latin America and other developing regions, a study on the possibilities for foreign trade co-operation with the African countries was presented at a joint meeting of governmental experts from the two regions (Addis Ababa, Ethiopia, 1-5 June).

Yearbook reference. [1]1981, p. 664.

Transport

In 1982, ECLA and the National Transport Planning Department of Argentina organized a Latin American transport planning seminar (Buenos Aires, 21-25 June). At the seminar, studies of the transport plans of Argentina, Bolivia, Brazil, Paraguay and Uruguay were examined and appraised.

At the request of the Latin American Integration Association, activities were carried out towards the establishment of an international transport information system to improve cargo transport planning. ECLA also participated in a South American conference on road transport convened by the International Road Transport Union and sponsored by Uruguay's Ministry of Transport and Public Works (Montevideo, 19-22 April). During the conference, a group of business associations from Argentina, Brazil, Chile, Colombia, Peru and Uruguay formed the South American International Transport Union to ensure a permanent co-operation mechanism. A working group on transportation planning met under the auspices of the Caribbean Development and Co-operation Committee (Trinidad and Tobago, 15-16 November).

Three seminars were held on co-operation among Latin American and Caribbean countries in the establishment of container repair and maintenance enterprises (Rio de Janeiro, Brazil, 15-16 April; Bogotá, Colombia, 19-20 April; Santo Domingo, Dominican Republic, 22-23 April).

Maritime rescue was the subject of three 1982 experts' meetings (Kingston, Jamaica, 6-8 October; Mexico City, 13-15 October; Port of Spain, Trinidad, 8-11 November).

Industrial development

Under a regional project on current production and prospects for the supply and production of capital goods in Latin America, leading industrial entrepreneurs met in 1982 to discuss systems of financing domestic sales, an area of deficiency in most of the countries (Santiago, Chile, 26-28 April). At this meeting, a study was made of reports on demand for iron and steel-making equipment, electrical generating equipment, maritime and railway transport equipment, and equipment for the production of cement, paper and pulp. An evaluation was also made of the productive capacity of eight medium-sized and small countries of South America and the members of the Central American Common Market. ECLA sponsored a November visit by Argentine businessmen to India and Indonesia to identify areas of possible industrial co-operation.

Natural resources

Mineral resources

Organized jointly by ECLA and the Colombian Mining Corporation, the first Meeting on Horizontal Co-operation for the Development of the Mineral Resources of Latin America (Bogotá, Colombia, 14-18 June)[1] discussed the development of the region's mining and metallurgical sector and the conditions of the international market. The Meeting agreed to establish an advisory committee and a co-ordinating secretariat to organize and promote co-operation for the development of mineral resources. The Meeting recommended that countries: make an inventory of mining and metallurgical studies and research; assess current and projected capacity of their mining equipment, communicate the desirability of minimizing shipping costs, promote the participation of private and/or public Latin American enterprises, co-operate in a proposed system of mining statistics and information, and support training in the mining sector. At the Meeting, nearly 100 proposals were presented for possible co-operation projects.

Advisory missions to promote horizontal co-operation projects for the development of mineral resources were carried out during 1982 in Bolivia and Peru. A seminar on policies and negotiations with transnational corporations on the mining and metallurgical sector of Bolivia was convened (La Paz, Bolivia, 17-21 May), as well as a meeting of southern hemisphere countries on mining technology (Rio de Janeiro, Brazil, 5-10 December). A group of African mining specialists visited Latin American countries in November in preparation for a joint project between ECLA and the Economic Commission for Africa on mineral resources development.

Report. [1]Meeting on development of mineral resources, E/CEPAL/G.1207-E/CEPAL/SEM.3/R.9/Rev.1.

Water

The Inter-Secretariat Working Group on Water Resources in Latin America (second meeting, Santiago, Chile, 16-17 August 1982)[1] met to review the co-ordination of activities begun in 1981 among organizations of the United Nations system. The Group agreed that ECLA should prepare and distribute to international organizations a questionnaire on their activities concerning water in Latin America in order to evaluate progress in implementing national plans on water resources.

The Second Latin American Seminar on Horizontal Co-operation for the International Drinking Water Supply and Sanitation Decade (Santo Domingo, Dominican Republic, 11-14 January 1982)[2] continued work begun in 1981[3] to encourage co-operation to achieve the targets of the 1981-1990 Decade (see Chapter IX of this section), with emphasis on social, economic and financial aspects. The participants adopted recommendations by which they: urged Governments to institutionalize horizontal co-operation by strengthening or establishing national operational machinery; called for horizontal co-operation at the subregional and regional levels and proposed means to achieve this; urged the United Nations system and intergovernmental organizations to give higher priority and more resources to water supply and sanitation; and suggested establishing national focal points to exchange information.

Advisory assistance was provided to Governments and institutions in such areas as water resources planning and management, and irrigation.

Reports. [1]Working Group on water resources, E/CEPAL/G.1225; [2]Seminar on drinking water and sanitation decade, E/CEPAL/G.1199.
Yearbook reference. [3]1981, p. 665.
Publication. Drinking Water Supply and Sanitation in Latin America, 1981-1990 (E/CEPAL/G.1238), Sales No. E/S.82.II.G.21.

Food and agriculture

ECLA in 1982 continued its research efforts in two related areas—the food and nutritional situation of the Latin American population, and the development of food output and the forces of production, with special emphasis on peasant agriculture and food security. A document on the food and nutritional aspects of intensive urbanization in Latin America was presented at a regional conference of the Food and Agriculture Organization of the United Nations (FAO) (Managua, Nicaragua, 30 August–10 September). In addition, ECLA co-operated with FAO in providing assistance to Governments on agricultural planning and policy, and missions were sent to Brazil, Costa Rica and Ecuador.

A project on peasant agriculture and development in the Andean countries, carried out jointly by ECLA and the Netherlands, included a regional seminar on agrarian policies and peasant survival in high-altitude ecosystems (see below).

Science and technology

A group of experts, jointly sponsored by ECLA and the United Nations Industrial Development Organization (UNIDO), convened a meeting on the implications of microelectronics for Latin America (Mexico City, 7-11 June 1982). The group's main recommendation was that ECLA and UNIDO prepare a draft Latin American programme of co-operation in microelectronics.

The ECLA Office for the Caribbean, serving as interim secretariat of the Caribbean Council on Science and Technology, provided support for a meeting of the Council's Executive Committee (Guyana, March) and a plenary session (Jamaica, November). A meeting was held on structures for the formulation and implementation of policies on science and technology in Latin America and the Caribbean (Mexico City, 27-30 April).

By the end of August a collaborative research programme on scientific and technological development in Latin America was completed. In its second (last) phase, the project prepared a number of studies examining the economic and technological behaviour of 50 metal-working companies in Argentina, Brazil, Colombia, Mexico, Peru and Venezuela.

Social and cultural development

In preparation for the July/August 1982 World Assembly on Aging (see Chapter XX of this section), ECLA convened a Latin American Regional Preparatory Meeting (San José, Costa Rica, 8-12 March), and a multidisciplinary seminar (Santiago, Chile, 28 June–2 July) was held to exchange information on aging among government agencies, non-governmental and international organizations, and experts.

In co-operation with the Latin American Institute for Economic and Social Planning (ILPES) and the United Nations Children's Fund, ECLA organized an International Seminar on Social Development Policies in Latin America and the Caribbean during the 1980s (Santiago, 12-15 April), at which it presented a document on the relationship between social and development policies. An *ad hoc* working group (Santiago, 22-24 November) met to consider changes in the social structure in Latin America and projections for the future. ECLA presented a study on the Latin American people's participation in development[1] at the International Seminar on Popular Participation (Ljubljana, Yugoslavia, 17-25 May) (see Chapter XIII of this section).

Study. [1]E/CEPAL/L.264.
Publications. Women and Development: Guidelines for Programme and Project Planning (E/CEPAL/G.1200), Sales No. E.82.II.G.8; *Five Studies on the Situation of Women in Latin America* (E/CEPAL/G.1217), Sales No. E.82.II.G.10.

Cultural property preservation and nature conservation

The Joint Inspection Unit (JIU), in a March 1982 report transmitted to the General Assembly by the Secretary-General,[1] reviewed the contribution of the United Nations system to the conservation and management of Latin American cultural and natural heritage. The report, prepared by Inspectors Toman Hutagalung and Joseph A. Sawe, examined the heritage to be protected and assessed United Nations training, research and monitoring capabilities for co-ordinated conservation and management activities. Regarding natural heritage, the study concentrated on the maintenance of ecological and life-support systems, preservation of genetic diversity and rational utilization of eco-systems. National parks, biosphere reserves and protected natural areas were the key instruments for conservation action. As for cultural heritage, the study was concerned foremost with properties such as architectural works, historical places and archaeological sites.

After examining current policies and practices, the Inspectors found that the international system was not fully attuned to the exigencies of a conservation-oriented approach to development. They recommended that: the United Nations make an effort to attract additional resources from multilateral, bilateral and other sources as well as from inside the system to support conservation projects; an intergovernmental forum, under ECLA auspices, be created to formulate conservation-oriented development leading to a comprehensive regional strategy and plan of action; the United Nations Environment Programme and ECLA set up a unit to co-ordinate regional conservation and environmental activities; United Nations organizations provide experts and information on conservation legislation and enforcement to facilitate adherence to international conventions on cultural property protection; and training programmes be organized to further conservation goals.

Report. [1]JIU, transmitted by S-G note, A/37/509.

Women

Among ECLA activities in 1982 for the integration of women into development, a regional training workshop on projects and programmes for women (Panama City, 18-27 January) was held with the financial backing of the Voluntary Fund for the United Nations Decade for Women. In addition, ECLA organized a regional seminar on the training of women and rural families through radio schools (Mexico, 8-12 November).

Population

The Latin American Demographic Centre (CELADE) continued in 1982 to assist countries with their census programmes for the 1980s, especially in regard to the inclusion of priority demographic topics, and to prepare or update population estimates and projections for individual countries. It carried out missions and provided advisory assistance to national agencies in such areas as research on international migration, fertility studies, statistics and demographic surveys, and metropolitan growth and its socio-economic implications. The Centre collaborated with ECLA and other organizations in activities and studies on critical poverty, agrarian policies and the peasant economy, labour migration, and aging. CELADE organized a seminar on indirect methods of measuring mortality (Santiago, Chile, June) and another on population projections (San José, Costa Rica, October).

Environment

ECLA activities. A regional seminar on agrarian policies and peasant survival in high-altitude ecosystems (Quito, Ecuador, 23-26 March 1982) was convened by the ECLA/Food and Agriculture Organization of the United Nations (FAO) Joint Agriculture Division, under its project on peasant agriculture in the development of the Andean countries.[5]

A permanent programme of co-operation among metropolitan authorities of Latin America, organized in part by ECLA, was also supported by the First Meeting of Mayors of Capital Cities of Iberoamerica (Madrid, Spain, 5-12 October 1982) and those Latin American mayors who participated in the ninth congress of mayors of large cities of the world (Caracas, Venezuela, 21-23 October). An expert meeting to prepare permanent horizontal co-operation machinery among metropolitan authorities of Latin America and the Caribbean (Santiago, 14-15 December) was convened at ECLA headquarters.

UNEP activities. With the support of the United Nations Environment Programme (UNEP), an Intergovernmental Regional Meeting on the Environment in Latin America and the Caribbean (Mexico City, 8-12 March 1982) was convened as a forum for Governments to develop policies guiding regional environmental activities.[4] The Regional Meeting made recommendations to the UNEP Governing Council, which took note of them on 18 May,[9] during its session of a special character held at Nairobi, Kenya.

By one of its resolutions,[7] the Meeting requested the Governing Council to authorize a government-nominated experts' meeting to elaborate a regional strategy for co-operation in environmental matters. In another,[8] the Meeting recommended that Latin American Governments convoke periodically experts' meetings to establish environmental policies, and that UNEP provide the necessary support for these meetings.

Acting on these recommendations at its regular annual session, the Governing Council, in a decision on UNEP regional activities adopted on 28 May,[2] authorized the UNEP Executive Director to convene a meeting of government-nominated experts to formulate a strategy for regional co-operation programmes on the environment. It recommended that the meeting take into account the strengthening of existing mechanisms for integration and the approval of specific agreements on environmental co-operation, and that UNEP develop guidelines for regional environmental programmes in consultation with Governments.

On 31 May,[1] the Governing Council invited Latin American and Caribbean Governments to consider convening periodic intergovernmental regional meetings to formulate environmental policies and to hold government-nominated experts' meetings enough in advance of Council sessions to allow review of the technical aspects of regional environmental programmes. It requested the Executive Director to provide secretariat support for such intergovernmental meetings through the Regional Office and authorized him to strengthen that Office by providing funds and staff.

Regarding environmental education, the Regional Meeting, in a resolution of 12 March,[6] reaffirmed its support for the establishment of the Environmental Training Network. It requested UNEP to reinforce support channels and advisory services in environmental training activities and to convoke a meeting in 1982 of the Network's Group of Advisers. It requested Latin American and Caribbean Governments' support in obtaining funds for the Network from UNEP and international agencies, and urged them to organize national agencies to implement the programme. The Meeting requested the UNEP Council to continue support of the International Centre for Training in Environmental Sciences, and requested ECLA and the Latin American Economic and Social Documentation Centre (CLADES) (see above) to conclude and disseminate an inventory of training institutions and their activities. It asked institutions comprising the Network to establish a fund to strengthen regional training activities.

The Council, on 31 May,[3] reaffirmed its support of the Network, and requested the Executive Director to launch its activities for two years and to support advisory services by other agencies concerned with environmental training. The Council urged the region's Governments to determine the form of their support and participation in the Network, and to designate national organizations to implement the programme and establish machinery to co-ordinate national agencies contributing to environmental training. It requested institutions to provide logistic support and international financing agencies to accord priority to environmental training projects. Declaring that the Network's activities should be directed towards all the region's countries, the Council requested the International Centre for Training in Environmental Sciences to meet the region's language requirements in developing training activities. The Executive Director was further requested to ensure the continuation of the Centre's activities beyond 1982.

Decisions. UNEP Council: [1]10/2, sect. III, 31 May; [2]10/3, 28 May; [3]10/25 B, 31 May.
Reports. [4]Meeting on environment, UNEP/IG.33/5; [5]Seminar on agrarian policies and peasant survival in high-altitude ecosystems, E/CEPAL/L.273.
Resolutions. Inter-Governmental Regional Meeting on Environment in Latin America and Caribbean, 12 Mar.: [6]1, [7]2, [8]3. [9]UNEP Council: V, 18 May.

Statistics

In 1982, the ECLA secretariat continued to organize and analyse specialized national data bases in the fields of national accounts, input-output, income distribution, consumption, prices, foreign trade, balance of payments, production, natural resources, population, social trends and employment. The two ECLA regional statistical advisers carried out nine advisory missions. A Regional Seminar of Experts on Comparisons of the System of National Accounts and the System of Balances of the National Economy in Latin America (Havana, Cuba, 6-11 May)[1] was organized by ECLA and held with the financial support of the Institute of Ibero-American Co-operation. A regional workshop on measurement of rural employment and income (Ixtapan de la Sal, Mexico, 24-28 May) was held in conjunction with two national institutions.

In the area of technical co-operation for household surveys, following an inter-agency meeting (Washington, D.C., 28-29 March), the Latin American component of the United Nations programme to develop national capacity for household surveys merged with the inter-American household surveys programme to form a regional programme. Within the context of the regional programme, a seminar was organized for heads of household surveys (Santiago, Chile, 22-24 September).

ECLA, in conjunction with the United Nations Development Programme, the Board of the Cartagena Agreement, and Mexico's Ministry of Planning and the Budget, sponsored a Latin American Seminar on National Accounts (Lima, Peru, 18-21 October) to exchange experience in the preparation of input-output tables and estimates of the quarterly product.

> *Report.* [1]Seminar of Experts on comparison of system of national accounts and system of balances of national economy, E/CEPAL/G.1213.
> *Publication. Statistical Yearbook for Latin America 1983* (E/CEPAL/G.1313), S/E.84.II.G.2.

Programme and administrative questions concerning ECLA

Work programme for 1984-1985

The 1984-1985 work programme of the ECLA system (including the Latin American Institute for Economic and Social Planning and the Latin American Demographic Centre) was approved by the ECLA Committee of the Whole on 3 December 1982, along with its calendar of conferences for 1982-1983.[1] The Committee requested the ECLA Executive Secretary to adjust the work programme in light of views to be expressed by delegations at the 1983 sessions of the Committee of the Whole and the Caribbean Development and Co-operation Committee (CDCC), and to submit a revised programme and budget proposals to the Secretary-General for consideration by bodies responsible for the overall United Nations programme. CDCC was invited to facilitate its consideration of the relevant aspects of future ECLA work programmes prior to consideration by ECLA.

Although the number of programmes and sub-programmes increased over the 1982-1983 biennium, the total amount of resources remained virtually constant. A new feature of the work programme was the inclusion of a subprogramme on co-operation with regional countries in the study of the application of the United Nations Convention on the Law of the Sea, signed in December 1982.

> *Resolution.* [1]ECLA Committee of Whole (report, E/CEPAL/G.1239), 449(PLEN.16), 3 Dec.

Strengthening the ECLA secretariat

On 3 December 1982,[1] the ECLA Committee of the Whole, noting the Secretary-General's efforts to transfer administrative and functional responsibilities to regional commissions as an efficiency measure, urged the General Assembly to provide the ECLA secretariat with sufficient resources to discharge its expanded functions and responsibilities. It requested the Executive Secretary to report in 1983 to CDCC and ECLA on the progress made towards decentralization and the assignment of budgetary resources.

The Economic and Social Council, on 30 July, requested the Secretary-General to consider certain measures so that CDCC would have the resources to implement fully the 1983 and 1984-1985 programme that it had proposed (see above).

> *Resolution.* [1]ECLA Committee of Whole (report, E/CEPAL/G.1239), 448(PLEN.16), 3 Dec.

Western Asia

ECWA activities. The Economic Commission for Western Asia (ECWA) held its ninth session at Baghdad, Iraq, from 8 to 12 May 1982,[1] adopting on 11 and 12 May a total of eight resolutions on various issues related to closer co-operation among the region's Arab States and aspects of future ECWA work.

The Commission urged its members to provide technical support to the food security projects of the region's least developed countries (LDCs). It linked the scale of assistance to the Palestine Liberation Organization to the scope of aid for the region's LDCs, urged States to provide information for a census of the Palestinian population, appealed for assistance to the flood-stricken areas of Democratic Yemen, adopted a document on aging persons and decided to convene a meeting in 1983 on the needs of youth in Western Asia.

On organizational questions, the Commission recommended to the Economic and Social Council the establishment of a Standing Committee for the Programme as the main ECWA subsidiary body—an action which the Council took in July. The Commission also endorsed a medium-term plan for 1984-1989.

During 1982, the Commission moved its headquarters from Beirut, Lebanon, to Baghdad, and asked that arrangements be made to establish an international school there for the children of its staff.

Expert group meetings were held on the reconstruction of agriculture in Lebanon and the development of the petrochemical industry in the region.

Implementation of the Commission's work programme in 1982 was described by the Executive Secretary in a report proposed for the 1983 ECWA session.[2]

> *Reports.* [1]ECWA, E/1982/22; [2]Executive Secretary, E/ECWA/162/Add.1.

Economic and social trends

Two major factors—a continuing recession in the developed countries and the emergence of a glut in the international oil market—affected the nations of Western Asia, according to a summary of the annual survey of economic and social developments in the ECWA region,[4] which the Economic and Social Council took note of on 30 July 1982.[1] Both factors adversely influenced development prospects in the region, with their impact proving ultimately to be more serious for the non-oil-producing countries and LDCs. These countries encountered particular difficulties as higher prices for manufactured goods and spiralling interest rates aggravated their already substantial balance-of-payments deficits.[3] Crude-oil production in the region dropped from 6.6 billion barrels in 1979 to 6.1 billion and 5.1 billion barrels in 1980 and 1981. The average real growth rate of gross domestic product for the region increased from 7.9 per cent in 1978 to 10.9 per cent in 1979; incomplete data for 1980 showed that the rate had slowed, with a further decline indicated for 1981.

A strategy for joint Arab economic development, adopted at an Arab summit conference held at Amman, Jordan, from 25 to 27 November 1980, had among its priorities manpower development, acquisition of technological capacity, food production, industrialization and military security. The text of the strategy was transmitted to the General Assembly by a letter of 26 November 1982 from Jordan.[2]

Decision (1982). [1]ESC: 1982/177, para. (d), 30 July.
Letter. [2]Jordan, 16 Nov., annexing strategy adopted by 11th Arab Summit Conference, A/37/638.
Report. [3]S-G, E/1982/88.
Survey. [4]E/1982/42.

Development policy

During 1982, ECWA began work on a model for the Jordanian economy and prepared a preliminary paper on the general framework of country models for planning purposes. The ECWA Development Planning Division drafted a programme of action for LDCs within the framework of the ECWA work programmes for 1982 through 1985. The Division helped to prepare a draft programme for the rehabilitation and reconstruction of areas in Democratic Yemen stricken by floods in 1981.

Technical co-operation

Expenditures on ECWA technical co-operation activities in 1982[1] totalled some $1.7 million, of which $672,000 was provided by the United Nations regular programme of technical co-operation. With support from the United Nations Development Programme, which supplied $331,000, ECWA provided advisory services to member States for the improvement of statistical operations, with special emphasis on the establishment of household survey capabilities, national accounts, and foreign trade, population and labour statistics. Advice was also given in the areas of development planning and finance, transport and communication, science and technology, social development and human settlements.

A regional training programme under the United Nations Financing System for Science and Technology for Development was organized at Amman, Jordan, to develop technological capabilities in petroleum-based industries. A nine-country survey was carried out with the aim of setting up a regional training institute for banking and financial studies. Fellowships from the Arab Planning Institute in Kuwait enabled candidates from various countries to study abroad.

Assistance from the United Nations Fund for Population Activities amounted to $248,000 for advisory services in demography and population statistics and for the publication of a guide for Arab students and researchers in the field of population, and of studies on population and development and on international migration in the Middle East. A report on the conditions of working women in Bahrain was prepared with assistance from the Voluntary Fund for the United Nations Decade for Women. The Fund also supported case studies on community self-help activities in disadvantaged urban areas of Amman, Alexandria (Egypt) and Damascus (Syrian Arab Republic). In addition, training was organized for 35 administrators of social services centres (Lebanon) as was a workshop on audio-visual materials for women extension workers (Jordan).

Report. [1]S-G, DP/1983/18/Add.1,2.

Transport, communications and tourism

In 1982, the ECWA secretariat, as part of an effort to achieve more efficient overland transport and speedier delivery of merchandise, sent a questionnaire to member countries on difficulties encountered by drivers at border crossings.

Tourism flows, payments and policies in the region were monitored. In order to formulate a new development strategy for tourism in Western Asia, the second part of a survey of the region's tourism potential was undertaken for the southern subregion;[1] the first, for the northern subregion, had been completed in 1981.

Survey. [1]E/ECWA/TCT/82/3.

Industrial development

During 1982, the *Ad Hoc* Technical Advisory Committee on the Petrochemical Industry in the ECWA Region (first meeting, Kuwait, 17 January)[1] considered areas of priority and complementarity for a proposed programme of studies as a basis for the development of the petrochemical industry in the region. The studies were to be submitted to an intergovernmental meeting in 1983. Co-sponsored by the Joint ECWA/UNIDO (United Nations Industrial Development Organization) Industry Division and the Arab Federation for Chemical Fertilizer Producers, with support from the Petrochemicals Industries Company of Kuwait, the meeting agreed that any study to be undertaken should be designed to cover all Arab

States and recommended that ECWA act as a focal point for the activities.

Under a joint ECWA/UNIDO project, country studies for the review and appraisal of industrial development in the region continued to be updated. As a first step towards a study on industrial financing, preparation of country monographs began, covering institutions providing such financing, starting with data collection in Saudi Arabia, for the period 1970-1980.

Report. [1]Advisory Committee on petrochemical industry, E/ECWA/ID/WG.5/7.

Natural resources

In 1982, the ECWA secretariat began work on a report analysing current consumption of and future demand for electrical energy in the region, existing and planned transmission networks in selected countries, and possibilities for multilateral co-operation.

A Surface Water Hydrology Symposium (Damascus, Syrian Arab Republic, 11-17 September) discussed national and regional studies and research work carried out on the subjects.

Food and agriculture

On 12 May 1982,[1] ECWA urged its members to consider regional food security as their common responsibility which should be fully reflected in their national policies; to intensify efforts to improve food production; and to provide technical assistance to food security projects, especially in the least developed countries. The Executive Secretary was asked to strengthen ECWA activities in this regard, in coordination with the Food and Agriculture Organization of the United Nations (FAO) and with the Arab Organization for Agricultural Development.

A Round-Table Conference on the Reconstruction and Development of Agriculture in Lebanon (Beirut, 11-13 January) endorsed a report containing a proposed strategy and policy options for agricultural development, a medium-term reconstruction and development programme, and a proposal for reorganizing agricultural administration. Jointly organized by ECWA, FAO and the United Nations Development Programme, the Conference was hosted by the Ministry of Agriculture of Lebanon.

Resolution (1982). [1]ECWA (report, E/1982/22): 113(IX), 12 May.

Science and technology

A case study on the role of consulting and engineering design in the development process[1] was completed and circulated by the ECWA secretariat in November 1982. The study examined the problems and implications of local versus foreign participation in industrial and infrastructural projects.

Report. [1]E/ECWA/NR/82/3.

Human settlements

Work was begun in 1982 on an analysis of the human settlements situation in Western Asia, with priority given to the preparation of country profiles on the least developed ECWA members, namely, Democratic Yemen and Yemen. Technical assistance was provided to Lebanon on housing policies and schemes.

Youth and aging persons

On 12 May 1982,[1] ECWA adopted a regional plan of action on aging[3] and requested its Executive Secretary to transmit it to the July/August World Assembly on Aging. Member countries were urged to participate fully in the Assembly's deliberations and formulation of the World Plan of Action on Aging, and to implement the Plan in every way possible. The Executive Secretary was asked to continue the secretariat's work on improving the well-being of elderly persons.

On the same date,[2] ECWA invited its member States to implement the specific programme of activities to be undertaken in connection with International Youth Year (1985). It urged its Executive Secretary to assist members in observing the Year, with emphasis on programmes to increase youth participation in national development, and asked him to convene a regional meeting in 1983 for the purpose of formulating a regional plan of action for the region's youth.

Resolutions (1982). ECWA (report, E/1982/22), 12 May: [1]111(IX), [2]112(IX).
Report. [3]ECWA Executive Secretary, E/ECWA/155.

Programme, organizational and administrative questions concerning ECWA

Establishment of a programme committee

By a resolution adopted without vote on 30 July 1982,[2] the Economic and Social Council established a Standing Committee for the Programme as the main subsidiary organ of ECWA for programme review, planning, programming and evaluation and co-ordination. The Committee was to be composed of all ECWA members.

The text, approved also without vote on 28 July by the Council's First (Economic) Committee, was submitted by a Vice-Chairman on the basis of informal consultations on an ECWA resolution of 12 May[1] recommending establishment of the Standing Committee.

Resolutions (1982). [1]ECWA (report, E/1982/22): 114(IX), 12 May. [2]ESC: 1982/64, 30 July, text following.
Meeting record. ESC, E/1982/SR.51 (30 July).

Economic and Social Council resolution 1982/64

30 July 1982   Meeting 51   Adopted without vote

Approved by First Committee (E/1982/96) without vote, 28 July (meeting 15); draft by Vice-Chairman (E/1982/C.1/L.33), based on informal consultations on ECWA recommendation (resolution 114(IX)); agenda item 9.

Establishment of a Standing Committee for the Programme of the Economic Commission for Western Asia

The Economic and Social Council

1. *Endorses* resolution 114(IX) of 12 May 1982 of the Economic Commission for Western Asia and decides to establish within the Commission a Standing Committee for the Programme, composed of all members of the Commission, as the main subsidiary organ of the Commission to assist it in the execution of its responsibilities for programme planning and review;

2. *Decides* that the Standing Committee shall function as the main subsidiary organ of the Commission for programme review, planning, programming, evaluation and co-ordination, and in that context, shall:

(a) Review the programmes of the Commission, as defined in the medium-term plan;

(b) Review the totality of the work programme of the Commission in the light of the availability of resources;

(c) Recommend an order of priority among the programmes and subprogrammes of the Commission, as defined in the medium-term plan;

(d) Give guidance to the Executive Secretary of the Commission on the design of the programme.

ECWA medium-term plan for 1984-1989

In 1982, the *Ad Hoc* Intergovernmental Expert Committee on the Medium-term Plan for 1984-1989 (Baghdad, 9-12 May)[1] reviewed the ECWA medium-term plan to determine programme and subprogramme priorities and recommended institutional arrangements in the form of a standing committee (see above) to assist ECWA in programme planning and review.

On 12 May,[2] ECWA, emphasizing that its programme planning and review processes should reflect more fully the development priorities and requirements of its member States, adopted the *Ad Hoc* Committee's report and its recommendations and endorsed the medium-term plan for 1984-1989.

Report. [1]Expert Committee on Medium-term Plan, E/ECWA/142 & Rev.1.
Resolution (1982). [2]ECWA (report, E/1982/22): 114(IX), 12 May.

Relocation of ECWA headquarters

The transfer of ECWA headquarters from Beirut, Lebanon, to Baghdad, authorized by the Economic and Social Council in 1976,[4] took place during the first six months of 1982, with the staff occupying temporary offices pending occupancy of permanent premises in 1983.

In anticipation of additional costs to be incurred in 1983 for the operation of the new premises, the Fifth (Administrative and Budgetary) Committee of the General Assembly, on 16 December 1982, approved by 69 votes to none, with 14 abstentions, a net additional appropriation of $2,274,500 in the programme budget for 1982-1983.[2]

The estimated additional appropriation which had been proposed by the Secretary-General[3] was $2,948,100. However, the Fifth Committee accepted a recommendation by the Advisory Committee on Administrative and Budgetary Questions that the amount be reduced by $673,600.[1]

Reports. [1]ACABQ, A/37/7/Add.22; [2]GA, 5th Committee, A/37/790; [3]S-G, A/C.5/37/65/Add.1.
Resolution. [4]ESC: 2045(LXI), 27 Oct. 1976 (YUN 1976, p. 506).

Proposed international school

On 12 May 1982,[1] ECWA requested the Secretary-General to proceed with arrangements for establishing a United Nations international school at Baghdad for the children of ECWA staff members. It also asked him to create a trust fund for the school, and called on Governments, international and national institutions and individuals to contribute.

Resolution (1982). [1]ECWA (report, E/1982/22): 110(IX), 12 May.

Chapter IX

Natural resources and cartography

Contents

Related topics:

Regional economic and social activities—Natural resources: Africa; Asia and the Pacific; Europe (Water); Latin America; Western Asia. Energy. Namibia: Protection of natural resources.

Natural resources exploration

Natural resources exploration, which included mineral exploration, mining feasibility studies and research on possible geothermal energy projects (see next chapter) was the focus in 1982 of the United Nations Revolving Fund for Natural Resources Exploration. The Fund, under the administration of the United Nations Development Programme (UNDP), was able to broaden its work and complete three projects despite financial constraints. On 18 June, the UNDP Governing Council authorized the Fund to extend its activities into geothermal exploration.

UN Revolving Fund for Natural Resources Exploration

Activities

The United Nations Revolving Fund for Natural Resources Exploration (UNRFNRE), a financing source for natural resources exploration activities in developing countries, continued its activities in that field during 1982, the Fund's eighth year of operations. The UNDP Administrator, in his annual report on the Fund's 1982 activities issued in April 1983,[5] described progress and effec-

tiveness in field activities and in the evaluation of new project requests. The report also presented the serious financial constraints of the UNRFNRE.

In the course of the year, there were 11 operational mineral exploration projects in various stages of development in Argentina, Benin, the Congo, Cyprus, Guyana, Kenya, Liberia, Mali, the Sudan, Suriname and the Upper Volta. In addition, UNRFNRE identified potential economic mineral discoveries in three countries—Argentina, Benin and Cyprus. It undertook further research in geothermal exploration to evaluate project proposals for generating energy from which it would propose a first geothermal project to the UNDP Governing Council for consideration. As part of its work in promoting natural resources exploration, UNRFNRE sought the financial and technical resources required for pre-investment work leading to mining development. Discussions were held between the Governments concerned, UNRFNRE, international and regional financial institutions and public and private sector mining groups in order to arrive at the most favourable arrangements for each case.

By the end of 1982, eight mineral exploration projects had been completed, three of them during the year (Benin, Philippines, Sudan). Evaluations of potential projects were made in Burundi,

Costa Rica, Honduras, Sierra Leone, the United Republic of Tanzania and Yemen, and UNRFNRE was considering 17 proposals, which were in various stages of evaluation. Requests for possible mineral projects were received from five Governments.

Field operations in Argentina for gold and silver exploration, with good by-product potential for copper, lead and zinc, were completed in May 1982 and a pre-investment report was prepared for potential private investors and lending institutions. In another pre-investment activity, UNRFNRE concluded offshore phosphate exploration work in the Congo and submitted a report on the first phase (minimum work) activities to the Government. Options were being discussed to determine the objectives and financial requirements for further work, which would begin in 1983 using funds already approved by the Governing Council. Fieldwork was completed in Cyprus where sufficient evidence of potential copper was obtained in three areas to allow UNRFNRE to declare them as reported mineral deposits. Although economic viability for copper mining there could not be proved, interest in additional exploration was generated with private mining groups.

Despite financial constraints, programme delivery in 1982 increased 33 per cent over 1981. Projects were selected on the basis of their technical and economic viability and of their potential for contributing to the requesting country's economic development. Discussions with user and donor countries, international financial institutions as well as public and private organizations led to co-financing and joint-financing proposals aimed at early development and returns, but they could not be regarded as a substitute for the Fund's basic programme.

The UNDP Governing Council, having considered the report of the Administrator for 1981 on UNRFNRE[3] and his report on geothermal energy,[4] adopted a decision on 18 June 1982,[2] authorizing UNRFNRE to extend its activities into geothermal exploration and calling for increased contributions.

The Economic and Social Council, on 28 July,[1] took note of the Governing Council's decision and the Administrator's report on UNRFNRE. The decision was adopted without vote, following similar approval by the Third (Programme and Co-ordination) Committee on 23 July of a draft proposed by its Chairman.

Decisions (1982). [1]ESC: 1982/158, 28 July, text following.
[2]UNDP Council (report, E/1982/16/Rev.1): 82/23, 18 June.
Reports. UNDP Administrator, [3]DP/1982/40, [4]DP/1982/41, [5]DP/1983/34.
Meeting record. ESC: E/1982/SR.49 (28 July).

Economic and Social Council decision 1982/158

Adopted without vote

Approved by Third Committee (E/1982/90) without vote, 23 July (meeting 16); draft by Chairman (E/1982/C.3/L.10); agenda item 19.

Report of the Administrator of the United Nations Development Programme on the United Nations Revolving Fund for Natural Resources Exploration

At its 49th plenary meeting, on 28 July 1982, the Council took note of the annual report of the Administrator of the United Nations Development Programme on the United Nations Revolving Fund for Natural Resources Exploration, and of decision 82/23, adopted on 18 June 1982 by the Governing Council of the Programme.

Contributions and expenditures

In 1982, contributions to UNRFNRE amounted to $4.5 million; expenditures totalled $7.6 million, which included $6.4 million for projects in 41 countries (see tables on next page).

In a report on the Fund's 1982 activities,[2] the UNDP Administrator noted a modest improvement in the level of voluntary contributions to UNRFNRE, as well as an increase in the number of countries financially supporting it. Because of the reduced programming resources at its disposal, UNRFNRE investigated additional financial resources which could be made available for its exploration programme as well as for pre-investment.

The Fund's cumulative resources as at 31 December 1982 totalled $46 million. Its programme commitments reached $27.3 million and, after other expenses were taken into account, funding availability for additional programming was approximately $10.8 million.

The UNDP Governing Council, in a decision of 18 June,[1] urged all countries to contribute, or increase their contributions, to UNRFNRE in order to enable it to respond adequately to the requests of the developing countries for assistance in natural resources exploration.

Decision (1982). [1]UNDP Council (report, E/1982/16/Rev.1): 82/23, para. 2, 18 June.
Report. [2]UNDP Administrator, DP/1983/34.

Mineral resources development

In addition to the natural resources survey work undertaken by UNRFNRE, the Department of Technical Co-operation for Development (DTCD), the Department of International Economic and Social Affairs and the regional commissions of the United Nations carried out project activities in mineral exploration, mining development, institution building and training support. Those activities were co-ordinated through the Committee for Programme and Co-ordination (CPC), which made recommendations on evaluating work in mineral resources. In 1982, DTCD supported 58 mineral projects in 43 countries, including exploration and investigation projects in nine

CONTRIBUTIONS TO UNRFNRE, 1982 AND 1983
(as at 31 December 1982; in US dollar equivalent)

Country	1982 payment	1983 pledge
Bangladesh	966	1,000
Belgium	110,497	102,041
Chile	5,000	5,000
Indonesia	—	10,000
Japan	4,000,000	—
Norway	422,535	—
Panama	—	1,000
Total	4,538,998	119,041

SOURCE: A/38/5/Add.1.

UNRFNRE PROJECT EXPENDITURES, 1982
(as at 31 December 1982; in thousands of US dollars)

Country	Amount
Angola	1
Argentina	342
Benin	195
Bolivia	1
Burma	1
Burundi	20
Chile	4
Colombia	4
Congo	246
Costa Rica	14
Cyprus	144
Djibouti	1
Dominican Republic	2
Ecuador	1
Egypt	6
Ethiopia	11
Gabon	2
Guatemala	21
Guyana	1,273
Haiti	12
Honduras	33
Indonesia	14
Kenya	907
Liberia	867
Mali	975
Mauritania	1
Mexico	13
Nicaragua	14
Panama	(56)
Papua New Guinea	2
Peru	23
Philippines	164
Rwanda	3
Sierra Leone	34
Sudan	21
Suriname	534
Turkey	10
United Republic of Tanzania	65
Upper Volta	480
Vanuatu	3
Yemen	16
Total	6,424

SOURCE: DP/1983/6/Add.4/Corr.1.

countries. Missions were carried out in 14 countries to estimate financial requirements for exploration and location of resources—six on mineral exploration requirements and eight in the energy field. Interregional advisers were sent on 91 missions in 50 countries. The Secretary-General described those activities in his annual report for 1982 on United Nations technical co-operation activities of DTCD issued in April 1983.[1]

Among the activities DTCD supported was an exploration project in the United Republic of Tanzania which discovered uranium and nickel sites. A search for gold continued in Haiti with en-couraging results. Institutional support activities included the establishment of an analytical and remote sensing facility in Benin, a mining documentation service in Mauritania, a chemical/petrographic/mineralographic laboratory in Pakistan, and a chemical laboratory in Angola. Geological surveys were conducted. Advanced drilling techniques and modern drilling equipment were the topics of an interregional seminar convened jointly by DTCD and Canada, and attended by participants from 26 developing countries.

Report. [1]S-G, DP/1983/18.
Publication. Sea-Bed Mineral Resources Development (ST/ESA/107/Add.1), Sales No. E.80.II.A.9/Add.1 [1980 data, published in 1982].

Programme evaluation

The Secretary-General, in response to a 1980 request by CPC, issued a report in March 1982[2] evaluating the United Nations programme in mineral resources including land-based and marine minerals, other than fuels, for the period 1976-1979. The report covered activities by a number of United Nations entities, at both the headquarters and regional levels, and was based on desk reviews, interviews with programme managers and interregional advisers and information from questionnaires sent to Member States, experts and national project personnel. The analysis showed that the overall quality and utility of research and analysis activities were judged favourably, but that the actual end-users were not necessarily the same as the primary target group of the relevant programme or subprogramme. With regard to technical co-operation activities (field projects, seminars, workshops and advisory services), the report stated that, despite problems with delivery and procurement procedures, the impact of the selected projects appeared to meet the needs of the recipient countries concerned.

CPC noted with great concern that in many cases the output of research and analysis activities was not reaching the policy-makers as the intended end-users and that secondary end-users appeared to be the chief beneficiaries. It concluded that deficiencies in the distribution mechanism were fundamental to the problem, but that poor programme design which failed to match output to the needs of identified end-users was also a factor. In the report on the work of its 1982 session to the General Assembly,[1] CPC stated that for future programmes it would scrutinize the definition of output and end-users and their relation to the stated objectives of programmes and subprogrammes, as those criteria had a bearing not only on the distribution of output but also on the ease with which their effectiveness and impact could be evaluated.

With regard to findings on technical assistance projects, CPC noted with concern that, due to financial limitations, United Nations activities seldom went beyond exploration. Being aware of the problem, DTCD had recently established an investment follow-up unit which, in co-operation with the United Nations Development Programme and the World Bank, offered advice to Governments on how to continue on to the production stage.

CPC decided to request the Secretary-General to submit his report to the 1983 session of the Committee on Natural Resources and to request that Committee to submit its reactions. With regard to the impact of the evaluation findings on planning at the Secretariat level, CPC requested the Secretary-General to inform the Assembly or CPC of any changes in the proposed medium-term plan for 1984-1989. Concerning co-ordination in the area of mineral resources at the organizational level, CPC requested the Administrative Committee on Co-ordination to develop means for achieving a clearer definition of tasks and a more integrated programme. As for the intergovernmental level, it requested the Committee on Natural Resources to review the matter in order to ensure effective co-ordination.

With regard to United Nations technical assistance in mineral resources development, CPC recommended that existing practices be re-examined with a view to facilitating the user's knowledge of and access to technical advisory services, improving the effectiveness of those services, and encouraging simple low-cost evaluation and better record-keeping. CPC recommended that the United Nations continue to monitor mineral deposits identified during its exploration activities and that it consider ways in which its activities might be extended to aid Governments to bring such deposits into production. Taking note of the continued delays in the implementation of technical co-operation projects caused by difficulties in equipment procurement and delivery and recruitment of experts, advisers and consultants, CPC reiterated its request that efforts to reduce the incidence of those problems be intensified.

Reports. [1]CPC, A/37/38; [2]S-G, E/AC.51/1982/5.

Water

The Governing Council of the United Nations Environment Programme (UNEP), by a resolution known as the Nairobi Declaration, adopted on 18 May 1982 at a special session commemorating the tenth anniversary of the United Nations Conference on the Human Environment at Stockholm, Sweden, decided on 10 environmental priority areas for United Nations action, including water.[1]

According to the Council, problems involving water were depletion and pollution of surface and ground water with increasing demand for drinking, agriculture and industry in most countries; continued acidification and eutrophication of fresh waters; environmental problems created by water development projects; inadequate water basin management; transboundary water pollution; and technical difficulties in management of water shared by States. To combat those problems, the Council called for action in the areas of: assistance in the implementation of the objectives of the International Drinking Water Supply and Sanitation Decade (1981-1990), proclaimed by the General Assembly in 1980,[2] and in the promotion of guidelines for environmentally sound water management, including transboundary water management and pollution and related environment aspects; management of inland fisheries and aquaculture; promotion of techniques for water management, including river basin management, pollution control, recycling of waste water, flood control and prevention of water waste; and promotion of assessment of the environmental impact of water resources development projects.

Resolution (1982). [1]UNEP Council (report, A/37/25): I, sect. III, para. 2 *(c)*, 18 May.
Resolution (prior). [2]GA: 35/18, 10 Nov. 1980 (YUN 1980, p. 712).
Publications. Ground Water in the Eastern Mediterranean and Western Asia (ST/ESA/112), Sales No. E.82.II.A.8; *Flood Damage Prevention and Control in China: Report of a Study Tour and Workshop in the People's Republic of China (16-31 October 1980)* (ST/ESA/119), Sales No. E.82.II.A.13.

Water resources

United Nations activities in water resources planning, management and policy formulation were concentrated in 1982 in the Department of Technical Co-operation for Development (DTCD), the regional commissions, the United Nations Development Programme and UNEP.

UN programme

Project activities carried out by DTCD covered development and management of ground- and surface-water resources, including river basin development, drilling, supply and demand management, exploration and assessment. Those activities in 1982 were described in the Secretary-General's annual report on DTCD activities (see below) issued in April 1983.[2] Following a July 1981 resolution by the Economic and Social Council,[4] DTCD commenced publication of a semi-annual newsletter on the activities and programmes of international river and lake organizations. Another publication, a briefing note entitled "The United Nations Organizations and Water", was produced by the Administrative Committee on Co-ordination (ACC) Inter-Secretariat Group for Water Resources, for circulation to resident co-ordinators, country representatives and field staff of the individual organizations.

The distribution of tasks and responsibilities between the regional commissions and other United Nations entities in the fields of water resources and the environment was the subject of a March 1982 report by the Secretary-General,[3] prepared in accordance with a 1981 decision of the Committee for Programme and Co-ordination (CPC).[6] In the analysis of mandates and activities in water resources, the Secretary-General said the Mar del Plata Action Plan,[5] adopted by the United Nations Water Conference in 1977 at Mar del Plata, Argentina, proved the most comprehensive system-wide action framework and was, along with related General Assembly and Economic and Social Council resolutions, the basis for his recommendations. The report suggested some basic principles for the distribution of responsibilities which were to be reflected in the 1984-1989 draft medium-term plans and in the 1982-1983 programme budget.

The regional commissions would continue to play leading roles in assisting Governments to establish the necessary institutional and legal structures, as well as policy formulation and planning procedures; to formulate recommendations on regional policies and techniques for assessment, development and management of water resources; to promote subregional, regional and interregional co-operation in the development of water resources; to collect information from Governments; and to follow up the implementation of the Action Plan.

DTCD would focus on the preparation of publications, manuals and guidelines to complement the programmes of the regional commissions. Both the commissions and DTCD would continue to convene conferences, seminars and *ad hoc* expert groups.

The Department of International Economic and Social Affairs (DIESA) and the regional commissions would formulate a standardized procedure for gathering the information from United Nations organizations, with DIESA playing a central role. Under arrangements with the ACC Inter-Secretariat Group, DTCD would make available the services of its regional advisers to the commissions for advisory missions, while regional advisers from one regional commission could be made available to other commissions or to Headquarters. In order to co-ordinate programme budgets and medium-term plans, it was envisaged that an annual meeting would be held in conjunction with the regular sessions of the Inter-Secretariat Group, attended by the regional commissions.

Reviewing the Secretary-General's report, CPC, in its 1982 report to the Assembly,[1] recommended that: the Secretary General take appropriate follow-up action to ensure that the regional commissions were in a position to implement effectively the tasks and responsibilities specified in his report; periodic consultations be held between the regional commissions and Headquarters to ensure complementarity of programmes and avoid duplication; a cross-organizational programme analysis be carried out for submission to CPC in 1983, in the context of the 1984-1985 programme budget; and the methodology followed in the Secretary-General's report be considered as a possible model for future analyses.

Reports. [1]CPC, A/37/38; [2]S-G, DP/1983/18, [3]E/AC.51/1982/7.
Resolution. [4]ESC: 1981/81, 24 July 1981 (YUN 1981, p. 686).
Yearbook references. [5]1977, p. 555; [6]1981, p. 686.

Water supply and sanitation

A major concern of the United Nations in the area of water resources was to ensure safe potable water and environmental sanitation in the developing countries. In 1982, the United Nations Children's Fund (UNICEF) provided assistance to water supply and sanitation programme components in 93 countries, involving expenditures of $60 million. According to the annual report of the UNICEF Executive Director issued in March 1983,[1] during 1982 an estimated 76,824 water systems—most of which were very simple, low-cost installations—were completed with UNICEF co-operation, benefiting 13.6 million people, and UNICEF helped in setting up excreta disposal systems which benefited about 1 million people. In several countries (including Bangladesh, Nepal, the United Republic of Tanzania and Zimbabwe), UNICEF co-operated with the United Nations Development Programme (UNDP)/World Bank global project for low-cost water supply and sanitation. National workshops to review ongoing programmes in sanitation and health education were held in Ethiopia, Mozambique and the Sudan.

The major constraint to providing safe water and sanitation was the lack of human resources development. UNICEF supported development of organizations, management and skills at intermediate (provincial and district) and village levels. It also supported training programmes for village pump operators/caretakers, sanitation/health promoters, and water-well diggers and drillers.

The lack of adequate water supply and sanitation contributed to the death of children in slums, shanty towns and infested city tenements, and for this reason water and sanitation were part of UNICEF co-operation in urban basic services programmes. Women's involvement in project development was emphasized because the access to safe and adequate water close to their homes was viewed as a major prerequisite for the advancement of women. Greater attention was given to issues of personal and food hygiene as well as to the design of water points, especially to ensuring adequate space and privacy for bath and laundry facilities. In the development of low-cost technology, UNICEF continued field testing of pumps and other methods and materials for improving water-well drilling and construction. An example of action in environmental sanitation was a village project in Bangladesh where 58,000 water-sealed latrines for families were produced and sold and 79 additional village sanitation manufacturing centres were established. In the emergency situation in Lebanon in 1982, UNICEF aid in water supply and sanitation constituted the only major external co-operation available. While warfare continued in West Beirut, UNICEF provided instant repairs for the water and sanitation systems.

UNICEF continued to play a part in the global exchange of information on low-cost water supply and sanitation technologies, which had increasingly become a joint effort between the United Nations and other organizations. UNICEF, the World Health Organization, UNDP and the World Bank were members of the Governing Board of the International Reference Centre for Community Water Supply and Sanitation at The Hague, Netherlands. Other UNICEF activities in the field of water resources included participation in publishing information materials, seminars and conferences, and generating donor interest and public awareness.

Three water resources projects were completed by DTCD in 1982. In Guinea-Bissau, a project involved sinking boreholes, running pump tests and installing pumps which resulted in water supply for 50,000 people and teams trained in water-well drilling. Follow-up activities focused on assistance to the Government in mobilizing funds, leading to 38 project proposals to be presented at a donors' "round table" scheduled for 1983. A similar project was completed in Mali. The third project, in the Bahamas, prepared an overall strategy for wellfield development, using a gravity system for abstraction of ground water, and improvements in storage facilities, transmission of water and construction techniques. When fully implemented, the gravity system was expected to reduce the number of pumps by 200, save several miles of pipes, and concentrate future treatment facilities at two locations.

The ongoing work of DTCD focused on rural water supply, especially in West Africa. Mali was helped in providing nearly 2,500 new water points for 80,000 inhabitants. Preparatory assistance was provided in Sierra Leone for development of a well digging programme, leading to approval of a new project. The Upper Volta was helped in drilling 530 village wells. Short-term missions were undertaken to advise Governments on water supply in Kenya and in countries of the Niger River basin. DTCD

was also involved in water resources legislation and administration, especially in Caribbean countries. The use of sub-surface space for water storage through artificial recharge was the topic of a workshop convened in co-operation with Sweden, which stressed the need for the United Nations to act as a clearing-house and co-ordinating agency for information on sub-surface development and related programme assistance.

Report. [1]UNICEF Executive Director, E/ICEF/698.

Cartography

Standardization of geographical names

The Fourth United Nations Conference on the Standardization of Geographical Names, convened at Geneva from 24 August to 14 September 1982,[1] was attended by 136 representatives and observers from 62 countries, 1 regional commission, 2 specialized agencies, 4 intergovernmental and international scientific organizations and 1 non-governmental organization. The Conference, the fourth of a series held every five years, established five technical committees dealing with specific items and five editorial groups and an editorial committee to assist the technical committees (for participants and officers, see APPENDIX III).

After considering progress reports by Governments, technical papers submitted by participants and reports of the United Nations Group of Experts on Geographical Names, the Conference on 14 September adopted 26 resolutions and its report. Its recommendations, summarized in a March 1983 report of the Secretary-General,[2] dealt with: the work programme of the Group of Experts; guidelines and a handbook for the standardization of geographical names; country, marine, region and outer space names; exonyms; linguistic questions, such as transliteration and an Arabic language glossary; the treatment of geographical names in data bases and data processing; education and training in toponymy; and the dates and place of the Fifth Conference (see below).

By one of its resolutions,[3] the Conference, recognizing that discrepancies in geographical names could cause confusion when used for transportation, tourism, economic studies and telecommunications, as well as the cultural and social importance of those names, recommended that their standardization be accelerated by all possible means.

Publication. [1]*Fourth United Nations Conference on the Standardization of Geographical Names, Geneva, 24 August-14 September 1982,* vol. I: *Report of the Conference* (E/CONF.74/3), Sales No. E.83.I.7.
Report. [2]S-G, E/1983/26 & Add.1.
Resolution (1982). [3]Conference on standardization of geographical names: 2, 14 Sep.

Work programme of the UN
Group of Experts on Geographical Names

At its close on 14 September 1982, the Fourth Conference adopted five resolutions on the United Nations Group of Experts on Geographical Names. By the first,[1] it recommended that the Group continue to standardize geographical names at the national and international levels, and that the Economic and Social Council express its appreciation of the experts' efforts which had made it possible to achieve the existing level of standardization.

By another resolution,[2] the Conference recommended that the Group examine the possibility of preparing a document combining and modifying, where appropriate, basic documents (United Nations decisions, *modus operandi*, aims and functions and rules of procedure) defining the Group's activities.

The Conference, by a third resolution,[3] recommended that the Group's activities be governed by the Group's statement, adopted at its February 1981 session, on steps to make its working groups more effective. Among those steps were: establishment of working groups only where the tasks assigned to them had a direct bearing on the aims of the Group of Experts; review of the need for the existence of working groups to determine whether to continue or terminate their mandates; and evaluation of conference proceedings and working group mandates.

With regard to the Group's geographical/linguistic divisions,[4] the Conference recommended that the Group continue to encourage the divisions to be more active in implementing the decisions of the United Nations conferences on the standardization of geographical names, in working out reporting schedules on their activities to all States within their divisions and to the Group. In addition, the Conference recommended that each division exchange information with the others and make available to them, as frequently as possible, the results of their work.

The Conference, by a resolution on funding support of the Group,[5] confirmed the requirement for its continued operation and recommended that the possibility of providing United Nations financing for Group meetings be investigated.

In 1982, the Group of Experts met at Geneva for its tenth session, on 23 August and 15 September.

Resolutions (1982). Conference on standardization of geographical names (report, E/CONF.74/3, Sales No. E.83.I.7), 14 Sep.: [1]21, [2]22, [3]23, [4]24, [5]25.

Guidelines and handbook

By three resolutions adopted on 14 September 1982, the Fourth Conference made recommendations on the preparation of geographic and cartographic reports to be used by countries in standardizing geographical names.

By one of those resolutions,[2] the Conference recommended that countries be encouraged to publish and keep up to date toponymic guidelines for map and other editors. The guidelines should contain certain information, including: the legal status of geographical names in the respective languages of multilingual countries; the alphabets of the language or languages and, in the case of non-Roman alphabets and scripts, the officially introduced romanization keys; and spelling rules for and aids to pronunciation of names. The Conference recommended that the toponymic guidelines submitted by Austria serve as a sample of format and content, and called for appointment of a correspondent to co-ordinate the development of national toponymic guidelines.

The Conference, by another resolution,[3] recommended that the Group of Experts, at its eleventh (1984) session, examine the possibility of developing a manual of simplified guidelines to assist Member States which were in the initial stages of national standardization.

By a third resolution,[1] the Conference, considering that substantial experience had been acquired in the standardization of geographical names and that the experience should be systematized, recommended that the Group of Experts initiate the systematization of that experience by preparing a handbook of general technical and methodological principles which could be used by interested countries as a guide in the elaboration of their own standardization procedures. It also recommended that the document be circulated to all participating countries and be examined at the next Conference.

Resolutions (1982). Conference on standardization of geographical names, 14 Sep.: [1]3, [2]4, [3]9.

Country, marine, region and outer space names

On 14 September 1982, the Conference made several recommendations on standardizing names of countries, marine features, regions and outer space areas.

Two resolutions concerned country names. By the first,[2] the Conference recommended that each country co-operate with a working group of the Group of Experts in preparing a list of country names. The Conference, by the other resolution,[3] recommended that the activities of the Group of Experts and the Documentation, Reference and Terminology Section (Translation Division, United Nations Department of Conference Services), which had similar programmes, be co-ordinated. It proposed that that Section be approached by the Cartography Section (Natural Resources and Energy Division, Department of

Technical Co-operation for Development), to assume full responsibility for maintenance of the list after it had been published.

The Conference, noting that a working group of the Group of Experts had completed its tasks in regard to undersea features and that work in maritime features had not been finished, recommended that the task of the working group be limited to maritime features and that the Group of Experts identify a point of contact to carry out essential liaison and communications regarding names of undersea features proposed by national bodies.[4]

Another resolution concerned standardization of physiogeographic names.[1] The Conference recommended that physiogeographic regions be registered and characterized unambiguously and be listed in surveys and other documents along with locations and dimensions of the features, and that the same procedures be followed with respect to regional features divided among two or more countries.

With regard to outer space names,[5] the Conference, noting that the naming of extraterrestrial features was done in a satisfactory way by the Working Group for Planetary System Nomenclature of the International Astronomical Union, recommended that the Working Group on Extraterrestrial Features of the Group of Experts be dissolved. In addition, the Conference recommended that the Chairman of the latter Working Group continue to maintain liaison between the Group of Experts and the former Working Group.

Resolutions (1982). Conference on standardization of geographical names, 14 Sep.: [1]7, [2]10, [3]11, [4]12, [5]13.

Exonyms

The Fourth Conference, by a resolution of 14 September 1982,[1] recommended that exonyms giving rise to international problems be used very sparingly and published in parentheses with the nationally accepted standard name. (The term "exonym" had been defined by a prior United Nations Conference as a name used in a certain language for a geographical entity situated outside the area where that language had official status and differing in form from the name used in the official language or languages of the area where the geographical entity was situated.)

Resolution (1982). [1]Conference on standardization of geographical names: 20, 14 Sep.

Linguistic questions

Transliteration

Three of the 26 resolutions adopted on 14 September 1982 by the Fourth Conference contained recommendations on transliteration of geographical terms.

By the first,[1] the Conference recommended that new romanization systems for international use be considered only on condition that the sponsoring nations implemented such systems on their cartographic products (maps and charts), and that States refrain from revising systems previously adopted for international use. By another resolution,[2] the Conference recommended that the Group of Experts, at its next session, request the Working Group on a Single Romanization System for Each Non-Roman Writing System to discuss any system that might be submitted to it and to report its findings to the Group of Experts. By a resolution on transliteration into Roman and Devanagari scripts,[3] the Conference, noting progress made and work required in the India Division, recommended that the Division undertake further studies in Urdu and Bangla in conjunction with the experts of Pakistan and Bangladesh, and suggested association in that regard with Bhutan, Nepal and Sri Lanka.

Resolutions (1982). Conference on standardization of geographical names, 14 Sep.: [1]15, [2]16, [3]17.

Arabic names

The Conference, in two resolutions adopted on 14 September 1982, made recommendations on geographical names in Arabic. Noting that Arabic was to be introduced as an official language of the Economic and Social Council and of United Nations conferences on the standardization of geographical names, the Conference recommended that the Documentation, Reference and Terminology Section (Translation Division, United Nations Department of Conference Services), in collaboration with the Arabic Service of the Translation Division, establish an Arabic version of the glossary of the terminology used in the standardization of geographical names.[1] English, French and Spanish versions of the glossary were currently available. The Conference also recommended that the United Nations Group of Experts consider the conversion of non-Arabic writing systems into Arabic script and, in particular, whether or not non-Roman writing systems should be converted into Arabic script through the medium of the Roman alphabet.[2]

Resolutions (1982). Conference on standardization of geographical names, 14 Sep.: [1]8, [2]14.

Data bases and processing

By a resolution of 14 September 1982,[1] the Fourth Conference, noting that it had become increasingly difficult to separate the subjects of automated data processing and gazetteers, recommended that future conferences as well as sessions of the Group of Experts consider both subjects under the single agenda item "Toponymic data files, (a) creation, (b) maintenance and (c) output, including gazetteer production". The Conference recognized that automated data processing was just one means of creating a names information file and that gazetteers were merely one product of such a file.

By another resolution of that date on automated data processing,[2] the Conference recommended that all countries send to the Cartography Section of the Natural Resources and Energy Division of the Department of Technical Co-operation for Development progress reports on the collection, treatment, writing and publishing of geographical names, especially in the field of automated data processing, so that a compendium of information could be produced on an annual basis.

Resolutions (1982). Conference on standardization of geographical names, 14 Sep.: [1]18, [2]19.

Training programmes

Another area of concern for the Conference was training and education in cartography. Noting a need for professional personnel with education in cartographic toponymy, it recommended that each country aim at providing training in that subject at the university or corresponding academic level.[2] That recommendation was among the resolutions adopted by the Conference on 14 September 1982.

A pilot training course in toponymy, held at Cisarua, Indonesia, from 7 to 18 June, was organized by the National Co-ordination Agency for Surveys and Mapping in Indonesia and was the first of its kind to be held under the aegis of the United Nations Cartography Section. The Agency co-operated closely with the Working Group on Training Courses in Toponymy of the United Nations Group of Experts on Geographical Names in setting up the course, which was attended by 29 students from Indonesia, Malaysia, Nepal, the Philippines and Thailand. A report on the course, prepared by F. J. Ormeling (Netherlands), Convenor of the Working Group, was presented in August.[1] The programme consisted of two parts: a series of lectures on geographical names standardization, including such topics as toponymy theory and functions, linguistics, global distribution of languages and scripts, exonyms, problems of geographical names collection and standardization, and applications of geographical names on maps and in gazetteers; and a series of field trips near Cisarua, during which the participants were exposed to actual field collection and verification of names in a region with a variety of topographic, hydrographic and cultural details.

Taking into account the success of the course, the Conference, by another resolution of 14 September,[3] recommended that similar courses and seminars be held in other geographic/linguistic divisions and that the Cartography Section make a submission on behalf of the Conference for the provision of the necessary funds.

Report. [1]Working Group on Training Courses in Toponymy, E/CONF.74/L.65.
Resolutions (1982). Conference on standardization of geographical names, 14 Sep.: [2]5, [3]6.

Dates and place of the Fifth UN Conference

The Fourth United Nations Conference on the Standardization of Geographical Names, in the first of its resolutions adopted on 14 September 1982,[1] expressed appreciation to Canada for its offer to host the Fifth Conference and recommended to the Economic and Social Council that it be held there not later than the second half of 1987.

Resolution (1982). [1]Conference on standardization of geographical names: 1, 14 Sep.

Thematic mapping through remote sensing

In co-operation with the Food and Agriculture Organization of the United Nations and the Government of Italy, the United Nations had organized since 1976 a series of international training courses for participants from developing countries in the use of aerial and satellite imagery in conjunction with topographic and land use maps for crop statistics and agriculture census, forestry, fisheries, water resources and hydrology, and pasture and rangeland development. The seventh course, held at Rome, Italy, from 30 August to 17 September 1982,[1] was devoted to the applications of satellite remote sensing to thematic mapping with special reference to land use, and was part of the United Nations Programme on Space Applications for 1982.

Report. [1]Training course on remote sensing for thematic mapping, A/AC.105/312.

Chapter X

Energy

Contents

Related topics:
Disarmament: Prevention of nuclear war; Protection of nuclear facilities. Peaceful uses of outer space: Use of nuclear power sources in outer space; Solar power transmission from satellites; Legal aspects of the use of nuclear power sources in outer space. Regional economic and social activities—Energy: Africa; Asia and the Pacific; Europe. Energy statistics. International Atomic Energy Agency.

Non-nuclear energy

Most United Nations activities during 1982 in the field of non-nuclear energy were related to the Nairobi Programme of Action for the Development and Utilization of New and Renewable Sources of Energy, adopted by the United Nations Conference on New and Renewable Sources of Energy in August 1981 and endorsed by the General Assembly in December of that year.[1] Aimed at finding alternatives to the world-wide dependence on depletable supplies of petroleum and gas, the Programme promoted the increased use of non-conventional power sources. Activities in this field by various United Nations organizations and entities were co-ordinated by the inter-agency Administrative Committee on Co-ordination (ACC). The Assembly called for the development of the energy resources of developing countries; the main organizations involved with assessing their energy needs and resources were the United Nations Development Programme (UNDP), the World Bank and the United Nations Conference on Trade and Development, and the United Nations Industrial Development Organization

(UNIDO) was the principal organization concerned with the industrial uses of energy (see below).

Resolution. [1]GA: 36/193, 17 Dec. 1981 (YUN 1981, p. 691).

Activities of the UN system

In a report issued in May 1982,[3] ACC described measures taken to ensure a United Nations system-wide approach in the field of energy. By a 1980 decision,[2] the Economic and Social Council had endorsed a review which would set out objectives for the system in the energy field, distribute the tasks involved in attaining those objectives among the various United Nations organizations and emphasize the need for co-ordination. Because the modalities for implementation of the 1981 Nairobi Programme of Action for the Development and Utilization of New and Renewable Sources of Energy[4] were under discussion at the intergovernmental level, as were the medium-term objectives of the individual organizations, ACC believed it was currently premature to propose system-wide objectives; therefore, it described steps being taken that would ensure a system-wide approach in energy and could lead to the formulation of joint objectives. It expected to report on those objectives at a later time.

The Nairobi Programme of Action set out a number of specific objectives with regard to various new and renewable sources of energy (charcoal and fuelwood; certain fossil fuels, particularly oil shale, tar sands and peat; non-conventional energy sources, including biomass, geothermal, marine, solar and wind; hydropower; and draught animals) as well as a number of general areas, such as comprehensive energy planning and assessment, and energy efficiency and conservation. Approximately 85 per cent of the 180 energy-related subprogrammes undertaken by the United Nations system—or about 45 per cent of the $121 million allocated to programme activities in energy during 1982-1983—were related to the Programme of Action.

Steps were being taken to translate the priorities set out in the Programme of Action into programme objectives for individual organizations. For the most part, those were being formulated in terms of proposals for or revisions of the medium-term plans or objectives of the organizations for 1984-1989 which were being considered by the appropriate intergovernmental bodies. The organizations of the United Nations system had decided to initiate joint planning in the field of energy and expected to clarify such objectives in the course of that process.

While it had not been possible to propose system-wide objectives at the time of the ACC report, some measures had been taken to ensure a co-ordinated approach. As a follow-up to the Programme of Action, an *Ad Hoc* Working Group, established by ACC in 1981,[5] at its second meeting (Geneva, 11 and 12 February 1982), analysed the extent to which current activities and medium-term plans of the system responded to the specific injunctions of the Programme and submitted the analysis to the Interim Committee on New and Renewable Sources of Energy, which in turn reported to the General Assembly on the need for co-ordination in the system to implement the Programme. The Working Group identified six areas for joint action and for which current levels of resources were inadequate. For each of the areas to be given immediate high priority, a co-ordinating agency was designated to organize the preparation of concrete proposals to the Interim Committee. Those areas were: assessment and planning (UNDP); integrated rural energy (Food and Agriculture Organization of the United Nations (FAO)); industrialization and energy (UNIDO); information systems (United Nations Educational, Scientific and Cultural Organization (UNESCO)); human resources (International Labour Organisation (ILO)); and evaluation, development and demonstration of priority sources, including solar, hydropower, geothermal and wind energy (United Nations Department of Technical Co-operation for Development (DTCD)).

ACC agreed that the general structure of the United Nations medium-term plan in energy could,

with appropriate amendments, also serve as an initial conceptual framework for further discussions of system-wide objectives. A number of joint activities were already under way which could help define future work. An example was a joint study undertaken by UNDP and the World Bank on the financial requirements for supporting actions and pre-investment activities (estimated at $14 billion) to implement the Nairobi Programme of Action. The study provided estimates for both the medium term (1982-1985) and the longer term (1986-1990).

By a decision of 28 July 1982[1] adopted without vote, the Economic and Social Council took note of the ACC report, on the recommendation of its Third (Programme and Co-ordination) Committee, which approved the draft on 19 July as proposed by its Chairman, also without vote.

Decision (1982). [1]ESC: 1982/162, 28 July, text following.
Decision (prior). [2]ESC: 1980/179, 25 July 1980 (YUN 1980, p. 993).
Report. [3]ACC, E/1982/67.
Yearbook references. 1981, [4]p. 689, [5]p. 702.
Meeting record. ESC: E/1982/SR.49 (28 July).

Economic and Social Council decision 1982/162

Adopted without vote

Approved by Third Committee (E/1982/91) without vote, 19 July (meeting 11); draft by Chairman (E/1982/C.3/L.3); agenda item 20.

Report of the Administrative Committee on Co-ordination on measures taken to ensure a system-wide approach in the field of energy

At its 49th plenary meeting, on 28 July 1982, the Council took note of the report of the Administrative Committee on Co-ordination on measures taken to ensure a system-wide approach in the field of energy.

Energy resources development

Energy resources development was part of the 1982 technical assistance programmes of several United Nations entities. Among them, FAO accounted for the largest number of programme activities in the general field of energy with 28 different subprogrammes; ILO had 18 subprogrammes and UNESCO had 17, while the World Meteorological Organization, UNIDO, the Economic Commission for Europe and the Economic and Social Commission for Asia and the Pacific each had 10 or more. FAO accounted for 26 per cent of the resources for programme activities in energy ($32 million), while UNIDO accounted for 10 per cent ($12 million). DTCD (see below) had 12 energy-related subprogrammes in 1982-1983, with a value of $5,897,000, but substantively supported 86 technical co-operation projects with a value of $46 million, of which 53 concerned new and renewable sources of energy. To assist the development of those sources of energy in the developing countries, the World Bank and UNDP carried out an extensive field investigation programme (see below).

DTCD activities. In 1982, DTCD carried out eight country missions to estimate financial requirements for exploration and location of energy resources. In the conventional energy field, requests for assistance increased to 24. Technical advisory or programming missions on petroleum were undertaken in nine countries, on petroleum legislation in four, and on coal in six. A workshop on geophysical methods in petroleum exploration was organized in co-operation with Norway, with participants from 31 developing countries. A meeting on oilfield development techniques, funded by the United Nations Regular Programme of Technical Co-operation in co-operation with China, included participants from 22 countries. The management and development of electric power was supported in 26 projects. A symposium on coal for electricity generation in developing countries, organized under the Regular Programme in co-operation with Australia, studied the economic, technical, commercial, financial and environmental aspects of the subject.

Energy planning and management projects were active in 20 countries and short-term missions were carried out in 12. Notable ones included those on statistics for energy production in Peru, and on consumption and related matters in Costa Rica, El Salvador, Nicaragua and Panama. A survey of energy resources and utilization was undertaken in Angola to formulate policy for integrated development. In Belize, Ethiopia and Panama, DTCD helped formulate national energy policies and short- and long-term energy development programmes. With funds provided by Sweden, DTCD undertook missions in energy planning to identify requirements in information, methodology and manpower training, and to identify projects for outside donors. A symposium was convened on energy supply management, in co-operation with France and funded by the Regular Programme, to examine policies and strategies in the light of changing conditions in energy supplies.

DTCD also provided assistance to projects in the field of new and renewable sources of energy (see below).

UNDP action. By a decision of 18 June 1982,[1] the Governing Council of UNDP commended the UNDP Administrator on his efforts to support energy development, especially through action supported by the UNDP Energy Account in 1981/82 and the conduct of surveys under the Energy Sector Assessment Programme undertaken jointly with the World Bank. It requested the Administrator to report in 1983 on the results of the surveys.

In a March 1982 report,[2] the Administrator informed the Governing Council of actions taken in respect to energy development programmes, including actions to implement the Nairobi Programme of Action for the Development and Utilization of New and Renewable Sources of Energy. The report included a summary of progress in raising funds for the Energy Account, as well as a description of the projects approved. The Programme of Action had invited the World Bank and UNDP to undertake a study of the financial requirements for supporting actions and pre-investment activities for implementing the Programme. Due to time constraints in preparing the study for the meeting of the Interim Committee on New and Renewable Sources of Energy held in June 1982 at Rome, Italy, the extensive field investigations at the country level of the new and renewable energy programmes of the developing countries were not completed. UNDP presented two papers to the Interim Committee and the Governing Council—one a supplementary policy statement by United Nations financial institutions, and the other a description of current activities and policies of other international financial institutions.

Five Governments responded positively to the Administrator's request to strengthen the UNDP financial resource base to assist energy projects. In addition to $2.8 million collected from those donors in 1982 (see table on next page), the Fund for International Development of the Organization of Petroleum Exporting Countries agreed to contribute 10 per cent of the funds received up to $6 million over three years. With the available resources, UNDP initiated 16 projects, half of which were studies for producing energy in particular developing countries and most of the others were general studies by United Nations organizations on certain energy aspects. Although the funds contributed to the Energy Account were limited, they were viewed by the Administrator as catalytic in initiating activities that would not otherwise have been possible. The initial operation of the Account indicated that with a modest input of resources from UNDP, the activities were capable of attracting additional funds from a variety of other multilateral, bilateral and private sources.

The major activity financed by the Energy Account was the UNDP/World Bank Energy Sector Assessment Programme, executed by the World Bank, analysing the energy requirements of 60 developing countries. According to the Administrator, the assessment surveys could be of great assistance to developing countries in setting priorities and future financing, planning and development of their energy resources. As the Administrator stated in his annual report for 1982,[3] missions had been completed in 16 countries, where it was frequently found that there was insufficient commitment, staff analysis or financial resources to deal effectively with the identified major issues. The Assessment Programme suggested ways in which national planning could be strengthened. The World Bank and UNDP were involved in ensuring that there was adequate follow-up to the surveys and that high-priority projects for both pre-investment and capital investment would be realized.

UNDP ENERGY ACCOUNT PROJECT EXPENDITURES, 1982
(in thousands of US dollars)

Country/Region	Amount
Barbados	23
Bolivia	57
Egypt	41
Jamaica	8
Niger	40
Subtotal	169
Latin America and the Caribbean	16
Interregional	1,345
Global	304
Subtotal	1,665
Total	1,834

SOURCE: DP/1983/6/Add.4/Corr.1.

CONTRIBUTIONS TO UNDP ENERGY ACCOUNT, 1982 AND 1983
(as at 31 December 1982; in US dollar equivalent)

Country	1982 payment	1983 pledge
Australia	527,650	—
Finland	421,053	363,636
Netherlands	1,000,000	—
New Zealand	36,232	36,232
Sweden	813,008	—
Total	2,797,943	399,868

SOURCE: A/38/5/Add.1.

An important activity which emerged from the assessments was the Energy Sector Management Programme, for which financing (an estimated $36 million for 1983-1986) was sought by the Administrator and the President of the World Bank. That Programme aimed at providing assistance to Governments in generating energy savings in such sectors as industry, transportation and power system losses. A pilot programme for rural/renewable energy resources proposed work regarding stoves and kilns, wind pumps, solar crop-driers and water-heaters, microhydro plants, peat for domestic use, biomass for power/heat and biogas. The First Meeting of Co-operating Institutions in Asia was held early in 1982 and similar meetings were foreseen for other regions.

Additional resources from the Energy Account in 1982 were used for a coal transportation study in Colombia which contributed to follow-up investment by the World Bank and a major multinational institution in the order of $400 million. In partnership with the World Bank, funding was provided by the United Nations and the United States Agency for International Development for a series of energy workshops to promote private investment in new and renewable sources of energy. A relatively modest contribution from the Energy Account financed two projects in Jamaica, one in Trinidad and Tobago, and one in Barbados.

They tested and demonstrated an energy-saving device which could introduce considerable savings in hotel energy consumption by automatically activating and cutting off the power supply when guests entered and left their rooms.

The United Nations Institute for Training and Research/UNDP Information Centre for Heavy Crude and Tar Sands, which became operational in late 1981 with a modest contribution from the Energy Account, received, at the second meeting of its Advisory Board at Caracas, Venezuela, in February 1982, a sufficient number of pledges from Governments and petroleum companies for five years.

Within UNDP itself, an Energy Policy Group was established to co-ordinate the overall policy activities of UNDP and its various associated funds and programmes. Energy activities financed by UNDP had expanded from $44.2 million in 1975 to $83.7 million in 1981. In 1982, expenditures under the Energy Account totalled $1.8 million (see table above).

General Assembly action. By a resolution of 21 December 1982,[4] the General Assembly requested the Secretary-General to report in 1983 on the development of the energy resources of the developing countries. The report would identify constraints to such development and review energy investment requirements and possible financing of such investment. Emphasizing the importance of increased concessional lending by multilateral financing institutions, in particular the World Bank—possibly with an energy affiliate—for developing energy resources in those countries, the Assembly urged the international community to provide more technical assistance to enable them to formulate energy and investment plans suited to their own needs. The Assembly called on the international community to stimulate the transfer of and research in appropriate technologies so that developing countries could develop their energy resources, and affirmed that special measures were required for the least developed countries. It requested the United Nations Conference on Trade and Development (UNCTAD) to submit in 1983 a report on strengthening the technological capacity of the developing countries.

Acting on the recommendation of its Second (Economic and Financial) Committee, the Assembly adopted the resolution by a recorded vote of 146 to 1. The Second Committee had approved the text, sponsored and revised by Bangladesh on behalf of the Group of 77 developing countries, on 13 December by a recorded vote of 127 to 1.

Introducing the draft, Bangladesh said its thrust was the development of the energy resources of developing countries and its provisions were to be implemented only in that context.

The United States said it opposed the resolution because the terms of reference of the requested report on energy resources development did not give sufficient attention to the private sector or to the need to study energy supply and demand and energy prices, and because the United States could not participate in an implicit call for an energy affiliate of the World Bank; furthermore, the sponsors had rejected its suggestions without discussing their merits. Responding to the United States, Bangladesh, on behalf of the Group of 77, said that the spirit of compromise and understanding of the Group of 77 had been duly reflected in the vote, which had clearly shown where responsibility lay for the failure to adopt the resolution by consensus.

Denmark, speaking on behalf of the States members of the European Economic Community, said they had voted in favour in the belief that the development of energy resources in energy-deficient developing countries was extremely important, not only for them but for the world community as a whole; in addition, they attached importance to the expansion of lending, including lending from private and commercial sources, to facilitate the exploration and development of energy resources. Japan stated that it had, reluctantly, voted for the resolution, which, with some modifications, could have provided a firm basis for reviewing how developing countries were being assisted in dealing with their energy problems and developing their own national plans; it added that the energy problems of one country or a group of countries could not be considered in isolation, but they had to be viewed in a broader global context with a view to finding a comprehensive solution.

Decision (1982). [1]UNDP Council (report, E/1982/16/Rev.1): 82/25, 18 June.
Reports. UNDP Administrator, [2]DP/1982/44 & Corr.1, [3]DP/1983/6/Add.3.
Resolution (1982). [4]GA: 37/251, 21 Dec., text following.
Meeting records. GA: 2nd Committee, A/C.2/37/SR.3, 5-8, 10, 13-26, 33, 40, *45, 48* (28 Sep.–13 Dec.); plenary, A/37/PV.115 (21 Dec.).

General Assembly resolution 37/251

21 December 1982   Meeting 115   146-1 (recorded vote)

Approved by Second Committee (A/37/680/Add.13) by recorded vote (127-1), 13 December (meeting 48); draft by Bangladesh, for Group of 77 (A/C.2/37/L.96/Rev.1); agenda item 71.

Development of the energy resources of developing countries

The General Assembly,

Recalling the Declaration and the Programme of Action on the Establishment of a New International Economic Order, contained in its resolutions 3201(S-VI) and 3202(S-VI) of 1 May 1974, the Charter of Economic Rights and Duties of States, contained in its resolution 3281(XXIX) of 12 December 1974, and resolution 3362(S-VII) of 16 September 1975 on development and international economic co-operation,

Recalling its resolution 35/56 of 5 December 1980, the annex to which contains the International Development Strategy for the Third United Nations Development Decade, which, *inter alia,* called, in paragraph 35, for the promotion of the exploration, development, expansion and processing of all energy resources of the developing countries at a rate commensurate with their development objectives and for the provision of adequate financial and technical resources for this purpose,

Recalling also the Nairobi Programme of Action for the Development and Utilization of New and Renewable Sources of Energy,

Recalling further section II.A of resolution 112(V) of 3 June 1979 of the United Nations Conference on Trade and Development concerning the strengthening of the technological capacity of the developing countries in the development of their energy resources, including that relating to transition from conventional sources to a more diversified pattern of energy consumption,

Aware that special measures are required in this regard for the least developed countries,

Aware that multilateral financial and technical assistance for the exploration, development, expansion and processing of the energy resources of the developing countries continues to be inadequate in relation to either their indigenous energy potential or the requirements commensurate with their development objectives,

Having regard to the situation of the developing countries, in particular the energy-deficient among them, which are unable to reduce energy use significantly without hindering their development and for which concerted and adequate measures are needed for the exploration and rational development of their energy resources,

Considering that the principal impediments to the realization of the indigenous energy potential of the developing countries are the scarcity of financial resources, insufficient analysis of exploration data, inadequate access to technology and a shortage of skills,

Emphasizing the importance of intensifying the capabilities of the United Nations in the collection, analysis and dissemination of information in the field of the development of energy resources in the developing countries,

Taking into account the fact that the development of their energy resources constitutes an important factor in the economic and social development of the developing countries,

Reaffirming that effective and urgent measures should be taken by the international community to assist and support the national efforts of the developing countries for developing the domestic energy resources of those countries, in particular the energy-deficient among them, in order to meet their needs through co-operation, assistance and investment in the field of conventional and of new and renewable sources of energy, consistent with their national plans and priorities, as called for in the International Development Strategy,

1. *Requests* the Secretary-General to prepare, within the context of the International Development Strategy for the Third United Nations Development Decade, a comprehensive report on the development of the energy resources of the developing countries, to be submitted to the Economic and Social Council at its second regular session of 1983 and to contain:

(a) An overview of the energy situation of the developing countries in regard to the development of their energy resources, including new and renewable sources of energy;

(b) An identification of the constraints to the development of energy resources in the developing countries, including constraints encountered in such fields as financing, both bilateral and multilateral, exploration and energy planning at the national level, information flows, education and training, research and development, and technology transfer;

(c) A review of the energy investment requirements of the developing countries and the possible and available mechanisms for the financing of such investment, and of the existing gaps and the prospective means of filling them, particularly in the field of energy exploration, taking into account desirable levels of increase in the ratio of energy consumption in those countries;

2. *Emphasizes* the importance of a substantial expansion in concessional lending, not merely a reallocation of existing resources, by multilateral financing and development institutions, in particular the World Bank, and the regional development banks, for the exploration and development of the energy resources of developing countries;

3. *Further emphasizes* the role which an energy affiliate for the development of energy resources of developing countries within the World Bank could play with a view to generating additional resources, stresses the importance of the consideration of other complementary frameworks for the mobilization of financial resources, to assure, on an urgent basis, the expenditures and investment needs of the developing countries, and calls upon Member States to make appropriate efforts to this end in the relevant forums;

4. *Urges* the international community to provide increased technical assistance to enable developing countries to formulate energy plans and investment programmes suited to their individual developmental needs, and to engage in the necessary pre-investment energy

development activities, consistent with the national plans and priorities of those countries;

5. *Recognizes* the importance of strengthening the technological capacities of the developing countries in the energy sector to facilitate the development of their energy resources and, in this regard, calls upon the international community to stimulate the transfer of appropriate technologies to the developing countries, to enhance financial and technical flows and to promote interdisciplinary research and analysis of the implications of, and requirements for, stepped-up energy exploration and development activities, as well as a gradual transition to a more diversified pattern of energy consumption, particularly in the developing countries;

6. *Affirms* that special measures are required for the least developed countries for the development of their energy resources;

7. *Welcomes* the work being done by the United Nations Conference on Trade and Development in the implementation of section II.A of its resolution 112(V), concerning the strengthening of the technological capacity of the developing countries in the development of their energy resources, and requests the Secretary-General of the Conference to submit a comprehensive report on that question to the General Assembly at its thirty-eighth session;

8. *Decides* to review at its thirty-eighth session the progress made in the implementation of the present resolution.

Recorded vote in Assembly as follows:

In favour: Afghanistan, Algeria, Angola, Argentina, Australia, Austria, Bahamas, Bahrain, Bangladesh, Barbados, Belgium, Benin, Bhutan, Bolivia, Botswana, Brazil, Bulgaria, Burma, Burundi, Byelorussian SSR, Canada, Cape Verde, Central African Republic, Chad, Chile, China, Colombia, Comoros, Congo, Costa Rica, Cuba, Cyprus, Czechoslovakia, Democratic Kampuchea, Democratic Yemen, Denmark, Djibouti, Dominican Republic, Ecuador, Egypt, El Salvador, Ethiopia, Fiji, Finland, France, Gabon, Gambia, German Democratic Republic, Germany, Federal Republic of, Ghana, Greece, Grenada, Guinea, Guinea-Bissau, Guyana, Honduras, Hungary, Iceland, India, Indonesia, Iran, Iraq, Ireland, Israel, Italy, Ivory Coast, Jamaica, Japan, Jordan, Kenya, Kuwait, Lao People's Democratic Republic, Lebanon, Lesotho, Liberia, Libyan Arab Jamahiriya, Luxembourg, Madagascar, Malawi, Malaysia, Maldives, Mali, Malta, Mauritania, Mauritius, Mexico, Mongolia, Morocco, Mozambique, Nepal, Netherlands, New Zealand, Nicaragua, Niger, Nigeria, Norway, Oman, Pakistan, Panama, Papua New Guinea, Paraguay, Peru, Philippines, Poland, Portugal, Qatar, Romania, Rwanda, Saint Lucia, Samoa, Sao Tome and Principe, Saudi Arabia, Senegal, Sierra Leone, Singapore, Solomon Islands, Somalia, Spain, Sri Lanka, Sudan, Suriname, Swaziland, Sweden, Syrian Arab Republic, Thailand, Togo, Trinidad and Tobago, Tunisia, Turkey, Uganda, Ukrainian SSR, USSR, United Arab Emirates, United Kingdom, United Republic of Cameroon, United Republic of Tanzania, Upper Volta, Uruguay, Vanuatu, Venezuela, Viet Nam, Yemen, Yugoslavia, Zaire, Zambia, Zimbabwe.

Against: United States.

Technology transfer

A Meeting of Governmental Experts on the Transfer, Application and Development of Technology in the Energy Sector was held at Geneva from 25 October to 2 November 1982.[1] As requested by the Trade and Development Board of UNCTAD in October 1981,[5] the UNCTAD Secretary-General, in cooperation with the UNIDO, DTCD, the International Atomic Energy Agency (IAEA) and other United Nations bodies, organized the Meeting to consider studies and reports submitted to it (among them an August 1982 report by the UNCTAD secretariat entitled "The energy sector in developing countries: issues in the transfer, application and development of technology"[2]) and the views of Governments and relevant United Nations bodies, and to examine issues concerning the transfer, application and development of technology in the energy sector. The Meeting considered the technological needs and development objectives of the developing countries and made recommendations to the UNCTAD Committee on Transfer of Technology, within the framework of the Nairobi Programme of Action for the Development and Utilization of New and Renewable Sources of Energy.

Among its recommendations, the Meeting proposed that all countries adopt strategies and policies within the context of their overall industrialization and development strategies that took into account the interrelationships between sources of energy (particularly those indigenous to the country), natural endowments, development priorities, energy conservation and the suitability of different energy technologies. The international community, the Meeting said, should adopt policies that would promote international co-operation in the energy sector under mutually beneficial terms and on a nondiscriminatory basis, taking into account the growing energy needs of the developing countries. The Meeting determined that energy was a fundamental requirement for the development and industrialization of developing countries, particularly the least developed of them, and those countries should be encouraged to adopt appropriate plans to develop their energy sector.

Many of the Meeting's recommendations concerned efforts at the national, regional and international levels to improve the access of the developing countries to energy technology and to strengthen their technological capacity in the energy sector. The Meeting recommended that the developing countries strengthen co-operative links among themselves on the basis of complementarity in technological and industrial capacity and their experience in that sector. Developed countries should contribute to strengthening the technological capacity of the developing countries in the energy sector by considering certain measures, including the transfer of technology through appropriate mechanisms in the public and private sectors, and expanding research and development programmes that were oriented towards the needs of developing countries.

The conclusions and recommendations of the Meeting were endorsed by the Committee on Transfer of Technology in a resolution of 10 December.[3]

The General Assembly, in a resolution of 21 December, called on the international community to stimulate the transfer of appropriate technologies in order to facilitate the development of the developing countries' energy resources.[4]

Reports. [1]Meeting of Governmental Experts on Transfer, Application and Development of Technology in Energy Sector, TD/B/C.6/94; [2]UNCTAD secretariat, TD/B/C.6/AC.9/2.
Resolutions (1982). [3]Committee on Transfer of Technology (report, TD/B/936): 18(IV), para. 2, 10 Dec. [4]GA: 37/251, para. 5, 21 Dec.
Yearbook reference. [5]1981, p. 699.

Industrial uses of energy

Industry was central to the energy problem, since about 35 per cent of the world energy supply was used directly in industry, and the energy needed for the utilization of capital and consumer goods delivered by industry accounted for another 50 per cent of total energy consumption.

The energy-related activities of UNIDO increased in volume and diversity in 1982, increasing awareness of problems and opportunities and leading to identification of priorities. Technical co-operation energy-related projects implemented by UNIDO covered industrial energy planning, management and conservation; production of energy-related equipment; training aspects; utilization of conventional and new and renewable sources of energy; and industrial production of synthetic fuels.

During 1982, UNIDO had 63 energy-related activities in the pipeline, with a value of about $34 million, including some large-scale projects proposed on a cost-sharing basis. In addition, there were 55 ongoing technical co-operation activities, valued at about $13 million. During the year, over 50 documents relating to the use of energy in industry and as feedstock were issued.

In the area of energy planning and management, UNIDO pursued efforts to strengthen government bodies dealing with overall energy assessment, planning and policy formulation for the improved use of energy resources. A project was initiated in the Niger to assist the Ministry of Mines and Industry in the formulation of industrial development plans, with emphasis on the development of energy for the needs of the industrial sector. In the Philippines, a project was started to establish an energy management consultancy service which would conduct energy audits of enterprises in different branches of industry, recommend energy-saving measures, assist in their implementation, train technical staff and assist individual enterprises in more efficient utilization of energy.

Projects in Brazil and Thailand focused on energy conservation in the industrial sector. After a preliminary study to identify the fields in which the best energy savings could be achieved, UNIDO provided assistance to the Electrical Research Institute of Turkey.

Energy training projects were given special emphasis in 1982. Two regional seminars on effective industrial energy management were held—one in the Philippines in January for the members of the Association of South-East Asian Nations (ASEAN) and the other at São Paulo, Brazil, in October for Latin American and Caribbean countries. The seminars were attended by over 300 leaders from Governments and industry in 32 countries. As a result of the ASEAN seminar, project proposals were submitted and the Philippines agreed to provide, in co-operation with UNIDO, training in energy management to least developed countries.

Similar follow-up was under way for the seminar in Brazil.

In view of escalating energy costs and in order to stimulate energy conservation and management, UNIDO launched several workshops and training courses in various industrial subsectors, focusing on energy-demanding industries such as glass, ceramics, metallurgy and petrochemicals. In some training programmes, such as the in-plant group training in electric welding held in the USSR and in diesel engines held in Czechoslovakia, new methods and techniques of energy management and conservation were introduced. In co-operation with two other international organizations, UNIDO organized an interregional training course on solar energy application which was held in Yugoslavia and attended by scientists from developing countries.

In 1982, a number of innovative energy projects were launched. One, for example, aimed at evaluating and testing different sea-water desalination technologies for which solar energy was used. As part of that project, UNIDO sponsored a pilot plant in Australia using solar stills. The results of the project were expected to be of direct relevance to many countries, including those in the Sudano-Sahelian region of Africa.

Projects in new and renewable sources of energy included assistance to a Malian laboratory for solar energy, the establishment of a pilot plant in the Comoros for the development of solar energy distillation of oil from the ylang-ylang flower, and technical support to a mini–hydropower centre in China. In the conventional energy field, UNIDO assisted Rwanda in the renovation of a methane gas extraction and purification plant and in ensuring consistent processing capacity to provide uninterrupted supplies to industrial consumers of methane. Assistance to the Petroleum Development Centre in Angola continued during 1982, with the aim of gradually increasing the number of Angolan nationals employed in the petroleum industry. In Hungary, preparatory assistance was provided for the use of low-grade and secondary raw materials in metallurgy and of types of coal of low calorific value. UNIDO assisted the Indian petroleum refining industry in developing oil technology and management.

UNIDO assisted Bangladesh, Bulgaria, China, India, Poland and the United Republic of Tanzania in various projects concerned with developing biological and synthetic fuels. Several of those projects addressed research and development problems of interest to other developing countries which would share the results under arrangements for technical co-operation among developing countries. In Poland, for example, the first phase of a project was completed which assisted the Government in the use of bituminous and brown coal resources for producing liquid and gaseous fuels through the development of technologies for coal gasification, pyrolysis and liquefaction.

Particular areas of the UNIDO energy programme received support from certain donor countries: large-scale generation of biogas from industrial wastes (Federal Republic of Germany); biofuels and synfuels, energy conservation (Australia); and fuel alcohol (Finland, Sweden).

With regard to energy-related technology and equipment, UNIDO collected and organized information which was made available in the form of a card index on the main primary and secondary sources of energy (coal, oil-gas, electricity, solar). Each card index contained a description of the production process, the required equipment, skill requirements, and the conditions of commercial access to each production process. The Industrial and Technological Information Bank of UNIDO handled some 250 inquiries on energy-related matters.

In addition, UNIDO carried out various general studies, research and promotion activities relating to industrial technology which could be useful to Governments, covering such subjects as investment requirements for developing power industries, biofuels and synfuels, the petrochemical industry, solar and wind energy and hydroelectric mini-power-plants.

As a result of work for and follow-up to the 1981 United Nations Conference on New and Renewable Sources of Energy[1] at Nairobi, Kenya, and the Programme of Action adopted there, UNIDO became even more involved in 1982 in the co-ordination of United Nations activities in the field of energy.

UNIDO participated with other United Nations entities in the preparation of an April report on current and planned activities of the United Nations system to implement the Nairobi Programme of Action, submitted to the Interim Committee on New and Renewable Sources of Energy in June, and participated in the elaboration of the chapter on energy of the proposed medium-term plan for 1984-1989. Co-operation in the energy field was discussed during regular joint meetings of UNIDO, the United Nations Educational, Scientific and Cultural Organization (UNESCO), the Food and Agriculture Organization of the United Nations and the International Labour Organisation (ILO). Consultations were held regarding studies and meetings to be organized jointly by UNIDO and the United Nations Institute for Training and Research.

In April 1982, one of a series of high-level meetings of Vienna-based organizations concerned with energy development and utilization was organized at the invitation of the UNIDO Executive Director and attended by the Austrian Foreign Minister and the executive heads and directors of IAEA, the International Institute for Applied Systems Analysis and the Organization of Petroleum Exporting Countries. As a follow-up, in October, IAEA convened a meeting of experts of the same organizations, together with representatives of Austrian ministries and institutes, to discuss co-operation in the fields of energy data banks, energy systems modelling, and training in energy management.

Most of the work to define a comprehensive, integrated and balanced UNIDO energy programme was completed in 1982 with the publication of a report on energy development and industrialization, which reflected work carried out by UNIDO from mid-1980 to mid-1982, in particular in connection with the 1981 Conference on new and renewable energy sources and follow-up activities. The report contained a blueprint for future activities and set out relevant facts, concepts, goals, guidelines and proposals for action on energy-related industrial development activities. An attempt was made to identify activity areas requiring priority attention by UNIDO.

Within UNIDO, a Special Advisory Group on Energy was responsible for efforts to increase awareness of the energy/industry interdependence, improve co-ordination, examine substance and priorities of energy-related activities, formulate a comprehensive and balanced UNIDO energy programme and follow up on the Nairobi Programme of Action. The Group was also responsible for evaluating requirements and availability of energy for industry and for assisting developing countries in adopting strategies and policies to cope with their energy needs.

Yearbook reference. [1]1981, p. 689.

New and renewable energy sources

Implementation of the Nairobi Programme of Action

While energy problems had long been a concern of the United Nations, the Organization in 1982 began to implement the Nairobi Programme of Action for the Development and Utilization of New and Renewable Sources of Energy, endorsed by the General Assembly in December 1981,[8] which promoted the use of various non-conventional energy sources, including solar and wind power, geothermal energy, ocean energy, biomass conversion, fuelwood and charcoal, oil shale and tar sands, peat, draught animal power and hydropower. Most of the action planned in accordance with the Programme was a continuation of previous activities.

ACC Reports. Current and planned activities of the United Nations system to implement the Nairobi Programme of Action were described in an April 1982 report submitted to the Interim Committee on New and Renewable Sources of Energy by the Administrative Committee on Co-ordination (ACC).[2] Proposals for programmes which could be initiated in the following two to three years, with emphasis on identifying areas for immediate action, were made in another report to the Committee in May.[3] That report was prepared by the ACC *Ad Hoc* Working Group on Inter-agency Follow-up to the Nairobi Programme of Action, but was not reviewed by ACC. The Working Group, at its second meeting on 11 and 12 February at Geneva,[6] reviewed energy activities on a system-wide basis and identified 68 areas for specific programmes to be carried out by co-ordinated United Nations action, with a value of more than $242 million. In addition, 29 regional and subregional programmes (most of them in Africa and Latin America) were proposed, totalling $72 million. ACC suggested that the financial requirements for these activities be met through increases in the regular United Nations budget or through increased voluntary contributions.

Of the over 850 subprogrammes in the 1982-1983 work programmes of the United Nations system, 180 were energy related, of which 152 related to the Nairobi Programme of Action, estimated at $56.4 million, i.e., 45 per cent of all energy-related activities; among them, 26 subprogrammes with a value of $14.7 million were completely devoted to issues relating to new and renewable sources of energy.

In accordance with the four areas for priority action set out in the Nairobi Programme of Action, energy assessment and planning was an element of 44 per cent of the United Nations subprogrammes; research, development and demonstration of 27 per cent; transfer, adaptation and application of mature technologies of 29 per cent; and information flows, education and training of 31 per cent. Another area of priority concern—mobilization of financial resources—was addressed by 7 per cent of the subprogrammes. Some activities were designed to meet one or more of the Programme's priorities.

The United Nations system responded to national requirements in terms of the Nairobi Programme of Action in 192 specific technical co-operation projects with new and renewable sources of energy components, which were requested by 88 Governments or groups of Governments and were implemented by 13 organizations with extrabudgetary funding from the United Nations Development Programme (UNDP) and other sources. The majority of those projects had been requested prior to the Nairobi Conference.

There were 10 regional and 61 country projects in 47 countries on energy assessment and planning. About half of the activities dealt with the establishment of national infrastructure; others dealt with

international or sectoral planning and resource assessment. The main activity in this area was a World Bank/UNDP 60-country Energy Sector Assessment Programme (see above). Twenty projects in 16 countries and one region were to evaluate and examine specific applications of alternative technologies.

In the area of research, development and demonstration, some 69 projects in three regions and 39 countries were executed by eight United Nations agencies. Activities involved general or sectoral assessment of research programmes in technologies for new and renewable sources of energy for rural, urban and industrial uses. Programmes carried out and planned included support for geothermal research centres and to national centres, with priority to those participating in regional networks. Other such projects included research in solar ponds, solar photovoltaic battery power units, wind turbine-diesel electric-power units, gasifier–internal combustion engine power units, wind- and solar-powered deep-well pumps, water desalination by reverse osmosis, and mini-hydropower units.

In the area of rural energy development, United Nations activities included projects on several energy sources (biogas, draught animal power, solar and wind power, and fuelwood) to increase food and agricultural production. Among projects in energy and industrialization were a programme to enable developing countries to produce hydroelectric power-station equipment and another to establish facilities for producing biofuels (methane, methanol, ethanol, charcoal, modified vegetable oils and fuel gas).

Activities concerned with transfer, adaptation and application of mature technologies—80 projects in 45 countries and seven regional projects—included support to centres involved with technology transfer or improvement of manufacturing equipment necessary for the use of new and renewable sources of energy. UNIDO support for the production of such equipment was the largest activity related to the latter objective. Another example was the provision of advisory services by ILO on the dissemination of fuel-saving techniques and devices for cooking.

Most subprogrammes in information flows, education and training—39 projects in 27 countries, and 11 regional or interregional projects—were courses, training or workshops on new and renewable sources of energy. The most significant project in this area was the development by UNESCO of a global information network on such energy sources. In response to the Nairobi Programme of Action, the 1984-1989 medium-term plan of the United Nations system established energy as a major programme, giving higher priority to new and renewable sources.

Interim Committee activities. The Interim Committee on New and Renewable Sources of

Energy, established by the General Assembly in December 1981[8] for the immediate launching of the implementation of the Nairobi Programme of Action, met at Rome, Italy, from 7 to 18 June 1982 and adopted several conclusions which were included in its report on the session.[4] The Committee stated that the Programme constituted the basic framework of reference for action by the international community and its fundamental objective was to promote concerted action in the development and utilization of new and renewable sources of energy, with a view to meeting future overall energy requirements, especially those of developing countries.

In the Committee's view, the primary responsibility for promoting the development and utilization of new and renewable energy sources rested with individual countries, but international cooperation was indispensable and should be directed towards assisting and strengthening national efforts. Specialized intergovernmental organizations in the energy field were invited to cooperate.

The Committee held that an exchange of detailed information on current and future programmes was essential for effective implementation of the Programme. It recommended that the United Nations system continue to provide information on its activities and invited countries engaged in bilateral assistance to provide information on theirs. As stipulated in the Programme, particular attention should be given to the energy needs of the least developed countries and developing countries whose needs were greatest. Sociocultural, environmental, energy efficiency and other factors related to development of energy sources should be given consideration and the specific circumstances of each country or region needed to be reflected in programmes and projects.

The Committee considered the ACC proposals for action-oriented plans and programmes for carrying out the Nairobi Programme of Action (see above) to be a useful framework for agency and inter-agency follow-up, and suggested that they be reviewed and adjusted, in particular in view of proposals by the developing countries.

In addition to general comments and policy guidelines, the Committee made recommendations on co-ordination of energy activities in the United Nations system, regional action and the financing of energy research and development.

Economic and Social Council action. By a decision of 29 July 1982,[1] the Economic and Social Council took note of the Interim Committee's report and decided to transmit it to the General Assembly. The Council expressed its appreciation to Italy for having acted as host to the Committee in such an exemplary manner.

The decision was adopted, without vote, on the recommendation of the First (Economic) Committee which approved it in a similar way on 23 July as orally proposed by its Chairman.

General Assembly action. In a resolution of 21 December,[7] the General Assembly reaffirmed the importance of the Nairobi Programme of Action and called for its early implementation. Noting with regret that the Interim Committee had not fully succeeded in immediately launching implementation of the Programme, the Assembly decided that the ACC recommendations on action-oriented plans and programmes provided a useful framework for agency and inter-agency follow-up. It requested the United Nations system's organizations and bodies to participate fully in and support implementation in the short-, medium- and long-term context, in particular for the benefit of developing countries. The Assembly called on specialized intergovernmental organizations in the field of new and renewable sources of energy to co-operate in implementing the Programme, and invited non-governmental organizations to support it. The Secretary-General was requested to report in 1983 on implementation of the resolution.

The Assembly, by other sections of the resolution, established an intergovernmental Committee on the Development and Utilization of New and Renewable Sources of Energy; decided that the secretariat support arrangements on the subject of new and renewable sources of energy should include both co-ordination functions and support services for the Committee; requested the Secretary-General to make proposals on improving co-ordination in that field within the United Nations system; reiterated that the regional commissions should perform a major role in promoting the development and utilization of new and renewable sources of energy; and called for action to mobilize resources for such energy sources.

The resolution was adopted by a recorded vote of 136 to 10, following its approval by the Second (Economic and Financial) Committee on 17 December by a recorded vote of 108 to 9. The text, revised in writing, was sponsored by Bangladesh, on behalf of the Group of 77, and by Denmark.

Introducing the revised draft, Bangladesh said development and utilization of new and renewable energy sources was important to the Group of 77, which consequently attached importance to full implementation of the Nairobi Programme of Action.

Explaining its negative vote, the United States said the resolution had unnecessary financial implications; it also believed that the development of alternative energy sources should form part of national plans involving both private enterprise and multilateral assistance.

Bulgaria, speaking also on behalf of the Byelorussian SSR, Czechoslovakia, the German Democratic Republic, Hungary, Mongolia, Poland, the Ukrainian SSR and the USSR, which also cast a negative vote, said they believed that the Programme of Action should be implemented primarily through national efforts, merely supported by United Nations measures; developing countries should mobilize their own resources to meet their energy needs.

Japan welcomed the text as a first positive step of the United Nations in the transition from conventional to alternative sources of energy. Kenya expressed disappointment that, although the text had been extensively revised, no consensus had been reached; in view of the energy crisis, all Governments surely attached importance to the harnessing of renewable sources of energy.

In an October report to the Assembly on development and international economic co-operation in the field of new and renewable energy sources,[5] the Secretary-General discussed secretariat arrangements to facilitate the work of the international community, inter-agency co-ordination and mobilization of resources (see below).

Decision 1982. [1]ESC: 1982/169, 29 July, text following.
Reports. ACC, [2]A/AC.215/2, [3]A/AC.215/5; [4]Interim Committee, A/37/47 & Corr.1; [5]S-G, A/37/574; [6]Working Group on inter-agency follow-up to Nairobi Programme of Action, ACC/1982/3.
Resolution (1982). [7]GA: 37/250, 21 Dec., text following.
Resolution (prior). [8]GA: 36/193, 17 Dec. 1981 (YUN 1981, p. 691).
Financial implications. 5th Committee report, A/37/784; S-G statements, A/C.2/37/L.98/Rev.1, A/C.5/37/104.
Meeting records. ESC: E/1982/SR.50 (29 July). GA: 2nd Committee, A/C.2/37/SR.3, 5-8, 20-26, 33, 40, *43, 50* (28 Sep.–17 Dec.); 5th Committee, A/C.5/37/SR.76 (18 Dec.); plenary, A/37/PV.115 (21 Dec.).

Economic and Social Council decision 1982/169

Adopted without vote

Approved by First Committee (E/1982/106) without vote, 23 July (meeting 14); oral proposal by Chairman; agenda item 18.

Report of the Interim Committee on New and Renewable Sources of Energy

At its 50th plenary meeting, on 29 July 1982, the Council:

(a) Expressed its appreciation to the Government of Italy for having acted as host, in such an exemplary manner, to the Interim Committee on New and Renewable Sources of Energy at its session held at Rome from 7 to 18 June 1982;

(b) Took note of the report of the Interim Committee on that session;

(c) Decided to transmit the report to the General Assembly at its thirty-seventh session.

General Assembly resolution 37/250

21 December 1982   Meeting 115   136-10 (recorded vote)

Approved by Second Committee (A/37/680/Add.11) by recorded vote (108-9), 17 December (meeting 50); 2-nation draft (A/C.2/37/L.74/Rev.1); agenda item 71 *(n)*.

Sponsors: Bangladesh (for Group of 77), Denmark.

Immediate implementation of the Nairobi Programme of Action for the Development and Utilization of New and Renewable Sources of Energy

The General Assembly,

Recalling its resolutions 3201(S-VI) and 3202(S-VI) of 1 May 1974, containing the Declaration and the Programme of Action on the Establish-

ment of a New International Economic Order, 3281(XXIX) of 12 December 1974, containing the Charter of Economic Rights and Duties of States, and 3362(S-VII) of 16 September 1975 on development and international economic co-operation,

Recalling also its resolution 35/56 of 5 December 1980, the annex to which contains the International Development Strategy for the Third United Nations Development Decade,

Recalling further its resolutions 33/148 of 20 December 1978, 34/190 of 18 December 1979 and 35/204 of 16 December 1980 and Economic and Social Council resolutions 2119(LXIII) of 4 August 1977, 1978/61 of 3 August 1978 and 1979/66 of 3 August 1979 and Council decision 1980/187 of 25 July 1980 regarding the convening of and preparation for the United Nations Conference on New and Renewable Sources of Energy,

Convinced of the importance of developing new and renewable sources of energy in order to contribute to meeting requirements for continued economic and social development, particularly in the developing countries, through, *inter alia*, the transition from the present international economy based primarily on hydrocarbons to one based increasingly on new and renewable sources of energy,

Reaffirming that the primary responsibility for promoting the development and utilization of new and renewable sources of energy rests with individual countries, that in this regard international co-operation is indispensable and should be directed to assist and support national efforts, that developed countries bear a special responsibility to contribute actively to this end and that other countries in a position to do so should also continue to promote efforts in this regard,

Further reaffirming that the United Nations system should fully participate in and support the implementation of the Nairobi Programme of Action for the Development and Utilization of New and Renewable Sources of Energy through adequate institutional arrangements and additional and adequate resources, and that it is imperative to increase the responsiveness of the system in this respect,

Cognizant of the need to take urgent and concerted measures for the mobilization of additional and adequate resources necessary for the implementation of the Nairobi Programme of Action and to ensure for this purpose the co-operation and effective co-ordination of the activities of the organs, organizations and bodies of the United Nations system, as well as of all specialized agencies and institutions in the field of new and renewable sources of energy,

Recalling that specialized intergovernmental organizations and institutions in the field of new and renewable sources of energy are invited to extend their co-operation in order to strengthen the co-operative action of the international community and to ensure that further resources are made available for the development of new and renewable sources of energy, that national private entities in interested countries, as appropriate, have a role to play and that, in certain countries, non-governmental entities will also have a significant role to play,

Recalling its resolution 36/193 of 17 December 1981, in which it, *inter alia*, endorsed the Nairobi Programme of Action, urged all Governments, as well as organs, organizations and bodies of the United Nations system, to take effective action for the implementation of the Programme and stressed the necessity for taking, at its thirty-seventh session, the final decision on adequate institutional arrangements for the implementation of the Programme,

Emphasizing the importance of the subregional, regional and interregional efforts for implementing the Nairobi Programme of Action,

Taking note of the report of the Interim Committee on New and Renewable Sources of Energy, which met in Rome from 7 to 18 June 1982,

Taking note also of the report of the Secretary-General called for under General Assembly resolution 36/193,

I

Nairobi Programme of Action for the Development and Utilization of New and Renewable Sources of Energy

1.   *Reaffirms* the significance and importance of the Nairobi Programme of Action for the Development and Utilization of New and Renewable Sources of Energy and calls for the early and effective implementation of the Programme as stipulated in General Assembly resolution 36/193;

2.   *Expresses its appreciation and thanks* to the Government and people of Italy for the excellent facilities and generous hospitality provided for the session of the Interim Committee on New and Renewable Sources of Energy, held in Rome from 7 to 18 June 1982;

3.   *Notes with regret* that the Committee did not fully succeed in its fundamental purpose of the immediate launching of the implemen-

tation of the Nairobi Programme of Action, as called for under section II, paragraph 3, of resolution 36/193;

4. *Decides* that the proposals and recommendations made by the Administrative Committee on Co-ordination on action-oriented plans and programmes for carrying out the Nairobi Programme of Action provide a useful framework for agency and inter-agency follow-up to the Programme within the United Nations system;

5. *Requests* the organs, organizations and bodies of the United Nations system to participate fully in and support the implementation of the Nairobi Programme of Action in the short-term, medium-term and long-term context, in particular for the benefit of developing countries in accordance with their national plans and priorities;

6. *Calls upon* all specialized intergovernmental organizations and institutions in the field of new and renewable sources of energy to extend their co-operation in the implementation of the Nairobi Programme of Action;

7. *Invites* all non-governmental organizations concerned, in both the developing and developed countries, to support and contribute to the implementation of the Nairobi Programme of Action;

II

Committee on the Development and Utilization
of New and Renewable Sources of Energy

1. *Decides* to establish an intergovernmental Committee on the Development and Utilization of New and Renewable Sources of Energy, which shall be open to the participation of all States as full members;

2. *Endorses* the recommendation of the United Nations Conference on New and Renewable Sources of Energy that representation of Member States in the Committee should be at a high level;

3. *Decides* that the Committee shall meet once every two years in even years, but that, exceptionally, it shall hold its first regular session in the second quarter of 1983;

4. *Decides also* that the Committee shall submit its reports and recommendations to the General Assembly through the Economic and Social Council, which may transmit to the Assembly such comments on the reports as it may deem necessary;

5. *Decides* that the Committee shall assist the General Assembly in, *inter alia*, the following functions:

(a) Recommending policy guidelines for different organs, organizations and bodies of the United Nations system in regard to new and renewable sources of energy, on the basis of the Nairobi Programme of Action;

(b) Formulating and recommending action-oriented plans and programmes for carrying out the Nairobi Programme of Action in accordance with the priorities identified in paragraphs 47 to 56 thereof;

(c) Keeping under review and modifying as may be necessary the priorities established in paragraphs 47 to 56 of the Nairobi Programme of Action;

(d) Reviewing and assessing trends and policy measures related to the development and utilization of new and renewable sources of energy, with a view to increasing their contributions to meeting future overall energy requirements;

(e) Promoting the mobilization of the resources required in the implementation of the Nairobi Programme of Action;

(f) Recommending guidelines to the financial organs, organizations and bodies of the United Nations system in the financing of the activities related to the implementation of the measures of the Nairobi Programme of Action, and helping to ensure the implementation of the measures listed in section III of the Programme relating to financial resources;

(g) Monitoring the implementation and helping to ensure co-ordination of the measures established in the Nairobi Programme of Action as well as of the activities of the organs, organizations and bodies of the United Nations system in the field of new and renewable sources of energy;

(h) Being informed of, drawing upon and contributing to the work and expertise of governmental and intergovernmental institutions in the field of new and renewable sources of energy;

(i) Reviewing the activities of the United Nations system in the field of new and renewable sources of energy and the implementation of the Nairobi Programme of Action, and where necessary making recommendations on the adaptation of the Programme;

6. *Invites* all organs, organizations and bodies concerned within the United Nations system to participate actively in the work of the Committee;

7. *Invites also* all intergovernmental and non-governmental organizations concerned to participate in the work of the Committee;

III

Secretariat for new and renewable sources of energy

1. *Welcomes* in principle the report of the Secretary-General on secretariat support arrangements on the subject of new and renewable sources of energy;

2. *Decides* that the secretariat support arrangements should include both co-ordination functions and support services for the Committee on the Development and Utilization of New and Renewable Sources of Energy:

(a) The co-ordination function shall comprise:

(i) Assisting the Director-General for Development and International Economic Co-operation in the co-ordination functions assigned to him in paragraph 63 of the Nairobi Programme of Action;

(ii) Co-ordinating activities at the secretariat level relating to new and renewable sources of energy within the United Nations system;

(iii) Assisting in promoting the development and utilization of new and renewable sources of energy, in particular in promoting and facilitating responsiveness by all appropriate organs, organizations and bodies of the United Nations system, especially to the specific needs and requirements of the developing countries;

(iv) Assisting in identifying areas for consultative meetings and providing services and co-ordination for such meetings;

(b) The secretariat support services for the Committee shall comprise:

(i) Providing support to the Committee in accordance with paragraph 60 of the Nairobi Programme of Action;

(ii) Developing and implementing work programmes in accordance with the specific requirements of the Committee;

(iii) Serving as a focal point for information on multilateral, bilateral and other programmes in the area of new and renewable sources of energy;

(iv) Monitoring and reporting on resources for the financing of the implementation of the Nairobi Programme of Action;

3. *Requests* the Secretary-General to provide such support arrangements in the office of the Director-General for Development and International Economic Co-operation, through the appointment of a special co-ordinator, and in the Department of International Economic and Social Affairs of the Secretariat through the establishment of a small, separate and identifiable unit;

IV

Mobilization of resources for new and renewable sources of energy

1. *Emphasizes* that the early implementation of the Nairobi Programme of Action requires the mobilization of additional and adequate resources and that each country will continue to bear the main responsibility for the development of its new and renewable sources of energy, which will require vigorous measures for a fuller mobilization of its domestic financial and other resources;

2. *Calls*, to this end, for the urgent implementation of the measures for the mobilization of financial resources as enumerated in paragraphs 76 to 95 of the Nairobi Programme of Action, as well as in paragraphs 93, 94 and 96 to 102 of the report of the Interim Committee on New and Renewable Sources of Energy, and calls upon all countries, particularly the developed countries and other countries in a position to do so, for the provision of additional and adequate financial resources to the relevant organs, organizations and bodies of the United Nations system;

3. *Stresses* the significant role which consultative meetings, as called for in paragraph 91 of the Nairobi Programme of Action and paragraph 98 of the report of the Interim Committee on New and Renewable Sources of Energy, can play in the mobilization of additional financial resources for new and renewable sources of energy, and decides that they should be convened in this field, as required, by the appropriate entities in the United Nations system, with the participation of multilateral and bilateral donors and interested recipient countries, at the national, subregional, regional and global levels, within the framework of the Nairobi Programme of Action, taking into account national plans and priorities and operating on a non-disciminatory basis;

4. *Emphasizes* that such meetings should be consistent with existing procedures, for example, along the lines of the round-tables held by the United Nations Development Programme and the consultative

groups convened by the World Bank, and reiterates the role which the United Nations system must continue to play at the national level through the resident co-ordinators of the operational activities for development of the United Nations system, at the request of the countries concerned, at the regional level through the regional commissions and at the global level, through the Director-General for Development and International Economic Co-operation, by the relevant organs, organizations and bodies of the United Nations system;

5. *Reaffirms*, in this context, that specific and additional resources should be directed through such channels as the United Nations Development Programme, the United Nations Revolving Fund for Natural Resources Exploration, the long-term financial arrangements for the United Nations Financing System for Science and Technology for Development, the United Nations Development Programme Energy Account and others directly or indirectly involved, in accordance with national plans and priorities;

6. *Further emphasizes* the role which an energy affiliate for the development of energy resources of developing countries within the World Bank could play with a view to generating additional resources, and stresses the importance of the consideration of other complementary frameworks for the mobilization of financial resources to assure, on an urgent basis, the expenditures and investment needs of the developing countries, and calls upon Member States to make appropriate efforts to this end in the relevant forums;

V
Co-ordination within the United Nations system

1. *Reiterates the call* made in its resolution 36/193 for enhancing co-operation and co-ordination within the United Nations system in the field of new and renewable sources of energy;

2. *Reaffirms* the role of the Director-General for Development and International Economic Co-operation, within the framework of his mandate as defined by the General Assembly in its resolutions 32/197 of 20 December 1977 and 33/202 of 29 January 1979 and paragraph 63 of the Nairobi Programme of Action, in providing overall co-ordination in the field of new and renewable sources of energy within the United Nations system;

3. *Endorses* the recommendation of the Interim Committee on New and Renewable Sources of Energy regarding the establishment of an appropriate mechanism for co-ordination, and requests the Director-General for Development and International Economic Co-operation to convene an *ad hoc* inter-agency meeting in early 1983 in order to establish an *ad hoc* inter-agency group and to define its terms of reference;

4. *Requests* the Secretary-General, taking into account the Nairobi Programme of Action, the conclusions and recommendations of the Interim Committee on New and Renewable Sources of Energy and the provisions of the present resolution, to submit a report to the Committee on the Development and Utilization of New and Renewable Sources of Energy at its first regular session, in 1983, which will contain, *inter alia*, practical proposals regarding:

(a) Guidelines for the relevant organs, organizations and bodies of the United Nations system on the preparation and convening of consultative meetings, bearing in mind the provisions of paragraph 4 of section IV above;

(b) Ways and means of improving the effectiveness of inter-agency co-ordination through the Administrative Committee on Co-ordination in the field of new and renewable sources of energy;

(c) Further ways and means of mobilizing financial resources for new and renewable sources of energy;

VI
Regional and subregional action

Reiterates that the regional commissions shall perform a major role, at the regional level, in promoting the development and utilization of new and renewable sources of energy, as defined in paragraph 71 of the Nairobi Programme of Action;

VII
Report of the Secretary-General

Requests the Secretary-General to report to the General Assembly at its thirty-eighth session, through the Economic and Social Council at its second regular session of 1983, on the implementation of the present resolution.

Recorded vote in Assembly as follows:

In favour: Afghanistan, Algeria, Angola, Argentina, Australia, Austria, Bahamas, Bahrain, Bangladesh, Barbados, Belgium, Benin, Bhutan, Bolivia, Botswana, Brazil, Burma, Burundi, Canada, Cape Verde, Central African Republic, Chad, Chile, China, Colombia, Comoros, Congo, Costa Rica, Cuba, Cyprus, Democratic Kampuchea, Democratic Yemen, Denmark, Djibouti, Dominican Republic, Ecuador, Egypt, El Salvador, Ethiopia, Fiji, Finland, France, Gabon, Gambia, Germany, Federal Republic of, Ghana, Greece, Grenada, Guinea, Guinea-Bissau, Guyana, Honduras, Iceland, India, Indonesia, Iran, Iraq, Ireland, Israel, Italy, Ivory Coast, Jamaica, Japan, Jordan, Kenya, Kuwait, Lao People's Democratic Republic, Lebanon, Lesotho, Liberia, Libyan Arab Jamahiriya, Luxembourg, Madagascar, Malawi, Malaysia, Maldives, Mali, Malta, Mauritania, Mauritius, Mexico, Morocco, Mozambique, Nepal, Netherlands, New Zealand, Nicaragua, Niger, Nigeria, Norway, Oman, Pakistan, Panama, Papua New Guinea, Paraguay, Peru, Philippines, Portugal, Qatar, Romania, Rwanda, Saint Lucia, Samoa, Sao Tome and Principe, Saudi Arabia, Senegal, Sierra Leone, Singapore, Solomon Islands, Somalia, Spain, Sri Lanka, Sudan, Suriname, Swaziland, Sweden, Syrian Arab Republic, Thailand, Togo, Trinidad and Tobago, Tunisia, Turkey, Uganda, United Arab Emirates, United Kingdom, United Republic of Cameroon, United Republic of Tanzania, Upper Volta, Uruguay, Vanuatu, Venezuela, Yemen, Yugoslavia, Zaire, Zambia, Zimbabwe.

Against: Bulgaria, Byelorussian SSR, Czechoslovakia, German Democratic Republic, Hungary, Mongolia, Poland, Ukrainian SSR, USSR, United States.

Establishment of the intergovernmental Committee

By its resolution of 21 December 1982 on implementation of the Nairobi Programme of Action,[1] the General Assembly established a Committee on the Development and Utilization of New and Renewable Sources of Energy, open to all States, which would report to the Assembly through the Economic and Social Council and meet once every two years in even years, with the exception of 1983 when it would hold its first regular session. The Committee's functions included: recommending policy guidelines for United Nations entities in regard to new and renewable sources of energy; formulating plans for carrying out the Nairobi Programme of Action; modifying as necessary the Programme's priorities; assessing trends and policy measures; mobilizing resources; recommending guidelines for financing Programme activities; monitoring and co-ordinating Programme measures; and contributing to the work of governmental and intergovernmental institutions in the field. The Assembly invited United Nations, intergovernmental and non-governmental organizations to participate in the Committee's work.

By another section of the resolution, the Assembly decided that support services for the Committee be provided by a special unit to be established in the United Nations Secretariat.

Explaining the Eastern European countries' negative vote on the resolution, Bulgaria said they opposed the establishment of an intergovernmental Committee and considered its administrative and financial implications unjustified. The United States would have wanted the Committee's mandate to be more explicit, and Turkey thought that it would eventually be necessary to set up a central unit within the United Nations system, with full administrative and executive powers, to deal with the various aspects of new and renewable sources of energy. Japan regarded establishment of the Committee as very important, and Kenya expected the Committee to give serious consideration particularly to the periodicity of meetings and the review and appraisal of the Programme of Action.

Resolution (1982). (1)GA: 37/250, sect. II, 21 Dec.

Secretariat unit

By its resolution of 21 December 1982 on implementation of the Nairobi Programme of Action,[2] the General Assembly decided that the secretariat support arrangements on new and renewable sources of energy should include co-ordination functions and support services for the Committee on the Development and Utilization of New and Renewable Sources of Energy. The co-ordination functions would include: assisting the Director-General for Development and International Economic Co-operation in the functions assigned to him by the Programme; co-ordinating secretariat activities in that field; promoting the development and utilization of those sources of energy; and identifying areas for consultative meetings and providing services for them. Secretariat support services would include: developing and implementing work programmes to meet the Committee's requirements; serving as a focal point for information on multilateral, bilateral and other programmes; and reporting on financial resources for implementing the Programme. The Assembly requested the Secretary-General to provide support arrangements in the Director-General's office, through the appointment of a special co-ordinator, and in the Department of International Economic and Social Affairs (DIESA) through the establishment of a separate unit.

The Assembly's decisions were based on recommendations in the Secretary-General's October report on secretariat support arrangements for new and renewable sources of energy.[1] Secretariat services, the Secretary-General stated, should facilitate concerted action by the international community and, in particular, by United Nations organizations. As much as possible, secretariat support should draw on existing United Nations entities in providing required services. Additional functions identified by the Interim Committee on New and Renewable Sources of Energy should be part of the responsibilities for secretariat support. Specific modalities for carrying out those functions would be formulated in consultations with United Nations entities, interested Governments and intergovernmental organizations.

The Secretary-General noted that current arrangements for secretariat support services had been established on an interim basis and that it was understood that more permanent arrangements would be made by the Assembly in 1982. With regard to financing, efforts would be made to meet personnel requirements from existing resources.

The establishment of a unit in DIESA was opposed by the Eastern European countries, as stated by Bulgaria, while Kenya regarded the establishment of separate financial and administrative arrangements as imperative. Every effort to improve the relevant support services must be made, Japan said.

Report. (1)S-G, A/37/574.
Resolution (1982). (2)GA: 37/250, sect. III, 21 Dec.

Co-ordination in the UN system

In its resolution of 21 December 1982 on implementation of the Nairobi Programme of Action,[3] the General Assembly, reiterating its call for enhancing co-ordination within the United Nations system in the field of new and renewable sources of energy, reaffirmed the role of the Director-General for Development and International Economic Co-operation in providing overall co-ordination, and endorsed the recommendation of the Interim Committee on New and Renewable Sources of Energy to establish an appropriate mechanism for that purpose. The Assembly requested the Director-General to convene an *ad hoc* inter-agency meeting in early 1983 in order to establish an *ad hoc* inter-agency group and to define its terms of reference. The Secretary-General was requested to submit in 1983 to the Committee on the Development and Utilization of New and Renewable Sources of Energy practical proposals on: guidelines for United Nations bodies on the preparation and convening of consultative meetings; ways of improving the effectiveness of inter-agency co-ordination through the Administrative Committee on Co-ordination in the field of new and renewable sources of energy; and ways of mobilizing financial resources.

The Assembly's decisions were based on recommendations by the Secretary-General in an October report on development and international economic co-operation in the field of new and renewable sources of energy.[2]

The need for continuing co-ordination and increased responsiveness of the system was also stressed by the Interim Committee at its June session. To that end, the Committee recommended[1] that focal points for new and renewable sources of energy be maintained or established; an appropriate inter-agency mechanism for co-ordination be established, making full use of existing resources and mechanisms; and the Director-General continue to carry out his responsibilities for overall co-ordination in implementing the Programme of Action. In this context, the Committee considered essential the exchange of information on and assessment of United Nations activities and bilateral assistance.

Reports. [1]Interim Committee, A/37/47; [2]S-G, A/37/574.
Resolution (1982). [3]GA: 37/250, sect. V, 21 Dec.

Regional action

The General Assembly, in its 21 December 1982 resolution on implementation of the Nairobi Programme of Action,[2] reiterated that the regional commissions should perform a major role in promoting the development and utilization of new and renewable sources of energy.

The Interim Committee on New and Renewable Sources of Energy, in its report to the Assembly,[1] stated that regional and subregional dimensions were very important in implementing the Programme. It recommended that the United Nations system assist the regional commissions and other regional bodies in formulating and implementing regional plans and programmes in accordance with the Programme, stressing that complementarity of action and mutual reinforcement should be pursued.

Report. [1]Interim Committee, A/37/47.
Resolution (1982). [2]GA: 37/250, sect. VI, 21 Dec.

Financing research and development

Emphasizing that the early implementation of the Nairobi Programme of Action required additional and adequate resources and that each country had the main responsibility for the development of its new and renewable sources of energy, the General Assembly, in a resolution of 21 December 1982,[5] called for urgent implementation of measures for the mobilization of financial resources and called on countries to provide the necessary resources. Stressing the significant role which consultative meetings could play in this regard, it decided that they should be convened by appropriate United Nations bodies, with the participation of donors and recipient countries. In this context, the Assembly reiterated the role the United Nations system must play at the national, regional and global levels, through the resident co-ordinators of the operational activities for development, the regional commissions and the Director-General for Development and International Economic Co-operation, respectively. Reaffirming that additional resources should be directed through United Nations channels, the Assembly emphasized the role which an energy affiliate within the World Bank could play in generating resources and the importance of considering other complementary frameworks for this purpose.

Supporting the resolution, Turkey said the establishment of a world energy bank would be the only solution in the long run to mobilize the required resources.

The convening of consultative meetings was recommended by the Interim Committee on New and Renewable Sources of Energy at its June ses-

sion, and by the Secretary-General in his October report on development and international economic co-operation in the field of new and renewable sources of energy.[4] The Secretary-General suggested that such meetings be held at different levels. National meetings should focus on national priorities and could be modelled on the round-tables held by the United Nations Development Programme (UNDP) with developing countries and the consultative groups convened by the World Bank. Subregional and regional meetings could focus on the mobilization of resources for specific programmes and projects, and on the identification of areas for action. In the Secretary-General's view, a global approach might be necessary or appropriate in areas such as research, development and demonstration, planning, information, training and development of specific energy sources. The United Nations Secretariat would provide support services for the meetings and serve as a focal point for information.

Similar suggestions were made by the Interim Committee.[1] Though stating that each country would continue to bear the main responsibility for the development of its new and renewable sources of energy which would require fuller mobilization of its domestic financial and other resources, the Committee felt that implementation of the Programme of Action required additional and adequate international financial resources, both public and private, from all developed countries and international organizations. The Committee recommended that efforts be made to increase concessional flows for the financing of projects and programmes, through channels such as UNDP, the United Nations Revolving Fund for Natural Resources Exploration and the United Nations Financing System for Science and Technology for Development. Besides an energy affiliate of the World Bank, the Committee suggested possible establishment of a new financing mechanism within the United Nations system, funded on a voluntary basis.

At its June session, the Interim Committee also considered two reports by the Secretary-General on the role of United Nations, regional and other financial institutions in the field of new and renewable sources of energy, and a World Bank/UNDP study on financial requirements for supporting actions and pre-investment activities for the development and utilization of such energy sources in developing countries during the 1980s.

In a report issued in April,[2] the Secretary-General reviewed the response of United Nations financial institutions—the World Bank, UNDP and six associated funds and programmes, and the International Fund for Agricultural Development—to the energy requirements of developing countries. The information provided showed that all of them had taken some steps for an increased role in promoting new and renewable sources of energy. In UNDP, for example, an Energy Policy Group and an Energy Projects Review Committee had been established to ensure co-ordination of UNDP-financed programmes and projects, and to provide guidance to regional bureaux and other units in the financing of energy development.

In a May report,[3] the Secretary-General discussed the role, in the field of new and renewable sources of energy, of regional and subregional banks—the African Development Bank, the Asian Development Bank, the Inter-American Development Bank and the Caribbean Development Bank—other financial institutions—such as the Fund for International Development of the Organization of Petroleum Exporting Countries (OPEC) and the European Development Fund—and a number of subregional and interregional financing institutions. The Secretary-General stated that none of them dealt exclusively with energy; developing countries seeking assistance in that field had to rely on institutions providing general financial development assistance. Available financial resources were limited and requests for pre-investment and capital assistance in the energy field competed with requests for other economic, social and technical assistance. Regional banks and other financial institutions, however, had increased their assistance programmes in energy, including new and renewable sources, in order to meet the growing requirements of developing countries. As an example, the report noted that the lending programmes of the Asian Development Bank, the Inter-American Development Bank and the OPEC Fund for International Development in the energy sector had more than doubled during the previous five years.

Total annual financial commitments of regional institutions were estimated at $1.6 billion in 1982, and it was estimated that in 1985 the level of commitments in the energy field would reach $2.2 billion. An analysis of the lending pattern of those institutions showed that hydropower projects accounted for more than two thirds of the total financing made available to the energy sector. Some institutions had expanded their operations to include other new and renewable sources of energy, such as geothermal and biomass.

The World Bank/UNDP study,[7] submitted to the Interim Committee at the Assembly's December 1981 request,[6] covered all developing countries but concentrated on the requirements of the energy-deficient ones. The study estimated the total financial requirements for support actions—energy assessment and planning, establishment or strengthening of national institutional infrastructure, research, data collection, and training and education—and pre-investment activities—

including feasibility studies, design and engineering—in the development and utilization of new and renewable sources of energy in developing countries at $14 billion during 1982-1990, with about $9 billion, or 65 per cent of the total, for large-scale hydropower. Large-scale new energy sources, including geothermal energy, oil shale, tar sands and peat, were calculated at $1.3 billion or 9 per cent of the total. Other renewable energy sources, including small hydro, fuelwood, biomass, draught animal power, and solar, wind and ocean energies, were estimated at $3.5 billion, or 25 per cent. Pre-investment activities accounted for 75 per cent ($10.6 billion) of the total estimate, while support actions were estimated to require 25 per cent (3.6 billion). As for geographical distribution of the financial requirements, developing countries of Africa, excluding North Africa, would account for 15 per cent of the total; Asia and the Pacific, 35 per cent; Latin America and the Caribbean, 35 per cent; and the Middle East, North Africa and Europe, 15 per cent.

Reports. [1]Interim Committee, A/37/47; S-G, [2]A/AC.215/3, [3]A/AC.215/6, [4]A/37/574.
Resolution (1982). [5]GA: 37/250, sect. IV, 21 Dec.
Resolution (prior). [6]GA: 36/193, 17 Dec. 1981 (YUN 1981, p. 691).
Study. [7]UNDP/World Bank, A/AC.215/4.

Exploration for geothermal energy

The Governing Council of UNDP, by a decision of 18 June 1982,[1] authorized the United Nations Revolving Fund for Natural Resources Exploration to extend its activities into the field of geothermal exploration.

The Council took that decision on the recommendation of the UNDP Administrator in an April report.[2] Noting an immediate demand by a number of developing countries for additional financing and technical assistance for the various stages of geothermal development, the Administrator regarded the Fund as particularly well adapted for pre-feasibility and exploration drilling programmes. In his view, the Fund could provide an additional source of funding to that available from the indicative planning figure (the projected expenditure by UNDP for a particular country) and the UNDP Energy Account (see above), which would continue to be used for all categories of geothermal activities. Although the Fund did not have an adequate financial reserve to undertake large-scale geothermal projects in the order of $10 million each, it was hoped that authorizing the Fund's extension of activities into the field would be an impetus for additional contributions. The report concluded that the approval of one project per year over the next few years appeared to be a reasonable target.

Assistance to geothermal energy projects (eight country projects in 1982) and advisory services for geothermal resources assessment were also provided by the United Nations Department of Technical Co-operation for Development (DTCD).

Decision 1982. [1]UNDP Council (report, E/1982/16/Rev.1): 82/23, para. 1, 18 June.
Report. [2]UNDP Administrator, DP/1982/41.

Solar power

The Second United Nations Conference on the Exploration and Peaceful Uses of Outer Space, held at Vienna, Austria, from 9 to 21 August 1982,[1] reported that, among the major new applications of space technology, probably none had drawn as much attention as proposals for a space solar power system. This concept could be particularly relevant in the context of diminishing conventional energy resources.

The Conference noted that the economics and advantages of the solar power system relative to other methods of energy production had by no means been established. However, if and when technological breakthroughs changed that situation, and provided that implications such as long-term effects on living organisms were solved to the satisfaction of all countries affected, the system would be an ideal project for co-operative international effort. Its magnitude, technological challenges, financial and material requirements, potential benefits and vulnerability would make international efforts not only worth while, but probably necessary. The Conference suggested that the feasibility of undertaking a joint international effort and the means of sharing the resulting benefits should be examined. While such a solar power system might be in the distant future, the Conference advised initiating international efforts immediately so that a mechanism for international participation could be found.

Among the United Nations entities assisting solar energy projects were DTCD and the United Nations Industrial Development Organization (UNIDO) (see above). UNIDO also organized an international training course on solar energy application, in co-operation with two other international organizations.

Report. [1]Conference on outer space, A/CONF.101/10.

Nuclear energy

Most of the United Nations technical work in nuclear energy was carried out by the International Atomic Energy Agency (IAEA), which submitted its annual report to the General Assembly. After considering the report for 1981, the Assembly, in November 1982, urged all States to strive for international co-operation in carrying out the Agency's work and to implement strictly its statute. The Assembly affirmed its confidence in the role of IAEA in the application of nuclear energy for peaceful purposes.

The Preparatory Committee for the United Nations Conference for the Promotion of International Co-operation in the Peaceful Uses of Nuclear Energy held two sessions in 1982 but was unable to reach agreement on an agenda or rules of procedure for the Conference. As a result, the Assembly, in December, decided that the Preparatory Committee would meet twice in 1983 to complete preparations; after the first of those meetings, the Assembly would take a decision on the date of the Conference.

The Assembly also adopted resolutions dealing with nuclear aspects of disarmament issues and outer space. It called for negotiations for an agreement on measures to prevent nuclear war, and for continued efforts to prohibit armed attacks and threats against nuclear facilities, and decided that the sub-committees of the Committee on the Peaceful Uses of Outer Space should continue consideration of the use of nuclear power sources in outer space and of the possibility of supplementing the norms of international law relevant to the use of such power sources.

Report of IAEA

The report of IAEA for 1981 was submitted to the 1982 General Assembly session by a note of the Secretary-General dated 12 August.[1]

Introducing the report to the Assembly on 18 November and updating the information it contained on the work of IAEA in 1981,[4] the IAEA Director General stated that 291 nuclear power reactors were in operation in 24 countries; in 1981, reactors had generated 9 per cent of the world's electricity, by 1990 they were expected to generate 18 per cent, and by the end of the century perhaps as much as 25 per cent, thus relieving some of the pressure on the world's limited oil resources.

Despite its favourable record, the Director General said, the nuclear option was facing many obstacles in industrialized countries and there was a declining demand for new plants. Due to the fact that electricity demands and grids in developing countries were too limited for large-size nuclear reactors, nuclear energy was a less attractive alternative for them. The Director General held it essential that all countries with nuclear power programmes be able to cope effectively with a nuclear emergency, with IAEA serving as a clearing-house for emergency assistance.

With regard to nuclear waste problems, there was reasonably good assurance that until 1990 adequate provision would exist for dealing with spent fuel through either interim storage or reprocessing. Although waste management was still a national responsibility, there was a need for regional and international approaches. Noting the advantages in regional or international co-operation in dealing with waste management and disposal, the Director General said it had been difficult to secure multinational co-operation in this area. This was one technical issue which would be dealt with at an IAEA international conference on radioactive waste management, scheduled to take place at Seattle, United States, in May 1983.

For many member States, support for IAEA work was mainly centred on the Agency's involvement in problems they regarded as vital, namely, food, health and water. Of the IAEA technical co-operation programmes, between 15 and 20 per cent were projects for introducing nuclear power for electricity generation in developing countries, but the bulk was devoted to helping those countries in applying nuclear science in agriculture, medicine and hydrology. There were projects to improve crop yields, develop new crop varieties, sterilize insects, reduce the need for artificial fertilizers, preserve food, treat cancer, control and improve industrial output, and map water resources in arid regions.

With regard to activities relating to international security, the Director General reported that IAEA had for seven years not detected any discrepancy that would indicate diversion of safeguarded nuclear material or misuse of safeguarded nuclear facilities. That conclusion in 1981 was subject to one reservation, namely, that pending the installation of certain additional safeguards equipment, IAEA was unable in two cases to perform fully adequate verification.

According to the Director General, about 98 per cent of the nuclear power plants outside the nuclear-weapon States were under IAEA safeguards and there were five nuclear-weapon States with steadily expanding stocks and sophistication of nuclear weapons and delivery systems. The Director General warned that if the number of nuclear-weapon States or States having tested nuclear explosive devices increased, it could have incalculable consequences for escalation and international security. On the other hand, he considered it possible to make progress in assuring no further proliferation and securing commitments to that effect, whether through the 1968 Treaty on the Non-Proliferation of Nuclear Weapons[3] (NPT) or otherwise. Beyond the five nuclear-weapon States and the four "threshold" States (States operating or building unsafeguarded facilities capable of making weapon-usable materials), there were perhaps 15 other countries that had the technical capability to make nuclear weapons but had bound themselves by treaty or by policy not to do so. That number was expected to grow.

While it was important to improve and refine the Agency's safeguards system, the Director

General stated, it was essential that its limitations be understood. The system was available for application to States which had not accepted safeguards over all their nuclear activities. Four of the five nuclear-weapon States had invited IAEA to perform safeguards inspections, the latest among them the USSR. These inspections demonstrated that nuclear-weapon States, too, were prepared to accept inspection of their peaceful nuclear activities and that safeguards did not lead to commercial disadvantage. The potential usefulness of those precedents should not be overlooked in arms control and disarmament negotiations. IAEA, as the technical operator of the only existing global safeguards system, had a potential that was not exhausted and possessed experience that could be drawn upon.

General Assembly action. By a resolution of 19 November 1982,[2] the General Assembly, taking note of the IAEA report, urged States to strive for effective and harmonious international co-operation in carrying out the work of IAEA and to implement strictly the mandate of its statute, in promoting the use of nuclear energy and the application of nuclear science and technology for peaceful purposes, in strengthening technical assistance and co-operation for developing countries, and in ensuring the effectiveness of the safeguards system. The Assembly considered that Israel's threat to repeat its 1981 armed attack against nuclear facilities as well as any other armed attack against such facilities constituted a serious threat to the role and activities of IAEA in the development and promotion of nuclear energy for peaceful purposes. Affirming its confidence in the Agency's role in that area, the Assembly requested the Secretary-General to transmit to the IAEA Director General the records of the Assembly's 1982 session relating to IAEA activities.

The resolution, sponsored by Czechoslovakia, Italy and Venezuela, was adopted, as amended, by a recorded vote of 105 to 2, with 25 abstentions. The orginal draft, as corrected by the sponsors, did not include paragraphs 3 and 4 of the final version by which the Assembly considered Israel's threat to repeat its armed attack against nuclear facilities a serious threat to IAEA activities and affirmed its confidence in the IAEA role in applying nuclear energy for peaceful purposes.

These two paragraphs were based on an amendment by Iraq, which was sub-amended by the United States and further orally sub-amended by Iraq. Under the United States proposal, the Assembly, instead of mentioning Israel's threat to repeat its armed attack against nuclear facilities, would have considered that any military attack against peaceful nuclear facilities in violation of the Charter of the United Nations constituted a serious threat to the IAEA role and activities in developing and promoting nuclear energy for peaceful purposes. Iraq's oral sub-amendment to the United States proposal incorporated the specific Israeli attack with the general phrase about any other armed attack.

After rejecting, by a recorded vote of 49 to 25, with 40 abstentions, a United States motion to give priority to its sub-amendment, the Assembly adopted the Iraqi oral sub-amendment by a recorded vote of 116 to 2, with 11 abstentions, and then, by a recorded vote of 120 to 2, with 7 abstentions, adopted the United States sub-amendment as amended. Next, the Assembly adopted operative paragraph 4 proposed in the Iraqi amendment by a recorded vote of 128 to none. That vote was followed by another on the full text of the Iraqi amendment (both paragraphs) which was adopted, as a whole as amended, by a recorded vote of 122 to 2, with 4 abstentions.

The Assembly then adopted amendments by Argentina, Brazil and India by a recorded vote of 93 to none, with 35 abstentions, following separate votes on each of the three amendments. Submitting the amendments, Brazil said the changes— to operative paragraph 2, and to the third and fourth preambular paragraphs—were more in line with the language and spirit of the IAEA statute and left no margin for doubt as to the basic function of the organization in the promotion of the peaceful uses of nuclear energy, technical assistance programmes being its most critical aspect.

The amendment to the third preambular paragraph, adopted by a recorded vote of 116 to none, with 11 abstentions, had the Assembly recognize the importance of the work of and the relevance for IAEA (instead of recognizing only the relevance) to promote further the application of nuclear energy for peaceful purposes, as envisaged in its statute, and to improve further its technical assistance and promotional programmes (instead of only its technical assistance programmes) for the benefit of developing countries.

The amendment to the fourth preambular paragraph was adopted by a recorded vote of 85 to 21, with 18 abstentions. Instead of stressing the Agency's role in improving the effectiveness of the safeguards system, the Assembly emphasized the importance of the work of IAEA in ensuring that the assistance provided by it, at its request or under its supervision or control was not used in such a way as to further any military purpose, as stated in article II of its statute (dealing with the objectives of IAEA).

The amendment to operative paragraph 2, urging States to strive for international co-operation in carrying out IAEA work, was adopted by a recorded vote of 89 to none, with 37 abstentions. The amended text urged States to co-operate in strengthening (instead of in continuing to provide) technical assistance and co-operation for developing countries, and in ensuring (instead of improving) the effectiveness of the safeguards system.

In explanation of its negative vote on the amended resolution, Israel said the amendment by Iraq was a clear attempt to introduce for partisan purposes controversial elements into what had always been a common position, thus politicizing the matter by injecting its version of the Arab-Israeli conflict. The amended resolution was totally incompatible with the original draft; it could only damage IAEA and its relationship with the Assembly, and it would not contribute to the solution of problems facing IAEA. Iraq was following the pattern set by it and its supporters after the unlawful rejection of Israel's credentials at the September 1982 session of the IAEA General Conference.

Also opposing the resolution, the United States said it would have voted for it had it not contained the Iraqi amendment singling out a particular Member State; the United States also objected to the fifth preambular paragraph—taking note of the decision of the IAEA General Conference on 20 September 1982 to grant IAEA membership to Namibia, represented by the United Nations Council for Namibia—in line with its long-standing reservation with regard to membership in United Nations bodies of entities other than nations.

Speaking on behalf of the 10 member States of the European Community (EC), which abstained in the vote on the resolution and objected to the manner of its adoption, Denmark said they had voted for the Iraqi amendment as a whole although they considered that, being of a political nature, it had no proper place in a resolution on the IAEA report; they also opposed the change in the fourth preambular paragraph to the reference to the Agency's safeguards system, which they believed should be improved and extended geographically. Finland and New Zealand said they had abstained for similar reasons—the original text, which represented a negotiated consensus, was amended in a manner they could not accept, and they regretted the weakening of the reference to the safeguards system. New Zealand added that the introduction into technical agencies such as IAEA of extraneous political subjects threatened the support and membership that had contributed to the Agency's achievements; New Zealand supported the principle of universal membership in IAEA and other United Nations organs.

Explaining its abstention, Australia expressed the view that the Agency's work was of such fundamental importance that an Assembly resolution relating to it should be a consensus text, carefully negotiated in full consultation with all interested delegations, but the text as adopted represented an unbalanced reflection of IAEA tasks; Australia had voted for the Iraqi amendment because it opposed any threats to attack nuclear installations, but it regretted that Iraq had sought to introduce a controversial political subject into the text, especially since that issue was dealt with in an Assembly resolution of 16 November on armed Israeli aggression against Iraqi nuclear installations.

Canada said the principal purpose that should be served by the resolution was found in the original draft, and it did not believe that the Assembly was the appropriate body to set IAEA policy and direction; accordingly it regretted the Iraqi and three-nation amendments because they entered into matters of substance and politics, thus breaking the consensus. Also abstaining, Japan stated that IAEA could best carry out its important work in a tranquil atmosphere without political complications; in that regard, Japan emphasized that IAEA was an international organization of a highly technical and specialized nature which its members should strive to preserve.

Among those voting in favour, Colombia reaffirmed that IAEA must maintain its strictly technical function and remain totally free from any political interference, which would divert it from its purpose of peaceful international co-operation. Guatemala, stating that the peaceful use of nuclear energy, with proper safeguards, contributed to the progress of developing and developed countries, supported the text because it recognized the importance of IAEA and urged States to strive for effective international co-operation in its work.

Introducing the original draft in the Assembly, Czechoslovakia expressed the sponsors' conviction that it provided a constructive and carefully balanced basis for the continued positive development of the Agency's work, reflecting the views of the overwhelming majority of United Nations Members. Expressing the sponsors' hope that the text would be adopted by consensus, Czechoslovakia said they welcomed the steps and measures proposed by IAEA for the further development of its activities, mainly in the fields of safeguards, nuclear energy and nuclear safety, and its efforts concerning the non-proliferation of nuclear weapons, the peaceful uses of nuclear energy and the search for new ways to assist developing countries in such uses. IAEA, through its safeguards system, played an irreplaceable role in the implementation of the relevant provisions of NPT.

During the Assembly's debate on the IAEA report, most speakers praised the report and the Agency's activities. Brazil and India, however, expressed reservations. The report made use of expressions or references which did not belong in the IAEA statute, Brazil said, since the statute did not allow any discrimination between member States,

whether or not parties to any particular treaty, nor did it endorse a non-proliferation régime which was not universally acceptable and applicable. India regretted that the report, when dealing with safeguards, tended to present a distorted and discriminatory picture in the treatment of some members which were not party to NPT; it added that as long as nuclear-weapon programmes in nuclear-weapon States continued unabated, safeguards would have little meaning, were wasteful of IAEA resources and tended to legitimize non-peaceful uses of nuclear energy in those States.

Many countries, however, most of them Eastern European and developed countries, emphasized the importance of the IAEA role in assuring the effectiveness of safeguards and the need to improve the safeguards system. Australia, Bulgaria and the USSR agreed that priority should be given to the Agency's responsibility in strengthening the régime of non-proliferation of nuclear weapons through the safeguards system. Austria, Canada, Chile, Czechoslovakia, Denmark (for the EC members), Egypt, Finland, the German Democratic Republic, Hungary, Poland and the United States emphasized this responsibility or called for strengthening of the system. The German Democratic Republic and others regarded that system as an important factor in the striving for disarmament and international co-operation. Several of those countries—Australia, Austria, Bulgaria, Czechoslovakia, Egypt, Finland, the German Democratic Republic, Hungary, Poland and the USSR—mentioned NPT, which gave added responsibilities to IAEA in regard to the safeguards system, and called on States that had not done so to accede to it. Australia, the German Democratic Republic and Poland welcomed the decision of the USSR to submit its nuclear power plants to IAEA safeguards. Bulgaria and the USSR expressed special concern over the non-participation in NPT of Israel and South Africa because of their technical knowledge or location in crisis areas. The German Democratic Republic welcomed the IAEA statement that it had not detected misuse of nuclear materials or facilities, and believed the existing system should be further improved by appointing a sufficient number of inspectors, by shortening the reaction time in nuclear incidents, by making the reporting system more effective and by using the latest scientific technical equipment. Canada called for upgrading the effectiveness of the safeguards system, taking into account the latest technological advances.

Austria, Canada, Denmark (for the EC members), the German Democratic Republic, Mexico and others praised IAEA activities in setting nuclear safety standards, mentioning such programmes as waste management, the annual review of nuclear safety, safety codes and the information system. Austria proposed establishing a demonstration facility for the disposal of nuclear waste, for which IAEA would provide financial and technical aid in exchange for a nation sharing the data and expertise resulting from the facility's operation. Finland, which welcomed IAEA work in technical co-operation programmes and on nuclear safety, regretted that the whole international plutonium storage scheme seemed to be in jeopardy because of differences of opinion on some basic principles of that plan. Denmark, for the EC members, said the decision to issue an annual review of nuclear safety might make an important contribution to improved safety.

Austria, Finland and Hungary were among the countries stressing the need to ensure for all States secure supplies and availability of nuclear materials and technology. In Hungary's view, this goal should not impair the operation of a non-proliferation régime. The USSR said the system of assurances of supply could be established only within the framework of that régime. Denmark, for the EC members, said the close relationship between assurance of non-proliferation and assurance of supplies had proved fundamental for measures to facilitate international nuclear trade and co-operation. Austria emphasized that any improvement in the area of supplies must not take place at the expense of international security and had to be accompanied by measures to strengthen the safeguards system.

Most speakers praised the Agency's work in technical co-operation and assistance to promote the peaceful uses of nuclear energy. Brazil, India and Mexico considered that to be the primary function of IAEA; and Canada, Chile, Egypt, the German Democratic Republic and Pakistan also emphasized that aspect of IAEA responsibilities. Brazil and Egypt said safeguards should not be strengthened to the detriment of those activities. Australia, on the other hand, stressed the overriding importance of the non-proliferation dimension and Hungary felt that the commitment to technical assistance could not be viewed in isolation from actual economic possibilities. Finland believed that there was nothing contradictory between broader co-operation in the peaceful uses of nuclear energy and a more effective safeguards system and a non-proliferation régime. Pakistan, which reported on its recent negotiations with IAEA to place its nuclear plant at Karachi under additional safeguards, said nuclear non-proliferation could be achieved through political will and consensus rather than by confining the benefits of nuclear technology to a group of privileged States; it added that developing countries had an inherent right to benefit from peaceful nuclear technology on a universal and non-discriminatory basis.

Substantial progress in the provision of technical assistance to developing countries in recent years was noted by the USSR. Austria, Brazil, Egypt and Pakistan said the technical assistance programme required additional financial resources. Czechoslovakia expressed agreement with the adoption of the indicative data for computing the volume and contributions to the IAEA Technical Assistance Fund, but India expressed reservations in this regard. Denmark, for the EC members, noted that the establishment of an annual target and indicative planning figures had led to an increase in the Fund's size.

Canada and Mexico suggested that IAEA activities could improve the public perception of the safety of nuclear energy and enhance the acceptability of nuclear power as an energy alternative. Mexico said the difficulty in obtaining licences for nuclear plants and public resistance to nuclear energy stemmed from concern about lack of safety, including nuclear waste and its possible effects on health and the environment, and about the proliferation of nuclear weapons. Egypt suggested that IAEA study the various energy options available, not only nuclear, so that States could choose the most appropriate one; as demonstrated by the implementation of NPT, IAEA could play an important part in the conclusion of agreements, in particular in relation to the establishment of a nuclear-weapon-free zone in the Middle East.

Emphasizing the technical aspects of IAEA work, several countries—among them Australia, Canada, Israel and the United States—expressed opposition to a growing trend towards politicization in IAEA. Chile, Denmark, for the EC members, Mexico and the United States stressed the importance of universal membership. Australia held it necessary to reduce political controversy so that full attention and priority could be given to specialized and technical matters for which IAEA was responsible.

Concerning the decision of the IAEA General Conference at its September session to reject the credentials of the Israeli delegation, Iraq, Poland and the USSR expressed agreement with the move. Iraq said only pressure tactics and blackmail by the United States had prevented suspension of Israel's membership, which would have been perfectly legal in view of Israel's persistent violation of the IAEA statute. As for the United States, it said the illegal rejection of the credentials had compelled it to reassess the extent and nature of its participation in IAEA and to withdraw from the General Conference in protest. According to Israel, the decision to prevent it from participating in the Conference was arbitrary, discriminatory, illegal and designed to deny an IAEA member one of its basic rights.

Report. [1]IAEA, transmitted by S-G note, A/37/382.
Resolution (1982). [2]GA: 37/19, 19 Nov., text following.
Resolution (prior). [3]GA: 2373(XXII), annex, 12 June 1968 (YUN 1968, p. 17).

Yearbook references. (4)1981, p. 711.
Meeting records. GA: A/37/PV.71-73 (18, 19 Nov.).

General Assembly resolution 37/19

19 November 1982   Meeting 73   105-2-25 (recorded vote)

3-nation draft (A/37/L.29 and Corr.1), amended by Iraq (A/37/L.34, sub-amended by United States (A/37/L.37, as orally sub-amended by Iraq)) and by 3 nations (A/37/L.35/Rev.1); agenda item 14.

Sponsors of draft: Czechoslovakia, Italy, Venezuela.
Sponsors of 3-nation amendment: Argentina, Brazil, India.

Report of the International Atomic Energy Agency

The General Assembly,

Having received the report of the International Atomic Energy Agency to the General Assembly for the year 1981,

Taking note of the statement by the Director General of the International Atomic Energy Agency of 18 November 1982, which provides additional information on developments in the Agency's activities during 1982,

Recognizing the importance of the work of and the relevance for the International Atomic Energy Agency to promote further the application of nuclear energy for peaceful purposes, as envisaged in its statute, and to improve further its technical assistance and promotional programmes for the benefit of developing countries,

Conscious of the importance of the work of the International Atomic Energy Agency in the implementation of the relevant provisions of the Treaty on the Non-Proliferation of Nuclear Weapons and other international treaties, conventions and agreements designed to achieve similar objectives, as well as in ensuring, so far as it is able, that the assistance provided by the Agency or at its request or under its supervision or control is not used in such a way as to further any military purpose, as stated in article II of its statute,

Taking note of the decision of the General Conference of the International Atomic Energy Agency of 20 September 1982 to grant membership of the Agency to Namibia, represented by the United Nations Council for Namibia, in conformity with the request contained in General Assembly resolution 36/121 D of 10 December 1981,

Conscious of the useful outcome of the Conference on Nuclear Power Experience, held at Vienna from 13 to 17 September 1982 by the International Atomic Energy Agency,

Aware that on 29 July 1982 twenty-five years had elapsed since the International Atomic Energy Agency came into being,

1. *Takes note* of the report of the International Atomic Energy Agency;

2. *Urges* all States to strive for effective and harmonious international co-operation in carrying out the work of the International Atomic Energy Agency and to implement strictly the mandate of its statute, in promoting the use of nuclear energy and the application of nuclear science and technology for peaceful purposes; in strengthening technical assistance and co-operation for developing countries; and in ensuring the effectiveness of the Agency's safeguards system;

3. *Considers* that Israel's threat to repeat its armed attack against nuclear facilities as well as any other armed attack against such facilities constitute, *inter alia*, a serious threat to the role and activities of the International Atomic Energy Agency in the development and further promotion of nuclear energy for peaceful purposes;

4. *Affirms* its confidence in the role of the International Atomic Energy Agency in the application of nuclear energy for peaceful purposes;

5. *Requests* the Secretary-General to transmit to the Director General of the International Atomic Energy Agency the records of the thirty-seventh session of the General Assembly relating to the Agency's activities.

Recorded vote in Assembly as follows:

In favour: Afghanistan, Albania, Algeria, Angola, Argentina, Bahrain, Bangladesh, Barbados, Benin, Bhutan, Brazil, Bulgaria, Burundi, Byelorussian SSR, Cape Verde, Central African Republic, Chad, Chile, Colombia, Congo, Cuba, Cyprus, Czechoslovakia, Democratic Yemen, Dominican Republic, Ecuador, Egypt, Equatorial Guinea, Ethiopia, Fiji, Gabon, Gambia, German Democratic Republic, Ghana, Guatemala, Guinea, Guinea-Bissau, Guyana, Honduras, Hungary, India, Indonesia, Iraq, Ivory Coast, Jamaica, Jordan, Kenya, Kuwait, Lao People's Democratic Republic, Lebanon, Libyan Arab Jamahiriya, Madagascar, Malaysia, Maldives, Mali, Malta, Mauritania, Mauritius, Mexico, Mongolia, Morocco, Mozambique, Nepal, Nicaragua, Niger, Nigeria, Oman, Pakistan, Panama, Papua New Guinea, Peru, Philippines, Poland, Qatar, Romania, Saint

Lucia, Samoa, Sao Tome and Principe, Saudi Arabia, Senegal, Sierra Leone, Singapore, Solomon Islands, Somalia, Sri Lanka, Sudan, Suriname, Syrian Arab Republic, Thailand, Togo, Trinidad and Tobago, Tunisia, Uganda, Ukrainian SSR, USSR, United Arab Emirates, United Republic of Cameroon, United Republic of Tanzania, Uruguay, Vanuatu, Venezuela, Viet Nam, Yemen, Yugoslavia, Zambia.

Against: Israel, United States.

Abstaining: Australia, Austria, Belgium, Canada, Denmark, Finland, France, Germany, Federal Republic of, Greece, Iceland, Ireland, Italy, Japan, Liberia, Luxembourg, Malawi, Netherlands, New Zealand, Norway, Paraguay, Portugal, Spain, Sweden, Turkey, United Kingdom.

Preparations for the Conference on nuclear energy

Preparatory Committee activities. The Preparatory Committee for the United Nations Conference for the Promotion of International Co-operation in the Peaceful Uses of Nuclear Energy, established by the General Assembly in 1980,[5] held its second and third sessions at Vienna, Austria, from 21 to 30 June and from 27 October to 2 November 1982, respectively, and reported on those sessions to the Assembly.[1]

Despite extensive negotiations at both sessions on the agenda for the Conference, based on various proposals submitted to the Committee, and although there was a degree of convergence of views, no agreement could be reached. The Committee also took up the question of the Conference's rules of procedure but again it was unable to finalize the matter. In this situation, the matter was left for further consideration by the Assembly. Four separate proposals on the Conference agenda by groups of States were annexed to the Committee's report along with statements by seven countries (China, India, Mexico for the Group of 77, Netherlands, Philippines, USSR, United States).

On 24 June, the Committee decided on the invitations to the Conference and, on 2 November, it took two decisions: one on documentation for the Conference and expressing the hope that United Nations organizations and bodies would continue to contribute to the Conference preparations; and another recommending that the Assembly make the necessary arrangements concerning the Committee's future programme of work, including schedule, venue and provisional agenda of its next session.

In a June report,[2] the Secretary-General informed the Committee of the status of Conference preparations. He reported that, following the Assembly's request in December 1981,[6] he had arranged for the establishment of a small secretariat, with a total appropriation in 1982 of $359,300. He had designated his Personal Representative for Special Missions to serve also as Secretary-General of the Conference, who would head the secretariat, and had arranged with IAEA for the temporary loan of a senior official to act as Deputy Secretary-General, to be in charge of the technical preparations for the Conference and of the Conference secretariat staff. An executive assistant would also be appointed. Once the Preparatory Committee had made sufficient progress in the development of the substantive work programme in preparation for the Conference, the remainder of the appropriations approved by the Assembly could be converted into temporary posts and other Conference secretariat staff, particularly substantive technical staff, could be appointed.

With regard to Member States' contributions to the Conference preparations, the Secretary-General reported that, as at 4 June, 26 Governments had replied to his request for views on the opening day, duration, venue and agenda of the Conference and on other matters relevant to its organization, and those statements had been forwarded to the Preparatory Committee. In addition, the Assembly had urged all States to make available information on their scientific and technological achievements and practical experiences in the field of peaceful uses of nuclear energy, and had invited IAEA and other United Nations entities to inform the Committee of relevant work under way. (In response to the Assembly's invitation, IAEA provided working papers on its activities for the second and third sessions of the Committee and began work on papers for the Conference itself.)

In view of the limited time prior to the Conference, the Secretary-General regarded it as urgent that the general considerations put forward by the Assembly on Conference preparations be translated into specific guidelines. He suggested that the Committee first address the items relating to the agenda and documentation for the Conference and then revert, in the light of the conclusions reached, to elaborating substantive as well as organizational guidelines for future preparatory work. The Secretary-General also suggested that the Committee might wish to give attention to the convening of *ad hoc* expert group meetings prior to the Conference.

General Assembly action. By a resolution of 17 December 1982,[3] the General Assembly decided that the Preparatory Committee should meet twice in 1983 and requested the Committee and the Secretary-General of the Conference, in order to speed up preparations, to make appropriate arrangements, including through intersessional work by Committee members, regional efforts and public information activities. The Assembly decided to take decisions on the Conference date in the light of the results of the Committee's first 1983 session, and that the necessary resources should be provided to ensure successful preparations, including adequate secretariat staffing and the availability of expert support. It invited IAEA to contribute to the Conference, and urged States to co-operate actively in the preparation and the holding of the Conference and to observe the principles set forth in its 1977 resolution on the peaceful use of nuclear energy for economic and social development.[4]

The Assembly adopted the resolution, as sponsored and revised by Bangladesh, on behalf of the Group of 77, by a recorded vote of 111 to 26, with 7 abstentions.

After the two 1982 sessions of the Preparatory Committee, negotiations were resumed among various groups in an effort to reach a text that could be adopted by consensus, as had been the case with all previous Assembly resolutions relating to the Conference, but the consultations failed to produce common ground, much less an agreement. The general sense of the position of those supporting the resolution of the Group of 77 was that nuclear energy could play a significant role in the economic and industrial progress of the developing countries; therefore, the establishment of universally acceptable principles for co-operation in the peaceful uses of nuclear energy should be the main purpose of the Conference and non-proliferation concerns should not be an overriding issue. Those opposed to the resolution considered it as unbalanced, not properly reflecting non-proliferation considerations and prejudging the outcome of the Conference. As a result, the Assembly, by its 1982 resolution, decided to reconsider the Conference date.

Introducing the draft in the Assembly, Bangladesh said the Group of 77 was concerned at the lack of progress in the Preparatory Committee. The Group, after proposing a draft, had consulted with members of other groups with a view to accommodating their viewpoints; however, it had not been possible to reach a consensus text. The revised text did not fully reflect the Group's position but it reflected the attempt to meet the concerns expressed by other States without compromising the Group's basic stand on the issue.

The different positions were reflected in the explanations of vote. Among those opposing the text, Australia, Czechoslovakia, Finland, the USSR and the United States expressed regret that it downgraded the importance of the non-proliferation régime and IAEA safeguards. With regard to the Agency's role in preparing for the Conference, Czechoslovakia, Denmark for the EC members, the USSR and the United States felt the resolution did not make adequate provision for its participation; they also agreed that the resolution prejudged the outcome of the Conference. The lack of consensus was a concern of Australia, Canada, Denmark (for the EC members), Finland, the USSR and the United States.

Explaining its negative vote, Australia objected that some delegations had sought to expand the aims of the Conference in a manner not originally envisaged and not acceptable to others, adding that unless consensus could be achieved on such a basic issue there was little prospect of a successful conference. Canada was concerned that the resolution implied the establishment of an *ad hoc* bureaucracy of an apparently open-ended nature without specific rules of procedure or defined control mechanisms; in its view, any conference must take into account existing structures, such as the IAEA Committee on Assurances of Supply, the International Nuclear Fuel Cycle Evaluation and NPT, but the resolution tended to move in the direction of providing the Conference with a mandate to seek new principles of international co-operation in peaceful uses of nuclear energy which would replace them. Similar reservations were voiced by Czechoslovakia and Denmark for the EC members. Czechoslovakia believed that the Conference must contribute to the full implementation of NPT.

Denmark, speaking on behalf of the EC members which opposed the resolution, said they had a positive attitude to the convening of a conference, but they believed that a resolution on the Conference's preparation should have dealt solely with procedural questions; the question of intersessional work and other organizational matters should have been decided upon by the Preparatory Committee itself. Expressing hope that the Conference would be held in 1983, Finland said the two goals of peaceful use of nuclear energy and the international non-proliferation régime should be pursued concurrently if the Conference were to succeed; Finland objected to the resolution because it contained no binding reference to the IAEA Committee on Assurances of Supply—a crucial omission, it felt, and an unwarranted departure from earlier consensus resolutions.

The USSR believed that the resolution did not adequately reflect the need for effective preparation of the Conference and did not take into consideration the positions of all the States concerned; it felt that IAEA and other United Nations organizations connected with the peaceful uses of nuclear energy should submit reports to the Conference, whose content and thrust they should determine.

The United States objected to the resolution because it felt that moving ahead with substantive preparations without agreement on an agenda and procedures was premature, that there was no need to move the Committee meetings to New York, and that the necessary resources should be provided from the 1982-1983 United Nations programme budget. It objected, in particular, to the fourth preambular paragraph (reaffirming the responsibility of States advanced in the nuclear field to promote fulfilment of the nuclear energy needs of developing countries); due to its objections, the United States found it increasingly difficult to justify its Conference participation.

Voting in favour, Turkey stressed that, in its understanding, universally acceptable principles for international co-operation in this field were embodied within the IAEA safeguards system and the non-proliferation régime. Yugoslavia said the members of the Group of 77 were hopeful that, on the basis of the resolution, the Preparatory Committee would be able to undertake substantive Conference preparations; its understanding was that the Assembly, at its resumed session in 1983, would take a decision with regard to the date in the light of the results of the next two sessions of the Preparatory Committee. India regarded the resolution as a significant attempt to meet the concerns of all groups. Indonesia believed that the resolution was consistent with earlier Assembly decisions and provided the best possible basis for the Conference preparations.

During the Assembly debate, several countries—among them Argentina, Egypt, India, Indonesia, Mexico, Nigeria and Yugoslavia—said that one of the main purposes of the Conference was the adoption of principles on the regulation of international co-operation in peaceful uses of nuclear energy, which would include assurances of supply and transfer of technology to developing countries. Such principles, Argentina added, would tend to establish balances in international economic relations, and Egypt believed that, with the convening of the Conference, international co-operation in the field would enter a new phase.

In Mexico's view, the convening of the Conference was urgent owing to the failure of all other efforts to establish efficient means and procedures to promote international co-operation in the field. Brazil said the agenda should cover all political and economic issues relevant to the peaceful uses of nuclear energy with the determination to achieve internationally agreed approaches for the transfer of technology.

Pakistan believed that the preparatory work must continue in a spirit of accommodation and must be completed by the Preparatory Committee if the Conference were to be successful. Similar views were expressed by Egypt, India, Nigeria and Yugoslavia. Nigeria could not subscribe to the holding of the Conference without substantive preparations and felt that adequate resources should be provided by the Assembly. According to Pakistan, the resolution of the Group of 77 provided for the necessary procedural arrangements for adequate preparation of the Conference and it was flexible on the dates for convening it. Argentina and India called on the Assembly to give precise guidelines to the Preparatory Committee in order to enable the Conference to achieve substantive results.

Finland regretted the results of the last session of the Preparatory Committee and hoped that the differences on the agenda and procedures could be settled; it emphasized its conviction that the method of consensus which had been traditionally applied on similar occasions should be accepted as a basis for the Conference's work. Indonesia, however, believed that the principle of consensus should be continued if possible but, if not, then the reservations of a few should not block progress towards wider international co-operation in the field.

Egypt said that, although the Preparatory Committee focused on organizational matters, it should not be prevented from touching on substantive issues. Over-emphasis on the question of nuclear non-proliferation to the detriment of developing countries' access to nuclear energy for peaceful uses would be a retrogressive development, Pakistan felt. In Yugoslavia's view, the developed countries were attempting to distort the Conference concept, trying to make non-proliferation the main issue. Czechoslovakia, on the other hand, said the Conference could contribute significantly to further development of the peaceful uses of nuclear energy, provided that due regard was given to strengthening the non-proliferation régime and the IAEA safeguards system, a view shared by several other speakers. The German Democratic Republic, India and others affirmed that the experience and capabilities of IAEA should be used in organizing a successful Conference. Egypt expressed the view that the next session of the Preparatory Committee, in early 1983, should be in New York because the Group of 77 did not have appropriate representation in Vienna.

Reports. [1]Preparatory Committee, A/37/48; [2]S-G, A/CONF.108/PC.4.
Resolution (1982). [3]GA: 37/167, 17 Dec., text following.
Resolutions (prior). GA: [4]32/50, 8 Dec. 1977 (YUN 1977, p. 106); [5]35/112, 5 Dec. 1980 (YUN 1980, p. 164); [6]36/78, 9 Dec. 1981 (YUN 1981, p. 715).
Financial implications. ACABQ report, A/37/7/Add.20; S-G statement, A/C.5/37/85.
Meeting records. GA: plenary, A/37/PV.71-73, *110* (18 Nov.–17 Dec.); 5th Committee, A/C.5/37/SR.66, 73 (13, 16 Dec.).

General Assembly resolution 37/167

17 December 1982   Meeting 110   111-26-7 (recorded)

Draft by Bangladesh, for Group of 77 (A/37/L.40/Rev.1); agenda item 27.

United Nations Conference for the Promotion of International Co-operation in the Peaceful Uses of Nuclear Energy
The General Assembly,

Reaffirming the principles and provisions of its resolutions 32/50 of 8 December 1977, 33/4 of 2 November 1978, 34/63 of 29 November 1979, 35/112 of 5 December 1980 and 36/78 of 9 December 1981 regarding the United Nations Conference for the Promotion of International Co-operation in the Peaceful Uses of Nuclear Energy and the relevant paragraphs of the Final Document of the Tenth Special Session of the General Assembly,

Taking note with satisfaction of the appointment of the Secretary-General of the Conference,

Recalling the experience gained during the last three decades of applications of nuclear energy and technology for power production and other uses,

Reaffirming the responsibility of States that are advanced in the nuclear field to promote the fulfilment of the legitimate nuclear energy needs of the developing countries by participating in the fullest possible transfer of nuclear equipment, materials and technology under agreed and appropriate international safeguards applied through the International Atomic Energy Agency on a non-discriminatory basis in order to prevent effectively the proliferation of nuclear weapons,

Having considered the report of the Preparatory Committee for the Conference on its second and third sessions,

Expressing concern at the lack of progress and recognizing the pressing need to speed up and complete substantive preparations for the Conference, its provisional agenda, its documentation and its rules of procedure, so as to ensure a successful conference which would achieve the objectives envisaged in General Assembly resolutions 32/50 and 35/112,

1. *Decides* that the Preparatory Committee for the United Nations Conference for the Promotion of International Co-operation in the Peaceful Uses of Nuclear Energy shall meet twice during 1983, once early in the year for ten working days in New York and, subsequently, for an appropriate duration prior to the Conference,

2. *Requests* the Preparatory Committee and the Secretary-General of the Conference, in order to speed up substantive preparations, to make appropriate arrangements, including as necessary through intersessional work by States members of the Committee under the guidance of its Chairman and also through regional efforts and appropriate public information activities, with a view to ensuring meaningful results from the Conference;

3. *Decides* to take suitable decisions in regard to the date of the Conference in the light of the results of the session of the Preparatory Committee to be held early in 1983;

4. *Reiterates* that the aim of the Conference is to promote international co-operation in the peaceful uses of nuclear energy and, to this end, to establish universally acceptable principles for such co-operation in accordance with the objectives contained in General Assembly resolution 32/50;

5. *Reaffirms* the provision of paragraph 4 of General Assembly resolution 36/78 that the outcome of the Conference should be embodied in appropriate documents, in a suitable format, pertaining, *inter alia*, to ways and means of promoting such international co-operation in the peaceful uses of nuclear energy;

6. *Decides* that the necessary resources should be provided to ensure successful preparations for the Conference, including adequate staffing of the secretariat and the availability of expert support in the substantive fields to be covered by the Conference;

7. *Invites* the International Atomic Energy Agency to contribute to the Conference in terms of paragraph 3 of resolution 32/50 and paragraph 11 of resolution 36/78 in accordance with its responsibilities under its statute;

8. *Urges* all States to co-operate actively in the preparation and the holding of the Conference and to respect and observe the principles set forth in resolution 32/50;

9. *Decides* to include in the provisional agenda of its thirty-eighth session an item entitled "United Nations Conference for the Promotion of International Co-operation in the Peaceful Uses of Nuclear Energy".

Recorded vote in Assembly as follows:

In favour: Afghanistan, Algeria, Angola, Antigua and Barbuda, Argentina, Bahamas, Bahrain, Bangladesh, Barbados, Benin, Bhutan, Bolivia, Botswana, Brazil, Burma, Burundi, Cape Verde, Chad, Chile, China, Colombia, Comoros, Congo, Costa Rica, Cuba, Cyprus, Democratic Kampuchea, Democratic Yemen, Djibouti, Dominica, Dominican Republic, Ecuador, Egypt, El Salvador, Ethiopia, Gabon, Gambia, Ghana, Grenada, Guatemala, Guinea, Guinea-Bissau, Guyana, Haiti, Honduras, India, Indonesia, Iran, Iraq, Ivory Coast, Jamaica, Jordan, Kenya, Kuwait, Lebanon, Lesotho, Liberia, Libyan Arab Jamahiriya, Madagascar, Malawi, Malaysia, Maldives, Malta, Mauritania, Mauritius, Mexico, Morocco, Mozambique, Nepal, Nicaragua, Niger, Nigeria, Oman, Pakistan, Panama, Papua New Guinea, Paraguay, Peru, Philippines, Qatar, Romania, Saint Lucia, Saint Vincent and the Grenadines, Samoa, Sao Tome and Principe, Saudi Arabia, Senegal, Sierra Leone, Singapore, Solomon Islands, Somalia, Sri Lanka, Sudan, Suriname, Thailand, Togo, Trinidad and Tobago, Tunisia, Turkey, Uganda, United Arab Emirates, United Republic of Cameroon, United Republic of Tanzania, Upper Volta, Uruguay, Vanuatu, Venezuela, Yemen, Yugoslavia, Zaire, Zambia.

Against: Australia, Austria, Belgium, Bulgaria, Byelorussian SSR, Canada, Czechoslovakia, Denmark, Finland, German Democratic Republic, Germany, Federal Republic of, Hungary, Iceland, Ireland, Japan, Luxembourg, Mongolia, Netherlands, New Zealand, Norway, Poland, Ukrainian SSR, USSR, United Kingdom, United States, Viet Nam.[a]

Abstaining: France, Greece, Israel, Italy, Portugal, Spain, Sweden.

[a]Later advised the Secretariat it had intended to abstain.

Chapter XI

Food

Contents

Related topics:

Industrial development: Food industry. Regional economic and social activities—Food and agriculture: Africa; Asia and the Pacific; Europe; Latin America; Western Asia. Health: Nutrition. Children: Nutrition.

Food problems

WFC activities. The World Food Council (WFC) held its eighth ministerial session from 21 to 24 June 1982 at Acapulco, Mexico.[5] The 36-member Council, the world's highest political body dealing exclusively with food problems, adopted conclusions and recommendations on national food policies and strategies, direct measures for eradicating hunger, international development assistance, the African food problem and the role of international agencies, and world food security and trade issues.

Reviewing the international food situation, WFC characterized the year as one of large crop and stock accumulation in some major countries, bringing global stocks to satisfactory levels. In many developing countries, however, food production had grown at a slower rate than demand and, in some instances, had even declined. WFC expressed particular concern about the African food situation and the hunger and malnutrition that were at unacceptable levels and increasing.

WFC noted the adverse effect of the current world economic recession on the international food situation: increased production costs and high interest rates had seriously hampered efforts in many countries to accelerate food production. The Council called for priority to be given to transforming the food sector in order to create food supplies and provide the foundation for expanding industry and modern services. Deep concern was also expressed over the continued diversion of substantial world resources to armaments, to the detriment of international security and of efforts to achieve the new international economic order and to solve food problems.

WFC was encouraged by the number of developing countries preparing national food policies and strategies—widely supported as means for increasing production and combating hunger in international forums such as the October 1981 International Meeting on Co-operation and Development (Cancún, Mexico).[12] Observing that strategies already completed could not be properly implemented for lack of resources, WFC urged full international support, calling on the World Bank and the United Nations Development Programme (UNDP) to lead in financing such strategies. The technical assistance and action programmes of the Food and Agriculture Organization of the United Nations and other agencies could achieve full potential within national policies.

WFC also urged integration of direct measures for eradicating hunger in national strategies to supplement production programmes. It would review progress in this regard in 1983, taking into account the 1982 work of the Committee on Food Aid Policies and Programmes (CFA) (see below). It recommended more attention to improving job and income opportunities, thereby effecting more equitable food distribution. Reiterating support for the Programme of Action of the 1979 World Conference on Agrarian Reform and Rural Development (WCARRD),[9] WFC also recommended:

stepped-up aid for rural development to reach smallholder producers, particularly women; reforms to ensure food-purchasing power for poor landless families; increased investment in human capital; further promotion of farm co-operatives; and a Council review in 1984 of the WCARRD Programme of Action.

Noting a shortfall in external resources required for agricultural development for 1975-1980—estimated at $8.36 billion a year at 1975 prices—WFC called for increased international development assistance in support of developing countries' efforts and stressed prompt replenishment of the International Development Association and the International Fund for Agricultural Development. It also called on donors to strengthen their programming and co-ordination, focusing more sharply on technical and financial aid to expand the food-investment capacity of developing countries and to improve food-production technologies. International organizations concerned with agriculture and food were asked to use resources more effectively, improve efficiency and avoid duplication of work through co-ordination. At the country level, co-ordination was best carried out by the Government, which might avail itself of the services of the UNDP resident co-ordinator for development assistance rendered by the United Nations system.

To alleviate food deficits in Africa, WFC stated, Governments of the region would have to make policy adjustments within the framework of the 1980 Lagos Plan of Action for the Implementation of the Monrovia Strategy for the Economic Development of Africa[11]—a plan based on collective self-reliance and self-sustainment. For improved co-ordination of efforts at all levels, coherent food policies were essential. Accelerated action by African countries and international agencies was recommended—taking into account the conclusions of the African Ministers for Food and Agriculture at the WFC Regional Consultation for Africa (Nairobi, Kenya, March 1982)—in the following areas: national food-strategy implementation and financing, with emphasis on improving producer incentives and raising rural living standards; training in food-policy planning and investment preparation and management; technical and resource support for adaptive research, technology and related services to farmers; and food-security infrastructure, including transport, storage and marketing.

In efforts to achieve world food security, WFC, in addition to its sustained support for more comprehensive national food strategies, called for the elimination of import barriers and adverse export trading practices. It also asked the General Agreement on Tariffs and Trade (GATT) to examine, at its November ministerial session, the inter-connection between trade possibilities and the development capacity of countries. The progress made in international arrangements for coping with food emergencies—including achievement of the annual minimum target of 500,000 metric tons of grain for the International Emergency Food Reserve (IEFR) in 1981[13]—needed to be supplemented by a fully supported World Food Programme and by achievement of the internationally agreed annual target of 10 million tons of food aid (see below).

In the absence of an agreement on a new Wheat Trade Convention and as a protection against instability in domestic and international grain markets, WFC urged international support for the establishment of national grain reserves in developing countries. It requested its Executive Director to propose ways of building such reserves, taking into account the linkage between national food security and balance-of-payment positions and between food strategies and storage policies; the availability of concessional financing, including access to the compensatory cereal financing and buffer-stock facilities of the International Monetary Fund (IMF); the need for assistance to defray the cost of food-security reserves; guidelines for the creation and utilization of national reserves; the possible formation of a consultative group of development agencies to review requirements for storage and related infrastructure; and manpower training and development programmes.

WFC also decided that in 1984 it would prepare a special assessment of progress made and of future tasks to achieve the objectives of the 1974 World Food Conference.[8]

Economic and Social Council action. Food problems were considered by the Economic and Social Council at its July 1982 session. Owing to a lack of time, no agreement was reached on a draft resolution[2] submitted by Algeria, on behalf of the Group of 77 developing countries, to the Council's First (Economic) Committee.

By a decision of 30 July,[1] the Council took note of the WFC conclusions and recommendations and the report of CFA on its 1981 activities, and decided to transmit the draft resolution to the General Assembly's 1982 regular session. In considering the draft, the Assembly was to take into account the comments made on it at the Council's July session. The decision was adopted, without vote, on the recommendation of the First Committee, which had similarly approved it on 29 July on the Chairman's oral proposal.

General Assembly action. By a resolution of 21 December,[6] the Assembly, welcoming the WFC recommendations, reaffirmed that food was a human right and should not be used as an instrument of political pressure. It affirmed that world food security could best be established by successful national programmes for attaining food self-reliance, invited integration of direct hunger-reduction measures in those programmes and stressed the desirability of co-ordinating efforts in solving world food problems. Developed countries, international institutions and others were asked to increase and improve their assistance to the food sector in developing countries. WFC was asked to consider in 1983 the proposals it had requested of its Executive Director on ways of building developing country–owned food-security reserves. The Assembly again called for urgent action against agricultural trade barriers and urged developed countries to make their markets accessible to exports from developing countries. It also urged implementation of the 1979 resolution on international food trade of the United Nations Conference on Trade and Development (UNCTAD).[10]

Other provisions of the resolution concerned CFA activities, achievement of the 1974 World Food Conference and IEFR targets, and increased aid to Africa.

The text, adopted without vote by the Assembly, had been similarly approved by the Second (Economic and Financial) Committee on 20 December. It had been submitted by a Committee Vice-Chairman, based on informal consultations on the draft resolution transmitted by the Economic and Social Council and orally amended by the Committee Chairman to add the words *inter alia* in paragraph 27.

In addition to the oral amendment and drafting changes, the adopted resolution differed from the text transmitted by the Council in a number of ways.

Added were provisions calling for agrarian reform and rural development (paragraph 4); reaffirming enhancement of multilateral aid (paragraph 5); urging particular account of the problems of food-producing and -exporting developing countries (paragraph 6); recognizing the need for increased food self-reliance and food production and the transitional role of food aid (paragraph 16); urging aid agencies to strengthen their capacities in agro-scientific research and promote the transfer of agro-technology to developing countries (paragraph 19); stressing the desirability of co-ordination (paragraph 30); and welcoming the intention of WFC to assess progress in achieving the 1974 Conference objectives (paragraph 31).

Paragraph 21, on the proposed developing country–owned reserve, was reworded. The Group of 77's text would have had the reserve give priority to the food-security needs of individual developing countries based on concessional financing being made available when international grain supplies were ample and prices low, utilizing, *inter alia*, the

IMF buffer-stock facility for stock acquisition. The text would have also called on WFC to explore ways for urgently bringing the reserve into operation.

A request to developed countries to eliminate protectionist measures affecting food and agricultural exports of developing countries was rephrased to call for urgent action to reduce and eliminate trade barriers in the different negotiating forums. Instead of the adopted paragraphs on GATT, the Group's draft would have called on both GATT and UNCTAD to review long-standing problems in international trade in agricultural products adversely affecting developing countries' production and exports. In the paragraph noting the downward trend in prices of commodities exported by developing countries, the Group's draft would have characterized the trend as one of the results of high interest rates in the international financial markets.

Also reworded was the paragraph on achieving food aid targets (see below).

Other activities. On 17 May, Italy sent a letter to the Secretary-General[3] giving details of a Rome Meeting to Fight Hunger in the World, sponsored by Italy, which was held from 26 to 29 April and attended by representatives of 44 countries, 15 international organizations and 7 development banks and funds. Organized at a technical working level, the Meeting examined general and emergency food aid, food security, national agri-food strategies, sectoral action themes, and harmonization and co-ordination of aid. Among the Meeting's broad conclusions were that there should be greater emphasis on programme and policy support for developing countries; more pragmatic approaches to donor- and recipient-country co-ordination; and continued efforts to enhance food-security mechanisms, including more judicious use of food aid.

The question of food and agriculture was also discussed at the Joint Meetings of the Committee for Programme and Co-ordination and the Administrative Committee on Co-ordination (Geneva, 6 and 7 July).[4] The debate focused on the need for: urgent massive investment in agriculture to step up production in developing countries; coherent food-sector strategies and increased support for those formulated by developing countries; ensuring adequate food aid progressively adapted to requirements; ensuring emergency relief quickly and on a fully multilateral basis; strengthening inter-agency co-ordination, both multilaterally and bilaterally; and strengthening food security, implementing agreements already made and exploring new approaches.

The right to adequate food as a human right was the subject of a draft resolution which the Sub-Commission on Prevention of Discrimination and Protection of Minorities on 7 September[7] recommended for adoption by the Commission on Human Rights. By the draft, the Commission would recommend that the Economic and Social Council authorize the Sub-Commission to prepare a study on the subject.

Decision (1982). [1]ESC: 1982/176, 30 July, text following.
Draft resolution not pressed. [2]Algeria, for Group of 77, E/1982/C.1/L.27 (transmitted to GA by Secretariat note, A/C.2/37/L.5).
Letter. [3]Italy, 17 May, A/37/260.
Reports. [4]CPC and ACC chairmen, E/1982/84; [5]WFC, A/37/19.
Resolutions (1982). [6]GA: 37/247, 21 Dec., text following. [7]SCPDPM (report, E/CN.4/1983/4): 1982/7, 7 Sep.
Yearbook references. [8]1974, p. 491; 1979, [9]p. 500, [10]p. 561; [11]1980, p. 548; 1981, [12]p. 379, [13]p. 729.
Meeting records. ESC: E/1982/SR.51 (30 July). GA: 2nd Committee, A/C.2/37/SR.3, 6, 7, 13-19, 33, 40, *51* (28 Sep.–20 Dec.); plenary, A/37/PV.115 (21 Dec.).

Economic and Social Council decision 1982/176

Adopted without vote

Approved by First Committee (E/1982/102) without vote, 29 July (meeting 17); oral proposal by Chairman; agenda item 14.

Food problems

At its 51st plenary meeting, on 30 July 1982, the Council:

(a) Expressed its appreciation to the Government and people of Mexico for acting as hosts to the World Food Council at its eighth ministerial session, held at Acapulco, Mexico, from 21 to 24 June 1982, and for the generous hospitality accorded to the participants;

(b) Took note with appreciation of the conclusions and recommendations adopted by the World Food Council at that session;

(c) Also took note with appreciation of the seventh annual report of the Committee on Food Aid Policies and Programmes;

(d) Decided to transmit the draft resolution annexed hereto to the General Assembly at its thirty-seventh session for consideration, taking into account the comments made thereon during the second regular session of 1982 of the Economic and Social Council.

ANNEX
Food problems

The General Assembly,

Recalling the Declaration and the Programme of Action on the Establishment of a New International Economic Order, contained in its resolutions 3201(S-VI) and 3202(S-VI) of 1 May 1974, the Charter of Economic Rights and Duties of States, contained in its resolution 3281(XXIX) of 12 December 1974, General Assembly resolution 3362(S-VII) of 16 September 1975 on development and international economic co-operation, and the International Development Strategy for the Third United Nations Development Decade, contained in Assembly resolution 35/56 of 5 December 1980,

Recalling the Universal Declaration on the Eradication of Hunger and Malnutrition adopted by the World Food Conference and the Programme of Action adopted by the World Conference on Agrarian Reform and Rural Development,

Having considered the report of the World Food Council on its eighth ministerial session and the seventh annual report of the Committee on Food Aid Policies and Programmes,

Expressing its appreciation to the Government and people of Mexico for acting as hosts to the World Food Council at its eighth ministerial session, held at Acapulco, Mexico, from 21 to 24 June 1982, and for the generous hospitality accorded to the participants,

Concerned that progress towards food-policy objectives is impeded by the prolonged world recession and inflation and by growing international political tension and the increasing expenditure on armaments,

Recognizing that a substantial increase in the export earnings of developing countries is essential for the adequate financing of their overall economic development and their imports of food and agricultural inputs,

Expressing its concern that trade barriers constitute a serious handicap to the efforts of developing countries, in particular their efforts to realize their economic potential, and reiterating the need for deve-

loped countries to adopt policies designed to eliminate the obstacles which distort international trade in agricultural products and to facilitate the access to international markets of agricultural exports, especially those of developing countries,

Recognizing that the lasting solution to the problems of food in developing countries depends on the attainment of self-reliance through increased food and agricultural production and investment, as part of the overall development of those countries and as an expression of their sovereign political determination,

Emphasizing that, within the framework of national economic development, priority must be given to the development of the food sector in order to lay a sound foundation for expanding industry and modern services,

Deeply concerned about the precarious nature of the food situation and the alarming trend towards the growing food-import dependency of developing countries, especially the least developed countries,

Emphasizing that African countries, in particular, require the strongest support of the international community for their efforts to reverse the trend of deteriorating food production and of growing hunger and malnutrition in that region,

Concerned about the continuing instability of international grain markets, involving increased food-security risks for many developing countries,

Deploring the fact that international assistance to the food and agricultural sector in developing countries has been decreasing since 1979 and is now lagging far behind the internationally agreed targets,

1. *Takes note with appreciation* of the conclusions and recommendations adopted by the World Food Council at its eighth ministerial session;

2. *Also takes note with appreciation* of the seventh annual report of the Committee on Food Aid Policies and Programmes;

3. *Commends* those developing countries that have achieved increased food self-sufficiency through their determined application of appropriate policies, resources and technology;

4. *Reaffirms* that the right to food is a universal human right and that food should not be used as an instrument of political pressure;

5. *Expresses its satisfaction* at the growing number of countries that are adopting a more integrated approach to food policy, including food-sector strategies, as one of the means for interested developing countries to translate their own priorities into effective action and to mobilize, within the context of their national plans and priorities, increased technical and financial resources and co-operation from international development assistance agencies;

6. *Requests* the developed countries and international institutions concerned to increase the volume of international assistance for food production substantially in real terms, and to improve its quality, on a sustained and predictable basis, so as to meet, as soon as possible, the estimated needs of external assistance of $8.3 billion, which will increase to $12.5 billion in 1990;*

7. *Welcomes* the efforts of the International Labour Organisation, the United Nations Development Programme and donor countries in mobilizing technical and financial support in favour of special labour-intensive public works programmes in developing countries, particularly in the least developed countries, which help to mobilize their food production potential, expand employment opportunities and generate incomes in the rural sector;

8. *Urges* the Food and Agriculture Organization of the United Nations, the International Fund for Agricultural Development, the World Bank and the United Nations Development Programme to take measures to assist developing countries in the implementation of their food strategies, plans and programmes;

9. *Invites* Governments concerned to adopt direct hunger-reduction measures integrated with productive development within the framework of national strategies and policies, including, *inter alia*, more assistance to rural development to reach smallholder producers, special attention to the needs of women farmers, investment in human capacities through programmes for mothers and children, the creation of productive employment for poor landless families and an increase in food aid;

10. *Welcomes* the decision of the World Food Council to pay particular attention to progress in integrating food aid more directly in national plans to overcome hunger, and to more effective ways of achieving higher levels of food production, taking into account the report of the Committee on Food Aid Policies and Programmes;

11. *Urges* present and potential donor countries to achieve without delay the minimum target of 10 million tons of cereals annually and to ensure that the minimum target of 500,000 tons of grains for the International Emergency Food Reserve is reinforced and placed on a fully multilateral basis, and that the World Food Programme target of $1 billion in 1981-1982 and $1.2 billion in 1983-1984 is attained;

12. *Urges* that, in the implementation of food aid policies and programmes, a greater volume of food and agricultural products be acquired from food-exporting developing countries, including a greater volume through triangular transactions;

13. *Urges* the international community to provide increased assistance in support of essential policy adjustments by African Governments, within the framework of the Lagos Plan of Action for the Implementation of the Monrovia Strategy for the Economic Development of Africa, to alleviate food deficits in Africa, taking into account the conclusions and recommendations adopted by the African Ministers of Food and Agriculture at the World Food Council Regional Consultation for Africa, held at Nairobi on 16 and 17 March 1982, and endorsed by the Council at its eighth ministerial session, in particular through:

(a) The speeding up of national food-strategy implementation and financing;

(b) Stepped-up training in food-policy planning and investment preparation and management;

(c) Substantially increased technical and resource support for adaptive research, technology and related services to farmers;

(d) Improved food-security infrastructure, including transport, storage and marketing;

14. *Further urges* developed countries to assist developing countries in meeting their needs for technological progress in food and agricultural matters and the development of agro-industries related to food problems;

15. *Affirms* that a sound basis for world food security can best be established by successful national programmes for attaining food self-reliance through increased food and agricultural production and investment in developing countries, as well as more open and stable world trade flows and assurance of supplies;

16. *Notes with appreciation* the support given by the World Food Council at its eighth ministerial session to the proposal for a developing country–owned reserve giving priority to the food-security needs of individual developing countries based on concessional financing being made available to interested developing countries when international grain supplies are ample and prices are low, and utilizing, *inter alia*, the buffer-stock facility of the International Monetary Fund for stock acquisition, and calls upon the World Food Council to explore possible ways for bringing the reserve into operation on an urgent basis;

17. *Requests* developed countries to eliminate existing import barriers, export subsidies and other protectionist measures and mechanisms which disrupt trade, seriously affect the food and agricultural exports of developing countries, and are detrimental to an equitable distribution of resources and to the ability of developing countries to resolve their food and development problems;

18. *Notes with great concern* the steady downward trend in the prices of commodities exported by developing countries as one of the results of the prevailing high interest rates in the international financial markets;

19. *Calls upon* the Contracting Parties to the General Agreement on Tariffs and Trade, at their forthcoming ministerial meeting, and the United Nations Conference on Trade and Development, at its sixth session, to review the long-standing problems in international trade in agricultural products which adversely affect production in developing countries and their exports, the solution of which could make an important contribution to improving overall food production in the world;

20. *Urges* developed countries to make serious efforts to adjust those sectors of their agricultural economies protected against exports from developing countries, thus facilitating more efficient patterns of production;

21. *Urges* the international community to implement resolution 105(V) of 1 June 1979 of the United Nations Conference on Trade and Development on international food trade;

22. *Requests* the international institutions concerned, especially the Food and Agriculture Organization of the United Nations, the International Fund for Agricultural Development, the World Bank and the United Nations Development Programme, and the developed countries to assist the developing countries in the implementation of programmes and projects of economic co-operation among developing countries in the sectors of food production, food security and food trade;

23. *Stresses* the desirability of co-ordinating the efforts being made, in the various international forums concerned, with regard to world food problems.

---

*Both amounts in 1975 prices.

General Assembly resolution 37/247

21 December 1982   Meeting 115   Adopted without vote

Approved by Second Committee (A/37/680/Add.5) without vote, 20 December (meeting 51); draft by Vice-Chairman (A/C.2/37/L.127), based on informal consultations on draft transmitted by Economic and Social Council decision 1982/176 and orally amended by Chairman; agenda item 71 *(f)*.

Food problems

The General Assembly,

Recalling the Declaration and the Programme of Action on the Establishment of a New International Economic Order, contained in its resolutions 3201(S VI) and 3202(S-VI) of 1 May 1974, the Charter of Economic Rights and Duties of States, contained in its resolution 3281(XXIX) of 12 December 1974, resolution 3362(S-VII) of 16 September 1975 on development and international economic co-operation, and the International Development Strategy for the Third United Nations Development Decade, contained in the annex to its resolution 35/56 of 5 December 1980,

Recalling the Universal Declaration on the Eradication of Hunger and Malnutrition adopted by the World Food Conference and the Programme of Action adopted by the World Conference on Agrarian Reform and Rural Development,

Recalling its resolutions 34/110 of 14 December 1979 and 35/68 of 5 December 1980 on the report of the World Food Council and 35/69 of 5 December 1980 on the situation of food and agriculture in Africa, as well as its resolutions 36/185 and 36/186 of 17 December 1981,

Having considered the report of the World Food Council on the work of its eighth ministerial session and the seventh annual report of the Committee on Food Aid Policies and Programmes,

Expressing its appreciation to the Government and people of Mexico for acting as host to the World Food Council at its eighth ministerial session, held at Acapulco, from 21 to 24 June 1982, and for the generous hospitality accorded to the participants,

Concerned that progress towards realizing food-policy objectives, particularly in developing countries, is impeded by the prolonged world recession, growing production costs, high interest rates and inflation and by growing international political tension,

Expressing its deep concern at the fact that a substantial part of world resources, material as well as human, continues to be diverted to armaments with a detrimental effect on international security and on efforts to achieve the new international economic order, including the solution of food problems, and calling upon Governments to take effective measures in the field of real disarmament that would increase the possibilities of allocation of the resources now being used for military purposes to economic and social development, especially development of developing countries, and to upgrading their food conditions,

Recognizing that a substantial increase in the export earnings of developing countries is essential for the adequate financing of their overall economic development and their imports of food and agricultural inputs,

Noting the need for all countries, particularly the developed countries, to adopt policies designed to bring about the reduction and elimination of obstacles in order to avoid disruption of international trade in agricultural products and to facilitate access to international markets of agricultural exports, especially those of developing countries,

Urging all countries to consider improvements in the generalized system of preferences, including the inclusion of additional agricultural products, especially those of export interest to least developed countries,

Recognizing that the lasting solution to the problems of food and agriculture in developing countries depends on progress towards the attainment of self-reliance through increased food and agricultural production and investment as part of the overall development of those countries within the framework of structural changes in international economic relations,

Emphasizing that, within the framework of national economic development, due priority must be given to the development of the food sector,

Deeply concerned about the precarious nature of the food situation and the alarming trends of the growing food-import dependency in many of the developing countries, particularly the least developed countries, while noting the increase in world food production in the past year,

Emphasizing that African countries, in particular, require the strongest assistance of the international community for their efforts to reverse the trend of deteriorating food production and of growing hunger and malnutrition in their region, in support of essential policy adjustments by African Governments within the framework of the Lagos Plan of Action for the Implementation of the Monrovia Strategy for the Economic Development of Africa,

Concerned with the continuing instability of food supply occasioned by fluctuating production and prices in international grain markets and with increased food-security risks for many developing countries and reduced self-reliance engendered by uncertain returns to domestic producers,

Regretting the fact that international assistance to the food and agricultural sector in developing countries has been decreasing since 1979 and is now lagging far behind the internationally estimated requirements,

1. *Welcomes* the conclusions and recommendations adopted by the World Food Council at its eighth ministerial session;

2. *Takes note with appreciation* of the seventh annual report of the Committee on Food Aid Policies and Programmes;

3. *Commends* the developing countries that have achieved increased food self-reliance through a determined application of policies, resources and technology and urges that such efforts should be continued;

4. *Calls upon* the Governments concerned to implement agrarian reform and rural development within the framework of their national plans and objectives and in accordance with the recommendations adopted by the World Conference on Agrarian Reform and Rural Development;

5. *Reaffirms* the importance of enhancing the role of multilateral assistance in support of food production and agricultural development in the developing countries;

6. *Urges* the international community, in adopting multilateral measures in the food sector, to take particularly into account the problems and interests of food-producing and food-exporting developing countries;

7. *Reaffirms* that food is a universal human right which Governments endeavour to guarantee their people and, in that context, stresses its belief in the general principle that food should not be used as an instrument of political pressure;

8. *Expresses its satisfaction* at the growing number of countries that are adopting a more integrated approach to food policy, including food-sector strategies, as one of the means for interested developing countries to translate their own priorities into effective action and to mobilize, within the context of their national plans and priorities, increased technical and financial resources and co-operation from international development assistance agencies;

9. *Requests* the developed countries, international institutions and others able to provide development assistance to increase the volume substantially and to improve the quality of international assistance to the food sector in developing countries, for which the estimated necessary element of external assistance is $8.3 billion, growing to $12.5 billion by 1990, both figures at 1975 prices;

10. *Welcomes* the efforts of the International Labour Organisation, the United Nations Development Programme, the World Food Programme and donor countries in mobilizing technical and financial support in favour of special labour-intensive public works programmes in developing countries, particularly in the least developed countries, which help to mobilize their food production potential, expand employment opportunities and generate incomes in the rural sector;

11. *Urges* the Food and Agriculture Organization of the United Nations, the International Fund for Agricultural Development, the World Food Programme, the World Bank, the United Nations Development Programme, other international organizations concerned and donor countries to expand measures to assist developing countries in the implementation of their food strategies, plans and programmes;

12. *Invites* Governments concerned to adopt direct hunger-reduction measures integrated with productive development within the

framework of national strategies and policies, including, *inter alia*, more assistance to rural development to reach smallholder producers and co-operatives, special attention to the needs of women farmers, investment in human capacities through programmes for mothers and children, the creation of productive employment for poor landless families and an increase in food aid;

13. *Welcomes* the recommendation of the World Food Council to pay particular attention to progress in integrating food aid more directly in national plans to overcome hunger, and to more effective ways of achieving higher levels of food production, taking into account the report of the Committee on Food Aid Policies and Programmes;

14. *Urges* present and new donor countries to achieve without delay the minimum target of the 1974 World Food Conference of 10 million tons of cereal aid annually and to ensure that the minimum annual target of 500,000 tons of grains for the International Emergency Food Reserve is reached, as in 1981, and to ensure that the World Food Programme target of $1.2 billion in 1983-1984 is fulfilled;

15. *Urges* that, in the implementation of food aid policies and programmes, a greater volume of food and agricultural products be acquired from food-exporting developing countries, where appropriate, including through triangular transactions;

16. *Recognizes* the need for increased food production and food self-reliance of developing countries to overcome hunger and malnutrition and, in this context, also recognizes the transitional role of food aid;

17. *Urges* the international community to provide increased assistance in support of essential policy adjustments by African Governments, within the framework of the Lagos Plan of Action for the Implementation of the Monrovia Strategy for the Economic Development of Africa, to alleviate food deficits in Africa, taking into account the conclusions and recommendations adopted by the African Ministers for Food and Agriculture at the World Food Council Regional Consultation for Africa, held at Nairobi on 16 and 17 March 1982, and endorsed by the Council at its eighth ministerial session, in particular through:

(a) The speeding up of national food-strategy implementation and financing, with emphasis on policies, particularly those improving producer incentives and raising the standard of living of the rural population;

(b) Stepped-up training in food-policy planning and investment preparation and management;

(c) Substantially increased technical and resource support for adaptive research, technology and related services to farmers, with emphasis on early low-cost improvement in cultivation practices;

(d) Improved food-security infrastructure, including transport, storage and marketing;

18. *Further urges* developed countries, and others in a position to do so, to increase assistance to developing countries in meeting their needs for technological progress in food and agricultural matters and the development of agro-industries related to food problems;

19. *Affirms* the important role of agro-scientific research in the promotion of agriculture and food production, processing, storage and reduction of food and grain losses, and urges all States, relevant international organizations and agencies to strengthen their capacities in agro-scientific research and to take effective measures aimed at promoting transfer of agro-technology to the developing countries;

20. *Affirms* that a sound basis for world food security can best be established by successful national programmes for attaining food self-reliance through increased food and agricultural production and investment in developing countries, as well as more open and more stable world trade and assurance of supplies;

21. *Notes with interest* the appreciation expressed by the World Food Council at its eighth ministerial meeting on the proposal for a developing country–owned reserve, giving priority to the food-security needs of individual developing countries and to enhance grain market stability and, in that context, calls upon the World Food Council to consider, at its ninth session, the proposals it has requested of its Executive Director on possible ways of building food-security reserves;

22. *Expresses concern* at the lack of sufficient progress in different negotiating forums in connection with proposals to bring about the reduction and elimination of the various types of barriers to trade in agricultural products, in particular in relation to those of export interest to developing countries, and calls for urgent action in this regard in those forums, thus facilitating, *inter alia*, more efficient patterns of production;

23. *Notes with great concern* the continued instability and downward trends in prices of agricultural commodities exported in particular by developing countries, which are adversely affecting the production of these commodities in those countries;

24. *Notes* that the Contracting Parties to the General Agreement on Tariffs and Trade, at their recent ministerial meeting, in recognition of the urgent need to find lasting solutions to the problems of trade in agricultural products, agreed to establish a committee on trade in agriculture to examine, *inter alia*, all measures affecting trade, market access and competition and supply in agricultural products, with full account being taken of the special needs of developing countries in the light of the provisions of the General Agreement on Tariffs and Trade providing for differential and more favourable treatment for such contracting parties;

25. *Notes further* that the Contracting Parties to the General Agreement on Tariffs and Trade, at that meeting, did not succeed in reconciling divergent views on certain substantial issues of agricultural trade;

26. *Notes with deep concern* that only limited progress has been achieved towards the solution of the long-standing problems of international trade in agricultural products, including access to international markets of agricultural exports, which adversely affect production and exports, particularly of developing countries, and the solution to which could make an important contribution to improving overall food production in the world;

27. *Urges* developed countries to make their best efforts to adjust those sectors of their agricultural and manufacturing economies which, for those countries, require support with regard to exports from developing countries, thus facilitating, *inter alia*, access to markets of food and agricultural products;

28. *Urges* the international community to implement resolution 105(V) of 1 June 1979 of the United Nations Conference on Trade and Development on international food trade and, in this context, invites the Conference, at its sixth session, to review progress in this regard;

29. *Requests* the international organizations concerned, especially the Food and Agriculture Organization of the United Nations, the International Fund for Agricultural Development, the World Bank, the World Food Programme and the United Nations Development Programme, and the developed countries to assist further the developing countries in their efforts to implement programmes and projects of economic co-operation among developing countries in the sectors of food production, food security and food trade;

30. *Stresses* the desirability of co-ordinating the efforts being made, in the various international forums concerned, with regard to world food problems;

31. *Welcomes* the decision of the World Food Council that its tenth session in 1984 would be the occasion to prepare a special assessment of progress made and the tasks ahead to achieve the objectives of the 1974 World Food Conference and requests the Council to report to the General Assembly at its thirty-eighth session on progress in the arrangements being made for the convening of the tenth session.

General Assembly decision 37/448

Adopted without vote

Approved by Second Committee (A/37/680/Add.5) without vote, 20 December (meeting 51); oral proposal by Vice-Chairman based on informal consultations; agenda item 71*(f)*.

Food and agriculture

At its 115th plenary meeting, on 21 December 1982, the General Assembly, on the recommendation of the Second Committee, decided to refer to its thirty-eighth session, for consideration, the draft resolution entitled "Food and agriculture".*

*For text of draft resolution, see YUN 1981, p. 724.

Food processing

During 1982, the United Nations Industrial Development Organization gave its support to a variety of food processing projects in a number of countries and organized a third Latin American seminar on the science and technology of food processing. In June, an expert meeting convened by UNCTAD examined ways of strengthening the technological capacity of developing countries in the food processing sector.

Food aid

World Food Programme

The World Food Programme (WFP), a joint undertaking of the United Nations and the Food and Agriculture Organization of the United Nations (FAO), continued during 1982 to provide food aid to developing countries in support of development projects and to meet emergency needs.

Since coming into operation in 1963,[3] WFP had, by the end of 1982, committed some $5.3 billion of assistance to over 1,100 development projects in 114 developing countries. It was estimated that about 170 million people had benefited from WFP development and emergency aid. Of that total, some 67 million had been helped through various types of development projects. In addition, relief assistance had been provided to over 100 million people through almost 600 emergency operations in 103 countries, involving about $1.1 billion in food aid.

The governing body of WFP, the 30-member Committee on Food Aid Policies and Programmes (CFA), presented annual reports to the Economic and Social Council and the FAO Council, covering 1981[1] and 1982.[2]

Reports. CFA, [1]E/1982/73, [2]E/1983/92.
Yearbook reference. [3]1963, p. 211.

WFP activities

The CFA annual report[4] stated that 1982 marked a significant expansion in WFP activities and resources. Almost 2 million metric tons of food were shipped, including deliveries on behalf of bilateral donors, the highest annual level ever achieved and about 35 per cent more than in 1981. Commitments amounting to $613 million—13 per cent more than the previous year—were made for 68 development projects. Some $193 million of food aid was approved for 68 emergency operations to provide about 537,000 metric tons of food commodities to over 7 million people. WFP acted as co-ordinator of food aid operations for international relief in the Thai/Kampuchean border areas, for Afghan refugees in Pakistan, for refugees in Somalia, for the famine-afflicted of Uganda and in Lebanon and for refugees and displaced persons in Central America. The major part (about 69 per cent) of WFP emergency food aid went to refugees and displaced persons in the aftermath of man-made disasters.

WFP aid continued to focus on the neediest countries. About 40 per cent was committed to countries in Africa south of the Sahara. Over 70 per cent of new development assistance was earmarked for agricultural and rural development projects.

CFA activities. The thirteenth and fourteenth sessions of CFA were held in 1982 at Rome, Italy, from 19 to 29 April[1] and from 11 to 18 October.[2]

Following its seventh annual review of food aid policies and programmes in April, CFA submitted its conclusions[4] to the Economic and Social Council, pointing out that cereal food aid shipments had declined and allocations by donors for 1981/82 at 8.9 million tons fell substantially short of the 10-million-ton target. CFA also considered: the general approach for a review of food aid requirements and targets in the 1980s, to be undertaken at its fifteenth (May 1983) session; a report—whose recommendations CFA approved unanimously—prepared in co-operation with FAO on ways of increasing the use of fishery products in food aid and describing how WFP assistance could help fisheries development in developing countries; and improving the effectiveness of emergency operations—CFA agreed that normally emergency food aid should be a temporary, short-term measure, but that there were situations where prolonged relief assistance would have to be provided.

In October, CFA considered a number of steps to mark the twentieth anniversary of WFP in 1983. It authorized the Executive Director to invite the Universal Postal Union to approach its member Governments to issue special stamps and/or frankings. It also announced that a seminar would be held in 1983, the conclusions of which were expected to help articulate new directions in food aid.

In its 21 December 1982 resolution concerning the activities of the World Food Council, the General Assembly took note of the CFA report covering 1981[3] and urged that, in implementing food aid policies and programmes, a greater volume of food and agricultural products be acquired from food-exporting developing countries, including through triangular transactions.[5]

Reports. CFA; [1]WFP/CFA:13/20, [2]WFP/CFA:14/18, [3]E/1982/73, [4]E/1983/92.
Resolution (1982). [5]GA: 37/247, paras. 2 & 15, 21 Dec.

Development assistance

During 1982, CFA approved 37 new assistance projects for economic and social development and the Executive Director approved an additional 11, bringing the total of projects approved to 48 at a total commitment value of over $485 million. (For list of development projects approved, see table below.) A significant proportion of WFP-assisted projects approved in 1982 involved external assistance from other United Nations agencies, bilateral and non-governmental organizations and development banks.

The majority of WFP commitments were concentrated on low-income, food-deficit countries, for which commitments exceeded 80 per cent of the total for development projects. Assistance to coun-

tries identified by the United Nations as least developed rose to 37 per cent, compared with 35 per cent for 1981. In 1982, a high proportion (about 40 per cent) of WFP development resources continued to be committed to African countries south of the Sahara. Commitments for agricultural and rural development exceeded 70 per cent.

Emergency operations

During 1982, food assistance was approved for 68 emergency operations, including additional aid to operations previously approved in 37 countries. Over 7 million people were provided with about 537,000 tons of food commodities at a total cost to WFP of some $193 million, surpassing the previous record level of $191.5 million reached in 1980.

About 69 per cent of the value of the aid went to refugees and displaced persons following man-made disasters, 20 per cent to people affected by drought and 11 per cent to victims of sudden natural disasters. More than half (57 per cent) of the aid went to 20 operations in Asia and the Pacific, 25 per cent to 25 operations in Africa south of the Sahara, 13 per cent for 12 operations in north Africa and the Near East, and 5 per cent for 11 operations in Latin America and the Caribbean. (For list of emergency operations approved, see table below.)

Throughout 1982, WFP was involved in a number of large-scale emergency operations. It continued co-ordinating the procurement and delivery of food aid to Kampuchea and relief operations along the Thai/Kampuchean border, which by year's end amounted to $314 million. It also assumed the role of lead agency for the delivery and monitoring of emergency food aid to over 200,000 people along that border, in close collaboration with 13 non-governmental organizations, and helped to co-ordinate international relief efforts concerning health, education, water supplies and shelter. In Pakistan, the total WFP commitment to the humanitarian relief operation for Afghan refugees since October 1979 reached some 593,000 tons of food by the end of 1982, estimated at $196 million. In 1982, WFP provided three basic commodities—wheat, edible oil/fats and dried skim milk—and co-ordinated the food shipments of other donors.

In Somalia, emergency food aid for 1 million refugees reached some 63,000 tons at a value of $39 million since the operation began in 1979, including 22,000 tons valued at $12 million approved in 1982. Following the outbreak of hostilities in Lebanon in 1982, WFP responded to a Government request by providing 22,319 tons of food valued at $9.4 million for 600,000 people.

Renewed unrest in Uganda caused fresh refugee flows into southern Sudan in 1982, displacement of persons within Uganda and a mass exodus to Rwanda, seriously disrupting those countries' fragile infrastructure and straining their limited resources. WFP responded by providing basic food commodities for 135,000 beneficiaries. Continuing strife in Central America, particularly in El Salvador, increased the number of displaced persons and refugees in the region. Some 14,000 tons of food valued at $6 million was supplied by WFP to 370,000 persons.

WFP resources

Contributions and pledges

The report of the Committee on Food Aid Policies and Programmes (CFA)[1] pointed out that, during 1982, total WFP resources reached a record level of $1,449 million. This amount consisted of pledges to regular resources totalling $1,061 million, including $993 million for the 1983-1984 biennium (see below); contributions of $273 million to the International Emergency Food Reserve (IEFR) channelled through WFP and of $90 million under the Food Aid Convention; and other resources amounting to $25 million.

By the end of 1982, 99 donors had pledged $838 million for the biennium 1981-1982 (see table below), or 84 per cent of the target of $1 billion set by the General Assembly for that period.[2] At the WFP Pledging Conference held in New York on 2 March 1982, for the 1983-1984 biennium, 48 donors announced pledges to the regular resources totalling $679.8 million. By the end of 1982, 59 donors had pledged $993 million—the highest amount ever pledged—or 83 per cent of the $1.2-billion target established for that biennium[3] (see table below).

Report. [1]CFA, E/1983/92.
Resolutions. GA: [2]34/108, 14 Dec. 1979 (YUN 1979, p. 670); [3]36/202, 17 Dec. 1981 (YUN 1981, p. 728).
Meeting records. Pledging Conference, A/CONF.111/SR.1,2 (2 Mar.).

Other resources

Earnings from cash deposits and bank accounts amounted to $25 million in 1982. Cash contributions of recipient Governments towards local operating costs totalled $600,000.

Contributions under the 1980 Food Aid Convention

The 1980 Food Aid Convention,[3] extended in 1981 until June 1983,[4] established minimum annual contributions in wheat and other grains for each of its parties and had as its objective the achievement of the 1974 World Food Conference target of at least 10 million metric tons of food aid annually.[2] The CFA report[1] announced that,

for the crop year 1981/82, contributions under the Convention channelled through WFP amounted to 309,841 tons of grain valued at $54.7 million. Contributors also provided cash grants for transportation and other expenses of almost $18 million. By the end of 1982, contributions announced for the 1982/83 crop year totalled 190,000 tons valued at over $34.5 million; cash for transportation and related costs were announced as $11.4 million (see table below). All figures excluded contributions for IEFR (see below).

Report. [1]CFA, E/1983/92.
Yearbook references. [2]1974, p. 496; [3]1980, p. 691; [4]1981, p. 729.

Contributions under IEFR

Contributions to IEFR in 1982 (see table below) were much higher than previously and reached over 505,000 metric tons of grains and other foods, of which about 15,000 tons were supplied bilaterally, CFA stated.[2] Some 454,000 tons of cereals and 51,000 tons of other commodities (vegetable oils, dried skim milk, pulses, sugar and canned meat) were contributed. Eighteen donors channelled their IEFR contributions through WFP in 1982.

Noting the achievement of the IEFR 500,000-ton target, the World Food Council (WFC) stressed the need for dealing with supply shortfalls in individual developing countries, supplemented by a fully supported WFP and by achievement of the minimum annual target of 10 million tons of food aid set by 1974 World Food Conference (see above).

In its 21 December resolution concerning the activities of WFC, the General Assembly urged donor countries to achieve without delay the 10-million-ton target and to ensure that the minimum annual target of 500,000 tons of grain for IEFR was reached and the WFP target of $1.2 billion in 1983-1984 fulfilled.[3] The draft of this resolution had been formulated in the Assembly's Second (Economic and Financial) Committee and was based on informal consultations on a text submitted to the Economic and Social Council by the Group of 77 and forwarded to the Assembly for its consideration (see above). By the Group's text, the Assembly would have urged that the IEFR target be reinforced and placed on a fully multilateral basis and, in addition to the adopted wording on the WFP target, would have also urged attainment of the target of $1 billion for 1981-1982.[1]

Decision (1982). [1]ESC: 1982/176, annex, para. 11, 30 July.
Report. [2]CFA, E/1983/92.
Resolution (1982). [3]GA: 37/247, para. 14, 21 Dec.

FOOD AID FOR DEVELOPMENT

(Projects approved in 1982 by CFA and the WFP Executive Director)

Country	Field of activity	Amount (in US dollars)	Country	Field of activity	Amount (in US dollars)
Algeria	Promotion and encouragement of women in production	1,185,000	Madagascar	Forestry and regional development	3,029,800
Angola	Rehabilitation of coffee production	14,165,000	Mali	Food security, price stabilization and restructuring of cereal marketing	8,455,000
	Assistance to Namibian refugees	6,492,000	Mauritania	Gorgol Noir irrigation and settlement scheme	6,609,000
Benin	Multi-purpose rural development	13,427,000	Morocco	Assistance in developing milk production	17,045,000
Bolivia	Promotion of dairy development modules for small producers	7,181,600	Mozambique	Primary boarding-school feeding	15,980,500
China	Land protection and wood production through forestry development, Shandong and Sichuan provinces	8,427,900		Dairy development	14,889,300
				Food security reserve	1,901,500
	Development of fishery resources. Hongze county, Jiangsu province	9,442,500	Nepal	National dairy development	2,760,500
				Road construction, Naudanda-Beni	989,800
	Xingpuzichuan irrigation project, Jiangyuan county, Gasu province	9,853,300	Niger	Assistance to school canteen programme	8,884,000
				Multi-purpose rural development	2,131,300
	Nan Shan Taixhi irrigation project, Zhongwei county, Ningxia Hui autonomous region	6,323,300	Pakistan	Assistance to Tarbela and Mangla watersheds	18,558,800
			Paraguay	Nutrition education programme and sanitation improvement	8,279,000
	Agricultural development through drainage, irrigation and salinity control, Hebei province	1,573,000	Philippines	Rehabilitation of malnourished pre-school children and supportive self-help pilot schemes	6,506,600
Democratic Yemen	Multi-sectoral project for agricultural, social and rural community development	17,275,700		Rural drinking water supply/sanitation development	5,066,800
Ecuador	Construction of rural infrastructure and support to productive activities for peasant communities	15,250,000		Assistance to victims of typhoons "Andy" and "Dinang"*	980,200
Equatorial Guinea	Primary school feeding	5,667,600	Sao Tome and Principe	Assistance to primary schools and kindergartens	3,221,600
Ethiopia	Rehabilitation of forest, grazing and agricultural lands	88,334,000	Senegal	Assistance to school canteens and rural training centres	1,811,000
Gambia	School feeding and nutrition education	7,704,000	Sri Lanka	Excavation of monuments and sites in the "cultural triangle"*	1,615,400
Guinea	Assistance to agricultural production and training centres	1,410,500		Kirindi Oya settlement project	3,027,200
Guyana	Feeding programme in nursery schools	2,830,100	Sudan	Water-related disease control in irrigation schemes	6,669,700
India	Social and economic development through forestry activities, Maharashtra	17,899,000	Syrian Arab Republic	Reforestation and establishment of green belt	20,464,000
	Rural development, Mahendergarh district, Haryana	974,500	Tonga	Food assistance to schools and establishment of school gardens*	360,600
Indonesia	Regional development through transmigration, Riau province, Sumatra	20,827,000	Tunisia	Erosion and desertification control	19,408,000
			Uganda	Multi-purpose rural development, Karamoja region*	14,065,200
Jordan	Development of highland agricultural regions	10,336,500	Viet Nam	Food assistance to vulnerable groups	23,989,300
			Zambia	Forestry assistance	1,784,100
			Total		485,062,700

*Approved by WFP Executive Director, but only $1,384,200 of the total cost of the Uganda project.

SOURCE: WFP/CFA:13/20 and 14/18, updated by WFP.

EMERGENCY ALLOCATIONS APPROVED IN 1982

Country or region	Nature of emergency	Amount (in US dollars) IEFR	WFP	Country or region	Nature of emergency	Amount (in US dollars) IEFR	WFP
Benin	Drought	672,500	65,700	Democratic Yemen	Floods	500,000	921,400
Bolivia	Floods	247,500	—		Floods	2,362,300	919,000
Botswana	Drought	1,603,900	211,900	Egypt	Drought	520,300	273,200
Central America*	Refugees	—	752,100	El Salvador	Refugees	2,540,700	—
Chad	Drought	4,370,000	770,000		Flood	545,400	—
	Refugees	5,889,300	1,181,000†	Ethiopia	Drought	2,129,500	1,290,500
Costa Rica	Refugees	296,300	—	Ghana	Drought	689,500	—
Cuba	Flood	—	1,172,800	Guatemala	Refugees	2,019,700	—
Democratic Kampuchea	Refugees	2,100,000	—	Guinea-Bissau	Refugees	—	200,700
	Refugees	2,360,000	—	Indonesia	Refugees	480,700	140,400
	Refugees	1,354,000	—		Eruption	3,738,200	—
	Refugees	185,000	—	Jordan	Drought	1,393,200	—
	Refugees	2,100,000	—	Lebanon	War	—	11,445,800
	Refugees	220,000	—	Madagascar	Refugees	—	246,000
	Refugees	1,293,000	—				

Country or region	Nature of emergency	Amount (in US dollars)		Country or region	Nature of emergency	Amount (in US dollars)	
		IEFR	WFP			IEFR	WFP
Mauritania	Drought	2,234,400	1,367,400	Sri Lanka	Drought	3,024,100	—
Mozambique	Drought	674,700	229,600	Sudan	Refugees	378,100	894,400
	Drought	—	2,100,000		Refugees	698,800	258,800
	Drought	1,025,000	—		Refugees	811,400	626,500
	Drought	72,600	3,000	Swaziland	Drought	939,800	234,000
Nepal	Drought	3,680,000	—	Syrian Arab			
Nicaragua	Floods	—	118,000	Republic	Refugees	108,000	34,700
	Flood	—	308,400	Tonga	Cyclone	339,600	156,800
	Refugees	—	131,700	Tunisia	Drought	2,540,000	—
	Drought	—	2,309,000		Flood	1,083,600	—
Pakistan	Refugees	5,135,700	—	Uganda	Drought	1,809,600	—
	Refugees	5,773,200	—		Drought	417,700	—
	Refugees	18,492,100	—		Refugees	678,000	220,700
	Refugees	5,808,000	1,134,100	United Republic			
	Refugees	37,155,300	—	of Tanzania	Floods	530,400	—
	Refugees	3,656,000	—	Viet Nam	Typhoon	5,094,800	1,021,200
Rwanda	Refugees	36,000	174,600		Typhoon	1,719,000	—
	Refugees	362,100	406,500‡	Yemen	Earthquake	452,300	521,700
	Refugees	182,000	106,000	Zambia	Drought	1,356,900	648,000
Somalia	Refugees	2,796,700	—				
	Refugees	1,676,000	—	Total		158,054,400	32,595,600
	Refugees	7,701,500	—				

*Expansion of the subregional operation, covering Salvadoran refugees in Honduras.

†Includes $380,000 for food and $801,000 for freight, funded under the International Conference on Assistance to Refugees in Africa (ICARA).

‡Includes $91,200 for food and $46,000 for freight, funded under ICARA.

SOURCE: WFP/CFA:14/4 and 15/9.

CONTRIBUTIONS UNDER THE FOOD AID CONVENTION MADE AVAILABLE TO WFP

(as at 31 December 1982; in US dollars)

CONTRIBUTOR	CROP YEAR 1981/82			CROP YEAR 1982/83		
	Commodity (metric tons)	Value	CASH	Commodity (metric tons)	Value	CASH
Food Aid Convention net						
Australia	80,000	14,640,000	5,039,564	120,000	21,840,000	7,200,000
Belgium	13,000	2,379,000	741,000	—	—	—
Finland	28,307	3,660,000	1,200,000	—	—	—
Germany, Federal Republic of	35,000	6,405,000	2,100,000	—	—	—
Ireland	6,004	746,640	244,800	—	—	—
Netherlands	25,000	4,575,000	1,500,000	—	—	—
Norway	30,667	5,490,000	1,800,000	30,000	5,460,000	1,800,000
Sweden	40,000	7,320,000	2,400,000	40,000	7,280,000	2,400,000
Switzerland	1,863	340,931	108,800	—	—	—
United Kingdom	50,000	9,150,000	2,822,580	—	—	—
Subtotal	309,841	54,706,571	17,956,744	190,000	34,580,000	11,400,000
IEFR through the Convention*						
Australia	39,672	7,412,450	2,139,164	45,000	8,235,000	3,150,000
EEC	30,000	5,490,000	2,910,900	—	—	—
Switzerland	14,484	2,650,572	1,404,948	10,000	1,830,000	970,000
Switzerland	—	—	—	3,297†	631,923	202,115
United Kingdom	5,000	915,000	485,000	—	—	—
Subtotal	89,156	16,468,022	6,940,012	58,297	10,696,923	4,322,115
Total	398,997	71,174,593	24,896,756	248,297	45,276,923	15,722,115

*Under IEFR, donor countries cover all transportation costs.

†1,075 metric tons of maize, and 1,600 metric tons of wheat flour equivalent to 2,222 metric tons of wheat.

SOURCE: WFP/CFA:15/4 Add.1.

CONTRIBUTIONS UNDER THE INTERNATIONAL EMERGENCY FOOD RESERVE
(as at 31 December 1982)

Contributor	Contribution	Quantity (in metric tons)	Estimated value (including costs for transportation) (in US dollars)	Contributor	Contribution	Quantity (in metric tons)	Estimated value (including costs for transportation) (in US dollars)
Multilateral				Sweden	Grain	30,000	7,716,700
Australia	Grain	45,000	11,385,000		Vegetable oil	1,250	1,250,000
Austria	Grain	5,000	1,025,000	Switzerland	$US 250,000	1,075	252,625
Canada	$Can 6,500,000	18,873	5,284,553		Grain	10,312	1,989,284
Denmark	DKr 16,000,000	8,050	1,868,395		Wheat flour	1,600	584,038
EEC	Grain	50,000	14,000,000		Dried skimmed milk	450	921,097
Finland	Dried skimmed milk	330	1,238,558		Maize	650	117,650
	Vegetable oil	391	554,700	United Kingdom	Grain	5,000	1,400,000
	Fmk 9,200,000	7,224	2,022,720	United States	Various com-		
	Sugar	30	117,600		modities	197,645	72,341,900
France	Grain	20,000	4,839,300	Subtotal		490,266	154,584,963
Germany, Federal							
Republic of	Grain	25,000	7,000,000	*Bilateral*			
India	Sugar	303	108,578	Austria	Grain	5,000	1,400,000
Italy	Grain	25,000	7,820,000	Finland	Canned meat	90	180,000
Japan	$US 1,375,000	5,341	1,375,000	Sweden	Grain	10,000	2,800,000
Netherlands	f. 5,000,000	3,188	1,978,200	Subtotal		15,090	4,380,000
Norway	Grain	9,034	2,394,065				
OPEC	$US 5,000,000	19,518	5,000,000	Total		505,354	158,964,963

SOURCE: WFP/CFA:15/4 Add.1.

STATEMENT OF PLEDGES TO THE WORLD FOOD PROGRAMME FOR 1981-1982 AND 1983-1984
(as at 31 December 1982; in US dollar equivalent)

Contributor	1981-1982 Commodities	1981-1982 Cash and services	1981-1982 Total	1983-1984 Commodities	1983-1984 Cash and services	1983-1984 Total
Afghanistan	—	3,000	3,000	—	3,000	3,000
Algeria	—	132,250	132,250	—	—	—
Antigua and Barbuda	—	—	—	—	500	500
Argentina	2,500,000	—	2,500,000	—	—	—
Australia	6,886,567	6,345,240	13,231,807	77,117,123	27,963,964	105,081,087
Austria	4,500,000	500,000	5,000,000	5,400,000	600,000	6,000,000
Bahamas	—	500	500	—	—	—
Bangladesh	600,000	—	600,000	660,000	—	660,000
Barbados	—	13,000	13,000	—	—	—
Belgium	1,531,915	863,859	2,395,774	—	—	—
Benin	—	4,500	4,500	—	—	—
Bhutan	—	1,000	1,000	—	1,250	1,250
Bolivia	—	—	—	—	10,000	10,000
Botswana	—	15,090	15,090	—	—	—
Brazil	50,000	300,000	350,000	—	—	—
Burundi	—	1,675	1,675	—	1,787	1,787
Canada	145,886,158	18,665,619	164,551,777	173,553,719	33,057,851	206,611,570
Canadian Mennonite Committee	379,090	—	379,090	—	—	—
Central African Republic	—	2,241	2,241	—	2,353	2,353
Chile	—	30,000	30,000	—	—	—
China	—	400,000	400,000	—	600,000	600,000
Colombia	400,000	20,527	420,527	500,000	—	500,000
Costa Rica	—	20,000	20,000	—	—	—
Cuba	2,500,000	—	2,500,000	2,500,000	—	2,500,000
Cyprus	—	2,011	2,011	—	1,689	1,689
Democratic People's Republic of Korea	—	100,000	100,000	—	100,000	100,000
Democratic Yemen	—	8,554	8,554	—	11,000	11,000
Denmark	21,506,428	12,522,523	34,028,951	24,482,013	12,227,848	36,709,861
Djibouti	—	—	—	—	2,000	2,000
Ecuador	—	50,000	50,000	—	50,000	50,000
Egypt	400,000	—	400,000	400,000	—	400,000
Ethiopia	—	2,000	2,000	—	—	—
EEC	94,599,532	14,447,250	109,046,782	118,674,000	16,990,000	135,664,000
Fiji	—	4,000	4,000	—	4,000	4,000
Finland	5,196,586	602,439	5,799,025	4,126,954	1,003,478	5,130,432
France	—	3,886,524	3,886,524	—	—	—
Germany, Federal Republic of	24,344,377	12,513,285	36,857,662	28,085,106	14,042,554	42,127,660
Greece	200,000	—	200,000	250,000	—	250,000

Contributor	1981-1982			1983-1984		
	Commodities	Cash and services	Total	Commodities	Cash and services	Total
Guyana	—	3,333	3,333	—	—	—
Honduras	—	10,000	10,000	—	—	—
Hungary	400,000	—	400,000	440,000	—	440,000
Iceland	6,000	21,000	27,000	—	40,000	40,000
India	1,310,000	—	1,310,000	1,570,000	—	1,570,000
Indonesia	395,900	—	395,900	—	—	—
Iraq	266,667	133,333	400,000	—	—	—
Ireland	1,440,142	748,429	2,188,571	2,122,572	1,061,285	3,183,857
Israel	—	10,000	10,000	—	10,000	10,000
Italy	21,228,668	4,957,122	26,185,790	—	—	—
Ivory Coast	—	45,440	45,440	—	—	—
Jamaica	—	10,103	10,103	—	10,000	10,000
Japan	8,330,000	4,170,000	12,500,000	10,333,330	5,166,670	15,500,000
Jordan	—	54,238	54,238	—	75,000	75,000
Kenya	—	948	948	—	—	—
Kuwait	—	500,000	500,000	—	—	—
Lao People's Democratic Republic	—	1,000	1,000	—	—	—
Lebanon*	—	45,000	45,000	—	—	—
Liberia	—	4,000	4,000	—	—	—
Libyan Arab Jamahiriya	—	100,000	100,000	—	100,000	100,000
Luxembourg	—	33,100	33,100	—	—	—
Madagascar	—	11,929	11,929	—	—	—
Malawi	—	10,824	10,824	—	1,600	1,600
Malaysia	17,241	8,771	26,012	17,544	8,772	26,316
Malta	—	2,200	2,200	—	2,600	2,600
Mauritania	—	4,980	4,980	—	—	—
Mauritius	4,400	—	4,400	—	—	—
Morocco	—	27,045	27,045	—	30,769	30,769
Nepal	—	6,000	6,000	—	—	—
Netherlands	26,724,530	14,214,508	40,939,038	32,367,044	14,853,234	47,220,278
New Zealand	825,579	412,699	1,238,278	410,256	205,128	615,384
Nigeria	—	250,000	250,000	—	250,000	250,000
Norway	29,029,401	11,386,675	40,416,076	26,428,572	13,214,284	39,642,856
OPEC	16,700,000†	—	16,700,000	—	—	—
Pakistan	900,000	—	900,000	750,000	—	750,000
Panama	—	2,000	2,000	—	—	—
Paraguay	—	10,000	10,000	—	—	—
Peru	—	20,000	20,000	—	—	—
Philippines	—	84,869	84,869	—	88,050	88,050
Portugal	—	90,000	90,000	—	—	—
Qatar	—	50,000	50,000	—	—	—
Rwanda	—	1,500	1,500	—	—	—
Saudi Arabia	25,000,000	30,000,000	55,000,000	27,500,000	27,500,000	55,000,000
Somalia	—	3,210	3,210	—	—	—
Spain	—	400,000	400,000	—	400,000	400,000
Sri Lanka	95,891	—	95,891	121,359	—	121,359
Sudan	10,000	—	10,000	—	10,000	10,000
Suriname	—	7,500	7,500	—	—	—
Sweden	14,636,641	8,214,729	22,851,370	18,086,957	9,043,478	27,130,435
Switzerland	4,721,558	2,025,346	6,746,904	5,172,105	2,481,492	7,653,597
Syrian Arab Republic	—	102,564	102,564	—	128,205	128,205
Thailand*	30,000	—	30,000	35,000	—	35,000
Togo	—	—	—	—	5,000	5,000
Trinidad and Tobago	—	3,273	3,273	—	—	—
Tunisia	—	23,250	23,250	—	55,000	55,000
Turkey	180,000	—	180,000	—	216,000	216,000
Uganda	—	—	—	—	1,000	1,000
United Kingdom	2,438,879	1,304,685	3,743,564	—	—	—
United Republic of Cameroon	—	30,159	30,159	—	—	—
United Republic of Tanzania	—	19,935	19,935	—	—	—
United States	165,000,000	55,000,000	220,000,000	188,000,000	62,000,000	250,000,000
Upper Volta	—	3,631	3,631	—	—	—
Venezuela	—	93,457	93,457	—	—	—
Viet Nam	—	10,000	10,000	—	10,000	10,000
Yemen	—	6,032	6,032	—	—	—
Yugoslavia	452,737	—	452,737	540,000	—	540,000
Total	631,624,887	206,145,904	837,770,791	749,643,654	243,640,841	993,284,495

*Subject to legislative approval.

†Cash for purchase and transportation of commodities.

SOURCE: WFP/CFA:15/19, updated by WFP.

Chapter XII

Science and technology

Contents

Related topics:

Peaceful uses of outer space: Space technology applications. Law of the sea: Marine scientific research; Marine technology development and transfer. Industrial development: Industrial technology. Regional economic and social activities—Science and technology: Africa; Asia and the Pacific; Europe; Latin America; Western Asia. Energy: technology transfer. Environment: Environmental monitoring. Women: Women and science and technology.

For resolutions and decisions of major organs mentioned but not reproduced, refer to INDEX OF RESOLUTIONS AND DECISIONS.

Vienna Programme of Action

During 1982, United Nations efforts in the area of science and technology focused on implementing the Vienna Programme of Action on Science and Technology for Development, adopted in 1979 by the United Nations Conference on Science and Technology for Development.[1] The efforts were based on the operational plan approved in June 1981 by the Intergovernmental Committee on Science and Technology for Development.[2] Following the structure of United Nations activities as defined in the Programme, the plan suggested programme areas to help make the advantages of science and technology more accessible to developing countries.

Steps to promote and execute the Vienna Programme continued to be taken through the Intergovernmental Committee, open to all States, and its 28-member Advisory Committee on Science and Technology for Development. The Director-General for Development and International Economic Co-operation (DIEC) continued to be responsible for overall co-ordination in science and technology within the United Nations system.

The Intergovernmental Committee held its fourth session in New York in two parts, from 24 May to 4 June, and from 8 to 10 September. The Advisory Committee held its second session in New York from 9 to 19 February.

Yearbook references. [1]1979, p. 636; [2]1981, p. 735.

Implementation of the Programme

Report of the Director-General. Concrete proposals for optimizing United Nations activities, with particular attention to strengthening the scientific and technical infrastructures of developing countries, were submitted to the Intergovernmental Committee by the DIEC Director-General in an April 1982 report on implementation of the Vienna Programme of Action,[4] as requested by the Committee in June 1981.[8] Part I of the report described efforts of the United Nations system, especially through the Task Force on Science and Technology for Development of the Administrative Committee on Co-ordination (ACC) and its four working groups, to design and carry out a number of joint activities under the eight major programme areas of the operational plan and the 31 areas of concentration established by the Committee. In part II, specific proposals for further action were outlined.

The Director-General suggested that a framework of constant interaction with developing countries was needed, particularly in information evaluation and assessment. Accordingly, he proposed that the Committee invite a group of developing countries to assess the impact of United Nations programmes on their endogenous capacity-building in the area of science and technology for development, and that individual organizations do the same with regard to their own activities. He suggested that, as a programme basis, Governments and non-governmental organizations be informed about specific activities endorsed by the Committee and, at the United Nations level, that the different bodies co-ordinate their scientific and technological activities in the 1984-1989 medium-term plan.

Task Force action. At its February 1982 session, the ACC Task Force established four working groups to identify and formulate, in the framework of the operational plan for implementation of the Vienna Programme, joint activities aimed at building the endogenous capacity of developing countries in science and technology for development. The working groups dealt with: assessment of new scientific and technological developments; national science and technology policies and support to developing countries in the choice of technology; upgrading traditional technologies; and science and technology and the productive sector—commercialization of research and development for the benefit of developing countries, and acquisition and transfer of technology.

Concerning the Director-General's biennial review of progress in implementing the operational plan and the Secretary-General's annual report on United Nations activities in science and technology for development, the Task Force observed overlapping elements and agreed that the United Nations Centre for Science and Technology for Development consider formulating a common format which could be applied to the information provided by United Nations organizations. Information on the Task Force's session and its proposals were contained in a March report to the Intergovernmental Committee.[3]

Advisory Committee consideration. Suggestions for implementing the Vienna Programme and the operational plan, in particular at the regional level, were made by the Advisory Committee at its February session. In its March report to the Intergovernmental Committee,[2] the Advisory Committee organized the eight programme areas of the operational plan into the following three groups: policy-making, financing and co-operation; infrastructure, human resources, and research and development linked to production; and choice, acquisition and transfer of technology and information. Within each of the three groups, the Advisory Committee made a number of proposals for further action.

Intergovernmental Committee action. By a resolution of 4 June,[6] the Intergovernmental Committee, welcoming the DIEC Director-General's report, invited Member States to comment not later than the end of 1982 on the proposals made, so that the Director-General, assisted by the Centre for science and technology, could propose guidelines to the Committee in 1983 for the formulation of specific projects aimed at strengthening the endogenous scientific and technological capacities in developing countries.

The Committee requested United Nations organizations and bodies to co-ordinate their individual and joint activities in science and technology, within available resources, taking into account the Director-General's proposals. It also requested Governments to take these proposals into account in formulating programmes, and invited the relevant United Nations bodies, when providing guidelines to individual entities in formulating their medium-term plans, to ensure the promotion, co-ordination and optimization of the activities relevant to the Vienna Programme.

In addition, the Committee requested United Nations entities to give attention to joint planning, and the Centre to take into account the need for an updated assessment of United Nations financing of science and technology for development.

By another resolution of the same date,[7] the Committee took note of the annual report of the Secretary-General on 1981 activities of the United Nations system in the field of science and technology for development, submitted in April 1982 and based on information from 30 United Nations entities including the five regional commissions.[5] In other sections, the resolution dealt with follow-up to the May 1981 study of the efficiency of the United Nations system in science and technology; activities of the Centre; financing; proposals of the Advisory Committee; and the Director-General's report on the level of attainment of scientific and technological development among different countries.

Other action. The Committee on Transfer of Technology of the United Nations Conference on Trade and Development (UNCTAD), on 10 December 1982,[1] requested the UNCTAD Secretary-General to take steps to implement the Vienna Programme of Action in accordance with the UNCTAD mandate and to report back in 1983. The Committee also requested him to participate actively in the 1983 session of the Intergovernmental Committee. Other provisions of the decision dealt with unresolved issues.

Decision (1982). [1]Committee on Transfer of Technology (report, TD/B/936): 22(IV), 10 Dec.
Reports. [2]Advisory Committee, A/CN.11/30; [3]Task Force, ACC/1982/2; [4]DIEC Director-General, transmitted by S-G note, A/CN.11/23; [5]S-G, A/CN.11/24.
Resolutions (1982). Intergovernmental Committee (report, A/37/37), 4 June: [6]1(IV); [7]3(IV), sect. VI.
Yearbook reference. [8]1981, p. 735.

Programme areas of the operational plan

The operational plan for implementation of the Vienna Programme of Action was divided into eight major programme areas: scientific and technological policies and plans for development; creation and strengthening of scientific and technological infrastructure; choice, acquisition and transfer of technology; development of human resources; financing; information; research and development and their linkage to the productive system; and strengthening international co-operation.

Science and technology policy

Under programme area I—scientific and technological policies and plans for development— technical advisory services relating to development of such policies continued to be provided to de-veloping countries in 1982 by organizations of the United Nations system. They were described by the Secretary-General in his April 1983 report on 1982 United Nations activities in science and technology for development.[3] National science and technology policies and plans and support to developing countries in the choice of technology was the subject of one of the four working groups of the Task Force on Science and Technology for Development.

UN activities. United Nations activities under programme area I focused on improving policy-making and planning, institutional arrangements, monitoring of scientific and technological developments, country studies, training of planning and management specialists, international co-operation, and information exchange and publication of reference documents.

The United Nations Financing System for Science and Technology for Development (UNFSSTD) concluded a preparatory assistance project in China to promote scientific and technological capabilities ($54,000) and started a project executed by the United Nations Development Programme (UNDP) to promote policy choices in science and technology ($203,000). In Africa, it continued to provide advisory services to the Organization of African Unity ($475,000), particularly in relation to the 1980 Lagos Plan of Action for the Implementation of the Monrovia Strategy for the Economic Development of Africa. It also supported preparatory assistance for the development of a national science and technology programme in Panama ($60,000).

Within the framework of its water resources programme, the United Nations Educational, Scientific and Cultural Organization (UNESCO) assisted States in developing comprehensive water-resources management plans. The International Maritime Organization (IMO) offered the services of nine technical experts to advise and assist Governments in implementing international technical standards and procedures concerning maritime safety, maritime training and prevention of pollution from ships. At their request, the United Nations Conference on Trade and Development (UNCTAD) provided assistance to developing countries in the formulation and implementation of policies, laws, regulations, procedures and mechanisms for the transfer and development of technology, particularly in the pharmaceutical, agro-industrial and energy sectors. The regional advisory committees on medical research of the World Health Organization (WHO) promoted collective formulation of science and technology policies in the field of health.

UNCTAD and the United Nations Environment Programme (UNEP) co-operated in a number of country sectoral studies on housing, pharmaceutical technology and the food-processing industry. The United Nations Industrial Development Organization (UNIDO) continued to examine the national policies of several countries and the feasibility of their adopting integrated technology policies and plans. The World Bank drew up the terms of reference for a study to delineate the science and technology policies of industrializing countries. UNESCO prepared a model legal statute governing the responsibilities and rights, working conditions and career structures of scientific researchers, and continued work on an international prospective study on science and technology policy.

UNIDO published quarterly bulletins on microelectronics and on genetic engineering and biotechnology. At a meeting at Belgrade, Yugoslavia, in December, UNIDO presented a five-year plan for a proposed international centre to support national efforts in genetic engineering and biotechnology.

In Mexico in March, a UNIDO/UNFSSTD project introduced a national system to monitor technological perspectives, with a view to providing inputs to industrial, technological and commercial policy formulation and decision-making on large industrial projects. The first meeting on cooperation between the scientific and industrial sectors in micro-electronics at the national level was held in Mexico as was a UNIDO/Economic Commission for Latin America (ECLA) expert group meeting (June) on the implications of microelectronics for the ECLA region. At the international level, UNIDO sent an expert mission to several countries to promote selective applications of micro-electronics and software development. Reports were prepared for an international conference on technology for development (Cairo, Egypt, November). UNIDO also held an expert preparatory meeting for an international forum on technological advances and developments in Moscow in November/December.

With the assistance of UNESCO and UNEP, the microbiological resources centres established in several countries initiated application of microbiological technologies and were conducting extensive regional training programmes. The relationship between environment, technology and development was the subject of a seminar convened by UNEP in Brazil in December.

The International Labour Organisation carried out case studies on the development of the capital goods industry; small, low-cost electronics-controlled machinery; and the effects on employment of new technologies in the printing industry.

Regional commissions also carried out work in science and technology planning. Among them, the Economic and Social Commission for Asia and the Pacific (ESCAP) helped prepare the Second Regional Conference of Ministers Responsible for the Application of Science and Technology to Development (Manila, Philippines, March). Other ESCAP activities included: preparation of a regional survey on scientific and technological development in the context of the Vienna Programme of Action, covering all eight programme areas and focusing on areas that needed to be strengthened; an advisory mission to develop measures for strengthening technology transfer arrangements; and advisory services concerning economic development policies and regulation of foreign business and investment.

The Economic Commission for Africa participated in planning meetings for science and technology policy training workshops—convened by the International Development Research Centre (Ottawa, Canada, August) and by the German Foundation for International Development (Bonn, Federal Republic of Germany, December)—as part of its efforts to study and mobilize the technological potential of the metal-working branch of the informal sector in a few African countries. The Economic Commission for Europe conducted reviews of changes in national policies, priorities and institutions in the region, including orientation and administration of research in various areas of science and technology, which might be of interest to developing countries. ECLA prepared a paper on the relations between science and technology policies and global economic and social development.

In the field of space science and technology, the International Civil Aviation Organization (ICAO) studied the application of satellite and space technology to the needs of international civil aviation. UNIDO presented a study on the potential applications of space-related technologies in developing countries as its contribution to the Second United Nations Conference on the Exploration and Peaceful Uses of Outer Space in August. The Department of Technical Co-operation for Development (DTCD) carried out studies on the application of remote sensing technology in developing countries. The Food and Agriculture Organization of the United Nations, in co-operation with the European Space Agency, the World Meteorological Organization, UNEP and the Office of the United Nations Disaster Relief Co-ordinator, organized training courses in the application of remote sensing in areas such as mapping of agro-ecological zones, drought and flood monitoring, surveys of range forest lands, desertification and desert locust control.

In another area of science and technology, the United Nations Centre on Transnational Corporations continued to assist Governments on matters related to policies, laws and regulations concerning such corporations.

Proposals of the Director-General. The Director-General for Development and International Economic Co-operation (DIEC), in his April report to the Intergovernmental Committee on Science and Technology for Development on the operational plan,[2] presented specific proposals for further action on scientific and technological policies and plans for development, in line with the three areas of concentration established under programme area I by the Intergovernmental Committee in June 1981.[4] Emphasizing that each country should develop its own scientific and technological policy, he suggested that the United Nations provide, at the request of Governments, advisory services to national agencies. Among the proposed United Nations activities was a progress review every five years of the structure and operations of such policy-making bodies. The first such review could be completed by 1985 by the Centre for Science and Technology for Development in co-operation with relevant United Nations organizations. The Director-General also proposed that training seminars, expert meetings and interregional symposia be held on policy-making in order to exchange experience.

With regard to the operational plan's proposal for an advance monitoring system for new science and technology through a network of specialized research centres in different countries, the Director-General proposed pilot projects in selected areas to test the system before extending it to a broader range of sectors. For 1982-1983, he proposed the following specific activities: continuation of contacts with international and regional organizations, research institutions and experts, with regard to the selection of areas for pilot projects, such as micro-electronics, robotics, biotechnology, remote sensing and other satellite technologies, and new technologies for energy, food, new materials, communications, transport and environment protection; and preparation of a feasibility study to be presented to the Intergovernmental Committee in 1983 for launching a few pilot projects in 1984.

Under the concentration area relating to support methods and analytical techniques, the Director-General proposed training programmes for developing national capacities in science and technology statistics, and development of suitable scientific and technological indicators. The Centre for science and technology, in co-operation with UNESCO, the United Nations Statistical Office and other organizations, could consider measures for that purpose during 1983 and 1984.

Advisory Committee consideration. The Advisory Committee on Science and Technology for Development, in the report on its February 1982 session,[1] also submitted proposals to the Intergovernmental Committee on specific action for im-

plementation of the Vienna Programme of Action. In the area of advisory services to national science and technology agencies, the Committee pointed out that the thrust of the Programme should be conveyed not only to ministers for science and technology but also to sectoral (industry, agriculture, transport, health) authorities. In providing advisory services, the Committee considered it important to stress the high returns, at both the macro- and micro-economic levels, of investment in science and technology. Based on these considerations, the Committee recommended that inter-agency consultations within the United Nations system be conducted to achieve an integrated approach to advisory services, and that training seminars and expert meetings on scientific and technological policy-making be organized at the national, subregional and regional levels. With regard to the Director-General's proposal on pilot projects for early identification and assessment of new scientific and technological developments, the Committee considered that a regional approach and the selection of specialized fields might be the most effective, and suggested that United Nations organizations submit project proposals in 1982.

Reiterating the Director-General's belief in the need for statistics and indicators of progress in the implementation of scientific and technological policies in individual developing countries, the Committee suggested that the United Nations continue to support countries in establishing national machinery and defining such indicators while, at the same time, recognizing the unique socioeconomic and cultural circumstances of individual countries.

For ministers in charge of science and technology and top-level policy makers, the Advisory Committee proposed the organization by United Nations and other organizations of management appreciation panels. The Committee established an *ad hoc* panel of specialists to discuss human resources development for the planning, management and implementation of science and technology programmes in developing countries.

Reports. [1]Advisory Committee, A/CN.11/30; [2]DIEC Director-General, transmitted by S-G note, A/CN.11/23; [3]S-G, A/CN.11/35.
Yearbook reference. [4]1981, p. 744.

Scientific and technological infrastructure

Activities in 1982 under programme area II— creation and strengthening of scientific and technological infrastructure—described by the Secretary-General in his report to the Intergovernmental Committee,[3] focused on: establishment of policy and planning machinery and of education and training institutions; assessment of science and technology functions of such institutions; intercountry facilities for these institutions in key development sectors; establishment of advanced national, regional and international research and development facilities; and assessment of the needs for standardization and quality control. They included a broad range of programmes carried out by specialized agencies and others. For example, the World Intellectual Property Organization assisted developing countries in adopting new or improving existing laws and in modernizing their industrial property institutions. The World Bank was preparing operational guidelines for strengthening countries' scientific and technological infrastructure.

UNFSSTD financed activities in Botswana, Djibouti, Guinea-Bissau, Mongolia and Sierra Leone, aimed at creating and strengthening scientific and technological infrastructure.

ICAO developed plans for the nine air navigation regions with a view to ensuring provision of air navigation facilities and services.

The International Fund for Agricultural Development (IFAD) extended technical assistance particularly for strengthening institutional capacities for the delivery of inputs, extension services, training, credit, marketing and development of social services. In addition to assistance in the establishment and management of health system infrastructures, WHO helped strengthen research institutions through training in research methodology and management.

UNESCO finalized a feasibility study on setting up an international institute for planning scientific and technological development, and supported the planning and development of educational and research institutions. Various UNESCO activities were related to its interregional research and training project leading to the integrated management of coastal systems.

In the area of training infrastructure, IMO launched a project for establishment of a World Maritime University to provide specialized training for maritime administrators, surveyors and inspectors, accident investigators and maritime lecturers of developing countries. The World Bank, with financing by UNDP, was developing training and research centres dealing with environmental management science and policy, while UNEP was establishing a network of high-level training institutions in environmental issues in Latin America and the Caribbean.

In the United Nations Secretariat, DTCD assisted in a UNFSSTD-funded project on strengthening national planning capabilities in science and technology. The Department of International Economic and Social Affairs (DIESA) organized a special expert group meeting on institutional arrangements for marine resources development to consider the integration of a country's marine potential into the national economy.

At the regional level, UNIDO assisted in the establishment of the Caribbean Technological Consultancy Service. UNCTAD co-operated with the Caribbean Community, the Economic Community of West African States and the Association of South-East Asian Nations in developing technology policies for pharmaceuticals and establishing institutional arrangements for implementing them. The ESCAP Regional Centre for Technology Transfer proceeded with the implementation of a UNFSSTD-financed regional project to assist member countries in strengthening their policy and institutional framework for science and technology.

Proposals of the Director-General. The DIEC Director-General, in his April 1982 report[2] to the Intergovernmental Committee on implementation of the operational plan of the Vienna Programme of Action, made proposals on scientific and technological infrastructure, in line with the areas of concentration established by the Committee. In view of the constraints facing developing countries in terms of human and financial resources, he proposed that regional and global research centres be established on a shared basis and existing research institutions be compared; possible approaches through the United Nations system could be considered in 1983 in order to demonstrate the feasibility of specific mechanisms by 1985. With regard to upgrading traditional technologies and promoting their dissemination, he suggested that in 1982 an *ad hoc* panel of specialists of the Advisory Committee on science and technology examine ways of applying emerging and traditional technologies in an integrated fashion, with the United Nations supporting national measures aimed at giving the informal sector access to services such as research and development, design and engineering, testing and quality control.

In order to popularize science and technology, the Director-General proposed the development of software for social communications and of delivery systems, such as the mass media, working-model museums, science fairs and mobile polytechnological clinics. In that connection, he suggested that the Advisory Committee's *ad hoc* panel on the role of regional organizations in strengthening research and development and in the popularization of science and technology examine those aspects in 1983, as a basis for the formulation in 1984-1985 of specific approaches. In order to assess the needs of Governments and to assist them in allocating resources for establishing or upgrading infrastructure, the Director-General suggested national reviews and feasibility studies, on a continuing basis and with United Nations support.

Noting that recent advances in technological areas, such as micro-electronics, material sciences and energy, had major implications for development strategies of developing countries, the Director-General proposed that the United Nations help provide access to research and training centres and assist in designing curricula and organizing courses. In addition, he suggested that the United Nations assist in training for use and maintenance of equipment and facilities and support regional harmonization of standards for metrology and quality control.

Advisory Committee consideration. Recommendations on infrastructure were also made by the Advisory Committee at its February 1982 session.[1] Among them was that each country have a policy-making body for science and technology, directly responsible to the political administration at the highest level. In this context, the Advisory Committee proposed a review, every five years, of the structure and operations of developing countries' science and technology policy-making bodies, including an assessment of the science and technology potential.

Concerning the popularization of science and technology, the Advisory Committee's suggestions were similar to those of the Director-General (see above). Because of the fundamental aspect of the subject, the Committee established an *ad hoc* panel of experts which was to meet in 1983.

Reports. [1]Advisory Committee, A/CN.11/30; [2]DIEC Director-General, transmitted by S-G note, A/CN.11/23; [3]S-G, A/CN.11/35.

Training of personnel

In his report to the Intergovernmental Committee on 1982 United Nations activities in science and technology,[3] the Secretary-General stated that in programme area IV—the development of human resources for science and technology—DTCD conducted research on management techniques and management training for scientific and technical personnel, and prepared a research/training project to improve management skills among senior scientific and technical personnel in public service.

The International Labour Organisation (ILO) proceeded with the preparation of guidelines for rural training at the grass-roots level and studied various methodologies for training and retraining workers in selected manufacturing and engineering industries to ensure successful technological innovation.

WHO continued to promote career policies and working conditions providing incentives to workers. It also assisted in the planning and management of manpower resources in order to improve training in health services.

Under the sponsorship of UNIDO, the First Consultation on the Training of Industrial Manpower was held at Stuttgart, Federal Republic of Germany, in November. In co-operation with the African Regional Centre for Technology and the Organization of African Unity, UNIDO published an inventory of technological manpower and institutions in Africa. During a conference of administrators of African institutions of higher learning (Addis Ababa, Ethiopia, January), the Economic Commission for Africa presented proposals for the establishment of pilot training and production workshops in various engineering disciplines in African least developed countries.

To update professional and technical skills, DIESA organized training in marine and coastal affairs to assist government agencies in marine and coastal development.

IMO assisted in the development of regional maritime training academies and the organization of seminars and symposia. ILO organized workshops on the training of engineers and technicians in labour-intensive technology for road construction and maintenance, as well as a regional seminar for senior African engineers (Gaborone, Botswana, March).

UNEP held training courses in pest management, malaria control, and air quality and water resource management, and organized regional training workshops on environmental management in the pulp and paper industry. Attention was given to the integration of the environmental dimension into education programmes, the development of curricula, and the preparation of textbooks and training activities focusing on environmental management.

Post-graduate education and training were provided by several United Nations organizations. The United Nations University continued to grant fellowships for advanced research-based training with the objective of strengthening the competence of the leadership in developing countries in building research institutions and organizing their own training programmes. In 1982, fellowships were granted under three subprogrammes: food, nutrition and poverty; resource policy and management; and energy systems and policy. The Food and Agriculture Organization of the United Nations (FAO) granted fellowships for advanced research in selected fields of food and agriculture of special interest to developing countries. The United Nations Children's Fund continued to provide fellowships and arranged exchange visits for plant-operating and maintenance staff in order to promote local manufacturing and processing of food and health-related products. Grants and loans by IFAD were directed towards projects for human and institutional development, such as training, agricultural extension, monitoring and evaluation and special studies. UNESCO provided support for the development of teaching materials and equipment for science and technology education as well as improvement of curricula and teaching methods.

UNFSSTD assisted in preparatory activities for the establishment of a research and training institute in Sri Lanka ($194,000), and financed a project for the upgrading of pre-university science training in Zambia ($794,000), jointly executed by the Government and UNESCO. It also financed the establishment in China of the Beijing Institute for Software Research and Training, executed by UNDP ($1,306,000), and the strengthening of the Magister Programme in Peru, executed by the Government ($97,000).

Under a joint project by the Economic Commission for Western Asia and UNFSSTD—a regional training programme for the development of technological capabilities in petroleum-based industries—an international team was engaged to supervise the preparation of case studies and substantive material for workshops. A workshop on technology and process design update in petrochemicals, fertilizers and oil and gas processing (October) and a symposium on plastic technologies and applications (December) were organized at Amman, Jordan.

Other United Nations activities dealt with women in scientific and technological development and the problem of reverse transfer of technology, known as the "brain drain".

Proposals of the Director-General. The DIEC Director-General, in his April report on implementation of the Vienna Programme of Action,[2] said that action for the development of human resources for science and technology should cover the whole population spectrum, from illiterate persons to high-level management experts and policy makers. He proposed that attention be directed towards non-formal education, particularly for artisans and peasants, through special training institutions; open universities and apprenticeship institutions for specialists; symposia and seminars on teaching methods, aids and curricula and textbook improvement, emphasizing the incorporation of data on new changes; and access for women to scientific, technological, managerial, and policy- and decision-making careers.

Implementation of most of those activities, the Director-General stated, would fall within the scope of Governments individually or collectively, with the United Nations and intergovernmental and non-governmental organizations providing expertise and assistance. He proposed that progress in strengthening human resources development for science and technology be assessed in 1985 to determine subsequent measures.

Advisory Committee consideration. The Advisory Committee on Science and Technology for Development, at its February 1982 session,[1] made suggestions similar to those of the DIEC Director-General. It identified the lack of adequately trained technicians as a major bottle-neck

in the application of science and technology to development. To address the problem and reverse the brain drain, the Committee proposed: utilizing available facilities for training technicians on a subregional or regional basis; adapting personnel policies at the institutional level to create greater incentives, including career advancement, status and financial rewards; and establishing arrangements between small institutes or universities and larger, better equipped institutions, for sharing or "borrowing" technicians.

For immediate action to strengthen science and technology education and training, the Advisory Committee proposed that the United Nations system increase support and fellowships for study abroad and augment support for study trips, and that developed countries help defray education costs in their institutions for students from developing countries.

With regard to extension services for knowledge transfer outside educational institutions, the Advisory Committee recommended that: the United Nations provide assistance in designing methods to ensure greater predictability and increase the opportunity for feedback; extension services be adapted to local needs and conditions; software development for the effective use of mass media receive priority; and national institutes of rural management be established.

Reports. [1]Advisory Committee, A/CN.11/30; [2]DIEC Director-General, transmitted by S-G note, A/CN.11/23; [3]S-G, A/CN.11/35.

Scientific and technological information

United Nations activities in 1982 under programme area VI—scientific and technological information were described by the Secretary-General in his report on science and technology activities.[3] They concentrated on the following: provision of access to bibliographical information sources and know-how information; establishment and management of national scientific and technological information capabilities; creation and strengthening of problem-oriented information and advisory services within the United Nations; national training programmes for information users; and establishment of a global network for scientific and technological information exchange.

UNESCO carried out preparations for regional pilot projects for specialized information systems in education, culture and communication, and the natural and social sciences, and executed a UNFSSTD-financed project in Kenya for a scientific and technological information and documentation service ($119,000).

Another UNESCO project, completed in 1982, was a world-wide inventory of information services on research in progress and an inventory of data sources in science and technology. UNESCO maintained an inventory of software packages in the information field and prepared lists of scientific journals. It initiated pilot projects on the use of small-scale computers and on numerical data services at the national level, made a study of telecommunication services for information transfer, and supported training courses on scientific and technological information.

UNIDO made efforts to identify data bases on appropriate technologies to add to over 150 accessible data bases at the Library of the Vienna International Centre. The World Meteorological Organization published a guide on the Global Data-processing System, a three-level system comprising world, regional and national meteorological centres connected by the Global Telecommunication System.

UNDP was developing an information referral system for collecting and disseminating information on capabilities of public and private organizations of developing countries with a view to promoting technical co-operation among themselves and national self-reliance.

Information activities in 1982 included environment issues. UNEP published a major study on the state of the global environment, reviewing progress in scientific and technological methods of environmental management. Its international referral system for sources of environmental information, with 117 countries participating in its network, continued to provide referral services to users. In the related field of hydrology and the water sciences, UNESCO began work on a world-wide system of information exchange.

In its third year of operation, the UNIDO Industrial and Technological Information Bank increased the sources of information. The United Nations Centre on Transnational Corporations continued to provide information services on policies, laws and regulations relating to foreign investment, as well as on the role of transnational corporations in developing countries. FAO and IFAD expanded their information systems. DIESA continued to compile references to sources of information in ocean economics and technology. UNFSSTD financed phase one of a project executed by the Government of Egypt for a national health information system ($50,000).

Proposals of the Director-General. The DIEC Director-General, in his April report to the Intergovernmental Committee,[2] included proposals on scientific and technological information. Emphasizing that the growing volume of information and its role as a decision-making tool underlined the importance of problem-oriented information and advisory services, he proposed that: United Nations organizations undertake a study on areas in developing countries where information services could be effective, and assist countries in the formulation of national information centres; assistance be provided to developing countries in establishing subregional and regional data bases on alternate technological options; and assistance and advisory services be provided to national information focal points.

Concerning establishment of a global network of scientific and technological information systems, the Director-General said it could facilitate use of problem-solving information resources, particularly for developing countries. Among preparatory activities to be financed within existing resources, he proposed that an analytical study be prepared on approaches to establishing such a network in the light of new technological advances; that expert meetings be convened for selecting information priority sectors; that feasibility studies be made on the establishment of a network in selected priority sectors; and that representatives of national, regional and international information centres meet to begin an experimental network. According to the Director-General, those activities could be carried out by 1985 through the participation of several national, intergovernmental and non-governmental bodies as well as United Nations organizations.

Advisory Committee consideration. At its February 1982 session,[1] the Advisory Committee on Science and Technology for Development also made recommendations on problem-oriented information and advisory services, as well as on the establishment of a global scientific and technological information network. With regard to the former, the Advisory Committee proposed preparation of manuals and teaching materials for information personnel and the scientific community in developing countries; assistance, including guidelines, to national information focal points in the establishment and strengthening of scientific and technological information centres; organization of training courses for information personnel and users; and a study of existing channels for dissemination of United Nations documents on scientific and technological issues, with a view to proposing mechanisms for wider distribution by governmental organizations, scientific and technical personnel, and private and public enterprises.

The Advisory Committee suggested proceeding with the creation of the global network through a consecutive sectoral approach (e.g. in the field of energy, followed by agro-industry, etc.). The information channelled through such a network could be enhanced if tailored to the specific needs of the users, including policy makers, planners, research and development professionals, engineers, manufacturers and entrepreneurs. As for specific proposals on establishing a network, the Committee's suggestions were similar to those of the Director-General.

Reports. (1)Advisory Committee, A/CN.11/30; (2)DIEC Director-General, transmitted by S-G note, A/CN.11/23; (3)S-G, A/CN.11/35.

Scientific research and development

Activities of United Nations organizations in 1982 to promote scientific and technological research and development in and for developing countries and their linkage to the productive system—programme area VII of the Vienna Programme of Action—were described by the Secretary-General in his annual report to the Intergovernmental Committee on implementation of the Programme.[4]

Among activities to help formulate and execute national research and development programmes was extensive research by the United Nations Centre on Transnational Corporations covering various aspects of scientific and technological trends and developments in selected sectors or on an intersectoral basis. To consider joint activities in the field, the Task Force on Science and Technology for Development of the Administrative Committee on Co-ordination, at its February 1982 session, established a working group.

FAO devoted increased effort to strengthening national capacities for planning and managing national research services. A workshop on research organization and allocation was held, as were several research management training workshops. To promote intercountry research co-operation, FAO organized a workshop to plan a series of multidisciplinary co-operative research networks along agro-ecological zones for selected countries and research institutions in Africa. IFAD continued to support activities of international agricultural research centres, and the International Labour Organisation (ILO) prepared working papers on the role of such centres, farmers' organizations, agricultural credit societies, extension agencies, machinery suppliers, consulting engineering organizations and information centres in the generation and diffusion of innovations.

The International Centre for Theoretical Physics (Trieste, Italy), jointly operated by the International Atomic Energy Agency (IAEA) and UNESCO, organized six workshops and courses in applied physics. The Centre, as well as the specialized laboratories of IAEA, continued to foster research and training for research in various disciplines of advanced science. The World Bank, UNDP and the World Health Organization (WHO) sponsored a programme in research and training in tropical diseases. UNFSSTD continued to execute with UNESCO a project to strengthen postgraduate training and research in the chemistry of natural products in Paraguay ($339,000).

With a view to strengthening linkages between research and the productive sector, the Centre for Human Settlements prepared a study on the contribution of the construction industry to national development goals. UNIDO prepared a book on the linkage between research and development systems and productive sectors of third world economies.

The Economic and Social Commission for Asia and the Pacific (ESCAP) conducted preparatory work for the organization of a joint venture with UNIDO—a symposium on contracts for the construction of oil and gas pipelines, scheduled for March 1983; it also produced a regional study on production of fuel ethanol from agro-products. About 10 per cent of the work programme of the Economic Commission for Europe related to scientific and technological research, concentrated on engineering, industries, agriculture, timber, energy and chemicals, with potential applications in developing countries. UNESCO continued work on regional programmes in Africa, the Arab States, and Latin America and the Caribbean, concerning research and development of technologies for water resources in rural areas. It also carried out the second round of an international comparative study on organization and performance of research units.

UNFSSTD gave assistance to a natural drug research centre in Bangladesh ($1,130,000), and approved assistance to a metallurgical institute in Bolivia ($111,000) and a mineral-processing project in Cuba ($59,000). It supported a project in Haiti to improve fish production through research and development executed by FAO ($289,000) and a project in Papua New Guinea on sago starch hydrolysis and fermentation ($76,744). It also approved the first phase of a project for establishing in Mozambique a laboratory to conduct research in metals, to be executed by UNIDO ($73,000).

Proposals of the Director-General. Specific proposals for strengthening research and development in and for developing countries were made by the DIEC Director-General.[2] He pointed out that most activities were within the scope of national action, and relevant international organizations could provide the means for exchange of knowledge and experience.

The Director-General proposed that United Nations organizations identify missing links between research and development and the production system, such as scaling up laboratory research through demonstration projects and pilot plants, and carrying out economic feasibility studies. Other proposals called for assistance in the design of a teaching method and the development of software for the use of mass media in extending relevant knowledge. He suggested the establishment of national institutes to extend management skills to rural professions, and of demonstration projects for model interactions between universities and enterprises.

To promote research and development activities and technological capabilities in the production sector, the Director-General suggested that: courses be developed at different levels for the training and organization of rotating and travelling seminars, and institutions in agriculture, industry and service sectors be established by 1986 and encouraged to develop special management training programmes related to science and technology. In addition, he proposed fellowships, study trips and workshops on research and development management.

Advisory Committee consideration. Recommendations on research and development were also made by the Advisory Committee on Science and Technology for Development.[1] Recognizing the severe constraints facing developing countries in terms of resources, the Committee stressed the value of sharing and creating regional networks. Proposed activities included: establishing an inventory of research institutions and a network of regional and global research centres in selected disciplines; and sharing of equipment, facilities and grants.

Noting that standardization, metrology and quality control were essential for purposes of external trade, protection of local consumers and the development of endogenous industries, the Committee suggested a number of activities, in co-operation with international governmental and non-governmental organizations.

In attempting to link research and development to the productive system, the Committee held it necessary to disseminate research information through demonstration projects and carry out economic feasibility studies to assess their potential commercial impact. It decided to convene an *ad hoc* panel of specialists on that subject in 1983. To encourage stronger links between university research and commercial enterprises, the Committee proposed that: assistance be provided to universities for the establishment of consultancy groups; senior and graduate students be encouraged to work in industry-related research; the United Nations assist Governments in making funds available to universities for demonstration projects, pilot plants and economic feasibility studies; and government planning include steps for promoting universities' involvement in developmental work.

Ad hoc **panel.** Noting a high potential for applying new scientific and technological techniques to the further development and upgrading of traditional technologies, the Advisory Committee, at its February 1982 session, established an *ad hoc* panel of specialists on the integrated application of emerging and traditional technologies for development. The panel met at Los Baños, Philippines, from 13 to 16 December.[3] To help achieve a beneficial blend of these technologies, the panel

recommended: that Governments establish an institutional mechanism to assess traditional technologies and monitor emerging ones; that United Nations bodies, regional and international non-governmental organizations, and public and private industries play a catalytic role in promoting the successful integration of traditional and new technologies; that every country identify a few areas for pioneer project initiation, in such fields as biotechnology, micro-electronics, space science, computer technology and materials science; and that a mechanism be established, using a network of existing institutions and United Nations agencies, for alerting Governments and policy makers, scientists and technologists about emerging scientific and technological developments.

Another *ad hoc* panel concerning the expansion of economic activities based on technological services and innovation was to be convened in 1983.

Reports. [1]Advisory Committee, A/CN.11/30; [2]DIEC Director-General, transmitted by S-G note, A/CN.11/23; [3]Panel of specialists, A/CN.11/AC.1/III/2; [4]S-G, A/CN.11/35.

International co-operation

United Nations activities in 1982 under programme area VIII of the Vienna Programme of Action—on strengthening international co-operation in science and technology—were described by the Secretary-General in his report to the Intergovernmental Committee.[3] They concentrated on the following areas: strengthening policy and institutional support; intercountry communication, through information sharing and exchange, seminars and meetings; co-operation of institutions and enterprises; co-operative arrangements; joint acquisition of technology; and promotional measures.

Several regional meetings were held. For example, UNIDO, under its System of Consultations, held meetings to mobilize co-operation among developing countries in the industrial sector, in particular on iron and steel, industrial financing and training of industrial manpower. A number of regional seminars on various scientific and technological subjects were sponsored by UNESCO and the United Nations Children's Fund.

Many United Nations programmes supported co-operation in specific sectors. UNIDO implemented a co-operative programme in the food-processing industry and made a proposal for a programme in small metalworking and light engineering plants. The United Nations Conference on Trade and Development (UNCTAD) followed up the recommendations of an October 1981 workshop on trade and technology policies in the pharmaceutical sector for French-speaking African countries,[4] with actions relating to the establishment of integrated and national pharmaceutical policies, the practice of bulk buying of pharmaceuticals at the subregional level, and the establishment of a fund for pharmaceuticals as well as a code on pharmaceuticals at the international level. WHO implemented an interregional project, financed by UNFSSTD ($90,000), entitled "Urban growth, employment and health: model of observed linkages in relation to development policy and planning". UNFSSTD also financed an interregional project on strengthening industrial and technological research institutes through linkages and other international co-operative arrangements ($60,000).

The United Nations Department of International Economic and Social Affairs undertook numerous co-operative programmes, jointly with international and regional organizations.

At the regional level, the Economic Commission for Latin America (ECLA) produced a study on the experiences of developing countries in exporting, consulting and engineering services to other developing countries. The Economic Commission for Africa (ECA) participated in discussions with the Organization of African Unity and UNIDO, reviewing proposals for the development of industrial and technological manpower in Africa. At an ECA/ECLA meeting of government experts (Addis Ababa, Ethiopia, June), attention was drawn to the need to formulate bilateral and multilateral plans within the context of the Vienna Programme of Action. Acting on the recommendations of the meeting, ECLA initiated interregional mining activities.

ESCAP implemented, in co-operation with UNIDO, a regional programme for developing industrial consultancy. The UNCTAD Advisory Service on Transfer of Technology continued to co-operate with various regional technology centres in strengthening linkages among them. A manual was completed by ILO on hand-operated animal-drawn farm equipment innovations, to facilitate exchange on technical information and research among African countries. In addition, ILO was preparing five country profiles and a regional overview of farm equipment innovations in Africa.

Proposals of the Director-General. Proposals to strengthen international co-operation, in line with the areas of concentration established by the Intergovernmental Committee and similar to the recommendations of the Advisory Committee, were made by the DIEC Director-General.[2] To promote effective communication and information exchange, he suggested that countries train specialists for analysis of scientific and technical data, using different networks of existing institutions under a common umbrella; assign scientific and technological personnel to embassies and missions; and diversify channels of intercountry communication through direct professional contacts in different sectors. United Nations organizations, acting with interested countries, could explore different means of strengthening co-operation through co-operative arrangements, joint acquisition of technology, promotion of joint ventures, legal and financial arrangements, strengthening the scope of national institutions, and commodity groups.

Joint ventures and scientific and technological co-operation between developing and developed countries should be expanded through global research and development projects to build up endogenous capacities; programmes of economic co-operation between the two groups of countries in specific commodity areas that included scientific and technological components; and exchange of staff and students at academic and research or industrial enterprises.

To enhance the transfer of technology among developing countries, the Director-General proposed: that assessment studies on programmes involving technical co-operation among developing countries be widely disseminated; that multilateral projects which benefited the least developed countries be launched; and that United Nations organizations, in co-operation with Governments, develop specific TCDC activities.

Advisory Committee consideration. At its February 1982 session,[1] the Advisory Committee on Science and Technology for Development described three perspectives with regard to strengthening co-operation: a regional approach, where common problems were jointly tackled; a problem-oriented approach, where countries could combine forces to address a common problem; and a non-governmental approach, where professionals from different countries could interact independently. Activities in those categories included training of specialists, research, and joint evaluation and analysis of data of common interest. In particular, the Committee recommended the use of different institutions in developing and developed countries under a common institutional umbrella. Sending scientific attachés to embassies and missions was another suggestion to promote co-operation. The Committee also recommended that an evaluation be made of co-operative projects within and outside the United Nations system, with particular attention to the least developed countries and their lack of infrastructure.

Reports. [1]Advisory Committee, A/CN.11/30; [2]DIEC Director-General, transmitted by S-G note, A/CN.11/23; [3]S-G, A/CN.11/35.
Yearbook reference. [4]1981, p. 597.

National focal points

Further efforts were made in 1982 to encourage the establishment of national focal points—originally set up to prepare for the 1979 United

Nations Conference on Science and Technology for Development—and to integrate them into the national system for science and technology, as called for by the operational plan for the implementation of the Vienna Programme of Action.

The United Nations Centre for Science and Technology for Development continued to interact regularly with the network of national focal points. At a meeting on the structures for science and technology policy formulation and implementation in Latin America and the Caribbean (Mexico City, 27-30 April), held under the Centre's auspices, a series of recommendations were adopted on the role of the focal points in implementing the Vienna Programme and its operational plan.[1]

The Intergovernmental Committee on Science and Technology for Development, by a resolution of 4 June,[2] took note with appreciation of the results of the Mexico City meeting and recommended that similar meetings be organized in other regions, in the framework of existing resources, to define the role of national focal points and other science and technology structures in the implementation of the Vienna Programme and their interaction with the Centre. The Committee requested the Centre to establish and maintain an up-to-date registry of all national focal points and to make it available to Member States as a document of the Committee.

In pursuance of that resolution, the Centre, with the co-operation of the Congo, organized a meeting on the strengthening of science and technology capacities of African countries (Brazzaville, 24-26 November), with special emphasis on the role of national focal points.

Report. [1]S-G, A/CN.11/40.
Resolution (1982). [2]Intergovernmental Committee (report, A/37/37): 2(IV), 4 June.

Assessment of levels of attainment

In a March 1982 report to the Intergovernmental Committee on Science and Technology for Development, the Director-General for Development and International Economic Co-operation summarized the activities of United Nations organizations—in particular the United Nations Educational, Scientific and Cultural Organization (UNESCO) and the regional commissions—in relation to the levels of attainment of scientific and technological development among different countries.[1] The report, prepared in accordance with a June 1981 request by the Committee,[3] included brief descriptions of the programmes concerning statistical information on scientific and technological activities (such as research and experimental development, scientific and technical education and training, and scientific and technological services), and science and technology indicators.

The collection, analysis and dissemination of statistical information were regularly carried out by many United Nations bodies. The statistics programme of the Department of International Economic and Social Affairs covered a range of topics wide enough to allow comparative analysis of essential aspects of economic and social development. It included data on economic performance and productivity, relative level of economic development, structure of economy, output of major industries, agriculture and transportation, growth and structure of external trade, and development of resources. The economic statistics were supplemented by data needed for the analysis of social progress, such as growth and structure of population, employment, distribution of income, housing, and medical and cultural services.

The regional commissions carried out statistical activities in co-operation with the United Nations Statistical Office, specialized agencies and other national and regional organizations. They were primarily concerned with economic, social, demographic, trade and financial information. For 17 years, UNESCO had organized the collection, analysis, publication and standardization of data on science and technology, especially on research and development. A data base covering 80 countries had been built up, which was included in the statistical yearbooks of UNESCO and the United Nations, and the methodology used in the surveys had been progressively developed.

The report also described the work achieved in developing science and technology indicators, which was related to the intended assessment of changes or progress in achievement of specific goals through statistical information. UNESCO and the Organisation for Economic Co-operation and Development were working on such indicators.

Sufficient progress had been made in the international standardization of statistics on science and technology, the Director-General noted, but it was necessary to increase national capabilities, particularly in the developing countries, for the collection and communication of such statistics by training personnel as well as incorporating in national systems the standard practices relating to science and technology statistics. The expertise of UNESCO would be valuable in that process. The development of science and technology indicators would require more careful examination, particularly in the context of measurement of levels of attainment of scientific and technological development in developing countries. In the mean time, "input" indicators relating to research and development could be useful for the measurement of selected science and technology activities. In this context, the Director-General recommended that the Centre for Science and Technology for Development, in co-operation with UNESCO, the United Nations Statistical Office and other United Nations organizations, promote the development of suitable indicators, with special reference to the measurement of the levels of attainment of scientific and technological capability within the context of the goals and objectives of the Vienna Programme of Action.

The Intergovernmental Committee, by a resolution of 4 June,[2] took note with appreciation of the report and decided to consider it further in 1983.

Report. [1]DIEC Director-General, transmitted by S-G note, A/CN.11/25.
Resolution (1982). [2]Intergovernmental Committee (report, A/37/37): 3(IV), sect. V, 4 June.
Yearbook reference. [3]1981, p. 744.

Proposed amendments to the Programme

Intergovernmental Committee action. The Intergovernmental Committee on science and technology, by a decision of 4 June 1982,[2] deferred the agenda item "Action to be taken on issues left unresolved by the United Nations Conference on Science and Technology for Development" to its 1983 session for consideration by an in-sessional working group, and requested the Secretary-General to bring up to date his report on the state of negotiations in other United Nations forums on issues left unresolved by the Conference.

The unresolved issues included aspects of technology transfer, and scientific and technological information systems and co-operation.

Other action. After reviewing information on unresolved issues related to activities of the United Nations Conference on Trade and Development (UNCTAD), the UNCTAD Committee on Transfer of Technology, on 10 December 1982, requested the UNCTAD Secretary-General to submit such information to the 1983 session of the Intergovernmental Committee.[1]

Decisions (1982). [1]Committee on Transfer of Technology (report, TD/B/936): 22(IV), 10 Dec. [2]Intergovernmental Committee (report, A/37/37): 1(IV), 4 June.

Financing

Methods for financing science and technology for development, at the national, regional and international levels, were described under programme area V of the operational plan for implementation of the Vienna Programme of Action, approved in June 1981 by the Intergovernmental Committee on Science and Technology for Development.[1]

A central role in financing was assigned to the United Nations Financing System for Science and Technology for Development, which became oper-

ative on 1 January 1982, replacing the United Nations Interim Fund for Science and Technology for Development. Financing was also provided by other United Nations agencies.

Suggestions for national and regional financing were made by the Advisory Committee on Science and Technology for Development.

Yearbook reference. [1]1981, p. 734.

UN Financing System

As of 1 January 1982, the United Nations Financing System for Science and Technology for Development (UNFSSTD) became operative, as decided by the General Assembly in December 1981.[10] The System, designed to help developing countries strengthen their scientific and technological capacities, was originally proposed in the 1979 Vienna Programme of Action.

In December 1982, the Assembly established the financial, institutional and organizational arrangements for the System,[7] deciding that it be organized on a voluntary and universal basis with a 1983-1985 target of $300 million in core resources and an equivalent amount in non-core resources. The Intergovernmental Committee on science and technology was to continue as the directing and policy-making body, and an Executive Board was to be responsible for the operation and conduct of UNFSSTD, including financial planning and approval of projects. The secretariat of UNFSSTD was to be under the overall supervision of the Administrator of the United Nations Development Programme (UNDP), who would report to the Executive Board on its activities. He would also report, in consultation with the Director-General for Development and International Economic Co-operation (DIEC), to the Intergovernmental Committee on the activities and progress of UNFSSTD.

UNFSSTD integrated its activities administratively and operationally within the United Nations machinery for development co-operation and used, under co-operative arrangements, UNDP administrative and support services in appraising, evaluating and implementing projects. In accordance with defined procedures, UNFSSTD relied on technical comments by United Nations agencies, the Centre for Science and Technology for Development, UNDP bureaux and independent consultants. The Administrator was to report annually to the UNDP Governing Council on co-operation between UNDP and UNFSSTD and on other matters of mutual interest.

Despite financial constraints, UNFSSTD was able to respond, through the co-operation of UNDP and other United Nations entities, to requests of developing countries for aid in scientific and technological projects.

The resources generated during the interim period (1980-1981) amounted to about $35 million.

At a Pledging Conference for UNFSSTD, held in March 1982, 13 countries pledged $4.5 million for 1982, while 22 others stated they would announce pledges at a later date. Cumulative pledges for 1980-1982 totalled $39.5 million.

The UNDP Administrator, under his authority as head of the Interim Fund, had approved 65 projects, from over 900 project proposals from Governments, with an average cost of about $500,000. In 1982, he approved an additional 18 projects which, in view of financial constraints, were mainly smaller than original project requests. Discussions continued with potential donors to establish co-financing arrangements for some 40 projects, which had been fully developed and were awaiting financing. At the end of 1982, there were 83 projects amounting to $37.9 million under implementation, of which nearly half were executed by Governments themselves.

The Administrator, in consultation with the DIEC Director-General, submitted in May 1982 to the Intergovernmental Committee a report[6] describing operations of the Interim Fund, established in 1979,[9] from its inception in May 1980 up to its termination on 31 December 1981, and of UNFSSTD from the point it became operational on 1 January 1982. Upon termination of the Interim Fund, its resources, organization, management and procedures were transferred to UNFSSTD.

The report included examples of the 65 ongoing projects in Africa, the Arab States, Asia and the Pacific, and Latin America and the Caribbean. Among those activities was a project aimed at improving the living conditions of 60,000 Somali nomads in settlement schemes through technology programmes in housing, water supply and agriculture. A project in Jordan would result in the development of improved techniques for low-cost and self-help housing using specially designed and locally manufactured production methods. A national remote sensing system project in China would train 200 technicians, establish a research programme and set up a central repository for remote sensing data. A project in Brazil was to result in production of carbon fibre material from local raw materials for use in advanced industrial production, such as the aircraft industry, with the general purpose of saving energy and expanding research.

Reporting to the Governing Council on 1982 operations of UNFSSTD,[5] the Administrator noted that the System had been able to establish the managerial and operational machinery necessary for its work. It had developed a specialized body of technical knowledge, a network of contacts with scientific and financial institutions, and a set of operational procedures.

Activities of the *Ad Hoc* Group. Recommendations on the institutional, organizational and financial arrangements for UNFSSTD were prepared by the *Ad Hoc* Intergovernmental Group on the United Nations Financing System for Science and Technology for Development, in accordance with a General Assembly decision of December 1981.[10] The Group held its first session in New York from 1 to 5 March 1982, and a second session from 12 to 20 April, which was resumed from 24 to 26 May. At these sessions, the Group held six formal meetings, but conducted most of its work in informal consultations.

In order to assist consultations, the Chairman prepared two informal papers, dated 15 April and 20 May, which were annexed to the Group's report to the Intergovernmental Committee.[3]

Intergovernmental Committee action. By a resolution of 4 June 1982,[8] the Intergovernmental Committee took note with appreciation of the report of the UNDP Administrator on the operations of the Interim Fund and UNFSSTD and of the report of the *Ad Hoc* Intergovernmental Group. It requested that the Group's report and the comments thereon be taken as a basis for further negotiations. The Committee noted with deep concern the insufficient pledges announced at the March Pledging Conference and urged that consultations be intensified, taking into account the increasing needs of the developing countries.

At the resumed fourth session of the Intergovernmental Committee (8-10 September), the Chairman reported that he had conducted informal consultations in July and September on institutional and financial issues relating to UNFSSTD. In a statement on the progress made, incorporated by the Committee in its 1982 report to the General Assembly,[4] the Chairman noted that there was convergence of views on the following financial issues: UNFSSTD should be endowed with core and non-core resources, core resources (the basis of the System) to be derived from government contributions in freely convertible currencies; there would be an overall global target for 1983-1985, with a target in core resources of $100 million for 1983; and the level of resources would be reviewed periodically, with the first review in 1985. It was the understanding of the Chairman that further discussion was needed on contributions and non-core resources.

The Chairman noted that, during the informal consultations, a group of Eastern European countries had reiterated their view that UNFSSTD should operate on the principle of unqualified voluntariness with regard to the participation of countriesand to the extent and nature of their contributions. They also did not agree to the division of the System's finances into core and non-core components, and were of the view that the existing United Nations institutions should be fully utilized.

Concerning institutional issues, discussion focused on the System's secretariat as a separate entity, and a paper on that proposition was submitted, providing what the Chairman suggested was a viable basis for further negotiations. Under that proposal, the Committee would be the directing and policy-making body of UNFSSTD, while a new executive body would be established for its operation and conduct, a function currently assigned to the UNDP Governing Council. Overall supervision of the System's management would be entrusted to the UNDP Administrator who would be accountable, in that function, to the executive body. The UNDP Governing Council would deal mainly with co-operative arrangements between UNFSSTD and UNDP.

CPC and ACC consideration. At Joint Meetings at Geneva on 6 and 7 July, the Committee for Programme and Co-ordination (CPC) and the Administrative Committee on Co-ordination (ACC) discussed how the United Nations system could respond in a more efficient and appropriate manner to economic and social problems. As stated in the Chairmen's report to the Economic and Social Council,[2] members of both committees expressed the hope that the consultations which were to take place during the July session of the Council would lead to agreement and would result in the establishment by the General Assembly in 1982 of long-term arrangements for a mature financing system for science and technology.

The Council took note of the report in a decision of 28 July.[1]

General Assembly action. By a resolution of 21 December 1982,[7] the General Assembly established long-term financial and institutional arrangements for UNFSSTD, open to all States and endowed with core and non-core resources to dispense grants and loans. Core contributions would be voluntary within the framework of a three-year financing plan. Non-core resources would include co-financing, multilateral and bilateral contributions, cost-sharing, joint ventures, equity participation and trust funds. UNFSSTD would aim to establish an equivalence between core and non-core resources in order to obtain $600 million for 1983-1985. Its institutional arrangements would consist of the Intergovernmental Committee, serving as the directing and policy-making body, a 21-member Executive Board and a secretariat. Responsible for the System's operation and conduct, the Board would mobilize resources, approve projects, decide on financial planning, recommend levels of resources, and approve administrative and financial arrangements. The secretariat would be supervised by the UNDP

Administrator, who would be accountable in that responsibility to the Board. Co-ordination with other United Nations bodies would be the responsibility of the DIEC Director-General. The Assembly decided that the Intergovernmental Committee would meet in special session in February or March 1983 to assess the resource situation of UNFSSTD for 1983, together with the outlook for the following two years.

The Assembly adopted the resolution by a recorded vote of 137 to none, with 9 abstentions, following its approval on 20 December by the Second (Economic and Financial) Committee by a recorded vote of 108 to none, with 9 abstentions. The draft resolution was originally submitted by a Committee Vice-Chairman, who orally revised it by specifying the number of Executive Board members. In the light of a request by the USSR for a vote on the draft, as orally revised, the Vice-Chairman withdrew the text, which was reintroduced by Austria, also on behalf of Egypt, Guinea, Jordan, Morocco, Sierra Leone, Sweden and Tunisia.

Decision (1982). [1]ESC: 1982/166, para. *(a)*, 28 July.
Reports. [2]CPC and ACC Chairmen, E/1982/84; [3]Group on financing system, A/CN.11/27; [4]Intergovernmental Committee, A/37/37; [5]UNDP Administrator, DP/1983/36; [6]UNDP Administrator, in consultation with DIEC Director-General, A/CN.11/28.
Resolutions (1982). [7]GA: 37/244, 21 Dec., text following. [8]Intergovernmental Committee: 3(IV), sect. III, 4 June.
Resolutions (prior). GA: [9]34/218, 19 Dec. 1979 (YUN 1979, p. 644); [10]36/183, 17 Dec. 1981 (YUN 1981, p. 740).
Meeting records. GA: 2nd Committee, A/C.2/37/SR.3, 6, 7, 10, 13-19, *51* (28 Sep.-20 Dec.); plenary, A/37/PV.115 (21 Dec.).

General Assembly resolution 37/244

21 December 1982   Meeting 115   137-0-9 (recorded vote)

Approved by Second Committee (A/37/680/Add.4) by recorded vote (108-0-9), 20 December (meeting 51); 8-nation draft (A/C.2/37/L.128), orally amended by Vice-Chairman; agenda item 71 *(e)*.
Sponsors: Austria, Egypt, Guinea, Jordan, Morocco, Sierra Leone, Sweden, Tunisia.

Long-term financial and institutional arrangements for the United Nations Financing System for Science and Technology for Development

The General Assembly,

Recalling its resolution 34/218 of 19 December 1979 by which it endorsed the Vienna Programme of Action on Science and Technology for Development,

Recalling also resolution 36/183 of 17 December 1981 in which the General Assembly, in considering the long-term arrangements for the United Nations Financing System for Science and Technology for Development, requested the Intergovernmental Committee on Science and Technology for Development to submit its recommendations, through the Economic and Social Council, to the General Assembly at its thirty-seventh session for consideration and decision,

Taking note of the report of the Intergovernmental Committee on its fourth session, in particular of paragraph 7 on institutional and financial arrangements, and of the statement of understanding of the Chairman incorporated therein,

1. *Decides* that, in accordance with its resolution 36/183, the long-term financial and institutional arrangements for the United Nations Financing System for Science and Technology for Development shall be as follows:

Long-term financial and institutional arrangements
for the United Nations Financing System for
Science and Technology for Development

I. Financial arrangements
1. The United Nations Financing System for Science and Technology for Development shall be organized on a voluntary and universal basis, open to the participation of all States as full members.
2. The Financing System shall be endowed with substantial resources and shall be composed of two types of resources: core and non-core.
3. Contributions to the core component of the Financing System shall be voluntary within the framework of a financing plan, covering a period of three years at a time.
4. The target for core resources for the period 1983-1985 shall be at least $300 million based on a progressive build-up of resources.
5. The core resources of the Financing System for the period 1983-1985 shall be provided by developed and developing countries in freely convertible currencies.
6. Developed countries and developing countries shall contribute to the core resources of the Financing System. The pattern of contributions of both developed and developing countries will be determined in the financing plan, which will reflect a mutual and joint undertaking.
7. Non-core resources will represent an important element of the Financing System and shall consist of a variety of resources, including co-financing, multilateral and bilateral contributions, cost-sharing, joint ventures, equity participation, trust funds and the like. The Intergovernmental Committee on Science and Technology for Development will evolve policy orientations for the mobilization and use of the non-core resources.
8. The Financing System shall aim to establish a reasonable equivalence between the levels of its core and non-core resources in order to ensure an overall global target for the Financing System of not less than $600 million for 1983-1985.
9. The Financing System shall dispense both grants and loans, which shall be provided on such terms as the Financing System deems appropriate in the light of the economic situation, the prospects of the recipient country and the nature and requirements of the activity concerned. Combinations of loans and grants may also be made where appropriate. The proportion of the resources of the Financing System to be committed in any financial year for financing operations shall be decided by the Executive Board of the United Nations Financing System for Science and Technology for Development with due regard to the long-term viability of the Financing System and the need for continuity in its operations. Loans will be provided on concessionary terms. Grants should be extended mainly to the least developed countries and for the support of a number of high-risk research and development projects in developing countries. The secretariat of the Financing System shall submit projects and programmes to the Executive Board for consideration and approval.
II. Institutional arrangements
10. The institutional arrangements of the Financing System shall consist of the Intergovernmental Committee on Science anad Technology for Development, the Executive Board of the United Nations Financing System for Science and Technology for Development and a secretariat.
A. *Intergovernmental Committee on Science and Technology for Development*
11. The Intergovernmental Committee on Science and Technology for Development shall continue to be the directing and policy-making body. Its principal functions shall be the following:
(a) General policy orientation of, and direction for, the Financing System;
(b) Decisions on policy proposals, including recommendations on levels of resources;
(c) General review and evaluation of the activities of the Financing System;
(d) Election of members to the Executive Board in accordance with the criteria stated in paragraph 13 below;
(e) Consideration of reports of the Executive Board.
B. *Executive Board of the United Nations Financing System for Science and Technology for Development*
12. The Financing System shall have its own Executive Board as an identifiable and separate entity, to be responsible for its operation and conduct. The functions of the Executive Board shall include:

(a) Mobilization of resources;
(b) Utilization of the resources of the Financing System, particularly approval of projects, programmes and activities of the System;
(c) Formulation of recommendations on levels of resources of the Financing System;
(d) Decisions on financial planning;
(e) Approval of administrative and financial arrangements involving the Financing System;
(f) Monitoring of the operations of the System in relation to its objectives.
13. The Executive Board shall be an effective body and its composition shall reflect an appropriate balance between developed and developing countries as well as between donors and recipients. It shall be composed of 21 directors, to be elected by the Intergovernmental Committee on Science and Technology for Development for a period of three years, one third to be drawn from developed countries and two thirds from developing countries reflecting an appropriate balance between donors and recipients.
C. *Secretariat arrangements*
14. The Financing System will have its own secretariat to process and monitor projects and to carry out other activities mandated by the Intergovernmental Committee on Science and Technology for Development and the General Assembly. The arrangements shall be as follows:
(a) The overall supervision of the management of the Financing System shall be entrusted to the Administrator of the United Nations Development Programme, who shall be accountable in the exercise of this responsibility to the Executive Board of the United Nations Financing System for Science and Technology for Development;
(b) The Administrator will report to the Executive Board on the operations and activities of the Financing System and bring forward projects for approval by the Executive Board;
(c) In order to ensure close and continuous interaction between the Centre for Science and Technology for Development and the Financing System, the Director-General for Development and International Economic Co-operation or his representative will be invited on a permanent basis to meetings of the Executive Board;
(d) The Director-General for Development and International Economic Co-operation, assisted by the Executive Director of the Centre for Science and Technology for Development, will submit an annual report to the Executive Board on, *inter alia*, matters of mutual concern to the Centre and the Financing System;
(e) The Director-General, in respect of both his responsibility for overall co-ordination of operational activities in the United Nations system and his oversight of the Centre, shall be entrusted by the General Assembly and by agreement with the Administrative Committee on Co-ordination with the co-ordination with other organizations and bodies of the United Nations system, including the United Nations Development Programme and the Centre for Science and Technology for Development, of the work relating to the Financing System. Such co-ordination activities shall be carried out through the existing mechanisms of the Administrative Committee on Co-ordination, particularly the Task Force on Science and Technology for Development;
(f) The Centre for Science and Technology for Development shall assist the Director-General in fulfilling the responsibilities assigned to him in the Vienna Programme of Action on Science and Technology for Development, particularly in providing the necessary substantive support to the Intergovernmental Committee, including its work relating to the Financing System;
(g) In view of the expectations of continued use of the services and field network of the United Nations Development Programme, the focus of the Governing Council of the Programme will in future be mainly on the co-operative arrangements between the Financing System and the Programme. Accordingly, the Administrator of the Programme will provide an annual report to the Governing Council containing information on co-operation between the two organizations and on other matters of common interest;
(h) The Administrator, in consultation with the Director-General, will report annually to the Intergovernmental Committee on the activities and progress of the Financing System;
(i) The Centre for Science and Technology for Development will play a meaningful role and, in line with its mandate and role, will, through appropriate arrangements and when required, co-operate with the secretariat of the Financing System in preparing, formulating and bringing to the attention of the Financing System suitable projects and

in appraising, evaluating and assessing projects financed by the Financing System in the context of the Vienna Programme of Action;

(j) There will be arrangements for exchange of detailed information between the Financing System and the United Nations Development Programme, especially where a common interest exists in specific programmes and projects. This collaboration may extend to co-financing arrangements as well as to technical areas in order to enable the two organizations to draw upon each other's special skills and experience;

(k) The co-operation of the secretariat of the Financing System will be sought by the Centre for Science and Technology for Development in elaborating the relevant major programme areas of the Operational Plan for the Implementation of the Vienna Programme of Action and in supporting the Intergovernmental Committee in the promotion of the optimum mobilization of financial resources to carry out the Vienna Programme of Action;

(l) The secretariat will be small, reflecting its use of the facilities of other organizations according to agreed procedures; its administrative and support costs will continue to be met from voluntary contributions;

(m) The secretariat, under the overall supervision of the Administrator, will have an executive head;

(n) The executive head of the secretariat will be appointed by the Secretary-General on the recommendation of the Director-General for Development and International Economic Co-operation and the Administrator of the United Nations Development Programme;

(o) The executive head will be responsible for the day-to-day management of the Financing System and for such other activities as may be necessary to ensure effective operations of the System for both core and non-core resource activities; the secretariat of the System will provide secretariat support to the Executive Board;

(p) Arrangements will be established with the United Nations Development Programme for the provision of administrative services; the nature and terms of such arrangements will be reviewed and evaluated as the operations of the Financing System expand;

(q) Reports to appropriate secretariat and intergovernmental bodies on financial audit and accounting matters will continue to be provided in accordance with United Nations and United Nations Development Programme procedures and requirements;

15. The required level of resources and functioning of the Financing System shall be reviewed periodically, taking into account the increasing needs of developing countries. The first of such reviews will be held in 1985.

2. *Also decides* that the foregoing agreement on the long-term financial and institutional arrangements for the Financing System shall take effect as soon as the provisions of the financing plan have been established together with institutional arrangements for decision-making of the Executive Board, in accordance with paragraph 3 below; in the mean time, the existing operating procedures of the System shall continue;

3. *Further decides* that the following special arrangements will be necessary in early 1983:

(a) The Intergovernmental Committee on Science and Technology for Development will meet in special session for a period of one week in February or March 1983 for the purpose of:

(i) Assessment of the resource situation for the Financing System for the year 1983 together with the outlook for the two following years;

(ii) Establishment of the provisions of the financing plan and, in this context, rules for the voting pattern of the Executive Board;

(iii) Confirmation (final pledges) of contributions for 1983 and, if possible, indications for 1984 and 1985;

(b) At its fifth session in June 1983, the Intergovernmental Committee on Science and Technology for Development will, *inter alia*, proceed to elect members to the Executive Board of the United Nations Financing System for Science and Technology for Development.

Recorded vote in Assembly as follows:

In favour: Afghanistan, Algeria, Angola, Argentina, Australia, Austria, Bahamas, Bahrain, Bangladesh, Barbados, Belgium, Benin, Bhutan, Bolivia, Betswana, Brazil, Burma, Burundi, Canada, Cape Verde, Central African Republic, Chad, Chile, China, Colombia, Comoros, Congo, Costa Rica, Cuba, Cyprus, Democratic Kampuchea, Democratic Yemen, Denmark, Djibouti, Dominican Republic, Ecuador, Egypt, El Salvador, Ethiopia, Fiji, Finland, France, Gabon, Gambia, Germany, Federal Republic of, Ghana, Greece, Grenada, Guinea, Guinea-Bissau, Guyana, Honduras, Iceland, India, Indonesia, Iran, Iraq, Ireland, Israel, Italy, Ivory Coast, Jamaica, Japan, Jordan, Kenya, Kuwait, Lao People's Democratic Republic, Lebanon, Lesotho, Liberia, Libyan Arab Jamahiriya, Luxembourg, Madagascar, Malawi, Malaysia, Maldives, Mali, Malta, Mauritania, Mauritius, Mexico, Morocco, Mozambique, Nepal, Netherlands, New Zealand, Nicaragua, Niger, Nigeria, Norway, Oman, Pakistan, Panama, Papua New Guinea, Paraguay, Peru, Philippines, Portugal, Qatar, Romania, Rwanda, Saint Lucia, Samoa, Sao Tome and Principe, Saudi Arabia, Senegal, Sierra Leone, Singapore, Solomon Islands, Somalia, Spain, Sri Lanka, Sudan, Suriname, Swaziland, Sweden, Syrian Arab Republic, Thailand, Togo, Trinidad and Tobago, Tunisia, Turkey, Uganda, United Arab Emirates, United Kingdom, United Republic of Cameroon, United Republic of Tanzania, Upper Volta, Uruguay, Vanuatu, Venezuela, Viet Nam, Yemen, Yugoslavia, Zaire, Zambia, Zimbabwe.

Against: None.

Abstaining: Bulgaria, Byelorussian SSR, Czechoslovakia, German Democratic Republic, Hungary, Poland, Ukrainian SSR, USSR, United States.

Contributions and expenditures

A Pledging Conference for the United Nations Financing System for Science and Technology for Development was held at United Nations Headquarters on 30 March 1982. The Secretary-General, having convened the Conference in accordance with a December 1981 request of the General Assembly,[3] invited all States to participate and to announce their contributions for 1982. During the year, 28 countries contributed a total of $8,034,416, and 17 countries pledged $281,153 for 1983. Expenditures in 1982 of UNFSSTD on projects in 48 countries, as well as several regions, totalled $10,537,000.

The Intergovernmental Committee on Science and Technology for Development, in a resolution of 4 June,[2] noted with deep concern the insufficient pledges announced during the Conference.

In its resolution of 21 December on financial and institutional arrangements for UNFSSTD, the Assembly established a financial plan for voluntary contributions to UNFSSTD by Governments, known as core resources, with a target of $300 million for 1983-1985.[1]

Resolutions (1982). [1]GA: 37/244, sect. I, paras. 3-6, 21 Dec. [2]Intergovernmental Committee (report, A/37/37): 3(IV), sect. III, para. 2, 4 June.
Resolution (prior). [3]GA: 36/183, 17 Dec. 1981 (YUN 1981, p. 740).
Meeting record. Pledging Conference: A/CONF.112/SR.1 (30 Mar.).

Other aspects of science and technology financing

UN activities

The Secretary-General, in a report issued in April 1983,[1] described 1982 United Nations activities for financing science and technology for development.

The United Nations Conference on Trade and Development convened the Second Meeting of Multilateral and Bilateral Financial and Technical Assistance Institutions with Representatives of the Least Developed Countries (LDCs) in October. The purpose of the Meeting was to review and assess requirements and progress of LDCs and the problems arising in the co-ordination and implementation of assistance programmes on both

CONTRIBUTIONS TO THE UN FINANCING SYSTEM FOR SCIENCE AND
TECHNOLOGY FOR DEVELOPMENT, 1982 AND 1983
(as at 31 December 1982; in US dollar equivalent)

Country	1982 payment	1983 pledge
Australia	1,060,900	—
Austria	960,452	—
Bangladesh	2,000	2,000
Belgium	77,348	—
Bhutan	—	1,200
Congo	—	2,915
Cuba	—	32,506
Denmark	696,203	—
Egypt	12,170	12,170
Fiji	1,000	1,000
Finland	888,889	—
France	147,059	—
Guyana	2,684	—
Honduras	2,000	2,000
India	200,000	100,000
Indonesia	12,000	12,000
Jordan	17,000	—
Lao People's Democratic Republic	1,000	—
Lesotho	—	500
Madagascar	6,667	—·
Malawi	1,000	879
Morocco	5,000	—
Netherlands	2,737,555	—
Panama	—	2,000
Philippines	10,000	10,000
Seychelles	500	—
Singapore	1,000	—
Sri Lanka	10,000	15,000
Sweden	1,000,000	—
Thailand	75,000	25,000
Tunisia	50,000	—
United Republic of Cameroon	3,341	—
Zambia	53,648	54,171
Zimbabwe	—	7,812
Total	**8,034,416**	**281,153**

SOURCE: A/38/5/Add.1.

EXPENDITURES OF THE UN FINANCING SYSTEM FOR SCIENCE AND
TECHNOLOGY FOR DEVELOPMENT BY COUNTRY OR AREA, 1982
(as at 31 December 1982; in thousands of US dollars)

Country/area	Amount
Bangladesh	(3)
Botswana	24
Brazil	406
Burundi	41
China	946
Costa Rica	203
Democratic Yemen	4
Djibouti	15
Dominican Republic	239
Egypt	47
Ethiopia	234
Fiji	71
Gambia	7
Guinea	164
Guinea-Bissau	2
Haiti	115
Honduras	64
India	155
Indonesia	188
Ivory Coast	42
Jamaica	368
Jordan	553
Kenya	268
Lao People's Democratic Republic	144
Lesotho	79
Madagascar	11
Malawi	157
Mauritius	163
Mexico	22
Nepal	14
Nigeria	414
Pakistan	1,117
Panama	(1)
Papua New Guinea	37
Paraguay	157

Country/area (cont.)	Amount
Philippines	355
Republic of Korea	237
Senegal	7
Seychelles	17
Sri Lanka	18
Sudan	233
Swaziland	178
Thailand	120
Tunisia	533
United Republic of Tanzania	172
Uruguay	72
Yemen	2
Zambia	1
Subtotal	**8,412**
Regional Africa	128
Regional Latin America and the Caribbean	387
Regional Arab States	370
Regional Asia and the Pacific	622
Interregional	631
Global	(13)
Subtotal	**2,125**
Total	**10,537**

NOTE: Figures in parentheses are negative amounts representing adjustments
from prior years' expenditures.

SOURCE: DP/1983/6/Add.4/Corr.1.

the donor and recipient sides, with the aim of
agreeing on specific proposals for a more rapid increase in the growth and welfare of LDCs.

The operational plan for implementation of the
Vienna Programme of Action called on the United
Nations to support governmental action in financing
science and technology for development; however,
information made available by United Nations organizations revealed that activities in that area did
not exist above a minimum level. The Secretary-
General's report noted that activities in programme
area V, financing of science and technology for development, overlapped with those in programme
area I, science and technology policy, and that in
assisting in the formulation of such policy, policies
on financing would also be dealt with.

In a resolution of 4 June,[2] the Intergovernmental
Committee on Science and Technology for Development requested the Centre for Science and Technology for Development, in drawing up reports for
consideration by the Committee, to take into account the need for an updated assessment of the
financing of science and technology in the United
Nations system, an assessment which should indicate the distribution of resources between the different areas of the operational plan and between the
principal fields of application of science and technology to economic and social development.

Report. [1]S-G, A/CN.11/35.
Resolution (1982). [2]Intergovernmental Committee (report,
A/37/37): 1(IV), para. 6, 4 June.

National and regional financing

The Advisory Committee on Science and Technology for Development, in the report on its February
1982 session,[1] made suggestions on national targets
for scientific and technological financing, as pro-

posed in the operational plan.[2] Re-emphasizing the importance of setting quantitative targets for public and private expenditures, the Committee stated that, while 1 per cent of gross national product for the allocation of resources to science and technology might not necessarily be the most suitable level of funding for a particular developing country, it should be retained unless and until some other tangible indicator became available.

Whatever the level of funding, the Committee felt that it was useful to establish a "distribution profile" to serve as a guideline for analysing alternate allocations of funds among different areas; for example, a breakdown into three categories of technical work (basic research, applied research, and technology) and national objectives (pursuing social goals and industrial development, training scientific and engineering personnel, and discovering new knowledge) could be helpful in framing priorities for funding. The Committee also stressed that well-directed research would more than pay for its costs by increasing productivity; therefore, it recommended that Governments create a separate budget for research and development.

Conditions among developing countries, and between developing and developed countries, varied too widely for uniform approaches to financing to be successful, but the Committee recommended that successful approaches be publicized, so that Governments could benefit from them. In addition, the Committee proposed that direct incentives be given to public authorities at decentralized local levels or to firms, and that host countries consider obtaining assistance from transnational enterprises in financing science and technology. Such assistance could include support for local research and development as well as the training of local scientists and engineers.

The Committee saw considerable potential in the regional development banks and other mechanisms for providing financial incentives for science and technology; it suggested that the United Nations, in co-operation with financing institutions, review information on sources and mechanisms for financing at the subregional level, and called on United Nations organizations, in co-operation with regional and subregional organizations, to establish an informal framework of consultations with regional development banks.

Report. [1]Advisory Committee, A/CN.11/30.
Yearbook reference. [2]1981, p. 737.

Activities of the UN system

Co-ordination in the system

The Task Force on Science and Technology for Development, set up by the Administrative Com-
mittee on Co-ordination (ACC) as the mechanism of inter-agency co-operation in implementing tasks assigned to the Intergovernmental Committee on Science and Technology for Development, held its third session in New York from 2 to 5 February 1982.[2] Its discussions focused on the operational plan for implementation of the Vienna Programme of Action and the efficiency of the United Nations system in responding to the plan.

In order to study joint activities and formulate specific proposals, the Task Force established four working groups: Working Group 1—early identification and assessment of new scientific and technological developments, and global network of scientific and technological information; Working Group 2—national science and technology policies and plans, and support to developing countries in the choice of technology; Working Group 3—upgrading traditional technologies; and Working Group 4—science and technology and the productive sector, commercialization of research and development for the benefit of developing countries, and acquisition and transfer of technology.

The working groups were open to all United Nations organizations and bodies, with the Centre for Science and Technology for Development ensuring adequate co-ordination. For each working group, an agency was selected as chairman, responsible for preparing documents and convening meetings, and a provisional list of core members was identified.

The Task Force agreed that each working group would formulate proposals for joint activities; identify the roles of United Nations entities in implementing these proposals; determine the resources required; and aim at completing its work in time for the Centre to consider its report before submitting its own report to the Intergovernmental Committee in 1983.

The four working groups held their first meetings in April 1982 and formulated proposals for further consideration and submission to the Task Force in early 1983. The Task Force was expected to submit its conclusions to the Intergovernmental Committee in May 1983.

With regard to the Secretary-General's annual report on United Nations activities in science and technology for development and the biennial review of progress in implementing the Vienna Programme of Action by the Director-General for Development and International Economic Co-operation (DIEC), required by the Intergovernmental Committee, the Task Force agreed that the Centre for science and technology should consider formulating a common format or guidelines, which could be applied to the information provided by United Nations organizations. It was also suggested that the Centre should issue, on a periodical basis, a comprehensive world report on science and technology for development.

By a decision of 6 April 1982,[1] ACC appointed Abdul-Razzak Kaddoura, Assistant Director-General for Science at the United Nations Educational, Scientific and Cultural Organization (UNESCO), as Chairman of the ACC Task Force for one year, on the basis of the principle of rotation.

Intergovernmental Committee action. The Intergovernmental Committee, in a resolution of 4 June,[4] requested United Nations organs, organizations and bodies, including the regional commissions, to give attention to the need for joint planning in science and technology for development, in order to improve co-ordination in their medium- and long-term plans.

On the same date,[5] the Committee proposed that the joint activities identified by the ACC Task Force be financed from the regular budget of the concerned United Nations organizations; stressed the need for the Task Force's working groups to accelerate their work; and requested the Centre for science and technology to include in its annual report to the Committee information on the progress in implementing United Nations joint activities.

ACC and CPC consideration. At Joint Meetings at Geneva on 6 and 7 July,[3] ACC and the Committee for Programme and Co-ordination considered how the United Nations could better respond to economic and social problems. On the topic of science and technology for development, they expressed the hope that negotiations on a mature financing system would result in the establishment of long-term arrangements by the General Assembly. They stated that they attached utmost importance to speedy implementation of the Vienna Programme of Action and expressed satisfaction at the progress made by the working groups of the ACC Task Force in identifying areas for joint activities.

Decision (1982). [1]ACC: 1982/8, 6 Apr.
Reports. [2]Task Force, ACC/1982/2; [3]CPC and ACC Chairmen, E/1982/84.
Resolutions (1982). Intergovernmental Committee (report, A/37/37), 4 June: [4]1(IV), para. 3; [5]3(IV), sect. I, paras. 3 & 4, & sect. II, para. 3 (b).

Efficiency of the system

Report of the Director-General. The DIEC Director-General, as requested by the General Assembly in December 1981,[1] prepared action-oriented recommendations, with cost estimates, as a follow-up to the proposals presented by the Secretary-General in his May 1981 study of the efficiency of the United Nations system in the field of science and technology for development.[5] The Director-General's recommendations on United Nations activities—dealing with both administra-

tive questions relating to operational activities and specific programme questions—were submitted in a March 1982 report to the Intergovernmental Committee.[3]

The Director-General suggested implementing the Secretary-General's proposals on programme evaluation and assessment continuously so that adjustments could be made taking account of experience and changing needs; the criteria used for evaluation and assessment should be the impact of science and technology activities on building endogenous capacity. Two ways of undertaking such an evaluation were mentioned—by the recipient Member States themselves and by the executing agencies concerned. The Director-General proposed that an evaluation be undertaken by 12 developing countries every two years, the countries to be selected according to equitable geographical distribution.

With regard to the Secretary-General's proposal on setting up, within the United Nations framework, an international institute for science policy training and study, the Director-General pointed out that UNESCO was examining the feasibility of such an institute, which would pool experience, research and training. He recommended that any further action await the completion of the UNESCO study.

Concerning support to consultancy, engineering and design organizations, as called for by the Secretary-General, the Director-General pointed out that no system existed to classify such organizations (estimated to number between 1,000 and 2,000 in developing countries) by size and function. As for the call to expand and diversify the means of programme action—traditionally experts, fellowships/training and equipment—the Director-General recommended that the Centre for science and technology, in consultation with the ACC Task Force, submit proposals to the Intergovernmental Committee.

With regard to establishment of a data base describing all approved programme activities in science and technology within the United Nations system, the Director-General recommended: that the Centre, in consultation with the ACC Task Force, develop a set of criteria for the selection of activities to be incorporated in the data base; and that it establish a data base of approved science and technology programmes, based on information provided annually by United Nations organizations.

ACC Task Force consideration. The ACC Task Force, at its February 1982 session, after considering a working paper on follow-up to the Secretary-General's system-wide efficiency study, made suggestions similar to some of the Director-General's recommendations. It endorsed the suggestion that a selected number of Governments be requested to evaluate the impact of United Nations activities.[2] As also proposed by the DIEC Director-General (see above), it suggested that the Intergovernmental Committee might wish to invite organizations to evaluate the extent to which their projects contributed to strengthening the scientific and technological capacities of developing countries, and to report on the results to the Centre on science and technology; and to invite the Centre to present the information to the Intergovernmental Committee as part of its annual report.

The Task Force agreed that the proposal to establish an international institute for science policy training and study should await the results of the UNESCO feasibility study, and that its Working Group 4 should consider the proposal on consultancy, engineering and design organizations. It also supported the proposal that the Centre establish a data base on approved programmes.

Intergovernmental Committee action. The Intergovernmental Committee, in a resolution of 4 June 1982,[4] welcomed with interest the Director-General's recommendations and deferred their consideration to its 1983 session.

Decision. [1]GA: 36/442, 17 Dec. 1981 (YUN 1981, p. 751).
Reports. [2]ACC Task Force, ACC/1982/2; [3]DIEC Director-General, transmitted by S-G note, A/CN.11/26.
Resolution (1982). [4]Intergovernmental Committee (report, A/37/37): 3(IV), sect. I, 4 June.
Yearbook reference. [5]1981, p. 750.

International machinery

Intergovernmental Committee on science and technology

Participation of NGOs

The Intergovernmental Committee on Science and Technology for Development, on 4 June 1982,[1] deferred consideration of a draft resolution on the participation of non-governmental organizations (NGOs) in its work to its 1983 session. It also decided to continue applying the provisional procedure for participation adopted in June 1981.[4]

Under the draft resolution, annexed to the Committee's report,[2] the following procedures would be adopted: NGOs in consultative status with the Economic and Social Council and other concerned organizations which had participated in the 1979 United Nations Conference on Science and Technology for Development[3] might be invited to participate as observers; and NGOs whose names had been submitted by the Secretary-General might be equally invited if the Committee so approved. Before submitting names of NGOs to the Committee for approval, the Secretary-General would apply the following criteria: the organization concerned should be a recognized non-profit national or international NGO; it should either have an active international programme or be involved in activities related to the Committee's work; and its activities should be of a nature that made them transferrable for use in other countries.

Decision (1982). [1]Intergovernmental Committee: 2(IV), 4 June.
Report. [2]Intergovernmental Committee, A/37/37.
Yearbook references. [3]1979, p. 635; [4]1981, p. 751.

Report of the Committee

The report of the Intergovernmental Committee on its 1982 session (New York, 24 May–4 June and 8-10 September)[2] was submitted to the General Assembly.

By a decision of 27 July,[1] adopted without vote, the Economic and Social Council noted the Committee's report on the first part of its session, and transmitted it to the Assembly. It authorized the Secretary-General to transmit directly to the Assembly the report on the Committee's resumed session.

Acting on the recommendation of its First (Economic) Committee, the Council combined two draft decisions, orally proposed by the Committee Chairman and approved without vote on 16 and 20 July,.

Decision (1982). [1]ESC: 1982/155, 27 July, text following.
Report. [2]Intergovernmental Committee, A/37/37.
Meeting record. ESC: E/1982/SR.48 (27 July).

Economic and Social Council decision 1982/155

Adopted without vote

Approved by First Committee (E/1982/105) without vote, 16 and 20 July (meetings 8 and 10); oral proposals by Chairman; agenda item 17.

Report of the Intergovernmental Committee on Science and Technology for Development

At its 48th plenary meeting, on 27 July 1982, the Council:

(a) Took note of the report of the Intergovernmental Committee on Science and Technology for Development on the first part of its fourth session;

(b) Decided to transmit that report to the General Assembly for consideration, in accordance with paragraph 3 of section II of Assembly resolution 34/218 of 19 December 1979;

(c) Decided also to authorize the Secretary-General to transmit directly to the General Assembly, at its thirty-seventh session, the report of the Intergovernmental Committee on Science and Technology for Development on its resumed fourth session, to be held from 8 to 10 September 1982.

Advisory Committee on science and technology

The Advisory Committee on Science and Technology for Development held its second session in New York from 9 to 19 February 1982 and submitted a report to the Intergovernmental Committee.[1] In a letter of transmittal, the Chairman expressed the Advisory Committee's belief that many developing countries had, at that time, a unique opportunity to integrate some of the most recent developments in technology with traditional skills and occupations, particularly in the rural areas. On the other hand, the technological gap between developed and developing countries continued to widen and, unless urgent steps were taken to accelerate the pace of the development and transfer of technology, global disparities in harnessing the tools of science and technology for improving the quality of life would grow. The Committee therefore established a panel of specialists to consider the question of integrating emerging and traditional technology in a mutually beneficial manner (see below).

Three sessional working groups were established to deal with specific programme areas and problems. The Committee made specific recommendations for further implementation of the Vienna Programme of Action and of the operational plan; for national targets for scientific and technological financing and for national financing institutions; for regional advisory bodies; on the choice, acquisition and transfer of technology and information; and on ways to involve women.

Efforts to improve the quality of life through science and technology should be made at the national level through bilateral or multilateral programmes and United Nations agencies, and in regional and global collaborative action programmes, the Committee stated. At the international level, the Committee considered it useful to develop within the United Nations system, through the Centre for Science and Technology for Development, a mechanism to alert Governments to potential developments in technology and their possible socio-economic impact. The Committee also proposed holding seminars for scientific policy makers from developing countries so as to sensitize them to global developments and emerging technologies. Another suggestion was to develop common codes relating to scientific and technological activities which raised ethical issues, such as the conduct of experiments, particularly involving human subjects, and the use of experimental drugs and pesticides.

The Committee decided on the following topics for four *ad hoc* panels of specialists: Panel I, which met from 13 to 16 December 1982, on the integrated application of emerging and traditional technologies for development; Panel II, scheduled to meet in January 1983, on human resources development for the planning, management and implementation of science and technology programmes in developing countries; Panel III, to meet in April 1983, on the role of regional associations and organizations in strengthening research and development and in the popularization of science and technology in developing countries; and Panel IV, to meet in October 1983, on a subject area related to the expansion of economic activities based on technology and technological services and innovation—the precise topic to be determined subject to the review of the recommendations of Panel I.

Noting the proposals of the Advisory Committee, the Intergovernmental Committee, in a resolution of 4 June 1982,[2] decided to examine them at its 1983 session, in particular the proposals on the establishment of a global network of scientific and technological information, of national information systems and of regional advisory bodies. The Intergovernmental Committee supported the suggestions relating to women and science and technology and took note of the suggestions relating to science and technology and the future. It also noted the establishment of the four *ad hoc* panels and agreed with the choice of the items to be discussed by each.

Report. [1]Advisory Committee, A/CN.11/30.
Resolution (1982). [2]Intergovernmental Committee (report, A/37/37): 3(IV), sect. IV, 4 June.

Centre for science and technology

The United Nations Centre for Science and Technology for Development continued in 1982 to assist the Director-General for Development and International Economic Co-operation in implementing the Vienna Programme of Action, particularly in providing substantive support to the Intergovernmental Committee and in promoting and co-ordinating United Nations science and technology activities at the secretariat level.

The Intergovernmental Committee, in a resolution of 4 June,[4] took note with satisfaction of the report on the Centre's activities for the period April 1981–March 1982.[1] Taking note of the Centre's updated work programme for 1982-1983, the Committee requested the Centre to intensify its efforts in the field of national and regional activities and to include in its annual report to the Committee information on the progress in carrying out United Nations joint activities.

In response to another Committee resolution of 4 June,[3] the Centre sent a questionnaire to Governments for background information necessary to develop guidelines for the formulation of specific projects to strengthen the endogenous scientific and technological capacities in developing countries. Based on one of the areas of concentration established by the Committee in June 1981[5] for implementation of the Vienna Programme, the Centre prepared proposals for the establishment of an advance technology alert system to identify scientific and technological developments which might adversely affect developing countries. It continued establishing a computerized data base on science and technology indicators and socio-economic indicators of particular relevance to science and technology activities so that guidelines could be developed for the evaluation of programmes and information exchange.

Other activities included monitoring of short- and long-term financial arrangements, and co-operation with the United Nations Financing System for Science and Technology for Development in the appraisal of projects.

To promote national and regional activities, the Centre held consultations with government officials and regional organizations, and maintained liaison with national focal points, the scientific community, and non-governmental and regional intergovernmental organizations. It continued to publish its newsletter *UPDATE* which reported on progress in implementing the Vienna Programme.

The Centre continued to provide substantive secretariat services to the Advisory Committee on Science and Technology for Development and participated in the work of the Task Force on Science and Technology for Development and its four working groups.

Information on the Centre's activities from April 1982 was provided by the Secretary-General in a May 1983 report.[2]

Note. [1]S-G, A/CN.11/29.
Report. [2]S-G, A/CN.11/40 & Corr.1.
Resolution (1982). Intergovernmental Committee (report, A/37/37), 4 June: [3]1(IV), para. 1; [4]3(IV), sect. II.
Yearbook reference. [5]1981, p. 734.

Proposed regional advisory bodies

The Advisory Committee on Science and Technology for Development, at its February 1982 session,[1] expressed the view that proper consideration of scientific and technological problems confronting the various regions within the context of their identified priorities could best be undertaken by the appropriate bodies at the regional level. To a large extent, this was already being done through the regional structures of the United Nations, as well as by regional intergovernmental bodies.

The Committee recommended the establishment of an advisory mechanism to assist governmental bodies at the regional level. It suggested that the composition of such an advisory body, from 7 to 10 persons serving in their individual capacity, be equitably distributed among the countries and disciplines relevant to the regions. Linkage between the regional advisory bodies and the Advisory Committee could be established through two members (one from within the region, the other from outside) who were members of both bodies.

The Intergovernmental Committee, in a resolution of 4 June,[2] noted with interest the Advisory Committee's proposals and decided to examine them thoroughly in 1983.

Report. [1]Advisory Committee, A/CN.11/30.
Resolution (1982). [2]Intergovernmental Committee (report, A/37/37): 3(IV), sect. IV, para. 3, 4 June.

Technology transfer

United Nations organizations continued in 1982 to provide advisory services on the choice, acquisition and transfer of technology to developing countries. Those activities, related to programme area III of the operational plan of the Vienna Programme of Action, were described by the Secretary-General in a report issued in April 1983[5] on 1982 activities of the United Nations system in the field of science and technology for development.

The bodies most directly concerned with technology transfer were the United Nations Conference on Trade and Development (UNCTAD) and the United Nations Industrial Development Organization (UNIDO) (see below). The United Nations Department of Technical Co-operation for Development (DTCD) provided assistance in the application of new technology in the collection, compilation and processing of statistical data with a view to improving the decision-making capacity of developing countries. Activities in this area were also carried out by the regional commissions; for example, the Economic and Social Commission for Asia and the Pacific prepared a report on the status and trends in national regulation of technology transfer within the region.

Several activities were aimed at establishing information bases on technological alternatives and decision-making. For example, the United Nations Centre on Transnational Corporations provided information on technology transfer through various industry studies on the activities of transnational corporations and profiles of individual corporations.

To help strengthen developing countries' technological capability, DTCD implemented technical assistance programmes to promote the use of microcomputers as user-oriented data-processing facilities particularly helpful in transferring technology owing to their low-key technical characteristics. The International Labour Organisation (ILO), jointly with donor and recipient Governments, carried out an evaluation of a project on the use of appropriate technology in the forestry sector. The United Nations Children's Fund, mostly through the provision of supplies and equipment, supported innovative scientific and technological activities related to food processing, water pumping and storage, biogas production, development and testing of vaccines, ironation or iodination of salt and production of oral rehydration salts.

Several organizations assisted national centres for the transfer of technology. Among them, ILO provided technical assistance to rural technology centres, in addition to advisory services for the establishment of institutional machinery for technology transfer, development, formulation and implementation of specific products and processes. The United Nations Financing System for Science and Technology for Development financed several projects involving technology transfer in Africa, Asia and Latin America.

Other United Nations activities included: assistance in formulating corporate and contractual arrangements and patent laws; advisory services on codes, conventions, and international agreements; study of the role of small and medium-sized enterprises in the transfer of technology; project appraisals; training programmes and seminars; and co-operation with subregional and regional organizations.

The Advisory Committee on Science and Technology for Development, at its February session,[2] made recommendations on the choice, acquisition and transfer of technology and scientific and technological information, having considered the two related programme areas together in recognition of the reciprocity between access to information and the ability to choose technologies. The Committee recommended establishment of a comprehensive data base, including an inventory of existing technological information facilities in both developed and developing countries; and advisory services and technical and financial assistance to technology information centres in developing countries for the identification, compilation and standardization of registries of technological alternatives in selected industries.

The Committee made proposals on support to national enterprises of developing countries in the choice, acquisition and transfer of technology, including: a cross-organizational study of United Nations activities to assess the degree to which investment projects promoted engineering and management capabilities in national enterprises; a study on co-operative schemes for technology transfer among private and/or public enterprises of developed and developing countries; and promotion and support of subregional, regional, interregional and international co-ordination among national centres in charge of technology transfer, such as identifying existing networks of these centres, and organizing a task force in each region to identify priorities.

As a means of training nationals of developing countries in negotiation and management of scientific and technological agreements, the Advisory Committee suggested: preparation of training manuals on national legislation, contractual and regulatory mechanisms and negotiation techniques; organization of training seminars, through regional centres for technology transfer and at the national level, on such topics as negotiating skills and contractual alternatives; and training workshops in developed countries for experts from developing countries.

UNCTAD activities. The Committee on Transfer of Technology of UNCTAD held its fourth session from 29 November to 10 December 1982 at Geneva. Annexed to the Committee's report[3] were seven resolutions and two decisions adopted on 10 December, and two draft resolutions on development aspects of the reverse transfer of technology.

The resolutions dealt with the Advisory Service on Transfer of Technology (ASTT); issues in three individual sectors of critical importance to developing countries; the work programme of UNCTAD in the development and transfer of technology; a strategy for the technological transformation of developing countries; aspects of the industrial property system in the transfer of technology; laws and regulations; and the role of small and medium-sized enterprises in technology transfer. Under the two decisions, the Committee requested the UNCTAD Secretary-General to take steps to implement the Vienna Programme of Action, and to report to the Committee in 1984 on the implementation of the 1979 UNCTAD resolution[15] on strengthening the technological capacity of developing countries and accelerating their technological transformation.[1]

By one resolution,[11] the Committee endorsed the conclusions and recommendations of three governmental meetings, held during 1982 at Geneva, on the transfer, application and development of technology in the following three sectors: food processing (1-10 June); capital goods and industrial machinery (7-16 July); and energy (25 October–2 November). The Committee requested follow-up studies by the UNCTAD secretariat. To consider that follow-up work, together with the views and comments by United Nations bodies, and to examine problems and policy issues of developing countries relating to the transfer, application and development of technology in the three sectors, the Committee agreed to convene a sessional committee during its next 1984 session.

By another resolution,[12] The Committee noted with satisfaction the progress and achievements described in a report on the UNCTAD work programme in the development and transfer of technology.[6] It requested the UNCTAD Secretary-General, before proposing examination of new issues and areas relevant to the technological transformation of developing countries, to take into account: subprogrammes concluded; the need for increasing the efficacy of UNCTAD in the field; and the need to avoid overlap with other United Nations bodies. In addition, the Committee requested him to submit information on ongoing UNCTAD work in technology, as well as proposals for future work, including by ASTT, bearing in mind the need to focus on specific issues.

By a third resolution, on ASTT,[10] the Committee requested the UNCTAD Secretary-General to ensure that ASTT assisted developing countries in formulating and implementing technology strategies and policies, as well as laws, regulations and mechanisms for technology transfer and development, and in establishing institutional infrastructure. The Committee requested that ASTT place greater emphasis on increasing the endogenous technological capacities of developing countries in sectors of critical importance, and invited the UNCTAD Secretary-General to prepare handbooks, manuals and guidelines, to assist developing countries in the acquisition and optimum utilization of technology. It requested him to encourage co-operation between ASTT and the subregional and regional centres for the transfer and development of technology, and to submit to the Trade and Development Board for further action a proposal on interregional linkages among those centres, and urged him to continue ASTT training activities. The Committee requested ASTT to respond especially to requests for assistance from the least developed countries, and urged all countries and United Nations and other international organizations and programmes to provide the necessary financing for ASTT projects.

Technical and operational assistance by ASTT was described in an October report by the UNCTAD secretariat[8] and in the report on the UNCTAD work programme. Activities in 1982 focused on the following areas: responding to initiatives of developing countries in the formulation and implementation of technology policies, plans, laws and regulations; subregional and regional co-operation; measures in sectors of critical importance; training programmes and exchanges of experience among developing countries. Special attention was given to the problems of the least developed, land-locked and island developing countries.

Established by UNCTAD in 1976,[14] ASTT continued in 1982 to send country missions with a view to preparing recommendations on technology transfer and development. As a result of a mission report, a technology centre in Iraq began operations in 1982. Proposals for national technology centres or mechanisms were made for submission to financing institutions by Rwanda, Somalia, the Sudan and the United Republic of Tanzania.

Advisory missions in the area of pharmaceuticals were sent to several countries and, in the case of Ethiopia, an outline of a technology plan in that sector for 1982-1991 was issued. At the subregional level, ASTT continued support to the Caribbean Centre for Pharmaceuticals and assisted in the formulation of a technology plan in that sector for the subregion. Programmes in the food processing, capital goods and energy sectors were being developed.

ASTT provided on-the-job, in-house and in-the-field training and exchange programmes in technology transfer and development. On-the-job training programmes for Indian officials were organized at Calcutta and New Delhi in March/April.

In its training programmes, ASTT gave priority to requests from least developed countries, 18 of which had been covered in one way or another by ASTT activities.

Recommendations on the main lines to be followed in ASTT operational activities in the energy sector were made by the October/November Meeting of Governmental Experts on the Transfer, Application and Development of Technology in the Energy Sector, which called for an expansion of technical assistance and training programmes.

The technological capacity of developing countries was to be strengthened by a twofold approach—planning and policies, as well as development of crucial sectors. A strategy for technological transformation of developing countries by reducing their external dependence and strengthening their national capacity for autonomous technological development, as an integral part of each country's long-term development strategy, was outlined in a September report of the UNCTAD secretariat.[7] As essential elements in the process, the report described nine main goals: to formulate technology plans and policies; to foster the technological development of sectors of critical significance, particularly capital goods and skills which embodied technology; to establish institutional arrangements and infrastructure; to strengthen research and development and technological innovation, and to increase the financial and human resources devoted to them; to establish a legal framework to regulate transfer of technology and foster its national development; to promote technical co-operation among developing countries; to undertake special measures for the least developed countries; to establish a framework of co-operation with the developed countries to supplement developing countries' efforts; and to create a suitable international environment through co-operation.

When translated into policies and quantitative measure, those goals, UNCTAD stated, could be used as criteria for ascertaining the progress in technological transformation, with the resources and socio-economic conditions of each country determining the emphasis on specific goals and the methods to attain them.

By a resolution of 10 December,[13] the Committee on Transfer of Technology requested the UNCTAD Secretary-General to transmit the report on a technological transformation strategy, together with the comments made by Governments at the Committee's session, to the 1983 UNCTAD session.

UNIDO activities. The activities of UNIDO in technology acquisition, described in the 1982 annual report of its Executive Director,[9] were aimed at strengthening the negotiating capacity of the developing countries. Those activities were reviewed at the Seventh Meeting of Heads of Technology Transfer Registries (New Delhi, 7-10 December). The Meeting also reviewed trends in technology acquisition, particularly in the participating countries, and the impact of relevant legislation on technology transfer flows.

During 1982, UNIDO completed a review of the experience of selected developing countries in technology regulation. It was preparing a manual for the negotiation of joint venture agreements; a training manual for the acquisition of technology, including joint ventures and engineering services; and guidelines for developing countries on provisions for guarantees and warranties in technology transfer agreements.

UNIDO activities included an advisory mission to Saudi Arabia on technology transfer negotiation policies. Preliminary assistance was given to Ethiopia in assessing information needs for a more co-ordinated government involvement in the importation of technology. Venezuela was assisted in the design of a contract evaluation information system, particularly with regard to the introduction of a microcomputer. Advice was given to Thailand on technology regulation with a view to the possible establishment of a technology transfer board.

Assistance was given to Egypt in the negotiation of a joint venture and turnkey delivery of a plant for the production of glass containers for the pharmaceutical industry, and to Malaysia in a reappraisal of policy regarding technical assistance and contracts for motor vehicle assembly and component manufacturing plants. Discussions continued with China on streamlining the inflow of foreign technology into the country's economy and expert advice was provided on a draft technology transfer law. Training workshops to strengthen negotiation capabilities were held in China and the Philippines, and study tours to technology transfer registries were organized for officials from Nigeria and from member countries of the Association of South-East Asian Nations.

The UNIDO Technological Information Exchange System (TIES) continued to expand its activities in the exchange of information among technology transfer registries, responding to requests from participating countries for information on contracts for specific technologies. The number of contracts registered reached 7,000 in 1982. With Ethiopia and Poland joining during the year, the number of TIES participants and observers totalled 32. A coding manual, prepared for the exchange of information on service agreements, went into full operation in July. A new methodology for the evaluation of technology payments being developed by UNIDO was tested among selected TIES countries. UNIDO provided TIES members with guidelines for software licensing agreements. A programme of co-operation with the Andean Technological Information System was developed, paving the way for regular information exchange between the two systems.

As part of a joint programme with ILO, technical memoranda on the tanning of hides and skins and on small-scale footwear manufacturing were published, as was a guide to low-cost vehicles for rural communities in developing countries. Sectoral and regional directories of industrial and technological research institutes were prepared to serve as a basis for co-operation among the institutes.

Commending the progress achieved by the UNIDO secretariat in the field, the Industrial Development Board of UNIDO, at its May 1982 session,[4] reaffirmed the high priority it attached to the development and transfer of technology to developing countries and to efforts to strengthen their technological capabilities. It drew attention to the need to strengthen existing institutional arrangements so as to increase the capacity of UNIDO to meet the needs of developing countries in a pragmatic way, and to bring the benefits of appropriate and advanced technologies to those countries. The Board requested the UNIDO secretariat to give consideration to the potential of co-operation among developing countries when implementing its programme, and urged it to co-operate closely with the United Nations and other bodies dealing with the transfer of technology. In addition, the Board requested the Executive Director to report in 1983 on progress in the secretariat's work on development and transfer of technology.

Decision (1982). [1]Committee on Transfer of Technology: 23(IV), 10 Dec.
Reports. [2]Advisory Committee, A/CN.11/30; [3]Committee on Transfer of Technology, TD/B/936; [4]IDB, A/37/16; [5]S-G, A/CN.11/35; UNCTAD secretariat, [6]TD/B/C.6/85, [7]TD/B/C.6/90, [8]TD/B/C.6/93 & Add.1; [9]UNIDO Executive Director, ID/B/300.
Resolutions (1982). Committee on Transfer of Technology, 10 Dec.: [10]17(IV), [11]18(IV), [12]24(IV), [13]25(IV).
Yearbook references. [14]1976, p. 397; [15]1979, p. 595.
Publications. Control of Restrictive Practices in Transfer of Technology Transactions: Selected Principal Regulations, Policy Guidelines and Case Law at the National and Regional Levels (TD/B/C.6/72), Sales No. E.82.II.D.8; *Guidelines on Technology Issues in the Pharmaceutical Sector in the Developing Countries* (UNCTAD/TT/49), Sales No. E.82.II.D.15.

Draft code of conduct

No agreement was reached in 1982 on the remaining issues involved in a code of conduct to govern technology transfer transactions across national borders. The General Assembly, in December, called for completion of negotiations so that it could adopt the code in 1983. Negotiations on the remaining issues were conducted in 1982 by the Interim Committee of the United Nations Conference on an International Code of Conduct on the Transfer of Technology. The Conference itself, initially convened in 1978 under the auspices of UNCTAD,[4] did not meet in 1982.

UNCTAD activities. The Interim Committee of the Conference on a code of conduct, established by the Assembly in December 1981[3] to seek agreement on the remaining issues involved in the code, held three sessions in 1982, at Geneva: 1-5 March, 17-21 May and 20 September–1 October. In its report to the Conference,[1] the Interim Committee proposed texts on the outstanding issues, based on suggestions by the President of the Conference, having also considered informal texts submitted by the chairmen of the Committee's two working groups and by the spokesmen for the regional groups.

The President of the Conference, in his capacity as Chairman of the Committee, stated at the close of the September/October session that measured progress had been achieved towards the solution of the outstanding issues. While he believed that the Committee's work would facilitate the Conference's task in finalizing the code, he stressed that, in the months before the Conference, consultations should be held among delegations in an effort to find solutions, with particular attention paid to the issues in the chapters on restrictive practices and on applicable law and settlement of disputes.

Among other proposals, the Committee invited the UNCTAD Secretary-General to convene the fifth session of the Conference at a date to be fixed in consultation with the regional groups.

General Assembly action. Recognizing that the adoption of an international code of conduct on the transfer of technology was in the interest of all countries, the General Assembly, by a resolution of 20 December 1982,[2] called for intensified efforts to complete negotiations during the fifth session of the Conference, so that the Assembly could adopt the code in 1983. The Assembly invited the UNCTAD Secretary-General and the President of the Conference, in consultation with regional groups and Governments, and, if necessary, with the assistance of a meeting of governmental representatives, to undertake the necessary work, including the identification of negotiating parameters, and the preparation of recommendations on outstanding issues, for submission to UNCTAD members before the fifth session of the Conference. The Assembly requested the UNCTAD Secretary-General to convene the fifth session in 1983 in time for it to report to the Assembly that year.

The resolution was adopted without vote, following similar approval on 13 December by the Second (Economic and Financial) Committee of a draft submitted by the Committee Chairman.

Report. [1]Interim Committee of United Nations Conference on International Code of Conduct on Transfer of Technology, TD/CODE TOT/35.
Resolution (1982). [2]GA: 37/210, 20 Dec., text following.
Resolution (prior). [3]GA: 36/140, 16 Dec. 1981 (YUN 1981, p. 756).
Yearbook reference. [4]1978, p. 503.
Meeting records. GA: 2nd Committee, A/C.2/37/SR.3, 5-8, 20-26, 33, 40, *48* (28 Sep.–13 Dec.); plenary, A/37/PV.113 (20 Dec.).

General Assembly resolution 37/210

20 December 1982   Meeting 113   Adopted without vote

Approved by Second Committee (A/37/680/Add.2) without vote, 13 December (meeting 48); draft by Chairman (A/C.2/37/L.115); agenda item 71 *(c)*.

United Nations Conference on an International Code of Conduct on the Transfer of Technology

The General Assembly,

Recalling its resolution 36/140 of 16 December 1981 on the United Nations Conference on an International Code of Conduct on the Transfer of Technology,

Taking note of the work accomplished by the Interim Committee of the United Nations Conference on an International Code of Conduct on the Transfer of Technology towards the solution of the issues outstanding in the draft international code of conduct on the transfer of technology,

1. *Recognizes* that the expeditious conclusion of the negotiations on the code of conduct and its adoption is in the interest of all countries;

2. *Calls* for intensified efforts aimed at the successful completion of the negotiations during the fifth session of the United Nations Conference on an International Code of Conduct on the Transfer of Technology, with the objective of enabling the General Assembly at its thirty-eighth session to adopt the international code of conduct on the transfer of technology;

3. *Invites* the Secretary-General of the United Nations Conference on Trade and Development and the President of the United Nations Conference on an International Code of Conduct on the Transfer of Technology, in consultation with regional groups and Governments, as appropriate, and, if necessary, with the assistance of a meeting of governmental representatives to be agreed to in consultation with regional groups, to undertake all the necessary work, including the identification of negotiating parameters, and the preparation of appropriate recommendations on all the issues outstanding in the draft code for submission to all members of the United Nations Conference on Trade and Development at least six weeks before the fifth session of the United Nations Conference on an International Code of Conduct on the Transfer of Technology;

4. *Requests* the Secretary-General of the United Nations Conference on Trade and Development to take the necessary measures for convening the fifth session of the United Nations Conference on an International Code of Conduct on the Transfer of Technology in the second half of 1983, in time to report to the General Assembly at its thirty-eighth session.

Other aspects of technology transfer

Industrial property

The Group of Governmental Experts on the Economic, Commercial and Developmental Aspects of Industrial Property in the Transfer of Technology to Developing Countries met at Geneva from 1 to 10 February 1982, as requested by the UNCTAD Committee on Transfer of Technology in 1980.[6] While UNCTAD had been involved in the question of patents and industrial property in the transfer of technology since its inception, concrete directives for its work in the revision of the patent system and the formulation of new national patent laws and policies were given in 1972.[3] Since then, two previous expert groups, meeting in 1975[4] and 1977,[5] had examined trade marks in developing countries and the need for achieving an equitable balance between public and private interests.

The Group considered three studies by the UNCTAD secretariat on: recent trends in patents in developing countries; the role of trade marks in the promotion of exports from developing countries; and trade marks and generic names of pharmaceuticals and consumer protection.

Introducing the first report, an UNCTAD representative noted that the changes made by some developing countries in their patent laws had altered the balance in favour of public benefit as opposed to private rights, by limiting the patentability of some items, by insisting on the domestic exploitation of patents, by excluding importation from the definition of patent exploitation and by affecting the duration of protection. Although the data compiled was insufficient to draw conclusions, it appeared that the changes had resulted in a decline in the registration of foreign patents but not in the volume of the transfer of technology. The report on the role of trade marks in the promotion of exports pointed to the need to strengthen the quality identification role of trade marks in relation to exports from developing countries. The report on trade marks of pharmaceuticals stated that almost 40 per cent of registered trade marks related to those products and that developing countries spent a much higher proportion of their health care budget on pharmaceuticals than did developed countries.

Based on the Group's conclusions and recommendations annexed to its report,[1] the Committee on Transfer of Technology, by a resolution of 10 December,[2] recommended that: the UNCTAD Secretary-General continue studying the effects of new patent policies in developing countries in relation to technology transfer, direct foreign investment and industrial development, paying particular attention to extending the coverage of countries and period of time, and to relevant industrial sectors; trading companies of developing countries explore the possibilities of concentrating their marketing efforts on a number of trade marks originating in those countries with a view to promoting exports of manufactured goods; that **measures be considered securing equal quality standards for the goods coming from different sources and to be marketed under the same trade** marks; and the Group continue consideration of the study on trade marks and generic names of pharmaceuticals and consumer protection, with States and interested intergovernmental organizations being given the opportunity to make written comments. It requested the UNCTAD Secretary-General to convene a further meeting of the Group and to report to the Committee in 1984.

In its resolution, the Committee did not include, as recommended by the Group and as called for by the developing countries and Group D (centrally planned economies), a request to the UNCTAD Secretary-General to examine possible measures including the formulation of international norms on promotion, distribution, trade and technology in the pharmaceutical sector. It also made no mention of the developing countries' wish that the UNCTAD Secretary-General examine such topics as: publication of a periodic report on trends in industrial property; study of the economic, commercial and developmental implications of plant breeders' rights; measures to minimize the effects of territorial restrictions in licensing agreements; and the examination of economic, developmental and commercial aspects of innovations and know-how of multilaterally financed research projects and the way in which their findings could be made available to developing countries.

Report. [1]Group of Governmental Experts on Economic, Commercial and Developmental Aspects of Industrial Property in Transfer of Technology to Developing Countries, TD/B/C.6/76.
Resolution (1982). [2]Committee on Transfer of Technology (report, TD/B/936): 21(IV), 10 Dec.
Yearbook references. [3]1972, p. 279; [4]1975, p. 462; [5]1977, p. 483; [6]1980, p. 634.

Laws and regulations

In October 1982, the UNCTAD secretariat submitted to the Committee on Transfer of Technology a report on common approaches to laws and regulations on the transfer and acquisition of technology,[1] as requested by the Trade and Development Board in October 1981.[3] The approaches would apply in general to all countries, particularly developing ones, which might make use of them globally or partially in introducing relevant laws and regulations.

The report analysed the scope of application of national transfer of technology laws, their basic elements and general requirements, and examined the rights and obligations of parties to transactions and the regulation of restrictive practices. In addition, it analysed the types of institutional mechanisms and legislative structures for the transfer of technology, such as a single governmental institution, an inter-ministerial body or division of the functions among different ministries and agencies.

It was found that, although transactions on transfer of technology were expressly dealt with by a relatively small number of national laws, most countries had some legislation affecting the transfer process, albeit often indirectly. National development plans or programmes also had an indirect bearing. Of more direct effect were national legislation and case law on foreign investment, industrial property and commercial transactions, particularly in the area of contracts, as well as protection of competition, or anti-trust law.

With many variations in scope and emphasis, the report stated, national legislation had been enacted to achieve such goals as control over and reduction of costs of technology transfers, the fulfilment of technology transfer arrangements, control of restrictions, and the development of the technological capabilities of the acquiring party and country.

Similarities were found in laws enacted in various countries—they extended mainly to international contracts, control was usually exerted through prior approval and registration, and the areas of control were principally pricing, restrictive practices, duration and applicable law.

With the number of laws in developing countries still growing and legal experience in those countries still limited, the report considered the development of common approaches to the regulation of technology transfer to be feasible, with the international code of conduct on the transfer of technology, when adopted, providing the background for effective international harmonization and setting standards for national legislation and administration.

The Committee on Transfer of Technology, by a resolution of 10 December 1982,[2] invited the UNCTAD Secretary-General to transmit the report, together with views expressed at the Committee's 1982 session, to UNCTAD members for comments and to seek the views of relevant United Nations bodies. The Committee requested him: to continue studying national laws and regulations relating to the transfer, application and development of technology, taking those views into account; and to prepare a manual reviewing policies and instruments on the promotion and encouragement of technological innovation in order to assist developing countries in formulating policies.

The Committee invited Governments to continue to inform the UNCTAD Secretary-General of new laws and regulations dealing with transfer and development of technology. It requested him to submit periodic reports to the Committee on such action, and invited him to complete an empirical analysis of the effects of legislation and regulations on technology transfer for submission to the Committee in 1984.

Report. [1]UNCTAD secretariat, TD/B/C.6/91.
Resolution (1982). [2]Committee on Transfer of Technology (report, TD/B/936): 20(IV), 10 Dec.
Yearbook reference. [3]1981, p. 757.

Role of small enterprises

The Committee on Transfer of Technology, by a resolution of 10 December 1982,[2] took note with great satisfaction of two studies commissioned by the UNCTAD secretariat in response to a 1980 Committee request:[5] "Organizational forms of transfer of technology to developing countries by small and medium-sized enterprises: a case study of equity joint ventures and technology agreements in Latin America"[3] and "Promotion of transfers of technology by small and medium-sized enter-

prises to developing countries: public policy implications and applicable instruments".[4] The Committee requested the UNCTAD Secretary-General to undertake further studies and invited him to submit to all member States those studies which had been completed. The Committee recommended appropriate action on them at its 1984 session, including the convening of seminars or workshops.

The study on equity joint ventures and technology agreements in Latin America was confined to the experience in a number of Latin American countries of some small and medium-sized enterprises (employing a maximum of 500 people) based primarily in Western Europe. The study on promotion of technology transfers by small and medium-sized enterprises in developed countries to developing countries evaluated such transfers, and methods and instruments used by industrialized countries to promote such transfers. The report concluded that fuller participation in technology transfers by that category of enterprises called for a strategy; it suggested that international consultations under United Nations auspices might bring together all the parties and national and international institutions concerned with a view to strengthening the technological co-operation of small and medium-sized enterprises, and to mobilizing the necessary financial and human resources.

In another resolution of 10 December,[1] the Committee requested the UNCTAD Secretary-General, in co-ordination with other United Nations bodies, to assist developing countries in obtaining access to information on the range and sources of technologies available from small and medium-sized public and private enterprises in developed and developing countries, taking into account existing work within the United Nations.

Resolutions (1982). Committee on Transfer of Technology (report, TD/B/936), 10 Dec.: [1]17(IV), para. 3; [2]19(IV). *Studies.* [3]TD/B/C.6/77, [4]TD/B/C.6/79. *Yearbook reference.* [5]1980, p. 634.

Brain drain

Measures to deal with the negative economic, political and social effects of the reverse transfer of technology—the so-called brain drain of skilled personnel from developing to developed countries—were considered in 1982 by UNCTAD and the General Assembly.

One of the ways the United Nations worked to halt this process was by improving training of human resources in developing countries. An UNCTAD expert group continued its work towards initiating the measurement of skilled human resource flows, but was unable to agree on a consensus text. The Assembly requested the establishment of an inter-agency group of United Nations organizations and requested UNCTAD to recommend measures to mitigate the adverse consequences of the brain drain.

Among other United Nations activities to help reduce the reverse transfer of technology were: technical reports by the United Nations Department of Technical Co-operation for Development (DTCD) to assist countries in collecting and improving annual statistics of immigration and migration, and a comprehensive study by DTCD on the feasibility of measuring human resource flows. The United Nations Financing System for Science and Technology for Development funded a project on the establishment of a data base on Arab migrant professionals to be executed by the Governments of the League of Arab States.

In an April report on implementation of the Vienna Programme of Action on Science and Technology for Development, the Director-General for Development and International Economic Co-operation made several proposals to reverse the brain drain, utilize the expertise of expatriates and provide incentives for the return of scientists and skilled personnel, with the United Nations providing practical assistance.[5] Similar proposals were made in February by the Advisory Committee on Science and Technology for Development.[1]

UNCTAD activities. An Intergovernmental Group of Experts on the Feasibility of Measuring Human Resource Flows was convened at Geneva from 30 August to 6 September 1982 to consider a study on the subject submitted in May,[8] in accordance with a March 1981 resolution of the UNCTAD Trade and Development Board.[9] As the different regional groups were unable to reach a consensus, the Group's report to the Committee on Transfer of Technology[3] included three annexes—draft conclusions and recommendations submitted by the Group of 77 developing countries, by Group B (developed market economies) and by the Chairman.

Introducing the report to the Committee, the Group's Chairman expressed the belief that his text constituted a basis for a compromise on which all groups could agree without sacrificing their main positions. Under its terms, the Group would conclude that international migration of economically active persons, regardless of their skills, constituted a transfer of productive resources and that international migration of such persons had economic and social effects, which were still not fully understood, for sending and receiving countries.

The Chairman's proposal pointed to the different views highlighted during discussion of the UNCTAD study; because of those differences, further work on the requirements for the practical measurement of human resource flows was needed, such as: studies on the full economic effects of international human resource transfers; the formulation of guidelines for the methodology of measurement; the data needed to perform the valuation; and the practicality of obtaining the data. Under the Chairman's text, the Group would recommend that the Committee: authorize UNCTAD to carry out that work; invite UNCTAD to establish contact with all interested Governments and relevant intergovernmental bodies in the preparation of the studies and guidelines; authorize a Group meeting for the adoption of guidelines; and consider enlarging the Group's terms of reference to include the formulation of policies.

After discussing the Group's work, the Trade and Development Board on 17 September[4] took note of the oral progress report by the Group's Chairman and commented that the Group's report would be considered fully by the Committee on Transfer of Technology at its November/December session.

On 10 December, the Committee decided that two draft resolutions—one by the Group of 77 and Group D (centrally planned economies), and the other by Group B—on development aspects of the reverse transfer of technology be annexed to its report and transmitted to the Trade and Development Board for consideration in 1983.[2]

Under the first draft, the Committee would take note of the Group's report and the UNCTAD study, and would recommend that the Board in 1983 take action in the light of developments at the 1982 General Assembly session.

By the Group B text, which endorsed the Chairman's text, the Committee would request the UNCTAD Secretary-General to carry out the work proposed by the Chairman; all Governments and appropriate intergovernmental organizations would be invited to participate in the next Group meeting for the adoption of guidelines; the Group's report would be submitted to the Trade and Development Board in 1984 so as to enable the Board to decide on the practical application of the conclusions, and the Committee would request UNCTAD to provide assistance in studies, policy formulation and institution strengthening, when so requested by developing countries.

General Assembly action. By a resolution of 20 December 1982,[6] the General Assembly recommended that the Member States concerned and international organizations consider formulating policies with a view to mitigating the adverse consequences of the reverse transfer of technology. It recommended that developed countries assist developing countries in fully utilizing their own trained personnel. The Assembly requested the Secretary-General to establish an inter-agency group to co-ordinate measures on the reverse transfer of technology and to enhance the effectiveness of the United Nations in responding to the countries concerned. The Assembly requested the UNCTAD Secretary-General to convene meetings of governmental experts to make recommendations on policies and measures to the Trade and Development Board in 1983, including the establishment of an international labour compensatory facility. The Secretary-General was requested to make recommendations on international co-operation in the field to the Assembly in 1983.

The resolution was adopted by a recorded vote of 127 to 21, with 1 abstention, following its approval by the Second (Economic and Financial) Committee on 13 December by a recorded vote, requested by the United States, of 106 to 21, with 1 abstention. The draft, submitted by Bangladesh on behalf of the Group of 77, was orally revised by the sponsors.

Introducing the revised text, Bangladesh said the issues raised were extremely important to the Group of 77, which considered that the Assembly should adopt policy guidelines; work on policy measures had been in abeyance for some time, and the time had come to make a new start.

Explaining its abstention, Greece said more information was needed before policy recommendations were made and measures taken; the measurement of human resource flows was likewise not adequately defined. Bulgaria, on behalf of the Eastern European States which supported the resolution, said the main cause of the brain drain lay in the economic inequality between the developed capitalist countries and developing countries, as well as in the activities of transnational corporations; the socialist countries believed that the United Nations should seek solutions to that problem within the framework of the 1974 Charter of Economic Rights and Duties of States.[7] China believed that a solution lay in the establishment of a new international economic order and that the developed countries should work with developing countries towards an acceptable solution.

Reports. [1]Advisory Committee on science and technology, A/CN.11/30; [2]Committee on Transfer of Technology, TD/B/936; [3]Group of Experts on Feasibility of Measuring Human Resource Flows, TD/B/C.6/89; [4]TDB, A/37/15, vol. II; [5]DIEC Director-General, transmitted by S-G note, A/CN.11/23.
Resolution (1982). [6]GA: 37/207, 20 Dec., text following.
Resolution (prior). [7]GA: 3281(XXIX), 12 Dec. 1974 (YUN 1974, p. 403).
Study. [8]UNCTAD, TD/B/C.6/AC.8/2.
Yearbook reference. [9]1981, p. 757.
Meeting records. GA: 2nd Committee, A/C.2/37/SR.3, 5-8, 20-26, *33*, 40, *48* (28 Sep.–13 Dec.); plenary, A/37/PV.113 (20 Dec.).

General Assembly resolution 37/207

20 December 1982   Meeting 113   127-21-1 (recorded vote)

Approved by Second Committee (A/37/680/Add.2) by recorded vote (106-21-1), 13 December (meeting 48); draft by Bangladesh, for Group of 77 (A/C.2/37/L.24), orally revised; agenda item 71 *(c)*.

Development aspects of the reverse transfer of technology

The General Assembly,

Recalling its resolutions 3201(S-VI) and 3202(S-VI) of 1 May 1974, containing the Declaration and the Programme of Action on the Establishment of a New International Economic Order, 3281(XXIX) of 12 December 1974, containing the Charter of Economic Rights and Duties of States, and 3362(S-VII) of 16 September 1975 on development and international economic co-operation,

Recalling also its resolution 35/56 of 5 December 1980, the annex to which contains the International Development Strategy for the Third United Nations Development Decade,

Reaffirming its resolutions 32/192 of 19 December 1977, 33/151 of 20 December 1978, 34/200 of 19 December 1979, 35/62 of 5 December 1980 and 36/141 of 16 December 1981, concerning the reverse transfer of technology,

Reaffirming also resolution 102(V) of 30 May 1979 adopted by the United Nations Conference on Trade and Development, the Vienna Programme of Action on Science and Technology for Development and the resolutions and decisions of the Trade and Development Board on the reverse transfer of technology, in particular decision 193(XIX) of 20 October 1979 and resolutions 219(XXI) of 27 September 1980 and 227(XXII) of 20 March 1981,

Noting the Economic Declaration adopted by the Sixth Conference of Heads of State or Government of Non-Aligned Countries, held at Havana from 3 to 9 September 1979,

Noting also the proposals contained in the Arusha Programme for Collective Self-Reliance and Framework for Negotiations, adopted by the Fourth Ministerial Meeting of the Group of Seventy-seven,

Convinced that the availability in the developing countries of their properly trained, skilled and professional personnel and of opportunities for their employment in their respective fields of competence is an essential factor in the economic and social development of developing countries,

Expressing its concern regarding the adverse effects of the reverse transfer of technology on the capacity and potential of scientific and technological development in the developing countries and, thus, on their economic and social development,

Reiterating the urgent need to reduce, as part of the efforts of the international community towards the establishment of the new international economic order, the reverse transfer of technology and to obviate its adverse effects on the developing countries,

Convinced that the United Nations system should play an active role in the alleviation of the adverse effects of the reverse transfer of technology,

Taking note of the report on the meeting of the Intergovernmental Group of Experts on the Feasibility of Measuring Human Resource Flows, convened by the Secretary-General of the United Nations Conference on Trade and Development at Geneva from 30 August to 6 September 1982, referred to in the report of the Trade and Development Board on its twenty-fifth session,

1. *Recommends* that the Member States concerned and the competent international organizations should, as a matter of urgency, give due consideration to the formulation of policies with a view to mitigating the adverse consequences of the reverse transfer of technology;

2. *Recommends* to the developed countries that they should assist and support the efforts of the developing countries towards the full utilization of their own trained personnel in promoting their economic and social development;

3. *Expresses its regret* that the Intergovernmental Group of Experts on the Feasibility of Measuring Human Resource Flows did not reach agreed conclusions and recommendations to mitigate the adverse effects of the reverse transfer of technology;

4. *Requests* the Secretary-General to establish an inter-agency group comprising representatives of the United Nations Conference on Trade and Development, the International Labour Organisation, the United Nations Educational, Scientific and Cultural Organization, the World Health Organization, the United Nations Institute for Training and Research, the Statistical Office of the Secretariat and other appropriate organs and bodies of the United Nations system to co-ordinate measures on the question of the reverse transfer of technology and, in particular, to examine and enhance the effectiveness of the United Nations system in responding to the complex needs of the countries concerned, as well as any additional measures to that effect;

5. *Requests* the Secretary-General of the United Nations Conference on Trade and Development to convene the requisite meetings of governmental experts with the following terms of reference:

(a) To formulate recommendations on policies and concrete measures, with a view to mitigating the adverse consequences for the developing countries of the reverse transfer of technology, including the proposal for the establishment of an international labour compensatory facility;

(b) To submit their report to the Trade and Development Board at its twenty-seventh session for its thorough consideration;

6. *Urges* all Governments and appropriate organizations to participate actively in the meetings mentioned in paragraph 5 above;

7. *Requests* the Secretary-General to report to the General Assembly at its thirty-eighth session on the implementation of the present resolution, including recommendations on concrete measures for the development of broad international co-operation for the solution of the problems arising in this field.

Recorded vote in Assembly as follows:

In favour: Afghanistan, Algeria, Angola, Antigua and Barbuda, Argentina, Bahamas, Bahrain, Bangladesh, Barbados, Benin, Bhutan, Bolivia, Botswana, Brazil, Bulgaria, Burma, Burundi, Byelorussian SSR, Cape Verde, Central African Republic, Chad, Chile, China, Colombia, Comoros, Congo, Costa Rica, Cuba, Cyprus, Czechoslovakia, Democratic Kampuchea, Democratic Yemen, Djibouti, Dominican Republic, Ecuador, Egypt, El Salvador, Equatorial Guinea, Ethiopia, Fiji, Gabon, Gambia, German Democratic Republic, Ghana, Grenada, Guatemala, Guinea, Guinea-Bissau, Guyana, Haiti, Honduras, Hungary, India, Indonesia, Iran, Iraq, Ivory Coast, Jamaica, Jordan, Kenya, Kuwait, Lao People's Democratic Republic, Lebanon, Lesotho, Liberia, Libyan Arab Jamahiriya, Madagascar, Malawi, Malaysia, Maldives, Mali, Malta, Mauritania, Mauritius, Mexico, Mongolia, Morocco, Mozambique, Nepal, Nicaragua, Niger, Nigeria, Oman, Pakistan, Panama, Papua New Guinea, Paraguay, Peru, Philippines, Poland, Qatar, Romania, Rwanda, Saint Lucia, Samoa, Sao Tome and Principe, Saudi Arabia, Senegal, Sierra Leone, Singapore, Somalia, Sri Lanka, Sudan, Suriname, Swaziland, Syrian Arab Republic, Thailand, Togo, Trinidad and Tobago, Tunisia, Turkey, Uganda, Ukrainian SSR, USSR, United Arab Emirates, United Republic of Cameroon, United Republic of Tanzania, Upper Volta, Uruguay, Vanuatu, Venezuela, Viet Nam, Yemen, Yugoslavia, Zaire, Zambia, Zimbabwe.

Against: Australia, Austria, Belgium, Canada, Denmark, Finland, France, Germany, Federal Republic of, Iceland, Ireland, Italy, Japan, Luxembourg, Netherlands, New Zealand, Norway, Portugal, Spain, Sweden, United Kingdom, United States.

Abstaining: Greece.

Information science

Preparations for the Conference on informatics (1983)

In 1982, preparations continued for a Second Intergovernmental Conference on Strategies and Policies for Informatics (SPIN II), to be held at Havana, Cuba, in June 1983.

Report of the UNESCO Director-General. The Director-General of the United Nations Educational, Scientific and Cultural Organization (UNESCO) submitted to the Economic and Social Council a report on SPIN II.[2] The report, dated May, provided information on the implementation by UNESCO of the recommendations of the First Intergovernmental Conference on Strategies and Policies for Informatics held in

1978,[4] while an addendum, dated June, focused on the preparations for SPIN II.

Representatives of UNESCO and the Intergovernmental Bureau for Informatics (IBI), the two organizations which had jointly organized the 1978 Conference, met on several occasions in 1982. At a meeting on 6 April at Rome, Italy, of the Directors-General of the two organizations, the IBI Director-General mentioned the possibility that SPIN II might lead to the adoption of an international instrument on transborder data flow and to the launching of a special programme of information for development, which would draw on resources of $1 billion over five years. At the May session of the UNESCO Executive Board, however, it was noted that the problem of transborder data flow needed more study prior to consideration of an international instrument and the competence of IBI to draft such an instrument was questioned. The Board invited the UNESCO Director-General to continue to examine the procedures for holding SPIN II, including the possibility of organizing it jointly with IBI.

Economic and Social Council action. By a resolution of 28 July,[3] the Economic and Social Council took note with appreciation of the UNESCO Director-General's report and an oral report of an IBI representative. The Council invited the Directors-General of the two organizations to continue their consultations, in order to determine the arrangements for co-operation, so as to guarantee the full success of SPIN II.

The resolution was adopted without vote, following similar approval on 19 July by the Third (Programme and Co-ordination) Committee, where the draft was introduced by Cuba also on behalf of Argentina, Ethiopia, Italy, Jordan, Mexico, Nicaragua, the Syrian Arab Republic, Tunisia and Venezuela.

Consideration by the Council of the UNESCO Director-General's report had been requested by the UNESCO Executive Board in a decision adopted at its September/October 1981 session, transmitted to the Council by a United Nations Secretariat note of 22 January 1982.[1]

Note. [1]Secretariat, E/1982/6.
Report. [2]UNESCO Director-General, E/1982/89 & Add.1.
Resolution (1982). [3]ESC: 1982/52, 28 July, text following.
Yearbook reference. [4]1978, p. 1100.
Meeting record. ESC: E/1982/SR.49 (28 July).

Economic and Social Council resolution 1982/52

28 July 1982   Meeting 49   Adopted without vote

Approved by Third Committee (E/1982/91) without vote, 19 July (meeting 11); 10-nation draft (E/1982/C.3/L.2); agenda item 20.
Sponsors: Argentina, Cuba, Ethiopia, Italy, Jordan, Mexico, Nicaragua, Syrian Arab Republic, Tunisia, Venezuela.

Second Intergovernmental Conference on Strategies and Policies for Informatics

The Economic and Social Council,

Recalling its resolution 1978/43 of 1 August 1978 on the application of computer science and technology to development, in which it invited the Director-General of the United Nations Educational, Scientific and Cultural Organization, in co-operation with the Director-General of the Intergovernmental Bureau for Informatics, to report to the Economic and Social Council on the results of the Intergovernmental Conference on Strategies and Policies for Informatics, held at Torremolinos, Spain, from 28 August to 6 September 1978,

Recalling also its resolution 1979/73 of 3 August 1979, in which it invited the United Nations Educational, Scientific and Cultural Organization, in co-operation with the Intergovernmental Bureau for Informatics, to continue to carry out programmes adopted by them in support of the recommendations of the Intergovernmental Conference on Strategies and Policies for Informatics,

Recalling further its resolution 1981/52 of 22 July 1981, in which it took note of the decision of the General Assembly of the Intergovernmental Bureau for Informatics to convene a second intergovernmental conference on strategies and policies for informatics at Havana in June 1983,

Having considered the report of the Director-General of the United Nations Educational, Scientific and Cultural Organization on the Second Intergovernmental Conference on Strategies and Policies for Informatics and having heard the oral report of the representative of the Intergovernmental Bureau for Informatics,

Emphasizing the crucial importance of informatics for the development of all countries and the need to assist the developing countries in their efforts to apply its results for their economic and social development, and conscious of the importance of a Second Conference for that purpose,

Gratified by the consultations between the Director-General of the United Nations Educational, Scientific and Cultural Organization and the Director-General of the Intergovernmental Bureau for Informatics regarding co-operation for the holding of the Second Conference, which has been postponed by the interested parties,

1. *Takes note with appreciation* of the report of the Director-General of the United Nations Educational, Scientific and Cultural Organization and the oral report of the representative of the Intergovernmental Bureau for Informatics on the Second Intergovernmental Conference on Strategies and Policies for Informatics;

2. *Invites* the Director-General of the United Nations Educational, Scientific and Cultural Organization and the Director-General of the Intergovernmental Bureau for Informatics to continue the consultations, with a view to determining the most appropriate arrangements for co-operation, within the framework of the relations existing between the two organizations, so as to guarantee the full success of the Conference.

Marine science and technology

The Third United Nations Conference on the Law of the Sea adopted by consensus on 30 April 1982 a resolution submitted by Peru on behalf of the Group of 77 developing countries.[1] Expressing the view that the maximum use of the new opportunities for economic and social development offered by the new Convention on the Law of the Sea would be facilitated through action aimed at strengthening national capabilities in marine science, technology and ocean services, particularly in developing countries, the Conference urged industrialized countries, United Nations organizations and multilateral funding agencies to assist those countries in the preparation and implementation of their marine science, technology and ocean service development programmes. The text of the resolution was transmitted to the General Assembly by the Secretary-General by a note of 24 November.[2]

The Convention on the Law of the Sea, also adopted on 30 April, dealt with international co-operation in the conduct and promotion of marine scientific research and development of marine technology, and contained provisions on the establishment of national and regional marine scientific and technological centres. It established rules to be followed by research and coastal States, particularly with regard to research in the exclusive economic zone and on the continental shelf, and dealt with the transfer of technology and scientific knowledge relating to sea-bed activities.

Draft resolution. [1]Peru, for Group of 77, A/CONF.62/L.127. *Resolution (1982).* [2]Conference on Law of Sea: transmitted by S-G note, A/37/566 & Corr.1.

Chapter XIII

Social and cultural development

Contents

Related topics:
Development and international economic and social policy: Economic and social conditions and trends; Rural and urban development. Regional economic and social activities—Social and cultural development: Asia and the Pacific; Latin America. Statistics: Social and demographic statistics.

Social development and welfare

Social survey

Reports on the social situation. The *1982 Report on the World Social Situation*[1] was the tenth in the series prepared by the United Nations since 1952. The *Report* differed from preceding ones, the last of which was prepared in 1978,[9] in that, as required by a 1979 General Assembly resolution,[6] it sought to identify emerging social trends of international concern and to contribute to the discussion of relationships among major development issues which had both international and national dimensions. Information relating to the implementation of the 1969 Declaration on Social Progress and Development,[5] previously reported on independently, was integrated into the chapters of the *1982 Report*.

The report had a triple function: (1) to provide an overview of living conditions in the world, based on information gathered by United Nations organizations, especially the specialized agencies and regional commissions; (2) to identify and analyse issues of international concern requiring international action; and (3) to provide the elements for a synthesis of socio-economic trends as a context in which more specific problems could be viewed in perspective. Part One presented an overview of living conditions in a period marked by uncertainty and economic set-backs. It examined poverty and equity, the family, social security and employment. Part Two discussed changes and trends in elements of well-being, examining food and nutrition, health, education and training, working conditions, housing and the environment. Part Three discussed removing obstacles to social progress. It focused on aspects of social progress as affected by participation (the involvement of citizens in political, economic and social affairs and organizations which affect their lives), agrarian reform, science and technology, disarmament and development, and civil and political rights.

The *1982 Report* showed that living conditions in many parts of the world were far below the standards judged acceptable by the international community and that the major objectives of the International Development Strategy for the Third United Nations Development Decade[8] were far from being achieved, in spite of some progress in such areas as food, nutrition, health, housing and employment. It also indicated that the international economic crisis was hindering the fight against poverty and having a direct effect on living conditions, particularly in the developing countries, while also aggravating existing structural imbalances and inequities.

The *Report* attempted to demonstrate the interplay of short- and long-term changes which shaped the evolution of societies; for example, the composition of the labour force, demographic trends and the role of the family were affected by even short-term changes in economic variables, while they, in turn, shaped the course of long-term economic development. A better understanding of that interaction was essential for the elaboration and implementation, at the national and international levels, of policies directed towards more balanced socio-economic development.

On 7 December 1982, the Secretary-General reported to the Economic and Social Council on social trends in developing countries and the influence of current economic conditions.[2] This report, to be discussed by the Council in 1983, was submitted in response to a 1981 Council request.[4] In discussing the elements of long-term social change in developing countries, as well as the main features of the current economic situation and of the impact of the recession on social change in those countries, the Secretary-General noted that the existing economic recession was straining the fragile social structure of many developing countries already under stress because of rapid long-term changes in society. There had been a reduction in the already meagre level of income and consumption for large sections of the population. The growth of employment opportunities had slowed considerably, militating against powerful forces in the long-term transformation of society, such as urbanization and the growth of new social groups and their aspirations. Public spending on the social sectors, including education and health, had also ceased to grow or had been reduced, thus further setting back long-term social development.

General Assembly action. Following its review of the *1982 Report on the World Social Situation*, the General Assembly, in a resolution[3] adopted without vote on 3 December, reaffirmed that the social development goals were an integral part of overall development and their implementation must take into account national priorities, economic development levels and cultural values. The Assembly emphasized the importance of the new international economic order for achieving social progress and reaffirmed the urgent need to implement the socio-economic development objectives in the third International Development Strategy, including those related to nutrition, health, employment, population, education and the participation of women in development. It called on Member States to formulate and implement interrelated policy measures to achieve priority goals in those areas as well as in housing, child welfare, equal opportunities for the disabled and aged, and the participation of youth in development. (Italy orally amended the text in the Assembly to include crime prevention among these goals.) United Nations bodies and organizations were called upon to take measures to

achieve the main objectives of the Declaration on Social Progress and Development and the Strategy.

The Assembly asked the Commission for Social Development to examine the *1982 Report* and submit its views to the 1983 sessions of the Economic and Social Council and the Assembly. Member States were also invited to comment on the *Report* to facilitate preparation of the next one in 1985. The Secretary-General was requested to transmit the *Report* to other United Nations bodies concerned with operational activities and to the regional commissions. The 1985 report was to include an analysis of the implementation of the Declaration, taking into account the objectives of the Strategy, oral and written comments received in the intervening years, and recommendations to improve the methodology for preparing the report.[7] It was to include also an analysis of the co-ordination between the United Nations and the specialized agencies in collecting social statistics and reporting on social issues. Bodies of the United Nations system were invited to make information available for future reports, which were to be widely disseminated.

The Assembly noted with great concern the rapidly deteriorating economic and social situation and the lack of implementation of the Declaration on social progress and the goals of the Development Strategy. The need to implement the socio-economic objectives of the Substantial New Programme of Action for the 1980s for the Least Developed Countries, adopted in 1981,[10] was reaffirmed, and the need for greater financial and technological contributions to national development efforts was re-emphasized.

The resolution was approved by the Assembly's Third (Social, Humanitarian and Cultural) Committee without vote on 22 November. It was introduced and orally revised by Bangladesh on behalf of the Group of 77 developing countries. Ireland, supported by Italy, orally suggested but did not press the addition, in the last preambular paragraph, of an expression of appreciation to the Secretary-General for his report.

Publication. [1]*Report on the World Social Situation* (E/CN.5/1983/3 & Corr.1,2), Sales No. E.82.IV.2 & corrigenda.
Report. [2]S-G, E/1983/4.
Resolution (1982). [3]GA: 37/54, 3 Dec., text following.
Resolutions (prior). [4]ESC: 1981/19, 6 May 1981 (YUN 1981, p. 768). GA: [5]2542(XXIV), 11 Dec. 1969 (YUN 1969, p. 433), [6]34/152, 17 Dec. 1979 (YUN 1979, p. 757), [7]*ibid.,* sect. II (p. 758), [8]35/56, annex, 5 Dec. 1980 (YUN 1980, p. 503).
Yearbook references. [9]1979, p. 750; [10]1981, p. 406.
Meeting records. GA: 3rd Committee, A/C.3/37/SR.27-29, *42, 49* (29 Oct.-22 Nov.); plenary, A/37/PV.90 (3 Dec.).

General Assembly resolution 37/54

3 December 1982   Meeting 90   Adopted without vote

Approved by Third Committee (A/37/640) without vote, 22 November (meeting 49); draft by Bangladesh, for Group of 77 (A/C.3/37/L.27), orally revised in Committee, and orally amended by Italy in Assembly; agenda item 78.

World social situation

The General Assembly,

Recalling its resolutions 33/48 of 14 December 1978 on world social development, 34/59 of 29 November 1979 on the implementation of the Declaration on Social Progress and Development and 34/152 of 17 December 1979 on the world social situation,

Recalling its resolutions 3201(S-VI) and 3202(S-VI) of 1 May 1974, containing the Declaration and the Programme of Action on the Establishment of a New International Economic Order, 3281(XXIX) of 12 December 1974, containing the Charter of Economic Rights and Duties of States, 3362(S-VII) of 16 September 1975 on development and international economic co-operation, 35/56 of 5 December 1980, containing the International Development Strategy for the Third United Nations Development Decade, and 36/194 of 17 December 1981, in which it endorsed the Substantial New Programme of Action for the 1980s for the Least Developed Countries,

Recalling also its resolution 35/136 of 11 December 1980 on the World Conference of the United Nations Decade for Women,

Recalling further its resolution 36/28 of 13 November 1981 on the International Youth Year: Participation, Development, Peace,

Recalling its resolutions 37/52 and 37/53 of 3 December 1982 on the World Programme of Action concerning Disabled Persons,

Recalling also its resolution 37/51 of 3 December 1982 on the World Assembly on Aging,

Recalling further its resolution 32/197 of 20 December 1977, in which it, *inter alia*, requested the Secretariat to prepare, on a regular basis, global economic and social surveys and projections,

Bearing in mind that social progress and development are founded on respect for the dignity and value of the human person,

Bearing in mind also that the ultimate aim of development is the constant improvement of the well-being of the entire population on the basis of its full participation in the process of development and a fair distribution of the benefits therefrom, and that the pace of development in the developing countries as a whole should be accelerated substantially in order to enable them to achieve this goal,

Mindful that the existing inequities and imbalances in international economic relations are widening the gap between developed and developing countries, and thereby constitute a major obstacle to the development of the developing countries and adversely affect international relations and the promotion of world peace and security,

Conscious that each country has the inalienable right to adopt the economic and social system that it deems the most appropriate and that each Government has a primary role in ensuring the social progress and well-being of its people,

Reaffirming that economic growth must go hand in hand with qualitative and structural changes, the reduction of social and economic disparities and the adoption of measures to ensure the effective participation of all peoples in the preparation and execution of national policies for economic and social development,

Convinced of the necessity rapidly and completely to eliminate colonialism, neo-colonialism, racism, racial discrimination, *apartheid*, aggression, foreign occupation and alien domination and all other forms of inequality, exploitation and subjugation of peoples which constitute major obstacles to economic and social progress as well as to the promotion of world peace and security,

Reaffirming the existence of the undeniable link between peace and development and the imperative need to halt the arms race, thereby releasing valuable additional resources which could be used for the development of the developing countries and could contribute to the well-being and prosperity of all,

Re-emphasizing that the primary responsibility for the development of developing countries rests upon themselves, but that, however great their own efforts, these will not enable them to achieve the desired development goals as expeditiously as they must unless just and equitable economic and commercial relations between developed and developing countries are established and, to that end, increasing financial resources and technological know-how are assured,

Having considered the *1982 Report on the World Social Situation*,

1. `Notes with deep concern* that the economic and social situation in the world today is not only disturbing but is also deteriorating rapidly;

2. *Notes also with great concern* the lack of implementation of the Declaration on Social Progress and Development and of the objectives and overall development goals adopted and reaffirmed in the International Development Strategy for the Third United Nations Development Decade;

3. *Reaffirms* that the social aspects and goals of development are an integral part of the overall development process and their implementation must take into account national priorities, levels of economic development and cultural tradition and values;

4. *Emphasizes again* the importance of the establishment of the new international economic order for the achievement of social progress;

5. *Reaffirms* the urgent need to implement the socio-economic development objectives established by the international community and contained in the International Development Strategy for the Third United Nations Development Decade, *inter alia*, the elimination of hunger and malnutrition, the achievement of full employment by the year 2000, health for all by the year 2000, appropriate population policies, the reduction of the infant mortality rate, the availability of safe water and adequate sanitary facilities by 1990, the attainment of a life expectancy of 60 years as a minimum by the year 2000, universal primary school enrolment by the year 2000 and the securing of the full participation of women, both as agents and beneficiaries, in all sectors and at all levels of the development process;

6. *Reaffirms also* the need to implement the socio-economic objectives of the Substantial New Programme of Action for the 1980s for the Least Developed Countries;

7. *Calls upon* all Member States to promote economic growth and social progress by the formulation and implementation of an interrelated set of policy measures to achieve their goals and objectives, within the framework of national priorities and interests, in the fields of employment, education, health, nutrition, housing facilities, crime prevention, the well-being of children, equal opportunities for the disabled and the aged, full participation of youth in the development process and the full integration and participation of women in development;

8. *Calls upon* the relevant organs, organizations and bodies of the United Nations system to mobilize the necessary resources so as to undertake measures aimed at improving social conditions and achieving the main objectives set forth in the Declaration on Social Progress and Development and in the International Development Strategy for the Third United Nations Development Decade;

9. *Emphasizes again* that rapid socio-economic progress of developing countries requires substantially enhanced multilateral and bilateral financial and technological contributions to national development efforts, rendered within the framework of the development plans of developing countries;

10. *Requests* the Commission for Social Development at its twenty-eighth session to give high priority to the examination and discussion of the *1982 Report on the World Social Situation* and to submit its views and observations to the General Assembly at its thirty-eighth session through the Economic and Social Council;

11. *Requests* the Secretary-General to transmit the *1982 Report on the World Social Situation* to other United Nations bodies concerned with operational activities and to the regional commissions for their consideration;

12. *Invites* Member States to convey to the Secretary-General their comments on the *1982 Report on the World Social Situation* so as to facilitate the preparation of the 1985 report;

13. *Requests* the Secretary-General to issue the 1985 report on the world social situation, taking into consideration the provisions of the present resolution and including an analysis of the implementation of the Declaration on Social Progress and Development in the light of the goals and objectives of the International Development Strategy for the Third United Nations Development Decade, and taking into account the comments of delegations on this question made during the thirty-seventh session of the General Assembly and to be expressed during the thirty-eighth session as well as the comments received by the Secretary-General from Member States and the observations made by the Commission for Social Development, through the Economic and Social Council;

14. *Also requests* the Secretary-General, in preparing the 1985 report on the world social situation, to take into account the recommendations made in section II of General Assembly resolution 34/152 and to report thereon periodically to the Economic and Social Council;

15. *Further requests* the Secretary-General, when presenting the 1985 report on the world social situation, to submit an analysis of the co-ordination between the United Nations and the specialized

agencies in the collection of social statistics and the preparation of reports on social issues;

16. *Invites* the organs, organizations and bodies of the United Nations system to co-operate fully with the Secretary-General in the preparation of future reports by making available all relevant information pertaining to their respective areas of competence;

17. *Requests* the Secretary-General to make the necessary arrangements for the wide dissemination of all future reports;

18. *Decides* to include in the provisional agenda of its thirty-eighth session the item entitled "World social situation".

Social aspects of UN development activities

In response to a 1981 Economic and Social Council decision,[2] the Secretary-General submitted a note[3] to the Council on 2 April 1982 commenting on the feasibility and programme, co-ordination and resource implications of the main recommendations of the *Ad Hoc* Working Group on the Social Aspects of the Development Activities of the United Nations, presented and discussed in 1981 but whose further consideration was postponed.[6] The Group had been established in 1979[5] to recommend ways to improve the Organization's effectiveness in dealing with social development issues.

The Secretary-General said it had not been possible in the time available to provide the detailed comments requested on the various implications of all of the more than 100 proposals contained in the report but he would continue to undertake consultations on them, taking into account the Council's views expressed at its April/May 1982 session, in order to prepare a response. He pointed out that the 1982-1983 budget programmes in social development and humanitarian affairs and in development issues and policies were constructed with a view to strengthening the integrated approach to development issues, to undertaking new and practical approaches to social aspects of development and to ensuring that the social component of development was given due recognition and not considered an appendage to economic issues, thus responding to resolutions and decisions within the United Nations system with respect to the social aspects of development.

On 4 May, the Council decided, without vote, to continue in 1983 its consideration of the recommendations of the *Ad Hoc* Working Group, together with comments of the Secretary-General, to be submitted to the General Assembly later in 1982, on the feasibility and programme, co-ordination and resource implications of those recommendations.

The decision[1] was approved without vote by the Council's Second (Social) Committee on 26 April. It was introduced and orally revised by Yugoslavia on behalf of its 12 sponsors.

In a report of 8 November 1982,[4] the Secretary-General reviewed for the Assembly the steps taken to date regarding consideration of the recommendations of the *Ad Hoc* Working Group.

Decision (1982). [1]ESC: 1982/125, 4 May, text following.
Decision (prior). [2]ESC: 1981/176, 23 July 1981 (YUN 1981, p. 763).
Note. [3]S-G, E/1982/35.
Report. [4]S-G, A/37/500.
Resolution. [5]ESC: 1979/45, 11 May 1979 (YUN 1979, p. 763).
Yearbook reference. [6]1981, p. 761.
Meeting record. ESC: E/1982/SR.23 (4 May).

Economic and Social Council decision 1982/125

Adopted without vote

Approved by Second Committee (E/1982/58) without vote, 26 April (meeting 9); 12-nation draft (E/1982/C.2/L.5), orally revised; agenda item 11.

Sponsors: Algeria, Argentina, Bangladesh, India, Italy, Nigeria, Norway, Pakistan, Romania, United States, Venezuela, Yugoslavia.

Report of the *Ad Hoc* Working Group on the Social Aspects of the Development Activities of the United Nations

At its 23rd plenary meeting, on 4 May 1982, the Council decided:

(a) To continue, at its first regular session of 1983, its consideration of the measures to improve the work of the Council suggested in the report of the *Ad Hoc* Working Group on the Social Aspects of the Development Activities of the United Nations;

(b) To consider those measures at its first regular session of 1983, together with the comments of the Secretary-General, to be submitted to the General Assembly at its thirty-seventh session, on the feasibility, programme and co-ordination implications, as well as on the resource implications, of the main recommendations submitted by the *Ad Hoc* Working Group, and in the light of the consideration of the matter by the Assembly at that session.

Popular participation in development

Report of the Seminar. An International Seminar on Popular Participation was held at Ljubljana, Yugoslavia, from 17 to 25 May 1982 for the purpose of comparing policies, institutions and experiences of Member States in the participation by all sectors of society in national economic and social development, as well as collective bargaining, worker participation in management and workers' self-management. The Seminar, called for by the General Assembly in 1979,[3] was attended by 48 participants from 36 countries, 11 United Nations bodies and institutions and a non-governmental organization.

In a 22 September report[1] to the Assembly on the Seminar, the Secretary-General noted that popular participation was widely recognized as an important principle for socio-economic development, that there was a need for a clear definition of the concept as the basis for national policy measures, and that every State had the right to choose the institutions and policies for participation best suited to its circumstances and socio-political dynamics. The Seminar reviewed the question in terms of various areas and approaches instituted by Member States. These included citizen participation in formulating and implementing national development plans, decentralization and local government reforms, reorientation of public administration, education, information, health, and community and rural development, as well as motivation and incentives for participation, working people's participation and self-management in socio-economic activities, participation of women, and associating specific groups with public affairs directly relevant to their interests.

The Seminar put forward a number of conclusions and suggestions for action by national authorities and international institutions to promote popular participation in development. They included periodic reviews of their experiences, reforming ineffective partial policies in programmes of decentralization and democratization, paying particular attention to education and information, and involving trade unions, non-governmental organizations and community and civic groups in promoting participation. The Seminar recommended that the United Nations system should: include participatory aspects in global strategies; expedite global negotiations on international economic relations; provide technical co-operation to countries in this field; and promote exchanges of experience among countries at various levels and through publications and seminars. Periodic meetings should elaborate indicators for measuring levels of participation.

The Seminar felt that: the Assembly should periodically consider Member States' views on popular participation and workers' participation in management and self-management; the Secretary-General should prepare a study on the question and submit progress reports on conclusions and recommendations; and he should prepare a comparative study on normative regulations concerning those questions, based on the information supplied by countries. It was further suggested that: the Commission on Human Rights consider the human rights aspects of the results of the Seminar's deliberations; the United Nations system give special consideration to study and the question of workers' participation in managing economic and social structures; the Committee for Development Planning include the question as part of its review of the implementation of the International Development Strategy for the Third United Nations Development Decade[4]; United Nations organizations continue to study engaging in the promotion of popular and worker participation, building up a system of education for participation and ensuring dissemination of information, and encourage Member States' co-operation; and funding agencies and Member States give special consideration to supporting technical co-operation projects and intergovernmental institutions meant to promote popular participation. The International Centre for Public Enterprises was called upon to continue research in the functioning of participation in developing countries and the United Nations International Research and Training Institute for the Advancement of Women was asked to carry out studies on the role and participation of women in development.

General Assembly action. On 3 December, the General Assembly, by a resolution[2] adopted without vote, invited Member States to take the Seminar's recommendations into consideration in their development policies and programmes. The Secretary-General's report[1] on the Seminar was to be transmitted to them and to relevant United Nations bodies for their consideration. The Assembly called on organizations of the United Nations system to promote popular participation as appropriate in executing their programmes, and requested the Commission on Human Rights to consider, at its 1983 session, the question of popular participation in its various forms as an important factor in development and the realization of human rights, taking into account the Seminar's deliberations, and to submit to the Assembly, through the Economic and Social Council, suggestions for the more complete realization of human rights. The Secretary-General was asked to prepare a progress report for the Assembly in 1983 on the implementation of the resolution, taking into account the Commission's suggestions.

The resolution was approved without vote by the Assembly's Third (Social, Humanitarian and Cultural) Committee on 22 November. Yugoslavia introduced the text on 15 November and subsequently revised it on behalf of the 17 sponsors. An additional revision by the sponsors took account of an oral drafting amendment by Morocco.

Report. [1]S-G, A/37/442.
Resolution (1982). [2]GA: 37/55, 3 Dec., text following.
Resolutions (prior). GA: [3]34/152, 17 Dec. 1979 (YUN 1979, p. 757); [4]35/56, annex, 5 Dec. 1980 (YUN 1980, p. 503).
Meeting records. GA: 3rd Committee, A/C.3/37/SR.27-29, *42, 49* (29 Oct.-22 Nov.); plenary, A/37/PV.90 (3 Dec.).

General Assembly resolution 37/55

3 December 1982   Meeting 90   Adopted without vote

Approved by Third Committee (A/37/640) without vote, 22 November (meeting 49); 17-nation draft (A/C.3/37/L.28/Rev.1), orally revised; agenda item 78.

Sponsors: Algeria, Bangladesh, Benin, China, Cyprus, Guyana, India, Iraq, Madagascar, Mexico, Pakistan, Panama, Philippines, Romania, Sri Lanka, Syrian Arab Republic, Yugoslavia.

Popular participation in its various forms as an important factor in development and in the realization of human rights

The General Assembly,

Recalling its resolution 34/152 of 17 December 1979,

Recalling also the Declaration on Social Progress and Development, contained in General Assembly resolution 2542(XXIV) of 11 December 1969, in which, *inter alia,* it was emphasized that all peoples and all human beings have the right to live in dignity and freedom and to enjoy the fruits of social progress and should, on their part, contribute to it,

Bearing in mind that social progress and development are founded on respect for the dignity and value of the human person and should ensure the promotion of human rights and social justice,

Stressing the importance of the adoption of measures to ensure the effective participation, as appropriate, of all elements of society in the preparation and implementation of national economic and social development policies and of the mobilization of public opinion and the dissemination of relevant information in support of the principles and objectives of social progress and development,

Recognizing that popular participation, including the participation of workers in management and workers' self-management in countries where they exist, constitutes an important factor of socio-economic development as well as of respect for human rights and dignity of the human person,

Having considered the report of the Secretary-General on the International Seminar on Popular Participation, held at Ljubljana, Yugoslavia, from 17 to 25 May 1982,

1. *Takes note with appreciation* of the report of the Secretary-General;

2. *Invites* Member States to take into consideration in their development policies and programmes the recommendations of the International Seminar on Popular Participation, keeping in view their specific economic and social conditions;

3. *Calls upon* the organs and organizations of the United Nations system to promote, as appropriate, popular participation in the execution of their programmes to the extent and in the form appropriate to the nature of their work;

4. *Requests* the Secretary-General to transmit his report on the Seminar to Member States and the relevant United Nations bodies for their consideration;

5. *Requests* the Commission on Human Rights to consider at its thirty-ninth session the question of popular participation in its various forms as an important factor in development and in the realization of human rights, taking into account, *inter alia*, the results of the deliberations of the Seminar, as contained in the report of the Secretary-General, and to submit to the General Assembly, through the Economic and Social Council, appropriate suggestions for the more complete realization of human rights;

6. *Also requests* the Secretary-General to prepare a comprehensive progress report on the implementation of the present resolution, taking account of the suggestions made in the Commission on Human Rights, and to submit his report to the General Assembly at its thirty-eighth session;

7. *Decides* to include in the provisional agenda of its thirty-eighth session, under the item relating to the world social situation, a sub-item entitled "Popular participation in its various forms as an important factor in development and in the realization of human rights" in order to review the progress made in this field.

National experience with co-operative movements

As noted in the Secretary-General's report[1] on the Seminar on Popular Participation held at Ljubljana in May 1982, the Seminar reviewed national policies and experiences Member States had instituted to promote popular participation in national development, including working people's participation in management and self-management. Participants in the Seminar observed that co-operative organizations had become a vehicle for social ownership or participation in managing common activities under private ownership. In some countries, co-operative ventures and credit unions had been established to improve the economic lot of their members. In countries with private ownership of land, service co-operatives were effective in meeting the needs of members.

Report. [1]S-G, A/37/442.

UN Research Institute for Social Development

The United Nations Research Institute for Social Development (UNRISD) continued research in 1982 on food systems and society (with emphasis on the role of women), improving development data, popular participation in development and refugee settlement. On 21 June, the Institute's Director reported[2] to the UNRISD Board of Direc-

tors at its twentieth session, held at Geneva on 8 and 9 July, on the progress of the Institute's work in 1981 and 1982 and on its work programme for 1982-1983. A December report[1] by the Board to the Commission for Social Development further summarized progress made during 1981 and 1982.

Substantial progress was made in the food systems and society project approved by the Board in 1978,[3] aimed at explaining why food security—the sufficient supply of food—had declined for many countries, social groups and individuals. Scarcity of funds had, until 1982, limited the scope of research, but a UNRISD request for support for strengthening its ongoing research in China, India, the Ivory Coast, Mexico, Nicaragua, Senegal and the Upper Volta and to begin new studies in China and Nepal was approved in 1982 by the Governing Council of the United Nations Development Programme. The United Nations Environment Programme also made funds available for a study on the reduction of the vulnerability of food systems to the climate in eastern India. The second loan of a four-year programme of loans from the International Fund for Agricultural Development was processed to support investment projects to improve food security in Nicaragua.

UNRISD published two reports on issues being studied in China in the food systems project: one on participation in rural China and the other on systems at the household level. Work was completed on the UNRISD project, based in Senegal, on the impact of social change on the role and status of women in Africa south of the Sahara, and considerable research and feasibility studies on food systems were under way in several African countries, as well as on the South Asia subcontinent and in Mexico. A UNRISD-originated project at Kerala, India, to test a methodology for monitoring change in socio-economic conditions and for examining the interrelationship of various factors in the development process entered its fourth year. UNRISD assisted the United Nations Children's Fund and the regional government with a similar project monitoring social indicators in southern Sudan. As part of UNRISD work in popular participation, a seminar organized in Mexico allowed a first summing up of research and subdebate experiences in the study of social movements. In India, the comparative analysis of nine grass-roots organizations was the subject of a seminar in May. Regarding refugee settlement, research included field studies of the integration of refugees in East Africa. A related study was completed in Somalia on the food situation of Ethiopian refugees living in camps.

The Institute's 1981 deficit was repaid in full in 1982 among expenditures for the year of $1,195,365. Income for 1982 was $1,538,232. During the year, UNRISD received contributions totalling $947,235 from 10 countries, as follows: Australia—$52,835; Cyprus—$38,129; Denmark —$45,383; Finland—$66,284; Italy—$80,000; Mexico—$5,089; Netherlands—$105,555; Norway —$84,832; Sweden—$443,656; Switzerland— $25,472.

> Reports. [1]UNRISD Board, E/CN.5/1983/16; [2]UNRISD Director, UNRISD/82/C.13.
> Yearbook reference. [3]1978, p. 614.

Crime

The Economic and Social Council's Committee on Crime Prevention and Control held its seventh session at Vienna, Austria, from 15 to 24 March 1982.[1] The Committee approved four draft resolutions for action by United Nations bodies. Two of these, which the Council later adopted, concerned preparations and organizational arrangements for the Seventh (1985) United Nations Congress on the Prevention of Crime and the Treatment of Offenders, and enhancement of the Committee's functions in relation to the preparation of such congresses.

Examination of the proposed agenda items for the Seventh Congress had been entrusted to two working groups. Another working group was set up to examine the implementation of a 1979 Council resolution[2] which had entrusted the Committee with various functions, including those involved in preparations for crime congresses and in preparing and submitting for approval to those congresses and United Nations bodies programmes of international co-operation in crime prevention. The group established two teams, one to concentrate on the role and status of the Committee and the other to deal with its long-term programme of work. One of two resolutions proposed by the Committee for consideration by the Commission for Social Development in 1983 derived from discussion of this topic. The Committee thereby sought authorization to report directly to the Council, because of the need for timely action on its recommendations. By the other, it sought authorization to study the matter of summary executions. Guidelines guaranteeing a fair trial for those sentenced to death, previously submitted to the Sixth United Nations Congress on crime prevention in 1980,[3] were annexed to the Committee's report.

The Committee also adopted a decision on organizational arrangements for its eighth session, scheduled to be held in 1984.

Operational activities in the field of crime prevention and criminal justice in 1982 included support to United Nations–affiliated regional institutes, strengthened relations with regional commissions and a project for Namibia. Advisory mis-

sions were carried out at the request of five countries and the Latin American Institute for Crime Prevention and Treatment of Delinquents, in Costa Rica.

> Report. [1]Committee on crime, E/CN.5/1983/2.
> Resolution. [2]ESC: 1979/19, 9 May 1979 (YUN 1979, p. 782).
> Yearbook reference. [3]1980, p. 779.
> Publication. Crime Prevention and Criminal Justice Newsletter No. 7.

Preparations for UN congresses on crime

Seventh Congress (1985)

In April 1982, the Secretary-General reported to the Economic and Social Council on the preparations for the Seventh United Nations Congress on the Prevention of Crime and the Treatment of Offenders, to be held in 1985, and included a statement on the administrative and financial implications of the Congress.[6] The report had been requested by the Council in 1981.[1] The Secretary-General noted that the Committee on Crime Prevention and Control, at its March 1982 session,[4] had recommended, as topics for inclusion in the Congress's provisional agenda: new dimensions of criminality and crime prevention in the context of development; criminal justice processes and perspectives in a changing world; youth, crime and justice; victims of crime; and formulation and application of United Nations standards and norms in criminal justice.

The Committee also recommended that the Secretary-General be requested to undertake a number of preparatory activities which were reflected in two draft resolutions it had proposed for Council adoption. These included regional preparatory meetings, for which special financial provisions were needed to permit the attendance of the least developed countries; interregional meetings of experts selected by the Secretary-General, to be held on the agenda items; and an effective and wide-ranging public information programme, including pre-Congress and post-Congress phases.

Economic and Social Council action. On 4 May,[7] the Economic and Social Council approved the provisional agenda for the Seventh Congress, as recommended by the Committee on Crime Prevention and Control in March. It also endorsed the Committee's recommendations, including the convening of preparatory meetings in 1983 and 1984, and asked the Secretary-General to provide resources for least-developed-country participation in regional preparatory meetings and in the Congress itself and for an effective public information programme. It further asked him to provide additional resources to the Centre for Social Development and Humanitarian Affairs for preparatory activities. The Council encouraged Governments to prepare for the Congress with a view to formulating national position papers, invited

Member States to submit information on implementation of the recommendations of the Sixth Congress, held in 1980,[10] and invited regional commissions, institutes and intergovernmental and non-governmental organizations to become actively involved in the preparations. The Secretary-General was urged to undertake consultations within the Administrative Committee on Coordination to facilitate the work of the Committee on Crime and the Council in crime prevention and control and to take other measures to ensure successful preparatory activities. Provision was also to be made for the regional commissions to attend the Committee's next session.

The resolution, which originated in the Committee on crime and was transmitted to the Council by the Secretariat,[2] was approved by the Council's Second (Social) Committee on 29 April by 41 votes to none, with 4 abstentions. The Committee had accepted an oral amendment by Bangladesh specifically to include temporary assistance in the additional resources the Secretary-General was asked to provide to the Centre for Social Development and Humanitarian Affairs.

The Byelorussian SSR orally proposed amendments relating to item 7 of the Congress's provisional agenda, "Formulation and application of United Nations standards and norms in criminal justice": first to delete the item, then changed to delete the words "United Nations". It subsequently decided not to pursue the matter on the understanding that it would be considered by the Committee on crime.

General Assembly action. On 21 December, in a resolution[8] on questions relating to the programme budget for 1982-1983, the General Assembly authorized resources to permit representatives from the least developed countries to attend regional preparatory meetings for the Seventh Congress and the Congress itself, as the Economic and Social Council had requested in May.[7] This was to be an exception to the provisions of a 1962 Assembly resolution[9] restricting payment by the Organization of travel expenses to specific representatives. The Secretary-General had requested[5] $68,600 to cover travel expenses for the representatives in question. The Advisory Committee on Administrative and Budgetary Questions recommended a reduction to $62,000.[3]

The resolution was approved on 26 October by the Fifth (Administrative and Budgetary) Committee, on an oral recommendation of its Chairman, by 74 votes to 6, with 19 abstentions. The Assembly adopted it by a recorded vote, requested by the United States, of 141 to 3.

The United States, opposing the resolution, said in Committee that, given current conditions, the principles established by the 1962 resolution should continue to apply. Japan abstained, expressing concern that the exception might have serious implications in the future. The United Kingdom, the Federal Republic of Germany and Italy shared those concerns, and said they would vote against the proposal. Canada, which abstained, said that, while the 1962 resolution should be observed, it was desirable to provide assistance for the least developed countries, though on a case-by-case basis.

Algeria, Ethiopia and Ghana spoke in favour of the resolution. Bangladesh also favoured the proposal and cited precedents for the action; Mali and Nigeria supported its view. Cuba said that savings should not be achieved at the expense of the least developed countries.

Decision. [1]ESC: 1981/122, 6 May 1981 (YUN 1981, p. 774).
Note. [2]Secretariat, E/1982/C.2/L.1 (transmitting draft res. by Committee on crime).
Reports. [3]ACABQ, A/37/7/Add.4; [4]Committee on crime, E/CN.5/1983/2; S-G, [5]A/C.5/37/3, [6]E/1982/37 & Add.1/Rev.1.
Resolutions (1982). [7]ESC: 1982/29, 4 May, text following. [8]GA: 37/237, sect. II, 21 Dec., text following.
Resolution (prior). [9]GA: 1798(XVII), 11 Dec. 1962 (YUN 1962, p. 558).
Yearbook reference. [10]1980, p. 779.
Meeting records. ESC: E/1982/SR.23 (4 May), GA: 5th Committee, A/C.5/37/SR.19 (26 Oct.); plenary, A/37/PV.114 (21 Dec.).

Economic and Social Council resolution 1982/29

4 May 1982   Meeting 23   Adopted without vote

Approved by Second Committee (E/1982/58) by vote (41-0-4), 29 April (meeting 11); draft by Committee on crime (E/CN.5/1983/2), orally amended by Bangladesh; agenda item 11.

Preparations for the Seventh United Nations Congress on the Prevention of Crime and the Treatment of Offenders, with special reference to its agenda

The Economic and Social Council,

Considering that, in pursuance of General Assembly resolution 415(V) of 1 December 1950, the Seventh United Nations Congress on the Prevention of Crime and the Treatment of Offenders is to be convened in 1985,

Bearing in mind General Assembly resolutions 32/59 and 32/60 of 8 December 1977 and 35/171 of 15 December 1980, in which the Assembly noted the importance of the United Nations congresses in the field of crime prevention and criminal justice,

Recognizing the significant contributions of the congresses in the promotion and strengthening of international co-operation in this field,

Recalling its decision 1981/122 of 6 May 1981, in which the Secretary-General was requested, without prejudice to the established reporting procedures, to submit a comprehensive statement on the preparatory work for the Seventh Congress to the Economic and Social Council at its first regular session of 1982,

Recalling also General Assembly resolution 36/21 of 9 November 1981, in which the Secretary-General was requested to take into account the relevant recommendations made by the Committee on Crime Prevention and Control at its seventh session regarding the preparations for the Congress,

Emphasizing the importance of undertaking all the preparatory activities in a timely and concerted manner,

Acknowledging the need to create governmental, professional and public awareness of the issues related to crime prevention and criminal justice in the context of development, particularly in the preparatory phase of the Congress,

Conscious of the positive response of many countries to the Caracas Declaration and the recommendations of the Sixth Congress, and of the need to keep national authorities involved in the preparations for the Seventh Congress,

Having considered the relevant recommendations made by the Committee on Crime Prevention and Control at its seventh session, bearing in mind that, in accordance with paragraph 2 of General Assembly resolution 32/60, the Committee is entrusted with the function of preparing the quinquennial United Nations congresses on the prevention of crime and the treatment of offenders,

Taking note of the comprehensive statement of the Secretary-General and of the note on the continuation of preparations for the Seventh United Nations Congress on the Prevention of Crime and the Treatment of Offenders,

1. *Approves* the provisional agenda for the Seventh United Nations Congress on the Prevention of Crime and the Treatment of Offenders, as recommended by the Committee on Crime Prevention and Control at its seventh session, set out below:

''1. Opening of the Congress
''2. Organizational matters
''3. New dimensions of criminality and crime prevention in the context of development: challenges for the future
''4. Criminal justice processes and perspectives in a changing world
''5. Victims of crime
''6. Youth, crime and justice
''7. Formulation and application of United Nations standards and norms in criminal justice
''8. Adoption of the report of the Congress'';

2. *Endorses* the recommendations of the Committee, particularly the recommendation that item 3 should be discussed in plenary meetings, the remaining items being dealt with by two main committees;

3. *Encourages* Governments to make preparations for the Congress by all appropriate means, with a view to formulating national position papers;

4. *Invites* Member States to submit, for consideration by the Seventh Congress, information to the Secretary-General on the implementation of the recommendations of the Sixth Congress, in order to ensure continuity between the two Congresses in accordance with resolution 17 of the Sixth Congress;

5. *Also invites* the regional commissions, the regional and international institutes in the field of crime prevention and the treatment of offenders, the specialized agencies and other entities within the United Nations system, other intergovernmental organizations concerned and non-governmental organizations having consultative status with the Economic and Social Council to become actively involved in the preparations for the Seventh Congress;

6. *Urges* the Secretary-General to undertake the necessary interagency consultations within the machinery of the Administrative Committee on Co-ordination as a means of facilitating the work of the Committee on Crime Prevention and Control in its function of assisting the Council in co-ordinating activities in the field of crime prevention and control;

7. *Requests* the Secretary-General to take all necessary measures to ensure the successful undertaking of the preparatory activities for the Seventh Congress as well as the success of the Congress itself, including the convening of the regional preparatory meetings and interregional meetings of experts in 1983 and 1984, and the commissioning of experts and consultants, selected with due regard to equitable geographical representation, to assist in the preparation of the necessary documentation and in the professional conduct of the proceedings of the Congress, in accordance with past practice and with rule 58 of the provisional rules of procedure of the congresses;

8. *Also requests* the Secretary-General to provide the necessary additional resources, including temporary assistance, to the Centre for Social Development and Humanitarian Affairs of the Secretariat in order to enable its Crime Prevention and Criminal Justice Branch to undertake, in an effective and timely manner, all the preparatory activities for the Seventh Congress.

9. *Recommends* that adequate provision should be made for the attendance of the regional commissions at the next session of the Committee on Crime Prevention and Control and at the Congress;

10. *Requests* the Secretary-General to make available the necessary resources for the participation of the least developed countries in the regional preparatory meetings for the Congress and in the Congress itself;

11. *Further requests* the Secretary-General to provide additional resources, as required, to ensure a wide and effective programme of public information for the preparations for the Congress.

General Assembly resolution 37/237, section II

21 December 1982   Meeting 114   141-3 (recorded vote)

Approved by Fifth Committee (A/37/790) by vote (74-6-19), 26 October (meeting 19); oral proposal by Chairman; agenda item 103.

Travel of representatives from the least developed countries to attend regional preparatory meetings for the Seventh United Nations Congress on the Prevention of Crime and the Treatment of Offenders

[*The General Assembly . . .*]

Authorizes, as an exception to the provisions of paragraph 2 *(b)* of its resolution 1798(XVII) of 11 December 1962, the necessary resources for the implementation of paragraph 10 of Economic and Social Council resolution 1982/29 of 4 May 1982;

. . .

Recorded vote in Assembly as follows:

In favour: Afghanistan, Algeria, Angola, Argentina, Australia, Austria, Bahamas, Bahrain, Bangladesh, Barbados, Belgium, Benin, Bhutan, Bolivia, Botswana, Brazil, Bulgaria, Burma, Burundi, Byelorussian SSR, Canada, Cape Verde, Central African Republic, Chad, Chile, China, Colombia, Comoros, Congo, Costa Rica, Cuba, Cyprus, Czechoslovakia, Democratic Kampuchea, Democratic Yemen, Denmark, Dominican Republic, Ecuador, Egypt, Ethiopia, Fiji, Finland, France, Gabon, Gambia, German Democratic Republic, Ghana, Greece, Grenada, Guatemala, Guinea, Guinea-Bissau, Guyana, Honduras, Hungary, Iceland, India, Indonesia, Iran, Iraq, Ireland, Israel, Italy, Ivory Coast, Jamaica, Japan, Jordan, Kenya, Kuwait, Lao People's Democratic Republic, Lebanon, Lesotho, Liberia, Libyan Arab Jamahiriya, Luxembourg, Madagascar, Malawi, Malaysia, Maldives, Mali, Malta, Mauritania, Mexico, Mongolia, Morocco, Mozambique, Nepal, Netherlands, New Zealand, Nicaragua, Niger, Nigeria, Norway, Oman, Pakistan, Panama, Papua New Guinea, Paraguay, Peru, Philippines, Poland, Portugal, Qatar, Romania, Rwanda, Saint Lucia, Samoa, Sao Tome and Principe, Saudi Arabia, Senegal, Sierra Leone, Singapore, Solomon Islands, Somalia, Spain, Sri Lanka, Sudan, Suriname, Swaziland, Sweden, Syrian Arab Republic, Thailand, Togo, Trinidad and Tobago, Tunisia, Turkey, Uganda, Ukrainian SSR, USSR, United Arab Emirates, United Republic of Cameroon, United Republic of Tanzania, Upper Volta, Uruguay, Venezuela, Viet Nam, Yemen, Yugoslavia, Zaire, Zambia, Zimbabwe.

Against: Germany, Federal Republic of, United Kingdom, United States.

Functions of the Committee on crime

On 4 May 1982, the Economic and Social Council, convinced of the need to make more effective the methods of work of the Committee on Crime Prevention and Control, especially in preparing the United Nations congresses on crime prevention, decided, without vote, that the Chairman of that Committee could appoint from among its members persons to give advice on the regional and interregional preparatory meetings for the Seventh United Nations Congress on the Prevention of Crime and the Treatment of Offenders. The resolution[4] had been recommended by the Committee on 24 March[2] and transmitted to the Council by the Secretariat.[1] The Council also requested the Secretary-General to implement the decisions and recommendations of the Committee's March session, in accordance with the Committee's 1979 mandate[5] to prepare and submit for approval to United Nations bodies and congresses programmes of international co-operation in crime prevention.

The resolution, with written and oral amendments, was first approved without vote by the Council's Second Committee on 29 April. The Byelorussian SSR introduced two amendments in Committee: one substituted a preambular text observing that the Council had considered the April 1982 report[3] of the Secretary-General on preparations for the Congress rather than the report of the Committee on Crime Prevention and Control on its March session[2] on its agenda item on the implementation of the Council's 1979 resolution;[5] the second replaced operative paragraph 1, by which the Council would have decided that special consultants, to be appointed from among the Committee members by the Chairman, should serve as resource persons on behalf of the Committee in respect of the regional and interregional preparatory meetings. The Council instead decided that the Committee could appoint advisers on the preparatory meetings from among its members. A Belgian oral sub-amendment accepted by the Byelorussian SSR specified that the appointments would stem from the Committee Chairman.

Note. [1]Secretariat, E/1982/C.2/L.1 (transmitting draft res. by Committee on crime).
Reports. [2]Committee on crime, E/CN.5/1983/2; [3]S-G, E/1982/37.
Resolution (1982). [4]ESC: 1982/30, 4 May, text following.
Resolution (prior). [5]ESC: 1979/19, 9 May 1979 (YUN 1979, p. 782).
Meeting record. ESC: E/1982/SR.23 (4 May).

Economic and Social Council resolution 1982/30

4 May 1982   Meeting 23   Adopted without vote

Approved by Second Committee (E/1982/58) without vote, 29 April (meeting 11); draft by Committee on crime (E/CN.5/1983/2), amended by Byelorussian SSR (E/1982/C.2/L.9, orally sub-amended by Belgium); agenda item 11.

Enhancement of the functioning of the Committee on Crime Prevention and Control in relation to the preparation of United Nations congresses on the prevention of crime and the treatment of offenders

The Economic and Social Council,

Having considered the report of the Secretary-General on preparations for the Seventh United Nations Congress on the Prevention of Crime and the Treatment of Offenders,

Convinced of the need to make more effective the methods of work of the Committee on Crime Prevention and Control, especially in connection with its function of preparing the United Nations congresses on the prevention of crime and the treatment of offenders,

Desiring to enable the Committee to undertake its functions between sessions, in accordance with paragraph 1 *(a)* of Economic and Social Council resolution 1979/19 of 9 May 1979 and General Assembly resolution 32/60 of 8 December 1977, particularly in relation to its functions as a preparatory committee,

1. *Decides* that the Chairman of the Committee on Crime Prevention and Control may appoint persons from among the members of the Committee who may give advice in respect of the regional and interregional preparatory meetings for the Seventh United Nations Congress on the Prevention of Crime and the Treatment of Offenders;

2. *Requests* the Secretary-General to implement fully the decisions and recommendations made by the Committee on Crime Prevention and Control at its seventh session, in accordance with paragraph 2 of Economic and Social Council resolution 1979/19.

UN Trust Fund for Social Defence

In 1982, the United Nations Trust Fund for Social Defence supplied $375,594 to the United Nations Social Defence Research Institute in Rome, Italy. The Trust Fund was established pursuant to a 1965 resolution of the Economic and Social Council[1] to strengthen United Nations work in social defence.

During 1982, contributions to the Trust Fund totalled $621,130, from France ($18,705), Greece ($7,500), Italy ($359,947), Japan ($78,966), Nigeria ($4,399), Saudi Arabia ($141,000) and Switzerland ($10,613). Pledges for future payment were received from France ($41,958), Israel ($2,000), Italy ($346,021), Switzerland ($10,227) and Thailand ($1,000).

Resolution. [1]ESC: 1086 B (XXXIX), 30 July 1965 (YUN 1965, p. 409).

Crime and aging persons

The World Assembly on Aging, meeting at Vienna, Austria, from 26 July to 6 August 1982,[1] noted that growing crime in some countries against the elderly also victimized the many older persons who became afraid to leave their homes. The World Assembly recommended that efforts should be directed to law enforcement agencies and the elderly to increase their awareness of the extent and impact of such crimes.

Report. [1]World Assembly on Aging, A/CONF.113/31.

Chapter XIV

Population

Contents

Related topics:
  Regional economic and social activities—Population: Africa; Asia and the Pacific; Latin America. Statistics: Population and housing censuses.

For resolutions and decisions mentioned but not reproduced, refer to INDEX OF RESOLUTIONS AND DECISIONS.

UN Fund for Population Activities

UNFPA activities

The programmes of the United Nations Fund for Population Activities (UNFPA) received almost no additional resources in 1982, in spite of increased annual contributions. According to the Fund's Executive Director,[4] this was a result of the global inflation rate, currency devaluations and the strength of the United States dollar in relation to other currencies. Though tighter managerial and financial controls were instituted in 1982 as a result of a shortfall in resources in 1981, a major problem continued to be the Fund's capability of meeting all requests for assistance. Long-term assistance was being phased out in favour of assistance to countries, particularly the 53 priority countries with the most urgent problems (expanded from 40 in June 1982), which had received only minimal assistance in the past.

Project allocations in 1982 totalled $120.4 million. Expenditures were $123.7 million, including $69.2 million for country programmes, $32.5 million for intercountry programmes, $4.6 million for the budgets of UNFPA Deputy Representatives and Senior Advisers on Population, $6.7 million for over-

head payments, and $10.7 million for the administrative budget. By the end of the year, UNFPA was assisting 1,659 projects—1,257 country, 170 regional, 84 interregional and 148 global; 290 new projects were approved in 1982, amounting to $15.6 million, compared to 209 in 1981 amounting to $11.3 million. The 390 projects completed in 1982 brought the cumulative total to 1,766.

UNFPA assistance for family planning programmes, the number one priority area, totalled $48.8 million, or 40.5 per cent of total programme allocations, compared to $38.8 million, or 31.7 per cent of expenditures, in 1981. It emphasized extension of service delivery to rural areas, as well as the integration of family planning with maternal/child health-care services. It also focused attention on personnel development and training at the country level, preparation of training materials and methodologies, management and evaluation, and contraceptive and family planning research. On 29 and 30 March, UNFPA co-sponsored with the World Health Organization (WHO) a meeting in New York on natural family planning for representatives of international, regional and national organizations.

Activities in basic data collection totalled $19.5 million, or 16.2 per cent of total allocations. UNFPA supported over 100 of such projects in approximately

90 developing countries. The major contributions were for population censuses (70 per cent) and surveys (19 per cent).

Assistance to population dynamics totalled $14.2 million, or 11.8 per cent of allocations, compared to $13.2 million, or 10.7 per cent of expenditures, in 1981. About 70 countries were assisted in population research, demographic training, institution-building, and dissemination and utilization of research findings on specific population trends. The costs for the formulation and evaluation of population policies and programmes totalled $8 million, or 6.6 per cent of allocations, compared to $7.3 million, or 6 per cent, in 1981. Forty-five countries received assistance for the creation of national population units and to organize seminars, studies and other activities preparatory to the formulation of national population policy, as well as for country studies on population and development strategies and the management and co-ordination of population activities. For implementation of policies, allocations totalled $1 million, or 1 per cent, compared to $1.3 million, or 1.1 per cent, in 1981. In this respect, UNFPA supported the collection and analysis of migration data, conducted research on the causes and consequences of migration, and strengthened national capabilities to formulate and implement national policies and programmes, rather than actually implementing such programmes.

Assistance for special programme interests totalled $1.5 million, or 1.2 per cent of allocations, compared to $2.3 million, or 1.9 per cent of expenditures, in 1981, and included work on such projects as: enhancing women's participation in national population and development activities and helping to fund a research project of the International Labour Organisation on demographic change and the role of women in population and development; activities with an emphasis on youth, including family planning and family-life education projects and information, education and communication projects; and, in the field of aging, activities in connection with the 1982 World Assembly on Aging.

Funds for population education and communication totalled $14 million or 11.6 per cent of programme allocation, compared to $15.2 million, or 12.4 per cent of expenditures, the previous year.

On 18 June,[1] the Governing Council of the United Nations Development Programme (UNDP), serving as the governing body of UNFPA, took note of reports of the Fund's Executive Director on the evaluation of UNFPA projects[2] and on the implementation and monitoring of selected country programmes,[3] and requested that he supply more-analytical and -functional reports periodically, taking into account views of Council members. It asked him to update his 1981 report[5] on the role of UNFPA in the 1980s, incorporating decisions of the Council at its 1981 and 1982 sessions.

The Council endorsed a methodology for determining programmable resources and agreed on their distribution and allocation to countries, asked for implementation reports, decided on the support (up to 25 per cent) to be given to intercountry activities, endorsed guidelines for approving intercountry projects, asked for provision of assistance for regional commissions and demographic centres, specified reporting categories for intercountry activity reports, and endorsed continuation of the system of priority countries. It gave the Executive Director additional approval authority for up to $41 million for 1983 and $39.75 million for 1984. The Council directed the Fund to increase support for contraceptive research and development and asked for a joint report with WHO on the future United Nations role in family planning research. It approved $2 million from UNFPA for the WHO human reproduction programme and $2 million over two years from UNDP for the World Fertility Survey project. The Council also approved supplementary and other appropriations, and took other decisions concerning financial and administrative questions.

Operational activities. The Department of Technical Co-operation for Development participated in UNFPA-sponsored missions for population-needs assessment and project formulation and review. It began collation of software packages for data analysis and proposed further aid measures to UNFPA. Demographic analysis focused on study of the 1980 census data. Technical assistance included estimation of measures of fertility, mortality, migration and urbanization, and preparation of population projections.

Decision (1982). [1]UNDP Council (report, E/1982/16/Rev.1): 82/20, 18 June.
Reports. UNFPA Executive Director, [2]DP/1982/32, [3]DP/1982/33, [4]DP/1983/19.
Yearbook reference. [5]1981, p. 784.
UNFPA publications. Inventory of Population Projects in Developing Countries around the World, 1981/82 (yearly); *1982 Report by the Executive Director of the United Nations Fund for Population Activities*; *Population, UNFPA Newsletter,* vol. 8, Nos. 1-12 (monthly in Arabic, English, French & Spanish; every 2 months in Chinese); *Populi, Journal of the United Nations Fund for Population Activities,* vol. 9, Nos. 1-4 (quarterly).

Country and intercountry programmes

Of total UNFPA project allocations of $120.4 million in 1982 (see table), those for regional and country activities amounted to $100.8 million.

An allocation of $20.1 million was made for Africa south of the Sahara, where some 41 countries and 20 regional projects received assistance. Activities in the field of data collection represented 32.8 per cent of UNFPA allocations for the region, while 26 per cent was devoted to maternal and child health.[4] The greatest part of allocations for Asia and the Pacific ($51.6 million), Latin America and the Caribbean ($15.5 million) and the Middle East, the

Mediterranean and Europe ($13.7 million) also went for maternal and child health services and family planning.

Most of the UNFPA-supported interregional and global projects executed by the United Nations and the specialized agencies were in the third year of a four-year programming cycle during 1982. Allocations amounted to some $20 million, and efforts continued to bring the total, together with the regional-project total, closer to 25 per cent of total UNFPA allocations. Intercountry programmes (regional, interregional and global) represented 29.6 per cent of the total allocations, compared with 34.9 per cent of expenditures in 1981.

The Executive Director of UNFPA offered suggested guidelines for the approval of new and continuing intercountry projects in an April report to the UNDP Governing Council.[2] UNFPA would continue to support technical assistance and backstopping at the intercountry level, and to provide assistance for interregional and regional training programmes where country needs had been clearly demonstrated. It would continue to fund research in demographic and socio-economic issues and in family planning, concentrating on responding to demonstrated country needs, within a time-frame and aiming at producing a final product and ensuring its utilization. At the global level, emphasis would be on conceptual and methodological issues of value to a wide range of countries. UNFPA would continue to assist information-exchange activities, but at a lower level than in the past.

Also in April,[3] the Executive Director reported on the Fund's system of priority countries, which allowed UNFPA to concentrate its resources on countries with the most urgent needs and problems. The report reviewed the system in terms of resource distribution to priority, borderline and other countries, as well as among major programme areas by priority status of countries. It also contained a regional analysis of the system. No major modification of the system's criteria was recommended, except to substitute a country's annual increment in population size for its annual rate of growth. Among recommendations for designating priority countries was one which stipulated that countries must have a gross national product per capita of $500 or less. The distinction between priority and borderline countries should be eliminated.

On 18 June,[1] the UNDP Governing Council decided that the Fund's support of intercountry activities should not exceed 25 per cent of programme resources, and endorsed the Executive Director's new guidelines for the approval of new and continuing intercountry projects. It requested him to assist the regional commissions and demographic training and research centres, and asked that intercountry activities be reported by work plan category as well as functional category. It endorsed continuation of the system of priority countries, viewed with grave concern downward trends in assistance to those countries, reiterated that all efforts should be made to devote two thirds of country programme resources to them and endorsed modified criteria for determining them.

Decision (1982). [1]UNDP Council (report, E/1982/16/Rev.1): 82/20, sect. I, paras. 3 & 4, 18 June.
Reports. UNFPA Executive Director, [2]DP/1982/29 & Add.1, [3]DP/1982/30 & Add.1, [4]DP/1983/19 & Add.1-3.

Work programmes

The UNFPA work plan for 1983-1986,[3] prepared by the Executive Director, was based on the assumptions that income would increase by 10 per cent per annum to 1986, that support to intercountry activities would be 25 per cent of total programme resources and that two thirds of allocations for country projects would be for priority countries. By this document, the Executive Director requested approval authority for implementing the plan, which included increases to the operational reserve.

A review of the UNFPA programme for 1982-1985,[2] submitted for the UNDP Governing Council's approval, examined resource requirements, availability and use. The report made a proposal for the distribution of programmable resources between country and intercountry activities and for country allocation in that period.

UNFPA ALLOCATIONS BY MAJOR FUNCTION, 1982

	Amount (in millions of US dollars)	Per cent of total programme
Family planning	48.8	40.5
Basic data collection	19.5	16.2
Population dynamics	14.2	11.8
Communication and education	14.0	11.6
Multisector activities	13.5	11.1
Formulation and evaluation of population policies	8.0	6.6
Special programmes	1.5	1.2
Implementation of policies	1.1	1.0
Total*	120.4	100.0

*Total includes allocations for Deputy Representatives and Senior Advisers on Population, overhead for government-executed projects and infrastructure.
NOTE: Total may differ from sum of figures due to rounding.

SOURCE: DP/1983/19.

UNFPA ALLOCATIONS BY EXECUTING AGENCY, 1982

	Amount (in millions of US dollars)	Per cent of total programme
Governments (directly executed)	27.1	22.5
United Nations	24.7	20.6
WHO	19.5	16.2
UNFPA	17.3	14.3
Non-governmental organizations	9.6	8.0
ILO	6.2	5.1
Regional commissions	6.1	5.1
UNESCO	4.7	3.9
UNICEF	3.5	2.9
FAO	1.7	1.4
Total	120.4	100.0

NOTE: Total may differ from sum of figures due to rounding.

SOURCE: DP/1983/19.

UNFPA PROJECT ALLOCATIONS, 1982
(in US dollars)

COUNTRY, TERRITORY AND REGIONAL PROJECTS	ALLOCATION	COUNTRY, TERRITORY AND REGIONAL PROJECTS	ALLOCATION	COUNTRY, TERRITORY AND REGIONAL PROJECTS	ALLOCATION
Africa south of the Sahara		*Asia and the Pacific* (cont.)		*Latin America and the Caribbean* (cont.)	
Angola*	324,238	Hong Kong	27,273	Peru	585,869
Benin*	581,652	India*	10,714,554	St. Kitts–Nevis	44,465
Botswana	354,180	Indonesia*	3,057,753	Saint Lucia	75,500
Burundi*	321,676	Kiribati	154,221	Saint Vincent and the Grenadines	79,555
Cape Verde	152,892	Lao People's Democratic Republic*	85,021	Suriname	13,719
Central African Republic*	221,500	Malaysia	1,166,328	Uruguay	81,397
Comoros*	453,935	Maldives*	18,862	Regional	3,701,613
Congo	384,110	Mongolia	425,690		
Equatorial Guinea*	254,717	Nepal*	1,829,258	Subtotal	15,537,474
Ethiopia*	1,399,268	Pakistan*	3,229,884		
Gabon	29,884	Papua New Guinea	85,722	*Middle East and the Mediterranean*	
Gambia*	264,540	Philippines	975,849	Algeria	2,945
Ghana*	58,569	Republic of Korea	578,555	Bahrain	409,983
Guinea*	281,320	Samoa*	205,133	Cyprus	58,754
Guinea-Bissau	176,216	Singapore	33,888	Democratic Yemen*	933,289
Ivory Coast	90,653	Solomon Islands*	144,742	Djibouti	594,899
Kenya*	669,010	Sri Lanka*	1,594,360	Egypt*	1,279,319
Lesotho*	182,700	Thailand	2,014,427	Iraq	152,634
Liberia*	405,355	Tonga	83,679	Jordan	1,017,362
Madagascar*	391,077	Trust Territory of the Pacific Islands	195,258	Kuwait	77,300
Malawi*	226,724	Tuvalu	27,001	Malta	5,000
Mali*	340,929	Vanuatu	199,648	Morocco	1,019,065
Mauritania*	632,746	Viet Nam*	2,528,435	Somalia*	1,010,975
Mauritius	318,073	Regional	5,630,009	Sudan*	1,479,273
Mozambique*	874,311			Syrian Arab Republic	1,073,999
Niger*	100,000	Subtotal	51,555,478	Tunisia	690,721
Nigeria	774,285			Turkey	269,759
Rwanda*	393,213	*Latin America and the Caribbean*		United Arab Emirates	13,705
Sao Tome and Principe*	147,685	Anguilla	30,700	Yemen*	787,690
Senegal*	610,330	Antigua and Barbuda	27,550	Regional	1,665,650
Seychelles	39,113	Barbados	130,414		
Sierra Leone*	441,587	Belize	12,377	Subtotal	12,542,322
Swaziland	267,332	Bolivia	466,375		
Togo	256,146	Brazil	367,051	*Europe*	
Uganda*	21,226	British Virgin Islands	27,067	Albania	1,950
United Republic of Cameroon	349,121	Chile	1,700	Bulgaria	11,042
United Republic of Tanzania*	638,884	Colombia	576,760	Czechoslovakia	20,160
Upper Volta*	635,713	Costa Rica	63,384	Greece	17,905
Zaire*	716,267	Cuba	741,721	Hungary	15,733
Zambia*	579,410	Dominica*	21,112	Portugal	239,801
Zimbabwe*	253,000	Dominican Republic	680,979	Romania	19,800
Regional	4,458,218	Ecuador	919,560	Yugoslavia	160,391
		El Salvador	1,027,063	Regional	677,561
Subtotal	20,080,785	Guatemala	687,062		
		Haiti*	983,239	Subtotal	1,164,343
Asia and the Pacific		Honduras	650,425		
Afghanistan*	510,312	Jamaica	245,400	INTERREGIONAL AND GLOBAL PROJECTS	
Bangladesh*	3,656,683	Mexico	1,582,837	Interregional	8,268,885
Bhutan*	414,571	Nicaragua	481,284	Global	11,299,355
Burma*	57,658	Panama	441,678		
China*	11,527,189	Paraguay	789,618	Subtotal	19,568,240
Cook Islands	32,684				
Fiji	350,831			Total	120,448,642

*Classified as a priority country for UNFPA assistance.

SOURCE: DP/1983/19/Add.2,3

The Governing Council, in an 18 June 1982 decision,[1] endorsed the methodology for determining the amount of programmable resources, as set forth in the report, including a provision for over-programming by 5 per cent, inasmuch as there was always a degree of under-implementation. It agreed to the intended distribution of resources between country and intercountry activities, as well as the intended distribution of allocations to countries, and asked the Executive Director to report on plan implementation in future reports. The Council also gave the Executive Director addi-tional approval authority of $41 million for 1983, bringing the total for that year to $149 million, $39.75 million for 1984, bringing the 1984 total to 75 per cent of the 1983 level (or $111.75 million), 50 per cent of the 1983 level for 1985 (or $74.5 million) and 25 per cent of the 1983 level for 1986 (or $37.25 million).

Decision (1982). [1]UNDP Council (report, E/1982/16/Rev.1): 82/20, sect. I, paras. 2 & 7, 18 June.
Report. [2]UNFPA Executive Director, DP/1982/28.
Work plan. [3]UNFPA Executive Director, DP/1982/24.

Contraceptive methods

There were promising scientific leads for new and better contraceptives and their wide application in developing countries over the next 10 to 15 years, according to an April 1982 report of the Executive Director of UNFPA.[2] However, funding for research for improved technology was decreasing. Private-sector investment from the pharmaceutical industry had declined, and government research aimed at developing countries' needs had not kept pace with demand. Voluntary contributions to the Special Programme of Research, Development and Research Training in Human Reproduction of the World Health Organization (WHO) had also declined.

The report presented several policy options for action by the UNDP Governing Council on issues such as: identifying contraceptive research and development needs and opportunities as a category of activity; the percentage of the Fund's intercountry activities to be earmarked for research programmes to develop and improve contraceptive and natural family-planning methods; and the level of continued UNFPA support for the WHO and other research programmes. Background information on research and development needs and information on the current status of technology and on current funds and opportunities for future UNFPA support were also supplied.

The Executive Director noted two important areas of activity that were beyond the Fund's current capacity: fundamental research on human reproductive processes, and core support for long-term strengthening of research institutions. He suggested that the Governing Council might wish to consider these when deciding future levels of UNFPA funding.

Noting the Executive Director's report in its 18 June decision on UNFPA[1], the Council directed the Fund to increase its contribution and the effectiveness of its support for contraceptive research and development by stimulating research on methods, taking a more active role in deliberations of UNFPA-supported research organizations, and co-ordinating its aid with support from other organizations. It endorsed the need for support in this area through the WHO human reproduction programme (to which the Fund was to contribute at least $2 million in 1983) and appropriate organizations and institutions, and asked the Executive Director to prepare, jointly with the WHO Director-General and in consultation with the International Planned Parenthood Federation, a report on the future role of the United Nations system in family-planning research.

Decision (1982). [1]UNDP Council (report, E/1982/16/Rev.1): 82/20, sect. I, para. 6, 18 June.
Report. [2]UNFPA Executive Director, DP/1982/36 & Add.1.

World Fertility Survey

The UNDP Governing Council, in an 18 June decision,[1] approved a final contribution for the large-scale data-collection-and-analysis project, the "World Fertility Survey" (completion and assessment phase), in the amount of $2 million over two years.

Originally conceived as a five-year programme starting in January 1972, the programme—executed by the International Statistical Institute through a project staff in London—was extended for five years in January 1977. The Survey was expected to complete its activities, assess its achievements and terminate the project by June 1984.

Decision (1982). [1]UNDP Council (report, E/1982/16/Rev.1): 82/20, sect. I, para. 11, 18 June.

Financial and administrative questions

Administrative budgets

1982 budget

A supplementary appropriation of $1,374,407 for UNFPA administrative and programme support services for 1982 was approved on 18 June[2] by the UNDP Governing Council. This was to finance national income-tax reimbursement related to earnings during previous years, during which insufficient amounts had been appropriated, as well as to finance an increased amount requested by UNDP for providing support services to UNFPA for 1981 and 1982.

The Executive Director of UNFPA had recommended that the Council approve $1,505,087,[1] which would have increased the total appropriation for 1982 by 16.1 per cent, from $9,345,579 to $10,850,666. This included an additional $797,070 for UNDP support services during 1982; the Advisory Committee on Administrative and Budgetary Questions (ACABQ) recommended reducing that amount to $708,017, as the matter was still the subject of discussion between UNDP and UNFPA.[3] The amount of $1,374,407 which the Council appropriated was reached by agreement between UNFPA and UNDP.

Budget estimates. [1]UNFPA Executive Director, DP/1982/25.
Decision (1982). [2]UNDP Council (report, E/1982/16/Rev.1): 82/20, sect. II, para. 1, 18 June.
Report. [3]ACABQ DP/1982/26.

1983 budget

The UNDP Governing Council, in its decision of 18 June 1982 on UNFPA[2], approved appropriations of $11,171,573 for the 1983 administrative and programme support services of UNFPA, including the reclassification of two posts to the P-5 level and one to the D-1 level. Of the total appropriation, $6,174,056 was for programme planning, appraisal and monitoring; $3,593,878 for administrative and information support services; and $1,403,639 for executive direction and management.

CONTRIBUTIONS TO UNFPA, 1982 AND 1983
(as at 31 December 1982; in US dollar equivalent)

Country or territory	1982 payment	1983 pledge	Country or territory	1982 payment	1983 pledge
Afghanistan	1,000	2,000	Malta	476	—
Australia	1,530,185	1,923,077	Mexico	11,803	11,472
Austria	37,500	36,200	Mongolia	542	520
Bahamas	4,000	—	Morocco	4,000	4,000
Bangladesh	12,000	13,200	Nepal	3,000	—
Barbados	6,000	3,000	Netherlands	11,315,326	—
Belgium	1,464,537	408,163	New Zealand	258,685	—
Benin	—	2,000	Nigeria	35,920	—
Bhutan	—	1,510	Norway	14,220,383	11,084,507
Botswana	1,326	1,101	Oman	10,000	10,000
British Virgin Islands	500	500	Pakistan	300,000	—
Burma	6,667	6,369	Panama	—	1,000
Burundi	—	3,350	Papua New Guinea	—	1,316
Canada	7,794,128	—	Portugal	14,035	20,000
Chile	5,000	5,000	Qatar	30,000	30,000
China	200,000	330,000	Republic of Korea	41,000	41,000
Colombia	3,930	—	Romania	5,455	5,455
Democratic Yemen	—	1,733	Rwanda	—	1,000
Denmark	4,467,657	4,800,000	Saint Lucia	—	500
Djibouti	—	2,000	Samoa	—	794
Ecuador	40,000	20,000	Saudi Arabia	30,000	30,000
Egypt	182,553	228,921	Senegal	—	20,000
Fiji	2,000	2,000	Singapore	7,500	—
Finland	918,345	1,181,818	Solomon Islands	1,000	—
France	143,885	218,978	Somalia	664	—
Germany, Federal Republic of	13,410,904	—	Sri Lanka	7,518	7,500
Greece	20,000	5,000	Sudan	—	25,000
Guatemala	5,000	5,000	Suriname	—	2,500
Guyana	333	—	Sweden	7,185,613	6,486,486
Honduras	10,000	10,000	Switzerland	1,774,194	1,704,225
Hungary	11,429	11,242	Syrian Arab Republic	—	5,500
Iceland	3,700	—	Thailand	44,000	44,000
India	338,266	338,266	Tunisia	32,060	19,262
Indonesia	99,611	150,000	Turkey	42,942	5,000
Italy	140,845	2,047,782	Uganda	—	4,032
Japan	24,300,000	—	United Kingdom	4,662,913	—
Kenya	4,110	3,571	United Republic of Cameroon	4,829	—
Lao People's Democratic Republic	500	500	United States	33,760,000	—
Lesotho	—	1,500	Uruguay	5,700	—
Libyan Arab Jamahiriya	40,000	—	Viet Nam	1,000	1,000
Luxembourg	—	5,408	Yemen	—	2,500
Malawi	1,212	—	Zimbabwe	—	2,604
Malaysia	10,000	—			
Maldives	871	871	Total	129,028,552	31,341,233

SOURCE: A/38/5/Add.7.

The UNFPA Executive Director had estimated that administrative and programme support services would amount to $11,362,543,[1] or 7.6 per cent of the Fund's anticipated 1983 resources. He attributed the rise over the 1982 level ($9,345,579) to resource growth and inflation. ACABQ recommended that the Governing Council approve instead $10,561,573, a reduction of $800,970 in the amount estimated by UNFPA for reimbursing the United Nations and UNDP[3] for administrative and management services. However, the cost of these services continued to be the subject of discussion among the bodies. The amount the Council appropriated was reached by agreement between UNFPA and UNDP.

Budget estimates. [1]UNFPA Executive Director, DP/1982/25.
Decision (1982). [2]UNDP Council (report, E/1982/16/Rev.1): 82/20, sect. II, para. 2, 18 June.
Report. [3]ACABQ, DP/1982/26.

Contributions

In an 18 June 1982 decision on UNFPA[1], the UNDP Governing Council expressed deep concern at the decline in the Fund's resources. It urged all countries to contribute or to increase their contributions, bearing in mind the work plan contained in the Executive Director's review and reassessment of the Fund, in order to achieve the level of resources for 1982-1985 envisaged in a 1981 Council decision[2] which had assumed a 10 per cent annual increase.

During 1982, 67 countries and territories paid a total of $129,028,552 in voluntary contributions to UNFPA; pledges for 1983, from 63 countries and territories, totalled $31,341,233 as at 31 December 1982 (see table above).

Decision (1982). [1]UNDP Council (report, E/1982/16/Rev.1): 82/20, sect. I, para. 10, 18 June.
Yearbook reference. [2]1981, p. 784.

Accounts for 1981

The Board of Auditors reported[2] the total expenditures of UNFPA at $136,366,575 for the year ended 31 December 1981, with an excess of expenditure over income of $10,858,132. The Board called for intensified efforts to collect unpaid pledges by Governments, including some $2.9 million pledged and outstanding for 1981 and previous years. It also recommended that: control over allotments and expenditures in project budgets be strengthened; the procurement system and inventory control be improved; adequate internal audit coverage be given to all UNFPA activities; field office budgets be realistically prepared to avoid wide variations from estimates, caused in part by late reimbursement of income tax; and monitoring of field office budget procedures be strengthened.

The Advisory Committee on Administrative and Budgetary Questions (ACABQ) agreed[1] with the Board's suggestions regarding improved inventory control and field office budgets, and suggested that billing procedures be speeded up to avoid *ex post facto* requests by UNFPA.

The General Assembly, in a resolution of 16 November 1982 on the accounts of several United Nations funds and programmes for the year ended 31 December 1981,[3] accepted the financial report and accounts of UNFPA, along with the audit opinion of the Board of Auditors.[2]

Reports. [1]ACABQ, A/37/443; [2]Board of Auditors, and financial statements, A/37/5/Add.7 & Corr.1.
Resolution (1982). [3]GA: 37/12, 16 Nov.

Other financial and administrative questions

The UNDP Governing Council, in a decision[1] of 18 June 1982 on UNFPA, requested the Fund's Executive Director to report on the budget estimates for administrative and programme support services for 1984-1985, together with proposed amendments to the Financial Regulations and Rules of the Fund. It noted the Executive Director's statement that if changes in arrangements between UNFPA and UNDP for administrative support services were necessary, they would be submitted to the Council through ACABQ. It requested that such proposals be worked out with UNDP. It noted the Executive Director's intention to report on the UNFPA staffing pattern and manpower requirements, agreed that he be authorized to transfer credits between programmes of the approved 1982 and 1983 budget, with the concurrence of ACABQ, and took note of the audit reports of participating and executing agencies relating to UNFPA-allocated funds as at 31 December 1980.

Decision (1982). [1]UNDP Council (report, E/1982/16/Rev.1): 82/20, sect. II, paras. 3-7, 18 June.

Publications

In addition to the *Demographic Yearbook*[4] and the *Population Bulletin*,[3] the United Nations Department of International Economic and Social Affairs prepared publications, issued in or related to 1982, on: international migration policies;[1] countries' demographic indicators, as assessed in 1980;[2] and world population prospects, as assessed in 1982.[5]

Publications. [1]*International Migration Policies and Programmes: A World Survey* (ST/ESA/SER.A/80), Sales No. E.82.XIII.4; [2]*Demographic Indicators of Countries: Estimates and Projections as Assessed in 1980* (ST/ESA/SER.A/82 & Corr.1), Sales No. E.82.XIII.5 and corr.; [3]*Population Bulletin of the United Nations, No. 14—1982* (ST/ESA/SER.N/14), Sales No. E.82.XIII.6; [4]*Demographic Yearbook, 1982* (ST/ESA/STAT/SER.R/12), Sales No. E/F.83.XIII.1; [5]*World Population Prospects: Estimates and Projections as Assessed in 1982*, Sales No. E.83.XIII.5.

Other UN population activities

Preparations for the 1984 Conference on Population

On 30 April 1982,[3] the Economic and Social Council, without vote, welcomed an offer of Mexico to host the International Conference on Population in 1984. It decided to review later in 1982 financial estimates for the Conference and the status of preparatory activities, and urged Member States to provide the necessary assistance and financial support. The draft was introduced by Australia, also on behalf of Bangladesh, China, Japan, Mexico and Pakistan.

On 27 July,[4] by 45 votes to none, with 4 abstentions, the Council accepted Mexico's offer with gratitude and requested the Secretary-General of the Conference to report on its dates, site and other arrangements. It welcomed India's offer to host an Expert Group Meeting on Fertility and the Family, at New Delhi in 1982, and an offer by the Federal Republic of Germany to support holding an Expert Group Meeting on Population, Resources, Environment and Development in early 1983, and requested the Conference Secretary-General to finalize arrangements for the two meetings. It decided to schedule an open-ended session of the Population Commission in January 1984, serving as the Preparatory Committee for the Conference, and invited the regional commissions to consider the Preparatory Committee's report and to transmit suggestions and recommendations for regional implementation of the World Population Plan of Action[5] to the Conference. It recommended that in 1982 the General Assembly approve expenses for the Conference preparations in 1983, and requested the Conference Secretary-General to report to the Council later in 1982 on his efforts to raise extrabudgetary resources for it.

The text, once revised, was introduced in the Council's First (Economic) Committee by India on behalf of 13 nations and approved by 44 votes to none, with 4 abstentions. Paragraph 7 was orally revised to stipulate that the open-ended Population Commission session should be scheduled in January 1984 rather than the preceding October, when the Commission's regular session was originally scheduled.

On 26 October, the Secretary-General of the Conference, in an oral report to the Council, said the Government of Mexico had agreed to August 1984 as the date for the Conference. Tentative arrangements had been made for expert group meetings in 1983 on fertility and the family (New Delhi, January); population distribution, migration and development (Hammemet, Tunisia, March); population, resources, environment and development (Geneva, April); and mortality and health policy (Rome, Italy, May/June).

The Secretary-General was confident that the fund-raising targets for the Conference—$300,000 in 1982, $700,000 in 1983 and $500,000 in 1984— would be met. The Council had requested that the General Assembly in 1982 approve the necessary expenses for the Conference preparations within the context of an overall budget of $2.3 million. The Council had decided that total Conference resources from the United Nations regular budget should not exceed $800,000, which was to come to the maximum extent possible from existing resources. The Secretary-General said he was making every effort to ensure that preparations were based on an integrated approach and the Conference was organized with the utmost economy.

The Council took note[1] of the Secretary-General's oral report on 26 October without vote, on an oral proposal by its President.

The *Ad Hoc* Task Force on the International Conference on Population of the Administrative Committee on Co-ordination (ACC), established to help provide inter-agency input to and co-ordinate the participation of the regional commissions and specialized agencies in the Conference, met at Geneva from 18 to 21 May.[2] The ACC Consultative Committee on Substantive Questions (Programme Matters) considered its report in October and expressed general satisfaction with the activities reported.

Decision (1982). [1]ESC: 1982/181, 26 Oct., text following.
Report. [2]ACC Task Force on Conference on Population, ACC/1982/PG/7.
Resolutions (1982). ESC: [3]1982/7, 30 Apr., text following; [4]1982/42, 27 July, text following.
Yearbook reference. [5]1974, p. 552.
Meeting records. ESC: E/1982/SR.15, 18, 19 (26-30 Apr.), 48 (27 July), 53 (26 Oct.).

Economic and Social Council resolution 1982/7

30 April 1982   Meeting 19   Adopted without vote

6-nation draft (E/1982/L.28/Rev.1); agenda item 4.

Sponsors: Australia, Bangladesh, China, Japan, Mexico, Pakistan.

Convening of an International Conference on Population in 1984

The Economic and Social Council,

Recalling its resolution 1981/87 of 25 November 1981, in which it decided to convene an International Conference on Population in 1984,

Noting with appreciation the report of the Secretary-General of the Conference and the significant progress made towards obtaining the necessary extrabudgetary resources for the Conference, as requested in paragraph 9 of Council resolution 1981/87,

Noting with satisfaction the current status of preparations for the Conference,

1. *Welcomes* the offer of the Government of Mexico to act as host to the International Conference on Population in 1984;

2. *Decides* to include in the agenda of its second regular session of 1982 an item on the convening of an International Conference on Population in 1984 in order:

(a) Further to review the financial estimates for the Conference contained in the report of the Secretary-General in the light of the contributions pledged;

(b) To consider the status of the preparatory activities being undertaken;

3. *Urges* Member States to provide the necessary assistance and financial support in order to ensure the success of the preparatory activities and of the Conference.

Economic and Social Council resolution 1982/42

27 July 1982   Meeting 48   45-0-4

Approved by First Committee (E/1982/95) by vote (44-0-4), 21 July (meeting 12); 13-nation draft (E/1982/C.1/L.1/Rev.1), orally revised; agenda item 8.

Sponsors: Australia, Bangladesh, Benin, China, India, Japan, Kenya, Mexico, Nepal, Nigeria, Pakistan, Qatar, Yugoslavia.

Convening of an International Conference on Population in 1984

The Economic and Social Council,

Recalling its resolution 1981/87 of 25 November 1981, in which it decided to convene an International Conference on Population in 1984,

Recalling also its resolution 1982/7 of 30 April 1982 concerning the status of preparations for the Conference,

1. *Decides* to accept, with gratitude, the offer of the Government of Mexico to act as host to the International Conference on Population in 1984;

2. *Requests* the Secretary-General of the Conference, after consultation with the Government of Mexico, to report to the Council, not later than at its first regular session of 1983, on the dates, site and other arrangements proposed for the Conference;

3. *Welcomes* the offer by the Government of India to act as host to the Expert Group Meeting on Fertility and the Family, to be held at New Delhi towards the end of 1982, and requests the Secretary-General of the Conference, in consultation with the Government of India, to finalize the arrangements for that meeting;

4. *Also welcomes* the offer by the Government of the Federal Republic of Germany to support the holding of the Expert Group Meeting on Population, Resources, Environment and Development in early 1983 and requests the Secretary-General of the Conference to finalize the arrangements for that meeting;

5. *Recommends* that the General Assembly, at its thirty-seventh session, should approve the necessary expenses for the preparation of the Conference in 1983, bearing in mind that the total financial cost of the Conference has been estimated by the Secretary-General at $2.3 million and that the total amount of the resources to be provided from the United Nations regular budget for the Conference should not exceed $800,000, which will come, to the maximum extent possible, from existing resources;

6. *Requests* the Secretary-General of the Conference to report to the Council at its resumed second regular session of 1982 on the status of his efforts to raise extrabudgetary resources for the Conference;

7. *Decides* to schedule the open-ended session of the Population Commission, which will serve as the Preparatory Committee for the Conference, in January 1984, immediately following the twenty-second session of the Commission, and to consider the report of the Preparatory Committee at the first regular session of 1984 of the Council;

8. *Invites* the regional commissions to consider, at their annual sessions in 1984, the report of the Preparatory Committee for the Conference

on its meeting in 1984, with a view to formulating suggestions and recommendations for the further implementation of the World Population Plan of Action at the regional level, and to transmit those suggestions and recommendations to the Conference for its consideration.

Economic and Social Council decision 1982/181

Adopted without vote

Oral proposal by President; agenda item 8.

Convening of the International Conference on Population in 1984

At its 53rd plenary meeting, on 26 October 1982, the Council took note of the oral report by the Secretary-General of the International Conference on Population to be held in 1984, made pursuant to its resolution 1982/42 of 27 July 1982.

Financing of the Conference

The Secretary-General of the International Conference on Population, after his appointment in January 1982, established contacts with donor Governments to consider the possibility of their making special contributions to the United Nations Fund for Population Activities (UNFPA) to help meet the costs of the Conference. In his March report[1] to the Economic and Social Council, he recalled that the United Nations Secretary-General had informed the General Assembly in December 1981[6] that the estimated cost of the Conference and its preparations was $2,319,700, of which $1.5 million was anticipated from extrabudgetary resources. He noted that the 1974 World Population Conference[5] had cost $3,647,000. The utmost economy was required, he said, as well as financial support from as many Governments as possible.

As it had decided to do on 30 April,[3] when it had also urged Member States to provide financial support, the Council reviewed at its July 1982 session the financial estimates as reported by the Secretary-General in December 1981.

As the United Nations Secretary-General reported to the Assembly in November,[2] the Council, on 27 July,[4] had recommended that the Assembly approve expenses for Conference preparations, bearing in mind that the total amount from the United Nations regular budget should not exceed $800,000, which should come, to the maximum extent possible, from existing resources. It had requested the Conference Secretary-General to report to it at its October/November session on his efforts to raise extrabudgetary resources. He reported orally on 26 October.

The USSR orally proposed to delete the phrase "to the maximum extent possible", with reference to costs coming from existing resources. The proposal was rejected by 29 votes to 4, with 8 abstentions, in the Council's First Committee, and, by 36 votes to 4, with 9 abstentions, in the Council.

Bulgaria, on behalf of Eastern European States in the Council, said they regarded the appropriation from the regular budget as undermining the functions of the Assembly's Fifth (Administrative and Budgetary) Committee and unjustifiably high. Conference preparations should be funded from extrabudgetary resources as far as possible, and discussion should be postponed until the amount of such resources was known.

The United States felt the principle governing the Conference's financing scheme—use of extrabudgetary resource to the maximum extent possible—was worthy of emulation. Both it and France felt that $800,000 should be the maximum provided from the budget. The United Kingdom reaffirmed its views on zero growth in the budget and trusted the earmarked amount would be found through corresponding savings elsewhere.

Canada said it had accepted the compromise on the financing, but reiterated its position of principle that conferences agreed to by Member States should be financed from the budget. Norway supported this view.

Reports. [1]Conference S-G, E/1982/27; [2]S-G, A/C.5/37/59. *Resolutions (1982).* ESC: [3]1982/7, paras. 2 (a) & 3, 30 Apr.; [4]1982/42, paras. 5 & 6, 27 July.
Yearbook references. [5]1974, p. 550; [6]1981, p. 791.

Regional commission activities

The General Assembly, on 17 December 1982,[4] noted the June 1982 decision[1] of the Governing Council of the United Nations Development Programme endorsing guidelines for approving new and continuing intercountry projects. The guidelines called for UNFPA to discontinue infrastructural support to its project-executing agencies, including the regional commissions. The Assembly requested the Secretary-General, in consultation with the executive secretaries of the regional commissions, to consider including, in the draft 1984-1985 budget, proposals on modalities for continuing regional population activities.

The Assembly's resolution, submitted by a Vice-Chairman of the Second (Economic and Financial) Committee, was adopted without vote, having been similarly approved by the Committee on 2 December. The text had been prepared following informal consultations on a draft[2] transmitted to the Assembly by the Economic and Social Council.

The draft was contained in a resolution adopted by the Council on 30 July.[3] It had stemmed from concern expressed by Economic Commission for Africa (ECA) intergovernmental bodies over reduced funding for certain demographic activities in Africa. The Council had, in its resolution of transmittal, taken note of the decreasing assistance being made available by UNFPA and other donor agencies to ECA and its member States for demographic data collection, processing, evaluation, analysis and dissemination. The text transmitted to the Assembly would have had it request the Secretary-General and the UNFPA Executive

Director to take measures to alleviate the reduction in resources for the regional population programme, and allocate the necessary posts to ECA for meeting its increased responsibilities in the field of population.

Decision (1982). [1]UNDP Council (report, E/1982/16/Rev.1); 80/20, sect. I, para. 3, 18 June.
Note. [2]Secretariat, A/C.2/37/L.2.
Resolutions (1982). [3]ESC: 1982/65 B, 30 July. [4]GA: 37/136, 17 Dec., text following.
Financial implications. S-G statement, A/C.2/37/L.30.
Meeting records. GA: 2nd Committee, A/C.2/37/SR.3-12, 32, *46* (28 Sep.–11 Nov. & 2 Dec.); plenary, A/37/PV.109 (17 Dec.).

General Assembly resolution 37/136

17 December 1982   Meeting 109   Adopted without vote

Approved by Second Committee (A/37/679/Add.1) without vote, 2 December (meeting 46); draft by Vice-Chairman (A/C.2/37/L.102), based on informal consultations on draft transmitted by Economic and Social Council resolution 1982/65 B; agenda item 12.

Population activities in the regional commissions
The General Assembly

1. *Takes note* of decision 80/44 of 27 June 1980 of the Governing Council of the United Nations Development Programme on agency support costs and of section I, paragraph 3, of decision 82/20 of 18 June 1982, in which the Council endorsed the guidelines for the approval of new and continuing intercountry projects that, *inter alia*, called for the discontinuation by the United Nations Fund for Population Activities of infrastructural support to its project-executing agencies, including the regional commissions;

2. *Requests* the Secretary-General, in consultation with the executive secretaries of the regional commissions, to consider the inclusion in the draft programme budget for the biennium 1984-1985 of proposals on modalities for the continuation of activities in the field of population at the regional level.

Rules of procedure of the Committee for the UN Population Award

The Economic and Social Council, on 26 April 1982,[1] approved the rules of procedure of the Committee for the United Nations Population Award. The Award, established by the General Assembly in 1981,[3] was to be presented annually to an individual, individuals or an institution for the most outstanding contribution made to the awareness of population questions or to their solutions. The draft rules had been drawn up by the Secretariat.[2]

The rules established that the Committee would hold a regular meeting in February of each year at United Nations Headquarters to select the laureate or laureates. Special meetings could be convened. Honorary members could be selected, by secret ballot, to fill vacancies. *Ex officio* members could, if necessary, act in the Committee through representatives. Six of the 10 elected members would constitute a quorum. A majority of those present and voting would make decisions. A ballot resulting in a tie would be repeated. The Committee Secretary would present nominations for laureates. No more than two individuals could be selected. Committee meetings would be closed and proceedings reported to the Secretary-General. The rules could be suspended by Committee decision; procedural matters not covered by the rules would be settled in accordance with rules applicable to Council committees.

The decision was adopted without vote on an oral proposal of the Council President, as orally amended by Japan: rule 4, stipulating that *ex officio* members might act in the Committee through representatives, was amended to include the phrase "if necessary".

Japan also proposed changes, which were accepted, to the second paragraph of rule 7, which had originally stated that the Committee would first decide whether to make the Award to an institution before deciding on the maximum number of individuals, which was to be no more than two unless otherwise decided.

Decision (1982). [1]ESC: 1982/112, 26 Apr., text following.
Note. [2]Secretariat, annexing draft rules, E/1982/L.19.
Resolution. [3]GA: 36/201, 17 Dec. 1981 (YUN 1981, p. 792).
Meeting record. ESC: E/1982/SR.15 (26 Apr.).

Economic and Social Council decision 1982/112

Adopted without vote

Oral proposal by President; draft rules by Secretariat (E/1982/L.19), orally amended by Japan; agenda item 1.

Rules of procedure of the Committee for the United Nations Population Award
At its 15th plenary meeting, on 26 April 1982, the Council, pursuant to General Assembly resolution 36/201 of 17 December 1981, approved the rules of procedure of the Committee for the United Nations Population Award set out below:

Rules of procedure of the Committee for the United Nations Population Award

Meetings
Rule 1
1. The Committee shall hold a regular meeting in February of each year, to select the laureate or laureates of the year.
2. Special meetings may be convened with the agreement of six voting members of the Committee.
3. All meetings shall take place at United Nations Headquarters.

Chairman
Rule 2
1. The Committee shall elect a Chairman at each regular meeting, who shall serve until a successor is elected at the following regular meeting. The Chairman shall be eligible for re-election.
2. In the absence of the Chairman, the Secretary-General or his representative shall act as Chairman.

Selection of honorary members
Rule 3
1. Honorary members may be selected at any meeting of the Committee, whenever there is a vacancy or in anticipation of a vacancy during the following twelve months.
2. Honorary members selected to fill an unexpired term shall serve for the balance of that term.

Ex officio members
Rule 4
The *ex officio* members may, if necessary, act in the Committee through representatives.

Quorum
Rule 5
Representatives of six of the ten members of the Committee elected by the Economic and Social Council shall constitute a quorum.

Decisions

Rule 6

1.   Unless otherwise provided, decisions shall be made by a majority of the elected and *ex officio* members present and voting.

2.   Decisions under rule 3 or rule 7 shall be made by secret ballot.

3.   When one or more candidates are to be selected under rule 3 or rule 7, each voting member of the Committee may vote for as many candidates as there are places to be filled, and those candidates, in a number not exceeding the number of such places, obtaining in the first ballot a majority of the votes cast and the largest number of votes shall be considered selected.

4.   If the number of candidates selected under paragraph 3 above is less than the number of places to be filled, additional ballots shall be held on a basis similar to the first one, to fill the remaining places, provided that once one or more individual candidates have been selected pursuant to rule 7, paragraph 2, the Committee may decide not to select additional ones up to the maximum originally decided. From such additional ballots the candidate obtaining the least number of votes, or on the proposal of the Chairman several candidates having received few votes, shall be eliminated.

5.   If any ballot results in a tie vote among all candidates, it shall be repeated; if the tie persists for two such repeated ballots, the Chairman shall select a successful candidate by drawing lots.

Selection of laureates

Rule 7

1.   The Secretary of the Committee shall present to the Committee at the regular meeting all the nominations received during the previous year for laureates eligible for the United Nations Population Award.

2.   The Committee shall decide to make the Award either to an institution or to an individual or individuals; unless it decides otherwise, no more than two individuals shall be selected.

Privacy of meetings and reports

Rule 8

1.   The meetings of the Committee shall be closed.

2.   The proceedings of the Committee shall be reflected in a report to be submitted to the Secretary-General after each regular meeting, which report shall be attached to the annual report to be submitted to the General Assembly by the Executive Director of the United Nations Fund for Population Activities.

Rules of procedure

Rule 9

1.   Any of these rules may be suspended by a decision of two thirds of the elected and *ex officio* members present and voting, provided that such decision is not inconsistent with General Assembly resolution 36/201 or any other decision of the Assembly.

2.   Any procedural matter not covered by these rules shall be settled in accordance with the rules applicable to committees of the Economic and Social Council.

Chapter XV

Health and human resources

Contents

Related topics:

Africa: United Nations Educational and Training Programme for Southern Africa. Environment: Protection against harmful products. Human rights of disabled persons. Children: Nutrition.

For resolutions and decisions of major organs mentioned but not reproduced, refer to INDEX OF RESOLUTIONS AND DECISIONS.

Health

On 18 May 1982,[2] in identifying the major trends and problems affecting the environment (see next chapter), the Governing Council of the United Nations Environment Programme (UNEP) cited health as one of the priorities for United Nations action, specifically through the system-wide programme to be co-ordinated by UNEP during 1982-1992. The Council drew attention to the continued massive prevalence of infectious and parasitic diseases, malnutrition, inadequate safe water supplies and lack of sanitation and food safety in developing countries, and to the increased resistance of pathogens or their intermediary agents to chemical control, the increasing incidence of disease associated with development schemes, and the increasing number and prevalence of potentially toxic chemicals and residual micropollutants in the environment. Also cited were illnesses related to life-styles and the working environment, as well as the continued danger from trade in hazardous substances and from inadequacies in their safe disposal.

To combat these trends and problems, the Council recommended development of environ-

mental health measures, including: methods for the control of disease vectors and parasites; the improvement of sanitation in settlements and of hygiene, especially in developing countries; continued monitoring, notably in the Global Environmental Monitoring System; and development of procedures, principles and guidelines within the International Programme on Chemical Safety, and of guidelines for the safe trade, handling and transport of hazardous substances and disposal of hazardous wastes. A follow-up to the UNEP list of dangerous substances and processes was also recommended.

The Administrative Committee on Co-ordination (ACC) commented on health activities in its review of international co-operation and co-ordination within the United Nations system for 1981/82.[1] It pointed out that, to promote, co-ordinate and support implementation of the Global Strategy for Health for All by the Year 2000—adopted in 1981 by the World Health Assembly of the World Health Organization (WHO)[4] and endorsed by the General Assembly in November of that year[3]—the Health Assembly adopted in 1982 a general programme of work for 1984-1989, aimed at fostering national and international action so that each member State would have developed a national health strategy by

1984 and a plan of action for that strategy's implementation by 1985, to be fully operational by 1986 and at an advanced stage by 1989. In this context, ACC stated, primary health care had been identified as a main area for joint planning, with WHO as the co-ordinating agency.

Report. [1]ACC, E/1982/4.
Resolution (1982). [2]UNEP Council (report, A/37/25): I, sect. III, para. 2 (g), 18 May.
Resolution (prior). [3]GA: 36/43, 19 Nov. 1981 (YUN 1981, p. 803).
Yearbook reference. [4]1981, pp. 802 & 1418.

Disabled persons

Programme of Action

The highlight of activities on behalf of disabled persons in 1982 was the adoption by the General Assembly of a World Programme of Action concerning Disabled Persons—a follow-up to the International Year of Disabled Persons (IYDP) observed in 1981.[7] The Programme of Action was elaborated by the Advisory Committee for the International Year of Disabled Persons on the basis of a draft prepared by the IYDP secretariat. The text was finalized at the Committee's fourth session, held at Vienna, Austria, from 5 to 14 July 1982,[2] in the light of comments by Member States and intergovernmental and non-governmental organizations, and recommended to the Assembly.

The Programme comprised three main parts. The first part provided a statement of objectives; background information on the disabled; definitions of recognized types of disabilities—impairment, disability and handicap—and of the courses of action in response to those problems—prevention, rehabilitation and equalization of opportunities; and concepts adopted within the United Nations system. The second part gave an overview of the world situation of disabled persons. The third outlined proposals for realizing the Programme's objectives, to be carried out at the national, regional and international levels.

The Programme's purpose was to promote effective measures for the prevention of disability, for the rehabilitation of disabled persons and for the realization of the goals of their full participation in social life and development and of equality. This meant ensuring for the disabled opportunities equal to those of the whole population and an equal share in the improvement in living conditions resulting from social and economic development.

The Programme noted that, in the context of health experience, WHO characterized the disabled as suffering from impairment—loss or abnormality of psychological, physiological, or anatomical structure or function; or from disability—restriction or lack of ability, resulting from impairment, to perform an activity in the manner or wi-

thin the range considered normal; or from handicap—a disadvantage resulting from impairment or disability that limited or prevented fulfilment of a role considered normal. To meet the barriers encountered by this inhomogeneous group, the Programme proposed three types of action: prevention of the onset of mental, physical and sensory impairments, or of the negative physical, psychological and social consequences of impairment; rehabilitation, to enable the impaired to reach an optimum mental, physical and/or social functional level, which could involve technical aids to compensate for functional loss or limitation and thus facilitate social readjustment; and equalization of opportunities, to make accessible to all the general system of society—housing, transportation, social and health services, educational and work opportunities, sports and other recreational facilities.

According to the Programme, of the estimated 500 million disabled, as many as 80 per cent lived in isolated rural areas of developing countries. Special groups of disabled included children, displaced persons and refugees, the elderly, migrant workers, the victims of crime and torture, and women. Preventive measures cited as significantly reducing the incidence of physical and mental impairment were: improving primary health care, nutrition, education and the quality of the environment; counselling parents on genetic factors and pre-natal care; immunization; and accident prevention, including occupational safety programmes. The trend in rehabilitation services—traditionally provided by specialized institutions—was to integrate such services in public facilities and involve family and community support. More attention was being given to the local production of simple, low-cost rehabilitative technical aids. Equalization of opportunities in education and employment and full participation in society's basic units—the family, social groups and the community—could be achieved primarily through political and social actions, such as legislation and public education.

Crucial to implementation of the Programme's objectives were a consideration for the situation of developing countries, particularly the least developed among them; a multisectoral and multidisciplinary global strategy for co-ordinated policies and actions; and the participation of the disabled and their organizations.

At the national level, the Government bore ultimate responsibility for implementation to be carried out by local authorities and other bodies in the public and private sectors. A long-term programme of activities should be urgently integrated into the national policy for socio-economic development and a co-ordinating mechanism set up. To implement the Programme, it was necessary that each Member State plan, organize and finance activities at every level; establish the legal basis for implementation; mobilize public and private organizations; foster the growth of organizations of the disabled; disseminate information and educate the public on issues of the Programme; promote technical assistance and co-operation; and facilitate related research as well as the participation of disabled persons and their organizations in decisions concerning the Programme.

Recommended preventive action included the development and full utilization of technology to prevent and control most disablement; community-based primary health-care systems, particularly in rural areas and urban slums; and sustained education of professionals and the public on preventive measures, and of pregnant women against the imprudent use of medication, stimulants and depressants. Member States were called on to develop and ensure adequate rehabilitation services, community-based workers and social services personnel. Equalization of opportunities was to be achieved principally through legislation to eliminate discriminatory practices against the disabled and to guarantee access to public facilities, income, social security, education, training and employment.

Action at the international level required extensive consultations and close co-operation among Governments, organs and other bodies in the United Nations system, and intergovernmental and non-governmental organizations, including organizations of and for disabled persons. The areas for international action included human rights where priority was to be given to the use of United Nations covenants and other instruments protecting the rights of all persons; technical and economic co-operation at the regional and interregional levels, which would improve the response of the United Nations system to the Programme's challenge; and research, which was to focus on the socio-cultural aspects of disability, on the causes and types of disability and on developing improved technical aids.

Monitoring and evaluation of implementation efforts were to be carried out periodically at the national, regional and international levels.

The General Assembly, acting without vote on 3 December 1982,[5] adopted the World Programme of Action concerning Disabled Persons as recommended by the Advisory Committee for IYDP. The Assembly called on all Member States, non-governmental and disabled persons' organizations and the United Nations system to ensure early implementation of the Programme. It decided to evaluate the implementation in 1987 with the Secretary-General's help.

The resolution was recommended by the Assembly's Third (Social, Humanitarian and Cul-

tural) Committee, based on a 38-nation text introduced by Belgium as revised by its sponsors, which the Committee approved, also without vote, on 15 November.

By a further resolution of 3 December,[6] the Assembly made specific requests of the Secretary-General, Member States, the United Nations system, international organizations, funding bodies and WHO for the Programme's implementation.

The draft text of the Programme had earlier been examined at two inter-agency meetings on IYDP organized at Vienna. The first, held on 9 and 10 March,[3] stressed that the text should be written in clear language and incorporate relevant portions of the Leeds Castle Declaration on the Prevention of Disablement, adopted by the Conference on the Prevention of Disablement held in the United Kingdom in November 1981. The second meeting, held on 15 and 16 July 1982,[4] further discussed the draft Programme; took note of a proposal for the prevention of disablement, prepared jointly by the United Nations Children's Fund, the United Nations Development Programme and WHO; and discussed inter-agency co-operation on follow-up activities to IYDP, including the question of employment of disabled persons in the United Nations system.

By a note verbale of 18 March to the Secretary-General,[1] the Libyan Arab Jamahiriya transmitted two sets of resolutions, one issued by the General People's Committee in December 1981 and another by the General People's Committee for Social Security in February 1982. The resolutions entitled disabled persons who qualified to a monthly allowance and to exemptions from customs duty on rehabilitative aids and on appliances, equipment and vehicles for their use, and from income tax, stamp duty and other taxes.

Note verbale. [1]Libyan Arab Jamahiriya, 18 Mar., A/37/160.
Reports. [2]Advisory Committee on IYDP, transmitted by S-G report, A/37/351/Add.1 & Add.1/Corr.1; Inter-agency meeting on IYDP, [3]ACC/1982/PG/5, [4]ACC/1982/PG/8.
Resolutions (1982). GA, 3 Dec.: [5]37/52, text following; [6]37/53.
Yearbook reference. [7]1981, p. 795.
Meeting records. GA: 3rd Committee, A/C.3/37/SR.14-23, 25, 26, 29, 42 (18 Oct.–15 Nov.); plenary, A/37/PV.90 (3 Dec.).

General Assembly resolution 37/52

3 December 1982   Meeting 90   Adopted without vote

Approved by Third Committee (A/37/632) without vote, 15 November (meeting 42); 38-nation draft (A/C.3/37/L.19/Rev.1); agenda item 89.
Sponsors: Algeria, Australia, Bangladesh, Barbados, Belgium, Canada, Central African Republic, Chad, Congo, Costa Rica, Dominican Republic, Ecuador, Finland, Gabon, Germany, Federal Republic of, Guinea, Ireland, Kenya, Libyan Arab Jamahiriya, Mali, Malta, Morocco, Nepal, Netherlands, Nigeria, Norway, Pakistan, Philippines, Portugal, Qatar, Saudi Arabia, Somalia, Sweden, United Kingdom, United States, Uruguay, Yugoslavia, Zaire.

World Programme of Action concerning Disabled Persons
The General Assembly,
Recalling its resolutions 31/123 of 16 December 1976, by which it proclaimed the year 1981 International Year of Disabled Persons, 32/133 of 16 December 1977, by which it established the Advisory Committee for the International Year of Disabled Persons, 33/170 of 20 December 1978, 34/154 of 17 December 1979, in which it, *inter alia*, decided

to expand the theme of the International Year of Disabled Persons to "full participation and equality", 35/133 of 11 December 1980 and 36/77 of 8 December 1981,

Deeply concerned that no less than five hundred million persons are estimated to suffer from disability of one form or another, of whom four hundred million are estimated to be in developing countries,

Reiterating the continuing need to promote the realization of the right of disabled persons to participate fully in the social life and development of their societies and to enjoy living conditions equal to those of other citizens, as well as to share equally in improvements in living conditions resulting from social and economic development,

Recognizing that the International Year of Disabled Persons contributed to the acceptance by the community of the right of disabled persons to participate fully in the social life and development of their societies and to enjoy living conditions equal to those of their fellow citizens,

Convinced that the International Year of Disabled Persons gave a genuine and meaningful impetus to activities related to equalization of opportunities for disabled persons, as well as prevention and rehabilitation at all levels,

Expressing its satisfaction with the efforts of Member States during the International Year of Disabled Persons to improve the conditions and well-being of disabled persons and their willingness to involve disabled persons and their organizations in all matters of concern to them,

Also expressing its satisfaction with the initiatives taken by the specialized agencies and other organizations of the United Nations system, non-governmental organizations and, in particular, organizations of disabled persons,

Taking note of the emergence of organizations of disabled persons in all parts of the world and their positive influence on the image and condition of persons with a disability,

Having considered the Vienna Affirmative Action Plan adopted by the World Symposium of Experts on Technical Co-operation among Developing Countries and Technical Assistance in Disability Prevention and Rehabilitation of Disabled Persons,

Expressing its appreciation to the Advisory Committee for the International Year of Disabled Persons for the work it has done,

Having considered the report of the Advisory Committee for the International Year of Disabled Persons on its fourth session and its recommendations for a World Programme of Action concerning Disabled Persons,

Desirous of ensuring effective follow-up to the International Year of Disabled Persons and aware that, if this is to be achieved, Member States, organs, organizations and agencies of the United Nations system, non-governmental organizations and organizations of disabled persons must therefore be encouraged to continue the activities already undertaken and to initiate new programmes and activities,

Stressing that the primary responsibility for promoting effective measures for prevention of disability, rehabilitation and the realization of the goals of "full participation" of disabled persons in social life and development and of "equality" rests with individual countries and that international action should be directed towards assisting and supporting national efforts in this regard,

1. *Adopts* the World Programme of Action concerning Disabled Persons as set forth in recommendation 1(IV) of the Advisory Committee for the International Year of Disabled Persons;

2. *Calls upon* all Member States, all non-governmental organizations concerned and organizations of disabled persons and, through a reallocation of existing resources, calls also upon all organs, organizations and agencies of the United Nations system to ensure early implementation of the World Programme of Action concerning Disabled Persons;

3. *Decides* to evaluate at its forty-second session, with the help of the Secretary-General, the implementation of the World Programme of Action concerning Disabled Persons.

Implementation of the Programme

Advisory Committee recommendations. At its July 1982 session,[1] the Advisory Committee for IYDP recommended for General Assembly adoption a series of short-term activities with a view to early implementation of the World Programme of Action concerning Disabled Persons. The Assembly would request Member States to develop plans for the prevention of disability, the rehabilitation of disabled persons and equalization of opportunities for them. It would likewise request United Nations bodies, in particular the regional commissions, to formulate and undertake measures in their spheres of competence, ensuring consultation and co-ordination among them; and would urge them to undertake new measures or expedite existing ones to improve disabled persons' employment opportunities within those bodies and access to their buildings, facilities and information sources. United Nations bodies would also be asked, in their activities relating to International Youth Year (1985), to recognize disabled persons' needs. International organizations and funding bodies would be urged to give higher priority to human resources development, especially training in the prevention of disability and rehabilitation, and to enhance equalization of opportunities for the disabled.

The Secretary-General would be requested to assist in implementation of the Programme by ensuring its wide distribution and promotion; to establish inter-organizational task forces, within the existing arrangements for inter-agency co-ordination, to support activities in developing regions; and to provide the United Nations Centre for Social Development and Humanitarian Affairs with resources to enable it to ensure follow-up activities to IYDP and facilitate the Programme's implementation. WHO would be asked to review its definitions of impairment, disability and handicap in the light of IYDP experience and in consultation with disabled persons' organizations and other bodies.

General Assembly action. On 3 December, the Assembly adopted without vote a resolution on the Programme's implementation,[2] incorporating the provisions recommended by the Advisory Committee on IYDP (see above). In addition, the Assembly requested the Secretary-General to continue consultative services to Member States on the design of national programmes for disabled persons and to develop for consultants' use a practical check-list dealing with the equalization of opportunities for the disabled. To assist implementation activities, the Secretary-General was asked to disseminate information on available technical and financial resources and to examine the need of continuing the United Nations Trust Fund for the International Year of Disabled Persons. He was also requested to continue to give appropriate priority to activities related to disabled persons' organizations and to explore the possibility of convening in 1987 a meeting of experts, largely of disabled persons, to prepare a report to help him and the Assembly evaluate the Programme's implementation.

Another provision of the resolution concerned the proclamation of the United Nations Decade of Disabled Persons.

The resolution, recommended by the Third Committee, was based on a 30-nation draft introduced by the Philippines, as revised by its sponsors. The Committee approved the draft, also without vote, on 15 November, following a further oral revision.

Report. [1]Advisory Committee on IYDP, transmitted by S-G report, A/37/351/Add.1 & Add.1/Corr.1.
Resolution (1982). [2]GA: 37/53, 3 Dec., text following.
Financial implications. ACABQ report, A/37/7/Add.9; 5th Committee report, A/37/688; S-G statements, A/C.3/37/L.29/Rev.1, A/C.5/37/43.
Meeting records. GA: 3rd Committee, A/C.3/37/SR.14-23, 25, 26, *29, 42* (18 Oct.–15 Nov.); 5th Committee, A/C.5/37/SR.50 (1 Dec.); plenary, A/37/PV.90 (3 Dec.).

General Assembly resolution 37/53

3 December 1982   Meeting 90   Adopted without vote

Approved by Third Committee (A/37/632) without vote, 15 November (meeting 42); 30-nation draft (A/C.3/37/L.22/Rev.1), orally revised; agenda item 89.

Sponsors: Algeria, Argentina, Bangladesh, Belgium, Congo, Dominican Republic, Ecuador, Egypt, Guinea, Indonesia, Libyan Arab Jamahiriya, Mali, Malta, Morocco, Nepal, Nicaragua, Nigeria, Oman, Pakistan, Panama, Papua New Guinea, Peru, Philippines, Qatar, Romania, Saudi Arabia, Singapore, Sri Lanka, Uruguay, Yugoslavia.

Implementation of the World Programme of Action concerning Disabled Persons

The General Assembly,

Recalling its resolutions 31/123 of 16 December 1976, by which it proclaimed the year 1981 International Year of Disabled Persons, 32/133 of 16 December 1977, by which it established the Advisory Committee for the International Year of Disabled Persons, 33/170 of 20 December 1978, 34/154 of 17 December 1979, in which it, *inter alia*, decided to expand the theme of the International Year of Disabled Persons to "full participation and equality", 35/133 of 13 December 1980, 36/77 of 8 December 1981 and 37/52 of 3 December 1982, in which it adopted the World Programme of Action concerning Disabled Persons,

Recognizing that the International Year of Disabled Persons contributed to the acceptance by the community of the right of disabled persons to participate fully in the social life and development of their societies and to enjoy living conditions equal to those of their fellow citizens,

Convinced that the International Year of Disabled Persons gave a genuine and meaningful impetus to activities related to equalization of opportunities for disabled persons, as well as prevention and rehabilitation at all levels,

Expressing its appreciation to the Advisory Committee for the International Year of Disabled Persons for its work, in particular for its contribution to the formulation of the World Programme of Action concerning Disabled Persons,

Expressing its satisfaction with the efforts of Member States during the International Year of Disabled Persons to improve the conditions and well-being of disabled persons and their willingness to involve disabled persons and their organizations in all matters of concern to them,

Also expressing its satisfaction with the initiatives taken by the specialized agencies, other organs and organizations of the United Nations system, non-governmental organizations and, in particular, organizations of disabled persons,

Encouraged by the emergence of organizations of disabled persons in all parts of the world and their positive influence on the image and condition of persons with a disability,

Having considered with appreciation the Vienna Affirmative Action Plan adopted by the World Symposium of Experts on Technical Co-operation among Developing Countries and Technical Assistance in Disability Prevention and Rehabilitation of Disabled Persons, in which it was emphasized that, in developing countries, efforts to prevent disabilities should be intensified and standards of rehabilitation for disabled persons should be as high as possible,

Noting in particular the results of the meetings organized for the International Year of Disabled Persons by the regional commissions, which stressed the need for more efficient technical co-operation at the regional and subregional levels in the training of rehabilitation personnel and the production of prosthetic appliances and aids using locally available resources, and also stressed the need for an interregional exchange of experience in the elaboration of national programmes for the development of such services,

Stressing that the primary responsibility for promoting effective measures for prevention of disability, rehabilitation and the realization of the goals of full participation and equality of disabled persons rests with the individual countries and that, in this regard, international co-operation is highly desirable and should be directed towards assisting and supporting national efforts,

Believing that, in addition to national programmes, effective implementation of the World Programme of Action would be assisted by activities at the international level of the organs, organizations and agencies of the United Nations system, non-governmental organizations and organizations of disabled persons,

Recognizing that such activities will be difficult to finance at present and that every effort must be made to reallocate existing resources within the United Nations system,

1. *Requests* the Secretary-General to assist in the early implementation of the World Programme of Action concerning Disabled Persons by ensuring its wide distribution and promotion;

2. *Requests* Member States to develop plans for the equalization of opportunities for disabled persons, as well as for prevention and rehabilitation, and thereby ensure early implementation of the World Programme of Action concerning Disabled Persons;

3. *Requests* all organs, organizations and agencies of the United Nations system to formulate and undertake measures within their respective spheres of competence, through a reallocation of existing resources, to ensure early implementation of the World Programme of Action concerning Disabled Persons and requests, in particular, the regional commissions to implement suitable programmes, on the understanding that effective consultation and co-ordination between the various bodies are essential;

4. *Requests* the Secretary-General to establish inter-organizational task forces, as recommended by the Advisory Committee for the International Year of Disabled Persons at its third and fourth sessions, in order to provide support services, as described in paragraph 17 of General Assembly resolution 36/77, within the existing arrangements for inter-agency co-ordination in order to support national and regional activities in the developing regions in the fields of prevention of disability, rehabilitation and equalization of opportunities for disabled persons;

5. *Encourages* the Secretary-General to find the means to provide the Centre for Social Development and Humanitarian Affairs of the Secretariat with the necessary resources to enable it to ensure follow-up to the International Year of Disabled Persons and to facilitate the implementation of the World Programme of Action concerning Disabled Persons;

6. *Requests* the Secretary-General to continue consultative services to Member States concerning the design of national programmes for the prevention of disability, for rehabilitation and for equalization of opportunities for disabled persons, to develop a practical check-list dealing with the equalization of opportunities for disabled persons which could be used by consultants in discussion with Governments of Member States and to compile and distribute information on available technical and financial resources to assist developing countries in the prevention of disability, rehabilitation and the equalization of opportunities;

7. *Also requests* the Secretary-General to continue to give appropriate priority, within the programmes for disabled persons, to activities related to organizations of disabled persons;

8. *Again urges* all organs, organizations and agencies of the United Nations system to undertake new measures or expedite those already under way to improve employment opportunities for disabled persons within those bodies at all levels and to improve access to their buildings and facilities and to their information sources, and requests the Secretary-General to submit a report on these measures to the General Assembly at its thirty-ninth session;

9. *Requests* the Secretary-General, in consultation with Governments, to examine the need and possibility of continuing the United Nations Trust Fund for the International Year of Disabled Persons for

the purpose of assisting Governments, at their request, in the implementation of the World Programme of Action concerning Disabled Persons and to report thereon to the General Assembly at its thirty-eighth session;

10. *Requests* all Governments in a position to do so, the United Nations Development Programme and all relevant United Nations organs, organizations and agencies to assist Governments of developing countries, at their request, in the formulation of national policies and programmes for disabled persons;

11. *Proclaims* the period 1983-1992 United Nations Decade of Disabled Persons as a long-term plan of action, on the understanding that no additional resources from the United Nations system will be needed for this purpose, and encourages Member States to utilize this period as one of the means to implement the World Programme of Action concerning Disabled Persons;

12. *Encourages* Governments to proclaim national days for the disabled;

13. *Urges* international organizations and funding bodies to give higher priority to human resources development, in particular to training activities in the fields of prevention of disability and rehabilitation, and to enhance the equalization of opportunities and the participation of disabled persons;

14. *Requests* the organizations of the United Nations system to recognize the needs of disabled persons in their activities relating to the International Youth Year and in the international and regional congresses and meetings that they sponsor;

15. *Requests* the World Health Organization, in the light of the experience of the International Year of Disabled Persons, to review its definitions of impairment, disability and handicap in consultation with organizations of disabled persons and other appropriate bodies;

16. *Requests* the Secretary-General to explore the possibility of convening in 1987 a meeting of experts, consisting largely of disabled persons, to prepare a report that would enable him to help the General Assembly at its forty-second session to evaluate the implementation of the World Programme of Action concerning Disabled Persons, as provided for in paragraph 3 of resolution 37/52;

17. *Requests* the Secretary-General to report to the General Assembly at its thirty-ninth session on the implementation of the World Programme of Action concerning Disabled Persons.

Proclamation of the Decade of Disabled Persons (1983-1992)

In its resolution of 3 December 1982 on implementation of the World Programme of Action concerning Disabled Persons,[2] the General Assembly proclaimed the period 1983-1992 United Nations Decade of Disabled Persons as a long-term plan of action, on the understanding that no additional resources from the United Nations system would be needed for the purpose. The Assembly encouraged Member States to utilize the period as a means to implement the Programme.

The proclamation had its origin in actions taken by the Advisory Committee for IYDP at its July session.[1] Agreeing that the most vital task in following up IYDP was to find effective ways of implementing the Programme, the Committee on 12 July decided, without reaching consensus, that a majority favoured proclaiming the period 1983-1992 as the Decade. On 14 July, the Committee also decided that a majority favoured proclaiming a world day of disabled persons, provided it was developed in close co-operation with organizations of disabled persons and used to rally support for action in their favour on an international scale.

Report. [1]Advisory Committee on IYDP, transmitted by S-G report, A/37/351/Add.1.
Resolution (1982). [2]GA: 37/53, para. 11, 3 Dec.

Other UN system activities

In 1982, follow-up activities to IYDP were undertaken at the national, regional and international levels. They were described by the Secretary-General in a September report to the General Assembly.[2]

In addition to the Advisory Committee's finalizing the World Programme of Action and recommending short-term activities towards its early implementation, the United Nations Centre for Social Development and Humanitarian Affairs was preparing studies on the full participation of disabled persons in socio-economic life and, jointly with the United Nations Centre for Human Settlements and the Swedish International Development Authority, a manual of practical guidelines for planning and architects, all for completion in 1982. The Centre for Social Development began publication of the *Disabled Persons Bulletin*.[1] Accessibility guides to United Nations buildings in New York and Geneva were produced for the use of disabled persons.

In June, the Consultative Committee on Administrative Questions of the Administrative Committee on Co-ordination (ACC) decided that a study of the question of employment for disabled persons in United Nations organizations be conducted with the assistance of the International Labour Organisation (ILO), the World Health Organization (WHO) and United Nations medical advisers. Also in June, the Department of Public Information organized an international seminar on media portrayal of disabled persons, which adopted guidelines for the media and recommendations for the communications efforts of disabled persons' organizations. The Office of the United Nations High Commissioner for Refugees developed guidelines for the identification and assessment of the needs of disabled refugees and for the formulation of projects.

The Trust Fund for IYDP financed six promotional projects of international scope and two of national scope during 1981-1982. Projects in 1982 included the Expert Conference on Utilization of Local Manpower and Technology for Disability-related Services in Rural and Poverty Areas of the Asia and Pacific Region (Manila, Philippines, February); the Caribbean Symposium on Technical Co-operation and Technical Assistance (Kingston, Jamaica, 17 September–30 October); and the East and Southern African Conference on Rehabilitation (Mbabane, Swaziland, 8-19 November). In addition, the Fund financed activities of disabled persons' organizations, as follows: the International League of Societies for Persons with Mental Handicap, which organized an Asian Training Workshop in Family Management of Problems Arising from Mental Retardation (Hong Kong, 12-18 April); and the Leadership Training

Seminar of the West African Federation of Associations for the Advancement of Disabled Persons (Dakar, Senegal, 7-15 December). The Ljubljana Institute for Rehabilitation of Disabled Persons, in Yugoslavia, which organized an International Seminar on Community Services and Locally Produced Technical Aids for Disabled Persons (1-22 October) also received support.

Among the specialized agencies, ILO, at its 1982 Conference, discussed a proposed international instrument to supplement its Recommendation on the vocational rehabilitation and employment of disabled persons. The ILO special Information Service on the Rehabilitation and Employment of the Visually Handicapped (BLINDOC) was expanded through co-operation with the International Federation of the Blind, which agreed to publish BLINDOC issues in Braille. In June, WHO organized an interregional meeting on the promotion of the community concept of rehabilitation aimed at reaching the majority of the disabled. It distributed a revised manual on training the disabled in the community to its regional offices for trial and evaluation and to 10 developing countries where its application was being tested.

By a resolution of 7 September addressing the question of the enjoyment by disabled persons of universally proclaimed human rights,[3] the Sub-Commission on Prevention of Discrimination and Protection of Minorities of the Commission on Human Rights requested the Secretary-General to seek ways of promoting such enjoyment and recommended that Governments ensure it and strengthen procedures whereby disabled persons might effectively obtain action on allegations of human rights violations.

Publication. [1]*Disabled Persons Bulletin*, Nos. 1 and 2, January-December 1982.
Report. [2]S-G, A/37/351 & Corr.1.
Resolution (1982). [3]SCPDPM (report, E/CN.4/1983/4): 1982/1, 7 Sep.

Nutrition

The eighth session of the ACC Sub-Committee on Nutrition and its Advisory Group on Nutrition was held at Bangkok, Thailand, from 15 to 19 February 1982.[1] The Sub-Committee, stating there was improvement in nutrition in some regions but a marked decline in others, concluded that, overall, there had been no measurable progress. Substantial numbers continued to suffer from diseases resulting from iron and vitamin A deficiencies, despite the availability of low-cost technologies for overcoming such deficiencies. However, major inroads could be made with iron and vitamin A supplementation programmes integrated in primary health-care systems. Undernourishment could be alleviated with direct food-transfer programmes and child malnutrition by

modest changes in family food distribution or village redistribution schemes.

The Sub-Committee made a series of recommendations affecting such matters as agricultural development planning, research, primary health care and community participation in nutrition programmes. Agreement was reached on a $5-million, internationally financed research programme to cover agricultural and rural development, food price policies, income and food transfers, and integrated health and nutrition. The bulk of the research would be undertaken by local institutions in developing countries.

Recognizing that the essential food needs of many poor households in developing countries were not adequately met, the Sub-Committee decided that it would be valuable to establish a working group on food entitlements, to be entrusted with exploring methods for improving dietary consumption among the poor by enhancing their ability to command food.

Report. [1]ACC Sub-Committee on Nutrition and its Advisory Group, ACC/1982/12 & Corr.1.

Human resources

Human resources development

In a March 1982 report[3] to the Governing Council of the United Nations Development Programme (UNDP), the UNDP Administrator assessed the methods and mechanisms for the periodic dissemination of information on countries' experience in training qualified national personnel and enhancing their role in social and economic development.

The Administrator reviewed information received from Governments on their approaches and efforts in human resources development and the United Nations system's support of such efforts. He described the range of United Nations mechanisms for the exchange and dissemination of experience in training national personnel—research, international conferences and expert meetings, referral systems (data processing systems, bibliographies, directories, statistical information, print and *ad hoc* question-and-answer services), regional institutions and network arrangements, technical advisory services, group training, study tours and fellowships. The Administrator concluded that the need to support training of all types continued, as did the need to give effect to policies ensuring the most effective use of qualified personnel in national development. Concluding also that existing mechanisms in the United Nations system fully responded to the reporting requirements set out by the General Assembly in 1980,[5] the Administrator recommended that maximum advantage be taken of those mechanisms, cautioning against the creation of additional expensive mechanisms and duplication of effort.

Economic and Social Council action. Acting without vote on 28 July 1982, the Economic and Social Council took note of the UNDP Administrator's report and decided to transmit it to the General Assembly at its 1982 session.[1] The decision was prepared by the Chairman of the Council's Third (Programme and Co-ordination) Committee, which approved it, also without vote, on 23 July.

General Assembly action. On 20 December,[4] the General Assembly, taking note of the UNDP Administrator's report on the role of qualified personnel in the social and economic development of developing countries, requested the Secretary-General and the Administrator to monitor further implementation of the 1980 Assembly resolution on the subject. The Secretary-General was also requested to ensure, within available resources, the preparation and distribution among Member States of periodic analytical surveys of reports on countries' national experience in human resources development and on international co-operation in training qualified personnel. Governments were invited to make such reports available regularly to the Secretariat; developed countries and United Nations organizations were also invited to assist developing countries in the education and training of qualified personnel. The Secretary-General was asked to consult with all concerned on possible elements of general guidelines on principles, objectives and structures of personnel education and training for the further development of national systems.

The resolution, adopted without vote by the Assembly, was recommended by its Second (Economic and Financial) Committee, which had similarly approved it on 2 December. The text, introduced by a Committee Vice-Chairman, had been orally revised in informal consultations. It was based on a 17-nation draft resolution[2] introduced by Mongolia and later withdrawn.

Apart from minor drafting changes, the adopted text differed from the original in that the requests made of the Secretary-General were made of the Director-General for Development and International Economic Co-operation in the original; the proviso that the preparation and distribution of periodic analytical surveys were to be carried out within available resources was lacking in the original; and the request for consultation and report on possible elements of general guidelines, taking into account the need for further development of national systems, was, in the original, a simple request for the elaboration of such guidelines.

Decision (1982). [1]ESC: 1982/159, 28 July, text following.

Draft resolution withdrawn. [2]Afghanistan, Algeria, Angola, Bangladesh, Benin, Cuba, Democratic Yemen, Ethiopia, German Democratic Republic, Guinea, Hungary, Lao People's Democratic Republic, Mongolia, Mozambique, Nicaragua, Syrian Arab Republic, Viet Nam, A/C.2/37/L.80.
Report. [3]UNDP Administrator, DP/1982/9.
Resolution (1982). [4]GA: 37/228, 20 Dec., text following.
Resolution (prior). [5]GA: 35/80, 5 Dec. 1980 (YUN 1980, p. 595).
Meeting records. ESC: E/1982/SR.49 (28 July). GA: 2nd Committee, A/C.2/37/SR.4, 6, 7, 32-40, *43, 46* (30 Sep.–2 Dec.); plenary, A/37/PV.113 (20 Dec.).

Economic and Social Council decision 1982/159

Adopted without vote

Approved by Third Committee (E/1982/90) without vote, 23 July (meeting 16); draft by Chairman (E/1982/C.3/L.10); agenda item 19.

Report of the Administrator of the United Nations Development Programme on the role of qualified national personnel in the social and economic development of developing countries

At its 49th plenary meeting, on 28 July 1982, the Council took note of the report of the Administrator of the United Nations Development Programme on the role of qualified national personnel in the social and economic development of developing countries, and decided to transmit that report to the General Assembly at its thirty-seventh session.

General Assembly resolution 37/228

20 December 1982   Meeting 113   Adopted without vote

Approved by Second Committee (A/37/774) without vote, 2 December (meeting 46); draft by Vice-Chairman (A/C.2/37/L.104), based on informal consultations on 17-nation draft (A/C.2/37/L.80) and orally revised in informal consultations; agenda item 72 *(b)*.

Role of qualified national personnel in the social and economic development of developing countries

The General Assembly,

Referring to its resolutions 33/135 of 19 December 1978 and 35/80 of 5 December 1980 on the role of qualified national personnel in the social and economic development of developing countries,

Recalling its resolutions 3201(S-VI) and 3202(S-VI) of 1 May 1974, containing the Declaration and the Programme of Action on the Establishment of a New International Economic Order, and 3281(XXIX) of 12 December 1974, containing the Charter of Economic Rights and Duties of States,

Desiring to promote full implementation of the provisions of the International Development Strategy for the Third United Nations Development Decade concerning training of qualified personnel for the developing countries,

1. *Takes note* of the report of the Administrator of the United Nations Development Programme on the role of qualified national personnel in the social and economic development of developing countries;

2. *Requests* the Secretary-General and the Administrator of the United Nations Development Programme to ensure and monitor further implementation of General Assembly resolution 35/80;

3. *Further requests* the Secretary-General, in consultation with the executive heads of the organizations concerned, with a view to facilitating the exchange of information and experience, to ensure, within available resources, the preparation and distribution among Member States of periodic analytical surveys of national reports on the experience of all countries in the field of human resources development and international co-operation in training qualified personnel of developing countries;

4. *Invites* Governments of Member States to make available to the Secretariat, on a regular basis, information on their experience in establishing and developing their national systems of training of qualified personnel and on the implementation of the provisions of the relevant resolutions of the General Assembly;

5. *Invites* developed countries and relevant organizations of the United Nations system to direct their assistance to developing countries in the field of education and training of qualified personnel towards, *inter alia:*

(a) Establishing and developing national systems of education and training of personnel as an integral part of the social and economic development programmes of developing countries;

(b) Promoting the most effective use of qualified national personnel in national development;

(c) Implementing the provisions of General Assembly resolution 35/80, especially paragraph 5 thereof;

6. *Requests* the Secretary-General to consult with Member States and relevant organizations of the United Nations system on possible elements of general guidelines on principles, objectives and structures of education and training of personnel of developing countries, taking into account the need for further development of their national systems, and to report on his findings to the General Assembly at its thirty-ninth session;

7. *Also requests* the Secretary-General to submit a progress report on the implementation of the present resolution, including the proposed elements of the above-mentioned general guidelines, to the General Assembly at its thirty-ninth session, through the Economic and Social Council.

UN Institute for Training and Research

Activities of UNITAR

In 1982, the work programme of the United Nations Institute for Training and Research (UNITAR), an autonomous organization within the United Nations system, reflected the retrenchment planned during the previous year as part of the economy measures adopted to alleviate the Institute's financial crisis. Those measures, coupled with an exceptional increase in miscellaneous income, achieved for UNITAR a balanced budget by the end of 1982 (see below). The Institute's programmes and other activities, as well as its finances, were described by the Executive Director in his annual reports to the General Assembly for the periods from 1 July 1981 to 30 June 1982[1] and from 1 July 1982 to 30 June 1983[2] and in his introductory statement to the Assembly's Second Committee on 5 October 1982.

The two main categories of training programmes conducted by UNITAR—those for members of permanent missions in New York and Geneva and those other than for diplomats—were virtually halved in 1982. The staffing reduction at the Geneva Office of UNITAR also resulted in a curtailment of activities.

Among the training programmes organized by UNITAR, seminars for members of permanent missions of Member States to the United Nations covered: the workings of the United Nations system (New York, January); issues currently before the Third United Nations Conference on the Law of the Sea (New York, March); economic development and its international setting, sponsored jointly with the Economic Development Institute of the World Bank (Washington, D. C., 22 March–2 April); international negotiations, (New York, 26-29 April); the second regular session of the Economic and Social Council (Geneva, 7 July); negotiation and drafting techniques for new delegates to the 1982 Assembly session, and an overview of the major issues before it (New York,

15-17 September); and familiarization with the various Geneva-based bodies of the United Nations system and the tasks facing the Organization (Geneva, 16-22 November).

Training programmes other than for diplomats included: the UNITAR-administered fellowship programme in international law (The Hague, Netherlands, July/August) and a regional training and refresher course in international law for Asian and Pacific countries (Seoul, Republic of Korea, 18-29 October), both part of the United Nations Programme of Assistance in the Teaching, Study, Dissemination and Wider Appreciation of International Law; the sixth seminar on multilateral diplomacy and the new international economic order (Vienna, Austria, 21 June–2 July); and an inter-agency seminar on the international civil service (Geneva, 27-29 October).

In response to requests for training services by Member States, UNITAR continued to provide advisory assistance to the Institute of Diplomatic Studies of Saudi Arabia as well as to that of the Libyan Arab Jamahiriya. It held a seminar in Kuwait in January for officials from the Middle East on planning, programming and servicing international conferences and a briefing seminar in July in Zimbabwe for Government officials on the United Nations system and the development process.

Special training activities included a one-week programme on multilateral diplomacy and international economic co-operation for French-speaking diplomats, mostly from Africa (Geneva, December).

Under the UNITAR research programme, an analysis of population movements within the English-speaking Caribbean and their socio-economic implications was begun early in 1982, as was a study on legislative incentives for the development of small-scale energy sources. The 1980 UNITAR Conference on Regionalism and the New International Economic Order[9] resulted in a programme of regional and interregional co-operation in the 1980s, which concluded its preliminary phase with the establishment of a Panel of Eminent Persons to devise an integrated set of policy recommendations for the enchancement of such co-operation. The Panel met for the first time in May 1982 (Brussels, Belgium) and again in September (Sri Lanka) mainly to review research on subregional and regional co-operation in Asia.

Research projects co-sponsored by UNITAR in the USSR for participants from developing countries included a joint seminar with the USSR Academy of Sciences on the role of the public sector in the social and economic development of African countries (Moscow and Alma Ata, 14-25 September) and joint seminars with the International Labour Organisation on labour conditions and labour protection for development (Baku, October) and on social aspects of rural development (Tashkent, September).

The UNITAR Project on the Future, concentrating on long-term problems of socio-economic and technological transformation, continued work on two broad themes: policy choices related to implementing a new international economic order; and the meaning of physical limits and supply constraints to energy and natural resources. The most important development under the Project in 1982 was the study of the pricing of exhaustible resources, centred mainly on the evolution of oil policies. With the United States Department of Energy and the Alberta (Canada) Oil Sands Technology and Research Authority, UNITAR co-sponsored the Second International Conference on Heavy Crude and Tar Sands (Caracas, Venezuela, 7-17 February), during which the Advisory Board of the UNITAR/UNDP Information Centre on Heavy Crude and Tar Sands also held its second meeting. The Centre, which began operating in 1981,[10] had its financial administration transferred to UNDP in January 1982.

Although reduced to a small liaison unit, most of the activities of the UNITAR Geneva Office remained unchanged. In 1982, these included training, organization of assistance programmes to the Libyan Institute of International Relations and continuing research on the material remnants of the Second World War.

The United Nations Institute for Disarmament Research, established within the framework of UNITAR as an interim arrangement, was designated by the General Assembly in December 1982 as an autonomous institution within the United Nations as of January 1983 (p. 154).

Ten publications and two periodicals were published by UNITAR in 1982 (see list below). In September, the Board of Trustees set up a publications committee to reformulate the publications policy of UNITAR. Accordingly, the Executive Director decided to scale down publication activity until a comprehensive policy was approved.

General Assembly action. On 17 December 1982,[5] the General Assembly, taking note of the report of the 1981/82 UNITAR Executive Director and of his introductory statement, welcomed the continuing emphasis UNITAR placed on economic and social training and research and its inclusion of projects on problems in areas identified previously by the Assembly and in the International Development Strategy for the Third United Nations Development Decade.[7] The Assembly also welcomed the efforts of UNITAR to strengthen coordination of its activities, its co-operation with other United Nations bodies and the steps it was taking in accordance with Assembly resolutions

of 1980[6] and December 1981,[8] calling on it to organize its work programme and adjust administrative costs so that estimated expenditure did not exceed estimated revenue. Other provisions called for increased and early announcement of contributions and for an examination of all possibilities for funding UNITAR.

The resolution was adopted by a recorded vote of 133 to 8, with 1 abstention. The text, recommended by the Second Committee, was based on a 26-nation revised draft resolution introduced by Pakistan and approved by the Committee on 8 December by a recorded vote of 121 to 8, with 1 abstention.

In two further resolutions, adopted on 16 November, on the pattern of conferences[3] and on meeting records and documentation for subsidiary organs,[4] the Assembly authorized the UNITAR Board of Trustees to meet each year in the week preceding the Assembly's regular session and included the Board among the governing bodies entitled to receive summary records, in the Board's case in English only.

Reports. UNITAR Executive Director, [1]A/37/14, [2]A/38/14.
Resolutions (1982). GA: [3]37/14 A, para. 3, 16 Nov.; [4]37/14 C, annex, para. 1 (a), 16 Nov.; [5]37/142, 17 Dec., text following.
Resolutions (prior). GA: [6]35/53 B, 5 Dec. 1980 (YUN 1980, p. 1001); [7]35/56, annex, 5 Dec. 1980 (*ibid.*, p. 503); [8]36/75, 4 Dec. 1981 (YUN 1981, p. 806).
Yearbook references. [9]1980, p. 998; [10]1981, p. 708.
Meeting records. GA: 2nd Committee, A/C.2/37/SR.6, 7, 11-13, 25, 26, 47 (5 Oct.-8 Dec.); plenary, A/37/PV.109 (17 Dec.).
UNITAR publications (Sales No. in parentheses):
   The New International Economic Order: International Law in the Making? (E.82.XV.PE/6); *Diplomats' Views on the United Nations System: An Attitude Survey* (E.82.XV.PE/7); *Model Rules for Disaster Relief Operations* (E.82.XV.PE/8); *Assessing the United Nations Scale of Assessments: Is It Fair? Is It Equitable?* (E.82.XV.PE/9); *The United Nations Security Council: Towards Greater Effectiveness* (E.82.XV.CR/15); *Alternative Strategies for Desert Development and Management,* vols. I-IV (UNITAR/CR/16-19); *Long-term Energy Resources,* vols. I-III (UNITAR/CR/20-22); *A New International Economic Order: Selected Documents, 1977* (UNITAR/DS/3); *Scientific-Technological Change and the Role of Women in Development* (UNITAR/RR/27); *Science and Technology in a Changing International Order: The United Nations Conference on Science and Technology for Development* (UNITAR/RR/28); *Important for the Future,* vol. VII, nos. 1-4; *UNITAR News,* vol. XIV.

General Assembly resolution 37/142

17 December 1982   Meeting 109   133-8-1 (recorded vote)

Approved by Second Committee (A/37/741) by recorded vote (121-8-1), 8 December (meeting 47); 26-nation draft (A/C.2/37/L.15/Rev.1); agenda item 73 (a).
Sponsors: Bangladesh, Canada, China, Costa Rica, Ecuador, Egypt, India, Jamaica, Liberia, Nigeria, Norway, Oman, Pakistan, Panama, Peru, Philippines, Senegal, Sierra Leone, Singapore, Sri Lanka, Sweden, Syrian Arab Republic, Trinidad and Tobago, Tunisia, Uganda, United Arab Emirates.

United Nations Institute for Training and Research

The General Assembly,

Recalling its resolution 36/75 of 4 December 1981 on the United Nations Institute for Training and Research,

Acknowledging the value and usefulness of the research on the effectiveness of the activities of the United Nations and of the studies on the future concerning development strategies, undertaken by the United Nations Institute for Training and Research,

Recognizing the role of the United Nations Institute for Training and Research in assisting, through training and other services within its mandate, members of permanent missions to the United Nations and other national officials concerned with the work of the United Nations,

Aware of the continuing precarious financial situation of the United Nations Institute for Training and Research and drawing attention to the recommendations of the Joint Inspection Unit on the financing of the Institute,

1. *Takes note with appreciation* of the report of the Executive Director of the United Nations Institute for Training and Research and of his introductory statement on 5 October 1982;

2. *Welcomes* the continuing emphasis that the United Nations Institute for Training and Research is placing at present on economic and social training and research and the inclusion of specific projects on the problems that exist in the areas identified by the General Assembly at its sixth and seventh special sessions, in the relevant decisions adopted by the Assembly at its twenty-ninth and subsequent sessions, and in the International Development Strategy for the Third United Nations Development Decade, taking into consideration the statements on the programme of work of the Institute made at the current session;

3. *Welcomes also* the efforts of the United Nations Institute for Training and Research to strengthen the co-ordination of its activities and its co-operation with relevant organs and organizations within the United Nations system, in particular the United Nations University, and the continuation of those efforts;

4. *Welcomes further* the steps being taken by the United Nations Institute for Training and Research in accordance with General Assembly resolutions 35/53 B of 5 December 1980 and 36/75 of 4 December 1981 and calls upon the Institute to continue to organize its programme of work and activities and to adjust its administrative costs so as to ensure that estimated expenditure does not exceed estimated revenue;

5. *Urges* all States that have not yet contributed to the United Nations Institute for Training and Research to do so, and calls upon all donor countries, especially those that are not contributing at a level commensurate with their capacity, to increase their voluntary contributions in order to meet the needs of the Institute;

6. *Requests* Member States to announce their annual voluntary contributions early, if possible at the annual United Nations Pledging Conference for Development Activities;

7. *Requests* the Secretary-General to examine all possibilities for funding the United Nations Institute for Training and Research in order to place its financing on a more predictable, assured and continuous basis, and to report thereon to the General Assembly at its thirty-eighth session, keeping in mind article VIII of the statute of the Institute and the views expressed during the current session of the Assembly.

Recorded vote in Assembly as follows:

In favour: Afghanistan, Algeria, Angola, Argentina, Australia, Austria, Bahamas, Bahrain, Bangladesh, Barbados, Belgium, Benin, Bhutan, Bolivia, Botswana, Brazil, Burma, Burundi, Canada, Cape Verde, Central African Republic, Chad, Chile, China, Colombia, Comoros, Congo, Costa Rica, Cuba, Cyprus, Democratic Kampuchea, Democratic Yemen, Denmark, Djibouti, Dominica, Dominican Republic, Ecuador, Egypt, El Salvador, Ethiopia, Fiji, Finland, France, Gabon, Gambia, Germany, Federal Republic of, Ghana, Greece, Grenada, Guatemala, Guinea, Guinea-Bissau, Guyana, Honduras, Iceland, India, Indonesia, Iran, Iraq, Ireland, Israel, Italy, Ivory Coast, Jamaica, Japan, Jordan, Kenya, Kuwait, Lebanon, Lesotho, Liberia, Libyan Arab Jamahiriya, Luxembourg, Madagascar, Malawi, Malaysia, Maldives, Mali, Malta, Mauritania, Mauritius, Mexico, Morocco, Mozambique, Nepal, Netherlands, New Zealand, Nicaragua, Niger, Nigeria, Norway, Oman, Pakistan, Panama, Papua New Guinea, Paraguay, Peru, Philippines, Portugal, Qatar, Romania, Rwanda, Samoa, Sao Tome and Principe, Saudi Arabia, Senegal, Sierra Leone, Singapore, Somalia, Spain, Sri Lanka, Suriname, Swaziland, Sweden, Thailand, Togo, Trinidad and Tobago, Tunisia, Turkey, Uganda, United Arab Emirates, United Kingdom, United Republic of Cameroon, United Republic of Tanzania, Upper Volta, Uruguay, Vanuatu, Venezuela, Yemen, Yugoslavia, Zaire, Zambia, Zimbabwe.

Against: Bulgaria, Byelorussian SSR, Czechoslovakia, German Democratic Republic, Hungary, Ukrainian SSR, USSR, United States.

Abstaining: Poland.

Finances of UNITAR

The balanced budget displayed by UNITAR at the end of 1982 reflected considerable reduction in expenditures during the year, according to the UNITAR Executive Director.[1] In 1982, income for the General Fund amounted to $2,523,750, against expenditures, including adjustments, of $2,283,528, resulting in a net excess of income over expenditure of $240,222 as of 31 December. This surplus occurred even though in 1982 UNITAR did not receive a grant from the United Nations regular budget, which had provided $352,600 in 1981.[3] Given the decrease in contributions from $2,055,850 in 1981 to $1,454,385 in 1982, there would have been a deficit in 1982 had it not been for the reduction in expenditures and the exceptional increase in miscellaneous income, which the Executive Director reported was unlikely to recur.

Income from the Special Purpose Grants amounted to $1,604,744 as of 31 December 1982, while obligations, including adjustments, amounted to $2,362,999. The balance of the Special Purpose Fund as of 31 December was $2,693,904.

According to the Executive Director, the trend of governmental contributions to the General Fund since 1965 showed that less than one third of the Member States currently contributed and only about one half had ever contributed. Some of those which if assessed would be making the largest contributions were not among the most generous supporters of UNITAR and some did not even contribute to the Fund. The trend in expenditures over the past six years also showed that in 1982 the same level of expenditure was maintained as in 1978, indicating that, despite the higher inflation rate since then, UNITAR had had to reduce costs by adopting stringent economy measures, thus hampering its normal activities. The situation had to be remedied without delay, the Executive Director concluded, if the aims and objectives of UNITAR were to be achieved.

General Assembly action. In its resolution of 17 December 1982,[2] the General Assembly urged all States that had not contributed to UNITAR to do so, calling on them to increase their voluntary contributions and announce their pledges early. The Assembly requested the Secretary-General to examine all possibilities for UNITAR financing in order to place it on a predictable, assured and continuous basis and to report to the Assembly in 1983, keeping in mind the article of the UNITAR statute relating to finances and the views expressed at the current session.

Among those voting against the resolution, the USSR, besides considering unacceptable the preambular paragraphs referring to the value of research undertaken by UNITAR and to its continuing precarious financial situation, said that paragraph 7, requesting an examination of all possibilities for funding, was an ambiguous provision which could be used to change the voluntary nature of the current funding system. Czechoslovakia found that provision unacceptable, whose implicit aim was to charge UNITAR expenses to the United Nations regular budget or to other assessed contributions. The United States raised a similar objection, adding that the provision would delay adoption of measures to solve the financial problems of UNITAR until at least 1983.

Argentina explained that its affirmative vote in no way changed its position; namely, that UNITAR should be financed from voluntary contributions and not from the United Nations budget—a position Japan shared. Brazil, which also voted in favour, reiterated its opposition to the use of regular-budget resources for bodies created to be financed from voluntary contributions, adding that UNITAR should tailor its programmes to the resources at its disposal.

Report. [1]UNITAR Executive Director, A/38/14.
Resolution (1982). [2]GA: 37/142, paras. 5-7, 17 Dec.
Yearbook reference. [3]1981, p. 807.

Accounts for 1981

By a resolution of 16 November 1982,[3] on the 1981 accounts of various United Nations programmes and funds, the General Assembly accepted the UNITAR accounts for the year ended 31 December 1981 and requested action where required by the the Board of Auditors in its comments on the accounts.[2]

The Board, in its examination of the UNITAR accounts, found internal controls and accounting procedures to be generally satisfactory but recommended improvements in budgetary and inventory controls to ensure that expenditures did not exceed the funds available and appropriate recording of inventories, including the prompt disposal of unserviceable items. The Board observed that, as a result of subleasing part of the ground floor of the UNITAR building to a third party at $19,500 a year, UNITAR had been paying a yearly real estate tax of $74,372. UNITAR later reported that the sublease had been terminated; it would use the already vacated premises suitably and was exploring possibilities for tax exemption.

The Advisory Committee on Administrative and Budgetary Questions, considering the Board's comments and observations, reported[1] that, according to the Office of Legal Affairs, the tax paid by UNITAR was in fact a contractual payment to the building's owner as reimbursement for the taxes levied by law on the building and that it was unlikely that elimination of the sublease would affect the contractual obligation of the United Nations to its owner.

Reports. [1]ACABQ, A/37/443; [2]Board of Auditors, and financial statements, A/37/5/Add.4.
Resolution (1982). [3]GA: 37/12, 16 Nov.

CONTRIBUTIONS TO THE UNITAR GENERAL FUND, 1982
(as at 31 December 1982; in US dollar equivalent)

Country	Amount
Argentina	11,773
Australia	39,645
Austria	10,000
Bahamas	500
Belgium	103,093
Canada	76,271
Chile	5,000
Cyprus	500
Denmark	40,971
Egypt	2,100*
Finland	44,444
France	73,581
Germany, Federal Republic of	176,180
Greece	5,000
Hungary	(3,385)†
India	40,000
Indonesia	4,000
Ireland	5,514
Israel	3,000
Italy	33,997
Ivory Coast	17,742
Japan	60,000
Kuwait	20,000
Luxembourg	2,091
Malta	600
Netherlands	55,545
New Zealand	5,375
Norway	84,832
Oman	20,000
Pakistan	14,000‡
Philippines	10,000
Qatar	20,000
Republic of Korea	2,000
Saudi Arabia	20,000
Spain	(50,000)†
Sweden	127,447§
Switzerland	75,226
Trinidad and Tobago	4,146
Tunisia	2,520
USSR	40,000
United Republic of Tanzania	7,273§
United States	522,500
Total	1,733,481

*Pledge for future year paid in 1982.
†Transfer to Special Purpose Grant.
‡For 1981 and 1982.
§Received in 1981 for 1982.

SOURCE: A/38/5/Add.4.

Tribute to the Executive Director

By a resolution adopted without vote on 17 December 1982,[1] the General Assembly, noting that the UNITAR Executive Director, Davidson S. H. W. Nicol, would shortly be relinquishing his duties, expressed its appreciation to him for the effective and dedicated manner in which he had performed his functions and extended him its good wishes for success in his future undertakings.

The text, recommended by the Assembly's Second (Economic and Financial) Committee, was based on a 27-nation draft resolution introduced by Sierra Leone and approved, also without vote, by the Committee on 19 November.

Resolution (1982). [1]GA: 37/141, 17 Dec., text following.
Meeting records. GA: 2nd Committee, A/C.2/37/SR.6, 7, 11-13, 26, 41, 42 (5 Oct.–19 Nov.); plenary, A/37/PV.109 (17 Dec.).

General Assembly resolution 37/141

17 December 1982   Meeting 109   Adopted without vote

Approved by Second Committee (A/37/741) without vote, 19 November (meeting 41); 27-nation draft (A/C.2/37/L.14); agenda item 73 (a).

Sponsors: Austria, Bangladesh, China, Egypt, Gambia, Ghana, Guinea, Ivory Coast, Jamaica, Japan, Liberia, Madagascar, Malaysia, Mali, Nigeria, Pakistan, Senegal, Sierra Leone, Singapore, Somalia, Sudan, Swaziland, Trinidad and Tobago, Tunisia, Uganda, United Arab Emirates, United Republic of Tanzania.

Expression of appreciation to the Executive Director of the United Nations Institute for Training and Research

The General Assembly,

Noting that the incumbent Executive Director of the United Nations Institute for Training and Research will shortly be relinquishing his duties,

Recognizing the contribution made by the United Nations Institute for Training and Research under his guidance, through training and research, towards the achievement of the major objectives of the United Nations, in particular the maintenance of peace and security and the promotion of economic and social development,

1. *Expresses its sincere appreciation and thanks* to Mr. Davidson Nicol for the effective and dedicated manner in which he has performed his functions as Executive Director of the United Nations Institute for Training and Research;

2. *Extends its good wishes* to him for success in his future undertakings.

UN University

UNU activities

In 1982, the United Nations University (UNU) began implementing its programme of work according to the medium-term perspective, 1982-1987, adopted by the UNU Council in 1981.[9] Its research, training and dissemination of knowledge were thus conducted to assure the interlinking of the five themes defining the priority areas of concern, as described in the perspective.

Activities under the first theme—peace, security, conflict resolution and global transformation—were consolidated in the subprogramme on peace and global transformation, aimed at identifying the most dangerous trends threatening the survival of nature, societies and cultures. A project on socio-cultural development alternatives in a changing world, begun in 1978, was successfully completed and its results were being processed for publication.

Under the second theme of global economy, exploratory work continued on the establishment by UNU of a World Institute for Development Economics Research.

In response to the concerns of the third theme—hunger, poverty, resources and environment—work concentrated on four subprogrammes: energy systems and policy, involving projects on rural energy systems, energy planning and management, research and technology assessment, and dissemination of knowledge, mainly by expanding the publication *ASSET*;[7] resource policy and management, ongoing projects which dealt with arid lands management, highland-lowland and water-land interactive systems, agro-forestry systems and coastal resources; food, nutrition and poverty, including studies on the impact of chronic energy and iron deficiencies and of agricultural and food policies on the population's health; and the food-energy nexus, concerned with, among other matters, increasing the energy efficiency of the food-chain and the efficiency of integrated food-energy systems of diverse ecosystems.

Studies under the fourth theme—human and social development and coexistence of peoples, cultures and social systems—were on such topics as the search for theories of human and democratic development; participatory development, power structure and social movements; the human economy as an alternative to the production-consumption paradigm; the psycho-cultural dimensions of development; emerging social thought; perceptions of desirable societies in different religious and ethical systems; ethnic minorities and human and social development; the socio-cultural impact of large-scale human migration; and main technological trends and their impact in the third world. Other studies were on specific regional perspectives, on violence at the community level and on the changing relationships among household members.

Under the fifth theme—science and technology and their social and ethical implications—three research projects were completed during the year and the results were being prepared for publication. These concerned the sharing of traditional technology; research and development in rural settings; and technology transfer, transformation and development in the Japanese experience. In the area of biotechnology, preparations were under way to set up an International Institute for Biotechnology in Venezuela, based on a feasibility study by a task force.

Studies encompassing all themes were undertaken on the topics of the information society, its concepts, perceptions and issues, the problems of information overload and underuse, and information economics. Research was begun on the global commons and development of international law, and on the management of complexity in natural and social systems.

In 1982, UNU organized some 84 workshops, seminars, symposia and meetings. It granted fellowships in three programme areas—energy systems and policies; resource policy and management; and food, nutrition and poverty—with a total of 124 fellows in training at the end of June 1982 and 233 having completed training by 31 December 1981.

The work of UNU was described in the annual reports of its Council to the General Assembly, covering activities from 1 July 1981 to 30 June 1982[4] and from 1 July 1982 to 30 June 1983.[5]

The Economic and Social Council decided on 30 July 1982[1] to authorize the Secretary-General to transmit the UNU Council's 1981/82 report directly to the Assembly.

JIU report. In its six years of operation since 1975,[8] UNU, an institution of learning at once a United Nations organ and a world-wide network of advanced centres of academic and scientific research, had demonstrated the potential of its unique concept and, although falling short of what had been envisioned by its founders, was an achievement in itself. It remained for UNU to prove, however, that not only was it viable institutionally but also capable of ideas and solutions of value to the international community. The response to this challenge would determine whether UNU would become a pole of attraction for academic and scientific communities worldwide or just another marginal research institution. These were among the conclusions made by the Joint Inspection Unit (JIU) in a November 1981 report assessing the status of UNU and its prospects; it was transmitted to the 1982 session of the General Assembly by the Secretary-General, together with his comments.[3]

JIU made a series of recommendations, including maintaining the present character of UNU; strengthening its intellectual capacity, as well as its institutional and working relationships with the world academic community, incorporating only those institutions serving well-defined, long-term needs; maintaining the Council as the overall policy-making organ, leaving daily operations to the Rector and his staff; modifying the UNU structure to limit the position of Vice-Rector to one to avoid compartmentalization of research activities; establishment of a planning and evaluation unit reporting directly to the Rector; and staffing the UNU Centre in Tokyo with highly competent academic professionals and with administrative personnel seconded from within the United Nations system.

Apart from measures concerning the UNU finance and budget, other recommendations were for the establishment of a clear relationship between the UNU Centre and the University's associated institutions, policy statements on programming, restraint in the scale of training activities, emphasis on information and dissemination of research results, development of the current information retrieval system into a computer data bank, exploration of new political and economic issues, co-ordination with the University for Peace on related activities, and utilization of existing research institutions in the United Nations system, such as UNITAR and the United Nations Research Institute for Social Development.

The Secretary-General, welcoming the JIU report as generally positive and supportive of the new direction and broader intellectual concerns of UNU, concurred in general with the recommendations, with certain exceptions such as leaving to the Rector determination of the appropriate method for minimizing compartmentalization of research. The Secretary-General noted that the Inspectors had underlined that their report focused mainly on the structure and method of UNU and only in a limited way on the substance of its programmes; their report was but one of a series of related studies. He believed that there remained a need to assess the scholarly achievements of UNU and the extent to which it had succeeded in serving its global constituency.

As requested by the Secretary-General, the UNU Council, in its report for the period ended June 1982, commented on the observations of JIU, stating that certain of its judgements suggested an insufficient understanding of the fundamental nature of UNU as an international community of scholars. The Council emphasized that, ultimately, it was in the best position to evaluate the University's scientific work with the assistance of peer reviews and assessments made through external expert evaluation. As to the recommendations for one Council meeting yearly and for only one Vice-Rector, the Council stated that, for the foreseeable future, two meetings and maintaining the existing organizational structure were in the University's interest.

General Assembly action. On 17 December 1982,[6] the General Assembly took note of the JIU report and of the Secretary-General's comments. It also noted a renewed emphasis on the multidisciplinary and integrative approach to urgent global problems and that UNU had maintained its momentum in the original programmes and enlarged on the foundations built earlier. The Assembly welcomed the fact that research, postgraduate training and the dissemination of knowledge would be a single programme under the medium-term perspective, with subprogrammes responding to the five themes specified therein. Increased UNU co-operation with United Nations organs, particularly research and training institutions, was noted, and UNU was urged to continue its co-operation and co-ordinate its activities with those bodies and with international academic and scientific organizations; it was encouraged to explore innovative and varied institutional relationships. Recognizing the need for UNU to build up its Endowment Fund and other contributions, the Assembly appealed to Member States to contribute urgently and generously to the Fund and/or make operating contributions to UNU.

The resolution was adopted, without vote, on the recommendation of the Second Committee, which had similarly approved it on 19 November. The text was submitted by a Committee Vice-Chairman on the basis of informal consultations held on a 17-nation draft resolution introduced by Austria and later withdrawn.[2]

The adopted text differed from the original in that the Secretary-General's comments were taken note of; in paragraph 5, concerning co-operative activities with other United Nations organs and institutions, a phrase was added by which the Assembly urged UNU to strengthen "its co-operation, and the co-ordination of its activities, with those institutions and the appropriate organizational units of the United Nations Secretariat"; in paragraph 7, welcoming the dissemination of knowledge by UNU, the phrase "including its own research findings" was inserted; and in paragraph 9, the Assembly appealed to States to contribute "urgently" as well as generously to the Endowment Fund.

Decision (1982). [1]ESC: 1982/178, para. *(c)*, 30 July.
Draft resolution withdrawn. [2]Austria, Bangladesh, China, Ecuador, Egypt, France, Ghana, Iceland, India, Indonesia, Japan, Jordan, Pakistan, Philippines, Sierra Leone, Singapore, Thailand, A/C.2/37/L.13.
Reports. [3]JIU, transmitted by S-G note, A/37/111, and S-G comments, Add.1; UNU Council, [4]A/37/31, [5]A/38/31.
Resolution (1982). [6]GA: 37/143, 17 Dec., text following.
UNU Publication. [7]*ASSET (Abstracts of Selected Solar Energy Technology)*, vol. 4, Nos. 1-10; Index, vol. 4.
Yearbook references. [8]1975, p. 727; [9]1981, p. 811.
Meeting records. GA: 2nd Committee, A/C.2/37/SR.6, 7, 11-13, *26*, 41 (5 Oct.–19 Nov.); plenary, A/37/PV.109 (17 Dec.).
Other UNU publications. Pollitt, E. and R. L. Leibel, eds., *Iron Deficiency: Brain Biochemistry and Behavior*; New York, Raven Press, 1982. *Urban Geomorphology in Drylands*, by R. U. Cooke and others; Oxford, Oxford University Press, 1982. *UNU Newsletter*, vol. 6, No. 1; vol. 7, No. 1.

General Assembly resolution 37/143

17 December 1982   Meeting 109   Adopted without vote

Approved by Second Committee (A/37/741) without vote, 19 November (meeting 41); draft by Vice-Chairman (A/C.2/37/L.28), based on informal consultations on 17-nation draft (A/C.2/37/L.13); agenda item 73 *(b)*.

United Nations University

The General Assembly,

Recalling its resolutions 2951(XXVII) of 11 December 1972, 3081(XXVIII) of 6 December 1973, 3313(XXIX) of 14 December 1974, 3439(XXX) of 9 December 1975, 31/117 and 31/118 of 16 December 1976, 32/54 of 8 December 1977, 33/108 of 18 December 1978, 34/112 of 14 December 1979, 35/54 of 5 December 1980 and 36/45 of 19 November 1981,

Having considered the report of the Council of the United Nations University on the work of the University and the report on the University prepared by the Joint Inspection Unit,

Noting with appreciation that a site has been dedicated for the permanent headquarters of the United Nations University, thanks to the generous offer of the Tokyo Metropolitan Government, and that active steps are being taken by the Government of Japan towards the construction of a building that will house the permanent headquarters of the University as provided in the Agreement of 14 May 1976 between the United Nations and Japan regarding the Headquarters of the University,

Noting decision 5.2.3 adopted on 7 October 1982 by the Executive Board of the United Nations Educational, Scientific and Cultural Organization at its one hundred and fifteenth session,

1. *Takes note with satisfaction* of the report prepared by the Joint Inspection Unit, and of the comments of the Secretary-General thereon, which, *inter alia*, support the new directions of the United Nations University and its broader intellectual concerns as reflected in its medium-term perspective (1982-1987) under the following five themes:

(a) Peace, security, conflict resolution and global transformation;

(b) Global economy;

(c) Hunger, poverty, resources and the environment;

(d) Human and social development and coexistence of peoples, cultures and social systems;

(e) Science and technology and their social and ethical implications;

2. *Notes with satisfaction* that, with the adoption of the medium-term perspective, a renewed emphasis has been placed on the multidisciplinary and integrative approach to the search for solutions to urgent global problems, in accordance with the Charter of the United Nations University;

3. *Also notes with satisfaction* that, in keeping with its philosophy of continuity with change, the United Nations University has maintained its momentum in the original programmes and enlarged on the foundations built in the early years;

4. *Welcomes* the fact that research, post-graduate training and the dissemination of knowledge will be covered under the medium-term perspective as a single programme of the United Nations University with subprogrammes responding to the five themes;

5. *Notes with satisfaction* the increasing co-operative activities of the United Nations University with the United Nations, its organs and agencies, particularly United Nations research and training institutions, and urges the University to continue to strengthen its co-operation, and the co-ordination of its activities, with those institutions and the appropriate organizational units of the United Nations Secretariat, as well as its collaboration with international academic and scientific organizations;

6. *Encourages* the United Nations University to explore and expand innovative, fruitful and varied institutional relationships in accordance with its Charter, to assist in the effective implementation of the medium-term perspective and achieve wider outreach and increased decentralization, ensuring the continuing growth of vigorous academic and scientific communities everywhere and particularly in the developing countries;

7. *Welcomes* the increased attention being given by the United Nations University to the activities related to the dissemination of knowledge, including its own research findings, referred to in its Charter and, as a consequence, the promotion of a more informed awareness of global problems among all sectors and levels of the world community through the use of the new information and communications technology now available;

8. *Recognizes* that, over the medium term, the United Nations University needs to build up its Endowment Fund and other contributions in order to increase its core income;

9. *Earnestly appeals* to all Member States to take cognizance of the important developments at the United Nations University and to contribute urgently and generously to its Endowment Fund and, additionally or alternatively, to make operating contributions to the University to enable it to fulfil effectively its global mandate.

UNU Council activities

In 1982, the UNU Council held its nineteenth and twentieth sessions, in Tokyo, from 21 to 25 June[1] and from 6 to 10 December,[2] at which it reviewed the University's progress, particularly with respect to implementation of the six-year medium-term perspective, and received a report from the Rector on developments since the previous session. In June, the Council adopted a revised version of its rules of procedure, according to which a Committee on Institutional and Programmatic Development was set up and the functions of the Committee on Finance and Budget were redefined. In December, on the recommendation of its *Ad Hoc* Committee on Statutes and Rules, the Council adopted two sets of provisional statutes, on the appointment of UNU personnel and on institutional relations, and extended the *Ad Hoc* Committee's mandate to the end of its December 1983 session. It approved the proposed programme and budget for 1983 and designated four new associated institutions, in Argentina, China, France and Japan.

The first colloquium of the Council, aimed at allowing greater involvement by its members in the substance of UNU work, was held on 6 December 1982, on the theme of peace and global transformation.

Reports. UNU Council, [1]A/37/31, [2]A/38/31.

UNU finances

In its recommendations on the finances and budget of UNU,[1] the Joint Inspection Unit (JIU) recommended that, besides the long-term objective of increasing the Endowment Fund, UNU should concentrate on fund-raising efforts to elicit supplementary contributions for specific programme activites, including contributions in non-convertible currencies once avenues for the optimum utilization of such currencies had been identified. Contributions in kind by Member States and by governmental and non-governmental institutions should also be seriously investigated. Thought should be given to establishing a high-level fund-raising group or a committee of eminent persons from outside UNU, with possible support from a network of volunteers and a system of national committees. Finally, JIU recommended biennial budgeting, to start in 1984 at the latest, to be accompanied by stringent budgetary control procedures, including restraining measures on official travel and publications.

The Secretary-General, in concurring with the recommendations to devote more energy to fund-raising and to broaden the base and support for UNU funding, observed that academic freedom as partly a function of financial independence should be borne in mind; that it was vitally important that support of UNU be widely shared so as not to inhibit it from serving the needs and interests of all nations; and that prior identification be made of the use of non-convertible currencies to avoid administrative work required to maintain separate accounts for unused currencies. The Secretary-General added that formation of national councils for UNU had been initiated.

Report. [1]JIU, transmitted by S-G note, A/37/111, and S-G comments, Add.1.

Fund-raising activities

In 1982, a number of exploratory missions were undertaken in response to the medium-term perspective's call to increase the core income of UNU from $15 million in 1982 to $28 million in 1987. Indirect contributions in cash and in kind were made by a number of Governments and institutions for UNU work. Funds were also obtained for specific associated institutions and research and training units from host Governments.[1] In addition, a major effort got under way to increase the

involvement of institutions in the Eastern European countries in the work of UNU and to mobilize the necessary financial support.[2]

Contributions received during 1982 totalled $5,589,187 from 12 States to the Endowment Fund and $260,531 from 4 States to the General Operating Fund; as at 31 December 1982, 4 States had pledged $2,216,470 to the Endowment Fund for 1983 (see table below).

CONTRIBUTIONS TO UNU, 1982 AND 1983
(as at 31 December 1982; in US dollar equivalent)

COUNTRY	1982 payment	1983 pledge
Endowment Fund		
Austria	119,522	119,522*
Germany, Federal Republic of	809,069	—
Japan	1,000,000	—
Mexico	250,000	—
Netherlands	92,081	—
Nigeria	17,187	—
Senegal	123,622	—
Thailand	200,000	100,000
Tunisia	9,925	—
United Kingdom	1,956,947	1,956,948
United Republic of Tanzania	—	40,000
Venezuela	1,000,000	—
Zambia	10,834	—
Subtotal	5,589,187	2,216,470
General Operating Fund		
France	40,708	—
Greece	40,000	—
Norway	169,823	—
Philippines	10,000	—
Subtotal	260,531	—
Total	5,849,718	2,216,470

*Or 1.5 million Austrian schillings, which Austria had pledged to pay annually.

SOURCE: Interim United Nations financial statements for the 12-month period ended 31 December 1982 (unpublished).

Reports. UNU Council, [1]A/37/31, [2]A/38/31.

Accounts for 1980-1981

By a resolution of 16 November 1982,[3] on the 1981 accounts of various United Nations programmes and funds, the General Assembly accepted the UNU accounts for the year ended 31 December 1981 and requested action where required by the Board of Auditors in its comments on those accounts.[2]

In examining the UNU accounts, the Board found the overall financial reporting system significantly improved. To improve the system further, the Board recommended intensifying efforts to obtain the participation of more Member States in UNU fund-raising programmes and strengthening procedures for the collection of outstanding pledges. It agreed with the UNU Council decision to start biennial budgeting in 1984. On the UNU policy of restricting expenditure so as to build up an unencumbered balance—such as the 1981 balance of $2.4 million carried over to 1982 for the Programme Reserve Fund—the Board recommended a level of expenditure consistent with budgeted estimates to ensure optimum programme delivery. Also recommended were measures to regulate consultancy services and a yearly verification of all properties.

The Advisory Committee on Administrative and Budgetary Questions, reporting on the Board's comments and observations,[1] supported the Board's recommendations concerning unencumbered balances and the verification of non-expendable properties.

Reports. [1]ACABQ, A/37/443; [2]Board of Auditors, and financial statements, A/37/5, vol. III.
Resolution (1982). [3]GA: 37/12, 16 Nov.

Chapter XVI

Environment

Contents

Related topics:

Law of the sea: Protection of the marine environment. Regional economic and social activities—Environment: Africa; Asia and the Pacific; Europe; Latin America. Environment statistics.

For resolutions and decisions of major organs mentioned but not reproduced, refer to INDEX OF RESOLUTIONS AND DECISIONS.

General aspects

Two sessions[1] of the Governing Council of the United Nations Environment Programme (UNEP) were held in 1982, at Nairobi, Kenya. To commemorate the tenth anniversary of the United Nations Conference on the Human Environment,[3] a session of special character was held from 10 to 18 May, at which the Council adopted the Nairobi Declaration—expressing serious concern about the state of the environment and requesting intensified efforts to protect and improve it—and five substantive resolutions. At its tenth session, held from 20 to 31 May, the Council adopted 27 decisions on various aspects of the environment programme.

The activities of UNEP in 1982 were described in a report by its Executive Director to the Governing Council.[2]

Reports. [1]UNEP Council, A/37/25; [2]UNEP Executive Director, UNEP/GC.11/2.
Yearbook reference. [3]1972, p. 318.

Programme and finances of UNEP

Programme policy

Special session of the UNEP Governing Council

The UNEP Governing Council held a session of special character at Nairobi from 10 to 18 May 1982.[1] Open to all States, the session commemorated the tenth anniversary of the United Nations Conference on the Human Environment (Stockholm, Sweden, June 1972).[6]

The main result of the session—held in accordance with General Assembly resolutions of 1980[4] and 1981[5]—was the adoption by consensus on 18 May of the Nairobi Declaration, in which States expressed serious concern about the state of the environment and requested Governments and peoples to intensify efforts at every level to protect and improve it. States reaffirmed their commitment to the 1972 Declaration of the United Nations Conference on the Human Environment[7] and the Action Plan for the Human Environment,[8] as well as to the further strengthening and expansion of national efforts and international co-operation in environmental protection. They also reaffirmed their support for strengthening UNEP as the major catalytic instrument for global environmental co-operation and called for increased resources, particularly through the Environment Fund, to address environment problems. They urged all Governments and peoples to discharge their historical responsibility to ensure that the planet was passed over to future generations in a condition guaranteeing a life in human dignity for all.

Of six resolutions adopted on 18 May, one was on the state of the environment in 1982, by which the Governing Council examined the major achievements in implementing the 1972 Action Plan; identified the major environmental trends, potential problems and priorities for action by the United Nations system during 1982-1992, laid down the basic orientations of UNEP for that decade, and dealt with the planning and implementation of environmental activities; and expressed its views on institutional arrangements.

By section II of the same resolution,[3] the Council looked at perceptions of environmental issues that had evolved over the previous decade which, it considered, together with the Nairobi Declaration, complemented the principles contained in the 1972 Conference Declaration. The Council identified the following perceptions: disarmament and security issues deserved attention; the wise use of resources and enlightened conservation strategies should be considered prerequisites for sustainable growth; research into alternative consumption patterns, technological styles and land-use strategies was called for; interconnections between components and processes supporting life should be considered in development planning; environmental development and management should be planned flexibly and monitored for unexpected changes; development plans should take account of the stability of environmental systems; developments in the transfer of certain inappropriate technologies, export of toxic substances and hazardous materials and certain marketing arrangements, could endanger the environment; and the United Nations system, particularly UNEP, must address environmental problems of poverty and underdevelopment.

In its 20 December resolution on the UNEP special session, the General Assembly endorsed the Governing Council's identification of the perceptions of environmental issues that had evolved between 1972 and 1982.[2]

The other resolutions adopted at the special session dealt with: establishing a special commission on long-term environment strategies (p. 14); arms and the environment; the environmental consequences of an Israeli project to build a canal linking the Mediterranean to the Dead Sea (See POLITICAL AND SECURITY QUESTIONS, Chapter IX); and resolutions and recommendations of an Intergovernmental Regional Meeting on the Environment in Latin America and the Caribbean (See ECONOMIC AND SOCIAL QUESTIONS, Chapter VIII).

Report. [1]UNEP Council, A/37/25.
Resolutions (1982). [2]GA: 37/219, para. 5 *(b)* (i), 20 Dec. [3]UNEP Council: I, sect. II, 18 May.
Resolutions (prior). GA: [4]35/74, 5 Dec. 1980 (YUN 1980, p. 724); [5]36/189, 17 Dec. 1981 (YUN 1981, p. 821).
Yearbook references. 1972, [6]p.318, [7]p. 319, [8]p. 322.

Implementation of the recommendations of the 1972 Conference

In section I of its 18 May 1982 resolution on the state of the environment,[2] adopted at its special session, the UNEP Governing Council stated that it considered that a sector-by-sector review of the implementation of the Action Plan for the Human Environment[4]—109 recommendations adopted at the 1972 Conference on the Human Environment[3]—suggested a mixed record of achievement. Its overall assessment was that fair to good progress had been made in implementing some elements, with very modest progress in others. The Council listed what it felt were the major achievements and failures in implementing the Plan.

In the area of environmental assessment: the Global Environmental Monitoring System was operating and expanding although gaps persisted; the International Referral System for sources of environmental information was functioning but had not realized its objectives, particularly because of slow growth in user demand; assessments of the environmental impact of various energy sources had been published, as had a major report—*The World Environment, 1972-1982*. Other environmental assessments were made on atmospheric research, toxic substances and the International Programme on Chemical Safety.

Concerning environmental management, the Council felt that: there had been progress in formulating regional programmes and concluding global and regional agreements, though with some delays in implementation; world-wide efforts had expanded to combat desertification and improve water supply/management and human settlements, but progress remained slow; progress had been made in implementing international scientific programmes on the human environment; the World Conservation Strategy was increasingly used for national conservation programmes; progress had been made in conceptualizing environmental management objectives and in developing some of its tools; the need to consider the environment when evaluating development projects had been widely recognized; a moratorium on commercial whaling had been given effect although progress had been made in reducing whale-catch quotas; and inadequacies persisted in redressing environmental problems of poverty and underdevelopment. The Council also assessed the regional seas programme (p. 1022), the industry and environment programme and shared natural resources.

Regarding supporting measures, the Council noted that: international technical co-operation programmes had increasingly included environmental components; despite nearly universal observance of World Environment Day (5 June), the information programme was inadequate; and it was important to continue increasing public awareness of environmental issues. The Council also commented on assistance to developing countries (p. 999) and environmental education.

The Council noted that, together with the environment secretariat and the Environment Fund, it was co-ordinating the institutional and financial arrangements for international environmental co-operation.

The General Assembly endorsed the Governing Council's assessment in its 20 December resolution on the UNEP special session.[1]

Resolutions (1982). [1]GA: 37/219, para. 5 (a), 20 Dec. [2]UNEP Council (report, A/37/25): I, sect. I, 18 May. Yearbook references. 1972, [3]p. 318, [4]p. 322.

Work programme for 1982-1992

In section III of the 18 May 1982 resolution on the state of the environment,[2] adopted at the special session of the UNEP Governing Council, the major environmental trends, potential problems and priorities were identified for action by the United Nations system in general and by UNEP in particular during 1982-1992. Attention was directed to the atmosphere, the oceans, water, the lithosphere, terrestrial biota and bioproductive systems, population and human settlements, and energy, health (See ECONOMIC AND SOCIAL QUESTIONS, Chapter XV), industry and other economic development, and peace, security and the environment.

Setting out the basic orientations of UNEP for 1982-1992 in section IV of the resolution, the Council considered that it should focus its attention on three major areas: environmental assessment, environmental management and support measures.

The objectives of environmental assessment should include: improvement of early-warning indicators and of global and regional monitoring; production of concrete problem-assessment statements and better links between data-producing centres and projects; and promotion of reliable statistics and reporting.

Management objectives were to: promote environmentally sound development patterns and help implement the International Development Strategy for the Third United Nations Development Decade;[3] improve cost/benefit and cost/effectiveness evaluations; promote and publicize instruments to assess the effect of harmful activities and promote cost-effective solutions; develop guidelines for sound development planning; and promote and contribute to the systems's activities in interrelationships among population, resources, environment and development.

Support measures should include: strengthened arrangements for developing countries; promotion of institutional arrangements for assessing the environmental impact of development and management; promotion of education; encouragement of arrangements for information exchange on crucial and emerging issues; efforts to increase public participation in planning and implementation; encouragement of the development of legal instruments and monitoring of their implementation; and encouragement of examination of economic measures which might complement regulations.

In section V of the resolution, the Council urged Governments to strengthen mechanisms for identifying and assessing environment changes, integrate environmental considerations into development planning, and fit management techniques to environmental circumstances. It asked the UNEP Executive Director to ensure that: the basic orientations identified above were accorded high priority; planning and implementation responded to regional and subregional needs and national conditions and capabilities; and activities were concrete, had fixed priorities, were realistic, were undertaken collaboratively and, where possible, had an administratively simple framework and adequate support. The Council invited United Nations organizations to integrate the major trends over the next decade in their action plans, draw up environmental protection measures, and intensify their co-operation with the Executive Director in implementing programmes. He was invited to intensify co-operation with organizations outside the system, and donors were asked to increase technical and financial assistance.

In its 20 December resolution on the UNEP special session,[1] the General Assembly endorsed the identification of trends, problems and priorities, co-ordinated by UNEP in accordance with its catalytic mandate and role, and the basic orientation of UNEP for 1982-1992. The Assembly invited Governments and intergovernmental and nongovernmental organizations to ensure that the priorities for action were accorded high priority within their respective programmes at the national and regional levels. It also invited the governing bodies of United Nations organizations to integrate the major environmental trends over the next 10 years in their action plans and, based on those trends, to draw up measures for environmental protection, particularly in developing countries. The initial draft of this resolution had omitted the phrase "in accordance with its catalytic mandate and role" in reference to UNEP co-ordination.

Resolutions (1982). [1]GA: 37/219, 20 Dec. [2]UNEP Council (report, A/37/25): I, sects. III-V, 18 May.
Resolution (prior). [3]GA: 35/56, annex, 5 Dec. 1980 (YUN 1980, p. 503).

Environmental policy in developing countries

In its 18 May 1982 resolution on the state of the environment,[7] adopted at its special session, the UNEP Governing Council, in listing what it saw as the major achievements and failures in implementing the 1972 Action Plan for the Human Environment,[10] stated that despite extensive bilateral and multilateral aid to assist with development programmes, it was recognized that the priorities of developing countries for dealing with their serious environmental problems still did not receive adequate attention.

On 31 May, at its tenth session, the Governing Council adopted a "package" of three decisions whose main purpose was to enable UNEP to render more assistance to developing countries for dealing with their serious environmental problems. In his annual report,[4] the Executive Director said that by these actions he had been authorized to establish what amounted to a clearing-house for technical assistance to developing countries.

In one of the three decisions,[3] calling on Governments to supply additional resources to deal with serious environmental problems in developing countries, the Council requested the Executive Director to review arrangements between UNEP and the United Nations Development Programme and others in the United Nations system, financing institutions and donors to ensure that environmental considerations were more fully taken into account in development programmes; and to facilitate expert assistance for those countries for their priority programmes, and to solicit resources for that purpose.

By the second decision,[2] on the role of UNEP in implementing the resolutions adopted at the Council's special session, the Council expressed concern that currently it was difficult for UNEP to address fully the serious environmental problems arising from poverty and underdevelopment and and requested the Executive Director, after consulting with Governments, to report in 1983 on ways UNEP might more adequately address such problems in developing countries, especially those identified in a 1981 Council decision.[11]

The third Council decision[1] dealt with co-operation among developing countries to solve those problems and the funding needed to accomplish that end (p. 1028).

In a 29 July resolution on international environmental co-operation,[5] the Economic and Social Council welcomed the Governing Council's decision[3] on providing a mechanism within UNEP for assisting developing countries in dealing with their serious environmental problems, expressed appreciation to those Governments pledging to provide technical and/or financial assistance, urged similar steps by others and called on potential donors and recipients to help UNEP ensure the success of the decision.

The original text of this part of the resolution had expressed appreciation to Governments pledging only financial assistance. It would also have had the Council urge Governments to make available additional financial resources to the UNEP Fund in order to maximize the efforts of the clearing-house facility and call on potential donors and recipients to co-operate fully with UNEP to ensure the success of the facility's experimental stage.

In its 20 December resolution[6] on the subject, the General Assembly also welcomed the Governing Council's decisions on ways to assist developing countries address their serious environmental problems[2] and on a mechanism to help them deal with those problems[3] using voluntary resources additional to the Fund's. It urged Governments to provide assistance, expressing the hope that measures taken would contribute effectively to implementing provisions of its 1981 resolution[9] on international environmental co-operation and, in general, of the International Development Strategy for the Third United Nations Development Decade[8] regarding ecologically sustainable development.

As a result of informal discussions on the original draft of this text, the word "voluntary" was added, with reference to additional resources.

Decisions (1982). UNEP Council (report, A/37/25), 31 May: [1]10/4, [2]10/6, [3]10/26.
Report. [4]UNEP Executive Director, UNEP/GC.11/2.
Resolutions (1982). [5]ESC: 1982/56, para. 3, 29 July. [6]GA: 37/217, para. 4, 20 Dec. [7]UNEP Council (report, A/37/25): I, sect. I, para. 3 *(c)* (v), 18 May.
Resolutions (prior). GA: [8]35/56, annex, 5 Dec. 1980 (YUN 1980, p. 503); [9]36/192, 17 Dec. 1981 (YUN 1981, p. 816).
Yearbook references. [10]1972, p. 322; [11]1981, p. 819.

Environmental Perspective

As it had decided in 1981,[6] the UNEP Governing Council again took up in 1982 the question of preparing an environmental perspective to the year 2000 and beyond. It considered a report[2] of the Executive Director on the perspective's desirability, feasibility and financing, which gave the views of Governments and international organizations on the creation of an independent commission of eminent persons representing all regions to report on global environment perspectives to the year 2000 and beyond, on establishing an intergovernmental process, involving all States, the United Nations system and the world scientific community, to develop the perspective document, and on other possible options. While there was no overall consensus, the report stated, the common features of the views received were: the importance of the perspective process in reviving a sense of concern for the environment; a concern with the costs of the exercise; and an emphasis on the desirability of using the institutional mechanisms of UNEP.

On 18 May, at its special session, the UNEP Governing Council adopted a resolution[5] invit-

ing the Council, at its tenth session later that month, to recommend to the General Assembly that it establish a voluntarily financed special commission to propose environmental strategies to the year 2000 and beyond. The resolution was adopted by 40 votes to 14, with 8 abstentions.

On 31 May,[1] at its tenth session, the Council requested the Executive Director to continue the consultations with Governments and decided to review the future development of the document in 1983 in the light of their outcome.

In its 29 July resolution on international environmental co-operation,[3] the Economic and Social Council stressed the importance of developing the Environmental Perspective to the year 2000 and beyond.

The General Assembly, in its 20 December resolution on the UNEP special session,[4] also reiterated the importance of developing the Perspective and requested the Governing Council to make, based on a report by the Executive Director, recommendations in 1983 on the modalities for its preparation. As a result of informal consultations on the original draft, this provision was amended. The original text would have stated that the Assembly considered the commission of eminent persons as one of the vehicles in developing the Perspective, and that the recommendations should be based on a linked process of an intergovernmental committee and the commission.

Decision (1982). [1]UNEP Council (report, A/37/25): 10/5, 31 May.
Report. [2]UNEP Executive Director, UNEP/GC.10/2/Add.5 & Corr.1.
Resolutions (1982). [3]ESC: 1982/56, para. 7, 29 July. [4]GA: 37/219, para. 8, 20 Dec. [5]UNEP Council (report, A/37/25): II, 18 May.
Yearbook reference. [6]1981, p. 822.

Implementation of UNEP Council recommendations

On 20 December 1982, the General Assembly adopted a resolution[3] on the UNEP special session, expressing satisfaction with the UNEP Governing Council's report on that session[2] and with the high level of Government participation, and recognizing that it represented a unique opportunity for Governments to re-emphasize their commitment to the environment and to UNEP. Endorsing the Nairobi Declaration (p. 997), the Assembly invited governing bodies to draw up measures for environmental protection (p. 998), and supported the view that the human environment would greatly benefit from an international atmosphere of peace and security.

Other provisions of the resolution dealt with implementing the recommendations of the 1972 Conference on the Human Environment[4], the UNEP work programme for 1982-1992, developing the Environmental Perspective to the year 2000 and beyond, contributions to the UNEP Fund and institutional arrangements for UNEP.

The resolution was adopted without vote. On 2 December, the Second (Economic and Financial) Committee had approved the draft in the same manner. The text was proposed by a Vice-Chairman on the basis of informal consultations on a 19-nation draft introduced by Sweden and subsequently withdrawn.[1]

In addition to drafting changes, the adopted text differed from the 19-nation draft in that changes were made to the operative paragraphs on the UNEP work programme and on developing the Environmental Perspective.

Draft resolution withdrawn. [1]Argentina, Australia, Barbados, Burundi, Colombia, Egypt, Ethiopia, India, Kenya, Nepal, Netherlands, Nigeria, Norway, Pakistan, Sudan, Sweden, Uganda, United Republic of Tanzania, Yugoslavia, A/C.2/37/L.49.
Report. [2]UNEP Council, A/37/25.
Resolution (1982). [3]GA: 37/219, 20 Dec., text following.
Yearbook reference. [4]1972, p. 322.
Meeting records. GA: 2nd Committee, A/C.2/37/SR.3, 5-8, 20-26, 33, *40, 43, 46* (28 Sep.–2 Dec.); plenary, A/37/PV.113 (20 Dec.).

General Assembly resolution 37/219

20 December 1982   Meeting 113   Adopted without vote

Approved by Second Committee (A/37/680/Add.8) without vote, 2 December (meeting 46); draft by Vice-Chairman (A/C.2/37/L.103), based on informal consultations on 19-nation draft (A/C.2/37/L.49); agenda item 71 *(i)*.

Session of a special character of the Governing Council of the United Nations Environment Programme

The General Assembly,

Recalling its resolutions 35/74 of 5 December 1980 and 36/189 of 17 December 1981, in which it decided to convene a session of a special character of the Governing Council of the United Nations Environment Programme at Nairobi from 10 to 18 May 1982 to commemorate the tenth anniversary of the United Nations Conference on the Human Environment, held at Stockholm from 5 to 16 June 1972, and having considered the report of the Governing Council on its session of a special character,

Reaffirming its resolution 2997(XXVII) of 15 December 1972, in which it declared itself convinced of the need for prompt and effective implementation by Governments and the international community of measures designed to safeguard and enhance the environment for the benefit of present and future generations of man,

Taking into account the need to strengthen international co-operation in the field of the environment, particularly to deal with the most serious environmental problems of developing countries, in line with the International Development Strategy for the Third United Nations Development Decade,

Convinced that the principles of the Declaration of the United Nations Conference on the Human Environment are as valid today as they were in 1972 and, together with the Nairobi Declaration adopted at the session of a special character, provide basic guidance for effective and sustained progress in the protection and enhancement of the environment,

1. *Takes note with satisfaction* of the report of the Governing Council of the United Nations Environment Programme on its session of a special character;

2. *Expresses its appreciation* of the positive manner in which Governments responded to its invitation to participate in the session at the highest political level;

3. *Recognizes* that the session of a special character represented a unique opportunity for Governments to re-emphasize their continued commitment and support to the cause of the environment and the United Nations Environment Programme;

4. *Endorses* the Nairobi Declaration, in which the world community, *inter alia*, reaffirmed its commitment to the Declaration of the United Nations Conference on the Human Environment and the Action Plan for the Human Environment adopted at Stockholm, as well as its support for strengthening the United Nations Environment Programme as the major catalytic instrument for global environmental co-operation, and urged all Governments and peoples of the world to discharge their historical responsibility to ensure that planet Earth is passed over to future generations in a condition that guarantees a life in human dignity for all;

5. *Further endorses:*

(a) The assessment by the Governing Council of the United Nations Environment Programme at its session of a special character of the major achievements and failures in the implementation of the Action Plan for the Human Environment and its conclusions that fair to good progress had been made in implementing some of the elements of the Action Plan while, in respect of other elements, the record had been very modest;

(b) The identification at the above-mentioned session of:

(i) The perceptions of environmental issues that had evolved over the past decade;

(ii) The major environmental trends, potential problems and priorities for action by the United Nations system, during the period 1982-1992, co-ordinated by the United Nations Environment Programme in accordance with its catalytic mandate and role;

(c) The basic orientation of the United Nations Environment Programme for 1982-1992, as recommended by the Governing Council at the above-mentioned session;

(d) The conclusions reached at the above-mentioned session with respect to the institutional arrangements for the United Nations Environment Programme;

6. *Invites* all Governments, intergovernmental bodies and non-governmental organizations to ensure that the priorities for action, agreed upon by the Governing Council at its session of a special character in section III of its resolution I, are accorded high priority within their respective programmes at both the national and regional levels;

7. *Also invites* the governing bodies of the relevant organizations of the United Nations system to integrate the major environmental trends over the next ten years effectively in their action plans and, on the basis of those trends, in close co-operation with the United Nations Environment Programme, to draw up appropriate measures for environmental protection, particularly in developing countries, with due regard to available resources;

8. *Reiterates* the importance it attaches to the development of the Environmental Perspective to the year 2000 and beyond, and requests the Governing Council at its eleventh session to make, on the basis of a report by the Executive Director, concrete recommendations to the General Assembly at its thirty-eighth session, through the Economic and Social Council at its second regular session of 1983, on the modalities for preparing the Environmental Perspective;

9. *Supports* the view expressed at the session of a special character that the human environment would greatly benefit from an international atmosphere of peace and security, free from the threat of any war;

10. *Emphasizes* that the implementation of the priorities for action recommended by the Governing Council of the United Nations Environment Programme at its session of a special character requires adequate financial resources and, in view of this, appeals to all Governments, particularly of developed countries, to respond positively and increase their contribution to the Fund of the United Nations Environment Programme.

Other programme policy aspects

Economic and Social Council action. On 29 July 1982, the Economic and Social Council adopted a resolution on international environmental co-operation,[4] by which it noted the UNEP Governing Council's report on its tenth session (20-31 May)[3] and reports on co-operation between States sharing natural resources and on implementing the Plan of Action to Combat Desertification. It also noted the Governing Council's decision on environment and development, and welcomed other Council decisions on: providing a mechanism for helping developing countries deal with their serious environmental problems (p. 999); adopting a programme for developing and reviewing environmental law, and the 1984-1989 system-wide medium-term environment programme. The Economic and Social Council also stressed the importance of developing the Environmental Perspective to the year 2000 and beyond and reiterated appeals for increased contributions to the UNEP Fund. It also asked for cost implications of arrangements for a regional presence of UNEP.

The resolution was adopted without vote. On 28 July, the First (Economic) Committee had approved the draft, also without vote, proposed by a Vice-Chairman on the basis of informal consultations on a 12-nation draft introduced by Kenya and subsequently withdrawn.[2]

General Assembly action. On 20 December, the General Assembly, in a resolution on international environmental co-operation,[5] noted the UNEP Governing Council's report[3] and a report on shared natural resources. It welcomed the Council's decisions on environment and development; on ways of enabling UNEP to help developing countries with their serious environmental problems and on providing a mechanism for helping them to deal with those problems; on developing and reviewing environmental law; and on the 1984-1989 system-wide medium-term environment programme. The Assembly further took note of: the conclusions of a study of the legal aspects concerning the environment related to offshore mining and drilling (p. 1021); a decision covering seven programme matters (carbon dioxide, tropical forests, soils policy, environment and development, regional marine programmes, environmental law, and desertification control); and the Council's decisions on expanding and implementing the regional seas programme, and on the impact of *apartheid* on the environment. The Assembly also stated that arrangements for the regional presence of UNEP should take full account of the needs of the various regions, and appealed for contributions to the UNEP Fund.

The resolution was adopted without vote. On 8 December, the Second Committee had approved the draft in the same way. The text was proposed by a Vice-Chairman on the basis of informal consultations on an 18-nation draft introduced by Sweden and subsequently withdrawn.[1]

Draft resolutions withdrawn. [1]Argentina, Australia, Bangladesh, Barbados, Burundi, Canada, Denmark, Finland, France, Germany, Federal Republic of, Indonesia,

Kenya, Nepal, Netherlands, Norway, Senegal, Sweden, Uganda, A/C.2/37/L.46; [2]Argentina, Australia, Benin, Egypt, Germany, Federal Republic of, India, Kenya, Liberia, Nepal, Netherlands, Saint Lucia, Sweden, E/1982/C.1/L.15.
Report. [3]UNEP Council, A/37/25.
Resolutions (1982). [4]ESC: 1982/56, 29 July, text following. [5]GA: 37/217, 20 Dec., text following.
Meeting records. ESC: E/1982/SR.50 (29 July). GA: 2nd Committee, A/C.2/37/SR.3, 5-8, 20-26, 33, *40*, 43, *47* (28 Sep.–8 Dec.); plenary, A/37/PV.113 (20 Dec.).

Economic and Social Council resolution 1982/56

29 July 1982   Meeting 50   Adopted without vote

Approved by First Committee (E/1982/103) without vote, 28 July (meeting 15); draft by Vice-Chairman (E/1982/C.1/L.28), based on informal consultations on 12-nation draft (E/1982/C.1/L.15); agenda item 15.

International co-operation on the environment
The Economic and Social Council,

Bearing in mind the importance which the International Development Strategy for the Third United Nations Development Decade attaches to an ecologically sustainable development process and the need for further international co-operation in the field of the environment, and taking into account the fact that environmental considerations should be viewed in the context of national plans and priorities and development objectives of all countries, in particular the developing countries,

Recalling General Assembly resolution 36/192 of 17 December 1981, in which the Assembly reaffirmed the catalytic mandate and role of the United Nations Environment Programme and stressed the need for additional resources to be made available to the Fund of the United Nations Environment Programme for the developing countries to deal with their most serious environmental problems, such as soil degradation and deforestation, which are examples of very severe deterioration of natural resources that call for particular attention,

Noting with satisfaction from the introductory statement of the Executive Director of the United Nations Environment Programme and from statements made during the general discussion of the question at the second regular session of 1982 of the Economic and Social Council that the Governing Council of the United Nations Environment Programme, at its session of a special character, which was held at Nairobi from 10 to 18 May 1982 to commemorate the tenth anniversary of the United Nations Conference on the Human Environment, adopted the Nairobi Declaration, supporting and supplementing the Declaration of the United Nations Conference on the Human Environment, stressed the need to intensify efforts at every level to protect and improve the environment, identified major environmental trends to be acted upon over the next decade, and fixed priorities for action by the United Nations system to deal with them and, within these priorities, the areas in which the United Nations Environment Programme should concentrate its efforts,

Having considered the report of the Governing Council of the United Nations Environment Programme on its tenth session,

1. *Takes note* of the report of the Governing Council of the United Nations Environment Programme on its tenth session and transmits it to the General Assembly for consideration and action with regard to the decisions contained in the annex thereto;

2. *Also takes note with satisfaction* of decision 10/4 of 31 May 1982 of the Governing Council on environment and development, particularly its emphasis on technical co-operation among developing countries;

3. *Welcomes* decision 10/26 of 31 May 1982 of the Governing Council concerning the provision of a mechanism within the Programme for assisting developing countries in dealing with their serious environmental problems in line with the co-ordinating and catalytic role of the Programme, expresses its appreciation to those Governments that have pledged to provide technical assistance and/or additional financial resources to that mechanism, urges other Governments in a position to do so to take similar steps, and calls upon potential donors and recipients to co-operate fully with the Programme to ensure the successful implementation of Governing Council decision 10/26;

4. *Welcomes* the adoption by the Governing Council, in its decision 10/21 of 31 May 1982, of the programme for the development and

periodic review of environmental law, expresses the hope that the programme will be implemented in a manner commensurate with the importance attached to it by the Governing Council, and calls upon Governments, United Nations organizations and bodies and intergovernmental organizations outside the United Nations system, as well as nongovernmental organizations active in the field of the environment, to co-operate fully with the United Nations Environment Programme in the implementation of the programme;

5. *Takes note* of the progress report on co-operation in the field of the environment concerning natural resources shared by two or more States, and transmits it to the General Assembly, pursuant to Assembly resolution 34/186 of 18 December 1979, and in this context endorses section VI of decision 10/14 of 31 May 1982 of the Governing Council;

6. *Considers* that the system-wide medium-term environment programme for 1984-1989 could be a useful means to ensure better co-ordination within the United Nations system in the field of the environment, welcomes decision 10/13 of 31 May 1982 of the Governing Council, in which it approved the structure and objectives of the system-wide medium-term environment programme and endorsed the environmental trends and proposed priorities for action by the United Nations system, urges other organizations of the United Nations system to continue their close co-operation with the United Nations Environment Programme in the further refinement and implementation of the system-wide programme, and appeals to Governments to continue to give support to the development and implementation of that programme and to take the necessary decisions in this regard in the appropriate governing bodies of organizations in the United Nations system;

7. *Stresses* the importance it attaches to the development of the Environmental Perspective to the year 2000 and beyond, and notes that the Executive Director will submit a report thereon to the Governing Council at its eleventh session;

8. *Takes note with appreciation* of the report of the Governing Council on the implementation of the Plan of Action to Combat Desertification and transmits it to the General Assembly for consideration;

9. *Expresses its serious concern* at, on the one hand, the persistence and aggravation of the desertification process and, on the other, the rate at which the Plan of Action to Combat Desertification is being implemented, urges all Governments, organizations of the United Nations system, other intergovernmental bodies and non-governmental and all other organizations to increase their efforts to prevent and combat desertification in order to accelerate progress in implementing the recommendations of the Plan of Action, and calls upon all Governments to consider seriously the urgent need for additional resources to finance its implementation;

10. *Recommends* that the General Assembly should invite the Governing Council of the United Nations Environment Programme to present its views on the implementation in the Eastern and Southern African subregion of the Plan of Action to Combat Desertification and to advise on the necessity or the possibility of the establishment of institutional machinery responsible for combating drought and desertification in that subregion;

11. *Requests* the Executive Director of the United Nations Environment Programme to include the pertinent financial implications in his report to the Governing Council at its eleventh session on the progress in the implementation of Governing Council decision 10/2 of 31 May 1982 on the regional presence of the Programme;

12. *Expresses its appreciation* to Governments that have contributed to the Fund of the United Nations Environment Programme for the first time and to those that continue to contribute generously to it, particularly those that have maintained or increased the real value of their contributions;

13. *Reiterates* its appeals and those of the General Assembly at different sessions to Governments to increase their contributions to the Fund and appeals to all Governments that have not yet pledged contributions thereto for the years 1982 and 1983 to do so as soon as possible.

General Assembly resolution 37/217

20 December 1982   Meeting 113   Adopted without vote

Approved by Second Committee (A/37/680/Add.8) without vote, 8 December (meeting 47); draft by Vice-Chairman (A/C.2/37/L.110), based on informal consultations on 18-nation draft (A/C.2/37/L.46); agenda item 71 *(i)*.

International co-operation in the field of the environment

The General Assembly,

Having considered the report of the Governing Council of the United Nations Environment Programme on its tenth session,

Taking note of Economic and Social Council resolution 1982/56 of 29 July 1982 on international co-operation on the environment,

Taking into account the note by the Secretary-General on international conventions and protocols in the field of the environment,

Recalling its resolution 36/192 of 17 December 1981, in which it reaffirmed the catalytic mandate and role of the United Nations Environment Programme and stressed the need for additional resources to be made available to the Fund of the United Nations Environment Programme so that the developing countries may deal with their most serious environmental problems, such as soil degradation and deforestation, which are examples of very severe deterioration of natural resources calling for particular attention,

Bearing in mind the importance that the International Development Strategy for the Third United Nations Development Decade attaches to an ecologically sustainable development process and the need for further international co-operation in the field of the environment, and taking into account the fact that environmental considerations should be viewed in the context of national plans and priorities and development objectives of both developing and developed countries,

1. *Takes note* of the report of the Governing Council of the United Nations Environment Programme on its tenth session and the decisions contained therein;

2. *Welcomes* Governing Council decision 10/13 of 31 May 1982 by which the Council approved the structure and objectives of the system-wide medium-term environment programme and took note of its general content, appealed to Governments to continue to give support to the development and implementation of the programme and to take the necessary decisions in that regard in the appropriate governing bodies of the organizations of the United Nations system, and urged other organizations of the United Nations system to continue their close co-operation with the United Nations Environment Programme in the further refinement and implementation of the system-wide programme;

3. *Welcomes also* Governing Council decision 10/4 of 31 May 1982, in which the Council, *inter alia,* requested the Executive Director of the United Nations Environment Programme to identify areas for co-operation among developing countries in the field of the environment, and also to identify expertise and institutions in developing countries capable of fostering that co-operation, as well as developing activities for horizontal co-operation based on such identification;

4. *Welcomes further* Governing Council decisions 10/6 of 31 May 1982, concerning ways and means of enabling the United Nations Environment Programme to assist developing countries in addressing their serious environmental problems, and 10/26 of 31 May 1982, concerning the provision of a mechanism within the existing structure of the United Nations Environment Programme for assisting developing countries in dealing with their serious environmental problems using voluntary resources additional to those available to the Fund of the United Nations Environment Programme, *inter alia,* through counterpart contributions, urges Governments in a position to do so to provide assistance to that mechanism and expresses the hope that measures to be taken pursuant to those decisions will contribute to the effective implementation of the provisions of General Assembly resolution 36/192 and, in general, those of the International Development Strategy for the Third United Nations Development Decade with respect to ecologically sustainable development;

5. *Welcomes* the adoption by the Governing Council, in its decision 10/21 of 31 May 1982, of the programme for the development and periodic review of environmental law and the measures to be taken for the early effective implementation of that programme;

6. *Takes note* of Governing Council decision 10/14 of 31 May 1982 on programme matters, comprising seven specific sections, and in this context:

(a) Takes note of the progress report on co-operation in the field of the environment concerning natural resources shared by two or more States, reiterates the terms of its resolution 34/186 of 18 December 1979 as a whole, and requests the Governing Council to submit a further progress report on its implementation to the General Assembly at its fortieth session;

(b) Takes note of the conclusions of the study of the legal aspects concerning the environment related to offshore mining and drilling

within the limits of national jurisdiction, made by the Working Group of Experts on Environmental Law, and of the views of the Governments thereon, recommends that Governments should consider the guidelines contained in the conclusions when formulating national legislation or undertaking negotiations for the conclusion of international agreements for the prevention of pollution of the marine environment caused by offshore mining and drilling within the limits of national jurisdiction, and requests the Governing Council to submit to the General Assembly at its fortieth session a progress report on the use made of those conclusions;

(c) Takes note of the endorsement by the Governing Council, in section III of its decision 10/14, of the World Soils Policy, and invites Governments, organizations of the United Nations system and other appropriate international organizations to take into account the objectives of the World Soils Policy in formulating relevant national policies and programmes of work;

(d) Takes note of the action agreed by the Governing Council, in section I of its decision 10/14, on the future work with regard to the potential socio-economic impact of increased carbon dioxide concentration in the atmosphere;

7. *Also takes note* of Governing Council decision 10/20 of 31 May 1982 on expansion and implementation of the regional seas programme;

8. *Further takes note* of Governing Council decision 10/7 of 28 May 1982 on the impact of *apartheid* on the environment aimed at promoting public awareness of the plight of the victims of *apartheid;*

9. *Expresses the view* that arrangements for the regional presence of the United Nations Environment Programme should take fully into account the specific situations and needs of the various regions, in accordance with Governing Council decision 10/2 of 31 May 1982 on the regional presence of the Programme;

10. *Expresses its appreciation* to Governments that have contributed to the Fund of the United Nations Environment Programme, particularly those that have maintained or increased the real value of their contributions;

11. *Expresses its concern* over the continued decline, in real terms, of the resources available to the Fund of the United Nations Environment Programme and the increasing trend towards late payment of pledged contributions, reiterates its appeal to Governments to increase their contributions to the Fund and appeals to all Governments that have not yet pledged contributions to the Fund for the years 1982 and 1983 to do so as soon as possible.

Regional activities

In a March 1982 report to the UNEP Governing Council reviewing the regional presence of UNEP,[4] the Executive Director outlined three alternatives for the most cost-effective use of the limited financial resources that could be made available over the coming decade to support the regional infrastructure of UNEP: (1) that UNEP strengthen its presence in the various regions through its regional offices, with the regional commissions bearing their own institutional costs; (2) that joint UNEP/regional commission divisions be established, bearing in mind the direct and specific regional responsibilities of UNEP with countries and with United Nations bodies in each region; or (3) that the current coexistence of regional offices and environmental co-ordination units continue with lower outlays, reducing expenditure on both components.

With regard to the first alternative, the report stated that a logical arrangement would be to integrate fully the regional advisers and support staff into the regional office structure, and to merge of their separate budgets. On the second option, the report concluded that a joint division financed largely by UNEP but only partly under its influence would be undesirable. Concerning the third alternative, the report stated that regional offices and co-ordination units should remain structurally separate but continue working together and be financed largely by the UNEP Environment Fund. Revised terms of reference were proposed for both components and were annexed to the report.

Also in March 1982, the Secretary-General submitted a report[3] to the Committee for Programme and Co-ordination (CPC), in response to a 1981 CPC decision,[6] on the distribution of tasks and responsibilities between the regional commissions and other United Nations entities regarding water resources (See ECONOMIC AND SOCIAL QUESTIONS, Chapter IX) and the environment. The report analysed the mandates and activities of the bodies concerned and stated that for the UNEP Governing Council a main criterion in choosing between the above-mentioned options would be the degree to which it was possible to differentiate between the functions of the regional offices and the environmental co-ordination units and to define complementary roles and work programmes for them in each region. It appeared that there was considerable variation among regions in that respect. A general conclusion was that, where mutually supportive and complementary roles and relations had been established, a case could be made for continuing the current pattern, while in other cases the second option would be preferable. In the latter event, the co-ordination units of the regional commissions could be strengthened, while reducing or phasing out UNEP regional offices. One way to strengthen the role of both units and commissions was through advisory services.

At its April/May session, CPC recommended:[2] that the alternatives described in the Secretary-General's report be given further consideration by the Governing Council; that the Council's attention be drawn to the fact that other joint units between regional commissions and other organizations, in areas such as food and agriculture and industrial development, had been functioning satisfactorily; and that the question of the distribution of Professional staff between UNEP and the commissions should be examined with a view to further decentralization.

On 31 May,[1] the UNEP Governing Council stated that arrangements for the regional presence of UNEP should take into account the specific situations and needs of the various regions. It endorsed the views of the Executive Director with respect to integrating regional advisory and information support services into the regional offices of UNEP for Africa, Asia and the Pacific, and Latin America and the Caribbean, requesting him to continue relevant support to the commissions for those regions, and considered the proposed terms of reference to be appropriate. The Council requested him to restore financial support for the advisory services for Africa and for Asia and the Pacific, to consider using regional offices for consultations among Governments, to involve the scientific community and other professional groups to further co-operation, and to report in 1983 on the implementation of its decisions. The Council also acted to strengthen environmental co-operation in Latin America and the Caribbean and in Europe (See ECONOMIC AND SOCIAL QUESTIONS, Chapter VIII)

In its 20 December resolution on international environmental co-operation,[5] the General Assembly also expressed the view that arrangements for the regional presence of UNEP should take full account of the situations and needs of the various regions, in accordance with the Governing Council's decision on the topic.

Decision (1982). [1]UNEP Council (report, A/37/25): 10/2, 31 May.
Reports. [2]CPC, A/37/38; [3]S-G, E/AC.51/1982/7 & Add 1; [4]UNEP Executive Director, UNEP/GC.10/2/Add.2 & Corr.1.
Resolution (1982). [5]GA: 37/217, para. 9, 20 Dec.
Yearbook reference. [6]1981, p. 842.

Co-ordination in the UN system

In reports of November 1981[3] and May 1982[2] on co-ordination in the United Nations system (See ECONOMIC AND SOCIAL QUESTIONS, Chapter XXIV), the Administrative Committee on Co-ordination (ACC) reviewed progress since the 1972 United Nations Conference on the Human Environment.[4] It felt that the UNEP Fund was indispensable if UNEP was to maintain its catalytic role. Therefore it was essential that the resources and the use made of them should be commensurate with the magnitude of the tasks. It noted progress in joint environmental programming and felt that the 1984-1989 system-wide medium-term environment programme should be of interest to all United Nations governing bodies.

On 31 May 1982,[1] the UNEP Governing Council recommended to ACC that its subject for cross-organizational programme analysis should be, in 1984, activities related to environmental aspects of energy production and, in 1985, human settlements planning. The Council agreed with a proposal of the Executive Director regarding the joint meetings of the bureaux of the United Nations Centre for Human Settlements (Habitat) and UNEP.

Decision (1982). [1]UNEP Council (report, A/37/25): 10/1, sect. V, paras. 1-5, 31 May.
Reports. ACC, [2]E/1982/4, [3]UNEP/GC.10/4/Add.1.
Yearbook reference. [4]1972, p. 318.

System-wide medium-term programme for 1984-1989

In 1982, further progress was made in preparing the 1984-1989 system-wide medium-term environment programme—the basic document for the United Nations system in environmental planning and programming matters, being prepared by the whole system with UNEP and the ACC playing major roles. A report containing the programme, provisionally approved by the UNEP Governing Council in 1981,[7] was submitted to the Council in March 1982 by the Executive Director.[3] The document covered 15 programmes embracing the concerns and environmental activities of the United Nations system in the areas of: environment and development, environmental awareness, the atmosphere, the oceans, water, the lithosphere, natural disasters, terrestrial ecosystems, living resources, health and welfare, the working environment, human settlements, energy, industry and transportation, and the arms race and the environment. It set forth the objectives of the system in these fields and the strategies to implement them. The Executive Director intended to submit to the Council in 1983 a more detailed presentation of activities for the first biennium (1984-1985) of the system-wide programme period.

In its 18 May 1982 resolution[6] on the state of the environment, adopted at its special session, in a section addressing institutional arrangements for UNEP, the Governing Council requested the Executive Director, in preparing the 1984-1989 system-wide programme, to emphasize thematic joint programming, intensify consultations with various United Nations organizations and ensure a positive and constructive relationship between UNEP and its co-operating and supporting agencies.

On 31 May,[1] the Governing Council approved the structure and objectives of the programme, endorsed the environmental trends and priorities for action and requested the Executive Director to consult with the United Nations system on refining and elaborating the programme. The Council urged continued co-operation in the programme's preparation, appealed to Governments to support its development and implementation and requested the Executive Director to prepare for 1983 a programme-budget-type document showing a full breakdown of UNEP activities and priorities for 1984-1985.

Also on 31 May, the Council asked the Executive Director to plan an Environment Fund programme during the 1984-1989 period on a base figure of $42.5 million.[2]

In its 29 July resolution on international environmental co-operation,[4] the Economic and Social Council welcomed the UNEP decision of 31

May,[1] and echoed the UNEP Council's calls for continued programme co-operation.

As a result of informal consultations on the original text of this paragraph, the Council called for the programme's refinement "and implementation" and appealed for support, instead of "full" support, to its development and implementation.

The Council's provisions were restated by the General Assembly in its 20 December resolution on international environmental co-operation.[5]

Decisions (1982). UNEP Council (report, A/37/25), 31 May: [1]10/13; [2]10/27, para. 21.
Report. [3]UNEP Executive Director, UNEP/GC.10/7 and Corr.1.
Resolutions (1982). [4]ESC: 1982/56, para. 6, 29 July. [5]GA: 37/217, para. 2, 20 Dec. [6]UNEP Council (report, A/37/25): I, sect. VI, para. 5, 18 May.
Yearbook reference. [7]1981, p. 841.

Joint meetings with Habitat

In 1982, the Commission on Human Settlements (See ECONOMIC AND SOCIAL QUESTIONS, Chapter XVII) and the UNEP Governing Council took separate decisions requesting, for reasons of economy, that future annual joint meetings of their bureaux be held in conjunction with other meetings, preferably with the inter-sessional informal consultations between Governments and UNEP at Nairobi, Kenya.

The Commission took this action on 7 May[3] with the request addressed to the Executive Director of the United Nations Centre for Human Settlements (Habitat), while the Governing Council made the request of the UNEP Executive Director on 31 May,[2] agreeing[1] with his proposal to minimize costs by following that procedure.

Decisions (1982). UNEP Council (report, A/37/25), 31 May: [1]10/1, sect. V, para. 6; [2]10/10.
Resolution (1982). [3]Commission on Human Settlements (report, A/37/8): 5/11, 7 May.

UNEP Fund and trust funds

On 31 December 1982, resources available to the Fund of the United Nations Environment Programme (Environment Fund) were estimated to be $55.38 million—some $2 million lower than in 1981, due mainly to a fall in the dollar value of contributions.

During 1982, the Fund disbursed $21,874,994 for programme activities—not including $270,801 for activities under the programme reserve—in the following areas: human settlements and health, $2,744,050; support, $5,146,906; environment and development, $1,934,713; oceans, $1,737,121; energy, $449,223; environmental management and law, $434,953; terrestrial ecosystems, $3,191,063; natural disasters, $44,267; Earthwatch, $4,136,208; environmental data, $255,394; and arid and semi-arid lands, $1,801,096. Disbursements in 1982 for

staff and other general operating expenses, including grants and contributions, totalled $8,646,844.

On 31 May,[1] the UNEP Governing Council accepted with appreciation a pledge by the Japanese Shipbuilding Industry Foundation to contribute $1 million to endow an international environment prize and established a trust fund to finance the prize. The Council made several appeals concerning the level and quality of contributions to the Environment Fund, and reconfirmed its 1982-1983 appropriation and apportionment for Fund activities[2]—along with the percentage breakdown for the various programme areas—with the aim of keeping that budget within 33 per cent of estimated contributions for any given year, and the desirability of a target level of $120 million. The Council asked for a report in 1983 on problems in administering the revolving fund (information) and for a fund programme for 1984-1989 on a base figure of $42.5 million in 1982 prices and for 1984-1985 based on total contributions in those two years of $85 million. The Council also approved an increase in the financial reserve in 1982-1983 and continuation of the Mediterranean and Arab Gulf trust funds until the end of 1983 (p. 1022).

Decision (1982). [1]UNEP Council (report, A/37/25): 10/27, 31 May.
Yearbook reference. [2]1981, p. 817.

Contributions

In its 18 May 1982 resolution[6] on the state of the environment, adopted at its special session, the UNEP Governing Council, in considering the institutional arrangements for UNEP, stressed the importance of the Environment Fund and strongly appealed to Governments to ensure that their contributions were in line with the objectives and basic orientations of UNEP for 1982-1992. It requested the Executive Director to continue efforts to broaden participation in and increase contributions to the Fund, seek other funding modalities, continue consulting with the Secretary-General on distributing UNEP costs between the United Nations regular budget and the Fund, and ensure that budgetary measures were more responsive to regional, subregional and national needs.

On 31 May,[1] the Governing Council noted with concern that the value of contributions to the Fund in terms of 1978 purchasing power had continued declining, and recalled its 1981 appeal[7] for pledges and contribution increases, and similar appeals by the Economic and Social Council and the General Assembly.

On the same day,[2] the Council reiterated its appeal for pledges for 1982 and 1983, appealed for contributions to be made at the beginning of the year to which they related, and called for increases in 1984 and 1985 pledges. It renewed its appeal to those contributing in non-convertible currencies to pay a part in convertible currencies in 1982 and larger proportions thereafter.

In resolutions of 29 July[3] and 20 December[4] on international environmental co-operation, the Economic and Social Council and the General Assembly expressed appreciation to contributing Governments, particularly those maintaining or increasing the real value of their payments. The Assembly also expressed concern over the continued decline in real terms of Fund resources and the increasingly late payments, and both bodies reiterated appeals for pledges and increases in contributions for 1982 and 1983.

The original text of the Assembly's resolution would have had the Assembly express appreciation to those contributing "for the first time and to those that continue to contribute generously to" the Fund—employing the phrasing of the Council's July resolution. Also, the adopted text included a modifier expressing the Assembly's concern about the "continued" decline in real terms of the Fund's resources.

Also on 20 December, in its resolution on the UNEP special session,[5] the Assembly emphasized that implementing the Governing Council's priorities required finances and appealed, particularly to developed countries, for increases to the Fund.

Decisions (1982). UNEP Council (report, A/37/25), 31 May: [1]10/1, sect. VI; [2]10/27.
Resolutions (1982). [3]ESC: 1982/56, paras. 12 & 13, 29 July. GA, 20 Dec.: [4]37/217, paras. 10 & 11; [5]37/219, para. 10,. [6]UNEP Council (report, A/37/25): I, sect. VI, paras. 6 & 7, 18 May.
Yearbook reference. [7]1981, p. 818.

CONTRIBUTIONS TO THE UNEP FUND, 1982 AND FUTURE YEARS

(as at 31 December 1982; in US dollars)

Country	1982 payment	Pledges for future years	Country	1982 payment	Pledges for future years
Algeria	10,450	33,000	Liberia	1,808	—
Argentina	54,874	—	Libyan Arab Jamahiriya	992,219	—
Australia	448,925	721,154	Luxembourg	—	6,531
Austria	300,000	—	Malawi	4,360	—
Bahamas	2,000	—	Malaysia	—	45,000
Bangladesh	2,023	2,000	Malta	1,666	—
Barbados	1,000	1,000	Mauritius	849	—
Belgium	171,735	—	Mexico	150,253	75,000
Benin	—	2,000	Mongolia	986	917
Botswana	1,109	1,101	Morocco	10,277	—
Brazil	—	20,000	Netherlands	398,288	605,660
Bulgaria	11,737	11,737	New Zealand	72,912	—
Byelorussian SSR	18,233	18,233	Norway	914,417	—
Canada	805,000	805,000	Oman	10,000	10,000
Chile	5,000	—	Pakistan	5,000	5,000
China	108,467	103,627	Panama	4,000	4,000
Colombia	53,898	—	Peru	—	20,000
Congo	10,850	—	Philippines	44,031	20,000
Cyprus	3,000	2,000	Poland	—	45,181
Czechoslovakia	—	24,116	Qatar	90,000	—
Democratic Yemen	—	1,602	Republic of Korea	10,000	10,000
Denmark	406,619	—	Romania	5,455	—
Ecuador	—	5,000	Saudi Arabia	500,000	1,500,000
Egypt	—	15,000	Singapore	1,000	—
Finland	350,000	600,000	Somalia	664	651
France	823,353	875,912	Spain	200,000	—
Gabon	11,877	—	Sri Lanka	1,982	3,000
German Democratic Republic	159,373	—	Sudan	—	1,500
Germany, Federal Republic of	1,847,264	—	Sweden	2,500,000	2,500,000
Guinea-Bissau	2,000	—	Switzerland	506,567	487,113
Hungary	21,429	21,079	Syrian Arab Republic	1,000	—
Iceland	6,600	—	Thailand	10,000	10,000
India	149,177	100,000	Turkey	11,279	—
Indonesia	12,000	12,000	Ukrainian SSR	44,880	44,881
Ireland	26,316	—	USSR	3,677,419	3,677,420
Italy	1,172,641	327,645	United Kingdom	1,034,483	1,334,520
Ivory Coast	6,667	—	United Republic of Cameroon	—	8,746
Jamaica	3,745	—	United States	7,833,000	—
Japan	4,000,000	—	Yugoslavia	24,507	—
Kenya	32,287	45,000	Zaire	—	75,000
Kuwait	200,000	—	Zambia	24,609	10,834
Lao People's Democratic Republic	4,000	—	Zimbabwe	—	6,510
Lesotho	2,000	—	Total	30,333,560	14,255,670

SOURCE: UNEP/GC.11/L.2.

Accounts for 1980-1981

As at 31 December 1981,[2] the Environment Fund's obligated appropriations for the 1980-1981 biennium amounted to $69,070,038. Total income for the same period was $66,116,618, leaving an excess of expenditure over income of $2,953,420. As at 31 December 1982, the first year of the 1982-1983 biennium, the Fund had a total income of $31,891,401 and expenditures of $31,557,582.[3]

Commenting on the audited accounts,[2] the Board of Auditors recommended, with regard to the construction of new UNEP permanent headquarters at Nairobi, Kenya, that any extension of time or major modification required a written justification, and that procedures be established for authorizing minor variations without delay and for obtaining advice from the Committee on Contracts to approve major modifications. The Board said it had accepted an Administration request to assist in preparing contracts; most of the contract clauses it had recommended to protect United Nations interests had been inserted in the bills of quantities. The audit also revealed: weaknesses in electronic data-processing control, attributed to understaffing; excess expenditures for some suballotments; a decrease in accumulated non-convertible currencies—down to $13,047,030 at the end of 1981 compared with $16,768,490 at the end of the 1978-1979 biennium; and weaknesses in the inventory system.

In a September 1982 report,[1] the Advisory Committee on Administrative and Budgetary Questions (ACABQ), noting that review of contracts was the responsibility of the Office of Legal Affairs, said it had been told that the request in question involved help in establishing acceptable administrative procedures, rather than actually drafting contracts. ACABQ also called for strict application of existing inventory-control procedures and for improved inventory systems.

In its 16 November resolution[4] accepting the 1981 financial reports, accounts and audit opinions of various United Nations funds and programmes, including the Environment Fund, the General Assembly concurred with the comments of ACABQ and requested the Secretary-General to strengthen financial discipline in the Secretariat and remove the shortcomings mentioned; executive heads were requested to take the required remedial action.

Reports. [1]ACABQ, A/37/443; [2]Board of Auditors, and financial statements, A/37/5/Add.6; [3]UNEP Executive Director, UNEP/GC.11/L.2.
Resolution (1982). [4]GA: 37/12, 16 Nov.

Administrative and budgetary questions

Publications

On 28 May 1982,[1] the UNEP Governing Council requested the Executive Director to ensure that UNEP publications reflected the diversity of languages, cultures and knowledge of Member States and, so far as resources permitted, that authors had the necessary means to use the UNEP working language of their choice. Circulation of publications was to benefit the greatest possible number of people, having regard to language diversity, particularly in developing countries.

Decision (1982). [1]UNEP Council (report, A/37/25): 10/9 B, 28 May.

Documents distribution

On 28 May 1982,[1] the UNEP Governing Council, concerned at delays in distributing documents in the different official languages, requested the Executive Director to implement a 1981 General Assembly resolution[2] calling for such documents to be given simultaneous distribution.

Decision (1982). [1]UNEP Council (report, A/37/25): 10/9 A, 28 May.
Resolution. [2]GA: 36/117 B, 10 Dec. 1981 (YUN 1981, p. 1376).

Exhibition

On 28 May 1982,[1] the UNEP Governing Council, recognizing the importance of information programmes, art and cultural events in raising awareness of environmental problems, congratulated the Executive Director for calling on artists to participate in an art exhibition during the Council's special session, and asked him to increase contacts with artists with a view to making the exhibition permanent and available for loan. In December 1981, the General Assembly had agreed that there should be a special public information programme for the special session.[2]

Decision (1982). [1]UNEP Council (report, A/37/25): 10/11, 28 May.
Resolution. [2]GA: 36/189, 17 Dec. 1981 (YUN 1981, p. 821).

Organizational questions

Institutional arrangements

In its 18 May 1982 resolution[2] on the state of the environment, adopted at its special session, the UNEP Governing Council expressed its views on the institutional arrangements for UNEP. The Council considered that arrangements for international environmental co-operation were generally adequate—but encouraged Governments to keep them under continuing review—and that the UNEP role remained appropriate and would require the Council's continuing attention. The Council was invited, at its regular sessions, to: give overall policy guidance on global, contemporary and emerging issues; set priorities and assure funds for implementing approved programmes; and address itself more to governing bodies of other United Nations organizations dealing with the environment. The Council also called for emphasis on thematic joint programming in preparing the 1984-1989 system-wide medium-term environment programme and intensified consultations between UNEP and the United Nations system. It also acted to try to broaden participation in and increase contributions to the Environment Fund.

The Council's conclusions on institutional arrangements were endorsed by the General Assembly in its 20 December resolution on the special session.[1]

Resolutions (1982). [1]GA: 37/219, para. 5 (d), 20 Dec. [2]UNEP Council (report, A/37/25): I, sect. VI, paras. 1-4, 18 May.

Periodicity of Governing Council sessions

On 31 May 1982, in a decision[2] on programme policy and implementation, the UNEP Governing Council stated that consideration should be given to holding Council sessions every two years and arrangements be made to follow up implementation of its decisions between sessions. It postponed a final recommendation to the General Assembly until presentation of a report from the Executive Director in 1983.

In a 20 December decision[1] on restructuring the economic and social sectors of the United Nations system, the General Assembly took note of the Council's decision, invited other subsidiary intergovernmental bodies to consider similar possibilities and invited recommendations from the Economic and Social Council on the subject.

Decisions (1982). [1]GA: 37/442, sect. II, 20 Dec. [2]UNEP Council (report, A/37/25): 10/1, sect. III, 31 May.

Content and format of the environment report

In its 31 May 1982 decision[1] on programme policy and implementation, the UNEP Governing Council requested the Executive Director to supplement the annual state-of-the-environment report, as from 1983, with a section on the most important environmental events and emerging issues of the preceding year and to present future reports in a format appealing to both policymakers and the general public. The number of topics as from 1984 should be limited to one or two; the items for the 1983 report would be hazardous waste, acid rain and environmental aspects of energy forms.

Decision (1982). [1]UNEP Council (report, A/37/25): 10/1, sect. II, 31 May.

Relations with NGOs

On 31 May 1982, in its decision[1] on programme policy and implementation, the UNEP Governing Council, after expressing appreciation to all non-governmental organizations (NGOs) contributing to the cause of the environment, invited their closer co-operation and called on Governments to make use of their work, knowledge and resources. The Council expressed appreciation to the Executive Director for improving liaison with NGOs and requested him to facilitate further their participation in the development of UNEP programmes.

Decision (1982). [1]UNEP Council (report, A/37/25): 10/1, sect. IV, 31 May.

Environmental activities

Environmental monitoring

Protection against harmful products

UNEP action. A main concern of the Global Environmental Monitoring System (GEMS)—a collective effort of the world community to acquire the data needed for rational management of the environment—is the environmental perturbations affecting human health, particularly toxic chemicals. This subject was reviewed by a meeting of Government-designated experts on health-related monitoring (Geneva, 8-12 March 1982), which assessed the progress and future activities of the health-related component of GEMS and examined the monitoring networks, basic methodologies and a data base established by UNEP. The subject of quality assurance was also pursued. Government-designated experts convened by UNEP and the World Meteorological Organization (Geneva, 22-26 March) made a similar review of the climate-related component of GEMS.

Under a joint UNEP/World Health Organization (WHO) project on assessing human exposure to pollutants through biological monitoring, the results of the metals component were published during 1982 (Assessment of Human Exposure to Lead and Cadmium through Biological Monitoring). Ten countries participated in the project, whose first phase was devoted to training and technical assistance to ensure quality control in the co-operating institutions. Results achieved in the second (monitoring) phase revealed considerable variations in lead exposure between the various study sites. For cadmium, the values in blood and in kidney cortex were highly correlated with smoking. There were strong indications that lead in petrol might be an important source of exposure. Under the same project, the determination of organochlorine compounds in human milk was completed. Results showed that it would be feasible to carry out such a programme internationally, applying strict quality control. Major differences in the exposure of different populations were revealed, the most striking of which were the high exposure to DDT and the low exposure to polychlorinated biphenyls (PCBs) in developing countries, with the exact opposite in developed countries.

Within the food and animal-feed contamination-monitoring project, a summary and assessment of data on levels of organochlorine compounds for 19 countries was published. Generally very few reported levels exceeded residue limits or guidelines recommended under the joint WHO/Food and Agriculture Organization of the United Nations Food Standards Programme. In some cases, levels of DDT, aldrin and dieldrin in human milk exceeded the acceptable daily intake, but it was believed that short-term exposure presented a lesser risk to the infant than alternatives to breast-feeding. There were indications of downward trends in lead levels which were higher in tinned than in fresh fruits and vegetables; cadmium data revealed no clear trends in cereals and flours.

The co-operative programme for monitoring and evaluating long-range transport of pollutants in Europe continued to give data on pollutants which were transported from one country to another. UNEP also maintained a register of chemicals (p. 1012) and assessed their toxicity under a chemical safety programme.

On 31 May 1982,[2] in a decision on follow-up action to the 1981 *Ad Hoc* Meeting of Senior Government Officials Expert in Environmental Law, the UNEP Governing Council authorized the Executive Director to convene in 1983/1984, after consulting with Governments and international agencies, three meetings of government experts to consider guidelines or principles on: environmentally sound transport, handling (including storage) and disposal of toxic and dangerous wastes; the exchange of information relating to trade in and use and handling of potentially harmful chemicals, particularly pesticides; and marine pollution from land-based sources.

Economic and Social Council action. At the July 1982 session of the Economic and Social Council, Venezuela introduced a 12-nation draft resolution on protection against harmful or potentially harmful products.[3]

By this text, the Council would have urged countries that had prohibited the consumption, use and/or sale of harmful or potentially harmful products to ensure that they were not produced or exported by corporations or individuals having their main seat of business in their territory, or were otherwise liable to their jursidiction. The Secretary-General would have been requested: to continue ensuring United Nations assistance to strengthen the capacities of developing countries to protect themselves from the products; and to prepare, regularly update and make available to Governments a consolidated list of products whose consumption, use and/or sale had been prohibited by Governments or challenged by authoritative institutions. Venezuela orally revised the draft to add a further request that the Secretary-General suggest, to the Council's second regular 1983 session, ways to implement the resolution's purpose effectively.

The draft was subsequently orally revised further to have the Council urge countries that had banned or severely restricted the products in question to ensure that they were not produced or exported by corporations or individuals liable to their jurisdiction, and to make available information on them in order to ensure that importing countries could be protected against harmful effects. The requests to the Secretary-General concerning the provision of United Nations assistance and the list of products were retained, but the wording on those provisions was redrafted; the request for him to suggest ways of implementing the resolution was omitted, however, and the preambular paragraphs were revised.

On the understanding that the draft, as it read prior to revision, would be transmitted to the General Assembly for consideration at its 1982 regular session, Venezuela withdrew a request for a roll-call vote on the final revised version.

Therefore, by a decision of 30 July,[1] the Council, without vote, transmitted the original draft to the Assembly.

General Assembly action. On 17 December, the General Assembly, by a resolution on protection against products harmful to health and the environment,[4] agreed that domestically banned products judged to endanger health and the environment should be sold abroad only on request from the importing country or when their consumption was officially permitted in that country. Countries that had severely restricted or had not approved specific products, particularly pharmaceuticals and pesticides, should make available full information on them to the importing country. The Secretary-General was requested to continue providing United Nations information and assistance to strengthen developing countries' capacities to protect themselves from those products. He was further asked, based on ongoing work in intergovernmental organizations, to the maximum extent possible within existing resources, to prepare and update regularly a product list and to make it available by December 1983. The list was to contain both generic/chemical and brand names, manufacturers' names and the grounds for government decisions on them. The format of the list was to be kept under review and Governments and United Nations bodies were to provide the necessary information.

The resolution was adopted by a recorded vote of 146 to 1. On 8 December, the Second (Economic and Financial) Committee had approved a 23-nation revised draft, introduced by Venezuela, by a recorded vote, requested by the United States, of 132 to 1.

A United States oral amendment—to delete "to the maximum extent possible" from the phrase referring to preparing the product list "to the maximum extent possible within existing resources"— was rejected by 111 votes to 8, with 10 abstentions.

Explaining its negative vote, the United States said that, although it endorsed the text's underlying principles, the categorical and unfounded judgements in the first and third preambular paragraphs did not take into account specific situations or needs or the offsetting of dangers, in certain circumstances, by advantages. Some problems of definition and intent, as well as ambiguities, remained; the text did not clearly specify that Governments would not be required to provide information about certain proprietary products; and its financial implications constituted a serious problem.

Venezuela pointed out that the vast majority of States felt the draft was clear on definitions and proposed measures. Bulgaria, on behalf also of other Eastern European States and Mongolia, said that the problem of distributing harmful products had not arisen spontaneously, but resulted from the selfishness of transnational corporations and the weakness of national monitoring bodies; the draft might contribute towards a code of conduct for those corporations.

Decisions (1982). [1]ESC: 1982/180, 30 July, text following. [2]UNEP Council (report, A/37/25): 10/24, para. 1 *(b)* & *(c)*, 31 May.
Draft resolution not pressed. [3]Algeria, Argentina, Bangladesh, Cuba, India, Kenya, Nigeria, Pakistan, Peru, Sudan, Venezuela, Zaire, E/1982/L.46 (transmitted to GA by Secretariat note, A/C.2/37/L.3).
Resolution (1982). [4]GA: 37/137, 17 Dec., text following.
Financial implications. 5th Committee report, A/37/759; S-G statements, A/C.2/37/L.99, A/C.5/37/97.
Meeting records. ESC: E/1982/SR.31-44, *48, 51* (27, 30 July). GA: 2nd Committee, A/C.2/37/SR.3 12, 32, *12, 44, 47* (28 Sep.–8 Dec.); 5th Committee, A/C.5/37/SR.71 (15 Dec.); plenary, A/37/PV.109 (17 Dec.).

Economic and Social Council decision 1982/180

Adopted without vote

Oral proposal by Venezuela, for sponsors of 12-nation draft (E/1982/L.46); agenda item 3.

Protection against harmful or potentially harmful products

At its 51st plenary meeting, on 30 July 1982, the Council decided to transmit the draft resolution annexed hereto to the General Assembly at its thirty-seventh session, for consideration.

ANNEX
Protection against harmful or potentially harmful products
The General Assembly,

Considering the profound, widespread and often irreparable damage that continues to be caused by some manufactured products, in particular foodstuffs, pharmaceuticals, pesticides, clothing and synthetic packaging, to the people of the developing countries,

Considering that many of these products continue to be exported to developing countries, despite the fact that, owing to their harmfulness or potential harmfulness, their consumption, use and/or sale have been prohibited in the producing country,

Considering that many developing countries lack the necessary expertise to keep up with developments in this field,

Cognizant of the fact that almost all these products are manufactured and exported by corporations that have their main seat of business in a limited number of industrialized countries,

In pursuance of Economic and Social Council resolution 1981/62 of 23 July 1981,

1. *Urges* all countries that have prohibited the consumption, use and/or sale of harmful or potentially harmful products to ensure that these are not produced or exported by corporations or individuals that have their main seat of business in their territory, or are otherwise liable to their jurisdiction;

2. *Requests* the Secretary-General to continue to ensure the provision of the necessary assistance by the United Nations to strengthen the national capacities of developing countries in protecting themselves from the consumption and use of harmful or potentially harmful products;

3. *Also requests* the Secretary-General to prepare and regularly update a consolidated list of products whose consumption, use and/or sale have been prohibited by national Governments or challenged by authoritative institutions, and to make that list available to Governments.

General Assembly resolution 37/137

17 December 1982   Meeting 109   146-1 (recorded vote)

Approved by Second Committee (A/37/679/Add.1) by recorded vote (132-1), 8 December (meeting 47); 23-nation draft (A/C.2/37/L.65/Rev.1); agenda item 12.
Sponsors: Algeria, Argentina, Bangladesh, Colombia, Cuba, Ethiopia, Ghana, Guyana, Honduras, India, Iran, Nicaragua, Nigeria, Pakistan, Saudi Arabia, Senegal, Sudan, Trinidad and Tobago, Tunisia, Uganda, Venezuela, Viet Nam, Zimbabwe.

Protection against products harmful to health and the environment
The General Assembly,

Aware of the damage to health and the environment that the continued production and export of products that have been banned and/or permanently withdrawn on grounds of human health and safety from domestic markets is causing in the importing countries,

Aware that some products, although they present a certain usefulness in specific cases and/or under certain conditions, have been severely restricted in their consumption and/or sale owing to their toxic effects on health and the environment,

Aware of the harm to health being caused in importing countries by the export of pharmaceutical products ultimately intended also for consumption and/or sale in the home market of the exporting country, but which have not yet been approved there,

Considering that many developing countries lack the necessary information and expertise to keep up with developments in this field,

Considering the need for countries that have been exporting the above-mentioned products to make available the necessary information and assistance to enable the importing countries to protect themselves adequately,

Cognizant of the fact that almost all of these products are at present manufactured and exported from a limited number of countries,

Taking into account that the primary responsibility for consumer protection rests with each State,

Recalling its resolution 36/166 of 16 December 1981 and the report on transnational corporations in the pharmaceutical industry of developing countries, and acting in pursuance of Economic and Social Council resolution 1981/62 of 23 July 1981,

Bearing in mind in this context the work of the Food and Agriculture Organization of the United Nations, the World Health Organization, the International Labour Organisation, the United Nations Environment Programme, the General Agreement on Tariffs and Trade, the United Nations Centre on Transnational Corporations and other relevant intergovernmental organizations,

1. *Agrees* that products that have been banned from domestic consumption and/or sale because they have been judged to endanger health and the environment should be sold abroad by companies, corporations or individuals only when a request for such products is received from an importing country or when the consumption of such products is officially permitted in the importing country;

2. *Agrees* that all countries that have severely restricted or have not approved the domestic consumption and/or sale of specific products, in particular pharmaceuticals and pesticides, should make available full information on these products with a view to safeguarding the health and environment of the importing country, including clear labelling in a language acceptable to the importing country;

3. *Requests* the Secretary-General to continue to ensure the provision of the necessary information and assistance by the United Nations system in order to strengthen the national capacities of developing countries to protect themselves from the consumption and/or sale of banned, withdrawn, severely restricted or, in the case of pharmaceuticals, non-approved products;

4. *Requests* the Secretary-General, based upon the work already being done within the Food and Agriculture Organization of the United Nations, the World Health Organization, the International Labour Organisation, the United Nations Environment Programme, the General Agreement on Tariffs and Trade, the United Nations Centre on Transnational Corporations and other relevant intergovernmental organizations, to the maximum extent possible within existing resources, to prepare and regularly update a consolidated list of products whose consumption and/or sale have been banned, withdrawn, severely restricted or, in the case of pharmaceuticals, not approved by Governments, and to make this list available as early as possible and, in any case, not later than December 1983;

5. *Agrees* that the consolidated list referred to in paragraph 4 above should be easy to read and understand and should contain both generic/chemical and brand names in alphabetical order, as well as the names of all manufacturers and a short reference to the grounds and the decisions taken by Governments that have led to the banning, withdrawal or severe restriction of such products;

6. *Decides*, on the basis of the above-agreed criteria, to keep under review the format of the consolidated list with a view to its possible improvement;

7. *Requests* Governments and the relevant organs, organizations and bodies of the United Nations system to provide all the information and assistance necessary for the prompt and effective fulfilment of the task entrusted to the Secretary-General.

Recorded vote in Assembly as follows:

In favour: Afghanistan, Albania, Algeria, Angola, Argentina, Australia, Austria, Bahamas, Bahrain, Bangladesh, Barbados, Belgium, Benin, Bhutan, Bolivia, Botswana, Brazil, Bulgaria, Burma, Burundi, Byelorussian SSR, Canada, Cape Verde, Central African Republic, Chad, Chile, China, Colombia, Comoros, Congo, Costa Rica, Cuba, Cyprus, Czechoslovakia, Democratic Kampuchea, Democratic Yemen, Denmark, Djibouti, Dominica, Dominican Republic, Ecuador, Egypt, El Salvador, Ethiopia, Fiji, Finland, France, Gabon, Gambia, German Democratic Republic, Germany, Federal Republic of, Ghana, Greece, Grenada, Guatemala, Guinea, Guinea-Bissau, Guyana, Honduras, Hungary, Iceland, India, Indonesia, Iran, Iraq, Ireland, Israel, Italy, Ivory Coast, Jamaica, Japan, Jordan, Kenya, Kuwait, Lao People's Democratic Republic, Lebanon, Lesotho, Liberia, Libyan Arab Jamahiriya, Luxembourg, Madagascar, Malawi, Malaysia, Maldives, Mali, Malta, Mauritania, Mauritius, Mexico, Mongolia, Morocco, Mozambique, Nepal, Netherlands, New Zealand, Nicaragua, Niger, Nigeria, Norway, Oman, Pakistan, Panama, Papua New Guinea, Paraguay, Peru, Philippines, Poland, Portugal, Qatar, Romania, Rwanda, Samoa, Sao Tome and Principe, Saudi Arabia, Senegal, Sierra Leone, Singapore, Solomon Islands, Somalia, Spain, Sri Lanka, Suriname, Swaziland, Sweden, Thailand, Togo, Trinidad and Tobago, Tunisia, Turkey, Uganda, Ukrainian SSR, USSR, United Arab Emirates, United Kingdom, United Republic of Cameroon, United Republic of Tanzania, Upper Volta, Uruguay, Vanuatu, Venezuela, Viet Nam, Yemen, Yugoslavia, Zaire, Zambia, Zimbabwe.

Against: United States.

List of toxic substances

In 1982, the International Register of Potentially Toxic Chemicals (IRPTC) published two issues of the *IRPTC Bulletin*, giving data for evaluating hazards associated with such chemicals. By the end of the year, IRPTC had enlisted the aid of 104 national correspondents from 95 countries in its network. The IRPTC file, the "International Register of Potentially Toxic Chemicals—Part A", was updated and distributed, and computerized files were reorganized so that information and data profiles on selected chemicals and the physical characteristics, uses, concentrations, behaviour and toxic-

ity of some 350 chemicals stored in the IRPTC data bank were available on request.

The legal file of IRPTC containing data on regulatory measures for control of chemical hazards was also revised and expanded. The International Programme on Chemical Safety (IPCS), in conjunction with IRPTC, was to strengthen arrangements for information exchange on particularly hazardous chemicals, provide information on exposure limits and enhance publicity. A joint project of IRPTC and the International Labour Organisation (ILO) was initiated to establish a computerized data base on occupational exposure limits for airborne toxic substances; a compendium covering over 1,000 chemicals was scheduled to be published in 1983. At an international workshop (Moscow, 15-18 June 1982), IRPTC co-operated in designing a draft programme for a post-graduate training course for specialists from developing countries responsible for protecting human health and the environment against chemical pollution. IRPTC was also represented at the second high-level meeting on chemicals organized by the Organisation for Economic Co-operation and Development (OECD) in November. The meeting reviewed achievements in the OECD chemical programme over the previous two years and set directions for future work.

In its 18 May resolution on the state of the environment,[3] adopted at its special session, the UNEP Governing Council, in reviewing major achievements and failures in implementing the 1972 Action Plan for the Human Environment,[4] felt that IRPTC had begun to prove itself as an important centre for information on toxic chemicals.

At its 1982 regular session, the Governing Council had before it a report by the Executive Director[2] containing a list of environmentally dangerous chemical substances and processes with global impact. Submitted in response to a May 1981 Council request,[5] the report contained the recommendations of an expert meeting (Geneva, 10-22 January 1982) for further action on each of the substances and the processes during which they were produced or used. Seven chemicals and chemical groups were recommended for inclusion: cadmium, carbon dioxide, chlorofluorocarbons and related compounds, lead, mercury, nitrogen oxides and photochemical oxidants, and sulphur dioxide and derivatives. Four dangerous processes of global impact were also recommended: eutrophication, fossil-fuel combustion, oil production and transportation, and indiscriminate use of pesticides.

On 31 May,[1] the Governing Council requested the Executive Director to obtain the comments of Governments, the scientific community and other international organizations on his report, calling on Governments to give priority attention to the recommendations in it. He was to review it based on those comments and report again in 1984. As from 1984, the list was to be reviewed and updated periodically, preferably every three years.

Decision (1982). [1]UNEP Council (report, A/37/25): 10/15, 31 May.
Report. [2]UNEP Executive Director, UNEP/GC.10/5/Add.3.
Resolution (1982). [3]UNEP Council (report, A/37/25): I, sect. I, para. 3 (*a*) (iv), 18 May.
Yearbook references. [4]1972, p. 322; [5]1981, p. 825.

Activities of the
International Programme on Chemical Safety

During 1982, the International Programme on Chemical Safety—sponsored by ILO, the World Health Organization (WHO) and UNEP—provided toxicological assessments for an increasing number of substances, together with accelerated manpower development, guidelines for emergency response to chemical accidents and technical cooperation relating to control of toxic chemicals. The UNEP Governing Council made this observation in its 18 May 1982 resolution[2] on the state of the environment, adopted at its special session, reviewing the major achievements and failures in implementing the 1972 Action Plan for the Human Environment.[3]

At the third meeting of the Advisory Committee of IPCS (Kiev, Ukrainian SSR, June), the Committee made suggestions about the Programme's future work, observing that it should currently be in a position to increase its direct practical assistance to member States. The central unit of IPCS was also to strengthen chemical safety arrangements in conjunction with IRPTC.

On 31 May,[1] the Governing Council commended UNEP, ILO and WHO for their efforts to make IPCS responsive to Member States' needs, and recommended that close links be maintained or established within and outside the United Nations system to involve the whole international community in a common effort to assess the hazards of chemicals and so avoid duplication of effort. The Executive Director was requested, within existing resources, to make UNEP activities increasingly supportive of the needs of IPCS.

Decision (1982). [1]UNEP Council (report, A/37/25): 10/16, 31 May.
Resolution (1982). [2]UNEP Council (report, A/37/25): I, sect. I, para. 3 (*a*) (v), 18 May.
Yearbook reference. [3]1972, p. 322.

Atmosphere

In its 18 May 1982 resolution[2] on the state of the environment, adopted at its special session, the UNEP Governing Council, in reviewing major achievements and failures in implementing the 1972 Action Plan for the Human Environment,[3] noted that international studies of climatic change and variability and of the application of climate knowledge to human activity had been incorpo-

rated into the World Meteorological Organization's World Climate Programme. The Council considered that the trends and problems that should receive the United Nations system's attention were: urban air quality in developing countries and, in the case of some pollutants, in developed countries; long-range transport of air pollution, including emissions giving rise to acid rains; continued increase of carbon dioxide, other trace gases and particulates in the atmosphere; depletion of stratospheric ozone; effects of human activities on weather and climate; and extreme meteorological events such as tropical cyclones, floods and droughts. Priorities for action were: the monitoring of pollutants and their effects, and development and promotion of appropriate programmes; guidelines or conventions to respond to those problems; improvement of early-warning indicators for extreme meteorological events; and understanding of factors affecting climate, including ocean-atmosphere interactions.

At the Second United Nations Conference on the Exploration and Peaceful Uses of Outer Space (Vienna, Austria, 9-21 August),[1] it was pointed out that although space activities had given rise to some concern over their environmental effects, satellites had contributed substantially to the monitoring of those and other effects. The Conference recommended that such world-wide monitoring and any remedial action be coordinated by UNEP within the Global Environmental Monitoring System. Countries were therefore urged to provide UNEP with data for such monitoring.

Report. [1]Conference on outer space, A/CONF.101/10.
Resolution (1982). [2]UNEP Council (report, A/37/25): I, sect. I, para. 3 (*a*) (ii), & sect. III, para. 2 (*a*), 18 May.
Yearbook reference. [3]1972, p. 322.

Draft convention on protecting the ozone layer

In accordance with a May 1981 UNEP Governing Council decision,[5] the first session of the *Ad Hoc* Working Group of Legal and Technical Experts for the Elaboration of a Global Framework Convention for the Protection of the Ozone Layer was held at Stockholm, Sweden, from 20 to 28 January 1982.[4] The Group considered various aspects of ozone depletion and considered informally general objectives and approaches for an international convention, addressing four main categories of provisions: specific forms of co-operation; basic obligations; institutional arrangements; and structure, format and other provisions. It also adopted recommendations on possible future work.

On 31 May,[1] the Governing Council commended the *Ad Hoc* Working Group's efforts, approved the recommendations for its future work and urged support for it.

At the Second United Nations Conference on the Exploration and Peaceful Uses of Outer Space (Vienna, 9-21 August),[2] it was recognized that there had been some depletion in the protective ozone layer resulting in possible hazards to human, plant and aquatic life due to increased ultraviolet radiation. Research should be encouraged, the Conference recommended, and an integrated global ozone-observing system created.

The first part of the second session of the *Ad Hoc* Working Group was held at Geneva from 10 to 17 December.[3] A revised text of a preamble and articles 1-12 for a convention emerged from a second reading; amendments on which final agreement was not reached appeared between brackets. Written proposals were also submitted on other parts of the draft text. The Group's generally agreed recommendations for its future work included: revising the draft convention, based on comments at the current session and containing alternative provisions and commentaries; transmitting the text to States and inviting them to the session's second part; and preparing possible annexes and/or protocols on research and monitoring, scientific and technical co-operation, and a list of chemical substances/activities affecting the ozone layer. The Group also recommended that it next meet at Geneva in April 1983; that consideration be given to holding the sixth session of the Co-ordinating Committee on the Ozone Layer before the Group's next meeting, with the Committee transmitting its report and recommendations to the Group; and that broader participation in the Group's work be encouraged.

Decision (1982). [1]UNEP Council (report, A/37/25): 10/17, 31 May.
Reports. [2]Conference on outer space, A/CONF.101/10; [3]Working Group of experts for a convention for protection of ozone layer, UNEP/WG.78/8; [4]UNEP Executive Director, UNEP/GC.10/5/Add.4.
Yearbook reference. [5]1981, p. 824.

Carbon dioxide

In an April 1982 report[2] to the UNEP Governing Council, the Executive Director submitted a proposed approach to assessing the effects of carbon dioxide concentrations in the atmosphere and recommended creating an intergovernmental co-ordinating committee to monitor the problem. He reported on discussions that had been held with the International Council of Scientific Unions (ICSU) and the World Meteorological Organization (WMO), as mandated by UNEP in 1980.[4] The consensus was that the carbon dioxide issue could be divided into specific topics: projected release; cycle and projected concentrations; climate responses; effects on marine biota, natural terrestrial ecosystems, agriculture, the managed biosphere and human health; economic and geopolitical consequences; and social and institutional responses. The Executive Director planned to establish, as an interim measure, a five-expert advisory group to monitor the assessment of all topics.

On 31 May 1982,[1] the Governing Council endorsed the proposed approach and requested the Executive Director to consider the appropriate timing—in the light of progress by WMO and ISCU, in co-operation with the Food and Agriculture Organization of the United Nations and the United Nations Educational, Scientific and Cultural Organization, in assessing the scientific and physical aspects of climatic changes induced by carbon dioxide—for establishing a committee to co-ordinate research and information exchange, and to report in 1983.

In its 20 December resolution[3] on international co-operation on the environment, the General Assembly took note of the Council's decision on its future work in this area—by a provision which had been added during informal discussions on the original draft.

Decision (1982). [1]UNEP Council (report, A/37/25): 10/14, sect. I, 31 May.
Report. [2]UNEP Executive Director, UNEP/GC.10/5/Add.4.
Resolution (1982). [3]GA: 37/217, para. 6 *(d)*, 20 Dec.
Yearbook reference. [4]1980, p. 717.

Ecosytems

Terrestrial ecosystems

In its 18 May 1982 resolution[1] on the state of the environment, adopted at its special session, the UNEP Governing Council identified major environmental trends, potential problems and priorities in terrestrial ecosystems—the interdependent balance of plant and animal life within particular geographical contexts—for action by the United Nations system, co-ordinated by UNEP during 1982-1992.

Concerning the lithosphere, trends and problems were listed as: environmental impact of increased mineral extraction and waste disposal; and environmental hazards caused by earthquakes, volcanic eruptions, tidal waves and landslides. The priorities for action were: encouraging technology for economic use of minerals, including recycling; further developing environmental impact-assessment methods of mineral resource extraction; improving methods for rehabilitating land and disposing or reutilizing wastes; and developing early-warning systems for volcanic eruptions, earthquakes and tidal waves.

Regarding terrestrial biota and bioproductive systems, the trends and problems were seen as: mounting world food demand; soil degradation; loss of agricultural land; adverse effects of inappropriate agricultural practices; loss of potentially valuable genetic resources, including wild flora and fauna; adverse impact of fertilizers and pesticides;

and wetlands depletion. Priorities for action were: assessing land conditions in developing countries; monitoring tropical ecosystems; programming activities for sustainable management of soils, tropical forests and genetic resources and for combating desertification; developing environmentally sound farming and forestry practices; preventing post-harvest food losses; reutilizing agricultural and agro-industrial residues; developing international procedures for handling, using and trading in pesticides; promoting plans of action following the 1980 World Conservation Strategy;[2] protecting wetlands and designating biosphere reserves; and planning urban development, taking into account agricultural development needs and conservation of natural resources.

Trends and problems in population and human settlements were listed as: continued population growth; urbanization outstripping Governments' capacities to provide services; slum growth; disruption of rural communities and inadequacies in rural services; and environmental degradation due to distortion of traditional pastoral-nomadism patterns. Priorities for action were: research into the population growth/environment interrelationship; guidelines for sound planning of rural and urban settlements; improving methods of safe disposal and reuse of urban wastes; and social and environmental support for nomads.

Energy trends and problems were considered to be: environmental impact of increasing demand for fuelwood, expanding nuclear energy programmes and wastes; increasing coal usage; intensified development and use of new and renewable energy sources, and increased energy plantations; and some success in developing energy conservation. Priorities for action were: supporting reafforestation in developing countries; improving energy efficiency and conservation; guidelines for environmentally sound development of new and renewable energy sources and of nuclear energy; and global strategies for energy conservation and diversification.

Resolution (1982). [1]UNEP Council (report, A/37/25): I, sect. III, para. 2 *(d)-(f)* & *(h),* 18 May.
Yearbook reference. [2]1980, p. 717.

Arid zones

Desertification control

In 1982, in addition to aiding the Sudano-Sahelian region, UNEP organized a mission to Democratic Yemen, Lesotho, Oman and the United Republic of Tanzania to formulate or revise proposals for submission to the Consultative Group for Desertification Control. Support was also given to the second phase of a Transnational Green Belt Project in North Africa, which comprised national anti-desertification projects in Algeria, the Libyan Arab Jamahiriya and Tunisia

as well as subregional training programmes. Publications included two issues of the *Desertification Control* bulletin, together with a booklet and a monograph on the topic. A meeting of Government-designated experts on desertification in the Americas and the Caribbean was held at Cocoyoc, Mexico, from 8 to 12 February, and the first meeting of the Advisory Panel for the General Assessment of Progress in the Implementation of the Plan of Action to Combat Desertification[11]—adopted in 1977 by the United Nations Conference on Desertification—took place at Nairobi, Kenya, from 21 to 23 June.

Within the USSR/UNEP Co-operation Programme, three courses on sand-dune fixation techniques, on reclaiming irrigated saline soils and on rangeland productivity and management were held in the USSR during 1982, with 56 participants from African and Latin American developing countries. In Japan, the Defence of Green Earth Foundation was established in October to support programmes in developing countries suffering from severe deforestation and desertification.

In a March report to the Governing Council,[5] the Executive Director stated that progress in implementing the Plan of Action had fallen well short of the 1977 Conference's aspirations and that a shortage of finances remained the major constraint.

To harmonize activities in combating desertification in Africa (See ECONOMIC AND SOCIAL QUESTIONS, Chapter VIII), the Conference of Ministers of the Economic Commission for Africa in April 1982 authorized its Executive Secretary to assist members in setting up a regional intergovernmental committee for that purpose.[6]

Meeting at Geneva from 6 to 8 April, representatives of the General Secretariat of the Organization of African Unity and the secretariats of the United Nations system recommended that,[4] to accelerate implementation of the Plan of Action, States should be urged to give priority to desertification control, that United Nations organizations should strengthen co-operation within the system, that African research institutions should be encouraged to fill gaps in the knowledge of control techniques, and that all possible ways be sought to mobilize additional financial resources for anti-desertification activities.

In its 1981/82 annual overview report published in May,[3] the Administrative Committee on Coordination said its Inter-agency Working Group on Desertification had agreed on components for an action programme to achieve the objectives of the General Assembly's 1980 resolution on implementing the Plan.[9] The components were: a survey of ongoing research and training activities; an inventory of existing national and regional institutions and activities in research and training; draft science and technology programmes; draft training programmes; and proposals for operational methodologies for regional co-operation.

UNEP action. The UNEP Governing Council, on 31 May 1982,[1] urged Governments, the United Nations system and other intergovernmental bodies and organizations to augment their efforts to combat desertification in order to speed implementation of the Plan's recommendations for immediate action. Noting the results of the 1981 session of the Consultative Group for Desertification Control,[12] the Council urged it to intensify its efforts to assist the Executive Director in mobilizing resources for the Plan's implementation and in ensuring proper co-ordination of activities carried out with the Group's resources. It also took note of the Assembly's 1981 request for a study on financing the Plan[10] and urged Governments to respond favourably to the Secretary-General's inquiries in pursuance of that request. It requested the Executive Director to use the results of the Mexico expert meeting on desertification for future action.

Economic and Social Council action. By its 29 July resolution[7] on international environmental co-operation, the Economic and Social Council transmitted the UNEP report[5] to the General Assembly. It expressed serious concern about the desertification process and the rate of implementation of the Plan, urging the international community to increase efforts to prevent and combat desertification in order to accelerate implementing the Plan's recommendations, and calling on Governments to consider seriously the need for additional resources. The Council recommended that the Assembly invite the UNEP Governing Council to present its views on implementation of the Plan in the Eastern and Southern African subregion and to advise on the possibility of establishing institutional machinery for combating drought and desertification there.

General Assembly action. On 20 December, the General Assembly adopted a resolution[8] with provisions similar to those of the Council, noting the report and expressing concern at the slow implementation because of the lack of finances. It called on the Consultative Group for Desertification Control to intensify its efforts to assist the UNEP Executive Director in mobilizing resources. The Assembly urged the world community to augment its efforts to prevent and combat desertification and encouraged countries affected by desertification to accord high priority to combating it in their development plans and requests for development assistance.

The resolution was adopted without vote. On 29 November, the Second (Economic and Finan-

cial) Committee had approved the draft similarly. The text was proposed by a Committee Vice-Chairman based on informal consultations on a 12-nation draft introduced by Egypt and subsequently withdrawn.[2]

The 12-nation draft would have had the Assembly express deep concern at the low priority accorded to desertification by affected countries in their development plans and in their bilateral and multilateral development assistance negotiations; and urge, rather than encourage, affected countries to accord high priority to combating desertification.

Decision (1982). [1]UNEP Council (report, A/37/25): 10/14, sect. VII, 31 May.
Draft resolution withdrawn. [2]Bangladesh, Egypt, Ethiopia, Guinea, Guinea-Bissau, Kenya, Lesotho, Liberia, Nigeria, United Republic of Tanzania, Upper Volta, Yugoslavia, A/C.2/37/L.48.
Reports. [3]ACC, E/1982/4; [4]S-G, A/37/335; [5]UNEP Executive Director, UNEP/GC.10/9 and Corr.1 and Add.1.
Resolutions (1982). [6]ECA (report, E/1982/21): 446(XVII), para. 2, 30 Apr. [7]ESC: 1982/56, paras. 8-10, 29 July. [8]GA: 37/218, 20 Dec., text following.
Resolutions (prior). GA: [9]35/73, 5 Dec. 1980 (YUN 1980, p. 730); [10]36/191, 17 Dec. 1981 (YUN 1981, p. 828).
Yearbook references. [11]1977, p. 509; [12]1981, p. 827.
Meeting records. GA: 2nd Committee, A/C.2/37/SR.3, 5-8, 20-26, 33, 40, *42, 44* (28 Sep.–29 Nov.); plenary, A/37/PV.113 (20 Dec.).

General Assembly resolution 37/218

20 December 1982   Meeting 113   Adopted without vote

Approved by Second Committee (A/37/680/Add.8) without vote, 29 November (meeting 44); draft by Vice-Chairman (A/C.2/37/L.86), based on informal consultations on 12-nation draft (A/C.2/37/L.48); agenda item 71 *(i)*.

Implementation of the Plan of Action to Combat Desertification

The General Assembly,

Recalling its resolutions 32/172 of 19 December 1977, 33/89 of 15 December 1978, 34/184 and 34/185 of 18 December 1979 and 35/73 of 5 December 1980, dealing with the various aspects of the implementation of the Plan of Action to Combat Desertification,

Taking note of the relevant section of the report of the Governing Council of the United Nations Environment Programme on its tenth session, in particular section VII of Council decision 10/14 of 31 May 1982 on the implementation of the Plan of Action to Combat Desertification,

Taking into account paragraphs 8 to 10 of Economic and Social Council resolution 1982/56 of 29 July 1982,

Having considered the report of the Governing Council of the United Nations Environment Programme on the implementation of the Plan of Action to Combat Desertification, submitted in accordance with General Assembly resolution 35/73,

1. *Takes note with appreciation* of the report of the Governing Council of the United Nations Environment Programme on the implementation of the Plan of Action to Combat Desertification;

2. *Expresses its deep concern* at the slow implementation of the Plan of Action owing to the lack of adequate financial resources;

3. *Urges* all Governments, organizations of the United Nations system, other intergovernmental bodies, non-governmental and all other organizations to augment their efforts to prevent and combat desertification in order to accelerate progress in implementing the recommendations of the Plan of Action for immediate initial action;

4. *Encourages* Governments of countries affected by desertification to accord the combating of desertification high priority in their development plans and in their requests for development assistance;

5. *Calls upon* the Consultative Group for Desertification Control to intensify further its efforts to assist the Executive Director of the

United Nations Environment Programme in the mobilization of resources for the implementation of the Plan of Action.

Financing the Plan of Action

In its 31 May 1982 decision[1] on implementing the Plan of Action to Combat Desertification, the UNEP Governing Council took note of a December 1981 General Assembly resolution[5] concerning a study on financing the Plan and urged Governments to respond favourably and promptly to the Secretary-General's inquiries undertaken in pursuance of the resolution. The Secretary-General had asked for Member States' views on additional means of financing the Plan. By 20 October,[3] 16 replies had been received: six (Brazil, Burma, El Salvador, Finland, Pakistan, Senegal) were acknowledgements of receipt; one indicated that Mexico would not be able to contribute to the proposed independent corporation for the financing of the desertification-control projects; and nine (Austria, Ethiopia, France, Federal Republic of Germany, Italy, Norway, Sweden, USSR, United States) included substantive comments on additional financial measures and the possibility of such a corporation. Therefore, the Secretary-General concluded that the limited number of replies did not allow for the preparation of a comprehensive report on the topic.

General Assembly action. On 20 December, the General Assembly adopted a resolution[4] by which it took note again of the Secretary-General's 1981 report and the annexed feasibility studies on additional means of financing the Plan[6] as well as of his 1982 report.[3] It urged Member States that had not commented on those means to do so as soon as possible and again requested the Secretary-General to refer the 1981 experts' study for establishing an international financial corporation to finance non-commercial desertification measures to Member States for their views on its creation and their interest in participating financially therein.

The resolution was adopted without vote. On 2 December, the Second Committee had approved the draft in like manner. The text was proposed by a Committee Vice-Chairman based on informal consultations on a draft submitted by Egypt, Guinea, Jamaica and the Sudan, and subsequently withdrawn.[2]

In addition to drafting changes in both preambular and operative parts of the resolution, the adopted text omitted provisions by which the Assembly would have reiterated appreciation of the Secretary-General's 1981 report and annex, expressed disappointment at the paucity of replies and called for the replies to be submitted no later than 31 March 1983.

Decision (1982). [1]UNEP Council (report, A/37/25): 10/14, sect. VII, para. 4, 31 May.
Draft resolution withdrawn. [2]Egypt, Guinea, Jamaica, Sudan, A/C.2/37/L.71.

Reports. [3]S-G, A/37/424 & Add.1.
Resolution (1982). [4]GA: 37/220, 20 Dec., text following.
Resolution (prior). [5]GA: 36/191, 17 Dec. 1981 (YUN 1981, p. 828).
Yearbook reference. [6]1981, p. 827.
Meeting records. GA: 2nd Committee, A/C.2/37/SR.3, 5-8, 33, 40, *43, 46* (28 Sep.–2 Dec.); plenary, A/37/PV.113 (20 Dec.).

General Assembly resolution 37/220

20 December 1982   Meeting 113   Adopted without vote

Approved by Second Committee (A/37/680/Add.8) without vote, 2 December (meeting 46); draft by Vice-Chairman (A/C.2/37/L.97), based on informal consultations on 4-nation draft (A/C.2/37/L.71); agenda item 71 *(i)*.

Study on financing the Plan of Action to Combat Desertification

The General Assembly,

Recalling its resolutions 32/172 of 19 December 1977, 33/89 of 15 December 1978, 34/184 of 18 December 1979 and 36/191 of 17 December 1981, dealing with the implementation and financing of the Plan of Action to Combat Desertification,

Taking note of the relevant section of the report of the Governing Council of the United Nations Environment Programme on its tenth session, in particular paragraphs 2 and 4 of section VII of Governing Council decision 10/14 of 31 May 1982 on the implementation of the Plan of Action to Combat Desertification,

1. *Takes note again* of the report of the Secretary-General and the annex thereto, which contains feasibility studies on additional measures of financing the Plan of Action to Combat Desertification, prepared by a group of high-level experts;

2. *Takes note* of the report of the Secretary-General on financing the Plan of Action to Combat Desertification and of the fact that the number of replies received from Governments in response to the request made by the General Assembly in paragraphs 3 and 4 of its resolution 36/191 was too small to allow for preparation of the report requested of the Secretary-General in that resolution;

3. *Urges* all Member States that have not yet provided their comments to the Secretary-General on the feasibility studies and concrete recommendations for the implementation of the additional measures of financing, as well as on the modalities for obtaining financial resources as described in the annex to the report of the Secretary-General, to do so as soon as possible;

4. *Requests again* the Secretary-General to refer the experts' feasibility study and working plan for the establishment of an international financial corporation to finance non-commercial desertification measures, contained in chapter IV of the annex to his report, to Member States and to seek their views on:

(a) The establishment of the corporation;

(b) Their interest in participating financially therein;

5. *Also requests* the Secretary-General, in co-operation with the Executive Director of the United Nations Environment Programme, to report to the General Assembly at its thirty-eighth session on the implementation of the present resolution.

Assistance to the Sudano-Sahelian region

Several 1982 reports detailed the activities of the United Nations Sudano-Sahelian Office (UNSO)—a joint UNEP/United Nations Development Programme (UNDP) venture—in trying to implement the Plan of Action to Combat Desertification[11] in the Sudano-Sahelian region and adjacent African countries. Recovery programmes also continued to help the drought-stricken countries of the Sahel.

A UNEP Governing Council report, covering 1982 UNSO activities, was transmitted to the Economic and Social Council and the General Assembly by the Secretary-General in July 1983.[8] A similar report,[7] covering 1981 activities, was transmitted in September 1982.[12] The 1982 desertification control activities in the region were also contained in reports by the UNDP Administrator to the UNDP Governing Council, submitted in April[4] and May 1983.[5] The 1983 UNEP report indicated that the level of funds mobilized and allocated by UNSO for desertification control in 1982 amounted to $12.1 million, including $5.9 million for new activities. Another $6.8 million was mobilized by UNSO for additional inputs provided directly by donors. Nineteen countries continued to be covered by the UNSO desertification control mandate and 258 projects were identified with Governments of the region, requiring an investment of $710.2 million, of which $404.6 million had been committed from bilateral and multilateral sources. The main activities during the year included:

Forestry: in Benin, a $1.4-million multi-purpose tree-planting project; in the Niger, establishing a green belt around the city of Tahoua, and inducing and regenerating 300,000 soil-enriching saplings in Dosso; reforestation and woodlots projects in the Saponé region and in Koudougou, Upper Volta; in Ethiopia, fuelwood plantations for four towns; fuelwood plantations in Somalia; and ecological exploitation of the Casamance forest in Senegal.

Renewable alternatives to fuelwood: in Senegal, the marketing of fuel briquettes made from groundnut shells and peat; installation of wind turbines in Cape Verde; in the Niger, a World Bank mission, financed by UNSO and UNDP, to formulate an energy master plan; and a feasibility study in Mali for producing solar energy equipment.

Fuel-efficient stoves: production of improved cooking stoves in the Gambia, Mali, Mauritania and the Niger; and in the Upper Volta, improving the efficiency of wood-cooking stoves.

Bush-fire control: major projects formulated in the Gambia and the Bafata Gabu area of Guinea-Bissau; and missions scheduled for Benin and Guinea to formulate projects to protect woodlands and grasslands.

Range management: in the Sudan, a project for managing grazing resources around water supplies; pasture development and protection of lands around livestock watering-points in the Gambia; and in Senegal, a centre for producing pasture seed to reseed rangelands for protection against drought.

Water resource management: in Mauritania, constructing and rehabilitating small earthen dams; in the Gambia, formulation missions for developing a project to construct small dams along tributaries of the Gambia River and for the ecologically sound management and use of ground-water resources; continued support to the Fouta-Djallon Massif project in Guinea aimed at agro-sylvo-pastoral development and rehabilitating its natural resources, and formulation of a project to protect the Kakrima Valley; in Somalia, preparation of a project to rehabilitate rural reservoirs; and a mission to Mali to formulate a project to strengthen the department of natural resources for hydrogeological exploration and exploitation.

Sand-dune fixation: in Mauritania, a project to control sand movements, part of a regional sand-dune fixation programme which also included a project in the Brava area of Somalia and one for sand-dune stabilization and reclamation in the Darfur region of the Sudan; and a mission to the Niger to prepare a project to control sand-dune encroachment on the oases of the Bilma region.

Planning, co-ordinating and monitoring activities also took place in 1982, with help being given in preparing national plans for combating desertification in Djibouti, the Gambia and Senegal; a similar approach was used in the Upper Volta; and in Benin, Guinea and Guinea-Bissau, missions were to concentrate on soil erosion and general degradation problems.

Other activities included approval of a project for the integrated development of the Lake Region (Zone Lacustre) in Mali, and formulation of a project for the integrated development of the coastal plain of Djibouti.

UNDP action. On 18 June 1982,[1] the UNDP Governing Council requested the UNDP Administrator to continue UNDP support costs for the joint UNDP/UNEP venture. On the same day,[2] noting with concern that the UNEP contribution level was uncertain, it urged that the issue be resolved so as not to impair the ability of UNSO to carry out its expanded responsibilities in the region and reaffirmed that the UNDP contribution should be equal to that of UNEP.

In a 21 June report of the UNDP Budgetary and Finance Committee,[6] it was noted that agreement had been reached between UNDP and UNEP on additional resources for the expanded level of operations for UNSO for 1980-1981, and that UNDP had requested increased appropriations for that period; the expanded level of operations was also used as a basis for the budget estimates for UNSO for 1982-1983. However, the UNEP Executive Director had not included the corresponding revised estimates in the Environment Fund's budget proposals for 1980-1981; UNEP was not prepared to pay its share of the expanded operation and intended to provide a level of support for 1982-1983 below that appearing in the UNDP biennial budget estimates. Therefore, UNDP intended to secure reimbursement of the additional $130,500 for 1980-1981, to secure immediate payment of the UNEP contribution for 1982 and to negotiate a firm basis for the level of activities for 1982-1983 based on the UNDP Governing Council's decisions.

UNEP action. On 31 May,[3] the UNEP Governing Council welcomed the efforts made and results achieved by UNSO and urged it to continue its work in desertification control, but expressed concern at the aggravation of desertification in the region and at the slow implementation of the Plan of Action. It urged Governments, United Nations organizations and others to support the Sudano-Sahelian countries' efforts to combat the problem and authorized continuation of the UNEP share of 1982-1983 costs of UNSO. It also urged the UNEP Executive Director to provide additional resources to facilitate information and expertise exchange among the region's countries and between them and other African countries with similar problems. He was also requested to strengthen UNEP support for UNSO.

Economic and Social Council action. On 29 July, the Economic and Social Council adopted a resolution[9] expressing satisfaction at progress made by UNSO in helping Sudano-Sahelian countries implement the Plan of Action and welcoming the UNEP and UNDP decisions on continuing the joint venture. After expressing gratitude to those contributing to the Plan's implementation, the Council urged Governments to intensify their aid in response to the priority requirements of the region's countries.

The resolution was adopted without vote. On 28 July, the Council's First (Economic) Committee had similarly approved the draft, sponsored by 16 nations and introduced by the Sudan.

General Assembly action. On 20 December, the General Assembly adopted a resolution[10] reiterating provisions of the Economic and Social Council resolution but also inviting UNEP and UNDP to strengthen further their support for UNSO in order to enable it to respond more adequately to the pressing needs of the region's countries and requesting the UNEP Governing Council to continue reporting annually to the Assembly, through the Economic and Social Council, on the Plan's implementation.

The resolution was adopted without vote. On 29 November, the Second Committee had likewise approved the draft, sponsored by 25 nations and introduced by Egypt.

Decisions (1982). UNDP Council (report, E/1982/16/Rev.1), 18 June: [1]82/26, [2]82/28. [3]UNEP Council (report, A/37/25): 10/18, 31 May.

Reports. UNDP Administrator, [4]DP/1983/6/Add.3, [5]DP/1983/38; [6]UNDP Budgetary & Finance Committee, DP/1982/95; UNEP Council, transmitted by S-G notes, [7]A/37/397, [8]A/38/304.

Resolutions (1982). [9]ESC: 1982/55, 29 July, text following. [10]GA: 37/216, 20 Dec., text following.

Yearbook references. [11]1977, p. 509; [12]1981, p. 829.

Meeting records. ESC: E/1982/SR.50 (29 July). GA: 2nd Committee, A/C.2/37/SR.3, 5-8, 20-26, 33, 40, *42, 44* (28 Sep.–29 Nov.); plenary, A/37/PV.113 (20 Dec.).

Economic and Social Council resolution 1982/55

29 July 1982   Meeting 50   Adopted without vote

Approved by First Committee (E/1982/103) without vote, 28 July (meeting 15); 16-nation draft (E/1982/C.1/L.14); agenda item 15.

Sponsors: Algeria, Argentina, Bangladesh, Benin, Denmark, Germany, Federal Republic of, Kenya, Liberia, Libyan Arab Jamahiriya, Mali, Netherlands, Nigeria, Portugal, Senegal, Sudan, Tunisia.

Implementation in the Sudano-Sahelian region of the Plan of Action to Combat Desertification

The Economic and Social Council,

Recalling the relevant resolutions of the General Assembly and the Economic and Social Council, particularly Assembly resolutions 34/187 of 18 December 1979, 35/72 of 5 December 1980 and 36/190 of 17 December 1981 and Council resolution 1981/72 of 24 July 1981,

Recalling also decision 10/18 of 31 May 1982 of the Governing Council of the United Nations Environment Programme and decision 82/26 of 18 June 1982 of the Governing Council of the United Nations Development Programme,

Reiterating its concern about the seriousness of desertification in the Sudano-Sahelian region and the persistent critical situations resulting from it which hamper the economic and social development of the countries of the region,

Having considered the report of the Governing Council of the United Nations Environment Programme on the implementation in the Sudano-Sahelian region of the Plan of Action to Combat Desertification, and the report of the Governing Council of the United Nations Environment Programme on its tenth session,

1. *Takes note with appreciation* of the report of the Governing Council of the United Nations Environment Programme on the implementation in the Sudano-Sahelian region of the Plan of Action to Combat Desertification;

2. *Expresses its satisfaction* at the progress made by the United Nations Sudano-Sahelian Office, on behalf of the United Nations Environment Programme, in assisting the countries of the Sudano-Sahelian region in the implementation of the Plan of Action to Combat Desertification in a joint venture between the United Nations Environment Programme and the United Nations Development Programme;

3. *Welcomes* the decisions of the Governing Council of the United Nations Environment Programme and the Governing Council of the United Nations Development Programme on the further continuation of the joint venture of the two Programmes, aimed at ensuring the timely and effective provision of assistance to the group of designated countries by the United Nations Sudano-Sahelian Office, on behalf of the United Nations Environment Programme, in combating desertification in the Sudano-Sahelian region;

4. *Expresses its gratitude* to the Governments, agencies of the United Nations system and intergovernmental organizations that are contributing to the implementation in the Sudano-Sahelian region of the Plan of Action to Combat Desertification;

5. *Strongly urges* all Governments to intensify their assistance in response to the priority requirements of the countries of the Sudano-Sahelian region in the implementation of the Plan of Action to Combat Desertification.

General Assembly resolution 37/216

20 December 1982   Meeting 113   Adopted without vote

Approved by Second Committee (A/37/680/Add.8) without vote, 29 November (meeting 44); 25-nation draft (A/C.2/37/L.45); agenda item 71 *(i)*.

Sponsors: Algeria, Bangladesh, Cape Verde, Chad, Democratic Yemen, Egypt, Ethiopia, Gambia, Guinea, Guinea-Bissau, Ivory Coast, Liberia, Mali, Mauritania, Niger, Nigeria, Senegal, Sierra Leone, Somalia, Sudan, Sweden, Uganda, United Republic of Cameroon, Upper Volta, Yugoslavia.

Implementation in the Sudano-Sahelian region of the Plan of Action to Combat Desertification

The General Assembly,

Recalling its resolution 36/190 of 17 December 1981,

Recalling also Economic and Social Council resolution 1982/55 of 29 July 1982,

Noting decision 10/18 of 31 May 1982 of the Governing Council of the United Nations Environment Programme and decisions 82/26 and 82/28 of 18 June 1982 of the Governing Council of the United Nations Development Programme,

Having considered the report of the Governing Council of the United Nations Environment Programme on the implementation in the Sudano-Sahelian region of the Plan of Action to Combat Desertification,

Reiterating its concern about the continued negative impacts of desertification on the countries of the Sudano-Sahelian region, and emphasizing again the need to accelerate the implementation of the Plan of Action to Combat Desertification,

1. *Takes note* of the report of the Governing Council of the United Nations Environment Programme on the implementation in the Sudano-Sahelian region of the Plan of Action to Combat Desertification;

2. *Expresses its satisfaction* with the progress made by the United Nations Sudano-Sahelian Office, on behalf of the United Nations Environment Programme, in assisting the Governments of the region in implementing the Plan of Action to Combat Desertification in a joint venture between the United Nations Environment Programme and the United Nations Development Programme;

3. *Invites* the Governing Council of the United Nations Environment Programme and the Governing Council of the United Nations Development Programme to strengthen further their support for the United Nations Sudano-Sahelian Office in order to enable it to respond more adequately to the pressing needs of the countries of the Sudano-Sahelian region;

4. *Expresses its gratitude* to the Governments, agencies of the United Nations system, intergovernmental organizations and other organizations that have contributed to the implementation in the Sudano-Sahelian region of the Plan of Action to Combat Desertification;

5. *Urges* all Governments to respond favourably to requests for assistance from the Governments of the Sudano-Sahelian region in combating desertification;

6. *Requests* the Governing Council of the United Nations Environment Programme to continue to report annually to the General Assembly, through the Economic and Social Council, on the implementation in the Sudano-Sahelian region of the Plan of Action to Combat Desertification.

Forest management

On 31 May 1982,[1] the UNEP Governing Council requested the Executive Director to include in the system-wide medium-term programme for 1984-1989 activities designed to ensure—taking into account the responsibilities of the Food and Agriculture Organization of the United Nations (FAO) and the United Nations Educational, Scientific and Cultural Organization (UNESCO)—particularly in developing countries, the conservation, rational management and development of forests, which were also an effective means of combating erosion and desertification.

Decision (1982). [1]UNEP Council (report, A/37/25): 10/12, 31 May.

Management of tropical forests

In 1982, forest conservation, management and development was the subject of a thematic joint programming exercise organized by UNEP with participants from various United Nations agencies and organizations (Paris, September). As part of the tropical timber component of the Integrated Programme for Commodities of the United Nations Conference on Trade and Development (UNCTAD), four basic components of a draft international agreement—negotiations on which commenced in 1977[3]—were discussed: research and development; improvement of market intelligence; further and increased processing in developing countries; and reforestation and forest management.

Several initiatives were taken to mobilize additional resources for tropical forest activities. A global fund was set up in the Netherlands to help

non-governmental organizations provide training in the sustainable exploitation and rehabilitation of forests and their resources. In October, a joint International Union for the Conservation of Nature and Natural Resources (IUCN)/World Wildlife Fund Tropical Forests and Primates Programme was launched to try to secure resources for high-priority conservation areas in Brazil, Costa Rica, Ecuador, Indonesia, the Ivory Coast, Madagascar, Papua New Guinea, Peru, Thailand, the United Republic of Cameroon, and the United Republic of Tanzania.

Seventeen African countries participated in UNEP-assisted Economic Commission for Africa regional seminars and a workshop on combating desertification in Africa (Khartoum, Sudan, 23-28 October). A workshop on research and training programmes to combat desertification (Paris, 2-4 November) was attended by 24 participants. Together with the International Institute for Applied Systems Analysis, a project was initiated to prepare a report on deforestation of the Himalayan foothills and its impact on the lower flood plains of the Brahmaputra, Ganges and Indus river basins.

An international programme to support national efforts for the rational management of tropical forest resources was recommended by the Second Expert Meeting on Tropical Forests, jointly sponsored by UNEP, FAO and UNESCO (Rome, Italy, 12-15 January).[2] The meeting recommended: that international organizations and other agencies should co-ordinate their activities in developing programmes for tropical forests and in agriculture and forestry; that action to improve tropical forest management should also include activities to solve agricultural problems so as to lessen constraints and stresses due to poverty and lack of land and food of nearby populations; that national efforts be made to promote information, education and knowledge of such forests; that tropical countries be assisted in elaborating development programmes; that those countries define their priorities; and that existing capabilities in education and research be strengthened and applied in forest resources development projects.

The meeting also recommended increased co-operation and support for activities such as: the Global Environmental Monitoring System, the Man and the Biosphere programme of UNESCO, the tropical timber component of the UNCTAD Integrated Programme for Commodities, and the FAO/UNEP/UNESCO/IUCN effort to establish a network of representative protected samples of tropical forest ecosystems. International steps should include: elaborating a plan for launching activities, including the goals, scope and content of each activity; defining activities for the next five or 10 years; identifying national centres and institutions to participate in the activity; determining a network of participating regional and international centres and institutions; quantifying the activity (personnel, means and resources) and distributing responsibilities; and convening *ad hoc* working groups for carrying out these tasks in relation to proposals involving groups of related activities.

On 31 May 1982,[1] the UNEP Governing Council took note of the experts' recommendations and called on the Executive Director to consider using existing regional arrangements to further the programme. It requested him to transmit the recommendations to all Governments, multilateral agencies and other international and regional organizations, to consult with FAO, UNESCO and other agencies with a view to having the FAO Committee on Forest Development in the Tropics assume the role of continuing review of international activity on tropical forestry—a specific recommendation of the experts—and to report to the Council in 1983.

Decision (1982). [1]UNEP Council (report, A/37/25): 10/14, sect. II, 31 May.
Report. [2]UNEP Executive Director, UNEP/GC.10/5/Add.4.
Yearbook reference. [3]1977, p. 477.

Soil management

In 1982, an Expert Group Meeting on the Formulation of a Plan of Action to Implement the World Soils Policy (Geneva, 14-19 March) examined the recommendations of previous meetings on a World Soils Policy held in 1980[4] and 1981.[5] The Policy's objectives were to increase and apply knowledge, encourage and assist productivity, conservation and management improvements, reduce pollution and improve water and air quality, develop agricultural production systems, enlarge and improve arable land, slow the loss of agricultural and forest land, monitor changes in soil quality and quantity and land use, and create awareness of the extent of soil degradation. The Group recommended that the World Soils Policy be adopted. It finalized draft guidelines for formulating national policies, recommending their dissemination, and developed a plan of action to implement the Policy, singling out several specific activities for immediate action.

On 31 May,[1] the UNEP Governing Council endorsed the Policy and recommended that Governments, the United Nations system and other international organizations give effect to its objectives. The Executive Director was requested to transmit the draft plan of action for its implementation to FAO, UNESCO and other relevant organizations and to member Governments and multilateral assistance agencies for their comments and, in the light of those comments, to submit that plan, together with its financial implications, to the Council in 1983.

In its 20 December resolution[3] on international environmental co-operation, the General Assembly noted the Council's endorsement and invited Governments, the United Nations system and other international organizations to take into account the objectives of the World Soils Policy in formulating national policies and work programmes. This provision of the resolution had been amended and repositioned during informal discussions on the original draft, which did not specifically take note of the Council's endorsement.

The World Charter for Nature, adopted by the Assembly on 28 October,[2] proclaimed the principle that the productivity of soils was to be maintained or enhanced through measures safeguarding their long-term fertility and the process of organic decomposition, and preventing erosion and all other forms of degradation.

Decision (1982). [1]UNEP Council (report, A/37/25): 10/14, sect. III, 31 May.
Resolutions (1982). GA: [2]37/7, annex, para. 10 (b), 28 Oct.; [3]37/217, para. 6 (c), 20 Dec.
Yearbook references. [4]1980, p. 718; [5]1981, p. 831.

Freshwater ecosystems

On 31 May 1982,[1] the UNEP Governing Council urged the Executive Director to highlight environmental management for protecting and rehabilitating freshwater ecosystems in the activities identified in the 1984-1989 system-wide medium-term environment programme and requested him to ensure that Lake Managua (Nicaragua) was used as a case study for other developing countries affected by similar problems.

In accordance with the Council's decision, an international workshop on reclaiming and using Lake Managua was held (Managua, 29 November–2 December); it made recommendations for a pilot project for the Lake's reclamation.

Decision (1982). [1]UNEP Council (report, A/37/25): 10/19, 31 May.

Marine ecosystems

Protection of the marine environment

In a February 1982 report[4] to the UNEP Governing Council, the Executive Director summarized the comments he had received pursuant to a May 1981 Council request[7] for Governments' views on the conclusions of a study on offshore mining and drilling by the Working Group of Experts on Environmental Law. He reported that of 14 replies received, 11 supported the Group's conclusions while three did not comment on them.

In its 18 May 1982 resolution[6] on the state of the environment, adopted at its special session, the Governing Council identified the major environmental trends, potential problems and priorities for UNEP-co-ordinated action from

1982 to 1992. Trends and problems related to oceans were: increasing pollution from land-based sources and ships; pollution of estuaries and coastal waters; overfishing; and inappropriate exploitation of marine and coastal resources. Priorities for action were: development and application of methods for monitoring, assessing, reducing and preventing pollution of the seas and degradation of natural resources; programmes and conventions for protecting regional seas; plans for managing marine resources; development of mariculture and establishment of protected areas; and support for disaster mitigation.

On 31 May,[2] the Governing Council recorded its satisfaction at the results of the Third United Nations Conference on the Law of the Sea, specifically in respect of protecting and preserving the marine environment, as an essential contribution to the progressive development and codification of international environmental law. The Council adopted the decision on this topic by a roll-call vote, requested by Canada, of 45 to 1 (United States), with 5 abstentions.

On the same day,[1] the Council took note of the government views on the conclusions of the legal experts' study on offshore mining and drilling. It proposed that the General Assembly recommend: that States consider the guidelines contained therein when formulating national legislation or negotiating international agreements to prevent marine pollution caused by offshore mining and drilling; and that the Council submit in 1985 a progress report on the use made of the conclusions.

In its 20 December resolution[5] on international environmental co-operation, the Assembly also took note of the study's conclusions and the government views, and accepted the Governing Council's recommendations.

In a further 31 May decision,[3] on follow-up action to the 1981 *Ad Hoc* Meeting of Senior Government Officials Expert in Environmental Law[8], the Governing Council authorized the UNEP Executive Director to convene in 1983/1984, after preparation consultations with Governments and international agencies, meetings of government experts to consider guidelines or principles on, among other topics, marine pollution from land-based sources.

Decisions (1982). UNEP Council (report, A/37/25), 31 May: [1]10/14, sect. VI, paras. 5-7; [2]10/23; [3]10/24, para. 1 (*a*).
Report. [4]UNEP Executive Director, UNEP/GC.10/5.
Resolutions (1982). [5]GA: 37/217, para. 6 (*b*), 20 Dec.
[6]UNEP Council (report, A/37/25): I, sect. III, para. 2 (*b*), 18 May.
Yearbook references. 1981, [7]p. 832, [8]p. 839.

Regional programmes

The co-ordination of environmental activities under various regional action plans, involving 10 regions and over 120 coastal States, continued to be the responsibility of UNEP throughout 1982. Activities reported on under its regional seas programme included:

Caribbean. A regional convention and a protocol on co-operation in combating oil spills were negotiated, and several projects were initiated with the Food and Agriculture Organization of the United Nations (FAO), the International Maritime Organization (IMO) and the Caribbean Conservation Association.

East Africa. Elements of an action plan were drawn up through a workshop of regional experts; regional priorities were identified, including preparation of a regional convention and two protocols. Six reports of exploratory missions were prepared and a regional overview on protecting and developing the marine and coastal environment was published.

West and central Africa. Three major projects dealing with marine pollution, contingency planning for pollution emergencies, and coastal erosion were initiated with FAO, the International Atomic Energy Agency (IAEA), IMO, the Intergovernmental Oceanographic Commission (IOC), the United Nations Educational, Scientific and Cultural Organization (UNESCO), the United Nations Industrial Development Organization, the World Health Organization and the United Nations.

Kuwait Action Plan. UNEP continued to assist the Regional Organization for the Protection of the Marine Environment in implementing five major projects with FAO, UNESCO, IAEA, IOC and the International Union for the Conservation of Nature and Natural Resources.

Mediterranean. A long-term pollution monitoring and research programme was initiated; a co-ordinating unit was established at Athens, Greece; and a protocol on specially protected areas was adopted.

Red Sea and the Gulf of Aden. Support was given to marine pollution assessment activities through the Arab League Educational, Cultural and Scientific Organization. An action plan, convention and protocol were adopted in February.

South-east Pacific. A draft protocol and land-based sources of pollution were reviewed by a workshop of regional experts. A programme to monitor marine pollution from domestic, industrial and agricultural sources was prepared, as was a contingency plan to abate oil pollution in emergencies.

South-west Pacific. Several studies related to assessing the region's major environmental problems were initiated and a regional convention and two protocols were prepared.

In its 18 May resolution[7] on the state of the environment, adopted at its special session, the UNEP Governing Council, in reviewing major achievements and failures of environmental management in implementing the 1972 Action Plan for the Human Environment,[8] considered that the regional seas programme, covering environmental assessment, management, law and supporting measures, had been implemented satisfactorily but that sufficient resources, continued planning and sustained commitment were necessary to maintain and extend it.

In a 31 May decision[3] on the Environment Fund, the Governing Council approved continuation of two funds until 31 December 1983: the Trust Fund for the Protection of the Mediterranean Sea against Pollution and the Trust Fund for the Protection and Development of the Marine Environment and the Coastal Areas of Bahrain, Iran, Iraq, Kuwait, Oman, Qatar, Saudi Arabia and the United Arab Emirates.

A Meeting of Government Experts on Regional Marine Programmes (Nairobi, Kenya, 18-21 January)[4] made a number of recommendations to control land-based sources of marine pollution, which were contained in an April report[5] to the Governing Council. According to the experts, an approach should be adopted which evaluated and tried to resolve environmental problems generated by the use of marine and coastal resources. Other recommendations referred to: extending regional action plans, furthering environmental protection in national seas and establishing regional programmes; protecting, managing and developing the marine and coastal environment and coordinating national policy-making activities; strengthening United Nations technical and financial efforts in regional programmes; taking account, in establishing new regional agreements, of negotiations at the Third United Nations Conference on the Law of the Sea and existing conventions and instruments; basing international and regional efforts on full mobilization of national capabilities; developing technological means to meet requirements, and preparing and implementing management programmes, taking into account, in particular, the interests and capabilities of developing countries as well as education and training needs; continuing scientific and technical assistance to developing countries; UNEP providing a framework for consultation and co-operation among States and organizations and for information and experience exchanges; directing co-ordination towards promoting the synthesis of regional activities into the global picture; and the Governing Council ensuring adequate funding for ongoing and projected activities. A number of specific main areas of co-operation were identified.

The Governing Council endorsed the Meeting's recommendations on 31 May, when it adopted a decision[1] on programme matters.

Also on 31 May,[2] the Council urged States to adopt and ratify conventions and protocols for protecting and developing the regional marine environment and coastal areas, and invited them to contribute to regional action plans. It also urged Governments, the United Nations system and other organizations to support the countries concerned in their efforts to combat coastal erosion

and marine pollution, calling on the Executive Director to provide adequate funds to the regional seas programme. It also asked him to ascertain the views of States of the South Asia Co-operative Environment Programme on conducting a regional seas programme for that area.

In its 20 December resolution[6] on international environmental co-operation, the General Assembly took note of the Council's decision on expanding and implementing the regional seas programme.[2] This provision had been added to the resolution during informal discussions on the original draft.

Decisions (1982). UNEP Council (report, A/37/25), 31 May: [1]10/14, sect. V; [2]10/20; [3]10/27, para. 11.
Reports. [4]Meeting of Government Experts on Regional Marine Programmes, UNEP/WG.63/4; [5]UNEP Executive Director, UNEP/GC.10/5/Add.4.
Resolutions (1982). [6]GA: 37/217, para. 7, 20 Dec. [7]UNEP Council (report, A/37/25): I, sect. I, para. 3 *(b)* (viii), 18 May.
Yearbook reference. [8]1972, p. 322.

World Charter for Nature

Responding to an October 1981 General Assembly resolution,[5] the Secretary-General submitted to that body in September 1982 a report, with a later addendum,[3] containing the views of 15 States on a draft World Charter for Nature, aimed at protecting animals and plants and their environment. The report supplemented a 1981 report[6] also containing States' comments on the draft Charter and on a report by the *Ad Hoc* Group of Experts on the Draft World Charter for Nature, which in 1981 had put forward a draft text.

After the additional responses of States had been analysed by UNEP and further changes suggested, the Secretary-General recommended that the Assembly give favourable consideration to the revised draft.

General Assembly action. On 28 October 1982,[4] the General Assembly adopted the World Charter for Nature, which contained a preamble and sections on general principles, functions and implementation, and proclaimed the principles of conservation by which all human conduct affecting nature was to be guided and judged.

By the preamble, the Assembly expressed conviction of the need for measures at all levels to protect nature and promote international co-operation in that field. It stated the general principles that nature was to be respected and its essential processes were not to be impaired. The Assembly set out principles to be taken into account for decision-making and planning, and rules for the use of natural resources, and specified activities having an impact on nature that were to be controlled. The Charter's principles were to be reflected in both State and international law; further modalities for its implementation were also set out.

The resolution annexing the Charter was adopted by a recorded vote of 111 to 1, with 18 abstentions. The 36-nation draft was introduced by Zaire. Prior to the resolution's adoption, the Assembly rejected, by a recorded vote of 73 to 36, with 12 abstentions, a motion by the United States to postpone a vote on it.

Several States spoke in explanation of vote. The United States, voting against, said that more precision in the language of the Charter should have been aimed at, and cited paragraph 13 as an example, submitting that neither the United Nations nor man could prevent natural disasters; it also objected to the Charter's purporting to create obligations for individuals, as stated in paragraph 24.

Argentina said it had abstained because the text touched on subjects dealt with more specifically in existing instruments or falling within the purview of different United Nations organs, and it did not distinguish between the environmental problems of developed and developing countries. Brazil, explaining the abstentions also of Bolivia, Colombia, Ecuador, Guyana, Peru, Suriname and Venezuela, said that those countries found it difficult to understand why the Charter's drafting was done outside an intergovernmental process; the Amazonian countries considered the text non-mandatory and would treat it merely as a general indication of intentions which they might take into account if such guidelines were in conformity with national legislation and accepted international obligations.

Canada said that, although it had voted in favour, it would have preferred a number of stylistic changes to the text to reflect its aspirational character more clearly: the verb "shall", appearing in most paragraphs, could have been replaced by "shall endeavour to" or "should". Japan had reservations on the preamble, part of which it felt had no direct bearing on protecting nature, and on the reference to forsaking war and armaments which it believed should have referred to mankind forsaking war only. India felt that some of the provisions were unrealistic and would have preferred more consultations.

Two letters on the topic were received by the President of the Assembly. By the first, a right of reply dated 29 October,[2] Zaire said that Brazil had demonstrated open hostility towards any international instrument aspiring to govern activities involving environmental protection, nature conservation and maintaining the equilibrium of ecosystems, or any proposal for international co-operation on managing nature and resources shared by two or more countries. In a 9 November letter,[1] Bolivia, Brazil, Colombia, Ecuador, Guyana, Peru, Suriname and Venezuela stressed that Brazil's statement was the collective view of the eight Amazonian countries which translated

their responsibilities towards the world's largest single natural ecosystem into the Treaty for Amazonian Co-operation; suggestions offered to facilitate a consensus on the Charter had been ignored, they said.

Letters. [1]Bolivia, Brazil, Colombia, Ecuador, Guyana, Peru, Suriname, Venezuela, 9 Nov., A/37/610; [2]Zaire, 29 Oct., A/37/585.
Report. [3]S-G, A/37/398 & Add.1.
Resolution (1982). [4]GA: 37/7, 28 Oct., text following.
Resolution (prior). [5]GA: 36/6, 27 Oct. 1981 (YUN 1981, p. 835).
Yearbook reference. [6]1981, p. 834.
Meeting record. GA: A/37/PV.48 (28 Oct.).

General Assembly resolution 37/7

28 October 1982   Meeting 48   111-1-18 (recorded vote)

36-nation draft (A/37/L.4 and Add.1); agenda item 21.
Sponsors: Belgium, Benin, Burundi, Cape Verde, Central African Republic, Chad, Comoros, Costa Rica, Djibouti, Egypt, Equatorial Guinea, Gabon, Gambia, Guinea, Guinea-Bissau, Haiti, Ivory Coast, Kenya, Mali, Malta, Mauritania, Morocco, Mozambique, Niger, Pakistan, Rwanda, Senegal, Singapore, Somalia, Swaziland, Thailand, Togo, United Republic of Cameroon, Upper Volta, Yugoslavia, Zaire.

World Charter for Nature

The General Assembly,

Having considered the report of the Secretary-General on the revised draft World Charter for Nature,

Recalling that, in its resolution 35/7 of 30 October 1980, it expressed its conviction that the benefits which could be obtained from nature depended on the maintenance of natural processes and on the diversity of life forms and that those benefits were jeopardized by the excessive exploitation and the destruction of natural habitats,

Further recalling that, in the same resolution, it recognized the need for appropriate measures at the national and international levels to protect nature and promote international co-operation in that field,

Recalling that, in its resolution 36/6 of 27 October 1981, it again expressed its awareness of the crucial importance attached by the international community to the promotion and development of co-operation aimed at protecting and safeguarding the balance and quality of nature and invited the Secretary-General to transmit to Member States the text of the revised version of the draft World Charter for Nature contained in the report of the *Ad Hoc* Group of Experts on the Draft World Charter for Nature, as well as any further observations by States, with a view to appropriate consideration by the General Assembly at its thirty-seventh session,

Conscious of the spirit and terms of its resolutions 35/7 and 36/6, in which it solemnly invited Member States, in the exercise of their permanent sovereignty over their natural resources, to conduct their activities in recognition of the supreme importance of protecting natural systems, maintaining the balance and quality of nature and conserving natural resources, in the interests of present and future generations,

Having considered the supplementary report of the Secretary-General,

Expressing its gratitude to the *Ad Hoc* Group of Experts which, through its work, has assembled the necessary elements for the General Assembly to be able to complete the consideration of and adopt the revised draft World Charter for Nature at its thirty-seventh session, as it had previously recommended,

Adopts and solemnly proclaims the World Charter for Nature contained in the annex to the present resolution.

ANNEX
World Charter for Nature

The General Assembly,

Reaffirming the fundamental purposes of the United Nations, in particular the maintenance of international peace and security, the development of friendly relations among nations and the achievement of international co-operation in solving international problems of an economic, social, cultural, technical, intellectual or humanitarian character,

Aware that:

(a) Mankind is a part of nature and life depends on the uninterrupted functioning of natural systems which ensure the supply of energy and nutrients,

(b) Civilization is rooted in nature, which has shaped human culture and influenced all artistic and scientific achievement, and living in harmony with nature gives man the best opportunities for the development of his creativity, and for rest and recreation,

Convinced that:

(a) Every form of life is unique, warranting respect regardless of its worth to man, and, to accord other organisms such recognition, man must be guided by a moral code of action,

(b) Man can alter nature and exhaust natural resources by his action or its consequences and, therefore, must fully recognize the urgency of maintaining the stability and quality of nature and of conserving natural resources,

Persuaded that:

(a) Lasting benefits from nature depend upon the maintenance of essential ecological processes and life support systems, and upon the diversity of life forms, which are jeopardized through excessive exploitation and habitat destruction by man,

(b) The degradation of natural systems owing to excessive consumption and misuse of natural resources, as well as to failure to establish an appropriate economic order among peoples and among States, leads to the breakdown of the economic, social and political framework of civilization,

(c) Competition for scarce resources creates conflicts, whereas the conservation of nature and natural resources contributes to justice and the maintenance of peace and cannot be achieved until mankind learns to live in peace and to forsake war and armaments.

Reaffirming that man must acquire the knowledge to maintain and enhance his ability to use natural resources in a manner which ensures the preservation of the species and ecosystems for the benefit of present and future generations,

Firmly convinced of the need for appropriate measures, at the national and international, individual and collective, and private and public levels, to protect nature and promote international co-operation in this field,

Adopts, to these ends, the present World Charter for Nature, which proclaims the following principles of conservation by which all human conduct affecting nature is to be guided and judged.

I. General principles

1. Nature shall be respected and its essential processes shall not be impaired.

2. The genetic viability on the earth shall not be compromised; the population levels of all life forms, wild and domesticated, must be at least sufficient for their survival, and to this end necessary habitats shall be safeguarded.

3. All areas of the earth, both land and sea, shall be subject to these principles of conservation; special protection shall be given to unique areas, to representative samples of all the different types of ecosystems and to the habitats of rare or endangered species.

4. Ecosystems and organisms, as well as the land, marine and atmospheric resources that are utilized by man, shall be managed to achieve and maintain optimum sustainable productivity, but not in such a way as to endanger the integrity of those other ecosystems or species with which they coexist.

5. Nature shall be secured against degradation caused by warfare or other hostile activities.

II. Functions

6. In the decision-making process it shall be recognized that man's needs can be met only by ensuring the proper functioning of natural systems and by respecting the principles set forth in the present Charter.

7. In the planning and implementation of social and economic development activities, due account shall be taken of the fact that the conservation of nature is an integral part of those activities.

8. In formulating long-term plans for economic development, population growth and the improvement of standards of living, due account shall be taken of the long-term capacity of natural systems to ensure the subsistence and settlement of the populations concerned, recognizing that this capacity may be enhanced through science and technology.

9. The allocation of areas of the earth to various uses shall be planned and due account shall be taken of the physical constraints, the biological productivity and diversity and the natural beauty of the areas concerned.

10. Natural resources shall not be wasted, but used with a restraint appropriate to the principles set forth in the present Charter, in accordance with the following rules:

(a) Living resources shall not be utilized in excess of their natural capacity for regeneration;

(b) The productivity of soils shall be maintained or enhanced through measures which safeguard their long-term fertility and the process of organic decomposition, and prevent erosion and all other forms of degradation;

(c) Resources, including water, which are not consumed as they are used shall be reused or recycled;

(d) Non-renewable resources which are consumed as they are used shall be exploited with restraint, taking into account their abundance, the rational possibilities of converting them for consumption, and the compatibility of their exploitation with the functioning of natural systems.

11. Activities which might have an impact on nature shall be controlled, and the best available technologies that minimize significant risks to nature or other adverse effects shall be used; in particular:

(a) Activities which are likely to cause irreversible damage to nature shall be avoided;

(b) Activities which are likely to pose a significant risk to nature shall be preceded by an exhaustive examination; their proponents shall demonstrate that expected benefits outweigh potential damage to nature, and where potential adverse effects are not fully understood, the activities should not proceed;

(c) Activities which may disturb nature shall be preceded by assessment of their consequences, and environmental impact studies of development projects shall be conducted sufficiently in advance, and if they are to be undertaken, such activities shall be planned and carried out so as to minimize potential adverse effects;

(d) Agriculture, grazing, forestry and fisheries practices shall be adapted to the natural characteristics and constraints of given areas;

(e) Areas degraded by human activities shall be rehabilitated for purposes in accord with their natural potential and compatible with the well-being of affected populations.

12. Discharge of pollutants into natural systems shall be avoided and:

(a) Where this is not feasible, such pollutants shall be treated at the source, using the best practicable means available;

(b) Special precautions shall be taken to prevent discharge of radioactive or toxic wastes.

13. Measures intended to prevent, control or limit natural disasters, infestations and diseases shall be specifically directed to the causes of these scourges and shall avoid adverse side-effects on nature.

III. Implementation

14. The principles set forth in the present Charter shall be reflected in the law and practice of each State, as well as at the international level.

15. Knowledge of nature shall be broadly disseminated by all possible means, particularly by ecological education as an integral part of general education.

16. All planning shall include, among its essential elements, the formulation of strategies for the conservation of nature, the establishment of inventories of ecosystems and assessments of the effects on nature of proposed policies and activities; all of these elements shall be disclosed to the public by appropriate means in time to permit effective consultation and participation.

17. Funds, programmes and administrative structures necessary to achieve the objective of the conservation of nature shall be provided.

18. Constant efforts shall be made to increase knowledge of nature by scientific research and to disseminate such knowledge unimpeded by restrictions of any kind.

19. The status of natural processes, ecosystems and species shall be closely monitored to enable early detection of degradation or threat, ensure timely intervention and facilitate the evaluation of conservation policies and methods.

20. Military activities damaging to nature shall be avoided.

21. States and, to the extent they are able, other public authorities, international organizations, individuals, groups and corporations shall:

(a) Co-operate in the task of conserving nature through common activities and other relevant actions, including information exchange and consultations;

(b) Establish standards for products and manufacturing processes that may have adverse effects on nature, as well as agreed methodologies for assessing these effects;

(c) Implement the applicable international legal provisions for the conservation of nature and the protection of the environment;

(d) Ensure that activities within their jurisdictions or control do not cause damage to the natural systems located within other States or in the areas beyond the limits of national jurisdiction;

(e) Safeguard and conserve nature in areas beyond national jurisdiction.

22. Taking fully into account the sovereignty of States over their natural resources, each State shall give effect to the provisions of the present Charter through its competent organs and in co-operation with other States.

23. All persons, in accordance with their national legislation, shall have the opportunity to participate, individually or with others, in the formulation of decisions of direct concern to their environment, and shall have access to means of redress when their environment has suffered damage or degradation.

24. Each person has a duty to act in accordance with the provisions of the present Charter; acting individually, in association with others or through participation in the political process, each person shall strive to ensure that the objectives and requirements of the present Charter are met.

Recorded vote in Assembly as follows:

In favour: Afghanistan, Angola, Australia, Austria, Bahrain, Bangladesh, Barbados, Belgium, Benin, Bulgaria, Burundi, Byelorussian SSR, Canada, Cape Verde, Central African Republic, Chad, China, Comoros, Congo, Costa Rica, Cuba, Cyprus, Czechoslovakia, Democratic Kampuchea, Denmark, Djibouti, Egypt, El Salvador, Equatorial Guinea, Ethiopia, Finland, France, Gabon, Gambia, German Democratic Republic, Germany, Federal Republic of, Greece, Guinea, Guinea-Bissau, Honduras, Hungary, Iceland, India, Indonesia, Iran, Iraq, Ireland, Italy, Ivory Coast, Jamaica, Japan, Kenya, Kuwait, Lao People's Democratic Republic, Libyan Arab Jamahiriya, Luxembourg, Madagascar, Malawi, Malaysia, Maldives, Mali, Malta, Mauritania, Mongolia, Morocco, Mozambique, Nepal, Netherlands, New Zealand, Nicaragua, Niger, Nigeria, Norway, Oman, Pakistan, Papua New Guinea, Poland, Portugal, Qatar, Romania, Rwanda, Samoa, Sao Tome and Principe, Saudi Arabia, Senegal, Seychelles, Singapore, Solomon Islands, Somalia, Spain, Sri Lanka, Sudan, Swaziland, Sweden, Thailand, Togo, Tunisia, Turkey, Uganda, Ukrainian SSR, USSR, United Arab Emirates, United Kingdom, United Republic of Cameroon, United Republic of Tanzania, Upper Volta, Uruguay, Yemen, Yugoslavia, Zaire, Zambia.

Against: United States.

Abstaining: Algeria, Argentina, Bolivia, Brazil, Chile, Colombia, Dominican Republic, Ecuador, Ghana, Guyana, Lebanon, Mexico,[a] Paraguay, Peru, Philippines, Suriname, Trinidad and Tobago, Venezuela.

[a]Later advised the Secretariat it had intended to vote in favour.

Environmental aspects of the arms race

In its 18 May 1982 resolution[3] on the state of the environment, adopted at its special session, the UNEP Governing Council identified, among new perceptions of environmental issues which had evolved from 1972 to 1982, the issues of disarmament and security. The Council also listed, among trends and problems concerning peace, security and the environment during 1982-1992, the continuing increase in the production, stockpiling and risk of use of weapons of mass destruction and the development of new types of chemical and bacteriological weapons, which not only threatened life on earth, but also competed for limited resources. The Council identified as a priority for action by the United Nations system, specifically through UNEP-co-ordinated activities, support of the continuing efforts in the General Assembly to ensure that environmental implications of existing and new types of armaments and warfare were taken into account.

Also on 18 May, the Governing Council adopted a resolution[4] on arms and the environment, appealing to Governments and the world community as a whole to do the utmost to halt the arms race and thereby prevent a major threat to the environment. The Secretary-General was requested to bring the appeal to the attention of the Assembly at its special session on disarmament. The resolution was adopted by 56 votes to 4, with 15 abstentions.

At Geneva, a High-Level Expert Group Meeting on the Historical Responsibility of States for the Preservation of the Environment for Present and Future Generations reviewed government responses to a letter sent in 1981 by the Executive Director of UNEP, pursuant to a 1980 Assembly resolution[5] on possible measures to be taken at the international level for the protection of nature. The Group also discussed the environmental impact of arms production. Among their conclusions[1] were: statements that money spent on, and scientific and intellectual efforts diverted to, the military wasted limited resources; negative environmental consequences could be expected from probable future increases in military budgets because of increased demand on limited natural resources; the unproductive and often destructive military use of land and resources could not be afforded; nuclear-weapon tests in—or which vent radioactivity into—the atmosphere were of particular concern; military research into biological agents carried great potential for accidents; knowledge (which should be expanded) of the interaction between environment and development indicated risks of long-term effects jeopardizing the resource base for development; and use of space for military purposes carried great potential for environmental destruction, as did pollution of space by satellite debris.

The World Charter for Nature, adopted by the General Assembly on 28 October,[2] also proclaimed the principle that military activities damaging to nature were to be avoided.

Report. [1]S-G, A/S-12/9.
Resolutions (1982). [2]GA: 37/7, annex, para. 20, 28 Oct. UNEP Council (report, A/37/25), 18 May: [3]I, sect. II, para. 1 *(a)*, & sect. III, para. 2 *(j)*; [4]III.
Resolution (prior). [5]GA: 35/8, 30 Oct. 1980 (YUN 1980. p. 725).

Material remnants of war

On 28 May 1982, the UNEP Governing Council adopted a decision,[1] by a roll-call vote of 36 to 9 (Belgium, Canada, France, Federal Republic of Germany, Netherlands, New Zealand, Spain, United Kingdom, United States), with 6 abstentions, on the problem of the remnants of war. The Council was convinced that responsibility for eliminating the remnants of aggressive and colonial wars, and its costs, should be borne by countries that planted them. It called on the Executive Director to use his good offices with the responsible States in order to supply affected countries with information and maps for locating the remnants, and to conduct bilateral negotiations with affected States to solve the problem. The Council appealed to all States, particularly those responsible for remnants in developing countries, to co-operate with the Executive Director, and requested him to submit to the Secretary-General all relevant information received with a view to finding ways of solving the problem, including the possible holding of a United Nations conference, and to report on the matter in 1983.

Responding to a 1981 General Assembly request[4] to collate information received from States on the topic, the Secretary-General in a September 1982 report[2] stated that of 33 replies received, only 18 contained substantive comments. Of those, seven were from Governments which had submitted the same or similar comments included in a previous report.[5] The report concluded that: more time might be required for a more representative sample of opinions; the main divergences of opinion seemed to relate to United Nations involvement and to steps being taken to solve the problem; and the Assembly might wish to defer consideration pending additional responses.

General Assembly action. On 20 December, the General Assembly adopted a resolution[3] on the remnants of war, taking note of the report and regretting that no real measures had been taken to solve the problem. It reiterated its support of the just demands of affected States for compensation and appealed to all States, particularly those responsible for the presence of war remnants, to co-operate with the Secretary-General in solving the problem. He was requested, in co-operation with the UNEP Executive Director, to prepare a study on the problem, particularly mines, analysing: the economic and environmental problems of affected developing countries; the loss of life and property suffered, the affected States' specific demands and the extent to which responsible States were willing to compensate and assist them; the problem's legal status; the international co-operation required for a solution; and the United Nations role, including the possibility of a conference.

The resolution was adopted by a recorded vote of 125 to none, with 25 abstentions. On 19 November, the Second (Economic and Financial) Committee approved the 19-nation draft, also by a recorded vote, of 109 to none, with 25 abstentions. It was introduced by the Libyan Arab Jamahiriya.

A United States oral amendment, to have the Assembly authorize the activities approved under the resolution only to the extent that they could be financed without exceeding resources approved in the 1982-1983 programme budget, was rejected in Committee by 83 votes to 30, with 16 abstentions.

Decision (1982). [1]UNEP Council (report, A/37/25): 10/8, 28 May.
Report. [2]S-G, A/37/415.

Resolution (1982). [3]GA: 37/215, 20 Dec., text following.
Resolution (prior). [4]GA: 36/188, 17 Dec. 1981 (YUN 1981, p. 837).
Yearbook reference. [5]1981, p. 836.
Financial implications. 5th Committee report, A/37/740; S-G statements, A/C.2/37/L.64, A/C.5/37/52.
Meeting records. GA: 2nd Committee, A/C.2/37/SR.3, 5-8, 20-26, 33, *37*, 40, *41, 42* (28 Sep.–19 Nov.); 5th Committee, A/C.5/37/SR.45 (26 Nov.); plenary, A/37/PV.113 (20 Dec.).

General Assembly resolution 37/215

20 December 1982   Meeting 113   125-0-25 (recorded vote)

Approved by Second Committee (A/37/680/Add.8) by recorded vote (109-0-25), 19 November (meeting 41); 19-nation draft (A/C.2/37/L.25); agenda item 71 (i).

Sponsors: Afghanistan, Algeria, Cuba, Democratic Yemen, Ethiopia, Kuwait, Libyan Arab Jamahiriya, Madagascar, Maldives, Malta, Nicaragua, Oman, Qatar, Saudi Arabia, Syrian Arab Republic, Tunisia, United Arab Emirates, Viet Nam, Yemen.

Remnants of war

The General Assembly,

Recalling its resolutions 3435(XXX) of 9 December 1975, 35/71 of 5 December 1980 and 36/188 of 17 December 1981 concerning the problem of remnants of war,

Recalling also decisions 80(IV) of 9 April 1976, 101(V) of 25 May 1977, 9/5 of 25 May 1981 and 10/8 of 28 May 1982, of the Governing Council of the United Nations Environment Programme,

Recalling further resolution 32 of the Fifth Conference of Heads of State or Government of Non-Aligned Countries, held at Colombo from 16 to 19 August 1976, and resolution 26/11-P of the Eleventh Islamic Conference of Foreign Ministers, held at Islamabad from 17 to 22 May 1980,

Convinced that the responsibility for the removal of the remnants of war should be borne by the countries that planted them,

Recognizing that the presence of the material remnants of war, particularly mines, on the lands of developing countries seriously impedes their development efforts and causes loss of life and property,

1. *Takes note* of the report of the Secretary-General on the problem of remnants of war;

2. *Regrets* that no real measures have been taken to solve the problem of remnants of war despite the various resolutions and decisions adopted thereon by the General Assembly and the Governing Council of the United Nations Environment Programme;

3. *Reiterates its support* of the just demands of the States affected by the implantation of mines and the presence of other remnants of war on their lands for compensation from the States responsible for those remnants;

4. *Requests* the Secretary-General, in co-operation with the Executive Director of the United Nations Environment Programme, to prepare a factual study on the problem of remnants of war, particularly mines, which would include an analysis of the following aspects:

(a) The economic and environmental problems experienced by developing countries affected by remnants of war, the loss of life and property they have suffered, their specific demands in this respect and the extent to which the responsible States are willing to compensate the affected States and to assist them in solving the problem;

(b) The legal status of the problem;

(c) The international co-operation required to solve the problem;

(d) The role of the United Nations in this regard, including the possibility of convening a conference pursuant to General Assembly resolutions 35/71 and 36/188;

5. *Appeals* to all States, particularly those responsible for the presence of remnants of war, to co-operate with the Secretary-General in order to enable him to prepare the study requested in paragraph 4 above and to make specific and effective recommendations for solving the problem of remnants of war;

6. *Requests* the Secretary-General, in co-operation with the Executive Director of the United Nations Environment Programme, to submit the study in time for consideration by the General Assembly at its thirty-eighth session.

Recorded vote in Assembly as follows:

In favour: Afghanistan, Albania, Algeria, Angola, Antigua and Barbuda, Argentina, Bahamas, Bahrain, Bangladesh, Barbados, Benin, Bhutan, Bolivia, Botswana, Brazil, Bulgaria, Burma, Burundi, Byelorussian SSR,

Cape Verde, Central African Republic, Chad, Chile, China, Colombia, Comoros, Congo, Costa Rica, Cuba, Cyprus, Czechoslovakia, Democratic Kampuchea, Democratic Yemen, Djibouti, Dominican Republic, Ecuador, Egypt, El Salvador, Equatorial Guinea, Ethiopia, Fiji, Gabon, Gambia, German Democratic Republic, Ghana, Grenada, Guatemala, Guinea, Guinea-Bissau, Guyana, Haiti, Honduras, Hungary, India, Indonesia, Iran, Iraq, Jamaica, Jordan, Kenya, Kuwait, Lao People's Democratic Republic, Lebanon, Lesotho, Liberia, Libyan Arab Jamahiriya, Madagascar, Malawi, Malaysia, Maldives, Mali, Malta, Mauritania, Mauritius, Mexico, Mongolia, Mozambique, Nepal, Nicaragua, Niger, Nigeria, Oman, Pakistan, Panama, Papua New Guinea, Paraguay, Peru, Philippines, Poland, Qatar, Romania, Rwanda, Saint Lucia, Saint Vincent and the Grenadines, Samoa, Sao Tome and Principe, Saudi Arabia, Sierra Leone, Somalia, Sri Lanka, Sudan, Suriname, Swaziland, Syrian Arab Republic, Thailand, Togo, Trinidad and Tobago, Tunisia, Turkey, Uganda, Ukrainian SSR, USSR, United Arab Emirates, United Republic of Cameroon, United Republic of Tanzania, Upper Volta, Uruguay, Vanuatu, Venezuela, Viet Nam, Yemen, Yugoslavia, Zaire, Zambia, Zimbabwe.

Against: None.

Abstaining: Australia, Austria, Belgium, Canada, Denmark, Finland, France, Germany, Federal Republic of, Greece, Iceland, Ireland, Italy, Ivory Coast, Japan, Luxembourg, Morocco, Netherlands, New Zealand, Norway, Portugal, Senegal, Spain, Sweden, United Kingdom, United States.

Environmental aspects of *apartheid*

During 1982, while the major organs of the United Nations continued to be concerned with the political aspects of South Africa's policy of *apartheid* (See POLITICAL AND SECURITY QUESTIONS, Chapter V), the UNEP Governing Council examined the impact of that system on the environment. On 28 May, it adopted a decision[1] on the topic by a roll-call vote of 40 to 11 (Belgium, Canada, France, Federal Republic of Germany, Iceland, Netherlands, New Zealand, Spain, Switzerland, United Kingdom, United States), with 2 abstentions. The Council thereby reaffirmed its solidarity with the victims of *apartheid* and its condemnation of that system, and requested the Executive Director to continue monitoring *apartheid*'s environmental impact and reporting to the Council; while giving widest circulation to his reports, so as to promote public awareness of the plight of *apartheid* victims.

In its 20 December resolution[2] on international environmental co-operation, the General Assembly took note of the Governing Council's decision. This text—a shortened version of the original which had repeated provisions of the Council's decision on circulating the reports and promoting public awareness—was agreed on during informal discussions.

Decision (1982). [1]UNEP Council (report, A/37/25): 10/7, 28 May.
Resolution (1982). [2]GA: 37/217, para. 8, 20 Dec.

Environment and development

By a 31 May 1982 decision[1] on environment and development, the UNEP Governing Council requested the Executive Director to identify: areas where an exchange of experience among developing countries could be fruitful for environmentally sound development; and expertise and institutions in developing countries which could help or co-operate with others to integrate environmental considerations into development programmes and projects. It also requested him to provide financial support for this purpose, including funds from relevant components of the Environment Fund and additional resources decided upon during its current session in a decision dealing with serious environmental problems in developing countries. The Council called on Governments and international organizations to consider using these funding arrangements in operating technical and financial aid programmes.

Also on 31 May,[2] the Council requested the Executive Director to follow up on the implementation of recommendations in a consultant's report on a Kenyan Government/UNEP/United Nations Development Programme project on environment and development and their application to countries with similar conditions, and to secure the support of other United Nations organs in that respect.

A thematic joint programming meeting on environment and development was held at New York on 29 and 30 September to examine the interest in this programme by various organizations active in development issues. An ensuing proposed programme covered: analysis of the relationship between people, resources, environment and development; refinement of environmental management methods and techniques, public policies and institutional arrangements needed to promote environmentally sound development; and a wide range of technical assistance measures.

The Economic and Social Council took note with satisfaction of the Governing Council's decision on environment and development, particularly its emphasis on technical co-operation among developing countries, in adopting its 29 July resolution on international environmental co-operation.[3]

The General Assembly, in its 20 December resolution on the same subject,[4] also welcomed the UNEP Council's decision.

Decisions (1982). UNEP Council (report, A/37/25), 31 May: [1]10/4; [2]10/14, sect. IV.
Resolutions (1982). [3]ESC: 1982/56, para. 2, 29 July. [4]GA: 37/217, para. 3, 20 Dec.

Environment and industry

In its 18 May 1982 resolution[2] on the state of the environment, adopted at its special session, the UNEP Governing Council, in reviewing major achievements and failures of environmental management in implementing the 1972 Action Plan for the Human Environment,[3] felt that industry had reduced its adverse effects on the environment but environmental controls in many countries were still very weak, and industry still needed to assume fully a role commensurate with its capabilities. The United Nations had identified the environmental impact of a number of industries, and guidelines were being tested and applied; training programmes had been provided and a supportive information service was operative.

Trends and problems identified were: the risks of pollution and natural resource degradation from inappropriate industrial development; inefficiency in the use of natural resources and energy; and inadequate environmental considerations in the siting and technologies of activities and in international trade and investment. Priorities for action were considered to be developing guidelines for: the assessment of the impact of industrial development; the improvement of the human environment and the rational use of natural resources; the environmental management of industry for the transport, handling and disposal of toxic and dangerous waste; and the promotion of environmentally sound practices in international trade and investment. Other priorities were the integration of environmental considerations in the development process and improving access to technical achievements practical for managing the environment.

In his 1982 annual report,[1] the Executive Director of the United Nations Industrial Development Organization (UNIDO) reported that, under the environment and industry programme, a UNIDO/Hungary Joint Programme for Cooperation in Industrialization of Construction and its Environmental and Energy Implications had been established. As in previous years, the UNIDO industrial studies programme included work on environmental protection during the process of industrial development and on industrial water use and treatment practices. Among publications issued was one on environmental protection within the context of the work of UNIDO. Work was also under way on studying the environmental aspects of the wood and wood-processing industry, and a paper on water use and treatment practices was presented to the First International Symposium on Environmental Technology for Developing Countries (Istanbul, Turkey, July).

Report. [1]UNIDO Executive Director, ID/B/300.
Resolution (1982). [2]UNEP Council (report, A/37/25): I, sect. I, para. 3 (b) (ix) & (x), & sect. III, para. 2 (i), 18 May.
Yearbook reference. [3]1972, p. 322.

Shared natural resources

Responding to a May 1981 UNEP Governing Council request,[8] the Executive Director submitted a report—summarized in a Council report transmitted to the General Assembly in September 1982 by a note of the Secretary-General[2]—dealing with progress made in applying a 1979 Assembly resolution[6] on natural resources shared by two or more States. The Executive Director stated that the tenor of the 27 responses he had received on the topic indicated that progress was being made in applying the resolution, by which States had been requested to use, in formulating conventions, a set of 15 draft principles drawn up by a UNEP working group of experts for the guidance of States in conserving and utilizing shared natural resources.

In its 18 May 1982 resolution[5] on the state of the environment, adopted at its special session, the UNEP Governing Council, in reviewing major achievements and failures in the area of environmental management in implementing the 1972 Action Plan for the Human Environment,[7] pointed out that the draft principles had not been widely used by Governments.

On 31 May,[1] at its tenth session, the Governing Council recommended that the Assembly reiterate the terms of its 1979 resolution, including the requests to all States to use the principles as guidelines and recommendations in formulating agreements on shared natural resources.

In its 29 July resolution[3] on international environmental co-operation, the Economic and Social Council endorsed the Governing Council's recommendation and transmitted the Executive Director's report to the Assembly.

The Assembly, in its 20 December resolution[4] on the same subject, reiterated the terms of its 1979 resolution and requested the UNEP Council to submit a further progress report in 1985 on its implementation. This text was agreed on during informal discussions on the original draft, whose wording had followed more fully the UNEP Council's wording.

Decision (1982). [1]UNEP Council (report, A/37/25): 10/14, sect. VI, paras. 1-3, 31 May.
Report. [2]UNEP Council, transmitted by S-G note, A/37/396 & Corr.1.
Resolutions (1982). [3]ESC: 1982/56, para. 5, 29 July. [4]GA: 37/217, para. 6 (a), 20 Dec. [5]UNEP Council (report, A/37/25): I, sect. I, para. 3 (b) (xi), 18 May.
Resolution (prior). [6]GA: 34/186, 18 Dec. 1979 (YUN 1979, p. 697).
Yearbook references. [7]1972, p. 322; [8]1981, p. 839.

Environment and aging persons

The World Assembly on Aging (Vienna, Austria, 26 July–6 August 1982) recommended:[1] that urban rebuilding and development planning and law pay special attention to the problems of the aging and assist in their social integration; that Governments be encouraged to adopt housing policies taking account of the needs of the elderly and socially disadvantaged, and that a living environment to support them should be an integral part of guidelines for human settlements policies; that special attention be paid to environmental problems and to designing a living environment that would take into account the functional capacity of the elderly, provide adequate transport, and enable them to continue to live in locations familiar to them; and that the aging be involved in housing policies and programmes for the elderly.

Report. [1]World Assembly on Aging, A/CONF.113/31.

Environmental law

In a 31 May 1982 decision[1] on environmental law, the UNEP Governing Council made recommendations concerning the use of guidelines for conventions on natural resources shared by two or more States and on mining and drilling pollution of the marine environment, and took note of a report of the Executive Director on international conventions and protocols in the environment field. Other decisions on the topic are discussed below.

Decision (1982). [1]UNEP Council (report, A/37/25): 10/14, sect. VI, 31 May.

Recommendations of the 1981
Meeting on environmental law

In October/November 1981, the *Ad Hoc* Meeting of Senior Government Officials Expert in Environmental Law had outlined a draft programme for the development and periodic review of environmental law and adopted conclusions and recommendations for developing and acting on the guidelines.

On 31 May 1982,[1] the UNEP Governing Council adopted the experts' programme and endorsed their conclusions and recommendations, as contained in a December 1981 report.[4] It requested the Executive Director, in consultation with Governments and international organizations concerned, to take steps to implement the recommendations and to promote implementation of and provide resources for implementing the programme, within the 1984-1989 system-wide medium-term environment programme. The Council called on Governments and international organizations to pay particular attention, in the progressive development and application of environmental law, to the cultural heritage of developing countries and their requirements for technical co-operation and other assistance. It further called on United Nations bodies and other intergovernmental organizations, as well as nongovernmental organizations active in environmental law, to co-operate with UNEP in implementing the programme and requested the Executive Director to report to the Council in 1983.

Also on 31 May,[2] acting on other recommendations of the *Ad Hoc* Meeting, the Council authorized the Executive Director to convene in 1983/1984, after preparatory consultations with Governments and international agencies, meetings of government experts to consider guidelines or principles on marine pollution from land-based sources, and environmentally sound transport, handling (including storage) and disposal of toxic and dangerous wastes; and the exchange of information relating to trade in and use and handling of potentially harmful chemicals, particularly pesticides. The Executive Director was to report to the Council on the results.

On the same day, the Council decided to consider in 1983 the mandate, future work programme and composition of the UNEP Working Group of Experts on Environmental Law.

In its 29 July resolution[3] on international environmental co-operation, the Economic and Social Council welcomed the UNEP Council's adoption of the programme for the development and periodic review of environmental law, expressing the hope that it would be implemented in a manner commensurate with its importance, and echoed the call on Governments and other bodies to co-operate with UNEP in implementing the programme.

This paragraph of the resolution was agreed on after informal consultations on the original draft, which would have had the Council urge, rather than call on, Governments and other bodies to co-operate with UNEP and contribute to initiatives and other measures aimed at the programme's early implementation.

Decisions (1982). UNEP Council (report, A/37/25), 31 May: [1]10/21, [2]10/24.
Resolution (1982). [3]ESC: 1982/56, para. 4, 29 July.
Yearbook reference. [4]1981, p. 840.

Role of the Group of Experts

On 31 May 1982,[1] the UNEP Governing Council, recognizing the useful contribution its Working Group of Experts on Environmental Law could make in implementing the programme for the development and periodic review of environmental law, decided to consider in 1983 the Working Group's mandate, future work programme and composition.

Decision (1982). [1]UNEP Council (report, A/37/25): 10/22, 31 May.

International instruments

In August 1982, the Secretary-General transmitted to the General Assembly the annual reports of the UNEP Executive Director on international conventions and protocols in the environment field and on the UNEP register of such instruments.[2] Transmittal had been authorized by the UNEP Governing Council on 31 May.[1]

Three recent conventions were recorded during 1982: the Convention on Future Multilateral Co-operation in the Northwest Atlantic Fisheries (adopted 1978, entered into force 1 January 1979; depositary, Canada); and the European Convention for the Protection of Animals Kept for Farming Purposes (adopted 1976) and the European Convention for the Protection of Animals for Slaughter (adopted 1979), for both of which the depositary is the Council of Europe.

Decision (1982). [1]UNEP Council (report, A/37/25): 10/14, sect. VI, para. 4, 31 May.

Reports. [2]UNEP Executive Director, transmitted by S-G note, A/37/394.

Environmental education

In its 18 May 1982 resolution[2] on the state of the environment, adopted at its special session, the UNEP Governing Council, in reviewing major achievements and failures of support measures in implementing the 1972 Action Plan for the Human Environment,[3] said it felt that progress had been made in encouraging environmental education. Deficiencies persisted in training, however, and there had been insufficient attention to environ-

mental and public education, as well as to training of workers, technicians and managers. UNEP objectives for 1982-1992 should be to promote, coordinate and catalyse environmental education, training and public awareness activities, emphasizing particularly: new education methods and better teacher-training programmes; increased specialist training; better dissemination of information; and integration of an environmental component in the training of enterprise managers, technicians, skilled workers and decision-makers concerned with environmental and resource management.

On 31 May,[1] at its tenth session, the Governing Council adopted decisions in support of environmental education and training in Africa and in Latin America and the Caribbean (See ECONOMIC AND SOCIAL QUESTIONS, Chapter VIII).

Decision (1982). [1]UNEP Council (report, A/37/25): 10/25 A & B, 31 May

Resolution (1982). [2]UNEP Council (report, A/37/25): I, sect. I, para. 3 *(c)* (i), & sect. IV, para. 2 *(c)* (iii), 18 May.

Yearbook reference. [3]1972, p. 322.

Chapter XVII

Human settlements

Contents

Related topics:
Regional economic and social activities: Human settlements in Africa; Human settlements in Asia and the Pacific. Energy: Implementation of the Nairobi Programme of Action. Environment: Joint UNEP-UNCHS meetings.

For resolutions and decisions of major organs mentioned but not reproduced, refer to INDEX OF RESOLUTIONS AND DECISIONS.

General aspects

United Nations activities regarding human settlements during 1982 focused on direct assistance to developing countries through technical co-operation, research and development (including training) and information dissemination.

The United Nations Centre for Human Settlements (UNCHS), also known as Habitat, implemented its work programme for 1982-1983 as established by the Commission on Human Settlements. In 1982, UNCHS was responsible for executing 129 technical co-operation projects, funded by three main sources—the United Nations Habitat and Human Settlements Foundation, financed by voluntary contributions, the United Nations Development Programme and the United Nations regular budget—and other contributions.

At the intergovernmental level, the Commission on Human Settlements, which held its fifth session

at Nairobi, Kenya, from 26 April to 7 May, adopted 19 resolutions and seven decisions, based on the recommendations of two committees of the whole. Agenda items included the activities of UNCHS and its work programme and budget for 1984-1985, land for human settlements, and the International Year of Shelter for the Homeless (1987). Two resolutions were recommended for adoption by the General Assembly: they pertained to mobilization of financial resources for improving human settlements and the International Year. The Commission also decided to accept Finland's invitation to hold its next session (April/May 1983) at Helsinki.

Taking note of the Commission's report on its 1982 session, the Economic and Social Council in July urged the Commission and UNCHS to improve co-ordination of United Nations human settlements activities. In December, the Assembly commended the Commission on its work and urged it to continue to support technical co-operation among developing countries in implementing its human settlements programmes.

Programme and finances of UNCHS

Programme policy

Economic and Social Council action. By a resolution adopted without vote on 27 July 1982,[3] the Economic and Social Council took note of the report of the Commission on Human Settlements on the work of its fifth session, held at Nairobi in April/May, and recommended to the General Assembly, for consideration and decision, the resolutions and decisions adopted by the Commission which required action by the Assembly. The Council urged the Commission and UNCHS to improve co-ordination of human settlements activities in the United Nations system and called on the organizations of that system to co-operate with the Commission and UNCHS in those efforts. It also urged the Commission to continue to support technical co-operation among developing countries in its programmes.

The draft texts of two resolutions[1] on human settlements were introduced in the Council's First (Economic) Committee by Algeria, on behalf of the Group of 77 developing countries. Following informal consultations, a Vice-Chairman submitted revised drafts which added to the first a preambular reference to the 1976 Vancouver Declaration on Human Settlements, adopted by Habitat: United Nations Conference on Human Settlements.[8] The revised texts of both resolutions were approved without vote on 21 July and the originals were withdrawn by the sponsors. The second resolution pertained to the International Year of Shelter for the Homeless.[4]

General Assembly action. By a resolution of 20 December,[5] the General Assembly took note of the report of the Commission on its 1982 session and commended it on the effective manner in which it continued to discharge its mandate. The Assembly reaffirmed the importance of human settlements activities in the promotion of national economic and social development and in the enhancement of the quality of life for the poor and the disadvantaged, particularly in developing countries. It urged the Commission to continue to support technical co-operation among developing countries in the formulation and implementation of its programmes on human settlements.

The Assembly adopted the resolution without vote, following similar action by its Second (Economic and Financial) Committee on 19 November. The resolution was the first of three on human settlements, originally sponsored by Burundi, Canada, Ecuador, Finland, Kenya, Norway, the Philippines, Sweden and Uganda,[2] and subsequently resubmitted by a Committee Vice-Chairman following consultations. The others dealt with mobilization of funds for the development and improvement of human settlements[6] and co-ordination of human settlements programmes within the United Nations system.[7] All three resolutions were adopted together in both the Committee and the Assembly.

Draft resolutions withdrawn. [1]Algeria, for Group of 77, E/1982/C.1/L.5; [2]Burundi, Canada, Ecuador, Finland, Kenya, Norway, Philippines, Sweden, Uganda, A/C.2/37/L.47.

Resolutions (1982). ESC, 27 July: [3]1982/46 A, text following; [4]1982/46 B. GA, 20 Dec.: [5]37/223 A, text following; [6]37/223 B; [7]37/223 C.

Yearbook reference. [8]1976, p. 441.

Meeting records. ESC: E/1982/SR.48 (27 July). GA: 2nd Committee, A/C.2/37/SR.3, 5-8, 20-26, 33, 40, *42* (28 Sep.–19 Nov.); plenary, A/37/PV.113 (20 Dec.).

Economic and Social Council resolution 1982/46 A

27 July 1982	Meeting 48	Adopted without vote

Approved by First Committee (E/1982/101) without vote, 21 July (meeting 12); draft by Vice-Chairman (E/1982/C.1/L.11, part A), based on informal consultations on draft by Algeria, for Group of 77 (E/1982/C.1/L.5); agenda item 13.

International co-operation in the field of human settlements

The Economic and Social Council,

Recalling General Assembly resolutions 3201(S-VI) and 3202(S VI) of 1 May 1974, containing the Declaration and the Programme of Action on the Establishment of a New International Economic Order, 3281(XXIX) of 12 December 1974, containing the Charter of Economic Rights and Duties of States, and 3362(S-VII) of 16 September 1975 on development and international economic co-operation,

Recalling also the principles and aims stipulated in the Vancouver Declaration on Human Settlements, 1976, and the recommendations adopted by Habitat: United Nations Conference on Human Settlements, and General Assembly resolutions 32/162 of 19 December 1977 on institutional arrangements for international co-operation in the field of human settlements and 34/116 of 14 December 1979 on the strengthening of human settlements activities,

Recalling further Council resolution 1981/69 A of 24 July 1981 on international co-operation in the field of human settlements,

Reaffirming its belief that human settlements activities can be a major contributor to national economic and social development and should be viewed as such,

Reaffirming also the need for system-wide harmonization and co-ordination of the activities of the United Nations system in the field of human settlements,

Having considered the report of the Commission on Human Settlements on the work of its fifth session,

1. *Takes note* of the report of the Commission on Human Settlements on the work of its fifth session;

2. *Recommends* to the General Assembly, for consideration and decision at its thirty-seventh session, those resolutions and decisions adopted by the Commission at its fifth session which require action by the Assembly;

3. *Urges* the Commission on Human Settlements and the United Nations Centre for Human Settlements (Habitat) to accelerate their efforts to achieve greater harmonization and co-ordination of human settlements activities in the United Nations system, in accordance with their respective mandates under General Assembly resolution 32/162, and calls upon the competent specialized agencies and other bodies and organizations of the United Nations system to co-operate with the Commission and the Centre in these efforts;

4. *Urges further* the Commission on Human Settlements to continue to take account of and to provide adequate support to technical co-operation among developing countries in the formulation and implementation of its programmes on human settlements.

General Assembly resolution 37/223 A

20 December 1982	Meeting 113	Adopted without vote

Approved by Second Committee (A/37/680/Add.9 and Add.9/Corr.1) without vote, 19 November (meeting 42); draft by Vice-Chairman (A/C.2/37/L.68, part A), based on informal consultations on 9-nation draft (A/C.2/37/L.47); agenda item 71 *(j).*

Report of the Commission on Human Settlements

The General Assembly,

Recalling its resolutions 3201(S-VI) and 3202(S-VI) of 1 May 1974, containing the Declaration and the Programme of Action on the Establishment of a New International Economic Order, 3281(XXIX) of 12 December 1974, containing the Charter of Economic Rights and Duties of States, and 3362(S-VII) of 16 September 1975 on development and international economic co-operation,

Recalling also its resolutions 32/162 of 19 December 1977 on institutional arrangements for international co-operation in the field of human settlements and 34/116 of 14 December 1979 on the strengthening of human settlements activities,

Recalling further the principles and aims contained in the Vancouver Declaration on Human Settlements, 1976, and the other recommendations of Habitat: United Nations Conference on Human Settlements, as well as those contained in resolution 4/1, entitled "Manila Communiqué on a Human Settlements Movement", adopted on 6 May 1981 by the Commission on Human Settlements,

Taking note of Economic and Social Council resolution 1982/46 A of 27 July 1982 on international co-operation in the field of human settlements,

Having considered the report of the Commission on Human Settlements on the work of its fifth session,

1. *Takes note* of the report of the Commission on Human Settlements on the work of its fifth session;

2. *Reaffirms* the importance of human settlements activities in the promotion of national economic and social development and in the enhancement of the quality of life for the poor and the disadvantaged, particularly in the developing countries;

3. *Commends* the Commission on Human Settlements on the effective manner in which it continues to discharge its mandate in assisting Governments to tackle the serious problems of human settlements development;

4. *Urges* the Commission on Human Settlements to continue to take account of and to provide adequate support to technical co operation among developing countries in the formulation and implementation of its programmes on human settlements.

Other programme questions

Programme priorities

In the report on its 1981 session,[3] the Committee for Programme and Co-ordination (CPC) had recommended merging two subprogrammes (settlement policies and strategies, and settlement planning) of the UNCHS work programme and that the resources released go towards strengthening the human settlements capacities of the regional commissions.

The Commission on Human Settlements, in a 7 May 1982 resolution on the CPC report,[2] re-emphasized the importance of both subprogrammes and the need to maintain them separately at no less than the current level of activity. It requested that CPC take the resolution and the Commission's views into account when considering the Secretary-General's 1981 report,[1] reviewing the United Nations work programme, in which reduced activity was recommended in the two subprogrammes, and that the Economic and Social Council and the General Assembly take them into account when considering the 1982 CPC report.

Report. [1]S-G, A/36/658.
Resolution (1982). [2]Commission on Human Settlements (report, A/37/8): 5/17, 7 May.
Yearbook reference. [3]1981, p. 846.

Demonstration projects

In a resolution of 7 May 1982,[1] the Commission made recommendations on follow-up action on its 1981 Manila Communiqué on a Human Settlements Movement,[2] which stated that human settlements development should encompass co-ordinated efforts to improve the quality of life by satisfying basic human needs. The Commission recommended to the UNCHS Executive Director that demonstration projects in human settlements should be promoted, integrating basic human services within the framework of the Centre's work programme and funds available, and authorized him to take steps in this connection and to report to it in 1983 on implementation. The Commission called on Governments and international development and financial institutions to provide counterpart resources, particularly sites, funds and trained manpower and expertise.

Resolution (1982). [1]Commission on Human Settlements (report, A/37/8): 5/18, 7 May.
Yearbook reference. [2]1981, p. 850.

Dissemination of information on projects

By a resolution of 6 May 1982,[1] the Commission requested the UNCHS Executive Director to ensure that Governments were adequately informed between sessions of the Commission of the essentials of UNCHS projects, and of progress in implementing them, and to report to it on implementation of the resolution in 1983.

Resolution (1982). [1]Commission on Human Settlements (report, A/37/8): 5/5, 6 May.

Administrative and budgetary questions

Extrabudgetary resources

The UNCHS Executive Director, in a February 1982 report[2] to the Commission on Human Settlements, described the use of extrabudgetary resources by the Centre during the biennium 1980-1981 and projections for such use during 1982-1983. Apart from funds available to UNCHS from the United Nations regular budget and from the United Nations Habitat and Human Settlements Foundation, extrabudgetary resources in the form of programme and programme support funds came from three sources: programme support income from the execution of projects financed by the United Nations Development Programme (UNDP) and trust funds ($3,896,800 for 1980-1981); a subvention from the World Food Programme ($202,000); and programme support from the Fund of the United Nations Environment Programme ($80,700). Of the total ($4,179,500), $3,617,500 was spent, mostly for providing substantive and administrative support ($3,334,800 or 92 per cent) to field projects.

In addition, extrabudgetary funds for projects were received from two sources: contributions by

Governments to trust funds and contributions in support of specific projects. During the biennium, project funds amounted to $2,709,200. Belgium, Denmark, France, the Federal Republic of Germany, Italy, the Netherlands, Norway and Sweden provided funds enabling the recruitment of 32 associate experts in connection with various projects. In 1980-1981, pledges and contributions were received from Denmark, the Netherlands and Sweden for specific projects, and negotiations were under way for projects to be financed by Belgium, Finland and others.

The Commission on Human Settlements, in a decision of 7 May 1982,[1] took note of the Executive Director's report and requested him to prepare for all subsequent Commission sessions a report on the availability and use of all extrabudgetary resources, including those of the Foundation, broken down by source and activity.

Decision (1982). [1]Commission on Human Settlements (report, A/37/8): 5/22, paras. *(a)* & *(b),* 7 May.
Report. [2]UNCHS Executive Director, HS/C/5/7.

Technical co-operation support costs

On 7 May 1982,[1] the Commission on Human Settlements noted that UNCHS was not eligible for the support-cost flexibility arrangement provided by UNDP to smaller agencies,[2] under which UNCHS, based on its current volume of delivery, would be entitled to reimbursement of actual support costs or a minimum of 16 per cent of agency overheads, instead of the 13 per cent it currently received.

The Commission expressed satisfaction that the UNCHS Executive Director had already taken measures to keep administrative and overhead costs to a minimum, and asked him to continue such efforts consistent with the efficient discharge of the Centre's responsibilities in operational activities for development, keeping the Commission informed periodically of the results. It also noted its previous request that the Centre include in its technical co-operation projects a built-in evaluation element and other steps to improve efficiency.

Decision (1982). [1]Commission on Human Settlements (report, A/37/8): 5/23, 7 May.
Yearbook reference. [2]1981, p. 449.

UN Habitat and Human Settlements Foundation

Contributions

On 7 May 1982,[1] the Commission on Human Settlements endorsed an appeal of the UNCHS Executive Director for additional contributions to the United Nations Habitat and Human Settlements Foundation and requested Member States to consider not only contributing but increasing their contributions to the Foundation to ensure its continuation as a major source of funding for UNCHS activities.

The General Assembly, in a resolution of 20 December,[2] expressed its appreciation to Governments that had made financial contributions to the Centre's activities and reiterated its urgent appeal to Member States, particularly developed countries and others in a position to do so, to contribute and, if possible, to increase their contributions to the Foundation.

Contributions by 29 Governments were recieved in 1982, totalling $1,533,183, and pledges for future years from 36 countries totalled $1,836,518.

CONTRIBUTIONS TO THE UN HABITAT
AND HUMAN SETTLEMENTS FOUNDATION
(as at 31 December 1982; in US dollar equivalent)

Country	1982 payment	Pledges for future years
Algeria	—	8,500
Bangladesh	—	5,000
Barbados	—	1,000
Belgium	1,000	—
Benin	54,735	—
Botswana	—	1,835
Canada	2,126	243,903
Chile	123,967	5,000
Colombia	12,000	12,000
Cyprus	428	390
Denmark	—	207,251
Egypt	—	15,213
Finland	—	228,113
France	110,473	62,937
Gabon	—	7,500
India	51,883	100,000
Indonesia	20,012	10,000
Iraq	65,540	—
Italy	215,720	—
Jamaica	19,967	25,000
Jordan	1,500	—
Kenya	—	45,000
Kuwait	30,000	—
Lebanon	—	10,000
Lesotho	18,000	3,000
Malawi	—	901
Malaysia	10,000	—
Netherlands	200,178	276,400
Norway	148,019	97,222
Oman	10,000	—
Pakistan	5,000	5,000
Panama	1,000	—
Papua New Guinea	6,000	10,200
Qatar	30,000	30,000
Republic of Korea	40,000	20,000
Sri Lanka	26,000	4,000
Swaziland	—	2,500
Sweden	258,844	260,845
Trinidad and Tobago	—	1,005
Tunisia	66,000	30,000
Turkey	—	30,000
Uganda	—	1,910
United Republic of Cameroon	2,777	2,801
United Republic of Tanzania	—	2,092
Venezuela	—	70,000
Zambia	2,014	—
Total	**1,533,183**	**1,836,518**

Decision (1982). [1]Commission on Human Settlements (report, A/37/8): 5/22, para. *(c),* 7 May.
Resolution (1982). [2]GA: 37/223 B, paras. 1 & 5, 20 Dec.

Accounts for 1980-1981

The United Nations Board of Auditors submitted to the General Assembly in 1982 a financial report and audited financial statements of the United Nations Habitat and Human Settlements

Foundation for the biennium 1980-1981.[2] Expenditures for the two-year period totalled $3,785,015. Of that amount, $1,937,204 related to programme and programme support activities and $1,847,811 to project activities. The excess of income over expenditure amounted to $3,682,242. In addition, a saving from the liquidation of prior years' unliquidated obligations of $78,197 was realized as at 31 December 1981.

During the biennium, government pledges of $6,126,559 were recorded and $5,843,054 was collected, of which $340,535 was for prior years and $75,000 against future years. Pledged contributions of $674,704 remained unpaid as at 31 December 1981.

According to the Board of Auditors, its review of the electronic data-processing system revealed weaknesses in the data-processing control system, attributed to understaffing, and it recommended that control procedures be strengthened. The Board also recommended steps to improve the inventory system for control of expendable and non-expendable property.

The Advisory Committee on Administrative and Budgetary Questions (ACABQ), commenting on the Board's report in September,[1] noted the remark on expendable and non-expendable property. In its view, such property represented significant assets; proper management, and especially inventory control, was essential, and it trusted that control procedures in place would be strictly applied and inventory systems improved where necessary.

The Assembly, in a resolution of 16 November,[3] accepted the financial report and accounts and endorsed the audit opinions of the Board of Auditors. Concurring with the comments made by ACABQ, the Assembly requested the Board and ACABQ to continue to give greater attention to areas on which they had made comments, and requested the Secretary-General and the executive head of the Foundation to take remedial action.

Reports. [1]ACABQ A/37/443; [2]Board of Auditors, and financial statements, A/37/5/Add.8.
Resolution (1982). [3]GA: 37/12, 16 Nov.

Human settlements activities

The United Nations Centre for Human Settlements (Habitat) (UNCHS) was responsible for executing 129 technical co-operation projects in all developing regions, funded by the United Nations Development Programme, voluntary contributions by Governments to the Habitat and Human Settlements Foundation, and other sources. Those activities, part of the 1982-1983 work programme established by the Commission on Human Settlements, included projects covering such areas as national settlement policies and programmes, urban and regional planning, rural and urban housing development, upgrading of slums and squatter areas, low-cost building technology, appropriate technologies for urban and rural infrastructure for settlements, and the establishment or strengthening of government institutions concerned with human settlements.

The Centre conducted research studies and organized seminars, training workshops and expert group meetings on those and related issues, such as the efficient use of energy in human settlements, housing co-operatives, building codes and regulations, and the strengthening of public participation by low-income groups. Data management for urban and regional development was a relatively new activity, as was the establishment of a global information network in the field of human settlements. Audio-visual and printed materials were produced as part of UNCHS projects and training programmes.

The Centre played a central role in the preparation of the International Year of Shelter for the Homeless (1987), proclaimed by the General Assembly in December. The Assembly designated the Commission as the body responsible for organizing the Year and the Centre as the secretariat and as the lead agency for co-ordinating programmes and activities of other organizations and agencies.

Habitat Centre

Activities of the Centre

The Executive Director of UNCHS, in a December 1982 report to the Commission on Human Settlements,[1] described progress in implementing the Centre's 1982-1983 work programme, which was structured on the basis of six subject areas, or subprogrammes: settlement policies and strategies; settlement planning; shelter, infrastructure and services; land-use policy; public participation; and institutions and management.

Under the first subprogramme, UNCHS began to collect and analyse information on national policy trends and develop guidelines for incorporating human settlement elements into national development policies. Work continued on the quinquennial *Global Report on Human Settlements*, scheduled for publication in 1985. National economic development plans were being analysed to develop a classification of human settlement policy options. A project on global settlement analysis and system-wide policy formulation, co-ordination and co-operation would provide information on global policy issues. Other projects included reports on land policy and on human settlement policy in the Asia and Pacific region, wall charts for the United Nations Environment Programme, and a theme paper on training.

A major project under the subprogramme on settlement planning was a forecast of settlement conditions up to the year 2000 for which information was being collected and data analysed. Case studies were being prepared on the environmental impact of human settlements for producing guidelines on environmental planning, and a training course on environmental planning was being organized in the USSR. Regional planning (particularly population) issues were being analysed for producing guidelines, criteria and methodologies for integrated planning. Draft reports on settlement planning in Latin America and Asia and the Pacific were under review. Criteria were being developed by which investment allocations could be made for rural networks. Guidelines and case studies were being prepared, and work continued on road and electricity networks, settlement planning in arid and semi-arid areas, and a bibliography on settlement planning.

A project on shelter was examining constraints to the implementation of housing programmes, analysing decision-making issues in programme formulation and testing models and projects for housing programmes in developing countries. Replies by Governments to a questionnaire were to be used in formulating demonstration projects on upgrading slums and squatter settlements, particularly inner-city slums. Case studies were formulated and guidelines were being produced for slum improvement in order to demonstrate public-participation techniques, the use of innovative technologies to provide shelter, non-conventional financial mechanisms and community training and information activities. One component of this project was to assist low-income families in Africa to gain access to resources for housing improvement, and another was to evaluate rent control in Western Asia. Other activities included producing guidelines for and demonstrations of building technologies, in order to promote indigenous construction. In Latin America, a study was being made of technologies for upgrading slums and squatter settlements, and, in Africa, of the construction industry, including prospects for increasing productivity, producing building materials and choosing appropriate technologies, as well as problems in training construction workers. A computerized reference system for building materials and equipment was under way and scheduled for completion in 1983. Information was being compiled on the provision of infrastructure and services to low-income settlements, to define standards and technologies for such settlements. Special attention was given to problems of energy in human settlements and urban and rural transportation requirements.

The Centre's land-use policy work involved evaluating the effectiveness of national institutions in controlling land prices and use, recommending measures to provide land for low-income groups and recommending the improvement of land data systems.

Technical co-operation projects in public participation focused on self-help efforts in utilizing human resources in low-income settlements and on disseminating information on the financial, legal and administrative aspects of co-operatives. Two workshops were held on the topic. A preliminary workshop drafted a programme on public participation in national programmes to assist Governments in mobilizing human resources in low-income settlements by preparing training materials and testing them in field conditions.

An analysis of institutions and management produced a framework for a methodology for analysing human settlement policies and defining institutional systems for their implementation, still to be tested. Two training courses in management were held in 1982: at Colombo, Sri Lanka, in February/March and at Nairobi, Kenya, in November/December. Preliminary work was begun on a global survey of training needs. A project on information systems was to disseminate human settlements information throughout the world. UNCHS collaborated with the United Nations Educational, Scientific and Cultural Organization on microcomputer software for bibliographic exchange in developing countries; two reports were published on means of exchange. Three issues of *Habitat News* were published in 1982, including an insert on non-governmental organizations and an Arabic supplement. Twelve television and 50 radio programmes were produced, and general dissemination of audio-visual material continued.

Other activities included work in data-management assistance, involving training workshops, special advisory services (to 10 countries), project execution, software development and internal management support information and project monitoring. During 1982, two workshops were conducted—at Buenos Aires, Argentina, for 21 participants from Latin American countries, and at Titograd, Yugoslavia, for 15 planners of the regional planning project for Montenegro. The Centre developed and circulated an urban data-management software package for use in human settlements planning, answering requests from more than 25 countries.

The Centre continued to provide special interregional technical advisory services and training to developing countries, with emphasis on the least developed, land-locked and island developing countries. In 1982, over 35 missions to 28 countries were conducted, in such areas as innovative use of building materials and low-cost housing technologies, development of finance institutions and technical manpower.

Report. [1]UNHCS Executive Director, HS/C/6/2.

Training of personnel

Among the resolutions adopted by the Commission on Human Settlements in May 1982, two dealt with training of personnel. By the first,[1] adopted on 6 May, the Commission stressed the need for more appropriate training programmes related to human settlements, especially in developing countries. It emphasized the urgent need to strengthen national agencies dealing with human settlements and to establish national human settlements data banks. The Commission decided to include in the provisional agenda of its 1984 session a theme on training and information.

By the second resolution,[2] adopted on 7 May, the Commission requested the UNCHS Executive Director to continue to give priority to promoting the integration of training and information into the various sectors of human settlements development, in particular to enhance the capacity of developing countries to formulate and implement human settlements policies, programmes and projects. It decided to select as a special theme for its 1984 session a comprehensive approach to training and information as part of overall human settlements policy. The Commission asked the Executive Director to prepare a report on the subject, based on consultations, to continue consultations for clarifying the implications of the establishment of a UNCHS training centre in Greece, and to examine and report in 1983 on the possibility of establishing training institutions elsewhere.

Resolutions (1982). Commission on Human Settlements (report, A/37/8): [1]5/7, 6 May; [2]5/16, 7 May.

Technical co-operation

The 1982 technical co-operation projects of UNCHS, outlined in an April 1983 report of the Secretary-General,[1] concentrated on development of human settlements policies, formulation of development plans, low-cost shelter, infrastructure and supporting services, and the building up of institutions and their management. About 83 per cent of the Centre's resources expended on technical co-operation during 1982 were provided by the United Nations Development Programme (UNDP), including cost-sharing contributions to projects by recipient Governments: 82 projects were financed by UNDP in 56 countries, of which 14 were initiated in 1982; of those, 22 were also supplemented by trust fund contributions for associate experts.

Voluntary contributions to the Habitat and Human Settlements Foundation funded 72 small-scale projects and missions designed to meet human settlement needs arising from natural and man-made disasters, as well as longer-term development requirements. Those projects included low-cost housing design and construction, audio-visual materials for slum and squatter settlement upgrading, domestic energy requirements, building finance and material research, planning in disaster-prone areas, information systems and training. The Foundation's resources were generally used for preparatory assistance and for activities with a multiplier effect which were likely to have a significant effect on the overall development of human settlements.

Regular programme funds were used mainly for specialized short-term advisory services, training and field projects with emphasis on supporting human settlements activities in the least developed, land-locked and island developing countries. Short-term services by interregional advisers, which included 35 missions to 28 countries, resulted in two approved funds-in-trust projects and proposed projects for four countries. The Centre was co-operating in implementing the Nairobi Programme of Action for the Development and Utilization of New and Renewable Sources of Energy as it related to human settlements problems, as well as with the Committee on the Peaceful Uses of Outer Space in organizing training courses and workshops on the role of remote sensing in human settlements planning and management.

Report. [1]S-G, DP/1983/18/Add.1.

Financing human settlements

As requested by the General Assembly in 1979,[8] the UNCHS Executive Director, in a January 1982 report[3] to the Commission on Human Settlements, provided an analytical overview of financial and other assistance provided to developing countries for human settlements activities, to help Member States to gauge whether human settlements activities—as indicated by the amount of resources going to them—were proceeding as expected. The report presented, in statistical tables, information and data received from Member States, bilateral agencies and multilateral organizations. These data were compiled from replies to a questionnaire received from Member States or representatives in those countries who had co-operated with national ministries, United Nations bodies and other organizations. The report noted that studies had confirmed that the flow of resources to human settlements projects had not been as substantial as desired; in several developing countries, the amount of governmental expenditure devoted to specific sectors of human settlements development had declined considerably.

The tables showed the total number of projects per country, the sources of financial inputs (multilateral, bilateral and national), their amounts and their relative size in proportion to total reported financial inputs in all the projects in each country. Data on funding for projects under implementation, as at 30 June 1981, were discussed in terms of sources of financial assistance and in terms of the patterns of distribution of that assistance among the regions. In Africa, there were 236 projects costing $2.24 billion; in the Americas, 142 projects ($2.23 billion); in Asia and the Pacific, 163 projects ($3.54 billion); in Europe, 13 projects ($262 million); and in Western Asia, 22 projects ($459 million)—a total of 578 projects costing $8.53 billion. Fifty-three per cent ($4.51 billion) of that total was provided by multilateral and bilateral assistance: 39 per cent ($3.36 billion) multilateral and 14 per cent ($1.15 billion) bilateral. Of the total, 47 per cent ($4.02 billion) was derived from national contributions.

According to information received, multilateral agencies contributed about $3.36 billion to human settlements projects in the developing countries (39 per cent of all financial inputs). They contributed the highest proportions in Africa and in Asia and the Pacific (41 per cent each) and the Americas (39 per cent), and provided Western Asia with 30 per cent of its financial inputs and Europe with 25 per cent. The World Bank, including the International Development Association, was the leading contributor, providing $1.97 billion or 23 per cent of the total.

The report concluded that, since complete information could not be collected solely through questionnaires, the Commission might consider making the main basis of data collection the UNDP compendia of approved projects and the UNDP reports on development assistance published annually for each developing country. Information from recipient countries and international donors could be used for verifying and updating that material. Another suggestion concerned two biennial reports prepared in alternate years: the report on financial and other assistance provided to and among developing countries on human settlements activities of the United Nations system, and the progress report on the implementation of the recommendations for national action adopted by the 1976 United Nations Conference on Human Settlements.[9] The Executive Director proposed combining the two reports to provide more enlightening information about income and expenditure meeting human settlements needs, to be prepared every two years starting from 1984.

On 7 May, the Commission commended the Executive Director for his report. Also by that decision,[1] the Commission endorsed his proposals regarding the data collection methods to be used for the 1984 report on financial and other assistance provided to developing countries and the recognition of the close links between human settlements needs, policies, programmes and expenditures at the national level and the role of financial and technical assistance to and among

developing countries in that field. The Commission requested the Executive Director to harmonize the methodological approach, data collection methods and presentation of those reports, to be submitted for the Commission's consideration every two years starting from 1984, taking into account the importance of qualitative rather than quantitative comparisons.

By a resolution of the same date, the Commission requested the Executive Director to continue a feasibility study on the creation of an Asian human settlements bank.

The General Assembly, by a resolution of 20 December,[6] urged recipient countries, consistent with their own national priorities, to consider allocating some of the multilateral development aid they received to financing national human settlements projects, and donors and recipients to consider using parts of bilateral assistance funds to finance human settlements activities. The Assembly also appealed to financial institutions to allocate a portion of development aid to human settlements development and improvement in the developing countries, in accordance with the countries' priorities. Expressing its appreciation for contributions to UNCHS, the Assembly reiterated its appeal for contributions to the United Nations Habitat and Human Settlements Foundation.

The Assembly adopted the resolution, without vote, on the recommendation of its Second (Economic and Financial) Committee, which had approved the text in the same manner on 19 November. The text, submitted by Burundi, Canada, Ecuador, Finland, Kenya, Norway, the Philippines, Sweden and Uganda, was the second of three resolutions on human settlements,[2] subsequently withdrawn in favour of a text presented by a Committee Vice-Chairman following consultations. The draft was based on a text proposed by the Commission on Human Settlements in a resolution of 7 May.[4] By the Commission's text, the Assembly would have urged recipient countries (omitting the phrase "consistent with their own national priorities") to consider allocating an appropriate percentage of their UNDP-allotted (indicative planning figure) resources to the specific financing of national projects for the development and improvement of human settlements. Member States, rather than donor and recipient countries, would have been urged to consider utilizing assistance funds for human settlements activities. In the appeal to financial institutions, the Commission had included a specific reference to the World Bank and regional development banks.

The other two resolutions concerned coordination of human settlements programmes[7] and the report of the Commission.[5]

Decision (1982). [1]Commission on Human Settlements (report, A/37/8): 5/24, 7 May.

Draft resolution withdrawn. [2]Burundi, Canada, Ecuador, Finland, Kenya, Norway, Philippines, Sweden, Uganda, A/C.2/37/L.47.

Report. [3]UNCHS Executive Director, HS/C/5/6.

Resolutions (1982). [4]Commission on Human Settlements: 5/10, 7 May. GA, 20 Dec.: [5]37/233 A; [6]37/223 B, text following; [7]37/233 C.

Resolution (prior). [8]GA: 34/114, 14 Dec. 1979 (YUN 1979, p. 708).

Yearbook reference. [9]1976, p. 444.

Meeting records. GA: 2nd Committee, A/C.2/37/SR.3, 5-8, 20-26, 33, 40, *42* (28 Sep.–19 Nov.); plenary, A/37/PV.113 (20 Dec.).

General Assembly resolution 37/223 B

20 December 1982   Meeting 113   Adopted without vote

Approved by Second Committee (A/37/680/Add.9 and Add.9/Corr.1) without vote, 19 November (meeting 42); draft by Vice-Chairman (A/C.2/37/L.68, part B), based on informal consultations on 9-nation draft (A/C.2/37/L.47); agenda item 71 *(j)*.

Mobilization of financial resources for the development and improvement of human settlements

The General Assembly,

Recalling its resolution 32/162 of 19 December 1977 on institutional arrangements for international co-operation in the field of human settlements, by which it, *inter alia*, provided for the mobilization and utilization of resources in the various regions in the field of human settlements,

Bearing in mind other relevant resolutions of the General Assembly, including, in particular, resolutions 31/109 of 16 December 1976, 35/77 D of 5 December 1980 and 36/72 of 4 December 1981,

Recalling also its resolution 35/56 of 5 December 1980, the annex to which contains the International Development Strategy for the Third United Nations Development Decade, in particular paragraphs 159 and 160 of the Strategy on the development and improvement of human settlements,

Considering that human settlements policies are inseparable from the goals of social and economic development and that solutions to the problems of such settlements must, consequently, be conceived of as an integral part of the development process of individual countries and the world community,

Recalling Economic and Social Council resolution 1981/69 A of 24 July 1981, particularly paragraphs 4 and 5 thereof on the need for adequate financing for the projected activities of the United Nations Centre for Human Settlements (Habitat),

Disturbed by the current trends affecting the resources available for the development and improvement of human settlements, resources which are clearly insufficient to meet existing requirements,

Convinced of the need for urgent action to improve the living conditions of the masses of people in human settlements, particularly in the developing countries,

Recognizing that such action is primarily the responsibility of Governments at the national and local levels,

Recognizing also that the international community should provide, at both the global and regional levels, encouragement and support to Governments determined to take effective action to ameliorate conditions, especially for the most disadvantaged, in rural and urban human settlements,

1. *Expresses its appreciation* to those Governments that have so far made financial contributions to the activities of the United Nations Centre for Human Settlements (Habitat);

2. *Urges* recipient countries, consistent with their own national priorities, to give consideration to allocating an appropriate portion of the development aid resources they receive from multilateral sources to the specific financing of national projects for the development and improvement of human settlements;

3. *Urges also* donor and recipient countries to give consideration to the utilization of parts of bilateral assistance funds for the financing of human settlements activities of interest to them;

4. *Appeals* to international and regional financial institutions to allocate an appropriate portion of their development aid resources to the development and improvement of human settlements in the developing countries, in accordance with the priorities of the recipient countries;

5. *Reiterates its urgent appeal* to Member States, particularly developed countries and others in a position to do so, to contribute and, if possible, to increase their contributions to the United Nations Habitat and Human Settlements Foundation in support of the activities of the Centre.

International Year of Shelter for the Homeless (1987)

Action by the Commission on Human Settlements. Following the 1981 resolution[13] of the General Assembly designating 1987, in principle, as the International Year of Shelter for the Homeless, the UNCHS Executive Director reported to the Commission on Human Settlements in February 1982 on planned activities and preparations for the Year.[7] He described the issues to be addressed and constraints and opportunities for action, as well as the interrelationship between shelter and economic development. He noted that, despite increased attention, activities by Governments and the international community to improve shelter and related infrastructure remained small in scale compared with the magnitude of the problems. The report presented objectives, strategies, criteria and guidelines for national and international action. It was recognized that policies and programmes for providing shelter and related infrastructure should be viewed as an integral part of national development strategies, while specifying concrete measures at the national and international levels.

The main objective of the International Year was to improve the shelter and neighbourhoods of some of the poor by 1987 and to demonstrate ways of improving the shelter and neighbourhoods of all of the poor by the year 2000. The report pointed to the need to focus on three major goals: ensuring political priority for and commitment to improving the shelter of the poor; consolidating knowledge and experience of Governments and international organizations since the 1976 United Nations Conference on Human Settlements[14] so that policy-makers had a full range of alternatives for such improvement; and developing and demonstrating new approaches and methods as a basis for national policies and programmes. To achieve those goals, Governments should assess needs, adopt new policies, develop demonstration projects, training programmes and appropriate legislation, disseminate information, strengthen the capacity of the poor to participate in shaping their environment, and generate the necessary resources.

The activities of the Year were to be designed to implement shelter demonstration projects around the world and to develop realistic national shelter strategies and a world shelter strategy which supported them. It was expected that by 1987 every Member State would have implemented at least one shelter demonstration project, which would be evaluated by 15 February 1987 so that the results could be disseminated during the Year.

At the national level, priority attention should be paid to the need for equitable distribution of land, as well as to improving building codes with a view to increasing the number of affordable low-cost dwellings, the report said. At the regional level, action should focus on facilitating and supporting national activities in areas of common interest and concern to the region or subregion, while activities at the international level should focus on stimulating, facilitating and supporting national action, in particular in the developing countries. The Commission on Human Settlements would be responsible for co-ordinating the implementation of the specific measures for the Year. UNCHS would service the Commission and serve as the Secretariat focal point within the United Nations system, also maintaining contact with other intergovernmental as well as non-governmental organizations and disseminating information. The Centre's functions would include initiation, co-ordination and monitoring of technical assistance and advisory services, and, when requested, advising on the financing of national activities.

The Commission adopted, on 7 May, a resolution[8] endorsing the objectives, strategies and criteria as well as the guidelines for national, regional and international action contained in the Executive Director's report, and requesting him to transmit it, with the Commission's comments, to the Economic and Social Council. The Commission also proposed a resolution for adoption by the General Assembly, after consideration by the Council. Accordingly, the Secretariat, by a note of 9 June,[4] submitted the report and resolution to the Council along with the Commission's comments.

Economic and Social Council action. By a resolution adopted without vote on 27 July,[9] the Economic and Social Council endorsed the Commission's recommendations to the General Assembly on the International Year of Shelter for the Homeless, on the understanding that the criteria for financing international years, as set out by the Council in 1980,[11] would be complied with. The Council urged that proposals on a specific programme of activities accord with voluntary contributions. It further urged that the main thrust of specific activities be exerted at the national and local levels. The Council appealed to all Governments, especially those of developed countries and those in a position to do so, international financial institutions, inter- and non-governmental organizations and others to extend financial and other support to the programme. It recommended that provision be made in the agenda of each session of the Commission up to 1987 for donors to indicate their proposed support to the programme.

The Secretariat subsequently reported[5] that such provision had been made for the Commission's 1983 session. Governments were asked to consider making a single, significant pledge, preferably at that session and, if possible, to pay the pledge in a single instalment as early as possible.

The Commission's 1982 report was considered by the Council's First (Economic) Committee. The observer for Algeria, on behalf of the Group of 77, introduced two draft resolutions on human settlements,[2] the second of which concerned the International Year (the first dealt with international co-operation in the field of human settlements). Following informal consultations on the Group's draft, resulting in a revised text introduced by a Committee Vice-Chairman, the Committee approved the resolution without vote on 21 July; the Group's draft was subsequently withdrawn.

The adopted resolution differed most significantly from the original in that two paragraphs were added urging that proposals for activities conform to the availability of voluntary contributions and that the main thrust of the activities be exerted at the national and local levels. Another change moved the phrase on compliance with the Council's criteria for financing international years from a preambular paragraph to operative paragraph 1. By a third change, the Council appealed not only to all Governments, especially those of developed countries, to contribute but also to "others in a position to do so".

Report of the Secretary-General. The Secretary-General, as the General Assembly had requested in 1981,[13] reported in October 1982[6] on organizational matters regarding the holding of the International Year of Shelter for the Homeless in 1987, including the availability of voluntary funds.

The report summarized problems and issues to be addressed, noted constraints and opportunities for action, set out objectives and guidelines for national and international action and defined the role of UNCHS. Despite national and international efforts since 1976, the overall conditions of shelter and related infrastructure and services for the poor in the developing world and for a substantial number in many developed countries continued to deteriorate, the report stated. Stressing the need for a renewed political commitment to improving the shelter and neighbourhoods of the poor, to consolidate the knowledge gained since the 1976 Conference on Human Settlements and take account of new factors, and to develop new approaches and methods for national policies and programmes, the Secretary-General said it was necessary to address larger problems which had blocked efforts to improve the human settlements situation.

Among those constraints, the report cited access to land and tenure, the lack of appropriate institutional arrangements within and among the different levels of government, inappropriate laws and standards for planning and construction, unrealistic eligibility requirements for financial arrangements, and the lack of low-cost building materials and techniques. A major problem was that no lasting overall improvement in shelter could be achieved without increased employment possibilities and real incomes; consequently, housing and settlement programmes had to be integrated with national and regional economic and social development plans.

Implicit in the attainment of economic development goals was the development of physical infrastructure (utility systems, roads, bridges, ports, airports), other civil engineering works (dams, hydroelectric plants, irrigation projects) and buildings (industrial and commercial structures, schools, hospitals, housing). Multiplier effects of construction activity would be increased if techniques favoured local resources.

Activities connected with the Year would also contribute to the goals of the International Development Strategy for the Third United Nations Development Decade, adopted by the Assembly in 1980.[12] In general, the objectives and goals for the Year and the role of the Commission and UNCHS for implementing the activities, as described by the Secretary-General, were elaborations of those identified by the Commission, as were the guidelines for action at the national, regional and international levels.

The report included financial implications. Operational programme activities, which included demonstration projects, regional and expert meetings and support activities of non-governmental organizations, were costed at $2,954,000, to be financed from extrabudgetary sources. Additional costs for the Commission serving as the organizing body for the Year might be needed after 1985. Additional resources of $1,973,200 would be required to provide for substantive secretariat and programme support costs, to be covered by both the regular budget and extrabudgetary sources. Of the total estimated cost of $4,927,200, $4,264,600 was expected to be paid by extrabudgetary sources and $662,600 from the regular budget.

Acting without vote on 27 July,[1] the Council had authorized the Secretary-General to transmit his report directly to the General Assembly at its 1982 session. Based on an oral proposal by the First Committee Chairman, the decision was approved without vote by the Committee on 21 July.

General Assembly action. By a resolution of 20 December,[10] the General Assembly proclaimed 1987 International Year of Shelter for the Homeless, with the objective of improving the shelter of some of the poor by 1987, according to national priorities, and to demonstrate, by the year 2000, ways of improving the shelter and neighbourhoods of the poor and disadvantaged. Special attention was to be given before and during the Year to means of: securing renewed political commitment by the international community to the Year's objectives, consolidating and sharing knowledge gained since the 1976 Conference on Human Settlements, developing new approaches to augment present efforts in this regard and provide a basis for national policies, and exchanging experience and providing support to meet the objectives.

The Assembly urged that the main thrust of activities take place at the national and local levels. It endorsed, in principle, the programme in the Secretary-General's report, on the understanding that the Economic and Social Council's financing criteria for international years would be complied with and that the programme costs would be kept within funds voluntarily contributed, and asked him to report on programme implementation in 1983. The Assembly appealed for contributions and other support for the programme, and reiterated the recommendation that the Commission make provision in its agenda until 1987 for donors to indicate proposed support. The Assembly designated the Commission as the organizing body—which was also to review annually the Year's objectives, strategies, criteria and guidelines—and UNCHS as the secretariat for the Year and lead coordinating agency. The Assembly invited international and national support for the Commission's work and called for special efforts through 1987 to achieve the Year's goals.

The Assembly adopted the resolution, without vote, on the recommendation of its Second Committee. Bangladesh, on behalf of the members of the Group of 77, had introduced a text in the Committee,[3] based on a text recommended by the Commission on Human Settlements.[8] The Group's text was later withdrawn when, after informal consultations, a revised resolution was presented by a Committee Vice-Chairman. The Committee approved the text on 23 November, without vote.

The Group's text had requested that the Secretary-General report annually on programme implementation "during the period 1983-1987" rather than in 1983. Other changes included the addition of operative paragraph 7 recommending that the Commission review annually the objectives, strategies, criteria and guidelines for the Year.

Other additions, indicated in quotes, were: The Assembly endorsed "in principle" the programme of the Year contained in the Secretary-General's report, an endorsement made "on the understanding that the criteria for financing and organizing international years set forth in the annex to Economic and Social Council resolution 1980/67[11] will be complied with and that the programme of measures and activities to be undertaken prior to and during the Year will be adjusted in accordance with the availability of voluntary contributions". The appeal for contributions from all Governments, especially those of developed countries, was expanded to include "others in a position to do so", and the Commission was designated, "in the framework of its regular sessions", to act as the organizing body.

Decision (1982). [1]ESC: 1982/154, 27 July, text following.
Draft resolutions withdrawn. [2]Algeria, for Group of 77, E/1982/C.1/L.5; [3]Bangladesh, for Group of 77, A/C.2/37/L.23.
Notes. Secretariat, [4]E/1982/81, [5]HS/C/6/4/Add.1.
Reports. [6]S-G, A/37/527 & Add.1; [7]UNCHS Executive Director, HS/C/5/5.
Resolutions (1982). [8]Commission on Human Settlements (report, A/37/8): 5/14, 7 May. [9]ESC: 1982/46 B, 27 July, text following. [10]GA: 37/221, 20 Dec., text following.
Resolutions (prior). [11]ESC: 1980/67, 25 July 1980 (YUN 1980, p. 1029). GA: [12]35/56, annex, 5 Dec. 1980 (YUN 1980, p. 503); [13]36/71, 4 Dec. 1981 (YUN 1981, p. 855).
Yearbook reference. [14]1976, p. 441.
Meeting records. ESC: E/1982/SR.48 (27 July). GA: 2nd Committee, A/C.2/37/SR.3, 5-8, 20-26, *31*, 33, 40, *43* (28 Sep.-23 Nov.); plenary, A/37/PV.113 (20 Dec.).

Economic and Social Council resolution 1982/46 B

27 July 1982   Meeting 48   Adopted without vote

Approved by First Committee (E/1982/101) without vote, 21 July (meeting 12); draft by Vice-Chairman (E/1982/C.1/L.11, part B), based on informal consultations on draft by Algeria, for Group of 77 (E/1982/C.1/L.5); agenda item 13.

International Year of Shelter for the Homeless

The Economic and Social Council,

Recalling its resolution 1981/69 B of 24 July 1981 on the proposal to declare an international year of shelter for the homeless,

Recalling also General Assembly resolution 36/71 of 4 December 1981, in which the Assembly decided, in principle, to designate 1987 as the International Year of Shelter for the Homeless,

Having considered the report of the Executive Director of the United Nations Centre for Human Settlements (Habitat) containing proposals on a specific programme of measures and activities to be undertaken prior to and during the International Year of Shelter for the Homeless,

Noting that the Commission on Human Settlements, in its resolution 5/14 of 7 May 1982, unanimously welcomed and endorsed the Executive Director's proposals on strategies and criteria, as well as guidelines for national, regional and international action, and took note of the institutional and administrative arrangements proposed by the Executive Director as a cost-effective way to organize and co-ordinate the activities of the Year,

Welcoming in particular the proposal to carry out and co-ordinate the activities of the International Year of Shelter for the Homeless within the framework of existing institutions,

Convinced that the holding of an international year devoted to the problems of homeless people in urban and rural areas, particularly in the developing countries, would contribute significantly to economic development and social justice in conditions of international peace and security,

Having noted the views of the Commission on Human Settlements and the proposals outlined in the Executive Director's report, as reflected in Commission resolution 5/14,

1. *Endorses* the recommendations made by the Commission on Human Settlements in its resolution 5/14 to the General Assembly at its thirty-seventh session, on the understanding that the criteria for financing and organizing international years set out in the annex to Council resolution 1980/67 of 25 July 1980 will be complied with;

2. *Urges* that the proposals on a specific programme of measures and activities to be undertaken prior to and during the International Year of Shelter for the Homeless be adjusted in accordance with the availability of voluntary contributions;

3. *Further urges* that the main thrust of the specific programme of measures and activities to be undertaken prior to and during the Year be exerted at the national and local levels;

4. *Appeals* to all Governments, especially those of developed countries, and others in a position to do so, international financial institutions, intergovernmental and non-governmental organizations and others in the public and private sectors to extend generous financial and other appropriate support to the programme for the Year;

5. *Recommends* that provision be made in the agenda of each session of the Commission up to the year 1987 for such donors to indicate the nature and extent of the support which they propose to give to the programme for the International Year of Shelter for the Homeless.

Economic and Social Council decision 1982/154

Adopted without vote

Approved by First Committee (E/1982/101) without vote, 21 July (meeting 12); oral proposal by Chairman; agenda item 13.

Report of the Secretary-General on the financial and organizational implications of holding an International Year of Shelter for the Homeless

At its 48th plenary meeting, on 27 July 1982, the Council decided to authorize the Secretary-General to transmit directly to the General Asssembly at its thirty-seventh session his report on the financial and organizational implications of holding an International Year of Shelter for the Homeless.

General Assembly resolution 37/221

20 December 1982   Meeting 113   Adopted without vote

Approved by Second Committee (A/37/680/Add.9 and Add.9/Corr.1) without vote, 23 November (meeting 43); draft by Vice-Chairman (A/C.2/37/L.69), based on informal consultations on draft by Bangladesh, for Group of 77 (A/C.2/37/L.23); agenda item 71 *(j)*.

International Year of Shelter for the Homeless

The General Assembly,

Recalling its resolution 35/76 of 5 December 1980, in which it expressed the view that an international year devoted to the problems of homeless people in urban and rural areas of the developing countries could be an appropriate occasion to focus the attention of the international community on those problems,

Recalling also its resolution 36/71 of 4 December 1981 in which it decided, in principle, to designate 1987 as the International Year of Shelter for the Homeless, on the understanding that the criteria for financing and organizing international years set out in the annex to Economic and Social Council resolution 1980/67 of 25 July 1980 were complied with,

Taking note of the report of the Executive Director of the United Nations Centre for Human Settlements (Habitat) on the International Year of Shelter for the Homeless, together with the comments made thereon by the Commission on Human Settlements at its fifth session and the Economic and Social Council at its second regular session of 1982, and also the report of the Secretary-General on the organizational and financial aspects of holding the International Year, called for in General Assembly resolution 36/71,

Taking note also of Economic and Social Council resolution 1982/46 B of 27 July 1982 on the International Year of Shelter for the Homeless,

Seriously concerned that, despite the efforts of Governments at the national and local levels and of international organizations, the living conditions of the majority of the people in slums and squatter areas and rural settlements, especially in developing countries, continue to deteriorate in both relative and absolute terms,

Convinced that a special effort to address this fundamental issue will strengthen overall national economic and social development, in furtherance of the goals of the International Development Strategy for the Third United Nations Development Decade,

Having considered the recommendations of the Commission on Human Settlements, contained in its resolution 5/14 of 7 May 1982, Economic and Social Council resolution 1982/46 B and the report of the Secretary-General,

1. *Proclaims* the year 1987 International Year of Shelter for the Homeless;

2. *Decides* that the objective of activities before and during the Year will be to improve the shelter and neighbourhoods of some of the poor and disadvantaged by the end of 1987, particularly in the developing countries, according to national priorities, and to demonstrate by the year 2000 ways and means of improving the shelter and neighbourhoods of the poor and disadvantaged;

3. *Also decides* that special attention will be given, during the Year and the preparations therefor, to ways and means of:

(a) Securing renewed political commitment by the international community to the improvement of the shelter and neighbourhoods of the poor and disadvantaged and to the provision of shelter for the homeless, particularly in the developing countries, as a matter of priority;

(b) Consolidating and sharing all new and existing knowledge and relevant experience gained since Habitat: United Nations Conference on Human Settlements, held in 1976, in order to provide a full range of tested and practical alternatives for improving the shelter and neighbourhoods of the poor and disadvantaged and for providing shelter for the homeless;

(c) Developing and demonstrating new approaches and methods to assist directly and to augment the present efforts of the homeless, poor and disadvantaged to secure their own shelter and in order to provide a basis for new national policies and strategies for improving the shelter and neighbourhoods of the poor and disadvantaged by the year 2000;

(d) Exchanging experience and providing support among countries to meet the objectives of the Year;

4. *Urges* that the main thrust of the specific programme of measures and activities to be undertaken prior to and during the Year should take place at the national and local levels, in accordance with national plans and priorities;

5. *Endorses*, in principle, the programme for the Year contained in the report of the Secretary-General, on the understanding that the criteria for financing and organizing international years set forth in the annex to Economic and Social Council resolution 1980/67 will be complied with and that the programme of measures and activities to be undertaken prior to and during the Year will be adjusted in accordance with the availability of voluntary contributions;

6. *Designates* the Commission on Human Settlements, in the framework of its regular sessions, to act as the United Nations intergovernmental body responsible for organizing the Year, and the United Nations Centre for Human Settlements (Habitat) as the secretariat for the Year and as the lead agency for co-ordinating the relevant programmes and activities of other organizations and agencies concerned;

7. *Recommends* that the Commission on Human Settlements should review annually the objectives, strategies and criteria for the Year, as well as the guidelines referred to in paragraph 1 of Commission resolution 5/14;

8. *Invites* all Governments, organs, organizations and bodies of the United Nations system, as well as other intergovernmental bodies and non-governmental organizations concerned, including interested national institutions, to collaborate in support of the work of the Commission on Human Settlements and to make special efforts through existing and new programmes during the period 1983-1987 to help achieve the objectives and goals for the Year;

9. *Appeals* to all Governments, especially those of developed countries and others in a position to do so, to extend generous financial and other appropriate support to the programme for the Year;

10. *Also appeals* to international financial institutions and intergovernmental bodies and non-governmental organizations to extend generous financial and other appropriate support to the programme for the Year;

11. *Recommends* that provision should be made in the agenda for each session of the Commission on Human Settlements, up to the year 1987, for such donors to indicate the nature and extent of the support which they propose to give to the programme for the Year;

12. *Requests* the Secretary-General to submit to the General Assembly at its thirty-eighth session, through the Economic and Social Council, a report on the implementation of the approved programme of measures and activities to be undertaken prior to and during the Year;

13. *Decides* to include in the provisional agenda of its thirty-eighth session an item entitled "International Year of Shelter for the Homeless".

Organizational questions

Organizational questions related to human settlements activities included the question of co-ordination in the United Nations system. In December, the General Assembly called for UNCHS to participate in the work of the Administrative Committee on Co-ordination (ACC) in order to improve co-ordination. The Centre, in carrying out programmes at the regional level, co-operated with the regional commissions and other intergovernmental institutions in human settlements projects, particularly in training programmes. Co-operation was also enhanced by the deployment of some UNCHS staff to the commissions. The Commission on Human Settlements took action on other organizational questions—co-ordination with the United Nations Environment Programme (UNEP), the inclusion of Arabic in the Commission's working languages, limitation of the Commission's documents, the widest possible circulation of the Centre's publications and simultaneous distribution of documents in the working languages.

Co-ordination in the UN system

The General Assembly, by a resolution of 20 December 1982,[6] requested the Secretary-General to accelerate his efforts to arrange consultations with ACC members on UNCHS participation in all aspects of ACC work in order to strengthen the co-ordination of human settlements programmes within the United Nations system, and to report to the Assembly in 1983 on those efforts. The Assembly urged the Commission on Human Settlements and UNCHS to accelerate their efforts to achieve greater system-wide harmonization and co-ordination of human settlements activities, in accordance with their mandates, and called on United Nations agencies and bodies to co-operate in those efforts.

The Assembly adopted the resolution without vote; the Second (Economic and Financial) Committee had approved it in like manner on 19 November. The text, the third of three resolutions on human settlements, was submitted by a Committee Vice-Chairman based on informal consultations on a draft sponsored by Burundi, Canada, Ecuador, Finland, Kenya, Norway, the Philippines, Sweden and Uganda,[1] which in turn was based on a draft resolution recommended to the Assembly by the Commission.[3] The nine-nation draft was subsequently withdrawn. The major change was the addition of a phrase to explain that the Centre's participation in ACC work was "in order to strengthen the co-ordination of human settlements programmes within the United Nations system".

The other two resolutions dealt with the report of the Commission[4] and mobilization of financial resources.[5]

The Commission, by a resolution of 7 May,[2] requested the UNCHS Executive Director to ensure that the joint meetings of the bureaux of the Commission and UNEP were held in conjunction with other meetings for reasons of economy.

Draft resolution withdrawn. [1]Burundi, Canada, Ecuador, Finland, Kenya, Norway, Philippines, Sweden, Uganda, A/C.2/37/L.47.

Resolutions (1982). Commission on Human Settlements (report, A/37/8, 7 May): [2]5/11; [3]5/13. GA, 20 Dec.: [4]37/223 A; [5]37/223 B; [6]37/223 C, text following.

Meeting records. GA: 2nd Committee, A/C.2/37/SR.3, 5-8, 20-26, 33, 40, *42* (28 Sep.–19 Nov.); plenary, A/37/PV.113 (20 Dec.).

General Assembly resolution 37/223 C

20 December 1982   Meeting 113   Adopted without vote

Approved by Second Committee (A/37/680/Add.9 and Add.9/Corr.1) without vote, 19 November (meeting 42); draft by Vice-Chairman (A/C.2/37/L.68, part C), based on informal consultations on 9-nation draft (A/C.2/37/L.47); agenda item 71 *(j)*.

Co-ordination of human settlements programmes within the United Nations system

The General Assembly,

Recalling its resolution 35/77 C of 5 December 1980, in which it invited the Secretary-General to arrange, in consultation with the members of the Administrative Committee on Co-ordination, for the United Nations Centre for Human Settlements (Habitat) to participate in all aspects of the work of that Committee and its subsidiary machinery,

Recalling also section III, paragraphs 5 *(a)* and *(b)*, of its resolution 32/162 of 19 December 1977, in which it called upon the Centre to ensure the harmonization at the intersecretariat level of human settlements programmes planned and carried out by the United Nations system and to assist the Commission on Human Settlements in co-ordinating human settlements activities in the United Nations system, to keep them under review and to assess their effectiveness,

Recalling, in particular, section VI, paragraph 4, of its resolution 32/162, in which it decided that the existing mechanisms of the Administrative Committee on Co-ordination must be strengthened to ensure that co-ordination in the field of human settlements is effective throughout the United Nations system,

Convinced that the implementation of the mandates of the Commission on Human Settlements and the Centre with respect to the co-ordination and harmonization of human settlements activities in the United Nations system can be most efficiently assured through the Centre's participation in all aspects of the work of the Administrative Committee on Co-ordination and its subsidiary machinery,

Taking note of Economic and Social Council resolution 1982/46 A of 27 July 1982, particularly paragraph 3 thereof,

1.   *Requests* the Secretary-General to accelerate his efforts to arrange consultations with the members of the Administrative Committee on Co-ordination, with a view to arranging for the United Nations Centre for Human Settlements (Habitat) to participate in all aspects of the work of the Committee and its subsidiary machinery in order to strengthen the co-ordination of human settlements programmes within the United Nations system, and to report to the General Assembly at its thirty-eighth session on the results of those efforts;

2.   *Urges* the Commission on Human Settlements and the Centre to accelerate their efforts to achieve greater harmonization and co-ordination of human settlements activities in the United Nations system, in accordance with their respective mandates under General Assembly resolution 32/162, and calls upon the appropriate specialized agencies and other bodies and organizations of the United Nations system to co-operate with the Commission and the Centre in those efforts.

Regional co-operation

As requested by the Commission in 1981,[3] the Executive Director of UNCHS reported in February 1982[1] on UNCHS programmes at the regional level, on proposals for implementing the Centre's work programme for 1982-1983 with special reference to the regions, and on setting up joint human settlements units with the regional commissions. The report described the research, training, technical co-operation and information activities carried out by the Centre at the regional level in collaboration with Governments, United Nations and bilateral agencies and non-governmental organizations. It also discussed strengthened collaboration between UNCHS and the regional commissions, particularly the Economic Commission for Africa, including manpower, training, financing, energy and public-participation projects being executed in Africa. Those activities were carried out as elements of the Centre's biennial work programme approved by the Commission. No joint units were set up with the regional commissions, but *ad hoc* administrative arrangements had been made for co-ordination of the work.

In the area of manpower development, UNCHS continued to provide advice on requirements for subregional groupings of African countries. For example, Botswana, Lesotho, Malawi and Swaziland received assistance in formulating a subregional project for training architectural/engineering and surveying assistants, clerks of works and physical planning assistants. The Centre collaborated with the World Bank on a similar programme in human settlements disciplines for the East African subregion. It promoted the formation of regional institutions for financing human settlements in Africa and Asia. Activities included participation in meetings sponsored by the African Development Bank on establishing a housing development and finance institution called Shelter-Afrique. The Commission on Human Settlements, in a resolution of 6 May,[2] encouraged co-operation, especially for the exchange of information, between the Bank and UNCHS in view of the establishment of Shelter-Afrique. UNCHS also participated in meetings of an *ad hoc* group of experts on a feasibility study for an Asian human settlements bank.

Among the Centre's training projects were courses held in conjunction with the Economic Development Institute of the World Bank, focusing on improving the living conditions of low-income families in urban settlements through management training of government officials. In 1982, regional courses for Asia were held at Colombo (Sri Lanka) and Madras (India) from 8 February to 19 March. A workshop on data management for human settlements development at Buenos Aires (Argentina) in March introduced urban-planning personnel to new data-management concepts and their application. An *Ad Hoc* Expert Group Meeting on Human Settlements Management with Special Reference to the Rehabilitation of Existing Housing (New Delhi, India, 1-8 February) focused on strategies for rehabilitation programmes to improve low- and middle-income housing.

The Centre submitted to the United Nations Development Programme proposals for regional technical co-operation projects in Africa and Europe. For Africa, projects included training, building-research co-ordination, regional pre-disaster planning, use of soil as a building material, energy for human settlements and construction industry development; for Europe, industrial waste use for housing construction, interfaces between energy and human settlements, training and information exchange in Eastern Europe, and control of development on the Mediterranean coast. In applied research, the Centre established a demonstration project on biogas use in Kenya and a feasibility study in Burundi and supported building-materials research. Among its public-participation activities was a five-year project in association with the Danish International Development Agency to develop training programmes for mobilizing the urban poor in developing countries to participate in the construction, improvement and maintenance of their homes and neighbourhoods.

The information activities of the Centre were carried out by offices at Amman (Jordan) for Arabic-speaking countries, Bangkok (Thailand) for Asia and the Pacific, Mexico City for Latin America and the Caribbean, Nairobi (Kenya) for English-speaking Africa and Dakar (Senegal) for French-speaking Africa. Hungary established an information office serving Eastern Europe. Those offices disseminated information from UNCHS, encouraged the use of its audio-visual materials, and collaborated with academic institutions in training courses and similar activities.

The Centre carried out regional components of its work programme through staff deployment to the regions. Two staff members were deployed to the Economic and Social Commission for Asia and the Pacific to identify regional policy issues regarding human settlements development and to develop regional policy guidelines. A study on the methodological framework for human settlements planning in Latin America, formulation of planning guidelines based on Western Asia, and integration of physical with economic and social planning in Asia and the Pacific were to be carried out.

Staff were deployed to Asia and the Pacific to analyse and synthesize experience in projects for upgrading slums and squatter settlements, to prepare guidelines to deal with the problem, and to work on a technical report on the effectiveness of rent control. The Centre began collecting and analysing information on land-use policies of countries in the region, as an input to the quinquennial *Global Report on Human Settlements*. Preparations were to be made in the region for a seminar on public participation in national programmes, aimed at public and private planners and managers of human settlements.

In addition to work carried out by staff deployed to the regional commissions, the Centre provided resources to those commissions to contribute to important global reports such as the theme papers presented to the Commission.

Report. [1]UNCHS Executive Director, HS/C/5/2/Add.5.
Resolution (1982). [2]Commission on Human Settlements (report, A/37/8): 5/6, 6 May.
Yearbook reference. [3]1981, p. 859.

Commission on Human Settlements

Work programme

In a resolution adopted on 7 May 1982,[1] the Commission decided to designate two years in advance the special themes to be considered at its sessions. It requested the UNCHS Executive Director to ensure thorough preparation for each theme, providing for extensive consultations and substantive contributions from interested Governments and organizations. Without extending the Commission's sessions, he was to allow for meetings at which the draft documents could be discussed.

Resolution (1982). [1]Commission on Human Settlements (report, A/37/8): 5/15, 7 May.

Arabic language services

By a decision of 7 May 1982,[1] the Commission decided to include Arabic among its official and working languages. The normal process for changing the Commission's rules of procedure—requiring the setting up of a working group to report on an amendment—was suspended in this case.

Decision (1982). [1]Commission on Human Settlements (report, A/37/8): 5/25, 7 May.

Documentation

Report of the Commission

By a decision of 7 May 1982,[1] the Commission approved a recommendation of the UNCHS Executive Director that the Commission's official reports, forwarded to the General Assembly through the Economic and Social Council, should be action-oriented, containing only information on organizational matters, resolutions and decisions. Another report, containing a full account of the proceedings, was to be prepared for participants and other interested parties.

Decision (1982). [1]Commission on Human Settlements (report, A/37/8): 5/26, 7 May.

Publications

On 6 May 1982,[1] the Commission requested the UNCHS Executive Director to ensure that the Centre's publications reflected the diversity of languages, cultures and knowledge of Member States, and that their authors could employ the working language of their choice, within existing resources; circulation was to benefit the greatest possible number of people, particularly in developing countries. The Executive Director was to report on implementation in 1983.

Resolution (1982). [1]Commission on Human Settlements (report, A/37/8): 5/8, 6 May.

Documents distribution

By a resolution of 6 May 1982,[1] the Commission requested the UNCHS Executive Director to implement fully the General Assembly's 1981 decision[2] that documents should be distributed simultaneously in the United Nations official and working languages, and to report to it in 1983.

Document dissemination was also the subject of a recommendation by the Committee for Programme and Co-ordination (see ADMINISTRATIVE AND BUDGETARY QUESTIONS, Chapter IV).

Resolution (1982). [1]Commission on Human Settlements (report, A/37/8): 5/9, 6 May.
Resolution (prior). [2]GA: 36/117 B, 10 Dec. 1981 (YUN 1981, p. 1376).

Chapter XVIII

Human Rights

Contents

Discrimination

Elimination of racial discrimination

Decade for Action to Combat Racism and Racial Discrimination (1973-1983)

Implementation of the Programme for the Decade

The Commission on Human Rights, the Committee on the Elimination of Racial Discrimination (CERD), the Economic and Social Council and the General Assembly continued in 1982 to follow action taken to implement the Programme for the Decade for Action to Combat Racism and Racial Discrimination, launched by the Assembly in 1973.[8] Preparations continued for the Second World Conference to Combat Racism and Racial Discrimination scheduled for 1983.

As called for in the Programme, the Secretary-General submitted to the Economic and Social Council in March two reports on activities relating to the Decade. His annual report on this topic[3] summarized actions, suggestions and trends emerging from the work of United Nations bodies, specialized agencies and regional intergovernmental organizations, and transmitted information on activities by non-governmental organizations. In the second report with an addendum in April, he summarized replies from Governments on legislative, administrative and other measures they had taken under the Programme.[4] In an August report to the Assembly,[2] he supplied additional information on the topics covered in the two earlier reports.

Action by the Commission on Human Rights. By a resolution of 25 February on implementation of the Programme,[5] the Commission on Human Rights made several recommendations regarding the Second World Conference to Combat Racism and Racial Discrimination (see below).

CERD activities. In March and August, CERD reviewed activities relating to the Decade, including its own participation in seminars and other events.[1] It appointed an observer to participate in the work of the Preparatory Sub-Committee for the Second World Conference to Combat Racism and Racial Discrimination (see below), and reviewed progress in the preparation of two Conference studies.

Economic and Social Council action. On 5 May,[6] the Economic and Social Council took note of the Secretary-General's report on activities relating to the Decade[3] and recommended a draft resolution for adoption by the General Assembly (see below).

The Council's resolution was adopted by 31 votes to 11, with 4 abstentions, as introduced and orally revised by Zaire, on behalf of 10 nations.

Austria, in explanation of its negative vote, stated that the approach taken by the sponsors was unacceptable. France found a number of elements of the text recommended for Assembly action inadmissible. Belgium regarded the introduction of the Middle East problem into the context of the Decade as unacceptable, and Israel objected to paragraph 2 which condemned racism in South Africa and the occupied Arab territories. Belgium, the Federal Republic of Germany and Israel voiced reservations to paragraph 3 because it advocated armed struggle, and objected to paragraph 10. The United States registered its opposition to the financial implications in spite of its policy not to participate in debates relating to the Decade which it did not endorse. The United Kingdom said it had cast a negative vote for reasons similar to those expressed by Belgium; it also objected to the draft's financial implications.

Portugal explained that it had abstained because of paragraphs 3, 8, 10 and 11; it also objected to certain preambular provisions.

Though voting in favour, Argentina, Chile and Fiji objected to the reference to armed struggle and to the paragraph on collaboration with South Africa. Argentina and Chile also reserved their position on the call for sanctions against South Africa, while Fiji had strong reservations on paragraph 2. Reservations on paragraph 10 were voiced by Mexico.

Introducing the draft, Zaire said its adoption by consensus would reflect a renewed common commitment to intensified efforts towards attaining the goals of the Decade as quickly as possible.

General Assembly action. In adopting the text recommended by the Economic and Social Council, the General Assembly, on 3 December,[7] proclaimed that the elimination of racism and racial discrimination and the attainment of the objectives of the Programme and activities for the Decade were of high priority. The Assembly strongly condemned *apartheid* and racial discrimination in southern Africa, occupied Arab territories and elsewhere, including the denial of the right to self-determination (see below, under CIVIL AND POLITICAL RIGHTS). It reaffirmed its support for the national liberation struggle against racial discrimination, *apartheid*, colonialism and foreign domination and for self-determination by all available means, including armed struggle. It called on States to punish by law the dissemination of ideas based on racial superiority or hatred, and to outlaw organizations based on racial hatred and prejudice, including neo-Nazi and Fascist organizations. It invited the international community to strengthen its activities for the Decade.

The Assembly requested that the Security Council consider imposing full mandatory sanctions against South Africa and consider strengthening the arms embargo (see POLITICAL AND SECURITY QUESTIONS, Chapter V). It vigorously condemned collaboration with South Africa by certain Western States, Israel and other States and by transnational corporations and other organizations, and called on Governments to take measures aimed at putting an end to enterprises in that country. It condemned South Africa's aggression against States of the region, expressed solidarity with the front-line States; and reaffirmed the rights of the Namibian people (see TRUSTEESHIP AND DECOLONIZATION, Chapter III). With regard to the Second World Conference to Combat Racism and Racial Discrimination (see below), it asked the Secretary-General to appoint a Conference Secretary-General, invited Member States to co-operate on the Decade's Programme and on Conference preparations, and invited United Nations bodies to contribute to those preparations. The Assembly invited Member States and the United Nations to continue efforts to protect migrant workers and their families (see below).

The resolution was adopted by a recorded vote of 122 to 19, with 5 abstentions. It was approved by the Third (Social, Humanitarian and Cultural) Committee on 27 October by 113 votes to 19, with 5 abstentions.

Austria, explaining its negative vote, stated that it was unable to accept some of the assessments and measures proposed. The United Kingdom again reserved its position on the financial implications and believed it would have been more logical to include in a single text all the provisions relating to the World Conference.

Ireland believed that the political situation in the Middle East should be considered separately from that in southern Africa. The United States said the references to the Arab-Israeli conflict compounded the damage already done by equating zionism with racism, and if some countries were to be mentioned for trading with South Africa, then all countries engaging in such trade should be mentioned. The United States also rejected the view that investment by foreign corporations in South Africa was perpetuating the *apartheid* system or the continued South African presence in Namibia; it regarded as counter-productive the support for armed struggle and the call for sanctions, the latter being within the exlusive competence of the Security Council. With regard to paragraph 12 outlawing the dissemination of ideas based on racial superiority, the United States felt that democratic ends could not be pursued through anti-democratic means.

Speaking for the five Nordic States, Norway said they believed that the Middle East situation and the question of sanctions against South Africa should be dealt with in the competent United Nations organs. The support by the Assembly for armed struggle was inconsistent with the United Nations obligation to seek peaceful solutions, and the fact that certain States were accused arbitrarily was unacceptable.

Abstaining, Japan said it could not accept some concepts underlying the text. Portugal reiterated reservations made in the Council.

The Dominican Republic, which supported the resolution in the Assembly, stated its reservations concerning paragraph 10 singling out certain States for their collaboration with South Africa, as well as paragraph 3 which condoned armed struggle.

Voting in favour, Chile and Uruguay voiced reservations on paragraphs 2, 3, 8 and 10. In addition, Uruguay strongly opposed paragraphs 5 and 12. Turkey could not accept the mention of certain countries in paragraph 10 and in the preamble.

The USSR observed that the resolution, together with other texts adopted by the Third Committee, dealt with the most urgent problems relating to the struggle against racism and colonialism, the realization of the right of peoples to self-determination and the granting of independence to colonial countries and peoples.

Reports. [1]CERD, A/37/18; S-G, [2]A/37/338 & Add.1, [3]E/1982/24 & Add.1, [4]E/1982/25 & Add.1.
Resolutions (1982). [5]Commission on Human Rights (report, E/1982/12): 1982/11, 25 Feb. [6]ESC: 1982/31, 5 May, text following. [7]GA: 37/40, 3 Dec., text following.
Resolution (prior). [8]GA: 3057(XXVIII), annex, 2 Nov. 1973 (YUN 1973, p. 524).
Financial implications. ACABQ report, A/37/7/Add.8; 5th Committee report, A/37/685; S-G statements, A/C.3/37/L.8, A/C.5/37/31, E/1981/L.32 & Corr.1.
Meeting records. ESC: E/1982/SR.10-14, *22, 24* (19 Apr.-5 May). GA: 3rd Committee, A/C.3/37/SR.*3*, 4-13, *24, 25* (30 Sep.-27 Oct.); 5th Committee, A/C.5/37/SR.39, 45, *46* (19-29 Nov.); plenary, A/37/PV.90 (3 Dec.).

Economic and Social Council resolution 1982/31

5 May 1982   Meeting 24   31-11-4

10-nation draft (E/1982/L.23), orally revised; agenda item 2.

Sponsors: Algeria, Benin, Ethiopia, Kenya, Liberia, Libyan Arab Jamahiriya, Nigeria, Sudan, Yugoslavia, Zaire.

Implementation of the Programme for the Decade for Action to Combat Racism and Racial Discrimination

The Economic and Social Council,

Recalling General Assembly resolution 3057(XXVIII) of 2 November 1973, in which the Assembly proclaimed the Decade for Action to Combat Racism and Racial Discrimination and approved the Programme for the Decade,

Recalling also the other relevant General Assembly resolutions, particularly resolution 34/24 of 15 November 1979, in which the Assembly adopted the four-year programme of activities designed to accelerate progress in the implementation of the Programme for the Decade,

Bearing in mind General Assembly resolution 35/33 of 14 November 1980, in which the Assembly decided to hold in 1983, as an important event of the Decade, a second world conference to combat racism and racial discrimination, and invited the Economic and Social Council to begin the preparatory work for the conference at its first regular session of 1981,

Convinced that effective implementation of the Programme for the Decade will help to promote and encourage respect for human rights and fundamental freedoms for all, without distinction as to race, colour, descent or national or ethnic origin,

Recalling its resolutions 1980/7 of 24 April 1980 and 1981/30 of 6 May 1981,

1. *Takes note with satisfaction* of the report of the Secretary-General submitted in accordance with General Assembly resolution 3057(XXVIII);

2. *Recommends* to the General Assembly the adoption of the following draft resolution:

[Text as in General Assembly resolution 37/40 below.]

General Assembly resolution 37/40

3 December 1982   Meeting 90   122-19-5 (recorded vote)

Approved by Third Committee (A/37/595) by vote (113-19-5), 27 October (meeting 24); draft recommended by Economic and Social Council (resolution 1982/31); agenda item 76.

Implementation of the Programme for the Decade for Action to Combat Racism and Racial Discrimination

The General Assembly,

Reaffirming its resolve to bring about the total and unconditional eradication of racism, racial discrimination and *apartheid*, which still represent serious obstacles to further progress and to the strengthening of international peace and security,

Recalling that, in its resolution 3057(XXVIII) of 2 November 1973 and in the Programme for the Decade for Action to Combat Racism and Racial Discrimination annexed thereto, and in other relevant resolutions, it called upon all peoples, Governments and institutions to continue their efforts to eradicate racism, racial discrimination and *apartheid* and thus to promote respect for human rights and fundamental freedoms for all, without distinction as to race, colour, descent or national or ethnic origin,

Taking into account the Declaration and the Programme of Action adopted by the World Conference to Combat Racism and Racial Discrimination,

Recalling that, in the programme of activities to be undertaken during the second half of the Decade for Action to Combat Racism and Racial Discrimination, contained in the annex to its resolution 34/24 of 15 November 1979, it called upon all States, United Nations organs and intergovernmental and non-governmental organizations to intensify their efforts to achieve the speediest attainment of the objectives of the Decade, aimed at the complete and final elimination of all forms of racism and racial discrimination,

Expressing its serious concern at the situation prevailing in South Africa and throughout southern Africa as a result of the policies and actions of the *apartheid* régime, particularly its efforts to perpetuate and strengthen racist domination of the country, its policy of "bantustanization", its brutal repression of opponents of *apartheid* and its renewed acts of aggression against neighbouring States,

Reaffirming that *apartheid* is a crime against humanity,

Particularly concerned at the persistence of the illegal occupation of Namibia by the racist minority régime of South Africa,

Disappointed that the talks between the United Nations and the South African racist and illegal occupation régime aimed at reaching

a negotiated settlement of the question of Namibia have thus far failed because of the bad faith of that régime,

Reaffirming that any collaboration with the racist régime of South Africa constitutes a hostile act against the oppressed people of South Africa and a contemptuous defiance of the United Nations and the international community,

Considering that such collaboration strengthens the racist régime, encourages it to persist in its repressive and aggressive policy and seriously aggravates the situation in southern Africa, thus constituting a threat to international peace and security,

Seriously concerned at the fact that the principal Western and other trading partners of South Africa are continuing to collaborate with the racist régime and that their collaboration constitutes the main obstacle to the abolition of that régime and the elimination of the inhuman and criminal system of *apartheid*,

Alarmed at the persistent collaboration of certain Western States and Israel with the racist régime of South Africa in the nuclear field,

Aware of the constant need to mobilize world public opinion against any political, military, economic and other assistance granted to the racist régime of South Africa,

Aware of the need to promote solutions to the problems of discrimination facing migrant workers and their families,

Recalling its resolution 35/33 of 14 November 1980, in which it decided to hold in 1983 a Second World Conference to Combat Racism and Racial Discrimination, which, while reviewing and assessing the activities undertaken during the Decade, should have as its main purpose the formulation of ways and means and of specific measures aimed at ensuring the full and universal implementation of United Nations resolutions and decisions on racism, racial discrimination and *apartheid*,

Stressing the importance of attaining the objectives of the Decade,

Convinced that the Second World Conference to Combat Racism and Racial Discrimination will make a useful and constructive contribution to the attainment of those objectives,

1. *Proclaims* that the elimination of all forms of racism and of discrimination based on race and the attainment of the objectives of the Programme for the Decade for Action to Combat Racism and Racial Discimination and of the programme of activities to be undertaken during the second half of the Decade are matters of high priority for the international community and, therefore, for the United Nations;

2. *Strongly condemns* the policies of *apartheid*, racism and racial discrimination pursued in southern Africa, all occupied Arab territories and elsewhere, including the denial of the right of peoples to self-determination and independence;

3. *Reaffirms* its strong support for the national liberation struggle against racism, racial discrimination, *apartheid*, colonialism and foreign domination and for self-determination by all available means, including armed struggle;

4. *Reaffirms* the inalienable right of the Namibian people to self-determination and independence;

5. *Vigorously condemns* the repeated acts of aggression committed by South Africa against the States of the region, particularly Angola, Botswana, Mozambique, Seychelles and Zambia;

6. *Expresses its profound solidarity* with the front-line States that are victims of the racist aggression and destabilization attempts of the Pretoria régime;

7. *Once again invites* all Member States, United Nations organs, specialized agencies, intergovernmental organizations, national liberation movements, anti-*apartheid* and anti-racist organizations and other solidarity groups to strengthen and enlarge the scope of their activities in support of the objectives of the Programme for the Decade;

8. *Again requests* the Security Council to consider, as a matter of urgency, the imposition of full mandatory sanctions under Chapter VII of the Charter of the United Nations against the racist régime of South Africa and the strengthening of the embargo on arms, with a view to putting an end to all military and nuclear collaboration with South Africa;

9. *Reaffirms* the decision by which it approved the Declaration of the International Seminar on the Implementation and Reinforcement of the Arms Embargo against South Africa, held in London from 1 to 3 April 1981 under the auspices of the Special Committee against Apartheid;

10. *Vigorously condemns* the collaboration of certain Western States, Israel and other States and of transnational corporations and

other organizations which are maintaining or continuing to increase their collaboration with the racist régime of South Africa, particularly in the political, economic, military and nuclear fields, thereby encouraging that régime to persist in its inhuman and criminal policy of brutal oppression of the peoples of southern Africa and in its denial of human rights;

11. *Calls once again upon* all Governments that have not yet done so to take legislative, administrative and other measures in respect of their nationals and the bodies corporate under their jurisdiction that own enterprises in southern Africa in order to put an end to such enterprises;

12. *Calls upon* all States to adopt, as a matter of high priority, measures declaring punishable by law any dissemination of ideas based on racial superiority or hatred and outlawing organizations based on racial hatred and prejudice, including neo-Nazi and Fascist organizations and private clubs and institutions established on the basis of racial criteria or propagating ideas of racial discrimination and *apartheid*;

13. *Invites* Member States, the organs and bodies of the United Nations system and the specialized agencies to continue their efforts with a view to the protection of the rights of all migrant workers and their families;

14. *Takes note with appreciation* of the report of the Preparatory Sub-Committee for the Second World Conference to Combat Racism and Racial Discrimination on its first session;

15. *Requests* the Secretary-General to provide the Preparatory Sub-Committee with all necessary assistance;

16. *Further requests* the Secretary-General to appoint, after consultation with the regional groups, in 1982, a Secretary-General of the Second World Conference to Combat Racism and Racial Discrimination, who shall have the rank of Assistant Secretary-General and shall be responsible for the organization of the Conference and co-ordination with Member States, organs and bodies of the United Nations, specialized agencies and intergovernmental and non-governmental organizations;

17. *Invites* Member States to continue to co-operate with the Secretary-General as part of the Programme for the Decade and the preparations for the Conference;

18. *Invites* the appropriate organs and bodies of the United Nations system to contribute to the preparations for the Conference;

19. *Expresses its satisfaction* to the Committee on the Elimination of Racial Discrimination, the Special Committee against *Apartheid*, the United Nations Council for Namibia, the Special Committee on the Situation with regard to the Implementation of the Declaration on the Granting of Independence to Colonial Countries and Peoples, the Committee on the Exercise of the Inalienable Rights of the Palestinian People and the Commission on Human Rights, through its *Ad Hoc* Working Group of Experts on Southern Africa, for their contribution to the implementation of the Programme for the Decade and invites them to include in their activities the preparations for the Conference;

20. *Decides* to consider at its thirty-eighth session, as a matter of high priority, the item entitled "Implementation of the Programme for the Decade to Combat Racism and Racial Discrimination".

Recorded vote in Assembly as follows:

In favour: Albania, Algeria, Angola, Antigua and Barbuda, Argentina, Bahamas, Bahrain, Bangladesh, Barbados, Belize, Benin, Bhutan, Bolivia, Botswana, Brazil, Bulgaria, Burma, Burundi, Byelorussian SSR, Cape Verde, Central African Republic, Chad, Chile, China, Colombia, Comoros, Costa Rica, Cuba, Cyprus, Czechoslovakia, Democratic Kampuchea, Democratic Yemen, Djibouti, Dominican Republic, Ecuador, Egypt, El Salvador, Equatorial Guinea, Ethiopia, Fiji, Gabon, German Democratic Republic, Ghana, Grenada, Guinea, Guinea-Bissau, Guyana, Haiti, Hungary, India, Indonesia, Iran, Iraq, Ivory Coast, Jamaica, Jordan, Kenya, Kuwait, Lao People's Democratic Republic, Lebanon, Lesotho, Liberia, Libyan Arab Jamahiriya, Madagascar, Malaysia, Maldives, Mali, Malta, Mauritania, Mauritius, Mexico, Mongolia, Morocco, Mozambique, Nepal, Nicaragua, Niger, Nigeria, Oman, Pakistan, Panama, Papua New Guinea, Peru, Philippines, Poland, Qatar, Romania, Rwanda, Saint Lucia, Samoa, Sao Tome and Principe, Saudi Arabia, Senegal, Sierra Leone, Singapore, Solomon Islands, Somalia, Sri Lanka, Sudan, Suriname, Swaziland, Syrian Arab Republic, Thailand, Togo, Trinidad and Tobago, Tunisia, Turkey, Uganda, Ukrainian SSR, USSR, United Arab Emirates, United Republic of Tanzania, Upper Volta, Uruguay, Vanuatu, Venezuela, Viet Nam, Yemen, Yugoslavia, Zaire, Zambia, Zimbabwe.

Against: Austria, Bahamas, Belgium, Canada, Denmark, Finland, France, Germany, Federal Republic of, Iceland, Ireland, Israel, Italy, Luxembourg, Netherlands, New Zealand, Norway, Sweden, United Kingdom, United States.

Abstaining: Greece, Japan, Paraguay, Portugal, Spain.

NGO activities

The Economic and Social Council, by a resolution of 4 May 1982,[1] expressed its expectation that non-governmental organizations in consultative status with it would take account in their activities of Council and General Assembly resolutions on *apartheid*.

Resolution (1982). [1]ESC: 1982/16, 4 May.

Seminar for Asia and the Pacific

The Economic and Social Council, on 4 May 1982,[1] requested the Secretary-General to organize, under the Programme for the Decade, a seminar for the region of the Economic and Social Commission for Asia and the Pacific at Bangkok, Thailand, from 2 to 13 August.

This decision was taken without vote and was introduced by Pakistan, also on behalf of Bangladesh, China, India and Nepal.

The Seminar made several recommendations with regard to recourse procedures and other forms of protection for victims of racial discrimination, together with activities to be undertaken at the national and regional levels.[2]

Decision (1982). [1]ESC: 1982/120, 4 May, text following.
Report. [2]Seminar, ST/HR/SER.A/13.
Financial implications. S-G statement, E/1982/L.33.
Meeting record. ESC: E/1982/SR.22 (4 May).

Economic and Social Council decision 1982/120

Adopted without vote

5-nation draft (E/1982/L.29); agenda item 2.

Sponsors: Bangladesh, China, India, Nepal, Pakistan.

Seminar for the region of the Economic and Social Commission for Asia and the Pacific under the Programme for the Decade for Action to Combat Racism and Racial Discrimination

At its 22nd plenary meeting, on 4 May 1982, the Council, taking into account the recommendation of the Preparatory Sub-Committee for the Second World Conference to Combat Racism and Racial Discrimination that the seminar planned for the region of the Economic and Social Commission for Asia and the Pacific under the Programme for the Decade for Action to Combat Racism and Racial Discrimination should be held well in advance of the World Conference in order for its results to be made available to participants, requested the Secretary-General to take the necessary steps to organize the seminar at the headquarters of the Economic and Social Commission for Asia and the Pacific from 2 to 13 August 1982.

Preparations for the Second World Conference

Work of the Preparatory Sub-Committee. At its first session, held in New York from 15 to 26 March 1982,[3] the Preparatory Sub-Committee for the Second World Conference to Combat Racism and Racial Discrimination recommended that the Conference be held in a developing country. If no offer from a developing country was received, the Conference should be held at Geneva. The tentative dates of the Conference were 1 to 12 August 1983.

The Sub-Committee recommended the Conference's draft provisional agenda and the draft rules of procedure to the Economic and Social Council for consideration, and made recommendations concerning pre-session and in-session documentation. It asked that the United Nations Secretariat prepare a draft programme of action containing proposals for post-Conference activities.

Action by the Commission on Human Rights. On 25 February 1982,[4] the Commission on Human Rights recommended that the Preparatory Sub-Committee pay particular attention to seminars, round-table meetings and studies conducted during the second half of the Decade, and that the relevant reports and studies be among the basic Conference documents. The Commission urged the Secretary-General to appoint the Conference's Secretary-General as early as possible, and decided that the Chairman of the Commission's 1983 session would represent the Commission at the Conference. The resolution was adopted by a roll-call vote of 34 to none, with 8 abstentions.

Economic and Social Council action. The Economic and Social Council, on 5 May,[5] approved the Conference's draft provisional agenda and draft provisional rules of procedure. It recommended to the General Assembly that all States and the United Nations Council for Namibia be invited to participate in the Conference, and made recommendations on the observers to be invited. It decided that the Conference languages be all six official United Nations languages, and that Conference documentation should include pre-session and in-session documents. It authorized the Preparatory Sub-Committee to meet for one week in March 1983 and to report to the Council in May of that year. It requested the Secretary-General to submit to the Sub-Committee a draft programme of action and invited the Sub-Committee to submit its draft programme to the Conference, through the Council. It recommended that the offer of the Philippines to host the Conference be accepted, with half of the additional cost of holding the Conference there being defrayed from the United Nations regular budget, in accordance with a 1976 Assembly resolution[11] on the first World Conference. The Council recommended that the Conference be held from 1 to 12 August 1983, subject to adjustment after consultations with the Secretary-General.

The Council also recommended a draft resolution for adoption by the Assembly (see below).

The Council resolution was adopted by 38 votes to 1, with 12 abstentions; it was sponsored and orally revised by 13 nations. Paragraph 1 was adopted by a vote, requested by Denmark, of 32 to 10, with 7 abstentions.

Voting against the resolution as a whole because of its financial implications, the United States said it did not participate in the vote on paragraph 1 because of its position of principle on the Decade.

Abstaining on the text as a whole and voting against paragraph 1, Austria and France regretted that efforts to produce a resolution acceptable to all had failed. Australia said that departures from the guidelines for the holding of United Nations conferences away from Headquarters and the resultant financial implications could not be tolerated. Australia, as well as Italy, also had reservations about accepting the Philippine offer.

Denmark objected to paragraph 1 because of the draft provisional agenda's specific reference to the Middle East situation. Similar reservations were voiced by Belgium, Canada, Fiji, the Federal Republic of Germany, Italy, Portugal and the United Kingdom.

Norway expressed the hope that paragraph 1 would be discussed further by the Assembly with a view to achieving consensus; a similar opinion was expressed by Belgium and Canada.

Japan, which abstained in both votes, believed that the goals of the Decade would be achieved only when all Member States were convinced of the appropriateness of activities undertaken in its context; it regretted that the Council had failed to reach a compromise on the Conference preparations.

Chile abstained on paragraph 1 because it felt that certain controversial aspects of the draft provisional agenda could impede the attainment of the objectives of the Decade; however, it had voted in favour of the resolution as a whole in support for the aims of the Conference.

The Philippines, by a letter of 12 April 1982 to the Secretary-General,[1] offered to host the Second World Conference on the condition that the 1976 formula for defraying half of the additional cost from the United Nations regular budget be applied. By a letter of 29 April,[2] the Philippines expressed its agreement to holding the Conference at Manila from 1 to 12 August 1983 with the same stipulation on defraying the cost.

General Assembly action. On 3 December 1982,[7] the General Assembly expressed its appreciation to the Philippines for its offer, but decided to convene the Conference at Geneva from 1 to 12 August 1983. It endorsed the Economic and Social Council resolution of 5 May (see above) and requested the Secretary-General to invite all States and the United Nations Council for Namibia to participate in the Conference, and to invite observers, including those from national liberation movements, United Nations bodies, specialized agencies, and intergovernmental and nongovernmental organizations. It requested the Secretary-General to ensure maximum publicity for the Conference and to report in 1983 on its work. It called on States to participate actively in the Conference proceedings and urged them to cooperate in the preparatory work and to consider setting up national committees. Annexed to the resolution was the Conference's draft provisional agenda.

The resolution was adopted without vote, following its approval in the Third (Social, Humanitarian and Cultural) Committee on 2 November by 124 votes to 2. After informal consultations on the draft recommended by the Economic and Social Council in its resolution of 5 May (see above), the text was orally amended by the Committee Chairman to delete, in the draft provisional agenda, references to specific activities for the Decade which were to be reviewed and evaluated.

Following the Assembly's decision on the financing of the Conference (see below), the resolution was orally amended by Ghana and by Canada. Ghana proposed that, in paragraph 2, the Assembly express its appreciation to the Philippines for, rather than accept, its offer, and that, in paragraph 3, it decided to convene the Conference at Geneva, not at Manila as originally suggested. As proposed by Canada, the provision was deleted by which the Assembly would have agreed that half of the additional cost of holding the Conference in the Philippines would be defrayed from the United Nations regular budget.

By another 3 December resolution,[6] the Assembly noted with appreciation the report of the Preparatory Sub-Committee and requested the Secretary-General to provide the Sub-Committee with all necessary assistance. It requested that the Secretary-General appoint in 1982, after consultation with the regional groups, a Conference Secretary-General, with the rank of Assistant Secretary-General, responsible for organization of the Conference and co-ordination with Member States and other bodies. It invited Member States to co-operate and invited the United Nations system to contribute to the Conference preparations.

In another resolution of the same date,[8] the Assembly took note with appreciation of the contribution of the Committee on the Elimination of Racial Discrimination to the work of the Preparatory Sub-Committee and to the regional seminars held in implementation of the Programme for the Decade. It welcomed the Committee's decision to prepare a study for the Conference on the implementation of articles 4 and 7 of the International Convention on the Elimination of All Forms of Racial Discrimination[10] (on the condemnation of propaganda and organizations based on ideas of racial or ethnic superiority and the eradication of discrimination, and on measures to combat prejudices which lead to racial discrimination, respectively), and reiterated its request that the Committee explore the possibility of preparing a study on the implementation of article 5, subparagraph *(e)*, on economic, social and cultural rights.

In another 3 December resolution,[9] on the status of the International Convention on the Sup-

pression and Punishment of the Crime of *Apartheid*, the Assembly called on States to participate actively in the Conference and to contribute to achieving effective results.

Letters. Philippines: [1]12 Apr., E/1982/49; [2]29 Apr., E/1982/68.
Report. [3]Preparatory Sub-Committee, E/1982/26.
Resolutions (1982). [4]Commission on Human Rights (report, E/1982/12): 1982/11, 25 Feb. [5]ESC: 1982/32, 5 May, text following. GA, 3 Dec.: [6]37/40, paras. 14-19; [7]37/41, text following; [8]37/46, paras. 13 & 14; [9]37/47, para. 15.
Resolutions (prior). GA: [10]2106 A (XX), annex, 21 Dec. 1965 (YUN 1965, p. 440); [11]31/78, 13 Dec. 1976 (YUN 1976, p. 573).
Financial implications. ACABQ report, A/37/7/Add.8; Committee on Conferences observations, A/C.5/37/32/Add.1; 5th Committee report, A/37/685; S-G statements, A/C.3/37/L.10, A/C.5/37/32, E/1981/L.37.
Meeting records. ESC: E/1982/SR.10-14, 22, *24, 25* (19 Apr.–5 May). GA: 3rd Committee, A/C.3/37/SR.3-13, *31* (30 Sep.–2 Nov.); 5th Committee, A/C.5/37/SR.39, 45, *46*, 52 (19 Nov.–2 Dec.); plenary, A/37/PV.90 (3 Dec.).

Economic and Social Council resolution 1982/32

5 May 1982	Meeting 25	38 1 12

13-nation draft (E/1982/L.36), orally revised; agenda item 2.

Sponsors: Bangladesh, Bulgaria, Cuba, Ethiopia, India, Iraq, Mexico, Nigeria, Pakistan, Philippines, Syrian Arab Republic, Yugoslavia, Zimbabwe.

Second World Conference to Combat Racism and Racial Discrimination

The Economic and Social Council,

Recalling General Assembly resolutions 3057(XXVIII) of 2 November 1973, 33/99 and 33/100 of 16 December 1978, 34/24 of 15 November 1979, 35/33 of 14 November 1980 and 36/8 of 28 October 1981, and its resolution 1990(LX) of 11 May 1976,

Recalling also its decision 206(ORG-77) of 14 January 1977, its resolution 2046(S-III) of 23 February 1977 and its decision 1981/130 of 6 May 1981,

Having considered the report of the Preparatory Sub-Committee for the Second World Conference to Combat Racism and Racial Discrimination on its first session,

Noting with appreciation the offer of the Government of the Philippines to act as host to the Second World Conference to Combat Racism and Racial Discrimination,

Recognizing that the Philippines is one of the countries affected by the current world economic crisis and that, despite this, the Government of the Philippines is willing to make a substantial financial contribution towards the Conference,

1. *Approves* the draft provisional agenda and the draft provisional rules of procedure of the Second World Conference to Combat Racism and Racial Discrimination;

2. *Recommends* to the General Assembly that invitations to participate in the Conference should be extended to:

(a) All States;

(b) The United Nations Council for Namibia, in accordance with General Assembly resolution 31/149 of 20 December 1976;

3. *Recommends* to the General Assembly that the following should be invited to participate in the Conference as observers:

(a) Representatives of national liberation movements recognized in its region by the Organization of African Unity, in accordance with General Assembly resolution 3280(XXIX) of 10 December 1974;

(b) Representatives of organizations that have received a standing invitation from the General Assembly to participate in the sessions and the work of all international conferences convened under its auspices, in accordance with Assembly resolutions 3237(XXIX) of 22 November 1974 and 31/152 of 20 December 1976;

(c) The specialized agencies concerned, as well as interested organs and bodies of the United Nations;

(d) Interested intergovernmental organizations;

(e) The Special Committee against *Apartheid;*

(f) The Special Committee on the Situation with regard to the Implementation of the Declaration on the Granting of Independence to Colonial Countries and Peoples;

(g) The Committee on the Elimination of Racial Discrimination;

(h) The Commission on Human Rights;

(i) The Committee on the Exercise of the Inalienable Rights of the Palestinian People and the Special Committee to Investigate Israeli Practices Affecting the Human Rights of the Population of the Occupied Territories;

(j) Other interested committees of the United Nations;

(k) Non-governmental organizations in consultative status with the Economic and Social Council which have contributed to the achievement of the goals and objectives of the Decade for Action to Combat Racism and Racial Discrimination and to the implementation of the Programme of Action adopted by the first World Conference to Combat Racism and Racial Discrimination, taking into account also their record in the struggle against racism and racial discrimination;

4. *Decides* that the languages of the Conference shall be Arabic, Chinese, English, French, Russian and Spanish;

5. *Decides* that the documentation for the Conference shall include pre-session and in-session documents as indicated in paragraphs 63 to 78 of the report of the Preparatory Sub-Committee;

6. *Decides* to authorize the Preparatory Sub-Committee to hold a second session of one week in March 1983 and to submit its report to the Economic and Social Council at its first regular session of 1983;

7. *Requests* the Secretary-General to take appropriate steps as soon as possible to start the timely preparation of all the necessary documentation and to ensure that the documentation is available at least six weeks before the beginning of the Conference;

8. *Requests* the Secretary-General to submit to the Preparatory Sub-Committee for the Second World Conference to Combat Racism and Racial Discrimination a draft programme of action containing proposals for activities to be undertaken after the Conference as a follow-up to the programme of activities adopted for the second half of the Decade and the Programme of Action adopted by the first World Conference, taking into account the above-mentioned documents and the relevant resolutions and decisions of the United Nations regarding racism, racial discrimination and *apartheid*, and invites the Preparatory Sub-Committee, on the basis of the Secretary-General's draft, to submit to the Conference, through the Economic and Social Council, a draft programme of action;

9. *Also requests* the Secretary-General to report to the Preparatory Sub-Committee at its second session on the status of the documentation;

10. *Recommends* that the offer of the Government of the Philippines to act as host to the Conference should be accepted and that the formula decided upon by the General Assembly in its resolution 31/78 of 13 December 1976 regarding the cost involved in holding the first World Conference should apply to that offer;

11. *Requests* the Secretary-General to consult with the Government of the Philippines concerning arrangements for holding the Conference at Manila;

12. *Recommends* that the duration of the Conference should be two weeks, from 1 to 12 August 1983, these dates being subject to adjustment contingent upon the consultations with the Secretary-General;

13. *Recommends* to the General Assembly the adoption of the following draft resolution:

"*The General Assembly*,

"*Recalling* its resolution 3057(XXVIII) of 2 November 1973, by which it proclaimed the Decade for Action to Combat Racism and Racial Discrimination,

"*Mindful* of the Declaration and the Programme of Action adopted by the World Conference to Combat Racism and Racial Discrimination,

"*Recalling* paragraph 26 of the programme of activities to be undertaken during the second half of the Decade for Action to Combat Racism and Racial Discrimination annexed to its resolution 34/24 of 15 November 1979, by which the Assembly decided that an important feature of the second half of the Decade should be the holding of a second World Conference to Combat Racism and Racial Discrimination,

"*Bearing in mind* its resolution 35/33 of 14 November 1980, by which it decided to hold in 1983, as an important event of the Decade, a second World Conference to Combat Racism and Racial Discrimination, which, while reviewing and assessing the activities undertaken during

the Decade, should have as its main purpose the formulation of ways and means and of specific measures aimed at ensuring the full and universal implementation of United Nations resolutions and decisions on racism, racial discrimination and *apartheid*,

"*Bearing in mind also* the provisions of its resolution 36/8 of 28 October 1981 regarding the preparations for the Second World Conference to Combat Racism and Racial Discrimination,

"*Taking note* of Economic and Social Council resolution 1982/32 of 5 May 1982, containing recommendations regarding the organization of the Second World Conference to Combat Racism and Racial Discrimination,

"1. *Endorses* Economic and Social Council resolution 1982/32;

"2. *Accepts* the offer of the Government of the Philippines to act as host to the Second World Conference to Combat Racism and Racial Discrimination;

"3. *Decides* to convene the Conference at Manila from 1 to 12 August 1983;

"4. *Decides* to make an exception to its resolution 2609(XXIV) of 16 December 1969 on the pattern of conferences and agrees that half of the additional cost involved in holding the Conference in the Philippines shall be defrayed from the regular budget of the United Nations;

"5. *Requests* the Secretary-General to invite as participants in the Conference:

"*(a)* All States;

"*(b)* The United Nations Council for Namibia, in accordance with General Assembly resolution 31/149 of 20 December 1976;

"6 *Also requests* the Secretary-General to invite as observers to the Conference:

"*(a)* Representatives of national liberation movements recognized in its region by the Organization of African Unity, in accordance with General Assembly resolution 3280(XXIX) of 10 December 1974;

"*(b)* Representatives of organizations that have received a standing invitation from the General Assembly to participate in the sessions and the work of all international conferences convened under its auspices, in accordance with Assembly resolutions 3237(XXIX) of 22 November 1974 and 31/152 of 20 December 1976;

"*(c)* The specialized agencies concerned, as well as interested organs and bodies of the United Nations;

"*(d)* Interested intergovernmental organizations;

"*(e)* The Special Committee against *Apartheid;*

"*(f)* The Special Committee on the Situation with regard to the Implementation of the Declaration on the Granting of Independence to Colonial Countries and Peoples;

"*(g)* The Committee on the Elimination of Racial Discrimination;

"*(h)* The Commission on Human Rights;

"*(i)* The Committee on the Exercise of the Inalienable Rights of the Palestinian People and the Special Committee to Investigate Israeli Practices Affecting the Human Rights of the Population of the Occupied Territories;

"*(j)* Other interested committees of the United Nations;

"*(k)* Non-governmental organizations in consultative status with the Economic and Social Council which have contributed to the achievement of the goals and objectives of the Decade for Action to Combat Racism and Racial Discrimination and to the implementation of the Programme of Action adopted by the first World Conference, taking into account also their record in the struggle against racism and racial discrimination;

"7. *Requests* the Secretary-General, as part of the preparatory process, to take adequate steps to ensure that maximum publicity is given to the Conference and, to that end, to allocate the necessary resources from the regular budget;

"8. *Calls upon* all States to contribute to the success of the Decade for Action to Combat Racism and Racial Discrimination, in particular by their active participation in the Conference;

"9. *Urges* all States to co-operate with the Secretary-General of the Conference in the preparatory work and to consider the establishment of national committees for publicizing the aims and, eventually, the main results of the Conference;

"10. *Requests* the Secretary-General to report to the General Assembly at its thirty-eighth session on the work of the Conference;

"11. *Decides* to consider at its thirty-eighth session, as a matter of high priority, an item entitled 'Second World Conference to Combat Racism and Racial Discrimination'."

General Assembly resolution 37/41

3 December 1982 Meeting 90 Adopted without vote

Approved by Third Committee (A/37/595) by vote (124-2), 2 November (meeting 31); draft recommended by Economic and Social Council (resolution 1982/32), orally amended in Committee by Chairman following consultations; orally amended in Assembly by Canada and by Ghana; agenda item 76.

Second World Conference to Combat Racism and Racial Discrimination

The General Assembly,

Recalling its resolution 3057(XXVIII) of 2 November 1973, by which it proclaimed the Decade for Action to Combat Racism and Racial Discrimination,

Mindful of the Declaration and the Programme of Action adopted by the World Conference to Combat Racism and Racial Discrimination,

Recalling paragraph 26 of the programme of activities to be undertaken during the second half of the Decade for Action to Combat Racism and Racial Discrimination, contained in the annex to its resolution 34/24 of 15 November 1979, in which the Assembly decided that an important feature of the second half of the Decade should be the holding of a Second World Conference to Combat Racism and Racial Discrimination,

Bearing in mind its resolution 35/33 of 14 November 1980, in which it decided to hold in 1983, as an important event of the Decade, a Second World Conference to Combat Racism and Racial Discrimination, which, while reviewing and assessing the activities undertaken during the Decade, should have as its main purpose the formulation of ways and means of specific measures aimed at ensuring the full and universal implementation of United Nations resolutions and decisions on racism, racial discrimination and *apartheid,*

Bearing in mind also the provisions of its resolution 36/8 of 28 October 1981 regarding the preparations for the Conference,

Taking note of Economic and Social Council resolution 1982/32 of 5 May 1982, which contains recommendations regarding the organization of the Conference,

1. *Endorses* Economic and Social Council resolution 1982/32;

2. *Expresses its appreciation* to the Government of the Philippines for its offer to act as host to the Second World Conference to Combat Racism and Racial Discrimination;

3. *Decides* to convene the Conference at Geneva from 1 to 12 August 1983;

4. *Recommends* the draft provisional agenda for the Conference as contained in the annex to the present resolution;

5. *Requests* the Secretary-General to invite:

(a) All States to participate in the Conference;

(b) The United Nations Council for Namibia to participate in the Conference, in accordance with paragraph 3 of General Assembly resolution 32/9 E of 4 November 1977;

6. *Further requests* the Secretary-General to invite:

(a) Representatives of national liberation movements recognized in its region by the Organization of African Unity to participate in the Conference in the capacity of observer, in accordance with General Assembly resolution 3280(XXIX) of 10 December 1974;

(b) Representatives of organizations that have received a standing invitation from the General Assembly to participate in the sessions and the work of all international conferences convened under its auspices in the capacity of observers to participate in the Conference in that capacity in accordance with General Assembly resolutions 3237(XXIX) of 22 November 1974 and 31/152 of 20 December 1976;

(c) The specialized agencies concerned, as well as interested organs and bodies of the United Nations system, to be represented at the Conference;

(d) Interested intergovernmental organizations to be represented by observers at the Conference;

(e) The Special Committee against *Apartheid* to be represented by observers at the Conference;

(f) The Special Committee on the Situation with regard to the Implementation of the Declaration on the Granting of Independence to Colonial Countries and Peoples to be represented by observers at the Conference;

(g) The Committee on the Elimination of Racial Discrimination to be represented by observers at the Conference;

(h) The Commission on Human Rights to be represented by observers at the Conference;

(i) The Committee on the Exercise of the Inalienable Rights of the Palestinian People and the Special Committee to Investigate Israeli Practices Affecting the Human Rights of the Population of the Occupied Territories to be represented by observers at the Conference;

(j) Other interested committees of the United Nations to be represented by observers at the Conference;

(k) Non-governmental organizations in consultative status with the Economic and Social Council which have contributed to the achievement of the goals and objectives of the Decade for Action to Combat Racism and Racial Discrimination and to the implementation of the Programme of Action adopted by the first World Conference, taking into account also their record in the field of struggle against racism and racial discrimination, to be represented by observers at the Conference;

7. *Requests* the Secretary-General, as part of the preparatory process, to take adequate steps to ensure that maximum publicity shall be given to the Conference and, to that end, to allocate the necessary resources from the regular budget;

8. *Calls upon* all States to contribute to the success of the Decade for Action to Combat Racism and Racial Discrimination, in particular by their active participation in the Conference;

9. *Urges* all States to co-operate with the Secretary-General of the Conference in the preparatory work and to consider the setting up of national committees for publicizing the aims and, eventually, the main results of the Conference;

10. *Requests* the Secretary-General to report to the General Assembly at its thirty-eighth session on the work of the Conference;

11. *Decides* to consider at its thirty-eighth session, as a matter of high priority, an item entitled "Second World Conference to Combat Racism and Racial Discrimination".

ANNEX
Draft provisional agenda for the Second World Conference to Combat Racism and Racial Discrimination

1. Opening of the Conference.
2. Election of the President.
3. Opening addresses.
4. Adoption of the rules of procedure.
5. Election of other officers.
6. Credentials of representatives to the Conference:
(a) Appointment of the Credentials Committee;
(b) Report of the Credentials Committee.
7. Adoption of the agenda.
8. Organization of work.
9. Political, historical, economic, social and cultural factors leading to racism, racial discrimination and segregation and *apartheid.*
10. Review and evaluation of activities undertaken to achieve the goals and objectives of the Decade for Action to Combat Racism and Racial Discrimination at the national, regional and international levels and in implementation of the Programme of Action adopted at the first World Conference to Combat Racism and Racial Discrimination.
11. Main obstacles to the full eradication of racism, racial discrimination and *apartheid.*
12. Determination of further action-oriented national, regional and international measures to combat all forms of racism, racial discrimination and *apartheid:*
(a) Adoption of legislative, judicial, administrative and other measures at the national level to improve relations among racial groups and to prohibit racial discrimination, including dissemination of ideas based on racial superiority or hatred, and all racist organizations such as Nazi and neo-Nazi organizations;
(b) Action in the field of education, culture, research and information and the role of the mass media in the struggle against racism, racial discrimination and *apartheid* with the aim of combating prejudices which lead to racial discrimination and of promoting understanding, tolerance and friendship among nations and racial or ethnic groups;
(c) Measures aimed at ensuring the full and universal implementation of United Nations resolutions and decisions on racism, racial discrimination and *apartheid;*
(d) Universal ratification of, or accession to, the International Convention on the Elimination of All Forms of Racial Discrimination and other existing international instruments adopted under the aegis of the United Nations and the specialized agencies aimed at combating racism, racial discrimination and *apartheid;*

(e) Drawing up of new international measures to combat racism and racial discrimination;

(f) Continued support and assistance to peoples and movements struggling against racism, racial discrimination and *apartheid;* and ways and means of denying support to racist régimes and of ensuring their isolation.

13. Adoption of the report and final documents of the Conference.

Conference costs

With regard to the financing of the Second World Conference, the General Assembly agreed on 3 December 1982[1] not to make exception to a 1969 Assembly resolution[3] which stipulated that United Nations bodies could hold sessions away from their headquarters when the Government issuing the invitation agreed to defray the additional costs. The Assembly authorized additional expenditures for the Conference as detailed by the Advisory Committee on Administrative and Budgetary Questions (ACABQ) in a November report.[2]

The decision was adopted without vote, following approval by the Fifth (Administrative and Budgetary) Committee without objection on 29 November; the draft was sponsored by Canada.

ACABQ recommended additional expenditures of $186,100 for travel and planning missions, public information activities and hospitality, or $51,200 less than the Secretary-General's estimates. Those expenditures were in addition to the Secretary-General's conference-servicing estimates of $986,900.

Savings were achieved by holding the Conference at Geneva. According to the Secretary-General's estimates, total costs for holding the Conference at Manila, including public information, travel and other costs, would have been $2,575,700, or $1,351,500 more than at Geneva. If the formula under which half the additional cost of holding the Conference away from Headquarters were defrayed from the United Nations regular budget and half by the host Government had been approved, the United Nations share would have been $1,899,950 and the share of the Philippines, $675,750.

Decision (1982). [1]GA: 37/422, 3 Dec., text following.
Report. [2]ACABQ, A/37/7/Add.8.
Resolution. [3]GA: 2609(XXIV), 16 Dec. 1969 (YUN 1969, p. 834).
Meeting records. GA: 5th Committee, A/C.5/37/SR.39, 45, *46*, 47 (19-29 Nov.); plenary, A/37/PV.90 (3 Dec.).

General Assembly decision 37/422

Adopted without vote

Approved by Fifth Committee (A/37/685) without objection, 29 November (meeting 46); draft by Canada (A/C.5/37/L.29); agenda item 76.

Implementation of the Programme for the Decade for Action to Combat Racism and Racial Discrimination

At its 90th plenary meeting, on 3 December 1982, the General Assembly, on the recommendation of the Fifth Committee, decided, in connection with its resolution 37/41 of 3 December 1982, to authorize additional expenditures as detailed in annex II of the ninth report of the Advisory Committee on Administrative and Budgetary Questions, and that no exception should be made to paragraph 10 of General Assembly resolution 2609(XXIV) of 16 December 1969.

Observance of the International Day for the Elimination of Racial Discrimination

As in previous years, the International Day for the Elimination of Racial Discrimination was observed by the Special Committee against *Apartheid*, at two meetings held on 22 March 1982.[1] Statements were made by the President of the General Assembly, the Secretary-General, other United Nations officials, representatives of the regional groups of States and observers from national liberation movements. The Day commemorated the date (21 March 1960) when 69 demonstrators against the "pass laws" of the *apartheid* system were killed and 180 others were wounded at Sharpeville, South Africa.

Report. [1]Committee against *Apartheid*, A/37/22.

Convention on the Elimination of Racial Discrimination

Implementation of the Convention

CERD activities. The Committee on the Elimination of Racial Discrimination (CERD), set up under article 8 of the International Convention on the Elimination of All Forms of Racial Discrimination,[5] held two sessions in 1982: the twenty-fifth from 1 to 19 March at Geneva and the twenty-sixth from 2 to 20 August in New York.

At those sessions, CERD devoted three fifths of its meetings to an examination of reports and additional information submitted by 40 States parties under article 9 of the Convention, on measures taken to give effect to the provisions of the Convention (see below). The annual report of CERD to the General Assembly[3] summarized the Committee members' views on each country report and the statements by the representatives of the States parties concerned.

In addition, CERD examined copies of petitions, reports and other information concerning Trust and Non-Self-Governing Territories transmitted to it by the Trusteeship Council (see TRUSTEESHIP AND DECOLONIZATION, Chapter II) and the Special Committee on the Situation with regard to the Implementation of the Declaration on the Granting of Independence to Colonial Countries and Peoples. CERD submitted to the Assembly recommendations on implementation of the principles and objectives of the Convention in eight Territories: in Africa—Namibia and Western Sahara; in the Caribbean area—the British Virgin Islands, the Cayman Islands and the United States Virgin Islands; and in the Atlantic Ocean—Bermuda, St. Helena and the Turks and Caicos Islands.

During both 1982 sessions, CERD discussed its activities within the framework of the Decade against racial discrimination, and its participation in preparations for the Second World Conference to Combat Racism and Racial Discrimination (see above), including the preparation of studies.

On 17 March,[1] the Committee suggested that, in implementing article 7 of the Convention, States parties should provide information, under the headings of education and teaching, culture, and information, on measures they had taken to combat prejudices leading to racial discrimination and to promote understanding, tolerance and friendship among nations and racial and ethnic groups.

On 19 August,[2] the Committee requested that the Secretary-General, in consultation with the Philippines, explore the possibility of arranging for the Committee's twenty-eighth session to be held at Manila from 11 to 29 July 1983, immediately prior to the Second World Conference. It recommended that the Assembly consider extending the formula in a 1976 resolution on the first World Conference[6] with a view to enabling the Philippines to host the session. Under that formula, half of the additional cost for a conference away from Headquarters would be defrayed from the United Nations regular budget.

General Assembly action. On 3 December 1982,[4] the General Assembly took note of the CERD report, commended the Committee for its contribution to eliminating discrimination, and called on United Nations bodies and administering Powers to provide information on Non-Self-Governing Territories (see TRUSTEESHIP AND DECOLONIZATION, Chapter II). It noted the Committee's efforts to secure the prosperity of minorities and indigenous populations (see below) through implementation of the Convention, called on States parties to the Convention to protect their rights and commended the parties on measures taken for ensuring recourse procedures for victims of racial discrimination. It called for measures to eliminate or prevent discrimination, and invited States parties to furnish information on implementation of the Convention, including information on the demographic composition of their population and on their relations with South Africa.

The Assembly strongly condemned *apartheid* in South Africa and Namibia and urged Member States to adopt political, economic and other measures to eliminate that policy (see POLITICAL AND SECURITY QUESTIONS, Chapter V, and TRUSTEESHIP AND DECOLONIZATION, Chapter III). It commended CERD for its endeavours to eliminate *apartheid*, racism and racial discrimination in southern Africa, and to implement resolutions on the liberation and independence of Namibia. It expressed grave concern at the Israeli policy of defiance of the Convention, and called for the respect and preservation of the national and cultural identity of the Palestinian people. It welcomed the Committee's efforts to eliminate discrimination against migrant workers and their families, to promote their rights, and to achieve their full equality and the possibility of preserving their cultural

characteristics (see below). It noted the Committee's contribution to the work of the Preparatory Sub-Committee for the Second World Conference to Combat Racism and Racial Discrimination and to the regional seminars held in implementation of the Programme for the Decade for Action to Combat Racism and Racial Discrimination (see above). It requested CERD to explore the possibility of preparing for the Conference a study on economic, social and cultural rights, and noted the Committee's request that the Secretary-General explore the possibility of arranging for its July 1983 session to be held at Manila (see above).

The resolution was adopted by a recorded vote of 131 to 2, with 15 abstentions, following its approval in the Third (Social, Humanitarian and Cultural) Committee on 27 October by a recorded vote of 123 to 2, with 13 abstentions. The Committee approved, by recorded votes, paragraph 7 by 98 to 16, with 20 abstentions, and paragraph 12 by 111 to none, with 23 abstentions.

Casting a negative vote, Israel said that paragraph 7 was a clear example of hypocrisy, based on nothing but falsifications and introducing pure politics into what had been created as an instrument for the enhancement of human rights. The United States, which also voted against paragraph 7 and the resolution as a whole, believed that the reference to the Arab-Israeli conflict compounded the damage already done.

A number of countries which abstained on the resolution as a whole, among them Australia, Belgium, Canada, Finland (for the Nordic countries), the Federal Republic of Germany, Ireland, New Zealand and the United Kingdom, also objected to that paragraph. Ireland considered it inappropriate that the Assembly should intervene in relations between CERD and a State party. Chile, Costa Rica and Portugal abstained on the paragraph stating strong reservations. France and the Netherlands, which also abstained, said it dealt with a political problem not within the mandate of CERD. In Uruguay's opinion, political allusions might well have been omitted.

Abstaining on paragraph 12, Austria, Belgium and Portugal voiced reservations. The Federal Republic of Germany and the Netherlands believed the provision went beyond the scope of the Convention.

Though supporting the resolution as whole, Japan said it had abstained on paragraphs 7 and 12 as it was not a party to the Convention. In Italy's view, the Assembly should refrain from judging individual countries, since such action jeopardized the Convention.

Introducing the draft on behalf of 14 nations, Yugoslavia said with regard to paragraph 7 that it reflected the facts described in the CERD report; by respecting paragraph 12, States parties to the

Convention would help CERD carry out its mandate.

Belgium, Portugal and Uruguay, the last two voting in favour of the resolution, also expressed reservations in particular to paragraph 3. The Federal Republic of Germany insisted, in that context, on the division of the responsibilities of the Assembly and the Security Council. Finland, on behalf of the Nordic countries, stressed the importance of such a division. Costa Rica believed that the paragraph could be placed more appropriately in the resolution on the International Convention on the Suppression and Punishment of the Crime of *Apartheid*.

With regard to paragraph 5, the Federal Republic of Germany felt it distorted the Committee's work. Austria also reserved its position on that paragraph, as well as on paragraph 14 and on the third preambular paragraph.

In addition, the United Kingdom had serious reservations about meeting the additional expenditure of holding the 1983 CERD session at Manila from the United Nations regular budget, as implicitly suggested in paragraph 15. In view of the financial implications, Italy also questioned the advisability of holding a CERD session there.

Decisions (1982). CERD: [1]2(XXV), 17 Mar.; [2]1(XXVI), 19 Aug.
Report. [3]CERD, A/37/18.
Resolution (1982). [4]GA: 37/46, 3 Dec., text following.
Resolutions (prior). GA: [5]2106 A (XX), annex, 21 Dec. 1965 (YUN 1965, p. 440); [6]31/78, 13 Dec. 1976 (YUN 1976, p. 573).
Financial implications. S-G statement, A/C.3/37/L.18.
Meeting records. GA: 3rd Committee, A/C.3/37/SR.3-13, *18, 24, 25* (30 Sep.–27 Oct.); plenary, A/37/PV.90 (3 Dec.).

General Assembly resolution 37/46

3 December 1982   Meeting 90   131-2-15 (recorded vote)

Approved by Third Committee (A/37/581) by recorded vote (123-2-13), 27 October (meeting 24); 14-nation draft (A/C.3/37/L.14); agenda item 80 *(a)*.

Sponsors: Angola, Bangladesh, Cape Verde, Cuba, Cyprus, India, Jordan, Madagascar, Nigeria, Pakistan, Sierra Leone, Yugoslavia, Zambia, Zimbabwe.

Report of the Committee on the Elimination of Racial Discrimination

The General Assembly,

Recalling its resolutions 36/12 of 28 October 1981 on the report of the Committee on the Elimination of Racial Discrimination and 37/45 of 3 December 1982 on the status of the International Convention on the Elimination of All Forms of Racial Discrimination, as well as its other relevant resolutions on the implementation of the Programme for the Decade for Action to Combat Racism and Racial Discrimination,

Having considered the report of the Committee on the Elimination of Racial Discrimination on its twenty-fifth and twenty-sixth sessions, submitted under article 9, paragraph 2, of the International Convention on the Elimination of All Forms of Racial Discrimination,

Emphasizing the importance for the success of the struggle against all practices of racial discrimination, including vestiges and manifestations of racist ideologies wherever they exist, that all Member States be guided in their internal and foreign policy by the basic provisions of the Convention,

Mindful of the obligation of all States parties to comply fully with the provisions of the Convention,

Welcoming the continued co-operation of the Committee on the Elimination of Racial Discrimination with the competent specialized agencies, especially the United Nations Educational, Scientific and Cul-

tural Organization and the International Labour Organisation, and with other United Nations bodies,

Noting the decisions adopted and recommendations made by the Committee at its twenty-fifth and twenty-sixth sessions,

1. *Takes note with appreciation* of the report of the Committee on the Elimination of Racial Discrimination on its twenty-fifth and twenty-sixth sessions;

2. *Commends* the Committee for its contribution to the elimination of all forms of discrimination based on race, colour, descent or national or ethnic origin, wherever it exists;

3. *Strongly condemns* the policy of *apartheid* in South Africa and Namibia as the most abhorrent form of racial discrimination and urges all Member States to adopt effective political, economic and other measures in order to secure the elimination of that policy and to achieve full implementation of the relevant resolutions of the General Assembly, the Security Council and other United Nations bodies;

4. *Calls upon* the United Nations bodies concerned to ensure that the Committee is supplied with all relevant information on all the Territories to which General Assembly resolution 1514(XV) of 14 December 1960 applies and urges the administering Powers to co-operate with these bodies by providing all necessary information in order to enable the Committee to discharge fully its responsibilities under article 15 of the International Convention on the Elimination of All Forms of Racial Discrimination;

5. *Commends* the Committee for its continuous endeavours towards the elimination of *apartheid*, racism and racial discrimination in southern Africa and the implementation of the United Nations resolutions relating to the liberation and independence of Namibia;

6. *Takes note with satisfaction* of the efforts of the Committee aimed at securing the prosperity of national or ethnic minorities and indigenous populations through the implementation of the principles and provisions of the Convention;

7. *Expresses grave concern* at the Israeli policy of defiance of the basic principles and objectives of the Convention, as reflected in the report of the Committee, and calls for the respect and preservation of the national and cultural identity of the Palestinian people;

8. *Welcomes* the efforts of the Committee aimed at the elimination of all forms of discrimination against migrant workers and their families, the promotion of their rights on a non-discriminatory basis and the achievement of their full equality and of the possibility to preserve their cultural characteristics;

9. *Commends* the States parties to the Convention on the measures taken to ensure within their jurisdiction the availability of appropriate recourse procedures for the victims of racial discrimination;

10. *Calls upon* all Member States to adopt effective legislative, socio-economic and other necessary measures in order to ensure the elimination or prevention of discrimination based on race, colour, descent or national or ethnic origin;

11. *Calls upon* the States parties to the Convention to protect fully, by adoption of relevant legislative and other measures, the rights of national or ethnic minorities, as well as rights of indigenous populations;

12. *Reiterates its invitation* to the States parties to the Convention to furnish the Committee, in accordance with its general guidelines, with information on the implementation of the provisions of the Convention, including information on the demographic composition of their population and on their relations with the racist régime of South Africa;

13. *Takes note with appreciation* of the Committee's contribution to the work of the Preparatory Sub-Committee for the Second World Conference to Combat Racism and Racial Discrimination and to the regional seminars held in implementation of the Programme for the Decade for Action to Combat Racism and Racial Discrimination;

14. *Welcomes* the decision of the Committee to contribute to the Second World Conference by preparing a study on the implementation of articles 4 and 7 of the Convention and reiterates its request to the Committee to explore the possibility of also preparing for the Conference a study on the implementation of subparagraph *(e)* of article 5;

15. *Takes note* of decision 1(XXVI) of 19 August 1982 of the Committee on the Elimination of Racial Discrimination, in which the Committee requested the Secretary-General, in consultation with the Government of the Philippines, to explore the possibility of arranging for the twenty-eighth session of the Committee to be held at Manila immediately prior to the holding of the Second World Conference to Combat Racism and Racial Discrimination.

Recorded vote in Assembly as follows:

In favour: Albania, Algeria, Angola, Antigua and Barbuda, Argentina, Bahamas, Bahrain, Bangladesh, Barbados, Benin, Bhutan, Bolivia, Botswana, Brazil, Bulgaria, Burma, Burundi, Byelorussian SSR, Cape Verde, Central African Republic, Chad, Chile, China, Colombia, Comoros, Congo, Costa Rica, Cuba, Cyprus, Czechoslovakia, Democratic Kampuchea, Democratic Yemen, Djibouti, Dominican Republic, Ecuador, Egypt, El Salvador, Equatorial Guinea, Ethiopia, Fiji, France, Gabon, German Democratic Republic, Ghana, Greece, Grenada, Guinea, Guinea-Bissau, Guyana, Haiti, Hungary, Iceland, India, Indonesia, Iran, Iraq, Italy, Ivory Coast, Jamaica, Japan, Jordan, Kenya, Kuwait, Lao People's Democratic Republic, Lebanon, Lesotho, Liberia, Libyan Arab Jamahiriya, Madagascar, Malaysia, Maldives, Mali, Malta, Mauritania, Mauritius, Mexico, Mongolia, Morocco, Mozambique, Nepal, Netherlands, Nicaragua, Niger, Nigeria, Oman, Pakistan, Panama, Papua New Guinea, Peru, Philippines, Poland, Portugal, Qatar, Romania, Rwanda, Saint Lucia, Samoa, Sao Tome and Principe, Saudi Arabia, Senegal, Sierra Leone, Singapore, Solomon Islands, Somalia, Spain, Sri Lanka, Sudan, Suriname, Swaziland, Syrian Arab Republic, Thailand, Togo, Trinidad and Tobago, Tunisia, Turkey, Uganda, Ukrainian SSR, USSR, United Arab Emirates, United Republic of Cameroon, United Republic of Tanzania, Upper Volta, Uruguay, Vanuatu, Venezuela, Viet Nam, Yemen, Yugoslavia, Zaire, Zambia, Zimbabwe.

Against: Israel, United States.

Abstaining: Australia, Austria, Belgium, Belize,[a] Canada, Denmark, Finland, Germany, Federal Republic of, Ireland, Luxembourg, Malawi, New Zealand, Norway, Sweden, United Kingdom.

[a]Later advised the Secretariat it had intended to vote in favour.

Reports from Governments

At its March and August 1982 sessions, CERD examined reports and additional information submitted by 40 States parties under article 9 of the Convention, on measures they had adopted to give effect to the Convention's provisions.

Representatives of 34 of the 40 reporting States participated in the consideration of their respective reports.

The reports examined were from: Argentina, Australia, Austria, Barbados, Cape Verde, Costa Rica, Czechoslovakia, Ecuador, Egypt, Ethiopia, Fiji, Finland, Gabon, Gambia, German Democratic Republic, Greece, Haiti, Holy See, Hungary, Iceland, Israel, Jordan, Kuwait, Malta, Mauritius, Mexico, Mongolia, Nepal, Norway, Panama, Philippines, Qatar, Republic of Korea, Romania, Spain, Sudan, Tonga, USSR, United Arab Emirates, Uruguay.

On 15 March,[1] CERD, stating that no less than 89 initial or periodic reports were overdue from 62 States, and that 42 of them were overdue from 15 States, invited the General Assembly to take note of the situation and to use its authority to ensure that CERD could more effectively fulfil its obligations under the Convention.

At the end of the August CERD session, 78 reports were still overdue from 48 States, among them 5 initial reports due between 1973 and 1981.

The Assembly, on 3 December 1982,[2] appealed to States parties to the Convention to fulfil their obligations and submit their reports within the appropriate time. It requested the Secretary-General to invite the views and observations of States parties on the causes of the situation; to submit in 1983 an analysis of the replies received, together with suggestions for improving the situation; in preparing his report, to consider the situation in the framework of the reporting obligations of Member States under various other human rights instruments so that he could take into account similar problems; and to submit his report, together with the records of the Assembly's consideration of the matter, to the 1984 meeting of the States parties.

The resolution was adopted without vote, following similar approval by the Third Committee on 27 October. It was introduced and revised by Italy, also on behalf of Australia, Fiji, Finland, France, Mexico, the Netherlands and the United Kingdom.

Decision (1982). [1]CERD (report, A/37/18): 1(XXV), 15 Mar. *Resolution (1982).* [2]GA: 37/44, 3 Dec., text following. *Meeting records.* GA: 3rd Committee, A/C.3/37/SR.3-13, *18,* *24* (30 Sep.–27 Oct.); plenary, A/37/PV.90 (3 Dec.).

General Assembly resolution 37/44

3 December 1982   Meeting 90   Adopted without vote

Approved by Third Committee (A/37/581) without vote, 27 October (meeting 24); 8-nation draft (A/C.3/37/L.13/Rev.1); agenda item 80 *(a).*

Sponsors: Australia, Fiji, Finland, France, Italy, Mexico, Netherlands, United Kingdom.

Report of the Committee on the Elimination of Racial Discrimination: General recommendation VI

The General Assembly,

Taking note of decision 1(XXV) of 15 March 1982 of the Committee on the Elimination of Racial Discrimination entitled "General recommendation VI",

Acknowledging the burden which reporting obligations under international instruments places upon States parties, especially those with limited technical and administrative resources,

Convinced, none the less, that the value of international conventions relies upon the full and conscientious implementation of the obligations undertaken upon ratification or accession,

Noting with concern that many periodic reports due under article 9 of the International Convention on the Elimination of All Forms of Racial Discrimination are outstanding and that in some cases initial reports are several years overdue,

1. *Appeals* to all States parties to the International Convention on the Elimination of All Forms of Racial Discrimination to fulfil their obligations under article 9 of the Convention and to submit their reports within the appropriate time;

2. *Requests* the Secretary-General to invite the views and observations of States parties to the Convention on the causes of the situation described in general recommendation VI of the Committee on the Elimination of Racial Discrimination and to submit an analysis of the replies received in a report to the General Assembly at its thirty-eighth session, together with such suggestions as he might wish to make with a view to improving the situation;

3. *Also requests* the Secretary-General, in preparing his report, to consider the situation described in general recommendation VI of the Committee in the overall framework of reporting obligations that Member States have under the various human rights instruments in order to be able to take into account similar and related problems which may have arisen in compliance with such obligations;

4. *Further requests* the Secretary-General to submit his report, together with the records of the General Assembly's consideration thereof, to the ninth meeting of the States parties to the Convention, to be held in 1984.

Accessions and ratifications

As at 31 December 1982, there were 117 parties to the International Convention on the Elimination of All Forms of Racial Discrimination, adopted by the General Assembly in 1965.[4] In 1982, five States (Papua New Guinea, Portugal, Solomon Islands, Sri Lanka, Viet Nam) and Namibia (represented by the United Nations Council for Namibia) became parties.[1]

Article 14 of the Convention entered into force on 3 December 1982, following the deposit of the tenth declaration by a State party (Senegal), recognizing the competence of CERD to receive and consider communications from individuals or groups within their jurisdiction claiming to be victims of a violation by the State party concerned of any of the rights set forth in the Convention. The following 10 States parties—Costa Rica, Ecuador, France, Iceland, Italy, the Netherlands, Norway, Senegal, Sweden and Uruguay—had made such declarations.

In his annual report to the General Assembly on the status of the Convention, the Secretary-General listed the States which had signed, ratified, acceded or succeeded to it as at 1 September.[2]

By a resolution of 3 December,[3] the Assembly expressed satisfaction with the increase in the number of States that had ratified or acceded to the Convention. It reaffirmed its conviction that universal adherence to the Convention and implementation of its provisions were necessary to realize the objectives of the Decade for Action to Combat Racism and Racial Discrimination. It requested States that had not become parties to do so and called on parties to consider the possibility of making the declaration provided for in article 14.

The resolution was adopted, without vote, on the recommendation of the Third Committee, which approved the text on 27 October in the same manner. The 28-nation draft was introduced by Belgium. Amendments to the draft, introduced by Uruguay also on behalf of Costa Rica, Ecuador, France, Iceland, Italy, the Netherlands, Norway and Sweden, added a preambular paragraph welcoming the increase in the number of declarations made under article 14 of the Convention, and an operative paragraph calling on States parties to consider the possibility of making such a declaration. The amendments were adopted by 75 votes to 1, with 47 abstentions.

> *Publication.* [1]*Multilateral Treaties Deposited with the Secretary-General: Status as at 31 December 1982* (ST/LEG/SER.E/2), Sales No. E.83.V.6.
> *Report.* [2]S-G, A/37/148.
> *Resolution (1982).* [3]GA: 37/45, 3 Dec., text following.
> *Resolution (prior).* GA: [4]2106 A (XX), annex, 21 Dec. 1965 (YUN 1965, p. 440).
> *Meeting records.* GA: 3rd Committee, A/C.3/37/SR.3-13, *18, 24, 25* (30 Sep.–27 Oct.); plenary, A/37/PV.90 (3 Dec.).

General Assembly resolution 37/45

3 December 1982   Meeting 90   Adopted without vote

Approved by Third Committee (A/37/581) without vote, 27 October (meeting 24); 28-nation draft (A/C.3/37/L.7), amended by 9 nations (A/C.3/37/L.17); agenda item 80 *(b).*

Sponsors of draft: Algeria, Argentina, Australia, Bahamas, Bangladesh, Barbados, Belgium, Bulgaria, Cape Verde, Cuba, Cyprus, Egypt, Germany, Federal Republic of, Ghana, Hungary, India, Morocco, New Zealand, Nigeria, Pakistan, Portugal, Rwanda, Spain, Syrian Arab Republic, Upper Volta, Venezuela, Yugoslavia, Zaire.

Sponsors of amendments: Costa Rica, Ecuador, France, Iceland, Italy, Netherlands, Norway, Sweden, Uruguay.

Status of the International Convention on the Elimination of All Forms of Racial Discrimination

The General Assembly,

Recalling its resolutions 3057(XXVIII) of 2 November 1973, 3135(XXVIII) of 14 December 1973, 3225(XXIX) of 6 November 1974, 3381(XXX) of 10 November 1975, 31/79 of 13 December 1976, 32/11 of 7 November 1977, 33/101 of 16 December 1978, 34/26 of 15 November 1979, 35/38 of 25 November 1980 and 36/11 of 28 October 1981,

Welcoming the increase in the number of declarations made under article 14 of the Convention,

1.   *Takes note* of the report of the Secretary-General on the status of the International Convention on the Elimination of All Forms of Racial Discrimination;

2.   *Expresses its satisfaction* with the increase in the number of States which have ratified the Convention or acceded thereto;

3.   *Reaffirms once again its conviction* that ratification of or accession to the Convention on a universal basis and implementation of its provisions are necessary for the realization of the objectives of the Decade for Action to Combat Racism and Racial Discrimination;

4.   *Requests* States that have not yet become parties to the Convention to ratify it or accede thereto;

5.   *Calls upon* States parties to the Convention to consider the possibility of making the declaration provided for in article 14 of the Convention;

6.   *Requests* the Secretary-General to continue to submit to the General Assembly annual reports concerning the status of the Convention, in accordance with Assembly resolution 2106 A (XX) of 21 December 1965.

Measures against nazism and fascism

The Commission on Human Rights, on 11 March 1982,[1] decided to defer until 1983 further discussion and action on measures against Nazi, Fascist and neo-Fascist activities and other ideologies and practices based on racial intolerance, hatred and terror.

As requested by the General Assembly in December 1981,[5] the Secretary-General submitted in April 1982 a report (with an addendum in November) summarizing comments by 22 States and an international organization on problems in regard to this topic and their suggestions on national and international measures to eradicate nazism, fascism and related ideologies.[3]

The Economic and Social Council, on 7 May,[2] took note of the report and decided to transmit it to the Assembly. The decision, orally proposed by the Chairman of the Second (Social) Committee, was adopted without vote, following similar approval by the Committee on 3 May.

General Assembly action. By a resolution of 17 December,[4] the General Assembly condemned all totalitarian or other ideologies and practices, in particular Nazi, Fascist and neo-Fascist, based on racial or ethnic exclusiveness or intolerance, hatred, terror and systematic denial of human rights. It urged States to draw attention to the threats to democratic institutions by those ideologies and practices, and to consider taking measures to prohibit or otherwise deter activities by groups and organizations practising them. The Assembly appealed to States to become parties to relevant human rights instruments and invited them to adopt measures outlawing any dissemination of ideas based on racial superiority or hatred and of war propaganda. It also called on intergovernmental and non-governmental organizations to initiate or intensify measures against such ideologies and practices, and requested the Secretary-General to ensure that the United Nations Department of Public Information (DPI) paid attention to the dissemination of information exposing those ideologies and practices.

This action was taken without vote, following similar approval by the Third Committee on 9 December. The draft was introduced and orally revised by the German Democratic Republic, on behalf of 13 nations.

One of the revisions took account of a proposal by Belgium, deleting in paragraph 7, on dissemination of information by DPI, reference to proponents of those ideologies.

Decisions (1982). [1]Commission on Human Rights (report, E/1982/12): 1982/105, 11 Mar. [2]ESC: 1982/146, 7 May, text following.
Report [3]S-G, A/37/188 & Corr.1 & Add.1.
Resolution (1982). [4]GA: 37/179, 17 Dec., text following.
Resolution (prior). [5]GA: 36/162, 16 Dec. 1981 (YUN 1981, p. 876).
Meeting records. ESC: E/1982/SR.29 (7 May). GA: 3rd Committee, A/C.3/37/SR.62, 63, 64, 68-71, 72, 74 (3-10 Dec.); plenary, A/37/PV.110 (17 Dec.).

Economic and Social Council decision 1982/146

Adopted without vote

Approved by Second Committee (E/1982/59) without vote, 3 May (meeting 16); oral proposal by Chairman; agenda item 9.

Report of the Secretary-General on measures to be taken against Nazi, Fascist and neo-Fascist activities and all other forms of totalitarian ideologies and practices based on racial intolerance, hatred and terror

At its 29th plenary meeting, on 7 May 1982, the Council took note of the report of the Secretary-General on measures to be taken against Nazi, Fascist and neo-Fascist activities and all other forms of totalitarian ideologies and practices based on racial intolerance, hatred and terror and decided to transmit it to the General Assembly.

General Assembly resolution 37/179

17 December 1982   Meeting 110   Adopted without vote

Approved by Third Committee (A/37/745) without vote, 9 December (meeting 72); 13-nation draft (A/C.3/37/L.69), orally amended by Belgium and orally revised; agenda item 12.

Sponsors: Afghanistan, Angola, Bulgaria, Cuba, Czechoslovakia, German Democratic Republic, Hungary, Lao People's Democratic Republic, Nicaragua, Poland, Ukrainian SSR, Viet Nam, Zimbabwe.

Measures to be taken against Nazi, Fascist and neo-Fascist activities and all other forms of totalitarian ideologies and practices based on racial intolerance, hatred and terror

The General Assembly,

Recalling that the United Nations emerged from the struggle against nazism, fascism, aggression and foreign occupation, and that the peoples expressed their resolve in the Charter of the United Nations to save future generations from the scourge of war,

Bearing in mind the suffering, destruction and death of millions of victims of aggression, foreign occupation, nazism and fascism,

Reaffirming the purposes and principles laid down in the Charter, which are aimed at maintaining international peace and security, developing friendly relations among nations based on respect for the principle of equal rights and self-determination of peoples, and achieving international co-operation in promoting and encouraging respect for human rights and fundamental freedoms for all,

Emphasizing that all totalitarian or other ideologies and practices, in particular Nazi, Fascist and neo-Fascist, based on racial or ethnic

exclusiveness or intolerance, hatred, terror, systematic denial of human rights and fundamental freedoms, or which have such consequences, may jeopardize world peace and constitute obstacles to friendly relations between States and to the realization of human rights and fundamental freedoms,

Reaffirming that the prosecution and punishment of war crimes and crimes against peace and humanity, as laid down in General Assembly resolutions 3(I) of 13 February 1946 and 95(I) of 11 December 1946, constitute a universal commitment for all States,

Recalling its resolutions 2331(XXII) of 18 December 1967, 2438(XXIII) of 19 December 1968, 2545(XXIV) of 11 December 1969, 2713(XXV) of 15 December 1970, 2839(XXVI) of 18 December 1971, 34/24 of 15 November 1979, 35/200 of 15 December 1980 and 36/162 of 16 December 1981,

Recalling also the Declaration on Social Progress and Development, the United Nations Declaration on the Elimination of All Forms of Racial Discrimination, the Declaration on the Granting of Independence to Colonial Countries and Peoples and the Declaration on the Elimination of All Forms of Intolerance and of Discrimination Based on Religion or Belief,

Underlining the importance of the Universal Declaration of Human Rights, the International Covenants on Human Rights, the International Convention on the Elimination of All Forms of Racial Discrimination, the Convention on the Prevention and Punishment of the Crime of Genocide and other relevant international instruments,

Acknowledging the fact that a number of States have established legal regulations which are suited to prevent the activities of Nazi, Fascist and neo-Fascist groups and organizations,

Noting again with deep concern that the proponents of Fascist ideologies have, in a number of countries, intensified their activities and are increasingly co-ordinating them on an international scale,

1. *Again condemns* all totalitarian or other ideologies and practices, in particular Nazi, Fascist and neo-Fascist, based on racial or ethnic exclusiveness or intolerance, hatred, terror, systematic denial of human rights and fundamental freedoms, or which have such consequences;

2. *Urges* all States to draw attention to the threats to democratic institutions by the above-mentioned ideologies and practices and to consider taking measures, in accordance with their national constitutional systems and with the provisions of the Universal Declaration of Human Rights and the International Covenants on Human Rights, to prohibit or otherwise deter activities by groups or organizations or whoever is practising those ideologies;

3. *Calls upon* the appropriate specialized agencies, as well as intergovernmental and international non-governmental organizations, to initiate or intensify measures against the ideologies and practices described in paragraph 1 above;

4. *Invites* Member States to adopt, in accordance with their national constitutional systems and with the provisions of the Universal Declaration of Human Rights and the International Covenants on Human Rights, as a matter of high priority, measures declaring punishable by law any dissemination of ideas based on racial superiority or hatred and of war propaganda, including Nazi, Fascist and neo-Fascist ideologies;

5. *Appeals* to all States which have not yet done so to ratify or to accede to the International Covenants on Human Rights, the Convention on the Prevention and Punishment of the Crime of Genocide, the International Convention on the Elimination of All Forms of Racial Discrimination, the Convention on the Non-Applicability of Statutory Limitations to War Crimes and Crimes against Humanity and the International Convention on the Suppression and Punishment of the Crime of *Apartheid;*

6. *Calls once again upon* all States to provide the Secretary-General with their comments on this question;

7. *Requests* the Secretary-General to ensure that the Department of Public Information of the Secretariat pays attention to the dissemination of information exposing the ideologies and practices described in paragraph 1 above;

8. *Reiterates its request* to the Commission on Human Rights to consider this question at its thirty-ninth session under the title: "Measures to be taken against all totalitarian or other ideologies and practices, including Nazi, Fascist and neo-Fascist, based on racial or ethnic exclusiveness or intolerance, hatred, terror, systematic denial of human rights and fundamental freedoms, or which have such consequences";

9. *Requests* the Secretary-General to submit a report, through the Economic and Social Council, to the General Assembly at its thirty-

eighth session, in the light of the discussion that will take place in the Commission on Human Rights and on the basis of comments provided by States and international organizations.

Other aspects of discrimination

Implementation of the 1981 Declaration against religious intolerance

The Economic and Social Council, by a decision adopted without vote on 7 May 1982,[1] endorsed an 11 March request[4] of the Commission on Human Rights to the Secretary-General that he disseminate widely, as a matter of priority and in as many languages as possible, the Declaration on the Elimination of All Forms of Intolerance and of Discrimination Based on Religion or Belief, proclaimed by the General Assembly in November 1981.[9] The Council also endorsed the Commission's request that he issue a pamphlet, in the six official languages of the United Nations, with the Declaration text, together with relevant articles of the 1948 Universal Declaration of Human Rights[7] and the International Covenant on Civil and Political Rights, adopted in 1966.[8]

The Second Committee approved the text, which originated in the Commission, on 3 May, also without vote.

On 10 September,[6] the Sub-Commission on Prevention of Discrimination and Protection of Minorities requested the Secretary-General to submit to it in 1983 information on the problems of discrimination on grounds of religion or belief. Based on that information, it would consider, also in 1983, the updating of a study on discrimination in religious rights and practices, submitted in 1960.[10]

Endorsing the Council's 7 May decision, the General Assembly, on 18 December,[5] invited Governments to ensure wide publicity for the Declaration and requested the Secretary-General to bring the Declaration to the attention of United Nations agencies and bodies for the consideration of measures to implement it. It requested the Commission on Human Rights to consider measures to implement the Declaration and to encourage understanding, tolerance and respect in matters relating to freedom of religion or belief, and to report, through the Council, to the Assembly in 1983.

The resolution, was adopted without vote, following similar approval by the Third Committee on 7 December. The text was introduced and orally revised by Ireland, on behalf of 23 nations.

By letters of 16 August[2] and 12 October[3] to the Secretary-General, Israel drew attention to anti-Jewish acts of violence in various countries of Europe and elsewhere.

Decision (1982). [1]ESC: 1982/138, 7 May, text following.
Letters. Israel: [2]16 Aug., A/37/392; [3]12 Oct., A/37/542.
Resolutions (1982). [4]Commission on Human Rights (report, E/1982/12): 1982/41, 11 Mar. [5]GA: 37/187, 18 Dec., text

following. [6]SCPDPM (report, E/CN.4/1983/4): 1982/28, 10 Sep.
Resolutions (prior). GA: [7]217 A (III), 10 Dec. 1948 (YUN 1948-49, p. 535); [8]2200 A (XXI), annex, 16 Dec. 1966 (YUN 1966, p. 423); [9]36/55, 25 Nov. 1981 (YUN 1981, p. 881).
Yearbook reference. [10]1960, p. 349.
Meeting records. ESC: E/1982/SR.29 (7 May). GA: 3rd Committee, A/C.3/37/SR.47, 50-56, *64, 67* (18 Nov.–7 Dec.); plenary A/37/PV.111 (18 Dec.).

Economic and Social Council decision 1982/138

Adopted without vote

Approved by Second Committee (E/1982/59) without vote, 3 May (meeting 15); draft by Commission on Human Rights (E/1982/12); agenda item 9.

Further promotion and encouragement of human rights and fundamental freedoms, including the question of the programme and methods of work of the Commission on Human Rights; alternative approaches and ways and means within the United Nations system for improving the effective enjoyment of human rights and fundamental freedoms

At its 29th plenary meeting, on 7 May 1982, the Council, noting resolution 1982/41 of 11 March 1982 of the Commission on Human Rights, endorsed the Commission's request to the Secretary-General, within the world-wide programme for the dissemination of basic international instruments on human rights, to disseminate widely, as a matter of priority and in as many languages as possible, the Declaration on the Elimination of All Forms of Intolerance and of Discrimination Based on Religion or Belief. The Council also endorsed the Commission's request to the Secretary-General to issue, as soon as possible, a pamphlet containing the text of the Declaration, together with relevant articles of the Universal Declaration of Human Rights and the International Covenant on Civil and Political Rights, in the six official languages of the United Nations, and to give the widest dissemination to the pamphlet.

General Assembly resolution 37/187

18 December 1982   Meeting 111   Adopted without vote

Approved by Third Committee (A/37/715) without vote, 7 December (meeting 67); 23-nation draft (A/C.3/37/L.59/Rev.1), orally revised; agenda item 84.

Sponsors: Australia, Austria, Barbados, Canada, Colombia, Costa Rica, Dominican Republic, Fiji, France, Germany, Federal Republic of, Ireland, Italy, Morocco, Netherlands, Norway, Peru, Samoa, Senegal, Suriname, Sweden, Uganda, United States, Uruguay.

Elimination of all forms of religious intolerance
The General Assembly,

Reaffirming its resolution 36/55 of 25 November 1981, in which it proclaimed the Declaration on the Elimination of All Forms of Intolerance and of Discrimination Based on Religion or Belief,

Believing that further efforts are required to promote and protect the right to freedom of thought, conscience, religion or whatever belief,

Wishing to encourage understanding, tolerance and respect in matters relating to freedom of religion or belief,

Conscious of the need to implement the provisions of the Declaration,

Desiring that wide publicity be given to the Declaration,

1. *Endorses* Economic and Social Council decision 1982/138 of 7 May 1982, in which the Council requested the Secretary-General to disseminate widely, as a matter of priority and in as many languages as possible, the Declaration on the Elimination of All Forms of Intolerance and of Discrimination Based on Religion or Belief and to issue a pamphlet containing the text of the Declaration in the six official languages of the United Nations;

2. *Invites* all Governments to take the necessary measures to ensure wide publicity for the Declaration;

3. *Requests* the Secretary-General to bring the Declaration to the attention of the appropriate specialized agencies, including the United Nations Educational, Scientific and Cultural Organization, and other appropriate bodies within the United Nations system, for the consideration of measures to implement the Declaration, and to report to the Commission on Human Rights at its thirty-ninth session on the views expressed;

4. *Requests* the Commission on Human Rights to consider what measures may be necessary to implement the Declaration and to encourage understanding, tolerance and respect in matters relating to freedom of religion or belief and to report, through the Economic and Social Council, to the General Assembly at its thirty-eighth session;

5. *Decides* to include in the provisional agenda of its thirty-eighth session the item entitled "Elimination of all forms of religious intolerance" and to consider the report of the Commission on Human Rights in the context of that item.

Indigenous populations

The Economic and Social Council, on 7 May 1982,[4] authorized the Sub-Commission on Prevention of Discrimination and Protection of Minorities to establish annually a working group which would meet for up to five working days before the Sub-Commission's annual sessions to review developments pertaining to the promotion and protection of human rights and fundamental freedoms of indigenous populations, and to analyse information requested by the Secretary-General from Governments, specialized agencies, regional intergovernmental organizations and non-governmental organizations, particularly those of indigenous peoples. The Group was to submit its conclusions to the Sub-Commission, giving special attention to the evolution of standards concerning the rights of indigenous populations.

The resolution was adopted by 51 votes to none, with 1 abstention, following its approval by the Second Committee on 3 May by 38 votes to none, with 1 abstention. Adoption of the text was recommended on 10 March by the Commission on Human Rights,[3] in accordance with a September 1981 Sub-Commission proposal.[7]

The Working Group on Indigenous Populations met from 9 to 13 August 1982 for its first session[2] and, without making formal recommendations, discussed such matters as the definition of indigenous populations, and the examination and evaluation of standards for their rights. The Group agreed that a definition should be elaborated with or by the indigenous peoples themselves, and that a guide should be prepared containing information relating to their rights, including information on international and national human rights standards and conferences organized by or about indigenous organizations. Under the Working Group's mandate, the Secretary-General should call annually for the submission of information on developments in the field. The Working Group should examine the application of existing human rights standards involving indigenous peoples, with priority given to the most basic rights, including the right to life, freedom from torture, and equality before the law, and with special attention to any situation indicating genocide. The evolution of standards should concern: land and mineral rights; self-management, consultation, participation, self-government or self-determination; freedom of religion and traditional religious practices;

and the right to maintain their own culture, language and way of life.

The Working Group should encourage dialogue among indigenous populations, non-governmental organizations, intergovernmental agencies and Governments; assist in evolving standards; and encourage the establishment of a fund to make possible the participation in the Group of indigenous populations. The Working Group should hold sessions in regions where such populations were found.

At its 1982 session, the Sub-Commission considered part of a final report on discrimination against indigenous populations,[1] submitted by Special Rapporteur José R. Martínez Cobo (Ecuador) in accordance with a September 1981 Sub-Commission request.[7] The first part of the study was submitted in 1981. The part submitted in 1982 dealt with the following: definition of indigenous populations; administrative arrangements; housing; occupation, employment and vocational training; religious rights and practices; and action by United Nations agencies and the Organization of American States.

On 10 September,[5] the Sub-Commission requested the Special Rapporteur to continue his work and to submit in 1983 the last part of the final report as well as conclusions, proposals and recommendations, and invited him to place these at the disposal of the Working Group.

On the same date,[6] the Sub-Commission commended the Working Group on its provisional recommendations. It agreed that there should be continuity in the Group's membership and requested that this be borne in mind when appointing the Group's members. It also agreed with the Group in its preliminary identification of main areas of concern, its decision to emphasize the importance of defining indigenous populations from an international viewpoint, and the special and urgent attention to be paid to cases of genocide or ethnocide. It requested the Group to take account of the final report, particularly the Special Rapporteur's conclusions and recommendations, and decided to request the Commission and the Economic and Social Council to establish a fund to allow for participation of representatives of indigenous populations in the Working Group.

Reports. [1]Special Rapporteur, E/CN.4/Sub.2/1982/2 & Add.1-7; [2]Working Group on Indigenous Populations, E/CN.4/Sub.2/1982/33.
Resolutions (1982). [3]Commission on Human Rights (report, E/1982/12): 1982/19, 10 Mar. [4]ESC: 1982/34, 7 May, text following. SCPDPM (report, E/CN.4/1983/4), 10 Sep.: [5]1982/29, [6]1982/31.
Yearbook reference. [7]1981, p. 883.
Meeting record. ESC: E/1982/SR.28 (7 May).
Statement. NGO, E/1982/NGO/1.

Economic and Social Council resolution 1982/34

| 7 May 1982 | Meeting 28 | 51-0-1 |

Approved by Second Committee (E/1982/59) by vote (38-0-1), 3 May (meeting 15); draft by Commission on Human Rights (E/1982/12); agenda item 9.

Study of the problem of discrimination against indigenous populations

The Economic and Social Council,

Recalling its resolution 1589(L) of 21 May 1971, resolutions 22(XXXVII) of 10 March 1981 and 1982/19 of 10 March 1982 of the Commission on Human Rights and resolutions 8(XXIV) of 18 August 1971, 5(XXXIII) of 10 September 1980 and 2(XXXIV) of 8 September 1981 of the Sub-Commission on Prevention of Discrimination and Protection of Minorities,

Recognizing the urgent need to promote and to protect the human rights and fundamental freedoms of indigenous populations,

Bearing in mind the concerns expressed in this regard at the World Conference to Combat Racism and Racial Discrimination in 1978,

Believing that special attention should be given to appropriate avenues of recourse at the national, regional and international levels in order to advance the promotion and protection of the human rights and fundamental freedoms of indigenous populations,

Mindful of the conclusions of the Sub-Commission on Prevention of Discrimination and Protection of Minorities and of the Commission on Human Rights that the plight of indigenous peoples is of a serious and pressing nature and that special measures are urgently needed to promote and protect the human rights and fundamental freedoms of indigenous populations,

1. *Authorizes* the Sub-Commission on Prevention of Discrimination and Protection of Minorities to establish annually a working group on indigenous populations which shall meet for up to five working days before the annual sessions of the Sub-Commission in order to review developments pertaining to the promotion and protection of the human rights and fundamental freedoms of indigenous populations, including information requested by the Secretary-General annually from Governments, specialized agencies, regional intergovernmental organizations and non-governmental organizations in consultative status, particularly those of indigenous peoples, to analyse such materials, and to submit its conclusions to the Sub-Commission bearing in mind the report of the Special Rapporteur of the Sub-Commission;

2. *Decides* that the Working Group shall give special attention to the evolution of standards concerning the rights of indigenous populations, taking account of both the similarities and the differences in the situations and aspirations of indigenous populations throughout the world;

3. *Requests* the Secretary-General to assist the Working Group on Indigenous Populations and make all necessary arrangements to enable it to carry out its functions.

Migrant workers

Work continued in 1982 on an international convention on the protection of the rights of all migrant workers and their families, through the Commission on Human Rights, the Working Group on the drafting of the convention and the General Assembly.

Action by the Commission on Human Rights. On 11 March,[4] the Commission on Human Rights, by 39 votes to none, with 3 abstentions, welcomed the progress of the Working Group. It invited Member States to co-operate fully with the Group and expressed the hope that the General Assembly would complete the convention as soon as possible. It requested the Secretary-General to inform the Commission in 1983 of further progress.

Working Group action. The open-ended Working Group on the Drafting of an International Convention on the Protection of the Rights of All Migrant Workers and Their Families met at United Nations Headquarters from 10 to 21 May 1982[2] and from 18 October to 16 November,[3] as authorized by the General Assembly in December 1981.[8] During the May session, it concluded its first reading of part II of the draft convention, concerning the fundamental human rights of all migrant workers and members of their families, on the understanding that the text, which was provisionally agreed upon, would be examined further. Concluding its preliminary consideration of part I related to the convention's scope and definitions, the Group agreed to postpone further consideration of articles 2 and 4 dealing, respectively, with the definition of the term "migrant worker" and the application of the convention to persons who were undocumented or in an irregular situation.

At its October/November session, the Group considered part III of the convention, on additional rights of migrant workers and members of their families in a regular or lawful situation. It completed the first reading of articles 35 to 45 and agreed to postpone consideration of the remaining proposals for part III and the remaining parts of the convention until 1983.

General Assembly action. The General Assembly, on 17 December,[7] took note of the Working Group's report on its October/November session and expressed satisfaction with the substantial progress made. It decided that the Group should hold a two-week meeting in New York immediately after the first regular session of the Economic and Social Council in 1983, and another meeting during the 1983 Assembly session to complete, if possible, elaboration of the convention. It invited the Secretary-General to transmit the Group's report together with the results of the first 1983 meeting, to Governments, United Nations organs and international organizations.

The resolution was adopted without vote, following similar approval by the Third (Social, Humanitarian and Cultural) Committee on 2 December, where it was introduced by Algeria on behalf of 22 nations.

In its resolution of 3 December on implementation of the Programme for the Decade for Action to Combat Racism and Racial Discrimination,[5] the Assembly invited Member States, the United Nations organs and bodies and the specialized agencies to continue their efforts to protect the rights of all migrant workers and their families.

On the same date,[6] the Assembly welcomed the efforts of the Committee on the Elimination of Racial Discrimination to eliminate all forms of discrimination against migrant workers and their families, to promote their rights, and to achieve their full equality and the possibility of preserving their cultural characteristics.

Other action. The World Assembly on Aging, meeting at Vienna, Austria, from 26 July to 6 August,[1] recommended that measures be taken, particularly through bilateral or mutilateral conventions, to guarantee legitimate migrant workers full social coverage in the receiving country, as well as maintenance of their social security rights, especially with regard to pensions, if they returned to their country of origin. In returning to their countries, they should be afforded special conditions facilitating their reintegration, particularly with regard to housing (see Chapter XX of this section).

Publication. [1]*Report of the World Assembly on Aging, Vienna, 26 July to 6 August 1982* (A/CONF.113/31), Sales No. E.82.I.16.
Reports. Working Group on convention, [2]A/C.3/37/1, [3]A/C.3/37/7 & Corr.1,2.
Resolutions (1982). [4]Commission on Human Rights (report, E/1982/12): 1982/35, 11 Mar. GA: [5]37/40, para. 13, 3 Dec.; [6]37/46, para. 8, 3 Dec.; [7]37/170, 17 Dec., text following.
Resolution (prior). [8]GA: 36/160, 16 Dec. 1981 (YUN 1981, p. 886).
Financial implications. 5th Committee report, A/37/756; S-G statements, A/C.3/37/L.66, A/C.5/37/72.
Meeting records. GA: 3rd Committee, A/C.3/37/SR.*58, 61* (30 Nov., 2 Dec.); 5th Committee, A/C.5/37/SR.61 (9 Dec.); plenary, A/37/PV.110 (17 Dec.).

General Assembly resolution 37/170

17 December 1982   Meeting 110   Adopted without vote

Approved by Third Committee (A/37/745) without vote, 2 December (meeting 61); 22-nation draft (A/C.3/37/L.52 and Corr.1); agenda item 12.

Sponsors: Algeria, Argentina, Bangladesh, Barbados, Cape Verde, Ecuador, Finland, Greece, India, Italy, Jordan, Mali, Mexico, Morocco, Norway, Pakistan, Philippines, Portugal, Spain, Sweden, Turkey, Yugoslavia.

Measures to improve the situation and ensure the human rights and dignity of all migrant workers

The General Assembly,

Again reaffirming the permanent validity of the principles and standards embodied in the basic instruments regarding the international protection of human rights, in particular in the Universal Declaration of Human Rights, the International Covenants on Human Rights, the International Convention on the Elimination of All Forms of Racial Discrimination and the Convention on the Elimination of All Forms of Discrimination against Women,

Bearing in mind the principles and standards established within the framework of the International Labour Organisation and the United Nations Educational, Scientific and Cultural Organization, and the importance of the task carried out in connection with migrant workers and their families in other specialized agencies and in various organs of the United Nations,

Reiterating that, in spite of the existence of a body of principles and standards already established, there is need to make further efforts to improve the situation and ensure the human rights and dignity of all migrant workers and their families,

Recalling its resolution 34/172 of 17 December 1979, by which it decided to establish a working group open to all Member States to elaborate an international convention on the protection of the rights of all migrant workers and their families,

Recalling also its resolutions 35/198 of 15 December 1980 and 36/160 of 16 December 1981, by which it renewed the mandate of the Working Group on the Drafting of an International Convention on the Protection of the Rights of All Migrant Workers and Their Families and requested it to continue its work,

Having examined the progress made by the Working Group during its second inter-sessional meeting, held from 10 to 21 May 1982,

Having also examined the report of the Working Group during the current session of the General Assembly,

1. *Takes note* of the report of the Working Group on the Drafting of an International Convention on the Protection of the Rights of All Migrant Workers and Their Families and expresses its satisfaction with the substantial progress that the Working Group has so far made in the accomplishment of its mandate;

2. *Decides* that, in order to enable it to complete its task as soon as possible, the Working Group shall again hold an inter-sessional meeting of two weeks' duration in New York, immediately after the first regular session of 1983 of the Economic and Social Council;

3. *Invites* the Secretary-General to transmit to Governments the report of the Working Group so as to allow the members of the Group to continue their task during the inter-sessional meeting to be held in the spring of 1983, as well as to transmit the results obtained at that meeting in order that the General Assembly may consider them during its thirty-eighth session;

4. *Also invites* the Secretary-General to transmit the above-mentioned documents to the competent organs of the United Nations and to international organizations concerned, for their information, so as to enable them to continue their co-operation with the Working Group;

5. *Decides* that the Working Group shall meet during the thirty-eighth session of the General Assembly, preferably at the beginning of the session, to continue and, if possible, to complete the elaboration of an international convention on the protection of the rights of all migrant workers and their families.

Protection of minorities

At its February/March 1982 session, the Commission on Human Rights, through an informal working group open to all Commission members, continued work on a draft declaration on the rights of persons belonging to national, ethnic, religious and linguistic minorities. Basing its work on a revised draft prepared by its Chairman/Rapporteur and submitted to the Commission in 1981, the group continued the first reading of the text. It adopted provisionally the preamble of the draft declaration and began consideration of article 1.

The Commission on 11 March,[2] after receiving the working group's report which was appended to the Commission's report,[1] decided to establish at its 1983 session an open-ended working group to continue consideration of the revised draft declaration, originally proposed by Yugoslavia in 1978.[3]

Report. [1]Commission on Human Rights, E/1982/12/Add.1.
Resolution (1982). [2]Commission on Human Rights (report, E/1982/12): 1982/38, 11 Mar.
Yearbook reference. [3]1978, p. 722.

Draft declaration on the human rights of non-citizens

Work continued in 1982 on the drafting of a declaration on the human rights of individuals who were not citizens of the country in which they lived. A Working Group established by the General Assembly in December 1981,[4] open to all United Nations Members and chaired by Halima Embarek Warzazi (Morocco), held nine meetings between 4 October and 30 November 1982.[1] It provisionally adopted and agreed to six articles, in addition to articles 1 to 5, provisionally adopted by similar groups in 1980[6] and 1981.[7]

The discussion was based mainly on a revised draft declaration presented in 1979[5] by a Special Rapporteur of the Sub-Commission on Prevention of Discrimination and Protection of Minorities, the Baroness Elles (United Kingdom), transmitted to the Assembly in 1980 by the Economic and Social Council,[3] and on amendments and proposals submitted by several Governments and by the Group's Chairman in the light of informal consultations.

In 1982, the Group reopened consideration of article 1 (defining the term "alien") and agreed that it would set aside the article in order to allow further consultations. It provisionally adopted article 6, stating that aliens could not be subjected to torture or cruel, inhuman or degrading treatment or punishment, nor could they be subjected to medical or scientific experiments without their free consent; article 7, stating that an alien could be expelled only after a decision had been reached in accordance with law; article 9, stating that no alien should be arbitrarily deprived of his lawfully acquired assets; article 10, stating that any alien should have the right to communicate freely with the consulate or diplomatic mission of the State of which he was a citizen or a national; and a new, unnumbered article, stating the right of any State to establish differences between its nationals and aliens. The Group provisionally agreed on article 8, on aliens' economic and social rights.

By a resolution adopted without vote on 17 December,[2] the Assembly took note of the Working Group's report and of the fact that it had not concluded its task. It requested the Secretary-General to transmit the reports of the 1980, 1981 and 1982 working groups to Governments, United Nations organs and international organizations, and invited them to bring up to date their comments on the subject or to submit new comments by 30 June 1983. It decided to establish, at its 1983 session, an open-ended working group to conclude elaboration of the draft declaration, which it hoped would be adopted at that session.

The Third (Social, Humanitarian and Cultural) Committee approved the text on 2 December, also without vote. The draft was introduced by Morocco, also on behalf of Cyprus, Ghana, Greece, Jordan, Mexico, Pakistan and Spain. An oral amendment by the United States was accepted and orally revised by Morocco on behalf of the sponsors. The United States introduced the paragraph requesting transmittal of the working groups' reports and inviting comments, with Morocco specifying the date of submission. An oral amendment by Sweden, by which the Assembly would have decided to continue in 1983 elaboration of the draft declaration with a view to concluding the task, was rejected by 41 votes to 9, with 6 abstentions.

Report. [1]Working Group on draft declaration, A/C.3/37/8.
Resolution (1982). [2]GA: 37/169, 17 Dec., text following.
Resolutions (prior). [3]ESC: 1980/29, 2 May 1980 (YUN 1980, p. 882). [4]GA: 36/165, 16 Dec. 1981 (YUN 1981, p. 888).
Yearbook references. [5]1979, p. 816; [6]1980, p. 867; [7]1981, p. 888.
Financial implications. 5th Committee report, A/37/756; S-G statements, A/C.3/37/L.65, A/C.5/37/71.
Meeting records. GA: 3rd Committee, A/C.3/37/SR.*58, 61* (30 Nov., 2 Dec.); 5th Committee, A/C.5/37/SR.61 (9 Dec.); plenary, A/37/PV.110 (17 Dec.).

General Assembly resolution 37/169
17 December 1982   Meeting 110   Adopted without vote

Approved by Third Committee (A/37/745) without vote, 2 December (meeting 61); 8-nation draft (A/C.3/37/L.48), orally amended by United States and orally revised; agenda item 12.

Sponsors: Cyprus, Ghana, Greece, Jordan, Mexico, Morocco, Pakistan, Spain.

Question of the international legal protection of the human rights of individuals who are not citizens of the country in which they live

The General Assembly,

Bearing in mind Economic and Social Council resolutions 1790(LIV) of 18 May 1973 and 1871(LVI) of 17 May 1974 concerning the question of the international legal protection of the human rights of individuals who are not citizens of the country in which they live,

Recalling Commission on Human Rights resolutions 8(XXIX) of 21 March 1973, 11(XXX) of 6 March 1974, 16(XXXV) of 14 March 1979 and 19(XXXVI) of 29 February 1980, on the same subject,

Recalling also resolution 9(XXXI) of 13 September 1978 of the Sub-Commission on Prevention of Discrimination and Protection of Minorities,

Recalling that the Economic and Social Council, by its resolution 1980/29 of 2 May 1980, decided to transmit to the General Assembly at its thirty-fifth session the text of the draft declaration on the human rights of individuals who are not citizens of the country in which they live, prepared by the Special Rapporteur of the Sub-Commission on Prevention of Discrimination and Protection of Minorities, the Baroness Elles, and amended by the Sub-Commission, together with the comments on the text received from Member States in response to Council decision 1979/36 of 10 May 1979, and recommended that the Assembly should consider the adoption of a declaration on the subject,

Recalling also its resolutions 35/199 of 15 December 1980 and 36/165 of 16 December 1981, by which it decided to establish an open-ended working group for the purpose of concluding the elaboration of the draft declaration on the human rights of individuals who are not citizens of the country in which they live,

Having considered the report of the Working Group,

1. *Takes note* of the report of the Working Group and of the fact that, although the Working Group has done useful work, it has not had sufficient time to conclude its task;

2. *Requests* the Secretary-General to transmit to Governments, competent organs of the United Nations system and international organizations concerned the reports of the open-ended working groups established at the thirty-fifth, thirty-sixth and thirty-seventh sessions and to invite them to bring up to date the comments they submitted in accordance with Economic and Social Council decision 1979/36 or to submit new comments on the basis of the above-mentioned reports, by 30 June 1983;

3. *Decides* to establish, at its thirty-eighth session, an open-ended working group for the purpose of concluding the elaboration of the draft declaration on the human rights of individuals who are not citizens of the country in which they live;

4. *Expresses the hope* that a draft declaration on the human rights of individuals who are not citizens of the country in which they live will be adopted by the General Assembly at its thirty-eighth session.

Discrimination in criminal justice

In 1982, a Special Rapporteur of the Sub-Commission on Prevention of Discrimination and Protection of Minorities, Abu Sayeed Chowdhury (Bangladesh), submitted a final report on his study on discriminatory treatment of members of racial, ethnic, religious or linguistic groups at the various levels in the administration of criminal justice. The study, authorized by the Economic and Social Council in 1980,[3] dealt with: police, military, administrative and judicial investigations; arrest; detention; trial and execution of sentences; and ideologies or beliefs contributing or leading to racism in the administration of criminal justice.[1]

In his conclusions, the Special Rapporteur stated that discriminatory treatment against members of racial, ethnic, religious or linguistic groups was in a number of jurisdictions a fact of life. To provide the necessary safeguards, he recommended that: national legislation recognize the need for special protection for minorities; provision be made for effective remedies, reporting, complaint and investigative procedures, and conciliation machinery and processes; the special needs and circumstances of minority groups be considered in the administration of criminal justice; efforts be made to bring minority groups into government and administration, and to make them officers of criminal justice services, and to protect individuals who were vulnerable to court processes because of their ethnic backgrounds or language difficulties. Further recommendations included formulation of national codes of conduct for law enforcement officials, and of norms for the selection and training of police, arrest and detention, administrative procedures and military law.

By a resolution of 7 September,[2] the Sub-Commission decided to transmit the report to the Commission on Human Rights.

Report. [1]Special Rapporteur, E/CN.4/Sub.2/1982/7.
Resolution (1982). [2]SCPDPM (report, E/CN.4/1983/4): 1982/4, 7 Sep.
Resolution (prior). [3]ESC: 1980/28, 2 May 1980 (YUN 1980, p. 803).

Civil and political rights

Covenant on Civil and Political Rights and Optional Protocol

Accessions and ratifications

As at 31 December 1982, the International Covenant on Civil and Political Rights and the Optional Protocol thereto, which were adopted by the General Assembly in 1966[5] and entered into force in 1976,[6] had been ratified or acceded to by 72 and 28 States, respectively.

Bolivia, Egypt and Viet Nam acceded to the Covenant in 1982. Bolivia also acceded to the Optional Protocol.[1]

The Commission on Human Rights, on 9 March,[2] and the General Assembly, on 18 December,[3] again invited all States that had not done so to become parties to the International Covenants on Human Rights, including the Covenant on Civil and Political Rights and the Optional Protocol, and invited the parties to consider making the declaration under article 41. They emphasized the importance of the strictest compliance by States parties with their obligations under the Covenant and the Optional Protocol.

As at 31 December, 14 parties[8] had made the declaration under article 41 which entered into force in 1979,[7] recognizing the competence of the Human Rights Committee to receive and consider communications to the effect that a State party claimed that another State party was not fulfilling its obligations under the Covenant. During 1982, no party made such a declaration.

In another resolution of 18 December,[4] the Assembly requested the Commission to consider in 1983 and 1984 elaborating a draft of a second optional protocol to the Covenant, on the abolition of the death penalty (see below).

Publication. [1]*Multilateral Treaties Deposited with the Secretary-General: Status as at 31 December 1982* (ST/LEG/SER.E/2), Sales No. E.83.V.6.
Resolutions (1982). [2]Commission on Human Rights (report, E/1982/12): 1982/18, 9 Mar. GA, 18 Dec.: [3]37/191, [4]37/192.
Resolution (prior). [5]GA: 2200 A (XXI), annex, 16 Dec. 1966 (YUN 1966, p. 423).
Yearbook references. [6]1976, p. 609; [7]1979, p. 855, [8]1981, p. 889.

Implementation of the Covenant

The Commission on Human Rights, by a resolution of 9 March 1982 on the International Covenants on Human Rights,[3] expressed appreciation that the Human Rights Committee continued to strive for uniform standards in the implementation of the Covenant on Civil and Political Rights and the Optional Protocol. It noted the Committee's decisions on the periodicity and on guidelines for the form and content of reports from States parties under article 40 on measures adopted to give effect to civil and political rights and progress made in their enjoyment, as well as the Committee's adoption of general comments.

The Committee, established under article 28 of the Covenant,[6] held three sessions during 1982: the fifteenth at United Nations Headquarters from 22 March to 9 April, and the sixteenth and seventeenth at Geneva, from 12 to 30 July and from 11 to 29 October, respectively.

During those sessions, the Committee considered reports and additional information submitted by seven States parties—Australia, Guyana, Iceland, Iran, Mexico, Rwanda and Uruguay—under article 40 of the Covenant. The Committee also concluded consideration of 14 communications, submitted under article 2 of the Optional Protocol by individuals claiming to be victims of violations of civil and political rights, and adopted its views on the merits of those cases. The cases concerned Canada (two), Colombia (three), Finland (one) and Uruguay (eight). The Committee also discussed matters concerning publicity for its work.

On 30 July,[1] the Economic and Social Council authorized the Secretary-General to transmit the Committee's report on its sessions held between

October 1981 and July 1982[2] directly to the General Assembly.

In a resolution of 18 December,[4] the Assembly noted with appreciation the Committee's report and urged States parties to submit their reports as speedily as possible and to provide additional information when requested. It expressed appreciation that the Committee continued to strive for uniform implementation standards. It requested the Secretary-General to keep the Committee informed of the activities of the Commission on Human Rights, the Sub-Commission on Prevention of Discrimination and Protection of Minorities, the Committee on the Elimination of Racial Discrimination and the Committee on the Elimination of Discrimination against Women, and to transmit the Committee's annual reports to those bodies.

Elaboration of a second optional protocol to the Covenant, aimed at the abolition of capital punishment (see below), was considered by the Assembly in another resolution of 18 December.[5]

Decision (1982). [1]ESC: 1982/178, para. *(b)*, 30 July.
Report. [2]Human Rights Committee, A/37/40.
Resolutions (1982). [3]Commission on Human Rights (report, E/1982/12): 1982/18, para. 3, 9 Mar. GA, 18 Dec.: [4]37/191, [5]37/192.
Resolution (prior). [6]GA: 2200 A (XXI), annex, 16 Dec. 1966 (YUN 1966, p. 423).

Human Rights Committee documents

The Commission on Human Rights, by a resolution of 9 March 1982 on the International Covenants on Human Rights,[3] welcomed measures taken by the Secretary-General to improve publicity for the work of the Human Rights Committee, and took note of the General Assembly's November 1981 request[5] that the Secretary-General consider more appropriate steps for the publication of the Committee's documentation. It asked that he report to the 1982 Assembly session.

On 18 December,[4] the Assembly noted the request of the Committee that its official records be made available annually in bound volumes, one volume containing the summary records of the Committee's public meetings and a second the Committee's other public documents, including reports of States parties under article 40 of the Covenant. The Assembly requested the Secretary-General to consider making arrangements for the publications within existing resources.

In an October report to the Assembly,[2] the Secretary-General estimated the annual cost of printing the Committee's documentation in two volumes in English, French, Russian and Spanish, by publishers outside the United Nations, at approximately $146,759. The Committee having first issued documentation in 1977, there was a backlog of five years, amounting to three volumes of summary records and three volumes of other documents.

The Committee Chairman, by a letter of 25 October 1982 to the Secretary-General,[1] stated that the availability of the Committee's public documents in annual bound volumes was necessary for its continuing dialogue with States parties and to facilitate the work of national and non-governmental entities concerned with promoting human rights throughout the world.

Letter. [1]Human Rights Committee Chairman, 25 Oct., A/C.3/37/6.
Report. [2]S-G, A/37/490.
Resolutions (1982). [3]Commission on Human Rights (report, E/1982/12): 1982/18, para. 7, 9 Mar. [4]GA: 37/191, para. 13, 18 Dec.
Resolution (prior). [5]GA: 36/58, 25 Nov. 1981 (YUN 1981, p. 934).

Self-determination of peoples

Action by the Commission on Human Rights.

On 25 February 1982,[4] the Commission on Human Rights called on States to implement United Nations resolutions, in particular the 1960 Declaration on the Granting of Independence to Colonial Countries and Peoples,[8] and to take steps to enable the peoples of the territories concerned to exercise their right to self-determination. It reaffirmed that colonialism was incompatible with the Declaration (see TRUSTEESHIP AND DECOLONIZATION, Chapter I), the 1948 Universal Declaration of Human Rights[7] and the Charter of the United Nations, and that it posed a serious threat to international peace and security. The Commission condemned the activities of foreign interests which were impeding implementation of the Declaration, particularly with respect to Namibia. It reaffirmed the right to self-determination of the peoples of Namibia and South Africa, and the legitimacy of their struggle, including armed struggle (see below, under HUMAN RIGHTS VIOLATIONS). The Commission reaffirmed that the use of mercenaries against national liberation movements and States was a criminal act, and expressed appreciation of the work on a draft convention against mercenaries (see LEGAL QUESTIONS, Chapter II). It decided to give the right to self-determination high priority in 1983.

This resolution was adopted by a roll-call vote of 32 to 8 (Australia, Canada, Denmark, France, Germany, Federal Republic of, Italy, United Kingdom, United States), with 3 abstentions.

In February, the Commission also adopted resolutions on the self-determination of Afghanistan, Kampuchea, the Palestinian people and Western Sahara (see below).

On 11 March,[1] the Commission decided to postpone action on a draft resolution[2] reaffirming the right of all peoples to determine freely their political status, and stating that the alien subjugation of peoples and their domination, exploitation or foreign occupation constituted a violation of human rights.

General Assembly action. On 3 December,[5] the General Assembly reaffirmed that the realization of the right of all peoples, including those under colonial, foreign and alien domination, to self-determination was fundamental for the effective guarantee, observance, preservation and promotion of human rights. It declared its firm opposition to foreign military intervention, aggression and occupation, and called for their immediate cessation. It deplored the plight of millions of refugees and displaced persons and reaffirmed their right to return to their homes. It requested the Commission on Human Rights to continue to give special attention to violations of human rights, especially the right to self-determination, resulting from foreign military intervention, aggression or occupation.

The resolution was adopted without vote, following similar approval on 27 October by the Third (Social, Humanitarian and Cultural) Committee, where it was introduced by Pakistan on behalf of 17 nations.

Also on 3 December,[6] the Assembly reaffirmed the legitimacy of the struggle, including armed struggle, for independence, territorial integrity, national unity and liberation from colonial and foreign domination and occupation. It urged States, United Nations agencies and organizations to ensure full implementation of the Declaration on colonial countries and to intensify their support to peoples under foreign domination in their struggle for self-determination. It reaffirmed the right of the Namibians, Palestinians and all peoples under foreign colonial domination to self-determination, national independence, territorial integrity, national unity and sovereignty without external interference, and strongly condemned the continued violations of those peoples' human rights and the denial of their national rights. It strongly condemned Governments which did not recognize the right to self-determination and independence of peoples under foreign domination, notably those of Africa and the Palestinians. It demanded the immediate release of children in Namibian and South African prisons, as well as all persons detained or imprisoned as a result of their struggle for self-determination, full respect for their rights, and the observance of prohibitions against torture and cruel, inhuman or degrading treatment.

Under other provisions, the Assembly condemned South Africa's policy of "bantustanization", its massacres, its increased oppression of Namibians, and its use of armed terrorist groups against national liberation movements and neighbouring countries. It strongly reaffirmed its solidarity with those countries and movements and called for increased assistance to the victims of racism and *apartheid* through their liberation movements. In particular, it strongly condemned South Africa's invasion of Angola and the relations of Western and other countries with South Africa. The Assembly demanded application of the mandatory arms embargo against South Africa, noted with satisfaction the May 1981 Paris Declaration on Sanctions against South Africa[11] and demanded implementation of its September 1981 resolution on a Namibia settlement.[9] It recommended that the Security Council urgently appeal for clemency on behalf of three South African freedom fighters. The Assembly strongly condemned Israel's aggression against Lebanon and its expansionist activities and continuous bombing of Palestinians, in particular the September 1982 massacre in Beirut, and urged support to the Palestinians (see POLITICAL AND SECURITY QUESTIONS, Chapters V and IX).

The Assembly called on States to outlaw the use of mercenaries, noted again a June 1981 decision of the Organization of African Unity[12] to hold a referendum on Western Sahara (see below) and took note of the contacts between the Comoros and France concerning the Comorian island of Mayotte (see POLITICAL AND SECURITY QUESTIONS, Chapter V).

The resolution, sponsored by Guinea on behalf of the African Group of United Nations Member States, was adopted by a recorded vote of 120 to 17, with 6 abstentions, following its approval by the Third Committee on 27 October by 110 votes to 17, with 7 abstentions.

The Secretary-General submitted to the Assembly in July and November a report[3] on action taken pursuant to a November 1981 Assembly resolution,[10] on implementation of the right to self-determination, summarizing replies from 18 Governments, two intergovernmental organizations and seven non-governmental organizations.

Decision (1982). [1]Commission on Human Rights (report, E/1982/12): 1982/104, 11 Mar.
Draft resolution. [2]Algeria, Australia, Costa Rica, Fiji, Germany, Federal Republic of, E/CN.4/1982/L.21.
Report. [3]S-G, A/37/317 & Add.1.
Resolutions (1982). [4]Commission on Human Rights: 1982/16, 25 Feb. GA, 3 Dec., texts following: [5]37/42; [6]37/43.
Resolutions (prior). GA: [7]217 A (III), 10 Dec. 1948 (YUN 1948-49, p. 535); [8]1514(XV), 14 Dec. 1960 (YUN 1960, p. 49); [9]ES-8/2, 14 Sep. 1981 (YUN 1981, p. 1153); [10]36/52, 24 Nov. 1981 (*ibid.*, p. 1102).
Yearbook references. 1981, [11]p. 165, [12]p. 1193.
Meeting records. GA: 3rd Committee, A/C.3/37/SR.3-13, *18, 24, 25* (30 Sep.–27 Oct.); plenary, A/37/PV.90 (3 Dec.).

General Assembly resolution 37/42

3 December 1982   Meeting 90   Adopted without vote

Approved by Third Committee (A/37/580) without vote, 27 October (meeting 24); 17-nation draft (A/C.3/37/L.9); agenda item 79.

Sponsors: Chile, Costa Rica, Ecuador, Jordan, Kuwait, Malaysia, Morocco, Oman, Pakistan, Papua New Guinea, Philippines, Qatar, Saudi Arabia, Singapore, Somalia, Sudan, Thailand.

Universal realization of the right of peoples to self-determination

The General Assembly,

Reaffirming the importance, for the effective guarantee and observance of human rights, of the universal realization of the right of peoples to self-determination enshrined in the Charter of the United

Nations and embodied in the International Covenants on Human Rights, as well as in the Declaration on the Granting of Independence to Colonial Countries and Peoples, contained in General Assembly resolution 1514(XV) of 14 December 1960,

Welcoming the progressive exercise of the right to self-determination by peoples under colonial, foreign or alien occupation and their emergence into sovereign statehood and independence,

Deeply concerned at the continuation of acts or threats of foreign military intervention and occupation, which are threatening to suppress, or have already suppressed, the right to self-determination of an increasing number of sovereign peoples and nations,

Further expressing grave concern that, as a consequence of the persistence of such actions, millions of people have been and are being uprooted from their homes as refugees and displaced persons, and emphasizing the urgent need for concerted international action to alleviate their conditions,

Recalling the relevant resolutions regarding the violation of the right of peoples to self-determination and other human rights as a result of foreign military intervention, aggression and occupation, adopted by the Commission on Human Rights at its thirty-sixth, thirty-seventh and thirty-eighth sessions,

Reiterating its resolutions 35/35 B of 14 November 1980 and 36/10 of 28 October 1981,

Taking note of the note by the Secretary-General of 28 September 1982,

1. *Reaffirms* that the universal realization of the right of all peoples, including those under colonial, foreign and alien domination, to self-determination is a fundamental condition for the effective guarantee and observance of human rights and for the preservation and promotion of such rights;

2. *Declares* its firm opposition to acts of foreign military intervention, aggression and occupation, since these have resulted in the suppression of the right of peoples to self-determination and of other human rights in certain parts of the world;

3. *Calls upon* those States responsible to cease immediately their military intervention and occupation of foreign countries and territories, and to cease all acts of repression, discrimination, exploitation and maltreatment, particularly the brutal and inhuman methods reportedly employed for the execution of these acts against the peoples concerned;

4. *Deplores* the plight of the millions of refugees and displaced persons who have been uprooted by the aforementioned acts and reaffirms their right to return to their homes voluntarily in safety and honour;

5. *Requests* the Commission on Human Rights to continue to give special attention to the violation of human rights, especially the right to self-determination, resulting from foreign military intervention, aggression and occupation;

6. *Requests* the Secretary-General to report on this issue to the General Assembly at its thirty-eighth session, under the item entitled "Importance of the universal realization of the right of peoples to self-determination and of the speedy granting of independence to colonial countries and peoples for the effective guarantee and observance of human rights".

General Assembly resolution 37/43

3 December 1982   Meeting 90   120-17-6 (recorded vote)

Approved by Third Committee (A/37/580) by vote (110-17-7), 27 October (meeting 24); draft by Guinea, for African Group (A/C.3/37/L.11); agenda item 79.

Importance of the universal realization of the right of peoples to self-determination and of the speedy granting of independence to colonial countries and peoples for the effective guarantee and observance of human rights

The General Assembly,

Recalling its resolutions 2649(XXV) of 30 November 1970, 2955(XXVII) of 12 December 1972, 3070(XXVIII) of 30 November 1973, 3246(XXIX) of 29 November 1974, 3382(XXX) of 10 November 1975, 33/24 of 29 November 1978, 34/44 of 23 November 1979, 35/35 of 14 November 1980 and 36/9 of 28 October 1981, and Security Council resolutions 418(1977) of 4 November 1977 and 437(1978) of 10 October 1978,

Recalling also its resolutions 2465(XXIII) of 20 December 1968, 2548(XXIV) of 11 December 1969, 2708(XXV) of 14 December 1970,

3103(XXVIII) of 12 December 1973 and 3314(XXIX) of 14 December 1974 concerning the use and recruitment of mercenaries against national liberation movements and sovereign States, and also Security Council resolutions 496(1981) of 15 December 1981 and 507(1982) of 28 May 1982,

Recalling further its relevant resolutions on the question of Palestine, in particular resolutions 3236(XXIX) and 3237(XXIX) of 22 November 1974, 36/120 of 10 December 1981 and ES-7/6 of 19 August 1982,

Recalling also its resolutions on the question of Namibia, in particular resolution ES-8/2 of 14 September 1981,

Recalling the resolutions on Namibia adopted by the Council of Ministers of the Organization of African Unity at its thirty-seventh ordinary session, held at Nairobi from 15 to 26 June 1981, particularly resolutions CM/Res.855(XXXVII) and CM/Res.865(XXXVII),

Deeply concerned at the continued terrorist acts of aggression committed by the Pretoria régime against independent African States, in particular Angola, Botswana, Mozambique, Seychelles and Zambia,

Deeply angered by the occupation of part of the territory of Angola by the troops of the racist régime of South Africa,

Recalling the Political Declaration adopted by the First Conference of Heads of State and Government of the Organization of African Unity and the League of Arab States, held at Cairo from 7 to 9 March 1977,

Considering that the denial of the inalienable rights of the Palestinian people to self-determination, sovereignty, independence and return to Palestine and the repeated acts of aggression by Israel against the peoples of the region constitute a serious threat to international peace and security,

Deeply shocked and alarmed at the deplorable consequences of the Israeli invasion of Beirut on 3 August 1982, and recalling all the resolutions of the Security Council, in particular resolutions 520(1982) of 17 September 1982 and 521(1982) of 19 September 1982,

Reaffirming its faith in the importance of the implementation of the Declaration on the Granting of Independence to Colonial Countries and Peoples, contained in General Assembly resolution 1514(XV) of 14 December 1960,

Reaffirming the importance of the universal realization of the right of peoples to self-determination, national sovereignty and territorial integrity and of the speedy granting of independence to colonial countries and peoples as imperatives for the full enjoyment of all human rights,

Reaffirming that "bantustanization" is incompatible with genuine independence, national unity and sovereignty and has the effect of perpetuating the power of the white minority and the racist system of *apartheid* in South Africa,

Reaffirming the obligation of all Member States to comply with the principles of the Charter of the United Nations and the resolutions of the United Nations regarding the exercise of the right to self-determination by peoples under colonial and foreign domination,

Reaffirming also that the system of *apartheid* imposed on the South African people constitutes an inadmissible violation of the rights of that people and a constant threat to international security,

Reaffirming the national unity and territorial integrity of the Comoros,

Gravely concerned at the continuation of the illegal occupation of Namibia by South Africa and the continued violations of the human rights of the peoples still under colonial and foreign domination and alien subjugation,

1. *Calls upon* all States to implement fully and faithfully the resolutions of the United Nations regarding the exercise of the right to self-determination and independence by peoples under colonial and foreign domination;

2. *Reaffirms* the legitimacy of the struggle of peoples for independence, territorial integrity, national unity and liberation from colonial and foreign domination and foreign occupation by all available means, including armed struggle;

3. *Reaffirms* the inalienable right of the Namibian people, the Palestinian people and all peoples under foreign and colonial domination to self-determination, national independence, territorial integrity, national unity and sovereignty without outside interference;

4. *Notes again with satisfaction* resolution AHG/Res.103(XVIII) adopted by the Assembly of Heads of State and Government of the Organization of African Unity at its eighteenth ordinary session, held at Nairobi from 24 to 27 June 1981, and the decisions of its Implementation Committee to organize and conduct a general, free and regular referendum on self-determination in Western Sahara, and welcomes

the willingness of the United Nations to collaborate in the implementation of the process envisaged by the Organization of African Unity;

5. *Takes note* of the contacts between the Government of the Comoros and the Government of France in the search for a just solution to the integration of the Comorian island of Mayotte into the Comoros in accordance with the resolutions of the Organization of African Unity and the United Nations on this question;

6. *Condemns* the policy of "bantustanization" and reiterates its support for the oppressed people of South Africa in their just and legitimate struggle against the racist minority régime in Pretoria;

7. *Further condemns* South Africa for its increased oppression of the Namibian people, for the massive militarization of Namibia and for its armed attacks on the front-line States with the aim of destabilizing their Governments;

8. *Strongly condemns* the establishment and use of armed terrorist groups by South Africa with a view to pitting them against the national liberation movements and destabilizing the legitimate Governments of southern Africa, thus impeding effective implementation of General Assembly resolution 1514(XV);

9. *Strongly reaffirms* its solidarity with the independent African countries and liberation movements that are victims of the murderous acts of aggression of the Pretoria régime and of its attempts at destabilization;

10. *Strongly condemns once again* the invasion and occupation of part of the territory of Angola by troops of the racist Pretoria régime and demands the immediate withdrawal of those troops from Angolan territory;

11. *Reaffirms* that the practice of using mercenaries against sovereign States and national liberation movements constitutes a criminal act and that the mercenaries themselves are criminals, and calls upon the Governments of all countries to enact legislation declaring the recruitment, financing and training of mercenaries in their territories and the transit of mercenaries through their territories to be punishable offences, and prohibiting their nationals from serving as mercenaries, and to report on such legislation to the Secretary-General;

12. *Strongly condemns* the continued violations of the human rights of the peoples still under colonial and foreign domination and alien subjugation, the continuation of the illegal occupation of Namibia, and South Africa's attempts to dismember its territory, the perpetuation of the racist minority régime in southern Africa and the denial to the Palestinian people of their inalienable national rights;

13. *Also strongly condemns* the policies of those Western and other countries whose political, economic, military, nuclear, strategic, cultural and sports relations with the racist minority régime in South Africa encourage that régime to persist in its suppression of the aspirations of peoples to self-determination and independence;

14. *Again demands* the immediate application of the mandatory arms embargo against South Africa, imposed under Security Council resolution 418(1977), by all countries, particularly by those countries that maintain military and nuclear co-operation with the racist Pretoria régime and continue to supply it with related *matériel;*

15. *Takes note again with satisfaction* of the Paris Declaration on Sanctions against South Africa, the Special Declaration on Namibia and the reports of the technical and political commissions adopted by the International Conference on Sanctions against South Africa, held in Paris from 20 to 27 May 1981, convened jointly by the United Nations and the Organization of African Unity;

16. *Demands* the immediate implementation of General Assembly resolution ES-8/2 on Namibia;

17. *Calls* for a substantial increase in all forms of assistance given by all States, United Nations organs, specialized agencies and non-governmental organizations to the victims of racism, racial discrimination and *apartheid* through their national liberation movements recognized by the Organization of African Unity;

18. *Strongly condemns* those Governments that do not recognize the right to self-determination and independence of all peoples still under colonial and foreign domination and alien subjugation, notably the peoples of Africa and the Palestinian people;

19. *Strongly condemns* the increasingly widespread massacres of innocent and defenceless people, including women and children, by the racist minority Pretoria régime in its desperate attempt to thwart the legitimate demands of the people;

20. *Strongly condemns* the massacre of Palestinians and other civilians at Beirut on 17 September 1982;

21. *Strongly condemns* the expansionist activities of Israel in the Middle East and the continual bombing of Palestinian civilians, which constitute a serious obstacle to the realization of the self-determination and independence of the Palestinian people;

22. *Strongly condemns* the Israeli aggression against Lebanon in June 1982, which endangers stability, peace and security in the region, and reiterates its support for the efforts undertaken to implement the resolutions of the Security Council, in particular those demanding the immediate and unconditional withdrawal of Israeli forces from Lebanese territory to internationally recognized boundaries and respect for the sovereignty and territorial integrity of Lebanon;

23. *Urges* all States, competent organizations of the United Nations system, specialized agencies and other international organizations to extend their support to the Palestinian people through its sole and legitimate representative, the Palestine Liberation Organization, in its struggle to regain its right to self-determination and independence in accordance with the Charter of the United Nations;

24. *Demands* the immediate and unconditional release of all persons detained or imprisoned as a result of their struggle for self-determination and independence, full respect for their fundamental individual rights and the observance of article 5 of the Universal Declaration of Human Rights, under which no one shall be subjected to torture or to cruel, inhuman or degrading treatment;

25. *Recommends* that the Security Council should make urgent appeals for clemency to the South African authorities in order that the lives of the three African National Congress freedom fighters sentenced to death on 6 August 1982 may be saved in accordance with General Assembly resolution 37/1 of 1 October 1982;

26. *Demands* the immediate release of children detained in Namibian and South African prisons;

27. *Reiterates its appreciation* for the material and other forms of assistance that peoples under colonial rule continue to receive from Governments, United Nations agencies and intergovernmental organizations, and calls for a substantial increase in this assistance;

28. *Urges* all States, specialized agencies and competent organizations of the United Nations system to do their utmost to ensure the full implementation of the Declaration on the Granting of Independence to Colonial Countries and Peoples and to intensify their efforts to support peoples under colonial, foreign and racist domination in their just struggle for self-determination and independence;

29. *Requests* the Secretary-General to give maximum publicity to the Declaration on the Granting of Independence to Colonial Countries and Peoples and to give the widest possible publicity to the struggle being waged by oppressed peoples for the realization of their self-determination and national independence;

30. *Decides* to consider this item again at its thirty-eighth session on the basis of the reports that Governments, United Nations agencies and intergovernmental and non-governmental organizations have been requested to submit concerning the strengthening of assistance to colonial territories and peoples.

Recorded vote in Assembly as follows:

In favour: Albania, Algeria, Angola, Antigua and Barbuda, Argentina, Bahamas, Bahrain, Bangladesh, Barbados, Belize, Benin, Bhutan, Bolivia, Botswana, Brazil, Bulgaria, Burundi, Byelorussian SSR, Cape Verde, Central African Republic, Chad, Chile, China, Colombia, Comoros, Congo, Cuba, Cyprus, Czechoslovakia, Democratic Kampuchea, Democratic Yemen, Djibouti, Dominican Republic, Ecuador, Egypt, El Salvador, Equatorial Guinea, Ethiopia, Fiji, Gabon, German Democratic Republic, Ghana, Grenada, Guinea, Guinea-Bissau, Guyana, Haiti, Hungary, India, Indonesia, Iran, Iraq, Ivory Coast, Jamaica, Jordan, Kenya, Kuwait, Lao People's Democratic Republic, Lesotho, Liberia, Libyan Arab Jamahiriya, Madagascar, Malaysia, Maldives, Mali, Malta, Mauritania, Mauritius, Mexico, Mongolia, Morocco, Mozambique, Nepal, Nicaragua, Niger, Nigeria, Oman, Pakistan, Panama, Papua New Guinea, Peru, Philippines, Poland, Qatar, Romania, Rwanda, Saint Lucia, Samoa, Sao Tome and Principe, Saudi Arabia, Senegal, Sierra Leone, Singapore, Solomon Islands, Somalia, Sri Lanka, Sudan, Suriname, Swaziland, Syrian Arab Republic, Thailand, Togo, Trinidad and Tobago, Tunisia, Turkey, Uganda, Ukrainian SSR, USSR, United Arab Emirates, United Republic of Tanzania, Upper Volta, Uruguay, Vanuatu, Venezuela, Viet Nam, Yemen, Yugoslavia, Zaire, Zambia, Zimbabwe.

Against: Australia, Belgium, Canada, Denmark, Finland, France, Germany, Federal Republic of, Iceland, Israel, Italy, Luxembourg, Netherlands, New Zealand, Norway, Sweden, United Kingdom, United States.

Abstaining: Austria, Greece, Ireland, Japan, Portugal, Spain.

Afghanistan

On 25 February 1982, the Commission on Human Rights adopted, by a roll-call vote of 32 to 7 (Bulgaria, Byelorussian SSR, Cuba, Ethiopia, Poland, Syrian Arab Republic, USSR), with 4 abstentions, a resolution on the situation in Afghanistan[1] by which it reaffirmed its most profound concern that the people of Afghanistan continued to be denied their right to self-determination and to determine their own Government and choose their economic, political and social system free from outside intervention, subversion, coercion or constraint. The Commission called for the immediate withdrawal of foreign troops, for a political settlement on the basis of full respect for Afghanistan's independence, sovereignty, territorial integrity and non-aligned status, and strict observance of the principle of non-intervention and non-interference.

The Commission urged all concerned to work towards a settlement ensuring that the Afghan people would determine their destiny free from outside interference, and to co-operate with the Secretary-General in his efforts to resolve the situation. The Commission appealed for humanitarian assistance to Afghan refugees and affirmed their right to return home. It decided to consider the Afghanistan situation in 1983 with high priority (see POLITICAL AND SECURITY QUESTIONS, Chapter VI).

By a resolution of 8 September,[2] adopted by 14 votes to 3, with 3 abstentions, the Sub-Commission on Prevention of Discrimination and Protection of Minorities expressed its solemn view that the withdrawal of foreign forces from Afghanistan was essential for restoring human rights. It urged the Secretary-General, in seeking a political settlement, to widen his consultations and include representatives of all parties concerned. It invited the Commission to urge all parties concerned to co-operate with him. It invited him to bring to the attention of the Sub-Commission in 1983 any reports to the General Assembly or any of its committees on the use of illegal weapons in Afghanistan or against the Afghan people. It recommended that the Commission in 1983 give priority to the Afghanistan situation.

Resolutions (1982). [1]Commission on Human Rights (report, E/1982/12): 1982/14, 25 Feb. [2]SCPDPM (report, E/CN.4/1983/4): 1982/21, 8 Sep.

Kampuchea

Communications. On 12 January 1982,[3] Democratic Kampuchea transmitted to the Commission on Human Rights two letters it had submitted to the General Assembly in November and December 1981,[12] alleging the use of chemical weapons by Vietnamese authorities in Kampuchea.

By a letter dated 12 February,[5] Democratic Kampuchea took exception to statements, transmitted on 8 February by Viet Nam to the Commission Chairman,[7] by the Vietnamese Foreign Ministry and the Foreign Ministry of the People's

Republic of Kampuchea rejecting Assembly resolutions and the July 1981 International Conference on Kampuchea.[13]

On 16 July,[6] Democratic Kampuchea transmitted to the President of the Economic and Social Council a proclamation of Prince Norodom Sihanouk, stating the formulation of a coalition Government of Democratic Kampuchea on 22 June.

Review. Material on the human rights situation in Kampuchea,[11] reviewed during 1981 by a member of the Sub-Commission on discrimination and minorities, Asbjorn Eide (Norway), was transmitted to the 1982 Commission on Human Rights session, as requested by the Sub-Commission in September 1981.[14] In his review, Mr. Eide stated that the documentation from the Government of Democratic Kampuchea for the most part described alleged atrocities in the conduct of anti-guerrilla warfare by Vietnamese forces. The documents submitted by Viet Nam, and through it by the Government of the People's Republic of Kampuchea, contained further evidence of the brutalities of the Khmer Rouge during 1975-1978, including mass murders, and their long-term effect. The review stated that the documents submitted by non-governmental organizations substantiated the allegations made by both sides; it concluded, however, that no final judgement on their veracity could be passed and that, unless the situation was normalized, there was not much hope that human rights could be satisfactorily realized. What the human rights organs of the United Nations could do was to express their views on what seemed to be required from a human rights perspective, including implementation of the right to self-determination of the Kampucheans, with everyone equally entitled to participate. To that end, the review recommended: that a political process be set in motion by which the Kampucheans could freely choose their own representatives, safeguarded by the United Nations and without outside interference; that all foreign forces be withdrawn and all local armed conflict be brought to a halt, under United Nations supervision; that the right of all Kampuchean refugees to return be unconditionally accepted; and that the international community, through the United Nations, pledge to provide interim assistance required for the new Kampuchean authorities to safeguard the basic social and economic rights.

By a letter of 27 January,[4] Democratic Kampuchea objected to a statement in the review that the Kampucheans were the victims of a "nebulous legal situation", where the United Nations continued to recognize a régime it condemned and which did not appear to have any serious hold on the country, and did not recognize a régime it condemned just as much but which controlled the territory.

Action by the Commission on Human Rights. On 25 February 1982,[9] the Commission on Human Rights reiterated its condemnation of gross and flagrant violations of human rights in Kampuchea. It expressed its conviction that the withdrawal of all foreign forces, the restoration and preservation of Kampuchea's independence, sovereignty and territorial integrity, the right of the Kampucheans to determine their own destiny and the commitment by all States to non-interference and non-intervention in Kampuchea's internal affairs were the principal components of any just and lasting solution to the Kampuchea problem. The Commission reaffirmed that the persistence of foreign occupation was the primary violation of human rights in Kampuchea and prevented the people from exercising their right to self-determination. It called again for a cessation of hostilities and immediate and unconditional withdrawal of foreign forces, in order to allow the Kampucheans to decide their own future through free elections under United Nations supervision.

The Commission called on all parties to join in the search for a comprehensive solution and requested the Secretary-General to exercise his good offices to contribute to a settlement. The Commission requested the Sub-Commission to report in 1983 on the practices of the foreign forces affecting the human rights of the Kampucheans. It decided to keep the situation under review in 1983 as a high priority matter and recommended that the Economic and Social Council consider the situation.

The resolution was adopted by a roll-call vote of 28 to 8 (Bulgaria, Byelorussian SSR, Cuba, Ethiopia, India, Poland, Syrian Arab Republic, USSR), with 5 abstentions.

By a statement of 12 April 1982, transmitted by Viet Nam on 16 April,[8] the Vice-President of the Council of Ministers and Minister for Foreign Affairs of the People's Republic of Kampuchea rejected the resolution, saying that by feigning to know nothing about the real situation and by allowing genocidal criminals to lead it astray with a view to camouflaging their monstrous crimes, the Commission placed itself at the service of those criminals.

Economic and Social Council action. Endorsing the resolution of the Commission on Human Rights, the Economic and Social Council, on 7 May 1982,[1] expressed concern over the continuing activities of foreign forces in Kampuchea and welcomed the Secretary-General's efforts to achieve a peaceful solution. The decision was adopted by a recorded vote, requested by Thailand, of 38 to 8, with 3 abstentions, following its approval by a recorded vote of 36 to 7, with 3 abstentions, by the Second (Social) Committee on 3 May, where the 20-nation text was introduced by Thailand.

The USSR, also on behalf of Bulgaria, the Byelorussian SSR and Poland, objected to the text as an inadmissible interference in the internal affairs of Kampuchea, aimed at diverting the Council's attention from the real human rights problems; human rights violations in Kampuchea no longer existed and it was the imperialist enemies of the Kampucheans who wished to deny them their right to self-determination.

Voting in favour, China said the text was consonant with the situation in Kampuchea where human rights were violated by foreign occupation.

By a letter of 12 July,[2] 15 States, including Viet Nam, stated that they considered the presence of persons claiming to represent Kampuchea in the Council under the name of Democratic Kampuchea to be illegal; the legitimate representative was the People's Republic of Kampuchea.

Sub-Commission action. By a resolution of 8 September,[10] adopted by 12 votes to 5, with 2 abstentions, the Sub-Commission on discrimination and minorities requested that further material on human rights in Kampuchea, reviewed by Mr. Eide, be transmitted to the Commission on Human Rights in 1983. The Sub-Commission endorsed the call for an immediate withdrawal of all foreign forces, and called on the Commission to affirm the need for a political solution based on the self-determination of the Kampucheans and on respect for human rights. It invited the Commission to urge all concerned to ensure, following the withdrawal of foreign forces: that the Kampucheans chose their own representatives to a constitutional assembly; that all foreign States publicly declared their intention not to interfere with the internal political process; that the right of the Kampuchean refugees to return be recognized; and that the United Nations offered its expert services in the field of human rights and fundamental freedoms. It recommended that the Commission call for a pledge by all foreign States not to intervene with armed forces.

Decision (1982). [1]ESC: 1982/143, 7 May, text following.
Letters. [2]Bulgaria, Byelorussian SSR, Cuba, Czechoslovakia, Democratic Yemen, Ethiopia, German Democratic Republic, Hungary, Mongolia, Nicaragua, Poland, Syrian Arab Republic, Ukrainian SSR, USSR, Viet Nam: 12 July, E/1982/107. Democratic Kampuchea: [3]12 Jan., E/CN.4/1982/3; [4]27 Jan., E/CN.4/1982/7; [5]12 Feb., E/CN.4/1982/15; [6]16 July, E/1982/108. Viet Nam: [7]8 Feb., E/CN.4/1982/10; [8]16 Apr., A/37/201 (E/1982/51).
Resolutions (1982). [9]Commission on Human Rights (report, E/1982/12): 1982/13, 25 Feb. [10]SCPDPM (report, E/CN.4/1983/4): 1982/22, 8 Sep.
Review. [11]SCPDPM member, transmitted by Secretariat note, E/CN.4/1491.
Yearbook references. 1981, [12]p. 73, [13]p. 241, [14]p. 897.
Meeting records. ESC: E/1982/SR.28, *29* (7 May).

Economic and Social Council decision 1982/143

7 May 1982   Meeting 29   38-8-3 (recorded vote)

Approved by Second Committee (E/1982/59) by recorded vote (36-7-3), 3 May (meeting 15); 20-nation draft (E/1982/C.2/L.10); agenda item 9.

Sponsors: Australia, Belgium, Canada, Fiji, Germany, Federal Republic of, Italy, Japan, Malaysia, Netherlands, New Zealand, Pakistan, Philippines, Portugal, Samoa, Singapore, Solomon Islands, Sudan, Thailand, United Kingdom, Zaire.

The right of peoples to self-determination and its application to peoples under colonial or alien domination or foreign occupation

At its 29th plenary meeting, on 7 May 1982, the Council endorsed resolution 1982/13 of 25 February 1982 of the Commission on Human Rights, in which the Commission, *inter alia*, reaffirmed that the primary violation of human rights in Kampuchea at present was the persistence of foreign occupation, which prevented the people of Kampuchea from exercising their right to self-determination. The Council reaffirmed its decision 1981/154 of 8 May 1981, and endorsed the call for the withdrawal of all foreign forces from Kampuchea, as contained in the Declaration on Kampuchea adopted by the International Conference on Kampuchea on 17 July 1981, in order to allow the people of Kampuchea to exercise their fundamental freedoms and human rights, including the right to decide their own future through free and fair elections under United Nations supervision, without outside interference, subversion or coercion. The Council expressed its grave concern over the continuing activities of the foreign forces in Kampuchea, resulting in the loss of life and property of Kampucheans and forcing large numbers of Kampuchean civilians to flee their homes. The Council welcomed the continuing efforts of the Secretary-General aimed at achieving a peaceful solution to the situation in South-East Asia and endorsed the Commission's call to all parties concerned to join in the efforts to seek a comprehensive solution to the Kampuchean problems within the framework of the Declaration on Kampuchea of 17 July 1981, which was endorsed by the General Assembly in its resolution 36/5 of 21 October 1981, and to co-operate in the work of the *Ad Hoc* Committee of the International Conference on Kampuchea. The Council noted with appreciation the recent visit to the area by the Special Representative of the Secretary-General.

Recorded vote in Council as follows:

In favour: Argentina, Australia, Austria, Bahamas, Bangladesh, Belgium, Brazil, Canada, Chile, China, Colombia, Denmark, Fiji, France, Germany, Federal Republic of, Greece, Italy, Japan, Kenya, Liberia, Malawi, Nepal, Nigeria, Norway, Pakistan, Peru, Portugal, Saint Lucia, Sudan, Swaziland, Thailand, Tunisia, United Kingdom, United Republic of Cameroon, United States, Venezuela, Yugoslavia, Zaire.

Against: Benin, Bulgaria, Byelorussian SSR, Ethiopia, India, Nicaragua, Poland, USSR.

Abstaining: Burundi, Mali, Mexico.

Palestinians

By a resolution of 11 February 1982,[1] adopted by a roll-call vote of 24 to 8 (Australia, Canada, Denmark, Germany, Federal Republic of, Italy, Netherlands, United Kingdom, United States), with 10 abstentions, the Commission on Human Rights reaffirmed the inalienable right of the Palestinian people to self-determination without external interference and to establish a fully independent and sovereign State of Palestine. It reaffirmed their inalienable right to return to their homes and property, from which they had been displaced by Israel, and called for their return in the exercise of their right to self-determination. It recognized their right to regain their rights by all means in accordance with the United Nations Charter; reaffirmed that their future could only be decided with their full participation, through their representative, the Palestine Liberation Organization (PLO); and urged the international community to support them through PLO. It expressed strong opposition to all partial agreements and separate treaties, which it declared to be without validity in determining the future of the Palestinians and of the Palestinian territories occupied by Israel since 1967, including Jerusalem, and strongly rejected the continuation of negotiations on the question of "autonomy" within the framework of the "Camp David accords". The Commission requested the Secretary-General to make available to it and to its Sub-Commission on discrimination and minorities the reports, studies and publications prepared by the Special Unit on Palestinian Rights of the United Nations Secretariat.

In a resolution of 8 September[2] dealing mainly with Israeli policy in the occupied territories (see below, under HUMAN RIGHTS VIOLATIONS), the Sub-Commission recommended that the Commission call for the full exercise of the inalienable rights of the Palestinians to return to their homes and property, to self-determination without external interference and to establish their own sovereign and independent State.

Resolutions (1982). [1]Commission on Human Rights (report, E/1982/12): 1982/3, 11 Feb. [2]SCPDPM (report, E/CN.4/1983/4): 1982/18, para. 1 *(g)*, 8 Sep.

Western Sahara

By a resolution of 25 February 1982 on Western Sahara,[1] the Commission on Human Rights welcomed the decisions of the Organization of African Unity (OAU) and the United Nations to organize throughout the territory a referendum on self-determination (see TRUSTEESHIP AND DECOLONIZATION, Chapter IV). It urged that the two parties to the conflict, Morocco and the Frente Popular para la Liberación de Saguia el-Hamra y de Río de Oro, enter into direct negotiations with a view to concluding a cease-fire, an indispensable prerequisite for the referendum. It decided to follow closely the situation in Western Sahara and to consider the question as a matter of high priority in 1983.

This resolution was adopted by a roll-call vote of 27 to 3 (Senegal, United States, Zaire), with 13 abstentions.

By its resolution of 3 December on the right to self-determination,[2] the General Assembly noted again with satisfaction the June 1981 OAU decision[3] to organize a free referendum and welcomed the willingness of the United Nations to collaborate.

Resolutions (1982). [1]Commission on Human Rights (report, E/1982/12): 1982/15, 25 Feb. [2]GA: 37/43, para. 4, 3 Dec. *Yearbook reference.* [3]1981, p. 1193.

Rights of detained persons

A sessional Working Group on the human rights of persons subjected to any form of detention or imprisonment, established by a Sub-Commission decision of 19 August,[1] by 14 votes to 2, with 5 abstentions, held four meetings in August under the chairmanship of Benjamin Charles George Whitaker (United Kingdom).[3]

The Working Group's suggestions served as the basis for a Sub-Commission resolution of 7 September, adopted by 8 votes to 1, with 4 abstentions.[4] The Sub-Commission considered it desirable that the law set out clearly the grounds for detention, whether on suspicion of criminal activities or on preventive grounds for security reasons, and that it require the grounds to be made known to the persons concerned in specific terms at the time of arrest. The Sub-Commission deemed it important that the names of detainees be announced publicly, and that those arrested or detained be entitled to visits by their families and a lawyer of choice within 24 hours and regularly thereafter. It recommended that Governments adopt legislation whereby those arrested or detained should be tried within a fixed period or released from detention pending further proceedings.

The Sub-Commission considered that incommunicado detention should be discouraged and be forbidden for periods exceeding 24 hours from the time of arrest. It recommended that detainees be examined, preferably by a doctor of their choice, within 48 hours after arrest and regularly thereafter, and considered that they should have access to their defence lawyers, who should be free from fear of arrest for defending their clients. The Sub-Commission recommended that the option of education be made available to prisoners. Detained persons should have the right to be produced before an independent magistrate and asked if they had complaints. To be admissible, confession must be made only before an independent legal person such as a magistrate. There should be independent inspections, without prior notice, of places of detention and interrogation centres. In principle, trials should not be *in camera*, except when they involved State secrets or when witnesses were frightened to testify in public. The Sub-Commission urged that military jurisdiction be limited to military offences and personnel and not be waived even in states of emergency; persons before military tribunals should have independent legal defenders and the right to appeal to a civilian court against severe sentences.

The Secretary-General was requested to submit to the Sub-Commission in 1983 a preliminary survey of maximum detention periods under existing national laws and under the decisions of international organs. He was requested to invite the international community to submit information on such issues as: arrest and detention on vague grounds or without grounds; the duration of pretrial detention; procedural guarantees for preventive detention, especially under states of emergency; incommunicado detention; extraterritorial abduction; and suicides in detention. The Sub-Commission proposed that a special study be made on how to give effect to the concepts of international *habeas corpus* and anticipatory bail.

Other provisions of the resolution dealt with capital punishment, extrajudicial executions, and hearings on torture and other cruel, inhuman or degrading treatment or punishment (see below). The Sub-Commission decided that a greater number of meetings be devoted to the Working Group in 1983.

The Sub-Commission decided without vote on 31 August 1982[2] to request the Secretary-General to forward to the Commission on Human Rights, for transmission to the Government of Malawi, a text stating the Sub-Commission's concern about allegations that Orton Chirwa and his wife faced a capital charge of treason, before a court not composed of legally trained judges and without right of representation. The Sub-Commission also expressed concern about indications that they had been arrested in Zambia by Malawi police. It urged for a public enquiry into the circumstances of the arrest and for a trial before the high court.

Recommendations on the rights of detained persons in specific circumstances were made in two studies submitted to the Sub-Commission: a study on human rights in states of emergency (see below, under OTHER HUMAN RIGHTS QUESTIONS) and the final report on discriminatory treatment of members of racial, ethnic, religious or linguistic groups in the administration of criminal justice (see above, under DISCRIMINATION).

Decisions (1982). SCPDPM (report, E/CN.4/1983/4): [1]1982/4, 19 Aug.; [2]1982/8, 31 Aug.
Report. [3]Working Group on Detention, E/CN.4/Sub.2/1982/34 & Corr.1.
Resolution (1982). [4]SCPDPM: 1982/10, 7 Sep.

Capital punishment

The Sub-Commission on Prevention of Discrimination and Protection of Minorities, in a resolution of 7 September 1982[3] on the human rights of detained persons (see above), recommended that the United Nations communicate with Governments to avert or postpone carrying out capital punishment immediately after sentencing without allowing the person sentenced proper time or opportunity for appeal.

The General Assembly, on 18 December,[2] requested the Commission on Human Rights to consider in 1983 and 1984 elaboration of a draft second optional protocol to the International Covenant on Civil and Political Rights aimed at the abolition of the death penalty. The Assembly decided to resume at its own session in 1983 consideration of the subject.

The resolution was adopted without vote, following its approval by the Third (Social, Humanitarian and Cultural) Committee on 7 December, by a recorded vote, requested by Sierra Leone, of 52 to 23, with 53 abstentions. The revised text was introduced by the Federal Republic of Germany on behalf of 21 nations.

The Secretary-General reported in September on replies he had received from 16 Governments containing their observations and comments on the elaboration of a second optional protocol,[1] in pursuance of a November 1981 Assembly resolution.[4]

Report. [1]S-G, A/37/407 & Add.1.
Resolutions (1982). [2]GA: 37/192, 18 Dec., text following.
  [3]SCPDPM (report, E/CN.4/1983/4): 1982/10, para. 14, 7 Sep.
Resolution (prior). [4]GA: 36/59, 25 Nov. 1981 (YUN 1981, p. 900).
Meeting records. GA: 3rd Committee, A/C.3/37/SR.47, 50-53, 55, 56, *64, 67* (18 Nov.–7 Dec.); plenary, A/37/PV.111 (18 Dec.).

General Assembly resolution 37/192

18 December 1982   Meeting 111   Adopted without vote

Approved by Third Committee (A/37/718) by recorded vote (52-23-53), 7 December (meeting 67); 21-nation draft (A/C.3/37/L.60/Rev.1); agenda item 87.

Sponsors: Austria, Cape Verde, Costa Rica, Denmark, Dominican Republic, France, Germany, Federal Republic of, Greece, Honduras, Iceland, Italy, Luxembourg, Netherlands, Nicaragua, Norway, Panama, Portugal, Solomon Islands, Spain, Sweden, Uruguay.

Capital punishment

The General Assembly,

Recalling its decision 35/437 of 15 December 1980 and its resolution 36/59 of 25 November 1981 concerning the idea of elaborating a draft of a second optional protocol to the International Covenant on Civil and Political Rights, aiming at the abolition of the death penalty,

1. *Takes note* of the report of the Secretary-General;

2. *Requests* the Commission on Human Rights to consider the idea of elaborating a draft of a second optional protocol to the International Covenant on Civil and Political Rights, aiming at the abolition of the death penalty, at its thirty-ninth and fortieth sessions, taking into account the documents considered by the General Assembly on this subject as well as the views of Governments thereon, and to submit a report, through the Economic and Social Council, to the Assembly at its thirty-ninth session;

3. *Decides* to resume at its thirty-ninth session, under the item entitled "International Covenants on Human Rights", consideration of the idea of elaborating a draft of a second optional protocol to the International Covenant on Civil and Political Rights, aiming at the abolition of the death penalty, with a view to considering what steps may be taken in this area.

Summary executions

Action by the Committee on crime. At its March 1982 session,[1] the Committee on Crime Prevention and Control recommended to the Commission for Social Development for approval and submission to the Economic and Social Council a draft resolution strongly condemning and deploring the practice of summary executions in various parts of the world and its apparent increase. By the text, the Council would strongly condemn and deplore the lack or non-observance in certain cases of minimum legal guarantees and safeguards, which could lead to sham trials and arbitrary executions. It would request the Secretary-General to make available to the Committee in 1984 a report on the progress of the work by the Commission on Human Rights and its Sub-Commission.

The Council would decide that the Committee should further study the question of death penalties that did not meet the acknowledged minimum legal guarantees and safeguards, and would welcome the Committee's intention that this issue be discussed at the Seventh United Nations Congress on the Prevention of Crime and the Treatment of Offenders, to be held in 1985. The Council would request the Secretary-General to continue to obtain information on the development of legal provisions, the actual practice relating to the death penalty, and the arbitrary character of some executions, and to make his next report on capital punishment available to the 1985 Congress.

Economic and Social Council action. On 7 May 1982,[3] the Economic and Social Council strongly deplored the increasing number of summary or arbitrary executions in various parts of the world. It decided to appoint for one year a special rapporteur to examine such executions and requested the Chairman of the Commission on Human Rights to appoint an individual of recognized international standing. It considered that the Special Rapporteur might seek and receive information from Governments and intergovernmental and non-governmental organizations. It urged Governments and the Secretary-General to assist the Special Rapporteur; requested the Special Rapporteur to submit a report to the Commission in 1983 on the occurrence and extent of the practice of such executions, together with conclusions and recommendations; and requested the Commission to consider that year the question as a matter of high priority.

The resolution was adopted without vote, following similar approval by the Second (Social) Committee on 3 May. The text was recommended by the Commission on Human Rights on 11 March.[2]

Sub-Commission action. On 7 September,[6] the Sub-Commission on Prevention of Discrimination and Protection of Minorities expressed deep concern at the increasing number of summary or arbitrary executions often taking place on a massive scale. It endorsed the Council's request to Governments to assist the Special Rapporteur in preparing his report, and recommended that the Commission adopt effective measures to prevent such executions.

By a resolution of the same date on human rights of detained persons (see above), the Sub-Commission recommended that the United Nations take strong and effective measures to prevent extrajudicial executions and, in particular, that the Commission and its Special Rapporteur take steps to prevent summary or arbitrary executions.[5]

General Assembly action. Welcoming the Council's resolution of 7 May, the General Assembly on 17 December[4] requested all Governments to co-operate with and assist the Special Rapporteur in preparing his report, and requested the Commission on Human Rights to recommend action to combat and eventually eliminate summary or arbitrary executions.

The resolution was adopted without vote, following similar approval on 9 December by the Third Committee, where it was introduced by Denmark on behalf of 10 nations.

Report. [1]Committee on crime, E/CN.5/1983/2.

Resolutions (1982). [2]Commission on Human Rights (report, E/1982/12): 1982/29, 11 Mar. [3]ESC: 1982/35, 7 May, text following. [4]GA: 37/182, 17 Dec., text following. SCPDPM (report, E/CN.4/1983/4), 7 Sep.: [5]1982/10, para. 15; [6]1982/13.

Meeting records. ESC: E/1982/SR.28 (7 May). GA: 3rd Committee, A/C.3/37/SR.*64*, 65-71, *72* (6-9 Dec.); plenary, A/37/PV.110 (17 Dec.).

Economic and Social Council resolution 1982/35

7 May 1982   Meeting 28   Adopted without vote

Approved by Second Committee (E/1982/59) without vote, 3 May (meeting 15); draft by Commission on Human Rights (E/1982/12); agenda item 9.

Summary or arbitrary executions

The Economic and Social Council,

Recalling the Universal Declaration of Human Rights, which guarantees the right to life, liberty and security of person,

Having regard to the provisions of the International Covenant on Civil and Political Rights, in which it is stated that every human being has the inherent right to life, that this right shall be protected by law and that no one shall be arbitrarily deprived of his life,

Recalling General Assembly resolution 34/175 of 17 December 1979, in which the Assembly reaffirmed that mass and flagrant violations of human rights are of special concern to the United Nations and urged the Commission on Human Rights to take timely and effective action in existing and future cases of mass and flagrant violations of human rights,

Further recalling resolution 8(XXIII) of 16 March 1967 of the Commission on Human Rights concerning the question of violations of human rights and fundamental freedoms in any part of the world,

Mindful of General Assembly resolution 36/22 of 9 November 1981, in which the Assembly condemned the practice of summary executions and arbitrary executions,

Bearing in mind resolution 5, on extra-legal executions, of the Sixth United Nations Congress on the Prevention of Crime and the Treatment of Offenders,

Deeply alarmed about the occurrence of summary or arbitrary executions, including extra-legal executions, that are widely regarded as being politically motivated,

Convinced of the need to deal urgently with the question of summary or arbitrary executions,

1. *Strongly deplores* the increasing number of summary or arbitrary executions taking place in various parts of the world;

2. *Decides,* therefore, to appoint for one year a special rapporteur to examine the questions related to summary or arbitrary executions;

3. *Requests* the Chairman of the Commission on Human Rights, after consultations within the Bureau, to appoint an individual of recognized international standing as special rapporteur;

4. *Considers* that the special rapporteur in carrying out his mandate may seek and receive information from Governments, specialized agencies and other intergovernmental organizations, as well as non-governmental organizations in consultative status with the Economic and Social Council;

5. *Requests* the special rapporteur to submit a comprehensive report to the Commission on Human Rights at its thirty-ninth session on the occurrence and extent of the practice of such executions, together with his conclusions and recommendations;

6. *Urges* all Governments to co-operate with and assist the special rapporteur in the preparation of his report;

7. *Requests* the Secretary-General to provide all necessary assistance to the special rapporteur;

8. *Requests* the Commission on Human Rights to consider the question of summary or arbitrary executions as a matter of high priority at its thirty-ninth session under the agenda item entitled "Question of the violation of human rights and fundamental freedoms in any part of the world, with particular reference to colonial and other dependent countries and territories".

General Assembly resolution 37/182

17 December 1982   Meeting 110   Adopted without vote

Approved by Third Committee (A/37/745) without vote, 9 December (meeting 72); 10-nation draft (A/C.3/37/L.76); agenda item 12.

Sponsors: Belgium, Costa Rica, Cyprus, Denmark, Finland, Greece, Netherlands, Norway, Portugal, Sweden.

Summary or arbitrary executions

The General Assembly,

Recalling the provisions of the Universal Declaration of Human Rights, which states that every human being has the inherent right to life, liberty and security of person and that everyone shall be entitled to a fair and public hearing by an independent and impartial tribunal established by law,

Recalling also its resolution 34/175 of 17 December 1979, in which it reaffirmed that mass and flagrant violations of human rights are of special concern to the United Nations and urged the Commission on Human Rights to take timely and effective action in existing and future cases of mass and flagrant violations of human rights,

Recalling further its resolution 36/22 of 9 November 1981, in which it condemned the practice of summary or arbitrary executions,

Deeply alarmed at the occurrence on a large scale of summary or arbitrary executions, including extra-legal executions,

Taking note of resolution 1982/13 of 7 September 1982 of the Sub-Commission on Prevention of Discrimination and Protection of Minorities, in which the Sub-Commission recommended that effective measures should be adopted to prevent the occurrence of summary or arbitrary executions,

Convinced of the need for appropriate action to combat and eventually eliminate this practice, which represents a flagrant violation of the most fundamental human right, the right to life,

1. *Welcomes* Economic and Social Council resolution 1982/35 of 7 May 1982, in which it was decided to appoint for one year a special rapporteur to examine the questions related to summary or arbitrary executions and to submit to the Commission on Human Rights, at its thirty-ninth session, a comprehensive report on the occurrence and extent of the practice of such executions, together with his conclusions and recommendations;

2. *Requests* all Governments to co-operate with and to assist the Special Rapporteur of the Commission on Human Rights in the preparation of his report;

3. *Requests* the Commission on Human Rights at its thirty-ninth session, on the basis of the report of the Special Rapporteur to be prepared in conformity with Economic and Social Council resolution 1982/35, to make recommendations concerning appropriate action to combat and eventually eliminate the practice of summary or arbitrary executions.

Treatment of prisoners and detainees

Draft principles

A working group open to all members of the General Assembly's Sixth (Legal) Committee, established by the Committee on 6 October 1982, continued work on a draft Body of Principles for the Protection of All Persons under Any Form of Detention or Imprisonment. The Assembly had decided in December 1981 to establish such a group,[2] to continue work begun by a Sixth Committee working group in September 1981,[6] after an open-ended working group of the Third Committee had in 1980[5] begun reviewing a draft adopted in 1978 by the Sub-Commission on Prevention of Discrimination and Protection of Minorities.[4]

Working group action. The 1982 working group, chaired by Luigi Ferrari Bravo (Italy), held nine meetings between 12 October and 23 November. Following the examples of previous groups, it continued a first reading of the principles on the understanding that it would reconsider the texts once definitions had been accepted. Taking up where the earlier groups had left off, the working group provisionally adopted three further principles and a part of one other, which were set out in its report.[3]

The approved principles stated that anyone arrested must be informed, at the time of the arrest, of the reasons for it and of the charges (principle 9, formerly principle 10). A detained person and his counsel must receive prompt and full communication of any order of detention and the reasons for it (paragraph 2 of principle 10, formerly principle 9). The reasons for and time of the arrest must be recorded and communicated to the person or his counsel; the same must be done with regard to the time of taking the arrested person to a place of custody and of his first appearance before a judicial or other authority, the identity of the law enforcement officials involved, and precise information about the place of custody (principle 11). An arrested, detained or imprisoned person must be provided promptly with information on and an explanation of his rights (principle 12).

General Assembly action. Noting the report of the working group, the General Assembly on 16 December[1] decided to establish in 1983 a working group of the Sixth Committee to expedite finalization of the draft principles. It requested that the Secretary-General circulate the reports of the 1980, 1981 and 1982 working groups to Member States, which it invited to update previous comments or submit new ones.

The decision was adopted without vote, following similar approval by the Sixth Committee on 3 December. It was introduced by Sweden, also on behalf of Egypt, and was orally amended by the Committee and working group Chairmen. An amendment by the working group Chairman specified that the 1983 working group was of the Sixth Committee, while according to an amendment by the Committee Chairman, the working group should be established at the Assembly's 1983, rather than 1982, session.

Decision (1982). [1]GA: 37/427, 16 Dec., text following.
Decision (prior). [2]GA: 36/426, 10 Dec. 1981 (YUN 1981, p. 901).
Report. [3]Working group, A/C.6/37/L.16.
Yearbook references. [4]1978, p. 698; [5]1980, p. 842; [6]1981, p. 900.
Meeting records. GA: 6th Committee, A/C.6/37/SR.61, 62 (2, 3 Dec.); plenary, A/37/PV.107 (16 Dec.).

General Assembly decision 37/427

Adopted without vote

Approved by Sixth Committee (A/37/701 and Corr.1) without vote, 3 December (meeting 62); 2-nation draft (A/C.6/37/L.22), orally amended by Committee and working group Chairmen; agenda item 129.
Sponsors: Egypt, Sweden.

Draft Body of Principles for the Protection of All Persons under Any Form of Detention or Imprisonment
At its 107th plenary meeting, on 16 December 1982, the General Assembly, on the recommendation of the Sixth Committee:

(a) Took note with appreciation of the report of the Working Group on the Draft Body of Principles for the Protection of All Persons under Any Form of Detention or Imprisonment, established in accordance with General Assembly decision 36/426 of 10 December 1981 to elaborate a final version of the draft Body of Principles, a task which it has not been able to conclude;

(b) Decided that an open-ended working group of the Sixth Committee would be established at the outset of its thirty-eighth session with a view to expediting the finalization of the draft Body of Principles for the Protection of All Persons under Any Form of Detention or Imprisonment;

(c) Requested the Secretary-General to circulate to Member States the reports of the open-ended Working Groups established at the thirty-fifth, thirty-sixth and thirty-seventh sessions and to invite them to update the comments they submitted in accordance with Economic and Social Council resolution 1979/34 of 10 May 1979 or submit new comments on the basis of the above-mentioned reports;

(d) Decided to include in the provisional agenda of its thirty-eighth session the item entitled "Draft Body of Principles for the Protection of All Persons under Any Form of Detention or Imprisonment".

Principles of Medical Ethics

The General Assembly, by a resolution of 18 December 1982,[2] adopted Principles of Medical Ethics relevant to the role of health personnel, particularly physicians, in the protection of prisoners and detainees against torture and other cruel, inhuman or degrading treatment or punishment. It called on Governments to give those Principles the widest possible distribution, and invited intergovernmental and non-governmental organizations to bring them to the attention of the widest possible group of individuals, especially in the medical and paramedical field.

The Principles, annexed to the resolution, stated that prisoners and detainees had the same rights as others to the protection of their physical or mental health and treatment of disease. It was in contravention of medical ethics for health personnel to participate in torture or other cruel treatment, to be involved with prisoners or detainees in any relationship other than medical, to assist in interrogation, and to certify prisoners fit for punishment that might adversely affect their health. Participation of health personnel in restraining prisoners was not in conformity with medical ethics unless it was necessary for health or safety reasons. The final principle stated that there might be no derogation from the Principles on any ground, including public emergency.

The text was adopted without vote, following similar approval on 9 December by the Third Committee, where it was introduced by the Netherlands on behalf of 13 nations.

The Principles, in the form of a draft Code of Medical Ethics, had been endorsed by the Executive Board of the World Health Organization in 1979.[4] The revised draft Principles, annexed to a November 1981 Assembly resolution,[3] were finalized in 1982 on the basis of further comments and suggestions from Member States. Those received from 21 Governments were transmitted by the Secretary-General in June, September and November.[1]

Report. [1]S-G, A/37/264 & Add.1,2.
Resolution (1982). [2]GA: 37/194, 18 Dec., text following.
Resolution (prior). [3]GA: 36/61, 25 Nov. 1981 (YUN 1981, p. 904).
Yearbook reference. [4]1979, p. 843.
Meeting records. GA: 3rd Committee, A/C.3/37/SR.47, 50-53, 55, 56, *61, 72* (18 Nov.–9 Dec.); plenary, A/37/PV.111 (18 Dec.).

General Assembly resolution 37/194

18 December 1982   Meeting 111   Adopted without vote

Approved by Third Committee (A/37/727) without vote, 9 December (meeting 72); 13-nation draft (A/C.3/37/L.79/Rev.1); agenda item 88 *(b)*.

Sponsors: Australia, Austria, Canada, Costa Rica, Dominican Republic, Fiji, Greece, Ireland, Italy, Netherlands, New Zealand, Norway, United States.

Principles of Medical Ethics

The General Assembly,

Recalling its resolution 31/85 of 13 December 1976, in which it invited the World Health Organization to prepare a draft code of medical ethics relevant to the protection of persons subjected to any form of detention or imprisonment against torture and other cruel, inhuman or degrading treatment or punishment,

Expressing once again its appreciation to the Executive Board of the World Health Organization which, at its sixty-third session, in January 1979, decided to endorse the principles set forth in a report entitled "Development of codes of medical ethics" containing, in an annex, a draft body of principles prepared by the Council for International Organizations of Medical Sciences and entitled "Principles of medical ethics relevant to the role of health personnel in the protection of persons against torture and other cruel, inhuman or degrading treatment or punishment",

Bearing in mind Economic and Social Council resolution 1981/27 of 6 May 1981, in which the Council recommended that the General Assembly should take measures to finalize the draft Principles of Medical Ethics at its thirty-sixth session,

Recalling its resolution 36/61 of 25 November 1981, in which it decided to consider the draft Principles of Medical Ethics at its thirty-seventh session with a view to adopting them,

Alarmed that not infrequently members of the medical profession or other health personnel are engaged in activities which are difficult to reconcile with medical ethics,

Recognizing that throughout the world significant medical activities are increasingly being performed by health personnel not licensed or trained as physicians, such as physician-assistants, paramedics, physical therapists and nurse practitioners,

Recalling with appreciation the Declaration of Tokyo of the World Medical Association containing the Guidelines for Medical Doctors concerning Torture and Other Cruel, Inhuman or Degrading Treatment or Punishment in relation to Detention and Imprisonment, adopted by the twenty-ninth World Medical Assembly, held at Tokyo in October 1975,

Noting that in accordance with the Declaration of Tokyo measures should be taken by States and by professional associations and other bodies, as appropriate, against any attempt to subject health personnel or members of their families to threats or reprisals resulting from a refusal by such personnel to condone the use of torture or other forms of cruel, inhuman or degrading treatment,

Reaffirming the Declaration on the Protection of All Persons from Being Subjected to Torture and Other Cruel, Inhuman or Degrading Treatment or Punishment, unanimously adopted by the General Assembly in its resolution 3452(XXX) of 9 December 1975, in which it declared any act of torture or other cruel, inhuman or degrading treatment or punishment an offence to human dignity, a denial of the purposes of the Charter of the United Nations and a violation of the Universal Declaration of Human Rights,

Recalling that, in accordance with article 7 of the Declaration adopted in resolution 3452(XXX), each State shall ensure that the commission of all acts of torture, as defined in article 1 of that Declaration, or participation in, complicity in, incitement to or attempt to commit torture are offences under its criminal law,

Convinced that under no circumstances should a person be punished for carrying out medical activities compatible with medical ethics, regardless of the person benefiting therefrom, or be compelled to perform acts or to carry out work in contravention of medical ethics, but that, at the same time, contravention of medical ethics for which health personnel, particularly physicians, can be held responsible should entail accountability,

Desirous of setting further standards in this field which ought to be implemented by health personnel, particularly physicians, and by Government officials,

1. *Adopts* the Principles of Medical Ethics relevant to the role of health personnel, particularly physicians, in the protection of prisoners and detainees against torture and other cruel, inhuman or degrading treatment or punishment, set forth in the annex to the present resolution;

2. *Calls upon* all Governments to give the Principles of Medical Ethics, together with the present resolution, the widest possible distribution, in particular among medical and paramedical associations and institutions of detention or imprisonment, in an official language of the State;

3. *Invites* all relevant intergovernmental organizations, in particular the World Health Organization, and non-governmental organizations concerned to bring the Principles of Medical Ethics to the attention of the widest possible group of individuals, especially those active in the medical and paramedical field.

ANNEX
Principles of Medical Ethics relevant to the role of health personnel, particularly physicians, in the protection of prisoners and detainees against torture and other cruel, inhuman or degrading treatment or punishment

Principle 1

Health personnel, particularly physicians, charged with the medical care of prisoners and detainees have a duty to provide them with protection of their physical and mental health and treatment of disease of the same quality and standard as is afforded to those who are not imprisoned or detained.

Principle 2

It is a gross contravention of medical ethics, as well as an offence under applicable international instruments, for health personnel, particularly physicians, to engage, actively or passively, in acts which constitute participation in, complicity in, incitement to or attempts to commit torture or other cruel, inhuman or degrading treatment or punishment.*

Principle 3

It is a contravention of medical ethics for health personnel, particularly physicians, to be involved in any professional relationship with prisoners or detainees the purpose of which is not solely to evaluate, protect or improve their physical and mental health.

Principle 4

It is a contravention of medical ethics for health personnel, particularly physicians:

(a) To apply their knowledge and skills in order to assist in the interrogation of prisoners and detainees in a manner that may adversely affect the physical or mental health or condition of such prisoners or detainees and which is not in accordance with the relevant international instruments;†

(b) To certify, or to participate in the certification of, the fitness of prisoners or detainees for any form of treatment or punishment that may adversely affect their physical or mental health and which is not in accordance with the relevant international instruments, or to participate in any way in the infliction of any such treatment or punishment which is not in accordance with the relevant international instruments.

Principle 5

It is a contravention of medical ethics for health personnel, particularly physicians, to participate in any procedure for restraining a prisoner or detainee unless such a procedure is determined in accordance with purely medical criteria as being necessary for the protection of the physical or mental health or the safety of the prisoner or detainee himself, of his fellow prisoners or detainees, or of his guardians, and presents no hazard to his physical or mental health.

Principle 6

There may be no derogation from the foregoing principles on any ground whatsoever, including public emergency.

---

*See the Declaration on the Protection of All Persons from Being Subjected to Torture and Other Cruel, Inhuman or Degrading Treatment or Punishment (resolution 3452(XXX), annex), article 1 of which states:

"1. For the purpose of this Declaration, torture means any act by which severe pain or suffering, whether physical or mental, is intentionally inflicted by or at the instigation of a public official on a person for such purposes as obtaining from him or a third person information or confession, punishing him for an act he has committed or is suspected of having committed, or intimidating him or other persons. It does not include pain or suffering arising only from, inherent in or incidental to, lawful sanctions to the extent consistent with the Standard Minimum Rules for the Treatment of Prisoners.

"2. Torture constitutes an aggravated and deliberate form of cruel, inhuman or degrading treatment or punishment."

Article 7 of the Declaration states:

"Each State shall ensure that all acts of torture as defined in article 1 are offences under its criminal law. The same shall apply in regard to acts which constitute participation in, complicity in, incitement to or an attempt to commit torture."

†Particularly the Universal Declaration of Human Rights (resolution 217 A (III)), the International Covenants on Human Rights (resolution 2200 A (XXI), annex), the Declaration on the Protection of All Persons from Being Subjected to Torture and Other Cruel, Inhuman or Degrading Treatment or Punishment (resolution 3452(XXX), annex) and the Standard Minimum Rules for the Treatment of Prisoners *(First United Nations Congress on the Prevention of Crime and the Treatment of Offenders: report by the Secretariat* (United Nations publication, Sales No. 1956.IV.4), annex I.A).

Torture and other cruel treatment

Draft convention on the prohibition of torture

Work continued in 1982 in the Commission on Human Rights on a draft convention against torture and other cruel, inhuman or degrading treatment or punishment.

A working group open to all Commission members, meeting at Geneva from 25 to 29 January and during the Commission's session until 4 March, provisionally adopted three articles and revised or adopted portions of several others which it had considered in 1979,[6] 1980[7] and 1981.[8] The newly approved articles provided for a definition of torture (article 1), extradition for acts of torture or attempts to commit torture (article 8) and for compensation to the victims of torture (article 14, provisionally agreed to in 1981). The working group did not complete work on articles relating to prosecution of individuals alleged to have committed or attempted to commit torture (article 7) and to the establishment of State jurisdiction over acts of or attempts to commit torture (article 5, paragraph 2), nor did it complete work on provisions for implementing the future convention. Sixteen draft articles were transmitted to the Commission in the group's report, which was reproduced in the Commission's report to the Economic and Social Council.[1]

Economic and Social Council action. The Council, on 7 May 1982,[3] authorized a meeting of an open-ended working group for one week prior to the 1983 session of the Commission on Human Rights to complete work on the draft convention. The resolution was adopted without vote, following its approval in the Second (Social) Committee on 3 May in the same manner. Adoption of the resolution had been recommended by the Commission on 11 March.[2]

Sub-Commission action. By a resolution of 7 September[5] on the human rights of detained persons (see above), the Sub-Commission on Prevention of Discrimination and Protection of Minorities decided that the Working Group on Detention in 1983 should hear and receive information on torture or cruel, inhuman or degrading treatment or punishment, unless the Commission established a system for examining such information. It decided that such hearings should be conducted annually except for States becoming parties to a convention against torture.

General Assembly action. Welcoming the Economic and Social Council's resolution, the General Assembly on 18 December[4] requested the Commission on Human Rights to complete the drafting of the convention as a matter of high priority in 1983, including provisions for its implementation.

The Assembly adopted the resolution, without vote, on the recommendation of the Third Committee, which similarly approved on 7 December a 19-nation draft introduced by Sweden.

Report. [1]Working Group, E/1982/12/Add.1.
Resolutions (1982). [2]Commission on Human Rights (report, E/1982/12): 1982/44, 11 Mar. [3]ESC: 1982/38, 7 May, text following. [4]GA: 37/193, 18 Dec., text following. [5]SCPDPM (report, E/CN.4/1983/4): 1982/10, paras. 17 & 18, 7 Sep.
Yearbook references. [6]1979, p. 841; [7]1980, p. 845; [8]1981, p. 901.
Meeting records. ESC: E/1982/SR.28 (7 May). GA: 3rd Committee, A/C.3/37/SR.47, 50-53, 55, 56, *64, 67* (18 Nov.–7 Dec.); plenary, A/37/PV.111 (18 Dec.).

Economic and Social Council resolution 1982/38

7 May 1982	Meeting 28	Adopted without vote

Approved by Second Committee (E/1982/59) without vote, 3 May (meeting 15); draft by Commission on Human Rights (E/1982/12); agenda item 9.

Question of the human rights of all persons subjected to any form of detention or imprisonment, in particular torture and other cruel, inhuman or degrading treatment or punishment

The Economic and Social Council,

Recalling General Assembly resolution 36/60 of 25 November 1981, by which the Commission on Human Rights was requested to complete as a matter of highest priority, at its thirty-eighth session, the drafting of a convention against torture and other cruel, inhuman or degrading treatment or punishment, and Economic and Social Council resolution 1981/37 of 8 May 1981 by which the Council authorized a meeting of an open-ended working group for a period of one week prior to the thirty-eighth session of the Commission on Human Rights to complete the work on a draft convention against torture and other cruel, inhuman or degrading treatment or punishment,

Considering that it was not found possible to complete the work on the draft convention during the thirty-eighth session of the Commission on Human Rights,

Taking note of resolution 1982/44 of 11 March 1982 of the Commission on Human Rights,

1. *Authorizes* a meeting of an open-ended working group for a period of one week prior to the thirty-ninth session of the Commission on Human Rights to complete the work on a draft convention against torture and other cruel, inhuman or degrading treatment or punishment;

2. *Requests* the Secretary-General to transmit to the Commission on Human Rights at its thirty-ninth session all relevant material relating to the draft convention.

General Assembly resolution 37/193

18 December 1982   Meeting 111   Adopted without vote

Approved by Third Committee (A/37/727) without vote, 7 December (meeting 67); 19-nation draft (A/C.3/37/L.49); agenda item 88.

Sponsors: Australia, Austria, Canada, Costa Rica, Denmark, Ecuador, Finland, Ghana, Greece, Iceland, India, Italy, Netherlands, Nicaragua, Norway, Portugal, Senegal, Spain, Sweden.

Torture and other cruel, inhuman or degrading treatment or punishment

The General Assembly,

Recalling the Declaration on the Protection of All Persons from Being Subjected to Torture and Other Cruel, Inhuman or Degrading Treatment or Punishment, adopted by the General Assembly in its resolution 3452(XXX) of 9 December 1975,

Bearing in mind article 7 of the International Covenant on Civil and Political Rights,

Recalling also its resolution 32/62 of 8 December 1977, in which it requested the Commission on Human Rights to draw up a draft convention against torture and other cruel, inhuman or degrading treatment or punishment, in the light of the principles embodied in the Declaration, and its resolution 32/63 of 8 December 1977,

Recalling further that the Sixth United Nations Congress on the Prevention of Crime and Treatment of Offenders, in its resolution 11 of 5 September 1980, expressed the belief that the draft convention should be finalized at the earliest possible time,

Considering that it was not found possible to complete the work on the draft convention during the thirty-eighth session of the Commission on Human Rights,

1. *Welcomes* Economic and Social Council resolution 1982/38 of 7 May 1982, by which the Council authorized a meeting of an open-ended working group of the Commission on Human Rights for a period of one week prior to the thirty-ninth session of the Commission to complete the work on a draft convention on torture and other cruel, inhuman or degrading treatment or punishment;

2. *Requests* the Commission on Human Rights to complete as a matter of highest priority, at its thirty-ninth session, the drafting of a convention on torture and other cruel, inhuman or degrading treatment or punishment, with a view to submitting a draft, including provisions for the effective implementation of the future convention, to the General Assembly at its thirty-eighth session;

3. *Decides* to include in the provisional agenda of its thirty-eighth session the item entitled "Torture and other cruel, inhuman or degrading treatment or punishment".

Unilateral declarations

As at 30 September 1982, the Secretary-General had received, in accordance with a 1980 General Assembly resolution,[2] unilateral declarations against torture and other cruel, inhuman or degrading treatment from France, Rwanda, Saint Vincent and the Grenadines, and Sri Lanka. He transmitted the four declarations in a November 1982 report to the Assembly.[1]

Report. [1]S-G, A/37/263.
Resolution. [2]GA: 35/178, 15 Dec. 1980 (YUN 1980, p. 849).

UN Voluntary Fund for Victims of Torture

As at 31 December 1982, six countries (Cyprus, Denmark, Finland, Netherlands, Norway, Sweden) had contributed $421,066 to the United Nations Voluntary Fund for Victims of Torture (originally the United Nations Trust Fund for Chile, redesignated by the General Assembly in December 1981[3]).

On 11 March 1982,[2] the Commission on Human Rights called for favourable responses to requests for contributions to the Fund, and requested the Secretary-General to transmit this appeal to Governments.

The Secretary-General reported to the Assembly[1] that, on 11 November, he had appointed four members of the Fund's Board of Trustees for a three-year term, and that consideration was being given to the appointment of a fifth member. Consultations with the Board were being conducted to determine a suitable date for the Board's first session.

Report. [1]S-G, A/37/618.
Resolution (1982). [2]Commission on Human Rights (report, E/1982/12): 1982/43, 11 Mar.
Resolution (prior). [3]GA: 36/151, 16 Dec. 1981 (YUN 1981, p. 906).

Detention on grounds of mental illness

The Commission on Human Rights, on 19 February 1982,[3] requested the Sub-Commission on Prevention of Discrimination and Protection of Minorities to consider at its August/September session, as a matter of priority, a report on the protection of persons detained on grounds of mental ill-health or suffering from mental disorder, prepared by the Sub-Commission's Special Rapporteur, Mrs. Erica-Irene A. Daes (Greece). The Commission asked the Sub-Commission to submit its views and recommendations, including a draft body of guidelines, principles and guarantees, in 1983 when it would consider the Sub-Commission's report as a priority.

The Special Rapporteur's final report, submitted to the Sub-Commission in August 1982,[1] in accordance with a September 1981 Sub-Commission request,[6] contained a draft body of guidelines, principles and guarantees.

A sessional working group, established by the Sub-Commission on 19 August 1982, reported in September[2] that it had undertaken a first reading of the draft body. The group agreed that its work could only be of a preliminary nature in 1982 and that it would proceed in 1983 to a thorough analysis of each provision.

On 10 September 1982,[5] the Sub-Commission recommended that the Commission recommend to the Economic and Social Council adoption of a resolution requesting the Special Rapporteur to supplement her final report, taking into account the views of the Sub-Commission and the Commission and including any new replies from Governments or specialized agencies. Under the resolution, the Sub-Commission would be requested to establish a sessional working group to examine the principles, guidelines and guarantees elaborated by the Special Rapporteur, and to submit a revised final report to the Commission in 1984.

By a resolution of 18 December 1982,[4] adopted without vote, the General Assembly urged the Commission and, through it, the Sub-Commission to continue and expedite consideration of the protection of those detained on grounds of mental ill-health, with a view to submitting recommendations in 1984.

This text, introduced by the United Kingdom on behalf of 19 nations, was approved without vote by the Third (Social, Humanitarian and Cultural) Commitee on 7 December.

Reports. [1]Special Rapporteur, E/CN.4/Sub.2/1982/16; [2]Working group, E/CN.4/Sub.2/1982/17.
Resolutions (1982). [3]Commission on Human Rights (report, E/1982/12): 1982/6, 19 Feb. [4]GA: 37/188, 18 Dec., text following. [5]SCPDPM (report, E/CN.4/1983/4): 1982/34, 10 Sep.
Yearbook reference. [6]1981, p. 906.
Meeting records. GA: 3rd Committee, A/C.3/37/SR.47, 50-53, 55, 56, *64*, 67 (18 Nov.–7 Dec.); plenary, A/37/PV.111 (18 Dec.).

General Assembly resolution 37/188

18 December 1982   Meeting 111   Adopted without vote

Approved by Third Committee (A/37/716) without vote, 7 December (meeting 67); 19-nation draft (A/C.3/37/L.56); agenda item 85.

Sponsors: Bolivia, Chad, Costa Rica, Cyprus, Fiji, Gambia, Ghana, Italy, Mexico, Morocco, Netherlands, Nigeria, Norway, Panama, Senegal, Singapore, Sweden, United Kingdom, Upper Volta.

Implications of scientific and technological developments for human rights

The General Assembly,

Recalling its resolution 33/53 of 14 December 1978, in which it requested the Commission on Human Rights to urge the Sub-Commission on Prevention of Discrimination and Protection of Minorities to undertake, as a matter of priority, a study of the question of the protection of those detained on the grounds of mental ill-health, with a view to formulating guidelines,

Recalling also its resolutions 35/130 B of 11 December 1980 and 36/56 B of 25 November 1981, in which it welcomed and noted with satisfaction the work being undertaken by the Sub-Commission and requested the Commission on Human Rights to continue its consideration of this question in the light of the action being taken by the Sub-Commission, with a view to submitting a report to the General Assembly at its thirty-eighth session, through the Economic and Social Council,

Recalling further Commission on Human Rights resolution 1982/6 of 19 February 1982, in which the Commission requested the Sub-Commission, at its thirty-fifth session, to consider the question as a matter of high priority, with a view to submitting its views and recommendations, including a draft body of guidelines, principles and guarantees, to the Commission at its thirty-ninth session,

Noting that the Commission on Human Rights will not be in a position to submit a report to the General Assembly at its thirty-eighth session through the Economic and Social Council, as requested in Assembly resolution 36/56 B, because it was impossible for the Sub-Commission to conclude at its thirty-fifth session its consideration of the draft body of guidelines, principles and guarantees,

Reaffirming its conviction that detention of persons in mental institutions on account of their political views or on other non-medical grounds is a violation of their human rights,

Noting with satisfaction the progress made by the Sub-Commission on Prevention of Discrimination and Protection of Minorities in its consideration of the draft body of guidelines, principles and guarantees submitted to it,

Urges the Commission on Human Rights and, through it, the Sub-Commission on Prevention of Discrimination and Protection of Minorities to continue and expedite their consideration of this question with a view to the Commission submitting its views and recommendations to the General Assembly at its thirty-ninth session, through the Economic and Social Council.

Case of Ziad Abu Eain

By a January 1982 report on the question of human rights relating to the case of the Palestinian Ziad Abu Eain,[1] the Secretary-General transmitted information from Israel and the United States on steps taken to implement a December 1981 General Assembly resolution deploring his extradition from the United States to Israel and demanding his release.[2]

By a note verbale of 31 December 1981, annexed to the report, Israel stated that Mr. Abu Eain was accused of having planted a bomb in a market (on 14 May 1979 at Tiberias, Israel), causing death to two young boys and wounding 36 passers-by. He would be tried before a civil court of law and would be entitled to all the safeguards under Israeli law. As the bringing to justice of an individual accused of criminal offences was within the domestic jurisdiction of the prosecuting State, the Assembly resolution was in violation of the Charter of the United Nations.

By a note verbale of 4 January 1982, the United States called "demonstrably false" the Assembly's assertions that Mr. Abu Eain had been illegally detained in the United States and that the sole basis for probable cause against him was one statement in Hebrew; the United States, therefore, would take no action to implement the resolution. Appended to the note was a memorandum of decision by the United States Deputy Secretary of State on Mr. Abu Eain's extradition.

Report. [1]S-G, A/36/855.
Resolution. [2]GA: 36/171, 16 Dec. 1981 (YUN 1981, p. 910).

Disappearance of persons

Working Group report. The five-member Working Group on Enforced or Involuntary Disappearances, established in 1980,[9] met at Geneva on 22 Febrary 1982 to review information received since its November/December 1981 session.[10] In a report of the same date,[2] the Group informed the Commission on Human Rights that two of its members had visited Mexico from 11 to 13 January 1982 to establish contacts with government authorities and domestic organizations directly concerned with enforced or involuntary disappearances, in order to acquire a balanced account of the 43 reports on such disappearances. The Government stated that it was prepared to reopen closed files or carry out new investigations, and subsequently transmitted information on five reportedly missing persons.

In addition, the group had received information from El Salvador (23 reportedly missing persons),

Honduras (one), Nicaragua (10), the Philippines (two), Uganda (one) and Uruguay (four). With regard to disappearances, since the end of the Group's sixth session on 7 December 1981, the Group had transmitted reports to the Governments of El Salvador (62 missing persons), Guatemala (six) and Honduras (three).

Action by the Commission on Human Rights. Expressing appreciation to the Working Group, the Commission on Human Rights, on 10 March 1982,[4] extended the Group's mandate for another year and requested the Group to submit in 1983 a report with conclusions and recommendations. It requested the Group to discharge its mandate with discretion, to protect persons providing information, or to limit dissemination of information provided by Governments. The Commission renewed its request to the Secretary-General to appeal to Governments to co-operate with the Group in a spirit of complete confidence. It requested the Sub-Commission to continue studying the means for eliminating enforced or involuntary disappearances, with a view to making recommendations to the Commission in 1983, when it would again consider the question.

Economic and Social Council action. On 7 May 1982,[1] the Economic and Social Council approved the Commission's decision to extend the Working Group's mandate for a year, and requested the Secretary-General to continue to provide the Group with necessary assistance.

The decision was adopted without vote, following similar approval by the Second (Social) Committee on 3 May. The text originated in the Commission.

Sub-Commission action. On 7 September,[7] the Sub-Commission on Prevention of Discrimination and Protection of Minorities reiterated the right of families to know the fate of their relatives, strongly appealed for the reappearance of all detainees held in secret detention and expressed its conviction that, in view of the persistence of violations resulting from the many cases of disappearances, the extension of the Working Group's mandate was indispensable. It urged the Commission to give special attention to the protection of persons, including relatives, who actively sought the whereabouts of missing persons and who provided information on them. It recommended that the Commission give careful consideration to obtaining more information on the whereabouts or fate of missing persons, and decided to consider the question as a matter of the highest priority in 1983.

Also on 7 September,[8] the Sub-Commission recommended that the Commission recommend to the Economic and Social Council adoption of a resolution requesting the General Assembly to invite the International Law Commission to take into account when elaborating the draft code of offences against the peace and security of mankind (see LEGAL QUESTIONS, Chapter II) the comments by Sub-Commission members on the question of missing and disappeared persons. The Secretary-General would be requested to inform the Sub-Commission in 1983 of consideration given to this item by the Commission, the Council and the Assembly.

Working Group action (May-December). The Working Group on disappearances held its seventh, eighth and ninth sessions in 1982 (Geneva, 24-28 May, 27 September-1 October, 6-10 December) and adopted on 10 December a report to the Comission on Human Rights.[3]

Since the extension of its mandate on 10 March, the Working Group had received individual reports of some 2,430 disappearances. The Group transmitted more than 20 reports each of enforced or involuntary disappearances to Argentina, Bolivia, Cyprus, El Salvador, Guatemala, Honduras, Indonesia, Mexico, Nicaragua, the Philippines and Uruguay. A smaller number of allegations of disappearances had been received from Brazil, Chile, Ethiopia, Guinea, Iran, Lebanon, Lesotho, Morocco, Peru, the Syrian Arab Republic and Zaire. During its 1982 sessions, the Group met with representatives of Argentina, Bolivia, Cyprus, El Salvador, Guatemala, Iran, Morocco, Nicaragua, the Philippines and Zaire, and with a number of organizations concerned by reports of disappearances. The Group did not receive replies to requests for information on cases in South Africa and Namibia.

The report stated that the observance of the rule of law would preclude disappearances. In the absence of this, the Commission should encourage government inquiries to solve specific cases, and should support the reorganization of government procedures which would facilitate rapid responses to allegations of a disappearance.

General Assembly action. On 17 December,[5] the General Assembly welcomed the Commission's decision to extend the Working Group's mandate and expressed appreciation to the Group for its work and to the Governments that had co-operated with it. It called on the Commission to continue to study the question as a matter of priority and to take any step it deemed necessary to the pursuit of the Working Group's task. The Assembly appealed to all Governments to co-operate fully with the Working Group and the Commission, and renewed its request that the Secretary-General continue to provide the Group with the necessary assistance.

The resolution was adopted without vote, following its similar approval by the Third (Social, Humanitarian and Cultural) Committee on 9 December, where it was introduced and orally revised by France, on behalf of 10 nations.

By a resolution of the same date,[6] the Assembly invited the Working Group to follow developments and to assist the Committee on Missing Persons in Cyprus in its work.

Decision (1982). [1]ESC: 1982/131, 7 May, text following.
Reports. Working Group, [2]E/CN.4/1492/Add.1, [3]E/CN.4/1983/14.
Resolutions (1982). [4]Commission on Human Rights (report, E/1982/12): 1982/24, 10 Mar. GA, 17 Dec.: [5]37/180, text following; [6]37/181, para. 1. SCPDPM (report, E/CN.4/1983/4), 7 Sep.: [7]1982/5, [8]1982/12.
Yearbook references. [9]1980, p. 843; [10]1981, p. 912.
Meeting records. ESC: E/1982/SR.28 (7 May). GA: 3rd Committee, A/C.3/37/SR.62, 63, *64,* 65-71, *72* (3-9 Dec.); plenary, A/37/PV.110 (17 Dec.).

Economic and Social Council decision 1982/131

Adopted without vote

Approved by Second Committee (E/1982/59) without vote, 3 May (meeting 15); draft by Commission on Human Rights (E/1982/12); agenda item 9.

Question of the human rights of all persons subjected to any form of detention or imprisonment, in particular the question of missing and disappeared persons

At its 28th plenary meeting, on 7 May 1982, the Council, noting resolution 1982/24 of 10 March 1982 of the Commission on Human Rights, approved the Commission's decision to extend for one year the term of the mandate of the Working Group on Enforced or Involuntary Disappearances, as laid down in Commission resolution 20(XXXVI) of 29 February 1980, and requested the Secretary-General to continue to provide the Working Group with all necessary assistance, in particular the staff and resources it required to perform its functions in an effective and expeditious manner, and if necessary to make arrangements to ensure the continuity of the Secretariat's work.

General Assembly resolution 37/180

17 December 1982   Meeting 110   Adopted without vote

Approved by Third Committee (A/37/745) without vote, 9 December (meeting 72); 10-nation draft (A/C.3/37/L.70), orally revised; agenda item 12.

Sponsors: Austria, Costa Rica, France, Germany, Federal Republic of, Greece, Italy, Mexico, Senegal, Sweden, United Kingdom.

Question of enforced or involuntary disappearances
The General Assembly,

Recalling its resolution 33/173 of 20 December 1978, entitled "Disappeared persons", and its resolution 36/163 of 16 December 1981 on the question of enforced or involuntary disappearances,

Bearing in mind Commission on Human Rights resolution 1982/24 of 10 March 1982, by which the Commission decided to extend for one year the term of the mandate of the Working Group on Enforced or Involuntary Disappearances, and Economic and Social Council decision 1982/131 of 7 May 1982, by which the Council approved the Commission's decision,

Convinced that the action taken, in consultation with the Governments concerned, to promote the implementation of the provisions of General Assembly resolution 33/173 and other United Nations resolutions relevant to the plight of missing or disappeared persons should be continued,

Expressing its emotion at the anguish and sorrow of the families concerned, who should know the fate of their relatives,

1. *Welcomes* the decision of the Commission on Human Rights to extend for one year the term of the mandate of the Working Group on Enforced or Involuntary Disappearances, as laid down in Commission resolution 1982/24;

2. *Expresses its appreciation* to the Working Group for the work it has done and to those Governments that have co-operated with it;

3. *Calls upon* the Commission on Human Rights to continue to study this question as a matter of priority and to take any step it may deem necessary to the pursuit of the task of the Working Group when it considers the report to be submitted by the Group at its thirty-ninth session;

4. *Appeals* to all Governments to provide the Working Group and the Commission on Human Rights with the full co-operation warranted by their strictly humanitarian objectives and their working methods based on discretion;

5. *Renews its request* to the Secretary-General to continue to provide the Working Group with all necessary assistance.

Slavery

Action by the Commission on Human Rights. The Commission on Human Rights, on 10 March 1982,[5] following an invitation by the Government of Mauritania, authorized the Sub-Commission on discrimination and minorities to send a delegation of not more than two persons, to be appointed by the Sub-Commission Chairman in consultation with the Government, to Mauritania to study the situation and ascertain the country's needs with regard to the question of slavery and the slave trade.

The Commission requested the United Nations Department of Public Information to take measures to create greater awareness of the existence of slavery and slavery-like institutions and practices, and to mobilize international action for their eradication. The Commission requested the Secretary-General to transmit statements submitted to the Working Group on Slavery by the Anti-Slavery Society for the Protection of Human Rights, the Minority Rights Group and the International Abolitionist Federation containing allegations of slavery-like practices in certain countries, together with the Working Group's recommendations, to the Governments concerned and to intergovernmental organizations and agencies. It requested him to call on States parties to international conventions on slavery and the traffic in persons to submit regular reports on the situation in their countries, and to call on other States, intergovernmental and non-governmental organizations, United Nations agencies and the International Criminal Police Organization (INTERPOL) to supply relevant information.

The Commission appealed to Member States to take action against prostitution (see Chapter XIX of this section) and the slavery-like practice of *apartheid* (see below, under HUMAN RIGHTS VIOLATIONS).

The Commission's resolution was adopted by 34 votes to none, with 9 abstentions.

Economic and Social Council action. On 7 May,[1] the Economic and Social Council endorsed the Commission's decision to authorize a delegation to visit Mauritania.

This action was taken without vote, following similar approval by the Second Committee on 3 May. The text was recommended by the Commission on Human Rights.

On 27 August,[2] the Sub-Commission authorized its Chairman to appoint Marc Bossuyt (Belgium) and Mohamed Yousif Mudawi (Sudan) to visit Mauritania.

Working Group on Slavery. During its eighth session at Geneva from 9 to 12 August,[4] the Sub-Commission's Working Group on Slavery reviewed developments in slavery and the slave trade, debt bondage, the sale of children and exploitation of child labour, traffic in persons and prostitution, *apartheid* and colonialism. The Working Group recommended that allegations of slavery and other practices be brought to the attention of the States concerned for their comments, and that these States be invited to participate in the Group's discussions. States should be urged to take concrete measures againt debt bondage, exploitation of child labour and the sale of children.

Recommendations for United Nations activities included: the United Nations and specialized agencies should assist Governments requesting help; the United Nations Educational, Scientific and Cultural Organization should assist in educational and information campaigns; the United Nations Development Programme (UNDP) and the United Nations Centre for Social Development and Humanitarian Affairs (CSDHA), in particular, should be urged to co-operate in combating problems including prostitution and the sale of children; and CSDHA should be requested to study the problem of street children in the context of International Youth Year, 1985. Studies on the sale of children and on female circumcision should be carried out. In order to combat *apartheid*, South Africa should be isolated economically, politically and diplomatically.

Sub-Commission action. A report on slavery and on national and international action to counteract it[3] was submitted to the Sub-Commission by Special Rapporteur Benjamin Charles George Whitaker (United Kingdom) on 14 July. The report, updating a report prepared in 1966,[8] made a series of recommendations, most of which were included in a 7 September 1982 Sub-Commission resolution.[6]

Expressing its appreciation to the Special Rapporteur for his study, the Sub-Commission requested him to present it to the Commission on Human Rights in 1983. It recommended that the Commission transmit the report to United Nations agencies, in particular to the subsidiary organs of the Economic and Social Council and UNDP, requesting them to submit comments to the Secretary-General for transmission to the Special Rapporteur. The Sub-Commission recommended that the Commission recommend to the Council that the report be given the widest possible distribution, including in Arabic.

By another resolution of the same date,[7] the Sub-Commission requested the Commission to appeal to Member States to sign or ratify conventions relevant to slavery, or to explain in writing why they were unable to do so. It suggested that the United Nations and its agencies offer assistance to eliminate conditions conducive to slavery; UNDP should help in rehabilitating freed slaves, and the Economic and Social Council and its subsidiary bodies should monitor and set targets for ensuring the success of the work on slavery. UNDP and other agencies should be invited to inform the Working Group about including in their technical assistance programmes activities designed to eliminate slavery-like practices. National police forces and INTERPOL should be asked to co-operate in the fight against slavery-like practices.

The Sub-Commission considered that persons on the list of slavery experts should become more closely involved in the work on slavery by United Nations bodies, including attending meetings and accompanying assistance missions. It recommended that the Centre for Human Rights be given the resources to assist in attaining the Organization's goals in the field of slavery. Regional seminars with a practical orientation should be organized to speed effective reforms, non-governmental organizations should assist the United Nations in its work, sources of information on slavery should be expanded and improved, United Nations representatives should regularly report instances of slavery and a study on debt bondage should be undertaken without delay. Legal aid should be provided to slavery victims.

The Sub-Commission requested the Secretary-General to transmit to Governments, organizations and agencies allegations of slavery-like practices submitted to the Working Group on Slavery, and to ensure that States participated fully in the Group's work. It recommended that working groups be established in consultation with the Commission on the Status of Women to protect better the human rights of women and children. It recommended that a study of forms of exploitation of women be made and requested that a study on female sexual mutilation be prepared.

The Sub-Commission urged that the International Labour Office be requested to continue its study of indentured labour in South African mines, and that more concrete measures, including sanctions, be taken against the *apartheid* régime.

Decisions (1982). [1]ESC: 1982/129, 7 May, text following. [2]SCPDPM (report, E/CN.4/1983/4): 1982/7, 27 Aug.
Reports. [3]Special Rapporteur, E/CN.4/Sub.2/1982/20 & Add.1; [4]Working Group on Slavery, E/CN.4/Sub.2/1982/21 & Corr.1.
Resolutions (1982). [5]Commission on Human Rights (report, E/1982/12): 1982/20, 10 Mar. SCPDPM, 7 Sep.: [6]1982/9, [7]1982/15.
Yearbook reference. [8]1966, p. 478.
Meeting record. ESC: E/1982/SR.28 (7 May).

Economic and Social Council decision 1982/129

Adopted without vote

Approved by Second Committee (E/1982/59) without vote, 3 May (meeting 15); draft by Commission on Human Rights (E/1982/12); agenda item 9.

Question of slavery and the slave trade in all their practices and manifestations, including the slavery-like practices of *apartheid* and colonialism

At its 28th plenary meeting, on 7 May 1982, the Council, noting resolution 1982/20 of 10 March 1982 of the Commission on Human Rights, endorsed the Commission's decision, pursuant to an invitation by the Government of Mauritania, to authorize the Sub-Commission on Prevention of Discrimination and Protection of Minorities to send a delegation not exceeding two persons, to be appointed by the Chairman of the Sub-Commission in consultation with the Government of Mauritania, to visit Mauritania in order to study the situation and ascertain the country's needs with regard to the question of slavery and the slave trade.

Conscientious objectors

A June 1982 report submitted to the Sub-Commission on discrimination and minorities by Special Rapporteurs Asbjorn Eide (Norway) and Chama L. C. Mubanga-Chipoya (Zambia) analysed the concept and dimensions of conscientious objection to military service,[1] as well as relevant international standards. The preliminary report, prepared at a September 1981 Sub-Commission request,[3] examined information from Governments and intergovernmental and non-governmental organizations on grounds recognized as valid for conscientious objection, procedures used for obtaining the status of conscientious objector, the question of alternative service, and the status of conscientious objectors in countries where such objection was not permitted.

The Sub-Commission, on 10 September,[2] by 9 votes to 4, with 3 abstentions, requested the Special Rapporteurs to prepare a final report based on comments received on their preliminary report, and to develop principles with a view to: recognizing the right to refuse service in military or police forces used to enforce *apartheid*, to pursue wars of aggression, or to engage in any other illegal warfare; recognizing the right to refuse such service on grounds of conscience or deeply held personal conviction and to offer instead service in the social or economic field; and urging Member States to grant asylum or safe transit to persons compelled to leave their country because of conscientious objection. The Sub-Commission decided to consider the question again in 1983.

Report. [1]Special Rapporteurs, E/CN.4/Sub.2/1982/24.
Resolution (1982). [2]SCPDPM (report, E/CN.4/1983/4): 1982/30, 10 Sep.
Yearbook reference. [3]1981, p. 913.

Freedom of movement

The Sub-Commission on discrimination and minorities, on 8 September 1982,[1] by 11 votes to 2, with 6 abstentions, requested Mr. Mubanga-Chipoya to prepare an analysis of trends and developments concerning the right of everyone to leave any country, including his own, and to return to his country. This included the possibility of entering other countries without discrimination or hindrance, especially with regard to the right to

employment, while taking into account the need to avoid the "brain drain" from developing countries (see Chapter XII of this section) and the question of recompensing those countries for losses incurred. The study was to consider in particular the extent of restrictions permissible under the International Covenant on Civil and Political Rights, including those provided by law and those necessary to protect national security, public order, public health or morals or the rights and freedoms of others. The Rapporteur was to present recommendations in 1984.

Resolution (1982). [1]SCPDPM (report, E/CN.4/1983/4): 1982/23, 8 Sep.

Independence of the judicial system

The Sub-Commission on discrimination and minorities decided on 17 August 1982[1] to defer consideration of the question of the independence and impartiality of the judiciary, jurors and assessors, and the independence of lawyers, until 1983, when L. M. Singhvi (India), the Special Rapporteur, would submit his final report.

Decision (1982). [1]SCPDPM (report, E/CN.4/1983/4): 1982/1, 17 Aug.

Economic, social and cultural rights

Covenant on Economic, Social and Cultural Rights

Accessions and ratifications

As at 31 December 1982, the International Covenant on Economic, Social and Cultural Rights, adopted by the General Assembly in 1966[2] and in force since 1976,[3] had been ratified or acceded to by 75 States (Bolivia, Egypt, Solomon Islands and Viet Nam having adhered in 1982).[1]

Publication. [1]*Multilateral Treaties Deposited with the Secretary-General: Status as at 31 December 1982* (ST/LEG/SER.E/2), Sales No. E.83.V.6.
Resolution. [2]2200 A (XXI), annex, 16 Dec. 1966 (YUN 1966, p. 419).
Yearbook reference. [3]1976, p. 609.

Implementation of the Covenant

At its fourth session, held in New York from 5 to 23 April 1982, the Economic and Social Council's Sessional Working Group (of Governmental Experts) on the Implementation of the International Covenant on Economic, Social and Cultural Rights[4] considered 23 reports from 20 States parties on their implementation of specific provisions of the Covenant. On each report, the Group heard statements by, and put questions to, the respective State representative. Under a programme established by the Council in 1976,[6] reports required under the Covenant were to be submitted in three biennial cycles or stages, each stage covering a related group of articles.

For the first stage (due 1 September 1977), the Working Group examined reports submitted in 1982 by Barbados, Canada, Italy, the United Kingdom and Yugoslavia, concerning rights covered by articles 6 to 9 of the Covenant (the right to work and to favourable conditions of work, the rights of trade unionists and the right to social security). At the request of the Syrian Arab Republic, the Working Group deferred consideration of that State's report.

The Working Group considered second-stage reports (due 1 September 1979) on rights covered by articles 10 to 12 (protection of the family, mothers and children, an adequate living standard, and physical and mental health) from Barbados, Bulgaria, Panama, Spain and the Ukrainian SSR.

Reports relating to the third stage (due 1 September 1981) on rights covered by articles 13 to 15 (education, including compulsory education, and participation in cultural life) were received from Australia, the Byelorussian SSR, the Federal Republic of Germany, Hungary, Japan, Mexico, Mongolia, Norway, Romania, Sweden, the United Kingdom, the Ukrainian SSR and the USSR. Consideration of reports from the German Democratic Republic, Guyana and the Libyan Arab Jamahiriya was deferred at the request of those States.

The Secretary-General submitted to the Council a note listing the reports received from States on rights covered by articles 13 to 15.[1] In February, he transmitted the first report of the United Nations Educational, Scientific and Cultural Organization dealing with rights covered by those articles,[3] and in March the fifth report of the International Labour Organisation on the situation in certain countries with regard to articles 6 to 9.[2]

In considering the reports, the Working Group observed that some laws of States, especially those in the social security field, had become complicated to the degree that beneficiaries were at a great disadvantage in determining their entitlements and how to obtain them. With regard to improving the quality of reports, the Working Group recommended that they: contain up-to-date statistics accurately reflecting the degree to which the Covenant had been implemented; explain coordination between central and local authorities; deal with equal treatment of women; indicate where divergencies existed between laws of States and the Covenant; be submitted in a timely manner; be circulated in the official languages of the United Nations six weeks in advance of meetings;

and conform to guidelines established by the Secretary-General (annexed to his note transmitting State reports on articles 13 to 15).

Later in the year, the Group received reports on rights covered by articles 13 to 15 from Czechoslovakia, Denmark, Poland, Senegal and Spain.

On 18 December,[5] the General Assembly commended those States parties that had submitted reports and urged those that had not to submit reports as soon as possible.

Note. [1]S-G, E/1982/3 & Add.1-22.
Reports. [2]Committee of Experts on Application of Conventions and Recommendations of ILO, transmitted by S-G note, E/1982/41; [3]Committee on Conventions and Recommendations of Executive Board of UNESCO, transmitted by S-G note, E/1982/10; [4]Working Group, E/1982/56 & Corr.1.
Resolution (1982). [5]GA: 37/191, para. 4, 18 Dec.
Resolution (prior). [6]ESC: 1988(LX), 11 May 1976 (YUN 1976, p. 615).

Organizational questions concerning the Working Group

Change of name, membership and organization of work

In 1982, the Economic and Social Council renamed the Working Group the Sessional Working Group of Governmental Experts on the Implementation of the International Covenant on Economic, Social and Cultural Rights. While the Group's character and composition remained unchanged, the Council decided on the following: the Group's members would in future be elected by the Council; all States parties to the Covenant would be eligible, whether or not they were members of the Council; the Group's sessions could be prolonged if necessary and would begin two weeks, rather than one week, before the beginning of the first regular Council session; and members would be elected for three years, instead of being nominated every year by the President, on the basis of recommendations by the regional groups of Member States.

The Commission on Human Rights, by a resolution of 9 March[3] on the status of the International Covenants on Human Rights, took note of a May 1981 Council decision[1] to review in 1982 the composition, organization and administrative arrangements of the Working Group.

The Group reviewed these matters at its meetings on 21 and 22 April[2] but was unable to reach consensus due to differing points of view and lack of time.

On 6 May,[4] the Council renamed the Working Group and decided to elect the 15 members from among the States parties to the Covenant for a three-year term. One third of the Group's membership, comprising one member from each regional group, would be renewed each year. Persons designated by Governments to represent them in the Group would be experts with recognized competence in the human rights field. The Group would meet annually for three weeks, to be extended by the Council if required. It would report to the Council and make suggestions and recommendations based on its consideration of reports by States parties to the Covenant and by specialized agencies. The Council would review the composition, organization and administrative arrangements of the Group at its first regular session of 1985, and every three years thereafter.

The revised resolution was adopted by a roll-call vote, requested by the United Kingdom, of 29 to 3, with 7 abstentions. It was orally revised by France for the 10 sponsors. An oral proposal by India, accepted by the sponsors, that Group members be elected by those Council members also States parties to the Covenant, was rejected by a roll-call vote of 16 to 14, with 7 abstentions.

The Byelorussian SSR cast a negative vote saying it provided for changes in existing arrangements which would not facilitate implementation of the Covenant. The USSR voted against the text finding some of its provisions ambiguous.

Supporting the resolution, the Federal Republic of Germany expressed the hope that, despite difficulties in adopting it, it would be used by the Council and the Group to guide them in a spirit of understanding and co-operation.

Introducing the revised draft, France said it had deemed it necessary to enhance the Group's effectiveness so that the Council could perform its supervisory role effectively.

The General Assembly, on 18 December,[5] took note of the Council's resolution.

Decision. [1]ESC: 1981/162, 8 May 1981 (YUN 1981, p. 919).
Report. [2]Working Group, E/1982/56 & Corr.1.
Resolutions (1982). [3]Commission on Human Rights (report, E/1982/12): 1982/18, para. 2, 9 Mar. [4]ESC: 1982/33, 6 May, text following. [5]GA: 37/191, para. 5, 18 Dec.
Financial implications. S-G statement, E/1982/L.38.
Meeting records. ESC: E/1982/SR.20-22, *24*, 25, *27* (3-6 May).

Economic and Social Council resolution 1982/33

6 May 1982   Meeting 27   29-3-7 (roll-call vote)

10-nation draft (E/1982/L.35/Rev.1), orally revised; agenda item 8.

Sponsors: France, Germany, Federal Republic of, Italy, Japan, Libyan Arab Jamahiriya, Netherlands, Norway, Peru, United Kingdom, Venezuela.

Review of the composition, organization and administrative arrangements of the Sessional Working Group (of Governmental Experts) on the Implementation of the International Covenant on Economic, Social and Cultural Rights

The Economic and Social Council,

Recalling its resolution 1988(LX) of 11 May 1976, by which it noted the important responsibilities placed upon the Economic and Social Council by the International Covenant on Economic, Social and Cultural Rights, in particular those resulting from articles 21 and 22 of the Covenant, and expressed its readiness to fulfil those responsibilities,

Recalling its decision 1978/10 of 3 May 1978, by which it decided to establish a Sessional Working Group on the Implementation of the International Covenant on Economic, Social and Cultural Rights, for the purpose of assisting the Council in the consideration of reports submitted by States parties to the Covenant in accordance with Council

resolution 1988(LX), and determined the composition of the Working Group,

Recalling also its resolution 1979/43 of 11 May 1979, by which it approved the methods of work of the Sessional Working Group, and its decision 1981/158 of 8 May 1981, by which it incorporated certain changes in, and modified the methods of work of, the Sessional Working Group,

Recalling further its resolution 1980/24 of 2 May 1980, by which it noted that the Sessional Working Group, established in accordance with Council decision 1978/10, had encountered certain difficulties in discharging its responsibilities under the arrangements and requested the Secretary-General to solicit the views of members of the Council and all States parties to the Covenant on the future composition, organization and administrative arrangements of the Sessional Working Group and to submit a report thereon, together with any comments he might wish to make, to the Council at its organizational session for 1981, in order to assist the Council in reviewing its decision 1978/10,

Recalling its decision 1981/162 of 8 May 1981, by which it decided to review the composition, organization and administrative arrangements of the Sessional Working Group at its first regular session of 1982,

Having considered the report of the Sessional Working Group (of Governmental Experts) on the Implementation of the International Covenant on Economic, Social and Cultural Rights,

Decides that:

(a)   The Working Group established by Economic and Social Council decision 1978/10 and modified by Council decision 1981/158 shall be renamed "Sessional Working Group of Governmental Experts on the Implementation of the International Covenant on Economic, Social and Cultural Rights" (hereinafter referred to as "the Group of Experts");

(b)   The fifteen members of the Group of Experts shall be elected by the Economic and Social Council from among the States parties to the International Covenant on Economic, Social and Cultural Rights, in accordance with the geographical distribution established by the Council in paragraph (a) of its decision 1978/10, under the following conditions:

(i)   The members of the Group of Experts shall be elected for a term of three years and shall be eligible for re-election at the end of their terms;

(ii)   One third of the membership of the Group of Experts, comprising one member from each regional group, shall be renewed each year;

(iii) The first elections shall take place during the resumed second regular session of 1982 of the Economic and Social Council and the confirmation of the experts designated by Member States to represent them in the Group of Experts shall take place at the organizational session for 1983 of the Council; immediately after the first elections, the President of the Council shall choose by lot the name of one member from each regional group whose term shall expire at the end of one year and the name of another member from each regional group whose term shall expire at the end of two years;

(iv)   The terms of office of members elected to the Group of Experts shall begin on 1 January following their election and shall expire on 31 December following the election of members that are to succeed them as members of the Group of Experts;

(v)   Subsequent elections shall take place each year during the first regular session of the Council;

(vi)   Each Member State elected to the Group of Experts shall designate, in consultation with the Secretary-General and subject to confirmation by the Council, a qualified person to represent that Member State in the Group of Experts;

(vii) The person so designated by his or her Government shall be an expert with recognized competence in the field of human rights;

(c)   The Group of Experts shall meet annually for a period of three weeks, beginning two weeks before the first regular session of the Council; the duration of each session may be extended by the Council at its organizational session, if required, taking into account the number of reports to be examined by the Group of Experts in the course of its following session;

(d)   At the end of each of its sessions, the Group of Experts shall submit to the Economic and Social Council a report on its activities and shall make suggestions and recommendations of a general nature based on its consideration of reports submitted by States parties to the Covenant and by the specialized agencies, in order to assist the Council to fulfil, in particular, its responsibilities under articles 21 and 22 of the Covenant;

(e) The Secretary-General shall provide the Group of Experts with summary records of its proceedings; those summary records shall be made available to the Council at the same time as the report of the Group of Experts; the Secretary-General shall also provide the Group of Experts with appropriate conference facilities;

(f) The Economic and Social Council shall review the composition, organization and administrative arrangements of the Group of Experts at its first regular session of 1985, and subsequently every three years, taking into account the principle of equitable geographical distribution and the increase in the number of States parties to the Covenant;

(g) The procedures and methods of work established by the resolutions and decisions referred to in the preamble to the present resolution shall remain in force in so far as they are not modified by the present resolution.

Roll-call vote in Council as follows:

In favour: Australia, Austria, Bahamas, Bangladesh, Belgium, Canada, Denmark, Fiji, France, Germany, Federal Republic of, Greece, India, Iraq, Italy, Japan, Libyan Arab Jamahiriya, Mexico, Nigeria, Norway, Pakistan, Peru, Portugal, Romania, Tunisia, United Kingdom, United States, Venezuela, Yugoslavia, Zaire.

Against: Bulgaria, Byelorussian SSR, USSR.

Abstaining: Argentina, Benin, China, Nepal, Poland, Thailand, United Republic of Cameroon.

Work programme for 1983

On 3 May 1982,[1] the Economic and Social Council approved without vote the Working Group's provisional agenda for 1983, which called for consideration of reports by States parties on rights covered by articles 6 to 9, 10 to 12 and 13 to 15.

This decision had been recommended by the Working Group on 23 April.[2]

Decision (1982). [1]ESC: 1982/118, 3 May, text following.
Report. [2]Working Group, E/1982/56 & Corr.1.
Meeting record. ESC: E/1982/SR.20 (3 May).

Economic and Social Council decision 1982/118

Adopted without vote

Draft by Working Group (E/1982/56 and Corr.1); agenda item 8.

Provisional agenda for 1983 of the Sessional Working Group (of Governmental Experts) on the Implementation of the International Covenant on Economic, Social and Cultural Rights

At its 20th plenary meeting, on 3 May 1982, the Council approved the provisional agenda for 1983 of the Sessional Working Group (of Governmental Experts) on the Implementation of the International Covenant on Economic, Social and Cultural Rights set out below:

Provisional agenda for 1983 of the Sessional Working Group (of Governmental Experts) on the Implementation of the International Covenant on Economic, Social and Cultural Rights

1. Consideration of reports submitted in accordance with Council resolution 1988(LX) by States parties to the Covenant concerning rights covered by articles 6 to 9
   Documentation
   Syrian Arab Republic (E/1978/8/Add.25 and 31)
   Any other reports received by the Secretary-General
2. Consideration of reports submitted in accordance with Council resolution 1988(LX) by States parties to the Covenant concerning rights covered by articles 10 to 12
   Documentation
   Reports received by the Secretary-General
3. Consideration of reports submitted in accordance with Council resolution 1988(LX) by States parties to the Covenant concerning rights covered by articles 13 to 15
   Documentation
   Guyana (E/1982/3/Add.5)
   Libyan Arab Jamahiriya (E/1982/3/Add.6)

German Democratic Republic (E/1982/3/Add.15 and Corr.1)
Any other reports received by the Secretary-General
4. Consideration of the report of the Sessional Working Group (of Governmental Experts) on the Implementation of the International Covenant on Economic, Social and Cultural Rights.

Right to development

Working Group activities. In 1982, the Working Group of Governmental Experts on the Right to Development, established by the Commission on Human Rights in 1981,[16] continued considering the scope and content of the individual and collective right to development, national and international means to ensure realization of the economic, social and cultural rights contained in various international instruments, and the obstacles encountered by developing countries in their efforts to secure the enjoyment of human rights.

The 15-member Working Group held three sessions in 1982 at Geneva (18-22 January, 28 June–9 July, 22 November–3 December). In January,[6] it agreed on preparation of a draft declaration. In June/July, it considered guidelines and provisions for the preamble, and in November/December, it began to examine proposals for the operative part which, it decided, should comprise three main parts: principles and objectives, means, and general provisions. The proposals were appended to the Group's report to the Commission.[7]

Action by the Commission on Human Rights. By a resolution of 9 March,[8] adopted by 41 votes to none, with 1 abstention, the Commission on Human Rights noted with satisfaction the recommendations of the Working Group and requested it to submit proposals for a draft declaration in 1983. The Commission reiterated the need to create conditions for the full promotion and protection of the human rights of individuals and peoples. It expressed deep concern at the situation with regard to the attainment of the objectives of a new international economic order and its adverse effects on the full achievement of human rights, in particular the right to development. It reaffirmed the right of all nations to pursue freely their economic and social development and to exercise full sovereignty over their natural resources, and reiterated the need to ensure the realization of work, education, health and proper nourishment as a necessity for the full enjoyment of human rights. The Commission reaffirmed that foreign occupation, colonialism, *apartheid*, racism and the denial of the right to self-determination were serious impediments to economic and social progress. It noted the recommendations of the August 1981 seminar on relations between human rights, peace and development,[17] as well as the second part of the Secretary-General's study on the regional and national dimensions of the right to development as a human right.[15]

The study suggested that regional arrangements for the promotion and protection of human rights should receive more attention, among them the recognition in regional instruments of the right to development and the stationing of human rights officers at the regional commissions.

Economic and Social Council action. On 7 May 1982,[3] the Economic and Social Council approved the Commission's request that the Working Group hold two meetings of two weeks each at Geneva in 1982. It decided that the Group's members should continue to receive travel expenses and subsistence allowances, which should not constitute a precedent for other bodies. The decision was to be brought to the attention of the General Assembly.

The decision, recommended by the Commission, was adopted without vote, following similar approval by the Second (Social) Committee on 3 May. The text was orally amended by India to include the provision on payment of travel expenses and subsistence allowances, with the directive that this would not constitute a precedent. The Committee Chairman orally proposed that the decision be brought to the attention of the Assembly.

Sub-Commission action. On 7 September,[12] the Sub-Commission on discrimination and minorities emphasized the importance of promoting full respect for human rights by accelerating the development process. It urged bilateral and multilateral development co-operation agencies to make available to States the resources and expertise required to contribute to the strengthening of the rule of law in the development process, and requested the Secretary-General to report on technical assistance available for that purpose.

Another resolution of the same date[14] dealt with a study on the new international economic order and the promotion of human rights,[5] authorized in 1980.[4] The Sub-Commission requested the Special Rapporteur, Raúl Ferrero (Peru), to submit the last part of his final report in 1983. The Secretary-General was requested to transmit the report to the Working Group on the right to development.

Also on 7 September,[13] the Sub-Commission recommended that the Commission on Human Rights recommend to the Economic and Social Council that it authorize preparation of a study on the right to adequate food as a human right (see below).

General Assembly action. On 18 December,[11] the General Assembly commended the Commission on Human Rights and its Working Group for their continuing efforts in the study of the right to development. It considered that the promotion and protection of human rights should be accompanied by efforts to establish a new international economic order, and affirmed that everyone had

the right to participate in, and benefit from, the development process.

The Assembly did not act on a series of amendments sponsored by 10 nations,[1] among them one to replace "a" with "the" new international economic order; under another, the Assembly would have commended the Commission and its Working Group for their efforts in elaborating a draft declaration on (instead of commending them for their efforts in the study of) the right to development. In addition, a new paragraph would have been added reaffirming that the right to development was an inalienable human right belonging to all persons and peoples.

In another resolution of the same date,[10] the Assembly expressed deep concern at the situation with regard to the achievement of the objectives and goals for the establishment of the new international economic order and its adverse effects on the full realization of human rights, in particular the right to development. It reaffirmed that international peace and security were essential elements of that right, which it declared to be an inalienable human right. The Assembly emphasized that the United Nations should give attention not only to the human rights aspects of development but also to the developmental aspects of human rights. It requested the Commission to promote the right to development, taking into account the results of its Working Group, and welcomed the Commission's decision that the Group continue its work on a draft declaration.

An amendment, one of a set submitted by six nations,[2] which would have had the Assembly recognize that a central purpose of development should be the realization of the potentialities of the human person in harmony with the community, was not acted on by the Assembly.

In a resolution of 3 December,[9] the Assembly requested that the Commission consider in 1983 the question of popular participation as an important factor in development and in the realization of human rights, taking into account the results of the International Seminar on Popular Participation held in May 1982 (see Chapter XIII of this section). It requested that the Commission submit, through the Economic and Social Council, suggestions for the more complete realization of human rights.

Also in December, the Assembly adopted resolutions on the proposed establishment of a new international economic order and on a new international human order (see Chapter I of this section).

Amendments not acted upon. [1]Algeria, Argentina, Bolivia, Cuba, Ethiopia, India, Indonesia, Pakistan, Panama, Yugoslavia, A/37/L.56; [2]Australia, Belgium, Greece, Ireland, Italy, Netherlands, A/37/L.57.
Decision (1982). [3]ESC: 1982/141, 7 May, text following.

Decision (prior). [4]ESC: 1980/126, 2 May 1980 (YUN 1980, p. 880).
Reports. [5]Special Rapporteur, E/CN.4/Sub.2/1982/19/Rev.1 & Rev.1/Add.1; Working Group, [6]E/CN.4/1489, [7]E/CN.4/1983/11.
Resolutions (1982). [8]Commission on Human Rights (report, E/1982/12): 1982/17, 9 Mar. GA: [9]37/55, paras. 5-7, 3 Dec.; [10]37/199, [11]37/200, 18 Dec. SCPDPM (report, E/CN.4/1983/4), 7 Sep.: [12]1982/6, [13]1982/7, [14]1982/8.
Study. [15]S-G, E/CN.4/1488.
Yearbook references. 1981, [16]p. 922, [17]p. 973.
Meeting record. ESC: E/1982/SR.29 (7 May).

Economic and Social Council decision 1982/141

Adopted without vote

Approved by Second Committee (E/1982/59) without vote, 3 May (meeting 16); draft by Commission on Human Rights (E/1982/12), orally amended by India and Chairman; agenda item 9.

Question of the realization in all countries of the economic, social and cultural rights contained in the Universal Declaration of Human Rights and in the International Covenant on Economic, Social and Cultural Rights, and study of special problems which the developing countries face in their efforts to achieve these human rights

At its 29th plenary meeting, on 7 May 1982, the Council, noting resolution 1982/17 of 9 March 1982 of the Commission on Human Rights:

(a) Approved the Commission's request to the Working Group of Governmental Experts on the Right to Development to hold two meetings of two weeks each at Geneva, the first in June/July 1982 and the second in September/October 1982;

(b) Decided that the members of the Working Group of Governmental Experts should continue to be paid travel expenses and subsistence allowances relating to sessions of the Working Group by the United Nations, in conformity with the implementation of Council decision 1981/149 of 8 May 1981;

(c) Further decided that that should not constitute a precedent for other similar bodies and that the present decision should be brought to the attention of the General Assembly at its thirty-seventh session.

Trade union rights

The *Ad Hoc* Working Group of Experts on Southern Africa submitted to the Commission on Human Rights in January 1982 a progress report[1] on human rights violations in South Africa and Namibia, including those of black workers, and a report[2] on infringements of the rights of black trade unions there (see below, under HUMAN RIGHTS VIOLATIONS).

Reports. Group of Experts, [1]E/CN.4/1485, [2]E/CN.4/1486.

Puerto Rico

A report of the Panel of the Fact-Finding and Conciliation Commission on Freedom of Association of the International Labour Organisation (ILO), concerning a complaint of infringements of trade union rights in Puerto Rico, was transmitted to the Economic and Social Council on 2 February 1982.[3] The complaint, presented by the World Federation of Trade Unions in 1977, had been transmitted by the Council to the ILO Commission in 1978.[2]

On 7 May 1982,[1] the Council took note of the report which concluded that the allegations made by the complainant were without foundation.

The decision was adopted without vote, following similar approval by the Second (Social) Com-

mittee on 3 May. The text was proposed orally by the Committee Chairman and amended by the United States to add the report's conclusion.

Decision (1982). [1]ESC: 1982/144, 7 May, text following.
Decision (prior). [2]ESC: 1978/41, 21 July 1978 (YUN 1978, p. 730).
Report. [3]ILO Fact-Finding and Conciliation Commission, transmitted by Secretariat note, E/1982/7.
Meeting record. ESC: E/1982/SR.29 (7 May).

Economic and Social Council decision 1982/144

Adopted without vote

Approved by Second Committee (E/1982/59) without vote, 3 May (meeting 16); oral proposal by Chairman, orally amended by United States; agenda item 9.

Report of the Panel of the Fact-Finding and Conciliation Commission on Freedom of Association appointed by the Governing Body of the International Labour Office to examine the complaints of alleged infringements of trade union rights in the United States/Puerto Rico

At its 29th plenary meeting, on 7 May 1982, the Council, recalling its resolution 277(X) of 17 February 1950 and its decision 1978/41 of 21 July 1978, took note of the report of the Panel of the Fact-Finding and Conciliation Commission on Freedom of Association appointed by the Governing Body of the International Labour Office, which concluded that the allegations of infringements of trade union rights made by the complainant were without foundation.

Right to education

A report on activities to implement the right to education in the framework of the draft medium-term plan for 1984-1989 of the United Nations Educational, Scientific and Cultural Organization (UNESCO), prepared by the UNESCO Director-General, was transmitted to the General Assembly by the Secretary-General in October 1982,[1] in accordance with a December 1981 Assembly resolution.[3]

On 17 December 1982,[2] the Assembly took note of the conclusions in the report, commended UNESCO for including in its medium-term plan on a permanent basis the issue of the implementation of the right to education, and invited it to continue its efforts to promote that right. The Assembly invited all States to consider adopting measures to ensure full implementation of the right to universal education. Specialized agencies were invited to co-operate with UNESCO to ensure high priority for education. The Assembly appealed in particular to the developed countries to support the efforts of developing countries to educate and train national personnel.

The resolution was adopted without vote, following similar approval on 9 December by the Third (Social, Humanitarian and Cultural) Committee, where it was introduced by Romania on behalf of 56 nations.

The Economic and Social Council's Sessional Working Group (of Governmental Experts) on the Implementation of the International Covenant on Economic, Social and Cultural Rights considered reports by States parties on their implementation of rights concerning education (see above).

Report. (1)UNESCO Director-General, transmitted by S-G note, A/37/521.
Resolution (1982). (2)GA: 37/178, 17 Dec., text following.
Resolution (prior). (3)GA: 36/152, 16 Dec. 1981 (YUN 1981, p. 925).
Meeting records. GA: 3rd Committee, A/C.3/37/SR.62, 63, *64*, 65-71, *72, 74* (3-10 Dec.); plenary, A/37/PV.110 (17 Dec.).

General Assembly resolution 37/178

17 December 1982   Meeting 110   Adopted without vote

Approved by Third Committee (A/37/745) without vote, 9 December (meeting 72); 56-nation draft (A/C.3/37/L.64); agenda item 12.

Sponsors: Bangladesh, Barbados, Bhutan, Bolivia, Bulgaria, Cape Verde, Central African Republic, Colombia, Congo, Costa Rica, Cuba, Cyprus, Dominican Republic, Ecuador, Egypt, Ethiopia, Gabon, Guinea, Guinea-Bissau, Guyana, Hungary, Indonesia, Jordan, Liberia, Libyan Arab Jamahiriya, Madagascar, Mali, Mauritius, Morocco, Mozambique, Nepal, Nicaragua, Nigeria, Oman, Pakistan, Philippines, Poland, Qatar, Romania, Rwanda, Senegal, Somalia, Sri Lanka, Sudan, Suriname, Syrian Arab Republic, Togo, Trinidad and Tobago, Tunisia, Turkey, Upper Volta, Venezuela, Viet Nam, Yemen, Yugoslavia, Zaire.

The right to education

The General Assembly,

Recalling its resolutions 34/170 of 17 December 1979, 35/191 of 15 December 1980 and 36/152 of 16 December 1981 on the right to education,

Recalling the International Covenant on Economic, Social and Cultural Rights, adopted by its resolution 2200 A (XXI) of 16 December 1966, which recognizes the right of everyone to education,

Bearing in mind the importance of the Convention against Discrimination in Education, adopted on 14 December 1960 by the General Conference of the United Nations Educational, Scientific and Cultural Organization,

Reaffirming the paramount importance of the implementation of the right to education for the full development of the human personality and for the enjoyment of other fundamental human rights and freedoms,

Recognizing that for the effective implementation of the right to education the eradication of illiteracy has a particular priority and urgency,

Convinced that the educational process could bring a substantial contribution to social progress, national development, mutual understanding and co-operation among peoples and to strengthening peace and international security,

Recalling that the establishment of the new international economic order requires effective support for the improvement and expansion of educational systems and for the training of specialized personnel and qualified cadres for the economic development of developing countries,

Convinced of the topicality and urgency of the provisions on education contained in the International Development Strategy for the Third United Nations Development Decade,

Recalling that, since its establishment, the United Nations Educational, Scientific and Cultural Organization has constantly striven for the effective realization of the right to education and equality of educational opportunities for all, without distinction as to race, colour, sex, language, religion, political or other opinion, national or social origin, economic status or birth, and that, for many years past, activities directed towards securing the right to education and the extension and improvement of educational and training systems in member States, more particularly in the developing countries, have occupied a central place in that organization's programme,

Aware of the important contribution of the United Nations Educational, Scientific and Cultural Organization to the implementation of the International Development Strategy for the Third United Nations Development Decade with a view to fostering full implementation of the right to education,

Taking note with satisfaction of the interest shown by the Executive Board of the United Nations Educational, Scientific and Cultural Organization in the implementation of General Assembly resolutions 34/170, 35/191 and 36/152,

1. *Takes note* of the conclusions contained in the report of the Director-General of the United Nations Educational, Scientific and Cultural Organization on the right to education;

2. *Commends* the United Nations Educational, Scientific and Cultural Organization for including on a permanent basis, in its medium-term plan, the issue of the implementation of the right to education;

3. *Again invites* all States to consider the adoption of appropriate legislative, administrative and other measures, including material guarantees, in order to ensure full implementation of the right to universal education through, *inter alia*, free and compulsory primary education, universal and gradually free-of-charge secondary education, equal access to all educational facilities and the access of the young generation to science and culture;

4. *Invites* all States to give all necessary attention to defining and determining in a more precise manner the means for implementing the provisions concerning the role of education in the International Development Strategy for the Third United Nations Development Decade;

5. *Invites* all specialized agencies to co-operate with the United Nations Educational, Scientific and Cultural Organization to ensure education a high priority in the implementation of various programmes and projects within the framework of the International Development Strategy for the Third United Nations Development Decade;

6. *Appeals once again* to all States, in particular the developed countries, to support actively, through fellowships and other means, including the general increasing of resources for education and training, the efforts of the developing countries in the education and training of national personnel needed in industry, agriculture and other economic and social sectors;

7. *Expresses its thanks* to the Director-General of the United Nations Educational, Scientific and Cultural Organization for his report on the right to education, submitted in accordance with General Assembly resolution 36/152;

8. *Invites* the United Nations Educational, Scientific and Cultural Organization to continue its intensive efforts for the promotion at the universal level of the right to education and to inform the General Assembly, in appropriate forms, of the progress achieved in this field.

Right to food

On 7 September 1982,(1) the Sub-Commission on Prevention of Discrimination and Protection of Minorities recommended that the Commission on Human Rights recommend to the Economic and Social Council that it authorize the Sub-Commission to request Asbjorn Eide (Norway) to prepare a study on the right to adequate food as a human right. The Special Rapporteur should take into account relevant work by the United Nations system and consult with its organs and agencies and non-governmental organizations. He should give special attention to the normative content of the right to food and its significance in relation to the establishment of the new international economic order.

The Special Rapporteur would be requested to submit a preliminary report to the Sub-Commission in 1983 and a final report in 1984.

Resolution (1982). (1)SCPDPM (report, E/CN.4/1983/4): 1982/7, 7 Sep.

Advancement of human rights

On 18 December 1982,(3) the General Assembly again requested the Commission on Human Rights to continue work on alternative approaches and ways for improving the enjoyment of human rights and fundamental freedoms. It affirmed that efforts by the United Nations and its Members to promote civil and political rights as well as economic, social and cultural rights should continue. Emphasizing the contribution of international and national stability to the human rights of peoples and individuals, the Assembly considered it necessary that Members promote international co-operation based on respect for each State's independence, including the right to choose its own socio-economic and political system. It reaffirmed the necessity to promote the right to education, work, health and proper nourishment through national and international measures, including the establishment of the new international economic order.

The Assembly also reaffirmed the importance of Member States' adherence to international human rights instruments, and said that standard-setting work within the United Nations should be encouraged and that the international community should accord priority to the search for solutions to violations of human rights of peoples and individuals. It emphasized that the United Nations should give attention to the developmental aspects of human rights and requested the Commission to promote the right to development (see above, under ECONOMIC, SOCIAL AND CULTURAL RIGHTS).

The resolution was adopted by a recorded vote of 113 to 1, with 26 abstentions, following its approval by the Third (Social, Humanitarian and Cultural) Committee on 1 December by a recorded vote of 104 to 1, with 24 abstentions. The draft was orally revised in Committee by the sponsors, taking into account an oral proposal by Morocco. By this revision, paragraph 10, which would have emphasized the need to ensure economic and political stability at the national and international levels for the full enjoyment of human rights, was changed to state that such stability would contribute to their full enjoyment.

In another resolution of 18 December,[4] the Assembly affirmed that all human rights were indivisible and interrelated and that the promotion of one category of rights should never exempt States from the promotion of others. It emphasized that foreign occupation, colonialism, *apartheid*, racism and racial discrimination and the denial of the right to self-determination were serious impediments to peace and development. The Assembly recognized the purpose of development to be realization of individual potentialities in harmony with the community and stressed Governments' duty to secure the rights of the vulnerable or disadvantaged. It requested the Secretary-General to include an overview of trends and problems in his study on international conditions and human rights, requested by the Assembly in December 1981 for submission in 1983.[7]

The Assembly noted that mass and flagrant violations in one State might threaten the peace and development of neighbouring States, and reaffirmed that violations were of concern to the United Nations wherever they occurred. It considered that efforts to promote human rights should be accompanied by efforts to establish a new international economic order and affirmed everyone's right to participate in development. The Assembly requested Member States to consider adhering to human rights conventions and urged all States to co-operate with the Commission in studying human rights violations. The Commission was requested to continue its efforts to improve the United Nations capacity to act in cases of serious violations, bearing in mind the proposals for a draft mandate of a High Commissioner for Human Rights. The Secretary-General was requested to take measures to strengthen the United Nations Centre for Human Rights (see below).

Adopted by a recorded vote of 81 to 38, with 20 abstentions, the orally revised draft had been approved by the Third Committee on 1 December by a recorded vote of 75 to 30, with 22 abstentions. Five of the paragraphs were approved in Committee by separate recorded votes: the eleventh preambular paragraph by 61 to 23, with 40 abstentions; the eighteenth preambular paragraph by 55 to 25, with 37 abstentions; operative paragraph 11 by 69 to 17, with 33 abstentions; paragraph 12 by 65 to 32, with 26 abstentions; and paragraph 13 by 70 to 24, with 28 abstentions.

A set of amendments for each resolution was submitted to the Assembly, which, on 18 December, by a recorded vote of 80 to 52, decided to take no action on them. Australia, Belgium, Greece, Ireland, Italy and the Netherlands proposed 10 amendments to the first resolution,[2] four of them calling for the addition of preambular paragraphs by which the Assembly would have: recognized that human rights violations, wherever they existed, were of concern to the United Nations; emphasized that lack of peace or constraints on development did not exempt a State from its obligation to ensure respect for human rights; borne in mind that mass and flagrant human rights violations might threaten international peace and development; and stated its awareness of the need to allocate resources to strengthen the Centre for Human Rights.

Other amendments would have added new operative paragraphs to have the Assembly: emphasize that promotion of certain human rights could not justify the denial of others; urge States to co-operate with the Commission in studying human rights violations; recognize that a central purpose of development should be the realization of individual potentialities in harmony with the community; request the Commission to continue in 1983 its efforts to improve the capacity of the United Nations to act in cases of serious human rights violations; and request the Secretary-General to take measures to strengthen the Centre for Human Rights. Finally, in paragraph 4, the Assembly would have affirmed the need for intensified rather than continued efforts by the United Nations and its Members to promote human rights.

A set of 19 amendments to the second resolution was submitted by 10 nations.[1] Those affecting the preamble would have had the following effect: to add a reference to the equal rights of large and small nations (first paragraph); to add freedom from want as another primary aim of international co-operation (third paragraph); to delete the word "social" from a phrase stating that social development must be based on respect for the dignity of man (fifth paragraph); to state that mass and flagrant human rights violations might threaten "international peace and development" rather than "the peace and development of neighbouring States, of a region or of the international community as a whole" (ninth paragraph); to specify that "mass and flagrant" human rights violations rather than simply human rights violations were of concern to the United Nations wherever they occurred (tenth paragraph); to delete the eleventh paragraph; to allocate "adequate" rather than "additional" resources to the Centre for Human Rights (eighteenth paragraph); and to reaffirm rather than recall a 1977 Assembly resolution (stating the indivisibility and interdependence of human rights and according high priority to solutions for mass and flagrant violations)[6] (nineteenth paragraph).

Other amendments in this set would have modified several operative paragraphs: to add to a clause listing serious impediments to peace and development mention of aggression and the threat or use of force against the territorial integrity or political independence of any State (paragraph 3); to reword paragraph 6 to state that development's ultimate aim was the improvement of the population's well-being and a distribution of the benefits; and to delete the words "a duty to take special measures" from paragraph 9. A paragraph reaffirming the right to development as an inalienable right of all individuals and peoples would have been added (see above, under ECONOMIC, SOCIAL AND CULTURAL RIGHTS). Other amendments would have emphasized the new international economic order and the right to development, stressed the search for solutions for mass and flagrant violations, and requested adequate resources for the Centre for Human Rights.

Introducing the motion to take no action on the amendments, Singapore described the two resolutions as complementary and compatible, whose balance would be upset by the proposed amendments.

Introducing the first resolution on behalf of 23 nations, Cuba expressed the opinion that balance had been achieved by reiterating the indivisibility and interdependence of human rights; Cuba said the right to development was inalienable and international peace was essential to its realization, and declared necessary the achievement of the objectives of the new international economic order for the full realization of human rights.

Explaining its negative vote, the United States termed the resolution an attempt to shift attention from individual to collective rights. It also voiced reservations on the provisions concerning the right to development, as did Australia, Austria, Canada, Finland (for the Nordic States), the Federal Republic of Germany, the Netherlands and the United Kingdom, which abstained.

Also abstaining, Ireland said the resolution concentrated excessively on collective and economic and social rights at the expense of individual and civil and political rights. Canada regarded both types of rights as inseparable. Australia, Italy, New Zealand and Turkey expressed concern at what they perceived to be the resolution's lack of balance between individual and collective aspects of human rights. France said it was unable to agree to giving some categories of human rights precedence over others. Sweden agreed with Costa Rica's contention that, as a declaration on the right to development, the resolution was an attempt to undermine the 1948 Universal Declaration of Human Rights[5] and could be used as a pretext for not promoting the individual's human rights. Turkey considered that the resolution should stress the independence of human rights from all other factors.

Voting in favour, Brazil hoped that the resolution would not interfere with the prerogatives of States concerning adherence to international instruments. Greece agreed with its basic principles but stated that it lacked balance and should have included other aspects of human rights.

Panama, on the other hand, considered the lack of progress in eliminating poverty and injustice to be indicative of an approach emphasizing the rights of the individual to the detriment of those of the group. Tunisia felt that the right of individuals to development was hampered by material insecurity, underdevelopment and political instability; it hoped that the discussion of the right to development could be pursued in all United Nations bodies. By voting in favour, Morocco said, it showed its belief in both collective and individual rights.

Introducing the second resolution, also on behalf of Australia, Belgium, Greece, Italy and the

Netherlands, Ireland said its purpose was to chart a general course for the United Nations in promoting and protecting human rights.

Argentina, Ethiopia, India and Yugoslavia explained that, although the resolution contained positive elements, they felt compelled to vote against it because they had not been allowed for procedural reasons to express their views as contained in the amendments. A similar view was expressed by Cuba. Pakistan said it would have liked to amend the resolution to protect and promote human rights in a comprehensive manner. Bulgaria stated that the resolution took a unilateral approach, was unbalanced and inconsistent with many international instruments and tried to prejudge the work of the Commission. The Byelorussian SSR, terming the resolution's objectives diffuse, said it contained no specific proposals for solving human rights problems. The USSR categorically opposed the text as being designed to cancel out important provisions relating to the international economic order and the 1977 Assembly resolution on the interdependence of human rights.[6] In India's view, a number of paragraphs bore no relation to any international instrument or Assembly resolution.

Indonesia, which abstained in the Committee but cast a negative vote in the Assembly, and the Philippines, which abstained, stated difficulties in particular with paragraphs 11 and 12, as well as paragraph 2.

Though voting in favour, Chile expressed the belief that the resolution detracted from the importance of the right to development; it further objected that the Commission on Human Rights was portrayed as non-discriminatory, whereas Chile believed that the Commission treated cases selectively, on political grounds.

Turkey believed that the balance between individual and collective rights, and civil and political rights and economic and social rights, was well maintained in the resolution. The United States regarded the text as a constructive approach to improving the enjoyment of human rights. Canada, Finland (for the Nordic countries) and the United Kingdom believed that the text offered a broad and comprehensive approach.

Amendments not acted upon. [1]Algeria, Argentina, Bolivia, Cuba, Ethiopia, India, Indonesia, Pakistan, Panama, Yugoslavia, A/37/L.56; [2]Australia, Belgium, Greece, Ireland, Italy, Netherlands, A/37/L.57.
Resolutions (1982). GA, 18 Dec., texts following: [3]37/199, [4]37/200.
Resolutions (prior). GA: [5]217 A (III), 10 Dec. 1948 (YUN 1948-49, p. 535); [6]32/130, 16 Dec. 1977 (YUN 1977, p. 734); [7]36/133, 14 Dec. 1981 (YUN 1981, p. 928).
Meeting records. GA: 3rd Committee, A/C.3/37/SR.38-40, *49, 59-61* (10 Nov.–2 Dec.); plenary, A/37/PV.110, *111* (17, 18 Dec.).

General Assembly resolution 37/199

18 December 1982   Meeting 111   113-1-26 (recorded vote)

Approved by Third Committee (A/37/693) by recorded vote (104-1-24), 1 December (meeting 60); 23-nation draft (A/C.3/37/L.31/Rev.1), orally revised; agenda item 94.

Sponsors: Algeria, Angola, Argentina, Bangladesh, Benin, Cape Verde, Cuba, Democratic Yemen, Ethiopia, Guinea-Bissau, Guyana, India, Libyan Arab Jamahiriya, Madagascar, Nicaragua, Pakistan, Panama, Romania, Syrian Arab Republic, Uganda, Viet Nam, Yugoslavia, Zimbabwe.

Alternate approaches and ways and means within the United Nations system for improving the effective enjoyment of human rights and fundamental freedoms

The General Assembly,

Recalling that in the Charter of the United Nations the peoples of the United Nations declared their determination to reaffirm faith in fundamental human rights, in the dignity and worth of the human person and in the equal rights of men and women and of nations large and small and to employ international machinery for the promotion of the economic and social advancement of all peoples,

Recalling also the purposes and principles of the Charter to achieve international co-operation in solving international problems of an economic, social, cultural or humanitarian character, and in promoting and encouraging respect for human rights and for fundamental freedoms for all without distinction as to race, sex, language or religion,

Emphasizing the importance of the Universal Declaration of Human Rights and of the International Covenants on Human Rights in promoting respect for and observance of human rights and fundamental freedoms,

Recalling its resolution 32/130 of 16 December 1977, in which it decided that the approach to the future work within the United Nations system with respect to human rights questions should take into account the concepts set forth in that resolution,

Recalling also its resolutions 34/46 of 23 November 1979, 35/174 of 15 December 1980 and 36/133 of 14 December 1981,

Reiterating once again that the establishment of the new international economic order is an essential element for the effective promotion and the full enjoyment of human rights and fundamental freedoms for all,

Reiterating also its profound conviction that all human rights and fundamental freedoms are indivisible and interdependent and that equal attention and urgent consideration should be given to the implementation, promotion and protection of both civil and political rights and economic, social and cultural rights,

Underlining the need for the creation of conditions at the national and international levels for the promotion and full protection of the human rights of individuals and peoples,

Welcoming the report of the Working Group of Governmental Experts on the Right to Development, established by the Commission on Human Rights, and the progress it has made to date,

Underlining that the right to development is an inalienable human right,

Recognizing that international peace and security are essential elements for the full realization of human rights, including the right to development,

Considering that the resources which would be released by disarmament could contribute significantly to the development of all States, in particular of the developing countries,

Recognizing also that co-operation among all nations on the basis of respect for the independence and sovereignty of each State, including the right of each people to choose its own socio-economic system, is essential for the promotion of peace and development,

Acknowledging the progress achieved by the international community in the promotion and protection of human rights and fundamental freedoms,

Convinced that the primary aim of such international co-operation must be the achievement by each human being of a life of freedom and dignity and freedom from want,

Affirming that the ultimate aim of development is the constant improvement of the well-being of the entire population on the basis of its full participation in the process of development and a fair distribution of the benefits therefrom,

1. *Reiterates its request* that the Commission on Human Rights continue its current work on the overall analysis with a view to further

promoting and improving human rights and fundamental freedoms, including the question of the Commission's programme and working methods, and on the overall analysis of the alternative approaches and ways and means for improving the effective enjoyment of human rights and fundamental freedoms, in accordance with the provisions of General Assembly resolution 32/130 and the concepts set forth therein, bearing in mind also other relevant texts;

2. *Reaffirms* that it is of paramount importance for the promotion of human rights and fundamental freedoms that Member States should undertake specific obligations through accession to, or ratification of, international instruments in this field and, consequently, that the standard-setting work within the United Nations system in the field of human rights and the universal acceptance and implementation of the relevant international instruments should be encouraged;

3. *Reiterates* that the international community should accord, or continue to accord, priority to the search for solutions to mass and flagrant violations of human rights of the peoples and individuals affected by situations such as those described in paragraph 1 *(e)* of its resolution 32/130, paying due attention also to other situations of violations of human rights;

4. *Affirms* that the efforts of the United Nations and its Member States to promote and to protect civil and political rights as well as economic, social and cultural rights should continue;

5. *Expresses its deep concern* at the present situation with regard to the achievement of the objectives and goals for the establishment of the new international economic order and its adverse effects on the full realization of human rights and, in particular, the right to development;

6. *Reaffirms* that international peace and security are essential elements in the full realization of the right to development;

7. *Declares* that the right to development is an inalienable human right;

8. *Emphasizes* that the United Nations should give attention not only to the human rights aspects of development but also to the developmental aspects of human rights;

9. *Considers* it necessary that all Member States promote international co-operation on the basis of respect for the independence and sovereignty of each State, including the right of each people to choose its own socio-economic and political system, with a view to resolving international problems of an economic, social and humanitarian character;

10. *Emphasizes* that economic and political stability at the national and international levels will contribute to the full enjoyment, promotion and observance of the human rights of peoples and individuals;

11. *Reaffirms also* that, in order to ensure the full enjoyment of all rights and complete personal dignity, it is necessary to promote the right to education and the right to work, health and proper nourishment, through adoption of measures at the national level, including those that provide for the right of workers to participate in management, as well as adoption of measures at the international level, including the establishment of the new international economic order;

12. *Requests* the Commission on Human Rights to take the necessary measures to promote the right to development, taking into account the results achieved by the Working Group of Governmental Experts on the Right to Development, and welcomes the decision of the Commission, in its resolution 1982/17 of 9 March 1982, that the Working Group should continue its work with the aim of presenting as soon as possible a draft resolution on the right to development;

13. *Decides* to include in the provisional agenda of its thirty-eighth session the item entitled "Alternative approaches and ways and means within the United Nations system for improving the effective enjoyment of human rights and fundamental freedoms".

Recorded vote in Assembly as follows:

In favour: Afghanistan, Algeria, Angola, Argentina, Bahamas, Bahrain, Bangladesh, Barbados, Benin, Bhutan, Bolivia, Botswana, Brazil, Bulgaria, Burma, Burundi, Byelorussian SSR, Cape Verde, Central African Republic, Chad, Chile, China, Colombia, Congo, Cuba, Cyprus, Czechoslovakia, Democratic Kampuchea, Democratic Yemen, Djibouti, Dominican Republic, Ecuador, Egypt, El Salvador, Ethiopia, Fiji, Gabon, Gambia, German Democratic Republic, Ghana, Greece, Grenada, Guatemala, Guinea, Guyana, Honduras, Hungary, India, Indonesia, Iran, Iraq, Ivory Coast, Jordan, Kenya, Kuwait, Lao People's Democratic Republic, Lebanon, Lesotho, Liberia, Libyan Arab Jamahiriya, Madagascar, Malaysia, Maldives, Mali, Malta, Mauritania, Mauritius, Mexico, Mongolia, Morocco, Mozambique, Nepal, Nicaragua, Niger, Nigeria, Oman, Pakistan, Panama, Papua New Guinea, Peru, Philippines, Poland, Qatar, Romania, Samoa, Sao Tome and

Principe, Senegal, Sierra Leone, Singapore, Solomon Islands, Somalia, Sri Lanka, Sudan, Suriname, Syrian Arab Republic, Thailand, Togo, Trinidad and Tobago, Tunisia, Ukrainian SSR, USSR, United Arab Emirates, United Republic of Cameroon, United Republic of Tanzania, Upper Volta, Uruguay, Venezuela, Viet Nam, Yemen, Yugoslavia, Zaire, Zambia, Zimbabwe.

Against: United States.

Abstaining: Australia, Austria, Belgium, Canada, Denmark, Finland, France, Germany, Federal Republic of, Iceland, Ireland, Israel, Italy, Jamaica, Japan, Luxembourg, Malawi, Netherlands, New Zealand, Norway, Paraguay, Portugal, Saudi Arabia, Spain, Sweden, Turkey, United Kingdom.

General Assembly resolution 37/200

18 December 1982   Meeting 111   81-38-20 (recorded vote)

Approved by Third Committee (A/37/693) by recorded vote (75-30-22), 1 December (meeting 60); 6-nation draft (A/C.3/37/L.41), orally revised; agenda item 94.

Sponsors: Australia, Belgium, Greece, Ireland, Italy, Netherlands.

Further promotion and protection of human rights and fundamental freedoms

The General Assembly,

Aware that in the Charter of the United Nations the peoples of the United Nations declared their determination to reaffirm faith in fundamental human rights, in the dignity and worth of the human person and in the equal rights of men and women and to promote social progress and better standards of life in larger freedom,

Conscious that it is a purpose of the United Nations and the duty of all Member States to achieve international co-operation in solving international problems of an economic, social, cultural or humanitarian character, and in promoting and encouraging respect for human rights and for fundamental freedoms for all without distinction as to race, sex, language or religion,

Convinced that a primary aim of such international co-operation must be the achievement by each human being of a life of freedom and dignity,

Aware that efforts to promote and protect human rights at the international level should be accompanied by efforts to establish a new international economic order,

Aware also that the promotion and protection of human rights are necessary conditions for the development of the human personality, whether in its individual or its social aspects, and that social development must be based on respect for the dignity of man from which all human rights derive their justification,

Considering that the advancement of development objectives is related to the promotion of harmonious relations within and among States,

Considering also that the great resources which would be released by disarmament could contribute significantly to the development of all States, especially those which are at present least developed,

Bearing in mind that the maintenance of international peace and security is vital for social and economic progress and for the full realization of human rights,

Bearing in mind also that mass and flagrant violations of human rights in one State may threaten the peace and development of neighbouring States, of a region or of the international community as a whole,

Recognizing that violations of human rights, wherever they exist, are of concern to the United Nations,

Emphasizing that the absence of peace or development can never exempt a State from its obligation to ensure respect for the human rights of its nationals and of other persons within its jurisdiction,

Reaffirming that everyone is entitled to all the rights and freedoms set forth in the Universal Declaration of Human Rights, without distinction of any kind, as to race, colour, sex, language, religion, political or other opinion, national or social origin, property, birth or other status,

Reaffirming also that nothing in the Universal Declaration of Human Rights may be interpreted as implying for any State, group or person any right to engage in any activity or perform any act aimed at the destruction of any of the rights and freedoms set forth therein,

Considering that regional arrangements for the promotion and protection of human rights can make a major contribution to the effective enjoyment of human rights and fundamental freedoms and that the exchange of information and experience in this field among the regions and within the United Nations system could be improved,

Underlining the obligation that Governments have to promote and protect human rights and to carry out the responsibilities that they have undertaken under various international instruments in the field of human rights,

Acknowledging the progress achieved by the international community in the promotion and protection of human rights and fundamental freedoms, particularly with respect to the setting of standards,

Acknowledging also the valuable efforts of the Commission on Human Rights in the study of violations of human rights and fundamental freedoms in any part of the world,

Aware of the need to allocate additional resources, including staff, to the Centre for Human Rights of the Secretariat,

Recalling its resolutions on this question, in particular its resolution 32/130 of 16 December 1977,

1. *Affirms* that a primary aim of international co-operation in the field of human rights is a life of freedom and dignity for each human being, that all human rights and fundamental freedoms are indivisible and interrelated and that the promotion and protection of one category of rights should never exempt or excuse States from the promotion and protection of the others;

2. *Notes* that mass and flagrant violations of human rights in one State may threaten the peace and development of neighbouring States, of a region or of the international community as a whole;

3. *Emphasizes* that foreign occupation, colonialism, *apartheid*, racism and racial discrimination and the denial of the right to self-determination of peoples and of all universally recognized human rights are serious impediments to peace and development;

4. *Reaffirms* that violations of human rights, wherever they exist, are of concern to the United Nations;

5. *Considers* that efforts to promote and protect human rights at the international level should be accompanied by efforts to establish a new international economic order;

6. *Recognizes* that the realization of the potentialities of the human person in harmony with the community should be seen as the central purpose of development;

7. *Affirms* that everyone has the right to participate in, as well as to benefit from, the development process;

8. *Commends* the Commission on Human Rights and its *ad hoc* working group, established by the Commission pursuant to its resolution 36(XXXVII) of 11 March 1981, for their continuing efforts in the study of the right to development;

9. *Stresses* that Governments have a duty to take special measures to secure the human rights of vulnerable or disadvantaged groups of individuals;

10. *Requests* Member States that have not yet done so to consider ratifying or acceding to the various conventions in the field of human rights;

11. *Urges* all States to co-operate with the Commission on Human Rights in its study of violations of human rights and fundamental freedoms in any part of the world;

12. *Requests* the Commission on Human Rights at its thirty-ninth session to continue its efforts to improve the capacity of the United Nations system to take urgent action in cases of serious violations of human rights, bearing in mind the proposals submitted by the Sub-Commission on Prevention of Discrimination and Protection of Minorities on possible terms of reference for the draft mandate of a High Commissioner for Human Rights;

13. *Requests* the Secretary-General to take appropriate measures to strengthen the Centre for Human Rights of the Secretariat;

14. *Also requests* the Secretary-General, in the light of the thirty-fifth anniversary of the Universal Declaration of Human Rights, to include in the updated study on international conditions and human rights, which the General Assembly, in its resolution 36/133 of 14 December 1981, requested him to submit to it at its thirty-eighth session, an overview of trends in the field of human rights with emphasis on the problems still being encountered;

15. *Decides* to include in the provisional agenda of its thirty-eighth session the item entitled "Alternative approaches and ways and means within the United Nations system for improving the effective enjoyment of human rights and fundamental freedoms".

Recorded vote in Assembly as follows:

In favour: Australia, Austria, Bahamas, Barbados, Belgium, Botswana, Burma, Burundi, Canada, Central African Republic, Chad, Chile, Colombia, Costa Rica, Cyprus, Democratic Kampuchea, Denmark, Djibouti, Dominican Republic, Ecuador, Egypt, El Salvador, Fiji, Finland, France, Gabon, Gambia, Germany, Federal Republic of, Ghana, Greece, Guatemala, Honduras, Iceland, Ireland, Israel, Italy, Ivory Coast, Jamaica, Japan, Kenya, Lebanon, Lesotho, Liberia, Luxembourg, Malaysia, Maldives, Mali, Malta, Mauritania, Mauritius, Mexico, Morocco, Nepal, Netherlands, New Zealand, Norway, Papua New Guinea, Paraguay, Peru, Portugal, Samoa, Senegal, Singapore, Solomon Islands, Somalia, Spain, Sudan, Suriname, Sweden, Thailand, Togo, Trinidad and Tobago, Tunisia, Turkey, United Kingdom, United Republic of Cameroon, United Republic of Tanzania, United States, Upper Volta, Uruguay, Venezuela.

Against: Afghanistan, Algeria, Angola, Argentina, Benin, Bolivia, Bulgaria, Byelorussian SSR, Cape Verde, Congo, Cuba, Czechoslovakia, Democratic Yemen, Ethiopia, German Democratic Republic, Guyana, Hungary, India, Indonesia, Iran, Lao People's Democratic Republic, Libyan Arab Jamahiriya, Madagascar, Mongolia, Mozambique, Nicaragua, Pakistan, Panama, Poland, Romania, Sao Tome and Principe, Syrian Arab Republic, Ukrainian SSR, USSR, Viet Nam, Yugoslavia, Zambia,[a] Zimbabwe.

Abstaining: Bahrain, Bangladesh, Bhutan, Brazil, China, Guinea, Iraq, Jordan, Malawi, Niger, Nigeria, Oman, Philippines, Qatar, Saudi Arabia, Sierra Leone, Sri Lanka, United Arab Emirates, Yemen, Zaire.

[a]Later advised the Secretariat it had intended to vote in favour.

UN machinery

Commission on Human Rights

Work programme

Action by the Commission on Human Rights. An informal open-ended working group of the Commission on Human Rights, similar to the one set up for the first time in 1981,[5] held five meetings between 11 February and 3 March 1982 on the question of the programme and work methods of the Commission.[3]

On 11 March,[4] the Commission, noting the group's report, recommended that the Economic and Social Council consider rescheduling the Commission's annual session—and, if necessary, the Sub-Commission's session—to later in the year. It decided to consider in 1983 the establishment of an informal group of 10 of its members to examine the possibility of rationalizing its 1984 agenda, the elaboration of its programme and work methods, the question of a time-limit on statements, and the organization and functioning of open-ended working groups. It decided to establish one such group to continue the overall analysis and to keep under consideration the proposal for the creation of the post of United Nations High Commissioner for Human Rights (see below).

Economic and Social Council action. On 7 May 1982,[1] the Economic and Social Council decided without vote to consider at its second 1982 session the possible rescheduling of the Commission's annual session to later in the year. This decision was approved without vote by the Second (Social) Committee on 3 May, on an oral proposal by its Chairman.

By a decision of 28 July,[2] orally proposed by its Secretary, the Council decided to consider the question at its second 1983 session, in the context of its consideration of the draft calendar of conferences and meetings for 1984-1985.

Decisions (1982). ESC: [1]1982/145, 7 May, text following; [2]1982/156, 28 July, text following.
Report. [3]Working Group, E/1982/12/Add.1.
Resolution (1982). [4]Commission on Human Rights (report, E/1982/12): 1982/40, 11 Mar.
Yearbook reference. [5]1981, p. 926.
Meeting records. ESC: E/1982/SR.29, 49 (7 May, 28 July).

Economic and Social Council decision 1982/145

Adopted without vote

Approved by Second Committee (E/1982/59) without vote, 3 May (meeting 16); oral proposal by Chairman; agenda item 9.

Scheduling of the annual session of the Commission on Human Rights

At its 29th plenary meeting, on 7 May 1982, the Council, taking note of resolution 1982/40 of 11 March 1982 of the Commission on Human Rights, in which, *inter alia*, the Commission recommended to the Economic and Social Council that it should consider the possibility of rescheduling the annual session of the Commission on Human Rights and, if necessary, of the Sub-Commission on Prevention of Discrimination and Protection of Minorities, with a view to enabling the Commission to meet later in the year, decided to consider the matter at its second regular session of 1982.

Economic and Social Council decision 1982/156

Adopted without vote

Oral proposal by Council Secretary; agenda item 6.

Scheduling of the annual session of the Commission on Human Rights

At its 49th plenary meeting, on 28 July 1982, the Council, in pursuance of its decision 1982/145 of 7 May 1982 and of resolution 1982/40 of 11 March 1982 of the Commission on Human Rights, decided to consider the question of rescheduling the annual session of the Commission on Human Rights at the second regular session of 1983 of the Council, in the context of its consideration of the draft calendar of conferences and meetings for the biennium 1984-1985.

Report on the 1982 session

On 7 May 1982,[1] the Economic and Social Council took note of the report of the Commission on Human Rights on its thirty-eighth session,[2] held at Geneva from 11 February to 12 March. The decision, recommended by the Commission, was adopted without vote, following similar approval by the Second Committee on 3 May.

Decision (1982). [1]ESC: 1982/142, 7 May, text following.
Report. [2]Commission on Human Rights, E/1982/12.
Meeting record. ESC: E/1982/SR.29 (7 May).

Economic and Social Council decision 1982/142

Adopted without vote

Approved by Second Committee (E/1982/59) without vote, 3 May (meeting 16); draft by Commission on Human Rights (E/1982/12); agenda item 9.

Report of the Commission on Human Rights

At its 29th plenary meeting, on 7 May 1982, the Council took note of the report of the Commission on Human Rights on its thirty-eighth session.

Sub-Commission on discrimination and minorities

Terms of reference and activities

On 10 March 1982,[1] the Commission on Human Rights called on the Sub-Commission on Prevention of Discrimination and Protection of Minorities to be guided in the fulfilment of its duties by relevant resolutions of the Commission, the Economic and Social Council and the General Assembly. It requested the Sub-Commission to take into account comments and suggestions made during the Commission's consideration of the Sub-Commission's report on its 1981 session, and to attach to future reports a list of studies under

preparation with information on their legislative authority and the timetable for completion.

It also considered that, when alternates were temporarily appointed in place of members, they must have the requisite expertise and qualifications. The appointment of a government official, it added, might sometimes not be in keeping with the character of the Sub-Commission as a body of experts.

Resolution (1982). [1]Commission on Human Rights (report, E/1982/12): 1982/23, 10 Mar.

Establishment of the Centre for Human Rights

On 18 December 1982,[3] acting without vote, the General Assembly, recalling a 1980 resolution[7] requesting the Secretary-General to keep under consideration the Secretariat's services relating to human rights, took note of his decision to redesignate the Division of Human Rights as the Centre for Human Rights effective 28 July 1982. Introduced and orally revised by Ireland and sponsored also by Italy and Senegal, the decision had been similarly approved by the Third (Social, Humanitarian and Cultural) Committee on 1 December.

Also on 18 December, in a resolution on the advancement of human rights,[5] the Assembly requested the Secretary-General to take measures to strengthen the Centre. The Third Committee had approved this provision on 1 December by a recorded vote of 70 to 24, with 28 abstentions. A proposed amendment would have reworded this paragraph to request the Secretary-General to ensure that adequate resources were made available to the Centre.[1]

Two amendments relating to the Centre[2] were also proposed to a second Assembly resolution of the same date on the advancement of human rights.[4] They would have inserted a new preambular paragraph expressing awareness of the need to allocate appropriate resources to strengthen the Centre and a new operative paragraph requesting the Secretary-General to take measures to strengthen it.

On 18 December, the Assembly decided to take no action on the proposed amendments (see above).

In a resolution of 21 December, relating to the United Nations programme budget for 1982-1983,[6] the Assembly approved the reclassification of the head of the Centre to Assistant Secretary-General.

Amendments not acted upon. [1]Algeria, Argentina, Bolivia, Cuba, Ethiopia, India, Indonesia, Pakistan, Panama, Yugoslavia, A/37/L.56; [2]Australia, Belgium, Greece, Ireland, Italy, Netherlands, A/37/L.57.
Decision (1982). [3]GA: 37/437, 18 Dec., text following.
Resolutions (1982). GA: [4]37/199, 18 Dec.; [5]37/200, para. 13, 18 Dec.; [6]37/237, sect. XII, para. *(b)* (ii), 21 Dec.
Resolution (prior). [7]GA: 35/194, 15 Dec. 1980 (YUN 1980, p. 872).
Meeting records. GA: 3rd Committee, A/C.3/37/SR.*49, 59, 60* (22 Nov.–1 Dec.); plenary, A/37/PV.111 (18 Dec.).

General Assembly decision 37/437

Adopted without vote

Approved by Third Committee (A/37/693) without vote, 1 December (meeting 60); 3-nation draft (A/C.3/37/L.42), orally revised; agenda item 94.

Sponsors: Ireland, Italy, Senegal.

Centre for Human Rights

At its 111th plenary meeting, on 18 December 1982, the General Assembly, on the recommendation of the Third Committee, recalling its resolution 35/194 of 15 December 1980, in which it requested the Secretary-General to keep under consideration the question of the services of the Secretariat concerned with human rights, with a view to redesignating the Division of Human Rights as a Centre for Human Rights when he deemed it appropriate, took note of the decision of the Secretary-General to redesignate the Division of Human Rights as the Centre for Human Rights.

Proposed post of UN
High Commissioner for Human Rights

The establishment of a post of United Nations High Commissioner for Human Rights, proposed for the first time in 1965 by Costa Rica,[9] was discussed again in 1982 by the Commission on Human Rights, its Sub-Commission on Prevention of Discrimination and Protection of Minorities and the General Assembly.

Action by the Commission on Human Rights. On 10 March,[4] the Commission on Human Rights requested the Sub-Commission to submit a first study on possible terms of reference for the mandate of a High Commissioner in 1983, when it would resume consideration of the matter. The Commission, which took up the matter in accordance with a December 1981 request by the General Assembly,[8] adopted its resolution by a roll-call vote of 29 to 8 (Bulgaria, Byelorussian SSR, Cuba, Ethiopia, Philippines, Poland, Syrian Arab Republic, USSR), with 6 abstentions.

On 11 March,[5] in a resolution on its future work programme (see above), the Commission decided to inform the Assembly, through the Economic and Social Council, that it intended to continue consideration of the proposal for a High Commissioner.

Sub-Commission action. On 10 September,[7] by 10 votes to 6, with 4 abstentions, the Sub-Commission submitted proposals to the Commission on the possible terms of reference for a High Commissioner. It suggested that he should have the following functions and responsibilities: to promote and protect human rights; to give special attention to ensuring civil, political, economic, social and cultural rights and others as recognized by the Charter of the United Nations and the Assembly; to initiate contacts with Governments to safeguard or assist in restoring human rights, especially in urgent situations; and to consider as areas of special concern massive violations such as *apartheid*, racism, racial discrimination, colonial domination, foreign occupation and alien subjugation.

The High Commissioner would make similar contacts with Governments in cases of mass and flagrant violations requiring urgent action, consult with the United Nations system, including the Centre for Human Rights, and establish a temporary inter-agency task force to facilitate co-ordinated action. He would carry out specific mandates assigned by the Assembly, the Economic and Social Council and the Commission, and report annually to those bodies. The Sub-Commission suggested that the officers of the Commission act as an advisory committee to the High Commissioner, and that he should be nominated by the Secretary-General and elected by the Assembly for a period of five years, serving no more than two consecutive terms. It also suggested that a Deputy High Commissioner, in principle from a different region, be elected in the same manner.

To assist the Sub-Commission in making its recommendations, an informal working group submitted a synopsis, prepared by the United Nations Secretariat, of proposals presented to the Commission and the Assembly.[3] The group had been set up by the Sub-Commission on 23 August by 9 votes to 5, with the object of preparing a report on possible terms of reference for the mandate of a High Commissioner.[2]

General Assembly action. In a resolution of 18 December,[6] the General Assembly requested the Commission to continue efforts in 1983 to improve the United Nations capacity for urgent action in cases of serious human rights violations, bearing in mind the Sub-Commission's proposals on possible terms of reference for the draft mandate of a High Commissioner. Based on a proposal by Morocco, the sponsors orally revised this paragraph to refer to the "draft" mandate.

The revised paragraph was approved by the Third Committee on 1 December by a recorded vote of 65 to 32, with 26 abstentions. Prior to the vote, Argentina and the Byelorussian SSR orally proposed that the paragraph be deleted. The Committee did not vote on these amendments after the Chairman ruled that they had been submitted too late.

Costa Rica said if those opposed to the establishment of a High Commissioner were to examine the possible mandate, they would not have to be concerned about selective accusations of individual States of human rights violations.

Voting against the paragraph, the Byelorussian SSR termed it vague and said it might prejudge the results of the Commission's work and no mandate had been established for a High Commissioner.

Abstaining, the Philippines said the paragraph was premature and should be deleted.

Among a set of amendments submitted to the Assembly by 10 countries,[1] one would have reworded the paragraph to request the Commission to continue consideration of mass and flagrant human rights violations, bearing in mind Assembly and Commission resolutions, omitting reference to the High Commissioner. The amendments were not acted on by the Assembly.

Amendments not acted upon. [1]Algeria, Argentina, Bolivia, Cuba, Ethiopia, India, Indonesia, Pakistan, Panama, Yugoslavia, A/37/L.56.
Decision (1982). [2]SCPDPM (report, E/CN.4/1983/4): 1982/5, 23 Aug.
Report. [3]Informal working group, E/CN.4/Sub.2/1982/36.
Resolutions (1982). Commission on Human Rights (report, E/1982/12): [4]1982/22, 10 Mar.; [5]1982/40, para. 8, 11 Mar. [6]GA: 37/200, para. 12, 18 Dec. [7]SCPDPM: 1982/27, 10 Sep.
Resolution (prior). [8]GA: 36/135, 14 Dec. 1981 (YUN 1981, p. 932).
Yearbook reference. [9]1965, p. 494.

International human rights instruments

International Covenants on Human Rights

As at 31 December 1982, the International Covenants on Economic, Social and Cultural Rights and on Civil and Political Rights, which were adopted by the General Assembly in 1966[4] and entered into force in 1976,[6] had been ratified or acceded to by 75 and 72 States, respectively. In 1982, four States became parties to the Covenant on Economic, Social and Cultural Rights, while three became parties to the Covenant on Civil and Political Rights. During the year, one State adhered to the Optional Protocol to the latter Covenant, raising to 28 the number of States parties to that instrument.

A report of the Secretary-General to the Assembly included a list of States which, as at 1 September 1982, had signed, ratified or acceded to the Covenants and the Optional Protocol.[1]

Action by the Commission on Human Rights. On 9 March,[2] the Commission on Human Rights reaffirmed the importance of the Covenants in promoting human rights. Emphasizing the importance of strict compliance, it urged States to become parties to the Covenants and to accede to the Optional Protocol. The Commission took note of a provision of a November 1981 Assembly resolution[5] requesting the Secretary-General to ensure the Division of Human Rights' ability to assist the Human Rights Committee and the Economic and Social Council in implementing their functions under the Covenants. It encouraged Governments to publish and distribute the texts of the Covenants, and requested the Secretary-General to report on their status in 1983, including information on the work of the Council and its Sessional Working Group on implementation of the International Covenant on Economic, Social and Cultural Rights. The Commission also took note of measures adopted to facilitate implementation of the Covenants and welcomed the Secretary-General's effort to improve publicity for the work of the Human Rights Committee.

General Assembly action. On 18 December 1982,[3] the General Assembly, again inviting States to become parties to the Covenants as well as to consider acceding to the Optional Protocol, emphasized the importance of States parties sending experts to present their reports under the Covenants. It requested the Secretary-General to continue to ensure the ability of the Centre for Human Rights to assist the Human Rights Committee and the Council in the implementation of their functions under the Covenants.

The Assembly urged States parties to the Covenants to submit their reports. Other provisions concerned a request for publishing the official records of the Human Rights Committee and arrangements for the Council's Sessional Working Group.

Adopted without vote by the Assembly, the 16-nation draft, introduced and orally revised by Denmark, had been similarly approved by the Third Committee on 7 December.

Report. [1]S-G, A/37/406.
Resolutions (1982). [2]Commission on Human Rights (report, E/1982/12): 1982/18, 9 Mar. [3]GA: 37/191, 18 Dec., text following.
Resolutions (prior). GA: [4]2200 A (XXI), annex, 16 Dec. 1966 (YUN 1966, p. 419); [5]36/58, 25 Nov. 1981 (YUN 1981, p. 934).
Yearbook reference. [6]1976, p. 609.
Meeting records. GA: 3rd Committee, A/C.3/37/SR.47, 50-53, 55, 56, *58, 67* (18 Nov.–7 Dec.); plenary, A/37/PV.111 (18 Dec.).
Publication. Human Rights: A Compilation of International Instruments (adopted up to 31 December 1982), Sales No. E.83.XIV.1.

General Assembly resolution 37/191

18 December 1982   Meeting 111   Adopted without vote

Approved by Third Committee (A/37/718) without vote, 7 December (meeting 67); 16-nation draft (A/C.3/37/L.51), orally revised; agenda item 87.

Sponsors: Australia, Canada, Central African Republic, Costa Rica, Cyprus, Denmark, Ecuador, Finland, Iceland, Italy, Netherlands, Nicaragua, Norway, Peru, Senegal, Sweden.

International Covenants on Human Rights
The General Assembly,
Recalling its resolutions 33/51 of 14 December 1978, 34/45 of 23 November 1979, 35/132 of 11 December 1980 and 36/58 of 25 November 1981,
Having noted the report of the Secretary-General on the status of the International Covenant on Economic, Social and Cultural Rights, the International Covenant on Civil and Political Rights and the Optional Protocol to the International Covenant on Civil and Political Rights,
Noting with appreciation that, following its appeal, more Member States have acceded to the International Covenants on Human Rights,
Bearing in mind the important responsibilities of the Economic and Social Council in relation to the International Covenants on Human Rights,
Recognizing the important role of the Human Rights Committee in the implementation of the International Covenant on Civil and Political Rights and the Optional Protocol thereto,
Taking into account the useful work of the Sessional Working Group of Governmental Experts on the Implementation of the International Covenant on Economic, Social and Cultural Rights,
Taking note of Economic and Social Council resolution 1980/30 of 2 May 1980 on the development of public information activities in the field of human rights and the report of the Secretary-General on publicity for the work of the Human Rights Committee,

1. *Notes with appreciation* the report of the Human Rights Committee on its fourteenth, fifteenth and sixteenth sessions, and expresses satisfaction at the serious and constructive manner in which the Committee is continuing to perform its functions;

2. *Expresses its appreciation* to those States parties to the International Covenant on Civil and Political Rights that have extended their co-operation to the Human Rights Committee in submitting their reports under article 40 of the Covenant and urges States parties that have not yet done so to submit their reports to the Committee as speedily as possible;

3. *Urges* those States parties to the International Covenant on Civil and Political Rights that have been requested by the Human Rights Committee to provide additional information to comply with that request;

4. *Commends* those States parties to the International Covenant on Economic, Social and Cultural Rights that have submitted their reports under article 16 of the Covenant and urges States that have not yet done so to submit their reports as soon as possible;

5. *Takes note* of Economic and Social Council resolution 1982/33 of 6 May 1982 concerning the review of the composition, organization and administrative arrangements of the Sessional Working Group of Governmental Experts on the Implementation of the International Covenant on Economic, Social and Cultural Rights;

6. *Emphasizes* the importance of States parties sending experts to present their reports under the International Covenants on Human Rights;

7. *Again invites* all States that have not yet done so to become parties to the International Covenant on Economic, Social and Cultural Rights and the International Covenant on Civil and Political Rights as well as to consider acceding to the Optional Protocol to the International Covenant on Civil and Political Rights;

8. *Invites* the States parties to the International Covenant on Civil and Political Rights to consider making the declaration provided for in article 41 of the Covenant;

9. *Appreciates* that the Human Rights Committee continues to strive for uniform standards in the implementation of the provisions of the International Covenant on Civil and Political Rights and of the Optional Protocol thereto;

10. *Emphasizes* the importance of strictest compliance by States parties with their obligations under the International Covenant on Civil and Political Rights and, where applicable, the Optional Protocol thereto;

11. *Requests* the Secretary-General to continue to keep the Human Rights Committee informed of the activities of the Commission on Human Rights, the Sub-Commission on Prevention of Discrimination and Protection of Minorities, the Committee on the Elimination of Racial Discrimination and the Committee on the Elimination of Discrimination against Women and also to transmit the annual reports of the Human Rights Committee to those bodies;

12. *Requests* the Secretary-General to submit to the General Assembly at its thirty-eighth session a report on the status of the International Covenant on Economic, Social and Cultural Rights, the International Covenant on Civil and Political Rights and the Optional Protocol to the International Covenant on Civil and Political Rights;

13. *Takes note with appreciation* of the request of the Human Rights Committee that its official records be made available annually in bound volumes—one volume to contain the summary records of public meetings of the Committee and a second volume to contain other public documents of the Committee, including reports of States parties under article 40 of the Covenant—and requests the Secretary-General to consider making, within existing resources, the arrangements which he deems most suitable and economical for publishing those annual volumes;

14. *Requests* the Secretary-General to continue to take all possible steps to ensure that the Centre for Human Rights of the Secretariat is able effectively to assist the Human Rights Committee and the Economic and Social Council in the implementation of their respective functions under the International Covenants on Human Rights, taking into account General Assembly resolutions 3534(XXX) of 17 December 1975 and 31/93 of 14 December 1976.

Accessions and ratifications

A sessional Working Group on the Encouragement of Universal Acceptance of Human Rights Instruments, established in pursuance of a 1979 decision of the Sub-Commission on discrimination and minorities[11] and composed of five of its members, met from 23 to 26 August 1982 at Geneva to examine ways of encouraging government adherence and information on obstacles to such adherence.[1] The Group examined replies by 22 Governments to the Secretary-General's notes verbales inviting adherence to international human rights instruments, such as: the International Covenants, the International Convention on the Elimination of All Forms of Racial Discrimination,[8] the Convention on the Prevention and Punishment of the Crime of Genocide,[5] the International Convention on the Suppression and Punishment of the Crime of *Apartheid*,[9] the 1926 Slavery Convention and the 1953 Protocol amending it,[7] and the 1956 Supplementary Convention on the Abolition of Slavery, the Slave Trade, and Institutions and Practices Similar to Slavery.[10]

On 7 September,[4] the Sub-Commission expressed appreciation to those Governments which had conveyed information on their adherence to human rights instruments and took note of the Working Group's report. As recommended by the Group, the Sub-Commission requested the Secretary-General to invite Governments to submit information on the circumstances preventing them from becoming parties and requested him to prepare an analysis of replies. It decided to include the 1949 Convention for the Suppression of the Traffic in Persons and of the Exploitation of the Prostitution of Others[6] in the list of instruments whose universal acceptance was to be encouraged.

The General Assembly, by a resolution of 18 December on measures for the advancement of human rights,[2] reaffirmed that it was of paramount importance for human rights that Member States undertake specific obligations through adherence to international human rights instruments. It also reaffirmed that standard-setting work within the United Nations and the universal acceptance and implementation of international instruments should be encouraged.

In another 18 December resolution on the same topic, the Assembly requested Member States that had not done so to consider ratifying or acceding to the various human rights conventions.[3]

Report. [1]Working Group, E/CN.4/Sub.2/1982/22.
Resolutions (1982). GA, 18 Dec.: [2]37/199, para. 2; [3]37/200, para. 10. [4]SCPDPM (report, E/CN.4/1983/4): 1982/3, paras. 1-6, 7 Sep.
Resolutions (prior). GA: [5]260 A (III), annex, 9 Dec. 1948 (YUN 1948-49, p. 959); [6]317(IV), annex, 2 Dec. 1949 (*ibid.*, p. 613); [7]794(VIII), 23 Oct. 1953 (YUN 1953, p. 411); [8]2106 A (XX), annex, 21 Dec. 1965 (YUN 1965, p. 440); [9]3068(XXVIII), annex, 30 Nov. 1973 (YUN 1973, p. 103).
Yearbook references. [10]1956, p. 228; [11]1979, p. 854.
Publication. Human Rights International Instruments: Signatures, Ratifications, Accessions, etc., 1 July 1982, ST/HR/4/Rev.4.

Other measures to advance human rights

Advisory services

In 1982, as reported by the Secretary-General to the Commission on Human Rights,[1] a seminar for the Asian region was held under the United Nations programme of advisory services in the field of human rights (see below). No training course was held under the programme in 1982.

During the year, 32 individual human rights fellowships were granted to nationals of the following countries:

Argentina, Australia, Bahamas, China, Cuba, Cyprus, Czechoslovakia, Democratic Yemen, Ecuador, Egypt, Ethiopia, Fiji, Gabon, Greece, Honduras, Hungary, India, Israel, Italy, Madagascar, Nepal, Papua New Guinea, Poland, Portugal, Senegal, Sudan, Suriname, Thailand, USSR, United Republic of Tanzania, Uruguay, Viet Nam.

The fellowships included awards for study of human rights of indigenous populations; convicted and released offenders; immigrants and resident aliens; minorities; refugees and Stateless persons; children; youth; freedom of information; judiciary procedures; and other social and economic as well as civil and political factors.

In compliance with a request from Equatorial Guinea, the Secretary-General provided that Government with two experts to assist in the drafting of a new constitution. The Commission requested him to provide consultative advisory services to Uganda to help the Government take measures to guarantee human rights (see below).

Report. [1]S-G, E/CN.4/1983/30.

Equatorial Guinea

The Economic and Social Council, on 7 May 1982,[5] took note of a plan of action proposed by the Secretary-General in August 1981 for the restoration of human rights in Equatorial Guinea. Regretting the delay in implementing the plan, the Council requested the Secretary-General to discuss with Equatorial Guinea the role the United Nations could play in implementing it, and invited that Government to co-operate. The Secretary-General was further requested to report to the Council later in 1982 and the Commission on Human Rights in 1983.

The resolution, adopted without vote, originated in a draft approved on 11 March by the Commission[4] and by the Council's Second (Social) Committee on 3 May, also without vote.

The draft plan of action,[2] based on recommendations of a United Nations expert,[6] was submitted to the Commission's February/March session. The Secretary-General informed the Commission that, as at December 1981, no response from Equatorial Guinea had been received.

In a second report, submitted in November 1982,[3] the Secretary-General informed the Commission of steps taken to implement the plan of action. Two constitutional experts, Rubén Hernández-Valle (Costa Rica) and Jorge Mario Laguardia (Guatemala), had been appointed to assist the Equatorial Guinea National Commission in drafting a constitution. The Constitution's final text had been promulgated on 3 August and subsequently approved.

On 27 July,[1] acting without vote on an oral proposal by its President, the Council took note of an oral report presented that day by the Deputy Director of the Division of Human Rights, describing steps taken to implement the plan of action.

Decision (1982). [1]ESC: 1982/150, 27 July, text following.
Reports. S-G, [2]E/CN.4/1495, [3]E/CN.4/1983/17.
Resolutions (1982). [4]Commission on Human Rights (report, E/1982/12): 1982/34, 11 Mar. [5]ESC: 1982/36, 7 May, text following.
Yearbook reference. [6]1981, p. 938.
Meeting records. ESC: E/1982/SR.28, 48 (7 May, 27 July).

Economic and Social Council resolution 1982/36

7 May 1982   Meeting 28   Adopted without vote

Approved by Second Committee (E/1982/59) without vote, 3 May (meeting 15); draft by Commission on Human Rights (E/1982/12); agenda item 9.

Situation of human rights in Equatorial Guinea

The Economic and Social Council,

Recalling its resolution 1981/38 of 8 May 1981 and its decision 1981/167 of 16 July 1981,

Bearing in mind resolution 1982/34 of 11 March 1982 of the Commission on Human Rights,

Mindful of the role that the United Nations could play in the promotion, the protection and the restoration of human rights and fundamental freedoms in the world,

Conscious of the request of the Government of Equatorial Guinea for assistance in the restoration of human rights and fundamental freedoms in that country with a view to ensuring, in particular, the right of the population to participate in the management of public affairs in the country,

1. *Takes note* of the plan of action proposed by the Secretary-General on the basis of recommendations submitted by the expert appointed pursuant to resolution 33(XXXVI) of 11 March 1980 of the Commission on Human Rights;

2. *Regrets* the delay in the implementation of the measures envisaged in the plan of action;

3. *Requests* the Secretary-General, with expert assistance if necessary, to discuss with the Government of Equatorial Guinea the role that the United Nations could play in the implementation of the plan of action;

4. *Invites* the Government of Equatorial Guinea to co-operate with the Secretary-General in this respect;

5. *Requests* the Secretary-General to inform the Economic and Social Council at its second regular session of 1982 of the steps taken to implement the present resolution and to report further to the Commission on Human Rights at its thirty-ninth session;

6. *Requests* the Commission on Human Rights to review this question at its thirty-ninth session.

Economic and Social Council decision 1982/150

Adopted without vote

Oral proposal by President; agenda item 6.

Situation of human rights in Equatorial Guinea

At its 48th plenary meeting, on 27 July 1982, the Council took note of the oral report made by the representative of the Secretary-General in pursuance of Council resolution 1982/36 of 7 May 1982 on the situation of human rights in Equatorial Guinea.

Uganda

On 11 March 1982,[3] the Commission on Human Rights requested the Secretary-General to establish contact with the Government of Uganda to provide advisory services assisting it in guaranteeing human rights, especially with regard to restoring a law library for the High Court and Ministry of Justice; an expert to serve as Commissioner for the revision of Ugandan laws and the printing of revised laws; and the training of prison officers and police officials to secure application of recognized norms of treatment of prisoners. The Commission invited States, specialized agencies, United Nations organs, and humanitarian and non-governmental organizations to assist Uganda. It decided to review the question in 1983 in the light of the Secretary-General's report on the implementation of this resolution.

On 7 May,[1] the Economic and Social Council approved the Commission's decision. Originating in the Commission, the text was adopted without vote, following similar approval by the Second Committee on 3 May.

In December,[2] the Secretary-General reported on steps taken to provide the advisory services. He informed the Commission that he was awaiting Uganda's final proposal of possible projects for which assistance might be required.

Decision (1982). [1]ESC: 1982/139, 7 May, text following.
Report. [2]S-G, E/CN.4/1983/31.
Resolution (1982). [3]Commission on Human Rights (report, E/1982/12): 1982/37, 11 Mar.
Meeting record. ESC: E/1982/SR.29 (7 May).

Economic and Social Council decision 1982/139

Adopted without vote

Approved by Second Committee (E/1982/69) without vote, 3 May (meeting 15); draft by Commission on Human Rights (E/1982/12); agenda item 9.

Advisory services in the field of human rights: assistance to Uganda

At its 29th plenary meeting, on 7 May 1982, the Council approved the decision taken by the Commission on Human Rights, in its resolution 1982/37 of 11 March 1982, to request the Secretary-General, in response to the interest expressed by the Government of Uganda, to provide consultative advisory services and other forms of appropriate assistance to help the Government of Uganda to take measures to continue guaranteeing the enjoyment of human rights and fundamental freedoms, paying particular attention to the following areas: *(a)* the need for appropriate assistance to restore a law library for the High Court and Ministry of Justice; *(b)* the need for a qualified and experienced expert to serve as Commissioner for the revision of Ugandan laws in conformity with recognized norms of human rights and fundamental freedoms, and the printing of consolidated volumes of the revised laws; *(c)* the need for the training of prison officers with a view to securing the application of recognized norms of treatment of prisoners; and *(d)* the need for the training of police officials, particularly investigative and scientific experts.

Draft declaration on promotion of human rights

On 11 March 1982,[2] the Commission on Human Rights reiterated the right and responsibility of individuals, groups and organs of society to promote and protect the rights recognized in international human rights instruments. It emphasized that the individual was subject only to limitations determined in such instruments and that the imposition of limitations on, or persecution or punishment of, any individual or group exercising those rights was at variance with States' obligations. It requested the Secretary-General to present the Sub-Commission on Prevention of Discrimination and Protection of Minorities with elements for a draft body of principles on the right and responsibility of individuals, groups and organs of society to promote human rights. It requested the Sub-Commission to submit a report on those principles in 1984, when it would undertake work on a draft declaration.

On 8 September,[3] the Sub-Commission, noting the Secretary-General's report,[1] reiterated the right to promote rights recognized in international instruments and deplored all attempts to prevent or punish such promotion. The Sub-Commission requested one of its members, Erica-Irene A. Daes (Greece), to prepare and submit in 1983 draft principles, taking into account information from Governments, specialized agencies, and regional intergovernmental and non-governmental organizations.

Report. [1]S-G, E/CN.4/Sub.2/1982/12.
Resolutions (1982). [2]Commission on Human Rights (report, E/1982/12 & Corr.1): 1982/30, 11 Mar. [3]SCPDPM (report, E/CN.4/1983/4): 1982/24, 8 Sep.

Proposed establishment of a new international humanitarian order

On 18 December 1982,[2] the General Assembly requested Governments that had not done so to communicate their views to the Secretary-General on the proposal for the promotion of a new international humanitarian order, advanced by Jordan in October 1981.[4] Taking note of a September 1982 report of the Secretary-General,[1] requested by the Assembly in December 1981,[3] it invited him to provide a more comprehensive report in 1983.

The resolution was adopted without vote, following similar approval by the Third (Social, Humanitarian and Cultural) Committee on 10 December. The draft was introduced by Jordan, also on behalf of Australia, Djibouti, Iraq, Italy, Morocco, Oman, Pakistan and Romania.

In his report, the Secretary-General stated that, as at 10 July, 23 Governments had submitted their views on a new international humanitarian order. All had supported the intentions underlying the proposal and several had suggested practical measures. Most Governments had stressed the complexity of the issue, and five States had suggested setting up an international commission of experts and specialists to study the question.

Following a separate initiative by the Philippines, the Assembly, in December, referred to the

Economic and Social Council a proposal for the drafting of a declaration on a new international human order (see Chapter I of this section).

Report. [1]S-G, A/37/145.
Resolution (1982). [2]GA: 37/201, 18 Dec., text following.
Resolution (prior). [3]GA: 36/136, 14 Dec. 1981 (YUN 1981, p. 969).
Yearbook reference. [4]1981, p. 968.
Meeting records. GA: 3rd Committee, A/C.3/37/SR.15, *75* (19 Oct., 10 Dec.); plenary, A/37/PV.111 (18 Dec.).

General Assembly resolution 37/201

18 December 1982   Meeting 111   Adopted without vote

Approved by Third Committee (A/37/746) without vote, 10 December (meeting 75); 9-nation draft (A/C.3/37/L.80); agenda item 95.

Sponsors: Australia, Djibouti, Iraq, Italy, Jordan, Morocco, Oman, Pakistan, Romania.

New international humanitarian order

The General Assembly,

Recalling its resolution 36/136 of 14 December 1981,

Taking note of the report of the Secretary-General,

Bearing in mind that, as noted by the Secretary-General in his report, all Governments that provided their views on the proposal for the promotion of a new international humanitarian order supported the intentions underlying the proposal and the need for developing greater international awareness of humanitarian issues and more effective means of dealing with such issues,

Recognizing the need for again seeking the views of Governments that have not yet provided them to the Secretary-General,

Noting the proposal for the establishment, outside the framework of the United Nations, of an independent commission on international humanitarian issues, composed of leading personalities in the humanitarian field or having wide experience of government or world affairs,

Recognizing further that the deliberations of such a commission, if established, could be useful for further study of the proposal,

1. *Requests* Governments that have not yet done so to communicate their views on the proposal for the promotion of a new international humanitarian order to the Secretary-General;

2. *Invites* the Secretary-General to provide a more comprehensive report on the subject to the General Assembly at its thirty-eighth session;

3. *Decides* to review at its thirty-eighth session the question of a new international humanitarian order.

Regional arrangements

On 17 December 1982,[1] the General Assembly noted the progress achieved in promoting human rights at the regional level. It commended the Organization of African Unity (OAU) for its efforts to promote respect for human rights, and noted the African Charter on Human and Peoples' Rights (adopted by OAU in 1981). The Assembly requested the Secretary-General to submit in 1983 compiled, updated reports on the status of regional arrangements for the promotion of human rights, including a review of the exchanges of experience and information between the United Nations and regional organs and organizations, as well as ways to further those exchanges.

Adopted without vote, the 13-nation draft, introduced and orally revised by Belgium, had been similarly approved by the Third Committee on 9 December.

Resolution (1982). [1]GA: 37/172, 17 Dec., text following.
Meeting records. GA: 3rd Committee, A/C.3/37/SR.62, 63, *64, 65-71, 72, 74* (3-10 Dec.); plenary, A/37/PV.110 (17 Dec.).

General Assembly resolution 37/172

17 December 1982   Meeting 110   Adopted without vote

Approved by Third Committee (A/37/745) without vote, 9 December (meeting 72); 13-nation draft (A/C.3/37/L.72), orally revised; agenda item 12.

Sponsors: Australia, Belgium, Costa Rica, Cyprus, Egypt, France, Ghana, Guinea, Italy, Mali, Netherlands, Senegal, Togo.

Regional arrangements for the protection of human rights

The General Assembly,

Recalling its resolutions 32/127 of 16 December 1977, 33/167 of 20 December 1978, 34/171 of 17 December 1979, 35/197 of 15 December 1980 and 36/154 of 16 December 1981 concerning regional arrangements for the promotion and protection of human rights,

Noting the regional arrangements which exist in the African, American, Arab and European regions and also the efforts which are currently under way to initiate Commonwealth activities in the area of human rights,

Welcoming recent developments in the Asian region with a view to consideration of appropriate arrangements for the promotion and protection of human rights,

Noting that the United Nations and regional intergovernmental organizations exchange information and materials on the promotion and protection of human rights,

1. *Notes with satisfaction* the progress achieved so far in the promotion and protection of human rights at the regional level, under the auspices of the United Nations, the specialized agencies and the regional intergovernmental organizations;

2. *Commends* the Organization of African Unity for its continuing efforts to promote respect for the guarantees and norms of human rights and fundamental freedoms and notes with interest the African Charter on Human and Peoples' Rights and the efforts to obtain its early entry into force;

3. *Requests* the Secretary-General to compile and update his reports on the status of regional arrangements for the promotion and protection of human rights and to include therein a review of the exchanges of experience and information between the United Nations and regional organs and organizations for the promotion and protection of human rights, as well as ways and means to further these exchanges, and to report to the General Assembly at its thirty-eighth session.

Asia and the Pacific

From 21 June to 2 July 1982,[1] Sri Lanka hosted at Colombo a Seminar on National, Local and Regional Arrangements for the Promotion and Protection of Human Rights in the Asian Region. Organized by the Secretary-General under the United Nations programme of advisory services in human rights, this was the first such seminar held in Asia. It was arranged in line with past recommendations of the Commission on Human Rights and the General Assembly that seminars be held to discuss the establishment of regional human rights commission in regions lacking them. The agenda included an exchange of experience and information on national and local institutions for human rights promotion, discussion of existing or proposed regional arrangements elsewhere in the world, and consideration of further regional co-operation in the Asian region.

The Seminar recommended: that States members of the Economic and Social Commission for Asia and the Pacific (ESCAP) be encouraged to ratify the basic international human rights instruments; that the United Nations and other organizations consider ways of assisting Governments to prepare legislation enforcing those instruments;

that the United Nations, including ESCAP, carry out studies and research, organize seminars, symposia and conferences, and disseminate information on human rights, with the United Nations and the United Nations Educational, Scientific and Cultural Organization and United Nations information centres playing an important role.

On 17 December,[2] the Assembly took note of the Seminar's report and its conclusions and recommendations, adopted by consensus. It requested the Secretary-General to transmit the report to ESCAP members, to invite their comments, to submit the report with their comments to the Commission on Human Rights, and to report through the Economic and Social Council to the Assembly in 1984.

Adopted without vote following similar approval on 9 December by the Third Committee, the resolution was introduced by Sri Lanka on behalf of 14 countries.

Report, [1]Seminar, ST/HR/SER.A/12 (transmitted by S-G report, A/37/422).
Resolution (1982). [2]GA: 37/171, 17 Dec., text following.
Meeting records. GA: 3rd Committee, A/C.3/37/SR.*64, 72* (6, 9 Dec.); plenary, A/37/PV.110 (17 Dec.).

General Assembly resolution 37/171

17 December 1982   Meeting 110   Adopted without vote

Approved by Third Committee (A/37/745) without vote, 9 December (meeting 72); 14-nation draft (A/C.3/37/L.47); agenda item 12.

Sponsors: Australia, Bangladesh, Bhutan, Cyprus, India, Ireland, Kenya, Morocco, Nepal, New Zealand, Nigeria, Pakistan, Papua New Guinea, Sri Lanka.

Regional arrangements for the promotion and protection of human rights

The General Assembly,

Recalling its resolutions 34/171 of 17 December 1979 and 35/197 of 15 December 1980 on regional arrangements for the promotion and protection of human rights, as well as its resolution 36/154 of 16 December 1981, in which it requested the Secretary-General to organize a seminar at Colombo, in 1982, to consider appropriate arrangements for the promotion and protection of human rights in the Asian region and to report to the General Assembly at its thirty-seventh session,

Having considered the report of the Seminar on National, Local and Regional Arrangements for the Promotion and Protection of Human Rights in the Asian Region, held at Colombo from 21 June to 2 July 1982,

1. *Expresses its deep appreciation* to the Government of Sri Lanka for acting as host to the Seminar on National, Local and Regional Arrangements for the Promotion and Protection of Human Rights in the Asian Region, as well as for the excellent facilities provided;

2. *Takes note* of the report of the Seminar, as well as of the conclusions and recommendations which it adopted by consensus;

3. *Requests* the Secretary-General to transmit the report of the Seminar to States members of the Economic and Social Commission for Asia and the Pacific, to invite their comments thereon and to submit the report of the Seminar, together with the comments received thereon, to the Commission on Human Rights at its fortieth session for its consideration, and to report through the Economic and Social Council to the General Assembly at its thirty-ninth session;

4. *Decides* to consider this question further at its thirty-ninth session.

Public information activities

The Commission on Human Rights, on 11 March 1982,[1] requested Governments to continue consideration of action to facilitate publicity for United Nations human rights activities, with particular reference to the Commission's work in setting standards. It invited the Secretary-General to give increased attention to stimulating public interest in human rights promotion and to report to the Commission in 1983. The Commission welcomed the launching of a dissemination programme for international human rights instruments (planned by the Secretary-General to start in 1982-1983)[2] and requested him to report annually to the Commission on its implementation. It recommended that the United Nations compile translations of international instruments, including in those languages other than official United Nations ones, and invited Governments which had authorized translations to send copies to the United Nations Division on Human Rights.

The Commission requested the Secretary-General to consider establishing, in United Nations offices, particularly in developing countries, reference libraries containing material on human rights. It requested him to keep the Commission informed on the implementation of this request and other public information programmes.

Resolution (1982). [1]Commission on Human Rights (report, E/1982/12): 1982/42, 11 Mar.
Yearbook reference. [2]1981, p. 940.

Human rights violations

Situations involving alleged violations of human rights on a large scale in several countries (see below) were again examined in 1982 by the General Assembly, the Economic and Social Council and the Commission on Human Rights, as well as by special bodies and officials appointed to examine some of these situations. The Assembly and/or Council took action on South Africa and Namibia, as well as on Bolivia, Chile, El Salvador, Guatemala, Poland and the territories occupied by Israel. Situations in Cyprus, East Timor and Iran were raised before the Commission and its Sub-Commission on Prevention of Discrimination and Protection of Minorities. The problems of mass exoduses, genocide and procedures for examining human rights violations were also under study.

In addition, situations of alleged human rights violations involving the self-determination of peoples (see above) were discussed with regard to Afghanistan, Kampuchea and Western Sahara. The United Nations offered advisory services to Equatorial Guinea and Uganda, where human rights violations under former régimes had been reported.

Under a procedure established in 1970 by the Council to deal with communications alleging denial or violation of human rights,[13] the Commission held closed meetings between 1 and 12 March 1982 to study confidential documents, observations submitted by States and a confidential report by a working group which had examined this material. The Commission maintained all such action confidential. On 5 March,[3] the Commission decided to set up again a working group of five of its members to examine particular situations of human rights violations referred by the Sub-Commission and those which the Commission had decided to keep under review; the group was to meet one week prior to the Commission's 1983 session. The Council approved this decision without vote on 7 May,[4] following similar approval by its Second (Social) Committee on 3 May.

The Sub-Commission's five-member Working Group on Communications, at its annual session from 2 to 13 August, also examined on a confidential basis communications alleging human rights violations. After considering the Group's report at five closed meetings between 2 and 6 September, the Sub-Commission adopted on 10 September a confidential report communicating its findings to the Commission.

On 7 September,[5] the Sub-Commission deferred until 1983 consideration of a draft resolution and an amendment[7] proposing that, as its Working Group on Communications had encountered difficulties in scrutinizing the growing number of communications on alleged human rights violations, the Sub-Commission be authorized to establish a geographically balanced working group of up to eight members, while strictly preserving the confidential nature of procedures for dealing with such communications.

On the same date,[10] the Sub-Commission requested Council authorization to continue its consideration of the effects of gross human rights violations on international peace and security (see below, under OTHER HUMAN RIGHTS QUESTIONS).

By another resolution of 7 September,[11] the Sub-Commission requested the Commission to seek Council authorization for the Sub-Commission to send one or more of its members to visit any country for which reliable allegations of gross and consistent human rights violations had been received. The purpose of the visit would be to examine such situations at first hand and to report on them to the Sub-Commission.

By a decision of 8 September,[6] the Sub-Commission expressed the view that, in order to avoid inter-State recriminations detrimental to its work, observers for States, when invited to participate on the agenda item of human rights violations, should not implicate other States in a deliberately abusive manner.

On 10 September,[12] the Sub-Commission submitted to the Commission possible terms of refer-

ence for the mandate of a United Nations High Commissioner for Human Rights (see above, under ADVANCEMENT OF HUMAN RIGHTS), who would also deal with human rights violations.

The Assembly, in two resolutions of 18 December on alternate approaches for improving the enjoyment of human rights, dealt also with the United Nations role in examining human rights violations. In the first resolution,[8] the Assembly reiterated that the international community should continue to search for solutions to mass and flagrant violations, priority being given to those situations resulting from human rights violations as detailed by the Assembly in 1977:[14] *apartheid*, racial discrimination, colonialism, foreign domination and occupation, aggression and threats against national sovereignty, and the refusal to recognize the right to self-determination and every nation's right to sovereignty over its wealth and natural resources. In the second resolution,[9] the Assembly noted that mass and flagrant human rights violations might threaten the peace and development of neighbouring States. It reaffirmed that human rights violations, wherever existent, were of concern to the United Nations, and urged all States to co-operate with the Commission in its study of such violations. This last request (paragraph 11) was adopted by the Third (Social, Humanitarian and Cultural) Committee by a recorded vote of 69 to 17, with 33 abstentions.

Two sets of amendments to these resolutions were presented to the Assembly which, on 18 December, decided not to take action on them. One set,[2] sponsored by six States, would have added four paragraphs to the first resolution. In the preamble, the Assembly would have recognized that human rights violations were of concern to the United Nations wherever they existed and would have acknowledged that mass and flagrant violations might threaten international peace and development. Under two new operative provisions, States would have been urged to co-operate with the Commission in the study of violations and the Commission would have been requested to continue its efforts in 1983 to improve the United Nations capacity to act in cases of serious violations.

The second set of amendments,[1] sponsored by 10 nations, would have specified, in the tenth preambular paragraph and operative paragraph 4 of the second resolution, that the United Nations was concerned with "mass and flagrant" violations. The ninth preambular paragraph and paragraph 2, which stated that the human rights violations of one State might threaten the peace of neighbouring States, would have been reworded to have the Assembly note that human rights violations might threaten international peace. Paragraph 11 would have changed from urging States to co-operate with the Commission in its study of human rights violations to inviting them to co-operate with the existing structures of the United Nations system in the promotion and protection of human rights as well the study of situations of mass and flagrant violations. The Commission, which was requested in paragraph 12 to continue its efforts to improve the United Nations capacity to act in cases of serious human rights violations, instead would have been requested only to continue consideration of such cases.

An oral proposal by the Byelorussian SSR to delete paragraphs 11 and 12 was not acted on by the Third Committee. Deletion of paragraph 12 and an amendment to paragraph 2 (to delete "of neighbouring States, of a region") was suggested by Argentina. Morocco proposed that paragraph 12 be modified to reflect the true state of affairs.

In voting against the second resolution, the USSR, recalling the 1977 Assembly resolution[14] according priority to mass and flagrant human rights violations, stated that the resolution under consideration was an attempt to cancel out the provision that human rights of individuals and peoples were interrelated and indivisible. India said it had difficulties with paragraphs 2 and 11. Difficulties with the latter were stated by Indonesia which cast a negative vote in the Assembly after having abstained in the Committee. Reservations to both paragraphs were voiced by the Philippines which abstained. Austria, in support of the resolution, expressed serious concern about any kind of human rights violations, not only mass and flagrant ones, and stated that any limitations or conditions in regard to the protection of human rights were unacceptable.

Introducing the text in the Committee, Ireland said the statement in paragraph 2, that human rights violations in one State might threaten the peace and development of neighbouring States, was particularly true in the case of South Africa.

Amendments not acted upon. [1]Algeria, Argentina, Bolivia, Cuba, Ethiopia, India, Indonesia, Pakistan, Panama, Yugoslavia, A/37/L.56; [2]Australia, Belgium, Greece, Ireland, Italy, Netherlands, A/37/L.57.
Decisions (1982). [3]Commission on Human Rights (report, E/1982/12): 1982/103, 5 Mar. [4]ESC: 1982/140, 7 May, text following. SCPDPM (report, E/CN.4/1983/4): [5]1982/9, 7 Sep.; [6]1982/12, 8 Sep.
Draft resolution and amendment deferred. [7]Special Rapporteurs, E/CN.4/Sub.2/1982/L.6, E/CN.4/Sub.2/1982/L.31.
Resolutions (1982). GA, 18 Dec.: [8]37/199, para. 3; [9]37/200. SCPDPM: [10]1982/11, 7 Sep.; [11]1982/14, 7 Sep.; [12]1982/27, 10 Sep.
Resolutions (prior). [13]ESC: 1503(XLVIII), 27 May 1970 (YUN 1970, p. 530). [14]GA: 32/130, 16 Dec. 1977 (YUN 1977, p. 734).
Meeting record. ESC: E/1982/SR.28 (7 May).

Economic and Social Council decision 1982/140

Adopted without vote

Approved by Second Committee (E/1982/59) without vote, 3 May (meeting 15); draft by Commission on Human Rights (E/1982/12); agenda item 9.

General decision concerning the establishment of a working group of the Commission on Human Rights to examine situations referred to the Commission under Economic and Social Council resolution 1503(XLVIII) and those situations of which the Commission is seized

At its 29th plenary meeting, on 7 May 1982, the Council approved the decision taken by the Commission on Human Rights, in its decision 1982/103 of 5 March 1982, to set up a working group composed of five of its members to meet for one week prior to the thirty-ninth session of the Commission to examine such particular situations as might be referred to the Commission by the Sub-Commission on Prevention of Discrimination and Protection of Minorities at its thirty-fifth session under Economic and Social Council resolution 1503(XLVIII) of 27 May 1970 and those situations which the Commission had decided to keep under review.

Africa

South Africa and Namibia

Working Group report. The *Ad Hoc* Working Group of Experts on Southern Africa, established in 1967 by the Commission on Human Rights,[11] submitted a progress report in January 1982 on developments concerning policies and practices violating human rights in South Africa and Namibia.[3] The report was based mainly on information received in the form of testimony and written communications from individuals and organizations, as well as on the analysis of published information. No conclusions or recommendations were formulated since they were to be included in the final report in 1983.

Action by the Commission on Human Rights. By two resolutions of 25 February 1982, the Commission on Human Rights dealt with the human rights situation in South Africa and Namibia. By the first,[4] after examining the Working Group's progress report, it expressed deep indignation at the continuing human rights violations there. It condemned the so-called "granting of independence" to the Ciskei as a denial of the right of self-determination and the impediments South Africa had placed in the way of negotiations for an independent Namibia. With regard to the situation in South Africa, the Commission expressed profound indignation at child labour, torture and abuse of arrested and imprisoned persons, oppression of black women and children, violation of black workers' trade union rights, and torture and murder of political prisoners. It demanded that South Africa cease all human rights violations, especially in regard to black children and women. The Working Group was requested to continue its study of violations in South Africa and Namibia, and to report in 1983. The Secretary-General was requested to give wide publicity to the findings. This resolution was adopted by a roll-call vote of 42 to none, with 1 abstention.

By the second resolution,[5] the Commission reaffirmed the Namibian people's right to self-determination by free elections under United Nations supervision, as outlined in two 1978 Security Council resolutions,[10] and again welcomed the readiness of the South West Africa People's Organization to negotiate for Namibia's independence under United Nations auspices. It demanded that South Africa comply with all United Nations resolutions on Namibia, cease torture and ill-treatment of Namibian political detainees and prisoners, and grant captured combatants prisoner-of-war status. The Commission condemned the increasing atrocities against defenceless people, especially women and children. It requested South Africa to allow a first-hand investigation by the Working Group of the treatment of prisoners in South Africa and Namibia, and called on South Africa to cease violating the territorial integrity of Angola and other African States. This resolution was adopted by a roll-call vote of 37 to none, with 6 abstentions.

Aspects of the human rights situation in South Africa and Namibia were also dealt with in another 25 February resolution,[6] on the self-determination of peoples (see above, under CIVIL AND POLITICAL RIGHTS).

Sub-Commission action. The Sub-Commission on Prevention of Discrimination and Protection of Minorities, in a resolution of 7 September (see above, under CIVIL AND POLITICAL RIGHTS), urged that the International Labour Office be requested to continue its study of indentured labour in South Africa and that more concrete measures be taken against *apartheid*, including economic, commercial, political and diplomatic sanctions.[9]

On 25 August,[1] the Sub-Commission decided to transmit its condolences to the family of Ruth First, a South African national and an opponent of *apartheid* who had been assassinated in Mozambique on 17 August. The Sub-Commission, expressing its shock, dismay and profound sorrow on learning of her assassination, stated the conviction that her work would go on and that the ultimate elimination of *apartheid* would not be prevented by such contemptible acts.

General Assembly action. On 3 December, in a resolution on the self-determination of peoples,[7] the General Assembly strongly condemned the widespread massacres of defenceless people, including women and children, by South Africa, and demanded the immediate release of children detained in Namibian and South African prisons.

In a 9 December resolution,[8] South Africa was strongly condemned for the repression, torture and killings of workers, schoolchildren and other opponents of *apartheid* and for the imposition of death sentences on freedom fighters.

The Assembly and its Special Committee against *Apartheid* also dealt with a number of other human rights aspects of the situation in South Africa during their consideration of *apartheid* policies, including the effects of those policies on the country's internal situation (see POLITICAL AND SECURITY QUESTIONS, Chapter V). Several human rights matters were also raised in connection with Namibia (see TRUSTEESHIP AND DECOLONIZATION, Chapter III).

Other action. The Governing Council of the United Nations Environment Programme (UNEP), on 28 May,[2] reaffirmed its solidarity with the victims of *apartheid* and requested the UNEP Executive Director to continue to monitor developments pertaining to environmental impacts of *apartheid*.

Decisions (1982). [1]SCPDPM (report, E/CN.4/1983/4): 1982/6, 25 Aug. [2]UNEP Council (report, A/37/25): 10/7, 28 May.
Report. [3]Working Group of Experts, E/CN.4/1485.
Resolutions (1982). Commission on Human Rights (report, E/1982/12), 25 Feb.: [4]1982/8, [5]1982/9, [6]1982/16. GA: [7]37/43, paras. 19 & 26, 3 Dec.; [8]37/69 A, para. 1, 9 Dec. [9]SCPDPM: 1982/15, para. 10, 7 Sep.
Resolutions (prior). [10]SC: 435(1978), 29 Sep. 1978, and 439(1978), 13 Nov. 1978 (YUN 1978, pp. 915 & 916).
Yearbook reference. [11]1967, p. 509.

Foreign support of South Africa

Action by the Commission on Human Rights. On 25 February 1982,[4] by a roll-call vote of 32 to 4 (France, Germany, Federal Republic of, United Kingdom, United States), with 7 abstentions, the Commission on Human Rights adopted a resolution on the adverse consequences for the enjoyment of human rights of assistance to racist régimes in southern Africa. Affirming the South African and Namibian peoples' right to self-determination, it welcomed the declarations adopted by the May 1981 International Conference on Sanctions against South Africa[9] as well as the General Assembly's proclamation of 1982 as International Year of Mobilization for Sanctions against South Africa. The Commission again requested States to end collaboration and assistance, including military and nuclear supplies, to South Africa.

Having examined a July 1981 report of the Sub-Commission's Special Rapporteur, Ahmed Mohamed Khalifa (Egypt), updating a list of banks, transnational corporations (TNCs) and other organizations assisting South Africa,[10] the Commission appealed again to the countries in which those companies were based to end trading, manufacturing and investment in South Africa and Namibia. The Commission welcomed the Sub-Commission's September 1981 decision to mandate the Special Rapporteur to continue updating his report for annual review. States, specialized agencies and non-governmental and other organizations were again called upon to give the report wide publicity.

The Group of Three, set up under the 1973 International Convention on the Suppression and Punishment of the Crime of *Apartheid* (see below), was requested to examine whether the actions of

TNCs operating in South Africa came under the definition of the crime of *apartheid* and whether or not legal action could be taken under the Convention.

In another resolution of 25 February,[5] on the right of the South African and Namibian peoples to self-determination, the Commission condemned the actions of States, especially major trading partners, which had increased their political, economic and military collaboration with South Africa, despite United Nations decisions and international appeals. In a 10 March resolution on slavery,[6] the Commission, recognizing *apartheid* as a slavery-like practice, endorsed the call for mandatory economic sanctions against South Africa, appealing to the Security Council members to support such proposals.

Economic and Social Council action. On 7 May,[1] the Economic and Social Council approved the Sub-Commission's September 1981 decision[10] to give the Special Rapporteur a mandate to continue his update of the list of banks, TNCs and other organizations assisting the racist régimes of southern Africa and to submit the revised report to the Commission through the Sub-Commission. Adopted by 37 votes to 5, with 10 abstentions, the Council decision originated in a draft recommended by the Commission and was approved by the Second (Social) Committee on 3 May by a recorded vote of 29 to 5 (Belgium, France, Germany, Federal Republic of, United Kingdom, United States), with 9 abstentions.

Sub-Commission action. On 7 September,[8] the Sub-Commission, having considered the June 1982 report of its Special Rapporteur which updated the list,[3] emphasized the need for an annual update of the report, as mandated by a May 1981 Council decision.[2] The Special Rapporteur was invited to use all available material from the United Nations, States, specialized agencies and organizations to demonstrate the volume and nature of assistance to the South African régime. The Secretary-General was requested to provide funds and the use of computers to facilitate the annual update, and was invited to issue the report as a United Nations publication and give it the widest publicity and dissemination. The Sub-Commission decided to consider the adverse consequences of assistance to southern Africa as a high-priority matter in 1983.

General Assembly action. On 3 December,[7] by a recorded vote of 121 to 10, with 14 abstentions, the General Assembly reaffirmed the right of the peoples of southern Africa to self-determination, and appealed to all States to co-operate with the liberation movements recognized by the United Nations and the Organization of African Unity. It vigorously condemned the collaboration with South Africa by certain Western States, Israel and other States, as well as TNCs and other organizations, naming them as accomplices in *apartheid*. Affirming the importance of updating the Special Rap-

porteur's report, the Assembly called on the countries where the banks, TNCs and other organizations listed were based to stop their trading, manufacturing and investing in South Africa and Namibia. All specialized agencies, particularly the International Monetary Fund and the World Bank, were urgently requested to refrain from granting loans. The Assembly decided to give high priority in 1984 to consideration of the adverse consequences of assistance to South Africa.

The Security Council was urged to consider complete and mandatory sanctions against South Africa, including the prohibition of technological assistance or collaboration in the manufacture of arms, the cessation of all collaboration in the nuclear field, the prohibition of loans, investments and trade, and an oil embargo.

The text was approved on 27 October by the Third (Social, Humanitarian and Cultural) Committee by 113 votes to 10, with 15 abstentions.

Casting a negative vote, the Federal Republic of Germany said the resolution contained a number of unacceptable or difficult elements, in particular paragraph 12 which, it felt, seriously affected the integrity of specialized agencies.

Israel said its being singled out in paragraph 3 for alleged collaboration with South Africa made a farce of the resolution. The United States regarded the text, in particular the call for support of armed struggle, as counter-productive and as a rejection of black groups in South Africa working for peaceful change; it also rejected the view that foreign investment perpetuated *apartheid* or South Africa's presence in Namibia.

Also voting against the resolution, the United Kingdom believed that the Special Rapporteur's report had serious defects and that the Secretary-General's suggestion to eliminate it should be accepted. The Netherlands said the report was based on the assumption that the activities of Western enterprises in South Africa were detrimental to human rights in that country. The Netherlands also could not support some of the measures proposed and it felt that certain assertions in the tenth and eleventh preambular paragraphs were groundless.

Objections to the report were also voiced by Australia which abstained. Also abstaining, Portugal objected in particular to the resolution's tenth and eleventh preambular paragraphs and to operative paragraphs 3, 4, 5 and 12. Ireland could not accept the seventh to tenth preambular paragraphs and operative paragraphs 3, 4 and 12.

Though voting in favour, Botswana, Chile, Lesotho and Swaziland reserved their position on paragraph 12. Botswana, Lesotho and Swaziland also had reservations on the call for sanctions in paragraph 5, in particular the prohibition of loans and investments and a petroleum embargo. Brazil had reservations with regard to the Special Rapporteur's report and the call for a stop to trading, manufacturing and investment in South Africa and Namibia.

Costa Rica, Turkey and Uruguay reserved their position on paragraph 3 condemning the collaboration of certain States. Chile and the Dominican Republic voiced reservations on the paragraphs referring selectively to certain States. The United States said if some countries were referred to, all countries engaging in trade with South Africa should be mentioned; sanctions would not encourage a peaceful evolution away from *apartheid*, but would have the opposite effect.

The USSR, on the other hand, regarded the resolution as particularly significant in the struggle against racism and colonialism, and for realization of the right to self-determination.

Introducing the text on behalf of the African Group of Member States, Guinea said it reaffirmed major principles in various international instruments which argued in favour of total isolation of racist South Africa.

Decision (1982). [1]ESC: 1982/128, 7 May, text following.
Decision (prior). [2]ESC: 1981/141, 8 May 1981 (YUN 1981, p. 946).
Report. [3]Special Rapporteur, E/CN.4/Sub.2/1982/10.
Resolutions (1982). Commission on Human Rights (report, E/1982/12): [4]1982/12, 25 Feb.; [5]1982/16, para. 10, 25 Feb.; [6]1982/20, para. 5, 10 Mar. [7]GA: 37/39, 3 Dec., text following. [8]SCPDPM (report, E/CN.4/1983/4): 1982/16, 7 Sep.
Yearbook references. 1981, [9]p. 165, [10]p. 946.
Meeting records. ESC: E/1982/SR.28 (7 May). GA: 3rd Committee, A/C.3/37/SR.3-13, *18, 24, 25* (30 Sep.–27 Oct.); plenary, A/37/PV.90 (3 Dec.).

Economic and Social Council decision 1982/128

7 May 1982   Meeting 28   37-5-10

Approved by Second Committee (E/1982/59) by recorded vote (29-5-9), 3 May (meeting 15); draft by Commission on Human Rights (E/1982/12); agenda item 9.

Adverse consequences for the enjoyment of human rights of political, military, economic and other forms of assistance given to the colonial and racist régime in South Africa

At its 28th plenary meeting, on 7 May 1982, the Council took note of resolution 1982/12 of 25 February 1982 of the Commission on Human Rights, and approved the decision of the Sub-Commission on Prevention of Discrimination and Protection of Minorities to give a mandate to Mr. Ahmed Khalifa, Special Rapporteur, to continue to update the list of banks, transnational corporations and other organizations giving assistance to the racist and colonial régimes of southern Africa and to submit the revised report to the Commission through the Sub-Commission.

General Assembly resolution 37/39

3 December 1982   Meeting 90   121-10-14 (recorded vote)

Approved by Third Committee (A/37/579) by vote (113-10-15), 27 October (meeting 24); draft by Guinea, for African Group (A/C.3/37/L.15); agenda item 75.

Adverse consequences for the enjoyment of human rights of political, military, economic and other forms of assistance given to the racist and colonialist régime of South Africa
The General Assembly,

Recalling its resolutions 3382(XXX) and 3383(XXX) of 10 November 1975, 33/23 of 29 November 1978 and 35/32 of 14 November 1980,

Recalling also its resolutions 3201(S-VI) and 3202(S-VI) of 1 May 1974, containing the Declaration and the Programme of Action on the Establishment of a New International Economic Order, and 3281(XXIX)

of 12 December 1974, containing the Charter of Economic Rights and Duties of States,

Mindful of its resolution 3171(XXVIII) of 17 December 1973 relating to permanent sovereignty over natural resources of both developing countries and territories under colonial and foreign domination or subjected to the *apartheid* régime,

Recalling its resolutions on military collaboration with South Africa, as well as Security Council resolutions 418(1977) of 4 November 1977 and 421(1977) of 9 December 1977,

Taking into account, in particular, the relevant decisions adopted by the Council of Ministers of the Organization of African Unity at its thirty-seventh ordinary session, held at Nairobi from 15 to 26 June 1981,

Taking note of the revised report prepared by the Special Rapporteur of the Sub-Commission on Prevention of Discrimination and Protection of Minorities on the adverse consequences for the enjoyment of human rights of political, military, economic and other forms of assistance given to colonial and racist régimes in southern Africa,

Having noted with concern that the Secretary-General, in his report on the special review of the ongoing work programme of the United Nations, concluded that the annual updated report on the adverse consequences for the enjoyment of human rights of political, military, economic and other forms of assistance given to colonial and racist régimes in southern Africa had been identified for termination in the proposed programme budget for the biennium 1982-1983,

Reaffirming that any collaboration with the racist régime of South Africa constitutes a hostile act against the oppressed peoples of southern Africa in their struggle for freedom and independence and a contemptuous defiance of the United Nations and of the international community,

Considering that such collaboration enables South Africa to acquire the means necessary to carry out acts of aggression and blackmail against independent African States,

Deeply concerned that the major Western and other trading partners of South Africa continue to collaborate with the racist régime and that their collaboration constitutes the main obstacle to the liquidation of that racist régime and the elimination of the inhuman and criminal system of *apartheid,*

Alarmed at the continued collaboration of certain Western States and Israel with the racist régime of South Africa in the nuclear field,

Regretting that the Security Council has not been in a position to take binding decisions to prevent any collaboration in the nuclear field with South Africa,

Recognizing that the highest priority must be accorded to international action to secure the full implementation of the resolutions of the United Nations for the eradication of *apartheid* and the liberation of the peoples of southern Africa,

Conscious of the continuing need to mobilize world public opinion against the political, military, economic and other assistance given to the racist régime of South Africa,

1. *Reaffirms* the inalienable right of the oppressed peoples of southern Africa to self-determination, independence and the enjoyment of the natural resources of their territories;

2. *Again reaffirms* the right of those same peoples to dispose of those resources for their greater well-being and to obtain just reparation for the exploitation, depletion, loss or depreciation of those natural resources, including reparation for the exploitation and abuse of their human resources;

3. *Vigorously condemns* the collaboration of certain Western States, Israel and other States, as well as the transnational corporations and other organizations which maintain or continue to increase their collaboration with the racist régime of South Africa, especially in the political, economic, military and nuclear fields, thus encouraging that régime to persist in its inhuman and criminal policy of brutal oppression of the peoples of southern Africa and denial of their human rights;

4. *Reaffirms once again* that States and organizations which give assistance to the racist régime of South Africa become accomplices in the inhuman practices of racial discrimination, colonialism and *apartheid* perpetrated by that régime, as well as in acts of aggression against the liberation movements and neighbouring States;

5. *Requests* the Security Council urgently to consider complete and mandatory sanctions under Chapter VII of the Charter of the United Nations against the racist régime of South Africa, in particular:

(a) The prohibition of all technological assistance or collaboration in the manufacture of arms and military supplies in South Africa;

(b) The cessation of all collaboration with South Africa in the nuclear field;

(c) The prohibition of all loans to, and all investments in, South Africa and the cessation of any trade with South Africa;

(d) An embargo on the supply of petroleum, petroleum products and other strategic goods to South Africa;

6. *Appeals* to all States, specialized agencies and non-governmental organizations to extend all possible co-operation to the liberation movements of southern Africa recognized by the United Nations and the Organization of African Unity;

7. *Expresses its appreciation* to the Special Rapporteur of the Sub-Commission on Prevention of Discrimination and Protection of Minorities for his revised report;

8. *Affirms* that the updating of the report on the adverse consequences for the enjoyment of human rights of political, military, economic and other forms of assistance given to colonial and racist régimes in southern Africa is of the greatest importance to the cause of fighting *apartheid* and other violations of human rights in South Africa and Namibia and should continue to be an activity in the ongoing work programme for 1982-1983;

9. *Calls upon* the Secretary-General to give all necessary assistance to the Special Rapporteur with a view to making available to him the computer services essential for the more detailed updating of the list contained in his report;

10. *Calls upon* the Governments of the countries where the banks, transnational corporations and other organizations named and listed in the revised report are based to take effective action to put a stop to their trading, manufacturing and investing activities in the territory of South Africa as well as in the Territory of Namibia illegally occupied by the racist Pretoria régime;

11. *Requests* the Secretary-General to transmit the revised report to the Special Committee against *Apartheid*, the United Nations Council for Namibia, other bodies concerned within the United Nations system and regional international organizations;

12. *Urgently requests* all specialized agencies, particularly the International Monetary Fund and the World Bank, to refrain from granting loans of any type to the racist régime in South Africa;

13. *Calls upon* all States, specialized agencies and regional, intergovernmental and other organizations concerned to give wide publicity to the revised report;

14. *Invites* the Commission on Human Rights to give high priority at its thirty-ninth session to the consideration of the revised report;

15. *Decides* to consider at its thirty-ninth session, as a matter of high priority, the item entitled "Adverse consequences for the enjoyment of human rights of political, military, economic and other forms of assistance given to the racist and colonialist régime of South Africa", in the light of any recommendations which the Sub-Commission on Prevention of Discrimination and Protection of Minorities, the Commission on Human Rights, the Economic and Social Council and the Special Committee against *Apartheid* may wish to submit to it.

Recorded vote in Assembly as follows:

In favour: Albania, Algeria, Angola, Antigua and Barbuda, Argentina, Bahamas, Bahrain, Bangladesh, Barbados, Belize, Benin, Bhutan, Bolivia, Botswana, Brazil, Bulgaria, Burma, Burundi, Byelorussian SSR, Cape Verde, Central African Republic, Chad, Chile, China, Colombia, Comoros, Costa Rica, Cuba, Cyprus, Czechoslovakia, Democratic Kampuchea, Democratic Yemen, Djibouti, Dominican Republic, Ecuador, Egypt, El Salvador, Equatorial Guinea, Ethiopia, Fiji, Gabon, German Democratic Republic, Ghana, Grenada, Guinea, Guinea-Bissau, Guyana, Haiti, Hungary, India, Indonesia, Iran, Iraq, Jamaica, Jordan, Kenya, Kuwait, Lao People's Democratic Republic, Lebanon, Lesotho, Liberia, Libyan Arab Jamahiriya, Madagascar, Malaysia, Maldives, Mali, Malta, Mauritania, Mauritius, Mexico, Mongolia, Morocco, Mozambique, Nepal, Nicaragua, Niger, Nigeria, Oman, Pakistan, Panama, Papua New Guinea, Peru, Philippines, Poland, Qatar, Romania, Rwanda, Saint Lucia, Samoa, Sao Tome and Principe, Saudi Arabia, Senegal, Sierra Leone, Singapore, Solomon Islands, Somalia, Sri Lanka, Sudan, Suriname, Swaziland, Syrian Arab Republic, Thailand, Togo, Trinidad and Tobago, Tunisia, Turkey, Uganda, Ukrainian SSR, USSR, United Arab Emirates, United Republic of Tanzania, Upper Volta, Uruguay, Vanuatu, Venezuela, Viet Nam, Yemen, Yugoslavia, Zaire, Zambia, Zimbabwe.

Against: Belgium, Canada, France, Germany, Federal Republic of, Israel, Italy, Luxembourg, Netherlands, United Kingdom, United States.

Abstaining: Australia, Austria, Denmark, Finland, Greece, Iceland, Ireland, Ivory Coast, Japan, New Zealand, Norway, Portugal, Spain, Sweden.

1973 Convention against apartheid

As at 31 December 1982, there were 69 parties to the 1973 International Convention on the Suppression and Punishment of the Crime of *Apartheid*.[7]

During the year, three States (Algeria, Antigua and Barbuda, and Sri Lanka) and Namibia (represented by the United Nations Council for Namibia) became parties.[1]

Activities of the Group of Three. The Group of Three, established under article IX of the Convention to consider reports by States parties on measures they had adopted to implement the Convention's provisions, held its fifth session at Geneva from 25 to 29 January 1982.[2] The Group, consisting of Bulgaria, Mexico and Zaire for the 1982 session, considered first (initial) reports from Barbados, Mexico and Mongolia. Second periodic reports were filed by Iraq and Qatar, and third periodic reports by the German Democratic Republic, Hungary, the Syrian Arab Republic, the USSR and the United Arab Emirates.[4] Representatives of these States, except for Barbados, attended the meetings to supplement the information in the reports.

In its conclusions and recommendations, the Group again expressed the opinion that the presence of States' representatives at its meetings in connection with the consideration of reports should be continued. It urged States to submit reports that provided full information on the measures adopted to implement article IV of the Convention (on suppression or prevention of encouragement of *apartheid* and prosecution and punishment for the crime of *apartheid*), and to follow guidelines established by the Group regarding form and content.

The Group again appealed for the strengthening of international co-operation to implement fully the decisions of the Security Council and other United Nations organs aimed at preventing, suppressing and punishing *apartheid;* in that context, it drew attention to the importance of strengthening assistance to national liberation movements in southern Africa.

The Group reiterated the desirability of disseminating more information about the Convention, its implementation and the work of the Group. It again recommended that the list of individuals, organizations, institutions and State representatives responsible for crimes of *apartheid*, drawn up by the Commission on Human Rights in accordance with article X, be brought to the attention of all United Nations Members and given the widest publicity.

Action by the Commission on Human Rights. On 25 February,[5] the Commission on Human Rights again called on States to ratify or accede to the Convention. Taking note of the Group's conclusions and recommendations, it urged States to file their reports, following recommended guidelines. It called on States parties to strengthen their co-operation to implement United Nations resolutions on *apartheid* and stated the desirability of disseminating information on the Convention and the work of the Group. The Commission decided that the Group should meet for no more than five days before its 1983 session.

The resolution was adopted by a roll-call vote of 32 to none, with 11 abstentions.

General Assembly action. By a 3 December 1982 resolution,[6] the General Assembly, taking note of the Secretary-General's September report on the status of the Convention,[3] also appealed to States parties to submit their reports as soon as possible and appealed for additional ratifications. The Assembly called on States parties and United Nations organs to submit their views on the Group's recommendations for implementing the Convention's provisions. It invited the Commission to expand periodically the list of individuals and organizations deemed responsible for crimes of *apartheid*, and called on States parties to provide relevant information and to prosecute those responsible. The Assembly requested the Secretary-General to distribute the list, and invited the Special Committee against *Apartheid* and the Centre against *Apartheid* to publicize it. The Secretary-General was requested to disseminate information on the Convention and to submit a report on its implementation in 1983. The Assembly requested the Commission to take into account that States giving assistance to South Africa became accomplices in *apartheid*, and called on States to participate actively in the 1983 Second World Conference to Combat Racism and Racial Discrimination.

The resolution was adopted by a recorded vote of 124 to 1, with 22 abstentions, following approval of the orally revised text by the Third Committee on 27 October by a recorded vote of 112 to 1, with 22 abstentions. The draft had been orally amended by Nigeria to add a preambular paragraph expressing concern over the widespread torture and ill-treatment of political prisoners and trade unionists in South Africa leading to deaths in detention, and an operative paragraph inviting the Special Committee against *Apartheid* and the Centre against *Apartheid* to publicize the list of those deemed responsible for crimes of *apartheid*.

Casting a negative vote, the United States said it considered the Convention to be fatally flawed and could not encourage its ratification, nor could it accept the view that *apartheid* was a crime against humanity in the context of international law.

Explaining the abstentions of the European Community members, Denmark said they did not believe that the Convention contributed effectively to the elimination of *apartheid* because of various legal defects, including its very imprecise definition of possible violations. With regard to paragraphs 9 and 10 of the resolution which endowed a United Nations body with controversial responsibility for implementing the Convention, Denmark noted that the Convention was only applicable to States which had ratified it and their citizens.

Also abstaining, Portugal said the resolution contained provisions which were not consistent with Portugal's legal system. Australia said it encountered legal and constitutional problems which hampered the application of some Convention provisions, and Austria abstained because it was not a party to the Convention.

Though voting in favour, Turkey stated serious legal problems with the Convention, as did Uruguay, the latter with regard in particular to the legal competence of States parties in respect of acts by non-nationals committed outside the territory of those States and the mandate to implement the Convention conferred on a United Nations organ, many of whose members were not parties to the Convention.

Introducing the resolution on behalf of 31 nations, the German Democratic Republic said its main purpose was to enhance the Convention's effectiveness and to implement effective measures against the *apartheid* régime, including universal sanctions.

Publication. [1]*Multilateral Treaties Deposited with the Secretary-General: Status as at 31 December 1982* (ST/LEG/SER.E/2), Sales No. E.83.V.6.
Reports. [2]Group of Three, E/CN.4/1507; [3]S-G, A/37/149 & Corr.1; [4]States parties, E/CN.4/1505 & Add.1-10.
Resolutions (1982). [5]Commission on Human Rights (report, E/1982/12): 1982/10, 25 Feb. [6]GA: 37/47, 3 Dec., text following.
Resolution (prior). [7]GA: 3068(XXVIII), annex, 30 Nov. 1973 (YUN 1973, p. 103).
Meeting records. GA: 3rd Committee, A/C.3/37/SR.3-13, *18, 24, 25* (30 Sep.–27 Oct.); plenary, A/37/PV.90 (3 Dec.).

General Assembly resolution 37/47

3 December 1982   Meeting 90   124-1-22 (recorded vote)

Approved by Third Committee (A/37/581) by recorded vote (112-1-22), 27 October (meeting 24); 31-nation draft (A/C.3/37/L.12), orally amended by Nigeria and orally revised accordingly; agenda item 80 *(c)*.

Sponsors: Afghanistan, Algeria, Angola, Benin, Bulgaria, Cape Verde, Congo, Cuba, Czechoslovakia, Democratic Yemen, Ecuador, Ethiopia, German Democratic Republic, Ghana, Guinea-Bissau, Guyana, Hungary, Iraq, Lao People's Democratic Republic, Libyan Arab Jamahiriya, Madagascar, Mongolia, Mozambique, Rwanda, Syrian Arab Republic, Uganda, Ukrainian SSR, Viet Nam, Yugoslavia, Zambia, Zimbabwe.

Status of the International Convention on the Suppression and Punishment of the Crime of *Apartheid*

The General Assembly,

Recalling its resolution 3068(XXVIII) of 30 November 1973, by which it adopted and opened for signature and ratification the International Convention on the Suppression and Punishment of the Crime of *Apartheid*, and its subsequent resolutions on the status of the Convention,

Convinced that the Declaration and the Programme of Action adopted by the World Conference to Combat Racism and Racial Discrimination, as well as the programme of activities to be undertaken during the second half of the Decade for Action to Combat Racism and Racial Discrimination, adopted by the General Assembly in its resolution 34/24 of 15 November 1979, and their full implementation will contribute to the final eradication of *apartheid* and all other forms of racism and racial discrimination,

Reaffirming its conviction that apartheid constitutes a total negation of the purposes and principles of the Charter of the United Nations and is a gross violation of human rights and a crime against humanity, seriously threatening international peace and security,

Strongly condemning South Africa's continued policy of *apartheid*, repression and "bantustanization" and its continued illegal occupation of Namibia, thereby perpetuating on Namibian territory its odious policy of *apartheid*, racial discrimination and fragmentation,

Gravely concerned over the widespread torture and ill-treatment of political prisoners and trade unionists detained by the racist régime of South Africa, leading to the death in detention of many prisoners, including Neil Aggett, Tshifiwa Muofhe and Ernest Moabi Dipale,

Deeply concerned about South Africa's repeated acts of aggression against sovereign African States, which constitute a manifest breach of international peace and security,

Condemning the continued collaboration of certain States and transnational corporations with the racist régime of South Africa in the political, economic, military and other fields as an encouragement to the intensification of its odious policy of *apartheid*,

Underlining that the strengthening of the existing mandatory arms embargo and the application of comprehensive mandatory economic sanctions under Chapter VII of the Charter of the United Nations are vital in order to compel the racist régime of South Africa to abandon its policy of *apartheid*,

Recalling its resolutions 36/172 A to P of 17 December 1981, in particular resolution 36/172 B in which it proclaimed the year 1982 International Year of Mobilization for Sanctions against South Africa,

Stressing the need to disseminate on a wider basis more information on the crimes committed by the racist régime of South Africa, taking into consideration the recommendation contained in the documents adopted by the International Seminar on Publicity and the Role of Mass Media in the International Mobilization against *Apartheid*, held at Berlin, German Democratic Republic, from 31 August to 2 September 1981,

Firmly convinced that the legitimate struggle of the oppressed peoples in southern Africa against *apartheid*, racism and colonialism and for the effective implementation of their inalienable right to self-determination and independence demands more than ever all necessary support by the international community and, in particular, further action by the Security Council,

Commending the work of the Preparatory Sub-Committee for the Second World Conference to Combat Racism and Racial Discrimination and the recommendations contained in its report to the Economic and Social Council,

Underlining that ratification of and accession to the International Convention on the Suppression and Punishment of the Crime of *Apartheid* on a universal basis and the implementation of its provisions without any delay are necessary for its effectiveness and would be a useful contribution towards achieving the goals of the Decade for Action to Combat Racism and Racial Discrimination,

1. *Takes note* of the report of the Secretary-General on the status of the International Convention on the Suppression and Punishment of the Crime of *Apartheid;*

2. *Commends* those States parties to the Convention that have submitted their reports under article VII thereof, in particular those that have presented their second reports, and appeals to those States parties that have not yet done so to submit their reports as soon as possible;

3. *Appeals once again* to those States that have not yet done so to ratify or to accede to the Convention without further delay;

4. *Appreciates* the constructive role played by the Group of Three of the Commission on Human Rights, established in accordance with article IX of the International Convention on the Suppression and Punishment of the Crime of *Apartheid*, in analysing the periodic reports of States and in publicizing the experience gained in the international struggle against the crime of *apartheid;*

5. *Requests* States parties to the Convention to take fully into account the guidelines prepared by the Group of Three;

6. *Calls upon* all States parties to the Convention to implement fully article IV thereof by adopting legislative, judicial and administrative measures to prosecute, bring to trial and punish, in accordance with their jurisdiction, persons responsible for, or accused of, the acts enumerated in article II of the Convention;

7. *Again calls upon* all States parties to the Convention and the competent United Nations organs to consider the conclusions and recommendations of the Group of Three contained in its reports and to submit their views and comments to the Secretary-General;

8. *Requests* the Commission on Human Rights to continue to undertake the functions set out in article X of the Convention and invites the Commission to intensify, in co-operation with the Special Committee against *Apartheid*, its efforts to compile periodically the progressive list of individuals, organizations, institutions and representatives of States deemed responsible for crimes enumerated in article II of the Convention, as well as of those against whom or which legal proceedings have been undertaken;

9. *Requests* the Commission on Human Rights to take into account General Assembly resolutions 33/23 of 29 November 1978 and 35/32 of 14 November 1980, as well as relevant documents of the Commission and its subsidiary organs reaffirming, *inter alia*, that States giving assistance to the racist régime of South Africa become accomplices in the inhuman practices of racial discrimination and *apartheid;*

10. *Calls upon* all States parties to the Convention and competent United Nations organs to continue to provide the Commission on Human Rights, through the Secretary-General, with information relevant to the periodic compilation of the above-mentioned list, as well as with information concerning the obstacles that prevent the effective suppression and punishment of the crime of *apartheid;*

11. *Requests* the Secretary-General to distribute the above-mentioned list among all States parties to the Convention and all Member States and to bring such facts to the attention of the public by all means of mass communication;

12. *Invites* the Special Committee against *Apartheid* and the Centre against *Apartheid* of the Secretariat to publicize the above-mentioned list and related particulars as widely as possible;

13. *Appeals* to all States, United Nations organs, specialized agencies and international and national non-governmental organizations to step up their activities in enhancing public awareness through denouncing the crimes committed by the racist régime of South Africa;

14. *Requests* the Secretary-General to intensify his efforts, through appropriate channels, to disseminate information on the Convention and its implementation with a view to further promoting ratification of or accession to the Convention;

15. *Calls upon* all States to participate actively in the Second World Conference to Combat Racism and Racial Discrimination, to be held in 1983, and to contribute to achieving effective results at that Conference;

16. *Requests* the Secretary-General to include in his next annual report under General Assembly resolution 3380(XXX) of 10 November 1975 a special section concerning the implementation of the International Convention on the Suppression and Punishment of the Crime of *Apartheid*.

Recorded vote in Assembly as follows:

In favour: Albania, Algeria, Angola, Antigua and Barbuda, Argentina, Bahamas, Bahrain, Bangladesh, Barbados, Belize, Benin, Bhutan, Bolivia, Botswana, Brazil, Bulgaria, Burma, Burundi, Byelorussian SSR, Cape Verde, Central African Republic, Chad, Chile, China, Colombia, Comoros, Congo, Costa Rica, Cuba, Cyprus, Czechoslovakia, Democratic Kampuchea, Democratic Yemen, Djibouti, Dominican Republic, Ecuador, Egypt, El Salvador, Equatorial Guinea, Ethiopia, Fiji, Gabon, German Democratic Republic, Ghana, Grenada, Guinea, Guinea-Bissau, Guyana, Haiti, Hungary, India, Indonesia, Iran, Iraq, Ivory Coast, Jamaica, Jordan, Kenya, Kuwait, Lao People's Democratic Republic, Lebanon, Lesotho, Liberia, Libyan Arab Jamahiriya, Madagascar, Malaysia, Maldives, Mali, Malta, Mauritania, Mauritius, Mexico, Mongolia, Morocco, Mozambique, Nepal, Nicaragua, Niger, Nigeria, Oman, Pakistan, Panama, Papua New Guinea, Peru, Philippines, Poland, Qatar, Romania, Rwanda, Saint Lucia, Samoa, Sao Tome and Principe, Saudi Arabia, Senegal, Sierra Leone, Singapore, Solomon Islands, Somalia, Sri Lanka, Sudan, Suriname, Swaziland, Syrian Arab Republic, Thailand, Togo, Trinidad and Tobago, Tunisia, Turkey, Uganda, Ukrainian SSR, USSR, United Arab Emirates, United Republic of Cameroon, United Republic of Tanzania, Upper Volta, Uruguay, Vanuatu, Venezuela, Viet Nam, Yemen, Yugoslavia, Zaire, Zambia, Zimbabwe.

Against: United States.

Abstaining: Australia, Austria, Belgium, Canada, Denmark, Finland, France, Germany, Federal Republic of, Greece, Iceland, Ireland, Italy, Japan, Luxembourg, Malawi, Netherlands, New Zealand, Norway, Portugal, Spain, Sweden, United Kingdom.

Violations of trade union rights

In 1982, the *Ad Hoc* Working Group of Experts on Southern Africa continued to study allegations of infringements of trade union rights in South Africa, in response to a May 1981 resolution[7] of the Economic and Social Council. The Group submitted two reports to the Commission on Human Rights that included information—conveyed to the Council by Secretariat notes—on suppression of the right to organize trade unions and persecution of workers because of their activities, particularly as a consequence of strikes.

In the first report,[3] the Group studied the implications of the reforms proposed by the Wiehahn Commission on industrial relations and the subsequent enactment of the Industrial Conciliation Amendment Act of 1979, which for the first time recognized the right of black workers to join trade unions.

In the second report,[4] the Group dealt with allegations originating from the International Confederation of Free Trade Unions[8] and transmitted to it by the Council in May 1981.[1] After summarizing international standards and South African legislation, the Group examined specific incidents of detention, prohibition of fund raising, and police and State interference in industrial disputes. The Group concluded that South Africa, in each case examined, had violated international standards. It recommended that the Council demand that South Africa recognize trade union rights, release imprisoned trade unionists, lift the ban on fund raising by the Federation of South African Trade Unions, and ensure the impartiality of the Government and police in labour disputes.

The Commission on Human Rights, in its 25 February resolution[5] on human rights violations in southern Africa (see above), expressed its profound indignation over the violation of international standards concerning trade union rights for black workers in South Africa.

Economic and Social Council action. By a resolution of 7 May,[6] the Economic and Social Council, taking note of the reports of the Working Group, demanded the immediate recognition of trade union rights for the entire population of South Africa. It called again for the immediate release of all imprisoned trade unionists, and demanded the lifting of the ban on fund raising by the Federation of South African Trade Unions and the cessation of all government and police interference in labour disputes. The Council requested the Group to consult with the International Labour Organisation, the Special Committee against *Apartheid* and international and African trade union confederations.

Adopted without vote, the 15-nation draft, introduced by Nigeria, had been similarly approved by the Second (Social) Committee on 3 May. The draft was orally amended by the United Kingdom to state, in the fifth preambular paragraph, that certain trade union rights violations had "persisted" rather than "increased", and, in operative paragraph 4, to call for the release of "all the imprisoned trade unionists" rather than "all trade unionists in prison".

Report of the Committee against *Apartheid*. The Special Committee against *Apartheid*, in a special report to the General Assembly and the Security Council in November on trade union action against *apartheid*,[2] stated that despite legislation intended to exercise strict control over African trade unions, they had rapidly grown in strength in recent years. Stressing the need for urgent international action, the Committee recommended that the Assembly authorize the organization in 1983 of an international conference of trade unions on sanctions and other actions against the *apartheid* régime in South Africa, that it make financial provision for the conference, and that it appeal to all Governments and organizations to support the black trade union movement.

Decision. [1]ESC: 1981/155, 8 May 1981 (YUN 1981, p. 950).
Reports. [2]Committee against *Apartheid*, A/37/22/Add.2; Working Group of Experts, [3]E/CN.4/1485 (excerpts annexed to Secretariat note, E/1982/31), [4]E/CN.4/1486 (transmitted by Secretariat note, E/1982/17).
Resolutions (1982). [5]Commission on Human Rights (report, E/1982/12): 1982/8, para. 5 (*d*), 25 Feb. [6]ESC: 1982/40, 7 May, text following.
Resolution (prior). [7]ESC: 1981/41, 8 May 1981 (YUN 1981, p. 950).
Yearbook reference. [8]1981, p. 950.
Meeting record. ESC: E/1982/SR.28 (7 May).

Economic and Social Council resolution 1982/40

7 May 1982   Meeting 28   Adopted without vote

Approved by Second Committee (E/1982/59) without vote, 3 May (meeting 16); 15-nation draft (E/1982/C.2/L.12), orally amended by United Kingdom; agenda item 9.

Sponsors: Bangladesh, Benin, Bulgaria, Costa Rica, Ethiopia, India, Kenya, Liberia, Libyan Arab Jamahiriya, Mali, Nigeria, Pakistan, Sierra Leone, Sudan, Yugoslavia.

Report of the *Ad Hoc* Working Group of Experts of the Commission on Human Rights on allegations of infringements of trade union rights in the Republic of South Africa

The Economic and Social Council,

Recalling its resolution 1981/41 of 8 May 1981,

Recalling its decision 1981/155 of 8 May 1981, by which it transmitted to the *Ad Hoc* Working Group of Experts of the Commission on Human Rights, for consideration, the allegations regarding infringements of trade union rights in South Africa submitted by the International Confederation of Free Trade Unions,

Having examined the reports of the *Ad Hoc* Working Group of Experts,

Noting that the Government of South Africa continues to violate, by its legislation, international standards concerning trade union rights,

Noting further with grave concern that police and State interference in industrial disputes and repression against the independent black trade union movement has persisted,

1. *Takes note* of the report of the *Ad Hoc* Working Group of Experts prepared in accordance with Council resolution 1981/41;

2. *Takes note with appreciation* of the report of the *Ad Hoc* Working Group of Experts prepared in accordance with Council decision 1981/155, and of the conclusions contained therein;

3. *Demands* the immediate recognition of the unimpeded exercise of freedom of association and trade union rights by the entire population of South Africa, without discrimination of any kind;

4. *Calls once again* for the immediate release of all the imprisoned trade unionists and the lifting of all banning orders imposed on persons engaged in trade union activities;

5. *Demands* the lifting of the ban on fund-raising drives by the Federation of South African Trade Unions;

6. *Reiterates* its demand for the cessation of all government and police interference in labour disputes;

7. *Requests* the *Ad Hoc* Working Group of Experts to continue to study the situation and to report thereon to the Commission on Human Rights and the Council, as appropriate;

8. *Also requests* the *Ad Hoc* Working Group of Experts, in the discharge of its mandate, to consult with the International Labour Organisation and the Special Committee against *Apartheid*, as well as with international and African trade union confederations;

9. *Decides* to consider at its first regular session of 1983 the question of allegations of infringements of trade union rights in South Africa as a sub-item under the item entitled "Human rights questions".

Asia and the Pacific

East Timor

On 8 September 1982,[1] by 10 votes to 2, with 9 abstentions, the Sub-Commission on Prevention of Discrimination and Protection of Minorities deplored the lack of international attention to the situation in East Timor. It recommended that the Commission on Human Rights reaffirm the right of the people of East Timor to self-determination and, to that end, call on Portugal, the representatives of East Timor and Indonesia to co-operate with the United Nations to guarantee the exercise of that right. Expressing deep concern at the suffering of the people of East Timor, the Commission would call on the parties to facilitate the entry of international aid into that Territory.

Resolution (1982). [1]SCPDPM (report, E/CN.4/1983/4): 1982/20; 8 Sep.

Iran

The Commission on Human Rights, on 11 March 1982,[1] expressed deep concern at continuing reports of grave human rights violations, including summary and arbitrary executions, in Iran. Taking into account the concern for the welfare of the Baha'is expressed in September 1981 by the Sub-Commission on discrimination and minorities,[4] the Commission urged Iran to ensure the rights recognized in the International Covenant on Civil and Political Rights[3] to all individuals without distinction. It requested the Secretary-General to establish direct contacts with the Government of Iran—which was invited to co-operate with him—to determine the human rights situation, and to continue his efforts to ensure human rights in regard to the Baha'i community. The Commission asked him to report in 1983 and decided to keep the situation under consideration. The resolution was adopted by a roll-call vote of 19 to 9 (Algeria, Bulgaria, Byelorussian SSR, Cuba, Ethiopia, Pakistan, Poland, Syrian Arab Republic, USSR), with 15 abstentions.

On 8 September 1982,[2] by 12 votes to 4, with 3 abstentions, the Sub-Commission expressed concern at reports of continued human rights violations in Iran, including summary and arbitrary executions and religious intolerance. Noting the Commission's request that the Secretary-General establish direct contacts with the Government, it expressed the hope that they would result in improvements. The Sub-Commission determined that the human rights situation was serious enough to merit continued scrutiny by all United Nations bodies, including the Commission.

Resolutions (1982). [1]Commission on Human Rights (report, E/1982/12): 1982/27, 11 Mar. [2]SCPDPM (report, E/CN.4/1983/4): 1982/25, 8 Sep.
Resolution (prior): [3]GA: 2200 A (XXI), annex, 16 Dec. 1966 (YUN 1966, p. 423).
Yearbook reference. [4]1981, p. 965.

Europe and the Mediterranean area

Cyprus

The Commission on Human Rights, on 11 March 1982,[1] decided to postpone until 1983 the debate on the question of human rights in Cyprus, on the understanding that action required by previous Commission resolutions continued to remain operative, including a request to the Secretary-General to report on their implementation. It acted after having received such a report from him,[2] especially regarding missing persons (p. 377).

Decision (1982). [1]Commission on Human Rights (report, E/1982/12): 1982/102, 11 Mar.
Report. [2]S-G, E/CN.4/1982/8.

Poland

Action by the Commission on Human Rights. On 10 March 1982,[3] the Commission on Human Rights affirmed the right of the Polish people to pursue political, economic, social and cultural development, free from outside interference. It expressed deep concern at continued reports of widespread human rights violations, including massive arbitrary arrests and detentions, denial of the rights of freedom of expression and peaceful assembly, suspension of the right to form and join independent trade unions and imposition of severe punishment on persons accused of violating martial law.

Noting that Polish authorities had stated the intention to terminate those restrictive measures, the Commission expressed the hope that that intention would be realized in the near future, especially with regard to the release of detained persons, the review of severe prison sentences and the lifting of restrictions on the free flow of information. It emphasized the importance of international and national humanitarian organizations in Poland, and requested the Secretary-General or a person designated by him—with the co-operation of the

Polish Government—to study the human rights situation and report in 1983.

The resolution was adopted by a roll-call vote of 19 to 13 (Algeria, Bulgaria, Byelorussian SSR, Cuba, Ethiopia, Ghana, India, Poland, Syrian Arab Republic, USSR, Yugoslavia, Zambia, Zimbabwe), with 10 abstentions.

Economic and Social Council action. On 7 May 1982,[1] by a recorded vote, requested by the USSR, of 21 to 14, with 15 abstentions, the Economic and Social Council approved the Commission's decision to request a study of the human rights situation in Poland. The Second (Social) Committee approved the draft, recommended by the Commission, on 3 May by a recorded vote of 20 to 13, with 14 abstentions.

Casting a negative vote, Poland stated that the Council decision and the Commission resolution violated the Charter of the United Nations and the principles of non-interference in the internal affairs of States; such decisions proved that human rights questions were used to attain political goals, and the Polish Government would not co-operate in implementing the Commission resolution, which it regarded as legally null and void, morally two-faced and politically harmful. Bulgaria, the Byelorussian SSR and the USSR objected to what they regarded as an attempt by the United States and some members of the North Atlantic Treaty Organization to intervene in the internal affairs of an independent State, contrary to international law.

Explaining its abstention, Brazil stated that a human rights review should always follow the procedures established by the Council in 1970,[4] except when prejudiced by the intervention of foreign armed forces, which was not the case in Poland. Tunisia, also abstaining, said the way the decision was presented gave the impression of prejudging the results of the study.

Voting in favour, the United States said that renewed demonstrations were evidence of the Polish people's refusal to submit to martial law; it urged Poland to co-operate with the study, as a sign of willingness to resume the process of renewal. Poland, replying that all responsible political forces in Poland, including the Catholic Church, had condemned the recent riots, referred to a statement by the Polish Minister for Foreign Affairs expressing the desire to develop co-operation with the United States but only on the basis of respect for the principle of non-interference in internal affairs.

Sub-Commission consideration. On 8 September 1982,[2] by 9 votes to 3, with 6 abstentions, the Sub-Commission on discrimination and minorities decided to postpone until 1983 consideration of a draft resolution to have the Secretary-General inform the Sub-Commission of the results of his study on Poland.

Decisions (1982). [1]ESC: 1982/133, 7 May, text following.
[2]SCPDPM (report. E/CN.4/1983/4): 1982/11, 8 Sep.
Resolution (1982). [3]Commission on Human Rights (report, E/1982/12): 1982/26, 10 Mar.
Resolution (prior). [4]ESC: 1503(XLVIII), 27 May 1970 (YUN 1970, p. 530).
Meeting records. ESC: E/1982/SR.*28*, 29 (7 May).

Economic and Social Council decision 1982/133

21-14-15 (recorded vote)

Approved by Second Committee (E/1982/59) by recorded vote (20-13-14), 3 May (meeting 15); draft by Commission on Human Rights (E/1982/12); agenda item 9.

Situation of human rights and fundamental freedoms in Poland
At its 28th plenary meeting, on 7 May 1982, the Council, noting resolution 1982/26 of 10 March 1982 of the Commission on Human Rights, approved the Commission's decision to request the Secretary-General or a person designated by him to undertake a thorough study of the human rights situation in Poland.

Recorded vote in Council as follows:

In favour: Australia, Austria, Bahamas, Belgium, Canada, Chile, Denmark, Fiji, France, Germany, Federal Republic of, Greece, Italy, Japan, Kenya, Mexico, Norway, Peru, Portugal, United Kingdom, United States, Venezuela.
Against: Argentina, Benin, Bulgaria, Byelorussian SSR, Ethiopia, India, Iraq, Jordan, Libyan Arab Jamahiriya, Nicaragua, Poland, Romania, USSR, Yugoslavia.
Abstaining: Bangladesh, Brazil, Burundi, Colombia, Liberia, Malawi, Mali, Nepal, Nigeria, Pakistan, Sudan, Thailand, Tunisia, United Republic of Cameroon, Zaire.

Latin America

Bolivia
Action by the Commission on Human Rights. In February 1982,[2] Special Envoy Héctor Gros Espiell (Uruguay) transmitted to the Commission on Human Rights Bolivia's official reply to his December 1981 report on the human rights situation in that State, mandated by the Commission in March 1981. In his report, the Special Envoy had stated that grave, massive and persistent violations of human rights had been committed after 17 July 1980 (the date of the assumption of power by a military Government) but that the situation appeared to have improved in the months prior to September 1981.[4]

In its reply, Bolivia emphasized its will to co-operate with the international community, and noted that it had responded promptly to inquiries by the International Labour Organisation and the Organization of American States. It stressed its intent to draw up a timetable for the return to democratic institutions and the full exercise of human rights. It noted as important first steps the complete dissolution of the Special Security Service (whose activities the Special Envoy had characterized as inadmissible), the repeal of some emergency measures and the recognition of workers' right of association with a view to re-establishing free trade unions. Bolivia expressed deep regret concerning past acts of violence, but insisted that they had not reached the dimensions claimed by non-governmental organizations.

On 11 March 1982,[3] the Commission expressed both deep concern over the grave, massive and repeated human rights violations in Bolivia after 17 July 1980 and satisfaction at the situation's improvement since 4 September 1981. It urged Bolivia to take further practical measures to ensure human rights and requested the Secretary-General to provide advisory services and other assistance to aid government compliance. The Commission decided to extend the Special Envoy's mandate for another year, requesting a further report in 1983. The Government of Bolivia was invited to continue its active co-operation.

Economic and Social Council action. On 7 May 1982,[1] acting without vote, the Economic and Social Council approved the extension for another year of the Special Envoy's mandate and requested the Secretary-General to provide all necessary assistance. The decision, recommended by the Commission, was approved by the Second Committee on 3 May, also without vote.

Decision (1982). [1]ESC: 1982/137, 7 May, text following.
Note. [2]Special Envoy, E/CN.4/1500/Add.1.
Resolution (1982). [3]Commission on Human Rights (report, E/1982/12): 1982/33, 11 Mar.
Yearbook reference. [4]1981, p. 957.
Meeting record. ESC: E/1982/SR.29 (7 May).

Economic and Social Council decision 1982/137

Adopted without vote

Approved by Second Committee (E/1982/59) without vote, 3 May (meeting 15); draft by Commission on Human Rights (E/1982/12); agenda item 9.

Situation of human rights in Bolivia

At its 29th plenary meeting, on 7 May 1982, the Council, noting resolution 1982/33 of 11 March 1982 of the Commission on Human Rights, approved the Commission's decision to extend for another year the mandate of the Special Envoy appointed to carry out a thorough study of the human rights situation in Bolivia and requested the Secretary-General to give all necessary assistance to the Special Envoy.

Chile

Action by the Commission on Human Rights. In January 1982, Special Rapporteur Abdoulaye Diéye (Senegal) submitted to the Commission on Human Rights a report on developments in the human rights situation in Chile in 1981. Transmitted by a Secretariat note,[3] the document updated a November 1981 report to the General Assembly.[8]

On 10 March 1982,[5] the Commission reiterated its serious concern at the persistence and, in certain respects, deterioration of the human rights situation in Chile. Particularly noted were the expansion of emergency legislation and promulgation of the new Constitution (in March 1981), intensification of arbitrary detention, torture and unexplained deaths, and persecution, intimidation, imprisonment and banishment of trade unionists, academics and persons involved in cultural and humanitarian activities. The Commission also reiterated concern that *habeas corpus* or *amparo* were not effective because of a highly restricted judiciary.

The Commission repeated its urgent appeal to Chile to end the state of emergency and restore democratic institutions; to end arbitrary detentions, intimidations and prosecution of those exercising the right to freedom of expression; to respect the rights of persons detained for political reasons; to prevent persecution, torture and unexplained deaths in detention and punish those responsible; to investigate the fate of persons who had disappeared for political reasons; to restore trade union rights; to re-establish civil and political rights; and to end the practice of banishments.

The Commission rejected the Chilean authorities' lack of co-operation with the Special Rapporteur and lack of compliance with international human rights instruments. It extended the Special Rapporteur's mandate for another year, asked him to report to the General Assembly in 1982 and to the Commission in 1983 when it would consider human rights in Chile as a matter of high priority, and recommended that the Economic and Social Council authorize financial resources and staff.

The resolution was adopted by a roll-call vote of 28 to 6 (Argentina, Brazil, Pakistan, Philippines, United States, Uruguay), with 8 abstentions.

Economic and Social Council action. On 7 May 1982,[1] by a recorded vote, requested by Mexico, of 34 to 5, with 13 abstentions, the Economic and Social Council approved the extension of the Special Rapporteur's mandate for one year and requested the Secretary-General to provide resources and staff. Originating in the Commission, the draft was approved by the Second Committee on 3 May by a recorded vote of 32 to 5, with 9 abstentions.

Casting a negative vote, Chile stated that, for more than eight years, it had been singled out for biased treatment through the perpetuation of a special entity whose mandate and conclusions had no legal validity. Chile reiterated its readiness to co-operate with United Nations bodies through normal procedures.

Sub-Commission action. On 8 September,[7] the Sub-Commission on discrimination and minorities recommended that the Commission call on the Chilean authorities to respect and promote human rights and to co-operate fully in the implementation of measures repeatedly requested by the Commission and the Assembly. The Sub-Commission further recommended that the Commission maintain vigilance in relation to the evolution of human rights in Chile.

Report of the Special Rapporteur. In November 1982, the Secretary-General transmitted to the Assembly a report by the Special Rapporteur[4] on human rights in Chile, relating to events mainly between January and June. The Special Rapporteur stated that Chile had continued to refuse to co-operate, despite repeated communications. As in past reports, he had relied on official and other documents in the Chilean press, the testimony of witnesses, reports by organizations, and documents and letters from individuals in Chile and elsewhere.

In his conclusions and recommendations, the Special Rapporteur noted that there was persistent institutionalization of the emergency régime, once again extended in 1982, with all branches of government subject to supervision by the armed forces. He expressed concern at the increasing number of reports of torture and ill-treatment of detainees which, he said, had an institutional character and benefited from the tolerance of the administrative and judicial authorities. Judicial protection of the right to life and the right to physical and moral integrity continued to be inadequate, and the security organs enjoyed an impunity which presupposed multiple human rights violations. Procedural guarantees continued to be challenged by the application of the legal provisions concerning the extension of the competence of military courts.

Though arbitrary individual arrests had declined, three mass arrests in May and June had resulted in 6,756 persons being detained, and the number of detentions of groups of persons at public gatherings had increased. Illegal detentions continued. The fate of 635 persons who had disappeared since 1973 had not been cleared up, despite repeated United Nations appeals, and judicial investigations of their fate had faced considerable obstacles in 1982. Though fewer people had been prohibited from entering the country, exile or expulsion had continued.

Freedom of expression and freedom of information continued to be substantially curtailed. During 1982, there had been repeated violations of the right of peaceful assembly, and the right of association was suspended until 1989. Economic rights had suffered, as had working conditions, with the levels of remuneration existing in July 1979 established as the maximum limits for 1982 and trade union rights suspended. Large numbers of illegally employed children and young persons were reported. There was no improvement in the situation with regard to education and culture; legislation restricted the right of equal access to instruction in the context of general education. The rights of indigenous minorities were not duly respected, in particular with regard to the division of indigenous communal land and to the economic, social, cultural and health situation.

Summing up his observations, the Special Rapporteur stated that he could not report an improvement in the human rights situation in Chile since none of the international community's recommendations had been adopted in 1982. He recommended that the General Assembly call on Chile to co-operate with the United Nations, and that the Government end the state of emergency and re-establish the traditional democratic legal order. In the absence of such an improvement, the international community should use means it deemed most appropriate to ensure the restoration of human rights.

General Assembly action. On 17 December,[6] the General Assembly reiterated its grave concern at the persistence of human rights violations in Chile, in particular at the widening of emergency legislation, the enactment of a new Constitution restricting human rights, and the inefficacy of *habeas corpus* or *amparo* due to the restricted judiciary. It again requested Chile to lift the state of emergency, re-establish democratic institutions and ensure rights guaranteed in international instruments. Chile was urged to investigate the fate of persons who had disappeared for political reasons (see above, under CIVIL AND POLITICAL RIGHTS), to restore trade union rights and the right of Chileans freely to enter and leave the country, to put an end to arbitrary detentions, imprisonment in secret places and torture, and to respect the rights of the indigenous population. Chile was again called on to co-operate with the Commission on Human Rights and its Special Rapporteur. The Assembly, stating the necessity of continued consideration of the situation, requested the Commission to take appropriate steps, including the extension of the Special Rapporteur's mandate, and to report to the Assembly in 1983.

The resolution was adopted by a recorded vote of 85 to 17, with 41 abstentions. The draft was approved by the Third (Social, Humanitarian and Cultural) Committee on 10 December by a roll-call vote of 74 to 16, with 40 abstentions.

Before its vote on the resolution, the Assembly rejected, by a recorded vote of 65 to 53, with 19 abstentions, a motion by Belgium not to vote on an amendment, introduced in the Assembly by Mexico for the sponsors, reinserting in paragraph 12 the request to extend the mandate as one of the steps to be taken by the Commission. The amendment was adopted by a recorded vote of 62 to 35, with 44 abstentions.

The Committee on 9 December, by a roll-call vote of 46 to 42, with 42 abstentions, had approved an oral amendment by the United Kingdom, deleting a paragraph inviting the Commission to extend the Special Rapporteur's mandate and incorporating, in paragraph 12, a request that the Commission take the most appropriate steps.

Introducing its oral amendment, the United Kingdom expressed the belief that the resolution was unbalanced; the amendment would leave it to the Commission to decide on further action.

Mexico said the sponsors could not accept an amendment that deleted substantive text. Algeria, Cuba, Nicaragua, the USSR and Yugoslavia stressed the need to extend the mandate, on the grounds that the human rights situation in Chile had not improved. Ireland cited Chile's refusal to co-operate with the Special Rapporteur as its reason to vote against the amendment. Zambia considered the proposal superfluous since the Commission was free to decide on the mandate regardless of Assembly action.

Voting in favour of the amendment, Peru regarded the Commission as the proper forum to decide on an extension of the mandate. In Australia's view, the amendment would not prejudice Commission action.

Colombia felt that the amendment sought a way for the Commission to study effective means of solving the problem through dialogue with the Chilean Government. In Uruguay's opinion, the amendment was designed to create a climate of confidence, enabling Chile to collaborate again with the United Nations. Morocco also believed that the amendment would ensure government collaboration which was necessary if a solution to the human rights situation in Chile was to be found. A similar view was expressed by Belgium. Also supporting the amendment, the Federal Republic of Germany stated that, by extending the mandate, the draft perpetuated a selective approach to human rights problems. Portugal voted in favour in the belief that the case of Chile, while disquieting, should not overshadow other situations which were at least as serious.

Following approval of the draft resolution, Denmark and the Netherlands withdrew a similar draft by which the Assembly would have expressed concern about the lack of information on disappeared persons and about the banishment or forced exile of citizens, and strongly urged Chile to promote human rights, guarantee the rights of persons detained or imprisoned for political reasons and cooperate with the Special Rapporteur.[2]

The Netherlands said that, together with Denmark, it had attempted to produce a compromise text reflecting a more balanced viewpoint and giving the Commission a precise mandate; to avoid a procedural debate and give the widest support to the appeal to Chile, it would vote in favour of the resolution, as amended by the United Kingdom.

Introducing the sponsors' amendment in the Assembly, Mexico said that if no reference to the Special Rapporteur's mandate was made, the Assembly would be changing a practice it had followed for seven years, which could be erroneously interpreted as implying that conditions in Chile had improved.

The United Kingdom considered it an unwelcome practice to vote in the plenary Assembly on issues already decided in Committee, adding that the amendment—which would request, rather than invite, the Commission to extend the mandate—was even more objectionable because it implied a stronger prejudgement of Commission action.

Also voting against the sponsors' amendment, Chile reiterated that it had never recognized the Special Rapporteur's mandate, which was a discriminatory attempt to intervene in domestic matters. The United States said that, whereas the United Kingdom's amendment had been a small step towards balance, the amendment introduced by Mexico would turn the resolution into a punitive and highly political process. Morocco described the Special Rapporteur's work as useless since no dialogue existed with the Chilean Government.

Italy abstained on the amendment saying that a decision on extending the mandate should be left to the Commission.

Cuba, on the other hand, said the situation in Chile justified reintroduction of the request. Also voting in favour of the amendment, Iran dissociated itself from any political implications. Seychelles stated that any selectivity should be overcome not by eliminating existing measures such as the Special Rapporteur's mandate, but by extending them to a larger number of countries.

Chile objected to the resolution as a whole saying it contained unsubstantiated statements, distortions and hostile language and interfered in its internal affairs. Also casting a negative vote, Indonesia voiced concern that the text, under the guise of protecting human rights, could sanction interventions or interference in internal affairs. The United States, asserting that many States felt that human rights issues were characterized by selectivity and political considerations, saw the resolution as unbalanced and unmindful of improvements in Chile.

The United Kingdom said it abstained because of the resolution's selectivity and incorporation of the request to extend the Special Rapporteur's mandate. Colombia, also abstaining, criticized the Special Rapporteur's reports as not taking into account Chile's achievements, and termed resolutions based on such reports as serving specific political interests. The Federal Republic of Germany voiced concern at the political emphasis of the resolution which, it said, made assertions that were not based on evidence and did not mention improvements.

The text's selectivity was also deplored by Bhutan, the Dominican Republic, Ecuador, Peru and Singapore. Trinidad and Tobago called for the study of human rights violations in a global context. Oman said its abstention was based on its adherence to the principle of non-interference in internal affairs.

Voting in favour, Australia voiced reservations at what it regarded as the assertion of a total lack of improvement in Chile's human rights situation, an assertion not consistent with the Special Rapporteur's report. Spain said human rights violations should be condemned wherever they occurred. Portugal hoped that the United Nations would revise the criteria applied to violations, so that they could be considered impartially. Austria expressed willingness to co-operate in all United Nations efforts to promote respect for human rights in all places. Finland deplored what it termed the consistent political viewpoint of resolutions on human rights violations and, though it voted in favour, stated that it would not be able to support such drafts in future.

Sweden voted in favour on the grounds that there was no indication that the situation in Chile had changed for the better; the state of emergency, it added, was a particularly serious aspect. In the opinion of the USSR, the Special Rapporteur's report showed that the situation continued to deteriorate and therefore all possible measures must be taken. The Netherlands said the resolution basically reflected its concern over the seriousness of the situation in Chile.

Venezuela declared that it would not participate in the vote because of the resolution's selectivity. Costa Rica, which abstained in Committee, cited a similar reason for its non-participation in the Assembly's vote.

Introducing the text also on behalf of Algeria, Bolivia, Cuba and Yugoslavia, Mexico said that, after nine years, the situation in Chile had not improved and the Special Rapporteur's report made it clear that some methods of oppression continued to prevail.

Decision (1982). (1)ESC: 1982/132, 7 May, text following.
Draft resolution withdrawn. (2)Denmark, Netherlands, A/C.3/37/L.68.
Reports. Special Rapporteur: (3)transmitted by Secretariat note, E/CN.4/1484; (4)transmitted by S-G note, A/37/564.
Resolutions (1982). (5)Commission on Human Rights (report, E/1982/12): 1982/25, 10 Mar. (6)GA: 37/183, 17 Dec., text following. (7)SCPDPM (report, E/CN.4/1983/4): 1982/19, 8 Sep.
Yearbook reference. (8)1981, p. 951.
Meeting records. ESC: E/1982/SR.28 (7 May). GA: 3rd Committee, A/C.3/37/SR.62-69, *70*, 71, *72-74* (3-10 Dec.); plenary, A/37/PV.110 (17 Dec.).

Economic and Social Council decision 1982/132

34-5-13 (recorded vote)

Approved by Second Committee (E/1982/59) by recorded vote (32-5-9), 3 May (meeting 15); draft by Commission on Human Rights (E/1982/12); agenda item 9.

Question of human rights in Chile

At its 28th plenary meeting, on 7 May 1982, the Council, noting resolution 1982/25 of 10 March 1982 of the Commission on Human Rights, approved the Commission's decision to extend for one year the mandate of the Special Rapporteur on the situation of human rights in Chile and requested the Secretary-General to make arrangements for the provision of adequate financial resources and staff for the implementation of that resolution.

Recorded vote in Council as follows:

In favour: Australia, Austria, Belgium, Benin, Bulgaria, Byelorussian SSR, Canada, Denmark, Ethiopia, France, Germany, Federal Republic of, Greece, India, Iraq, Italy, Japan, Kenya, Liberia, Libyan Arab Jamahiriya, Malawi, Mali, Mexico, Nicaragua, Norway, Poland, Portugal, Romania, Sudan, Swaziland, Tunisia, USSR, United Kingdom, Venezuela, Yugoslavia.
Against: Argentina, Brazil, Chile, Pakistan, United States.

Abstaining: Bahamas, Bangladesh, Burundi, China, Colombia, Fiji, Nepal, Nigeria, Peru, Qatar, Thailand, United Republic of Cameroon, Zaire.

General Assembly resolution 37/183

17 December 1982   Meeting 110   85-17-41 (recorded vote)

Approved by Third Committee (A/37/745) by roll-call vote (74-16-40), 10 December (meeting 73); 5-nation draft (A/C.3/37/L.53), orally amended by United Kingdom; amended in Assembly by sponsors (A/37/L.60); agenda item 12.
Sponsors of draft and amendment: Algeria, Bolivia, Cuba, Mexico, Yugoslavia.

Situation of human rights and fundamental freedoms in Chile

The General Assembly,

Aware of its responsibility to promote and encourage respect for human rights and fundamental freedoms for all and determined to remain vigilant with regard to violations of human rights wherever they occur,

Emphasizing the obligation of Governments to protect and promote human rights and to carry out the responsibilities they have undertaken with respect to the various international instruments,

Recalling its resolutions 3219(XXIX) of 6 November 1974, 3448(XXX) of 9 December 1975, 31/124 of 16 December 1976, 32/118 of 16 December 1977, 33/175 of 20 December 1978, 34/179 of 17 December 1979, 35/188 of 15 December 1980 and 36/157 of 16 December 1981, all related to the situation of human rights in Chile, as well as its resolution 33/173 of 20 December 1978 on disappeared persons,

Recalling also the resolutions of the Commission on Human Rights dealing with the human rights situation in Chile, in particular resolution 1982/25 of 10 March 1982, by which the Commission decided, *inter alia*, to extend the mandate of the Special Rapporteur on the situation of human rights in Chile,

Deploring the fact that the Chilean authorities have consistently refused to co-operate with the Commission on Human Rights and its Special Rapporteur,

Expressing its deepest concern at the total lack of improvement in the human rights situation in Chile, as shown by the Special Rapporteur in his report,

Noting with increasing concern that the Chilean authorities continue to ignore the repeated appeals of the international community, made through a number of resolutions of the General Assembly, the Commission on Human Rights and various other international organs,

Reiterating its deep concern at the lack of information concerning the numerous persons who have disappeared in Chile for political reasons and at the fact that the Chilean authorities have not taken urgent and effective measures to investigate and clarify the fate of those persons,

Noting with great concern that the Constitution promulgated by the Chilean authorities on 11 March 1981 represents the institutionalization of the state of exception, with grave prejudice to the civil and political rights of the Chilean people and serious limitations to their economic, social and cultural rights,

1.   *Commends* the Special Rapporteur on the human rights situation in Chile for his report, submitted in accordance with resolution 1982/25 of the Commission on Human Rights;

2.   *Reiterates its grave concern* at the persistence of serious and systematic violations of human rights in Chile, as described by the Special Rapporteur, in particular at the subversion of the traditional democratic legal order and its institutions, through the maintenance and widening of emergency and exceptional legislation and the promulgation of a Constitution which does not reflect a freely expressed popular will and the provisions of which suppress, suspend or restrict the enjoyment and the exercise of human rights and fundamental freedoms;

3.   *Reiterates also its deep concern* at the inefficacy of the recourse of *habeas corpus* or *amparo* in view of the fact that the judiciary in Chile does not exercise its functions fully in this respect, except within considerable restrictions;

4.   *Once more urgently requests* the Chilean authorities to respect and promote human rights in conformity with the obligations undertaken under various international instruments and, in particular, to adopt the concrete measures contemplated in resolution 1982/25 of the Commission on Human Rights, especially the lifting of the state of emergency and the state of exception and the re-establishment of democratic institutions, by ensuring the full enjoyment and exercise of civil and political rights as well as the economic, social and cultural rights and fundamental freedoms of the Chilean people, as provided in those international instruments;

5. *Urges once more* the Chilean authorities to investigate and clarify the fate of all persons who have disappeared in Chile for political reasons, to inform their families of the results of such investigation and to punish those responsible for the disappearance;

6. *Further urges again* the Chilean authorities to restore the full enjoyment of trade union rights, in particular the right to organize trade unions, the right to collective bargaining and the right to strike;

7. *Urges* the Chilean authorities to respect, in conformity with the International Covenant on Civil and Political Rights, the right of Chilean nationals to live in and freely enter and leave Chilean territory, without restrictions or conditions of any kind, and to cease the practice of "relegation" (assignment of forced residence) and forced exile, in particular of those who participate in trade union activities, academic life or the defence of human rights;

8. *Also urges* the Chilean authorities to put an end to arbitrary detentions and imprisonment in secret places and the practice of torture and other forms of inhuman or degrading treatment which have resulted on occasion in unexplained deaths;

9. *Requests* the Chilean authorities to respect fully the economic, social and cultural rights of the Chilean population in general and of the indigenous population in particular;

10. *Concludes*, on the basis of the report of the Special Rapporteur, that it is necessary to keep under consideration the situation of human rights in Chile;

11. *Calls again* on the Chilean authorities to co-operate with the Commission on Human Rights and its Special Rapporteur and to submit commentaries on his report to the Commission on Human Rights at its thirty-ninth session;

12. *Requests* the Commission on Human Rights to study in depth the report of the Special Rapporteur at its thirty-ninth session, with a view to taking the most appropriate steps, in particular the extension of the mandate of the Special Rapporteur, and report on its consideration, through the Economic and Social Council, to the General Assembly at its thirty-eighth session.

Recorded vote in Assembly as follows:

In favour: Afghanistan, Algeria, Angola, Australia, Austria, Bahrain, Barbados, Belgium, Benin, Bolivia, Botswana, Bulgaria, Burundi, Byelorussian SSR, Canada, Cape Verde, Congo, Cuba, Cyprus, Czechoslovakia, Democratic Yemen, Denmark, Ethiopia, Finland, France, Gambia, German Democratic Republic, Ghana, Greece, Grenada, Guinea, Guinea-Bissau, Guyana, Hungary, Iceland, India, Iran, Iraq, Ireland, Italy, Jamaica, Kenya, Kuwait, Lao People's Democratic Republic, Lesotho, Libyan Arab Jamahiriya, Luxembourg, Madagascar, Maldives, Mali, Malta, Mauritania, Mauritius, Mexico, Mongolia, Mozambique, Netherlands, New Zealand, Nicaragua, Nigeria, Norway, Papua New Guinea, Poland, Portugal, Romania, Sao Tome and Principe, Senegal, Seychelles, Sierra Leone, Spain, Sri Lanka, Sudan, Sweden, Togo, Tunisia, Uganda, Ukrainian SSR, USSR, United Arab Emirates, United Republic of Tanzania, Vanuatu, Viet Nam, Yugoslavia, Zambia, Zimbabwe.

Against: Antigua and Barbuda, Argentina, Brazil, Chile, El Salvador, Guatemala, Haiti, Honduras, Indonesia, Israel, Lebanon, Morocco, Pakistan, Paraguay, Philippines, United States, Uruguay.

Abstaining: Bahamas, Bangladesh, Belize, Bhutan, Burma, Chad, China, Colombia, Democratic Kampuchea, Dominica, Dominican Republic, Ecuador, Egypt, Fiji, Gabon, Germany, Federal Republic of, Ivory Coast, Japan, Jordan, Liberia, Malawi, Malaysia, Nepal, Niger, Oman, Panama, Peru, Saint Lucia, Saint Vincent and the Grenadines, Samoa, Saudi Arabia, Singapore, Solomon Islands, Suriname, Thailand, Trinidad and Tobago, Turkey, United Kingdom, United Republic of Cameroon, Upper Volta, Zaire.

El Salvador

Action by the Commission on Human Rights.
In January 1982, Special Representative José Antonio Pastor Ridruejo submitted to the Commission on Human Rights a report on the human rights situation in El Salvador,[3] as requested by the General Assembly in December 1981.[8] Since his October 1981 interim report,[9] the Special Representative had analysed information from Governments, specialized agencies and intergovernmental and non-governmental organizations, and had interviewed a number of persons in New York and Madrid, Spain, including members of Salvadorian political, academic and educational institutions and organizations.

The Special Representative concluded that far-reaching reforms were necessary, especially in the agrarian sector, to counteract the inequitable distribution of wealth and insufficient essential public services. He noted that the agrarian reforms that had occurred had been planned by the Government with no participation by the peasants. He stated that there had been consistent gross human rights violations, with the State and violent rightist groups largely responsible for attempts on human life and violent leftist groups responsible for terrorist acts against public and private property.

In his recommendations, the Special Representative described as the ultimate objective the establishment of peace and social justice to enable the Salvadorian people to enjoy human rights and self determination without outside interference. He regarded the government plan for holding elections as perfectly legitimate if and when the elections could take place in a climate of social peace in which the rights of free expression, association and assembly were respected, a complete roll of voters was available, and the authenticity of the ballot and respect of the people's will were guaranteed.

To that end, the Special Representative recommended repeal of legal measures incompatible with international human rights instruments; effective government control of armed and security forces; adoption by the Government of legal measures to prevent and punish human rights violations; and a demonstrated flexibility regarding other measures that might lead to elections, not excluding dialogue with the opposition forces. He also suggested that the United Nations, the Organization of American States or some other impartial observer might monitor the electoral process.

On 11 March,[5] the Commission expressed deepest concern at the deteriorating situation and continued human rights violations in El Salvador, and affirmed the Salvadorian people's right to determine its political status and pursue its economic, social and cultural development without external interference. The Commission reiterated the Assembly's December 1981 appeals[8] for negotiations of all representative political forces in order to establish a democratically elected Government, and to States not to intervene and to suspend all military support. It called on all Salvadorian parties to co-operate with humanitarian organizations and requested them to apply a minimum standard of human rights protection and human treatment of civilians.

It strongly urged El Salvador to ensure human rights and called on it to co-operate with the

Special Representative, whose mandate was extended for another year. He was requested to report to the Assembly in 1982 and to the Commission in 1983, when the Commission would consider the question as a matter of high priority.

This resolution was adopted by a roll-call vote of 25 to 5 (Argentina, Brazil, Philippines, United States, Uruguay), with 13 abstentions.

Economic and Social Council action. On 7 May 1982,[1] by 24 votes to 4, with 18 abstentions, the Economic and Social Council approved the Commission's decision to extend the Special Representative's mandate for another year and approved the request that he submit his report on further developments in the human rights situation in El Salvador to the Assembly in 1982 and the Commission in 1983. The decision, recommended by the Commission, was approved by the Second Committee on 3 May 1982 by a recorded vote of 27 to 6 (Argentina, Brazil, Chile, Colombia, Pakistan, Venezuela), with 16 abstentions.

Brazil stated that El Salvador's internal affairs should be settled without outside interference and that the decision would not make a positive contribution to that objective.

In explanation of its abstention, Tunisia, noting the new political situation in El Salvador, said the way the decision was presented appeared to prejudge the results of the study. The United States, describing El Salvador's efforts to comply with international human rights standards as significant, said the Special Representative could make a positive contribution by substantiating improved conditions and recommending an end to special attention for El Salvador.

Sub-Commission action. On 8 September,[7] by 13 votes to 3, with 4 abstentions, the Sub-Commission on discrimination and minorities, deeply concerned at continued human rights violations in El Salvador, expressed regret that the parties in conflict had not heeded repeated appeals for peaceful settlement. It recommended that El Salvador apply the provisions of the 1949 Geneva Conventions applicable to non-international armed conflicts, requiring minimum standards of human rights protection. The Sub-Commission recalled the Assembly's appeal to States to abstain from intervention in El Salvador and to suspend all military support. It requested the Secretary-General to inform it in 1983 of the action of the Commission's Special Representative, as well as of any consideration by the Commission, the Assembly, the Economic and Social Council or the Security Council.

By a note verbale of 6 September,[2] transmitted to the Director of the Centre for Human Rights for circulation as a Sub-Commission document, El Salvador concluded that the situation had improved and that various measures adopted had led to a positive trend in human rights. Noting a substantial reduction in violence and terrorism, El Salvador stated that it had maintained an open attitude towards the initiatives of States and organizations seeking to contribute to a political solution, though it would continue to reject partiality or judgements indicative of interventionist positions.

Report of the Special Representative. In November 1982, the Commission's Special Representative submitted, in accordance with the Commission's request, a report on the human rights situation in El Salvador since March, transmitted to the Assembly by a note of the Secretary-General.[4]

As in his January report (see above), the Special Representative analysed information from Governments and intergovernmental and non-governmental organizations. During a visit to the country from 19 to 25 September, he interviewed a number of persons, including the President, members of the Salvadorian junta, and representatives of trade union organizations, the business community and the Catholic Church. He visited a prison and police detention cells where he was able to interview political prisoners. In Mexico and the United States, he talked with representatives of the El Salvador Commission on Human Rights and heard statements and testimony from refugees representing various organizations.

In his conclusions, the Special Representative stated that, due to the country's economic crisis and attacks on the economy by the guerrilla opposition, the Salvadorian people still did not enjoy significant economic, social and cultural rights. With regard to civil and political rights, serious and massive human rights violations had persisted because of the continuing civil conflict.

Regarding the judiciary, he considered the situation still unsatisfactory, but observed a slight increase in the punishment of human rights violations and noted the authorities' concern to encourage judiciary activity. The Special Representative stated that serious human rights violations were still being committed by violent groups of both right and left, but noted cases of humanitarian treatment by both sides to persons captured in combat. He expressed hope that the concern voiced in the country for protection of human rights would be speedily effected, especially regarding the right to life.

The Special Representative concluded that the full restoration of civil peace was the essential prerequisite to improving human rights, and specifically recommended the repeal of all laws incompatible with international human rights instruments; effective government control over armed and security forces; adoption of legal measures to punish human rights violations; the organization at all levels, including schools and mass media, of campaigns to respect human rights; the continuation of reforms, including agrarian reform; and consideration of the possibility of a dialogue with all political forces, including the left-wing opposition, to end armed confrontation.

General Assembly action. On 17 December,[6] by a recorded vote of 71 to 18, with 55 abstentions, the General Assembly expressed deepest concern at continued human rights violations in El Salvador and again requested all parties in conflict to apply a minimum standard of human rights protection. Reaffirming the right of the Salvadorian people to determine their future without interference or intimidation, it expressed regret that the Government had not attempted to negotiate a peaceful settlement with all political forces, and called on all parties to end acts of violence and not interfere with the activities of humanitarian organizations. The Assembly reiterated its appeals: to States to abstain from intervention; to the Government and other political forces in El Salvador to negotiate; and to the Government to ensure respect for human rights by its agencies, including its security forces. The judiciary was urged to punish those responsible for violations and the Government was called on to co-operate with the Commission's Special Representative. The Assembly decided to keep the subject under review in 1983 and requested the Commission to continue its examination.

The draft was approved by the Third Committee on 10 December by a roll-call vote of 67 to 19, with 49 abstentions.

In Committee, Canada proposed eight amendments to the draft, some of which were orally revised taking account of proposals by Denmark and Ireland. The only amendment approved in Committee, by 43 votes to 41, with 35 abstentions, merged paragraphs 4 and 7 to reaffirm the right of Salvadorians to determine their future without interference or intimidation, and deleted an appeal to the Government and other political forces to work together towards a peaceful settlement and free elections. However, the Assembly, on 17 December, adopted by a recorded vote of 62 to 32, with 45 abstentions, an amendment by the sponsors to reinstate the deleted paragraph 7 containing that appeal.

Six of the Canadian amendments were rejected by vote in Committee. By the first of these, rejected by 38 votes to 38, with 52 abstentions, the eighth preambular paragraph would have noted the inability, rather than failure, of the judiciary to fulfil its duties.

The second amendment would have had the Assembly state, in the ninth preambular paragraph, that since the March elections there had been little noticeable improvement in human rights,

replacing the assertion that elections had not led to improvements. Canada further revised this amendment to delete reference to the elections. The revised amendment was rejected by 42 votes to 29, with 46 abstentions.

The third amendment would have added a new preambular paragraph noting the creation of a national Commission on Human Rights and expressing the hope that it would be able to discharge its mandate. A later oral revision would have added that the Commission would contribute to the ending of human rights violations observed by the Special Representative. The revised amendment was rejected by 43 votes to 27, with 39 abstentions.

Canada proposed to amend operative paragraph 3 to note that the restoration of peace in El Salvador was a prerequisite to respect for human rights and gradual improvement of economic, social and cultural rights, thereby replacing the statement that the situation had its root causes in internal factors and that conditions for the exercise of human rights did not exist. That amendment was then orally revised to delete the reference to "gradual improvement" of economic, social and cultural rights in favour of a clause calling for their full exercise. The revised amendment was rejected by 44 votes to 35, with 37 abstentions.

An amendment to paragraph 5 would have had the Assembly urge the Government and other political forces to utilize the offers of friendly countries to establish a dialogue, instead of expressing regret that the Government had not responded to suggestions to negotiate a peaceful settlement with all representative political forces. The amendment, further revised to delete mention of the offers of friendly countries, was rejected by 45 votes to 36, with 36 abstentions.

The last of the rejected amendments, affecting paragraph 10, rather than have the Assembly urge the judiciary to assume its obligation to punish those responsible for violations, would have expressed concern over its inability to do so. The amendment was rejected by 44 votes to 30, with 43 abstentions.

One further amendment by Canada was withdrawn. Affecting the appeal in paragraph 8 that States abstain from intervening in El Salvador's internal affairs and suspend military assistance, it would have replaced the clause which cited the need to allow the establishment of a democratic system by the phrase "thus securing a democratic system".

Introducing the amendments, Canada described them as an attempt to make the resolution as well balanced as the Special Representative's report. Mexico, on behalf of the resolution's sponsors, said that they had not reached agreement on the amendments and would have to reject them. Bulgaria believed that the amendments did not balance the text so much as reduce its scope. Nicaragua felt that they altered the resolution's objectives; in particular, it could not accept a national Human Rights Commission of which the Director of Police would be a member. Cuba, also voting against the amendments, made a similar point and added that paragraph 5 should not be amended because the Salvadorian Government had rejected the offer for negotiations. Costa Rica, however, viewed the establishment of a national Human Rights Commission as positive.

Reintroducing the appeal for negotiations to bring about a peaceful settlement, Mexico stressed the importance of ending violence as a prerequisite to restoring human rights. El Salvador regarded the amendment as an attempt to manipulate the human rights issue, which would create a resolution lacking objectivity and balance. Morocco, also rejecting the amendment, termed it an encouragement to interfere in a country's internal political affairs, and the United States felt that its adoption would add to the resolution's political nature. Canada considered it neither helpful nor desirable to reintroduce in the plenary Assembly what had been deleted in Committee. Cuba and Nicaragua, on the other hand, considered it essential to restore the paragraph in order to bring about a peaceful settlement and conditions for the establishment of a Government in an atmosphere free from intimidation and terror. In the opinion of Seychelles, a negotiated settlement which took into account the representative political forces was the only solution to the conflict in El Salvador. Iran emphasized that it voted for the amendment with regard to human rights implications only and dissociated itself from any political implications.

El Salvador rejected the resolution, saying it contrasted the report of the Special Representative and distorted reality, disregarded the efforts of the highest authorities and attempted to intervene in the internal political process, disregarding the electoral results of 28 March. The text was part of a discriminatory strategy against Latin American countries and its partial bias encouraged violence by extremists. Despite the propaganda against it, El Salvador would continue its agrarian reform and was convinced that free elections would take place in 1984.

Also voting against the resolution, Brazil termed it unbalanced, contradictory and incapable of improving the human rights situation. In the opinion of the United States, the resolution did not reflect the attempt at balance inherent in the Special Representative's report but rather contradicted the report's findings. The United States also opposed any call for direct negotiations between the legitimate Government and a political front representing what it felt were unrepresentative guerrillas; in its view, the path to peace meant a halt to illegal, clandestine arms movement and the fostering of confidence through international supervision and inspection.

Saint Lucia, calling the text tendentious and selective, stated that it would vote against any human rights resolution that did not display greater impartiality. Indonesia cautioned that, under the guise of protecting human rights, the resolution could sanction interventions or interference in internal affairs.

Oman and Tunisia cited adherence to the principle of non-interference as a reason for their abstentions; Tunisia added that initiatives such as the March elections should be encouraged and dogmatic attitudes should not hamper processes that could restore unity and harmony. Australia and Portugal expressed regret that the resolution conveyed a one-sided view and, according to Australia, did not recognize the democratization that had begun after the elections. Belgium and the Federal Republic of Germany felt that the resolution placed the sole responsibility for the conflict on the Government, overlooked the efforts by the authorities to improve the situation and seemed to contest the results of the March elections. Colombia believed that the resolution ignored the very occurrence of elections along with the efforts made in the search for social justice.

Belgium, Bhutan, Colombia, the Dominican Republic and the Federal Republic of Germany objected to the singling out of a few countries for human rights violations, despite the fact that many others were responsible for such violations, at times on an even larger scale. Remarking that some of the worst human rights violations seemed to be immune from scrutiny, Singapore urged for a more objective way to defend human rights. Trinidad and Tobago called for the study of human rights violations in a global context.

Also abstaining, the United Kingdom said the resolution failed to reflect the thrust of the Special Representative's report or to recognize the Government's difficulties. Jamaica felt that, with the Canadian amendments not having been adopted, the resolution did not reflect the Special Representative's views or objectively describe the situation. Ecuador abstained, stating that it could not accept the first, second, third, fourth and seventh preambular paragraphs or operative paragraphs 2, 6, 8 and 11 to 14.

Though voting in favour of the text, Finland deplored its political perspective and stated that it would not be able to support such resolutions in the future. Spain said that a partial and discriminatory approach to human rights violations was unacceptable.

The USSR supported the resolution, considering it necessary to end human rights violations and to give the people in El Salvador a chance to decide their own fate. Seychelles said its positive vote was based on its concern over a conflict whose increasing regionalization made it imperative to find a peaceful political solution.

Objecting to the singling out of Latin American countries, Venezuela did not participate in the vote. Costa Rica, which cast a negative vote in Committee, cited a similar reason for its non-participation in the Assembly's vote.

Introducing the draft also on behalf of Algeria, France, Greece, Sweden and Yugoslavia, Mexico said the sponsors were convinced that the best way to safeguard human rights in Central America was to maintain international awareness of the excesses committed there and to promote political *rapproche-ment* for the re-establishment of peace in the interest of all Salvadorian people, not merely that of one party to the conflict.

Decision (1982). [1]ESC: 1982/134, 7 May, text following.
Note verbale. [2]El Salvador, 6 Sep., E/CN.4/Sub.2/1982/37.
Reports. Special Representative: [3]E/CN.4/1502; [4]transmitted by S-G note, A/37/611.
Resolutions (1982). [5]Commission on Human Rights (report, E/1982/12): 1982/28, 11 Mar. [6]GA: 37/185, 17 Dec., text following. [7]SCPDPM (report, E/CN.4/1983/4). 1982/26, 8 Sep.
Resolution (prior). [8]GA: 36/155, 16 Dec. 1981 (YUN 1981, p. 962).
Yearbook reference. [9]1981, p. 958.
Meeting records. ESC: E/1982/SR.28, *29* (7 May). GA: 3rd Committee, A/C.3/37/SR.57, 62-69, *70,* 71, *72-74* (29 Nov.–10 Dec.); plenary, A/37/PV.110 (17 Dec.).

Economic and Social Council decision 1982/134

24-4-18

Approved by Second Committee (E/1982/59) by recorded vote (27-6-16), 3 May (meeting 15); draft by Commission on Human Rights (E/1982/12); agenda item 9.

Situation of human rights in El Salvador

At its 29th plenary meeting, on 7 May 1982, the Council, noting resolution 1982/28 of 11 March 1982 of the Commission on Human Rights, approved the Commission's decision to extend for another year the mandate of the Special Representative on the situation of human rights in El Salvador and the Commission's request to the Special Representative to submit his report on further developments in the situation of human rights in El Salvador to the General Assembly at its thirty-seventh session and to the Commission on Human Rights at its thirty-ninth session.

General Assembly resolution 37/185

17 December 1982   Meeting 110   71-18-55 (recorded vote)

Approved by Third Committee (A/37/745) by roll-call vote (67-19-49), 10 December (meeting 74); 6-nation draft (A/C.3/37/L.77), amended by Canada (A/C.3/37/L.82, amendment 5); amended in Assembly by sponsors (A/37/L.61); agenda item 12.
Sponsors of draft and amendment: Algeria, France, Greece, Mexico, Sweden, Yugoslavia.

Situation of human rights and fundamental freedoms in El Salvador

The General Assembly,

Guided by the principles embodied in the Charter of the United Nations and in the Universal Declaration of Human Rights,

Conscious of its responsibility in all circumstances to promote and encourage respect for human rights and fundamental freedoms for all,

Reiterating that the Governments of all Member States have an obligation to promote and protect human rights and fundamental freedoms and to carry out the responsibilities they have undertaken under various international human rights instruments,

Determined to remain vigilant with regard to violations of human rights wherever they occur and to take measures to restore respect for human rights and fundamental freedoms,

Recalling that, in its resolutions 35/192 of 15 December 1980 and 36/155 of 6 December 1981, it expressed deep concern at the situation of human rights in El Salvador, especially in view of the death of thousands of people, the climate of violence and insecurity prevailing in that country and the impunity of paramilitary forces and other armed groups,

Bearing in mind Commission on Human Rights resolution 32(XXXVII) of 11 March 1981, in which the Commission decided to appoint a Special Representative on the situation of human rights in El Salvador, and resolution 1982/28 of 11 March 1982, whereby the Commission extended the mandate of the Special Representative for another year and requested him to report, *inter alia,* to the General Assembly at its thirty-seventh session,

Taking note of resolutions 10(XXXIV) of 9 September 1981 and 1982/26 of 8 September 1982 of the Sub-Commission on Prevention of Discrimination and Protection of Minorities,

Taking note with grave concern of the interim report of the Special Representative of the Commission on Human Rights, in which the unabated continuation of a climate of violence and insecurity in El Salvador with armed clashes, acts of terrorism and unbridled, large-scale and grave violations of human rights, as well as the failure of the judiciary to fulfil its duties to uphold the rule of law, are confirmed,

Observing that the elections which were held in El Salvador in March 1982 have not led to the cessation of violence or to any improvement in the situation of human rights and fundamental freedoms in that country,

1. *Expresses its deepest concern* at the continued and unbridled violations of human rights and at the resulting suffering of the Salvadorian people, and regrets that the appeals for the cessation of violence made by the General Assembly, the Commission on Human Rights and the international community in general have not been heeded;

2. *Again draws the attention* of all Salvadorian parties concerned to the fact that the rules of international law, as contained in article 3 common to the Geneva Conventions of 12 August 1949 on the laws of war, are applicable to armed conflicts not of an international character and requests all parties to the conflict to apply a minimum standard of protection of human rights and of human treatment to the civilian population;

3. *Notes* that the situation in El Salvador, as is clearly shown in the report of the Special Representative of the Commission on Human Rights, has its root causes in internal political, economic and social factors, and that conditions in El Salvador for the effective exercise of civil and political rights do not exist at present;

4. *Reaffirms* the right of the Salvadorian people freely to determine their political, economic and social future without interference from outside and in an atmosphere free from intimidation and terror from all parties;

5. *Regrets* that the Government of El Salvador has not responded to suggestions to initiate, through available channels, contacts to negotiate a peaceful settlement with all representative political forces in that country;

6. *Calls again upon* the parties in El Salvador to seek an end to all acts of violence in order to end the loss of life and the suffering of the people of El Salvador;

7. *Reiterates its appeal* to the Government and other political forces in El Salvador to work together towards a comprehensive negotiated political solution in order to bring about a peaceful settlement and appropriate conditions for the establishment of a Government through free and unhampered elections, in an atmosphere free from intimidation and terror;

8. *Reiterates its appeal* to all States to abstain from intervening in the internal situation in El Salvador and to suspend all supplies of arms and any type of military assistance, so as to allow the political forces in that country to restore peace and security and to permit the establishment of a democratic system;

9. *Strongly urges* the Government of El Salvador to fulfil its obligations towards its citizens and to assume its international responsibilities in this regard by taking the necessary steps to ensure that human rights and fundamental freedoms are fully respected by all its agencies, including its security forces and other armed organizations operating under its authority or with its permission;

10. *Urges* the judiciary in El Salvador to assume its obligation to uphold the rule of law and to prosecute and to punish those found responsible for assassinations, acts of torture and other forms of cruel, inhuman or degrading treatment;

11. *Reiterates its appeal* to all Salvadorian parties concerned to co-operate fully and not to interfere with the activities of humanitarian organizations dedicated to alleviating the suffering of the civilian population, wherever these organizations operate in El Salvador;

12 *Calls again upon* the Government of El Salvador, as well as all other parties concerned, to continue to co-operate with the Special Representative of the Commission on Human Rights;

13. *Requests* the Commission on Human Rights at its thirty-ninth session to continue to examine, as a matter of high priority, the situation in El Salvador on the basis of the report of its Special Representative;

14. *Decides* to keep under consideration, during its thirty-eighth session, the situation of human rights and fundamental freedoms in El Salvador, in order to examine this situation anew in the light of additional elements provided by the Commission on Human Rights and the Economic and Social Council.

Recorded vote in Assembly as follows:

In favour: Afghanistan, Algeria, Angola, Austria, Bahrain, Barbados, Benin, Botswana, Bulgaria, Byelorussian SSR, Cape Verde, Congo, Cuba, Cyprus, Czechoslovakia, Democratic Yemen, Denmark, Ethiopia, Finland, France, German Democratic Republic, Ghana, Greece, Grenada, Guinea, Guinea-Bissau, Guyana, Hungary, Iceland, India, Iran, Iraq, Ireland, Italy, Kenya, Kuwait, Lao People's Democratic Republic, Lesotho, Libyan Arab Jamahiriya, Madagascar, Mali, Malta, Mauritania, Mauritius, Mexico, Mongolia, Mozambique, Netherlands, Nicaragua, Nigeria, Norway, Papua New Guinea, Poland, Sao Tome and Principe, Senegal, Seychelles, Sierra Leone, Spain, Sweden, Syrian Arab Republic, Togo, Uganda, Ukrainian SSR, USSR, United Arab Emirates, United Republic of Tanzania, Vanuatu, Viet Nam, Yugoslavia, Zambia, Zimbabwe.

Against: Antigua and Barbuda, Argentina, Brazil, Chile, El Salvador, Guatemala, Haiti, Honduras, Indonesia, Israel, Morocco, Pakistan, Paraguay, Philippines, Saint Lucia, Solomon Islands, United States, Uruguay.

Abstaining: Australia, Bahamas, Bangladesh, Belgium, Belize, Bhutan, Bolivia, Burma, Burundi, Canada, Chad, China, Colombia, Democratic Kampuchea, Djibouti, Dominica, Dominican Republic, Ecuador, Egypt, Fiji, Gabon, Gambia, Germany, Federal Republic of, Ivory Coast, Jamaica, Japan, Jordan, Liberia, Luxembourg, Malawi, Malaysia, Maldives, Nepal, New Zealand, Niger, Oman, Panama, Peru, Portugal, Romania, Saint Vincent and the Grenadines, Samoa, Saudi Arabia, Singapore, Sri Lanka, Sudan, Suriname, Thailand, Trinidad and Tobago, Tunisia, Turkey, United Kingdom, United Republic of Cameroon, Upper Volta, Zaire.

Guatemala

Action by the Commission on Human Rights. On 11 March 1982,[3] by a roll-call vote of 29 to 2 (Argentina, Uruguay), with 12 abstentions, the Commission on Human Rights expressed profound concern at the continuing deterioration of human rights in Guatemala. It requested the appointment of a Special Rapporteur, with whom Guatemala was asked to co-operate, to study the human rights situation in that country and report to the Commission in 1983.

Economic and Social Council action. The appointment of a Special Rapporteur was approved by the Economic and Social Council on 7 May.[1] The Council adopted the decision by a recorded vote, requested by Chile, of 28 to 2, with 21 abstentions. The Second Committee approved the draft, recommended by the Commission, on 3 May by a recorded vote of 28 to 2, with 19 abstentions.

Before the vote, Guatemala stated that, under the new Government, human rights were no longer violated but rather guaranteed by a new legal order, those responsible for human rights violations in the past were being brought to justice,

and *habeas corpus* and *amparo* were being strictly observed. The Council might therefore reconsider the advisability of appointing a Special Rapporteur; Guatemala, for its part, was prepared to co-operate fully with the Council and the Commission in their efforts to protect human rights.

Colombia said it abstained because the decision involved selective treatment which placed political considerations first.

Tunisia cited as the main reason for its abstention the way the decision was presented which, it said, gave the impression of prejudging the results of any study.

Sub-Commission action. On 7 September,[5] the Sub-Commission on discrimination and minorities expressed concern at the persistence of human rights violations in Guatemala and at reports of massive repression against and displacement of the indigenous population, and emphasized that those violations made the effective exercise of civil and political rights impossible. It declared that only free elections, as guaranteed under the International Covenant on Civil and Political Rights,[6] would enable the Guatemalan people to determine its future. The Sub-Commission urged the Government to guarantee human rights so that conditions could be established for the exercise of civil and political rights. It welcomed the appointment of a Special Rapporteur and Guatemala's assurance of co-operation with him, and requested the Secretary-General to inform the Sub-Commission in 1983 of the results of the Special Rapporteur's mission.

General Assembly action. Noting the state of siege in force in Guatemala since 1 July 1982, the General Assembly, on 17 December,[4] by a recorded vote of 79 to 16, with 49 abstentions, expressed deep concern at the serious human rights violations, particularly reports of widespread displacement, repression and killing of rural and indigenous populations. It urged the Government to ensure respect for human rights by all its authorities, including security forces, and to allow the assistance of international humanitarian organizations. The Assembly appealed to all parties in Guatemala to end violence, inviting them to co-operate with the Special Rapporteur. It called on States to refrain from supplying military assistance to Guatemala, and requested the Commission to study the Special Rapporteur's report and consider further steps for securing human rights.

The Third Committee approved the text on 10 December, by a roll-call vote of 74 to 16, with 45 abstentions.

Introducing the draft also on behalf of Austria, Canada, Denmark, Ireland, the Netherlands and Norway, Sweden said that, despite encouraging statements from Guatemala, new information seemed to confirm continuing serious human rights violations. The lack of long-demanded reforms was one of the main factors behind the violence and it was to be hoped that Guatemala would do its utmost to find a solution to its social and economic problems; the Government's co-operation with the Special Rapporteur would be a positive step in that direction.

Guatemala termed the resolution as unjust, politically motivated and premature, since the Special Rapporteur's report had not yet been submitted. It rejected any attempt to condemn it for human rights violations which it did not recognize having committed; any analysis of the human rights situation not considering national realities and the problem of subversion lacked objectivity and practical worth.

Also casting a negative vote, Brazil agreed that the resolution was premature and unlikely to contribute to the cause of human rights. Indonesia considered that the resolution, under the guise of protecting human rights, could sanction intervention or interference in internal affairs. In the opinion of the United States, the resolution took no account of the changes since March 1982 when the new Government had come into power, ignored the violence of anti-Government guerrillas and sought to pass judgement before giving the Government a chance to act.

Abstaining, Ecuador expressed concern over the resolution's selectivity. The Dominican Republic stated that it did not wish to contribute to the singling out of human rights violations in Latin America. Singapore said the United Nations must find more objective ways to defend human rights. Trinidad and Tobago believed that human rights should be studied in a global context.

The Federal Republic of Germany termed the resolution inappropriate and untimely and said it took no account of the latest developments, did not encourage the new Government's efforts to improve human rights and ignored the fact that the Government was not solely to blame for violence. In Colombia's view, the resolution disregarded the announcement by the Government of the holding of elections to the Constituent Assembly and the establishment of a human rights commission. India felt that, pending the Special Rapporteur's report, Guatemala should be given an opportunity to improve the human rights situation. Oman explained that its abstention was consistent with its adherence to the principle of non-interference.

Though voting in favour, Finland deplored the trend of human rights violations being viewed from a political perspective, often in the context of a transient political situation, and stated that it would not be able to support such resolutions in the future. Spain considered a partial and discriminatory approach to be unacceptable, saying that human rights violations should be condemned

wherever they occurred. Belgium said it shared the concerns of the resolution's sponsors; however, it must be borne in mind that there were human rights violations elsewhere.

By a letter of 26 October,[2] Guatemala informed the Secretary-General that the Inter-American Commission on Human Rights had been invited for a visit to ascertain that human rights were being observed within the context of the national situation. After the Commission's visit from 20 to 26 September, Guatemala reported its decision to implement a Commission recommendation to suspend penalties imposed by special courts until the right of due process could be more effectively ensured.

Decision (1982). [1]ESC: 1982/135, 7 May, text following.
Letter. [2]Guatemala, 26 Oct., A/C.3/37/5.
Resolutions (1982). [3]Commission on Human Rights (report, E/1982/12): 1982/31, 11 Mar. [4]GA: 37/184, 17 Dec., text following. [5]SCPDPM (report, E/CN.4/1983/4): 1982/17, 7 Sep.
Resolution (prior), [6]2200 A (XXI), annex, 16 Dec. 1966 (YUN 1966, p. 423).
Meeting records. ESC: E/1982/SR.28, *29* (7 May). GA: 3rd Committee, A/C.3/37/SR.62, 63, *64,* 65-71, *72-74* (3-10 Dec.); plenary, A/37/PV.110 (17 Dec.).

Economic and Social Council decision 1982/135

28-2-21 (recorded vote)

Approved by Second Committee (E/1982/59) by recorded vote (28-2-19), 3 May (meeting 15); draft by Commission on Human Rights (E/1982/12); agenda item 9.

Situation of human rights in Guatemala

At its 29th plenary meeting, on 7 May 1982, the Council, noting resolution 1982/31 of 11 March 1982 of the Commission on Human Rights, approved the Commission's request to its Chairman to appoint, after consultation within the Bureau, a special rapporteur of the Commission whose mandate would be to make a thorough study of the human rights situation in Guatemala, based on all information which he might deem relevant, including any comments and information which the Government of Guatemala might wish to submit, to be presented to the Commission at its thirty-ninth session. The Council requested the Secretary-General to give all necessary assistance to the special rapporteur of the Commission.

Recorded vote in Council as follows:

In favour: Australia, Austria, Belgium, Benin, Bulgaria, Byelorussian SSR, Canada, Denmark, France, Germany, Federal Republic of, Greece, India, Iraq, Italy, Japan, Kenya, Libyan Arab Jamahiriya, Mexico, Nicaragua, Norway, Poland, Portugal, Romania, Swaziland, USSR, United Kingdom, Venezuela, Yugoslavia.
Against: Argentina, Chile.
Abstaining: Bahamas, Bangladesh, Brazil, Burundi, China, Colombia, Fiji, Jordan, Liberia, Mali, Nepal, Nigeria, Pakistan, Peru, Qatar, Sudan, Thailand, Tunisia, United Republic of Cameroon, United States, Zaire.

General Assembly resolution 37/184

17 December 1982   Meeting 110   79-16-49 (recorded vote)

Approved by Third Committee (A/37/745) by roll-call vote (74-16-45), 10 December (meeting 73); 7-nation draft (A/C.3/37/L.75); agenda item 12.

Sponsors: Austria, Canada, Denmark, Ireland, Netherlands, Norway, Sweden.

Situation of human rights and fundamental freedoms in Guatemala

The General Assembly,

Reiterating that the Governments of all Member States have an obligation to promote and protect human rights and fundamental freedoms,

Recalling Commission on Human Rights resolution 1982/31 of 11 March 1982, in which the Commission expressed its profound concern at the continuing deterioration in the situation of human rights and fundamental freedoms in Guatemala under the previous régime and in which it requested its Chairman to appoint a Special Rapporteur,

Taking into account General Assembly decision 36/435 of 16 December 1981,

Expressing its satisfaction at the declared willingness of the present Government of Guatemala to co-operate with the Special Rapporteur to be appointed pursuant to Commission on Human Rights resolution 1982/31 with a mandate to make a thorough study of the human rights situation in Guatemala,

Taking note of resolution 1982/17 of 7 September 1982 of the Sub-Commission on Prevention of Discrimination and Protection of Minorities, in which the Sub-Commission expressed alarm at reports of massive repression against and displacement of indigenous populations,

Disturbed about the large number of missing persons, who, despite appeals from various international organizations to the Government of Guatemala, remain unaccounted for,

Noting with concern the state of siege in force in Guatemala since 1 July 1982, under which basic human rights are abrogated and serious violations of human rights are reported to occur,

1. *Expresses its deep concern* at the serious violations of human rights reported to be taking place in Guatemala, particularly those reports of widespread repression, killing and massive displacement of rural and indigenous populations;

2. *Urges* the Government of Guatemala to ensure that human rights and fundamental freedoms are fully respected by all its authorities and agencies, including its security forces;

3. *Appeals* to the Government of Guatemala to allow international humanitarian organizations to give their assistance to those displaced;

4. *Appeals also* to all parties concerned in Guatemala to seek an end to all acts of violence;

5. *Calls upon* Governments to refrain from supplying arms and other military assistance as long as serious human rights violations in Guatemala continue to be reported;

6. *Invites* the Government of Guatemala and other parties concerned to co-operate with the Special Rapporteur of the Commission on Human Rights;

7. *Requests* the Commission on Human Rights to study carefully the report of its Special Rapporteur and to consider, in the light of that report, further steps for securing human rights and fundamental freedoms for all in Guatemala.

Recorded vote in Assembly as follows:

In favour: Afghanistan, Algeria, Angola, Australia, Austria, Bahrain, Barbados, Belgium, Benin, Botswana, Bulgaria, Byelorussian SSR, Canada, Cape Verde, Congo, Cuba, Cyprus, Czechoslovakia, Democratic Yemen, Denmark, Ethiopia, Finland, France, Gambia, German Democratic Republic, Ghana, Greece, Grenada, Guinea-Bissau, Guyana, Hungary, Iceland, Iran, Iraq, Ireland, Italy, Jamaica, Kenya, Kuwait, Lao People's Democratic Republic, Lesotho, Libyan Arab Jamahiriya, Luxembourg, Madagascar, Mali, Malta, Mauritania, Mauritius, Mexico, Mongolia, Mozambique, Netherlands, New Zealand, Nicaragua, Nigeria, Norway, Papua New Guinea, Poland, Portugal, Qatar, Sao Tome and Principe, Senegal, Seychelles, Sierra Leone, Spain, Sweden, Syrian Arab Republic, Togo, Uganda, Ukrainian SSR, USSR, United Arab Emirates, United Kingdom, United Republic of Tanzania, Vanuatu, Viet Nam, Yugoslavia, Zambia, Zimbabwe.

Against: Antigua and Barbuda, Argentina, Brazil, Chile, El Salvador, Guatemala, Haiti, Honduras, Indonesia, Israel, Morocco, Pakistan, Paraguay, Philippines, United States, Uruguay.

Abstaining: Bahamas, Bangladesh, Belize, Bhutan, Bolivia, Burma, Burundi, Chad, China, Colombia, Democratic Kampuchea, Dominica, Dominican Republic, Ecuador, Egypt, Fiji, Gabon, Germany, Federal Republic of, Guinea, India, Ivory Coast, Japan, Jordan, Liberia, Malawi, Malaysia, Maldives, Nepal, Niger, Oman, Panama, Peru, Romania, Saint Lucia, Saint Vincent and the Grenadines, Samoa, Saudi Arabia, Singapore, Solomon Islands, Sri Lanka, Sudan, Suriname, Thailand, Trinidad and Tobago, Tunisia, Turkey, United Republic of Cameroon, Upper Volta, Zaire.

Territories occupied by Israel

During 1982, the question of human rights violations in the territories occupied by Israel as a result of 1967 hostilities in the Middle East was again considered by the Commission on Human Rights, its Sub-Commission and the General Assembly. This was in addition to the consideration of political and other aspects by the Assembly, its Special Committee to Investigate Israeli Practices Affecting the Human Rights of the Population of the Occupied Territories and other bodies (see

POLITICAL AND SECURITY QUESTIONS, Chapter IX).

Action by the Commission on Human Rights. On 11 February, the Commission on Human Rights adopted two resolutions on human rights violations in the occupied Arab territories, and another on self-determination for the Palestinian people (see above, under CIVIL AND POLITICAL RIGHTS).

By the first resolution,[1] adopted by a roll-call vote of 32 to 3 (Australia, Canada, United States), with 7 abstentions, the Commission reaffirmed that occupation constituted a fundamental violation of the human rights of the civilian population in the territories. It expressed alarm that Israel's policy, based on the so-called "Homeland" doctrine envisaging a Jewish State including those territories, denied the right to self-determination and was a continuing source of human rights violations. It declared that Israel's grave breaches of the 1949 Geneva Convention relative to the Protection of Civilian Persons in Time of War (fourth Geneva Convention) were war crimes and an affront to humanity. It again rejected and condemned Israel's decision to annex Jerusalem and alter its character and status.

The Commission strongly condemned Israeli measures to promote and expand settler colonies and called for an end to the following specific practices: annexation of occupied territories, including Jerusalem; establishment and expansion of Israeli settlements on Arab lands; arming of settlers in the occupied territories and violence by the settlers, causing injury, death and damage to Arab property; evacuation, deportation and expulsion of Arabs and the denial of their right of return; confiscation and expropriation of Arab property and all other transactions for the acquisition of land in the occupied territories involving Israeli authorities; destruction and demolition of Arab houses; mass arrests, collective punishments, detention, ill-treatment, torture and inhuman prison conditions; pillaging of archaeological and cultural property; interference with religious freedoms and family customs; systematic repression against Palestinian universities; and illegal exploitaton of natural resources.

The Commission demanded that Israel desist from those policies and practices, and called on it to take immediate steps for the return of displaced Arabs to their homes and property; to implement resolutions on the return of the expelled Mayors of Hebron and Halhul; to cease all torture and ill-treatment of Arab detainees and prisoners; and to release all those imprisoned as a result of their struggle for self-determination. It renewed its request to the Secretary-General to collect information on detainees and make it available to the Commission in 1983. The Secretary-

General was further requested to give the resolution the widest possible publicity and to bring to the Commission's attention all United Nations reports appearing between Commission sessions on the situation of the population of the occupied territories. The Commission decided to hold a seminar at Geneva on human rights violations in the occupied territories (see below).

The Commission reiterated its call to States not to recognize any changes by Israel in the occupied territories and to avoid taking any action or extending aid which Israel might use in pursuit of its annexation and colonization policies. It called on Israel to report on implementation of the resolution and decided to give the question high priority in 1983.

By the second resolution,[2] adopted by a roll-call vote of 41 to 1 (United States), the Commission condemned Israel's failure to acknowledge the applicability to the occupied territories of the fourth Geneva Convention and expressed deep concern at the consequences of Israel's refusal to apply its provisions. The Commission called on Israel to abide by and respect its obligations under the Convention, the Charter of the United Nations and other international instruments, and urged States parties to the Convention to exert all efforts to ensure respect for and compliance with its provisions in the occupied territories.

After each resolution was adopted separately, the two resolutions were adopted together by a roll-call vote of 32 to 1 (United States), with 9 abstentions.

Sub-Commission action. On 8 September,[3] by 18 votes to 1, with 3 abstentions, the Sub-Commission on Prevention of Discrimination and Protection of Minorities recommended that the Commission declare as an affront to humanity Israel's breaches in Lebanon and the occupied Palestinian territories of the fourth Geneva Convention, and call on Israel to withdraw from all occupied territories and to implement United Nations resolutions.

The Sub-Commission also requested the Secretary-General to supply it in 1983 with a list of reports, documents, statistics and texts of United Nations resolutions and decisions on Palestine and other occupied Arab territories, including Lebanon. Recommending that the Commission and the Economic and Social Council take urgent measures to implement the resolution, the Sub-Commission also asked the Commission to condemn Israel's invasion of Lebanon and indiscriminate destruction of Lebanese cities and Palestinian refugee camps; urge Israel to grant prisoner-of-war status to Lebanese and Palestinian combatants, to release all detained civilians, and to comply with the Security Council resolutions asking for unconditional and immediate Is-

raeli withdrawal from Lebanon; and call for the full exercise of the rights of the Palestinians to self-determination and to return to their homes.

Resolutions (1982). Commission on Human Rights (report, E/1982/12), 11 Feb.: [1]1982/1 A, [2]1982/1 B. [3]SCPDPM (report, E/CN.4/1983/4): 1982/18, 8 Sep.

Seminar

From 29 November to 3 December 1982, a Seminar on violations of human rights in the Palestinian and other Arab territories occupied by Israel was organized at Geneva by the United Nations Centre for Human Rights.[2]

The Seminar affirmed the right of the Palestinians to self-determination; human rights violations in the territories would only cease when the Palestinians were allowed to enjoy that right. The Seminar characterized the Israeli occupation as resulting in demographic transformation and eventual annexation—the time factor was thus crucial.

The laws applicable in the territories had been totally eclipsed by military orders, establishing *de facto* a new legal régime. Palestinians and other Arabs in the territories were deprived of most kinds of protection. The establishment of Israeli settlements in the territories was a grave breach of the fourth Geneva Convention and inconsistent with Israel's status as an occupying Power. The economy of the territories was completely subjugated to the Israeli economy, and the cultural life was affected by restraints on freedom of movement, expression, assembly and religion and other restrictions.

The Seminar stated that the Palestinian people's right of return was interrelated with the right to self-determination and acknowledged the Palestine Liberation Organization as its sole legitimate representative. According to the Seminar, Palestinians had been denied their rights to participation, social welfare, economic well-being, education and development as a society. Affirming the applicability to all Israeli-occupied territories of the fourth Geneva Convention, the Seminar concluded that Israel had committed acts tantamount to genocide, had seriously contravened the Convention and had committed breaches of other international instruments. The Seminar condemned the Israeli invasion of Lebanon as an illegal act, and characterized Israeli acts committed in the course of that aggression as war crimes, crimes of genocide and crimes against humanity.

The Seminar made several recommendations to the Commission on Human Rights, among them that States parties to the fourth Geneva Convention should urge Israel to comply strictly with it and with United Nations resolutions and to withdraw from all Arab territories occupied in 1967. The Seminar recommended a conference of States parties to the Convention to study ways of implementing it in the occupied territories and the nomination by the international community of a Protecting Power to safeguard the rights of the Palestinians there. The Seminar recommended special consideration of the question of Palestinian and Lebanese prisoners detained by Israel, and revision of the mandate of the United Nations Relief and Works Agency for Palestine Refugees in the Near East to guarantee legal and physical protection to Palestinian refugees. All Member States should actively support the struggle of the Palestinians, should be made to realize that assistance to Israel prevented implementation of United Nations resolutions, and should consider imposing sanctions on Israel similar to those against South Africa.

The decision to convene the Seminar at Geneva had been taken by the Commission on 11 February 1982[3] in one of its resolutions on human rights in the occupied territories (see above). This decision was endorsed on 7 May by the Economic and Social Council,[1] which requested the Secretary-General to arrange for its organization and report to the Commission in 1983. The Council adopted the decision, recommended by the Commission, by a recorded vote, requested by Iraq, of 37 to 1, with 14 abstentions, following its approval by the Second (Social) Committee on 3 May by a recorded vote of 30 to 1, with 12 abstentions.

Expressing regret at the adoption of the decision, Israel, speaking as an observer, commented that the Commission's resolution, by condemning Israel, prejudged the outcome of the Seminar and would not contribute to a better understanding of the situation. The United States, casting a negative vote, reiterated that negotiations involving withdrawal from occupied territory in exchange for peace were the only sound framework for resolving conflict; the Seminar would only create further divisions and hinder peace prospects.

Decision (1982). [1]ESC: 1982/127, 7 May, text following.
Report. [2]Seminar, ST/HR/SER.A/14.
Resolution (1982). [3]Commission on Human Rights (report, E/1982/12): 1982/1 A, para. 15, 11 Feb.
Meeting record. ESC: E/1982/SR.28 (7 May).

Economic and Social Council decision 1982/127

37-1-14 (recorded vote)

Approved by Second Committee (E/1982/59) by recorded vote (30-1-12), 3 May (meeting 15); draft by Commission on Human Rights (E/1982/12); agenda item 9.

Question of the violation of human rights in the occupied Arab territories, including Palestine

At its 28th plenary meeting, on 7 May 1982, the Council, noting resolution 1982/1 A of 11 February 1982 of the Commission on Human Rights, endorsed the Commission's decision that a seminar on violations of human rights in the Palestinian and other Arab territories occupied by Israel should be held at the United Nations Office at Geneva and requested the Secretary-General to make the appropriate arrangements for the organization of the seminar and to report to the Commission on Human Rights at its thirty-ninth session.

Recorded vote in Council as follows:

In favour: Argentina, Bahamas, Bangladesh, Benin, Brazil, Bulgaria, Burundi, Byelorussian SSR, Chile, China, Ethiopia, Fiji, Greece, India, Iraq, Jordan, Kenya, Libyan Arab Jamahiriya, Mali, Mexico, Nepal, Nicaragua, Nigeria, Pakistan, Peru,

Poland, Qatar, Romania, Sudan, Swaziland, Thailand, Tunisia, USSR, United Republic of Cameroon, Venezuela, Yugoslavia, Zaire.
Against: United States.
Abstaining: Australia, Austria, Belgium, Canada, Denmark, France, Germany, Federal Republic of, Italy, Japan, Liberia, Malawi, Norway, Portugal, United Kingdom.

Golan Heights

On 11 February 1982,[1] the Commission on Human Rights resolutely condemned the December 1981 Israeli decision annexing the Syrian Golan Heights, occupied since 1967, through the imposition of its laws, jurisdiction and administration (see POLITICAL AND SECURITY QUESTIONS, Chapter IX), and demanded that Israel rescind its act. The Commission, declaring that decision null and void and without international legal effect, determined that Israel's persistent defiance of United Nations resolutions and its systematic human rights violations were a threat to international peace. It called on States, international institutions and United Nations agencies to comply with a General Assembly resolution of 5 February 1982,[2] refrain from supplying Israel with military assistance, suspend all economic, financial and technological assistance, sever diplomatic, trade and cultural relations, and isolate Israel in all fields.

The Commission resolution was adopted by a roll-call vote of 22 to 11 (Australia, Canada, Denmark, Fiji, France, Germany, Federal Republic of, Italy, Japan, Netherlands, United Kingdom, United States), with 7 abstentions.

Resolutions (1982). [1]Commission on Human Rights (report, E/1982/12): 1982/2, 11 Feb. [2]GA: ES-9/1, 5 Feb.

Lebanon

In a resolution of 8 September 1982[2] concerned with human rights violations in the territories occupied by Israel (see above), the Sub-Commission on Prevention of Discrimination and Protection of Minorities condemned Israel for its invasion of Lebanon and the indiscriminate destruction of Lebanese cities and Palestinian refugee camps, causing mass killings of civilians (see POLITICAL AND SECURITY QUESTIONS, Chapter IX). It urged Israel to grant, in accordance with the 1949 Geneva Conventions and the Additional Protocols, prisoner-of-war status to Lebanese and Palestinian combatants, to release detained civilians and to comply with the Security Council's calls for unconditional and immediate withdrawal from Lebanon.

By a decision of 17 August,[1] the Sub-Commission requested the Secretary-General to forward a message to the Chairman of the Commission on Human Rights for transmission to Israel. The text expressed the Sub-Commission's grave concern at the suffering of civilians caused by the invasion of Lebanon and the blockade and bombardment of Beirut, and its urgent wish that all military operations cease and that international humanitarian norms, especially the 1949 Geneva Conventions, be respected.

Decision (1982). [1]SCPDPM (report, E/CN.4/1983/4): 1982/2, 17 Aug.
Resolution (1982). [2]SCPDPM: 1982/18, para. 1, 8 Sep.

Mass exoduses

Action by the Commission on Human Rights. On 11 March 1982,[4] the Commission on Human Rights commended Special Rapporteur Sadruddin Aga Khan for his 1981 study on human rights and massive exoduses.[6] The Commission requested the Secretary-General to transmit the study to the General Assembly and to bring it to the attention of the Group of Governmental Experts on International Co-operation to Avert New Flows of Refugees (see Chapter XXI of this section). The Commission invited interested Governments, United Nations departments, specialized agencies, and international and non-governmental organizations to submit their views on the study and its recommendations to the Secretary-General. The Special Rapporteur was requested to explore the recommendations further with the Secretary-General and those interested parties, convey their observations with his comments to the Assembly and remain available for consultations with the Group of Governmental Experts.

Economic and Social Council action. On 7 May,[1] acting without vote, the Economic and Social Council approved the Commission's request that the Special Rapporteur explore further his recommendations on massive exoduses with the Secretary-General and interested parties, that he present their observations with his comments to the Assembly and that he remain available for consultations with the Group of Governmental Experts.

Originating in the Commission, the draft was approved by the Second (Social) Committee on 3 May, also without vote.

General Assembly action. As requested by the Commission, the Secretary-General transmitted the Special Rapporteur's study to the Assembly by a note of 30 June.[3]

Commending the Special Rapporteur for his study, the Assembly, on 17 December,[5] renewed the Commission's invitation to Governments, United Nations agencies and organizations to communicate their views. It requested the Secretary-General to ensure that these views be made available to the Commission in 1983 and to the Group of Governmental Experts, which were invited to consider those aspects of the study falling within their mandates. The Assembly requested the Secretary-General to examine the study's recommendations, taking into account the views communicated to him, the 1982 Assembly debates and the 1983 deliberations by the Commission and the Group, and to report to the Assembly in 1983.

The resolution was adopted without vote, following its similar approval by the Third (Social, Humanitarian and Cultural) Committee on 10 December, where the 12-nation draft was introduced and orally revised by Canada. Three of the revisions were based on proposals by other States: mass "movements" of population in the third and fourth preambular paragraphs was changed to "exoduses and displacements" (Ethiopia); the word "deeply" was added before the word "preoccupied" in the fourth preambular paragraph (Djibouti); and in paragraph 5, deliberations of the Group of Governmental Experts were also to be considered by the Secretary-General in conjunction with his examination of the Special Rapporteur's study (Cuba).

By a letter of 11 October to the Special Rapporteur,[2] the Secretary-General commended him for his study and said that some of the recommendations could be considered further and acted on within the United Nations system. In particular, he mentioned proposals for a reappraisal of developing countries' economic needs in relation to possible causes of mass exoduses, an international labour compensatory facility (to reimburse countries adversely affected by the brain drain of skilled personnel to developed countries) (see Chapter XII of this section), the standardization of international aid criteria, an integrated approach to multilateral and bilateral aid, and the use of multidisciplinary assessment teams. Concerning the Special Rapporteur's proposal for the establishment of a corps of "humanitarian observers", the Secretary-General shared his view that an international presence would have a stabilizing influence, but added that the proposal required the consent of the Governments concerned.

The Secretary-General termed as innovative the proposal to monitor and assess situations which might result in mass movements of population. He drew attention to his intent, as stated in his annual report on the work of the United Nations (p. 6), to develop a systematic capacity for fact-finding in potential conflict areas. He also expressed interest in learning whether the Assembly would expand the concept to include areas where human rights violations might lead to massive exoduses, thereby possibly inhibiting the deterioration of such situations. In relation to that issue, the Secretary-General expressed further interest in the attitude of Members towards the proposal that he appoint a special representative for humanitarian questions.

Decision (1982). [1]ESC: 1982/136, 7 May, text following.
Letter. [2]S-G, 11 Oct., A/C.3/37/9.
Note. [3]S-G, A/37/310.

Resolutions (1982). [4]Commission on Human Rights (report, E/1982/12): 1982/32, 11 Mar. [5]GA: 37/186, 17 Dec., text following.
Yearbook reference. [6]1981, p. 966.
Meeting records. ESC: E/1982/SR.28, 29 (7 May). GA: 3rd Committee, A/C.3/37/SR.57, 62, 63, *64*, 65-71, *72, 74* (29 Nov.–10 Dec.); plenary, A/37/PV.110 (17 Dec.).

Economic and Social Council decision 1982/136

Adopted without vote

Approved by Second Committee (E/1982/59) without vote, 3 May (meeting 15); draft by Commission on Human Rights (E/1982/12); agenda item 9.

Human rights and mass exoduses

At its 29th plenary meeting, on 7 May 1982, the Council, noting resolution 1982/32 of 11 May 1982 of the Commission on Human Rights, approved the Commission's request to the Special Rapporteur, in order to facilitate consideration by the General Assembly of his study on human rights and massive exoduses, to explore further with interested Governments, the Secretary-General, United Nations bodies and the specialized agencies, and other organizations, intergovernmental and non-governmental, the study and the recommendations contained therein, to convey their observations together with his comments to the General Assembly in the course of introducing his study, and to remain available for consultations with the Group of Governmental Experts on International Co-operation to Avert New Flows of Refugees as required.

General Assembly resolution 37/186

17 December 1982   Meeting 110   Adopted without vote

Approved by Third Committee (A/37/745) without vote, 10 December (meeting 74); 12-nation draft (A/C.3/37/L.74/Rev.1), orally revised; agenda item 12.

Sponsors: Australia, Canada, Costa Rica, Djibouti, Germany, Federal Republic of, Ghana, Greece, Japan, Jordan, Pakistan, Senegal, Somalia.

Human rights and mass exoduses

The General Assembly,

Mindful of its general humanitarian mandate under the Charter of the United Nations and its mandate to promote and encourage respect for human rights and fundamental freedoms for all,

Deeply disturbed by the increasing scale and magnitude of exoduses and displacements of populations in many regions of the world and by the human suffering of millions of refugees and displaced persons in all regions of the world,

Conscious that human rights violations are among the principal factors in the complex and multiple root causes of mass exoduses and displacements of population,

Deeply preoccupied by the increasingly heavy burden being imposed upon the international community as a whole, and more particularly on developing countries with limited resources of their own, by these sudden and mass exoduses and displacements of population,

Conscious of its obligations towards the millions of victims of mass exoduses and of displacements of population, and of its dual responsibility, under the Charter, to provide adequate international protection and assistance to such victims and to eliminate or mitigate the root causes of this phenomenon,

Recalling its resolution 36/136 of 14 December 1981 on a new international humanitarian order,

Recalling also its resolutions 35/124 of 11 December 1980 and 36/148 of 16 December 1981 on international co-operation to avert new flows of refugees, 35/196 of 15 December 1980 on mass exoduses, and Commission on Human Rights resolutions 29(XXXVII) of 11 March 1981 and 1982/32 of 11 March 1982,

Recalling further its resolution 32/130 of 16 December 1977 and Commission on Human Rights resolution 4(XXXIII) of 21 February 1977 on the full realization of economic, social and cultural rights,

Considering the study on human rights and massive exoduses by the Special Rapporteur of the Commission on Human Rights,

1. *Commends* the Special Rapporteur of the Commission on Human Rights for his study on human rights and massive exoduses;

2. *Renews* the invitation extended in Commission on Human Rights resolution 1982/32 to Governments, United Nations agencies or departments concerned, specialized agencies, international organizations and non-governmental organizations to communicate their views on the study and the recommendations contained therein to the Secretary-General;

3. *Requests* the Secretary-General to ensure that the views expressed to date on the study and the recommendations contained therein by all interested parties—Governments, United Nations agencies or departments concerned, specialized agencies, international organizations and non-governmental organizations—together with those to be received in the mean time, are made available to the Commission on Human Rights at its thirty-ninth session and to the Group of Governmental Experts on International Co-operation to Avert New Flows of Refugees to facilitate their further consideration of the study and its recommendations;

4. *Invites* the Commission on Human Rights at its thirty-ninth session, and the Group of Governmental Experts, at meetings to be held pursuant to General Assembly resolution 37/121 of 16 December 1982, to give careful consideration to those aspects of the study of the Special Rapporteur which fall within their respective mandates in the light of the views expressed by all interested parties;

5. *Requests* the Secretary-General to pursue his examination of the recommendations contained in the study, taking into account the views of Governments and other interested parties, as enumerated in paragraph 3 above, the debates in the General Assembly at its thirty-seventh session and the deliberations of the Commission on Human Rights at its thirty-ninth session, and of the Group of Governmental Experts, and to report thereon to the Assembly at its thirty-eighth session in order to enable it to continue its consideration of this matter;

6. *Decides* to review the question of human rights and mass exoduses at its thirty-eighth session.

Genocide

On 7 September 1982,[1] the Sub-Commission on Prevention of Discrimination and Protection of Minorities recommended that it be authorized to appoint a Special Rapporteur to revise and update its 1978 study on the prevention and punishment of the crime of genocide.[2] In a draft resolution submitted for adoption in 1983 by the Commission on Human Rights and the Economic and Social Council, the Sub-Commission proposed that the study, to be presented in 1984, take account of replies to a questionnaire that would be sent to Governments and organizations.

Resolution (1982). [1]SCPDPM (report, E/CN.4/1983/4): 1982/2, 7 Sep.
Yearbook reference. [2]1978, p. 723.

Other human rights questions

Additional Protocols I and II to the 1949 Geneva Conventions

On 16 December 1982,[3] the General Assembly reiterated its call for ratification of or accession to the two 1977 Protocols Additional to the Geneva Conventions of 12 August 1949 for the protection of war victims.[4] The Assembly also called on States becoming parties to Protocol I—on protection of victims of international armed conflicts—to consider making the declaration under article 90 (allowing States the option of recognizing the competence of a fact-finding commission to inquire into cases of grave breaches or serious violations). The Secretary-General was requested to report in 1984 on the status of the Protocols.

The resolution was adopted without vote, following similar approval on 19 November by the Sixth (Legal) Committee, where the 14-nation draft was introduced by Sweden.

The item on signatures and ratifications of the Protocols was placed on the Assembly's agenda at the request of Denmark, Finland, Norway and Sweden, in a letter of 6 July.[1] In an explanatory memorandum attached, they noted that only a small number of States had ratified the Protocols and expressed the view that it was appropriate for the Assembly to call again for States to adhere. They added that the International Red Cross Conference in November 1981 had reaffirmed its intention to do everything possible to aid universal acceptance of the Protocols and invited States to ratify or accede.

As at 31 December 1982, 27 States had ratified or acceded to Protocol I, as follows (names of States adhering in 1982 are italicized):

Austria, Bahamas, Bangladesh, Botswana, *Cuba*, Cyprus, *Denmark*, Ecuador, El Salvador, Finland, Gabon, Ghana, Jordan, Lao People's Democratic Republic, Libyan Arab Jamahiriya, Mauritania, *Mauritius*, Niger, Norway, *Republic of Korea*, *Saint Lucia*, Sweden, *Switzerland*, Tunisia, Viet Nam, Yugoslavia, *Zaire*.

All of these States, except Cuba, Cyprus, Viet Nam and Zaire, had also adhered to Protocol II, on protection of victims of non-international conflicts.

A list of States adhering to the Protocols as at 13 October was submitted by the Secretary-General to the Assembly.[2]

Letter. [1]Denmark, Finland, Norway, Sweden, 6 July, A/37/142.
Report. [2]S-G, A/INF/37/2 & Add.1.
Resolution (1982). [3]GA: 37/116, 16 Dec., text following.
Yearbook reference. [4]1977, p. 706.
Meeting records. GA: General Committee, A/BUR/37/SR.2 (22 Sep.); plenary, A/37/PV.4, 107 (24 Sep., 16 Dec.); 6th Committee, A/C.6/37/SR.18, 19, 51 (15 Oct., 19 Nov.).

General Assembly resolution 37/116

16 December 1982   Meeting 107   Adopted without vote

Approved by Sixth Committee (A/37/641) without vote, 19 November (meeting 51); 14-nation draft (A/C.6/37/L.10); agenda item 132.

Sponsors: Austria, Bahamas, Bangladesh, Denmark, Egypt, Finland, Ghana, Libyan Arab Jamahiriya, Netherlands, Norway, Sweden, Tunisia, Yugoslavia, Zaire.

State of signatures and ratifications of the Protocols Additional to the Geneva Conventions of 1949 and relating to the protection of victims of international armed conflicts (Protocol I) and the protection of victims of non-international armed conflicts (Protocol II)

The General Assembly,

Recalling its resolutions 32/44 of 8 December 1977 and 34/51 of 23 November 1979,

Having considered the report of the Secretary-General on the state of signatures and ratifications of the two Protocols Additional to the Geneva Conventions of 1949 and relating to the protection of victims of armed conflicts,

Taking note of resolution VII of the Twenty-fourth International Red Cross Conference, adopted on 13 November 1981,

Convinced of the continuing value of established humanitarian rules relating to armed conflict and the need to secure the full observance of human rights in armed conflicts pending the earliest possible termination of such conflicts,

Noting the virtually universal acceptance of the four Geneva Conventions of 12 August 1949 concerning the protection of victims of armed conflicts, and their binding character for all parties,

Noting further with appreciation the continuing efforts of the International Committee of the Red Cross to disseminate information about the two additional Protocols,

Concerned, however, at the fact that so far only a limited number of States have signed, ratified or acceded to the two Protocols,

Mindful of the need for continued improvement of the implementation, and for further expansion, of the body of humanitarian rules relating to armed conflicts,

1. *Reiterates its call*, contained in resolution 34/51, to all States to consider without delay the matter of ratifying or acceding to the two Protocols Additional to the Geneva Conventions of 1949 and relating to the protection of victims of armed conflicts;

2. *Calls upon* all States becoming parties to Protocol I to consider the matter of making the declaration provided for under article 90 of that Protocol;

3. *Requests* the Secretary-General to submit to the General Assembly at its thirty-ninth session a report on the status of the Protocols based on information received from Member States;

4. *Decides* to include in the provisional agenda of its thirty-ninth session an item entitled "Status of the Protocols Additional to the Geneva Conventions of 1949 and relating to the protection of victims of armed conflicts: report of the Secretary-General".

Rights of the child

Draft convention

Action by the Commission on Human Rights. An informal, open-ended working group of the Commission on Human Rights met at Geneva from 25 to 29 January 1982 to continue work on a draft convention on the rights of the child, begun in 1979.[8] In addition, the group met during the Commission's annual session, between 2 and 9 February and on 5 March, with Adam Lopatka (Poland) re-elected as Chairman/Rapporteur.[1]

The group adopted articles 6, 10, 11 and 11 *bis*, and the first sentence of paragraph 1 of article 12. These pertained to: parental care and circumstances permitting separation of children from their parents; special protection for children separated from their families; adoption and inter-country adoption; child refugees; and mentally and physically disabled children.

On 11 March,[2] the Commission decided to continue work on the draft convention with a view to completing it in 1983 for transmission to the General Assembly through the Economic and Social Council. To facilitate this work, it recommended that the Council authorize a one-week working group meeting prior to the 1983 Commission session.

Economic and Social Council action. On 7 May,[5] the Council authorized the actions recommended by the Commission. This resolution was adopted without vote, following similar approval on 3 May by the Second (Social) Committee of a draft recommended by the Commission.

In a separate action pertaining to parental kidnapping, also taken on 7 May,[6] the Council invited the Commission, when drafting the convention, to take into consideration the protection of the rights of the child in cases of unauthorized international removal. In addition, on 4 May, the Council called for action to combat abuses against women and children[3] and, with reference to the effects of *apartheid*, it appealed for contributions to assistance projects for refugee women and children from South Africa and Namibia.[4]

General Assembly action. On 18 December,[7] the General Assembly welcomed the Council's decision to authorize continuation of the working group and requested that the Commission give highest priority in 1983 to completing the draft convention, to which all Member States were invited to contribute.

The resolution was adopted without vote, following similar approval on 7 December by the Third (Social, Humanitarian and Cultural) Committee, where the draft was introduced by Poland on behalf of 45 countries.

Report. [1]Working Group, E/1982/12/Add.1.
Resolutions (1982). [2]Commission on Human Rights (report, E/1982/12): 1982/39, 11 Mar. ESC: [3]1982/22, para. 1, 4 May; [4]1982/24, para. 3, 4 May; [5]1982/37, 7 May, text following; [6]1982/39, para. 3, 7 May. [7]GA: 37/190, 18 Dec., text following.
Yearbook reference. [8]1979, p. 863.
Meeting records. ESC: E/1982/SR.28 (7 May). GA: 3rd Committee, A/C.3/37/SR.47, 50-53, 55, 56, 64, 67 (18 Nov.–7 Dec.); plenary, A/37/PV.111 (18 Dec.).

Economic and Social Council resolution 1982/37

7 May 1982	Meeting 28	Adopted without vote

Approved by Second Committee (E/1982/59) without vote, 3 May (meeting 15); draft by Commission on Human Rights (E/1982/12); agenda item 9.

Question of a convention on the rights of the child

The Economic and Social Council,

Recalling General Assembly resolutions 33/166 of 20 December 1978, 34/4 of 18 October 1979 and 35/131 of 11 December 1980, as well as resolution 36/57 of 25 November 1981, by which the Assembly requested the Commission on Human Rights to continue to give the highest priority to the question of completing the draft convention on the rights of the child, and Economic and Social Council resolutions 1978/18 of 5 May 1978 and 1978/40 of 1 August 1978 and decisions 1980/138 of 2 May 1980 and 1981/144 of 8 May 1981, by which the Council authorized a one-week session of an open-ended working group prior to the thirty-eighth session of the Commission to facilitate completion of the work on a draft convention on the rights of the child,

Considering that it was not found possible to complete the work on the draft convention during the thirty-eighth session of the Commission on Human Rights,

Taking note of resolution 1982/39 of 11 March 1982 of the Commission on Human Rights,

1. *Authorizes* a meeting of an open-ended working group for a period of one week prior to the thirty-ninth session of the Commission on Human Rights to facilitate the completion of the work on a draft convention on the rights of the child;

2. *Requests* the Secretary-General to transmit to the Commission on Human Rights at its thirty-ninth session all relevant material relating to the draft convention on the rights of the child.

General Assembly resolution 37/190

18 December 1982	Meeting 111	Adopted without vote

Approved by Third Committee (A/37/717) without vote, 7 December (meeting 67); 45-nation draft (A/C.3/37/L.46); agenda item 86.

Sponsors: Afghanistan, Angola, Argentina, Bhutan, Bolivia, Bulgaria, Byelorussian SSR, Central African Republic, Chad, Colombia, Cuba, Cyprus, Democratic

Yemen, Egypt, Ethiopia, German Democratic Republic, Guinea, Guinea-Bissau, Guyana, India, Jamaica, Jordan, Lao People's Democratic Republic, Libyan Arab Jamahiriya, Mali, Madagascar, Mongolia, Morocco, Mozambique, Nicaragua, Pakistan, Panama, Peru, Poland, Rwanda, Senegal, Sierra Leone, Suriname, Syrian Arab Republic, Uruguay, Venezuela, Viet Nam, Yemen, Yugoslavia, Zaire.

Question of a convention on the rights of the child

The General Assembly,

Recalling its resolutions 33/166 of 20 December 1978, 34/4 of 18 October 1979, 35/131 of 11 December 1980 and 36/57 of 25 November 1981,

Recalling also Commission on Human Rights resolutions 20(XXXIV) of 8 March 1978, 19(XXXV) of 14 March 1979, 36(XXXVI) of 12 March 1980, 26(XXXVII) of 10 March 1981 and 1982/39 of 11 March 1982 as well as Economic and Social Council resolutions 1978/18 of 5 May 1978, 1978/40 of 1 August 1978 and 1982/37 of 7 May 1982 and Council decisions 1980/138 of 2 May 1980 and 1981/144 of 8 May 1981,

Conscious of the importance of its task to contribute to the improvement of the situation of children in the world and to ensure their development and education in conditions of peace,

Bearing in mind the need to pursue effective action with a view to generating an international record of accomplishment such as that of the International Year of the Child,

Noting again the important role of the United Nations Children's Fund and the specialized agencies in promoting the well-being of children and their development,

Aware of the importance of an international convention on the rights of the child for more effective protection of children's rights,

Noting with appreciation that further progress has been made in the elaboration of a draft convention on the rights of the child prior to and during the thirty-eighth session of the Commission on Human Rights,

1. *Welcomes* Economic and Social Council resolution 1982/37, by which the Council authorized a meeting of an open-ended working group of the Commission on Human Rights for a period of one week prior to the thirty-ninth session of the Commission in order to facilitate completion of the work on a draft convention on the rights of the child;

2. *Invites* all Member States to offer their effective contribution to the elaboration of a draft convention;

3. *Requests* the Commission on Human Rights to give the highest priority at its thirty-ninth session to the question of completing a draft convention;

4. *Requests* the Secretary-General to provide all necessary assistance to the working group in order to ensure its smooth and efficient work;

5. *Decides* to include in the provisional agenda of its thirty-eighth session the item entitled "Question of a convention on the rights of the child".

Child labour

On 7 May 1982,[1] the Economic and Social Council endorsed the recommendation of the Commission on Human Rights, in a resolution of 10 March,[3] that the study on child labour submitted by Special Rapporteur Abdelwahab Bouhdiba (Tunisia) to the Sub-Commission on Prevention of Discrimination and Protection of Minorities in 1981[6] be given the widest possible distribution, including distribution in Arabic. The Council's decision, recommended by the Commission, was adopted without vote, following its similar approval by the Second Committee on 3 May.

In response to the Commission's invitation in its 10 March resolution to present a concrete programme of action against the exploitation of child labour, the Sub-Commission, on 10 September,[5] decided to submit for that purpose the Special Rapporteur's recommendations, some of which were reiterated in a note of 26 July.[2] In that note, the Special Rapporteur reaffirmed the importance of a global campaign against the exploitation of child labour, including the organization of a seminar and the celebration of a special "week". Stating that the appeal for extensive media coverage of the question had been answered mainly by the developed countries, he called for a renewal of that appeal. Referring to comments from various organizations, he stated that the information received indicated a slight improvement of the situation, with a great deal of research and studies being carried out.

In a 7 September resolution on slavery (see above, under CIVIL AND POLITICAL RIGHTS), the Sub-Commission considered that a report should be prepared on the sale of children, including commercially motivated (and especially transnational) adoptions.[4]

Decision (1982). [1]ESC: 1982/130, 7 May, text following.
Note. [2]Special Rapporteur, E/CN.4/Sub.2/1982/29.
Resolutions (1982). [3]Commission on Human Rights (report, E/1982/12): 1982/21, 10 Mar. SCPDPM (report, E/CN.4/1983/4): [4]1982/15, para. 14, 7 Sep.; [5]1982/33, 10 Sep.
Yearbook reference: [6]1981, p. 971.
Meeting record. ESC: E/1982/SR.28 (7 May).

Economic and Social Council decision 1982/130

Adopted without vote

Approved by Second Committee (E/1982/59) without vote, 3 May (meeting 15); draft by Commission on Human Rights (E/1982/12); agenda item 9.

Exploitation of child labour

At its 28th plenary meeting, on 7 May 1982, the Council, noting resolution 1982/21 of 10 March 1982 of the Commission on Human Rights, endorsed the Commission's recommendation that the study prepared by Mr. Abdelwahab Bouhdiba on the exploitation of child labour should be printed and given the widest possible distribution, including distribution in Arabic.

Parental kidnapping

Action by the Commission on the Status of Women. On 5 March 1982,[1] the Commission on the Status of Women decided, by 12 votes to 7, with 5 abstentions, to postpone until 1984 consideration of a draft resolution on the protection of the rights of parents and children in cases of the separation of couples of different nationalities. According to that proposal, the Economic and Social Council would request the Secretary-General: to invite agencies to give "full information" on the 1980 Hague Convention on the Civil Aspects of International Child Abduction and the 1980 European Convention on Recognition and Enforcement of Decisions concerning Custody of Children and on Restoration of Custody of Children; to ascertain the status of this problem world-wide and communicate such information to the Commission on Human Rights; and to invite the Commission to reaffirm the child's right to relations with both parents in the event of a couple's separation.

Economic and Social Council action. On 7 May,[2] the Economic and Social Council invited States to co-operate to prevent the removal and retention of children in the case of conflict between couples of different nationalities. To this end, it invited States to conclude bilateral arrangements or to accede to regional or international conventions. It invited the Commission on Human Rights, when drafting the convention on the rights of the child (see above), to take into consideration the protection of such rights in cases of unauthorized international removal. The Secretary-General was asked to consult with States on this issue and report his findings to the Commission in 1983.

The resolution was adopted without vote, following similar approval by the Second Committee on 3 May. The draft was introduced by France, also on behalf of Burundi, Greece and Zaire.

Report. [1]Commission on women, E/1982/14.
Resolution (1982). [2]ESC: 1982/39, 7 May, text following.
Meeting record. ESC: E/1982/SR.28 (7 May).

Economic and Social Council resolution 1982/39

7 May 1982   Meeting 28   Adopted without vote

Approved by Second Committee (E/1982/59) without vote, 3 May (meeting 15); 4-nation draft (E/1982/C.2/L.11); agenda item 9.

Sponsors: Burundi, France, Greece, Zaire.

Protection of the rights of children and parents in cases of removal or retention of children

The Economic and Social Council,

Bearing in mind the Declaration of the Rights of the Child proclaimed by the General Assembly in its resolution 1386(XIV) of 20 November 1959,

Recalling that, under the terms of principle 2 of that Declaration, the child shall enjoy special protection, and shall be given opportunities and facilities, by law and by other means, to enable him to develop physically, mentally, morally, spiritually and socially in a healthy and normal manner and in conditions of freedom and dignity,

Concerned about the proliferation of conflicts between couples of different nationalities and at the consequences which result therefrom for children, concerned particularly by their removal from the country of one spouse to the country of the other without the consent of one of the two spouses, and without or in violation of a judicial or administrative decision, and, lastly, concerned about the cases of child retention in which such situations sometimes end,

Noting the existence of a common interest in the elaboration of a full and detailed international convention on the rights of the child, as already evinced by the representatives of many countries and international organizations,

Recalling that the universally acknowledged standards and principles in the field of human rights impose on States the obligation to protect all individuals under their jurisdiction from infringements of their freedom and dignity by any private person,

1. *Calls the attention* of States to the proliferation of cases of removal and retention of children and invites them to co-operate actively with a view to preventing the occurrence of such cases and to solving them speedily, out of concern for the interest of the child;

2. *Invites* States to organize such co-operation through the conclusion of bilateral arrangements or through accession to regional conventions or international conventions such as the Hague Convention on the Civil Aspects of International Child Abduction of 25 October 1980, which is open to all States;

3. *Invites* the Commission on Human Rights, when drafting the convention on the rights of the child, to take into consideration the protection of the rights of the child in cases of unauthorized international removal;

4. *Requests* the Secretary-General to consult with Governments on this problem and to report to the Commission on Human Rights at its thirty-ninth session under the agenda item entitled "Question of a convention on the rights of the child".

Youth and human rights

Action by the Commission on Human Rights. In anticipation of International Youth Year (IYY) (1985), the Commission on Human Rights, on 11 March 1982,[1] called on States to take appropriate action enabling young people to exercise all human rights. The Secretary-General was requested to submit a progress report on implementation of the Specific Programme of Measures and Activities in connection with the Year, endorsed by the General Assembly in November 1981.[3] As it had done in March 1981,[5] the Commission emphasized the role of young people in their country's political, social and economic development. It decided to examine in 1984 the issue of youth and human rights, including the right to education and to work.

General Assembly action. Expressing its serious interest that IYY succeed in promoting increasing participation of youth in the socio-economic life of their country, the Assembly, on 3 December 1982,[2] called on States, governmental and non-governmental organizations, United Nations bodies and specialized agencies to continue implementing a November 1981 resolution[4] on the human rights of youth, particularly the right to education and work. It requested that the Advisory Committee for IYY give attention to that resolution and all relevant human rights instruments when drafting recommendations.

The resolution was adopted without vote, following its similar approval on 15 November by the Third (Social, Humanitarian and Cultural) Committee. The draft was introduced by Czechoslovakia on behalf of 22 States and was orally amended by Sweden to add to paragraph 1 a reference to "resolving the problem of youth unemployment". Sweden had originally used the word "employment" but the Committee accepted a sub-amendment by India to change this to "unemployment".

Resolutions (1982). [1]Commission on Human Rights (report, E/1982/12): 1982/36, 11 Mar. [2]GA: 37/49, 3 Dec., text following.
Resolutions (prior). GA, 13 Nov. 1981: [3]36/28 (YUN 1981, p. 1021); [4]36/29 (*ibid.*, p. 973).
Yearbook reference. [5]1981, p. 972.
Meeting records. GA: 3rd Committee, A/C.3/37/SR.14-23, 25, 26, *29, 42* (18 Oct.–15 Nov.); plenary, A/37/PV.90 (3 Dec.).

General Assembly resolution 37/49

3 December 1982   Meeting 90   Adopted without vote

Approved by Third Committee (A/37/629) without vote, 15 November (meeting 42); 22-nation draft (A/C.3/37/L.20/Rev.1), orally amended by Sweden and sub-amended by India; agenda item 77.

Sponsors: Afghanistan, Algeria, Angola, Benin, Bulgaria, Byelorussian SSR, Congo, Cuba, Czechoslovakia, Democratic Yemen, Ethiopia, German Democratic Republic, Guinea, Lao People's Democratic Republic, Madagascar, Mongolia, Mozambique, Nicaragua, Syrian Arab Republic, Venezuela, Viet Nam, Zimbabwe.

Efforts and measures for securing the implementation and the enjoyment by youth of human rights, particularly the right to education and to work

The General Assembly,

Recalling its resolution 36/29 of 13 November 1981, in which it, *inter alia,* recognized the need to intensify efforts and to adopt appropriate

measures for securing the implementation and the enjoyment by youth of human rights, particularly the right to education and to work,

Recalling also its resolution 34/151 of 17 December 1979, by which it decided to designate 1985 as International Youth Year: Participation, Development, Peace,

Convinced that it is necessary to ensure full enjoyment by youth of the rights stipulated in the Universal Declaration of Human Rights, the International Covenant on Economic, Social and Cultural Rights and the International Covenant on Civil and Political Rights, with special regard for the right to education and to work,

Aware of the fact that insufficient education and the unemployment of youth limits their ability to participate in the development process, and, in this regard, emphasizing the importance of secondary and higher education of youth, as well as of their access to appropriate technical, vocational guidance and training programmes,

Expressing its serious interest in the success of the forthcoming International Youth Year which should, *inter alia,* promote increasing participation of youth in the socio-economic life of their country,

1. *Calls upon* all States, all governmental and non-governmental organizations and the interested bodies of the United Nations and specialized agencies to pay continuous attention to the implementation of General Assembly resolution 36/29 relating to efforts aimed at the promotion of human rights and their enjoyment by youth, particularly the right to education and vocational training and to work, with a view to resolving the problem of youth unemployment;

2. *Requests* the Advisory Committee for the International Youth Year to give full attention to resolution 36/29 and to all relevant international human rights instruments in the preparation for and in the course of the International Youth Year, in particular in elaborating its recommendations concerning the Year.

Human rights of aging persons

The Advisory Committee for the World Assembly on Aging, on 17 February 1982, considered the desirability of a declaration on the rights of the aging. There was a general consensus that such a declaration was not only unnecessary but contrary to the objective of considering the question of aging within the context of society as a whole. The Committee decided in principle to consider adding a preamble to the international plan of action on aging, with its contents to be discussed at the appropriate time.[1]

Decision (1982). [1]Advisory Committee (report, A/CONF.113/11): 8(II), 17 Feb.

Human rights of disabled persons

The Sub-Commission on Prevention of Discrimination and Protection of Minorities, on 7 September 1982,[1] recommended that Governments give consideration to disabled persons' difficulties in enjoying human rights, as well as to the need to strengthen procedures whereby they could bring allegations of rights violations to an authoritative body or to the Government. The Sub-Commission requested the Secretary-General to invite the views of States, specialized agencies and organizations on ways of promoting the human rights of disabled persons. In this connection, it suggested that Governments, in their reports on follow-up action to the 1981 International Year of Disabled Persons,[2] provide information on how programmes to promote and protect such rights had been affected by reductions in spending for social programmes.

Resolution (1982). [1]SCPDPM (report, E/CN.4/1983/4): 1982/1, 7 Sep.
Yearbook reference. [2]1981, p. 797.

Emergency legislation

A study on the implications of human rights in countries under a state of emergency,[1] prepared by Special Rapporteur Nicole Questiaux (France), was submitted in 1982 to the Sub-Commission on discrimination and minorities. Her study had begun at the request of the Sub-Commission in 1977[5] and continued with authorization from the Economic and Social Council in 1979.[3] It analysed the *de facto* impact of states of emergency on human rights and examined the effectiveness of protective mechanisms and international surveillance, particularly in regard to detained or imprisoned persons.

While basic international laws and national legislation ideally limited State power and guaranteed human rights, states of emergency that were increasingly characterized by transformations undermining institutions and the rule of law had a serious effect on prisoners and detainees. The Special Rapporteur recommended measures to develop the role of international human rights surveillance organs, including the Sub-Commission, and suggested that human rights guarantees provided by international law be strengthened, particularly in such areas as imprisonment, the right to a fair trial and sentencing.

Endorsing the Special Rapporteur's conclusions and recommendations, the Sub-Commission on 10 September,[2] by 13 votes to 1 with 2 abstentions, decided to transmit the study in 1983 to the Commission. It recommended to the Commission that the study also be transmitted to United Nations agencies, the Human Rights Committee and the Committee on the Elimination of Racial Discrimination, and that it be published and given the widest possible distribution. The Sub-Commission further recommended that the Commission ask for Economic and Social Council authorization of a Sub-Commission study of the advisability of strengthening or extending the inalienability of rights as contained in the 1966 International Covenant on Civil and Political Rights.[4]

Report. [1]Special Rapporteur, E/CN.4/Sub.2/1982/15.
Resolution (1982). [2]SCPDPM (report, E/CN.4/1983/4): 1982/32, 10 Sep.
Resolutions (prior). [3]ESC: 1979/34, 10 May 1979 (YUN 1979, p. 846). [4]GA: 2200 A (XXI), annex, 16 Dec. 1966 (YUN 1966, p. 423).
Yearbook reference. [5]1977, p. 711.

Human rights of the individual and international law

In September 1982, Special Rapporteur Erica-Irene A. Daes (Greece) reported to the Sub-Commission on discrimination and minorities, outlining plans for her study on the status of the individual and contemporary international law, mandated by the Commission on Human Rights in March 1981[3] and authorized by the Economic and Social Council in May of that year.[1] The study was an outgrowth of a 1981 study on the duty of the individual to the community.

On 10 September 1982,[2] the Sub-Commission recommended that the Commission recommend to the Council that it request the Special Rapporteur to continue her work, with a view to submitting a final report to the Sub-Commission in 1983, if possible, and that it request the Secretary-General to remind Governments and organizations to submit their comments.

Decision. [1]ESC: 1981/142, 8 May 1981 (YUN 1981, p. 976).
Resolution (1982). [2]SCPDPM (report, E/CN.4/1983/4): 1982/35, 10 Sep.
Yearbook reference. [3]1981, p. 975.

Human rights and science and technology

Action by the Commission on Human Rights. On 19 February 1982,[2] by 31 votes to none, with 12 abstentions, the Commission on Human Rights again requested a study by the Sub-Commission on the use of scientific and technological achievements to ensure the right to work and development. The study, to be considered by the Commission in 1983, was originally requested in 1981.[9] The Commission stressed the importance of implementing the General Assembly's 1975 Declaration on the Use of Scientific and Technological Progress in the Interests of Peace and for the Benefit of Mankind,[7] and called on States to use scientific and technological achievements for peaceful economic, social and cultural development.

General Assembly action. On 18 December 1982,[6] by a resolution adopted by a recorded vote of 113 to none, with 21 abstentions, the Assembly also stressed the importance of implementing the Declaration and called for the use of scientific and technological achievements for peaceful development. It requested the Commission to give special attention to implementation of the Declaration, and United Nations agencies and organizations to take its provisions into account in their programmes. The Assembly noted a 1982 report by the Secretary-General,[1] requested in 1980,[8] containing information from nine States and seven United Nations organizations on action taken to implement the Declaration, and it invited others to provide such information.

Introduced by the Byelorussian SSR, the 28-nation draft was approved by the Third (Social, Humanitarian and Cultural) Committee on 7 December by 109 votes to none, with 23 abstentions.

In a 9 December resolution concerned with aspects of disarmament, the Assembly called on

States to ensure the use of scientific and techno-logical achievements for peaceful purposes.[3] It made a similar call on 18 December in a resolu-tion on human rights and peace.[5] Also in connec-tion with human rights and science and technol-ogy, the Assembly, on the same date,[4] urged the Sub-Commission to continue its study of the pro-tection of persons detained on grounds of mental ill-health, for the purpose of formulating guidelines.

Report. [1]S-G, A/37/330 & Add.1.
Resolutions (1982). [2]Commission on Human Rights (report, E/1982/12): 1982/4, 19 Feb. GA: [3]37/77 B, 9 Dec.; [4]37/188, 18 Dec.; [5]37/189 A, para. 5, 18 Dec.; [6]37/189 B, 18 Dec., text following.
Resolutions (prior). GA: [7]3384(XXX), 10 Nov. 1975 (YUN 1975, p. 631); [8]35/130 A, 11 Dec. 1980 (YUN 1980, p. 878).
Yearbook reference. [9]1981, p. 976.
Meeting records. GA: 3rd Committee, A/C.3/37/SR.47, 50-53, 55, 56, 64, 67 (18 Nov.–7 Dec.); plenary, A/37/PV.111 (18 Dec.).

General Assembly resolution 37/189 B

18 December 1982   Meeting 111   113-0-21 (recorded vote)

Approved by Third Committee (A/37/716) by vote (109-0-23), 7 December (meet-ing 67); 28-nation draft (A/C.3/37/L.73); agenda item 85.

Sponsors: Afghanistan, Angola, Argentina, Bangladesh, Benin, Bulgaria, Byelorus-sian SSR, Chad, Cuba, Cyprus, Czechoslovakia, Democratic Yemen, Ecuador, German Democratic Republic, Guyana, Hungary, Lao People's Democratic Repub-lic, Madagascar, Mali, Mongolia, Morocco, Nicaragua, Panama, Poland, Roma-nia, Viet Nam, Zambia, Zimbabwe.

The General Assembly,

Noting that scientific and technological progress is one of the im-portant factors in the development of human society,

Noting once again the great importance of the Declaration on the Use of Scientific and Technological Progress in the Interests of Peace and for the Benefit of Mankind, adopted by the General Assembly in its resolution 3384(XXX) of 10 November 1975,

Considering that implementation of the said Declaration will con-tribute to the strengthening of international peace and the security of peoples and to their economic and social development, as well as to international co-operation in the field of human rights,

Seriously concerned that the results of scientific and technological progress could be used for the arms race to the detriment of interna-tional peace and security and social progress, human rights and fun-damental freedoms, and the dignity of the human person,

Recognizing that the establishment of the new international eco-nomic order calls in particular for an important contribution to be made by science and technology to economic and social progress,

Bearing in mind that the exchange and transfer of scientific and tech-nological knowledge is one of the important ways to accelerate the social and economic development of the developing countries,

Noting with satisfaction the report of the Secretary-General on human rights and scientific and technological developments,

1. Stresses the importance of the implementation by all States of the provisions and principles contained in the Declaration on the Use of Scientific and Technological Progress in the Interests of Peace and for the Benefit of Mankind in order to promote human rights and fun-damental freedoms;

2. Calls upon all States to make every effort to use the achieve-ments of science and technology in order to promote peaceful social, economic and cultural development and progress;

3. Requests the specialized agencies and other organizations of the United Nations system to take into account in their programmes and activities the provisions of the Declaration;

4. Invites those Member States, specialized agencies and other or-ganizations of the United Nations system that have not yet done so to submit their information pursuant to General Assembly resolution 35/130 A of 11 December 1980;

5. Requests the Commission on Human Rights to give special at-tention, in its consideration of the item entitled "Human rights and

scientific and technological developments", to the question of the im-plementation of the provisions of the Declaration;

6. Decides to include in the provisional agenda of its thirty-eighth session the item entitled "Human rights and scientific and technologi-cal developments".

Recorded vote in Assembly as follows:

In favour: Afghanistan, Algeria, Angola, Argentina, Bahamas, Bahrain, Ban-gladesh, Barbados, Benin, Bhutan, Bolivia, Botswana, Brazil, Bulgaria, Burma, Burundi, Byelorussian SSR, Cape Verde, Central African Republic, Chad, Chile, China, Colombia, Congo, Costa Rica, Cuba, Czechoslovakia, Democratic Kam-puchea, Democratic Yemen, Djibouti, Dominican Republic, Ecuador, Egypt, El Salvador, Ethiopia, Fiji, Gabon, Gambia, German Democratic Republic, Ghana, Greece, Guatemala, Guinea, Guyana, Hungary, India, Indonesia, Iran, Iraq, Ivory Coast, Jamaica, Japan, Jordan, Kenya, Kuwait, Lao People's Democratic Repub-lic, Lebanon, Lesotho, Liberia, Libyan Arab Jamahiriya, Madagascar, Malaysia, Maldives, Mali, Malta, Mauritania, Mexico, Mongolia, Morocco, Mozambique, Nepal, Nicaragua, Niger, Nigeria, Oman, Pakistan, Panama, Papua New Guinea, Paraguay, Peru, Philippines, Poland, Qatar, Romania, Samoa, Saudi Arabia, Sene-gal, Sierra Leone, Singapore, Somalia, Sri Lanka, Sudan, Suriname, Syrian Arab Republic, Thailand, Togo, Trinidad and Tobago, Tunisia, Turkey, Ukrainian SSR, USSR, United Arab Emirates, United Republic of Cameroon, United Republic of Tanzania, Upper Volta, Uruguay, Venezuela, Viet Nam, Yemen, Yugoslavia, Zaire, Zambia, Zimbabwe.

Against: None.

Abstaining: Australia, Austria, Belgium, Canada, Denmark, Finland, France, Germany, Federal Republic of, Iceland, Ireland, Israel, Italy, Luxembourg, Nether-lands, New Zealand, Norway, Portugal, Spain, Sweden, United Kingdom, United States.

Human rights and peace

Action by the Commission on Human Rights.

On 19 February 1982,[4] by a roll-call vote of 32 to none, with 11 abstentions, the Commission on Human Rights requested a study by the Sub-Commission on discrimination and minorities, for consideration in 1984, on the negative conse-quences of the arms race (see POLITICAL AND SECURITY QUESTIONS, Chapter I), particularly the nuclear arms race. Stressing the need for the international community to achieve general and complete disarmament under effective interna-tional control, the Commission called on States to ensure that scientific and technological achieve-ments were used exclusively in the interests of peace, for the benefit of mankind and for promot-ing human rights. The Commission decided to stress in its future activities the need to ensure everyone's right to life.

In conformity with the Commission's request to bring this resolution to the attention of the Eco-nomic and Social Council, the General Assembly and other United Nations bodies, the Secretary-General transmitted it to the Assembly by a note of 8 June.[3]

Sub-Commission action.

On 7 September,[8] the Sub-Commission on discrimination and minorities recommended that the Economic and Social Council: authorize continuation of the Sub-Commission's consideration of the effects of gross human rights violations on international peace and security, with a view to preparing principles; re-quest the Assembly to invite the International Law Commission to take flagrant human rights viola-tions and the Sub-Commission's comments on them into account when drafting a code of offences against peace and security (see LEGAL QUES-TIONS, Chapter II); and request the Security

Council to consider effective means of dealing with human rights violations that threatened international peace and security.

Also on 7 September,[1] the Sub-Commission decided to defer until 1983 consideration of a draft resolution[2] expressing the hope that States would avoid threats to peace by promoting human rights, including releasing all persons detained for their views who had not advocated or used violence.

General Assembly action. Expressing its firm conviction that all peoples and individuals had a right to life, the safeguarding of which was an essential condition for the enjoyment of other rights, the General Assembly, on 18 December 1982,[6] stressed the need for the international community to achieve general and complete disarmament under international control. It further stressed the importance of implementing practical measures of disarmament to release resources for social and economic development, particularly in developing countries. The Assembly called on States to prohibit by law any propaganda for war, and called on them, as well as on United Nations agencies and intergovernmental and non-governmental organizations, to take measures to ensure the peaceful uses of scientific and technological achievements (see above). The Commission on Human Rights was requested to stress in its future activities the need to ensure the right of everyone to life, liberty, security and peace.

The resolution was adopted by a recorded vote of 110 to none, with 24 abstentions. Introduced by the USSR, the 21-nation draft was approved by the Third Committee on 7 December by 102 votes to none, with 28 abstentions. The approved text incorporated oral revisions by the sponsors, two of them based on suggestions by other States. On the proposal of Oman, the phrase "and prevent violations of the principles of the Charter of the United Nations regarding the sovereignty and territorial integrity of States and self-determination of peoples" was added in paragraph 2. At the suggestion of the United States, the phrase "liberty and security of person, and to live in peace" was added to paragraph 6. A similar amendment was made to the second preambular paragraph.

In a resolution of 16 December, the Assembly stated that respect for human rights and the strengthening of international peace and security mutually reinforced each other.[5] On 18 December, it noted that mass and flagrant human rights violations in one State might threaten the peace of neighbouring States, a region or the international community.[7]

Decision (1982). [1]SCPDPM (report, E/CN.4/1983/4): 1982/10, 7 Sep.
Draft resolution deferred. [2]Special Rapporteurs, E/CN.4/Sub.2/1982/L.22.
Note. [3]S-G, A/S-12/AC.1/2.

Resolutions (1982). [4]Commission on Human Rights (report, E/1982/12): 1982/7, 19 Feb. GA: [5]37/118, para. 10, 16 Dec.; [6]37/189 A, 18 Dec., text following; [7]37/200, para. 2, 18 Dec. [8]SCPDPM: 1982/11, 7 Sep.
Meeting records. GA: 3rd Committee, A/C.3/37/SR.47, 50-53, 55, 56, *64,* 67 (18 Nov.–7 Dec.); 1st Committee, A/C.1/37/PV.59 (9 Dec.); plenary, A/37/PV.111 (18 Dec.).

General Assembly resolution 37/189 A

18 December 1982   Meeting 111   110-0-24 (recorded vote)

Approved by Third Committee (A/37/716) by vote (102-0-28), 7 December (meeting 67); 21-nation draft (A/C.3/37/L.71), orally amended by Oman and orally revised; agenda item 85.

Sponsors: Angola, Benin, Bulgaria, Byelorussian SSR, Cape Verde, Cuba, Democratic Yemen, Ethiopia, Ghana, Guinea-Bissau, India, Lao People's Democratic Republic, Mongolia, Mozambique, Nigeria, Poland, Romania, Syrian Arab Republic, Ukrainian SSR, USSR, Viet Nam.

The General Assembly,

Reaffirming the determination of the peoples of the United Nations to save succeeding generations from the scourge of war, to reaffirm faith in the dignity and worth of the human person, to maintain international peace and security, to develop friendly relations among peoples and international co-operation in promoting and encouraging universal respect for human rights and for fundamental freedoms,

Recalling the provisions of the Universal Declaration of Human Rights, according to which everyone has the right to life, liberty and security of person, the International Covenant on Economic, Social and Cultural Rights and the International Covenant on Civil and Political Rights, article 6 of which states that every human being has the inherent right to life,

Recalling also its resolutions 3281(XXIX) of 12 December 1974, containing the Charter of Economic Rights and Duties of States, and 3201(S-VI) and 3202(S-VI) of 1 May 1974, containing the Declaration and the Programme of Action on the Establishment of a New International Economic Order,

Recalling further the Declaration on the Strengthening of International Security, the Declaration on the Use of Scientific and Technological Progress in the Interests of Peace and for the Benefit of Mankind, the Declaration on the Preparation of Societies for Life in Peace, the Declaration on the Prevention of Nuclear Catastrophe and General Assembly resolution 36/92 I of 9 December 1981, on the non-use of nuclear weapons and prevention of nuclear war,

Noting with appreciation Commission on Human Rights resolution 1982/7 of 19 February 1982,

Reaffirming the inherent right to life of all peoples and all individuals,

Deeply concerned that international peace and security continue to be threatened by the arms race, particularly the nuclear arms race, as well as by violations of the principles of the Charter of the United Nations regarding the sovereignty and territorial integrity of States and self-determination of peoples,

Aware that all horrors of past wars and all other calamities that have befallen people would pale in comparison with what is inherent in the use of nuclear weapons capable of destroying civilization on earth,

Noting the pressing need for urgent measures towards general and complete disarmament, particularly nuclear disarmament,

Bearing in mind that, in accordance with the International Covenant on Civil and Political Rights, any propaganda for war shall be prohibited by law,

Recalling the historic responsibility of the Governments of all countries of the world to remove the threat of war from the lives of people, to preserve civilization and ensure that everyone enjoys his inherent right to life,

Convinced that for no people in the world today is there a more important question than that of the preservation of peace and of ensuring the cardinal right of every human being, namely, the right to life,

1. *Expresses its firm conviction* that all peoples and all individuals have an inherent right to life, and that the safeguarding of this foremost right is an essential condition for the enjoyment of the entire range of economic, social and cultural, as well as civil and political, rights;

2. *Stresses* the urgent need for all possible efforts by the international community to strengthen peace, remove the threat of war, particularly nuclear war, halt the arms race and achieve general and complete disarmament under effective international control, and prevent violations of the principles of the Charter of the United Nations regard-

ing the sovereignty and territorial integrity of States and self-determination of peoples, thus contributing to assuring the right to life;

3. *Stresses further* the foremost importance of the implementation of practical measures of disarmament for releasing substantial additional resources, which should be utilized for social and economic development, particularly for the benefit of the developing countries;

4. *Calls upon* all States to take effective measures with a view to prohibiting by law any propaganda for war;

5. *Again calls upon* all States, appropriate organs of the United Nations, specialized agencies, and intergovernmental and non-governmental organizations concerned to take the necessary measures to ensure that the results of scientific and technological progress are used exclusively in the interests of international peace, for the benefit of mankind and for promoting and encouraging respect for human rights and fundamental freedoms without distinction as to race, sex, language or religion;

6. *Requests* the Commission on Human Rights in its future activities to stress the need to ensure the cardinal right of everyone to life, liberty and security of person, and to live in peace;

7. *Decides* to consider this matter further at its thirty-eighth session under the item entitled "Human rights and scientific and technological developments".

Recorded vote in Assembly as follows:

In favour: Afghanistan, Algeria, Angola, Argentina, Bahamas, Bahrain, Bangladesh, Barbados, Benin, Bhutan, Bolivia, Botswana, Brazil, Bulgaria, Burma, Burundi, Byelorussian SSR, Cape Verde, Central African Republic, Chad, Chile, Colombia, Congo, Costa Rica, Cuba, Czechoslovakia, Democratic Kampuchea, Democratic Yemen, Djibouti, Dominican Republic, Ecuador, Egypt, El Salvador, Ethiopia, Fiji, Gabon, Gambia, German Democratic Republic, Ghana, Greece, Guatemala, Guinea, Guyana, Hungary, India, Indonesia, Iran, Iraq, Ivory Coast,

Jamaica, Jordan, Kenya, Kuwait, Lao People's Democratic Republic, Lebanon, Lesotho, Liberia, Libyan Arab Jamahiriya, Madagascar, Malaysia, Maldives, Mali, Malta, Mauritania, Mexico, Mongolia, Morocco, Mozambique, Nepal, Nicaragua, Niger, Nigeria, Oman, Pakistan, Panama, Papua New Guinea, Paraguay, Peru, Philippines, Poland, Qatar, Romania, Samoa, Saudi Arabia, Senegal, Sierra Leone, Singapore, Somalia, Sri Lanka, Sudan, Suriname, Syrian Arab Republic, Thailand, Togo, Trinidad and Tobago, Tunisia, Ukrainian SSR, USSR, United Arab Emirates, United Republic of Cameroon, United Republic of Tanzania, Upper Volta, Uruguay, Venezuela, Viet Nam, Yemen, Yugoslavia, Zaire, Zambia, Zimbabwe.

Against: None.

Abstaining: Australia, Austria, Belgium, Canada, China, Denmark, Finland, France, Germany, Federal Republic of, Iceland, Ireland, Israel, Italy, Japan, Luxembourg, Netherlands, New Zealand, Norway, Portugal, Spain, Sweden, Turkey, United Kingdom, United States.

Iraq and Israel

The Commission on Human Rights, on 19 February 1982,[1] by a roll-call vote of 30 to 1 (United States), with 11 abstentions, adopted a resolution strongly condemning Israel for its aerial attack against an Iraqi nuclear reactor in June 1981, which, it said, was a dangerous escalation of Israeli violations of human rights and the right of States to scientific and technological progress (p. 425).

Resolution (1982). [1]Commission on Human Rights (report, E/1982/12): 1982/5, 19 Feb.

Chapter XIX

Women

Contents

Related topics:
Africa: Women and children under *apartheid*. Middle East: Situation of women and children in the occupied Arab territories. Human rights: Parental kidnapping.

For resolutions and decisions of major organs mentioned but not reproduced, refer to INDEX OF RESOLUTIONS AND DECISIONS.

Advancement of women

Decade for Women (1976-1985)

Implementation of the Programme for 1981-1985

In 1982, Governments and the United Nations system worked to implement the Programme of Action for the Second Half of the United Nations Decade for Women[4]—adopted by the World Conference of the United Nations Decade for Women: Equality, Development and Peace and endorsed by the General Assembly in 1980.[3] In an October 1982 report[1] to the Assembly, the Secretary-General noted that system-wide activities were designed to advance women's interests in collaboration with Governments and non-governmental organizations, with particular reference to: integrating women in development (see below);

disseminating information on matters concerning women and infrastructure support for documentation and communications; and developing or improving statistics and indicators on the situation of women for evaluating their role in all aspects of economic and social development.

Among these activities in 1982, the United Nations Centre for Social Development and Humanitarian Affairs (CSDHA), the focal point for the Programme's implementation, held an expert group meeting on Women and the International Development Strategy (Vienna, Austria, 6-10 September). The United Nations Educational, Scientific and Cultural Organization organized the third in a series of regional seminars on women and media decision-making (Mexico, March) and a course in social communication for women professionals in population programmes (Shanghai, China, 23 August–3 September).

General Assembly action. By a resolution adopted without vote on 3 December,[2] the General Assembly took note of the Secretary-General's report and welcomed steps taken towards realizing the Decade's objectives. It called on the international community to pay increased attention to the need to implement the recommendations of the Programme of Action and in particular to expand technical co-operation activities to ensure women's full and equal participation in development. The Assembly emphasized the role of CSDHA as the focal point for implementating United Nations activities, and requested the Secretary-General to report to the Assembly in 1983 on implementation of the current resolution.

Other provisions concerned contributions to the Decade's objectives by the Voluntary Fund for the United Nations Decade for Women and the International Research and Training Institute for the Advancement of Women, the ratification of the Convention on the Elimination of All Forms of Discrimination against Women, and the Committee on the Elimination of Discrimination against Women.

The text, recommended by the Assembly's Third (Social, Humanitarian and Cultural) Committee, had been introduced by Bangladesh on behalf of the Group of 77 Member States and approved, also without vote, by the Committee on 24 November, following an oral amendment to paragraph 3 by Denmark. The amendment called for increased attention to the need for practical measures to implement the relevant recommendations of the Programme of Action, rather than simply to implement the Programme.

Report. [1]S-G, A/37/458 & Add.1.
Resolution (1982). [2]GA: 37/58, 3 Dec., text following.
Resolution (prior). [3]GA: 35/136, 11 Dec. 1980 (YUN 1980, p. 905).
Yearbook reference. [4]1980, p. 890.
Meeting records. GA: 3rd Committee, A/C.3/37/SR.30, 32-37, 49, 54, 55 (2-26 Nov.); plenary, A/37/PV.90 (3 Dec.).

General Assembly resolution 37/58

3 December 1982   Meeting 90   Adopted without vote

Approved by Third Committee (A/37/676) without vote, 24 November (meeting 54); draft by Bangladesh, for Group of 77 (A/C.3/37/L.40), orally amended by Denmark; agenda item 91 *(a)*.

United Nations Decade for Women: Equality, Development and Peace

The General Assembly,

Bearing in mind its resolutions 3201(S-VI) and 3202(S-VI) of 1 May 1974, containing the Declaration and the Programme of Action on the Establishment of a New International Economic Order, 3281(XXIX) of 12 December 1974, containing the Charter of Economic Rights and Duties of States, and 3362(S-VII) of 16 September 1975 on development and international economic co-operation,

Recalling its resolutions 35/136 of 11 December 1980 and 36/126 of 14 December 1981, in which it endorsed the Programme of Action for the Second Half of the United Nations Decade for Women,

Affirming the role of the Centre for Social Development and Humanitarian Affairs of the Secretariat as the focal point for the organizations of the United Nations system with regard to activities undertaken in implementation of the Programme of Action for the Second Half of the United Nations Decade for Women,

Recalling also its resolution 36/128 of 14 December 1981 on the establishment of the International Research and Training Institute for the Advancement of Women and Economic and Social Council resolution 1982/27 of 4 May 1982 concerning the programmes and activities of the Institute,

Having considered the reports of the Secretary-General on the Voluntary Fund for the United Nations Decade for Women, on the status of the Convention on the Elimination of All Forms of Discrimination against Women and on the programmes and activities of the International Research and Training Institute for the Advancement of Women,

1. *Takes note with appreciation* of the report of the Secretary-General on the implementation of the Programme of Action for the Second Half of the United Nations Decade for Women;

2. *Welcomes* the steps taken by Governments and by the organizations of the United Nations system, including the regional commissions, to achieve progress towards the effective realization of the objectives of the United Nations Decade for Women: Equality, Development and Peace;

3. *Calls upon* Governments, the organizations of the United Nations system, including the regional commissions, intergovernmental bodies and non-governmental organizations to pay increased attention to the need to take practical measures to implement the relevant recommendations of the Programme of Action for the Second Half of the United Nations Decade for Women and, in particular, to expand technical co-operation activities which would ensure women's full and equal participation, as agents and as beneficiaries, in all sectors and at all levels of development;

4. *Emphasizes* the continuing role of the Centre for Social Development and Humanitarian Affairs as the focal point for the organizations of the United Nations system with regard to activities undertaken in implementation of the Programme of Action;

5. *Notes with satisfaction* the contribution made by the Voluntary Fund for the United Nations Decade for Women to the implementation of the Programme of Action, mainly through innovative and experimental projects at the grass-roots level;

6. *Notes with satisfaction* the commencement of the work of the International Research and Training Institute for the Advancement of Women and invites it to continue contributing to the objectives of the Decade;

7. *Notes with satisfaction* that, as at 1 November 1982, forty-five Member States had ratified or acceded to the Convention on the Elimination of All Forms of Discrimination against Women;

8. *Invites* all States that have not yet done so to become parties to the Convention;

9. *Welcomes* the commencement of the work of the Committee on the Elimination of Discrimination against Women, which held its first session at Vienna from 18 to 22 October 1982;

10. *Requests* the Secretary-General to report to the General Assembly at its thirty-eighth session on the steps taken to implement the present resolution;

11. *Also requests* the Secretary-General to report to the General Assembly at its thirty-eighth session on the status of the Convention;

12. *Decides* to include in the provisional agenda of its thirty-eighth session the item entitled "United Nations Decade for Women: Equality, Development and Peace".

National action

Activities undertaken by 42 Governments to implement the Programme of Action for the Second Half of the Decade for Women during 1980-1981 were summarized by the Secretary-General in a January 1982 report and in a later addendum,[1] submitted to the February/March session of the Commission on the Status of Women. The information was presented separately for developed market economies, centrally planned economies and developing economies.

Report. [1]S-G, E/CN.6/1982/2 & Corr.1 & Add.1.

Preparations for the Conference on the Decade for Women (1985)

Responding to a December 1981 request of the General Assembly,[6] the Secretary-General prepared a report for the Commission on the Status of Women[1] on the preparations for the World Conference to Review and Appraise the Achievements of the United Nations Decade for Women scheduled for 1985.[5] The report discussed two interrelated concerns: issues on which to base an agenda for the Conference, such as women and development, women and decision-making, and co-operation among countries and promotion of peace; and organizational arrangements, including the form and composition of the intergovernmental body to prepare for the Conference, its secretariat, organization of work, documentation, rules of procedure, public information activities and national, regional and sectoral preparations.

Economic and Social Council action. On 4 May 1982,[2] the Economic and Social Council, taking note of the Secretary-General's report, decided that the Commission on the Status of Women would be the preparatory body for the Conference, and the Advancement of Women Branch of CSDHA its secretariat. The Commission, which would operate on the basis of consensus, was to meet in 1983 and 1985 at Vienna, Austria, and extend its 1984 regular session to prepare for the Conference; it was to formulate a draft perspective on the status of women to the year 2000. The Council encouraged Member States to establish national committees to assist in preparations and invited them to submit their views on the Conference's goals and themes. Member States, organizations and regional commissions were asked for their views on other possible issues and themes, while the Secretary-General was asked to undertake inter-agency consultations on the topic.

This resolution was adopted without vote on the recommendation of the Council's Second (Social) Committee. The text, submitted by the Commission and orally amended by Kenya, had been similarly approved by the Committee on 26 April. By the amendments, the Council recommended that the Assembly make the necessary budgetary allocations "in the light of proposals made by the preparatory body at its first session", and decided to consider at its first 1983 session the Commission's report on its first session as preparatory body for the Conference.

General Assembly action. On 3 December 1982,[3] the General Assembly endorsed the Council's resolution and welcomed its decision that the Commission on the Status of Women be the Conference's preparatory body, to operate on the basis of consensus. Noting that the first preparatory session was to be held at Vienna, from 23 February to 4 March 1983, the Assembly also endorsed the Council's decision to invite the widest participation by States and hoped that representatives experienced in the area of women and development would be designated. The Secretary-General of the Conference was to be appointed at the level of Assistant Secretary-General, from outside the United Nations system and from a developing country, in accordance with a 1979 Assembly request.[4] The Assembly decided to include an item on the Conference preparations in the provisional agenda of its 1983 session, at which it would consider the Council's recommendations based on the preparatory body's report. It also took note of a report on a world survey on women in development.

This resolution was adopted without vote on the recommendation of the Assembly's Third (Social, Humanitarian and Cultural) Committee. The text, introduced and orally revised by Bangladesh on behalf of the Group of 77 Member States, had been similarly approved by the Committee on 24 November.

Report. [1]SG, E/CN.6/1982/8.
Resolutions (1982). [2]ESC, 1982/26, 4 May, text following; [3]GA, 37/60, 3 Dec., text following.
Resolutions (prior). GA: [4]33/189, 29 Jan. 1979 (YUN 1978, p. 750); [5]35/136, 11 Dec. 1980 (YUN 1980, p. 905); [6]36/126, 14 Dec. 1981 (YUN 1981, p. 982).
Meeting records. ESC: E/1982/SR.23 (4 May). GA: 3rd Committee, A/C.3/37/SR.30, 32-37, *49, 54, 55* (2-26 Nov.); plenary, A/37/PV.90 (3 Dec.).

Economic and Social Council resolution 1982/26

4 May 1982   Meeting 23   Adopted without vote

Approved by Second Committee (E/1982/57) without vote, 26 April (meeting 9); draft by Commission on women (E/1982/14), orally amended by Kenya; agenda item 10.

Preparations for the 1985 World Conference to Review and Appraise the Achievements of the United Nations Decade for Women

The Economic and Social Council,

Considering that the General Assembly, in its resolution 35/136 of 11 December 1980, decided to convene in 1985, at the conclusion of the United Nations Decade for Women: Equality, Development and Peace, a world conference to review and appraise the achievements of the Decade,

Recalling General Assembly resolution 36/126 of 14 December 1981, in which the Commission on the Status of Women was requested to give priority at its twenty-ninth session to the question of the preparations for the World Conference to Review and Appraise the Achievements of the United Nations Decade for Women, with a view to submitting to the Assembly at its thirty-seventh session, through the Economic and Social Council, specific proposals on that question,

Recalling also General Assembly resolution 35/10 C of 3 November 1980, by which the Assembly decided that preparatory committees should be established for special conferences only if that function could not be appropriately performed by an existing intergovernmental organ,

Emphasizing the importance of undertaking at the conclusion of the Decade a critical review and appraisal of progress at international, regional and national levels in the achievement of the goals of the Decade—equality, development and peace—and the subthemes of education, health and employment, and the obstacles encountered in the implementation of the World Plan of Action for the Implementation of the Objectives of the International Women's Year and the Programme of Action for the Second Half of the United Nations Decade for Women, and also of developing a forward-looking perspective on the status of women,

Emphasizing also the need to identify the most effective strategies and methods of work at the international level and to establish priorities for the United Nations system,

Bearing in mind the positive response of many Governments to the World Plan of Action, in the form of national mechanisms or legislation,

Also bearing in mind the need in the coming years to realize the full potential of those mechanisms or legislation to enable women to maintain and consolidate gains made during the Decade,

Taking note of the report of the Secretary-General on the preparations for the World Conference to Review and Appraise the Achievements of the United Nations Decade for Women, to be held in 1985,

1. *Decides* that the Commission on the Status of Women shall be the preparatory body for the World Conference to Review and Appraise the Achievements of the United Nations Decade for Women and shall operate on the basis of consensus, and invites the widest possible participation by Member States in the deliberations of the preparatory body;

2. *Recommends* that the Commission on the Status of Women, acting as the preparatory body for the Conference, should meet at Vienna in extraordinary session in 1983 and again in 1985 with conference preparations as the sole item of the agenda, and that its thirtieth regular session, in 1984, should be extended to allow additional time for conference preparations;

3. *Decides also* to recommend to the General Assembly that the Advancement of Women Branch of the Centre for Social Development and Humanitarian Affairs of the Secretariat should serve as the secretariat of the preparatory body, as well as of the Conference;

4. *Recommends also* that the General Assembly should make the necessary budgetary allocations, in the light of the proposals made by the preparatory body at its first session, to enable the Advancement of Women Branch to perform those duties;

5. *Recommends further* that, with a view to the achievement of the goals of the Decade, a forward-looking draft perspective on the status of women to the year 2000 should be prepared by the preparatory body for consideration by the Conference based on the experience gained in the implementation of the World Plan of Action for the Implementation of the Objectives of the International Women's Year and the Programme of Action for the Second Half of the United Nations Decade for Women;

6. *Encourages* Member States to consider establishing national committees to assist, for example, in national-level preparations for the Conference, consultations on issues and themes and the preparation of national reports;

7. *Invites* the regional commissions to conduct consultations, within existing resources, on issues and themes for the Conference and on organizational arrangements at the regional level to prepare for the Conference, and to submit the results of those consultations to the preparatory body;

8. *Invites* Member States to submit in writing, by 1 July 1982, their views on the proposed goals and specific themes of the Conference so that the Centre for Social Development and Humanitarian Affairs can prepare a report based on those views by 31 January 1983, for consideration by the Commission, in its capacity as preparatory body, at its extraordinary session in 1983;

9. *Also invites* non-governmental organizations having consultative status with the Economic and Social Council and intergovernmental organizations to submit their views, in writing, on their contributions to the Conference and on possible issues and themes for the Conference to the Centre for Social Development and Humanitarian Affairs, for consolidated presentation to the preparatory body;

10. *Requests* the Secretary-General to undertake inter-agency consultations on issues and themes for the Conference with a view to presenting an inter-agency report on the question to the preparatory body at its first session;

11. *Decides* to consider at its first regular session of 1983, in connection with the question of the United Nations Decade for Women: Equality, Development and Peace, the report of the Commission on the Status of Women on its first session as preparatory body for the World Conference.

General Assembly resolution 37/60

3 December 1982   Meeting 90   Adopted without vote

Approved by Third Committee (A/37/676) without vote, 24 November (meeting 54); draft by Bangladesh, for Group of 77 (A/C.3/37/L.34), orally revised; agenda item 91.

Preparations for the World Conference to Review and Appraise the Achievements of the United Nations Decade for Women

The General Assembly,

Recalling its resolution 3520(XXX) of 15 December 1975, in which it endorsed, *inter alia*, the action proposals contained in the World Plan of Action for the Implementation of the Objectives of the International Women's Year,

Recalling its resolution 3490(XXX) of 12 December 1975, in which it expressed its conviction that a comprehensive and thorough review and appraisal of progress made in meeting the goals of the World Plan of Action was of crucial importance for the success of the Plan and recognized that the results of the implementation of the Plan would contribute to the consideration of the review and appraisal of the International Development Strategy for the Second United Nations Development Decade and would consequently promote the role of women in the development process,

Recalling also its resolution 35/136 of 11 December 1980, in which it endorsed the Programme of Action for the Second Half of the United Nations Decade for Women as adopted at the World Conference of the United Nations Decade for Women, and decided to convene in 1985, at the conclusion of the Decade, a World Conference to Review and Appraise the Achievements of the United Nations Decade for Women,

Recalling further that the International Development Strategy for the Third United Nations Development Decade stressed that the important set of measures to improve the status of women, contained in the World Plan of Action adopted at Mexico City in 1975, and the important agreed measures relating to the International Development Strategy in the Programme of Action for the Second Half of the United Nations Decade for Women, adopted at Copenhagen in 1980, should be implemented,

Recalling its resolution 36/126 of 14 December 1981, in which it requested the Commission on the Status of Women, at its session to be held in 1982, to give priority to the question of the preparations for the Conference,

Noting that the Economic and Social Council, at its first regular session of 1982, considered the recommendations of the Commission on the Status of Women as set forth in its report and adopted, on 4 May 1982, resolution 1982/26 on the preparations for the Conference,

Bearing in mind all its relevant resolutions and decisions regarding preparations for special conferences, in particular its resolution 33/189 of 29 January 1979,

1. *Endorses* Economic and Social Council resolution 1982/26 on the preparations for the World Conference to Review and Appraise the Achievements of the United Nations Decade for Women, to be held in 1985;

2. *Welcomes* the decision of the Economic and Social Council that the Commission on the Status of Women should be the preparatory body for the Conference and that it should operate on the basis of consensus;

3. *Endorses* the decision of the Economic and Social Council to invite the widest possible participation by States in the preparatory meetings for the Conference and expresses the hope that they will designate representatives who will have the background and experience in the area of women and development;

4. *Notes* that the first session of the Commission on the Status of Women as the preparatory body of the Conference is to be held at Vienna from 23 February to 4 March 1983 and that the report on that session will be considered by the Economic and Social Council at its first regular session of 1983;

5. *Requests* the Secretary-General to take into account paragraph 9 of General Assembly resolution 33/189 when appointing the Secretary-General of the Conference;

6. *Decides* to consider at its thirty-eighth session the recommendations of the Economic and Social Council at its first regular session of 1983 based on the report of the first session of the Commission on the Status of Women as the preparatory body for the Conference, together with the observations, if any, of the Secretary-General;

7. *Takes note with appreciation* of the report of the Secretary-General on the progress made in the preparation of a world survey on the role of women in development and recommends that the survey should be submitted to the Conference;

8. *Decides* to include in the provisional agenda of its thirty-eighth session an item entitled "Preparations for the World Conference to Review and Appraise the Achievements of the United Nations Decade for Women".

Voluntary Fund

The Voluntary Fund for the United Nations Decade for Women, which was extended by the General Assembly in 1975[5] to provide during 1976-1985 financial and technical assistance with special attention to rural and poor urban women, ended its fifth year of operation in 1982. By that time, 75 projects of a total of 294 supported by the Fund were completed.[2] Distribution of the projects by subject area was as follows: employment, 31 per cent; human development, 30; planning, 24; energy, 9; and information, 6.

Of the more than 170 projects for which Fund support was requested in 1982, 75 were approved on the recommendation of the Consultative Committee on the Voluntary Fund; 43 of them were valued at a total of $3.8 million, and the 32 others consisted of small-scale projects valued at less than $20,000 each, or additional inputs to ongoing activities. Ten programming missions undertaken jointly by the Fund and the United Nations Development Programme (UNDP) were completed, resulting in proposals, to be financed by UNDP indicative planning figures, for the reorientation of large-scale projects to ensure consideration of women and for the development of new ones specifically directed to women.

In 1982, the proportion of country-level projects—all of which were UNDP-administered—rose to 88 per cent of total Fund-supported projects. Fund-assisted projects executed by non-governmental organizations (NGOs) showed a significant upward trend, to 48 per cent of all such projects.

In 1982, contributions pledged to the Fund by Governments totalled $1.8 million. Non-governmental contributions amounted to $41,000.

The Fund's activities from October 1981 to September 1982, its financial situation and needs, and a summary of the Consultative Committee's recommendations at its eleventh (March/April 1982) and twelfth (August) sessions were detailed in a November report of the Secretary-General to the General Assembly.[1]

The Committee, reiterating that the Fund should find its own role and not overlap other funds, referred many projects to more appropriate funding agencies. Stressing that the choice of projects for Fund approval be left to the requesting country, the Committee encouraged a positive response to requests for strengthening national machineries, given the many Fund-financed projects under execution by such machineries. The Committee recommended that, in case of a delay in obtaining financing from other sources for future project stages, especially where programmes were at risk, consideration could be given to financing by the Fund. Support for regional commission posts for senior women programme officers was to continue through 1983. The Committee hoped that the Secretary-General would ensure the Fund's efficient management, including adequate staff support.

General Assembly action. On 3 December 1982,[4] the Assembly, taking note of the Secretary-General's report and the Consultative Committee's recommendations, considered that the Fund had a unique contribution to make in the technical assistance field to implementation of the goals of the United Nations Decade for Women; and that project evaluation was important in enabling the Fund to fulfil its objectives, as were fund-raising and information activites in maintaining and increasing its effectiveness and financial viability. The Assembly, noting the increasing number of Fund-financed projects and the appointment within regular budget resources of senior women programme officers by the regional commissions, urged further strengthening of their programmes for women. It requested the Secretary-General to continue to report annually on the Fund's progress and include it in the annual United Nations Pledging Conference for Development Activities.

Two other provisions concerned the level of Fund contributions.

This resolution was adopted without vote on the recommendation of the Assembly's Third (Social, Humanitarian and Cultural) Committee. The text, introduced by the United Kingdom on behalf also of the German Democratic Republic, India, Jamaica and Nigeria, had been similarly approved by the Committee on 24 November.

By a further resolution of 3 December, on the United Nations Decade for Women,[3] the Assembly noted the Fund's contribution to implementation of the Programme of Action for the Second Half of the Decade for Women, mainly through innovative and experimental projects at the grass-roots level.

Reports. (1)S-G, A/37/421; (2)UNDP Administrator, DP/1983/6/Add.3.
Resolutions (1982). GA, 3 Dec.: (3)37/58, para. 5; (4)37/62, text following.
Yearbook reference. (5)1975, p. 661.
Meeting records: GA: 3rd Committee, A/C.3/37/SR.30, 32-37, *49, 54* (2 Nov.–24 Nov.); plenary, A/37/PV.90 (3 Dec.).

General Assembly resolution 37/62

3 December 1982　　　　Meeting 90　　　　Adopted without vote

Approved by Third Committee (A/37/676) without vote, 24 November (meeting 54); 5-nation draft (A/C.3/37/L.24); agenda item 91 *(b).*

Sponsors: German Democratic Republic, India, Jamaica, Nigeria, United Kingdom.

Voluntary Fund for the United Nations Decade for Women
The General Assembly,

Recalling its resolution 31/133 of 16 December 1976, containing the criteria and arrangements for the management of the Voluntary Fund for the United Nations Decade for Women,

Recalling also its resolution 36/129 of 14 December 1981,

Welcoming the contributions made by Member States and non-governmental organizations towards the implementation of the goals of the United Nations Decade for Women: Equality, Development and Peace,

Taking note with appreciation of the report of the Secretary-General on the Fund,

1. *Takes note with satisfaction* of the recommendations of the Consultative Committee on the Voluntary Fund for the United Nations Decade for Women at its eleventh and twelfth sessions;

2. *Considers* that the Fund has a unique contribution to make in the technical assistance field to the implementation of the goals of the United Nations Decade for Women: Equality, Development and Peace;

3. *Considers further* that the evaluation of projects has an important role to play in enabling the Fund to fulfil its objectives;

4. *Notes with satisfaction* the continuing increase in the number of projects submitted to and financed by the Fund, and the catalytic role played by the Fund in promoting the adoption of innovative and experimental activities by Governments and other funds;

5. *Notes* the appointment of senior women's programme officers at the regional commissions within regular budget resources available to them, and recognizes the valuable contribution that this is making to the work of the Fund and thus to the implementation of the goals of the Decade;

6. *Urges* the executive secretaries of the regional commissions to take further action to use available financial and personnel resources to strengthen their programmes for women;

7. *Notes with concern* that contributions to the Fund have not been sufficient to enable it to take on all the worthwhile projects submitted to it;

8. *Considers* that fund-raising and information activities have a vital role to play in maintaining and increasing the financial viability and effectiveness of the Fund;

9. *Expresses its appreciation* for the support which national committees for the Fund, national United Nations associations and other non-governmental organizations have given to the work of the Fund;

10. *Expresses its appreciation also* for the voluntary contributions to the Fund pledged by Member States, and its hope that the overall level of such contributions will be maintained or increased;

11. *Notes* the view of the Consultative Committee on the Voluntary Fund for the United Nations Decade for Women, as expressed at its twelfth session, that there are still grounds for concern regarding administrative matters relating to the Fund, and its hope that specific and concrete measures will be taken by the Secretary-General on an urgent basis to ensure that these issues are studied and the necessary action is taken;

12. *Notes also* the assurance given to the Consultative Committee that the Secretary-General will do everything possible to ensure that the Fund is administered efficiently;

13. *Requests* the Secretary-General:

(a) To continue to report annually on the management of the Fund and on the progress of its activities;

(b) To continue to include the Fund, on an annual basis, as one of the programmes for which funds are pledged at the United Nations Pledging Conference for Development Activities.

Contributions and expenditures

In its 3 December resolution on the Voluntary Fund for the United Nations Decade for Women,[1] the General Assembly, noting that contributions had not been sufficient to enable the Fund to take on all the worthwhile projects submitted to it, expressed appreciation of voluntary contributions pledged by Member States and the hope that the overall contribution level would be maintained or increased.

As at 31 December 1982, contributions and pledges were as follows:

CONTRIBUTIONS TO THE VOLUNTARY FUND FOR THE UNITED NATIONS DECADE FOR WOMEN, 1982 AND 1983
(as at 31 December 1982; in US dollar equivalent)

Country	1982 payment	1983 pledge
Australia	112,610	116,948
Austria	21,000	21,000
Belgium	85,486	—
Botswana	—	4,587
Chile	5,000	5,000
China	—	20,000
Congo	—	2,801
Democratic Yemen	—	1,455
Denmark	44,412	100,000
Ecuador	—	2,000
Finland	112,360	90,909
France	35,398	27,972
Germany, Federal Republic of	21,739	—
Greece	3,500	3,500
Guinea-Bissau	7	—
Guyana	1,000	—
Iceland	9,200	—
India	20,000	20,000
Indonesia	7,000	—
Italy	254,237	207,612
Jamaica	—	2,247
Lesotho	—	1,000
Madagascar	225	—
Mexico	5,317	5,195
Netherlands	204,819	—
Norway	672,269	555,556
Oman	10,000	—
Pakistan	2,101	8,000
Panama	500	—
Papua New Guinea	1,471	—
Philippines	6,000	6,000
Portugal	—	3,500
Qatar	5,000	5,000
Republic of Korea	—	2,000
Senegal	—	1,000
Sweden	100,000	108,108
Togo	369	—
Trinidad and Tobago	—	1,008
Tunisia	1,161	—
Uganda	64	—
United Republic of Cameroon	696	2,801
Zimbabwe	5,000	6,510
Total	1,747,941	1,331,709

SOURCE: Interim United Nations financial statements for the 12-month period ended 31 December 1982: schedules of individual trust funds.

Resolution (1982). (1)GA, 37/62, paras. 7 & 10, 3 Dec.

1979 Convention on Discrimination against Women

Implementation of the Convention

Action by the meeting of States parties. The first meeting of the States parties to the 1979 Convention on the Elimination of All Forms of Discrimination against Women[6] was held in New York on 16 April 1982.[1] By secret ballot, the meeting elected the 23 members of the Committee on the Elimination of Discrimination against Women.

Economic and Social Council action. By a resolution adopted without vote on 4 May 1982,[3] the Economic and Social Council welcomed the Convention's entry into force in September 1981[8] and expressed interest in the early commencement of the Committee's work, in particular to consider national reports on the Convention's implementation. The Secretary-General was asked to transmit the Committee reports to the Commission on the Status of Women and to consider spreading knowledge of the Convention. Its ratification was urged and a review of its status recommended.

The text, recommended by the Council's Second (Social) Committee, had been submitted by the Commission and approved by the Committee also without vote on 23 April, after an oral amendment by Argentina to add the phrase "for its information" to paragraph 4.

Activities of the Committee on discrimination against women. The Committee on the Elimination of Discrimination against Women held its first regular session at Vienna, Austria, from 18 to 22 October.[2] The Committee proposed dates for its 1983 session and postponed consideration of the draft guidelines on the form and content of the reports on implementation of the Convention, to be submitted by States parties under article 18 of that text.[7]

In two resolutions of 3 December 1982, on the Status of the Convention[5] and on the Decade for Women,[4] the General Assembly welcomed the elections to the Committee and commencement of its work.

Note. [1]Secretariat, CEDAW/SP/4.
Report. [2]Committee on discrimination against women, A/38/45.
Resolutions (1982). [3]ESC: 1982/17, 4 May, text following. GA, 3 Dec.: [4]37/58, para. 9; [5]37/64, para. 4.
Resolution (prior). [6]GA: 34/180, annex, 18 Dec. 1979 (YUN 1979, p. 895).
Yearbook references. [7]1979, p. 899; [8]1981, p. 994.
Meeting record. ESC, E/1982/SR.22 (4 May).

Economic and Social Council resolution 1982/17

4 May 1982   Meeting 22   Adopted without vote

Approved by Second Committee (E/1982/57) without vote, 23 April (meeting 7); draft by Commission on women (E/1982/14), orally amended by Argentina; agenda item 10.

Convention on the Elimination of All Forms of Discrimination against Women

The Economic and Social Council,

Recalling General Assembly resolution 34/180 of 18 December 1979, in which the Assembly adopted the Convention on the Elimination of All Forms of Discrimination against Women contained in the annex thereto,

Recalling also General Assembly resolution 35/140 of 11 December 1980,

Recalling further General Assembly resolution 36/131 of 14 December 1981,

Stressing the central role of the Commission on the Status of Women in considering within the United Nations matters relating to the achievement of the objectives of the United Nations Decade for Women: Equality, Development and Peace,

Reaffirming its conviction that the ratification of, or accession to, the Convention on the Elimination of All Forms of Discrimination against Women and the implementation of its provisions are important for the attainment of the three objectives of the United Nations Decade for Women: Equality, Development and Peace,

1. *Welcomes with great satisfaction* the entry into force on 3 September 1981 of the Convention on the Elimination of All Forms of Discrimination against Women;

2. *Urges* States that have not yet become parties to the Convention to ratify it or to accede to it;

3. *Expresses its interest* in the earliest possible commencement of the work of the Committee on the Elimination of Discrimination against Women provided for in part V of the Convention, in particular with a view to considering national reports on the implementation of the Convention in accordance with article 18 thereof;

4. *Requests* the Secretary-General to transmit the reports of the Committee to the Commission on the Status of Women for its information;

5. *Recommends* that the Commission on the Status of Women should include the question of the status of the Convention in the agenda of its thirtieth session;

6. *Recommends* to the Secretary-General that he should consider a concerted information effort to spread knowledge regarding the Convention.

Ratifications, accessions and signatures

As at 31 December 1982, the following 45 States had ratified or acceded to the 1979 Convention on the Elimination of All Forms of Discrimination against Women (the 13 in italics acted in 1982):

Austria, Barbados, Bhutan, *Bulgaria*, Byelorussian SSR, Canada, Cape Verde, China, *Colombia*, *Congo*, Cuba, *Czechoslovakia*, Dominica, *Dominican Republic*, Ecuador, Egypt, El Salvador, Ethiopia, German Democratic Republic, *Guatemala*, *Guinea*, Guyana, Haiti, Hungary, Lao People's Democratic Republic, Mexico, Mongolia, Nicaragua, Norway, Panama, *Peru*, Philippines, Poland, Portugal, *Romania*, Rwanda, *Saint Lucia*, Saint Vincent and the Grenadines, Sri Lanka, Sweden, Ukrainian SSR, USSR, Uruguay, *Viet Nam*, *Yugoslavia*.

In a report and a later addendum, the Secretary-General submitted to the Assembly a list of States which had signed, ratified or acceded to the Convention as at 13 September, together with reservations made at the time of ratification.[1]

In its resolution of 4 May on the Convention,[2] the Economic and Social Council urged States not parties to the Convention to ratify or accede to it and recommended that the Commission on the Status of Women include the question of the Convention's status in its 1984 agenda.

On 3 December,[4] the General Assembly, noting that an increasing number of Member States had ratified or acceded to and signed the Convention, invited those that had not done so to become parties to it and requested the Secretary-General to report on the Convention's status in 1983. The Assembly also welcomed the election of the Committee on the Elimination of Discrimination against Women.

This resolution was adopted without vote by the Assembly. The 32-nation text was introduced by Sweden in the Assembly's Third (Social, Humanitarian and Cultural) Committee, which had approved it also without vote on 24 November.

By a further resolution of 3 December, on the United Nations Decade for Women,[3] the Assembly noted that, as at 1 November, 45 Member States had ratified or acceded to the Convention. It invited States that had not done so to become parties to the Convention and requested the Secretary-General to report to it in 1983 on the Convention's status.

Report. [1]S-G, A/37/349 & Add.1.
Resolutions (1982). [2]ESC: 1982/17, paras. 2 & 5, 4 May. GA, 3 Dec.: [3]37/58; [4]37/64, text following.
Meeting records. GA: 3rd Committee, A/C.3/37/SR.30, 32-37, *49, 54, 55* (2-26 Nov.); plenary, A/37/PV.90 (3 Dec.).

General Assembly resolution 37/64

3 December 1982   Meeting 90   Adopted without vote

Approved by Third Committee (A/37/677) without vote, 24 November (meeting 54); 32-nation draft (A/C.3/37/L.35); agenda item 92.

Sponsors: Austria, Bhutan, Bulgaria, Canada, Cape Verde, China, Costa Rica, Cuba, Denmark, Dominican Republic, Ecuador, Egypt, Finland, German Democratic Republic, Greece, Guyana, Hungary, Iceland, Mexico, Mongolia, Netherlands, Norway, Philippines, Poland, Portugal, Rwanda, Sri Lanka, Sweden, USSR, Uruguay, Viet Nam, Yugoslavia.

Status of the Convention on the Elimination of All Forms of Discrimination against Women

The General Assembly,

Considering that one of the purposes of the United Nations, as stated in Articles 1 and 55 of the Charter, is to promote universal respect for human rights and fundamental freedoms without distinction of any kind, including any distinction as to sex,

Reaffirming that women and men should, on a basis of equality, participate in and contribute to the social, economic and political processes of development and should share equally in improved conditions of life,

Recalling its resolution 34/180 of 18 December 1979, by which it adopted the Convention on the Elimination of All Forms of Discrimination against Women,

Recalling also its resolutions 35/140 of 11 December 1980 and 36/131 of 14 December 1981,

Recalling that the Convention entered into force on 3 September 1981,

Having taken note of the report of the Secretary-General on the status of the Convention,

1. *Notes with appreciation* that an increasing number of Member States have ratified or acceded to the Convention on the Elimination of All Forms of Discrimination against Women;

2. *Notes further* that an important number of Member States have signed the Convention;

3. *Invites* all States that have not yet done so to become parties to the Convention by ratifying or acceding to it;

4. *Welcomes* the election, in accordance with article 17 of the Convention, of the twenty-three members of the Committee on the Elimination of Discrimination against Women on 16 April 1982, as well as the fact that the Committee has already commenced its work, having held its first session at Vienna from 18 to 22 October 1982;

5. *Requests* the Secretary-General to report to the General Assembly at its thirty-eighth session on the status of the Convention.

UN Research and Training Institute for the Advancement of Women

The International Research and Training Institute for the Advancement of Women (INSTRAW), which the Economic and Social Council decided to establish in 1976,[6] continued in 1982 to develop its organizational procedures. It began implementing its substantive work programme for 1982-1983 on a wider scope than had been envisaged. As reported by the Secretary-General in March 1982 to the Council on INSTRAW activities,[3] negotiations to establish the Institute's permanent headquarters at Santo Domingo, the Dominican Republic, continued with the host Government, which said that it was endeavouring to complete the premises.

The Institute's major activities in 1982, described by its Board of Trustees in a report to the Council,[2] included work on the first phase of a programme to improve statistics and indicators on the situation of women, undertaken jointly with the United Nations Statistical Office and nearly completed, with two draft technical reports completed for review in 1983. Having become a full member of the Steering Committee for Cooperative Action of the International Drinking Water Supply and Sanitation Decade, INSTRAW assumed joint responsibility with the United Nations Children's Fund for the secretariat of an inter-agency task force on women and the Decade.

Projects were developed in collaboration with various United Nations bodies, notably the United Nations Industrial Development Organization (UNIDO), to elaborate guidelines for incorporating women's issues into the UNIDO small-scale and rural industry programmes and to enhance the training of women entrepreneurs in industrial activities; and with the United Nations Institute for Training and Research, on women's role in the New International Economic Order[7] and in the International Development Strategy for the Third United Nations Development Decade[8] to link the position of women to overall world economic trends. Information activities, which depended heavily on existing information facilities within United Nations Headquarters, were aimed at strengthening relations with non-governmental organizations.

The INSTRAW Board of Trustees held its second session in New York from 25 to 29 January.[1] After reviewing the Director's progress report on the Institute, the Board made recommendations on the Institute's status and authority and approved the proposals for its organizational structure, authorizing the Director to decide on all administrative questions arising between Board meetings and on all substantive questions in consultation with the Board's President. It endorsed the desirability of close co-operation with the Commission on the Status of Women. It urged the

Council to invite contributions from Member States and requested the Director to explore further the possibilities of securing contributions in kind and contributions from non-governmental sources, including an annual pledging conference.

The Board also approved the Institute's proposed programme budget for 1982-1983 and, in principle, the network concept as a mode of operation, that is, programme execution through a series of co-operative arrangements with organizations within and outside the United Nations system. It emphasized that research and training should be related to practical and specific objectives and aim at strengthening the links between issues affecting women and mainstream development activities at all levels.

Economic and Social Council action. By a resolution adopted without vote on 4 May,[4] the Economic and Social Council requested the Secretary-General to ensure the transition of IN-STRAW to its headquarters in the Dominican Republic. The Council emphasized that INSTRAW research and training activities should aim at strengthening links between women's issues and development activities, endorsed the network concept for executing its programmes, and reiterated the need for continued co-operation between the United Nations system and other organizations and INSTRAW, particularly in research and training leading to increased technical co-operation for development. The Council requested the United Nations system to co-operate with and support IN-STRAW, and the Secretary-General to report on its activities and programme to the General Assembly's 1982 session. Member States were called on to contribute to the Trust Fund for INSTRAW or to co-operate in other ways.

The 16-nation text was introduced by Argentina in the Council's Second (Social) Committee, which had approved it also without vote on 25 April.

General Assembly action. On 3 December,[5] the Assembly, taking note of the progress made in implementing the INSTRAW work programme, repeated those provisions of the Council's resolution on the network concept, research and training, co-operation, contributions, and the 1983 report. In addition, the Assembly reiterated that research and training be carried out so as to lead to a better understanding of women's role in development, to more effective methods for enhancing that role and to increased activities for women's fuller participation especially in technical co-operation for development.

This resolution, adopted without vote by the Assembly, was based on a 38-nation text introduced by Argentina in the Assembly's Third (Social, Humanitarian and Cultural) Committee, which had similarly approved it on 24 November.

Reports. [1]E/1982/11, [2]E/1983/31; [3]S-G, E/1982/33.
Resolutions (1982). [4]ESC, 1982/27, 4 May, text following; [5]GA, 37/56, 3 Dec., text following.
Resolutions (prior). [6]ESC: 1998(LX), 12 May 1976 (YUN 1976, p. 620); GA: [7]3201(S-VI), 1 May 1974 (YUN 1974, p. 324), [8]35/56, annex, 5 Dec. 1980 (YUN 1980, p. 503).
Meeting records. ESC: E/1982/SR.23 (4 May). GA: 3rd Committee, A/C.3/37/SR.30, 32-37, *49, 54* (2-24 Nov.); plenary, A/37/PV.90 (3 Dec.).

Economic and Social Council resolution 1982/27

4 May 1982	Meeting 23	Adopted without vote

Approved by Second Committee (E/1982/57) without vote, 25 April (meeting 8); 16-nation draft (E/1982/C.2/L.3); agenda item 10.

Sponsors: Algeria, Argentina, Bangladesh, Colombia, Denmark, Egypt, France, India, Japan, Morocco, Nicaragua, Nigeria, Norway, Pakistan, Yugoslavia, Zaire.

International Research and Training Institute for the Advancement of Women

The Economic and Social Council,

Recalling its resolutions 1998(LX) of 12 May 1976 and 1981/13 of 6 May 1981 on the International Research and Training Institute for the Advancement of Women,

Having considered the report of the Secretary-General on developments relating to the organizational aspects of the Institute,

Taking note with satisfaction of the report of the Board of Trustees of the International Research and Training Institute for the Advancement of Women on its second session,

Expressing its satisfaction with the approved programme and activities of the Institute for 1982-1983,

Taking note with appreciation of the host country's effort to ensure the completion of the Institute's premises at Santo Domingo by June 1982,

1. *Requests* the Secretary-General to take all necessary measures to ensure the transition of the functioning of the International Research and Training Institute for the Advancement of Women to its headquarters in the Dominican Republic;

2. *Emphasizes* that the research and training activities of the Institute should aim at strengthening the links between issues affecting women and mainstream development activities at all levels;

3. *Endorses* the network concept to be developed in stages with the organizations of the United Nations system and regional and national institutions as a mode of operation for the execution of the programmes of the Institute;

4. *Reiterates* the need for close and continued co-operation between the United Nations system and other organizations and the Institute, particularly in research and training, which would lead to increased technical co-operation for development;

5. *Requests* the regional commissions, the specialized agencies and other organizations and bodies in the United Nations system to co-operate fully and to give support to the Institute, particularly in the programming and implementation of joint activities;

6. *Calls upon* all Member States to contribute to the United Nations Trust Fund for the International Research and Training Institute for the Advancement of Women or to co-operate in other ways with the Institute so as to ensure regular and effective financing for its programme development;

7. *Requests* the Secretary-General to inform the General Assembly at its thirty-seventh session of the activities and programme of the Institute.

General Assembly resolution 37/56

3 December 1982	Meeting 90	Adopted without vote

Approved by Third Committee (A/37/676) without vote, 24 November (meeting 54); 38-nation draft (A/C.3/37/L.33); agenda item 91.

Sponsors: Algeria, Angola, Argentina, Bahamas, Belgium, Bolivia, Colombia, Congo, Costa Rica, Cuba, Denmark, Dominican Republic, Ecuador, Egypt, El Salvador, France, Greece, Guatemala, Guinea, India, Jamaica, Japan, Jordan, Morocco, Nicaragua, Nigeria, Norway, Pakistan, Panama, Peru, Philippines, Tunisia, United Republic of Cameroon, Uruguay, Venezuela, Yugoslavia, Zaire, Zimbabwe.

International Research and Training Institute for the Advancement of Women

The General Assembly,

Recalling its resolution 36/128 of 14 December 1981, in which it underlined the importance of the contributions of the International Research and Training Institute for the Advancement of Women to the work of all United Nations bodies, agencies and institutions involved in the advancement of women,

Also recalling Economic and Social Council resolution 1982/27 of 4 May 1982, in which the Council, *inter alia*, took note with satisfaction of the report of the Secretary-General on developments relating to the organizational aspects of the Institute and the report of the Board of Trustees of the Institute on its second session and expressed its satisfaction with the approved programme and activities of the Institute for 1982-1983,

1. *Takes note with satisfaction* of the progress made in the implementation of the programme of work of the International Research and Training Institute for the Advancement of Women;

2. *Endorses* the network concept to be developed in stages with the organizations of the United Nations system and regional and national institutions as a mode of operation for the implementation of the programme of the Institute;

3. *Reiterates* the need for the Institute to carry out research and training which lead particularly to a better understanding of the role of women in development, more effective methods for enhancing the role of women in development and an increase in activities for the fuller participation of women in development, especially in the field of technical co-operation;

4. *Reaffirms* that the research and training activities of the Institute should aim at strengthening the links between issues affecting women and mainstream development activities at all levels;

5. *Calls upon* the regional commissions, the specialized agencies and other organizations and bodies of the United Nations system to continue to co-operate with the Institute and to ensure its participation in the activities relevant to women in development;

6. *Stresses* the need for all Member States to consider contributing financially to the United Nations Trust Fund for the International Research and Training Institute for the Advancement of Women or co-operating in other ways with the Institute in order to assure its regular and effective financing so as to facilitate the implementation of its programme;

7. *Invites* the Secretary-General to report to the General Assembly at its thirty-eighth session on the programme activities of the Institute;

8. *Decides* to include in the provisional agenda of its thirty-eighth session an item entitled "International Research and Training Institute for the Advancement of Women".

INSTRAW finances

Expenditures from the United Nations Trust Fund for INSTRAW in 1982 totalled $449,137. Income exceeded expenditures by $304,271, making possible implementation of some programmes proposed under the section on future programme development of the approved programme budget. As at 31 December 1982, the Fund showed an unencumbered balance of $2,783,864.

In 1982, a total of $409,270 was paid to the Fund by 13 States, while $510,701 was pledged by 12 States for 1983 (see table).

A call for contributions to the Fund, both financially and in kind, was made by the Economic and Social Council on 4 May,[1] and the need for such contributions stressed by the General Assembly on 3 December,[2] in order to assure the Institute's regular and effective financing.

Resolutions (1982). [1]ESC: 1982/27, 4 May. [2]GA: 37/56, 3 Dec.

Status of women

In two resolutions of 4 May 1982, on the situation of women and children in the occupied Arab

territories[2] and under *apartheid*,[3] the Economic and Social Council appealed for solidarity with the Palestinian women and people in their drive to end Israel's human rights violations in the occupied territories (see POLITICAL AND SECURITY QUESTIONS, Chapter IX) and with the liberation struggle of women in South Africa and Namibia (see POLITICAL AND SECURITY QUESTIONS, Chapter V), welcoming in this connection the International Conference on Women and *Apartheid*, at Brussels, Belgium. Also on 4 May, the Chairman of the Commission on the Status of Women was designated observer to that Conference by the Council.[1]

The Sub-Commission on Prevention of Discrimination and Protection of Minorities of the Commission on Human Rights recommended on 7 September[4] that a comprehensive study be made in conjunction with the Commission on the Status of Women, of the most serious forms of exploitation of women; and that working groups be created, in consultation with that Commission, for the better protection of the human rights of women and children. At the same time the Sub-Commission requested its members, Mohamed Yousif Mudawi (Sudan) and Halima Embarek Warzazi (Morocco), to conduct a study on the problem of female sexual mutilation, the extent and causes of the problem, and its remedies (see Chapter XVIII of this section).

The Commission on the Status of Women, at its February/March session, postponed until 1984 consideration of a draft resolution on the protection of the rights of parents and children in cases of the separation of couples of different nationalities (see Chapter XVIII of this section).

CONTRIBUTIONS TO THE INTERNATIONAL RESEARCH AND TRAINING INSTITUTE FOR THE ADVANCEMENT OF WOMEN, 1982 AND 1983
(as at 31 December 1982; in US dollar equivalent)

Country	1982 payment	1983 pledge
Algeria	10,000	—
Austria	11,800	7,000
Barbados	—	1,000
Chile	5,000	—
China	—	3,000
Cuba	—	1,478
Denmark	88,732	50,000
France	106,195	83,916
Greece	—	2,000
Guinea-Bissau	7	—
Indonesia	1,000	—
Jamaica	—	1,124
Mexico	5,889	—
Nigeria	10,991	—
Norway	168,067	353,175
Pakistan	1,051	4,000
Panama	500	—
Philippines	—	3,000
Trinidad and Tobago	—	1,008
Uganda	38	—
Total	**409,270**	**510,701**

SOURCE: Interim United Nations financial statements for the 12-month period ended 31 December 1982: schedules of individual trust funds.

Decision (1982). [1]ESC: 1982/121, 4 May.
Resolutions (1982). ESC, 4 May: [2]1982/18, [3]1982/24.
[4]SCPDM (report, E/CN.4/1983/4): 1982/15, 7 Sep.

Aging women

On 4 May 1982,[2] the Economic and Social Council urged that elderly women's special problems—income security, education, employment, housing, health and community support services—be given full attention by the World Assembly on Aging scheduled for July/August (see Chapter XX of this section) and be dealt with in the plan of action to be adopted. It requested Member States to include women in the preparations for and delegations to the Assembly; and, along with relevant United Nations bodies, to continue collecting data on the situation of elderly women to formulate policy and implement programmes on their behalf. Governments, national and international organizations, and the mass media were urged to strengthen efforts to adopt or change national laws to ensure equal opportunities for elderly women to live in health, dignity, self-reliance and self-fulfilment.

This resolution was adopted without vote. The text, submitted by the Commission on the Status of Women, had been similarly approved on 23 April by the Council's Second (Social) Committee.

Chief among the concerns covered by the Vienna International Plan of Action on Aging,[1] which the World Assembly adopted, were income security and employment, considered in the context of a demographic projection that women would increasingly constitute the majority of the aging population and would face an employment situation favouring the young and men, with women's salaries generally lower than men's and their employment often broken up by maternity and family responsibilities. These circumstances raised acute problems for women, whose longer life expectancy might mean an old age aggravated by economic need and isolation, with little or no income security or prospects for paid employment. The Plan recommended that Governments ensure an appropriate minimum income for all older persons and direct long-term policies towards social security systems permitting women as well as men to acquire their own rights.

Publication. [1]*Report of the World Assembly on Aging, Vienna, 26 July to 6 August 1982* (A/CONF.113/31), Sales No. E.82.I.16.
Resolution (1982). [2]ESC, 1982/23, 4 May, text following.
Meeting record. ESC, E/1982/SR.23 (4 May).

Economic and Social Council resolution 1982/23

4 May 1982   Meeting 23   Adopted without vote

Approved by Second Committee (E/1982/57) without vote, 23 April (meeting 7); draft by Commission on women (E/1982/14); agenda item 10.

Elderly women and the World Assembly on Aging

The Economic and Social Council,

Recalling General Assembly resolutions 32/131 of 16 December 1977, 33/52 of 14 December 1978, 34/153 of 17 December 1979 and 35/129 of 11 December 1980,

Recalling also resolution 13, entitled "Social security and family security for women, including the elderly and the handicapped", adopted by the World Conference of the International Women's Year, and resolution 4, entitled "Elderly women and economic security", adopted by the World Conference of the United Nations Decade for Women: Equality, Development and Peace,

Emphasizing the fact that, because the increasing life expectancy of women exceeds that of men in many developing and more developed societies, elderly women are a rapidly increasing segment of the national population,

Aware that elderly women have suffered from past discrimination and lack of opportunity and that in many countries the economic plight of elderly women is becoming more serious,

Concerned that this situation is further complicated by increased migration of family members and other cultural phenomena resulting in socioeconomic hardships for the aging,

Bearing in mind the Convention on the Elimination of All Forms of Discrimination against Women,

1. *Urges* that the special problems faced by elderly women, such as income security, education, employment, housing, health and community support services, should be given explicit and full attention by the World Assembly on Aging to be held at Vienna from 26 July to 6 August 1982, and should be dealt with in the plan of action to be adopted by the World Assembly;

2. *Requests* Member States to ensure that women are included in the preparations for the World Assembly on Aging and are appointed as members of their delegations to that Assembly;

3. *Requests* Member States and the relevant United Nations bodies to continue to collect data on the situation of elderly women to serve as a basis for formulating and implementing policies and programmes to define their special economic and social planning needs;

4. *Urges* all Governments, national and international organizations, both governmental and non-governmental, the mass media, educational bodies and all individuals concerned to strengthen their efforts to adopt or change national laws to ensure that elderly women have equal opportunities to live in health, dignity, self-reliance and self-fulfilment.

Battered women

By a resolution adopted without vote on 4 May 1982,[1] the Economic and Social Council called on Member States to combat immediately such social evils as kidnapping, abduction, forced child labour, battered women and children, violence in the family, rape and prostitution, which resulted in mental and physical problems. It requested the Secretary-General to compile a study on the action taken, for possible submission to the 1985 World Conference to Review and Appraise the Achievements of the United Nations Decade for Women.

The text, submitted by the Commission on the Status of Women, had been approved also without vote on 23 April by the Council's Second Committee.

Resolution (1982). [1]ESC: 1982/22, 4 May, text following.
Meeting record. ESC: E/1982/SR.23 (4 May).

Economic and Social Council resolution 1982/22

4 May 1982   Meeting 23   Adopted without vote

Approved by Second Committee (E/1982/57) without vote, 23 April (meeting 7); draft by Commission on women (E/1982/14); agenda item 10.

Abuses against women and children

The Economic and Social Council,

Taking note of the continued and consistent concern expressed by the international community at the blatant and inhuman abuses of women and children,

Recognizing the evils of such abuses as kidnapping, abduction, forced child labour, battered women and children, violence in the family, rape, prostitution, and the inevitable serious problems of mental and physical health,

Appalled by the resultant exploitation, oppression and violence to human dignity,

Believing that the abuse of women and children is an intolerable offence to the dignity of the human being and is a harsh indictment of any claim to be civilized,

1. *Calls upon* Member States to take immediate and energetic steps to combat these social evils and to inform the Secretary-General of the action taken;

2. *Requests* the Secretary-General to compile a study on the action taken by Member States for submission as a report to the World Conference to Review and Appraise the Achievements of the United Nations Decade for Women to be held in 1985, if the Preparatory Committee for the Conference so decides.

Elimination of prostitution and illicit traffic in women

On 10 March 1982, the Commission on Human Rights, acting on the question of slavery and the slave trade in all their practices and manifestations,[2] appealed to Member States to: ratify the 1949 Convention for the Suppression of the Traffic in Persons and of the Exploitation of the Prostitution of Others[7] or implement its provisions; take concerted action against prostitution and traffic in persons; and intensify research into the causes of prostitution and pimping and promote the social reintegration of the victims. The Commission invited the Voluntary Fund for the United Nations Decade for Women to consider supporting projects to rehabilitate prostitutes in poor areas, and to inform the August session of the Working Group on Slavery of its decision (see Chapter XVIII of this section).

On 4 May 1982,[3] the Economic and Social Council requested the Secretary-General to appoint a special rapporteur to make a synthesis, within existing budgetary resources, of past and current surveys and studies, within and outside the United Nations system, on the traffic in persons and the exploitation of prostitution. The synthesis, together with proposed measures against such practices, was to be presented to the Council's first 1983 session.

This resolution, adopted without vote, had been submitted by the Commission on the Status of Women to the Council's Second Committee, which similarly approved it on 26 April, after being amended by France. The amendments provided for inclusion in the seventh preambular paragraph of the United Nations Educational, Scientific and Cultural Organization among the agencies to consult and co-ordinate on the problem of traffic in persons, and, in the operative paragraph, for the appointment of a special rapporteur by the Secretary-General to make a synthesis of the surveys and studies for presentation in 1983, rather than for the Assembly's Third (Social, Humanitarian and Cultural) Committee to have before it a proposal for the appointment of a rapporteur to submit an in-depth analysis of the situation.

The Sub-Commission on Prevention of Discrimination and Protection of Minorities of the

Commission on Human Rights took two separate actions on the topic on 7 September 1982. By the first,[4] it included the 1949 Convention for the Suppression of the Traffic in Persons and of the Exploitation of the Prostitution of Others in a list of instruments whose universal acceptance was to be encouraged. By the second,[5] it considered that the 1959 publication *Study on Traffic in Persons and Prostitution* should be updated. (See Chapter XVIII of this section.)

Pursuant to a Council request of May 1981,[6] the Secretary-General reported in September 1982[1] that 26 Member States, 2 international and 7 non-governmental organizations had replied to a questionnaire on the status of the question of combating the traffic in persons and prostitution, a summary of which was submitted to the General Assembly.

Report. [1]S-G, A/37/412.
Resolutions (1982). [2]Commission on Human Rights (report, E/1982/12): 1982/20, paras. 3 & 4, 10 Mar. [3]ESC: 1982/20, 4 May, text following. SCPDM (report, E/CN.4/1983/4), 7 Sep.: [4]1982/3, para. 7; [5]1982/15, para. 13.
Resolutions (prior). [6]ESC: 1981/40, 8 May 1981 (YUN 1981, p. 915). [7]GA: 317(IV), annex, 2 Dec. 1949 (YUN 1948-49, p. 613).
Meeting record. ESC, E/1982/SR.23 (4 May).

Economic and Social Council resolution 1982/20

4 May 1982	Meeting 23	Adopted without vote

Approved by Second Committee (E/1982/57) without vote, 26 April (meeting 8); draft by Commission on women (E/1982/14), amended by France (E/1982/C.2/L.6); agenda item 10.

Suppression of the traffic in persons and of the exploitation of the prostitution of others

The Economic and Social Council,

Considering the terms of General Assembly resolution 317(IV) of 2 December 1949,

Referring to resolution 1(XXVII) of 4 April 1978 of the Commission on the Status of Women,

Recalling its resolutions 1980/4 of 16 April 1980 and 1981/40 of 8 May 1981,

Taking into account the work of the Sub-Commission on Prevention of Discrimination and Protection of Minorities and the report on its thirty-fourth session,

Having taken note of the report presented orally to the Commission on the Status of Women at its twenty-ninth session,.

Aware of the contribution that the Centre for Social Development and Humanitarian Affairs can make by reason of its interdisciplinary competence,

Convinced that the scope of the problem raised by the traffic in persons, in particular women and children, requires consultation and co-ordination by all the competent agencies in the United Nations system or outside the system—the regional commissions, the Office of the United Nations High Commissioner for Refugees, the World Health Organization, the International Labour Organisation, the United Nations Children's Fund, the United Nations Educational, Scientific and Cultural Organization, the World Tourism Organization, INTERPOL and non-governmental organizations interested in this problem,

Requests the Secretary-General to appoint a special rapporteur who, within existing budgetary resources, will make a synthesis of the surveys and studies on the traffic in persons and the exploitation of the prostitution of others that have been or are being carried out within the agencies in the United Nations system or outside the system, and will present that synthesis and propose appropriate measures to prevent and suppress those practices that are contrary to the fundamental rights of human beings at the first regular session of 1983 of the Council.

Rural areas

The General Assembly, acting without vote on 3 December 1982,[1] called on Member States to improve the economic and social conditions of rural women and requested greater attention to the problem of elevating their status from the Commission on the Status of Women, the regional commissions and other United Nations bodies, particularly the Food and Agriculture Organization of the United Nations. The Assembly also requested the Secretary-General to report to it in 1984 on national experience in improving rural women's situation and to consider holding, within the framework of the Programme of Action for the Second Half of the United Nations Decade for Women and as a matter of priority, an interregional seminar on the subject, with special emphasis on developing countries' problems.

The resolution, recommended by the Assembly's Third Committee, was based on an 18-nation draft text introduced and orally revised by Mongolia on behalf of the sponsors. By the amended sixth preambular paragraph, the Assembly took account of an Argentine and Indian proposal to replace "are consequently those who suffer most from negative effects of agricultural expansion" with "and suffer most from the exploitation of agricultural labour". After approval of the revised paragraph by 75 votes to 1, with 43 abstentions, the Committee approved the text as a whole without vote on 24 November.

Resolution (1982). [1]GA: 37/59, 3 Dec., text following.
Meeting records. GA: 3rd Committee, A/C.3/37/SR.30, 32-37, 49, 54, 55 (2-26 Nov.); plenary, A/37/PV.90 (3 Dec.).

General Assembly resolution 37/59

3 December 1982   Meeting 90   Adopted without vote

Approved by Third Committee (A/37/676) without vote, 24 November (meeting 54); 18-nation draft (A/C.3/37/L.32), orally amended by Morocco and orally revised; agenda item 91.

Sponsors: Afghanistan, Algeria, Angola, Benin, Cape Verde, Cuba, Democratic Yemen, Ethiopia, German Democratic Republic, Lao People's Democratic Republic, Madagascar, Mali, Mongolia, Mozambique, Nicaragua, Sierra Leone, Syrian Arab Republic, Viet Nam.

Improvement of the situation of women in rural areas

The General Assembly,

Bearing in mind the objectives of the United Nations Decade for Women: Equality, Development and Peace,

Recalling its resolution 35/136 of 11 December 1980, in which it endorsed the Programme of Action for the Second Half of the United Nations Decade for Women,

Reaffirming the importance attached in the International Development Strategy for the Third United Nations Development Decade to the need to improve the status of women and ensure their full participation in the development process as agents and beneficiaries of development,

Reaffirming further the importance attached in the Programme of Action for the Second Half of the United Nations Decade for Women, as well as in the Convention on the Elimination of All Forms of Discrimination against Women, to the need to improve the situation of women in rural areas in many parts of the world,

Recalling the Declaration of Principles and the Programme of Action adopted by the World Conference on Agrarian Reform and Rural Development, particularly with regard to the integration of women in rural development,

Bearing in mind that a majority of women, particularly in developing countries, live and work in rural areas and suffer most from the exploitation of agricultural labour, in particular by transnational corporations,

Convinced that the eradication of *apartheid*, all forms of racial discrimination, colonialism, neo-colonialism, aggression and foreign occupation and domination is essential to the further improvement of the situation of rural women,

Considering that the strengthening of international peace and cooperation is one of the most important conditions for further improving the situation of rural women,

Convinced also that the effective implementation of fundamental human rights is essential for the improvement of the situation of rural women,

Recognizing the urgent need to take additional appropriate measures aimed at further improving the situation of women in rural areas,

Recognizing also the importance of exchanging experiences in this field among States,

1. *Calls upon* Member States to take additional appropriate measures for further improving the economic and social conditions of women in rural areas;

2. *Requests* the Economic and Social Council, the Commission on the Status of Women, the regional commissions and other bodies of the United Nations system, in particular the Food and Agriculture Organization of the United Nations, to devote greater attention to the problem of elevating the status of rural women;

3. *Requests* the Secretary-General to prepare, within the framework of the integrated reporting system on the status of women which the Economic and Social Council, in its resolution 1980/38 of 2 May 1980, decided to continue, a comprehensive report containing the observations and comments received from Governments on national experience relating to the improvement of the situation of women in rural areas, paying special attention to such aspects as social insurance, mother and child care, health facilities, training, education and employment opportunities;

4. *Also requests* the Secretary-General to consider holding, within the framework of the Programme of Action for the Second Half of the United Nations Decade for Women, as a matter of priority, an interregional seminar on national experience relating to the improvement of the situation of women in rural areas, with special emphasis on the problems of developing countries;

5. *Further requests* the Secretary-General to submit to the General Assembly at its thirty-ninth session, through the Commission on the Status of Women and the Economic and Social Council, the report requested in paragraph 3 above.

Support

By a resolution adopted without vote on 4 May 1982,[1] the Economic and Social Council, considering that, in the case of divorce and separation, recovery of maintenance for a spouse and children was practically impossible when the debtor spouse resided abroad, requested the Secretary-General to provide full information on the 1956 Convention on the Recovery Abroad of Maintenance,[2] and the States parties to it to study possible improvements in the light of their experience. The Council invited those parties, in conformity with the Convention, to accord the highest priority to the transfer of maintenance funds or to cover expenses in respect of proceedings, and expressed the wish that States which had not done so would ratify the Convention as soon as possible.

The text, submitted by the Commission on the Status of Women, was approved, also without vote, on 23 April by the Council's Second (Social) Committee.

Resolution (1982). [1]ESC: 1982/21, 4 May, text following.
Yearbook reference. [2]1956, p. 386.
Meeting record: ESC, E/1982/SR.23 (4 May).

Economic and Social Council resolution 1982/21

4 May 1982   Meeting 23   Adopted without vote

Approved by Second Committee (E/1982/57) without vote, 23 April (meeting 7);
  draft by Commission on women (E/1982/14); agenda item 10.

Action to be taken to ensure the recovery abroad of maintenance

The Economic and Social Council,

Noting that in many countries the number of divorces and separations has continually increased during recent years,

Taking note of the fact that judicial or administrative decisions taken on the occasion of divorces and separations often include the payment of maintenance intended to meet, at least partly, the needs of the spouse and the children, as issue of the union, for whom the spouse is responsible, taking into consideration existing legislation in the countries of the two spouses,

Considering that the recovery of such maintenance, which is already difficult within the national territory, becomes practically impossible when the debtor spouse resides abroad,

Emphasizing the extreme prejudicial situation of creditors in respect of maintenance due who are injured in this way,

Emphasizing also the important progress constituted, for the States that have ratified it, by the Convention on the Recovery Abroad of Maintenance, done at New York on 20 June 1956,

1. *Requests* the Secretary-General to provide full information on the Convention on the Recovery Abroad of Maintenance, done at New York on 20 June 1956; in addition, States parties could study possible improvements in the light of their experience with regard to that Convention;

2. *Expresses the wish* that States which have not yet done so should ratify the Convention as soon as possible, in view of its undeniable humanitarian scope;

3. *Invites* the States parties to that Convention, in conformity with article 10 thereof, to accord the highest priority to the transfer of funds payable as maintenance or to cover expenses in respect of proceedings under that Convention.

Women refugees from Democratic Kampuchea

On 4 May 1982,[1] the Economic and Social Council expressed grave concern at the plight of Kampuchean women and children, including many thousands who had been forced to flee as refugees. It called on the international community to continue to share the burden of assisting Kampuchean refugees and displaced persons.

This resolution, adopted without vote, was based on a text submitted by the Commission on the Status of Women and similarly approved on 23 April by the Council's Second Committee.

Resolution (1982). [1]ESC: 1982/25, 4 May, text following.
Meeting record. ESC: E/1982/SR.23 (4 May).

Economic and Social Council resolution 1982/25

4 May 1982   Meeting 23   Adopted without vote

Approved by Second Committee (E/1982/57) without vote, 23 April (meeting 7);
  draft by Commission on women (E/1982/14); agenda item 10.

Women and children refugees

The Economic and Social Council,

Considering the agony and suffering of the Kampuchean refugees in South-East Asia,

Considering the special problems of women refugees, particularly with regard to physical safety,

1. *Expresses grave concern* at the plight of Kampuchean women and children, including the many thousands who have been forced to flee to other countries as refugees;

2. *Calls upon* the international community to continue to share the burden of assisting refugees and displaced persons from Kampuchea.

Women and society

Women in development

UNDP action. In 1982, the United Nations Development Programme (UNDP) made progress in institutionalizing, throughout the United Nations development system, the concern for women's interests in the planning and implementation of projects through staff training and through procedures and guidelines designed to ensure women's participation in project activities. It also improved the data base for planning such participation and implementing action proposals and reported that there had been a significant decline in 1981 in the number of projects involving women. These developments were described by the UNDP Administrator in an April report[4] to the Governing Council at its June session.

Taking note of the Administrator's report, the Governing Council on 18 June[1] endorsed his recommendation to strengthen ongoing efforts to institutionalize the concern for women's interests. To that end, the Council recommended that advantage be taken of existing and additional measures, and that a concerted effort be made in the following three years to provide interested Governments with special programming assistance. The Council also recommended that the Administrator and Governments reverse the downward trend in the number of projects involving women and decided that evaluation studies should be submitted to the Council in 1984 for presentation to the 1985 World Conference to Review and Appraise the Achievements of the United Nations Decade for Women.

UNIDO action. During 1982, the Interdivisional Working Group on Integration of Women in Industrial Development of the United Nations Industrial Development Organization (UNIDO) continued to promote awareness of the need for greater emphasis on women's integration in development. Participation of women was increased in UNIDO fellowship programme, study tours and group training, in addition to an expanded range of technical co-operation activities. The Group evaluated ways to enhance women's involvement in such activities and continued discussions with the International Research and Training Institute for the Advancement of Women (INSTRAW) on joint programmes. The UNIDO Executive Director described these activities in his report to the 1983 session of the Industrial Development Board.[3]

Technical co-operation activities for women comprised: general projects impacting on women's employment and advancement; and projects tailored to promote women's integration in development. In the first category were three garment industry projects providing expertise to the South Indian Textile Research Association, to the Textile Development Centre in Alexandria (Egypt) and to the Société d'Economie Mixte (Senegal); and a large-scale project in Viet Nam to improve maintenance and production management procedures in textile factories. The second category included: a project to develop ceramic technologies for rural areas in the United Republic of Tanzania; a seminar/workshop on industrial planning and management (Ouagadougou, Upper Volta, 20-25 September); and a project proposal for organizing seminars in the United Republic of Tanzania, to upgrade the skills of women entrepreneurs.

Having reviewed the Executive Director's report, the Board on 28 May[2] reiterated that the integration of women was intrinsic to all UNIDO activities. Noting that the Interdivisional Working Group's work bore limited results and that no follow-up had been made to the 1978 Preparatory Meeting on the Role of Women in Industrialization in Developing Countries, the Board requested the Executive Director to strengthen the Group and to follow up on the Meeting's recommendations. The Board asked UNIDO to promote women's industrial training and employment, taking account of equal pay for like work. It stressed the need for accelerating women's participation and recruitment in UNIDO activities at the Professional and higher levels and requested the Executive Director to report to its 1983 session on the subject.

UNICEF action. In 1982, the United Nations Children's Fund (UNICEF), aware that women's economic condition was crucial to children's welfare, continued to orient its programming approach towards improving women's participation in economic activities, including small-scale entrepreneurship and formal-sector employment. For the most part, UNICEF co-operation in this area continued to focus on support of small-scale endeavours, mostly handicrafts and sewing, and on such potentially productive and economically viable activities as animal husbandry, fish farming, food processing and poultry raising. In a number of countries, UNICEF facilitated women's access to formal credit; strengthened entrepreneurial development and promoted employment; transferred traditional activities to the market economy; and trained women for the modern productive sector. Details of these activities were given by the UNICEF Executive Director in a report to the Executive Board's 1983 session.[5]

Economic and Social Council action. By a resolution adopted without vote on 4 May 1982,[6] the Economic and Social Council recommended that the General Assembly request all specialized agencies and other organizations, in particular UNDP, to consider including special financial components, within budgetary resources, in their technical co-operation programmes for women's development in the economic field, particularly in the co-operative and non-traditional sectors and in developing countries. The Council requested the Secretary-General to report to the Commission on the Status of Women in 1983 on implementation of this resolution.

The text, submitted by the Commission, was approved also without vote on 23 April by the Council's Second (Social) Committee.

In another action, also taken on 4 May,[7] the Council emphasized that INSTRAW research and training should aim to strengthen links between women's issues and development activities.

General Assembly action. On 3 December,[9] the General Assembly called on the Secretary-General to encourage specialized agencies and regional commissions which had not done so to develop comprehensive policies regarding women's concerns in technical co-operation and development activities and a strategy to ensure that women were an integral part of those activities. It urged those organizations, within existing resources, to monitor implementation of such policies and strategies and to help disseminate information about them on request. The Secretary-General was asked to report to the Assembly in 1983 on his progress in carrying out, within existing resources, the request made.

This resolution was adopted without vote. It was based on a 16-nation text introduced by the United States as revised by its sponsors in the Assembly's Third (Social, Humanitarian and Cultural) Committee, which similarly approved it on 24 November.

By two further resolutions of 3 December, on INSTRAW[8] and on the United Nations Decade for Women,[10] the Assembly reiterated the need for more effective enhancement of women's role in development and called for international community action to ensure women's participation in all development sectors at all levels.

Decision (1982). [1]UNDP Council (report, E/1982/16/Rev.1): 82/12, 18 June.
Reports. IDB, [2]A/37/16, [3]ID/B/298; [4]UNDP Administrator, DP/1982/16; [5]UNICEF Executive Director, E/ICEF/698.
Resolutions (1982). ESC, 4 May: [6]1982/19, text following; [7]1982/27, para. 2. GA, 3 Dec.: [8]37/56, paras. 3-5; [9]37/57, text following; [10]37/58, para. 3.
Meeting records. ESC: E/1982/SR.23 (4 May). GA: 3rd Committee, A/C.3/37/SR.30, 32-37, *49, 54* (2-24 Nov.); plenary, A/37/PV.90 (3 Dec.).
Statement. NGO, E/1982/NGO/4.

Economic and Social Council resolution 1982/19

4 May 1982   Meeting 23   Adopted without vote

Approved by Second Committee (E/1982/57) without vote, 23 April (meeting 7); draft by Commission on women (E/1982/14); agenda item 10.

Role of women in economic development

The Economic and Social Council,

Recalling General Assembly resolution 35/136 of 11 December 1980, in which the Assembly endorsed the Programme of Action for the Second Half of the United Nations Decade for Women,

Bearing in mind General Assembly resolutions 3201(S-VI) and 3202(S-VI) of 1 May 1974, containing the Declaration and the Programme of Action on the Establishment of a New International Economic Order, 3281(XXIX) of 12 December 1974, containing the Charter of Economic Rights and Duties of States, and 3362(S-VII) of 16 September 1975 on development and international economic co-operation,

Emphasizing the importance of women's full participation in the development process as agents and beneficiaries of development,

Aware that improvement in the economic condition and role of women is a necessary prerequisite for an improvement in the status of women,

Aware that at present women are not equal beneficiaries of the fruits of economic and social development,

1. *Recommends* that the General Assembly should request all specialized agencies and other relevant organizations, in particular the United Nations Development Programme, to consider including special financial components, within existing budgetary resources, in their technical co-operation programmes for the development of women in the economic field, enhancing the entrepreneurial and technological capacity of women, particularly in the co-operative and non-traditional sectors and in developing countries;

2. *Requests* the Secretary-General to report to the Commission on the Status of Women at its thirtieth session on the implementation of the present resolution.

General Assembly resolution 37/57

3 December 1982   Meeting 90   Adopted without vote

Approved by Third Committee (A/37/676) without vote, 24 November (meeting 54); 16-nation draft (A/C.3/37/L.36/Rev.1); agenda item 91.

Sponsors: Colombia, Costa Rica, Denmark, Indonesia, Italy, Japan, Jordan, Kenya, Lesotho, Morocco, Nepal, Norway, Philippines, Trinidad and Tobago, United Kingdom, United States.

Integration of women in development

The General Assembly,

Recalling paragraphs 190 to 196 of the World Plan of Action for the Implementation of the Objectives of the International Women's Year, in which the relevant agencies of the United Nations and intergovernmental, interregional and regional bodies were called upon to scrutinize all existing plans and projects with a view to extending their sphere of activities to include women and to develop new and innovative projects to include women,

Bearing in mind that development is one of the themes of the United Nations Decade for Women,

Recalling paragraphs 233 and 234 of the Programme of Action for the Second Half of the United Nations Decade for Women, in which it was recommended that numerous actions should be taken in the areas of technical co-operation, training and advisory services,

Also recalling paragraph 51 of the International Development Strategy for the Third United Nations Development Decade, which stated that full and effective participation by the entire population at all stages of the development process should be ensured,

Looking ahead to the world conference on women to be held in 1985, at which the achievements of the United Nations Decade for Women and the need to continue such achievements beyond the end of the Decade will be reviewed and appraised,

Convinced of the importance of integrating women fully into all areas of development, both as participants and as beneficiaries,

Aware that greater co-ordination and knowledge of activities in this area within the specialized agencies of the United Nations and the regional commissions and by Member States and non-governmental organizations would facilitate an exchange of experiences and concepts and be beneficial to all,

Expressing its appreciation to those organizations which have made regular reports on the implementation of the objectives of the World Plan of Action and the Programme of Action,

1. *Calls upon* the Secretary-General to encourage specialized agencies and regional commissions which have not yet done so to develop a comprehensive policy regarding the concerns of women, both as participants and as beneficiaries, in technical co-operation and development activities and to develop a strategy to ensure that women are an integral part of these activities;

2. *Urges* those organizations to take every appropriate action within existing resources to monitor the implementation of the above-mentioned policies and strategies and to help disseminate this information upon request to Member States and other interested parties;

3. *Requests* the Secretary-General to carry out all the activities called for in the present resolution within existing resources and to submit a progress report to the General Assembly at its thirty-eighth session for its consideration, bearing in mind Assembly resolution 36/127 of 14 December 1981 entitled "Consideration within the United Nations of questions concerning the role of women in development".

Survey

In a September report to the 1982 session of the General Assembly on progress in preparing a world survey on women's role in development,[2] the Secretary-General stated that, in response to an Assembly request of December 1981,[5] the Commission on the Status of Women had considered the subject, following which a revised annotated outline was prepared. The proposed structure and content were as recommended by the Assembly,[4] and would be followed by chapters examining women's role in: agriculture, industry and trade; the use, conservation and development of energy resources; money and finance; and the development and application of science and technology. Each chapter would contain sections examining the current role of women, benefits accruing to them, ways of improving their role, and the potential impact of such improvement on development goals. The survey would provide a thorough but concise review of the most significant aspects of the situation in both developed and developing countries.

In addition to ongoing inter-agency consultations on the survey preparations, the Secretary-General had asked specialized agencies and other United Nations bodies to consider the revised outline for suggestions on specific issues and on their collaboration.

Acting without vote on 21 December,[1] the Assembly took note of the Secretary-General's report. The draft decision was similarly approved by the Assembly's Second (Economic and Financial) Committee on 13 December, on the Chairman's oral proposal.

The Assembly had taken note of the same report earlier, on 3 December,[3] recommending that the survey be submitted to the World Conference to Review and Appraise the Achievements of the United Nations Decade for Women.

Decision (1982). [1]GA: 37/449, 21 Dec., text following.
Report. [2]S-G, A/37/381.
Resolution (1982). [3]GA: 37/60, para. 7, 3 Dec.
Resolution (prior). GA: [4]36/74, 4 Dec. 1981 (YUN 1981, p. 989); [5]36/127, 14 Dec. 1981 (*ibid.*, p. 990).
Meeting records: GA: 2nd Committee, A/C.2/37/SR.3, 6, 7, 10-19, 33, 40, *48* (28 Sep.–13 Dec.); plenary, A/37/PV.115 (21 Dec.).

General Assembly decision 37/449

Adopted without vote

Approved by Second Committee (A/37/680/Add.10) without vote, 13 December (meeting 48); oral proposal by Chairman; agenda item 71 *(k).*

At its 115th plenary meeting, on 21 December 1982, the General Assembly, on the recommendation of the Second Committee, took note of the report of the Secretary-General on the progress made in the preparation of a world survey on the role of women in development.

Declaration on Women and Peace

On 3 December 1982,[3] the General Assembly proclaimed the Declaration on the Participation of Women in Promoting International Peace and Co-operation. The Declaration was first elaborated by the Commission on the Status of Women in response to a 1977 Assembly request[4] that it consider drafting, as a contribution to the 1980 World Conference of the United Nations Decade for Women,[5] a text on the participation of women in the struggle for the strengthening of international peace and security, and against colonialism, racism, racial discrimination, foreign aggression and occupation and all forms of foreign domination. The World Conference requested the Assembly to elaborate a draft declaration based on Governments' views on the nature and content of such a text. Later in 1980, 29 nations submitted a text to the Assembly, which held extensive discussions on the matter the following year, but postponed final action until 1982.

The two-part Declaration comprised 14 articles. Part I (articles 1 to 5) stated that: women and men had an equal interest in contributing to international peace and co-operation and, to that end, women must be enabled to participate equally with men in economic, social, cultural, civil and political affairs; full participation depended on an equitable distribution of roles between men and women in the family and society; women's increased participation would contribute to international peace and co-operation; their participation in promoting peace would contribute to eradicating *apartheid* and racial discrimination, aggression, foreign occupation and interference; and special measures were necessary to increase women's participation in international relations.

Part II (articles 6 to 14) provided for measures to: intensify national and international efforts to permit women's participation in promoting international peace and co-operation, promote the exchange of experience in this regard, give effective publicity to such participation, pay tribute to it and provide opportunities for it, encourage women to participate in organizations concerned with strengthening international peace and security, render support to women victims of human rights violations, and establish legal protection of women's rights on an equal basis with men. The final article urged all to promote and implement the Declaration's principles.

This resolution, with the annexed Declaration, was adopted without vote. The 24-nation text was introduced in the Assembly's Third (Social, Humanitarian and Cultural) Committee by the German Democratic Republic, which orally revised it. It was further orally amended by Morocco and by the United States and thereafter approved, also without vote, by the Committee on 24 November.

The Moroccan amendment concerned article 12 (*d*) on the employment of women in the United Nations system, replacing a phrase "taking account of their efficiency, professional competence and integrity and in accordance with the principle of equitable geographical distribution", by the phrase "in conformity with Article 101 of the Charter of the United Nations". The United States amendment inserted "all" in article 9 on the support for women victims of human rights violations.

In a September report and a later addendum,[2] the Secretary-General reported to the Assembly on the replies to his invitation for Government views on the draft Declaration, issued in accordance with an Assembly decision of December 1981.[1] Of the 25 Member States which had replied, 6 confirmed their previous position and made no specific comment, 6 expressed support for the draft and 12 expressed reservations on the Declaration's need.

Decision. [1]GA: 36/428, 14 Dec. 1981 (YUN 1981, p. 992).
Report: [2]S-G, A/37/144 & Corr.1 & Add.1.
Resolution (1982). [3]GA: 37/63, 3 Dec., text following.
Resolution (prior). [4]GA:32/142, 16 Dec. 1977 (YUN 1977, p. 756).
Yearbook reference. [5]1980, p. 886.
Meeting records: GA: 3rd Committee, A/C.3/37/SR.30, 32-37, 49, 54, 55 (2-26 Nov.); plenary, A/37/PV.90 (3 Dec.).

General Assembly resolution 37/63

3 December 1982   Meeting 90   Adopted without vote

Approved by Third Committee (A/37/676) without vote, 24 November (meeting 54); 24-nation draft (A/C.3/37/L.38), orally amended by Morocco and by United States, and orally revised; agenda item 91 (c).

Sponsors: Afghanistan, Algeria, Angola, Bulgaria, Cape Verde, Cuba, Czechoslovakia, Democratic Yemen, Ethiopia, German Democratic Republic, Guinea-Bissau, Hungary, Iraq, Lao People's Democratic Republic, Libyan Arab Jamahiriya, Madagascar, Mali, Mongolia, Mozambique, Nicaragua, Nigeria, Syrian Arab Republic, Ukrainian SSR, Viet Nam.

Declaration on the Participation of Women in Promoting International Peace and Co-operation

The General Assembly,

Considering that the Charter of the United Nations expresses the determination of the peoples of the United Nations to reaffirm faith in the equal rights of men and women and to practise tolerance and live together in peace with one another as good neighbours,

Considering also that the Universal Declaration of Human Rights proclaims that recognition of the inherent dignity and of the equal and inalienable rights of all members of the human family is the foundation of freedom, justice and peace in the world,

Considering further that the International Covenants on Human Rights provide for the equal right of men and women to the enjoyment of all economic, social, cultural, civil and political rights,

Reaffirming the objectives of the United Nations Decade for Women: Equality, Development and Peace,

Taking into account the resolutions, declarations, conventions, programmes and recommendations of the United Nations and the specialized agencies and international conferences designed to eliminate all forms of discrimination and to promote equal rights for men and women,

Recalling that the Declaration of Mexico on the Equality of Women and their Contribution to Development and Peace, 1975, states that women have a vital role to play in the promotion of peace in all spheres of life: in the family, the community, the nation and the world,

Recalling that the Convention on the Elimination of All Forms of Discrimination against Women declares that discrimination against women violates the principles of equality of rights and respect for human dignity, is an obstacle to the participation of women, on equal terms with men, in the political, social, economic and cultural life of their countries and makes more difficult the full development of the potentialities of women in the service of their countries and of humanity,

Recalling also that the Convention on the Elimination of All Forms of Discrimination against Women affirms that the strengthening of international peace and security, the relaxation of international tension, mutual co-operation among all States irrespective of their social and economic systems, general and complete disarmament, in particular nuclear disarmament under strict and effective international control, the affirmation of the principles of justice, equality and mutual benefit in relations among countries and the realization of the right of peoples under alien and colonial domination and foreign occupation to self-determination and independence, as well as respect for national sovereignty and territorial integrity, will promote social progress and development and as a consequence will contribute to the attainment of full equality between men and women,

Recognizing that the Convention on the Elimination of All Forms of Discrimination against Women obligates States Parties to take all appropriate measures to eliminate discrimination against women in all its forms and in every field of human endeavour, including politics, economic activities, law, employment, education, health care and domestic relations,

Noting that, despite progress towards the achievement of equality between men and women, considerable discrimination against women continues to exist, thereby impeding the active participation of women in promoting international peace and co-operation,

Welcoming the contribution which women have nevertheless made towards promoting international peace and co-operation, the struggle against colonialism, *apartheid*, all forms of racism and racial discrimination, foreign aggression and occupation and all forms of alien domination, and towards the unrestricted and effective enjoyment of human rights and fundamental freedoms,

Welcoming also the contribution of women towards a just restructuring of international economic relations and the achievement of a new international economic order,

Convinced that women can play an important and increasing role in these areas,

Solemnly proclaims the Declaration on the Participation of Women in Promoting International Peace and Co-operation set forth in the annex to the present resolution.

ANNEX
Declaration on the Participation of Women in Promoting International Peace and Co-operation

PART I

Article 1

Women and men have an equal and vital interest in contributing to international peace and co-operation. To this end, women must be enabled to exercise their right to participate in the economic, social, cultural, civil and political affairs of society on an equal footing with men.

Article 2

The full participation of women in the economic, social, cultural, civil and political affairs of society and in the endeavour to promote international peace and co-operation is dependent on a balanced and equitable distribution of roles between men and women in the family and in society as a whole.

Article 3

The increasing participation of women in the economic, social, cultural, civil and political affairs of society will contribute to international peace and co-operation.

Article 4

The full enjoyment of the rights of women and men and the full participation of women in promoting international peace and co-operation will contribute to the eradication of *apartheid*, of all forms of racism, racial discrimination, colonialism, neo-colonialism, aggression, foreign occupation and domination and interference in the internal affairs of States.

Article 5

Special national and international measures are necessary to increase the level of women's participation in the sphere of international relations so that women can contribute, on an equal basis with men, to national and international efforts to secure world peace and economic and social progress and to promote international co-operation.

PART II

Article 6

All appropriate measures shall be taken to intensify national and international efforts in respect of the participation of women in promoting international peace and co-operation by ensuring the equal participation of women in the economic, social, cultural, civil and political affairs of society through a balanced and equitable distribution of roles between men and women in the domestic sphere and in society as a whole, as well as by providing an equal opportunity for women to participate in the decision-making process.

Article 7

All appropriate measures shall be taken to promote the exchange of experience at the national and international levels for the purpose of furthering the involvement of women in promoting international peace and co-operation and in solving other vital national and international problems.

Article 8

All appropriate measures shall be taken at the national and international levels to give effective publicity to the responsibility and active participation of women in promoting international peace and co-operation and in solving other vital national and international problems.

Article 9

All appropriate measures shall be taken to render solidarity and support to those women who are victims of mass and flagrant violations of human rights such as *apartheid*, all forms of racism, racial discrimination, colonialism, neo-colonialism, aggression, foreign occupation and domination and of all other violations of human rights.

Article 10

All appropriate measures shall be taken to pay a tribute to the participation of women in promoting international peace and co-operation.

Article 11

All appropriate measures shall be taken to encourage women to participate in non-governmental and intergovernmental organizations concerned with the strengthening of international peace and security, the development of friendly relations among nations and the promotion of co-operation among States and, to that end, freedom of thought, conscience, expression, assembly, association, communication and movement, without distinction as to race, political or religious belief, language or ethnic origin, shall be effectively guaranteed.

Article 12

All appropriate measures shall be taken to provide practical opportunities for the effective participation of women in promoting international peace and co-operation, economic development and social progress including, to that end:

(a) The promotion of an equitable representation of women in governmental and non-governmental functions;

(b) The promotion of equality of opportunities for women to enter diplomatic service;

(c) The appointment or nomination of women, on an equal basis with men, as members of delegations to national, regional or international meetings;

(d) Support for increased employment of women at all levels in the secretariats of the United Nations and the specialized agencies, in conformity with Article 101 of the Charter of the United Nations.

Article 13

All appropriate measures shall be taken to establish adequate legal protection of the rights of women on an equal basis with men in order to ensure effective participation of women in the activities referred to above.

Article 14

Governments, non-governmental and international organizations, including the United Nations and the specialized agencies, as well as individuals, are urged to do all in their power to promote the implementation of the principles set forth in the present Declaration.

Political participation

Article 12 of the Declaration on women and peace (see above), proclaimed by the Assembly on 3 December 1982,[2] called for practical opportunities for women's participation in international peace and co-operation, economic development and social progress through equitable representation in governmental and non-governmental functions; equal opportunities for diplomatic service; appointment on an equal basis with men to membership in delegations to national, regional or international meetings; and support for increased employment at all levels in the secretariats of the United Nations system, in conformity with Article 101 of the Charter.

Acting without vote on 3 December,[1] the General Assembly noted that women were still not represented equally with men in decision-making positions in a majority of national and international institutions. It called on Member States to make special efforts, by the end of the United Nations Decade for Women in 1985, to nominate and appoint women to such positions on an equal basis with men, using the same professional criteria. A similar call was made with respect to decision-making positions in United Nations organizations, in conformity with the Charter of the United Nations (see ADMINISTRATIVE AND BUDGETARY QUESTIONS, Chapter III).

This resolution was based on an 18-nation text introduced in the Assembly's Third Committee by Canada, which orally revised it on behalf of the sponsors to take into account proposals by Kuwait, Pakistan, and Trinidad and Tobago with respect to paragraph 1. The revised text was approved, also without vote, by the Committee on 24 November.

As proposed by Kuwait and Trinidad and Tobago, paragraph 1 was revised to note with concern rather than with regret that women were not represented on an equitable basis with men in decision-making positions; and the parenthetical explication "(boards, committees, commissions, delegations etc.)" at the end was deleted—as proposed by Pakistan.

Resolutions (1982). GA: [1]37/61, 3 Dec., text following; [2]37/63, annex, art. 12, 3 Dec.
Meeting records: GA: 3rd Committee, A/C.3/37/SR.30, 32-37, 49, 54, 55 (2-26 Nov.); plenary, A/37/PV.90 (3 Dec.).

General Assembly resolution 37/61

3 December 1982   Meeting 90   Adopted without vote

Approved by Third Committee (A/37/676) without vote, 24 November (meeting 54); 18-nation draft (A/C.3/37/L.37), orally revised to take also into account proposals by Kuwait and Trinidad and Tobago, and by Pakistan; agenda item 91.

Sponsors: Canada, Chile, Costa Rica, Denmark, Ethiopia, France, Germany, Federal Republic of, Greece, Iceland, Indonesia, Italy, Japan, Jordan, Morocco, Netherlands, New Zealand, Philippines, United States.

Women in public life

The General Assembly,

Reaffirming the objectives of the United Nations Decade for Women: Equality, Development and Peace,

Bearing in mind paragraphs 72 and 73 of the Programme of Action for the Second Half of the United Nations Decade for Women, in which equitable representation for women was called for at all levels in national government and in international bodies,

Recalling that in article 7 of the Convention on the Elimination of All Forms of Discrimination against Women it was agreed that States Parties should ensure that women have the right, on equal terms with men, to participate in the formulation and implementation of government policy and to hold public office,

Recalling further that in article 8 of the Convention it was agreed that States Parties should ensure to women, on equal terms with men, the opportunity to represent their Governments at the international level and to participate in the work of international organizations,

Recognizing that only three years remain before the end of the United Nations Decade for Women,

1. *Notes with concern* that women are still not represented on an equitable basis with men in decision-making positions in a majority of national and international institutions;

2. *Calls upon* all Member States, by the end of the United Nations Decade for Women in 1985, to make special efforts to nominate and appoint women, on an equal basis with men and taking due account of the same professional criteria, to decision-making positions in those national and international bodies in which they are not equitably represented;

3. *Calls upon* the Secretary-General and the executive heads of the specialized agencies and other organizations of the United Nations system to make, by the end of the United Nations Decade for Women in 1985, increased efforts to select and appoint women, in conformity with Article 101 of the Charter of the United Nations, to decision-making positions in the Secretariat and in the organs and agencies of the United Nations system.

Women and science and technology

During its February session,[1] the Advisory Committee on Science and Technology for Development discussed the under-utilization of women in scientific and technological endeavours in the light of studies on its causes (see Chapter XII of this section). The Committee suggested two broad categories of action to be taken at the national, regional and international levels—namely, science and technology for women and women in science and technology.

Suggestions under the first category were aimed at eliminating daily drudgery (such as fetching water and gathering fuelwood) and occupational hazards of women in developing countries. They included micro-level analysis of the occupational hazards posed by traditional occupations of rural women, so that remedies might be initiated. Monitoring the impact of technological change should be integrated into the planning process in order to retrain women displaced by new technologies. The Committee also believed that women's special skills should be a major consideration in technology development for rural occupations and could be put to use in small- and medium-scale, informal industrial activities (in textiles, woollen products, glassware, fashion goods), organized in small co-operative units or at home.

Under the second category, the Advisory Committee emphasized that education needed to be given the highest priority in order to enhance the role of women in science and technology. It called for public policies and monitoring mechanisms to ensure equal participation of women in scientific and technological efforts, a detailed analysis of human resources by sex for a reliable estimate of women's potential for contributing to those efforts, and promotion of equal development of men and women for important roles in national development. The Advisory Committee also suggested that its membership include adequate representation of qualified women.

At the close of its fourth session on 4 June,[2] the Intergovernmental Committee on Science and Technology for Development took note of the Advisory Committee's suggestions.

Report. [1]Advisory Committee on science and technology, A/CN.11/30.
Resolution (1982). [2]Intergovernmental Committee on science and technology (report, A/37/37): 3(IV), sect. IV, para. 4, 4 June.

Organizational questions

Procedures for communications received

On 4 May 1982,[1] the Economic and Social Council decided without vote to ask the Commission on Human Rights for its views on how communications relating to the status of women should be handled and to submit them to the Council's first 1983 session. The Council also decided to consider those views at that session when it considered a draft resolution on the subject recommended by the Commission on the Status of Women.[4]

The draft resolution referred to had been recommended by the Commission on the Status of Women by a roll-call vote, taken on 4 March, of 16 to 6 (Cuba, Czechoslovakia, German Democratic Republic, India, Ukrainian SSR, USSR), with 5 abstentions. By the draft, the Council would request the Secretary-General to submit to the Commission in 1983 a report on confidential and non-confidential communications on the status of women and would authorize the Commission to appoint a working group to consider all such communications and submit to it those appearing to reveal a consistent pattern of reliably attested injustice and discriminatory practices against women. The Secretary-General would be asked to provide, within existing budgetary resources, services and facilities to implement the resolution.

The 4 May decision of the Council was approved, also without vote, by its Second (Social) Committee on 26 April. The text, introduced by a Committee Vice-Chairman, was based on informal consultations held on the Commission draft resolution and on a draft decision[2] submitted by the Byelorussian SSR on behalf also of Bulgaria, which was later withdrawn.

The two-nation draft decision would have had the Council consider the Commission draft resolution on receipt of the views requested, without specifying any date.

Background information on existing procedures within the United Nations system for handling communications relating to the status of women, requested by the Council in 1980,[5] was provided by the Secretary-General in a note with later addenda[3] to the Council's April/May 1982 session.

Decision (1982). [1]ESC: 1982/122, 4 May, text following.
Draft decision withdrawn. [2]Bulgaria, Byelorussian SSR, E/1982/C.2/L.4.
Note. [3]S-G, E/1982/34 & Corr.1 & Add.1,2.
Report. [4]Commission on women, E/1982/14.
Resolution. [5]ESC: 1980/39, 2 May 1980 (YUN 1980, p. 923).
Meeting record: ESC: E/1982/SR.23 (4 May).

Economic and Social Council decision 1982/122

Adopted without vote

Approved by Second Committee (E/1982/57) without vote, 26 April (meeting 9); draft by Vice-Chairman (E/1982/C.2/L.7), based on informal consultations on draft by Commission on women (E/1982/14) and 2-nation draft (E/1982/C.2/L.4); agenda item 10.

Communications on the status of women

At its 23rd plenary meeting, on 4 May 1982, the Council, recalling its resolution 1980/39 of 2 May 1980, having considered the note by the Secretary-General containing background information regarding existing procedures on communications within the United Nations system, and taking note of draft resolution X contained in the report of the Commission on the Status of Women on its twenty-ninth session and also of the views expressed by delegations on the subject of communications on the status of women, decided:

(a) To request the Commission on Human Rights at its thirty-ninth session, in response to Economic and Social Council resolution 1980/39, to provide its views on how communications relating to the status of women should be handled, taking into account its own procedures, and to submit its views to the Council at its first regular session of 1983;

(b) To consider, at its first regular session of 1983, draft resolution X, entitled "Communications concerning the status of women", contained in the report of the Commission on the Status of Women on its twenty-ninth session, and the views expressed by the Commission on Human Rights in response to Council resolution 1980/39.

Commission agenda

The Economic and Social Council, on 4 May 1982,[1] approved the provisional agenda and documentation for the 1983 session of the Commission on the Status of Women. This decision, adopted without vote, was based on a draft submitted by the Commission and similarly approved by the Council's Second Committee on 26 April.

Decision (1982). [1]ESC: 1982/123, 4 May, text following.
Meeting record: ESC, E/1982/SR.23 (4 May).

Economic and Social Council decision 1982/123

Adopted without vote

Approved by Second Committee (E/1982/57) without vote, 26 April (meeting 9); draft by Commission on women (E/1982/14); agenda item 10.

Provisional agenda and documentation for the thirtieth session of the Commission on the Status of Women

At its 23rd plenary meeting, on 4 May 1982, the Council approved the provisional agenda and documentation for the thirtieth session of the Commission on the Status of Women set out below:

Provisional agenda and documentation for the thirtieth session
of the Commission on the Status of Women

1. Election of officers
2. Adoption of the agenda and other organizational matters
3. Review and appraisal of progress achieved in the implementation
   of the World Plan of Action for the Implementation of the Objectives of the International Women's Year and the Programme of Action for the Second Half of the United Nations Decade for Women
   during the period 1982-1983
   (a) Review and appraisal of progress made at the national level
   (Legislative authority: General Assembly resolutions 3490(XXX),
   35/78, 35/136 and 36/74 and Economic and Social Council resolutions 2060(LXII) and 1981/12)
   Documentation
       Report of the Secretary-General (fifth biennial report to the Com-
       mission on the Status of Women on review and appraisal of
       the implementation of the World Plan of Action for the Im-
       plementation of the Objectives of the International Women's
       Year and the Programme of Action for the Second Half of
       the United Nations Decade for Women (1982-1983))
       Report of the Secretary-General on progress made in the prepa-
       ration of a world survey on the role of women in development
   (b) Measures taken by the United Nations system of organizations and by intergovernmental organizations, progress made
   in the implementation of new strategies for women and work
   aimed at the follow-up and harmonization of actions of various bodies of the United Nations system
   (Legislative authority: General Assembly resolution 36/126 and Economic and Social Council resolutions 48 B (IV), 154 F (VII),
   821 IV B (XXXII), 1978/34, 1980/3 and 1980/38)
   Documentation
       Report of the Secretary-General on United Nations activities dur-
       ing the biennium 1982-1983
       Progress report of the Secretary-General on the implementation
       of new strategies for women and work aimed at the follow-
       up and harmonization of action of the various bodies of the
       United Nations system
       Progress report of the Secretary-General on the development
       of statistics and indicators on the situation of women
       Report of the International Labour Organisation on its activities
       of special interest to women
       Report of the United Nations Educational, Scientific and Cul-
       tural Organization on its activities of special interest to women
       Report of the Food and Agricultural Organization of the United
       Nations on its activities of special interest to women
       Report of the World Health Organization on its activities of spe-
       cial interest to women
       Report of the Inter-American Commission of Women
       Report of the Commission on the Status of Arab Women
       Information on the activities of the International Research and
       Training Institute for the Advancement of Women
4. Preparations for the World Conference to Review and Appraise
   the Achievements of the United Nations Decade for Women
   (Legislative authority: General Assembly resolutions 35/136 and
   36/123 and Economic and Social Council resolution 1982/26)
   Documentation
       Report of the Secretary-General on preparations for the World
       Conference to Review and Appraise the Achievements of the
       United Nations Decade for Women

5. Convention on the Elimination of All Forms of Discrimination
   against Women
   (Legislative authority: General Assembly resolution 34/180)
   Documentation
       Note by the Secretary-General on the status of the Convention
       on the Elimination of All Forms of Discrimination against
       Women
       Report of the Committee on the Elimination of Discrimination
       against Women to the General Assembly through the Eco-
       nomic and Social Council, transmitted by the Secretary-
       General for the information of the Commission
6. Communications concerning the status of women
   (Legislative authority: Economic and Social Council resolutions
   76(V) and 304 I (XI))
   Documentation
       Note by the Secretary-General transmitting a non-confidential
       list containing a brief summary of communications dealing
       with the principles relating to the promotion of women's rights
       in the political, economic, civil, social and educational fields
       Note by the Secretary-General transmitting a confidential list of
       communications concerning the status of women
7. Participation of women in the struggle for the strengthening of international peace and security and against colonialism, racism, racial discrimination, foreign aggression and occupation, and all
   forms of foreign domination
   (Legislative authority: decision of the Commission and General Assembly resolutions 3318(XXIX) and 34/24)
   Documentation
       Report of the Secretary-General on the situation of women and
       children living under racist minority régimes and in the oc-
       cupied Arab territories and other occupied territories
8. Programme of future work, including a draft provisional agenda
   for the thirty-first session
9. Adoption of the report of the Commission on its thirtieth session

Report of the Commission

On 4 May 1982,[1] the Economic and Social
Council took note of the report of the Commission on the Status of Women on its 1982 session.[2] This decision, adopted without vote, was
similarly approved by the Council's Second Committee on 26 April on an oral proposal by the
Chairman.

Decision (1982). [1]ESC: 1982/124, 4 May, text following.
Report. [2]Commission on Women, E/1982/14.
Meeting record. ESC: E/1982/SR.23 (4 May).

Economic and Social Council decision 1982/124

Adopted without vote

Approved by Second Committee (E/1982/57) without vote, 26 April (meeting 9);
oral proposal by Chairman; agenda item 10.

Report of the Commission on the Status of Women
At its 23rd plenary meeting, on 4 May 1982, the Council took note
of the report of the Commission on the Status of Women on its twenty-
ninth session.

Chapter XX

Children, youth and aging persons

Contents

Related topics:

Africa: Women and children under *apartheid*. Middle East: International Day of Innocent Children Victims of Aggression; Aging persons in Lebanon. Human rights: Draft convention on the rights of the child.

For resolutions and decisons of major organs mentioned but not reproduced, refer to INDEX OF RESOLUTIONS AND DECISIONS.

Children

UN Children's Fund

In 1982, the United Nations Children's Fund (UNICEF) co-operated in programmes in 112 countries, with a total child population under 16 years of age of approximately 1.3 billion. Total expenditure on programmes and budgetary support came to $289 million, making the average UNICEF expenditure per child 22 cents, compared with 23 cents in 1981. Support was given to basic maternal and child health services in 104 countries, and to water supply (93 countries), child nutrition (90), social welfare services (99), and formal (94) and non-formal (85) education. Of the total expenditure by main category of programme,

28 per cent was spent for water supply and sanitation, 24 for basic child health, 10 for formal education, 10 for planning and project support services, 9 for child nutrition, 8 for emergency relief, 7 for social welfare services for children, and 4 for non-formal education.

In addition, UNICEF expended $28 million from funds received in trust, mainly for reimbursable procurement of goods and services, and distributed donations in kind through its field network for a value of $7 million.[4]

The UNICEF Executive Board met three times in 1982: on 16 April for a special session,[2] at which it considered increasing its membership to 41 members; from 10 to 21 May for its regular session;[1] and on 28 June,[3] to elect officers to serve from 1 August 1982 to 31 July 1983.

At its regular session, the Board approved programme commitments for multiyear implementation totalling $226.2 million net and "noted" projects (those financed by specific-purpose contributions) totalling $252 million. It noted that the financial position of UNICEF had strengthened significantly in 1982 compared to 1981, increasing by 30 per cent to a total income of $378 million. The Board adopted by consensus a message to the General Assembly at its second special session devoted to disarmament, appealing for reduction of arms expenditures so that a portion of the savings could be channelled through national or multinational programmes towards meeting the minimum needs of children everywhere—adequate nutrition, safe water, primary health care and suitable education.

Reports. UNICEF Board, [1]E/1982/17, [2]E/ICEF/694, [3]E/ICEF/696; [4]UNICEF Director, E/ICEF/698 & Corr.1.

Programme policy decisions

UNICEF Executive Board consideration. At its May 1982 session,[2] the UNICEF Executive Board endorsed the trend towards greater co-operation in area-specific programmes at the intermediate and local levels in developing countries, as well as the expansion and strengthening of urban basic services. It also endorsed a new five-year programme to reduce child and maternal malnutrition and a complementary project to provide essential drugs, both to be undertaken jointly by UNICEF and the World Health Organization. Emphasizing the catalytic role of UNICEF, the Board urged continued and strengthened collaboration with other United Nations and international aid agencies, local institutions and non-governmental organizations (NGOs) to enhance programme convergence.

The Board approved the objectives and priorities of the medium-term work plan, which emphasized the promotion and use of low-cost effective measures to benefit the most disadvantaged children and women. It also approved the financial plan of the work plan as a framework of projections for 1982-1985 and agreed that the Executive Director could prepare $383 million in programme and budget commitments from general resources for submission to the Board in 1983.

Economic and Social Council action. By a resolution adopted without vote on 28 July 1982,[3] the Economic and Social Council endorsed the policies, actions and conclusions adopted by the Board in May. The Council commended organizations supporting UNICEF activities, notably the UNICEF national committees and NGOs, as well as other United Nations organizations, and urged intensified co-operation. The Council also commended the Fund's energetic and imaginative efforts to enlarge its income, expressed appreciation to Governments that had responded to the Fund's needs and appealed for increased contributions. The text, introduced by Yugoslavia on behalf of 15 countries, had been approved without vote on 23 July by the Council's Third (Programme and Co-ordination) Committee.

General Assembly action. On 20 December,[4] the General Assembly, acting without vote, commended UNICEF policies and activities, endorsed the Council's 28 July resolution, reaffirmed the Fund's role as the United Nations lead agency for co-ordinating the follow-up activities of the International Year of the Child (1979)[5] and urged the Fund's Executive Director and secretariat to continue and intensify their innovative efforts to adapt the basic-services approach for children in the light of the current economic crisis, in accordance with the Executive Board's decisions. Like the Council, the Assembly commended UNICEF for its imaginative efforts to enlarge its income, expressed appreciation to Governments that had responded to its needs and appealed for increased contributions.

This resolution, based on informal consultations on an 18-nation text which had been introduced in the Assembly's Second (Economic and Financial) Committee by the Netherlands and later withdrawn,[1] was submitted by a Vice-Chairman. It was approved by the Committee without vote, on 8 December.

Draft resolution withdrawn. [1]Bangladesh, Belgium, Bhutan, China, Denmark, Finland, France, India, Lebanon, Nepal, Netherlands, Nigeria, Norway, Sweden, United Kingdom, United States, Venezuela, Yugoslavia, A/C.2/37/L.87.
Report. [2]UNICEF Board, E/1982/17.
Resolutions (1982). [3]ESC: 1982/51, 28 July, text following. [4]GA: 37/231, 20 Dec., text following.
Yearbook reference. [5]1979, p. 908.
Meeting records. ESC: E/1982/SR.49 (28 July). GA: 2nd Committee, A/C.2/37/SR.7, 32-40, *44, 47* (5 Oct.–8 Dec.); plenary, A/37/PV.113 (20 Dec.).

Economic and Social Council resolution 1982/51

28 July 1982   Meeting 49   Adopted without vote

Approved by Third Committee (E/1982/90) without vote, 23 July (meeting 16); 15-nation draft (E/1982/C.3/L.9); agenda item 19.

Sponsors: Austria, Bangladesh, Benin, India, Italy, Mali, Nepal, Nigeria, Norway, Pakistan, Peru, Sweden, Venezuela, Yugoslavia, Zaire.

Report of the Executive Board of the United Nations Children's Fund

The Economic and Social Council,

Recalling General Assembly resolution 36/197 of 17 December 1981 and Council resolution 1981/56 of 22 July 1981, in which, *inter alia,* the principles and guidelines for the programme activities of the United Nations Children's Fund, as laid down by its Executive Board, in particular the field-oriented and action-oriented approach of the Fund, were reaffirmed,

Having considered the decisions and conclusions adopted by the Executive Board of the United Nations Children's Fund at its session held at United Nations Headquarters from 10 to 21 May 1982, in particular concerning the policy reviews on the co-operation of the Fund in urban basic services and at intermediate and local levels in developing countries,

Deeply concerned that the present global economic situation adversely affects both the ability of developing countries to implement plans for the extension of basic services to children and mothers and the level of contributions to the Fund and other organizations concerned for those purposes,

Noting with appreciation the exceptional efforts that have recently been made by certain Governments to increase their contributions to the Fund,

Taking note of the message adopted by consensus by the Executive Board and addressed to the General Assembly at its second special session devoted to disarmament, in which the Board appealed for a reduction of expenditures on armaments so that a portion of the savings could be channelled through national or multinational programmes towards meeting the minimum needs of children everywhere,

Aware that significant progress can be made in alleviating the situation of children and mothers in developing countries with relatively modest increases in contributions to the Fund and to other organizations sharing similar concern, pending progress in the implementation of the new international economic order,

1. *Endorses* the policies, actions and conclusions of the Executive Board of the United Nations Children's Fund as adopted at its session held from 10 to 21 May 1982;

2. *Commends* the Executive Director and the secretariat of the Fund for their energetic and imaginative efforts to enlarge the income of the Fund during the past year;

3. *Also commends* all organizations concerned in supporting the activities of the Fund, notably the national committees for the Fund and the co-operating non-governmental organizations, as well as other organizations of the United Nations system, and urges them to intensify such co-operation;

4. *Expresses its appreciation* to Governments that have responded to the needs of the Fund and hopes that more Member States will follow their example;

5. *Appeals* to all Governments to increase their contributions, if possible on a multiyear basis, so that, in the current global economic situation, the Fund may be able to strengthen its co-operation with developing countries and respond to the urgent needs of the children in those countries.

General Assembly resolution 37/231

20 December 1982   Meeting 113   Adopted without vote

Approved by Second Committee (A/37/774) without vote, 8 December (meeting 47); draft by Vice-Chairman (A/C.2/37/L.112), based on informal consultations on 18-nation draft (A/C.2/37/L.87); agenda item 72 *(h).*

United Nations Children's Fund

The General Assembly,

Taking note of Economic and Social Council resolution 1982/51 of 28 July 1982,

Having considered the report of the Executive Board of the United Nations Children's Fund on its session held at United Nations Headquarters from 10 to 21 May 1982,

Reaffirming the principles and guidelines for programme activities established by the Executive Board of the United Nations Children's Fund, in particular its basic-services approach and its efforts to reach the most disadvantaged as part of a comprehensive field-oriented and action-oriented development policy, and the maintenance of a low ratio of administration to programme costs,

Acutely aware that the present global economic situation both adversely affects the ability of developing countries to implement efforts to extend basic services and makes the need for those services all the more critical,

Concerned that the situation regarding financing for development, including in particular the situation of multilateral agencies depending upon voluntary contributions, has been adversely affected by a number of unfavourable factors,

1. *Commends* the policies and activities of the United Nations Children's Fund;

2. *Endorses* Economic and Social Council resolution 1982/51;

3. *Reaffirms* the role of the United Nations Children's Fund as the lead agency in the United Nations system responsible for co-ordinating the follow-up activities of the International Year of the Child related to the goals and objectives concerning children set forth in the International Development Strategy for the Third United Nations Development Decade;

4. *Urges* the Executive Director and the secretariat of the United Nations Children's Fund to continue and intensify their innovative efforts to adapt the basic-services approach for children in the light of the current economic crisis, in accordance with the relevant decisions of the Executive Board of the Fund;

5. *Commends* the Executive Director and the secretariat of the United Nations Children's Fund for their imaginative efforts to enlarge the income of the Fund so that it may respond to the needs of developing countries;

6. *Expresses its appreciation* to Governments that have responded to the needs of the United Nations Children's Fund and expresses the hope that more Member States will follow their example;

7. *Appeals* to all Governments, especially to those whose voluntary contributions may not reflect their capacity to contribute, to increase their contributions, preferably the contributions to the general resources, if possible on a multiyear basis, so that, in the light of the present economic situation, the United Nations Children's Fund may meet its responsibilities to developing countries in responding to the urgent needs of children.

Medium-term plan for 1982-1985

At its May 1982 session,[2] the Executive Board approved the programme objectives of the 1982-1985 medium-term work plan[1] as UNICEF contributions towards attainment of the goals of the International Development Strategy for the Third United Nations Development Decade[3]—to eradicate mass illiteracy and strive for universal access to primary education, eradicate mass hunger and malnutrition, and reduce infant mortality rates to 50 or less per 1,000 by the year 2000.

The plan's objectives were to direct programmes to the most disadvantaged children, particularly in regions and countries most seriously affected by the economic recession and where expenditures on social services had stagnated or deteriorated; to promote low-cost activities in such areas as infant and child feeding, child immunization, the provision of essential drugs, diarrhoeal diseases control, women's functional literacy and the education of girls, and multidimensional water projects; and to strengthen UNICEF capacity and management.

In endorsing the plan's priorities, the Board stressed that programme delivery was to be the main focus. Primary health care (PHC) orientation of services outside the health sector and education of out-of-school children and youth would receive special attention, as would specific aspects of child nutrition such as breast-feeding.

Medium-term plan. [1]E/ICEF/691 & Corr.1.
Report. [2]UNICEF Board, E/1982/17.
Resolution. [3]GA: 35/56, annex, 5 Dec. 1980 (YUN 1980, p. 503).

Programme delivery at the local levels

The Executive Board, at its May 1982 session,[1] welcomed the main findings of a UNICEF secretariat report on programme co-operation at the intermediate and local levels and endorsed the trend towards greater co-operation in the introduction and strengthening of institutions and services benefiting children at those levels. PHC, basic services and income-generating activities for women were cited as effective entry points for community participation, while the non-governmental sector was identified as an effective channel for stimulating, encouraging and sustaining such participation.

UNICEF experience reviewed by the report supported the policy of co-operation in area-specific programmes (those limited to a geographically defined area). It moreover suggested that opportunities should be sought for increased subnational co-operation focusing on special groups, as on children of disadvantaged minorities or nomads, and that supporting programmes capable of being replicated and translated into national policy should be emphasized.

Report. [1]UNICEF Board, E/1982/17.

Maurice Pate Memorial Award

The Executive Board, in approving the 1982 commitments at its May session, approved the Executve Director's recommendation that, for the year, the Maurice Pate Memorial Award, established to commemorate the first Executive Director of UNICEF, be awarded to the University of the West Indies to support activities of its Department of Social and Preventive Medicine, in recognition of the University's increasingly important role in that field.[1] That Department had been engaged in several outreach training programmes over the previous two decades, including those for paramedical personnel in community medicine, and had developed the first community training programme for health aides in the region, producing a manual for the basic training and continuing education of such personnel.

Recommendation. [1]UNICEF Director, E/ICEF/P/L.2143(REC).

UNICEF programmes by region

In 1982, programme expenditures were roughly maintained at previous levels for all geographical regions,[1] except the Middle East (eastern Mediterranean) where, due principally to emergency relief in Lebanon, expenditures increased to $31 million, compared with $17.5 million in 1981. The tables on the following pages show expenditures and commitments for 1982, and commitments and "notings" (awaiting funding) approved by the Executive Board in May.[2]

Reports. [1]Board of Auditors, and financial statements, A/38/5/Add.2; [2]UNICEF Board, E/1982/17.

Africa

In eastern Africa,[1] primary health care (PHC) development continued in 1982, with greater emphasis on training and planning. A regional workshop was held on the subject (Ethiopia, February), as were several intercountry workshops. UNICEF assistance in education continued to focus on curriculum development and teacher training, in co-operation with the United Nations Educational, Scientific and Cultural Organization. Interregional workshops were organized on diarrhoeal and sexually transmitted diseases. An adviser on water and environmental sanitation visited the region, and funding was arranged for a regional project on improved sanitation and health education in water delivery schemes. Case studies were made of projects designed to integrate appropriate technology into basic services (Burundi, Ethiopia, Kenya, Swaziland). To ensure the operation of programme vehicles, UNICEF provided transport-maintenance support in the form of spare parts, tools and equipment to 10 of the 19 east African countries. Assistance was also provided for the production of information materials on breast-feeding, such as newsletters, slides, posters and press briefings.

In west and central Africa,[2] where the economic situation and the drought cycle continued to constrain assistance programmes, some progress was nevertheless reported in establishing national PHC systems, providing drinking water and adequate diet, improving sanitation and expanding immunization programmes. Co-operation in food production was mainly at the family and village levels. UNICEF focused on strengthening field offices, improving logistic services, training staff, and carrying out advocacy activities directed at national officials in the policy-making and technical fields.

The Fund continued its emergency assistance to Chad, distributing enriched food supplies, essential drugs, vaccines and school materials for children. A programme was begun to rehabilitate primary schools and health and social centres to include projects in preventive child care, nutrition and income-producing activities for women such as food-gardening and sewing. Other emergency aid was provided for refugee children and

(continued on p. 1169)

1982 EXPENDITURE AND MULTIYEAR COMMITMENTS BY COUNTRY AND REGION

(as at 31 December 1982; in US dollars)

COUNTRY	Expenditure	Approved new commitment
Africa		
Algeria	174,464	—
Angola	1,859,808	—
Benin	865,376	—
Botswana	294,220	—
Burundi	911,665	2,862,366
Cape Verde	123,352	253,242
Central African Republic	581,303	—
Chad	1,050,407	—
Comoros	95,633	189,000
Congo	168,278	—
Djibouti	720,712	—
Equatorial Guinea	87,075	—
Ethiopia	10,029,924	—
Gabon	56	—
Gambia	209,190	—
Ghana	1,154,064	2,463,000
Guinea	919,589	—
Guinea-Bissau	720,450	232,445
Ivory Coast	382,191	2,006,000
Kenya	952,240	—
Lesotho	175,850	—
Liberia	729,276	1,189,220
Madagascar	912,274	—
Malawi	1,056,475	—
Mali	1,083,848	8,812,000
Mauritania	578,476	1,995,000
Mauritius	212,715	—
Morocco	1,423,000	—
Mozambique	1,072,754	—
Niger	1,369,930	—
Nigeria	4,060,592	—
Rwanda	1,492,530	—
Sao Tome and Principe	78,544	—
Senegal	513,178	—
Seychelles	59,023	—
Sierra Leone	234,077	1,427,000
Somalia	2,798,665	—
Swaziland	314,915	—
Togo	159,218	—
Tunisia	160,457	—
Uganda	4,385,841	—
United Republic of Cameroon	544,342	—
United Republic of Tanzania	4,453,367	13,427,000
Upper Volta	1,316,313	—
Zaire	2,762,940	10,166,000
Zambia	485,671	—
Zimbabwe	1,582,152	—
Regional projects	881,798	—
Subtotal	56,198,215	45,022,273
Americas		
Antigua	12,385	—
Barbados	22,431	—
Belize	37,370	—
Bolivia	525,134	—
Brazil	1,149,263	1,260,000
Chile	67,000	—
Colombia	1,925,347	—
Costa Rica	109,353	—
Cuba	85,097	—
Dominica	12,941	94,992
Dominican Republic	265,625	—
Ecuador	546,672	—
El Salvador	275,959	—
Grenada	23,904	—
Guatemala	490,223	2,518,000
Guyana	114,284	—
Haiti	745,274	5,114,000

COUNTRY	Expenditure	Approved new commitment
Americas (cont.)		
Honduras	477,599	—
Jamaica	83,399	—
Mexico	428,172	—
Nicaragua	638,612	—
Panama	58,473	—
Paraguay	237,443	665,000
Peru	1,238,952	3,000,000
St. Kitts–Nevis–Anguilla	9,490	—
Saint Lucia	27,491	—
Saint Vincent and the Grenadines	34,087	—
Suriname	12,323	—
Regional projects	1,466,578	—
Subtotal	11,120,881	12,651,992
East Asia and Pakistan		
Bangladesh	10,602,609	50,000,000
Burma	3,344,847	27,000,000
China	4,069,385	20,163,000
Democratic Kampuchea	9,631,803	—
Indonesia	13,025,142	—
Lao People's Democratic Republic	1,140,991	4,256,000
Malaysia	318,337	1,062,000
Pacific island Territories	388,128	283,669
Pakistan	11,840,070	—
Papua New Guinea	247,001	193,000
Philippines	2,746,247	—
Republic of Korea	622,703	2,716,000
Thailand	2,943,789	14,740,000
Viet Nam	4,475,739	27,142,000
Regional projects	145,786	—
Subtotal	65,542,576	147,555,669
South Central Asia		
Afghanistan	1,265,596	—
Bhutan	712,547	—
India	35,285,031	—
Maldives	505,126	159,000
Mongolia	38,093	—
Nepal	4,359,039	12,710,000
Sri Lanka	3,069,540	—
Subtotal	45,234,972	12,869,000
Eastern Mediterranean		
Bahrain	106,797	—
Democratic Yemen	552,588	—
Egypt	3,084,684	4,972,000
Jordan	722,311	547,000
Lebanon	15,267,321	—
Oman	315,055	—
Sudan	8,449,213	—
Syrian Arab Republic	259,904	1,460,000
Yemen	1,770,491	—
Palestine children and mothers	263,612	—
Regional projects	191,012	—
Subtotal	30,982,988	6,979,000
Europe		
Poland	107,390	—
Turkey	154,014	460,000
Subtotal	261,404	460,000
Interregional	3,755,223	1,065,034
Savings (cancellation)	—	(446,961)
Total	213,096,259	226,156,007

NOTES: Approved new commitments include the following to cover over-expenditures incurred in previous commitments: Burundi, $5,366; Cape Verde, $1,242; Guinea-Bissau, $39,445; Liberia, $9,220; Dominica, $11,992; and Pacific island Territories, $6,669. Left over from a previous commitment and recommended for cancellation were: Egypt, $136,817; Jordan $12,516; Maldives, $41,123; and Turkey, $26,906.

SOURCES: A/38/5/Add.2, E/1982/17.

COMMITMENTS AND "NOTINGS" APPROVED BY THE EXECUTIVE
BOARD IN 1982 FOR INTERREGIONAL PROJECTS
(in US dollars)

	Period	Approved commitments	Approved for "notings"
Maurice Pate Memorial Award	1982-1983	15,000	—
International Children's Centre	1983-1985	700,000	—
Supplementary funds for support for primary health care	1982-1983	—	5,000,000
Provision for essential drugs for primary health care in Africa	1982-1983	—	15,000,000
WHO/UNICEF programme of action for the improvement of nutrition	1982-1986	—	85,300,000
Commitment to cover over-expenditure		350,034	—
Total		1,065,034	105,300,000

NOTE: No regional projects were considered in 1982.
SOURCE: E/1982/17.

displaced persons (Rwanda, Uganda) and for victims of drought (Botswana, Cape Verde, Mauritania, Mozambique), flood (Benin, Madgascar) and an outbreak of meningitis (Zambia).

Reports. UNICEF regional offices for: [1]Eastern Africa, E/ICEF/L.1458; [2]West and central Africa, E/ICEF/L.1459.

Americas

Steps were taken in the Americas[1] during 1982 to achieve co-ordinated action by Governments and organizations in implementing the regional plan of action for PHC formulated in 1980. In collaboration with the World Health Organization (WHO), UNICEF continued to support the related programmes for immunization and control of diarrhoeal diseases, a leading cause of infant death. Focusing on prevention and family-based treatment of diarrhoea, it assisted in a study of prevention methods, for the purpose of designing a technical co-operation project among the five Andean Pact countries—Bolivia, Colombia, Ecuador, Peru and Venezuela. With the Fund's help, a plant was built in Colombia for the production of oral rehydration salts for low-cost treatment of diarrhoeal diseases.

Besides support for breast-feeding programmes, nutrition surveillance systems were established within national health services (Colombia, Cuba, Nicaragua, St. Kitts–Nevis–Anguilla), and adequate child nutrition was promoted through food production at the family and community levels (Bolivia, Dominican Republic, Mexico, Peru). New approaches to early childhood development, many involving parents and trained community workers or volunteers, were carried out (Barbados, Colombia, Dominican Republic, Ecuador, Haiti, Mexico, Panama, Peru). In Chile, UNICEF co-operated with the Centre for Development and Psychosocial Stimulation on a study of emotional and behavioural disorders affecting the young.

Report. [1]UNICEF regional office for Americas, E/ICEF/L.1460.

Asia

During 1982, medium- and long-term programmes of co-operation submitted by seven countries in the east Asia and Pakistan region[1] (Bangladesh, Burma, Lao People's Democratic Republic, Malaysia, Republic of Korea, Thailand, Viet Nam) and approved by the UNICEF Executive Board at its May session were under implementation. Towards the end of the year, joint annual reviews of programme implementation were held with Indonesia, Malaysia, Pakistan, the Republic of Korea and Viet Nam, and plans of action for 1983 were finalized.

Burma and Papua New Guinea were selected for a study aimed at supporting PHC in countries committed to its development and learning how UNICEF and WHO could best collaborate in providing support. Increased efforts were made to develop urban PHC programmes for selected cities—Jakarta and Surabaya (Indonesia), Kuala Lumpur (Malaysia), Manila (Philippines), Seoul (Republic of Korea) and Bangkok (Thailand).

Under the joint UNICEF/WHO five-year nutrition programme, Burma and Pakistan were chosen for intensive support. The Fund's participation in another nutrition project in Indonesia involved nutrition education; distribution of vitamin A capsules, iron-folate tablets and oral rehydration salts; supplementary feeding for malnourished children; and food production. In Thailand, where some 53 per cent of pre-school children suffered from protein deficiency, and weaning mothers from malnutrition, the Fund co-operated with national ministries in nutrition surveillance, educational and training activities (training some 13,725 trainees at various levels in 1982) and promoting food production. Jointly with the World Food Programme, UNICEF was developing the first food aid project for vulnerable groups in Viet Nam. In the Lao People's Democratic Republic, it extended support to a food processing plant for weaning foods.

Regional services in supply, procurement and logistics continued in 1982. By the end of October, purchase orders, including those for Kampuchea where the Fund played an important role in relief operations, totalled $5.6 million. Cement, iron pipes and school supplies were among the major items procured.

In south central Asia,[2] emphasis was laid on the control of diarrhoeal diseases, anaemia and goitre, with the Fund co-operating in such measures as oral rehydration therapy and immunization, the use of iron-fortified salt for anaemia and iodinated oil injections during pregnancy where goitre was endemic. Response to the goitre problem shifted from funding salt-iodization plants towards advocacy—persuading Governments, the medical profession and teaching institutions to give the problem priority in terms of urgency and resource allocation.

Reports. UNICEF regional offices for: [1]East Asia and Pakistan, E/ICEF/L.1461; [2]South Central Asia, E/ICEF/L.1462.

Mediterranean area

During 1982, UNICEF submitted proposals for two programme areas—drinking water supply and sanitation, and women's activities—for adoption by the Arab Gulf Programme for the United Nations Development Organizations (AGFUND), which had pledged approximtely $20 million to the Fund for the fiscal year starting in 1982.[1] UNICEF also co-operated with the Arab Fund for Economic and Social Development, which granted a $23-million concessional loan to eight Arab countries—Democratic Yemen, Djibouti, Jordan, Mauritania, Morocco, the Sudan, Tunisia and Yemen—in support of rural drinking water programmes; arrangements for UNICEF co-operation in these projects were in the final stage of negotiation, whereby the recipient countries would channel the proceeds of the projects to UNICEF.

Within hours of the outbreak of fighting in Beirut, Lebanon, on 6 June, UNICEF became involved in relief operations in that country. Response to the Executive Director's $5-million appeal for an initial 90-day programme of intensive relief and rehabilitation assistance was immediate, and the goal was met by Governments. Despite persisting hostilities and tensions, the reconstruction programme in south Lebanon continued. By year's end, 198 projects in health, water supply, education and community self-help had been completed; another 49 were being implemented, 7 were under procurement and 44 in preparation. Following a major earthquake in Yemen in December, an AGFUND emergency reserve released $201,000 for relief supplies delivered and distributed by UNICEF.

Report. [1]UNICEF regional office for Middle East and North Africa, E/ICEF/L.1463.

UNICEF programmes by sector

As in the previous four years, child health (see below) accounted for the largest portion of the Fund's expenditures in 1982.[2] Other major programmes dealt with water supply and sanitation, nutrition, social welfare services and education. The table below gives details of 1982 expenditures and commitments by programme sector.[1]

Reports. UNICEF Board, [1]E/1982/17, [2]E/1983/21.

Child welfare in urban areas

At its May 1982 session,[1] the Executive Board reviewed UNICEF work in urban basic services[2] and, in the light of growing urban populations and the increasing magnitude of the problems of children and women of the urban poor, adopted a new urban programme strategy for the remainder of the 1980s. The strategy, aimed at strengthening government efforts to implement solutions, continued to give priority to the critical areas of malnutrition, pre-school care and early childhood development, abandoned and disabled children, responsible parenthood and family planning, water supply and sanitation, and women's situation. The Board's action paved the way for the Fund to expand urban programmes to meet the needs identified in country-by-country analyses in projects such as sites-and-services, slum upgrading, water and sanitation, post-disaster settlements, and physical infrastructure for small and medium-sized towns and cities.

In Central America, UNICEF collaboration in urban basic services included technical assistance and seed money through the Central American Bank for Economic Integration for the institutionalization of a system of loans and technical assistance; this resulted, for example, in the creation of employment opportunities and income-generating activities for women in Costa Rica. In five urban areas in Guatemala, UNICEF, in co-operation with the Government and a local consortium of non-governmental organizations, provided financial, material and technical support for community-based projects in education and training, health and nutrition, income-generating activities, legal aid and urban infrastructure.

UNICEF made a commitment to add its resources to $400,000 made available by Mexico's National Bank for the Development of Physical Infrastructure for the World Bank's second urban and regional development project, for low-income urban communities in the states of Tabasco, Chiapas and Vera Cruz, designed to provide training and technical assistance for enhancing institutional co-operation and arranging credit.

1982 UNICEF EXPENDITURE AND COMMITMENTS,
BY MAIN FIELD OF CO-OPERATION
(in thousands of US dollars)

	1982 expenditure	*Approved commitments*
Child health	111,028	67,808
Water supply/sanitation	—	45,177
Child nutrition	19,013	13,070
Social welfare services for children	15,647	21,250
Formal education	20,560	41,602
Non-formal education	8,571	12,933
Emergency relief*	16,263	—
General	22,014	24,339
Programme support services†	39,551	—
Total	252,647	226,179

*Expenditures for rehabilitation of facilities damaged or destroyed in emergency situations, distributed among the appropriate programme sectors, would have brought the total to $18,117,288.

†Not comparable with previous years' figures due to changes in the 1982-1983 budget presentation.

Applied workshops aimed at strengthening government and UNICEF capacities were organized. One such workshop in Sri Lanka reviewed management experience in urban basic services programmes in Asia, particularly water and sanitation services in slums and shanty towns; another, held in Haiti in November, reviewed programmes to reduce urban malnutrition in Africa, Asia and Latin America. An international conference on primary health care (PHC) for poor urban areas of the Andean Pact countries, organized by the Colombian Ministry of Health and UNICEF, was held in Colombia.

Reports. [1]UNICEF Board, E/1982/17; [2]UNICEF Executive Director, E/ICEF/L.1440 & Corr.1.

Education

In 1982, UNICEF activities classified as formal and non-formal education—excluding education in health, nutrition, sanitation and other programmes—accounted for $29.1 million, or 14 per cent of total programme expenditure, compared with 15 per cent in 1981. Assistance in education was in four main areas: pre-school care and education; primary education; non-formal education (educational opportunities for youth and women outside the school system, including vocational training); and education in basic health services (training of childbirth attendants, PHC workers and construction and maintenance workers in water supply and sanitation facilities; workshops and seminars on specific aspects of programme development, implementation and evaluation). Recipient countries numbered 102: 46 in Africa, 26 in Asia, 22 in the Americas and 8 in the Middle East region (including Turkey).

Following a meeting in April 1982 between the Director-General of the United Nations Educational, Scientific and Cultural Organization (UNESCO) and the UNICEF Executive Director, a joint UNESCO/UNICEF working group prepared a programme to foster universal primary education and literacy for consideration by the Executive Board in 1983. The programme was to be implemented within the framework of UNICEF country programmes, with UNESCO technical support. Under the first phase, a five-year period of assistance was to be provided for activities in Bangladesh, Ethiopia, Nepal, Nicaragua and Peru.

Nutrition

In 1982, UNICEF co-operated in nutrition programmes in 90 countries—41 in Africa, 22 in Asia, 21 in the Americas and 6 in the Middle East—with a total expenditure of $19 million, an increase of $5 million over 1981. These activities accounted for 9 per cent of all programme costs. The Fund continued to support national and community activities for the improvement of food production, education and training in nutrition, and nutritional monitoring and evaluation.

At its May session,[1] the Executive Board approved a five-year (1982-1986) nutrition support programme to reduce malnutrition among children and women through PHC. To be jointly undertaken by the World Health Organization (WHO) and UNICEF, the programme included promotion of breast-feeding, improvement of weaning practices and nutrition education, control of specific deficiencies as in iodine and vitamin A, environmental health, and food production and distribution.[2] The Board also examined another proposed UNICEF/WHO project to increase the supply of essential drugs to least developed countries, to be limited initially to five such countries. These joint undertakings were to be funded as complementary "noted" projects, for which the Government of Italy had already pledged $100 million ($85 million of which was for the five-year nutrition support programme).

Reports. [1]UNICEF Board, E/1982/17; [2]UNICEF and WHO secretariats, E/ICEF/L.1441 & Add.1.

Infant feeding

In 1982, as in previous years, the campaign to halt and reverse the decline of breast-feeding in the developing world received the Fund's moral and material support, based on the fact that breast-feeding yielded improvement in the child's survival and health prospects. Irresponsible advertising of infant-formula products and practices of health clinics and hospitals continued to be campaign targets. While only a few countries had formally adopted the 1981 International Code of Marketing of Breast-milk Substitutes[1] by year's end, 12 had banned advertising of substitutes and more than 20 were developing national regulatory measures modelled on the Code. In 24 of the countries with which the Fund co-operated, breast-feeding was promoted through surveys, studies, national workshops and consultations with government and health officials.

Information on the benefits of breast-feeding was disseminated through the mass media, and education and training on young child feeding was encouraged. A document clarifying the position of UNICEF and WHO on the Code was sent to the field offices of those agencies. Efforts were also made to assist on an individual basis all groups—Governments, non-governmental organizations (NGOs) and infant-formula manufacturers—committed to the Code's implementation. UNICEF participated in four NGO conferences on infant feeding—in South-East Asia, east Africa and the Caribbean (two)—which discussed the mother's right to choose the best feeding method for her infant based on strategies to promote breast-feeding.

Yearbook reference. [1]1981, p. 1419.

Primary health care

In 1982, UNICEF addressed itself to five major problems identified in primary health care (PHC) implementation: lack of political support and therefore of the necessary community organization for the effective delivery of health services; failure to involve the community sufficiently in decision making and programme management; poor integration of health services; the need for information and monitoring systems within those services; and the need to give priority to mothers' and children's health within PHC programmes. Co-operation in maternal and child health services continued to be the largest field of activity of UNICEF, with programmes totalling $111 million.

Accordingly, the Fund gave considerable attention to PHC advocacy at the national level, as in Nepal and Sri Lanka where efforts were made to raise political awareness. Ways of co-operation were sought in refashioning health service infrastructures, including transportation, for increased coverage particularly in rural areas; and in orienting community health workers towards the PHC approach. Communications and education programmes to foster community involvement were undertaken, as in Bangladesh, Jamaica and the Philippines, in connection with child immunization. Special training sessions for government officials drawn from different programme sectors at local and regional levels promoted intersectoral collaboration in Costa Rica, Nigeria and the United Republic of Cameroon; integrated area approaches, such as those under way in India, Oman and Pakistan, helped to focus on intrasectoral liaison and joint planning. Assistance was provided for regular evaluation of PHC programmes and, where necessary, for reorientation and restructuring of services, as in Angola, Ecuador, Lesotho and the United Republic of Tanzania.

As part of its PHC programmes, UNICEF included an essential drugs component. For example, jointly with WHO, UNICEF undertook a $30-million project for the United Republic of Tanzania to provide a regular supply of drug kits for community health workers at clinics. Each kit was packaged to meet the particular needs of the area and designed to ensure an adequate supply of essential drugs for up to three months.

The Fund supported diarrhoeal diseases control programmes in 22 countries and supplied more than 40 with oral rehydration salts for home treatment. Approximately 25 million packets were distributed and assistance was given for local production and packaging of another 25 million.

The Fund also supported related programmes in immunization, health education, monitoring of child growth, and water and sanitation. Under the WHO-assisted immunization programme, it supplied vaccines against tuberculosis, diphtheria, tetanus, typhoid, measles and poliomyelitis to approximately 80 countries in Asia, Africa and the Middle East. It additionally provided the necessary cold-chain equipment (refrigerators, cold boxes, transport) and assisted in their maintenance as well as in maintenance training. An emerging part of UNICEF involvement was participation in national evaluations of immunization programmes which helped to determine reasons for low coverage in some areas.

UNICEF finances

Despite severe contraints on resources available for international development assistance, the financial position of UNICEF improved significantly during 1982 due to increased contributions, so that, for the first time in four years, its income exceeded expenditure.[1] Total income was $378 million (including $41 million for the Lebanon emergency and reconstruction programme), a 30 per cent increase over 1981, while total expenditure was $289 million ($75 million in cash, $138 million in supplies, and $76 million in programme support and administration), a decrease of approximately 1.4 per cent.

In 1982, virtually all major donors increased their contributions to the Fund, with Italy, which had quadrupled its contribution to $10 million, becoming the second largest contributor of overall multiyear commitments. In terms of general resources, the Arab Gulf Programme for the United Nations Development Organizations, a new major source of funding, ranked second and Italy fourth.

The rate of increase in cash balances in 1982 was slower than had been envisaged in the year's financial plan. As at the end of December, general resources cash balances were $14 million, against the planned level of $33 million. An estimated $14 million of the difference was due to the strengthened exchange value of the United States dollar; a further factor was the phasing of payments by donors for adopted projects according to implementation rather than in the year of pledge. None the less, general resources cash balances increased by $9 million over the very low 1981 level. In addition, supplementary funds income in 1982 was higher than had been anticipated.

Report. [1]UNICEF Board, E/1983/21.

Financial plan for 1982-1985

The UNICEF financial plan for 1982-1985, set out in the medium-term work plan, had projected a 1982 income of $385 million, compared to the actual income of $378 million. The annual income projections for the next three years were $410 million, $450 million and $500 million. Projection levels on expenditure were kept lower to allow for liquidity build-up: $322 million for 1982, compared to the actual expenditure of $289 million, $354 million for 1983, $408 million for 1984 and $465 million for 1985.

The planned programme commitments from general resources for 1982 totalled $226.2 million, approved by the Executive Board at its May session[1] on the recommendation of its Programme Committee. Also approved were 36 "noted" projects, valued at $252 million, for financing through specific-purpose contributions, including two large projects of $100 million, already pledged, for nutrition and essential drugs. Planned programme and budget commitments totalled $383 million for 1983, $278 million for 1984 and $497 million for 1985.

The Executive Director introduced the medium-term work plan as reflecting severe financial stringencies imposed by the prevailing economic recession. He stressed that the income projections were based on identified sources and firm pledges for 1982-1983 and on cautious estimates for 1984-1985. The Board found the projections to be realistic.

Report. [1]UNICEF Board, E/1982/17.

Contributions

In its resolution of 28 July 1982 on the report of the Executive Board of UNICEF,[3] the Economic and Social Council commended the UNICEF Executive Director and secretariat for their energetic and imaginative efforts to enlarge the Fund's income, and expressed appreciation to those Governments that had responded to the Fund's needs. It appealed to all Governments to increase their contributions, if possible on a multiyear basis, so as to enable the Fund in the prevailing global economic situation to strengthen its response to the urgent needs of children in developing countries.

The General Assembly, in a resolution of 20 December on the Fund,[4] took essentially the same action, but in addition appealed especially to those Governments whose contributions might not reflect their capacity to contribute to increase their contributions, preferably to the general resources.

The original 18-nation text on which the Assembly resolution was based[1] would have commended the Executive Director and secretariat simply for their efforts to enlarge the Fund's income and would have directed its appeal in general to all Governments to increase their regular contributions.

The contributions received in or pledged for 1982 to the UNICEF general resources and supplementary funds totalled $351,757,337, after a deduction of $539,403 in adjustments to prior years' income. Of this amount, $298,417,656 came from Governments and intergovernmental agencies outside the United Nations, $45,452,863 from non-governmental sources, and $7,886,818 from the United Nations (see table below).[2]

Draft resolution withdrawn. [1]Bangladesh, Belgium, Bhutan, China, Denmark, Finland, France, India, Lebanon, Nepal, Netherlands, Nigeria, Norway, Sweden, United Kingdom, United States, Venezuela, Yugoslavia, A/C.2/37/L.87.
Report. [2]Board of Auditors, and financial statements, A/38/5/Add.2.
Resolutions (1982). [3]ESC: 1982/51, 28 July. [4]GA: 37/231, paras. 5-7, 20 Dec.

CONTRIBUTIONS TO UNICEF
(INCLUDING GENERAL RESOURCES AND SUPPLEMENTARY FUNDS)
(as at 31 December 1982; in US dollar equivalent)

Country or organization	Received in or pledged for 1982 Governmental	Received in or pledged for 1982 Non-governmental	Pledged for 1983 Governmental	Country or organization	Received in or pledged for 1982 Governmental	Received in or pledged for 1982 Non-governmental	Pledged for 1983 Governmental
Afghanistan	30,000	—	30,000	Central African Republic	25,568	—	—
Algeria	150,789	220	142,500	Chile	235,000	—	150,000
Antigua	301	—	—	China	270,000	—	300,000
Argentina	90,193	301	—	Colombia	431,625	51,023	—
Australia	11,744,282	464,732	3,632,075	Congo	14,610	290	7,003
Austria	2,022,781	290,712	979,802	Costa Rica	11,020	—	—
Bahamas	2,960	—	—	Cuba	139,699	—	117,730
Bahrain	7,500	526	15,000	Cyprus	—	7,343	—
Bangladesh	16,293	105	6,000	Czechoslovakia	81,037	—	81,037
Barbados	5,000	—	5,000	Democratic Yemen	5,819	—	6,400
Belgium	1,179,724	397,076	714,286	Denmark	19,939,229	70,587	16,673,184
Benin	11,836	—	2,000	Djibouti	2,000	—	2,000
Bhutan	2,530	—	3,030	Dominica	499	—	—
Bolivia	16,000	—	16,000	Ecuador	27,066	—	51,051
Botswana	9,007	—	9,174	Egypt	72,107	—	72,107
Brazil	122,222	353	100,000	Ethiopia	49,215	60	42,275
British Virgin Islands	149	—	—	Fiji	2,000	—	2,000
Bulgaria	58,685	—	—	Finland	2,912,304	1,083,431	3,636,364
Burma	215,115	—	50,374	France	1,740,609	5,251,329	3,671,329
Burundi	1,675	—	3,350	Gambia	5,045	—	—
Byelorussian SSR	78,892	—	75,503	German Democratic Republic	117,155	—	110,236
Canada	12,192,650	5,489,645	—				

Country or organization	Received in or pledged for 1982 Governmental	Non-governmental	Pledged for 1983 Governmental
Germany, Federal Republic of	6,246,170	3,423,387	925,000
Ghana	—	105	—
Greece	130,000	2,487	135,000
Grenada	992	—	—
Guatemala	37,335	5	30,000
Guinea	38,838	—	—
Guyana	4,508	—	—
Holy See	1,000	—	1,000
Honduras	20,000	—	—
Hong Kong	16,750	—	—
Hungary	21,429	422	21,079
Iceland	21,061	—	21,350
India	1,945,355	6,784	1,691,332
Indonesia	670,096	132	—
Iran	10,000	—	—
Iraq	121,600	—	—
Ireland	316,456	119,147	—
Israel	50,000	—	50,000
Italy	31,102,989	287,853	21,089,219
Ivory Coast	63,636	57	—
Jamaica	9,551	195	9,551
Japan	9,200,608	5,454,783	10,200,000
Jordan	27,972	—	—
Kenya	23,963	2	23,318
Kuwait	350,000	—	200,000
Lao People's Democratic Republic	5,000	—	5,000
Lebanon	9,334,507	1,653	50,000
Lesotho	2,100	—	2,500
Liberia	20,000	4,003	—
Libyan Arab Jamahiriya	1,000,000	40	—
Luxembourg	17,347	27,324	17,347
Madagascar	7,895	—	—
Malawi	3,660	—	3,777
Malaysia	98,400	8	78,000
Maldives	3,000	—	3,000
Malta	5,016	—	—
Mauritius	3,794	—	—
Mexico	290,263	34,055	267,637
Monaco	3,478	—	3,497
Mongolia	3,500	—	3,500
Morocco	100,000	—	100,000
Mozambique	5,026	—	—
Nepal	8,015	100	—
Netherlands	18,048,783	1,234,743	—
New Zealand	538,462	23,450	—
Nicaragua	—	1,795	—
Nigeria	270,344	—	439,883
Norway	19,000,716	174,989	15,492,958
Oman	1,050,000	—	50,000
Pakistan	130,200	9	59,800
Panama	22,000	—	22,000
Philippines	516,969	5	413,700
Poland	78,930	—	78,930
Portugal	15,000	5,536	15,000
Qatar	200,000	—	200,000
Republic of Korea	147,000	—	147,000
Romania	13,636	—	13,636
Rwanda	8,154	—	4,000

SOURCES: A/38/5/Add.2 and UNICEF.

Country or organization	Received in or pledged for 1982 Governmental	Non-governmental	Pledged for 1983 Governmental
St. Kitts–Nevis–Anguilla	749	—	—
Saint Vincent and the Grenadines	749	—	—
San Marino	4,625	62	—
Saudi Arabia	7,000,000	5,461	1,000,000
Senegal	30,303	1,691	3,000
Seychelles	1,000	—	—
Singapore	1,395	476	—
Solomon Islands	500	—	500
Somalia	3,987	—	—
Spain	259,920	1,589,609	282,715
Sri Lanka	12,568	35	10,766
Sudan	35,000	—	35,000
Swaziland	5,763	—	—
Sweden	30,216,957	112,889	22,351,352
Switzerland	7,082,151	2,081,846	4,478,447
Syrian Arab Republic	25,641	—	—
Thailand	297,871	14,363	203,352
Togo	8,746	—	—
Trinidad and Tobago	10,417	—	10,417
Tunisia	60,412	—	38,844
Turkey	168,501	—	169,492
Uganda	1,923	1,068	1,786
Ukrainian SSR	157,784	—	157,007
USSR	852,034	—	815,436
United Arab Emirates	799,498	58,977	—
United Kingdom	10,341,031	504,399	—
United Republic of Cameroon	76,164	—	72,829
United Republic of Tanzania	29,289	7,155	29,812
United States	54,600,000	14,209,086	—
Venezuela	200,000	13,272	—
Viet Nam	4,398	88	5,000
Yemen	22,298	—	—
Yugoslavia	250,000	9,673	—
Zaire	13,000	—	—
Zambia	19,502	—	—
Zimbabwe	5,031	4,188	32,550
Subtotal	268,020,964	42,525,141	112,274,129
Intergovernmental agencies			
Arab Fund for Economic and Social Development	318,750	—	—
Arab Gulf Programme for UN Development Organizations	24,250,000	2,973,715	—
European Community	3,858,010	—	—
OPEC	2,365,000		
Subtotal	30,791,760	2,973,715	—
United Nations system	7,977,390	7,771	—
Adjustments to prior years' income	(485,639)	(53,764)	—
Total	306,304,474	45,452,863	112,274,129

Accounts

1980

On the recommendation of its Committee on Administration and Finance, the UNICEF Executive Board, at its May 1982 session,[1] noted the observations of the United Nations Board of Auditors and the Advisory Committee on Administrative and Budgetary Questions (ACABQ) on the 1980 UNICEF financial report and the financial report on the Greeting Card Operation (GCO) for the 1980/81 season. It also noted the Executive Director's response to those observations. The Executive Director, in a December 1981 report,[2] had stated that modifications to the accounting system were being made as suggested by the Auditors, but that suggestions on GCO budgetary practices needed to be studied. He also made recommendations on administrative issues.

Report. [1]UNICEF Board, E/1982/17.
Yearbook reference. [2]1981, p. 1008.

1981

Following an audit of the financial reports of UNICEF for 1981[4]—noted and submitted by the

Executive Board in May 1982[3] on the recommendation of its Committee on Administration and Finance—and of GCO for the 1980/81 season, the Board of Auditors made a series of recommendations.[2] These called for improvements in budgetary control for field offices; field office management; project monitoring; and procurement procedures, particularly the inclusion of quality controls and a penalty clause for late delivery in contracts and compliance with regulations on competitive bidding. In connection with matters raised in the 1980 report, the Auditors noted that certain obligations and expenditures continued to be excluded from the 1981 GCO financial statement and that arrangements for hiring manual labour staff for the UNICEF Packing and Assembly Centre at Copenhagen, Denmark,[6] had yet to be formalized.

In a September 1982 report to the General Assembly on financial and Auditors' reports,[1] ACABQ noted the Auditors' comments and UNICEF response. It agreed with the Office of Legal Affairs that, on the question of the penalty clause for late delivery, specification of damages in the event of a breach of contract should be considered on an individual basis. ACABQ also welcomed UNICEF action in establishing procedures to broaden competitive bidding so as to ensure procurement of the best products at the lowest possible cost.

The financial reports were accepted by the Assembly in a resolution of 16 November,[5] when it accepted various 1981 United Nations financial reports and accounts and endorsed the Auditors' opinions, concurred with the ACABQ observations and requested the executive heads to take such remedial action as might be required by the Auditors.

Reports. [1]ACABQ, A/37/443; [2]Board of Auditors, A/37/5/Add.2; [3]UNICEF Board, E/1982/17; [4]UNICEF Director, E/ICEF/AB/L.239.
Resolution (1982). [5]GA: 37/12, 16 Nov.
Yearbook reference. [6]1981, p. 1008.

Organizational questions

Greeting Card Operation

During the 1981 GCO season (1 May 1981–30 April 1982),[1] 115 million cards, 497,000 calendars, 292,000 packs of stationery and other related items were sold in 137 countries. Compared to the previous season, 2 million fewer cards were sold; gross proceeds from all sales totalled $46.8 million, a decrease of 0.9 per cent; operational expenditures were $18.7 million, or 4.1 per cent less; and net income was $16.7 million, or 9.2 per cent lower ($9.6 million below the projected revenue for 1981). The decreased income was due both to a lower volume of sales and to a loss of $2.2 million from exchange rate fluctuations.

Reproduction rights were given by 183 artists and museums from 33 countries. Sixty-nine designs were used for calendars and 165 designs for cards.

Report. [1]UNICEF Director, E/ICEF/AB/L.245.

1982/83 budget

On the recommendation of its Committee on Administration and Finance, the Executive Board, at its May 1982 session,[2] approved the budget estimates for the 1982 GCO season (1 May 1982–30 April 1983) and advance costs for the 1983 season, as recommended by the Executive Director.[1] Gross operational expenditures were estimated at $25.8 million, and gross revenue at $50.2 million. The Board welcomed the secretariat's intention to revise the GCO budget format so as to reflect more fully the commercial nature of the operation.

Recommendations. [1]UNICEF Director, E/ICEF/AB/L.241 & Corr.1.
Report. [2]UNICEF Board, E/1982/17.

Relations with NGOs

UNICEF continued to foster close relationships with non-governmental organizations (NGOs), an increasingly important channel of advocacy for the Fund's programmes and fund-raising. In 1982, the membership of the NGO Committee on UNICEF rose to 134 international professional and voluntary groups, involved directly or indirectly with children and holding consultative status with the Fund. A roster of international and national correspondents, particularly from developing countries, was also growing. In all, some 400 organizations participated in UNICEF activities and shared information through the Fund's NGO liaison offices in New York and Geneva.

This larger, more diverse constituency allowed for greater concentration on issue-oriented programming (emergency situations, primary health care, water and sanitation) and thus for a more effective response by UNICEF to NGO needs and requests.

Public information

In 1982, UNICEF strengthened international and national capabilities in project support communications. In partnership with local media and communications agencies, this involved support for advocacy campaigns aimed at changing policy in favour of children, such as campaigns to promote breast-feeding and focus attention on possibilities for reducing infant mortality. A wide variety of mass media materials produced for this endeavour included posters, press advertisements, radio spots, cartoon stickers, and reference texts and training manuals.

In an effort to disseminate the work of UNICEF its annual report, *The State of the World's Children 1982-1983*, was given extensive radio, television and newspaper coverage, directly reaching some 12,000 newspapers published in 20 languages. Beginning with the *1982 UNICEF Annual Report*, it was redesigned to include profiles on selected development situations and more graphic presentation. The first French edition of the quarterly *UNICEF News* was published during the year.

Information support was also provided for fundraising activities, including special events such as a soccer game televised from the United States, a number of film *premières*, benefit concerts held in Austria and Spain, and exhibits on certain aspects of UNICEF work mounted in Europe. The Goodwill Ambassadors for UNICEF—Danny Kaye, Liv Ullmann and Peter Ustinov—continued to draw attention to the needs of children during tours to several countries.

In addition to producing or co-producing audiovisual materials for the purposes of advocacy, fundraising and development education, UNICEF distributed during the year three new feature documentaries—titled "Herbal Medicine: Fact or Fiction", "A Child's Horizon" (on childhood blindness) and "A Kind of Paradise" (on the state of children in the Caribbean)—and some 2,000 copies of films in 10 languages.

Increase in membership of the Executive Board

The General Assembly, acting without vote on 28 April 1982,[5] enlarged the membership of the UNICEF Executive Board from 30 to 41 members. It determined the distribution of 40 of the seats among the five regional groups, as well as the rotation among them of the remaining seat, and requested the Economic and Social Council to elect the additional 11 members at its first 1982 regular session.

This resolution was recommended by the Council in a decision of 22 April,[1] adopted without vote and transmitted to the Assembly by a letter of the same date from the Council President.[2]

The enlargement of the Board had been discussed by it since 1980. On 16 April 1982, at a special session held on the question,[4] the Board reached a consensus on a draft resolution, which its Chairman transmitted to the Council President by a letter of 21 April[3] and which served as the basis for the text adopted by the Assembly.

The additional 11 members were elected by the Council on 6 May (see APPENDIX III).

Decision (1982). [1]ESC: 1982/111, 22 Apr., text following.
Letters. [2]ESC President, 22 Apr., A/36/872; [3]UNICEF Board Chairman, 21 Apr., E/1982/55.
Report. [4]UNICEF Board, E/ICEF/694.
Resolution (1982). [5]GA: 36/244, 28 Apr., text following.
Meeting records. ESC: E/1982/SR.13 (22 Apr.). GA: A/36/PV.110 (28 Apr.).

Economic and Social Council decision 1982/111

Adopted without vote

Draft by UNICEF Board (E/1982/55, annex); agenda item 1.

Enlargement of the Executive Board of the United Nations Children's Fund

At its 13th plenary meeting, on 22 April 1982, the Council decided to recommend to the General Assembly the adoption of the following draft resolution:

[Text as in General Assembly resolution 36/244 below.]

General Assembly resolution 36/244

28 April 1982   Meeting 110   Adopted without vote

Draft recommended by Economic and Social Council (decision 1982/111); agenda item 70 *(h)*.

Enlargement of the Executive Board of the United Nations Children's Fund

The General Assembly,

Convinced that a strengthened and expanded United Nations Children's Fund necessitates the increased participation of Member States in the work of the Executive Board of the Fund,

Recalling its resolution 417(V) of 1 December 1950, which established the importance of constituting the Executive Board with due regard to geographical distribution and to the representation of the major contributing and recipient countries,

Noting that the composition of the Executive Board was last considered by the General Assembly at its eleventh session, when the Assembly adopted resolution 1038(XI) of 7 December 1956, replacing paragraph 6 *(a)* of resolution 417(V),

1. *Decides*, without prejudice to arrangements which may be made in other bodies, to enlarge the membership of the Executive Board of the United Nations Children's Fund to forty-one members, to be elected from States Members of the United Nations or members of specialized agencies or of the International Atomic Energy Agency, subject to the following conditions:

   (a) Nine seats for African States;

   (b) Nine seats for Asian States;

   (c) Four seats for Eastern European States;

   (d) Six seats for Latin American States;

   (e) Twelve seats for Western European and other States;

   (f) One seat to be rotated among the five regional groups, in the following order:

   (i)   African States;

   (ii)   Latin American States;

   (iii) Asian States;

   (iv)   Western European and other States;

   (v)   Eastern European States

   (g) Without prejudice to the terms of the States already elected, elections to these forty-one seats shall be for a term of three years and retiring members shall be eligible for re-election;

2. *Requests* the Economic and Social Council to elect, at its first regular session of 1982, the additional eleven members of the Executive Board.

Draft declaration on adoption and foster placement

By a resolution of 16 December 1982,[3] the General Assembly, acting without vote, requested the Secretary-General to circulate to Member States, for their views, the draft Declaration on Social and Legal Principles relating to the Protection and Welfare of Children, with Special Reference to Foster Placement and Adoption Nationally and Internationally, as well as the conclusions contained in his 1980 report[5] on the draft.

The text was approved, also without vote, on 3 December, by the Sixth (Legal) Committee following an oral revision by Sweden, which had introduced the text also on behalf of Colombia, Iceland, Norway and Uruguay.

In its consideration of the item, the Assembly had before it an October report by the Secretary-General[2] reproducing the comments of 40 Member States on the draft Declaration, submitted in response to a 1979 request of the Economic and Social Council.[4] Also before it were the comments of the Holy See,[1] expressing gratification with the draft Declaration's explicit recognition of the family as the best environment for the welfare of children and drawing attention, therefore, to the duty of Governments to support families in difficulty so that they could bring up their own children. In the event of adoption or foster placement, the Holy See said, account should be taken of the child's rights and those of the adoptive and natural parents; the important role of private charitable agencies, including churches; and the child's cultural and religious heritage.

Comments. [1]Holy See, A/C.6/37/6.
Report. [2]S-G, A/37/146.
Resolution (1982). [3]GA: 37/115, 16 Dec., text following.
Resolution (prior). [4]ESC: 1979/28, 9 May 1979 (YUN 1979, p. 769).
Yearbook reference. [5]1980, p. 777.
Meeting records. GA: 6th Committee, A/C.6/37/SR.27, *60, 62* (26 Oct. & 2, 3 Dec.); plenary, A/37/PV.107 (16 Dec.).

General Assembly resolution 37/115

16 December 1982   Meeting 107   Adopted without vote

Approved by Sixth Committee (A/37/710) without vote, 3 December (meeting 62); 5-nation draft (A/C.6/37/L.23), orally revised; agenda item 128.

Sponsors: Colombia, Iceland, Norway, Sweden, Uruguay.

Draft Declaration on Social and Legal Principles relating to the Protection and Welfare of Children, with Special Reference to Foster Placement and Adoption Nationally and Internationally

The General Assembly,

Recalling its resolution 36/167 of 16 December 1981, whereby it decided, *inter alia*, that appropriate measures should be taken to finalize the draft Declaration on Social and Legal Principles relating to the Protection and Welfare of Children, with Special Reference to Foster Placement and Adoption Nationally and Internationally,

Noting, in this connection, the current efforts of the Commission on Human Rights to elaborate a draft Convention on the Rights of the Child,

Taking note of the decisions taken by the Economic and Social Council on the draft Declaration on Social and Legal Principles relating to the Protection and Welfare of Children, with Special Reference to Foster Placement and Adoption Nationally and Internationally,

Bearing in mind the reports of the Secretary-General, of 8 September 1980 and 19 October 1982, which contain the views of Member States on the text of the draft Declaration,

Noting that section VI of the first of the above-mentioned reports contains some proposed amendments and reformulations of certain articles based on comments by Member States,

Fully aware of the sovereign right of Governments to define their national and international policies as regards the protection and welfare of children, including foster placement and adoption,

Recognizing that it is the reponsibility of Governments to determine the adequacy of their national services for children and to recognize those children whose needs are not being met by existing services,

Noting the usefulness of regional co-operation in matters regarding the well-being of children,

Recognizing that the best child welfare is good family welfare and that when family care is unavailable or inappropriate, substitute family care should be considered, in conformity with national legislation,

Convinced that adoption of the draft Declaration will promote the well-being of children with special needs,

Noting that the further views of Member States on the draft Declaration as well as on the amendments and reformulations of certain articles contained in section VI of the report of the Secretary-General would provide helpful guidance for further efforts to elaborate a generally agreed draft Declaration,

1.   *Requests* the Secretary-General:

(a) To circulate to Member States, for their views, the draft Declaration on Social and Legal Principles relating to the Protection and Welfare of Children, with Special Reference to Foster Placement and Adoption Nationally and Internationally as well as the conclusions contained in the report of the Secretary-General;

(b) To submit to the General Assembly at its thirty-eighth session a report containing the views of Member States;

2.   *Decides* to resume consideration of this item at its thirty-eighth session and to determine at that session the most appropriate course of further action.

Youth

In a December 1982 report on the situation of youth in the 1980s,[1] prepared in response to a 1979 request of the Economic and Social Council,[2] the Secretary-General stated that the world youth population, defined as persons aged between 15 and 24 years, was currently estimated at 857 million, or 20 per cent of the total population. Over 75 per cent of them lived in developing countries, and projections for the remainder of the century indicated that the youth population would continue to rise in those countries and decline in developed nations. Current trends in practically all regions indicated that there would be dramatically increased numbers of unemployed young people.

Young people in the 1980s were faced with an economic recession and rising unemployment, coupled with social changes of family disintegration, rapid urbanization and industrialization, and conflict between traditional and modern values. As a major constituent of the population flow from rural to urban areas, of the unemployed, and of the insufficiently or inappropriately educated, youth was severely affected by the inequities of the prevailing economic order. Juvenile delinquency, crime and widespread drug abuse were additional problems of young people linked to the economic recession.

According to the Secretary-General, a more equitable distribution of the fruits of progress through implementation of the new international economic order, participation of youth in national development, and education and vocational training appropriate to available work would help youth perform a constructive social role and face a future that, for the first time since the end of the Second World War, seemed one of shrinking opportunities. In addition, the promotion of international understanding and peace would be of special service to youth. The Secretary-General concluded that action on behalf of youth needed to be adapted to the specific needs of each country. Action by the United Nations system and its member States was required to analyse the situation of youth around the world and to propose practical programmes at the international, regional and national levels. Preparation for the International Youth Year (1985) (IYY) provided an opportunity for increasing the realization among member States and non-governmental organizations of the seriousness of the problem that would be confronting youth and societies in the 1980s.

Report. [1]S-G, E/1983/3.
Resolution. [2]ESC: 1979/16, 9 May 1979 (YUN 1979, p. 986).

Activities of the UN system

Responding to a May 1981 request of the Economic and Social Council,[4] the Secretary-General issued a report in March 1982 on co-ordination and information in the field of youth,[1] in which he presented the views of United Nations bodies and specialized agencies on the needs and situation of youth. They agreed that adoption of policy measures aimed at the fullest possible mobilization and integration of youth in development should be among the primary objectives of inter-agency collaboration. The report described arrangements made to ensure co-ordination of efforts, through an informal inter-agency working group, within the United Nations system and to implement the Specific Programme of Measures and Activities for IYY.[5]

Acting without vote on 4 May 1982,[2] the Council endorsed the conclusions of the Secretary-General and requested that, in the documentation to be submitted to the June session of the Advisory Committee for the International Youth Year, he take account of the ideas expressed for improving co-ordination and information activities on youth. The Council invited all United Nations bodies and intergovernmental, as well as non-governmental, organizations to pay particular attention to such improvement.

This resolution originated in a 27-nation text introduced by Romania in the Council's Second (Social) Committee, which approved it without vote on 23 April.

The General Assembly, in a resolution of 3 December on IYY,[3] requested the Secretary-General to continue, through communications media at his disposal, to give widespread publicity to United Nations activities in the field of youth and to increase the dissemination of information on youth.

Report. [1]S-G, E/1982/36.
Resolutions (1982). [2]ESC: 1982/28, 4 May, text following.
[3]GA: 37/48, para. 8, 3 Dec.
Resolution (prior). [4]ESC: 1981/25, 6 May 1981 (YUN 1981, p. 1016).
Yearbook reference. [5]1981, p. 1019.
Meeting record. ESC: E/1982/SR.23 (4 May).

Economic and Social Council resolution 1982/28

4 May 1982   Meeting 23   Adopted without vote

Approved by Second Committee (E/1982/58) without vote, 23 April (meeting 7); 27-nation draft (E/1982/C.2/L.2); agenda item 11.

Sponsors: Algeria, Argentina, Bangladesh, Colombia, Djibouti, Egypt, France, Germany, Federal Republic of, Greece, Indonesia, Japan, Madagascar, Mali, Mexico, Morocco, Nepal, Nigeria, Pakistan, Philippines, Romania, Rwanda, Saint Lucia, Senegal, Syrian Arab Republic, Venezuela, Yugoslavia, Zaire.

Co-ordination and information in the field of youth

The Economic and Social Council,

Recalling its resolutions 1979/27 of 9 May 1979, 1980/25 of 2 May 1980 and 1981/25 of 6 May 1981 on co-ordination and information in the field of youth,

Recalling also resolution 34/151 of 17 December 1979, by which the General Assembly decided to designate 1985 as International Youth Year: Participation, Development, Peace, and resolution 36/28 of 13 November 1981, by which the Assembly endorsed the Specific Programme of Measures and Activities to be undertaken prior to and during the International Youth Year,

Noting that the Advisory Committee for the International Youth Year will hold its second session at Vienna from 14 to 23 June 1982,

Considering that the implementation of the Specific Programme of Measures and Activities to be undertaken prior to and during the International Youth Year will contribute to intensifying and improving the co-ordination of the activities of the United Nations and specialized agencies relating to youth,

Convinced of the importance of giving widespread publicity to the activities of the United Nations in the field of youth and of increasing the dissemination of information about youth, especially in the context of the preparations for the International Youth Year,

Recalling the conclusions contained in the report of the Committee for Programme and Co-ordination on the work of its twenty-first session regarding the cross-organizational programme analysis of the youth activities of the United Nations system,

Taking note of the report of the Secretary-General on co-ordination and information in the field of youth,

1. *Endorses* the conclusions contained in the report of the Secretary-General on co-ordination and information in the field of youth;

2. *Requests* the Secretary-General to take into account the ideas expressed in the Economic and Social Council on ways and means for improving the activities of co-ordination and information in the field of youth in the preparation of the documentation to be submitted to the Advisory Committee for the International Youth Year at its second session;

3. *Invites* all United Nations bodies, specialized agencies, regional commissions and other international intergovernmental organizations, as well as non-governmental organizations concerned, to pay particular attention to the improvement of co-ordination and information in the field of youth in the context of the implementation of the Specific Programme of Measures and Activities to be undertaken prior to and during the International Youth Year;

4. *Decides* to consider at its first regular session of 1983, on the basis of a report of the Secretary-General, the progress achieved in co-ordination and information in the field of youth.

Strengthening channels of communication between youth and the United Nations

In a September 1982 report to the General Assembly,[2] submitted in accordance with a November 1981 Assembly request,[5] the Secretary-General reviewed implementation of the guidelines adopted in 1977[4] and 1981[6] for the improvement of communication channels between the United Nations and youth and youth organizations.

Among United Nations measures to reach out to young people and their organizations were participation in and organization of meetings on youth, distribution of documentation, promotion of exchange of information through United

Nations publications, such as the quarterly *Youth Information Bulletin*,[1] and replies to oral and written queries from youth. While reporting increased interest in youth issues and recognition of young people's contribution to the solution of world problems, the Secretary-General said that the United Nations had not achieved its target of generating among young people awareness concerning the Organization's work. The Secretary-General observed a lack of balance between United Nations efforts to reach out to young people and the feedback from them. He therefore recommended that additional channels of communication be sought, such as educational institutions and the mass media, so as to reach the largest possible number of young people.

By a resolution adopted without vote on 3 December,[3] the Assembly requested Member States, specialized agencies and other intergovernmental organizations, as well as the Advisory Committee for IYY, to promote further implementation of the 1977 and 1981 guidelines. The Assembly asked the Secretary-General to give full support to inter-agency co-operation in information activities in the context of IYY, to develop additional channels of communication and to improve the functioning of existing ones. It invited Member States, specialized agencies, regional commissions, intergovernmental organizations and non-governmental youth organizations to communicate and offer suggestions for further development of communication channels; it also invited youth and youth organizations to contribute to the formulation of United Nations policies and programmes on youth.

The 33-nation text, introduced in the Assembly's Third (Social, Humanitarian and Cultural) Committee by Egypt, was approved without vote by the Committee on 15 November.

Publication. [1]*Youth Information Bulletin*, Nos. 42-45 (quarterly).
Report. [2]S-G, A/37/401.
Resolution (1982). [3]GA: 37/50, 3 Dec., text following.
Resolutions (prior). GA: [4]32/135, annex, 16 Dec. 1977 (YUN 1977, p. 801); [5]36/17, 9 Nov. 1981 (YUN 1981, p. 1017); [6]*ibid.*, annex, (p. 1018).
Meeting records. GA: 3rd Committee, A/C.3/37/SR.14-23, 25, 26, *29, 42* (18 Oct.–15 Nov.); plenary, A/37/PV.90 (3 Dec.).

General Assembly resolution 37/50

3 December 1982   Meeting 90   Adopted without vote

Approved by Third Committee (A/37/630) without vote, 15 November (meeting 42); 33-nation draft (A/C.3/37/L.23); agenda item 81.

Sponsors: Bangladesh, Bolivia, Chile, Costa Rica, Denmark, Dominican Republic, Ecuador, Egypt, El Salvador, Fiji, Greece, Guatemala, Kenya, Malta, Morocco, Nepal, Netherlands, Nicaragua, Nigeria, Norway, Pakistan, Philippines, Romania, Rwanda, Sudan, Suriname, Sweden, Togo, United Republic of Cameroon, Uruguay, Venezuela, Zaire, Zambia.

Channels of communication between the United Nations and youth and youth organizations

The General Assembly,

Recalling its resolutions 32/135 of 16 December 1977 and 36/17 of 9 November 1981, in which it adopted guidelines for the improvement of the channels of communication between the United Nations and youth and youth organizations,

Recalling also Economic and Social Council resolutions 1980/25 of 2 May 1980 and 1981/25 of 6 May 1981 concerning co-ordination and information in the field of youth,

Taking note of the report of the Secretary-General of 8 September 1982,

Convinced of the need to improve further the efforts of the United Nations and the specialized agencies with regard to the participation of youth in achieving the objectives of the Charter of the United Nations,

Equally convinced of the valuable contribution that youth can make in promoting co-operation among States and in implementing the new international economic order and the International Development Strategy for the Third United Nations Development Decade,

Bearing in mind the importance of the existence of channels of communication between the United Nations and youth and youth organizations for the proper information of youth and youth organizations and their effective participation in the United Nations and the specialized agencies at the national, regional and international levels,

Taking note of the efforts in inter-agency co-operation to promote and strengthen channels of communication between the United Nations and youth and youth organizations within the context of International Youth Year: Participation, Development, Peace,

Convinced that the existence and the proper functioning of channels of communication between the United Nations and youth and youth organizations form a basic prerequisite of the active involvement of young people and thus of the successful preparation for, celebration of and follow-up to International Youth Year,

1. *Requests* Member States, specialized agencies and other intergovernmental organizations to promote, in co-operation with youth organizations in consultative status with the Economic and Social Council and other youth organizations concerned, further implementation of the guidelines adopted in General Assembly resolution 32/135 and the additional guidelines adopted in its resolution 36/17;

2. *Requests* the Advisory Committee for the International Youth Year to continue to promote the implementation of the additional guidelines, together with the guidelines adopted in resolution 32/135, during the preparation for and celebration of International Youth Year;

3. *Requests* the Secretary-General to give full co-operation and support to inter-agency co-operation and co-ordination in promotional and information activities within the context of International Youth Year;

4. *Invites* Member States, specialized agencies, regional commissions, intergovernmental organizations and non-governmental youth organizations to communicate and further promote the guidelines and additional guidelines for the improvement of channels of communication between the United Nations and youth and youth organizations and to offer additional suggestions for their further development;

5. *Requests* the Secretary-General to give special attention to developing additional channels of communication through such means as the mass media and educational institutions in order to reach the largest possible number of young people in different regions of the world;

6. *Invites* youth and youth organizations to act as disseminators of and contributors to the formulation of United Nations policies and programmes directed to youth;

7. *Requests* the Secretary-General to strengthen and improve the functioning of existing channels of communication between the United Nations and youth and youth organizations, such as the quarterly publication *Youth Information Bulletin* produced by the Secretariat;

8. *Requests* the Secretary-General, on the basis of the reports of Member States, specialized agencies and other intergovernmental organizations, as well as non-governmental youth organizations, to report to the General Assembly at its thirty-eighth session on the implementation of the guidelines and additional guidelines for the improvement of the channels of communication between the United Nations and youth and youth organizations, and to include information on measures being taken to strengthen those channels of communication.

Preparations for International Youth Year (1985)

In accordance with a November 1981 General Assembly request,[7] the Secretary-General submitted in May 1982 a progress report on implementation of the Specific Programme of Measures and

Activities for IYY by Member States, United Nations bodies and intergovernmental and nongovernmental organizations.[2] The report outlined current trends in implementation, as well as major United Nations activities including: participation in establishing regional and national plans of action on youth issues and special funds to implement them; development of youth-related schemes and projects, and mechanisms for their coordination; organization of special events celebrating youth and drawing attention to the Year; dissemination of information on policy and strategies for bringing youth into the mainstream of development; research and studies on specific youth problems; and information and promotional activities on the Year.

Among the conferences, meetings, seminars and workshops organized in 1982 were an inter-agency working group meeting and the *Ad Hoc* Interagency Consultation on Preparations for IYY (Vienna, Austria: 18 and 19 March; 10 and 11 June); an International Labour Organisation workshop on youth unemployment (Geneva, 13 and 14 May); an *ad hoc* regional meeting and a technical meeting of youth experts on the Year (Thailand: Bangkok, 23-26 November; Chiangmai, 29 November–5 December) organized by the Economic and Social Commission for Asia and the Pacific; and a meeting on the role of youth and changes in the social structure under the auspices of the Economic Commission for Latin America (November).

In conclusion, the report suggested further activities at the national, regional and international levels and proposed additional guidelines for implementation of the Programme in the areas of criminal justice and youth, disabled youth, young migrant workers and children of migrant workers, and young women.

Advisory Committee activities. At its second session, held at Vienna from 14 to 23 June 1982,[4] the Advisory Committee for IYY recommended that the Assembly consider organizing five regional meetings in 1983 and that it request the Secretary-General to consult Governments and interested organizations on the launching of a world-wide campaign for tree-planting during the Year.

The Committee requested the Secretary-General to transmit to all concerned a draft declaration on the rights and responsibilities of youth (appended to the Committee's report) and prepare a working document on comments received; to review his report on public information activities to highlight IYY in the light of the Committee's comments (see below); to report on Secretariat arrangements for observance of IYY, including making the Youth Unit within the United Nations Centre for Social Development and Humanitar-

ian Affairs (CSDHA) the secretariat for the Year; and to transmit periodically to Member States a list of international conferences connected with IYY. In addition, the Committee recommended that all States set up national co-ordinating committees for activities during the Year.

Other recommendations called for: government action to establish co-ordinating committees to prepare national plans of action for IYY and provide them with technical assistance and financial support, to encourage youth participation in those committees, and to mobilize the media for promotional activities on IYY; regional commission action to support preparations for IYY and to conduct research and studies on problems relating to the integration of youth in the development process, with special attention to the needs of specific groups; and action by all United Nations agencies to encourage governmental preparations for the Year's activities and to identify possible areas for collaboration in implementing decisions relating to it. Participation of Committee members in related activities was also recommended, as was the development of projects by CSDHA.

In regard to additional guidelines for implementing the Specific Programme, the Committee proposed that Governments and international organizations review their policies and programmes and report to CSDHA so as to enable it to suggest improvements and adjustments to the Programme. Other guidelines proposed were similar to the Secretary-General's proposals (see above), plus the suggestion that attention be given to the roles of youth for development and for peace.

General Assembly action. On 3 December,[5] the General Assembly endorsed the Advisory Committee's recommendations for the further implementation of the Programme for IYY and requested the Secretary-General to transmit them to all States and organizations concerned for early implementation. It invited States that had not done so to establish national co-ordinating committees or other forms of co-ordination for IYY, and stressed the importance of direct participation of youth organizations in activities organized for it at the local, national, regional and international levels. The Assembly requested the Secretary-General to take measures to ensure the success of the regional meetings devoted to IYY and the co-ordination of the Programme's implementation, and to convene the third session of the Advisory Committee during the first half of 1984. The Assembly appealed for additional voluntary contributions to supplement the funds provided by the United Nations regular budget for the costs of the Programme.

This resolution was adopted, without vote, on the recommendation of the Third Committee, which had approved the 88-nation draft, introduced by Romania, on 15 November by a recorded vote of 133 to 1.

An amendment, sponsored by the United States,[1] had been rejected by a recorded vote of 75 to 22, with 26 abstentions. The amendment, as orally revised by its sponsor and sub-amended by Australia, would have added an operative paragraph to the draft, authorizing the Secretary-General to implement the activities approved in the resolution without exceeding, during the current budget period, the level of resources approved in the 1982-1983 programme budget. The rejection of this amendment led the United States to cast the only vote against the resolution.

Although voting in favour in the Third Committee, Brazil said that application of the Advisory Committee's recommendations, as endorsed by the Assembly, would be contingent upon Brazil's examination of them, which had not been possible due to the late distribution of the report; it also stated that the recommended support and professional technical back-stopping to be provided by CSDHA for national and regional projects should be provided only at the request of States. As to the Committee's recommendation that an international instrument on youth rights and responsibilities be drawn up, the Netherlands felt it was unnecessary because existing international instruments already dealt with the rights of special groups such as youth.

Australia, concerned about the way in which the issue of financial implications had been handled, said it would have preferred adoption of the United States amendment. Also expressing support for the amendment, New Zealand stated that it wanted to place on record its concern at the continued tendency to overlook the need for financial stringency with regard to programmes, adding, however, that its concern in no way affected its support for the programmes. The Federal Republic of Germany said funding should be within budgetary resources or through voluntary contributions. The USSR said it acknowledged the work of the Secretariat to reduce required resources, but added that it could not accept the financial implications for CSDHA because the Secretariat was departing from the understanding reached by the Advisory Committee that its recommendations should not entail new requirements for the United Nations regular budget. The United Kingdom, which supported the Centre's work, also expressed concern at the financial implications.

In a further resolution of 3 December, on human rights of youth,[6] the Assembly requested the Advisory Committee to give full attention to the Assembly's 1981 resolution on the same topic[8] and to all relevant international human rights instruments in its preparation for IYY, particularly when elaborating recommendations.

For its consideration of the item on IYY, the Assembly had before it the Secretary-General's revised report on public information activities to highlight the Year,[3] submitted at the Advisory Committee's request (see above). The report outlined a core programme for implementation within available human and financial resources, proposed additional activities in case voluntary contributions for their implementation became available, identified target audiences and ways to reach them, outlined resource requirements, and proposed establishment of a Joint United Nations Information Committee task force to consider activities of particular interest to youth.

Owing to a lack of time, the report could not be considered by the Assembly in 1982; consequently, the Third Committee requested the Secretary-General to transmit it to the Committee on Information in 1983 for consideration.

Amendment rejected. [1]United States, A/C.3/37/L.39
Reports. S-G, [2]A/37/237, [3]A/37/348/Add.2; [4]S-G and Advisory Committee, A/37/348 & Add.1.
Resolutions (1982). GA, 3 Dec.: [5]37/48, text following; [6]37/49, para. 2.
Resolutions (prior). GA, 13 Nov. 1981: [7]36/28 (YUN 1981, p. 1021); [8]36/29 (*ibid.*, p. 973).
Financial implications. ACABQ report, A/37/7/Add.9; 5th Committee report, A/37/688; S-G statements, A/C.3/37/L.25/Rev.1, A/C.5/37/42.
Meeting records. GA: 3rd Committee, A/C.3/37/SR.14-23, 25, 26, *29, 42* (18 Oct.–15 Nov.); 5th Committee, A/C.5/37/SR.50 (1 Dec.); plenary, A/37/PV.90 (3 Dec.).

General Assembly resolution 37/48

3 December 1982   Meeting 90   Adopted without vote

Approved by Third Committee (A/37/629) by recorded vote (133-1), 15 November (meeting 42); 88-nation draft (A/C.3/37/L.16); agenda item 77.

Sponsors: Afghanistan, Algeria, Angola, Argentina, Bangladesh, Barbados, Benin, Bhutan, Bolivia, Botswana, Burundi, Cape Verde, Central African Republic, Chad, Chile, Colombia, Congo, Costa Rica, Cuba, Cyprus, Democratic Yemen, Djibouti, Dominican Republic, Ecuador, Egypt, El Salvador, Equatorial Guinea, Ethiopia, Gabon, Gambia, Greece, Guatemala, Guinea, Guinea-Bissau, Guyana, Honduras, Indonesia, Ivory Coast, Jamaica, Jordan, Kenya, Lebanon, Lesotho, Liberia, Libyan Arab Jamahiriya, Madagascar, Malawi, Maldives, Mali, Malta, Mauritania, Morocco, Mozambique, Nepal, Nicaragua, Niger, Nigeria, Pakistan, Peru, Philippines, Qatar, Romania, Rwanda, Saint Lucia, Samoa, Senegal, Sierra Leone, Singapore, Somalia, Sri Lanka, Sudan, Suriname, Syrian Arab Republic, Togo, Trinidad and Tobago, Tunisia, Turkey, Uganda, United Arab Emirates, Upper Volta, Uruguay, Venezuela, Viet Nam, Yemen, Yugoslavia, Zaire, Zambia, Zimbabwe.

International Youth Year: Participation, Development, Peace

The General Assembly,

Recalling its resolutions 34/151 of 17 December 1979 and 35/126 of 11 December 1980, by which it decided to designate and observe 1985 as International Youth Year: Participation, Development, Peace,

Recalling also its resolution 36/28 of 13 November 1981, by which it endorsed the Specific Programme of Measures and Activities to be undertaken prior to and during the International Youth Year,

Recalling further its decision 35/318 of 11 December 1980 on the appointment of the members of the Advisory Committee for the International Youth Year,

Recognizing the profound importance of the direct participation of youth in shaping the future of mankind and the valuable contribution that youth can make in the implementation of the new international economic order based on equity and justice,

Considering it necessary to disseminate among youth the ideals of peace, respect for human rights and fundamental freedoms, human solidarity and dedication to the objectives of progress and development,

Convinced of the imperative need to harness the energies, enthusiasms and creative abilities of youth to the tasks of nation-building, the struggle for self-determination and national independence, in accordance with the Charter of the United Nations, and against foreign domination and occupation, for the economic, social and cultural advancement of peoples, the implementation of the new international economic order, the preservation of world peace and the promotion of international co-operation and understanding,

Emphasizing again that the United Nations should give more attention to the role of young people in the world of today and to their demands for the world of tomorrow,

Recalling the topicality of assessing the needs and aspirations of youth, and reaffirming the importance of current and projected United Nations activities designed to increase the opportunities for young people and for their active participation in national development activities,

Believing that it is urgently desirable to consolidate the efforts of all States in carrying out specific programmes concerning youth and to improve the activities of the United Nations and the specialized agencies in the field of youth, including youth exchanges in the cultural, sporting and other fields,

Aware of the valuable contribution which the United Nations Educational, Scientific and Cultural Organization is making to the promotion of international co-operation in the field of youth,

Reaffirming the necessity of better co-ordination of efforts in dealing with specific problems confronting young people and in examining the manner in which those problems are being treated by the specialized agencies and by various United Nations bodies,

Convinced that the preparation for and observance in 1985 of the International Youth Year with the motto "Participation, Development, Peace" will offer a useful and significant opportunity for drawing attention to the situation and specific needs and aspirations of youth, for increasing co-operation at all levels in dealing with youth issues, for undertaking concerted action programmes in favour of youth and for involving young people in the study and resolution of major national, regional and international problems,

Confident that the International Youth Year will serve to mobilize efforts at the local, national, regional and international levels in order to promote the best educational, professional and living conditions for young people, to ensure their active participation in the overall development of society and to encourage the preparation of new national and local policies and programmes in accordance with each country's experience, conditions and priorities,

Recognizing that the preparation for and observance of the International Youth Year will contribute to the reaffirmation of the goals of the new international economic order and to the implementation of the International Development Strategy for the Third United Nations Development Decade,

Recalling also in this connection its decision 35/424 of 5 December 1980 and Economic and Social Council resolution 1980/67 of 25 July 1980 on the question of guidelines for international years and anniversaries,

Aware that, for the International Youth Year to be successful and to maximize its impact and practical efficiency, adequate preparation and the widespread support of Governments, all specialized agencies, international intergovernmental and non-governmental organizations and the public will be required,

Noting with great satisfaction the interest of Member States, various United Nations bodies and specialized agencies, as well as youth organizations, in the implementation of the Specific Programme of Measures and Activities to be undertaken prior to and during the International Youth Year,

Taking note of the report of the Advisory Committee for the International Youth Year on its second session, held at Vienna from 14 to 23 June 1982, as well as of the report of the Secretary-General,

1.   *Endorses* the recommendations made by the Advisory Committee for the International Youth Year for the further implementation of the Specific Programme of Measures and Activities to be undertaken prior to and during the International Youth Year;

2.   *Requests* the Secretary-General to transmit the recommendations of the Advisory Committee to all States, United Nations bodies, specialized agencies and regional commissions, as well as to the international intergovernmental and non-governmental organizations concerned, with a view to their early implementation;

3.   *Invites* all States that have not already done so to establish national co-ordinating committees or other forms of co-ordination for the International Youth Year;

4.   *Requests* the Secretary-General to take all necessary organizational measures to ensure the success of the regional meetings devoted to the International Youth Year;

5.   *Stresses again* the importance of active and direct participation of youth organizations in the activities organized at the local, national, regional and international levels for the preparation for and observance of the International Youth Year;

6.   *Requests* the Secretary-General to continue to take the necessary measures to ensure the proper co-ordination of the implementation of and follow-up to the Specific Programme of Measures and Activities, including the provision of information, and to report to the General Assembly at its thirty-eighth session on the implementation of the present resolution;

7.   *Also requests* the Secretary-General to convene the third session of the Advisory Committee during the first half of 1984, to provide it with all necessary assistance and to submit to it a progress report on the implementation of the Specific Programme of Measures and Activities and of the recommendations made by the Advisory Committee at its second session;

8.   *Further requests* the Secretary-General to continue to take concrete measures, through all the communications media at his disposal, to give widespread publicity to the activities of the United Nations system in the field of youth and to increase the dissemination of information on youth;

9.   *Welcomes* the voluntary contributions so far made for the International Youth Year, expresses its appreciation to all contributors and again appeals to all States, to international governmental and non-governmental organizations and to the public to make in due time generous voluntary contributions to supplement funds provided under the regular budget of the United Nations for the costs of the Specific Programme of Measures and Activities and requests the Secretary-General to take all appropriate measures for obtaining such voluntary contributions;

10.   *Decides* to include in the provisional agenda of its thirty-eighth session the item entitled "International Youth Year: Participation, Development, Peace" and to grant it high priority.

Aging persons

World Assembly on Aging

The World Assembly on Aging was held at Vienna from 26 July to 6 August 1982.[1] Convened in accordance with a 1978 General Assembly resolution,[2] the World Assembly served as a forum to assess the significance of aging trends for national development and to launch an international action programme aimed at guaranteeing to the growing number of older persons economic and social security and opportunities for contributing to national development. Its objectives were to promote awareness of major demographic shifts in progress, to identify the wide-ranging impact of those shifts on socio-economic development, particularly in developing countries, and to clarify their practical implications for those entrusted with planning necessary adjustments to economic and social infrastructure.

On 6 August, the World Assembly adopted by consensus an International Plan of Action on Aging, recommended by its Main Committee whose task had been to review and modify the Plan's text. The Assembly also adopted two resolutions. By one, it expressed appreciation to the Government and people of Austria for hosting the

Assembly and decided that, to mark the association of Austria's capital with the Plan's elaboration, the Plan would be known as the Vienna International Plan of Action on Aging, 1982. The other resolution concerned aging people in Lebanon (see POLITICAL AND SECURITY QUESTIONS, Chapter IX).

The World Assembly was attended by representatives of 124 States and the United Nations Council for Namibia, the Secretariat, regional commissions, specialized agencies, other United Nations bodies, and intergovernmental and non-governmental organizations (for participants and officers, see APPENDIX III).

Publication. [1]*Report of the World Assembly on Aging, Vienna, 26 July to 6 August 1982* (A/CONF.113/31), Sales No. E.82.I.16. *Resolution.* [2]GA: 33/52, 14 Dec. 1978 (YUN 1978, p. 799).

Preparations for the Assembly

Work of the Advisory Committee. At its second session, held in New York from 16 to 22 February 1982,[2] the Advisory Committee for the World Assembly on Aging continued to examine the draft international plan of action on aging. In addition, it recommended a provisional agenda and approved the draft rules of procedure for the World Assembly, and made a series of recommendations on participants, topics for plenary meetings, the Main Committee's work, and the financing by the United Nations Trust Fund for the World Assembly of the least developed countries' participation in intergovernmental regional meetings and in the Assembly itself.

Taking note of documentation for the Assembly, the Advisory Committee decided against a separate declaration on the rights of the aging as had been suggested by the 1981 *Ad Hoc* Inter-agency Meeting on Aging,[12] but agreed to the inclusion of a preamble to the draft plan of action.

At its third session, held at Vienna from 3 to 7 May,[3] the Advisory Committee agreed on the text of the revised draft plan of action as a whole, subject to certain reservations. It revised the Assembly's provisional agenda and made recommendations on the allocation of agenda items, the Credentials Committee membership, additional rules for the conduct of meetings, an outline of the Assembly's report and the method for electing the Main Committee officers. The Advisory Committee recommended that non-governmental organizations (NGOs) not in consultative status with the Economic and Social Council but meeting the criteria for participation in the Assembly be invited. It also requested its Chairman to explore ways of improving public information activities for the Assembly.

Other activities. As suggested in the Secretary-General's 1980 draft programme for the World Assembly on Aging,[11] three regional intergovernmental meetings were organized in 1982 by the regional commissions in collaboration with the United Nations Centre for Social Development and Humanitarian Affairs (CSDHA). The meetings, which were in addition to the 1981 meeting organized by the Economic and Social Commission for Asia and the Pacific, were held under the auspices of the Economic Commission for Africa (ECA) at Addis Ababa, Ethiopia, from 1 to 5 March; the Economic Commission for Latin America at San José, Costa Rica, from 8 to 12 March; and the Economic Commission for Europe at Vienna from 26 to 30 April.

At each of these meetings, a regional plan of action on aging was approved.[1] The ECA plan was endorsed by that Commission on 30 April with a request that its Executive Secretary bring it to the attention of Governments.[8] The Economic Commission for Western Asia, which could not organize a meeting, also prepared a regional plan, which it adopted on 12 May[9] for transmittal to the World Assembly's Secretary-General.

Common to the plans were principles and guidelines governing regional action and suggestions for national action on issues relating to the aging. The issues were broadly classified into those concerned with the implications for national strategies and programmes for economic and social development of the aging segment of populations; and the humanitarian issues of education and training for and about the aging, employment, family support and care, institutional care, health and social welfare services, housing and social security. The plans recommended research and collection of statistical data on actual situations of the aging on which to base national programmes, as well as programme co-ordination, monitoring and evaluation.

Notable among the preparatory activities for the World Assembly was a forum on aging, held at Vienna from 29 March to 2 April[6] by NGOs in consultative status with the Economic and Social Council. Attended by 336 delegates from 43 countries and representing 159 NGOs, the forum made recommendations for action by Governments to provide for the needs of the aging.

In a related area, the Economic and Social Council, on 4 May,[10] urged that the special problems of elderly women be given full attention by the Assembly and treated in the plan of action that it was to adopt.

The *Ad Hoc* Inter-agency Meeting on Aging convened in New York on 25 and 26 February[4] and again at Vienna on 10 and 11 May,[5] for its third and fourth meetings, to review the co-ordination of preparations for the Assembly, including the status of documentation. After the Meeting's review of the draft international plan of action, a text urging recognition of the needs of elderly refugees was proposed and annexed to the Meeting's report.

As decided by the Advisory Committee at its third session, pre-conference consultations were held at Vienna on 24 and 25 July, at which procedural and organizational matters for the Assembly were further considered.[7]

Regional plans of action. [1]A/CONF.113/26.
Reports. Advisory Committee, [2]A/CONF.113/11, [3]A/CONF.113/24; Inter-agency Meeting on Aging, [4]ACC/1982/PG/3, [5]ACC/1982/PG/6; [6]NGO forum, transmitted by 13 May letter from Austria, A/CONF.113/27; [7]Pre-conference consultations, A/CONF.113/L.1.
Resolutions (1982). [8]ECA (report, E/1982/21): 448(XVII), 30 Apr. [9]ECWA (report, E/1982/22): 111(IX), 12 May; [10]ESC: 1982/23, para. 1, 4 May.
Yearbook references. [11]1980, p. 1016; [12]1981, p. 1024.

Work of the Assembly

Plan of Action

The Vienna International Plan of Action on Aging,[5] conceived as the instrument for carrying out the basic mandates of the World Assembly, contained a preamble, a foreword and four main sections. Its primary aims were to strengthen the capacities of countries to deal with the aging of their populations and with the needs of the elderly, and to promote an international response through action for the establishment of the new international economic order and increased international technical co-operation, particularly among developing countries. The introductory section provided information on demographic trends in developed and developing regions and defined the developmental and humanitarian aspects of aging; section II set forth the principles on which the Plan was based; section III presented recommendations for action, covering the impact of aging on development, specific areas of concern to the aging, and promotion of policies and programmes; and section IV recommended measures for the Plan's implementation at the national, regional and international levels, including periodic review and appraisal.

The preamble articulated the belief that the rights enshrined in the Universal Declaration of Human Rights[7] applied fully and undiminishedly to the aging, and recognized that the aging should be enabled to enjoy a life of fulfilment, health, security and contentment as an integral part of society.

The foreword stated that the Plan should be considered an integral component of major international, regional and national strategies and programmes in response to world problems and needs, and should also be considered within the framework of other international instruments. The foreword outlined the Plan's objectives as follows: to promote understanding of the economic, social and cultural implications, as well as the humanitarian and developmental issues, of population aging; to stimulate action-oriented policies and programmes to guarantee social and economic security for the elderly and provide opportunities for their participation in development and in its benefits; to present policy alternatives consistent with national values and goals and with internationally recognized principles; and to encourage appropriate education and research on aging and foster international exchange of relevant skills and knowledge.

To give perspective to the impact of the aging population, the Plan described demographic trends according to which, from 1975 to 2025, the number of persons aged 60 years and over throughout the world would increase from 350 million to over 1,100 million, or by 315 per cent. This compared with a total world population growth of 102 per cent. By 2025, the aging would constitute 13.7 per cent of the population. This trend was indicative of the gradually decreasing ratio between the economically active and employed sectors of society and those dependent on the resources provided by those sectors.

The Plan grouped the issues affecting the aging into two categories: the developmental issues arising from the socio-economic implications of a growing population of elderly for production, consumption, savings, investment and general social conditions; and the humanitarian issues related to their specific concerns, namely, health and nutrition, housing and environment, the family, social welfare, income security, employment, retirement and education.

The main principles underlying concerted action as recommended by the Plan to tackle these issues were: development for improving the well-being of the entire population; the right of participation in development; the creation of conditions of peace, security, freedom and respect for human rights in order to find solutions to problems of older people; the central importance of the family; public, private and individual responsibility to support the elderly; and the preparation of the entire population for old age as an integral part of social policies.

The Plan's general policy recommendations were aimed at a shift from policies and practices limited to providing protection and care to a vulnerable and declining minority to policies based on a positive, active and developmentally oriented view of aging. Stressing activity in old age, the recommendations identified the following avenues for self-expression and contribution to society: participation in family and kinship systems, volunteer work, continued formal and informal learning, work with arts and crafts, participation in community organizations, recreation and travel, religious activities, part-time work and involvement in the political process as informed citizens.

In pursuit of the Plan's realization, full use was urged of opportunities existing for technical co-operation between developed and developing countries in three areas: data collection and analysis by means of censuses and surveys or statistics systems; training and education; and research on the developmental and humanitarian aspects of aging as identified by the Plan. Educational institutions of gerontology, geriatrics and geriatric psychology, as well as international exchange of research data, were recommended to advance research efforts, particularly in the biological, mental and social fields.

The text of the Plan had evolved over a two-year period. A draft was prepared by the Secretary-General in consultation with Member States,[4] as requested by the Economic and Social Council in 1980.[6] It was considered and revised at three sessions by the Advisory Committee on the World Assembly, which recommended inclusion of a preamble and, at its May 1982 session, agreed to the draft text as a whole, subject to reservations on suggestions on which consensus was not achieved.[2] One was the addition of a paragraph recommending that the Secretary-General study the impact of removing the retirement-age limitations from the United Nations Staff Regulations. Two others, under the section on international and regional co-operation, concerned the addition of the concept of a decade for the aging and of a sentence to the effect that CSDHA be given executing-agency status by the United Nations Development Programme (UNDP) in order to carry out technical assistance projects for the aging.

A text urging recognition of the needs of elderly refugees, particularly in health, housing and social services, was proposed for inclusion in the Plan by the United Nations Relief and Works Agency for Palestine Refugees in the Near East, together with the United Nations High Commissioner for Refugees, during the *Ad Hoc* Inter-agency Meeting in May.

The regional commissions provided their input by holding preparatory meetings (under the auspices of CSDHA and reporting to the World Assembly).[1] Also taken into account were the views of delegations, which were given an opportunity for further input during consideration and final modification of the Plan's text by the Assembly's Main Committee.[3]

Regional plans of action. [1]A/CONF.113/26.
Reports. [2]Advisory Committee, A/CONF.113/24; [3]Main Committee, A/CONF.113/30; [4]S-G, A/CONF.113/22; [5]World Assembly on Aging, A/CONF.113/31 (Sales No. E.82.I.16).
Resolutions. [6]ESC: 1980/26, 2 May 1980 (YUN 1980, p. 1018). [7]GA: 217 A (III), 10 Dec. 1948 (YUN 1948-49, p. 535).

Implementation of the Plan

In the recommendations for implementation included in the Plan of Action on Aging,[2] the role of Governments was defined, as were the mechanisms for international and regional co-operation, technical co-operation and the exchange of information and experience. Governments were urged to design national strategies responsive to their own particular needs, with established priorities and objectives for the short, medium and long terms; to set up multisectoral machinery within government to ensure integration of the issues of aging in national development plans; to co-ordinate activities through co-operation between those in positions of responsibility with representatives of the aging; and to use national mechanisms that had been set up for the World Assembly for planning, implementation and evaluation of activities recommended in the Plan.

International co-operation in the form of bilateral and multilateral technical and financial assistance was recommended. The plan was to be brought to the attention of United Nations bodies responsible for preparations for the International Conference on Population (1984) so that it could be taken into account in proposals for further implementation of the 1974 World Population Plan of Action.[4] As implementation was primarily at the national level, the Secretary-General was requested, within existing United Nations resources, to give consideration to providing increased resources. The Administrative Committee on Co-ordination was to continue inter-agency co-ordination of activities; guidelines were to be kept under review; and Governments and international, governmental and non-governmental organizations were urged to maintain channels of communication with the elderly on policies and programmes affecting their lives.

The United Nations—in particular UNDP and the Department of Technical Co-operation for Development—and its specialized agencies were to carry out technical co-operation activities with CSDHA support. Aging being a population issue affecting development, the United Nations Fund for Population Activities (UNFPA) was urged, in co-operation with all organizations concerned with international population assistance, to continue and strengthen its assistance in that field, particularly in developing countries.

The Plan suggested meetings and seminars at all levels as forums for information exchange. It recommended that CSDHA promote and co-ordinate information activities and that standardization of definitions, terms and research methodologies be undertaken to achieve compatibility of international data.

Institutions with regional mandates were urged to contribute to the Plan's implementation. The

United Nations regional commissions and their members were asked to conduct a periodic review of regional and national plans on the aging. The Commission for Social Development was recommended as the intergovernmental body to review implementation of the Plan every four years and to make proposals for updating the Plan; it was to transmit its findings to the General Assembly through the Economic and Social Council. To assist it in its work, the Commission was to be provided with periodic progress reports on the Plan's implementation by the United Nations system. CSDHA was to serve as co-ordinator of this process.

General Assembly action. By a resolution of 3 December 1982,[3] adopted by a recorded vote of 149 to none, the General Assembly endorsed the Plan of Action on Aging, called on Governments to implement its principles and recommendations and urged the Secretary-General to implement the recommendations on international co-operation and assessment of implementation. It requested the Secretary-General to ensure sufficient resources for the Plan's implementation and to strengthen the international network of information, research and training centres on aging, as well as technical co-operation within the various regions. The Assembly urged UNFPA to strengthen its assistance in the field of aging and requested the Economic and Social Council to report on the Plan's implementation every four years from 1985. It invited specialized agencies to co-operate in the implementation, and intergovernmental and non-governmental organizations to co-ordinate their work on aging with the United Nations.

The draft of this resolution, sponsored by 38 nations, was introduced in the Third (Social, Humanitarian and Cultural) Committee by Malta, which orally revised paragraph 5 to add a request that the Secretary-General make every effort to reallocate existing global resources in ensuring sufficient resources for the Plan's implementation. The revised text was approved by the Committee on 15 November by a recorded vote of 121 to 1, with 7 abstentions.

Prior to approving the text, the Committee rejected an amendment proposed by the United States[1] by a recorded vote of 67 to 23, with 32 abstentions. The amendment would have added an operative paragraph by which the Assembly would have decided that implementation of the resolution's provisions would be carried out within existing global resources or with voluntary contributions that might become available from the Trust Fund.

Amendment rejected. [1]United States, A/C.3/37/L.30.
Report. [2]World Assembly on Aging, A/CONF.113/31 (Sales No. E.82.I.16).
Resolution (1982). [3]GA: 37/51, 3 Dec. text following.
Yearbook reference. [4]1974, p. 552.

Financial implications. ACABQ report, A/37/7/Add.9; 5th Committee report, A/37/688; S-G statements, A/C.3/37/L.26, A/C.5/37/44.
Meeting records. GA: 3rd Committee, A/C.3/37/SR.14-23, 25, 26, *29, 42* (18 Oct.–15 Nov.); 5th Committee, A/C.5/37/SR.50 (1 Dec.); plenary, A/37/PV.90 (3 Dec.).

General Assembly resolution 37/51

3 December 1982　　　　　　Meeting 90　　　　　149-0 (recorded vote)

Approved by Third Committee (A/37/631) by recorded vote (121-1-7), 15 November (meeting 42); 38-nation draft (A/C.3/37/L.21), orally revised; agenda items 82 and 83.

Sponsors: Argentina, Australia, Austria, Bolivia, Chile, Colombia, Costa Rica, Cyprus, Dominican Republic, Ecuador, Egypt, France, Greece, Guatemala, Guinea, Guyana, Indonesia, Jordan, Lebanon, Liberia, Madagascar, Mali, Malta, Mauritania, Morocco, Nepal, Nigeria, Pakistan, Philippines, Romania, Sierra Leone, Spain, Suriname, Thailand, Togo, United Arab Emirates, Uruguay, Venezuela.

Question of aging

The General Assembly,

Recalling its resolution 33/52 of 14 December 1978, in which it decided to convene a World Assembly on Aging to call world-wide attention to the serious problems besetting a growing portion of the population of the world and to provide a forum to launch an international programme of action aimed at guaranteeing economic and social security to older persons, as well as opportunities for them to contribute to national development,

Recognizing that increasing longevity is an achievement of biology and a sign of progress, and that the aged are an asset and not a liability to society because of the invaluable contribution they can make by virtue of their accumulated wealth of knowledge and experience,

Bearing in mind that the States gathered in the World Assembly on Aging, held at Vienna from 26 July to 6 August 1982, reaffirmed their belief that the fundamental and inalienable rights enshrined in the Universal Declaration of Human Rights apply fully and undiminishedly to the aging, and recognized that the quality of life was no less important than longevity, and that the aging should therefore, as far as possible, be enabled to enjoy in their own families and communities a life of fulfilment, health, security and contentment, appreciated as an integral part of society,

Convinced that the International Plan of Action on Aging adopted by the World Assembly on Aging must lead to developing and applying, at the international, regional and national levels, policies designed to enhance the lives of the aging as individuals and to mitigate, by appropriate measures, any negative effects resulting from the impact of the aging of populations on development,

Recognizing that the Plan of Action should be considered an integral component of the major international, regional and national strategies and programmes formulated in response to important world problems and needs,

Recalling its resolution 35/129 of 11 December 1980, in pursuance of which the United Nations Trust Fund for the World Assembly on Aging was established to finance preparatory and follow-up activities in connection with the World Assembly, and its resolution 36/20 of 9 November 1981, in which it requested the Secretary-General to use the Trust Fund to encourage further interest in the field of aging among developing countries, particularly the least developed among them, within the context of the conclusions and recommendations of the World Assembly on Aging,

Acknowledging the role played by the United Nations and the specialized agencies through their efforts in the field of aging and the need to strengthen this role in order to make the implementation of the recommendations of the Plan of Action effective,

Emphasizing the importance of the Plan of Action and stressing the spirit of co-operation that prevailed during the World Assembly on Aging,

Expressing appreciation to the Government of Austria for acting as host to the World Assembly on Aging,

Having considered the *Report of the World Assembly on Aging,*

1. *Takes note* of the *Report of the World Assembly on Aging;*

2. *Endorses* the International Plan of Action on Aging, adopted by consensus at the World Assembly on Aging;

3. *Affirms* that aging should be considered in the context of economic, social and cultural development, as well as in the context of international strategies and plans;

4. *Calls upon* Governments to make continuous efforts to implement the principles and recommendations contained in the Plan of Action in accordance with their national structures, needs and objectives;

5. *Requests* the Secretary-General to take the necessary steps to ensure that sufficient resources within reasonable limits are made available for the effective implementation of, and follow-up action to, the Plan of Action, as well as to maintain the momentum generated by the World Assembly on Aging; in doing so, the Secretary-General should make every effort to reallocate existing global resources;

6. *Also requests* the Secretary-General to take such steps as may be appropriate for the necessary strengthening of activities in the field of aging at the central and regional levels of the United Nations, as set forth in the Plan of Action;

7. *Further requests* the Secretary-General to strengthen the international network of existing information, research and training centres in the field of aging in order to encourage and facilitate the exchange of knowledge, skills and experiences, as well as technical co-operation between countries within the various regions;

8. *Urges* the Secretary-General to implement the recommendations concerning international co-operation with respect to aging, as well as those concerning the assessment, review and appraisal of the implementation of the Plan of Action, using the Centre for Social Development and Humanitarian Affairs of the Secretariat as the focal point;

9. *Requests* the Secretary-General to continue to use the United Nations Trust Fund for the World Assembly on Aging to meet the rapidly increasing needs of the aging in the developing countries, in particular in the least developed countries;

10. *Also requests* the Secretary-General to use the Trust Fund to encourage greater interest among developing countries in matters related to aging and to assist Member States, at their request, in formulating and implementing policies and programmes for the elderly; further requests the Secretary-General to use the Trust Fund for technical co-operation and research related to the aging of populations and for promoting co-operation among developing countries in the exchange of relevant information and technology;

11. *Appeals* to Member States to make voluntary contributions to the Trust Fund;

12. *Urges* the United Nations Fund for Population Activities, in co-operation with all organizations responsible for international population assistance, to strengthen its assistance, within its mandate, in the field of aging, particularly in developing countries;

13. *Requests* the Economic and Social Council, through the Commission for Social Development, to review the implementation of the Plan of Action every four years, beginning in 1985, and to transmit its findings to the General Assembly;

14. *Invites* the specialized agencies concerned to co-operate with the Secretary-General in the implementation of the Plan of Action within their fields of competence;

15. *Invites* the intergovernmental organizations and non-governmental organizations concerned to continue to give attention to major issues related to aging and to co-ordinate their work with the United Nations, particularly in view of the need for well co-ordinated activities for the implementation of the Plan of Action;

16. *Requests* the Secretary-General to report to the General Assembly at its thirty-eighth session on the progress achieved in implementing and following up the Plan of Action and to include in his report an account of project activities financed by the Trust Fund;

17. *Decides* to include in the provisional agenda of its thirty-eighth session a single item entitled "Question of aging" to replace the items entitled "Question of the elderly and the aged" and "World Assembly on Aging".

Recorded vote in Assembly as follows:

In favour: Albania, Algeria, Angola, Antigua and Barbuda, Argentina, Australia, Austria, Bahamas, Bahrain, Bangladesh, Barbados, Belgium, Belize, Benin, Bhutan, Bolivia, Botswana, Brazil, Bulgaria, Burma, Burundi, Byelorussian SSR, Canada, Cape Verde, Central African Republic, Chad, Chile, China, Colombia, Comoros, Congo, Costa Rica, Cuba, Cyprus, Czechoslovakia, Democratic Kampuchea, Democratic Yemen, Denmark, Djibouti, Dominican Republic, Ecuador, Egypt, El Salvador, Equatorial Guinea, Ethiopia, Fiji, Finland, France, Gabon, German Democratic Republic, Germany, Federal Republic of, Ghana, Greece, Grenada, Guinea, Guinea-Bissau, Guyana, Haiti, Honduras, Hungary, Iceland, India, Indonesia, Iran, Iraq, Ireland, Israel, Italy, Ivory Coast, Jamaica, Japan, Jordan, Kenya, Kuwait, Lao People's Democratic Republic, Lesotho, Liberia, Libyan Arab Jamahiriya, Luxembourg, Madagascar, Malawi, Malaysia, Maldives, Mali, Malta, Mauritania, Mauritius, Mexico, Mongolia, Morocco, Mozambique, Nepal, Netherlands, New Zealand, Nicaragua, Niger, Nigeria, Norway, Oman, Pakistan, Panama, Papua New Guinea, Paraguay, Peru, Philippines, Poland, Portugal, Qatar, Romania, Rwanda, Saint Lucia, Samoa, Sao Tome and Principe, Saudi Arabia, Senegal, Sierra Leone, Singapore, Solomon Islands, Somalia, Spain, Sri Lanka, Sudan, Suriname, Swaziland, Sweden, Syrian Arab Republic, Thailand, Togo, Trinidad and Tobago, Tunisia, Turkey, Uganda, Ukrainian SSR, USSR, United Arab Emirates, United Kingdom, United Republic of Cameroon, United Republic of Tanzania, United States, Upper Volta, Uruguay, Vanuatu, Venezuela, Viet Nam, Yemen, Yugoslavia, Zaire, Zambia, Zimbabwe.

Against: None.

UN Trust Fund

In a September 1982 report to the General Assembly on United Nations activities on aging,[1] the Secretary-General stated that the United Nations Trust Fund for the World Assembly on Aging, established in response to a 1980 Assembly request,[1] had been used to finance activities in three areas—secretariat support for the preparatory work for the World Assembly, including costs associated with the post of that Assembly's Secretary-General; participation of least developed countries in a regional meeting for Africa and in the Assembly itself; and public information for the Assembly. As at 31 December, the Fund's total income, from pledged contributions by Governments, public donations and interest, came to $485,308; expenditures totalled $336,450, leaving a balance of $148,858.

The Secretary-General also stated that, should the General Assembly endorse the Plan of Action on Aging,[2] he would use the Fund to provide financial support for achieving the Plan's objectives.

The Plan recommended that the Fund be used to meet the increasing needs of the aging in developing countries, particularly in the least developed countries (LDCs); to encourage greater interest among those countries in matters related to aging; and to assist Member States, at their request, in formulating and implementing policies and programmes for the elderly. The Fund should further be used for technical co-operation and research related to the aging segment of populations and to promote co-operation among developing countries in the exchange of relevant information and technology. It should be administered by CSDHA and contributions to it should be encouraged.

In its 3 December resolution on the question of aging,[3] the Assembly requested the Secretary-General to continue to use the Fund to meet the rapidly increasing needs of the aging in developing countries, in particular in LDCs, and to encourage their interest in matters related to aging. He was also requested to assist Member States, at their request, in formulating and implementing policies and programmes for the elderly; and to use the Fund for technical co-operation and research in this field and for promoting information and technology exchange among developing countries. The Assembly appealed to Member

States to make voluntary contributions to the Fund.

Reports. (1)S-G, A/37/435; (2)World Assembly on Aging, A/CONF.113/31 (Sales No. E.82.I.16).
Resolution (1982). (3)GA: 37/51, paras. 9-11, 3 Dec.
Resolution (prior). (4)GA: 35/129, 11 Dec. 1980 (YUN 1980, p. 1019).

Social welfare of aging persons

The Vienna International Plan of Action on Aging,(4) drawing attention to the interrelation of all aspects of aging, called for co-ordination of both policy and research on the topic. The Plan urged adoption of preventive measures to combat the detrimental effects of premature aging, such as educational programmes on the physiology of aging, life-styles to promote health, appropriate working conditions and adaptation of the individual to his work and vice versa, including job flexibility so that the aging might better adjust to personal, social and cultural, as well as technological and economic, changes.

The Secretary-General, in a March 1982 report(2) submitted to the World Assembly on Aging, gave broad coverage to the social welfare issues confronting the aging in terms of the humanitarian problems of aging and the family, income security, health and continuing care, housing and environment, social welfare services and education. In a subsequent report issued in May,(3) he discussed the social welfare services required by aging persons, with emphasis on the question of adequacy and appropriateness of existing services. Outlining the needs of the aging, the report suggested a number of alternatives for progress in providing services.

By a letter of 15 October to the Secretary-General, Viet Nam transmitted extracts of its 26 July report to the World Assembly on the situation of its elderly, giving information on demographic trends, national policy on the care of the elderly, social welfare services and areas for future action.(1)

Letter. (1)Viet Nam, 15 Oct., A/C.3/37/4.
Reports. S-G, (2)A/CONF.113/9, (3)A/CONF.113/12; (4)World Assembly on Aging, A/CONF.113/31 (Sales No. E.82.I.16).

Education

The Plan of Action on Aging recommended expansion of educational structures to respond to the needs of an entire life-span, including continued opportunities for education for the aging; exchanges of skills, knowledge and experience in dealing with issues of aging as areas for international co-operation and technical co-operation among developing countries, to involve elderly people's organizations; establishment of practical training centres for the training of personnel in the field of aging, especially in developing countries, to serve also as links with developed countries and with United Nations agencies and facilities; research and study on the integration of issues of aging in policy formulation and management at the national, regional and international levels; and increased training in gerontology and geriatrics.

In a report on humanitarian issues submitted in March 1982 to the World Assembly,(1) the Secretary-General, underscoring the informational and related social obsolescence of older persons in societies characterized by rapid technological and social change and by information explosion, drew attention to the need for a life-span approach to education for all. This approach should include mid-career education, continuing education in the middle and later years, retraining of older persons who had become unemployed due to technological changes and training of those entering the work force for the first time, and educational programmes drawing on the experiences and skills of older persons.

A report submitted to the Assembly on the same topic by the United Nations Educational, Scientific and Cultural Organization concentrated on education for, by, with and about the elderly, aimed at promoting development of the human person and tapping unused intelligence and energy for the benefit of society.(2) It examined various programmes aimed at involving the elderly in education and suggested ways to expand such education.

Reports. (1)S-G, A/CONF.113/9; (2)UNESCO, A/CONF.113/20.

Employment

The Plan of Action on Aging, noting the prevalence of age discrimination in employment practices, recommended that Governments facilitate the participation of older persons in the economic life of society by eliminating age discrimination in the labour market, securing for older workers job security under satisfactory working conditions, gearing health services to the needs particular to older workers and to occupational hazards, creating new employment possibilities through training, making pension age flexible, ensuring the application of international standards governing employment of older workers and guaranteeing full social coverage for migrant workers.

A February 1982 report of the International Labour Organisation (ILO) prepared for the World Assembly(1) reviewed the problems of employment for older workers, as well as existing employment policies and practices. The report highlighted two concerns shared by the majority of countries—that older workers should not be subjected to discrimination because of age; and that, on the contrary, they should be accorded protection so as to achieve the best possible fit between their capacities and their conditions of employment. The report reiterated a 1980 ILO Recommendation on a code of good conduct towards older workers, based on the fundamental principles of social justice and respect for the needs and aspirations of the aging.

Report. [1]ILO, A/CONF.113/15.

Retirement

Noting that most people could expect to survive their own retirement by a substantial number of years, the Plan of Action on Aging stated that preparation for retirement should be a matter not of last-minute adaptation but of concern from adulthood onwards and for society at large. The Plan proposed measures to facilitate the transition from employment to retirement and suggested that the varieties of personal preference could be taken into account in a system of elastic retirement plans catering to the individual. This would allow for choice of voluntary early retirement with reduced benefits, extended employment or part-time work.

A February 1982 ILO report on transition from professional life to retirement,[1] prepared for the World Assembly, highlighted end-of-career arrangements at the work place for a gradual transition to retirement—modification of work and working hours, medical surveillance, a system of remuneration to accommodate reduced work time and diminished capacities, and programmes to prepare employees for retirement. The report also raised questions for further examination in developing transition measures.

Report. [1]ILO, A/CONF.113/16.

Family

The Plan of Action on Aging, recognizing the family as a fundamental unit of society that had traditionally provided care for its elderly members, made a series of recommendations to enable the family to continue in that vital role. Among them were government promotion of social policies encouraging family solidarity and appropriate support in terms of social services for the family, especially for low-income families engaged in caring for their elderly members. The Plan stressed the contribution of non-governmental organizations in this endeavour.

The Secretary-General, in an April 1982 report on aging in the family context,[1] prepared for the World Assembly, suggested that the United Nations and its Member States make policy declarations affirming the family's importance and its viability as an instrument for the care of the young as well as the aging. He also suggested that social policies include support for families caring for their older members, and other forms of aid, such as income maintenance schemes, for families in that situation.

Report. [1]S-G, A/CONF.113/10.

Health and nutrition

The recommendations on health and nutrition of the Plan of Action on Aging were primarily aimed at achieving the highest degree of well-being of the elderly so that they might be able to live and function as independently and for as long as possible within the family or community. Thus, the recommendations laid stress on preventive health care to encompass physical, mental, social, spiritual and environmental factors; primary health care and maintenance administered to the extent possible within the home environment by social services and community health workers; curative measures, including early diagnosis, medical treatment and adequate hospital care, and rehabilitation geared to returning the patient to the community; and appropriate nutrition.

In support of these measures, the Plan also recommended education for the elderly in self-care; basic training for families in home care for the aging; education in correct nutrition and eating habits; and development and organization of adequate health care and allied services such as day-care centres, out-patient clinics, day hospitals, paramedical, nursing and domestic services, and technical and emergency facilities. The Plan additionally called on Governments to undertake measures to ensure that food products and household installations and equipment conformed to standards of safety, taking into account the vulnerability of the aged; to facilitate the availability of medications, hearing aids, dentures, glasses and other prosthetic devices to the elderly; and to regulate the promotional and marketing techniques aimed at exploiting the elderly.

The Secretary-General, in his report on the humanitarian issues of aging prepared for the World Assembly,[1] stated that health for the aging went beyond the concepts of the absence of disease and of optimal social functioning; it involved complex, interrelated biomedical, psychological and social factors, some of which were related to organic, physiological changes caused by normal aging, others to disease, and still others to social-environmental situations such as poverty, lack of environmental sanitation and social roles and purposes. The report continued that, as a result, greater emphasis needed to be given to preventive and primary health care services, including: continuing assessment of functional capacity and treatment for the restoration of function to the highest possible extent; community health care systems financed and organized for effective delivery to respond to health care needs outside hospitals and institutions for the elderly; the pursuit of health as an integral part of development and therefore of national policies and programmes; early prevention and life-long attention to general health and nutrition; and continuing education in the process of aging for the public at large and for policy makers, the medical profession and health service practitioners in particular.

In a March 1982 report prepared for the World Assembly, the World Health Organization elaborated guidelines for the establishment of health and social policies on aging.[2] It included a statement addressed principally to decision makers, stating that the keystone of such policies was the commitment by all sectors of government, non-governmental organizations, the professions engaged in health care and individuals to programmes for the promotion of health and maintenance of functioning within society during aging.

Reports. [1]S-G, A/CONF.113/9; [2]WHO, A/CONF.113/19.

Housing and environment

The World Assembly on Aging, conscious that the home was the centre of the elderly's activities, incorporated into the Plan of Action on Aging a number of recommendations on housing designed to facilitate their ability to live independently. These included national policies aimed at helping the aged to continue to live in their own homes for as long as possible; improving inadequate dwellings to include facilities and practical aids adapted to the diminished mobility of the aged; adapting transportation to their needs; providing housing to suit varying degrees of self-sufficiency and located in traffic-safe environments; and securing social integration of the aged through urban development planning and law. Housing policies should be co-ordinated with health, social, cultural and communications policies. The Plan additionally recommended that law enforcement agencies and the elderly then.selves be made aware of crime against older persons, which was on the rise in some countries.

The Secretary-General, addressing the issue of housing and environment for the aging in his report on humanitarian issues prepared for the World Assembly,[1] stated that, in the context of inadequate, overcrowded housing and housing lacking sanitary water supply and waste disposal, the aged were particularly vulnerable and often victimized. Social factors, such as the trend towards urbanization and the migrations of the young, were physically and socially isolating the aged. Housing policies should therefore meet not only the need for minimum adequacy, security, and access to transportation, community health and social welfare services but also the integrative needs of the aging.

In a supplementary report on housing for the aging issued in April 1982, the Secretary-General provided additional information, including recommendations for national programmes for improving housing and environmental conditions of the aging.[2] In addition, he urged local governments, private voluntary organizations and the residents of low-income communities to participate in providing home services.

The findings in a May report of the United Nations Centre for Human Settlements (Habitat) to the World Assembly[3] pointed to the diversity of housing and environmental conditions which called for different approaches. The vast majority of older persons required conveniently accessible community services; the infirm and those with limited mobility needed help in housekeeping and household maintenance; and others needed institutional care. To meet these needs, government action was urged. Local governments, private voluntary organizations and individuals, including the aging themselves, were called on to participate in providing home services. International agencies were urged to assist developing countries in formulating national policies and programmes for the improvement of housing and environmental conditions for the aging.

Reports. S-G, [1]A/CONF.113/9, [2]A/CONF.113/13; [3]UNCHS, A/CONF.113/25.

Social security

The Plan of Action on Aging noted that social security schemes had been established in most developed countries but were limited, if they existed at all, in most developing ones. The Plan recommended that Governments ensure a minimum income for all older persons through social security programmes to meet their essential needs and guarantee their independence. Where this was not feasible, other approaches such as payment of benefits in kind or for direct assistance to families and local co-operative institutions should be tried. Such programmes should include special coverage for elderly women, who generally earned less than men and were employed for shorter periods. Ways were to be found to protect the purchasing power of social security benefits and savings of the elderly.

The Secretary-General, in his report on humanitarian issues to the World Assembly,[3] noted a lack of universal coverage in many social security systems. Also lacking was a unified system for income security, maintenance and protection in old age in the majority of countries. Work and retirement policies, social security benefits and private pension schemes were inflexible, and the limited incomes of older persons were being eroded by inflation. Among options suggested were public policies and programmes ensuring an adequate minimum income for all older persons, a periodic adjustment of benefits to increases in national productivity and cost of living, international agreements to assure migrant workers continuity of social security coverage, and assistance programmes in kind, such as subsidized housing and reduced transportation fees and food prices.

The International Labour Organisation, in a March 1982 report on income security for the elderly,[1] identified for the World Assembly two categories of problems. The first related to the different national approaches to income security, the scope and level of protection provided by national social security legislation and the contingencies limiting such protection. The second category involved financial problems of different income support programmes and the impact on those programmes of aging populations, which were progressively increasing and drawing on these support systems, often before reaching normal pensionable age, without a corresponding increase in contributions to those systems.

A report on the contribution of social security to the protection of the elderly was also submitted to the World Assembly by the International Social Security Association.[2]

Reports. [1]ILO, A/CONF.113/17; [2]International Social Security Association, A/CONF.113/18 & Corr.1,2; [3]S-G, A/CONF.113/9.

Social services

The Plan of Action on Aging stated that social welfare services could be instruments of national policy whose goal should be to maximize the social functioning of the aging. They should be community-based and encompass a broad range of preventive, remedial and developmental services.

The Plan suggested that, in countries lacking organized social welfare services, co-operatives and non-governmental organizations (NGOs) could play important roles in providing those services. A partnership should be formed between Governments and NGOs, designed to ensure a comprehensive, integrated, co-ordinated and multipurpose approach to meeting the social welfare needs of the elderly. The participation of youth in this effort was to be encouraged with a view to promoting inter-generational ties. The Plan also recommended that Governments endeavour to eliminate fiscal or other constraints on informal and voluntary social welfare activities and to set minimum standards for the institutional care of the elderly. Also to be encouraged was group action by the elderly so that they could participate in social service agencies to make known their wishes, use their knowledge and enhance their sense of belonging.

Aging persons and development

The Vienna International Plan of Action on Aging[5] recommended that attention be given to the vast and multifaceted impact which the aging of populations was bound to have on the structure, functioning and further development of all societies. Chief among the problems identified by the Plan was the deteriorating ratio between the economically productive sectors of society and those dependent on the resources generated by these sectors. At the same time, the number of dependent elderly was growing and traditional care-providing structures, such as the extended family, were undergoing radical change in many parts of the world. Another problem was the political and psychological one related to perceptions of the relative urgency of meeting the needs of population groups not involved in production or public life. Pointing out that security for older people would be most acute in rural areas, the Plan said efforts should be made to improve socio-economic conditions in those areas and rural development should be promoted.

In a March 1982 report on developmental issues,[2] prepared for the World Assembly on Aging, the Secretary-General highlighted the effects of demographic change on aging as it related to development, the tendency of development processes to create problems by segregating the old from the rest of the population, and how government planning and action should be adapted to meet the problems of old age.

In a supplementary report issued in April on the implications of aging populations for economic development,[3] the Secretary-General stated that prudent public policies, such as reducing early retirement incentives and facilitating the growth of the female work force, could mitigate the adverse effects of population growth of those aged 60 and over and the decline of the fertility rate. A close monitoring of the changing age structure of the population would enable Governments gradually to shift their emphasis from youth-oriented social services to those oriented towards older people.

In another April report,[4] the Secretary-General explored how the situation of aging populations could be improved through social development and discussed socio-economic and political issues that called for specific as well as general policy considerations, with a view to proposing feasible policy options.

The Food and Agriculture Organization of the United Nations, in a February report analysing the condition of aging populations in the developing world,[1] noting the need for more data on the topic, recommended new policies for an integrated rural development strategy to provide improved technologies to assist older farmers and home-based productive activities for older rural women.

Reports. [1]FAO, A/CONF.113/8; S-G, [2]A/CONF.113/5, [3]A/CONF.113/6, [4]A/CONF.113/14; [5]World Assembly on Aging, A/CONF.113/31 (Sales No. E.82.I.16).

Population trends

The Plan of Action on Aging described demographic trends according to which, from 1975 to

2025, the number of persons aged 60 years and over throughout the world would more than treble. Life expectancies were increasing, with a higher expectancy for women than for men; thus women in most cases were expected to make up a majority of the older population.

These trends were supported by estimates included in a report of the Secretary-General on demographic considerations[1] provided to the World Assembly. The report described trends over time of the elderly population and the relative proportion of the elderly in the total population, in order to assist decision makers when dealing with problems relating to aging.

Report. [1]S-G, A/CONF.113/4.

Migration

The Plan of Action on Aging described the particular needs of aging migrants, in particular an improvement in the continuity of social benefits such as pensions. This could be achieved through bilateral and multilateral social security arrangements. Besides recommending guarantees for social coverage, including continuous social security credits, the Plan also recommended special assistance for the migrant worker upon repatriation, particularly with respect to housing, to facilitate reintegration. It urged co-ordinated efforts by the mass media to highlight the effects of migration on the relative aging of populations of rural areas and its effects on agricultural production and living conditions in those areas.

The Secretary-General, in a June 1982 report on migration and aging[1] prepared for the World Assembly, described problems linked to migration and suggested that policy makers take account of considerations in this regard, such as the rights of elderly migrant workers; the importance of the use of remittances sent by migrants for investment and the development process; measures to encourage continued relationships between younger migrants and the elderly they had left behind, as well as measures to enable the elderly to rejoin their children or maintain contact with them; and research on migration to provide decision makers

with information necessary for policy and programme formulation.

Report. [1]S-G, A/CONF.113/7.

National days

The Vienna International Plan of Action on Aging[2] invited all States to consider designating a national Day for the Aging in conformity with a General Assembly resolution of November 1981.[3] In a September report to the Assembly,[1] the Secretary-General stated that, of the 21 Member States which had replied to the invitation, three had indicated their hesitation to designate a specific day, another three would communicate their decision at a later date and the remaining 15 indicated their support for the idea.

Reports. [1]S-G report, A/37/408; [2]World Assembly on Aging, A/CONF.113/31 (Sales No. E.82.I.16).
Resolution. [3]GA: 36/20, 9 Nov. 1981 (YUN 1981, p. 1023).

Other activities of the UN system

The February 1982 *Ad Hoc* Inter-agency Meeting on Aging[1] suggested that, as an alternative mechanism for co-ordinating implementation of the Vienna International Plan of Action on Aging, a separate inter-agency secretariat or consortium, to which agency staff could be seconded, could be established, as could a task force on aging within the Administrative Committee on Co-ordination, with the Centre for Social Development and Humanitarian Affairs (CSDHA) as the focal point.

The May Meeting[2] recommended that the inter-agency arrangements which had been set up for co-ordinating the preparations for the World Assembly on Aging should serve as the mechanism for the Plan's implementation, with CSDHA acting as the focal point. It also recommended that CSHDA convene an informal inter-agency meeting to decide on the next *Ad Hoc* Inter-agency Meeting and that organizations take the Plan into account when preparing future programmes and budgets, particularly for the 1984-1985 biennium.

Reports. Inter-agency Meeting on Aging, [1]ACC/1982/PG/3, [2]ACC/1982/PG/6.

Chapter XXI

Refugees

Contents

Related topics:

Africa: Lesotho and South Africa. Middle East: Protection of Palestine refugees and civilians in Lebanon; Activities of UNRWA. Economic Assistance, Disasters and Emergency Relief: Lebanon.

For resolutions and decisions of major organs mentioned but not reproduced, refer to INDEX OF RESOLUTIONS AND DECISIONS.

General aspects

In 1982, despite some encouraging developments, the world-wide problem of refugees and displaced persons remained serious, especially in Africa, Asia and Latin America, and the Office of the United Nations High Commissioner for Refugees (UNHCR) continued to respond to their immediate and long-term needs.

In recognition of the valuable work carried out by UNHCR, the General Assembly decided to continue that Office for a further period of five years from 1 January 1984, and also elected Poul Hartling, serving a five-year term as High Commissioner since 1978, for a further three-year term beginning on 1 January 1983.

Programme and finances of UNHCR

Programme policy

Executive Committee action. At its thirty-third session at Geneva from 11 to 20 October 1982,[1] the Executive Committee for the Programme of the United Nations High Commissioner for Refugees took note with satisfaction of the evolution of many major activities from their emergency or relief phase to the promotion of self-reliance leading to durable solutions.

It welcomed the continued attention paid to voluntary repatriation—particularly through the expanded programme for Ethiopian returnees, the recently completed programme in Chad and the ongoing programmes for Indo-Chinese returnees—and took note of the relative stabilization of the refugee problem in the Horn of Africa and the Sudan. At the same time, the Committee expressed concern over the refugee situation in Central America and in Lebanon, and urged the High Commissioner to continue or expand assistance there within his competence. Further, it noted with appreciation the progress made in the assistance programme in Pakistan.

The Executive Committee took note of the resettlement activities, and stressed the importance of Governments continuing to admit refugees who had no other durable solution, or those with special needs such as emergency cases or disabled refugees. It noted with concern the significant decrease in resettlement opportunities for Indo-Chinese refugees, urged Governments to maintain the momentum of resettlement based on equitable international burden-sharing and those connected with the Orderly Departure Programme from Viet Nam to facilitate its implementation and expansion. It also urged Governments to provide resettlement opportunities to the growing number of world-wide refugees from the Middle East.

General Assembly action. By a resolution adopted without vote on 18 December,[2] the General Assembly commended the work of UNHCR, and urged intensified efforts to provide humanitarian assistance to refugees and displaced persons, especially in Africa, Asia and Latin America. It reaffirmed the need for co-operation between UNHCR and Governments, and for the latter to uphold relevant legal instruments and to observe the principles of asylum and _non-refoulement_. The Assembly called on the international community to share the burden of providing durable solutions to the problems of refugees and displaced persons, taking into account residual problems as well as the absorption capacity of the countries concerned. It urged Governments to support the High Commissioner's humanitarian programmes.

The Assembly urged continued examination of problems in providing temporary refuge to asylum seekers in situations of large-scale influx, with a view to finding durable solutions. It urged adapting management practices to the increased UNHCR workload, and requested that humanitarian assistance efforts be co-ordinated with those of United Nations and other bodies concerned in accordance with relevant decisions of the Organization.

At the same time, the Assembly deplored the continued violations of the basic rights of refugees and displaced persons in southern Africa and elsewhere, requested the High Commissioner to continue participation in the follow-up activities of the 1981 International Conference on Assistance to Refugees in Africa[3] and to intensify his assistance to refugees in Africa, and stressed maintenance of relief and resettlement efforts for South-East Asian cases.

The 19-nation text, introduced by Sweden, had been approved by the Assembly's Third (Social, Humanitarian and Cultural) Committee on 1 December, also without vote.

Report. [1]UNHCR Executive Committee, A/37/12/Add.1.
Resolution (1982). [2]GA: 37/195, 18 Dec., text following.
Yearbook reference. [3]1981, p. 1039.
Meeting records. GA: 3rd Committee, A/C.3/37/SR.41, 43-46, 58, 59 (15 Nov.–1 Dec.); plenary, A/37/PV.111 (18 Dec.).

General Assembly resolution 37/195

18 December 1982   Meeting 111   Adopted without vote

Approved by Third Committee (A/37/692) without vote, 1 December (meeting 59); 19-nation draft (A/C.3/37/L.44); agenda item 90 _(a)._

Sponsors: Australia, Belgium, Canada, Costa Rica, Denmark, Djibouti, Finland, Greece, Iceland, Italy, Madagascar, New Zealand, Norway, Pakistan, Portugal, Sudan, Sweden, Thailand, United Republic of Tanzania.

Report of the United Nations High Commissioner for Refugees
The General Assembly,
Having considered the report of the United Nations High Commissioner for Refugees on the activities of his Office, as well as the report of the Executive Committee of the Programme of the High Commissioner on the work of its thirty-third session, and having heard the state-

ment made by the High Commissioner before the Third Committee on 15 November 1982,

Recalling its resolutions 36/124 and 36/125 of 14 December 1981,

Reaffirming the eminently humanitarian and non-political character of the activities of the Office of the High Commissioner on behalf of refugees, returnees and displaced persons of concern to the Office,

Expressing deep concern that the problems of refugees and displaced persons remain distressingly serious, especially in Africa, Asia and Latin America,

Considering that, despite some encouraging developments, substantial efforts continue to be needed to aid refugees and displaced persons of concern to the Office of the High Commissioner, in particular through the promotion of durable and speedy solutions to their problems in accordance with the statute of the Office,

Welcoming the increasing number of accessions by States to the 1951 Convention and the 1967 Protocol relating to the Status of Refugees,

Noting with deep concern that serious violations of the basic rights of refugees and displaced persons of concern to the Office have continued,

Deploring, in particular, the instances of military attacks on refugee camps in southern Africa and elsewhere,

Noting that many assistance programmes have evolved from the emergency phase to a state of consolidation,

Noting with great appreciation the positive responses of Governments to the problems of refugees and displaced persons of concern to the Office of the High Commissioner through offers of asylum, voluntary repatriation, rehabilitation, local settlement, resettlement and financial contributions, as well as the generous support given to the Office in its humanitarian task,

Noting with appreciation the report of the Secretary-General on the International Conference on Assistance to Refugees in Africa,

1. *Commends* the United Nations High Commissioner for Refugees and his staff for the valuable work that the Office of the High Commissioner continues to perform on behalf of refugees, returnees and displaced persons of concern to the Office;

2. *Reaffirms* the fundamental nature of the High Commissioner's function to provide international protection and the need for Governments to co-operate fully with him to facilitate the effective exercise of this essential function, in particular by acceding to and fully implementing the relevant international and regional instruments and by scrupulously observing the principles of asylum and *non-refoulement*;

3. *Deplores* the continued serious violations of the basic rights of refugees and displaced persons of concern to the Office of the High Commissioner, in particular through military attacks on refugee camps and settlements in southern Africa and elsewhere, *refoulement* and arbitrary detention, and stresses the need to strengthen measures to protect them against such violations;

4. *Welcomes*, within the context of the efforts of the international community to share the burden of caring for refugees, the work of the High Commissioner in examining the problems associated with providing refuge on a temporary basis to asylum seekers in situations of large-scale influx with a view to finding durable solutions, and requests him to continue the work in this regard;

5. *Notes with appreciation* the major contribution by countries in giving asylum to, or otherwise accepting on a temporary basis, and assisting large numbers of refugees and displaced persons of concern to the Office of the High Commissioner;

6. *Stresses* the High Commissioner's role in promoting durable and speedy solutions, in consultation and agreement with the countries concerned, to the problems of refugees and displaced persons facing his Office, through voluntary repatriation or return and, whenever appropriate, subsequent assistance in rehabilitation of returnees, resettlement in other countries or integration in countries of asylum, and urges Governments to extend the necessary co-operation to support the High Commissioner's efforts in this regard;

7. *Urges* the High Commissioner to intensify his efforts to provide humanitarian assistance to refugees and displaced persons of concern to his Office, especially to the large numbers of them in Africa, Asia and Latin America;

8. *Stresses* the importance of maintaining relief efforts and the resettlement momentum for boat and land cases in South-East Asia, where large numbers of refugees and displaced persons have been admitted on a temporary basis, including the Programme of Orderly Departure;

9. *Takes note* of the efforts already made by the High Commissioner to adapt the management practices and staffing policy of his Office to the vastly increased tasks and invites him to continue these efforts in line with the relevant resolutions of the General Assembly and decisions of the Executive Committee of the Programme of the High Commissioner;

10. *Requests* the High Commissioner to co-ordinate closely the efforts of his Office in the field of humanitarian assistance with those of other bodies concerned both within and outside the United Nations system, in accordance with the relevant resolutions and decisions of the General Assembly, the Economic and Social Council and the Administrative Committee on Co-ordination;

11. *Also requests* the High Commissioner to continue participating in the follow-up activities to the International Conference on Assistance to Refugees in Africa and to intensify his assistance to refugees in Africa;

12. *Calls upon* the international community to share the burden of providing appropriate durable solutions to the problems of refugees and displaced persons of concern to the Office of the High Commissioner the world over, taking into account residual problems as well as the economic and demographic absorption capacity of the countries concerned;

13. *Urges* all Governments in a position to do so to support and contribute generously to the High Commissioner's humanitarian programmes.

Continuation of UNHCR

Considering the valuable work accomplished by UNHCR in providing international protection and assistance to refugees and displaced persons and in promoting permanent solutions to their problems, the General Assembly, by an 18 December 1982 resolution adopted without vote,[1] decided to continue the Office for five more years from 1 January 1984. It invited the High Commissioner to continue to report to, and be guided by, the Executive Committee of the Programme of the High Commissioner which, in turn, would remain responsible for determining the general policies for UNHCR activities and for ensuring the efficient use of funds and the successful administration and management of programmes. The Assembly decided to review, not later than at its 1987 session, the arrangements for the Office to determine its future beyond 31 December 1988.

The Third Committee had approved, in a similar fashion on 1 December, the 25-nation text introduced by Sweden.

Resolution (1982). [1]GA: 37/196, 18 Dec., text following.
Meeting records. GA: 3rd Committee, A/C.3/37/SR.*41*, 43-46, *58, 59* (15 Nov.–1 Dec.); plenary, A/37/PV.111 (18 Dec.).

General Assembly resolution 37/196

18 December 1982   Meeting 111   Adopted without vote

Approved by Third Committee (A/37/692) without vote, 1 December (meeting 59); 25-nation draft (A/C.3/37/L.45); agenda item 90 *(b)*.

Sponsors: Australia, Bangladesh, Belgium, Canada, Costa Rica, Denmark, Ethiopia, Finland, France, Germany, Federal Republic of, Iceland, Italy, Japan, Malaysia, Netherlands, New Zealand, Norway, Pakistan, Sudan, Sweden, Thailand, United Kingdom, United Republic of Cameroon, United Republic of Tanzania, United States.

**Continuation of the Office of the United Nations
High Commissioner for Refugees**

The General Assembly,

Having considered the report of the United Nations High Commissioner for Refugees on the activities of his Office,

Recalling its resolution 32/68 of 8 December 1977, in which it decided to review, not later than at its thirty-seventh session, the arrangements for the Office of the High Commissioner with a view to determining whether the Office should be continued beyond 31 December 1983,

Recalling further its resolutions 1166(XII) of 26 November 1957 and 1673(XVI) of 18 December 1961 and Economic and Social Council resolution 672(XXV) of 30 April 1958 on the establishment of the Executive Committee of the Programme of the United Nations High Commissioner for Refugees,

Recognizing the great continuing need for international action on behalf of refugees and displaced persons of concern to the High Commissioner,

Expressing its concern at the persistence and gravity of the problems of refugees and displaced persons of concern to the High Commissioner in all parts of the world, particularly in different parts of Africa, Asia and Latin America,

Considering the valuable work accomplished by the Office of the High Commissioner in providing international protection and assistance to refugees and displaced persons of concern to the High Commissioner and in promoting permanent solutions to their problems,

1. *Decides* to continue the Office of the United Nations High Commissioner for Refugees for a further period of five years from 1 January 1984;

2. *Requests* the High Commissioner to continue to discharge his basic functions of protection, assistance and the promotion of durable solutions in accordance with the statute of the Office and the relevant General Assembly resolutions;

3. *Invites* the High Commissioner to continue to report to and be guided by the Executive Committee of the Programme of the High Commissioner in accordance with the Committee's terms of reference and its decisions, as set forth in General Assembly resolution 1166(XII) and Economic and Social Council resolution 672(XXV);

4. *Reiterates* that the responsibilities of the Executive Committee of the Programme of the High Commissioner shall continue to cover the determination of the general policies by means of periodic review of programmes, operations, management and activities under which the High Commissioner shall plan, develop and administer the programmes and projects;

5. *Urges*, in this regard, the Executive Committee of the Programme of the High Commissioner, when fulfilling the functions and the responsibilities entrusted to it by the relevant resolutions of the General Assembly and the Economic and Social Council, to ensure the efficient use of funds and to give special attention to the successful administration and management of programmes;

6. *Takes note* of the efforts already made by the High Commissioner to adapt the management of his services to the vastly increased tasks and invites him to undertake his efforts in accordance with the principles and guidelines set by the General Assembly, and in the light of the guidance given to him by the Executive Committee of the Programme of the High Commissioner;

7. *Decides* to review, not later than at its forty-second session, the arrangements for the Office of the United Nations High Commissioner for Refugees with a view to determining whether the Office should be continued beyond 31 December 1988.

Financial and administrative questions

In 1982, total expenditure by the UNHCR Office for all programmes was $420.2 million. Of that amount, $318.9 million was allocated under General Programmes, $88.1 million under Special Programmes and $13.2 million under the United Nations regular budget.

Total income for 1982 was $444.4 million.

Contributions

In 1982, contributions from governmental and private sources amounted to $354.8 million against the total UNHCR income for 1982 of $444.4 million.[1]

The Executive Committee of the Programme of UNHCR, at its October 1982 session,[2] reaffirmed the need for more equitable and widespread financial support within the international community for UNHCR programmes, thanked donor Governments and non-governmental organizations for their generosity, and urged Governments to announce, at the November 1982 pledging conference, sufficient substantial unearmarked pledges for 1983 to ensure early availability of funds and orderly implementation of programmes.

At the 19 November 1982 meeting of the *Ad Hoc* Committee of the General Assembly for the Announcement of Voluntary Contributions to the 1983 UNHCR Programme, 43 countries announced pledges totalling $105,972,366 towards General Programmes and $4,660,861 towards Special Programmes.

For contributions paid or pledged in 1982, see table on next page.

Reports. [1]Board of Auditors, and financial statements, A/38/5/Add.5; [2]UNHCR Executive Committee, A/37/12/Add.1.
Meeting record. Ad Hoc Committee of GA for voluntary contributions to 1983 UNHCR programme, A/AC.217/SR.1 (19 Nov.).

Financing of administrative expenses

Report of the Secretary-General. Based on the joint survey with the High Commissioner involving a post-by-post review of his Office's 1,053 established posts as at the beginning of 1982, including those of 57 field representatives and chargés de mission covering 120 countries, the Secretary-General, in a July 1982 report,[3] pointed to the need to rationalize the current apportionment of the UNHCR administrative expenditure between regular funds and extrabudgetary resources. He proposed, in that regard, that 65 Professional posts currently charged to voluntary funds be transferred to the regular programme budget, and that 45 General Service posts be transferred from the regular budget to extrabudgetary funds. The proposed redistribution of posts was estimated to incur additional regular-budget costs of $4.1 million a year (at 1982 rates).

The Secretary-General suggested, for General Assembly endorsement, that there be a joint annual review, starting in 1983, on establishing and financing of new posts, and the information reported to the Advisory Committee on Administrative and Budgetary Questions (ACABQ) and the Assembly; unless unforeseen situations arose, no further transfers of posts would be made before the 1990-1991 biennium.

ACABQ report. Commenting on the Secretary-General's report in September,[2] ACABQ recalled that, according to the UNHCR Statute,[6] only "administrative expenditures relating to the functioning

CONTRIBUTIONS PAID OR PLEDGED TO UNHCR ASSISTANCE PROGRAMMES, 1982
(as at 31 December 1982; in US dollar equivalent)

Country	1982 payment or pledge	Country	1982 payment or pledge	Country	1982 payment or pledge
Algeria	50,000	Japan	46,293,353	Swaziland	2,139
Argentina	39,400	Jordan	10,000	Sweden	14,696,373
Australia	14,173,931	Kenya	659	Switzerland	5,162,798
Austria	101,406	Kuwait	130,000	Syrian Arab Republic	1,000
Bahamas	5,454	Lao People's Democratic Republic	6,000	Thailand	10,000
Bangladesh	1,006	Lebanon	10,000	Tunisia	7,000
Barbados	1,000	Liberia	5,000	Turkey	111,000
Belgium	1,977,649	Liechtenstein	14,151	Uganda	11,798
Benin	4,675	Luxembourg	70,440	United Kingdom	8,381,751
Bermuda	10,000	Madagascar	1,316	United Republic of Cameroon	3,790
Botswana	1,486	Malaysia	20,000	United Republic of Tanzania	4,184
Brazil	15,000	Malta	1,000	United States	121,935,254
Burma	10,000	Mauritius	1,500	Upper Volta	1,458
Burundi	1,675	Mexico	50,435	Viet Nam	880
Canada	14,825,758	Monaco	831	Yugoslavia	54,705
Chile	20,000	Morocco	9,099	Zaire	20,000
China	232,000	Netherlands	8,103,448	Zambia	4,396
Colombia	17,586	New Zealand	144,758	Zimbabwe	31
Cyprus	3,595	Nicaragua	1,000		
Denmark	12,852,183	Norway	10,227,224	Subtotal	284,313,431
Finland	1,864,362	Oman	6,000		
France	1,173,530	Pakistan	9,343	*Intergovernmental contributions*	
Germany, Federal Republic of	16,250,132	Panama	1,000		
Greece	92,948	Philippines	5,817	European Economic Community	59,341,711
Holy See	2,500	Portugal	102,500	International Year of the Child Committee	664,229
Iceland	53,300	Qatar	35,000	UNICEF	22,403
India	10,000	Republic of Korea	10,000	United Nations Trust Fund for Southern Africans	300,000
Indonesia	8,000	San Marino	13,652		
Ireland	210,065	Saudi Arabia	10,000	Subtotal	60,328,343
Israel	15,000	Senegal	3,000		
Italy	3,261,668	Spain	1,318,110	Total	344,641,774
Ivory Coast	2,621	Sudan	2,308		

SOURCE: A/38/5/Add.5.

of the Office" could be borne by the United Nations regular budget; all other expenditures were to be financed by voluntary contributions. ACABQ did not dispute that there might be need to charge some additional posts to the regular budget; however, the number and nature of such posts to be transferred in a given biennium would require an Assembly decision based on careful examination of the data, and should be taken on a case-by-case basis in the context of the Secretary-General's proposed programme budgets for 1984-1985 and subsequent biennia.

Executive Committee action. By a note of 26 October,[1] the Secretary-General transmitted to the General Assembly a decision[4] taken earlier that month by the Executive Committee for the High Commissioner's Programme, recommending that the Assembly note the ACABQ comments and approve the principles outlined in the Secretary-General's report which formed the basis of an equitable apportionment of the administrative costs of UNHCR between the regular budget and voluntary funds.

General Assembly action. By a 21 December resolution,[5] the General Assembly took note of the Secretary-General's report, concurred in the ACABQ comments, and endorsed its opinion that decisions on the transfer of posts should be taken on a case-by-case basis.

The Assembly adopted the text by a recorded vote, requested by the USSR, of 122 to 9, with 10 abstentions. The Assembly's Fifth (Administrative and Budgetary) Committee had approved, without vote on 29 October, the text introduced by Lebanon also on behalf of Sweden.

Speaking in explanation of position, Cyprus, Jordan and Nigeria endorsed the Secretary-General's report, and agreement with the ACABQ recommendations was expressed by Cyprus, Iran, Nigeria, Morocco and the Syrian Arab Republic. Spain particularly agreed with those recommendations on the detailed review of administrative costs. The Sudan called the resolution constructive.

Iran supported financing UNHCR activities from both the regular budget and voluntary contributions, and asserted that the Office's management should be carefully reviewed in the light of refugees' needs. In a similar vein, Nigeria hoped that the administrative costs would be kept to the minimum so that more resources could be devoted to refugee relief, while the Syrian Arab Republic believed the text would improve the apportionment of the UNHCR administrative expenditure.

Denmark, speaking on behalf of the 10 member States of the European Community, agreed with the Secretary-General's call for rationalizing apportionment of costs between the budget and contributions, and endorsed the ACABQ case-by-case recommendation. Brazil and Ghana, which opposed transferring posts financed from extrabudgetary funds to the regular budget, supported, as did Japan, the text in the light of that recommendation. Similarly, Iraq stressed the importance of close examination of such transfers, and urged completion of the ongoing study of the way UNHCR activities were organized.

The United Kingdom considered the estimated cost to be high. The USSR, from its position of principle with regard to posts financed from extrabudgetary funds, said it was unable to approve either the recommendation in the Secretary-General's report or that of ACABQ, but withdrew a proposal to have the text put to a vote in the Committee.

Note. (1)S-G, A/C.5/37/22.
Reports. (2)ACABQ, A/37/7/Add.3; (3)S-G, A/C.5/37/1 & Corr.1; (4)UNHCR Executive Committee, A/37/12/Add.1.
Resolution (1982). (5)GA: 37/238, 21 Dec., text following.
Resolution (prior). (6)GA: 428(V), annex, 14 Dec. 1950 (YUN 1950, p. 585).
Meeting records. GA: 5th Committee, A/C.5/37/SR.*20-22* (27-29 Oct.); plenary, A/37/PV.114 (21 Dec.).

General Assembly resolution 37/238

21 December 1982   Meeting 114   122-9-10 (recorded vote)

Approved by Fifth Committee (A/37/790) without vote, 29 October (meeting 22); 2-nation draft (A/C.5/37/L.19); agenda item 103.

Sponsors: Lebanon, Sweden.

Review of the financing of the administrative costs of the Office of the United Nations High Commissioner for Refugees

The General Assembly,

Having considered the report of the Secretary-General on the review of the financing of the administrative costs of the Office of the United Nations High Commissioner for Refugees and the related report of the Advisory Committee on Administrative and Budgetary Questions,

1. *Takes note* of the report of the Secretary-General;

2. *Endorses* the opinion of the Advisory Committee on Administrative and Budgetary Questions that decisions on the proposals of the Secretary-General concerning the transfer of posts should be taken on a case-by-case basis in the context of his proposed programme budgets for the 1984-1985 and subsequent bienniums;

3. *Concurs* in the other comments and observations of the Advisory Committee in its report.

Recorded vote in Assembly as follows:

In favour: Algeria, Angola, Argentina, Australia, Austria, Bahamas, Bahrain, Bangladesh, Barbados, Benin, Bhutan, Bolivia, Botswana, Brazil, Burma, Burundi, Canada, Central African Republic, Chad, Chile, China, Colombia, Comoros, Congo, Costa Rica, Cyprus, Democratic Kampuchea, Democratic Yemen, Denmark, Ecuador, Egypt, El Salvador, Ethiopia, Fiji, Finland, Gabon, Gambia, Ghana, Greece, Grenada, Guatemala, Guinea, Guinea-Bissau, Guyana, Honduras, Iceland, India, Indonesia, Iran, Iraq, Ireland, Israel, Ivory Coast, Jamaica, Jordan, Kenya, Kuwait, Lebanon, Lesotho, Liberia, Libyan Arab Jamahiriya, Madagascar, Malawi, Malaysia, Maldives, Mali, Malta, Mauritania, Mexico, Morocco, Mozambique, Nepal, Netherlands, New Zealand, Nicaragua, Niger, Nigeria, Norway, Oman, Pakistan, Panama, Papua New Guinea, Paraguay, Peru, Philippines, Portugal, Qatar, Romania, Rwanda, Saint Lucia, Samoa, Sao Tome and Principe, Saudi Arabia, Senegal, Sierra Leone, Singapore, Solomon Islands, Somalia, Spain, Sri Lanka, Sudan, Suriname, Swaziland, Sweden, Syrian Arab Republic, Thailand, Togo, Trinidad and Tobago, Tunisia, Turkey, Uganda, United Arab Emirates, United Republic of Cameroon, United Republic of Tanzania, Upper Volta, Uruguay, Venezuela, Yemen, Yugoslavia, Zaire, Zambia, Zimbabwe.

Against: Bulgaria, Byelorussian SSR, Czechoslovakia, German Democratic Republic, Hungary, Mongolia, Poland, Ukrainian SSR, USSR.

Abstaining: Afghanistan, Belgium, Dominican Republic, France, Germany, Federal Republic of, Italy, Japan, Luxembourg, United Kingdom, United States.

Accounts of voluntary funds for 1981

The audited financial statements for the year ended 31 December 1981 including the voluntary funds administered by UNHCR showed a total expenditure of $474.3 million, and total income of $506.8 million.

After examining the financial statement, the Board of Auditors recommended in its report(2) to the General Assembly that UNHCR should provide more detailed information on programme support and administrative expenditures. It recommended that "overall allocations", large amounts of which were transferred to country programmes, be limited and used for the purposes intended.

The Board felt that UNHCR representatives and field officers should be more attentive to proper application of the administrative and financial provisions of agreements with the implementing partners. It believed that a currently-used glossary of standard clauses for agreements was too general in terms, and recommended that UNHCR develop a field-office procurement manual for the economical use of funds in awarding procurement contracts and purchase orders. The Board also suggested that Governments be required to notify UNHCR in advance of the closure of a refugee camp.

The Advisory Committee on Administrative and Budgetary Questions (ACABQ), commenting on the Board's audit in a September report,(1) said it agreed with the UNHCR Executive Committee on the need to provide for overall allocations in the programme budget to cover small projects, and concurred with the Board's suggestion regarding a manual for local procurement.

The Executive Committee in October(3) took note of the 1981 financial accounts and the reports of the Board and ACABQ.

By a 16 November resolution(4) accepting the financial reports of several United Nations organizations and programmes, and endorsing the Board's audit opinions, including those on UNHCR, the General Assembly requested the Board and ACABQ to give greater attention to areas regarding which they had made comments. It also requested the Secretary-General to remove the shortcomings referred to and asked executive heads to take remedial action.

Reports. (1)ACABQ, A/37/443; (2)Board of Auditors, and financial statements, A/37/5/Add.5; (3)UNHCR Executive Committee, A/37/12/Add.1.
Resolution (1982). (4)GA: 37/12, 16 Nov.

Organizational questions

Representation of Namibia in the Executive Committee

The Economic and Social Council, by a decision of 16 April 1982,(2) granted Namibia, represented by the United Nations Council for

Namibia, full membership in the Executive Committee of the Programme of UNHCR, thus enlarging the membership to 41. The text, orally proposed by Zaire and based on a recommendation by the Group of African States, was adopted by 35 votes to 2, with 12 abstentions.

Introducing the text, Zaire observed that Namibia was already a full member in a number of United Nations bodies and specialized agencies and therefore a precedent was not being created; this view was shared by Benin and Senegal. Greece supported the decision, maintaining that, since UNHCR was the only international organ entrusted with protecting refugees, close co-operation between the Council for Namibia and UNHCR was essential.

Portugal said the decision raised legal questions which should have been clarified; it abstained in the light of its reservations concerning the broadening of the mandate of the Council for Namibia. Brazil voted for the decision, but stressed that it was against giving an organization equality with a Member State; in its view the decision could not be regarded as creating a legal or political precedent.

The Federal Republic of Germany, speaking also on behalf of Canada, France, the United Kingdom and the United States—members of the Contact Group pursuing consultations with the parties to negotiations on Namibia—said those countries opposed the precedent inherent in the decision. They—as well as Norway and Denmark, which abstained—pointed out that the Council was already invited to the Executive Committee as an observer.

On 5 February 1982,[1] at its organizational session for the year, the Council, on an oral proposal of its President, had decided to take action on the membership question at its first regular session of the year, in pursuance of a December 1981 request by the General Assembly.[3]

Decisions (1982). ESC: [1]1982/104, 5 Feb., text following; [2]1982/110, 16 Apr., text following.
Resolution (prior). [3]GA, 36/121 D, 10 Dec. 1981 (YUN 1981, p. 1164).
Meeting records. ESC: E/1982/SR.*4*, 8, *9* (5 Feb. & 15, 16 Apr.).

Economic and Social Council decision 1982/104

Adopted without vote

Draft orally proposed by President, based on recommendation by Bureau; agenda item 2.

Membership of Namibia, represented by the United Nations Council for Namibia, in the Executive Committee of the Programme of the United Nations High Commissioner for Refugees

At its 4th plenary meeting, on 5 February 1982, the Council decided to defer until its first regular session of 1982, for final consideration and decision, the question concerning the membership of Namibia, represented by the United Nations Council for Namibia, in the Executive Committee of the Programme of the United Nations High Commissioner for Refugees, in pursuance of the request made by the General Assembly in its resolution 36/121 D of 10 December 1981.

The Council also agreed to consider this question under item 1 of the provisional agenda for the first regular session of 1982, entitled "Adoption of the agenda and other organizational matters".

Economic and Social Council decision 1982/110

35-2-12

Draft orally proposed by Zaire, based on recommendation by African Group; agenda item 1.

Membership of Namibia, represented by the United Nations Council for Namibia, in the Executive Committee of the Programme of the United Nations High Commissioner for Refugees

At its 9th plenary meeting, on 16 April 1982, the Council, pursuant to the request made by the General Assembly in paragraph 7 of its resolution 36/121 D of 10 December 1981, decided:

(a) To enlarge the membership of the Executive Committee of the Programme of the United Nations High Commissioner for Refugees to forty-one members so as to enable Namibia, represented by the United Nations Council for Namibia, to participate in the Committee as a full member;

(b) To grant membership in the Committee to Namibia, represented by the United Nations Council for Namibia.

Extension of the High Commissioner's term

By a decision adopted without vote on 18 December 1982,[1] the General Assembly, on the proposal of the Secretary-General,[3] elected Poul Hartling United Nations High Commissioner for Refugees for a further three-year term beginning on 1 January 1983. Mr. Hartling had been serving as High Commissioner since 1 January 1978.[2]

On the same date, the Assembly continued the Office of the High Commissioner for five years from 1 January 1984.[4]

Decision (1982). [1]GA: *37/319*, 18 Dec., text following.
Decision (prior). [2]GA: 32/314, 8 Dec. 1977 (YUN 1977, p. 625).
Note. [3]S-G, A/37/769.
Resolution (1982). GA: [4]37/196, 18 Dec.
Meeting record. GA: A/37/PV.111 (18 Dec.).

General Assembly decision 37/319

Adopted without vote

Proposal by Secretary-General (A/37/769); agenda item 16 *(g)*.

Election of the United Nations High Commissioner for Refugees

At its 111th plenary meeting, on 18 December 1982, the General Assembly, on the proposal of the Secretary-General, elected Mr. Poul Hartling United Nations High Commissioner for Refugees for a further three-year term beginning on 1 January 1983.

Public information

The Public Information Section of UNHCR continued trying to promote greater public awareness of refugee problems by producing and distributing written and audio-visual information materials and through direct co-operation with information sources and outlets.

In September, a quarterly colour supplement to the monthly English- and French-language tabloid, *Refugees*, was introduced. Some 60,000 photographs and three documentary films—*Sanctuary: an African Epic, Nueva Esperanza,* and *Rwanda Influx*—were distributed to media, schools and non-governmental organizations. Co-productions of refugee films with television companies were intensified, and radio programmes were produced and distributed to radio stations around the world or via regional disseminators.

Four seminars were held for journalists in Central America, the Horn of Africa and the Sudan, Pakistan and South-East Asia. Films, photographs, posters, printed material, calendars and kits were provided to voluntary agencies to support their fund-raising projects and information campaigns.

Activities for refugees

Assistance to refugees

The 1982 UNHCR expenditure in assistance programmes totalling some $407 million—as compared with $474 million in 1981 and $497 million in 1980 at the time of dramatic refugee influxes in Africa and Asia—reflected the progression of relative stabilization of most major programmes beyond a strictly emergency phase.[2]

Of some $5.8 million obligated for emergency assistance in 1982, $2.25 million was used to provide immediate relief to persons affected by the events in Lebanon, and another $2.1 million to cover the short-term emergency relief requirements of needy Lebanese who had left the country (see POLITICAL AND SECURITY QUESTIONS, Chapter IX); by the end of 1982, many had returned. Some $1.4 million was made available for emergency assistance to Rwandese refugees and affected persons within Rwanda or in Uganda (see below). Special measures taken because of large increases in arrivals in Honduras and southern Sudan were not necessary by year's end. Increased emergency preparedness was reflected in the completion of a *Handbook on Emergencies* and of rosters of technical experts who could be called on.

Intermediate aid in the form of care and maintenance (food, shelter, water, health services, education) accounted for some 59 per cent of the total General Programmes expenditure, a reduction from 1981 (63 per cent). The programme for Afghan refugees in Pakistan remained the largest single UNHCR care and maintenance programme ($94 million), followed by $60 million for Indo-Chinese refugees and $29 million for Somalia. Activities for promoting self-sufficiency either began or were expanded in most such programmes, and community counselling services were provided through 53 projects in 46 countries. Essential educational assistance, including elementary and advanced education as well as technical or skills training, amounted to some $11.9 million in 1982.

Durable solutions remained the primary objective, and continued efforts were made to achieve voluntary repatriation, local integration in the country of first asylum, or resettlement to another country when other alternatives were not feasible.

Almost $66 million, or some 20 per cent of the total UNHCR General Programmes expenditure, financed such local settlement activities as large-scale agricultural programmes in Africa—notably in the Sudan, the United Republic of Tanzania and Zaire—and smaller initial projects in Central America—in Belize, Costa Rica, Nicaragua and Panama. In China, a large-scale settlement programme for Indo-Chinese refugees had reached the final stage, while substantial aid was given to Indo-Chinese individuals and small groups in Argentina and in Europe.

Some 109,000 Indo-Chinese were resettled in 1982 in third countries, and another 10,000 Vietnamese were reunited with families abroad through the Orderly Departure Programme (see below). While the majority of refugees in Central America were permitted to settle in the region, only a few countries had formal programmes for the resettlement of refugees from the Middle East and South-West Asia.

UNHCR found resettlement opportunities for more than 500 disabled refugees and their families who could not be admitted otherwise. Assistance to handicapped refugees increased appreciably during 1982, partly as a consequence of the establishment of a new Trust Fund for Handicapped Refugees with the proceeds of the Nobel Peace Prize awarded to the Office in 1981.[3] Specific measures financed under the Trust Fund and General Programme helped 1,858 handicapped refugees meet the costs of surgery, physiotherapy, special equipment and psychological counselling.

Special arrangements were made at Nairobi (Kenya) and Cairo (Egypt) for the treatment of disabled refugees from various parts of Africa, and steps taken to establish similar arrangements at Dakar (Senegal). Assistance continued in Spain and Venezuela to refugees suffering from trauma, and projects for disabled refugees were undertaken or ongoing in a number of countries in Africa, Asia and Latin America. In 1982, $473,340 was obligated from both General and Special Programmes for the treatment and rehabilitation of handicapped and elderly refugees (see below).

Several assistance programmes, as in Chad and Zambia, were phased out during 1982, and responsibilities for further assistance transferred to host Governments. Other promising developments included the establishment of a Tripartite Commission involving Ethiopia, Djibouti and UNHCR to facilitate the voluntary repatriation of Ethiopian refugees in Djibouti, progress in a rural project in Costa Rica, and successful local integration in China of more than 260,000 refugees.

The following table shows 1982 programme expenditure by country or area.[1]

UNHCR EXPENDITURE IN 1982 BY COUNTRY OR AREA*
(in thousands of US dollars)

Country or area	Local settlement	Resettlement	Voluntary repatriation	Relief † and other assistance	Total
AFRICA					
Algeria	1,708.1	—	—	92.0	1,800.1
Angola	3,423.1	9.8	97.0	681.7	4,211.6
Botswana	682.3	4.0	50.0	100.5	836.8
Burundi	1,483.7	1.1	—	2.4	1,487.2
Djibouti	3,227.2	11.8	0.3	207.7	3,447.0
Egypt	2,662.5	146.4	0.4	234.0	3,043.3
Ethiopia	631.1	91.5	4,084.8	70.1	4,877.5
Kenya	1,569.1	20.1	5.0	445.6	2,039.8
Lesotho	299.8	45.0	—	328.7	673.5
Nigeria	859.6	—	11.6	—	871.2
Rwanda	346.4	1.4	—	5,343.5	5,691.3
Senegal	601.3	—	—	64.3	665.6
Somalia	6,489.2	0.7	1.6	24,496.0	30,987.5
Sudan	23,474.3	171.2	215.5	1,161.8	25,022.8
Swaziland	2,292.2	13.6	—	136.4	2,442.2
Uganda	196.0	3.6	548.0	559.6	1,307.2
United Republic of Cameroon	3,977.7	—	0.6	105.2	4,083.5
United Republic of Tanzania	6,684.7	2.4	2.0	85.6	6,774.7
Zaire	15,424.5	2.0	29.4	33.1	15,489.0
Zambia	2,803.2	—	0.5	311.1	3,114.8
Zimbabwe	266.9	1.4	—	68.0	336.3
Other	2,796.2	34.8	4,781.3	35.5	7,647.8
Follow-up on recommendations of Pan-African Conference on Refugees	—	—	—	287.2	287.2
Subtotal	81,899.1	560.8	9,828.0	34,850.0	127,137.9
AMERICAS					
Argentina	951.2	198.0	75.2	713.9	1,938.3
Costa Rica	1,287.1	16.0	23.0	1,477.0	2,803.1
Peru	493.2	30.0	4.0	41.0	568.2
Other northern Latin America	2,964.4	203.2	96.0	16,421.0	19,684.6
Other north-western South America	351.8	—	23.6	122.0	497.4
Other southern Latin America	620.3	300.0	—	582.3	1,502.6
North America	11.5	6.5	36.0	56.8	110.8
Subtotal	6,679.5	753.7	257.8	19,414.0	27,105.0
EAST AND SOUTH ASIA AND OCEANIA					
Australia	0.1	—	—	0.2	0.3
China	10,942.6	187.9	—	3.9	11,134.4
Hong Kong	—	1,114.6	0.1	3,970.5	5,085.2
Indonesia	—	1,301.2	—	7,475.6	8,776.8
Lao People's Democratic Republic	432.3	—	720.2	—	1,152.5
Malaysia	1,861.8	553.7	—	6,199.4	8,614.9
Philippines	3.5	764.2	0.7	9,985.4	10,753.8
Thailand	0.9	4,564.4	1.9	34,316.6	38,883.8
Viet Nam	1,150.0	2,400.0	0.2	—	3,550.2
Other	402.2	1,064.1	2,603.7	6,594.9	10,664.9
Subtotal	14,793.4	11,950.1	3,326.8	68,546.5	98,616.8
EUROPE					
Austria	166.7	54.0	0.5	1,210.8	1,432.0
France	243.7	59.4	40.4	329.8	673.3
Germany, Federal Republic of	92.4	34.0	0.1	356.8	483.3
Greece	481.0	170.4	0.8	150.1	802.3
Italy	123.0	94.1	2.4	528.0	747.5
Portugal	716.9	3.4	8.0	203.5	931.8
Spain	1,343.8	10.8	13.3	904.4	2,272.3
Turkey	462.2	291.6	—	6.3	760.1
United Kingdom	156.3	4.3	84.3	69.7	314.6
Yugoslavia	2.5	75.8	—	1,356.0	1,434.3
Other	311.0	19.1	38.5	646.1	1,014.7
Subtotal	4,099.5	816.9	188.3	5,761.5	10,866.2
MIDDLE EAST AND SOUTH-WEST ASIA					
Cyprus	9,153.8	1.8	—	382.7	9,538.3
Lebanon	78.9	10.0	—	3,318.1	3,407.0
Pakistan	205.0	1,531.5	—	91,228.7	92,965.2
Western Asia	218.5	37.0	—	592.0	847.5
Subtotal	9,656.2	1,580.3	—	95,521.5	106,758.0
GLOBAL AND REGIONAL	323.4	234.9	5.7	528.0	1,092.0
Total	117,451.1	15,896.7	13,606.6	224,621.5	371,575.9

*Not including expenditure for programme support and administration.
†Including donations in kind, such as food.
SOURCE: A/38/12.

Reports. [1]Board of Auditors, and financial statements, A/38/5/Add.5; [2]UNHCR, A/38/12, Corr. and Add.1. *Yearbook reference.* [3]1981, p. 1028.

Africa

UNHCR report. In 1982, UNHCR assistance programmes in Africa, focusing primarily on the Horn of Africa, the Sudan, Zaire and Angola and countries in southern Africa, amounted to some $134.7 million—$103.5 million under General Programmes and $31.2 million under Special Programmes.

Although an increased number of refugees from Africa was resettled in 1982, the need for resettlement remained slight as UNHCR worked with African Governments to encourage repatriation or local integration. A repatriation programme for Chadian refugees was successfully concluded and preliminary discussions were held with Governments on voluntary repatriation for Ugandans in Zaire, Ethiopians in Djibouti, and Ugandans in Rwanda.

In 1982, more than 20,000 South African refugees were assisted by UNHCR in the eight countries of first asylum (Angola, Botswana, Lesotho, Mozambique, Swaziland, the United Republic of Tanzania, Zambia and Zimbabwe). Those elsewhere in Africa received scholarships or subsistence assistance. UNHCR assisted over 75,000 Namibian refugees during the year, including some 70,000 in Angola, 4,700 in Zambia and the remainder in various countries in Africa. Special assistance was also given to disabled African refugees (see above).

On 19 July, the High Commissioner orally informed the Economic and Social Council that the refugee problem remained grave and showed no sign of receding, placing a heavy burden on many host countries, some the poorest in the world. All but some $12 million of the pledges worth $573 million made at the April 1981 International Conference on Assistance to Refugees in Africa (ICARA)[10] had, at the express wish of donors, been channelled bilaterally or through various agencies and organizations.

By a decision of 27 July,[1] the Council took note of the High Commissioner's oral report.

Follow-up to the 1981 Conference. In response to a December 1981 request of the General Assembly,[9] the Secretary-General presented to the Economic and Social Council at its second regular session of 1982 a report, dated 10 June 1982,[4] transmitting an interim report by the ICARA Steering Committee. The Steering Committee, comprising the representatives of each of the ICARA sponsoring organizations (the Organization of African Unity (OAU), the United Nations and UNHCR), had been established after the 1981 Conference (Geneva, 9 and 10 April) to ensure implementation of the Conference conclusions.

In its interim report, the Steering Committee stated that the vast majority of African refugees lived in rural areas, and that refugees and returnees were concentrated in the Horn of Africa (Djibouti, Ethiopia, Somalia and Sudan), where the existing infrastructure, already inadequate, showed clear signs of strain. In central and southern Africa, the returnee population was unevenly distributed, with the largest concentrations in Angola, the United Republic of Tanzania and Zaire; in western Africa, refugees were concentrated in Ghana, Liberia, Nigeria, Senegal and the United Republic of Cameroon. Per capita costs for settling refugees or returnees varied from $300 in non-irrigated agricultural areas in the savannah region to over $1,300 in irrigated areas.

At its meeting at Nairobi on 5 February 1982, the Committee had noted with regret that funding had not yet been provided for the first group of ICARA priority projects, worth $38 million, that had been submitted to the donor community on 22 December 1981. Even ongoing programmes were not fully covered by pledges made at the Conference; however, work continued with the assistance of United Nations development agencies to refine project proposals submitted by African countries. The OAU Council of Ministers, at its February/March 1982 session, asked that the desirability of convening another conference be examined.

Reporting in August to the General Assembly[2] on the meeting held at Geneva from 6 to 8 April 1982 between the representatives of OAU and various United Nations offices and bodies (see POLITICAL AND SECURITY QUESTIONS, Chapter V), the Secretary-General noted the OAU proposals that UNHCR ascertain which assistance requests submitted to ICARA were projects within its area of competence, that the remainder be submitted to the international community for possible funding, and that United Nations agencies assist countries in preparing project documents for consideration by funding agencies. OAU also stressed that additional assistance for refugee-related projects should not be provided at the expense of the host country's own development needs. Some funding agencies pointed out that their ability to provide developmental assistance in the context of refugee problems depended on the initiative of the host country.

In an October report to the Assembly[3] on ICARA, the Secretary-General identified the United Nations Centre for Human Settlements (Habitat) and the United Nations Environment Programme as having prepared the documentation for several of the ICARA priority projects falling within their areas of competence; several other United Nations organizations, though willing to act as implementing partners if project funds were made available, were unable to prepare project documents because of a shortage of resources. The October report also contained information on the use made by Governments and organizations of the $573 million pledged at ICARA.

General Assembly action. Noting that the assistance resulting from ICARA had fallen short of expectations, the General Assembly, by a resolution of 18 December 1982,[8] requested the Secretary-General, in co-operation with the OAU Secretary-General and UNHCR, to convene a second ICARA at Geneva in 1984, to consult with and report on the situation in each African country concerned so the Conference would have an up-to-date assessment of the needs of the refugees/returnees and of the countries, and, for that purpose, to reallocate existing resources.

The 1984 Conference was to review the results of the 1981 ICARA as well as the progress of projects submitted to it; consider the continuing need for assistance with a view to providing, as necessary, additional assistance to refugees and returnees in Africa; and assist the countries concerned in strengthening their social and economic infrastructure so as to enable them to deal with large numbers of refugees and returnees.

The Assembly appealed to the international community for strong support for the Conference with a view to offering maximum financial and material assistance to refugees and returnees in Africa, while stressing that refugee-related assistance should not be provided at the expense of the countries' development needs.

The adoption of the text as a whole, without vote, followed the retention by a recorded vote of 127 to none, with 9 abstentions, of paragraph 5 concerning the decision to convene, and the scope of, a second ICARA. Introduced by Kenya on behalf of the Group of African States, the text as a whole, as orally revised by the Libyan Arab Jamahiriya on behalf of sponsors, had been approved by the Third (Social, Humanitarian and Cultural) Committee without vote on 2 December, following separate adoption of paragraph 5 by 105 votes to none, with 4 abstentions. The vote was requested by the United States.

The paragraph had been amended by the sponsors, before the vote in Committee, to replace one of the purposes of the new Conference to read "to consider the continuing need for assistance with a view to providing, as necessary," additional assistance to refugees and returnees in Africa— rather than simply "to provide" such assistance. Also, taking into account a Moroccan proposal, the sponsors added, to the provision requesting a report on required assistance, the clause "and, for that purpose, to reallocate existing resources".

The question of refugees in Africa was also dealt with in a number of other General Assembly resolutions in 1982. By a 16 November resolution on co-operation between the United Nations and OAU,[5] the Assembly urged the international community to continue its support of African refugee programmes and to provide material and economic assistance to help the host countries cope with the heavy burden imposed on their limited resources and weak infrastructures. By a 17 December resolution on assistance to student refugees in southern Africa,[6] the Assembly appealed to UNHCR, the United Nations Development Programme, and the United Nations Educational, Scientific and Cultural Organization, as well as other international and non-governmental bodies, to continue providing humanitarian and development assistance to expedite the resettlement and integration of refugee families from South Africa that had been granted asylum in Botswana, Lesotho and Zambia. Further, the Assembly, in a resolution of 18 December on the report of UNHCR,[7] requested the High Commissioner to continue participating in ICARA follow-up activities and to intensify his assistance to refugees in Africa.

Decision (1982). [1]ESC: 1982/151, para. *(a)* (iii), 27 July.
Reports. S-G, [2]A/37/335, [3]A/37/522; [4]S-G and ICARA Steering Committee, E/1982/76 & Corr.1.
Resolutions (1982). GA: [5]37/15, para. 17, 16 Nov.; [6]37/177, para. 7, 17 Dec.; [7]37/195, para. 11, 18 Dec.; [8]37/197, 18 Dec., text following.
Resolution (prior). [9]GA: 36/124, 14 Dec. 1981 (YUN 1981, p. 1041).
Yearbook reference. [10]1981, p. 1039.
Financial implications. 5th Committee report, A/37/757; S-G statements, A/C.3/37/L.61, A/C.5/37/94.
Meeting records. ESC: E/1982/SR.46, 47 (19, 20 July). GA: 3rd Committee, A/C.3/37/SR.*41*, 43-46, *58*, 59, 60, *61*, *62* (15 Nov.–3 Dec.); 5th Committee, A/C.5/37/SR.69 (14 Dec.); plenary, A/37/PV.111 (18 Dec.).

General Assembly resolution 37/197

18 December 1982   Meeting 111   Adopted without vote

Approved by Third Committee (A/37/692) without vote, 2 December (meeting 61); draft by Kenya, for African Group (A/C.3/37/L.43), orally revised; agenda item 90 *(c)*.

International Conference on Assistance to Refugees in Africa

The General Assembly,

Recalling its resolutions 35/42 of 25 November 1980 and 36/124 of 14 December 1981 relating to the International Conference on Assistance to Refugees in Africa, held at Geneva on 9 and 10 April 1981,

Having considered the reports of the Secretary-General on the Conference and the report of the United Nations High Commissioner for Refugees on the activities of his Office,

Gravely concerned at the present influx of refugees on the African continent, who now constitute over half the population of refugees in the world,

Noting that, while the Conference succeeded in raising world consciousness with regard to the plight of refugees and returnees in Africa, as well as the problems of asylum countries, the overall results of the Conference in terms of financial and material assistance have fallen short of the expectations of the African countries,

Aware of the economic and social burden imposed on African countries of asylum by the growing influx of refugees and its consequences for their development and of the heavy sacrifices made by them, despite their limited resources, to alleviate the plight of those refugees,

Considering, therefore, the need of the countries of asylum for adequate human, technical and financial assistance to enable them properly to shoulder their increased responsibilities and assume the additional burden that the presence of refugees represents for their economies,

Considering further the need similarly to assist the countries of origin in the voluntary repatriation and resettlement of returnees, in accordance with the procedures of the Office of the United Nations High Commissioner for Refugees,

Recognizing, therefore, the need to review further, with the African Governments concerned, the burden imposed on their national economies by refugees and returnees,

1. *Commends* the Secretary-General for his reports on the International Conference on Assistance to Refugees in Africa, which were prepared in pursuance of paragraphs 6 and 9 of General Assembly resolution 36/124;

2. *Expresses its appreciation* to all donor countries, the United Nations High Commissioner for Refugees and the international community at large for their continued support and assistance to African refugees, including their efforts to facilitate the process of voluntary repatriation to the countries of origin;

3. *Expresses its concern* that the assistance currently being provided under existing refugee-related programmes falls short of the urgent needs of refugees and returnees in Africa and does not provide sufficient resources to permit the implementation of projects designed to ensure adequate care and relief for the refugees and to expedite the process of rehabilitation and resettlement;

4. *Expresses its appreciation* to the countries of asylum for the great contribution that they are making in alleviating the plight of refugees and urges the international community to give the assistance necessary to enable those countries to provide essential services and facilities for the refugees;

5. *Requests* the Secretary-General, in close co-operation with the Secretary-General of the Organization of African Unity and the United Nations High Commissioner for Refugees, to convene at Geneva in 1984 a second International Conference on Assistance to Refugees in Africa:

(a) To review thoroughly the results of the Conference held in 1981 as well as the state of progress of the projects submitted to it;

(b) To consider the continuing need for assistance with a view to providing, as necessary, additional assistance to refugees and returnees in Africa for the implementation of programmes for their relief, rehabilitation and resettlement;

(c) To consider the impact imposed on the national economies of the African countries concerned and to provide them with the assistance required to strengthen their social and economic infrastructure so as to enable them to cope with the burden of dealing with large numbers of refugees and returnees;

6. *Also requests* the Secretary-General, in close co-operation with the Secretary-General of the Organization of African Unity and the United Nations High Commissioner for Refugees, to consult with the African countries concerned with regard to their needs for dealing adequately with the problem of refugees and returnees and to submit a report on the situation in each country so as to enable the proposed Conference to have an up-to-date assessment, by priority, of the humanitarian, rehabilitation and resettlement needs of the refugees and returnees, and the assistance required by the countries concerned to strengthen existing services, facilities and infrastructure and, for that purpose, to reallocate existing resources;

7. *Calls upon* the competent specialized agencies and organizations of the United Nations system, including the development-oriented organizations, to provide all necessary co-operation and support to the Secretary-General in respect of the report called for in paragraph 6 above, to be prepared for the Conference to be held in 1984;

8. *Requests* the Secretary-General to ensure that adequate financial and budgetary arrangements are made to cover the expenses involved in the preparation of the report, as well as those for the organization of the Conference in 1984;

9. *Appeals* to the international community, all Member States, the specialized agencies and regional, intergovernmental and non-governmental organizations to provide the utmost support for the Conference with a view to offering maximum financial and material assistance to refugees and returnees in Africa;

10. *Invites* the executive bodies of the specialized agencies and intergovernmental and non-governmental organizations to bring the present resolution to the attention of their members and to consider, within their respective spheres of competence, various ways and means substantially to increase assistance to African refugees and returnees;

11. *Stresses* that any additional assistance provided for refugee-related projects should not be at the expense of the development needs of the countries concerned;

12. *Requests* the Secretary-General to report to the General Assembly at its thirty-eighth session on the implementation of the present resolution.

Algeria

In 1982, the refugee population in Algeria remained unchanged at some 2,000—about half were Latin Americans, one fourth were elderly of various European origin, and the remainder from Africa, Asia and the Middle East.

In addition, UNHCR continued to assist a group identified by Algerian authorities as Sahrawi refugees, some 165,000 of whom were living in 22 camps. One-time grants totalling $80,000 were made available by the High Commissioner from the Emergency Fund to assist 378 Lebanese in Algeria who were in a refugee-like situation and had appealed for temporary relief assistance.

Angola

The arrival of some 600 South Africans during 1982 brought the total number of refugees in Angola to 96,200: 70,000 Namibians, 20,000 Zairians and 6,200 South Africans. The UNHCR assistance programme for Namibians shifted its emphasis from relief to medium-term projects designed to improve living standards. The resettlement of Zairians to more viable sites continued. Assistance to South African refugees was directed at improving agricultural production in the 6,000 hectares made available by the Government.

Botswana

The total number of refugees in Botswana remained unchanged in 1982—at some 1,300 Angolans, South Africans and Namibians. With UNHCR assistance, 120 refugee students of various nationalities were enrolled in educational institutions in Botswana, and 82 Angolan refugees were repatriated.

Burundi

In 1982, some 58,000 refugees in Burundi needed UNHCR assistance: 50,000 Rwandese in rural areas and 8,000 Rwandese or Zairians in the capital. The most needy urban refugees received education and counselling.

An inter-agency mission to Burundi in April led to a programme to improve infrastructure and training facilities in refugee settlements.

Chad

The repatriation programme for Chadian refugees was successfully completed in 1982, and UNHCR provided assistance to over 200,000 persons in N'Djamena, including returnees and displaced persons. By July, following political changes in Chad, over 5,000 additional refugees had repatriated from the Central African Republic, Nigeria, and the United Republic of Cameroon. Later in the year, 13,000 new returnees were benefiting under an expanded UNHCR assistance programme; in all, some $5.07 million was obligated in 1982 for rehabilitation activities in Chad.

Djibouti

In 1982, the number of refugees in Djibouti, almost all of whom were Ethiopians, was estimated at 35,000, half of them under the age of 15, and most with pastoral backgrounds. The arid climate, sparse natural resources and lack of infrastructure made long-term rural settlement impractical for the refugees (over 10 per cent of the local population), and their voluntary repatriation seemed the only feasible long-term solution.

A Tripartite Commission composed of representatives of the Governments of Ethiopia and Djibouti and the UNHCR was established to facilitate the voluntary repatriation of Ethiopian refugees in Djibouti. Meanwhile, UNHCR continued its care and maintenance programme during 1982, totalling $4,071,000.

The Secretary-General, in a September 1982 report,[1] stated that vocational/technical training for some 100 urban refugees was to commence that month. UNHCR covered the running costs of the training centre, located at Ali Sabieh. Efforts were under way to establish primary education in refugee camps, and other projects provided food, medical assistance, housing, scholarships and establishment of handicrafts co-operation.

Economic and Social Council action. By a 27 April 1982 resolution[2] adopted without vote, the Economic and Social Council requested UNHCR to intensify humanitarian assistance to the refugees in Djibouti, and to maintain close contact with Member States, organizations and voluntary agencies to mobilize aid for the Government so it could cope with the situation. The Council also requested the Secretary-General, in co-operation with UNHCR, to evaluate the scope of assistance needed for the relief and rehabilitation programmes and to report to the General Assembly later in the year.

The 29-nation draft, introduced by Zaire, and revised by the sponsors, was adopted by the Council without vote.

General Assembly action. By a resolution[3] adopted without vote on 17 December 1982, the General Assembly requested UNHCR, in co-operation with the Secretary-General, to send an inter-agency mission to Djibouti to evaluate the aid required to finance refugee relief and rehabilitation programmes, and to report to the Economic and Social Council and to the Assembly in 1983. Member States, the United Nations system, and

organizations were called on to continue to support Djibouti's efforts to cope with the ever-growing refugee population and other drought victims. The Assembly also took note of the report of the Secretary-General and UNHCR, invited the High Commissioner to intensify his humanitarian assistance programme in the country, and expressed appreciation for the assistance provided.

The 56-nation text, introduced by Zaire and twice revised by the sponsors, had been approved without vote by the Third (Social, Humanitarian and Cultural) Committee on 9 December.

Report. [1]S-G, A/37/420.
Resolutions (1982). [2]ESC: 1982/3, 27 Apr., text following. [3]GA: 37/176, 17 Dec., text following.
Meeting records. ESC: E/1982/SR.13, 14, *16*, *17* (22-27 Apr.).
   GA: 3rd Committee, A/C.3/37/SR.41, 57, 58, 62, 63, *64*, 65, 66, 68-71, *72* (15 Nov.–9 Dec.); plenary, A/37/PV.110 (17 Dec.).

Economic and Social Council resolution 1982/3

27 April 1982   Meeting 17   Adopted without vote

29-nation draft (E/1982/L.26/Rev.1); agenda item 3.

Sponsors: Bangladesh, Benin, Burundi, China, Democratic Yemen, Djibouti, France, Italy, Jordan, Kenya, Libyan Arab Jamahiriya, Madagascar, Malawi, Mali, Mauritania, Morocco, Nigeria, Pakistan, Qatar, Senegal, Somalia, Sudan, Swaziland, Tunisia, United Republic of Cameroon, United States, Yugoslavia, Zaire, Zimbabwe.

Humanitarian assistance to refugees in Djibouti

The Economic and Social Council,

Recalling its resolutions 1980/11 of 28 April 1980, 1980/44 of 23 July 1980 and 1981/4 of 4 May 1981,

Recalling also General Assembly resolutions 35/182 of 15 December 1980 and 36/156 of 16 December 1981,

Having heard the oral report of the representative of the Secretary-General on the refugee situation in Djibouti,

Having heard also the statement of the delegation of Djibouti on the refugee situation in that country,

Appreciating the determined efforts of the Government of Djibouti to cope with the refugee situation, despite its limited economic resources,

Aware of the social and economic burden placed on the Government and people of Djibouti as a result of the influx of refugees and of its impact on the development and infrastructure of the country,

Deeply concerned about the persistence of the food shortage in the country, which has been aggravated by the devastating effects of the prolonged drought,

Noting with satisfaction the concern and continued efforts of the United Nations High Commissioner for Refugees, the United Nations Development Programme, the United Nations Children's Fund, the World Health Organization, the World Food Programme, the Food and Agriculture Organization of the United Nations, other intergovernmental organizations, as well as the non-governmental organizations and voluntary agencies which have worked closely with the Government of Djibouti in the implementation of the relief and rehabilitation programme for the refugees in Djibouti,

1. *Takes note with appreciation* of the oral report of the representative of the Secretary-General on the refugee situation in Djibouti;

2. *Appreciates* the efforts made by the United Nations High Commissioner for Refugees to keep the refugee situation in Djibouti under constant review;

3. *Requests* the United Nations High Commissioner for Refugees to intensify his programme of humanitarian assistance to the refugees in Djibouti;

4. *Requests* all Member States, the specialized agencies and other organizations of the United Nations system, and other intergovernmental and non-governmental organizations, to continue to support the efforts made by the Government of Djibouti to meet the needs of the refugees and the other victims of the drought;

5. *Requests* the United Nations High Commissioner for Refugees to continue to ensure that adequate assistance programmes are

organized for the refugees in Djibouti and to maintain close contact with Member States and intergovernmental and non-governmental organizations and voluntary agencies concerned to mobilize the necessary assistance to the Government of Djibouti so as to enable it to cope effectively with the refugee situation, which has been further aggravated by the debilitating effects of the drought;

6. *Requests* the Secretary-General, in co-operation with the United Nations High Commissioner for Refugees, to evaluate the needs and the scope of the assistance necessary to finance the relief and rehabilitation programmes for the refugees and to report to the General Assembly, at its thirty-seventh session, on the progress achieved in the implementation of the present resolution;

7. *Decides* to keep the question under review.

General Assembly resolution 37/176

17 December 1982   Meeting 110   Adopted without vote

Approved by Third Committee (A/37/745) without vote, 9 December (meeting 72); 56-nation draft (A/C.3/37/L.57/Rev.2); agenda item 12.

Sponsors: Algeria, Bahrain, Bangladesh, Benin, Botswana, Cape Verde, Central African Republic, Chad, China, Comoros, Democratic Yemen, Djibouti, France, Gambia, Ghana, Guinea-Bissau, India, Indonesia, Italy, Ivory Coast, Jordan, Kenya, Kuwait, Lesotho, Liberia, Libyan Arab Jamahiriya, Madagascar, Malawi, Mali, Mauritania, Morocco, Niger, Oman, Pakistan, Panama, Qatar, Saudi Arabia, Senegal, Singapore, Somalia, Sri Lanka, Sudan, Swaziland, Syrian Arab Republic, Thailand, Togo, Tunisia, Turkey, United Arab Emirates, United Republic of Cameroon, United Republic of Tanzania, Upper Volta, Yemen, Zaire, Zambia, Zimbabwe.

Humanitarian assistance to refugees in Djibouti

The General Assembly,

Recalling its resolutions 35/182 of 15 December 1980 and 36/156 of 16 December 1981 on humanitarian assistance to refugees in Djibouti,

Recalling also Economic and Social Council resolution 1982/3 of 27 April 1982,

Having heard the statement made before the Third Committee on 15 November 1982 by the United Nations High Commissioner for Refugees,

Having considered with satisfaction the report of the Secretary-General on humanitarian assistance to refugees in Djibouti,

Appreciating the determined efforts made by the Government of Djibouti, despite its limited economic resources, to cope with the growing needs of the refugees,

Aware of the consequences of the social and economic burden placed on the Government and people of Djibouti as a result of the influx of refugees and the subsequent impact on the national development and infrastructure of the country,

Deeply concerned about the continuing plight of the refugees and displaced persons in the country, which has been aggravated by the devastating effects of the prolonged drought,

Noting with appreciation the concern and unremitting efforts of the Office of the United Nations High Commissioner for Refugees, the United Nations Development Programme, the United Nations Children's Fund, the World Health Organization, the World Food Programme, the Food and Agriculture Organization of the United Nations, the intergovernmental and non-governmental organizations and the benevolent organizations which have worked closely with the Government of Djibouti in the relief and rehabilitation programme for the refugees in that country,

1. *Takes note with appreciation* of the report of the Secretary-General on humanitarian assistance to refugees in Djibouti and of the report of the United Nations High Commissioner for Refugees;

2. *Appreciates* the efforts made by the High Commissioner to keep the situation of the refugees in Djibouti under constant review and invites him to intensify his programme of humanitarian assistance to the refugees in the country;

3. *Requests* the High Commissioner to continue to organize adequate programmes of assistance for the refugees in Djibouti and to maintain close contact with Member States, intergovernmental and non-governmental organizations and benevolent organizations concerned to mobilize the necessary assistance to the Government of Djibouti to enable it to cope effectively with the refugee situation, which has been aggravated by the debilitating effects of the drought;

4. *Appreciates* the assistance provided thus far by Member States and intergovernmental and non-governmental organizations to the relief and rehabilitation programmes for the refugees and displaced persons in Djibouti;

5. *Calls upon* all Member States, the organizations of the United Nations system, the specialized agencies and intergovernmental and non-governmental organizations to continue to support the efforts being made by the Government of Djibouti to cope with the ever-growing needs of the refugee population and other victims of drought;

6. *Requests* the United Nations High Commissioner for Refugees, in co-operation with the Secretary-General, to send an inter-agency mission to Djibouti to evaluate the needs and the magnitude of the aid required to finance the relief and rehabilitation programmes for the refugees and to report to the Economic and Social Council at its second regular session of 1983, and to the General Assembly at its thirty-eighth session, on the progress achieved in the implementation of the present resolution.

Egypt

No significant change occurred in 1982 in the refugee situation in Egypt. Of the estimated 5,500, some 1,700 received UNHCR assistance, mainly in education; most were African students, the majority from Ethiopia, and elderly Armenian refugees who had lived in Egypt for a number of years.

Ethiopia

As part of its regional approach in the Horn of Africa, UNHCR continued, in co-operation with the Governments concerned, to promote an orderly and voluntary return of an estimated 35,000 Ethiopian refugees from Djibouti, over half of whom were dependent children.

On 30 April 1982, the High Commissioner, after consulting Ethiopia's Relief and Rehabilitation Commission and on the recommendations of two fact-finding missions, issued a special appeal for basic relief assistance to an estimated 110,000 to 126,000 returnees in the Eritrea and Hararghe regions. A Special Programme of Assistance to Ethiopian Refugees was launched in September by UNHCR with a $20 million budget for 105,100 refugees who had spontaneously returned to those regions. While Ethiopia held overall responsibility for the programme, the League of Red Cross Societies joined UNHCR in June as a principal implementing partner. The first phase of the programme, mainly procurement of relief items and transport vehicles, was carried out during 1982, with the second and the third phases expected to focus on rehabilitation.

Ethiopia in 1982 hosted some 11,000 refugees who had lived there for the previous 10 to 12 years, the majority of whom were of rural Sudanese origin; approximately 5,500 were self-supporting, while some 5,350 continued to receive UNHCR assistance.

Economic and Social Council action. By a resolution[2] adopted without vote on 27 April, the Economic and Social Council appealed again to the international community to contribute generously to Ethiopia in providing relief and rehabilitation to the displaced persons and voluntary returnees. The Council commended United Nations efforts in mobilizing assistance and requested

UNHCR to intensify such efforts for voluntary returnees, in view of their increasing number.

General Assembly action. By a 17 December resolution[3] adopted without vote, the General Assembly reiterated its appeals for generous contributions to assist Ethiopia in providing relief and rehabilitation for displaced persons. It requested UNHCR to intensify efforts in mobilizing humanitarian assistance for the relief, rehabilitation and resettlement of voluntary returnees and for displaced persons. Various organs and specialized agencies of the United Nations were commended for mobilizing assistance.

The Third (Social, Humanitarian and Cultural) Committee had approved on 9 December, also without vote, the 31-nation draft, introduced by Zaire and orally revised by the sponsors, taking into account an amendment proposed by Somalia to delete, in paragraph 3, the words "the large number of", characterizing the displaced persons to whom Ethiopia provided relief and rehabilitation; the sponsors deleted reference to voluntary returnees in the same paragraph. The sponsors also deleted reference in a preambular paragraph to the "growing" number of voluntary returnees to Ethiopia. They did not accept the deletion of "voluntary returnees" used in describing, in paragraph 1, the subject of the appeals of the Secretary-General, the Assembly and the Council, nor the addition of the words "of concern to his [the High Commissioner's] Office", at the end of paragraph 4, referring to those for whom humanitarian assistance was to be mobilized. Somalia withdrew its amendments.[1]

Amendments withdrawn. [1]Somalia, A/C.3/37/L.67.
Resolutions (1982). [2]ESC: 1982/2, 27 Apr., text following. [3]GA: 37/175, 17 Dec., text following.
Meeting records. ESC: E/1982/SR.13, *16, 17* (22-27 Apr.). GA: 3rd Committee, A/C.3/37/SR.41, 57, 62, 63, *64,* 65-71, *72* (15 Nov.–9 Dec.); plenary, A/37/PV.110 (17 Dec.).

Economic and Social Council resolution 1982/2

27 April 1982   Meeting 17   Adopted without vote

23-nation draft (E/1982/L.25); agenda item 3.

Sponsors: Bangladesh, Benin, Burundi, China, Democratic Yemen, Egypt, Ethiopia, German Democratic Republic, Kenya, Liberia, Libyan Arab Jamahiriya, Madagascar, Malawi, Nepal, Nigeria, Pakistan, Sierra Leone, Swaziland, Tunisia, Yugoslavia, Zaire, Zambia, Zimbabwe.

Assistance to displaced persons in Ethiopia

The Economic and Social Council,

Recalling its resolution 1980/54 of 24 July 1980 and General Assembly resolution 36/161 of 16 December 1981,

Having heard the statements of the representative of the Secretary-General and of the United Nations Deputy High Commissioner for Refugees,

Taking into account the report of the Secretary-General on assistance to displaced persons in Ethiopia, prepared pursuant to Council resolution 1980/8 of 28 April 1980,

Recalling the appeal of the Secretary-General in his note verbale of 11 November 1980,

Recognizing the growing number of voluntary returnees in Ethiopia,

Deeply concerned that the appeals of the Secretary-General, the General Assembly and the Council have yet to give rise to an adequate response,

1. *Endorses once again* the appeals of the Secretary-General and the General Assembly;

2. *Appeals once again* to the Governments of Member States and to intergovernmental and non-governmental organizations and all voluntary agencies to contribute generously to the Government of Ethiopia in its effort to provide relief and rehabilitation to the displaced persons and voluntary returnees;

3. *Commends* the effort made by various organs and specialized agencies of the United Nations in mobilizing assistance to displaced persons and voluntary returnees in Ethiopia;

4. *Requests* the United Nations High Commissioner for Refugees to intensify his efforts in mobilizing humanitarian assistance for the relief, rehabilitation and resettlement of voluntary returnees, in view of their increasing number;

5. *Decides* to keep the matter under review.

General Assembly resolution 37/175

17 December 1982   Meeting 110   Adopted without vote

Approved by Third Committee (A/37/745) without vote, 9 December (meeting 72); 31-nation draft (A/C.3/37/L.55), orally revised; agenda item 12.

Sponsors: Afghanistan, Algeria, Angola, Bangladesh, Benin, Botswana, Cape Verde, Central African Republic, Congo, Cyprus, Democratic Yemen, Djibouti, Egypt, Ethiopia, Guinea-Bissau, India, Jamaica, Kenya, Lesotho, Liberia, Libyan Arab Jamahiriya, Madagascar, Malawi, Morocco, Nepal, Nigeria, Sierra Leone, Viet Nam, Zaire, Zambia, Zimbabwe.

Assistance to displaced persons in Ethiopia

The General Assembly,

Recalling its resolutions 35/91 of 5 December 1980 and 36/161 of 16 December 1981 and Economic and Social Council resolutions 1980/54 of 24 July 1980 and 1982/2 of 27 April 1982,

Recalling the report of the Secretary-General on assistance to displaced persons in Ethiopia, prepared pursuant to Economic and Social Council resolution 1980/8 of 28 April 1980,

Recalling also the appeal of the Secretary-General in his note verbale of 11 November 1980, as well as those of the General Assembly and the Economic and Social Council,

Having heard the statements made before the Third Committee by the United Nations High Commissioner for Refugees and by the representative of the Secretary-General on 15 November and 3 December 1982, respectively,

Recognizing the number of persons who have returned voluntarily to Ethiopia,

Deeply concerned that the repeated appeals of the Secretary-General, the General Assembly and the Economic and Social Council have yet to give rise to an adequate response,

1. *Endorses once again* the appeals of the Secretary-General, the General Assembly and the Economic and Social Council concerning assistance to displaced persons and voluntary returnees in Ethiopia;

2. *Commends* the efforts made by various organs of the United Nations and specialized agencies in mobilizing humanitarian assistance to the displaced persons and voluntary returnees in Ethiopia;

3. *Appeals once again* to the Governments of Member States and to intergovernmental and non-governmental organizations and all voluntary agencies to contribute generously to assist the Government of Ethiopia in its efforts to provide relief and rehabilitation for the displaced persons;

4. *Requests* the United Nations High Commissioner for Refugees to intensify his efforts in mobilizing humanitarian assistance for the relief, rehabilitation and resettlement of numbers of voluntary returnees, as well as for displaced persons;

5. *Requests* the Secretary-General, in co-operation with the United Nations High Commissioner for Refugees, to report to the Economic and Social Council at its second session of 1983 and to the General Assembly at its thirty-eighth session on the implementation of the present resolution.

Kenya

In 1982, an influx of over 1,000 Ugandans brought the total number of refugees in Kenya to 5,200, including 1,800 Ugandans, 1,600 Ethiopians and 1,400 Rwandese. Immediate needs of new arrivals led to an overall increase in the UNHCR programme in Kenya. As in previous years, assistance focused on facilitating local integration through job placement, vocational training and support to small businesses. A large number of refugees remained unemployed, and efforts continued for suitable income-generating activities.

Lesotho

Lesotho estimated that 11,500, mainly South African, refugees were residing in Maseru and other towns in 1982. Some 1,300 persons, registered with UNHCR, received various forms of assistance.

On 9 December, South African forces attacked Maseru, killing 42 persons, of whom 23 were refugees (see POLITICAL AND SECURITY QUESTIONS, Chapter V). The Security Council, on 15 December,[1] requested Member States to extend economic assistance to Lesotho to strengthen its capacity to receive and maintain South African refugees, and asked the Secretary-General to enter into immediate consultations with Lesotho and United Nations agencies to ensure the welfare of the refugees in Lesotho in a manner consistent with their security.

Resolution (1982). [1]SC: 527(1982), 15 Dec.

Morocco

As in previous years, UNHCR provided local integration assistance, supplementary aid and educational assistance to 500 refugees in Morocco, who were mainly elderly Europeans and African students.

Mozambique

Approximately 150 refugees in Mozambique, mostly from South Africa and Malawi, living in Maputo, received UNHCR assistance on an individual basis. Work began on construction of a residential and training centre in Marrucuene, 30 kilometres from Maputo.

Nigeria

With the return to their homeland in the course of 1982 of many thousands of Chadian refugees, the refugee population in Nigeria decreased to an estimated 5,000 by the end of the year, including some 4,000 Chadians who chose to remain in Nigeria, and a small number of refugees from South Africa. The departure of the Chadians, 3,500 of them assisted by UNHCR, meant a decrease in the UNHCR programme in the country, especially in terms of local settlement assistance.

Rwanda

The refugee population in Rwanda, before October 1982, was 18,000, mainly of Burundi origin and living in rural communities. The influx of displaced persons in October, following the events in the Mbarara district of Uganda, was estimated at 44,000 persons; UNHCR estimated that 35,000 would need care and maintenance and 9,000 would be helped to settle locally.

The High Commissioner made an initial allocation of $1 million from the Emergency Fund to provide for immediate needs; a further appeal to the international community on 26 October for $5 million for emergency assistance was met with rapid response.

Somalia

Review mission report. In response to a December 1981 request of the General Assembly,[7] a United Nations mission, led by the Joint Coordinator for Special Economic Assistance Programmes, visited Somalia from 28 January to 3 February 1982 to review the refugee situation. Its findings, annexed to a March report of the Secretary-General,[4] pointed to the persistence of massive problems facing Somalia due to the large refugee population.

The mission noted that, since early 1981, the relatively small refugee inflow had resulted in empty or closed reception centres, and the population of many of the refugee camps had decreased. Nevertheless, there were more young men in evidence than a year earlier, but frequent movements in and out of camps made estimations of the refugee population difficult. Following discussions between the Government, donor countries and nongovernmental organizations, the mission recommended that the 1982 international relief programme be based on a camp population of 700,000 and that, in the more stable situation that had emerged, programmes should move from care and maintenance towards self-support and self-sustaining activities.

While some success in meeting the basic needs was recorded, the mission noted severe ecological damage caused by the refugees' demands for domestic fuel. Afforestation programmes, therefore, had a high priority, and kerosene cookers and fuel were urgently needed.

The mission concluded that voluntary repatriation remained the only foreseeable solution to the refugee problems in Somalia. In addition to 1982 requirements estimated at some $138 million, Somalia needed large-scale aid for accelerated development programmes as well as $45 million to meet its national food deficit.

Economic and Social Council action. By a resolution[5] adopted without vote on 27 April, the Economic and Social Council appealed for material, financial and technical assistance to enable Somalia to meet the needs of the refugees. It noted with satisfaction the help given by the international community and thanked the Secretary-General and UNHCR for their efforts.

The 28-nation text was introduced by Zaire.

On 19 July, the High Commissioner orally recapitulated to the Council the findings of the review mission, adding that discussions between the Government and the inter-agency mission had led, for instance, to the removal of restrictions for refugees to engage in agriculture, an agreement on relocation of some camps to more economically viable areas, and plans to bring some 15,000 hectares under cultivation by 1983. Action had been initiated to conserve and meet the demand for domestic fuel, and a programme of afforestation, well advanced in the south, was to be expanded. The Council, by a decision of 27 July,[1] took note of this information.

Report of the Secretary-General. In a September report[3] on assistance to refugees in Somalia, the Secretary-General stated that the majority were of Somali ethnic background, largely nomadic, and lived in 35 camps in the regions of Hiran, Gedo, the North-West, and Lower Shebelle. The demographic breakdown was 80 per cent women and children and 20 per cent adult men—not 10 per cent as earlier estimated. While all parties agreed on repatriation as the most appropriate solution, the Government pledged to help lead the refugees towards self-sustenance while they remained in Somalia.

A network of transport and logistical facilities had helped overcome most of the problems associated with commodity delivery and the flow of food supplies, and the general nutritional and health situation of refugees was comparatively satisfactory. A joint United Nations Children's Fund/UNHCR well-drilling project to provide 20 litres of potable water per refugee per day ended in May with partial success. Over 6,000 refugee families were cultivating close to 3,000 hectares of land placed at their disposal by the Government, and an agricultural workshop at Mogadishu in March made recommendations on expanded crop farming. Other income-generating activities were also under way.

General Assembly action. By a 17 December resolution[6] adopted without vote, the General Assembly appealed to the international community for maximum assistance to Somalia in its efforts to assist the refugees. The Assembly requested UNHCR, in consultation with the Secretary-General, to review the overall needs of the refugees, including settlement and rehabilitation aspects.

The Third (Social, Humanitarian and Cultural) Committee had approved, in a similar fashion on 9 December, the 41-nation draft, which had been introduced by Zaire and orally revised by the sponsors. As a result of the revision, Ethiopia withdrew a series of amendments[2] it had proposed.

The sponsors amended the wording in two preambular paragraphs that Ethiopia had proposed deleting, and accepted an Ethiopian amendment to paragraph 4 by deleting the phrase "until such time as they are able to return to their homeland in safety and dignity", which had originally qualified the duration of assistance. The sponsors did not act on an Ethiopian proposal to delete paragraphs 5 and 6, asking UNHCR for a comprehensive review of refugee needs and for a report thereon to the Council.

Decision (1982). [1]ESC: 1982/151, para. *(a)* (iii), 27 July.
Amendments withdrawn. [2]Ethiopia, A/C.3/37/L.81.
Reports. S-G, [3]A/37/419, [4]E/1982/40 & Corr.1.
Resolutions (1982). [5]ESC: 1982/4, 27 Apr., text following.
[6]GA: 37/174, 17 Dec., text following.
Resolution (prior). [7]GA: 36/153, 16 Dec. 1981 (YUN 1981, p. 1048).
Meeting records. ESC: E/1982/SR.*16, 17,* 18, *46* (26, 27 Apr. & 1-19 July). GA: 3rd Committee, A/C.3/37/SR.62, 63, *64,* 65-71, *72* (15 Nov.–9 Dec.); plenary, A/37/PV.110 (17 Dec.).

Economic and Social Council resolution 1982/4

27 April 1982   Meeting 17   Adopted without vote

28-nation draft (E/1982/L.27); agenda item 3.

Sponsors: Bangladesh, Benin, Burundi, China, Djibouti, Egypt, Jordan, Kuwait, Liberia, Madagascar, Malawi, Mauritania, Morocco, Nigeria, Oman, Pakistan, Qatar, Saudi Arabia, Senegal, Sierra Leone, Somalia, Sudan, Tunisia, United Arab Emirates, United States, Yemen, Zaire, Zambia.

Assistance to refugees in Somalia

The Economic and Social Council,

Recalling its resolution 1981/31 of 6 May 1981 and General Assembly resolution 36/153 of 16 December 1981, on the question of assistance to refugees in Somalia,

Taking into account the report of the Secretary-General, to which was annexed the report of the review mission to Somalia on the situation of the refugees in Somalia, containing an assessment of their overall needs as well as the amount and type of assistance required to strengthen support services and facilities,

Aware of the consequences of the social and economic burden placed on the Government and people of Somalia as a result of the influx of refugees and the subsequent impact on the national development and the infrastructure of the country,

1. *Takes note* of the report of the Secretary-General;

2. *Expresses its appreciation* to the Secretary-General and to the United Nations High Commissioner for Refugees for their continued efforts to mobilize international assistance on behalf of the refugees in Somalia;

3. *Notes with satisfaction* the assistance rendered to the refugees in Somalia by various Member States, the United Nations High Commissioner for Refugees, the World Food Programme, the United Nations Children's Fund and other intergovernmental organizations concerned;

4. *Also notes with satisfaction* the valuable services and assistance being contributed to the refugee programme in Somalia by various voluntary agencies and non-governmental organizations;

5. *Appeals* to Member States, international organizations and voluntary agencies to render all possible material, financial and technical assistance to the Government of Somalia to enable it to meet the needs of the refugees, including those aspects relating to their education, self-help activities and community development and to the strengthening of support services and facilities;

6. *Requests* the Secretary-General, in co-operation with the United Nations High Commissioner for Refugees, to report to the Economic and Social Council, at its second regular session of 1982, on the refugee situation in Somalia and on the progress made in implementing the recommendations contained in the report of the review mission;

7. *Further requests* the Secretary-General, in co-operation with the United Nations High Commissioner for Refugees, to submit a report to the General Assembly at its thirty-seventh session on the progress achieved in the implementation of the present resolution.

General Assembly resolution 37/174

17 December 1982   Meeting 110   Adopted without vote

Approved by Third Committee (A/37/745) without vote, 9 December (meeting 72); 41-nation draft (A/C.3/37/L.54/Rev.1), orally revised; agenda item 12.

Sponsors: Bahrain, Bangladesh, Barbados, Botswana, Canada, Central African Republic, Chad, China, Comoros, Djibouti, Egypt, Indonesia, Italy, Jordan, Kenya, Kuwait, Lesotho, Liberia, Malaysia, Mauritania, Morocco, Nepal, Oman, Pakistan, Philippines, Qatar, Saudi Arabia, Senegal, Sierra Leone, Singapore, Solomon Islands, Somalia, Sudan, Thailand, Tunisia, Turkey, United Arab Emirates, Yemen, Zaire, Zambia, Zimbabwe.

Assistance to refugees in Somalia

The General Assembly,

Recalling its resolutions 35/180 of 15 December 1980 and 36/153 of 16 December 1981 on the question of assistance to refugees in Somalia,

Recalling also Economic and Social Council resolutions 1981/31 of 6 May 1981 and 1982/4 of 27 April 1982,

Taking note of the report of the Secretary-General and the report of the United Nations High Commissioner for Refugees on the situation of the refugees in Somalia,

Having heard the statement made before the Third Committee on 15 November 1982 by the United Nations High Commissioner for Refugees,

Considering the fact that the refugee problem has not yet been resolved,

Recognizing the need to continue to provide assistance to the refugees in Somalia,

Aware of the consequences of the social and economic burden placed on the Government and people of Somalia as a result of the continued presence of refugees and the consequent impact on the national development and the infrastructure of the country,

1. *Takes note* of the reports of the Secretary-General and of the United Nations High Commissioner for Refugees on the situation of refugees in Somalia;

2. *Expresses its appreciation* to the Secretary-General and the High Commissioner for their continued efforts to mobilize international assistance on behalf of the refugees in Somalia;

3. *Takes note with satisfaction* of the assistance rendered to refugees in Somalia by various Member States, the Office of the United Nations High Commissioner for Refugees, the World Food Programme, the United Nations Children's Fund and other intergovernmental and non-governmental organizations concerned;

4. *Appeals* to Member States, international organizations and voluntary agencies to render maximum material, financial and technical assistance to the Government of Somalia in its efforts to provide all necessary assistance to the refugees;

5. *Requests* the High Commissioner, in consultation with the Secretary-General, to make a comprehensive review of the overall needs of the refugees, including those aspects relating to their settlement and rehabilitation;

6. *Also requests* the High Commissioner, in consultation with the Secretary-General, to submit a report on the proposed review of the refugee situation in Somalia to the Economic and Social Council at its second regular session of 1983;

7. *Further requests* the High Commissioner, in consultation with the Secretary-General, to report to the General Assembly at its thirty-eighth session on the progress achieved in the implementation of the present resolution.

Sudan

The Sudan estimated that at the end of 1982 there were 637,000 refugees in the country, including 460,000 Ethiopians, 170,000 Ugandans, 2,000 Chadians and 5,000 Zairians; a substantial increase over 1981, due to the continued influx of refugees from Uganda, which more than compensated for the repatriation of over 13,000 refugees to Chad.

The refugee situation was studied by a United Nations inter-agency mission, which visited the Sudan in January/February 1982, and by a joint review mission in November by the Sudanese Government and UNHCR, which formulated recommendations for improving the economic viability of refugee settlements. The International Labour Organisation conducted a number of UNHCR-funded studies on refugee skills, potential labour markets and prospects for self-reliance in eastern Sudan. An emergency situation persisted due partly to the movement of refugees from the border areas into the settlements and transit centres initially created for temporary accommodation.

Inter-agency mission report. In response to a December 1981 General Assembly resolution,[5] an Inter-agency Mission on Education and Social Development/Welfare Services for Refugees in the Sudan, organized by the Economic Commission for Africa and including the representatives of UNICEF, the United Nations Educational, Scientific and Cultural Organization, and UNHCR, visited the Sudan from 21 January to 19 February. It conducted three technical feasibility studies relating to planning for social development and welfare services, the educational system and training.

Its findings and recommendations, annexed to a report[2] of 15 April by the Secretary-General, pointed to the need to evolve, and to involve governmental agencies in the co-ordinated delivery of, comprehensive educational and social services to meet the needs of the refugees and the local population, in view of the strain the refugees' presence exerted on already overstretched services. To that end, the mission proposed five educational and six social development/welfare services projects costing some $6 million.

Economic and Social Council action. By a 27 April resolution,[3] the Economic and Social Council endorsed the mission's report and recommendations and urgently appealed to the international community to help the Sudan implement the envisaged development assistance projects. It requested the Secretary-General, in co-operation with UNHCR and specialized agencies, to make available the human, technical and financial resources to that Government for immediate implementation of the recommendations of various inter-agency missions.

The 20-nation text, introduced by Zaire, was adopted without vote.

Report of the Secretary-General. In an October report on humanitarian assistance to refugees in the Sudan,[1] requested by the Council, the Secretary-General reviewed the progress made in implementing the recommendations of the seven technical feasibility missions undertaken in 1981 and 1982 by various United Nations bodies on new settlements, integrated housing programmes, other social development/welfare services, strengthened educational system, health-delivery system, training programmes, and agricultural projects in refugee zones.

The report stated that the Government relocated unemployed refugees in urban areas and newly arrived refugees to settlements where opportunities to achieve self-sufficiency would be created. Nine new settlements had been created, bringing the total number of assisted refugees in settlements at mid-1982 to 177,000.

General Assembly action. By a resolution adopted without vote on 17 December,[4] the General Assembly thanked all parties concerned for assisting the refugees in the Sudan, endorsed the mission's recommendations, and appealed to the international community for resources to help the Sudan implement the development assistance projects and strengthen its social and economic infrastructure. The Assembly requested the Secretary-General to mobilize assistance to implement recommendations of the various inter-agency missions, and asked UNHCR to co-ordinate with specialized agencies on essential services to the refugees in the settlements.

The Third Committee had approved, in like manner on 9 December, the 39-nation text introduced by Zaire.

Reports. [1]S-G, A/37/519; [2]S-G and Inter-agency Mission, A/37/178.
Resolutions (1982). [3]ESC: 1982/1, 27 Apr., text following. [4]GA: 37/173, 17 Dec., text following.
Resolution (prior). [5]GA: 36/158, 16 Dec. 1981 (YUN, p. 1050).
Meeting records. ESC: E/1982/SR.13, *16, 17* (22-27 Apr.). GA: 3rd Committee, A/C.3/37/SR.57, 62, 63, *64,* 65-71, *72* (29 Nov.–9 Dec.); plenary, A/37/PV.110 (17 Dec.).

Economic and Social Council resolution 1982/1

27 April 1982   Meeting 17   Adopted without vote

20-nation draft (E/1982/L.24); agenda item 3.

Sponsors: Bangladesh, China, Djibouti, Egypt, Italy, Jordan, Kenya, Morocco, Nigeria, Pakistan, Qatar, Senegal, Somalia, Sudan, Syrian Arab Republic, Tunisia, United States, Yugoslavia, Zaire, Zambia.

Situation of refugees in the Sudan

The Economic and Social Council,

Recalling its resolution 1981/5 of 4 May 1981 on the situation of refugees in the Sudan,

Recalling further General Assembly resolutions 35/181 of 15 December 1980 and 36/158 of 16 December 1981,

Having considered the report of the Secretary-General, to which was annexed the report of the United Nations inter-agency mission on education and social development/welfare services for refugees in the Sudan,

Having heard the statement delivered by the United Nations Deputy High Commissioner for Refugees before the Council on 22 April 1982,

Recognizing the heavy burden placed on the Government of the Sudan in caring for the refugees and the need for adequate international assistance to continue its efforts to render services to the refugees,

Appreciating the measures which the Government of the Sudan, a least developed country, is taking in order to provide shelter, food and other services to the growing number of refugees in the Sudan,

1. *Endorses* the report of the United Nations inter-agency technical follow-up mission to the Sudan and the recommendations contained therein;

2. *Expresses its appreciation* to the Secretary-General, the United Nations High Commissioner for Refugees, donor countries and voluntary agencies for their efforts to assist the refugees in the Sudan;

3. *Requests* the Secretary-General, in close co-operation with the United Nations High Commissioner for Refugees and the relevant specialized agencies, to make available the necessary human, technical and financial resources to the Government of the Sudan so that the recommendations of various inter-agency missions can be implemented immediately;

4. *Appeals urgently* to Member States, the United Nations High Commissioner for Refugees, the United Nations organizations concerned and voluntary agencies to provide the Government of the Sudan with the resources necessary for the prompt implementation of the development assistance projects envisaged in the annex to the report of the Secretary-General;

5. *Requests* the Secretary-General, in co-operation with the United Nations High Commissioner for Refugees, to submit a comprehensive report to the General Assembly at its thirty-seventh session on the progress made in the implementation of the recommendations of the inter-agency technical follow-up missions as well as on the implementation of the present resolution.

General Assembly resolution 37/173

17 December 1982   Meeting 110   Adopted without vote

Approved by Third Committee (A/37/745) without vote, 9 December (meeting 72); 39-nation draft (A/C.3/37/L.50); agenda item 12.

Sponsors: Algeria, Bahrain, Bangladesh, Canada, Central African Republic, Chad, Chile, China, Cyprus, Djibouti, Egypt, India, Indonesia, Italy, Jamaica, Jordan, Kenya, Kuwait, Liberia, Malawi, Mauritania, Morocco, Nepal, Oman, Pakistan, Philippines, Qatar, Romania, Senegal, Singapore, Somalia, Spain, Sudan, Thailand, Tunisia, Turkey, United Arab Emirates, Zaire, Zambia.

Situation of refugees in the Sudan

The General Assembly,

Recalling its resolutions 35/181 of 15 December 1980 and 36/158 of 16 December 1981 on the situation of refugees in the Sudan,

Recalling further Economic and Social Council resolutions 1981/5 of 14 May 1981 and 1982/1 of 27 April 1982,

Having considered the report of the Secretary-General, the annex to which contains the report of the inter-agency technical follow-up mission on education and social development/welfare services for refugees in the Sudan, as well as the report of the Secretary-General on humanitarian assistance to refugees in the Sudan,

Taking note of the ever-increasing number of refugees arriving in the Sudan,

Recognizing the heavy burden placed on the Government of the Sudan in caring for the refugees and the need for adequate international assistance to enable it to continue its efforts to provide assistance to the refugees,

Expressing its appreciation for the assistance rendered to the Sudan by Member States and intergovernmental and non-governmental organizations in support of refugee programmes,

1. *Endorses* the report of the inter-agency technical follow-up mission to the Sudan and the recommendations contained therein;

2. *Expresses its appreciation* to the Secretary-General, the United Nations High Commissioner for Refugees, donor countries and voluntary agencies for their efforts to assist the refugees in the Sudan;

3. *Appreciates* the measures which the Government of the Sudan is taking to provide shelter, food and other services to the refugees;

4. *Requests* the Secretary-General to mobilize the necessary financial and material assistance for the implementation of the recommendations of the various inter-agency missions;

5. *Appeals* to Member States, the appropriate organs, organizations and programmes of the United Nations and other intergovernmental and non-governmental organizations and the international financial institutions to provide the Government of the Sudan with the necessary resources for the implementation of the development assistance projects envisaged in the report of the inter-agency mission and to strengthen its social and economic infrastructure so that essential services and facilities for refugees can be strengthened and expanded;

6. *Requests* the United Nations High Commissioner for Refugees to co-ordinate with the appropriate specialized agencies in order to consolidate and ensure the continuation of essential services to the refugees in their settlements;

7. *Further requests* the Secretary-General, in co-operation with the United Nations High Commissioner for Refugees, to submit a comprehensive report to the General Assembly at its thirty-eighth session on the progress made in the implementation of the recommendations of the inter-agency technical follow-up missions as well as on the implementation of the present resolution.

Swaziland

Refugees in Swaziland, according to a 1982 Government census, were estimated to total 7,000 by year's end, 95 per cent of whom were South Africans living in the Ndzevane rural settlement in south-eastern Swaziland.

UNHCR assistance continued to concentrate on developing the Ndzevane settlement, with refugees' participation in much of the construction work and in community development.

Uganda

In the aftermath of the events in the Mbarara district of Uganda in October 1982, when over 75,000 people were uprooted, an accurate estimate of needy refugees was not available. However, some 116,000 persons were considered of immediate concern to UNHCR, including 48,000 Rwandese in established settlements, 32,000 Zairians and 1,000 refugees of Ethiopian or Sudanese origin. In addition to those who fled to neighbouring Rwanda during the events in Mbarara, 35,000 were internally displaced; of those, 31,000 moved into two existing settlements, while the rest were located near the Rwandese border. Pending a comprehensive plan for the displaced, assistance was provided with a $400,000 allocation from the Emergency Fund.

United Republic of Cameroon

The large-scale repatriation of Chadian refugees from the United Republic of Cameroon which took place towards the end of 1981 was followed by continued spontaneous movement back to Chad during 1982. At the end of the year, 3,500 refugees remained in the country, including 3,300 Chadian refugees and 200 of other origin—mainly Namibian students in educational institutions.

The Chadian refugees choosing to stay behind were transferred to a new settlement in the Poli region, where they were encouraged to engage in agricultural activity.

United Republic of Tanzania

There were 159,000 refugees at the end of 1982 in the United Republic of Tanzania, including 148,000 from Burundi, 9,500 Zairians and some 1,500 others of various origins. UNHCR assistance focused on integrating rural settlements, once they achieved self-reliance, into the national economy. During 1982, assistance to individual urban or semi-urban cases was directed to more durable solutions, particularly local settlement.

Zaire

In 1982, the refugee population of 301,200 in Zaire included 215,000 Angolans, 60,000 Ugandans and 26,200 others of various origins, most of whom were long-time settlers in border or urban areas. Spontaneous movement of Ugandan refugees had been a noteworthy phenomenon since November 1982; some 10,000 arrived during the year.

In early 1982, the emphasis of the assistance programme for Ugandan refugees in the six rural settlements shifted from emergency aid to care and maintenance. Based on the findings of a multidisciplinary technical mission in November, the programme was reoriented towards self-sufficiency and local integration.

Zambia

A determination that some of the Angolans and Zairians who had spontaneously settled in western Zambia were of concern to UNHCR brought the number of refugees in its programme up to 89,000 in 1982, comprising 71,400 Angolans, 9,000 Zairians, 4,900 Namibians and 2,800 South Africans; the remainder were of various nationalities living in urban centres. Assistance focused on education, health, agriculture and emergency relief. Famine and drought in the western part of the country necessitated extra relief supplies.

The Meheba settlement for 11,000 refugees reached an adequate level of self-sufficiency and became the Government's responsibility in April.

Zimbabwe

At the end of 1982, there were only 177 refugees registered with UNHCR in Zimbabwe, most of whom were urban South Africans. An estimated 20,000 Mozambicans who sought asylum in eastern Zimbabwe were cared for by the Government, and UNHCR provided supplementary relief assistance worth $42,000 from its Emergency Fund. A reception centre was established in Harare, capable of accommodating 70 refugees.

Southern African student refugees

In an oral report to the Economic and Social Council on 19 July, the United Nations High Commissioner for Refugees said educational assistance was vital in fostering self-reliance and leading to durable solutions to refugee problems; at the same time, UNHCR prepared refugee students from Namibia and South Africa to become useful citizens upon their return to their places of origin. On 27 July,[1] the Council took note of the High Commissioner's statement.

In an October report,[2] submitted in accordance with a December 1981 General Assembly request,[4] the Secretary-General stated that the United Nations programme of assistance to student refugees in southern Africa had helped improve their condition and alleviate the burden carried by Botswana, Lesotho, Swaziland and Zambia; the situation, however, required constant review. According to the report, the estimated number of Namibian and South African student refugees, as at mid-1982, stood at 134 in Botswana, 1,022 in Swaziland, and 2,541 in Zambia. Of the total 11,500 refugees in Lesotho, approximately 1,050 were of concern to UNHCR; of the latter group, 114 were registered in schools under UNHCR sponsorship. Pending a report by the Government, no estimate was available of the total number of student refugees. Government contributions received by July, in response to an appeal by the High Commissioner in 1977 and earmarked for those countries, amounted to some $16 million, with various other contributions of $8.7 million, in addition to scholarships.

General Assembly action. By a resolution[3] of 17 December 1982, the General Assembly requested the Secretary-General, in co-operation with the High Commissioner, to continue to organize and implement educational and other assistance for student refugees from Namibia and South Africa who had taken asylum in Botswana, Lesotho, Swaziland and Zambia. It thanked host Governments for granting asylum and making educational and other facilities available to the students, and for co-operating with the Secretary-General and the High Commissioner concerning the welfare of those refugees. The Assembly endorsed the recommendations contained in the Secretary-General's report, noted with appreciation the support provided by the international community, and urged contributions to the programmes. It also appealed for continued assistance to expedite the resettlement and integration of refugee families from South Africa that had been granted asylum in four bordering countries.

The Assembly adopted the resolution without vote. Its Third (Social, Humanitarian and Cultural) Committee had approved, in a similar fashion on 9 December, the 18-nation draft, introduced by Lesotho.

Decision (1982). [1]ESC: 1982/151, para. *(a)* (iii), 27 July.
Report. [2]S-G, A/37/495 & Corr.1.
Resolution (1982). [3]GA: 37/177, 17 Dec., text following.
Resolution (prior). [4]GA: 36/170, 16 Dec. 1981 (YUN 1981, p. 211).
Meeting records. ESC: E/1982/SR.46 (19 July). GA: 3rd Committee, A/C.3/37/SR.57, 62, 63, *64,* 65-71, *72* (29 Nov.-9 Dec.); plenary, A/37/PV.110 (17 Dec.).

General Assembly resolution 37/177

17 December 1982   Meeting 110   Adopted without vote

Approved by Third Committee (A/37/745) without vote, 9 December (meeting 72); 18-nation draft (A/C.3/37/L.62); agenda item 12.

Sponsors: Algeria, Angola, Benin, Botswana, Djibouti, Egypt, Ethiopia, Kenya, Lesotho, Liberia, Somalia, Swaziland, Togo, Trinidad and Tobago, Uganda, United Republic of Tanzania, Yugoslavia, Zambia.

Assistance to student refugees in southern Africa

The General Assembly,

Recalling its resolution 36/170 of 16 December 1981, in which it, *inter alia,* requested the Secretary-General, in co-operation with the United Nations High Commissioner for Refugees, to continue to organize and implement an effective programme of educational and other appropriate assistance for student refugees from Namibia and South Africa who had taken asylum in Botswana, Lesotho, Swaziland and Zambia,

Having considered the report of the Secretary-General containing the review by the High Commissioner of assistance programmes for student refugees from Namibia and South Africa,

Noting with appreciation that some of the projects recommended in the report on assistance to student refugees in southern Africa have been successfully completed,

Noting with concern the continued influx into Botswana, Lesotho, Swaziland and Zambia of student refugees from South Africa, as well as from Namibia,

Convinced that the discriminatory policies and repressive measures being applied in Namibia and South Africa will lead to a further exodus of student refugees from those countries,

Conscious of the burden placed on the limited financial, material and administrative resources of the host countries by the presence of those student refugees,

Appreciating the efforts of the host countries both to deal adequately with their present student refugee populations and to be prepared to meet any new emergency by sharing the responsibilities and obligations with the international community,

1. *Endorses* the assessments and recommendations contained in the report of the Secretary-General and commends him and the United Nations High Commissioner for Refugees for their efforts to mobilize resources and organize the programme of assistance for student refugees in the host countries of southern Africa;

2. *Expresses its appreciation* to the Governments of Botswana, Lesotho, Swaziland and Zambia for continuing to grant asylum and make educational and other facilities available to the student refugees in spite of the pressure which the continuing influx of those refugees exerts on facilities in their countries;

3. *Also expresses its appreciation* to the Governments of Botswana, Lesotho, Swaziland and Zambia for the co-operation which they have extended to the Secretary-General and to the High Commissioner on matters concerning the welfare of those refugees;

4. *Notes with appreciation* the financial and material support provided for the student refugees by Member States, the Office of the United Nations High Commissioner for Refugees, other bodies of the United Nations system and intergovernmental and non-governmental organizations;

5. *Requests* the Secretary-General, in co-operation with the High Commissioner, to continue to organize and implement an effective programme of educational and other appropriate assistance for student refugees from Namibia and South Africa who have taken asylum in Botswana, Lesotho, Swaziland and Zambia;

6. *Urges* all Member States and intergovernmental and non-governmental organizations to continue contributing generously to the assistance programmes for the student refugees, through financial support of the regular programmes of the High Commissioner, of the projects identified in the report of the Secretary-General and of the projects and programmes, including unfunded projects, submitted to the International Conference on Assistance to Refugees in Africa;

7. *Appeals* to the Office of the United Nations High Commissioner for Refugees, the United Nations Development Programme and the United Nations Educational, Scientific and Cultural Organization, as well as other international and non-governmental bodies, to continue providing humanitarian and development assistance to expedite the resettlement and integration of refugee families from South Africa that have been granted asylum in Botswana, Lesotho, Swaziland and Zambia;

8. *Calls upon* all agencies and programmes of the United Nations system to continue co-operating with the Secretary-General and the High Commissioner in the implementation of humanitarian programmes of assistance for the student refugees in southern Africa;

9. *Requests* the Secretary-General, in co-operation with the High Commissioner, to continue to keep the matter under review, to apprise the Economic and Social Council, at its second regular session of 1983, of the current status of the programmes and to report to the General Assembly at its thirty-eighth session on the implementation of the present resolution.

Asia and the Pacific

In 1982, the assistance programme for 2.2 million refugees in Pakistan remained the largest single programme of UNHCR, with obligations for the year totalling $94 million; there were signs of gradual stabilization of the refugee situation and a trend among the refugees towards closer integration into the local economy.

Developments in Lebanon in mid-1982 necessitated UNHCR emergency aid to the internally displaced persons and over 20,000 others who left Lebanon to find temporary asylum in the Syrian Arab Republic (see POLITICAL AND SECURITY QUESTIONS, Chapter IX). In 1982, a total of $108.1 million was obligated for assistance activities in the Middle East and South-West Asia.

Though the situation of Indo-Chinese refugees continued to command attention, their numbers had decreased by 28,577 in the course of 1982, to 204,589. Those arriving by boat in the area declined from 74,754 in 1981 to 43,825 in 1982. Total resettlement departures from countries of first asylum dropped from 168,501 in 1981 to 75,891 in 1982, while durable solutions within the region were neither immediately evident nor easily formulated. UNHCR obligations in East and South Asia and Oceania during the year amounted to $103.2 million, almost 60 per cent of which was absorbed by care and maintenance operations.

The General Assembly, by an 18 December resolution[1] on the report of UNHCR, stressed the importance of maintaining relief efforts and the resettlement momentum for boat and land cases in South-East Asia, where large numbers of refugees and displaced persons had been admitted on a temporary basis.

Resolution (1982). [1]GA: 37/195, para. 8, 18 Dec.

Burma

The major part of the UNHCR special programme of assistance to some 187,000 returnees to Burma from Bangladesh was completed, but logistical and access problems had prevented its conclusion. In 1982, progress was made with the remaining construction of schools and delivery of supplies and equipment to several hospitals.

China

By the end of 1982, Indo-Chinese refugees in China totalled some 272,000, taking into account 2,850 new arrivals and 435 departures. Refugees were settled on 209 state farms in southern provinces, and UNHCR assistance promoted local integration by creating employment opportunities through expanded economic activities in the communities. Such measures benefiting some 68,900 refugees included land reclamation, the development of water resources and plantations, as well as promotion of local industry.

Hong Kong

By the end of 1982, Hong Kong had 12,624 Vietnamese refugees, the highest number of "boat people" in the region. New arrivals recorded in 1982 totalled 7,937, against 9,193 departures for resettlement in third countries.

In early May, crowded living conditions led to the opening of a second UNHCR-supported centre. The continued arrival of new groups and the stagnating resettlement rate led Hong Kong authorities to institute a new policy in July, confining new arrivals to "closed" centres, thus preventing them from seeking local employment; the new arrivals received care and maintenance from UNHCR. The slower rate of resettlement meant an extended waiting period: at the end of 1982, over 70 per cent of the case-load had been residing in Hong Kong for over three years.

India

During 1982, the number of persons in India of concern to UNHCR continued to increase; by year's end, 5,006 persons were registered with UNHCR—living mainly in private accommodations in large cities—of whom 3,425 were Afghans, 1,476 Iranians and 105 from other countries. Assistance took the form of bimonthly subsistence allowances, medical care, education and counselling.

Indonesia

During 1982, 7,835 Vietnamese refugees arrived by boat in Indonesia. A first asylum case-load of 7,274 Indo-Chinese boat refugees remained in the Galang Island camp at the end of 1982, after departure of 5,160 refugees for resettlement or transfer to the Refugee Processing Centre. The population in the Centre, which accepted Indo-Chinese refugees who had been guaranteed resettlement in third countries, numbered 5,952, after the movement of 9,949 arrivals and 13,033 departures during the year.

As in the past, care and maintenance of refugees awaiting resettlement accounted for the major part of the UNHCR assistance programme in Indonesia.

Iran

Iran, which estimated the number of Afghans within its borders at 1.5 million, outlined in 1982 a programme for 50,000 Afghan refugees to become self-supporting, and requested UNHCR financial participation in establishing 10 settlements to accommodate that group. The majority of the Afghan refugees, however, achieved economic and social integration and required no further assistance.

The Government estimated that there were 100,000 persons of other origins in the country.

Japan

In 1982, 954 Indo-Chinese refugees rescued at sea found first asylum in Japan. With the departure of 1,002 refugees for resettlement, 1,905 remained by the end of the year. Over 500 asylum-seekers of various nationalities applied for refugee status following the entry into force in Japan in early 1982 of the 1951 Convention relating to the Status of Refugees (see below); UNHCR provided advice and assistance, including interpreter services.

Indo-Chinese refugees were housed in over 30 centres run by voluntary agencies or at a government reception centre, and UNHCR provided funds for assistance, including food and medical care. A pilot project was launched in 1982 to promote local integration through Japanese language training.

Lao People's Democratic Republic

UNHCR activities in the Lao People's Democratic Republic focused on some 3,500 Kampuchean refugees, mostly in southern Laos, and Lao nationals who had repatriated voluntarily from Thailand. There were 1,069 new arrivals in the latter group who received UNHCR assistance; in addition, over 1,000 spontaneous returnees were provided with resettlement kits and transportation to their places of origin.

Lebanon

The events occurring in Lebanon in June 1982 (see POLITICAL AND SECURITY QUESTIONS, Chapter IX) resulted in the departure of an estimated 33,000 persons from Lebanon for the Syrian Arab Republic, not counting Syrian nationals who returned. UNHCR participated in the emergency relief programme (see Chapter III of this section), and allocated $2,250,000 from the Emergency Fund to transport relief supplies and rehabilitate social and medical institutions taking care of the most vulnerable groups, including orphans, the elderly and the handicapped.

During the year UNHCR also continued its regular assistance activities to some 2,900 refugees living in Lebanon, the majority of whom were Ethiopians and stateless Assyrians.

Malaysia

During 1982, 14,855 Vietnamese refugees arrived in Malaysia, compared to the 1981 total of 23,113. The number resettled in third countries also fell—to 16,253, as compared to 25,652 in 1981—thus leaving an asylum case-load of 8,440 Vietnamese refugees at year's end. Care and maintenance assistance was provided to a monthly average of some 9,000 Vietnamese refugees awaiting resettlement. In addition, about 800 other Indo-Chinese refugees were settled in Malaysia during 1982, after undergoing language training and cultural orientation.

Projects were undertaken in 1982, at the request of the Government, to promote the self-sufficiency and local integration of the estimated 90,000 Filipino refugees in the east Malaysian state of Sabah.

Pakistan

The number of Afghan refugees in Pakistan remained relatively stable in 1982 although the influx did not come to a halt (see POLITICAL AND SECURITY QUESTIONS, Chapter VI). In addition to the basic food rations furnished by the World Food Programme, UNHCR provided supplementary food for some 2.2 million persons in 340 refugee villages in the Northwest Frontier Province and Baluchistan. To relieve the pressure resulting from such large numbers, the Government began planning in mid-1982 the relocation of some of the refugees in the Province to western Punjab.

In refugee villages, more permanent housing gradually replaced tents, and economic activity gathered momentum; the International Labour Organisation was requested to examine the potential for income-generating projects for refugees, in addition to the ongoing handicrafts and vocational training programme. A Memorandum of Understanding was signed with the World Bank in September/October for a $20 million pilot project to provide employment opportunities for refugees and some local inhabitants and develop viable economic assets.

Philippines

A total of 3,288 Vietnamese refugees arrived in the Philippines in 1982, while 6,166 left for countries of permanent resettlement. At the end of the year, 3,861 refugees were awaiting a durable solution in a first asylum camp. A case-load of 10,557 Indo-Chinese refugees remained at a refugee processing centre.

An increasing number of non-Indo-Chinese refugees, mainly Iranian students, were receiving UNHCR assistance in Manila; 293 such persons were registered during the year.

Singapore

In 1982, 2,749 Vietnamese refugees rescued at sea were permitted to disembark in Singapore against written resettlement and departure (within three months) guarantees by third countries. With the departure of 2,784 persons during 1982, the refugee population at year's end stood at 480, as compared with 539 a year earlier.

Thailand

At the end of 1982, there were 168,909 Indo-Chinese refugees and displaced persons of concern to UNHCR in Thailand, comprising 83,951 Kampucheans, 76,055 Lao and 8,903 Vietnamese. This compared with a total of 192,998 in 1981. Although arrivals (11,261) were the lowest since 1975, departures (33,090) for resettlement were only one third of the 1981 figure. In addition, 1,069 Lao refugees from Thailand were voluntarily repatriated.

A number of camps in Thailand were closed during the year because of the reduced case-load and the Government's policy of camp consolidation. UNHCR continued to concentrate on basic care and maintenance while more durable solutions were being sought. Funds were also made available to the Government for its anti-piracy programme aimed at limiting attacks on refugee boats in the Gulf of Siam (see below).

Viet Nam

UNHCR activities in Viet Nam continued to focus on the implementation of the Orderly Departure Programme and on assistance to Kampuchean refugees, whose number, according to Government estimates, had decreased from 30,000 at the end of 1981 to 28,000 in 1982, partly as a result of 1,090 departures for resettlement in third countries.

Under the Orderly Departure Programme, 10,057 Vietnamese left for resettlement abroad in 1982. By a letter[1] dated 18 October to the Secretary-General, Viet Nam transmitted a joint Vietnamese/UNHCR communiqué issued at Geneva on 8 October, in which the two sides noted that the number of departures could be increased over the current monthly average of 1,000 if all parties co-operated in overcoming the existing obstacles; they also agreed that the resettlement of Kampuchean refugees should be promoted according to the refugees' wishes.

Communiqué. [1]UNHCR–Viet Nam, transmitted by 18 Oct. letter from Viet Nam, A/37/557.

Western Asia

Following the events in Lebanon in June 1982 (see POLITICAL AND SECURITY QUESTIONS, Chapter IX), the UNHCR assistance programme in the region shifted its emphasis to emergency relief, mainly for those who left Lebanon (see above) for the Syrian Arab Republic. An estimated 15,000 persons, both Lebanese and Palestinians not registered with the United Nations Relief and Works Agency for Palestine Refugees in the Near East, benefited from the programme.

In addition, assistance activities continued for an estimated 70,000 non-Palestinian refugee population in the region, many of whom faced difficulties in local integration.

Europe

In 1982, the number of asylum-seekers in Europe fell to 91,350 from the 1981 figure of 123,700, despite the increase of asylum-seekers in southern Europe from the Middle East and South-West Asia. Increasingly restrictive criteria were introduced by the traditional countries of resettlement; several Governments adopted measures to prevent abuse of asylum procedures by economically motivated applicants. Consequently, UNHCR increased appropriations for the promotion of resettlement and for care and maintenance of refugees awaiting a durable solution in Greece, Italy, Turkey and Yugoslavia. It obligated $10.4 million, or $2 million more than in 1981, for expenditure in Europe under General Programmes.

In Austria, the majority of asylum-seekers who had arrived there in 1981 were granted local settlement or were resettled in third countries during 1982, and the refugee population at year's end was 29,000; the refugee population in France remained stable at 150,000, while that in the Federal Republic of Germany changed little—an estimated 100,000, including some 24,000 from Indo-China. The number in Greece also remained stable at 4,000, including 2,400 from the Middle East, and Italy hosted 13,600 refugees, a small increase over 1981.

In Portugal, the number of persons of concern to UNHCR remained at 7,600, the majority of them from Angola and Mozambique, with an increase in arrivals from Zaire and Iran in late 1982. As from January 1982, the Portuguese Government undertook sole responsibility for the care and maintenance of asylum-seekers, while UNHCR provided such assistance to recognized refugees.

The number of refugees in Spain increased by 2,000 to 23,500, largely due to the arrival of 1,353 Iranians, making it necessary to double the care and maintenance appropriation and more than triple legal assistance obligations.

Turkey accepted for permanent resettlement 3,815 Afghan refugees of Turkish ethnic origin who had previously found asylum in Pakistan. UNHCR contributed to their travel and initial settlement, and 3,500 of them acquired Turkish nationality before the end of the year. The rate of asylum-seekers from Iran also increased and, by year's end, the total number of registered refugees stood at 1,177.

In the United Kingdom, the number of refugees decreased from 146,000 in 1981 to 143,000 in 1982, while the number of asylum-seekers increased from 2,904 to 4,167; in addition, 879 mostly Indo-Chinese refugees were resettled.

In Yugoslavia, while the resident refugee population decreased slightly to some 1,700, almost 3,000 asylum-seekers arrived, mostly from Eastern Europe, the majority of them in transit pending resettlement.

Elsewhere in Europe, the number of refugees at year's end was as follows: Belgium, 21,000; the Netherlands, 14,000; and Switzerland, 43,000.

Cyprus

UNHCR continued to act as Co-ordinator of United Nations Humanitarian Assistance for Cyprus (see POLITICAL AND SECURITY QUESTIONS, Chapter VIII), assisting the displaced and needy in the country. Ongoing projects included promotion of agricultural activities, provision of educational facilities and vocational training, special assistance to the handicapped and construction of low-cost housing to replace temporary shelters.

Latin America

In 1982, the number of refugees in Central America exceeded 300,000, mainly from El Salvador, Guatemala and Nicaragua, of whom 80,000 received UNHCR assistance. The principal countries affected were Mexico (160,000) and Honduras (34,500). In most other countries, the refugee situation remained relatively stable, actually declining in some countries through repatriation, notably to Bolivia.

UNHCR obligated $29.6 million for assistance activities in the Americas.

Argentina, which accommodated 11,500 refugees of concern to UNHCR (5,000 of European origin, 5,000 of Latin American origin and 1,500 Indo-Chinese), in September gave Indo-Chinese refugees the option to acquire Argentine nationality. In Costa Rica, economic difficulties hindered the integration of 15,000 refugees. Salvadorians and Nicaraguans comprised the majority of the Honduran refugee population, 30,000 of whom received aid mainly in UNHCR-assisted camps and settlements. Mexico's refugee population of 160,000 included some 120,000 Salvadorians and 30,000 Guatemalans, the latter having increased tenfold during the year. In Nicaragua, which had an estimated 18,500 refugees, the monthly average of those requiring UNHCR assistance was 4,000; the special assistance programme for Nicaraguan returnees and internally displaced persons, launched in 1979, was successfully completed in 1982. The number of refugees in Peru decreased from 1,500 to 1,200 (500 of Latin American origin, and 700, mostly elderly, of European origin) due partly to the voluntary repatriation of 190 Bolivians and the resettlement of 160 other refugees.

The total refugee population in Belize, Cuba, the Dominican Republic, El Salvador, Guatemala, Haiti and Panama was estimated at some 80,500 at year's end, including some 73,000 Salvadorians; about 3,500 received regular UNHCR assistance. El Salvador and Guatemala each estimated the number of internally displaced persons at 150,000 to 200,000; for statutory reasons, they remained outside the scope of the UNHCR assistance programme.

In Colombia, Ecuador and Venezuela, 1,744 refugees, mostly of European or Latin American origin, were registered with voluntary agencies co-operating with UNHCR.

In Bolivia, Brazil, Chile, Paraguay and Uruguay, the total refugee population, previously estimated at 28,500 persons, could not be ascertained: most of them were elderly refugees of European origin who did not seek UNHCR assistance. The number whose status could be confirmed stood at some 8,500, of whom 5,400 were in Brazil.

North America

Canada received 18,123 refugees and displaced persons in 1982—8,196 from Eastern Europe, 9,594 from Indo-China and 333 from Latin America—and granted asylum to 626 of a total 7,000 direct asylum-seekers. The number admitted to the United States decreased from 154,063 in 1981 to 88,944 in 1982: 69,351 from South-East Asia, 13,192 from Eastern Europe, 3,089 from the Near East and South Asia, 3,292 from Africa and 20 from Latin America. In addition, 36,923 aliens applied directly for asylum; 3,996 of such requests were approved during 1982, bringing pending requests to 140,000.

Except for some special assistance on a case-by-case basis, UNHCR offered no regular assistance programmes for refugees in North America, where support was provided by voluntary agencies and government services.

Refugee protection

In 1982, military attacks on refugee camps or settlements occurred in Lebanon, Central America and South-East Asia, while in Lesotho refugee groups living in local communities fell victim to military incursions by neighbouring armed forces. Refugees were vulnerable to other forms of violence both within and outside the camps. A UNHCR/Thai Government anti-piracy programme was established in 1982 to deal with the continuing attacks against asylum-seekers in the South China Sea.

UNHCR continued to provide refugees and asylum-seekers with various measures of protection, against a growing trend among States to be restrictive in granting asylum; in almost all parts of the world, UNHCR was confronted with requests for the resettlement of refugees who had been admitted temporarily to countries of asylum pending the search for a durable solution elsewhere. The principle of *non-refoulement*—whereby asylum-seekers would not be forcibly returned to countries where they faced persecution or death—was almost universally respected, and in one country a UNHCR presence was established to determine the *bona fide* character of asylum requests in critical border areas, in agreement with the authorities concerned. However, the practice continued in some States of detaining asylum-seekers for illegal entry or presence or on other grounds.

Cases of mass expulsion or displacement of aliens which could have involved refugees occurred during 1982. In one of those cases, assurances were given by the expelling authorities that persons of concern to UNHCR would not be affected; in another instance involving the forced internal displacement of some 85,000 persons, a large number of refugees, mostly of foreign origin and not fully integrated, were uprooted and compelled to flee from their homes.

Widespread recessionary trends, and increasing legal and other restrictions, added to the difficulties encountered by refugees in obtaining employment, or in enjoying economic rights and entitlements.

There was growing recognition among States of the importance of appropriate documentation; UNHCR printed 75,000 refugee identity cards at the request of various Governments and contributed to the cost of producing such cards in several other countries. In addition, it provided Governments with 16,000 Convention Travel Documents, and offered assistance in cases where such documents had been issued without return clauses or with return clauses of insufficient duration.

The Executive Committee of the High Commissioner's Programme, at its October 1982 session,[2] reiterated the importance of international protection as a primary task entrusted to the High Commissioner under the statute of his Office, and expressed concern over the growing seriousness of the problems relating to international protection and over violations of the basic rights of refugees and asylum-seekers. It hoped that large-scale refugee flows and current recessionary trends would not lead to restrictive practices in granting asylum or in the application of the refugee concept, or to an undermining of the principles of international protection.

The Executive Committee took note of a preliminary report by Felix Schnyder (Switzerland), who had been requested by the High Commissioner to carry out a survey of the problem of military attacks on UNHCR-assisted refugee camps and settlements, and called for the final report by September 1983. It also stressed the international obligation to rescue asylum-seekers in distress at sea, and asked UNHCR to examine a series of suggestions made by the Working Group of Experts on the Rescue of Asylum-Seekers at Sea, which had met from 5 to 7 July 1982.

The Committee recognized the need for measures to deal with the problem of manifestly unfounded or abusive applications for refugee sta-

tus, and stated that a decision that an application was manifestly unfounded or abusive should only be taken after reference to the authority competent to determine refugee status. It suggested the establishment of procedural safeguards to ensure sound decisions, and felt that its Sub-Committee of the Whole on International Protection should examine the question further on the basis of a study to be prepared by UNHCR. The Sub-Committee had held its Seventh Meeting between 7 and 12 October,[1] just prior to the Executive Committee's session. The Committee hoped that an informal meeting of the Sub-Committee would be held as soon as possible in 1983 to consider further the question of military attacks on refugee camps and settlements and related questions.

By a provision in its 18 December resolution on the report of UNHCR,[3] the General Assembly deplored the continued serious violations of the basic rights of refugees and displaced persons of concern to UNHCR, in particular through military attacks on refugee camps and settlements in southern Africa and elsewhere, *refoulement* and arbitrary detention, and emphasized the need to strengthen measures to protect them against such violations.

Reports. [1]Sub-Committee of Whole on International Protection, A/AC.96/613; [2]UNHCR Executive Committee, A/37/12/Add.1.
Resolution (1982). [3]GA: 37/195, para. 3, 18 Dec.

International instruments

As at 31 December 1982, the 1951 Convention relating to the Status of Refugees[1] (which entered into force on 22 April 1954)[2] and its 1967 Protocol[3] (which entered into force on 4 October 1967)[4] had been ratified or acceded to by 91 and 90 States, respectively.

By year's end, the following States (those adhering in 1982 are italicized) had ratified or acceded to the Convention:[5]

Algeria, Angola, Argentina, Australia, Austria, Belgium, Benin, *Bolivia*, Botswana, Brazil, Burundi, Canada, Central African Republic, Chad, Chile, *China*, Colombia, Congo, Costa Rica, Cyprus, Denmark, Djibouti, Dominican Republic, Ecuador, Egypt, Ethiopia, Fiji, Finland, France, Gabon, Gambia, Germany, Federal Republic of, Ghana, Greece, Guinea, Guinea-Bissau, Holy See, Iceland, Iran, Ireland, Israel, Italy, Ivory Coast, Jamaica, Japan, Kenya, Lesotho, Liberia, Liechtenstein, Luxembourg, Madagascar, Mali, Malta, Monaco, Morocco, Netherlands, New Zealand, Nicaragua, Niger, Nigeria, Norway, Panama, Paraguay, Peru, Philippines, Portugal, Rwanda, Sao Tome and Principe, Senegal, Seychelles, Sierra Leone, Somalia, Spain, Sudan, Suriname, Sweden, Switzerland, Togo, Tunisia, Turkey, Uganda, United Kingdom, United Republic of Cameroon, United Republic of Tanzania, Upper Volta, Uruguay, Yemen, Yugoslavia, Zaire, Zambia, Zimbabwe.

The Protocol had been ratified or acceded to by the following States (those adhering in 1982 are italicized):

Algeria, Angola, Argentina, Australia, Austria, Belgium, Benin, *Bolivia*, Botswana, Brazil, Burundi, Canada, Central African Republic, Chad, Chile, *China*, Colombia, Congo, Costa Rica, Cyprus, Denmark, Djibouti, Dominican Republic, Ecuador, Egypt, Ethiopia, Fiji, Finland, France, Gabon, Gambia, Germany, Federal Republic of, Ghana, Greece, Guinea, Guinea-Bissau, Holy See, Iceland, Iran, Ireland, Israel, Italy, Ivory Coast, Jamaica, *Japan*, Kenya, Lesotho, Liberia, Liechtenstein, Luxembourg, Mali, Malta, Morocco, Netherlands, New Zealand, Nicaragua, Niger, Nigeria, Norway, Panama, Paraguay, Philippines, Portugal, Rwanda, Sao Tome and Principe, Senegal, Seychelles, Sierra Leone, Somalia, Spain, Sudan, Suriname, Swaziland, Sweden, Switzerland, Togo, Tunisia, Turkey, Uganda, United Kingdom, United Republic of Cameroon, United Republic of Tanzania, United States, Upper Volta, Uruguay, Yemen, Yugoslavia, Zaire, Zambia, Zimbabwe.

There were no further accessions to the 1954 Convention relating to the Status of Stateless Persons, nor to the 1961 Convention on the Reduction of Statelessness, and the number of States parties to those instruments remained at 32 and 10, respectively.

Other intergovernmental legal instruments of benefit to refugees were the 1969 Convention Governing the Specific Aspects of Refugee Problems in Africa, as adopted by the Organization of African Unity, the 1957 Agreement relating to Refugee Seamen, the 1973 Protocol to the Agreement relating to Refugee Seamen, the 1959 European Agreement on the Abolition of Visas for Refugees, the 1980 European Agreement on Transfer of Responsibility for Refugees, and the 1969 American Convention on Human Rights Pact of San José, Costa Rica.

In 1982, government officials from 27 countries attended a two-week lecture course on the promotion of international protection and of refugee laws, held in co-operation with the International Institute of Humanitarian Law at San Remo, Italy.

Yearbook references. [1]1951, p. 520; [2]1954, p. 256; [3]1967, p. 769; [4]1967, p. 770.
Publication. [5]*Multilateral Treaties Deposited with the Secretary-General* (ST/LEG/SER.E/2), Sales No.E.83.V.6.

Aging refugees

In a report submitted to the 1982 World Assembly on Aging[2] (see Chapter XX of this section), UNHCR estimated that 3 per cent of the 10 million or so refugees in the world were between 60 and 92 years of age, and the number was increasing. The majority lived with their families in camps or elsewhere: those living alone numbered fewer than 10,000. In addition to the general problems that came with aging, elderly refugees had added problems which impeded durable solutions, and a small number of them were mentally depressed or disturbed because of their physical condition and social isolation.

The ongoing UNHCR projects which provided material assistance to elderly refugees had been enlarged in scope, and an assessment was being made of the existing UNHCR-assisted facilities for further improvement in physical amenities, medical care and social services. A Social Services Section was established at UNHCR headquarters in January 1982 as the focal point for development and co-ordination of services for elderly and other vulnerable refugee groups, statistics were collected and compiled on the numbers and needs of elderly refugees, and guidelines for establishing programmes were developed.

The World Assembly recommended that as far as possible groups of refugees accepted by a country should include elderly persons, and efforts should be made to keep family groups intact and ensure that appropriate housing and services were provided.[1]

As part of the follow-up to the World Assembly, UNHCR organized a workshop on elderly refugees, at Cairo, Egypt, in November 1982. It also made a substantial contribution to the construction of a home for aged and disabled persons in Yugoslavia, which opened in December.

Programmes for elderly refugees in Greece, Lebanon, and the Syrian Arab Republic were continued as in Argentina and elsewhere in Latin America. A review was made of their situation in Latin America and steps were taken to ensure adequate assistance for them, many of whom had long resided in their countries of asylum without being able to obtain naturalization and finding themselves without pension or retirement benefits.

Publication. [1]*Report of the World Assembly on Aging, 26 July–6 August 1982*, A/CONF.113/31 (Sales No. E.82.I.16).
Report. [2]UNHCR, A/CONF.113/21 & Add.1.

International co-operation to avert new refugee flows

The General Assembly, by a resolution of 16 December 1982,[4] enlarged from 17 to 24 the membership of the Group of Governmental Experts on International Co-operation to Avert New Flows of Refugees. Members would be appointed by the Secretary-General, in accordance with the Assembly's decision of December 1981[6] to establish the Group. The Assembly reaffirmed the Group's mandate, stressing the need for a constructive, future-oriented approach and for reaching general agreement whenever it was significant for the outcome of its work. It called on the Group to hold, as soon as possible, the meetings already arranged, and to report to the Secretary-General in 1983. Member States which had not conveyed their comments on the question were asked to do so, and the Secretary-General was asked to compile those replies and provide facilities to the Group for its work.

The Assembly adopted the text without vote. The Special Political Committee had approved the draft, introduced by Senegal on behalf of 44 sponsoring nations, in like manner on 6 December.

In a note dated 18 October,[1] the Secretary-General had reported to the Assembly that he had not been able to nominate the experts, due to the wish of several regional groups to nominate more experts than was possible with membership limited to 17. One possibility suggested during his consultations was enlarging the membership to 24.

The Secretary-General, in a September report and an addendum,[2] submitted to the Assembly the observations of nine Member States (Bangladesh, Democratic Kampuchea, Ecuador, Pakistan, Philippines, Rwanda, Sri Lanka, USSR, Viet Nam) and three specialized agencies on international co-operation to avert new refugee flows.

In a related action in 1982, the Assembly, by a 3 December resolution,[3] deplored the plight of the millions of refugees and displaced persons uprooted by foreign military intervention, aggression and occupation, and reaffirmed their right to return to their homes voluntarily in safety and honour.

By a resolution of 17 December,[5] the Assembly commended the Special Rapporteur of the Commission on Human Rights for his study on human rights and mass exoduses, and invited comments from Governments and organizations.

Note. [1]S-G, A/SPC/37/3.
Report. [2]S-G, A/37/416 & Add.1.
Resolutions (1982). GA: [3]37/42, para. 4, 3 Dec.; [4]37/121, 16 Dec., text following; [5]37/186, paras. 1, 2, 18 Dec.
Resolution (prior). [6]GA, 36/148, 16 Dec. 1981 (YUN 1981, p. 1053).
Financial implications. 5th Committee report, A/37/748; S-G statements, A/SPC/37/L.37 & Corr.1, A/C.5/37/91.
Meeting records. GA: SPC, A/SPC/37/SR.*41, 42,* 43, *45,* 46, 48 (1-8 Dec.); 5th Committee, A/C.5/37/SR.66 (13 Dec.); plenary, A/37/PV.108 (16 Dec.).

General Assembly resolution 37/121
16 December 1982   Meeting 108   Adopted without vote

Approved by SPC (A/37/712) without vote, 6 December (meeting 45); 44-nation draft (A/SPC/37/L.36/Rev.1); agenda item 66.

Sponsors: Australia, Austria, Bangladesh, Belgium, Canada, Chad, Comoros, Costa Rica, Denmark, Djibouti, Egypt, France, Gambia, Germany, Federal Republic of, Honduras, Iceland, Indonesia, Ireland, Italy, Japan, Jordan, Luxembourg, Malaysia, Mali, Netherlands, Norway, Pakistan, Philippines, Qatar, Rwanda, Saint Lucia, Samoa, Senegal, Sierra Leone, Singapore, Somalia, Spain, Sudan, Thailand, Togo, United Kingdom, United Republic of Cameroon, United States, Zaire.

International co-operation to avert new flows of refugees

The General Assembly,

Having examined the report of the Secretary-General,

Taking note of the comments and suggestions submitted by Member States, organs and organizations of the United Nations and specialized agencies in response to General Assembly resolutions 35/124 of 11 December 1980 and 36/148 of 16 December 1981,

Stressing the importance of adopting a constructive and future-oriented approach in considering the question of international co-operation to avert new massive flows of refugees,

1. *Takes note* of the report of the Secretary-General;

2. *Reaffirms* its resolution 36/148 on international co-operation to avert new flows of refugees;

3. *Welcomes* the comments and suggestions submitted in response to General Assembly resolutions 35/124 and 36/148 by Member States, organs and organizations of the United Nations and specialized agencies;

4. *Decides* to enlarge the Group of Governmental Experts on International Co-operation to Avert New Flows of Refugees, established in accordance with paragraph 4 of resolution 36/148, from seventeen to twenty-four members;

5. *Reaffirms* the mandate of the Group of Governmental Experts as defined by resolution 36/148 by stressing the need for members of the Group to embark upon the study in question in the framework of a constructive, future-oriented approach and in conformity with the spirit which must form the basis of friendly relations and close co-operation among Member States;

6. *Requests* the Group of Governmental Experts to be mindful of the importance of reaching general agreement whenever that has significance for the outcome of its work;

7. *Renews its call* upon Member States that have not yet conveyed to the Secretary-General their comments and suggestions on this item to do so as soon as possible;

8. *Requests* the Secretary-General to prepare a compilation of the replies received in accordance with paragraph 7 above and to provide the Group of Governmental Experts with all necessary assistance and facilities for the completion of its task;

9. *Calls upon* the Group of Governmental Experts to hold, as soon as possible, the meetings which had already been arranged and to submit a report to the Secretary-General in time for deliberation by the General Assembly at its thirty-eighth session;

10. *Decides* to include in the provisional agenda of its thirty-eighth session the item entitled "International co-operation to avert new flows of refugees".

Chapter XXII

Drugs of Abuse

Contents

General aspects

In 1982, the Commission on Narcotic Drugs held its seventh special session, at Vienna, Austria, from 2 to 8 February. The International Narcotics Control Board held two sessions at Vienna—17 to 28 May (thirty-first session) and 5 to 22 October (thirty-second session).

International Control

Implementation of the International Drug Abuse Control Strategy

In 1982, the Commission on Narcotic Drugs, by a resolution[4] of 8 February, provisionally established a task force to facilitate its work in implementing the 1981 International Drug Abuse Control Strategy and the five-year programme of action for 1982-1986, as called for by the General Assembly.[8] Until further review in February 1983, the group would be composed of the Commission's Steering Committee and of representatives of the International Narcotics Control Board (INCB), the United Nations Division of Narcotic Drugs, the United Nations Development Programme (UNDP), the United Nations Fund for Drug Abuse Control (UNFDAC) and the World Health Organization (WHO). The Commission recommended that the General Assembly approve a number of projects proposed for 1983 (see below), and asked the Secretary-General to include in the 1984/1985 budget estimates a list of projects envisaged for that biennium under the programme of action to be reviewed by the task force and the Commission in 1983.

Acting on the recommendation, the Economic and Social Council on 3 May[5] recommended for Assembly adoption a draft resolution by which the Assembly would approve the projects recommended by the Commission and request that body to report to the Assembly through the Council in 1983. It would urge the international community and organizations concerned to strengthen their participation in and support for activities related to the Strategy and the programme of action, and would urge Member States to increase contributions to UNFDAC.

The Council adopted without vote the text which had been recommended by the Commission after it was orally amended by the United States to request the Commission to report to the Assembly in 1983 rather than then and "annually thereafter".

The Commission proposed to continue in 1983 seven projects begun in 1982:[2] study of the possible merging of the 1961 Single Convention on Narcotic Drugs and the 1971 Convention on Psychotropic Substances (see below); approaches to drug abuse reduction; INCB monitoring of psychotropic substances; establishing a system of voluntary reports by Governments on their estimated requirements for specific psychotropic substances; research on the characteristics of seized heroin to trace its origins; developing a network of laboratories for information exchange; and a feasibility study on establishing a computerized data base for the Division of Narcotic Drugs.

In addition, the Commission gave priority to four study projects for implementation in 1983: measures to deprive drug traffickers of illegally acquired assets, and to counter bank secrecy of drug-related assets; chemical composition of drugs of abuse; curbing illicit traffic in transit countries; and the impact of heavy penalties for drug-related offences.

Other priority projects for financing from extrabudgetary sources in 1983 included: multisectoral country programmes, including income substitution and rural development, to reduce the illicit supply of narcotic raw materials; drug identification or quick-testing kits; strengthening of narcotics laboratories in developing countries; regional seminars on the use of community resources to reduce drug demand; fellowships, study programmes, and courses for law enforcement personnel; and meetings of operational heads of law enforcement agencies.

On 17 December,[6] the Assembly adopted without vote the text recommended to it by the Council. The text had met similar approval in the Third (Social, Humanitarian and Cultural) Committee on 2 December after it had been orally amended by the United States to add at the end of paragraph 1 "within available United Nations resources and to the extent possible in order of priority".

Bolivia, in a letter of 14 June 1982,[1] appealed to the Secretary-General to suggest to those con-

cerned that they immediately implement the Assembly's December 1981 resolution on the International Drug Abuse Control Strategy,[7] particularly with regard to establishing a United Nations task force for the campaign.

In a report, dated 29 October[3] on international drug abuse control, submitted in response to a 1979 General Assembly request,[7] the Secretary-General gave details of activities undertaken by the United Nations Division of Narcotic Drugs, INCB, UNFDAC, United Nations Centre for Social Development and Humanitarian Affairs, United Nations Social Defence Research Institute, International Labour Organisation, Food and Agriculture Organization of the United Nations, United Nations Educational, Scientific and Cultural Organization and WHO.

Letter. [1]Bolivia, 14 June, A/37/292.
Reports. [2]Commission on Narcotic Drugs, E/1982/13; [3]S-G, A/37/556.
Resolutions (1982). [4]Commission on Narcotic Drugs (report, E/1982/13): 1(S-VII), 8 Feb. [5]ESC: 1982/13, 3 May, text following. [6]GA: 37/168, 17 Dec., text following.
Resolutions (prior). GA: [7]34/177, 17 Dec. 1979 (YUN 1979, p. 933); [8]36/168, 16 Dec. 1981 (YUN 1981, p. 1058).
Financial implications. S-G statement, A/C.3/37/L.6.
Meeting records. ESC: E/1982/SR.17-19, *20, 21* (27 Apr.–3 May). GA: 3rd Committee, A/C.3/37/SR.57, 58, *61,* 62-64, 66, 68, 69 (29 Nov.–8 Dec.); plenary, A/37/PV.110 (17 Dec.).
Publication. International Strategy and Policies for Drug Control, NAR/INF/1982/3.

Economic and Social Council resolution 1982/13

3 May 1982   Meeting 20   Adopted without vote

Draft by Commission on Narcotic Drugs (E/1982/13), orally amended by United States; agenda item 12.

Strategy and policies for drug control

The Economic and Social Council,

Taking note of resolution 1(S-VII) of 8 February 1982 of the Commission on Narcotic Drugs,

Recommends to the General Assembly the adoption of the following draft resolution:

"*The General Assembly,*

"*Recalling* its resolution 36/168 of 16 December 1981, by which it adopted the International Drug Abuse Control Strategy and the basic five-year programme of action dealt with in resolution 1(XXIX) of 11 February 1981 of the Commission on Narcotic Drugs, transmitted to the General Assembly by the Economic and Social Council in accordance with its decision 1981/113 of 6 May 1981,

"*Recalling also* that in paragraph 3 of resolution 36/168 the Commission on Narcotic Drugs was requested to establish, within available resources, a task force to review, monitor and co-ordinate the implementation of the International Drug Abuse Control Strategy and the programme of action,

"*Recalling further* its resolutions 32/124 of 16 December 1977, 33/168 of 20 December 1978, 34/177 of 17 December 1979 and 35/195 of 15 December 1980,

"*Noting with satisfaction* the establishment on a provisional basis by the Commission on Narcotic Drugs of the task force requested,

"*Taking note* of Economic and Social Council resolution 1982/13 of 3 May 1982 and resolution 1(S-VII) of 8 February 1982 of the Commission on Narcotic Drugs,

"1. *Approves* the projects recommended by the Commission on Narcotic Drugs in its resolution 1(S-VII), as set out in the report of the Commission on its seventh special session, for implementation in 1983;

"2. *Requests* the Commission on Narcotic Drugs to review the reports of its task force and to report thereon, through the Economic and Social Council, to the General Assembly at its thirty-eighth session;

"3. *Urges* all Member States, non-member States parties to the international drug control treaties, specialized agencies and other international organizations and private institutions concerned with the drug abuse problem to strengthen their participation in and support for activities related to the International Drug Abuse Control Strategy and the programme of action;

"4. *Also urges* Member States to contribute or increase their contributions to the United Nations Fund for Drug Abuse Control in order to ensure success of the International Drug Abuse Control Strategy and to give firm impetus to the world community's battle against international drug traffickers and against drug abuse;

"5. *Requests* the Secretary-General to transmit the text of the present resolution and related documents to all Member States, non-member States parties to the international drug control treaties, and all relevant international, intergovernmental and non-governmental organizations."

General Assembly resolution 37/168

17 December 1982   Meeting 110   Adopted without vote

Approved by Third Committee (A/37/745) without vote, 2 December (meeting 61); draft recommended by Economic and Social Council (resolution 1982/13), amended by United States (A/C.3/37/L.63, orally revised); agenda item 12.

Strategy and policies for drug control

The General Assembly,

Recalling its resolution 36/168 of 16 December 1981, by which it adopted the International Drug Abuse Control Strategy and the basic five-year programme of action dealt with in Commission on Narcotic Drugs resolution 1(XXIX) of 11 February 1981, which the Economic and Social Council, by its decision 1981/113 of 6 May 1981, decided to transmit to the General Assembly,

Recalling also that in paragraph 3 of resolution 36/168 the Commission on Narcotic Drugs was requested to establish, within available resources, a task force to review, monitor and co-ordinate the implementation of the International Drug Abuse Control Strategy and the programme of action,

Recalling further its resolutions 32/124 of 16 December 1977, 33/168 of 20 December 1978, 34/177 of 17 December 1979 and 35/195 of 15 December 1980,

Noting with satisfaction the establishment on a provisional basis by the Commission on Narcotic Drugs of the task force requested,

Taking note of Economic and Social Council resolution 1982/13 of 3 May 1982 and Commission on Narcotic Drugs resolution 1(S-VII) of 8 February 1982,

1. *Approves* the projects recommended by the Commission on Narcotic Drugs in its resolution 1(S-VII), as set out in the report of the Commission on its seventh special session, for implementation in 1983, within available United Nations resources and to the extent possible in order of priority;

2. *Requests* the Commission to review the reports of its task force and to report thereon, through the Economic and Social Council, to the General Assembly at its thirty-eighth session;

3. *Urges* all Member States, non-member States parties to the international drug control treaties, specialized agencies and other international organizations and private institutions concerned with the drug abuse problem to strengthen their participation in and support for activities related to the International Drug Abuse Control Strategy and the programme of action;

4. *Also urges* Member States to contribute or to increase their contributions to the United Nations Fund for Drug Abuse Control in order to ensure the success of the International Drug Abuse Control Strategy and to give firm impetus to the world community's battle against international drug traffickers and against drug abuse;

5. *Requests* the Secretary-General to transmit the text of the present resolution and related documents to all Member States, non-member States parties to the international drug control treaties and all relevant international, intergovernmental and non-governmental organizations.

UN Fund for Drug Abuse Control

In 1982, the United Nations Fund for Drug Abuse Control (UNFDAC) devoted 79 per cent of its resources to 12 country programmes, comprising 27 projects.[1] These development-oriented country programmes were concentrated in regions with major narcotics control problems. Centralized research and training projects which supplement United Nations drug control activities also received UNFDAC resources.

On 17 December 1982,[2] the General Assembly urged Member States to contribute to UNFDAC to ensure the success of the International Drug Abuse Control Strategy and to give impetus to the battle against international drug traffickers.

The Assembly repeated the call for contributions to UNFDAC in an 18 December resolution.[3]

In 1982, 42 countries and one Territory contributed some $6.8 million to UNFDAC and 22 countries pledged some $2.5 million for 1983 (see table below).

CONTRIBUTIONS TO THE UNITED NATIONS FUND
FOR DRUG ABUSE CONTROL, 1982 AND 1983
(As at 31 December 1982; in US dollar equivalents)

Country or Territory	1982 payment	1983 pledge
Argentina	7,882	—
Australia	143,078	141,509
Austria	72,990	84,746
Bahamas	1,000	—
Barbados	250	250
Benin	1,667	—
Bolivia	—	2,000
Brazil	10,000	5,000
Canada	204,918	—
Chile	4,000	5,000
Denmark	20,428	213,837
Egypt	1,000	1,000
Finland	5,074	—
France	101,770	139,860
Germany, Federal Republic of	2,284,827	1,496,063
Greece	2,000	—
Hong Kong	17,129	—
Iceland	3,200	—
India	14,000	7,000
Iran	4,000	—
Italy	—	103,806
Ivory Coast	309	—
Jamaica	561	562
Japan	300,000	—
Kenya	4,615	—
Malawi	—	474
Malaysia	5,000	—
Malta	506	—
Mexico	2,063	4,000
Morocco	6,000	3,000
New Zealand	27,692	—
Norway	1,056,328	138,889
Philippines	2,000	2,000
Qatar	20,000	—
Republic of Korea	2,000	—
Saudi Arabia	50,000	50,000
Singapore	1,000	—
South Africa	4,397	—
Sweden	176,856	—
Switzerland	96,602	40,909
Tunisia	2,711	—
Turkey	10,000	10,000
United Kingdom	89,500	—
United Republic of Cameroon	1,767	2,801
United States	2,000,000	—
Venezuela	2,000	—
Total	**6,761,720**	**2,452,706**

SOURCE: Interim financial statements for the 12-month period ended 31 December 1982 - Individual trust funds.

Report. [1]UNFDAC, E/CN.7/1983/15.
Resolutions (1982). GA: [2]37/168, para. 4, 17 Dec.; [3]37/198, para. 3, 18 Dec.

UN Narcotics Laboratory

The Narcotics Laboratory Section of the United Nations Division of Narcotic Drugs trained scientists from developing countries in methods of identifying and analysing drugs of abuse seized in illicit traffic. It provided technical information, chemicals and equipment to a number of countries to strengthen national narcotics laboratories, and expanded its collection of scientific literature on drugs and drug abuse.

An expert group met at Vienna, Austria, from 28 September to 1 October 1982, in accordance with a project proposed under the 1981 International Strategy for Drug Abuse Control and programme of action, to discuss co-ordination of research by the Narcotics Laboratory on the physical and chemical characteristics of heroin to trace its origin and movement in the illicit traffic.

It recommended that resources should be made available for technical assistance to national laboratories of developing countries and that there should be continuing research and collaboration on development of heroin profiles by national laboratories, as well as periodical reviews of advances in research and assessment of findings.

International Control in the Andean area

The Economic and Social Council, on 3 May 1982,[1] called on the Commission on Narcotic Drugs to give higher priority to the problems of illicit production, trafficking and abuse of narcotic drugs, including in particular coca, in the Andean subregion and to formulate, with United Nations narcotics agencies, a more specific strategy and programmes for that subregion. It requested the Secretary-General, through UNFDAC, to assist in co-ordinating international narcotics control efforts in the Andean subregion and to consider establishing a regional office at Lima, Peru. It requested the international community's collaboration and urged Governments to contribute to UNFDAC.

The 14-nation text introduced by Peru was adopted without vote after incorporation of an oral correction by Peru on behalf of the sponsors which referred to problems of "narcotic drugs" rather than "cocaine" in the region, and replaced the original phrase "particularly coca" with "including in particular coca".

Resolution (1982). [1]ESC: 1982/14, 3 May, text following.
Meeting record. ESC: E/1982/SR.20 (3 May).

Economic and Social Council resolution 1982/14

| 3 May 1982 | Meeting 20 | Adopted without vote |

14-nation draft (E/1982/L.34); agenda item 12.

Sponsors: Argentina, Bahamas, Bolivia, Canada, Colombia, Costa Rica, France, Italy, Nigeria, Pakistan, Peru, Portugal, United States, Yugoslavia.

Establishment of a regional office at Lima for co-ordinating narcotics control

The Economic and Social Council,

Recalling the resolutions on the problem of drug abuse control adopted in recent years by the General Assembly, the Economic and Social Council, the Commission on Narcotic Drugs, the World Health Organization and other competent bodies,

Recalling, in particular, General Assembly resolution 36/168 of 16 December 1981, by which the Assembly adopted the International Drug Abuse Control Strategy and the basic five-year programme of action dealt with in resolution 1(XXIX) of 11 February 1981 of the Commission on Narcotic Drugs, transmitted to the Assembly by the Economic and Social Council in accordance with its decision 1981/113 of 6 May 1981,

Convinced that greater control of the production and distribution of narcotics and a reduction of the demand for illicit narcotics are necessary prerequisites for reducing the illicit traffic in narcotic drugs and psychotropic substances,

Conscious of the links between drug trafficking and serious problems of a socio-economic nature, which are reflected in an intensification of organized crime, the illegal acquisition of firearms, exchange-control violations, customs offences and various other forms of criminality,

Acknowledging that constraints of an economic and technical nature are obstacles for many developing countries in their fight against drug trafficking,

Drawing attention to the need for developing country producers of narcotic drugs to receive more assistance from Governments and international organizations concerned, so that they will be able to facilitate drug abuse control by implementing policies of crop substitution and programmes of industrial and rural development,

Taking into account United Nations programmes related to combating the problem of drug trafficking, in particular the International Drug Abuse Control Strategy, which recognize the need to encourage activities at the regional level, *inter alia,* by grouping together geographical areas with similar social, economic and cultural characteristics and by preparing one or more strategies for those areas which should be effective in the short term,

Considering that the increase in coca production in the Andean subregion is assuming alarming proportions, owing to the growing illicit demand for cocaine throughout the world, and that it is therefore necessary to deal globally with the problem in all its manifestations,

1. *Calls upon* the Commission on Narcotic Drugs to give higher priority to the problems of illicit production of narcotic drugs and the trafficking in and abuse of narcotic drugs in the Andean subregion, including in particular coca, and to formulate, with the participation of the United Nations narcotics agencies, a more specific strategy and programmes for the subregion within its regular budget and through voluntary contributions;

2. *Requests* the Secretary-General, through the United Nations Fund for Drug Abuse Control, to assist in co-ordinating international narcotics control efforts in the Andean subregion, and to consider the establishment of a regional office at Lima, taking into account the recommendations concerning regional activities outlined in the International Drug Abuse Control Strategy, as agreed to in General Assembly resolution 36/168;

3. *Requests* the specialized agencies, Member States and non-governmental organizations to assist in the implementation of the present resolution and to collaborate in any projects and activities which may become part of the programme;

4. *Urges* Governments to support United Nations efforts in the Andean subregion by contributing to the United Nations Fund for Drug Abuse Control.

Drug abuse

The International Narcotics Control Board (INCB) stated in its 1982 report[1] that the current drug abuse situation required innovative and concerted action and that governments should fully implement the controls in existing treaties, while complying voluntarily with additional measures suggested by INCB for detecting diversion. Once widely accepted, the INCB-suggested measures should be formalized in treaty amendments.

In its 1982 annual report[2] to the Economic and Social Council, INCB noted the need for data collection on the dimensions, distribution and changing trends of drug abuse within populations, along with the importance of constant review of prevention and treatment approaches.

An Expert Group on Drug Abuse Reduction, meeting at Vienna, Austria, from 6 to 10 September 1982,[3] recommended that all concerned bodies be encouraged to direct more resources to solving drug abuse problems, and governments and specialized agencies should re-examine mobilization of existing programmes and resources. Approaches to reducing drug abuse should be continuously evaluated and monitored. The prevention and reduction of illicit demand for controlled drugs would be enhanced if concurrent emphasis were placed on reducing the use of socially accepted substances, such as alcohol and tobacco.

Publication. [1]*Report of the International Narcotics Control Board for 1982* (E/INCB/61), Sales No. E.83.XI.1.
Reports. [2]INCB, E/1983/6 (summary); [3]Commission on Narcotic Drugs, E.CN.7/1983/2/Add.3.

Proposed International Year

The Economic and Social Council, on 30 April,[1] invited Governments to submit to the Commission on Narcotic Drugs, for consideration at its February 1983 session, comments on a proposed International Year against Drug Abuse. The Commission was asked to transmit to the Council at its May 1983 session an analysis of comments received in order for a recommendation to be submitted to the 1983 General Assembly.

This action was incorporated into a resolution which was adopted by 32 votes to none, with 11 abstentions. The vote was taken at the request of the USSR on a draft which originated in the Commission on Narcotic Drugs.

Resolution (1982). [1]ESC: 1982/10, 30 Apr., text following.
Meeting record. ESC: E/1982/SR.19 (30 Apr.).

Economic and Social Council resolution 1982/10

30 April 1982	Meeting 19	32-0-11

Draft by Commission on Narcotic Drugs (E/1982/13); agenda item 12.

International Year against Drug Abuse
The Economic and Social Council,
Having considered the report of the International Narcotics Control Board for 1981,
Noting with deep concern the Board's conclusion that, despite the international community's efforts to date, drug abuse throughout most of the world has not decreased — on the contrary, the situation has continued to deteriorate, afflicting more and more countries, both developing and developed, victimizing adolescents and even children, and leading to the availability of drugs of ever greater potency capable of being consumed in more hazardous ways,
Noting also the Board's call for the stimulation of action at all levels, from international to local, involving families, communities, neighbourhoods, schools, religious institutions, and public, private and voluntary associations and organizations,

Convinced that the holding within the near future of an International Year against Drug Abuse could serve as a catalyst for renewed world-wide awareness of the serious drug situation in many parts of the world and for stimulating the wide range of national and international activities required in the battle against drug abuse and illicit traffic,
Bearing in mind its resolution 1980/67 of 25 July 1980, by which it established guidelines for future international years,
1. *Invites* all Governments to submit, through the Secretary-General, their comments on the proposed proclamation of an International Year against Drug Abuse to the Commission on Narcotic Drugs for consideration at its thirtieth session;
2. *Invites* the Commission on Narcotic Drugs to transmit to the Council at its first regular session of 1983 an analysis of those comments, together with a recommendation thereon, in order that an appropriate recommendation may be submitted to the General Assembly at its thirty-eighth session;
3. *Requests* the Secretary-General to transmit the text of the present resolution to all Governments for consideration and action as appropriate.

Economic and social consequences

The Commission on Narcotic Drugs decided, on 8 February 1982,[1] to consider at its February 1983 session measures to assess the nature and extent of drug abuse and the health, social and economic consequences of such abuse.

Decision. [1]Commission on Narcotic Drugs (report, E/1982/13), 2(S-VII), 8 Feb.

Supply and demand

The International Narcotics Control Board (INCB), in its 1982 report,[1] stated that the international control system for the licit trade of narcotics operated for the most part in a satisfactory manner, and that a fragile balance was attained in 1982 between supply and demand of opiates for medical and scientific needs, due mainly to reduced cultivation by the four main producing countries, in co-operation with INCB. World-wide demand for opiates remained within forecasts made by INCB based on data furnished by Governments.

Report. [1]INCB, E/INCB/61 (Sales No. E.83.XI.1).

Production control to meet world requirements

On 30 April 1982,[2] the Economic and Social Council, concerned that large stocks of opiate raw materials held by traditional supplier countries were a heavy financial and other burden for them, urged Governments to implement its 1979,[3] 1980[4] and 1981[5] resolutions and to take other steps to achieve a world-wide balance between demand and supply of opiates for medical and scientific purposes. The Council appealed to those which had not cultivated *papaver bracteatum* to refrain from its commercial cultivation and asked the Secretary-General to transmit the resolution to Governments, inviting them to bring it to the attention of their authorities.

The text, which originated in the Commission on Narcotic Drugs, was adopted without vote.

An expert group to study the possibility of an international buffer stock of opiate raw materials which met at Vienna, Austria, from 20 to 24 September 1982,[1] stated that the buffer stock technique did not deal satisfactorily with problems of managing existing stocks and bringing production into line with current and future demand. The current supply-and-demand situation could be improved by various exceptional and temporary measures, such as examination by producers and consumers of recent technological changes, shifts in demand patterns, disposal of excess stocks, and removal of artificial commodity barriers; provision of timely statistical reports; introduction of substitute crops in regions of traditional licit opium poppy cultivation; and conversion of excess stocks of opiate raw materials into codeine.

Report. [1]Expert group on international buffer stock of opiate raw material, E/CN.7/1983/2.
Resolution (1982). [2]ESC: 1982/12, 30 Apr., text following.
Resolutions (prior). ESC: [3]1979/8, 9 May 1979 (YUN 1979, p. 932); [4]1980/21, 30 Apr. 1980 (YUN 1980, p. 963); [5]1981/8, 6 May 1981 (YUN 1981, p. 1060).
Meeting record. ESC: E/1982/SR.19 (30 Apr.).
Publications. Estimated World Requirements of Narcotic Drugs in 1982 (E/INCB/57), Sales No. E/F/S.82.XI.2; *Supplements Nos. 1-12* (E/INCB/57/Supp.1-11), Sales No. E/F/S.82.XI.2/Supp.1-12).

Economic and Social Council resolution 1982/12

30 April 1982   Meeting 19   Adopted without vote

Draft by Commission on Narcotic Drugs (E/1982/13); agenda item 12

Demand and supply of opiates for medical and scientific needs
The Economic and Social Council,

Recalling its resolutions 1979/8 of 9 May 1979, 1980/20 of 30 April 1980, 1981/8 of 6 May 1981, and resolution 1(XXIX) of 11 February 1981 of the Commission on Narcotic Drugs, entitled "Strategy and policies for drug control",

Taking note of the supplement to the report of the International Narcotics Control Board for 1980, entitled *Demand and Supply of Opiates for Medical and Scientific Needs*, and of the recommendations contained therein,

Reaffirming that a world-wide balance is essential between the supply of opiate raw materials and the demand for opiates for medical and scientific purposes,

Noting with satisfaction that a number of major importing, manufacturing and consuming countries have responded positively to the above-mentioned resolutions,

Concerned that large stocks of opiate raw materials held by the traditional supplier countries constitute a heavy financial and other burden for them,

1. *Urges* the Governments of those countries that have not already done so to take effective steps to implement the above-mentioned resolutions, and also to consider taking other steps, including those recommended by the International Narcotics Control Board, to achieve a world-wide balance between demand and supply of opiates for medical and scientific purposes;

2. *Appeals* to Governments which have not cultivated *papaver bracteatum* to consider possibilities for refraining from embarking on the commercial cultivation of *papaver bracteatum*;

3. *Requests* the Secretary-General to transmit the present resolution to all Governments, inviting them to bring it to the attention of their competent authorities.

Illicit traffic

According to a 1982 report by the International Narcotics Control Board,[2] illicit production, traffic and abuse of cannabis, cocaine and opium were prevalent over wide areas. Cannabis culti-

vation was increasing and spreading to new countries, traffickers in opium could easily procure quantities for morphine and heroine manufacture, and the staggering oversupply of coca leaves facilitated the traffic of cocaine and coca paste in greater quantities.

A two-part review of illicit traffic in narcotic drugs and psychotropic substances during 1981 was issued by the Commission on Narcotic Drugs in November and December 1982.[4] It analysed world trends, suggested countermeasures, and included country reports, an analysis by region, and statistical tables of drugs seized.

Economic and Social Council action. The Economic and Social Council, on 30 April 1982,[5] urged Governments to strengthen customs and drug control bodies to promote the interdiction of substances diverted to illicit channels. The Council appealed to States to develop more effective monitoring of controlled drug shipments within and across borders, and called on them to pass and enforce laws making the deliberate misrepresentation or mislabelling of controlled narcotic drugs or psychotropic substances punishable offences, or to take other suitable measures. It invited Governments to make a list of precursors and reagents most widely used in the illicit manufacture of narcotic drugs and psychotropic substances, for submission to the Secretary-General and for the attention of police, customs and other control authorities.

The Council approved the draft, which originated in the Commission on Narcotic Drugs, without vote.

In response to a December 1981 General Assembly request[5] for comments on an international campaign against drug traffic, the Secretary-General received replies from 28 Member States, four United Nations organs, three non-governmental and two inter-governmental organizations.[3] Due to time constraints, the Council, by a 3 May 1982 decision,[1] waived its examination of the replies and requested the Secretary-General to report directly to the Assembly.

General Assembly action. On 18 December,[6] the Assembly urged the United Nations system and Member States with resources and expertise, to continue granting assistance, especially in the training of law enforcement professionals, to countries most affected by the illicit production of and traffic in drugs and drug abuse. It called on Member States to ratify international drug control treaties (see below) and to contribute to the United Nations Fund for Drug Abuse Control (UNFDAC). The Assembly also requested the Secretary-General, through the Commission on Narcotic Drugs, to explore co-ordination mechanisms for drug law enforcement, give priority to alleviating problems of transit States, and consider convening in 1986 an interregional meeting of heads of national drug law enforcement agencies. It requested him to devote a special issue of the *Bulletin on Narcotic Drugs* to the campaign against drug trafficking and to report to the Assembly in 1983 on the resolution's implementation.

This action was taken without vote following similar approval in the Third (Social, Humanitarian and Cultural) Committee on 9 November. The 16-nation text was introduced by the Bahamas.

Decision. [1]ESC: 1982/117, 3 May, text following.
Reports. [2]INCB, E/INCB/61 (Sales No. E.83.XI.1); [3]S-G, A/37/530; [4]Commission on Narcotic Drugs, E/CN.7/1983/10 (Parts one and two).
Resolutions (1982). [5]ESC: 1982/8, 30 Apr., text following. [6]GA: 37/198, 18 Dec., text following.
Meeting records. ESC: E/1982/SR.19, 20 (30 Apr., 3 May). GA: 3rd Committee, A/C.3/37/SR.57, 62-65, *66*, 68, 69, *72* (29 Nov.-9 Dec.); plenary, A/37/PV.111 (18 Dec.).

Economic and Social Council resolution 1982/8

30 April 1982　　　　Meeting 19　　　　Adopted without vote

Draft by Commission on Narcotic Drugs (E/1982/13); agenda item 12.

Measures to improve international co-operation in the interdiction of illicit drug traffic

The Economic and Social Council,

Recalling the need for close co-operation among law enforcement authorities in investigating the illicit traffic in narcotics and psychotropic substances,

Bearing in mind resolutions 2(S-V) of 22 February 1978, 5(XXVIII) of 21 February 1979, 4(S-VI) of 20 February 1980 and 3(XXXIX) of 10 February 1981 of the Commission on Narcotic Drugs, as well as the relevant provisions of the international Conventions,

Firmly believing that, to be effective in combating and interdicting the illicit traffic, measures employed by customs and drug control administrations must be given wide international support,

1. *Urges* all Governments, whenever necessary, to strengthen their customs and drug control bodies with a view to promoting the interdiction of substances diverted to illicit channels, by means which include the provision of timely, relevant information and co-operation to the fullest extent possible with national and international organizations working in this area;

2. *Appeals* to all States to develop means of monitoring more effectively shipments of controlled drugs within and across their borders, particularly within free trading zones;

3. *Calls upon* States, subject to their constitutional limitations, their legal systems and domestic law, to pass and enforce laws that make the deliberate misrepresentation or mislabelling of controlled narcotic drugs or psychotropic substances punishable offences, or to take other suitable measures for their control;

4. *Invites* all Governments to respond positively to the suggestion of the International Narcotics Control Board that a list should be made of the precursors and reagents most widely used in the illicit manufacture of narcotic drugs and psychotropic substances by submitting this information to the Secretary-General at his request and bringing the list to the attention of their police, customs and other control authorities;

5. *Requests* the Secretary-General to transmit the text of the present resolution to all Governments and to invite them to bring it to the attention of their competent authorities in order to ensure the implementation of its provisions.

Economic and Social Council decision 1982/117

　　　　　　　　　　　　　　　　　　　Adopted without vote

Oral proposal by President; agenda item 12.

International campaign against traffic in drugs

At its 20th plenary meeting, on 3 May 1982, the Council decided to authorize the Secretary-General to submit the report on an international campaign against traffic in drugs, requested by the General Assembly in its resolution 36/132 of 14 December 1981, directly to the Assembly at its thirty-seventh session.

General Assembly resolution 37/198

18 December 1982　　　　Meeting 111　　　　Adopted without vote

Approved by Third Committee (A/37/728) without vote, 9 December (meeting 72); 16-nation draft (A/C.3/37/L.78), orally revised; agenda item 93.

Sponsors: Australia, Bahamas, Barbados, Costa Rica, Egypt, Grenada, Jamaica, Morocco, Nigeria, Pakistan, Peru, Philippines, Saint Lucia, Singapore, Thailand, Trinidad and Tobago.

International campaign against traffic in drugs

The General Assembly,

Recalling its resolutions 36/132 of 14 December 1981, in which it recognized the need, within the context of the International Drug Abuse Control Strategy, for an effective international campaign against traffic in drugs, and 36/168 of 16 December 1981, in which it adopted the Strategy and the basic five-year programme of action;

Taking note of Economic and Social Council resolutions 1982/8 and 1982/9 of 30 April 1982,

Having considered the report of the Secretary-General,

Reaffirming the need to improve regional and interregional co-operation and co-ordination, particularly in the field of law enforcement, to eradicate illicit traffic,

Acknowledging that many countries, including developing countries, continue to divert substantial human, financial and other resources to control international drug trafficking,

Recognizing, in particular, the dilemma of transit States, which have no control over the production of and demand for illicit narcotics, yet are seriously affected both at the domestic and international levels by the movement of illicit drugs,

Noting the significant role of the international drug control treaties in the development of effective countermeasures in combating the illicit supply, demand and traffic in drugs,

Considering the important role of the United Nations Fund for Drug Abuse Control in the implementation of various drug control programmes, particularly in developing countries, and the necessity of increasing contributions to the Fund to permit it to continue its most valuable work,

1. *Takes note with appreciation* of the report of the Secretary-General;

2. *Calls upon* Member States that have not yet done so to ratify the international drug control treaties and, until such time, to endeavour to abide by the provisions thereof;

3. *Encourages* Member States to contribute, or to continue to contribute, to the United Nations Fund for Drug Abuse Control so that it may pursue its useful programmes in the field of drug abuse control;

4. *Urges* organizations and programmes within the United Nations system, as well as Member States with available resources and expertise, to continue to grant technical and other forms of assistance, especially in the area of training of law enforcement professionals, to countries most affected by the illicit production of and traffic in drugs and drug abuse;

5. *Requests* the Secretary-General, through the Commission on Narcotic Drugs, to explore all avenues leading to further improving regional and international co-ordination of activities against drug trafficking and drug abuse, in particular:

(a) To explore the feasibility of establishing, on a continuing basis, co-ordination mechanisms for drug law enforcement in regions where these do not exist;

(b) To give adequate priority to measures designed to alleviate the special problems of transit States;

(c) To consider convening in 1986 an interregional meeting of heads of national drug law enforcement agencies;

6. *Also requests* the Secretary-General to devote a special issue of the *Bulletin on Narcotic Drugs*, published by the Division of Narcotic Drugs of the Secretariat, to an analysis of the campaign against drug trafficking;

7. *Further requests* the Secretary-General to prepare a report, for review by the General Assembly at its thirty-eighth session, on the progress achieved in the implementation of the present resolution;

8. *Decides* to include in the provisional agenda of its thirty-eighth session the item entitled "International campaign against traffic in drugs".

Drug law enforcement

The Commission on Narcotic Drugs decided on 8 February 1982[1] that the United Nations Division of Narcotic Drugs should ask Governments and international bodies to provide details—including the advantages or disadvantages—of legislative or other measures to effect the drug law enforcement technique of controlled delivery, by which detected illicit consignments were allowed to proceed under strict surveillance; the Division was asked to present the information along with appropriate recommendations to the Commission at its February 1983 session.

In 1982, the Division of Narcotic Drugs executed projects totalling more than $3 million under extra-budgetary financing.[2] In co-operation with Member States and intergovernmental organizations, it organized four training seminars on drug law enforcement and related matters (Malaysia, May; Argentina, August; Nepal, August; Sri Lanka, December). The Division provided audio-visual and other training material to developing countries, organized 14 study tours and awarded 18 fellowships. It also participated in international meetings and conferences, and intensified collaborative work with the Customs Co-operation Council and with the International Criminal Police Organization (ICPO/Interpol), and published *Bulletin on Narcotics* (quarterly) and *Information Letter* (bimonthly).

Decision. [1]Commission on Narcotic Drugs (report, E/1982/13): 1(S-VII), 8 Feb.
Report. [2]S-G, A/37/556.

Asia and the Pacific

The Ninth Meeting of Operational Heads of Narcotics Law Enforcement Agencies, Far East Region, was held at Manila, Philippines from 22 to 26 November 1982,[1] in accordance with a 1974 resolution of the Economic and Social Council.[2] The meeting recommended that the region's Governments continue or adopt measures to prevent and reduce illicit demand for drugs and give priority to developing legislative, administrative and other measures to deprive drug traffickers, their organizers and financiers of illicitly acquired assets. Member States, especially major manufacturing and exporting countries, were urged to adhere to the 1971 Convention on Psychotropic Substances. The Meeting requested the Commission on Narcotic Drugs to approve a joint meeting between the Heads of National Narcotics Law Enforcement Agencies, Far East and the Sub-Commission on Illicit Drug Traffic and Related Matters in the Near and Middle East, in view of the adverse impact of drug traffic emanating from parts of these regions. It also recommended improved bilateral extradition arrangements for offenders in serious drug-related cases.

Report. [1]Commission on Narcotic Drugs, E/CN.7/1983/12.
Resolution (prior). [2]ESC: 1845(LVI), 15 May 1974 (YUN 1974, p. 615).

Latin America and Caribbean area

The Economic and Social Council, on 30 April 1982,[1] requested the United Nations Fund for Drug Abuse Control (UNFDAC) to consider favourably, within available financial resources, requests from countries in Central and South America and the Caribbean region for assistance in strengthening action against illicit drug traffic. It requested the Division of Narcotic Drugs, in co-operation with the International Criminal Police Organization (ICPO/Interpol) and the Customs Co-operation Council, to give priority to organizing, and to consider financing, drug law enforcement training seminars in the region, using training facilities and expertise available within the area or from other countries affected by the drug traffic which emanated from, or passed through, the region.

The text, which originated in the Commission on Narcotic Drugs, was adopted without vote.

In related action, on 3 May, the Economic and Social Council requested the Secretary-General to consider establishing a regional office at Lima, Peru, to co-ordinate narcotics control efforts in the Andean subregion.[2]

Resolutions (1982). ESC: [1]1982/9, 30 Apr., text following; [2]1982/14, 3 May.
Meeting record. ESC: E/1982/SR.19 (30 Apr.).

Economic and Social Council resolution 1982/9

30 April 1982   Meeting 19   Adopted without vote

Draft by Commission on Narcotic Drugs (E/1982/13); agenda item 12.

Concerted action against the illicit drug traffic in Central and South America and the Caribbean region

The Economic and Social Council,

Recalling General Assembly resolution 36/132 of 14 December 1981,

Recognizing that, to be more effective, measures against the illicit drug traffic must be so co-ordinated that all affected States, including those not producers or significant consumers of illicit drugs, will be able to strengthen their countermeasures against such traffic nationally, regionally and internationally,

Aware of the urgent need to strengthen co-ordinated efforts in parts of Central and South America and the Caribbean region, having due regard to the special problems of this area in so far as drug law enforcement is concerned,

1. *Requests* the United Nations Fund for Drug Abuse Control to give favourable consideration, within the limits of the financial resources available, to reasonable requests for assistance in strengthening effective action against the illicit drug traffic which may be received from countries in Central and South America and the Caribbean region;

2. *Requests* the Division of Narcotic Drugs, in co-operation with INTERPOL and the Customs Co-operation Council, to attach high priority to organizing drug law enforcement training seminars in Central and South America and the Caribbean region, making full use of the training facilities and expertise that may be available within the area or from countries in other regions affected by the traffic in drugs emanating from, or passing through, Central and South America and the Caribbean region, and requests the United Nations Fund for Drug Abuse Control to consider financing such seminars.

Middle East

The Sub-Commission on Illicit Drug Traffic and Related Matters in the Near and Middle East,[1] meeting at Vienna, Austria, from 4 to 6 October 1982, noted the increased illicit demand for and supply of drugs and recommended a series of measures to counter that trend, among them, the development of rapid communication for action against drug traffickers and establishment of guidelines on the severity of penalties for drug-related offences. It suggested the convening of a second inter-regional meeting of heads of national narcotic law enforcement agencies in the region as well as some countries of Europe, and stated that it would welcome initiatives by the region's Governments that would enable drug law enforcement agencies to meet within parts of the region most affected by illicit traffic.

The Sub-Commission believed that the Western European, North American and other countries should contribute more resources through UNFDAC to support drug law enforcement agencies in the region, and that all should support an expert group meeting scheduled for 1983 on measures to deprive drug traffickers of illegally acquired assets.

Report. [1]Sub-Commission on Illicit Drug Traffic and Related Matters in Near and Middle East, E/CN.7/1983/11.

Reduction of illicit demand

The Commission on Narcotic Drugs, in its 1982 report[3] to the Economic and Social Council, endorsed the conclusions reached in the Secretary-General's October/November 1981 note[1] on preventive and treatment measures found effective for reducing illicit demand for drugs based on replies by 47 Governments to a 1981 Secretariat questionnaire. Measures to prevent the emergence of illicit demand included continued controls to reduce availability of drugs for abuse, involvement of volunteer organizations, dissemination of accurate information, and development of programmes based on such information. The Secretary-General also recommended in-built evaluation of the effects of preventive programmes, community involvement and drug education programmes for youth.

As regards counter measures, the Commission endorsed the concept that realistic treatment should be based on an individual's motivation and needs, on ability to improve, and the potential for achieving a drug-free existence. Detoxification should be linked to treatment, rehabilitation, aftercare and social reintegration, involving the participation of peer groups, families and local communities. Activities to motivate individuals or groups away from drug abuse and to prevent the emergence of a drug sub-culture should be reinforced.

The Commission also examined a January 1982 summary of World Health Organization activities for preventing and treating drug dependence, and a summary of measures undertaken by 66 Governments to reduce illicit demand for drugs.[2].

The International Narcotics Control Board (INCB) stated in its 1982 report[4] that information on the dimensions, distribution and changing trends of drug abuse was essential in coping with illicit demand. Continuing research and review of prevention and treatment approaches were also necessary.

Note. Secretariat: [1]E/CN.7/673 (Parts One & Two); [2]E/CN.7/673 (Part Two)/Add.1,2.
Reports. [3]Commission on Narcotic Drugs, E/1982/13; [4]INCB, E/INCB/61 (Sales No. E.83.XI.1).

Psychotropic substances

INCB stated in its 1982 report,[1] that despite the increase in the number of parties to the 1971 Convention on Psychotropic Substances, its effective application depended on adherence to it and on the implementation of national legislation by all manufacturing, exporting and importing countries. Voluntary submission by countries to INCB of their assessments of legitimate requirements and trade statistics for substances would enable the Board to monitor the situation better and to stop diversion into illicit traffic. The Board noted that, while some psychotropic substances were manufactured illegally in clandestine laboratories or were being diverted from licit retail trade, the illicit traffic was also supplied by a substantial spillover of substances, licitly manufactured in and exported by developed countries to developing countries.

Report. [1]INCB, E/INCB/61 (Sales No. E.83.XI.1).

Implementation of the 1971 Convention

The Economic and Social Council, on 30 April 1982,[3] invited INCB, with the co-operation of Governments, to continue to monitor international trade substances listed under Schedule II of the 1971 Convention on Psychotropic Substances in order to curtail significant diversion of substances into illicit channels. It appealed to manufacturing and exporting countries to refrain from exporting Schedule II substances, when a suspicious pattern existed, until the legitimacy of shipments was established; Governments of importing countries were invited to send copies of import certificates to the Governments of exporting countries. It called attention to Governments possibly protecting themselves against the import of unwanted substances and the need to ensure that no exports of such substances to prohibiting countries took place.

This action was taken without vote on the recommendation of the Commission on Narcotic Drugs.

On 8 February, the Commision[2] requested the World Health Organization, when reviewing substances for scheduling under the 1971 Convention, to continue to collect and analyse data on each substance with regard to the extent or likelihood of abuse, the degree of seriousness of public health and social problems associated with such abuse, and the usefulness of the substance in medical therapy.

An expert group to study the functioning, adequacy and enhancement of the Convention met at Vienna, Austria, from 18 to 22 October 1982.[1] The group considered that a number of shortcomings in the Convention were often connected with control measures applicable to substances in Schedules III and IV; the Convention also lacked provisions for reasonable identification of actual medical and scientific needs on a global basis. The group pointed to the advisability of identifying lacunae in the Convention's general reporting system.

Among topics discussed by the group were the scope of control, adequacy of classification system, method for scheduling substances in the Convention, system of import/export authorizations, restrictions in free port areas, measures for greater adherence to the Convention, and the possibility of merging the Convention with the 1961 Single Convention on Narcotic Drugs and its 1972 Protocol.

Report. [1]Expert group to study functioning and enhancement of Convention on Psychotropic Substances, E/CN.7/1983/2/Add.2.
Resolutions (1982). [2]Commission on Narcotic Drugs (report, E/1982/13): 2(S-VII), para. 5, 8 Feb. [3]ESC: 1982/11, 30 Apr., text following.
Meeting record. ESC: E/1982/SR.19 (30 Apr.).

Economic and Social Council resolution 1982/11

30 April 1982   Meeting 19   Adopted without vote

Draft by Commission on Narcotic Drugs (E/1982/13); agenda item 12.

Co-operation with the International Narcotics Control Board concerning Schedule II of the 1971 Convention on Psychotropic Substances

The Economic and Social Council,

Noting with deep concern the increasing diversion from international commerce of psychotropic substances controlled under Schedule II of the 1971 Convention on Psychotropic Substances, notably amphetamine, methamphetamine and methaqualone,

Commending the International Narcotics Control Board for the manner in which it is actively carrying out its mandate under the 1971 Convention with a view to promoting effective international control,

Bearing in mind the observations made by the Board in its report for 1981 concerning the international situation and the need for action by Governments,

Recalling the need for Governments to apply strictly to Schedule II substances the export and import authorization system provided for in article 12, paragraph 1, of the 1971 Convention,

1. *Invites* the International Narcotics Control Board to continue to monitor international trade substances listed in Schedule II of the 1971 Convention on Psychotropic Substances, to maintain dialogues with Governments and to exercise its good offices with a view to facilitating the earliest possible identification of instances of significant diversion and the prompt adoption of measures to curtail such diversion;

2. *Invites* Governments to co-operate with the Board and provide it promptly with the information it requests in order to enable it effectively to monitor international trade and identify diversion of Schedule II substances;

3. *Also invites* Governments of importing countries to send to Governments of exporting countries copies of import certificates, as suggested by the Board in its report for 1981;

4. *Appeals* to manufacturing/exporting countries to refrain from exporting Schedule II substances in the event of the Board advising them that a suspicious pattern exists until further inquiries establish the legitimacy of the purposes for which the shipment is intended;

5. *Reminds* Governments of the need, in pursuance of article 12, paragraph 3, subparagraph *(a)*, of the 1971 Convention, to exercise in free ports and zones the same supervision and control of Schedule II substances as is applied in other parts of their territories;

6. *Calls attention* to the possibility of Governments availing themselves of the protection against the import of unwanted substances afforded by article 13 of the 1971 Convention and to the need to implement the necessary measures to ensure that no exports of such substances to the prohibiting countries take place;

7. *Requests* the Secretary-General to transmit the present resolution to all Governments for urgent consideration and action as appropriate.

Conventions

On 18 December 1982,[2] the General Assembly called on Member States that had not done so to ratify international drug control treaties and, until that time, to endeavour to abide by them.

INCB, in its 1982 report,[1] expressed the hope that States not adhering to the 1961 Single Convention on Narcotic Drugs or its 1972 Protocol would become parties at an early date, and that the few States not participating in the international drug control system would assist the world community by developing *de facto* co-operation. INCB hoped its relations with China would be further advanced, and said it would welcome collaboration with Viet Nam and the Democratic People's Republic of Korea.

In 1981, the Solomon Islands acceded to the 1961 Single Convention on Narcotic Drugs, bringing to 114 the total number of parties to that instrument. No additional State adhered to the Convention as amended by the 25 March 1972 Protocol, and the number of parties remained at 76. As a result of Australia's ratification, the number of parties to the 1971 Convention on Psychotropic Substances rose to 76.

Report. [1]INCB, E/1982/61.
Resolution (1982). [2]GA: 37/198, para. 2, 18 Dec.

1961 Single Convention

An expert group convened to study the functioning, adequacy and enhancement of the 1961 Single Convention on Narcotic Drugs, met at Vienna, Austria, from 11 to 15 October 1982.[1]. It observed that, while the Convention had instituted a good regulatory system, problems had arisen, particularly with regard to the balance between supply and demand, the fight against illicit traffic and the implementation of provisions by States parties.

Topics discussed included control of various substances, adequacy of methods for scheduling substances in the Convention, improvements in national implementation measures and other control measures. Among other things, the group agreed that it was impracticable, due to varying legal and constitutional systems, to institute in the Single Convention a provision on mandatory extradition of offenders; greater international co-operation should, however, be encouraged in view of insufficient bilateral treaties on drug offences.

> *Report.* [1]Expert group to study functioning and enhancement of Single Convention on Narcotic Drugs, 1961, E/CN.7/1983/2/Add.1.

Proposed amendments to Schedules

The Commission on Narcotic Drugs, on 8 February 1982,[2] requested the World Health Organization (WHO) to inform the Commission of substances it planned to review for scheduling and the time of such review. It decided to take note, at each session, of WHO review plans and, if appropriate, indicate subjects requiring WHO's attention. Further, it requested WHO, when reviewing substances for possible scheduling under the 1961 Single Convention on Narcotic Drugs, and the Convention as amended by the 1972 Protocol, to continue to collect and analyse data on each substance concerning liability to abuse, ill effects, convertibility into a drug, recoverability and therapeutic advantages.

The Commission requested parties to international drug control treaties to provide information promptly when requested by the Secretary-General and invited Member States to respond to the Secretary-General's requests for information on abuse of substances being considered for scheduling and on the drugs' illicit trafficking.

In 1982, the Commission[1] noted a recommendation of the WHO Director-General that pentazocine should not be added to Schedule I or II annexed to the Single Convention and the amended Convention. A number of delegations expressed concern over the pentazocine abuse situation and requested WHO to seek additional data for further review. The Commission considered the status of specific substances in a number of countries, and decided to postpone until 1983 consideration of WHO recommendations that twelve substances be added to Schedule IV of the 1971 Convention on Psychotropic Substances.

> *Report.* [1]Commission on Narcotic Drugs, E/1982/13.
> *Resolution (1982).* [2]Commission on Narcotic Drugs (report, E/1982/13): 2(S-VII), 8 Feb.

Organizational questions

Duration and periodicity of Commission sessions

On 3 May 1982,[1] the Economic and Social Council decided, without vote, to defer until May 1983 consideration of a draft resolution by the Commission on Narcotic Drugs[2] that would allow that body to meet annually in a regular session of no fewer than eight working days.

In its draft, the Commission asserted that the need for yearly sessions had been established by the fact that it had met annually in regular and special sessions since 1946 (except for 1967 and 1972), and that regular annual sessions were more cost-effective and would allow it to fulfil its functions better.

> *Decision (1982).* [1]ESC: 1982/114, 3 May, text following.
> *Report.* [2]Commission on Narcotic Drugs, E/1982/13, draft resolution IV.
> *Meeting record.* ESC: E/1982/SR.20 (3 May).

Economic and Social Council decision 1982/114

Adopted without vote

Oral proposal by President; agenda item 12.

Duration and periodicity of sessions of the Commission on Narcotic Drugs

At its 20th plenary meeting, on 3 May 1982, the Council decided to defer consideration of draft resolution IV, entitled "Duration and periodicity of sessions of the Commission on Narcotic Drugs", contained in the report of the Commission on Narcotic Drugs on its seventh special session, until its first regular session of 1983, with a view to taking a decision on the matter in the context of its consideration of the report of the Commission on its thirtieth session.

Commission on Narcotic Drugs

By a decision of 3 May 1982,[1] adopted without vote, the Economic and Social Council took note of the report of the Commission on Narcotic Drugs on its seventh special session, held in February 1982. It did so on the Commission's recommendation.

> *Decision (1982).* [1]ESC: 1982/116, 3 May, text following.
> *Meeting record.* ESC: E/1982/SR.20 (3 May).

Economic and Social Council decision 1982/116

Adopted without vote

Draft by Commission on Narcotic Drugs (E/1982/13); agenda item 12.

Report of the Commission on Narcotic Drugs

At its 20th plenary meeting, on 3 May 1982, the Council took note of the report of the Commission on Narcotic Drugs on its seventh special session.

International Narcotics Control Board

The Economic and Social Council, in a decision adopted without vote on 3 May 1982,[1] took note of the 1981 report of the International Narcotics Control Board (INCB). The Council acted on the recommendation of the Commission on Narcotic Drugs.

In its report for 1982,[2] INCB—composed of 13 members serving in their personal capacities—discussed drug abuse, drug supply and demand, illicit traffic, reduction of illicit demand for psychotropic substances, and international drug control conventions.

> *Decision (1982).* [1]ESC: 1982/115, 3 May, text following.
> *Report.* INCB, [2]E/INCB/61 (Sales No. E.83.XI.1).
> *Meeting record.* ESC: E/1982/SR.20 (3 May).

Economic and Social Council decision 1982/115

Adopted without vote

Draft by Commission on Narcotic Drugs (E/1982/13); agenda item 12.

Report of the International Narcotics Control Board

At its 20th plenary meeting, on 3 May 1982, the Council took note of the report of the International Narcotics Control Board for 1981.

Chapter XXIII

Statistics

Contents

Related topics:
Energy, Population, Environment.

Economic statistics

Energy statistics

During 1982, the work of the Statistical Office of the United Nations in energy statistics[1] was expanded in the areas of new and renewable sources of energy, as a result of the adoption of the Nairobi Programme of Action for the Development and Utilization of New and Renewable Sources of Energy in August 1981.[3] Follow-up action was taken on a May 1981 Economic and Social Council resolution,[2] requesting improved and more timely international energy statistics, and urging developing countries to participate in developing national statistics according to international guidelines and to seek technical assistance in that regard, if needed.

Although there were no specific requests in 1982 from developing countries for technical assistance, the Statistical Office discussed the 1981 Council resolution with participants at the Pacific Subregional Workshop on Energy Statistics (Suva, Fiji, 2-8 February). As a result, some countries indicated willingness to develop their energy statistics further and to seek technical assistance in the field, if needed, in the future.

The Statistical Office and other bodies within and outside the United Nations continued to co-operate in exchanging energy data and to hold energy statistics workshops. In addition to issuing publications, the Office added to its computerized file which included information on most countries and nearly all energy commodities.

Report. [1]S-G, E/CN.3/1983/11.
Resolution. [2]ESC: 1981/2, 4 May 1981 (YUN 1981, p. 1069).
Yearbook references. [3]1981, p. 689.

Publications. Concepts and Methods in Energy Statistics with Special Reference to Energy Accounts and Balances: A Technical Report (ST/ESA/STAT/SER.F/29 & Corr.1), Sales No. E.82.XVII.13 & Corr.1; 1982 Energy Statistics Yearbook (ST/ESA/STAT/SER.J/26), Sales No. E/F.84.XVII.4; Energy Balances and Electricity Profiles, 1982 (ST/ESA/STAT/SER.W/2), Sales No. E.85.XVII.7.

Environment statistics

In response to a 1981 request of the Statistical Commission,[3] the Statistical Office in 1982 continued its work on environment statistics in three areas: developing methodology; exchanging information, in particular by updating the directory of environment statistics; and organizing training programmes and workshops for national statisticians. These activities were described by the Secretary-General in a July progress report on environment statistics.[2]

The *Survey of Environment Statistics: Frameworks, Approaches and Statistical Publications*, published in 1982, described efforts by national and international agencies to develop methodological frameworks, related models and approaches and to prepare statistical compendiums of environment statistics.[1] The Regional Workshop on Environmental and Natural Resource Statistics (Nairobi, Kenya, 25-29 January) was held to bring together users and producers of environment statistics in order to identify major environmental concerns in the region.

Publication. [1]Survey of Environment Statistics: Frameworks, Approaches and Statistical Publications (ST/ESA/STAT/SER.M/73), Sales No. E.82.XVII.4.
Report. [2]S-G, E/CN.3/1983/19.
Yearbook reference. [3]1981, p. 1071.

Industrial statistics

During 1982, preparations were made for the 1983 World Programme of Industrial Statistics, which the Statistical Commission had approved in 1979 as a means of obtaining an overall perspective of world-wide industrial activity, with emphasis on accelerating industrial statistics programmes in developing countries to provide reliable and timely information on their industrialization.[5] Recommendations for countries' participation in the Programme,[6] adopted by the Commission and distributed in English in 1981, were also issued in French and Spanish in early 1982. The Statistical Office in 1982 surveyed all countries in order to ascertain the extent of their anticipated participation in the Programme, which involved collecting information and conducting an industrial census. Of the 81 replies received by May 1982,[3] 60 countries indicated that they planned to participate.

The Economic Commission for Africa, in co-operation with other organizations, convened a Regional Industrial Census Workshop for the English-speaking developing countries of Africa (Addis Ababa, Ethiopia, 11 January–13 February) to contribute to training in industrial census-taking and to discuss proposals for the Programme. The Federal Republic of Germany provided the Economic and Social Commission for Asia and the Pacific, for one year beginning in January, with an expert on industrial statistics to assist countries of the region, on request, in improving industrial surveys and in their participation in the Programme.

In April,[2] the Secretary-General submitted proposals to the Statistical Commission on revising the 1968 International Recommendations for Industrial Statistics,[4] dealing with methods for conducting industrial surveys.

The Statistics and Survey Unit of the United Nations Industrial Development Organization (UNIDO) was established in July to provide a central reference point for statistical activities within the Division for Industrial Studies. The Unit worked on improving the available industrial statistics as well as the associated industrial data base in support of studies carried out both within and outside UNIDO. UNIDO and the United Nations Statistical Office co-operated in the area of industrial statistics, in particular on preparations for the 1983 World Programme. In addition to publishing studies on the world industrial situation, UNIDO completed work on a *Handbook of Industrial Statistics*[1] with indicators permitting international comparisons and analyses of industrial progress.

Publication. [1]*Handbook of Industrial Statistics* (ID/284), Sales No. E.82.II.B.2.
Reports. S-G, [2]E/CN.3/1983/9, [3]E/CN.3/1983/10.

Yearbook references. [4]1968, p. 462; [5]1979, p. 747; [6]1981, p. 1068.
Other publications. *Yearbook of Construction Statistics, 1972-1979* (ST/ESA/STAT/SER.U/8), Sales No. E.82.XVII.2; *1982* (ST/ESA/STAT/SER.U/11), Sales No. E.84.XVII.9. *Industrial Statistics Yearbook 1982*, vol. I: *General Industrial Statistics* (ST/ESA/STAT/SER.P/21, vol. I), Sales No. E.84.XVII.7; vol. II: *Commodity Production Data, 1973-1982* (ST/ESA/STAT/SER.P/21, vol. II), Sales No. E/F.84.XVII.8.

National accounts

In 1982, the Statistical Office continued its work on updating, clarifying and harmonizing the United Nations System of National Accounts (SNA), a framework for establishing standards for statistics. It took into consideration the views of an Expert Group Meeting on the Review and Development of SNA (New York, 22-26 March), which recommended that a working group be established to guide the preparatory work for revising SNA and mobilizing necessary resources. In the Group's view, the revision should not be undertaken as a continuous adjustment but should be accomplished by a single target date, possibly 1990. The Group reviewed a consultant's report on reviewing major issues and proposals for future work and short-term changes, which was also considered by an *Ad Hoc* Meeting on National Accounts (Paris, 17-19 May), convened by the Organisation for Economic Co-operation and Development, and by a Working Party on National Accounts and Balances of the Conference of European Statisticians (Geneva, 1-4 June). In a July report to the Statistical Commission on the development of SNA,[2] the Secretary-General said that organizations directly involved with statistics standards needed to co-ordinate their work, and that the participation of experts from different countries would be useful.

Progress in establishing links between SNA and the United Nations System of Balances of the National Economy (MPS), as described by the Secretary-General in a September report to the Commission,[3] was achieved by accelerating work on illustrative calculations of gross domestic product (GDP) for countries using MPS and of net material product for countries using SNA. The report included drafts of conversion tables designed to derive GDP for countries with centrally planned economies. A publication on conversion of aggregates of SNA to MPS and vice versa, issued in March, contained the results and a description of the methods used in the intersystem conversions for 10 countries.[1] The Statistical Office also initiated a new round of calculations for 20 countries in order to increase the number of countries involved or to update previous estimates. The Economic Commission for Latin America, in co-operation with the Institute for Ibero-American Co-operation of Spain and the Government of

Cuba, organized a seminar on comparisons of SNA and MPS in Latin America (Havana, Cuba, 6-11 May).

Publication. [1]*Comparisons of the System of National Accounts and the System of Balances of the National Economy, Part Two: Conversion of Aggregates of SNA to MPS and vice versa for Selected Countries,* Sales No. E.81.XVII.15.
Reports. S-G, [2]E/CN.3/1983/5, [3]E/CN.3/1983/8.
Other publications. National Accounts Statistics: Main Aggregates and Detailed Tables, 1982 (replaces *1982 Yearbook of National Accounts Statistics,* vol. I (Parts 1 & 2), *Individual Country Data*) (ST/ESA/STAT/SER.X/1), Sales No. E.85.XVII.3; *Analysis of Main Aggregates, 1982* (replaces *1982 Yearbook of National Accounts Statistics,* vol. II, *International Tables*) (ST/ESA/STAT/SER.X/2), Sales No. E.85.XVII.4; *Government Accounts and Tables, 1982* (ST/ESA/STAT/SER.X/3), Sales No. E.85.XVII.5.

Price statistics

In 1982, the Statistical Office accelerated its work on price statistics. After the Secretary-General issued a report in May on the development of an inter-agency price statistics programme,[1] the subject was again placed on the agenda of the Statistical Commission. It was reintroduced after several years because of increasing concern for the improvement of price statistics at both international and national levels and because of the nature of steps being taken by the Statistical Office and international agencies to co-ordinate the improvement. Work in this field involved the development of specific price indexes, such as consumer price indexes or wholesale price indexes, and the adjustment of national accounting flows using those indexes. Price statistics were used for assessing the relative economic development of countries through the International Comparison Project.[2] Phase III of the Project was completed in 1982, increasing the coverage to 34 countries of statistics on national products and purchasing power, and work proceeded on data collection and analysis for additional countries.

Reports. S-G, [1]E/CN.3/1983/13, [2]E/CN.3/1983/14.
Publication. Strategies for Price and Quantity Measurement in External Trade (ST/ESA/STAT/SER.M/69), Sales No. E.82.XVII.3.

Trade statistics

In order to obtain trade statistics useful for comparison purposes from existing customs administration systems, the Statistical Office prepared a draft of the third revision of the Standard International Trade Classification (SITC),[2] as requested in 1981 by the Statistical Commission.[3] An expert group meeting[1] (New York, 15-19 March 1982) discussed the SITC revision and decided to circulate the text to competent bodies so that their comments could be taken into consideration before the revision's submission to the Commission in March 1983.

Reports. [1]Expert group meeting, ESA/STAT/AC.14/3; [2]S-G, E/CN.3/1983/12.

Yearbook reference. [3]1981, p. 1070.
Publications. Maritime Transport Study for the Years 1975-1978: Commodity Trade (by Sea) Statistics; Analysis by Type of Goods Moved during 1975-1978 between Regions of the World (ST/ESA/STAT/SER.D/75-78), Sales No. E.82.XVII.10. *International Trade Statistics: Concepts and Definitions* (ST/ESA/STAT/SER.M/52/Rev.1), Sales No. E.82.XVII.14. *1982 Yearbook of International Trade Statistics,* vol. I: *Trade by Country;* vol. II: *Trade by Commodity: Commodity Matrix Tables* (ST/ESA/STAT/SER.G/31 & Add.1), Sales No. E/F.84.XVII.6, vols. I & II. *Commodity Trade Statistics,* Statistical Papers, Series D, vol. XXVII (1977 data), No. 24; vol. XXVIII (1978 data), No. 26; vol. XXIX (1979 data), Nos. 24-26; vol. XXX (1980 data), Nos. 21-26; vol. XXXI (1981 data), Nos. 1, 3-7, 9-22; vol. XXXII (1982 data), Nos. 6, 8, 13-15, 17-21.

Social and demographic statistics

Migration statistics

Statistical work on international migration focused in 1982 on the international co-operative programme on immigrant stock data, in conjunction with 1980 population censuses, and technical publications designed to help countries compile migration statistics.[1] Two technical reports on migration statistics were substantially completed for publication in 1983. One included several country studies on national experience and issues in implementing United Nations recommendations, as well as the illustrative phased national programme for collecting, tabulating and publishing international migration statistics. The second dealt with special categories of international population movements and with a system of consolidated statistics of all international arrivals and departures.

The regional commissions continued to collect and analyse data on migration. For example, the Economic Commission for Europe (ECE) issued a document with data on long-term migrants among ECE and selected other countries, which was considered by the Conference of European Statisticians in June. The Economic Commission for Latin America was among the sponsors of a seminar (Bridgetown, Barbados, 19-21 May) on the development of methodology to measure emigration. The Economic Commission for Africa (ECA) published a study on classification of nomadic populations within the framework of the United Nations work on statistics of international arrivals and departures.

In collaboration with the United Nations Conference on Trade and Development (UNCTAD), the Statistical Office prepared a study on measuring international flows of human resources, which was submitted to the UNCTAD Committee on Transfer of Technology.

Report. [1]S-G, E/CN.3/1983/17.

National Household Survey Capability Programme

Progress was made during 1982 in expanding the National Household Survey Capability

Programme (NHSCP), a technical co-operation project bringing together national donors and international agencies to assist developing countries in producing socio-economic and demographic statistics needed for their development plans. As at the end of May, 57 countries had expressed an interest in NHSCP, 49 of which had invited project formulation missions.[1] Project proposals for 35 countries had been formulated, and 24 of those had been approved by the Governments—13 in Africa, 5 in Latin America, 3 in South-East Asia and 3 in Western Asia. The projects were of an average duration of five years at an average cost of $5.8 million. The recipient countries met most of the cost of their survey programmes, with an average of over 70 per cent.

The Second Consultative Meeting on NHSCP (Geneva, 2 June), chaired by the United Nations Development Programme, was attended by, among others, 20 bilateral and multilateral donor agencies, the five regional commissions, three specialized agencies and six developing countries. Many donors indicated their readiness to help selected developing countries financially and technically. Welcoming the willingness of developing countries to commit substantial resources to survey programmes, the Meeting endorsed the institutional arrangements for the Programme's management and the work plan for the next few years. Arrangements for implementing NHSCP were discussed by the Programme Review Committee (New York, 18 February), which welcomed the decision by the United Nations Children's Fund to become a co-sponsor of NHSCP. The role of NHSCP in providing health information in developing countries was discussed at a meeting organized by the World Health Organization and the United Nations (Geneva, 3 and 4 June).

The Joint Conference of African Planners, Statisticians and Demographers (Addis Ababa, Ethiopia, 8-17 March) emphasized the importance of the African regional component of NHSCP as an essential element of national development planning and called for a more vigorous mobilization of resources from bilateral and multilateral sources. On the recommendation of the Joint Conference, the ECA Conference of Ministers in April adopted a resolution in support of the African Household Survey Capability Programme. In March, the Economic and Social Commission for Asia and the Pacific endorsed suggestions for building up the survey capabilities of member countries. An inter-agency meeting (Washington, D. C., 29 March) agreed that the Inter-American Household Survey Programme and NHSCP should be merged and that the joint programme should concentrate on methodological development and training.

Report. [1]S-G, E/CN.3/1983/20.

Population and housing censuses

By mid-1982, most countries had participated in the 1980 World Population and Housing Census Programme and the number of countries expected to participate in the 1975-1984 census decade was larger than in previous decades. In the remaining two and a half years of the census decade, 19 countries were expected to join the 175 nations which had already taken censuses, leaving 19 countries which were not expected to take such action. The results were obtained by the United Nations Statistical Office through questionnaires for use in its analyses and publications.[1]

Report. [1]S-G, E/CN.3/1983/16.
Publications. Provisional Guidelines on Standard International Age Classifications (ST/ESA/STAT/SER.M/74), Sales No. E.82.XVII.5; *Demographic Yearbook, 1982* (ST/ESA/STAT/SER.R/12), Sales No. E/F.83.XIII.l; *Population and Vital Statistics Report*, vol. XXXIV, Nos. 1-4 (data available as of 1 Jan., 1 Apr., 1 July, 1 Oct. 1982), ST/ESA/STAT/SER.135-138.

Social indicators

During 1982, the Statistical Office continued its work on social indicators for integration and international co-ordination of social, demographic and related economic statistics. Many United Nations organizations contributed to work on such indicators as: population projections and household size; educational services; earning activities; distribution of income, consumption and accumulation; social security and welfare services; health services and nutrition; housing and environment; public order and safety; productivity and leisure time; culture; and social stratification and mobility.[1]

As part of its efforts to assess agrarian reform and rural development, the Food and Agriculture Organization of the United Nations held workshops in developing regions to discuss the results of pilot studies for testing and refining indicators in that field and to prepare guidelines on socio-economic indicators. The World Bank continued publishing annual reports on population, per capita product and growth rates, as well as on world development, which included social indicators covering population, demography, the labour force, urbanization, life expectancy, health, education and income distribution. The United Nations Educational, Scientific and Cultural Organization (UNESCO) prepared a review of social indicators in the field of education, mainly in the European region, for a meeting on statistics on education of the Conference of European Statisticians and UNESCO (Geneva, September). It also carried out the first comprehensive international survey of public expenditure on cultural activities.

Report. [1]S-G, E/CN.3/1983/18.

Technical co-operation

In 1982, the United Nations Department of Technical Co-operation for Development (DTCD), in co-operation with the Statistical Office, supported 151 country projects in statistics, of which 67 were in Africa, 34 in Asia and the Pacific, 27 in Latin America and the Caribbean, and 23 in the Middle East and Western Asia.[3] Technical co-operation activities emphasized censuses and strengthening institutions and capacities for compiling data. With DTCD assistance, censuses were conducted in 12 countries in 1982, including China. In this largest census ever, project support included purchasing hardware and software for 21 computer centres, training computer technicians, advisory services on planning the census and processing its results, fellowships and study tours.

Among projects in statistical data processing,[2] materials were devised to process population data. Installation of small computing equipment for data processing was continued, providing a user-oriented, educational environment for technology transfer. Interregional advisers and other staff assisted countries in demographic and social statistics, computer methods, economic statistics and assessment of requirements for strengthening statistical services and developing national accounts. The United Nations Development Programme and the United Nations Fund for Population Activities continued to fund the bulk of projects for establishing and improving the computer-related capabilities of developing countries to process their statistical data.

The United Nations regional commissions and the specialized agencies included statistical training activities as part of their effort to promote technical co-operation among developing countries.[1]

For example, the Statistical Institute for Asia and the Pacific sought financial assistance in order to hold joint courses on household surveys (see above) dealing with sampling, statistical methods and statistical operations with the Economic and Social Commission for Asia and the Pacific, as part of the National Household Survey Capability Programme (NHSCP). A project in India that would include regional training for NHSCP was developed and a meeting was convened by the South Pacific Commission to discuss the involvement of South Pacific countries in NHSCP.

Reports. S-G, [1]E/CN.3/1983/22, [2]E/CN.3/1983/23; [3]UNDP Administrator, DP/1983/18.

Co-ordination in the UN system

The Sub-Committee on Statistical Activities, of the Administrative Committee on Co-ordination, decided at its sixteenth session (Vienna, Austria, 3-7 May 1982) to establish a technical working group on statistical data bases to meet as soon as possible and that the International Computing Centre at Geneva should be asked to participate.[1] The Sub-Committee also agreed on a document outlining and co-ordinating future statistical work plans of the United Nations organizations, which put together such plans of all the organizations for the first time. The Sub-Committee recommended that co-ordination in selected areas relating to statistics must begin on the basic level of adopting standard codes and terminology. Suggestions were made regarding statistics on the situation of women, tourism, international trade and transport, prices, energy, and state and local government finances.

Report. [1]ACC Sub-Committee on Statistical Activities, ACC/1982/24.

Chapter XXIV

Organizational questions

Contents

Related topics:

Regional economic and social activities: Strengthening of regional commissions; Restructuring of ECA. United Nations finances: Appropriations for 1982-1983. United Nations programmes.

For resolutions and decisions of major organs mentioned but not reproduced, refer to INDEX OF RESOLUTIONS AND DECISIONS.

Co-ordination in the UN system

ACC activities. In 1982, the Administrative Committee on Co-ordination (ACC) focused on co-ordination of information systems among United Nations organizations, approaches to joint planning by those organizations, support activities for international conferences and years, and methods for preparing cross-organizational analyses of programmes.

In its 1981/82 annual overview report[7] submitted in May to the Economic and Social Council, ACC reiterated its concern about the state of the international economy and its impact on developing countries; the trend among member States to retreat from multilateral approaches and to seek national or bilateral solutions to international economic and social problems; and the deteriorating situation facing United Nations organizations with regard to the declining level of resources available for development activities.

ACC stated that if United Nations efforts to support member States in promoting economic and social development were to succeed, these States must make use of the United Nations potential and guide the work of ACC; the international community needed to provide the resources necessary to carry out the activities that it requested the organizations to undertake. ACC recognized its responsibility to improve the image of the United Nations so as to reassure Governments and the public of its effectiveness in dealing with issues of concern to the international community.

In order to enhance its functioning and that of its subsidiary machinery, ACC streamlined its work programme and limited documentation. Measures taken to expedite inter-agency work concerned the presentation of the work programme, the preparation of a handbook as a guide to ACC decisions, and rules for documentation from inter-agency meetings.

Acting without vote on 28 July,[2] the Economic and Social Council took note of the ACC report.

The decision was recommended by the Council's Third (Programme and Co-ordination) Committee, which approved without vote on 19 July a proposal by its Chairman.

At its three 1982 regular sessions, ACC adopted 33 decisions—12 at the first session (Rome, Italy, 5 and 6 April); 4 at the second (Geneva, 5 July); and 17 at the third (New York, 1-3 November).

The principal subsidiary bodies of ACC met as follows in 1982:

Consultative Committee on Administrative Questions (CCAQ) (Personnel and General Administrative Questions) (fifty-sixth session, Geneva, 22 February–12 March; special session, Geneva, 1-4 June; fifty-seventh session, New York, 30 June–23 July); CCAQ (Financial and Budgetary Questions) (fifty-sixth session, Paris, 8-12 March; special session, Geneva, 1 and 2 June; fifty-seventh session, New York, 30 August–3 September; Consultative Committee on Substantive Questions (CCSQ) (Programme Matters) (first regular session, Geneva, 22-25 March; second regular session, New York, 11-14 October); CCSQ (Operational Activities) (first regular session, Rome, 7 and 8 April; informal meeting, Geneva, 22 and 23 June; second regular session, New York, 15-20 October). The ACC Organizational Committee met in New York, 2-4 February; Geneva, 26 and 27 March, and 24 and 25 June; and New York, 21-23 October and 3 November.

ACC bodies on specific subjects met as follows:

Panel on People's Participation of the Task Force on Rural Development, Geneva, 19-21 January; *ad hoc* inter-agency consultations on the cross-organizational programme analysis on marine affairs, Rome, 27 and 28 January; Task Force on Science and Technology for Development, New York, 2-5 February, and informal meeting, 25 May (four working groups of the Task Force met in November and December); *ad hoc* working group on inter-agency follow-up to the Nairobi Programme of Action, Geneva, 11 and 12 February and 29 March–2 April; Sub-Committee on Nutrition, eighth session, Bangkok, Thailand, 15-19 February; Task Force on Long-Term Development Objectives, ninth session, Geneva, 24-26 February, and tenth session, New York, 22-24 November (a technical energy group met in June and December and a working group met in July); *ad hoc* inter-agency meeting on aging, New York, 25 and 26 February, and Vienna, Austria, 10 and 11 May; inter-agency meeting on the International Year of Disabled Persons, Vienna, 9 and 10 March, and 15 and 16 July; *ad hoc* inter-agency meeting on strengthening the capacity of the United Nations system to respond to emergencies, New York, 15 and 16 March; Task Force on Rural Development, tenth session, Rome, 15-17 March; inter-agency meeting on strengthening the co-ordination of information systems in the United Nations system, Geneva, 16 and 17 March and 25-27 May; meeting of the Organization of African Unity secretariat and secretariats of the United Nations and other organizations of the United Nations system, Geneva, 6-8 April; *ad hoc* inter-agency meeting on co-ordination of disarmament-related activities in the United Nations system, Geneva, 15 April; Joint

United Nations Information Committee, ninth session, Geneva, 19-23 April; Sub-Committee on Statistical Activities, sixteenth session, Vienna, 3-7 May; *Ad Hoc* Task Force on the International Conference on Population (1984), Geneva, 18-21 May; inter-agency consultations on the follow-up to the Substantial New Programme of Action for the Least Developed Countries, Geneva, 25 and 26 May; informal inter-agency meeting on the United Nations Conference on the Law of the Sea, Geneva, 13-15 July; inter-agency meeting on outer space activities, Rome, 22-24 September; Inter-Secretariat Group for Water Resources, third session, Paris, 4-8 October; *Ad Hoc* Working Group on Population Estimates and Projections, Geneva, 8-10 November.

In June, ACC reported to the Economic and Social Council on expenditures of the United Nations system in relation to programmes.[8] The report was based on the interorganization classification of programmes developed by ACC in consultation with Governments and other interested parties and showed expenditures of regular budget and extrabudgetary funds for 1980-1981 and estimated expenditures for 1982-1983 (see ADMINISTRATIVE AND BUDGETARY QUESTIONS, Chapter II).

CPC activities. The Committee for Programme and Co-ordination (CPC), meeting in New York, held an organizational meeting on 9 March 1982 and its twenty-second session from 19 April to 29 May.[9]

The Committee devoted most of the session to the proposed United Nations medium-term plan for 1984-1989 covering 24 programme areas (see ADMINISTRATIVE AND BUDGETARY QUESTIONS, Chapter II). In regard to the plan, it considered the content and timing of programme performance reports; procedures for review of the programme budget; and draft rules governing programme planning, the programme aspects of the budget, the monitoring of implementation and the methods of evaluation. CPC also discussed the continuation of the Information Systems Unit in the United Nations Department of International Economic and Social Affairs (see Chapter I of this section), and co-ordination of United Nations public information activities (see POLITICAL AND SECURITY QUESTIONS, Chapter X). It examined a cross-organizational programme analysis of public administration and finance activities of the United Nations system, and selected two subjects for future analyses (see below). A report by the Secretary-General on programme evaluation of mineral resources activities in the United Nations for 1976-1979 was also examined. CPC endorsed the design of a study on technical co-operation activities of the United Nations Industrial Development Organization in manufactures, as outlined in a report by the Secretary-General. In regard to regional co-operation and development, CPC examined the distribution of responsibilities between global and regional bodies for work on water resources and the environment.

By a decision of 28 July,[1] the Economic and Social Council, acting without vote, took note with appreciation of the CPC report on its 1982 session, endorsed its recommendations, and transmitted the report to the General Assembly. The decision was approved without vote by the Council's Third Committee on 23 July. By the original draft, proposed by the Committee Chairman on 15 July, the Council would have taken note of the relevant sections of the CPC report and transmitted them to the Assembly.[6] The Committee postponed consideration of the decision until it had concluded discussion on the medium-term plan. The final version of the decision was also sponsored by the Chairman.

Joint meetings of CPC and ACC. CPC and ACC held their seventeenth series of Joint Meetings at Geneva on 6 and 7 July to consider how the United Nations system could respond in a more co-ordinated, appropriate and efficient manner to economic and social problems.[10] The Meetings examined two areas selected by CPC—food and agriculture, and science and technology.

The Economic and Social Council, by a decision[3] adopted without vote on 28 July, took note of the report of the Chairmen of CPC and ACC on the Meetings, and requested ACC to include information on follow-up measures concerning specific suggestions made at the Meetings in its annual overview report for 1982/83. The Third Committee approved the text, submitted by its Chairman, without vote on 23 July.

Report of the Secretary-General. In October, the Secretary-General reported to the General Assembly on the restructuring of the economic and social sectors of the United Nations system,[11] a process initiated by the Assembly in 1977[12] which was welcomed by ACC as an opportunity to reappraise the direction of United Nations activities, strengthen institutional relationships and co-operative arrangements, and increase the impact of the Organization's response to the objectives of the international community. Prepared after consultation with entities of the system, the report described the results of ACC efforts to restructure and streamline its subsidiary machinery so that it could assist in the preparatory work for intergovernmental decisions, in the implementation of such decisions and in their translation into joint programme activities. The report reviewed organizational arrangements; assistance in planning programme activities; and operational, administrative and budgetary activities.

According to the report, ACC believed that its restructured machinery, after three years of operation, had made a positive contribution to inter-agency co-ordination at the inter-secretariat level. Possi-

bilities for further improvement included a clearer distinction between managerial and substantive issues in ACC discussions, increased use of informal arrangements for in-depth discussion of major substantive issues, and improved secretariat support. Of particular concern were improvements to enhance the Committee's capacity to identify and explore emerging issues, particularly in the development field.

On 20 December,[4] the Assembly took note of the Secretary-General's report. Under the original version of the decision,[5] the Assembly would have welcomed the Secretary-General's report and requested him to submit in 1984 a further progress report, including proposals for further action, as well as similar reports on restructuring the economic and social sectors of: United Nations forums for negotiations other than the Assembly and the Council, the regional commissions, the operational activities of the system for development, and the planning, programming, budgeting and evaluation processes within the system.

Decisions (1982). ESC, 28 July: [1]1982/160, text following; [2]1982/161, text following; [3]1982/166, text following. [4]GA: 37/442, sect. IV, 20 Dec.
Draft decisions. [5]Algeria, Argentina, Belgium, Canada, Denmark, Jamaica, Nigeria, Philippines, Sudan, Sweden, Trinidad and Tobago, Uganda, Yugoslavia, A/C.2/37/L.72 (withdrawn); [6]ESC 3rd Committee Chairman, E/1982/C.3/L.3 (superseded).
Reports. ACC, [7]E/1982/4, [8]E/1982/87; [9]CPC, A/37/38; [10]CPC and ACC Chairmen, E/1982/84; [11]S-G, A/37/439.
Resolution. [12]GA: 32/197, 20 Dec. 1977 (YUN 1977, p. 438).
Meeting record. ESC: E/1982/SR.49 (28 July).

Economic and Social Council decision 1982/160

Adopted without vote

Approved by Third Committee (E/1982/91) without vote, 23 July (meeting 16); draft by Chairman (E/1982/C.3/L.11); agenda item 20.

Report of the Committee for Programme and Co-ordination on the work of its twenty-second session

At its 49th plenary meeting, on 28 July 1982, the Council:

(a) Took note with appreciation of the report of the Committee for Programme and Co-ordination on the work of its twenty-second session;

(b) Decided to endorse the conclusions and recommendations of the Committee, taking fully into account the comments made by members of the Council;

(c) Decided also to transmit the report to the General Assembly at its thirty-seventh session.

Economic and Social Council decision 1982/161

Adopted without vote

Approved by Third Committee (E/1982/91) without vote, 19 July (meeting 11); draft by Chairman (E/1982/C.3/L.3); agenda item 20.

Annual overview report of the Administrative Committee on Co-ordination for 1981/82

At its 49th plenary meeting, on 28 July 1982, the Council took note of the annual overview report of the Administrative Committee on Co-ordination for 1981/82.

Economic and Social Council decision 1982/166

Adopted without vote

Approved by Third Committee (E/1982/91) without vote, 23 July (meeting 16); draft by Chairman (E/1982/C.3/L.11); agenda item 20.

Report of the Chairmen of the Committee for Programme and Co-ordination and the Administrative Committee on Co-ordination on the Joint Meetings of the two Committees

At its 49th plenary meeting, on 28 July 1982, the Council:

(a) Took note of the report of the Chairmen of the Committee for Programme and Co-ordination and the Administrative Committee on Co-ordination on the Joint Meetings of the two Committees;

(b) Decided to request the Administrative Committee on Co-ordination to include information on follow-up measures concerning specific suggestions made at the seventeenth series of Joint Meetings in its annual overview report for 1982/83.

Cross-organizational programme analyses

In its overview report for 1981/82,[1] ACC noted that system-wide analyses of programmes had become increasingly common in reporting to inter-governmental bodies. It suggested that to improve the reports, known as cross-organizational programme analyses, the organizations concerned should be involved in their design and in defining the main issues to be addressed. Computerized programme reference files were being increasingly used to establish an initial central data base, which could be augmented by the organization concerned. Inter-agency co-operation in the preparation of a system-wide analysis of public administration and finance activities, requested by CPC for its April/May session, included informal prior consultations on the 1982-1983 programme budgets in public administration and finance of the concerned organizations.

To provide the necessary two-year preparation time for future analyses, ACC recommended that CPC decide in 1982 on topics for its 1984 and 1985 sessions with possible alternative areas for future analyses, and that analyses be oriented towards specific priority problems being addressed by the system rather than solely to areas involving issues of institutional structure. CPC decided that human settlements should be the subject of an analysis at its 1984 session and economic and technical co-operation among developing countries at its 1985 session.[2]

Reports. [1]ACC, E/1982/4; [2]CPC, A/37/38.

Economic and Social Council

Rationalization of work

Economic and Social Council action. On 28 July 1982, the Economic and Social Council, without vote, adopted measures concerning its programme and organization of work, and its documentation and calendar of meetings.[10] Among those measures, the Council decided to: identify priority issues for its work; draw up recommendations for General Assembly action on economic and social issues; submit its own recommendations to the Assembly on the relevant sections of the proposed United Nations medium-term plan and programme budget; ensure compatibility of United Nations activities; recommend to the Assembly priorities for activities in the economic and social fields; review operational activities throughout the United Nations system; review regional co-operation; take steps to limit documentation; begin its first regular session on the first Tuesday of May each year; and refrain from establishing new subsidiary bodies. The Council endorsed the Secretary-General's recommendations on its revitalization, which were annexed to the resolution, and recommended that the Assembly do likewise.

The Secretary-General's recommendations, contained in a note of 30 March,[9] were that: the Council decide on ways to consider the reports it had requested, whether by direct submission to it or through its subsidiary machinery; subsidiary bodies refrain from requesting the Secretary-General to submit reports directly to the Council; on subjects covered by a subsidiary body, only that body's report be before the Council; the documentation and work programme of the Council's and Assembly's subsidiary bodies be streamlined; the Assembly not request reports for submission to the Council at its first regular session of the following year, and the Council not request, at its first regular session, reports for its second regular session; and progress reports be presented orally.

The draft resolution on revitalizing the Council was submitted by its President following informal consultations. The United States orally proposed that, in paragraph 1 *(d)*, the phrase "the Council shall formulate conclusions and recommendations" would be replaced by "the Council may formulate, as appropriate, conclusions and recommendations". Later, the President orally revised that phrase to read "the Council may formulate appropriate conclusions and recommendations". In the light of the President's revision, the United States withdrew its amendment.

At its organizational session on 4 February,[1] the Council had decided, without vote, to include in the agenda of its first and second 1982 regular sessions the item on the Council's revitalization and to request the President to continue consultations with the regional groups on the matter and report to the Council at its first regular session. By another decision adopted without vote on the same date,[2] the Council requested the Secretary-General to submit to it at its first regular session proposals for the consideration of some items on a biennial or triennial basis and suggestions for ensuring a better distribution of items between the Assembly and the Council, as requested by the Council in July 1981.[11] The draft decisions were proposed by the President, based on informal consultations.

In a letter of 20 April,[8] the Acting Chairman of the Committee on Conferences informed the President that, as requested by the Assembly in December 1981,[12] the Committee had reviewed the 1982-1983 calendar of conferences, with a view to adjusting it to the servicing capacities within the Secretariat, taking into account the time needed for processing and distribution of documents. For this purpose, the Committee suggested postponing the Council's first regular session by two weeks and that the Assembly should avoid requests for reports to be submitted at the first regular session of the following year. These suggestions were incorporated in the Council's 28 July resolution.

On 30 July,[3] the Council decided to identify, at its annual organizational session, a subject relating to interregional co-operation, of common interest to all regions, for detailed consideration under the agenda item on regional co-operation.

General Assembly action. In a decision of 20 December on restructuring the economic and social sectors of the United Nations system,[4] the General Assembly welcomed the Council's 28 July resolution and requested the Assembly President, in co-ordination with the Council President, to undertake consultations regarding the organization and rationalization of work of the United Nations intergovernmental bodies in the economic and social fields. The Assembly referred to its 1984 session a draft resolution originally submitted in 1980,[6] by which the Assembly, *inter alia*, would amend the Charter of the United Nations so that the Council would consist of all United Nations Members, and would discontinue several of its subsidiary bodies.

By an earlier version of this decision, introduced and later withdrawn by Jamaica on behalf of 13 States,[7] the Assembly would have requested consultations "on the subject" (meaning restructuring of the economic and social sectors of the United Nations) rather than on organization and rationalization of the work of its bodies, and, after deciding to consider the 1980 draft resolution in 1984, would have called for taking into consideration further consultations by the Council President and further experience of the Assembly and the Council.

On 21 December 1982,[5] the Assembly, acting without vote, endorsed the recommendations of the Secretary-General as contained in the annex to the Council's 28 July resolution. The decision was approved without objection on 18 December by the Assembly's Fifth (Administrative and Budgetary) Committee, on an oral proposal by its Chairman.

Decisions (1982). ESC: [1]1982/102, 4 Feb., text following; [2]1982/103, 4 Feb., text following; [3]1982/174, para. *(a)*, 30 July. GA: [4]37/442, sect. I, 20 Dec.; [5]37/445, 21 Dec., text following.
Decision (prior). [6]GA: 35/439, annex, 16 Dec. 1980 (YUN 1980, p. 573).
Draft decision withdrawn. [7]Algeria, Argentina, Belgium, Canada, Denmark, Jamaica, Nigeria, Philippines, Sudan,

Sweden, Trinidad and Tobago, Uganda, Yugoslavia, A/C.2/37/L.72.
Letter. [8]Committee on Conferences Acting Chairman, 20 Apr., E/1982/60.
Note. [9]S-G, E/1982/28.
Resolution (1982). [10]ESC: 1982/50, 28 July, text following.
Resolutions (prior). [11]ESC: 1981/83, 24 July 1981 (YUN 1981, p. 1090). [12]GA: 36/117 A, 10 Dec. 1981 (*ibid.*, p. 1364).
Meeting records. ESC: E/1982/SR.2, 3 (4, 5 Feb.), 45, *48, 49* (19-28 July). GA: 5th Committee, A/C.5/37/SR.76 (18 Dec.); plenary, A/37/PV.114 (21 Dec.).

Economic and Social Council decision 1982/102

Adopted without vote

Draft by President (E/1982/L.12), based on informal consultations; agenda item 4.

Revitalization of the Economic and Social Council

At its 2nd plenary meeting, on 4 February 1982, the Council decided to include in the agenda of its first and second regular sessions of 1982 the item entitled "Revitalization of the Economic and Social Council" and to request the President of the Economic and Social Council to continue his consultations with the regional groups on this matter and report thereon to the Council at its first regular session of 1982.

Economic and Social Council decision 1982/103

Adopted without vote

Draft by President (E/1982/L.12), based on informal consultations; agenda item 4.

Rationalization of the agenda and programme of work of the Economic and Social Council

At its 2nd plenary meeting, on 4 February 1982, the Council decided to request the Secretary-General to submit to the Council, at its first regular session of 1982, the report called for in paragraph 4 of its resolution 1981/83 of 24 July 1981.

Economic and Social Council resolution 1982/50

28 July 1982	Meeting 49	Adopted without vote

Draft by President (E/1982/L.48), orally revised following informal consultations; agenda item 7.

Revitalization of the Economic and Social Council

The Economic and Social Council,

Recalling General Assembly resolutions 3201(S-VI) and 3202(S-VI) of 1 May 1974, containing the Declaration and the Programme of Action on the Establishment of a New International Economic Order, 3281(XXIX) of 12 December 1974, containing the Charter of Economic Rights and Duties of States, and 3362(S-VII) of 16 September 1975 on development and international economic co-operation,

Recalling also General Assembly resolution 35/56 of 5 December 1980, containing the International Development Strategy for the Third United Nations Development Decade,

Recalling further General Assembly resolution 32/197 of 20 December 1977 on the restructuring of the economic and social sectors of the United Nations system,

Recalling Council resolutions 1156(XLI) of 5 August 1966, 1622(LI) and 1623(LI) of 30 July 1971, 1768(LIV) of 18 May 1973 and 1981/83 of 24 July 1981,

Fully aware of the urgent need to revitalize the Council in order to enable it, under the authority of the General Assembly, to exercise effectively its functions and powers as set out in the Charter of the United Nations and in relevant resolutions of the Assembly and the Council,

Reaffirming its desire to continue the process of the restructuring of the economic and social sectors of the United Nations system, and recognizing that the revitalization of the Council requires its continuous attention,

Having considered the note by the Secretary-General on the revitalization of the Economic and Social Council,

Having heard statements by the President of the Economic and Social Council and by Member States on the revitalization of the Council as the principal organ of the United Nations under the Charter in the economic and social fields,

1. *Decides* to adopt, without prejudice to future decisions which the General Assembly or the Council may wish to take, the following

measures concerning its programme and organization of work, and its documentation and calendar of meetings:

(a) In formulating its biennial programme of work, the Council shall identify issues which will require its priority consideration, and shall organize its work in such a manner as to enable it to focus its attention on a limited number of carefully selected major policy issues, to be studied in depth with a view to elaborating concrete action-oriented recommendations; the Council shall, in this context, review at each of its regular sessions the programme of work for the ensuing session; it shall also decide on the manner in which it will consider those issues, including the possibility of devoting parts of its sessions to specific subjects or of convening, if necessary, special sessions, in accordance with rule 4 of its rules of procedure, to deal with specific subjects or issues;

(b) The Council shall assist in the preparation of the work of the General Assembly in the economic, social and related fields through the drawing up of suggestions, for consideration by the Assembly, regarding the latter's documentation and organization of work, and of recommendations for action by the Assembly on substantive issues;

(c) The Council shall consolidate similar or related issues under a single agenda item, in order to consider and to take action on them in an integrated manner;

(d) As part of its annual general discussion of international economic and social policy, including regional and sectoral developments, the Council may formulate appropriate conclusions and recommendations thereon addressed to the General Assembly, States Members of the United Nations and organs, organizations and bodies of the United Nations system concerned;

(e) The Council shall examine the relevant sections of the proposed medium-term plan and proposed programme budget of the United Nations on the basis of the recommendations of the Committee for Programme and Co-ordination on the matter, and shall submit its own recommendations thereon to the General Assembly;

(f) The Council shall enhance its role in co-ordinating the activities of the United Nations system in the economic and social sectors; in this context, it shall consider, on a cross-sectoral basis, the activities and programmes of the organs, organizations and bodies of the United Nations system, in order to ensure that the work programmes of the United Nations and its agencies are compatible and mutually complementary, and shall recommend to the General Assembly relative priorities for activities of the United Nations system in the economic and social fields; to that end, beginning at its second regular session of 1983, the Council shall review, every six years, selected major issues in the proposed medium-term plans of the organizations of the United Nations system;

(g) The Council shall, in accordance with General Assembly resolution 32/197, carry out comprehensive policy reviews of operational activities throughout the United Nations system, bearing in mind the need for balance, compatibility and conformity with the priorities established by the Assembly for the system as a whole; the Council shall undertake such a review in 1983 and every three years thereafter and shall submit its recommendations to the General Assembly, in order to assist and prepare the Assembly for its work in this regard, in accordance with Assembly resolution 35/81 of 5 December 1980;

(h) The Council shall henceforth also concentrate on the policy review and co-ordination of activities in the area of regional co-operation, particularly in respect of issues of common interest to all regions and matters relating to interregional co-operation;

(i) The Council shall review at its annual organizational session, in the context of its consideration of its draft basic programme of work, all its recurrent and other documentation requested under an existing legislative authority, in order to determine whether any document has become redundant, has lost its usefulness or could be issued at less frequent intervals; the Secretary-General is requested to submit his recommendations in this regard to the Council, together with the draft basic programme of work;

(j) All the subsidiary bodies of the Council are urged to exercise the utmost restraint in making requests of the Secretary-General for new reports and studies and to implement fully the provisions of the decisions of the Council and of the General Assembly with respect to the control and limitation of documentation;

(k) The Council shall henceforth begin its first regular session on the first Tuesday of May of each year;

(l) The Secretary-General is requested, in proposing future draft calendars of conferences, to ensure that meetings of subsidiary bodies of the Council, to the extent possible, will end at least eight weeks before the Council session at which their reports are to be considered; the Committee on Conferences is also requested to act accordingly;

(m) The Council shall, to the maximum extent possible, refrain from establishing new subsidiary bodies; it shall make every effort to meet the need for any new bodies by holding sessions as envisaged in paragraph 1 *(a)* above;

2. *Endorses* the recommendations of the Secretary-General as contained in the annex to the present resolution, and recommends to the General Assembly that it should also endorse those recommendations;

3. *Decides* to request the President of the Economic and Social Council to continue consultations with Member States on other questions relating to all aspects of the implementation of section II of the annex to General Assembly resolution 32/197 and to report all the results of those consultations to the Council in 1983.

ANNEX
Recommendations of the Secretary-General concerning the revitalization of the Economic and Social Council

1. The Economic and Social Council, at its annual organizational session, should decide on ways to consider all the reports which have been requested for submission to it and/or its subsidiary machinery. In principle, all reports on subjects which are within the purview of an established subsidiary body should, in the first instance, be submitted to that body.* The subsidiary body should include, in a separate chapter in its report to the Council and/or the General Assembly, specific recommendations on issues requiring action by the Council and/or the Assembly. Such recommendations should, whenever appropriate, be in the form of draft resolutions and/or decisions for action by the Council and/or the Assembly.

2. As a general rule, all subsidiary bodies of the Council and the General Assembly should refrain from requesting the Secretary-General to submit reports directly to the Council and/or the Assembly. They should also refrain, to the extent possible, from transmitting reports submitted to them for consideration to the Council and/or the Assembly.

3. Accordingly, on all subjects covered by a subsidiary body, the Council should have before it, as a general rule, only the report of that subsidiary body. In the consideration of such reports, the Council should, in order to avoid repetitious debates, confine its consideration as far as possible to matters which require its guidance and decisions. The same procedure should also apply to the consideration of reports of subsidiary bodies of the Assembly which are transmitted through the Council.

4. The documentation and programme of work of the subsidiary bodies of the Council and the General Assembly should also be streamlined in order to enable them to perform effectively the functions entrusted to them. The Council and the Assembly should continue to review, in accordance with Council resolution 1979/41 of 10 May 1979 and Assembly resolution 34/50 of 23 November 1979, the provisional agenda for their subsidiary bodies, together with the list of requested documentation, in order, *inter alia*, to establish greater consistency in the overall request for documentation and its orderly consideration at the intergovernmental level, taking fully into account the medium-term plan and the programme budget. In doing so, the Council and the Assembly should also take into account the need for the consolidation of items and documentation for their subsidiary machinery.

5. In order to enable the Council and the General Assembly to have the necessary time to prepare for their work, the Assembly, as a general rule, should not request reports for submission to the Council at its first regular session of the following year. The Council, likewise, should refrain from requesting at its first regular session reports for submission to it at its second regular session.†

6. Reports on the progress of work for the information of the Council or the Assembly should, as a general rule, be presented orally rather than in written form.

---

*According to this principle, even when there are legislative mandates for the submission of Secretariat or expert reports directly to the Council or through the Council to the General Assembly, the Council should in the first instance transmit such reports to the subsidiary body concerned for consideration.

†For the same reason, it would also be desirable for the Council at its second regular session to avoid requesting reports for submission to the General Assembly in the same year. This rule, however, may need to be applied with some flexibility, since the Council considers different sets of issues at its first and second regular sessions, and also on account of possible administrative and financial implications requiring action by the Assembly.

General Assembly decision 37/445

Adopted without vote

Approved by Fifth Committee (A/37/783) without objection, 18 December (meeting 76); oral proposal by Chairman; agenda item 12.

Revitalization of the Economic and Social Council

At its 114th plenary meeting, on 21 December 1982, the General Assembly, on the recommendation of the Fifth Committee, endorsed the recommendations of the Secretary-General as contained in the annex to Economic and Social Council resolution 1982/50 of 28 July 1982 dealing with the revitalization of the Council.

Relations with NGOs

The Economic and Social Council's Committee on Non-Governmental Organizations (NGOs) met twice in 1982—in New York on 14 April,[2] and at Geneva on 7 July[3]—to review requests from NGOs in consultative status with the Council to be heard by the Council or its committees in connection with items on the Council's agenda (see below). As the Committee did not take action in 1982 on any NGO requests for consultative status with the Council, the 646 NGOs with such status (see list below)[1] remained the same as in 1981. They were divided into three groups:

category I, organizations representative of major population segments in a large number of countries, involved with the economic and social life of the areas they represented; category II, international organizations having special competence in a few of the Council's fields of activity; and organizations on the Roster, considered able to make occasional and useful contributions to the Council's work.

In a series of documents issued between February and April,[4] the Secretary-General forwarded, for consideration by the Committee, quadrennial reports submitted by 165 NGOs in categories I and II consultative status on their United Nations–related activities during 1978-1981.

By a resolution of 4 May, the Council expressed its expectation that NGOs in consultative status with it would take account of the relevant Council and General Assembly resolutions condemning South Africa's *apartheid* policy and requested the Committee on NGOs to examine that question.[5]

NGOs in consultative status with the Economic and Social Council
(as at 31 December 1982)

Category I

International Alliance of Women—Equal Rights, Equal Responsibilities
International Association of French-Speaking Parliamentarians
International Chamber of Commerce
International Confederation of Free Trade Unions
International Co-operative Alliance
International Council of Voluntary Agencies (ICVA)
International Council of Women
International Council on Social Welfare
International Federation of Agricultural Producers
International Federation of Business and Professional Women
International Organization for Standardization (IOS)
International Organization of Consumers Unions (IOCU)
International Organization of Employers
International Planned Parenthood Federation
International Social Security Association (ISSA)
International Union of Local Authorities (IULA)
International Youth and Student Movement for the United Nations (ISMUN)
Inter-Parliamentary Union
League of Red Cross Societies
Muslim World League
Organization of African Trade Union Unity (OATUU)
Society for International Development (SID)
United Towns Organization
Women's International Democratic Federation
World Assembly of Youth (WAY)
World Confederation of Labour
World Federation of Democratic Youth (WFDY)
World Federation of Trade Unions (WFTU)

World Federation of United Nations Associations (WFUNA)
World Muslim Congress
World Veterans Federation

Category II

Afro-Asian Peoples' Solidarity Organization (AAPSO)
AFS International/Intercultural Programs, Inc. (formerly American Field Service)
Agudas Israel World Organization
Airport Associations Co-ordinating Council (AACC)
All-India Women's Conference
All Pakistan Women's Association
Amnesty International
Anti-*Apartheid* Movement, The
Anti-Slavery Society for the Protection of Human Rights, The
Arab Lawyers Union
Associated Country Women of the World
Association for Childhood Education International
Association for the Study of the World Refugee Problem
Bahá'i International Community
Baptist World Alliance
CARE (Cooperative for American Relief Everywhere, Inc.)
Caritas Internationalis (International Confederation of Catholic Charities)
Carnegie Endowment for International Peace
Catholic Relief Services—United States Catholic Conference, Inc.
Chamber of Commerce of the United States of America
Christian Democratic World Union
Christian Peace Conference

Church World Service, Inc.

Commission of the Churches on International Affairs of the World Council of Churches

Commonwealth Human Ecology Council (CHEC)

Conference of European Churches (CEC)

Consultative Council of Jewish Organizations

Co-ordinating Board of Jewish Organizations (CBJO)

Co-ordinating Committee for International Voluntary Service

Council of European and Japanese National Shipowners Association, The (CENSA)

Democratic Youth Community of Europe

Eastern Regional Organization for Public Administration (EROPA)

Environment Liaison Centre

European Association of National Productivity Centres

European Insurance Committee

European League for Economic Co-operation

European Organization for Quality Control (EOQC)

Experiment in International Living, The

Federation for the Respect of Man and Humanity

Federation of Arab Economists, The

Federation of Arab Scientific Research Councils

Foundation for the Peoples of the South Pacific, Inc., The

Friends World Committee for Consultation

Howard League for Penal Reform

Ibero-American Institute of Aeronautic and Space Law and Commercial Aviation

Institute for Policy Studies—Transnational

Institute of Electrical and Electronic Engineers, Inc.

Inter-American Federation of Public Relations Associations (IFPRA)

Inter-American Federation of Touring and Automobile Clubs (FITAC)

Inter-American Planning Society

Inter-American Press Association

Inter-American Statistical Institute

International Air Transport Association

International Association against Painful Experiments on Animals

International Association for Religious Freedom (IARF)

International Association for Social Progress

International Association for the Protection of Industrial Property

International Association for Water Law (IAWL)

International Association of Democratic Lawyers

International Association of Educators for World Peace

International Association of Juvenile and Family Court Magistrates

International Association of Penal Law

International Association of Ports and Harbours (IAPH)

International Association of Schools of Social Work

International Astronautical Federation

International Automobile Federation (FIA)

International Bar Association

International Cargo Handling Co-ordination Association

International Catholic Child Bureau

International Catholic Migration Commission

International Catholic Union of the Press

International Centre for Industry and the Environment (ICIE)

International Centre for Local Credit

International Centre of Social Gerontology

International Chamber of Shipping

International Christian Union of Business Executives (UNIAPAC)

International Civil Airports Association

International College of Surgeons

International Commission of Jurists

International Commission on Irrigation and Drainage

International Committee for European Security and Co-operation

International Committee of the Red Cross

International Co-operation for Socio-Economic Development (CIDSE)

International Co-ordinating Committee of Financial Analysts' Associations

International Council for Adult Education (ICAE)

International Council for Building Research, Studies and Documentation

International Council of Environmental Law

International Council of Jewish Women

International Council of Monuments and Sites (ICOMOS)

International Council of Scientific Unions

International Council of Societies of Industrial Design (ICSID)

International Council on Alcohol and Addictions

International Council on Jewish Social and Welfare Services

International Defence and Aid Fund for Southern Africa

International Electrotechnical Commission

International Federation for Home Economics (IFHE)

International Federation for Housing and Planning

International Federation of Beekeepers' Associations

International Federation of Human Rights

International Federation of Journalists

International Federation of Landscape Architects

International Federation of Resistance Movements

International Federation of Senior Police Officers

International Federation of Settlements and Neighbourhood Centres

International Federation of Social Workers

International Federation of University Women

International Federation of Women in Legal Careers

International Federation of Women Lawyers

International Federation on Aging

International Fellowship of Reconciliation

International Hotel Association

International Indian Treaty Council

International Institute for Vital Registration and Statistics (IIVRS)

International Institute of Administrative Sciences

International Islamic Federation of Student Organizations

International Law Association

International League for Human Rights

International League of Societies for Persons with Mental Handicap

International Movement ATD Fourth World

International Movement for Fraternal Union among Races and Peoples (UFER)

International Organization for the Elimination of All Forms of Racial Discrimination (EAFORD)

International Organization—Justice and Development

International Organization of Journalists

International Organization of Supreme Audit Institutions (INTOSAI)

International Petroleum Industry Environmental Conservation Association IPIECA)

International Prisoners Aid Association
International Road Federation
International Road Transport Union
International Rural Housing Association
International Savings Banks Institute
International Senior Citizens Association, Inc., The
International Social Service
International Society for Criminology
International Society of Social Defence
International Statistical Institute
International Touring Alliance
International Union for Child Welfare
International Union for Conservation of Nature and Natural Resources
International Union for Inland Navigation
International Union for the Scientific Study of Population
International Union of Architects
International Union of Building Societies and Savings Associations
International Union of Family Organizations
International Union of Latin Notariat
International Union of Lawyers
International Union of Producers and Distributors of Electrical Energy
International Union of Public Transport
International Union of Young Christian Democrats (IUYCD)
International Young Christian Workers
Jaycees International
Latin American Association of Finance Development Institutions (ALIDE)
Latin American Iron and Steel Institute
Law Association for Asia and the Western Pacific (LAWASIA)
Lions International—The International Association of Lions Clubs
Lutheran World Federation
Mutual Assistance of the Latin American Government Oil Companies (ARPEL)
Organization for International Economic Relations (IER)
OXFAM (Oxford Committee for Famine Relief)
Pan-African Institute for Development
Pan-African Women's Organization
Pan American Federation of Engineering Societies (UPADI)
Pan-Pacific and South-East Asia Women's Association
Pax Christi, International Catholic Peace Movement
Pax Romana
 (International Catholic Movement for Intellectual and Cultural Affairs)
 (International Movement of Catholic Students)
Permanent International Association of Road Congresses (PIARC)
Rädda Barnen's Riksförbund (Save the Children)
Rehabilitation International
St. Joan's International Alliance
Salvation Army, The
Save the Children Federation
Socialist International
Socialist International Women (SIW)
Société internationale de prophylaxie criminelle
Society for Comparative Legislation
Soroptimist International

Studies and Expansion Society—International Scientific Association (SEC)
Third World Foundation
Union of Arab Jurists
Union of International Associations
Union of International Fairs
United Kingdom Standing Conference on the Second United Nations Development Decade
Universal Federation of Travel Agents Associations
Vienna Institute for Development
War Resisters International
Women's International League for Peace and Freedom
Women's International Zionist Organization
World Alliance of Young Men's Christian Associations
World Association of Former United Nations Interns and Fellows
World Association of Girl Guides and Girl Scouts
World Association of World Federalists
World Confederation of Organizations of the Teaching Profession
World Conference on Religion and Peace
World Council for the Welfare of the Blind
World Council of Credit Unions, Inc. (WOCCU)
World Council of Indigenous Peoples (WCIP)
World Council of Management
World Energy Conference
World Federation for Mental Health
World Federation of Catholic Youth
World Federation of the Deaf
World Jewish Congress
World Leisure and Recreation Association
World Movement of Mothers
World Organization of the Scout Movement (World Scout Bureau)
World Peace Through Law Centre
World Population Society
World Society for the Protection of Animals
World Student Christian Federation
World Trade Centers Association
World Union for the Safeguard of Youth
World Union of Catholic Women's Organizations
World University Service
World Women's Christian Temperance Union
World Young Women's Christian Association
Zonta International

Roster

Organizations included by action
of the Economic and Social Council

African Medical and Research Foundation
Altrusa International, Inc.
American Foreign Insurance Association
American Foreign Law Association, Inc.
American Society for Engineering Education (ASEE)
Asian Development Center (ADC)
Asian Youth Council
Association for World Education
Battelle Memorial Institute
Bureau international de la récupération
Caribbean Conservation Association
Catholic International Union for Social Service
Center for Inter-American Relations
Commission to Study the Organization of Peace

Committee for Economic Development
Committee for European Construction Equipment (CECE)
Confederation of Asian Chambers of Commerce
Congress of Racial Equality (CORE)
Council of European National Youth Committees (CENYC)
Council on Religion and International Affairs (CRIA)
Data for Development (DFD)
Economic Research Committee of the Gas Industry (COMETEC-GAZ)
Engineers Joint Council
Environmental Coalition for North America (ENCONA)
European Alliance of Press Agencies
European Association of Refrigeration Enterprises (AEEF)
European Confederation of Woodworking Industries
European Container Manufacturers' Committee
European Federation for the Welfare of the Elderly (EURAG)
European Liquefied Petroleum Gas Association
European Mediterranean Commission on Water Planning
European Union of Women
Ex-Volunteers International
Federation of European Manufacturers of Friction Materials
Federation of National Committees in the International Christian Youth Exchange
Foster Parents Plan International (PLAN)
Foundation for the Establishment of an International Criminal Court, The
Friedrich Ebert Foundation
Gray Panthers
Habitat International Council
Help the Aged
Indian Law Resource Centre
Institute of International Container Lessors
International Abolitionist Federation
International Association for Bridge and Structural Engineering
International Association for Community Development
International Association for Housing Science
International Association for Hydrogen Energy
International Association for Research into Income and Wealth
International Association for the Child's Right to Play
International Association for the Defence of Religious Liberty
International Association for the Exchange of Students for Technical Experience
International Association for the Promotion of Democracy under God (Pro Deo)
International Association of Airport and Seaport Police
International Association of Chiefs of Police
International Association of Gerontology
International Association of the Soap and Detergent Industry
International Board of Co-operation for the Developing Countries (EMCO)
International Bureau of Motor-Cycle Manufacturers
International Center for Dynamics of Development
International Committee against *Apartheid*, Racism and Colonialism in Southern Africa
International Committee of Outer Space Onomastics (ICOSO)

International Confederation for Disarmament and Peace
International Confederation of Associations of Experts and Consultants
International Container Bureau
International Council for Commercial Arbitration
International Council for Game and Wildlife Conservation
International Council of Psychologists
International Federation for Documentation
International Federation of Chemical Energy and General Workers' Unions
International Federation of Free Journalists
International Federation of Freight Forwarders Associations
International Federation of International Furniture Removers
International Federation of Operational Research Societies
International Federation of Pedestrians
International Federation of Rural Adult Catholic Movements
International Federation of Surveyors
International Federation of the Blind
International Fiscal Association
International Hydatidological Association
International Inner Wheel
International Institute of Public Finance
International Institute of Rural Reconstruction (IIRR)
International Iron and Steel Institute
International Juridical Organization (IJO)
International League for the Rights and Liberation of Peoples
International League of Surveillance Societies, The
International Olive Growers Federation
International Organization of Experts (ORDINEX)
International Peace Academy
International Peace Bureau
International Permanent Bureau of Automobile Manufacturers
International Police Association
International Press Institute (IPI)
International Prevention of Road Accidents
International Progress Organization (IPO)
International Public Relations Association (IPRA)
International Real Estate Federation
International Research Institute for Immigration and Emigration Politics
International Schools Association
International Shipping Federation (ISF)
International Society for Prosthetics and Orthotics
International Solar Energy Society
International Textile Manufacturers Federation
International Union of Judges
International Union of Marine Insurance
International Union of Police Federations
International Union of Social Democratic Teachers
International Union of Tenants
International Working Group for the Construction of Sports and Leisure Facilities
La Leche League International, Inc. (LLLI)
Latin American Confederation of Tourist Organizations (COTAL)
Latin American Official Workers' Confederation (CLATE)
Liberation

Minority Rights Group
Movement against Racism and for Friendship between
 Peoples
Movement for a Better World
National Organization for Women (NOW)
National Parks and Conservation Association
OISCA International (Organization for Industrial,
 Spiritual and Cultural Advancement International)
Open Door International (for the Economic Emanci-
 pation of the Woman Worker)
Overseas Education Fund of the League of Women
 Voters
Pan American Development Foundation
Permanent International Association of Navigation Con-
 gresses
Pio Mansú International Research Centre for Environ-
 mental Structures, The
Planetary Citizens
Population Council, The
Procedural Aspects of International Law Institute
Program for the Introduction and Adaptation of Con-
 traceptive Technology (PIACT)
Quota International Incorporated
Romani Union
Rotary International
SERVAS International
Society for Social Responsibility in Science
Survival International Ltd.
Transfrigoroute Europe
United Nations of Yoga (UNY)
United Schools International
United Way International
Universal Esperanto Association
World Alliance of Reformed Churches
World Association for Christian Communication
World Confederation for Physical Therapy
World Development Movement
World Environment and Resources Council (WERC)
World Federation of Christian Life Communities
World Federation of Health Agencies for the Advance-
 ment of Voluntary Surgical Contraception
World Mining Congress
World Union for Progressive Judaism
Young Lawyers' International Association (AIJA)

Organizations included by action
of the Secretary-General

American Association for the Advancement of Science
Asian Environmental Society
Association for the Advancement of Agricultural
 Sciences in Africa
Center for Research on the New International Economic
 Order, The
Center of Concern
Committee for International Co-operation in National
 Research in Demography (CICRED)
Council for Development of Economic and Social
 Research in Africa, The (CODESRIA)
Fauna Preservation Society, The
Foresta Institute for Ocean and Mountain Studies
Friends of the Earth (FOE)
Institut de la vie
International Advisory Committee on Population and
 Law

International Association against Noise
International Association on Water Pollution Research
 (IAWPR)
International Educational Development, Inc.
International Institute for Environment and De-
 velopment
International Ocean Institute
International Society for Community Development
International Studies Association
International Union of Anthropological and Ethnolog-
 ical Sciences
National Audubon Society
Natural Resources Defence Council, Inc.
Population Crisis Committee
Population Institute
Sierra Club
Trilateral Commission, The
World Education
World Society for Ekistics

Organizations included because of
consultative status with specialized agencies
or other United Nations bodies

Organization	In consultative status with
African Centre for Monetary Studies	UNCTAD
Arab Federation for Engineering Industries	UNCTAD
Arab Federation of Chemical Fertilizer Producers	UNIDO
Arab Iron and Steel Union (AISU)	UNIDO
Association of African Universities	UNESCO
Association of Arab Universities	UNESCO
Association of European Jute Industries	UNCTAD
Association of Partially and Wholly French-Language Universities	UNESCO
Association of West European Builders, The (AWES)	IMO
Baltic and International Maritime Conference, The	IMO, UNCTAD
B'nai B'rith International Council	UNESCO
Catholic International Education Office	UNESCO, UNICEF
Centre Europe–Tiers Monde (CETIM)	UNCTAD
Centre for Latin American Monetary Studies	UNCTAD
Club de Dakar	FAO, UNIDO
Committee on Space Research (COSPAR)	ITU
Confederation of International Trading Houses Associations	UNCTAD

Organization	In consultative status with	Organization	In consultative status with
Co-ordination Committee for the Textile Industries in the European Common Market (COMITEXTIL)	UNCTAD	International Association for Educational Assessment	UNESCO
Council for International Organizations of Medical Sciences (CIOMS)	UNESCO, WHO	International Association for Mass Communication Research	UNESCO
Engineering Committee on Oceanic Resources (ECOR)	IMO	International Association for Suicide Prevention	WHO
European Association for Animal Production	FAO	International Association for the Study of the Liver	WHO
European Broadcasting Union	ITU, UNESCO	International Association of Agricultural Economists	FAO, UNCTAD
European Centre for International Co-operation (CECI)	UNIDO	International Association of Agricultural Librarians and Documentalists	FAO
European Computer Manufacturers Association	ITU	International Association of Art (IAA)	UNESCO
European Confederation of Agriculture	FAO, IAEA, UNESCO	International Association of Cancer Registries	WHO
		International Association of Classification Societies	IMO
European Council of Chemical Manufacturers' Federations	FAO, ICAO, ILO, IMO, UNCTAD	International Association of Conference Interpreters	ILO, UNESCO
European Federation of National Associations of Engineers	UNESCO, UNIDO	International Association of Crafts and Small and Medium-sized Enterprises	UNIDO
		International Association of Drilling Contractors (IADC)	IMO
European Oceanic Association	UNIDO	International Association of Dry Cargo Shipowners	UNCTAD
European Tea Committee	FAO	International Association of Fish Meal Manufacturers	FAO
European Tugowners Association	IMO	International Association of Horticultural Producers	FAO
European Union of Public Relations	UNIDO	International Association of Lighthouse Authorities	IMO, ITU
Federación Latinoamericana de Periodistas	UNESCO	International Association of Literary Critics	UNESCO
Federation of Afro-Asian Insurers and Reinsurers (FAIR)	UNCTAD	International Association of Logopedics and Phoniatrics	UNESCO, UNICEF, WHO
General Union of Chambers of Commerce, Industry and Agriculture for Arab Countries	UNCTAD	International Association of Medical Laboratory Technologists (IAMLT)	WHO
Institute of Air Transport	ICAO	International Association of Microbiological Societies	WHO
Institute of International Law	ICAO	International Association of Mutual Insurance Companies	UNCTAD
Institute on Man and Science	UNESCO		
Inter-American Association of Broadcasters	ITU, UNESCO	International Association of Students in Economics and Management	UNESCO
International Academy of Pathology	WHO	International Association of the Third Age Universities	ILO, UNESCO
International Aeronautical Federation	ICAO	International Association of Universities	UNESCO
International Agency for the Prevention of Blindness (Vision International)	UNICEF, WHO	International Association of University Professors and Lecturers	UNESCO
International Amateur Radio Union	ITU	International Baccalaureate Office	UNESCO
International Association for Cereal Chemistry (ICC)	FAO, UNIDO	International Board on Books for Young People	UNESCO, UNICEF

Organization	In consultative status with	Organization	In consultative status with
International Bureau of Social Tourism	ILO, UNESCO	International Falcon Movement	UNESCO
International Centre of Films for Children and Young People	UNESCO, UNICEF	International Federation for Information Processing	ITU, UNESCO, WHO
International Cocoa Trades Federation	UNCTAD	International Federation for Medical and Biological Engineering	WHO
International Commission on Illumination	ICAO, ILO	International Federation for Parent Education	UNESCO, UNICEF
International Commission on Radiological Protection (ICRP)	WHO	International Federation of Air Line Pilots Associations	ICAO, WMO
International Committee for Plastics in Agriculture	UNIDO	International Federation of Automatic Control	UNIDO
International Confederation of European Beet Growers	UNCTAD	International Federation of Catholic Universities	UNESCO
International Confederation of Midwives	ILO, UNICEF, WHO	International Federation of Children's Communities	UNESCO
International Conference of Historians of the Labour Movement	UNESCO	International Federation of Clinical Chemistry	WHO
International Copyright Society	UNESCO	International Federation of Film Archives	UNESCO
International Council for Correspondence Education	UNESCO	International Federation of Gynecology and Obstetrics	WHO
International Council for Philosophy and Humanistic Studies	UNESCO	International Federation of Health Records Organizations	WHO
International Council of Aircraft Owner and Pilot Associations	ICAO	International Federation of Library Associations and Institutions (IFLA)	UNESCO
International Council of Marine Industry Associations (ICOMIA)	IMO	International Federation of Margarine Associations	FAO
International Council of Nurses	ILO, UNESCO, WHO	International Federation of Medical Student Associations	WHO
		International Federation of Multiple Sclerosis Societies	WHO
International Council of Sport and Physical Education	UNESCO	International Federation of Musicians	UNESCO
International Council on Archives	UNESCO	International Federation of Newspaper Publishers	UNESCO
International Council on Education for Teaching	UNESCO	International Federation of Organizations of School Correspondence and Exchanges	UNESCO
International Cystic Fibrosis (Mucoviscidosis) Association	WHO	International Federation of Pharmaceutical Manufacturers Associations	UNCTAD, UNIDO, WHO
International Dairy Federation	FAO		
International Dental Federation	WHO		
International Diabetes Federation	WHO	International Federation of Physical Medicine and Rehabilitation	WHO
International Epidemiological Association	WHO	International Federation of Plantation, Agricultural and Allied Workers	FAO
International Ergonomics Association	ILO, WHO		

Organization	In consultative status with
International Federation of Popular Travel Organizations	UNESCO
International Federation of Purchasing and Materials Management (IFPMM)	UNCTAD
International Federation of Surgical Colleges	WHO
International Federation of the Periodical Press	UNESCO
International Federation of Translators	UNESCO
International Federation of Travel Journalists and Writers	UNESCO
International Food Policy Research Institute	FAO, UNCTAD
International Gas Union	ITU
International Hospital Federation–IHF	WHO
International Humanist and Ethical Union	UNESCO
International Institute for Audio-Visual Communication and Cultural Development (MEDIACULT)	UNESCO
International Institute for Peace	UNESCO
International League against Rheumatism	WHO
International Leprosy Association	WHO
International Maritime Pilots' Association	IMO
International Organization against Trachoma	WHO
International Organization for Co-operation in Health Care	WHO
International Paediatric Association	WHO
International Peace Research Association	UNCTAD, UNESCO
International PEN	UNESCO
International Pharmaceutical Federation	WHO
International Phosphate Industry Organization	FAO, IMO, UNCTAD, UNIDO
International Political Science Association	UNESCO
International Press Telecommunications Council	ITU
International Publishers Association	UNESCO
International Round Table for the Advancement of Counselling (IRTAC)	ILO, UNESCO
International Scientific Film Association	UNESCO
International Secretariat of Catholic Technologists, Agriculturists and Economists	ILO

Organization	In consultative status with
International Shipowners' Association	IMO, UNCTAD
International Social Science Council	ILO, UNESCO
International Society and Federation of Cardiology	WHO
International Society for Burn Injuries	WHO
International Society for Human and Animal Mycology	WHO
International Society for Photogrammetry	UNESCO
International Society of Citriculture	FAO
International Society of Endocrinology	WHO
International Society of Haematology	WHO
International Society of Radiographers and Radiological Technicians	WHO
International Society of Soil Science	FAO, UNESCO, WMO
International Sociological Association	UNESCO, WHO
International Time Bureau	ITU
International Transport Workers' Federation	ICAO
International Union against Tuberculosis	ILO, WHO
International Union for Health Education	UNESCO, WHO
International Union of Aviation Insurers	ICAO
International Union of Biological Sciences	WHO
International Union of Forestry Research Organizations	FAO
International Union of Geodesy and Geophysics	ICAO
International Union of Independent Laboratories	UNIDO
International Union of Nutritional Sciences	FAO, WHO
International Union of Pure and Applied Chemistry	FAO, WHO
International Union of School and University Health and Medicine	UNESCO, WHO
International Union of Socialist Youth	ILO, UNESCO
International Union of Students	UNESCO
International Water Supply Association	WHO
International Young Catholic Students	UNESCO
International Youth Hostel Federation	UNESCO
Inter-Union Commission on Frequency Allocations for	

Organization	In consultative status with	Organization	In consultative status with
Radio Astronomy and Space Science	ITU	World Confederation of Teachers	UNESCO
Latin American Social Science Council	UNESCO	World Crafts Council	UNESCO
Latin American Federation of Pharmaceutical Industries	UNIDO	World Education Fellowship, The	UNESCO
Liaison Office of the Rubber Industries of the European Economic Community	UNCTAD	World Federation for Medical Education	WHO
Licensing Executives Society International	UNCTAD, UNIDO	World Federation of Agricultural Workers	FAO
Medical Women's International Association	WHO	World Federation of Associations of Clinical Toxicology Centres and Poison Control Centres	WHO
Miners' International Federation	UNCTAD	World Federation of Engineering Organizations	UNESCO, UNIDO
Oil Companies' International Marine Forum (OCIMF)	IMO	World Federation of Foreign-Language Teachers' Associations	UNESCO
Organization for Flora Neotropica	UNESCO	World Federation of Neurosurgical Societies	WHO
Pacific Science Association	UNESCO, WMO	World Federation of Nuclear Medicine and Biology	WHO
Permanent Commission and International Association on Occupational Health	ILO, WHO	World Federation of Occupational Therapists	WHO
Société internationale de télécommunications aéronautiques (SITA)	ITU	World Federation of Public Health Associations	WHO
Sri Aurobindo Society	UNESCO	World Federation of Scientific Workers	UNESCO
Standing Conference of Rectors and Vice-Chancellors of the European Universities	UNESCO	World Federation of Societies of Anaesthesiologists	WHO
Trade Unions International of Agricultural, Forestry and Plantation Workers	FAO	World Federation of Teachers' Unions	UNESCO
UNDA—Catholic International Association for Radio and Television	UNESCO	World Federation of Workers of Food, Tobacco and Hotel Industries	FAO
Union of Industries of the European Community (UNICE)	UNCTAD, UNIDO	World Future Studies Federation	UNESCO
United Seamen's Service, Inc.	ILO	World Medical Association	ILO
United States Trademark Association, The	UNCTAD	World Movement of Christian Workers	ILO, UNESCO
World Association for Element Building and Prefabrication	UNIDO	World Organization for Early Childhood Education	UNESCO
World Association for the School as an Instrument of Peace	UNESCO	World Organization of Former Students of Catholic Teaching	UNESCO
World Association of Industrial and Technological Research Organizations	UNIDO	World ORT Union	ILO
		World Packaging Organization	UNIDO
		World Peace Council	UNCTAD, UNESCO
World Association of Societies of Pathology	WHO	World Poultry Science Association	FAO
		World Psychiatric Association	WHO

List of NGOs. [1]E/1982/INF.9.
Reports. Committee on NGOs, [2]E/1982/50 & Add.1, [3]E/1982/79; [4]S-G, E/C.2/1982/2 & Add.1-8.
Resolution (1982). [5]ESC: 1982/16, 4 May.

Hearings

The Committee on NGOs, at its 1982 meetings, heard requests from organizations in categories I and II consultative status wishing to address the Economic and Social Council or its committees in connection with items on the Council's agenda. On 14 April, it recommended that three be heard on specific agenda items[1] and, on 7 July, it recommended that a further eight be heard.[2] In addition, the Council received statements[3] submitted in 1982 by four NGOs concerning specific areas of its work.

Reports. Committee on NGOs, [1]E/1982/50 & Add.1, [2]E/1982/79.

Statements. [3]NGOs, E/1982/NGO/1-4.
Meeting records. ESC: E/1982/SR.9, 11 (16, 20 Apr.).

Work programme for 1982-1983

At its organizational session for 1982 (New York, 2-5 February), the Economic and Social Council, having considered the draft basic programme of work for 1982-1983 submitted by the Secretary-General,[3] approved its basic work programme for 1982, allocating the agenda items for consideration at its sessions.

The Council held its first regular session (13 April-7 May) in New York, during which its Second (Social) Committee and its Sessional Working Group (of Governmental Experts) on the Implementation of the International Covenant on Economic, Social and Cultural Rights met. During the second regular session (Geneva, 7-30 July), the Council's First (Economic) and Third (Programme and Co-ordination) Committees met. The Council also held a resumed second regular session (New York, 25-27 October and 9-11 November).

The 1982 work programme was approved without vote by the Council on 5 February.[1] By that decision, the Council also noted a list of questions for inclusion in its work programme for 1983 and decided to refer a series of 1981 General Assembly resolutions to the Commission on Human Rights, the Commission for Social Development, the Commission on the Status of Women, the Commission on Narcotic Drugs, the Committee on Crime Prevention and Control, the Commission on Human Settlements and the regional commissions. The Council acted on a proposal[5] made by its President on the basis of informal consultations on his earlier text.[4] The decision as adopted incorporated some changes in the agenda items.

By a decision adopted without vote, on an oral proposal of the President, the Council, on 30 July[2] authorized the Secretary-General to transmit directly to the Assembly the annual reports of the Trade and Development Board, the Human Rights Committee and the Council of the United Nations University.

Decisions (1982). ESC: [1]1982/100, 5 Feb. (no text); [2]1982/178, 30 July, text following.
Draft basic work programme. [3]S-G, E/1982/1.
Draft decisions. ESC President, [4]E/1982/L.11 (superseded), [5]E/1982/L.14 (adopted).
Meeting records. ESC: E/1982/SR.3, 51 (5 Feb., 30 July).

Economic and Social Council decision 1982/178

Adopted without vote

Oral proposal by President; agenda item 2.

Transmittal of reports to the General Assembly for consideration

At its 51st plenary meeting, on 30 July 1982, the Council decided to authorize the Secretary-General to transmit directly to the General Assembly the following annual reports, for consideration:

(a) The report of the Trade and Development Board;

(b) The report of the Human Rights Committee;

(c) The report of the Council of the United Nations University.

Agenda of 1982 sessions

The Economic and Social Council approved on 5 February 1982 the provisional agenda for its first regular session of the year.[2] On 7 May, it approved the draft provisional agenda for its second regular session and the proposed organization of work for that session.[3]

Six items were considered by the Council at its February organizational session.[4] The 14 items of the provisional agenda for the first regular session were listed in a February report[5] which provided background information on each item. The agenda of the second regular session had 29 items, of which 6 were considered at the resumed session. (For lists of agenda items, see APPENDIX IV.)

The Council also decided on 5 February[1] that, beginning in 1983, the item on "Special economic, humanitarian and disaster relief assistance" should be considered at its second regular session, unless circumstances warranted earlier consideration.

Decisions (1982). ESC: [1]1982/101, 5 Feb.; [2]1982/109, 5 Feb. (no text); [3]1982/148, 7 May (no text).
Provisional agenda. ESC, [4]E/1982/2 & Add.1, [5]E/1982/30 & Add.1.

Calendar of meetings

The Economic and Social Council, acting without vote on a proposal of its President, decided on 10 November 1982 to discontinue the practice of holding resumed second regular sessions as of 1983.[2]

On 7 May, the Council postponed until its second regular session in July consideration of the possibility of rescheduling the annual session of the Commission on Human Rights.[1]

Decisions (1982). ESC: [1]1982/145, 7 May; [2]1982/189, 10 Nov., text following.
Meeting record. ESC: E/1982/SR.57 (10 Nov.).

Economic and Social Council decision 1982/189

Adopted without vote

Oral proposal by President; agenda item 2.

Discontinuation of resumed second regular sessions of the Economic and Social Council

At its 57th plenary meeting, on 10 November 1982, the Council decided to discontinue the practice of holding resumed second regular sessions of the Economic and Social Council as from 1983.

Discontinuance of summary records for sessional committees

On 4 February 1982, the Economic and Social Council decided without vote to discontinue, for an experimental period of two years, providing summary records for its three sessional committees and to keep the existing format of the reports of those committees.[1]

The decision was submitted by the President on the basis of informal consultations.

Decision (1982). [1]ESC: 1982/105, 4 Feb., text following.
Meeting record. ESC: E/1982/SR.2 (4 Feb.).

Economic and Social Council decision 1982/105

Adopted without vote

Draft by President (E/1982/L.11), based on informal consultations; agenda item 3.

Discontinuance of summary records for the sessional committees of the Economic and Social Council

At its 2nd plenary meeting, on 4 February 1982, the Council, recalling its resolution 1981/83 of 24 July 1981, decided:

(a) To discontinue, for an experimental period of two years, the provision of summary records for its sessional committees (First (Economic) Committee, Second (Social) Committee and Third (Programme and Coordination) Committee);

(b) To keep the existing format of the reports of the sessional committees.

Arabic language services

The Economic and Social Council included Arabic among its official languages by a decision of 15 April 1982.[1] It took this action, effective 1 January 1983, without vote on an oral proposal of the President; its rules of procedure were amended accordingly. The Council had decided in May 1981 to pursue such arrangements.[2]

Decision (1982). [1]ESC: 1982/147, 15 Apr., text following.
Decision (prior). [2]ESC: 1981/135, 8 May 1981 (YUN 1981, p. 1092).
Meeting record. ESC: E/1982/SR.8 (15 Apr.).
Publications. Rules of Procedure of the Economic and Social Council (E/5715/Rev.1), Sales No. E.83.I.9; *Rules of Procedure of the Functional Commissions of the Economic and Social Council* (E/5975/Rev.1), Sales No. E.83.I.10.

Economic and Social Council decision 1982/147

Adopted without vote

Oral proposal by President; agenda item 1.

Inclusion of Arabic among the official languages of the Economic and Social Council

At its 8th plenary meeting, on 15 April 1982, the Economic and Social Council, in pursuance of General Assembly resolution 35/219 A of 17 December 1980, decided to include Arabic among its official languages, with effect from 1 January 1983, and to amend rule 32 of its rules of procedure accordingly.

Financial implications of resolutions and decisions

Acting without vote on an oral proposal by its President, the Economic and Social Council, on 30 July 1982,[1] took note of the Secretary-General's report[7] on estimates of programme budget implications of resolutions and decisions adopted during the Council's first and second 1982 regular sessions. The estimates totalled $5,290,100 for 1982-1983, including conference servicing costs at Geneva and New York in the amount of $3,756,400, most of which was subsequently absorbed within the United Nations conference services appropriation of the 1982-1983 programme budget.[3]

As later approved by the General Assembly on the recommendation of its Fifth (Administrative and Budgetary) Committee,[3] the net addition to the 1982-1983 budget resulting from the Council's 1982 resolutions and decisions—excluding conference servicing costs—amounted to $1,146,200, of which $592,600 related to 1982 and $553,600 to 1983. The 1982 figure was included in the package of budget revisions[6] approved by the Fifth Committee on 17 December in connection with the Secretary-General's budget performance report (see ADMINISTRATIVE AND BUDGETARY QUESTIONS, Chapter I). The 1983 figure consisted of $453,600 relating to Council decisions through July 1982, approved by the Fifth Committee on 26 October by 92 votes to 2, with 6 abstentions, and $100,000 in travel costs for advisers at a meeting, authorized by the Council in October, on the draft code of conduct on transnational corporations, with funding approved by the Fifth Committee on 3 December by 73 votes to 10, with 9 abstentions.

The 1983 figure of $453,600 was reduced from the Secretary-General's estimate of $566,000[4] and the $525,000 recommended by the Advisory Committee on Administrative and Budgetary Questions (ACABQ).[2] The Secretary-General's estimate of $130,000 for travel costs[5] was reduced by $30,000 on an oral recommendation of ACABQ.

Decision (1982). [1]ESC: 1982/179, 30 July, text following.
Reports. [2]ACABQ, A/37/7/Add.4; [3]5th Committee, A/37/790; S-G, [4]A/C.5/37/3 & Corr.1 (revised estimates), [5]A/C.5/37/3/Add.1 (revised estimates), [6]A/C.5/37/65, [7]E/1982/109.
Meeting record. ESC: E/1982/SR.51 (30 July).

Economic and Social Council decision 1982/179

Adopted without vote

Oral proposal by President.

Summary of estimates of programme budget implications of resolutions and decisions adopted by the Economic and Social Council during its first and second regular sessions of 1982

At its 51st plenary meeting, on 30 July 1982, the Council took note of the report of the Secretary-General containing the summary of estimates of programme budget implications of resolutions and decisions adopted by the Council during its first and second regular sessions of 1982.

Report for 1982

The work of the Economic and Social Council at its organizational session and two regular sessions in 1982 was summarized in its annual report to the General Assembly.[3] By a decision adopted without vote on 16 November, the Assembly took note of the parts of the report allocated to plenary meetings.[1] Acting without vote on 21 December, the Assembly took note of those parts allocated to the Fifth Committee.[2] The first action was taken on an oral proposal by the Assembly President; the second was approved by the Fifth Committee without objection on 18 December, on an oral proposal of the Chairman. Other parts of the Council's report were considered by the Second

(Economic and Financial) Committee,[4] Third (Social, Humanitarian and Cultural) Committee[5] and Fourth Committee.[6]

Decisions (1982). GA: [1]37/409, 16 Nov., text following; [2]37/446, 21 Dec., text following.
Reports. [3]ESC: A/37/3. GA: [4]2nd Committee, A/37/679 & Add.1; [5]3rd Committee, A/37/745; [6]4th Committee, A/37/625.
Meeting records. GA: plenary, A/37/PV.*69, 114* (16 Nov., 21 Dec.); 5th Committee, A/C.5/37/SR.76 (18 Dec.).

General Assembly decision 37/409

Adopted without vote

Oral proposal by President; agenda item 12.

Report of the Economic and Social Council

At its 69th plenary meeting, on 16 November 1982, the General Assembly took note of chapters I, III (section E), VI (section D), VIII and IX (sections A to C, F, G and H) of the report of the Economic and Social Council.

General Assembly decision 37/446

Adopted without vote

Approved by Fifth Committee (A/37/783) without objection, 18 December (meeting 76); oral proposal by Chairman; agenda item 12.

Report of the Economic and Social Council

At its 114th plenary meeting, on 21 December 1982, the General Assembly, on the recommendation of the Fifth Committee, took note of chapters II, III (sections A to G and K), IV (sections A to C and E to K), V, VI (sections A to C and E), VII, VIII and IX (sections C, E, H, J and K) of the report of the Economic and Social Council.

Restructuring the economic and social sectors of the UN system

Two reports were submitted in 1982 to the General Assembly on specific aspects of the ongoing process of restructuring the economic and social sectors of the United Nations system, initiated by the Assembly in 1977.[8] The first, by the Joint Inspection Unit (JIU),[4] contained recommendations for programming, operational and other issues confronting the Economic Commission for Africa (ECA) (see Chapter VIII of this section). The second report, by the Secretary-General,[5] described action taken to improve inter-agency co-ordination (see above).

By a decision of 30 July 1982,[1] the Economic and Social Council took note of two 1981 documents on restructuring submitted by the Secretary-General:[9] one described arrangements put into effect for streamlining United Nations economic and social activities, and the other commented on a JIU report on the relationships between the Director-General for Development and International Economic Co-operation and United Nations Secretariat entities.

The General Assembly, in a decision adopted without vote on 20 December,[2] requested the Secretary-General to implement the 1981 JIU recommendations on the Director-General's relationships with other Secretariat entities along the

lines he had indicated in his comments. It decided to review restructuring again in 1984 and every three years thereafter, and requested the Secretary-General to propose further action on the subject. Noting a suggestion made in May by the Governing Council of the United Nations Environment Programme that the Council meet biennially rather than annually (see Chapter XVI of this section), the Assembly invited its other subsidiary bodies in the economic and social fields to consider similar possibilities, and invited the Economic and Social Council to submit recommendations on the matter in 1984.

On other aspects of restructuring, the Assembly: requested its President to undertake consultations on the organization and rationalization of work of United Nations intergovernmental bodies in the economic and social fields (see above); endorsed a July Economic and Social Council resolution on regional programming, operations, restructuring and decentralization issues with respect to ECA;[6] and noted the Secretary-General's report on improving inter-agency co-ordination.

This decision was approved without vote by the Assembly's Second Committee on 13 December. It was submitted by a Committee Vice-Chairman on the basis of informal consultations on a 13-nation draft[3] introduced by Jamaica and later withdrawn.

The approved decision omitted a sentence in the original draft by which the Assembly would have decided to review the implementation of its 1977 call to improve its effectiveness in the economic and social fields. Also omitted was a request that the Secretary-General report on implementation of the JIU recommendations and make proposals for further action. The final version added the request for a report by the Secretary-General on restructuring, stipulated that the issue would be considered every three years instead of every two, and specified that the triennial review was without prejudice to future decisions on the periodicity of such consideration.

Other changes concerned improving inter-agency co-ordination and restructuring of ECA.

The Assembly, in a resolution of 20 December[7] on regional programming, restructuring and decentralization issues affecting ECA and other United Nations organizations, approved several measures to improve their functioning and called for a study of new approaches to regional and subregional programming and management.

Decisions (1982). [1]ESC: 1982/177, paras. *(i)* & *(j)*, 30 July. [2]GA: 37/442, 20 Dec., text following.
Draft decision withdrawn. [3]Algeria, Argentina, Belgium, Canada, Denmark, Jamaica, Nigeria, Philippines, Sudan, Sweden, Trinidad and Tobago, Uganda, Yugoslavia, A/C.2/37/L.72.

Reports. (4)JIU, A/37/119; (5)S-G, A/37/439.
Resolutions (1982). (6)ESC: 1982/63, 30 July. (7)GA: 37/214, 20 Dec.
Resolution (prior). (8)GA: 32/197, 20 Dec. 1977 (YUN 1977, p. 438).
Yearbook reference. (9)1981, p. 1093.
Meeting records. GA: 2nd Committee, A/C.2/37/SR.20-26, *43, 48* (25 Oct.–13 Dec.); plenary, A/37/PV.113 (20 Dec.).

General Assembly decision 37/442

Adopted without vote

Approved by Second Committee (A/37/680/Add.7) without vote, 13 December (meeting 48); draft by Vice-Chairman (A/C.2/37/L.120), based on informal consultations on 13-nation draft (A/C.2/37/L.72); agenda item 71 *(h)*.

Restructuring of the economic and social sectors of the United Nations system

At its 113th plenary meeting, on 20 December 1982, the General Assembly, on the recommendation of the Second Committee, having considered the draft resolution on the implementation of section II of the annex to its resolution 32/197—the consideration of which it had referred, during its thirty-sixth session, to its thirty-seventh session—the report of the Economic and Social Council on revitalization of the Council, the reports of the Joint Inspection Unit entitled "Relationships between the Director-General for Development and International Economic Co-operation and entities of the United Nations Secretariat" and "Economic Commission for Africa: regional programming, operations, restructuring and decentralization issues", together with the comments of the Secretary-General thereon, the report of the Secretary-General on the implementation of section VII of the annex to resolution 32/197, Economic and Social Council resolution 1982/63 of 30 July 1982 on regional programming, operations, restructuring and decentralization issues with respect to the Economic Commission for Africa, as well as the report of the Secretary-General on the implementation of section VIII of the annex to resolution 32/197, decided:

I

(a) To welcome Economic and Social Council resolution 1982/50 of 28 July 1982;

(b) To request the President of the General Assembly, in close co-ordination with the President of the Economic and Social Council, to undertake consultations regarding the organization and rationalization of work of the intergovernmental bodies of the United Nations system in the economic and social fields, and to submit a report thereon to the Assembly at its thirty-ninth session;

(c) To refer to its thirty-ninth session, for consideration, the draft resolution on the implementation of section II of the annex to General Assembly resolution 32/197;

II

(a) To take note of section III of decision 10/I adopted on 31 May 1982 by the Governing Council of the United Nations Environment Programme;

(b) To invite its other subsidiary intergovernmental organs and bodies in the economic and social fields, if they deem it desirable, also to consider similar possibilities and to submit their views and recommendations to the Economic and Social Council for consideration at its second regular session of 1984;

(c) To invite the Economic and Social Council to submit to the General Assembly, at its thirty-ninth session, concrete recommendations on this section of the present decision, having due regard to its own measures for revitalization and in the light of its consideration of the views and recommendations requested above;

III

To endorse Economic and Social Council resolution 1982/63 on regional programming, operations, restructuring and decentralization issues with respect to the Economic Commission for Africa;

IV

To take note of the report of the Secretary-General on the implementation of section VII of the annex to General Assembly resolution 32/197;

V

(a) To take note of the recommendations of the Joint Inspection Unit with respect to relationships between the Director-General for Development and International Economic Co-operation and entities of the United Nations Secretariat, and of the comments of the Secretary-General thereon, as well as of the report of the Secretary-General on the implementation of section VIII of the annex to General Assembly resolution 32/197;

(b) To request the Secretary-General to undertake implementation of the aforementioned recommendations along the lines indicated in his comments;

VI

(a) To review the implementation of all aspects of General Assembly resolution 32/197 during its next consideration of the subject of restructuring of the economic and social sectors of the United Nations system, which will be undertaken at its thirty-ninth session and thereafter only once every three years, without prejudice to its future decisions regarding the periodicity of such consideration;

(b) To request the Secretary-General, in this regard, to submit to the General Assembly at its thirty-ninth session a report including, as appropriate, proposals for further action on the implementation of sections III to VIII of the annex to resolution 32/197.

Trusteeship and decolonization

Chapter I

General questions relating to colonial countries

Contents

General aspects

In 1982, the General Assembly's Special Committee on the Situation with regard to the Implementation of the Declaration on the Granting of Independence to Colonial Countries and Peoples continued consideration of the implementation by international organizations of the Assembly's 1960 Declaration[2], foreign interests impeding implementation of the Declaration, military bases, information dissemination, information on the Territories supplied by their administering Powers and visiting missions of the Committee. In addition, it urged the United States to adopt measures for the transfer of all powers to the people of Puerto Rico.

Aside from the general questions on decolonization, the Committee examined the situations pertaining to the following individual Territories: Trust Territory of the Pacific Islands, Namibia,

Falkland Islands (Malvinas), East Timor, Western Sahara, American Samoa, Anguilla, Bermuda, British Virgin Islands, Brunei, Cayman Islands, Cocos (Keeling) Islands, Gibraltar, Guam, Montserrat, Pitcairn, St. Helena, St. Kitts–Nevis, Tokelau, Turks and Caicos Islands, United States Virgin Islands.

The 25-member Committee held two sessions in 1982 at United Nations Headquarters—from 1 March to 1 July and from 2 August to 20 September—and also held an extra-sessional meeting on 8 November to consider the report of its visiting mission to Montserrat. The Committee's subsidiary bodies, the Sub-Committee on Petitions, Information and Assistance and the Sub-Committee on Small Territories, met between 3 May and 6 August and between 4 May and 29 July, respectively.

In its report submitted in September to the General Assembly,[1] the Committee made a series of recommendations for action by the assembly.

Report. [1]Committee on colonial countries. A/37/23/Rev.1.
Resolution. [2]GA: 1514(XV), 14 Dec. 1960 (YUN 1960, p. 49).

Implementation of the 1960 Declaration on colonial countries

By a resolution of 23 November[3] on the implementation of the Declaration, the Assembly again called on administering Powers to enable dependent peoples to exercise their right to self-determination and independence, termed the continuation of colonialism a serious threat to international peace and security, and called for the speedy eradication of colonialism in all its forms, including racism, *apartheid*, economic exploitation and the suppression of national liberation movements. These views had also been affirmed in a resolution[2] on the self-determination of peoples adopted on 25 February by the Commission on Human Rights. The Assembly also reaffirmed recognition of the legitimacy of the struggle, by all necessary means, of peoples under colonial and alien domination to exercise their right to self-determination and independence.

Calling on States to give effect to the recommendations of the Committee on colonial countries, the Assembly requested the Committee to formulate proposals for the elimination of the remaining manifestations of colonialism. The Committee was also asked to make suggestions to the Security Council with regard to developments in colonial Territories that were likely to threaten international peace and security, to continue to examine compliance by Member States with resolutions on decolonization, to pay particular attention to the needs of the small Territories and to enlist world-wide support for the implementation of United Nations resolutions regarding decolonization.

The Assembly also condemned the activities of foreign interests impeding decolonization, particularly in Namibia; called for a halt to collaboration with South Africa; requested that all States withhold assistance from that Government until Namibia exercised self-determination; called for the withdrawal of military bases from colonial Territories; urged all States to provide assistance to the people of Namibia; and requested the administering Powers to strengthen the economies of the Territories under their administration. Those Powers were also called on to permit access of United Nations visiting missions to the Territories to secure first-hand information.

The resolution, sponsored by 28 nations and introduced by Trinidad and Tobago, was adopted by a recorded vote of 141 to 2, with 8 abstentions.

In another resolution, of 3 December, on the self-determination of peoples,[4] the Assembly urged all States to intensify support for peoples under colonial domination in their struggle for self-determination and independence.

Austria, Colombia, the Netherlands, New Zealand, Norway (on behalf of the five Nordic countries) and Portugal expressed reservations on paragraph 4 of the 23 November resolution concerning the legitimacy of the self-determination struggle by all means at the disposal of the people concerned; they felt that the United Nations should encourage only peaceful settlement of disputes.

Reservations on other points were expressed by the following: the Netherlands on the wording of paragraph 2; Iraq, the Netherlands and Portugal on collaboration with South Africa; and Ireland, the Netherlands, New Zealand, Norway (for the Nordic States), Portugal and Turkey on military bases in colonial countries. Japan could not support parts of the Committee's report[1] and therefore reserved its position on paragraph 5 of the resolution approving the report.

In the Assembly's plenary debate preceding adoption of the 23 November resolution, many speakers praised the significant advances made towards decolonization during the past two decades, while being critical of South Africa for not having allowed this process to take place in Namibia. Cyprus said that, since the adoption of the 1960 Declaration, more than 70 million people had attained independence—and Algeria noted that 57 new States had joined the United Nations—but there were still more than 4 million people in the remaining colonial Territories. Czechoslovakia added that some 0.3 per cent of the current world population was subject to colonial oppression, as was almost 1 per cent of its territory. According to the Syrian Arab Republic, over 4 million people in more than 20 countries were still deprived of autonomy, 4 million Palestinians were denied self-determination in their own land, and some 20 million Africans in South Africa and Namibia remained subject to persecution and military occupation.

Poland believed efforts could be made to mark the year 1985, the twenty-fifth anniversary of the adoption of the Declaration, with the final eradication of colonialism or with considerable progress made towards attaining that goal.

Cyprus, India, the Syrian Arab Republic and Tunisia called the situation of the Palestinians a colonial issue, while Algeria, Czechoslovakia, the Lao People's Democratic Republic, Liberia, Madagascar, the United Republic of Tanzania and Zambia said that attention must also be given to the peoples of the small Territories awaiting self-determination and independence.

India stressed the need for educating the people of Non-Self-Governing Territories in respect of the options available to them for their future, and Sierra Leone spoke of the duty of the Organization to help those people determine their own destiny. The Libyan Arab Jamahiriya and Tunisia saw use or abuse of the veto in the Security Council as preventing full implementation of the Declaration.

The United States asserted that it had redoubled its efforts to bring about a stable, negotiated independence for Namibia and had sought to ensure the right of self-determination for the people of American Samoa, Guam, Micronesia, the United States Virgin Islands and Puerto Rico; it charged that a small group of politically motivated States led by the USSR sought to impose on the Committee on colonial countries and on the Assembly its ideological views, including the inaccurate premise that self-determination could only result in independence.

The USSR replied that the Western countries were trying to impose rules on the Committee that would allow the colonial Powers to block any Committee actions with which they did not agree; it asserted that the United States aided South Africa and tried to annex Micronesia (see Chapter II of this section), and that colonialism persisted because of the United States.

The United Kingdom said there was a strain in the Committee's tradition of consensus as a result of departures from procedure in the handling of certain contentious texts and the tendency to seek out new problems with divisive and confrontational impact which would more properly be dealt with by other bodies; it wondered if some members of that Committee were more concerned with their own politicking than with the welfare of the peoples whose interests and aspirations they were meant to be serving. The Committee Chairman, in response, denied that there had been any change in the Committee's procedures and stated that the Committee had dealt only with items clearly covered by its mandate, allowing ample time for debate. Bulgaria said the colonial Powers continued their attempts to downgrade the Committee's contribution and to foil its efforts to implement the Declaration in all colonial Territories.

Report. [1]Committee on colonial countries, A/37/23/Rev.1.
Resolutions (1982). [2]Commission on Human Rights (report, E/1982/12): 1982/16, paras. 1 & 13, 25 Feb. GA: [3]37/35, 23 Nov., text following; [4]37/43, para. 28, 3 Dec.
Financial implications. 5th Committee report, A/37/636; S-G statement, A/C.5/37/47.
Meeting records. GA: 4th Committee, A/C.4/37/SR.9-15, 17-24 (26 Oct.-16 Nov.); 5th Committee, A/C.5/37/SR.41 (22 Nov.); plenary, A/37/PV.74-76, 77 (22, 23 Nov.).

General Assembly resolution 37/35

23 November 1982   Meeting 77   141-2-8 (recorded vote)

28-nation draft (A/37/L.32 and Add.1); agenda item 18.

Sponsors: Algeria, Barbados, Bulgaria, Byelorussian SSR, Congo, Cuba, Cyprus, Czechoslovakia, Ethiopia, German Democratic Republic, Grenada, Guyana, Hungary, India, Lao People's Democratic Republic, Madagascar, Mali, Mongolia, Poland, Saint Lucia, Sierra Leone, Syrian Arab Republic, Trinidad and Tobago, Ukrainian SSR, United Republic of Tanzania, Viet Nam, Yugoslavia, Zambia.

Implementation of the Declaration on the Granting of Independence to Colonial Countries and Peoples

The General Assembly,

Having examined the report of the Special Committee on the Situation with regard to the Implementation of the Declaration on the Granting of Independence to Colonial Countries and Peoples,

Recalling its resolutions 1514(XV) of 14 December 1960, containing the Declaration on the Granting of Independence to Colonial Countries and Peoples, 2621(XXV) of 12 October 1970, containing the programme of action for the full implementation of the Declaration, and 35/118 of 11 December 1980, the annex to which contains the Plan of Action for the Full Implementation of the Declaration,

Recalling all its previous resolutions concerning the implementation of the Declaration, in particular resolution 36/68 of 1 December 1981, as well as the relevant resolutions of the Security Council,

Recalling the relevant provisions of the Special Declaration on Namibia, adopted by the International Conference on Sanctions against South Africa,

Condemning the continued colonialist and racist repression of millions of Africans, particularly in Namibia, by the Government of South Africa through its persistent, illegal occupation of the international Territory and its intransigent attitude towards all efforts being made to bring about an internationally acceptable solution to the situation obtaining in the Territory,

Deeply conscious of the urgent need to take all necessary measures to eliminate forthwith the remaining vestiges of colonialism, particularly in respect of Namibia where desperate attempts by South Africa to perpetuate its illegal occupation have brought untold suffering and bloodshed to the people,

Strongly condemning the policies of those States which, in defiance of the relevant resolutions of the United Nations, have continued to collaborate with the Government of South Africa in its domination of the people of Namibia,

Conscious that the success of the national liberation struggle and the resultant international situation have provided the international community with a unique opportunity to make a decisive contribution towards the total elimination of colonialism in all its forms and manifestations in Africa,

Noting with satisfaction the work accomplished by the Special Committee with a view to securing the effective and complete implementation of the Declaration and the other relevant resolutions of the United Nations,

Noting also with satisfaction the co-operation and active participation of the administering Powers concerned in the relevant work of the Special Committee, as well as the continued readiness of the Governments concerned to receive United Nations visiting missions in the Territories under their administration,

Reiterating its conviction that the total eradication of racial discrimination, *apartheid* and violations of the basic human rights of the peoples of colonial Territories will be achieved most expeditiously by the faithful and complete implementation of the Declaration, particularly in Namibia, and by the speediest possible complete elimination of the presence of the illegal occupying régimes therefrom,

1. *Reaffirms* its resolutions 1514(XV), 2621(XXV) and 36/68 and all other resolutions on decolonization and calls upon the administering Powers, in accordance with those resolutions, to take all necessary steps to enable the dependent peoples of the Territories concerned to exercise fully and without further delay their inalienable right to self-determination and independence;

2. *Affirms once again* that the continuation of colonialism in all its forms and manifestations—including racism, *apartheid*, the exploitation by foreign and other interests of economic and human resources and the waging of colonial wars to suppress national liberation movements—is incompatible with the Charter of the United Nations,

the Universal Declaration of Human Rights and the Declaration on the Granting of Independence to Colonial Countries and Peoples and poses a serious threat to international peace and security;

3. *Reaffirms its determination* to take all necessary steps with a view to the complete and speedy eradication of colonialism and to the faithful and strict observance by all States of the relevant provisions of the Charter, the Declaration on the Granting of Independence to Colonial Countries and Peoples and the guiding principles of the Universal Declaration of Human Rights;

4. *Affirms once again* its recognition of the legitimacy of the struggle of the peoples under colonial and alien domination to exercise their right to self-determination and independence by all the necessary means at their disposal;

5. *Approves* the report of the Special Committee on the Situation with regard to the Implementation of the Declaration on the Granting of Independence to Colonial Countries and Peoples covering its work during 1982, including the programme of work envisaged for 1983;

6. *Calls upon* all States, in particular the administering Powers, and the specialized agencies and other organizations of the United Nations system to give effect to the recommendations contained in the report of the Special Committee for the speedy implementation of the Declaration and the other relevant resolutions of the United Nations;

7. *Condemns* the continuing activities of foreign economic and other interests which are impeding the implementation of the Declaration with respect to the colonial Territories, particularly Namibia;

8. *Strongly condemns* all collaboration, particularly in the nuclear and military fields, with the Government of South Africa and calls upon the States concerned to cease forthwith all such collaboration;

9. *Requests* all States, directly and through their action in the specialized agencies and other organizations of the United Nations system, to withhold assistance of any kind from the Government of South Africa until the inalienable right of the people of Namibia to self-determination and independence within a united and integrated Namibia, including Walvis Bay, has been restored, and to refrain from taking any action which might imply recognition of the legitimacy of the illegal occupation of Namibia by that régime;

10. *Calls upon* the colonial Powers to withdraw immediately and unconditionally their military bases and installations from colonial Territories and to refrain from establishing new ones;

11. *Urges* all States, directly and through their action in the specialized agencies and other organizations of the United Nations system, to provide all moral and material assistance to the oppressed people of Namibia and, in respect of the other Territories, requests the administering Powers, in consultation with the Governments of the Territories under their administration, to take steps to enlist and make effective use of all possible assistance, on both a bilateral and a multilateral basis, in the strengthening of the economies of those Territories;

12. *Requests* the Special Committee to continue to seek suitable means for the immediate and full implementation of General Assembly resolution 1514(XV) in all Territories that have not yet attained independence and, in particular:

(a) To formulate specific proposals for the elimination of the remaining manifestations of colonialism and to report thereon to the General Assembly at its thirty-eighth session;

(b) To make concrete suggestions which could assist the Security Council in considering appropriate measures under the Charter with regard to developments in colonial Territories that are likely to threaten international peace and security;

(c) To continue to examine the compliance of Member States with the Declaration and with other relevant resolutions on decolonization, particularly those relating to Namibia;

(d) To continue to pay particular attention to the small Territories, including the sending of visiting missions thereto, as appropriate, and to recommend to the General Assembly the most suitable steps to be taken to enable the populations of those Territories to exercise their right to self-determination, freedom and independence;

(e) To take all necessary steps to enlist world-wide support among Governments, as well as national and international organizations having a special interest in decolonization, in the achievement of the objectives of the Declaration and in the implementation of the relevant resolutions of the United Nations, particularly as concerns the oppressed people of Namibia;

13. *Calls upon* the administering Powers to continue to co-operate with the Special Committee in the discharge of its mandate and, in

particular, to permit the access of visiting missions to the Territories to secure first-hand information and ascertain the wishes and aspirations of their inhabitants;

14. *Requests* the Secretary-General to provide the Special Committee with the facilities and services required for the implementation of the present resolution, as well as of the various resolutions and decisions on decolonization adopted by the General Assembly and the Special Committee.

Recorded vote in Assembly as follows:

In favour: Afghanistan, Albania, Algeria, Angola, Antigua and Barbuda, Argentina, Australia, Austria, Bahamas, Bahrain, Bangladesh, Barbados, Belize, Benin, Bhutan, Bolivia, Botswana, Brazil, Bulgaria, Burma, Burundi, Byelorussian SSR, Cape Verde, Central African Republic, Chad, Chile, China, Colombia, Congo, Costa Rica, Cuba, Cyprus, Czechoslovakia, Democratic Kampuchea, Democratic Yemen, Denmark, Djibouti, Dominica, Dominican Republic, Ecuador, Egypt, El Salvador, Ethiopia, Fiji, Finland, Gabon, Gambia, German Democratic Republic, Ghana, Greece, Grenada, Guinea, Guinea-Bissau, Guyana, Haiti, Honduras, Hungary, Iceland, India, Indonesia, Iran, Iraq, Ireland, Ivory Coast, Jamaica, Japan, Jordan, Kenya, Kuwait, Lao People's Democratic Republic, Lebanon, Lesotho, Liberia, Libyan Arab Jamahiriya, Madagascar, Malaysia, Maldives, Mali, Malta, Mauritania, Mauritius, Mexico, Mongolia, Morocco, Mozambique, Nepal, Netherlands, New Zealand, Nicaragua, Niger, Nigeria, Norway, Oman, Pakistan, Panama, Papua New Guinea, Peru, Philippines, Poland, Portugal, Qatar, Romania, Rwanda, Saint Lucia, Samoa, Sao Tome and Principe, Saudi Arabia, Senegal, Seychelles, Sierra Leone, Singapore, Solomon Islands, Somalia, Spain, Sri Lanka, Sudan, Suriname, Swaziland, Sweden, Syrian Arab Republic, Thailand, Togo, Trinidad and Tobago, Tunisia, Turkey, Uganda, Ukrainian SSR, USSR, United Arab Emirates, United Republic of Cameroon, United Republic of Tanzania, Upper Volta, Uruguay, Vanuatu, Venezuela, Viet Nam, Yemen, Yugoslavia, Zaire, Zambia, Zimbabwe.

Against: United Kingdom, United States.

Abstaining: Belgium, Canada, France, Germany, Federal Republic of, Israel, Italy, Luxembourg, Malawi.

Implementation by international organizations

In response to a series of calls by the General Assembly for implementation of its 1960 Declaration, a number of specialized agencies and organizations in the United Nations system continued in 1982 to provide assistance to peoples of colonial countries and their national liberation movements, particularly in Namibia and the rest of southern Africa. In a resolution adopted on 23 November,[7] the Assembly continued to encourage such activity while expressing concern that the level of assistance was inadequate to the task.

Such assistance activities in 1981 were described in a report by the Secretary-General in April 1982 (with later addenda)[3] which summarized replies by 18 United Nations organizations in response to a November 1981 request of the Assembly[10] for information on action taken by them to implement the Declaration and other Assembly resolutions on decolonization. While most of the activities related to southern Africa, a number of programmes were intended for refugees from colonial Territories, or for Non-Self-Governing Territories and newly independent countries.

Among the 1982 activities, the Food and Agriculture Organization of the United Nations emphasized the development of food self-sufficiency in refugee communities and the training of personnel for the formulation of agricultural policies. The International Labour Organisation increased the regular budgetary resources allocated to technical assistance activities for the front-line and neighbouring States and the liberation movements recognized by the Organization of African Unity (OAU). The United Nations Educational, Scientific and Cultural Organization sponsored a series of meetings on the themes of education, human rights and racial prejudice, including a seminar in Paris from 29 March to 2 April on the history of resistance in South Africa.

The total 1982 allocation by the United Nations Development Programme (UNDP) for development assistance to national liberation movements amounted to approximately $2.5 million, of which some $400,000 was from the United Nations Trust Fund for Assistance to Colonial Countries and Peoples. Allocation from the Fund went to health assistance training and for movements' representation at meetings convened by UNDP; other UNDP assistance included education and training programmes for members of national liberation movements in southern Africa, including some in countries of asylum such as the United Republic of Tanzania. The Fund received no additional contributions in 1982.[4]

Co-ordination of assistance by the United Nations system to colonial countries and peoples was again the subject of consultations between the President of the Economic and Social Council and the Chairman of the Committee on colonial countries. The latest of these meetings, held annually in recent years, had been requested by the General Assembly in November 1981.[10] In a May 1982 report to the Council,[2] the Council President summarized his discussions with the Committee Chairman, which focused principally on assistance to southern African liberation movements. They called for increased flow of funds in support of assistance programmes for Namibia, expressed satisfaction that national liberation movements continued to be represented at relevant meetings of United Nations organizations, hoped that further steps would be taken to strengthen co-ordination of assistance to these movements and agreed that measures to withhold assistance from the Government of South Africa should be strengthened.

On 7 May, at its fifth session, the Commission on Human Settlements strongly condemned the South African Government's racial policies, its occupation of Namibia and its aggression against neighbouring States, and urged the Executive Director of the United Nations Centre for Human Settlements to intensify efforts to assist the victims of *apartheid*.[5]

Economic and Social Council action. At its second regular session of 1982, the Economic and Social Council, by a 27 July resolution,[6] endorsed the observations and suggestions contained in its President's May report and recommended that all Governments intensify efforts in the specialized agencies and other organizations within the United Nations system of which they were members to ensure the full and effective implementation of the Declaration and other relevant resolutions.

The Council reaffirmed that the United Nations system of organizations should extend all the necessary moral and material assistance to the colonial peoples and their national liberation movements, and ensure financially and otherwise participation of movement representatives in relevant meetings. It urged that those organizations include in the agenda of their governing bodies a separate item on the implementation of decolonization resolutions, and that their executive heads give priority to drawing up concrete proposals in that regard, with OAU co-operation. It requested continued consultations between its President and the Chairman of the Committee on colonial countries, as well as a follow-up report by the Secretary-General in 1983.

The Council also called for increased assistance to Namibians, intensified support for the oppressed peoples of South Africa, and membership of the United Nations Council for Namibia in United Nations organizations.

The 26-nation resolution, introduced by Nigeria, was adopted by 43 votes to 1, with 7 abstentions, following its approval in the Council's Third (Programme and Co-ordination) Committee on 21 July by 23 votes to 1, with 7 abstentions.

Explaining its vote against the resolution, the United States said that, while it felt that implementation of a 1978 Security Council resolution[11] was the only constructive means to end the conflict in southern Africa, it continued to oppose United Nations assistance to national liberation movements, including the South West Africa People's Organization (SWAPO), which it did not regard as the sole and authentic representative of the Namibian people.

Among those which abstained, Canada said that it could not support the trend towards financing liberation movements from the United Nations regular budget. France felt that it was not the mission of United Nations agencies to assist liberation movements, particularly through initiatives which appeared to be selective and discriminatory. The Federal Republic of Germany said that there were references in the text unsuited to the tasks of the agencies, while Portugal viewed some references as discriminatory, including the mention of certain General Assembly resolutions. The United Kingdom cited reservations it had expressed in connection with the Council's 1981 resolution,[9] namely provisions on Namibia and language used with regard to South Africa.

Austria said its support for the resolution could not prejudge its position on the autonomy of the specialized agencies. Japan stated that, although it had voted in favour, it could not accept some of the resolution's provisions, and Colombia expressed reservations about references to SWAPO as the sole legitimate representative of the Namibian people.

Action by the Committee on colonial countries. By a resolution of 20 August,[(1)] the Committee on colonial countries reaffirmed the role of the specialized agencies and other organizations of the United Nations system in assisting the colonial peoples and their national liberation movements. In addition to those paragraphs similar in substance to the text adopted by the Economic and Social Council, the Committee's 25-paragraph resolution called for termination of what it called the persistent collaboration between the International Monetary Fund (IMF) and South Africa, urged that body to discuss its relations with South Africa at its annual meeting in September 1982, and recommended the sending in 1983 of a high-level mission to IMF which, subject to the agreement of the other bodies involved, would be composed of the Chairman of the Committee on colonial countries, the President of the United Nations Council for Namibia and the Chairman of the Special Committee against *Apartheid*.

By this text, which was adopted by 22 votes to none, with 2 abstentions, the Committee on colonial countries also expressed concern that the assistance given by certain agencies and organizations of the United Nations system to the Namibian people and SWAPO had been inadequate, and requested them to discontinue all support to the Government of South Africa until that régime restored to the Namibians their right to self-determination and independence.

The Committee's Sub-Committee on Petitions, Information and Assistance, in its conclusions and recommendations submitted to the parent body, had urged intensification of assistance to the colonial peoples and their national liberation movements, expressed concern at what it said was the lack of proper communication between some national liberation movements and certain specialized agencies and other United Nations organizations, and called on the latter to withhold financial, economic, technical or other assistance from the Government of South Africa. It recommended that the Committee request the General Assembly to hold accountable those agencies and organizations which continued to extend assistance to that Government.

Other parts of the Sub-Committee's conclusions and recommendations dealt with developments in Namibia and the relationship between IMF and South Africa.

General Assembly action. On 23 November, the General Assembly adopted a resolution[(7)] recommending that the specialized agencies and other organizations and institutions of the United Nations system continue to render moral and material assistance to colonial peoples and their national liberation movements, as well as to newly independent and emerging States. It called for these organizations to broaden contacts with colonial peoples and their liberation movements, to provide them with speedy assistance in their struggle for self-determination and independence, and to enable their representatives to participate as observers in relevant meetings of these bodies. It also urged United Nations organizations to extend substantial material assistance to the front-line States in order to enable them to support the struggle of the Namibian people for independence.

The Assembly requested the Secretary-General to continue to assist those organizations to implement the Declaration and related resolutions, called for continued consultations between the Economic and Social Council and the Committee on colonial countries on means to improve coordination of activities in that sphere, and asked for reports in 1983 from both the Committee and the Secretary-General.

Further, the Assembly urged the United Nations agencies and organizations to increase assistance to SWAPO and to the United Nations Institute for Namibia and the Nationhood Programme for Namibia, requested that all support to South Africa from the United Nations system be withheld until Namibia was independent and called for an end to collaboration between IMF and South Africa.

The Assembly adopted the resolution by a recorded vote of 128 to 4, with 20 abstentions; the seventh preambular paragraph, containing a reference to support to the Pretoria régime by the United States and other Western States and mentioning SWAPO as the sole and authentic representative of the people of Namibia, was adopted by a recorded vote of 87 to 26, with 27 abstentions.

The text, recommended by the Committee on colonial countries, had been approved on 16 November by the Assembly's Fourth Committee by a recorded vote, requested by the United States, of 110 to 4, with 21 abstentions. In the course of its debate on the subject, the Fourth Committee granted a request for hearing and subsequently heard a statement on 19 October by Jim Morrell of the Center for International Policy.

In a related action, the Assembly, in a 3 December resolution on the self-determination of peoples,[(8)] called for a substantial increase in assistance to those under colonial rule.

Explaining in the Assembly plenary its negative vote on the 23 November resolution, the United States objected to the recognition of SWAPO as the sole authentic representative of the Namibian people in the absence of free elections;

viewed as inappropriate the call for United Nations agencies to provide aid to SWAPO or to other national liberation movements, particularly those engaged in warfare, as such action politicized the agencies, undermined their effectiveness and jeopardized support to them; and termed the seventh preambular paragraph an irresponsible accusation, totally contrary to its continuing search for negotiated independence in Namibia.

While voting in favour of the text as a whole, Botswana and Samoa had reservations regarding the wording of paragraphs 6 and 7 on collaboration between IMF and South Africa. Bolivia and Samoa expressed reservations on the seventh preambular paragraph.

Ghana, which voted in favour, said certain IMF member States with great power and influence used that body to serve their political motives and designs in the third world; the agencies and organizations within the United Nations system had the duty not to participate in the crime of *apartheid* but to promote implementation of the Declaration on colonial countries.

In explanation of vote in the Fourth Committee, Belgium and the United Kingdom, voting against the text, said it contained provisions contrary to the principle of universality and respect for independence of the specialized agencies. Similar views were expressed by Finland (for the Nordic countries), France, the Federal Republic of Germany and the Netherlands, which all abstained, and by Chile, which voted in favour.

Belgium and the United Kingdom especially objected to the paragraphs questioning South Africa's membership in the World Bank and IMF and containing criticisms of the activities of those organizations. Objections to those paragraphs were also made by France, the Federal Republic of Germany, Ireland and the Netherlands, which all abstained. Although voting in favour of the resolution, reservations on these paragraphs were made by Chile, Colombia, the Dominican Republic, Fiji, Greece, Malawi and Uruguay.

Belgium and the United Kingdom, joined by Finland (for the Nordic countries), the Federal Republic of Germany and the Netherlands, rejected what they called the arbitrary and unjustified attacks made on certain Member States accused as being responsible for the policy followed by South Africa. Although voting for the resolution, Greece, the Sudan and Turkey voiced similar reservations.

The Netherlands asserted that the Namibian people should be allowed to choose their own representatives in free and fair elections under United Nations supervision and control in accordance with the Security Council's 1978 resolution.[11] The United Kingdom and Uruguay shared that view. Belgium stated that conflicts between nations must be solved on the basis of the rule of international law.

Kenya, voting in favour, and the United Kingdom, voting against, expressed appreciation of the assistance provided by the specialized agencies to the Non-Self-Governing Territories. Although voting affirmatively, Sri Lanka had reservations on certain paragraphs.

Reports. [1]Committee on colonial countries, A/37/23/Rev.1; [2]ESC President, E/1982/65; [3]S-G, A/37/177 & Add.1-3; [4]UNDP Administrator, DP/1983/6/Add.3.

Resolutions (1982). [5]Commission on Human Settlements (report, A/37/8): 5/19, 7 May. [6]ESC: 1982/47, 27 July, text following. GA: [7]37/32, 23 Nov., text following; [8]37/43, para. 27, 3 Dec.

Resolutions (prior). [9]ESC: 1981/54, 22 July 1981 (YUN 1981, p. 1101). [10]GA: 36/52, 24 Nov. 1981 (*ibid.*, p. 1102). [11]SC: 435(1978), 29 Sep. 1978, (YUN 1978, p. 915).

Meeting records. ESC: E/1982/SR.48 (27 July). GA: 4th Committee, A/C.4/37/SR.9-11, 13, 14, 17-23, *24* (26 Oct.–16 Nov.); plenary, A/37/PV.77 (23 Nov.).

Economic and Social Council resolution 1982/47

27 July 1982   Meeting 48   43-1-7

Approved by Third Committee (E/1982/93) by vote (23-1-7), 21 July (meeting 13); 26-nation draft (E/1982/C.3/L.5); agenda items 22 and 23.

Sponsors: Algeria, Bahamas, Bangladesh, Benin, Cuba, Egypt, Ethiopia, India, Iraq, Jordan, Kenya, Liberia, Libyan Arab Jamahiriya, Nepal, Nigeria, Pakistan, Qatar, Saint Lucia, Senegal, Sudan, Swaziland, Trinidad and Tobago, Tunisia, Venezuela, Yugoslavia, Zaire.

Implementation of the Declaration on the Granting of Independence to Colonial Countries and Peoples by the specialized agencies and the international institutions associated with the United Nations and assistance to the oppressed people of South Africa and their national liberation movement by agencies and institutions within the United Nations system

The Economic and Social Council,

Having examined the report of the Secretary-General and the reports of the President of the Economic and Social Council concerning the items entitled "Implementation of the Declaration on the Granting of Independence to Colonial Countries and Peoples by the specialized agencies and the international institutions associated with the United Nations" and "Assistance to the oppressed people of South Africa and their national liberation movement by agencies and institutions within the United Nations system",

Having heard the statements of the Chairman of the Special Committee on the Situation with regard to the Implementation of the Declaration on the Granting of Independence to Colonial Countries and Peoples and the Acting Chairman of the Special Committee against *Apartheid,*

Recalling General Assembly resolution 1514(XV) of 14 December 1960, containing the Declaration on the Granting of Independence to Colonial Countries and Peoples, and all other resolutions adopted by United Nations bodies on this subject, including in particular Assembly resolution 36/52 of 24 November 1981 and Council resolution 1981/54 of 22 July 1981,

Reaffirming the responsibility of the specialized agencies and other organizations within the United Nations system to take all effective measures, within their respective spheres of competence, to ensure the full and speedy implementation of the Declaration on the Granting of Independence to Colonial Countries and Peoples and other relevant resolutions of United Nations bodies,

Deeply conscious of the continuing critical need of the people of Namibia and their national liberation movement, the South West Africa People's Organization, for concrete assistance from the specialized agencies and the international institutions associated with the United Nations in their struggle for liberation from the illegal occupation of their country by the racist minority régime in South Africa,

Deeply concerned that, while progress has been maintained through the continuing efforts of the United Nations High Commissioner for

Refugees in the extension of assistance to refugees from southern Africa, the action taken thus far by the organizations and agencies concerned in the provision of assistance generally to the people of Namibia is still far from adequate to meet their urgent and growing needs,

Noting with satisfaction the continuing efforts of the United Nations Development Programme in the extension of assistance to the national liberation movements concerned and commending the initiative taken by that organization in establishing channels for closer, periodic contacts and consultations between the specialized agencies and United Nations institutions and the Organization of African Unity and the national liberation movements in the formulation of assistance programmes, including in particular the holding at Dar es Salaam, from 8 to 11 December 1981, of an Inter-agency Consultative Meeting on Assistance to African National Liberation Movements Recognized by the Organization of African Unity,

1. *Takes note* of the reports of the President of the Economic and Social Council and endorses the observations and suggestions contained therein;

2. *Reaffirms* that the recognition by the General Assembly, the Security Council and other United Nations organs of the legitimacy of the struggle of colonial peoples to exercise their right to self-determination and independence entails, as a corollary, the extension by the United Nations system of organizations of all the necessary moral and material assistance to the peoples of the colonial territories and their national liberation movements;

3. *Expresses its appreciation* to those specialized agencies and organizations within the United Nations system which have continued to co-operate in varying degrees with the United Nations and the Organization of African Unity in the implementation of the Declaration on the Granting of Independence to Colonial Countries and Peoples and other relevant resolutions of United Nations bodies, and urges all the specialized agencies and other organizations within the United Nations system to accelerate the full and speedy implementation of the relevant provisions of those resolutions;

4. *Requests* the specialized agencies and other organizations within the United Nations system, in the light of the intensification of the liberation struggle in Namibia, to do everything possible as a matter of urgency to render, in consultation with the Organization of African Unity and the United Nations Council for Namibia, increased assistance to the people of Namibia, in particular in connection with the Nationhood Programme for Namibia;

5. *Requests also* the specialized agencies and other organizations within the United Nations system to continue to take, in accordance with the relevant resolutions of the General Assembly and the Security Council, all necessary measures to withhold any financial, economic, technical or other assistance to the Government of South Africa until that Government restores to the people of Namibia their inalienable right to self-determination and independence, and to refrain from taking any action which might imply recognition of, or support for, the illegal occupation of Namibia by that régime;

6. *Requests further* the specialized agencies and other organizations within the United Nations system, in accordance with the relevant resolutions of the General Assembly and the Security Council on the *apartheid* policy of the Government of South Africa, to intensify their support for the oppressed people of South Africa and to take such measures as will isolate the *apartheid* régime and mobilize world public opinion against *apartheid;*

7. *Notes with satisfaction* the inclusion of Namibia, represented by the United Nations Council for Namibia, in the membership of the Executive Committee of the Programme of the United Nations High Commissioner for Refugees, in accordance with General Assembly resolution 36/121 D of 10 December 1981, and urges the specialized agencies and other organizations of the United Nations system which have not yet granted full membership to the United Nations Council for Namibia ·to do so without delay;

8. *Notes with satisfaction* the arrangements made by several specialized agencies and United Nations institutions which enable representatives of the national liberation movements recognized by the Organization of African Unity to participate fully as observers in the proceedings relating to matters concerning their respective countries, and calls upon those international institutions which have not yet done so to follow this example and make the necessary arrangements without delay, including arrangements to defray the cost of the participation of those representatives;

9. *Recommends* that all Governments should intensify their efforts in the specialized agencies and other organizations within the United Nations system of which they are members to ensure the full and effective implementation of the Declaration on the Granting of Independence to Colonial Countries and Peoples and other relevant resolutions of United Nations bodies;

10. *Urges* those specialized agencies and organizations within the United Nations system which have not already done so to include in the agenda of the regular meetings of their governing bodies a separate item on the progress made by those organizations in their implementation of the Declaration on the Granting of Independence to Colonial Countries and Peoples and other relevant resolutions of United Nations bodies;

11. *Further urges* the executive heads of the specialized agencies and other organizations within the United Nations system to formulate, with the active co-operation of the Organization of African Unity, and to submit, as a matter of priority, to their governing and legislative organs concrete proposals for the full implementation of the relevant United Nations decisions;

12. *Draws the attention* of the Special Committee on the Situation with regard to the Implementation of the Declaration on the Granting of Independence to Colonial Countries and Peoples to the present resolution and to the discussions on the subject at the second regular session of 1982 of the Council;

13. *Requests* the President of the Economic and Social Council to continue consultations on these matters with the Chairman of the Special Committee on the Situation with regard to the Implementation of the Declaration on the Granting of Independence to Colonial Countries and Peoples and the Chairman of the Special Committee against *Apartheid* and to report thereon to the Council;

14. *Requests* the Secretary-General to follow the implementation of the present resolution and to report thereon to the Council at its second regular session of 1983;

15. *Decides* to keep these questions under continuous review.

General Assembly resolution 37/32

23 November 1982   Meeting 77   128-4-20 (recorded vote)

Approved by Fourth Committee (A/37/625 and Corr.1) by recorded vote (110-4-21), 16 November (meeting 24); draft by Committee on colonial countries (A/37/23/Rev.1); agenda items 99 and 12.

Implementation of the Declaration on the Granting of Independence to Colonial Countries and Peoples by the specialized agencies and the international institutions associated with the United Nations

The General Assembly,

Having examined the item entitled "Implementation of the Declaration on the Granting of Independence to Colonial Countries and Peoples by the specialized agencies and the international institutions associated with the United Nations",

Recalling the Declaration on the Granting of Independence to Colonial Countries and Peoples, contained in its resolution 1514(XV) of 14 December 1960, and the Plan of Action for the Full Implementation of the Declaration, contained in the annex to its resolution 35/118 of 11 December 1980, as well as all other relevant resolutions adopted by the General Assembly on this subject, in particular resolution 36/52 of 24 November 1981,

Recalling also its resolution ES-8/2 of 14 September 1981 on the question of Namibia,

Having examined the reports submitted on the item by the Secretary-General, the Economic and Social Council and the Special Committee on the Situation with regard to the Implementation of the Declaration on the Granting of Independence to Colonial Countries and Peoples,

Taking into account the relevant provisions of the Arusha Declaration and Programme of Action on Namibia adopted by the United Nations Council for Namibia on 13 May 1982 at its extraordinary plenary meeting held at Arusha, United Republic of Tanzania,

Bearing in mind the relevant provisions of the final communiqué and other documents of the Ministerial Meeting of the Co-ordinating Bureau of the Non-Aligned Countries, held at Havana from 31 May to 5 June 1982,

Aware that the struggle of the people of Namibia is in its most crucial stage and has sharply intensified as a consequence of the stepped-up aggression of the illegal colonialist régime of Pretoria against the people of the Territory and the increased general support rendered to that régime by the United States of America and other Western States, coupled with efforts to deprive the Namibian people of their hard-won victories in the liberation struggle, and that it is therefore incumbent upon the entire international community decisively to intensify concerted action in support of the people of Namibia and their sole and authentic representative, the South West Africa People's Organization, for the attainment of their goal,

Deeply conscious of the critical need of the Namibian people and their national liberation movement, the South West Africa People's Organization, and of the peoples of other colonial Territories for concrete assistance from the specialized agencies and other organizations of the United Nations system in their struggle for liberation from colonial rule and in their efforts to achieve and consolidate their national independence,

Reaffirming the responsibility of the specialized agencies and other organizations of the United Nations system to take all the necessary measures, within their respective spheres of competence, to ensure the full and speedy implementation of the Declaration on the Granting of Independence to Colonial Countries and Peoples and other relevant resolutions of the United Nations, particularly those relating to the provision of moral and material assistance, on a priority basis, to the peoples of the colonial Territories and their national liberation movements,

Deeply concerned that, although there has been progress in the extension of assistance to refugees from Namibia, the actions taken hitherto by the organizations concerned in providing assistance to the people of the Territory through their national liberation movement, the South West Africa People's Organization, still remain inadequate to meet the urgent needs of the Namibian people,

Expressing its confident hope that closer contacts and consultations between the specialized agencies and other organizations of the United Nations system and the Organization of African Unity and the national liberation movement concerned will help to overcome procedural and other difficulties which have impeded or delayed the implementation of some assistance programmes,

Recalling its resolution 36/121 D of 10 December 1981, in which it requested all specialized agencies and other organizations and conferences of the United Nations system to grant full membership to the United Nations Council for Namibia as the legal Administering Authority for Namibia,

Expressing its appreciation to the General Secretariat of the Organization of African Unity for the continued co-operation and assistance extended by it to the specialized agencies and other organizations of the United Nations system in connection with the implementation of the relevant resolutions of the United Nations,

Expressing its appreciation also to the Governments of the front-line States for the steadfast support extended to the people of Namibia and their national liberation movement, the South West Africa People's Organization, in their just and legitimate struggle for the attainment of freedom and independence despite increased armed attacks by the forces of the racist régime of South Africa, and aware of the particular needs of those Governments for assistance in that connection,

Noting with satisfaction the intensified efforts of the United Nations Development Programme in the extension of assistance to the national liberation movements and commending its initiative in establishing channels for closer periodic contacts and consultations between the specialized agencies and other organizations of the United Nations system and the Organization of African Unity and the national liberation movements in the formulation of assistance programmes,

Noting also the support given by the specialized agencies and other organizations of the United Nations system to the implementation of the Nationhood Programme for Namibia, in accordance with General Assembly resolution 32/9 A of 4 November 1977,

Gravely concerned at the continued collaboration between the International Monetary Fund and the Government of South Africa in disregard of relevant General Assembly resolutions,

Noting with satisfaction the Meeting between representatives of the General Secretariat of the Organization of African Unity and the secretariats of the United Nations and other organizations of the United Nations system, held at Geneva from 6 to 8 April 1982 in accordance with General Assembly resolution 36/80 of 9 December 1981,

Mindful of the necessity of keeping under continuous review the activities of the specialized agencies and other organizations of the

United Nations system in the implementation of the various United Nations decisions relating to decolonization,

1. *Approves* the chapter of the report of the Special Committee on the Situation with regard to the Implementation of the Declaration on the Granting of Independence to Colonial Countries and Peoples relating to the question;

2. *Reaffirms* that the specialized agencies and other organizations and institutions of the United Nations system should continue to be guided by the relevant resolutions of the United Nations in their efforts to contribute, within their spheres of competence, to the full and speedy implementation of the Declaration on the Granting of Independence to Colonial Countries and Peoples, contained in General Assembly resolution 1514(XV);

3. *Reaffirms also* that the recognition by the General Assembly, the Security Council and other United Nations organs of the legitimacy of the struggle of colonial peoples to exercise their right to self-determination and independence entails, as a corollary, the extension by the specialized agencies and other organizations of the United Nations system of all the necessary moral and material assistance to those peoples and their national liberation movements;

4. *Expresses its appreciation* to those specialized agencies and other organizations of the United Nations system which have continued to co-operate in varying degrees with the United Nations and the Organization of African Unity in the implementation of the Declaration and other relevant resolutions of the United Nations, and urges all the specialized agencies and other organizations of the United Nations system to accelerate the full and speedy implementation of the relevant provisions of those resolutions;

5. *Expresses its concern* that the assistance extended thus far by certain specialized agencies and other organizations of the United Nations system to the colonial peoples, particularly the people of Namibia and their national liberation movement, the South West Africa People's Organization, is far from adequate in relation to the actual needs of the peoples concerned;

6. *Regrets*, notwithstanding the statement of the representative of the World Bank of 17 May 1982 that the Bank has terminated business relations with the régime of South Africa, that the World Bank and the International Monetary Fund continue to maintain links with the racist régime of Pretoria as exemplified by the continued membership of South Africa in both agencies;

7. *Deeply deplores* the persistent collaboration between the International Monetary Fund and South Africa, in disregard of repeated resolutions to the contrary by the General Assembly, and calls upon the International Monetary Fund to put an end to such collaboration;

8. *Urges* the executive heads of the World Bank and the International Monetary Fund to draw the particular attention of their governing bodies to the present resolution with a view to formulating specific programmes beneficial to the peoples of the colonial Territories, particularly Namibia;

9. *Requests* the specialized agencies and other organizations of the United Nations system to render or continue to render, as a matter of urgency, all possible moral and material assistance to the colonial peoples struggling for liberation from colonial rule;

10. *Requests once again* the specialized agencies and other organizations of the United Nations system to continue to provide all moral and material assistance to the newly independent and emerging States;

11. *Reiterates its recommendation* that the specialized agencies and other organizations of the United Nations system should initiate or broaden contacts and co-operation with the colonial peoples and their national liberation movements, directly or, where appropriate, through the Organization of African Unity, and review and introduce greater flexibility in their procedures with respect to the formulation and preparation of assistance programmes and projects so as to be able to extend the necessary assistance without delay to help the colonial peoples and their national liberation movements in their struggle to exercise their inalienable right to self-determination and independence in accordance with General Assembly resolution 1514(XV);

12. *Notes with satisfaction* that the South West Africa People's Organization continues to be the beneficiary of a number of programmes established within the framework of the United Nations Institute for Namibia at Lusaka and that the United Nations Council for Namibia, in co-operation with the South West Africa People's Organization, continues to represent the people of Namibia at meetings

of the specialized agencies and other organizations and institutions of the United Nations system, and urges those agencies and organizations to increase their assistance to the South West Africa People's Organization, as well as to the United Nations Institute for Namibia and the Nationhood Programme for Namibia;

13. *Urges* the specialized agencies and other organizations of the United Nations system which have not already done so to include in the agenda of the regular meetings of their governing bodies a separate item on the progress they have made in the implementation of the Declaration and the other relevant resolutions of the United Nations;

14. *Requests* the specialized agencies and other organizations of the United Nations system, in accordance with the relevant resolutions of the General Assembly and the Security Council, to take all necessary measures to withhold any financial, economic, technical or other assistance from the Government of South Africa, to discontinue all support to that Government until it restores to the people of Namibia their inalienable right to self-determination and independence and to refrain from taking any action which might imply recognition of, or support for, the legitimacy of the domination of the Territory by that régime;

15. *Notes with satisfaction* the arrangements made by several specialized agencies and other organizations of the United Nations system which enable representatives of the national liberation movements recognized by the Organization of African Unity to participate fully as observers in the proceedings relating to matters concerning their respective countries and calls upon those agencies and organizations that have not yet done so to follow this example and to make the necessary arrangements without delay;

16. *Urges* the specialized agencies and other organizations of the United Nations system that have so far not granted full membership to the United Nations Council for Namibia to do so without delay;

17. *Urges* the specialized agencies and other organizations and institutions of the United Nations system to extend, as a matter of priority, substantial material assistance to the Governments of the front-line States in order to enable them more effectively to support the struggle of the people of Namibia for freedom and independence and to resist the violation of their territorial integrity by the armed forces of the racist régime of South Africa, directly or, as in Angola, through puppet traitor groups in the service of Pretoria;

18. *Urges* the specialized agencies and other organizations and institutions of the United Nations system to assist in accelerating progress in all sectors of the national life of the small Territories, particularly in the development of their economies;

19. *Recommends* that all Governments should intensify their efforts in the specialized agencies and other organizations of the United Nations system of which they are members to ensure the full and effective implementation of the Declaration and other relevant resolutions of the United Nations and, in that connection, should accord priority to the question of providing assistance on an emergency basis to the peoples of the colonial Territories and their national liberation movements;

20. *Reiterates its proposal*, under article III of the Agreement between the United Nations and the International Monetary Fund, for the urgent inclusion in the agenda of the Board of Governors of the Fund of an item dealing with the relationship between the Fund and South Africa and further reiterates its proposal that, in pursuance of article II of the Agreement, the relevant organs of the United Nations should participate in any meeting of the Board of Governors called by the Fund for the purpose of discussing the item;

21. *Recommends* the sending in 1983 of a high-level mission to the International Monetary Fund which, subject to the agreement of the United Nations bodies involved, would be composed of the Chairman of the Special Committee on the Situation with regard to the Implementation of the Declaration on the Granting of Independence to Colonial Countries and Peoples, the President of the United Nations Council for Namibia and the Chairman of the Special Committee against *Apartheid;*

22. *Draws the attention* of the specialized agencies and other organizations of the United Nations system to the Plan of Action for the Full Implementation of the Declaration on the Granting of Independence to Colonial Countries and Peoples, contained in the annex to General Assembly resolution 35/118, and in particular to the provisions of paragraph 19 calling on the agencies and organizations to render all possible moral and material assistance to the peoples of the colonial Territories and their national liberation movements;

23. *Urges* the executive heads of the specialized agencies and other organizations of the United Nations system, having regard to the provisions of paragraphs 11 and 22 above, to formulate, with the active co-operation of the Organization of African Unity where appropriate, and to submit, as a matter of priority, to their governing and legislative organs concrete proposals for the full implementation of the relevant United Nations decisions, in particular specific programmes of assistance to the peoples of the colonial Territories and their national liberation movements;

24. *Requests* the Secretary-General to continue to assist the specialized agencies and other organizations of the United Nations system in working out appropriate measures for implementing the relevant resolutions of the United Nations and to prepare for submission to the relevant bodies, with the assistance of those agencies and organizations, a report on the action taken since the circulation of his previous report in implementation of the relevant resolutions, including the present resolution;

25. *Requests* the Economic and Social Council to continue to consider, in consultation with the Special Committee on the Situation with regard to the Implementation of the Declaration on the Granting of Independence to Colonial Countries and Peoples, appropriate measures for the co-ordination of the policies and activities of the specialized agencies and other organizations of the United Nations system in implementing the relevant resolutions of the General Assembly;

26. *Requests* the Special Committee to continue to examine this question and to report thereon to the General Assembly at its thirty-eighth session.

Recorded vote in Assembly as follows:

In favour: Afghanistan, Albania, Algeria, Angola, Antigua and Barbuda, Argentina, Bahamas, Bahrain, Bangladesh, Barbados, Belize, Benin, Bhutan, Bolivia, Botswana, Brazil, Bulgaria, Burma, Burundi, Byelorussian SSR, Cape Verde, Central African Republic, Chad, Chile, China, Colombia, Congo, Costa Rica, Cuba, Cyprus, Czechoslovakia, Democratic Kampuchea, Democratic Yemen, Djibouti, Dominica, Dominican Republic, Ecuador, Egypt, El Salvador, Ethiopia, Fiji, Gabon, Gambia, German Democratic Republic, Ghana, Greece, Grenada, Guinea, Guinea-Bissau, Guyana, Haiti, Honduras, Hungary, India, Indonesia, Iran, Iraq, Jamaica, Jordan, Kenya, Kuwait, Lao People's Democratic Republic, Lebanon, Lesotho, Liberia, Libyan Arab Jamahiriya, Madagascar, Malawi, Malaysia, Maldives, Mali, Malta, Mauritania, Mauritius, Mexico, Mongolia, Morocco, Mozambique, Nepal, Nicaragua, Niger, Nigeria, Oman, Pakistan, Panama, Papua New Guinea, Peru, Philippines, Poland, Qatar, Romania, Rwanda, Saint Lucia, Samoa, Sao Tome and Principe, Saudi Arabia, Senegal, Seychelles, Sierra Leone, Singapore, Solomon Islands, Somalia, Sri Lanka, Sudan, Suriname, Swaziland, Syrian Arab Republic, Thailand, Togo, Trinidad and Tobago, Tunisia, Turkey, Uganda, Ukrainian SSR, USSR, United Arab Emirates, United Republic of Cameroon, United Republic of Tanzania, Upper Volta, Uruguay, Vanuatu, Venezuela, Viet Nam, Yemen, Yugoslavia, Zaire, Zambia, Zimbabwe.

Against: Belgium, Israel, United Kingdom, United States.

Abstaining: Australia, Austria, Canada, Denmark, Finland, France, Germany, Federal Republic of, Iceland, Ireland, Italy, Ivory Coast, Japan, Luxembourg, Netherlands, New Zealand, Norway, Paraguay, Portugal, Spain, Sweden.

Foreign interests impeding implementation of the Declaration on colonial countries

On 23 November 1982, the General Assembly adopted a resolution on foreign economic and other interests impeding decolonization,[(3)] by which it reaffirmed the right of peoples of dependent Territories to dispose of their natural resources in their best interests, and reiterated that any administering or occupying Power which subordinated those peoples' rights to foreign economic and financial interests violated its obligations under the Charter of the United Nations.

The Assembly reaffirmed that the activities of foreign economic, financial and other interests currently operating in the colonial Territories, particularly in southern Africa, constituted a major obstacle to political independence by the indigenous population; condemned the policies of Governments that supported or collaborated with those interests whose exploitation of the Territories obstructed decolonization; and requested the Committee on colonial countries to continue to monitor the situation. The Assembly called on Governments to put an end to enterprises owned by their nationals that were detrimental to the interests of the Territories' inhabitants and to prevent new investments counter to those interests. It invited all Governments and United Nations organizations to ensure that the permanent sovereignty of the colonial Territories over their natural resources was safeguarded, and called on the administering Powers to abolish discriminatory wage systems in the Territories concerned. The Assembly also requested a continued United Nations information campaign on the pillaging of natural resources in colonial Territories.

Under other provisions of the text, the Assembly condemned the collusion of some Governments with the Pretoria régime in the nuclear field, strongly condemned Western and other countries and transnational corporations (TNCs) which invested in South Africa, and called on States to terminate all collaboration with that country. Reiterating that South Africa's exploitation of the natural resources of Namibia was illegal, the Assembly called on States to discontinue economic relations with South Africa, including the supply of crude oil and petroleum products.

In considering the item, the Assembly had before it a report by the United Nations Centre on Transnational Corporations,[1] transmitted in an October 1982 note by the Secretary-General in response to a November 1981 Assembly request[5] that the Centre prepare a register of the profits TNCs derived from their activities in colonial Territories. The Centre reported that, as at 1 August 1982, it had identified 2,099 TNC affiliates operating in 15 of the 21 Territories with which the Committee on colonial countries was concerned. The Centre had circulated a questionnaire to 600 parent companies with affiliates in the Territories concerned; 80 companies had replied as at 1 August and 20 had expressly declined co-operation. Profit data were provided by only 16 companies and were available from public sources for 15 more, the report stated, but more time and data would be needed for preparation of a preliminary register. The Assembly, in its resolution on foreign economic interests, requested the Centre to complete the register and to report to the Committee on colonial countries and to the Assembly in 1983.

The resolution was adopted by a recorded vote of 128 to 7, with 16 abstentions. The text originated in the Committee on colonial countries, which approved it on 20 August, and was then approved by the Assembly's Fourth Committee

on 26 October by a recorded vote of 99 to 6, with 17 abstentions.

In another 23 November resolution, on implementing the Declaration on colonial countries, the Assembly condemned the continuing activities of foreign economic and other interests impeding implementation of the Declaration, particularly in Namibia.[4] A similar condemnation had been included in a resolution on the self-determination of peoples, adopted on 25 February by the Commission on Human Rights.[2]

Among those voting against the resolution on foreign interests, Canada and the Netherlands objected to the implication that foreign economic activity as such impeded implementation of the Declaration, and to the failure to distinguish between unfair exploitation and legitimate commercial activity; the United Kingdom added that the assumption implicit in the text that the peoples of dependent Territories should not have access to the capital, technology and know-how of TNCs was in direct contravention of their right to take their own decisions. A number of delegations expressed similar reservations, namely, Denmark, France, the Federal Republic of Germany and Japan, which abstained; and Australia, Chile, Fiji and Uruguay, which voted in favour. Ireland and Sweden, which abstained, and New Zealand, which voted in favour, stated that, under reasonable control, foreign investment and trade could be the key to development or an important factor in achieving independence.

A number of those abstaining in the vote, among them Denmark, France, Ireland and Sweden, viewed the text as an improvement over the corresponding 1981 resolution,[5] in that it did not contain selective condemnation of particular countries. Chile and Uruguay, which voted affirmatively, made similar observations. However, the Federal Republic of Germany viewed the text still lacking in balance, as did the Netherlands, which found the wording hostile in tone towards foreign economic interests in general and the Western countries in particular. New Zealand and the United Kingdom shared those views, while recognizing the efforts made to introduce more balance in the text. Despite its affirmative vote, Turkey had reservations concerning certain condemnatory references to a specific region.

Bulgaria, however, maintained that the foreign economic and other activities in colonial Territories constituted a major obstacle, that those activities were the root cause of the illegal colonial situations, and that the text should have included the names of countries collaborating with the Pretoria régime. Iraq agreed, adding that the omission of specific names would also encourage the Zionist collaboration with Pretoria. Czechoslovakia said the text was weaker than that of the previous year and failed to reflect the growing co-operation between certain Western countries and South Africa. Also regretting the omission of names, the USSR said the text appeared to favour the activities of TNCs in colonial territories and, as such, was contrary to previous Assembly resolutions. Zimbabwe regarded all collaboration with South Africa as bad in itself, and added that the only way to eliminate *apartheid* was to put an end to all foreign economic aid and collaboration.

While Canada regretted the presence in the text of questionable suppositions and generalizations and cast a negative vote, Australia, though participating in the consensus in the Committee on colonial countries and voting in favour in the Assembly, said it would be unable in 1983 to support a text which stretched its tolerance any further. Sweden considered the language of the text far too sweeping.

Reservations on other paragraphs were expressed by Zimbabwe, on the text's failure to mention the threat to international peace and security posed by South Africa's arms build-up, and by Botswana, regarding trade relations with South Africa including the supply of oil and the call for economic and other sanctions. Bulgaria had reservations in respect of paragraphs 6 and 9 dealing with nuclear and other collaboration with South Africa.

Ireland said the text did not adequately address the complex range of issues confronting the remaining small Non-Self-Governing Territories. New Zealand said the paragraphs referring to the Pacific region, such as the seventeenth preambular paragraph, drew conclusions that were not justified by the facts; the criticism of administering Powers in the text did not apply to New Zealand's administration of Tokelau.

Canada observed that the text contained calls for measures which specifically violated the principle, espoused by the Group of 77, that home Governments of TNCs should not exercise their national laws in an extraterritorial manner. The Netherlands objected to the call for a register of profits derived by TNCs from operations in colonial Territories and to the equation of *apartheid* with a colonial situation.

Denmark and Sweden expressed reservations with regard to a number of paragraphs which failed to take into account the provisions of the United Nations Charter concerning the division of competence between the General Assembly and the Security Council.

In the Assembly debate, many countries, among them Bulgaria, the Byelorussian SSR, Cuba, Czechoslovakia, the German Democratic Republic, Hungary, the Lao People's Democratic Republic, Mongolia, Poland, the Ukrainian SSR, the USSR, the United Republic of Tanzania and Viet Nam, asserted that economic domination by colonial Powers served as obstacles to decolonization in southern Africa and in a number of small Territories. India called on the administering Powers not to engage in exploitative economic activities.

Cuba said the number of TNCs making funds available to South Africa had increased from 1,883 in 1978 to 3,035 in 1981, with 80 per cent of the investments being made by five Western countries; Bulgaria and the Byelorussian SSR added that the amount of foreign investment there exceeded $35 billion. Czechoslovakia, Mongolia and the USSR attributed the continuance of the *apartheid* policy to various kinds of assistance from a number of Western countries, primarily the United States, and from their transnational monopolies.

Madagascar, Mongolia, Sierra Leone, the Ukrainian SSR and the USSR were among those which called on the Security Council to enact comprehensive mandatory sanctions against South Africa.

Report. [1]Centre on TNCs, transmitted by S-G note, A/37/405.
Resolutions (1982). [2]Commission on Human Rights (report, E/1982/12): 1982/16, para. 7, 25 Feb. GA, 23 Nov.: [3]37/31, text following; [4]37/35, para. 7.
Resolution (prior). [5]GA: 36/51, 24 Nov. 1981 (YUN 1981, p. 1108).
Financial implications. S-G statement, A/C.4/37/L.3.
Meeting records. GA: 4th Committee, A/C.4/37/SR.2-8, *9* (11-26 Oct.); plenary, A/37/PV.77 (23 Nov.).

General Assembly resolution 37/31

23 November 1982   Meeting 77   128-7-16 (recorded vote)

Approved by Fourth Committee (A/37/624) by recorded vote (99-6-17), 26 October (meeting 9); draft by Committee on colonial countries (A/37/23/Rev.1); agenda item 98.

Activities of foreign economic and other interests which are impeding the implementation of the Declaration on the Granting of Independence to Colonial Countries and Peoples in Namibia and in all other Territories under colonial domination and efforts to eliminate colonialism, *apartheid* and racial discrimination in southern Africa

The General Assembly,

Having considered the item entitled "Activities of foreign economic and other interests which are impeding the implementation of the Declaration on the Granting of Independence to Colonial Countries and Peoples in Namibia and in all other Territories under colonial domination and efforts to eliminate colonialism, *apartheid* and racial discrimination in southern Africa",

Having examined the chapter of the report of the Special Committee on the Situation with regard to the Implementation of the Declaration on the Granting of Independence to Colonial Countries and Peoples relating to this question,

Taking into consideration the relevant chapters of the report of the United Nations Council for Namibia,

Taking note of the progress report of the United Nations Centre on Transnational Corporations, relating to the preparation of a register indicating the profits which transnational corporations derive from their activities in colonial Territories, submitted in pursuance of General Assembly resolution 36/51 of 24 November 1981,

Recalling its resolutions 1514(XV) of 14 December 1960, containing the Declaration on the Granting of Independence to Colonial Countries and Peoples, 2621(XXV) of 12 October 1970, containing the programme of action for the full implementation of the Declaration, and 35/118 of 11 December 1980, the annex to which contains the Plan of Action for the Full Implementation of the Declaration, as well as all other resolutions of the United Nations relating to the item,

Reaffirming the solemn obligation of the administering Powers under the Charter of the United Nations to promote the political, economic, social and educational advancement of the inhabitants of the Territories under their administration and to protect the human and natural resources of those Territories against abuses,

Bearing in mind the relevant resolutions adopted by the Council of Ministers of the Organization of African Unity at its thirty-seventh ordinary session, held at Nairobi from 15 to 26 June 1981, and endorsed by the Assembly of Heads of State and Government of the Organization of African Unity at its eighteenth ordinary session, held at Nairobi from 24 to 27 June 1981,

Taking into account the relevant provisions of the Special Declaration on Namibia, adopted by the International Conference on Sanctions against South Africa,

Reaffirming that any economic or other activity which impedes the implementation of the Declaration on the Granting of Independence to Colonial Countries and Peoples and obstructs efforts aimed at the elimination of colonialism, *apartheid* and racial discrimination in southern Africa and other colonial Territories is in direct violation of the rights of the inhabitants and of the principles of the Charter and all relevant resolutions of the United Nations,

Reaffirming that the natural resources of all Territories under colonial and racist domination are the heritage of the peoples of those Territories and that the exploitation and depletion of those resources by foreign economic interests, in particular in Namibia, in association with the occupying régime of South Africa, constitute a direct violation of the rights of the peoples and of the principles of the Charter and all relevant resolutions of the United Nations,

Bearing in mind the relevant provisions of the final communiqué and other documents of the Ministerial Meeting of the Co-ordinating Bureau of the Non-Aligned Countries, held at Havana from 31 May to 5 June 1982,

Taking into account the relevant provisions of the Arusha Declaration and Programme of Action on Namibia, adopted by the United Nations Council for Namibia on 13 May 1982 at its extraordinary plenary meeting held at Arusha, United Republic of Tanzania,

Noting with profound concern that the colonial Powers and certain States, through their activities in the colonial Territories, have continued to disregard United Nations decisions relating to the item and that they have failed to implement in particular the relevant provisions of General Assembly resolutions 2621(XXV) and 36/51, by which the Assembly called upon all Governments that had not yet done so to take legislative, administrative or other measures in respect of their nationals and the bodies corporate under their jurisdiction that own and operate enterprises in colonial Territories, particularly in Africa, which are detrimental to the interests of the inhabitants of those Territories, in order to put an end to such enterprises and to prevent new investments that run counter to the interests of the inhabitants of those Territories,

Condemning the intensified activities of those foreign economic, financial and other interests which continue to exploit the natural and human resources of the colonial Territories and to accumulate and repatriate huge profits to the detriment of the interests of the inhabitants, particularly in the case of Namibia, thereby impeding the realization by the peoples of the Territories of their legitimate aspirations for self-determination and independence,

Strongly condemning the support which the racist minority régime of South Africa continues to receive from those foreign economic, financial and other interests which are collaborating with it in the exploitation of the natural and human resources of the international Territory of Namibia, in the further entrenchment of its illegal racist domination over the Territory and in the strengthening of its system of *apartheid,*

Strongly condemning the investment of foreign capital in the production of uranium and the collaboration of certain Western States and other States with the racist minority régime of South Africa in the nuclear field which, by providing that régime with nuclear equipment and technology, enable it to develop nuclear and military capabilities and to become a nuclear Power, thereby promoting South Africa's continued illegal occupation of Namibia,

Concerned about the conditions in other colonial Territories, including certain Territories in the Caribbean and the Pacific regions, where foreign economic, financial and other interests continue to deprive the indigenous populations of their rights over the wealth of their countries, and where the inhabitants of those Territories continue to suffer from a loss of land ownership as a result of the failure of the administering Powers concerned to restrict the sale of land to foreigners, despite the repeated appeals of the General Assembly,

Conscious of the continuing need to mobilize world public opinion against the involvement of foreign economic, financial and other interests in the exploitation of natural and human resources, which impedes the independence of colonial Territories and the elimination of racism, particularly in southern Africa,

1. *Reaffirms* the inalienable right of the peoples of dependent Territories to self-determination and independence and to the enjoyment of the natural resources of their Territories, as well as their right to dispose of those resources in their best interests;

2. *Reiterates* that any administering or occupying Power that deprives the colonial peoples of the exercise of their legitimate rights over their natural resources or subordinates the rights and interests of those peoples to foreign economic and financial interests violates the solemn obligations it has assumed under the Charter of the United Nations;

3. *Reaffirms* that, by their depletive exploitation of natural resources, the continued accumulation and repatriation of huge profits and the use of those profits for the enrichment of foreign settlers and the entrenchment of colonial domination and racial discrimination in the Territories, the activities of foreign economic, financial and other interests operating at present in the colonial Territories, particularly in southern Africa, constitute a major obstacle to political independence and racial equality as well as to the enjoyment of the natural resources of those Territories by the indigenous inhabitants;

4. *Condemns* the activities of foreign economic and other interests in the colonial Territories impeding the implementation of the Declaration on the Granting of Independence to Colonial Countries and Peoples, contained in General Assembly resolution 1514(XV), and the efforts to eliminate colonialism, *apartheid* and racial discrimination;

5. *Condemns* the policies of Governments that continue to support or collaborate with those foreign economic and other interests engaged in exploiting the natural and human resources of the Territories, including in particular illegally exploiting Namibia's marine resources, violating the political, economic and social rights and interests of the indigenous peoples and thus obstructing the full and speedy implementation of the Declaration in respect of those Territories;

6. *Strongly condemns* the collusion of the Governments of certain Western States and other States with the racist minority régime of South Africa in the nuclear field and calls upon those and all other Governments to refrain from supplying that régime, directly or indirectly, with installations that might enable it to produce uranium, plutonium and other nuclear materials, reactors or military equipment;

7. *Requests* the Special Committee on the Situation with regard to the Implementation of the Declaration on the Granting of Independence to Colonial Countries and Peoples to continue to monitor closely the situation in other Non-Self-Governing Territories so as to ensure that all economic activities in those Territories are aimed at strengthening and diversifying their economies in the interests of the indigenous peoples and their speedy accession to independence, and that those peoples are not exploited for political, military and other purposes detrimental to their interests;

8. *Strongly condemns* those Western States and all other States, as well as the transnational corporations, which continue their investments in, and supply of armaments and oil and nuclear technology to, the racist régime of South Africa, thus buttressing it and aggravating the threat to world peace;

9. *Calls upon* all States, in particular certain Western States, to take urgent, effective measures to terminate all collaboration with South Africa in the political, diplomatic, economic, trade, military and nuclear fields and to refrain from entering into other relations with the racist régime of South Africa in violation of the relevant resolutions of the United Nations and of the Organization of African Unity;

10. *Calls once again upon* all Governments that have not yet done so to take legislative, administrative or other measures in respect of their nationals and the bodies corporate under their jurisdiction that own and operate enterprises in colonial Territories, particularly in Africa, which are detrimental to the interests of the inhabitants of those Territories, in order to put an end to such enterprises and to prevent new

investments that run counter to the interests of the inhabitants of those Territories;

11. _Calls upon_ all States to terminate, or cause to have terminated, any investments in Namibia or loans to the racist minority régime of South Africa and to refrain from any agreements or measures to promote trade or other economic relations with that régime;

12. _Requests_ all States that have not yet done so to take effective measures to end the supply of funds and other forms of assistance, including military supplies and equipment, to the racist minority régime of South Africa, which uses such assistance to repress the people of Namibia and their national liberation movement;

13. _Strongly condemns_ South Africa for its continued exploitation and plundering of the natural resources of Namibia, in complete disregard of the legitimate interests of the Namibian people, for the creation in the Territory of an economic structure dependent essentially upon its mineral resources and for its illegal extension of the territorial sea and its proclamation of an economic zone off the coast of Namibia;

14. _Calls upon_ those oil-producing and oil-exporting countries that have not yet done so to take effective measures against the oil companies concerned so as to terminate the supply of crude oil and petroleum products to the racist régime of South Africa;

15. _Reiterates_ that the exploitation and plundering of the natural resources of Namibia by South African and other foreign economic interests, including the activities of those transnational corporations which are engaged in the exploitation and export of the Territory's uranium ores and other resources, in violation of the relevant resolutions of the General Assembly and the Security Council and of Decree No. 1 for the Protection of the Natural Resources of Namibia, enacted by the United Nations Council for Namibia on 27 September 1974, are illegal and contribute to the maintenance of the illegal occupation régime;

16. _Calls once again upon_ all States to discontinue all economic, financial and trade relations with the racist minority régime of South Africa concerning Namibia and to refrain from entering into any relations with South Africa, purporting to act on behalf of or concerning Namibia, which may lend support to its continued illegal occupation of that Territory;

17. _Invites_ all Governments and organizations of the United Nations system, having regard to the relevant provisions of the Declaration on the Establishment of a New International Economic Order, contained in General Assembly resolution 3201(S-VI) of 1 May 1974, and of the Charter of Economic Rights and Duties of States, contained in Assembly resolution 3281(XXIX) of 12 December 1974, to ensure, in particular, that the permanent sovereignty of the colonial Territories over their natural resources is fully respected and safeguarded;

18. _Calls upon_ the administering Powers to abolish all discriminatory and unjust wage systems and working conditions prevailing in the Territories under their administration and to apply in each Territory a uniform system of wages to all the inhabitants without any discrimination;

19. _Requests_ the Secretary-General to continue, through the Department of Public Information of the Secretariat, a sustained and broad campaign with a view to informing world public opinion of the facts concerning the pillaging of natural resources in colonial Territories and the exploitation of their indigenous populations by foreign monopolies and, in respect of Namibia, the support they render to the racist minority régime of South Africa;

20. _Appeals_ to all non-governmental organizations to continue their campaign to mobilize international public opinion for the enforcement of economic and other sanctions against the Pretoria régime;

21. _Requests_ the United Nations Centre on Transnational Corporations to complete the register called for in General Assembly resolution 36/51, indicating the profits that transnational corporations derive from their activities in colonial Territories, and to report thereon to the Special Committee on the Situation with regard to the Implementation of the Declaration on the Granting of Independence to Colonial Countries and Peoples at its session in 1983 and to the Assembly at its thirty-eighth session;

22. _Requests_ the Special Committee to continue to examine this question and to report thereon to the General Assembly at its thirty-eighth session.

Recorded vote in Assembly as follows:

In favour: Afghanistan, Albania, Algeria, Angola, Antigua and Barbuda, Argentina, Australia, Bahamas, Bahrain, Bangladesh, Barbados, Belize, Benin, Bhutan, Bolivia, Botswana, Brazil, Bulgaria, Burma, Burundi, Byelorussian SSR, Cape Verde, Central African Republic, Chad, Chile, China, Colombia, Congo, Costa Rica, Cuba, Cyprus, Czechoslovakia, Democratic Kampuchea, Democratic Yemen, Djibouti, Dominica, Dominican Republic, Ecuador, Egypt, El Salvador, Ethiopia, Fiji, Gabon, Gambia, German Democratic Republic, Ghana, Grenada, Guinea, Guinea-Bissau, Guyana, Haiti, Hungary, India, Indonesia, Iran, Iraq, Ivory Coast, Jamaica, Jordan, Kenya, Kuwait, Lao People's Democratic Republic, Lebanon, Lesotho, Liberia, Libyan Arab Jamahiriya, Madagascar, Malaysia, Maldives, Mali, Malta, Mauritania, Mauritius, Mexico, Mongolia, Morocco, Mozambique, Nepal, New Zealand, Nicaragua, Niger, Nigeria, Oman, Pakistan, Panama, Papua New Guinea, Peru, Philippines, Poland, Qatar, Romania, Rwanda, Saint Lucia, Samoa, Sao Tome and Principe, Saudi Arabia, Senegal, Seychelles, Sierra Leone, Singapore, Solomon Islands, Somalia, Sri Lanka, Sudan, Suriname, Swaziland, Syrian Arab Republic, Thailand, Togo, Trinidad and Tobago, Tunisia, Turkey, Uganda, Ukrainian SSR, USSR, United Arab Emirates, United Republic of Cameroon, United Republic of Tanzania, Upper Volta, Uruguay, Vanuatu, Venezuela, Viet Nam, Yemen, Yugoslavia, Zaire, Zambia, Zimbabwe.

Against: Belgium, Canada, Honduras, Luxembourg, Netherlands, United Kingdom, United States.

Abstaining: Austria, Denmark, Finland, France, Germany, Federal Republic of, Greece, Iceland, Ireland, Israel, Italy, Japan, Malawi, Norway, Portugal, Spain, Sweden.

Military bases in colonial countries

Military activities and arrangements by colonial Powers in Territories under their administration which might impede implementation of the 1960 Declaration on colonial countries were the subject of a 1982 General Assembly decision and of provisions in four Assembly resolutions relating to its implementation.

By a 23 November decision,[1] the Assembly deplored that colonial Powers had taken no steps to implement past resolutions asking them to withdraw military bases and installations from colonial Territories and to refrain from establishing new ones. It reiterated its conviction that, in many instances, military activities and arrangements seriously impeded the full and speedy implementation of the Declaration, and condemned all such activity which denied people the right to self-determination and independence. The Assembly again called on colonial Powers to terminate military activities and eliminate bases in the Territories under their administration, called for a United Nations publicity campaign on the problem, and requested the Committee on colonial countries to continue its consideration of the item and to report in 1983. It deprecated the continued alienation of land in colonial Territories for military installations, stating that the large-scale utilization of local economic and manpower resources for such purposes diverted resources which could be more beneficially used for the Territories' economic development.

Referring to the effects on Namibia, the Assembly condemned South Africa for its increasing military build-up in Namibia and declared null and void all measures by the illegal régime to enforce military conscription there. It also condemned the continuing co-operation of certain Western and other countries supplying that régime with military arms and technology, and called on those States to end nuclear co-operation with South Africa.

The decision was adopted by a recorded vote of 123 to 11, with 15 abstentions. The draft originated in the Committee on colonial countries,[2] which requested the Assembly's Fourth Committee to consider the text under agenda item 98 on foreign interests impeding implementation of the Declaration. The Fourth Committee Chairman agreed to that procedure, stating that, although the Committee could take up the text under any of the agenda items on decolonization, it would be most appropriate, in keeping with its long-standing practice, to be guided by the indication given by the Committee on colonial countries. The Fourth Committee approved the text on 26 October by a recorded vote of 94 to 10, with 16 abstentions.

In its resolution of 23 November on implementation of the Declaration,[6] the Assembly again called on colonial Powers to withdraw immediately and unconditionally their military bases and installations from colonial Territories and to refrain from establishing new ones.

In resolutions on Bermuda,[4] Guam[3] and the Turks and Caicos Islands,[5] also adopted on 23 November, the Assembly reaffirmed its conviction that the administering Power must ensure that military bases and installations did not interfere with the right of the population of the Territory to self-determination and independence, and urged the administering Power to comply fully with relevant United Nations resolutions.

Several States, in explaining their votes on the decision, expressed reservations concerning the procedure by which the draft had been introduced for consideration. Speaking for the European Community members—including France and the Federal Republic of Germany, which voted against, and Ireland, which abstained—Denmark cited concern that the topic had not been assigned to the Fourth Committee by the Assembly, that there had been no formal introduction of the text nor substantive discussion in the Committee and that there was no justification for voting on the decision under agenda item 98. States taking a similar view included Canada (against), Turkey (abstained) and Uruguay (in favour).

The United Kingdom had objections of substance to justify its negative vote, but would not go into them as the status of the text itself was doubtful. The United States called the procedure sloppy and inconsistent with the Charter of the United Nations, while the Netherlands said such procedural irregularities would hurt the Committee's credibility. Agreeing that the procedure violated United Nations practice, Australia said it had reluctantly agreed to the new arrangements for the transmission to the Fourth Committee of texts agreed on by consensus in the Committee on colonial countries, but had explicitly dissociated itself from the arrangement in respect of texts not approved by consensus; it abstained in the vote on the draft, as it had done in the Committee on colonial countries.

As regards the substance of the text, the United States objected to what it called the USSR-inspired premise on which the text was based; to the non-germane references to trade, nuclear co-operation and the call for a total boycott of South Africa in all fields; and to the rhetorical excesses embodied in the text, which did not usefully support those struggling to change the system. In a similar vein, the Netherlands expressed reservations on portions of the text dealing with comprehensive sanctions against South Africa, unwarranted and selective condemnation of Western countries for alleged violation of the mandatory arms embargo, the endorsement of armed struggle and a publicity campaign, adding that in its view the paragraph dealing with military activities in the Territories went beyond the consensus language of previous years.

Voting for the decision, Czechoslovakia considered the text well-balanced and felt that the consideration of the matter under item 98 was fully within the Committee's competence. The USSR observed that Western attempts to cast doubt on the relevance of the decision to item 98 had been refuted by the result of the vote.

Among other States supporting the decision, Botswana reserved its position on a paragraph dealing with military relations with South Africa and Fiji said it did not subscribe to the view that military activities necessarily constituted an obstacle to self-determination, while Zimbabwe emphasized the importance of ending all collaboration with South Africa.

During the Assembly's debate on implementation of the Declaration (see above), those describing military activities and bases in colonial Territories as obstacles to self-determination included Bulgaria, Cuba, Czechoslovakia, the German Democratic Republic, Hungary, the Lao People's Democratic Republic, the Libyan Arab Jamahiriya, Mongolia, Poland, the Ukrainian SSR, the USSR, the United Republic of Tanzania, Viet Nam and Zambia. The Byelorussian SSR said military bases and activities were diametrically opposed to the vital interests of colonial peoples.

The German Democratic Republic charged that Diego Garcia, Guam, Micronesia and Puerto Rico were being misused as military bases; in that light, the Ukrainian SSR said the need for their speedy decolonization was thus ever more acute. The USSR said the military bases of the Western Powers located in such Territories were advance posts for the stifling of the national liberation struggles of people under colonial oppression. The Lao People's Democratic Republic favoured unconditional elimination of such bases and activities, and the Syrian Arab Republic accused the colonial Powers, and particularly the United States, of delaying independence of the Territories in order to preserve military interests. India deemed it incumbent on the administering Powers to refrain from engaging in exploitative military activities.

The United Kingdom said the attacks, by certain members of the Committee on colonial countries, on territorial Governments for providing friends with defence facilities were motivated by their own strategic or ideological preoccupations, rather than their concern for the plight of the peoples of the remaining small Territories.

Decision (1982). [1]GA: 37/420, 23 Nov., text following.
Report. [2]Committee on colonial countries, A/37/23/Rev.1.
Resolutions (1982). GA, 23 Nov.: [3]37/21, para. 6; [4]37/22, para. 8; [5]37/25, para. 9; [6]37/35, para. 10.
Meeting records. GA: 4th Committee, A/C.4/37/SR.2-8, *9* (11-26 Oct.); plenary, A/37/PV.77 (23 Nov.).

General Assembly decision 37/420

123-11-15 (recorded vote)

Approved by Fourth Committee (A/37/624) by recorded vote (94-10-16), 26 October (meeting 9); draft by Committee on colonial countries (A/37/23/Rev.1); agenda item 98.

Military activities and arrangements by colonial Powers in Territories under their administration which might be impeding the implementation of the Declaration on the Granting of Independence to Colonial Countries and Peoples

At its 77th plenary meeting, on 23 November 1982, the General Assembly, on the recommendation of the Fourth Committee, adopted the following text:

"1. The General Assembly, having considered the chapter of the report of the Special Committee on the Situation with regard to the Implementation of the Declaration on the Granting of Independence to Colonial Countries and Peoples relating to an item on the Special Committee's agenda entitled 'Military activities and arrangements by colonial Powers in Territories under their administration which might be impeding the implementation of the Declaration on the Granting of Independence to Colonial Countries and Peoples', deplores the fact that the colonial Powers concerned have taken no steps to implement the requests repeatedly addressed to them by the Assembly, most recently in paragraph 10 of its resolution 36/68 of 1 December 1981, and also in paragraph 9 of the annex to its resolution 35/118 of 11 December 1980, containing the Plan of Action for the Full Implementation of the Declaration on the Granting of Independence to Colonial Countries and Peoples, to withdraw immediately and unconditionally their military bases and installations from colonial Territories and to refrain from establishing new ones.

"2. The General Assembly, in reaffirming the inalienable right of the peoples of all colonial and dependent Territories to self-determination and independence in accordance with the Declaration on the Granting of Independence to Colonial Countries and Peoples, contained in its resolution 1514(XV) of 14 December 1960, reiterates its conviction that military activities and arrangements in the Territories concerned constitute, in a great number of instances, a serious impediment to the full and speedy implementation of the Declaration with respect to those Territories.

"3. The General Assembly deplores the fact that South Africa and the colonial Powers continue to engage in activities and dispositions of a military character and to establish and maintain bases and other military installations in Namibia and other colonial Territories in violation of the purposes and principles of the Charter of the United Nations and of Assembly resolution 1514(XV).

"4. The General Assembly condemns all military activities and arrangements in colonial Territories which deny the peoples concerned their right to self-determination and independence.

"5. The General Assembly notes that, in southern Africa, an extremely serious situation continues to prevail owing to the persistent manoeuvres by the racist minority régime of Pretoria aimed at transferring power to illegitimate groups subservient to its interests in order to perpetuate its illegal occupation of Namibia. The illegal occupying régime has resorted to desperate measures in order to suppress by force the legitimate aspirations of the people and to maintain its control over the Territory. In its escalating war against the people of Namibia and their national liberation movement, the South West Africa People's Organization, struggling for freedom and independence, the régime has repeatedly committed acts of armed aggression against the neighbouring independent African countries, particularly Angola and Zambia, which have caused extensive loss of human life and destruction of the economic infrastructure.

"6. The General Assembly, noting that in Namibia the South African Government has continued to expand its network of military bases and to carry out a massive build-up of its military forces, condemns the continuing co-operation of certain Western countries and other States with South Africa in supplying it with arms and military equipment as well as technology, including technology and equipment in the nuclear field capable of being utilized for military purposes. The Assembly condemns South Africa for its ever-increasing military build-up in Namibia, its recruitment and training of Namibians for tribal armies, the expansion of the so-called SWA/Namibia Territory Force, the use of mercenaries to carry out its policy of military attacks against independent African States, particularly Angola and Zambia, and its threats and acts of subversion and aggression against those countries, as well as its illegal use of Namibian territory to commit such acts. The Assembly is particularly mindful in that regard of the relevant resolutions of the Organization of African Unity.

"7. The General Assembly, accordingly, demands the immediate cessation of the war of oppression waged by the racist minority régime against the people of Namibia and their national liberation movement, as well as the urgent dismantling of all military bases in the Territory. Reaffirming the legitimacy of the struggle of the people of Namibia to achieve their freedom and independence, the Assembly appeals to all States to increase their moral and material assistance to the oppressed people of Namibia and their national liberation movement.

"8. The General Assembly condemns the continued military collaboration and support which certain Western countries and other States render to the Government of South Africa, and calls upon all States to cease such collaboration and support to that Government, particularly the sale of weapons and other *matériel*, which increases South Africa's capacity to wage wars against neighbouring African States. In particular, the Assembly calls upon all Governments to comply strictly with the provisions of Security Council resolution 418(1977) of 4 November 1977, by which the Council, acting under Chapter VII of the Charter, decided to apply specific sanctions against South Africa. In that connection, the General Assembly draws particular attention to the relevant provisions of its resolution 36/121 of 10 December 1981 and the Arusha Declaration and Programme of Action on Namibia, adopted by the United Nations Council for Namibia on 13 May 1982 at its extraordinary plenary meeting held at Arusha, United Republic of Tanzania, as well as the conclusions and recommendations adopted by the Seminar on the Military Situation in and relating to Namibia, held at Vienna from 8 to 11 June 1982 under the auspices of the United Nations Council for Namibia.

"9. The General Assembly condemns the continued nuclear co-operation by certain Western countries and other States with South Africa. It calls upon the States concerned to end all such co-operation and, in particular, to halt the supply to South Africa of equipment, technology, nuclear materials and related training, which increase its nuclear capability.

"10. The General Assembly, noting that the militarization of Namibia has led to the forced conscription of Namibians, to a greatly intensified flow of refugees and to a tragic disorganization of the family life of the Namibian people, strongly condemns the forcible and wholesale displacement of Namibians from their homes for military and political purposes and the introduction of compulsory military service for Namibians and declares that all measures by the illegal occupation régime to enforce military conscription in Namibia are null and void.

"11. The General Assembly recalls its resolution ES-8/2 of 14 September 1981, by which it strongly urged States to cease forthwith, individually and collectively, all dealings with South Africa in order totally to isolate it politically, economically, militarily and culturally.

"12. The General Assembly deplores the establishment and maintenance by colonial Powers and their allies of military bases and other installations in the colonial Territories under their administration which impede the implementation of the Declaration on the Granting of Independence to Colonial Countries and Peoples and which are incompatible with the purposes and principles of the Charter and of Assembly resolution 1514(XV).

"13. The General Assembly reiterates its condemnation of all military activities and arrangements by colonial Powers in Territories under their administration which are detrimental to the interests and rights of the colonial peoples concerned, especially their right to self-determination and independence. The Assembly once again calls upon the colonial Powers concerned to terminate such activities and eliminate such military bases in compliance with its relevant resolutions and in particular with paragraph 9 of the annex to its resolution 35/118, containing the Plan of Action for the Full Implementation of the Declaration on the Granting of Independence to Colonial Countries and Peoples.

"14. The General Assembly deprecates the continued alienation of land in colonial Territories for military installations. While it has been argued that the servicing of such installations creates employment, nevertheless, the large-scale utilization of local economic and manpower resources for this purpose diverts resources that could be more beneficially utilized in promoting the economic development of the Territories concerned and is thus contrary to the interests of their populations.

"15. The General Assembly requests the Secretary-General, through the Department of Public Information of the Secretariat, to undertake an intensified campaign of publicity with a view to informing world public opinion of the facts concerning the military activities and arrangements in colonial Territories which are impeding the implementation of the Declaration on the Granting of Independence to Colonial Countries and Peoples, contained in Assembly resolution 1514(XV).

"16. The General Assembly requests the Special Committee to continue its consideration of the item and to report thereon to the Assembly at its thirty-eighth session."

Recorded vote in Assembly as follows:

In favour: Afghanistan, Albania, Algeria, Angola, Antigua and Barbuda, Argentina, Bahamas, Bahrain, Bangladesh, Barbados, Belize, Benin, Bhutan, Bolivia, Botswana, Brazil, Bulgaria, Burma, Burundi, Byelorussian SSR, Cape Verde, Central African Republic, Chad, China, Colombia, Congo, Costa Rica, Cuba, Cyprus, Czechoslovakia, Democratic Kampuchea, Democratic Yemen, Djibouti, Dominica, Dominican Republic, Ecuador, Egypt, El Salvador, Ethiopia, Fiji, Gabon, Gambia, German Democratic Republic, Ghana, Grenada, Guinea, Guinea-Bissau, Guyana, Haiti, Hungary, India, Indonesia, Iran, Iraq, Ivory Coast, Jamaica, Jordan, Kenya, Kuwait, Lao People's Democratic Republic, Lebanon, Lesotho, Liberia, Libyan Arab Jamahiriya, Madagascar, Malaysia, Maldives, Mali, Malta, Mauritania, Mauritius, Mexico, Mongolia, Morocco, Mozambique, Nepal, Nicaragua, Niger, Nigeria, Oman, Pakistan, Panama, Papua New Guinea, Peru, Philippines, Poland, Qatar, Romania, Rwanda, Saint Lucia, Samoa, Sao Tome and Principe, Saudi Arabia, Senegal, Seychelles, Sierra Leone, Singapore, Solomon Islands, Somalia, Sri Lanka, Sudan, Suriname, Swaziland, Syrian Arab Republic, Thailand, Togo, Trinidad and Tobago, Tunisia, Uganda, Ukrainian SSR, USSR, United Arab Emirates, United Republic of Cameroon, United Republic of Tanzania, Upper Volta, Vanuatu, Venezuela, Viet Nam, Yemen, Yugoslavia, Zaire, Zambia, Zimbabwe.

Against: Belgium, Canada, France, Germany, Federal Republic of, Honduras, Italy, Japan, Luxembourg, Netherlands, United Kingdom, United States.

Abstaining: Australia, Austria, Denmark, Finland, Greece, Iceland, Ireland, Israel, Malawi, New Zealand, Norway, Portugal, Spain, Sweden, Turkey.

Information dissemination

Action by the Committee on colonial countries. On 5 August 1982, the Committee on colonial countries[1] approved a report of its Sub-Committee on Petitions, Information and Assistance, thereby reiterating the importance of information dissemination to further the aims of the 1960 Declaration on colonial countries. The Sub-Committee considered it imperative for the United Nations to intensify its public information activities in view of the disturbing situation in Namibia due to the intransigence of the Pretoria authorities, the increased support to that régime by certain Western countries and the attempts from certain quarters to misrepresent as terrorism the struggle for independence in southern Africa.

The Sub-Committee attached importance to the work of the Information Unit on Decolonization in the Secretariat's Department of Political Affairs, Trusteeship and Decolonization, and considered valuable the Unit's studies and monographs in the *Decolonization* series. It recommended that the Department of Public Information (DPI), in consultation with the Unit, intensify publicity on decolonization, with particular attention paid to the activities of the South West Africa People's Organization (SWAPO) as the sole and authentic representative of the Namibian people, and requested DPI to inform the Sub-Committee of the relevant activities of United Nations information centres for evaluation of their effectiveness. The Sub-Committee regretted that decolonization information supplied by DPI received only limited media coverage in western Europe and the Americas, and requested that an analysis of the problem be presented at the Committee's 1983 session. It further recommended that the Unit, in co-operation with DPI, undertake speaking engagements on colonial issues at university campuses across North America, with particular emphasis on Namibia, and reiterated its appeal to non-governmental organizations (NGOs) to intensify their campaigns in support of colonial peoples, especially those in southern Africa.

General Assembly action. By a 23 November resolution,[3] the General Assembly reaffirmed the importance of effecting the widest possible dissemination of information on the evils of colonialism, on the efforts of the colonial peoples to achieve self-determination and independence and on the assistance provided by the international community towards the elimination of colonialism. It approved the relevant chapter of the report of the Committee on colonial countries and requested the Secretary-General to continue to collect, prepare and disseminate material relating to decolonization, seeking the full co-operation of the administering Powers and working closely with the Organization of African Unity. The Assembly also requested him to intensify the activities of United Nations information centres, particularly those in western Europe and the Americas, and to enlist the support of NGOs having a special interest in the issue. It invited all States and United Nations organizations to participate in the effort.

The resolution, sponsored by 24 nations and introduced by Trinidad and Tobago, was adopted by a recorded vote of 148 to none, with 5 abstentions.

The question of information dissemination on decolonization was also dealt with in other 1982 Assembly resolutions. In a 3 December resolution on the self-determination of peoples,[4] the Assembly requested the Secretary-General to give maximum publicity to the Declaration and to the struggle by oppressed peoples for self-determination and national independence.

On 23 November, in a resolution on the activities of foreign economic and other interests impeding implementation of the Declaration,[2] the Assembly requested the Secretary-General to continue to inform world public opinion of the pillaging of natural resources and the exploitation of indigenous populations in colonial Territories by foreign monopolies.

Report. [1]Committee on colonial countries, A/37/23/Rev.1.
Resolutions (1982). GA: [2]37/31, para. 19, 23 Nov.; [3]37/36, 23 Nov., text following; [4]37/43, para. 29, 3 Dec.
Financial implications. 5th Committee report, A/37/636; S-G statement, A/C.5/37/47.
Meeting records. GA: 4th Committee, A/C.4/37/SR.9-15, 17-23 (26 Oct.–15 Nov.); 5th Committee, A/C.5/37/SR.41 (22 Nov.); plenary, A/37/PV.74-76, 77 (22, 23 Nov.).

General Assembly resolution 37/36

23 November 1982   Meeting 77   148-0-5 (recorded vote)

24-nation draft (A/37/L.33 and Add.1); agenda item 18.

Sponsors: Afghanistan, Algeria, Barbados, Congo, Cyprus, Czechoslovakia, Ethiopia, Grenada, Guyana, India, Jamaica, Lao People's Democratic Republic, Madagascar, Mali, Romania, Saint Lucia, Sierra Leone, Syrian Arab Republic, Trinidad and Tobago, Tunisia, United Republic of Tanzania, Viet Nam, Yugoslavia, Zambia.

Dissemination of information on decolonization

The General Assembly,

Having examined the chapter of the report of the Special Committee on the Situation with regard to the Implementation of the Declaration on the Granting of Independence to Colonial Countries and Peoples relating to the question of publicity for the work of the United Nations in the field of decolonization,

Recalling its resolution 1514(XV) of 14 December 1960, containing the Declaration on the Granting of Independence to Colonial Countries and Peoples, and all other resolutions and decisions of the United Nations concerning the dissemination of information on decolonization, in particular General Assembly resolution 36/69 of 1 December 1981,

Reiterating the importance of publicity as an instrument for furthering the aims and purposes of the Declaration and mindful of the continuing pressing need to take all possible steps to acquaint world public opinion with all aspects of the problems of decolonization with a view to assisting effectively the peoples of the colonial Territories to achieve self-determination, freedom and independence,

Aware of the increasingly important role being played in the widespread dissemination of relevant information by a number of non-governmental organizations having a special interest in decolonization, and noting with satisfaction the intensified efforts of the Special Committee in enlisting the support of those organizations in that regard, including the dispatch of a special mission to Europe in 1982,

1. *Approves* the chapter of the report of the Special Committee on the Situation with regard to the Implementation of the Declaration on the Granting of Independence to Colonial Countries and Peoples relating to the question of dissemination of information on decolonization and of publicity for the work of the United Nations in the field of decolonization;

2. *Reaffirms* the importance of effecting the widest possible dissemination of information on the evils and dangers of colonialism, on the determined efforts of the colonial peoples to achieve self-determination, freedom and independence and on the assistance being provided by the international community towards the elimination of the remaining vestiges of colonialism in all its forms;

3. *Requests* the Secretary-General, having regard to the suggestions of the Special Committee, to continue to take concrete measures through all the media at his disposal, including publications, radio and television, to give widespread and continuous publicity to the work of the United Nations in the field of decolonization, and, *inter alia:*

(a) To continue, in consultation with the Special Committee, to collect, prepare and disseminate basic material, studies and articles relating to the problems of decolonization and, in particular, to continue to publish the periodical *Objective: Justice* and other publications, special articles and studies, including the *Decolonization* series, and to select from them appropriate material for wider dissemination by means of reprints in various languages;

(b) To seek the full co-operation of the administering Powers concerned in the discharge of the tasks referred to above;

(c) To intensify the activities of all United Nations information centres, particularly those located in Western Europe and the Americas;

(d) To maintain a close working relationship with the Organization of African Unity by holding periodic consultations and by systematically exchanging relevant information with that organization;

(e) To enlist the support of non-governmental organizations having a special interest in decolonization in the dissemination of the relevant information;

(f) To ensure the availability of the necessary facilities and services in this regard;

(g) To report to the Special Committee on the measures taken in implementation of the present resolution;

4. *Invites* all States, the specialized agencies and other organizations of the United Nations system and non-governmental organizations having a special interest in decolonization to undertake or intensify, in co-operation with the Secretary-General and within their respective spheres of competence, the large-scale dissemination of the information referred to in paragraph 2 above;

5. *Requests* the Special Committee to follow the implementation of the present resolution and report thereon to the General Assembly at its thirty-eighth session.

Recorded vote in Assembly as follows:

In favour: Afghanistan, Albania, Algeria, Angola, Antigua and Barbuda, Argentina, Australia, Austria, Bahamas, Bahrain, Bangladesh, Barbados, Belgium, Belize, Benin, Bhutan, Bolivia, Botswana, Brazil, Bulgaria, Burma, Burundi, Byelorussian SSR, Canada, Cape Verde, Central African Republic, Chad, Chile, China, Colombia, Congo, Costa Rica, Cuba, Cyprus, Czechoslovakia, Democratic Kampuchea, Democratic Yemen, Denmark, Djibouti, Dominica, Dominican Republic, Ecuador, Egypt, El Salvador, Ethiopia, Fiji, Finland, Gabon, Gambia, German Democratic Republic, Ghana, Greece, Grenada, Guatemala, Guinea, Guinea-Bissau, Guyana, Haiti, Honduras, Hungary, Iceland, India, Indonesia, Iran, Iraq, Ireland, Israel, Italy, Ivory Coast, Jamaica, Japan, Jordan, Kenya, Kuwait, Lao People's Democratic Republic, Lebanon, Lesotho, Liberia, Libyan Arab Jamahiriya, Madagascar, Malawi, Malaysia, Maldives, Mali, Malta, Mauritania, Mauritius, Mexico, Mongolia, Morocco, Mozambique, Nepal, Netherlands, New Zealand, Nicaragua, Niger, Nigeria, Norway, Oman, Pakistan, Panama, Papua New Guinea, Paraguay, Peru, Philippines, Poland, Portugal, Qatar, Romania, Rwanda, Saint Lucia, Samoa, Sao Tome and Principe, Saudi Arabia, Senegal, Seychelles, Sierra Leone, Singapore, Solomon Islands, Somalia, Spain, Sri Lanka, Sudan, Suriname, Swaziland, Sweden, Syrian Arab Republic, Thailand, Togo, Trinidad and Tobago, Tunisia, Turkey, Uganda, Ukrainian SSR, USSR, United Arab Emirates, United Republic of Cameroon, United Republic of Tanzania, Upper Volta, Uruguay, Vanuatu, Venezuela, Viet Nam, Yemen, Yugoslavia, Zaire, Zambia, Zimbabwe.

Against: None.

Abstaining: France, Germany, Federal Republic of, Luxembourg, United Kingdom, United States.

Observance of the Week of Solidarity with the colonial peoples of southern Africa

The Week of Solidarity with the Colonial Peoples of Southern Africa Fighting for Freedom, Independence and Equal Rights, observed annually in the week beginning 25 May—Africa Liberation Day—was marked in 1982 by a series of activities, including the issuance of a statement on 24 May by the Chairman of the Committee on colonial countries. In it, the Chairman paid tribute to those who had given their lives to the cause of freedom and justice for colonial peoples, commended SWAPO's efforts to bring about fair elections in

Namibia, and requested that Member States mobilize maximum support for the peoples of southern Africa struggling for independence and equal rights by effecting the widest possible dissemination of information on their cause.

By a letter of 2 November,[2] the Chairman informed the President of the General Assembly that, after consideration by the Committee in 1981[4] and 1982[3] of the possibility of extending the commemoration of the Week to the peoples of all the remaining dependent Territories, and following consultations with the presiding officers of the Special Committee against *Apartheid* and the United Nations Council for Namibia, an agreement had been reached by the three bodies to recommend to the Assembly that the title of the Week should be changed to "Week of Solidarity with the Peoples of Namibia and All Other Colonial Territories, as well as those in South Africa, Fighting for Freedom, Independence and Human Rights".

Acting without vote on 23 November, the Assembly adopted that recommendation.[1]

Decision (1982). [1]GA: 37/421, 23 Nov., text following.
Letter. [2]Committee on colonial countries Chairman, 3 Nov., A/37/594.
Report. [3]Committee on colonial countries, A/37/23/Rev.1.
Yearbook reference. [4]1981, p. 1113.
Meeting records. GA: A/37/PV.74-76, 77 (22, 23 Nov.).

General Assembly decision 37/421

Adopted without vote

Recommendation by Committee against *Apartheid*, Committee on colonial countries and Council for Namibia (A/37/594); agenda item 18.

Week of Solidarity with the Peoples of Namibia and All Other Colonial Territories, as well as those in South Africa, Fighting for Freedom, Independence and Human Rights
At its 77th plenary meeting, on 23 November 1982, the General Assembly adopted the recommendation of the Special Committee on the Situation with regard to the Implementation of the Declaration on the Granting of Independence to Colonial Countries and Peoples, the Special Committee against *Apartheid* and the United Nations Council for Namibia that the title of the Week of Solidarity with the Colonial Peoples of Southern Africa Fighting for Freedom, Independence and Equal Rights should be changed to "Week of Solidarity with the Peoples of Namibia and All Other Colonial Territories, as well as those in South Africa, Fighting for Freedom, Independence and Human Rights".

Role of non-governmental organizations

The Sub-Committee on Petitions, Information and Assistance of the Committee on colonial countries, in its 1982 report to the Committee, noted once again the important role played by non-governmental organizations (NGOs) in disseminating information on decolonization, urged continued consultations between the Sub-Committee and relevant NGOs, and appealed to them to intensify their campaigns in support of colonial peoples and their national liberation movements, especially in southern Africa. In so doing, the Sub-Committee recommended that those NGOs should strive to counteract the hostile and negative propaganda that liberation movements in

southern Africa were terrorists. It also recommended that the Secretary-General be requested to maintain an updated list of NGOs active in the decolonization field to help facilitate its contact with them and that the Secretariat's Information Unit on Decolonization continue to co-operate with the Department of Public Information in providing briefings to NGOs and student groups at United Nations Headquarters as well as outside New York. The Sub-Committee's report was approved by the Committee on 5 August.[1]

In addition, the Committee sent a mission to London, The Hague (Netherlands), Brussels (Belgium), Geneva, and Prague (Czechoslovakia) from 4 to 22 September, which consulted with 54 NGOs having headquarters outside New York and with the directors of the United Nations information centres in the capitals visited (except The Hague), concerning the dissemination of information on decolonization.

Reporting on its findings to the Committee,[2] the five-member mission confirmed that NGOs played an important role, particularly by monitoring the activities of foreign economic interests impeding decolonization and by offering programmes of assistance to colonial peoples and their liberation movements. It called on the Committee and the Secretariat to increase the supply of information to NGOs to help them inform and mobilize public opinion, particularly in western Europe, and reported that there was agreement between the mission and the NGOs on the merits of organizing several joint activities. The mission recommended to the Committee that a seminar be held in 1983 to strengthen co-operation between NGOs and to co-ordinate their information dissemination activities. A member of the mission expressed reservations to parts of the report dealing with East Timor, and another did likewise as regards the proposed seminar.

On 8 November, the Committee approved the mission's report, endorsed its conclusions and recommendations, and agreed that further consultations should be held on the particulars of the proposed seminar.

Reports. [1]Committee on colonial countries, A/37/23/Rev.1; [2]Mission to NGOs, A/AC.109/L.1457 & Add.1.

Puerto Rico

Action by the Committee on colonial countries. In connection with its review of the list of Territories to which the 1960 Declaration was applicable, the Committee on colonial countries adopted a resolution on 4 August 1982,[3] by which it reaffirmed the inalienable right of the people of Puerto Rico to self-determination and independence in accordance with the Declaration and the document's full applicability with respect to Puerto Rico. Recalling the resolutions and decisions it had adopted on the subject since 1972, the Committee again urged the United States Government to adopt measures for the full transfer of sovereign powers to the people of Puerto Rico, to assist the Committee in applying resolutions relative to Puerto Rico and to co-operate in sending a fact-finding mission of the Committee to visit the territory. The Committee deplored the United States decision to prohibit Puerto Rican citizens from attending the Fourteenth Central American and Caribbean Games scheduled for 1983 at Caracas, Venezuela, and again recommended that the General Assembly examine the question of Puerto Rico as a separate item at its 1982 session.

The resolution was adopted by 12 votes to 2, with 9 abstentions, following adoption of paragraph 2—on consideration of the question as a separate item—by 10 votes to 3, with 9 abstentions. Before adopting the text, the Committee heard 19 representatives of organizations from Puerto Rico and considered a report,[4] prepared by its Rapporteur in response to its August 1981 request,[7] containing updated information on the territory and the opinions of the political parties, social, cultural and labour organizations and other institutions concerned.

General Assembly action. On 24 September 1982, the General Assembly decided, by a roll-call vote of 70 to 30, with 43 abstentions, not to include the question of Puerto Rico as a separate item on the agenda of its 1982 session.

That action came when Cuba requested the reversal of the 22 September decision of the Assembly's General Committee—by a roll-call vote of 11 to 7, with 8 abstentions—not to include the item on the Assembly's agenda.[5]

The proposal for inclusion of the question in the Assembly's agenda had been made by the Minister for Foreign Affairs of Cuba in his letter of 17 August to the Secretary-General,[1] in which he cited the 1981 and 1982 resolutions of the Committee on colonial countries recommending that the Assembly consider the question of Puerto Rico as a separate item in 1982, and asserted that the statements made before the Committee by representatives of various organizations in Puerto Rico had unequivocally demonstrated the dissatisfaction of the people of "that Latin American nation" with their present political status and the desire to change it.

In the General Committee, the United States asserted that there was no basis for overturning the Assembly's 1953 resolution[6] endorsing the results of a 1952 referendum by which the people of Puerto Rico had chosen the status of a self-governing commonwealth in association with the United States; to do so would constitute an intervention in the affairs of the United States. The

Puerto Rican people had not chosen thus far to change the status of their relationship with the United States and the international community should respect the right of the Puerto Ricans to determine their future for themselves.

Cuba stated in the Assembly that the presence of the Mayor of San Juan on the United States delegation was proof that Puerto Rico was a colony; it further asserted that that individual favoured annexation of the territory and was proud to be with those who oppressed his people. The United States, by a letter to the President of the Assembly dated 24 November,[2] transmitted a reply by the Mayor stating that as a Puerto Rican he had all the rights of an American citizen and the absolute freedom to determine his future—a freedom, he said, the Cuban people did not have.

Letters. [1]Cuba, 17 Aug., A/37/194; [2]United States, 24 Nov., A/37/645.
Reports. [3]Committee on colonial countries, A/37/23/Rev.1; [4]Committee on colonial countries Rapporteur, A/AC.109/L.1436; [5]General Committee, A/37/250 *(item 137)*.
Resolution. [6]GA: 748(VIII), 27 Nov. 1953 (YUN 1953, p. 539).
Yearbook reference. [7]1981, p. 1113.
Meeting records. GA: General Committee, A/BUR/37/SR.2 (22 Sep.); plenary, A/37/PV.4, 74-77 (24 Sep. & 22, 23 Nov.); 4th Committee, A/C.4/37/SR.9-15, 17-23 (26 Oct.-15 Nov.).

Other general questions concerning NSGTs

Fellowships and scholarships

In a report to the General Assembly covering the year ended 30 September 1982,[1] the Secretary-General said the following 32 States had offered to make scholarships and fellowships available to persons from Non-Self-Governing Territories (NSGTs) for secondary, vocational and postgraduate studies: Austria, Brazil, Bulgaria, Cyprus, Czechoslovakia, Egypt, German Democratic Republic, Federal Republic of Germany, Ghana, Greece, Hungary, India, Iran, Israel, Italy, Libyan Arab Jamahiriya, Malawi, Malta, Mexico, Pakistan, Philippines, Poland, Romania, Sri Lanka, Syrian Arab Republic, Tunisia, Turkey, Uganda, USSR, United Arab Emirates, United States, Yugoslavia. He reported that the United Nations Secretariat had received queries from 344 students and had transmitted two completed application forms from students to the States offering fellowships; other applications had gone directly to the States concerned.

After considering the Secretary-General's report, the Assembly adopted on 23 November, without vote, a resolution[2] by which it expressed appreciation to Member States that made scholarships available, and invited all States to make or continue to make generous offers of study and training facilities to inhabitants of NSGTs, providing travel funds whenever possible. The Assembly also urged the administering Powers to ensure widespread and continuous dissemination of such offers in the Territories under their administration, and to provide facilities to enable students to take advantage of them.

This resolution was approved without objection by the Fourth Committee on 16 November on the basis of a proposal sponsored by 37 nations.

Report. (1)S-G, A/37/539 & Add.1.
Resolution (1982). (2)GA: 37/34, 23 Nov., text following.
Meeting records. GA: 4th Committee, A/C.4/37/SR.9-15, 17-23, *24* (26 Oct.–16 Nov.); plenary, A/37/PV.77 (23 Nov.).

General Assembly resolution 37/34

23 November 1982   Meeting 77   Adopted without vote

Approved by Fourth Committee (A/37/627) without objection, 16 November (meeting 24); 37-nation draft (A/C.4/37/L.10); agenda item 101.

Sponsors: Algeria, Angola, Australia, Austria, Bangladesh, Barbados, Congo, Cyprus, Egypt, Ethiopia, Fiji, Greece, Guinea, Guinea-Bissau, Guyana, India, Ivory Coast, Jamaica, Liberia, Madagascar, Mali, Mauritania, New Zealand, Nigeria, Qatar, Romania, Senegal, Sudan, Syrian Arab Republic, Trinidad and Tobago, Tunisia, Turkey, Uganda, United Republic of Tanzania, Yugoslavia, Zambia, Zimbabwe.

Offers by Member States of study and training facilities for inhabitants of Non-Self-Governing Territories
The General Assembly,

Recalling its resolution 36/54 of 24 November 1981,

Having examined the report of the Secretary-General on offers by Member States of study and training facilities for inhabitants of Non-Self-Governing Territories, prepared under General Assembly resolution 845(IX) of 22 November 1954,

Considering that more scholarships should be made available to the inhabitants of Non-Self-Governing Territories in all parts of the world and that steps should be taken to encourage applications from students in those Territories,

1. *Takes note* of the report of the Secretary-General;

2. *Expresses its appreciation* to those Member States that have made scholarships available to the inhabitants of Non-Self-Governing Territories;

3. *Invites* all States to make or continue to make generous offers of study and training facilities to the inhabitants of those Territories that have not yet attained self-government or independence and, whenever possible, to provide travel funds to prospective students;

4. *Urges* the administering Powers to take effective measures to ensure the widespread and continuous dissemination in the Territories under their administration of information relating to offers of study and training facilities made by States and to provide all the necessary facilities to enable students to avail themselves of such offers;

5. *Requests* the Secretary-General to report to the General Assembly at its thirty-eighth session on the implementation of the present resolution;

6. *Draws the attention* of the Special Committee on the Situation with regard to the Implementation of the Declaration on the Granting of Independence to Colonial Countries and Peoples to the present resolution.

Information to the United Nations

In accordance with Chapter XI, Article 73 *e*, of the Charter of the United Nations, Member States responsible for the administration of Territories which had not attained a full measure of self-government were obligated to send each year to the Secretary-General information on economic, social and educational conditions in those Territories, subject to security and constitutional limitations. The reports received in 1982 also contained information on political and constitutional developments.

During 1982, information was transmitted to him with respect to the following NSGTs(2):

Australia: Cocos (Keeling) Islands
New Zealand: Tokelau
United Kingdom: Bermuda, British Virgin Islands, Cayman Islands, Falkland Islands (Malvinas), Gibraltar, Montserrat, Pitcairn, St. Helena, Turks and Caicos Islands
United States: American Samoa, Guam, United States Virgin Islands

In a note verbale dated 26 February,(1) Portugal informed the Secretary-General that it had nothing to add to the information provided in a 1979 note (stating that conditions in East Timor had prevented it from assuming its responsibilities for the Territory's administration).(5)

In an October 1982 report to the General Assembly listing the reports submitted on NSGTs,(2) the Secretary-General noted that, with respect to Western Sahara, Spain had informed him in 1976 that with the termination of its presence in the Territory it considered itself exempt from any international responsibility in connection with the administration of the Territory.(4) Further, the United Kingdom considered that transmission of information was no longer appropriate for Brunei and St. Kitts–Nevis because they had achieved full self-government, and that Anguilla had been formally separated from St. Kitts–Nevis in December 1980.

On 23 November, the Assembly adopted a resolution(3) deploring the fact that some Member States responsible for NSGTs had ceased to transmit information, and reaffirming that, in the absence of a decision by the Assembly that a Territory had attained full self-government, the administering Power concerned should continue to transmit the information prescribed in Article 73 *e* of the Charter, as well as the fullest possible information on political and constitutional developments in the Territory, within a maximum of six months following expiration of the administrative year.

This resolution was adopted by a recorded vote of 148 to none, with 3 abstentions. It originated in the Committee on colonial countries, which approved it on 5 August, and was approved by the Fourth Committee on 15 November by a recorded vote of 144 to none, with 5 abstentions.

Note verbale. (1)Portugal, 26 Feb., A/37/113.
Report. (2)S-G, A/37/501.
Resolution (1982). (3)GA: 37/29, 23 Nov., text following.
Yearbook references. (4)1976, p. 738; (5)1979, p. 1117.
Meeting records. GA: 4th Committee, A/C.4/37/SR.9-15, 17-22, *23* (26 Oct.–15 Nov.); plenary, A/37/PV.77 (23 Nov.).

General Assembly resolution 37/29

23 November 1982   Meeting 77   148-0-3 (recorded vote)

Approved by Fourth Committee (A/37/622) by recorded vote (144-0-5), 15 November (meeting 23); draft by Committee on colonial countries (A/37/23/Rev.1); agenda item 96.

Information from Non-Self-Governing Territories transmitted under Article 73 *e* of the Charter of the United Nations

The General Assembly,

Having examined the chapter of the report of the Special Committee on the Situation with regard to the Implementation of the Declaration on the Granting of Independence to Colonial Countries and Peoples relating to the information from Non-Self-Governing Territories transmitted under Article 73 *e* of the Charter of the United Nations and the action taken by the Committee in respect of that information,

Having also examined the report of the Secretary-General on the question,

Recalling its resolution 1970(XVIII) of 16 December 1963, in which it requested the Special Committee to study the information transmitted to the Secretary-General in accordance with Article 73 *e* of the Charter and to take such information fully into account in examining the situation with regard to the implementation of the Declaration,

Recalling also its resolution 36/49 of 24 November 1981, in which it requested the Special Committee to continue to discharge the functions entrusted to it under resolution 1970(XVIII),

Deploring the fact that some Member States having responsibilities for the administration of Non-Self-Governing Territories have ceased to transmit information under Article 73 *e* of the Charter,

1. *Approves* the chapter of the report of the Special Committee on the Situation with regard to the Implementation of the Declaration on the Granting of Independence to Colonial Countries and Peoples relating to the information from Non-Self-Governing Territories transmitted under Article 73 *e* of the Charter of the United Nations;

2. *Reaffirms* that, in the absence of a decision by the General Assembly itself that a Non-Self-Governing Territory has attained a full measure of self-government in terms of Chapter XI of the Charter, the administering Power concerned should continue to transmit information under Article 73 *e* of the Charter with respect to that Territory;

3. *Requests* the administering Powers concerned to transmit, or continue to transmit, to the Secretary-General the information prescribed in Article 73 *e* of the Charter, as well as the fullest possible information on political and constitutional developments in the Territories concerned, within a maximum period of six months following the expiration of the administrative year in those Territories;

4. *Requests* the Special Committee to continue to discharge the functions entrusted to it under General Assembly resolution 1970(XVIII), in accordance with established procedures, and to report thereon to the Assembly at its thirty-eighth session.

Recorded vote in Assembly as follows:

In favour: Afghanistan, Albania, Algeria, Angola, Antigua and Barbuda, Argentina, Australia, Austria, Bahamas, Bahrain, Bangladesh, Barbados, Belgium, Belize, Benin, Bhutan, Bolivia, Botswana, Brazil, Bulgaria, Burma, Burundi, Byelorussian SSR, Canada, Cape Verde, Central African Republic, Chad, Chile, China, Colombia, Congo, Costa Rica, Cuba, Cyprus, Czechoslovakia, Democratic Kampuchea, Democratic Yemen, Denmark, Djibouti, Dominican Republic, Ecuador, Egypt, El Salvador, Ethiopia, Fiji, Finland, Gabon, Gambia, German Democratic Republic, Germany, Federal Republic of, Ghana, Greece, Grenada, Guatemala, Guinea, Guinea-Bissau, Guyana, Haiti, Honduras, Hungary, Iceland, India, Indonesia, Iran, Iraq, Ireland, Israel, Italy, Ivory Coast, Jamaica, Japan, Jordan, Kenya, Kuwait, Lao People's Democratic Republic, Lebanon, Lesotho, Liberia, Libyan Arab Jamahiriya, Luxembourg, Madagascar, Malawi, Malaysia, Maldives, Mali, Malta, Mauritania, Mauritius, Mexico, Mongolia, Morocco, Mozambique, Nepal, Netherlands, New Zealand, Nicaragua, Niger, Nigeria, Norway, Oman, Pakistan, Panama, Papua New Guinea, Paraguay, Peru, Philippines, Poland, Portugal, Qatar, Romania, Rwanda, Samoa, Sao Tome and Principe, Saudi Arabia, Senegal, Seychelles, Sierra Leone, Singapore, Solomon Islands, Somalia, Spain, Sri Lanka, Sudan, Suriname, Swaziland, Sweden, Syrian Arab Republic, Thailand, Togo, Trinidad and Tobago, Tunisia, Turkey, Uganda, Ukrainian SSR, USSR, United Arab Emirates, United Republic of Cameroon, United Republic of Tanzania, Upper Volta, Uruguay, Vanuatu, Venezuela, Viet Nam, Yemen, Yugoslavia, Zaire, Zambia, Zimbabwe.

Against: None.

Abstaining: France, United Kingdom, United States.

UN visiting missions

In 1982, the Committee on colonial countries sent a visiting mission to one NSGT—a three-member group which visited Montserrat in August at the invitation of the United Kingdom.

The Committee adopted on 5 August a resolution on the question of visiting missions, stressing the need to continue to dispatch missions to colonial Territories, calling on the administering Powers to permit access by those missions to Territories under their administration, and requesting the Committee Chairman to consult with the administering Powers and report back as appropriate.[1]

In June 1982, the Chairman submitted a report in response to a similar request made by the Committee in August 1981[3] concerning consultations with administering Powers on the subject of visiting missions. Noting with satisfaction the continued co-operation of these Powers, he re-emphasized the importance of dispatching such missions to colonial Territories. He further noted that the representatives of Australia, New Zealand, the United Kingdom and the United States had reiterated their Governments' readiness to receive missions in Territories under their administration. His report was annexed to the Committee's report to the General Assembly;[1] an appendix listed the 25 visiting missions sent by the Committee or the Assembly between 1965 and 1981.

In its resolution of 23 November on implementation of the Declaration on colonial countries,[2] the Assembly called on the administering Powers to continue to co-operate with the Committee and to permit access of visiting missions to the Territories to secure first-hand information and ascertain the wishes and aspirations of their inhabitants.

Report. [1]Committee on colonial countries, A/37/23/Rev.1. *Resolution (1982).* [2]GA: 37/35, para. 13, 23 Nov. *Yearbook reference.* [3]1981, p. 1116.

Chapter II

International Trusteeship System

Contents

General aspects

The Trusteeship Council continued during 1982 to supervise, on behalf of the Security Council, the one Trust Territory remaining under the International Trusteeship System—the Trust Territory of the Pacific Islands, a strategic Territory administered by the United States—and dispatched a visiting mission there in July.

The Council, at its forty-ninth session held at United Nations Headquarters from 17 May to 11 June 1982, examined the conditions in the Territory, taking into account the annual report of the Administering Authority,[3] petitions and communications, and statements made in the Council by the Special Representatives of the Administering Authority and Advisers—representatives of the Territory attached to the Administering Authority's delegation. Following a general debate in which Council members gave their opinions on conditions in the Territory, the Council adopted a report[2] to the Security Council containing its conclusions and recommendations.

At its fifteenth special session held from 16 to 20 December, also in New York, the Council decided, at the invitation of the Administering Authority, to dispatch a series of missions starting in early 1983 to Palau, the Marshall Islands and the Federated States of Micronesia, to observe the plebiscites there.

Of the Council's five members (China, France, USSR, United Kingdom, United States), China did not participate in the Council's 1982 sessions.

Conclusions and recommendations pertaining to the Trust Territory were also made, to the General Assembly, by its Special Committee on the Situation with regard to the Implementation of the Declaration on the Granting of Independence to Colonial Countries and Peoples.[1]

Reports. [1]Committee on colonial countries, A/37/23/Rev.1; [2]TC, S/15705; [3]United States, transmitted by S-G note, S/15094 (T/1837).

Trust Territory of the Pacific Islands

Conditions in the Territory

The Trust Territory of the Pacific Islands, designated as a strategic area and administered by the United States in accordance with the Trusteeship Agreement approved by the Security Council in 1947,[9] included more than 2,100 islands and atolls (about 100 of which were inhabited) scattered over an area of some 7.8 million square kilometres of the western Pacific Ocean, north of the Equator.

The population of the Territory, also known as Micronesia, totalled 132,988 as at the 1980 census.

There were four administrative entitites within the Territory—the Federated States of Micronesia, the Marshall Islands, the Northern Mariana Islands and Palau. As a result of referendums, each had its own constitution and popularly elected legislature and executive head.

Trusteeship Council action. At its 1982 regular session, the Trusteeship Council considered the annual report, for the year ending 30 September 1981,[6] submitted by the United States as Administering Authority for the Trust Territory, and presented its report[5] containing conclusions and recommendations to the Security Council.

These conclusions and recommendations, prepared by its Drafting Committee (composed of France and the United Kingdom) on the basis of the Council's discussions, dealt with self-determination and independence, politics and government, economic conditions, social conditions, education, war and post-war damage claims, radioactive waste management, resettlement of the Bikini and Enewetak populations and the United States military base. The Drafting Committee was also asked to make recommendations concerning the chapter on conditions in the Territory for inclusion in the Council's report.

On 11 June, the Council adopted by 2 votes to 1, with 1 abstention, the conclusions and recommendations contained in the annex to the report of the Drafting Committee,[3] before adopting that report as a whole by 3 votes to 1. It also adopted, on the Drafting Committee's recommendation, a working paper prepared by the Secretariat on conditions in the Territory[8] as the basic text for the relevant sections of its report to the Security Council.

The United States, which voted in favour of the report as a whole, explained that it had abstained in the vote on the conclusions and recommendations inasmuch as they were addressed to it as the Administering Authority; it would study them carefully and try, to the extent possible, to implement the recommendations for the benefit of the peoples of Micronesia. The USSR, explaining its negative vote, said the report failed to reflect the deficient performance of the Administering Authority, and a number of passages in the report could only be interpreted as encouragement for that Authority to continue the policy of fragmenting and militarizing the Territory and turning it into its own colonial appendage.

Action by the Committee on colonial countries. The General Assembly's Committee on colonial countries[2] adopted, by 17 votes to none, with 3 abstentions, on 10 August, a series of conclusions and recommendations, made by its Sub-Committee on Small Territories, concerning the Trust Territory of the Pacific Islands.

Stating with regret that the Administering Authority repeatedly declined participation and refused co-operation with the Committee, the 25-member body called on the United States to have its representative present at Committee meetings to provide information. It drew the attention of the relevant United Nations organs to Article 83 of the Charter of the United Nations, which empowered the Security Council to exercise all United Nations functions relating to strategic areas, with the Trusteeship Council's assistance on political, economic, social and educational matters.

The Committee reaffirmed the inalienable right of the people of the Trust Territory to self-determination and independence, and reiterated that factors such as size, geographical location, population and limited natural resources should not delay the implementation of the General Assembly's 1960 Declaration on the Granting of Independence to Colonial Countries and Peoples[7]. It also recalled that the Administering Authority was duty-bound to transfer all power to the freely elected representatives of the Territory, called for increased economic assistance thereto and reaffirmed that the people of Micronesia should receive all benefits from the Territory's 200-mile exclusive economic zone.

The Chairman transmitted the Committee's conclusions to the Security Council by a letter of 10 August.[1]

General Assembly consideration. On 20 September, the Committee on colonial countries requested its Rapporteur to reformulate the conclusions and recommendations into a draft resolution for submission to the General Assembly. On 16 November, the Chairman of the Assembly's Fourth Committee suggested, on the basis of consultations with the Chairman of the Committee on colonial countries and with delegations, that the Committee not take any action at the current session on the draft resolution. The Fourth Committee, without objection, agreed to the Chairman's suggestion.[4]

Letter. [1]Committee on colonial countries Chairman, transmitting Committee conclusions and recommendations, 10 Aug., S/15351.
Reports. [2]Committee on colonial countries, A/37/23/Rev.1; [3]Drafting Committee, T/L.1229; [4]GA 4th Committee, A/37/621 & Corr.1; [5]TC, S/15705; [6]United States, transmitted by S-G note, S/15094 (T/1837).
Resolution. [7]GA: 1514(XV), 14 Dec. 1960 (YUN 1960, p. 49).
Working paper. [8]Secretariat, T/L.1228 & Add.1-3.
Yearbook reference. [9]1946-47, p. 398.
Compilations of resolutions and decisions. TC: 49th session, T/1842; 15th special session, T/1859.
Meeting records. TC: T/PV.1523-1531, 1533, 1535-1539 (17 May–11 June). GA: 4th Committee, A/C.4/37/SR.9-15, 17-23, 24 (26 Oct.-16 Nov.); plenary, A/37/PV.74-77 (22, 23 Nov.).

Publications. Index to Proceedings of the Trusteeship Council, Forty-ninth session—1982 (ST/LIB/SER.B/T.43), Sales No. E.82.I.18; *Fifteenth Special Session—1982, Fiftieth Session—1983* (ST/LIB/SER.B/T.44 & Corr.1), Sales No. E.84.I.2 & Corr.

Self-determination and independence

Trusteeship Council action. In its conclusions and recommendations adopted on 11 June 1982 (see above), the Trusteeship Council reaffirmed the right of the Micronesian people to self-determination, including the right to independence, and noted that, following the 1981 inauguration of a constitutional government in Palau, each of the political components of the Trust Territory had achieved full functional self-government under the Trusteeship Agreement.

It noted with interest the statements of the representatives of the constitutional governments emphasizing their desire to maintain preferential and close relations with the Administering Authority after the termination of the Agreement, and trusted that the negotiations would lead to a mutually satisfactory outcome which respected the personality of every party. The Council understood that the Administering Authority intended to invite the international community to observe, through the appropriate United Nations organs, the plebiscite to be held simultaneously in each of the areas to which the compact of free association applied (see below). As in previous years, the Council refrained from making precise recommendations on the future political status of the various Micronesian entities and reiterated its view that free association was not incompatible with the Trusteeship Agreement, provided that the population concerned freely accepted it. In that regard, the Council favoured a political education programme.

The Council noted that the United States had reaffirmed its intention to proceed in a manner consistent with the Charter of the United Nations and to take up the matter of termination of the Trusteeship Agreement at the appropriate time with the Trusteeship Council and the Security Council. It again expressed hope that the Micronesians would take all necessary steps to establish, after termination of the Agreement, the all-Micronesian entity which they had agreed upon in 1977.

In the Trusteeship Council debate, the United States said the parties were entering the final phase of negotiations, and it expected in the near future the signing and subsequent official submission to the Council of the compact of free association and related agreements by the Administering Authority, the Federated States of Micronesia, the Marshall Islands and Palau. The negotiation process had served to educate the people of the Territory on the political status options and had pre-

pared them to exercise self-determination. The United States expected that when these four governments committed the signed documents to their respective domestic approval processes, the Administering Authority would be able, in consultation with the other parties concerned, to establish a date for the plebiscite and request the Council to organize a mission to observe that act (see below).

France welcomed the progress made towards self-government for the population as well as the Administering Authority's concurrence with the governments of all the entities of the Territory on the need for a speedy termination of the Trusteeship Agreement; the choice before the electorate in a referendum should not be confined to mere approval of the status of free association but should also include the possibility of opting for independence.

The United Kingdom supported the Trusteeship Council's view that free association was an option compatible with the Trusteeship Agreement, provided that the populations concerned had freely accepted it; the Micronesian people should be fully informed, before the referendum, of the various choices available to them as regards their political future.

The USSR said that the Administering Authority, having dismembered the Territory politically and leaving it in a disastrous economic and social situation, pursued a policy intended to perpetuate United States domination over the Territory and transform it into a military-strategic springboard in the western Pacific; instead of improvement, all the signs indicated the further worsening of the situation in the Territory.

Representatives of the Federated States of Micronesia, the Marshall Islands and Palau expressed the support of their peoples for the initialled compacts of free association and the former two, along with the representative of the Northern Mariana Islands, reiterated the eagerness of their peoples for a speedy termination of the Trusteeship Agreement.

Action by the Committee on colonial countries. In its conclusions and recommendations, adopted on 10 August, the Committee on colonial countries reaffirmed the right of the people of the Territory to self-determination and independence in conformity with the United Nations Charter and the Assembly's 1960 Declaration on colonial countries. Reiterating the Administering Authority's obligation to create conditions that would enable the people to exercise that right freely, it urged the Authority to undertake a programme of political education to that end. It noted the Administering Authority's intention to seek termination of the Trusteeship Agreement at the earliest possible date and called on the United

States to preserve the Territory's unity until the people had exercised their right to self-determination and independence.

Communications. By a letter dated 18 November,[2] the United States informed the President of the Trusteeship Council of the completion of the Territory's political status negotiations through the signing of the compact of free association and a series of subsidiary or related agreements with the constitutional governments of the Marshall Islands on 30 May, Palau on 26 August and the Federated States of Micronesia on 1 October. The compact and the related agreements were to be committed to an approval process in each constitutional entity; the United Nations would be formally invited to observe the plebiscite, the timing of which was under consultation.

The Trusteeship Council President sent a telegram on 17 November[1] to two senators of the Palau National Congress, who had requested, in an 8 November telegram, information on the United Nations position regarding the wording of the ballot on the compact of free association. The President expressed the view that the parties concerned should agree on the wording of the ballot in accordance with the objectives of the Trusteeship System as laid down in the Charter.

Letter and telegram (t). [1]TC President, 17 Nov., T/1843 *(t)*; [2]United States, 18 Nov., T/1845.

Politics and government

The United States reported to the Trusteeship Council in 1982 that constitutional governments were fully functioning in the Federated States of Micronesia, the Marshall Islands, the Northern Mariana Islands and Palau, headed, and assisted in key administrative posts, by Micronesians.

Trusteeship Council action. Under the heading "Political Advancement", the Trusteeship Council, in its report, noted with satisfaction the increasing confidence and competence with which each of the governments in the Trust Territory handled all aspects of full, functional self-government, and their continuing efforts to increase contacts with other nations in the region and to develop links with regional agencies. The Council also noted the substantial efforts made by the Administering Authority to transfer all possible responsibility and authority to the new governments, and the reduction in the number of activities and the staff of the Trust Territory Headquarters.

The Council, however, expressed concern over the size of the civil service and the heavy burden it placed on budgets throughout the Trust Territory, and urged the Administering Authority to help create private-sector jobs so that the civil service could be reduced without exacerbating unemployment.

The Council also remained concerned about the generally slow pace of the political education programme in preparation for the plebiscite. While welcoming the Administering Authority's invitation to the constitutional governments to enact legislation for such programmes and for the future plebiscite, the Council expressed the view that various island communities throughout the Trust Territory should be consulted on the programme's form and scope.

The Council noted with satisfaction the progress made in the Territory in the establishment and advancement of the judicial system.

In the Council's debate, the United Kingdom stressed the importance of a political education programme clarifying the options for Micronesians, while France noted the efforts made to inform them of the negotiations under way in respect of the compact of free association.

The United States expressed readiness to fulfil its obligation under the Trusteeship Agreement to ensure that any act of self-determination, particularly a plebiscite on future political status, was preceded by a fair, open and comprehensive public information programme covering the alternatives.

Action by the Committee on colonial countries. In its conclusions and recommendations of 10 August, the Committee on colonial countries noted that responsibility for administrative matters throughout the Trust Territory was exercised by local authorities but regretted that the High Commissioner of the Territory maintained the power, although rarely invoked, to suspend certain legislation. The Committee recalled that the Administering Authority was duty-bound to transfer all power to the Territory's freely elected representatives

Economic conditions

Trusteeship Council action. In its 1982 report, the Trusteeship Council noted with regret that the Territory's economy could not provide sufficient funds to cover the administrative and social expenditure of the constitutional governments. The structural imbalances in the economy had not been reduced and the Territory had suffered from the effects of the deteriorating world economic situation. Substantial economic assistance was more than ever necessary, the Council stated, noting at the same time the efforts by the Administering Authority to help local governments develop their economic activities.

In view of the large deficit in the Territory's balance of trade, the Council called on the Administering Authority to promote the development of the kinds of production that could satisfy local needs, especially for food. It noted that the Authority was assisting the constitutional governments to develop local products, thereby discouraging purchases of similar products abroad. The Council welcomed the completion, as at 1 January 1982, of 18 projects totalling $25 million, under the five-year capital improvement programme, and expressed the hope that attention would be paid in the second phase of that programme to the development of the outer islands.

Further, the Council noted that the constitutional governments were given the opportunity to determine their own priorities for the 1983 budgetary year; that the Administering Authority had provided them with $7.4 million during fiscal year 1981 to help cover their expenses during the transitional period; and that various financial systems were being rationalized, with the governments consulted on the matter and on budget preparation procedures and accounting transfers. The Council also noted that taxes and duties fell within the competence of these governments, under the agreement on free trade within the Territory, and reiterated that the Territory's tax system should be designed to discourage the import of goods and services that were locally available.

The Council welcomed the development of relations between the local leadership and other States in the region, as well as with various regional and international programmes; welcomed the progress made in the operation of the Economic Development Loan Fund; noted the transfer of public land as well as agricultural responsibility to the constitutional governments; and urged the Administering Authority to help expand agricultural and livestock production to meet the local needs and to encourage export-oriented agriculture. It also noted with satisfaction that the maritime authorities of the Federated States of Micronesia, the Marshall Islands and Palau were working to strengthen their legislation on the protection of the 200-mile oceanic zones; and that the Administering Authority was paying constant attention to projects for improving the exploitation of marine resources.

The Council reiterated that the development of tourism in the Territory should be based on a carefully prepared overall plan, with due regard paid to safeguarding the local interests and social structures and preserving the environment.

In the view of the Council, transport and communications continued to be a serious problem in the Territory, although progress had been made in the transfer of ownership of most of the ships and aircraft from the Trust Territory Government to the constitutional governments. It welcomed projects for improving telecommunications within and outside the Territory, such as the signing of agreements between the constitutional governments and COMSAT, the Communications Satellite Corporation, for the installation of land satel-

lite stations to go into operation between autumn 1982 and the end of 1983.

In the discussion, France noted the Territory's insufficient infrastructure, lack of job opportunities and outside economic dependence, and added that the Administering Authority could make an additional effort to help the local administration and the public services to meet the needs of the people and to create the conditions for balanced economic development. The United Kingdom welcomed the growth in the Territory's relations with its Pacific neighbours.

The USSR said the United States had not met its obligations under the Charter and the Trusteeship Agreement to promote the economic progress and self-reliance of the Territory; it asked if the Administering Authority intended to keep Micronesia economically and socially underdeveloped in order to claim the Territory unprepared for independence. Further, the Authority used for military purposes the land it took from the local population.

The United States said it recognized the need for additional efforts to improve the economic situation in the Territory and expressed its intention to continue working with the constitutional governments in installing basic infrastructures that would make self-sustaining economic growth possible; it fully intended to continue assistance in that regard in the post-trusteeship period.

Action by the Committee on colonial countries. In its conclusions and recommendations of 10 August (see above), the Committee on colonial countries called for increased economic assistance to help the Micronesian people achieve economic independence and reduce the structural imbalances of the Territory's economy. It noted that the Administering Authority's role was increasingly restricted to overseeing the capital improvement programme and expenditure of funds appropriated by the United States Congress.

The Committee urged the Administering Authority to continue to safeguard and guarantee, in co-operation with the authorities of the Territory, the right of the people of Micronesia to own and to dispose freely of the natural resources and to establish and maintain control of their future development. It noted the efforts of the Territory's maritime authorities to strengthen existing legislation concerning the exploitation, management and conservation of a 200-mile exclusive economic zone, and reaffirmed that Micronesia's right over such a zone should be respected. It also noted with satisfaction the material assistance provided to the Territory by certain international and regional bodies and encouraged the Territory's leadership to develop relations with such agencies, particularly those in the United Nations system.

Social conditions

Trusteeship Council action. In the section of its 1982 report dealing with "Social advancement", the Trusteeship Council stated its concern that the health services in Micronesia had only two qualified Micronesian doctors. However, it noted the increasing number of Micronesians entering medical school, and suggested that the Territory's governments might consider offering incentives to encourage young people to study medicine. The Council was satisfied to note that several medical facilities in the Territory were being renovated, that one new hospital was fully operational and that the World Health Organization had offered to provide leprosy drugs free of charge. It also noted the improvement made in health care in the Northern Mariana Islands due to the provision of physicians from the United States Public Health Service, and the co-operation between the government of the Northern Mariana Islands and the United States Department of Health and Human Services to upgrade medical facilities.

The Council hoped that the people of Micronesia would recognize the need to participate more actively in community development projects, and expressed regret that the Administering Authority had not examined, with Micronesian representatives, ways to study the effects of trusteeship in preparing future social and cultural programmes. The Council continued to be deeply concerned by the serious unemployment problem and the imbalance between wage-earners in the public and private sectors. It also remained concerned about youth problems in the Trust Territory, particularly with respect to unemployment and juvenile delinquency, and urged the Administering Authority to view sympathetically requests from the constitutional governments for assistance and technical support.

In the debate, France said it saw considerable progress made in many sectors, especially as regards respect for human rights and fundamental freedoms. The USSR disagreed, saying that the Administering Authority paid little respect for human rights and turned the Territory into a testing ground for weapons of mass destruction; the state of medical care and the training of medical personnel was disastrous, and the young people were the main victims of the high rate of crime and suicides.

Education

In the section of its 1982 report dealing with "Educational advancement", the Trusteeship Council considered that the Administering Authority had served the Trust Territory well in providing a system of universal primary schooling throughout the islands. It welcomed the high rate of secondary school attendance and hoped that higher educational and vocational training schemes would be improved in preparation for termination of the Trusteeship Agreement. The Council also noted the transfer to local governments of jurisdiction over education matters.

The Council continued to attach importance to the existence and future development of the College of Micronesia, the only higher education institution in the Territory, and welcomed the operation in the Northern Mariana Islands of a junior community college which co-ordinated practical training at the post-secondary level. It stressed the importance of the acquisition of technical skills by young people as an essential factor in the Territory's economic development, and hoped that the co-operation among the constitutional governments in that regard would permit concerted preparation of training programmes and satisfactory correspondence between the youth training and manpower needs throughout the Territory.

In addition to the Administering Authority's efforts to improve the level of teachers' qualifications, the Council welcomed the efforts of all concerned to preserve and promote the indigenous languages and cultures.

Claims

The Trusteeship Council dealt in its 1982 report with the question of war damage claims brought against the Japanese Government, mainly for damages sustained by Micronesians during the Second World War, and of post-war claims against the United States Government. The Council reiterated its concern that the claims had not been fully settled, as determined by the Micronesian Claims Commission, and called on the parties concerned to resolve the issues before the termination of the Trusteeship Agreement.

Radioactive waste management

The Trusteeship Council, in the section of its 1982 report devoted to "Land and people", noted the continuing concern expressed by Micronesian representatives about the possible dangers of dumping nuclear waste in the Pacific region, along with the stated intention of the Administering Authority not do so in the Trust Territory or in its adjacent waters. The Council noted Japan's assurances that it would continue efforts to obtain the understanding of the countries and Territories concerned with regard to Japan's low-level nuclear waste disposal plans. It also noted that the Administering Authority had not sought a dialogue with Japan on the proposed dumping, contending that such proposals were in accordance with existing international law.

In a letter dated 2 June to the President of the Trusteeship Council,[1] Japan stressed that it proposed to dispose of low-level radioactive wastes—not high-level radioactive wastes or "spent nuclear fuel", the sea disposal of which was prohibited—at a site selected in accordance with the international standards established by the International Atomic Energy Agency; Japan was the nation nearest that site. Fully convinced of the environmental safety of its proposal on the basis of extensive experiments, it would continue its efforts at obtaining the understanding of its Pacific neighbours, taking into account their sentiments and sensitivities on the issue.

In the Council debate, representatives of the Northern Mariana Islands reaffirmed their peoples' total opposition to the dumping of nuclear waste in the Pacific Ocean. The United States said Japan's proposed dumping site was part of the high seas, as defined by international law and the draft Convention on the Law of the Sea. Japan was a party to the Convention on the Prevention of Marine Pollution by Dumping of Wastes and Other Matter, and intended to become a party to the consultations and surveillance mechanism of the Nuclear Energy Agency, which monitored ocean disposal activities. While the United States itself had no intention of disposing of nuclear wastes in the Trust Territory or in the adjacent waters, it had no basis on which to oppose the test dumping so long as Japan abided by those international standards.

Letter. [1]Japan, 2 June, T/1841.

Military base

In the section of its 1982 report dealing with "Population movements", the Trusteeship Council reiterated its concern over the social, cultural and economic difficulties of the people living on the island of Ebeye arising primarily from overpopulation, and urged the Administering Authority to seek mutually satisfactory solutions to specific problems arising from the presence of the United States military facility on Kwajalein Atoll.

In the discussion, the USSR said the Administering Authority had used the Trust Territory for atomic and nuclear-weapon testing and for deployment of its military and support bases; through the proposed additional military agreements, which constituted an integral part of the compact of free association, the United States intended to use the Territory for transporting, deploying, maintaining and testing nuclear, chemical and bacteriological weapons, and for modernizing its strategic missile system.

The United States said it was entirely within its rights under the Trusteeship Agreement in utilizing portions of the Territory for strategic purposes and had done so openly for many years. So long as current international circumstances continued,

the United States would take whatever steps were necessary to prepare for contingencies and, to that end, would continue to use the Kwajalein Missile Range in accordance with leases and agreements with individual landowners and the Marshall Islands government.

Resettlement of the
Bikini and Enewetak populations

In the section of its 1982 report entitled "Population movements", the Trusteeship Council dealt with the situation of the people of Bikini and Enewetak atolls in the Marshall Islands who had had to relocate to other islands because of radioactive contamination from nuclear-weapon tests three decades earlier.

The Council reiterated its concern about the quality of medical care available to these displaced people and regretted that a health programme proposed under United States legislation had not been implemented. It asserted that resettlement proposals for the Bikini and Enewetak populations should take into account any remaining health hazards, and recommended that the Administering Authority continue to ensure the removal of radiation hazards threatening the inhabitants of the Marshall Islands.

The Council noted with satisfaction the March 1982 opening of the airstrip on Kili Island, home of the displaced Bikinians, and the provision of regular air service thereto by the government of the Marshall Islands; it hoped that efforts would be made to improve living conditions for the displaced people of Bikini and that further consideration would be given to the problems of their current location on that island.

In the debate, the United Kingdom accepted that the Bikinians had a genuine cause for concern and hoped that the Administering Authority would continue to do its utmost to allow the early and safe return home of those displaced people and, in the mean time, to improve the living conditions of those living on Ebeye and Kili Islands. France called for continued efforts by the Administering Authority to alleviate the damage caused by its military experiments and facilities; while displacements of the population were necessary and had been useful to the United States Government, the Administering Authority must provide equitable compensation to the displaced population. The USSR said the inhabitants of Bikini and Enewetak had become life-long victims of the United States nuclear experiments and military plans, which failed to eliminate for the Micronesians the results of nuclear testing and violated their fundamental rights and freedoms.

The United States said it had acknowledged, through earlier legislation and in the recent initialled compact of free association, its obligations towards the displaced people of Bikini and Enewetak as well as towards others in the northern Marshall Islands who had suffered personal injury and damage to property; it intended to meet those obligations, to improve the living conditions of those who might not yet return to their home atolls, or islands within given atolls, due to continuing high levels of radiation in the soil and the food-chain, and to provide ultimately for the resettlement of those who had been displaced.

Visiting missions

Visiting Mission in 1982

Acting without vote on 11 June 1982,[2] the Trusteeship Council, decided to dispatch in July a periodic visiting mission to the Trust Territory of the Pacific Islands, composed of the Council members wishing to participate, with the Administering Authority providing an escort officer. By the same resolution, the Council requested the Visiting Mission to investigate the steps taken in the Territory towards realizing the objectives of the Charter of the United Nations regarding the Territory's future; to give attention to issues raised in the annual reports on the administration of the Territory, the relevant petitions, the reports of previous missions and the Administering Authority's observations thereon; to receive petitions and conduct on-the-spot investigation where warranted; and to report its findings to the Council.

At the same time, the Council agreed to its President's suggestion that the nominations for the mission's membership would be approved automatically when received.

The resolution was introduced by France also on behalf of the United Kingdom. In May, the United States had suggested that the Council consider dispatching such a mission in 1982. The USSR did not object to the text's adoption on the understanding that the Visiting Mission would be a periodic mission such as those dispatched to the Trust Territory in the past for the purpose of appraising the situation there, and that it would not have any additional terms of reference beyond the regular mandate of such missions.

The Council's 1982 Visiting Mission,[1] composed of one representative each from France and the United Kingdom, began its visit to the Trust Territory at Kolonia, Ponape, in the Federated States of Micronesia on 4 July and ended it on 31 July at Majuro, Marshall Islands.

Report. [1]Visiting Mission to Trust Territory of Pacific Islands, T/1850.
Resolution (1982). [2]TC: 2173(XLIX), 11 June, text following.
Financial implications. S-G statement, T/L.1232.
Meeting records. TC: T/PV.1537-1540 (8-11 June).

Trusteeship Council resolution 2173(XLIX)

11 June 1982   Meeting 1539   Adopted without vote

2-nation draft (T/L.1231); agenda item 6.
Sponsors: France, United Kingdom.

Terms of reference of the United Nations Visiting Mission to the Trust Territory of the Pacific Islands, 1982

The Trusteeship Council,

Having decided to dispatch a periodic visiting mission to the Trust Territory of the Pacific Islands in 1982,

Having decided that the Visiting Mission should be composed of members of the Council wishing to participate, except the Administering Authority, which will provide an escort officer,*

Having decided that the Visiting Mission should visit the Trust Territory in July 1982 for a period of approximately four weeks,

1. *Directs* the Visiting Mission to investigate and report as fully as possible on the steps taken in the Trust Territory of the Pacific Islands towards the realization of the objectives set forth in Article 76 *b* of the Charter of the United Nations and to pay special attention to the question of the future of the Territory, in the light of the relevant Articles of the Charter and the Trusteeship Agreement;

2. *Directs* the Visiting Mission to give attention, as may be appropriate in the light of discussion in the Trusteeship Council and of resolutions adopted by it, to issues raised in connection with the annual reports on the administration of the Territory, in the petitions received by the Council concerning the Territory, in the reports of the previous periodic visiting missions to the Territory and in the observations of the Administering Authority on those reports;

3. *Directs* the Visiting Mission to receive petitions, without prejudice to its action in accordance with the rules of procedure of the Council, and to investigate on the spot such of the petitions as, in its opinion, warrant special investigation;

4. *Requests* the Visiting Mission to submit to the Council as soon as practicable a report on its visit to the Trust Territory of the Pacific Islands containing its findings, with such observations, conclusions and recommendations as it may wish to make;

5. *Requests* the Secretary-General to provide the necessary staff and facilities to assist the Visiting Mission in the performance of its functions.

---

*At its 1539th meeting, on 11 June 1982, the Council decided that the nominations to be submitted would automatically be approved when received.

Visiting missions in 1983 for plebiscites in Palau, the Marshall Islands and the Federated States of Micronesia

On 20 December 1982, the Trusteeship Council, at the invitation of the Administering Authority, decided to send visiting missions of approximately two weeks duration each to Palau, the Marshall Islands and the Federated States of Micronesia, to observe the plebiscites and to report their observations, conclusions and recommendations to the Council.[4]

The Council took this action at a special session convened at the request of the United States, submitted in a letter of 18 November addressed to the Secretary-General.[3]

Acting by 3 votes to 1 on the text proposed by the United Kingdom, the Council also decided that the mission to Palau, to be composed of not more than four members, would begin on or about 1 February 1983 and end after the declaration of the plebiscite results. The dates of the other missions—the one to the Marshall Islands, composed of not more than five members, and another to the Federated States of Micronesia, composed of not more than six members—would be decided by the Council President in consultation with the Administering Authority and the other Council members.

The Council considered it desirable to include in such missions representatives of the region which were not Council members, and decided that the proposed missions would be composed of representatives of France and the United Kingdom, which had declared their readiness in the Council debate, as well as those of Fiji[1] and Papua New Guinea,[2] which, in letters dated 17 December, had informed the Council President of their willingness to participate. Papua New Guinea had also expressed its understanding that independence would be offered as an option in the plebiscites.

In the debate, the United States informed the Council that the Administering Authority had signed the compact of free association, together with a series of related agreements, with the Marshall Islands on 30 May, with Palau on 26 August and with the Federated States of Micronesia on 1 October, thus allowing the four signatory governments to submit the documents for public approval, including a plebiscite constituting an act of self-determination in each of the Micronesian jurisdictions. It also informed the Council that the Administering Authority and Palau had agreed on 10 February 1983 as the most convenient date for the plebiscite there, and similar consultations were under way with the other two entities; the political education campaign had begun in Palau on 9 September 1982. In inviting the Council to observe the plebiscites, the United States welcomed inclusion of other States of the Pacific region in such missions and requested its President to consult with such States to ascertain their willingness in that regard.

The United States also told the Council that, if any of the peoples of Micronesia were to reject the compact of free association as negotiated by their representatives, the United States Government would accept that decision and negotiate an alternative arrangement for the termination of the trusteeship. It added that, under the terms of the compact of free association, the status could be changed unilaterally at any time.

France noted, and the United Kingdom welcomed, the fact that the people in the three entities would have the opportunity to choose as alternatives to free association the negotiation of their independence or a closer relationship with the United States. France and the United Kingdom believed that, if the three plebiscites could not be held simultaneously, they should be held consecutively, as closely together as possible; they also supported, as clearly permissible under the Council's rules, the inclusion of representatives

of the Pacific region in the visiting missions. The United Kingdom expected the missions to find the answers to such questions as the political education programme and the language of the ballot paper.

The USSR objected to the sending of missions and to the proposed inclusion of non-Council members in such endeavours, as attempts by the United States to give a semblance of legitimacy to its illegal actions and impose on the United Nations the role of assistant in annexing a Trust Territory and transforming it into a colony. In that regard, the USSR asserted that any change in Micronesia's status must take place only with the agreement of the Security Council, that the plebiscites were instruments of an illegitimate dismemberment of a Trust Territory in violation of the Trusteeship Agreement and of the Declaration on the Granting of Independence to Colonial Countries and Peoples, and that these acts would be carried out, not under conditions of free choice but under the total dependence of the population of the Territory on the powers of the Administering Authority.

The United States called the USSR accusations groundless and polemical, and termed them insulting to the intelligence and integrity of the Micronesians and their self-governing, constitutional and freely elected governments; the Council was discussing not the question of a change in the trusteeship, but that of observing the acts of self-determination by Micronesians who had been offered the full range of future political options.

Letters. [1]Fiji, 17 Dec., T/1848; [2]Papua New Guinea, 17 Dec., T/1849; [3]United States, 18 Nov., T/1844.
Resolution (1982). [4]TC: 2174(S-XV), 20 Dec., text following.
Financial implications. S-G statement, T/L.1234.
Meeting records. TC: T/PV.1541-1543 (16-20 Dec.).

Trusteeship Council resolution 2174(S-XV)

20 December 1982   Meeting 1543   3-1

Draft by United Kingdom (T/L.1233); agenda item 3.

Arrangements for the dispatch of visiting missions to observe the plebiscites in Palau, the Marshall Islands and the Federated States of Micronesia, Trust Territory of the Pacific Islands

The Trusteeship Council,

Aware of the plebiscites which are to be held in Palau, the Marshall Islands and the Federated States of Micronesia, Trust Territory of the Pacific Islands,

Having been invited by the Administering Authority to dispatch missions to observe the plebiscites,

Considering that it would be desirable to include in such missions representatives of countries of the region which are not members of the Trusteeship Council,

1. *Decides* to send visiting missions, of approximately two weeks duration in each case, to Palau, the Marshall Islands and the Federated States of Micronesia, the mission to Palau to begin on or about 1 February 1983 and to end as soon as practicable after the declaration of the results of the plebiscite, and the other missions to take place at dates to be decided by the President of the Trusteeship Council in consultation with the Administering Authority and the other members of the Council;

2. *Further decides* that the visiting mission to Palau should be composed of not more than four members, that to the Marshall Islands of not more than five members and that to the Federated States of Micronesia of not more than six members, the members of the missions to be representatives of Fiji, France, Papua New Guinea and the United Kingdom of Great Britain and Northern Ireland;*

3. *Directs* the visiting missions to observe the plebiscites, including the campaign and polling arrangements, the casting of votes, the closure of voting, the counting of ballots and the declaration of results;

4. *Requests* the visiting missions to submit to the Trusteeship Council as soon as practicable reports on their observations of the plebiscites, containing such conclusions and recommendations as they may wish to make;

5. *Requests* the Secretary-General to provide the necessary staff and facilities to assist the visiting missions in the performance of their functions.

---

*At its 1543rd meeting, on 20 December 1982, the Council decided that the nominations to be submitted would automatically be approved when received.

Hearings

During its 1982 examination of the annual report of the Administering Authority on the Trust Territory of the Pacific Islands,[2] the Trusteeship Council[1] heard the following 15 petitioners whose requests for oral hearings had been previously circulated: Douglas Faulkner, of the Republic of Palau; Pedro R. Guerrero, of Micronesia; Roman Tmetuchl, Governor of the State of Airai, one of the largest of the 16 subdivisions of Palau; Ibedul Y. M. Gibbons, one of the Paramount Chiefs of Palau; Moses Uludong, representative of Koror State and member of the Senate of Palau's National Congress; Ismael John, representative of the Council of Enewetak and member of the Marshall Islands Senate; Glenn Alcalay and Roger S. Clark, of the International League for Human Rights; Henchi Balos, on behalf of the people of Bikini; Jonathan M. Weisgall, Legal Counsel for the people of Bikini; the Reverend Paul Gregory, of the Focus on Micronesia Coalition, National Council of the Churches of Christ in the United States; Ataji Balos, on behalf of the people of Kwajalein Atoll; Imada Kabua, on behalf of the landowners of Kwajalein Atoll; Richard Gery, of the Marshall Islands Atomic Testing Litigation Project; and George Allen, Legal Counsel for the landowners of Kwajalein Atoll.

Reports. [1]TC, S/15705; [2]United States, transmitted by S-G note, S/15094 (T/1837).

Petitions, communications and observations

The Trusteeship Council, at its 1982 regular session,[3] examined 4 of the 13 petitions and all 6 communications received,[1] along with the observations of the Administering Authority where applicable. In addition, it received 3 petitions and 3 communications at its special session in December,[2] and a further petition and a communication before the end of the year.

Lists of petitions and communications. [1]T/1836/Add.1, [2]T/1846/Add.1.
Report. [3]TC, S/15705.

Other aspects of the International Trusteeship System

Fellowships and scholarships

Under a programme initiated by the General Assembly in 1952,[2] 11 Member States had in past years made offers of scholarships to students from Trust Territories: Czechoslovakia, Hungary, Indonesia, Italy, Mexico, Pakistan, Philippines, Poland, Tunisia, USSR, Yugoslavia. In a May 1982 report, with later addenda,[1] to the Trusteeship Council covering the period from 25 May 1981 to 13 May 1982, the Secretary-General recalled having requested those States in April 1982 for up-to-date information on the scholarships offered and the extent of their utilization. In response, Czechoslovakia reported that the 20 university and college scholarships it offered annually under the programme had not been fully utilized, as demonstrated by the enrolment of only one scholarship holder in the 1981/82 academic year; all past applicants had been from southern Africa. Poland informed the Secretary-General that it had granted three scholarships to candidates from the Trust Territory of the Pacific Islands and two scholarships for the disposal of the Secretary-General in the 1982/83 academic year. Indonesia did not currently provide scholarships to students from the Trust Territory of the Pacific Islands, and none was studying in the USSR.

In the Council debate, the United States said many Trust Territory students were enrolled in programmes abroad, including those offered in the Western and South Pacific; most of the Micronesian students at university level continued to enrol in United States educational institutions. Because of language barriers, scholarship offers from non-English-speaking States had not been fully utilized.

Representatives of the Trust Territory informed the Council that their students were enrolled at various levels and in diverse fields in educational institutions and programmes in Fiji, Japan, the Netherlands, New Zealand, Papua New Guinea and the Philippines, as well as in the United States. A representative of the Federated States of Micronesia thanked the Government of the Netherlands for providing educational opportunities in its programmes in the Philippines and in the Netherlands itself.

The USSR said the Council should take note of the fact that the people of the Territory, which had only two Micronesian medical doctors among them, had not fully utilized the fellowships offered by States other than the United States and a small number of others, as was the case with the large number of scholarships offered by Czechoslovakia.

On 27 May, the Trusteeship Council, without objection, took note of the Secretary-General's report and the first addendum on the scholarship programme. On 8 June, the Council likewise took note of another addendum containing information submitted by Czechoslovakia.

Report. [1]S-G, T/1839 & Add.1-3.
Resolution. [2]GA: 557(VI), 18 Jan. 1952 (YUN 1951, p. 788).
Meeting records. TC: T/PV.1534, 1537 (27 May, 8 June).

Information dissemination

A report of the Secretary-General covering the period 1 May 1981 to 30 April 1982[1] described activities by the United Nations Department of Public Information (DPI) in distributing United Nations documents, official records and information materials throughout the Trust Territory, including its legislatures, libraries, offices of administrators and the information media. The United Nations Information Centre in Tokyo distributed information published by DPI and other United Nations organs, including material relating to the International Trusteeship System, decolonization, disarmament and economic and social development. Its counterpart in Washington, D. C., provided the people of the United States with updated information on developments concerning the Trust Territory. Radio programmes produced by the United Nations were being used extensively and United Nations films kept at the library of the College of Micronesia were available for loan throughout the Territory. Special information was issued in relation to United Nations Day.

A Special Representative of the Administering Authority told the Trusteeship Council that United Nations Day was a legal holiday in the Territory, deeply appreciated and widely observed throughout.

On 27 May, the Council, without objection, took note of the Secretary-General's report and decided to publish, as an annex to that report, a list of United Nations publications and films distributed in the Trust Territory, as furnished to the Council by DPI. On 8 June the Council took note of that DPI document.

Report. [1]S-G, T/1838 & Add.1.
Meeting records. TC: T/PV.1532-1534, 1537 (25 May–8 June).

Trusteeship Council

At its forty-ninth session, held at United Nations Headquarters from 17 May to 11 June 1982, the Trusteeship Council examined the following items on its agenda,[2] which it adopted on 17 May: annual report of the Administering Authority for the Trust Territory of the Pacific Islands, petitions, arrangements for the dispatch of a periodic visiting mission to the Territory, offers by Member States of study and training facilities for inhabitants of Trust Territories, information dissemination, co-operation with the Committee on the Elimination of Racial Discrimination and the Decade for Action to Combat Racism and Racial Discrimination, attainment of self-government or independence by the Trust Territories, co-operation with the Special Committee on the Situation with regard to the Implementation of the Declaration on the Granting of Independence to Colonial Countries and Peoples, and adoption of its report to the Security Council.

At its fifteenth special session,[1] convened in New York from 16 to 20 December at the urging of the United States, the Trusteeship Council discussed the request by the Administering Authority for organization and dispatch by the Council of a mission or series of missions to observe the plebiscites in Palau, the Marshall Islands and the Federated States of Micronesia. The agenda for that session, which also included examination of petitions, was adopted on 16 December.

Provisional agenda. [1]15th special session, T/1846; [2]49th session, T/1836.
Meeting records. TC: T/PV.1523, 1541 (17 May, 16 Dec.).

Co-operation with the Committee on colonial countries

At its 1982 regular session,[1] the Trusteeship Council considered together the questions of attainment of self-government or independence and co-operation with the Special Committee on the Situation with regard to the Implementation of the Declaration on the Granting of Independence to Colonial Countries and Peoples.

In the debate, the United States maintained that the Council was under no obligation to assist the Committee, as Article 83 of the Charter of the United Nations explicitly prescribed the functions of the Security and Trusteeship Councils in regard to strategic Trust Territories; the Trusteeship Council reported to the Security Council, not to the General Assembly, with regard to those Territories.

France and the United Kingdom shared that view, stating that Article 83 conferred on the Security Council all functions of the United Nations in regard to strategic Trust Territories, and that the Trusteeship Council had no responsibility to assist the Committee on colonial countries with regard to the Trust Territory of the Pacific Islands. The United Kingdom added that, while the Council had in the past assisted the Committee in relation to the former non-strategic Trust Territories, it was no longer called upon to do so as such Territories no longer existed.

The USSR maintained that the provisions of the General Assembly's 1960 Declaration applied to the Trust Territory of the Pacific Islands, that the Assembly exercised a certain function with respect to that Territory, and that the Administering Authority was obliged to co-operate with the Assembly and its subsidiary bodies. It added that, under Article 83, only the Security Council, not the Administering Authority acting unilaterally, could change the status of a Trust Territory.

On 11 June, the Trusteeship Council decided to draw the Security Council's attention to the conclusions and recommendations adopted at its 1982 regular session, along with the statements by its members, on the attainment of self-government or independence by the Trust Territory in accordance with the relevant provisions of the Charter.

Report. [1]TC, S/15705.
Meeting records. TC: T/PV.1535, 1537-1539 (28 May–11 June).

Co-operation with CERD and the Decade against racial discrimination

In 1982, the Trusteeship Council[1] considered together the question of co-operation with the Committee on the Elimination of Racial Discrimination (CERD) and the Decade for Action to Combat Racism and Racial Discrimination (1973-1983).

In the debate, the United States reported the absence, by law and by practice, of racial discrimination in the Trust Territory; it took pride in the favourable treatment given by CERD to information on the Territory's human rights situation. While it continued not to participate in the activities of the Decade for well-known reasons, it supported all genuine efforts to end racism and racial discrimination.

The USSR reiterated its regret that the Trusteeship Council, in view of the positions taken by its Western members, refused to participate in the Decade's activities; it urged the Council to demand from the Administering Authority all relevant information, full co-operation with CERD and more attention and concern to the protection of human rights in the Territory. It asserted that the Administering Authority violated the rights of the Micronesians by driving them out of their land, which it then used as a nuclear testing range.

On 28 May, the Council took note, without objection, of the statements made.

Report. [1]TC, S/15705.
Meeting record. TC: T/PV.1535 (28 May).

Chapter III

Namibia

Contents

For resolutions and decisions of major organs mentioned but not reproduced, refer to INDEX OF RESOLUTIONS AND DECISIONS.

General aspects

In a continuing effort towards Namibia's independence, negotiations resumed in New York in July 1982, with the participation of the representatives of the front-line States, Nigeria, the South West Africa People's Organization (SWAPO), the members of the Western "contact group" (Canada, France, Federal Republic of Germany, United Kingdom, United States) and South Africa, on arrangements for the implementation of the United Nations settlement plan and on the roles of the United Nations and the United Nations Transition Assistance Group (UNTAG). The Secretary-General reported to the Security Council that substantial progress had been made in the discussions.

The United Nations Council for Namibia, at a series of extraordinary plenary meetings held at Arusha, United Republic of Tanzania, adopted on 13 May the Arusha Declaration and Programme of Action on Namibia. By the Declaration, the Council asserted that South Africa's defiance continued due to the increasing support it received from its major Western trading partners, by the misuse of the veto by the three Western permenent members of the Security Council, and by the reluctance of the Western contact group to apply sufficient pressure on South Africa to comply with the United Nations decisions.

Among a series of resolutions adopted in 1982 on the question, the General Assembly, by one text, reiterated that a 1978 Security Council resolution, in which the Council had endorsed the United Nations plan for the independence of Namibia, formed the only basis for a peaceful settlement of the Namibia question and called for its immediate and unconditional implementation without qualification or modification.[1]

Resolution (1982). [1]GA: 37/233 B, 20 Dec.

Namibia question

Communications. By a letter of 21 January 1982 to the Secretary-General on the Namibia question and *apartheid*,[5] South Africa's Minister for Foreign Affairs and Information considered equal treatment of all political parties essential for the successful implementation of any settlement proposal on Namibia, and declared it imperative for the Secretary-General to demonstrate his impartiality by dissociating himself from the General Assembly's commitment to SWAPO as the sole and authentic representative of the Namibian people. In South Africa's view, the January 1981 Geneva meeting[30] had been inconclusive because the United Nations had remained extensively pro-SWAPO in its stance.

By a letter of 12 July,[4] the members of the "contact group"—the five Western States (Canada, France, Federal Republic of Germany, United Kingdom, United States) that had originally proposed the 1978 settlement plan[29]—transmitted to the Secretary-General a set of principles, which they said had been accepted by all parties to the negotiation, concerning the constituent assembly and the constitution for an independent Namibia. While the text of the principles contained certain conditions, such as the provision that every adult Namibian would be eligible to vote, campaign and stand for election, and the voting would be by secret ballot, the group believed that the method of electing the assembly must be determined in accordance with the provisions of the 1978 Security Council resolution endorsing the settlement plan.[27]

The Secretary-General reported to the Security Council[12] that negotiations resumed in New York during the second half of July, with representatives of the front-line States, Nigeria, SWAPO, the Western contact group and South Africa, to finalize arrangements for the plan's implementation in 1982 and discuss the roles of the United Nations and UNTAG. The Secretary-General stated that the discussions led to substantial progress on outstanding issues, including the composition and deployment of the military component of UNTAG, and to an agreement that UNTAG would monitor SWAPO bases in Angola and Zambia and that the system for electing the constituent assembly, to be settled according to the terms of the 1978 Council resolution, would be based either on proportional representation or single-member constituencies.

In response to a December 1981 General Assembly request,[23] the Secretary-General submitted a report on 28 April 1982,[11] with later addenda, transmitting information provided by 20 States on action taken or envisaged by them in support of Namibia.

Activities of the UN Council for Namibia. Throughout 1982, the United Nations Council for Namibia continued to act both as a policy-making organ of the United Nations and as the legal Administering Authority for Namibia until independence, the role assigned to it by the General Assembly in 1967.[21]

From 10 to 14 May, the Council, in response to a December 1981 Assembly request,[24] held a series of extraordinary plenary meetings at Arusha, United Republic of Tanzania, and adopted, on 13 May, the Arusha Declaration and Programme of Action on Namibia. The text was transmitted to the Secretary-

General by a letter of 14 May from the Council President[3] and included in the Council's report to the Assembly.[9]

By the Declaration, the Council condemned South Africa for its continued illegal occupation of Namibia and for its militarization and use of that Territory for launching armed attacks against neighbouring States, particularly Angola. It asserted that South Africa's defiance continued due to the increasing support given it by its major Western trading partners, by the misuse of the veto by the three Western permanent members of the Security Council, and by the reluctance of the Western contact group to apply sufficient pressure on South Africa to comply with the United Nations decisions.

Reaffirming its support for the Namibian people's armed liberation struggle under the leadership of SWAPO, their sole and authentic representative, the Council declared that the question of Namibia, being one of decolonization, had to be resolved according to the Assembly's 1960 Declaration on the Granting of Independence to Colonial Countries and Peoples,[20] and that the attempts to link it with irrelevant issues, such as that of co-operation between Angola and certain other countries, were designed to justify the illegal occupation and thus delay Namibia's independence. It again declared that the United Nations plan, as set forth in Security Council resolutions of 1976[25] and 1978,[27] was the only basis for a negotiated settlement, to be implemented without modification; that Namibia must accede to independence with its territorial integrity intact, including Walvis Bay and the offshore islands; and that Namibia's natural resources were its inviolable heritage.

By the Programme of Action, the Council called anew for the imposition of comprehensive mandatory sanctions against South Africa by the Security Council and for international assistance, including military assistance, to SWAPO in its liberation struggle. It called on all Member States to work towards a negotiated settlement based on the United Nations plan, including United Nations–supervised free elections, and to support the SWAPO proposal to convene a conference under United Nations auspices, similar to that held at Geneva in 1981,[30] to resolve outstanding issues on the basis of relevant United Nations resolutions. Governments were also urged to impose voluntary sanctions, including economic sanctions and arms and oil embargoes; to adopt legislation to prevent the recruitment of mercenaries for service in Namibia; and to support the 4 May 1982 communiqué issued by the Foreign Ministers of the front-line States, Kenya and Nigeria and the SWAPO President.

The Council decided actively to protect the needs of Namibian refugees, demanded the release of all Namibian political prisoners, and declared that it would determine Namibia's maritime zones and protect its natural resources, specifically from their exploitation by transnational and other corporations including State-controlled corporations. The Council also declared its determination to intensify its efforts towards the early decolonization of Namibia by mobilizing international public opinion, taking measures to preserve Namibia's territorial integrity and safeguarding its interests in international forums, dispatching missions of consultation to Governments and broadening contacts with national parliaments, intergovernmental and non-governmental organizations, liberation-support and solidarity groups, trade unions and other organizations in all States.

Earlier in the year, the Council dispatched a consultation mission—composed of Botswana, Cyprus, Guyana (Chairman), India, the USSR, the United Republic of Cameroon and SWAPO—to Cyprus (28—31 March), Sri Lanka (1-6 April) and Bangladesh (9-13 April). Following consultations with foreign affairs officials, the Council issued joint communiqués with the Governments of Bangladesh and Cyprus and a joint press statement with the Government of Sri Lanka, by which they reaffirmed their commitment to Namibia's cause and rejected any attempts to present the liberation struggle in Namibia as part of an East-West confrontation and as so-called international terrorism.

In efforts to implement its 1974 Decree No. 1 for the Protection of the Natural Resources of Namibia,[28] the Council dispatched a mission to London and Frankfurt, Federal Republic of Germany, from 30 June to 9 July to inform corporations operating in Namibia of the illegality of their activities and urging them to withdraw from Namibia until independence. The Council held a seminar at Vienna, Austria, from 8 to 11 June on South Africa's military installations and operations in Namibia.

As in the past, the Council participated in the ministerial meetings of the Organization of African Unity and of the Movement of Non-Aligned Countries and in a number of international conferences.

In 1982, Namibia, represented by the Council, was granted full membership in the Executive Committee of the Programme of the United Nations High Commissioner for Refugees (UNHCR), the International Atomic Energy Agency (IAEA) and the International Telecommunication Union (ITU), and the right to become party to the United Nations Convention on the Law of the Sea and to join the Preparatory Commission for the International Sea-Bed Authority and for the International Tribunal for the Law of the Sea.

The Council reported to the General Assembly at its 1982 regular session on developments concerning the Territory and on the Council's activities from 1 September 1981 to 31 August 1982.[9]

The Assembly approved the report on 20 December in two resolutions: one on the Namibia question (see below) and another on the Council's work programme, in which it also supported the efforts of the Council as the legal Administering Authority for Namibia.

Activities of the Committee on colonial countries. By a consensus text adopted on 20 August,[8] the Special Committee on the Situation with regard to the Implementation of the Declaration on the Granting of Independence to Colonial Countries and Peoples rejected all manœuvres by South Africa designed to bring about a sham independence in Namibia, and reaffirmed the need to hold without further delay free elections under United Nations supervision and control in the whole of Namibia as one political entity, in accordance with the 1976[25] and 1978[27] Security Council resolutions. The Committee deprecated any attempt to undermine the international consensus embodied in the Council's 1978 resolution which, it declared, constituted the only acceptable basis for a peaceful transition of Namibia to independence.

The Committee expressed support for the struggle, by all available means, of the people of Namibia and their national liberation movement, SWAPO, and condemned South Africa for its intensified military build-up in Namibia, including the recruitment of Namibians into the so-called South West Africa/Namibia Territory Force, and its use of mercenaries as well as of Namibian territory for acts of aggression against neighbouring African States. The Committee recommended that the Security Council act decisively against South Africa's dilatory manœuvres and fraudulent schemes aimed at frustrating Namibia's legitimate struggle; widen the scope of its 1977 resolution on an arms embargo against South Africa;[26] and impose forthwith comprehensive mandatory sanctions against South Africa under the terms of Chapter VII of the Charter of the United Nations. The Secretary-General was requested to mobilize world public opinion against South Africa's policy on Namibia.

By a letter of 24 August,[2] the Committee Chairman transmitted the 19-paragraph consensus text to the Security Council President.

Action by the Commission on Human Rights. In a resolution of 25 February dealing with the right of peoples to self-determination,[13] the Commission on Human Rights reaffirmed the inalienable right of the people of Namibia to self-determination and the legitimacy of their struggle, including armed struggle, against the illegal occupation of South Africa. It declared that occupation an act of aggression against the Namibians and a threat to international peace and security (See ECONOMIC AND SOCIAL QUESTIONS, Chapter XVIII).

General Assembly action. Of five resolutions on the Namibian question adopted by the General Assembly on 20 December, one dealt with the general aspects resulting from South Africa's illegal occupation of the Territory, and another with implementation of the Security Council's 1978 resolution[27] endorsing the United Nations settlement plan.

By the first resolution,[18] the Assembly reaffirmed that the genuine independence of Namibia could be achieved only with the direct and full participation of SWAPO, the sole and authentic representative of the Namibian people, and that the only parties to the conflict in Namibia were South Africa and the Namibian people under SWAPO leadership. It also reaffirmed that the Security Council's 1978 resolution, together with one of 1976,[25] was the only basis for a peaceful settlement of the Namibia question and called for its immediate and unconditional implementation without qualification or modification. In that regard, the Assembly rejected the manœuvres by one member of the Western contact group, characterizing them as being aimed at undermining the international consensus embodied in the 1978 resolution.

The Assembly condemned South Africa for its continued illegal occupation of Namibia and for its attempts at undermining the territorial integrity and unity of Namibia as well as perpetuating the systematic plunder of the Territory's natural resources. It also condemned South Africa for its military build-up in Namibia and for its introduction of compulsory military service for Namibians, use of mercenaries for suppression and for military attacks against neighbouring States, and forcible displacement of Namibians. The Assembly described as threats to international peace and security South Africa's acts of aggression and repression, its policies of *apartheid* and its development of nuclear weapons. The Secretary-General was requested to report to the Assembly in 1983 on the text's implementation.

The resolution also included provisions containing a call for international assistance to SWAPO and to the front-line States; a demand for the release of all political prisoners and an accounting of "disappeared" Namibians; a request for the withdrawal of foreign economic interests from Namibia and adoption of measures for the protection of its natural resources; a call for an end to nuclear collaboration and to collaboration by the International Monetary Fund (IMF), the effective isolation of South Africa in all respects by all States, and comprehensive mandatory sanctions by the Security Council; and a request for co-operation with the Council for Namibia.

The Assembly adopted the resolution by a recorded vote of 120 to none, with 23 abstentions. The text, recommended by the Council for Namibia, was introduced in the Assembly by Guyana.

By the second resolution,[19] the Assembly reaffirmed United Nations responsibility for Namibia until achievement of genuine national independence. It reiterated that the Security Council's 1978 resolution, endorsing the United Nations plan for Namibia's independence, was the only basis for a peaceful settlement of the Namibia question and called for its immediate implementation without qualification or modification. The Assembly firmly rejected what it called persistent attempts by the United States and South Africa to establish any linkage between the independence of Namibia and extraneous issues, in particular the withdrawal of Cuban forces from Angola, which it emphasized would only retard the decolonization process and constitute interference in Angola's internal affairs. The Assembly requested the Council to exercise its authority for implementation of its 1978 resolution so as to bring about Namibia's independence without delay.

The Assembly adopted the resolution by a recorded vote of 129 to none, with 17 abstentions. The text, also recommended by the Council for Namibia, was introduced in the Assembly by Nigeria.

The Namibia question was also dealt with in a number of other 1982 Assembly resolutions.

By the first of two resolutions adopted on 23 November on implementation of the 1960 Declaration on the Granting of Independence to Colonial Countries and Peoples,[14] the Assembly requested the specialized agencies and other organizations of the United Nations system to withhold all assistance from, and discontinue all support to, the Government of South Africa until restoration of the Namibians' right to independence, and to refrain from action that might imply recognition of the legitimacy of the domination of the Territory by that régime. It urged those bodies to grant full membership to the Council for Namibia if they had not done so. The text's adoption followed a decision to retain the seventh preambular paragraph, by a recorded vote of 87 to 26, with 27 abstentions; the vote was requested by the United States, which objected to what it called an irresponsible accusation contained in the paragraph against the United States and other Western countries for working against Namibian independence.

By the second resolution on the Declaration,[15] the Assembly requested all States, directly and through action in the specialized agencies and other organizations of the United Nations system, to withhold all assistance from the South African

Government until Namibia's right to self-determination had been restored and its independence in a united Namibia achieved; and to refrain from action which might imply recognition of the legitimacy of South Africa's illegal occupation of Namibia. The Assembly also requested the Committee on colonial countries to continue to examine Member States' compliance with the Declaration and other resolutions on decolonization, particularly those relating to Namibia.

In its resolution of 3 December on the Decade for Action to Combat Racism and Racial Discrimination (1973-1983),[16] the Assembly reaffirmed the inalienable right of the Namibian people to self-determination and independence. In another resolution of 3 December, on right to self-determination,[17] the Assembly condemned South Africa for its increased oppression of the Namibian people, its massive militarization of Namibia and its armed attacks on the front-line States with the aim of destabilizing their Governments; and demanded immediate implementation of the resolution on Namibia adopted at its September 1981 emergency special session.[23]

On 13 December, the Assembly, acting without vote on an oral proposal by its President,[1] took note of the report of its Fourth Committee on the hearing it had granted on 15 October to the Reverend G. Michael Scott of the International Fellowship of Reconciliation;[10] the Committee heard his statement on 11 November.

In explanation of vote on the 20 December resolutions, France, also on behalf of the other members of the Western contact group, said they abstained to avoid jeopardizing the group's role in the negotiations; they had reservations on numerous aspects of the texts, which they viewed as having failed in form and substance to recognize the seriousness of the situation or the opportunity that existed for a peaceful solution. The group denounced violence from any source for whatever reason and called on the international community to support the effort for a negotiated settlement.

With respect to the first resolution, on general aspects of the Namibia question, most of those abstaining reiterated their commitment to Namibia's independence through a negotiated settlement based on the 1978 Security Council resolution. Australia, though a member of the Council for Namibia, could not support what it described as the extravagant formulations and tendentious language in the text. Portugal objected to what it called insufficiently realistic appreciation of the situation, which contributed little to implementing the independence plan. In a similar vein, the Ivory Coast viewed the text's wording to be inappropriate and untimely, as did Brazil, which voted in favour.

Denmark, on behalf of the 10 member countries of the European Community (EC), regretted the text's failure to take account of efforts being made in accordance with the 1978 resolution and of the substantial progress achieved following resumption of the negotiations initiated by the Western contact group. Similarly, Uruguay, which voted in favour, would have liked the text to refer to the progress made to date through negotiations. Australia, abstaining, commended the contact group for its continuing efforts, while Senegal called on the group to show greater firmness in regard to South Africa.

Many delegations, among them Australia, Austria, Denmark (for the EC members), Japan, Norway (speaking also for Denmark, Finland, Iceland and Sweden) and Portugal, considered the singling out by name of individual countries for condemnation to be arbitrary, divisive, inappropriate and unjustified. In a similar vein, Ireland noted that one of those condemned, as a member of the Western contact group, had been engaged in major negotiating efforts; for the Netherlands, that condemnation raised doubts as to the real motive of those who insisted on including unfounded accusations in the resolution. Although voting in favour of the text, Burma, Fiji, the Gambia, Greece, Peru, Samoa, Thailand, Turkey and Uruguay objected to the selective condemnation. Chile, not participating in the vote, said the name-calling detracted from achieving a climate of co-operation essential for a negotiated solution.

Sri Lanka also objected to condemnation by name of specific institutions, as did the Netherlands, which rejected attempts at politicizing the specialized agencies. Uruguay further observed that international economic and financial bodies were governed by their respective statutes, and Botswana expressed reservations on the paragraph deploring the relations of IMF with South Africa.

Along with Austria and Norway (for the Nordic countries), which rejected formulations prejudicial to the outcome of free elections, Denmark (for the EC members) and the Netherlands asserted that none of the participants in the proposed elections should be designated in advance as the sole and authentic representative of the Namibian people. Japan and Ireland, although appreciative of the role of SWAPO in seeking Namibia's independence, were of the understanding that the Namibians themselves would freely elect their representatives. While voting in favour, Uruguay shared that view. For the Libyan Arab Jamahiriya, those opposing reference to SWAPO as the sole legitimate representative of the Namibian people thereby supported South Africa.

Austria, Ireland, Japan, the Netherlands and Norway (for the Nordic countries) rejected the United Nations endorsement of armed struggle and calls for military assistance, and Denmark (for the EC countries) observed that the United Nations obligation was to encourage peaceful solutions. Similar reservations were expressed by Fiji, Peru and Uruguay, which all voted in favour. However, the Libyan Arab Jamahiriya said that opposing the Namibians' recourse to armed struggle amounted to telling them to acquiesce in persecution, oppression and murder.

Commitment to the United Nations Charter and the division of competence was expressed by Denmark (for the EC countries), as well as by Austria, the Netherlands and Norway (for the Nordic countries), which said the text failed to take into account that only the Security Council could adopt decisions binding on Member States. Uruguay asserted that only the Council had the competence to limit or restrict the sovereign right of States to conduct relations with one another.

Japan doubted, under the prevailing circumstances, whether comprehensive and mandatory sanctions against South Africa would be the most effective and expeditious means of achieving the desired end. The Netherlands opposed measures for the total isolation of South Africa for fear it would only inflict added suffering and hardship on the people of South Africa and neighbouring countries. Botswana had reservations on the paragraphs requesting continued monitoring of the boycott of South Africa and urging comprehensive mandatory sanctions.

Austria, Ireland, the Netherlands and Norway (for the Nordic countries) said they could not accept those provisions with sweeping financial implications.

Albania declared that its affirmative vote demonstrated its support for the just cause of the Namibian people and their struggle for freedom and independence. The Libyan Arab Jamahiriya said a negative vote was tantamount to supporting the racist régime's occupation of Namibia. Iran declared its support for all liberation movements and anti-imperialist struggles, and regretted that the Zionist nature of the *apartheid* régime had not been clearly recognized and defined. Vanuatu said the Namibian people had been compelled to wage an armed struggle against South Africa and that those who had the power to bring South Africa to its senses through non-violent means had chosen not to use that power.

With respect to the second resolution of 20 December, Belgium explained its abstention by stating that, despite its appreciation of the United States efforts, it rejected establishment of a linkage between the withdrawal of Cuban troops from Angola and the achievement of Namibian independence, considering it unwise to set any pre-conditions to implementation of the plan as approved by the Security Council. Albania, voting in favour, supported the text's condemnation of United States and South African efforts to establish such a linkage, although it regarded as inadmissible the continued foreign military presence in Angola.

The Netherlands, abstaining, and Turkey, voting in favour, objected to paragraph 3, which contained reference to the United States attempts to establish a linkage. Similarly, despite their affirmative votes, Chile, Thailand and Uruguay had reservations on that paragraph, and Greece would have abstained if a separate vote was taken on it. Ireland said those trying to negotiate implementation of the 1978 resolution must be given a certain latitude, including separate efforts to resolve other issues, but without changing the terms of the plan; its affirmative vote, therefore, should not be taken as endorsement of the excessively categorical statement about delaying the decolonization process or as specific criticism of the United States efforts to secure implementation of the 1978 resolution. In addition, objections to the name-calling of Member States were again voiced by some, among them Australia, Denmark (for the EC members), Fiji, Japan, the Netherlands, Norway (for the Nordic countries), Portugal and Sri Lanka.

During the General Assembly debate on the question of Namibia, a majority of the speakers—mostly from the developing or Eastern European countries—expressed frustration and disappointment at the manner in which the negotiations on the Namibia question had thus far proceeded: at each stage of imminent implementation of the settlement plan, South Africa would make a new demand to bring negotiations to a halt. They asserted that through this dilatory tactic, South Africa, while appearing to be involved in serious negotiations—but using them as a loophole to gain time, as Romania put it—was actually entrenching itself more firmly in Namibia. The speakers maintained that economic, military and nuclear collaboration with South Africa, instead of being curtailed, was blatantly expanding, and that the Assembly should, therefore, immediately impose comprehensive mandatory sanctions, under Chapter VII of the United Nations Charter, to compel South Africa to implement the settlement plan. Kuwait said South Africa derived comfort from the lack of enforcement measures against it. In the absence of collective sanctions, Djibouti urged all Governments to comply individually with the Charter provisions.

In Madagascar's view, the people of Namibia were being held hostage while South Africa and its supporters obtained satisfaction regarding a plan which had no concern or interest for that people. Zimbabwe rejected attempts to blame Angola for the stalemate in the international efforts to have the Security Council's 1978 resolution implemented.

Poland rejected what it called the manoeuvres by certain members of the contact group aimed at undermining the 1978 Council resolution and, along with others including Argentina, Liberia, Malaysia, Mauritania and Pakistan, urged its implementation without prevarication, qualification, modification or delay. Czechoslovakia condemned certain members of the contact group for trying to impose on Namibians a decision that would limit their right to self-determination.

Ethiopia said that so long as the Security Council's Western members felt their economic and military interests to be better served by the perpetuation of racism and colonialism in southern Africa, it would be futile to expect a meaningful Council contribution towards Namibian independence. Benin and Iraq condemned those States which used the veto to block the Council's adoption of concrete political and economic measures. Kenya remained concerned that the Council had been so frustrated, and Qatar regretted that the will of the international community thus yielded to the will of a single Member State which had the right of veto. Democratic Kampuchea, Indonesia, Sweden and Zimbabwe, among others, urged the Council to act expeditiously and decisively by exercising its authority in accordance with the Charter.

A large number of developing and Eastern European States shared the view that South Africa was encouraged in its continued defiance of relevant United Nations decisions by the extensive support it enjoyed from its Western allies, principally the United States, whose economic and military interests decisively influenced their policy towards Namibia and South Africa. Angola called South Africa's supporters the absentee occupiers. Nigeria found it disturbing that some Member States pursued short-term economic interests and so-called strategic considerations at the expense of Namibia's independence. Colombia urged the major Powers to realize that Namibia was not a geographical whim, nor an economic booty or a strategic enclave.

India and Kenya called the operation of foreign economic interests in Namibia illegal and inimical, asserting that the economic stake perhaps accounted for the ambivalent attitude of some of South Africa's supporters. Mozambique said the intensified activities in Namibia of the leading Western countries and other members of the North Atlantic Treaty Organization and their position concerning a settlement of the Namibia question could be explained by their greed and military, strategic and political interests.

It was understandable, Benin and Czechoslovakia said, for the members of the Western contact group to strengthen their alliance with Pretoria rather than compel it to abide by the international decisions, since their transnational corporations played a leading role in the rapacious plunder of Namibia's natural resources. Sharing that view, the German Democratic Republic and the USSR said that 53 out of the 88 transnational corporations of imperialist States operating in Namibia had their headquarters in countries of the contact group. Angola and the Libyan Arab Jamahiriya asserted that the trade between South Africa and each member State of the contact group had registered an increase in recent years.

Yugoslavia said those members of the contact group engaged in economic and other co-operation with South Africa bore a special responsibility. Iraq concluded that, having placed their interests above all other considerations, they had no serious intention of solving the Namibia problem.

While reaffirming the prime responsibility of the Security Council in implementing the United Nations settlement plan, some countries—among them Bangladesh, Burundi, Gabon, Guinea-Bissau, Nepal, Nicaragua, Romania, Sao Tome and Principe, Senegal, Sweden and Togo—underscored the contact group's special role in making that a reality. They urged the members of the group, either collectively or individually, to use the means and influence at their disposal to pressure South Africa into accepting the international consensus and implement the plan without further delay.

The Byelorussian SSR asserted that the contact group applied pressure on SWAPO rather than on South Africa, so as to have the Namibia question settled outside the United Nations. Behind its slogan of restraint, Czechsolovakia said, the group continued to support Pretoria's policy of delaying tactics. For Albania, the Western Powers' plans to solve the Namibia question themselves constituted the delaying tactics.

In Zambia's view, France, which had explained the group's position, had not addressed the heart of the problem: South African intransigence encouraged by the United States position. Algeria wondered whether the group really intended to honour the commitment it had freely assumed, adding that the five Western countries had refused to demonstrate firmness and thus encouraged South Africa to persist in intransigence. Ethiopia held South Africa and the contact group responsible for the imminent collapse of the process of implementing the United Nations plan. Albania asserted that American imperialism and its allies pursued neo-colonialist interests in Namibia and in southern Africa, while creating a false impression that the negotiations under their patronage could lead to a speedy solution of the Namibia question. The Syrian Arab Republic spoke similarly. Chile called Namibia an international struggle and expressed perplexity at the position of those who wished to assume sole responsibility for the

Namibian cause. Japan, however, expressed its firm support for the efforts of the contact group.

The South African demand for Cuban troop withdrawal from Angola as a condition for Namibia's independence was condemned and rejected as an extraneous element by a majority of speakers, including the Congo, calling it an absolutely unfounded legal quibbling, and the United Republic of Tanzania, extortionist manoeuvres in furtherance of the cold-war rivalry.

Angola rejected the linkage as not part of the 1978 Security Council resolution, which South Africa had accepted, and said the Cubans were in Angola at the express invitation of that sovereign Government. Similarly, others, among them Cuba, Cyprus, Czechoslovakia, the German Democratic Republic, Guinea-Bissau, Hungary, India, Mongolia, Togo and Venezuela, said the presence of Cuban troops in Angola was solely the concern of the two sovereign States. Such linkage therefore constituted an encroachment on State sovereignty, said a number of speakers, including Antigua and Barbuda, Benin, Botswana, the Byelorussian SSR, the Congo, Ethiopia, Mali, Mozambique, Pakistan, Sao Tome and Principe, Sierra Leone, the Syrian Arab Republic, the Ukrainian SSR, the USSR, the United Republic of Tanzania, Yugoslavia and Zimbabwe.

Several speakers drew attention to a declaration issued in November by 31 African heads of State and Government at Tripoli, Libyan Arab Jamahiriya, rejecting the linkage and any other question alien to the 1978 Security Council resolution, and to a communiqué by the front-line States, similarly condemning the linkage as contrary to that resolution and as inadmissible interference in Angola's internal affairs.

Brazil and Norway said that, while nobody might be happy with the presence of foreign forces in southern Africa, that circumstance could not be used to prevent a settlement of the Namibia question. Brazil observed, in this connection, that the Foreign Ministers of Angola and Cuba had reiterated in the 1982 Assembly general debate their pledge that those troops would be withdrawn once Namibia became independent. Sweden found it unfortunate that Pretoria had gained support for its demand, asserting that it was South African aggression in southern Angola that had invited the foreign troops in that sovereign country. Norway added that, if the idea of the parallel withdrawal of Cuban troops from Angola and South African troops from Namibia, or expanded demilitarized zones, could point the way out of the current impasse, it would welcome that.

Cuba called the linkage not a South African requirement but an imperialist machination to further United States counter-revolutionary strategy in Africa, aimed at establishing a puppet government in Namibia under South African manage-

ment and overthrowing the Government of Angola to bring that country under an imperialist neo-colonial system. Zambia said South Africa and the United States wanted to hold the Namibian people hostage to their own ideological perceptions and preoccupations, and the Byelorussian SSR urged the United Nations to unmask and foil what it called the cynical scheming of those two countries. Similarly, the Libyan Arab Jamahiriya and the United Republic of Tanzania called the linkage a time-buying tactic to enable South Africa, faced with the collapse of the Democratic Turnhalle Alliance and other so-called ethnic alternatives to SWAPO, to prop up new puppet factions in Namibia.

Bangladesh, Peru and Venezuela also rejected the introduction of additional elements into the initial agreements, and Austria considered such elements better suited for direct discussion between the interested Governments. Mexico called the linkage interference in international decisions regarding Namibia, and hoped that the almost universal opposition to the demand would make its sponsors give it up.

Egypt noted with satisfaction that France, a member of the Western contact group, had rejected the linkage, and Kuwait regretted that the United States had not acted likewise. The United Republic of Tanzania regretted that a party to the negotiations which was expected to play the role of honest broker was actively fuelling and sustaining the intransigence of the *apartheid* régime. Zambia urged the rest of the group to bring pressure on the United States to drop its insistence.

The SWAPO representative blamed the United States for inventing the linkage issue, which it said South Africa merely seized upon as an excuse to avoid free elections in Namibia; he endorsed the call by African States and the Movement of Non-Aligned Countries for an early meeting of the Security Council to resume its responsibilities under the Charter and set its own time-frame for the implementation of the United Nations plan for Namibia.

Objections were raised by a number of speakers, including the Congo, Iraq, the Lao People's Democratic Republic, Nicaragua, Senegal and Uganda, over what they believed to be South African attempts at making the Namibia question part of the East-West geopolitical conflict. The United Republic of Tanzania said South Africa had arrogated to itself the role of defender of democracy in southern Africa, by exploiting the cold-war fixations of the West. Similarly, Togo saw South Africa posing as the last bastion against communist expansion in that region for the purpose of receiving from certain States more direct military commitment, or at least a complicity of silence. Albania believed the question to have been complicated by the rivalry between the USSR and the United States, which competed for the position of advantage throughout Africa.

Concern was also voiced over possible South African attempts at an internal settlement in Namibia. Pretoria's extension of the mandate of the Namibian assembly and provisional government beyond the expiration date of 21 November led Nicaragua to wonder whether this was preparatory to a surreptitious establishment of a colonial-style independence. Sweden agreed that South Africa was trying to reshape the constellation of internal parties in Namibia with the idea of an internal solution—referred to as a disguised colonial régime by Viet Nam. Uganda called the measure a racist arrangement that only replaced South Africa's white surrogate with a black puppet. Madagascar, fearing a *fait accompli*, urged swift action by the Security Council to prevent what might prove irreparable. Mexico asserted that South Africa and its allies had resorted to various subterfuges to impose an internal administration which was an unacceptable substitute for the attributes of genuine sovereignty. On behalf of the EC members, Denmark reiterated their rejection of attempts to impose an internal settlement or a solution that was not internationally acceptable and could condemn Namibia to isolation.

In Kuwait's view, South Africa had been given licence by the United States, which claimed interest in solving the Namibia problem but whose so-called policy of constructive engagement had led to increased collaboration with the Pretoria régime—a view shared by Ethiopia and Zambia. That policy heralded renewed all-round co-operation with South Africa, the United Republic of Tanzania said, and was being complemented by a massive campaign by certain other Western countries to rehabilitate that régime. Egypt appealed to the United States to review its policy of "constructive engagement", which Egypt believed was being exploited by South Africa to gain time.

A number of developing countries deplored the decision of IMF to grant a credit of 1 billion special drawing rights to South Africa as directly helping that régime's policy of repression and aggression. The United Republic of Tanzania said the supporters of the loan, by applying narrow legal interpretations to the workings of IMF, thus subsidized the South African military interventionist policies. The Ukrainian SSR said the loan exactly covered South Africa's military expenditure for the 1980-1982 period, while the Syrian Arab Republic asserted that the loan enabled the Pretoria régime to meet the deficit resulting from the increase in its military expenditures.

The loan application, whose speedy approval had been ensured by South Africa's powerful friends, should have provided an excellent oppor-

tunity to bring pressure on South Africa, asserted Trinidad and Tobago. The contact group shunned its responsibility, Kuwait commented, when it chose to encourage IMF to grant the loan. The United Arab Emirates called the action irresponsible, regardless of the justifications made for it. Nicaragua, doubting the validity of the argument that IMF was a technical body whose decisions were based on purely economic considerations, wondered if that was why the United States had prevented IMF from granting loans to Nicaragua and Viet Nam, but approved loans to El Salvador. Gabon expressed surprise that respect for human rights, which for certain important IMF members was among the criteria for determining allocation of the Fund's resources, had not been applied in the case of South Africa, whose *apartheid* policies constituted the very negation of human rights. Togo and Poland deplored the support given to South Africa by some international organizations and institutions.

A number of countries saw the United Nations credibility at stake. The Central African Republic said the total deadlock had seriously harmed the prestige of the Organization and Colombia called into question its effectiveness as an instrument to settle conflicts. For Antigua and Barbuda, Namibia symbolized the United Nations failure; South Africa's success in scoffing at United Nations efforts was a sad confirmation of the Organization's impotence, and the fact that some Members had intrigued to create that impotence was a damning blow to the concept of a world body. Bangladesh called on the United Nations to face effectively and expeditiously the challenge of South Africa's open rejection of United Nations decisions and Charter principles, and Ecuador said the Organization should not tolerate the dilatory tactics that had led to the present stalemate. Morocco called for a new and decisive impulse to the 1978 peace process. Indonesia believed that the Arusha Declaration and Programme of Action constituted the most expeditious means of forcing Pretoria to negotiate a settlement.

Echoing the Congo's impression of the powerlessness of the international community, Tunisia said the unfulfilled promises of the contact group and the latest South African demand had produced the greatest scepticism; given the uncertainty of a political solution, the only alternative was intensification of struggle, including armed struggle, for which no one could reproach SWAPO. Romania, the Sudan and Togo made a similar observation. Others, among them Ethiopia, Romania, Tunisia and the United Republic of Tanzania, also supported armed struggle in the face of what they viewed as total deadlock, fruitless diplomatic struggle, the Security Council's inability to fulfil its responsibility and South Africa's determination to dominate and enslave Namibia. Iraq called the armed struggle by SWAPO an acknowledged and legitimate right, and the Sudan viewed such struggle inevitable. Mozambique said various intergovernmental bodies had reaffirmed the justice of the Namibian people's armed struggle for national liberation. Finland, however, viewed negotiations as the only peaceful and realistic way to achieve settlement.

A number of countries paid tribute to SWAPO, as well as to the front-line States, for showing statesmanship and restraint in the protracted negotiations on the Namibia question. Algeria stressed the need to reaffirm the legitimacy of SWAPO as the representative of the Namibian people. The USSR said the internationally recognized position of SWAPO could not be detracted from any political intrigue. Without participation of this political movement, Sweden said, there could be no real solution to the Namibia question. Mexico found unacceptable the assertion being made to the effect that the United Nations position favoured one group in Namibia, or that it was directed against the legitimate interests of one country or another.

Further communications. Referring to the Assembly resolutions of 20 December, the Minister for Foreign Affairs and Information of South Africa, by a letter of 21 December transmitted on the same date to the Secretary-General,[7] reiterated the South African position on resolutions on Namibia—that they hampered the ongoing negotiations, created suspicion as to the United Nations position on the question and undermined the trust essential in negotiations.

Referring also to the Angolan Foreign Minister's 4 October statement in the Assembly, on the right of the Namibian people to self-determination and independence, the Foreign Minister of South Africa, by an 8 October letter,[6] transmitted on the same date to the Assembly President, stated that real progress had been made towards achievement of Namibian independence over the past two years. He pointed to the proposals put forward by the members of the Western contact group, stressing that what remained to be resolved were conditions of security in the region, which were imperative for implementing the third phase of the settlement process.

Decision (1982). [1]GA: 37/426, 13 Dec., text following.
Letters. [2]Committee on colonial countries Chairman: 24 Aug., S/15374. [3]Council for Namibia President, transmitting Arusha Declaration and Programme of Action: 14 May, A/37/230-S/15089. [4]Canada, France, Germany, Federal Republic of, United Kingdom, United States: 12 July, S/15287. South Africa: [5]21 Jan., A/37/74-S/14843; [6]8 Oct., A/37/532; [7]21 Dec., A/37/789-S/15538.
Reports. [8]Committee on colonial countries, A/37/23/Rev.1; [9]Council for Namibia, A/37/24; [10]GA 4th Committee, A/37/619; S-G, [11]A/37/203/Rev.1 & A/37/203/Add.1-4, [12]S/15776.

Resolutions (1982). [13]Commission on Human Rights (report, E/1982/12): 1982/16, paras. 2 & 9, 25 Feb. GA: [14]37/32, paras. 14 & 16, 23 Nov.; [15]37/35, paras. 9 & 12 *(c)*, 23 Nov.; [16]37/40, para. 4, 3 Dec.; [17]37/43, paras. 7 & 16, 3 Dec.; [18]37/233 A, 20 Dec., text following; [19]37/233 B, 20 Dec., text following.
Resolutions (prior). GA: [20]1514(XV), 14 Dec. 1960 (YUN 1960, p. 49); [21]2248(S-V), sect. II, 19 May 1967 (YUN 1967, p. 709); [22]ES-8/2, 14 Sep. 1981 (YUN 1981, p. 1153); [23]36/121 B, 10 Dec. 1981 *(ibid.,* p. 1157); [24]36/121 C, 10 Dec. 1981 *(ibid.,* p. 1163). SC: [25]385(1976), 30 Jan. 1976 (YUN 1976, p. 782); [26]418(1977), 4 Nov. 1977 (YUN 1977, p. 161); [27]435(1978), 29 Sep. 1978 (YUN 1978, p. 915).
Yearbook references. [28]1974, p. 152; [29]1978, p. 882; [30]1981, p. 1126.
Financial implications. 5th Committee report, A/37/782; S-G statement, A/C.5/37/102.
Meeting records. GA: 4th Committee, A/C.4/37/SR.3, 19 (15 Oct., 11 Nov.); plenary, A/37/PV.77, 84, *101*, 102-106, *113* (23 Nov.–20 Dec.); 5th Committee, A/C.5/37/SR.76 (18 Dec.).

General Assembly decision 37/426

Adopted without vote

Oral proposal by President; agenda item 32.

Question of Namibia

At its 101st plenary meeting, on 13 December 1982, the General Assembly took note of the report of the Fourth Committee.

General Assembly resolution 37/233 A

20 December 1982   Meeting 113   120-0-23 (recorded vote)

Draft by Council for Namibia (A/37/24); agenda item 32.

Situation in Namibia resulting from the illegal occupation of the Territory by South Africa

The General Assembly,

Having examined the report of the United Nations Council for Namibia and the relevant chapters of the report of the Special Committee on the Situation with regard to the Implementation of the Declaration on the Granting of Independence to Colonial Countries and Peoples,

Recalling its resolution 1514(XV) of 14 December 1960 containing the Declaration on the Granting of Independence to Colonial Countries and Peoples,

Recalling, in particular, its resolutions 2145(XXI) of 27 October 1966 and 2248(S-V) of 19 May 1967 and subsequent resolutions of the General Assembly and the Security Council relating to Namibia, as well as the advisory opinion of the International Court of Justice of 21 June 1971, delivered in response to the request addressed to it by the Security Council in its resolution 284(1970) of 29 July 1970,

Recalling also its resolutions 3111(XXVIII) of 12 December 1973 and 31/146 and 31/152 of 20 December 1976, by which it, *inter alia,* recognized the South West Africa People's Organization as the sole and authentic representative of the Namibian people and granted observer status to it,

Recalling further its resolutions ES-8/2 of 14 September 1981 and 36/121 B of 10 December 1981, by which it called upon States to cease forthwith, individually and collectively, all dealings with South Africa in order totally to isolate it politically, economically, militarily and culturally,

Recalling the Paris Declaration on Sanctions against South Africa and the Special Declaration on Namibia, adopted by the International Conference on Sanctions against South Africa,

Taking into consideration the Arusha Declaration and Programme of Action on Namibia, adopted by the United Nations Council for Namibia on 13 May 1982 at its extraordinary plenary meeting held at Arusha, United Republic of Tanzania,

Strongly reiterating that the continuing illegal and colonial occupation of Namibia by South Africa, in defiance of repeated General Assembly and Security Council resolutions, constitutes an act of aggression against the Namibian people and a challenge to the authority of the United Nations, which has direct responsibility for Namibia until independence,

Stressing the grave responsibility of the international community to take all possible measures in support of the Namibian people in their liberation struggle under the leadership of their sole and authentic representative, the South West Africa People's Organization,

Reaffirming its full support for the armed struggle of the Namibian people under the leadership of the South West Africa People's Organization to achieve self-determination, freedom and national independence in a united Namibia,

Indignant at South Africa's refusal to comply with repeated resolutions of the Security Council, in particular resolutions 385(1976) of 30 January 1976, 435(1978) of 29 September 1978 and 439(1978) of 13 November 1978 and at its manoeuvres aimed at perpetuating its brutal domination and exploitation of the Namibian people, as repeatedly manifested in the course of the consultations for the implementation of the United Nations plan for the independence of Namibia,

Commending the front-line States and the South West Africa People's Organization for the statesmanlike and constructive attitude which they have displayed throughout the consultations to implement Security Council resolution 435(1978),

Strongly condemning South Africa's continued illegal occupation of Namibia, its brutal repression of the Namibian people and its ruthless exploitation of the people and resources of Namibia, as well as its attempts to destroy the national unity and territorial integrity of Namibia,

Strongly condemning the racist régime of South Africa for its efforts to develop a nuclear capability for military and aggressive purposes,

Deeply concerned at the increasing militarization of Namibia, the forceful conscription of Namibians, the creation of tribal armies and the use of mercenaries for internal repression and external aggression,

Noting with grave concern that, as a result of the Security Council's failure on 31 August 1981, on account of the veto of the United States of America, to exercise its responsibilities, unprovoked massive armed aggression against Angola continues,

Expressing its strong condemnation of South Africa's continuing acts of aggression against independent African States, particularly Angola, which have caused extensive loss of human life and destruction of economic infrastructures,

Reaffirming that the resources of Namibia are the inviolable heritage of the Namibian people and that the exploitation of those resources by foreign economic interests under the protection of the illegal colonial administration, in violation of the Charter of the United Nations, of the relevant resolutions of the General Assembly and the Security Council and of Decree No. 1 for the Protection of the Natural Resources of Namibia, enacted by the United Nations Council for Namibia on 27 September 1974, and in disregard of the advisory opinion of the International Court of Justice of 21 June 1971, is illegal and contributes to the maintenance of the illegal occupation régime,

Deeply deploring the continued collaboration with South Africa of certain Western States, in particular the United States of America, as well as that of Israel, in disregard of the relevant resolutions of the General Assembly and the Security Council,

Deeply concerned at the continued assistance rendered to the racist Pretoria régime by certain international organizations and institutions, in particular the International Monetary Fund, in disregard of the relevant resolutions of the General Assembly,

Indignant at the continuing arbitrary imprisonment and detention of political leaders and followers of the South West Africa People's Organization, the killing of Namibian patriots and other acts of brutality, including the wanton beating, torture and murder of innocent Namibians, and the arbitrary inhuman measures of collective punishment and measures designed to intimidate the Namibian people and to destroy their will to fulfil their legitimate aspirations for self-determination, freedom and national independence in a united Namibia,

Noting with grave concern that the Security Council has been prevented on several occasions from taking effective action against South Africa in the discharge of its responsibilities under Chapter VII of the Charter on account of the vetoes cast by one of more of the Western permanent members of the Security Council,

Commending the efforts of the United Nations Council for Namibia in the discharge of the responsibilities entrusted to it under the relevant resolutions of the General Assembly as the legal Administering Authority for Namibia until independence,

1. *Approves* the report of the United Nations Council for Namibia;

2. *Reaffirms* the inalienable right of the people of Namibia to self-determination, freedom and national independence in a united Namibia, in accordance with the Charter of the United Nations and as recognized in General Assembly resolutions 1514(XV) and 2145(XXI) and in subsequent resolutions of the Assembly relating to Namibia, as well as the legitimacy of their struggle by all means at their disposal, including armed struggle, against the illegal occupation of their territory by South Africa;

3. *Reiterates* that, in accordance with its resolution 2145(XXI), Namibia is the direct responsibility of the United Nations until genuine self-determination and national independence are achieved in the Territory and, for this purpose, reaffirms the mandate given to the United Nations Council for Namibia as the legal Administering Authority for Namibia until independence under resolution 2248(S-V) and subsequent resolutions of the General Assembly;

4. *Reaffirms* that the South West Africa People's Organization, the national liberation movement of Namibia, is the sole and authentic representative of the Namibian people;

5. *Solemnly reaffirms* that the genuine independence of Namibia can be achieved only with the direct and full participation of the South West Africa People's Organization in all efforts to implement the resolutions of the United Nations relating to Namibia and further reaffirms that the only parties to the conflict in Namibia are, on the one hand, South Africa, as the illegal occupying Power, and, on the other, the Namibian people under the leadership of the South West Africa People's Organization, their sole and authentic representative;

6. *Strongly condemns* the South African régime for its continued illegal occupation of Namibia in defiance of the resolutions of the United Nations relating to Namibia;

7. *Declares* that South Africa's illegal occupation of Namibia constitutes an act of aggression against the Namibian people in terms of the Definition of Aggression contained in General Assembly resolution 3314(XXIX) of 14 December 1974 and supports the armed struggle of the Namibian people, under the leadership of the South West Africa People's Organization, to achieve self-determination, freedom and national independence in a united Namibia;

8. *Reiterates* that, in accordance with the resolutions of the United Nations, in particular Security Council resolution 432(1978) of 27 July 1978 and General Assembly resolutions S-9/2 of 3 May 1978 and 35/227 A of 6 March 1981, Walvis Bay and the offshore islands of Namibia are an integral part of Namibia and that all attempts by South Africa to annex them are therefore illegal, null and void;

9. *Reaffirms* that Security Council resolution 435(1978), together with Council resolution 385(1976), is the only basis for a peaceful settlement of the question of Namibia and calls for its immediate and unconditional implementation without qualification or modification;

10. *Firmly rejects* the manoeuvres by one member of the Western contact group aimed at undermining the international consensus embodied in Security Council resolution 435(1978) and at depriving the oppressed people of Namibia of their hard-won victories in the struggle for national liberation;

11. *Expresses its appreciation* to the front-line States and the South West Africa People's Organization for their statesmanlike and constructive attitude throughout the consultations to implement Security Council resolution 435(1978);

12. *Strongly condemns* South Africa for obstructing the implementation of Security Council resolutions 385(1976), 435(1978) and 439(1978) and for its manoeuvres, in contravention of those resolutions, designed to consolidate its colonial and neo-colonial interests at the expense of the legitimate aspirations of the Namibian people for genuine self-determination, freedom and national independence in a united Namibia;

13. *Denounces* all fraudulent constitutional and political schemes through which the illegal racist régime of South Africa may attempt to perpetuate its colonial domination in Namibia and, in particular, calls upon the international community, especially all Member States, to continue to refrain from according any recognition or extending any co-operation to any régime which the illegal South African administration may impose upon the Namibian people in disregard of the present resolution, of Security Council resolutions 385(1976), 435(1978) and 439(1978) and of other relevant resolutions of the General Assembly and the Council;

14. *Strongly urges* the Security Council to act decisively against any dilatory manoeuvres and fraudulent schemes of the illegal occupation régime aimed at frustrating the legitimate struggle of the Namibian people, under the leadership of the South West Africa People's Organization, for self-determination and national liberation, as well as at negating the achievements of their just struggle;

15. *Declares* that all so-called laws and proclamations issued by the illegal occupation régime in Namibia are illegal, null and void;

16. *Calls upon* Member States and the specialized agencies and other international organizations associated with the United Nations to render sustained and increased support as well as material, financial, military and other assistance to the South West Africa People's Organization so as to enable it to intensify its struggle for the liberation of Namibia;

17. *Deeply deplores* the increased assistance rendered by certain Western States to South Africa in the political, economic, military and cultural fields, expresses its conviction that this assistance should be exposed before the world public at large and demands that it be immediately terminated;

18. *Strongly condemns* South Africa for its military build-up in Namibia, its introduction of compulsory military service for Namibians, its recruitment and training of Namibians for tribal armies and the use of mercenaries to suppress the Namibian people and to carry out its military attacks against independent African States, its threats and acts of subversion and aggression against those States and the forcible displacement of Namibians from their homes;

19. *Strongly condemns* South Africa for its persistent acts of subversion and aggression against Angola, including the occupation of a part of its territory, and calls upon South Africa to cease all acts of aggression against and withdraw all its troops from that country;

20. *Calls upon* the international community to extend, as a matter of urgency, full support and assistance, including military assistance, to the front-line States in order to enable them to defend their sovereignty and territorial integrity against the repeated acts of aggression by South Africa;

21. *Requests* the Secretary-General to continue to develop, in consultation with the United Nations Development Programme, a comprehensive programme of assistance to States which are neighbours of South Africa and Namibia, on the understanding that such assistance should not only envisage the overcoming of short-term difficulties but be designed to enable those States to move towards complete self-reliance, and requests the Secretary-General to report to the General Assembly at its thirty-eighth session on the development of this programme;

22. *Reiterates its call* upon all States to take legislative and other appropriate measures to prevent the recruitment, training and transit of mercenaries for service in Namibia;

23. *Strongly condemns* the illegal South African administration for its massive repression of the people of Namibia and their national liberation movement, the South West Africa People's Organization, with the intention of establishing an atmosphere of intimidation and terror for the purpose of imposing upon the Namibian people a political arrangement aimed at undermining the territorial integrity and unity of Namibia as well as perpetuating the systematic plunder of the natural resources of the Territory;

24. *Demands* that South Africa immediately release all Namibian political prisoners, including all those imprisoned or detained under the so-called internal security laws, martial law or any other arbitrary measures, whether such Namibians have been charged or tried or are being held without charge in Namibia or South Africa;

25. *Demands* that South Africa account for all "disappeared" Namibians and release any who are still alive and declares that South Africa shall be liable for damages to compensate the victims, their families and the future lawful Government of an independent Namibia for the losses sustained;

26. *Strongly condemns* the collusion by the Governments of certain Western and other States, particularly those of the United States of America and Israel, with the racist régime of South Africa in the nuclear field and calls upon France and all other States to refrain from supplying the racist minority régime of South Africa, directly or indirectly, with installations that might enable it to produce uranium, plutonium or other nuclear materials, reactors or military equipment;

27. *Strongly condemns* the activities of all foreign economic interests operating in Namibia under the illegal South African adminis-

tration which are illegally exploiting the resources of the Territory and demands that transnational corporations engaged in such exploitation comply with all relevant resolutions of the United Nations by immediately refraining from any new investment or activities in Namibia, by withdrawing from the Territory and by putting an end to their co-operation with the illegal South African administration;

28. *Requests once again* all Member States to take all appropriate measures, including legislation and enforcement action, to ensure the full application of, and compliance with, the provisions of Decree No. 1 for the Protection of the Natural Resources of Namibia;

29. *Declares* that, by their depletive exploitation of natural resources and continued accumulation and repatriation of huge profits, the activities of foreign economic, financial and other interests operating at present in Namibia constitute a major obstacle to its political independence;

30. *Requests* the Governments of the Federal Republic of Germany, the Netherlands and the United Kingdom of Great Britain and Northern Ireland, which operate the Urenco uranium-enrichment plant, to have Namibian uranium specifically excluded from the Treaty of Almelo, which regulates the activities of Urenco;

31. *Deeply deplores* the continued collaboration of the International Monetary Fund with South Africa, as exemplified by the recent grant of a credit of one billion special drawing rights in disregard of General Assembly resolution 37/2 of 21 October 1982, and calls upon the Fund to put an end to such collaboration;

32. *Reiterates its request* to all States to take legislative, administrative and other measures, as appropriate, in order effectively to isolate South Africa politically, economically, militarily and culturally, in accordance with General Assembly resolutions ES-8/2 and 36/121 B;

33. *Requests* the United Nations Council for Namibia to continue to follow the implementation of the provisions of paragraph 32 above on the basis of information received from States as well as other sources;

34. *Requests* the United Nations Council for Namibia, in implementation of paragraph 15 of resolution ES-8/2 and of the provisions of resolution 36/121 B, to continue to monitor the boycott of South Africa and to submit to the General Assembly at its thirty-eighth session a comprehensive report on all contacts between all States and South Africa, containing an analysis of the information received from Member States and other sources on the continuing political, economic, financial and other relations of States and their economic and other interest groups with South Africa and of measures taken by States to terminate all dealings with the racist régime of South Africa;

35. *Requests* all States to co-operate fully with the United Nations Council for Namibia in the fulfilment of its tasks concerning the implementation of General Assembly resolutions ES-8/2 and 36/121 B and to report to the Secretary-General by the thirty-eighth session of the Assembly on the measures taken by them in implementation of those resolutions;

36. *Declares* that South Africa's defiance of the United Nations, its illegal occupation of the Territory of Namibia, its war of repression against the Namibian people, its persistent acts of aggression launched from bases in Namibia against independent African States, its policies of *apartheid* and its development of nuclear weapons constitute a serious threat to international peace and security;

37. *Strongly urges* the Security Council, in the light of the serious threat to international peace and security posed by South Africa, to respond positively to the overwhelming demand of the international community by immediately imposing against that country comprehensive mandatory sanctions, as provided for in Chapter VII of the Charter of the United Nations;

38. *Requests* the Secretary-General to report to the General Assembly at its thirty-eighth session on the implementation of the present resolution.

Recorded vote in Assembly as follows:

In favour: Afghanistan, Albania, Algeria, Angola, Antigua and Barbuda, Argentina, Bahamas, Bahrain, Bangladesh, Barbados, Benin, Bhutan, Bolivia, Botswana, Brazil, Bulgaria, Burma, Burundi, Byelorussian SSR, Cape Verde, Central African Republic, Chad, China, Colombia, Comoros, Congo, Costa Rica, Cuba, Cyprus, Czechoslovakia, Democratic Kampuchea, Democratic Yemen, Djibouti, Dominican Republic, Ecuador, Egypt, Equatorial Guinea, Ethiopia, Fiji, Gabon, Gambia, German Democratic Republic, Ghana, Greece, Grenada, Guinea, Guinea-Bissau, Guyana, Haiti, Hungary, India, Indonesia, Iran, Iraq, Jamaica, Jordan, Kenya, Kuwait, Lao People's Democratic Republic, Lebanon, Liberia, Libyan Arab Jamahiriya, Madagascar, Malaysia, Maldives, Mali, Malta, Mauritania, Mauritius,

Mexico, Mongolia, Morocco, Mozambique, Nepal, Nicaragua, Niger, Nigeria, Oman, Pakistan, Panama, Papua New Guinea, Peru, Philippines, Poland, Qatar, Romania, Rwanda, Saint Lucia, Saint Vincent and the Grenadines, Samoa, Sao Tome and Principe, Saudi Arabia, Senegal, Seychelles, Sierra Leone, Somalia, Sri Lanka, Sudan, Syrian Arab Republic, Thailand, Togo, Trinidad and Tobago, Tunisia, Turkey, Uganda, Ukrainian SSR, USSR, United Arab Emirates, United Republic of Cameroon, United Republic of Tanzania, Upper Volta, Uruguay, Vanuatu, Venezuela, Viet Nam, Yemen, Yugoslavia, Zaire, Zambia, Zimbabwe.

Against: None.

Abstaining: Australia, Austria, Belgium, Canada, Denmark, Finland, France, Germany, Federal Republic of, Iceland, Ireland, Italy, Ivory Coast, Japan, Luxembourg, Malawi, Netherlands, New Zealand, Norway, Portugal, Spain, Sweden, United Kingdom, United States.

General Assembly resolution 37/233 B

20 December 1982   Meeting 113   129-0-17 (recorded vote)

Draft by Council for Namibia (A/37/24); agenda item 32.

Implementation of Security Council resolution 435(1978)

The General Assembly,

Reaffirming the imperative need to proceed without any further delay with the implementation of Security Council resolution 435(1978) of 29 September 1978, which, together with Council resolution 385(1976) of 30 January 1976, is the only basis for a peaceful settlement of the question of Namibia,

Taking note of the consultations which have been held with a view to achieving the implementation of Security Council resolution 435(1978) and noting that those consultations have so far failed to bring about its implementation,

Condemning the attempts to link the independence of Namibia with totally extraneous issues, in particular the withdrawal of Cuban troops from Angola, an issue which falls within the exclusive domestic jurisdiction of a sovereign Member State,

1. *Reaffirms* the direct responsibility of the United Nations for Namibia pending its achievement of genuine self-determination and national independence;

2. *Reiterates* that Security Council resolution 435(1978), in which the Council endorsed the United Nations plan for the independence of Namibia, is the only basis for a peaceful settlement of the question of Namibia and calls for its immediate and unconditional implementation without qualification or modification;

3. *Firmly rejects* the persistent attempts by the United States of America and South Africa to establish any linkage or parallelism between the independence of Namibia and any extraneous issues, in particular the withdrawal of Cuban forces from Angola, and emphasizes unequivocally that the persistence of such attempts would only retard the decolonization process in Namibia as well as constitute interference in the internal affairs of Angola;

4. *Requests* the Security Council to exercise its authority for the implementation of its resolution 435(1978) so as to bring about the independence of Namibia without further delay.

Recorded vote in Assembly as follows:

In favour: Afghanistan, Albania, Algeria, Angola, Antigua and Barbuda, Argentina, Austria, Bahamas, Bahrain, Bangladesh, Barbados, Benin, Bhutan, Bolivia, Botswana, Brazil, Bulgaria, Burma, Burundi, Byelorussian SSR, Cape Verde, Central African Republic, Chad, Chile, China, Colombia, Comoros, Congo, Costa Rica, Cuba, Cyprus, Czechoslovakia, Democratic Kampuchea, Democratic Yemen, Djibouti, Dominican Republic, Ecuador, Egypt, El Salvador, Equatorial Guinea, Ethiopia, Fiji, Finland, Gabon, Gambia, German Democratic Republic, Ghana, Greece, Grenada, Guinea, Guinea-Bissau, Guyana, Haiti, Honduras, Hungary, India, Indonesia, Iran, Iraq, Ireland, Ivory Coast, Jamaica, Jordan, Kenya, Kuwait, Lao People's Democratic Republic, Lebanon, Liberia, Libyan Arab Jamahiriya, Madagascar, Malawi, Malaysia, Maldives, Mali, Malta, Mauritania, Mauritius, Mexico, Mongolia, Morocco, Mozambique, Nepal, Nicaragua, Niger, Nigeria, Oman, Pakistan, Panama, Papua New Guinea, Peru, Philippines, Poland, Qatar, Romania, Rwanda, Saint Lucia, Saint Vincent and the Grenadines, Samoa, Sao Tome and Principe, Saudi Arabia, Senegal, Seychelles, Sierra Leone, Somalia, Sri Lanka, Sudan, Sweden, Syrian Arab Republic, Thailand, Togo, Trinidad and Tobago, Tunisia, Turkey, Uganda, Ukrainian SSR, USSR, United Arab Emirates, United Republic of Cameroon, United Republic of Tanzania, Upper Volta, Uruguay, Vanuatu, Venezuela, Viet Nam, Yemen, Yugoslavia, Zaire, Zambia, Zimbabwe.

Against: None.

Abstaining: Australia, Belgium, Canada, Denmark, France, Germany, Federal Republic of, Iceland, Italy, Japan, Luxembourg, Netherlands, New Zealand, Norway, Portugal, Spain, United Kingdom, United States.

Work programme of the UN Council for Namibia

On 20 December 1982, the General Assembly adopted a resolution on the programme of work of the United Nations Council for Namibia for 1983.[1]

The Assembly decided that the Council should, *inter alia:* undertake a concerted effort to counter attempts to link Namibia's decolonization with extraneous issues; secure Namibia's territorial integrity; contact specialized agencies, IMF in particular, with a view to protecting Namibia's interests; organize regional symposia, aimed at intensifying support for Namibia, and prepare reports on all aspects of the Namibia situation; and accede to the 1949 Geneva Conventions on the law of war and to other appropriate international instruments. It welcomed the recent admission of Namibia, represented by the Council, as a full member of IAEA and of ITU, as well as its membership in the Executive Committee of the Programme of UNHCR. It took note of the signing by the Council of the United Nations Convention on the Law of the Sea.

Other tasks of the Council were defined in regard to the conduct of hearings on the exploitation of Namibia's resources by South Africa and by other foreign economic interests, completion of the index of transnational corporations operating in Namibia and preparations for the 1983 International Conference in Support of the Struggle of the Namibian People for Independence.

The resolution, recommended by the Council for Namibia and introduced in the Assembly by India, was adopted by a recorded vote of 139 to none, with 8 abstentions.

Speaking also on behalf of other members of the Western contact group—Canada, the Federal Republic of Germany, the United Kingdom and the United States—France said the group abstained in the vote so as simply to avoid jeopardizing its role in the negotiations. Australia, a member of the Council for Namibia, said the text's extravagant formulations left it no alternative but to abstain.

While voting in favour, the Netherlands doubted the usefulness of the proposed Conference, objected to the paragraph calling on the Council to counteract attempts to establish a linkage between Namibia's decolonization and extraneous issues, and expressed reservations about conferring on the Council the same rights and privileges in international organizations as those reserved for States. Ireland said it had difficulties with certain Council recommendations and reservations about that body's powers in regard to certain issues. Japan declared that its affirmative vote should not be construed as support for all of the paragraphs. Portugal voted in favour despite its reservations about the resolution's financial implications.

In the debate, China said the Council had contributed greatly to the enhancement of international support for the Namibian struggle. India commended the Council for its efforts to fulfil its mandate despite the indifference and open hostility of certain quarters. Cuba believed the Council should enjoy the total support and commitment of Member States.

Resolution (1982). [1]GA: 37/233 C, 20 Dec., text following.
Financial implications. 5th Committee report, A/37/782; S-G statement, A/C.5/37/102.
Meeting records. GA: plenary, A/37/PV.101-106, *113* (13-20 Dec.); 5th Committee, A/C.5/37/SR.76 (18 Dec.).

General Assembly resolution 37/233 C

20 December 1982   Meeting 113   139-0-8 (recorded vote)

Draft by Council for Namibia (A/37/24); agenda item 32.

Programme of work of the United Nations Council for Namibia

The General Assembly,

Having examined the report of the United Nations Council for Namibia,

Reaffirming that Namibia is the direct responsibility of the United Nations and that the Namibian people must be enabled to attain self-determination and independence in a united Namibia,

Recalling its resolution 2248(S-V) of 19 May 1967, by which it established the United Nations Council for Namibia as the legal Administering Authority for Namibia until independence,

Taking into consideration the Arusha Declaration and Programme of Action on Namibia, adopted by the United Nations Council for Namibia on 13 May 1982 at its extraordinary plenary meeting held at Arusha, United Republic of Tanzania,

Convinced of the need for continued consultations with the South West Africa People's Organization in the formulation and implementation of the programme of work of the United Nations Council for Namibia as well as in any matter of interest to the Namibian people,

Recalling paragraph 18 of its resolution 36/121 C of 10 December 1981, in which it requested the Secretary-General, after consulting the United Nations Council for Namibia regarding its assessment of the situation pertaining to Namibia, to carry out preparatory work with a view to organizing, at an appropriate time, an international conference in support of the struggle of the Namibian people for independence,

Deeply conscious of the urgent and continuing need to press for the termination of South Africa's illegal occupation of Namibia and to put an end to its repression of the Namibian people and its exploitation of the natural resources of the Territory,

Bearing in mind the constructive results achieved by the International Conference in Support of the Peoples of Zimbabwe and Namibia, held at Maputo from 16 to 21 May 1977,

1. *Approves* the report of the United Nations Council for Namibia, including the recommendations contained therein, and decides to make adequate financial provision for their implementation;

2. *Expresses its strong support* for the efforts of the United Nations Council for Namibia in the discharge of the responsibilities entrusted to it both as the legal Administering Authority for Namibia and as a policy-making organ of the United Nations;

3. *Requests* all Member States to co-operate fully with the United Nations Council for Namibia in the discharge of the mandate entrusted to it under the provisions of General Assembly resolution 2248(S-V) and subsequent resolutions of the Assembly;

4. *Decides* that the United Nations Council for Namibia, in the discharge of its responsibilities as the legal Administering Authority for Namibia until independence, shall:

(a) Continue to mobilize international support in order to press for the speedy withdrawal of the illegal South African administration from Namibia in accordance with the resolutions of the United Nations relating to Namibia;

(b) Counter the policies of South Africa against the Namibian people and against the United Nations, as well as against the United Nations Council for Namibia as the legal Administering Authority for Namibia;

(c) Denounce and seek the rejection by all States of all fraudulent constitutional or political schemes through which South Africa may attempt to perpetuate its presence in Namibia;

(d) Ensure non-recognition of any administration or entity installed at Windhoek not issuing from free elections in Namibia conducted under the supervision and control of the United Nations, in accordance with the relevant resolutions of the Security Council;

(e) Undertake a concerted effort to counter the attempts to establish any linkage or parallelism between the decolonization of Namibia and extraneous issues;

5. *Decides* that the United Nations Council for Namibia shall:

(a) Consult Governments in order to further the implementation of United Nations resolutions relating to Namibia and to mobilize support for the cause of Namibia;

(b) Represent Namibia in United Nations conferences and intergovernmental and non-governmental organizations, bodies and conferences to ensure that the rights and interests of Namibia shall be adequately protected;

6. *Decides* that Namibia, represented by the United Nations Council for Namibia, shall participate as a full member in all conferences and meetings organized by the United Nations to which all States or, in the case of regional conferences and meetings, all African States are invited;

7. *Requests* all committees and other subsidiary bodies of the General Assembly and of the Economic and Social Council to continue to invite a representative of the United Nations Council for Namibia to participate whenever the rights and interests of Namibians are discussed, and to consult closely with the Council before submitting any draft resolution which may involve the rights and interests of Namibians;

8. *Reiterates its request* to all specialized agencies and other organizations and conferences of the United Nations system to grant full membership to Namibia, represented by the United Nations Council for Namibia as the legal Administering Authority for Namibia, so that the Council may participate in the work of those agencies, organizations and conferences;

9. *Reiterates its request* to all specialized agencies and other organizations of the United Nations system that have not yet done so to grant a waiver of the assessment of Namibia during the period in which it is represented by the United Nations Council for Namibia;

10. *Again requests* all intergovernmental organizations, bodies and conferences to ensure that the rights and interests of Namibia are protected and to invite Namibia, represented by the United Nations Council for Namibia, to participate as a full member whenever such rights and interests are involved;

11. *Welcomes* the recent admission of Namibia, represented by the United Nations Council for Namibia, as a full member of the International Atomic Energy Agency and of the International Telecommunication Union, as well as Economic and Social Council decision 1982/110 of 16 April 1982 to grant membership to Namibia, represented by the United Nations Council for Namibia, in the Executive Committee of the Programme of the United Nations High Commissioner for Refugees;

12. *Takes note* of the accession by the United Nations Council for Namibia, in its capacity as the legal Administering Authority for Namibia, to the International Convention on the Elimination of All Forms of Racial Discrimination and the International Convention on the Suppression and Punishment of the Crime of *Apartheid* and requests the Council to accede to the Geneva Conventions of 12 August 1949 and the Additional Protocols thereto and to such other international conventions as it may deem appropriate;

13. *Takes note* of the signing by the United Nations Council for Namibia, on behalf of Namibia, of the United Nations Convention on the Law of the Sea and the Final Act of the Third United Nations Conference on the Law of the Sea;

14. *Decides* that the United Nations Council for Namibia shall:

(a) Review the progress of the liberation struggle in Namibia in its political, military and social aspects and prepare periodic reports related thereto;

(b) Consider the compliance of Member States with the relevant United Nations resolutions relating to Namibia, taking into account the advisory opinion of the International Court of Justice of 21 June 1971;

(c) Consider the activities of foreign economic interests operating in Namibia with a view to recommending appropriate policies to the General Assembly in order to counter the support which those foreign economic interests give to the illegal South African administration in Namibia;

(d) Continue to examine the exploitation of and trade in Namibian uranium by foreign economic interests and report on its findings to the General Assembly at its thirty-eighth session;

(e) Notify the Governments of States whose corporations, whether public or private, operate in Namibia of the illegality of such operations;

(f) Send missions of consultation to Governments whose corporations have investments in Namibia in order to review with them all possible action to discourage the continuation of such investments;

(g) Contact administering and managing bodies of foreign corporations operating in Namibia regarding the illegal basis on which they are operating in the Territory;

(h) Contact specialized agencies and other international organizations associated with the United Nations, in particular the International Monetary Fund, with a view to protecting Namibia's interests;

(i) Draw the attention of the specialized agencies to Decree No. 1 for the Protection of the Natural Resources of Namibia, enacted by the United Nations Council for Namibia on 27 September 1974;

(j) Take all measures to ensure compliance with the provisions of Decree No. 1 for the Protection of the Natural Resources of Namibia, including consideration of the institution of legal proceedings in the domestic courts of States and other appropriate bodies;

(k) Conduct hearings, seminars and workshops in order to obtain relevant information on the exploitation of the people and resources of Namibia by South African and other foreign interests and to expose such activities;

(l) Organize regional symposia on the situation in Namibia with a view to intensifying active support for the Namibian cause;

(m) Prepare and publish reports on the political, economic, military, legal and social situation in and relating to Namibia;

(n) Secure the territorial integrity of Namibia as a unitary State, including Walvis Bay and the offshore islands of Namibia;

15. *Requests* the Secretary-General to complete, in accordance with the guidelines established by the United Nations Council for Namibia, the preparation of an indexed reference book on transnational corporations operating in Namibia;

16. *Decides* to make adequate financial provision in the section of the programme budget of the United Nations relating to the United Nations Council for Namibia to finance the office of the South West Africa People's Organization in New York in order to ensure appropriate representation of the people of Namibia through the South West Africa People's Organization at the United Nations;

17. *Decides* to continue to defray the expenses of representatives of the South West Africa People's Organization, whenever the United Nations Council for Namibia so decides;

18. *Requests* the United Nations Council for Namibia to continue to consult with the South West Africa People's Organization in the formulation and implementation of its programme of work, as well as in any matter of interest to the Namibian people;

19. *Requests* the Secretary-General, in order to facilitate financial reporting to the United Nations Council for Namibia, to ensure that, within the section of the programme budget of the United Nations relating to the Council, the accounts shall reflect closely the activities of the Council as described in the report of the Council to the General Assembly at its thirty-seventh session;

20. *Further requests* the Secretary-General to ensure the establishment of an appropriate accounting system which will enable the Council, in its capacity as the legal Administering Authority for Namibia, to receive speedy and comprehensive financial data on projects for which the Council is directly responsible;

21. *Requests* the Secretary-General, in consultation with the President of the United Nations Council for Namibia, to review the requirements of personnel and facilities of all units which service the Council so that the Council may fully and effectively discharge all tasks and functions arising out of its mandate;

22. *Requests* the Secretary-General to provide the Office of the United Nations Commissioner for Namibia with the necessary resources in order for it to strengthen, under the guidance of the United Nations Council for Namibia, the assistance programmes and services for Namibians, the implementation of Decree No. 1 for the Protection of

the Natural Resources of Namibia, the preparation of economic and legal studies and the existing activities of dissemination of information undertaken by that Office;

23. *Requests* the United Nations Council for Namibia, in the discharge of its responsibilities as the legal Administering Authority for Namibia, to hold plenary meetings away from Headquarters whenever it deems it necessary, and requests the Secretary-General to defray the cost of these meetings and to provide the necessary staff and services for them;

24. *Decides* that an International Conference in Support of the Struggle of the Namibian People for Independence shall be held at the headquarters of the United Nations Educational, Scientific and Cultural Organization in Paris during 1983;

25. *Requests* the Secretary-General to organize the above-mentioned Conference in co-operation with the United Nations Council for Namibia and in consultation with the Organization of African Unity and to this end to appoint, in consultation with the United Nations Council for Namibia, a Secretary-General of the Conference and provide other necessary staff and services for the Conference.

Recorded vote in Assembly as follows:

In favour: Afghanistan, Albania, Algeria, Angola, Antigua and Barbuda, Argentina, Austria, Bahamas, Bahrain, Bangladesh, Barbados, Benin, Bhutan, Bolivia, Botswana, Brazil, Bulgaria, Burma, Burundi, Byelorussian SSR, Cape Verde, Central African Republic, Chad, Chile, China, Colombia, Comoros, Congo, Costa Rica, Cuba, Cyprus, Czechoslovakia, Democratic Kampuchea, Democratic Yemen, Denmark, Djibouti, Dominican Republic, Ecuador, Egypt, El Salvador, Equatorial Guinea, Ethiopia, Fiji, Finland, Gabon, Gambia, German Democratic Republic, Ghana, Greece, Grenada, Guinea, Guinea-Bissau, Guyana, Haiti, Honduras, Hungary, Iceland, India, Indonesia, Iran, Iraq, Ireland, Italy, Ivory Coast, Jamaica, Japan, Jordan, Kenya, Kuwait, Lao People's Democratic Republic, Lebanon, Liberia, Libyan Arab Jamahiriya, Luxembourg, Madagascar, Malawi, Malaysia, Maldives, Mali, Malta, Mauritania, Mauritius, Mexico, Mongolia, Morocco, Mozambique, Nepal, Netherlands, Nicaragua, Niger, Nigeria, Norway, Oman, Pakistan, Panama, Papua New Guinea, Peru, Philippines, Poland, Portugal, Qatar, Romania, Rwanda, Saint Lucia, Saint Vincent and the Grenadines, Samoa, Sao Tome and Principe, Saudi Arabia, Senegal, Seychelles, Sierra Leone, Singapore, Somalia, Spain, Sri Lanka, Sudan, Sweden, Syrian Arab Republic, Thailand, Togo, Trinidad and Tobago, Tunisia, Turkey, Uganda, Ukrainian SSR, USSR, United Arab Emirates, United Republic of Cameroon, United Republic of Tanzania, Upper Volta, Uruguay, Vanuatu, Venezuela, Viet Nam, Yemen, Yugoslavia, Zaire, Zambia, Zimbabwe.

Against: None.

Abstaining: Australia, Belgium, Canada, France, Germany, Federal Republic of, New Zealand, United Kingdom, United States.

Information dissemination

In 1982, the United Nations Council for Namibia[4] continued its efforts, through its Standing Committee III working with the United Nations Department of Public Information (DPI), to keep international public opinion informed of its objectives and functions and of the Namibian people's struggle under the leadership of the South West Africa People's Organization (SWAPO).

Through press releases available at Headquarters and at United Nations information centres around the world, DPI publicized all public Council meetings, including the extraordinary meetings at Arusha, United Republic of Tanzania, the June Seminar on the Military Situation in and relating to Namibia and its consultation mission to Asia, as well as all other events and major United Nations reports on Namibia. Work of the United Nations concerning Namibia was also publicized in DPI publications, including periodicals, books and general reference works. Arrangements continued to be made for audio-visual coverage as well.

The Council President and the United Nations Commissioner for Namibia attended the Mass

Media Leaders Round Table held by DPI at Budapest, Hungary, from 8 to 10 February, where one session was devoted to the problems of South Africa and Namibia. Similar meetings were held at Arusha, Bangkok (Thailand), London, Paris and Quito (Ecuador) as well as in many United States cities. The 1982 United Nations graduate student intern programme, with some 100 persons from 55 countries participating, gave attention to the Organization's activities concerning Namibia.

The Commissioner's Office continued to prepare the substantive parts of the quarterly *Namibia Bulletin*[1] and to publish *Namibia in the News*,[2] a weekly newsletter distributed to Member States and non-governmental organizations (NGOs). The Office also gave briefings on Council activities to NGOs, support organizations and student groups.

The Council held its annual commemorations of Namibia Day and of the Week of Solidarity with the People of Namibia and their Liberation Movement, SWAPO, on 26 August and 27 October,[5] respectively, holding on the latter date two special meetings in New York that were addressed by United Nations officials and representatives of regional groups and organizations.

The Special Committee on the Situation with regard to the Implementation of the Declaration on the Granting of Independence to Colonial Countries and Peoples[3] adopted on 5 August the report of its Sub-Committee on Petitions, Information and Assistance, recommending, among other things, that the United Nations intensify its information activities to counter the misrepresentation of the Namibia liberation struggle as terrorism and make the international community aware of United Nations recognition of the legitimacy of that struggle, with emphasis on SWAPO activities. By a consensus of 20 August, the Committee reiterated the request it had made of the Secretary-General to intensify information dissemination in this regard.

General Assembly action. By a resolution of 20 December,[6] the General Assembly requested the Council for Namibia to continue to consider ways of increasing information dissemination in support of Namibia and, deciding to intensify its campaign to expose the collusion of certain Western States with South Africa, asked the Council to formulate a programme that would include publications on the political, economic, military and social consequences of the illegal occupation of Namibia, as well as radio and television broadcasts, films, advertisements, posters, and press releases and briefings. The Council was also asked to produce and disseminate a comprehensive economic map of Namibia, an indexed reference book on transnational corporations operating in Namibia and a booklet on implementation of its 1974 Decree No. 1 for the Protection of the Natural Resources of Namibia.[8]

In requesting the Secretary-General to give wide publicity to the 1983 International Conference in Support of the Struggle of the Namibian People for Independence, the Assembly also asked the Council to organize, on the occasion of that Conference, an international seminar of media leaders to alert them to the need for increased publicity on Namibia and a workshop for NGOs to consider their contribution towards implementing the Conference decisions. It called on the Council to enlist NGO co-operation in mobilizing international public opinion in support of Namibia and SWAPO, and allocated $200,000 to the Council's programme of co-operation with NGOs. The Assembly also requested Member States to broadcast programmes and publish material in their official news media on the Namibia situation, and requested NGOs and support groups to intensify international action in support of the Namibian liberation struggle, including assistance to the Council in monitoring the boycott of South Africa called for by the Assembly in September 1981.[7]

The resolution, recommended by the Council for Namibia and introduced in the Assembly by Bulgaria, was adopted by a recorded vote of 127 to none, with 20 abstentions.

Speaking also for the other members of the Western contact group—Canada, the Federal Republic of Germany, the United Kingdom and the United States—France said the group abstained in the vote in order to avoid jeopardizing its role in the negotiations. Australia, a member of the Council for Namibia, abstained in objection to what it called the extravagant formulations of the text, citing tendentious language and name-calling. Also abstaining, Japan said it was imperative that the information to be disseminated be accurate, fair and balanced and that close co-operation be maintained between the Council and DPI, to utilize more effectively the limited financial and human resources available.

Reservation was voiced by some on paragraph 5 of the text, by which the Assembly requested the Council to carry out a number of tasks aimed at exposing and denouncing the collusion of certain Western States with South Africa. Abstaining, Ireland considered it unacceptable and harmful, and the Netherlands feared that entrusting a United Nations subsidiary organ with tasks inimical to a group of Member States could detract from the Organization's ability to resolve the problem. While voting in favour, Turkey disagreed with that paragraph's reference to Western States, as did Greece, which said it would have abstained had a separate vote been taken on that paragraph. Portugal said it voted in favour despite its reservations about that paragraph and paragraph 13 (on intensified NGO action, in co-operation with the Council, in support of the Namibian liberation struggle) and the text's financial implications.

During the Assembly debate, Colombia said it was necessary more vigorously to mobilize public opinion on the Namibia question, using more powerful methods. Malaysia made similar observations. Togo suggested that the public in certain countries, if better informed of the Namibia problem, might be able to influence Government policy in favour of Namibia.

Publications. (1)*Namibia Bulletin*, No. 1/82; (2)*Namibia in the News*, Nos. 1/82-13/82.
Reports. (3)Committee on colonial countries, A/37/23/Rev.1; Council for Namibia, (4)A/37/24, (5)A/38/24.
Resolution (1982). (6)GA: 37/233 D, 20 Dec., text following.
Resolution (prior). (7)GA: ES-8/2, 14 Sep. 1981 (YUN 1981, p. 1153).
Yearbook reference. (8)1974, p. 152.
Financial implications. 5th Committee report, A/37/782; S-G statement, A/C.5/37/102.
Meeting records. GA: plenary, A/37/PV.101-106, *113* (13-20 Dec.); 5th Committee, A/C.5/37/SR.76 (18 Dec.).

General Assembly resolution 37/233 D

20 December 1982   Meeting 113   127-0-20 (recorded vote)

Draft by Council for Namibia (A/37/24); agenda item 32.

Dissemination of information and mobilization of international public opinion in support of Namibia

The General Assembly,

Having examined the report of the United Nations Council for Namibia,

Recalling its resolutions 36/121 A to F of 10 December 1981 and all other relevant resolutions and decisions of the United Nations relating to Namibia,

Taking into consideration the Arusha Declaration and Programme of Action on Namibia, adopted by the United Nations Council for Namibia on 13 May 1982 at its extraordinary plenary meeting held at Arusha, United Republic of Tanzania,

Stressing the urgent need to intensify efforts to mobilize international public opinion on a continuous basis with a view to assisting effectively the people of Namibia, under the leadership of the South West Africa People's Organization, in their legitimate struggle for self-determination, freedom and independence in a united Namibia,

Recognizing the important role that non-governmental organizations are playing in the dissemination of information on Namibia and in the mobilization of international public opinion in support of the Namibian cause,

Reiterating the importance of publicity as an instrument for furthering the mandate given by the General Assembly to the United Nations Council for Namibia and mindful of the pressing need for the Department of Public Information of the Secretariat to intensify its efforts to acquaint world public opinion with all aspects of the question of Namibia, in accordance with policy guidelines formulated by the Council,

1. *Requests* the United Nations Council for Namibia, in pursuance of its international campaign in support of Namibia, to continue to consider ways and means of increasing the dissemination of information relating to Namibia;

2. *Requests* the Secretary-General to ensure that the Department of Public Information of the Secretariat, in all its activities of dissemination of information on the question of Namibia, follows the policy guidelines laid down by the United Nations Council for Namibia as the legal Administering Authority for Namibia;

3. *Requests* the Secretary-General to direct the Department of Public Information, in addition to its responsibilities relating to southern Africa, to assist, as a matter of priority, the United Nations Council for Namibia in the implementation of its programme of dissemination of information in order that the United Nations may intensify its efforts to generate publicity and disseminate information with a view to mobilizing public support for the independence of Namibia, particularly in the Western States;

4. *Requests* the Secretary-General to give the widest possible publicity to the forthcoming International Conference in Support of the Struggle of the Namibian People for Independence, convened pursuant to paragraph 24 of resolution C above, through all the means at his disposal, including special publications, press releases and radio and television broadcasts;

5. *Decides* to intensify its international campaign in support of the cause of Namibia and to expose and denounce the collusion of certain Western States with the South African racists and, to this end, requests the United Nations Council for Namibia to include in its programme of dissemination of information for 1983 the following activities:

(a) Preparation and dissemination of publications on the political, economic, military and social consequences of the illegal occupation of Namibia by South Africa, as well as on legal matters and on the question of the territorial integrity of Namibia;

(b) Production and dissemination of radio programmes in English, French, German and Spanish designed to draw the attention of world public opinion to the current situation in Namibia;

(c) Production of material for publicity through radio and television broadcasts;

(d) Placement of advertisements in newspapers and magazines;

(e) Production of films, film-strips and slide sets on Namibia;

(f) Production and dissemination of posters;

(g) Full utilization of the resources related to press releases, press conferences and press briefings in order to maintain a constant flow of information to the public on all aspects of the question of Namibia;

(h) Production and dissemination of a comprehensive economic map of Namibia;

(i) Preparation and wide dissemination of booklets, containing:

(i)   Official declarations of the Council;

(ii) Joint communiqués and press releases issued by missions of consultation of the Council;

(iii) Resolutions of the General Assembly and the Security Council relating to Namibia, together with relevant portions of Assembly resolutions on the question of foreign economic interests operating in Namibia and on military activities in Namibia;

(j) Publicity for and distribution of an indexed reference book on transnational corporations operating in Namibia;

(k) Preparation and dissemination of a booklet based on a study on the implementation of Decree No. 1 for the Protection of the Natural Resources of Namibia, enacted by the Council on 27 September 1974;

(l) Acquisition of books, pamphlets and other materials relating to Namibia for further dissemination;

6. *Requests* the United Nations Council for Namibia, on the occasion of the International Conference in Support of the Struggle of the Namibian People for Independence, to organize, in co-operation with the Department of Public Information, an international seminar of media leaders with a view to alerting the mass media to the need to increase publicity on the question of Namibia, particularly in its political, economic and military aspects;

7. *Requests* the Secretary-General to allocate, in consultation with the United Nations Council for Namibia, sales numbers to publications on Namibia selected by the Council;

8. *Requests* the Secretary-General to provide the United Nations Council for Namibia with the work programme of the Department of Public Information for the year 1983 covering the activities of dissemination of information on Namibia, followed by periodic reports on the programmes undertaken, including details of expenses incurred;

9. *Requests* the Secretary-General to group under a single heading, in the section of the proposed programme budget of the United Nations for the biennium 1984-1985 relating to the Department of Public Information, all the activities of the Department related to the dissemination of information on Namibia;

10. *Requests* Member States to broadcast programmes on their national radio and television networks and to publish material in their official news media, informing their populations about the situation in Namibia and the obligation of Governments and peoples to assist in the struggle of Namibians for independence;

11. *Calls upon* the United Nations Council for Namibia to enlist the support of non-governmental organizations in its efforts to mobilize international public opinion in support of the liberation struggle of the Namibian people and of their liberation movement, the South West Africa People's Organization;

12. *Requests* the United Nations Council for Namibia to organize, at the conclusion of the International Conference in Support of the Struggle of the Namibian People for Independence, a workshop for

non-governmental organizations concerned with the question of Namibia at which those organizations will consider their contribution to the implementation of the decisions of the Conference;

13. *Requests* those non-governmental organizations and support groups that are actively engaged in supporting the struggle of the Namibian people under the leadership of the South West Africa People's Organization, their sole and authentic representative, to intensify, in co-operation with the United Nations Council for Namibia, international action in support of the liberation struggle of the Namibian people, including assistance to the Council in the monitoring of the boycott of South Africa called for in General Assembly resolution ES-8/2 of 14 September 1981;

14. *Decides* to allocate the sum of $200,000 to be used by the United Nations Council for Namibia for its programme of co-operation with non-governmental organizations, including support to conferences in solidarity with Namibia arranged by those organizations, dissemination of conclusions of such conferences and support to such other activities as will promote the cause of the liberation struggle of the Namibian people, subject to decisions of the Council in each individual case on the recommendation of the South West Africa People's Organization.

Recorded vote in Assembly as follows:

In favour: Afghanistan, Albania, Algeria, Angola, Antigua and Barbuda, Argentina, Bahamas, Bahrain, Bangladesh, Barbados, Benin, Bhutan, Bolivia, Botswana, Brazil, Bulgaria, Burma, Burundi, Byelorussian SSR, Cape Verde, Central African Republic, Chad, Chile, China, Colombia, Comoros, Congo, Costa Rica, Cuba, Cyprus, Czechoslovakia, Democratic Kampuchea, Democratic Yemen, Djibouti, Dominican Republic, Ecuador, Egypt, El Salvador, Equatorial Guinea, Ethiopia, Fiji, Gabon, Gambia, German Democratic Republic, Ghana, Greece, Grenada, Guinea, Guinea-Bissau, Guyana, Haiti, Honduras, Hungary, India, Indonesia, Iran, Iraq, Ivory Coast, Jamaica, Jordan, Kenya, Kuwait, Lao People's Democratic Republic, Lebanon, Liberia, Libyan Arab Jamahiriya, Madagascar, Malawi, Malaysia, Maldives, Mali, Malta, Mauritania, Mauritius, Mexico, Mongolia, Morocco, Mozambique, Nepal, Nicaragua, Niger, Nigeria, Oman, Pakistan, Panama, Papua New Guinea, Peru, Philippines, Poland, Portugal, Qatar, Romania, Rwanda, Saint Lucia, Saint Vincent and the Grenadines, Samoa, Sao Tome and Principe, Saudi Arabia, Senegal, Seychelles, Sierra Leone, Singapore, Somalia, Sri Lanka, Sudan, Syrian Arab Republic, Thailand, Togo, Trinidad and Tobago, Tunisia, Turkey, Uganda, Ukrainian SSR, USSR, United Arab Emirates, United Republic of Cameroon, United Republic of Tanzania, Upper Volta, Uruguay, Vanuatu, Venezuela, Viet Nam, Yemen, Yugoslavia, Zaire, Zambia, Zimbabwe.

Against: None.

Abstaining: Australia, Austria, Belgium, Canada, Denmark, Finland, France, Germany, Federal Republic of, Iceland, Ireland, Italy, Japan, Luxembourg, Netherlands, New Zealand, Norway, Spain, Sweden, United Kingdom, United States.

Preparations for the 1983 Conference on Namibian independence

In its 20 December 1982 resolution on the work programme of the United Nations Council for Namibia,[2] the General Assembly decided that an International Conference in Support of the Struggle of the Namibian People for Independence be held in 1983 in Paris. It requested the Secretary-General, in co-operation with the Council and in consultation with the Organization of African Unity, to organize the Conference, appoint its Secretary-General and provide other necessary staff and services.

The Netherlands, while voting in favour of the text, doubted the usefulness of the proposed Conference, stating that the efforts of the Western contact group seemed to hold out the best prospects for the early, internationally recognized independence for Namibia.

In the course of its May meetings at Arusha, the Council had approved a provisional agenda for the Conference, and later in the year assigned to its Steering Committee the co-ordination of arrangements for the Conference.[1]

Report. [1]Council for Namibia, A/37/24.
Resolution (1982). [2]GA: 37/233 C, paras. 24 & 25, 20 Dec.

Military aspects

The United Nations Council for Namibia, on the basis of its decision of 1 February 1982, conducted a Seminar on the Military Situation in and relating to Namibia, at Vienna, Austria, from 8 to 11 June.[3] It was attended by a nine-member delegation of the Council, four representatives of the South West Africa People's Organization (SWAPO) and 23 experts.

In its conclusions submitted to the Council, the Seminar noted the continuing supply of military-related materials to South Africa and the wide-ranging military collaboration with it, and considered as a major problem the lack of effective implementation of the existing arms embargo, especially by France, the Federal Republic of Germany, the United Kingdom and the United States. The Seminar observed that South Africa remained heavily dependent on a variety of foreign supplies, despite Western countries' assistance to enable it to become self-sufficient in arms production. It drew attention to what it perceived as Israel's increasingly open military collaboration; to certain Latin American countries' collaboration that was developing into a *de facto* military alliance; to collaboration in South Africa's nuclear programme through such bodies as the joint Working Group on Uranium Extraction of the International Atomic Energy Agency and the Nuclear Energy Agency of the Organisation for Economic Co-operation and Development; and to the expanded assistance to South Africa's nuclear development.

The Seminar expressed concern at the rising level of mercenary activity in South Africa and Namibia, naming the United Kingdom and the United States as the leading recruitment centres. It noted violations of the oil embargo, imposed by the Organization of Arab Petroleum Exporting Countries and other oil-producing countries, by major oil companies whose Governments were ignoring the violations. Attention was drawn to specific transnational corporations (TNCs) engaged in the militarization of Namibia's economy and in assisting South Africa's occupation by their revenue contributions and military-related contracts and by arming South African–controlled "civilian" forces.

The Seminar recommended that the Council for Namibia continue to resist attempts by certain Western Governments to diminish the role of SWAPO and even to exclude it from negotiations on Namibian independence; to request reactivation of the Security Council committee established in 1977 to monitor the arms embargo;[5] to pursue a ban on all nuclear collaboration with South Africa; and to press for the establishment of a nuclear-weapon-free zone in Africa. It asked the Council to promote the elaboration of a convention to outlaw the recruitment of mercenaries specifically for deployment in South Africa and Namibia; to continue to enlist the good will and support of all non-governmental organizations to bring pressure on Governments and TNCs to stop all military and nuclear collaboration with South Africa; and to enlist the co-operation of the Organization of Petroleum Exporting Countries and all countries registering oil tankers bound for South Africa in implementing the oil embargo against it.

The Seminar recommended that the Council enact a decree on war reparations payable to a future lawful Government of Namibia by those TNCs operating illegally in Namibia. It urged the Council to secure the release of combatants of the People's Liberation Army of Namibia, the Cassinga detainees and all other Namibian refugees and citizens of the front-line States. The Seminar asked the Council to encourage material and humanitarian assistance to the Namibian people and the front-line States and, in co-operation with the United Nations Educational, Scientific and Cultural Organization, to undertake a wide-ranging programme of public education on Namibia, using the mass media and drawing on information from the Seminar.

Along with a number of studies by expert participants, the Seminar had before it a report prepared by the Council's Standing Committee II on the military situation in and relating to Namibia,[4] which included a military map and a list of military bases and units permanently stationed in Namibia.

Responding to a remark made by one of the participants at the Seminar, Argentina, by a letter of 24 November to the Secretary-General,[1] requested circulation in the General Assembly of its letter of 19 November addressed to the President of the Council for Namibia. In it, Argentina denied the existence of a South Atlantic Treaty Organization and hence its alleged participation in that body, declared that Argentina had neither military nor political ties with South Africa, and expressed regret that the Council had been used as a means of disseminating false and inaccurate statements on Argentina's foreign policy based on what it called tendentious information put about in bad faith and taken up by an individual in his private capacity.

Action by the Committee on colonial countries. By a decision of 20 August,[2] the Special Committee on the Situation with regard to the Implementation of the Declaration on the Granting of Independence to Colonial Countries and Peoples, noting South Africa's persistent manœuvres aimed at transferring power to illegitimate groups

subservient to its interests in order to perpetuate its illegal occupation of Namibia, condemned South Africa for its military build-up there, its recruitment and training of Namibians for tribal armies, expansion of the so-called South West Africa/Namibia Territory Force, its use of mercenaries to carry out military attacks against independent African States and its forcible displacement of Namibians from their homes for military and political purposes.

The Committee demanded the immediate cessation of South Africa's war of oppression and the dismantling of its military bases in Namibia. It condemned the continued military collaboration with South Africa and support extended to it by certain Western and other States, particularly in the sale of weapons and other *matériel*.

Letter. [1]Argentina, 24 Nov., A/37/678.
Reports. [2]Committee on colonial countries, A/37/23/Rev.1; [3]Seminar on Military Situation in and relating to Namibia, A/AC.131/L.268; [4]Standing Committee II, A/AC.131/L.251/Rev.1 & Rev.1/Corr.1.
Resolution. [5]SC: 421(1977), 9 Dec. 1977 (YUN 1977, p. 162).

UN Commissioner for Namibia

Activities of the Commissioner

In 1982, the Office of the United Nations Commissioner for Namibia[1] continued to collect and analyse information relating to Namibia and followed internal political and legal developments in South Africa concerning Namibia. In its continuing effort to implement the 1974 Decree No. 1 for the Protection of the Natural Resources of Namibia,[3] the Office prepared the north American portion of a reference book on TNCs operating in Namibia; consulted with government experts in investigation into the shipment and sale of Namibian products by foreign economic interests; and reviewed documentation and recommendations of the panel for hearings on Namibian uranium.

The Office continued to administer assistance programmes for Namibians under the United Nations Fund for Namibia, composed of the General Account, the Nationhood Programme for Namibia and the United Nations Institute for Namibia. Arrangements had been made for the Office also to administer the scholarship programme under the Fund. As co-ordinating authority for implementation of the Nationhood Programme, the Office organized a workshop on mining, industries, trade and economic planning, at Harare, Zimbabwe, in March/April 1982. As in previous years, it issued or renewed travel and identity documents to Namibians in different parts of the world.

The Commissioner participated in August meetings in New York with the Chairman of the SWAPO Committee on the Nationhood

Programme and with the Institute's Senate, and in a November meeting of 31 African States at Tripoli, Libyan Arab Jamahiriya.

The Commissioner's Regional Office at Lusaka, Zambia, co-ordinated the placement of Namibians in training programmes in various countries, provided facilities and services to consultants under the Nationhood Programme and issued or renewed travel and identity documents. The Office at Gaborone, Botswana, assisted in the placement of the third group of 10 Namibian students from the Institute in a practical training programme in Botswana in February. It participated in a Seminar on Law and Human Rights in Development (Gaborone, 24-29 May) and in sessions of the Co-ordinating Committee for the Liberation of Africa and of the Co-ordinating Committee of the Bureau for the Placement and Education of African Refugees, both of the Organization of African Unity (Arusha, United Republic of Tanzania, 7-11 and 14-18 June). In response to a December 1981 General Assembly request,[2] a Regional Office of the Commissioner was opened at Luanda, Angola, on 26 August 1982, to coincide with the observance of Namibia Day.

Report. [1]Council for Namibia, A/37/24.
Resolution. [2]GA: 36/121 C, 10 Dec. 1981 (YUN 1981, p. 1163).
Yearbook reference. [3]1974, p. 152.

Appointment of the Commissioner

On 29 March 1982,[1] the General Assembly, acting without vote on the Secretary-General's proposal, as contained in his note of 25 March,[4] appointed Brajesh Chandra Mishra United Nations Commissioner for Namibia for a nine-month term beginning on 1 April. He was reappointed for a further year, beginning on 1 January 1983, by an Assembly decision of 20 December 1982.[2] The decision was adopted, also without vote, on the Secretary-General's proposal of 16 December.[5]

Following the Assembly's March action, the Minister for Foreign Affairs and Information of South Africa, by a 13 April letter to the Secretary-General,[3] stressed that his Government did not and would not recognize the United Nations Council for Namibia and its Commissioner. It viewed the latter's appointment as provocative and illustrative of the United Nations lack of desire to depart from its course of favouring SWAPO to the exclusion of the other parties of the Territory. He warned that South Africa could not be held responsible for any detrimental effect which the appointment might have on the delicate negotiations under way.

Decisions (1982). GA: [1]36/325, 29 Mar., text following; [2]37/324, 20 Dec., text following.
Letter. [3]South Africa, 13 Apr., A/37/176-S/14977.
Notes. SG, [4]A/36/870, [5]A/37/772.
Meeting records. GA: A/36/PV.109 (29 Mar.), A/37/PV.113 (20 Dec.).

General Assembly decision 36/325

Adopted without vote

Proposal by Secretary-General (A/36/870); agenda item 18 *(i)*.

Appointment of the United Nations Commissioner for Namibia

At its 109th plenary meeting, on 29 March 1982, the General Assembly, on the proposal of the Secretary-General, appointed Mr. Brajesh Chandra Mishra United Nations Commissioner for Namibia for a nine-month term beginning on 1 April 1982.

General Assembly decision 37/324

Adopted without vote

Proposal by Secretary-General (A/37/772); agenda item 17 *(k)*.

Appointment of the United Nations Commissioner for Namibia

At its 113th plenary meeting, on 20 December 1982, the General Assembly, on the proposal of the Secretary-General, appointed Mr. Brajesh Chandra Mishra as United Nations Commissioner for Namibia for a one-year term beginning on 1 January 1983.

Economic and social conditions

Foreign investments

Action by the UN Council for Namibia. By its Arusha Declaration and Programme of Action on Namibia, the Council for Namibia, in connection with the protection of Namibia's natural resources from continued illegal exploitation, called on all States to prohibit corporations from investing or obtaining concessions in Namibia, with an advisory that such investments would not be protected against claims by the Council or by a future lawful Government of Namibia.[2]

As part of the work programme outlined for it by the General Assembly in December 1981,[11] the Council sent a mission, consisting of representatives of Botswana, China, Venezuela and SWAPO, to London and to Frankfurt, Federal Republic of Germany, from 30 June to 9 July 1982, formally to notify corporations with interests in Namibia of the illegality of their operations.[3] The mission concluded that it had achieved its purpose in so far as the discussions provided the first opportunity for such formal notification, although the company officials contacted defended their involvement in Namibia as legal, apolitical and beneficial to the Namibian people. The mission considered it important for the Council to persist in its efforts to change the attitude of corporations.

The Council's Standing Committee II stated, in its report on the activities of foreign economic interests in Namibia,[4] that some 88 transnational corporations (TNCs) operated in Namibia, of which 35 were based in South Africa, 25 in the United Kingdom, 15 in the United States, 8 in the Federal Republic of Germany, 3 in France and 2 in Canada. The Committee recommended, among other things, that the Council reiterate its demand for termination of co-operation between South Africa and those exploiting Namibia's resources, send missions of consultation to Governments and contact corporations, conduct hearings and seminars, mobilize public opinion, and urge Member States to enact national legislation prohibiting the entry of Namibian goods.

Economic and Social Council action. In its 27 October resolution on activities of TNCs in southern Africa,[5] the Economic and Social Council, asserting that such activities reinforced the illegal occupation of Namibia and threatened its future political and economic independence, reaffirmed a 1971 Security Council resolution[12] calling on States not to enter into economic relations with South Africa in respect of Namibia and declaring that rights, titles or contracts granted by South Africa following termination of its Mandate in 1966[10] could not be protected against the claims of a future lawful Government of Namibia.

General Assembly action. In its 23 November resolution on foreign interests impeding decolonization,[6] the General Assembly called on all States to terminate, or cause to have terminated, any investments in Namibia or loans to the South African régime and to refrain from or discontinue economic, financial and trade relations with that régime, concerning Namibia which might support the illegal occupation. On 20 August, the Special Committee on the Situation with regard to the Implementation of the Declaration on the Granting of Independence to Colonial Countries and Peoples had adopted a resolution with identical provisions.[1]

In addition, the Assembly, in its resolution of 20 December on general aspects of the Namibia question,[7] condemned the activities of all foreign economic interests which were illegally exploiting Namibia's resources, and demanded that TNCs so engaged comply with all relevant United Nations resolutions by refraining from any new investment or activities, withdrawing from the Territory and putting an end to their co-operation with the illegal South African administration.

Also on 20 December, the Assembly included in the work programme of the Council for Namibia[8] measures to counter such activities, such as dispatching missions of consultation to Governments whose corporations operated in Namibia so as to review with them possible action to discourage continuation of such illegal operations and investments; contacting managing bodies of foreign corporations concerned regarding the illegality of their operations; and conducting hearings, seminars and workshops in order to obtain information on South African and other foreign exploitation of Namibian resources and to expose such activities. The Assembly requested the Secretary-General to complete the preparation of an indexed reference book on TNCs operating in Namibia and, under another resolution, on information dissemination,[9] requested the Council for Namibia to give that book publicity and distribution.

Reports. [1]Committee on colonial countries, A/37/23/Rev.1; [2]Council for Namibia, A/37/24; [3]Mission to corporations, A/AC.131/L.271; [4]Standing Committee II, A/AC.131/L.250 & Corr.1.
Resolutions (1982). [5]ESC: 1982/69, para. 12, 27 Oct. GA: [6]37/31, paras. 11 & 16, 23 Nov.; [7]37/233 A, para. 27, 20 Dec.; [8]37/233 C, paras. 14 & 15, 20 Dec.; [9]37/233 D, para. 5 (j), 20 Dec.
Resolutions (prior). GA: [10]2145(XXI), 27 Oct. 1966 (YUN 1966, p. 605); [11]36/121 C, 10 Dec. 1981 (YUN 1981, p. 1163). [12]SC: 301(1971), 20 Oct. 1971 (YUN 1971, p. 560).

Protection of natural resources

In its Arusha Declaration and Programme of Action on Namibia,[2] the United Nations Council for Namibia, reaffirming that Namibia's natural resources were the inviolable heritage of its people, stated that their rapid depletion, particularly uranium, owing to their systematic plunder by South Africa's Western trading partners, threatened the integrity and prosperity of an independent Namibia. In deciding to promote the speedy implementation of its 1974 Decree No. 1 for the Protection of the Natural Resources of Namibia,[10] the Council declared its readiness to initiate legal action in appropriate courts against the violators of the Decree. Guidelines for a study on the possibility of instituting such action in domestic courts were subsequently outlined by the Council's Standing Committee II.[4]

As regards uranium exploitation, the Council held Western European parties to the 1970 Treaty of Almelo—the Federal Republic of Germany, the Netherlands and the United Kingdom— responsible for processing Namibian uranium, owing to their failure to identify the source of the uranium processed into uranium hexafluoride at the Urenco uranium-enrichment plant at Almelo, Netherlands. It would pursue its policy of denouncing all multinational corporations, such as the British Rio Tinto Zinc Corporation, Ltd., which continued to exploit Namibia's basic resources in disregard of United Nations decisions and the 1971 advisory opinion of the International Court of Justice.[9]

Also under the Arusha Declaration and Programme of Action, the Council declared null and void South African actions relating to Namibia's marine zones, and stated that it would determine the extent of Namibia's territorial sea and contiguous zone, proclaim its exclusive economic zone, delimit its continental shelf and sign and ratify on its behalf the United Nations Convention on the Law of the Sea. At the final part of the eleventh session of the Third United Nations Conference on the Law of the Sea (Montego Bay, Jamaica, 6-10 December),[3] the Council

President signed the Final Act of the Conference and the Convention on behalf of Namibia on 10 December.

The General Assembly, in its resolution of 23 November on foreign interests impeding decolonization,[5] condemned South Africa for its continued exploitation and plunder of Namibia's natural resources in disregard of the legitimate interests of the Namibians, for its creation of an economic structure dependent essentially on its mineral resources and for its illegal extension of the territorial sea and proclamation of an economic zone off the Namibian coast. The Assembly reiterated that such exploitation and plunder by South African and other foreign economic interests contributed to the maintenance of the illegal occupation régime. A resolution with identical provisions had been adopted on 20 August by the Committee on colonial countries.[1]

The Assembly further dealt with the protection of Nambia's natural resources in three 20 December resolutions—on general aspects of the Namibia question,[6] on the Council's 1983 work programme[7] and on information dissemination in support of Namibia.[8]

By the first of these resolutions, the Assembly again requested all Member States to take appropriate measures, including legislation and enforcement action, to ensure the full application of, and compliance with, Decree No. 1; declared the activities of foreign economic, financial and other interests in Namibia a major obstacle to its political independence; and requested the Federal Republic of Germany, the Netherlands and the United Kingdom to exclude Namibian uranium from the Treaty of Almelo, which governedUrenco's activities. By the second resolution, the Assembly asked the Council to continue to examine the exploitation of, and trade in, Namibian uranium by foreign economic interests and report its findings to the Assembly; to draw the attention of the specialized agencies to Decree No. 1; and to ensure compliance with its provisions, including consideration of the institution of legal proceedings in domestic courts and other appropriate bodies. By the third resolution, the Council was also asked to prepare and disseminate a study on the Decree's implementation.

During the Assembly debate, Japan called the Council's report inaccurate in its reference to Japan, stating there was no record of the importation of Namibian uranium into that country and that, in response to steps taken by the Government, a contract for the purchase of such uranium by a private company had been recently cancelled.

Reports. [1]Committee on colonial countries, A/37/23/Rev.1; [2]Council for Namibia, A/37/24; [3]Delegation to 11th session of Conference on Law of Sea, A/AC.131/L.272; [4]Standing Committee II, A/AC.131/L.254.

Resolutions (1982). GA: [5]37/31, paras. 13 & 15, 23 Nov.; [6]37/233 A, paras. 28-30, 20 Dec.; [7]37/233 C, para. 14, 20 Dec.; [8]37/233 D, para. 5 *(k),* 20 Dec.
Yearbook references. [9]1971, p. 585; [10]1974, p. 152.

Human rights

The Commission on Human Rights, in its 25 February 1982 resolution on human rights violations in southern Africa,[3] reaffirmed the right of the Namibian people to self-determination and demanded South Africa's compliance with all United Nations resolutions on Namibia. It also demanded that South Africa immediately cease all acts of torture and ill-treatment of Namibian political detainees and prisoners, grant the captured combatants prisoner-of-war status and treatment according to the 1949 Geneva Conventions on the law of war and allow the Commission's *Ad Hoc* Working Group of Experts to make an on-the-spot investigation of prison conditions. The Commission dealt with other aspects of the Namibia question in its resolutions, also of 25 February, on the widespread violations of human rights in South Africa and Namibia[2] and on peoples' right to self-determination.[4]

Besides repeating the demand for prisoner-of-war status on behalf of captured combatants and three freedom fighters of the South West Africa People's Organization (SWAPO) who had been charged under South Africa's Terrorism Act, the United Nations Council for Namibia,[1] in its Arusha Declaration and Programme of Action on Namibia, also demanded the immediate and unconditional release of all Namibian political prisoners held at Robben Island and in jails and detention centres in South Africa and Namibia.

The General Assembly, in its 20 December resolution on general aspects of the Namibia question,[5] reiterated the demand for the release of all Namibian political prisoners, including those imprisoned or detained under the so-called internal security laws, martial law or any other arbitrary measures. It also demanded that all "disappeared" Namibians be accounted for and those still alive released. It declared that South Africa would be liable for damages to compensate the victims, their families and the future lawful Government of Namibia for the losses sustained.

Report. [1]Council for Namibia, A/37/24.
Resolutions (1982). Commission on Human Rights (report, E/1982/12), 25 Feb.: [2]1982/8; [3]1982/9; [4]1982/16, paras. 2 & 9. [5]GA: 37/233 A, paras. 24 & 25, 20 Dec.

International assistance

United Nations assistance to Namibia, rendered to Namibians outside the Territory, continued in 1982 through the United Nations Institute for Namibia and the Nationhood Programme for Namibia. These two programmes received financing mainly from the United Nations Fund for Namibia (see below) and the United Nations Development Programme, supported by voluntary contributions.

The United Nations Council for Namibia,[2] in its Arusha Declaration and Programme of Action on Namibia, decided to strengthen its overall assistance to the Namibian people and SWAPO, and to protect the needs of Namibian refugees by participating in the Executive Committee of the Programme of the United Nations High Commissioner for Refugees (UNHCR).

The Special Committee on the Situation with regard to the Implementation of the Declaration on the Granting of Independence to Colonial Countries and Peoples, in a 20 August resolution,[1] expressed concern that the assistance extended to colonial peoples, particularly Namibians, by certain United Nations organizations was far from adequate. It urged those bodies to increase their assistance to SWAPO, the Namibia Institute and the Nationhood Programme, as well as to the front-line States; and requested them to withhold or discontinue any support to South Africa until it restored to Namibians their right to self-determination.

The General Assembly called for assistance to the Namibians in two resolutions adopted on 23 November. By the first,[3] it repeated the request for increased assistance by United Nations organizations to SWAPO, the Namibia Institute and the Nationhood Programme. By the second,[4] it urged all States, directly or through action in United Nations bodies, to provide moral and material assistance to the oppressed people of Namibia.

The Assembly, in its 20 December resolution on general aspects of the Namibia question,[5] called on Member States, specialized agencies and other international organizations associated with the United Nations to render increased support as well as material, financial, military and other assistance to SWAPO so as to enable it to intensify its liberation struggle. In its 20 December resolution on the Council's work programme,[6] the Assembly decided to make adequate financial provision in the United Nations programme budget to finance the SWAPO office in New York to ensure appropriate representation of the Namibian people at the United Nations, and decided to continue to defray the expenses of SWAPO representatives whenever the Council for Namibia so decided.

Explaining its vote against the Assembly's first 23 November resolution, the United States, which objected to the continued recognition of SWAPO as the sole authentic representative of the Namibian people in the absence of free and fair elections, considered it inappropriate for United Nations

agencies to provide aid to national liberation movements, particularly those engaged in warfare or other forms of violence; it drew attention to United States legislation forbidding the use for SWAPO of the United States share of contributions to international organizations and programmes.

During the Assembly debate on the Namibia question, Norway said its extensive assistance to several front-line States, aimed at lessening their technical dependence on South Africa, was its way of contributing to the peaceful solution of the question. Finland and Sweden pledged continued humanitarian assistance to SWAPO and all Namibians, both bilaterally and through the United Nations, and hoped their assistance would develop into long-term economic and technical cooperation once Namibia achieved independence.

Reports. [1]Committee on colonial countries, A/37/23/Rev.1; [2]Council for Namibia, A/37/24.
Resolutions (1982). GA: [3]37/32, para. 12, 23 Nov.; [4]37/35, para. 11, 23 Nov.; [5]37/233 A, para. 16, 20 Dec.; [6]37/233 C, paras. 16 & 17, 20 Dec.

UN Fund for Namibia

Activities of the Fund

The United Nations Council for Namibia reported[1] that the United Nations Fund for Namibia, which became operative in 1972[3] and for which the Council was trustee, continued to serve in 1982 as the main vehicle through which the Council channelled its assistance. The Fund financed three main programmes: the United Nations Institute for Namibia; the Nationhood Programme for Namibia; and educational, social and relief assistance to Namibians.

While the Institute and the Nationhood Programme were set up with particular reference to the future attainment of independence, including the establishment of State machinery and the assumption of administrative responsibilities by Namibians, the third programme emphasized the immediate needs and welfare of Namibians. This programme was administered by the Office of the United Nations Commissioner for Namibia and financed from the Fund's General Account.

Under this programme, 12 of the students on scholarships completed their studies, 3 were withdrawn and 114 continued studies in 10 countries during the year ended 31 August 1982. The General Account financed four training projects: broadcasting, English language improvement, law enforcement training and vocational training. Individual Namibians in need received emergency medical treatment and other forms of humanitarian assistance.

Fund expenditures for the three programmes in 1982 were: $2,051,654 for the Nationhood

Programme; $4,442,184 for the Institute; and $2,259,136 for educational, social and relief assistance.

By a resolution of 20 December on the Fund,[2] the General Assembly, taking note of the relevant sections of the Council's report,[1] decided that the Fund be the primary source of assistance to Namibians and that they continue to be eligible for assistance through the United Nations Educational and Training Programme for Southern Africa and the United Nations Trust Fund for South Africa. The Assembly requested the United Nations system to initiate new assistance measures in the context of the Institute and the Nationhood Programme, and to execute the Programme's projects in a manner to reflect the Council's role as the legal Administering Authority for Namibia. It also requested UNHCR to expand assistance to Namibian refugees and asked the Council to carry out, in consultation with the Office of the Commissioner for Namibia, a demographic study of Namibia and a study of its educational needs. It decided that the Council continue to formulate policies of assistance to Namibians, co-ordinate assistance provided by the United Nations system, administer and manage the Fund, and consult with SWAPO on assistance programmes for Namibians.

Other provisions of the resolution related to the Fund's financing, the Nationhood Programme, the Institute and amendments to its Charter.

The resolution, recommended by the Council for Namibia and introduced by Venezuela, was adopted by the Assembly by a recorded vote of 141 to none, with 5 abstentions.

Among those voting in favour, Ireland felt that the Fund performed a valuable function. France explained the abstention by the five members of the Western contact group (Canada, France, Federal Republic of Germany, United Kingdom, United States) as purely procedural, to avoid jeopardizing their role in the negotiations.

Report. [1]Council for Namibia, A/37/24.
Resolution (1982). [2]GA: 37/233 E, 20 Dec., text following.
Yearbook reference. [3]1972, p. 616.
Financial implications. 5th Committee report, A/37/782; S-G statement, A/C.5/37/102.
Meeting records. GA: plenary, A/37/PV.101-106, *113* (13-20 Dec.); 5th Committee, A/C.5/37/SR.76 (18 Dec.).

General Assembly resolution 37/233 E

20 December 1982   Meeting 113   141-0-5 (recorded vote)

Draft by Council for Namibia (A/37/24); agenda item 32.

United Nations Fund for Namibia

The General Assembly,

Having examined the sections of the report of the United Nations Council for Namibia relating to the United Nations Fund for Namibia,

Recalling its resolution 2679(XXV) of 9 December 1970, by which it decided to establish the United Nations Fund for Namibia,

Recalling also its resolution 3112(XXVIII) of 12 December 1973, by which it appointed the United Nations Council for Namibia trustee of the United Nations Fund for Namibia,

Recalling its resolution 31/153 of 20 December 1976, by which it decided to launch the Nationhood Programme for Namibia,

Recalling further its resolution 34/92 A of 12 December 1979, by which it approved the Charter of the United Nations Institute for Namibia,

1. *Takes note* of the relevant sections of the report of the United Nations Council for Namibia;

2. *Expresses its appreciation* to all States, specialized agencies and other organizations of the United Nations system, governmental and non-governmental organizations and individuals that have made voluntary contributions to the United Nations Fund for Namibia, the United Nations Institute for Namibia and the Nationhood Programme for Namibia, and calls upon them to increase their assistance to Namibians through those channels;

3. *Decides* to allocate as a temporary measure to the United Nations Fund for Namibia the sum of $1 million from the regular budget of the United Nations for 1983;

4. *Urges* the organizations of the United Nations system to waive programme-support costs in respect of projects in favour of Namibians financed from the United Nations Fund for Namibia and other sources;

5. *Requests* the Secretary-General and the President of the United Nations Council for Namibia to intensify appeals to Governments, intergovernmental and non-governmental organizations and individuals for generous voluntary contributions to the General Account of the United Nations Fund for Namibia and to the Trust Funds for the Nationhood Programme for Namibia and the United Nations Institute for Namibia and, in this connection, emphasizes the need for contributions in order to increase the number of scholarships awarded to Namibians under the United Nations Fund for Namibia;

6. *Invites* Governments to appeal once more to their national organizations and institutions for voluntary contributions to the United Nations Fund for Namibia;

7. *Decides* that the United Nations Fund for Namibia, including the Trust Funds for the Nationhood Programme for Namibia and the United Nations Institute for Namibia, shall be the primary source of assistance to Namibians;

8. *Decides* that Namibians shall continue to be eligible for assistance through the United Nations Educational and Training Programme for Southern Africa and the United Nations Trust Fund for South Africa;

9. *Requests* the specialized agencies and other organizations and bodies of the United Nations system, when planning and initiating their new measures of assistance to Namibians, to do so within the context of the Nationhood Programme for Namibia and the United Nations Institute for Namibia;

10. *Requests* the specialized agencies and other organizations and bodies of the United Nations system, in the light of the urgent need to strengthen the programme of assistance to the Namibian people, to make every effort to expedite the execution of Nationhood Programme for Namibia projects and other projects in favour of Namibians and to execute these projects on the basis of procedures which will reflect the role of the United Nations Council for Namibia as the legal Administering Authority for Namibia;

11. *Expresses its appreciation* for the efforts of the United Nations High Commissioner for Refugees to assist Namibian refugees and requests him to expand these efforts in view of the substantial increase in the number of Namibian refugees;

12. *Decides* that the United Nations Council for Namibia shall:

(a) Continue to formulate policies of assistance to Namibians and co-ordinate assistance for Namibia provided by the specialized agencies and other organizations and bodies of the United Nations system;

(b) Continue to act as trustee of the United Nations Fund for Namibia and, in this capacity, administer and manage the Fund;

(c) Continue to provide broad guidelines and formulate the principles and policies for the United Nations Institute for Namibia;

(d) Continue to co-ordinate, plan and direct the Nationhood Programme for Namibia in consultation with the South West Africa People's Organization, with the aim of consolidating all measures of assistance by the specialized agencies and other organizations and bodies of the United Nations system into a comprehensive assistance programme;

(e) Continue to consult with the South West Africa People's Organization in the formulation and implementation of assistance programmes for Namibians;

(f) Report to the General Assembly at its thirty-eighth session on activities in respect of the United Nations Fund for Namibia, the United Nations Institute for Namibia and the Nationhood Programme for Namibia;

13. *Approves* the amendments to the Charter of the United Nations Institute for Namibia adopted by the United Nations Council for Namibia at its 391st meeting, on 10 November 1982;

14. *Commends* the United Nations Institute for Namibia for the effectiveness of its training programmes for Namibians and its research activities on Namibia, which contribute substantially to the struggle for freedom of the Namibian people and to the establishment of an independent State of Namibia;

15. *Requests* the United Nations Council for Namibia to complete the preparation of and publish at an early date, through the United Nations Institute for Namibia, a comprehensive reference book on Namibia covering all aspects of the question of Namibia as considered by the United Nations since its inception, in accordance with the outline prepared by the Council;

16. *Commends* the progress made in the implementation of the pre-independence components of the Nationhood Programme for Namibia and requests the United Nations Council for Namibia to elaborate and consider in due course policies and contingency plans regarding the transitional and post-independence phases of the Programme;

17. *Requests* the United Nations Institute for Namibia to prepare, in co-operation with the South West Africa People's Organization, the Office of the United Nations Commissioner for Namibia and the United Nations Development Programme, a comprehensive document on all aspects of economic planning in an independent Namibia, and requests the Secretary-General to provide substantive support through the Office of the Commissioner for the preparation of that document;

18. *Requests* the United Nations Council for Namibia to carry out, in consultation with the Office of the United Nations Commissioner for Namibia, a demographic study of the Namibian population and a study of its educational needs;

19. *Urges* the specialized agencies and other organizations and bodies of the United Nations system to co-operate closely with the United Nations Institute for Namibia in strengthening its programme of activities;

20. *Expresses its appreciation* to those specialized agencies and other organizations and bodies of the United Nations system that have contributed to the Nationhood Programme for Namibia and calls upon them to continue their participation in the Programme by:

(a) Implementing projects approved by the United Nations Council for Namibia;

(b) Preparing new project proposals at the request of the Council;

(c) Allocating funds from their own financial resources for the implementation of the projects approved by the Council;

21. *Expresses its appreciation* to the United Nations Development Programme for its contribution to the financing and administration of the Nationhood Programme for Namibia and calls upon it to continue to allocate, at the request of the United Nations Council for Namibia, funds from the indicative planning figure for Namibia, for the implementation of the projects within the Nationhood Programme and to increase the indicative planning figure for Namibia;

22. *Requests* the Secretary-General to continue to provide the Office of the United Nations Commissioner for Namibia with the necessary resources for the performance of the responsibilities entrusted to it by the United Nations Council for Namibia as the co-ordinating authority in the implementation of the Nationhood Programme for Namibia.

Recorded vote in Assembly as follows:

In favour: Afghanistan, Albania, Algeria, Angola, Antigua and Barbuda, Argentina, Australia, Austria, Bahamas, Bahrain, Bangladesh, Barbados, Belgium, Benin, Bhutan, Bolivia, Botswana, Brazil, Bulgaria, Burma, Burundi, Byelorussian SSR, Cape Verde, Central African Republic, Chad, Chile, China, Colombia, Comoros, Congo, Costa Rica, Cuba, Cyprus, Czechoslovakia, Democratic Kampuchea, Democratic Yemen, Denmark, Djibouti, Dominican Republic, Ecuador, Egypt, El Salvador, Ethiopia, Fiji, Finland, Gabon, Gambia, German Democratic Republic, Ghana, Greece, Grenada, Guinea, Guinea-Bissau, Guyana, Haiti, Honduras, Hungary, Iceland, India, Indonesia, Iran, Iraq, Ireland, Italy, Ivory Coast, Jamaica, Japan, Jordan, Kenya, Kuwait, Lao People's Democratic Republic, Lebanon, Liberia, Libyan Arab Jamahiriya, Luxembourg, Madagascar, Malawi,

Malaysia, Maldives, Mali, Malta, Mauritania, Mauritius, Mexico, Mongolia, Morocco, Mozambique, Nepal, Netherlands, New Zealand, Nicaragua, Niger, Nigeria, Norway, Oman, Pakistan, Panama, Papua New Guinea, Peru, Philippines, Poland, Portugal, Qatar, Romania, Rwanda, Saint Lucia, Saint Vincent and the Grenadines, Samoa, Sao Tome and Principe, Saudi Arabia, Senegal, Seychelles, Sierra Leone, Singapore, Somalia, Spain, Sri Lanka, Sudan, Sweden, Syrian Arab Republic, Thailand, Togo, Trinidad and Tobago, Tunisia, Turkey, Uganda, Ukrainian SSR, USSR, United Arab Emirates, United Republic of Cameroon, United Republic of Tanzania, Upper Volta, Uruguay, Vanuatu, Venezuela, Viet Nam, Yemen, Yugoslavia, Zaire, Zambia, Zimbabwe.

Against: None.

Abstaining: Canada, France, Germany, Federal Republic of, United Kingdom, United States.

Financing of the Fund

In 1982, 34 States made a total contribution of $3,520,334 to the United Nations Fund for Namibia (see table). Other income included $1,176 from public donations and $1 million from the United Nations budget, as authorized by the General Assembly in December 1981.[4] Funding for assistance projects was also provided by the United Nations Development Programme (UNDP) and the executing agencies.

Two fund-raising missions were conducted in 1982, in response to the Assembly's December 1981 request.[4] Between 9 February and 12 March, a mission composed of three Council members visited Austria, Belgium, Canada, Denmark, Finland, France, the Federal Republic of Germany, the Netherlands, Norway, Sweden and the headquarters of the European Economic Community.[1] Additional fund-raising activities were undertaken by the United Nations Commissioner for Namibia in Bahrain, Egypt, Oman, Qatar and the United Arab Emirates between 19 November and 5 December.[2]

The General Assembly, in its 20 December resolution on the Fund,[3] decided to provide the Fund with a temporary allocation of $1 million from the United Nations 1983 budget and urged organizations of the United Nations system to waive programme-support costs in respect of projects for Namibians financed from the Fund and other sources. It expressed appreciation to, and called for increased assistance by, the contributors to the Fund, the Namibia Institute and the Nationhood Programme. The Assembly asked the Secretary-General and the President of the Council for Namibia to intensify appeals for contributions, emphasizing the need to increase the number of scholarships under the Fund. Governments were invited to appeal once more to their national organizations for voluntary contributions.

Among those voting in favour of this resolution, Japan expressed reservations regarding the allocation to the Fund from the United Nations regular budget, recalling that the Fund had been established as a voluntary fund.

Reports. Council for Namibia, [1]A/37/24, [2]A/38/24.
Resolution (1982). [3]GA: 37/233 E, paras. 2-6, 20 Dec.
Resolution (prior). [4]GA: 36/121 F, 10 Dec. 1981 (YUN 1981, p. 1173).

CONTRIBUTIONS TO THE UN FUND FOR NAMIBIA, 1982
(as at 31 December 1982)

Amount *(in US dollar equivalent)*

Country	General Account	Nationhood Programme	Institute for Namibia
Argentina	4,093	–	–
Austria	16,700	–	–
Bahamas	1,000	–	–
Brazil	5,000	20,000	10,000
Canada	–	–	165,289
China	20,000	–	–
Cyprus	225	225	225
Denmark	–	119,048	238,095
Egypt	–	–	3,000
Finland	55,054	789,795	176,173
France	158,333	–	15,408
Germany, Federal Republic of	–	–	72,340
Greece	4,500	–	5,500
Iceland	4,400	–	–
Indonesia	4,500	–	–
Ireland	4,902	4,902	4,902
Italy	–	–	1,295
Japan	10,000	–	210,000
Kuwait	100,000	–	–
Liberia	3,000	–	–
Mali	309	–	309
Mexico	5,000	–	–
Netherlands	134,084	–	46,459
New Zealand	3,696	–	–
Norway	–	166,667	200,000
Pakistan	3,000	–	–
Panama	1,000	–	–
Philippines	2,000	–	500
Republic of Korea	–	–	50,000
Suriname	1,000	1,000	1,000
Sweden	–	–	670,535
Togo	31	–	31
United Republic of Cameroon	309	–	–
Zimbabwe	5,500	–	–
Total	547,636	1,101,637	1,871,061

SOURCE: Interim United Nations financial statements for the 12-month period ended 31 December 1982—Individual trust funds (unpublished).

Nationhood Programme

The Nationhood Programme for Namibia, launched by the General Assembly in 1976,[5] continued in 1982 to finance training programmes and surveys of the Namibian economy in preparation for independence.

The United Nations Council for Namibia[2] reported that, for the period 1 September 1981 to 31 August 1982, one group of students entered the third phase of training in the administration of public enterprises and another group began preparatory studies for a mining engineering course; a group of eight studying railways operations commenced, in August, one year's in-service training with Sudan Railways. The United Nations Commissioner for Namibia told a meeting of the Committee on the United Nations Fund for Namibia[1] in July that, under two new projects launched in 1982, 230 Namibians began law enforcement training in the United Republic of Tanzania and 70 were enrolled in various vocational training programmes in Denmark. Training continued in food science and economics, nutrition, radio programme production and equipment maintenance.

The United Nations Vocational Training Centre, under construction in Angola to provide training to Namibians, began offering preparatory courses in late 1981, and the third meeting of the Centre's Governing Board took place in June 1982 with the Council's participation.

Of the sectoral surveys envisaged by the Programme, draft reports were submitted on the protection of food supplies and nutrition, land suitability, maritime transportation and training, and civil aviation. The last in a series of four workshops requested by the Council in 1980, a workshop on mining, industries, trade and economic planning was organized at Harare, Zimbabwe, in March/April 1982. The three earlier workshops had been held in Mozambique and the United Republic of Tanzania in August 1980 and in Ethiopia in April 1981.

On 22 July 1982, the Committee on the Fund, after considering the Commissioner's reports on the Nationhood Programme and educational, social and relief activities of the Fund, as well as on the organization of sectoral planning workshops,[1] recommended to the Council that the Institute for Namibia prepare a comprehensive document on all aspects of economic planning in an independent Namibia, to form the basis for a fifth workshop. This recommendation was approved by the Council on 13 October.[3]

In its resolution on the Fund of 20 December,[4] the General Assembly decided that the Council for Namibia continue to co-ordinate, plan and direct the Nationhood Programme in consultation with SWAPO. It commended the progress made in implementation of the Programme's pre-independence components and requested the Council to elaborate policies and contingency plans for the transitional and post-independence phases. Expressing appreciation to the United Nations agencies and organizations that had contributed to the Programme, the Assembly called on them to continue implementing the Programme's projects, preparing new proposals and allocating funds from their own resources for project implementation. The Assembly also thanked UNDP for its contribution, and asked it to continue allocating funds from its indicative planning figure for Namibia and to increase that figure. The Secretary-General was requested to continue providing the necessary resources to the Office of the Commissioner for Namibia, the co-ordinating authority in the Nationhood Programme's implementation.

Reports. [1]Committee on UN Fund for Namibia, A/AC.131/L.258; [2]Council for Namibia, A/37/24.
Resolutions (1982). Council for Namibia (A/AC.131/89): [3]A & B, 13 Oct. [4]GA: 37/233 E, 20 Dec.
Resolution (prior). [5]GA: 31/153, 20 Dec. 1976 (YUN 1976, p. 791).

United Nations Institute for Namibia

The United Nations Institute for Namibia, inaugurated in 1976[3] to undertake research, training, planning and related activities, continued in 1982 to develop human resources in anticipation of Namibia's independence.

The Institute, located at Lusaka, Zambia, and open only to persons of Namibian origin who fulfilled the admission requirements of the Institute's Senate, had a student body of 415.[1] Its expanded curriculum included teacher training courses, secretarial instruction and special preparatory courses in English, statistics and mathematics. On 16 January, the third group of students, numbering 74, graduated from the Institute with diplomas in management and development studies, bringing the total number of graduates to 220. Twenty students also graduated from the secretarial course, to which 58 new ones were admitted.

As part of its applied research programme, intended to make available basic documentation for policy formulation by the future Government of an independent Namibia, the Institute completed and published studies on agrarian reform, constitutional options, a language policy, a legal system, manpower requirements and development implications. Work continued for a comprehensive reference book covering aspects of the Namibia question as considered by the United Nations since its inception.

In 1982, the Institute's Namibian Extension Unit, which became operational in November 1981, was serving some 40,000 Namibians in Zambia and Angola who had limited access to formal education.

In its 20 December resolution on the United Nations Fund for Namibia,[2] the General Assembly commended the Institute for the effectiveness of its training programmes and research activities, and requested it to prepare, in co-operation with SWAPO, the Office of the United Nations Commissioner for Namibia and UNDP, a comprehensive document on all aspects of economic planning in an independent Namibia. The Assembly decided that the Council continue to formulate policies for the Institute and requested it to complete the preparation and publication, through the Institute, of the comprehensive reference book on Namibia. It also urged the United Nations system to co-operate with the Institute in strengthening its programme and took action on the Institute's Charter (see below).

Report. [1]Council for Namibia, A/37/24.
Resolution (1982). [2]GA: 37/233 E, 20 Dec.
Yearbook reference. [3]1976, p. 779.

Amendments to the Institute Charter

In its resolution of 20 December 1982 on the Fund,[2] the General Assembly approved the amendments to the Charter of the United Nations Institute for Namibia, as adopted by the Council for Namibia on 10 November.[1]

Article 6 of the original Charter, which had been approved by the Council in 1979,[3] provided for a Senate membership of 15. The number was amended to 16, the additional member to be the Vice-Chancellor of the University of Zambia or a representative nominated by him.

Report. [1]Council for Namibia, A/37/24.
Resolution (1982). [2]GA: 37/233 E, para. 13, 20 Dec.
Yearbook reference. [3]1979, p. 1090.

Other UN assistance

UN Educational and Training Programme for Southern Africa. In a September 1982 report to the General Assembly,[2] the Secretary-General stated that for the 1981/82 academic year, the United Nations Educational and Training Programme for Southern Africa granted 24 new scholarship awards to Namibians and extended 111, making a total of 135 scholarship holders studying in 13 countries. Fourteen of the new awards were financed by the United Nations Fund for Namibia.

In a resolution of 23 November, the Assembly appealed for greater financial and other support to the Programme.[6]

UNIDO activities. In 1982, the United Nations Industrial Development Organization (UNIDO) completed three priority projects of assistance for Namibia, based on its Industrial Development Board's 1978 comprehensive blueprint of technical assistance for Namibia's pre-independence, transitional and post-independence periods. The projects, financed jointly with the United Nations Development Programme (UNDP), included a secondment of Namibian students to UNIDO projects, a study tour in India, Kenya and the United Republic of Tanzania, and secondment of Namibian officials to UNIDO headquarters at Vienna, Austria.

In the absence of a final decision from the Council for Namibia, other projects for implementation in the pre-independence phase were suspended. Five further project proposals, resulting from a UNIDO programming mission to Dar es Salaam, United Republic of Tanzania, and Lusaka, Zambia, in March 1982, could not be accommodated due to constraints faced by UNDP. In the mean time, UNIDO allocated $80,000 from the United Nations Industrial Development Fund for its pre-independence assistance to Namibia, which was expected to lead to co-operation with the Institute for Namibia in the industrial and technological fields.[5]

At its sixteenth session, on 28 May, the Industrial Development Board[1] took note of the UNIDO Executive Director's report on technical to the Namibian people.[4] It emphasized the need for effective delivery of such assistance, taking into account the priority areas within the industrial sector as defined in the programme for the Industrial Development Decade for Africa, and the importance of close co-operation between the UNIDO secretariat, the Council and the South West Africa People's Organization (SWAPO) in project formulation and execution. The Board called on the Council and UNDP to act on the UNIDO project proposals already submitted to them.

The Board adopted these conclusions by a roll-call vote of 34 to 1 (United States), with 7 abstentions.

UNDP activities. During 1982, SWAPO benefited from two UNDP projects, aimed at providing technical and physical infrastructures for the education of SWAPO children in Angola and Zambia.[3] The project in Angola provided the salaries of 21 primary school teachers and 3 support personnel, and fellowships for the upgrading of 4 teachers, all of whom were Namibians. The project in Zambia assisted the Namibia Education Centre at Nyango—which provided for 2,500 children at the primary and secondary school levels—in the form of educational equipment and salaries for 2 teaching consultants, 21 Namibian teachers and some support personnel.

Reports. [1]IDB, A/37/16; S-G, [2]A/37/436, [3]A/38/111/Add.1; UNIDO Executive Director, [4]ID/B/276 & Corr.1 & Add.1, [5]ID/B/293 & Corr.1.
Resolution (1982). [6]GA: 37/33, para. 5, 23 Nov.

Chapter IV

Other colonial Territories

Contents

Related topic:

Treaty for the Prohibition of Nuclear Weapons in Latin America (Treaty of Tlatelolco).

For resolutions and decisions of major organs mentioned but not reproduced, refer to INDEX OF RESOLUTIONS AND DECISIONS.

General aspects

In April 1982, Argentina and the United Kingdom alerted the Security Council to a deteriorating situation in the South Atlantic, where a dispute concerning sovereignty over the Falkland Islands (Malvinas) resulted in an outbreak of armed hostilities between the two countries. Despite Security Council action, intensive negotiations by the Secretary-General and mediation efforts by individual countries, fighting lasted until the military commanders of both sides signed a cease-fire agreement in mid-June.

On 4 November, the General Assembly requested the two parties to resume negotiations towards a peaceful solution of their sovereignty dispute and requested the Secretary-General to undertake a renewed mission of good offices to assist them in that task.[(2)]

The Falkland Islands (Malvinas), consisting of two large islands (East Falkland and West Falkland)

and some 200 smaller ones with a total area of about 12,000 square kilometres, lie in the South Atlantic, some 772 kilometres north-east of Cape Horn. The Falkland Islands (Malvinas) dependencies consist of South Georgia, situated about 1,300 kilometres east-south-east of the Falkland Islands (Malvinas) group, and the uninhabited South Sandwich Islands, some 756 kilometres east-south-east of South Georgia. At the census held in December 1980, the population of the Territory, excluding the dependencies, numbered 1,813, of whom just over 1,000 lived in Stanley, the capital on East Falkland.

The extent of progress towards self-determination and independence in other individual Non-Self-Governing Territories was again examined in 1982 by the General Assembly and its Special Committee on the Situation with regard to the Implementation of the Declaration on the Granting of Independence to Colonial Countries and Peoples.

For most of the Territories, the United Nations Secretariat prepared working papers for the Committee, outlining recent developments. The Committee, and usually its Sub-Committee on Small Territories, examined the situation in each Territory, hearing further information in most cases from a representative of the administering Power. A set of conclusions and recommendations was approved for each Territory, and these were set out in the Committee's report to the Assembly,[(1)] where the situation in the Territories was discussed mainly in the Fourth Committee.

Report. [(1)]Committee on colonial countries, A/37/23/Rev.1. *Resolution (1982).* [(2)]GA: 37/9, 4 Nov.

Status of the Falkland Islands (Malvinas)

Security Council action (April). In a letter to the President of the Security Council dated 1 April 1982,[(126)] the United Kingdom requested an immediate meeting of the Council, saying it had good reason to believe that Argentina's armed forces were about to invade the Falkland Islands. By a letter of the same date,[(8)] Argentina informed the Council that a situation of grave tension existed between it and the United Kingdom, citing news reports that British warships had been sent to the South Atlantic region because of a dispute involving Argentine workers in the South Georgia Islands.

At a Council meeting that day, the United Kingdom stated that an Argentine Navy cargo vessel was reported anchored on 19 March at Leith harbour, South Georgia—a dependency of the Falklands Islands—over which the United Kingdom had exercised sovereignty since its discovery by Captain Cook in 1775, that a large party of Argentines were setting up camp and that the Argentine flag had been hoisted. The Commander of the British Antarctic survey base on South Georgia told the men they had no right to land without seeking permission from the British authorities and ordered them either to seek the necessary clearance or to leave. While Argentina withdrew on 21 March all but about 10 of the party, purported to be non-military personnel working for a commercial company, an Argentine naval transport vessel arrived at the harbour on 25 March to deliver further supplies to the men ashore. When requested again to remove the personnel or request proper authorization, Argentina pressed on 28 March for talks on the wider sovereignty issue. The British efforts to engage that Government in the search for a diplomatic solution had been rebuffed. At the same time, it had noted Argentine press reports, supported by government statements, concerning the country's naval movements in preparation for operations in the South Atlantic; there had also been unauthorized flights over the Falklands on 30 March by at least two aircraft of the Argentine Air Force. The

United Kingdom rejected any attempt to change the situation by force and asked the Council to call on Argentina to refrain from the use of force.

Argentina told the Council that the United Kingdom's threat of the use of force against workers engaged in peaceful commercial activity in South Georgia constituted an act of aggression. Argentina did not seek that incident; the crisis resulted from the perpetuation of, and the irrational rejection of a search for a logical solution to, the colonial situation. Argentina said that during lengthy negotiations between the two Governments since the British seizure of the Malvinas by force in 1833, the United Kingdom had consistently rejected Argentine proposals, while Argentina provided uninterrupted assistance to the Islands' inhabitants. The Malvinas question, Argentina said, was that of the right of a State to territorial integrity; the principle of self-determination was inapplicable to that question because of the forced displacement and replacement of the islanders with subjects of the occupying Power. Argentina would not pursue negotiations without prior recognition by the United Kingdom of Argentine sovereignty over the islands. In the face of the latest act of aggression, Argentina asserted, it would be obliged to act in self-defence, to protect its territory and citizens.

Following consultations among the members of the Security Council, its President made the following statement at the end of the Council meeting on 1 April:[(199)]

"The Security Council has heard statements from the representatives of the United Kingdom and Argentina about the tension which has recently arisen between the two Governments.

The Security Council has taken note of the statement issued by the Secretary-General, which reads as follows:

'The Secretary-General, who has already seen the representatives of the United Kingdom and Argentina earlier today, renews his appeal for maximum restraint on both sides. He will, of course, return to Headquarters at any time, if the situation demands it.'

The Security Council, mindful of its primary responsibility under the Charter of the United Nations for the maintenance of international peace and security, expresses its concern about the tension in the region of the Falkland Islands (Islas Malvinas). The Council accordingly calls on the Governments of Argentina and the United Kingdom to exercise the utmost restraint at this time and, in particular, to refrain from the use or threat of force in the region and to continue the search for a diplomatic solution.

The Security Council will remain seized of the question."

The United States expressed its support for the statement and its readiness to help in the search for a diplomatic solution.

The Secretary-General left New York for Rome, Italy, on the evening of 1 April, on his first trip away from Headquarters since taking office in January. After presiding at a meeting of the Administrative Committee on Co-ordination at Rome, he travelled to Geneva, but left there for New York on 12 April, thus postponing official visits to Berne (Switzerland), Austria and Yugoslavia.

By a letter of 2 April,[(127)] the United Kingdom informed the Security Council President that Argentine armed forces were invading the Falkland Islands and requested an immediate meeting of the Council.

Following two meetings on 2 April, the Council adopted, by 10 votes to 1, with 4 abstentions, a resolution on 3 April,[(195)] demanding an immediate cessation of hostilities and a withdrawal of Argentine forces from the Falkland Islands (Malvinas). The Council called on the two Governments to seek a diplomatic solution to their differences and to respect the purposes and principles of the Charter of the United Nations. The text had been proposed by the United Kingdom and subsequently revised to include after each mention of the Falkland Islands a parenthetical reference to Islas Malvinas, the Argentine nomenclature for the islands in question.

Introducing the draft on 2 April, the United Kingdom condemned the Argentine invasion as a blatant violation of international law and as an attempt at imposing by force a foreign and unwanted control over 1,900 Falkland Islanders who had chosen in fair elections to maintain their links with the United Kingdom.

Argentina responded that the sovereignty question had been taken up directly with the United Kingdom but never with the islanders, and that it could not accept the description or interpretation of the events as given by the United Kingdom. It informed the Council that it had recovered on 2 April its national sovereignty over Islas Malvinas and its dependencies—South Georgia and the South Sandwich Islands—in self-defence against acts of aggression by the United Kingdom. It affirmed its readiness to negotiate, but stated that the sovereignty issue itself was not negotiable.

Argentina's Minister for External Relations and Worship told the Council on 3 April that the Malvinas question was a colonial issue; he rejected the British argument invoking the wishes of the local population, adding that the only inhabitants of the South Sandwich Islands and South Georgia were seals, while those of the Malvinas were largely British government officials or employees of the Falkland Islands Company, a colonial firm. Military preparations and the dispatch of warships to the region by the United Kingdom explained and justified Argentina's actions in defence of its rights.

Argentina considered it strange that the United Kingdom, the party which had taken the Islands through an illegitimate act of force, should call for the withdrawal of the Argentine troops which recovered the Malvinas for national sovereignty.

The United Kingdom, speaking in right of reply, asserted that the current crisis originated from Argentina's armed invasion of the Falklands, not from the relatively trivial incident of the illegal presence of 10 Argentine workers on South Georgia. To argue that this was not an invasion because the Islands belonged to Argentina, the United Kingdom stated, flew in the face of the fact that the United Nations—including the Committee on colonial countries—had accepted the United Kingdom as the administering Power. It contended that the people of the Falkland Islands were entitled to enjoy the protection of international law and to have their freely expressed wishes respected.

Prior to the vote on the United Kingdom draft, Panama asked for a ruling by the Council President on whether the proposed text fell under Chapter VI (relating to pacific settlement of disputes) or Chapter VII (breaches of the peace and acts of aggression) of the United Nations Charter, observing that, according to Article 27 of the Charter, a party to a dispute must abstain from voting in decisions taken under Chapter VI. The United Kingdom declared that Article 40 of the Charter applied to its proposal relating to a breach of the peace. The Council decided without objection that the matter fell under Chapter VII and proceeded to the vote.

Speaking in explanation of its negative vote, Panama said the text failed to recognize the colonial aspect of the problem; because the Malvinas were the sovereign territory of Argentina, it was wrong to speak of an invasion or a breach of the peace.

Poland, Spain and the USSR abstained in the vote, asserting that the text ignored the decolonization aspect. Also abstaining, China hoped that negotiations between the two parties would continue.

Among those voting in favour, France, Guyana, Togo and Uganda deplored the use of force in international relations, as did Ireland which called for a strict observance of the Charter and the principle of the peaceful settlement of disputes. Uganda and Zaire endorsed the position of the Movement of Non-Aligned Countries which recognized Argentina's claim to the Malvinas while urging negotiations between the two parties. Guyana, Ireland, Togo and Zaire stressed that their votes were not meant to prejudice the merits of the underlying problem.

During the Council debate on 3 April, Panama proposed, but did not press after adoption of the United Kingdom text, a draft resolution[(3)] calling on the United Kingdom to cease its hostile conduct and refrain from the threat or use of force, and requesting Argentina and the United Kingdom to proceed immediately to negotiations based on respect for Argentina's sovereignty over the Malvinas Islands, South Georgia and the South Sandwich Islands. Spain said it could not support the text, which neglected to mention the violent action resorted to by Argentina.

At their request, Australia, Canada and New Zealand, on 2 April, and Bolivia, Brazil, Paraguay and Peru, on 3 April, were invited to participate in the discussion without the right to vote.

In the debate, Australia, France, Guyana, Ireland, Japan, Jordan, New Zealand, Togo and Zaire deplored the invasion as a violation of the Charter's provision on the non-use of force in international relations. Canada joined them in observing that Argentina acted in disregard of the appeals made by the Council and the Secretary-General.

Japan, New Zealand and Zaire feared that the armed action would increase the tension in the region and make the search for a peaceful solution more difficult; Australia, France and New Zealand called on Argentina to withdraw its troops. Australia, Canada, New Zealand and the United States supported the Council's call for restraint and the United Kingdom text.

Panama, however, expressed the view that an action carried out in assertion of national sovereignty over its own territory could not be considered an illegitimate use of force. It was joined by Bolivia, Jordan, Paraguay, Peru and the USSR in seeing a colonial situation. Brazil, Jordan, Uganda and Zaire also supported Argentina's claim to the Malvinas, while endorsing the principle of the peaceful settlement of disputes, and appealed to both countries to act with moderation.

Ireland and Togo stressed that their position was in relation to the immediate situation existing in the region, without passing judgement on the merits of the underlying issue. New Zealand hoped that negotiations would lead to a settlement that reflected the wishes of the inhabitants of the territory.

Communications (3 April–21 May). Between 3 April and 21 May, the President of the Security Council and the Secretary-General received a number of communications, mostly from Argentina and the United Kingdom. The United Kingdom also transmitted to the Council communications it had had with the Argentine Government through the Embassy of Switzerland at Buenos Aires; Argentina's responses were for the most part addressed to the Council President. (The following were addressed to the Council President except as otherwise noted.)

On 3 April,[104] Belgium transmitted a joint statement of 2 April by the 10 States members of the European Community (EC) condemning Argentina's armed intervention in the Falkland Islands, and urgently appealing to that Government to withdraw its forces immediately, to refrain from the use of force and to continue to search for a diplomatic solution.

In a telegram of 5 April,[182] addressed to the Secretary-General, Dominica called for respect for the right of the Falkland Islanders to self-determination, and deplored Argentine acts of aggression as threatening to the sense of security of small States, particularly in the Caribbean.

On 9 April,[9] Argentina conveyed an 8 April communication from the United Kingdom declaring a 200-nautical-mile maritime exclusion zone around the Falkland Islands; Argentina also conveyed the text of its reply, by which it maintained that the United Kingdom's communication constituted "a notification of blockade", an act defined as aggression in the General Assembly's 1974 Definition of Aggression,[198] and stated that Argentina would exercise its right of self-defence under Article 51 of the Charter.

In a letter dated 9 April,[128] the United Kingdom stated that because Argentina continued to reinforce its armed forces in the Falkland Islands, it would establish a 200-nautical-mile maritime exclusion zone around the Falklands as from 0400 hours Greenwich mean time (GMT) on 12 April, beyond which time any Argentine warships and naval auxiliaries found within that zone were liable to be attacked by British forces.

Responding to Argentina's letter of 9 April, the United Kingdom, in a letter dated 11 April,[129] stated that its declaration of the maritime exclusion zone fell short of the concept of blockade as understood in international law. The Definition of Aggression cited by Argentina referred to the blockade of the coasts of another State and was therefore not relevant to the zone the United Kingdom had declared around its own territory; a more relevant portion of the Definition stated that the "first use of armed force by a State in contravention of the Charter shall constitute *prima facie* evidence of an act of aggression", it having been determined that Argentina had been the first to use armed force.

On 13 April,[105] Belgium transmitted a joint statement issued on 10 April by the EC members announcing their decision to apply a total embargo on the exports of arms and military equipment to Argentina and to prohibit all imports of Argentine origin into the Community; they called on other Governments to act likewise in order to ensure prompt and full implementation of the Council resolution of 3 April.

Expressing its concern about the possibility of an imminent outbreak of hostilities, Peru sent a telegram on 11 April to the Foreign Ministers of

Argentina, the United Kingdom and the United States, the text of which was transmitted to the Security Council on 12 April,[123] formally proposing a 72-hour truce between Argentina and the United Kingdom pending the exercise of good offices, accepted by both parties, being provided by the United States.

Responding to the Peruvian proposal by a telegram dated 13 April, which was transmitted to the Security Council that day,[131] the United Kingdom stated that since Argentina had initiated the armed confrontation, the first requirement for any solution was the withdrawal of Argentine forces from the Islands and their dependencies, in accordance with the Council resolution of 3 April. Argentina's reply to Peru, also transmitted to the Council on 13 April,[11] was that it had no intention of initiating or provoking hostilities; that it was the United Kingdom that committed an act of armed aggression by decreeing a naval blockade with the participation of warships and nuclear submarines; and that if the United Kingdom established a blockade it would respond in self-defence.

Saying that the situation was becoming more alarming by the hour, Peru again requested the United Kingdom by a letter of 14 April, which was transmitted to the Council the following day,[124] to agree to a 72-hour truce in order to create the optimal conditions for finding a diplomatic solution. The United Kingdom's reply, transmitted to the Council on 19 April,[132] was that the right conditions for a negotiated solution would exist only when Argentina withdrew its troops.

In a letter dated 12 April,[10] Argentina stated its readiness to withdraw its forces as called for under the 3 April Council resolution, on condition that the United Kingdom ceased hostilities and did not attempt to use the resolution to justify a return to the previous colonial situation; it also asserted that the United Kingdom had unilaterally taken a series of measures which constituted "economic aggression", thereby violating the 1974 Charter of Economic Rights and Duties of States,[197] and had induced other States to act likewise.

In a letter dated 13 April,[130] the United Kingdom referred to Argentina's letter of 12 April, stating that while it welcomed Argentina's preparedness to comply with the Council's call for the withdrawal of forces, that resolution had to be read as a whole, including the preamble which determined that Argentina had breached the peace; in violation of that resolution, Argentina had invaded South Georgia on 4 April and continued to increase its forces in the region. It rejected Argentina's charge of economic aggression and said it would continue to take all necessary measures in exercise of its right of self-defence.

By a letter dated 16 April,[5] the Secretary-General of the Organization of American States (OAS) transmitted to the United Nations Secretary-General the text of a resolution adopted by the OAS Permanent Council at an extraordinary session held on 13 April, in which it offered its co-operation in the peace efforts already under way.

Panama, in a letter of 14 April,[118] reiterated its support for Argentina's position; expressed concern and indignation at what it called the punitive expedition by the United Kingdom whose naval combat forces, inluding nuclear submarines, were on their way to the Argentine territorial waters; and requested the Council President urgently to convene informal consultations among the Council members. The Minister for External Relations of Venezuela, in a statement of 13 April transmitted to the Council the next day,[171] reaffirmed his Government's solidarity with Argentina and deplored the fact that the alarming movement of British armed forces was being observed in silence by the Council, further accentuating the scepticism with which that body was viewed.

By a letter dated 16 April,[12] Argentina reaffirmed its readiness to comply with the 3 April Council resolution and claimed that the mobilization of the fleet and the blockade by the United Kingdom constituted acts of war and demonstrated that country's lack of readiness to comply with the Council's call for a cessation of hostilities; Argentina therefore had no alternative but to defend itself. In response, the United Kingdom, in a letter dated 20 April,[133] stated that it would continue to take whatever measures were necessary for self-defence in the face of Argentina's unlawful invasion of British territory and violations of the rights of the people of the Falkland Islands.

In a communiqué of 23 April to Argentina, which was transmitted to the Council the next day,[134] the United Kingdom declared that appropriate action would be taken against any Argentine aircraft or warships which threatened to interfere with the mission of the British forces in the South Atlantic, and that all Argentine aircraft, including civil aircraft engaging in surveillance of the British forces, would be regarded as hostile and dealt with accordingly. Argentina, in a letter dated 24 April,[13] stated that the communiqué demonstrated the British extension of its threat of aggression beyond a specific zone and even against civil aircraft, and its lack of intention to comply with the Security Council's call for a cessation of hostilities.

Argentina informed the Security Council by a letter of 25 April[14] that, while negotiations with the participation of the United States Secretary of State were still open, the British naval units and armed helicopters that day fired on an Argentine submarine at Grytviken and ground positions on the South Georgia Islands for four hours until the defence capability of the small Argentine naval force stationed there was exhausted. In a letter dated 26 April,[135] the United Kingdom announced that its forces had re-established British authority on South Georgia on 25 April; that it had acted in self-defence; and that the only casualty was an injured Argentine seaman.

By a letter of 26 April,[184] Japan transmitted a statement of the same date by its Minister for Foreign Affairs calling for the immediate cessation of hostilities and withdrawal of Argentine forces, and expressing Japan's intention to make further efforts to prevent enlargement of the dispute.

Acting on a 19 April request by Argentina, the Permanent Council of OAS adopted a resolution on 21 April, transmitted the same day,[6] agreeing to convene on 26 April the Twentieth Meeting of Consultation of Ministers of Foreign Affairs of its member States to consider what it termed the grave situation in the South Atlantic.

On 26 April,[113] Cuba transmitted to the Secretary-General a communiqué issued that day by the Co-ordinating Bureau of the Movement of Non-Aligned Countries, which had met at Argentina's request. The Bureau reaffirmed its support for Argentine sovereignty over the Malvinas Islands, requested the parties to seek a peaceful solution of their dispute and said the use of force in international relations was contrary to the Movement's principles. The United Kingdom commented in a letter dated 28 April[137] that it shared the Co-ordinating Bureau's concern over developments in the region, and asserted that Argentina's use of force was contrary to the principles of the Movement as well as those of the United Nations Charter; it emphasized the right of self-determination of the Islands' inhabitants who, it noted, had expressed their wishes regarding their political status in free elections, as recently as October 1981. The letter carried an annex tracing the history of the settlement of the Falkland Islands from 1592 to 1981.

On 28 April,[175] the President of the Twentieth Meeting of Consultation of Ministers of Foreign Affairs of OAS transmitted a resolution adopted that day urging the United Kingdom to cease the hostilities and Argentina to refrain from taking any action that might exacerbate the situation. By that resolution, OAS also urged the two parties to call a truce and to resume negotiations, taking into account the Argentine sovereignty over the Malvinas and the interests of the Islanders, and urged the EC and other States to lift coercive political and economic measures they had taken against Argentina. In a letter dated 29 April,[138] the United Kingdom expressed surprise that the OAS resolution had failed to mention Argentina's armed invasion of the Falkland Islands or urge Argentina

to withdraw its forces, rejected the criticism against legitimate political and economic countermeasures, and reaffirmed the British sovereignty over the Territory and the right to self-determination of its inhabitants.

On 28 April,[136] the United Kingdom conveyed the text of its announcement on that date, declaring the establishment of a total exclusion zone around the Falkland Islands as from 1100 hours GMT on 30 April, the outer limit of which would be the same as for the maritime exclusion zone established on 12 April, and which would apply to any ship or aircraft, military or civil, operating in support of the illegal Argentine occupation; as of that time, the Port Stanley Airport would be closed and any aircraft on the ground in the Falkland Islands would be liable to attack. The United Kingdom asserted that its action was necessitated by Argentina's failure to comply with the 3 April Council resolution and the need to exercise its right to self-defence under Article 51 of the Charter.

Argentina, in a letter dated 28 April,[15] described as a new act of aggression the United Kingdom's declaration of a total exclusion zone; called the British use of armed force an unjustified act of reprisal aimed at restoring colonial occupation of the Argentine islands; and asserted that it was impossible for the United Kingdom to claim the right of self-defence, under Article 51, in islands situated 8,000 miles from British territory.

On 29 April,[16] Argentina conveyed the text of a message it had received from the United Kingdom announcing that all Argentine vessels, including merchant or fishing vessels, apparently engaged in surveillance of, or intelligence-gathering activities against, British forces in the South Atlantic would be regarded as hostile and dealt with accordingly; Argentina charged that by these acts the United Kingdom was unleashing a new colonialist war.

The United Kingdom, in transmitting that declaration on 30 April,[139] reasserted that the unprovoked attacks on, and the continuing illegal military occupation of, the British territory gave the United Kingdom the right to use force in self-defence. By another letter of the same date,[140] the United Kingdom responded to Argentina's letter of 29 April, describing as preposterous the allegation that the United Kingdom was unleashing a colonialist war and saying that it was Argentina that was attempting to subject the Islanders to alien domination and sweep away, by acts of aggression, their democratically chosen institutions and way of life.

On 30 April, Argentina issued a statement, which was transmitted that day,[17] declaring that as of that day all British ships, including merchant and fishing vessels, operating within the 200-mile zone of the Argentine sea, of the Malvinas Islands, South Georgia and the South Sandwich Islands, would be considered hostile, and that any British aircraft, military or civil, which flew through Argentine airspace would be considered hostile and treated accordingly.

Referring to the United Kingdom's letter of 26 April, Argentina, in a letter dated 30 April,[18] said its forces continued their resistance on the South Georgia Islands, contrary to the United Kingdom's claim to the restoration of its authority in those territories; and asserted that, despite its declared intention to comply with the Security Council resolution of 3 April, the continuation of the United Kingdom's punitive actions compelled Argentina to exercise its right of self-defence which, under the Charter, allowed it to repel any armed attack endangering its territorial integrity and its existence as a State. In a letter of 1 May,[19] Argentina charged that United Kingdom aircraft had attacked Puerto Argentino (Port Stanley) in the Malvinas Islands at 0440 hours that day, in violation of the Council resolution of 3 April. The United Kingdom, in a letter dated 4 May,[145] refuted the allegations contained in Argentina's letters of 30 April and 1 May, stating that South Georgia had long been British territory and nothing in international law prohibited a State from exercising sovereignty over more than one island, irrespective of distance or their constitutional or other status; and that it was exercising its right of self-defence, not arrogating to itself "a police power" as Argentina claimed, in the face of Argentina's first use of force and contining illegal military occupation.

In another letter of 1 May,[20] Argentina reported having acted in self-defence and having repulsed successive attacks by the British Air Force against Puerto Argentino, during which two British aircraft had been shot down and a third hit; it added that the United Kingdom action was threatening to unleash an armed conflict of unknown dimensions and unforeseeable implications for international peace and security.

On 1 May,[141] the United Kingdom conveyed the text of a statement issued by its Ministry of Defence that day, stating that a total exclusion zone had been enforced since noon, London time, on 30 April, and that action had been taken on the morning of 1 May to deny the Argentines the use of the airstrip at Port Stanley. The Ministry, in a statement of 2 May transmitted the same day,[142] reported that before dawn on 1 May, British aircraft had damaged the runway at Port Stanley airfield and the surrounding military installations, as well as the airstrip at Goose Green and Argentine military aircraft parked in the vicinity; later that day Argentine aircraft had mounted ineffective bombing

raids on British ships and positions, sustaining loss or damage to four of their aircraft without causing the British side serious damage or casualties.

Brazil, on 1 May,[106] conveyed to the Security Council a 30 April communication from its Minister of External Relations to the Secretary-General, calling on the United Nations to take prompt and effective measures, including those of a preventive nature, to ensure implementation of the Council resolution of 3 April, in the light of the worsening crisis in the South Atlantic. Venezuela's Minister for External Relations issued a statement on 30 April, which was transmitted on 3 May,[172] regretting the 30 April decision of the United States, an OAS member, to support the British position in the conflict and saying that this development placed an even greater responsibility on the Security Council to ward off the possibility of war by having its resolution implemented in its entirety—which, he said, Argentina was ready to do, while the United Kingdom was not.

On 2 May,[21] Argentina transmitted the text of a letter informing the Chairman of the Twentieth Meeting of Consultation of Ministers of Foreign Affairs of OAS that the United States was suspending military exports to Argentina and imposing a series of economic sanctions against it, while offering support in the form of *matériel* to the forces of the aggressor.

On 2 May, the British Defence Ministry announced that, at approximately 2000 hours London time that day, torpedoes fired from a British submarine had caused what was believed to be severe damage to the Argentine cruiser *General Belgrano*, which had posed a significant threat to the British task force maintaining the total exclusion zone; it announced on 3 May that at about 0400 hours London time that day British helicopters sunk one and damaged a second armed Argentine patrol boat which had fired on a British aircraft. Both statements were transmitted on 3 May,[143] stating that the actions had been taken in exercise of Britain's right to self-defence.

In a letter of 3 May,[22] Argentina stated that the *General Belgrano*, while positioned outside the 200-mile exclusion zone, had been torpedoed on 2 May by a nuclear-powered British submarine and sunk; the number of survivors among the 1,042 men aboard was not known. On 6 May,[24] Argentina conveyed a communiqué issued by its Joint General Staff, stating that its dispatch boat *Alférez Sobral*, while on a rescue mission, had been attacked by British helicopters on 3 May and had suffered considerable damage and some casualties. Argentina reported, in a communiqué conveyed by a letter of 7 May,[27] that eight of the ship's crew had been killed and six wounded in the attack.

The United Kingdom, on 4 May,[144] conveyed a statement issued by its Ministry of Defence that day, announcing that its destroyer *Sheffield* had been hit within the total exclusion zone by an Argentine missile, had caught fire and had been abandoned by its crew; in a separate action that day over the Port Stanley airfield, one British aircraft had been shot down and the pilot killed.

Argentina confirmed, in a letter dated 6 May,[25] that its Air Force had attacked the *Sheffield* in self-defence. On 5 May,[23] Argentina conveyed two communiqués issued on 4 and 5 May by its Joint General Staff, reporting that, following the British air raid on Puerto Argentino, it had carried out an air mission against the British task force situated 60 miles south-east of the Malvinas, and had shot down two intruding aircraft during a subsequent British air raid at Port Darwin.

Ireland issued a statement on 2 May, transmitted the next day,[115] expressing concern at the escalating military situation in the South Atlantic and emphasizing that the possibilities offered by the United Nations should be fully exploited and further military escalation avoided. In a further statement on 4 May, conveyed by a letter of the same date,[117] Ireland said that it was appalled by the outbreak of what amounted to open war in the South Atlantic; that the United Nations should become involved immediately to resolve the conflict, and that it would seek withdrawal of economic sanctions by EC, considering those measures to be no longer appropriate.

On 4 May, a call for a meeting of the Security Council was made by Ireland in a letter to the Council President,[116] and by Colombia in a telegram to the Secretary-General,[109] both calling for a cessation of hostilities. In the telegram, the President of Colombia expressed his support for the Secretary-General's peace-making efforts in what the former called the absurd dispute, condemned the military take-over of the Malvinas by Argentina and equally denounced the British attack on the Argentine cruiser *General Belgrano* outside the exclusion zone.

On 5 May, following consultations of the Council, the Council President issued the following statement:[200]

> "The members of the Security Council express deep concern at the deterioration of the situation in the region of the Falkland Islands (Islas Malvinas) and the loss of lives.
> The members of the Security Council also express strong support for the efforts of the Secretary-General with regard to his contacts with the two parties.
> The members of the Security Council have agreed to meet for further consultations tomorrow, Thursday, 6 May 1982."

On 5 May,[114] Cuba transmitted to the Secretary-General a communiqué issued that day by the Co-ordinating Bureau of the Movement of Non-Aligned Countries, which had met at Argentina's request, expressing regret at the loss of life in the conflict, reaffirming its support for Argentine sovereignty over the Malvinas, and appealing to the parties to find a peaceful solution in accordance with the Security Council resolution of 3 April.

On 6 May,[186] Saint Vincent and the Grenadines, as Chairman of the Latin American Group at the United Nations for that month, transmitted a statement issued by the Group on 5 May, expressing its regret at the increasing loss of life in the conflict, calling for a cessation of all hostile acts in the region and urging the parties concerned to initiate negotiations with a view to achieving a solution.

Denmark, Finland, Iceland, Norway and Sweden, by a letter of 6 May to the Secretary-General,[181] conveyed a joint statement they had issued on that date, in which they expressed regret that the hostilities had led to loss of life, appealed to both parties to comply with the Council resolution of 3 April and expressed support for the Secretary-General's efforts to resolve the conflict.

In a letter dated 7 May,[26] Argentina reported having received information from London, on the United Kingdom's decision to impose a blockade as of that date on every Argentine warship or military aircraft which departed beyond 12 nautical miles from the continental and island territory of Argentina; it asserted that this action demonstrated the British insistence on a military solution and desire to obstruct the diplomatic option then under consideration with the Secretary-General.

On 8 May,[146] the United Kingdom transmitted the announcement of 7 May by its Ministry of Defence referred to in Argentina's letter of the same date, stating that the announcement was aimed at reducing the possibility of misunderstanding about the United Kingdom's intentions with regard to how it would exercise its right of self-defence in the Falklands and to give further precision to the circumstances in which Argentine forces would be regarded as a threat.

In transmitting the text of that Ministry announcement, Argentina, by a letter dated 8 May,[28] asserted that this latest action by the United Kingdom constituted a qualitative escalation of its aggression against Argentina and proof of its bad faith in the diplomatic field at a time when the Secretary-General was engaged in a peace move known to the Council. On 11 May,[31] Argentina conveyed a communiqué issued that day by its Joint General Staff, stating that, in view of the United Kingdom's persistent aggressive attitude and in the exercise of its right of self-defence, it would consider as hostile and take appropriate action against any vessel flying the British flag and navigating towards the area of operations or presumed to constitute a threat to Argentina's national security.

Peru, on 10 May,[125] transmitted a communiqué of 7 May, in which it considered as a matter of the utmost gravity the extension of the conflict to waters that were part of South American continental territory, repeated its call for a truce and expressed support for the efforts being made by the Secretary-General.

Argentina informed the Council, by a letter dated 9 May,[29] that at 0140 hours Argentine time that day British forces had carried out a simultaneous attack on Puerto Argentino and Puerto Darwin lasting 35 minutes, while the Secretary-General was taking steps with both Governments to reach a settlement. In a communiqué by its Joint General Staff, conveyed on 9 May,[30] Argentina announced that at 0921 hours that day a British aircraft had attacked and sunk a fishing vessel, *Narval*, engaged in normal fishing activity 66 nautical miles south of Puerto Argentino, and another British aircraft had machine-gunned the vessel's lifeboats.

The United Kingdom confirmed the attack on the *Narval* in a letter dated 10 May,[147] but rejected as groundless the allegation that its aircraft had machine-gunned the vessel's lifeboats; the *Narval* had been shadowing the British task force for some days within the total exclusion zone, and the documents found on board together with the presence among the crew of an Argentine naval officer constituted irrefutable evidence that the ship had been engaged in surveillance. Of the 25 people on board, it reported, 1 was killed and 13 injured, 1 seriously; the survivors would be treated and repatriated and the ship kept in the custody of the Royal Navy. By the same letter, the United Kingdom reported additional military activity on 9 May near the Port Stanley airfield, said that an Argentine helicopter had been downed over the Falklands later that day, and commented on Argentina's letters of 7, 8 and 9 May.

The Argentine Air Force issued a communiqué on 10 May listing the names of 10 dead and 4 missing and said that 18 others had been wounded as a result of the air battle of the Malvinas; the Argentine Joint General Staff, in a communiqué of the same date, announced that on 9 and 10 May its forces had repelled acts of aggression against Puerto Argentino and the airport area. Both communiqués were transmitted on 11 May.[32]

Argentina, on 12 May,[33] transmitted a communiqué by its Joint General Staff, announcing that one of its helicopters on a search and rescue mission in connection with the *Narval* had been shot down by British aircraft. In a letter dated 14 May,[149] the United Kingdom replied that there had been no reason to believe that the Argentine helicopter had been on such a mission, as it had been flying towards the British task force, bearing no markings to suggest any role other than military.

The Argentine Joint General Staff, in a communiqué issued on 12 May and transmitted on 13 May,[34] reported that its aircraft had attacked and damaged two British frigates shelling Puerto Argentino, its land-based personnel had shot down a British helicopter in the area and two Argentine aircraft had been shot down in the action. The United Kingdom, in a letter dated 13 May,[148] said its Ministry of Defence had announced that on 12 May two Royal Navy ships in the course of enforcing the total exclusion zone had been attacked by Argentine aircraft, two of which had been shot down and a third had flown into the sea while taking evasive action; one of the British ships sustained comparatively minor damage.

On 15 May,[35] Argentina conveyed the following, dated 14 May: an Air Force communiqué listing two personnel as disappeared in combat; an announcement by the Joint General Staff that, following the sinking of the *General Belgrano*, 790 persons had been recovered, of whom 20 were found dead, while 301 persons remained missing; and another Joint General Staff announcement that two British aircraft had bombed Puerto Argentino on 14 May but were driven off by anti-aircraft fire.

On 14 May, according to an announcement of 15 May by the British Ministry of Defence transmitted that day,[150] British aircraft attacked Port Stanley airfield and associated military installations, and carried out that evening a raid on the Pebble Island airstrip on West Falkland destroying a number of aircraft on the ground and a large ammunition dump; all planes returned safely, it reported, with only two minor casualties.

The Argentine Joint General Staff announced on 15 May that British surface units shelled Puerto Calderón that day damaging three aircraft on the ground; the communiqué was transmitted by a letter dated 15 May,[36] pointing out that those acts of military aggression took place when the negotiations initiated through the good offices of the Secretary-General were in progress.

On 18 May,[37] Argentina conveyed four communiqués issued on 16 and 17 May by its Joint General Staff regarding a series of attacks carried out by the British task force, resulting in damage to three unarmed transport vessels supplying foodstuffs, medicines and fuel to the civilian population of the Malvinas Islands and damage to a number of civilian installations at Fox Bay; Argentina charged that these acts demonstrated the United Kingdom's hypocrisy in asserting its responsibility to protect the Islanders.

The United Kingdom replied in a letter of 20 May[151] that, contrary to Argentine assertions, actions by British forces had been directed against military targets; Argentina could best demonstrate its concern for the population of the islands by withdrawing its forces. By the same letter, it transmitted a statement issued that day by its Ministry of Defence, reporting that the task force had bombed Argentine military positions near Stanley on 19 May and that no operational contact with the Argentine forces had occurred on 20 May.

Argentina, on 21 May,[38] conveyed five communiqués issued by its Joint General Staff concerning military developments: on 19 May it reported a bombing attack that day by two British aircraft 7 miles from Puerto Argentino; no warlike activity was recorded on 20 May apart from harassment shelling by a British surface unit near Puerto Argentino; later on 20 May it confirmed the sinking of the transport vessel *Isla de los Estados*, which had been attacked a few days earlier; also on 20 May, it noted a report from Chile that a downed British helicopter had been found 18 kilometres south of Punta Arenas, Chile; and on 21 May it reported that its forces were resisting a British landing at Puerto San Carlos Bay.

The President of Panama, in a telegram dated 10 May[119] requesting the Secretary-General to intensify his "highly important moves" to achieve a peaceful settlement, condemned the United Kingdom's escalating aggression against Argentina as a collective affront to Latin America and asserted that the United Kingdom was seeking to establish a blockade without Security Council authority and had violated a number of international conventions and the Treaty for the Prohibition of Nuclear Weapons in Latin America (Treaty of Tlatelolco).

In a statement transmitted to the Secretary-General on 11 May,[179] Austria appealed to all concerned to seek a peaceful solution of the conflict on the basis of the Security Council resolution of 3 April, and expressed support for the efforts of the Secretary-General to bring about a negotiated settlement.

By a letter dated 12 May to the Secretary-General,[173] Viet Nam transmitted a statement of 29 April by its Ministry of Foreign Affairs reaffirming its recognition of Argentine sovereignty over the Malvinas Archipelago and demanding that the United Kingdom implement the United Nations resolutions on decolonization of the Malvinas and stop its military acts against Argentina. In a statement of 4 May, transmitted to the Secretary-General on 13 May,[174] Viet Nam condemned the British acts of aggression and what it termed the complicity of the United States against Argentina, and demanded that those countries cease those acts and respect the sovereignty and territorial integrity of Argentina.

The Lao People's Democratic Republic, on 17 May,[185] transmitted to the Secretary-General a statement issued on 12 May by its Ministry of Foreign Affairs condemning the United Kingdom's acts of aggression, supported by the United States, and demanding that Britain immediately cease its military operations in the Malvinas and respect Argentine independence and sovereignty.

The Foreign Minister of Costa Rica, in a communiqué of 15 May transmitted on 17 May,[111] recognized Argentine sovereignty over the Malvinas, but expressed regret that the claim had culminated in an act of force; urged both parties to halt their military activities and agree to a negotiated settlement; and expressed support for the Secretary-General's peace efforts.

Brazil's Minister for External Relations issued a message on 19 May, transmitted the same day,[107] reiterating his Government's support for the efforts undertaken by the Secretary-General and appealing for abstention from any military action that might thwart those efforts.

In a letter dated 20 May,[176] the Secretary-General informed the Security Council that, although substantial progress towards a diplomatic solution had been achieved in the preceding two weeks, the necessary accommodations needed to end the conflict had not been forthcoming. He added that, in his judgement, the efforts in which he had been engaged, with the support of the Council, did not currently offer the prospect of bringing about an end to the crisis nor of preventing the intensification of the conflict.

By a letter dated 21 May,[120] Panama requested a meeting of the Security Council, in view of the serious situation existing in the region of the Malvinas Islands and the Secretary-General's letter of the previous day.

Security Council action (May). In response to the request of 4 May by Ireland and that of 21 May by Panama, the Security Council met from 21 to 26 May.

Recounting his negotiation efforts, the Secretary-General informed the Council that he had met separately with the two sides and with the United States on 19 April and outlined to them the assistance the United Nations could render upon request. In another separate meeting with the two sides on 2 May, the Secretary-General proposed to them a series of measures that included simultaneous mutual withdrawal of forces and commencement of negotiations for a diplomatic solution. Some 30 additional separate meetings were held between 7 and 21 May so as to assist the parties in reaching an agreement along those lines.

He told the Council of his assessment that, at the end of the second week in May, essential agreement had been reached on the following points: the agreement sought would be of an interim nature, without prejudice to the rights, claims or positions of the parties and it would include a cease-fire, phased mutual withdrawal of forces under United Nations supervision, termination of exclusion zones and economic measures, interim administration of the Territory under the United Nations authority, and negotiations towards a settlement under the auspices of the Secretary-General. Crucial differences remained, he reported, concerning certain aspects of the interim administration, the time-frame for completion of negotiations, the mutual withdrawal of forces and the geographical area to be covered by the terms of the interim agreement.

The Secretary-General informed the Council that, in his view, the drafts of an interim agreement—the United Kingdom's draft of 17 May and that of Argentina of the night of 18/19 May—which were exchanged through him, had failed to reflect the progress achieved previously. On 19 May, the Secretary-General spoke by telephone with the President of Argentina and with the Prime Minister of the United Kingdom to suggest certain specific ideas to assist the parties at that critical stage; both agreed to give them consideration. He subsequently presented to the two sides that same day a further aide-mémoire listing the points of agreement and disagreement and containing suggestions and formulations which he thought might satisfactorily meet their preoccupations on the unresolved issues without prejudice to the rights, claims or positions of either. By the evening of 20 May, the necessary accommodations had not been made, however, and the Secretary-General so informed the Council President at 9 p.m. that day.

The Secretary-General called for continued efforts to put an end to the conflict and the loss of lives, and reiterated his personal commitment to lend assistance towards the lasting solution of the problem.

Argentina asserted that its will to negotiate was constantly threatened by the British military aggression, and that the United Kingdom had introduced during the negotiating process new demands aimed at impeding the withdrawal of military forces from the region, rejected certain ideas on the maintenance of communications and certain services between the Islands and Argentina during the interim administration, and placed pre-conditions on substantive issues by insisting on a United Nations administration that would retain the colonial administrative structure. The United Kingdom, it added, also wished to maintain the provisional United Nations administration indefinitely, thus drawing out the negotiations for as long as the United Kingdom desired. Argentina had understood that an exclusively United Nations administration would be considered, while the Argentine flag flew in the Islands during the

brief period of the negotiations, expected to last approximately one year; it had been prepared not to place any pre-conditions on the negotiations in view of its confidence in its legitimate stand. It also stated that the United Kingdom would not accept any references to General Assembly resolutions concerning decolonization of the Malvinas, and had attempted to divide the Territory by submitting to negotiation only one archipelago while keeping the two dependencies.

The United Kingdom said it had given to the Secretary-General on 17 May its final position in the form of a draft interim agreement which showed its maximum flexibility without abandoning certain principles. It had been prepared to contemplate a parallel mutual withdrawal under United Nations supervision, followed by a short interim administration by the United Nations, Argentine representation in the Territory's democratic institutions and the presence of an Argentine observer during the interim period. Argentina's response was unsatisfactory, especially in its insistence on including the Falklands' two dependencies in the agreement and on unequal withdrawal of forces, its rejection of the continuance of the Territory's democratic institutions during the interim period, the idea of parity in numbers of advisers between the Argentine population of 30 and the British population of about 1,800 on the Islands, the requirement of freedom of access to residents and property during the interim period (which, the United Kingdom believed, would have allowed Argentina to change the demographic status of the Islands) and the formulation of how and when the negotiations should be concluded.

By a resolution adopted unanimously on 26 May,[(196)] the Security Council, reaffirming its resolution of 3 April, requested the Secretary-General to renew his mission of good offices; to contact the parties immediately in order to negotiate mutually acceptable terms for a cease-fire, including, if necessary, the dispatch of United Nations observers to monitor compliance; and to submit an interim report to the Council within seven days. The Council also urged the parties to the conflict to co-operate with the Secretary-General with a view to ending hostilities.

The text was introduced by Uganda, also on behalf of Guyana, Ireland, Jordan, Togo and Zaire.

Speaking in explanation of vote, China, Panama, Spain and the USSR said they would have preferred that Council order an immediate cease-fire. Spain added that the Secretary-General should have been given more specific terms of reference. Panama and the USSR said the text should have contained reference to the fundamental question of decolonization of the Malvinas. Panama also regretted that the text did not ask all

Member States to abstain from providing military supplies to either side. The United States offered assurances that it wished to live in peace with its neighbours in the hemisphere and pledged continued support for the Secretary-General's efforts.

The United Kingdom said it supported the draft for its reaffirmation of the resolution of 3 April, asserted that it would no longer accept a parallel troop withdrawal in view of the changed situation since the Secretary-General reported to the Council on 21 May, and named the withdrawal of Argentine troops as the only acceptable condition for a cease-fire. Argentina, participating without the right to vote, said the intransigence and pressures of more than one of the permanent members of the Council had prevented that body from calling for a cease-fire; it would enter the resumed negotiations without pre-conditions, but without giving up any of its rights.

The Secretary-General told the Council that the resolution's terms of reference might not provide him or the parties with sufficiently clear and precise guidance; as a first step in his new effort, however, he would urge both parties to recognize that a lasting solution could only be achieved through negotiations, the first requirement for which was a cessation of armed conflict.

Ireland, which had earlier submitted a draft,[1] subsequently joined the five non-aligned members of the Council in sponsoring the text finally adopted, which it called the revised version of its original proposal. The Irish proposal, while essentially the same as the one adopted, would have had the Council call for a suspension of hostilities for 72 hours as a first step in the Secretary-General's renewed mission, and mandate that mission to be consistent with its 3 April resolution and with the outline the Secretary-General had presented to it on 21 May. Ireland had introduced the draft, saying that the text sought to achieve a return to negotiations by successive stages of confidence-building measures, would give the Secretary-General a formal mandate from the Council, and help preserve the measure of agreement that the Secretary-General had already achieved; those negotiations, it added, should neither betray the principles which one side was defending nor ignore the sense of grievance of the other.

Similarly, Japan did not press to a vote a draft resolution[2] it had earlier proposed, saying that its main ideas had been incorporated in the consensus text adopted. The Japanese draft would have had the Council request the Secretary-General to renew his mission of good offices on the basis of his efforts as reported to the Council on 21 May, with a view to achieving the earliest cessation of hostilities, realizing a peaceful settlement of the dispute, and securing the implementation of the Council resolution of 3 April.

In addition to Argentina, States participating in the discussions without the right to vote were: Antigua and Barbuda, Australia, Belgium, Bolivia, Brazil, Canada, Chile, Colombia, Cuba, Ecuador, El Salvador, Equatorial Guinea, Federal Republic of Germany, Greece, Guatemala, Honduras, India, Indonesia, Italy, Kenya, Lao People's Democratic Republic, Liberia, Mexico, Netherlands, New Zealand, Nicaragua, Paraguay, Peru, Uruguay, Venezuela, Yugoslavia.

In the debate, most speakers expressed concern over the escalation of hostilities and the tragic loss of life, appreciation for the Secretary-General's efforts to negotiate a solution, and the need to abide by the provisions of the Charter of the United Nations concerning the non-use of force and peaceful settlement of disputes.

Spain and Togo listed the cessation of hostilities, negotiation and peace as the priorities of the Council's action, as did several other speakers who urged the Council to call for an immediate cease-fire. Jordan asserted that the Council should not resign itself to the role of onlooker while blood was being shed, and Brazil said the Council was duty-bound to prevent a worsening of the situation. Greece said the Council's prestige would be enhanced if it unequivocally condemned all invasions and breaches of the Charter provisions. Colombia asserted that the United Nations would emerge greatly weakened if it failed to enforce international law and maintenance of international peace and security, while the United States considered that the Organization had functioned in the crisis in the manner foreseen by its founders and its Charter.

Argentina said the United Kingdom had broken off negotiations by its negative reply to every Argentine proposal: Britain insisted on Argentina's remaining 150 miles from the Islands and on excluding the dependencies from negotiations, and rejected admission of Argentine citizens to the Islands during the interim administration or entrusting the General Assembly with the future of the Islands if the negotiations had not been concluded within a reasonable period. Several countries, among them Brazil, Cuba, Ecuador, Nicaragua, Panama, Uruguay and Venezuela, held the United Kingdom responsible for blocking the negotiating efforts. China said the negotiations had broken down due to a tough stand taken by the party with superior military strength. Bolivia asserted that any peace effort would be doomed to failure as long as the United Kingdom persisted in its equivocal stand. Panama and the USSR said the United Kingdom had resorted to the language of ultimatums and virtually broken off negotiations by resorting to the use of force.

The United Kingdom rejected the charge that it had issued ultimatums or that it had brought the last round of negotiations to an unsuccessful conclusion, and stated that it had shown a maximum degree of flexibility without abandoning certain principles. Antigua and Barbuda believed the United Kingdom had made genuine attempts to reach a negotiated settlement. The United States said the United Kingdom had indicated its willingness to consider, but Argentina had rejected or chosen not to consider, first the United States proposal and subsequently the Peruvian peace plan, both based on the Council's 3 April resolution. New Zealand said it was Argentina's obduracy and rigidity that had frustrated and blocked the Secretary-General's efforts just when it looked as if an agreement was within reach.

Peru recounted its mediation efforts, including its introduction on 20 May of a new formula by which the two parties would separately agree to comply with those provisions of the Secretary-General's proposal on which there had been common ground; as that Peruvian plan had not been rejected by either party, Peru considered it desirable to preserve the gains the Secretary-General had achieved thus far. Ireland said the Council could not afford to lose what the Secretary-General had achieved in his negotiating efforts, and Mexico, Spain and Togo urged that the Secretary-General's proposal be taken up and built upon.

Indonesia and Uruguay proposed that the Council give the Secretary-General a formal mandate to resume negotiations, conserving the six points on which agreement between the two sides had been reached. Cuba, France and Italy also felt that the Secretary-General's negotiation efforts contained the key elements for a peaceful solution. In a similar vein, several countries, among them Colombia, El Salvador, Equatorial Guinea, Greece, Guyana, India, Ireland, Paraguay and Yugoslavia, favoured giving the Secretary-General a formal mandate to continue efforts. Chile, declaring its strict neutrality in the conflict, also favoured such a move. China hoped that the Secretary-General, with the support of the Council, would continue to play an active part.

Ecuador and Peru said the mandate to the Secretary-General should be wide-ranging, clear and practical. The Federal Republic of Germany, Guyana, Jordan, Uganda and Zaire believed the mandate should be based on the Council's 3 April resolution. Panama cautioned that such a mandate could be carried out only when there had been a cease-fire and a separation of forces.

A call for the full implementation of the Council's 3 April resolution was made by a number of speakers, among them Brazil, Colombia, Cuba, El Salvador, Italy, Japan and Jordan; in addition, Canada, France, the Federal Republic of Germany, Greece, Guyana, India, Indonesia, Jordan, the Netherlands, Paraguay, Uganda, the United States, Yugoslavia and Zaire said that resolution continued to provide the basis for a diplomatic settlement.

Cuba and Peru were among those which called that resolution faulty for not recognizing the colonial origin of the problem, while Zaire said the text did not prejudge the substance of the problem concerning Argentina's claims over the Islands. Venezuela commented that, while complete compliance with that resolution by both sides would have made possible a peaceful settlement, the United Kingdom had violated the provisions by claiming to act in self-defence. Argentina and Panama shared that view, saying that the resolution should not have been understood as authorizing the United Kingdom to become the world's policeman and to use force. Mexico asserted that there was no case for invoking the right to self-defence to justify the use of force by either side because such an argument presupposed that the sovereignty question had been resolved; further, only the Council could take measures to maintain or restore international peace and security.

Australia said Argentina's invocation of paragraph 1 of the 3 April resolution in accusing the United Kingdom of hostile action was a perverted reading of that text, as that paragraph, it said, was directed to the state of armed conflict caused by the Argentine seizure of the Falklands. New Zealand shared that view, adding that Argentina set unacceptable pre-conditions to the implementation of that text. Belgium and Guyana urged Argentina to comply with the resolution.

The question of sovereignty and the right to self-determination was again raised in the debate. Citing decolonization resolutions by the United Nations or other intergovernmental bodies, the majority of Latin American countries, along with China, Equatorial Guinea, the Lao People's Democratic Republic, Poland, the USSR, Yugoslavia and Zaire, supported Argentina's territorial claim, while endorsing efforts to find a peaceful solution to the dispute. El Salvador asserted that Argentina's occupation of the Islands was in accordance with its lawful title to them, which led Panama to state that there had been no breach of peace on 3 April, when Argentina recovered the Islands.

Belgium and Kenya said territorial claims should not be allowed to override the interests of peoples in choosing democratically their own destinies. Australia considered that Argentina had been insistent on loaded arrangements in the Falklands which, if accepted, would lead to conceding its demand of sovereignty and ignoring the rights of the Falklanders; if Argentina's aggression was allowed to persist, it would itself amount to colonialism. In a similar vein, Kenya said Argentina could not claim any right to impose its own form of colonialism on the Islands' inhabitants. New Zealand added that the two aggrieved parties in the crisis were the United Kingdom and the people of the Falklands. In contrast, Panama called it illogical to talk of the right to self-determination—the right of the oppressed—in the Malvinas case, when the inhabitants of the Islands were dependents of a British colonial company; to do so, Argentina said, would mean giving the colonizers an opportunity to legitimize their settlement in a territory that did not belong to them. Colombia, noting that the United Kingdom's policy of decolonization had allowed the independence of many countries by means of negotiations, believed it reasonable to expect that the Malvinas case could also be solved in that manner. Zaire also noted the United Kingdom's past record of decolonization, and wondered if the current problem arose not from the issue of decolonizing but from seeing its hand forced militarily in contravention of Charter provisions.

Uganda and Zaire, while supporting the Argentine claim of sovereignty over the Malvinas, rejected the use of force in international relations and called for a negotiated settlement. Kenya stated that the principle of the peaceful settlement of disputes had been brushed aside by Argentina, and added that the support of the non-aligned countries could not be invoked as support for aggression or military settlement. The Netherlands felt that Argentina's resort to force could not be justified in terms of international law. Antigua and Barbuda said that, as a small island State dependent for its security on the United Nations, it had to deplore Argentina's illegal use of force in seizing the Falklands in defiance of the Council. In a similar vein, Guyana rejected the attitude of those which held aloft the action of 2 April as an example to be emulated, and said aggression should not be rewarded.

The Council debate also centred around what had started the current conflict, with Argentina and its supporters pointing to what they called the United Kingdom's illegal possession of the Islands, and the United Kingdom and its supporters holding as responsible Argentina's illegal presence there.

Venezuela said the crisis was caused by the warlike conduct of the United Kingdom, which Nicaragua and Uruguay said had impeded Argentina from fully abiding by the Council's 3 April resolution. Poland deplored what it viewed as the unilateral escalation of hostilities on the part of the United Kingdom. Argentina, Bolivia, Nicaragua and Peru said no aggression should be rewarded, and that the act of aggression first committed by the United Kingdom against Argentina in 1833 thus needed to be resolved; Argentina added that colonialism was an act of force and permanent aggression. Similarly, the USSR said the conflict had been caused by the United Kingdom's refusal to abide by the General Assembly resolutions on decolonization of the Malvinas.

Ireland said the immediate cause of conflict was not the underlying issue of sovereignty, but the effort by one side to resolve that dispute in its favour by the use of force in breach of the rule of law. Canada and Togo said Argentina had initiated the hostilities in occupying the Islands unilaterally, and Kenya rejected what it called the perverted reasoning by some that aggression started when the British forces moved to the Falkland Islands. Australia said that, since it was the Argentine invasion which had started the crisis, it must be an Argentine withdrawal that would end it; it was not the British obstinacy but Argentine recklessness that accounted for the widening conflict. Belgium, the Federal Republic of Germany and New Zealand spoke similarly.

Criticism of economic sanctions against Argentina was expressed by some, including Panama, Poland and the USSR, which called that measure a violation of the Charter. El Salvador called it an act of economic aggression. Nicaragua appealed to the EC countries to end their economic sanctions, asserting that their policy only strengthened Britain's warlike attitude; it commended Denmark, Ireland and Italy for deciding against extending the sanctions upon expiration. Belgium, rejecting the argument that Article 41 of the Charter gave the Security Council a monopoly on deciding on sanctions, said it had joined in the economic sanctions to demonstrate in specific form the grave view it took of Argentina's violation of the Charter as well as to support the diplomatic efforts then under way to find a negotiated solution. Canada said it was compelled to impose such sanctions in order to uphold the rule of law embodied in the Charter. Ireland said it decided not to extend its sanctions beyond 17 May, as it considered the measures part of the war rather than means of reinforcing a diplomatic effort for a peaceful settlement.

The Lao People's Democratic Republic, Panama and Peru deplored the United States pledge of political and material support to the United Kingdom.

The United Kingdom said that, contrary to certain assertions by Nicaragua and Panama, it was inconceivable that it would use nuclear weapons in the dispute with Argentina over the Falklands.

Communications (22 May-2 June). On 22 May,[39] Argentina transmitted to the Security Council six communiqués issued on 21 and 22 May by the Joint General Staff of its Armed Forces reporting that, on 21 May, in response to an attack by United Kingdom forces in the San Carlos Channel of the Malvinas Islands, its forces had damaged several British ships and aircraft while suffering the loss of six aircraft and three helicopters; in a second letter of the same date,[40] it specified that three British aircraft and two helicopters had been shot down, eight British frigates damaged, and a ninth sunk.

In eight communiqués issued by its Joint General Staff between 22 and 25 May, transmitted on 25 May,[41] Argentina said that beginning on 22 May the United Kingdom had landed 2,000 men and *matériel* in the Puerto San Carlos area, eventually establishing a beachhead there, and that in the fighting a British troop carrier and frigate had been damaged and a Sea Harrier aircraft lost, while two Argentine aircraft had been shot down; it also reported that in separate actions a British aircraft had been shot down over Puerto Darwin on 22 May and another apparently downed over Puerto Argentino on 24 May.

In a communiqué of 26 May transmitted that day,[42] Argentina announced that its coastguard vessel *Río Iguazú* had been attacked by two United Kingdom aircraft, that one crew member had been killed and two wounded, and that one of the attacking aircraft had been shot down. In a second communiqué of that date, also conveyed on 26 May,[43] Argentina said its aircraft had sunk the British destroyer *Coventry* and the aircraft transport vessel *Atlantic Conveyor*.

On 27 May,[45] Argentina transmitted a communiqué issued on 26 May by its Joint General Staff stating that 22 surface naval units and 30 aircraft of the United Kingdom had been affected by Argentine military actions taken in self-defence between 1 and 26 May; listed as sunk were the destroyers *Sheffield* and *Coventry*, the frigates *Ardent* and *Antelope*, an unidentified frigate and the *Atlantic Conveyor*; seriously damaged were three destroyers or frigates and a large carrier; damaged were 10 destroyers or frigates, a troop carrier and an unidentified vessel; and 21 Sea Harrier aircraft were reportedly shot down and 12 helicopters lost.

Five more communiqués, issued by the Joint General Staff on 27 and 28 May and transmitted on 28 May,[46] described the following military actions: downing of two British helicopters and inflicting serious damage to two others; Argentine troops' harassment activities against the British forces reportedly hemmed into a pocket of some 150 square kilometres; some action on 26 May in the area of Puerto Argentino, Fox Bay and Puerto San Carlos without Argentine losses; bombing on 27 May of the British beachhead at Puerto San Carlos; and downing of a British aircraft in the course of British air attacks near Howard, Puerto Argentino and Darwin on 27 May. In the 28 May communiqué, Argentina called on the United Kingdom to cease on the *Uganda* all activities not related to the specific function of that hospital ship

and to remove it from the San Carlos Strait. On 29 May,[48] Argentina transmitted another communiqué of 28 May, reporting that in action near Darwin on that date its Air Force had shot down two British helicopters and damaged a frigate-type vessel.

In a communiqué issued on 30 May, conveyed on that date,[49] Argentina reported its total casualties between 2 April and 30 May as 82 dead, 106 wounded and 342 missing.

On 30 May, Argentina announced in four communiqués forwarded on 31 May[52] that its Air Force had attacked and seriously damaged the main British naval force, putting out of action an aircraft carrier while suffering the loss of two of its aircraft; it further reported hostilities in the area of Puerto Darwin on that day, as well as in Puerto Argentino where it said two British aircraft were shot down and a third damaged.

Seven more communiqués, issued on 31 May and 1 June by the Argentine Joint General Staff and transmitted on 2 June,[55] described further military action around San Carlos, Darwin and Goose Green; noted British troop movements near Puerto Argentino and reported the downing of a British aircraft there; announced a bombing attack by its Air Force on Isla Soledad; and updated its count of losses on the United Kingdom side through 31 May—25 Harrier aircraft destroyed, 22 helicopters destroyed or seriously damaged, one aircraft carrier out of action, two destroyers sunk and three damaged, two frigates sunk and eight or nine damaged, two landing craft damaged and one container ship (with the aircraft aboard) sunk.

In a letter dated 23 May,[152] the United Kingdom reported the following military operations: on 20 May it bombarded military land targets, including Fox Bay on West Falkland; on 21 May, a major amphibious landing took place, unopposed, near San Carlos on East Falkland, as well as a series of landing raids and bombardments involving Goose Green and Port Stanley airfields and other areas, which resulted in some casualties and the loss of three helicopters and one Harrier aircraft; in an air-sea battle later that day, Argentina lost 20 aircraft while the United Kingdom suffered damage to four warships and the loss of the frigate *Ardent* in the night of 21/22 May; on 22 May, British aircraft attacked and damaged an Argentine patrol boat to the south of Port Stanley, and also attacked military installations in the Goose Green area.

Developments since 22 May were described in a letter from the United Kingdom dated 27 May[154] as follows: on 23 May three Argentine helicopters were destroyed in action over the Falkland Sound, while an Argentine attack on British ships in San Carlos Water resulted in the British frigate *Antelope* damaged (and sunk the following day) and at least seven Argentine aircraft shot down; on 24 May, an air-sea battle in San Carlos Water left two British support vessels damaged and eight Argentine aircraft destroyed; and on 25 May, British aircraft continued their attacks on Port Stanley airfield while in several air-sea battles five Argentine aircraft were shot down and the British ships *Coventry* and *Atlantic Conveyor* were destroyed.

The Argentine Joint General Staff, in a communiqué issued on 26 May and conveyed the same day,[44] said it had notified the United Kingdom that it could not guarantee the safety of the British hospital ship *Uganda*, whose presence near the zone of operations was interfering with the activities of the Argentine forces. The United Kingdom replied in a letter dated 28 May[155] that the *Uganda* was acting in accordance with the relevant Geneva Convention (Geneva Convention for the Amelioration of the Condition of Wounded, Sick and Shipwrecked Members of the Armed Forces at Sea, of 12 August 1949), that it had briefly entered Middle Bay of East Falkland on 27 May in order to take on board both British and Argentine casualties and that the ship could be inspected by the International Committee of the Red Cross (ICRC) at any time.

On 29 May,[47] Argentina conveyed the text of a 28 May communication it had transmitted to the United Kingdom through the Embassy of Brazil, stating that if by zero hours on 29 May the *Uganda* and other hospital ships had not withdrawn to a distance which left no doubt about their use, they would be treated as hostile vessels. In a statement issued on 30 May by its Ministry of Defence, transmitted the next day,[156] the United Kingdom rejected as unfounded Argentina's charge that the hospital ships were being used for military purposes, stated that it had notified Argentine authorities of the ships' movements, and declared its intention to use them when and where appropriate in accordance with the Geneva Convention, with a warning that any Argentine military action against them would constitute a breach of that Convention. In a letter dated 31 May,[51] Argentina stated its preparedness to allow ICRC officials to embark on hospital ships of both sides to confirm compliance with the Convention.

In a communiqué of 1 June, transmitted on 2 June,[53] Argentina announced that its hospital ship *Bahía Paraíso* would receive the wounded Argentines from Puerto Argentino and subsequently from the *Uganda*, at a place to be determined, before returning to Argentina. Also on 2 June,[54] Argentina conveyed three messages dated 26, 27 and 28 May, which it had transmitted to the United Kingdom through the Brazilian Government, in which it claimed having verified the military use of the *Uganda* and repeated its declaration that hospital ships not having withdrawn to a certain distance would be considered hostile as of zero hours 29 May.

On 24 May,[188] the USSR transmitted a 23 May statement by its news agency TASS, charging that the United Kingdom was responsible for having caused the situation in the Falkland Islands (Malvinas) through years of opposition to the Islands' decolonization, and for having obstructed efforts to avert a military clash and abandoned negotiations despite Argentina's wish to continue them; further, the responsibility for the armed invasion was shared by the United States and others who had openly sided with the United Kingdom and encouraged a military solution; it concluded with a call for an end to the bloodshed and a return to negotiations.

Brazil, in a letter dated 24 May,[108] suggested the following points which it believed might form the basis of a Council resolution for peace: immediate cessation of hostilities, simultaneous withdrawal of Argentine and British forces, appointment by the Secretary-General of a provisional administration for the Islands, and establishment under Article 29 of the Charter of a committee presided over by the Secretary-General and composed of the two parties and four other Member States, with the mandate of conducting urgent negotiations leading to a permanent settlement of the question.

In a statement of 23 May, transmitted the next day,[189] Uruguay recognized Argentina's sovereignty over the Malvinas, condemned the armed attack against the Islands, declared as unreasonable the invocation of the right of self-defence for that action, and called for an immediate cessation of hostilities and a negotiated solution.

Suriname, by a letter of 24 May,[187] expressed support for Argentina's struggle to restore sovereignty, deplored the military and economic actions taken against Argentina and urgently called on the United Kingdom to withdraw its troops and resume negotiations.

Costa Rica issued a statement on 25 May, transmitted the same day,[112] saying that in the light of the deteriorating situation it was imperative that the Council call on the parties to cease warlike activities immediately and give the Secretary-General the broadest and clearest mandate to seek a peaceful settlement.

In a telegram dated 21 May,[183] Ecuador requested that the Council be convened, with the urgency required by the situation, in order to adopt measures for the immediate cessation of hostilities and achieve a peaceful solution to the problem.

Colombia transmitted on 26 May[110] the texts of letters exchanged between its President and the Prime Minister of the United Kingdom; in his letter of 21 May, the Colombian President offered his Government's co-operation in whatever peace formula best met the interests of both sides; in her reply of 25 May, the British Prime Minister said the decision to end the conflict rested with Argentina which had resorted to force and that a compliance with the 3 April Council resolution for Argentine troop withdrawal was an essential first stage for a negotiated solution; she asked the Colombian President to help bring home that message to Argentina.

In a joint declaration made in New York on 24 May, which was transmitted the same day,[178] the Foreign Ministers of Argentina, Nicaragua, Panama and Venezuela rejected what they called the United Kingdom's military offensive against the South American continent; protested the British decision, as communicated to Uruguay, to extend military action to the River Plate; rejected the EC decision, with the exception of Ireland and Italy, to extend indefinitely its economic sanctions against Argentina; and expressed alarm that the Security Council had taken no action thus far to re-establish peace.

In a letter dated 25 May,[153] the United Kingdom replied that it had assured Uruguay of its intention not to engage in any military activities inshore of the line at the mouth of the River Plate as established by the Treaty of the Rio de la Plata of 1973 between Argentina and Uruguay and that it would not infringe Uruguay's rights and interests.

Argentina, on 31 May,[50] transmitted a resolution adopted at Washington, D. C., on 29 May by the Twentieth Meeting of Consultation of Ministers of Foreign Affairs of OAS. By that resolution, the Meeting demanded the immediate cessation of the British acts of war, expressed support for the mandate the Security Council had given to the Secretary-General, called for an end to military and economic moves against Argentina and reaffirmed the principle of the peaceful settlement of disputes. The same text was transmitted to the Secretary-General of the United Nations by the OAS Secretary-General on 29 May.[7]

The United Kingdom commented on the OAS resolution in a letter dated 1 June,[157] observing that the text did not refer to the Security Council resolutions of 3 April and 26 May, thereby failing to take into account the Argentine invasion of the Falkland Islands on 2 April and the Council's demand for the withdrawal of Argentine troops; rather than acts of war, as charged, the United Kingdom had taken proportionate measures in exercise of its right of self-defence. It said a peaceful settlement would permit the lifting of the economic measures against Argentina.

In his interim report[192] submitted on 2 June in response to the Council resolution of 26 May, the Secretary-General said he had met separately with the parties on the day the Council adopted that resolution giving him a mandate to negotiate, and had requested each to provide within 24 hours a statement of the terms it considered acceptable for a cease-fire. Both sides complied but, after extensive exchanges with them continuing through the morning of 2 June, it was his judgement that the positions of the two sides did not offer the possibility of developing at that time mutually acceptable terms for a cease-fire.

Security Council consideration (June). The Security Council met on 2, 3 and 4 June, in response to a request made by Panama, by a letter of 31 May,[121] for the urgent convening of the Council to continue studying the situation in the Falkland Islands (Islas Malvinas).

Argentina, Brazil and Honduras, at their request, were invited to participate in the Council discussions without the right to vote.

Owing to the negative vote of a permanent member, the Council, on 4 June, by 9 votes to 2 (United Kingdom, United States), with 4 abstentions, failed to adopt a twice-revised draft resolution submitted by Panama and Spain,[4] by which the Council would have requested the parties to the dispute to cease fire immediately and to observe simultaneously the implementation of its resolutions of 3 April and 26 May. Further, the Council would have authorized the Secretary-General to verify compliance with the resolution, submit an interim report to the Council within 72 hours and keep the Council informed.

Spain had introduced the original draft on 2 June, saying that an immediate cease-fire could be followed by the withdrawal of the forces and speedy negotiations on full compliance with the Council resolutions. While it was joined by Panama in asking the Council to vote on the text that same day, a vote was postponed until the next day, 3 June, at Japan's request. The 2 June draft simply called for a cease-fire without it being linked to simultaneous implementation of the Council's April and May resolutions, an element which was added in the first revision put forward on 3 June.

When that revision was proposed and the United Kingdom requested time to give it consideration, Spain, also on behalf of Panama, asked for a two-hour suspension of the meeting until 3.30 p.m., to be followed by a vote on the text. Jordan requested a postponement until 5 p.m. in order to allow delegations to seek instructions from their Governments. The United States also appealed for more time for consultations, saying that the proposed revision substantially altered the substance of the text. Jordan's proposal of a postponement to 5 p.m., on which Spain requested action, was rejected by 5 votes to none, with 10 abstentions, and the President declared the meeting suspended until 3.30 p.m. The meeting resumed at 6.10 p.m. only to adjourn until 4 p.m., 4 June, at the request of several members and with the consent of the sponsors of the draft resolution.

On 4 June, the sponsors made further revisions, authorizing the Secretary-General to verify compliance with the resolution, rather than with the cease-fire, and adding a request that he keep the Council informed concerning its implementation.

Explaining its vote against the resolution, the United Kingdom said the text did not make a direct and inseparable link between the cease-fire and immediate Argentine withdrawal within a fixed time-limit, and that its wording would enable Argentina to reopen the endless process of negotiation while leaving Argentine armed forces in illegal occupation of parts of the Islands. The United States said its veto affirmed the principle that force should not be allowed to triumph, but it wanted to record the fact that, if it were possible, it would have changed its vote to an abstention.

France, which abstained, considered it understandable that one of the parties to the conflict felt it essential to obtain certain safeguards against continued non-compliance with the 3 April resolution; consensus should have been reached regarding its effective implementation. Similarly, Guyana abstained, saying that, while Argentine non-compliance with the 3 April resolution was both the cause and consequence of the current level of armed hostilities in the South Atlantic, the text failed to make an explicit link between a cease-fire and withdrawal of Argentine forces within a clearly defined time-frame. Japan supported the resolution with the understanding that Argentina would withdraw its forces within a reasonable period of time.

Panama said the British veto had deprived the Security Council of a new chance to demonstrate its effectiveness, and had put that body back into a state of absolute impotence. Spain said the non-adoption of what it considered to be a highly balanced text represented a failure for peace. Ireland and Uganda felt the text clearly linked full implementation of the previous resolutions with the call for a cease-fire. Zaire supported the text as it called for the implementation of the previous Council resolutions. China also voted in favour, saying the Council should call for an unconditional cease-fire, resumption of negotiations and, at the same time, extend the Secretary-General's mandate.

In the Council debate, Argentina asserted that the United Kingdom was bent on re-establishing colonial imperialism in the Americas and ensuring its military predominance in the South Atlantic; it claimed Britain was proposing an international security agreement on the Islands which would include the participation of United States forces. Argentina said the British Government had systematically rejected alternative formulae for a cease-fire and had insisted that it would not withdraw militarily until it had successfully repossessed the Islands, restored its administration of them, undertaken reconstruction and consulted with the inhabitants.

The United Kingdom told the Council that, while respecting the confidence of the negotiations carried out through the Secretary-General, an acceptance of Argentine pre-conditions would have led to more procrastination and evasion on Argentina's part. Reasserting that it was Argentina which had launched an act of aggression, and thus rejecting a call for an unconditional immediate cease-fire, the United Kingdom commended to the Council as essential elements of a cease-fire resolution the reaffirmation of the resolutions of 3 April and 26 May, reiteration of the demand for Argentine withdrawal and a call for a cease-fire to come into effect as soon as watertight arrangements existed for that withdrawal within a fixed period. It stated that the only reason for requiring adequate long-term security arrangements in the Falkland Islands was to shield the Islanders against the threat or actuality of further aggression.

Most speakers praised the Secretary-General's efforts to find a peaceful solution to the conflict and expressed frustration that his mission had not led to the cessation of hostilities. Panama said the domineering and intransigent attitude of the United Kingdom had prevented the Secretary-General from giving the Council an encouraging report. The USSR agreed, stating that the United Kingdom had virtually struck out everything positive that the Secretary-General had achieved, and had used the negotiating process as a smoke-screen for a military operation aimed at restoring colonialism on the Islands. China said that one of the parties, relying on its superior military strength, had no intention of effecting a cease-fire.

Also charging the United Kingdom with breaking off negotiations, Brazil asserted that the Secretary-General's chances of success had been limited by the vague mandate given him under the Council's 26 May resolution; it added that if the United Kingdom felt the 3 April resolution remained unimplemented, it should have returned to the Council, rather than assume unilaterally the task of ensuring implementation. Spain called it improper to refer exclusively to paragraph 2 of the 3 April resolution, which demanded the withdrawal of Argentine forces, when the resolution should be implemented in full.

Panama observed that the dispute had gone on too long, threatening international peace and security, and Jordan said it was not too late to contain the conflict, save numerous lives and restore goodwill. Brazil and China both declared it time for the Council to decide on an immediate cease-fire.

Communications (2 June–August). On 4 June,[56] Argentina transmitted to the Security Council the text of an agreement adopted at Caracas, Venezuela, on 2 June by high-level government representatives of the Latin American Economic System, calling for the immediate discontinuation of what it termed the illegal coercive economic measures taken against Argentina by the United Kingdom and other States, extending to Argentina economic co-operation to deal with the effects of these measures and recommending formulation of a strategy to defend Latin American security and economic independence through greater regional economic integration and development.

The Argentine Armed Forces Joint General Staff issued a communiqué on 3 June, transmitted on 4 June,[57] reporting an exchange of artillery fire in the Mount Kent area, with no losses on its side. In two communiqués of 4 June, transmitted on 5 June,[58] the Joint General Staff reported a decline in Britain's air operations, while its Air Force conducted intensive bombing raids in the Mount Kent area. Further communiqués, conveyed on 6 June,[60] said that the British Defence Ministry's announcement of 3 June on damage to four of its naval units, including the destroyer *Glasgow* and the frigate *Argonaut*, demonstrated the truthfulness of Argentine reports which had previously been denied or not admitted by the United Kingdom; military activity remained limited on 5 June.

The relatively static military situation persisted until 7 June, according to three Argentine communiqués issued on 6 and 7 June and transmitted on the latter date;[62] the Argentine hospital ship *Bahía Paraíso* transported wounded personnel from several points, including 47 from the British counterpart *Uganda*, to the Argentine mainland on 5 June, it was also reported. In two additional communiqués issued on 7 June, forwarded the following day,[63] Argentina said that its ice-breaker *Almirante Irizar* was undertaking new duties as a hospital ship and that some exchanges with United Kingdom air and ground forces had taken place on 7 June.

A landing was attempted by the British forces near Puerto Argentino on 8 June, Argentina said in a communiqué of that date forwarded on 9 June,[65] and all four British naval craft involved in the operation were damaged by Argentine aircraft. A second landing attempt near Puerto Argentino later that day was reported in a 9 June communiqué transmitted on 10 June;[66] intense ground combat and violent artillery duels had

taken place near Mount Kent at 2230 hours, 8 June, and several British aircraft had been shot down or damaged on 9 June.

In a communiqué of 10 June, conveyed the following day,[68] Argentina stated that its Air Force had carried out numerous attacks on 9 June in the Fitzroy area, its Army had conducted artillery attacks in the Mount Kent vicinity, and Britain's 8 June landing attempt had been repulsed. In a second communiqué of 10 June as well as two issued on 11 June, all of which were transmitted on 12 June,[69] Argentina reported on continued military activities as well as evacuation of the wounded by hospital ships and charged that United Kingdom reports were minimizing British losses while exaggerating Argentina's.

Argentina reported heavy fighting on 12 June near Puerto Argentino following a landing at daybreak of approximately 4,500 British troops, armed with sophisticated weapons, which managed to penetrate Argentine defence lines by 3.5 kilometres; the details were provided in two communiqués issued that day and transmitted on 12 June[72] and 13 June.[75] There were no infantry confrontations that night or the morning of 13 June, according to an Argentine communiqué of 13 June conveyed by a letter dated 14 June.[77] In two more communiqués transmitted by that same letter, three by a second letter of 14 June[79] and two more by a third letter of that date,[80] all issued on 14 June, Argentina described heavy fighting in the hills outside Puerto Argentino and the continued advance of United Kingdom troops, followed by a *de facto* cease-fire; talks between the military commanders of the two sides were reported to have taken place at 1600 hours, 14 June.

In a communiqué of 16 June, transmitted on 17 June,[82] Argentina presented its analysis of the fighting at Puerto Argentino that led to a *de facto* cease-fire at 1500 hours on 14 June, and said that the United Kingdom had broken its defences in a pre-dawn attack with the aid of high-technology weapons, including infra-red equipment for night viewing, portable missile-launchers and laser aiming systems; that consequently the Malvinas had been transformed into a test site for these weapons, many of which were unknown even on the international arms market; that the fact that this market had been closed to Argentina had a basic impact on the outcome; and that the United States had provided logistical support.

Argentina said in a letter dated 6 June[59] that the United Kingdom had acknowledged the presence on 27 May of the *Uganda* in a place where fighting had been going on and had further reported that a British vessel had boarded and inspected the Argentine hospital ship *Bahía Paraíso* without finding any violations of the Geneva Convention; by the same letter, it transmitted a communiqué of 5 June which said that the two ships had had a rendezvous on 4 June in order to transfer wounded personnel.

In a letter dated 10 June from its Foreign Minister to ICRC, which was transmitted to the Council on 12 June,[70] Argentina said it had inspected the United Kingdom hospital ship *Hydra* on 7 June and was analysing information to the effect that military spare parts had been found on an aircraft delivering medical supplies to that ship.

On 12 June,[71] Argentina conveyed two communiqués issued on 11 and 12 June reporting that on 11 June its hospital ship *Bahía Paraíso*, which was moored in the Puerto Argentino area with crew, injured personnel and ICRC officials aboard, was nearly hit by two missiles fired by British aircraft, and that indiscriminate bombing in the harbour area had resulted in two civilians killed and four wounded; Argentina asserted that the modern weapons systems used by the United Kingdom ruled out the possibility that the incident had been caused by an error. Argentina's protest on the attack on its hospital ship was conveyed in an 11 June letter, transmitted through Brazilian authorities to the United Kingdom; the text of the letter was sent to the Council on 12 June.[73]

In two communiqués issued on 12 June and transmitted the same day,[74] the Argentine Joint General Staff announced that its Air Force had attacked and put out of action a United Kingdom frigate, which it said was bombarding the civilian population of Puerto Argentino, and provided the identities of civilians wounded or killed there by British naval units the day before. It announced in a communiqué of 13 June, transmitted that day,[76] that it had further protested to the United Kingdom Government through the Brazilian authorities the bombardment of the hospital ship and of the civilian population, calling it inappropriate for the British Government to expect Argentina to assume responsibility for the protection of the civilians which the British forces were attacking.

In a letter dated 17 June,[161] the United Kingdom refuted Argentina's allegations concerning the attack on Port Stanley, saying that its forces had been instructed to keep clear of the hospital ship and pointing out that under the relevant Geneva Convention such ships acted "at their own risk" during a military engagement; the ultimate responsibility for incidents such as the alleged civilian casualties at Port Stanley, on which it awaited authoritative reports, lay with Argentina which had resorted to an act of unprovoked aggression on 2 April and which should have arranged for the evacuation of civilians and facilitated access by ICRC.

In response to press reports that captive Argentine soldiers had been compelled to locate and deactivate explosives in the area of Goose Green and Port Darwin, Argentina issued a communiqué on 5 June, transmitted on 6 June,[61] saying that, if confirmed, such action would constitute a violation of the Geneva Convention relative to the Treatment of Prisoners of War. In a communiqué of 7 June, conveyed on 8 June,[64] Argentina announced that the United Kingdom had replied through Brazilian authorities that a box of munitions had exploded while in transport, killing five prisoners and injuring seven others; further clarification was being sought, Argentina said, in order to prevent the recurrence of such actions.

In a letter dated 11 June,[158] the United Kingdom said it knew of no facts to support reports or Argentine allegation that prisoners were made to clear minefields but was investigating the matter, denied that its account of prisoner casualties communicated to Argentina implied a violation of Geneva Conventions, asserted that its treatment of prisoners was in full accord with those Conventions, and added that further loss of life could be avoided if Argentina agreed to an immediate withdrawal of its forces from the Islands according to a firmly agreed timetable.

Replying to an ICRC request for information, in a letter of 8 June transmitted on 11 June,[67] Argentina said the development of the hostilities, the imposition of the exclusion zone and the indiscriminate attacks on population centres prompted it to declare that the United Kingdom bore sole responsibility for the consequences that might result from certain shortages and limitations in meeting the needs of the civilian population of the Malvinas. In another letter to ICRC, transmitted to the Council on 14 June,[78] Argentina said that on the basis of talks with ICRC representatives on 10 and 11 June, and in accordance with the relevant Geneva Convention, it was designating an area around the cathedral in Puerto Argentino as a neutral zone for the shelter of civilians, the sick and the wounded.

On 14 June, Brigadier-General Mario Benjamín Menéndez, the Commander of Argentine Land, Sea and Air Forces in the Malvinas, signed an Instrument of Surrender with Major-General Jeremy J. Moore, Commander of the British Land Forces in the Falkland Islands, to enter into effect from 2059 hours local time (2359 hours GMT) on that day. The text of the Instrument, transmitted by the United Kingdom on 17 June,[160] stated that the surrender was to include those Argentine Forces deployed "in and around Port Stanley, those others on East Falkland, West Falkland and all the outlying islands".

Argentina, on 17 June,[81] transmitted communications it had exchanged with the United Kingdom through the Brazilian authorities. In a message delivered on 15 June, the United Kingdom expressed its readiness to commence repatriation of Argentine personnel, provided it received assurance of a total cessation of hostilities and a guarantee of safe passage for ships and planes used for that purpose; once total cessation of hostilities was confirmed, the United Kingdom would propose lifting economic measures and exclusion zones instituted by both parties and would ask other nations to lift their economic sanctions against Argentina. In response, Argentina stated its readiness to receive its personnel as soon as possible and hoped that the United Kingdom would apply the procedure used during the conflict with the co-operation of Uruguay and ICRC, but that any attempt to impose conditions of a political nature would be unacceptable.

In a communiqué issued on 17 June and transmitted the following day,[85] Argentina reported that a total of 549 wounded personnel had been transported from the Islands to the mainland since the conflict had begun and that the transfer operation was continuing normally.

In a letter of 17 June,[83] Argentina charged that the United Kingdom warship *Endurance* had threatened to use force to remove Argentine personnel from the scientific station "Corbeta Uruguay" which Argentina had maintained on an island in the South Sandwich archipelago since 1977 and which constituted no military threat.

In a letter dated 18 June,[84] Argentina stated that on 14 June the Commander of the Argentine forces defending the Malvinas Islands had had to surrender, owing to the military superiority of the British forces; a total cessation of hostilities would be achieved, it said, only when the United Kingdom lifted its military blockade and economic sanctions against Argentina and withdrew its military forces from the Islands. It stated further that only negotiations within the United Nations framework could lead to a final settlement of the dispute and eliminate a situation of illegal colonial domination by force.

Argentina informed the Council, by a letter dated 19 June,[86] that United Kingdom helicopters had fired shots at the "Corbeta Uruguay" station that day in violation of the cessation of hostilities. The United Kingdom replied in a letter dated 21 June[162] that its forces had recovered possession of the South Sandwich Islands, over which it had first proclaimed its sovereignty in 1775, and that 11 Argentine naval and air force personnel at the illegally-established station had formally surrendered on 20 June without any shots having been fired by British forces. Argentina responded in a letter of 24 June[87] that it had never accepted the British claim to sovereignty over the South Sandwich Islands; that the unarmed personnel at the "Corbeta Uruguay" were scientific personnel of the Argentine armed forces, which were respon-

sible for all Antarctic and sub-Antarctic logistical operations; and that this station was officially registered with the World Meteorological Organization and recognized as an Argentine station.

In a letter dated 23 June,[163] the United Kingdom, referring to the Argentine letter of 18 June, asserted that it was none other than Argentina which had committed an act of aggression; rejected Argentine attempts at imposing pre-conditions for a total cessation of hostilities, including the withdrawal of British forces from the Islands; stated that the Falkland Islanders had resented the Argentine invasion and welcomed their liberation by British forces; and expressed readiness to implement its 15 June proposals once Argentina accepted a total end of hostilities.

In exercise of its right of reply to a statement made on 14 June by the President of Panama at the Twelfth Special Session of the General Assembly devoted to disarmament, the United Kingdom addressed a letter of the same date[159] to the Assembly President taking issue with the Panamanian charge that the introduction of British nuclear submarines in the South Atlantic had made a mockery of the Treaty for the Prohibition of Nuclear Weapons in Latin America (Treaty of Tlatelolco). That Treaty, the United Kingdom said, prohibited nuclear weapons in the region but not nuclear-powered submarines; it was inconceivable, it added, that it would use nuclear weapons against Argentina.

Panama observed in a 17 June letter to the Assembly President[122] that the United Kingdom did not declare its non-use of nuclear weapons against Argentina but simply called such action inconceivable; that the presence in the South Atlantic of the British nuclear submarines on military missions, with the possibilities of their destruction and consequent environmental contamination, threatened the safety of the States of the region; and that the United Kingdom should submit its submarines to inspection by the International Atomic Energy Agency so as to dispel apprehension.

Taking issue with other arguments put forward by Panama in its 17 June letter, the United Kingdom said in a letter of 30 June[164] that the right of self-determination as defined by the United Nations applied not only to the so-called oppressed but to all peoples, including the Falkland Islanders; and that a 1980 census had shown 1,360 of the 1,813 inhabitants to have been born in the Falklands, many of whom were descendants of nineteenth-century immigrants from Europe, belying Panama's charge that the population had been artificially installed.

Argentina, in a letter of 23 July to the Assembly President,[88] referred to the United Kingdom letter of 30 June, asserting that the principle of self-determination did not apply to the occupying population of the Malvinas which had been established there through an act of force by the colonial Power and which consisted in many cases of transitory employees of the United Kingdom Government or of the British-based Falkland Islands Company. The United Kingdom, in a 13 August letter to the Secretary-General,[166] called that argument tendentious and said that historical evidence did not support Argentina's contention that a settled Argentine population had been forcibly displaced by the United Kingdom in the nineteenth century.

On 22 July,[165] the United Kingdom conveyed a statement made by its Prime Minister that day, announcing the lifting of the total exclusion zone of 200 nautical miles around the Falkland Islands and adding that, in order to minimize the risk of inadvertent clashes, it had asked Argentina, via the Swiss Government, to ensure that its warships and military aircraft did not enter a zone of 150 miles around the Islands. Referring to this statement in a letter dated 26 July,[90] Argentina declared that it did not accept the existence of limits of any kind in seas within its jurisdiction; that the British attitude demonstrated the existence in the zone of only a *de facto* suspension, rather than a final cessation, of hostilities; and that genuine peace could be achieved only if the United Kingdom abrogated the military and economic measures it had taken and agreed to negotiate within the framework of the United Nations.

On 26 July,[89] Argentina transmitted a letter of 20 July addressed to the President of the Commission of the European Communities protesting the EC decision to grant the United Kingdom's request for emergency assistance for the Malvinas Islands, arguing that the action constituted inadmissible interference and could be construed as disregard for Argentina's legitimate rights over the archipelagos. On 7 October,[180] Denmark, as current President of the Council of the European Communities, transmitted a letter dated 23 August from the President of the Commission of the European Communities in reply to Argentina's letter of 20 July, stating that EC aid had been granted to the Falklands in the past and that therefore the current action did not constitute a change of any kind, that by EC policy such aid did not prejudge the status of the countries or territories which received it and that the Commission considered as inadmissible criticism by third States of the legality of its actions.

On 13 August,[91] Argentina informed the Security Council that, on 5, 8 and 10 August, its fishing vessels had been forced to withdraw from waters lying within its jurisdiction by British warships and military aircraft enforcing the 150-mile "protection zone" imposed by the United Kingdom; that act of aggression interfered with the

right of free navigation and exploitation of its marine resources, Argentina said, adding that an effective and just peace could be attained only when the United Kingdom ceased to enforce the protection zone and the economic sanctions, withdrew its forces and undertook negotiations within the United Nations framework.

The United Kingdom, in a letter dated 20 August,[167] denied having used force against Argentine fishing boats; stated that it had never accepted Argentina's claim to fisheries or continental shelf jurisdiction beyond the median line between the Falkland Islands and Argentina and that it reserved the rights of the Falkland Islands over their own maritime resources; called the protection zone for the defence of the Islands necessary in view of Argentina's unwillingness to declare a definite end to hostilities; and stated that Argentine conduct since 2 April had deprived the international community of any certainty that that country could be trusted to negotiate in good faith, and that it would be a long time before confidence in Argentine intentions could be re-established to the point where the prospect of negotiations could be discussed.

Argentina complained that United Kingdom aircraft had been harassing its fishing vessels while they were operating outside the protection zone; in a letter dated 24 August,[92] it said that five ships had been buzzed by British helicopters on 14 and 15 August, and in a letter dated 27 August,[93] it informed the Council that two of the same ships had been buzzed on 18 August. The United Kingdom, in a letter dated 27 August,[168] confirmed that its naval forces had had encounters with five Argentine vessels on 14 and 15 August but denied that there had been any threat or use of force.

Consideration by the Committee on colonial countries. The Special Committee on the Situation with regard to the Implementation of the Declaration on the Granting of Independence to Colonial Countries and Peoples considered the Territory of the Falkland Islands (Malvinas) at meetings between 29 April and 20 August,[190] during which it heard statements by the United Kingdom as the administering Power, by Argentina and by Committee members. It also heard statements by those not members of the Committee which had requested to participate (Bolivia, Brazil, Colombia, Ecuador, Panama, Peru, Uruguay) and by two members of the Territory's Legislative Council. On 20 August, the Committee decided without objection to continue consideration of the item at its 1983 session, subject to any directives by the General Assembly.

Communications (September-November). Replying to the United Kingdom's letter of 20 August, Argentina, in a letter dated 20 September,[94] said that the imposition of the protection zone violated the right of freedom of navigation; it could not allow the United Kingdom, by the use of fallacious arguments, to continue the colonial aggression in a part of Argentine territory and extend it to waters under Argentine jurisdiction or to attempt to perpetuate that situation by declining to negotiate an end to the dispute.

In a letter of 23 September,[95] Argentina complained of further harassment of its fishing vessels, citing 19 incidents of overflight and buzzing by United Kingdom aircraft between 24 August and 15 September, all but one of which, it said, had taken place outside the protection zone.

On 8 October,[169] the United Kingdom responded to the Argentine letters of 20 and 23 September, stating that Argentina bore sole responsibility for the failure of the Council resolution of 3 April to bring about a peaceful resolution of the dispute; that by Argentina's own account the 19 encounters with Argentine fishing vessels consisted of no more than overflight by British aircraft for the purpose of identification or to request that they leave the protection zone; and that Argentine civilian vessels with legitimate reason to enter the zone should continue to seek British agreement in advance, as they were known, it said, to have been used as cover for naval personnel or equipment for intelligence purposes.

Argentina, in a letter dated 1 November,[99] summarized its arguments in rejection of the United Kingdom's imposition of a protection zone, and charged that the United Kingdom was maintaining the climate of tension in the area and ignoring the mandate in United Nations resolutions to negotiate urgently with Argentina on the dispute over sovereignty.

By a letter of 18 October,[96] Argentina requested circulation as a General Assembly document of an overview of the question of the Malvinas Islands, summarizing its view of the history of the Territory and consideration of it by the United Nations; included were the texts of several Latin American and United Nations decisions and statements by the Movement of Non-Aligned Countries on the question. On 1 November[98] and 2 November,[101] Argentina submitted additional historical material. The United Kingdom, in a letter dated 28 October,[170] stated that the Argentine document repeated numerous tendentious claims which it had refuted earlier, and annexed copies of its letters of 28 April and 13 August which set out its position concerning the historical record and the substantive issues.

In letters dated 20 October,[97] 1 November[100] and 17 November,[102] Argentina reported 50 further acts of harassment by British vessels and aircraft against Argentine fishing vessels outside the protection zone occurring between 10 September and 7 November.

General Assembly action (November). On 4 November, the General Assembly requested Argentina and the United Kingdom to resume negotiations towards a peaceful solution of their sovereignty dispute over the Falkland Islands (Malvinas), calling on the Secretary-General to undertake a renewed mission of good offices to assist the parties in this task and asking him to report in 1983 on progress made in implementing the resolution.[194]

The resolution, sponsored by 20 Latin American States, was adopted by a recorded vote of 90 to 12, with 52 abstentions. The request for inclusion of the question as a supplementary item on the agenda of the 1982 Assembly session came in a letter dated 16 August[177] signed by the Foreign Ministers of the same 20 States, who hoped for a peaceful settlement through negotiations conducted under United Nations auspices.

In deciding on 24 September to consider the question directly in plenary meetings, the Assembly, by a recorded vote of 41 to 33, with 24 abstentions, agreed to a proposal by the United Kingdom that the interested parties would be heard in the Fourth Committee. Among those casting the negative votes were 17 Latin American countries joined by several Eastern European and other socialist countries. The Fourth Committee subsequently heard on 2 November [191] the following petitioners:[193] Anthony T. Blake and John E. Cheek, members of the Legislative Council of the Falkland Islands (Malvinas); and Alexander Jacob Betts, Susan Coutts de Maciello, Bárbara Minto de Pennissi and Reynaldo Ernesto Reed, all residents or former residents of the Islands. The General Assembly took note of the Committee's action in a decision of 3 November.[201]

In explanation of vote, absence in the text of an explicit reference to the principle of self-determination or respect for the freely expressed wishes of the inhabitants of the Falkland Islands (Malvinas) was cited by many, among them Antigua and Barbuda, Fiji, the Gambia and Solomon Islands, which voted against; Jamaica, Lesotho, Norway, Sweden and Zaire, which abstained; and Liberia, which voted in favour. New Zealand voted negatively, and the Netherlands abstained, saying that the Islanders were entitled to have a say in their own future.

Along with the United Kingdom, which voted against, Belgium, abstaining, said the text should have referred not only to the interests but also to the aspirations of the Islanders. Botswana, Ghana, Israel and the United States, supporting the text, and Sweden, abstaining, said the negotiations should take into account the Islanders' rights and aspirations. Australia, abstaining, said the text referred to the rights of the inhabitants in a highly qualified way. However, Mexico said in support of the resolution that an inclusion in the text of a reference to the principle of self-determination of peoples would tend to disguise colonial domination with supposedly moral arguments and give rise to confusion. The United Kingdom called it ridiculous to rest the case on the Argentine version of what had happened in the eighteenth and nineteenth centuries in disregard of the wishes of the current inhabitants. Saint Lucia, abstaining, was not convinced that the argument against self-determination was valid in respect of the timeframe in question.

The United Kingdom, joined by Luxembourg and the Netherlands, both of which abstained, said the text failed to recognize the obligations of the United Kingdom as the administering Power or the rights of the Falklanders under Article 73 (relating to Non-Self-Governing Territories) of the Charter of the United Nations. Sierra Leone, abstaining, called the question one of self-determination and decolonization and, as such, fell within the purview of that Article.

A number of those supporting the text reaffirmed their belief in Argentine sovereignty over the Falkland Islands (Malvinas). The Libyan Arab Jamahiriya saw the Malvinas as Argentina's natural geographic and historic extension and, joined by Afghanistan and Viet Nam, called for the defence of the territorial integrity and the United Kingdom's immediate withdrawal.

Mexico said deleting the concept of sovereignty from the text would make the controversy devoid of substance and cause the negotiations to be diverted to secondary and even banal questions. Such a deletion, Peru said, would have meant ignoring all the United Nations resolutions which had described the Malvinas question as a dispute concerning sovereignty. Brazil appealed to the parties to proceed directly to what it called the fundamental question of whose claim to sovereignty was more legitimate. Chile, while supporting Argentina's claim of sovereignty over the Islands, cautioned against going back into history to stir up memories of facts which might sharpen differences or deepen unhealed wounds. Mexico, on the other hand, asserted that the text did not expressly affirm the background information in support of the legitimacy of Argentina's claim over the Islands. The United Kingdom denied, however, that Argentina had inherited title to the Falklands from Spain, that Argentina had ever established sovereignty or a permanent settlement there by 1833 or that Britain had used force in reoccupying the Islands that year.

A number of speakers expressed fear that the resolution's terms prejudged the outcome of negotiations. France, Italy and the Netherlands abstained for that reason, as did Luxembourg and Samoa, which considered the text as having failed

to place the envisaged negotiations in a neutral context. Similarly, Belgium feared the adoption of the text might exacerbate the differences and prove prejudicial to the negotiations. Sharing that view, Saint Lucia said the Assembly should not be used to suit any State's convenience by ignoring Charter principles when those principles were at variance with the perceived self-interest of that State. Ireland said it would have preferred a more open and flexible approach to the questions at issue, adding that the text tilted towards the position of one of the parties. The United Kingdom rejected the emphasis in paragraph 1 on the sovereignty dispute as prejudging the negotiations, and Australia concurred. Belize cast a negative vote, saying that the text failed to cover adequately the subject of negotiations.

Turkey regretted that it had not been possible to formulate a consensus resolution on which the resumption of the negotiations could safely be based. Senegal asserted that an appeal for negotiations should not contain formulations subject to different interpretations by the two parties, and the Federal Republic of Germany called on both sides to search for a basis for negotiations, without asking the international community to prejudge the outcome and without setting pre-conditions.

Also abstaining in the vote, Saint Lucia and the Sudan considered that certain elements in the text might have created obstacles to negotiations towards a solution that would ensure the fulfilment of the aspirations of the population; Sierra Leone saw the text falling short of recognizing that self-determination, independence and sovereignty were inseparable in that negotiation. New Zealand and the United Kingdom opposed the text, as they questioned the effectiveness of calling for negotiations without clearly setting forth the principles involved. Although agreeing with the need for negotiations, the Bahamas, abstaining, said it could not support the deficient modalities and guiding principles which underpinned the resolution, including presenting the Secretary-General with tools that were not equal to the task. While Hungary and Uruguay supported as timely the call for the Secretary-General's renewed mission of good offices, Antigua and Barbuda voted against the text, as it saw no practical purpose being served by instructing the Secretary-General to undertake a mission in the renewed tension which the resolution could produce. Solomon Islands, which voted similarly, called on Argentina to change its attitude completely before coming to the United Nations to ask for the support of the international community.

Among those voting in favour, Austria agreed that the call for negotiations should not prejudice the outcome, and Tunisia said that to advocate the right to self-determination as the only basis for a settlement of the conflict might result in prejudging the content of negotiations. Botswana said its affirmative vote should not be construed as support for one party or to prejudge the outcome of negotiations; to do so, Japan said, would only intensify hostilities and diminish the chance of a peaceful settlement. The United States said the resolution did not legally prejudice the position of either party or prejudge the result of negotiations; in fact, the text aimed at creating a negotiating framework on an impartial basis, Mexico said. Chile, Costa Rica, El Salvador and Nicaragua also maintained that the text did not prejudge the outcome of the proposed negotiations, and Hungary considered the text constructive and well-balanced. Albania, while supporting the text, said it had no confidence that the United Kingdom would renounce its colonial position if the negotiations were resumed with Argentina. Madagascar felt that the resolution took into account the interests of the inhabitants and would not prejudice the sovereignty question.

The timing of acting on the resolution in 1982 was questioned by some. In the United Kingdom's assessment, many delegations were troubled at being obliged to vote on the text; they felt it a mistake for Argentina to have pressed the matter to a vote so soon after invading the Islands, and it would be a tragedy if the Assembly vote encouraged Argentina into thinking that the Assembly was prepared to ignore its act of aggression seven months earlier. Antigua and Barbuda, which cast a negative vote, said the text had the potential to reopen wounds too fresh to be properly healed, to encourage acrimony when sensitivity was required and to whip up emotions when a period of somber reflection would be more helpful; it would have preferred the matter to be aired in a debate rather than have a vote on a resolution. Belize, voting negatively, and Belgium and Sierra Leone, abstaining, shared that view. Jamaica, which had appealed to the sponsors for a one-year deferment of the draft for that reason, abstained in the vote.

Canada, which also abstained, said it would have preferred a simple resolution expressing concern over the tragedy, urging the parties to resume negotiations at the earliest possible moment and offering appropriate assistance through the Secretary-General. Similarly, Australia believed the United Nations, at some appropriate time, should urge the parties to resume discussions in a less emotionally charged atmosphere. Ghana voted in favour, saying that the sooner the negotiations began the greater the chances of their success, and the Dominican Republic appealed to the United Kingdom to support the resolution so that negotiations could get under way as soon as possible.

Among those abstaining, Australia, Guyana, and Trinidad and Tobago considered some important basic elements either missing or inadequately addressed in the text, and Malta, although voting in favour, shared that view. Similarly, Zaire said the resolution must avoid the temptation to amalgamate inconsistent elements; defining the very nature of the dispute as exactly as possible would in itself be a way of helping towards a solution. Maldives and Sierra Leone abstained because of the importance they attached to the principle of the non-use or threat of force, as did Kuwait, which affirmed its belief also in decolonization, self-determination, sovereignty and territorial integrity; Austria voted in favour with the understanding that the resolution was based on such fundamental principles of international conduct. Tunisia supported the text for advocating the peaceful settlement of disputes; the Central African Republic and Israel expressed a similar view. While voting in favour, Liberia said it would have preferred more specific reference to denunciation of the use of force.

The issue of a formal, lasting cessation of hostilities was not adequately covered in the text, said Belize and Solomon Islands, both of which voted against, and France, which abstained. The United Kingdom said its negative vote signified resistance to any renewed Argentine pressure on the Falklands, and asserted that the phrase about a *de facto* cessation of hostilities was carefully drafted so as to contain no commitment at all. Liberia, voting in favour, appealed to the two parties to proceed to the cessation of all hostilities, which Ghana, voting in favour, and Lesotho, abstaining, considered as an essential basis for negotiations; the Federal Republic of Germany, abstaining, considered it necessary for the restoration of normal relations between the parties. Among those voting in favour, Japan appealed to Argentina to respect the principle of the non-use of force, and Greece expected from Argentina a definite commitment not to resume hostilities, so as to ensure just negotiations. The Netherlands, abstaining, said it welcomed Argentina's declared intention not to resume hostilities. Brazil and Peru said all those sponsoring the text, including Argentina, were committed to the cessation of hostilities; Chile said the text put the cessation of hostilities in a legal framework, leading to *de jure* cessation.

War was imposed on Latin America, Suriname asserted, and the text's objective was restoration of peace; Ghana and Venezuela voted for the text as an act of faith in the United Nations capacity to restore peace. Uruguay believed the peace initiative by the 20 sponsors established Latin America anew in the United Nations as a stable and calming force. The Assembly had to take a more active role in the search for a peaceful solution, Ethiopia said in support of the text, in order to avert a possible repetition of the tragedy. Albania, despite reservations concerning what it called omission of fact and reference to certain documents, supported the resolution because it believed the maintenance of colonial situations to be incompatible with the ideal of international peace. Bolivia likewise said that to vote for the text was to vote for the Charter principle against colonialism. For Tunisia, the issue was conflict over sovereignty caused by a continuing colonial situation, and Ghana called the question that of decolonization.

China and Haiti believed that the recommendations put forward by the sponsors constituted the most viable formula for a peaceful solution. Honduras said the text provided the United Kingdom with an honourable way out.

During the debate, most speakers lamented the loss of life and the material damage caused by the armed confrontation between two Member States. Several urged the United Nations to provide an adequate framework for a peaceful solution to the dispute, and complimented the Secretary-General for his efforts at mediation. Support was repeatedly expressed for the principles of the non-use or threat of use of force in international relations and the peaceful settlement of disputes.

Belize, Guyana, Norway and the United Kingdom said they regretted the abrupt interruption of the negotiating process at the end of March and Argentine resort to the use of force in April; the United Kingdom asserted that a military and political confrontation had been forced upon it. In addition to the invasion, Liberia regretted the British military response to it as contravention of the two Security Council resolutions, while New Zealand regretted Argentine refusal to comply with the Council's demand for troop withdrawal.

As both sides counted their dead and assessed the damage, India observed, they must have realized the value of diplomacy, dialogue and negotiation. Poland concurred, saying that the cost of gunboat diplomacy, when measured in human lives, was enormous. China said that the momentary success of the militarily stronger party could not lead to a settlement of the dispute. Many speakers shared Brazil's view that serious negotiations were the only way to achieve a just and lasting settlement. Yugoslavia asserted that a successful negotiating process had to take into account the rights of Argentina and the interests of the population of the Malvinas. The United Kingdom rejected the idea that negotiations could have only one outcome, that of the transfer of sovereignty from Britain to Argentina.

Mexico rejected the United Kingdom's contention that the bloodshed was too fresh for negotiations to be reopened; on the contrary, the more

recent the hostilities, the more urgent the need to find a peaceful solution. Cuba agreed, saying that the victims of the conflict deserved an effort for a negotiated solution. The urge to remember the sacrifices made should not prevent the efforts for a peaceful settlement, said Uruguay, and Nicaragua said that any attempt to delay or prevent negotiations would run counter to the Charter and to United Nations resolutions. Malta cautioned that time would be needed for the wounds to heal and that hasty efforts might be counterproductive, although it also observed that deliberate delay on one side could be provocative. The aftermath of the conflict was an understandable constraint on the normalization of relations, Canada said, but the international community had an interest in an early settlement as well. India hoped both parties could find the necessary confidence to negotiate.

Several speakers dwelt on the effectiveness of the United Nations in the peaceful settlement of disputes. Equatorial Guinea expressed concern over the failure of the negotiating efforts and numerous resolutions to stop the military hostilities in the Falkland Islands (Malvinas). Chile advocated reactivating the Organization's preventive function for the timely avoidance of conflict. Peru said the proposed resolution meant negotiations to strengthen the United Nations role in maintaining international peace and security. The tragic conflict was not due to a failure of the United Nations, Finland asserted, but to a breach of its Charter by those which acted on political expediency and narrowly conceived national interests.

Some questioned the validity of the right to veto in the Security Council. Suriname wondered whether the Council could function effectively when one of the parties to the dispute was a permanent member with the option of blocking any decisions that were not to its liking. Venezuela considered the Council's 3 April resolution as partial and pro-colonialist, because it reproduced verbatim the proposal made by one of the parties to the conflict; Panama said the United Kingdom, in addition to its right to veto, behaved as if it could act outside the Charter framework with impunity, as demonstrated by its imposition of a blockade. Honduras said the Malvinas issue offered a clear example of the veto power making a mockery of the principle of the sovereign equality of all United Nations Member States.

There was frequent reference to the Assembly decisions taken since 1965 as having recognized the colonial character of the dispute between Argentina and the United Kingdom, and several speakers endorsed Argentina's claim to sovereignty over the Territory as consistent with positions adopted by the United Nations, the Movement of

Non-Aligned Countries or other intergovernmental bodies. Cuba said Argentina's sovereignty over the Malvinas had the support of history, geography and international law. Colombia felt that the statements and replies by petitioners from the Malvinas and the related debate in the Fourth Committee favoured Argentina's claim.

Given the history of its willingness to decolonize, the United Kingdom should have been able to approach the problem with serenity, Zaire stated, while Argentina should have realized that the resort to force was unlikely to create conditions favourable to a negotiated settlement. A speeding up of the negotiating process towards restoring Argentina's territorial integrity would have prevented an unwarranted war, Spain said, a view that was shared by the Congo. Fiji felt that the United Kingdom had fulfilled its obligations under the Charter as administering Power of the Falkland Islands (Malvinas), had respected the rights and wishes of the Islanders and should be allowed to continue to do so; the decolonization process should continue in accordance with Article 73 of the Charter.

Several speakers took issue with the contention of the United Kingdom that the right of self-determination applied to Falkland Islanders, who should not be compelled against their will to become citizens of another country, and moreover a country which, it said, had already ill-treated them so harshly; it termed as specious and unsubstantiated the Argentine claim that the Assembly had specifically excluded the right of self-determination for the Falkland Islanders. Luxembourg called the right to self-determination a corollary of the principle of decolonization, and Australia asserted that it was Argentina, not Britain, that was attempting to impose an alien rule.

Argentina stated that the right of self-determination could not be used to transform illegitimate occupation into full sovereignty under the protective umbrella of the United Nations; that the non-aligned Movement had declared non-applicability of the right to self-determination in the Malvinas case; and that only the Argentine people were legitimately entitled to self-determination in the question. Mexico and Spain supported that position, as did Ecuador, which called the United Kingdom's reasoning neo-colonial, since it implied that any State could be dismembered by the introduction of settlers, occupation forces or missions. To do so, according to Madagascar, was analogous to allowing the Jewish settlers in the occupied Arab territories by their votes to determine the territories' sovereignty. Similar views were expressed by several Latin American countries, joined by Albania, Czechoslovakia and Equatorial Guinea. Tunisia stated that the implementation of the principle of self-

determination by itself could not resolve the sovereignty dispute.

Panama said the United Kingdom's concern for the Islanders' rights was paradoxical as it had displaced the indigenous inhabitants from the Indian Ocean island of Diego Garcia to accomodate a United States military base there; several other speakers concurred with that view.

Costa Rica asserted that the United Kingdom had changed its position since 1968—when it had first considered the possibility of recognizing Argentine sovereignty over the Islands within 4 to 10 years—possibly due to the territory's potential strategic importance for control of the South Atlantic. Algeria said that the Islands' privileged geostrategic position and the large economic interests that might arise from application of the new Convention on the Law of the Sea could have explained the slow negotiations. The German Democratic Republic also commented that the Islands' location at the crossroads of the major sea lanes made the territory a springboard for the Antarctic and a potential operational base against the people of the region.

The Latin American countries, said Peru, viewed with concern the existence in the Malvinas of a military base with 4,000 men equipped with sophisticated war *matériel*. Argentina said the United Kingdom had installed a powerful military base on the Malvinas, while Panama and the USSR asserted that plans had now emerged for a significant expansion of military structures and installations there. Czechoslovakia charged that by establishing a naval base the United Kingdom was turning the Islands into a strategic stronghold, creating a hotbed of tension in the region.

The USSR asserted that the United Kingdom had used peace efforts within the Security Council as a diplomatic cover for military preparations, and that the United States support for Britain showed that country's aspiration to strengthen its own military-political springboard in Latin America and to include the North Atlantic Treaty Organization (NATO) bloc in its policies in the western hemisphere. Similar views were expressed by Bulgaria, the Byelorussian SSR, the Lao People's Democratic Republic, Mongolia and the Ukrainian SSR. The German Democratic Republic said NATO practically took part in the conflict as a military alliance, using the occasion for testing the logistic and telecommunication links and the efficiency of its weapons systems and ocean warfare.

The United States called the USSR allegations against NATO a perversion of truth, an attempt to score propaganda points from a tragic conflict and an insult to the parties and the Latin American States. Albania, while critical of the NATO countries, charged that the USSR also tried to profit from the conflict; the USSR pretended to be a defender of Argentine sovereignty, it said, but when the British were bombarding the Falklands, the Soviets were bombarding Afghanistan. The Congo said that the South Atlantic must not become like its northern counterpart where rival military blocs confronted each other.

Suriname charged that the swiftness with which some countries supported the United Kingdom's military action prompted that country to seek a military solution. The Byelorussian SSR criticized as hypocrisy economic sanctions imposed on Argentina by a group of Western European and other countries which, meanwhile declined to implement the arms embargo against South Africa called for by the Security Council.

Argentina said the debate showed Latin American support for a peaceful settlement of the sovereignty dispute, while the United Kingdom sought to consolidate a colonial situation; the United Kingdom asserted that, while Argentina stressed legalism and sovereignty over land, it stressed natural law, fundamental rights and the rights of the people.

In a letter to the Secretary-General of 23 December, transmitted on 30 December,[103] Argentina accepted his renewed good offices mission and expressed its readiness to settle what it called the sovereignty dispute.

Draft resolutions (1982). [1]Ireland, S/15106 (superseded). [2]Japan, S/15112; and [3]Panama, S/14950 (not pressed). [4]Panama and Spain, S/15156/Rev.2 (not adopted).

Letters, notes verbales (nv) and telegrams (t).
OAS S-G: [5]16 Apr., S/15023; [6]21 Apr., S/15001 (t); [7]29 May, S/15155 (t).

Argentina: [8]1 Apr., S/14940; [9]9 Apr., S/14961; [10]12 Apr., S/14968; [11]13 Apr., S/14975; [12]16 Apr., S/14984; [13]24 Apr., S/14998; [14]25 Apr., S/14999; [15]28 Apr., S/15009; [16]29 Apr., S/15014; 30 Apr., [17]S/15018, [18]S/15021; 1 May, [19]S/15022, [20]S/15026; [21]2 May, S/15028; [22]3 May, S/15032; [23]5 May, S/15046; 6 May, [24]S/15049, [25]S/15053; 7 May, [26]S/15055, [27]S/15057; [28]8 May, S/15059; 9 May, [29]S/15060, [30]S/15061; 11 May, [31]S/15069, [32]S/15070; [33]12 May, S/15074; [34]13 May, S/15078; 15 May, ^{35}S/15083, [36]S/15085;. [37]18 May, S/15092; [38]21 May, S/15101; 22 May, [39]S/15102, [40]S/15103; [41]25 May, S/15117; 26 May, [42]S/15125, [43]S/15128, [44]S/15129; [45]27 May, S/15131; [46]28 May, S/15136; 29 May, [47]S/15139, [48]S/15140; [49]30 May, S/15142; 31 May, [50]S/15143, [51]S/15146, [52]S/15147; 2 June, [53]S/15152, [54]S/15153, [55]S/15154; 4 June, [56]S/15159, [57]S/15160; [58]5 June, S/15169; 6 June, [59]S/15172, [60]S/15173, [61]S/15176; [62]7 June, S/15177; 8 June, [63]S/15181, [64]S/15182; [65]9 June, S/15189; [66]10 June, S/15192; 11 June, [67]S/15199, [68]S/15201; 12 June, [69]S/15202, [70]S/15203, [71]S/15204, [72]S/15205, [73]S/15206, [74]S/15207; 13 June, [75]S/15212, [76]S/15213; 14 June, [77]S/15214, [78]S/15215, [79]S/15217, [80]S/15218; 17 June, [81]S/15228, [82]S/15229, [83]S/15230; 18 June, [84]S/15234, [85]S/15237; [86]19 June, S/15241; [87]24 June, S/15253; [88]23 July, A/37/353; 26 July, [89]A/37/362, [90]S/15313; [91]13 Aug., S/15361; [92]24 Aug., S/15373; [93]27 Aug., S/15377; [94]20 Sep., S/15409; [95]23 Sep., S/15427; [96]18 Oct., A/37/553 & Corr.1; [97]20 Oct., S/15464; 1 Nov., [98]A/37/553/Add.1, [99]S/15474, [100]S/15475; [101]2 Nov., A/37/553/Add.2 (nv); [102]17 Nov., S/15496; [103]30 Dec., A/38/70.

Belgium: [104]3 Apr., S/14949; [105]13 Apr., S/14976.

Brazil: [106]1 May, S/15024; [107]19 May, S/15097; [108]24 May, S/15108.

Colombia: [109]4 May, S/15045 (t); [110]26 May, S/15126.

Costa Rica: [111]17 May, S/15090; [112]25 May, S/15116.

Cuba: [113]26 Apr., S/15003; [114]5 May, S/15048.

Ireland: [115]3 May, S/15036; 4 May, [116]S/15037, [117]S/15044.

Panama: [118]14 Apr., S/14978; [119]10 May, S/15068 (t); [120]21 May, S/15100; [121]31 May, S/15145; [122]17 June, A/S-12/30.

Peru: [123]12 Apr., S/14966; [124]15 Apr., S/14981; [125]10 May, S/15071.

United Kingdom: [126]1 Apr., S/14942; [127]2 Apr., S/14946; [128]9 Apr., S/14963; [129]11 Apr., S/14964; 13 Apr., [130]S/14973, [131]S/14974; [132]19 Apr., S/14987; [133]20 Apr., S/14988; [134]24 Apr., S/14997; [135]26 Apr., S/15002; 28 Apr., [136]S/15006, [137]S/15007; [138]29 Apr., S/15010; 30 Apr., [139]S/15016 & Corr.1, [140]S/15017; [141]1 May, S/15025; [142]2 May, S/15027; [143]3 May, S/15031; 4 May, [144]S/15040, [145]S/15041; [146]8 May, S/15058; [147]10 May, S/15063; [148]13 May, S/15081; [149]14 May, S/15082; [150]15 May, S/15084; [151]20 May, S/15098; [152]23 May, S/15104; [153]25 May, S/15119; [154]27 May, S/15134; [155]28 May, S/15137; [156]31 May, S/15144; [157]1 June, S/15148; [158]11 June, S/15198; [159]14 June, A/S-12/29; 17 June, [160]S/15231, [161]S/15232 & Corr.1; [162]21 June, S/15246; [163]23 June, S/15249; [164]30 June, A/S-12/31; [165]22 July, S/15307; [166]13 Aug., A/37/389; [167]20 Aug., S/15369; [168]27 Aug., S/15378; [169]8 Oct., S/15452; [170]28 Oct., A/37/582.

Venezuela: [171]14 Apr., S/14979; [172]3 May, S/15030.

Viet Nam: [173]12 May, A/37/225-S/15076; [174]13 May, A/37/226-S/15077.

Others: [175]OAS consultation meeting President: 28 Apr., S/15008. [176]S-G: 20 May, S/15099. [177]Argentina, Bolivia, Brazil, Chile, Colombia, Costa Rica, Cuba, Dominican Republic, Ecuador, El Salvador, Guatemala, Haiti, Honduras, Mexico, Nicaragua, Panama, Paraguay, Peru, Uruguay, Venezuela: 16 Aug., A/37/193. [178]Argentina, Nicaragua, Panama, Venezuela: 24 May, S/15111 (nv). [179]Austria: 11 May, S/15073. [180]Denmark: 7 Oct., A/37/531. [181]Denmark, Finland, Iceland, Norway, Sweden: 6 May, S/15052. [182]Dominica: 5 Apr., S/14956 (t). [183]Ecuador: 21 May, S/15123 (t). [184]Japan: 26 Apr., S/15000. [185]Lao People's Democratic Republic: 17 May, A/37/227-S/15088. [186]Saint Vincent and the Grenadines: 6 May, S/15050 (nv). [187]Suriname: 24 May, S/15115. [188]USSR: 24 May, S/15105. [189]Uruguay: 24 May, S/15110.

Reports. [190]Committee on colonial countries, A/37/23/Rev.1; [191]GA 4th Committee, A/37/592; [192]S-G, S/15151.

Requests for hearing. [193]A/C.4/37/9 & Add.1-4.

Resolutions (1982). [194]GA: 37/9, 4 Nov., text following. SC: [195]502(1982), 3 Apr., text following; [196]505(1982), 26 May, text following.

Resolutions (prior). GA: [197]3281 (XXIX), 12 Dec. 1974 (YUN 1974, p. 403); [198]3314 (XXIX), annex, 14 Dec. 1974 (ibid., p. 847).

Statements. SC President, [199]S/14944, [200]S/15047.

Decision (1982). [201]GA: 37/404, 3 Nov., text following.

Meeting records. SC: S/PV.2345, 2346, 2349, *2350*, 2360, 2362-2364, 2366, *2368*, 2371-2373 (1-3 Apr. & 21 May-4 June). GA: General Committee, A/BUR/37/SR.2 (22 Sep.); plenary, A/37/PV.4, 51, *52*, 53, 54, *55* (24 Sep. & 2-4 Nov.); 4th Committee, A/C.4/37/SR.10-12 (29 Oct.-2 Nov.).

General Assembly decision 37/404

Adopted without vote

Oral proposal by President; agenda item 135.

Question of the Falkland Islands (Malvinas)
At its 52nd plenary meeting, on 3 November 1982, the General Assembly took note of the report of the Fourth Committee.

Security Council resolution 502(1982)

3 April 1982   Meeting 2350   10-1-4

Draft by United Kingdom (S/14947/Rev.1).

The Security Council,

Recalling the statement made by the President of the Security Council at the 2345th meeting of the Council on 1 April 1982 calling on the Governments of Argentina and the United Kingdom of Great Britain and Northern Ireland to refrain from the use or threat of force in the region of the Falkland Islands (Islas Malvinas),

Deeply disturbed at reports of an invasion on 2 April 1982 by armed forces of Argentina,

Determining that there exists a breach of the peace in the region of the Falkland Islands (Islas Malvinas),

1. *Demands* an immediate cessation of hostilities;

2. *Demands* an immediate withdrawal of all Argentine forces from the Falkland Islands (Islas Malvinas);

3. *Calls* on the Governments of Argentina and the United Kingdom of Great Britain and Northern Ireland to seek a diplomatic solution to their differences and to respect fully the purposes and principles of the Charter of the United Nations.

Vote in Council as follows:

In favour: France, Guyana, Ireland, Japan, Jordan, Togo, Uganda, United Kingdom, United States, Zaire.

Against: Panama.

Abstaining: China, Poland, Spain, USSR.

Security Council resolution 505(1982)

26 May 1982   Meeting 2368   Adopted unanimously

6-nation draft (S/15122).

Sponsors: Guyana, Ireland, Jordan, Togo, Uganda, Zaire.

The Security Council,

Reaffirming its resolution 502(1982),

Noting with the deepest concern that the situation in the region of the Falkland Islands (Islas Malvinas) has seriously deteriorated,

Having heard the statement made by the Secretary-General at its 2360th meeting, on 21 May 1982, as well as the statements made in the debate by the representatives of Argentina and the United Kingdom of Great Britain and Northern Ireland,

Concerned to achieve, as a matter of the greatest urgency, a cessation of hostilities and an end to the present conflict between the armed forces of Argentina and the United Kingdom,

1. *Expresses appreciation* to the Secretary-General for the efforts that he has already made to bring about an agreement between the parties, to ensure the implementation of resolution 502(1982), and thereby to restore peace to the region;

2. *Requests* the Secretary-General, on the basis of the present resolution, to undertake a renewed mission of good offices, bearing in mind resolution 502(1982) and the approach outlined in his statement of 21 May 1982;

3. *Urges* the parties to the conflict to co-operate fully with the Secretary-General in his mission with a view to ending the present hostilities in and around the Falkland Islands (Islas Malvinas);

4. *Requests* the Secretary-General to enter into contact immediately with the parties with a view to negotiating mutually acceptable terms for a cease-fire, including, if necesssary, arrangements for the dispatch of United Nations observers to monitor compliance with the terms of the cease-fire;

5. *Requests* the Secretary-General to submit an interim report to the Security Council as soon as possible and, in any case, not later than seven days after the adoption of the present resolution.

General Assembly resolution 37/9

4 November 1982   Meeting 55   90-12-52 (recorded vote)

20-nation draft (A/37/L.3/Rev.1); agenda item 135.

Sponsors: Argentina, Bolivia, Brazil, Chile, Colombia, Costa Rica, Cuba, Dominican Republic, Ecuador, El Salvador, Guatemala, Haiti, Honduras, Mexico, Nicaragua, Panama, Paraguay, Peru, Uruguay, Venezuela.

Question of the Falkland Islands (Malvinas)

The General Assembly,

Having considered the question of the Falkland Islands (Malvinas),

Aware that the maintenance of colonial situations is incompatible with the United Nations ideal of universal peace,

Recalling its resolutions 1514(XV) of 14 December 1960, 2065(XX) of 16 December 1965, 3160(XXVIII) of 14 December 1973 and 31/49 of 1 December 1976,

Recalling also Security Council resolutions 502(1982) of 3 April 1982 and 505(1982) of 26 May 1982,

Taking into account the existence of a *de facto* cessation of hostilities in the South Atlantic and the expressed intention of the parties not to renew them,

Reaffirming the need for the parties to take due account of the interests of the population of the Falkland Islands (Malvinas) in accordance with the provisions of General Assembly resolutions 2065(XX) and 3160(XXVIII),

Reaffirming also the principles of the Charter of the United Nations on the non-use of force or the threat of force in international relations and the peaceful settlement of international disputes,

1. *Requests* the Governments of Argentina and the United Kingdom of Great Britain and Northern Ireland to resume negotiations in order to find as soon as possible a peaceful solution to the sovereignty dispute relating to the question of the Falkland Islands (Malvinas);

2. *Requests* the Secretary-General, on the basis of the present resolution, to undertake a renewed mission of good offices in order to assist the parties in complying with the request made in paragraph 1 above, and to take the necessary measures to that end;

3. *Requests* the Secretary-General to report to the General Assembly at its thirty-eighth session on the progress made in the implementation of the present resolution;

4. *Decides* to include in the provisional agenda of its thirty-eighth session the item entitled "Question of the Falkland Islands (Malvinas)".

Recorded vote in Assembly as follows:

In favour: Afghanistan, Albania, Algeria, Angola, Argentina, Austria, Benin, Bolivia, Botswana, Brazil, Bulgaria, Burundi, Byelorussian SSR, Cape Verde, Central African Republic, Chile, China, Colombia, Comoros, Congo, Costa Rica, Cuba, Cyprus, Czechoslovakia, Democratic Kampuchea, Democratic Yemen, Dominican Republic, Ecuador, El Salvador, Equatorial Guinea, Ethiopia, Gabon, German Democratic Republic, Ghana, Greece, Grenada, Guatemala, Guinea, Guinea-Bissau, Haiti, Honduras, Hungary, India, Indonesia, Iran, Iraq, Israel, Ivory Coast, Japan, Lao People's Democratic Republic, Liberia, Libyan Arab Jamahiriya, Madagascar, Malaysia, Mali, Malta, Mexico, Mongolia, Morocco, Mozambique, Nicaragua, Nigeria, Pakistan, Panama, Paraguay, Peru, Philippines, Poland, Romania, Rwanda, Sao Tome and Principe, Spain, Suriname, Syrian Arab Republic, Togo, Tunisia, Uganda, Ukrainian SSR, USSR, United Arab Emirates,[a] United Republic of Tanzania, United States, Upper Volta, Uruguay, Venezuela, Viet Nam, Yemen, Yugoslavia, Zambia, Zimbabwe.

Against: Antigua and Barbuda, Belize, Dominica, Fiji, Gambia, Malawi, New Zealand, Oman, Papua New Guinea, Solomon Islands, Sri Lanka, United Kingdom.

Abstaining: Australia, Bahamas, Bahrain, Bangladesh, Barbados, Belgium, Bhutan, Burma, Canada, Chad, Denmark, Egypt, Finland, France, Germany, Federal Republic of, Guyana, Iceland, Ireland, Italy, Jamaica, Jordan, Kenya, Kuwait, Lebanon, Lesotho, Luxembourg, Maldives, Mauritania, Mauritius, Nepal, Netherlands, Niger, Norway, Portugal, Qatar, Saint Lucia, Saint Vincent and the Grenadines, Samoa, Saudi Arabia, Senegal, Sierra Leone, Singapore, Somalia, Sudan, Swaziland, Sweden, Thailand, Trinidad and Tobago, Turkey, United Republic of Cameroon, Vanuatu, Zaire.

[a]Later advised the Secretariat it had intended to abstain.

East Timor question

Action by the Committee on colonial countries. In 1982, the question of East Timor was considered at two meetings of the Special Committee on the Situation with regard to the Implementation of the Declaration on the Granting of Independence to Colonial Countries and Peoples.[4] On 1 July, the Committee granted a request for a hearing to a representative of the Frente Revolucionária de Timor Leste Independente (FRETILIN) and heard a statement in that connection by Indonesia.

On 20 August, after hearing statements by Portugal, as the administering Power, Indonesia and FRETILIN, as well as by Cape Verde, Mozambique, Nicaragua, Sao Tome and Principe and Zimbabwe, the Committee decided to continue consideration of the question in 1983, subject to any directives by the General Assembly.

Action by the Sub-Commission on discrimination and minorities. On 8 September 1982,[8] the Sub-Commission on Prevention of Discrimination and Protection of Minorities recommended that its parent body, the Commission on Human Rights, reaffirm the right of the people of East Timor to self-determination, and call on Portugal, Indonesia and the representatives of the East Timorese people to co-operate with the United Nations with a view to guaranteeing that right.

General Assembly action. On 23 November, the General Assembly, by a recorded vote of 50 to 46, with 50 abstentions, adopted a resolution on the East Timor question.[7] Expressing concern at the humanitarian situation prevailing in the Territory, it requested the Secretary-General to explore with the parties directly concerned ways to achieve a comprehensive settlement of the problem and to report at its 1983 session. It also requested the Committee on colonial countries to keep the matter under consideration and called on United Nations organizations to assist the East Timorese people, in close consultation with Portugal, as the administering Power. The resolution was recommended by the Fourth Committee, having been introduced by Portugal on behalf of 18 sponsors and approved on 15 November by a recorded vote of 48 to 42, with 54 abstentions.

In his 14 October report[5] regarding implementation of the Assembly's 1981 resolution on East Timor,[9] which had called on United Nations organizations to provide famine relief to the Territory, the Secretary-General informed the Assembly that the World Food Programme had received no request for assistance as at 2 March; the United Nations Children's Fund, on 8 June, had submitted information on relevant activities.

During its debate, the Fourth Committee heard the following petitioners:[6] Lord Avebury, Chairman, United Kingdom Parliamentary Human Rights Group; Michael A. Chamberlain, East Timor Human Rights Committee; Roger S. Clark, International League for Human Rights; Thomas Hammarberg, Amnesty International; J. A. Manusama; Gordon McIntosh, member of the Australian Senate Foreign Affairs and Defence Committee, but speaking as a private petitioner sponsored by the Human Rights Council of Australia and the Australian Council for Overseas Aid; José Ramos-Horta, FRETILIN; Susanne Roff, Minority Rights Group; Ernst Utrecht, Permanent People's Tribunal in Rome; and E. Gough Whitlam, former Prime Minister of Australia. Jacob Xavier, Movimento Nacional para a Libertação e Independência de Timor-Díli, although his request for a hearing had been granted, did not appear before the Committee.

The Chairman of the Fourth Committee received five letters from Indonesia in October and November[2] opposing the participation of these petitioners in the Committee's deliberations, and asserting that the colonial status of East Timor had been terminated with its integration into the Republic of Indonesia on 17 July 1976; consideration of the question by the Committee would, therefore, constitute interference in the internal affairs of a sovereign State.

Portugal, in a note verbale dated 26 February,[3] informed the Secretary-General that it had nothing to add to the information it had supplied in 1979 in compliance with its obligation under the Charter of the United Nations to provide information each year on colonial Territories under its administration.

In a note verbale of 7 October addressed to the Secretary-General,[1] Indonesia criticized a 1982 Secretariat working paper on East Timor as unbalanced, tendentious and based on unsubstantiated evidence. It objected to the impression created by the paper that the Territory was famine-stricken, subjected to major military operations against civilians and the scene of widespread human rights violations; and argued that, had these allegations been true, they would have been reported by the many United Nations and other agencies working in East Timor.

Explaining its vote against the Assembly resolution, Indonesia reiterated that the people of East Timor had completed the decolonization process by exercising their right to self-determination and choosing integration with Indonesia. It added that the number of countries supporting Indonesia on the question had shown a steady increase, that the large number of abstentions indicated that an overwhelming majority of States questioned the relevance of continued consideration of the item, and that the time had come to view East Timor on the basis of facts and realism rather than of baseless accusations and wishful thinking.

Also voting against the text, Australia said one could not ignore the reality that the Territory had become part of Indonesia and that the Timorese could better be served by donations of needed aid. Iraq voted against the draft because it mentioned resolutions which Iraq had not supported.

Among those abstaining, the Federal Republic of Germany and Italy considered it essential to promote a dialogue between the Indonesian Government and the other parties concerned in order to overcome the remaining obstacles; they saw as a positive element in the resolution the request for the use of the good offices of the Secretary-General. While agreeing with the latter point, Guatemala, which abstained in the Fourth Committee but voted against in the Assembly, observed that the veracity of the new facts presented to the Committee could not currently be ascertained. The United Kingdom, viewing the text as more constructive than in previous years, called on Indonesia and Portugal to settle the problem through diplomatic negotiations.

Portugal said it co-sponsored the resolution on the East Timor question for the first time because, having been unable to fulfil its functions as administering Power, it had to respond in that manner to the appeals made to it by the inhabitants of the Territory to safeguard their inalienable rights on moral and constitutional grounds; it hoped the text, calling for a peaceful and negotiated solution to the problem, would offer real possibilities for the people of East Timor to exercise freely the right to decide their own future.

Rwanda said its affirmative vote demonstrated its support for the principle of self-determination and its opposition to the policies of *fait accompli* and of might makes right. Vanuatu supported the resolution as a matter of conscience; if it did not protest Indonesia's actions in East Timor, it said, there would be no moral ground to condemn aggression by other States.

Letters and notes verbales (nv). Indonesia: [1]7 Oct., A/C.4/37/6 & Corr.1 *(nv)*; [2]14 Oct., A/C.4/37/8 & Add.1 (20 Oct.), 2 (28 Oct.), 3 (1 Nov.) & 4 (8 Nov.). [3]Portugal: 26 Feb., A/37/113 *(nv)*.
Reports. [4]Committee on colonial countries, A/37/23/Rev.1; [5]S-G, A/37/538.
Requests for hearing. [6]A/C.4/37/3 & Add.1-10.
Resolutions (1982). [7]GA: 37/30, 23 Nov., text following. [8]SCPDPM (report, E/CN.4/1983/4): 1982/20, 8 Sep.
Resolution (prior). [9]GA: 36/50, 24 Nov. 1981 (YUN 1981, p. 1185).
Meeting records. GA: General Committee, A/BUR/37/SR.2 (22 Sep.); plenary, A/37/PV.4, 77 (24 Sep., 23 Nov.); 4th Committee, A/C.4/37/SR.3, 5, 6, 8-11, 13-18, *19*, 20-22, *23* (15 Oct.–15 Nov.).

General Assembly resolution 37/30

23 November 1982   Meeting 77   50-46-50 (recorded vote)

Approved by Fourth Committee (A/37/623) by recorded vote (48-42-54), 15 November (meeting 23); 18-nation draft (A/C.4/37/L.8); agenda item 97.

Sponsors: Angola, Barbados, Belize, Benin, Brazil, Cape Verde, Grenada, Guinea-Bissau, Malawi, Mozambique, Nicaragua, Portugal, Sao Tome and Principe, Seychelles, Swaziland, Trinidad and Tobago, Vanuatu, Zimbabwe.

Question of East Timor

The General Assembly,

Recognizing the inalienable right of all peoples to self-determination and independence in accordance with the principles of the Charter of the United Nations, the Declaration on the Granting of Independence to Colonial Countries and Peoples, contained in its resolution 1514(XV) of 14 December 1960, and other relevant United Nations resolutions,

Having examined the chapter of the report of the Special Committee on the Situation with regard to the Implementation of the Declaration on the Granting of Independence to Colonial Countries and Peoples relating to East Timor and other relevant documents,

Taking note of the report of the Secretary-General on the question of East Timor,

Taking note of resolution 1982/20 adopted on 8 September 1982 by the Sub-Commission on Prevention of Discrimination and Protection of Minorities,

Having heard the statement of the representative of Portugal, as the administering Power,

Having heard the statement of the representative of Indonesia,

Having heard the statements of the representative of the Frente Revolucionária de Timor Leste Independente and of various petitioners, as well as of the representatives of non-governmental organizations,

Bearing in mind that Portugal, the administering Power, has stated its full and solemn commitment to uphold the right of the people of East Timor to self-determination and independence,

Bearing in mind also its resolutions 3485(XXX) of 12 December 1975, 31/53 of 1 December 1976, 32/34 of 28 November 1977, 33/39 of 13 December 1978, 34/40 of 21 November 1979, 35/27 of 11 November 1980 and 36/50 of 24 November 1981,

Concerned at the humanitarian situation prevailing in the Territory and believing that all efforts should be made by the international community to improve the living conditions of the people of East Timor and to guarantee to them the effective enjoyment of their fundamental human rights,

1. *Requests* the Secretary-General to initiate consultations with all parties directly concerned, with a view to exploring avenues for achieving a comprehensive settlement of the problem and to report thereon to the General Assembly at its thirty-eighth session;

2. *Requests* the Special Committee on the Situation with regard to the Implementation of the Declaration on the Granting of Independence to Colonial Countries and Peoples to keep the situation in the Territory under active consideration and to render all assistance to the Secretary-General with a view to facilitating the implementation of the present resolution;

3. *Calls upon* all specialized agencies and other organizations of the United Nations system, in particular the World Food Programme, the United Nations Children's Fund and the Office of the United Nations High Commissioner for Refugees, immediately to assist, within their respective fields of competence, the people of East Timor, in close consultation with Portugal, as the administering Power;

4. *Decides* to include in the provisional agenda of its thirty-eighth session the item entitled "Question of East Timor".

Recorded vote in Assembly as follows:

In favour: Afghanistan, Albania, Algeria, Angola, Barbados, Belize, Benin, Brazil, Burundi, Byelorussian SSR, Cape Verde, China, Congo, Cuba, Cyprus, Democratic Yemen, Ethiopia, Ghana, Greece, Grenada, Guinea-Bissau, Guyana, Iceland, Ireland, Kenya, Lao People's Democratic Republic, Lesotho, Madagascar, Malawi, Mali, Mauritius, Mexico, Mozambique, Nicaragua, Portugal, Rwanda, Sao Tome and Principe, Seychelles, Sierra Leone, Swaziland, Togo, Trinidad and Tobago, Uganda, Ukrainian SSR, USSR, United Republic of Tanzania, Vanuatu, Viet Nam, Zambia, Zimbabwe.

Against: Antigua and Barbuda, Argentina, Australia, Bahrain, Bangladesh, Canada, Chad, Chile, Democratic Kampuchea, Egypt, El Salvador, Fiji, Gambia, Guatemala, Honduras, India, Indonesia, Iraq, Japan, Jordan, Kuwait, Liberia, Malaysia, Maldives, Morocco, New Zealand, Oman, Pakistan, Papua New Guinea, Paraguay, Philippines, Qatar, Saint Lucia, Saudi Arabia, Singapore, Solomon Islands, Sudan, Suriname, Syrian Arab Republic, Thailand, Tunisia, Turkey, United Arab Emirates, United States, Uruguay, Yemen.

Abstaining: Austria, Bahamas, Belgium, Bhutan, Bolivia, Botswana, Burma, Central African Republic, Colombia, Costa Rica, Czechoslovakia, Denmark, Dominica, Dominican Republic, Ecuador, Finland, France, Gabon, Germany, Federal Republic of, Guinea, Haiti, Hungary, Israel, Italy, Ivory Coast, Jamaica, Lebanon, Luxembourg, Mauritania, Nepal, Netherlands, Niger, Nigeria, Norway, Panama, Peru, Poland, Romania, Samoa, Senegal, Somalia, Spain, Sri Lanka, Sweden, United Kingdom, United Republic of Cameroon, Upper Volta, Venezuela, Yugoslavia, Zaire.

Western Sahara question

The General Assembly, in November 1982, reaffirmed its intention to co-operate with the Organization of African Unity (OAU) in organizing a referendum on self-determination for the people of Western Sahara and appealed to Morocco and Frente Popular para la Liberación de Saguia el-Hamra y de Río de Oro (Frente POLISARIO) to negotiate a cease-fire. The Secretary-General reported to the Assembly that no decision had been reached on the United Nations role in the conduct of the referendum. Morocco opposed a role for the Organization and also objected to a decision by OAU to seat at one of its meetings in February the Saharan Arab Democratic Republic, established in 1976 and backed by POLISARIO.

Co-operation with OAU. In November 1982, the Secretary-General submitted to the General Assembly a report on Western Sahara,[12] pursuant to the Assembly's 1981 resolution[17] and decision[4] requesting him to co-operate with OAU in organizing a referendum in the Territory. He informed the Assembly that a United Nations team had travelled to Nairobi, Kenya, in early February 1982 at the invitation of the OAU Secretary-General, for consultations with the OAU Ministerial Consultative Committee on technical questions relating to the proposed cease-fire and referendum. That Committee, composed of the Ministers for Foreign Affairs of Guinea, Kenya, Mali, Nigeria, Sierra Leone, the Sudan and the United Republic of Tanzania, met on 6 and 7 February to discuss these issues as well as the role of the United Nations in the process.

The Consultative Committee referred three documents to the OAU Implementation Committee on Western Sahara, which met at Nairobi on 8 and 9 February and took decisions on two of them, leaving undecided the question of the United Nations role. By the first of these, a cease-fire would come into force on a date to be fixed by the Implementation Committee after consultation with the parties concerned, a peace-keeping force would be stationed in the Territory, and troops would be withdrawn and prisoners of war exchanged. By the second, an Interim Administration would be set up to organize the referendum and a Commissioner would be appointed to carry out the preparatory work for it.

By a letter dated 23 February to the Secretary-General,[7] Morocco transmitted the texts of three letters it had sent that day to OAU officials, protesting the OAU recognition of the Saharan Arab Democratic Republic as that body's new member. By the first, addressed to the OAU Chairman, King Hassan II called a fatal blow to the credibility of OAU its decision allowing participation of that so-called Republic as a constituent member in the thirty-eighth session of the Council of Ministers being held at Addis Ababa, Ethiopia. In a letter to the OAU Secretary-General, the King described as an abuse of power the recognition given by one of the administrative units of OAU to that so-called Republic as a new member and asked that the measure be revoked. Morocco's Minister of State for Foreign Affairs, in a letter to the Chairman of the OAU Council of Ministers,

said that the decision was contrary to agreements reached at earlier OAU meetings, that it was a violation of the OAU Charter and that Morocco therefore considered it null and void.

In a letter dated 3 March,[8] Morocco informed the United Nations Secretary-General that 19 States (Central African Republic, Comoros, Djibouti, Equatorial Guinea, Gabon, Gambia, Guinea, Ivory Coast, Liberia, Mauritius, Morocco, Niger, Senegal, Somalia, Sudan, Tunisia, United Republic of Cameroon, Upper Volta, Zaire) had withdrawn in protest from the February OAU meeting at Addis Ababa. Appended to the letter was the text of a message from the Secretary for Foreign Affairs of Zaire, on behalf of the 19 States, to the Chairman of that meeting protesting that the Council had continued its work in the absence of a quorum and saying that the decisions taken were considered null and void. In a note verbale dated 1 April,[10] the United Republic of Cameroon transmitted to the United Nations Secretariat a statement saying that the Assembly of Heads of State and Government, the highest body of OAU, had the exclusive competence to decide on the question of admission of the Saharan Arab Democratic Republic.

Morocco, by a letter dated 4 November,[9] transmitted to the Secretary-General a note charging that the OAU Secretary-General had taken it upon himself to invite the so-called Republic to participate as a member State in the February meeting, and then omitted transmitting to the United Nations Secretariat the text of the decision of the Implementation Committee concerning a referendum in Western Sahara, in order to sabotage the Committee's action. However, a 4 November addendum to the Secretary-General's report on Western Sahara carried the text of that decision as transmitted to the United Nations on 2 November by the OAU Executive Secretary.

Action by the Commission on Human Rights. By a resolution of 25 February on the right of peoples to self-determination and its application to peoples under colonial or alien domination or foreign occupation,[14] the Commission on Human Rights welcomed OAU and United Nations decisions to organize a referendum in Western Sahara and urged Morocco and POLISARIO to negotiate a cease-fire.

Action by the Committee on colonial countries. The question of Western Sahara was considered by the Committee on colonial countries on 1 July and 20 August.[11] At its August meeting, it heard statements by Cuba, Iran, Nicaragua and Zimbabwe and by a representative of POLISARIO before deciding, without objection, to continue consideration of the question in 1983, subject to any directives of the General Assembly.

General Assembly action. On 23 November 1982,[15] the General Assembly reaffirmed the right of the people of Western Sahara to self-determination and independence and welcomed the OAU efforts to promote a just and definitive solution to the question. The Assembly expressed its conviction that only negotiation between Morocco and POLISARIO could guarantee the fair conduct of a referendum on self-determination in the Territory and appealed to these two parties to negotiate a cease-fire.

Reaffirming the United Nations determination to co-operate with OAU in organizing the referendum, the Assembly requested the Secretary-General to ensure effective participation of the United Nations in that endeavour and to report to the Assembly and the Security Council on the subject and on the measures requiring a Council decision. The Secretary-General was urged to co-operate with the OAU Secretary-General in implementing the pertinent OAU decisions and the 1982 Assembly resolution. The Assembly requested the Committee on colonial countries to give priority to the Western Sahara question and to report in 1983.

The Assembly adopted the resolution, by a recorded vote of 78 to 15, with 50 abstentions, on the recommendation of the Fourth Committee, which had approved the text on 12 November by a recorded vote of 74 to 12, with 55 abstentions. The draft was introduced by Mexico and sponsored by 37 States.

Also on 23 November, the Assembly, by a decision[3] adopted without vote, requested the Secretary-General to assist the OAU Implementation Committee in the discharge of its mandate on Western Sahara and to report to the Assembly and the Security Council as appropriate.

Introduced by Kenya as current OAU Chairman, the draft decision had been approved by the Fourth Committee without objection on 12 November, when an earlier text was withdrawn. The 14-nation draft,[5] introduced by Senegal, was essentially the same in content as the Kenyan text, except that the former specified the role of the Implementation Committee as that of monitoring the establishment of a cease-fire and the organization of a referendum. As the 14-nation text was withdrawn, no action was taken on the proposed amendments thereto by 16 States (to specify the referendum as that on self-determination for the people of Western Sahara, and to add reference to the statements made by POLISARIO),[2] on a revision by the original 14 States (to add reference to the decisions adopted by the Implementation Committee at Nairobi in August 1981 and February 1982),[6] and on further amendments proposed by 24 States (to add reference to statements made by POLISARIO, and to specify the task of the Implementation Committee as that of organizing and conducting a referendum on self-determination).[1]

In a related action, the Assembly, in its 3 December resolution on the self-determination of peoples,[16] noted with satisfaction the OAU resolution establishing the Implementation Committee and the decisions of the Committee to conduct a referendum in Western Sahara, and welcomed the willingness of the United Nations to collaborate with OAU in the process.

Morocco, which voted against the resolution of 23 November, said the United Nations initiatives could only be detrimental to the process of peaceful settlement being pursued by OAU. The wording of the resolution whose sponsors included Algeria, Morocco said, was not consistent with the African consensus as it prejudged who was to benefit from the referendum, and paragraphs 3 and 4, calling for a cease-fire to be negotiated between Morocco and the POLISARIO, violated the OAU decisions by imposing conditions which its Implementation Committee had never endorsed. Chile also cast a negative vote, stating that the draft was not in line with the OAU appeal to the parties concerned and that the solution to the dispute lay in the self-determination of the people of Western Sahara.

Austria, which abstained in the Committee, but voted in favour in the Assembly, said it supported the OAU efforts and felt that a peaceful settlement could be brought about only through negotiations involving all parties concerned.

Among others abstaining, Jordan said that in the Western Sahara question the principle of self-determination was being abused while well-defined national interests were at play, undermining the very existence of OAU. The role of the United Nations was to create a climate conducive to the cessation of hostilities, Maldives commented, and the draft was unlikely to serve that purpose. Norway did not want adoption of a text that might impair the peace process envisaged by OAU. Somalia thought it preferable to leave it to the OAU Implementation Committee to continue the process that had been started. The Sudan said it had abstained in order to remain impartial as a member of the Implementation Committee.

Argentina and Fiji voted in favour of the resolution and joined the consensus on the decision because they backed OAU efforts in support of self-determination for the people of Western Sahara. Finland and Sweden also supported both texts, although they would have preferred to vote on one text rather than two; Finland did not believe the resolution reflected the OAU spirit of Nairobi, and Sweden regretted that it did not reflect in detail some important elements of the OAU decisions.

Supporting the consensus decision, Denmark, on behalf of the members of the European Community (EC), pointed out that EC had welcomed the OAU decision to seek a referendum in Western

Sahara because it paved the way for a peaceful solution. Somalia welcomed the consensus decision.

During its debate, the Fourth Committee granted a request for a hearing by a petitioner from POLISARIO,[13] having heard Morocco object on the ground that OAU had already found a process for settlement of the question which was no longer one of decolonization. The POLISARIO representative told the Committee that, despite Morocco's attempt to annex the Territory with the support of the United States, the Saharan Arab Democratic Republic exercised effective sovereignty over virtually all of Western Sahara, that its admission to OAU testified to its support among a majority of African nations and that he welcomed United Nations consideration of what he called a purely colonial question.

Amendments not acted upon. [1]Afghanistan, Algeria, Angola, Benin, Burundi, Cape Verde, Congo, Cuba, Cyprus, Democratic Yemen, Guinea-Bissau, Iran, Lao People's Democratic Republic, Madagascar, Mali, Mauritania, Mauritius, Mozambique, Nicaragua, Rwanda, Sao Tome and Principe, Vanuatu, Viet Nam, Zimbabwe, A/C.4/37/L.13 (to 14-nation revised draft, A/C.4/37/L.5/Rev.1); [2]Algeria, Benin, Burundi, Cape Verde, Cuba, Cyprus, Democratic Yemen, Guinea-Bissau, Madagascar, Mauritania, Mauritius, Mozambique, Nicaragua, Rwanda, Sao Tome and Principe, Zimbabwe, A/C.4/37/L.12 (to 14-nation draft, A/C.4/37/L.5).
Decision (1982). [3]GA: 37/411, 23 Nov., text following.
Decision (prior). [4]GA: 36/406, 24 Nov. 1981 (YUN 1981, p. 1197).
Draft decisions withdrawn. Chad, Comoros, Equatorial Guinea, Gabon, Gambia, Guinea, Ivory Coast, Liberia, Morocco, Niger, Senegal, United Republic of Cameroon, Upper Volta, Zaire, [5]A/C.4/37/L.5, [6]A/C.4/37/L.5/Rev.1.
Letters and note verbale (nv). Morocco: [7]23 Feb., A/37/99; [8]3 Mar., A/37/107; [9]4 Nov., A/37/602. [10]United Republic of Cameroon: 1 Apr., A/37/167 *(nv).*
Reports. [11]Committee on colonial countries, A/37/23/Rev.1; [12]S-G, A/37/570/Rev.2 & Rev.2/Corr.1.
Requests for hearing. [13]A/C.4/37/2 & Add.1 & Add.1/Corr.1.
Resolutions (1982). [14]Commission on Human Rights (report, E/1982/12): 1982/15, 25 Feb. GA: [15]37/28, 23 Nov., text following; [16]37/43, para. 4, 3 Dec.
Resolution (prior). [17]GA: 36/46, 24 Nov. 1981 (YUN 1981, p. 1196).
Financial implications. 5th Committee report, A/37/637; S-G statements, A/C.4/37/L.9, A/C.5/37/46.
Meeting records. GA: 4th Committee, A/C.4/37/SR.3, 9-15, *17*, 18, *19, 20*, 21, *22*, 23 (15 Oct.–15 Nov.); 5th Committee, A/C.5/37/SR.41 (22 Nov.); plenary, A/37/PV.74-76, 77 (22, 23 Nov.).

General Assembly resolution 37/28

23 November 1982   Meeting 77   78-15-50 (recorded vote)

Approved by Fourth Committee (A/37/621) by recorded vote (74-12-55), 12 November (meeting 22); 37-nation draft (A/C.4/37/L.6/Rev.1); agenda item 18.

Sponsors: Afghanistan, Algeria, Angola, Belize, Benin, Botswana, Burundi, Cape Verde, Congo, Cuba, Cyprus, Democratic Yemen, Ethiopia, Grenada, Guinea-Bissau, Guyana, Iran, Jamaica, Lao People's Democratic Republic, Lesotho, Libyan Arab Jamahiriya, Madagascar, Mali, Mauritania, Mexico, Mozambique, Nicaragua, Panama, Rwanda, Sao Tome and Principe, Seychelles, Uganda, Vanuatu, Viet Nam, Yugoslavia, Zambia, Zimbabwe.

Question of Western Sahara

The General Assembly,

Having considered in depth the question of Western Sahara,

Recalling the inalienable right of all peoples to self-determination and independence in accordance with the principles set forth in the Charter of the United Nations and in General Assembly resolution 1514(XV) of 14 December 1960, containing the Declaration on the Granting of Independence to Colonial Countries and Peoples,

Recalling its resolutions 35/19 of 11 November 1980 and 36/46 of 24 November 1981 on the question of Western Sahara,

Having considered the relevant chapter of the report of the Special Committee on the Situation with regard to the Implementation of the Declaration on the Granting of Independence to Colonial Countries and Peoples,

Having heard the statements made on the question of Western Sahara, in particular the statement of the representative of the Frente Popular para la Liberación de Saguia el-Hamra y de Río de Oro,

Recalling its resolution 36/80 of 9 December 1981 on co-operation between the United Nations and the Organization of African Unity,

Recalling all the decisions of the Organization of African Unity on the question of Western Sahara,

Recalling also the decision of the Assembly of Heads of State and Government of the Organization of African Unity at its eighteenth ordinary session, held at Nairobi from 24 to 27 June 1981, to organize throughout the Territory of Western Sahara a general and free referendum on self-determination,

Taking note of the various decisions adopted by the Implementation Committee on Western Sahara of the Organization of African Unity concerning the establishment of appropriate machinery to enable the people of Western Sahara to express themselves freely and democratically on their future,

1. *Reaffirms* the inalienable right of the people of Western Sahara to self-determination and independence in accordance with the Charter of the United Nations, the Charter of the Organization of African Unity and the objectives of General Assembly resolution 1514(XV), as well as with the relevant resolutions of the Assembly and the Organization of African Unity;

2. *Welcomes* the efforts of the Organization of African Unity with a view to promoting a just and definitive solution to the question of Western Sahara;

3. *Remains convinced* that only negotiation between Morocco and the Frente Popular para la Liberación de Saguia el-Hamra y de Río de Oro could create the objective conditions for the return of peace in north-west Africa and would guarantee the fair conduct of a general, free and orderly referendum on self-determination in Western Sahara;

4. *Appeals,* to that end, to the two parties to the dispute, Morocco and the Frente Popular para la Liberación de Saguia el-Hamra y de Río de Oro, to enter into negotiations with a view to achieving a cease-fire in accordance with General Assembly resolution 36/46 and the decisions of the Organization of African Unity;

5. *Reaffirms* the determination of the United Nations to co-operate fully with the Organization of African Unity in the fair and impartial organization of the referendum;

6. *Requests,* to that end, the Secretary-General to take the necessary steps to ensure that the United Nations participates effectively in the organization and conduct of the referendum and to report to the General Assembly and the Security Council on this subject and on the measures requiring a decision by the Council;

7. *Urges* the Secretary-General to co-operate closely with the Secretary-General of the Organization of African Unity with a view to the implementation of the pertinent decisions of the Organization of African Unity and of the present resolution;

8. *Requests* the Special Committee on the Situation with regard to the Implementation of the Declaration on the Granting of Independence to Colonial Countries and Peoples to continue to consider the situation in Western Sahara as a matter of priority and to report thereon to the General Assembly at its thirty-eighth session.

Recorded vote in Assembly as follows:

In favour: Afghanistan, Albania, Algeria, Angola, Antigua and Barbuda, Argentina, Australia, Austria, Bahamas, Barbados, Belize, Benin, Bhutan, Bolivia, Botswana, Brazil, Bulgaria, Burundi, Byelorussian SSR, Cape Verde, Colombia, Congo, Costa Rica, Cuba, Cyprus, Czechoslovakia, Democratic Yemen, Dominica, Ecuador, Ethiopia, Fiji, Finland, German Democratic Republic, Ghana, Greece, Grenada, Guinea-Bissau, Guyana, Hungary, India, Iran, Jamaica, Lao People's Democratic Republic, Lesotho, Libyan Arab Jamahiriya, Madagascar, Mali, Malta, Mauritania, Mauritius, Mexico, Mongolia, Mozambique, Nicaragua, Panama, Peru, Poland, Rwanda, Saint Lucia, Sao Tome and Principe, Seychelles, Sierra Leone, Sri Lanka, Suriname, Swaziland, Sweden, Syrian Arab Republic, Trinidad and Tobago, Uganda, Ukrainian SSR, USSR, United Republic of Tanzania, Vanuatu, Venezuela, Viet Nam, Yugoslavia, Zambia, Zimbabwe.

General Assembly decision 37/411

Adopted without vote

Approved by Fourth Committee (A/37/621) without objection, 12 November (meeting 22); draft by Kenya (A/C.4/37/L.14); agenda item 18.

Question of Western Sahara

At its 77th plenary meeting, on 23 November 1982, the General Assembly, on the recommendation of the Fourth Committee, recalling its decision 36/406 of 24 November 1981 and taking into account the resolution adopted by the Assembly of Heads of State and Government of the Organization of African Unity at its eighteenth ordinary session, held at Nairobi from 24 to 27 June 1981, by which it decided, *inter alia,* to establish an Implementation Committee on Western Sahara, as well as the decisions adopted by the Implementation Committee, decided to request the Secretary-General to give assistance, in consultation and co-operation with the Organization of African Unity, to the Implementation Committee in the discharge of its mandate relating to the question of Western Sahara arising from the above-mentioned resolution and decisions and to report thereon to the General Assembly and the Security Council, as appropriate.

Other Territories

American Samoa

On 23 November 1982, the General Assembly adopted without vote a resolution[(2)] by which it reaffirmed the inalienable right of American Samoans to self-determination and independence, and called on the United States, as the administering Power, to keep the people fully informed of that right and to expedite the process of decolonization of the Territory.

Reaffirming the responsibility of the administering Power for the economic and social development of the Territory, the Assembly asked it to continue to help strengthen and diversify the Samoan economy in order that the Territory might achieve self-sufficiency. The Assembly also recommended changes in the Territory's judicial system, urged closer relations with neighbouring communities in order to enhance economic welfare, and called for the safeguarding of the Territory's natural resources. In so doing, the Assembly approved the relevant chapter of the report of the Committee on colonial countries, requested the Committee to continue to examine the question and to report in 1983, and decided to keep under review the possibility of sending a visiting mission to the Territory.

The resolution was approved without objection by the Fourth Committee on 15 November. The draft originated in the Committee on colonial countries, which had approved it on 16 September, following its approval on 5 August of the conclusions and recommendations of its Sub-Committee on Small Territories.[(1)]

Report. [(1)]Committee on colonial countries, A/37/23/Rev.1.
Resolution (1982). [(2)]GA: 37/20, 23 Nov., text following.
Meeting records. GA: 4th Committee, A/C.4/37/SR.9-15, 17-22, *23* (26 Oct.–15 Nov.); plenary, A/37/PV.74-76, *77* (22, 23 Nov.).

General Assembly resolution 37/20

23 November 1982   Meeting 77   Adopted without vote

Approved by Fourth Committee (A/37/621) without objection, 15 November (meeting 23); draft by Committee on colonial countries (A/37/23/Rev.1); agenda item 18.

Question of American Samoa

The General Assembly,

Having considered the question of American Samoa,

Having examined the relevant chapters of the report of the Special Committee on the Situation with regard to the Implementation of the Declaration on the Granting of Independence to Colonial Countries and Peoples,

Recalling its resolution 1514(XV) of 14 December 1960, containing the Declaration on the Granting of Independence to Colonial Countries and Peoples, and all other resolutions and decisions of the United Nations relating to American Samoa,

Taking into account the statement of the representative of the administering Power,

Conscious of the need to promote progress towards the full implementation of the Declaration in respect of American Samoa,

Noting with appreciation the continued active participation of the administering Power in the work of the Special Committee in regard to American Samoa, thereby enabling it to conduct a more informed and meaningful examination of the situation in the Territory, with a view to accelerating the process of decolonization for the purpose of the full implementation of the Declaration,

Considering that it remains the obligation of the administering Power to carry out a thorough programme of political education so as to ensure that the people of American Samoa are made fully aware of their inalienable right to self-determination and independence in accordance with General Assembly resolution 1514(XV),

Noting with interest that the Office of Economic Development and Planning of the Government of American Samoa is now implementing a five-year economic development plan, focusing on economic diversification, land use, housing, banking and tourism, for the benefit of the people of the Territory,

Aware of the special circumstances of the geographical location and economic conditions of American Samoa and stressing the necessity of diversifying the economy of the Territory as a matter of priority in order to reduce its dependence on fluctuating economic activities,

Mindful that United Nations visiting missions provide an effective means of ascertaining the situation in the small Territories and expressing its satisfaction at the willingness of the administering Power to receive visiting missions in the Territories under its administration,

Welcoming the fact that American Samoa was the host for the 1982 South Pacific Conference of the South Pacific Commission,

1. *Approves* the chapter of the report of the Special Committee on the Situation with regard to the Implementation of the Declaration on the Granting of Independence to Colonial Countries and Peoples relating to American Samoa;

2. *Reaffirms* the inalienable right of the people of American Samoa to self-determination and independence in conformity with the Declaration on the Granting of Independence to Colonial Countries and Peoples, contained in General Assembly resolution 1514(XV);

3. *Reiterates* the view that such factors as territorial size, geographical location, size of population and limited natural resources should in no way delay the speedy implementation of the Declaration contained in General Assembly resolution 1514(XV), which fully applies to American Samoa;

4. *Calls upon* the Government of the United States of America, as the administering Power, to take all necessary steps, taking into

account the freely expressed wishes of the people of American Samoa, to expedite the process of decolonization of the Territory in accordance with the relevant provisions of the Charter of the United Nations and the Declaration;

5. *Reaffirms* that it is the responsibility of the administering Power to ensure that the people of American Samoa are kept fully informed of their inalienable right to self-determination and independence in accordance with General Assembly resolution 1514(XV);

6. *Recommends* that, in accordance with the wishes of the people of American Samoa, the Chief Justice and Associate Justices should be appointed by the Governor and approved by the Legislature, a procedure now facilitated by the growing number of American Samoans who are qualified lawyers, and that the recommendation of the second temporary Political Status Commission for a change in the judicial system should be acted upon;

7. *Reaffirms* the responsibility of the administering Power, under the Charter, for the economic and social development of the Territory;

8. *Calls upon* the administering Power, in co-operation with the territorial Government and within the framework of the five-year economic development plan, to continue to help to strengthen and diversify the economy of the Territory in order to achieve self-sufficiency;

9. *Urges* the administering Power to continue to facilitate close relations and co-operation between the people of the Territory and the neighbouring island communities and the regional institutions in order to enhance further their economic welfare;

10. *Urges* the administering Power, in co-operation with the freely elected representatives of American Samoa, to safeguard the inalienable right of the people of the Territory to the enjoyment of their natural resources by taking effective measures to ensure their right to own and dispose of those resources and to establish and maintain control of their future development;

11. *Considers* that the possibility of sending a further visiting mission to American Samoa at an appropriate time should be kept under review;

12. *Requests* the Special Committee to continue the examination of this question at its next session, including the possible dispatch of a further visiting mission to American Samoa at an appropriate time and in consultation with the administering Power, and to report thereon to the General Assembly at its thirty-eighth session.

Anguilla

The Committee on colonial countries decided without objection on 20 August 1982 to consider the question of Anguilla at its 1983 session, subject to any directives by the General Assembly.[2] On the recommendation of the Fourth Committee, as orally proposed by its Chairman and approved without vote on 15 November, the Assembly decided without vote on 23 November[1] to defer consideration of the question until 1983.

Decision (1982). [1]GA: 37/419, 23 Nov., text following.
Report. [2]Committee on colonial countries, A/37/23/Rev.1.
Meeting records. GA: 4th Committee, A/C.4/37/SR.9-15, 17-22, *23* (26 Oct.–15 Nov.); plenary, A/37/PV.74-76, *77* (22, 23 Nov.).

General Assembly decision 37/419

Adopted without vote

Approved by Fourth Committee (A/37/621) without vote, 15 November (meeting 23); oral proposal by Chairman; agenda item 18.

Question of Anguilla

At its 77th plenary meeting, on 23 November 1982, the General Assembly, on the recommendation of the Fourth Committee, decided to defer until its thirty-eighth session consideration of the question of Anguilla.

Bermuda

The General Assembly reaffirmed the inalienable right of the people of Bermuda to self-determination and independence on 23 November 1982, when it

adopted without vote a resolution[2] stating that it was ultimately for Bermudians themselves to decide their future political status. By so doing, it reiterated that the administering Power, the United Kingdom, should foster an awareness among Bermudians of the possibilities open to them in the exercise of that right.

The Assembly called on the administering Power to receive a visiting mission in the Territory, and urged it to comply with United Nations resolutions relating to military bases in colonial Territories and to guarantee the right of Bermudians to dispose of their natural resources. It reaffirmed the need to foster national unity and a national identity, welcomed the local authorities' efforts to establish a human rights commission and called for greater localization of the public service. Urging diversification of the economy, the Assembly called on United Nations organizations to pay special attention to Bermuda's development needs, and requested the Committee on colonial countries to continue examining the situation in the Territory and to report in 1983.

The resolution was approved without objection by the Fourth Committee on 15 November. The draft originated in the Committee on colonial countries which approved it on 16 September, based on the report of its Sub-Committee on Small Territories which the Committee adopted on 5 August.[1]

Report. [1]Committee on colonial countries, A/37/23/Rev.1.
Resolution (1982). [2]GA: 37/22, 23 Nov., text following.
Meeting records. GA: 4th Committee, A/C.4/37/SR.9-15, 17-22, *23* (26 Oct.–15 Nov.); plenary, A/37/PV.74-76, *77* (22, 23 Nov.).

General Assembly resolution 37/22

23 November 1982   Meeting 77   Adopted without vote

Approved by Fourth Committee (A/37/621) without objection, 15 November (meeting 23); draft by Committee on colonial countries (A/37/23/Rev.1); agenda item 18.

Question of Bermuda

The General Assembly,

Having considered the question of Bermuda,

Having examined the relevant chapters of the report of the Special Committee on the Situation with regard to the Implementation of the Declaration on the Granting of Independence to Colonial Countries and Peoples,

Recalling its resolution 1514(XV) of 14 December 1960, containing the Declaration on the Granting of Independence to Colonial Countries and Peoples, and all other resolutions and decisions of the United Nations relating to Bermuda,

Taking into account the statement of the representative of the administering Power, in which he said that his Government would fully respect the wishes of the people of Bermuda in determining the future constitutional status of the Territory,

Conscious of the need to ensure the full and speedy implementation of the Declaration in respect of the Territory,

Noting with appreciation the continued active participation of the administering Power in the work of the Special Committee in regard to Bermuda, thereby enabling it to conduct a more informed and meaningful examination of the situation in the Territory, with a view to accelerating the process of decolonization for the purpose of the full implementation of the Declaration,

Recalling all relevant resolutions of the United Nations relating to military bases and installations in colonial and Non-Self-Governing Territories,

Noting that the economy of the Territory continues to depend heavily on tourism and international company business,

Aware of the special circumstances of the geographical location and economic conditions of the Territory and bearing in mind the necessity of diversifying and strengthening further its economy as a matter of priority in order to promote economic stability,

Mindful that United Nations visiting missions provide an effective means of ascertaining the situation in the small Territories, acquiring adequate first-hand information on the situation prevailing in those Territories and ascertaining the views of the peoples concerning their future political status,

1. *Approves* the chapter of the report of the Special Committee on the Situation with regard to the Implementation of the Declaration on the Granting of Independence to Colonial Countries and Peoples relating to Bermuda;

2. *Reaffirms* the inalienable right of the people of Bermuda to self-determination and independence in conformity with the Declaration on the Granting of Independence to Colonial Countries and Peoples, contained in General Assembly resolution 1514(XV);

3. *Reiterates* the view that such factors as territorial size, geographical location, size of population and limited natural resources should in no way delay the speedy exercise by the people of the Territory of their inalienable right as set out in the Declaration contained in General Assembly resolution 1514(XV), which fully applies to Bermuda;

4. *Urges* the administering Power, taking into account the freely expressed will and desire of the people of Bermuda, to continue to take all necessary steps to ensure the full and speedy implementation of General Assembly resolution 1514(XV);

5. *Reiterates* that it is the obligation of the administering Power to create such conditions in the Territory as will enable the people of Bermuda to exercise freely and without interference their inalienable right to self-determination and independence in accordance with General Assembly resolution 1514(XV) and, in that connection, reaffirms the importance of fostering an awareness among the people of Bermuda of the possibilities open to them in the exercise of that right;

6. *Reaffirms* that, in accordance with the relevant provisions of the Charter of the United Nations and the Declaration contained in General Assembly resolution 1514(XV), it is ultimately for the people of Bermuda themselves to decide on their future political status;

7. *Reaffirms* the importance of the need to foster national unity and a national identity and, in that regard, welcomes the steps taken by the local authorities towards the establishment of a human rights commission;

8. *Reaffirms its strong conviction* that the administering Power must ensure that military bases and installations do not hinder the population of the Territory from exercising its right to self-determination and independence in conformity with the purposes and principles of the Charter and urges the administering Power to take all necessary measures to comply fully with the relevant resolutions of the United Nations relating to military bases and installations in colonial and Non-Self-Governing Territories;

9. *Urges once again* the administering Power, in co-operation with the territorial Government, to continue to take all effective measures to guarantee the right of the people of Bermuda to own and dispose of their natural resources and to establish and maintain control of their future development;

10. *Strongly urges* the administering Power, in consultation with the Government of Bermuda, to make every effort to diversify the economy of Bermuda, including increased efforts to promote agriculture and fisheries;

11. *Welcomes* the role being played in the Territory by the United Nations Development Programme and the Food and Agriculture Organization of the United Nations, specifically in programmes of agriculture and fisheries, and urges the specialized agencies and all other organizations of the United Nations system to continue to pay special attention to the development needs of Bermuda;

12. *Reiterates its call* upon the administering Power, in co-operation with the local authorities, to continue to expedite the process of "bermudianization" in the Territory and, in that connection, urges that particular attention be paid to greater localization of the public service;

13. *Calls upon* the Government of the United Kingdom of Great Britain and Northern Ireland to receive a visiting mission in the Territory at an appropriate time;

14. *Requests* the Special Committee to continue the examination of this question at its next session, including the possible dispatch of

a visiting mission to Bermuda at an appropriate time and in consultation with the administering Power, and to report thereon to the General Assembly at its thirty-eighth session.

British Virgin Islands

The General Assembly adopted without vote on 23 November 1982 a resolution[2] reaffirming the inalienable right of the people of the British Virgin Islands to self-determination and independence. It stressed the importance of fostering an awareness among the people of the Territory of the possibilities open to them in the exercise of that right and stated that it was ultimately for them to decide their future political status.

The Assembly called on the United Kingdom, as the administering Power, to safeguard the right of the people to own and dispose of the Territory's natural resources and to intensify efforts at economic diversification. Further, it urged United Nations organizations to accelerate progress in the Territory's social and economic sectors, decided to keep under review the possibility of sending a visiting mission to the Territory, and requested the Committee on colonial countries to continue examining the situation there and to report in 1983.

The Fourth Committee approved the text without objection on 15 November. The draft originated in the Committee on colonial countries which approved it on 16 September, based on the report of its Sub-Committee on Small Territories which the Committee adopted on 28 June.[1]

Report. [1]Committee on colonial countries, A/37/23/Rev.1. *Resolution (1982).* [2]GA: 37/23, 23 Nov., text following.
Meeting records. GA: 4th Committee, A/C.4/37/SR.9-15, 17-22, 23 (26 Oct.–15 Nov.); plenary, A/37/PV.74-76, 77 (22, 23 Nov.).

General Assembly resolution 37/23

23 November 1982   Meeting 77   Adopted without vote

Approved by Fourth Committee (A/37/621) without objection, 15 November (meeting 23); draft by Committee on colonial countries (A/37/23/Rev.1); agenda item 18.

Question of the British Virgin Islands

The General Assembly,

Having considered the question of the British Virgin Islands,

Having examined the relevant chapters of the report of the Special Committee on the Situation with regard to the Implementation of the Declaration on the Granting of Independence to Colonial Countries and Peoples,

Recalling its resolution 1514(XV) of 14 December 1960, containing the Declaration on the Granting of Independence to Colonial Countries and Peoples, and all other resolutions and decisions of the United Nations relating to the British Virgin Islands,

Taking into account the statement of the representative of the administering Power, in which he said that his Government would fully respect the wishes of the people of the British Virgin Islands in determining the future political status of the Territory,

Conscious of the need to ensure the full and speedy implementation of the Declaration in respect of the Territory,

Noting with appreciation the continued active participation of the administering Power in the work of the Special Committee in regard to the British Virgin Islands, thereby enabling it to conduct a more informed and meaningful examination of the situation in the Territory, with a view to accelerating the process of decolonization for the purpose of the full implementation of the Declaration,

Reaffirming the responsibility of the administering Power for the economic and social development of the Territory,

Taking note of the fact that positive economic developments have occurred during the period under review, including the achievement of a sustained growth in the tourist, real estate and construction industries,

Aware of the special circumstances of the geographical location and economic conditions of the Territory and bearing in mind the necessity of diversifying and strengthening further its economy as a matter of priority in order to promote economic stability,

Noting that the United Nations Development Programme has made budgetary provisions for the Territory amounting to $240,000 for the period 1982-1986,

Mindful that United Nations visiting missions provide an effective means of ascertaining the situation in the small Territories and expressing its satisfaction at the willingness of the administering Power to receive visiting missions in the Territories under its administration,

1. *Approves* the chapter of the report of the Special Committee on the Situation with regard to the Implementation of the Declaration on the Granting of Independence to Colonial Countries and Peoples relating to the British Virgin Islands;

2. *Reaffirms* the inalienable right of the people of the British Virgin Islands to self-determination and independence in conformity with the Declaration on the Granting of Independence to Colonial Countries and Peoples, contained in General Assembly resolution 1514(XV);

3. *Reiterates* the view that such factors as territorial size, geographical location, size of population and limited natural resources should in no way delay the speedy implementation of the Declaration contained in General Assembly resolution 1514(XV), which fully applies to the British Virgin Islands;

4. *Reiterates* that it is the responsibility of the administering Power to create such conditions in the Territory as will enable the people of the British Virgin Islands to exercise freely and without interference their inalienable right to self-determination in accordance with General Assembly resolution 1514(XV), as well as all other relevant resolutions of the Assembly;

5. *Reaffirms* that it is ultimately for the people of the British Virgin Islands themselves to determine their future political status in accordance with the relevant provisions of the Charter of the United Nations and the Declaration and reaffirms the importance of fostering an awareness among the people of the Territory of the possibilities open to them in the exercise of their right to self-determination;

6. *Calls upon* the administering Power, in consultation with the freely elected authorities of the territorial Government, to take all necessary steps to ensure the full and speedy attainment of the objectives of decolonization set out in the Charter and the Declaration and all other relevant resolutions of the United Nations;

7. *Notes* the continuing commitment of the territorial Government to the goal of economic diversification, particularly in the areas of agriculture, fisheries and small industries, and calls upon the administering Power, in consultation with the local authorities, to intensify its efforts in this regard in order to offset the recent decline in agricultural production;

8. *Urges* the administering Power, in co-operation with the territorial Government, to safeguard the inalienable right of the people of the Territory to the enjoyment of their natural resources by taking effective measures to ensure their right to own and dispose of those resources and to establish and maintain control of their future development;

9. *Urges* the specialized agencies and other organizations of the United Nations system, as well as regional institutions such as the Caribbean Development Bank, to take measures to accelerate progress in the social and economic life of the British Virgin Islands;

10. *Considers* that the possibility of sending a further visiting mission to the British Virgin Islands at an appropriate time should be kept under review;

11. *Requests* the Special Committee to continue the examination of this question at its next session, including the possible dispatch of a visiting mission to the British Virgin Islands at an appropriate time and in consultation with the administering Power, and to report thereon to the General Assembly at its thirty-eighth session.

Brunei

The Committee on colonial countries decided without objection on 20 August 1982 to consider the question of Brunei at its 1983 session, subject to any directives by the General Assembly.[2] On the recommendation of the Fourth Committee, which approved without vote an oral proposal by its Chairman on 15 November, the Assembly decided in like manner on 23 November[1] to defer consideration of the question until 1983 and asked the Committee on colonial countries to keep the situation in the Territory under review.

Decision (1982). [1]GA: 37/417, 23 Nov., text following.
Report. [2]Committee on colonial countries, A/37/23/Rev.1.
Meeting records. GA: 4th Committee, A/C.4/37/SR.9-15, 17-22, *23* (26 Oct.–15 Nov.); plenary, A/37/PV.74-76, *77* (22, 23 Nov.).

General Assembly decision 37/417

Adopted without vote

Approved by Fourth Committee (A/37/621) without vote, 15 November (meeting 23); oral proposal by Chairman; agenda item 18.

Question of Brunei

At its 77th plenary meeting, on 23 November 1982, the General Assembly, on the recommendation of the Fourth Committee, decided to defer until its thirty-eighth session consideration of the question of Brunei and requested the Special Committee on the Situation with regard to the Implementation of the Declaration on the Granting of Independence to Colonial Countries and Peoples to continue to keep the situation in the Territory under review and to report thereon to the Assembly.

Cayman Islands

On 23 November 1982,[2] the General Assembly adopted without vote a resolution reaffirming the inalienable right of the people of the Cayman Islands to self-determination and independence. It reiterated that the United Kingdom, as administering Power, must create conditions in the Territory to enable the people to exercise freely that right and stated that it was ultimately for the people of the Territory to decide their future political status. Reaffirming the responsibility of the administering Power for economic and social development of the Territory, the Assembly urged continued efforts to diversify the economy and to safeguard the right of the people to own and dispose of the Territory's natural resources. It decided to keep under review the possibility of sending a visiting mission to the Cayman Islands and requested the Committee on colonial countries to continue examining the situation there and to report in 1983.

The resolution was approved without objection by the Fourth Committee on 15 November. The draft originated in the Committee on colonial countries which approved it on 16 September, based on the report of its Sub-Committee on Small Territories which the Committee adopted on 28 June.[1]

Report. [1]Committee on colonial countries, A/37/23/Rev.1.
Resolution (1982). [2]GA: 37/24, 23 Nov., text following.
Meeting records. GA: 4th Committee, A/C.4/37/SR.9-15, 17-22, *23* (26 Oct.–15 Nov.); plenary, A/37/PV.74-76, *77* (22, 23 Nov.).

General Assembly resolution 37/24

23 November 1982   Meeting 77   Adopted without vote

Approved by Fourth Committee (A/37/621) without objection, 15 November (meeting 23); draft by Committee on colonial countries (A/37/23/Rev.1); agenda item 18.

Question of the Cayman Islands

The General Assembly,

Having considered the question of the Cayman Islands,

Having examined the relevant chapters of the report of the Special Committee on the Situation with regard to the Implementation of the Declaration on the Granting of Independence to Colonial Countries and Peoples,

Recalling its resolution 1514(XV) of 14 December 1960, containing the Declaration on the Granting of Independence to Colonial Countries and Peoples, and all other resolutions and decisions of the United Nations relating to the Cayman Islands,

Noting the statement of the representative of the administering Power, in which he said that his Government would fully respect the wishes of the people of the Cayman Islands in determining the future constitutional status of the Territory,

Conscious of the need to ensure the full and speedy implementation of the Declaration in respect of the Territory,

Noting that, in the period under review, the economy of the Territory has continued to sustain sound rates of growth, especially in the tourist, international finance and real estate industries,

Mindful that United Nations visiting missions provide an effective means of ascertaining the situation in the small Territories and expressing its satisfaction at the willingness of the administering Power to receive visiting missions in the Territories under its administration,

Aware of the special circumstances of the geographical location and economic conditions of the Territory and bearing in mind the necessity of diversifying and strengthening further the economy as a matter of priority in order to promote economic stability,

1. *Approves* the chapter of the report of the Special Committee on the Situation with regard to the Implementation of the Declaration on the Granting of Independence to Colonial Countries and Peoples relating to the Cayman Islands;

2. *Reaffirms* the inalienable right of the people of the Cayman Islands to self-determination and independence in conformity with the Declaration on the Granting of Independence to Colonial Countries and Peoples, contained in General Assembly resolution 1514(XV);

3. *Reiterates* the view that such factors as territorial size, geographical location, size of population and limited natural resources should in no way delay the speedy implementation of the process of self-determination in accordance with the Declaration contained in General Assembly resolution 1514(XV), which fully applies to the Cayman Islands;

4. *Notes with appreciation* the active participation of the administering Power in the work of the Special Committee in regard to the Cayman Islands, thereby enabling it to conduct a more informed and meaningful examination of the situation in the Territory, with a view to accelerating the process of decolonization for the purpose of the full implementation of the Declaration;

5. *Reiterates* that it is the responsibility of the administering Power to create such conditions in the Territory as will enable the people of the Cayman Islands to exercise freely and without interference their inalienable right to self-determination in accordance with General Assembly resolution 1514(XV), as well as all other relevant resolutions of the Assembly;

6. *Reaffirms* that it is ultimately for the people of the Cayman Islands themselves to determine their future political status in accordance with the relevant provisions of the Charter of the United Nations and the Declaration and reaffirms the importance of fostering an awareness among the people of the Territory of the possibilities open to them in the exercise of their right to self-determination;

7. *Reaffirms* the responsibility of the administering Power for the economic and social development of the Territory and urges it, in co-operation with the territorial Government, to render continuing support, to the fullest extent possible, to the development of programmes of economic diversification which will benefit the people of the Territory;

8. *Urges* the administering Power, in co-operation with the territorial Government, to safeguard the inalienable right of the people of the Territory to the enjoyment of their natural resources by taking effective measures to ensure their right to own and dispose of those resources and to establish and maintain control of their future development;

9. *Urges* the specialized agencies and other organizations of the United Nations system, as well as regional institutions such as the Caribbean Development Bank, to take measures to accelerate progress in the social and economic life of the Cayman Islands;

10. *Welcomes* the continuing assistance provided to the Territory by the United Nations Development Programme, amounting to $448,000 for the period 1982-1986;

11. *Considers* that the possibility of sending a further visiting mission to the Cayman Islands at an appropriate time should be kept under review;

12. *Requests* the Special Committee to continue the examination of this question at its next session, including the possible dispatch of a visiting mission to the Cayman Islands at an appropriate time and in consultation with the administering Power, and to report thereon to the General Assembly at its thirty-eighth session.

Cocos (Keeling) Islands

On 23 November 1982,[1] the General Assembly adopted without vote a decision on the Cocos (Keeling) Islands by which it reaffirmed the responsibility of Australia, as the administering Power, to create conditions for self-determination and noted Australia's continued commitment to the political, social and economic advancement of the people of the Territory. The Assembly also welcomed Australia's willingness to receive United Nations visiting missions in the Territory, decided to keep under review the need to send a further mission and requested the Committee on colonial countries to continue to examine the question.

The Fourth Committee approved the text without objection on 15 November. The draft originated in the Committee on colonial countries which approved it on 16 September, based on the report of its Sub-Committee on Small Territories which the Committee adopted on 5 August.[3]

By a letter dated 1 December,[2] Australia transmitted to the Chairman of the Committee on colonial countries a statement of 29 November by its Minister of Home Affairs and Environment concerning his discussions with leaders of the Cocos (Keeling) Islands. According to the statement, the islanders would choose, in an act of self-determination, between independence, free association with Australia and integration with Australia, probably in mid-1983.

Decision (1982). [1]GA: 37/413, 23 Nov., text following.
Letter. [2]Australia, 1 Dec., transmitting statement of 29 Nov. from Minister for Home Affairs and Environment, A/AC.109/723.
Report. [3]Committee on colonial countries, A/37/23/Rev.1.
Meeting records. GA: 4th Committee, A/C.4/37/SR.9-15, 17-22, *23* (26 Oct.–15 Nov.); plenary, A/37/PV.74-76, *77* (22, 23 Nov.).

General Assembly decision 37/413

Adopted without vote

Approved by Fourth Committee (A/37/621) without objection, 15 November (meeting 23); draft by Committee on colonial countries (A/37/23/Rev.1); agenda item 18.

Question of the Cocos (Keeling) Islands

At its 77th plenary meeting, on 23 November 1982, the General Assembly, on the recommendation of the Fourth Committee, having examined the relevant chapters of the report of the Special Committee on the Situation with regard to the Implementation of the Declaration on the Granting of Independence to Colonial Countries and Peoples, and having heard the statement of the representative of Australia with regard to the Cocos (Keeling) Islands, noted with appreciation the continuing co-operation of the Government of Australia, as the administering Power, with regard to the implementation of the Declaration on the Granting of Independence to Colonial Countries and Peoples, contained in General Assembly resolution 1514(XV) of 14 December 1960, in respect of the Territory. The Assembly reaffirmed that it was the responsibility of the administering Power to create conditions under which the people of the Cocos (Keeling) Islands would be able to determine freely their own future in conformity with resolution 1514(XV) as well as other relevant resolutions of the Assembly. In this respect, the Assembly noted the positive and continuing commitment of the administering Power to the political, social and economic advancement of the people of the Territory so that they might be able, as quickly as possible, to exercise fully their inalienable rights. The Assembly welcomed the continuing willingness of the administering Power to receive visiting missions in the Cocos (Keeling) Islands and, in that regard, reaffirmed that the need to send a further mission to the Territory at an appropriate time should be kept under review. The Assembly requested the Special Committee to continue to examine the question at its next session, including the possible dispatch of a visiting mission to the Cocos (Keeling) Islands at an appropriate time and in consultation with the administering Power, and to report thereon to the Assembly at its thirty-eighth session.

Gibraltar

On 20 August 1982, the Committee on colonial countries, taking into account the continuing negotiations between the parties on the question of Gibraltar, decided without objection to continue consideration of the question at its 1983 session, subject to any General Assembly directives.[2]

The Assembly, acting without vote on 23 November,[1] noted that Spain and the United Kingdom had signed a declaration in 1980 by which they had agreed to initiate negotiations on the problem of Gibraltar and simultaneously re-establish communications in the region; on 8 January 1982, they had fixed 20 April for the declaration's implementation. The Assembly noted that, although both Governments had subsequently agreed to postpone those arrangements, they intended to keep alive the process and set a new date for its implementation. In that light, the Assembly urged the two parties to initiate negotiations as envisaged in the Assembly's 1973 consensus,[3] with the object of reaching a lasting solution.

The decision was recommended by the Fourth Committee, which on 29 October approved the text, without objection, in the form of a draft consensus.

Decision (1982). [1]GA: 37/412, 23 Nov., text following.
Report. [2]Committee on colonial countries, A/37/23/Rev.1.
Yearbook reference. [3]1973, p. 699.
Meeting records. GA: 4th Committee, A/C.4/37/SR.9-15, 17-22, *23* (26 Oct.–15 Nov.); plenary, A/37/PV.74-76, *77* (22, 23 Nov.).

General Assembly decision 37/412

Adopted without vote

Approved by Fourth Committee (A/37/621) without objection, 29 October (meeting 10); draft consensus (A/C.4/37/L.4); agenda item 18.

Question of Gibraltar

At its 77th plenary meeting, on 23 November 1982, the General Assembly, on the recommendation of the Fourth Committee, noting that the Governments of Spain and the United Kingdom of Great Britain and Northern Ireland had signed a declaration on 10 April 1980 at Lisbon, intending, in accordance with the relevant resolutions of the United Nations, to resolve the problem of Gibraltar, agreeing to that end to start negotiations aimed at overcoming all the differences between them on Gibraltar, agreeing also to the re-establishment of direct communications in the region, the Government of Spain having decided to suspend the application of the measures at present in force, and both Governments agreeing to base future co-operation on reciprocity and full equality of rights, noting that both Governments had agreed on 8 January 1982 in London to fix the date of 20 April 1982 for the full implementation of the Lisbon Declaration, including the initiation of negotiations and the simultaneous re-establishment of direct communications in the region, and noting that, when it had subsequently been agreed to postpone these arrangements, both Governments had expressed their determination to keep alive the process initiated by the Lisbon Declaration, in the spirit of the letters exchanged in London on 8 January 1982, and their intention to set a new date for its implementation, decided to urge both Governments to make possible the initiation of the negotiations as envisaged in the consensus adopted by the Assembly on 14 December 1973, with the object of reaching a lasting solution to the problem of Gibraltar in the light of the relevant resolutions of the Assembly and in the spirit of the Charter of the United Nations.

Guam

Noting that a referendum on political status was held in Guam on 30 January 1982, the General Assembly, by a resolution adopted without vote on 23 November,[2] reaffirmed the right of the people of Guam to self-determination and independence, and reiterated that the United States, as the administering Power, was responsible for creating conditions conducive to the free exercise of that right.

The Assembly again stated its conviction that the administering Power should ensure that military bases and installations did not hinder the population of the Territory from exercising its right to self-determination and urged compliance with relevant United Nations resolutions. It called on the administering Power to accelerate the transfer of land to the people of the Territory, remove constraints to economic development and safeguard the people's right to their natural resources. It further urged promotion of the language and culture of the Chamorro people, who made up more than half the population of Guam. The Assembly decided to keep under review the possibility of sending a visiting mission to the Territory and requested the Committee on colonial countries to report to the Assembly on Guam in 1983.

The resolution was recommended by the Fourth Committee, which approved on 15 November without objection the draft submitted to it by the Committee on colonial countries. That Committee had approved the text on 16 September, based on the report of its Sub-Committee on Small Territories which the Committee adopted on 5 August.[1]

Report. [1]Committee on colonial countries, A/37/23/Rev.1.
Resolution (1982). [2]GA: 37/21, 23 Nov., text following.
Meeting records. GA: 4th Committee, A/C.4/37/SR.9-15, 17-22, *23* (26 Oct.–15 Nov.); plenary, A/37/PV.74-76, *77* (22, 23 Nov.).

General Assembly resolution 37/21

23 November 1982   Meeting 77   Adopted without vote

Approved by Fourth Committee (A/37/621) without objection, 15 November (meeting 23); draft by Committee on colonial countries (A/37/23/Rev.1); agenda item 18.

Question of Guam

The General Assembly,

Having considered the question of Guam,

Having examined the relevant chapters of the report of the Special Committee on the Situation with regard to the Implementation of the Declaration on the Granting of Independence to Colonial Countries and Peoples,

Recalling its resolution 1514(XV) of 14 December 1960, containing the Declaration on the Granting of Independence to Colonial Countries and Peoples, and all other resolutions and decisions of the United Nations relating to Guam,

Having heard the statement of the representative of the administering Power,

Noting with appreciation the continued active participation of the administering Power in the work of the Special Committee in regard to Guam, thereby enabling it to conduct a more informed and meaningful examination of the situation in the Territory, with a view to accelerating the process of decolonization for the purpose of the full implementation of the Declaration,

Noting that a referendum on political status was held in the Territory on 30 January 1982,

Recalling all relevant resolutions of the United Nations relating to military bases and installations in colonial and Non-Self-Governing Territories,

Bearing in mind that an obstacle to the economic development of the Territory has been the uncertainty concerning land held by the federal authorities,

Aware of the special circumstances of the geographical location and economic conditions of Guam and the necessity of diversifying the economy of the Territory as a matter of priority and noting the great potential for diversification offered by commercial fishing, agriculture and the development of the transportation industry,

Mindful that United Nations visiting missions provide an effective means of ascertaining the situation in the small Territories and expressing its satisfaction at the willingness of the administering Power to receive visiting missions in the Territories under its administration,

1. *Approves* the chapter of the report of the Special Committee on the Situation with regard to the Implementation of the Declaration on the Granting of Independence to Colonial Countries and Peoples relating to Guam;

2. *Reaffirms* the inalienable right of the people of Guam to self-determination and independence in conformity with the Declaration on the Granting of Independence to Colonial Countries and Peoples, contained in General Assembly resolution 1514(XV);

3. *Reaffirms its conviction* that such factors as territorial size, geographical location, size of population and limited natural resources should in no way delay the implementation of the Declaration contained in General Assembly resolution 1514(XV), which fully applies to Guam;

4. *Recalls* that the United States of America, as the administering Power, has the responsibility under the Charter of the United Nations to ensure that the people of the Territory are kept fully informed of their inalienable right to self-determination and independence, in accordance with General Assembly resolution 1514(XV);

5. *Reiterates* that it is the responsibility of the administering Power to create such conditions in the Territory as will enable the people of Guam to exercise freely and without interference their inalienable right to self-determination and independence in accordance with General Assembly resolution 1514(XV);

6. *Reaffirms its strong conviction* that the administering Power must ensure that military bases and installations do not hinder the population of the Territory from exercising its right to self-determination and independence in conformity with the purposes and principles of the Charter and urges the administering Power to take all necessary measures to comply fully with the relevant resolutions of the United Nations relating to military bases and installations in colonial and Non-Self-Governing Territories;

7. *Reaffirms* the responsibility of the administering Power, under the Charter, for the economic and social development of Guam and calls upon the administering Power to take all necessary steps to strengthen and diversify the economy of the Territory;

8. *Calls upon* the administering Power, in co-operation with the local authorities, to accelerate the transfer of land to the people of the Territory;

9. *Reiterates its call* upon the administering Power, in co-operation with the territorial Government, to remove the constraints which limit growth in the economic development of the Territory, particularly with regard to commercial fishing, agriculture and the transportation industry;

10. *Urges* the administering Power, in co-operation with the territorial Government, to continue to take effective measures to safeguard and guarantee the right of the people of Guam to their natural resources and to establish and maintain control over their future development and requests the administering Power to take all necessary steps to protect the property rights of the people of the Territory;

11. *Urges* the administering Power to strengthen its efforts to develop and promote the language and culture of the Chamorro people, who comprise more than half of the population of the Territory;

12. *Considers* that the possibility of sending a further visiting mission to Guam at an appropriate time should be kept under review;

13. *Requests* the Special Committee to continue the consideration of this question at its next session, including the possible dispatch of a further visiting mission to Guam at an appropriate time and in consultation with the administering Power, and to report thereon to the General Assembly at its thirty-eighth session.

Montserrat

Action by the Committee on colonial countries. On 28 June 1982,[1] the Committee on colonial countries adopted without objection the conclusions and recommendations of its Sub-Committee on Small Territories concerning Montserrat, whereby the Committee reaffirmed the inalienable right of the people of that Territory to self-determination and independence. Noting the increasing economic viability of the Territory, the Committee called on the United Kingdom, as the administering Power, to continue to strengthen and diversify the economy, to safeguard the right of the people to own and dispose of their natural resources and to intensify training programmes for an efficient public service. United Nations organizations were urged to help accelerate economic and social progress in the Territory. In addition, the Committee agreed to keep under review the possibility of sending a further visiting mission there, in view of the fact that the last such mission took place in May 1975.

In response to a July invitation by the United Kingdom, the Committee decided to send to Montserrat a visiting mission composed of the Ivory Coast (as Chairman), the United Republic of Tanzania and Venezuela. The mission visited the Territory from 23 to 27 August and consulted with the United Kingdom Government in London on 7 September.

In its report,[2] introduced to and adopted without objection by the Committee on 8 November, the mission concluded that the population, while regarding independence as inevitable, did not feel the Territory was ready in the current circumstances to accede to independence. The mission recommended that political education should be intensified and that the question of an interim constitutional advance should be left to the administering Power, in consultation with the local Government. The administering Power should try to instil in the population national pride and self-confidence and to appoint Monserratians to fill the remaining senior posts in the public service.

The mission noted a widespread fear of attaining independence before prevailing economic and social problems—deriving from a lack of natural resources, trained manpower and appropriate infrastructure—had been overcome and a concern that foreign capital would be more difficult to attract if the political status of the Territory were to change. The mission's recommendations included greater economic diversification, development of infrastructure and encouraging investment capital; education to encourage young people to engage in agriculture; expansion of tourist and transportation facilities; and the training of local medical staff.

General Assembly action. Acting without vote on 23 November,[3] the General Assembly reaffirmed the inalienable right of the people of Montserrat to self-determination and independence and called on the United Kingdom, in co-operation with the Government of Montserrat, to launch programmes of political education to inform the people of the options available to them in the exercise of that right. The Assembly commended the conclusions and recommendations of the visiting mission to the Government of the United Kingdom and Montserrat and called on the former to expand its aid programme in order to accelerate the development of the Territory's economic and social infrastructure and to enlist the assistance of United Nations organizations in diversifying the Territory's economy. The Committee on colonial countries was asked to continue examination of the situation in the Territory and to report to the Assembly in 1983.

The Fourth Committee on 15 November had approved the draft resolution without objection, as submitted to it by the Committee on colonial countries on 8 November.

Reports. [1]Committee on colonial countries, A/37/23/Rev.1; [2]Visiting mission, A/AC.109/722.
Resolution (1982). [3]GA: 37/27, 23 Nov., text following.
Meeting records. GA: 4th Committee, A/C.4/37/SR.9-15, 17-22, *23* (26 Oct.–15 Nov.); plenary, A/37/PV.74-76, *77* (22, 23 Nov.).

General Assembly resolution 37/27

23 November 1982   Meeting 77   Adopted without vote

Approved by Fourth Committee (A/37/621) without objection, 15 November (meeting 23); draft by Committee on colonial countries (A/37/23/Rev.1); agenda item 18.

Question of Montserrat

The General Assembly,

Having considered the question of Montserrat,

Having examined the relevant chapters of the report of the Special Committee on the Situation with regard to the Implementation of the Declaration on the Granting of Independence to Colonial Countries and Peoples,

Having also examined the report of the United Nations visiting mission dispatched to the Territory in August 1982, at the invitation of the Government of the United Kingdom of Great Britain and Northern Ireland as the administering Power,

Recalling its resolution 1514(XV) of 14 December 1960, containing the Declaration on the Granting of Independence to Colonial Countries and Peoples,

Recalling also its resolution 36/62 of 25 November 1981 on the question of five Territories, including Montserrat,

Having heard the statement of the representative of the administering Power,

Mindful of the responsibility of the United Nations to help the people of Montserrat to realize their aspirations in accordance with the objectives set forth in the Declaration,

Recalling that the administering Power has the responsibility to ensure that the people of Montserrat are kept fully informed of their inalienable right to self-determination and independence, in accordance with the Declaration,

Aware of the special problems facing the Territory by virtue of its isolation, small size, limited resources and lack of infrastructure,

1. *Approves* the chapter of the report of the Special Committee on the Situation with regard to the Implementation of the Declaration on the Granting of Independence to Colonial Countries and Peoples relating to Montserrat;

2. *Approves also* the report of the United Nations visiting mission to Montserrat in 1982;

3. *Reaffirms* the inalienable right of the people of Montserrat to self-determination and independence in conformity with the Declaration on the Granting of Independence to Colonial Countries and Peoples;

4. *Reiterates* the view that such factors as size, geographical location, size of population and limited natural resources should in no way delay the speedy implementation of the process of self-determination in accordance with the Declaration, which fully applies to Montserrat;

5. *Commends*, for appropriate action, the conclusions and recommendations of the visiting mission to the Government of the United Kingdom of Great Britain and Northern Ireland, as the administering Power, and to the Government of Montserrat;

6. *Expresses its appreciation* to the members of the visiting mission for the constructive work accomplished and to the administering Power, the territorial Government, the Legislative Council and the people of the Territory for the close co-operation and assistance extended to the mission;

7. *Calls upon* the administering Power to take the necessary measures to promote the political, economic and social development of Montserrat;

8. *Calls upon* the administering Power, in co-operation with the Government of Montserrat, to launch programmes of political education so that the people of the Territory may be fully informed of the options available to them in the exercise of their right to self-determination and independence;

9. *Urges* the administering Power to continue to intensify and expand its programme of aid in order to accelerate the development of the economic and social infrastructure of the Territory;

10. *Requests* the administering Power, in the light of the conclusions and recommendations of the visiting mission, to continue to enlist the assistance of the specialized agencies and other organizations of the United Nations system, as well as other regional and international bodies, in the strengthening, development and diversification of the economy of the Territory;

11. *Requests* the Special Committee to continue the examination of this question at its next session, including the possible dispatch of a further visiting mission to Montserrat at an appropriate time and in consultation with the administering Power, and to report thereon to the General Assembly at its thirty-eighth session.

Pitcairn

Acting without vote on 23 November 1982,[1] the General Assembly reiterated its call on the United Kingdom, as the administering Power, to continue to safeguard the interests of the people of Pitcairn. Taking note of the United Kingdom's willingness to discuss any change of constitutional status with the people of the Territory whenever the latter so desired, and its statement that it was encouraging local initiative and enterprise, the Assembly observed that the current size of the population (numbering 53 at the end of 1982) continued to raise the question of the capacity of the islanders to maintain essential services in education and health care as well as the launching of long boats on which their trade with passing ships depended.

The Fourth Committee on 15 November approved without objection the text originating in the Committee on colonial countries. That Committee on 16 September had adopted the text based on a draft consensus submitted by its Sub-Committee on Small Territories, which the Committee had approved on 28 June.[2]

Decision (1982). [1]GA: 37/415, 23 Nov., text following.
Report. [2]Committee on colonial countries, A/37/23/Rev.1.
Meeting records. GA: 4th Committee, A/C.4/37/SR.9-15, 17-22, *23* (26 Oct.–15 Nov.); plenary, A/37/PV.74-76, *77* (22, 23 Nov.).

General Assembly decision 37/415

Adopted without vote

Approved by Fourth Committee (A/37/621) without objection, 15 November (meeting 23); draft by Committee on colonial countries (A/37/23/Rev.1); agenda item 18.

Question of Pitcairn

At its 77th plenary meeting, on 23 November 1982, the General Assembly, on the recommendation of the Fourth Committee, having examined the relevant chapter of the report of the Special Committee on the Situation with regard to the Implementation of the Declaration on the Granting of Independence to Colonial Countries and Peoples, took note of the statement of the representative of the United Kingdom of Great Britain and Northern Ireland affirming the policy of his Government to encourage as much local initiative and enterprise as possible, so that the people of Pitcairn could make the most of their own way of life. The Assembly, further noting the willingness of the administering Power to discuss any change of constitutional status with the people of the Territory whenever the latter so desired, and that the current size of the population continued to raise the question of the capacity of the islanders to maintain the essential services of education, medical welfare and the launching of long boats, on which their trade with passing ships depended, called once again upon the administering Power to continue to take the necessary measures to safeguard the interests of the people of Pitcairn. The Assembly requested the Special Committee to continue to examine the question at its next session, and to report thereon to the Assembly at its thirty-eighth session.

St. Helena

In 1982, the General Assembly reaffirmed the inalienable right of the people of St. Helena to self-determination and independence, and urged the United Kingdom, as the administering Power and in consultation with the people's elected representatives, to take steps to ensure the speedy implementation in that Territory of the 1960 Declaration on the Granting of Independence to Colonial Countries and Peoples.[3] The Assembly reaffirmed the importance of development assistance from the administering Power and the international community for developing the Territory's economic potential, and expressed the hope that the United Kingdom would continue to implement infrastructure and community projects and to encourage local intitiative and enterprise.

Noting the administering Power's positive attitude towards United Nations visiting missions, the Assembly decided to keep under review the possibility of dispatching such a mission to St. Helena at an appropriate time and requested the Committee on colonial countries to continue to examine the question and to report in 1983.

The Assembly adopted the decision without vote on 23 November 1982;[1] the Fourth Committee had approved the draft without objection on 15 November. The text originated in the Committee on colonial countries as a draft consensus adopted on 16 September, based on the report of its Sub-Committee on Small Territories which the Committee had approved on 28 June.[2]

Decision (1982). [1]GA: 37/416, 23 Nov., text following.
Report. [2]Committee on colonial countries, A/37/23/Rev.1.
Resolution. [3]GA: 1514(XV), 14 Dec. 1960 (YUN 1960, p. 49).
Meeting records. GA: 4th Committee, A/C.4/37/SR.9-15, 17-22, *23* (26 Oct.–15 Nov.); plenary, A/37/PV.74-76, *77* (22, 23 Nov.).

General Assembly decision 37/416

Adopted without vote

Approved by Fourth Committee (A/37/621) without objection, 15 November (meeting 23); draft by Committee on colonial countries (A/37/23/Rev.1); agenda item 18.

Question of St. Helena

At its 77th plenary meeting, on 23 November 1982, the General Assembly, on the recommendation of the Fourth Committee, having examined the relevant chapters of the report of the Special Committee on the Situation with regard to the Implementation of the Declaration on the Granting of Independence to Colonial Countries and Peoples, and having heard the statement of the representative of the United Kingdom of Great Britain and Northern Ireland, as the administering Power, reaffirmed the inalienable right of the people of St. Helena to self-determination and independence in conformity with the Declaration on the Granting of Independence to Colonial Countries and Peoples, contained in Assembly resolution 1514(XV) of 14 December 1960. The Assembly noted the commitment of the Government of the United Kingdom to respect the wishes of the people of the Territory and, in that regard, urged the administering Power, in consultation with the freely elected representatives of the people of St. Helena, to continue to take all necessary steps to ensure the speedy implementation of the Declaration in respect to that Territory. The Assembly expressed the hope that the administering Power would continue to implement infrastructure and community projects aimed at improving the general welfare of the community and to encourage local initiative and enterprise, particularly in the area of the local handicrafts industry. The Assembly noted that, despite the economic improvement in these sectors, the commercial sector still remained affected by world inflation. The Assembly reaffirmed that continued development assistance from the administering Power, together with any assistance that the international community might be able to provide, constituted an important means of developing the economic potential of the Territory and of enhancing the capacity of its people to realize fully the goals set forth in the relevant provisions of the Charter of the United Nations for the improvement of economic conditions in the Territory. Noting the positive attitude of the administering Power with respect to the question of receiving United Nations visiting missions in the Territories under its administration, the Assembly considered that the possibility of dispatching such a mission to St. Helena at an appropriate time should be kept under review. The Assembly requested the Special Committee to continue to examine the question at its next session, including the possible dispatch of a visiting mission to St. Helena, at an appropriate time and in consultation with the administering Power, and to report thereon to the Assembly at its thirty-eighth session.

St. Kitts-Nevis

The Committee on colonial countries decided without objection on 20 August 1982 to consider the question of St. Kitts–Nevis at its 1983 session, subject to any directives by the General Assembly.[2] On the recommendation of the Fourth Committee, approved without vote on 15 November on an oral proposal by its Chairman, the Assembly decided in like manner on 23 November to defer consideration of the question until 1983.[1]

Decision (1982). [1]GA: 37/418, 23 Nov., text following.
Report. [2]Committee on colonial countries, A/37/23/Rev.1.
Meeting records. GA: 4th Committee, A/C.4/37/SR.9-15, 17-22, *23* (26 Oct.–15 Nov.); plenary, A/37/PV.74-76, *77* (22, 23 Nov.).

General Assembly decision 37/418

Adopted without vote

Approved by Fourth Committee (A/37/621) without vote, 15 November (meeting 23); oral proposal by Chairman; agenda item 18.

Question of St. Kitts-Nevis

At its 77th plenary meeting, on 23 November 1982, the General Assembly, on the recommendation of the Fourth Committee, decided to defer until its thirty-eighth session consideration of the question of St. Kitts–Nevis.

Tokelau

In a decision adopted without vote on 23 November 1982,[1] the General Assembly, reaffirming the inalienable right of the people of Tokelau to self-determination, noted the wish of the people not to review for the time being their existing relationship with New Zealand, the administering Power. The Assembly welcomed the assurances by the administering Power that it would continue to be guided by the people's wishes as to their future status, and called on that Power to continue its programme of political education while preserving the identity and cultural heritage of the Tokelauans. The Assembly also noted New Zealand's efforts to promote economic development and to safeguard the peoples' right to their natural resources, and felt that development aid to the Territory should be expanded. It decided to keep under review the possibility of sending a visiting mission to Tokelau and requested the Committee on colonial countries to report on the Territory in 1983.

The Fourth Committee had approved the draft without objection on 15 November. The text originated in the Committee on colonial countries as a draft consensus adopted on 16 September, based on the report of its Sub-Committee on Small Territories which the Committee approved on 28 June.[2]

Decision (1982). [1]GA: 37/414, 23 Nov., text following.
Report. [2]Committee on colonial countries, A/37/23/Rev.1.
Meeting records. GA: 4th Committee, A/C.4/37/SR.9-15, 17-22, *23* (26 Oct.–15 Nov.); plenary, A/37/PV.74-76, *77* (22, 23 Nov.).

General Assembly decision 37/414

Adopted without vote

Approved by Fourth Committee (A/37/621) without objection, 15 November (meeting 23); draft by Committee on colonial countries (A/37/23/Rev.1); agenda item 18.

Question of Tokelau

At its 77th plenary meeting, on 23 November 1982, the General Assembly, on the recommendation of the Fourth Committee, having examined the relevant chapters of the report of the Special Committee on the Situation with regard to the Implementation of the Declaration on the Granting of Independence to Colonial Countries and Peoples, and having heard the statement of the representative of New Zealand with regard to Tokelau, noted with appreciation the willingness of the administering Power to maintain its close co-operation with the United Nations in the exercise of its responsibility towards Tokelau. The Assembly reaffirmed the inalienable right of the people of Tokelau to self-determination in conformity with the Declaration on the Granting of Independence to Colonial Countries and Peoples, contained in Assembly resolution 1514(XV) of 14 December 1960, and reaffirmed further that it was the responsibility of the administering Power to keep the people of Tokelau fully informed of this right. In that regard, the Assembly noted that the people of the Territory had expressed the view that, for the time being, they did not wish to review the nature of the existing relationship between Tokelau and New Zealand. The Assembly welcomed the assurances of the administering Power that it would continue to be guided solely by the wishes of the people of Tokelau as to the future status of the Territory. The Assembly noted also that the administering Power had assured the people of Tokelau of its continuing assistance in the event that they should desire to change their status. The Assembly called upon the administering Power to continue its programme of political education within the context of its efforts to ensure the preservation of the identity and cultural heritage of the people of Tokelau. The Assembly recognized that the economic development of Tokelau was an important element in the process of self-determination. The Assembly noted the continuing efforts of the administering Power to promote the economic development of the Territory and the measures it had taken to safeguard and guarantee the rights of the peoples of Tokelau to all their natural resources and the benefits derived therefrom. The Assembly was of the opinion that the administering Power should continue to expand its programme of budgetary support and development aid to the Territory. The Assembly noted with appreciation the continuing efforts of the administering Power to make improvements in the fields of public health, public works and education. The Assembly reiterated its expression of appreciation to the specialized agencies and other organizations of the United Nations system, as well as to the regional organizations, for their assistance to Tokelau, and called upon those bodies to continue providing assistance to the Territory. Mindful of the effective means provided by United Nations visiting missions to assess the situation in the Territories, the Assembly was of the opinion that the possibility of sending a further visiting mission to the Territory at an appropriate time should be kept under review, taking into account, in particular, the wishes of the people of Tokelau. The Assembly requested the Special Committee to continue to examine the question at its next session, including the possible dispatch of a further visiting mission to Tokelau, at an appropriate time and in consultation with the administering Power, and to report thereon to the Assembly at its thirty-eighth session.

Turks and Caicos Islands

The General Assembly, by a 23 November 1982 resolution[2] adopted without vote, reaffirmed the obligation of the United Kingdom, as the administering Power for the Turks and Caicos Islands, to enable the people of the Territory to exercise freely their right to self-determination and independence. It urged the United Kingdom, in consultation with the territorial Government, to promote the Territory's economic and social development, guarantee the people's right to own and dispose of their natural resources, and continue to train local personnel in skills essential to development. United Nations organizations were asked to pay attention to the Territory's development needs. Further, the Assembly urged the administering Power to abide by United Nations resolutions relating to military bases in Non-Self-Governing Territories. It agreed to keep under review the possibility of sending a visiting mission to the Territory and requested the Committee on colonial countries to report on the question in 1983.

The Fourth Committee had approved the text without objection on 15 November. The draft originated in the Committee on colonial countries which had approved it on 16 September, based on the report of its Sub-Committee on Small Territories which the Committee adopted on 5 August.[1]

Report. [1]Committee on colonial countries, A/37/23/Rev.1. *Resolution (1982).* [2]GA: 37/25, 23 Nov., text following. *Meeting records.* GA: 4th Committee, A/C.4/37/SR.9-15, 17-22, 23 (26 Oct -15 Nov); plenary, A/37/PV 74-76, 77 (22, 23 Nov.).

General Assembly resolution 37/25

23 November 1982   Meeting 77   Adopted without vote

Approved by Fourth Committee (A/37/621) without objection, 15 November (meeting 23); draft by Committee on colonial countries (A/37/23/Rev.1); agenda item 18.

Question of the Turks and Caicos Islands

The General Assembly,

Having considered the question of the Turks and Caicos Islands,

Having examined the relevant chapters of the report of the Special Committee on the Situation with regard to the Implementation of the Declaration on the Granting of Independence to Colonial Countries and Peoples,

Recalling its resolution 1514(XV) of 14 December 1960, containing the Declaration on the Granting of Independence to Colonial Countries and Peoples, and all other resolutions and decisions of the United Nations relating to the Turks and Caicos Islands,

Taking into account the statement of the representative of the administering Power, in which he said that his Government would fully respect the wishes of the people of the Turks and Caicos Islands in determining the future constitutional status of the Territory, and bearing in mind the importance of fostering an awareness among the people of the Territory of the possibilities open to them,

Conscious of the need to ensure the full and speedy implementation of the Declaration in respect of the Territory,

Noting with appreciation the continued active participation of the administering Power in the work of the Special Committee in regard to the Turks and Caicos Islands, thereby enabling it to conduct a more informed and meaningful examination of the situation in the Territory, with a view to accelerating the process of decolonization for the purpose of the full implementation of the Declaration,

Aware of the special circumstances of the geographical location and economic conditions of the Territory and bearing in mind the necessity of diversifying and strengthening further its economy as a matter of priority in order to promote economic stability and to develop a wider economic base for the Territory,

Recalling all relevant resolutions of the United Nations relating to military bases and installations in colonial and Non-Self-Governing Territories,

Noting the arrangements made for university training abroad and for vocational training in the Territory,

Mindful that United Nations visiting missions provide an effective means of ascertaining the situation in the small Territories and expressing its satisfaction at the willingness of the administering Power to receive visiting missions in the Territories under its administration,

1. *Approves* the chapter of the report of the Special Committee on the Situation with regard to the Implementation of the Declaration on the Granting of Independence to Colonial Countries and Peoples relating to the Turks and Caicos Islands;

2. *Reaffirms* the inalienable right of the people of the Turks and Caicos Islands to self-determination and independence in conformity with the Declaration on the Granting of Independence to Colonial Countries and Peoples, contained in General Assembly resolution 1514(XV);

3. *Reiterates* the view that such factors as territorial size, geographical location, population and limited natural resources should in no way delay the speedy exercise by the people of the Territory of their inalienable right as set out in the Declaration contained in General Assembly resolution 1514(XV), which fully applies to the Turks and Caicos Islands;

4. *Reiterates* that it is the obligation of the administering Power to create such conditions in the Territory as will enable the people of the Turks and Caicos Islands to exercise freely and without interference their inalienable right to self-determination and independence in accordance with General Assembly resolution 1514(XV), as well as all other relevant resolutions of the Assembly;

5. *Reaffirms* that it is the responsibility of the administering Power under the Charter of the United Nations to develop its dependent Territories economically and socially and urges the administering Power, in consultation with the territorial Government, to take the necessary measures to promote the economic and social development of the Turks and Caicos Islands and, in particular, to intensify and expand its programme of assistance in order to accelerate the development of the economic and social infrastructure of the Territory;

6. *Emphasizes* that greater attention should be paid to diversification of the economy, particularly in the promotion of agriculture and fisheries, for the benefit of the people of the Territory;

7. *Recalls* that it is the responsibility of the administering Power, in accordance with the freely expressed wishes of the people, to safeguard, guarantee and ensure the inalienable right of the people of the Territory to the enjoyment of their natural resources by taking effective measures to guarantee their right to own and dispose of those resources and to establish and maintain control of their future development;

8. *Urges* the specialized agencies and other organizations of the United Nations system, as well as regional institutions such as the Caribbean Development Bank, to continue to pay special attention to the development needs of the Turks and Caicos Islands;

9. *Reaffirms its strong conviction* that the administering Power must ensure that military bases and installations do not hinder the people of the Territory from exercising their right to self-determination and independence in conformity with the purposes and principles of the Charter and urges the administering Power to take all necessary measures to comply fully with the relevant resolutions of the United Nations relating to military bases and installations in colonial and Non-Self-Governing Territories;

10. *Requests* the administering Power, in consultation with the territorial Government, to continue to provide the assistance necessary for the training of qualified local personnel in the skills essential to the development of various sectors of the society of the Territory;

11. *Considers* that the possibility of sending a further visiting mission to the Turks and Caicos Islands at an appropriate time should be kept under review;

12. *Requests* the Special Committee to continue the examination of this question at its next session, including the possible dispatch of a further visiting mission to the Turks and Caicos Islands at an appropriate time and in consultation with the administering Power, and to report thereon to the General Assembly at its thirty-eighth session.

United States Virgin Islands

Acting without vote on 23 November 1982,[2] the General Assembly reaffirmed the right of the people of the United States Virgin Islands to self-determination and independence and called on the United States, as the administering Power, to enable the people of the Territory to exercise freely that right. In so doing, the Assembly asked the administering Power to facilitate the work of the Status Commission, set up in 1980 to study options for the future political status of the Territory, and to ensure that the people were informed of the relevant discussions.

The United States was urged to expedite passage by its Congress of legislation concerning the problem of aliens in the Territory, help diversify the Islands' economy, develop its infrastructure, safeguard the people's right to their natural resources and pay particular attention to the problems of unemployment, public housing, health care, education and crime. The Assembly decided to keep under review the possibility of sending a visiting mission to the Territory and requested the Committee on colonial countries to report on the Islands in 1983.

The Fourth Committee had approved the text without objection on 15 November. The draft originated in the Committee on colonial countries, which adopted on 16 September a text based on the report of its Sub-Committee on Small Territories, which the Committee had adopted on 5 August.[1]

Report. [1]Committee on colonial countries, A/37/23/Rev.1.
Resolution (1982). [2]GA: 37/26, 23 Nov., text following.
Meeting records. GA: 4th Committee, A/C.4/37/SR.9-15, 17-22, 23 (26 Oct.–15 Nov.); plenary, A/37/PV.74-76, 77 (22, 23 Nov.).

General Assembly resolution 37/26

23 November 1982   Meeting 77   Adopted without vote

Approved by Fourth Committee (A/37/621) without objection, 15 November (meeting 23); draft by Committee on colonial countries (A/37/23/Rev.1); agenda item 18.

Question of the United States Virgin Islands

The General Assembly,

Having considered the question of the United States Virgin Islands,

Having examined the relevant chapters of the report of the Special Committee on the Situation with regard to the Implementation of the Declaration on the Granting of Independence to Colonial Countries and Peoples,

Recalling its resolution 1514(XV) of 14 December 1960, containing the Declaration on the Granting of Independence to Colonial Countries and Peoples, and all other resolutions and decisions of the United Nations relating to the United States Virgin Islands,

Noting with appreciation the continued active participation of the administering Power in the work of the Special Committee in regard to the United States Virgin Islands, thereby enabling it to conduct a more informed and meaningful examination of the situation in the Territory and expressing its satisfaction at the willingness of the administering Power to receive visiting missions in the Territories under its administration,

Having heard the statement of the representative of the administering Power,

Taking note of the fact that the proposed constitution submitted to a referendum on 3 November 1981 after an extensive debate was not accepted by the people of the Territory,

Bearing in mind that the territorial Government has taken positive steps by adopting legislation designed to solve the problem of aliens in the Territory,

Noting that the territorial Government has pursued its efforts to diversify the economy and noting also the progress achieved in the fields of construction and manufacturing, including developments in oil refining and the production of alumina and rum,

Noting with satisfaction the efforts to revitalize health care programmes and to discourage juvenile delinquency, the measures to improve crime prevention and the action taken to expand and upgrade school facilities,

1. *Approves* the chapter of the report of the Special Committee on the Situation with regard to the Implementation of the Declaration on the Granting of Independence to Colonial Countries and Peoples relating to the United States Virgin Islands;

2. *Reaffirms* the inalienable right of the people of the United States Virgin Islands to self-determination and independence in conformity with the Declaration on the Granting of Independence to Colonial Countries and Peoples, contained in General Assembly resolution 1514(XV);

3. *Reiterates* the view that such factors as territorial size, geographical location, size of population and limited natural resources should in no way delay the speedy implementation of the Declaration contained in General Assembly resolution 1514(XV), which fully applies to the United States Virgin Islands;

4. *Calls upon* the administering Power, taking into account the freely expressed wishes of the people of the United States Virgin Islands, to take all necessary steps to expedite the process of decolonization in accordance with the relevant provisions of the Charter of the United Nations and the Declaration, as well as all other relevant resolutions of the General Assembly;

5. *Reaffirms* that it is the obligation of the administering Power, in consultation with the territorial Government, to inform the local people of the possibilities open to them, so as to enable them to exercise freely and without interference their inalienable right to self-determination and independence in accordance with General Assembly resolution 1514(XV) and, in this respect, calls upon the administering Power to facilitate the work of the recently established Status Commission and to ensure that the people are fully informed of the discussions concerning the future political status of the Territory;

6. *Urges* the administering Power to expedite the passage of legislation currently before the Congress of the United States of America concerning the problem of aliens in the Territory;

7. *Reaffirms* the responsibility of the administering Power under the Charter for the economic and social development of the Territory;

8. *Urges* the administering Power, in co-operation with the territorial Government, to strengthen the economy of the Territory by taking additional measures of diversification in all fields and developing an adequate infrastructure;

9. *Urges* the administering Power, in co-operation with the Government of the United States Virgin Islands, to safeguard the inalienable right of the people of the Territory to the enjoyment of their natural resources by taking effective measures which guarantee the right of the people to own and dispose of those resources and to establish and maintain control of their future development;

10. *Urges* the administering Power, in co-operation with the territorial Government, to continue to improve social conditions and to pay particular attention to overcoming problems of unemployment, public housing, health care, education and crime;

11. *Considers* that the possibility of sending a further visiting mission to the United States Virgin Islands at an appropriate time should be kept under review;

12. *Requests* the Special Committee to continue the examination of this question at its next session, including the possible dispatch of a further visiting mission to the United States Virgin Islands at an appropriate time and in consultation with the administering Power, and to report thereon to the General Assembly at its thirty-eighth session.

Legal questions

Chapter I

International Court of Justice

Contents

General aspects

Two contentious cases and a request for an advisory opinion were before the International Court of Justice in 1982 and, in January, a special chamber of the Court was established to deal with a third dispute.[1]

Publications. [1]*International Court of Justice Yearbook 1981-1982*, No. 36, I.C.J. Sales No. 479; *International Court of Justice Yearbook 1982-1983*, No. 37, I.C.J. Sales No. 488; *International Court of Justice: Reports of Judgments, Advisory Opinions and Orders, Index 1982*, I.C.J. Sales No. 482; *Bibliography of the International Court of Justice*, No. 36/37, *1982/83*, I.C.J. Sales No. 495.

Judicial work of the Court

Continental shelf delimitation between the Libyan Arab Jamahiriya and Tunisia

On 24 February 1982, the International Court of Justice delivered at a public sitting its Judgment in the case concerning the delimitation of the continental shelf between the Libyan Arab Jamahiriya and Tunisia.[1] The case had been referred to the Court under the terms of a Special Agreement drawn up by the disputing parties in 1977 and submitted to the Court in 1978[2] and 1979.[3] Memorials (initial written pleadings), submitted by each State, were filed with the Court and exchanged between the parties in 1980.[4] In 1981, after an application by Malta for permission to

intervene in the case had been refused by the Court, the oral arguments of the parties were heard.[5]

In its Judgment, the Court found that the physical data presented did not enable it to ascertain the natural prolongation of each party's land territory, inasmuch as the delimitation to be effected would in fact concern one continuous continental shelf. Accordingly, after examining as requested the new accepted trends in the Third United Nations Conference on the Law of the Sea, the Court based itself on some further factors which the Special Agreement had requested it take into consideration, namely equitable principles and relevant circumstances characterizing the area.

The operative part of the Judgment read as follows:

The Court,

By ten votes to four,

Finds that:

A. The principles and rules of international law applicable for the delimitation, to be effected by agreement in implementation of the present Judgment, of the areas of continental shelf appertaining to the Republic of Tunisia and the Socialist People's Libyan Arab Jamahiriya respectively, in the area of the Pelagian Block in dispute between them as defined in paragraph B, subparagraph 1, below, are as follows:

1. the delimitation is to be effected in accordance with equitable principles, and taking account of all relevant circumstances;

2. the area relevant for the delimitation constitutes a single continental shelf as the natural prolongation of the land territory of both Parties, so that in the present case, no criterion for delimitation of shelf areas can be derived from the principle of natural prolongation as such;

3. in the particular geographical circumstances of the present case, the physical structure of the continental shelf areas is not such as to determine an equitable line of delimitation.

B. The relevant circumstances referred to in paragraph A, subparagraph 1, above, to be taken into account in achieving an equitable delimitation include the following:

1. the fact that the area relevant to the delimitation in the present case is bounded by the Tunisian coast from Ras Ajdir to Ras Kaboudia and the Libyan coast from Ras Ajdir to Ras Tajoura and by the parallel of latitude passing through Ras Kaboudia and the meridian passing through Ras Tajoura, the rights of third States being reserved;

2. the general configuration of the coasts of the Parties, and in particular the marked change in direction of the Tunisian coastline between Ras Ajdir and Ras Kaboudia;

3. the existence and position of the Kerkennah Islands;

4. the land frontier between the Parties, and their conduct prior to 1974 in the grant of petroleum concessions, resulting in the employment of a line seawards from Ras Ajdir at an angle of approximately 26° east of the meridian, which line corresponds to the line perpendicular to the coast at the frontier point which had in the past been observed as a *de facto* maritime limit;

5. the element of a reasonable degree of proportionality, which a delimitation carried out in accordance with equitable principles ought to bring about between the extent of the continental shelf areas appertaining to the coastal State and the length of the relevant part of its coast, measured in the general direction of the coastlines, account being taken for this purpose of the effects, actual or prospective, of any other continental shelf delimitation between States in the same region.

C. The practical method for the application of the aforesaid principles and rules of international law in the particular situation of the present case is the following:

1. the taking into account of the relevant circumstances which characterize the area defined in paragraph B, subparagraph 1, above, including its extent, calls for it to be treated, for the purpose of its delimitation between the Parties to the present case, as made up of two sectors, each requiring the application of a specific method of delimitation in order to achieve an overall equitable solution;

2. in the first sector, namely in the sector closer to the coast of the Parties, the starting point for the line of delimitation is the point where the outer limit of the territorial sea of the Parties is intersected by a straight line drawn from the land frontier point of Ras Ajdir through the point 33° 55′N, 12° E, which line runs at a bearing of approximately 26° east of north, corresponding to the angle followed by the north-western boundary of Libyan petroleum conces-

sions numbers NC 76, 137, NC 41 and NC 53, which was aligned on the south-eastern boundary of Tunisian petroleum concession "Permis complémentaire offshore du Golfe de Gabès" (21 October 1966); from the intersection point so determined, the line of delimitation between the two continental shelves is to run north-east through the point 33° 55′N, 12° E, thus on that same bearing, to the point of intersection with the parallel passing through the most westerly point of the Tunisian coastline between Ras Kaboudia and Ras Ajdir, that is to say, the most westerly point on the shoreline (low-water mark) of the Gulf of Gabes;

3. in the second sector, namely in the area which extends seawards beyond the parallel of the most westerly point of the Gulf of Gabes, the line of delimitation of the two continental shelves is to veer to the east in such a way as to take account of the Kerkennah Islands; that is to say, the delimitation line is to run parallel to a line drawn from the most westerly point of the Gulf of Gabes bisecting the angle formed by a line from that point to Ras Kaboudia and a line drawn from that same point along the seaward coast of the Kerkennah Islands, the bearing of the delimitation line parallel to such bisector being 52° to the meridian; the extension of this line northeastwards is a matter falling outside the jurisdiction of the Court in the present case, as it will depend on the delimitation to be agreed with third States.

In favour: Acting President Elias; Judges Lachs, Morozov, Nagendra Singh, Mosler, Ago, Sette Câmara, El-Khani, Schwebel and Judge *ad hoc* Jiménez de Aréchaga.

Against: Judges Forster, Gros, Oda and Judge *ad hoc* Evensen.

Judges Ago, Schwebel and Jiménez de Aréchaga appended separate opinions to the Judgment. Judges Gros, Oda and Evensen appended dissenting opinions.

(For list of members of the Court, see APPENDIX III.)

Publication. [1]*Case concerning the Continental Shelf* (Tunisia/Libyan Arab Jamahiriya), *Judgment of 24 February 1982*, I.C.J. Sales No. 473.
Yearbook references. [2]1978, p. 944; [3]1979, p. 1121; [4]1980, p. 1121; [5]1981, p. 1201.

Continental shelf delimitation between the Libyan Arab Jamahiriya and Malta

On 26 July 1982, the Libyan Arab Jamahiriya and Malta instituted proceedings by joint notification to the Court of a Special Agreement signed on 23 May 1976 and in force since an exchange on 20 March 1982 of instruments of ratification (See POLITICAL AND SECURITY QUESTIONS, Chapter VIII). The Agreement requested the Court to indicate the principles and rules applicable to delimitation of the continental shelf between the parties and the practical method for their application.

On 27 July 1982, the Vice-President of the Court, having regard to a provision of the Special Agreement, made an Order[1] fixing 26 April 1983 as the time-limit for the filing of a Memorial by each party.

> *Publication.* [1]*Case concerning the Continental Shelf* (Libyan Arab Jamahiriya/Malta), *Order of 27 July 1982,* I.C.J. Sales No. 476.

Maritime boundary delimitation between Canada and the United States

On 25 November 1981, Canada and the United States had notified the Court of a Special Agreement, signed on 29 March 1979 and in force as from 20 November 1981, by which they submitted to a chamber of the Court a question concerning the course of the maritime boundary dividing the continental shelf and fisheries zones in the Gulf of Maine area. Subsequently, the President of the Court had requested the Parties to provide further explanations on several points.[5]

After considering their joint reply of 6 January 1982, the Court, on 20 January, adopted, by 11 votes to 2 (Judges Morozov and El-Khani), an Order[1] whereby it constituted a Chamber of five members to deal with the case while noting that, by application of Article 31, paragraph 4, of its Statute, one of the Judges elected for the purpose would yield his place to a Judge *ad hoc.*

The Chamber, the first of its kind in the Court's history, consisted of Judges André Gros (France), Hermann Mosler (Federal Republic of Germany), Roberto Ago (Italy), Stephen M. Schwebel (United States) and Maxwell Cohen (Judge *ad hoc* chosen by Canada). On 29 January, the Chamber elected Judge Ago as its President and held its first public sitting.

On 1 February, the Court, after consulting the Chamber, adopted by 10 votes to 2 (Judges Morozov and El-Khani) an Order[2] fixing 26 August as the time-limit for the filing of Memorials. On 28 July, the President of the Chamber, at the request of one party, extended the limit to 27 September.[3] On 5 November, the Memorials having been duly filed, the President fixed 28 June 1983 as the time-limit for the filing of Counter-Memorials.[4]

> *Publications. Case concerning Delimitation of the Maritime Boundary in the Gulf of Maine Area* (Canada/United States of America): [1]*Order of 20 January 1982,* I.C.J. Sales No. 471; [2]*Order of 1 February 1982,* I.C.J. Sales No. 472; [3]*Order of 28 July 1982,* I.C.J. Sales No. 477; [4]*Order of 5 November 1982,* I.C.J. Sales No. 480.
> *Yearbook reference.* [5]1981, p. 1202.

Review of a judgement by the UN Administrative Tribunal

On 20 July 1982, the International Court of Justice delivered at a public sitting its advisory opinion in regard to Judgement No. 273 of the United Nations Administrative Tribunal.[1]

On 28 July 1981, it had received a request by the General Assembly's Committee on Applications for Review of Administrative Tribunal Judgements for an advisory opinion in regard to Judgement No. 273 delivered by the Tribunal, in Geneva on 15 May 1981 in the case of Ivor Peter Mortished v. the Secretary-General.[4] By that judgement, the Tribunal had determined that Mr. Mortished was entitled, by invoking an acquired right, to receive a repatriation grant under a provision of the Staff Rules which had no longer been in force on the date of his separation from the Secretariat. The provision in question had been revised pursuant to a 1979 Assembly resolution determining that no staff member would be entitled to any part of the grant unless evidence was provided of relocation away from the country of the last duty station.[3]

The question put to the Court by the Committee, on an application by the United States, was whether the judgement had been warranted in determining that the Assembly resolution could not be given immediate effect in requiring, for the payment of repatriation grants, evidence of relocation to a country other than the country of the staff member's last duty station.

The Court had received written statements on the question from France and the United States, as well as from the United Nations on behalf of Mr. Mortished.

The Court decided that written comments on those statements might be submitted by 15 April 1982. Such comments were received from France and the United States. After deciding to dispense with oral proceedings, the Court proceeded to its deliberation.

Finding itself bound to interpret the question put to it in terms of the grounds for review enumerated in Article 11 of the Statute of the Administrative Tribunal, the Court (in paragraph 48 of its advisory opinion) concluded that it was required to determine whether the Tribunal had erred on a question of law relating to the provisions of the Charter of the United Nations or exceeded its jurisdiction or competence. As to its own competence, the Court found that it fell short of any retrial of the case. It therefore refrained from considering whether the provision found by the Tribunal to have conferred an acquired right on Mr. Mortished had in fact had that effect. It found that the Tribunal had only attempted to apply to his case the relevant Staff Regulations and Rules made under the Assembly's authority and had clearly not erred on a question of law relating to the provisions of the Charter. As for the alleged excess of jurisdiction or competence, the Court found that the Tribunal had neither endeavoured to impose the judicial review of an Assembly resolution nor anywhere strayed outside the limits defined by Article 2 of its Statute, which entitled it to consider the meaning and effect of Staff Regulations and Rules in force at material times.

The operative part of the Court's advisory opinion[2] read as follows:

> The Court,
> 1. By nine votes to six,
> *Decides* to comply with the request for an advisory opinion;
> In favour: President Elias; Vice-President Sette Câmara; Judges Nagendra Singh, Mosler, Ago, Schwebel, Sir Robert Y. Jennings, de Lacharrière and M'Baye;
> Against: Judges Lachs, Morozov, Ruda, Oda, El-Khani and Bedjaoui.
> 2. With respect to the question as formulated in paragraph 48 above, *is of the opinion:*
> A. By ten votes to five,
> *That* the Administrative Tribunal of the United Nations in Judgement No. 273 did not err on a question of law relating to the provisions of the Charter of the United Nations;
> In favour: President Elias; Vice-President Sette Câmara; Judges Nagendra Singh, Ruda, Mosler, Oda, Ago, Sir Robert Y. Jennings, de Lacharrière and M'Baye;
> Against: Judges Lachs, Morozov, El-Khani, Schwebel and Bedjaoui.
> B. By twelve votes to three,
> *That* the Administrative Tribunal of the United Nations in Judgement No. 273 did not commit any excess of the jurisdiction or competence vested in it.
> In favour: President Elias; Vice-President Sette Câmara; Judges Lachs, Nagendra Singh, Ruda, Mosler, Oda, Ago, Sir Robert Y. Jennings, de Lacharrière, M'Baye and Bedjaoui;
> Against: Judges Morozov, El-Khani and Schwebel.

Judges Nagendra Singh, Ruda, Mosler and Oda appended separate opinions to the advisory opinion. Judges Lachs, Morozov, El-Khani and Schwebel appended dissenting opinions.

Publications. [1]*Application for Review of Judgement No. 273* (Mortished v. The Secretary-General) *of the United Nations Administrative Tribunal: Advisory Opinion of 20 July 1982*, I.C.J. Sales No. 475; *Pleadings, Oral Arguments, Documents*, I.C.J. Sales No. 484.
Report. [2]ICJ, A/37/4.
Resolution. [3]GA: 34/165, sect. II, 17 Dec. 1979 (YUN 1979, p. 1170).
Yearbook reference. [4]1981, p. 1202.

Organizational questions

Judges of the Court

Elections

On 19 March 1982, the General Assembly[1]— at its resumed thirty-sixth session—and the Security Council held elections to fill a vacancy in the International Court of Justice caused by the death of Judge Abdullah Ali El-Erian (Egypt) on 12 December 1981. This course of action had been decided by the Assembly on 18 December 1981[2]

and by the Council on 21 December.[3] Voting independently, both bodies elected Mohammed Bedjaoui (Algeria) to complete Judge El-Erian's term of office, due to expire on 5 February 1988.

Decision (1982). [1]GA: 36/309 B, 19 Mar. (no text).
Decision (prior). [2]GA: 36/461, 18 Dec. 1981 (YUN 1981, p. 350).
Resolution. [3]SC: 499(1981), 21 Dec. 1981 (YUN 1981, p. 1203).
Meeting records. GA: A/36/PV.107 (19 Mar.). SC: S/PV.2333 (19 Mar.).

Travel remuneration

In 1982, the General Assembly approved revised Travel and Subsistence Regulations for the members of the International Court of Justice.[3] The Regulations[4]—in force since 1947—had been amended effective 1 January 1969[5] to make the subsistence allowance rates correspond to those payable to members of organs and subsidiary organs of the United Nations.

Having received representations from the Court on the urgent need to update the Regulations, the Secretary-General, in a November note to the Assembly,[1] proposed that the Regulations be revised. He pointed out that for a number of years the Court's annual work programme had consisted of two two-to-three-month sessions and, under the current Regulations, those Judges not remaining at The Hague, Netherlands (the seat of the Court), between sessions had to pay travel costs to one of them. In view of increases in international travel costs since 1947, this was neither reasonable nor in line with practices followed for sessions of other United Nations organs, the note stated. Moreover, the travel of *ad hoc* Judges and members of Chambers of the Court was not covered, nor was there provision for reimbursing the removal costs of Judges taking up residence at The Hague, although this had been the practice based on arrangements applied to members of the Permanent Court of International Justice under the League of Nations.

Stating that it was difficult to predict the exact arrangements that each Judge would make regarding resident status, the Secretary-General estimated the financial implications at $70,000 for 1983, of which $33,000 represented non-recurring costs for removal and installation. Additional expenditures would be dealt with in the context of the second programme budget performance report, to be submitted to the Assembly in 1983.

Reporting on the programme budget for the 1982-1983 biennium, the Advisory Committee on Administrative and Budgetary Questions (ACABQ) stated that it agreed with the need to revise the Regulations[2]. However, since it had been established that members of the Court not residing at The Hague were not paid subsistence while attending sessions at the seat of the Court, and that it was not intended to change that practice, ACABQ felt that the text should be redrafted to avoid any ambiguity on that point. With regard to a suggestion by the Court that the level of subsistence allowance payable to the Court President be payable under the conditions and at rates for officials of the United Nations Secretariat, plus 50 per cent, ACABQ recalled that in all cases subsistence paid to chairmen and members of principal and subsidiary organs was paid at the same rate. Therefore, it recommended that the Secretary-General's proposal to fix the figure at "plus 40 per cent" be adopted.

General Assembly action. The General Assembly, by a resolution adopted without vote on 21 December 1982, approved the revised Regulations for the members of the Court.[3] On 8 December, the Fifth (Administrative and Budgetary) Committee had approved without objection its Chairman's oral proposal that it accept the Secretary-General's recommendations, as revised by ACABQ.

In the Committee, a draft decision orally proposed by the United States was rejected by a recorded vote, requested by Belgium, of 41 to 20, with 17 abstentions. By this draft, the Assembly would have taken note of the ACABQ report and decided that the additional expenditures incurred in 1983, if any, resulting from revision of the Regulations should be absorbed within the programme budget for 1982-1983.

Note. [1]S-G, A/C.5/37/50.
Report. [2]ACABQ, A/37/7/Add.13.
Resolution (1982). [3]GA: 37/240, 21 Dec., text following.
Resolutions (prior). GA: [4]85(I), annex, 11 Dec. 1946 (YUN 1946-47, p. 238); [5]2491(XXIII), 21 Dec. 1968 (YUN 1968, p. 901).
Meeting records. GA: 5th Committee, A/C.5/37/SR.60 (8 Dec.); plenary, A/37/PV.114 (21 Dec.).

General Assembly resolution 37/240

21 December 1982   Meeting 114   Adopted without vote

Approved by Fifth Committee (A/37/790) without objection, 8 December (meeting 60); oral proposal by Chairman to approve recommendations by Secretary-General (A/C.5/37/50, annex II), as revised on ACABQ suggestion (A/37/7/Add.13, annex); agenda item 103.

Travel and Subsistence Regulations of the International Court of Justice

The General Assembly,

Recalling its resolution 85(I) of 11 December 1946,

Approves the revised Travel and Subsistence Regulations of the International Court of Justice as contained in the annex to the present resolution.

ANNEX
Travel and Subsistence Regulations of the International Court of Justice

Article I
Travel expenses

1. The United Nations shall pay, subject to the conditions of these Regulations, the travel expenses of the members of the International Court of Justice necessarily incurred on duly authorized journeys. The following shall be deemed to be duly authorized journeys:

(a) For members of the Court and one close relative residing with them to attend sessions at the seat of the Court;

(b) For members of the Court and one close relative residing with them to attend a session which is held at a place other than the seat of the Court;

(c) In the case of the President of the Court, who by virtue of Article 22 of the Statute must reside at the seat of the Court:

(i) At the time of his election to the Presidency, a journey from his home to the seat of the Court in connection with any transfer of residence;

(ii) In the calendar year following that of his election to the Presidency, a return journey from the seat of the Court to his home at the time of that election;

(iii) At the end of his term of office as President, a journey from the seat of the Court to his home at the time of his election to that office, or to any other place provided that the cost of the journey is no greater.

Where the spouse and/or dependent children of the President reside with him at the seat of the Court, the United Nations shall reimburse their travel expenses for journeys undertaken in conjunction with (i), (ii) and (iii) above;

(d) Notwithstanding the provisions of subparagraph *(a)* above, in the case of any member of the Court other than the President who takes up residence at the seat of the Court in compliance with Article 23 of its Statute, solely:

(i) A journey from his home, at the time of appointment, to the seat of the Court, in connection with the transfer of his residence;

(ii) A return journey every second calendar year after the year of appointment from the seat of the Court to his home at the time of appointment;

(iii) A journey upon termination of appointment from the seat of the Court to his home at the time of appointment, or to any other place provided that the cost of the journey is not greater than the cost of the journey to his home at the time of appointment.

Where the spouse and/or dependent children of the member of the Court reside with him at the seat of the Court, the United Nations shall reimburse the travel expenses for journeys undertaken in conjunction with (i), (ii) and (iii) of the present subparagraph;

(iv) Any journey within the meaning of subparagraph *(b)* above;

(e) Journeys of any *ad hoc* judge chosen under Article 31 of the Statute of the Court and one close relative residing with him, in accordance with subparagraphs *(a)* and *(b)* above, when his presence is certified by the President as necessary for official business;

(f) Other journeys on official business, undertaken with the authority of the President.

2. In all cases, payment by the United Nations of travel expenses shall comprise the cost of journeys actually undertaken, subject to the following maximum entitlements:

(a) Payment of travel expenses by the United Nations shall comprise the cost of first-class accommodation and shall include expenses normally incidental to transportation, e.g., taxi-cab fares from station. The cost of transportation of baggage in excess of the weight or size carried free by transportation companies will not be allowable as an expense unless the excess is necessarily carried for official business reasons;

(b) Travel shall be by air, rail, private car or any other means of transport authorized by the President of the Court for special reasons;

(c) All travel will be by the most direct route, provided that travel by other routes may be allowed under written authority of the President when the official necessity therefor is satisfactorily established, but in other cases the travel expenses and subsistence allowance payable shall not exceed the amounts which would have been payable had the journey been by the most direct route.

Article 2
Subsistence allowances

1. A daily subsistence allowance shall be paid to the members of the Court while in official travel status under article 1, paragraph 1, subparagraphs *(b)*, *(c)* (i) and (iii), *(d)* (i), (iii) and (iv) and *(f)* of these Regulations. The allowance will be regarded as covering all charges for meals, lodging and gratuities, and other personal expenses.

2. The allowance will be payable under the conditions and at rates equivalent to the standard travel subsistence allowance rates applied to officials of the United Nations Secretariat, plus 40 per cent, provided that the President of the Court may reduce this rate in the event of the provision of board and/or lodging by a host Government. The allowance shall normally be payable in local currency.

3. Where the President of the Court or another member of the Court undertaking an official journey under article 1, paragraph 1 *(c)* or *(d)* of these Regulations is accompanied by a spouse and/or

dependent children, a subsistence allowance of one half of the appropriate rate payable to the President or member concerned in respect of that journey will be payable in respect of each dependant; where these dependants are travelling unaccompanied on an authorized journey, the full rate of subsistence allowance will be payable in respect of one adult and one half of that rate in respect of each other dependant.

Article 3
Removal and installation

1.   The President of the Court, who by virtue of Article 22 of its Statute shall reside at the seat of the Court, and any other member of the Court who takes up residence at the seat of the Court in compliance with Article 23 of the Statute, shall be entitled:

(a)   In conjunction with article 1, paragraph 1 *(c)* (i) or *(d)* (i), of these Regulations:

(i)   To full removal costs of household goods and personal effects to the seat of the Court from his home at the time of appointment (or any country other than that where the Court has its seat if less expenditure is entailed);

(ii)   To an amount corresponding to the installation grant provisions applicable to the senior officials of the Secretariat of the United Nations;

(b)   In conjunction with article 1, paragraph 1 *(c)* (iii) or *(d)* (iii), of these Regulations:

To full removal costs of household goods and personal effects from the seat of the Court to his home at the time of appointment (or any other country where he may choose to have his residence if less expenditure is entailed).

2.   The President may authorize, in the case of other members of the Court:

(a)   The reimbursement of reasonable costs of partial removal of household goods and personal effects between their principal place of residence and the seat of the Court upon taking up their appointment and upon separation;

(b)   An amount not exceeding one half of the installation grant provisions applicable to the senior officials of the Secretariat of the United Nations.

Article 4
Submission and payment of accounts

A detailed expense account must be rendered in support of each claim for reimbursement of travel expenses or subsistence allowance as soon as possible after completion of the travel or removal. The claims should show every item of expense, except where such expenses are to be covered by a subsistence allowance, and every advance drawn from any United Nations source, and must, as far as possible, be supported by receipts showing the service to which the payment is related. All expenses must be shown in the actual currency in which they were made and must be certified as having been necessarily and solely incurred in the discharge of the official business of the Court. No reimbursement shall be made without the written authorization of the President of the Court, countersigned by the Registrar.

Article 5
Travel and subsistence allowance of the Registrar

The travel and subsistence provisions applicable to the Registrar of the Court shall be as set out in the Staff Regulations of the United Nations for officials of comparable rank, subject to any exceptions authorized by the President of the Court.

Article 6
Applicability

These Regulations shall enter into force on 1 January 1983.

Reports of the Court

The 1982 activities of the International Court of Justice were contained in two reports to the General Assembly, covering the periods 1 August 1981 to 31 July 1982[2] and 1 August 1982 to 31 July 1983.[3]

On 17 December 1982, by a decision [1] adopted without vote on an oral proposal by its President, the Assembly took note of the 1981/82 report.

Decision (1982). [1]GA: 37/436, 17 Dec., text following.
Reports. ICJ, [2]A/37/4, [3]A/38/4.
Meeting record. GA: A/37/PV.110 (17 Dec.).

General Assembly decision 37/436

Adopted without vote

Oral proposal by President; agenda item 13.

Report of the International Court of Justice

At its 110th plenary meeting, on 17 December 1982, the General Assembly took note of the report of the International Court of Justice.

Chapter II

Legal aspects of international political relations

Contents

For resolutions and decisions of major organs mentioned but not reproduced, refer to INDEX OF RESOLUTIONS AND DECISIONS.

Manila Declaration on dispute settlement

In November 1982, the General Assembly approved the Manila Declaration on the Peaceful Settlement of International Disputes, the draft of which had been finalized, in accordance with the Assembly's December 1981 requests,[6] by the Special Committee on the Charter of the United Nations and on the Strengthening of the Role of the Organization.

The idea of such a declaration had been suggested by Romania in 1979,[7] and in 1980 at Manila, Philippines, the 47-member Special Committee began working on the draft.[9] In 1981, both the Special Committee and the Assembly's Sixth (Legal) Committee had formulated further elements of the text.[10]

Special Committee consideration. The draft Manila declaration on dispute settlement was one of two main questions considered by the Special Committee at its 1982 session, held at Geneva from 22 February to 19 March. The other topic was a list of proposals concerning the maintenance of international peace and security.

To consider both questions, the Committee established an open-ended Working Group—which met from 2 to 12 March on the draft declaration—while the Group, in turn, established a Drafting Group to solve certain pending points on that topic. In June, the Committee submitted its report,[3] containing the finalized version of the draft declaration, to the General Assembly.

General Assembly action. On 15 November, the General Assembly adopted a resolution[4] approving the Manila Declaration and urging efforts to have it generally known and fully observed and implemented. The Declaration, comprising a preamble, two main sections and concluding paragraphs, was annexed to the resolution.

Section I set out principles to be observed by States, covering such matters as good-faith action to avoid disputes, peaceful settlement by free choice of means appropriate to the circumstances, observance of obligations under international law, recourse to regional or other means of settlement before reference to the Security Council, avoidance of action which might aggravate a situation, the use of agreements and provisions on peaceful settlement, the use of direct negotiations, good-faith implementation of settlement agreements, and the possible recourse to peaceful settlement procedures in order to facilitate exercise of the right of peoples to self-determination. By section II, concerned with the United Nations role in dispute settlement, the Assembly declared that Member States should make full use of the Charter, fulfil in good faith their Charter obligations, reaffirm the Assembly's role, strengthen the Security Council's role, and refer legal disputes as a general rule to the International Court of Justice. The Secretary-General's role was also discussed.

The resolution was adopted without vote. On 27 October, the Sixth Committee had approved the draft, sponsored by 40 States and introduced by Romania, by consensus.

Also on 27 October, on an oral proposal by Romania for the sponsors of the 40-nation draft, the Committee, without vote, recommended that the Assembly include the item on peaceful settlement of disputes between States in the provisional agenda of its 1983 session. On 15 November, the Assembly adopted a decision to that effect without vote.[1]

In its 16 December resolution on the work of the Special Committee,[5] the Assembly welcomed the Declaration's adoption as a significant achievement of the Committee and requested it to continue in 1983 work on the peaceful settlement of disputes by considering the remaining proposals it had listed in 1979.[8]

In a letter of 16 November 1982 to the Secretary-General,[2] Venezuela, referring to its 1981 comments on the Declaration,[11] pointed out that, regarding the references to the International Court of Justice, Venezuela's Constitution provided that in its international agreements there should be a clause whereby the parties would undertake to decide by peaceful means recognized in international law or other agreed means any disputes that might arise between the parties concerning their interpretation or execution.

Decision (1982). [1]GA: 37/407, 15 Nov., text following.
Letter. [2]Venezuela, 16 Nov., A/37/633.
Report. [3]Committee on Charter and role of United Nations, A/37/33.
Resolutions (1982). GA: [4]37/10, 15 Nov., text following; [5]37/114, paras. 2 & 5 (*b*), 16 Dec.
Resolutions (prior). [6]GA: 36/110, 10 Dec. 1981 (YUN 1981, p. 1211) and 36/122, 11 Dec. 1981 (*ibid.*, p. 1239).
Yearbook references. 1979, [7]p. 150, [8]p. 160; [9]1980, p. 189; 1981, [10]p. 1208, [11]p. 1210.
Meeting records. GA: 6th Committee, A/C.6/37/SR.20-28, *29, 30* (18-28 Oct.); plenary, A/37/PV.68 (15 Nov.).

General Assembly resolution 37/10

15 November 1982　　　　Meeting 68　　　　Adopted without vote

Approved by Sixth Committee (A/37/590) by consensus, 27 October (meeting 29); 40-nation draft (A/C.6/37/L.2); agenda item 122.

Sponsors: Australia, Bahamas, Bangladesh, Chile, Congo, Costa Rica, Cyprus, Ecuador, Egypt, Ethiopia, Finland, German Democratic Republic, Greece, Guinea, Guinea-Bissau, Guyana, Indonesia, Italy, Japan, Madagascar, Mali, Mexico, Morocco, Nigeria, Philippines, Romania, Rwanda, Sierra Leone, Singapore, Spain, Sri Lanka, Sudan, Togo, Uganda, United Republic of Cameroon, Upper Volta, Uruguay, Yugoslavia, Zaire, Zambia.

Manila Declaration on the Peaceful Settlement of International Disputes

The General Assembly,

Having examined the item entitled "Peaceful settlement of disputes between States",

Recalling its resolutions 34/102 of 14 December 1979, 35/160 of 15 December 1980 and 36/110 of 10 December 1981,

Reaffirming the need to exert utmost efforts in order to settle any conflicts and disputes between States exclusively by peaceful means and to avoid any military action and hostilities, which can only make more difficult the solution of those conflicts and disputes,

Considering that the question of the peaceful settlement of disputes should represent one of the central concerns for States and for the United Nations and that the efforts to strengthen the process of the peaceful settlement of disputes should be continued,

Convinced that the adoption of the Manila Declaration on the Peaceful Settlement of International Disputes should enhance the observance of the principle of peaceful settlement of disputes in relations between States and contribute to the elimination of the danger of recourse to force or to the threat of force, to the relaxation of international tensions, to the promotion of a policy of co-operation and peace and of respect for the independence and sovereignty of all States, to the enhancing of the role of the United Nations in preventing conflicts and settling them peacefully and, consequently, to the strengthening of international peace and security,

Considering the need to ensure a wide dissemination of the text of the Declaration,

1. *Approves* the Manila Declaration on the Peaceful Settlement of International Disputes, the text of which is annexed to the present resolution;

2. *Expresses its appreciation* to the Special Committee on the Charter of the United Nations and on the Strengthening of the Role of the Organization for its important contribution to the elaboration of the text of the Declaration;

3. *Requests* the Secretary-General to inform the Governments of the States Members of the United Nations or members of specialized agencies, the Security Council and the International Court of Justice of the adoption of the Declaration;

4. *Urges* that all efforts be made so that the Declaration becomes generally known and fully observed and implemented.

ANNEX
Manila Declaration on the Peaceful Settlement of International Disputes

The General Assembly,

Reaffirming the principle of the Charter of the United Nations that all States shall settle their international disputes by peaceful means in such a manner that international peace and security, and justice, are not endangered,

Conscious that the Charter of the United Nations embodies the means and an essential framework for the peaceful settlement of international disputes, the continuance of which is likely to endanger the maintenance of international peace and security,

Recognizing the important role of the United Nations and the need to enhance its effectiveness in the peaceful settlement of international disputes and the maintenance of international peace and security, in accordance with the principles of justice and international law, in conformity with the Charter of the United Nations,

Reaffirming the principle of the Charter of the United Nations that all States shall refrain in their international relations from the threat or use of force against the territorial integrity or political independence of any State, or in any other manner inconsistent with the purposes of the United Nations,

Reiterating that no State or group of States has the right to intervene, directly or indirectly, for any reason whatsoever, in the internal or external affairs of any other State,

Reaffirming the Declaration on Principles of International Law concerning Friendly Relations and Co-operation among States in accordance with the Charter of the United Nations,

Bearing in mind the importance of maintaining and strengthening international peace and security and the development of friendly relations among States, irrespective of their political, economic and social systems or levels of economic development,

Reaffirming the principle of equal rights and self-determination of peoples as enshrined in the Charter of the United Nations and referred to in the Declaration on Principles of International Law concerning Friendly Relations and Co-operation among States in accordance with the Charter of the United Nations and in other relevant resolutions of the General Assembly,

Stressing the need for all States to desist from any forcible action which deprives peoples, particularly peoples under colonial and racist régimes or other forms of alien domination, of their inalienable right to self-determination, freedom and independence, as referred to in the Declaration on Principles of International Law concerning Friendly Relations and Co-operation among States in accordance with the Charter of the United Nations,

Mindful of exisiting international instruments as well as respective principles and rules concerning the peaceful settlement of international disputes, including the exhausting of local remedies whenever applicable,

Determined to promote international co-operation in the political field and to encourage the progressive development of international law and its codification, particularly in relation to the peaceful settlement of international disputes,

Solemnly declares that:

1. All States shall act in good faith and in conformity with the purposes and principles enshrined in the Charter of the United Nations with a view to avoiding disputes among themselves likely to affect friendly relations among States, thus contributing to the maintenance of international peace and security. They shall live together in peace with one another as good neighbours and strive for the adoption of meaningful measures for strengthening international peace and security.

2. Every State shall settle its international disputes exclusively by peaceful means in such a manner that international peace and security, and justice, are not endangered.

3. International disputes shall be settled on the basis of the sovereign equality of States and in accordance with the principle of free choice of means in conformity with obligations under the Charter of the United Nations and with the principles of justice and international law. Recourse to, or acceptance of, a settlement procedure freely agreed to by States with regard to existing or future disputes to which they are parties shall not be regarded as incompatible with the sovereign equality of States.

4. States parties to a dispute shall continue to observe in their mutual relations their obligations under the fundamental principles of international law concerning the sovereignty, independence and territorial integrity of States, as well as other generally recognized principles and rules of contemporary international law.

5. States shall seek in good faith and in a spirit of co-operation an early and equitable settlement of their international disputes by any of the following means: negotiation, inquiry, mediation, conciliation, arbitration, judicial settlement, resort to regional arrangements or agencies or other peaceful means of their own choice, including good offices. In seeking such a settlement, the parties shall agree on such peaceful means as may be appropriate to the circumstances and the nature of their dispute.

6. States parties to regional arrangements or agencies shall make every effort to achieve pacific settlement of their local disputes through such regional arrangements or agencies before referring them to the Security Council. This does not preclude States from bringing any dispute to the attention of the Security Council or of the General Assembly in accordance with the Charter of the United Nations.

7. In the event of failure of the parties to a dispute to reach an early solution by any of the above means of settlement, they shall continue to seek a peaceful solution and shall consult forthwith on mutually agreed means to settle the dispute peacefully. Should the parties fail to settle by any of the above means a dispute the continuance of which is likely to endanger the maintenance of international peace and security, they shall refer it to the Security Council in accordance with the Charter of the United Nations and without prejudice to the functions and powers of the Council set forth in the relevant provisions of Chapter VI of the Charter.

8. States parties to an international dispute, as well as other States, shall refrain from any action whatsoever which may aggravate the situation so as to endanger the maintenance of international peace and security and make more difficult or impede the peaceful settlement of the dispute, and shall act in this respect in accordance with the purposes and principles of the United Nations.

9. States should consider concluding agreements for the peaceful settlement of disputes among them. They should also include in bilateral agreements and multilateral conventions to be concluded, as appropriate, effective provisions for the peaceful settlement of disputes arising from the interpretation or application thereof.

10. States should, without prejudice to the right of free choice of means, bear in mind that direct negotiations are a flexible and effective means of peaceful settlement of their disputes. When they choose to resort to direct negotiations, States should negotiate meaningfully, in order to arrive at an early settlement acceptable to the parties. States should be equally prepared to seek the settlement of their disputes by the other means mentioned in the present Declaration.

11. States shall in accordance with international law implement in good faith all the provisions of agreements concluded by them for the settlement of their disputes.

12. In order to facilitate the exercise by the peoples concerned of the right to self-determination as referred to in the Declaration on Principles of International Law concerning Friendly Relations and Co-operation among States in accordance with the Charter of the United Nations, the parties to a dispute may have the possibility, if they agree to do so and as appropriate, to have recourse to the relevant procedures mentioned in the present Declaration, for the peaceful settlement of the dispute.

13. Neither the existence of a dispute nor the failure of a procedure of peaceful settlement of disputes shall permit the use of force or threat of force by any of the States parties to the dispute.

II

1. Member States should make full use of the provisions of the Charter of the United Nations, including the procedures and means provided for therein, particularly Chapter VI, concerning the peaceful settlement of disputes.

2. Member States shall fulfil in good faith the obligations assumed by them in accordance with the Charter of the United Nations. They should, in accordance with the Charter, as appropriate, duly take into account the recommendations of the Security Council relating to the peaceful settlement of disputes. They should also, in accordance with the Charter, as appropriate, duly take into account the recommendations adopted by the General Assembly, subject to Articles 11 and 12 of the Charter, in the field of peaceful settlement of disputes.

3. Member States reaffirm the important role conferred on the General Assembly by the Charter of the United Nations in the field of peaceful settlement of disputes and stress the need for it to discharge effectively its responsibilities. Accordingly, they should:

(a) Bear in mind that the General Assembly may discuss any situation, regardless of origin, which it deems likely to impair the general welfare or friendly relations among nations and, subject to Article 12 of the Charter, recommend measures for its peaceful adjustment;

(b) Consider making use, when they deem it appropriate, of the possibility of bringing to the attention of the General Assembly any dispute or any situation which might lead to international friction or give rise to a dispute;

(c) Consider utilizing, for the peaceful settlement of their disputes, the subsidiary organs established by the General Assembly in the performance of its functions under the Charter;

(d) Consider, when they are parties to a dispute brought to the attention of the General Assembly, making use of consultations within the framework of the Assembly, with a view to facilitating an early settlement of their dispute.

4. Member States should strengthen the primary role of the Security Council so that it may fully and effectively discharge its responsibilities, in accordance with the Charter of the United Nations, in the area of the settlement of disputes or of any situation the continuance of which is likely to endanger the maintenance of international peace and security. To this end they should:

(a) Be fully aware of their obligation to refer to the Security Council such a dispute to which they are parties if they fail to settle it by the means indicated in Article 33 of the Charter;

(b) Make greater use of the possibility of bringing to the attention of the Security Council any dispute or any situation which might lead to international friction or give rise to a dispute;

(c) Encourage the Security Council to make wider use of the opportunities provided for by the Charter in order to review disputes or situations the continuance of which is likely to endanger the maintenance of international peace and security;

(d) Consider making greater use of the fact-finding capacity of the Security Council in accordance with the Charter;

(e) Encourage the Security Council to make wider use, as a means to promote peaceful settlement of disputes, of the subsidiary organs established by it in the performance of its functions under the Charter;

(f) Bear in mind that the Security Council may, at any stage of a dispute of the nature referred to in Article 33 of the Charter or of a situation of like nature, recommend appropriate procedures or methods of adjustment;

(g) Encourage the Security Council to act without delay, in accordance with its functions and powers, particularly in cases where international disputes develop into armed conflicts.

5. States should be fully aware of the role of the International Court of Justice, which is the principal judicial organ of the United Nations. Their attention is drawn to the facilities offered by the International Court of Justice for the settlement of legal disputes, especially since the revision of the Rules of the Court.

States may entrust the solution of their differences to other tribunals by virtue of agreements already in existence or which may be concluded in the future.

States should bear in mind:

(a) That legal disputes should as a general rule be referred by the parties to the International Court of Justice, in accordance with the provisions of the Statute of the Court;

(b) That it is desirable that they:

(i) Consider the possibility of inserting in treaties, whenever appropriate, clauses providing for the submission to the International Court of Justice of disputes which may arise from the interpretation or application of such treaties;

(ii)   Study the possibility of choosing, in the free exercise of their sovereignty, to recognize as compulsory the jurisdiction of the International Court of Justice in accordance with Article 36 of its Statute;
(iii) Review the possibility of identifying cases in which use may be made of the International Court of Justice.

The organs of the United Nations and the specialized agencies should study the advisability of making use of the possibility of requesting advisory opinions of the International Court of Justice on legal questions arising within the scope of their activities, provided that they are duly authorized to do so.

Recourse to judicial settlement of legal disputes, particularly referral to the International Court of Justice, should not be considered an unfriendly act between States.

6.   The Secretary-General should make full use of the provisions of the Charter of the United Nations concerning the responsibilities entrusted to him. The Secretary-General may bring to the attention of the Security Council any matter which in his opinion may threaten the maintenance of international peace and security. He shall perform such other functions as are entrusted to him by the Security Council or by the General Assembly. Reports in this connection shall be made whenever requested to the Security Council or the General Assembly.

Urges all States to observe and promote in good faith the provisions of the present Declaration in the peaceful settlement of their international disputes;
Declares that nothing in the present Declaration shall be construed as prejudicing in any manner the relevant provisions of the Charter or the rights and duties of States, or the scope of the functions and powers of the United Nations organs under the Charter, in particular those relating to the peaceful settlement of disputes;
Declares that nothing in the present Declaration could in any way prejudice the right to self-determination, freedom and independence, as derived from the Charter, of peoples forcibly deprived of that right and referred to in the Declaration on Principles of International Law concerning Friendly Relations and Co-operation among States in accordance with the Charter of the United Nations, particularly peoples under colonial and racist régimes or other forms of alien domination; nor the right of these peoples to struggle to that end and to seek and receive support, in accordance with the principles of the Charter and in conformity with the above-mentioned Declaration;
Stresses the need, in accordance with the Charter, to continue efforts to strengthen the process of the peaceful settlement of disputes through progressive development and codification of international law, as appropriate, and through enhancing the effectiveness of the United Nations in this field.

General Assembly decision 37/407

Adopted without vote

Approved by Sixth Committee (A/37/590) without vote, 27 October (meeting 29); oral proposal by Romania for sponsors of 40-nation draft, A/C.6/37/L.2; agenda item 122.

Peaceful settlement of disputes between States

At its 68th plenary meeting, on 15 November 1982, the General Assembly, on the recommendation of the Sixth Committee, decided to include in the provisional agenda of its thirty-eighth session the item entitled "Peaceful settlement of disputes between States".

Non-use of force in international relations

In December 1982, the General Assembly decided that its Special Committee on Enhancing the Effectiveness of the Principle of Non-Use of Force in International Relations should continue drafting a world treaty on that principle.

Special Committee consideration. In response to a November 1981 General Assembly resolution,[6] the 35-member Special Committee on Enhancing the Effectiveness of the Principle of Non-Use of Force in International Relations—established in 1977[5] to consider suggestions towards drafting

a world treaty on that principle—met at United Nations Headquarters from 29 March to 23 April 1982 and submitted a report on its work to the Assembly.[2]

The Committee had before it a draft world treaty on the non-use of force submitted in 1976 by the USSR;[7] a working paper put forward in 1979 by Belgium, France, the Federal Republic of Germany, Italy and the United Kingdom;[8] and a 1981 revised working paper from 10 non-aligned countries (Benin, Cyprus, Egypt, India, Iraq, Morocco, Nepal, Nicaragua, Senegal, Uganda).[9] Also before the Committee were comments by Botswana, the Central African Republic, Czechoslovakia, Democratic Kampuchea, Egypt and Iran submitted in reply to a renewed Assembly invitation in 1981 for States' observations.[6] These comments, together with those of Venezuela, were forwarded to the Assembly by the Secretary-General in August 1982.[3]

The Committee re-established an open-ended Working Group with the same mandate and officers as the Committee. The Group held nine meetings, between 12 and 19 April, at which it considered the revised working paper by the non-aligned States.

On 20 April, the Committee Chairman proposed a set of ideas in the form of a very informal working paper which he suggested should be explored to see whether it could serve to facilitate the Committee's future work. The paper, which was subsequently discussed in a preliminary manner, contained proposals and suggestions made in the Committee and grouped under the headings of: manifestations, scope and dimensions of the threat or use of force; general prohibition of its threat or use; consequences of threat or use; legitimate use; peaceful settlement of disputes; United Nations role; and disarmament and confidence-building measures.

On 23 April, the Committee approved the Working Group's report. Since the Committee had not completed its work, it generally recognized the desirability of further consideration of the questions before it. While most members were in favour of renewing the Committee's mandate, some were not; others thought the mandate should be reviewed.

General Assembly action. On 16 December, the General Assembly adopted a resolution[4] on the work of the Special Committee, by which it decided that the Committee should continue work on drafting, as soon as possible, a world treaty on the non-use of force in international relations as well as the peaceful settlement of disputes or any other recommendations as it deemed appropriate. In order to ensure further progress, the Committee was requested to begin, in 1983, elaborating the formulas of the working paper containing the main elements of the principle of non-use of force in international relations, taking into account the proposals submitted to it and the efforts made at its 1982 session. The Assembly invited the Committee to report in 1983 and again invited comments from Governments.

The resolution was adopted by a recorded vote of 119 to 15, with 8 abstentions. On 29 November, the Sixth Committee had approved the draft, sponsored by 33 States, by a recorded vote, requested by the USSR, of 87 to 15, with 9 abstentions.

Several States explained their votes in the Sixth Committee. Norway (against) said the principle of the non-use of force was already embodied in the United Nations Charter. Australia (abstaining) shared that view and was joined by the Netherlands (against) in stating that the draft did not take account of the views of some members of the Special Committee. The latter added that the Committee's terms of reference remained too narrow since it was charged with elaborating a world treaty which would not contribute to settling international problems.

Introducing the draft, Mongolia said the text was procedural reproducing the Assembly's 1981 resolution, although it did contain an innovation in that the Special Committee was requested to begin elaborating the formulas of the working paper.

Other developments. The conclusion of a world treaty on the non-use of force in international relations was also considered in conjunction with a proposed comprehensive programme of disarmament[1] which was examined, but not adopted, at the General Assembly's 1982 special session devoted to disarmament.

Reports. [1]*Ad Hoc* Committee of 12th special session, A/S-12/32; [2]Committee on non-use of force, A/37/41; [3]S-G, A/37/375.
Resolution (1982). [4]GA: 37/105, 16 Dec., text following.
Resolutions (prior). GA: [5]32/150, 19 Dec. 1977 (YUN 1977, p. 118); [6]36/31, 13 Nov. 1981 (YUN 1981, p. 1207).
Yearbook references. [7]1976, p. 105; [8]1979, p. 153; [9]1981, p. 1204.
Financial implications. 5th Committee report, A/37/737; S-G statements, A/C.5/37/78, A/C.6/37/L.14.
Meeting records. GA: 6th Committee, A/C.6/37/SR.31-40, *57* (29 Oct.-29 Nov.); 5th Committee, A/C.5/37/SR.61 (9 Dec.); plenary, A/37/PV.107 (16 Dec.).

General Assembly resolution 37/105

16 December 1982　　　Meeting 107　　　119-15-8 (recorded vote)

Approved by Sixth Committee (A/37/721) by recorded vote (87-15-9), 29 November (meeting 57); 33-nation draft (A/C.6/37/L.11); agenda item 118.

Sponsors: Afghanistan, Angola, Benin, Bulgaria, Byelorussian SSR, Cuba, Cyprus, Czechoslovakia, Democratic Yemen, Ecuador, Egypt, Ethiopia, German Democratic Republic, Grenada, Hungary, India, Iraq, Lao People's Democratic Republic, Libyan Arab Jamahiriya, Madagascar, Mali, Mongolia, Morocco, Mozambique, Nicaragua, Poland, Romania, Syrian Arab Republic, Uganda, Ukrainian SSR, USSR, Venezuela, Viet Nam.

Report of the Special Committee on Enhancing the Effectiveness of the Principle of Non-Use of Force in International Relations

The General Assembly,

Recalling its resolution 31/9 of 8 November 1976, in which it invited Member States to examine further the draft World Treaty on the Non-Use of Force in International Relations as well as other proposals made during the consideration of this item,

Recalling also its resolution 32/150 of 19 December 1977, by which it established the Special Committee on Enhancing the Effectiveness of the Principle of Non-Use of Force in International Relations,

Recalling, in particular, its resolutions 33/96 of 16 December 1978, 34/13 of 9 November 1979, 35/50 of 4 December 1980 and 36/31 of 13 November 1981, in which it decided that the Special Committee should continue its work,

Taking note of the statement made by the Chairman of the Special Committee at its session in 1982,

Having considered the report of the Special Committee,

Taking into account that the Special Committee has not completed the mandate entrusted to it,

Reaffirming the need for universal and effective application of the principle of the non-use of force in international relations and for assistance by the United Nations in this endeavour,

Expressing the hope that the Special Committee will, on the basis of the proposals before it, complete the mandate entrusted to it as soon as possible,

1. *Takes note* of the report of the Special Committee on Enhancing the Effectiveness of the Principle of Non-Use of Force in International Relations;

2. *Decides* that the Special Committee shall continue its work with the goal of drafting, at the earliest possible date, a world treaty on the non-use of force in international relations as well as the peaceful settlement of disputes or such other recommendations as the Committee deems appropriate;

3. *Requests* the Special Committee, in order to ensure further progress in its work, to begin at its forthcoming session, as the next step, the elaboration of the formulas of the working paper containing the main elements of the principle of non-use of force in international relations, taking duly into account the proposals submitted to it and, in particular, the efforts undertaken at its session in 1982;

4. *Invites* the Governments that have not yet done so to communicate their comments or suggestions or to bring them up to date, in accordance with General Assembly resolution 31/9;

5. *Requests* the Special Committee to be mindful of the importance of reaching general agreement whenever it has significance for the outcome of its work;

6. *Requests* the Secretary-General to provide the Special Committee with the necessary facilities and services;

7. *Invites* the Special Committee to submit a report on its work to the General Assembly at its thirty-eighth session;

8. *Decides* to include in the provisional agenda of its thirty-eighth session the item entitled "Report of the Special Committee on Enhancing the Effectiveness of the Principle of Non-Use of Force in International Relations".

Recorded vote in Assembly as follows:

In favour: Afghanistan, Algeria, Angola, Argentina, Bahamas, Bahrain, Bangladesh, Barbados, Belize, Benin, Bhutan, Bolivia, Brazil, Bulgaria, Burma, Burundi, Byelorussian SSR, Central African Republic, Chad, Chile, Colombia, Comoros, Congo, Costa Rica, Cuba, Cyprus, Czechoslovakia, Democratic Yemen, Djibouti, Dominican Republic, Ecuador, Egypt, El Salvador, Ethiopia, Fiji, Finland, Gabon, Gambia, German Democratic Republic, Ghana, Greece, Grenada, Guatemala, Guinea, Guyana, Honduras, Hungary, India, Indonesia, Iran, Iraq, Ivory Coast, Jamaica, Jordan, Kenya, Kuwait, Lao People's Democratic Republic, Lebanon, Lesotho, Libyan Arab Jamahiriya, Madagascar, Malawi, Malaysia, Maldives, Mali, Malta, Mauritania, Mauritius, Mexico, Mongolia, Morocco, Mozambique, Nepal, Nicaragua, Niger, Nigeria, Oman, Pakistan, Panama, Papua New Guinea, Paraguay, Peru, Philippines, Poland, Qatar, Romania, Rwanda, Samoa, Sao Tome and Principe, Saudi Arabia, Senegal, Sierra Leone, Singapore, Solomon Islands, Somalia, Sri Lanka, Sudan, Suriname, Syrian Arab Republic, Thailand, Togo, Trinidad and Tobago, Tunisia, Uganda, Ukrainian SSR, USSR, United Arab Emirates, United Republic of Cameroon, United Republic of Tanzania, Upper Volta, Uruguay, Vanuatu, Venezuela, Viet Nam, Yemen, Yugoslavia, Zaire, Zambia, Zimbabwe.

Against: Belgium, Canada, Denmark, France, Iceland, Israel, Italy, Japan, Luxembourg, Netherlands, Norway, Portugal, Spain, United Kingdom, United States.

Abstaining: Australia, Austria, China, Germany, Federal Republic of, Ireland, New Zealand, Sweden, Turkey.

Draft code of offences against peace and security

With a view to elaborating the draft Code of Offences against the Peace and Security of Mankind, the International Law Commission

(ILC), in July 1982, resumed work on it, in response to a December 1981 General Assembly request.[7] In December 1982, the Assembly invited ILC to continue that work.

Prepared by ILC in 1954[8] in response to a 1947 Assembly resolution,[6] the draft Code defined offences which were crimes under international law and for which the responsible individual was to be punished. Also by the 1947 resolution, ILC had been directed to formulate the principles of international law recognized in the Charter of the Nürnberg Tribunal and in the judgement of the Tribunal, before which the Nazi war crimes trials were held after the Second World War.

ILC action. At its 1982 session, held at Geneva from 3 May to 23 July,[1] ILC appointed Doudou Thiam (Senegal) as Special Rapporteur for the topic and established a Working Group which met on 20 July. On the Group's recommendation, ILC decided to accord priority to the draft Code within its five-year programme and stated that it intended to proceed, early in its 1983 session, to a general debate in plenary meetings based on a first report to be submitted by the Special Rapporteur. The conclusions of the debate would be presented to the Assembly in 1983. To assist the Special Rapporteur, ILC requested the Secretariat for a compendium of relevant international instruments and an updated version of a 1981 analysis of the written or oral comments of Member States.[9]

During its consideration of the topic, ILC had before it the comments of eight Member States (Barbados, Byelorussian SSR, Czechoslovakia, Finland, German Democratic Republic, Ukrainian SSR, USSR, Uruguay) received in reply to a December 1981 Assembly request.[7] These comments were also forwarded to the Assembly by the Secretary-General in August 1982.[2]

Other actions. On 7 September, the Sub-Commission on Prevention of Discrimination and Protection of Minorities recommended two draft resolutions to its parent body, the Commission on Human Rights, for adoption.

By these text, on the effects of gross violations of human rights on international peace and security,[4] and on the human rights of persons subjected to any form of detention or imprisonment,[5] the Sub-Commission recommended that the Assembly be requested by the Economic and Social Council to invite ILC to take into account, when elaborating the draft Code, mass and flagrant violations of human rights and the comments by Sub-Commission members on such violations, and Sub-Commission members' comments on the question of missing or disappeared persons with a view to declaring as a crime against humanity the practice of persons being rendered missing and disappeared involuntarily.

General Assembly action. On 16 December 1982,[3] the General Assembly invited ILC to continue its work with a view to elaborating the 1954 draft Code and requested it to submit a preliminary report to the Assembly in 1983 on the draft's scope and structure. The Assembly requested the Secretary-General to reiterate an invitation to Member States and international intergovernmental organizations to present or update their comments on the draft with a view to submitting them to ILC.

The resolution was adopted by a recorded vote of 126 to none, with 17 abstentions. On 7 December, the Sixth Committee had approved the text, sponsored by 25 countries and introduced by Zaire, by 82 votes to none, with 17 abstentions.

At the request of the United States, a separate vote was taken in the Committee on paragraph 4, by which the Assembly decided to include the item on the draft Code in its 1983 agenda. The paragraph was approved by 72 votes to 13, with 13 abstentions.

Explaining their votes against retaining the paragraph, and their consequent abstention in the vote on the text as a whole, France, Japan and the United Kingdom considered the resolution unnecessary in view of the fact that ILC was currently seized with the subject on the instruction of the Assembly. The United Kingdom added that once the subject had been referred to ILC, the Sixth Committee should not give the impression that it did not trust that body to carry out the mandate or that it was putting pressure on ILC, either of a political nature or with regard to priorities in its work programme. The United States considered improper the proposed inclusion of the topic as a separate agenda item. Japan considered that the retention of paragraph 4 created an undesirable precedent, as did Australia, which abstained in the votes on the paragraph and the text as a whole.

Norway, speaking for the Nordic countries, said they had voted in favour of the text as a whole, as they welcomed continued consideration of the subject by ILC, but did not see any reason for retaining it as a separate agenda item of the Assembly; the matter could well be discussed by the Committee under the general item on the ILC report.

Australia, France, Japan, Norway (for the Nordic countries) and the United States expressed reservations as regards the text's suggestion of particular importance and urgency of the subject.

Reports. [1]ILC, A/37/10; [2]S-G, A/37/325.
Resolutions (1982). [3]GA: 37/102, 16 Dec., text following. SCPDPM (report, E/CN.4/1983/4), 7 Sep.: [4]1982/11; [5]1982/12.
Resolutions (prior). GA: [6]177(II), 21 Nov. 1947 (YUN 1947-48, p. 215); [7]36/106, 10 Dec. 1981 (YUN 1981, p. 1214).
Yearbook references. [8]1954, p. 411; [9]1981, p. 1212.

Meeting records. GA: 6th Committee, A/C.6/37/SR.52-55, *63, 64* (22 Nov.–7 Dec.); plenary, A/37/PV.107 (16 Dec.).

General Assembly resolution 37/102

16 December 1982   Meeting 107   126-0-17 (recorded vote)

Approved by Sixth Committee (A/37/714) by vote (82-0-17), 7 December (meeting 64); 25-nation draft (A/C.6/37/L.26); agenda item 115.

Sponsors: Afghanistan, Algeria, Congo, Cuba, Cyprus, Egypt, German Democratic Republic, Ghana, Liberia, Mali, Mongolia, Morocco, Mozambique, Niger, Nigeria, Philippines, Rwanda, Sierra Leone, Sudan, Syrian Arab Republic, Thailand, Togo, Tunisia, Ukrainian SSR, Zaire.

Draft Code of Offences against the Peace and Security of Mankind

The General Assembly,

Mindful of Article 13, paragraph 1 *a*, of the Charter of the United Nations, which provides that the General Assembly shall initiate studies and make recommendations for the purpose of encouraging the progressive development of international law and its codification,

Recalling its resolution 177(II) of 21 November 1947, by which it directed the International Law Commission to prepare a draft code of offences against the peace and security of mankind,

Having considered the draft Code of Offences against the Peace and Security of Mankind prepared by the International Law Commission and submitted to the General Assembly in 1954,

Recalling its belief that the elaboration of a code of offences against the peace and security of mankind could contribute to strengthening international peace and security and thus to promoting and implementing the purposes and principles set forth in the Charter of the United Nations,

Recalling its resolution 36/106 of 10 December 1981, in which it invited the International Law Commission to resume its work with a view to elaborating the draft Code and to examine it with the required priority in order to review it, taking into account the results achieved by the process of the progressive development of international law,

Taking into account the views expressed during the debate on this item at the current session,

Noting with satisfaction the appointment of a special rapporteur for the draft Code,

Taking into account the importance and the urgency of the subject,

1.   *Invites* the International Law Commission to continue its work with a view to elaborating the draft Code of Offences against the Peace and Security of Mankind, in conformity with paragraph 1 of General Assembly resolution 36/106 and taking into account the decision contained in paragraph 255 of the report of the International Law Commission on the work of its thirty-fourth session;

2.   *Requests* the International Law Commission, in conformity with resolution 36/106, to submit a preliminary report to the General Assembly at its thirty-eighth session bearing, *inter alia*, on the scope and the structure of the draft Code;

3.   *Requests* the Secretary-General to reiterate his invitation to Member States and relevant international intergovernmental organizations to present or update their comments and observations on the draft Code with a view to their submission to the International Law Commission;

4.   *Decides* to include in the provisional agenda of its thirty-eighth session the item entitled "Draft Code of Offences against the Peace and Security of Mankind".

Recorded vote in Assembly as follows:

In favour: Afghanistan, Algeria, Angola, Argentina, Austria, Bahamas, Bahrain, Bangladesh, Barbados, Benin, Bhutan, Bolivia, Brazil, Bulgaria, Burundi, Byelorussian SSR, Central African Republic, Chad, Chile, China, Colombia, Comoros, Congo, Costa Rica, Cuba, Cyprus, Czechoslovakia, Democratic Kampuchea, Democratic Yemen, Denmark, Djibouti, Dominican Republic, Ecuador, Egypt, El Salvador, Ethiopia, Fiji, Finland, Gabon, Gambia, German Democratic Republic, Ghana, Greece, Grenada, Guatemala, Guinea, Guyana, Honduras, Hungary, Iceland, India, Indonesia, Iran, Iraq, Ivory Coast, Jamaica, Jordan, Kenya, Kuwait, Lao People's Democratic Republic, Lebanon, Lesotho, Libyan Arab Jamahiriya, Madagascar, Malawi, Malaysia, Maldives, Mali, Malta, Mauritania, Mauritius, Mexico, Mongolia, Morocco, Mozambique, Nepal, Nicaragua, Niger, Nigeria, Norway, Oman, Pakistan, Panama, Papua New Guinea, Paraguay, Peru, Philippines, Poland, Portugal, Qatar, Romania, Rwanda, Samoa, Sao Tome and Principe, Saudi Arabia, Senegal, Seychelles, Sierra Leone, Singapore, Solomon Islands, Somalia, Sri Lanka, Sudan, Suriname, Sweden, Syrian Arab Republic, Thailand, Togo, Trinidad and Tobago, Tunisia, Uganda, Ukrainian SSR, USSR, United Arab Emirates, United Republic of Cameroon, United Republic of Tanzania, Upper Volta, Uruguay, Vanuatu, Venezuela, Viet Nam, Yemen, Yugoslavia, Zaire, Zambia, Zimbabwe.

Against: None.

Abstaining: Australia, Belgium, Burma, Canada, France, Germany, Federal Republic of, Ireland, Israel, Italy, Japan, Luxembourg, Netherlands, New Zealand, Spain, Turkey, United Kingdom, United States.

Draft convention against mercenaries

In 1982, the General Assembly decided that its *Ad Hoc* Committee on the Drafting of an International Convention against the Recruitment, Use, Financing and Training of Mercenaries should continue its work towards that goal.

Work of the Committee against mercenaries. Responding to a December 1981 Assembly resolution,[11] the Committee against mercenaries held its second session at United Nations Headquarters from 25 January to 19 February 1982. Established in 1980 by the Assembly,[10] the Committee was to be composed of 35 Member States; in 1982, however, it had 34 members (see APPENDIX III).

In its 1982 report to the Assembly,[4] the Committee stated that, in order to distinguish between technical and political or controversial issues raised by the future convention, it had briefly reviewed a draft submitted by Nigeria in 1981[13] and then established two Working Groups: Group A to deal with issues of definition and the convention's scope; and Group B to deal with all other issues relevant to the future convention. Working Group A had before it proposals submitted by Cuba, the German Democratic Republic, Jamaica and Suriname. It also received a proposal by France, introduced late in the Group's stage of work, which was not discussed.

Two communications concerning the composition of the Committee against mercenaries were addressed to the President of the General Assembly in 1982.

In a letter of 17 February,[2] the Congo, as current Chairman of the Group of African States, announced that the States of the West African subregion which were Committee members had established a schedule for rotation of the seats they occupied, as follows: 1982—Benin, Nigeria, Senegal; 1983—Benin, Nigeria, Togo; 1984—Benin, Senegal, Togo; and 1985—Nigeria, Senegal, Togo.

In a note verbale of 9 December,[3] Senegal confirmed that Togo would be a candidate for the seat becoming vacant in 1983 following Senegal's withdrawal, on the understanding that Senegal would be a candidate to replace Nigeria in 1984.

General Assembly action. On 16 December 1982, the General Assembly decided that the Committee against mercenaries should continue its work towards drafting as soon as possible an international convention against them and that the Committee should hold its third session from 2 to 26 August 1983 and then report to the Assembly.[8]

The resolution was adopted without vote. On 26 November, the Sixth Committee had approved the 61-nation draft, introduced by Nigeria, by consensus.

In the Sixth Committee, the sponsors orally revised the draft to delete the venue, suggested as Geneva, for the third session of the Committee against mercenaries. They took this action after the United States proposed the addition of a paragraph[1] by which the Assembly would have authorized the Secretary-General to implement the activities approved only to the extent that they could be financed from resources approved in the programme budget for the 1982-1983 biennium.[12] The United States amendment was not pressed to a vote.

Other action. A number of other actions were taken in 1982 with regard to mercenaries.

A Security Council Commission of Inquiry, set up to investigate a November 1981 mercenary attack against Seychelles, made several recommendations[5] after visiting the area in January and February 1982. Since such aggression remained a grave threat to States, particularly small developing countries, the Commission recommended that the convention against mercenaries be concluded speedily, that the international community make every effort to prevent mercenary operations and, in co-operating towards preventing those activities, Governments and Member States having related information should immediately communicate it directly or through the Secretary-General to the Governments concerned.

The Security Council, in its 28 May resolution on the Commission's report,[9] condemned all forms of external interference in Member States' internal affairs, including the use of mercenaries to destabilize States and/or to violate their territorial integrity, sovereignty and independence.

The Commission on Human Rights, on 25 February,[6] and the Assembly, on 3 December,[7] in resolutions on the right of peoples to self-determination, reaffirmed that the practice of using mercenaries against national liberation movements and sovereign States constituted a criminal act and that the mercenaries themselves were criminals. They called on all Governments to enact legislation declaring the recruitment, financing and training of mercenaries in their territories and the transit of mercenaries through their territories to be punishable offences, and prohibiting their nationals from serving as mercenaries, and to report on such legislation to the Secretary-General. The Commission also expressed appreciation of the work of the Committee against mercenaries towards elaborating the draft convention and urged all States to contribute to its early adoption.

Amendment not pressed. [1]United States, A/C.6/37/L.15.
Letter (l) and note verbale. [2]Congo, 17 Feb., A/37/91 *(l)*; [3]Senegal, 9 Dec., A/37/749.
Reports. [4]Committee on drafting convention against mercenaries, A/37/43 & Corr.1; [5]SC Commission of Inquiry on Seychelles, S/14905.

Resolutions (1982). [6]Commission on Human Rights (report, E/1982/12): 1982/16, paras. 11 & 12, 25 Feb. GA: [7]37/43, para. 11, 3 Dec.; [8]37/109, 16 Dec., text following. [9]SC: 507(1982), para. 5, 28 May.
Resolutions (prior). GA: [10]35/48, 4 Dec. 1980 (YUN 1980, p. 1145); [11]36/76, 4 Dec. 1981 (YUN 1981, p. 1218); [12]36/240 A, 18 Dec. 1981 *(ibid.,* p. 1278).
Yearbook reference. [13]1981, p. 1215.
Financial implications. Committee on Conferences observations, A/C.5/37/73/Add.1; 5th Committee report, A/37/738; S-G statements, A/C.5/37/73, A/C.6/37/L.13.
Meeting records. GA: 6th Committee, A/C.6/37/SR.9-15, *53, 56* (5 Oct.–26 Nov.); 5th Committee, A/C.5/37/SR.61 (9 Dec.); plenary, A/37/PV.107 (16 Dec.).

General Assembly resolution 37/109

16 December 1982　　　　　Meeting 107　　　　　Adopted without vote

Approved by Sixth Committee (A/37/648) by consensus, 26 November (meeting 56); 61-nation draft (A/C.6/37/L.9), orally revised; agenda item 121.

Sponsors: Afghanistan, Algeria, Angola, Bahamas, Bangladesh, Barbados, Benin, Burundi, Congo, Cuba, Cyprus, Democratic Yemen, Egypt, Ethiopia, German Democratic Republic, Ghana, Guinea, Guinea-Bissau, Guyana, India, Iraq, Jamaica, Kenya, Lao People's Democratic Republic, Lesotho, Libyan Arab Jamahiriya, Madagascar, Malaysia, Mali, Mexico, Mongolia, Morocco, Mozambique, Nicaragua, Niger, Nigeria, Pakistan, Panama, Qatar, Romania, Rwanda, Sao Tome and Principe, Senegal, Sierra Leone, Somalia, Sudan, Suriname, Swaziland, Syrian Arab Republic, Togo, Trinidad and Tobago, Turkey, Uganda, Ukrainian SSR, United Republic of Tanzania, Uruguay, Viet Nam, Yugoslavia, Zaire, Zambia, Zimbabwe.

Drafting of an international convention against the recruitment, use, financing and training of mercenaries

The General Assembly,

Bearing in mind the need for strict observance of the principles of sovereign equality, political independence, territorial integrity of States and self-determination of peoples, as enshrined in the Charter of the United Nations and developed in the Declaration on Principles of International Law concerning Friendly Relations and Co-operation among States in accordance with the Charter of the United Nations,

Recalling its resolutions, particularly resolutions 2395(XXIII) of 29 November 1968, 2465(XXIII) of 20 December 1968, 2548(XXIV) of 11 December 1969, 2708(XXV) of 14 December 1970, 3103(XXVIII) of 12 December 1973 and its resolution 1514(XV) of 14 December 1960, as well as Security Council resolutions 405(1977) of 14 April 1977, 419(1977) of 24 November 1977, 496(1981) of 15 December 1981 and 507(1982) of 28 May 1982, in which the United Nations denounced the practice of using mercenaries, in particular against developing countries and national liberation movements,

Recalling in particular its resolution 36/76 of 4 December 1981, by which it renewed the mandate of the *Ad Hoc* Committee on the Drafting of an International Convention against the Recruitment, Use, Financing and Training of Mercenaries, composed of thirty-five Member States,

Having considered the report of the *Ad Hoc* Committee on its second session,

Recognizing that the activities of mercenaries are contrary to fundamental principles of international law, such as non-interference in the internal affairs of States, territorial integrity and independence, and seriously impede the process of self-determination of peoples struggling against colonialism, racism and *apartheid* and all forms of foreign domination,

Bearing in mind the pernicious impact that the activities of mercenaries have on international peace and security,

Considering that the progressive development and codification of the rules of international law on mercenaries would contribute immensely to the implementation of the purposes and principles of the Charter,

Taking account of the fact that, although the *Ad Hoc* Committee has made substantial progress, it has not yet fulfilled its mandate,

Reaffirming the need for the elaboration, at the earliest possible date, of an international convention against the recruitment, use, financing and training of mercenaries,

1. *Takes note* of the report of the *Ad Hoc* Committee on the Drafting of an International Convention against the Recruitment, Use, Financing and Training of Mercenaries and the progress made, especially during its second session;

2. *Decides* that the *Ad Hoc* Committee shall continue its work, with the goal of drafting, at the earliest possible date, an international convention against the recruitment, use, financing and training of mercenaries;

3. *Requests* the *Ad Hoc* Committee, in the fulfilment of its mandate, to consider the suggestions and proposals of Member States, bearing in mind the views and comments submitted to the Secretary-General and those expressed at the thirty-seventh session of the General Assembly during the debate in the Sixth Committee devoted to the consideration of the report of the *Ad Hoc* Committee;

4. *Requests* the Secretary-General to make available to the *Ad Hoc* Committee at its third session any up-to-date and relevant documentation on the subject;

5. *Also requests* the Secretary-General to provide the *Ad Hoc* Committee with any assistance and facilities it may require for the performance of its work;

6. *Decides* that the *Ad Hoc* Committee shall hold its third session for four weeks, from 2 to 26 August 1983;

7. *Requests* the *Ad Hoc* Committee to submit its report to the General Assembly at its thirty-eighth session;

8. *Decides* to include in the provisional agenda of its thirty-eighth session the item entitled "Report of the *Ad Hoc* Committee on the Drafting of an International Convention against the Recruitment, Use, Financing and Training of Mercenaries".

Draft articles on non-navigational uses of international watercourses

Responding to a December 1981 General Assembly recommendation that the International Law Commission (ILC) continue preparing draft articles on non-navigational uses of international watercourses,[3] ILC, at its 1982 session held at Geneva from 3 May to 23 July,[1] appointed Jens Evensen (Norway) as Special Rapporteur for the topic, in succession to Stephen M. Schwebel (United States) who had resigned in 1981.[5] Mr. Schwebel's third report, begun prior to his resignation, was circulated at the session, as were replies received from Bangladesh and Portugal to a questionnaire on the topic formulated by ILC in 1974.[4]

In its 16 December resolution on the work of ILC, the Assembly recommended that, taking into account Government comments, ILC should continue preparing the draft articles.[2]

Report. [1]ILC, A/37/10.
Resolution (1982). [2]GA: 37/111, para. 3, 16 Dec.
Resolution (prior). [3]GA: 36/114, 10 Dec. 1981 (YUN 1981, p. 1265).
Yearbook references. [4]1974, p. 837; [5]1981, p. 1222.

Chapter III

States and international law

Contents

For resolutions and decisions of major organs mentioned but not reproduced, refer to INDEX OF RESOLUTIONS AND DECISIONS.

Diplomatic relations

Protection of diplomats

As at 31 December 1982, the number of parties to the various international instruments relating to the protection of diplomats and to diplomatic and consular relations[1] was as follows: 140 States were parties to the 1961 Vienna Convention on Diplomatic Relations,[6] Indonesia, Kiribati and Tuvalu having adhered in 1982; 40 States were parties to the Optional Protocol concerning acquisition of nationality,[7] Indonesia having acceded in 1982; and 51 States were parties to the Optional Protocol concerning the compulsory settlement of disputes.[7]

The 1963 Vienna Convention on Consular Relations[8] had 104 States parties, Indonesia, Kiribati and Tuvalu having adhered in 1982; 33 States were parties to the Optional Protocol concerning the acquisition of nationality,[9] Indonesia having acceded in 1982; and 39 States were parties to the Optional Protocol concerning the compulsory settlement of disputes.[9]

The 1973 Convention on the Prevention and Punishment of Crimes against Internationally Protected Persons, including Diplomatic Agents,[4] had 57 States parties, Argentina, the Democratic People's Republic of Korea and Poland having adhered in 1982.

Pursuant to a November 1981 General Assembly resolution,[5] the Secretary-General submitted to that body in September 1982 a report, with later addenda,[2] containing information from States on serious violations of the protection, security and safety of diplomatic and consular missions and

representatives as well as on subsequent action taken by them to bring offenders to justice and prevent a repetition. Two countries updated information supplied to the Secretary-General in 1981:[10] Denmark reported on action it was taking following an attack on a Turkish diplomat at Copenhagen; and Sweden reported on measures taken against Iranian students who had occupied their country's Embassy near Stockholm. Turkey gave details of attacks on its diplomats between October 1981 and September 1982 in Bulgaria, Canada, France, Italy, the Netherlands, Portugal and the United States, while Canada, France and the United States informed of their actions in connection with those attacks. France also gave information on action it was taking following attacks, in Paris, on Israeli and United States diplomats between December 1981 and September 1982 and an August 1982 explosion at the Iraqi Embassy. The Federal Republic of Germany reported that in February 1982 one of its diplomats had been attacked in Iran, and Algeria gave details of what it called a Zionist incursion into its Embassy at Beirut, Lebanon, in September.

The Secretary-General's report also contained the views of 15 States (Barbados, Byelorussian SSR, Denmark, Ecuador, Finland, Indonesia, Kiribati, Kuwait, Lebanon, Spain, Sweden, Syrian Arab Republic, Ukrainian SSR, USSR, United States) on measures needed to enhance the protection of missions and representatives.

General Assembly action. On 16 December, the General Assembly adopted a resolution[3] by which it urged States to observe international law governing diplomatic and consular relations, and called on States that had not done so to become parties to such instruments as the 1961, 1963 and

1973 Conventions. Recommending that States co-operate closely to protect missions and diplomats and settle disputes peacefully, the Assembly invited them to report serious violations to the Secretary-General; States in which a violation occurred or where an alleged offender was present were invited to report promptly on measures taken to bring about justice and to prevent a repetition. The Secretary-General was requested, on receiving a report of a serious violation, to draw the attention of the States concerned to the reporting procedures. He was also requested to invite States to inform him of their views on measures needed to enhance the protection of missions and representatives.

The resolution was adopted without vote. On 30 November, the draft, sponsored by 17 nations, had been similarly approved by the Sixth (Legal) Committee.

Introducing the draft, Norway pointed out that most of the text was the same as the Assembly's 1981 resolution, except that the fourth preambular paragraph was new and a reference to exchange of information on serious violations had been included in paragraph 4.

Publication. (1)*Multilateral Treaties Deposited with the Secretary-General, Status as at 31 December 1982* (ST/LEG/SER.E/2), Sales No. E.83.V.6.
Report. (2)S-G, A/37/404 & Corr.1 & Add.1 & Add.1/Corr.1 & Add.2-5.
Resolution (1982). (3)GA: 37/108, 16 Dec., text following.
Resolutions (prior). GA: (4)3166(XXVIII), annex, 14 Dec. 1973 (YUN 1973, p. 775); (5)36/33, 13 Nov. 1981 (YUN 1981, p. 1225).
Yearbook references. 1961, (6)p. 512, (7)p. 516; 1963, (8)p. 510, (9)p. 512; (10)1981, p. 1223.
Meeting records. GA: 6th Committee, A/C.6/37/SR.14-17, *58* (12 Oct.–30 Nov.); plenary, A/37/PV.107 (16 Dec.).

General Assembly resolution 37/108

16 December 1982   Meeting 107   Adopted without vote

Approved by Sixth Committee (A/37/699) without vote, 30 November (meeting 58); 17-nation draft (A/C.6/37/L.18 and Corr.1); agenda item 120.

Sponsors: Argentina, Australia, Austria, Canada, Denmark, Ecuador, Finland, Germany, Federal Republic of, Iceland, Japan, Nigeria, Norway, Philippines, Sierra Leone, Sweden, Turkey, Uruguay.

Consideration of effective measures to enhance the protection, security and safety of diplomatic and consular missions and representatives

The General Assembly,

Having considered the report of the Secretary-General,

Emphasizing the duty of States to take all appropriate steps, as required by international law:

(a) To protect the premises of diplomatic and consular missions, as well as of missions to international intergovernmental organizations,

(b) To prevent any attacks on diplomatic and consular representatives, as well as on representatives to international intergovernmental organizations and officials of such organizations,

Deeply concerned about the continued large number of violations of, and failures to respect, the inviolability of diplomatic and consular missions and representatives, and about the serious threat presented by such violations to the maintenance of normal and peaceful international relations, which are necessary for co-operation among States,

Expressing its sympathy for the victims of illegal acts against diplomatic and consular representatives and missions as well as against representatives and missions to international intergovernmental organizations and officials of such organizations,

Noting that only a small number of States have so far, in response to the call by the General Assembly at its thirty-fifth and thirty-sixth sessions, become parties to the relevant conventions concerning the inviolability of diplomatic and consular missions and representatives,

Convinced that the reporting procedures established under General Assembly resolution 35/168 of 15 December 1980 and further elaborated in Assembly resolution 36/33 of 13 November 1981 are important steps in the efforts to enhance the protection, security and safety of diplomatic and consular missions and representatives,

Desiring to maintain and further strengthen those reporting procedures,

1.   *Takes note* of the report of the Secretary-General;

2.   *Strongly condemns* acts of violence against diplomatic and consular missions and representatives as well as against missions and representatives to international intergovernmental organizations and officials of such organizations;

3.   *Urges* States to observe and to implement the principles and rules of international law governing diplomatic and consular relations and, in particular, to take all necessary measures in conformity with their international obligations effectively to ensure the protection, security and safety of all diplomatic and consular missions and representatives officially present in territory under their jurisdiction, including practicable measures to prohibit in their territories illegal activities of persons, groups and organizations that encourage, instigate, organize or engage in the perpetration of acts against the security and safety of such missions and representatives;

4.   *Recommends* that States should co-operate closely, *inter alia* through contacts between the diplomatic and consular missions and the receiving State, with regard to practical measures designed to enhance the protection, security and safety of diplomatic and consular missions and representatives and with regard to exchange of information on the circumstances of all serious violations thereof;

5.   *Calls upon* States that have not yet done so to consider becoming parties to the instruments relevant to the protection, security and safety of diplomatic and consular missions and representatives, *inter alia* the Vienna Convention on Diplomatic Relations of 1961, the Vienna Convention on Consular Relations of 1963, and the respective optional protocols thereto, as well as the Convention of 1973 on the Prevention and Punishment of Crimes against Internationally Protected Persons, including Diplomatic Agents;

6.   *Calls upon* States, in cases where a dispute arises in connection with a violation of the principles and rules of international law concerning the inviolability of diplomatic and consular missions and representatives, to make use of the means for peaceful settlement of disputes, including the good offices of the Secretary-General;

7.   *Invites:*

(a) All States to report to the Secretary-General serious violations of the protection, security and safety of diplomatic and consular missions and representatives;

(b) The State in which the violation took place—and, where applicable, the State where the alleged offender is present—to report as promptly as possible on measures taken to bring the offender to justice and eventually to communicate, in accordance with its laws, the final outcome of the proceedings against the offender, and on measures adopted with a view to preventing a repetition of such violations;

8.   *Requests* the Secretary-General to circulate to all States, upon receipt, the reports received by him pursuant to paragraph 7 above, unless the reporting State requests otherwise;

9.   *Also requests* the Secretary-General to invite States to inform him of their views with respect to any measures needed to enhance the protection, security and safety of diplomatic and consular missions and representatives;

10.   *Further requests* the Secretary-General, when a serious violation has been reported pursuant to paragraph 7 (a) above, to draw the attention, when appropriate, of the States directly concerned to the reporting procedures set forth in paragraph 7 above;

11.   *Requests* the Secretary-General to submit to the General Assembly at its thirty-eighth session a report on the state of ratification of, and accessions to, the instruments referred to in paragraph 5 above, as well as the reports received and views expressed pursuant to paragraphs 7 and 9 above, and invites him to submit any views he may wish to express on these matters;

12.   *Decides* to include in the provisional agenda of its thirty-eighth session the item entitled "Consideration of effective measures to

enhance the protection, security and safety of diplomatic and consular missions and representatives: report of the Secretary-General".

Status of diplomatic bags and couriers

Responding to a December 1981 General Assembly recommendation,[3] the International Law
Commission (ILC), at its May-July 1982 session,
continued preparing draft articles on the status of
the diplomatic courier and the diplomatic bag not
accompanied by courier with a view to elaborating a legal instrument on the topic.[1]

The Commission had before it a third report[2]
by the Special Rapporteur, Alexander Yankov
(Bulgaria). Since draft articles 1 to 6 contained in
his previous report had not been considered by the
ILC Drafting Committee in 1981,[4] the Special
Rapporteur re-examined them in the light of the
1981 discussions in ILC and the Sixth Committee
and reintroduced them, as amended, in his third
report.

The report consisted of two parts containing 14
draft articles. Part I (general provisions) contained
six articles: scope of the articles (article 1), couriers and bags not within such scope (article 2),
use of terms (article 3), freedom of communication for all official purposes effected through diplomatic couriers and bags (article 4), duty to respect
international law and the laws and regulations of
receiving and transit States (article 5), and non-
discrimination and reciprocity (article 6). Part II
(status of the courier, the courier *ad hoc* and the
captain of a commercial aircraft or master of a ship
carrying a diplomatic bag) contained eight articles: proof of status (article 7), appointment of a
courier (article 8), appointment of the same person by two or more States as a courier (article 9),
the courier's nationality (article 10) and functions
(article 11), commencement of functions (article
12), end of function (article 13), and persons
declared *non grata* or not acceptable (article 14).

ILC requested the Secretariat: to update the collection of treaties on the topic and other materials
on diplomatic and consular relations, particularly
official communications exercised through couriers
and bags; to renew a 1981 request to States for information on national practices[4] (information
had been received from 13 States); to prepare a
preliminary analysis of State practice in accordance with a tentative list of issues and the structure of the draft articles; and to update a statement on the status of four multilateral conventions
on diplomatic law elaborated under United Nations auspices. At the conclusion of its debate on
the topic, ILC referred the 14 articles to its Drafting Committee.

Reports. [1]ILC, A/37/10; [2]Special Rapporteur, A/CN.4/359
& Add.1.
Resolution. [3]GA: 36/114, 10 Dec. 1981 (YUN 1981, p. 1265).
Yearbook reference. [4]1981, p. 1226.

State succession in respect of property, archives and debts

In 1982, the General Assembly took further action in preparation for an international conference
of plenipotentiaries to consider draft articles on
State succession in respect of property, archives
and debts and to conclude an international convention on the subject.

The Assembly had decided, in December
1981,[4] to convene the conference in early 1983
and had invited Member States to submit their
written comments on the draft articles, finalized
by ILC in 1981.[6] The comments of Austria,
Czechoslovakia, Hungary, the Philippines, Uruguay and Venezuela were forwarded to the Assembly by the Secretary-General in a September 1982
report with a later addendum.[2]

General Assembly action. On 15 November,[3]
the General Assembly decided to hold the United
Nations Conference on Succession of States in
respect of State Property, Archives and Debts at
Vienna, Austria, from 1 March to 8 April 1983.
The Secretary-General was requested to invite all
States and Namibia, represented by the United
Nations Council for Namibia, to participate. Or-
ganizations with standing invitations to participate
in United Nations conferences, national liberation
movements recognized by the Organization of
African Unity, the specialized agencies, the Inter-
national Atomic Energy Agency and interested
United Nations organs and intergovernmental or-
ganizations were to be invited as observers. The
Secretary-General was also requested to arrange
for the participation, as an expert, of the former
ILC Special Rapporteur on the topic, Mohammed
Bedjaoui (Algeria). The Assembly referred to the
Conference, as the basic proposal for considera-
tion, the draft articles adopted by ILC.

The resolution was adopted by a recorded vote
of 136 to 1, after an amendment,[1] proposed by
the United States, had been rejected by a recorded
vote of 103 to 2, with 26 abstentions. On 29 October, the Sixth Committee had approved the
draft, sponsored by 38 States and introduced by
Sierra Leone, by consensus.

The amendment would have added a paragraph
by which the Assembly would have authorized the
Secretary-General to implement activities approved under the resolution only to the extent that
they could be financed from the resources approved in the programme budget for the 1982-1983
biennium.[5] The United States said the amendment was not intended to single out the draft resolution in question but rather to highlight the need
for a rational and responsible financial manage-

ment of the United Nations and to put an end to the continuing upward spiral of its expenses.

Several States explained their votes on the amendment. Cuba, speaking on behalf of the Movement of Non-Aligned Countries, said that they had voted against as, in addition to creating technical difficulties for the Secretariat, the amendment would prevent national liberation movements from participating, thereby setting a dangerous precedent. Austria said that, since it needed an unequivocal decision on the holding of the Conference in order to be able to make the necessary arrangements, it had voted against, although it was sympathetic to efforts aimed at limiting the financial burden on Member States. Canada and the USSR shared the latter view, but abstained because a consensus had been reached in the Committee.

Amendment rejected. [1]United States, A/37/L.25.
Report. [2]S-G, A/37/454 & Corr.1 & Add.1.
Resolution (1982). [3]GA: 37/11, 15 Nov., text following.
Resolutions (prior). GA: [4]36/113, 10 Dec. 1981 (YUN 1981, p. 1230); [5]36/240 A, 18 Dec. 1981 (*ibid.*, p. 1278).
Yearbook reference. [6]1981, p. 1227.
Financial implications. Committee on Conferences observations, A/C.5/37/33/Add.1; 5th Committee report, A/37/603; S-G statements, A/C.5/37/33, A/C.6/37/L.4.
Meeting records. GA: 6th Committee, A/C.6/37/SR.30, *31, 41* (28 Oct.–10 Nov.); 5th Committee, A/C.5/37/SR.28 (18 Nov.); plenary, A/37/PV.68 (15 Nov.).

General Assembly resolution 37/11

15 November 1982   Meeting 68   136-1 (recorded vote)

Approved by Sixth Committee (A/37/593) by consensus, 29 October (meeting 31); 38-nation draft (A/C.6/37/L.3); agenda item 124.

Sponsors: Afghanistan, Algeria, Angola, Argentina, Benin, Burundi, Colombia, Congo, Cuba, Cyprus, Democratic Yemen, Egypt, German Democratic Republic, Greece, Guinea, India, Iraq, Jamaica, Kenya, Lebanon, Libyan Arab Jamahiriya, Mali, Mexico, Mongolia, Nigeria, Panama, Philippines, Romania, Senegal, Sierra Leone, Sudan, Thailand, Tunisia, Turkey, Venezuela, Yugoslavia, Zaire, Zambia.

United Nations Conference on Succession of States in respect of State Property, Archives and Debts

The General Assembly,

Recalling that, by its resolution 36/113 of 10 December 1981, it decided to convene a conference of plenipotentiaries in 1983 to consider the draft articles on succession of States in respect of State property, archives and debts, adopted by the International Law Commission at its thirty-third session, and to embody the results of its work in an international convention and such other instruments as it might deem appropriate,

Recalling further that, in paragraph 1 of the same resolution, it expressed its appreciation to the International Law Commission for its valuable work on the question of succession of States in respect of State property, archives and debts, and to the Special Rapporteur on the topic for his contribution to that work,

Believing that the draft articles adopted by the International Law Commission at its thirty-third session represent a good basis for the elaboration of an international convention and such other instruments as may be appropriate on the question of succession of States in respect of State property, archives and debts,

Taking note of the report of the Secretary-General, which contains the comments and observations submitted by a number of Member States in accordance with General Assembly resolution 36/113,

Mindful of Article 13, paragraph 1 *a*, of the Charter of the United Nations, which provides that the General Assembly shall initiate studies and make recommendations for the purpose of encouraging the progressive development of international law and its codification,

Believing that the successful codification and progressive development of the rules of international law governing succession of States in respect of State property, archives and debts would contribute to the development of friendly relations and co-operation among States, irrespective of their constitutional and social systems, and would assist in promoting and implementing the purposes and principles set forth in Articles 1 and 2 of the Charter,

Noting with appreciation that an invitation has been extended by the Government of Austria to hold the United Nations Conference on Succession of States in respect of State Property, Archives and Debts at Vienna,

1. *Decides* that the United Nations Conference on Succession of States in respect of State Property, Archives and Debts, referred to in General Assembly resolution 36/113, shall be held from 1 March to 8 April 1983 at Vienna;

2. *Requests* the Secretary-General to invite:

(a) All States to participate in the Conference;

(b) Namibia, represented by the United Nations Council for Namibia, to participate in the Conference, in accordance with paragraph 1 of General Assembly resolution 36/121 D of 10 December 1981;

(c) Representatives of organizations that have received a standing invitation from the General Assembly to participate in the sessions and the work of all international conferences convened under its auspices in the capacity of observer to participate in the Conference in that capacity, in accordance with Assembly resolutions 3237(XXIX) of 22 November 1974 and 31/152 of 20 December 1976;

(d) Representatives of the national liberation movements recognized in its region by the Organization of African Unity to participate as observers, in accordance with General Assembly resolution 3280(XXIX) of 10 December 1974;

(e) The specialized agencies and the International Atomic Energy Agency as well as interested organs of the United Nations and interested intergovernmental organizations to be represented by observers at the Conference;

3. *Refers to the Conference, as the basic proposal for its consideration, the draft articles on succession of States in respect of State property, archives and debts adopted by the International Law Commission at its thirty-third session;

4. *Decides* that the languages of the Conference shall be the official and working languages of the General Assembly, its committees and its sub-committees;

5. *Requests* the Secretary-General to submit to the Conference all relevant documentation and recommendations relating to its methods of work and procedures and to arrange for the necessary staff, facilities and services which it will require, including the provision of summary records;

6. *Requests* the Secretary-General to arrange for the participation at the Conference, as an expert, of the former Special Rapporteur of the International Law Commission on the topic of succession of States in respect of matters other than treaties, if he is available.

Recorded vote in Assembly as follows:

In favour: Afghanistan, Albania, Algeria, Angola, Argentina, Australia, Austria, Bahamas, Bahrain, Bangladesh, Barbados, Belgium, Benin, Bhutan, Brazil, Bulgaria, Burma, Burundi, Byelorussian SSR, Canada, Central African Republic, Chad, Chile, China, Colombia, Congo, Costa Rica, Cuba, Cyprus, Czechoslovakia, Democratic Kampuchea, Democratic Yemen, Denmark, Djibouti, Dominican Republic, Ecuador, Egypt, El Salvador, Equatorial Guinea, Ethiopia, Fiji, Finland, France, Gabon, German Democratic Republic, Germany, Federal Republic of, Ghana, Greece, Grenada, Guatemala, Guinea, Guyana, Haiti, Honduras, Hungary, Iceland, India, Indonesia, Iran, Iraq, Ireland, Israel, Italy, Ivory Coast, Jamaica, Japan, Jordan, Kenya, Kuwait, Lao People's Democratic Republic, Liberia, Libyan Arab Jamahiriya, Luxembourg, Madagascar, Malawi, Malaysia, Maldives, Mali, Malta, Mauritania, Mexico, Mongolia, Morocco, Mozambique, Nepal, Netherlands, New Zealand, Nicaragua, Niger, Nigeria, Norway, Oman, Pakistan, Panama, Papua New Guinea, Paraguay, Peru, Philippines, Poland, Portugal, Qatar, Romania, Rwanda, Sao Tome and Principe, Saudi Arabia, Senegal, Sierra Leone, Singapore, Somalia, Spain, Sudan, Suriname, Swaziland, Sweden, Syrian Arab Republic, Thailand, Togo, Trinidad and Tobago, Tunisia, Turkey, Uganda, Ukrainian SSR, USSR, United Arab Emirates, United Kingdom, United Republic of Cameroon, United Republic of Tanzania, Upper Volta, Uruguay, Venezuela, Viet Nam, Yemen, Yugoslavia, Zaire, Zambia, Zimbabwe.

Against: United States.

State immunities, liability and responsibility

In response to a December 1981 General Assembly resolution,[2] ILC, at its May-July 1982 session, continued drafting articles on three other aspects of international law concerning States: jurisdictional immunities of States and their property (see below), international liability for injurious consequences arising from acts not prohibited by international law and State responsibility for internationally wrongful acts.

In its 16 December resolution on the work of ILC, the Assembly recommended that, taking into account Government comments, ILC should continue preparing the draft articles.[1]

Resolution (1982). [1]GA: 37/111, 16 Dec.
Resolution (prior). [2]GA: 36/114, 10 Dec. 1981 (YUN 1981, p. 1265).

Draft articles on State immunities

In 1982, ILC continued preparing draft articles on the jurisdictional immunities of States and their property. Its work, detailed in its report,[2] was based on a fourth report by the Special Rapporteur,[3] Sompong Sucharitkul (Thailand), which dealt with part III of the draft articles concerning exceptions to State immunity and containing two articles—on the scope of part III (article 11), and on trading or commercial activity (article 12). The Rapporteur also indicated a tentative list of other possible exceptions that would form the basis for the whole of part III: contracts of employment; personal injuries and damage to property; ownership, possession and use of property; patents, trade marks and other intellectual properties; fiscal liabilities and customs duties; shareholdings and membership of bodies corporate; ships employed in commercial service; and arbitration.

With regard to article 11, ILC members generally felt it superfluous, since the basic principle with which it was concerned was already embodied in article 6 on State immunity, provisionally approved by ILC in 1980.[4] As presented, it was felt that article 11 merely served as a necessary link between parts II and III. After discussing the draft articles, ILC confirmed its 1981 referral of articles 7 to 10 to the Drafting Committee[5]—these had not been considered by that body in 1981 due to time constraints—and also referred to it articles 11 and 12. It also decided that article 6 should be re-examined by the Committee, as should articles 2 and 3 relevant to the problem of definition of "jusrisdiction" and "trading and commercial activities".

In 1982, ILC provisionally adopted draft articles on the scope of the topic (article 1), modalities for giving effect to State immunity (article 7), express consent to the exercise of jurisdiction (article 8), and effect of participation in a proceeding before a court (article 9). It also provisionally adopted a subparagraph, defining the term "court", of the draft article on use of terms (article 2). The texts of these articles were transmitted

to the Assembly in a September note by the Secretary-General.[1]

Note. [1]S-G, A/37/402.
Reports. [2]ILC, A/37/10; [3]Special Rapporteur, A/CN.4/357 & Corr.1.
Yearbook references. [4]1980, p. 1125; [5]1981, p. 1231.

Draft articles on State liability

In 1982, ILC continued preparing draft articles on international liability for injurious consequences arising from acts not prohibited by international law.[1] It had before it a third report by the Special Rapporteur,[2] Robert Q. Quentin-Baxter (New Zealand), containing two chapters, the first of which traced the relationship between a schematic outline and principles relevant to State liability already identified. The second chapter set out the schematic outline of the topic, covering such questions as scope, definitions, requirements of prior consultation and negotiation, factors to be considered in balancing the interests of the parties involved, and liability in the case of injury. Discussion in ILC concentrated on the schematic outline and the topic's future.

ILC requested the Codification Division of the Secretariat's Office of Legal Affairs to continue its research on the analyses of relevant bilateral agreements and judicial decisions, and on a collection and analytical study of agreements on prevention measures and liability to which entities other than States were also parties.

Reports. [1]ILC, A/37/10; [2]Special Rapporteur, A/CN.4/360 & Corr.1.

Draft articles on State responsibility

In 1982, ILC continued preparing draft articles on State responsibility for internationally wrongful acts,[1] and had before it a third report by the Special Rapporteur,[2] Willem Riphagen (Netherlands), which attempted to clarify some of the principles affecting the topic. After a revision of draft articles presented in his second report,[3] the Special Rapporteur analysed various "subsystems" of international law on State responsibility and their interrelationship. Based on the analysis, a catalogue of legal consequences was discussed. In relation to the concept of enforcement, a distinction was made between "self-enforcement by the author State", "enforcement by the injured State" and "international enforcement". Six draft articles were presented for inclusion in part II. The first of these (article 1) linked the draft articles with those in part I. The others dealt with: the requirement of "quantitative proportionality" (article 2), the residual character of the rules of part II other than articles 4, 5, and 6 on "peremptory subsystems" (article 3), *jus cogens* (article 4), the United Nations system (article 5) and international crimes (article 6).

After discussing the draft articles, ILC confirmed its 1981 referral of articles 1 to 3 to the Drafting Committee[4]—these had not been considered by that body in 1981 due to time constraints—and also referred to it draft articles 1 to 6 as proposed in the third (1982) report. ILC took this action on the understanding that the Committee would prepare framework provisions and consider whether a draft article along the lines of the new draft article 6 should have a place in those provisions.

Reports. [1]ILC, A/37/10; [2]Special Rapporteur, A/CN.4/354 & Corr.1 & Add.1.

Yearbook references. 1981, [3]p. 1232, [4]p. 1233.

Chapter IV

International organizations and international law

Contents

Strengthening the role of the United Nations

In 1982, the General Assembly took steps to try to strengthen the role of the United Nations. Expressing grave concern at the frequent disregard for the Charter of the United Nations, the Assembly emphasized the need to strengthen the Organization's role and effectiveness.[1] The Assembly also decided that, in 1983, the Special Committee on the Charter of the United Nations and on the Strengthening of the Role of the Organization should give priority to working on proposals on ways to maintain and consolidate international peace and security, including suggestions on the functioning of the Security Council.[2]

Resolutions (1982). GA: [1]37/67, 3 Dec.; [2]37/114, 16 Dec.

Report of the Secretary-General for 1981/82

The role and capacity of the United Nations as an instrument for peace and rational change, and how to strengthen them, was a central theme of the Secretary-General's September 1982 report to the General Assembly on the work of the Organization for 1981/82 (p. 3). Pointing out that the Charter of the United Nations had been born after six years of global war, he called for a conscious recommitment by Governments to that document, and urged the reconstruction of the Charter concept of collective action for peace and security so as to make the United Nations more capable of carrying out its primary function.

Too often the Security Council, as the Organization's primary organ for maintaining international peace and security, found itself unable to act decisively to resolve international conflicts, the Secretary-General said. In order to strengthen the system prescribed in the Charter, he called for more systematic, less last-minute use of the Council and for that organ to keep an active watch on dangerous situations and initiate discussions with the parties before they reached crisis point. It was neither wise nor responsible of the Council to leave matters to the judgement of the conflicting parties to the point where the Council's irrelevance became a matter of comment by world public opinion.

The Secretary-General stated that, although the Council's increasing use of informal consultations was valuable, there was a risk that this might become a substitute for action or an excuse for inaction by that body. In that connection, he thought the Council should reconsider reviewing and streamlining its procedures with a view to acting swiftly and decisively in crises. After stressing that the system of collective security envisaged by the Charter presupposed, as a minimum, a working relationship among the permanent members of the Council, he appealed to them to reassess their Charter obligations. Pointing out that the best resolution in the world would have little effect unless Member States followed up with appropriate support, he called for new ways to be considered of bringing the collective influence of the United Nations membership to bear on the problem at hand. Very often a Member State or group of States involved in negotiations undertaken at the behest of the Security Council could play an important reinforcing role in promoting understanding, he said.

With regard to the Secretary-General's role in bringing potentially dangerous situations to the Council's attention, he announced his intention to develop a wider and more systematic system for fact-finding in potential conflict areas. In that regard, he urged the Council to devise swifter measures for sending observers to such areas in order to resolve potential or incipient disputes by peaceful means.

General Assembly action. On 3 December 1982,[1] the General Assembly emphasized the imperative need to strengthen the role and effectiveness of the United Nations as indispensable for maintaining international peace and security, for settling international crises peacefully, for strengthening international co-operation based on sovereign equality and for promoting economic and social development and human rights. Solemnly reaffirming that genuine and stable peace and security could be achieved by strict adherence to the Charter and to international law and that States should fulfil in good faith their obligations, the Assembly called on United Nations organs to discharge fully and effectively their Charter responsibilities and on Member States to contribute actively to that end. The Security Council was requested to carry out the primary responsibility for maintaining international peace and security and to give due consideration to the Secretary-General's report. The Assembly urged him to continue his efforts towards strengthening the Organization's capacity to fulfil the role envisaged in the Charter, taking into account the views of Member States.

The resolution was adopted without vote. The draft, twice revised and sponsored by 49 States, was introduced by Yugoslavia.

Resolution (1982). [1]GA: 37/67, 3 Dec., text following.
Meeting record. GA: A/37/PV.91 (3 Dec.).

General Assembly resolution 37/67

3 December 1982   Meeting 91   Adopted without vote

49-nation draft (A/37/L.39/Rev.2); agenda item 10.

Sponsors: Algeria, Argentina, Australia, Austria, Bangladesh, Benin, Canada, Chile, Colombia, Congo, Cuba, Cyprus, Denmark, Ecuador, Egypt, Finland, Greece, Guyana, Iceland, India, Indonesia, Ireland, Jamaica, Japan, Kuwait, Lebanon, Libyan Arab Jamahiriya, Madagascar, Mali, Malta, Mexico, Netherlands, Nigeria, Norway, Pakistan, Panama, Peru, Philippines, Romania, Senegal, Sierra Leone, Singapore, Sri Lanka, Suriname, Sweden, Tunisia, Uganda, Yugoslavia, Zambia.

Report of the Secretary-General on the work of the Organization

The General Assembly,

Deeply disturbed by the continuing deterioration of international relations, the frequent recourse to the threat or use of force, the further escalation of the arms race, particularly in its nuclear dimension, the aggravation of global economic problems, widespread, mass and flagrant violations of human rights, all hindrances to the process of decolonization and the continued stalemate in the resolution of various fundamental international crises and their exacerbation,

Gravely concerned at the crisis in many multilateral negotiations and in co-operation, especially within the United Nations,

Noting with concern that the United Nations system of collective security has not been used effectively,

Gravely concerned at the frequent disregard shown for the provisions of the Charter and the resolutions of the United Nations,

Convinced that there is an urgent and imperative need for strict respect for the provisions of the Charter and for strengthening the role of the United Nations in the maintenance of international peace and security and in solving international problems in accordance with the purposes and principles of the Charter,

Recalling the Declaration on Principles of International Law concerning Friendly Relations and Co-operation among States in accordance with the Charter of the United Nations and the Manila Declaration on the Peaceful Settlement of International Disputes,

Bearing in mind the views expressed by Member States during the thirty-seventh session of the General Assembly,

1. *Takes note with appreciation* of the report of the Secretary-General on the work of the Organization;

2. *Solemnly reaffirms* that genuine and stable peace and security in the world can be achieved by strict adherence to the purposes and principles of the Charter of the United Nations and to international law and that all States should fulfil in good faith their obligations assumed in accordance therewith;

3. *Emphasizes* the imperative need to strengthen the role and effectiveness of the United Nations as indispensable for the maintenance of international peace and security, for the settlement of international disputes and crises by peaceful means, for the strengthening of international co-operation on the basis of sovereign equality and for the promotion of economic and social development and of human rights;

4. *Calls upon* all organs of the United Nations to discharge fully and effectively their responsibilities in accordance with the Charter and upon all Member States to contribute actively to that end;

5. *Requests* the Security Council to carry out the primary responsibility for the maintenance of international peace and security and to give due consideration to the report of the Secretary-General;

6. *Invites* the Secretary-General, in discharging his responsibilities under the Charter, to continue his efforts towards strengthening the capacity of the United Nations to fulfil the effective and decisive role envisaged for it in the Charter;

7. *Urges* that efforts to this end continue, taking into account the views expressed by Member States during the thirty-seventh session of the General Assembly as well as those which Member States may wish to offer, while views of institutions and eminent persons may also be taken into consideration as appropriate;

8. *Requests* the Secretary-General to keep the General Assembly informed on the implementation of the present resolution.

Activities of the Special Committee

The Special Committee on the Charter of the United Nations and on the Strengthening of the Role of the Organization met at Geneva from 22 February to 19 March 1982 to continue considering Member States' proposals on maintaining peace and security, and submitted a report on its work to the General Assembly.[3] The 47-member Committee, meeting in response to a December 1981 Assembly resolution,[6] also finalized the draft Manila Declaration on the Peaceful Settlement of International Disputes (see Chapter II of this section), the other of two main items on its agenda. Owing to lack of time, the Committee was unable to consider Member States' proposals on rationalizing United Nations procedures as it had been requested to do by the same 1981 resolution.

An open-ended Working Group of the Committee met from 23 February to 1 March and on 16 and 17 March 1982 to resume work on the informal compilation of 74 proposals regarding the maintenance of peace and security, submitted between 1976 and 1980, an assessment of which had been made by the Chairman of the 1981 Working Group.[8] The Group then turned its attention to a draft recommendation presented in 1981 by Egypt on behalf of Committee members belonging to the Movement of Non-Aligned Countries. By that text, the Committee would recommend that urgent efforts be made to enhance the Security Council's effectiveness. In the light of the Group's discussion, Egypt, for the non-aligned members, submitted a revised draft recommendation but it was not considered for lack of time.

The Group also had before it two proposals submitted by France, one in 1981 and the other in 1982. The first contained draft amendments to the General Assembly's rules of procedure concerning the convening of emergency special sessions of that body which, the sponsor said, involved modifications to provide more flexible procedures for holding such sessions. The sponsor stated that its second proposal would assist the Security Council to be better informed since it provided for it to hear, informally, the views of parties to a conflict.

General Assembly action. On 16 December,[5] the General Assembly decided that the Special Committee should continue examining current and future proposals with a view to according priority to those on which agreement seemed possible, and to make recommendations thereon. The Committee was requested to give priority to the proposals on maintaining international peace and security, to the revised draft recommendation presented on behalf of the Movement of Non-Aligned Countries and to other proposals on the subject, including those on the Security Council's functioning, and to consider Member States' proposals on rationalizing existing United Nations procedures. Reminding the Committee of the importance of reaching general agreement whenever that had significance for the outcome of its work, the Assembly urged Committee members to participate fully and decided that other Member States would be allowed to take part in Committee meetings as observers. Governments were invited to submit or update their comments on the topic. The Assembly also welcomed the adoption of the Manila Declaration and decided that the Committee should continue work on the peaceful settlement of disputes by considering the remaining proposals.

The resolution was adopted by a recorded vote of 125 to none, with 17 abstentions. On 1 December, the Sixth (Legal) Committee had approved the 49-nation draft, introduced by the Philippines, by a recorded vote of 99 to none, with 15 abstentions. Two separate Committee votes, requested by the USSR, preceded the approval of the draft: by 94 votes to 16, with 3 abstentions, the words

"and to make recommendations thereon" in paragraph 3 *(b)* were retained; and by 87 votes to 14, with 11 abstentions, paragraph 5 *(a)* was retained. Both votes were recorded.

The Committee rejected, by a recorded vote of 85 to 12, with 11 abstentions, a United States amendment[1] which would have added a paragraph to have the Assembly authorize the Secretary-General to implement the activities approved only to the extent that they could be financed from resources approved in the programme budget for the 1982-1983 biennium.[7]

Another draft resolution on the Special Committee's work was submitted to the Sixth Committee by Benin, Iran, the Libyan Arab Jamahiriya, Mali and Mauritania.[2] On Australia's suggestion, the Committee decided, by a recorded vote of 52 to 32, with 24 abstentions, not to vote on the draft.

Several States gave their reasons for voting against the words "and to make recommendations thereon". The United States said they were unnecessary and created problems. The USSR said they could be accepted only in the context of the Special Committee's overall mandate and subject to compliance with the reminder to that body about the importance of reaching general agreement. The German Democratic Republic said that progress in the Committee's work could be achieved only if all its members observed the Charter's provisions; the draft failed to take account of that, particularly the words in question and paragraph 5 *(a)*. Speaking on those provisions, France felt they were contrary to the spirit in which the Committee should work.

Explaining their negative votes on paragraph 5 *(a)*, France said all proposals should be treated equally and the United Kingdom believed that singling out and trying to force the pace on particular proposals could have seriously damaging effects on the Committee's work and cast doubt on the consensus rule referred to. The USSR said its reservations were well known—the text would create confrontation in the Committee and undermine Charter principles, especially the unanimity rule among the Security Council's permanent members. The German Democratic Republic spoke in like manner. The Netherlands abstained in the vote on the paragraph since it did not think it advisable to change Charter provisions with a view to improving the functioning of the United Nations, as proposed in the Non-Aligned Movement's text; the proposals therein should not be given priority as general agreement on them was unlikely.

Reasons were also given for abstaining in the vote on the draft as a whole. France and the USSR said they abstained because the provisions to which they objected had been included. The latter added that its position was based on the view that the Sixth Committee had taken a responsible approach to the question and had in effect rejected the five-nation draft. The United States said it abstained because of its negative positions taken in the separate votes and because of the rejection of its amendment. The United Kingdom said the draft's final form made it clear that proposals other than those of the Non-Aligned Movement qualified for priority treatment; that decision had been helped by the recognition, in paragraph 5 *(c)*, that other proposals must be given priority, as agreed at the Committee's 1982 session. The German Democratic Republic said the draft did not take into account that the Charter was the basic international document for ensuring peaceful coexistence between States with different social systems and that observance of all Charter provisions was an important pre-condition for maintaining international peace and security.

During its consideration of the question, the Assembly had before it the comments of Egypt, submitted in response to its 1981 request[6] and forwarded to it in September 1982 by the Secretary-General.[4]

Amendment rejected. [1]United States, A/C.6/37/L.21.
Draft resolution not voted upon. [2]Benin, Iran, Libyan Arab Jamahiriya, Mali, Mauritania, A/C.6/37/L.5/Rev.1.
Reports. [3]Committee on Charter and role of United Nations, A/37/33; [4]S-G, A/37/384.
Resolution (1982). [5]GA: 37/114, 16 Dec., text following.
Resolutions (prior). GA: [6]36/122, 11 Dec. 1981 (YUN 1981, p. 1239); [7]36/240 A, 18 Dec. 1981 (*ibid.*, p. 1278).
Yearbook reference. [8]1981, p. 1235.
Financial implications. 5th Committee report, A/37/739; S-G statements, A/C.5/37/82, A/C.6/37/L.20.
Meeting records. GA: 6th Committee, A/C.6/37/SR.20-29, 57, *58-60* (18 Oct.–2 Dec.); 5th Committee, A/C.5/37/SR.61 (9 Dec.), plenary, A/37/PV.107 (16 Dec.).

General Assembly resolution 37/114

16 December 1982   Meeting 107   125-0-17 (recorded vote)

Approved by Sixth Committee (A/37/722) by recorded vote (99-0-15), 1 December (meeting 59); 49-nation draft (A/C.6/37/L.19); agenda item 127.

Sponsors: Argentina, Australia, Bahamas, Barbados, Benin, Bolivia, Brazil, Chile, Colombia, Congo, Cyprus, Ecuador, Egypt, El Salvador, Germany, Federal Republic of, Ghana, Guyana, Indonesia, Italy, Jamaica, Japan, Kenya, Madagascar, Malaysia, Mali, Mauritania, Mexico, Nepal, New Zealand, Nigeria, Papua New Guinea, Paraguay, Philippines, Romania, Rwanda, Senegal, Sierra Leone, Singapore, Somalia, Spain, Suriname, Thailand, Trinidad and Tobago, Tunisia, Uruguay, Venezuela, Yugoslavia, Zaire, Zambia.

Report of the Special Committee on the Charter of the United Nations and on the Strengthening of the Role of the Organization

The General Assembly,

Reaffirming its support for the purposes and principles set forth in the Charter of the United Nations,

Recalling its resolutions 686(VII) of 5 December 1952, 992(X) of 21 November 1955, 2285(XXII) of 5 December 1967, 2552(XXIV) of 12 December 1969, 2697(XXV) of 11 December 1970, 2968(XXVII) of 14 December 1972 and 3349(XXIX) of 17 December 1974,

Recalling also its resolutions 2925(XXVII) of 27 November 1972, 3073(XXVIII) of 30 November 1973 and 3282(XXIX) of 12 December 1974 on the strengthening of the role of the United Nations,

Recalling especially its resolution 3499(XXX) of 15 December 1975, by which it established the Special Committee on the Charter of the United Nations and on the Strengthening of the Role of the Organiza-

tion, and its resolutions 31/28 of 29 November 1976, 32/45 of 8 December 1977, 33/94 of 16 December 1978, 34/147 of 17 December 1979, 35/164 of 15 December 1980 and 36/122 of 11 December 1981,

Welcoming the report of the Secretary-General on the work of the Organization,

Having considered the report of the Special Committee on the Charter of the United Nations and on the Strengthening of the Role of the Organization on the work of the session it held in 1982,

Noting that significant progress has been made in fulfilling the mandate of the Special Committee,

Noting the importance that pre-session consultations among the members of the Special Committee and other interested States may have in facilitating the fulfilment of its task,

Considering that the Special Committee has not yet completed the mandate entrusted to it,

1. *Takes note* of the report of the Special Committee on the Charter of the United Nations and on the Strengthening of the Role of the Organization;

2. *Welcomes* the adoption by the General Assembly, at its thirty-seventh session, of the Manila Declaration on the Peaceful Settlement of International Disputes as a significant achievement of the Special Committee;

3. *Decides* that the Special Committee should continue its work in pursuance of the following tasks with which it is entrusted:

(a) To list the proposals which have been made or will be made in the Committee and to identify those which have awakened special interest;

(b) To examine proposals which have been made or will be made in the Committee with a view to according priority to the consideration of those on which agreement seems possible and to make recommendations thereon;

4. *Also decides* that the Special Committee shall convene its next session from 11 April to 6 May 1983;

5. *Requests* the Special Committee at its next session:

(a) To accord priority in its work to the proposals regarding the question of the maintenance of international peace and security, to document A/AC.182/L.29/Rev.1 as well as to other proposals made in regard to this subject, including those relating to the functioning of the Security Council;

(b) To continue its work on the question of the peaceful settlement of disputes by considering the remaining proposals contained in the list prepared by the Special Committee in accordance with General Assembly resolution 33/94;

(c) To consider proposals made by Member States on the question of rationalization of existing procedures of the United Nations, as agreed by the Special Committee, and to consider any proposals under other relevant topics;

6. *Requests* the Special Committee to be mindful of the importance of reaching general agreement whenever that has significance for the outcome of its work;

7. *Urges* members of the Special Committee to participate fully in its work in fulfilment of the mandate entrusted to it;

8. *Decides* that the Special Committee shall accept the participation in its meetings of observers of Member States and, paying due regard to its efficiency and the time at its disposal, allow their participation in the meetings of its working groups;

9. *Invites* Governments to submit or to bring up to date, if they deem it necessary, their observations and proposals, in accordance with General Assembly resolution 3499(XXX);

10. *Requests* the Secretary-General to render all assistance to the Special Committee;

11. *Requests* the Special Committee to report on its work to the General Assembly at its thirty-eighth session;

12. *Decides* to include in the provisional agenda of its thirty-eighth session the item entitled "Report of the Special Committee on the Charter of the United Nations and on the Strengthening of the Role of the Organization".

Recorded vote in Assembly as follows:

In favour: Algeria, Angola, Antigua and Barbuda, Argentina, Australia, Austria, Bahamas, Bahrain, Bangladesh, Barbados, Belgium, Belize, Benin, Bhutan, Bolivia, Brazil, Burma, Burundi, Canada, Central African Republic, Chad, Chile, China, Colombia, Comoros, Congo, Costa Rica, Cyprus, Democratic Kampuchea, Democratic Yemen, Denmark, Djibouti, Dominican Republic, Ecuador, Egypt, El Salvador, Ethiopia, Fiji, Finland, Gabon, Gambia, Germany, Federal Republic of, Ghana, Greece, Guatemala, Guinea, Guyana, Honduras, Iceland, India, Indonesia, Iran, Iraq, Ireland, Italy, Ivory Coast, Jamaica, Japan, Jordan, Kenya, Kuwait, Lebanon, Lesotho, Libyan Arab Jamahiriya, Luxembourg, Madagascar, Malawi, Malaysia, Maldives, Mali, Malta, Mauritius, Mexico, Morocco, Mozambique, Nepal, Netherlands, New Zealand, Nicaragua, Niger, Nigeria, Norway, Oman, Pakistan, Panama, Papua New Guinea, Paraguay, Peru, Philippines, Portugal, Qatar, Romania, Rwanda, Samoa, Sao Tome and Principe, Saudi Arabia, Senegal, Sierra Leone, Singapore, Solomon Islands, Somalia, Spain, Sri Lanka, Sudan, Suriname, Sweden, Syrian Arab Republic, Thailand, Togo, Trinidad and Tobago, Tunisia, Turkey, Uganda, United Arab Emirates, United Republic of Cameroon, United Republic of Tanzania, Upper Volta, Uruguay, Vanuatu, Venezuela, Yemen, Yugoslavia, Zaire, Zambia, Zimbabwe.

Against: None.

Abstaining: Afghanistan, Bulgaria, Byelorussian SSR, Cuba, Czechoslovakia, France, German Democratic Republic, Grenada, Hungary, Israel, Lao People's Democratic Republic, Mongolia, Poland, Ukrainian SSR, USSR, United Kingdom, United States.

Publication of repertories of practice

Responding to a December 1981 General Assembly request,[2] that high priority be given to preparing and publishing supplements to the *Repertoire of the Practice of the Security Council* and the *Repertory of Practice of United Nations Organs* in order to bring both up to date, the Secretary-General reported in October 1982 on the progress made.[1]

With regard to the *Repertoire*, the report noted that the French version of the seventh supplement, covering 1972-1974, was scheduled to appear in the first half of 1983 and work on the eighth, covering 1975-1980 instead of 1975-1978 as reported in 1981,[3] was progressing. Concerning the *Repertory*, reprinting the French and Spanish versions of the original and Supplement No. 1 had not been possible as funds were not available from savings. In that regard, it was pointed out that interest in the English reprinted version had been negligible and that volumes I to IV of the original as well as Supplement No. 1 were available on microfiche in English, French and Spanish. Volume V of the original in those languages would be available in the near future. As to Supplement No. 4 (covering 1 September 1966 to 31 December 1969), publication in English of volume I (Charter Articles 1-54) and volume II (Articles 55-111) was expected in 1983; translation into French and Spanish had commenced. Work on Supplement No. 5 (covering 1970 to 1978) was progressing.

Report. [1]S-G, A/C.6/37/4.
Resolution. [2]GA: 36/123, 11 Dec. 1981 (YUN 1981, p. 1240).
Yearbook reference. [3]1981, p. 1240.
Publications. Repertory of Practice of United Nations Organs, Supplement No. 4 (covering the period 1 September 1966 to 31 December 1969), vol. I: *Articles 1-54 of the Charter*, Sales No. E.80.V.13; vol. II: *Articles 55-111 of the Charter*, Sales No. E.82.V.7.

Implementation of UN resolutions

In a letter of 25 October 1982 to the Secretary-General,[2] Cyprus proposed that an item on implementation of United Nations resolutions be included in the agenda of the General Assembly's thirty-seventh (1982) session. It said it fully shared the grave concern, regarding the implementation of those resolutions, expressed by the Secretary-General in his report on the work of the Organization and pledged support to his conviction that resolutions, particularly those unanimously adopted by the Security Council, should serve as a springboard for governmental support (p. 5).

The item was subsequently included in the agenda on the recommendation of the General Committee[3] and, on 21 December, the Assembly decided to retain the item among those to be considered when resuming the thirty-seventh session at a date to be announced.[1]

Decision (1982). [1]GA: 37/452 *(item 141)*, 21 Dec.
Letter. [2]Cyprus, 25 Oct., A/37/245.
Report. [3]General Committee, A/37/250/Add.2.
Meeting records. GA: General Committee, A/BUR/37/SR.4 (11 Nov.); plenary, A/37/PV.*68, 115* (15 Nov., 21 Dec.).

Host country relations

Improving the relations between New York City's diplomatic community and the local population continued to be a major focus of the work of the Committee on Relations with the Host Country in 1982, and the Committee's recommendations to that end were endorsed by the General Assembly.

Consideration by the Committee on host country relations. The 15-member Committee on host country relations met five times in 1982. Details of its work on various aspects of relations between the Headquarters diplomatic community and the host country—the United States—were contained in its 1982 report to the Assembly.[1]

The Committee considered several communications concerning the security of Member States' missions and the safety of their personnel.

According to the USSR, between 15 and 29 October some 3,000 "Zionist hooligans" had assembled daily near its Mission, attempting to break through barriers around the entrance and yelling insults. Asserting that it received telephone threats—as many as 270 a day—to blow up the building and diplomatic cars, the USSR demanded that the host country establish normal conditions for the Mission's work and observe international law.

The United States said it had met its obligations under such law, in that USSR personnel had not been prevented from entering or leaving the Mission and no physical attack against them or property damage had occurred. According to the police, student groups of no more than 50 persons had conducted daily vigils and only once had they moved into the protected area around the Mission, from where they had been removed. Regretting the telephone calls, the United States said these were under police investigation.

Stressing its efforts to provide maximum protection for the diplomatic community, the United States, in a letter to the Committee Chairman, pointed out that a terrorism task force which it had established in 1980 had arrested members of various terrorist groups. Fixed police posts had been put up outside missions where the threat potential was greatest, and others were patrolled by police cars. Concerning an attempt to assassinate a Cuban diplomat, the United States said a $2-million, two-year investigation resulting in arrests showed its commitment to protecting diplomats in New York.

The Committee decided, on the USSR's suggestion, to request the Secretariat to prepare a comparative study on mission security in Geneva, New York and Vienna, Austria.

The Committee also considered issues connected with implementing the 1947 Agreement between the United Nations and the United States of America regarding the Headquarters of the United Nations (the Headquarters Agreement).[3] Referring to a United States request for the departure of two members of the Cuban Mission on the grounds of abuse of privileges of residence, Cuba stated the action was contrary to the Headquarters Agreement and an offence against Cuba. The United States said that the diplomats had violated the Trading with the Enemy Act, thereby abusing their privileges of residence. Consequently, it had been compelled to ask for their departure.

Difficulties connected with the issuing of entry visas for non-governmental organizations (NGOs) during the June/July special session of the Assembly devoted to disarmament were also discussed. The USSR suggested that representatives of NGOs be heard to clarify the matter. The United States said that every individual United Nations invitee had been granted a visa and those not so invited were required to comply with the United States Immigration and Nationality Act; those unable to do so were denied visas.

The Committee also considered an alleged incident of sexual assault on a female by a male member of the Permanent Observer Mission of the Democratic People's Republic of Korea, which had resulted in the issuing of a warrant for his arrest by United States authorities. Denying that the accused had anything to do with the incident, the Democratic People's Republic of Korea stated that, in its view, permanent observer missions enjoyed complete immunity, hence also immunity from criminal jurisdiction of the host country. The United States pointed out that such missions enjoyed only functional immunity, namely, immunity from arrest resulting directly from the discharge of the specific functions for which the mission had been permitted into the United States.

Other matters considered by the Committee included accelerating immigration and customs procedures, tax exemption, possible establishment of a commissary at Headquarters, claims of financial indebtedness, housing and public relations.

By recommendations approved on 6 December, the Committee:

—noted assurances given and actions taken by the host country and urged it to continue preventing acts violating the security of diplomatic missions and the safety of their personnel or property, and to ensure normal conditions for their functioning;

—urged the host country to continue punishing those responsible for criminal acts against missions and called on those missions to co-operate fully with United States authorities in cases affecting security;

—called on the host country to avoid actions not consistent with its international obligations regarding Member States' privileges and immunities;

—welcomed the diplomatic community's readiness to co-operate with local authorities in solving traffic problems, noted the desirability of missions making efforts to utilize off-street parking, and appealed to the host country to review its diplomatic parking measures and to consider terminating the serving of summonses to diplomats;

—expressed the hope that the host country could ameliorate the housing situation causing problems for the diplomatic community and that efforts would be intensified to acquaint the people of New York City with the privileges and immunities of mission personnel and the importance of their international functions;

—suggested that the Secretariat and others work together to solve difficulties regarding the unpaid bills of certain missions and diplomats; and

—expressed appreciation to the New York City Commission for the United Nations and the Consular Corps and those bodies, particularly the New York City Police, contributing to its efforts to help the diplomatic community, provide hospitality and promote mutual understanding between the community and the local population.

General Assembly action. On 16 December,[2] the General Assembly endorsed the Committee's recommendations and requested it to continue its work. The Assembly strongly condemned acts violating the security of missions and the safety of their personnel and urged the host country to continue to ensure their protection. It urged the host country and missions, in cases in which problems arose regarding privileges and immunities, to use fully the good offices of the Secretary-General. The Assembly asked him to remain active in all aspects of host country relations.

The resolution was adopted without vote. On 10 December, the Sixth (Legal) Committee had approved the draft similarly after it had been introduced and orally revised by the Libyan Arab Jamahiriya on behalf also of Benin, Cuba, Madagascar, Nicaragua, the Syrian Arab Republic and Zimbabwe.

Report. (1)Committee on host country relations, A/37/26.
Resolution (1982). (2)GA: 37/113, 16 Dec., text following.
Resolution (prior). (3)GA: 169(II), 31 Oct. 1947 (YUN 1947-48, p. 199).
Meeting records. GA: 6th Committee, A/C.6/37/SR.66, 67, *68* (9, 10 Dec.); plenary, A/37/PV.107 (16 Dec.).

General Assembly resolution 37/113

16 December 1982   Meeting 107   Adopted without vote

Approved by Sixth Committee (A/37/752) without vote, 10 December (meeting 68); 7-nation draft (A/C.6/37/L.32), orally revised; agenda item 126.

Sponsors: Benin, Cuba, Libyan Arab Jamahiriya, Madagascar, Nicaragua, Syrian Arab Republic, Zimbabwe.

Report of the Committee on Relations with the Host Country

The General Assembly,

Having considered the report of the Committee on Relations with the Host Country,

Recalling Article 105 of the Charter of the United Nations, the Convention on Privileges and Immunities of the United Nations and the Agreement between the United Nations and the United States of America regarding the Headquarters of the United Nations,

Recalling further that the problems related to the privileges and immunities of all missions accredited to the United Nations, their security and the safety of their personnel are of great importance and concern to them, as well as the primary responsibility of the host country,

Noting with deep concern the continued acts violating the security of missions and the safety of the personnel of missions accredited to the United Nations,

Recognizing that effective measures should be taken by the competent authorities of the host country, in particular to prevent any acts violating the security of missions and the safety of their personnel,

1.   *Endorses* the recommendations of the Committee on Relations with the Host Country contained in paragraph 43 of its report;

2.   *Urges* the host country to continue to take all necessary measures effectively to ensure the protection, security and safety of the missions accredited to the United Nations and their personnel, including practicable measures to prohibit illegal activities of persons, groups and organizations that encourage, instigate, organize or engage in the perpetration of acts against the security and safety of such missions and representatives;

3.   *Strongly condemns* the acts violating the security of all missions accredited to the United Nations and the safety of their personnel;

4.   *Requests* the Secretary-General to remain actively engaged in all aspects of the relations of the United Nations with the host country and, in this context, to continue to stress to the host country the importance of effective measures to avoid any acts violating the security of missions and the safety of their personnel;

5.   *Urges* the host country and the missions concerned, in any cases in which problems arise regarding privileges and immunities of members of missions to the United Nations, to make full use of the good offices of the Secretary-General in pursuit of solutions satisfactory to the parties involved;

6.   *Requests* the Committee on Relations with the Host Country to continue its work, in conformity with General Assembly resolution 2819(XXVI) of 15 December 1971;

7.   *Decides* to include in the provisional agenda of its thirty-eighth session the item entitled "Report of the Committee on Relations with the Host Country".

Observer status of national liberation movements in international organizations

As it had decided in 1980,(3) the General Assembly took up in 1982 an item concerning two resolutions adopted by the 1975 United Nations Conference on the Representation of States in Their Relations with International Organiza-

tions.(4) The resolutions(6) dealt, respectively, with the observer status in international organizations of national liberation movements recognized by the Organization of African Unity and/or by the League of Arab States, and with the application of the Vienna Convention on the Representation of States in Their Relations with International Organizations of a Universal Character,(5) adopted by the Conference, in future activities of such organizations.

In July 1982, the Secretary-General submitted a report, with a later addendum,(1) containing the comments he had received from nine Governments—Byelorussian SSR, Cyprus, Egypt, German Democratic Republic, Mexico, Philippines, Uganda, Ukrainian SSR, USSR—on their implementation of the Assembly's 1980 resolution.

General Assembly action. On 16 December 1982, the General Assembly adopted a resolution(2) by which it noted that the Vienna Convention regulated only the representation of States in their relations with international organizations; it also noted the current practice of inviting national liberation movements to participate as observers in sessions of the Assembly, specialized agencies and other United Nations organizations and in conferences held under their auspices. This, the Assembly was convinced, helped to strengthen international peace and co-operation. The Assembly invited States that had not done so, particularly those hosting international organizations or conferences convened by, or held under the auspices of, international organizations of a universal character, to consider as soon as possible ratifying or acceding to the Convention. It again called on the States concerned to accord to the delegations of the liberation movements in question the facilities, privileges and immunities necessary for performing their functions in accordance with the Convention.

The resolution was adopted by a recorded vote of 110 to 10, with 17 abstentions. On 10 December, the Sixth Committee approved the draft, sponsored by 19 nations and introduced by the United Arab Emirates, by 76 votes to 10, with 16 abstentions.

A number of States explained their negative votes. Several, among them Canada, France, Israel, Italy, the Netherlands and the United States, pointed out that the Convention had not entered into force. Many of them recalled that the Convention had been adopted after a divided vote. Belgium, Canada, France and the United Kingdom added that the Convention's scope could not be extended by a resolution. Even if it had entered into force, France and Israel said, it would be applicable only to States. The Netherlands found it anomalous that privileges and immunities should be accorded to certain national liberation movements when provisions concerning their granting to States had not entered into force. Canada could not accept the idea of placing representatives of an entity other than a State on the same footing as representatives of States. The United States found that idea daunting and, together with Israel, Italy, the Netherlands and the United Kingdom, noted that most of the draft's sponsors were not parties to the Convention. The United Kingdom especially objected to the reference to host countries in paragraph 1. For that reason and the call in paragraph 2 to accord facilities, privileges and immunities to certain national liberation movements, Japan said it had abstained.

Mexico stressed that its positive vote was on the understanding that paragraph 2 could not be interpreted as imposing on any State an obligation to recognize a liberation movement or to grant privileges without the express consent of the host State.

Two sponsors explained their positions. Algeria said the fact that sponsors were not parties to the Convention was irrelevant, as the text in question would ultimately be an Assembly resolution addressed to all States, including the sponsors. The United Arab Emirates said it was obvious that those that had drawn attention to the fact that the draft's sponsors had not ratified the Convention would not in any event have voted in favour of the text because of their well-known political position on the national liberation movements in question.

Report. [1]S-G, A/37/326 & Add.1.
Resolution (1982). [2]GA: 37/104, 16 Dec., text following.
Resolution (prior). [3]GA: 35/167, 15 Dec. 1980 (YUN 1980, p. 1156).
Yearbook references. 1975, [4]p. 879, [5]p. 880, [6]p. 882.
Meeting records. GA: 6th Committee, A/C.6/37/SR.63, *64, 68* (6-10 Dec.); plenary, A/37/PV.107 (16 Dec.).

General Assembly resolution 37/104

16 December 1982   Meeting 107   110-10-17 (recorded vote)

Approved by Sixth Committee (A/37/750) by vote (76-10-16), 10 December (meeting 68); 19-nation draft (A/C.6/37/L.30); agenda item 117 *(a)*.

Sponsors: Algeria, Bahrain, Benin, Cuba, Democratic Yemen, Iran, Iraq, Kuwait, Libyan Arab Jamahiriya, Mali, Niger, Nigeria, Qatar, Saudi Arabia, Syrian Arab Republic, Tunisia, United Arab Emirates, Yemen, Yugoslavia.

Observer status of national liberation movements recognized by the Organization of African Unity and/or by the League of Arab States

The General Assembly,

Recalling its resolution 35/167 of 15 December 1980,

Taking note of the report of the Secretary-General,

Bearing in mind the resolution of the United Nations Conference on the Representation of States in Their Relations with International Organizations relating to the observer status of national liberation movements recognized by the Organization of African Unity and/or by the League of Arab States,

Noting that the Vienna Convention on the Representation of States in Their Relations with International Organizations of a Universal Character, of 14 March 1975, regulates only the representation of States in their relations with international organizations,

Taking into account the current practice of inviting the above-mentioned national liberation movements to participate as observers in the sessions of the General Assembly, specialized agencies and other organizations of the United Nations system and in the work of the conferences held under the auspices of such international organizations,

Convinced that the participation of the national liberation movements referred to above in the work of international organizations helps to strengthen international peace and co-operation,

Desirous of ensuring the effective participation of the above-mentioned national liberation movements as observers in the work of international organizations and of regulating, to that end, their status and the facilities, privileges and immunities necessary for the performance of their functions,

1. *Invites* all States that have not done so, in particular those that are hosts to international organizations or to conferences convened by, or held under the auspices of, international organizations of a universal character, to consider as soon as possible the question of ratifying, or acceding to, the Vienna Convention on the Representation of States in Their Relations with International Organizations of a Universal Character;

2. *Calls once more upon* the States concerned to accord to the delegations of the national liberation movements recognized by the Organization of African Unity and/or by the League of Arab States, and accorded observer status by international organizations, the facilities, privileges and immunities necessary for the performance of their functions in accordance with the provisions of the Vienna Convention on the Representation of States in Their Relations with International Organizations of a Universal Character;

3. *Requests* the Secretary-General to report to the General Assembly at its thirty-ninth session on the implementation of the present resolution.

Recorded vote in Assembly as follows:

In favour: Afghanistan, Albania, Algeria, Angola, Argentina, Bahamas, Bahrain, Bangladesh, Barbados, Belize, Benin, Bhutan, Bolivia, Brazil, Bulgaria, Burundi, Byelorussian SSR, Central African Republic, Chad, Chile, China, Colombia, Comoros, Congo, Cuba, Cyprus, Czechoslovakia, Democratic Kampuchea, Democratic Yemen, Djibouti, Ecuador, Egypt, Ethiopia, Gabon, Gambia, German Democratic Republic, Ghana, Greece, Grenada, Guinea, Guyana, Hungary, India, Indonesia, Iran, Iraq, Ivory Coast, Jamaica, Jordan, Kenya, Kuwait, Lao People's Democratic Republic, Lebanon, Lesotho, Libyan Arab Jamahiriya, Madagascar, Malawi, Malaysia, Maldives, Mali, Malta, Mauritania, Mauritius, Mexico, Mongolia, Morocco, Mozambique, Nepal, Nicaragua, Niger, Nigeria, Oman, Pakistan, Panama, Papua New Guinea, Peru, Philippines, Poland, Qatar, Romania, Rwanda, Sao Tome and Principe, Saudi Arabia, Senegal, Sierra Leone, Singapore, Somalia, Sri Lanka, Sudan, Syrian Arab Republic, Thailand, Togo, Trinidad and Tobago, Tunisia, Turkey, Uganda, Ukrainian SSR, USSR, United Arab Emirates, United Republic of Cameroon, United Republic of Tanzania, Upper Volta, Vanuatu, Venezuela, Viet Nam, Yemen, Yugoslavia, Zaire, Zambia, Zimbabwe.

Against: Belgium, Canada, France, Germany, Federal Republic of, Israel, Italy, Luxembourg, Netherlands, United Kingdom, United States.

Abstaining: Australia, Austria, Burma, Denmark, Fiji, Finland, Guatemala, Iceland, Ireland, Japan, New Zealand, Norway, Paraguay, Portugal, Spain, Sweden, Uruguay.

Draft rules of procedure for conferences

In a 1980 resolution,[5] the General Assembly had asked the Secretary-General to propose draft standard rules of procedure for special conferences of the United Nations, and he had presented a report on the topic to the Assembly in 1981.[6] On the Fifth (Administrative and Budgetary) Committee's recommendation, the Assembly had deferred consideration of the report until 1982, recommending that the Sixth Committee take up the matter.[2]

In April 1982, the Secretary-General submitted an updated report[3] containing a set of draft rules of procedure which followed closely those of United Nations conferences convened during the previous decade. Annexed to the report were guidelines for the preparation and distribution of conference documents and a model conference agreement. In October, he forwarded further revisions[4] to the draft proposals based on comments he had received and taking account of related developments.

On 16 December, the General Assembly decided without vote to defer consideration of the Secretary-General's reports until 1983, inviting Governments and concerned international organizations to comment on them and asking that he report on the question at that time.[1] The Sixth Committee had approved the draft by consensus on 10 December, as orally proposed by its Chairman.

Decision (1982). [1]GA: 37/428, 16 Dec., text following.
Decision (prior). [2]GA: 36/427, 10 Dec. 1981 (YUN 1981, p. 1370).
Reports. S-G, [3]A/37/163, [4]A/C.6/37/5.

Resolution. [5]GA: 35/10 C, 3 Nov. 1980 (YUN 1980, p. 1225).
Yearbook reference. [6]1981, p. 1370.
Meeting records. GA: 6th Committee, A/C.6/37/SR.67 (10 Dec.); plenary, A/37/PV.107 (16 Dec.).

General Assembly decision 37/428

Adopted without vote

Approved by Sixth Committee (A/37/753) by consensus, 10 December (meeting 67); draft orally proposed by Chairman; agenda item 130.

Draft standard rules of procedure for United Nations conferences

At its 107th plenary meeting, on 16 December 1982, the General Assembly, on the recommendation of the Sixth Committee:

(a) Decided to defer to its thirty-eighth session consideration of the reports of the Secretary-General on draft standard rules of procedure for United Nations conferences;

(b) Invited Governments and the international organizations concerned to communicate to the Secretary-General, by 1 May 1983, their observations on the above-mentioned reports;

(c) Requested the Secretary-General to submit to the General Assembly at its thirty-eighth session a report on draft standard rules of procedure for United Nations conferences.

Chapter V

Treaties and agreements

Contents

Drafting process for multilateral treaties

Six Governments (Australia, Colombia, Indonesia, Qatar, Republic of Korea, Switzerland) and two international organizations (International Telecommunication Union, World Intellectual Property Organization) replied to an invitation in a December 1981 General Assembly resolution[5] for observations on reports by the Secretary-General of 1980[6] and 1981[7] posing questions to be considered in examining the multilateral treaty-making process within the United Nations. These replies, contained in an October report with a later addendum,[2] were forwarded to the Assembly.

Also by its 1981 resolution, the Assembly had decided to establish a working group of the Sixth (Legal) Committee to consider the questions raised in the 1981 report, to assess the United Nations multilateral treaty-making process and to make recommendations, and had asked the Secretary-General for a provisional volume of the *United Nations Legislative Series* containing material listed in his 1981 report and an analysis of observations he had received.

The Working Group, which had before it the provisional volume,[1] held 14 meetings between 7 October and 3 December 1982,[3] basing its work on a four-phase approach to the multilateral treaty-making process set out in a working paper prepared by the Chairman at the Group's request. Because of the limited time available, the Group exchanged views on only two phases—initiating a treaty-making process and formulating a multilateral treaty. The two other phases not considered were adopting such a treaty, and post-adoption and entry into force. The Group concluded that the review should be continued during the Assembly's 1983 regular session.

General Assembly action. On 16 December 1982, the General Assembly adopted a resolution[4] by

which it decided to reconvene the Working Group in 1983 to complete its mandate and reiterated its 1981 request[5] to the Secretary-General to prepare and publish new editions of publications related to the multilateral treaty-making process—the 1957 *Handbook of Final Clauses* and the 1959 *Summary of the Practice of the Secretary-General as Depositary of Multilateral Agreements*.

The resolution was adopted without vote. On 9 December, the Sixth Committee had approved the 14-nation draft, introduced by Australia, in the same manner, having agreed to an oral amendment by the Ukrainian SSR to include in the first preambular paragraph a reference to multilateral treaties as an important means of ensuring co-operation among States.

Publication. [1]*United Nations Legislative Series No. 21* (provisional version), ST/LEG/SER.B/21, vols. I, II.
Reports. [2]S-G, A/37/444 & Add.1; [3]Working Group on Review of Multilateral Treaty-making Process, A/C.6/37/L.29.
Resolution (1982). [4]GA: 37/110, 16 Dec., text following.
Resolution (prior). [5]GA: 36/112, 10 Dec. 1981 (YUN 1981, p. 1247).
Yearbook references. [6]1980, p. 1139; [7]1981, p. 1245.
Meeting records. GA: 6th Committee, A/C.6/37/SR.9, 10 (5, 6 Oct.), 65, *66* (8, 9 Dec.); plenary, A/37/PV.107 (16 Dec.).

General Assembly resolution 37/110

16 December 1982   Meeting 107   Adopted without vote

Approved by Sixth Committee (A/37/751) without vote, 9 December (meeting 66); 14-nation draft (A/C.6/37/L.31), orally revised on suggestion of Ukrainian SSR; agenda item 123.

Sponsors: Argentina, Australia, Canada, Egypt, Fiji, Indonesia, Kenya, Mexico, Netherlands, Nigeria, Philippines, Senegal, Sudan, Uruguay.

Review of the multilateral treaty-making process

The General Assembly,

Bearing in mind that multilateral treaties are an important means of ensuring co-operation among States and an important primary source of international law,

Conscious, therefore, that the process of elaboration of multilateral treaties, directed towards the progressive development of international law and its codification, forms an important part of the work of the United Nations and of the international community in general,

Aware of the heavy burden which active involvement in the process of multilateral treaty-making places upon Governments,

Convinced that the most rational use should be made of the finite resources available for the elaboration of multilateral treaties,

Aware that the Asian-African Legal Consultative Committee has been reviewing certain aspects of multilateral treaty-making,

Taking note of the reports of the Secretary-General submitted to the General Assembly at its thirty-fifth, thirty-sixth, and thirty-seventh sessions, including the replies and observations made by Governments and international organizations on the review of the multilateral treaty-making process,

Having considered the report of the Working Group on the Review of the Multilateral Treaty-making Process, established pursuant to General Assembly resolution 36/112 of 10 December 1981, and noting that the Working Group will require more time to fulfil its mandate as provided in paragraph 2 of that resolution,

Taking into account the statements made at the current session in the debate in the Sixth Committee,

1. *Decides* to reconvene the Working Group at its thirty-eighth session with the aim of completing the examination of the matters referred to in paragraph 2 of resolution 36/112;

2. *Reiterates its request* to the Secretary-General to prepare and publish as soon as possible new editions of the *Handbook of Final Clauses* and the *Summary of the Practice of the Secretary-General as Depositary of Multilateral Agreements*, taking into account relevant new developments and practices in that respect;

3. *Decides* to include in the provisional agenda of its thirty-eighth session the item entitled "Review of the multilateral treaty-making process".

Treaties involving international organizations

In December 1982, the General Assembly decided that an international convention should be concluded on the law of treaties between States and international organizations or between such organizations. The convention was to be based on draft articles adopted by the International Law Commission (ILC).

ILC action. At its May-July 1982 session,[3] ILC adopted the final text of 80 draft articles and an annex on treaties concluded between States and international organizations or between international organizations.[2] The Commission recommended that the General Assembly convoke a conference to conclude a convention based on the draft articles. This aspect of the law of treaties had been under consideration by ILC since 1970[8] and was the subject of 11 reports by the Special Rapporteur, Paul Reuter (France), the first of which had been submitted in 1972.[9]

As had been recommended by the Assembly in December 1981,[6] ILC completed, in the light of comments by Governments and international organizations, its second reading of the draft articles. It based its 1982 work on the Special Rapporteur's eleventh report,[4] containing articles 27 to 41—examined by ILC in 1981 but not considered by its Drafting Committee for lack of time[13]—and a review of articles 42 to 80 and the annex, provisionally adopted by ILC in first reading in 1979[11] and 1980.[12] Articles 27 to 80 and the annex, a subparagraph of article 2, article 5 and a new paragraph of article 20 were first referred to the Drafting Committee. On that body's recommendation, ILC approved the title to be given to the set of draft articles and adopted the final text together with the annex.

The 80 draft articles, each with a detailed commentary, were divided into seven parts. Part I (articles 1 to 5) constituted the introduction. Part II was divided into three sections: section 1 (articles 6 to 18) dealt with the conclusion of treaties; section 2 (articles 19 to 23) was on reservations; and section 3 (articles 24 and 25) concerned entry into force and provisional application. Part III had four sections: section 1 (articles 26 and 27), observance; section 2 (articles 28 to 30), application; section 3 (articles 31 to 33), interpretation; and section 4 (articles 34 to 38), treaties and third States or third organizations. Part IV (articles 39 to 41) dealt with amendment and modification. Part V, on invalidity, termination and suspension of operation, comprised five sections: section 1 (articles 42 to 45), general provisions; section 2 (articles 46 to 53), invalidity; section 3 (articles 54 to 64), termination and suspension of operation; section 4 (articles 65 to 68), procedure; and section 5 (articles 69 to 72), consequences. Part VI (articles 73 to 75) concerned miscellaneous provisions. Part VII (articles 76 to 80) was on depositaries, notifications, corrections and registration. The annex dealt with arbitration and conciliation procedures established in application of article 66.

The Commission pointed to the close relationship between the draft articles and the 1969 Vienna Convention on the Law of Treaties;[7] the draft followed the same order as that document and any provision not corresponding to one in that Convention was numbered *bis* or *ter*. Stressing that the draft, however, was in form entirely independent of that document, ILC also pointed out that since the law of treaties was the subject of two conventions—that of 1969 and the 1978 Vienna Convention on Succession of States in Respect of Treaties[10]—it seemed logical to have a third as the final piece in the United Nations overall design.

ACC action. Two issues raised by the subject were contained in a decision[1] adopted by the Administrative Committee on Co-ordination (ACC) at its November 1982 session: the manner in which the articles would be made binding on international organizations and their participation in the final elaboration of the articles.

With regard to the first issue, ACC suggested four possibilities: embodying the articles in an international convention and enabling both States and international organizations to become parties thereto on the same footing; following the approach adopted regarding the various conventions on privileges and immunities whereby the organizations considered themselves bound by their terms; a variant of the foregoing—a "third party" approach whereby organizations would be invited to consent to a convention; and the General Assembly adopting the articles, not as an international convention but as a standard of reference for action designed to harden into customary law. A number of agencies had argued in favour of the last suggestion, ACC said.

Concerning the organizations participating in the final elaboration of the text, ACC outlined three possible forms of participation: with the same rights and on the same footing as States; as observers; and—the choice favoured by ACC—with full rights except voting, thus allowing the organizations to propose amendments.

General Assembly action. On 16 December,[5] the General Assembly decided that a convention should be concluded, based on the ILC draft articles, and invited States and international organizations to submit comments by 1 July 1983. The Assembly took note of the ILC recommendation that the Assembly should convoke a conference and agreed to decide in 1983 on the appropriate forum for adopting the convention in the light of the comments received.

The resolution was adopted without vote. On 6 December, the Sixth Committee had approved the 26-nation draft, introduced by Iraq, by consensus.

Decision (1982). [1]ACC: 1982/17, 3 Nov. (transmitted by Secretariat note, A/C.6/37/L.12).

Note. [2]S-G, A/37/402.

Reports. [3]ILC, A/37/10; [4]Special Rapporteur, A/CN.4/353.

Resolution (1982). [5]GA: 37/112, 16 Dec., text following.

Resolution (prior). [6]GA: 36/114, 10 Dec. 1981 (YUN 1981, p. 1265).

Yearbook references. [7]1969, p. 734; [8]1970, p. 801; [9]1972, p. 636; [10]1978, p. 952; [11]1979, p. 1124; [12]1980, p. 1125; [13]1981, p. 1248.

Meeting records. GA: 6th Committee, A/C.6/37/SR.37-52, *63* (4 Nov.–6 Dec.); plenary, A/37/PV.107 (16 Dec.).

General Assembly resolution 37/112

16 December 1982   Meeting 107   Adopted without vote

Approved by Sixth Committee (A/37/700) by consensus, 6 December (meeting 63); 26-nation draft (A/C.6/37/L.28); agenda item 125.

Sponsors: Algeria, Argentina, Austria, Belgium, Brazil, Egypt, France, Germany, Federal Republic of, Ghana, Greece, Iraq, Italy, Jordan, Kenya, Kuwait, Libyan Arab Jamahiriya, Niger, Nigeria, Philippines, Qatar, Sierra Leone, Spain, Thailand, Yemen, Yugoslavia, Zaire.

Convention on the Law of Treaties between States and International Organizations or between International Organizations

The General Assembly,

Recalling that, following consideration of a recommendation adopted by the United Nations Conference on the Law of Treaties, held at Vienna in 1968 and 1969, the General Assembly, by its resolution 2501(XXIV) of 12 November 1969, recommended that the International Law Commission should study, in consultation with the principal international organizations, as it may consider appropriate in accordance with its practice, the question of treaties concluded between States and international organizations or between two or more international organizations, as an important question,

Noting that, pursuant to General Assembly resolution 36/114 of 10 December 1981, the International Law Commission, taking into account the written comments of Governments and of principal international organizations as well as views expressed in debates in the Assembly, completed at its thirty-fourth session the second reading of the draft articles on the said question,

Noting that, as reflected in paragraph 57 of the report of the International Law Commission on the work of its thirty-fourth session, the Commission decided to recommend that the General Assembly should convoke

a conference to study the draft articles on the law of treaties between States and international organizations or between international organizations prepared by the Commission and to conclude a convention,

Recalling the adoption of the Vienna Convention on the Law of Treaties of 23 May 1969, the Vienna Convention on the Representation of States in Their Relations with International Organizations of a Universal Character of 14 March 1975 and the Vienna Convention on Succession of States in respect of Treaties of 23 August 1978,

Mindful of Article 13, paragraph 1 *a*, of the Charter of the United Nations, which provides that the General Assembly shall initiate studies and make recommendations for the purpose of encouraging the progressive development of international law and its codification,

Believing that the successful codification and progressive development of the rules of international law governing treaties between States and international organizations or between international organizations would contribute to the development of friendly relations and co-operation among States, irrespective of their differing constitutional and social systems, and would assist in promoting and implementing the purposes and principles set forth in Articles 1 and 2 of the Charter,

1. *Expresses its appreciation* to the International Law Commission for its valuable work on the law of treaties between States and international organizations or between international organizations and to the Special Rapporteur on the topic for his contribution to this work;

2. *Invites* States to submit, not later than 1 July 1983, their written comments and observations on the final draft articles on the law of treaties between States and international organizations or between international organizations, prepared by the International Law Commission, as well as on the questions referred to in paragraph 60 of the report of the Commission on the work of its thirty-fourth session;

3. *Invites also* the principal international intergovernmental organizations to submit within the same period their written comments and observations on the subject;

4. *Requests* the Secretary-General to circulate such comments so as to facilitate the discussion on the subject at the thirty-eighth session of the General Assembly;

5. *Decides* that an international convention shall be concluded on the basis of the draft articles adopted by the International Law Commission;

6. *Takes note* of the recommendation of the International Law Commission on the subject and agrees to decide at its thirty-eighth session upon the appropriate forum for the adoption of the convention in the light of the comments received in accordance with the present resolution;

7. *Decides* to include in the provisional agenda of its thirty-eighth session an item entitled "Convention on the Law of Treaties between States and International Organizations or between International Organizations".

Registration and publication of treaties by the United Nations

During 1982, some 1,227 international agreements and 351 subsequent actions were received by the Secretariat for registration or filing and recording. In addition, there were 263 registrations of formalities concerning agreements for which the Secretary-General performed depositary functions.

The texts of international agreements registered or filed and recorded are published in the United Nations *Treaty Series* in the original languages with translations into English and French where necessary. In 1982, 25 volumes of the *Treaty Series* covering treaties registered or filed and recorded in 1973, 1974 and 1975 were issued.[1]

Publication. [1]United Nations *Treaty Series*, vols. 880, 886/887, 897, 899/900, 907/908, 911/912, 925/926, 931/932, 936, 937, 938, 940, 941, 943, 944, 951, 952, 953, 954, 956, 957, 959/962, 963, 967, issued in 1982, covering treaties registered or filed and recorded in 1973, 1974 and 1975.

Other publication. Statement of Treaties and International Agreements, registered or filed with the Secretariat during 1982, ST/LEG/SER.A/419-430 (monthly).

Multilateral treaties

*New multilateral treaties
concluded under United Nations auspices*

The following treaties, concluded under United Nations auspices, were deposited with the Secretary-General during 1982:[1]

Agreement Establishing the African Development Bank,[2] done at Khartoum on 4 August 1963, as amended by resolution 05-79 adopted by the Board of Governors on 17 May 1979. Concluded at Lusaka on 7 May 1982
Charter of the Asian and Pacific Development Centre.[8] Adopted at Bangkok by the Economic and Social Commission for Asia and the Pacific on 1 April 1982
Convention on the Limitation Period in the International Sale of Goods.[12] Concluded at New York on 14 June 1974, as amended by the Protocol of 11 April 1980
Extension of the International Sugar Agreement, 1977[14] (until 31 December 1984). Approved by the International Sugar Council in decisions No. 13 of 20 November 1981 and No. 14 of 21 May 1982
International Agreement on Jute and Jute Products, 1982.[13] Concluded at Geneva on 1 October 1982
International Coffee Agreement, 1976.[9] Concluded at London on 3 December 1975, as extended until 30 September 1983 by the International Coffee Council in resolution No. 318 of 25 September 1981
International Coffee Agreement, 1983.[10] Adopted by the International Coffee Council on 16 September 1982
Regulation No. 51: Uniform provisions concerning the approval of motor vehicles having at least four wheels with regard to their noise emissions;[3] *Regulation No. 52: Uniform provisions concerning the construction of small capacity public service vehicles;*[4] *Regulation No. 53: Uniform provisions concerning the approval of motor cycles with regard to the installation of lighting and light-signalling devices;*[5] *Regulation No. 54: Uniform provisions concerning the approval of pneumatic tyres for commercial vehicles and their trailers;*[6] and *Regulation No. 55: Uniform provisions concerning the approval of mechanical coupling components of combinations of vehicles;*[7] all annexed to the *Agreement concerning the Adoption of Uniform Conditions of Approval and Reciprocal Recognition of Approval for Motor Vehicle Equipment and Parts*, done at Geneva on 20 March 1958
United Nations Convention on the Law of the Sea.[11] Concluded at Montego Bay, Jamaica, on 10 December 1982

Publication. [1]*Multilateral Treaties Deposited with the Secretary-General, Status as at 31 December 1982* (ST/LEG/SER.E/2), Sales No. E.83.V.6.

Treaty texts. [2]Agreement Establishing African Development Bank, ADB/BG/XV/05 Rev.II. Agreement on motor vehicle equipment and parts: [3]Regulation 51, E/ECE/324/Rev.1/Add.50; [4]Regulation 52, E/ECE/324/Rev.1/Add.51; [5]Regulation 53, TRANS/SC1/R.61 & Amend.1; [6]Regulation 54, TRANS/SC1/R.183 & Amend.1,2,3; [7]Regulation 55, TRANS/SC1/R.8/Rev.2. [8]Charter of Asian and Pacific Development Centre, ESCAP res. 225(XXXVIII) in E/1982/20. [9]Coffee agreement, 1976, United Nations, *Treaty Series*, vol. 1024. [10]Coffee agreement, 1983, International Coffee Council document EB-2142/82 & Add.1/Rev.1 & Add.2. [11]Convention on Law of the Sea (A/CONF.62/122 & Corr.1-11), Sales No. E.83.V.5. [12]Convention on Limitation Period in International Sale of Goods, amended by Protocol, Sales Nos. E.74.V.8 (Convention) and E.81.IV.3 (Protocol). [13]Jute agreement, 1982, TD/JUTE/EX/R.4. [14]Sugar agreement, 1977, TD/SUGAR/9/10.

*Multilateral treaties
deposited with the Secretary-General*

The number of multilateral treaties for which the Secretary-General performed depositary functions stood at 331 at the end of 1982. During the year, 194 signatures were affixed to such treaties and 433 instruments of ratification, accession, acceptance and approval or notifications were transmitted to him. In addition, the Secretary-General received 138 communications from States expressing observations on declarations and reservations made by certain States at the time of signature, ratification or accession.

The following multilateral treaties,[1] in respect of which the Secretary-General acts as depositary, came into force during 1982:

Protocol to the Agreement on the Importation of Educational, Scientific and Cultural Materials of 22 November 1950. Concluded at Nairobi on 26 November 1976; entered into force on 2 January 1982
International Natural Rubber Agreement, 1979. Concluded at Geneva on 6 October 1979; entered into force definitively on 15 April 1982
Amendments to the Convention on the International Maritime Organization. Adopted by the Assembly of the International Maritime Organization by resolutions A.358(IX) of 14 November 1975 and A.371(X) of 9 November 1977 (rectification of resolution A.358(IX)); entered into force on 22 May 1982 (excluding article 51) and on 28 July 1982 (in respect of article 51)
Convention on the Registration of Inland Navigation Vessels, with annexed Protocols. Concluded at Geneva on 25 January 1965; entered into force on 24 June 1982
International Tin Agreement, 1981. Concluded at Geneva on 26 June 1981; entered into force provisionally on 1 July 1982
Regulation No. 48: Uniform provisions concerning the approval of vehicles with regard to the installation of lighting and light-signalling devices (entered into force on 1 January 1982); *Regulation No. 49: Uniform provisions concerning the approval of diesel engines with regard to the emission of gaseous pollutants* (entered into force on 15 April 1982); *Regulation No. 50: Uniform provisions concerning the approval of front position lights, rear position lights, stop lights, direction indicators and rear-registration-plate illuminating devices for mopeds, motor cycles and vehicles treated as such* (entered into force on 1 June 1982); *Regulation No. 51: Uniform provisions concerning the approval of motor vehicles having at least four wheels with regard to their noise emissions* (entered into force on 1 October 1982); *Regulation No. 52: Uniform provisions concerning the construction of small capacity public service vehicles* (entered into force on 1 November 1982); all annexed to the *Agreement concerning the Adoption of Uniform Conditions of Approval and Reciprocal Recognition of Approval for Motor Vehicle Equipment and Parts*, done at Geneva on 20 March 1958

Publication. [1]*Multilateral Treaties Deposited with the Secretary-General, Status as at 31 December 1982* (ST/LEG/SER.E/2), Sales No. E.83.V.6.

Chapter VI

International economic law

Contents

	Page		Page

Related topics:

Development and international economic and social policy: Economic rights and duties of States. Industrial development: Industrial co-operation contracts.

For resolutions and decisions of major organs mentioned but not reproduced, refer to INDEX OF RESOLUTIONS AND DECISIONS.

General aspects

In 1982, the United Nations Commission on International Trade Law (UNCITRAL) held its fifteenth session in New York from 26 July to 6 August.[3] Among the items considered by the 36-member Commission were international commercial arbitration, international payments, uniform rules on liquidated damages and penalty clauses, co-ordination of trade law activities, training and assistance and the legal aspects of the new international economic order.

The 1982 report of UNCITRAL was considered and taken note of by the Trade and Development Board of the United Nations Conference on Trade and Development on 7 September[2]—an action reported to the General Assembly by the Secretary-General on 2 November.[1]

By a resolution of 16 December,[5] the Assembly also took note of the report and, reaffirming the importance of the UNCITRAL work programme and of the conventions emanating from its work, recommended that it continue work on the topics in its programme, commending its progress and efforts to enhance efficiency. The Assembly also reaffirmed the importance of the increasing role of the International Trade Law Branch of the Office of Legal Affairs as the substantive secretariat of UNCITRAL in helping implement the work programme. Other aspects of

the Assembly's resolution dealt with: international commercial arbitration, international payments, co-ordination of trade law activities, training programmes, and the legal aspects of the new international economic order.

The resolution was adopted without vote. On 11 November, the Sixth (Legal) Committee had approved the draft, sponsored by 31 nations and introduced by Austria, in like manner.

In its 16 November resolution dealing with meeting records and documentation for subsidiary organs, the Assembly—in deciding that, for a three-year experimental period, none of its subsidiary organs would be entitled to summary records—excepted a number of those organs including UNCITRAL.[4]

Note. [1]S-G, A/C.6/37/L.6.

Reports. [2]TDB, A/37/15, vol. II; [3]UNCITRAL, A/37/17 & Corr.1,2.

Resolutions (1982). GA: [4]37/14 C, para. 3 (f), 16 Nov.; [5]37/106, 16 Dec., text following.

Meeting records. GA: 6th Committee, A/C.6/37/SR.3-8, 43 (28 Sep.–11 Nov.); plenary, A/37/PV.107 (16 Dec.).

Publication. United Nations Commission on International Trade Law Yearbook, vol. XIII: 1982 (A/CN.9/SER.A/1982), Sales No. E.84.V.5.

General Assembly resolution 37/106

16 December 1982   Meeting 107   Adopted without vote

Approved by Sixth Committee (A/37/620) without vote, 11 November (meeting 43); 31-nation draft (A/C.6/37/L.7); agenda item 119.

Sponsors: Argentina, Australia, Austria, Belgium, Brazil, Canada, Chile, Cyprus, Egypt, Finland, France, Germany, Federal Republic of, Ghana, Greece, India, Italy, Jamaica, Japan, Kenya, Morocco, Netherlands, Nigeria, Philippines, Senegal, Singapore, Spain, Sweden, Thailand, Trinidad and Tobago, Turkey, Yugoslavia.

Report of the United Nations Commission on International Trade Law

The General Assembly,

Having considered the report of the United Nations Commission on International Trade Law on the work of its fifteenth session,

Recalling that the object of the United Nations Commission on International Trade Law is the promotion of the progressive harmonization and unification of international trade law,

Recalling, in this regard, its resolutions 2205(XXI) of 17 December 1966, by which it established the United Nations Commission on International Trade Law and defined the object and terms of reference of the Commission, 3108(XXVIII) of 12 December 1973, by which it increased the membership of the Commission, 34/142 of 17 December 1979, by which the co-ordinating function of the Commission in the field of international trade law was emphasized, and 36/32 of 13 November 1981, by which the importance of the participation of observers from all States and interested international organizations at sessions of the Commission and its Working Groups was affirmed, as well as its previous resolutions concerning the reports of the Commission on the work of its annual sessions,

Recalling also its resolutions 3201(S-VI) and 3202(S-VI) of 1 May 1974, 3281(XXIX) of 12 December 1974 and 3362(S-VII) of 16 September 1975,

Reaffirming its conviction that the progressive harmonization and unification of international trade law, in reducing or removing legal obstacles to the flow of international trade, especially those affecting the developing countries, would significantly contribute to universal economic co-operation among all States on a basis of equality, equity and common interests and to the elimination of discrimination in international trade and, thereby, to the well-being of all peoples,

Having regard for the need to take into account the different social and legal systems in harmonizing the rules of international trade law,

Bearing in mind its resolution 36/111 of 10 December 1981 concerning the draft articles on most-favoured-nation clauses,

Stressing the usefulness and importance of sponsoring symposia and seminars, including those organized on a regional basis, for promoting better knowledge and understanding of international trade law and, especially, for the training of lawyers from developing countries in this field,

1. *Takes note with appreciation* of the report of the United Nations Commission on International Trade Law on the work of its fifteenth session;

2. *Commends* the United Nations Commission on International Trade Law for the progress made in its work and for its efforts to enhance the efficiency of its working methods;

3. *Calls upon* the United Nations Commission on International Trade Law, in particular its Working Group on the New International Economic Order, to continue to take account of the relevant provisions of the resolutions concerning the new international economic order, as adopted by the General Assembly at its sixth and seventh special sessions;

4. *Takes note with appreciation* of the completion by the United Nations Commission on International Trade Law, through its Working Group on the New International Economic Order, of the examination of studies related to clauses in contracts for the supply and construction of large industrial works, preparatory to the commencement of work on drafting a legal guide identifying the legal issues involved in such contracts and suggesting possible solutions to assist parties, in particular from developing countries, in their negotiations;

5. *Notes* that the United Nations Commission on International Trade Law has adopted a provision for a universal unit of account for expressing monetary amounts in international transport and liability conventions and two alternative provisions for adjustment of the limits of liability in such conventions;

6. *Notes with appreciation* that the United Nations Commission on International Trade Law has approved recommended guidelines for arbitral institutions and other relevant bodies to assist them in adopting procedures for acting as appointing authority or for providing administrative services in cases to be conducted under the Commission's Arbitration Rules;

7. *Reaffirms* the mandate of the United Nations Commission on International Trade Law as the core legal body within the United Nations system in the field of international trade law to co-ordinate legal activities in this field in order to avoid duplication of efforts and to promote efficiency, consistency and coherence in the unification and harmonization of international trade law, and, in this connection:

(a) Recommends that the Commission should continue to maintain close co-operation with the other international organs and organizations active in the field of international trade law, in particular the United Nations Conference on Trade and Development, the International Law Commission, the United Nations Industrial Development Organization and the Commission on Transnational Corporations;

(b) Reaffirms the importance of the participation of observers from all States and interested international organizations at sessions of the Commission and its Working Groups;

8. *Reaffirms* the importance of bringing into effect the conventions emanating from the work of the United Nations Commission on International Trade Law for the global unification and harmonization of international trade law;

9. *Reaffirms also* the importance, in particular for the developing countries, of the work of the United Nations Commission on International Trade Law concerned with training and assistance in the field of international trade law and the desirability for the Commission to sponsor symposia and seminars, in particular those organized on a regional basis, to promote training and assistance in the field of international trade law, and, in this connection:

(a) Welcomes the decision of the Commission to continue to explore various possibilities of collaborating with other organizations and institutions in the organization of regional seminars and also to use those occasions for the promotion of legal texts emanating from its work;

(b) Expresses its appreciation to those States that have made financial contributions to be used towards the financing of symposia and seminars and of other aspects of the training and assistance programme of the Commission;

(c) Expresses its appreciation to those Governments and institutions that are arranging seminars or symposia in the field of international trade law, and endorses the request of the Commission that its secretariat be supplied with copies of papers or proceedings in connection with these seminars or symposia in order to assist in the further planning of regional seminars;

(d) Invites Governments, relevant United Nations organs, organizations, institutions and individuals to assist the secretariat of the Commission in financing and organizing symposia and seminars;

10. *Recommends* that the United Nations Commission on International Trade Law should continue its work on the topics included in its programme of work;

11. *Reaffirms* the importance of the programme of work of the United Nations Commission on International Trade Law;

12. *Reaffirms also* the importance of the increasing role of the International Trade Law Branch of the Office of Legal Affairs of the Secretariat as the substantive secretariat of the United Nations Commission on International Trade Law in assisting in the implementation of the work programme of the Commission;

13. *Requests* the Secretary-General to forward to the United Nations Commission on International Trade Law the records of the discussion at the thirty-seventh session of the General Assembly relating to the report of the Commission on the work of its fifteenth session.

International trade law

Unification of trade law

International commercial arbitration

Draft model law

Because of the increasing role of arbitration as a means of settling international commercial disputes, UNCITRAL had decided in 1981 to prepare a draft model law on international commercial arbitration to serve as a basis for modernizing national laws and practices on the subject.[4] The Commission entrusted this work to its 15-member

Working Group on International Contract Practices.

The Group began work on the project at its third session, held in New York from 16 to 26 February 1982, by considering the draft's possible features. It examined the concerns and underlying principles and discussed the various issues to be dealt with, including the scope of application, the arbitration agreement, arbitrators, arbitral procedure, the award and means of recourse.[2]

At its July/August session, UNCITRAL took note of the Working Group's report, requesting it to proceed with its work expeditiously.[1]

At its fourth session, held at Vienna, Austria, from 4 to 15 October,[3] the Working Group completed preliminary discussion of the model law and considered tentative draft articles prepared by the UNCITRAL secretariat. The Group requested that organ to redraft the articles in the light of the Group's discussions and decisions.

Reports. [1]UNCITRAL, A/37/17; Working Group on International Contract Practices, [2]A/CN.9/216, [3]A/CN.9/232.
Yearbook reference. [4]1981, p. 1253.

UNCITRAL Arbitration Rules

In 1981,[4] UNCITRAL had agreed on the desirability of issuing recommended guidelines to help arbitral institutions and other interested bodies, such as chambers of commerce, in adopting procedures for acting as appointing authority or for providing administrative services in cases to be conducted under the 1976 UNCITRAL Arbitration Rules.[3] At its July/August 1982 session, UNCITRAL finalized and approved a set of recommendations to this end and requested the Secretary-General to transmit them to Governments, arbitral institutions and other interested bodies.[1] These actions were taken after the UNCITRAL secretariat had redrafted the text, at the Commission's request, to reflect the views expressed during its 1982 session.

In its 16 December resolution on the work of UNCITRAL, the General Assembly noted with appreciation that that body had approved the recommended guidelines.[2]

Report. [1]UNCITRAL, A/37/17.
Resolution (1982). [2]GA: 37/106, para. 6, 16 Dec.
Yearbook references. [3]1976, p. 823; [4]1981, p. 1254.

International payments

Universal unit of account

In 1982, UNCITRAL continued to study the problem caused by erosion of the purchasing value of the maximum compensation recoverable under conventions specifying a limit of liability.

Responding to a 1981 UNCITRAL request,[5] the eight-member Working Group on International Negotiable Instruments, at its twelfth session (Vienna, 4-12 January 1982), took up the question of a universal unit of account for international trans-

port and liability conventions and recommended that a draft article be prepared for use in them, designating the special drawing right (SDR) of the International Monetary Fund as the unit of account for limitation of liability provisions.[2] The Group also drafted two alternative sample provisions for revising the limits of liability in such conventions: one whereby revision would be effected automatically in accordance with fluctuations in a price index; and another whereby revision would be effected through an expedited procedure to revise the limits of liability.

At its July/August session, UNCITRAL agreed that a preferred unit of account for international transport and liability conventions, particularly those for global application, should be the SDR and it prepared a text for incorporation into those conventions, as recommended by the Working Group.[1] In order to prevent the monetary amounts contained in such conventions from becoming inappropriate due to inflation or deflation, UNCITRAL also adopted the two alternative provisions. The Commission recommended that in preparing future international conventions containing limitation of liability provisions, or in revising existing conventions, the unit of account provision and one of the alternatives for adjusting the limitation of liability should be used. It requested the General Assembly to recommend use of those provisions.

General Assembly action. On 16 December, the General Assembly endorsed the recommendations of UNCITRAL when it adopted without vote a resolution on the subject.[4] On 11 November, the Sixth (Legal) Committee had approved by consensus the draft sponsored by 17 nations and introduced by Austria.

Also on 16 December, in its resolution on the work of UNCITRAL, the Assembly noted that that body had adopted the provision and the two alternatives.[3]

Reports. [1]UNCITRAL, A/37/17 & Corr.2; [2]Working Group on International Negotiable Instruments, A/CN.9/215.
Resolutions (1982). GA, 16 Dec.: [3]37/106, para. 5; [4]37/107, text following.
Yearbook reference. [5]1981, p. 1255.
Meeting records. GA: 6th Committee, A/C.6/37/SR.3-8, 43 (28 Sep.–11 Nov.); plenary, A/37/PV.107 (16 Dec.).

General Assembly resolution 37/107

16 December 1982   Meeting 107   Adopted without vote

Approved by Sixth Committee (A/37/620) by consensus, 11 November (meeting 43); 17-nation draft (A/C.6/37/L.8); agenda item 119.

Sponsors: Australia, Austria, Chile, Cyprus, Egypt, Finland, France, Germany, Federal Republic of, Greece, Japan, Kenya, Netherlands, Nigeria, Philippines, Singapore, Sweden, Thailand.

Provisions for a unit of account and adjustment of limitations of liability adopted by the United Nations Commission on International Trade Law

The General Assembly,

Recognizing that many international transport and liability conventions of both a global and a regional character contain limitation of liability provisions, wherein the limitation of liability is expressed in a unit of account,

Noting that the amount fixed in such a convention as the limitation of liability may become seriously affected over time by changes in monetary values, thereby destroying the intended balance of the convention as adopted,

Believing that a preferred unit of account for many conventions, particularly for those of global application, should be the special drawing right as determined by the International Monetary Fund,

Being of the opinion that the conventions should, in any event, contain a provision which would facilitate adjustment of the limit of liability to changes in monetary values,

Taking into consideration any preferential agreements between the States concerned,

Noting that the United Nations Commission on International Trade Law has adopted a provision for a universal unit of account for expressing monetary amounts in international transport and liability conventions and two alternative provisions for adjustment of the limits of liability in such conventions,

1. *Recommends* that, in the preparation of future international conventions containing limitation of liability provisions or in the revision of existing conventions, the unit of account provision adopted by the United Nations Commission on International Trade Law should be used;

2. *Recommends further* that in such conventions one of the two alternative provisions for adjustment of the limitation of liability adopted by the United Nations Commission on International Trade Law should be used.

Draft Conventions on bills of exchange and promissory notes, and on international cheques

At its July/August 1982 session,[5] UNCITRAL had before it two draft Conventions adopted in 1981 by its Working Group on International Negotiable Instruments: one on international bills of exchange and international promissory notes,[1] together with a commentary;[3] and the other on international cheques,[2] also accompanied by a commentary.[4]

These draft Conventions would establish comprehensive sets of uniform rules applicable to international instruments for optional use in international payments. Each draft dealt with the sphere of application and form of the instrument; interpretation; transfer; rights and liabilities; presentment, dishonour and recourse; discharge; lost instruments; and limitation of actions (prescription). The draft Convention on International Cheques also dealt with crossed cheques and cheques payable in account.

The texts had been circulated to Governments and interested international organizations with a request for written comments by 15 February 1983. However, as many UNCITRAL members felt the time-limit was too short, it was decided that it should be extended to 30 September 1983 and that a final decision on the future course of action on the draft Conventions would be taken by UNCITRAL in 1984.

Draft conventions. [1]Bills of exchange and promissory notes, transmitted by Secretariat note, A/CN.9/211; [2]International cheques, transmitted by Secretariat note, A/CN.9/212.
Reports. SG, [3]A/CN.9/213, [4]A/CN.9/214; [5]UNCITRAL, A/37/17.

Electronic funds transfer

At its July/August 1982 session,[1] UNCITRAL had before it a report of the Secretary-General describing some of the legal problems arising from the transfer of funds by electronic means and containing the recommendations of the Study Group on International Payments, a consultative body composed of representatives of banking and trade institutions entrusted by UNCITRAL in 1979 with considering the legal problems of the question. The report, submitted in response to a 1981 UNCITRAL secretariat request,[2] concluded that it would be premature to try to unify the law in respect of electronic funds transfers. What was needed was a guide to the legal problems arising from such transfers which would identify the legal issues, describe the various approaches, point out the advantages and disadvantages of each approach and suggest alternative solutions.

There was general agreement in UNCITRAL that a guide on the legal problems should be prepared. It was pointed out that in many States transfers took place in a legal vacuum and that there was no agreement on the rules governing international electronic funds transfers. It was suggested that the problems would soon become more important for developing countries with their increased participation in domestic and international funds transfers. The Commission decided that its secretariat should begin preparing a legal guide on the topic, in co-operation with the Study Group.

Report. [1]UNCITRAL, A/37/17.
Yearbook reference. [2]1981, p. 1255.

Draft uniform rules on international trade contracts

At its July/August 1982 session,[2] UNCITRAL again considered a set of draft uniform rules on liquidated damages and penalty clauses, preparation of which had been completed by its Working Group on International Contract Practices in 1981.[3] This draft text specified the circumstances and conditions under which a party to an international contract was entitled to recover or forfeit an agreed sum in the event of failure to perform or delay in performance. The rules would apply to both liquidated damages (where a contract sought to pre-estimate compensation payable on its breach) and penalty clauses.

UNCITRAL also had before it supplementary provisions, prepared by its secretariat, which might be required if the rules were to take the form of a convention or a model law, and a commentary;[1] and an analysis of the comments of Governments and international organizations submitted in response to a 1981 request.[3]

The Commission considered whether the rules should be embodied in a convention, a model law or in general contract conditions. Although the majority view favoured a model law, it was decided to defer a decision on the form to be adopted until

1983. Specific articles of the draft uniform rules were also discussed and UNCITRAL requested its secretariat to submit to its 1983 session a revised draft text taking into account the current discussions.

Reports. [1]S-G, A/CN.9/218; [2]UNCITRAL, A/37/17. *Yearbook reference.* [3]1981, p. 1256.

Co-ordination of trade law activities

In 1981, it had been suggested in UNCITRAL discussions that efforts be made to strengthen co-operation with other competent bodies so as to avoid both a duplication of work in international trade law and the adoption of conflicting regional conventions.[3] Therefore, UNCITRAL had decided that its secretariat should select a particular legal area of the subject for consideration and submit a report on the work of other organizations in that area.

The secretariat chose the topic of international transport documents; its subsequent report discussed the legal régime governing transport documentation requirements under the principal multilateral conventions and current developments. It foresaw a growing need for future harmonization of the rules on the subject. At its July/August 1982 session,[1] UNCITRAL welcomed a suggestion by the secretariat that it should continue monitoring developments in the area and UNCITRAL repeated its expressed desire that a report be submitted regularly on all the work of other organizations active in international trade law.

The Commission also considered a note by its secretariat describing progress made by the International Chamber of Commerce in revising the 1974 version of the Uniform Customs and Practice for Documentary Credits. The Secretary-General was requested to submit to a future UNCITRAL session a study on letters of credit and their operation in order to identify legal problems arising from their use, especially in connection with contracts other than those for the sale of goods.

In its 16 December resolution on the work of UNCITRAL,[2] the General Assembly reaffirmed that body's mandate to co-ordinate legal activities in international trade law and recommended that it continue maintaining close co-operation with others active in the field, particularly the United Nations Conference on Trade and Development, the International Law Commission, the United Nations Industrial Development Organization and the Commission on Transnational Corporations. The Assembly also reaffirmed the importance of the participation of observers from all States and interested international organizations at sessions of the Commission and its Working Groups.

Report. [1]UNCITRAL, A/37/17. *Resolution (1982).* [2]GA: 37/106, para. 7, 16 Dec. *Yearboook reference.* [3]1981, p. 1257.

Training programmes

At its July/August 1982 session,[1] UNCITRAL was informed that Yugoslavia had contributed $3,000 to UNCITRAL training programmes, while the Netherlands had made available 25,000 guilders for future seminars or symposia; Australia was conducting yearly international trade law seminars and was considering a future one relating specifically to Pacific region countries; Iraq was organizing for its officials a symposium dealing with the United Nations Convention on Contracts for the International Sale of Goods, and the work of UNCITRAL was being studied at the University of Baghdad; and an institute for the unification of trade law had been established at the University of Seville, Spain. It was decided by UNCITRAL that it would continue exploring possible collaboration with organizations and institutions in organizing regional seminars and that it would use those occasions to promote its legal texts.

In its 16 December resolution on the work of UNCITRAL,[2] the General Assembly reaffirmed the importance of training and assistance in international trade law, particularly for developing countries; welcomed the UNCITRAL decision; and invited Governments, United Nations bodies and individuals to help finance and organize seminars.

Report. [1]UNCITRAL, A/37/17. *Resolution (1982).* [2]GA: 37/106, para. 9, 16 Dec.

Legal aspects of the new international economic order

UNCITRAL Working Group action. In 1982, the UNCITRAL Working Group on the New International Economic Order (New York, 12-23 July) completed its work on industrial works contracts and agreed that a legal guide on the topic should be drawn up (See ECONOMIC AND SOCIAL QUESTIONS, Chapter VI).

UNITAR study. Pursuant to a December 1981 General Assembly resolution,[8] the Secretary-General submitted in October 1982 a report, with later addenda,[2] containing a progress report by the United Nations Institute for Training and Research (UNITAR) on its analytical study on the progressive development of the principles and norms of international law relating to the new international economic order—a study requested by the Assembly in 1980.[7] The addenda gave the comments of Argentina, Ecuador, the USSR and the United Kingdom. Phase I of the study—a compendium listing all possible sources of norms and principles evolving in the direction of law—had been forwarded to the Assembly in 1981.[12]

In its 1982 report, UNITAR gave details on phase II of its study, stating that it had completed analytical papers on several principles: preferential treatment for developing countries; stabilization of their export earnings; and permanent sovereignty over natural resources. Further analytical papers on other principles, and research on sources of international law-making and sources that evidenced State practice, would be carried out using the expertise of eminent persons in the field and submitted to the Secretary-General, marking the end of the third and final phase of work.

General Assembly action. On 16 December, the General Assembly adopted a resolution[3] by which it requested UNITAR to complete the final phase of its study in time for the Assembly's 1983 regular session. The Secretary-General was to submit a report on that study on a priority basis for consideration at the session. Member States were urged to submit, no later than 31 May 1983, relevant information, and United Nations organs and intergovernmental and non-governmental organizations active in the field were also asked for such information and to co-operate with UNITAR. The Assembly also invited UNITAR to select, based on equitable geographical representation and taking into account the world's different legal and economic systems, experts to help with the final phase.

The resolution was adopted by a recorded vote of 113 to 1, with 30 abstentions. On 2 December, the Sixth (Legal) Committee had approved the draft, sponsored by 14 nations and introduced by the Philippines, by 69 votes to 1, with 29 abstentions.

Also on 16 December, the Assembly, in its resolution on the work of UNCITRAL,[4] called on that body to continue taking account of the relevant provisions of resolutions on the new international economic order adopted at the Assembly's sixth (1974)[10] and seventh (1975)[11] special sessions.

An amendment to the draft dealing with the UNITAR study, proposed by the United States,[1] was rejected by 59 votes to 16, with 15 abstentions. By the text, the Assembly would have authorized the Secretary-General to implement activities approved under the resolution only to the extent that they could be financed by resources in the programme budget for the 1982-1983 biennium.[9]

Explaining its negative vote, the United States felt that, in the absence of political agreement on the new international economic order, there was no basis for considering the legal questions involved.

A number of States explained their abstentions. The Federal Republic of Germany felt that the legal principles relating to the order could derive only from generally accepted international law corresponding to State practice. Belgium believed codification of an evolving process was premature and said the systematization and progressive development of the principles and norms of inter-

national law should be based on the principle of interdependence and take into account the legitimate interests of the parties concerned. France could not accept the *a priori* judgements made by UNITAR on whether some of the principles of international law existed or were evolving, or its opinion about the juridical hierarchy of different sources of law. Argentina and Chile were unable to support some aspects of the UNITAR study. Australia held a similar view and noted that the proposed third phase was not what might have been expected in the light of earlier Secretariat documents on the question. Expressing disappointment over the first two phases of the study, Belgium feared the third would exhibit the same shortcomings because of the short time which UNITAR had been allowed. The United Kingdom said it had basic reservations on the study's methodological approach and even more serious reservations on the second phase; it was also shocked to see that completion of the study would cost an additional $127,400.

Bulgaria, speaking also for the Byelorussian SSR, Czechoslovakia, the German Democratic Republic, Hungary, Poland, the Ukrainian SSR and the USSR, said UNCITRAL was the most appropriate body to consider the subject as UNITAR was an organ in which Governments were not represented and it had no authority to pass judgements on questions requiring a concerted decision by States; further, a body funded by voluntary contributions should not carry out a study which had financial implications for the United Nations. Referring to the 1974 instruments mentioned in the preambular text—such as the Declaration on the Establishment of a New International Economic Order[5] and the Charter of Economic Rights and Duties of States[6]—Bulgaria said a study should have due regard for the diversity of economic relations among States and the position of the socialist States as expressed when those texts were adopted.

Austria said that although it had voted in favour it was not in full agreement with all aspects of procedure followed thus far or with the entire content of the studies, and recommended that, in future, State practice be taken into account to a greater degree. The Netherlands, also voting positively, asserted that the study in its existing form left much to be desired and hoped this would be taken into account by UNITAR in finalizing the study.

Amendment rejected. [1]United States, A/C.6/37/L.25.
Report. [2]S-G, A/37/409 & Add.1-3.
Resolutions (1982). GA, 16 Dec.: [3]37/103, text following; [4]37/106, para. 3.
Resolutions (prior). GA: [5]3201(S-VI), 1 May 1974 (YUN 1974, p. 324); [6]3281(XXIX), 12 Dec. 1974 (*ibid.,* p. 403); [7]35/166, 15 Dec. 1980 (YUN 1980, p. 532); [8]36/107, 10 Dec. 1981 (YUN 1981, p. 1263); [9]36/240 A, 18 Dec. 1981 (*ibid.,* p. 1278).
Yearbook references. [10]1974, p. 305; [11]1975, p. 329; [12]1981, p. 1261.

Financial implications. 5th Committee report, A/37/736; S-G statements, A/C.5/37/81, A/C.6/37/L.24.

Meeting records. GA: 6th Committee, A/C.6/37/SR.*55*, 56-60, *61* (26 Nov.–2 Dec.); 5th Committee, A/C.5/37/SR.61 (9 Dec.); plenary, A/37/PV.107 (16 Dec.).

General Assembly resolution 37/103

16 December 1982   Meeting 107   113-1-30 (recorded vote)

Approved by Sixth Committee (A/37/720) by vote (69-1-29), 2 December (meeting 61); 14-nation draft (A/C.6/37/L.17/Rev.1); agenda item 116.

Sponsors: Ecuador, Egypt, Equatorial Guinea, Ghana, India, Mexico, Nigeria, Pakistan, Philippines, Romania, Tunisia, Venezuela, Zaire, Zambia.

Progressive development of the principles and norms of international law relating to the new international economic order

The General Assembly,

Bearing in mind that, in accordance with the Charter of the United Nations, the General Assembly is called upon to initiate studies and make recommendations for the purpose of encouraging the progressive development of international law and its codification,

Recalling its resolutions 3201(S-VI) and 3202(S-VI) of 1 May 1974, containing the Declaration and the Programme of Action on the Establishment of a New International Economic Order, 3281(XXIX) of 12 December 1974, containing the Charter of Economic Rights and Duties of States, and 3362(S-VII) of 16 September 1975 on development and international economic co-operation,

Recalling its resolutions 34/150 of 17 December 1979 and 35/166 of 15 December 1980, entitled "Consolidation and progressive development of the principles and norms of international economic law relating in particular to the legal aspects of the new international economic order", and its resolution 36/107 of 10 December 1981, entitled "Progressive development of the principles and norms of international law relating to the new international economic order",

Taking note of the report of the Secretary-General, particularly of the progress report prepared by the United Nations Institute for Training and Research, of the analytical papers and analysis of texts of relevant instruments and of the views submitted by States in response to General Assembly resolution 36/107,

Taking note, in particular, of the recommendation that the United Nations Institute for Training and Research should complete the analytical study on the progressive development of the principles and norms of international law relating to the new international economic order, in accordance with the fifth preambular paragraph and paragraph 2 of resolution 36/107,

Recognizing the need for a systematic and progressive development of the principles and norms of international law relating to the new international economic order,

1. *Requests* the United Nations Institute for Training and Research to prepare the third and final phase of the analytical study and to complete it in time for the Secretary-General to submit it to the General Assembly at its thirty-eighth session;

2. *Urges* Member States to submit not later than 31 May 1983 relevant information with respect to the study, including proposals concerning further action to be taken on the final study to be submitted to the General Assembly at its thirty-eighth session;

3. *Requests* the United Nations Commission on International Trade Law, the United Nations Conference on Trade and Development, the United Nations Industrial Development Organization, the regional commissions, the United Nations Centre on Transnational Corporations and other relevant intergovernmental and non-governmental organizations active in this field, as determined by the United Nations Institute for Training and Research, to submit relevant information and to co-operate fully with the Institute in the implementation of the present resolution;

4. *Invites* the United Nations Institute for Training and Research to select, on the basis of equitable geographical representation, taking into account the different legal and economic systems of the world, experts who will help it to carry out the last phase of the study;

5. *Requests* the Secretary-General to submit to the General Assembly at its thirty-eighth session a report on the final study prepared by the United Nations Institute for Training and Research for its consideration, on a priority basis, under the item entitled "Progressive development of the principles and norms of international law relating to the new international economic order" to be included in the provisional agenda of that session.

Recorded vote in Assembly as follows:

In favour: Afghanistan, Algeria, Angola, Austria, Bahamas, Bahrain, Bangladesh, Barbados, Belize, Benin, Bhutan, Bolivia, Brazil, Burma, Burundi, Central African Republic, Chad, China, Colombia, Comoros, Congo, Costa Rica, Cuba, Cyprus, Democratic Kampuchea, Democratic Yemen, Djibouti, Dominican Republic, Ecuador, Egypt, El Salvador, Ethiopia, Fiji, Finland, Gabon, Gambia, Ghana, Greece, Grenada, Guatemala, Guinea, Guyana, Honduras, India, Indonesia, Iran, Iraq, Ivory Coast, Jamaica, Jordan, Kenya, Kuwait, Lebanon, Lesotho, Libyan Arab Jamahiriya, Madagascar, Malawi, Malaysia, Maldives, Mali, Malta, Mauritania, Mauritius, Mexico, Morocco, Mozambique, Nepal, Netherlands, Nicaragua, Niger, Nigeria, Oman, Pakistan, Panama, Papua New Guinea, Paraguay, Peru, Philippines, Qatar, Romania, Rwanda, Samoa, Sao Tome and Principe, Saudi Arabia, Senegal, Seychelles, Sierra Leone, Singapore, Solomon Islands, Somalia, Sri Lanka, Sudan, Suriname, Syrian Arab Republic, Thailand, Togo, Trinidad and Tobago, Tunisia, Turkey, Uganda, United Arab Emirates, United Republic of Cameroon, United Republic of Tanzania, Upper Volta, Uruguay, Vanuatu, Venezuela, Viet Nam, Yemen, Yugoslavia, Zaire, Zambia, Zimbabwe.

Against: United States.

Abstaining: Argentina, Australia, Belgium, Bulgaria, Byelorussian SSR, Canada, Chile, Czechoslovakia, Denmark, France, German Democratic Republic, Germany, Federal Republic of, Hungary, Iceland, Ireland, Israel, Italy, Japan, Lao People's Democratic Republic, Luxembourg, Mongolia, New Zealand, Norway, Poland, Portugal, Spain, Sweden, Ukrainian SSR, USSR, United Kingdom.

Chapter VII

Other legal questions

Contents

For resolutions and decisions of major organs mentioned but not reproduced, refer to INDEX OF RESOLUTIONS AND DECISIONS.

International Law Commission

In 1982, the International Law Commission (ILC), which held its thirty-fourth session at Geneva from 3 May to 23 July, continued work on the progressive development and codification of international law.[1]

Report. [1]ILC, A/37/10.

ILC work programme

The 1982 ILC session was devoted mainly to considering draft articles on various aspects of international law.[1] The Commission, which had been expanded from 25 to 34 members by the General Assembly in November 1981,[4] began its 1982 work programme with members elected for a five-year term beginning on 1 January (see APPENDIX III).

ILC adopted the final version of draft articles on treaties concluded between States and international organizations or between international organizations, and recommended that a convention be concluded based on those articles (see Chapter V of this section). It continued preparing draft articles on: the status of the diplomatic courier and the diplomatic bag not accompanied by courier (Chapter III); jurisdictional immunities of States and their property (*ibid.*); international liability for injurious consequences arising from acts not prohibited by international law (*ibid.*); and State responsibility for internationally wrongful acts (*ibid.*). The Commission also resumed work on the 1954 draft Code of Offences against the Peace and Security of Mankind (Chapter II) and took up the question of drafting articles on non-navigational uses of international watercourses (*ibid.*). It was not able to consider the second part of the topic on relations between States and international organizations—a further topic recommended by the Assembly in 1981. During 1982, ILC maintained co-operation with

other juridical bodies such as the Inter-American Juridical Committee and the European Committee on Legal Co-operation.

With regard to improving further its current procedures and methods of work, there was an initial exchange of views in ILC on such questions as: providing additional assistance to special rapporteurs; encouraging greater response from Member States to questionnaires; better use of available time, such as concentrating on fewer topics at any one session; and possible further expansion of research on ILC topics as well as other substantive servicing given by its secretariat and the Codification Division of the Office of Legal Affairs of the Secretariat. ILC stated its intention to consider these questions in greater detail at future sessions. It also reiterated a 1980 conclusion that continuing the ILC summary records was an inescapable requirement for its work and for codifying international law in general.

Concerning a December 1981 Assembly request[5] that reports of subsidiary organs be brief and not exceed 32 pages, ILC reaffirmed that it could not endorse that request as it felt its reports should be short or long according to its perception of the need to explain work accomplished and justify the draft articles contained therein. However, it would bear in mind the need for achieving economies. Noting that the practice of listing in each summary record of its meetings the members attending had been discontinued by the United Nations Office at Geneva, ILC requested that the practice be reinstated.

General Assembly action. On 16 December 1982, the General Assembly adopted a resolution on the work of ILC[3] recommending that it continue preparing drafts on all the topics in its current programme. The Assembly expressed satisfaction with the conclusions and intentions of ILC on its procedures and methods of work. Further, the Assembly reaffirmed its previous decisions concerning the increased role of the Codification Division and its wish that ILC continue co-operating with intergovernmental legal bodies.

The resolution was adopted without vote. On 6 December, the Sixth (Legal) Committee had likewise approved the 34-nation draft introduced by Argentina.

In its 16 November resolution dealing with the meeting records and documentation for subsidiary organs, the Assembly—in deciding that, for a three-year experimental period, none of its subsidiary organs would be entitled to summary records—excepted a number of those organs, including ILC.[2]

Report. [1]ILC, A/37/10.
Resolutions (1982). GA: [2]37/14 C, para. 3 *(c)*, 16 Nov.; [3]37/111, 16 Dec., text following.
Resolutions (prior). GA: [4]36/39, 18 Nov. 1981 (YUN 1981, p. 1266), [5]36/117 A, 10 Dec. 1981 *(ibid.,* p. 1364).
Meeting records. GA: 6th Committee, A/C.6/37/SR.37, 38-52, 63 (4 Nov.–6 Dec.); plenary, A/37/PV.107 (16 Dec.).
Publications. Yearbook of the International Law Commission, 1982, vol. I: *Summary Records of the Meetings of the Thirty-fourth Session, 3 May–23 July 1982* (A/CN.4/SER.A/1982), Sales No. E.83.V.2; vol. II, *Part One: Documents of the Thirty-fourth Session (Excluding the Report of the Commission to the General Assembly* & *Part Two: Report of the Commission to the General Assembly on the Work of Its Thirty-fourth Session* (A/CN.4/SER.A/1982/Add.1, Parts I, II), Sales No. E.83.V.3 (Parts I, II).

General Assembly resolution 37/111

16 December 1982	Meeting 107	Adopted without vote

Approved by Sixth Committee (A/37/700) without vote, 6 December (meeting 63); 34-nation draft (A/C.6/37/L.27); agenda item 125.

Sponsors: Algeria, Argentina, Australia, Austria, Bahamas, Brazil, Bulgaria, Canada, Chile, Colombia, Cyprus, Ecuador, Egypt, Germany, Federal Republic of, Greece, Iraq, Italy, Japan, Madagascar, Mexico, Netherlands, New Zealand, Nigeria, Panama, Philippines, Romania, Sierra Leone, Spain, Thailand, Turkey, Uruguay, Venezuela, Yugoslavia, Zaire.

Report of the International Law Commission

The General Assembly,

Having considered the report of the International Law Commission on the work of its thirty-fourth session,

Emphasizing the need for the progressive development of international law and its codification in order to make it a more effective means of implementing the purposes and principles set forth in the Charter of the United Nations and in the Declaration on Principles of International Law concerning Friendly Relations and Co-operation among States in accordance with the Charter of the United Nations and to give increasing importance to its role in relations among States,

Recognizing the importance of referring legal and drafting questions to the Sixth Committee, including topics which might be submitted to the International Law Commission, and of enabling the Sixth Committee and the Commission further to enhance their contributions to the progressive development of international law and its codification,

Welcoming the establishment of general objectives and priorities which will guide the study by the International Law Commission of the topics on its programme of work within the term of office of Commission members elected at the thirty-sixth session of the General Assembly,

Recalling the need to keep under review those topics of international law which, given their new or renewed interest for the contemporary international community, may be suitable for progressive development and codification of international law and therefore may be included in the future programme of work of the International Law Commission,

1. *Takes note* of the report of the International Law Commission on the work of its thirty-fourth session;

2. *Expresses its appreciation* to the International Law Commission for the work accomplished at that session and, in particular, for having completed the final reading of the draft articles on the law of treaties between States and international organizations or between international organizations;

3. *Recommends* that, taking into account the comments of Governments, whether in writing or expressed orally in debates in the General Assembly, the International Law Commission should continue its work aimed at the preparation of drafts on all the topics in its current programme;

4. *Expresses its satisfaction* with the conclusions and intention of the International Law Commission concerning its procedures and methods of work, as reflected in paragraphs 266 and 270 of its report;

5. *Reaffirms* its previous decisions concerning the increased role of the Codification Division of the Office of Legal Affairs of the Secretariat and approves the conclusions reached by the International Law Commission concerning summary records of its meetings and the application to its documentation of the thirty-two-page limit, as well as the request made by the Commission in paragraph 272 of its report;

6. *Appeals* to Governments and, as appropriate, to international organizations to respond as fully and expeditiously as possible to the requests of the International Law Commission for comments and observations on its draft articles and questionnaires and for materials on topics on its programme of work;

7. *Reaffirms its wish* that the International Law Commission will continue to enhance its co-operation with intergovernmental legal bodies whose work is of interest for the progressive development of international law and its codification;

8. *Expresses the wish* that seminars will continue to be held in conjunction with sessions of the International Law Commission and that an increasing number of participants from developing countries will be given the opportunity to attend those seminars;

9. *Requests* the Secretary-General to forward to the International Law Commission, for its attention, the records of the debate on the report of the Commission at the thirty-seventh session of the General Assembly and to prepare and distribute a topical summary of the debate.

International Law Seminar

Responding to the Assembly's 1981 wish,[3] the eighteenth session of the International Law Seminar—intended for advanced students and junior government officials dealing with international law—was held from 10 to 28 May 1982 at Geneva with 24 participants, all of different nationality and a great majority from developing countries.[1] The participants followed the work of ILC at its 1982 session and heard lectures given by its members and other eminent jurists. As in the past, none of the costs of the Seminar fell on the United Nations. Austria, Denmark, Finland, the Federal Republic of Germany, Jamaica, the Netherlands, Norway and Spain made fellowships available to participants from developing countries, and a private body, the Dana Fund for International and Comparative Legal Studies (United States), also made funds available.

In its 16 December resolution on the work of ILC,[2] the General Assembly expressed the wish that seminars would continue to be held in conjunction with ILC sessions and that increasing numbers of participants from developing countries would be given the opportunity to attend.

Report. [1]ILC, A/37/10.
Resolution (1982). [2]GA: 37/111, para. 8, 16 Dec.
Resolution (prior). [3]GA: 36/114, 10 Dec. 1981 (YUN 1981, p. 1265).

Co-operation between the United Nations and the Asian-African Legal Consultative Committee

On 29 October 1982, the General Assembly, by a resolution adopted without vote,[1] noted with deep satisfaction the close co-operation between the United Nations and the Asian-African Legal Consultative Committee in the progressive development and codification of international law and other areas of common interest and requested the Secretary-General to report in 1983 on the state of that co-operation.

The text, sponsored by 13 nations, was introduced by India.

Resolution (1982). [1]GA: 37/8, 29 Oct., text following.
Meeting record. GA: A/37/PV.49 (29 Oct.).

General Assembly resolution 37/8

29 October 1982   Meeting 49   Adopted without vote

13-nation draft (A/37/L.10 and Add.1); agenda item 26.

Sponsors: Bangladesh, Cyprus, Egypt, India, Indonesia, Iraq, Japan, Mongolia, Nigeria, Pakistan, Philippines, Sri Lanka, United Republic of Tanzania.

Co-operation between the United Nations and the Asian-African Legal Consultative Committee

The General Assembly,

Recalling its resolution 36/38 of 18 November 1981,

Having heard the statements of the Secretary-General of the United Nations and the Secretary-General of the Asian-African Legal Consultative Committee on further strengthening and widening the scope of the co-operation between the United Nations and the Committee,

1. *Notes with deep satisfaction* the ongoing close and effective co-operation between the United Nations and the Asian-African Legal Consultative Committee in the field of progressive development and codification of international law and other areas of common interest;

2. *Requests* the Secretary-General to report to the General Assembly at its thirty-eighth session on the state of the co-operation between the United Nations and the Asian-African Legal Consultative Committee;

3. *Decides* to include in the provisional agenda of its thirty-eighth session the item entitled "Co-operation between the United Nations and the Asian-African Legal Consultative Committee".

Administrative and budgetary questions

United Nations finances

Contents

UN regular budget

Programme budget for 1982-1983

The 1982-1983 programme budget, originally adopted in December 1981,[4] setting out the appropriations and income estimates for each programme covered by the United Nations regular budget, was reduced by $5.8 million (net) by the General Assembly in December 1982, primarily reflecting more favourable exchange rates for the United States dollar. The net reduction consisted of $33.3 million less in appropriations, partly offset by a $27.5 million reduction in income estimates. These amounts were included in a revised budget for the biennium[3] which also took account of the financial implications of actions taken by the Assembly during 1982, as well as reduced costs due to a lower rate of inflation than the Assembly had provided for when it adopted the initial budget.

The effects of inflation and altered exchange rates were calculated by the Secretary-General in his first performance report[2] to the Assembly on the 1982-1983 budget, which also contained other proposals

for budget revisions, some of them the result of actions by other United Nations bodies since the initial budget was adopted. These proposals, along with others presented to the Assembly during its 1982 session, were reviewed by the Assembly's Advisory Committee on Administrative and Budgetary Questions (ACABQ),[1] revised by the Fifth (Administrative and Budgetary) Committee and finally approved by the Assembly itself.

The following table shows expenditure and income figures, in thousands of United States dollars (negative amounts in parentheses), at various stages of this process (totals may differ from sums of figures because of rounding).

	Expenditure	Income
Revised estimates		
Amount proposed by the Secretary-General	(55,373)	(29,957)
Reduction recommended by Fifth Committee	(3,730)	(189)
Amount approved	(59,103)	(30,146)
Financial implications		
Amount proposed by the Secretary-General	32,246	3,506
Reduction recommended by Fifth Committee	(6,423)	(854)
Amount approved	25,823	2,653
Totals		
Amount proposed by the Secretary-General	(23,128)	(26,451)
Reduction recommended by Fifth Committee	(10,153)	(1,043)
Amount approved	(33,280)	(27,493)

Reports. (1)ACABQ, A/37/7 & Add.1-24; (2)S-G, A/C.5/37/65 & Add.1,2.
Resolutions (1982). (3)GA: 37/243 A-C, 21 Dec.
Resolutions (prior). (4)GA: 36/240 A-C, 18 Dec. 1981 (YUN 1981, pp. 1278-80).

Appropriations

By a resolution of 21 December 1982,(4) the General Assembly revised downward by $33,280,100 its 1981 appropriation for the 1982-1983 biennium, giving a new total of $1,472,961,700. The action was taken by a recorded vote of 117 to 14, with 12 abstentions, following approval on the previous day by the Fifth Committee by a recorded vote, requested by India, of 68 to 14, with 10 abstentions.

The main factor responsible for this reduction was variations in rates of exchange. According to calculations by the Secretary-General in his first performance report for the biennium,(2) dated 3 December, with subsequent addenda, a saving of nearly $71.3 million would be realized from a gradual appreciation of the United States dollar against the currencies of countries in which the United Nations operated, and a further gain of $1.8 million due to an inflation rate below projected levels. These savings were partly offset by $3.7 million in additional expenditure stemming from decisions of United Nations policy-making organs other than the General Assembly and from other changes. These estimates were accepted by ACABQ(1) and by the Fifth Committee.

The only proposed additional commitment in the performance report which exceeded $1 million was for staff travel and related costs in connection with the move of the headquarters of the Economic Commission for Western Asia (ECWA) from Beirut, Lebanon, to Baghdad, Iraq, during the first half of 1982. The final effect of the performance report was a decrease of $69.5 million in expenditure partly offset by a decrease of $30.9 million in income, for a net decrease of $38.6 million.

Other revised estimates approved by the Assembly in 1982 included additional appropriations of $5.4 million to relocate certain United Nations offices in the new United Nations Development Corporation building (UNDC II) at Headquarters (see Chapter IV of this section) and $2.4 million for servicing staff and equipment at the new ECWA headquarters. When these and other revised estimates were added to the budget appropriations, the savings recorded in the performance report were reduced; thus, the total of all revised estimates approved by the Assembly in 1982, including those in the performance report, resulted in a $54.1 million reduction from the amount approved in 1981.

The savings were further reduced by some $25.8 million in financial implications of the actions taken by the Assembly in 1982. Of the 41 items for which additional funds were appropriated, five exceeded $1 million (gross) each: conference servicing for additional meetings approved for 1983, $9.4 million; new activities pertaining to the law of the sea, $3.2 million, and to Namibia, $2.5 million; an expanded work programme of the United Nations Industrial Development Organization (UNIDO), including additional senior industrial development field advisers, $2.2 million; and the International Conference on the Question of Palestine, scheduled for 1983, $2 million.

Voting on these items in the Fifth Committee took place as follows. The amount of $9,370,000 gross ($8,300,000 net) for additional conference-servicing costs was approved on 18 December by a recorded vote, requested by Bangladesh, of 71 to 10. The financial implications ($3,156,900 gross, $2,728,500 net) of activities relating to the law of the sea, including the cost of convening the Preparatory Commission for the International Sea-Bed Authority and the International Tribunal for the Law of the Sea, were approved on 2 December by a recorded vote, requested by Turkey, of 92 to 3, with 19 abstentions. The financial implications ($2,514,600 gross, $2,421,800 net) of five resolutions pertaining to the Namibia question adopted on 20 December(3) were approved on 18 December by a recorded vote of 71 to 5, with 7 abstentions; Egypt had asked that, if a vote were taken, it be recorded. A sum for additional UNIDO activities ($2,191,700 gross, $1,990,700 net) was approved by the Committee on 17 December by a vote, requested by the United States, of 63 to 18, with 8 abstentions. The financial implications ($2,048,000 gross, $1,831,000 net) of an International Conference on the Question of Palestine were approved on 29 September by a roll-call vote of 63 to 2, with 12 abstentions; Israel had requested the vote.

The revised estimate ($5,378,300 gross, $5,141,100 net) for relocating Headquarters staff was approved by the Committee on 8 December by a recorded vote, requested by the United States, of 35 to 8, with 19 abstentions. An amount ($2,369,600 gross, $2,274,500 net) for additional posts, operating expenses and equipment for the new ECWA headquarters was approved by the Committee on 17 December by a vote, requested by the United States, of 69 to none, with 14 abstentions.

As a result of approval of additional financing, 142 new posts were created, in addition to the 11,580 authorized under the initial budget approved in 1981.

Explaining its opposition to the revised appropriations, the United Kingdom said the amounts were considerable, and the fact that shifts in currency exchange rates would cover the additional expenses was a matter of luck, not management. Australia, while abstaining, was in agreement, and warned that the reverse might easily happen. The United Kingdom was among those which considered that there was a need for a more rigorous examination of new and existing programmes to ensure the most effective use of resources. Italy, abstaining, agreed on the need for budgetary discipline, adding that new or expanded programmes should be financed through redeployment of existing resources, a view also held by France and the Netherlands, as well as by the Federal Republic of Germany, which voted against. Canada, which abstained, added that the minimal redeployment that had occurred did not offset the additional expenses; Spain added that, while it was aware of the Secretariat's efforts to enhance effectiveness, much remained to be done.

The United States objected to certain types of expenditure that it said had found their way into the regular budget in recent years: it was wrong, it said, to assess all Member States for the support of organizations committed to the destruction of a Member State, and neither expenditure on programmes previously funded by voluntary contributions nor expenditure related to a treaty body which not all States had joined should be included in the regular budget.

Brazil and France, both abstaining, said that the strong dollar had caused the expenses of the United Nations to be artificially reduced, but the full effect of the decisions on recruitment, promotion and construction would not be felt until the next biennium. France and the Netherlands were unable to support certain proposals whose financial implications they felt were unjustified or inflated, even though the objectives were commendable.

The Federal Republic of Germany, which voted against, and New Zealand, which abstained, said many of the additional expenses were greater than was reasonable in a time of world-wide economic stringency; the latter also regretted that it was taking so long to devise a workable method of ensuring that available resources were devoted to high-priority activities.

Israel opposed expenditure on a number of items, including the International Conference on the Question of Palestine, the issuing of special identity cards to Palestinian refugees and the Special Committee to Investigate Israeli Practices Affecting the Human Rights of the Population of the Occupied Territories.

The USSR noted with concern that many decisions were taken on beginning new kinds of activities using additional allocations, without due efforts being made during the budget period to re-evaluate priorities or redistribute resources saved through reduction or elimination of outdated or ineffective activities. Efforts to redeploy resources met with many obstacles, one of the most serious being the system of

permanent contracts for the majority of staff; fixed-term contracts would allow speedier reaction to changing mandates. It opposed the practice of transferring to the regular budget posts earlier financed through extrabudgetary sources, it did not intend to contribute to expenses involved in budget allocations for interest and principal payments on loans for activities it considered to be contrary to the Charter of the United Nations, and it maintained its position of principle that technical assistance should be excluded from the regular budget and merged with the United Nations Development Programme.

Voting in favour, Ireland held that, although the savings were fortuitous, it had always held that the Organization needed adequate financing to fulfil its objectives. Austria and Kenya felt that requests for funds must be considered on their merits and that resources used to further the purposes of the United Nations were well spent.

Ghana, India, Kenya and the United Republic of Cameroon said that, while financial prudence was certainly desirable, the Assembly had never required the Secretary-General to submit a zero-growth budget, and the United Nations should actually be spending much more than was currently the case. It was unreasonable to expect United Nations programmes not to grow, Ghana said, although it was opposed to the proliferation of posts in the Secretariat. Kenya could not agree that Member States should decide in advance whether to accept new programmes. Egypt warned that some measures proposed in support of zero growth and the redeployment of resources might backfire and actually decrease the effectiveness of the United Nations. Morocco, pointing out that staff costs and overheads consumed nearly 85 per cent of the budget, leaving only 15 per cent for programmes, said the budgetary policy advocated by the developed countries would reduce that amount even further, which was totally unacceptable.

The Dominican Republic supported the resolution but believed it was necessary to put an end to wars that required expensive peace-keeping forces. Chile expressed reservations with regard to certain items of expenditure contained in the section on public information, but said it would vote in favour. Turkey said it would withhold contributions earmarked for expenditure on activities relating to the law of the sea. China said it would have voted against the bond-issue expenditures if a separate vote had been taken.

Voting in favour, Finland, speaking also on behalf of Denmark, Iceland, Norway and Sweden, said there should be no arbitrarily restrictive budgetary framework into which Assembly decisions should be forced; the concept of zero growth was too blunt an instrument and could seriously undermine important programmes. Ireland agreed with those countries in continuing to support a budget policy characterized by financial restraint and economy, while stressing the importance of the principle of collective responsibility of Member States in meeting common expenditures.

Reports. (1)ACABQ, A/37/7/Add.23; (2)S-G, A/C.5/37/65 & Add.1,2.

Resolutions (1982). GA: (3)37/233 A-E, 20 Dec.; (4)37/243 A, 21 Dec., text following.

Meeting records. GA: 5th Committee, A/C.5/37/SR.3, 14, 19, 21, 22, 28, 30, 34, 38, 39, 41, 42, 45-47, 49, 50, 52-54, 59-62, 64, 66, 68-69, 71, 73-77 (29 Sep.–20 Dec.); plenary, A/37/PV.114 (21 Dec.).

Revised estimates. Reports of S-G (A/C.5/37/65 & Add.1,2) and ACABQ (A/37/7/Add.24):

Over $1 million. Accommodation at Headquarters, A/C.5/37/48; A/37/7/Add.12. ECWA, A/C.5/37/65/Add.1; A/37/7/Add.22.

Others. Changes in top echelon of Secretariat, A/C.5/37/62; A/37/7/Add.19. Child-care services at Headquarters, A/C.5/37/69; A/37/7/Add.21. ECA, A/C.5/37/13; A/C.5/37/67; A/37/7/Add.18. ESC decisions, A/C.5/37/3 & Corr.1 & Add.1; A/37/7 and Add.1-24, Add.4 & annex, paras. 1 & 2. First performance report, A/C.5/37/65 & Add.2 & Add.2/Corr.1; A/37/7/Add.23. ICSC, A/C.5/37/12 & Corr.1; A/37/7/Add.6; interorganization secretariat services for information systems, A/C.5/37/41; A/37/7 and Add.1-24, annex, paras. 20-23. Question of Palestine, A/C.5/37/64; A/37/7 and Add.1-24, annex, paras. 32-36.

General Assembly resolution 37/243 A

21 December 1982   Meeting 114   117-14-12 (recorded vote)

Approved by Fifth Committee (A/37/790, draft resolution VII A) by recorded vote (68-14-10), 20 December (meeting 77); agenda item 103.

Revised budget appropriations for the biennium 1982-1983
The General Assembly

Resolves that for the biennium 1982-1983 the amount of $US 1,506,241,800 appropriated by its resolution 36/240 A of 18 December 1981 shall be decreased by $US 33,280,100 as follows:

Section	Amount appropriated by resolution 36/240 A	Increase or (decrease)	Revised appropriation
		(US dollars)	
PART I. *Overall policy-making, direction and co-ordination*			
1. Overall policy-making, direction and co-ordination	34,175,000	4,674,500	38,849,500
Total, PART I	34,175,000	4,674,500	38,849,500
PART II. *Political and Security Council affairs; peace-keeping activities*			
2. Political and Security Council affairs; peace-keeping activities	72,862,000	11,464,800	84,326,800
Total, PART II	72,862,000	11,464,800	84,326,800
PART III. *Political affairs, trusteeship and decolonization*			
3. Political affairs, trusteeship and decolonization	18,774,200	2,332,500	21,106,700
Total, PART III	18,774,200	2,332,500	21,106,700
PART IV. *Economic, social and humanitarian activities*			
4. Policy-making organs (economic and social activities)	1,992,400	605,100	2,597,500
5A. Office of the Director-General for Development and International Economic Co-operation	3,228,900	51,600	3,280,500

	Amount appropriated by resolution 36/240 A	Increase or (decrease)	Revised appropriation
5B. Centre for Science and Technology for Development	3,658,100	(42,500)	3,615,600
6. Department of International Economic and Social Affairs	44,112,100	(442,400)	43,669,700
7. Department of Technical Co-operation for Development	16,030,300	(383,000)	15,647,300
8. Office of Secretariat Services for Economic and Social Matters	3,232,500	(32,000)	3,200,500
9. Transnational corporations	9,029,700	(29,400)	9,000,300
10. Economic Commission for Europe	26,178,800	(2,429,600)	23,749,200
11. Economic and Social Commission for Asia and the Pacific	28,166,400	989,300	29,155,700
12. Economic Commission for Latin America	60,365,300	(15,502,300)	44,863,000
13. Economic Commission for Africa	35,945,700	1,356,800	37,302,500
14. Economic Commission for Western Asia	16,283,100	3,219,400	19,502,500
15. United Nations Conference on Trade and Development	57,168,800	(4,757,100)	52,411,700
16. International Trade Centre	9,246,200	(952,500)	8,293,700
17. United Nations Industrial Development Organization	72,942,200	(1,159,800)	71,782,400
18. United Nations Environment Programme	10,235,400	1,169,200	11,404,600
19. United Nations Centre for Human Settlements (Habitat)	8,312,200	819,100	9,131,300
20. International drug control	6,141,600	(260,600)	5,881,000
21. Office of the United Nations High Commissioner for Refugees	30,270,700	(1,330,800)	28,939,900
22. Office of the United Nations Disaster Relief Co-ordinator	5,136,700	(280,500)	4,856,200
23. Human rights	10,517,300	272,300	10,789,600
24. Regular programme of technical co-operation	30,995,400	(151,500)	30,843,900
Total, PART IV	489,189,800	(19,271,200)	469,918,600
PART V. *International justice and law*			
25. International Court of Justice	8,675,300	281,400	8,956,700
26. Legal activities	13,145,900	(84,100)	13,061,800
Total, PART V	21,821,200	197,300	22,018,500
PART VI. *Public information*			
27. Public information	63,156,100	1,478,900	64,635,000
Total, PART VI	63,156,100	1,478,900	64,635,000
PART VII. *Common support services*			
28. Administration and management	274,557,900	(8,779,400)	265,778,500
29. Conference and library services	247,970,300	(2,746,800)	245,223,500
Total, PART VII	522,528,200	(11,526,200)	511,002,000
PART VIII. *Special expenses*			
30. United Nations bond issue	17,220,300	—	17,220,300
Total, PART VIII	17,220,300	—	17,220,300
PART IX. *Staff assessment*			
31. Staff assessment	229,525,500	(21,723,000)	207,802,500
Total, PART IX	229,525,500	(21,723,000)	207,802,500
PART X. *Capital expenditures*			
32. Construction, alteration, improvement and major maintenance of premises	36,989,500	(907,700)	36,081,800
Total, PART X	36,989,500	(907,700)	36,081,800
Grand total	1,506,241,800	(33,280,100)	1,472,961,700

Recorded vote in Assembly as follows:

In favour: Algeria, Angola, Argentina, Austria, Bahamas, Bahrain, Bangladesh, Barbados, Benin, Bhutan, Bolivia, Botswana, Burma, Burundi, Cape Verde, Central African Republic, Chad, Chile, China, Colombia, Comoros, Congo, Costa Rica, Cuba, Cyprus, Democratic Kampuchea, Democratic Yemen, Denmark, Dominican Republic, Ecuador, Egypt, El Salvador, Ethiopia, Fiji, Finland, Gabon, Gambia, Ghana, Greece, Grenada, Guinea, Guinea-Bissau, Guyana, Honduras, Iceland, India, Indonesia, Iran, Iraq, Ireland, Ivory Coast, Jamaica, Jordan, Kenya, Kuwait, Lebanon, Lesotho, Liberia, Libyan Arab Jamahiriya, Madagascar, Malawi, Malaysia, Maldives, Mali, Malta, Mauritania, Mexico, Morocco, Mozambique, Nepal, Nicaragua, Niger, Nigeria, Norway, Oman, Pakistan, Panama, Papua New Guinea, Paraguay, Peru, Philippines, Portugal, Qatar, Rwanda, Saint Lucia, Samoa, Sao Tome and Principe, Saudi Arabia, Senegal, Sierra Leone, Singapore, Solomon Islands, Somalia, Sri Lanka, Sudan, Suriname, Swaziland, Sweden, Syrian Arab Republic, Thailand, Togo, Trinidad and Tobago, Tunisia, Turkey, Uganda, United Arab Emirates, United Republic of Cameroon, United Republic of Tanzania, Upper Volta, Uruguay, Venezuela, Yemen, Yugoslavia, Zaire, Zambia, Zimbabwe.

Against: Bulgaria, Byelorussian SSR, Czechoslovakia, German Democratic Republic, Germany, Federal Republic of, Hungary, Israel, Japan, Mongolia, Poland, Ukrainian SSR, USSR, United Kingdom, United States.

Abstaining: Afghanistan, Australia, Belgium, Brazil, Canada, France, Italy, Luxembourg, Netherlands, New Zealand, Romania, Spain.

Financing of appropriations

By a resolution of 21 December 1982,[1] the General Assembly specified how the $719,840,800 in appropriations for 1983—consisting of half the gross budget for 1982-1983 initially approved in December 1981[2] less the $33,280,100 decrease in appropriations for 1983 (see above)—were to be financed: $685,315,089 from assessments on Member States; $20,358,000 from income other than staff assessment, composed of half the estimated income from these sources approved for the biennium by the Assembly in 1981[3] less a projected decrease of $5,220,100 (see below); $13,967,320 in unspent appropriations from years prior to 1982 (the surplus account); and $200,391 in contributions from new Member States for 1981-1982. The gross assessment on Members was to be partly offset by $96,967,300, representing their share in the Tax Equalization Fund (financed from staff assessment and used in part to reimburse staff members who paid national income tax). Consequently, net assessment on Member States totalled $588,347,789 for 1983.

The resolution was adopted by a recorded vote of 116 to 13, with 12 abstentions. The Fifth Committee had approved the draft on 20 December by a vote, taken at the request of the USSR, of 68 to 13, with 11 abstentions.

Resolution (1982). [1]GA: 37/243 C, 21 Dec., text following. *Resolutions (prior).* GA: [2]36/240 A, 18 Dec. 1981 (YUN 1981, p. 1278); [3]36/240 B, 18 Dec. 1981 (ibid., p. 1280). *Meeting records.* GA: 5th Committee, A/C.5/37/SR.77 (20 Dec.); plenary, A/37/PV.114 (21 Dec.).

General Assembly resolution 37/243 C

21 December 1982   Meeting 114   116-13-12 (recorded vote)

Approved by Fifth Committee (A/37/790, draft resolution VII C) by vote (68-13-11), 20 December (meeting 77); agenda item 103.

Financing of appropriations for the year 1983

The General Assembly

Resolves that for the year 1983:

1. Budget appropriations in a total amount of $US 719,840,800 consisting of $US 753,120,900, being half of the appropriations initially approved for the biennium 1982-1983 by General Assembly resolution 36/240 A of 18 December 1981, less $US 33,280,100, being the decrease in appropriations approved during the thirty-seventh session by resolution

A above, shall be financed in accordance with regulations 5.1 and 5.2 of the Financial Regulations of the United Nations as follows:

(a) $20,358,000, consisting of $25,578,100, being half of the estimated income other than staff assessment income approved for the biennium 1982-1983 by resolution 36/240 B of 18 December 1981 less $5,220,100, being the decrease in estimated income other than from staff assessment approved by resolution B above;

(b) $200,391 being contributions of new Member States for 1981 and 1982;

(c) $13,967,320 being the balance of the surplus account as at 31 December 1981;

(d) $685,315,089 being the assessment on Member States in accordance with General Assembly resolution 37/125 A of 17 December 1982 on the scale of assessments for the years 1983, 1984 and 1985;

2. There shall be set off against the assessment on Member States, in accordance with the provisions of General Assembly resolution 973(X) of 15 December 1955, their respective share in the Tax Equalization Fund in the total amount of $US 96,967,300 consisting of:

(a) $116,698,400 being half of the estimated staff assessment income approved by resolution 36/240 B;

(b) Less $22,273,000 being the estimated decrease in income from staff assessment approved by resolution B above;

(c) Plus $2,541,900 being the increase in actual income from staff assessment compared to the revised estimates for the biennium 1980-1981, approved by resolution 36/234 B of 18 December 1981.

Recorded vote in Assembly as follows:

In favour: Afghanistan, Algeria, Angola, Argentina, Austria, Bahamas, Bahrain, Bangladesh, Barbados, Benin, Bhutan, Bolivia, Botswana, Burma, Burundi, Cape Verde, Central African Republic, Chad, Chile, China, Colombia, Comoros, Congo, Costa Rica, Cyprus, Democratic Kampuchea, Democratic Yemen, Denmark, Dominican Republic, Ecuador, Egypt, El Salvador, Ethiopia, Fiji, Finland, Gabon, Gambia, Ghana, Greece, Grenada, Guatemala, Guinea, Guinea-Bissau, Guyana, Honduras, Iceland, India, Indonesia, Iran, Iraq, Ireland, Ivory Coast, Jamaica, Jordan, Kenya, Kuwait, Lebanon, Lesotho, Liberia, Libyan Arab Jamahiriya, Madagascar, Malawi, Malaysia, Maldives, Mali, Malta, Mauritania, Mexico, Morocco, Mozambique, Nepal, Niger, Nigeria, Norway, Oman, Pakistan, Panama, Papua New Guinea, Paraguay, Peru, Philippines, Portugal, Qatar, Rwanda, Saint Lucia, Samoa, Sao Tome and Principe, Saudi Arabia, Senegal, Sierra Leone, Singapore, Solomon Islands, Somalia, Sri Lanka, Sudan, Suriname, Swaziland, Sweden, Syrian Arab Republic, Thailand, Togo, Trinidad and Tobago, Tunisia, Turkey, Uganda, United Arab Emirates, United Republic of Cameroon, United Republic of Tanzania, Upper Volta, Uruguay, Venezuela, Yemen, Yugoslavia, Zaire, Zambia, Zimbabwe.

Against: Bulgaria, Byelorussian SSR, Czechoslovakia, German Democratic Republic, Germany, Federal Republic of, Hungary, Japan, Mongolia, Poland, Ukrainian SSR, USSR, United Kingdom, United States.

Abstaining: Australia, Belgium, Brazil, Canada, France, Israel, Italy, Luxembourg, Netherlands, New Zealand, Romania, Spain.

Income estimates

On 21 December 1982, the General Assembly approved revised estimates of income for 1982-1983—other than assessments on Member States—in the amount of $257,059,900, including $211,123,800 to be derived from staff assessment (a kind of internal income tax paid by United Nations staff members on salaries and wages), $32,194,500 in general income and $13,741,600 in revenue-producing activities.[2] The net amount represented a reduction of $27,493,100 from that originally approved by the Assembly in 1981.[3]

The resolution was adopted without vote, following its approval without objection by the Fifth Committee on 20 December.

In his first performance report, of 3 December 1982,[1] the Secretary-General submitted revised income estimates in the above three categories totalling $253,688,400, representing a reduction of $30,864,600 from the figure approved in 1981. Income from staff assessment, he reported, would fall short of projections by $25,199,500, while revenue-producing activities would produce $3,543,000 less than expected, primarily due to a decline in the sale of postage stamps.

Report. [1]S-G, A/C.5/37/65.
Resolution (1982). [2]GA: 37/243 B, 21 Dec., text following.
Resolution (prior). [3]GA: 36/240 B, 18 Dec. 1981 (YUN 1981, p. 1280).
Meeting records. GA: 5th Committee, A/C.5/37/SR.77 (20 Dec.); plenary, A/37/PV.114 (21 Dec.).

General Assembly resolution 37/243 B

21 December 1982   Meeting 114   Adopted without vote

Approved by Fifth Committee (A/37/790, draft resolution VII B) without objection, 20 December (meeting 77); agenda item 103.

Revised income estimates for the biennium 1982-1983
The General Assembly

Resolves that for the biennium 1982-1983 the estimates of income of $US 284,553,000 approved by its resolution 36/240 B of 18 December 1981 shall be decreased by $US 27,493,100 as follows:

Income section	Amount approved by resolution 36/240 A	Increase or (decrease)	Final estimates
		(US dollars)	
PART I. *Income from staff assessment*			
1. Income from staff assessment	233,396,800	(22,273,000)	211,123,800
Total, PART I	233,396,800	(22,273,000)	211,123,800
PART II. *Other income*			
2. General income	33,871,600	(1,677,100)	32,194,500
3. Revenue-producing activities	17,284,600	(3,543,000)	13,741,600
Total, PART II	51,156,200	(5,220,100)	45,936,100
GRAND TOTAL	284,553,000	(27,493,100)	257,059,900

Budget formulation, presentation, review and approval

Arrangements for budget formulation, presentation, review and approval were discussed inconclusively by the Fifth Committee in March 1982, following that Committee's consideration of the topic in December 1981.[5] The Committee took no action on a draft resolution that had been submitted in December by Algeria on behalf of the Group of 77 setting out a number of proposed directives, guidelines and procedures. Instead, it recommended—as proposed by the Committee Chairman following consultations and approval by consensus by the Committee on 18 March—that the General Assembly continue consideration of the item at its regular session beginning in September. The Assembly so decided without vote on 19 March.[3]

In an April report[2] the Secretary-General addressed procedures for review of the proposed programme budget, with special reference to the timing of budget presentation and the relationship between the two Committees principally concerned—the Committee for Programme and Co-ordination (CPC) and the Advisory Committee on Administrative and Budgetary Questions (ACABQ). With regard to timing, he described the difficulties faced by the Secretariat which prevented it from completing the proposed budget before April of the year it was to be adopted, and suggested that there was no need to change the timing of either its presentation or its review by the two Committees. With regard to their relationship in this review process, he mentioned the objective of ensuring that the Assembly had before it for simultaneous consideration both the CPC report on programme aspects and the ACABQ report on budgetary aspects.

After reviewing the Secretary-General's report, CPC decided that submission of the proposed programme budget for 1984-1985 should be made in staggered fashion, to be completed no later than April 1983; that the Secretary-General should charge the recently established Programme Planning and Budgeting Board with the task of rationalizing the process of preparing the proposed programme budget and with preparing a cross-sectional programme analysis; and that it would take up the matter again in 1983.[1]

On 21 December, the Assembly adopted a set of Regulations Governing Programme Planning, the Programme Aspects of the Budget, the Monitoring of Implementation and the Methods of Evaluation.[4] The Regulations included an article on programme aspects of the budget which stated, in part, that the proposed budget was to be considered first by CPC, whose report was to be communicated simultaneously to the Economic and Social Council and ACABQ, and that the reports of both Committees were to be considered simultaneously by the Assembly.

Reports. [1]CPC, A/37/38; [2]S-G, A/37/207.
Resolutions (1982). GA: [3]36/243, 19 Mar., text following; [4]37/234, sect. II & annex, 21 Dec.
Yearbook reference. [5]1981, p. 1286.
Meeting records. GA: 5th Committee, A/C.5/36/SR.84, *85* (17, 18 Mar.); plenary, A/36/PV.108 (19 Mar.).

General Assembly resolution 36/243

19 March 1982   Meeting 108   Adopted without vote

Approved by Fifth Committee (A/36/845/Add.1) by consensus, 18 March (meeting 85); draft by Chairman (A/C.5/36/L.52), based on informal consultations; agenda item 100.

Formulation, presentation, review and approval of programme budgets
The General Assembly,

Recalling section XX of its resolution 36/235 of 18 December 1981,

Decides to continue, at its thirty-seventh session, consideration of the question of the formulation, presentation, review and approval of programme budgets, including the draft resolution on this subject submitted on 14 December 1981, as orally revised.

Assessment of contributions

Scale of contributions

Scale for 1983-1984

The General Assembly's Committee on Contributions, at its forty-second session held in New

York from 8 June to 2 July 1982, drew up a three-year scale of assessments for contributions by Member States to the United Nations regular budget for the period 1983 to 1985, taking into account criteria laid down by the Assembly in 1981. After considering the Committee's report in October/November, the Assembly requested that the Committee re-examine the draft scale, which was then redrawn by the Committee at a special session in November before being adopted by the Assembly in December.

Action by the Committee on Contributions (June/July). In drafting the scale of assessments for 1983-1985 during its June/July session, the Committee on Contributions debated whether the criteria for the scale as defined by the General Assembly in December 1981[7] were binding.

The Assembly had requested that the Committee prepare a set of guidelines for the collection and presentation of national income and other economic data by Member States, that it study alternative methods of assessing the real capacity of Member States to pay; and that, pending completion of the study, specific criteria be observed in reviewing the scale of assessments: *(a)* that the statistical base period (range of calendar years) for calculating assessments be increased from 7 to 10 years; *(b)* that the upper limit of the low per capita income allowance formula (which under the current scale reduced the rates of countries with incomes below a certain figure) be raised from $1,800 to $2,100 and that the gradient of relief (a scale providing successively greater reductions in inverse proportion to national income) be increased from 75 to 85 per cent; *(c)* that increases in individual assessment rates be kept to a reasonable level and that special treatment be given to countries whose assessments were increased as a result of the previous review; and *(d)* that the individual rates of the least developed countries not be increased.

Upon receiving the advice of the United Nations Legal Counsel, whose opinion it had sought, the Committee decided that these criteria were binding on it.

The Committee then took up a country-by-country review of statistical data to determine per capita income, the principal criterion used in determining assessments. In January and February, the Committee had requested data from Member and non-member States for each of the years from 1969 to 1980. Although 110 Member States responded, only about half of them had provided complete sets of national income data, leading the Committee to state in its 1982 report[4] that its work was significantly hampered by lack of information from Member States. Estimates of national income for years for which data had not been supplied were made by the United Nations Statistical Office. The Committee explored in detail mechanisms for dealing with the problem of domestic inflation uncompensated for by exchange-rate adjustments, but could not agree on a systematic approach and so postponed to 1983 discussion of this issue as well as of the broader one of guidelines for the collection and presentation of data by Member States on a uniform and comparable basis.

The Committee arrived at a new scale of assessments which it deemed to be consistent with criteria *(a)*, *(b)* and *(d)*, but was unable to reach agreement on *(c)*, which called for limiting individual rate increases to "a reasonable level". Divergent opinions on this issue and on the general question of mitigation of changes in the scale resulted in the proposed scale being adopted with reservations expressed by four Committee members. Analysing the effects of applying criteria *(a)* and *(b)*, the Committee determined that the recommended changes would result in a shift of 3.5 per cent, or $25.3 million, from countries having a per capita income below $2,100 to countries above that level.

According to the recommended scale, 93 Member States (59 per cent of the membership) were assessed at or below the rate of 0.03 per cent of the total—75 at 0.01 per cent, 11 at 0.02 per cent and 7 at 0.03 per cent (89 Members were in this category in the previous scale adopted in 1979). For the Group of 77 developing countries as a whole, the proposed new scale represented a percentage increase since the 1978-1979 scale from 7.94 to 9.82, due mainly to the upward adjustment of the rate of assessment of those in the Organization of Petroleum Exporting Countries from 1.91 to 3.57 per cent. The rate of the member countries of the Organisation for Economic Co-operation and Development climbed from 68.37 to 73.60 per cent for that same period, while that of the countries with centrally planned economies, excluding Romania and Yugoslavia, dropped from 17.68 to 15.18 per cent, and China moved from 5.5 to 0.81 per cent.

The Committee also recommended rates of assessment for 1981 and 1982 for the three Member States admitted to the Organization in 1981—Antigua and Barbuda, Belize and Vanuatu—and for 1983, 1984 and 1985 for non-member States, which are required to contribute towards the expenses of United Nations activities in which they participate.

The Committee briefly examined a Secretariat paper on alternative methods of assessing the real capacity of Members to pay, but because of a lack of time deferred until 1983 its study on methodology.

General Assembly action (November). On 16 November,[1] the General Assembly requested the

Committee on Contributions to re-examine its proposed scale of assessments, bearing in mind discussions in the Fifth Committee during the 1982 session, and to report back by 3 December. The decision was adopted by a recorded vote of 106 to 15, with 18 abstentions. The Fifth Committee had approved the draft, introduced by Morocco on behalf of 26 sponsoring States, on 12 November by 90 votes to 18, with 17 abstentions.

Spain had orally proposed that the draft be amended to give the Committee on Contributions until 30 May 1983 to report while keeping the current scale in force until the end of that year. However, the Committee decided, by a recorded vote of 91 to 24, with 6 abstentions, to consider the Spanish amendment as a separate proposal, but took no action on it in the light of the adoption of the 26-nation text.

Explaining its vote against that text, the Dominican Republic said it felt that there was not enough time for the Committee on Contributions to re-evaluate Members' views and report back during the current session.

Several nations, including Canada, China, New Zealand and the USSR, said that, in the spirit of compromise, they had voted for, or refrained from voting against, the decision despite reservations: Austria said that by its action the Fifth Committee was virtually establishing the scale of assessments itself whereas it would have preferred the negotiations to have been conducted by the Committee on Contributions; the Bahamas, which abstained, felt that the action was a political decision; and Japan, which also abstained, held that the Fifth Committee should not seek to undermine the position of the Committee on Contributions. Mexico and Venezuela, both abstaining, commented that the decision should not establish a precedent.

Among those voting for the decision, Algeria hoped the Committee on Contributions would bring the scale in line with the Assembly request that increases for individual countries be kept at a reasonable level. Colombia felt the decision was fairer than proposals that would have left the existing scale in place. Indonesia viewed the compromise as a demonstration of the Fifth Committee's confidence in the Committee on Contributions, and hoped that that confidence would be rewarded by a new scale commanding broad support. Kuwait saw the decision as an opportunity to review the scale in a fairer manner.

Australia expressed reservations over the course of action adopted; it felt the Fifth Committee should have solved the political problems without referring the matter back to the Committee on Contributions, and felt an unfortunate precedent had been set.

Two draft resolutions were introduced in the course of the Committee's deliberations, on the understanding that they would not be discussed or voted upon at that stage. The first, sponsored by Brazil, Chile, the Dominican Republic, Ecuador, Mexico, Nigeria, Uruguay, Venezuela and Yugoslavia,[3] would have had the Assembly decide to keep the current scale in force until the Committee on Contributions completed its work. To that end, it would have allowed the Committee to extend its sessions and authorized the Secretary-General to contract for the services of statistical and economic institutions outside the United Nations; it would also have not allowed claims related to revisions of exchange rate and national income statistics to have retroactive effect. The Statistical Office could only accept data which were standardized as to methodology and basis. The second, sponsored by Australia,[2] would have had the Assembly accept the three-year scale as recommended and call on the Committee to complete the study on alternative methods of assessing the real capacity of States to pay, with the Secretary-General providing resources for the study, including consultants, as required.

Action by the Committee on Contributions (November). Meeting in special session in New York from 22 to 24 November, the Committee on Contributions, by 10 votes to 4, with 2 abstentions, recommended to the General Assembly a modified scale of assessments for 1983, 1984 and 1985.[5] The Chairman did not participate in the vote and one member did not attend the session.

Taking as its mandate the Assembly decision of 16 November (see above), the Committee reviewed the Fifth Committee debates held earlier in the session, during which 62 delegations had made statements. One member (from Morocco) said that he had taken it upon himself, with the co-operation of countries that had secured decreases under the July scale, and with the support of a majority of the Group of 77, to work out an alternative to the two opposite points of view—freezing the current scales or accepting the proposed one. According to this plan, nine countries would give up a total of 58 points (5.8 per cent) in reductions accorded them, on condition that a corresponding amount be distributed so as to reduce the assessments of the Group's members that had received the greatest increases under that scale. The 58 points were offered by the USSR (20), Poland (10), China and Canada (7 each), India and Australia (4 each), Hungary (3), Czechoslovakia (2) and Argentina (1).

The Committee discussed whether to interpret the Assembly decision as calling for a complete review of the scale, but most felt that they had been seized with a new situation as a result of the proposed compromise formula. The author of the plan was asked to submit his ideas on how the 58 points might be distributed. His suggestions were then modified when the Committee decided, by 10 votes to 3, with 3 abstentions, to take five additional points from the decrease in assessment for South Africa proposed in the Committee's July scale. The result was to reduce the assessments of the following States a total of 63 points: Algeria (2 points), Bahrain (1), Brazil (8), Chile, Ecuador, Egypt and Gabon (1 each), Iraq (3), Italy and Japan (1 each), Kuwait (3), the Libyan Arab Jamahiriya (2), Mexico (9), Morocco (1), Nigeria (3), Oman (1), Peru (2), Qatar (1), Saudi Arabia (5), Singapore (1), Spain (2), the Syrian Arab Republic, Trinidad and Tobago, and Turkey (1 each), the United Arab Emirates (3), the United Republic of Cameroon (1), Uruguay (1), Venezuela (3) and Yugoslavia (2). Six members offered separate opinions or explanations of vote on the modified scale.

General Assembly action (December). On 17 December,[(6)] the General Assembly adopted the modified scale of assessments for 1983, 1984 and 1985 by a recorded vote of 110 to 26, with 7 abstentions. The Fifth Committee had approved the draft resolution, submitted by the Committee on Contributions, on 3 December by a recorded vote, requested by Spain, of 84 to 25, with 8 abstentions, incorporating the redrawn scale.

The scale contained increases for 29 States and decreases for the same number compared with the scale in effect for 1980-1982. It increased by 20 per cent or more the rates for Kuwait (from 0.20 to 0.25 per cent), Saudi Arabia (from 0.58 to 0.86) and the United Arab Emirates (from 0.10 to 0.16). Other sizeable increases (in percentage points) were for Japan (up 0.74), France (up 0.25), the Federal Republic of Germany and Spain (each up 0.23) and the United Kingdom (up 0.21).

The new scale contained reductions for China (down 0.74 points), the USSR (down 0.56), Poland (down 0.52), Australia (down 0.26), India (down 0.24) and Canada (down 0.20). The rates of Sri Lanka, Zaire and Zambia were halved, from 0.02 to 0.01 per cent.

The nine largest contributors in the new scale, in descending order, were the United States, the USSR, Japan, the Federal Republic of Germany, France, the United Kingdom, Italy, Canada and Spain. Among the nine largest contributors in the 1980-1982 scale, only Australia changed its position, moving from ninth to eleventh place under the new scale.

Assessed at the minimum rate of 0.01 per cent were 78 countries, compared to 70 in the previously adopted scale. Besides Sri Lanka, Zaire and Zambia, the additions at the lower end of the scale were Antigua and Barbuda, Belize, Saint Lucia, Saint Vincent and the Grenadines, and Vanuatu, all admitted to the United Nations between 1979 and 1981. Ten States were given a rate of 0.02 per cent, while eight were assessed at 0.03 per cent.

Thus, 96 Member States, or about three fifths of the membership, were assessed at 0.03 per cent or less.

Explaining their votes against the revised scale, Brazil, Chile, Kuwait, the Libyan Arab Jamahiriya, Mexico and Spain said it did not comply fully with the 1981 Assembly resolution laying down criteria for the new scale. Uruguay and Yugoslavia, which abstained, and Algeria, Argentina, Cuba, Nigeria and Zaire, which voted in favour, urged future full compliance with the 1981 resolution.

A number of States disagreed with the procedure by which the scale was modified. Denmark, speaking for the 10 members of the European Community, called it profoundly unsatisfactory and potentially dangerous for the United Nations; it charged that the Committee on Contributions had merely rubber-stamped an agreement worked out in the Fifth Committee to redistribute points according to political rather than technical criteria, and its independent status and integrity had therefore been severely damaged. Sweden, speaking also on behalf of Denmark, Finland, Iceland and Norway, all of which opposed the resolution, called for a return to the practice of giving a broad mandate to the Committee as the only way of restoring its integrity and independent status.

Others expressing reservations concerning the procedure and the criteria used included Austria, the Dominican Republic, Kuwait, Singapore, Spain, Turkey, the United States and Venezuela, which voted against the resolution; Israel, Japan and Uruguay, which abstained; and Australia, Iran, Poland, Portugal and Zambia, which voted in favour. The Dominican Republic objected to the fact that its assessment was not to be reduced despite economic set-backs. Poland calculated that it had been over-assessed by more than 15 per cent and said that it could accept the new scale only on condition that future assessments were adjusted downward, based on its real capacity to pay.

China, Jordan, Pakistan and the USSR, while supporting the new scale, hoped the method used would not constitute a precedent; Bulgaria, Japan and Yugoslavia, among those abstaining, also expressed this view.

Several States objected to anomalies in the scale or said they found it otherwise unfair. These included Brazil, the Dominican Republic, Kuwait, the Libyan Arab Jamahiriya, Singapore, Spain, Turkey and Venezuela, which voted against; the Bahamas and Yugoslavia, which abstained; and Bangladesh, Iran and Nigeria, which voted in favour.

Morocco said the modified scale reflected the general consensus that the burden on developing countries should be lightened; Morocco did not consider that the integrity of the Committee on Contributions had been violated. Japan regretted that that Committee had had to take the unprecedented course of reaching a decision by vote, a view shared by Zambia; New Zealand and Pakistan, both voting in favour, would have preferred a procedure whereby the Committee on Contributions could have presented the Fifth Committee with a unified recommendation.

Canada said that, although the procedure by which the scale had been revised was extraordinary, it supported the new scale primarily so that the financing of the Organization could be ensured on a proper basis. Among those speaking for the resolution, though they might have had reservations regarding either criteria or procedure, were Cuba, Egypt, Ghana, Guinea, Hungary, India, Indonesia, Iran, Iraq, Jordan, Pakistan, the Philippines, Sierra Leone, the Syrian Arab Republic, Tunisia, Uganda, the United Arab Emirates and the United Republic of Cameroon. India added that it was unfair to have several low-income countries giving points when several States with high per capita incomes were to benefit.

Decision (1982). [1]GA: 37/408, 16 Nov., text following.
Draft resolutions not voted upon. [2]Australia, A/C.5/37/L.21; [3]Brazil, Chile, Dominican Republic, Ecuador, Mexico, Nigeria, Uruguay, Venezuela, Yugoslavia, A/C.5/37/L.20/Rev.1.
Reports. Committee on Contributions, [4]A/37/11, [5]A/37/11/Add.1 & Add.1/Corr.1.
Resolution (1982). [6]GA: 37/125 A, 17 Dec., text following.
Resolution (prior). [7]GA: 36/231 A, 18 Dec. 1981 (YUN 1981, p. 1292).
Meeting records. GA: plenary, A/37/PV.1, 14 (21 Sep., 1 Oct.), *69, 109* (16 Nov., 17 Dec.); 5th Committee, A/C.5/37/SR.4, 5, 7-16, *32-34,* 54, *55* (1 Oct.–3 Dec.).

General Assembly decision 37/408

106-15-18 (recorded vote)

Approved by Fifth Committee (A/37/617) by vote (90-18-17), 12 November (meeting 33); 26-nation draft (A/C.5/37/L.23); agenda item 110.

Sponsors: Bahrain, Canada, Costa Rica, Cuba, Czechoslovakia, Ecuador, Egypt, Ethiopia, Ghana, Hungary, India, Jordan, Kenya, Mauritania, Morocco, Oman, Panama, Peru, Philippines, Poland, Qatar, Romania, Sri Lanka, Syrian Arab Republic, Trinidad and Tobago, Zaire.

Scale of assessments for the apportionment of the expenses of the United Nations

At its 69th plenary meeting, on 16 November 1982, the General Assembly, on the recommendation of the Fifth Committee, decided to request the Committee on Contributions to re-examine the proposed scale of assessments for the apportionment of the expenses of the United Nations contained in its report and, bearing in mind the discussions on this agenda item at the current session, to submit its recommendations by 3 December 1982, so as to enable the Assembly at its thirty-seventh session to decide on the matter before it adjourned in December 1982.

Recorded vote in Assembly as follows:

In favour: Afghanistan, Algeria, Angola, Antigua and Barbuda, Argentina, Bahrain, Barbados, Benin, Bhutan, Bolivia, Botswana, Bulgaria, Burma, Burundi, Byelorussian SSR, Canada, Cape Verde, Central African Republic, China, Colombia, Comoros, Congo, Costa Rica, Cuba, Czechoslovakia, Democratic Kampuchea, Democratic Yemen, Djibouti, Ecuador, Egypt, El Salvador, Ethiopia, Fiji, Gabon, German Democratic Republic, Ghana, Grenada, Guatemala, Guinea-Bissau, Guyana, Haiti, Honduras, Hungary, India, Indonesia, Iran, Iraq, Ivory Coast, Jamaica, Jordan, Kenya, Kuwait, Lebanon, Lesotho, Liberia, Libyan Arab Jamahiriya, Madagascar, Malaysia, Maldives, Mali, Malta, Mauritania, Mauritius,

Mongolia, Morocco, Mozambique, Nepal, Nicaragua, Niger, Nigeria, Oman, Pakistan, Panama, Paraguay, Peru, Philippines, Poland, Qatar, Romania, Rwanda, Samoa, Sao Tome and Principe, Saudi Arabia, Senegal, Solomon Islands, Somalia, Sri Lanka, Sudan, Suriname, Swaziland, Syrian Arab Republic, Thailand, Togo, Trinidad and Tobago, Tunisia, Turkey, Ukrainian SSR, USSR, United Arab Emirates, United Republic of Cameroon, United Republic of Tanzania, Upper Volta, Viet Nam, Yemen, Zaire, Zambia.

Against: Belgium, Denmark, Dominican Republic, France, Germany, Federal Republic of, Greece, Ireland, Israel, Italy, Luxembourg, Netherlands, Portugal, Spain, United Kingdom, United States.

Abstaining: Australia, Austria, Bahamas, Brazil, Chile, Finland, Iceland, Japan, Mexico, New Zealand, Norway, Papua New Guinea, Sierra Leone, Singapore, Sweden, Uruguay, Venezuela, Yugoslavia.

General Assembly resolution 37/125 A

17 December 1982   Meeting 109   110-26-7 (recorded vote)

Approved by Fifth Committee (A/37/617/Add.1) by recorded vote (84-25-8), 3 December (meeting 55); draft by Committee on Contributions (A/37/11/Add.1); agenda item 110.

The General Assembly
Resolves that:

1. The scale of assessments for the contributions of Member States to the United Nations budget for the financial years 1983, 1984 and 1985 shall be as follows:

Member State	Per cent	Member State	Per cent
Afghanistan	0.01	Germany, Federal	
Albania	0.01	Republic of	8.54
Algeria	0.13	Ghana	0.02
Angola	0.01	Greece	0.40
Antigua and Barbuda	0.01	Grenada	0.01
Argentina	0.71	Guatemala	0.02
Australia	1.57	Guinea	0.01
Austria	0.75	Guinea-Bissau	0.01
Bahamas	0.01	Guyana	0.01
Bahrain	0.01	Haiti	0.01
Bangladesh	0.03	Honduras	0.01
Barbados	0.01	Hungary	0.23
Belgium	1.28	Iceland	0.03
Belize	0.01	India	0.36
Benin	0.01	Indonesia	0.13
Bhutan	0.01	Iran (Islamic Republic of)	0.58
Bolivia	0.01	Iraq	0.12
Botswana	0.01	Ireland	0.18
Brazil	1.39	Israel	0.23
Bulgaria	0.18	Italy	3.74
Burma	0.01	Ivory Coast	0.03
Burundi	0.01	Jamaica	0.02
Byelorussian Soviet		Japan	10.32
Socialist Republic	0.36	Jordan	0.01
Canada	3.08	Kenya	0.01
Cape Verde	0.01	Kuwait	0.25
Central African Republic	0.01	Lao People's Democratic	
Chad	0.01	Republic	0.01
Chile	0.07	Lebanon	0.02
China	0.88	Lesotho	0.01
Colombia	0.11	Liberia	0.01
Comoros	0.01	Libyan Arab Jamahiriya	0.26
Congo	0.01	Luxembourg	0.06
Costa Rica	0.02	Madagascar	0.01
Cuba	0.09	Malawi	0.01
Cyprus	0.01	Malaysia	0.09
Czechoslovakia	0.76	Maldives	0.01
Democratic Kampuchea	0.01	Mali	0.01
Democratic Yemen	0.01	Malta	0.01
Denmark	0.75	Mauritania	0.01
Djibouti	0.01	Mauritius	0.01
Dominica	0.01	Mexico	0.88
Dominican Republic	0.03	Mongolia	0.01
Ecuador	0.02	Morocco	0.05
Egypt	0.07	Mozambique	0.01
El Salvador	0.01	Nepal	0.01
Equatorial Guinea	0.01	Netherlands	1.78
Ethiopia	0.01	New Zealand	0.26
Fiji	0.01	Nicaragua	0.01
Finland	0.48	Niger	0.01
France	6.51	Nigeria	0.19
Gabon	0.02	Norway	0.51
Gambia	0.01	Oman	0.01
German Democratic		Pakistan	0.06
Republic	1.39	Panama	0.02
		Papua New Guinea	0.01

Member State	Per cent	Member State	Per cent
Paraguay	0.01	Togo	0.01
Peru	0.07	Trinidad and Tobago	0.03
Philippines	0.09	Tunisia	0.03
Poland	0.72	Turkey	0.32
Portugal	0.18	Uganda	0.01
Qatar	0.03	Ukrainian Soviet Socialist	
Romania	0.19	Republic	1.32
Rwanda	0.01	Union of Soviet Socialist	
Saint Lucia	0.01	Republics	10.54
Saint Vincent and the		United Arab Emirates	0.16
Grenadines	0.01	United Kingdom of Great	
Samoa	0.01	Britain and Northern	
Sao Tome and Principe	0.01	Ireland	4.67
Saudi Arabia	0.86	United Republic of	
Senegal	0.01	Cameroon	0.01
Seychelles	0.01	United Republic of	
Sierra Leone	0.01	Tanzania	0.01
Singapore	0.09	United States of America	25.00
Solomon Islands	0.01	Upper Volta	0.01
Somalia	0.01	Uruguay	0.04
South Africa	0.41	Vanuatu	0.01
Spain	1.93	Venezuela	0.55
Sri Lanka	0.01	Viet Nam	0.02
Sudan	0.01	Yemen	0.01
Suriname	0.01	Yugoslavia	0.46
Swaziland	0.01	Zaire	0.01
Sweden	1.32	Zambia	0.01
Syrian Arab Republic	0.03	Zimbabwe	0.02
Thailand	0.08		100.00

2. In accordance with rule 160 of the rules of procedure of the General Assembly, the scale of assessments given in paragraph 1 above shall be reviewed by the Committee on Contributions in 1985, when a report shall be submitted to the Assembly for consideration at its fortieth session;

3. Notwithstanding the terms of regulation 5.5 of the Financial Regulations of the United Nations, the Secretary-General shall be empowered to accept, at his discretion and after consultation with the Chairman of the Committee on Contributions, a portion of the contributions of Member States for the calendar years 1983, 1984 and 1985 in currencies other than United States dollars;

4. For the year 1981, Vanuatu, Belize and Antigua and Barbuda, which became Members of the United Nations on 15 September, 25 September and 11 November 1981, respectively, shall contribute amounts equal to one ninth of 0.01 per cent;

5. For the year 1982, Vanuatu, Belize and Antigua and Barbuda shall contribute amounts equal to 0.01 per cent;

6. The contributions of the three new Member States for 1981 and 1982 shall be applied to the same basis of assessment as for other Member States, except that in the case of appropriations approved under General Assembly resolutions 35/45 A of 1 December 1980 and 36/66 A of 30 November 1981 for the financing of the United Nations Disengagement Observer Force and Assembly resolutions 35/115 A of 10 December 1980 and 36/138 A of 16 December 1981 for the financing of the United Nations Interim Force in Lebanon, the contributions of those States, in accordance with the group of contributors to which they may be assigned by the Assembly, shall be calculated in proportion to the calendar year;

7. In accordance with rule 160 of the rules of procedure of the General Assembly, States which are not Members of the United Nations but which participate in certain of its activities shall be called upon to contribute towards the 1983, 1984 and 1985 expenses of such activities on the basis of the following rates:

Non-member State	Per cent
Democratic People's Republic of Korea	0.05
Holy See	0.01
Liechtenstein	0.01
Monaco	0.01
Nauru	0.01
Republic of Korea	0.18
San Marino	0.01
Switzerland	1.10
Tonga	0.01

the following countries being called upon to contribute:

(a) *To the International Court of Justice:* Liechtenstein, San Marino, Switzerland;

(b) *To international drug control:* Holy See, Liechtenstein, Monaco, Republic of Korea, Switzerland, Tonga;

(c) *To the Economic and Social Commission for Asia and the Pacific:* Republic of Korea;

(d) *To the Economic Commission for Europe:* Switzerland;

(e) *To the United Nations Conference on Trade and Development:* Democratic People's Republic of Korea, Holy See, Liechtenstein, Monaco, Republic of Korea, San Marino, Switzerland, Tonga;

(f) *To the United Nations Industrial Development Organization:* Holy See, Liechtenstein, Monaco, Republic of Korea, Switzerland;

(g) *To the United Nations Environment Programme:* Switzerland.

Recorded vote in Assembly as follows:

In favour: Afghanistan, Albania, Algeria, Angola, Argentina, Australia, Bahrain, Bangladesh, Barbados, Benin, Bhutan, Bolivia, Botswana, Burma, Burundi, Byelorussian SSR, Canada, Cape Verde, Central African Republic, Chad, China, Colombia, Comoros, Congo, Costa Rica, Cuba, Czechoslovakia, Democratic Yemen, Djibouti, Dominica, Ecuador, Egypt, El Salvador, Ethiopia, Fiji, Gabon, Gambia, German Democratic Republic, Ghana, Grenada, Guatemala, Guinea-Bissau, Guyana, Hungary, India, Indonesia, Iran, Iraq, Ivory Coast, Jamaica, Jordan, Kenya, Lao People's Democratic Republic, Lebanon, Lesotho, Liberia, Madagascar, Malawi, Malaysia, Maldives, Mali, Malta, Mauritania, Mauritius, Mongolia, Morocco, Mozambique, Nepal, New Zealand, Niger, Oman, Pakistan, Panama, Papua New Guinea, Paraguay, Peru, Philippines, Poland, Portugal, Qatar, Romania, Rwanda, Samoa, Sao Tome and Principe, Saudi Arabia, Senegal, Sierra Leone, Solomon Islands, Somalia, Sri Lanka, Sudan, Suriname, Swaziland, Syrian Arab Republic, Thailand, Togo, Trinidad and Tobago, Tunisia, Uganda, Ukrainian SSR, USSR, United Arab Emirates, United Republic of Cameroon, United Republic of Tanzania, Upper Volta, Viet Nam, Yemen, Zaire, Zambia, Zimbabwe.

Against: Austria, Belgium, Brazil, Chile, Denmark, Dominican Republic, Finland, France, Germany, Federal Republic of, Greece, Iceland, Ireland, Italy, Kuwait, Libyan Arab Jamahiriya, Luxembourg, Mexico, Netherlands, Norway, Singapore, Spain, Sweden, Turkey, United Kingdom, United States, Venezuela.

Abstaining: Bahamas, Bulgaria, Cyprus, Israel, Japan, Uruguay, Yugoslavia.

Criteria for future scales

By a resolution of 17 December 1982,[1] the General Assembly reconfirmed that the real capacity to pay of Member States was the fundamental criterion on which the scale of assessments was to be based. It also decided that the Committee on Contributions should complete the study requested by the Assembly in December 1981[2] on alternative means of determining future scales of assessments, as well as the guidelines for the collection and presentation of data on Member States, for submission to the Assembly in 1984. The Committee was asked, in so doing, to study ways of avoiding excessive variations in rates.

The resolution was adopted by consensus, having been approved by the Fifth Committee, on 13 December, also by consensus. The draft was introduced by a Committee Vice-Chairman following informal consultations. The Committee accepted without objection an oral amendment by the United States, as sub-amended by Morocco, to delete the words "under the Charter" from the sixth preambular paragraph, which originally referred to "the obligation of Member States under the Charter to bear the expenses of the Organization as apportioned by the General Assembly according to the capacity to pay".

Resolution (1982). [1]GA: 37/125 B, 17 Dec., text following.
Resolution (prior). [2]GA: 36/231 A, 18 Dec. 1981 (YUN 1981, p. 1292).
Meeting records. GA: 5th Committee, A/C.5/37/SR.4, 5, 7-16 (1-20 Oct.), 66 (13 Dec.); plenary, A/37/PV.109 (17 Dec.).

STATUS OF CONTRIBUTIONS TO THE UN REGULAR BUDGET

(amounts in US dollars)

Member State	1982 scale of assessments (per cent)	Collections in 1982	Contributions outstanding as at 31 Dec. 1982	Assessment for 1983
Afghanistan	0.01	162,783	6,000	58,834
Albania	0.01	69,738	36,000	58,834
Algeria	0.12	685,186	40,198	764,853
Angola	0.01	—	106,071	58,834
Antigua and Barbuda	—	—	—	58,834
Argentina	0.78	3,080,822	2,310,593	4,177,271
Australia	1.83	11,062,099	—	9,237,061
Austria	0.71	4,291,852	—	4,412,610
Bahamas	0.01	60,449	—	58,834
Bahrain	0.01	60,449	—	58,834
Bangladesh	0.04	241,794	—	176,504
Barbados	0.01	39,000	21,449	58,834
Belgium	1.22	6,733,531	2,106,732	7,530,853
Belize	—	—	—	58,834
Benin	0.01	58,027	110,756	58,834
Bhutan	0.01	60,449	—	58,834
Bolivia	0.01	—	95,935	58,834
Botswana	0.01	60,449	—	60,694
Brazil	1.27	4,492,895	8,438,975	8,178,035
Bulgaria	0.16	1,041,674	862,496	1,059,027
Burma	0.01	60,449	—	58,834
Burundi	0.01	—	60,449	58,834
Byelorussian SSR	0.39	2,248,407	1,781,815	2,118,053
Canada	3.28	19,860,095	—	18,121,113
Cape Verde	0.01	51,128	117,655	58,834
Central African Republic	0.01	78,128	130,447	58,834
Chad	0.01	42,502	182,532	58,834
Chile	0.07	423,141	—	411,843
China	1.62	9,653,194	4,103,323	5,177,461
Colombia	0.11	—	664,935	647,183
Comoros	0.01	—	158,240	58,834
Congo	0.01	51,535	61,794	58,834
Costa Rica	0.02	38,511	184,802	117,670
Cuba	0.11	—	664,935	529,514
Cyprus	0.01	60,449	—	58,834
Czechoslovakia	0.83	4,913,544	2,289,798	4,471,444
Democratic Kampuchea	0.01	—	164,863	58,834
Democratic Yemen	0.01	117,577	—	58,834
Denmark	0.74	4,473,198	—	4,412,610
Djibouti	0.01	60,449	51,206	58,834
Dominica	0.01	39,067	137,149	58,834
Dominican Republic	0.03	117,802	370,730	176,504
Ecuador	0.02	90,374	87,545	117,670
Egypt	0.07	670,737	—	411,843
El Salvador	0.01	—	168,783	58,834
Equatorial Guinea	0.01	—	108,092	58,834
Ethiopia	0.01	60,449	—	58,834
Fiji	0.01	60,449	—	58,834
Finland	0.48	2,901,534	—	2,824,070
France	6.26	38,359,960	4,357,157	38,301,442
Gabon	0.02	121,277	207,539	117,670
Gambia	0.01	117,577	30,563	58,834
German Democratic Republic	1.39	8,515,093	2,714,970	8,178,035
Germany, Federal Republic of	8.31	50,232,815	—	50,245,432
Ghana	0.03	181,346	—	117,670
Greece	0.35	1,905,702	210,000	2,353,392
Grenada	0.01	42,200	185,072	58,834
Guatemala	0.02	120,897	—	117,670
Guinea	0.01	187,137	—	58,834
Guinea-Bissau	0.01	—	168,783	58,834
Guyana	0.01	17,031	65,456	58,834
Haiti	0.01	126,898	41,820	58,834
Honduras	0.01	—	60,449	58,834
Hungary	0.33	1,202,000	1,866,337	1,353,201
Iceland	0.03	181,346	—	176,504
India	0.60	3,579,255	47,662	2,118,053
Indonesia	0.16	967,179	—	764,853
Iran	0.65	2,784,020	8,540,601	3,412,418
Iraq	0.12	—	725,384	706,019
Ireland	0.16	967,179	—	1,059,027
Israel	0.25	1,280,143	2,939,415	1,353,201
Italy	3.45	20,854,778	—	22,004,208
Ivory Coast	0.03	125,239	158,432	176,504
Jamaica	0.02	120,897	—	117,670
Japan	9.58	57,909,791	—	60,717,492
Jordan	0.01	60,449	—	58,834
Kenya	0.01	49,644	12,618	58,834
Kuwait	0.20	1,208,972	—	1,470,870
Lao People's Democratic Republic	0.01	60,449	—	58,834
Lebanon	0.03	292,703	364,061	117,670
Lesotho	0.01	51,000	66,577	58,834
Liberia	0.01	60,449	47,056	58,834
Libyan Arab Jamahiriya	0.23	1,390,319	—	1,529,705
Luxembourg	0.05	302,243	—	353,010
Madagascar	0.01	71,565	46,012	58,834
Malawi	0.01	60,449	—	58,834
Malaysia	0.09	544,038	—	529,514
Maldives	0.01	45,206	72,371	58,834
Mali	0.01	25,357	92,220	58,834
Malta	0.01	60,449	—	58,834
Mauritania	0.01	—	152,476	58,834
Mauritius	0.01	60,449	—	58,834
Mexico	0.76	6,754,923	—	5,177,461
Mongolia	0.01	58,727	55,950	58,834
Morocco	0.05	302,243	—	294,544
Mozambique	0.01	89,013	—	58,834
Nepal	0.01	60,449	—	58,834
Netherlands	1.63	9,853,126	—	10,472,592
New Zealand	0.27	1,632,113	—	1,529,705
Nicaragua	0.01	58,921	173,577	58,834
Niger	0.01	—	75,854	58,834
Nigeria	0.16	976,105	853,481	1,117,862
Norway	0.50	3,022,431	—	3,000,575
Oman	0.01	60,449	—	58,834
Pakistan	0.07	459,814	22,301	353,010
Panama	0.02	132,742	—	117,670
Papua New Guinea	0.01	60,259	190	58,834
Paraguay	0.01	46,604	113,577	58,834
Peru	0.06	306,767	684,376	411,843
Philippines	0.10	397,547	245,579	529,514
Poland	1.24	3,256,000	17,351,561	4,236,105
Portugal	0.19	1,198,220	—	1,059,027
Qatar	0.03	181,346	—	176,504
Romania	0.21	1,074,000	1,562,719	1,117,862
Rwanda	0.01	60,449	—	58,834
Saint Lucia	0.01	—	61,449	58,834
Saint Vincent and the Grenadines	0.01	123,267	—	58,834
Samoa	0.01	—	117,577	58,834
Sao Tome and Principe	0.01	60,449	—	58,834
Saudi Arabia	0.58	3,506,020	—	5,059,792
Senegal	0.01	64,569	—	58,834

STATUS OF CONTRIBUTIONS *(cont.)*

Member State	1982 scale of assessments (per cent)	Collections in 1982	Contributions outstanding as at 31 Dec. 1982	Assessment for 1983
Seychelles	0.01	60,449	—	58,834
Sierra Leone	0.01	207,242	16,951	58,834
Singapore	0.08	483,589	—	529,514
Solomon Islands	0.01	117,577	—	58,834
Somalia	0.01	69,000	48,577	58,834
South Africa	0.42	—	16,710,177	2,412,227
Spain	1.70	4,495,677	5,780,590	11,355,114
Sri Lanka	0.02	120,897	—	58,834
Sudan	0.01	—	109,768	58,834
Suriname	0.01	60,449	—	58,834
Swaziland	0.01	117,577	—	58,834
Sweden	1.31	7,918,770	—	7,766,192
Syrian Arab Republic	0.03	—	181,346	176,504
Thailand	0.10	604,486	—	470,680
Togo	0.01	46,110	106,878	58,834
Trinidad and Tobago	0.03	181,346	—	176,504
Tunisia	0.03	181,346	12,256	176,504
Turkey	0.30	2,067,307	—	1,889,409
Uganda	0.01	60,558	—	59,334
Ukrainian SSR	1.46	8,417,113	5,653,884	7,766,192
USSR	11.10	65,543,118	40,389,362	62,011,858
United Arab Emirates	0.10	604,486	—	941,358
United Kingdom	4.46	26,960,090	—	27,475,843
United Republic of Cameroon	0.01	51,449	66,128	58,834
United Republic of Tanzania	0.01	57,666	71,751	64,143
United States	25.00	201,144,160	3,402,899	171,328,773
Upper Volta	0.01	—	60,758	58,834
Uruguay	0.04	—	241,794	235,341
Vanuatu	—	—	—	58,834
Venezuela	0.50	2,515,492	506,939	3,235,914
Viet Nam	0.03	155,059	271,288	117,670
Yemen	0.01	314	60,135	58,834
Yugoslavia	0.42	1,770,877	3,919,663	2,706,401
Zaire	0.02	—	222,220	58,834
Zambia	0.02	241,394	—	58,834
Zimbabwe	0.02	246,533	—	117,670
Total	100.04	630,814,101	147,948,884	612,604,877

SOURCE: ST/ADM/SER.B/264, ST/ADM/SER.B/265.

ASSESSMENT OF NON-MEMBER STATES FOR 1982 EXPENSES OF UN ACTIVITIES IN WHICH THEY PARTICIPATED
(amounts in US dollars)

Non-member State	Rate of assessment	Amount
Democratic People's Republic of Korea	0.05	35,358
Holy See	0.01	7,775
Liechtenstein	0.01	5,681
Monaco	0.01	5,259
Nauru	0.01	1,710
Republic of Korea	0.15	127,872
San Marino	0.01	5,646
Switzerland	1.05	1,656,722
Tonga	0.01	6,613
Total		1,852,636

NOTE: Activities and organizations for which non-member States were assessed were: the International Court of Justice, the Economic and Social Commission for Asia and the Pacific, the Economic Commission for Europe, international drug control, the United Nations Conference on Trade and Development, the United Nations Industrial Development Organization, the United Nations Environment Programme, transnational corporations, the United Nations High Commissioner for Refugees, human rights, the Intergovernmental Committee on Science and Technology for Development, the World Assembly on Aging, the Third United Nations Conference on the Law of the Sea and the United Nations Conference on the Exploration and Peaceful Uses of Outer Space.
SOURCE: ST/ADM/SER.B/267 and Corr.1.

General Assembly resolution 37/125 B

17 December 1982   Meeting 109   Adopted by consensus

Approved by Fifth Committee (A/37/617/Add.1) by consensus, 13 December (meeting 66); draft by Vice-Chairman (A/C.5/37/L.44/Rev.1) based on informal consultations, orally amended by United States, as sub-amended by Morocco; agenda item 110.

The General Assembly,

Recalling its resolutions 14(I) of 13 February 1946, 1927(XVIII) of 11 December 1963, 2118(XX) of 21 December 1965, 2961 C and D (XXVII) of 13 December 1972, 31/95 A and B of 14 December 1976 and 34/6 B of 25 October 1979,

Recalling also its resolution 36/231 A of 18 December 1981,

Having examined the report of the Committee on Contributions and the addendum thereto,

Recognizing once again the need for an improved methodology to assess the real capacity to pay of Member States, in order to increase the fairness and equity of the scale of assessments,

Taking into account the difficult economic and financial situation of Member States, in particular developing countries,

Mindful of the obligation of Member States to bear the expenses of the Organization as apportioned by the General Assembly according to the capacity to pay,

Noting the views expressed by Member States on the new scale as well as on the integrity of the Committee on Contributions,

1. *Reconfirms* that the real capacity to pay of Member States is the fundamental criterion on which the scale of assessments is based;

2. *Decides* that the Committee on Contributions may extend its sessions, as necessary, in order to:

(a) Submit to the General Assembly at its thirty-ninth session the study called for in paragraph 3 of resolution 36/231 A, together with its proposals for methods which it should use in determining future scales of assessments;

(b) Submit to the General Assembly not later than at its thirty-ninth session a set of guidelines for the collection and presentation of data as requested in paragraph 2 of resolution 36/231 A, taking into account the views expressed by a number of delegations concerning in particular the comparability of national income data;

3. *Invites* the Secretary-General to provide the Committee on Contributions with the facilities it requires to carry out its work and, if requested by the Committee, necessary supplementary assistance;

4. *Requests* the Committee on Contributions, in carrying out its mandate pursuant to resolution 36/231 A, to pay attention, *inter alia,* to the following:

(a) The need to ensure that the Statistical Office of the Secretariat receives or obtains standardized data and statistics in respect of methodology and technical bases, including those on exchange rates and national income expressed in current prices;

(b) The need to study ways and means of avoiding excessive variations by utilizing objective criteria when finalizing the scale of assessments;

5. *Requests* the Committee on Contributions to report to the General Assembly at its thirty-eighth session on the progress made in carrying out the work called for in the present resolution.

Status of contributions

The total of contributions to the United Nations regular budget payable by Member States in 1982 was $778,762,985, of which $633,994,175 was assessed for 1982 in accordance with the scale of assessments adopted in 1979 for the years 1980, 1981 and 1982[9] and $144,768,810 was payable for prior years. Of this total, $630,814,101 was collected and $147,948,884 remained outstanding as at 31 December 1982 (see table above). Nine non-member States were assessed a total of $1,852,636 for 1982 expenses of United Nations activities and organizations in which they participated (see table above). Net assessments on Member States for 1983, due early in that year, totalled $612.6 million, in accordance with a scale for 1983-1985 approved by the General Assembly in December 1982.[8]

At the opening of the ninth emergency special session of the Assembly on 29 January 1982, the Secretary-General, in a letter of that date,[1] informed the Assembly President that four Member States (Central African Republic, Chad, Grenada, South Africa) were more than two years in arrears in the payment of their financial contributions to the regular United Nations budget. By 2 February,[2] Grenada had made the necessary payment. Under Article 19 of the Charter of the United Nations, a Member in arrears to the extent of contributions due for the preceding two full years shall have no vote in the Assembly but the Assembly can permit such a Member to vote if it is satisfied that failure to pay was due to conditions beyond the State's control.

When the Assembly resumed its thirty-sixth regular session on 16 March, the Secretary-General announced[3] that only two Member States (Central African Republic, South Africa) were in arrears under Article 19, a situation which persisted throughout the Assembly's seventh emergency special session in April,[4] its twelfth special session in June[5] and into its thirty-seventh regular session which opened in September.[6] However, in a letter of 1 October,[7] the Secretary-General informed the Assembly that the Central African Republic had made the necessary payment under Article 19; only South Africa remained in arrears for the duration of 1982.

Letters. S-G: [1]29 Jan., A/ES-9/3; [2]2 Feb., A/ES-9/3/Add.1; [3]16 Mar., A/36/867; [4]20 Apr., A/ES-7/15; [5]7 June, A/S-12/25; [6]21 Sep., A/37/461; [7]1 Oct., A/37/461/Add.1.
Resolution (1982). [8]GA: 37/125 A, 17 Dec.
Yearbook reference. [9]1979, p. 1207.
Meeting records. GA: A/ES-7/PV.12 (20 Apr.), A/37/PV.1 (21 Sep.).

UN financial situation

In response to a December 1981 request by the General Assembly,[12] the Secretary-General in October 1982 submitted to the Assembly's Fifth (Administrative and Budgetary) Committee a progress report[7] giving details on the extent, rate of increase and composition of the United Nations deficit, and an account of the issuance of special revenue-producing postage stamps.

The Secretary-General stated that despite the Assembly's appeal to Member States to pay contributions in a timely manner, the rate of payment for 1982 had decreased to the lowest level of any recent year. By 30 June, only 29.4 per cent of the assessed contributions for the year had been received; by 30 September payments had reached only 48.65 per cent of the total amount due. These levels represented a serious decline since 1978, when the June figure had been 56.86 and the September figure 71.94 per cent. Of 154 Member States assessed in 1982 (three new Members had not yet been assessed), 50 had paid their full contribution at the time the report was written, 30 had paid only a part, and the remaining 74 had made no payment, of which 58 were in arrears for prior years' assessments as well. United Nations specialized agencies had also experienced a worsening rate of payment.

The short-term deficit of the Organization, projected to 31 December, would amount to $303.2 million, the Secretary-General reported—an increase of $29.1 million, or 10.6 per cent, over the deficit at the end of 1981. The bulk of the increase was the result of continued withholding of contributions from peace-keeping activities; the United Nations Interim Force in Lebanon accounted for most of the increase, or $28.8 million. The amount withheld from the regular budget by Member States because of positions of principle was projected to increase by $7 million to a total of $84.8 million, while the cumulative total of funds withheld from peace-keeping operations in the Middle East was projected at $150.5 million (see table below).

CUMULATIVE WITHHOLDINGS OF ASSESSED CONTRIBUTIONS
BY MEMBER STATES
*(estimated as at end of 1982 financial periods;
in thousands of US dollars)*

Member State	Regular budget	UNEF/ UNDOF	UNIFIL
Albania	36.0	20.2	12.7
Algeria	—	—	142.1
Benin	—	9.8	6.1
Bulgaria	575.9	27.5	195.5
Byelorussian SSR	1,224.1	566.7	2,536.0
China	4,103.1	—	—
Cuba	—	—	140.3
Czechoslovakia	1,759.4	397.7	5,325.0
Democratic Kampuchea	70.6	20.2	—
Democratic Yemen	—	4.5	6.1
France	4,357.1	—	—
German Democratic Republic	2,585.8	1,223.7	8,748.1
Hungary	968.6	—	421.4
Iraq	—	92.0	135.5
Lao People's Democratic Republic	—	—	6.1
Libyan Arab Jamahiriya	—	181.5	262.6
Mongolia	54.2	8.7	12.7
Poland	2,556.8	—	8,254.6
Romania	885.7	—	—
South Africa	16,710.2	2,719.9	2,683.4
Syrian Arab Republic	—	27.0	33.7
Ukrainian SSR	5,537.2	2,123.7	9,483.2
USSR	42,794.5	18,826.8	85,795.8
United States	612.6	—	—
Viet Nam	—	10.6	38.1
Yemen	—	9.4	—
Total	84,831.8	26,269.9	124,239.0

NOTES: Estimated withholdings from the regular budget, projected to 31 December 1982, consisted of $41,628,800 relating to the 1961 United Nations bond issue, $20,125,100 relating to the regular programme of technical assistance and $23,077,900 relating to other budget items. Estimated withholdings in regard to the Middle East peace-keeping forces, declared by the States concerned to be for reasons of principle, related to (1) the second United Nations Emergency Force (UNEF) from its inception in 1973 through its liquidation in 1979 and the inception of UNDOF in 1974 to 30 November 1982; and (2) UNIFIL inception from 1978 to 18 October 1982.

SOURCE: A/C.5/37/15 and Corr.1.

As authorized by the Assembly in December 1981,[12] a $9.9 million surplus arising from the unobligated balance of appropriations for the 1980-1981 biennium—which, after meeting certain obligations, was reduced to approximately $5.4 million—was retained by the United Nations, but would have no effect on the cash shortage situation since it was to be credited to Member States against their 1983 assessed contributions. Of the $60 million assessed increase in the Working Capital Fund authorized at the same time, $57.5 had been collected as at 30 September. However, as the Financial Regulations of the United Nations stipulated that payments be credited first to the Fund and then to contributions due, the intended benefit of the increase, the Secretary-General concluded, had not been achieved.

When the Fifth Committee in September and October examined the United Nations accounts for 1980-1981, the USSR submitted a draft decision[4] proposing that the $2,533,100 added to the budget when the Assembly revised it in December 1981[13] should be credited to Member States so as to reduce their 1982 assessments, rather than being retained by the United Nations. It withdrew the proposal after the United Nations Controller explained that the amount requested at that time was regarded as a new appropriation not affected by the suspension of financial regulations affecting unspent appropriations, and would therefore be credited to Member States.

The Secretary-General further estimated that the United Nations Special Account, set up to record voluntary contributions aimed at resolving the financial difficulties of the Organization, would have a balance of $62 million at year's end. A total of 28 Member States had contributed $42.6 million to the Account since the Assembly first called for such contributions in 1965;[9] the remainder of the balance consisted of income earned on that amount.

The Secretary-General also reported that United Nations postage stamps on the subject of conservation and protection of nature, the issuance of which had been requested by the Assembly in 1980,[11] were to be issued in November and were expected to generate net sales revenue of $2 million.

The Chairman of the Advisory Committee on Administrative and Budgetary Questions (ACABQ), commenting orally on the Secretary-General's report in the Fifth Committee on 27 October,[6] said ACABQ had discussed with representatives of the Secretary-General implementation of the portion of the 1981 Assembly resolution which authorized suspension of certain financial regulations to permit the United Nations to retain unobligated funds remaining at the end of a biennium. Pointing out that appropriations were revised each year in the light of programme performance reports, the Chairman said the Secretary-General and ACABQ had

to ensure that the estimates recommended to the Assembly were not inflated so as to secure a larger surplus, as that would be contrary to the spirit of the financial regulations.

In a statement transmitted to the Fifth Committee by the Secretary-General in November,[5] the Administrative Committee on Co-ordination (ACC), consisting of the executive heads of United Nations organizations and bodies, expressed concern over the worsening situation with regard to the problems of incomplete payment and delayed payment of contributions. It noted that four organizations—the International Labour Organisation, the World Health Organization, the International Civil Aviation Organization and the World Intellectual Property Organization—like the United Nations itself, had shown a deficit at the end of their last financial period.

While most of the specialized agencies fixed a 30-day deadline for payment of assessed contributions, a survey of 11 agencies showed that as at 30 June 1982 only two had received more than 59 per cent of their assessed contributions for that year. Both exceptions, the International Telecommunication Union and the Universal Postal Union, which had received over 90 per cent, levied interest on contributions that remained unpaid at the beginning of the financial year.

The statement pointed to a tendency among some of the largest contributors to remit payment at later dates. Such delays, ACC said, placed an unfair burden on those members which met their obligations promptly and in full. Of particular importance was the intention announced by the largest contributor (United States) to postpone, as a matter of legislative policy, payment of its assessed contributions until the last quarter of each calendar year.

Organizations and funds financed by voluntary contributions faced similar problems, according to the statement. Unpredictability of pledges and late payment led to a climate of uncertainty which hampered effective planning. The five largest recipients of voluntary funds (United Nations Environment Programme, United Nations Children's Fund, United Nations Development Programme, United Nations Relief and Works Agency for Palestine Refugees in the Near East, United Nations Fund for Population Activities) had received only between 36 and 56 per cent of their total 1982 funding by 30 June. Unlike organizations funded through assessments, those bodies had no borrowing power, and the operational effects of delayed payment were severe. The statement concluded with an appeal to the organizations' member States to pay their assessed and voluntary contributions in full, on time and in a consistent manner.

The statement was drafted by the ACC Consultative Committee on Administrative Questions

(Financial and Budgetary Questions) pursuant to an April decision[1] of ACC requesting the Consultative Committee to meet in special session to prepare a synthesis of the positions of the organizations with regard to problems of cash flow and liquidity. In July,[2] ACC called for revisions of a draft before approving the final text in November.[3]

General Assembly action. By a resolution[8] of 16 November on the financial emergency of the United Nations, the General Assembly renewed its appeal to Member States to pay early each year their full assessed contributions and advances to the Working Capital Fund. Noting that the already serious cash-flow problems had been aggravated by delayed and partial payment, the Assembly requested the Secretary-General to approach Members to encourage expeditious payment. It invited Members to provide information on their expected pattern of payments in order to facilitate financial planning. The Assembly requested the Secretary-General to submit in 1983 details on the deficit and on the pattern of Members' payments, and to report on the progress of the postage stamp project, including proposals for using part of the revenue to further the cause of the protection of nature. The Negotiating Committee on the Financial Emergency of the United Nations (established in 1975[10] but inactive since it last met in 1976[14]) was requested to keep the matter under review and to report as appropriate.

The resolution was adopted by a recorded vote of 112 to none, with 18 abstentions. The Fifth Committee had approved the text on 10 November by 68 votes to none, with 17 abstentions. The draft was introduced by Pakistan and sponsored by 16 States.

Decisions (1982). ACC: [1]1982/10, 6 Apr.; [2]1982/15, 5 July; [3]1982/31, 3 Nov.
Draft decision withdrawn. [4]USSR, A/C.5/37/L.3.
Note. [5]S-G, transmitting ACC statement, A/C.5/37/30.
Reports. [6]ACABQ, A/37/7, annex; [7]S-G, A/C.5/37/15 & Corr.1.
Resolution (1982). [8]GA: 37/13, 16 Nov., text following.
Resolutions (prior). GA: [9]2053 A (XX), 15 Dec. 1965 (YUN 1965, p. 24); [10]3538(XXX), 17 Dec. 1975 (YUN 1975, p. 957); [11]35/113, 10 Dec. 1980 (YUN 1980, p. 1220); [12]36/116 B, 10 Dec. 1981 (YUN 1981, p. 1298); [13]36/234 A, 18 Dec. 1981 (*ibid.*, p. 1283).
Yearbook reference. [14]1976, p. 889.
Meeting records. GA: 5th Committee, A/C.5/37/SR.13, 20-22, 24, 25, *29, 30* (15 Oct.–10 Nov.); plenary, A/37/PV.69 (16 Nov.).

General Assembly resolution 37/13

16 November 1982   Meeting 69   112-0-18 (recorded vote)

Approved by Fifth Committee (A/37/612) by vote (68-0-17), 10 November (meeting 30); 16-nation draft (A/C.5/37/L.22); agenda item 105.

Sponsors: Australia, Canada, Denmark, Egypt, Finland, Ghana, Iceland, Ireland, Jamaica, Nigeria, Norway, Pakistan, Philippines, Sierra Leone, Sweden, Zaire.

Financial emergency of the United Nations

The General Assembly,

Having considered the report of the Secretary-General on the analysis of the financial situation of the United Nations, and the statement adopted by the Administrative Committee on Co-ordination on 3 November 1982,

Recalling its resolutions 3049 A (XXVII) of 19 December 1972, 3538(XXX) of 17 December 1975, 32/104 of 14 December 1977, 35/113 of 10 December 1980 and 36/116 B of 10 December 1981,

Noting with concern that the short-term deficit of the Organization is expected to exceed $300 million as at 31 December 1982,

Noting with deep regret that, in spite of repeated appeals to Member States, delays and partial payment of assessed contributions have aggravated the already serious cash-flow problems of the Organization,

Considering the possibility that for many Member States administrative considerations, including a lack of synchronization of the national fiscal year with that of the Organization, may be responsible for the delay in the payment of assessed contributions,

1. *Reaffirms* its commitment to seek a comprehensive and lasting solution to the financial problems of the United Nations, based on the principle of collective financial responsibility of Member States;

2. *Renews its appeal* to all Member States to make their best efforts to overcome constraints to the prompt payment early each year of full assessed contributions and of advances to the Working Capital Fund;

3. *Expresses its appreciation* to all Member States which pay their assessed contributions in full within thirty days of the receipt of the Secretary-General's request, in accordance with regulation 5.4 of the Financial Regulations of the United Nations;

4. *Requests* the Secretary-General, in addition to his official communications to the permanent representatives of Member States, to approach, as and when appropriate, the Governments of Member States for the purpose of encouraging expeditious payment in full of assessed contributions, in compliance with regulation 5.4 of the Financial Regulations of the United Nations;

5. *Invites* Member States also to provide, in response to the Secretary-General's official communication and consistent with regulation 5.4 of the Financial Regulations of the United Nations, information regarding their expected pattern of payments, in order to facilitate the financial planning by the Secretary-General;

6. *Requests* the Negotiating Committee on the Financial Emergency of the United Nations to keep the financial situation of the Organization under review and to report, as appropriate, to the General Assembly;

7. *Requests* the Secretary-General to submit to the General Assembly at its thirty-eighth session:

(a) Detailed information relating to the extent, rate of increase and composition of the deficit of the Organization, the pattern of payments of Member States, the reasons for delays in such payments as known to the Secretary-General, the cash-flow situation and voluntary contributions received from Member States and other sources pursuant to General Assembly resolutions 2053 A (XX) of 15 December 1965 and 3049 A (XXVII) of 19 December 1972;

(b) A progress report on the status of the project on the issue of special postage stamps, including proposals to use a portion of the revenues to further the cause of the protection of nature;

8. *Further requests* the Secretary-General to include in his report a study of suggestions and proposals put forward by Member States during the discussions of this item at the thirty-seventh session of the General Assembly;

9. *Decides* to include in the provisional agenda of its thirty-eighth session the item entitled "Financial emergency of the United Nations: report of the Negotiating Committee on the Financial Emergency of the United Nations".

Recorded vote in Assembly as follows:

In favour: Algeria, Antigua and Barbuda, Argentina, Australia, Austria, Bahrain, Barbados, Belgium, Benin, Bhutan, Botswana, Brazil, Burma, Burundi, Canada, Cape Verde, Central African Republic, Chile, China, Colombia, Comoros, Congo, Costa Rica, Cyprus, Democratic Kampuchea, Democratic Yemen, Denmark, Djibouti, Dominican Republic, Ecuador, Egypt, El Salvador, Ethiopia, Fiji, Finland, France, Gabon, Germany, Federal Republic of, Ghana, Greece, Guatemala, Guinea, Guinea-Bissau, Guyana, Haiti, Honduras, Iceland, India, Indonesia, Ireland, Israel, Italy, Ivory Coast, Jamaica, Japan, Jordan, Kenya, Kuwait, Lebanon, Lesotho, Luxembourg, Madagascar, Malaysia, Maldives, Mali, Malta, Mauritania, Mauritius, Mexico, Nepal, Netherlands, New Zealand, Niger, Nigeria, Norway, Oman, Pakistan, Panama, Papua New Guinea, Paraguay, Peru, Philippines, Portugal, Qatar, Rwanda, Samoa, Saudi Arabia, Senegal, Sierra Leone, Singapore, Solomon Islands, Somalia, Spain, Sri Lanka, Sudan, Sweden, Thailand, Togo, Trinidad and Tobago, Tunisia, Turkey, United Arab Emirates, United

Kingdom, United Republic of Cameroon, United Republic of Tanzania, Upper Volta, Uruguay, Venezuela, Yemen, Yugoslavia, Zaire, Zambia.

Against: None.

Abstaining: Afghanistan, Bahamas, Bulgaria, Byelorussian SSR, Cuba, Czechoslovakia, German Democratic Republic, Grenada, Hungary, Mongolia, Mozambique, Poland, Romania, Syrian Arab Republic, Ukrainian SSR, USSR, United States, Viet Nam.

Effects of currency instability and inflation

In a November 1982 report,[3] the Secretary-General responded to a General Assembly request of December 1981[5] for an analysis of the impact of inflation and monetary instability on the United Nations regular budget, including a calculation of the amounts which, over the last three bienniums, had resulted from those factors in the developed countries where United Nations organizations had their headquarters.

Citing difficulties inherent in the attempt to make such a calculation, the Secretary-General limited his study to an examination of the evolution, in New York, Geneva and Vienna, Austria, from 1976 to 1981, of expenditures for staff costs. The study showed a close correlation between increases in these costs, which comprised approximately 77 per cent of the regular budget, and the combined effects of inflation and monetary fluctuations. During the three bienniums, increases in the net remuneration of New York staff in the Professional and higher categories, for example, had been due solely to adjustments based on a cost-of-living index. The average cost per post in New York for all categories for the 1980-1981 biennium had increased by 42.8 per cent over 1976-1977 levels. As the consumer price index over this period had moved up 37.5 per cent, the real increase in staff costs was 3.8 per cent. The comparable number for Vienna was 3.7 per cent, while staff costs at Geneva had declined by 10 per cent due primarily to dollar depreciation and the effects of a lower salary scale for General Service staff introduced in 1978.

In a resolution of 17 December,[4] adopted by a recorded vote of 94 to 25, with 22 abstentions, the Assembly, by the preamble, expressed concern at the increased cost of goods and services to the United Nations system as a result of inflation and monetary instability in those developed countries in which the Organization made its expenditures, said it was convinced that many Member States were not responsible for the budgetary losses thereby incurred, and stressed the need for a continuing review of procedures to meet the cost of such losses. By the operative paragraphs, it took note of the Secretary-General's report and requested a more penetrating, extensive and detailed study to be submitted in 1984.

The Fifth Committee had approved the text, as introduced and orally revised by Cuba and sponsored by 10 nations, on 6 December by 64 votes to 22, with 21 abstentions.

In the course of debate, Canada put forward an amendment, on behalf also of France and the Netherlands,[1] that would have replaced the operative paragraphs, except that taking note of the Secretary-General's report, with one requesting him to identify and suggest possible solutions to operational or budgetary problems caused or worsened by inflation and to report in 1984. Cuba had already agreed to delete from the 10-nation draft a request that the Secretary-General include in the new study additional criteria, procedures and guidelines, allowing sufficient flexibility in the budget process to determine more precisely the cost of inflation so that such cost might be distributed more appropriately among Member States.

Italy, on behalf also of the United Kingdom, submitted an amendment[2] that would have replaced the first four preambular paragraphs with two, noting that inflation was a world-wide problem with which all Governments and international organizations had to deal and stating the Assembly's conviction that the United Nations should plan, forecast and manage its expenditures so as better to deal with it.

Both amendments were opposed by the sponsors of the original draft. By recorded votes of 51 to 30, with 21 abstentions, and 54 to 29, with 21 abstentions, respectively, the Committee decided not to consider them as amendments. The Chairman subsequently informed the Committee that the sponsors of the proposals had notified him that they did not intend to press for a vote on them as separate proposals.

Egypt orally proposed compromise language in both the preambular and operative paragraphs but did not press for a vote on them after the resolution's sponsors said they were not acceptable. Among other things, they would have deleted reference to "those developed countries in which the United Nations makes its expenditures" from the second preambular paragraph, deleted the third preambular paragraph, and changed wording in operative paragraph 2 to describe the new study as "comprehensive" rather than "more penetrating, extensive and detailed". A subsequent Egyptian motion to take separate votes on those three paragraphs was opposed by Cuba and defeated by a recorded vote, requested by the United Kingdom, of 48 to 42, with 17 abstentions.

Explaining votes against the resolution, Denmark, on behalf of the 10 European Community members, said that developed countries alone were not responsible for inflation and monetary instability and that the real thrust of the draft was not financial but political. Canada, voting against, said the text consisted primarily of polemics and failed to come to grips with the real issues. Egypt opposed the resolution on the ground that some of its language created problems for many delegations and would have preferred a consensus adoption. New Zealand said it would have preferred more balance—a point also made by Singapore, and Trinidad and Tobago—and Tunisia, voting affirmatively, would have preferred more appropriate wording for certain ideas. The United States, which also voted against the text, felt that the changes agreed to by the sponsors did not go far enough and regretted the decision not to allow separate votes on different paragraphs and that much of the polemical language remained.

Several States cited the Egyptian proposals in explaining their vote. Canada said the refusal to allow voting on specific provisions constituted a denial of freedom of expression. Pakistan, which abstained, felt that several delegations would have supported the resolution as a whole if they had been able to abstain on particular paragraphs. Sierra Leone, which voted in favour, and Singapore, which abstained, indicated that they would have supported the Egyptian amendments, and Trinidad and Tobago regretted that the Egyptian compromise had not been given a chance.

The Bahamas said it had abstained because it could not support inefficient use of United Nations resources; study of the problem was already being carried out by other United Nations bodies. New Zealand, which opposed the draft, was in agreement. Brazil argued that the text was superfluous, since countries which, according to its sponsors, bore responsibility for inflation paid 75 per cent of the budget and were therefore already penalized.

Ghana, which abstained, favoured the study but felt that the wording of the draft prejudged the outcome. Pakistan thought that a portion of the draft was inconsistent with the principle of collective financial responsibility; also, because the United Nations made expenditures in practically all developed countries, it had difficulty with the paragraph which singled out certain of them.

Supporting the resolution, the USSR said the draft recognized the need for a new procedure to establish the responsibility of certain Governments for additional costs to the United Nations resulting from inflation and monetary instability, thereby filling a gap in the Secretary-General's report. The Libyan Arab Jamahiriya, also voting in favour, said it hoped the requested study would shed light on the subject of inflation, which caused tremendous suffering among developing countries.

Amendments not to be considered amendments. (1)Canada, France, Netherlands, A/C.5/37/L.34; (2)Italy, United Kingdom, A/C.5/37/L.35.
Report. (3)S-G, A/C.5/37/39.
Resolution (1982). (4)GA: 37/130, 17 Dec., text following.
Resolution (prior). (5)GA: 36/230, 18 Dec. 1981 (YUN 1981, p. 1301).
Meeting records. GA: 5th Committee, A/C.5/37/SR.27, 36, 39, 42, *50*, 52, *57*, *58* (5 Nov.–6 Dec.); plenary, A/37/PV.109 (17 Dec.).

General Assembly resolution 37/130

17 December 1982   Meeting 109   94-25-22 (recorded vote)

Approved by Fifth Committee (A/37/766) by vote (64-22-21), 6 December (meeting 57); 10-nation draft (A/C.5/37/L.31), orally revised; agenda item 106 *(b)*.

Sponsors: Burundi, Costa Rica, Cuba, Dominican Republic, Ethiopia, Guinea-Bissau, Madagascar, Mexico, Nigeria, Panama.

Impact of inflation and monetary instability on the regular budget of the United Nations

The General Assembly,

Recalling its resolution 36/230 of 18 December 1981,

Deeply concerned at the increased cost of the goods and services associated with the operation of the United Nations and the United Nations system as a whole as a result of the persistence of inflation and monetary instability in those developed countries in which the United Nations makes its expenditures,

Convinced that many Member States are not responsible for the losses that the budget of the United Nations experiences as a result of the monetary phenomena referred to in the preceding paragraph,

Stressing that, in order to cover the substantial losses caused by inflation and monetary instability, there is a need for a continuing review of procedures that could help meet the above-mentioned budget costs in the most appropriate way,

Having considered the study prepared by the Secretary-General on the impact of inflation and monetary instability on the regular budget of the United Nations, contained in his report on the subject,

Convinced of the need to analyse more thoroughly all aspects of the increased costs of the goods and services associated with the operation of the United Nations,

1. *Takes note* of the report of the Secretary-General on the impact of inflation and monetary instability on the regular budget of the United Nations;

2. *Requests* the Secretary-General to prepare a more penetrating, extensive and detailed study on the impact of inflation and monetary instability on the regular budget of the United Nations, taking duly into consideration the content of the preambular paragraphs of resolution 36/230 and the present resolution, together with the opinions of the Member States concerned, and to submit it to the General Assembly at its thirty-ninth session.

Recorded vote in Assembly as follows:

In favour: Afghanistan, Algeria, Angola, Argentina, Bahrain, Benin, Bhutan, Bolivia, Botswana, Bulgaria, Burma, Burundi, Byelorussian SSR, Cape Verde, Chile, Colombia, Comoros, Congo, Costa Rica, Cuba, Cyprus, Czechoslovakia, Democratic Yemen, Djibouti, Dominican Republic, Ecuador, El Salvador, Ethiopia, Gabon, Gambia, German Democratic Republic, Grenada, Guatemala, Guinea, Guinea-Bissau, Honduras, Hungary, India, Indonesia, Iran, Iraq, Ivory Coast, Jordan, Kenya, Kuwait, Lao People's Democratic Republic, Lesotho, Libyan Arab Jamahiriya, Madagascar, Mali, Malta, Mauritius, Mexico, Mongolia, Morocco, Mozambique, Nicaragua, Niger, Nigeria, Oman, Panama, Papua New Guinea, Paraguay, Peru, Philippines, Poland, Qatar, Romania, Rwanda, Sao Tome and Principe, Saudi Arabia, Senegal, Sierra Leone, Somalia, Sri Lanka, Sudan, Suriname, Swaziland, Syrian Arab Republic, Togo, Trinidad and Tobago, Tunisia, Uganda, Ukrainian SSR, USSR, United Arab Emirates, Upper Volta, Venezuela, Viet Nam, Yemen, Yugoslavia, Zaire, Zambia, Zimbabwe.

Against: Australia, Austria, Belgium, Canada, Denmark, Egypt, Finland, France, Germany, Federal Republic of, Greece, Iceland, Ireland, Israel, Italy, Japan, Luxembourg, Netherlands, New Zealand, Norway, Portugal, Spain, Sweden, Turkey, United Kingdom, United States.

Abstaining: Bahamas, Bangladesh, Barbados, Brazil, Central African Republic, Chad, China, Dominica, Fiji, Ghana, Jamaica, Malawi, Malaysia, Mauritania, Nepal, Pakistan, Samoa, Singapore, Solomon Islands, United Republic of Cameroon, United Republic of Tanzania, Uruguay.

Accounts and auditing

Accounts for 1980-1981

On 31 March 1982, the Secretary-General transmitted to the United Nations Board of Auditors his financial report on the accounts for the 1980-1981 biennium ended 31 December 1981,(4) including a statement of income and expenditure, as shown in the table below (in millions of United States dollars).

Account	Income	Expenditures
General Fund	1,352.9	1,331.8
Other General Fund–related activities	9.2	–
Peace-keeping missions	505.8	389.7
Technical co-operation activities	599.6	608.5
General and special purpose trust funds	151.7	126.7
Special accounts for programme support costs	84.7	75.2

SOURCE: A/37/5.

By a resolution of 16 November 1982,[5] the General Assembly accepted the financial reports and accounts for the biennium ended 31 December 1981, as well as the audit opinions of the Board of Auditors,[4] for the United Nations and the following programmes, funds and organs: the United Nations Development Programme, the United Nations Children's Fund, the United Nations Relief and Works Agency for Palestine Refugees in the Near East, the United Nations Institute for Training and Research, the voluntary funds administered by the United Nations High Commissioner for Refugees, the Fund of the United Nations Environment Programme, the United Nations Fund for Population Activities and the United Nations Habitat and Human Settlements Foundation.

The Assembly concurred with observations and comments by the Advisory Committee on Administrative and Budgetary Questions (ACABQ),[2] requested the Board of Auditors and ACABQ to continue to give greater attention to areas on which they had made observations and comments, and requested the Secretary-General to strengthen financial discipline in the Secretariat and to remove the shortcomings referred to in the reports of the Board and ACABQ. The executive heads of the organizations and programmes concerned were requested to take remedial action in areas within their competence as might be required by the Board's comments.

The resolution was adopted without vote, following approval without objection by the Fifth Committee on 6 October. The text, submitted by the Committee Chairman, was orally revised on a proposal by Ghana to have the Assembly endorse with appreciation the Board's audit opinions. The paragraph requesting the Secretary-General to take steps to strengthen financial discipline in the Secretariat and remove shortcomings was added on a proposal by the Byelorussian SSR, adopted without objection after the sponsor, following consultations, revised it orally to request that "necessary" rather than "urgent" and effective steps be taken.

A draft decision by the USSR,[1] later withdrawn, proposed to approve crediting to Member States the uncommitted balance remaining from 1980-1981 appropriations (see above, under UN FINANCIAL SITUATION).

The Board of Auditors, on 16 June, transmitted to the Assembly its audit opinion on the financial statements submitted to it by the Secretary-General. The Board's opinion was reviewed and commented upon by ACABQ in a report of 20 September.[3] The United Nations accounts covered by the Board included those of the International Trade Centre and the United Nations University.

In the area of procurement practices, the Board observed that, despite significant improvement at Headquarters, certain activities, such as the streamlining of the processing of purchase orders, registration of vendors to assist in their selection and evaluation, and improving delivery procedures, were being hampered by delay in implementation of the Automated Purchase and Payment System, which was more than two years behind schedule. ACABQ shared the Board's concern. The Board, referring to certain procurement practices by the Office of the United Nations Disaster Relief Co-ordinator, the Economic Commission for Western Asia and the Economic Commission for Africa, also recommended that the United Nations Financial Regulations and Rules be strictly adhered to.

The Board's review of capital assets concentrated on contracting for additions and alterations to Headquarters premises in New York. It saw ambiguities in provisions of contracts with architects which would permit additional substantial claims for services, and it recommended use of a detailed standard contract form, modified to meet United Nations needs. ACABQ observed that some $785,000 more than the contract price had been paid for architects' services, due to an underestimation by the United Nations and its consultants of the project's complexity and cost.

The Board cited as an example of delayed implementation of trust fund projects the Trust Fund for the United Nations Special Emergency Operation, set up in 1974[6] to help developing countries most seriously affected by economic crisis to maintain essential imports. After seven years, large portions of the amounts allocated to some developing countries had not been spent by them. ACABQ was informed that the amount involved was approximately $6.9 million and that the Administration was undertaking a complete review of this Fund. The Board also reported considerable delays in the approval of budget proposals for the Trust Fund for the United Nations Institute for Namibia; ACABQ was informed that the delays were due to late approval of the budget by the Institute's Council and that procedures would be reviewed in order to correct the situation. The Board further observed that the records of the Office of Financial Services were not up to date, making it difficult to determine outstanding pledges to trust fund accounts.

With regard to cash management, the Board saw satisfactory progress in implementing the recommendations made in its 1978-1979 report. However, it commented on some worsening problems with cash management by the United Nations Industrial Development Organization, and ACABQ advised prompt corrective action.

ACABQ noted that, as reported by the Board, a staff management resources system was under study that would streamline the personnel and payroll systems, although it might take two to three years to implement. The Board also commented that United Nations procedures for use of consultants were not being fully complied with.

Draft decision withdrawn. [1]USSR, A/C.5/37/L.3.
Reports. ACABQ, [2]A/37/7, [3]A/37/443 & Corr.1; [4]Board of Auditors, and financial statements, A/37/5, vols. I-III & Add.1 & Add.1/Corr.1, Add.2-7 & Add.7/Corr.1 & Add.8.
Resolution (1982). [5]GA: 37/12, 16 Nov., text following.
Resolution (prior). [6]GA: 3202(S-VI), 1 May 1974 (YUN 1974, p. 326).
Meeting records. GA: 5th Committee, A/C.5/37/SR.3-7 (29 Sep.-6 Oct.); plenary, A/37/PV.69 (16 Nov.).

General Assembly resolution 37/12

16 November 1982   Meeting 69   Adopted without vote

Approved by Fifth Committee (A/37/533) without objection, 6 October (meeting 7); draft by Chairman (A/C.5/37/L.4), orally revised on proposal by Ghana and amended by Byelorussian SSR (A/C.5/37/L.5, orally revised); agenda item 102.

Financial reports and accounts, and reports of the Board of Auditors

The General Assembly,

Having considered the financial reports and accounts for the financial period ended 31 December 1981 of the United Nations, the United Nations Development Programme, the United Nations Children's Fund, the United Nations Relief and Works Agency for Palestine Refugees in the Near East, the United Nations Institute for Training and Research, the voluntary funds administered by the United Nations High Commissioner for Refugees, the Fund of the United Nations Environment Programme, the United Nations Fund for Population Activities and the United Nations Habitat and Human Settlements Foundation, the audit opinions of the Board of Auditors and the report of the Advisory Committee on Administrative and Budgetary Questions,

Taking into account the views expressed by delegations during the debate in the Fifth Committee,

1. *Accepts* the financial reports and accounts and endorses with appreciation the audit opinions of the Board of Auditors;

2. *Concurs* with the observations and comments made by the Advisory Committee on Administrative and Budgetary Questions in its report;

3. *Requests* the Board of Auditors and the Advisory Committee on Administrative and Budgetary Questions to continue to give greater attention to areas regarding which they have made observations and comments;

4. *Requests* the Secretary-General to take necessary and effective steps further to strengthen financial discipline in all departments of the Secretariat and to remove the shortcomings referred to in the reports of the Board of Auditors and the report of the Advisory Committee on Administrative and Budgetary Questions;

5. *Further requests* the executive heads of the organizations and programmes concerned to take such remedial action in areas falling within their competence as may be required by the comments and observations made by the Board of Auditors in its reports.

Chapter II

United Nations programmes

Contents

Programme planning

The main work of the Committee for Programme and Co-ordination (CPC) at its twenty-second session, held in New York from 19 April to 29 May 1982, was drafting the proposed medium-term plan for the period 1984-1989 (see below). In addition to examining and making proposals on specific activities of the United Nations system, divided into 24 programme areas (or chapters), CPC, in its report to the General Assembly,[2] made general recommendations on the process of programme planning (see REGULATIONS FOR PROGRAMME PLANNING AND EVALUATION, below).

The Committee recommended that the Secretary-General consider further measures to rationalize the process of programme planning, budgeting, monitoring and evaluation in the United Nations. He was requested to ensure that the policy guidelines, priorities and programmatic content of the medium-term plan, as adopted by the Assembly, were accurately reflected in the budget-formulating process during the plan period. The preparations of the proposed budget and medium-term plan, CPC said, should be conducted in the context of the activities of the United Nations system as a whole, taking fully into account the programmed activities of the specialized agencies. Every effort should be made to ensure a thorough review of the plan by the appropriate regional, sectoral and functional intergovernmen-

tal organs and that all United Nations organizations, including those without medium-term plans, participate in the joint planning exercise.

Commenting on approaches to joint planning by organizations of the United Nations system, the inter-agency Administrative Committee on Co-ordination (ACC) said that, since the Assembly had called in 1977[5] for joint planning to be one of the tasks on which co-ordination at the inter-secretariat level should concentrate, ACC had pursued increased use of joint planning as a means for joint action within the system. In reviewing this issue, the ACC Consultative Committee on Substantive Questions (Programme Matters) noted that such planning could enhance the efficiency, effectiveness and general impact of the system's activities. In its annual overview report on international co-operation and co-ordination within the system for 1981/82,[1] ACC observed that joint planning should not be undertaken for its own sake, but should grow as programmes developed and acquired inter-agency dimensions. Non-formalized channels for joint activities already existed, including the preparation of cross-organizational programme analyses, prior consultation arrangements, and certain activities based on agreements or letters of understanding between organizations.

ACC welcomed the idea of entrusting small teams of programming officials with joint planning in selected areas and endorsed the suggestion of designating one organization with primary responsibility in the selected area as the co-ordinating agency. It also supported expanding and strengthening programme consultations at the regional level between the regional commissions and agencies having regional programmes.

ACC noted the joint planning arrangements already made in the fields of science and technology for development and new and renewable sources of energy. It decided to initiate joint planning in the following areas (the co-ordinating agency is in parentheses): primary health care (World Health Organization (WHO)); aging (WHO and United Nations Centre for Social Development and Humanitarian Affairs); research and training in energy assessment, planning and utilization (United Nations Department of Technical Co-operation for Development); and harmonization of information systems for energy (United Nations Educational, Scientific and Cultural Organization).

The Committee of Governmental Experts to Evaluate the Present Structure of the Secretariat in the Administrative, Finance and Personnel Areas, in its 1982 report to the Assembly,[3] commented on the adequacy of the structure to undertake programme planning in relation to budget preparation and resource allocation. The Secretary-General had indicated that he regarded the establishment of the Programme Planning and Budgeting Board as a step towards enhancing the integration of the programme planning and budgeting functions, in order to reflect, as much as possible, the wishes of Member States in regard to the work programme as expressed in Assembly decisions; he intended to assess resulting developments and draw conclusions regarding further measures at a later stage.

While it saw some merit in the establishment of the Board, the Committee felt that the Board, as constituted, could not replace the need for integration of the whole system of programme planning, budgeting, monitoring and reporting, and it stressed the need for a single responsibility for such a system. It hoped that the experience gained with current arrangements, and the modalities existing in other United Nations organizations, would be taken into account in deciding on how such responsibility would be established.

General Assembly action. By a resolution of 21 December,[4] the General Assembly adopted the 1984-1989 medium-term plan, which it considered to be the principal policy directive of the United Nations, and the Regulations Governing Programme Planning, the Programme Aspects of the Budget, the Monitoring of Implementation and the Methods of Evaluation (see below) annexed to the resolution. It accepted the revisions and recommendations of CPC and the Economic and Social Council on the plan and endorsed other CPC recommendations. It requested the Secretary-General to issue rules to implement the Regula-

tions, which outlined procedures for the periodic review of all United Nations programmes. The process was intended to allow reflection, before choosing the type of action, by all participants in the action, especially Member States and the Secretariat. The process was also aimed at determining feasible objectives which were politically acceptable to Member States as a whole. In carrying out those aims, the United Nations was to use such instruments as the medium-term plan, the programme budget, the programme performance report and the evaluation system.

The resolution was adopted without vote, following approval by consensus of the text, sponsored by 13 nations, by the Fifth (Administrative and Budgetary) Committee on 15 December. It was introduced and orally revised by the United Republic of Cameroon on behalf of the sponsors. Among the revisions was the addition to the sixth preambular paragraph of mention of the intention expressed by the Secretary-General at the Assembly's 1982 session (in addition to that expressed at the resumed 1981 session in March 1982) to improve the effectiveness of the programme planning, budgeting, monitoring and evaluation system.

Reports. [1]ACC, E/1982/4; [2]CPC, A/37/38; [3]Committee on Secretariat structure in administrative, finance and personnel areas, A/37/44.
Resolution (1982). [4]GA: 37/234, 21 Dec., text following.
Resolution (prior). [5]GA: 32/197, annex, 20 Dec. 1977 (YUN 1977, p. 439).
Meeting records. GA: 5th Committee, A/C.5/37/SR.13 (15 Oct.), 37, 38, 41, 42, 44, 45, 48, 51, 56, *71-73* (17 Nov.–16 Dec.); 3rd Committee, A/C.3/37/SR.16 (20 Oct.); 4th Committee, A/C.4/37/SR.10 (29 Oct.); SPC, A/SPC/37/SR.14 (1 Nov.); 6th Committee, A/C.6/37/SR.46 (16 Nov.); plenary, A/37/PV.114 (21 Dec.).

General Assembly resolution 37/234

21 December 1982	Meeting 114	Adopted without vote

Approved by Fifth Committee (A/37/776) by consensus, 15 December (meeting 71); 13-nation draft (A/C.5/37/L.49), orally revised; agenda item 104.

Sponsors: Egypt, Finland, Ghana, India, Japan, Mauritania, Mexico, Morocco, Netherlands, Norway, Sweden, Trinidad and Tobago, United Republic of Cameroon.

Programme planning

The General Assembly,

Recalling its resolution 3043(XXVII) of 19 December 1972, in which it approved the new form of presentation of the United Nations budget,

Recalling also its resolutions 3199(XXVIII) of 18 December 1973, 31/93 of 14 December 1976, 32/197 of 20 December 1977, 32/206 of 21 December 1977, 33/118 of 19 December 1978, 34/224 of 20 December 1979, 35/9 of 3 November 1980 and 36/228 of 18 December 1981, in which it elaborated further on the establishment of an integrated programme planning, budgeting, monitoring and evaluation system in the United Nations,

Having considered the report of the Committee for Programme and Co-ordination on the work of its twenty-second session, chapter VI, section C, of the report of the Economic and Social Council for the year 1982, and the reports of the Advisory Committee on Administrative and Budgetary Questions on the draft regulations and rules governing programme planning, the programme aspects of the budget, the monitoring of implementation and methods of evaluation and on the review of the Financial Rules and Regulations in the light of the restructuring of the economic and social sectors of the United Nations and on the proposed medium-term plan for the period 1984-1989,

Having also considered the proposed medium-term plan for the period 1984-1989, the reports of the Secretary-General on the draft regulations and rules governing programme planning, the programme aspects of the budget, the monitoring of implementation and the methods of evaluation, on the review of the Financial Rules and Regulations in the light of the restructuring of the economic and social sectors of the United Nations, on the procedures for the proposed programme budget review, on the programme performance of the United Nations for the biennium 1980-1981 and on the updating of the special review of the ongoing work programme of the United Nations, and the report of the Joint Inspection Unit entitled "Elaboration of regulations for the planning, programming and evaluation cycle of the United Nations",

Having also considered the note by the Chairman of the Fifth Committee reporting on the review of the proposed medium-term plan for the period 1984-1989 by the other Main Committees of the General Assembly,

Recalling that the Secretary-General, at the resumed thirty-sixth session and at the thirty-seventh session of the General Assembly, had expressed the intention to improve the effectiveness of the programme planning, budgeting, monitoring and evaluation system,

Bearing in mind the observations contained in the report of the Committee of Governmental Experts to Evaluate the Present Structure of the Secretariat in the Administrative, Finance and Personnel Areas on the need to integrate the whole system of programme planning, budgeting, monitoring and reporting, taking into account modalities existing in other organizations of the United Nations system,

Noting the establishment of the Programme Planning and Budgeting Board and of the Central Monitoring Unit,

I
Medium-term plan

1. *Adopts* the proposed medium-term plan for the period 1984-1989, as revised by the recommendations of the Committee for Programme and Co-ordination at its twenty-second session and the Economic and Social Council at its second regular session of 1982, taking into account the views of Main Committees of the General Assembly, with the exception of subprogramme 5 of programme 1 of chapter 21, which requires further revision and approval;

2. *Considers* the medium-term plan, as adopted, to be the principal policy directive of the United Nations;

3. *Requests* the Secretary-General to issue the medium-term plan for the period 1984-1989, as adopted, as a single-volume printed document;

4. *Further requests* the Secretary-General to make the necessary methodological improvements to the medium-term plan for the period 1984-1989 in the context of its first revision and in the light of the observations at the second regular session of 1982 of the Economic and Social Council and by the Committee for Programme and Co-ordination at its twenty-second session, as well as the views expressed during the thirty-seventh session of the General Assembly;

II
Programme planning, the programme aspects of the budget, the monitoring of implementation and the methods of evaluation

1. *Adopts* the Regulations Governing Programme Planning, the Programme Aspects of the Budget, the Monitoring of Implementation and the Methods of Evaluation recommended by the Committee for Programme and Co-ordination in its report on its twenty-second session, as revised and set out in the annex to the present resolution, and the related changes to the Financial Regulations of the United Nations, as amended by the Committee for Programme and Co-ordination;

2. *Notes* that the draft set of rules submitted by the Secretary-General does not conform fully with all the stipulations of the Regulations Governing Programme Planning, the Programme Aspects of the Budget, the Monitoring of Implementation and the Methods of Evaluation;

3. *Requests* the Secretary-General to issue rules in implementation of and in conformity with those Regulations and with the recommendations of the Committee for Programme and Co-ordination at its twenty-second session, taking into consideration comments made in the Fifth Committee during its review of the draft Regulations, and to submit those rules to the Committee for Programme and Co-ordination at its twenty-third session and to the General Assembly at its thirty-eighth session;

4. *Confirms* the understanding of the Secretary-General that, when appropriating resources for the implementation of the programme budget, the General Assembly also decides that the programme elements and output citations in the proposed programme budget, as revised by the Assembly, shall constitute the commitments against which programme performance is to be reported and assessed;

5. *Notes* that the Secretary-General intends to issue revisions to the Financial Rules and to submit them to the General Assembly through the Advisory Committee on Administrative and Budgetary Questions;

6. *Requests* the Secretary-General to take further steps to improve the effectiveness of programme monitoring, in accordance with section I, paragraph 2 *(b)*, of General Assembly resolution 36/228 A;

7. *Requests* the Secretary-General:

(a) To report to the Committee for Programme and Co-ordination, at its twenty-third session, on methods and procedures which will be used to provide the General Assembly with programme implications, together with administrative and financial implications of draft resolutions being considered by the General Assembly;

(b) To take the necessary measures to provide the General Assembly, at its thirty-eighth session, with programme implications of draft resolutions being considered by the Assembly;

8. *Requests* the Secretary-General to submit, through the Committee for Programme and Co-ordination at its twenty-third session, to the General Assembly at its thirty-eighth session, an evaluation programme and a timetable for intergovernmental review of evaluation studies, together with the proposed programme budget for the biennium 1984-1985;

9. *Requests* the Secretary-General to report to the General Assembly at its thirty-eighth session, through the Committee for Programme and Co-ordination at its twenty-third session and through the Advisory Committee on Administrative and Budgetary Questions, on the measures which he has considered appropriate to take, bearing in mind the views expressed on the matter by delegations, to further integrate the programme planning, budgeting, monitoring and evaluation functions in the Secretariat;

III
Other conclusions and recommendations of the Committee for Programme and Co-ordination

1. *Notes with satisfaction and endorses* the other conclusions and recommendations of the Committee for Programme and Co-ordination at its twenty-second session;

2. *Requests* the Secretary-General to comment on those recommendations of the Joint Inspection Unit on the regulations for planning, programming and evaluation in the United Nations which have not yet been reflected in the Regulations for consideration by the Committee for Programme and Co-ordination at its twenty-third session;

3. *Requests* the Committee for Programme and Co-ordination at its twenty-third session to report to the General Assembly at its thirty-eighth session on the need to amend the programme planning Regulations and Financial Regulations of the United Nations in the light of the recommendations of the Joint Inspection Unit and the comments thereon by the Secretary-General, as well as in the light of the discussion on this subject in the Fifth Committee at the thirty-seventh session.

ANNEX
Regulations Governing Programme Planning, the Programme Aspects of the Budget, the Monitoring of Implementation and the Methods of Evaluation

Preamble

1. The planning, programming, budgeting, monitoring and evaluation cycle established in the United Nations by decisions of the General Assembly aims at the following:

(a) To subject all programmes of the Organization to periodic and thorough reviews;

(b) To afford an opportunity for reflection before choices among the various types of action possible are made in the light of all existing conditions;

(c) To associate in that reflection all participants in the Organization's actions, especially Member States and the Secretariat;

(d) To assess what is feasible and derive from this assessment objectives which are both feasible and politically acceptable to Member States as a whole;

(e) To translate those objectives into programmes and work plans where the responsibilities and tasks of those who are to implement them are specified;

(f) To indicate to Member States the resources needed to design and implement activities and to ensure that those resources are utilized according to legislative intent and in the most effective and economic manner;

(g) To provide a framework for setting priorities among activities;

(h) To establish an independent and effective system for monitoring implementation and verifying the effectiveness of the work actually done;

(i) To evaluate periodically the results achieved, with a view either to confirming the validity of the orientations chosen or to reshaping the programmes towards different orientations.

2. In pursuance of the above aims, the following instruments are to be utilized in the Organization:

(a) The introduction to the medium-term plan and the medium-term plan itself, whereby orientations are given to the Organization's activities;

(b) The programme budget and the programme performance report, where the Secretariat is committed to precise work plans involving delivery of output and where implementation thereof is monitored and reported;

(c) The evaluation system, which allows for continuing critical review of achievements, collective thinking thereon and formulation of subsequent plans.

Article 1
Applicability

Regulation 1.1. These regulations shall govern the planning, programming, monitoring and evaluation of all activities undertaken by the United Nations, irrespective of their source of financing.

Article 2
Instruments of integrated management

Regulation 2.1. Activities undertaken by the United Nations shall be submitted to an integrated management process reflected in the following instruments:

(a) Medium-term plans;

(b) Programme budgets;

(c) Reports on programme performance;

(d) Evaluation reports.

Each of these instruments corresponds to one phase in a programme-planning cycle and, consequently, shall serve as a framework for the subsequent phases.

Regulation 2.2. The planning, programming, budgeting and evaluation cycle shall form an integral part of the general policy-making and management process of the Organization. The instruments referred to in regulation 2.1 above shall be used to ensure that activities are coordinated and that available resources are utilized according to legislative intent and in the most effective and economic manner.

Article 3
Medium-term plan

Regulation 3.1. A medium-term plan shall be proposed by the Secretary-General.

Regulation 3.2. The medium-term plan shall be a translation of legislative mandates into programmes. Its objectives and strategies shall be derived from the policy orientations and goals set by the intergovernmental organs. It shall reflect Member States' priorities as set out in legislation adopted by functional and regional intergovernmental bodies within their spheres of competence and by the General Assembly, on advice from the Committee for Programme and Co-ordination. In this context, subsidiary intergovernmental and expert bodies should, accordingly, refrain from making recommendations on the relative priorities of the major programmes as outlined in the medium-term plan and should instead propose, through the Committee, the relative priorities to be accorded to the various subprogrammes within their respective fields of competence. The medium-term plan shall clearly identify new activities.

Regulation 3.3. After adoption by the General Assembly, the medium-term plan shall constitute the principal policy directive of the United Nations which:

(a) States the medium-term objectives to be attained in the plan period;

(b) Describes the strategy to be followed to that effect and the means of action to be used;

(c) Gives an indicative estimate of the necessary resources.

Regulation 3.4. The medium-term plan shall serve as a framework for the formulation of the biennial programme budgets within the period covered by the plan.

Regulation 3.5. The plan shall cover all activities, substantive and servicing, including those to be financed partially or fully from extrabudgetary resources.

Regulation 3.6. The plan shall be presented by programme and objective and not by organizational unit. It shall emphasize the description of objectives and strategies; the presentation and format of the analysis provided therein shall vary according to the type and nature of activities; to this end a distinction shall be made between substantive and servicing activities; objectives shall be time-limited as far as possible, and the plan shall be objective-based in all programmes where that is feasible. The medium-term plan shall identify:

(a) Major programmes, consisting of all activities conducted in a sector;

(b) Programmes, consisting within a major programme, of all activities in a sector which are under the responsibility of a distinct organizational unit, normally at the division level;

(c) Subprogrammes, consisting, within a programme, of all activities that are directed at the accomplishment of one medium-term objective or several closely related objectives.

Regulation 3.7. The plan shall be preceded by an introduction, which will constitute a key integral element in the planning process and shall:

(a) Highlight, in a co-ordinated manner, the policy orientations of the United Nations system;

(b) Indicate the medium-term objectives and strategy and trends deduced from mandates which reflect priorities set by intergovernmental organizations;

(c) Contain the Secretary-General's proposals on priorities.

Regulation 3.8. In order to facilitate the planning process, the Secretary-General shall request the executive heads of the voluntary funds to indicate the likely future volume of extrabudgetary funds sufficiently in advance for this information to be taken into consideration in the preparation of the medium-term plan.

Regulation 3.9. The medium-term plan shall cover a six-year period and be submitted to the General Assembly one year before the submission of the proposed programme budget covering the first biennium of the plan period.

Regulation 3.10. Sectoral, functional and regional programme-formulating organs shall refrain from undertaking new activities not programmed in the medium-term plan, unless a pressing need of an unforeseeable nature arises, as determined by the General Assembly.

Regulation 3.11. The medium-term plan shall be revised as necessary every two years to incorporate required programme changes; revisions to the plan shall be considered by the General Assembly one year before the submission of the programme budget providing for implementation of the changes. The proposed revisions shall be as detailed as required to incorporate the programme implications of the resolutions and decisions adopted by the intergovernmental organs or international conferences since the adoption of the plan.

Regulation 3.12. The chapters of the proposed medium-term plan shall be reviewed by the relevant sectoral, functional and regional intergovernmental bodies, if possible during the regular cycle of their meetings prior to their review by the Committee for Programme and Coordination, the Economic and Social Council and the General Assembly. The Committee for Programme and Co-ordination and the Advisory Committee on Administrative and Budgetary Questions shall consider the proposed medium-term plan in accordance with their terms of reference.

Regulation 3.13. The participation of sectoral, functional and regional organs in the formulation of the plan shall be achieved by means of an appropriate preparation period. To that end, the Secretary-General shall provide proposals for the co-ordination of their calendars of meetings.

The activities in the medium-term plan shall be co-ordinated with those of the concerned specialized agencies through prior consultations.

Regulation 3.14. The General Assembly shall consider the proposed medium-term plan in the light of the comments and recommendations of the Economic and Social Council, the Committee for Programme and Co-ordination and the Advisory Committee on Administrative and Budgetary Questions. The Assembly shall decide to accept, curtail, reformulate or reject each of the subprogrammes proposed in the plan.

Regulation 3.15. The establishment of priorities among both substantive programmes and common services shall form an integral part of the general planning and management process without prejudice to arrangements and procedures now in force or to the specific character of servicing activities. Such priorities shall be based on the importance of the objective to Member States, the Organization's capacity to achieve it and the real effectiveness and usefulness of the results.

Regulation 3.16. Intergovernmental and expert bodies shall, when reviewing the relevant chapters of the proposed medium-term plan, recommend priorities among subprogrammes in their field of competence. They shall refrain from making recommendations on priority among major programmes. The Committee for Programme and Co-ordination, when making recommendations, and the Secretary-General, when making proposals on programme priorities, shall take into account the views of the above-mentioned bodies.

Regulation 3.17. On the basis of the Secretary-General's proposals and of the recommendations of the Committee for Programme and Co-ordination, the General Assembly shall designate, among the subprogrammes it accepts, those which are of the highest and lowest priority.

Regulation 3.18. Priorities as determined by the General Assembly in the medium-term plan shall guide the allocation of budgetary and extrabudgetary resources in the subsequent programme budgets. After the medium-term plan has been adopted by the Assembly, the Secretary-General shall bring the decisions on priorities to the attention of Member States and the governing boards of the voluntary funds.

Article 4
Programme aspects of the budget

Regulation 4.1. The medium-term plan as adopted and revised by the General Assembly shall serve as the framework for the formulation of the biennial programme budget. In order to facilitate this relationship, the programme budget shall have financial information corresponding to at least one of the three programming levels in the medium-term plan.

Regulation 4.2. The programme proposals in the budget shall aim at implementing the strategy in the plan and, therefore, shall be derived from its strategy statements. Programme proposals that are not derived from the plan strategies shall be submitted only as a result of legislation passed subsequent to the adoption of the plan or its last revision.

Regulation 4.3. In the proposed programme budget, requested resources shall be justified in terms of the requirements of output delivery. The highest-priority subprogrammes, as decided by the General Assembly, shall have first claim on resources, if budgetary needs are demonstrated, and, if possible, through redeployment in the event that low-priority activities are curtailed or terminated by intergovernmental decision.

Regulation 4.4. The proposed programme budget shall be divided into parts, sections and programmes. Programme narratives shall set out subprogrammes, programme elements, output and users. The proposed programme budget shall be preceded by a statement explaining the main changes made in the content of the programme and the volume of resources allocated to them in relation to the previous biennium and indicating the progress envisaged for all activities with time-limited objectives in implementing the plan. The proposed programme budget shall be accompanied by such information annexes and explanatory statements as may be requested by or on behalf of the General Assembly and such further annexes or statements as the Secretary-General may deem necessary and useful.

Regulation 4.5. All activities for which resources are requested in the proposed programme budget shall be programmed.

Regulation 4.6. Within the proposed programme budget the Secretary-General shall provide the General Assembly with:

(a) A list of programme elements and output included in the previous budgetary period which, in his judgement, can be discontinued and, as a consequence, have not been included in the proposed programme budget;

(b) An identification within each programme of programme elements of high and low priority, each category representing approximately 10 per cent of the resources requested.

Regulation 4.7. The Secretary-General shall provide the Committee for Programme and Co-ordination and the Advisory Committee on Administrative and Budgetary Questions with advance copies of the proposed programme budget by the end of April of the year preceding the budgetary period.

Regulation 4.8. The Committee for Programme and Co-ordination shall prepare a report on the proposed programme budget, containing its programme recommendations and its general assessment of the related resource proposals. It shall receive a statement by the Secretary-General on the programme budget implications of its recommendations. The report of the Committee for Programme and Co-ordination shall be communicated simultaneously to the Economic and Social Council and to the Advisory Committee on Administrative and Budgetary Questions. The Advisory Committee shall receive the report of the Committee for Programme and Co-ordination and study the statement by the Secretary-General. The reports of the Committee for Programme and Co-ordination and the Advisory Committee on each section of the proposed programme budget shall be considered simultaneously by the General Assembly.

Regulation 4.9. No Council, Commission or other competent body shall take a decision involving either a change in the programme budget approved by the General Assembly or the possible requirement of expenditure unless it has received and taken account of a report from the Secretary-General on the programme budget implications of the proposal.

Article 5
Monitoring of programme implementation

Regulation 5.1. The Secretary-General shall monitor the delivery of output scheduled in the approved programme budget through a central unit in the Secretariat. After the completion of the biennial budget period, the Secretary-General shall report to the General Assembly, through the Committee for Programme and Co-ordination, on programme performance during that period.

Regulation 5.2. An entire subprogramme shall not be reformulated nor a new programme introduced in the programme budget without the prior approval of an intergovernmental body and the General Assembly. The Secretary-General may make such proposals for review by the relevant intergovernmental body if he considers that circumstances so warrant.

Regulation 5.3. The Secretary-General shall transmit the biennial programme performance report to all Member States by the end of the first quarter following the completion of the biennial budget period.

Article 6
Evaluation

Regulation 6.1. The objective of evaluation is:

(a) To determine as systematically and objectively as possible the relevance, efficiency, effectiveness and impact of the Organization's activities in relation to their objectives;

(b) To enable the Secretariat and Member States to engage in systematic reflections, with a view to increasing the effectiveness of the main programmes of the Organization by altering their content and, if necessary, reviewing their objectives.

Regulation 6.2. All activities programmed shall be evaluated over a fixed time period. An evaluation programme as well as a timetable for intergovernmental review of evaluation studies shall be proposed by the Secretary-General and approved by the General Assembly at the same time as the proposed medium-term plan.

Regulation 6.3. Evaluation shall be internal and/or external. The Secretary-General shall develop internal evaluation systems and seek the co-operation of Member States in the evaluation process, as appropriate. Evaluation methods shall be adapted to the nature of the programme being evaluated. The General Assembly shall invite such bodies as it sees fit, including the Joint Inspection Unit, to perform *ad hoc* external evaluations and to report on them.

Regulation 6.4. The findings of intergovernmental review of evaluations shall be reflected in subsequent programme design, delivery and policy directives. To this end, a brief report summarizing the conclusions of the Secretary-General on all evaluation studies conducted in the established evaluation programme shall be submitted to the General Assembly at the same time as the text of the proposed medium-term plan.

Medium-term plan for 1984-1989

The medium-term plan for 1984-1989[6] covered the entire range of United Nations activities, both global and regional. It described those activities in 24 major programmes, or chapters covering a broad sectoral area, which themselves were broken down into numerous programmes and sub-programmes. The activities were designated to be carried out by various organizations within the United Nations system—the Secretariat, the regional commissions and United Nations agencies. The plan covered (a) political, legal and humanitarian, (b) public information and (c) economic and social sectors, providing the framework within which the United Nations programme budgets for the periods 1984-1985, 1986-1987 and 1988-1989 would be prepared.

In the introduction to the plan, the Secretary-General highlighted the policy orientations of the United Nations. He stated that the overriding task during the six years of the medium-term plan was to develop and strengthen the United Nations in a more systematic, orderly and efficient manner, so as to translate the purposes and principles of the Charter into reality. The various concrete programmes and activities would then fall into place as parts of a complex process towards a viable international order. Structured around objectives, the plan and its various programmes and subprogrammes were intended to show the strategies which should be followed if those objectives were to be achieved within the resources available.

United Nations political activities concerned with international peace and security, according to the Secretary-General, were bound to continue to focus on two problems—disarmament and the management of conflict. Increasing attention would have to be paid to the problems of nuclear proliferation and the extension of the arms race. United Nations peace-keeping operations and the good offices missions of the Secretary-General had been among the more innovative and fruitful contributions by the Organization in deterring conflict. The United Nations would continue to help develop and codify public international law and international trade law, as well as ensure that inhabitants of dependent territories were given the opportunity to excercise their right to self-determination. A major effort would have to be initiated to ensure world-wide public understanding of and support for its objectives.

The interrelated objectives in the humanitarian, economic and social sectors, as elaborated in the International Development Strategy for the Third United Nations Development Decade[11] (the 1980s), concerned improving the quality of life at the national level and, at the international level, involved a collective commitment to increased resource transfers, a more open trading environment and the creation of conditions which would facilitate and support domestic action. Based on the development objectives and specific policy measures outlined in the Strategy, the medium-term plan described future economic and social activities in the sectors of energy, environment,

food and agriculture, human settlements, industrial development, trade and development finance, natural resources, population, public administration, science and technology, social development and humanitarian aid (including disaster relief, human rights, international drug control and refugee aid), statistics, transnational corporations, and transport and communications.

In recognition of the importance the international community had attached to international trade as a driving force of development, the medium-term plan envisaged extensive activities in that sector, in such areas as manufactures, prevention of the spread of protectionism, development of rules governing restrictive business practices, and expansion of trade. Activities were also designed to assist developing countries to build up their industrial base within an integrated framework of national development. The alleviation of hunger would remain one of the international community's most urgent tasks.

Ensuring adequate financial resources for development efforts was likely to remain a major problem. Accordingly, several programmes would focus on: research and analysis concerning trends in financial flows, and measures to increase their volume; debt problems of developing countries; adequacy of balance-of-payments financing facilities; and the interrelationships between trade, development finance and the international monetary system. Technical co-operation was recognized as an important means in furthering development and therefore was a component of several major programmes.

As the medium-term plan provided the framework for the biennial programme budgets, no request would be made in those budgets for substantive activities that were not part of the plan without subsequent authorization by the General Assembly. The intention was to incorporate in the budgetary proposals reductions in and redeployments of resources for subprogrammes that the Assembly identified as of low priority, obsolete or of marginal usefulness. The plan had been drawn up under the assumption that the process of redeployment of resources would continue and that the real resources of the Organization would increase moderately over that period. Some increase would be indispensable in order for the Organization to carry out the proposed activities and those which were likely to be added by the Assembly. However, if the current financing trends continued, almost 50 per cent of the resources needed to carry out the plan would depend on extrabudgetary financing, for which no commitments had been made and which fluctuated considerably from year to year.

CPC action. The Committee for Programme and Co-ordination, at its April/May 1982 session, considered the proposed medium-term plan for 1984-1989. In its report to the Assembly,[8] CPC made numerous recommendations for changes in the plan, and recommended that it be reviewed by the Economic and Social Council and the Assembly, which would request the Secretary-General to make revisions.

The Committee proposed changes in almost all chapters of the plan, and suggested that future introductions should follow more closely the guidelines found in various Assembly resolutions. Other recommendations included a suggestion to revise the information on authorized Professional posts contained in each programme section on Secretariat organization to reflect the situation as at 1 January 1982, thereby indicating the comparative distribution of posts to the relevant units, the distribution between those funded from the regular budget and those funded from extrabudgetary resources, and, where appropriate, the sources of extrabudgetary funding. In general, CPC added and deleted only a few subprogrammes described in the plan. Many revisions, both substantive and drafting changes, were made refining the narrative descriptions of activities. Those descriptions included the legislative authority, objectives, problems addressed and strategy for each subprogramme.

Recognizing the lack of agreement on substantial portions of chapter 16 (international trade and development finance), CPC took note of, and transmitted through the Economic and Social Council to the Assembly, the chapter plan and the reports of intergovernmental bodies on its individual programmes. Unable also to reach a consensus on subprogramme 5 (participation of women in international affairs and strengthening of peace) of a programme on global development issues in chapter 21 (social development and humanitarian affairs), it followed the same procedure.

The Committee felt that it was not in a position to frame conclusions on the general orientation of chapter 15 (industrial development), and programmes 1 (policy co-ordination of the United Nations Industrial Development Organization (UNIDO)), 2 (industrial studies and research of UNIDO) and 6 (industrial development in Latin America) and subprogramme 4, on pre-investment activities, of programme 3 (UNIDO industrial operations), and remitted those sections to the Council. Chapter 20 (science and technology), programme 2 (transfer of technology—the United Nations Conference on Trade and Development (UNCTAD)), and chapter 24 (transport, communications and tourism), programme 2 (shipping— UNCTAD), were transmitted for decision to the Assembly through the Council.

Economic and Social Council action. After considering the proposed medium-term plan and

the CPC revisions, the Economic and Social Council, by a decision adopted without vote on 29 July,[1] recommended that the General Assembly adopt the proposed plan, incorporating the Council's proposed revisions and those recommended by CPC, taking into account the views expressed by Council members at the July session. The Council transmitted two programmes of the proposed plan to the Assembly for consideration in 1982: chapter 16, programme 5 (trade among countries having different economic and social systems—UNCTAD); and chapter 21, programme 1 (global social development issues—Department of International Economic and Social Affairs), subprogramme 5.

The Council's decision was based on a recommendation of the Third (Programme and Co-ordination) Committee, which had established an open-ended working group to conduct consultations on the proposed plan, under the chairmanship of a Vice Chairman. He introduced and orally revised a draft decision to which were annexed the group's proposed revisions to chapters 15, 16, 20 and 24. The changes to chapter 15 included new introductory paragraphs on the general orientation of industrial development. Numerous substantive and editorial changes were made to other paragraphs in that chapter, as well as to provisions of the other three chapters. The Committee approved the decision without vote on 28 July.

General Assembly action. By a resolution of 21 December on programme planning,[10] the General Assembly adopted the medium-term plan for 1984-1989 as revised by CPC and the Council, except for subprogramme 5 of programme 1 of chapter 21, which required further revision. The Assembly considered the medium-term plan, as adopted, to be the principal policy directive of the United Nations and requested the Secretary-General to publish it. The Assembly also requested him to make the necessary methodological improvements to the plan in the context of its first revision and in the light of the observations made by CPC and at the Council's July 1982 session, as well as views expressed during the Assembly's 1982 session.

The sponsors of the resolution in the Assembly's Fifth Committee had orally revised the section on the medium-term plan to delete words in paragraph 1 excepting programme 5 (trade among countries having different economic and social systems) from those adopted, and to add a reference in paragraph 4 to the observations made at the Council's July session.

In a note of 20 November,[7] the Fifth Committee Chairman recalled that on 24 September the Assembly had decided that each chapter of the proposed medium-term plan should be submitted to the appropriate Main Committee before being adopted as a whole by the Assembly. (In letters of 5 October to the Chairmen of the Special Political,[5] Second (Economic and Financial)[3] and Fourth[4] Committees, the Assembly President had reminded them that the Fifth Committee would be considering the plan in the near future, adding that comments from the Committees would be appreciated.) The Chairman's November note contained the replies that he had received to letters informing the Chairmen of the Assembly's decision. The First, Special Political and Sixth (Legal) Committees had no comments on the plan. The Chairman of the Third (Social, Humanitarian and Cultural) Committee reported that Nepal, the Philippines and Romania had expressed certain observations concerning the International Youth Year (1985), but he concluded that there were no views on the plan that could be submitted as the views of the Third Committee. The Fourth Committee forwarded a correction to a statement in the plan, requested by the Chairman of the Special Committee on the Situation with regard to the Implementation of the Declaration on the Granting of Independence to Colonial Countries and Peoples.

After considering the sections of the plan submitted to it, the Second Committee had approved, without vote, a draft decision[2] on 1 November recommending to the Fifth Committee the approval of those sections, incorporating the revisions recommended by CPC and those proposed by the Council, taking into account the views and reservations expressed by some members of the Second Committee. The text had been presented by a Committee Vice-Chairman on the basis of informal consultations. He accepted an oral amendment by Denmark, on behalf of the European Community members, to reword the last clause, by which the Committee would have taken into account the views expressed by the members of the Committee, to reflect that members had reservations on some parts of the medium-term plan; this was sub-amended by Jamaica to indicate that "some" members had expressed views and reservations.[9]

Decision (1982). [1]ESC: 1982/173, 29 July, text following.
Draft decision adopted. [2]GA 2nd Committee Vice-Chairman, A/C.2/37/L.16, as orally amended.
Letters. GA President, 5 Oct.: [3]A/C.2/37/L.12, [4]A/C.4/37/L.2, [5]A/SPC/37/L.2.
Medium-term plan. [6]A/37/6 & Corr.1 & Add.1.
Note. [7]GA 5th Committee Chairman, A/C.5/37/53.
Reports. [8]CPC, A/37/38; [9]GA 2nd Committee, A/37/679.
Resolution (1982). [10]GA: 37/234, sect. I, 21 Dec.
Resolution (prior). [11]35/56, annex, 5 Dec. 1980 (YUN 1980, p. 503).
Meeting records. ESC: E/1982/SR.50 (29 July). GA: 2nd Committee, A/C.2/37/SR.26 (1 Nov.).

Economic and Social Council decision 1982/173

Adopted without vote

Approved by Third Committee (E/1982/92) without vote, 28 July (meeting 17); draft by Vice-Chairman (E/1982/C.3/L.13), based on informal consultations and orally revised; agenda item 21.

Proposed medium-term plan for the period 1984-1989

At its 50th plenary meeting, on 29 July 1982, the Council decided:

(a) To transmit the following programmes of the proposed medium-term plan for the period 1984-1989 to the General Assembly at its thirty-seventh session for consideration:

(i) Chapter 16, programme 5;

(ii) Chapter 21, programme 1, subprogramme 5;

(b) To recommend that the General Assembly, at its thirty-seventh session, should adopt the proposed medium-term plan for the period 1984-1989, incorporating the revisions thereto recommended by the Committee for Programme and Co-ordination at its twenty-second session and the revisions proposed by the Council, taking into account the views expressed by members of the Council at the second regular session of 1982.

Regulations for programme planning and evaluation

The General Assembly, by a resolution of 21 December 1982,[6] adopted Regulations Governing Programme Planning, the Programme Aspects of the Budget, the Monitoring of Implementation and the Methods of Evaluation, as well as related changes to the Financial Regulations of the United Nations. The Assembly requested the Secretary-General: to issue rules for implementing the new Regulations; to improve programme monitoring; to report on procedures to provide the Assembly with programme implications, as well as administrative and financial implications of draft resolutions, and provide data on such implications for those currently being considered; to submit an evaluation programme and timetable for intergovernmental review of evaluation studies with the proposed 1984-1985 programme budget; to report on measures to integrate the programme planning, budgeting, monitoring and evaluation functions in the Secretariat; and to comment on the recommendations of the Joint Inspection Unit (JIU) on the planning, programming and evaluation regulations that had not yet been considered by CPC. The Assembly asked CPC to report on the need to amend planning and financial regulations in the light of the JIU recommendations, the Secretary-General's comments and the Fifth Committee's discussions.

The Regulations Governing Programme Planning were annexed to the resolution. The planning, programming, budgeting and evaluation cycle set out therein was to form an integral part of the general policy-making and management process of the United Nations. The system of programme planning was intended to ensure the accountability of the Secretariat for delivering the programmed activities and services and, in so doing, establish the standards against which their implementation could be judged. It was also designed to facilitate the evaluation of completed programmes against the objectives and work plans set out in the medium-term plan and the programme budget as reviewed and approved by intergovernmental bodies.

The Regulations were aimed at subjecting all United Nations activities, irrespective of their source of financing, to periodic reviews and evaluation, and at affording an opportunity for examination by all participants, especially Member States and the Secretariat, before choices on action were made. The process would allow assessment of what was feasible and politically acceptable to Member States as a whole, provide a framework for setting priorities among activities, and indicate required resources. In pursuing those aims, the Organization would use the following instruments: medium-term plans, which indicated orientations of United Nations activities and translated legislative mandates into programmes; programme budgets, by which requested resources were justified in terms of the requirements of delivery; programme performance reports, which monitored implementation through a central Secretariat unit; and evaluation reports, which reviewed achievements and allowed for formulation of subsequent plans. Those instruments would be used to ensure that activities were co-ordinated and that available resources were utilized most effectively according to legislative intent.

Before approval of the draft resolution in the Fifth Committee, the sponsors orally revised it. One revision pertained to the section by which the new Regulations were adopted: in paragraph 3, requesting the Secretary-General to issue rules in implementation of and in conformity with the Regulations, a phrase was added to have the rules also conform to the CPC recommendations at its April/May 1982 session.[2]

CPC had considered a report of the Secretary-General,[4] dated 27 April, containing the draft Regulations—the culmination of seven years of effort by CPC, JIU, its Inspector Maurice Bertrand, and the Secretariat. Once the Assembly had adopted them, the report said, the Secretary-General would propose rules for their implementation, as the Assembly had requested in 1981.[8] The report also proposed certain revisions to the Financial Regulations which covered closely related issues, and included references to legislative mandates on which the Regulations were based.

During its discussions, CPC, noting that the report contained only draft Regulations whereas the Assembly had requested both draft regulations and rules, stressed the importance of having the rules before it in order to determine whether or not additional material should be inserted.

As for the substance of the draft Regulations, CPC noted omissions relating to the specification of the functions of the monitoring unit called for by the Assembly in 1981, the procedures and methodology of evaluation, and the treatment of obsolete or marginally useful activities. Certain structural imbalances were identified. Imperfections in the current system were noted, such as little follow-up of the implementation of plans and programme budgets, once approved. After a

detailed review, CPC formulated revised Regulations for Assembly review and adoption, agreeing that the Assembly would have to examine them in the light of the rules to be provided by the Secretary-General later in the year and of a forthcoming report by JIU, requested by CPC, to assist the Assembly in its consideration of the question. CPC recommended that the Assembly consider, adjust as necessary, and adopt the draft Regulations together with the proposed revisions to the Financial Regulations. It asked the Secretary-General to submit to the Assembly in 1982 a comprehensive list of revisions to the Financial Rules and Regulations which might be required as a consequence of the restructuring of the economic and social sectors of the United Nations called for by the Assembly in 1977.[7]

In an addendum to his April report, dated 4 October, the Secretary-General put forward draft rules governing programme planning, budgeting, monitoring and evaluation—in implementation of the proposed new Regulations—as an aid to decisions on the Regulations. The rules were prepared after consultations with all programme managers in the Secretariat who would be responsible for their implementation. Changes suggested by JIU in September[3] (see below) had not been incorporated. The Programme Planning and Budgeting Board would be responsible for the administration of the rules, on behalf of the Secretary-General.

Under the draft rules, requests and directives to the Secretary-General contained in decisions of United Nations intergovernmental organs were to constitute legislative mandates for proposed activities. Regarding programme aspects of the budget, the proposed rules stated that financial information was to be provided in the proposed programme budget, and financial data as a rule would be linked to the medium-term plan at the programme level. Budget submissions to the Secretary-General were to provide data on resources required, such as professional work-months, travel, consultants and other relevant items of expenditure for use in formulating internal budgets. Heads of organizational units were to submit programme proposals and budget estimates in time for the Secretary-General to conclude a proposed programme budget by the end of April of the year preceding the budgetary period, and to identify elements considered obsolete, of marginal usefulness or ineffective which could be proposed for termination.

Monitoring of programme implementation, a responsibility of the Secretary-General, would be carried out by the Programme Planning and Budgeting Board. It would examine changes made during the biennium in the approved work programme, determine the actual delivery of final output in comparison with the commitments set out in the programme narratives of the budget, and report to the Assembly through CPC, based on biennial performance reports by heads of departments or offices. The evaluation system would include periodic self-evaluation of all activities. This process would be conducted by programme managers advised by a central evaluation unit and guided by a methodological manual. The evaluation system would provide for monitoring the follow-up of evaluation conclusions and recommendations.

In response to a May request of CPC, the Secretary-General submitted to the Assembly a report dated 27 October[5] concerning the Financial Rules and Regulations of the United Nations which might need to be revised in the light of the restructuring of economic and social sectors. He said the requested review of the Financial Regulations had been undertaken and this had raised two substantive issues: the status of the programme narratives in the budget, and the treatment of the programme aspects of supplementary proposals. Regarding the first, it was the Secretary-General's understanding that the adoption of the budget applied to the programme narratives as well. With respect to the second issue, treating supplementary proposals in a manner equivalent to initial budget proposals would entail a review by CPC during each Assembly session. The Secretary-General observed that he had instituted further changes in budget preparation procedures in 1982, and that the functions of the Programme Planning and Budgeting Board might require the revision of several financial rules. He intended to issue revisions as soon as practicable after the Assembly approved the revised Financial Regulations.

JIU, as requested by CPC, reported to the Assembly to assist it in its consideration of the draft Regulations Governing Programme Planning. Prepared by Mr. Bertrand, the report on the elaboration of regulations for the planning, programming and evaluation cycle was transmitted to the Assembly by a note of 20 September from the Secretary-General.[3] The draft Regulations taken into account were those which were amended by CPC. The author concluded that the current conception of the planning-programming-evaluation cycle had reached a considerable level of precision which required only a few touches and additions to provide the Organization with an instrument for constantly improving its effectiveness. However, the system was neither properly understood nor satisfactorily applied. It was therefore essential to examine how the draft Regulations could be revised in order to make them more readily applicable, and to consult those who were to apply the Regulations, informing them of the true objectives of the reforms and asking for their views.

In his view, the review of the Regulations needed to focus on three areas: (1) the distinction to be made between three different kinds of activity—support for negotiations, joint action on matters on which there was a certain degree of consensus among Member States, and administrative management; (2) adaptation of the evaluation exercises to those different kinds of activity and their integration into the timetable for the preparation of the medium-term plan; and (3) adaptation of the presentation of the medium-term plan for those three kinds of activity. Recommendations for amendments were made on specific paragraphs of the Regulations and suggestions offered for drafting rules supplementing the new Regulations.

After receiving the reports of JIU and the Secretary-General, the Advisory Committee on Administrative and Budgetary Questions (ACABQ) also submitted to the Assembly, on 26 November,[1] a report on the draft Regulations and rules governing programme planning and on the review of the Financial Rules and Regulations. ACABQ pointed out that one rule attempted to categorize United Nations activities by substantive services, common services and conference services, whereas previously conference services had always been considered a common service. It cautioned that if conference services were to be treated separately and reviewed by the Committee on Conferences, a similar procedure could be adopted for public information with respect to the Committee on Information. A draft regulation on the form of the proposed programme budget dealt with an area already regulated by a financial regulation and might better be cross-referenced; this also applied to a rule on decisions of bodies which involved expenditure or a change in the approved budget. ACABQ also felt that proposed procedures for reporting on budget implications of such proposed changes were too complicated and could result in delays.

Regarding the regulation stating that CPC would assess related resource proposals, ACABQ said it assumed that what was meant was that CPC would determine whether resources had been allocated in accordance with priorities, rather than determine the actual resources required for any particular programme, a function performed by ACABQ. As to the Secretary-General's understanding that the adoption of the programme budget by the Assembly applied to the programme narratives, ACABQ believed that this would lead to undesirable rigidities whereby all changes, including changes in the narratives, would require unnecessary legislative action.

Its observations made it clear to ACABQ that there were several areas where fundamental concepts had not been adequately translated into practical guidelines for action. The Office of Legal Affairs had found a number of difficulties with the draft regulations and rules involving ambiguity of terminology and lack of specificity with regard to what was being regulated. The Office had informed ACABQ that such shortcomings might be unavoidable because of the special nature of programme planning and the inherent limitations with regard to its legal regulation. ACABQ had also been informed that the new Regulations and rules would have limited impact on the 1984-1985 programme budget, already in an advanced stage of preparation.

Reports. [1]ACABQ, A/37/650; [2]CPC, A/37/38; [3]JIU, transmitted by S-G note, A/37/460; S-G, [4]A/37/206 & Add.1 & Add.1/Corr.1, [5]A/C.5/37/25.
Resolution (1982). [6]GA: 37/234, 21 Dec.
Resolutions (prior). GA: [7]32/197, 20 Dec. 1977 (YUN 1977, p. 438); [8]36/228 A, 18 Dec. 1981 (YUN 1981, p. 1308).

Programme priorities

At its April/May 1982 session,[4] CPC made recommendations on the review of the ongoing United Nations work programme. It recommended that the Assembly request the Secretary-General to issue an updated version of his 1981 report[10] on the topic, to be submitted to CPC with the proposed 1984-1985 programme budget in 1983. It urged him, when presenting any revised estimates in 1982, to point out any activities listed in his 1981 report which might be considered of low priority, as well as high-priority activities; similar reviews should become part of the regular budget preparation process.

CPC also requested the Secretary-General to establish, as soon as possible, the central monitoring unit the Assembly had called for in 1981,[8] recommending that it be entrusted with continuous programme review, ensuring independence, objectivity and effective accountability for the implementation of the United Nations work programme as a whole. The Secretariat was urged to ensure greater consistency in document presentation for the programme planning, budgeting and monitoring process, to facilitate CPC cross-referencing and comparative analysis and review.

In a report of 30 July,[2] ACABQ also commented on the Secretary-General's review of the ongoing work programme. As requested by the Assembly in 1981,[9] ACABQ reported on the administrative and financial implications of the Secretary-General's proposals, including those arising out of CPC recommendations on those proposals.

ACABQ agreed with CPC that the Secretary-General's report, which identified activities of low and high priority, needed updating and should be available to the Assembly in 1982. The updated report should indicate activities which the Secretary-General proposed to terminate on his authority, with an estimate of the resources involved, and activities, though of low priority, he felt should be continued. Regarding activities re-

quired by legislative mandates whose termination or curtailment called for intergovernmental-organ decisions, ACABQ recommended that the Secretary-General identify separately those he proposed for termination or curtailment, with an estimate of resources, and those he regarded as being of low priority, leaving Member States to propose termination or curtailment.

ACABQ suggested that if the updated review was to be referred to the competent Main Committees of the 1982 Assembly session, the General Committee would first have to determine the areas for immediate decision and those where views of intergovernmental organs would be sought.

In response to the ACABQ report, the Secretary-General submitted on 24 November an updated review of the ongoing work programme.[5] The annex listed 162 programme elements and activities which he had identified in the 1981 special review as being of low priority, each assigned to one of eight categories (A to H) according to priority. The largest group of low-priority activities (category E—37 per cent of the total) comprised activities which the Secretary-General could terminate but which he considered sufficiently useful to warrant continuation in their entirety; and the second largest group (category B—34 per cent of the total) were low-priority activities which he proposed to curtail, but not terminate. Action taken by the Secretary-General on his own authority had resulted in the redeployment of over $3.5 million from low-priority to high-priority activities, and a budgetary saving of $82,000.

ACABQ commented on the Secretary-General's updated review on 8 December.[3] While noting that there was no direct correlation between the number of programme elements to be terminated or curtailed and the volume of resources, it believed that a more critical approach by the Secretary-General to low-priority activities would have resulted in the release of substantially more resources for redeployment.

ACABQ had been informed that the resources related to activities in category D (required by legislative mandates but which the Secretary-General regarded as being of low priority) were estimated at $4 million a year. It suggested that the Fifth Committee could either request the Secretary-General, when preparing the programme budget, not to include resources for those activities and inform the competent intergovernmental organs of that action so they might reinstate them, if desired; or let CPC, at its early 1983 session, make recommendations to the Assembly on the programmatic aspects of those activities.

Regarding activities in categories B and E, ACABQ urged the Secretary-General, when preparing the 1984-1985 budget, to subject them to critical review, so that the maximum possible resources would be redeployed to activities of higher priority. It agreed that further *ad hoc* examinations of the ongoing work programme were not necessary; action on eliminating or curtailing obsolete, marginally useful or ineffective activities would be reported in the context of future programme budget proposals or performance reports.

The General Assembly, by a resolution of 21 December 1982,[6] endorsed the Secretary-General's decision to terminate or curtail, on his own authority, the activities so identified in his November report.[5] The Assembly requested him to refer category D activities to the competent intergovernmental organs for their views, if possible prior to Assembly consideration of the proposed 1984-1985 budget. The Assembly also requested the Secretary-General to report, in the introductions to that and subsequent budgets, on the steps he had taken and proposals he would make to terminate or curtail low-priority activities. The Secretary-General's report was transmitted to CPC for consideration during its budget examination so that it could make recommendations to the Assembly in 1983.

The resolution was adopted without vote, following approval by the Fifth Committee without objection on 15 December. The text was introduced by Canada, also on behalf of Japan, and orally revised by the sponsors. They deleted reference to reporting, in the introduction to future medium-term plans, on steps taken and intended to terminate or curtail obsolete activities, and added the words "if possible" to the request that views be submitted in time for Assembly consideration of the 1984-1985 budget. The request that the Secretary-General refer category D activities to the competent organs was substituted for one requesting him, when preparing his 1984-1985 budget proposals, not to include in them any resources for the activities in that category and to inform the competent intergovernmental organs so as to enable them, if they desired, to request that the activities be reinstated.

Panama also submitted a draft resolution,[1] by which the Assembly would have requested the Secretary-General to contribute further to trying to achieve a more balanced rationale on identification of completed, obsolete and marginally useful or ineffective activities, in compliance with a 1980 resolution.[7] In addition, the Assembly would have requested him to give high priority to and conclude certain activities—pertaining to four regional commissions and the United Nations Conference on Trade and Development—to include them in the next programme budget, and report in 1984. Panama withdrew the draft in favour of the two-nation text.

Draft resolution withdrawn. [1]Panama, A/C.5/37/L.47.
Reports. ACABQ [2]A/37/7/Add.1, [3]A/37/7/Add.14; [4]CPC, A/37/38; [5]S-G, A/C.5/37/51.
Resolution (1982). GA: [6]37/242, 21 Dec., text following.
Resolutions (prior). GA: [7]35/209, 17 Dec. 1980 (YUN 1980, p. 1209); [8]36/228 A, 18 Dec. 1981 (YUN 1981, p. 1308); [9]36/239, 18 Dec. 1981 (*ibid.*, p. 1310).
Yearbook reference. [10]1981, p. 1309.
Meeting records. GA: 5th Committee, A/C.5/37/SR.49, 62, 67, 68, *70, 72* (30 Nov.–15 Dec.); plenary, A/37/PV.114 (21 Dec.).

General Assembly resolution 37/242

21 December 1982   Meeting 114   Adopted without vote

Approved by Fifth Committee (A/37/790) without objection, 15 December (meeting 72); 2-nation draft (A/C.5/37/L.51), orally revised; agenda item 103.

Sponsors: Canada, Japan.

Special review of the ongoing work programme of the United Nations

The General Assembly,

Recalling its resolution 36/239 of 18 December 1981 on the special review of the ongoing work programme of the United Nations,

Having considered the reports of the Secretary-General and the related reports of the Advisory Committee on Administrative and Budgetary Questions as well as the report of the Committee for Programme and Co-ordination,

1. *Endorses* the decision of the Secretary-General to terminate or curtail the activities listed in categories A and B, as contained in his report;

2. *Requests* the Secretary-General to refer category D (activities which are required by legislative mandates but which the Secretary-General regards as being of a low priority and for the termination or curtailment of which he leaves it to the initiative of Member States to make proposals) to the competent intergovernmental organs for their views thereon, if possible prior to the consideration by the General Assembly of the proposed programme budget for the biennium 1984-1985;

3. *Requests* the Secretary-General to report, in the introduction to the proposed programme budget for the biennium 1984-1985 and those of subsequent bienniums, on the specific steps he has taken and decisions he intends to propose to the General Assembly to terminate or curtail activities of low priority;

4. *Decides* to transmit the report of the Secretary-General to the Committee for Programme and Co-ordination at its twenty-third session and to request that Committee to consider the report in the context of its examination of the programme aspects of the proposed programme budget for the biennium 1984-1985 and to make recommendations thereon to the General Assembly at its thirty-eighth session.

Programme evaluation

The General Assembly, by a resolution of 21 December 1982,[3] adopted Regulations Governing Programme Planning, the Programme Aspects of the Budget, the Monitoring of Implementation and the Methods of Evaluation. One of the articles contained Regulations on evaluating United Nations activities. The evaluation procedure, aimed at determining the relevance, efficiency, effectiveness and impact of the Organization's activities in relation to their objectives, was to be internal and/or external. The Secretary-General was to develop internal evaluation systems, adapting methods to the nature of the programme being evaluated. The Assembly could invite bodies it saw fit, including the Joint Inspection Unit (JIU), to perform *ad hoc* external evaluations. The findings of intergovernmental review of evaluations would be reflected in subsequent programme design, delivery and policy directives. A brief report summarizing the Secretary-General's conclusions on all evaluation studies would be submitted to the Assembly together with the medium-term plan.

The Secretary-General reported on 2 November[2] on major JIU recommendations on several topics which had not been implemented, and the reasons therefor. He stated that, in accordance with a 1981 JIU report on the status of internal evaluation in the organizations of the United Nations system,[4] the Evaluation Unit in the Department of International Economic and Social Affairs (DIESA), before the end of 1982, would be strengthened by another Professional post redeployed from elsewhere, and that the DIESA Unit and the Programme Analysis and Evaluation Unit of the Department of Administration and Management continued to collaborate on methodologies.

In implementation of a second 1981 JIU report on evaluation,[5] the Secretary-General reported that DIESA was developing concepts, methodologies and procedures to facilitate built-in evaluation in all activities and improve managerial capacity, was preparing an evaluation manual and guidelines relating to the decision-making process and standards for the conduct, content and process of evaluation, and was developing the design and methodology for studies on minerals and on technical assistance activities in manufactures to ensure they represented "true" evaluations and not merely assessments or reviews. CPC had instituted a new procedure whereby managers whose programmes might be affected by evaluation findings were asked to incorporate in their medium-term plan and budget drafts any changes arising therefrom, and had instituted biennial reviews of implementation (see below). Governments' views on particular programme outputs or activities were currently a basic feature of evaluation.

At its April/May 1982 session,[1] CPC had considered an evaluation of United Nations activities in the field of mineral resources for the period 1976-1979, as well as in-depth evaluation of the technical co-operation activities of the United Nations Industrial Development Organization in the field of manufactures.

With respect to the first, CPC recognized that deficiencies in the planning and design of programme-element output impaired and often precluded assessment of impact. It decided to give the matter particular attention in its forthcoming review of the 1984-1985 budget. It reaffirmed the need for greater precision in specifying programme-element output at the planning and budgeting levels, taking into account the necessary resource adjustments made during the budget

cycle and the uncertainty of extrabudgetary funds. To strengthen the evaluation function, CPC decided to establish triennial reviews of the implementation of its decisions on the basis of in-depth evaluation studies. It reiterated that a close relationship should be established between output producers and disseminators. It recognized that, in order to improve the quality of future evaluations, it would have to provide guidelines regarding the scope and coverage of the topic selected for evaluation.

On evaluation methodology, CPC recommended that the existing planning and design criteria be applied more rigorously to project and programme proposals submitted for approval. Noting the problem of ensuring that output reached targeted recipients, CPC recommended that the Secretariat specify, in programme planning, the appropriate type and quantity of output and intended end-users, and that the circulation of United Nations publications be expanded among policy-level officials and other end-users. It reiterated that a study of the document dissemination system should be made and submitted to it in 1984 by the Secretariat. Moreover, Governments should be invited to strengthen existing mechanisms for responding to requests for information for evaluation purposes, disseminating information to respondents and expediting replies. It also recommended that the evaluation report on mineral resources should be submitted to the Committee on Natural Resources.

Reports. [1]CPC, A/37/38; [2]S-G, A/C.5/37/28.
Resolution (1982). [3]GA: 37/234, annex, 21 Dec.
Yearbook references. 1981, [4]p. 1310, [5]p. 1311.

Joint Inspection Unit

The Joint Inspection Unit, composed of 11 Inspectors, drew up its 1982 work programme[8] taking into account requests and suggestions by participating organizations—the United Nations and its affiliated bodies, and 11 specialized agencies and the International Atomic Energy Agency. The World Intellectual Property Organization became a participating organization on 1 January 1982. The work programme included new and continued studies in five broad areas: restructuring of the economic and social sectors of the United Nations system, development co-operation, personnel policy, programme budgeting, and management questions. At the request of the General Assembly, the Inspectors included a study of the organization, budget and operations of the United Nations Relief and Works Agency for Palestine Refugees in the Near East, and, at the request of CPC, a report to aid the Assembly in its consideration of rules and regulations governing programme planning, the programme aspects of the budget and evaluation procedures (see above).

In April 1982, a JIU-arranged four-day informal inter-agency evaluation meeting, attended by evaluation specialists of participating organizations and representatives of other organizations, discussed, among other things, feedback of evaluation results, the relationship of evaluation to the management process, issues related to the United Nations Development Programme (UNDP), common problems of evaluation systems, and support for evaluation by legislative bodies and executive heads. Also in April, JIU discussed with the Advisory Committee on Administrative and Budgetary Questions (ACABQ) four JIU reports under preparation on subjects of concern to ACABQ. The JIU Chairman attended meetings in March of the International Civil Service Commission (ICSC), discussing studies that were being carried out by ICSC and JIU on career development in United Nations organizations (see Chapter III of this section).

In 1982, JIU issued 11 reports. (They are discussed in the relevant chapters of this volume.) Nine of them concerned management and administration: equitable geographical distribution of United Nations Secretariat staff; organization and procedures for preparation of United Nations special conferences; the career concept; status of women in the Professional category and above; communications in the United Nations system; official travel; use of consultants and experts in the United Nations; and elaboration of regulations on the planning, programming and evaluation cycle. The ninth report, on equitable geographical distribution of the secretariat staff of the United Nations Educational, Scientific and Cultural Organization, was sent for action in December to the Director-General of that organization.

Two reports dealt with substantive regional activities: the Economic Commission for Africa—regional programming, operations, restructuring and decentralization issues; and the contribution of the United Nations to the conservation and management of the Latin American cultural and natural heritage. JIU summarized and made recommendations and comments on reports it had concluded before July 1982 in its report on its activities during the period 1 July 1981 to 30 June 1982.[2] Information on reports concluded during the second half of 1982 was contained in the subsequent annual report.[3]

JIU completed several reports in 1981 which were considered by various United Nations bodies in 1982. A report on co-ordination of public information activities within the United Nations system was considered by the Administrative Committee on Co-ordination.[9] The Governing Council of UNDP considered three 1981 JIU reports, the one on co-ordination of public information activities, and two on the status of internal evaluation of United Nations organizations.[12] The General Assembly con-

sidered a JIU report on the United Nations University.

In his annual report on implementation of JIU recommendations, submitted to the Fifth (Administrative and Budgetary) Committee in November 1982,[4] the Secretary-General remarked on the status of implementation of JIU proposals, which had not been completely carried out, contained in eight 1981 reports on: subregional offices for Central America and Panama and for the Caribbean of the Economic Commission for Latin America;[10] methods of determining staff requirements;[13] status of internal evaluation in United Nations organizations (two reports);[12] co-ordination of public information activities within the United Nations system;[9] management services in the system;[15] building construction procedures of United Nations organizations;[14] and relationships between the Director-General for Development and International Economic Co-operation and entities of the Secretariat.[11]

The above reports are discussed in the relevant chapters elsewhere in this volume.

The General Assembly, in a resolution of 17 December 1982,[5] noted with appreciation the JIU annual report, and welcomed the intention of JIU to undertake an assessment of its own work, including methods of increasing the effectiveness of its recommendations, and to make proposals for improving the process whereby the intergovernmental organs took decisions on those recommendations. It reiterated its 1972 request[6] that the Secretary-General submit an annual report on JIU recommendations which had not been implemented, as well as its 1977 decision[7] that those reports should provide information only on JIU reports determined to be of interest to the Assembly, its Main Committees or other subsidiary organs. The Assembly requested the Secretary-General, when submitting comments on JIU reports, to include summaries indicating which JIU recommendations should or should not be implemented.

The Assembly adopted the resolution without vote, following approval without objection by the Fifth Committee on 30 November. Barbados, on behalf also of Guyana and Panama, had introduced and revised the text.

Also on 17 December,[1] the Assembly decided that JIU members be given the option of membership in the United Nations Joint Staff Pension Fund, despite the fact that they were not staff members.

Decision (1982). [1]GA: 37/429, 17 Dec.
Reports. JIU, [2]A/37/34, [3]A/38/34; [4]S-G, A/C.5/37/28.
Resolution (1982). [5]GA: 37/124, 17 Dec., text following.
Resolutions (prior). GA: [6]2924 B (XXVII), 24 Nov. 1972 (YUN 1972, p. 733); [7]32/199, 21 Dec. 1977 (YUN 1977, p. 1053).
Work programme. [8]JIU, transmitted by S-G note, A/37/103.
Yearbook references. 1981, [9]p. 370, [10]p. 668, [11]p. 1093, [12]p. 1310, [13]p. 1362, [14]p. 1372, [15]p. 1378.
Meeting records. GA: 5th Committee, A/C.5/37/SR.*25*, 26-28, 30, 32, 38, 39, *49* (3-30 Nov.); plenary, A/37/PV.109 (17 Dec.).

General Assembly resolution 37/124
17 December 1982   Meeting 109   Adopted without vote

Approved by Fifth Committee (A/37/767) without objection, 30 November (meeting 49); 3-nation draft (A/C.5/37/L.25/Rev.1), orally revised; agenda item 107.

Sponsors: Barbados, Guyana, Panama.

Joint Inspection Unit

The General Assembly,

Having considered the report of the Joint Inspection Unit on its activities during the period 1 July 1981 to 30 June 1982, the work programme of the Joint Inspection Unit for 1982 and the report of the Secretary-General on the implementation of the recommendations of the Joint Inspection Unit,

1. *Notes with appreciation* the report of the Joint Inspection Unit;

2. *Welcomes* the intention of the Joint Inspection Unit to undertake an assessment of its own work, including methods of increasing the effectiveness of its recommendations, and to make proposals for improving the process whereby the intergovernmental organs take decisions on those recommendations;

3. *Reiterates* the request made in paragraph 7 of its resolution 2924 B (XXVII) of 24 November 1972 and the decision contained in the operative part of its resolution 32/199 of 21 December 1977;

4. *Requests* the Secretary-General, when submitting comments on reports of the Joint Inspection Unit, to include summaries indicating which recommendations of the Unit should or should not be implemented, in accordance with General Assembly decision 36/454 of 18 December 1981.

Programme performance, 1980-1981

The Secretary-General submitted to the General Assembly in March 1982 a report on the programme performance of the United Nations for the biennium 1980-1981,[2] in accordance with a 1978 Assembly resolution calling for the monitoring of programme performance and for improving identification of output in the programme budget.[3] The second exercise of this type, the report used as a frame of reference the text of the proposed programme budget for 1980-1981, incorporating recommendations by CPC and ACABQ made after considering the first programme performance report for 1978-1979, including a greater degree of precision and homogeneity in the programme narratives (i.e., descriptions of programme elements and outputs).

The report included tables completed by the 26 submitting units, giving a comprehensive picture in terms of the number of outputs produced in the biennium for each programme within a department or equivalent organizational unit. The tables indicated the number of activities: as programmed in the 1980-1981 budget; implemented as programmed; reformulated but executed; postponed; terminated; and implemented although not originally programmed. Explanations were given for all departures from programme commitments. The report was described as transitional, since a codification of output descriptions in the programme budget was introduced only in the 1982-1983 budget.

Two options were put forward in the report for the timing of future programme performance reports: to continue the current practice of issuing the report in the first quarter of the year following the biennium; or to issue the report in the third quarter of the biennium so that it could be considered during the Assembly debate on the proposed programme for the subsequent biennium. The second option would necessitate a supplemental report in the first quarter after the biennium, but would afford the possibility of taking account of the performance during the current biennium in the debate on allocations for the biennium under consideration.

CPC, at its April/May 1982 session,[1] pointed to the need in such reports, for: quantitative information, which should be supported by information on the resource situation in each programme; pre-costing of activities at the programme-element level in the proposed budget; information on both regular and extrabudgetary resources; and data on administrative and common services.

The Committee called for the establishment of a central programme monitoring unit which would monitor the delivery of output as described in the programme narratives, and which would prepare a report for submission to the Assembly, through CPC, on programme implementation for the United Nations as a whole. Two additional output areas needed to be presented more clearly: output specifically required by a legislative decision subsequent to the formulation or approval of a programme budget; and output added at the discretion of the programme manager. The low implementation rates by some of the regional commissions in several areas, such as natural resources, energy, industrial development, and science and technology, should be thoroughly explained, including resource constraints, staffing problems and overprogramming. Possibilities of underprogramming, overfinancing and overstaffing should not be overlooked in cases of high implementation rates.

Future programme performance reports should contain more precise information regarding the termination of planned output and the disposal of the resources thus released, as well as output carried over to the next biennium. The number of high-priority and low-priority outputs should be indicated in the tables, for each category of output implementation. CPC welcomed the involvement of the Internal Audit Division in the monitoring of programme performance.

Reports. [1]CPC, A/37/38; [2]S-G, A/37/154 & Corr.1,2.
Resolution. [3]GA: 33/118, 19 Dec. 1978 (YUN 1978, p. 1031).

Administrative and budgetary co-ordination in the UN system

In October 1982, ACABQ issued its annual report[1] reviewing and comparing the finances of the following organizations whose agreements with the United Nations provided for a review by the General Assembly: the International Labour Organisation

(ILO), the Food and Agriculture Organization of the United Nations (FAO), the United Nations Educational, Scientific and Cultural Organization (UNESCO), the World Health Organization (WHO), the International Civil Aviation Organization (ICAO), the Universal Postal Union (UPU), the International Telecommunication Union (ITU), the World Meteorological Organization (WMO), the International Maritime Organization (IMO), the World Intellectual Property Organization (WIPO), the International Fund for Agricultural Development (IFAD) and the International Atomic Energy Agency (IAEA).

According to the 1983 budget figures given in the report, the regular budgets of those organizations, excluding IFAD, would amount to $1.6 billion, of which $1.5 billion would be covered by assessed contributions. Those figures were essentially the same as those for 1982. The number of established posts authorized or requested under the regular budgets of the United Nations, the specialized agencies (excluding IFAD) and IAEA for 1983 totalled 24,099 (of which 11,580 were United Nations staff). The total number of participants in the United Nations Joint Staff Pension Fund, which covered all staff members with contracts of at least one year, was 42,490 as at 31 December 1981.

The total of contributions outstanding, to the United Nations, the specialized agencies and IAEA, as at 30 September 1982, was $839,272,000; that figure compared with $713,617,000 a year earlier. The total outstanding as at that date equalled 55.7 per cent of total net contributions of member States actually payable in respect of 1982. In their meetings with ACABQ, representatives of the organizations voiced concern at the impact of the delays in the receipt of contributions on the cash flow in their organizations.

The General Assembly, by a resolution of 17 December,[3] noted with appreciation the ACABQ report, which it referred to the organizations concerned along with the comments made in the Assembly's Fifth (Administrative and Budgetary) Committee. The Assembly requested the Secretary-General to refer to the executive heads of the United Nations organizations, through the Administrative Committee on Co-ordination (ACC), matters arising out of the ACABQ report and the related debate in the Fifth Committee that called for their attention and action. The Assembly transmitted the ACABQ report to the Board of Auditors, the Panel of External Auditors, CPC, the International Civil Service Commission and the Joint Inspection Unit for their information. It requested the Secretary-General to consult with United Nations organizations on identifying obsolete or ineffective programmes that might result in the release of resources for financing new ac-

tivities. It drew the attention of Member States to the problems resulting from delays in payments, and invited United Nations organizations to encourage them to make timely payments.

The Assembly adopted the resolution without vote; the Fifth Committee had approved the text without objection on 29 November. The draft, introduced by Barbados on behalf also of Australia, Cuba and Sweden, was orally revised by the sponsors to delete a preambular paragraph recalling a November 1982 resolution on the financial emergency of the United Nations.[2]

Two other Assembly resolutions were adopted on 17 December to strengthen administrative and budgetary co-ordination in the United Nations system. By one,[5] the Assembly requested a study on the impact of inflation and monetary instability on the United Nations budget; by the other,[4] it requested continuation of consultations on the statutes, rules and practices of the Administrative Tribunals of ILO and the United Nations.

Report. [1]ACABQ, A/37/547 & Corr.1.
Resolutions (1982). GA: [2]37/13, 16 Nov.; [3]37/128, 17 Dec., text following; [4]37/129, 17 Dec.; [5]37/130, 17 Dec.
Meeting records. GA: 5th Committee, A/C.5/37/SR.13, 27, 36, 39, 42, *46, 47* (15 Oct. & 5-29 Nov.); plenary, A/37/PV.109 (17 Dec.).

General Assembly resolution 37/128

17 December 1982   Meeting 109   Adopted without vote

Approved by Fifth Committee (A/37/766 and Corr.1) without objection, 29 November (meeting 47); 4-nation draft (A/C.5/37/L.28), orally revised; agenda item 106 (a).

Sponsors: Australia, Barbados, Cuba, Sweden.

Administrative and budgetary co-ordination of the United Nations with the specialized agencies and the International Atomic Energy Agency

The General Assembly,

Concerned at the need for effective administrative and budgetary co-ordination within the framework of the United Nations system,

Recalling its decision of 15 December 1975 to consider in depth the item entitled "Administrative and budgetary co-ordination of the United Nations with the specialized agencies and the International Atomic Energy Agency" normally in off-budget years,

Recalling also its resolutions 33/142 A of 20 December 1978, 35/114 of 10 December 1980 and 36/229 of 18 December 1981,

1. *Notes with appreciation* the report of the Advisory Committee on Administrative and Budgetary Questions on the administrative and budgetary co-ordination of the United Nations with the specialized agencies and the International Atomic Energy Agency;

2. *Refers* to the organizations concerned the report of the Advisory Committee as well as the comments and observations made in the course of its consideration in the Fifth Committee;

3. *Requests* the Secretary-General to refer to the executive heads of the organizations of the United Nations system, through the Administrative Committee on Co-ordination, matters arising out of the report of the Advisory Committee and of the related debate in the Fifth Committee that call for their attention and necessary action;

4. *Transmits* the report of the Advisory Committee to the Board of Auditors, the Panel of External Auditors, the Committee for Programme and Co-ordination, the International Civil Service Commission and the Joint Inspection Unit for their information;

5. *Requests* the Secretary-General to consult with the executive heads of the organizations of the United Nations system on experience gained in identifying programmes that are obsolete, ineffective or of marginal usefulness that might result in the release of resources for financing new programmes and other types of activities;

6. *Invites* legislative organs of the specialized agencies, of the International Atomic Energy Agency and of other organizations in the United Nations system to continue their efforts towards the achievement of more effective and economical use of the resources of the organizations;

7. *Draws the attention* of States Members of the United Nations or members of specialized agencies or the International Atomic Energy Agency to the serious problems being encountered as a result of delays in payments of contributions;

8. *Invites* the legislative organs of the specialized agencies, of the International Atomic Energy Agency and of other organizations in the United Nations system to encourage Member States to make timely payments to the budgets of those organizations;

9. *Requests* the Secretary-General and the executive heads of those organizations to transmit to Member States relevant extracts of the present resolution when notifying them in connection with their contributions.

Expenditure in relation to programmes

In June 1982, ACC issued its biennial report on expenditures of the United Nations system in relation to programmes.[3] The report, submitted to the Economic and Social Council, was based on an interorganization classification of programmes developed by ACC in consultation with individual Governments and other interested parties. Presented for the most part in tables, data showed expenditures of regular budget and extrabudgetary funds for 1980 and 1981 and estimated expenditures of those funds for 1982 and 1983. Where approved expenditure estimates were not available for 1983, figures were based on projections.

The organizations represented in the report were the United Nations, the United Nations Children's Fund, the United Nations Development Programme, the World Food Programme, the United Nations Relief and Works Agency for Palestine Refugees in the Near East, the United Nations Fund for Population Activities, ILO, FAO, UNESCO, WHO, ICAO, UPU, ITU, WMO, IMO, WIPO and IAEA.

The report comprised four types of tables: total expenditures of all the organizations considered, by biennium and main source of funds; total expenditures of those organizations, by biennium and main source of funds and by sector of the interorganization classification of programmes; total expenditures of the organizations, by organization and by sector, for all sources of funds; and expenditures by organization and by subsector and biennium, for all sources of funds. In order to present a full picture of the expenditures involved for the various programme sectors and subsectors, the cost of non-substantive work, such as the organizations' management and support activities, was distributed to programme headings. Expenditures for policy-making organs, on the other hand, were shown separately.

The estimated 1982-1983 expenditure of the United Nations was $3,276.4 million, of which $1,515.7 million came from regular budget funds and $1,760.7 million from extrabudgetary funds. The total figure represented an increase of 17.5 per cent over 1980-1981. The total expenditure projected for 1982-1983 for all the organizations listed (including the United Nations) was $10,125.9 million, a 15.9 per cent increase over 1980-1981. Of that amount, $3,527.7 million came from regular budget funds and $6,598.2 million from extrabudgetary funds. The sectors for which 1982-1983 projected expenditures were greatest were, in descending order: health ($1,587.4 million); agriculture, forestry and fisheries ($1,308.2 million); humanitarian aid and relief ($1,261.5 million); and political affairs ($873.5 million).

The Third (Programme and Co-ordination) Committee of the Economic and Social Council, on 23 July, approved without vote a recommendation proposed by the Chairman that the Council consider the ACC report at its resumed second regular session of 1982; the Council adopted it without vote on 28 July.[1] At the resumed session, on 27 October,[2] the Council, on an oral proposal by its President, took note without vote of the report.

Decisions (1982). ESC: [1]1982/167, 28 July, text following; [2]1982/186, 27 Oct., text following.
Report. [3]ACC, E/1982/87.
Meeting records. ESC: E/1982/SR.49, 54 (28 July, 27 Oct.).

Economic and Social Council decision 1982/167

Adopted without vote

Approved by Third Committee (E/1982/91) without vote, 23 July (meeting 16); draft by Chairman (E/1982/C.3/L.11); agenda item 20.

Report of the Administrative Committee on Co-ordination on expenditures of the United Nations system in relation to programmes

At its 49th plenary meeting, on 28 July 1982, the Council decided to consider the report of the Administrative Committee on Co-ordination on expenditures of the United Nations system in relation to programmes at its resumed second regular session of 1982.

Economic and Social Council decision 1982/186

Adopted without vote

Oral proposal by President; agenda item 20.

Report of the Administrative Committee on Co-ordination on expenditures of the United Nations system in relation to programmes

At its 54th plenary meeting, on 27 October 1982, the Council took note of the report of the Administrative Committee on Co-ordination on expenditures of the United Nations system in relation to programmes.

Chapter III

United Nations officials

Contents

For resolutions and decisions of major organs mentioned but not reproduced, refer to INDEX OF RESOLUTIONS AND DECISIONS.

Composition of the Secretariat

The Secretary-General, in his annual report on the composition of the Secretariat, submitted to the General Assembly in September 1982,[1] described progress in the attainment of the objectives set by the Assembly for a more equitable distribution of staff in the Professional category by nationality and region, by sex and by types of appointment.

The report showed that, as at 30 June, the total number of staff in the United Nations Secretariat was 16,155, as compared with 15,318 a year earlier. This figure included all staff members financed from both the regular budget and extrabudgetary sources with appointments for a year or more, covering staff in the Professional and higher categories, technical co-operation project personnel, and General Service personnel and those in related categories. In addition, staff assigned to the secretariats of other United Nations organs numbered: United Nations Development Programme, 5,580; Office of the United Nations High Commissioner for Refugees, 1,268; United Nations Children's Fund, 2,676; United Nations Institute for Training and Research, 51; United Nations Relief and Works Agency for Palestine Refugees in the Near East, 93 (UNRWA also had 16,777 area personnel paid from voluntary funds); International Trade Centre, 272; International Civil Service Commission, 42; International Court of Justice, 33; and United Nations University, 97. The overall total of staff members was 26,267, excluding area personnel of UNRWA.

Report. [1]S-G, A/37/143.

Geographical distribution

Report of the Secretary-General. In his 1982 annual report on the composition of the United Nations Secretariat,[3] the Secretary-General described the distribution of staff by nationality and by region in posts subject to geographical distribution. The system of desirable ranges of posts for Member States—showing how many Professionals and higher-level posts should ideally be held by nationals of a Member State—established by the General Assembly in 1980[6] as a guideline for the geographical distribution of staff, applied to these posts. Secretariat staff in posts defined as subject to geographical distribution were in the Professional category and above holding appointments for one year or more. Excluded from that group were those in posts with special language requirements (mainly translators and interpreters); staff appointed for mission service; staff serving with the United Nations Environment Programme; staff appointed to posts financed on an inter-agency basis; technical co-operation project personnel; staff of the secretariats of United Nations organs with special appointment procedures; staff who had permanent resident status in, but not the nationality of, the country of their duty station; and staff in the General Service and related categories.

The representation of each Member State in Secretariat posts subject to geographical distribution was compared with the desirable range and the related mid-point for that State. At the beginning of the reporting year, on 30 June 1981, there were 19 Member States that were not represented by any of their nationals in geographical posts; by 30 June 1982, there were 17 unrepresented Member States (Albania, Bahrain, Djibouti, Equatorial Guinea, Gabon, Guinea-Bissau, Kuwait, Maldives, Mongolia, Papua New Guinea, Qatar, Saint Lucia, Samoa, Sao Tome and Principe, Solomon Islands, Suriname, Vanuatu).

At the beginning of the reporting year, 26 Member States were underrepresented (those whose nationals in geographical posts numbered fewer than the lower limit of their desirable range); a year later, there were 24 (Antigua and Barbuda, Bhutan, Cape Verde, Central African Republic, Czechoslovakia, Dominica, German Democratic Republic, Federal Republic of Germany, Israel, Ivory Coast, Japan, Luxembourg, Mozambique, Norway, Oman, Saint Vincent and the Grenadines, Saudi Arabia, Seychelles, Spain, Swaziland, Ukrainian SSR, USSR, United Arab Emirates, Venezuela).

Of the 2,995 staff members in geographical posts as at 30 June 1982, 682 were from Western Europe, 638 from North America and the Caribbean, 494 from Asia and the Pacific, 439 from Africa, 312 from Eastern Europe, 248 from Latin America, and 145 from the Middle East. There were 37 others, including stateless persons.

The report showed the distribution of staff in geographical posts in four groups: developed market economies (48.5 per cent); developing countries in Africa, Asia and the Middle East (30.7 per cent); developing countries of Latin America and the Caribbean (10.8 per cent); and socialist countries of Eastern Europe (10 per cent). The 10 socialist countries occupied fewer geographic posts than the lower limit of the group's combined desirable range, as had been the case for the previous four years.

JIU report. Three members of the Joint Inspection Unit (JIU) prepared an addendum[1] to their 1981 report[7] on the application of the principle of equitable geographical distribution of the staff of the Secretariat. The authors, Alexander S. Bryntsev, Joseph Adolph Sawe and Zakaria Sibahi, updated information on their own recommendations and commented on the Secretary-General's follow-up remarks[7] on the 1981 report.

Despite some progress in a more equitable distribution of staff, they said there was little evidence of measurable improvement or that the predominance of nationals from a certain group of developed countries had been eliminated. The report gave the number and percentage of Professional staff in 11 departments, in three categories—those from 25 developed countries, from 118 developing countries and from 11 Eastern European countries—as at 30 June 1981. The group of developed market-economy countries had a clear predominance in those departments both in the total number of Professional-and-above staff and in the number of heads of sections. In the Inspectors' view, the major obstacle to equitable geographical distribution of posts was the reluctance of some high officials to consider the necessity of recruiting candidates from unrepresented and underrepresented countries and the principle should be applied not only to the Secretariat as a whole but to each entity of the Organization, except the regional commissions, in which a maximum of 75 per cent of the staff might be from the region.

The Inspectors believed that the "flexibility" exercised in recruiting "on as wide a geographical basis as possible" should not be unlimited. The emphasis on the "efficiency" of the candidates as against equitable geographical distribution, used to explain why some Member States were unrepresented or underrepresented, was, in their opinion, unwarranted and in fact discriminatory in regard to candidates from those countries.

The Inspectors commented that the data for the period from 30 June to 31 December 1981 indicated that the changes (appointments and separations) in the composition of the Secretariat had no significant bearing on the equitable geographical distribution of the staff. At the current rate of change, it would take four years for unrepresented and underrepresented countries to reach their minimum desirable ranges and nine years to reach mid-point. Therefore, the Inspectors recommended again that special efforts be made to recruit staff from those countries.

Reiterating their recommendation to reduce the number of permanent appointments (currently about two thirds of the Professional-and-above staff), they suggested that in future the majority of Secretariat staff in geographical posts should have fixed-term appointments.

The Inspectors again drew attention to their proposal for the introduction of a new type of interruptible (rotation) fixed-term contract, involving periodic secondment of staff for four to six years from national organizations, with similar intervals between secondments.

They said that misinterpretation of their recommendation that vacancy announcements be issued simultaneously for internal and external candidates had led to an excessive slant towards filling vacant posts by internal reassignments. Figures showed that, as at 30 June 1981, only one third of all staff subject to geographical distribution were recruited from outside, while two thirds were promoted; at the P-4, P-5 and D-1 levels, the percentage of staff promoted accounted for about 75 per cent.

In conclusion, the report said that the data indicated that there had been no significant change either in the quantitative or qualitative distribution of the staff over the previous year. The principle of geographical distribution had not been fully observed in many departments and offices. The Secretariat had not eliminated factors previously described by the Inspectors as hindering the application of that principle—appointment of nationals from overrepresented countries, extensive use of permanent contracts, filling vacancies preferably by internal reassignments, and deficiencies in geographical distribution of staff in senior posts. In order to achieve equitable geographical distribution quickly, the Inspectors said mandatory measures were needed, and they reaffirmed their recommendations made in the 1981 report as a basis for a true solution.

Commenting in October on the JIU report,[2] the Secretary-General said that 90 Member States (57.3 per cent) were within their desirable range, an increase of 11 for the year ending 30 June 1982 and of 40 over the previous five years. During the five-year period, 30 Member States that were overrepresented had come within their desirable range, only 26 (16.6 per cent) were still overrepresented, the number of unrepresented Member States dropped from 23 to 17, staff from developing countries increased from 37.8 per cent to 41.5 per cent, and nationals from developing countries at the senior and policy-making levels (D-1 and above) increased from 40 to 48.2 per cent.

The Secretary-General stated that the one area of disagreement was on whether specific targets of geographical distribution should be applied only for the Secretariat as a whole or for each unit. He reaffirmed his view that the application of numerical targets within each organizational unit was inappropriate, as it would hinder mobility, career development and the exercise of his responsibilities, and might hinder progress towards improved geographical distribution in the Secretariat as a whole. Regarding specific targets for recruiting staff from unrepresented and underrepresented countries, the Secretary-General said the 40 per cent target established by the Assembly had been achieved.

The Secretary-General reiterated his belief that the determination of the proper ratio between fixed-term and permanent contracts must relate primarily to operational needs; establishment of any particular percentage would limit his ability to offer the type of appointment most in the interest of the Organization in the individual circumstances. Commenting on the proposals for a new type of interruptible fixed-term contract, he said that, as an initial step, the Staff Rules had been amended to permit recognition of the seniority in grade of seconded officials during a previous period of service to be counted towards their eligibility for promotion during a subsequent period of service. He pointed out that the practice of promoting staff with experience of the Organization was a normal exercise of personnel administration. Regarding geographical distribution of staff in senior and policy-formulating posts, he observed that, apart from the region of North America and the Caribbean, the situation at those levels compared with the mid-point of the desirable range of each region continued to improve.

He believed that steady progress had been made in both the quantitative and qualitative distribution of staff over the past five years. His objective would continue to be an efficient and effective Secretariat representing all Member States and geographically distributed in a way that was considered equitable by them.

The Secretariat staff unions and associations expressed their view on the JIU recommendation on rotating staff between the Secretariat and governmental ministries or organizations in a report submitted to the Fifth (Administrative and Budgetary) Committee in October through the Secretary-General.[4] In their opinion, this would destroy the impartiality, integrity, independence, competence and ability to function of the international civil service. Therefore, they rejected the plan and urged the Committee to do likewise.

General Assembly action. In a resolution of 21 December,[5] the General Assembly reaffirmed the principles and procedures it had set out in 1980[6] for recruiting staff for Secretariat posts subject to geographical distribution. It stressed the importance of having the largest possible number of Member States represented at the higher levels of the Secretariat (D-2 and above). The Assembly welcomed the Secretary-General's intention to monitor progress in applying the principle of wide geographical representation in departments and main offices, and asked him to include in his annual reports on the composition of the Secretariat information on progress in improving geographical distribution in the Secretariat, particularly at the higher levels. It welcomed his intention to develop and apply a medium-term plan of recruitment in order to bring the number of staff from unrepresented and underrepresented countries within their desirable ranges by 1985, and a

medium-term plan for career development, asking him to report in 1984 on progress on all aspects of personnel policy reform.

The Assembly adopted the resolution without vote; the Fifth Committee had approved the text by consensus on 11 December. The text was introduced by a Committee Vice-Chairman following informal consultations.

Reports. [1]JIU, transmitted by S-G note, A/37/378, and [2]S-G comments, Add.1 & Add.1/Corr.1; [3]S-G, A/37/143; [4]Staff unions and associations, transmitted by S-G note, A/C.5/37/24.
Resolution (1982). [5]GA: 37/235 A, 21 Dec., text following.
Resolution (prior). GA: [6]35/210, 17 Dec. 1980 (YUN 1980, p. 1164).
Yearbook reference. [7]1981, p. 1318.
Meeting records. GA: 5th Committee, A/C.5/37/SR.13, 23, 25-34, 36-38, 40, 41, 43, 47, *63, 65* (15 Oct. & 1 Nov.–11 Dec.); plenary, A/37/PV.114 (21 Dec.).

General Assembly resolution 37/235 A

21 December 1982   Meeting 114   Adopted without vote

Approved by Fifth Committee (A/37/764) by consensus, 11 December (meeting 65); draft by Vice-Chairman (A/C.5/37/L.30), based on informal consultations; agenda item 111.

The General Assembly,

Recalling its resolutions 33/143 of 20 December 1978 and 35/210 of 17 December 1980 on personnel questions,

Recalling its decisions 36/456 and 36/457 of 18 December 1981 on the application of the principle of equitable geographical distribution and on the concept of career, types of appointment, career development and related questions,

Having examined the reports of the Secretary-General on the composition of the Secretariat and on the implementation of personnel policy reforms,

Having considered the study by the International Civil Service Commission on the concept of career, types of appointment, career development and related questions,

Taking note of the following reports of the Joint Inspection Unit and the related comments of the Administrative Committee on Co-ordination and of the Secretary-General:

(a) Personnel policy options and comments of the Secretary-General;

(b) Second report on the career concept and comments of the Administrative Committee on Co-ordination;

(c) Application of the principle of equitable geographical distribution of the staff of the United Nations Secretariat and comments of the Secretary-General;

(d) Second progress report on the status of women in the Professional category and above and comments of the Administrative Committee on Co-ordination,

Conscious of paragraph 1 of Article 101 of the Charter of the United Nations which states that "The staff shall be appointed by the Secretary-General under regulations established by the General Assembly",

Bearing in mind paragraph 3 of Article 101 of the Charter, which states that "The paramount consideration in the employment of the staff and in the determination of the conditions of service shall be the necessity of securing the highest standards of efficiency, competence and integrity. Due regard shall be paid to the importance of recruiting the staff on as wide a geographical basis as possible",

Convinced that the principle of equitable geographical distribution is fully compatible with the necessity of securing the highest standards of efficiency, competence and integrity,

Noting that some limited progress has been made with respect to the situation of unrepresented and underrepresented Member States and towards a balanced and equitable geographical distribution of staff in the Secretariat,

1. *Reaffirms* the principles and procedures set forth in General Assembly resolution 35/210, in particular in its section I, paragraphs 1 to 5, and section III;

2. *Stresses* the importance of having the largest possible number of Member States represented at the higher levels of the Secretariat, that is, the D-2 level and above;

3. *Reiterates* the principle of wide geographical representation throughout the Secretariat and welcomes the intention of the Secretary-General to monitor progress towards that objective in departments and main offices;

4. *Requests* the Secretary-General to include in his annual reports on the composition of the Secretariat information on progress made in respect of improvement of geographical distribution in the Secretariat, particularly at the higher levels;

5. *Welcomes* the intention of the Secretary-General to develop and apply a medium-term plan of recruitment in order to bring the number of staff from unrepresented and underrepresented countries within their desirable ranges by 1985 at the latest;

6. *Also welcomes* the intention of the Secretary-General to develop and apply a medium-term plan for career development;

7. *Recommends* that career planning be based upon clearly defined occupational groups for the Professional and General Service categories;

8. *Requests* the Secretary-General to report to the General Assembly at its thirty-ninth session on progress made in the implementation of all aspects of personnel policy reform.

Recruitment

JIU made recommendations on objective methods of recruitment in its second report on the career concept, transmitted by the Secretary-General to the General Assembly in October 1982.[3] The report, prepared by Inspectors Maurice Bertrand and Moustapha Ould Khalifa, concluded the two-part report on personnel policy options, the first part of which was issued in August 1981.[9] The two documents, intended for all organizations of the United Nations system, dealt with policy issues regarding the overall approach to the international civil service.

Noting that written and oral tests were the objective means generally practised in national civil services for recruitment, JIU proposed that all United Nations organizations adopt a common methodology applying those methods for recruitment of staff in the Professional category. The United Nations had already begun to shape such a policy, and special or simplified methods could be established for the smaller agencies or for certain highly technical occupational groups.

For the junior level (P-2), JIU proposed the more formal, objective and equitable method of competitive examination, accompanied by adequate publicity. Less sophisticated methods for P-3 and P-4 would be based on written and oral tests. Appointment at the P-5, D-1 and D-2 levels would be based on an examination of the candidates' work and on systematic interviews. To ensure overall consistency and equitable treatment of candidates, the panels of examiners should be made up at least partly of the same persons for each occupational group. For the General Service category, JIU said objective methods of recruitment would be determined later.

First steps should include determination of the occupational groups for which experiments in instituting objective recruitment methods would be

the easiest. Over the medium term, JIU suggested that, in the case of the largest occupational groups, many organizations join together in holding common competitive examinations.

The Administrative Committee on Co-ordination (ACC) commented on the JIU recommendations in October.[4] Appended was a statement submitted by it to the International Civil Service Commission (ICSC) containing the views of the executive heads of the United Nations organizations as to what was desirable and feasible with regard to the concept of career, types of appointment, career development and related questions.

ACC, while endorsing the Inspectors' call for systematic and rigorous methods of recruitment, remarked that, given the nature of their functions and the high degree of specialization of staff for certain posts, most organizations were obliged to recruit primarily in terms of specifications established for a particular post. Most organizations believed that the number of instances where written examinations for junior entry grades would be applicable was too small to warrant the considerable work and expense entailed, and they doubted that even special or simplified methods would prove satisfactory for highly technical groups. ACC agreed that systematic methods of assessment, interviewing and selection should be used at all levels.

In their statement to ICSC, the executive heads said that the criteria of professional aptitude applied would vary for those who, by the nature of their specialization, were expected to serve for a limited period (who normally would be fully qualified at the outset of their recruitment), and for those who were expected to serve for a longer period (whose aptitude to perform work at a higher level might be more important than their initial assignment). They believed that the requirements of equitable geographical distribution must be met at the recruitment stage, but that this objective was not incompatible with the highest standards of competence and efficiency. According to them, there were two prerequisites to putting improved methods of recruitment into practice: first, a system of anticipating vacancies through improved manpower planning and management, and second, more resources for recruitment.

The Secretary-General, in a September report to the General Assembly on implementation of personnel policy reforms,[5] described improvements in recruitment policy based on guidelines set by the Assembly. First priority was given to nationals of unrepresented and underrepresented Member States and women, for whom numerical objectives had been established. Also taken into account was the concern of the Assembly that no post should be considered the exclusive preserve of any Member State or group of States and that posts subject to geographical distribution should not be successively encumbered by nationals of the same Member State. However, replacement by nationals of the same Member State was permitted for States whose nationals served primarily on fixed-term contracts.

The target of 40 per cent of all vacancies in geographical posts, established in 1980[8] for the appointment of nationals of unrepresented and underrepresented countries, was met by June 1982. Other measures were taken, such as inviting a number of underrepresented States to nominate candidates for posts at the entry levels for which examinations would not be held, and recruiting and publicity missions. Candidates were interviewed for current vacancies as well as for placement on the roster for future consideration, which was to become the main tool of recruitment. An occupational structure to categorize candidates had been developed, and a review procedure—established to obtain updated background information on qualifications, work experience and availability—and new computer programmes were being developed to expand information retrieval capability and monitoring.

The suggested transitional plan for competitive examinations at the P-1 and P-2 (entry) levels had been implemented. Examinations were held in six unrepresented or underrepresented Member States (Brazil, Federal Republic of Germany, Italy, Ivory Coast, Mauritania, Suriname) in four occupational groups. The proportion of P-1 and P-2 vacancies filled through external examinations was 63.2 per cent during the reporting year, although the Assembly had set an objective of 70 per cent. One of the difficulties encountered was that the need to identify and reserve available posts before the examinations meant that the posts remained vacant for about a year.

The Secretariat had identified 14 occupational groups for use in recruitment planning: administration, economics, electronic data processing, engineering and architecture, finance, language, legal, library, political affairs, public information, publishing and printing, science and technology, social development, and statistics. A comprehensive occupational coding scheme was being developed to categorize posts and staff members by occupation, for a more accurate determination of vacancies by occupational group and to facilitate placement, mobility and career development.

In its 1982 report to the Assembly,[2] ICSC commented on the role of recruitment in career development (see below, under PERSONNEL QUESTIONS), stressing that it was the quality of the recruitment process that determined the quality and potential of the staff. It listed in an appendix 14 recommendations it had previously made to im-

prove the recruitment process, preliminary to a full examination of all major aspects of recruitment ICSC intended to complete in 1984.

The Commission asked organizations to reflect before adopting competitive examinations as the sole selection instrument for recruitment at the junior Professional level, as recommended by JIU; it believed that first an evaluation of United Nations experience in the matter was important. In its view, a recruitment process that screened out candidates before taking into account past performance, ability to function in an international setting, motivation, managerial skills, articulateness and similar qualities might not identify true quality and potential. Organizations needed to allocate sufficient funds for a well-equipped recruitment programme, with adequate and timely vacancy information, broad contacts with recruitment sources, up-to-date rosters, trained interviewers, travel funds and staff.

The Federation of International Civil Servants' Associations (FICSA), representing some staff associations of the United Nations system, expressed its views on recruitment in a November document transmitted to the Fifth Committee by the Secretary-General.[1] It shared the ICSC view that competitive examinations as a recruitment option should be treated with caution and other options needed to be fully explored. The staff of the specialized agencies did not support the extension of the examinations, at least until the United Nations experience had been fully analysed in cost-benefit terms. FICSA had grave reservations about the JIU idea that recruitment and selection procedures should become progressively less rigorous for senior staff. It endorsed the ICSC proposal that organizations inform staff before or at the time of recruitment about the career prospects of a job, and it called for the completion of the ICSC study on this subject.

The staff unions and associations of the Secretariat which were not members of FICSA expressed their views on recruitment to the Fifth Committee in October, in a document transmitted by the Secretary-General,[6] and when commenting on an ICSC study on career development (see below, under PERSONNEL QUESTIONS). They said the use of competitive examinations as the sole screening instrument for recruitment would be premature before a thorough evaluation of the results achieved so far. They recommended that examinations for external recruitment at the junior Professional level, already scheduled, be open to serving staff in other categories who had the requisite academic qualifications and were nationals of unrepresented or underrepresented countries.

The associations believed that an over-emphasis on formal academic education would fail to test for such qualities as adaptability to an intercultural environment, motivation and managerial skills, and could put candidates from developing countries at a disadvantage. If it proved essential to earmark posts for certain groups or for women, it must be done openly under established criteria drawn up with staff participation, requiring well-advertised recruitment campaigns and objective screening by trained interviewers.

The Assembly, in a resolution of 17 December,[7] noted the ICSC intention to undertake an evaluation of competitive examinations and other elements of recruitment policy.

Note. [1]S-G, transmitting FICSA comments, A/C.5/37/29.
Reports. [2]ICSC, A/37/30; [3]JIU, transmitted by S-G note, A/37/528, and [4]ACC comments, Add.1; [5]S-G, A/C.5/37/5; [6]Staff unions and associations, transmitted by S-G note, A/C.5/37/24.
Resolution (1982). [7]GA: 37/126, sect. IV, para. 6, 17 Dec.
Resolution (prior). [8]GA: 35/210, 17 Dec. 1980 (YUN 1980, p. 1164).
Yearbook reference. [9]1981, p. 1325.

Employment of women

In response to a 1980 request by the General Assembly,[11] JIU issued in September 1982 a second progress report[2] on the status of women in the Professional category and above in the United Nations system, i.e. progress in increasing the proportion of women in the Secretariat and in posts subject to geographical distribution (25 per cent by 1982 was the target for the latter).

The report reviewed actions taken in the United Nations and 11 related intergovernmental organizations since the first JIU progress report in July 1980.[12] These included measures on setting targets, ensuring equality of opportunity for promotion and career development, investigating claims of discrimination and harassment, implementing policy directives and establishing day-care facilities for children. Since 1976, when the percentage of women staff at the Professional level and above (excluding field representatives) was 17.7, the percentage had risen slightly by the end of 1981 to 19.6. Some organizations had made a significant improvement since 1976, particularly the United Nations (a 33.7 per cent increase), the International Civil Aviation Organization (up 41.3 per cent) and the International Atomic Energy Agency (up 31.4 per cent); however, the proportion of women to men was still unsatisfactory. The United Nations continued to lead all other organizations in the percentage of women in the Professional category (24.4 per cent).

There had been an increase in the number of women at the upper levels up to D-1; above that, women had made little progress. The report recommended that efforts be made to select women for the highest Professional levels. Concerning female Professional staff by nationality, 110 countries were represented in 1980 as compared to 103 in 1978, and there was a clear trend towards recruiting more women from developing countries.

The 1982 report mentioned that the recommendations made in the first progress report were still valid, and it re-emphasized six of them: executive heads and legislative bodies should follow the problem closely and review measures for bringing about an equitable balance between men and women at the Professional level; organizations should press Member States to propose more women candidates; organizations should re-examine established targets and set new ones; organizations should review promotion procedures and practices as well as training in order to ensure equal advancement opportunities for women; personnel offices should make an effort to present at least one qualified woman among candidates for posts; and ACC should monitor regularly the status of women and report regularly, suggesting corrective measures.

Commenting on the JIU report in October,[3] ACC said the executive heads of United Nations organizations were continuing to establish procedures for increasing the participation of women on equal terms with men in the work of the secretariats. They noted the recognition given to the responsibility of Member States in achieving this goal, and accepted the recommendation that personnel offices work closely with government representatives in order to reach qualified women candidates.

The proportion of women recruited in several organizations was around 25 per cent, corresponding approximately to the target figure adopted by several of them. In some organizations, targets would be of limited use, the availability of qualified women often being limited by the small number of women in some specialized disciplines. Geographical distribution considerations further limited efforts to improve the proportion of women. Promotion review procedures, training for women, and inclusion of at least one qualified woman in the lists of candidates were procedures already in practice in most organizations.

With regard to training and career development opportunities for women, ACC, while warning of the pitfall of "reverse discrimination", endorsed the recommendation that in cases where disparate treatment of any group of staff existed, training programmes to enable them to compete on an equal footing might be instituted. ACC endorsed the suggestion that organizations should explore the possibility of establishing day-care facilities where needed.

ACC suggested that the Assembly take note of the JIU report and the organizations' efforts to achieve greater participation of women on equal terms with men, that it again invite Member

States to co-operate further in the recruitment of women, and that it request the Secretary-General, as Chairman of ACC, to report to the Assembly at suitable intervals on progress made.

The Secretary-General, in his September 1982 report on the composition of the Secretariat,[4] included figures on the proportion of men and women in posts subject to geographical distribution. As at 30 June 1982, the percentage of women was 22.2, an increase of 4.4 percentage points over a period of three and a half years. The Secretary-General also gave comparative figures for posts with special language requirements, of which 33.5 per cent were held by women, as compared with 30.3 per cent in 1972.

The Secretary-General said that he had taken vigorous steps, as requested by the Assembly, to increase the proportion of women in the Secretariat, particularly at senior levels. Commenting on the situation in his September report on implementation of personnel policy reforms,[5] he stated that, since assuming his functions in January 1982, he had appointed three women to posts at the Assistant Secretary-General and Under-Secretary-General levels. The proportion of women in those posts had increased from 4.3 per cent on 30 June 1981 to 7.8 per cent a year later. In addition, many individual organizational units had achieved or exceeded the 25 per cent target for women in geographical posts. Priority in recruitment was given to women candidates, especially nationals of States not overrepresented.

The proportion of women on promotion registers had steadily increased. Promotion registers for P-4 showed that 25.4 per cent of the staff members in 1980 were women, 27.6 per cent in 1981, and 29.8 per cent in 1982. For the P-5 registers, the percentages were 11.5, 14 and 20.4. The Secretary-General had also appointed women to preside over the three boards which advised him on recruitment and promotion. The overall percentage of women in personnel advisory and administrative boards at Headquarters was 38 per cent.

He had approved measures to introduce part-time employment in the Secretariat for staff in the General Service and related categories to improve the recruitment of women, and was studying extending such employment and flexible working hours to other categories. He noted that few candidates nominated by Member States were women. As at 30 June 1982, the number of candidates on the recruitment roster was 13,301, of whom 1,181, or 8.9 per cent, were women.

Views of the staff on the status of women in the United Nations were presented to the Assembly's Fifth Committee by two bodies: FICSA, in a document transmitted by the Secretary-General in November,[1] and the staff unions and associations

of the Secretariat, in one transmitted in October.[6]

FICSA believed that the JIU report on the status of women in the Professional category, updating previous reports, had recommended no innovative measures to ease the chronic underrepresentation of women in all United Nations secretariats, and indicated that its former recommendations remained unimplemented. Targets had still not been set in all organizations of the system. FICSA recommended that grade and divisional/departmental targets and profiles be established in addition to overall targets.

FICSA said it was imperative to mount an effort to locate qualified women, and to take other measures to reconcile the two objectives of equitable geographical distribution and equitable representation of women. It urged more vigorous action by the organizations, including actively encouraging Member States to submit applications of qualified women. FICSA supported the JIU recommendation that organizations review again the possibility of delegating a person or panel to monitor progress in the recruitment and promotion of women, and agreed on the need for child-care facilities and part-time work for all categories in all agencies. It felt that recurrent and regular reporting on the issue at two- or three-year intervals was essential.

The staff unions and associations of the United Nations Secretariat said the situation of women in the Secretariat had not improved substantially and the 25 per cent target had not been met. They pointed out that the 22.2 per cent figure for women in Secretariat posts subject to geographical distribution was a mere 0.6 per cent increase over the 1981 figure, less than the annual average increase of 1.1 per cent since the target was established in 1978. They suggested that new targets be set to ensure real progress—30 per cent by 1985 and 40 per cent by 1990—and called for more targets within organizational units. The proportion of senior women was still extremely small (8 women and 130 men above the D-1 level, only two more women than in 1981, and there were seven fewer women at the P-5 level). There were five fewer women recruited than in 1981, the percentage of women recruits (20.5) was the lowest in three years, and 71 per cent of women in posts subject to geographical distribution were at the P-3 level and below compared with 33.5 per cent of men staff members. More needed to be done to move women up from the P-3 level. There was a need for up-to-date statistics and for publicizing personnel policy objectives in order to monitor progress. According to the staff associations, discrimination against women was particularly acute in the General Service, where 57.9 per cent of staff were women.

General Assembly action. In a resolution of 21 December,[9] the General Assembly requested the Secretary-General to intensify efforts to implement the provisions of 1978[10] and 1980[11] resolutions which were intended to ensure that women had equal opportunity for advancement and appointment, keeping in mind that the 25 per cent target for the number of women in geographical posts should not be viewed as a limit. The Assembly called on him to report annually on the number and percentage of women promoted and on promotion registers and appointment lists. Each United Nations organization was to be invited to provide updated information on the recruitment, promotion and assignment of women, to take concrete steps to ensure compliance with policy directives on recruitment, promotion, career development and training of women, and to examine additional measures for attaining policy directives. Member States were asked to nominate more women candidates and assist United Nations recruitment efforts.

The Assembly adopted the resolution without vote. The text, introduced by Ireland on behalf of 16 countries, was approved by the Fifth Committee without objection on 11 December. After considering proposals made by various delegations, the sponsors had orally revised the text: in operative paragraph 1, a statement indicating that there was currently a lower than average percentage of women was deleted; in paragraph 2, the Secretary-General's report was to identify the number and percentage of women "by nationality" on all promotion registers and appointment lists; in paragraph 4, Member States were requested, rather than called upon, to support United Nations efforts; and in paragraph 7, in examining additional measures to attain policy objectives, legislative bodies were asked to bear in mind the United Nations Charter's provision on the need to secure the highest standards of efficiency, competence and integrity, in addition to the principle of equitable geographical distribution.

By a resolution of 3 December,[7] the Assembly called on the Secretary-General and the executive heads of other United Nations organizations to make, by the end of the United Nations Decade for Women in 1985, increased efforts to select and appoint women, in conformity with Charter principles, to decision-making positions.

The Assembly, by another resolution of 3 December,[8] proclaimed a Declaration on the Participation of Women in Promoting International Peace and Co-operation, which, among other things, called for appropriate measures to provide practical opportunities for the participation of women in promoting international peace and co-operation, economic development and social progress. One such measure was support for increased employment of women at all levels in the secretariats of the United Nations system, in conformity with Charter principles.

Note. [1]S-G, transmitting FICSA comments, A/C.5/37/29.
Reports. [2]JIU, transmitted by S-G note, A/37/469, and [3]ACC comments, Add.1; S-G, [4]A/37/143, [5]A/C.5/37/5; [6]Staff unions and associations, transmitted by S-G note, A/C.5/37/24.
Resolutions (1982). GA: [7]37/61, para. 3, 3 Dec.; [8]37/63, annex, art. 12 *(d),* 3 Dec.; [9]37/235 B, 21 Dec., text following.
Resolutions (prior). GA: [10]33/143, 20 Dec. 1978 (YUN 1978, p. 988); [11]35/210, 17 Dec. 1980 (YUN 1980, p. 1164).
Yearbook reference. [12]1980, p. 1160.
Meeting records. GA: 5th Committee, A/C.5/37/SR.13, 23, 25-34, 36-38, 40, 41, 43, 47, *63, 65* (15 Oct. & 1 Nov.–11 Dec.); plenary, A/37/PV.114 (21 Dec.).

General Assembly resolution 37/235 B

21 December 1982   Meeting 114   Adopted without vote

Approved by Fifth Committee (A/37/764) without objection, 11 December (meeting 65); 16-nation draft (A/C.5/37/L.39), orally revised; agenda item 111.

Sponsors: Bahamas, Barbados, Belgium, Denmark, Dominican Republic, Egypt, Finland, Ghana, Ireland, Mexico, Netherlands, Norway, Sweden, Trinidad and Tobago, United States, Venezuela.

The General Assembly,

Conscious of Article 8 of the Charter of the United Nations on the equality of opportunity for men and women to participate in the work of the Organization,

Recalling resolution 24 adopted by the World Conference of the United Nations Decade for Women,

Noting the progress made towards the target set in section III of General Assembly resolution 33/143 of 20 December 1978 that the number of women in posts subject to geographical distribution should be increased to 25 per cent of the total by 1982,

Reaffirming section III of General Assembly resolution 33/143 and section V of Assembly resolution 35/210 of 17 December 1980,

Having considered the second progress report of the Joint Inspection Unit on the status of women in the Professional category and above,

Recalling that the forthcoming medium-term recruitment plan is intended, *inter alia,* to improve the representation of women in the Secretariat,

1. *Requests* the Secretary-General to intensify his efforts to implement fully section III of General Assembly resolution 33/143 and section V of Assembly resolution 35/210, keeping in mind that the 25 per cent target set should not be viewed as a limit on the number of women employed and paying particular attention to those areas of the United Nations where compliance with the resolution has lagged behind;

2. *Calls upon* the Secretary-General to include in his annual report on the composition of the Secretariat statistical analyses on the number and percentage of women by nationality on all promotion registers and appointment lists, identifying both *ad hoc* and accelerated promotions as well as normal promotions and specifying what percentage of those eligible for promotion, actually promoted and appointed from outside, within each grade, are women with a view to ensuring that women have equal opportunity for advancement and appointment, particularly at the higher levels;

3. *Requests* the Secretary-General, in his capacity as Chairman of the Administrative Committee on Co-ordination, to invite organizations to continue to provide updated information on the recruitment, promotion and assignment of women in each organization, for submission to the General Assembly at its thirty-ninth session;

4. *Requests* Member States to continue to support the efforts of the United Nations and the specialized agencies to increase the proportion of women in the Professional category and above by nominating more women candidates and by assisting in recruitment efforts by the Secretary-General and the executive heads of the agencies;

5. *Urges* the Secretary-General to take concrete steps to ensure compliance throughout the United Nations with policy directives

concerning the recruitment, promotion, career development and training of women as well as other aspects of the employment of women;

6. *Requests* the Secretary-General to invite, through the Administrative Committee on Co-ordination, the executive heads of the other organizations of the United Nations system that have not already done so similarly to take concrete steps to guarantee compliance;

7. *Requests* the Secretary-General and the executive heads of all the other organizations in the United Nations system to examine additional measures that will advance the attainment of the policy directives of the appropriate legislative bodies concerning the appointment, promotion and assignment of women in the organizations in the United Nations system, bearing in mind paragraph 3 of Article 101 of the Charter of the United Nations and the principle of equitable geographical distribution;

8. *Requests* the International Civil Service Commission, in its ongoing work programme, to keep these questions under continuing review and to report thereon as appropriate to the General Assembly.

Personnel questions

International Civil Service Commission

The International Civil Service Commission (ICSC), established by the General Assembly in 1974[5] to regulate and co-ordinate conditions of service in the United Nations system, held two sessions in 1982: its fifteenth, at Geneva from 1 to 19 March, and its sixteenth, in New York from 12 to 30 July. In its report to the Assembly,[2] ICSC described its work and action taken on Assembly decisions concerning various personnel matters. It made recommendations for action by the Assembly and the legislative organs of the 11 other participating organizations on such matters as the procedure for adjusting cost-of-living differential factors applicable to certain retirees and the determination of the remuneration of the Professional and higher categories (see below, under REMUNERATION), and career development (see above).

The Assembly adopted on 17 December a five-part resolution[4] on the ICSC report. By section I, the Assembly approved the procedure for adjusting cost-of-living differential factors for certain retirees. By section II, it requested ICSC to review the basis for determining the level of remuneration of the Professional and higher categories. Section III dealt with the children's allowance, the education grant, rental subsidies and staff health insurance (see below, under REMUNERATION), and the assignment allowance (see below, under FIELD PERSONNEL). The Assembly, in section IV, recommended application of a new job classification system (see below), and, in section V, requested the system's bodies to co-ordinate personnel proposals closely with ICSC.

The text was introduced in the Fifth Committee, and subsequently revised, by Canada, also on behalf of Denmark, Finland, Ghana, Norway, Pakistan, Panama and Sweden. The sponsors then orally revised provisions in section III pertaining to the education grant (see below, under REMUNERATION), before the Committee approved the text

on 13 December by a vote, requested by the United States, of 79 to 10, with 6 abstentions. The Assembly adopted the resolution by a recorded vote of 123 to 11, with 6 abstentions.

Speaking in explanation of vote, the USSR, which opposed the resolution, said it was unable to endorse certain paragraphs either because they were inappropriate or because they would lead to unwarranted growth in United Nations expenditure. The United States also opposed the text, because it would lead to increased costs to be borne by Member States.

Egypt found the text to be an acceptable compromise, and New Zealand supported it because it represented a delicate balance between the economic concerns of Member States and the technical arguments put forward by ICSC in favour of selective improvements in the conditions of service of international civil servants.

When considering requests by the Secretary-General[3] for supplementary funds for the programme budget for 1982-1983 (see this section, Chapter I, under PROGRAMME PLANNING), and accepting the recommendation of the Advisory Committee on Administrative and Budgetary Questions on revised estimates for ICSC expenses,[1] the Fifth Committee approved on 29 October, by 69 votes to 9, with 3 abstentions, an additional appropriation of $158,800 for ICSC. The additional costs were needed for computerization of the work of the Cost-of-Living Division, the reclassification of posts in the ICSC secretariat, and staff travel costs. Of that total, $11,400 would be offset by an increase of the same amount from income from staff assessment, and $95,000 would be offset by the reimbursement by the specialized agencies of their share (59.8 per cent) of the additional ICSC costs. The total 1982-1983 budget previously approved for new ICSC activities was $5,741,400 (regular budget and extrabudgetary funds).

Reports. [1]ACABQ, A/37/7/Add.6; [2]ICSC, A/37/30; [3]S-G, A/C.5/37/12 and Corr.1.
Resolution (1982). [4]GA: 37/126, 17 Dec., text following.
Resolution (prior). [5]GA: 3357(XXIX), 18 Dec. 1974 (YUN 1974, p. 875).
Financial implications. ACABQ report, A/37/7/Add.11; S-G statement, A/C.5/37/37.
Meeting records. GA: 5th Committee, A/C.5/37/SR.13, 28, 29, 31, 35, 36, 40, 42-44, *63-65, 67* (15 Oct. & 8 Nov.–13 Dec.); plenary, A/37/PV.109 (17 Dec.).

General Assembly resolution 37/126

17 December 1982   Meeting 109   123-11-6 (recorded vote)

Approved by Fifth Committee (A/37/768) by vote (79-10-6), 13 December (meeting 67); 8-nation draft (A/C.5/37/L.38/Rev.1), orally revised; agenda item 112.

Sponsors: Canada, Denmark, Finland, Ghana, Norway, Pakistan, Panama, Sweden.

Report of the International Civil Service Commission

The General Assembly,

Taking note with appreciation of the eighth annual report of the International Civil Service Commission,

Reaffirming the importance of the acknowledged role of the Commission in the development of a single, unified, international civil service through the application of common personnel standards, methods and arrangements as stated in article 9 of its statute,

Reaffirming the importance of respect for these common standards, methods and arrangements by all member organizations of the common system,

Noting the difficulties in reaching a consensus in the Commission on the interpretation and application of the Noblemaire Principle,

Aware of the difficult global economic situation affecting Member States, in particular developing countries,

Desirous of ensuring adequate financial support for programme delivery,

I

1. *Approves* the procedure for adjusting cost-of-living differential factors applicable to retirees from the Professional and higher categories where those factors are applied and where the rates of taxation are zero or lower than those implicit in the amounts of base pensions provided under the United Nations staff pension scheme;

2. *Approves* the recommendation of the International Civil Service Commission and of the United Nations Joint Staff Pension Board that no reduction factor be applied to the retirees from the General Service and related categories;

II

1. *Takes note* of the current status of the comparison between the total compensation in the comparator civil service and that in the United Nations common system;

2. *Calls the attention* of Member States to the fact that the practice of supplementary payments or deductions is inconsistent with the provisions of the Staff Regulations of the United Nations and, therefore, inappropriate;

3. *Notes* the results of the review by the International Civil Service Commission of the purposes and operation of the post adjustment system and the need to continue to improve the system, and in particular invites the Commission to continue to improve the methodology for cost-of-living measurements;

4. *Requests* the Commission to review further the basis for the determination and level of remuneration of the Professional and higher categories, with a view to making recommendations thereon to the General Assembly at its thirty-ninth session, and thereafter periodically on the level of remuneration;

III

1. *Takes note* of the general methodology for surveys of best prevailing conditions of service of the staff in the General Service and related categories approved by the International Civil Service Commission for application to headquarters duty stations;

2. *Notes* that the Commission has started a comprehensive review of conditions of service in the field;

3. *Decides* that the children's allowance for the Professional and higher categories shall be increased to $700 as from 1 January 1983, and that the currency floor measures designed to ensure an equitable level of the allowance everywhere be maintained, based on the twelve-month average exchange rate ending 30 June 1982, for all duty stations;

4. *Decides* that the education grant shall remain an expatriate benefit to be granted to all United Nations expatriate officials but that nationals returning to duty stations in their home country following an assignment elsewhere may receive the grant for the balance of a school year, not exceeding one full school year after their return from expatriate service;

5. *Requests* the Commission to keep the question of the education grant under review, particularly in regard to the situation of officials subject to rotation between headquarters and other duty stations and taking account of the views expressed by delegations during the debate;

6. *Notes* the Commission's decision to increase the provisions of the assignment allowance by 50 per cent and to double the lump sum portion of the installation grant received by field staff;

7. *Requests* the Commission to complete on an urgent basis its study of the need for a rental subsidy arrangement in headquarters duty stations of organizations of the United Nations common system, particularly with regard to newcomers and staff transfers, and to report to the General Assembly, at its thirty-eighth session, on action taken;

8. *Requests* the Commission to examine the need for raising the ratio of contributions by organizations of the United Nations common system for health insurance of staff members and the question of applying appropriate retroactivity;

IV

1. *Welcomes* the study on the concept of career, types of appointment, career development and related questions submitted by the International Civil Service Commission;

2. *Considers* that the overall concept of integrated personnel management based on human resources planning as envisaged by the Commission will assist organizations in achieving their programme objectives in an efficient manner, while providing improved conditions for career development to all categories of staff in the common system, whether they serve on career or fixed-term appointments;

3. *Recommends* that the three-tiered job classification system developed by the Commission, based on a Master Standard of common system job classification standards, be applied to ensure optimal equity in remuneration as well as a sound basis for human resources planning and career development, and that personnel policies of organizations of the common system be harmonized with the job classification system promulgated by the Commission;

4. *Recommends further* that organizations should establish their needs for permanent and fixed-term staff on a continuing basis in conjunction with the human resources planning process, taking into account the criteria considered by the Commission for this purpose;

5. *Decides* that staff members on fixed-term appointments upon completion of five years of continuing good service shall be given every reasonable consideration for a career appointment;

6. *Notes* the Commission's intention to undertake an evaluation of competitive examinations and other elements of recruitment policy;

7. *Requests* the Commission to pursue its programme under articles 13 and 14 of its statute as scheduled;

V

Requests all bodies making proposals for action on personnel matters affecting the United Nations common system to co-ordinate those proposals closely with the International Civil Service Commission, which shall give its recommendations thereon to the General Assembly and other legislative organs in the common system and thereby avoid duplication of efforts.

Recorded vote in Assembly as follows:

In favour: Algeria, Angola, Argentina, Australia, Austria, Bahamas, Bahrain, Bangladesh, Barbados, Belgium, Benin, Bhutan, Bolivia, Botswana, Brazil, Burma, Burundi, Canada, Central African Republic, Chad, Chile, Colombia, Comoros, Congo, Costa Rica, Cyprus, Democratic Yemen, Denmark, Djibouti, Dominica, Dominican Republic, Ecuador, Egypt, Ethiopia, Fiji, Finland, France, Gabon, Gambia, Ghana, Greece, Guatemala, Guinea, Guinea-Bissau, Guyana, Honduras, Iceland, India, Indonesia, Iran, Iraq, Ireland, Israel, Italy, Ivory Coast, Jamaica, Jordan, Kenya, Kuwait, Lebanon, Lesotho, Liberia, Libyan Arab Jamahiriya, Luxembourg, Madagascar, Malawi, Malaysia, Maldives, Mali, Malta, Mauritania, Mauritius, Mexico, Morocco, Mozambique, Nepal, Netherlands, New Zealand, Niger, Norway, Oman, Pakistan, Panama, Papua New Guinea, Paraguay, Peru, Philippines, Portugal, Qatar, Rwanda, Samoa, Sao Tome and Principe, Saudi Arabia, Senegal, Sierra Leone, Singapore, Solomon Islands, Somalia, Spain, Sri Lanka, Sudan, Suriname, Swaziland, Sweden, Syrian Arab Republic, Thailand, Togo, Trinidad and Tobago, Tunisia, Turkey, Uganda, United Arab Emirates, United Kingdom, United Republic of Cameroon, United Republic of Tanzania, Upper Volta, Uruguay, Venezuela, Yemen, Yugoslavia, Zaire, Zambia, Zimbabwe.

Against: Bulgaria, Byelorussian SSR, Czechoslovakia, German Democratic Republic, Hungary, Mongolia, Poland, Ukrainian SSR, USSR, United States, Viet Nam.

Abstaining: Afghanistan, Cuba, Germany, Federal Republic of, Grenada, Japan, Romania.

Staff administration

Career development

In response to a 1980 request by the General Assembly,[9] both ICSC and the Joint Inspection Unit (JIU) submitted reports on career concepts, types of appointment, career development and related questions, preliminary reports on which had been submitted in 1981.[10]

ICSC report. In its 1982 annual report,[2] ICSC described the action it had taken regarding human resources planning and career development.

It considered an analysis by its secretariat of the role of human resources planning and its importance for individual staff, the organizations and the common system, describing the components of the planning process and making recommendations to facilitate further review of the issue. ICSC briefly outlined the views of three organizations also concerned with personnel questions: the Consultative Committee on Administrative Questions (CCAQ) of the Administrative Committee on Co-ordination (ACC), and two bodies representing staff members—the Federation of International Civil Servants' Associations (FICSA) and the Co-ordinating Committee for Independent Staff Unions and Associations of the United Nations System (CCISU).

Both FICSA and CCISU agreed on the need for human resources planning. Expressing the hope that the application of such planning would be seen as an urgent necessity, FICSA said it would review the question and make specific comments and proposals in 1983. CCISU said it would like to see a programme of action developed for enhancing the career prospects of women and nationals from underrepresented States so that the organizations could simultaneously develop their own personnel and serve as a training ground for an international civil service. It had reservations on the use of special remuneration, as it felt the legitimate need to attract and retain qualified staff should be weighed against the danger of creating a group with special privileges.

ICSC questioned to what extent it would be desirable or possible to apply such human resources planning to the system as a whole in common fields of work, and why there had been little progress in that area at the level of individual organizations. The Commission decided to transmit its study to United Nations organizations and staff representatives for further analysis and comment, and to request CCAQ to provide a synopsis of the relevant practices in existence, to provide information on organizations' personnel data systems, to identify factors hampering progress in the field, and to indicate whether an interorganizational approach would be desirable and possible in fields where common jobs existed.

An ICSC study on the concept of career, types of appointment, career development and related questions was annexed to the 1982 report. It was aimed at placing broad principles for the determination of service—as reflected in the United Nations Charter and Staff Regulations and in the corresponding instruments of the other organizations—within the context of human resources management by identifying their inter-action with related questions, such as recruitment, job classification, promotion policy and training. The study took into account the views of JIU, the position of the organizations as formulated by CCAQ and ACC, the position of FICSA, the views expressed by Member States in the Assembly's Fifth Committee, and a number of related studies.

The principles set out in the study for the determination of conditions of service were meant to be equally valid for General Service and related categories of staff as well as for the Professional and higher categories. Emphasizing that efficient human resources management required a comprehensive approach, ICSC said its recommendations needed to be translated into a distinct recruitment policy, common job classification standards, a common salary system, a promotion policy, a contractual policy, a training policy, a budgetary planning system linked to job classification and, above all, a human resources planning system to transform the policies into action. It recommended that the Assembly and the organizations consider the concept of human resources as a basis for a systematic approach to integrated personnel management and that they pursue the development of a planning process based on the particular needs of organizations in close co-ordination with the Commission's further study programme in that area.

ICSC had been attempting to set common job classification standards (see below) for Professionals and above as a basis for analysing management systems, determining salaries and controlling budgetary processes, as well as for providing a data base for other elements of an integrated system aimed at career development. The Commission recommended that organizations maintain the necessary flexibility to implement classification decisions within a given budgetary period, and that they maintain adequate links between their job classification activities and their budgetary processes, recruitment and training programmes, human resources and career planning programmes, and promotion machinery, to ensure that the job information was used to maximum advantage.

Noting the advantages of a career service, yet aware of concerns expressed, ICSC recommended that, on the basis of forecasts, organizations reassess their needs for permanent and fixed-term staff. Organizations should inform staff, at the time of recruitment, what was intended for their period of employment. Granting successive fixed-term contracts over an extended period of time was unsound; ICSC recommended that, after five years of service, each employee be given every reasonable consideration for a career appointment. Organizations should have the flexibility to determine their ratio of permanent staff and fixed-term staff according to their needs. The Commission requested organizations to reflect before they adopted the use of competitive examinations as the sole selection instrument for recruitment at the P-1 and P-2 levels, and to allocate sufficient resources to their recruitment programmes.

Commenting on an appraisal system for performance evaluation, put into effect in 1982 after a three-year study, ICSC recommended that the organizations should study providing appropriate performance awards. It also urged organizations to ensure that promotion processes were aligned with their career development policy, and requested them to pursue that goal in co-ordination with ICSC. It recommended that the concepts of lateral movement and job mobility be applicable to all staff, in accordance with the nature of their functions, through job rotation for locally recruited staff and through moves between duty stations for internationally recruited staff. Organizations should stimulate assessment of staff training needs by furthering supervisor-staff dialogue to identify realistic objectives.

Commenting on the study, CCAQ said the conclusion that the objective of establishing systematic career development for all categories in the common system could only be met through systematic human resources management based on integrated policies in a number of areas was too categorical and needed to reflect that the situation varied among organizations. In addition, the organizations could not accept an interpretation of the concept of job classification identifying stepping-stones on the career path as constituting some kind of guarantee for individual staff members to be promoted. It also urged ICSC not to take a decision that would ban linked grades as a means of identifying posts.

FICSA felt that, while it believed in the need for an integrated approach, a career development programme built step by step must be capable of being modified where necessary and be subject to regular review; it maintained that a substantial proportion of the system's officials should hold permanent contracts. Staff on fixed-term contracts should be limited to 25 per cent of the total, although the actual proportion should be determined by the work pattern of each organization, according to clearly defined criteria, and the practice of employing staff on a series of fixed-term appointments should be halted. To alleviate the difficulties of staff in that position, ICSC should recommend an end-of-service grant. FICSA supported staff mobility at all levels.

The staff associations of the Secretariat also agreed on the need for a system-wide approach to career development. CCISU suggested that a system-wide computerized roster be established to inventory skills. It underlined the need to iden-

tify career paths and define occupations, and took strong issue with the concept of linked grades. It emphasized that preference in recruitment should be given to qualified internal candidates, in accordance with staff regulations, and that a scrutiny of the results of competitive examinations was needed before applying them more broadly. CCISU recommended that national examinations for Professional posts be open to qualified candidates within the General Service category, that the ceiling on the number of posts allocated for promotion to the Professional category be raised and that the ratio of such posts be fixed. Concern was also expressed at the growing use of fixed-term contracts for extended periods of time, agreeing that they should be limited to 25 per cent of the total, and endorsing the recommendation that a career appointment be granted to staff members completing five years of service.

Staff views on career development were also presented by the Secretariat associations and FICSA in documents transmitted to the Fifth Committee by the Secretary-General in October[6] and November.[1] Both groups expressed concern at the lack of career development planning in the United Nations organizations. FICSA shared the ICSC view that job function should determine the contractual status of the staff member and favoured the establishment of career development and counselling units in all organizations. It felt it was time to analyse the effectiveness of the year-old vacancy announcement bulletin in increasing inter-agency mobility, and proposed linking it to computerized rosters.

The staff associations said that, in order to develop a system of career planning, a Secretariat-wide career development unit with well-defined functions should be established. They stressed that full consideration should be given to internal candidates for vacant posts, and were gratified that both ICSC and JIU (see below) recognized the need to define a clear policy and uniform application of the use of different-length contracts.

JIU report and ACC comments. JIU submitted to the General Assembly in October, through the Secretary-General, its second report[3] on the career concept, prepared by Inspectors Maurice Bertrand and Moustapha Ould Khalifa, thus completing their 1981 report on personnel policy options.[10] The report, completed in March, dealt with policy issues regarding the overall approach to the international civil service and was addressed to all the United Nations organizations. The Inspectors found several aspects of personnel policy unsatisfactory, which they said was characterized by the lack of objective recruitment, performance appraisal and promotion methods. They found an absence of professionalism and of any career development system organized on occupational lines.

The report stressed the need for common principles in order to ensure the highest standards of efficiency, and to create a satisfying climate of work with both job security and reasonable opportunities for advancement. While stressing the need for unity in the system, JIU suggested that methods and reforms could be implemented for the larger organizations but would have to be adapted and simplified for those with smaller secretariats.

The Inspectors recommended that career development in the international civil service should be based on practices in national civil services, with a career system based on standard career paths in clearly defined occupational groups, objective methods of recruitment, prospects of career development and an average rate of advancement that was known beforehand for each occupational group, methods of punishing staff members who did not give satisfaction, procedures enabling staff to take part in determining how their career would be shaped, and recruitment mainly at the junior level. JIU urged organizations to establish a list of occupational groups, defined on the basis of qualifications required for entry, and to view them as standard career paths with a defined average rate of advancement for each.

The Inspectors suggested that organizations determine the desirable percentages for external recruitment for each grade, increase recruitments at the P-2 level and considerably reduce those at the P-3 level, and link the largest number of P-3 with P-2 posts and P-4 with P-3 posts. Geographical distribution should be given greater weight in recruitment, and systems be adopted for consulting staff on career development and planning. Current appointment and promotion committees should be replaced by special committees for each occupational group. In-service training activities were suggested as a part of career development policy. Precise criteria for granting permanent appointments should be established, and rules worked out on arrangements for secondment of national officials who served alternately with their Governments and with United Nations organizations.

ACC submitted to the Assembly in October[4] its comments on both the 1981 and 1982 JIU reports, including a statement ACC had submitted to ICSC containing the views of the executive heads of United Nations organizations as to what they considered desirable and feasible with regard to the concept of career, types of appointment, career development and related questions.

In general, ACC welcomed the Inspectors' recognition that personnel reforms must take account of the differences between the organizations. Despite the differences, the executive heads believed that there was much common ground, and any changes should expand the common ground.

However, they did not fully share the Inspectors' emphasis on occupational groups and on the practices of national civil services as the keys to remedies. They considered that the international civil service had characteristics peculiar to it and that the work could not be confined within the traditional definitions of professions. They agreed to continue to co-operate with ICSC in studying improvements.

Regarding the career concept, ACC said most organizations required a large proportion of specialists with advanced qualifications and experience before recruitment, who therefore could not be appointed at the junior entry grade and whose useful employment was often limited to a few years. For these reasons, it was not feasible for some organizations to accept a large proportion of their staff members for permanent appointment. ACC said that an excessively compartmentalized concept of professionalism, within which specific career paths were identified by occupational groups, was not the concept most relevant to the needs of the specialized agencies and therefore its significance as the framework for career development should not be over-emphasized. Moreover, occupational groups defined by one organization were unlikely to coincide with those of other organizations.

The executive heads agreed that career development prospects for serving staff would be enhanced if external recruitment above entry level were limited. While encouraging maximum use of junior grades for recruitment, ACC said it would not be consistent with the recruitment policies of most organizations to establish limits for external recruitment at higher levels, particularly of qualified specialists. The organizations questioned the feasibility of drawing up long-term career planning. They concurred that professional specialists should continue to be involved in selection and review bodies, but did not agree that panels constituted within professional groups should entirely replace existing consultative machinery. They did not accept the proposal that extensions of fixed-term contracts should be limited, and recommended that ICSC study the whole question of secondment, including its legal, contractual and administrative aspects.

Report of the Secretary-General. The Secretary-General, in his September report[5] to the Assembly on personnel policy reforms, commented on progress in carrying out Assembly requests concerning career development. Currently, he noted, staff reassignment and movement were mostly initiated by the staff member rather than by the Organization, resources being available to meet only the most urgent needs for reassignment. The United Nations was, however, establishing machinery to facilitate reassignment and staff mobility, consisting of review of all vacancies and recruitment objectives as well as the availability of candidates, and issuing vacancy notices.

A roster of internal candidates had been developed along the same lines as the roster of external candidates, and staff were currently being categorized by occupational groups, according to the 14-group structure developed for the Secretariat (see above, under RECRUITMENT), thus facilitating the matching of post requirements with qualifications of staff.

General Assembly action. In a resolution of 17 December on the ICSC report,[7] the Assembly welcomed the ICSC study on the concept of career, types of appointment, career development and related questions. It considered that the concept of integrated personnel management based on human resources planning as envisaged by ICSC would assist organizations in achieving their programme objectives in an efficient manner, while providing improved conditions for career development to all categories of staff, whether on career or fixed-term appointments. The Assembly recommended that organizations establish their needs for permanent and fixed-term staff on a continuing basis in conjunction with the human resources planning process, taking into account the criteria considered by ICSC for that purpose. It decided that staff members on fixed-term appointments upon completion of five years of continuing good service would be given every reasonable consideration for a career appointment.

By the same resolution, the Assembly recommended that a job classification system (see below) developed by ICSC be applied to ensure equity in remuneration and a basis for human resources planning and career development. It also noted the ICSC intention to evaluate competitive examinations and other elements of recruitment policy (see above, under COMPOSITION OF THE SECRETARIAT).

Speaking in explanation of vote, Japan expressed reservations on the paragraph pertaining to career appointment consideration after five years.

The Assembly, in a resolution of 21 December,[8] welcomed the intention of the Secretary-General to develop and apply a medium-term plan for career development and recommended that career planning be based on clearly defined occupational groups for the Professional and General Service categories.

Note. [1]S-G, transmitting FICSA comments, A/C.5/37/29. *Reports.* [2]ICSC, A/37/30; [3]JIU, transmitted by S-G note, A/37/528, and [4]ACC comments, Add.1; [5]S-G, A/C.5/37/5; [6]Staff unions and associations, transmitted by S-G note, A/C.5/37/24. *Resolutions (1982).* GA: [7]37/126, sect. IV, 17 Dec.; [8]37/235 A, paras. 6 & 7, 21 Dec.

Resolution (prior). [9]GA: 35/210, 17 Dec. 1980 (YUN 1980, p. 1164). *Yearbook reference.* [10]1981, p. 1325.

Language staff

In a December 1982 addendum[2] to a first performance report on the 1982-1983 budget, the Secretary-General reported to the General Assembly on job classification and career development of language staff. This was in implementation of a plan adopted by the Assembly in 1980[4] which envisaged a progressive adjustment over the period from 1981 to 1983 of the manning tables for translators, interpreters, verbatim reporters, editors, copy-preparers and proof-readers, providing for reclassification of those posts to reflect the increasingly complex and specialized nature of their assignments. Adjustments for Headquarters and Geneva had been dealt with in 1981.[5]

Describing the results of a review undertaken in 1982 of the United Nations Industrial Development Organization (UNIDO) language staff at Vienna, Austria, where UNIDO headquarters was located, he recommended changes in the grade structure of that staff, most of which would involve upgrading posts, entailing additional costs of $20,800 for 1983, which he believed could be offset by an equivalent reduction of temporary assistance for meetings.

The Advisory Committee on Administrative and Budgetary Questions orally approved[1] the Secretary-General's recommendations. On its proposal and as orally proposed by the Fifth Committee Chairman, the Committee, without vote on 14 December, recommended that the Assembly take note of the Secretary-General's report. The Assembly did so without vote on 21 December.[3]

Reports. [1]ACABQ, A/37/7 and Add.1-24, annex, para. 37; [2]S-G, A/C.5/37/65/Add.2 & Add.2/Corr.1. *Resolution (1982).* [3]GA: 37/237, sect. XIII, 21 Dec., text following. *Resolution (prior).* [4]GA: 35/225, 17 Dec. 1980 (YUN 1980, p. 1195). *Yearbook reference.* [5]1981, p. 1328. *Meeting records.* GA: 5th Committee, A/C.5/37/SR.70 (14 Dec.); plenary, A/37/PV.114 (21 Dec.).

General Assembly resolution 37/237, section XIII

21 December 1982   Meeting 114   Adopted without vote

Approved by Fifth Committee (A/37/790) without vote, 14 December (meeting 70); oral proposal by Chairman; agenda item 103.

Job classification and career development of language staff

[*The General Assembly . . .*]

Takes note of the report of the Secretary-General on the job classification and career development of language staff;

. . .

Job classification

The International Civil Service Commission (ICSC), at its two 1982 sessions,[4] considered the progress of the United Nations and the specialized agencies in putting into effect the Master

Standard (Tier I) formulated in 1980[7] as the first part of a three-tiered system of job classification standards, and considered the draft Tier II standards for certain occupational fields. The Master Standard incorporated a point-factor rating system to measure the relative importance of jobs.

Statistics covering 80 per cent of Professional posts in the United Nations system indicated that the Master Standard had been applied to about 15 per cent of the total posts. While slower than anticipated, progress was considered satisfactory taking into account difficulties encountered by some organizations. ICSC requested organizations to continue providing annual statistics and instructed the secretariats to carry out a comprehensive study on the implementation of the Master Standard after the first three years (1981-1983).

In 1982, ICSC established the Tier II standards for two fields of work—technical co-operation administration and electronic data processing—and approved their promulgation. Tier II described duties and responsibilities at each level within an occupational group, using the rating system of the Master Standard. The ICSC secretariat issued a job classification users' manual for administrators.

The Co-ordination Committee for Development of Classification Standards for the General Service Category in New York, established in February 1981, which included representatives of the administrations and staff of the United Nations, the United Nations Development Programme and the United Nations Children's Fund, unanimously recommended the adoption of the job classification standards it had developed for a seven-level grade structure for General Service posts, to replace the current five levels. ICSC decided that the proposed structure should be established in the three New York–based organizations.

The ICSC decision also took into account the work of the Sub-Committee on Job Classification, a sub-committee of the Consultative Committee on Administrative Questions of the Administrative Committee on Co-ordination (ACC). The Sub-Committee held two sessions in 1982—its seventh, from 24 to 28 May at Geneva,[2] and its eighth, from 8 to 12 November at Vienna[3]—and reported to ACC. It called for a study of classification of General Service posts in non-Headquarters duty stations. At the Vienna session, it examined a draft Tier II standard for civil engineers and decided to separate the standards to be developed for the fields of accounting and finance officers, auditors and budget analysts.

In his September report[5] to the General Assembly on implementation of personnel policy reforms, the Secretary-General described progress in implementing the classification standards. As at 30 June, 1,054 Professional posts had been classified, of which 896 (85 per cent) had been con-firmed at their previous levels, 79 (7.5 per cent) upgraded and 79 downgraded. The Classification Appeals and Review Committee, established in April 1981 to provide recourse on the results of the classification analysis, had examined five cases, and revised two classifications. The classification of new and vacant posts according to the Master Standard (Tier I) and occupational standards (Tier II) continued at the rate of approximately 65 posts each month. In addition, occupational or organizational surveys were carried out, with the object of developing benchmark-level definitions. Progress was made in the occupational groups of administration, economics, language and related work, and library and related work.

Standards for classification of General Service posts at Headquarters in seven levels, as approved by ICSC, would be applied beginning in 1983; standards for jobs in related categories were to be completed by December 1982. Job descriptions and post evaluations for a classification scheme for the General Service at United Nations offices at Geneva were nearly completed; the scheme was expected to be put into effect before the end of 1982. At Vienna, 66.9 per cent (523) of the General Service posts at UNIDO had been classified. Classification schemes were being developed for staff of the Economic Commissions for Africa and for Latin America.

The staff unions and associations of the Secretariat, in an October document[6] transmitted to the Assembly's Fifth Committee by the Secretary-General, viewed job classification as an essential tool to career development, but warned against rigidity in implementating ICSC policies, particularly evident in the application of the point rating system, resulting in manipulation of information in order to change the level of posts to accommodate specific individuals, thus leading to "grade creep". Job classification had been introduced without an overall framework of human resources planning, and related policies of personnel management—training, mobility, interorganizational exchange—and financial planning had not been simultaneously developed.

Similar views on classification were expressed to the Fifth Committee by the Federation of International Civil Servants' Associations (FICSA) in a November document.[1] FICSA believed that classification was valuable as a part of human resources planning but that its implementation must go hand in hand with efforts in other areas of human resources development. Calling for greater flexibility than envisaged by ICSC in the use of personal promotions to adjust shortcomings in a rigid points-factor system, FICSA said that ideally the budgetary organs or legislative bodies should not have to scrutinize upgradings.

Note. [1]S-G, transmitting FICSA comments, A/C.5/37/29.
Reports. CCAQ Sub-Committee on Job Classification, [2]ACC/1982/PER/26, [3]ACC/1983/PER/2; [4]ICSC, A/37/30; [5]S-G, A/C.5/37/5; [6]Staff unions and associations, transmitted by S-G note, A/C.5/37/24.
Yearbook reference. [7]1980, p. 1169.

Competitive examinations
for General Service staff

The Secretary-General, in his September 1982 report[1] to the General Assembly on implementation of personnel policy reforms, observed that the second competitive examination for the promotion of staff in the General Service and related categories to the Professional category had been held in 1981 at 12 centres. Of the 459 candidates who sat for it, 30 successful candidates were promoted as at March 1982.

The third examination took place in October 1982 for posts in administration, economics, finance, political affairs, social development and nursing. Some changes had been made in the format of and marking procedures for the third examination, based on the experience gained and after consultations with staff and management representatives. In addition, a more flexible approach had been adopted for identifying posts for those promoted, and the views of the departments and offices concerned were taken into consideration in assigning them.

The staff unions and associations of the United Nations Secretariat, in a report to the Fifth Committee transmitted by the Secretary-General in October,[2] said the 1981 examination had presented some recurring problems—delays in marking papers, resistance from departments in accepting successful candidates, introduction of *ex post facto* requirements, and encumbrance of some posts earmarked for the candidates by General Service staff with special post allowances. Training was needed both to prepare candidates for the examination and to prepare successful candidates for their new posts, and, despite the problems, the examination should continue on an annual basis. However, the 30 per cent quota of Professional posts at the entry (P-1/P-2) level reserved for successful candidates should be raised to 50 per cent to improve career prospects.

The Assembly, by a resolution of 21 December,[3] requested the Secretary-General to permit General Service candidates participating in competitive examinations for promotion to P-1 and P-2 to take the examination in any of the working languages of the regional commissions, with due regard to the proficiency requisite of the working languages of the Secretariat.

The resolution was adopted without vote, following its consensus approval by the Fifth Committee on 14 December. It was introduced by Panama, also on behalf of 12 other sponsors, and orally revised to indicate that the promotion referred to was to the Professional category at "the P-1 and P-2 levels".

Reports. [1]S-G, A/C.5/37/5; [2]Staff unions and associations, transmitted by S-G note, A/C.5/37/24.
Resolution (1982). [3]GA: 37/235 D, 21 Dec., text following.
Meeting records. GA: 5th Committee, A/C.5/37/SR.13, 23, 25-34, 36-38, 40, 41, 43, 47, *70* (15 Oct. & 1 Nov.–14 Dec.); plenary, A/37/PV.114 (21 Dec.).

General Assembly resolution 37/235 D

21 December 1982   Meeting 114   Adopted without vote

Approved by Fifth Committee (A/37/764) by consensus, 14 December (meeting 70); 13-nation draft (A/C.5/37/L.46), orally revised; agenda item 111.

Sponsors: Costa Rica, Cuba, Dominican Republic, Ecuador, Ethiopia, Iraq, Jordan, Libyan Arab Jamahiriya, Panama, Peru, Spain, Uruguay, Venezuela.

The General Assembly,

Recalling its resolutions 33/143 of 20 December 1978 and 35/210 of 17 December 1980 on personnel questions,

Requests the Secretary-General to permit candidates participating in competitive examinations for passage from the General Service category to the P-1 and P-2 levels of the Professional category to take the examination in any of the working languages of the regional commissions, with due regard to the proficiency requisite of the working languages of the Secretariat.

Staff training

The International Civil Service Commission (ICSC), at its March 1982 session, continued to study inter-agency co-operation in the field of training, as requested by the General Assembly in 1981,[5] and the usefulness of training activities in the United Nations system, particularly in management. It presented in its report to the Assembly[3] the views of the Consultative Committee on Administrative Questions (CCAQ) of the Administrative Committee on Co-ordination and the views of the Federation of International Civil Servants' Associations (FICSA).

CCAQ felt that the principal function of ICSC in this area was the formulation of policy guidelines. United Nations organizations raised the question of the appropriateness of requesting ICSC to carry out a study to be applied to the activities of other organizations without having first consulted them, but CCAQ was prepared to co-operate in the studies on training.

ICSC agreed that CCAQ should be requested to pursue its work in training and that the existing mandate of the secretariat should be renewed to enable further consultations to be carried out. It decided to consider the issues that the Assembly had raised in 1981 at a later session.

FICSA stressed two concerns: the need for increased funds for training and the need for a strong linkage between training and career development. Training funds and activities should be divided equitably between Headquarters and the field, and field staff should be brought to Headquarters for training when feasible. FICSA felt that evaluation of existing training facilities should not be a high-priority item for ICSC, since the agencies were undertaking that exercise.

FICSA also presented its views in a November document transmitted to the Fifth Committee by the Secretary-General.[1] It pointed out that United Nations organizations spent more than 70 per cent of their budget on staff costs, yet none allocated even 1 per cent to staff development, nor in most was there any systematic identification of training needs. It proposed increases in the resources allocated to training, calculated as a specific percentage of staff costs. Measures such as sabbatical leave, study-time entitlement, twinning arrangements with entities outside the United Nations system (universities, industry, etc.) and wider use of staff resources for training and counselling should be explored.

Staff views on training were also presented to the Fifth Committee by the staff unions and associations of the United Nations Secretariat in October.[4] The associations stated that training deserved greater financial and human resources. Priorities needed to be established, with special attention given to field staff through such means as rotational training teams, video-taped training courses and sending staff to headquarters duty stations for training. For headquarters staff, one of the main concerns was the lack of incentives for further study and training. Lifting of some of the restrictions imposed on outside activities, such as authorship, additional training, refresher courses or teaching, would enhance professional development, as would providing salary advances for study, granting study leave and recognition for completion of courses.

The Sub-Committee on Staff Training of CCAQ (Personnel and General Administrative Questions), whose members were representatives of the training services of United Nations organizations, continued to study, compare and co-ordinate the training activities in the system at its ninth session held at Geneva from 11 to 14 October.[2]

Note. [1]S-G, transmitting FICSA comments, A/C.5/37/29.
Reports. [2]CCAQ(PER) Sub-Committee on Staff Training, ACC/1983/PER/3; [3]ICSC, A/37/30; [4]Staff unions and associations, transmitted by S-G note, A/C.5/37/24.
Resolution. [5]GA: 36/233, 18 Dec. 1981 (YUN 1981, p. 1323).

Status of language teachers

The Secretary-General, in response to a 1981 request by the General Assembly,[4] submitted in December 1982 a report[2] on the contractual status of language teachers, expanding on his 1981 proposal[5] to give language teachers at Headquarters the status of staff members. He also outlined a plan for providing pension coverage to the teachers within the existing contractual arrangements.

Should Headquarters teachers be granted staff member status, the Secretary-General said, then about 28 full-time teachers serving at other duty stations might expect the same treatment. He proposed creating a separate group of locally-recruited staff to be called "language teachers", who would be remunerated in accordance with the best prevailing conditions of employment in the locality. Pending determination of the appropriate salary level, he proposed to pay Headquarters teachers a salary equivalent to that of the G-5 level of the General Service category. The proposal would require an additional appropriation of $310,300 for 1983.

The Advisory Committee on Administrative and Budgetary Questions (ACABQ) commented on the Secretary-General's proposals in December 1982.[1] It had considerable difficulty with the proposal to change the teachers' status and expressed scepticism that their schedule could be effectively adapted to the normal work schedule of United Nations staff. In its view, the necessary job security could be accorded to them by devising a new contract, whose provisions could include: a term of one to three years, remuneration calculated on an annual basis at the current level of payment, a requirement of at least 15 hours teaching time per week for at least 10 months per year, provision for sick and maternity leave, and post-employment benefits. The ACABQ proposal would have no financial implications other than $106,000 for pension benefits through the United Nations Joint Staff Pension Fund.

The General Assembly, in a resolution of 21 December,[3] took note of the reports of the Secretary-General and ACABQ. It adopted, on an interim basis, the ACABQ recommendations and decided to consider the matter again in 1983 on the basis of an updated report by the Secretary-General.

The resolution was adopted without vote, following its approval without objection by the Fifth Committee on 17 December. The text was proposed orally by the Chairman on a suggestion by Egypt. At the same meeting, the Committee approved, without objection, an additional appropriation of $106,000 under the 1982-1983 budget to implement the recommendations.

Reports. [1]ACABQ, A/37/7/Add.24; [2]S-G, A/C.5/37/63.
Resolution (1982). [3]GA: 37/237, sect. XV, 21 Dec., text following.
Resolution (prior). [4]GA: 36/235, sect. XV, 18 Dec. 1981 (YUN 1981, p. 1333).
Yearbook reference. [5]1981, p. 1332.
Meeting records. GA: 5th Committee, A/C.5/37/SR.75 (17 Dec.); plenary, A/37/PV.114 (21 Dec.).

General Assembly resolution 37/237, section XV

21 December 1982   Meeting 114   Adopted without vote

Approved by Fifth Committee (A/37/790) without objection, 17 December (meeting 75); oral proposal by Chairman on suggestion by Egypt; agenda item 103.

Contractual status of language teachers

[*The General Assembly ...*]

1. *Takes note* of the report of the Secretary-General on the contractual status of language teachers at Headquarters, Geneva, Vienna, Nairobi and the headquarters of regional commissions and the related report of the Advisory Committee on Administrative and Budgetary Questions;

2. *Adopts,* on an interim basis, the recommendations made by the Advisory Committee in its report;

3. *Decides* to consider fully the question of the contractual status of language teachers at its thirty-eighth session on the basis of an updated report to be submitted by the Secretary-General.

Amendments to the Staff Regulations and Rules

The General Assembly, by a two-part resolution of 21 December 1982,[5] amended two articles and an annex of the Staff Regulations of the United Nations which concerned the procedure for amending or supplementing the Regulations and Rules, staff relations and the repatriation grant. The Assembly also endorsed recommendations of ACABQ on the repatriation grant (see below, under REMUNERATION).

Annexed to the resolution were the amendments to the Regulations. Under the amended article XII, pertaining to general provisions, the regulations could be supplemented or amended by the Assembly, without prejudice to the acquired rights of staff members. Such staff rules and amendments that the Secretary-General might make to implement the regulations would be provisional until approved by the Assembly. The full text of provisional staff rules and amendments would be reported annually to the Assembly by the Secretary-General and, if approved, would enter into force on 1 January the year after the report was made to the Assembly.

These changes flowed from other changes in the Regulations dealing with entitlement to the repatriation grant.

The Assembly adopted section I without vote; it had been similarly approved by the Fifth Committee on 11 December; it outlined the procedure for supplementing or amending the Regulations and clarified eligibility for the repatriation grant. Section II amended regulations on relations between the Secretary-General and the staff (see below).

The text of section I was proposed by ACABQ in a November report on the repatriation grant.[3] The United States introduced an amendment, which the Fifth Committee adopted without vote, to insert the words "The full text of" in regulation 12.3, preceding the statement that "provisional staff rules and amendments shall be reported annually" to the Assembly. The United States withdrew a second amendment[1] calling for those rules and amendments to go into effect on 1 January following the year in which the report was "considered by" rather than "made to" the Assembly. The USSR orally proposed and subsequently withdrew an amendment to add a statement in the resolution to the effect that the validity of rules which gave rise to different opinions in the Assembly, but on which it had taken no decision, would be temporarily suspended. The USSR withdrew its amendment on the understanding that however the Secretary-General reported on provisional rules or amendments, the

Assembly should take action to note them with approval, withhold approval or suspend their application.

By a decision of 21 December,[2] the Assembly took note of the Secretary-General's August report[4] on the amendments he had made to the Staff Rules, since his last report in 1981,[6] to implement the Staff Regulations. Those amendments dealt with such areas as termination indemnity, repatriation grant, commutation of accrued annual leave, last day for pay purposes, official holidays, re-employment, official travel, resignation procedure, and revised salary scales for the Field Service staff and those in the General Service and related categories.

The Assembly adopted the decision without vote; the Fifth Committee had approved it without objection on 14 December on an oral proposal by its Chairman.

Amendment withdrawn. [1]United States, A/C.5/37/L.36, para. 2.
Decision (1982). [2]GA: 37/447, 21 Dec., text following.
Reports. [3]ACABQ, A/37/675; [4]S-G, A/C.5/37/6 & Corr.1.
Resolution (1982). [5]GA: 37/235 C, 21 Dec., text following.
Yearbook reference. [6]1981, p. 1334.
Meeting records. GA: 5th Committee, A/C.5/37/SR.49, 53, 56, 58, 63, 65, 70 (30 Nov.–14 Dec.); plenary, A/37/PV.114 (21 Dec.).

General Assembly resolution 37/235 C

21 December 1982   Meeting 114   Section I adopted without vote
Section II, 128-9-3 (recorded vote)

Approved by Fifth Committee (A/37/764): sections I and II and annex, paragraphs 1 and 2, without vote, 11 December (meeting 65), and annex, paragraph 3, by vote (76-10-7), 14 December (meeting 70); draft by ACABQ (A/37/675, annex II), amended by United States (A/C.5/37/L.36, paragraph 1); agenda item 111.

The General Assembly,

I

Bearing in mind that Article 101 of the Charter of the United Nations provides that the staff shall be appointed by the Secretary-General under regulations established by the General Assembly,

Mindful of Judgement No. 273 of the United Nations Administrative Tribunal and the advisory opinion of 20 July 1982 of the International Court of Justice reviewing that judgement,

1. *Takes note* of the note by the Secretary-General on the repatriation grant and the related report of the Advisory Committee on Administrative and Budgetary Questions;

2. *Endorses* the comments and recommendations of the Advisory Committee as contained in its report;

3. *Decides* that, with effect from 1 January 1983, article XII of the Staff Regulations of the United Nations and the introductory paragraph of annex IV to the Staff Regulations shall be amended as shown in paragraphs 1 and 2 of the annex to the present resolution;

II

Having considered the note of the Secretary-General on an amendment to the Staff Regulations of the United Nations,

Decides that article VIII of the Staff Regulations of the United Nations shall be amended as shown in paragraph 3 of the annex to the present resolution.

ANNEX
Amendments to the Staff Regulations of the United Nations

1. Article XII (General provisions) of the Staff Regulations shall read as follows:

"*Regulation 12.1:* These regulations may be supplemented or amended by the General Assembly, without prejudice to the acquired rights of staff members.

"*Regulation 12.2:* Such staff rules and amendments as the Secretary-General may make to implement these regulations shall be provisional until the requirements of regulations 12.3 and 12.4 below have been met.

"*Regulation 12.3:* The full text of provisional staff rules and amendments shall be reported annually to the General Assembly by the Secretary-General. Should the Assembly find that a provisional rule and/or amendment is inconsistent with the intent and purpose of the Regulations, it may direct that the rule and/or amendment be withdrawn or modified.

"*Regulation 12.4:* The provisional rules and amendments reported by the Secretary-General, taking into account such modifications and/or deletions which may be directed by the General Assembly, shall enter into full force and effect on 1 January following the year in which the report is made to the Assembly.

"*Regulation 12.5:* Staff rules shall not give rise to acquired rights within the meaning of regulation 12.1 while they are provisional."

2. The introductory paragraph of annex IV (Repatriation grant) of the Staff Regulations shall be amended to read:

"In principle, the repatriation grant shall be payable to staff members whom the Organization is obligated to repatriate. The repatriation grant shall not, however, be paid to a staff member who is summarily dismissed. Staff members shall be entitled to a repatriation grant only upon relocation outside the country of the duty station. Detailed conditions and definitions relating to eligibility and requisite evidence of relocation shall be determined by the Secretary-General. The amount of the grant shall be proportional to the length of service with the United Nations, as follows:".

3. Article VIII (Staff relations) of the Staff Regulations shall read as follows:

"*Regulation 8.1: (a)* The Secretary-General shall establish and maintain continuous contact and communication with the staff in order to ensure the effective participation of the staff in identifying, examining and resolving issues relating to staff welfare, including conditions of work, general conditions of life and other personnel policies.

"*(b)* Staff representative bodies shall be established and shall be entitled to initiate proposals to the Secretary-General for the purpose set forth in *(a)* above. They shall be organized in such a way as to afford equitable representation to all staff members, by means of elections that shall take place at least biennially under electoral regulations drawn up by the respective staff representative body and agreed to by the Secretary-General.

"*Regulation 8.2:* The Secretary-General shall establish joint staff/management machinery at both local and Secretariat-wide levels to advise him regarding personnel policies and general questions of staff welfare as provided in regulation 8.1."

Recorded vote in Assembly as follows:

In favour: Algeria, Angola, Argentina, Australia, Austria, Bahamas, Bahrain, Bangladesh, Barbados, Belgium, Benin, Bhutan, Bolivia, Botswana, Brazil, Burma, Burundi, Canada, Central African Republic, Chad, Chile, China, Colombia, Comoros, Congo, Costa Rica, Cuba, Democratic Kampuchea, Democratic Yemen, Denmark, Dominican Republic, Ecuador, Egypt, El Salvador, Ethiopia, Fiji, Finland, France, Gabon, Gambia, Germany, Federal Republic of, Ghana, Greece, Grenada, Guatemala, Guinea, Guinea-Bissau, Guyana, Honduras, Iceland, India, Indonesia, Iran, Iraq, Ireland, Israel, Italy, Ivory Coast, Jamaica, Jordan, Kenya, Kuwait, Lebanon, Lesotho, Liberia, Libyan Arab Jamahiriya, Luxembourg, Madagascar, Malawi, Malaysia, Maldives, Mali, Malta, Mauritania, Mexico, Morocco, Mozambique, Nepal, Netherlands, New Zealand, Nicaragua, Niger, Nigeria, Norway, Oman, Pakistan, Panama, Papua New Guinea, Paraguay, Peru, Philippines, Portugal, Qatar, Rwanda, Saint Lucia, Samoa, Sao Tome and Principe, Saudi Arabia, Senegal, Sierra Leone, Singapore, Solomon Islands, Somalia, Spain, Sri Lanka, Sudan, Suriname, Swaziland, Sweden, Syrian Arab Republic, Thailand, Togo, Trinidad and Tobago, Tunisia, Turkey, Uganda, United Arab Emirates, United Kingdom, United Republic of Cameroon, United Republic of Tanzania, United States, Upper Volta, Uruguay, Venezuela, Yemen, Yugoslavia, Zaire, Zambia.

Against: Bulgaria, Byelorussian SSR, Czechoslovakia, German Democratic Republic, Hungary, Mongolia, Poland, Ukrainian SSR, USSR.

Abstaining: Afghanistan, Japan, Romania.

General Assembly decision 37/447

Adopted without vote

Approved by Fifth Committee (A/37/764) without objection, 14 December (meeting 70); oral proposal by Chairman; agenda item 111.

Amendments to the Staff Rules

At its 114th plenary meeting, on 21 December 1982, the General Assembly, on the recommendation of the Fifth Committee, took note of the report of the Secretary-General on the amendments to the Staff Rules.

Staff-management relations

By section II of a two-part resolution of 21 December 1982,[7] the General Assembly amended article VIII of the Staff Regulations of the United Nations, which dealt with staff relations. Under the new article, the Secretary-General would establish and maintain continuous contact and communication with the staff in order to ensure its participation in identifying, examining and resolving issues relating to staff welfare, including conditions of work, general conditions of life and other personnel policies. Staff representative bodies were to be established and entitled to initiate proposals to the Secretary-General for those purposes. Those bodies were to afford equitable representation to all staff members, by means of (at least biennial) elections under regulations drawn up by the respective staff representative body and agreed to by the Secretary-General, who was to establish joint staff/management machinery at both local and Secretariat-wide levels to advise him regarding personnel policies and general questions of staff welfare.

The amendment was made on the recommendation of the Secretary-General in a note to the Assembly dated 20 November,[4] following a comprehensive review of the subject undertaken with staff participation. He said it was aimed at ensuring a more active and constant staff participation in resolving staff welfare issues, recognizing staff representative bodies and establishing joint staff/management machinery at other duty stations besides Headquarters, and allowing for less frequent elections to them if desired.

Section II of the resolution was adopted separately by the Assembly by a recorded vote of 128 to 9, with 3 abstentions. In the Fifth Committee, the USSR proposed that consideration of the amendments to article VIII be deferred until 1983. By 51 votes to 15, with 18 abstentions, the Committee rejected the proposal. The Committee then approved on 14 December the draft amendments to article VIII by 76 votes to 10, with 7 abstentions.

The Federation of International Civil Servants' Associations (FICSA), in comments transmitted to the Fifth Committee in November by a note from the Secretary-General,[3] complained of the exclusion of union representatives from the decision-making process at all levels in the United Nations system, and proposed fuller staff participation in the deliberations of the International Civil Service Commission (ICSC).

In an October document,[6] the staff unions and associations of the Secretariat said that the Staff Rules and Regulations, written 30 years earlier, needed to be updated, to recognize the right of staff representative bodies to negotiate with the Secretary-General and to have regular dialogue with the Assembly. They suggested reforms to speed up grievance machinery and give its decisions full force and effect. To enhance the decision-making process at Geneva and Vienna, they proposed a greater degree of decentralization, particularly in the annual promotion review which would require appropriate staff representation through local appointment and promotion bodies. Another issue of primarily local concern was the reclassification of posts.

During the Fifth Committee's debate on personnel questions, on a proposal by Sweden, the Committee decided, without vote on 1 November, to extend an invitation to a staff representative to make an oral presentation before the Committee.

At another meeting, Jordan introduced a draft amendment[1] to the 1980 Assembly resolution[8] which outlined the procedure for presentation of the staff's views to the Fifth Committee. The proposed amendment would have had the effect of allowing the designated representative of the Coordinating Committee for Independent Staff Unions and Associations of the United Nations System (CCISU) to make its views known to the Assembly and the Committee in the same manner as FICSA. After several reservations had been expressed about the legality of amending a previously adopted resolution or about the advisability of the Committee's interjecting itself into internal staff affairs, Jordan withdrew its proposal but reserved its right to present a new draft decision at a suitable time.

The Administrative Committee on Coordination (ACC), on 3 November, adopted a decision[2] endorsing a proposal by the Secretary-General that its Consultative Committee on Administrative Questions (CCAQ) be invited to conclude a study on determining the conditions under which ACC might accept requests for hearing by staff representatives and report on its findings to the next ACC session. ACC agreed to hear a representative of CCISU during its current session.

The CCAQ/FICSA Joint Working Party on Staff-Management Relations, which had been constituted in 1975 to explore ways of improving the working climate of the international civil service, held its third meeting at Geneva from 15 to 19 February. In a report to CCAQ,[5] the Working Party presented its ideas on confidential files, staff access to governing bodies, measures to prevent discrimination against staff representatives, and grievance and recourse procedures.

Amendment withdrawn. [1]Jordan, A/C.5/37/L.24.
Decision (1982). [2]ACC: 1982/18, 3 Nov.
Notes. S-G, [3]A/C.5/37/29 (transmitting FICSA comments), [4]A/C.5/37/54.
Reports. [5]CCAQ/FICSA Working Party on Staff-Management Relations, ACC/1982/PER/15; [6]Staff unions and associations, transmitted by S-G note, A/C.5/37/24.
Resolution (1982). [7]GA: 37/235 C, sect. II, & annex, para. 3, 21 Dec.
Resolution (prior). [8]GA: 35/213, 17 Dec. 1980 (YUN 1980, p. 1196).

Retirement

The General Assembly, by a resolution of 17 December 1982,[8] requested ICSC, in co-operation with the United Nations Joint Staff Pension Board, to undertake a study of the age of separation and retirement in all member organizations, and to submit proposals based thereon to the Assembly in 1983.

The Pension Board, in its 1982 report to the Assembly,[7] had proposed a draft resolution calling for measures to improve the actuarial balance of the Pension Fund, among them that age 62 be established in all its member organizations as the statutory age of separation and that, in the mean time, executive heads of the organizations be granted discretionary authority to extend service to at least age 62. During discussions on the Pension Board's report by the Fifth Committee, a Committee Vice-Chairman, following informal consultations, proposed replacing the paragraph by one requesting ICSC to study the question. The text proposed by the Vice-Chairman[1] would have called for a study of a "uniform" age of separation and retirement, but he agreed to an oral amendment by Ghana and Kenya deleting reference to a uniform age, and a Ghanaian suggestion to add a phrase to indicate that the views expressed in the Fifth Committee were also to be taken into account. The Fifth Committee approved the draft resolution as a whole by 85 votes to 1, with 15 abstentions (see section below on UN JOINT STAFF PENSION FUND, under REMUNERATION).

In arriving at its proposal, the Pension Board studied various suggestions offered in the Fifth Committee in 1981,[9] including increasing the age of separation beyond the current age of 60, without reducing entitlements linked to age currently established. Arguments advanced for raising the retirement age included actuarial savings and bringing United Nations practice more in line with that of the comparator civil service system. The Board also had before it the outcome of consideration of the matter by ICSC at its March 1982 session:[4] i.e. that it could not pronounce itself on the actuarial benefit of the proposal at that time—noting that the Pension Board had not yet taken a position on the deferment of the retirement age—and recommending that the Assembly not take any decision on the matter until ICSC had examined the issue in the broader context of an overall retirement policy.

The Board noted with regret that ICSC had been unable to pronounce itself on the personnel policy aspects of such a change but instead proposed to study the entire question. Nevertheless, the Board believed that it had the responsibility to come to a clear-cut conclusion on the matter, towards improving the Fund's actuarial balance; therefore, it recommended raising the mandatory separation age to 62, the age already set by the Food and

Agriculture Organization of the United Nations. Entitlements to rights currently existing on separation before that age would continue to be maintained.

The Advisory Committee on Administrative and Budgetary Questions, commenting in a November report[3] to the Assembly on the United Nations pension system and on measures the Board had proposed to improve the Fund's actuarial balance, said that representatives of the Board had informed it that savings would arise not only because staff members older than 60 would continue contributing to the Fund, but also because they would draw retirement benefits for fewer years. The right to retire with full benefits at age 60 was not questioned but, by staying on to age 62, staff members could increase their retirement payments.

In a September report[5] on the implementation of personnel policy reforms, the Secretary-General described current retirement policy. Extensions of service beyond age 60 were granted up to six months solely for finding replacements for retiring staff. (Some flexibility was applied to staff in posts with special language requirements, General Service staff with special technical skills and General Service staff already employed prior to December 1978 and who would have less than 20 years' contributory service to the Fund at age 60.) As at 30 June 1982, there were 79 staff members over age 60 retained in service; in 1978 there had been 132.

The staff unions and associations of the United Nations Secretariat, in an October document,[6] rejected the proposal to change the retirement age. Retirement policy must be consistent with staff welfare, career development, the acquired rights of those already in service, and the need to improve geographical distribution and to lower the average age of the Secretariat, as well as with the interests of the Organization; it could not be determined on actuarial grounds. The associations supported the ICSC proposal to collect more information on the issue.

FICSA also rejected discussion of the retirement age in the context of the actuarial deficit of the Pension Fund. Stressing the importance of equity in a November document,[2] FICSA said it did not oppose giving the staff the option of working until age 62, provided that this option was available to staff at all levels, that it was exercised by choice of the staff member, and that existing rights to earlier retirement were not affected. It supported deferral of a decision and urged that the ICSC study of retirement age be undertaken in conjunction with its study on recruitment policy, including the desirability and feasibility of recruitment of staff at a younger age.

Amendment adopted. [1]5th Committee Vice-Chairman, based on informal consultations, A/C.5/37/L.40/Rev.1, para. 1.

Note. [2]S-G, transmitting FICSA comments, A/C.5/37/29.
Reports. [3]ACABQ, A/37/674; [4]ICSC, A/37/30; [5]S-G, A/C.5/37/5; [6]Staff unions and associations, transmitted by S-G note, A/C.5/37/24; [7]UNJSPB, A/37/9 & Corr.1-4.
Resolution (1982). [8]GA: 37/131, sect. I, para. 2, 17 Dec.
Yearbook reference. [9]1981, p. 1353.

Field personnel

Assignment allowance and installation grant. The General Assembly, in a resolution of 17 December 1982,[7] noted that ICSC had started a comprehensive review of conditions of service in the field. It also noted an ICSC decision to increase the provisions of the assignment allowance by 50 per cent (to $600 for staff members and dependants; maximum, $2,400 per family) and to double the lump-sum portion of the installation grant received by field staff. The Assembly's action took effect on 1 January 1983.

ICSC, during its two 1982 sessions,[5] began a review of conditions of service in the field, which could encompass a comprehensive review of allowances, benefits and salary elements paid to field staff, job classification, security of personnel (see below), career development and the problems of mobility. At the request of the Administrative Committee on Co-ordination (ACC), it had also reviewed the levels and applicability of two field staff allowances: the installation grant and the assignment allowance.

The installation grant was paid to staff members who travelled to a new duty station on an assignment for at least a year and was intended to cover the initial expenses. It consisted of the equivalent of 30 days of subsistence allowance and half of that rate for each accompanying dependant; it could be extended at a reduced rate up to 90 days under certain conditions. At some duty stations (in general, those outside Europe and North America), the amount was a lump sum of $300 for the staff member and for each dependant (maximum, $1,200). The assignment allowance compensated, for up to five years, Professional-and-above staff outside their home country whose household effects were not shipped, to enable them to purchase essential household equipment and furnishings. The amount paid ranged from $800 to $2,400 depending on grade, duty station and marital status.

The Chairman of the Consultative Committee on Administrative Questions (CCAQ), presenting the views of ACC on the installation grant and assignment allowance, stressed the need to increase both allowances. He presented a series of proposals for other changes, which included the establishment of a pre-departure allowance to defray certain costs on transfer or assignment, and a quarters allowance to cover housing costs outside the post adjustment system.

FICSA felt that increases were long overdue, supported the proposal for the pre-departure allowance, and mentioned areas where improvements in conditions of field staff should be made, including housing costs, security measures, crisis management, career development, training and job classification.

ICSC members agreed to defer consideration of any innovations (such as the payment of pre-departure hotel expenses, extension of the lump sum to headquarters staff in certain circumstances and approval of a regressive scale for the assignment allowance) until its examination of the comprehensive review of field conditions at a future session. It approved a programme of studies on the conditions of field staff and decided to include field service staff in its programme.

Other aspects of conditions of service in the field. ICSC considered other aspects of conditions of service in the field on the basis of comments by CCAQ and FICSA—as well as the recommendations of an ICSC working group on a scheme for classifying duty stations according to conditions of life and work. The new scheme, replacing a plan which had granted rest and recuperation leave, classified duty stations in groups with certain entitlements, according to conditions. As an interim measure, ICSC gave its Chairman authority to establish entitlements of duty stations which had not previously been examined, giving them provisional ratings that would be reviewed by the working group.

ICSC also continued its work in developing a methodology for establishing salary scales for national Professional staff—i.e. locally recruited for duty stations away from Headquarters. It decided to defer its discussion of the issues raised until after the completion of its review of the general methodology of salary surveys in field duty stations, meanwhile asking CCAQ for additional statistics.

By its decision of 6 April[1] to seek an increase in the installation grant, ACC had also recommended that executive heads of United Nations organizations consider seeking, in appropriate cases, the approval of legislative and governmental bodies for the purchase or construction of housing in field duty stations where suitable housing was lacking. It urged ICSC to review the way housing costs were met, including the possibility of separating them from the post adjustment system, and requested CCAQ to continue studying the problem of staff members transferring from duty stations with high post adjustment classes to those with low classes.

In its annual overview report for 1981/82 submitted to the Economic and Social Council in May 1982,[3] ACC said that, while the United Nations system did provide benefits and entitlements specifically designed for service in the field and/or for staff movement between duty stations, prompt and remedial action was required in other areas such as housing, installation grants, cost-of-living and post adjustments, shipment and insurance of personal effects and assignment allowances. The conditions of service of national staff in the field were also of major concern to ACC.

The conditions of the General Service staff in the field had also been considered by the ACC Working Party on Conditions of Service of General Service Staff in the Field, which met at Geneva from 15 to 19 February 1982.[4] It considered several problems of staff in this category, in particular the lack of security of employment, ways to improve recruitment practices, the limited possibilities for career development, the need for and difficulties in providing training, the lack of uniformity in the application of staff rules, performance appraisal, medical evacuation and insurance, reassignment, security, and difficult working environments.

In a November document,[2] FICSA said that the remuneration of field staff was considerably less attractive than that offered by many comparable employers, such as national civil services and bilateral aid agencies. It welcomed the ICSC decision to undertake an overall review of conditions of service in the field; priority should be given to those areas in which ICSC could develop policy guidelines at the inter-agency level and to review of the remuneration package.

The staff unions and associations of the United Nations Secretariat, in an October report,[6] suggested that the following points should be addressed by the Fifth Committee and then referred to ICSC for further study: review of the maximum compensation for losses and procedures to ensure prompt processing of claims; extension of health and life insurance coverage to local staff; increased benefits at difficult duty stations; re-examination of the entire system of allowances to provide for improvements in the assignment allowance, installation grant, and mobility incentives.

Decision (1982). [1]ACC: 1982/4, 6 Apr.
Note. [2]S-G, transmitting FICSA comments, A/C.5/37/29.
Reports. [3]ACC, E/1982/4; [4]ACC Working Party on Conditions of General Service Staff in Field, ACC/1982/PER/11; [5]ICSC, A/37/30; [6]Staff unions and associations, transmitted by S-G note, A/C.5/37/24.
Resolution (1982). [7]GA: 37/126, sect. III, paras. 2 & 6, 17 Dec.

Security

The staff unions and associations of the United Nations Secretariat, in an October 1982 report,[2] said that current *ad hoc* security arrangements for staff serving in the field were inadequate. The Organization needed a well-conceived contingency security plan to cope with emergencies as well as more specialized experts in security planning to evaluate the needs of individual duty stations. Staff members being sent to the field should be briefed about possible dangers, local conditions and general background for their work. The staff associations recommended that the Office of Co-ordination for Security Measures at Headquarters co-operate in this matter with the Emergency Co-ordination Unit of the United Nations Development Programme and a representative of the Secretary-General.

In a November document,[1] FICSA also pointed to increasing outbreaks of violence and civil unrest and called for measures to ensure the protection and safety of United Nations personnel. In its view, staff security suffered from inadequate inter-agency funding and priority should be given to a review of the system's security needs, based not on expenditures but on requirements, and a review of emergency measures and evacuation plans for all staff.

In a resolution of 21 December,[3] the General Assembly welcomed measures approved by the Secretary-General to enhance the safety and protection of international civil servants (see section on PRIVILEGES AND IMMUNITIES below).

Note. [1]S-G, transmitting FICSA comments, A/C.5/37/29.
Report. [2]Staff unions and associations, transmitted by S-G note, A/C.5/37/24.
Resolution (1982). [3]GA: 37/236 A, para. 3, 21 Dec.

Day-care services

In a report on child-care services at United Nations Headquarters,[3] submitted to the General Assembly in December 1982, the Secretary-General said that, in the light of the 1981 Assembly decision[5] to study alternatives to his proposal for a day-care centre at Headquarters, he had established a task force of staff and administration representatives to review possible options for child care in New York. It had conducted a survey of 129 day-care facilities in the vicinity of Headquarters to determine the type of care and space available to children of staff and mission personnel, and engaged day-care specialists to conduct a professional assessment of needs. The Day Care Council of New York, which found a clear need for child-care assistance, presented its report and recommendations to the task force in November 1982.

Based on the study, the task force made proposals, which were endorsed by the Secretary-General. It called for the establishment of a crèche for up to 50 infants. The $372,600 cost would be offset by fees paid by parents, approximately $85 per child per week, leaving an estimated deficit of $185,600.

For pre-school and school-age children, the task force proposed using a network of existing family day-care homes, licensed and supervised in accordance with New York State law. A co-ordinator would be needed to assist staff members and evalu-

ate programmes, at a cost of $44,100 for six months.

The Advisory Committee on Administrative and Budgetary Questions (ACABQ), commenting on the Secretary-General's proposals,[2] recommended that he continue to explore, with interested parents and others, the establishment of a crèche as an independent incorporated entity; as such, there would be no contractual relationship with the United Nations nor would the Organization assume any responsibility to underwrite the operating deficits. Once the crèche had been established, United Nations assistance should be in the form of a grant, not to exceed a lump sum of $100,000. Rather than establishing a separate function of co-ordinator, ACABQ preferred strengthening the Staff Counsellor's Office in the Office of Personnel for advising staff on day care, at a cost of $18,100.

FICSA, in a November document,[1] said it was pleased that the provision of child-care facilities was now a matter of social policy and that organizations had agreed that they should provide assistance for such facilities in duty stations where need was demonstrated.

The need for a social policy to include provision of child-care facilities at various duty stations was also stressed by the staff unions and associations of the United Nations Secretariat in October,[4] which urged that action be taken to establish such facilities at Headquarters.

The Assembly's Fifth (Administrative and Budgetary) Committee considered the question on 14 December. The United States proposed that the Assembly take note of the reports of the Secretary-General and ACABQ and request an updated report, to be submitted to the Assembly in 1983, on the feasibility and financial implications of the recommendations contained in them. The Committee rejected this proposal by 73 votes to 18, with 11 abstentions. It then decided, by 83 votes to 5, with 16 abstentions, to recommend that the Assembly take note of the two reports and concur with the comments and recommendations of ACABQ. It approved the appropriation of $18,100 that such action would entail.

Note. [1]S-G, transmitting FICSA comments, A/C.5/37/29.
Reports. [2]ACABQ, A/37/7/Add.21; [3]S-G, A/C.5/37/69; [4]Staff unions and associations, transmitted by S-G note, A/C.5/37/24.
Resolution. [5]36/235, sect. XVI, 18 Dec. 1981 (YUN 1981, p. 1334).
Meeting record. GA: 5th Committee, A/C.5/37/SR.69 (14 Dec.).

Privileges and immunities

By a resolution of 21 December 1982,[6] the General Assembly took note with concern of a report[4] submitted to it by the Secretary-General on behalf of the Administrative Committee on Co-ordination (ACC), which showed a marked deterioration in the observance of the principles related to privileges and immunities of officials of the United Nations and the specialized agencies and related organizations. Welcoming measures approved by the Secretary-General to enhance the safety and protection of international civil servants, as outlined in his report, the Assembly invited him, as ACC Chairman, to suggest in his 1983 annual report on this issue further steps to alleviate the situation.

The resolution was adopted without vote, having been similarly approved by the Fifth Committee on 14 December. The Netherlands introduced the draft on behalf of 16 sponsors.

By a related resolution[7] adopted on the same day, the Assembly called for measures to be taken with a view to obtaining the release of officials of the United Nations Relief and Works Agency for Palestine Refugees in the Near East (UNRWA) arrested in Lebanon.

The Secretary-General, in his 1982 annual report on privileges and immunities of United Nations officials, listed cases of arrest and detention of staff members of the United Nations and its related organizations and described other violations of conventions on privileges and immunities, such as searches by agents of airlines, opening of diplomatic pouches, travel restrictions and withdrawal of duty-free privileges. The report, approved and submitted by ACC to the Assembly in November,[1] was based on information received from United Nations subsidiary organs, offices or missions and specialized or related agencies.

The largest number of arrests and detentions during the reporting period, from 1 July 1981, was reported by UNRWA—194 cases. The United Nations Development Programme reported 11 cases of arrest and detention, and the United Nations Children's Fund one case of detention; a staff member from each organ remained under detention since before the reporting period. Two cases of arrest and temporary detention of staff family members were reported by the United Nations Industrial Development Organization, and three cases of arrest and detention by the Economic Commission for Africa (bringing the total to six). Two staff members of the Economic Commission for Latin America previously reported detained had not been released, and the United Nations Educational, Scientific and Cultural Organization described a case in which a staff member was believed to have been prevented by his Government from returning to work in Paris.

In May 1982, the Secretary-General appointed a task force composed of representatives of the administration and the staff to prepare proposals concerning the security, safety and independence of the international civil service. On the basis of the group's proposals and other recommendations, he approved the following measures: issuance of an instruction setting out the procedures for reporting to Headquarters cases of arrest or detention, disappearance or death of any employee or family member; improvement of the security system at each duty station through designating wardens and providing training and equipment; system-wide sharing of information on security problems arising from natural disasters or conflict situations; and regular review of contingency plans. The Secretary-General would continue his efforts, including personal contacts with Governments or designating a representative to act on his behalf, to ensure that staff members were accorded treatment in conformity with international law and with the applicable bilateral agreements with the host country.

In October,[5] the staff unions and associations of the United Nations Secretariat also gave an accounting of staff members arrested, detained or missing. According to their figures, the number of those staff members increased to 21 since September 1981. In most cases, a representative of the Secretary-General had been denied access to them, in contravention of the 1946 Convention on the Privileges and Immunities of the United Nations,[8] and a case was cited to demonstrate that the Secretary-General's personal attention in such matters could make a difference. The associations supported the proposals of the task force on staff security and appealed to Member States to respect agreements in this regard.

FICSA, in November,[3] said there had not been any progress in the settlement of a number of outstanding cases of arbitrary arrest, detention and disappearance of staff. It appealed to States to grant the Secretary-General or his representative the right to visit the staff members concerned, to be informed of charges and to ensure that they were given due legal process. It appealed to States, on humanitarian grounds, to reveal the whereabouts of staff in cases of disappearance and facilitate the speedy conclusion of investigations in cases of death.

In a letter of 11 November to the Secretary-General,[2] Mozambique described why it had detained a staff member of the Food and Agriculture Organization of the United Nations and said he had been expelled from the country in September.

Decision (1982). [1]ACC: 1982/30, 3 Nov.
Letter. [2]Mozambique, 11 Nov., A/C.5/37/45.
Note. [3]S-G, transmitting FICSA comments, A/C.5/37/29.
Reports. [4]S-G, A/C.5/37/34 & Corr.1; [5]Staff unions and associations, transmitted by S-G note, A/C.5/37/24.
Resolutions (1982). GA, 21 Dec.: [6]37/236 A, text following; [7]37/236 B.
Resolution (prior). [8]GA: 22 A (I), annex, 13 Feb. 1946 (YUN 1946-47, p. 100).
Meeting records. GA: 5th Committee, A/C.5/37/SR.13, 23, 25, 34, 36-38, 40, 41, 43, 47, *63, 70,* 77 (15 Oct. & 1 Nov.-20 Dec.); plenary, A/37/PV.114 (21 Dec.).

General Assembly resolution 37/236 A

21 December 1982   Meeting 114   Adopted without vote

Approved by Fifth Committee (A/37/764) without vote, 14 December (meeting 70); 16-nation draft (A/C.5/37/L.37); agenda item 111 *(b)*.

Sponsors: Australia, Barbados, Belgium, Canada, Denmark, Germany, Federal Republic of, Ghana, Ireland, Italy, Jamaica, Netherlands, New Zealand, Nigeria, Norway, Spain, Sweden.

The General Assembly,

Recalling its resolutions 35/212 of 17 December 1980 and 36/232 of 18 December 1981,

1. *Takes note with concern* of the report submitted to the General Assembly by the Secretary-General on behalf of the Administrative Committee on Co-ordination, which showed, *inter alia*, a marked deterioration in the observance of the principles related to privileges and immunities of officials of the United Nations and the specialized agencies and related organizations;

2. *Reaffirms* the above-mentioned resolutions;

3. *Welcomes* the measures approved by the Secretary-General to enhance the safety and protection of international civil servants as outlined in his report;

4. *Invites* the Secretary-General, as Chairman of the Administrative Committee on Co-ordination, to suggest in his annual report on this issue to be submitted to the General Assembly at its thirty-eighth session further steps designed to alleviate the present situation.

Remuneration

The General Assembly, in a five-part resolution of 17 December 1982[2] on the report of the International Civil Service Commission (ICSC), noted the results of an ICSC review of the post adjustment system applied to salaries of staff members in the Professional category and invited ICSC to continue to improve the methodology for cost-of-living measurements and to make recommendations in 1984 on the basis for determining Professional remuneration. The Assembly noted the methodology for surveys of best prevailing conditions of service of General Service staff at headquarters duty stations, and that ICSC had started a review of conditions of service in the field (see section above on FIELD PERSONNEL, under PERSONNEL QUESTIONS). Regarding staff salaries, the Assembly pointed out to Member States that the practice of supplementary payments or deductions was inappropriate.

The Assembly decided that the education grant would remain an expatriate benefit. It also increased the children's allowance for the Professional category, and noted ICSC decisions to increase the assignment allowance and the installation grant for field staff (see FIELD PERSONNEL above). It approved a procedure for adjusting cost-of-living differential factors applicable to certain retirees of the Professional category and agreed that no reduction factor would be applied to retirees from the General Service and related categories. It requested ICSC to complete in 1983 a study of the need for a rental subsidy in headquarters duty stations and to examine the need for raising organizations' contributions for health insurance.

A United States amendment[1]—proposed during the discussions of the ICSC report in the Assembly's Fifth Committee—to add a sixth section to the resolution, by which the Assembly would have authorized the Secretary-General to implement the provisions of the resolution only to the extent to which the resultant costs could be financed without exceeding the 1982-1983 budget, was not acted upon.

Amendment not acted upon. [1]United States, A/C.5/37/L.43. *Resolution (1982).* [2]GA: 37/126, sects. I-III, 17 Dec.

Salary system

Salaries of the Professional category

The General Assembly, in its resolution[8] of 17 December 1982 on the report of ICSC, took note of the current status of the comparison between the total compensation in the comparator civil service (the United States federal civil service) and that in the United Nations common salary system. It asked ICSC to review further the basis for the determination and level of remuneration of the Professional and higher categories, with a view to making recommendations to the Assembly in 1984, and thereafter periodically on remuneration levels.

In taking this action on Professional salary scales, the Assembly considered a proposal of the executive heads of the United Nations organizations to increase those salaries by 5 per cent. It also took into account the fact that a majority of ICSC members favoured an increase, but had been unable to reach a consensus on the size. Subsequently, the Assembly, at its 1982 session, decided not to make any change in the salary scales at that time.

During 1982, ICSC continued to examine the salary system of the Professional and higher categories of the United Nations staff (levels P-1 to D-2) and to compare it with the remuneration levels of the United States federal civil service. The comparisons were adjusted for the cost-of-living differences between New York and Washington, D. C., and were averaged over 12 months. For comparison purposes, the United Nations salary figures included post adjustment, a salary supplement used to compensate for cost-of-living changes and differences between duty stations. In its September report to the Assembly,[6] ICSC noted the following developments during the previous year in the comparator service: an increase in base salary; changes in rates of federal taxation; further implementation of the higher-grades (Senior Executive Service) system; bonuses and performance awards issued to higher grades; and implementation of a merit-pay system. The remuneration system of the United Nations, meanwhile, had one development—an increase in the post adjustment for New York with effect from 1 October 1981 and an expected increase to take effect from 1 September 1982.

In determining salary levels, the United Nations had for more than 30 years applied the Noblemaire Principle, whereby salaries in the Professional and higher categories were based on the best paid national civil service. A "margin" was added to the base scale to compensate for the predominantly expatriate character of the United Nations service, but the margin level had never been defined.

The margin by which United Nations salaries exceeded those of the United States Government for the period of October 1981 to September 1982 at matching grades was an average ratio of 118.2 (or 18.2 per cent), as compared with 117.8 a year earlier (United States civil service salaries = 100). Widening of the margin had been due mainly to the fact that the salary increases of the United States civil service had not kept pace with the movement in the cost of living, and, although real income of United Nations officials continued to decline, losses in real income experienced by the United States civil service employees were greater than those of United Nations officials.

In comparing compensation, ICSC took into account the differences between the two services in average length of service (greater in the United States, thus increased pension annuities) and mandatory retirement age (60 for most United Nations organizations; no limitation in the comparator service) (see section on RETIREMENT, under PERSONNEL QUESTIONS above). It instructed its secretariat to collect additional information for analysing further whether the mandatory retirement age was an advantage or disadvantage for staff.

The Commission agreed that the comparison of total compensation should not only be based on non-expatriate elements of compensation but that it should also take into account expatriate benefits on both sides. More resources would be needed if the Assembly wished ICSC to develop a methodology for comparing those benefits.

Due to problems encountered in applying the Noblemaire Principle, the ICSC secretariat considered two alternative approaches. The first proposal called for full pay comparability between United States private as well as public sectors. Under the second, the comparison would be made with United States levels as they would have evolved had full pay comparability between the private and public sectors been established. If the latter system had been used, the margin between the United Nations and United States would have been 108.1. After examining information in this regard, ICSC reaffirmed the validity of the Noblemaire Principle and that the United States should remain the comparator service. It decided to consider the matter at a future date.

Throughout 1982, the Administrative Committee on Co-ordination (ACC) had continued to view with concern the erosion in the purchasing power of Professional salaries. An ACC body, the Consultative Committee on Administrative Questions (Personnel and General Administrative Questions) (CCAQ(PER)), at a February/March meeting at Geneva, had concluded a report for ACC on the remuneration of the Professional and higher categories.[5] The report dealt with possible ways of applying the Noblemaire Principle and suggested one approach as the most promising: determining the percentage of salary increase by splitting the difference between the rate of increase in the United States civil service and the rate in the non-governmental sector of the United States. In a decision of 6 April,[1] ACC requested CCAQ(PER) to elaborate proposals on the level of remuneration of the Professional and higher categories for submission by ACC to ICSC at its July session, and to continue exploring possible alternatives and remedies for the particular problems existing in certain duty stations by virtue of anomalies in the post adjustment system.

After considering the CCAQ report on its special session at Geneva from 1 to 4 June, ACC adopted on 5 July[2] a statement on the level of Professional remuneration and transmitted it to ICSC. That statement presented the views of ACC on the loss in purchasing power, the United Nations/United States margin, a comparison between the United Nations and real income movements in other national civil services and international organizations, the application of the Noblemaire Principle, total compensation comparison and expatriation benefits. The CCAQ Chairman informed ICSC, at the latter's July session, that ACC considered that the periodic review of the level of base remuneration, which was intended to correct the effect of the regressive feature of the post adjustment system, should not be further postponed, considering that almost eight years had elapsed since the last adjustment of base salary. It felt that an increase of the net salary scale by 5 per cent, with effect from 1 January 1983, would be fair and reasonable. The cost for all organizations and sources of funds was estimated at $45.5 million (1.3 per cent of total expenditures).

The two organizations representing staff associations—the Federation of International Civil Servants' Associations (FICSA) and the Co-ordinating Committee for Independent Staff Unions and Associations of the United Nations System (CCISU)—expressed their view to ICSC that an increase of 10 per cent was necessary. FICSA suggested that the increase should be across the board, without differentiation by grade, while CCISU proposed that the increase should be applied only from the P-1 to P-5 levels on a retrogressive scale.

FICSA reiterated its views in a document transmitted by the Secretary-General to the Fifth Committee in November,[4] in which it urged a 10 per cent interim adjustment, pending completion of the long-term studies on methodology for fixing remuneration, and a return to regular Professional salary reviews.

While most ICSC members agreed that an increase was justified, they were unable to reach a consensus on its size. Accordingly, it agreed to transmit the various views on the matter to the Assembly for decision.

By a decision of 3 November,[3] ACC adopted another statement on the level of remuneration of Professional staff members, elaborating on the considerations which had led the executive heads to recommend a 5 per cent salary increase. It expressed disappointment that ICSC had not made a specific recommendation on this question.

Supplementary payments to international civil servants. Responding to a 1981 request[9] by the Assembly to study supplementary payments to international civil servants and related matters, ICSC considered the findings of CCAQ on the question—that little concrete evidence existed on staff member salary supplements and deductions made by Governments. Observing that it did not have direct relations with Member States and therefore was not in a position to undertake a comprehensive survey, ICSC again proposed that the Assembly point out that the practice was inappropriate, undesirable, and inconsistent with the Staff Regulations of the United Nations.

Both FICSA and the staff unions and associations of the United Nations Secretariat stated, in November[4] and October[7] respectively, that supplementary payments were inconsistent with the spirit of the Charter of the United Nations and the provisions of the Staff Regulations, and constituted a threat to the independence and integrity of the international civil service.

In its resolution of 17 December[8] on the report of ICSC, the Assembly called the attention of Member States to the fact that the practice of supplementary payments or deductions was inconsistent with the Staff Regulations and, therefore, inappropriate. Australia said that, despite its positive vote, it had reservations on that paragraph. Japan and the Federal Republic of Germany abstained because of reservations on it.

Decisions (1982). ACC: [1]1982/5, 6 Apr.; [2]1982/14, 5 July; [3]1982/32, 3 Nov.
Note. [4]S-G, transmitting FICSA comments, A/C.5/37/29.
Reports. [5]CCAQ(PER), ACC/1982/5; [6]ICSC, A/37/30; [7]Staff unions and associations, transmitted by S-G note, A/C.5/37/24.
Resolution (1982). [8]GA: 37/126, sect. II, 17 Dec.
Resolution (prior). [9]GA: 36/233, 18 Dec. 1981 (YUN 1981, p. 1323).

Post adjustment

ICSC reviewed in 1982 the purposes and operation of the post adjustment system, which provided supplements to the base salaries of staff in the Professional-and-above categories to compensate for cost-of-living changes and differences between duty stations. In its 1982 report to the General Assembly,[3] ICSC identified a number of issues relating to the operation of the post adjustment system which had been considered by its Advisory Committee on Post Adjustment Questions (ACPAQ).

ICSC discussed preparations under way for the use of a new methodology for cost-of-living measurement in a number of duty stations where United Nations headquarters or regional offices were located. Both ACPAQ and ICSC considered the problem of housing costs faced by newcomers at some duty stations which were currently excluded from the application of the rental subsidy scheme; ICSC agreed that a working group should study the effects of extension of the scheme to such duty stations and report to it in 1983. ICSC requested its secretariat to continue studies on the effects of currency fluctuations and inflation on the post adjustment system, to eliminate distortions, and approved a number of modifications to procedures for the administration of the system which would have the effect of providing relief in situations of abrupt currency devaluations and excessive inflation.

ICSC continued to classify duty stations for the purpose of applying post adjustments. It considered post adjustment for Geneva at the request of the staff unions and associations there, which had protested a decision to lower the post adjustment for Geneva by 5 per cent on the grounds that it was based on two technically controversial surveys.

In view of the complexity of the problem, ICSC decided that its secretariat should continue to study the matter and that, in the mean time, in all countries where local currency had recently appreciated, a remuneration correction factor should be applied. It agreed that the interim measure should be used for modifying post adjustment at affected duty stations, with effect from 1 August 1982. Such adjustments should continue to be made until a permanent solution could be found or the results of place-to-place surveys were implemented.

This action was based on a recommendation by ACPAQ made at its seventh session (Vienna, 17-28 May),[2] when it also considered the issues of housing problems of newcomers to duty posts (see above) and a special index for pensioners (see INDEXATION OF COST-OF-LIVING ADJUSTMENT TO INCOME TAX RATES below).

FICSA, in comments transmitted to the Assembly in November,[1] said it was monitoring closely the results of the cost-of-living surveys being carried out at major duty stations on the basis of the revised methodology and it welcomed the imminent publication of a descriptive booklet and technical manual on the post adjustment system. It also looked forward in particular to completion of the study on measures to ease the housing problems of newcomers at headquarters duty stations.

By its resolution[4] of 17 December on the ICSC report, the Assembly noted the results of the ICSC review of the purposes and operation of the post adjustment system and the need to continue to improve the system, and in particular invited ICSC to continue to improve the methodology for cost-of-living measurements.

Note. [1]S-G, transmitting FICSA comments, A/C.5/37/29.
Reports. [2]ACPAQ, ACC/1982/23; [3]ICSC, A/37/30.
Resolution (1982). [4]GA: 37/126, sect. II, para. 3, 17 Dec.

Income tax

The Administrative Committee on Co-ordination (ACC), in a decision of 6 April 1982,[1] requested the Secretary-General, in his capacity as ACC Chairman, to prepare, and after appropriate consultations to transmit to the United States Secretary of State, a statement on the question of the reimbursement of income taxes levied on salaries of United States nationals. The ACC action was based on the report of its Consultative Committee on Administrative Questions (Financial and Budgetary Questions) (CCAQ(FB)) on its session in Paris from 8 to 12 March.[2] ACC authorized the Chairman of CCAQ to constitute a team of senior officials to conduct discussions with the United States Government on this subject if this were found necessary or appropriate.

In 1981, the United States had approached several United Nations organizations with respect to amending agreements with them regarding reimbursement of income taxes levied on United States nationals serving on their staff.[3] The proposal would involve changing the modalities of reimbursing income taxes paid by international staff. Because such a change raised questions about the equality of treatment of officials of different nationalities and about the financial responsibilities of the United Nations organizations, CCAQ(FB) had proposed that the Secretary-General send such a statement to the Secretary of State, explaining the issues in detail.

Decision (1982). [1]ACC: 1982/12, 6 Apr.
Report. [2]CCAQ(FB), ACC/1982/6.
Yearbook reference. [3]1981, p. 1342.

Salaries of the General Service category

Following several years of work in conducting surveys to determine the best prevailing conditions of employment for the General Service and other locally recruited staff, the International Civil Service Commission (ICSC) reported in 1982[2] on progress in the promulgation of a comprehensive methodology. The objective of the general methodology was to apply the same principles at all headquarters duty stations and, with some modification, to all non-headquarters duty stations while allowing for flexibility in the application to account for local conditions. The first phase of the review was the establishment of a general methodology for surveys of several best employers at the duty stations. In the second phase, the review was to include salaries and other conditions of service in field duty stations and periodic adjustments to salaries, other allowances, staff assessment and pensionable remuneration for staff at all duty stations. The third phase would include social security, salary scales for other locally recruited categories, overtime and shift differentials, and other methods for determining the best prevailing conditions.

The Commission approved the general methodology developed by its secretariat for headquarters duty stations and described the procedure in its 1982 report to the General Assembly. It postponed consideration of a final general methodology for non-headquarters duty stations until 1983.

As part of the second phase of a comprehensive study on the conditions of employment for the General Service and other locally recruited staff, ICSC studied the question of periodic adjustments to their salaries, between surveys of best prevailing conditions. It endorsed the principle of automatic adjustments between salary surveys in headquarters duty stations. For the application of the principle, it approved a methodology based on an appropriate index or combination of indexes (wage or price). Adjustments to salary scales would be made when the reference index moved by 5 per cent or more; in the event that the index did not move 5 per cent within 12 months, an adjustment would be made on the basis of the movement that did occur. Changes in local taxation would be taken into account when such adjustments were made.

The Commission studied a report prepared for it by the Centre d'étude de technique et d'évaluation legislatives of the University of Geneva on the differences in remuneration for men and women in Geneva. The Commission concluded that although the study had confirmed the incidence of sex discrimination in the Geneva labour market, it had failed to provide a precise measure of the level of that difference. The divergent views in ICSC led members to conclude that it was not possible to arrive at a figure of the percentage differential in male/female remuneration for work of equal value on the basis of purely objective means; however, ICSC decided to increase mean salaries for such jobs by 10 per cent, retroactive to March 1980.

The views of the Federation of International Civil Servants' Associations (FICSA) on General Service salaries were transmitted by the Secretary-General to the Fifth (Administrative and Budgetary) Committee in November.[1] Noting that those salaries were fixed according to the principle of "best prevailing local conditions", FICSA said the ICSC methodology for salary surveys, to be used at all headquarters duty stations, should be applied with the greatest flexibility, given the diversity of conditions and concerns. It was not satisfied that the concerns at the various headquarters duty stations had been adequately taken into account, and it reserved its position on the methodology, pending further review by ICSC. As for the methodology for non-headquarters duty stations, FICSA believed that priority should be given to major existing problems at field duty stations, namely, delays in the salary survey process and the inadequacy of interim adjustments.

The General Assembly, by its resolution of 17 December[3] on the ICSC report, took note of the general methodology for surveys of best prevailing conditions of service of the staff in the General Service and related categories approved by ICSC for application to headquarters duty stations.

Note. [1]S-G, transmitting FICSA comments, A/C.5/37/29. *Report.* [2]ICSC, A/37/30.
Resolution (1982). [3]GA: 37/126, sect. III, para. 1, 17 Dec.

Allowances

Education grant

The General Assembly, in a resolution of 17 December 1982,[3] decided that the education grant would remain an expatriate benefit to be granted to all United Nations expatriate officials, but that nationals returning to duty stations in their home country might receive the grant for the balance of a school year. The Assembly requested ICSC to keep the question of the education grant under review, particularly in regard to the situation of officials subject to rotation between headquarters and other duty stations, and taking account of the views expressed by delegations.

The sponsors of the draft resolution in the Fifth Committee, following consultations, orally revised the paragraph by which it was decided that the grant would "remain" rather than "be solely" an expatriate benefit, and added words to specify that nationals returning "to duty stations" in their home country could receive the grant for the balance of the school year.

Reporting to the Assembly in accordance with a 1981 request[5] that it review the scope and purpose of the education grant, ICSC pointed out that the grant had always been regarded as an expatriate element of compensation—established to help parents meet some of the extra costs involved in educating their children in such a way that they did not become alienated from their national system of education. It noted that the Consultative Committee on Administrative Questions (CCAQ), a subsidiary body of the Administrative Committee on Co-ordination, was preparing data on education costs, the adequacy of the grant and the purpose for which it was being used, but it had not completed its work. CCAQ favoured extending the grant to those formerly expatriated staff who had returned for a tour of duty to their home country and were therefore ineligible for the grant, although often facing schooling problems stemming from their former expatriate service. In its view, such extension would enhance staff mobility.

ICSC concluded that the grant should remain solely an expatriate benefit to be granted to all United Nations expatriate officials and it should not be extended, except for expatriate staff members who returned to their home country for reassignment.[2]

FICSA had requested ICSC to abandon the current reimbursement formula and return to the 75 per cent reimbursement scheme, because of rising education costs. It offered justification for extending the grant to non-expatriate Professional staff and locally recruited General Service staff. Calling for a study on a duty-station-by-duty-station basis, FICSA proposed that the grant be payable for pre-primary education and that the upper age-limit be extended in deserving cases. The Co-ordinating Committee for Independent Staff Unions and Associations of the United Nations System also called for extending the grant to all staff without discrimination.

In a November document,[1] FICSA expressed disappointment at the lack of progress made on the education grant in 1982, and called on the Assembly to refer the matter of extending the grant to all staff back to ICSC for further study.

The Assembly, by a resolution of 21 December,[4] decided to consider the question of the education grant for certain full-time non-Secretariat officials as part of an overall review in 1983 of the conditions of service of those officials.

Note. [1]S-G, transmitting FICSA comments, A/C.5/37/29. *Report.* [2]ICSC, A/37/30.
Resolutions (1982). GA: [3]37/126, sect. III, paras. 4 & 5, 17 Dec.; [4]37/237, sect. XIV, 21 Dec.
Resolution (prior). [5]GA: 36/233, 18 Dec. 1981 (YUN 1981, p. 1323).

Repatriation grant

By a resolution of 21 December 1982,[3] the General Assembly decided that, with effect from 1983, article XII of the United Nations Staff Regulations (outlining procedures for supplementing or amending the Regulations (see above, under PERSONNEL QUESTIONS)) and the introductory paragraph of annex IV to the Regulations (on the repatriation grant) would be amended.

The new introductory paragraph stated that, in principle, the repatriation grant would be payable to eligible staff members; it would not, however, be paid to a staff member who was summarily dismissed. Staff members would be entitled to such a grant only upon relocation outside the country of the duty station, and the Secretary-General would determine conditions and definitions of eligibility and requisite evidence of relocation. The amount of the grant would be proportional to the length of service with the United Nations.

At the same time, the Assembly took note of the Secretary-General's note[1] on the repatriation grant and the related report of the Advisory Committee on Administrative and Budgetary Questions (ACABQ)[2] and endorsed the ACABQ comments and recommendations. The ACABQ position was not to contest the Secretary-General's proposed action to apply a judgement—Judgement No. 273 of the United Nations Administrative Tribunal, which was the subject of an advisory opinion by the International Court of Justice on 20 July 1982 *(Mortished v. the Secretary-General of the United Nations)*—to similar claims by staff members who had accrued qualifying service for a repatriation grant prior to 1 July 1979. In that judgement, the Tribunal recognized that the applicant was entitled to receive a repatriation grant on the terms defined in the staff rules, despite the fact that the relevant rule was no longer in force on the date of his separation from the United Nations. Accordingly, a repatriation grant would be payable to staff members with qualifying service, without the need to provide evidence of relocation. However, ACABQ proposed, and annexed to its report, amendments to the Regulations to reflect the specific intent of the Assembly concerning the repatriation grant—that the grant should only be paid to former staff members who relocated. This text was approved by the Fifth Committee. ACABQ also proposed changes to the general provisions of the Regulations pertaining to methods for supplementary or amending procedures in any case where the evolution of a practice resulted in a departure from the Assembly's original intent.

Note. [1]S-G, A/C.5/37/26.
Report. [2]ACABQ, A/37/675.
Resolution (1982). [3]GA: 37/235 C, sect. I, & annex, para. 2, 21 Dec.

Other allowances

The General Assembly, in a resolution of 17 December,[4] took action on the children's allowance, a study for a rental subsidy and health insurance. It decided that the children's allowance for the Professional and higher categories would be increased to $700 as from 1 January 1983, and that the currency floor measures designed to ensure an equitable level of the allowance everywhere be maintained, based on the 12-month average exchange rate ending 30 June 1982, for all duty stations. It requested the International Civil Service Commission (ICSC) urgently to complete its study of the need for a rental subsidy arrangement in headquarters duty stations of organizations of the United Nations common system, particularly with regard to newcomers and staff transfers, and asked it to examine the need for raising the ratio of contributions by those organizations for staff health insurance, including the question of applying retroactivity. In addition, the Assembly noted an ICSC decision to increase the assignment allowance and the installation grant received by field staff.

ICSC, in its 1982 report to the Assembly,[2] had reviewed the children's allowance for all categories of staff, as requested by the Assembly in 1981.[5] With respect to the General Service category, ICSC said that in most cases the children's allowance was based on practices prevailing at the local duty station as determined by periodic surveys of best prevailing local conditions. With regard to the Professional category, the secretariat suggested that a more systematic procedure be used to determine the amount of the allowance in view of the fact that the current amount of $450 was largely determined on a judgemental basis.

The Consultative Committee on Administrative Questions expressed the view that a differentiation between children's allowances in the two categories should continue to be made because of the difference in the principles governing their salaries and allowances. It supported a universal rate of children's allowance for staff in the Professional and higher categories, but considered that the calculation of that rate should be based not only on the situation in a single comparator country but also on progressive social policy in other countries. The President of the Federation of International Civil Servants' Associations (FICSA) indicated that organization's preference for a unified system of dependency allowances for all categories. It supported the proposal for a floor for the allowances where there was no local practice or where such practice resulted in insignificant amounts. FICSA recalled its earlier proposal that the allowance for Professional staff be increased to $750 in the light of cost-of-living movements and the development of social legislation as well as tax practices in the seven headquarters duty stations.

Having considered those views, ICSC decided that the children's allowance should remain a social benefit for all staff and should continue to be differentiated between the General Service and the Professional categories. For General Service staff, it agreed that a floor amount should be set for areas where local practices allowed for a smaller amount; in those areas where local practice provided for larger allowances, the local amount would prevail. The flat-rate allowance would be determined on the basis of 3 per cent of the mid-point of the salary scale of each duty station, as opposed to the current practice based on the minimum of the salary scale.

For the Professional category, ICSC recommended the action subsequently taken by the Assembly in its resolution of 17 December.[4] The United States, explaining its negative vote on that resolution, said it would have been able to accept the paragraph establishing the children's allowance if the additional costs could have been absorbed from within available resources. Japan, which voted for the resolution, also expressed reservations about that paragraph.

In 1982, ICSC reviewed other allowances for the General Service category, although it recommended no changes in current practice. It began a review of dependency allowances for all categories of staff, examined the language allowance for proven proficiency in an official language other than the mother tongue, and discussed the establishment of the spouse allowance as a benefit available at all duty stations. It also studied the non-resident's allowance, which was granted in cases where local salaries were not sufficiently high to attract qualified staff from other countries with the required qualifications. It requested its secretariat to make proposals in 1983 on guidelines concerning the administration and the amount of the non-resident's allowance.

FICSA expressed its views on dependency allowances to the Fifth Committee in November.[1] It felt that an increase in the level of the children's allowance for Professional staff had been overdue for several years. FICSA said the methodology adopted by ICSC for determining the General Service allowance, based on the mid-point of the local salary scale, was flawed since it penalized low-income staff.

In comments transmitted to the Fifth Committee in October,[3] the staff unions and associations of the United Nations Secretariat expressed concern at the rising cost of health care, which was reflected in increased health insurance premiums. Noting that the United States was paying 75 per cent of health insurance costs for federal civil servants and a number of diplomatic services provided even better medical coverage, the associations said that urgent action was needed to improve the health insurance subsidy system in the United Nations.

Note. [1]S-G, transmitting FICSA comments, A/C.5/37/29.
Reports. [2]ICSC, A/37/30; [3]Staff unions and associations, transmitted by S-G note, A/C.5/37/24.
Resolution (1982). [4]GA: 37/126, sect. III, paras. 3 & 6-8, 17 Dec.
Resolution (prior). [5]GA: 36/233, 18 Dec. 1981 (YUN 1981, p. 1323).

UN Joint Staff Pension Fund

The number of participants in the United Nations Joint Staff Pension Fund declined from 51,048 on 31 December 1981 to 50,966 as at 31 December 1982. During the same period the principal of the Fund increased from $2,458,365,968 to $2,763,185,751, and income from interest and dividends, less investment management costs, was $188,727,000, as compared with $166,638,000 in 1981. At the end of 1982, the Fund was paying 6,458 retirement benefits, 6,407 early and deferred retirement benefits, 2,213 widows' and widowers' benefits, 3,467 children's benefits, 417 disability benefits and 36 secondary dependants' benefits. In the course of the year, it also paid 4,055 lump-sum withdrawal and other settlements. Fourteen member organizations of the United Nations system belonged to the Fund in 1982.

The United Nations Joint Staff Pension Board, which administered the Fund, held its thirtieth session at Geneva from 9 to 20 August 1982. The major item dealt with by the Board was an analysis of all possible measures to improve the actuarial balance of the Fund, which the General Assembly in 1981[5] had asked the Board to carry out, in co-operation with ICSC. At its 1982 session, the Board also considered investments of the Fund, the financial statements of the Fund and report of the Board of Auditors, a special index for pensioners, proof of residence by pensioners, financial obligations of pensioners to their spouses or former spouses, methodology and assumptions for the actuarial valuation of the Fund as from 1983, admission to membership in the Fund, administrative expenses and the Emergency Fund.

The Board's annual report to the Assembly, issued in November,[3] contained recommendations for action by the Assembly, as well as the report of the Board of Auditors, financial statements for 1981, a summary of the Fund's investments and an accounting of administrative expenses.

Following consideration of the Board's recommendations, the Assembly on 17 December 1982 adopted a six-part resolution dealing with aspects of the Board's report.[4] The Assembly approved measures to improve the actuarial balance of the Fund by amending the Fund's Regulations (see section on RETIREMENT, under PERSONNEL QUESTIONS above), admitted the European and Mediterranean Plant Protection Organization to membership in the Fund, authorized the Board to supplement contributions to the Emergency Fund, approved administrative expenses, requested the Board to continue studying financial obligations of pensioners to their spouses or former spouses, and requested the Board to submit proposals for eliminating the possibility of excluding staff members from participation in the Fund.

The resolution was adopted by a recorded vote of 129 to 1, with 12 abstentions. The Fifth Committee had approved the text on 13 December by a vote, requested by the United States, of 85 to 1, with 15 abstentions. The text was based on a draft included in the Board's report and included amendments introduced by a Vice-Chairman of the Committee following informal consultations.

Two amendments concerned a study of retirement age (see above, under PERSONNEL QUESTIONS), and exception from pension coverage of non-Secretariat officials (see below, under OTHER UN OFFICIALS). The latter amendment[1] was rejected.

Two other amendments added sections on benefits for spouses of pensioners and on eliminating exclusions from participating in the Fund (see below).

The Advisory Committee on Administrative and Budgetary Questions (ACABQ) issued its own report on the pension system in November,[2] commenting in particular on the Board's proposals on measures to improve the actuarial balance of the Fund, the extension of pension coverage to officials other than staff members, and administrative expenses.

Amendment rejected. [1]5th Committee Vice-Chairman, A/C.5/37/L.40/Rev.1, para. 2.
Reports. [2]ACABQ, A/37/674; [3]UNJSPB, A/37/9 & Corr.1-4.
Resolution (1982). [4]GA: 37/131, 17 Dec., text following.
Resolution (prior). [5]GA: 36/118 B, 10 Dec. 1981 (YUN 1981, p. 1345).
Financial implications. S-G notes, A/C.5/37/90 & Add.1.
Meeting records. GA: 5th Committee, A/C.5/37/SR.45, 48, 51, 58, *63*, 67 (26 Nov.–13 Dec.); plenary, A/37/PV.109 (17 Dec.).

General Assembly resolution 37/131

17 December 1982   Meeting 109   129-1-12 (recorded vote)

Approved by Fifth Committee (A/37/761) by vote (85-1-15), 13 December (meeting 67); draft by UNJSPB (A/37/9), amended by Vice-Chairman (A/C.5/37/L.40/Rev.1: paragraph 1 as orally sub-amended by Ghana and by Kenya; and paragraph 3); agenda item 113.

Report of the United Nations Joint Staff Pension Board
The General Assembly,

Having considered the report of the United Nations Joint Staff Pension Board to the General Assembly and to the member organizations of the United Nations Joint Staff Pension Fund for 1982, chapter III of the report of the International Civil Service Commission and the related report of the Advisory Committee on Administrative and Budgetary Questions,

Noting, in particular, the unanimous proposals made by the Board in response to the request of the General Assembly to undertake a comprehensive analysis of all possible measures to improve the actuarial balance of the Fund, bearing in mind the views expressed in the Fifth Committee,

Noting further that a co-operative effort by member organizations, participants and beneficiaries—sharing equitably the burdens such measures may impose on them—is required if the actuarial imbalance is to be reduced significantly,

I

Measures to improve the actuarial balance of the
United Nations Joint Staff Pension Fund

1. *Approves* the measures designed to improve the actuarial balance of the United Nations Joint Staff Pension Fund which are con-

tained in section III.A of the report of the United Nations Joint Staff Pension Board;

2. *Requests* the International Civil Service Commission, in co-operation with the United Nations Joint Staff Pension Board, to undertake the study of the age of separation and of retirement in all member organizations, bearing in mind all the relevant resolutions of the General Assembly together with the views expressed in the Fifth Committee, and to submit proposals based thereon to the General Assembly at its thirty-eighth session;

3. *Amends,* with effect from 1 January 1983, the Regulations of the United Nations Joint Staff Pension Fund, without retroactive effect, as set forth in annex XII of the report of the Board, and the pension adjustment system in accordance with annexes IX and X thereof;

II

Admission to membership in the United Nations Joint
Staff Pension Fund of the European and
Mediterranean Plant Protection Organization

Decides to admit the European and Mediterranean Plant Protection Organization to membership in the United Nations Joint Staff Pension Fund, in accordance with article 3 of the Regulations of the Fund, with effect from 1 January 1983;

III

Emergency Fund

Authorizes the United Nations Joint Staff Pension Board to supplement the voluntary contributions to the Emergency Fund, for a further period of one year, by an amount not exceeding $100,000;

IV

Administrative expenses

Approves expenses, chargeable directly to the United Nations Joint Staff Pension Fund, totalling $5,955,300 (net) for 1983 and reductions of $205,400 (net) for 1982 for the administration of the Fund;

V

Financial obligations of pensioners to their spouses or former spouses

1. *Takes note* of section III.F of the report of the United Nations Joint Staff Pension Board concerning the absence of effective measures for dealing with the financial obligations of a pensioner to his or her spouse or former spouse which, in some cases, might give rise to serious hardship;

2. *Requests* the Board to pursue the search for such measures along the lines indicated in paragraph 84 of its report or by any other methods and to report thereon to the General Assembly at its thirty-eighth session;

3. *Also requests* the Board to examine the effects of the dissolution of a marriage on survivors' entitlements, together with the possibility of granting such benefits to spouses whose marriage was contracted after the service of a participant had ceased, and to report thereon to the General Assembly not later than at its thirty-ninth session;

4. *Further requests* the Board, in formulating proposals with regard to the above, to bear in mind that these should have no financial implications for the Fund;

VI

Elimination of the possibility of excluding or preventing
staff members from participation in
the United Nations Joint Staff Pension Fund

1. *Takes note* of the views expressed by the United Nations Joint Staff Pension Board in paragraphs 24 and 25 of its report;

2. *Requests* member organizations of the United Nations Joint Staff Pension Fund to furnish to the Board, without delay, information regarding exclusions of members of their staff from participation in the Fund;

3. *Requests* the Board, in the light of such information, to submit proposals to the General Assembly at its the thirty-eighth session for removing the exclusion provision from article 21 of the Regulations of the Fund.

Recorded vote in Assembly as follows:

In favour: Afghanistan, Algeria, Angola, Argentina, Australia, Austria, Bahamas, Bahrain, Bangladesh, Barbados, Belgium, Benin, Bhutan, Bolivia, Botswana, Brazil, Burma, Burundi, Canada, Central African Republic, Chad, Chile, China, Colombia, Comoros, Congo, Costa Rica, Cuba, Cyprus, Democratic Yemen, Denmark, Djibouti, Dominica, Dominican Republic, Ecuador, Egypt, El Salvador, Ethiopia, Fiji, Finland, France, Gabon, Gambia, Germany, Federal Republic of, Ghana, Greece, Grenada, Guatemala, Guinea, Guinea-Bissau, Honduras, Iceland, India,

Indonesia, Iran, Iraq, Ireland, Israel, Italy, Ivory Coast, Jamaica, Jordan, Kenya, Kuwait, Lebanon, Lesotho, Liberia, Libyan Arab Jamahiriya, Luxembourg, Madagascar, Malawi, Malaysia, Maldives, Mali, Malta, Mauritania, Mauritius, Mexico, Morocco, Mozambique, Nepal, Netherlands, New Zealand, Niger, Nigeria, Norway, Oman, Pakistan, Panama, Papua New Guinea, Paraguay, Peru, Philippines, Portugal, Qatar, Rwanda, Samoa, Sao Tome and Principe, Saudi Arabia, Senegal, Sierra Leone, Singapore, Solomon Islands, Somalia, Spain, Sri Lanka, Sudan, Suriname, Swaziland, Sweden, Syrian Arab Republic, Thailand, Togo, Trinidad and Tobago, Tunisia, Turkey, Uganda, United Arab Emirates, United Kingdom, United Republic of Cameroon, United Republic of Tanzania, Upper Volta, Uruguay, Venezuela, Yemen, Yugoslavia, Zaire, Zambia, Zimbabwe.

Against: United States.

Abstaining: Bulgaria, Byelorussian SSR, Czechoslovakia, German Democratic Republic, Hungary, Japan, Mongolia, Poland, Romania, Ukrainian SSR, USSR, Viet Nam.

Finances of the Fund

The General Assembly, by its resolution of 17 December 1982 on the report of the United Nations Joint Staff Pension Board,[3] approved the measures designed to improve the actuarial balance of the United Nations Joint Staff Pension Fund which were contained in the Board's 1982 report,[2] except for a proposal that the retirement age be raised from 60 to 62.

The Board submitted recommendations for action on this matter in response to a 1981 Assembly request.[4] It concluded that, while the situation required immediate corrective measures, it was not at that time advisable to invoke article 27 of the Fund's Regulations which mandated extra payments to the Fund by member organizations if it should be unable to meet its liabilities. While the measures proposed were not intended immediately to remove the total imbalance (7.3 per cent of pensionable remuneration), they were designed to reduce it by 3.8 per cent and set a course towards re-establishing an actuarial balance.

The measures proposed were part of a package affecting: the personnel policies of the member organizations; the Fund's benefit and adjustment system; and the system of contributions. The recommendations regarding benefits and contributions would require amendments to the Regulations of the Fund (see below).

Among the proposals affecting personnel policies were raising the age of mandatory separation from service from 60 to 62 (for a 0.35 per cent saving in terms of pensionable remuneration), hiring staff at a younger age, eliminating the possibility of excluding or preventing certain staff members from participating in the Fund, requiring timely payments of contributions during leave without pay if that period was to be counted as contributory service, and extension of pension coverage to officials who were paid by member organizations for services but were not staff members.

With regard to expected savings through changes in the benefit system, a reduction for new participants in the rate of accumulation to a retirement benefit during the first 10 years of contributory service would yield a saving of 1.84 per cent of pensionable remuneration, while changes in the system of pension adjustments and in the interest rate used in the lump-sum commutations were estimated to result in a saving of 1.09 per cent. The abolition of article 26 of the Regulations (which provided for the return to the employing organization of one half of the contributions made for a staff member who, on separation from service after less than five years, became entitled to a withdrawal settlement) would result in a 0.52 per cent saving.

ACABQ, in November,[1] commented on the Board's recommendations. It noted that, to correct fully the 7.3 per cent imbalance, the current rate of contribution (21 per cent, of which 14 per cent was payable by the member organizations and 7 per cent by the participants) would have to be raised to 28.3 per cent—higher than the Board's 1981 estimates.

One proposal with cost implications for member organizations was the proposed elimination of article 26 of the Fund's Regulations. Noting that the proposed measures, if approved in their entirety, were expected to reduce the actuarial imbalance by about one half, ACABQ agreed in the current circumstances with the gradual approach to eliminating the deficit and had no objection to the measures recommended by the Board.

Reports. [1]ACABQ, A/37/674; [2]UNJSPB, A/37/9 & Corr.1-4.
Resolution (1982). [3]GA: 37/131, sect. I, para. 1, 17 Dec.
Resolution (prior). [4]GA: 36/118 B, 10 Dec. 1981 (YUN 1981, p. 1345).

Administrative expenses

By its resolution of 17 December 1982,[3] on the Pension Board's report,[2] the General Assembly approved expenses, chargeable directly to the Pension Fund, totalling $5,955,300 (net) for 1983 and reductions of $205,400 (net) for 1982 for the administration of the Fund. Those amounts were based on estimates submitted by the Board.

The Board noted that the administrative costs (as distinguished from investment costs) for 1983 were estimated at $2,418,300, or 0.12 per cent of the anticipated 1983 pensionable remuneration, and were therefore within the 0.14 per cent limit established by its Pension Review Group. Of the total, $1,374,500 would be spent on staff salaries, 16 per cent more than in 1982. The Board estimated that actuarial consulting services would increase 43 per cent, to $165,000. Data processing costs included a one-time provision of $12,000 required for relocating the secretariat and $10,000 for new equipment.

Investment costs, estimated to total $3,537,000 in 1983, consisted principally of the fees payable to the two financial institutions engaged to provide advisory and custodial services in the management of the Fund's investments. Those costs would rise by 13.5 per cent to $2,950,000. The remaining net increase was mainly due to additional posts for a newly established Investment Management Section and to common staff costs—offset by decreases in temporary assistance and the corresponding common staff costs, overtime and investment consultants' fees.

The reductions in the original 1982 cost estimates were mainly due to the delay in filling some vacancies, reduced overtime and travel requirements and a decrease in investment advisory services.

In its November report,[1] ACABQ said that it had no objection to the proposed changes in estabished posts or to the Board's estimates.

Reports. [1]ACABQ, A/37/674; [2]UNJSPB, A/37/9 & Corr.1-4.
Resolution (1982). [3]GA: 37/131, sect. IV, 17 Dec.

Investments

The market value of the Pension Fund's investments as at 31 March 1982 was $2,393 million, down from $2,495 million a year earlier. Reflecting depressed securities markets, the market value was $38 million below the book value, according to the Secretary-General in an October report[3] to the General Assembly on the Fund's investments. He described the economic conditions which prevailed during the year ending 31 March 1982, their impact on the broad investment strategy and the results obtained. It was a period of almost world-wide recession, he noted, with reduced demand for imports, slow capital spending, sluggish consumer demand, high real interest rates and falling inflation rates. That contrasted with the previous year, when the main problems were high inflation and continued escalation in energy and other commodity prices.

The investment return, or total return, on the Fund's investments for the year was minus 7.85 per cent (the lowest since 1974) compared with a total return of plus 26.6 per cent the preceding year. The rate, he said, should be viewed in a proper perspective: the rates of return for the total portfolio had been relatively stable for 22 years, with an average compound return being 5.78 per cent a year. Currency fluctuations and the appreciation of the United States dollar had resulted in nearly 70 per cent of the overall negative return.

Income yield for 1981 was 7.49 per cent, more than 70 per cent higher than five years earlier. By the end of 1981, the total assets of the Fund (contributions less benefit payments, reinvested interest, dividends, and capital gains less investment expenses) had grown to $2,458 million, a compound rate of about 20 per cent a year since 1950. After deduction of expenses, the net funds available for investment during 1981 were $304 million.

As at 31 March 1982, 60 per cent of the long-term investments of the Fund were domiciled outside the United States (55 per cent a year earlier).

Equity investment outside the United States was 44 per cent; investments were held in 46 (23 developing) countries and in 21 different currencies.

Further work was done to increase investments in Africa ($28 million as at 30 June 1982), but two major constraints continued to hinder these efforts: because of high interest rates, the international and domestic bond markets continued to be unattractive to African and other Governments, and restrictions existed which made it difficult for foreign portfolio investors to utilize the African domestic capital markets. Total investments in developing countries or development-related securities as at 30 June 1982 were $480,883,000.

In its 1982 report to the Assembly,[4] the Pension Board noted that the short-term results would have to be interpreted with caution because a large part of the negative return was attributable to adverse currency movements and volatile security markets, and it noted that the long-term results were positive. Over the 22 years to 31 March 1982, United States equities furnished an average return of 6.1 per cent per year, equities outside the United States provided 7.33 per cent, and bonds yielded 4.92 per cent.

The Board endorsed the continuing policy of the Secretary-General to diversify, to the extent possible, the assets of the Fund by type, geographical location and currency, and welcomed the progress in increasing investments in developing countries. It pointed out that, as at 31 March 1982, investments in development-related securities were 32 per cent higher than a year earlier. Investments Committee members recommended maintaining or increasing fixed-income investments for as long as the real rate of return remained far above historical norms.

Commenting on the Fund's investments, ACABQ said[2] it had been informed that, if the report had covered the 12-month period to 30 September 1982, it would have shown a positive return of approximately 10 per cent. It recalled that it had noted the Board's statement that the criteria of safety, profitability, liquidity and convertibility would be applied equally to investments in both the developed and the developing world and, where those criteria were equally satisfied, priority should be given to investment in developing countries.

The Assembly, in a decision of 17 December, took note of the Secretary-General's report on Fund investments.[1] The Fifth (Administrative and Budgetary) Committee had approved the text on 13 December, as introduced by a Vice-Chairman following informal consultations. Both bodies took their action without vote.

Decision (1982). [1]GA: 37/430, 17 Dec., text following.
Reports. [2]ACABQ, A/37/674; [3]S-G, A/C.5/37/16; [4]UNJSPB, A/37/9 & Corr.1-4.
Meeting records. GA: 5th Committee, A/C.5/37/SR.45, 48, 51, 58, 63, 67 (26 Nov.-13 Dec.); plenary, A/37/PV.109 (17 Dec.).

Adopted without vote

Approved by Fifth Committee (A/37/761) without vote, 13 December (meeting 67); draft by Vice-Chairman (A/C.5/37/L.41), based on informal consultations; agenda item 113.

Investments of the United Nations Joint Staff Pension Fund

At its 109th plenary meeting, on 17 December 1982, the General Assembly, on the recommendation of the Fifth Committee, recalling its resolution 36/119 of 10 December 1981, took note of the report of the Secretary-General on the investments of the United Nations Joint Staff Pension Fund.

Amendments to the Regulations

Indexation of cost-of-living adjustment to income tax rates

In 1980, the General Assembly had approved[1] the application of cost-of-living differential factors to increase the initial pension in local currency of a pensioner residing in a country whose cost of living was substantially higher than that at the base of the system; it had requested the International Civil Service Commission (ICSC), in co-operation with the United Nations Joint Staff Pension Board, to elaborate a special index for pensioners which would take into account the impact of national taxation.

The Pension Board, at its 1982 session,[4] agreed with a scheme, recommended by ICSC at its 1982 session,[3] for recalculating pensions of all retirees in countries where the cost-of-living differential factors were applied. The Board drew up procedures, contained in an annex to its report, for applying the special index to existing pensioners and to effect a transition from the provisions of the previous system to the revised system of cost-of-living factors.

Only one reduction factor would be calculated for each country. National, state and local taxes applicable in cities having a United Nations headquarters or a regional office would be taken into account. If no such organization was there, then the national, state and local taxes applicable in the capital city would be considered. Base pension would be based on an average of exchange rates over the previous 36 months.

Staff views on the special index for pensioners were expressed by the Federation of International Civil Servants' Associations (FICSA) in a November document transmitted to the Fifth Committee.[2] While realizing that a special index had merit in establishing equity among pensioners, FICSA said it believed that the matter must be approached comprehensively; it was regrettable that a single element, namely, the effect of taxation, was considered in isolation and from the point of view of deductions from pensions of those who paid low or no taxes on pensions, with no concomitant compensation for those who paid higher taxes.

The General Assembly, by its resolution[5] of 17 December on the report of Pension Board, approved, effective 1 January 1983, amendments to the pension adjustment system contained in the annex to the Board's report. It thereby amended the procedure for adjusting cost-of-living differential factors applicable to retirees from the Professional and higher categories where those factors were applied and where the rates of taxation were zero or lower than those implicit in the amounts of base pensions provided under the United Nations pension scheme. The Assembly also approved a recommendation of ICSC and the Board that no reduction factor be applied to the retirees from the General Service and related categories.

Decision. [1]GA: 35/447, 17 Dec. 1980 (YUN 1980, p. 1186). *Note.* [2]S-G, transmitting FICSA comments, A/C.5/37/29. *Reports.* [3]ICSC, A/37/30; [4]UNJSPB, A/37/9 & Corr.1-4. *Resolution (1982).* [5]GA: 37/126, sect. I, 17 Dec.

Other amendments

The Pension Board, at its 1982 session, agreed on a package of measures for remedial action to improve the actuarial balance of the Fund, which it said should be accepted in its entirety. Besides proposals affecting personnel policies such as raising the retirement age, hiring members at a younger age and entitlement of all staff members to participation in the Fund, the Board made recommendations for changing benefits and contributions to the Fund which would require amending the Fund's Regulations. The Board also proposed other measures to improve the actuarial balance: the elimination of the possibility of member organizations excluding certain staff members from participation in the Fund (see below) and extending participation in the Fund to certain United Nations officials who were not staff members (see below, under OTHER UN OFFICIALS).

One change related to the arrangements under which special leave without pay could be made to count as contributory service for entitlement to pension benefits. For that purpose, instead of allowing payment after the leave, the amended regulation would require that the Fund be contributed to on a current basis during the leave.

Several measures involved reductions in future benefits, including: revision of the benefit formula for new participants, thereby reducing the benefits of future participants with less than 10 years of contributory service; raising the interest rate used in calculating the lump-sum actuarial equivalent of a pension from 4 to 4.5 per cent, thus reducing the amount payable as a one-third lump sum; reduction of the frequency of cost-of-living adjustments from quarterly to biannually and raising the trigger point for the pension adjustment from 3 to 5 per cent; delay in adjusting deferred pensions until the former participant reached age 50, then adjusting the entitlement according to the consumer price index until payment of the pension commenced; elimination of article 26 of the Regulations which provided for the refund to the employing organization of one half of the contributions it had made for a participant who left the organization with less than five years of contributory service and therefore was entitled to only a withdrawal settlement; reduction of the one-year employment requirement for participation to six months; and limiting the restoration of prior contributory service to those former participants with less than five years of service on separation, who, after returning to the organization, elected to restore prior contributions.

The Advisory Committee on Administrative and Budgetary Questions (ACABQ) commented on the Board's proposals in a November report.[1] It noted that the measure having the largest impact on reducing the actuarial imbalance related to changes in the rate of accumulation for future participants in the Fund. Under the revised formula for pension benefits, the accumulation rate would be 1.5 per cent during the first five years of service and 1.75 per cent for the following five years, instead of 2 per cent for every year of service. The change with the second largest impact was the calculation of lump-sum commutations.

The cost of the proposal to abolish article 26 for the system as a whole would be of the order of $8 million a year (at 1981 rates), which would have to be financed by assessment of Member States.

Expected savings through changes in the benefit system, and additional comments by ACABQ on those changes are outlined above under FINANCES OF THE FUND.

The General Assembly, in a resolution of 17 December,[3] approved the Board's proposed measures designed to improve the actuarial balance of the Pension Fund (see above), except for a recommendation on extending the mandatory age of separation (see section on RETIREMENT, under PERSONNEL QUESTIONS above). It did so in amending, with effect from 1 January 1983, the Regulations of the Fund and the pension adjustment system, as set forth in the Board's report.[2]

At the time of the vote on the resolution, Egypt said it objected in particular to the provision in the amended regulations by which the rate of accumulation for future participants was changed, which it said unjustly reduced the pension of a staff member joining after 1982.

The United States opposed the resolution because of the financial implications of the deletion of article 26 of the Fund's regulations, which would result in the loss of several million dollars to the United Nations and member organizations.

Reports. [1]ACABQ, A/37/674; [2]UNJSPB, A/37/9 & Corr.1-4.
Resolution (1982). [3]GA: 37/131, sect. I, paras. 1 & 3, 17 Dec.

Other action relating to the Pension Fund

Protection of spouses

In section V of a resolution of 17 December 1982,[3] the General Assembly noted the absence in Pension Fund Regulations of rules concerning the financial obligations of a pensioner to his or her spouse or former spouse which, in some cases, might give rise to serious hardship. The Assembly requested the Joint Staff Pension Board to pursue the search for such measures along the lines suggested in its report or by any other methods and to report thereon to the Assembly in 1983. It requested the Board to examine the effects of the dissolution of a marriage on survivors' entitlements, together with the possibility of granting such benefits to spouses whose marriage was contracted after the service of a participant had ceased, and to report on the matter not later than 1984. In formulating those proposals, the Board was to bear in mind that they should have no financial implications for the Fund.

This section of the six-part resolution on the 1982 report of the Pension Board[2] was proposed in the Fifth (Administrative and Budgetary) Committee by a Vice-Chairman[1] following informal consultations, as an addition to a draft resolution which had been proposed by the Board. This amendment was approved without vote on 13 December.

After studying the issue in 1982, in accordance with a 1981 Assembly request,[4] the Board agreed that, desirable though it might be to use the entitlements of a pensioner to discharge his or her obligations, legal and moral, to a spouse or former spouse, the Fund could not enforce such an obligation unless procedures were established to determine its validity and extent. The Board believed that it was not equipped or qualified to serve as the arbiter for resolving such questions in instances where no legal judgement was involved. Although it examined proposals to overcome those difficulties, it could not devise such an arrangement or suggest another remedy. Pending the elaboration of a satisfactory method for ascertaining when reductions in a pensioner's benefit could be justified, the Board recommended that the guidelines of the Emergency Fund should be broadened to deal with hardship cases.

Amendment adopted. [1]5th Committee Vice-Chairman, A/C.5/37/L.40/Rev.1, para. 3.
Report. [2]UNJSPB, A/37/9 & Corr.1-4.
Resolution (1982). [3]GA: 37/131, sect. V, 17 Dec.
Resolution (prior). [4]GA: 36/118 C, 10 Dec. 1981 (YUN 1981, p. 1348).

Participation in the Fund

In section VI of its resolution of 17 December 1982[3] on the report of the United Nations Joint Staff Pension Board,[2] the General Assembly took note of views expressed by the Board on practices relating to excluding or preventing certain staff members from participating in the Pension Fund. It requested the Fund's member organizations to furnish information on such instances, and the Board, in the light of such information, was to submit proposals to the Assembly in 1983 for removing the exclusion provision from the Fund's Regulations.

This section of the six-part resolution was presented to the Fifth Committee by a Vice-Chairman,[1] after informal consultations, as an amendment to the text suggested by the Board in its report. The addition was approved without vote on 13 December.

Commenting on information received from member organizations on the topic, the Board noted the varying use in different organizations of exclusions from the Fund and the different practices by which individuals or entire categories were prevented from becoming participants or were classified in such a way as not to acquire the status of staff members. The information it had received was insufficient to quantify the actuarial impact on the Fund of such practices, and organizations were asked to provide data for costing. The Board did determine, however, that such practices adversely affected the Fund's "open group" concept, whereby an increase in the entire work force spread the cost of benefits being paid. In that regard, the Board also suggested expanding participation in the Fund to certain non-Secretariat officials (see below, under OTHER UN OFFICIALS). It recommended a change in article 21 of the Regulations to reduce the period required to qualify for participation in the Fund from one year to six months.

Amendment adopted. [1]5th Committee Vice-Chairman, A/C.5/37/L.40/Rev.1, para. 3.
Report. [2]UNJSPB, A/37/9 & Corr.1-4.
Resolution (1982). [3]GA: 37/131, sect. VI, 17 Dec.

Admission of the European and Mediterranean Plant Protection Organization

The General Assembly, on 17 December 1982,[2] decided to admit the European and Mediterranean Plant Protection Organization (EPPO) to membership in the Pension Fund, with effect from 1 January 1983.

The decision was unanimously recommended by the Pension Board at its 1982 session,[1] after being informed that EPPO had adopted, as from 1 August 1982, staff regulations and staff rules patterned after those of the United Nations Educational, Scientific and Cultural Organization, and had satisfied the necessary conditions of participation in the United Nations common system.

Report. [1]UNJSPB, A/37/9 & Corr.1-4.
Resolution (1982). [2]GA: 37/131, sect. II, 17 Dec.

Contributions to the Emergency Fund

On 17 December 1982,[2] the General Assembly authorized the Pension Board to supplement up to $100,000 the voluntary contributions to the Emergency Fund for another year. The text was recommended by the Board.[1]

The Emergency Fund, established from voluntary contributions by member organizations, staff associations and individual contributors to alleviate the distress caused to the recipients of small pensions by currency fluctuations and cost-of-living increases, had been used since 1975 to relieve hardship in emergency cases of illness, infirmity or similar causes. Since then, the Assembly had authorized the Board annually to supplement the Emergency Fund by $100,000. Payments by the Fund during 1982 amounted to $55,600.

Report. [1]UNJSPB, A/37/9 & Corr.1-4.
Resolution (1982). [2]GA: 37/131, sect. III, 17 Dec.

Pensionable remuneration

The International Civil Service Commission, in its 1982 report,[1] informed the General Assembly that the pensionable remuneration for staff members in the Professional and higher categories—the portion of their pay counted in calculating their pension benefits and contributions—would increase by 7.1 per cent over the previous levels with effect from 1 October 1982. The adjustment was due to an equal percentage increase in the United States consumer price index. The increase was implemented for both benefits and contributions purposes.

Report. [1]ICSC, A/37/30.

Management of the Secretariat

Proposed restructuring of the Secretariat

The Committee of Governmental Experts to Evaluate the Present Structure of the Secretariat in the Administrative, Finance and Personnel Areas, established by the General Assembly in 1980,[3] submitted its final report to the Assembly in November 1982.[1] After submitting an interim report to the Assembly in 1981,[5] it held four meetings from 15 to 20 September 1982 and, as agreed by the Assembly on 8 October, five additional meetings between 18 and 22 October. The Secretary-General, as requested by the Assembly in 1981,[4] met with the Committee Chairman on 11 March 1982, and informally with available Committee members, to discuss questions outlined in the interim report. He submitted his views in written form to the Committee in August.

The Committee noted the intention of the Secretary-General to keep the effectiveness of the administrative structure under continuous review and to make every effort towards an improved, unified and coherent administration. Recognizing that the Secretary-General, as the Chief Administrative Officer of the United Nations, was primarily responsible for the structure of the Secretariat, unless political considerations made legislative action desirable, the Committee noted that the Assembly had the opportunity to provide overall policy guidance to him and to modify the structure. Believing that the issues identified in its 1981 report formed a useful framework for a thorough review and evaluation of the current structure of the Secretariat, the Committee decided to make no recommendations to the Assembly, but put forward certain suggestions regarding responsibility for different areas of administration, finance and personnel.

In order to enhance policy coherence in those areas, the Secretary-General considered it essential that there be one official who, as the Secretary-General's surrogate in administrative matters, was responsible for providing clear guidance in the Department of Administration and Management. He believed that the current structure of a unified, integrated department of administration should continue. The Committee did not propose any alternative structure, but recognized that some modifications within the structure could be considered.

The Secretary-General stated that it was the responsibility of the Office of Personnel Services (OPS) to administer the staff, to develop and maintain a coherent personnel policy and to ensure implementation of personnel measures decided by the Assembly. It was the responsibility of the Under-Secretary-General for Administration and Management to provide impulse and top policy guidance to those endeavours. The Secretary-General believed that the authority of OPS could be exercised within the existing structure. The Committee attached importance to the relationship of OPS with the substantive departments, particularly in regard to recruitment and ability to implement personnel policies established by the Assembly, and stressed its role in the training and development of staff.

The Secretary-General pointed out that there was a clear distinction between the staff functions of his Executive Office and the line functions of any department, including the Department of Administration and Management. It was the general view of the Committee that, perhaps with the exception of the Internal Audit Division, the promotion of policy coherence and the enhancement of effectiveness in administration would not be well served by expanding the role of the Executive Office. It suggested the alternative of establishing those functions directly under the Secretary-General.

Concerning the capacity of the structure to achieve a proper balance between administrative decentralization and central control and co-ordination, the Secretary-General agreed that the question was not whether to decentralize, but rather how rapidly and under what conditions, so that it did not weaken coherent overall policies. He believed that the existing administrative structure was fully capable of developing and monitoring a clear policy of decentralization. The Committee welcomed his statement that the matter was under study and noted his intention to issue appropriate instructions to decentralize decision-making in administrative matters within established guidelines.

In connection with the adequacy of the structure to integrate programme planning with programme budget preparation and resource allocation, the Secretary-General said he regarded the establishment of the Programme Planning and Budgeting Board as an initial, promising step, whose results he intended to assess to determine possible further measures. The Committee felt that the Board, as constituted, could not replace the need for integration of the whole system of programme planning, budgeting, monitoring and reporting, and highlighted the need for a single responsibility for such a system.

The Committee agreed that the United Nations needed to strengthen its efforts in utilizing new management technology, with structures, personnel policies, leadership and participation considered in an interrelated context. In this connection, the Secretary-General said he had asked the Under-Secretary-General for Administration and Management to review the role and effectiveness of the Administrative Management Service and the Electronic Data Processing and Information Systems Division.

General Assembly action. In a resolution of 21 December,[(2)] the General Assembly took note with appreciation of the Committee's final report and commended it to the Secretary-General. It requested him to take into account the Committee's suggestions, as well as the related views of the Fifth (Administrative and Budgetary) Committee, in his consideration of the administrative structure of the Secretariat and his current review on decentralizing the decision-making in administrative matters referred to in the report. He was requested to submit in 1984, within the context of the programme budget for 1984-1985, a report on the major issues identified by the Committee, including changes in the administrative structure that he considered appropriate. The USSR agreed not to press an oral amendment in the Fifth Committee to delete the final phrase.

The Assembly adopted the resolution without vote, following the Fifth Committee's approval of the text without objection on 2 December. The text was introduced by Sweden, also on behalf of 12 other countries. The sponsors orally revised operative paragraph 3, which originally referred to the Secretary-General's review on decentralizing the decision-making in administrative matters "which he has assigned to the Under-Secretary-General for Special Assignments"; the adopted paragraph deleted that phrase but included a reference to the relevant paragraphs in the Committee's report.

Report. [1]Committee on Secretariat structure in administrative, finance and personnel areas, A/37/44.
Resolution (1982). [2]GA: 37/239, 21 Dec., text following.
Resolutions (prior). GA: [3]35/211, 17 Dec. 1980 (YUN 1980, p. 1194); [4]36/238, 18 Dec. 1981 (YUN 1981, p. 1378).
Yearbook reference. [5]1981, p. 1376.
Meeting records. GA: 5th Committee, A/C.5/37/SR.13, 45, 46, 49, 50, *53* (15 Oct. & 26 Nov.–2 Dec.); plenary, A/37/PV.114 (21 Dec.).

General Assembly resolution 37/239

21 December 1982   Meeting 114   Adopted without vote

Approved by Fifth Committee (A/37/790) without objection, 2 December (meeting 53); 13-nation draft (A/C.5/37/L.33), orally revised; agenda item 103.

Sponsors: Barbados, Denmark, Finland, Ghana, Kenya, Norway, Pakistan, Panama, Philippines, Sudan, Sweden, Trinidad and Tobago, United States.

Report of the Committee of Governmental Experts to Evaluate the Present Structure of the Secretariat in the Administrative, Finance and Personnel Areas

The General Assembly

1. *Takes note with appreciation* of the final report of the Committee of Governmental Experts to Evaluate the Present Structure of the Secretariat in the Administrative, Finance and Personnel Areas;

2. *Commends* the report of the Committee to the Secretary-General;

3. *Requests* the Secretary-General to take into account the suggestions highlighted in paragraph 39 of the report of the Committee, as well as the related views of the Fifth Committee thereon, in his consideration of the administrative structure of the Secretariat and his present review on decentralizing the decision-making in administrative matters referred to in paragraph 25 and in annex I, paragraph 15, of the report;

4. *Requests* the Secretary-General to submit to the General Assembly, at its thirty-ninth session, within the context of the programme budget for the biennium 1984-1985, a report on the major issues identified by the Committee, including changes in the administrative structure that he considers appropriate.

Classification of posts at the top echelon

By a resolution of 21 December 1982[3] on the 1982-1983 programme budget, the General Assembly approved the reclassification of two posts to the level of Under-Secretary-General (the Director-General of the United Nations Office at Vienna and the Commissioner-General of the United Nations Relief and Works Agency for Palestine Refugees in the Near East (UNRWA)), and two to the level of Assistant Secretary-General (the head of the Centre against *Apartheid* and the head of the Centre for Human Rights).

The Assembly adopted the section on these changes in the top echelon of the Secretariat by a recorded vote of 108 to 22, with 9 abstentions. The Fifth Committee had approved the text by 51 votes to 16, with 17 abstentions, on 13 December. The vote was requested by Peru and the United States.

In a December report[2] on revised estimates for proposed changes in the top echelon, the Secretary-General said that during 1982 he had introduced a number of staff changes at that level, on a temporary basis pending Assembly action; he gave the reasons for his decisions and indicated the financial implications. While most costs would be met by redeployment of resources, the total additional costs for all his proposed changes would require an additional appropriation of $1,126,900 for the 1982-1983 biennium.

The Advisory Committee on Administrative and Budgetary Questions (ACABQ) also submitted revised estimates in December[1] on the proposed changes. Recalling its previous recommendation that any submissions for upward reclassification be made in the context of the proposed programme budget for a given biennium, it recommended that the Secretary-General resubmit his reclassification requests in the context of the proposed 1984-1985 budget. After reviewing the other proposals, it decided that economics could be made: net additional requirements recommended by ACABQ amounted to $646,300, after accounting for savings through redeployment. That figure was approved by the Fifth Committee by 59 votes to 13, with 15 abstentions.

Speaking in explanation of vote in the Fifth Committee, Canada said that the reclassifications were in no way immediately necessary, had nothing to do with efficiency, were essentially political, and should have been carefully studied in the context of the 1984-1985 budget. The Federal Republic of Germany and Italy said they opposed the reclassifications for budgetary reasons and out of consideration for ACABQ which was the competent body on the subject; however, had a separate vote been taken on reclassifying the post of the head of the Centre for Human Rights, they would have supported it, for that body should have the necessary political weight. The United States explained that its negative vote was based purely on a concern for efficiency and the desire to avoid grade creep and not because the personal qualities of the occupants of the posts were being questioned; in particular, the United States approved the activities of the Commissioner-General of UNRWA and of the Centre for Human Rights.

Brazil said it would have preferred the Fifth Committee to go along with the ACABQ recommendations. Ghana said it voted in favour because it believed that the Fifth Committee should have confidence in the Secretary-General to conduct his administration in an effective manner; it also believed the reclassifications would pay tribute of the Commissioner-General of UNRWA and to the

Centre for Human Rights. Zambia had voted in favour, considering it essential that the Centre against *Apartheid* should have the resources necessary to strengthen its means of action.

Reports. [1]ACABQ, A/37/7/Add.19; [2]S-G, A/C.5/37/62.
Resolution (1982). [3]GA: 37/237, sect. XII, 21 Dec., text following.
Meeting records. GA: 5th Committee, A/C.5/37/SR.68 (13 Dec.); plenary, A/37/PV.114 (21 Dec.).

General Assembly resolution 37/237, section XII

21 December 1982   Meeting 114   108-22-9 (recorded vote)

Approved by Fifth Committee (A/37/790) by vote (51-16-17), 13 December (meeting 68); reclassifications proposed by Secretary-General (A/C.5/37/62); agenda item 103.

Changes in the top echelon of the Secretariat

[*The General Assembly* . . .]

Approves, with effect from 1 January 1983, the following reclassifications:

(a)   To the level of Under-Secretary-General, the posts of:
(i)   Director-General of the United Nations Office at Vienna;
(ii) Commissioner-General of the United Nations Relief and Works Agency for Palestine Refugees in the Near East;
(b)   To the level of Assistant Secretary-General, the posts of:
(i)   Head of the Centre against *Apartheid* of the Department of Political and Security Council Affairs;
(ii) Head of the Centre for Human Rights;
    . . .

Recorded vote in Assembly as follows:

In favour: Afghanistan, Algeria, Angola, Argentina, Austria, Bahrain, Bangladesh, Barbados, Benin, Bhutan, Bolivia, Botswana, Brazil, Burma, Burundi, Central African Republic, Chad, Chile, China, Colombia, Comoros, Congo, Costa Rica, Cuba, Cyprus, Democratic Kampuchea, Democratic Yemen, Dominican Republic, Ecuador, Egypt, Ethiopia, Fiji, Gabon, Gambia, Ghana, Grenada, Guatemala, Guinea-Bissau, Guyana, Honduras, India, Indonesia, Iran, Iraq, Ivory Coast, Jamaica, Jordan, Kenya, Kuwait, Lebanon, Lesotho, Liberia, Libyan Arab Jamahiriya, Madagascar, Malawi, Malaysia, Maldives, Mali, Malta, Mauritania, Mexico, Morocco, Mozambique, Nepal, Nicaragua, Niger, Nigeria, Oman, Panama, Papua New Guinea, Paraguay, Peru, Philippines, Portugal, Qatar, Romania, Rwanda, Saint Lucia, Samoa, Sao Tome and Principe, Saudi Arabia, Senegal, Sierra Leone, Singapore, Solomon Islands, Somalia, Sri Lanka, Sudan, Suriname, Swaziland, Syrian Arab Republic, Thailand, Togo, Trinidad and Tobago, Tunisia, Turkey, Uganda, United Arab Emirates, United Republic of Cameroon, United Republic of Tanzania, Upper Volta, Uruguay, Venezuela, Yemen, Yugoslavia, Zaire, Zambia, Zimbabwe.

Against: Australia, Belgium, Bulgaria, Byelorussian SSR, Canada, Czechoslovakia, Denmark, France, German Democratic Republic, Germany, Federal Republic of, Hungary, Japan, Luxembourg, Mongolia, Netherlands, New Zealand, Poland, Spain, Ukrainian SSR, USSR, United Kingdom, United States.

Abstaining: Bahamas, Finland, Greece, Iceland, Ireland, Israel, Italy, Norway, Sweden.

Management services

The Secretary-General, in a November 1982 report[1] to the General Assembly on implementation of the recommendations of the Joint Inspection Unit (JIU), commented on the status of implementation of the 1981 JIU recommendations[2] on management services in the United Nations system. He agreed that United Nations organizations should foster closer links among their management services, and he had requested the Consultative Committee on Administrative Questions, a subsidiary body of the Administrative Committee on Coordination (ACC), to play a co-ordinating role in the matter. The Secretary-General also agreed, in principle, that any management service should spend the bulk of its time on its basic and continuing functions. In that connection, he noted that the roles

and effectiveness of the Administrative Management Service and the Electronic Data Processing and Information Systems Division were being reviewed by the Under-Secretary-General for Administration and Management as part of the measures being taken to improve the administrative efficiency of the Secretariat.

Report. [1]S-G, A/C.5/37/28.
Yearbook reference. [2]1981, p. 1378.

Methods of determining staff requirements

In his November 1982 report[1] on implementing JIU recommendations, the Secretary-General described the work of the Secretariat to improve methods of determining staff requirements, in particular the 1981 JIU recommendations[2] that central management services play a greater role in assessing those requirements and that work measurement systems and analytical estimating techniques be introduced.

According to the Secretary-General, the Secretariat was using work measurement techniques, as appropriate, in the studies conducted by the Administrative Management Service. As for the recommendation that legislative bodies be provided with information in their draft budgets to permit better assessment of staffing proposals, he reported that data on estimated work-months for individual programme elements were prepared as part of the budget-formulation process and were available to budget-reviewing bodies upon request. While interagency consultations on work-measurement norms had not yet taken place, the organizations intended to do so through the established machinery of ACC.

Report. [1]S-G, A/C.5/37/28.
Yearbook reference. [2]1981, p. 1362.

UN Administrative Tribunal

Activities of the Tribunal

The United Nations Administrative Tribunal, which adjudicated staff grievances against the administration, held two sessions in 1982—a special plenary session at Geneva on 13 May and its annual plenary session in New York on 7 October. It also held two panel sessions, one at Geneva from 26 April to 14 May and one in New York from 20 September to 15 October, at which it considered 20 complaints. During the year, the Tribunal delivered 20 judgements, listed in a note submitted by the Secretary-General to the General Assembly in November.[1]

Note. [1]Administrative Tribunal, transmitted by S-G note, A/INF/37/6.

Proposed harmonization with the ILO Administrative Tribunal

The General Assembly, in a resolution of 17 December 1982,[3] requested the Secretary-General to continue the consultations necessary for a progressive harmonization and further development of the statutes, rules and practices of the Administrative Tribunal of the International Labour Organisation and of the United Nations Administrative Tribunal, with a view to strengthening the common system and to reducing, to the extent possible, the associated administrative costs. He was to report on his findings at a future session, upon completion of the consultations, and to submit interim progress reports at intervening sessions.

Acting on the recommendation of its Fifth (Administrative and Budgetary) Committee, which had approved the Barbados-sponsored text without objection on 29 November, the Assembly adopted the resolution without vote.

Since the question of establishing a single tribunal was first proposed by the Assembly in 1979,[1] it had been pursued in consultations with intergovernmental organizations. In an October 1982 report,[2] the Secretary-General outlined elements in a study undertaken by the Secretariat of the statutes, rules and practices of the two Tribunals which should be taken into account, including: their membership and structure; the possible extension of jurisdiction to additional classes of applicants, to additional kinds of claims and to other types of proceedings, such as the rendering of advisory opinions at the request of executive heads of United Nations organizations; the requirements for filing applications; tribunal procedures; necessary proceedings to uphold judgements; review procedures; and possible methods of co-operation and co-ordination between Tribunals.

In view of the numerous questions to be examined and the need to consult many entities, the Secretary-General said he was not yet in a position to make proposals to the Assembly and suggested that the question be considered when proposals were advanced for a reform of the review procedures.

Decision. [1]GA: 34/438, 17 Dec. 1979 (YUN 1979, p. 1223).
Report. [2]S-G, A/C.5/37/23.
Resolution (1982). [3]GA: 37/129, 17 Dec., text following.
Meeting records. GA: 5th Committee, A/C.5/37/SR.27, 46, 47 (5, 29 Nov.); plenary, A/37/PV.109 (17 Dec.).

General Assembly resolution 37/129

17 December 1982   Meeting 109   Adopted without vote

Approved by Fifth Committee (A/37/766) without objection, 29 November (meeting 47); draft by Barbados (A/C.5/37/L.27); agenda item 106 *(c)*.

Feasibility of establishing a single administrative tribunal

The General Assembly

1. *Takes note* of the report of the Secretary-General on the feasibility of establishing a single administrative tribunal;

2. *Requests* the Secretary-General:

(a) To continue the consultations necessary for a progressive harmonization and further development of the statutes, rules and practices of the Administrative Tribunal of the International Labour Organisation and of the United Nations Administrative Tribunal, with a view to strengthening the common system and to reducing, to the extent possible, the associated administrative costs;

(b) To report thereon to the General Assembly at a future session, upon completion of the consultations, with interim reports on the progress of the consultations being submitted at intervening sessions of the Assembly.

Other UN officials

Experts and consultants

In a July 1982 report,[4] the Joint Inspection Unit (JIU) assessed the status of the implementation of the guidelines established by the General Assembly in 1974[8] for the use of consultants and experts from outside the United Nations system, reporting on efforts to identify existing problems and deficiencies and recommending changes. The report was prepared by Inspectors Alexander S. Bryntsev and Joseph Adolph Sawe. Because the principles and guidelines had not been fully observed, they said, an increasing proportion of budget appropriations had been used for consultants and experts—a 16.4-fold increase from 1962 to 1981, while the total regular budget appropriations had increased 7.8-fold.

One of the main difficulties in implementing Assembly decisions in this regard was the lack of a clear definition of "consultant", "expert", "contractor" and "temporary staff", and the absence of adequate reporting procedures on their use, leading to a lack of effective control. Other factors hindering observance of the guidelines were an absence of productivity norms for most categories of the regular staff, an absence of precise methods for determining requirements for consultants, an inadequate mechanism for assessing requests for consultants, a lack of uniformity in determining the level of their remuneration, and deficiences in the recruitment of consultants on as wide a geographical basis as possible.

JIU reaffirmed the principles and guidelines established in 1974 and proposed issuance of a new administrative instruction with clear definitions of those four above-mentioned terms. It suggested establishing productivity norms for corresponding categories of regular staff, where feasible. Methods were needed to determine consultant requirements associated with the approved budget, similar to those used to determine staff requirements. Assessments of all candidates considered and reasons for a particular choice should be submitted to the Office of Personnel Services, and rosters of candidates from a wide range of countries by specific fields should be established.

In determining remuneration for consultants who were former staff members receiving pensions, a rule should be considered covering assignments of longer than one month, whereby the consultancy fee plus pension together should not be greater than the last pay level of the staff member, or the current rule by which pension payments ceased when a pensioner was re-employed might be applied, even if the staff member did not resume participation in the Pension Fund. In the view of JIU, adequate reporting procedures on the use of outside expertise common to all Secretariat units were needed, providing financial and personnel information.

The Secretary-General commented on the JIU recommendations in November.[5] In general, he did not share the conclusion that the principles and guidelines for the use of consultants and experts had not been fully observed. New instructions were about to be issued, however, on policies to be followed for obtaining the services of consultants and experts, defining the terms of temporary staff, individual contractors, consultants and participants in expert groups.

The Secretary-General did not agree that it would be worth while, or in many cases feasible, to establish productivity norms for regular staff, nor did recourse to outside expertise absolve staff from making every effort to achieve maximum results. The recommendation that methods for determining consultant requirements be interrelated with those of determining staff requirements was currently being implemented, and adequate reporting procedures common to all Secretariat units had been introduced. He agreed that units should assess each consultant candidate and explain their choices, and that rosters of candidates by field should be maintained by each large user of consultancy services. The Secretary-General could not support the proposal limiting remuneration for re-employed retired staff since it would be discriminatory.

In another November report[6] to the Assembly, the Secretary-General presented data on the use of experts and consultants in the United Nations, for the period 1980-1981, to permit the monitoring of the existing practice on their use in the light of Assembly guidelines. As a result of improvements in the reporting procedures followed by departments and offices, he said, it was possible to correlate the financial and personnel information for the first time. The report included the appropriations for experts employed on an *ad hoc* basis for expert group and other advisory meetings, the purposes for which consultants were hired, travel costs and geographical and age distribution.

The main purposes for which consultants were hired in 1981 were analytical studies, the preparation of meetings and seminars, drafting documents and manuscripts, and programme implementation. The total cost for consultants in 1980 was $8,575,100, and $9,128,100 in 1981. In 1981, the cost for consultants paid from the regular budget was $6,880,300, of which $1,340,200 was for travel; from extrabudgetary sources, $2,247,800

was paid, $277,800 of it for travel. In 1980, the number of individual participants in meetings of experts was 527 compared with 871 the following year. Round trips numbered 717 in 1980 and 1,012 in 1981, and 1,046 contracts commenced, compared to 1,608. The number of former staff members engaged as consultants was 110, or 6.8 per cent of the total, of whom 35 were under age 60 and 75 had reached retirement age.

Their services were normally limited to six months in any 12-month period. The percentage of contracts of one month or less was 61.9 during 1980-1981, 29.4 per cent were between one and three months and 8.7 per cent were for longer periods. Nationals of 122 Member States participated in advisory meetings during that period, of which 87 were developing countries.

The Advisory Committee on Administrative and Budgetary Questions (ACABQ) commented on the subject in a December report.[2] It agreed that the data reported for 1981 were much higher in quality than those for previous years and recommended that the next report be made in 1984. Aware that departures from the guidelines might on occasion be necessary, ACABQ nevertheless expected the Secretary-General to ensure that they would occur only in exceptional circumstances and be fully explained.

While agreeing that even if productivity norms for staff could be established they would have little effect on the need for experts—who by definition would possess special skills or knowledge not normally possessed by regular staff—ACABQ believed that the Secretary-General should explore the feasibility of establishing such norms wherever possible.

In the view of ACABQ, the proposal to limit the level of remuneration for consultants who were retired staff members might help to ensure that abuses did not occur. Future reports should include information on the employment of former staff members. Should evidence of abuse come to light, ACABQ would consider how the JIU recommendation should be applied.

The Board of Auditors found that consultants had been engaged without due regard for the principle that outside experts should be used only when expertise was lacking within regular staff resources. The Board stated this conclusion in its financial report and audited financial statements for the biennium ended 31 December 1981.[3] ACABQ, which issued in September its own report on the Auditors' findings,[1] pointed out that the Secretary-General had introduced, as of 1 January 1982, different expenditure codes designed to isolate expenditure for consultants on the basis of common and generally accepted criteria and noted his intention to issue new definitions of terms related to this question.

General Assembly action. By a resolution of 21 December,[7] the General Assembly took note of the reports and comments on the use of consultants and experts as submitted by JIU, the Secretary-General and ACABQ. It requested the Secretary-General to include in future reports detailed information on the employment of former staff members, including their date of separation, the period of post-separation employment and the amount paid to them. As an interim measure, no former staff member who was receiving a pension from the United Nations would receive from the United Nations emoluments exceeding $12,000 in any one calendar year for work under contract or special service agreement. The Assembly decided to review the situation in 1984 in the light of the additional information to be provided by the Secretary-General.

Acting on the recommendation of its Fifth Committee, the Assembly adopted this section of the resolution without vote. The Fifth Committee had approved the draft, sponsored by the United States, without objection on 15 December.

Reports. ACABQ, [1]A/37/443 & Corr.1, [2]A/37/684; [3]Board of Auditors, A/37/5; [4]JIU, transmitted by S-G note, A/37/358 & Corr.2, and [5]S-G comments, Add.1; [6]S-G, A/C.5/37/27.
Resolution (1982). [7]GA: 37/237, sect. VIII, 21 Dec., text following.
Yearbook reference. [8]1974, p. 933.
Meeting records. GA: 5th Committee, A/C.5/37/SR.54, 56, 57, 68, *72* (3-15 Dec.); plenary, A/37/PV.114 (21 Dec.).

General Assembly resolution 37/237, section VIII

21 December 1982   Meeting 114   Adopted without vote

Approved by Fifth Committee (A/37/790) without objection, 15 December (meeting 72); draft by United States (A/C.5/37/L.52); agenda item 103.

Use of consultants and experts in the United Nations
[*The General Assembly . . .*]

1. *Takes note* of the report of the Joint Inspection Unit, the comments thereon of the Secretary-General and the related report of the Advisory Committee on Administrative and Budgetary Questions;

2. *Requests* the Secretary-General to include in his future reports on consultants and experts detailed information on the employment of former staff members, including the date of separation from service, the period of post-separation employment and the amount paid to the former staff member;

3. *Decides* that, as an interim measure, no former staff member who is in receipt of a pension benefit from the United Nations Joint Staff Pension Fund shall receive from United Nations funds, regular budget or extrabudgetary, for work performed by him or her under contract or a special service agreement, emoluments in a total amount exceeding $12,000 in any one calendar year;

4. *Decides further* to review the situation at its thirty-ninth session in the light of the additional information to be provided by the Secretary-General in response to the request addressed to him in paragraph 2 above;

. . .

Education grant for non-Secretariat officials

The General Assembly, in a resolution of 21 December 1982,[1] decided to consider the question of an education grant for certain full-time officials other than members of the Secretariat as part of an overall review of compensation and other conditions of service of those officials. The review was to be carried out in 1983 on the basis of a report by the Secretary-General.

The Assembly adopted this section of the resolution without vote, following the Fifth Committee's approval of the text without objection on 16 December. Pakistan, also on behalf of Burundi, Kenya and Malawi, had introduced and revised the text, which had originally set out *ad hoc* arrangements for an education grant for the Chairman and Vice-Chairman of the International Civil Service Commission (ICSC) and the Chairman of ACABQ.

Resolution (1982). [1]GA: 37/237, sect. XIV, 21 Dec., text following.
Meeting records. GA: 5th Committee, A/C.5/37/SR.*71, 73* (15, 16 Dec.); plenary, A/37/PV.114 (21 Dec.).

General Assembly resolution 37/237, section XIV

21 December 1982   Meeting 114   Adopted without vote

Approved by Fifth Committee (A/37/790) without objection, 16 December (meeting 73); 4-nation draft (A/C.5/37/L.50/Rev.1); agenda item 103.

Sponsors: Burundi, Kenya, Malawi, Pakistan.

Education grant for certain full-time officials other than members of the Secretariat
[*The General Assembly . . .*]

1. *Takes note* of the views expressed by Member States on the question of the education grant for certain full-time officials other than members of the Secretariat;

2. *Decides* to consider this question as part of an overall review of compensation and other conditions of service of the full-time officials other than members of the Secretariat;

3. *Further decides* that this review shall be carried out at its thirty-eighth session on the basis of a report by the Secretary-General;

. . .

Participation in the Pension Fund by non-Secretariat officials

The Secretary-General issued a note to the General Assembly in December 1982[2] on the financial implications of extending participation in the United Nations Joint Staff Pension Fund to officials other than staff members, as had been proposed by the United Nations Joint Staff Pension Board in its 1982 report[4] to the Assembly and examined by ACABQ.[3] The Secretary-General provided information on the proposed participation in the Fund of the members of the Joint Inspection Unit (JIU), the Chairmen of ICSC and ACABQ, and the Vice-Chairman of ICSC.

The Pension Board recommended an addition to the Regulations of the Fund—a supplementary article B—which would extend participation to officials covered by the Conventions on the Privileges and Immunities of the United Nations and of the Specialized Agencies who performed functions for member organizations of the Fund which, if provided by their staff members, would be considered as full- or part-time employment. The Board recalled its earlier proposal to grant coverage to JIU members (see below).

ACABQ said the proposed change in the Fund's Regulations was so broad that it might cover most consultants and all short-term employees of member organizations, and perhaps others. ACABQ believed that before the Assembly decided on the proposal, it should be provided with an analysis of its full impact, including financial implications. It gave some preliminary consideration to those implications, noting that none were attached to extension of pensions to JIU members unless past services were to be covered, since the Assembly had already approved their retirement benefits.[5] As for the other three officials, the financial implications would depend on the level of the pensionable remuneration established for them, since their annual compensation was set out in net terms and they had no entitlement to post-retirement benefits at that time.

The Assembly's Fifth Committee, at a meeting on 13 December, voted on a draft resolution recommended by the Pension Board which, among other things, would amend the Fund's Regulations as the Board had proposed. Amendments were put forward by a Committee Vice-Chairman following informal consultations. By one of these,[1] the Assembly, instead of amending the Regulations as suggested by the Board, would have added a clause to except from adoption the proposed supplementary article B which would be further studied by the Board in the light of ACABQ comments on the need for a full-impact analysis and report in 1983. The amendment was rejected by 31 votes to 31, with 24 abstentions; thus pension coverage was extended to officials covered by the Conventions on Privileges and Immunities who performed the functions specified.

The United Republic of Cameroon said that the reservations expressed by ACABQ were not sufficient to prevent the officials in question from joining the Fund if they so wished; moreover, the opportunity to join the Fund should not be restricted to them alone. Noting the recommendation to extend pension coverage to certain officials, the USSR said any additional financial requirements for United Nations organizations should be covered within the appropriations for the 1982-1983 biennium.

Amendment rejected. [1]5th Committee Vice-Chairman, A/C.5/37/L.40/Rev.1, para. 2.
Note. [2]S-G, A/C.5/37/90.
Reports. [3]ACABQ, A/37/674; [4]UNJSPB, A/37/9.
Resolution. [5]GA: 31/193 A, 22 Dec. 1976 (YUN 1976, p. 923).
Meeting record. GA: 5th Committee, A/C.5/37/SR.67 (13 Dec.).

Participation by JIU members

On 17 December 1982,[1] the General Assembly, without vote, decided that two transitional provisions relating to pension benefits would apply to current Inspectors in JIU: they would have the option of membership in the United Nations Joint Staff Pension Fund or remaining in the Provident Fund for JIU members; those who decided to join the Pension Fund would have the option of joining either with effect from 1 January 1983 or from the date their service with the Unit began, on the understanding that, if an Inspector chose the former option, the amounts credited to him in the Provident Fund for service prior to 1983, plus his *pro rata* share of the residual interest earnings, would be paid to him.

The decision, orally proposed by the Chairman of the Fifth Committee, was approved without vote by the Committee on 13 December.

JIU Inspectors had expressed their view on Pension Fund participation in a cable dated 7 December which the Secretary-General conveyed in a note to the Fifth Committee the next day.[2] They unanimously considered that their participation in the Fund would be undesirable. However, if the Assembly decided that they should join the Pension Fund, some transitional measures would be necessary because of their existing contractual arrangement with the Provident Fund, which provided them with retirement benefits. JIU proposed the two transitional measures which were included in the Assembly's decision.

Decision (1982). [1]GA: 37/429, 17 Dec., text following.
Note. [2]S-G, A/C.5/37/90/Add.1.
Meeting records. GA: 5th Committee, A/C.5/37/SR.45, 48, 51, 58, 67 (26 Nov.–13 Dec.); plenary, A/37/PV.109 (17 Dec.).

General Assembly decision 37/429

Adopted without vote

Approved by Fifth Committee (A/37/761) without vote, 13 December (meeting 67); oral proposal by Chairman to approve JIU recommendations (A/C.5/37/90Add.1); agenda item 113.

Transitional measures for serving members of the Joint Inspection Unit

At its 109th plenary meeting, on 17 December 1982, the General Assembly, on the recommendation of the Fifth Committee, decided that the following provisions would apply with regard to persons currently serving as Inspectors in the Joint Inspection Unit:

(a) Serving Inspectors shall have the option of membership in the United Nations Joint Staff Pension Fund or remaining in the Provident Fund for members of the Unit;

(b) Serving Inspectors who decide to join the United Nations Joint Staff Pension Fund shall have the option of joining either with effect from 1 January 1983 or from the date their service with the Unit began, on the understanding that, if an Inspector opts to join the United Nations Joint Staff Pension Fund from 1 January 1983, the amounts credited to him in the Provident Fund for his service prior to 1 January 1983, plus his *pro rata* share of the residual interest earnings, shall be paid to him.

Travel of staff members and other officials

In a report prepared by Inspector Miljenko Vukovic on organization and methods for official travel, transmitted by the Secretary-General to the General Assembly in July 1982,[4] JIU made specific proposals for cost savings. At that time, the organizations of the United Nations system were spending about $150 million per year on official travel (mainly daily subsistence allowance and tickets) plus some $100 million for indirect costs, such as cost of staff time while on official missions and cost of processing travel authorizations and claims. The cost of tickets alone was estimated at $85 million per year, not incuding $47 million for tickets purchased by the World Bank and the International Monetary Fund. About 95 per cent of travel was by air. Travel costs for United Nations organizations amounted to 5 per cent of total expenditures of the system, whose organizations had been remiss in adopting measures for reducing costs, according to the report.

Among the JIU recommendations were the termination of the contract with the commercial travel agency used by the United Nations and the establishment of an in-plant travel unit serving organizations located in New York, with eventual extension to other major duty stations, and investigation of the possibility of owning and operating its own travel agency.

Another recommendation called for negotiations with air carriers for discounts in view of the high volume of business the United Nations provided. Efforts to obtain the lowest suitable fares should involve the traveller, the originating department and the travel unit of the Secretariat. Information should be provided and rules issued to facilitate the search for the lowest suitable fares. Consultants, Under-Secretaries-General, Assistant Secretaries-General and delegates should travel by business class or equivalent, when available. Procedures for controlling costs could include requiring justification for the duration of each trip and simplifying the processing of travel authorizations. The Inspector suggested that the Secretary-General should call the attention of the Administrative Committee on Co-ordination (ACC) to the problems and report thereon to the Assembly in 1983.

The Secretary-General commented on the recommendations in November.[5] He stated that, given the ramifications of the project and its financial implications, the review of proposals and negotiations for new arrangements for travel was not expected to be completed before January 1983. Current regulations of air traffic regulatory bodies made the possibility of a client-owned travel agency operating on a viable basis at Headquarters remote.

The Secretary-General stated that in future it was intended that any new contractual agreement with a travel agent should include a provision under which the agent would guarantee the lowest fare, a guarantee that would be subject to spot-check audit to assure compliance. Since the recommendations on simplifying travel claim procedures would involve a major departure from the current financial and administrative practices, cost estimates and actual reimbursements would be analysed to determine whether simplified procedures could be adopted.

Suggestions for negotiating for favourable high-volume airline rates and for block ticket purchases would be pursued. The Secretary-General suggested a number of arrangements which might apply regarding the standard of travel; they were based on the rank of the official, duration of the flight, duration of the meetings to be attended, and purpose of the travel. He added that current procedures for review and spot-checking of official travel would be reviewed in the light of the JIU recommendations.

In a report issued in December,[3] the Advisory Committee on Administrative and Budgetary Questions (ACABQ) also commented on the JIU recommendations, finding them timely and useful. It requested that it be informed at its first 1983 session of the outcome of efforts to revise and improve current arrangements for travel services. The Secretary-General had informed ACABQ that he would keep the issue of a United Nations–owned travel agency under review. Noting that ACC had requested its Consultative Committee on Administrative Questions to pursue matters of inter-agency concern in the JIU report, ACABQ recommended that, in his next report on official travel, the Secretary-General should include a special section on the implementation of the JIU recommendations concerning matters which could be pursued by the United Nations on its own.

In October, the Secretary-General issued his annual report on first-class travel in the United Nations.[6] He reported savings of $407,143 achieved through utilization of economy and other air fares during the period from 1 July 1981 to 30 June 1982, through the application of the established rule limiting first-class travel to more-than-nine-hour flights. Exceptions were made during the period to allow first-class travel by 37 officials, including six cases for medical reasons. In addition, the Secretary-General listed six cases in which first-class travel had been permitted, for which in future similar cases the guidelines might need clarification.

In that connection, the ACABQ Chairman, commenting on the Secretary-General's report in the Assembly's Fifth Committee, said that, in the opinion of ACABQ, persons on official travel who were serving in their individual capacity on organs or subsidiary organs established after the adoption of the 1977 guidelines[12] were covered by the resolution establishing those guidelines. Accordingly, ACABQ recommended that the Fifth Committee endorse the Secretary-General's interpretation of the provision—he had said that such cases would no longer be reported as exceptions. The Chairman's comments were included in an annex to the ACABQ reports[2] on the programme budget for 1982-1983.

General Assembly action. In a resolution of 21 December,[11] the General Assembly concurred with the JIU recommendations that the United Nations select a commercial travel agency under an in-plant or other arrangement through international competitive bidding at appropriate intervals, and that the Secretary-General negotiate with air carriers or with interested Governments which sponsored carriers to obtain discounts in countries where permitted or to relax conditions which were an obstacle to obtaining the most economical fares. The Assembly called on the Secretary-General to keep the possibility of establishing a United Nations travel agency under review and to report to the Assembly in 1983, and to study the possibility of in-plant travel arrangements for United Nations duty stations other than New York and implementation of the JIU recommendations on travel procedures. The Assembly hoped that, by sharing his experience in introducing improved travel arrangements among United Nations organizations, a co-ordinated approach to travel arrangements could be developed, as proposed by JIU.

The resolution was adopted without vote, following its approval by the Fifth Committee on 14 December without objection. By the original draft, introduced by Barbados, also on behalf of Norway, the USSR and the United States, the Assembly would have reaffirmed, in operative paragraph 6, its 1977 resolution which provided that travel expenses would be limited to the least costly airfare structure regularly available, with the exception that Under-Secretaries-General, Assistant Secretaries-General and delegates previously entitled under special circumstances to first-class travel should travel under the same circumstances by business class or equivalent, when available, on all trips.

Morocco proposed[1] a new paragraph 6 by which the Assembly would have reaffirmed that resolution, with two provisos: that those officials at the highest level and some others previously entitled (State representatives attending sessions, persons serving in their individual capacity, chairmen of intergovernmental committees) would continue to be entitled to first-class travel when the duration of a flight exceeded nine hours, and to the class immediately below first for all other flights; and staff members at the D-2 level and below would be entitled to the class immediately below first for official travel, except for travel related to servicing or participating in conferences, seminars and other meetings of established bodies, when the duration of the meetings justified the use of excursion rates.

The United Republic of Cameroon then proposed the paragraph which was subsequently adopted; it had been accepted by the four sponsors and by Morocco, which withdrew its proposal.

Thus the Assembly reaffirmed the 1977 resolution which provided that travel expenses were to be limited to the least costly airfare structure, taking into account the nature of the mission and the conditions of travel.

The Assembly, in another resolution of 21 December,[9] took note of the Secretary-General's report on first-class travel in the United Nations and the related oral report of ACABQ. It concurred with the Secretary-General's interpretation of its 1977 resolution in respect of the travel of members of Assembly-established bodies whose members served in their individual capacities and chairmen of intergovernmental committees who travelled at United Nations expense.

This section of the resolution was adopted without vote, following its approval by the Fifth Committee without objection on 29 October. The Chairman had suggested that, in the light of the ACABQ recommendations, the Committee should recommend the action to the Assembly.

Two other sections of this resolution concerned official travel. The Assembly limited travel and subsistence costs for members of intergovernmental preparatory bodies for special conferences[7] and provided travel funds for representatives from the least developed countries to attend regional preparatory meetings for the Seventh (1985) United Nations Congress on the Prevention of Crime and the Treatment of Offenders, as well as the Congress itself.[8]

By another 21 December resolution, the Assembly approved revised Travel and Subsistence Regulations of the International Court of Justice.[10]

Amendment withdrawn. [1]Morocco, A/C.5/37/L.48.
Reports. ACABQ, [2]A/37/7 and Add.1-24, annex, paras.9 & 10, [3]A/37/7/Add.15; [4]JIU, transmitted by S-G note, A/37/357 & Corr.1, and [5]S-G comments, Add.1; [6]S-G, A/C.5/37/18 & Corr.1.
Resolutions (1982). GA, 21 Dec.: 37/237, [7]sect. I, [8]sect. II, [9]sect. III, text following; [10]37/240, [11]37/241, text following.
Resolution (prior). [12]GA: 32/198, 21 Dec. 1977 (YUN 1977, p. 1004).
Meeting records. GA: 5th Committee, A/C.5/37/SR.*22*, 61, 62, *68, 70* (29 Oct.–14 Dec.); plenary, A/37/PV.114 (21 Dec.).

General Assembly resolution 37/237, section III

21 December 1982   Meeting 114   Adopted without vote

Approved by Fifth Committee (A/37/790) without objection, 29 October (meeting 22); oral proposal by Chairman; agenda item 103.

First-class travel in the United Nations
[*The General Assembly* . . .]

1. *Takes note* of the report of the Secretary-General on first-class travel in the United Nations and the related oral report of the Advisory Committee on Administrative and Budgetary Questions;

2. *Concurs* with the interpretation of paragraph 2 *(b)* of its resolution 32/198 of 21 December 1977 proposed by the Secretary-General in his report, in respect of the travel of members of organs, subsidiary organs or other bodies established by the General Assembly whose membership consists of persons serving in their individual capacities and chairmen of intergovernmental committees who travel at United Nations expense;

. . .

General Assembly resolution 37/241

21 December 1982   Meeting 114   Adopted without vote

Approved by Fifth Committee (A/37/790) without objection, 14 December (meeting 70); 4-nation draft (A/C.5/37/L.45), orally amended by United Republic of Cameroon; agenda item 103.

Sponsors: Barbados, Norway, USSR, United States.

Organization and methods for official travel

The General Assembly,

Recalling its resolutions 3198(XXVIII) of 18 December 1973 and 32/198 of 21 December 1977 on the standards of accommodation for official travel of United Nations staff and members of organs and subsidiary organs of the United Nations,

1. *Takes note* of the report of the Joint Inspection Unit on organization and methods for official travel, the comments of the Secretary-General thereon and the related report of the Advisory Committee on Administrative and Budgetary Questions;

2. *Concurs* with the recommendation of the Joint Inspection Unit that the United Nations should select a commercial travel agency under an in-plant or other arrangement through widespread international competitive bidding at appropriate intervals;

3. *Concurs* with the recommendations of the Joint Inspection Unit that the Secretary-General should undertake negotiations with air carriers or with the interested Governments which sponsor carriers to obtain discounts in countries where this is permitted or to relax conditions which are an obstacle to obtaining the most economical fares;

4. *Calls upon* the Secretary-General to keep the possibility of establishing a United Nations travel agency under review and to report accordingly to the General Assembly at its thirty-eighth session;

5. *Calls upon* the Secretary-General to study the possibility of in-plant travel arrangements for United Nations offices at duty stations other than New York;

6. *Reaffirms* its resolution 32/198 which provided that travel expenses shall be limited to the least costly airfare structure, taking into account the nature of the mission and the conditions of travel;

7. *Calls upon* the Secretary-General to examine further for possible implementation the recommendations of the Joint Inspection Unit on travel procedures;

8. *Endorses* the intention of the Secretary-General to share his experience in introducing improved travel arrangements with other members of the Administrative Committee on Co-ordination and hopes that these exchanges will lead to a co-ordinated approach to travel arrangements by the organizations of the United Nations system as proposed by the Joint Inspection Unit;

9. *Requests* the Secretary-General to report on the implementation of the present resolution to the General Assembly at its thirty-eighth session.

Chapter IV

Other administrative and management questions

Contents

For resolutions and decisions of major organs mentioned but not reproduced, refer to INDEX OF RESOLUTIONS AND DECISIONS.

Conferences and meetings

The work of the 22-member Committee on Conferences in 1982 focused on seven main areas: calendar of conferences for 1982-1983; Secretariat organization for United Nations special conferences; control and limitation of documentation; special review of the ongoing work programme of the United Nations; future requirements for conference services, facilities and documentation; co-ordination of United Nations conferences; and utilization of conference resources. Meanwhile work also continued towards drafting a set of rules of procedure for special conferences (see LEGAL QUESTIONS, Chapter IV).

The Committee held nine meetings between 18 February and 27 August to deal with specific problems pertaining to the 1982 calendar of con-

ferences, in particular to consider departures from the approved calendar. Two series of meetings to consider various substantive questions were also held (19 and 20 April and 10-19 May).

In its August report,[1] the Committee made eight recommendations to the General Assembly (see below).

Report. [1]Committee on Conferences, A/37/32 & Corr.1.

Pattern of conferences

On 16 November 1982,[3] the General Assembly, taking note of the report of the Committee on Conferences, authorized the Advisory Committee on the United Nations Programme of Assistance in the Teaching, Study, Dissemination and Wider Appreciation of International Law to hold its future sessions in December in even years and in October in uneven years and the Board of Trustees of the United Nations Institute for Training and Research to meet each year during the week preceding the beginning of the Assembly's regular session. The Assembly also approved a draft revised calendar of conferences for 1983.

The resolution was adopted, without vote, on the recommendation of the Assembly's Fifth (Administrative and Budgetary) Committee. The draft stemmed from recommendations 1, 2 and 3 of the Committee on Conferences.[2] On 26 October, on an oral proposal by its Chairman, the Fifth Committee approved the preambular paragraph and paragraph 1 without objection. Paragraphs 2 to 4 had been approved by consensus the previous day.

An amendment, to a draft resolution on limiting documentation recommended by the Committee on Conferences, was proposed in the Fifth Committee but was subsequently withdrawn.[1] Introduced by the United States on behalf also of Belgium, Japan, Turkey and the United Kingdom, it would have added a request to the Secretary-General, in submitting his proposed 1984-1985 programme budget, to consider and, if possible, provide for a reduction in the number of scheduled conference days compared with the number of conference days in the 1982-1983 biennium.

Amendment withdrawn. [1]Belgium, Japan, Turkey, United Kingdom, United States, A/C.5/37/L.7.
Report. [2]Committee on Conferences, A/37/32.
Resolution (1982). [3]GA: 37/14 A, 16 Nov., text following.
Meeting records. GA: 5th Committee, A/C.5/37/SR.5, 9-11, 13-17, *18, 19* (4-26 Oct.); plenary, A/37/PV.69 (16 Nov.).

General Assembly resolution 37/14 A

16 November 1982   Meeting 69   Adopted without vote

Approved by Fifth Committee (A/37/605): paragraphs 2-4 by consensus, 25 October (meeting 18), and preamble and paragraph 1 without objection, 26 October (meeting 19); recommendations by Committee on Conferences (A/37/32) and draft orally proposed by Chairman; agenda item 108.

Report of the Committee on Conferences

The General Assembly,

Having considered the report of the Committee on Conferences,

1. *Takes note with appreciation* of the report of the Committee on Conferences;

2. *Authorizes* the Advisory Committee on the United Nations Programme of Assistance in the Teaching, Study, Dissemination and Wider Appreciation of International Law to hold its future sessions in December in even years and in October in uneven years;

3. *Authorizes* the Board of Trustees of the United Nations Institute for Training and Research to meet each year during the week preceding the beginning of the regular session of the General Assembly;

4. *Approves* the draft revised calendar of conferences and meetings of the United Nations for 1983 as submitted by the Committee on Conferences.

Calendar of conferences

Changes in the 1982 calendar

In accordance with its 1974 mandate,[2] redefined in 1977,[3] the Committee on Conferences approved changes requested by three bodies in places or dates of their 1982 sessions.[1] All re-

quests were approved on the understanding that any additional expenditure could be met within approved budgetary appropriations for 1982-1983. It agreed to the holding of a session of the Drafting Committee of the Third United Nations Conference on the Law of the Sea at Geneva from 12 July to 13 August, with an option for one additional week, and a resumed eleventh session of the Conference in New York from 22 to 24 September. The Committee also agreed to change the venue and dates for a meeting of the *Ad Hoc* Committee on the Indian Ocean (from New York, 9-20 August, to Geneva, 3-20 August). The Committee requested that the *Ad Hoc* Committee limit its requirements for summary records to minimize expenditures connected with holding the session at Geneva.

Report. [1]Committee on Conferences, A/37/32.
Resolutions. GA: [2]3351(XXIX), 18 Dec. 1974 (YUN 1974, p. 922); [3]32/72, 9 Dec. (YUN 1977, p. 1039).

General Assembly subsidiary organs

On 24 September, 8 and 14 October and 2 December 1982, the General Assembly decided, without vote, to permit 11 of its subsidiary organs to meet during its 1982 regular session.[1]

On 22 September, 8 October and 1 December, the General Committee had similarly recommended that those organs meet in the light of recommendations to the President of the Assembly by the Committee on Conferences. Those recommendations had been made in letters of 14 September,[2] 22 September[3] and 1 October[4] from the Committee's Acting Chairman and in letters of 12 October[5] and 15 November[6] from the Chairman.

Decision (1982). [1]GA: 37/403, 24 Sep., 8 & 14 Oct. & 2 Dec., text following.
Letters. Committee on Conferences Chairman (C) and Acting Chairman: [2]14 Sep., A/37/450; [3]22 Sep., A/37/450/Add.1; [4]1 Oct., A/37/450/Add.2; [5]12 Oct., A/37/450/Add.3 (C); [6]15 Nov., A/37/450/Add.4 (C).
Meeting records. GA: General Committee, A/BUR/37/SR.1, 3 (22 Sep., 8 Oct.), 5 (1 Dec.); plenary, A/37/PV.4 (24 Sep.), 24, 31 (8, 14 Oct.), 88 (2 Dec.).

General Assembly decision 37/403

Adopted without vote

Approved by General Committee (A/37/250 and Add.1,3) without vote, 22 September, 8 October and 1 December (meetings 1, 3 and 5); proposals by Committee on Conferences (A/37/450 and Add.1-4); agenda item 8 (b).

Meetings of subsidiary organs during the thirty-seventh session

At its 4th, 24th, 31st and 88th plenary meetings, on 24 September, 8 and 14 October and 2 December 1982, the General Assembly, on the recommendations of the Committee on Conferences and of the General Committee, decided that the following subsidiary organs should be authorized to hold meetings during the thirty-seventh session:

(a) *Ad Hoc* Committee on the Indian Ocean;

(b) Committee of Governmental Experts to Evaluate the Present Structure of the Secretariat in the Administrative, Finance and Personnel Areas;

(c) Committee on Relations with the Host Country;

(d) Committee on the Exercise of the Inalienable Rights of the Palestinian People;

(e) Disarmament Commission;

(f) Preparatory Committee for the International Conference on the Question of Palestine;

(g) Special Committee against *Apartheid;*

(h) Special Committee on the Situation with regard to the Implementation of the Declaration on the Granting of Independence to Colonial Countries and Peoples;

(i) Special Committee to Investigate Israeli Practices Affecting the Human Rights of the Population of the Occupied Territories;

(j) United Nations Council for Namibia;

(k) Working Group on the Financing of the United Nations Relief and Works Agency for Palestine Refugees in the Near East.

Calendar for 1983

On 16 November 1982,[4] the General Assembly approved the draft revised calendar of conferences and meetings of the United Nations for 1983, as suggested in recommendation 3 of the Committee on Conferences.[3] The draft calendar had been forwarded to the Assembly by a 17 September Secretariat note.[2] Subsequently, the revised calendar adopted by the Assembly was annexed to a Secretariat note of 4 February 1983.[1] A total of 244 meetings of United Nations bodies were scheduled, as were 34 meetings of the principal organs of the specialized agencies, the International Atomic Energy Agency and the General Agreement on Tariffs and Trade.

Notes. Secretariat, [1]A/AC.172/84, [2]A/C.5/37/7 & Corr.1. *Report.* [3]Committee on Conferences, A/37/32. *Resolution (1982).* [4]GA: 37/14 A, para. 4, 16 Nov.

Conference and meeting services

On 16 November 1982,[5] the General Assembly, without vote, endorsed the programme of replacement and upgrading of electronic equipment in the Headquarters conference rooms, as recommended by the Secretary-General in a 4 August note by the Secretariat,[2] and requested him to submit further proposals for phased equipment replacement and upgrading during coming bienniums.

The resolution was recommended by the Fifth (Administrative and Budgetary) Committee which, on 26 October, approved by consensus recommendation 8 of the Committee on Conferences.[4]

In the 4 August note to the Fifth Committee,[2] the Secretary-General had reported that, in response to a 1981 request for the upgrading programme,[6] he had reviewed the capacity of existing facilities to meet expanding conference requirements. He said that the proposals outlined, as well as those he would submit over coming budget bienniums, would offer accelerated programmes designed to compress the first cycle of modernization and upgrading to approximately eight years. He noted that great care was required to ensure that the choices in modification and upgrading of equipment would

meet the Organization's needs for an extended period and that substantive conference and committee work was subjected to minimum disruption. With that in mind, a modern multiplex system had been installed in one conference room as a pilot project. The Secretary-General described improvements planned for another room and the Economic and Social Council Chamber to provide Arabic language facilities and to provide interpreters' booths to the General Assembly Hall, all within available resources.

In its report on the programme budget for the biennium 1982-1983,[3] the Advisory Committee on Administrative and Budgetary Questions (ACABQ) submitted to the Assembly its observations on an analysis by the Secretary-General,[1] requested in 1981 by the Assembly,[6] of the way in which conference-servicing costs were calculated and presented in statements of administrative and financial implications, in the consolidated statement of conference-servicing costs presented near the close of each Assembly session, and in the programme budget. ACABQ concluded that the "full-costing" method used to estimate conference costs, despite several drawbacks, was preferable to the "incremental" approach of the past and recommended that the system be refined. Further, in the case of inter-sessional departures from the approved calendar of conferences, related statements of administrative and financial implications should contain incremental as well as full costs.

Two bodies included Arabic among their official languages in 1982: the Security Council (see POLITICAL AND SECURITY QUESTIONS, Chapter XI) and the Commission on Human Settlements (see ECONOMIC AND SOCIAL QUESTIONS, Chapter XVII).

Financial implications. [1]S-G statement, A/C.5/37/103. *Note.* [2]Secretariat, A/C.5/37/2. *Reports.* [3]ACABQ, A/37/7; [4]Committee on Conferences, A/37/32. *Resolution (1982).* [5]GA: 37/14 E, 16 Nov., text following. *Resolution (prior).* [6]GA: 36/117 A, 10 Dec. 1981 (YUN 1981, p. 1364). *Meeting records.* GA: 5th Committee, A/C.5/37/SR.5, 9-11, 13-18, *19* (4-26 Oct.), *76* (18 Dec.); plenary, A/37/PV.69 (16 Nov.).

General Assembly resolution 37/14 E

16 November 1982   Meeting 69   Adopted without vote

Approved by Fifth Committee (A/37/605) by consensus, 26 October (meeting 19); recommendation by Committee on Conferences (A/37/32); agenda item 108.

Electronic equipment in the conference rooms at United Nations Headquarters

The General Assembly

1. *Endorses* the programme of systematic and progressive replacement and upgrading of the electronic equipment in the conference rooms at United Nations Headquarters, as contained in the report of the Secretary-General;

2. *Requests* the Secretary-General to submit further proposals for a phased programme of equipment replacement and upgrading during the next bienniums.

Guidelines for conferences

In a resolution of 16 November 1982, the General Assembly approved guidelines on Secretariat organization for United Nations special conferences.[4] The guidelines, annexed to the resolution, called for the establishment of a Secretariat-level conference management committee to meet during the preparatory period; plan, schedule, monitor and co-ordinate departmental activities and conference preparations; provide for inter-agency consultations; prepare progress reports to intergovernmental organs; formulate proposals for involving non-Secretariat participants to increase international support; make proposals for harmonizing documentation needs; report to the Committee on Conferences after the end of a conference and recommend future improvements; ensure that detailed cost and servicing estimates were prepared; and ensure early agreement between the United Nations and the host country, and that servicing requirements were economical and realistic. The guidelines further directed that conference secretariats should, to the extent possible, be existing Secretariat machinery, temporarily strengthened, and that standards of staffing requirements should be developed for Secretariat units involved. To provide guidance for conferences on economic and social matters, the Director-General for Development and International Economic Co-operation was encouraged to set up a steering committee, under his chairmanship and with the participation of the heads of the United Nations entities most directly concerned.

In the resolution, the Assembly also encouraged conference host countries to advance payment to the United Nations for the estimated conference costs (see below).

The resolution was adopted by 136 votes to none. It had been recommended by the Fifth Committee on 25 October and was based on a recommendation of the Committee on Conferences.[1] The preambular paragraph, operative paragraph 1 and the annex were approved without objection. In the Fifth Committee, several amendments were proposed to the annex. At the end of guideline 11, "in consultation with the host country" was added (Philippine amendment, approved without objection). Added to guideline 8 was that a closing evaluation should also take into account, in the case of conferences held at the invitation of a host country, views offered or reports prepared by host country authorities (Austrian amendment, approved without objection). In guideline 4, the word "will" replaced "have the opportunity to" (USSR amendment, approved by 60 votes to 11, with 28 abstentions). In guideline 9, "preferably" was deleted before "prior to the date" (USSR amendment, approved without ob-

jection). Deleted was a guideline calling for the career development and training of secretarial staff so that they might be assigned to conferences related to their chosen area of activity (USSR amendment, approved by 52 votes to 25, with 34 abstentions).

In a February 1982 report to the Assembly,[2] the Joint Inspection Unit (JIU) reviewed arrangements for recent and planned special conferences, including two held in 1981, and found that there were problems in harmonizing the contributions of the 23 different groups participating in conference organization and preparation. The Inspectors concluded that no one was clearly in charge, comprehensive planning and control processes had not been established at an early date and preparations had not been emphasized and supervised. They recommended changes which concerned: establishing for each conference a Secretariat management committee with authority and control over preparations, supplemented by standard guidelines and by developing basic servicing requirements; merging the functions of the conference secretary with that of the executive or administrative officer; seeking new approaches to increase non-Secretariat involvement; establishing more promptly and carefully arrangements for conferences held away from established headquarters and specific conference-servicing requirements; and assessing the preparatory experience as a basis for improving future conferences. The Economic and Social Council and the General Assembly should consider adopting guidelines for future special conferences.

Commenting on the JIU recommendations,[3] the Secretary-General welcomed the proposal to establish a conference management committee. He did not see merit in merging the functions of conference secretary and executive or administrative officer since he felt that the administrative officer's functions were distinctly different. Concerning standard guidelines, the Secretary-General believed that basic ones already existed, but felt that the Assembly might wish to adopt further guidelines. He agreed that new approaches should be devised to increase non-Secretariat involvement. The Secretary-General pointed out that it was current Secretariat practice to send a planning and review mission to assist Governments hosting conferences away from established headquarters and that he also intended to implement a 1981 Assembly resolution on limiting documentation.[5] Regarding servicing requirements, the Secretary-General said the recommendation was in line with current Secretariat practice. He agreed that the conference management committee should complete its work with an assessment report to the Committee on Conferences, but believed it would be preferable to gain experience with the guidelines adopted in the past two years before the Assembly and the Council developed new ones.

Reports. [1]Committee on Conferences, A/37/32; [2]JIU, transmitted by S-G note, A/37/112, and [3]S-G comments, Add.1.

Resolution (1982). [4]GA: 37/14 B, 16 Nov., text following.

Resolution (prior). [5]GA: 36/117 D, 10 Dec. 1981 (YUN 1981, p. 1374).

Meeting records. GA: 5th Committee, A/C.5/37/SR.5, 9-11, 13-15, *16-18* (4-25 Oct.); plenary, A/37/PV.69 (16 Nov.).

General Assembly resolution 37/14 B

16 November 1982   Meeting 69   136-0

Approved by Fifth Committee (A/37/605): preamble, paragraph 1 and annex without objection, and paragraph 2 by vote (80-19-10), 25 October (meeting 18); draft by Committee on Conferences (A/37/32), amended by Austria (A/C.5/37/L.13), by Philippines (A/C.5/37/L.10) and by USSR (A/C.5/37/L.18), and recommendation by Committee on Conferences, amended by Egypt (A/C.5/37/L.12); agenda item 108.

Secretariat organization for United Nations special conferences

The General Assembly,

Recalling its resolutions 35/10 C of 3 November 1980 and 36/117 D of 10 December 1981,

1. *Approves* the guidelines on Secretariat organization for United Nations special conferences contained in the annex to the present resolution;

2. *Decides* that, following acceptance of the invitation to act as host to a special conference, the Government of the host country may, at its option, decide to make an advance payment to the United Nations of part of the estimated total additional cost to be borne by the Government in order to cover early preparatory expenses, including in particular the cost of the planning and review mission.

ANNEX
Guidelines on Secretariat organization for
United Nations special conferences

1. Once an intergovernmental organ has decided to convene a special conference, the Secretary-General should establish at the Secretariat level a Conference Management Committee. The Committee should guide and co-ordinate all Secretariat activities during the preparatory phase of the conference and, after the conclusion of the conference, prepare a comprehensive and critical evaluation of the success and problems of the conference.

2. The Committee should be composed of representatives of all Secretariat departments and offices involved in the preparation and organization of the conference, including its logistical arrangements, and should meet regularly throughout the preparatory period under the chairmanship of the Special Representative of the Secretary-General or, where appointed, the secretary-general or executive secretary of the conference.

3. In its planning for the preparatory process, the Committee should institute disciplined management techniques for the detailed planning, scheduling, monitoring and co-ordination of both the departmental activities and the conference preparations as a whole.

4. Early provision should be made for inter-agency consultations to ensure that interested and concerned organizations of the United Nations system will contribute to the substantive preparations for the conference.

5. The Committee should be responsible for the preparation and submission of progress reports to intergovernmental organs on the status of preparations for the conference, including all financial, administrative and organizational arrangements and substantive and programme matters.

6. The Committee should, where appropriate, formulate proposals for the involvement of non-Secretariat participants in order to increase international support for the objectives of the conference and the likelihood of effective follow-up action outside the framework of the United Nations.

7. The Committee should, at an early date, also formulate proposals in line with General Assembly resolution 36/117 D of 10 December 1981 for harmonizing documentation needs with the design of the conference, taking into account all existing rules and instructions on the control and limitation of documentation. The Committee should further monitor, on a regular basis, the implementation of all documentation plans, particularly with regard to the timely submission of documents.

8. After completion of the conference, the Committee should submit a report to the Committee on Conferences, assessing its experience in the preparation and holding of the conference and, where appropriate, submitting recommendations for future improvement. Such evaluation should also take into account, in the case of conferences held at the invitation of a host country, views offered or reports prepared by host country authorities.

9. If it is proposed that the conference should take place at a venue away from established United Nations headquarters, at the invitation of a host country in accordance with General Assembly resolution 31/140 of 17 December 1976, the Committee should ensure that a planning and review mission, whose composition would be determined in consultation with the host country, is dispatched to that country at the earliest possible time. Based on the findings of the mission, detailed cost and servicing estimates should be prepared and discussed with the Government concerned, prior to the date when an offer to act as host is formally made and accepted.

10. The Committee should, where applicable, ensure that early arrangements are made for the conclusion of an agreement between the United Nations and the host country.

11. All servicing requirements for the conference should be as economical as possible and determined on a realistic and detailed basis, preferably by the Committee, as soon as it is established, in consultation with the host country.

12. In line with General Assembly resolution 35/10 C of 3 November 1980, the secretariats for conferences should, to the extent possible, be provided by existing Secretariat machinery, with such temporary strengthening as may be required for their effective functioning, allowing for the necessary mix of technical, substantive, administrative and conference-servicing skills.

13. In consultation with the competent intergovernmental organs, standards of staffing requirements should be developed for all Secretariat units involved in the preparation and servicing of conferences and should be kept under constant review.

14. In the case of United Nations conferences dealing with economic and social matters, the Director-General for Development and International Economic Co-operation may also set up a steering committee, under his chairmanship and with the participation of the heads of all the United Nations entities most directly concerned, to provide guidance on major policy issues affecting the substantial direction of conference preparations and, in particular, to ensure conformity of the preparatory work with the general strategies and priorities established by the General Assembly and the Economic and Social Council, as well as the substantive co-ordination of such work with related activities undertaken within the United Nations system.

Contributions of host countries

On 16 November 1982, the General Assembly decided, in its resolution on United Nations special conferences, that, after accepting to act as host to such a conference, the host country might make advance payment to the United Nations of part of the estimated total additional cost to be borne by the Government to cover early preparatory expenses, particularly the planning and review mission's cost.[3] This paragraph was an amended version of recommendation 5 of the Committee on Conferences[2] which the Fifth Committee approved on 25 October by 80 votes to 19, with 10 abstentions. The amendment, sponsored by Egypt,[1] replaced a phrase suggesting that the host country "should make" an advance payment by "may, at its option, decide to make" such payment.

Amendment adopted. (1)Egypt, A/C.5/37/L.12.
Report. (2)Committee on Conferences, A/37/32.
Resolution (1982). (3)GA: 37/14 B, para. 2, 16 Nov.

Travel costs of members of preparatory bodies

On 21 December 1982, the General Assembly decided without vote that, unless it decided otherwise, the United Nations would not pay the travel and subsistence expenses or honorariums of members of an existing commission, committee or other intergovernmental body designated as the preparatory body for a special conference, even though the members would normally be entitled to such payments when they attended that body's regular sessions.[3]

The Fifth Committee approved without objection on 18 October the text recommended by the Advisory Committee on Administrative and Budgetary Questions (ACABQ).[1] The matter had been raised by the Secretary-General in an August report[2] on revised budget estimates resulting from 1982 decisions of the Economic and Social Council, regarding preparations for the 1985 World Conference to Review and Appraise the Achievements of the United Nations Decade for Women. The Commission on the Status of Women had been designated by the Council in 1982 as the preparatory body for the Conference and was to hold special sessions in 1983 and 1985 solely for that purpose (see ECONOMIC AND SOCIAL QUESTIONS, Chapter XIX). The Secretary-General said in his report that, according to the Assembly's 1962 guidelines,[4] Commission members attending the 1983 preparatory session would be entitled to travel and subsistence reimbursement of $71,400, although States not members of the Commission would not have the same entitlement. In recommending that no participants in preparatory bodies receive the entitlement, ACABQ observed that granting it to some but not to others would give rise to inequities. The $71,400 in question was therefore not approved by the Fifth Committee.

Reports. (1)ACABQ, A/37/7/Add.4; (2)S-G, A/C.5/37/3 & Corr.1.
Resolution (1982). (3)GA: 37/237, sect. I, 21 Dec., text following.
Resolution (prior). (4)GA: 1798(XVII), 11 Dec. 1962 (YUN 1962, p. 558).
Meeting records. GA: 5th Committee, A/C.5/37/SR.14 (18 Oct.); plenary, A/37/PV.114 (21 Dec.).

General Assembly resolution 37/237, section I

21 December 1982   Meeting 114   Adopted without vote

Approved by Fifth Committee (A/37/790) without objection, 18 October (meeting 14); draft by ACABQ (A/37/7/Add.4); agenda item 103.

Travel and subsistence costs in respect of members of intergovernmental preparatory bodies for special conferences

The General Assembly . . .]

Decides that, when a commission, committee or other intergovernmental body, the members of which are entitled, under the relevant resolutions of the General Assembly, to payment from United Nations funds of any or all travel expenses, subsistence allowance and honorariums in connection with their attendance at sessions of the said body, is designated as the preparatory body for a special conference, the members' entitlement to such payments shall not extend to sessions at which the body in question acts as the preparatory body for the special conference, unless the Assembly decides otherwise;

. . .

Documentation

Limitation of documentation

During 1982, the General Assembly demonstrated continued concern over the excess of United Nations documentation when it adopted two resolutions.

Subsidiary organs. In a 16 November resolution on meeting records and documentation for its subsidiary organs,[4] the Assembly urged those organs not entitled to written meeting records to observe existing guidelines for succinct reports by confining the contents to: draft resolutions and decisions recommended for Assembly adoption with concise supporting or opposing statements; matters meriting special Assembly attention; voting details; decisions relevant to the subsidiary organ's own activities not requiring Assembly action; and organization of work and brief opening statements. Organs receiving written meeting records were requested to avoid including summaries of discussions, unless they were indispensable, by referring to the meeting records and, particularly those receiving written meeting records, were urged to keep reports within 32 pages.

The Assembly also requested subsidiary organs whose reports exceeded 32 pages to submit to the Committee on Conferences reasons for non-compliance, and the Committee to report to the Assembly in 1983 on improving the implementation of the 32-page rule and to recommend measures designed to relieve overloaded conference services. The Secretary-General was invited to continue using contractual services for translating and printing when that was most effective and economical. The Assembly also asked its subsidiary organs, and recommended to other United Nations bodies, to consider the recommendations of the Committee on Conferences[3] and submit their comments on implementing them in 1983.

By the same resolution, the Assembly took action on reducing and monitoring the volume of meeting records for its subsidiary bodies (see below).

The resolution was adopted by 138 votes to 1, following its approval by the Fifth Committee on 25 October by 93 votes to 1, with 4 abstentions. The text, based on recommendation 6 of the Committee on Conferences, incorporated five amendments or sets of amendments put forward in the Fifth Committee.

The first of these was introduced by the United States, also on behalf of Belgium, the Dominican Republic, France, Japan, Turkey and the United Kingdom. Following an oral sub-amendment by Canada, accepted by the sponsors, the amendments,[1] which added paragraphs 15 to 17, were approved by 90 votes to 3, with 14 abstentions.

The second set of amendments was sponsored and twice revised by the USSR. It added paragraphs 18 (approved by 72 votes to none, with 32 abstentions) and 19 (approved by 93 votes to none, with 12 abstentions). A third USSR amendment,[2] rejected by a recorded vote of 57 to 25, with 21 abstentions, would have had the Assembly invite subsidiary organs and the Secretary-General to reduce the overall volume of 1983 documentation, having in mind a 5-per-cent target, without detriment to implementing programmes approved by the Assembly.

Lebanon proposed and later withdrew a sub-amendment, which would have replaced in paragraph 18 "when it is the most effective and economical method" by "when he considers it useful and more economical".[6]

Three other amendments approved by the Fifth Committee concerned meeting records for specific committees (see below).

JIU and ACC comments. On 16 November,[5] the General Assembly, without vote, took note of a report of the Joint Inspection Unit (JIU) on control and limitation of documentation in the United Nations system, together with the related comments of the Administrative Committee on Co-ordination and the Secretary-General. The report and comments had been submitted to the Assembly in 1981.[7]

The resolution was recommended by the Fifth Committee on 26 October when it approved by consensus recommendation 7 of the Committee on Conferences. In reviewing the 1981 JIU report, the Committee on Conferences noted that 11 of the 18 JIU recommendations conformed to existing Secretariat practice. The Committee could not support one recommendation calling for a separate document reviewing adherence to the 32-page rule. It also rejected a recommendation that its title be changed to the Committee on Conferences and Documentation in the belief that its established identity would not be enhanced by lengthening its name. Regarding a recommendation to introduce a documents quota system, the Committee recalled its 1979 consideration of the topic when it had stated that it favoured regulatory rather than mandatory measures. The Committee took note of a recommendation that United Nations in-service training programmes provide courses in drafting skills and editing and reiterated the importance of such programmes.

Amendments. [1]Belgium, Dominican Republic, France, Japan, Turkey, United Kingdom, United States, A/C.5/37/L.6/Rev.1; [2]USSR, A/C.5/37/L.9/Rev.2, para. 1 (rejected).
Report. [3]Committee on Conferences, A/37/32.
Resolutions (1982). GA, 16 Nov., texts following: [4]37/14 C, [5]37/14 D.
Sub-amendment withdrawn. [6]Lebanon, A/C.5/37/L.16 (to USSR amendment, A/C.5/37/L.9/Rev.2, para. 2).
Yearbook reference. [7]1981, p. 1370.
Meeting records. GA: 5th Committee, A/C.5/37/SR.5, 9-11, 13, 14, *15-19* (4-26 Oct.); plenary, A/37/PV.69 (16 Nov.).

General Assembly resolution 37/14 C

16 November 1982   Meeting 69   138-1

Approved by Fifth Committee (A/37/605) by vote (93-1-4), 25 October (meeting 18); draft by Committee on Conferences (A/37/32), amended by USSR (A/C.5/37/L.9/Rev.2, paras. 2 and 3), by 7 nations (A/C.5/37/L.6/Rev.1), by 24 nations (A/C.5/37/L.11), by 14 nations (A/C.5/37/L.15) and by 8 nations (A/C.5/37/L.14); agenda items 109 and 8 *(b).*

Sponsors of amendments: Belgium, Dominican Republic, France, Japan, Turkey, United Kingdom, United States (A/C.5/37/L.6/Rev.1); Benin, Cuba, Egypt, Ethiopia, Ghana, Guinea, Kenya, Lebanon, Mali, Mexico, Niger, Nigeria, Senegal, Sierra Leone, Somalia, Sri Lanka, Togo, Tunisia, Uganda, United Republic of Tanzania, Yugoslavia, Zaire, Zambia, Zimbabwe (A/C.5/37/L.11); Benin, Egypt, Ethiopia, Guinea, Lebanon, Mali, Niger, Senegal, Sierra Leone, Somalia, Sri Lanka, Syrian Arab Republic, Togo, Tunisia (A/C.5/37/L.15); Egypt, Ethiopia, Guinea, Lebanon, Somalia, Sri Lanka, Togo, Tunisia (A/C.5/37/L.14).

Meeting records and documentation for subsidiary organs

The General Assembly,

Recalling its resolutions 2292(XXII) of 8 December 1967, 2538(XXIV) of 11 December 1969, 3415(XXX) of 8 December 1975, 34/50 of 23 November 1979, 35/10 B of 3 November 1980 and 36/117 A and D of 10 December 1981 and its decision 33/419 of 15 December 1978,

Mindful of the action taken by the Economic and Social Council in its resolution 1979/69 of 2 August 1979 and its decision 1982/105 of 4 February 1982,

1. *Reaffirms* that no United Nations body or organ shall have both verbatim and summary records for the same meeting;

2. *Confirms* the present arrangements in regard to the provision of meeting records for the General Assembly, its Main Committees and the General Committee;

3. *Decides* that, for an experimental period of three years, no subsidiary organ of the General Assembly shall be entitled to summary records, with the exception of the following:

(a) *Ad Hoc* Committee on the Indian Ocean;

(b) Committee on the Exercise of the Inalienable Rights of the Palestinian People;

(c) International Law Commission;

(d) Legal Sub-Committee of the Committee on the Peaceful Uses of Outer Space;

(e) Special Committee against *Apartheid;*

(f) United Nations Commission on International Trade Law;

(g) United Nations Council for Namibia;

4. *Decides* that summary records shall continue to be provided to regular and special sessions of governing bodies of United Nations organs and programmes listed in paragraph 1 of the annex to the present resolution and to pledging conferences or meetings of *ad hoc* bodies established for the announcement of voluntary contributions by States and determines that this entitlement shall not extend to any of their subsidiary organs;

5. *Further decides* that the exceptions granted to the subsidiary organs listed in paragraphs 3 and 4 above shall not apply to any of their subsidiary organs;

6. *Reaffirms* that any further exception shall require the explicit approval of the General Assembly in a pertinent resolution or decision;

7. *Requests* all its subsidiary organs entitled to written meeting records to keep their requirements for such records to a reasonable minimum, to dispense with them whenever possible, and to make wider use of sound recordings;

8. *Confirms* that summary records shall not be provided to special conferences and their preparatory organs, with the exception of legal codification conferences, for which the needs will be determined in each case;

9. *Decides* that those subsidiary organs that are entitled to receive written meeting records for all or some of their meetings shall receive them when meeting away from recognized United Nations conference centres only if there is a specific decision by the General Assembly for each case;

10. *Requests* the Secretary-General to arrange for sound recordings, in the appropriate working languages, for all proceedings of those organs no longer entitled to written meeting records in accordance with the present resolution, so that tapes may be made available with easy access to interested delegations in accordance with the established practice of the Secretariat;

11. *Confirms* the present entitlements to verbatim records of its subsidiary organs as set out in paragraph 2 of the annex to the present resolution and reiterates that no subsidiary organ shall be entitled to receive verbatim records unless the General Assembly has explicitly so approved in a relevant resolution;

12. *Urges* all its subsidiary organs not entitled to written meeting records to observe more widely the present guidelines on the format and contents of their reports, as approved by the General Assembly in its resolution 34/50, which are aimed at fostering the clear and succinct presentation of such information which the Assembly needs for a meaningful review of the work of its subsidiary organs and for taking action on their recommendations, by confining the contents of such reports to the following elements:

(a) Draft resolutions and draft decisions recommended for adoption by the General Assembly with, as necessary, concise statements supporting or opposing the recommendations;

(b) Matters meriting the special attention of the Assembly;

(c) Details of voting, where appropriate;

(d) Decisions relevant to the subsidiary organ's own activities and procedures, which do not require action by the Assembly;

(e) Organization of work and, where applicable, brief mention of opening statements;

13. *Requests* those subsidiary organs that receive written meeting records to avoid including summaries of discussions in their reports, unless such summaries are indispensable as part of the elements referred to in paragraph 12 *(a)*, *(b)* and *(d)* above, by referring instead to the relevant meeting records;

14. *Reiterates* that, in preparing their reports, subsidiary organs, particularly those receiving written meeting records, should strive to keep such reports within the desirable limit of thirty-two pages;

15. *Requests* all subsidiary organs whose reports exceed thirty-two pages to submit to the Committee on Conferences, prior to its next session, reasons for non-compliance;

16. *Requests* the Committee on Conferences to report to the General Assembly at its thirty-eighth session on improving the effective implementation of the thirty-two-page rule;

17. *Requests* the Committee on Conferences to examine further the measures listed in paragraph 27 of its report and make concrete recommendations to the General Assembly at its thirty-eighth session on the possible implementation of these measures designed to relieve the overloading of conference services;

18. *Invites* the Secretary-General to continue to make use of contractual services for the translation and printing of United Nations documents, when it is the most effective and economical method;

19. *Requests* its subsidiary organs and recommends to other United Nations bodies to consider, at their meetings, the recommendations of the Committee on Conferences contained in paragraph 85 of its report and, through it, to submit their comments on the implementation of those recommendations for the consideration of the General Assembly at its thirty-eighth session.

ANNEX
Organs entitled to summary or verbatim records
1. The following governing bodies of United Nations organs and programmes are entitled to receive summary records:

(a) Board of Trustees of the United Nations Institute for Training and Research (in English only);

(b) Executive Board of the United Nations Children's Fund;

(c) Executive Committee of the Programme of the United Nations High Commissioner for Refugees;

(d) Governing Council of the United Nations Development Programme;

(e) Industrial Development Board;

(f) Trade and Development Board.

2. The following subsidiary organs of the General Assembly are entitled to receive verbatim records:

(a) Committee on Applications for Review of Administrative Tribunal Judgements;

(b) Committee on the Peaceful Uses of Outer Space;

(c) Disarmament Commission;

(d) Special Committee on the Situation with regard to the Implementation of the Declaration on the Granting of Independence to Colonial Countries and Peoples;

(e) Special Committee to Investigate Israeli Practices Affecting the Human Rights of the Population of the Occupied Territories (when hearing witnesses);

(f) United Nations Administrative Tribunal (when holding hearings, only in the language of the speaker).

Verbatim records are further provided to the Committee on Disarmament (on the understanding that the Committee receives verbatim records from full statements as delivered and checked by the delegations concerned but without the use of verbatim reporters) and to subsidiary organs of the General Assembly when holding meetings in observance of international days of solidarity proclaimed by the Assembly.

General Assembly resolution 37/14 D

16 November 1982   Meeting 69   Adopted without vote

Approved by Fifth Committee (A/37/605) by consensus, 26 October (meeting 19); recommendation by Committee on Conferences (A/37/32), agenda item 109.

Control and limitation of documentation
The General Assembly

Takes note of the report of the Joint Inspection Unit on control and limitation of documentation in the United Nations system, together with the comments of the Administrative Committee on Co-ordination and the Secretary-General thereon.

Meeting records

By its 16 November 1982 resolution on meeting records and documentation for subsidiary organs,[7] the General Assembly reaffirmed that no United Nations body should have both verbatim and summary records for the same meeting. It confirmed existing arrangements for providing meeting records for the Assembly, its Main Committees and the General Committee, and decided that, for a three-year experimental period, no Assembly subsidiary organ should have summary records except for seven bodies it listed; the exceptions were not to apply to any of those bodies' subsidiary organs, while further exceptions would require Assembly approval. It also decided to continue summary records for pledging conferences or meetings of *ad hoc* bodies where States announced voluntary contributions and for sessions of six United Nations governing bodies which were listed in an annex to the resolution. Organs entitled to written meeting records were requested to minimize those requirements and use sound recordings. The Assembly confirmed that summary records should not be provided to special conferences and preparatory organs, except for legal codification conferences. It decided that organs entitled to written meeting records should receive them when meeting away from United Nations conference centres only by a specific Assembly decision. Stating that no subsidiary organ should receive verbatim records unless the Assembly had so approved, it confirmed entitlement to those records for seven bodies, under certain circumstances; these bodies were also listed in the resolution's annex.

By the same resolution, the Assembly took a number of steps to try to limit the size of reports made by its subsidiary bodies (see above).

In the Fifth Committee, the list of subsidiary organs entitled to summary records, suggested by the Committee on Conferences in its recommendation 6,[6] was amended to include three additional organs. The Special Committee against *Apartheid* was added by an amendment introduced by Nigeria on behalf also of 23 other States (approved by 92 votes to 1, with 11 abstentions).[1] The importance of maintaining summary records for the Special Committee, whose work was followed closely by many non-governmental organizations and anti-*apartheid* movements world-wide, had been stressed in a 14 October letter[4] to the President of the Assembly, transmitted to the Fifth Committee Chairman the next day, from the Special Committee Chairman. The *Ad Hoc* Committee on the Indian Ocean was added by an amendment introduced by Sri Lanka on behalf also of Egypt, Ethiopia, Guinea, Lebanon, Somalia, Togo and Tunisia (approved by 87 votes to 1, with 18 abstentions).[3] Also added was the Committee on the Exercise of the Inalienable Rights of the Palestinian People. The amendment effecting this action was introduced by the Syrian Arab Republic on behalf of 13 other States (approved by 86 votes to 2, with 16 abstentions).[2] The Chairman of the Committee on Palestinian rights, in a 20 October letter to the Assembly President, transmitted to the Fifth Committee Chairman the same day,[5] stated that during the preceding five years the Committee on Palestinian rights had been provided with summary records in recognition of the political importance of its work.

Amendments adopted. [1]Benin, Cuba, Egypt, Ethiopia, Ghana, Guinea, Kenya, Lebanon, Mali, Mexico, Niger, Nigeria, Senegal, Sierra Leone, Somalia, Sri Lanka, Togo, Tunisia, Uganda, United Republic of Tanzania, Yugoslavia, Zaire, Zambia, Zimbabwe, A/C.5/37/L.11; [2]Benin, Egypt, Ethiopia, Guinea, Lebanon, Mali, Niger, Senegal, Sierra Leone, Somalia, Sri Lanka, Syrian Arab Republic, Togo, Tunisia, A/C.5/37/L.15; [3]Egypt, Ethiopia, Guinea, Lebanon, Somalia, Sri Lanka, Togo, Tunisia, A/C.5/37/L.14.
Letters. GA President: [4]15 Oct., A/C.5/37/L.8 (transmitting 14 Oct. letter from Committee against *Apartheid* Chairman); [5]20 Oct., A/C.5/37/L.17 (transmitting 20 Oct. letter from Committee on Palestinian rights Chairman).
Report. [6]Committee on Conferences, A/37/32.
Resolution (1982). [7]GA: 37/14 C, paras. 1-11, 16 Nov.

Documents distribution

The problem of ensuring that United Nations output reached targeted recipients was examined by the Committee for Programme and Co-ordination (CPC) in 1982. In its report to the General Assembly on the work of its April/May session,[1] CPC recommended that the Secretariat specify for all programmes the appropriate type and number of output and intended end-users in planning and designing programmes and that an effort be made to broaden the circulation of United Nations publications and documents among policy-level officials and other concerned end-users. CPC also recommended that a study of the document dissemination system should be undertaken for submission to the Committee in 1984 by the appropriate Secretariat unit and that it should include an examination of distribution channels of the United Nations and of Member States. An evaluation of other United Nations activities was also considered by CPC (see Chapter II of this section).

In a September 1982 report on simultaneous distribution of documents in the different languages of the United Nations,[2] called for in a 1981 Assembly resolution,[4] the Secretary-General noted that, since the resolution's adoption, greater emphasis had been placed on strict compliance with the simultaneous distribution requirement, established in 1966.[3] He stated that no suspensions of the requirement had been allowed, even where storage difficulties had been cited, and steps were being taken to make more space available for documents being held for simultaneous release.

In May 1982, the Commission on Human Settlements requested the Executive Director of the United Nations Centre for Human Settlements (Habitat) to implement the Assembly's 1981 resolution and to report to the Commission in 1983 on the matter, and the Governing Council of the United Nations Environment Programme made a similar request to its Executive Director (see ECONOMIC AND SOCIAL QUESTIONS, Chapters XVI and XVII).

Reports. [1]CPC, A/37/38; [2]S-G, A/C.5/37/11.
Resolutions. GA: [3]2247(XXI), 20 Dec. 1966 (YUN 1966, p. 948); [4]36/117 B, 10 Dec. 1981 (YUN 1981, p. 1376).

UN premises

Headquarters

The General Assembly's Fifth (Administrative and Budgetary) Committee, on 8 December 1982, approved by 35 votes to 8, with 19 abstentions, an appropriation package totalling $5,341,100 for relocating and consolidating offices in the second United Nations Development Corporation building (UNDC II) (located across United Nations Plaza from the main Headquarters buildings in

New York). The sum had been recommended by the Advisory Committee on Administrative and Budgetary Questions (ACABQ)[1] after it had reviewed an 18 November report by the Secretary-General on Headquarters office accommodation.[2] The Secretary-General had recommended that $6,919,300 be appropriated to cover the cost of relocating offices, including some rented in commercial buildings, to the UNDC I and UNDC II buildings. Included in these costs were items such as modification of office space, overtime, temporary assistance, furnishings, communications facilities, cleaning, additional staff and rental of premises.

The Secretary-General had projected in a 1981 report[3] that in the long term some 300,000 square feet of rented space for the United Nations and the United Nations Development Programme (UNDP) would be required in addition to that already available in UNDC I. However, in May 1982, he was informed that UNDP had made alternative arrangements and would not take up its option for 100,000 square feet of that space, thus providing an opportunity for the Secretariat to consolidate, over a period of time, almost all the outside rentals in the two UNDC buildings.

The most advantageous arrangement was to bring together in UNDC II all offices of the Department of International Economic and Social Affairs. The Secretary-General suggested that, in view of the history of United Nations space requirements, it would be wise to retain control of the rentals in one of the commercial buildings being used. In reducing the Secretary-General's calculations for costs associated with the move, ACABQ recommended that estimates of rental income be reduced by $70,000 and felt that he should try to absorb more of the anticipated expenses within already approved resources. Because the consolidation of staff, currently in four buildings, into UNDC II should lead to economies in staff services, ACABQ also recommended that fewer General Service posts be approved.

Reports. [1]ACABQ, A/37/7/Add.12; [2]S-G, A/C.5/37/48.
Yearbook reference. [3]1981, p. 1380.
Meeting records. GA: 5th Committee, A/C.5/37/SR.59, *60* (8 Dec.).

Addis Ababa

The adequacy of the conference facilities of the Economic Commission for Africa at Addis Ababa, Ethiopia, was considered by both the Economic and Social Council and the General Assembly in 1982 (see ECONOMIC AND SOCIAL QUESTIONS, Chapter VIII).

Nairobi

Construction

The Secretary-General described, in a November 1982 report to the General Assembly's Fifth (Administrative and Budgetary) Committee,[2] the progress made in constructing permanent headquarters facilities for the United Nations Environment Programme (UNEP) and the United Nations Centre for Human Settlements (UNCHS), also known as Habitat, and accommodation for other United Nations offices at Nairobi, Kenya. In 1981, the Assembly had approved a revised construction project at Nairobi and had requested the Secretary-General to report on commitments he had entered into and on the results of tendering of bids.[4]

From 19 final bids received by the Executive Director of UNEP in January, the UNEP Committee on Contracts (Building) had unanimously recommended that the fourth lowest bid be accepted and that guarantees be incorporated into the contract to ensure that construction was completed to the required standard, at the prices quoted and on time.

After the UNEP Executive Director had approved these recommendations in February, the contract was concluded and building began on 19 April. The estimated cost, including furniture and equipment in conference and catering facilities, was $15,842,133.

The Secretary-General reported that, as at 30 September, the work was on schedule and that new space requirements had been confirmed by the regional offices of the United Nations Children's Fund and the United Nations Educational, Scientific and Cultural Organization, as well as by UNEP, UNCHS and the United Nations Information Centre, while the International Civil Aviation Organization had also decided to set up a regional office in the complex.

Pointing out that it would be economical to undertake further construction while the contractor was on the premises, thus utilizing the discount price, the Secretary-General recommended that an additional office block and a visitors' and tours pavilion be added to the project which, along with furniture and equipment, would require an additional estimated $1,651,905.

Commenting on these suggestions in a December report to the Assembly,[1] the Advisory Committee on Administrative and Budgetary Questions (ACABQ) agreed with the Secretary-General's recommendations for additional buildings. ACABQ also recommended that the Assembly request the Secretary-General to report to ACABQ as soon as possible on his negotiations with the contractor on the proposed additional construction and that he seek the concurrence of ACABQ before proceeding with the project if the estimate proved inadequate.

On 21 December, the Assembly, without vote, took note of both reports and approved the Secretary-General's proposals subject to the ACABQ conditions.[3] This action had been recommended by the Fifth Committee on 11 December when it approved without objection a draft proposed orally by the Chairman.

Reports. (1)ACABQ, A/37/7/Add.17; (2)S-G, A/C.5/37/66.
Resolution (1982). (3)GA: 37/237, sect. IX, 21 Dec., text following.
Resolution (prior). (4)GA: 36/235, sect. IX, 18 Dec. 1981 (YUN 1981, p. 1380).
Meeting records. GA: 5th Committee, A/C.5/37/SR.64 (11 Dec.); plenary, A/37/PV.114 (21 Dec.).

General Assembly resolution 37/237, section IX

21 December 1982   Meeting 114   Adopted without vote

Approved by Fifth Committee (A/37/790) without objection, 11 December (meeting 64); draft orally proposed by Chairman; agenda item 103.

United Nations accommodation at Nairobi

[*The General Assembly* . . .]

1. *Takes note* of the report of the Secretary-General on United Nations accommodation at Nairobi and the related report of the Advisory Committee on Administrative and Budgetary Questions;

2. *Approves* the proposals of the Secretary-General as described in paragraphs 24 and 27 of his report, subject to the conditions specified in paragraph 10 of the report of the Advisory Committee;

. . .

Common services

Guidelines on organizational arrangements for a number of administrative functions of Secretariat entities located at Nairobi—UNEP and UNCHS—were described in a 19 November 1982 report by the Secretary-General to the Fifth Committee.(2) The Executive Directors of the two bodies had agreed in 1981 that 11 administrative functions should be administered by a common organizational unit and that further consultation would be required in 1982 on the arrangements for the six remaining functions. The guidelines resulted from those consultations.

It was agreed in 1982 with the Executive Directors that certain functions should become part of the common services unit: personnel administration and recruitment; electronic data processing; financial services; contracting and procurement; transportation, travel and freight; and conference services. Consultations were to continue in 1983 on four other functions: project and trust fund accounting; approving officer functions; translation activities; and editing. In addition, the final organizational structure, staffing and job descriptions, operating procedures and budgetary aspects were to be developed.

In a 10 December report to the Assembly,(1) ACABQ, commenting on the Secretary-General's report, recommended that he re-examine the proposals for common organizational arrangements, particularly those showing potential for duplication and additional expense. Establishing a common services unit should not lead to creating semi-autonomous or autonomous structures, ACABQ added.

On 21 December, the General Assembly, without vote, took note of the reports and concurred with the ACABQ recommendations.(3)

The resolution, approved without objection by the Fifth Committee on 11 December, was orally proposed by the Committee Chairman on the basis of an ACABQ recommendation.

Reports. (1)ACABQ, A/37/7/Add.17; (2)S-G, A/C.5/37/49.
Resolution (1982). (3)GA: 37/237, sect. X, 21 Dec., text following.
Meeting records. GA: 5th Committee, A/C.5/37/SR.64 (11 Dec.); plenary, A/37/PV.114 (21 Dec.).

General Assembly resolution 37/237, section X

21 December 1982   Meeting 114   Adopted without vote

Approved by Fifth Committee (A/37/790) without objection, 11 December (meeting 64); oral proposal by Chairman based on ACABQ recommendation; agenda item 103.

Common services at the United Nations accommodation at Nairobi

[*The General Assembly* . . .]

1. *Takes note* of the report of the Secretary-General on common services at the United Nations accommodation at Nairobi and of the related report of the Advisory Committee on Administrative and Budgetary Questions;

2. *Concurs* with the observations and recommendations of the Advisory Committee contained in paragraphs 15 and 16 of its report;

. . .

Building construction procedures

In a November 1982 report to the Fifth Committee on implementing recommendations made by the Joint Inspection Unit (JIU), the Secretary-General commented on the building construction procedures of United Nations organizations.(1) In 1981, JIU had made specific recommendations on those procedures.(2)

The Secretary-General reported that the Headquarters construction project (see above) was too far advanced to permit practical changes in those procedures not already consistent with the JIU recommendations. On the Nairobi project (see above), tenders had already been requested before the 1981 JIU report was considered by the Assembly; however, the procedures used were consistent with most of the JIU recommendations. The Secretary-General added that he would report separately on planning and management controls for the proposed expansion of conference facilities at the headquarters of the Economic Commission for Africa at Addis Ababa, Ethiopia (see ECONOMIC AND SOCIAL QUESTIONS, Chapter VIII).

Report. (1)S-G, A/C.5/37/28.
Yearbook reference. (2)1981, p. 1382.

Computers and information systems

Co-ordination of information systems

ACC activities. In a July 1982 report,(9) the Administrative Committee on Co-ordination (ACC) recommended measures to enhance inter-agency co-ordination of United Nations information systems, pursuant to a July 1981 Economic and Social Council resolution.[15] By this resolution, the Council had also requested ACC to propose means of ensuring cost-effective compatibility of computerized information systems and to reconsider its 1981 decision[16] to terminate the operational functions and abolish the secretariat of the Inter-Organization Board for Information Systems (IOB), a body composed of representatives of the United Nations and a number of specialized agencies.

In its report, ACC proposed a new institutional structure to replace IOB and its secretariat, including an inter-agency advisory committee and secretariat to co-ordinate information systems. It also recommended that specialized panels be set up to examine: inter-agency use of common communications systems; tools to be developed to improve organization and Member State awareness of information in the United Nations; harmonizing co-ordination methods by identifying areas of information handling where the application of existing or proposed new standards was necessary; a common, generic vocabulary for indexing and retrieving United Nations information; the impact of new technology for handling and transfer of information; and an information system on United Nations development activities. ACC further suggested that the Council convene a meeting of government and secretariat representatives to ascertain countries' views on strengthening the co-ordination of information systems.

The ACC report, adopted on 5 July,[2] was based on recommendations by an *ad hoc* inter-agency meeting (Geneva, 25-27 May).[10] At the meeting, the report of two experts, appointed in October 1981 to assist in formulating proposals, was considered. Their report, annexed to that of ACC,[9] was submitted in May 1982, following a 6 April decision[1] by which ACC requested them to complete their work prior to the inter-agency meeting.

By a decision of 3 November,[3] ACC recommended provisional appropriations for 1982-1983 to continue interorganization secretariat services for information systems at the same real level as embodied in the 1980-1981 budget of the IOB secretariat.

Economic and Social Council action. On 27 April 1982,[4] the Economic and Social Council, acting on an oral proposal of its President, decided without vote to take note of an oral progress report on the ongoing work of the experts by the Assistant Secretary-General for Programme Planning and Co-ordination. He reported that they had reached the preliminary conclusion that Member States were the most important users of United Nations information systems as opposed to the view of IOB that intergovernmental organizations were the main users.

On 29 July.[5] the Council decided without vote to postpone consideration of the ACC report until later in the year. The adopted text was an orally amended version of a draft submitted by the Third (Programme and Co-ordination) Committee. By the Committee draft, proposed by the Chairman and approved without vote on 19 July, the Council would have noted the ACC report, transmitted it to the General Assembly and organized a meeting of government and secretariat representatives pursuant to the ACC recommendation. The draft had been orally amended by the USSR to add that the proposed meeting would be financed within the framework of allocations for the Assembly's 1982 regular session.

On 10 November,[12] the Council urged that a small central mechanism in ACC advise on proposals to create new information systems or revise existing ones; determine the needs of users, especially those in developing countries, and develop a register of development activities within a year; compile, update and popularize indexing vocabularies at the generic level and formulate standards; and monitor the development of information technology and ensure its application in the United Nations system. The Council stressed the importance of associating United Nations technical experts with the users and suppliers of information for maximum benefit. It also stressed that the work should involve no costs for 1983 additional to those proposed to ACC and that work in future years should be cost-effective. It invited ACC to ensure the continuation of activities supporting the co-ordination of information systems and to submit a report on the resolution's implementation to the Council at its second regular 1983 session.

This action was incorporated in a resolution adopted by 47 votes to 5, with 2 abstentions. The text originated from a draft submitted by a Third Committee Vice-Chairman to the Council which was based on informal consultations.[7] The Council also had before it a note by the United Nations Secretariat[8] on the related administrative and financial implications. The United States orally proposed an amendment to paragraph 3 of the draft by which the work in 1983, in addition to involving no costs additional to the ACC estimates, would be funded out of existing resources. The Vice-Chairman then withdrew his draft because he could not accept the proposed amendment and, as the representative of the Sudan, reintroduced it on behalf of 12 nations. Subsequently, the United States proposed the same amendment, which the Council rejected by 31 votes to 9, with 11 abstentions.

General Assembly action. In a resolution of 21 December[14] relating to the 1982-1983 programme budget, the General Assembly approved, without vote, the ACC proposal whereby interorganization secretariat services for information systems were to be continued in 1983 at the same real level as in the budget of the IOB secretariat for 1980-1981.

The Fifth (Administrative and Budgetary) Committee, which had before it a report of the Secretary-General giving revised estimates on the United Nations share of those services,[11] had approved this section of the resolution without objection on 23 November. The Committee acted on an oral proposal by its Chairman based on the recommendation of ACC.

In a resolution of 20 December[13] on operational activities for development of the United Nations system, the Assembly reiterated the Council's request that ACC develop the register of development activities within a year. The original draft of this resolution, submitted by Bangladesh for the Group of 77 and subsequently withdrawn,[6] did not include the provision on the register of development activities.

Decisions. ACC: [1]1982/2, 6 Apr.; [2]1982/13, 5 July; [3]1982/21, 3 Nov. ESC: [4]1982/113, 27 Apr., text following; [5]1982/170, 29 July, text following
Draft resolutions withdrawn. [6]Bangladesh, for Group of 77, A/C.2/37/L.92; [7]ESC 3rd Committee Vice-Chairman, E/1982/L.55, based on informal consultations.
Note. [8]Secretariat, E/1982/L.56.
Reports. [9]ACC, E/1982/85; [10]Inter-agency meeting, ACC/1982/18; [11]S-G, A/C.5/37/41.
Resolutions (1982). [12]ESC: 1982/71, 10 Nov., text following. GA: [13]37/226, para. 23, 20 Dec.; [14]37/237, sect. VII, 21 Dec., text following.
Resolution (prior). [15]ESC: 1981/63, 23 July 1981 (YUN 1981, p. 1385).
Yearbook reference. [16]1981, p. 1386.
Meeting records. ESC: E/1982/SR._17_ (27 Apr.), _49, 50_ (28, 29 July), 52, _56, 57_ (25 Oct., 10 Nov.). GA: 5th Committee, A/C.5/37/SR.42 (23 Nov.); plenary, A/37/PV.114 (21 Dec.).

Economic and Social Council decision 1982/113

Adopted without vote

Draft orally proposed by President; agenda item 6.

Strengthening of the co-ordination of information systems

At its 17th plenary meeting, on 27 April 1982, the Council took note of the oral progress report made by the representative of the Secretary-General pursuant to Council resolution 1981/63 of 23 July 1981 on the strengthening of the co-ordination of information systems.

Economic and Social Council decision 1982/170

Adopted without vote

Approved by Third Committee (E/1982/91) without vote, 19 July (meeting 11); draft by Chairman (E/1982/C.3/L.4), orally amended by USSR; further orally amended in Council by Secretary; agenda item 20.

Report of the Administrative Committee on Co-ordination on the strengthening of the co-ordination of information systems in the United Nations system

At its 50th plenary meeting, on 29 July 1982, the Council decided to consider the report of the Administrative Committee on Co-ordination on the strengthening of the co-ordination of information systems in the United Nations system at its resumed second regular session of 1982.

Economic and Social Council resolution 1982/71

10 November 1982   Meeting 57   47-5-2

12-nation draft (E/1982/L.55); agenda item 20.

Sponsors: Bangladesh, India, Jordan, Kenya, Liberia, Nigeria, Norway, Pakistan, Sudan, Sweden, Tunisia, Yugoslavia.

Strengthening of the co-ordination of information systems in the United Nations system

The Economic and Social Council,

Conscious that information is one of the most valuable resources at the disposal of the United Nations system,

Emphasizing the need for facilitating the access of developing countries to the United Nations information systems,

Recognizing the need to co-ordinate and harmonize the information systems in the United Nations system and the need to undertake this from the perspective of the needs of users at the national level,

Bearing in mind the conclusions contained in the report of the Administrative Committee on Co-ordination and the recommendations set forth in the final report of the independent experts on the strengthening of the co-ordination of information systems in the United Nations system, and stressing the need for further consideration of that report,

Recalling its resolution 1981/63 of 23 July 1981,

1. _Urges_ that a small central mechanism in the Administrative Committee on Co-ordination for the co-ordination of information systems, whose aims would be to ensure the more efficient operation of existing or planned United Nations information systems from the perspective of users at the national level and to enhance the capacity of the United Nations system to collect, store, retrieve and disseminate information, should:

_(a)_ Review and advise on at an early stage proposals for the creation of new information systems or for the substantial modification of existing ones, when such proposals might be of interest to more than one organization, with a view to avoiding unnecessary duplication and to ensuring compatibility of information systems in the same or related fields, and stresses that such advisory opinions should be presented to the governing bodies of organizations, together with the proposals of those organizations, before decisions are taken to create new information systems or substantially modify existing ones;

_(b)_ Give priority in its work programme to determining the needs of users, in particular those in developing countries; to identifying the areas, especially those related to operational activities, in which coherent information should be made available, especially at the level of the United Nations system; and to developing, within a year, a meaningful register of development activities;

_(c)_ Compile, update and popularize common indexing vocabularies at the generic level and formulate standards, drawing upon the technical expertise of the appropriate organs, organizations and bodies of the United Nations system;

_(d)_ Monitor the development of information technology and ensure its application in the United Nations system in an effective and co-ordinated manner;

2. _Stresses_ the importance of associating the technical experts of the United Nations system with the suppliers and users of information in the discharge of the functions outlined in paragraph 1 above, in order to ensure that information users at the national level obtain maximum benefit from the information systems of the United Nations system;

3. _Stresses further_ that such work should involve no costs additional to those foreseen in the estimates proposed to the Administrative Committee on Co-ordination for 1983 and that, in future years, work of this nature should be carried out with maximum cost-effectiveness;

4. _Invites_ the Administrative Committee on Co-ordination to take appropriate action to ensure the continuation of current activities supporting the co-ordination of information systems and to strengthen and reorient them so as to achieve the above objectives;

5. _Invites_ the Administrative Committee on Co-ordination to submit to it, through the Committee for Programme and Co-ordination at its twenty-third session, a report on the implementation of the present resolution for consideration at its second regular session of 1983.

General Assembly resolution 37/237, section VII

21 December 1982   Meeting 114   Adopted without vote

Approved by Fifth Committee (A/37/790) without objection, 23 November (meeting 42); oral proposal by Chairman based on ACC recommendation; agenda item 103.

Interorganization secretariat services for information systems

[The General Assembly . . .]

Approves the proposal made by the Administrative Committee on Co-ordination at its third regular session in 1982 for the continuation in 1983 of interorganization secretariat services in the field of information systems at the same real level as embodied in the budget of the secretariat of the Inter-Organization Board for Information Systems for the biennium 1980-1981;

. . .

Budget estimates of the International Computing Centre for 1983

The General Assembly, on 21 December 1982,[3] approved without vote 1983 budget estimates in the amount of $5,580,200 for the International Computing Centre (ICC), an international facility at Geneva financed by the United Nations and 12 other participating United Nations organizations and programmes.

The Fifth Committee recommended this action without objection on 23 November as proposed orally by its Chairman based on a recommendation by the Advisory Committee on Administrative and Budgetary Questions (ACABQ).[1]

The budget estimates were submitted by the Secretary-General in November,[2] following review by representatives of organizations using ICC services.

The United Nations share of the 1983 budget came to $1.6 million.

Reports. [1]ACABQ, A/37/7; [2]S-G, A/C.5/37/40.
Resolution (1982). [3]GA: 37/237, sect. VI, 21 Dec., text following.
Meeting records. GA: 5th Committee, A/C.5/37/SR.42 (23 Nov.); plenary, A/37/PV.114 (21 Dec.).

General Assembly resolution 37/237, section VI

21 December 1982   Meeting 114   Adopted without vote

Approved by Fifth Committee (A/37/790) without objection, 23 November (meeting 42); oral proposal by Chairman based on ACABQ recommendation; agenda item 103.

International Computing Centre

[The General Assembly . . .]

Approves the 1983 budget estimates of the International Computing Centre, amounting to $5,580,200, as contained in the report of the Secretary-General;

. . .

Communications

In response to a request from one of its participating organizations, the Joint Inspection Unit (JIU) undertook, in 1981, a study on communications in the United Nations system. The report on the study, an update of a similar study undertaken by JIU in 1972, was transmitted to the General Assembly by the Secretary-General in August 1982.[1]

The report examined how existing communications services in the United Nations system, whose annual global costs were estimated at $100 million in 1982, could be utilized more effectively and what new technologies could best complement the traditional communications media to enhance their effectiveness. JIU noted that in the United Nations system there had been many developments in communications in recent years, including computer conferencing, electronic mail and "memory" telephones, and some modernization had taken place, but mail, pouch, telex and telephones still constituted the backbone of communications. JIU felt that United Nations organizations should adopt a broader communications philosophy in which the systems and media operated should be seen as instruments of development geared to the needs of developing countries. The issue was one of strategy and policy rather than technical or budgetary, the report added.

JIU recommended that, within the Administrative Committee on Co-ordination (ACC), the Secretary-General set up an *ad hoc* inter-agency committee on communications in which top-level administrators could review proposals for a long-term system-wide communications plan but with the immediate objective of facilitating discussions between communications experts of the system. On specific issues concerning the United Nations, JIU recommended an outside expert evaluation of the telephone system; a study on the advisability of upgrading the cable, telex and teleprinter network; and examining the pouch system, including working conditions, the accounting system, and reducing the volume of material transmitted.

Concerning the United Nations system in general, JIU recommended that services offered by public telecommunications authorities be kept under review; greater use of facsimile; continued experimentation with computer-controlled communications techniques; telecommunications as an alternative to travel, particularly voice teleconferencing and computer conferencing; increased use of radio communications; and studying the communications needs of field duty stations before modernizing the existing radio network. JIU also made a recommendation on the United Nations possibly acquiring its own communications satellite system (see below).

Commenting on the report,[2] the Secretary-General said that, although he agreed that it had become necessary to pay greater attention to developing the Organization's communications facilities, the statement that the issue was one of strategy and policy rather than technical or budgetary underestimated the fact that the problem was a combination of those factors. With regard to the

JIU comments on telephone, cables, the telex and teleprinter network and the pouch system, the Secretariat had to a large extent already identified the problems and measures were in place or contemplated in line with the recommendations. On the United Nations system in general, the Secretary-General said he agreed with the proposals and measures on some of them had been undertaken. He also said he would pursue the recommendation to create an *ad hoc* inter-agency committee on communications in consultation with ACC.

ACC commented[3] that the JIU report was generally viewed as containing important guidelines which United Nations organizations should largely follow. Reservations were expressed by the World Health Organization (WHO) which considered that organizations did follow developments and that new methods were used according to requirements; and by WHO and the International Labour Organisation which cautioned that voice conferencing would be difficult because of different cultural patterns and thought processes. ACC said there was also broad agreement concerning satellite facilities (see below). Regarding the creation of an *ad hoc* committee, it would be preferable that the technical aspects of those questions be reviewed within the existing mechanisms for inter-agency co-ordination.

Speaking in the Fifth Committee, the ACABQ Chairman said that, assuming that none of the JIU recommendations required immediate action, ACABQ recommended that the report be accepted.

On 21 December,[4] the General Assembly, without vote, took note of the JIU report and the related comments. On 23 November, the Fifth Committee had approved without objection the draft orally proposed by the Chairman.

Report. [1]JIU, transmitted by S-G note, A/37/372, and [2]S-G comments, Add.1, and [3]ACC comments, Add.2.
Resolution (1982). [4]GA: 37/237, sect. V, 21 Dec., text following.
Meeting records. GA: 5th Committee, A/C.5/37/SR.28, *39, 42* (8-23 Nov.); plenary, A/37/PV.114 (21 Dec.).

General Assembly resolution 37/237, section V

21 December 1982   Meeting 114   Adopted without vote

Approved by Fifth Committee (A/37/790) without objection, 23 November (meeting 42); oral proposal by Chairman; agenda item 103.

Communications in the United Nations system

[*The General Assembly* . . .]

Takes note with appreciation of the report of the Joint Inspection Unit entitled "Communications in the United Nations system", of the comments thereon of the Secretary-General and of the Administrative Committee on Co-ordination, as well as of the related oral report of the Advisory Committee on Administrative and Budgetary Questions;

. . .

Communications satellite

In an April 1982 note to the Committee on Information,[1] the Secretary-General responded to a 1981 General Assembly resolution[7] approving recommendations of the Committee, including one requesting him to explore the possibility of the United Nations acquiring its own communications satellite. He pointed out that the question should be viewed in the light of its broad implications for the Organization's work to avoid piecemeal decisions. The cost of a communications satellite system was prohibitive, particularly because of current budgetary restraints, and preliminary calculations indicated that one-time costs of a limited system between the Middle East, Western Europe and North America would be $175 million, plus annual operational costs of $1.75 million. The Secretariat was exploring more cost-effective methods of providing a rapid, flexible and responsive broad-based network to major areas of interest to the United Nations. The Secretary-General said he would address the question further following consideration of an upcoming JIU report.

In an August report,[3] JIU said that, instead of acquiring its own communications satellite system, organizations should negotiate with the International Telecommunication Satellite Consortium (INTELSAT) or similar consortia and with Governments of host countries to acquire communications channels at preferential rates.

Commenting on the JIU report, the Secretary-General[4] said that measures in line with the recommendation had already been taken. He felt that endorsement of the JIU recommendation by the General Assembly would facilitate future negotiations.

In November,[5] ACC said it broadly agreed with JIU that it would be unnecessarily expensive for the United Nations to acquire its own earth stations; its preference was for leasing.

The Committee on Information recommended[2] that the Secretary-General be requested to present to the Committee in 1983 a new detailed report on acquiring a satellite. The report should study the alternatives and analyse existing administrative costs for telephone, telex, radio, video, document processing, the holding of conferences and travel of interpreters and, while projecting seven-year operational goals, compare them with the cost of a United Nations satellite. The study should also take into account all uses by the United Nations system and present financing and self-maintenance alternatives. The Committee would also take into account a JIU report on communications.

The General Assembly, on 10 December, adopted the Committee's recommendation in a resolution on questions relating to information.[6]

Note. [1]S-G, A/AC.198/51.
Reports. [2]Committee on Information, A/37/21; [3]JIU, transmitted by S-G note, A/37/372, and [4]S-G comments, Add.1, and [5]ACC comments, Add.2.
Resolution (1982). [6]GA: 37/94 B, para. 20, 10 Dec.
Resolution (prior). [7]GA: 36/149 B, 16 Dec. 1981 (YUN 1981, p. 363).

UN Postal Administration

In 1982, gross revenue of the United Nations Postal Administration from the sale of philatelic items at United Nations Headquarters and at overseas offices totalled more than $13 million. Revenue derived from the sale of stamps for philatelic purposes was retained by the United Nations; revenue from stamps used for postage from Headquarters was retained by the United States Postal Service under an agreement between the United Nations and the United States Government. Similarly, revenue from stamps used for postage from the Palais des Nations, Geneva, and from the Vienna International Centre was retained by the Swiss and Austrian postal authorities, respectively, in accordance with agreements between the Organization and the Swiss and Austrian Governments.

Six definitive stamps, four postal cards, two air letters, four commemoratives and two souvenir cards were issued.

On 22 January, six definitives were issued in denominations of 17, 28 and 40 cents, 0.30 and 1.00 Swiss francs (SwF) and 3 Austrian schillings (S).

The theme of the first commemorative stamp, issued on 19 March, was "Human Environment". The stamp was issued in denominations of 20 and 40 cents, SwF 0.40 and 1.20, and S 5 and 7. A souvenir card was also issued.

Six pieces of stationery were issued on 28 April. The issue consisted of four postal cards in denominations of 13 and 28 cents and S 3 and 5, as well as two air letters in values of 30 cents and S 9.

The second commemorative issue, on 11 June, was for "Exploration and Peaceful Uses of Outer Space", in denominations of 20 cents, SwF 0.80 and 1.00, and S 5. A souvenir card accompanied this issue.

On 24 September, the third group of 16 stamps was issued in the commemorative "Flag Series" in denominations of 20 cents each.

The fourth and final commemorative, issued on 19 November, was on the theme "Conservation and Protection of Nature". The stamps were issued in denominations of 20 and 28 cents, SwF 0.40 and 1.50, and S 5 and 7.

The number of first-day covers serviced for the various issues in 1982 was as follows:

Definitives	17, 28, 40 cents	243,073
	SwF 0.30, 1.00	199,347
	S 3	203,872
Stationery		
Postal cards	13 cents	59,200
	28 cents	58,700
	S 3	93,010
	S 5	89,502
Air letters	30 cents	61,400
	S 9	120,650
Human Environment		727,452
Exploration and Peaceful Uses of Outer Space		513,625
Flag Series		3,202,744
Conservation and Protection of Nature		656,200

Responding to a December 1981 General Assembly request,[3] the Secretary-General informed the Assembly in October 1982 of a publicity programme which was to accompany the issuing of the Conservation and Protection of Nature stamps.[1]

In its 16 November resolution[2] on the financial emergency of the United Nations, the Assembly asked the Secretary-General to submit to it in 1983 a progress report on the issue of special postage stamps, including proposals to use some revenue to further the cause of protecting nature.

Report. [1]S-G, A/C.5/37/15.
Resolution (1982). [2]GA: 37/13, para. 7 *(b),* 16 Nov.
Resolution (prior). [3]GA: 36/116 B, 10 Dec. 1981 (YUN 1981, p. 1298).

PART TWO

Intergovernmental organizations related to the United Nations

Chapter I

International Atomic Energy Agency (IAEA)

In 1982, the International Atomic Energy Agency (IAEA) continued its activities to accelerate and enlarge the contribution of atomic energy to peace, health and prosperity throughout the world and to ensure that the assistance provided was not used for military purposes. Continued emphasis was placed on safeguards, the safety of nuclear power stations, nuclear fuel-cycle services and the management of nuclear waste, and the provision of technical assistance to member States, particularly the developing countries.

IAEA celebrated its twenty-fifth anniversary in 1982, its statute having entered into force on 29 July 1957. To mark this event, a conference on technical and economic experience gained with nuclear power was held (Vienna, Austria, 13-17 September 1982) and a meeting on the role of nuclear power in energy planning was convened during the twenty-sixth session of the General Conference of IAEA (Vienna, 20-24 September).

At the end of 1982, the Treaty on the Non-Proliferation of Nuclear Weapons[a] (Non-Proliferation Treaty) had 118 non-nuclear-weapon States parties (Nauru, Papua New Guinea, Uganda and Viet Nam became parties during the year). The Agency continued its efforts to improve the effectiveness and efficiency of its international safeguards system, which aimed at deterring the proliferation of nuclear weapons by early detection, while respecting States' sovereign rights. Work also continued on assuring supplies of nuclear material, equipment and technology and fuel-cycle services, on possible schemes for international storage of plutonium and on the international management of spent fuel.

Work neared completion on an up-to-date set of internationally agreed safety standards for nuclear power plants—IAEA Nuclear Safety Standards (NUSS)—and the Agency increased assistance to member States in implementing NUSS recommendations through advisory missions. In 1982, IAEA produced its first annual nuclear safety review, which outlined world-wide trends in nuclear safety and described related Agency activities. The review concluded that recent research and operating experience had not revealed a need for significant changes with regard to nuclear safety.

Membership of IAEA remained at 110 in 1982. On 20 September, the IAEA General Conference approved the application of Namibia, represented by the United Nations Council for Namibia, for membership. Neither Namibia nor Zimbabwe, which was admitted in 1981, had deposited their instruments of acceptance as at 31 December 1982.

At its 1982 session, the General Conference decided not to accept the credentials of Israel, following a number of roll-call votes. The Conference decided to request the IAEA Board of Governors—its executive organ—to recommend proposed amendments to its statute. One proposal concerned representation on the Board of the areas of Africa, the Middle East and South Asia; another would ensure that technical assistance was funded through the IAEA regular budget or through other assured resources and that funds were increased to respond to growing requirements; and a third would request the Director General to increase staff from developing areas, particularly at the higher levels.

The Board of Governors met four times during 1982, once in February and June and twice in September, at Vienna.

Agency safeguards responsibilities

As at 31 December 1982, 118 non-nuclear-weapon States and three nuclear-weapon States (USSR, United Kingdom, United States) had ratified or acceded to the Non-Proliferation Treaty. Safeguards agreements with IAEA, concluded under article III of the Treaty, had entered into force for 74 non-nuclear-weapon States parties. On 20 December, the safeguards agreement with Colombia pursuant to the Treaty for the Prohibition of Nuclear Weapons in Latin America (Treaty of Tlatelolco)—by which States parties are required to enter into safeguards agreements with the Agency—entered into force.

---

[a]See YUN 1968, p. 17, text of Treaty, annexed to General Assembly resolution 2373(XXII) of 12 June 1968.

Agency safeguards were applied under other agreements in 10 non-nuclear-weapon States not party to the Non-Proliferation Treaty, but having substantial nuclear activities, namely Argentina, Brazil, Chile, Cuba, the Democratic People's Republic of Korea, India, Israel, Pakistan, South Africa and Spain. In seven of these States, all substantial nuclear activities known to IAEA were covered by a network of individual safeguards agreements.

At the end of 1982, safeguards applied by IAEA covered material in 143 power reactors; in 177 research reactors and critical assemblies; in six conversion, 39 fuel fabrication, six reprocessing and four enrichment plants; and in 469 other nuclear installations.

Technical assistance

During 1982, 74 countries received IAEA technical assistance in the form of expert services or equipment or both. Eleven additional countries received assistance under the Agency's training programmes. A total of 592 fellows were carrying out individual field studies, and 1,019 persons—including 158 whose costs were met from other sources—participated in 36 group training projects. Technical assistance provided by IAEA in 1982 exceeded $23 million in value, 9.8 per cent higher than in 1981.

The Agency served as executing agency for 25 large-scale projects financed by the United Nations Development Programme (UNDP). Among these were: nuclear engineering (Argentina); exploration for nuclear minerals (Chile, Colombia, Ecuador, Madagascar); nuclear manpower training and development of agriculture through nuclear technology (Brazil); a centre for isotope applications (Bulgaria); introduction of nuclear techniques (Cuba, Ethiopia, Senegal); a national centre for radiation technology (Egypt); application of isotopes and radiation to increase agricultural production (Indonesia); a pilot demonstration plant for radio-sterilization and other applications of radiation technology (Iran); nuclear techniques in animal production (Nigeria); nuclear energy (Peru); manpower development in nuclear power (Philippines); nuclear technology and assistance for nuclear power stations (Romania); radioactive tracer techniques for studying coastal sedimentation (Sri Lanka); industrial application of high-energy ionizing radiation (Yugoslavia); strengthening the regional centre for nuclear studies at Kinshasa (Zaire); industrial application of isotopes and radiation technology (regional, Asia and the Pacific); and modern techniques in physics (interregional).

The Agency also continued to provide large-scale assistance to projects in Bangladesh and India for the use of nuclear techniques in agricultural research, financed by Sweden. Two new large-scale projects were begun in 1982: eradication of the Mediterranean fruit fly in Egypt, funded by Italy and Austria as well as by in-kind assistance from Mexico; and interregional research on micro-organisms to degrade cellulose, funded by Italy.

The target for member States' voluntary contributions to the IAEA regular programme was $16 million in 1982, of which $14.9 million was pledged. Other sources of support for the technical co-operation programme were UNDP funds ($4.6 million), extrabudgetary contributions ($4.5 million) and assistance in kind ($2.5 million).

Nuclear power

At the end of 1982, 297 nuclear power plants with a total capacity of 173,040 megawatts (electrical) (MW(e)) accounted for around 8 per cent of the world's electricity-generating capacity. The record of operating nuclear power plants continued to be excellent: over 2,800 reactor years had accumulated without any significant spread of radioactivity to the environment or any radiation-induced fatality.

The Agency continued to assist its developing member States to introduce nuclear-powered electricity-generating plants with planning surveys, feasibility studies and the evaluation of technical bids. It also continued preparing a series of guidebooks, for example, on manpower development for nuclear power, on technical evaluation of bids for nuclear power plants, on the introduction of nuclear power, on the interaction of grid characteristics with the design and performance of nuclear power plants, and on nuclear power plant instrumentation and control.

In 1982, 10 interregional training courses, four of which focused on special aspects of nuclear power plant safety, were attended by 270 participants from developing countries. IAEA continued to develop its energy data bank and to collect and disseminate information on nuclear technology and the reliability of nuclear power plants. A computerized power-reactor information system was further developed as a systematic source of operating-experience data for nuclear power plants.

Environment

Because the future growth of nuclear power was felt to depend to a large extent on providing evidence of the capability to manage radioactive waste safely, IAEA continued to attach importance to its waste management programme, addressing the technological, environmental, safety and regulatory aspects of the treatment and disposal of radioactive waste. Four technical reports reviewing site investigations for repositories were published as well as a report in a safety series—in collaboration with the World Health Organization—on nuclear power, the environment and man.

Among 1982 activities related to radioactive waste management, IAEA issued a provisional code of practice on the management of radioactive waste from nuclear power plants and a technical report on radio-nuclides at nuclear facilities. In collaboration with the Nuclear Energy Agency of the Organisation for Economic Co-operation and Development, IAEA organized a symposium on the management of wastes from uranium mining and milling (Albuquerque, United States, May) and published a report on uranium resources, production and demand.

At the Agency's request and within its responsibilities under the 1975 Convention on the Prevention of Marine Pollution by Dumping of Wastes and Other Matter, a United Nations joint group of experts on the scientific aspects of marine pollution completed its assessment of oceanographic models to review the definition of high-level radioactive waste under the Convention.

Nuclear safety

The Agency continued developing its safety standards and regulations for nuclear power plants: 46 of 57 planned safety guides were completed. An extensive effort to implement those standards was under way by means of training courses, seminars and visits by experts to member States. The first annual safety review, dealing with the status of nuclear power-plant safety world-wide and the Agency's safety activities, was presented to the Board of Governors in June. The Basic Safety Standards for Radiation Protection of workers and the general public, developed by IAEA and revised in 1981 to reflect recommendations of the International Commission on Radiological Protection, were published in 1982.

Advisory services continued throughout the year to member States with developing nuclear programmes; missions to member States dealt with a wide spectrum of safety issues, from general questions such as problems of organizing a national regulatory authority to those which involved specific details such as mechanical problems with a particular nuclear power-plant component.

Information exchange continued to be emphasized. The Agency transmitted safety information through world-wide training courses and worked to develop an international system for collecting information on incidents of safety significance occurring at nuclear power plants.

The Agency also maintained its radiological assistance plan, involving about 20 duty officers ready to deal with radiation-release accidents. New publications and training courses strengthened the programme of emergency preparedness planning, and special assistance missions were sent to member States to develop, evaluate and improve their emergency plans.

Nuclear information

The International Nuclear Information System, with 68 participating countries and 14 international organizations, provided a comprehensive nuclear information and abstracting service from its file of some 800,000 items.

Life sciences

In co-operation with the World Health Organization (WHO), IAEA continued in 1982 to promote the use of nuclear techniques in medicine, biology and health-related environmental research and to conduct research on techniques for improving the accuracy of radiation dosimetry.

Radio-immunoassay and related medical procedures were the subject of a symposium (Vienna, Austria) and an interregional training course. Three national workshops (Latin America) and a seminar (Asia and the Pacific region) were held on quality assurance of nuclear medicine instruments. Advisory groups treated: quality control of *in vivo* radio-nuclide procedures and biomedical neutron activation analysis; the future of the dose inter-comparison service for radio-therapy; review and updating of the IAEA recommended code of practice for radiosterilization of medical supplies; and nuclear techniques in environmental health studies of mineral pollutants.

In 1982, China and Portugal each nominated a dosimetry laboratory for membership in the IAEA/WHO network of Secondary Standard Dosimetry Laboratories (SSDLs), raising the number of member laboratories to 45. The Agency assisted in setting up SSDLs in Algeria, Colombia, Ecuador, Malaysia, the Philippines, Portugal, the Republic of Korea, Thailand, Turkey and Uruguay. Sixteen co-ordinated research programmes were carried out during 1982. These related to: maintenance plans for nuclear laboratories; quality control of radio-assay techniques in nuclear medicine; trace elements in nutrition and in environmental pollution; high dose standardization and inter-comparison; preparation of irradiated vaccines; improved methods of radio-therapy; comparative biological hazards from low-level radiation and major chemical pollutants; radiation-induced chromosomal changes; and biological hazards of low-level ionizing radiation.

Physical sciences and laboratories

The role of IAEA in co-ordinating the international effort in controlled fusion was reflected in the continuation of the International Tokamak Reactor Workshop, in which scientists from the major fusion laboratories of the European Atomic Energy Community, Japan, the USSR and the United States participated. Work on optimization of the design and cost/benefit/risk analysis of design alternatives continued in 1982.

Nuclear analytical techniques in mineral exploration, mining and processing were reviewed at an international seminar. Renewed emphasis was given to programmes on chemical aspects of fusion reactor technology and on radiation degradation of organic materials and components used in reactor environments. Within the isotope hydrology programme, isotope techniques were used in more than 30 member States in projects varying from assistance in establishing environmental isotope analytical facilities to applied field studies solving hydrological problems. An advisory group assessed the current status of the use of tracer methods in hydrology.

The Agency continued to provide nuclear data services to member States, primarily to 40 developing countries, and responded to more than 700 requests, over 10 per cent more than in 1981. In co-ordinated research programmes, the Agency reviewed the accuracy and validity of atomic collision data and improvements in measuring and evaluating isotope decay data, and established a comprehensive computer library of evaluated neutron nuclear data. With the aim of training scientists from developing countries to perform accurate nuclear measurements and use nuclear techniques, IAEA held an interregional training course on using neutron generators and assisted nuclear data training and research programmes in 21 developing countries.

The International Laboratory of Marine Radioactivity in Monaco, with the co-operation of the United Nations Environment Programme and the United Nations Educational, Scientific and Cultural Organization, conducted studies in the occurrence, distribution and behaviour of radio-nuclides and other pollutants. The laboratory also organized co-ordinated research programmes and intercalibration of pollutant measurements in member States.

The IAEA Laboratory at Seibersdorf, Austria, supported an agricultural biotechnology programme, with projects in fertilizer utilization, plant breeding, pest control, agrochemicals and animal production. Medical programmes included a study on trace elements in human milk and development of a counting system for nuclear medicine. The medical applications and dosimetry laboratory continued its postal dose calibration service for member States.

The Safeguards Analytical Laboratory continued to analyse nuclear fuel-cycle samples collected by IAEA safeguards inspectors. In 1982, the Laboratory worked to maximum capacity, and plans were drawn up to extend its premises.

Food and agriculture

Under joint programmes of the Food and Agriculture Organization of the United Nations and IAEA, work continued through 27 co-ordinated research programmes on the application of isotope and radiation techniques in order to increase agricultural production, improve the quality of food, reduce food losses and minimize pollution of food and the environment. Support was given to over 100 technical assistance projects in some 46 developing member States during 1982.

Work continued on insect control, particularly the control of the Mediterranean fruit fly in Peru and Egypt and the tsetse fly in Nigeria. Other projects were designed to improve crop and livestock production.

Secretariat

As at the end of 1982, 1,718 staff members were employed by IAEA. Of these, 610—drawn from 72 countries—were in the Professional and higher categories and 1,108 were in the General Service and Maintenance and Operatives Service categories.

Budget

The General Conference of IAEA at its September 1982 session adopted a regular budget of $91,561,000 for 1983. The target for voluntary contributions to finance the Agency's technical co-operation programme for 1983 was set at $19 million.

Annex I.   MEMBERSHIP OF THE INTERNATIONAL ATOMIC ENERGY AGENCY AND CONTRIBUTIONS

(Membership as at 31 December 1982; contributions as assessed for 1982 and 1983)

MEMBER	CONTRIBUTION FOR 1982		CONTRIBUTION FOR 1983	
	Percentage	Net amount (in US dollars)	Percentage	Net amount (in US dollars)
Afghanistan	0.00766	5,927	0.00731	5,924
Albania	0.00766	5,927	0.00731	5,924
Algeria	0.08381	64,823	0.07995	64,790
Argentina	0.56655	438,194	0.54047	437,973
Australia	1.91026	1,477,472	1.91762	1,553,965
Austria	0.74345	575,016	0.74632	604,788
Bangladesh	0.03119	24,125	0.02976	24,113
Belgium	1.27006	982,318	1.27496	1,033,177
Bolivia	0.00766	5,927	0.00731	5,924
Brazil	0.89162	689,617	0.85056	689,258
Bulgaria	0.11367	87,918	0.10844	87,873
Burma	0.00802	6,202	0.00765	6,199
Byelorussian SSR	0.41303	319,462	0.41462	335,991
Canada	3.42814	2,651,460	3.44136	2,788,740
Chile	0.05348	41,360	0.05101	41,340
Colombia	0.08112	62,739	0.07738	62,708
Costa Rica	0.01435	11,100	0.01369	11,095
Cuba	0.07845	60,679	0.07484	60,648
Cyprus	0.00766	5,927	0.00731	5,924
Czechoslovakia	0.86736	670,851	0.87071	705,585
Democratic Kampuchea	0.00766	5,927	0.00731	5,924
Democratic People's Republic of Korea	0.03655	28,268	0.03487	28,254
Denmark	0.77443	598,975	0.77741	629,986
Dominican Republic	0.02104	16,273	0.02007	16,265
Ecuador	0.01435	11,100	0.01369	11,095
Egypt	0.05215	40,331	0.04974	40,311
El Salvador	0.00766	5,927	0.00731	5,924
Ethiopia	0.00766	5,927	0.00731	5,924
Finland	0.50596	391,331	0.50791	411,591
France	6.53619	5,055,347	6.56139	5,317,087
Gabon	0.02065	15,973	0.02073	16,800
German Democratic Republic	1.45593	1,126,073	1.46154	1,184,374
Germany, Federal Republic of	8.67361	6,708,516	8.70706	7,055,850
Ghana	0.02184	16,892	0.02084	16,884
Greece	0.24874	192,386	0.23729	192,288
Guatemala	0.01471	11,375	0.01403	11,370
Haiti	0.00766	5,927	0.00731	5,924
Holy See	0.01032	7,985	0.01037	8,400
Hungary	0.25784	199,425	0.24598	199,333
Iceland	0.03098	23,958	0.03110	25,200
India	0.46303	358,122	0.44172	357,951
Indonesia	0.11589	89,635	0.11056	89,590
Iran	0.46437	359,160	0.44298	358,975
Iraq	0.08248	63,793	0.07868	63,760
Ireland	0.16521	127,782	0.16585	134,398
Israel	0.25815	199,659	0.25914	209,997
Italy	3.60368	2,787,227	3.61757	2,931,538
Ivory Coast	0.02104	16,273	0.02007	16,265
Jamaica	0.01460	11,289	0.01392	11,284
Japan	10.00563	7,738,751	10.04421	8,139,427
Jordan	0.00766	5,927	0.00731	5,924
Kenya	0.00766	5,927	0.00731	5,924
Kuwait	0.20651	159,726	0.20731	167,997
Lebanon	0.02140	16,548	0.02041	16,540
Liberia	0.00766	5,927	0.00731	5,924
Libyan Arab Jamahiriya	0.23749	183,685	0.23841	193,197
Liechtenstein	0.01032	7,985	0.01037	8,400
Luxembourg	0.05163	39,933	0.05183	42,000
Madagascar	0.00766	5,927	0.00731	5,924
Malaysia	0.06330	48,960	0.06039	48,935
Mali	0.00766	5,927	0.00731	5,924
Mauritius	0.00766	5,927	0.00731	5,924
Mexico	0.55451	428,878	0.52898	428,662
Monaco	0.01032	7,985	0.01037	8,400
Mongolia	0.00766	5,927	0.00731	5,924
Morocco	0.03611	27,925	0.03444	27,911
Namibia*	—	—	—	—
Netherlands	1.70375	1,317,744	1.71032	1,385,971
New Zealand	0.27880	215,632	0.27987	226,796
Nicaragua	0.00766	5,927	0.00731	5,924
Niger	0.00766	5,927	0.00731	5,924
Nigeria	0.11145	86,202	0.10632	86,157
Norway	0.52661	407,302	0.52864	428,390
Pakistan	0.05348	41,360	0.05101	41,340
Panama	0.01435	11,100	0.01369	11,095
Paraguay	0.00766	5,927	0.00731	5,924
Peru	0.04324	33,441	0.04125	33,424
Philippines	0.07532	58,253	0.07185	58,225
Poland	0.97909	757,269	0.93405	756,919
Portugal	0.13418	103,781	0.12800	103,728
Qatar	0.03098	23,958	0.03110	25,200
Republic of Korea	0.10521	81,372	0.10036	81,330
Romania	0.15421	119,275	0.14711	119,216
Saudi Arabia	0.60922	471,193	0.61157	495,589
Senegal	0.00766	5,927	0.00731	5,924
Sierra Leone	0.00766	5,927	0.00731	5,924
Singapore	0.05528	42,758	0.05274	42,735
South Africa	0.31068	240,292	0.29638	240,172
Spain	1.77603	1,373,649	1.78287	1,444,768
Sri Lanka	0.01471	11,375	0.01403	11,370
Sudan	0.00791	6,116	0.00754	6,113
Sweden	1.37332	1,062,182	1.37862	1,117,176
Switzerland	1.09453	846,551	1.09875	890,380
Syrian Arab Republic	0.02104	16,273	0.02007	16,265
Thailand	0.07177	55,506	0.06846	55,478
Tunisia	0.02104	16,273	0.02007	16,265
Turkey	0.21397	165,490	0.20411	165,406
Uganda	0.00766	5,927	0.00731	5,924
Ukrainian SSR	1.52821	1,181,976	1.53410	1,243,173
USSR	11.58546	8,960,659	11.63014	9,424,600
United Arab Emirates	0.10326	79,864	0.10366	83,999
United Kingdom	4.65690	3,601,834	4.67486	3,788,320
United Republic of Cameroon	0.00766	5,927	0.00731	5,924
United Republic of Tanzania	0.00766	5,927	0.00731	5,924
United States	25.81431	19,965,819	25.91386	20,999,553
Uruguay	0.02942	22,752	0.02806	22,740
Venezuela	0.35576	275,155	0.33937	275,012
Viet Nam	0.02273	17,578	0.02168	17,570
Yugoslavia	0.30313	234,456	0.28918	234,336
Zaire	0.01460	11,289	0.01392	11,284
Zambia	0.01435	11,100	0.01369	11,095
Zimbabwe*	—	—	—	—
Total	100.00000	77,344,000	100.00000	81,036,000

*Namibia, represented by the United Nations Council for Namibia, and Zimbabwe had not deposited their instruments of acceptance as at 31 December 1982.

Annex II.   OFFICERS AND OFFICES OF THE INTERNATIONAL ATOMIC ENERGY AGENCY

BOARD OF GOVERNORS
(For period October 1982–October 1983)

OFFICERS
Chairman: Emil Keblusek (Czechoslovakia).
Vice-Chairmen: Luigi Noe (Italy), Adolfo R. Taylhardat (Venezuela).

MEMBERS
Algeria, Argentina, Australia, Bangladesh, Brazil, Bulgaria, Canada, Colombia, Czechoslovakia, Denmark, Egypt, France, Germany, Federal Republic of, India, Indonesia, Italy, Japan, Kenya, Libyan Arab Jamahiriya, Mexico, Netherlands, Pakistan, Panama, Portugal, Republic of Korea, Romania, Spain, Thailand, USSR, United Kingdom, United States, Venezuela, Zaire, Zambia.

MAIN COMMITTEES OF THE BOARD OF GOVERNORS

ADMINISTRATIVE AND BUDGETARY COMMITTEE
   Participation in the Administrative and Budgetary Committee is open to all members of the Board of Governors.

TECHNICAL ASSISTANCE COMMITTEE
   Participation in the Technical Assistance Committee is open to all members of the Board of Governors.

SCIENTIFIC ADVISORY COMMITTEE
K. Beckurts (Federal Republic of Germany), D. Beninson (Argentina), A. Bennini (Algeria), Floyd L. Culler (United States), H. Dunster (United Kingdom), G. Fernández de la Garza (Mexico), L. Gutiérrez Jodra (Spain), J. Jennekens (Canada), Malu wa Kalenga (Zaire), J. Minczewski (Poland), W. Murata (Japan), R. Ramanna (India), I. Ursu (Romania), A. A. Vasiliev (USSR), G. Vendryes (France).

SENIOR SECRETARIAT OFFICERS

Director General: Hans Blix.
Deputy Director General for Safeguards: Hans Gruemm.
Deputy Director General for Technical Operations: Boris Semenov.

Deputy Director General for Administration: Nelson F. Sievering, Jr.
Deputy Director General for Technical Co-operation: Carlos Vélez Ocón.
Deputy Director General for Research and Isotopes: Maurizio Zifferero.

HEADQUARTERS AND OTHER OFFICE

HEADQUARTERS
International Atomic Energy Agency
Vienna International Centre
Wagramerstrasse 5, P. O. Box 100
A-1400 Vienna, Austria
   Cable address: INATOM VIENNA
   Telephone: (222) 2360-1270
   Telex: 1-12645

LIAISON OFFICE
International Atomic Energy Agency
   Liaison Office at the United Nations
United Nations Headquarters, Room DC1-1155
New York, N. Y. 10017, United States
   Telephone: (212) 754-6010, 754-6011

Chapter II

International Labour Organisation (ILO)

During 1982, the International Labour Organisation (ILO) continued activities in six major programme areas: promotion of policies to create employment and satisfy basic human needs; development of human resources; improvement of working and living conditions and environment; promoting social security; strengthening of industrial relations and tripartite (government/employer/worker) co-operation; and the advancement of human rights in the social and labour fields. The main instruments of action continued to be standard-setting, technical co-operation activities, research and publishing.

Membership in ILO rose to 150 during the year, with the admission of Antigua and Barbuda (16 February), Sao Tome and Principe (1 June), Dominica (17 June) and San Marino (18 June).

Meetings

The sixty-eighth session of the International Labour Conference, held at Geneva from 2 to 23 June 1982, was attended by over 1,800 delegates, advisers and observers from 138 countries. The Conference had before it the annual report of the ILO Director-General and the eighteenth special report on the effect of *apartheid* on labour and employment in South Africa.

The Conference adopted an International Labour Convention on the maintenance of rights in social security, and a Convention and Recommendation on terminating employment at the employer's initiative. It also adopted a protocol revising the Plantations Convention, 1958 (No. 110), and held a first discussion on vocational rehabilitation and employment, with a view to adopting a Recommendation on this theme at its 1983 session.

In accordance with usual practice, a tripartite Conference committee examined the application by member States of the 156 Conventions and 165 Recommendations adopted since 1919, and reviewed the application of ILO standards concerning tripartite consultation.

Ratification of ILO Conventions registered during the Conference raised their total to 4,985.

The Conference also adopted the report and conclusions—in the form of recommendations—of its Committee on *Apartheid* aimed at ensuring implementation of the June 1981 ILO Declaration on the policy of *apartheid* in South Africa.[a]

Pope John Paul II and President François Mitterrand of France addressed special sittings of the Conference.

The eleventh session of the Coal Mines Committee (Geneva, 20-29 April) adopted conclusions and resolutions aimed at improving safety and health in mines, and ensuring more effective training of personnel and conditions of access to the best possible retirement benefits for mineworkers.

The ninth session of the Chemical Industries Committee (Geneva, 21-30 September) reached conclusions designed to help accelerate the creation of a skilled work-force for these industries—especially in developing countries—and to promote effective industrial relations. Occupational health and trade union freedom were subjects of resolutions adopted.

Ways to improve the quality and comparability of data on jobs, injuries and wages were proposed by the thirteenth International Conference of Labour Statisticians (Geneva, 18-29 October).

The Committee on Work on Plantations (Geneva, 7-16 December) adopted conclusions on training and on occupational safety and health, and resolutions on freedom of association and collective bargaining, women workers, and living and working conditions.

Working environment

The International Programme for the Improvement of Working Conditions and Environment, approved by the ILO Governing Body in 1976,[b] continued to encourage member States to set definite objectives. The Programme included standard-setting and operational activities, studies and tripartite meetings, clearing-house activities in occupational safety and health and conditions of work, the operation of an international alert system to detect potential hazards to the health of workers—for which 100 Governments had designated national focal points—and the dispatch of multidisciplinary teams of experts to member States. At the end of 1982, visits by such teams had been made to 16 countries, and two large-scale comprehensive projects for the improvement of working conditions and environment were launched. Training activities were stepped up and a number of tripartite seminars and symposia were held during the year in various parts of the world, while the introduction to a major reference book for use by trainers in the field of working conditions and environment was completed.

Collaboration with the World Health Organization (WHO) and other United Nations agencies in the field of workers' health continued, and included participation in the International Programme on Chemical Safety, in conjunction with the United Nations Environment Programme and WHO, as well as close co-operation with the International Atomic Energy Agency and WHO on protecting workers against ionizing radiation.

World Employment Programme

The World Employment Programme was launched in 1969[c] to assist Governments to reshape their policies and plans in order to generate increased employment and income. Work under this Programme continued to be guided by the Declaration of Principles and the Programme of Action adopted by the 1976 World Employment Conference[d] and by a 1979 resolution of the International Labour Conference.[e]

Operational activities and advisory missions at the country and regional levels remained important elements of the Programme. Much of the work was carried out by the Programme's regional arms, four employment teams located in Africa and southern Africa, Asia and Latin America.

Field activities

During 1982, ILO spent more than $103 million on technical co-operation activities (a decline of about 3.3 per cent compared with 1981) to promote employment, development of human resources and social institutions, and improvement in living and working conditions.

Most of this expenditure ($52.3 million) continued to be financed by the United Nations Development Programme (UNDP). The ILO regular programme provided $5.2 million in 1982 while expenditure funded from multi-bilateral arrangements and other special programmes rose to $40.5 million. Activities financed by the United Nations Fund for Population Activities (UNFPA) accounted for $5 million.

A breakdown of expenditure by field of activities showed that training received the largest share

[a]See YUN 1981, p. 1397.
[b]See YUN 1976, p. 943.
[c]See YUN 1969, p. 854.
[d]See YUN 1976, pp. 346 and 942.
[e]See YUN 1979, p. 1245.

of funds ($41.1 million), followed by employment planning and promotion ($31.9 million), sectoral activities ($16.9 million), industrial relations and labour administration ($3.2 million), working conditions and environment ($2.7 million), workers' activities ($2.4 million), regional services ($1.1 million) and social security ($0.9 million); other activities received $3 million.

A breakdown of expenditure on technical cooperation by field of activity, source of funds, and country, territory, region or organization is shown in the tables below.

ASSISTANCE IN 1982 BY ACTIVITY AND SOURCE OF FUNDS
(Excluding programme support costs; in US dollars)

Activity	Regular budget	UNDP	Trust funds (including UNFPA)	Total
Training	1,324,062	27,905,799	11,821,893	41,051,754
Employment and development	1,077,648	10,318,087	20,456,620	31,852,355
Sectoral activities	307,644	9,028,622	7,590,968	16,927,234
Industrial relations and labour administration	518,808	1,356,533	1,362,716	3,238,057
Working conditions and environment	481,370	1,892,589	304,885	2,678,844
Workers' activities	584,627	821,667	1,038,882	2,445,176
Regional and other services	—	10,624	1,045,701	1,056,325
Personnel, budget and finance, internal administration	—	—	1,050,308	1,050,308
Social security	99,549	446,600	315,406	861,555
International Institute for Labour Studies	—	431,130	102,985	534,115
Statistics and special studies	361,254	89,981	26,938	478,173
Employers' activities	260,264	—	87,951	348,215
Promotion of equality	80,775	3,299	165,375	249,449
International labour standards	128,042	—	48,539	176,581
Programming and management	—	—	86,462	86,462
Total	5,224,043	52,304,931	45,505,629	103,034,603

COUNTRIES, TERRITORIES, REGIONS AND ORGANIZATIONS AIDED BY ILO IN 1982

COUNTRY, TERRITORY OR OTHER	No. of experts provided	No. of fellowships awarded	ILO regular programme	UNDP*	UNFPA	Trust funds	Total
						EXPENDITURES ON AID GIVEN BY SOURCE OF FUNDS (in US dollars)	
Afghanistan	—	24	—	295,951	7,400	—	303,351
Algeria	7	11	—	538,504	—	16,758	555,262
Angola	12	30	58,485	816,451	—	—	874,936
Antigua	5	1	309	271,064	—	—	271,373
Argentina	2	14	379	248,346	—	—	248,725
Australia	—	1	—	—	—	—	—
Bahamas	2	—	—	69,064	—	31,733	100,797
Bahrain	1	5	15,887	107,779	—	—	123,666
Bangladesh	44	18	17,091	2,234,430	137,983	1,887,043	4,276,547
Barbados	3	1	21,125	49,874	—	11,512	82,511
Belgium	—	6	—	—	—	—	—
Belize	—	4	2,286	12,132	—	—	14,418
Benin	14	7	—	1,056,840	—	292,034	1,348,874
Bermuda	1	—	3,250	—	—	—	3,250
Bhutan	1	3	—	7,917	—	—	7,917
Bolivia	2	7	1,752	11,821	58,213	1,320	73,106
Botswana	15	9	398	316,603	—	602,895	919,896
Brazil	10	23	4,389	557,456	—	80,161	642,006
Bulgaria	—	—	149	45,885	2,389	—	48,423
Burma	11	18	5,810	1,339,233	—	49,160	1,394,203
Burundi	18	5	165,538	632,223	—	640,431	1,438,192
Cape Verde	7	—	3,137	330,966	—	375,434	709,537
Caribbean islands	—	—	31,111	141,558	—	—	172,669
Cayman Islands	—	2	—	8,281	—	—	8,281
Central African Republic	9	4	—	500,319	—	—	500,319
Chad	—	—	—	(2,000)†	—	—	(2,000)†

			EXPENDITURES ON AID GIVEN BY SOURCE OF FUNDS (in US dollars)				
COUNTRY, TERRITORY OR OTHER	No. of experts provided	No. of fellowships awarded	ILO regular programme	UNDP*	UNFPA	Trust funds	Total
Chile	—	2	—	3,543	—	52,492	56,035
China	—	4	—	—	—	—	—
Colombia	—	13	5,451	75,053	—	26,660	107,164
Comoros	2	—	2,619	7,063	—	—	9,682
Congo	14	29	24,401	1,100,607	84,355	136,022	1,345,385
Costa Rica	8	13	11,328	73,426	—	146,318	231,072
Cuba	1	8	—	177,216	—	—	177,216
Cyprus	2	4	9,020	88,654	22,829	—	120,503
Democratic Yemen	14	6	9,849	496,992	180,418	476,184	1,163,443
Djibouti	4	4	5,986	140,300	—	15,597	161,883
Dominica	5	1	—	—	—	466,953	466,953
Dominican Republic	6	6	328	176,695	—	303,500	480,523
Dubai	—	3	—	—	—	—	—
Ecuador	3	12	9,549	241,211	—	—	250,760
Egypt	18	183	14,739	774,486	136,891	527,249	1,453,365
El Salvador	—	3	—	—	—	3,782	3,782
Equatorial Guinea	4	1	—	62,345	—	—	62,345
Ethiopia	21	26	22,750	1,484,980	—	36,499	1,544,229
Fiji	9	2	25,727	89,482	—	325,872	441,081
France	—	20	—	—	—	—	—
Gabon	7	5	12,600	151,009	6,486	204,366	374,461
Gambia	11	6	—	501,104	—	266,432	767,536
Germany, Federal Republic of	—	2	—	—	—	—	—
Ghana	1	2	2,592	—	—	55,225	57,817
Greece	—	3	3,003	—	—	—	3,003
Guatemala	3	5	—	3,063	208,581	—	211,644
Guinea	4	5	3,008	337,042	—	—	340,050
Guinea-Bissau	5	5	3,791	253,435	—	1,144,254	1,401,480
Haiti	16	—	—	929,649	—	52,002	981,651
Honduras	4	10	9,059	508,875	—	—	517,934
Hong Kong	1	1	—	13,093	21,457	—	34,550
India	28	86	75,661	3,396,737	—	641,285	4,113,683
Indonesia	27	54	41,563	1,075,974	—	1,063,046	2,180,583
Iran	1	—	—	185,582	—	—	185,582
Iraq	55	17	14,667	299,486	—	3,856,596	4,170,749
Israel	—	1	4,750	—	—	—	4,750
Italy	—	258	—	—	—	—	—
Ivory Coast	6	8	—	11,662	—	489,556	501,218
Jamaica	3	2	847	—	—	42,923	43,770
Japan	—	1	—	—	—	—	—
Jordan	14	9	11,279	727,544	70,126	—	808,949
Kenya	17	44	11,900	659,372	—	598,493	1,269,765
Kiribati	—	1	—	4,626	14,886	—	19,512
Kuwait	4	1	19,161	289,039	—	24,528	332,728
Lao People's Democratic Republic	1	—	—	91,547	—	—	91,547
Lebanon	5	3	10,356	130,618	—	43,151	184,125
Lesotho	4	1	871	64,617	—	15,480	80,968
Liberia	5	7	—	101,676	—	155,739	257,415
Libyan Arab Jamahiriya	10	3	—	521,311	—	443,660	964,971
Madagascar	9	8	3,976	446,242	—	194,751	644,969
Malawi	16	4	—	1,200,306	—	48,668	1,248,974
Malaysia	3	24	18,000	98,717	—	213,562	330,279
Maldives	2	—	—	82,009	—	—	82,009
Mali	6	8	5,576	214,263	3,571	312,221	535,631
Malta	1	4	13,719	66,751	—	—	80,470
Mauritania	11	2	15,560	580,047	—	321,821	917,428
Mauritius	2	2	—	83,220	—	—	83,220
Mexico	9	17	23,698	432,337	—	136,268	592,303
Mongolia	6	7	—	145,009	—	—	145,009
Montserrat	—	1	—	—	—	—	—
Morocco	1	7	—	15,615	—	—	15,615

EXPENDITURES ON AID GIVEN BY SOURCE OF FUNDS
(in US dollars)

COUNTRY, TERRITORY OR OTHER	No. of experts provided	No. of fellowships awarded	ILO regular programme	UNDP*	UNFPA	Trust funds	Total
Mozambique	6	11	750	—	—	294,959	295,709
Namibia	3	5	—	506,043	—	589,589	1,095,632
National liberation movements‡	—	5	49,986	57,538	—	—	107,524
Nepal	8	17	2,239	1,166,130	1,450	17,128	1,186,947
Netherlands	—	8	—	—	—	—	—
Netherlands Antilles	13	4	143	870,620	—	—	870,763
Nicaragua	5	9	5,235	177,888	—	145,597	328,720
Niger	5	21	8,505	255,526	—	405,629	669,660
Nigeria	9	65	52,273	599,657	—	49,002	700,932
Niue	1	—	—	37,613	—	—	37,613
Oman	—	1	6,158	—	—	—	6,158
Pakistan	23	21	34,184	851,698	73,719	725,765	1,685,366
Panama	5	11	10,836	34,066	—	51,874	96,776
Papua New Guinea	7	—	6,900	144,956	—	206,905	358,761
Paraguay	3	6	669	93,864	—	149,513	244,046
Peru	10	13	26,984	273,600	162,534	295,182	758,300
Philippines	15	43	103,159	299,086	—	471,123	873,368
Poland	—	—	1,540	—	—	—	1,540
Portugal	1	14	—	202,006	—	—	202,006
Qatar	1	1	5,560	—	—	68,143	73,703
Republic of Korea	2	4	—	109,927	—	—	109,927
Romania	—	—	—	5,782	—	—	5,782
Rwanda	3	2	—	96,369	—	39,217	135,586
Saint Lucia	—	1	—	31,894	—	—	31,894
Saint Vincent and the Grenadines	—	1	—	30,123	—	—	30,123
Samoa	—	—	—	14,462	—	—	14,462
Saudi Arabia	1	44	—	19,316	—	194,349	213,665
Senegal	20	15	20,800	587,436	—	614,667	1,222,903
Seychelles	1	—	9,126	49,677	—	—	58,803
Sierra Leone	6	3	2,007	13,200	149,666	372,546	537,419
Singapore	1	5	—	98,865	—	—	98,865
Solomon Islands	10	—	—	338,787	—	—	338,787
Somalia	8	13	2,717	566,269	81,376	204,627	854,989
South Africa	—	—	5,000	—	—	—	5,000
Spain	—	1	—	—	—	—	—
Sri Lanka	3	11	16,786	319,038	44,502	116,136	496,462
Sudan	26	50	55,208	2,038,165	89,406	1,564,618	3,747,397
Suriname	4	—	4,685	118,283	—	—	122,968
Swaziland	5	3	52,429	196,579	—	19,026	268,034
Sweden	—	1	—	—	—	—	—
Switzerland	1	7	—	—	—	56,658	56,658
Syrian Arab Republic	8	4	4,793	530,689	—	—	535,482
Thailand	33	34	59,510	831,161	—	526,893	1,417,564
Togo	9	2	21,758	309,102	—	229,028	559,888
Tokelau	—	—	—	59	—	—	59
Tonga	1	—	271	67,385	—	—	67,656
Trinidad and Tobago	3	3	3,759	112,363	—	68,577	184,699
Trust Territory of the Pacific Islands	—	—	—	9,784	—	—	9,784
Tunisia	3	20	58,838	101,686	—	—	160,524
Turkey	5	59	49,367	396,143	—	—	445,510
Tuvalu	1	—	183	61,270	—	—	61,453
Uganda	19	27	6,936	1,464,165	—	—	1,471,101
United Arab Emirates	6	—	—	266,079	—	138,685	404,764
United Republic of Cameroon	25	10	—	1,431,879	132,663	639,090	2,203,632
United Republic of Tanzania	12	50	8,261	489,123	—	727,103	1,224,487
United States	2	2	—	—	—	37,168	37,168
Upper Volta	11	5	—	458,286	—	982,149	1,440,435
Uruguay	2	3	4,704	9,988	—	49,021	63,713
Vanuatu	2	—	8,019	121,644	—	40,428	170,091

COUNTRY, TERRITORY OR OTHER	No. of experts provided	No. of fellowships awarded	EXPENDITURES ON AID GIVEN BY SOURCE OF FUNDS (in US dollars)				
			ILO regular programme	UNDP*	UNFPA	Trust funds	Total
Venezuela	1	3	14,385	84,085	—	(215)†	98,255
Yemen	—	1	—	—	—	—	—
Yugoslavia	—	2	—	—	10,865	—	10,865
Zaire	16	83	—	1,292,371	—	100,469	1,392,840
Zambia	11	42	7,080	2,738	6,893	418,135	434,846
Zimbabwe	6	55	82,575	206,157	—	107,023	395,755
Subtotal	955	1,978	1,592,798	46,655,217	1,708,659	27,545,383	77,501,847
INTERCOUNTRY REGIONAL PROJECTS§							
Africa	62	—	813,393	1,191,494	359,351	7,157,771	9,522,009
Asia	58	—	1,270,257	1,413,623	713,319	2,022,580	5,419,779
Europe	1	—	—	283,773	—	—	283,773
Latin America and the Caribbean	36	—	1,096,463	781,021	290,104	1,002,435	3,170,023
Arab States in the Middle East	5	—	78,447	63,601	—	—	142,048
Subtotal	162	—	3,258,560	3,733,512	1,362,774	10,182,786	18,537,632
INTERREGIONAL PROJECTS	77	—	372,685	2,047,890	1,969,797	7,170,752	11,561,124
Total	1,194	1,978	5,224,043	52,436,349	5,041,230	44,898,981	107,600,603
Deduct programme support costs	—	—	—	(131,418)	—	(4,434,582)	(4,566,000)
GRAND TOTAL	1,194	1,978	5,224,043	52,304,931	5,041,230	40,464,399	103,034,603

*Includes projects for which ILO acted as executing agency.

†Adjustment on figures previously reported.

‡Liberation movements of South Africa.

§Number of fellowships awarded included in the list above by country or territory.

Educational activities

The International Institute for Labour Studies at Geneva, an ILO centre for advanced study in the labour and social fields, included in its 1982 programme six educational activities for 146 participants, 54 of whom were from workers' organizations, 48 from government institutions, 18 from employers' groups and 26 from other institutions such as universities.

The annual International Internship Course (Geneva, 20 April–2 June) was attended by 23 participants from 18 countries in Africa, Asia, Europe and Latin America. The course's subject was the formulation and implementation of social policies founded on the principle of solidarity and it focused on social and labour policies currently in force in industrialized and developing countries; labour and social requirements of a new world order; new emerging solidarity groups and the concept of the solidarity contract; and the International Labour Office and the promotion of greater social justice in development.

A course on industrial relations was given at Harare, Zimbabwe, from 13 to 30 July for some 30 new officials in the Ministry of Labour and focused on relations between social partners (employers and their organizations, trade unions, the State), collective bargaining, disputes and methods of resolving them (including conciliation and arbitration) and the role of industrial relations in development.

A seminar on social aspects of rural development and the role of women (Tallin, Estonia, USSR, 13-24 September) was the third in a series carried out in collaboration with the All-Union Central Council of Trade Unions of the USSR and the United Nations Institute for Training and Research. The 26 participants, from English-speaking countries of Africa, Asia and the Caribbean, discussed economic and social conditions facilitating rural development, the application of science and technology to rural development, and the objectives of rural development.

For the third time, the Institute organized (Geneva, 5-22 October) a course on labour-management relations in the petroleum industry for 22 participants from Governments, employers' organizations and trade unions in 10 countries.

Topics examined were: the economic and social "environment" of the industry and its impact on industrial relations; specific labour-management relations themes, such as trade union and employer organizations, and recognition of collective bargaining, labour disputes and workers' participation in management; and certain substantive labour questions relating to remuneration systems, the personnel function, multinational enterprises, manpower and conditions of work.

As part of the joint activities of the Institute and the University of Geneva, seminars were conducted during the 1981/82 academic year at the Institut universitaire d'études européennes. Some 20 students attended the seminars which focused on social policy in the countries of Eastern Europe.

As in 1980 and 1981, the Institute and the Ambekar Institute for Labour Studies (Bombay, India) organized a joint seminar on labour studies training for 25 trade unionists from India and neighbouring countries. Participants in the seminar (Bombay, 6-18 December) studied simple research methods, elementary statistics and statistical analysis, and economic concepts of particular interest to trade unions.

International Centre for Advanced Technical and Vocational Training

In 1982, the ILO International Centre for Advanced Technical and Vocational Training at Turin, Italy, designed and implemented training programmes, training placements and seminars for nearly 2,000 participants, a significant proportion of whom were from Africa.

In response to developing countries' requests, the Centre offered international training programmes in the specialized fields of: educational technology (curriculum development, training methodology and audio-visual aids technology); functional management (as applied to such sectors as training institutions, small enterprises, energy resources and energy saving, maintenance, co-operatives, hotels and tourism); technical and industrial skills for trainers and specialized personnel; labour policies (labour relations, labour administration, working conditions and environment, international labour standards, workers' education, employment and co-operatives development); and new renewable sources of energy. In addition, courses were developed in computerized information systems and microcomputer applications to training for implementation in 1983.

Responding to requests from Governments, institutions and large enterprises, the Centre also organized tailor-made programmes based on its training capacities in those specialized fields which comprised a major proportion of the Centre's 1982 activities.

Publications

Published ILO research covered a wide range of topical social and labour questions. New publications issued in 1982 included: *Safety and Health in the Construction of Fixed Offshore Installations in the Petroleum Industry: An ILO Code of Practice; New Technologies: Their Impact on Employment and the Working Environment; Employment Opportunities and Equity in a Changing Economy: Egypt in the 1980s; Negotiating Development: Labour Relations in Southern Asia; The Practice of Entrepreneurship; Work-force Reductions in Undertakings: Policies and Measures for the Protection of Redundant Workers in Seven Industrialised Market-Economy Countries; Deterrence and Compensation: Legal Liability in Occupational Safety and Health; Workers' Management in Yugoslavia: Recent Development and Trends; Cottage Industries and Handicrafts: Some Guidelines for Employment Promotion;* and the first five titles in the new *Women, Work and Development* series.

The 1982 *Yearbook of Labour Statistics* was published, and regular periodicals and technical series continued to appear, including the bimonthly *International Labour Review,* the quarterly *Social and Labour Bulletin* and the biannual *Legislative Series.*

Secretariat

As at 31 December 1982, the total number of full-time staff under permanent, fixed-term and short-term appointments at ILO headquarters and elsewhere was 3,036. Of these, 1,532 were in the Professional and higher categories (drawn from 111 nationalities), and 1,504 were in the General Service or Maintenance categories. Of the Professional staff, 738 were assigned to technical co-operation projects.

Budget

In June 1982, the International Labour Conference adopted a revised budget for 1982-1983 totalling $242,407,945, increased from the $230,033,000 approved by the Conference in 1981.

MAIN CATEGORIES OF EXPENDITURE IN 1982

	Amount (in US dollars)
Staff costs	69,437,290
Refund to the Working Capital Fund	7,884,428
General operating expenses	6,272,443
Operational activities	5,224,043
Fellowships, grants and contributions	4,323,535
Travel on official business	3,434,410
Acquisition and improvement of premises	2,692,510
Contractual services	2,149,154
Supplies and materials	993,001
Joint activities within the United Nations system	676,584
Acquisition of furniture and equipment	332,934
Total	103,420,332

Annex I. MEMBERSHIP OF THE INTERNATIONAL LABOUR ORGANISATION AND CONTRIBUTIONS

(Membership as at 31 December 1982; contributions as assessed for 1983)

MEMBER	Percentage	Gross amount (in US dollars)
Afghanistan	0.01	12,338
Algeria	0.12	148,062
Angola	0.01	12,338
Antigua and Barbuda*	0.01	12,338
Argentina	0.77	950,063
Australia	1.82	2,245,602
Austria	0.70	863,693
Bahamas	0.01	12,338
Bahrain	0.01	12,338
Bangladesh	0.04	49,354
Barbados	0.01	12,338
Belgium	1.21	1,492,955
Belize*	0.01	12,338
Benin	0.01	12,338
Bolivia	0.01	12,338
Botswana	0.01	12,338
Brazil	1.26	1,554,648
Bulgaria	0.16	197,416
Burma	0.01	12,338
Burundi	0.01	12,338
Byelorussian SSR	0.39	481,201
Canada	3.25	4,010,004
Cape Verde	0.01	12,338
Central African Republic	0.01	12,338
Chad	0.01	12,338
Chile	0.07	86,370
China	1.61	1,986,494
Colombia	0.11	135,724
Comoros	0.01	12,338
Congo	0.01	12,338
Costa Rica	0.02	24,677
Cuba	0.11	135,724
Cyprus	0.01	12,338
Czechoslovakia	0.82	1,011,755
Democratic Kampuchea	0.01	12,338
Democratic Yemen	0.01	12,338
Denmark	0.73	900,709
Djibouti	0.01	12,338
Dominicat	–	–
Dominican Republic	0.03	37,016
Ecuador	0.02	24,677
Egypt	0.07	86,370
El Salvador	0.01	12,338
Equatorial Guinea	0.01	12,338
Ethiopia	0.01	12,338
Fiji	0.01	12,338
Finland	0.47	579,909
France	6.21	7,662,192
Gabon	0.02	24,677
German Democratic Republic	1.38	1,702,710
Germany, Federal Republic of	8.25	10,179,240
Ghana	0.03	37,016
Greece	0.35	431,847
Grenada	0.01	12,338
Guatemala	0.02	24,677
Guinea	0.01	12,338
Guinea-Bissau	0.01	12,338
Guyana	0.01	12,338
Haiti	0.01	12,338
Honduras	0.01	12,338
Hungary	0.33	407,170
Iceland	0.03	37,016
India	0.59	727,970
Indonesia	0.16	197,416
Iran	0.64	789,663
Iraq	0.12	148,062
Ireland	0.16	197,416
Israel	0.25	308,462
Italy	3.42	4,219,758
Ivory Coast	0.03	37,016
Jamaica	0.02	24,677
Japan	9.51	11,733,888
Jordan	0.01	12,338
Kenya	0.01	12,338
Kuwait	0.20	246,770
Lao People's Democratic Republic	0.01	12,338
Lebanon	0.03	37,016
Lesotho	0.01	12,338
Liberia	0.01	12,338
Libyan Arab Jamahiriya	0.23	283,785
Luxembourg	0.05	61,693
Madagascar	0.01	12,338
Malawi	0.01	12,338
Malaysia	0.09	111,047
Mali	0.01	12,338
Malta	0.01	12,338
Mauritania	0.01	12,338
Mauritius	0.01	12,338
Mexico	0.75	925,386
Mongolia	0.01	12,338
Morocco	0.05	61,693
Mozambique	0.01	12,338
Namibia	0.01	12,338
Nepal	0.01	12,338
Netherlands	1.62	1,998,833
New Zealand	0.27	333,139
Nicaragua	0.01	12,338
Niger	0.01	12,338
Nigeria	0.16	197,416
Norway	0.49	604,585
Pakistan	0.07	86,370
Panama	0.02	24,677
Papua New Guinea	0.01	12,338
Paraguay	0.01	12,338
Peru	0.06	74,031
Philippines	0.10	123,385
Poland	1.23	1,517,632
Portugal	0.19	234,431
Qatar	0.03	37,016
Romania	0.21	259,108
Rwanda	0.01	12,338
Saint Lucia	0.01	12,338
San Marino‡	–	–
Sao Tome and Principe*	0.01	12,338
Saudi Arabia	0.57	703,293
Senegal	0.01	12,338
Seychelles	0.01	12,338
Sierra Leone	0.01	12,338
Singapore	0.08	98,708
Somalia	0.01	12,338
Spain	1.69	2,085,202
Sri Lanka	0.02	24,677
Sudan	0.01	12,338
Suriname	0.01	12,338
Swaziland	0.01	12,338
Sweden	1.30	1,604,002
Switzerland	1.04	1,283,201
Syrian Arab Republic	0.03	37,016
Thailand	0.10	123,385
Togo	0.01	12,338
Trinidad and Tobago	0.03	37,016
Tunisia	0.03	37,016
Turkey	0.30	370,155
Uganda	0.01	12,338
Ukrainian SSR	1.45	1,789,079
USSR	11.02	13,596,997
United Arab Emirates	0.10	123,385
United Kingdom	4.43	5,465,944
United Republic of Cameroon	0.01	12,338
United Republic of Tanzania	0.01	12,338
United States	25.00	30,846,181
Upper Volta	0.01	12,338
Uruguay	0.04	49,354
Venezuela	0.49	604,585
Viet Nam	0.03	37,016
Yemen	0.01	12,338
Yugoslavia	0.42	518,216
Zaire	0.02	24,677
Zambia	0.02	24,677
Zimbabwe	0.01	12,338
Total	100.03	123,421,737

*On 15 June 1982, the ILO Conference decided that the financial contributions of Antigua and Barbuda, Belize, and Sao Tome and Principe would be assessed at the rate of 0.01 per cent. This accounts for the percentage total of 100.03.

†Became a member on 17 June 1982.

‡Became a member on 18 June 1982.

Annex II. OFFICERS AND OFFICES OF THE INTERNATIONAL LABOUR ORGANISATION

(As at 31 December 1982)

MEMBERSHIP OF THE GOVERNING BODY OF THE INTERNATIONAL LABOUR OFFICE

Chairman: Aída González Martínez (Mexico).

Vice-Chairmen: Jean-Jacques Oechslin (France), Employers' Group; Gerd Muhr (Federal Republic of Germany), Workers' Group.

REGULAR MEMBERS

Government members
Australia, Bahrain, Bangladesh, Barbados, Brazil,* Bulgaria, Canada,* China,*

Colombia, Ecuador, Egypt, France,* German Democratic Republic, Germany, Federal Republic of,* India,* Italy,* Japan,* Kenya, Mali, Mexico, Mozambique, Netherlands, Niger, Nigeria, Philippines, Senegal, USSR,* United Kingdom,* United States,* Venezuela.

Employers' members

Frank Bannerman-Menson (Ghana), Murat Eurnekian (Argentina), Daniel J. Flunder (United Kingdom), Henri Georget (Niger), Abderrahim Gharbaoui (Morocco), David L. Grove (United States), Wolf-Dieter Lindner (Federal Republic of Germany), Marwan Nasr (Lebanon), Jean-Jacques Oechslin (France), George Polites (Australia), Naval H. Tata (India), Albert Verschueren (Belgium), Horatio G. Villalobos (Venezuela), Koh Yoshino (Japan).

Workers' members

Irving Brown (United States), Shirley Carr (Canada), Cliff O. Dolan (Australia), José González Navarro (Venezuela), Abdul M. Issifu (Ghana), Glynn Lloyd (United Kingdom), Elias J. Mashasi (Republic of Tanzania), Kanti Mehta (India), Gerd Muhr (Federal Republic of Germany), Vassily I. Prokhorov (USSR), Alfonso Sánchez Madariaga (Mexico), Moussa D. Sow (Mauritania), John Svenningsen (Denmark), Yoshikazu Tanaka (Japan).

*Member holding a non-elective seat as a State of chief industrial importance.

DEPUTY MEMBERS

Government deputy members

Algeria, Angola, Argentina, Belgium, Burma, Cuba, Denmark, Ethiopia, Ghana, Hungary, Indonesia, Madagascar, Mongolia, Panama, Portugal, Ukrainian SSR, Uruguay, Zimbabwe.

Employers' deputy members

Agil Al-Jassem (Kuwait), Sidney B. Chambers (Jamaica), Albert Deschamps (Canada), Jairo Escobar Padrón (Colombia), Johan von Holten (Sweden), J. M. Lacasa Aso (Spain), Felix Moukoko Kingue (United Republic of Cameroon), Munga-wa-Nyasa (Zaire), Tom D. Owuor (Kenya), Aurelio Periquet (Philippines), Najib Said (Tunisia), Lucia Sasso-Mazzufferi (Italy), Fanuel C. Sumbwe (Zambia), Fernando Yllanes Ramos (Mexico).

Workers' deputy members

Jerome Abondo (United Republic of Cameroon), Nangbog Barnabo (Togo), Gideon Ben-Israel (Israel), Marc Blondel (France), Youcef Briki (Algeria), Tulio E. Cuevas (Colombia), V. David (Malaysia), Heribert Maier (Austria), Democrito T. Mendoza (Philippines), Agus Sudono (Indonesia), Jozsef Timmer (Hungary), Raffaele Vanni (Italy), Frank Walcott (Barbados), Newstead Zimba (Zambia).

SENIOR OFFICIALS OF THE INTERNATIONAL LABOUR OFFICE

Director-General: Francis Blanchard.

Deputy Directors-General: Bertil Bolin, Surendra K. Jain, Albert Tévoédjrè.*

*As Director of the International Institute for Labour Studies.

Assistant Directors-General: André Aboughanem,† Antoinette Béguin, Salih Burgan, Vladimir G. Chkounaev, Julio Galer, Elimane Kane, Francis Wolf, Kazuo F. Yoshimura.

†As Director of the International Centre for Advanced Technical and Vocational Training, Turin, Italy.

HEADQUARTERS, REGIONAL, LIAISON AND OTHER OFFICES

HEADQUARTERS

International Labour Office
4 Route des Morillons
1211 Geneva 22, Switzerland
Cable address: INTERLAB GENEVA
Telephone: (022) 99 61 11
Telex: 22271

REGIONAL OFFICES

International Labour Organisation Regional Office for Africa
P. O. Box 2788
Addis Ababa, Ethiopia
Cable address: INTERLAB ADDISABABA

International Labour Organisation Regional Office for the Americas
Apartado Postal 3638
Lima 1, Peru
Cable address: INTERLAB LIMA

International Labour Organisation Regional Office for Asia and the Pacific
P. O. Box 1759
Bangkok 2, Thailand
Cable address: INTERLAB BANGKOK

International Labour Organisation Regional Office for Europe
1211 Geneva 22, Switzerland
Cable address: INTERLAB GENEVA

LIAISON OFFICES

International Labour Organisation Liaison Office with the European Communities and the Benelux
40 Rue Aimé Smekens
B-1040 Brussels, Belgium

International Labour Organisation Liaison Office with the United Nations
300 East 44th Street, 18th floor
New York, N. Y. 10017, United States

International Labour Organisation Liaison Office with the United Nations Economic Commission for Latin America
Casilla de Correo 2353
Santiago, Chile

OTHER OFFICES

International Labour Organisation Office
01-Boîte Postale 3960
Abidjan 01, Ivory Coast

International Labour Organisation Office
Boîte Postale 226
Alger-Gare, Algeria

International Labour Organisation Office
P. K. 407
Ankara, Turkey

International Labour Organisation Office
Boîte Postale 683
Antananarivo, Madagascar

International Labour Organisation Office
Boîte Postale 114-5096
Beirut, Lebanon

International Labour Organisation Office
Hohenzollernstrasse 21
D-5300 Bonn 2, Federal Republic of Germany

International Labour Organisation Office
Caixa Postal 04-401/403
70 312 Brasilia DF, Brazil

International Labour Organisation Office
Avenida Julio A. Roca 710 (3er piso)
Buenos Aires, Argentina

International Labour Organisation Office
9 Dr. Taha Hussein Street
Zamalek
Cairo, Egypt

OTHER OFFICES *(cont.)*

International Labour Organisation Office
Boîte Postale 414
Dakar, Senegal

International Labour Organisation Office
P. O. Box 9212
Dar es Salaam, United Republic of Tanzania

International Labour Organisation Office
P. O. Box 2061
Dhaka, Bangladesh

International Labour Organisation Office
P. O. Box 1047
Islamabad, Pakistan

International Labour Organisation Office
P. O. Box 75
Jakarta, Indonesia

International Labour Organisation Office
Boîte Postale 7248
Kinshasa I, Zaire

International Labour Organisation Office
P. O. Box 20275 SAFAT
Kuwait, Kuwait

International Labour Organisation Office
P. O. Box 2331
Lagos, Nigeria

International Labour Organisation Office
96/98 Marsham Street
London SW1P 4LY, England

International Labour Organisation Office
P. O. Box 2181
Lusaka, Zambia

International Labour Organisation Office
P. O. Box 2965
Manila, Philippines

Chapter III

Food and Agriculture Organization of the United Nations (FAO)

The 49-member Council of the Food and Agriculture Organization of the United Nations (FAO), the organization's governing body between biennial meetings of the FAO Conference, expressed concern, during its eighty-second session (Rome, Italy, 22 November to 3 December 1982), at the continuing bleak situation of the world economy. Farm incomes were adversely affected and protectionist pressures in certain developed countries were becoming stronger.

The Council urged that greater attention be given to establishing adequate cereal stocks in developing importing countries and that they be given the assistance needed for that purpose. It stressed that, notwithstanding increased stocks of cereals and the establishment of the International Monetary Fund food facility, there had not been sufficient improvement in world food security. Resumption was urged of negotiations towards a new International Wheat Agreement, an essential step in strengthening and stabilizing world food supplies.

The Council underlined the need for pricing systems and incentives to induce more food production without harming low-income consumers or marginal smallholders.

It also stressed the need for more resources to be devoted to agricultural research in developing countries to facilitate higher food and agricultural production, and called on developed countries to continue to foster methods of sharing agricultural, scientific and technical knowledge with developing countries.

Expressing particular concern at the decline in multilateral assistance and the greater decline in bilateral assistance to agriculture, the Council urged donors to maintain their earlier record of growth in development assistance.

The Council welcomed a proposal by the FAO Director-General that the Committee on Food Security should reappraise the concept of world food security and the Committee's role, as this action met Government anxieties about persisting food security difficulties and apparent duplication and overlapping of various fora dealing with these issues. The Council agreed that the Committee provided the appropriate consultative forum for Governments to analyse the problem from all aspects and make recommendations on world food security, and considered that FAO should continue to play its role in co-ordinating food security efforts.

The Council expressed grave concern at the resource situation of the United Nations Development Programme (UNDP), the major source of funds for the FAO field programme.

During 1982, membership of FAO remained unchanged at 152 countries.

World food and agricultural situation

World food and agricultural production together increased by about 2 per cent in 1982 following a better than average year in 1981, when food and agricultural production increased by about 2.7 per cent and 3 per cent, respectively. Preliminary estimates revealed that although food production had increased, output of non-food commodities had declined. It was estimated that the slight increase in food production resulted from greater production of crops, rather than livestock, particularly in developed countries. Cereal production remained largely unchanged in 1982, with larger wheat and coarse grain crops, particularly in North America, Western Europe, and Latin America, being partially offset by lower rice production. The relatively large cereal harvest, combined with continuing weak demand, was expected to increase cereal stocks for 1982/83 by some 20 per cent to 330 million tons. Total carryover stocks of cereals were expected to reach 21 per cent of annual consumption by the end of the 1982/83 season. Cereal prices continued to decline.

Funding

FAO provides advice and assistance in the field through its field programme, funded largely from external sources such as UNDP and various trust funds provided by donor governments. Funds available from UNDP were expected to drop from $182 million in 1981 to around $141 million in 1982, a reduction in real terms of about 25 per cent. UNDP's share of FAO's field programme costs declined from 87 per cent in 1972 to less than 50 per cent in 1982. The fall in UNDP funds was partially offset by increases in trust funds and in funds available through the Technical Co-operation Programme (TCP), funded from FAO's own regular programme budget. Trust fund delivery in 1982

was expected to be about $120 million. TCP delivery in 1982 accounted for some $18 million, an increase of about 20 per cent over the previous year. Total field programme delivery in 1982 was approximately $280 million, a decrease of about 10 per cent in real terms.

Activities in 1982

Field programmes

FAO devotes a large proportion of its field and regular programme resources to increasing production of crops, livestock and foodfish. Activities range from research support through the supply of seeds and semen, to the provision of technical advice and assistance to field projects. Emphasis is placed on assisting developing countries to plan and carry out their own programmes and on encouraging technical co-operation among those countries.

Crops. In crop production FAO activities covered conserving genetic resources, improving seed quality and distributing and preventing losses before harvest, as well as introducing new cultivation practices.

More than 100 field projects on seeds were operational during the year in the areas of variety evaluation, seed production, quality control and supply. Other field projects involved training technicians and national seed campaigns. Information on seed development was improved with the establishment of the International Seed Information System.

Priority was given to increasing production of food legumes, roots and tubers—important staples in much of the developing world. In cereals, FAO has helped to develop varieties of wheat and barley suited to arid conditions. In African countries the emphasis was on maize, sorghum, millet and rice. FAO was also involved in some 100 projects in the horticultural sector.

Plant diseases remained one of the major checks on crop production. FAO-supported research was aimed at breeding varieties with durable or long-term resistance. This would represent a breakthrough in stabilizing resistance to pests and diseases in crops of developing countries.

Livestock. Many developing countries were enhancing the genetic potential of indigenous dairy herds with support from FAO's Artificial Insemination and Breeding Development Programme. Providing semen was a major activity and in 1982 some 50,000 doses were supplied in 15 countries.

Livestock planning assistance was provided through the International Scheme for the Co-ordination of Dairy Development and the International Meat Development Scheme. Some $25 million was generated in 1982 for projects under these schemes.

A global network of reference laboratories for major infectious diseases was being developed. Together with centres for diseases transmissible from animals to humans, these laboratories were able to provide diagnostic services for both developed and developing countries. Work to control African animal trypanosomiasis—spread by the tsetse fly—in sub-Saharan countries of Africa contributed to developing economical and environmentally acceptable methods of control.

Fisheries. During 1982, FAO's Fisheries Programme focused on small-scale fisheries development, aquaculture, market information, training and resources surveys. A total of 195 fisheries projects were ongoing in 1982 with a budget of $39.9 million. The problems and opportunities presented to developing coastal States by the establishment of exclusive economic zones continued to be an important aspect of FAO's work in marine fisheries.

Land and water development. As the cost of bringing new land under cultivation increased, more attention was given to intensifying production on land already under cultivation. FAO advised and assisted farmers, Governments and non governmental organizations on overcoming soil and land degradation, and increasing productivity of land.

Concern over the critical food situation in Africa resulted in more attention being given to developing small-scale irrigation in that region. FAO assisted countries to plan, execute and manage systems which could be run by farmers and which normally used simple technology involving relatively small investment.

Investment in agriculture. FAO continued to help countries in formulating viable investment projects to attract external financing for increased food production, to raise farmers' incomes and strengthen rural economies. By the end of 1982, FAO's Investment Centre had channelled over $22 billion of foreign and domestic capital to developing countries since its establishment in 1966. During the year, staff worked on 131 projects involving 182 missions to 67 countries.

Joint activities with the three regional development banks increased considerably, as did FAO's support for national development banks. FAO continued to help prepare projects for financing by the International Fund for Agricultural Development (IFAD). Since IFAD was established in 1978, FAO has prepared six out of every ten projects financed entirely by the Fund. A major cause for concern in 1982 was the curtailment of funds available for lending by the World Bank, and particularly its concessional lending agency, the International Development Association. The World Bank is the single most important financing institution for investment projects prepared by FAO.

Information for agriculture. Increasing expectations of agriculture created a growing demand for information on natural resources and advances in food and agricultural production. FAO had a major role in monitoring the state ,of natural resources. It supported research efforts in developing countries; provided technical information for specialists through an active publishing programme and advanced data processing facilities; and prepared training material for use in developing countries.

The Second United Nations Conference on the Exploration and Peaceful Uses of Outer Space, held in Vienna in August 1982 confirmed FAO's lead role in applying remote sensing to renewable resources such as land, water, forests, grassland and fishery resources and the monitoring of crops, pests, drought and soil degradation. In this context, FAO's Remote Sensing Centre provided advice or assistance to over 50 countries in the developing world.

Improving distribution. In order to improve distribution of agricultural products, FAO was involved at every stage in the agricultural cycle—from preventing food losses to attempting to bring about a more equitable régime of international trade. Programmes were mounted to prevent post-harvest losses, to assist the development of marketing skills in developing countries, to bolster food security, and to assist producers and exporters of agricultural products to obtain a fair return for their products.

Storage and the prevention of food losses. During 1982, post-harvest losses accounted for about 70 million tons of grains or 10 per cent of the food production of developing countries. A major reason was the lack of dry, pest-free storage facilities. As a result, FAO's Special Action Programme for the Prevention of Food Losses focused on the drying of grains before storage throughout 1982.

Promoting food security. In 1982, the Committee on Food Security recommended increased action at the regional level to supplement national and global arrangements for food security as part of efforts to implement FAO's 1979 Plan of Action on World Food Security.[a]

Contributions to FAO's Food Security Assistance Scheme (FSAS) in 1982 amounted to $5.3 million, bringing the total value of projects funded by donors since the scheme's inception in 1976 to $50.3 million. One project was completed during the year while eleven new ones valued at $2.6 million became operational. Seven projects worth $5.2 million were submitted to potential donors for possible funding.

[a] See YUN 1979, p. 1253.

The FAO Global Information and Early Warning System continued to monitor developments in food demand and supply during 1982. Special reports identified countries threatened by shortages to guide potential donors. FSAS also helped to establish national and regional early warning systems linked to the global system.

Emergency assistance for agriculture. Over 70 emergency projects with a total budget of $47 million were underway in 1982 through FAO's Office of Special Relief Operations. Supplies and equipment provided included seeds, fertilizers, pesticides, livestock supplies and equipment, and logistic support.

Promoting rural development. FAO continued to act as the United Nations lead agency for implementing the Programme of Action approved by the 1979 World Conference on Agrarian Reform and Rural Development (WCARRD).[b] FAO assistance to countries ranged from high-level missions on agrarian reform to ensuring that the principles of WCARRD were embodied in field projects. During the year, FAO undertook 115 field projects related to agrarian reform, land tenure improvement, production structure improvement and land settlement.

Forestry. In 1982, FAO started an action programme on forestry and rural energy to mobilize resources for developing countries with major fuelwood deficits. The programme was designed to mobilize extra-budgetary support for projects aimed at strengthening the capacity of national institutions to boost fuelwood production and to encourage rural development generally. Other programmes encouraged and supported forestry activities contributing to basic needs such as food, fuel and housing materials, and which increased the incomes and quality of life of rural people.

Nutrition. A long-term FAO programme was begun in 1982 to raise nutritional standards in the poorest countries by applying guidelines on nutrition to development projects.

Popular participation. Participation by people in providing their own food continued to be stressed in FAO development activities, with both World Food Day (16 October) and the Freedom from Hunger/Action for Development programme endeavouring to involve people in food and agriculture issues on the broadest possible level in both developing and developed countries.

Co-operation for self-reliance. FAO continued to assist developing countries to strengthen and manage their agricultural sector. In 1982, planning assistance, mostly funded by UNDP, was provided to about 45 countries. Some 55 countries were given help to train national staff in project analysis and planning. The developing countries' share in the allocation of experts, fellowships, study

places, equipment and contractual services increased significantly during the year. Governments were also encouraged to carry out for themselves projects funded externally.

A network of FAO Representatives was established in developing member countries as part of a policy of decentralization. The representatives were active in identifying local capacities which could strengthen Technical Co-operation among Developing Countries, a crucial element of efforts to increase self-reliance.

World Food Programme. As at 31 December 1982, the World Food Programme (WFP), a joint venture of FAO and the United Nations, had completed almost 20 years of operations and committed a total of $5.3 billion to over 1,100 projects in 114 countries. In addition, some 600 emergency relief operations had been provided to 103 countries. Pledges by member Governments for 1983/1984 reached $993 million, 83 per cent of the $1.2 billion target, by the end of 1982. Resources pledged for the 1981/1982 biennium had reached $838 million, 16 per cent short of the $1 billion target, at the end of the year.

Contributions channelled through the Programme under the Food Aid Convention (FAC) for 1981/82 amounted to some 310,000 tons of grain valued at $54.7 million; cash grants for transportation and other expenses amounted to almost $18 million. Contributions to the International Emergency Food Reserve (IEFR) reached 505,000 tons of grain and other foods by the end of 1982.

During 1982, shipments of commodities from WFP and IEFR pledges and from FAC resources exceeded 1.7 million tons. WFP assistance continued to be heavily concentrated in the least developed countries and those most seriously affected by adverse economic conditions. New projects approved in 1982 represented a total commitment value of some $485 million. The Programme provided food aid totalling an unprecedented $193 million for 68 emergency operations in 37 countries during 1982. A high proportion of contributions went to refugees and persons displaced by man-made disasters.

Secretariat

At 31 December 1982, Professional staff including consultants and short-term staff totalled 3,404; General Service staff totalled 3,536.

Budget

The twenty-first session of the FAO Conference, in November 1981, approved a budget of $366.6 million for 1982-1983.

[b]See YUN 1979, p. 500.

Annex I. MEMBERSHIP OF THE FOOD AND AGRICULTURE ORGANIZATION AND CONTRIBUTIONS
(Membership as at 31 December 1982; contributions as assessed for 1982 and 1983)

MEMBER	CONTRIBUTION Percentage	Net amount (in US dollars)	MEMBER	CONTRIBUTION Percentage	Net amount (in US dollars)	MEMBER	CONTRIBUTION Percentage	Net amount (in US dollars)
Afghanistan	0.01	17,619	Ghana	0.04	70,476	Panama	0.02	35,238
Albania	0.01	17,619	Greece	0.43	757,617	Papua New Guinea	0.01	17,619
Algeria	0.15	264,285	Grenada	0.01	17,619	Paraguay	0.01	17,619
Angola	0.01	17,619	Guatemala	0.02	35,238	Peru	0.07	123,333
Argentina	0.95	1,673,805	Guinea	0.01	17,619	Philippines	0.12	211,428
Australia	2.24	3,946,656	Guinea-Bissau	0.01	17,619	Poland	1.52	2,678,088
Austria	0.87	1,532,853	Guyana	0.01	17,619	Portugal	0.23	405,237
Bahamas	0.01	17,619	Haiti	0.01	17,619	Qatar	0.04	70,476
Bahrain	0.01	17,619	Honduras	0.01	17,619	Republic of Korea	0.18	317,142
Bangladesh	0.05	88,095	Hungary	0.40	704,760	Romania	0.26	458,094
Barbados	0.01	17,619	Iceland	0.04	70,476	Rwanda	0.01	17,619
Belgium	1.49	2,625,231	India	0.73	1,286,187	Saint Lucia	0.01	17,619
Benin	0.01	17,619	Indonesia	0.20	352,380	Samoa	0.01	17,619
Bhutan	0.01	17,619	Iran	0.80	1,409,520	Sao Tome and Principe	0.01	17,619
Bolivia	0.01	17,619	Iraq	0.15	264,285	Saudi Arabia	0.71	1,250,949
Botswana	0.01	17,619	Ireland	0.20	352,380	Senegal	0.01	17,619
Brazil	1.55	2,730,945	Israel	0.31	546,189	Seychelles	0.01	17,619
Bulgaria	0.20	352,380	Italy	4.22	7,435,218	Sierra Leone	0.01	17,619
Burma	0.01	17,619	Ivory Coast	0.04	70,476	Somalia	0.01	17,619
Burundi	0.01	17,619	Jamaica	0.02	35,238	Spain	2.08	3,664,752
Canada	4.01	7,065,219	Japan	11.72	20,649,468	Sri Lanka	0.02	35,238
Cape Verde	0.01	17,619	Jordan	0.01	17,619	St. Vincent and the Grenadines	0.01	17,619
Central African Republic	0.01	17,619	Kenya	0.01	17,619	Sudan	0.01	17,619
Chad	0.01	17,619	Kuwait	0.24	422,856	Suriname	0.01	17,619
Chile	0.09	158,571	Lao People's Democratic Republic	0.01	17,619	Swaziland	0.01	17,619
China	1.98	3,488,562	Lebanon	0.04	70,476	Sweden	1.60	2,819,040
Colombia	0.13	229,047	Lesotho	0.01	17,619	Switzerland	1.28	2,255,232
Comoros	0.01	17,619	Liberia	0.01	17,619	Syrian Arab Republic	0.04	70,476
Congo	0.01	17,619	Libyan Arab Jamahiriya	0.28	493,332	Thailand	0.12	211,428
Costa Rica	0.02	35,238	Luxembourg	0.06	105,714	Togo	0.01	17,619
Cuba	0.13	229,047	Madagascar	0.01	17,619	Tonga	0.01	17,619
Cyprus	0.01	17,619	Malawi	0.01	17,619	Trinidad and Tobago	0.04	70,476
Czechoslovakia	1.02	1,797,138	Malaysia	0.11	193,809	Tunisia	0.04	70,476
Democratic Kampuchea	0.01	17,619	Maldives	0.01	17,619	Turkey	0.37	651,903
Democratic People's Republic of Korea	0.06	105,714	Mali	0.01	17,619	Uganda	0.01	17,619
Democratic Yemen	0.01	17,619	Malta	0.01	17,619	United Arab Emirates	0.12	211,428
Denmark	0.91	1,603,329	Mauritania	0.01	17,619	United Kingdom	5.45	9,602,355
Djibouti	0.01	17,619	Mauritius	0.01	17,619	United Republic of Cameroon	0.01	17,619
Dominica	0.01	17,619	Mexico	0.93	1,638,567	United Republic of Tanzania	0.01	17,619
Dominican Republic	0.04	70,476	Mongolia	0.01	17,619	United States	25.00	45,547,500
Ecuador	0.02	35,238	Morocco	0.06	105,714	Upper Volta	0.01	17,619
Egypt	0.09	158,571	Mozambique	0.01	17,619	Uruguay	0.05	88,095
El Salvador	0.01	17,619	Namibia	0.01	17,619	Venezuela	0.61	1,074,759
Equatorial Guinea	0.01	17,619	Nepal	0.01	17,619	Viet Nam	0.04	70,476
Ethiopia	0.01	17,619	Netherlands	1.99	3,506,181	Yemen	0.01	17,619
Fiji	0.01	17,619	New Zealand	0.33	581,427	Yugoslavia	0.51	898,569
Finland	0.59	1,039,521	Nicaragua	0.01	17,619	Zaire	0.02	35,238
France	7.66	13,496,154	Niger	0.01	17,619	Zambia	0.02	35,238
Gabon	0.02	35,238	Nigeria	0.20	352,380	Zimbabwe	0.02	35,238
Gambia	0.01	17,619	Norway	0.61	1,074,759			
Germany, Federal Republic of	10.16	17,900,904	Oman	0.01	17,619			
			Pakistan	0.09	158,571	Total	100.00	177,690,000*

*The total sum for the 1982-1983 biennium was $355,380,000.

Annex II. MEMBERS OF THE COUNCIL OF THE FOOD AND AGRICULTURE ORGANIZATION

Holding office until 31 December 1982: Argentina, Bangladesh, China, Germany, Federal Republic of, Indonesia, Ivory Coast, Japan, Malaysia, Panama, Portugal, Syrian Arab Republic, Thailand, United Republic of Cameroon, Venezuela, Yugoslavia, Zambia.

Holding office until conclusion of twenty-second session of the FAO Conference, November 1983: Afghanistan, Angola, Barbados, Brazil, Canada, Colombia, Congo, Cuba, Ireland, Kenya, Lebanon, Mexico, Morocco, Nigeria, Poland, Romania, United States.

Holding office until 31 December 1984: Cape Verde, Ecuador, Egypt, Ethiopia, France, India, Italy, Lesotho, New Zealand, Norway, Pakistan, Philippines, Saudi Arabia, Sudan, United Kingdom, Upper Volta.

Annex III. OFFICERS AND OFFICES OF THE FOOD AND AGRICULTURE ORGANIZATION

OFFICERS

OFFICE OF THE DIRECTOR-GENERAL
Director-General: Edouard Saouma.
Deputy Director-General: Edward M. West.
Executive Director, World Food Programme: James C. Ingram.
Co-ordinator, Freedom from Hunger Campaign/Action for Development: A. Peña-Montenegro.

DEPARTMENTS
Officer-in-Charge, Administration and Finance Department: A. G. Georgiadis.
Assistant Director-General, Agriculture Department: D. F. R. Bommer.
Assistant Director-General, Development Department: R. Lignon.
Assistant Director-General, Forestry Department: M. A. Flores Rodas.
Assistant Director-General, Department of General Affairs and Information: A. Sylla.

Assistant Director-General, Economic and Social Department: N. Islam.
Officer-in-Charge, Fisheries Department: A. Labon.

REGIONAL REPRESENTATIVES OF THE DIRECTOR-GENERAL
Director, Liaison Office for North America: D. C. Kimmel.
Representative, Liaison Office with the United Nations: G. S. Saab.
Assistant Director-General and Regional Representative for the Near East: S. Jum'a.
Assistant Director-General and Regional Representative for the Far East: S. S. Puri.
Assistant Director-General and Regional Representative for Latin America: M. E. Jalil.
Assistant Director-General and Regional Representative for Africa: J. A. C. Davies.
Regional Representative for Europe: S. Stampach.

HEADQUARTERS AND REGIONAL OFFICES

HEADQUARTERS

Food and Agriculture Organization
Via delle Terme di Caracalla
Rome 00100, Italy
  Cable address: FOODAGRI ROME
  Telephone: 57971
  Telex: 610181

REGIONAL AND OTHER OFFICES

Food and Agriculture Organization Regional
Office for Africa
United Nations Agency Building
North Maxwell Road
Post Office Box 1628
Accra, Ghana

REGIONAL AND OTHER OFFICES *(cont.)*

Food and Agriculture Organization Regional
Office for Asia and the Pacific
Maliwan Mansion
Phra Atit Road
Bangkok 2, Thailand

Food and Agriculture Organization Regional Office for
the Near East
Via delle Terme di Caracalla
Rome 00100, Italy

Food and Agriculture Organization Regional Office for
Europe
Via delle Terme di Caracalla
Rome 00100, Italy

REGIONAL AND OTHER OFFICES *(cont.)*

Food and Agriculture Organization Regional Office for
Latin America and the Caribbean
Avenida Santa Maria 6700
Casilla de correo 10095
Santiago, Chile

Food and Agriculture Organization Liaison Office with
the United Nations
United Nations Headquarters, Room DC1-1125
New York, N.Y. 10017, United States

Food and Agriculture Organization Liaison Office for
North America
1776 F Street, N. W., Suite 101
Washington, D. C. 20437, United States

Chapter IV

United Nations Educational, Scientific and Cultural Organization (UNESCO)

During 1982, the United Nations Educational, Scientific and Cultural Organization (UNESCO) continued a broad range of activities in education, natural and social sciences, culture and communication.

In 1982, Bhutan (13 April), Belize (10 May) and Antigua and Barbuda (15 July) joined UNESCO, bringing the membership to 158.

Education

The 1982 UNESCO education programme continued to promote the right to education, international understanding and respect for human rights, the struggle against all forms of discrimination, and the establishment of a new international economic order.

Literacy continued to be a main concern. The UNESCO Director-General noted on International Literacy Day (8 September) that despite the continuing drop in the illiteracy rate, the absolute number of illiterates was increasing due to the population growth; in addition, some 123 million children between 6 and 11 years of age, deprived of access to primary education, could swell the size of the illiterate population. Emphasis was placed in 1982 on a comprehensive approach linking adult literacy with the extension of primary education.

The fourth extraordinary session of the UNESCO General Conference (Paris, 23 November–3 December) adopted its second medium-term plan which included three main educational programmes: universal education, including development of primary education, continuing education for adults, and education for women, rural inhabitants and other groups; implementation of educational policies and strengthening of national capabilities in educational planning and administration; and education, training and society, stressing education in culture, communication, science, technology and other areas.

On the regional level, a conference of African education ministers and ministers for economic planning (Harare, Zimbabwe, 28 June–3 July) and a consultative committee on regional co-operation in education in Asia and the Pacific (second session, Manila, Philippines, 16-22 August) reviewed current efforts and examined future activities for the development of education.

A special committee of governmental experts (Paris, 6-10 December) met to develop a plan for regional agreement on the mutual recognition of studies and certificates, diplomas, degrees and other credentials of higher education in Asia and the Pacific. The plan, to be submitted in 1983 for approval by an intergovernmental conference, was the sixth and last such regional agreement, others having been formulated for Africa, the Americas and the Caribbean, Arab States, Arab and European countries bordering on the Mediterranean, and European States.

Reflecting the decentralization policy of UNESCO, an increasing number of activities in education were carried out by its four regional offices for education, in Africa, the Arab states, Asia and the Pacific and Latin America and the Caribbean. Regional centres for higher education at Caracas (Venezuela) and Bucharest (Romania) continued to contribute to regional co-operation. The International Bureau of Education at Geneva, the International Institute for Educational Planning at Paris and the Institute for Education at Hamburg (Federal Republic of Germany) strengthened their research and training activities at national, regional and international levels.

During 1982, UNESCO took part in 400 projects in education, financed by various sources including the United Nations Development Programme (UNDP), the United Nations Fund for Population Activities, the International Bank for Reconstruction and Development (World Bank) and regional development banks. Activities carried out in co-operation with other United Nations organizations included 49 regional, 12 interregional and 2 global projects, involving 308 experts, 279 consultants and 31 associate experts. Efforts were made to strengthen project preparation, management and evaluation.

Natural sciences

In 1982, UNESCO continued helping to use scientific and technological resources for development by assisting member States in planning, training and research activities. The Second Conference of Ministers Responsible for the Application of Science and Technology to Development and those Responsible for Economic Planning in Asia and the Pacific was convened at Manila, the Philippines, from 22 to 30 March, while preparatory work continued for similar meetings for the Arab region and Latin America.

The International Geological Correlation Programme, a joint enterprise of UNESCO and the International Union of Geological Sciences, observed its tenth year of operation in 1982. With national committees in 81 countries, the Programme had undertaken 87 projects, 49 of which were still in progress at the end of the year. In the framework of a regional project on geology for development, geological units in Burundi, United Republic of Tanzania and Zambia carried out several programmes; a training course on the geology of the Precambrian was held at Bujumbura, Burundi in July/August; and a regional workshop on geological interpretation of remote sensing data met at Nairobi, Kenya, in September/October.

By the end of 1982, the intergovernmental Man and the Biosphere Programme had established national committees in 101 countries, with over 1,000 field research projects under way in 79 countries, together with an international network of biosphere reserves on 226 sites in 62 countries.

In co-operation with the Food and Agriculture Organization of the United Nations, the United Nations Environment Programme and the United Nations Industrial Development Organization, UNESCO reinforced a network of microbiological centres in Brazil, Egypt, Guatemala, Kenya, Senegal and Thailand, as well as with the United Kingdom and the United States. In that framework, the World Data Centre of Micro-organisms was established in Australia under the auspices of the World Federation of Culture Collections.

Research and development in engineering were promoted through grants to institutions in developing countries and support for training activities, particularly for teaching staff and maintenance technicians. Further progress was made on the establishment of regional networks of engineering schools in Africa, the Arab States, Asia and Latin America.

The International Hydrological Programme, in its second phase (1981-1983), focused on assessment, planning and management of water resources, backed by 129 national committees and focal points. In addition to several symposia and workshops, UNESCO sponsored 19 post-graduate and other training courses, including a three-month course for African hydrology technicians (Lusaka, Zambia, July/September). Three regional projects—for Africa, the Arab States, and Latin America and the Caribbean—for water resources management in rural areas emphasized conservation and renovation of traditional works and the use of appropriate low-cost technologies for improved utilization of resources.

The UNESCO Division of Marine Sciences and the Intergovernmental Oceanographic Commission (IOC), an autonomous body within UNESCO, co-operated with non-governmental marine scientific organizations in sponsoring a Joint Oceanographic Assembly (Halifax, Canada, 2-13 August) and the Third International Marine Geosciences Workshop (Heidelberg, Federal Republic of Germany, 19-24 July). In addition to its Comprehensive Plan for a major assistance programme to enhance the marine science capabilities of developing countries, IOC promoted global programmes under the Long-term and Expanded Programme of Oceanic Exploration and Research: ocean dynamics and climate, marine pollution research and monitoring, ocean science in relation to living and non-living resources, and ocean-floor mapping.

Seminars and training courses in earth sciences continued, and UNESCO worked jointly with the Office of the United Nations Disaster Relief Coordinator and others on programmes to mitigate risks arising from natural hazards, including a feasibility study on earthquake risk in the Arab region.

Other activities during 1982 included courses and workshops by the International Centre for Theoretical Physics, a joint undertaking with the International Atomic Energy Agency; research and training programmes by the International Organization for Chemical Sciences in Development, created by UNESCO in 1981; designing of a pilot project for establishing microprocessor laboratories and minicomputer centres in developing countries; and an international forum on new technologies of coal utilization, a seminar on training of energy planning specialists, and training courses in new and renewable energy sources.

Social sciences

During 1982, UNESCO encouraged discussion on the tasks and challenges for the social sciences in the 1980s at national, regional and international levels. It continued to support the development of social sciences in all regions directly and indirectly through international professional non-governmental organizations, regional centres and associations. Its broad range of activities included training, research, theory and methodology, information and documentation services, international exchanges and publications.

Studies for development dealt with new styles of development and peoples' participation in the development process; socio-cultural inequalities between and within nations; socio-cultural impact of transnational corporations; socio-cultural aspects of rural development; and the situation and role of children in different cultures and environments.

Activities in socio-economic analysis and development planning included: the use of relevant indicators to examine and deal with problems associated with rapid socio-economic change, and the social integration of the disabled; research on planning methods, including modelling, and the strengthening of national capacity to use the UNESCO Educational Simulation Model; and studies on evaluation methods and their use in different countries. Training of planners in developing countries continued in 1982.

Environmental activities emphasized research on rural habitat and public participation, training "barefoot" architects and human settlement planners and administrators, rehabilitation of historic centres, and the UNESCO mass media programme to inform the public of environmental issues.

Population activities dealt with the demographic, socio-cultural and economic aspects of internal and international migration; the interrelationship between population, resources and development; assistance to member States to develop strategies for peoples' participation in developing and implementing population policies and programmes; the integration of human rights and development considerations in population communication programmes; training in social communication techniques; women's regional press feature services in Asia and Latin America and the Caribbean; and the training of journalists.

The organization continued to analyse human rights violations and conditions for a constructive peace. Courses in human rights were set up for universities and organizations, and information and documentation for teachers and researchers was improved.

Preparations began for a survey of teaching and research in philosophy in Asia and the Pacific, while research continued on comparative philosophical studies on the changing relationship of science and society, philosophical perspectives on the concept of environment, and studies on the process of change in a culture and the concept of a transcultural universal.

Other activities dealt with the status of women and their participation in development and youth-related projects in developing countries, including those benefiting disadvantaged youth.

Culture

In 1982, the World Conference on Cultural Policies, meeting at Mexico City from 26 July to 6 August 1982, gave new impetus to efforts carried out since the end of the 1960s under the aegis of UNESCO to promote international reflection on problems of culture in the contemporary world. Confirming the understanding of culture as a fundamental dimension and objective of global development, the Conference adopted the Mexico Declaration on Cultural Policies which enumerated principles for promoting cultural activities and enhancing the cultural dimension of development.

Study programmes continued on African, Arab, Arctic, Asian, Caribbean, Latin American, Oceanic, Southeast European and Slavic cultures, and the programme on intercultural studies was expanded. Work continued on the *General History of Africa* and publications on Islamic culture. Work began on the *History of the Civilizations of Central Asia* and preparations began for the *General History of the Caribbean*. Over thirty translations of the world's literature were published in Arabic, English, French and Spanish.

In 1982, a new international campaign was launched to establish the Nubia Museum in Aswan and the National Museum of Egyptian Civilization in Cairo, Egypt. The international campaign to save the Temple of Borobudur (Indonesia) was successfully completed. Preservation work continued for Venice (Italy), four ancient sites in Mauritania, monuments of Hué (Viet Nam), Moenjodaro (Pakistan), Sukhothai (Thailand), monuments and sites in the "Cultural Triangle" (Sri Lanka), monuments in Haiti, the island of Gorée (Senegal), Fez (Morocco), Montenegro (Yugoslavia), Carthage (Tunisia), the Hanuman Dhoka Palace complex at Kathmandu (Nepal) and the Acropolis at Athens (Greece).

The number of States parties to the 1972 International Convention concerning the Protection of the World Cultural and Natural Heritage increased to 71 in 1982. Under the Convention, 24 sites in 15 countries were designated as having outstanding universal value. Technical co-operation amounting to $1 million, including $400,000 for training, was provided to States parties from the World Heritage Fund, the annual income of which totalled $700,000. The World Heritage Committee held its sixth session in Paris from 13 to 17 December.

Communications

In 1982, UNESCO continued to promote a free flow and wider and better balanced dissemination of information, study the role of communication in society, assist member States in formulating national and regional communication policies, and reinforce communication systems in developing countries. A meeting of experts was held at Amman, Jordan, in preparation for the 1984 Intergovernmental Conference on Communication Policies in the Arab States.

The Intergovernmental Council of the International Programme for the Development of Communications (IPDC) held its second and third sessions in 1982 (Acapulco, Mexico, January; Paris, December), and allocated funds for regional and interregional projects, including a global experiment in the use of satellites for television news exchange. At the third session, the Council, in addition to approving financing of regional and interregional projects, approved for the first time IPDC funding of national projects, 15 in all.

The UNESCO programme in communication included activities aimed at developing national news agencies and organizing regional news agency exchanges. Projects launched or developed with funding from the United Nations Development Programme (UNDP), IPDC, funds-in-trust donors and UNESCO included the Pan African News Agency, the West and Central African News Agency Development, the Caribbean News Agency, the Asian Pacific News Network and the Latin American Agency for Special Services of Information. In addition, assistance was provided for developing communication infrastructures—including rural newspapers, radio, television, film production and audio-visual archives—in 23 developing countries.

With support given for the regional exchange of films and television programmes, preparations were made in Asia for organizing regional audio-visual depositories, an audio-visual training resource base and a method for standardizing and computerizing film and audio-visual material for cataloguing and retrieval purposes. The Union of National Radio and Television Organizations of Africa and the Caribbean Broadcasting Union also received assistance to strengthen programme exchange activities.

An interregional research project on the international flow of television news and programmes was begun in 1982, and projects continued for television news exchange by satellite between Africa, Asia and the Arab States, and for reducing telecommunication tariffs. Studies continued on such subjects as: the right to communicate and the democratization of communication, media education, and the nature, scope and impact of advertising in different regions in the world. An abridged version of *Many Voices, One World*, the final report of the International Commission for the Study of Communication Problems, was prepared.

Research in new technology produced a low-cost, low-power FM transmitter which was successfully tested at Homa Bay, Kenya. Other experiments dealt with solar-powered radio and television receivers, upgraded video recorders, monochrome video field cameras, and digital signal processors.

In 1982, the UNESCO World Congress on Books (London, 7-11 June) marked the tenth anniversary of the 1972 International Book Year. The Congress, attended by over 300 participants and observers from 92 countries, adopted the London Declaration, and endorsed the following six targets for action under the slogan "Towards a reading society—targets for the 80s": formulation of a national book strategy, recognition of the book industry as a vital industry, integration of new technologies into the book chain, creation of a reading environment throughout society, stimulation of international co-operation for building national book capacities, and increasing the international exchange of books.

General Information Programme

The UNESCO General Information Programme provided services at the national, regional and international levels for the development and promotion of information systems in scientific and technological information, documentation, libraries and archives.

The programme emphasized: the needs of users requiring information to contribute to the development process; a user-oriented approach in designing and developing information systems and services; the special needs of the least developed countries; maximum utilization of local information resources; encouragement of creativity and innovation; facilitation of use and adaptation of advanced technology for information handling by member States; and the importance of evaluating and sharing experiences among member States.

Technical assistance

Assistance in 1982 under UNESCO Participation Programme

As at 31 December 1982, the allocations approved by the Director-General under the UNESCO Participation Programme, through which member States and organizations participated in technical assistance activities, amounted to $5,265,000. Of the total of $15,048,800 the General Conference had approved for the Programme in the 1981-1983 regular budget, some $9,400,000 had been allocated in 1981 for the first of two budget instalments for the three-year period. The amounts by sector and by region are as follows (in thousands of United States dollars):

Sector	Allocation
General development issues, policies and planning	1,413
Education	1,193
Culture and communication	1,149
Social conditions equity	828
Science and technology	456
Natural resources	142
Human settlements	84
Total	5,265

Region	
Africa	1,680
Latin America and the Caribbean	921
Europe	684
Asia and the Pacific	615
Arab States	472
Global and interregional	893
Total	5,265

Projects executed for UNDP and UNFPA

As at 31 December 1982, amounts obligated in 1982 for projects for which UNESCO served as executing agency for the United Nations Development Programme (UNDP) and the United Nations Fund for Population Activities (UNFPA) totalled some $48.5 million, as shown in the tables below (in thousands of United States dollars).

PROJECTS EXECUTED BY UNESCO
FOR UNDP IN 1982

Sector	Amount obligated
Education	24,671
Natural sciences	13,287
Culture	2,102
General Information Programme	2,100
Communication	1,517
Social sciences	620
Statistics	206
Total	44,503

Region	
Africa	17,462
Asia and the Pacific	13,588
Arab States	6,204
Latin America and the Caribbean	5,587
Europe and North America	1,542
Interregional and global	120
Total	44,503

PROJECTS EXECUTED BY UNESCO
FOR UNFPA IN 1982

Sector	Amount obligated
Education	2,573
Social sciences	1,210
Infrastructure and backstopping	257
Statistics	9
Total	4,049

Region	
Asia and the Pacific	1,102
Latin America and the Caribbean	872
Africa	791
Arab States	777
Infrastructure and backstopping	257
Global and interregional activities	250
Total	4,049

Secretariat

As at 31 December 1982, the total number of full-time staff employed by UNESCO on permanent, fixed- and short-term appointments was 3,495, drawn from 129 nationalities. Of these, 1,435 were in the Professional or higher categories and 2,060 were in the General Service and Maintenance Worker categories.

Of the Professional staff, 515 were serving in the field, as were 548 General Service staff.

Budget

The twenty-first (1980) session of the UNESCO General Conference approved a budget of $625.4 million for the three-year period 1981-1983. The Conference fixed the level of the Working Capital Fund at $20 million; amounts to be advanced by member States were to be calculated according to their percentage contribution. Amounts allocated are shown in the table on the following page.

Annex I. MEMBERSHIP OF THE UNITED NATIONS EDUCATIONAL, SCIENTIFIC AND CULTURAL ORGANIZATION AND CONTRIBUTIONS

(Membership as at 31 December 1982;
annual contributions as assessed for 1981-1983)

MEMBER	Percentage	Amount (in US dollars)
Afghanistan	0.01	19,916
Albania	0.01	19,916
Algeria	0.12	238,992
Angola	0.01	19,916
Antigua and Barbuda	0.01	19,916
Argentina	0.77	1,533,532
Australia	1.81	3,604,796
Austria	0.70	1,394,120
Bahamas	0.01	19,916
Bahrain	0.01	19,916
Bangladesh	0.04	79,664
Barbados	0.01	19,916
Belgium	1.21	2,409,836
Belize	0.01	19,916
Benin	0.01	19,916
Bhutan	0.01	19,916
Bolivia	0.01	19,916
Botswana	0.01	19,916
Brazil	1.26	2,509,416
Bulgaria	0.16	318,656
Burma	0.01	19,916
Burundi	0.01	19,916
Byelorussian SSR	0.38	756,808
Canada	3.24	6,452,784
Cape Verde	0.01	19,916
Central African Republic	0.01	19,916
Chad	0.01	19,916
Chile	0.07	139,412
China	1.60	3,186,560
Colombia	0.11	219,076
Comoros	0.01	19,916
Congo	0.01	19,916
Costa Rica	0.02	39,832
Cuba	0.11	219,076
Cyprus	0.01	19,916
Czechoslovakia	0.82	1,633,112
Democratic Kampuchea	0.01	19,916
Democratic People's Republic of Korea	0.05	99,580
Democratic Yemen	0.01	19,916
Denmark	0.73	1,453,868
Dominica	0.01	19,916
Dominican Republic	0.03	59,748
Ecuador	0.02	39,832
Egypt	0.07	139,412
El Salvador	0.01	19,916
Equatorial Guinea	0.01	19,916
Ethiopia	0.01	19,916
Finland	0.47	936,052
France	6.19	12,328,004
Gabon	0.02	39,832
Gambia	0.01	19,916
German Democratic Republic	1.37	2,728,492
Germany, Federal Republic of	8.22	16,370,952
Ghana	0.03	59,748
Greece	0.35	697,060
Grenada	0.01	19,916
Guatemala	0.02	39,832
Guinea	0.01	19,916
Guinea-Bissau	0.01	19,916
Guyana	0.01	19,916
Haiti	0.01	19,916
Honduras	0.01	19,916
Hungary	0.33	657,228
Iceland	0.03	59,748
India	0.59	1,175,044
Indonesia	0.16	318,656
Iran	0.64	1,274,624
Iraq	0.12	238,992
Ireland	0.16	318,656
Israel	0.25	497,900
Italy	3.41	6,791,356
Ivory Coast	0.03	59,748
Jamaica	0.02	39,832
Japan	9.48	18,880,368
Jordan	0.01	19,916
Kenya	0.01	19,916
Kuwait	0.20	398,320
Lao People's Democratic Republic	0.01	19,916
Lebanon	0.03	59,748
Lesotho	0.01	19,916
Liberia	0.01	19,916
Libyan Arab Jamahiriya	0.23	458,068
Luxembourg	0.05	99,580
Madagascar	0.01	19,916
Malawi	0.01	19,916
Malaysia	0.09	179,244
Maldives	0.01	19,916
Mali	0.01	19,916
Malta	0.01	19,916
Mauritania	0.01	19,916
Mauritius	0.01	19,916
Mexico	0.75	1,493,700
Monaco	0.01	19,916
Mongolia	0.01	19,916
Morocco	0.05	99,580
Mozambique	0.01	19,916
Namibia*	–	–
Nepal	0.01	19,916
Netherlands	1.61	3,206,476
New Zealand	0.27	537,732
Nicaragua	0.01	19,916
Niger	0.01	19,916
Nigeria	0.16	318,656
Norway	0.49	975,884
Oman	0.01	19,916
Pakistan	0.07	139,412
Panama	0.02	39,832
Papua New Guinea	0.01	19,916
Paraguay	0.01	19,916
Peru	0.06	119,496
Philippines	0.10	199,160
Poland	1.23	2,449,668
Portugal	0.19	378,404
Qatar	0.03	59,748
Republic of Korea	0.15	298,740
Romania	0.21	418,236
Rwanda	0.01	19,916
Saint Lucia	0.01	19,916
Samoa	0.01	19,916
San Marino	0.01	19,916
Sao Tome and Principe	0.01	19,916
Saudi Arabia	0.57	1,135,212
Senegal	0.01	19,916
Seychelles	0.01	19,916
Sierra Leone	0.01	19,916
Singapore	0.08	159,328
Somalia	0.01	19,916
Spain	1.68	3,345,888
Sri Lanka	0.02	39,832
Sudan	0.01	19,916
Suriname	0.01	19,916
Swaziland	0.01	19,916
Sweden	1.30	2,589,080
Switzerland	1.04	2,071,264
Syrian Arab Republic	0.03	59,748
Thailand	0.10	199,160
Togo	0.01	19,916
Tonga	0.01	19,916
Trinidad and Tobago	0.03	59,748
Tunisia	0.03	59,748
Turkey	0.30	597,480
Uganda	0.01	19,916
Ukrainian SSR	1.44	2,867,904
USSR	10.98	21,867,768
United Arab Emirates	0.10	199,160
United Kingdom	4.41	8,782,956
United Republic of Cameroon	0.01	19,916
United Republic of Tanzania	0.01	19,916
United States	25.00	49,790,000
Upper Volta	0.01	19,916
Uruguay	0.04	79,664
Venezuela	0.49	975,884
Viet Nam	0.03	59,748
Yemen	0.01	19,916
Yugoslavia	0.41	816,556
Zaire	0.02	39,832
Zambia	0.02	39,832
Zimbabwe	0.02	39,832
Total†	100.07	199,299,412
ASSOCIATE MEMBER		
British Eastern Caribbean Group	0.01	19,916

*Namibia's assessment remained suspended in 1982.

†Includes contributions assessed for Bahamas, Samoa and Zimbabwe, admitted as members in 1981, and for Antigua and Barbuda, Belize and Bhutan, admitted as members in 1982, after assessments for the period 1981-1983 had been set by the 1980 Session of the UNESCO General Conference.

Annex II.   OFFICERS AND OFFICES OF THE UNITED NATIONS
EDUCATIONAL, SCIENTIFIC AND CULTURAL ORGANIZATION
(As at 31 December 1982)

MEMBERS OF THE EXECUTIVE BOARD

Chairman: Victor Massuh (Argentina).

Vice-Chairmen: Aziz Al-Hajj Ali Haidar (Iraq), Barnabé Karorero (Burundi), Guillermo Putzeys Alvarez (Guatemala), Nikolai I. Smirnov (USSR), Kaw Swasdi Panich (Thailand), François Valery (France).

Members: Daniel Arango (Colombia), Mario Cabral (Guinea-Bissau), Estrella Z. de Carazo (Costa Rica), Cu-Huy-Can (Viet Nam), Georges-Henri Dumont (Belgium), Mohammed El Fasi (Morocco), Dafalla El Hag Yousif (Sudan), Salvador Garcia de Pruneda (Spain), Jean B. S. Gerard (United States), Alfredo Guevara (Cuba), Erdal Inonu (Turkey), Triloki Nath Kaul (India), Mumtaz Ali Kazi (Pakistan), Mamadi Keita (Guinea), Donald J. Kirkness (United Kingdom), Donald M. Kusenha (United Republic of Tanzania), Jean-Félix Loung (United Republic of Cameroon), Mahmoud Messadi (Tunisia), Peter Mod (Hungary), Karl Moersch (Germany, Federal Republic of), A. Bola Olaniyan (Nigeria), Masami Ota (Japan), Demodetdo Y. Pendje (Zaire), Gian Franco Pompei (Italy), Abdellatif Rahal (Algeria), Hubert de Ronceray (Haiti), Saeed Abdullah Salman (United Arab Emirates), Patrick K. Seddoh (Ghana), Ladislav Smid (Czechoslovakia), Sulaiman Haji Daud (Malaysia), Hanne Sondergaard (Denmark), Thomas Sohl Thelejane (Lesotho), Iba der Thiam (Senegal), Gleb N. Tsvetkov (Ukrainian SSR), Fred Turnovsky (New Zealand), José Israel Vargas (Brazil), Hector L. Wynter (Jamaica), Yang Bozheng (China).

PRINCIPAL OFFICERS OF THE SECRETARIAT

Director-General: Amadou Mahtar M'Bow.

Director, Executive Office of the Secretary-General: Chikh Bekri.

Assistant Directors-General: Gérard Bolla, Abdul-Razzak Kaddoura, John Borema Kaboré, Jean Knapp, Henri Lopes, Makaminan Makagiansar, Zala Lusibu N'Kanza, George F. Saddler, Sema Tanguiane, Tien-Chang Young.

HEADQUARTERS AND OTHER OFFICE

HEADQUARTERS
UNESCO House
7 Place de Fontenoy
75700 Paris, France
  Cable address: UNESCO PARIS
  Telephone: 577-16-10
  Telex: 204461

NEW YORK OFFICE
United Nations Educational, Scientific and
  Cultural Organization
United Nations Headquarters, Room S-2401
New York, N. Y. 10017, United States
  Cable Address: UNESCORG NEWYORK
  Telephone: (212) 754-5981

Chapter V

World Health Organization (WHO)

The thirty-fifth World Health Assembly met at Geneva, from 3 to 14 May 1982, and approved a plan of action for implementing the Global Strategy for Health for All by the Year 2000, adopted in 1981.[a] The plan called on member States to review their health policies and develop national strategies in light of the Global Strategy. The regional committees of the World Health Organization (WHO) were asked to bring up to date and adapt strategies as necessary, and prepare regional plans of action. To assist member States, the Director-General of WHO prepared a "common framework and format" for monitoring and reporting on the implementation of health strategies.

The Assembly also approved the Seventh General Programme of Work covering the period 1984-1989. The Programme divided WHO's work into four main categories: direction, co-ordination and management of WHO policy and its general programme; establishment of health system infrastructure; health research, science and technology; and programme support, including administrative, financial and information activities.

Bhutan became a member of WHO on 8 March 1982. Thus, as at 31 December, WHO had 158 members and one associate member.

Emergency Assistance

During 1982, WHO continued and expanded its emergency assistance in disaster situations. With donor countries, institutions and non-governmental organizations, WHO provided health services and medical supplies to the victims of natural disasters, epidemics, famine, war and civil strife. It took part in more than 50 emergency operations at a cost of some $10 million, mostly from extrabudgetary sources.

Health system development

Information

The Director-General decided in 1982 to redefine the scope of traditional programmes of vital and health statistics and epidemiological surveillance. A new programme to assess health situations

[a]See YUN 1981, p. 1418.

and trends and provide information for implementing and evaluating health strategies was established.

WHO helped to develop health information support in several areas of the Americas, South-East Asia, the Eastern Mediterranean and Western Pacific. For example, it supported the development of hospital record systems in a number of countries in the Americas and the Western Pacific. In addition, WHO collaborated with several countries in carrying out morbidity and mortality surveys and various studies on health status.

An interregional workshop on primary health care information was held in Beijing, China in October 1982, and discussions were begun on a common system for reporting health information in the islands of the Indian Ocean.

Research

Health system research provides a basis for policy-making, planning and implementation of not only the system but health care delivery itself. An interregional workshop, held in July 1982 in New Delhi, concluded that a combination of research approaches would offer the best results. Approaches ranged from the experimental use of simulation and quasi-experimental design methods to statistical survey, documentary analysis and descriptive case study.

A WHO study group, meeting in October in Geneva, reviewed the concept of health system research and upheld its value in the delivery of care.

The advantages of the "partnership" approach were stressed by the WHO Advisory Committee on Medical Research (ACMR). Its subcommittee on health services research pointed out that in this approach WHO fosters the allocation by other agencies of resources for carrying out research in accordance with national priorities.

Development

In 1982, WHO published the first substantial review of primary health care development since the 1978 International Conference on Primary Health Care (Alma-Ata, USSR).[b] Highlighting both positive trends and problems encountered, it described the efforts of 70 countries to develop primary care facilities.

WHO gave particular attention to strengthening primary health care programmes in urban areas. It sponsored inter-city workshops and seminars in Latin America, Europe, Asia and the Pacific. Several countries in the South-East Asia region—India, Indonesia, Sri Lanka and Thailand—completed case studies on health care in the slums and fringe areas of major cities. In the European region, a working group explored the delivery of primary health care services in rapidly changing urban settings.

Health manpower

Health manpower policies in China, Indonesia, Viet Nam, Zambia and Zimbabwe were studied, and priority needs identified. Those most frequently mentioned were: development of job profiles to improve manpower planning; improvement in research capability; training of personnel at the peripheral level of health services, including teacher training; management of health staff to improve utilization, efficiency and effectiveness; and community-oriented medical education.

A preliminary investigation on women as providers of health care was carried out by WHO, with the support of the United Nations Fund for Population Activities (UNFPA), as part of a continuing project to implement policies to enhance the status of women as health care providers. Seventeen countries took part—Brazil, Colombia, Egypt, Ethiopia, France, Hungary, India, Indonesia, Jamaica, Mali, Nigeria, Pakistan, the Philippines, Switzerland, Thailand, the USSR and Zimbabwe.

WHO also developed a guide for monitoring and evaluating health manpower, which was tested in countries in Africa and South-East Asia.

Public information and education for health

Public information and health education activities were combined by WHO in 1982. Strategies were to be formulated to include an information and education component in all programmes. They were to be promoted at the country level through WHO's regional offices.

World Health Day 1982 (7 April) was designated World Day for the Aged, with the theme, "Add Life to Years". In his message for the day, the Director-General spoke of a new image of old age—basically healthy, experienced individuals with a variety of useful roles to play in the community. Broadcasts and articles also marked the occasion. Special celebrations were held in Paris and in London, the latter with a round-table on aging. Later in the year the United Nations World Assembly on Aging was held at Vienna, Austria.

Health Science and Technology

The WHO Advisory Committee on Medical Research held its twenty-fourth session in October 1982 at Geneva. It reviewed progress made in WHO's global and regional research, and endorsed the programme on cancer control, including prevention, early detection, and pain relief. It also endorsed the proposals of the scientific planning group on an expanded programme of research and training in the bio-behavioural sciences and mental health.

[b]See YUN 1978, p. 1107.

Family health

Family planning programmes were supported by WHO in more than 80 countries during 1982, most in co-operation with UNFPA. Guidelines were published on contraceptive technology, including oral contraceptives, injectable hormonal contraceptives, and intrauterine devices.

A workshop, jointly sponsored with the United States National Research Council (Geneva, February), concluded that there was urgent need for adoption in many countries of a consistent national policy on family planning as well as on breast-feeding.

Malnutrition remained a major public health problem in both developing and industrialized countries. A five-year plan to improve the nutrition of mothers and children, developed with the United Nations Children's Fund in 1981, was launched in 1982 with a pledge of $85.3 million from Italy.

Disease prevention and control

Blindness

Technical co-operation with Member States focused on developing national programmes for the prevention of blindness. Such programmes existed in 24 countries. Activities included preparing guidelines for simple, low-cost surveys of blindness and its main causes, a multi-language poster on eye care, a publication entitled *Strategies for the Prevention of Blindness in National Programmes: A Primary Health Care Approach*, studies in several countries on providing low-cost spectacles to schoolchildren and patients operated on for cataract, manuals on the screening of schoolchildren for visual defects and on basic optics.

Cancer

Primary cancer of the liver was singled out for prevention by the WHO Advisory Committee on Medical Research. It was agreed that for the first time an unprecedented opportunity existed to prevent a common cancer—primary hepatocellular carcinoma—by vaccination. It was estimated that about 80 per cent of liver cancers occur as a result of infection by hepatitis B virus. The WHO Regional Office for the Western Pacific organized a scientific group on viral hepatitis B and related liver diseases (Nagasaki, Japan, September-October 1982), which recommended *inter alia* the establishment of a network of WHO-designated laboratories.

The International Agency for Research on Cancer was developing a major programme on the role of dietary factors in cancer. A number of studies were in progress; among them were investigations of diet in the etiology of large-bowel cancer in Belgium and in Greece.

Cardiovascular diseases

Despite reports that mortality from coronary heart disease was declining in some countries (for example, Australia, Japan and the United States), death rates in most industrialized countries were stationary or rising. In developing countries such as Malaysia, Singapore and Sri Lanka, the incidence had reached unacceptable levels. Reasons for the trends were not known and the WHO MONICA (multinational monitoring of trends and determinants in cardiovascular diseases) project was designed to illuminate the question. Forty centres in 25 countries were taking part in the project, which was planned to continue for 10 years.

Cardiovascular community control programmes continued in all regions, co-ordinated by WHO. A European group of investigators met in October 1982 at Heidelberg, Federal Republic of Germany, to review progress. The group concluded that the programmes had been of benefit, especially in promoting the control of hypertension and smoking. In Europe, attempts were being made to enlarge the scope of the community programmes to include diabetes, chronic lung diseases and cancer.

Immunization

In 1982, the Director-General reported that much progress had been achieved in the Expanded Programme on Immunization, but warned that it would have to be accelerated in order to meet the goal of providing immunizations for all children of the world by 1990.

The World Health Assembly accordingly urged member States to take action on a five-point programme involving promotion of immunization in the context of primary health care, investment of adequate resources, evaluation and adaptation of programmes, and research.

Leprosy

In the past few years, the leprosy problem had become more complex, particularly because of an alarming situation created by increased resistance of *Mycobacterium leprae* to the drug dapsone. Consequently, the use of multidrug regimens had become mandatory. This was in line with recommendations made in October 1982 by the WHO Study Group on Chemotherapy of Leprosy for Control Programmes. Multidrug therapy for leprosy control would have to be implemented as soon as possible if the leprosy problem was not to become unmanageable. The new treatment policy had important operational implications, including a substantial cost increase.

Recommendations for mobilizing additional resources for leprosy control were drawn up at a WHO meeting (New Delhi, India, August) by representatives of: the United Nations Children's

Fund, Swedish International Development Authority, Japan Shipbuilding Industry Foundation, International Leprosy Association, International Federation of Anti-Leprosy Associations, officers from five WHO regional offices, and other leprosy experts. The Damien Foundation (Belgium) established a drug fund with an initial endowment of $400,000 to support projects receiving WHO's approval.

Malaria

The number of clinical malaria cases in the world in 1982 was estimated to be about 90 million.

Malaria continued to be one of the main causes of high morbidity and mortality in Africa, where obstacles to reducing the number of cases included a shortage of antimalarial drugs and difficulties in their distribution. In June 1982, WHO signed a two-year agreement with the Arab Gulf Programme for United Nations Development Organizations to make antimalarial drugs available to 10 of the least developed African countries.

In November 1982, Singapore was added to the register of areas where malaria had been eradicated.

Other parasitic diseases

The major protozoal and helminthic infections were still highly prevalent on a global scale and in numerous areas presented serious public health problems. Some infections were lethal, for example, African trypanosomiasis, disseminated amoebiasis, complicated strongyloidiasis, and neurocysticercosis. Others, the majority, produced the chronic disease syndromes of the tropics and control was complicated by their complex epidemiologies and their intimate relationships to the environment, human behavioural factors, animal reservoirs, and above all, socio-economic deprivation. Technical advances in control were frequently only effective on a large scale when basic improvements were made in the public health infrastructure and the environment, including the provision of safe water supplies, adequate sanitary facilities and continuing health education.

Although little change in the distributions of parasitic diseases could be discerned, it was noted that in two areas in particular, schistosomiasis and gastrointestinal protozoan and helminthic infections, excellent results in controlling morbidity could be achieved. Highly effective therapeutic drugs of minimal toxicity were available.

Mental health

Recognizing the magnitude of psychosocial and mental health problems and the importance of utilizing knowledge from the bio-behavioural sciences in health care, WHO's Advisory Committee on Medical Research in October 1982 endorsed the preparation of a detailed programme in three fields—adaptation to rapid societal and technological change, alcoholism, and promotion of child and family health through bio-behavioural principles.

Sexually transmitted diseases

Resistance of certain causative agents to an increasing range of antibiotics—a serious problem in treating sexually transmitted diseases—led to a rise in treatment failures and higher rates of transmission and complications. Continuous adjustment of treatment in the light of the resistance pattern of local strains was called for. A WHO consultative group (Geneva, November) suggested options for treating specific infections that would be effective for various resistance patterns in different geographical areas. The options would help health administrations to select regimens for inclusion in their national treatment standards. On the basis of the suggested regimens, the International Union against the Venereal Diseases and the Treponematoses formulated options for the treatment of sexually transmitted diseases in Africa.

Smoking and health

A WHO survey revealed that in 1976 only about 20 countries had legislation aimed at controlling tobacco smoking but that by 1982 the number had increased to about 60. Many countries had established either government or government-approved committees on smoking and health. The smoking habit was decreasing in most industrialized countries, particularly among middle-aged men of medium-to-high socio-economic levels. The same trend was becoming apparent among women and adolescents. However, in developing countries, prevalence was increasing, owing to heavy promotion by the tobacco industry.

A WHO Expert Committee on Smoking Control Strategies in Developing Countries met (Geneva, November 1982) to provide guidelines for action by health authorities of those countries. Among circumstances considered were diseases involved, absence of smoking control legislation in most developing countries, and the paucity of health education programmes.

Vector control

The World Health Assembly reiterated in a 1982 resolution the importance of giving special attention to health implications of large-scale socio-economic development schemes. The resolution was circulated to member States, 36 bilateral assistance agencies, development banks and donors. Responses revealed widespread concern about this problem.

Surveys of urban vector control services, carried out in 26 cities in all WHO regions, showed that the current global expenditure on urban vector and pest control was probably as much as $600 million annually, including some $100 million spent on insecticides and rodenticides. The quality of control, however, was not always equivalent to the funds expended; on the basis of the surveys, WHO made recommendations for improvements.

WHO published a practical manual in 1982 to provide guidance on environmental measures to control mosquitos in connection with water resources development projects.

Secretariat

As at 31 December 1982, the total number of full-time staff employed by WHO stood at 4,403 on permanent and fixed-term contracts. Of these, 1,563 staff members, drawn from 116 nationalities, were in the Professional and higher categories and 2,840 were in the General Service category. Of the total number of staff, 186 were in posts financed by the United Nations Development Programme, United Nations Environment Programme, United Nations Fund for Drug Abuse Control, and UNFPA.

Budget

The thirty-fourth World Health Assembly (1981) approved an effective working budget of $468,900,000 for the financial period 1982-1983. This compared with $427,290,000 for the two years 1980 and 1981.

It also authorized the use of casual income up to a maximum of $20 million for 1982-1983 in order to meet any net additional costs under the regular

budget resulting from differences in the exchange rate between the Swiss franc and the United States dollar. At the same time, the Director-General was requested to transfer to casual income any net savings resulting from such differences, provided that such net savings need not exceed $20 million.

The budget was allocated as follows:

Purpose of appropriation	Amount (in US dollars)
Development of comprehensive health services	88,493,400
Disease prevention and control	86,054,200
General services and support programmes	85,865,300
General programme development, management and co-ordination	63,362,100
Health manpower development	60,056,100
Health information and literature	44,525,900
Promotion of environmental health	30,927,800
Policy organs	9,615,200
Total	468,900,000

INTEGRATED INTERNATIONAL HEALTH PROGRAMME OBLIGATIONS BY SOURCE OF FINANCING FOR THE TWO-YEAR PERIOD 1982-1983

Source	Amount (in US dollars)
Regular budget	468,900
Pan American Health Organization	165,411
International Agency for Research on Cancer	23,040
Other sources	
Voluntary Fund for Health Promotion	84,353
Sasakawa Health Trust Fund	5,563
United Nations sources	
UNICEF	315
UNDP	53,133
UNEP	2,439
UNFDAC	628
UNFPA	36,911
Trust funds	108,061
Special Account for Servicing Costs	7,384
Total	956,138

Annex I.   MEMBERSHIP OF THE WORLD HEALTH ORGANIZATION AND CONTRIBUTIONS

(Membership as at 31 December 1982; contributions as assessed for 1983)

MEMBER	CONTRIBUTION Percentage	Amount* (in US dollars)	MEMBER	CONTRIBUTION Percentage	Amount* (in US dollars)	MEMBER	CONTRIBUTION Percentage	Amount* (in US dollars)
Afghanistan	0.01	23,920	Canada	3.22	7,719,215	Ecuador	0.02	47,835
Albania	0.01	23,920	Cape Verde	0.01	23,920	Egypt	0.07	167,425
Algeria	0.12	287,020	Central African Republic	0.01	23,920	El Salvador	0.01	23,920
Angola	0.01	23,920	Chad	0.01	23,920	Equatorial Guinea	0.01	23,920
Argentina	0.77	1,841,715	Chile	0.07	167,425	Ethiopia	0.01	23,920
Australia	1.80	4,305,305	China	1.59	3,803,020	Fiji	0.01	23,920
Austria	0.70	1,674,285	Colombia	0.11	263,100	Finland	0.47	1,124,165
Bahamas	0.01	23,920	Comoros	0.01	23,920	France	6.15	15,105,805
Bahrain	0.01	23,920	Congo	0.01	56,920	Gabon	0.02	47,835
Bangladesh	0.04	95,670	Costa Rica	0.02	47,835	Gambia	0.01	23,920
Barbados	0.01	23,920	Cuba	0.11	263,100	German Democratic		
Belgium	1.20	2,870,205	Cyprus	0.01	23,920	Republic	1.37	3,276,815
Benin	0.01	23,920	Czechoslovakia	0.82	1,961,305	Germany, Federal		
Bhutan†	0.01	29,993	Democratic Kampuchea	0.01	23,920	Republic of	8.17	19,541,315
Bolivia	0.01	23,920	Democratic People's			Ghana	0.03	71,755
Botswana	0.01	23,920	Republic of Korea	0.05	119,590	Greece	0.34	813,225
Brazil	1.25	2,989,795	Democratic Yemen	0.01	30,420	Grenada	0.01	23,920
Bulgaria	0.16	382,695	Denmark	0.73	1,746,040	Guatemala	0.02	47,835
Burma	0.01	23,920	Djibouti	0.01	23,920	Guinea	0.01	23,920
Burundi	0.01	23,920	Dominica‡	0.01	23,920	Guinea-Bissau	0.01	23,920
Byelorussian SSR	0.38	908,900	Dominican Republic	0.03	71,755	Guyana	0.01	23,920

MEMBER	CONTRIBUTION Percentage	Amount* (in US dollars)	MEMBER	CONTRIBUTION Percentage	Amount* (in US dollars)	MEMBER	CONTRIBUTION Percentage	Amount* (in US dollars)
Haiti	0.01	23,920	Morocco	0.05	119,590	Suriname	0.01	23,920
Honduras	0.01	23,920	Mozambique	0.01	23,920	Swaziland	0.01	23,920
Hungary	0.32	765,385	Nepal	0.01	23,920	Sweden	1.29	3,085,470
Iceland	0.03	71,755	Netherlands	1.60	3,826,940	Switzerland	1.03	2,463,590
India	0.59	1,411,185	New Zealand	0.26	621,875	Syrian Arab Republic	0.03	71,755
Indonesia	0.16	382,695	Nicaragua	0.01	23,920	Thailand	0.10	239,180
Iran	0.64	1,530,775	Niger	0.01	23,920	Togo	0.01	23,920
Iraq	0.12	287,020	Nigeria	0.16	382,695	Tonga	0.01	23,920
Ireland	0.16	382,695	Norway	0.49	1,172,000	Trinidad and Tobago	0.03	71,755
Israel	0.24	574,040	Oman	0.01	23,920	Tunisia	0.03	71,755
Italy	3.39	8,108,330	Pakistan	0.07	167,425	Turkey	0.29	693,630
Ivory Coast	0.03	71,755	Panama	0.02	47,835	Uganda	0.01	23,920
Jamaica	0.02	47,835	Papua New Guinea	0.01	23,920	Ukrainian SSR	1.44	3,444,250
Japan	9.42	22,531,110	Paraguay	0.01	23,920	USSR	10.91	26,094,945
Jordan	0.01	23,920	Peru	0.06	143,510	United Arab Emirates	0.10	239,180
Kenya	0.01	23,920	Philippines	0.10	239,180	United Kingdom	4.38	10,476,250
Kuwait	0.20	478,365	Poland	1.22	2,918,040	United Republic of Cameroon	0.01	23,920
Lao People's Democratic Republic	0.01	23,920	Portugal	0.19	454,450	United Republic of Tanzania	0.01	23,920
Lebanon	0.03	71,755	Qatar	0.03	71,755	United States	25.00	63,794,950
Lesotho	0.01	23,920	Republic of Korea	0.15	358,775	Upper Volta	0.01	23,920
Liberia	0.01	23,920	Romania	0.20	478,365	Uruguay	0.04	95,670
Libyan Arab Jamahiriya	0.22	526,205	Rwanda	0.01	23,920	Venezuela	0.49	1,172,000
Luxembourg	0.05	119,590	Samoa	0.01	23,920	Viet Nam	0.03	71,755
Madagascar	0.01	23,920	San Marino	0.01	23,920	Yemen	0.01	23,920
Malawi	0.01	23,920	Sao Tome and Principe	0.01	23,920	Yugoslavia	0.41	980,650
Malaysia	0.09	215,265	Saudi Arabia	0.57	1,363,345	Zaire	0.02	47,835
Maldives	0.01	23,920	Senegal	0.01	23,920	Zambia	0.02	47,835
Mali	0.01	23,920	Seychelles	0.01	23,920	Zimbabwe	0.01	23,920
Malta	0.01	23,920	Sierra Leone	0.01	23,920			
Mauritania	0.01	23,920	Singapore	0.08	191,345	ASSOCIATE MEMBER		
Mauritius	0.01	23,920	Somalia	0.01	23,920	Namibia	0.01	23,920
Mexico	0.75	1,793,880	South Africa	0.41	980,650			
Monaco	0.01	23,920	Spain	1.67	3,994,370	Total	100.02	243,689,713
Mongolia	0.01	23,920	Sri Lanka	0.02	47,835			
			Sudan	0.01	23,920			

NOTE: Table includes contributions for countries which became members of WHO in 1981 and 1982. Their 1983 assessments were set by the thirty-fifth World Health Assembly on 11 May 1982.

*Adjusted to take into account the actual amounts paid to staff as reimbursement for taxes levied by member countries on the WHO emoluments of their nationals.

†Became a member on 8 March 1982.

‡Became a member on 13 August 1981.

Annex II.   OFFICERS AND OFFICES OF THE WORLD HEALTH ORGANIZATION
(As at 31 December 1982)

OFFICERS OF THE THIRTY-FIFTH WORLD HEALTH ASSEMBLY

President: M. Diop (Senegal).
Vice-Presidents: Dr. M. Calles (Mexico), Dr. N. Jogezai (Pakistan), L. von Manger-Koenig (Federal Republic of Germany), Dr. C. Nyamdorj (Mongolia), Dr A. Tarutia (Papua New Guinea).
Chairman, Committee A: A. M. Fadl (Sudan).
Chairman, Committee B: N. N. Vohra (India).

MEMBERS OF THE EXECUTIVE BOARD*

Chairman: Dr. Maureen M. Law (Canada)
Vice-Chairmen: Dr. D. Fuejo (Spain), M. M. Hussain (Maldives), Dr. A. H. Taweel (Iraq).
Rapporteurs: Dr. M. H. Abdulla (United Arab Emirates), Dr. S. J. Dias, (Guinea-Bissau).

Members were designated by: Brazil, Bulgaria, Chile, China, France, Gabon, Gambia, Guatemala, Japan, Kuwait, Malaysia, Mongolia, Morocco, Mozambique, Pakistan, Romania, Sao Tome and Principe, Seychelles, Trinidad and Tobago, USSR, United Kingdom, United States, Yemen, Zimbabwe.

*The Board consists of thirty persons designated by as many member States which have been elected for such purpose by WHO.

SENIOR OFFICERS OF THE SECRETARIAT

Director-General: Dr. Halfdan Mahler.

Deputy Director-General: Dr. T. A. Lambo.
Assistant Directors-General: Warren W. Furth, Dr. J. Hamon, Dr. S. K. Litvinov, Dr. Lu Rushan, Dr. David Tejada-de-Rivero.
Director, Regional Office for Africa: Dr. Comlan A. A. Quenum.

Director, Regional Office for the Americas (Pan American Sanitary Bureau): Dr. Héctor R. Acuña.
Director, Regional Office for South-East Asia: Dr. U Ko Ko.
Director, Regional Office for Europe: Dr. Leo A. Kaprio.
Director, Regional Office for the Eastern Mediterranean: Dr. Hussein A. Gezairy.
Director, Regional Office for the Western Pacific: Dr. Hiroshi Nakajima.

HEADQUARTERS AND OTHER OFFICES

HEADQUARTERS
World Health Organization
20 Avenue Appia
1211 Geneva 27, Switzerland
  Cable address: UNISANTE GENEVE
  Telephone: 91 21 11
  Telex: 27821

LIAISON OFFICE WITH THE
  UNITED NATIONS
World Health Organization
New York, N. Y. 10017, United States
  Cable address: UNISANTE NEWYORK
  Telephone: (212) 754-6004, 754-6005
  Telex: 234292

REGIONAL OFFICE FOR THE EASTERN
  MEDITERRANEAN
World Health Organization
P. O. Box 1517
Alexandria 21511, Egypt
  Cable address: UNISANTE ALEXANDRIA
  Telephone: 802318, 807843
  Telex: 54028

REGIONAL OFFICE FOR EUROPE
World Health Organization
8 Scherfigsvej
DK-2100 Copenhagen O, Denmark
  Cable address: UNISANTE COPENHAGEN
  Telephone: 29 01 11
  Telex: 15348

REGIONAL OFFICE FOR SOUTH-EAST ASIA
World Health Organization
World Health House
Indraprastha Estate, Mahatma Gandhi Road
New Delhi 110002, India
  Cable address: WHO NEWDELHI
  Telephone: 27 01 81 88
  Telex: 312241, 312195

REGIONAL OFFICE FOR AFRICA
World Health Organization
P. O. Box No. 6
Brazzaville, Congo
  Cable address: UNISANTE BRAZZAVILLE
  Telephone: 81 38 60-65
  Telex: 5217, 5278

REGIONAL OFFICE FOR THE WESTERN
  PACIFIC
World Health Organization
P. O. Box 2932
12115 Manila, Philippines
  Cable address: UNISANTE MANILA
  Telephone: 59 20 41, 59 37 21
  Telex: 27652, 40365, 63260

REGIONAL OFFICE FOR THE AMERICAS/
  PAN AMERICAN SANITARY BUREAU
World Health Organization
525 23rd Street, N. W.
Washington, D. C. 20037, United States
  Cable address: OFSANPAN WASHINGTON
  Telephone: (202) 861-3200
  Telex: 248338

Chapter VI

International Bank for Reconstruction and Development (World Bank)

The International Bank for Reconstruction and Development (World Bank) and its affiliate, the International Development Association (IDA), continued their efforts, during the fiscal year 1 July 1981 to 30 June 1982, to assist developing countries raise their standards of living by channelling financial resources to them from developed countries.

Lending commitments by the Bank, credit approvals from IDA, and investment commitments by another Bank affiliate, the International Finance Corporation (IFC), amounted to $13,628 million—up $526 million from the previous year.

Membership in the Bank rose to 144 during 1982, with the admission of Belize on 19 March, Hungary on 7 July and St. Vincent and the Grenadines on 30 August.

On 1 July 1981, A.W. Clausen became the sixth president of the World Bank.

Lending operations

In the fiscal year ending 30 June 1982, the World Bank made 150 loans amounting to $10,330 million to 43 countries, an increase of $1,521 million over fiscal 1981. This brought the cumulative

total of loan commitments by the Bank since its inception in 1946 to $78,480.3 million.

The table on the following pages summarizes World Bank lending in fiscal 1982 by area and by purpose.

Agriculture and rural development

The Bank continued its commitment to rural development, making 41 loans in fiscal 1982 amounting to $2,180.2 million in 24 countries. Efforts continued in support of projects directly benefiting the rural poor.

Mexico received $355 million, of which $180 million was for the development of irrigated agriculture on 280,000 hectares, benefiting 15,000 farm families. India received $210.3 million, of which $190 million was to strengthen agricultural credit institutions which help farmers invest in irrigation, land development, plantations and horticulture, livestock and fisheries.

Of $190.1 million lent to Indonesia, $70 million was for an irrigation project in East Java.

Other loans went for agricultural research and extension services, and projects in agro-industry, forestry, livestock, fisheries and various rural works programmes.

WORLD BANK LOANS APPROVED BY REGION/COUNTRY AND PURPOSE, 1 JULY 1981–30 JUNE 1982
(in millions of US dollars)

REGION/COUNTRY	Agriculture and rural development	Development finance companies	Education	Energy	Industry	Non-project	Population, health and nutrition	Small-scale enterprises	Technical assistance	Telecommunications	Transportation	Urbanization	Water supply and sewerage	Total
Eastern Africa														
Botswana	—	—	20.0	—	—	—	—	—	—	—	—	—	—	20.0
Kenya	21.5	—	—	4.0	—	—	—	—	—	44.7	—	—	—	70.2
Mauritius	—	6.0	—	—	—	—	—	—	—	—	—	—	—	6.0
Zambia	—	—	—	6.6	5.1	—	—	—	—	—	—	—	—	11.7
Subtotal	21.5	6.0	20.0	10.6	5.1	—	—	—	—	44.7	—	—	—	107.9
Western Africa														
Ivory Coast	13.0	—	—	101.5	—	150.0	—	—	16.0	—	—	51.0	43.0	374.5
Liberia	—	—	—	—	20.0	—	—	—	—	—	—	—	—	20.0
Nigeria	147.0	—	—	100.0	—	—	—	—	—	—	—	—	67.0	314.0
United Republic of Cameroon	67.8	—	—	—	—	—	—	—	—	7.5	70.0	—	—	145.3
Subtotal	227.8	—	—	201.5	20.0	150.0	—	—	16.0	7.5	70.0	51.0	110.0	853.8
East Asia and Pacific														
Indonesia	190.1	—	105.0	380.0	—	—	—	—	—	—	251.0	—	—	926.1
Malaysia	25.4	—	40.6	86.3	—	—	—	—	—	—	—	—	—	152.3
Papua New Guinea	6.0	—	—	—	—	—	—	—	—	—	—	—	—	6.0
Philippines	138.5	—	—	17.0	157.4	—	132.0	—	—	—	—	8.0	—	452.9
Republic of Korea	50.0	30.0	—	—	50.0	250.0	—	—	—	—	—	—	90.0	470.0
Thailand	142.0	—	75.0	90.0	—	150.0	—	—	—	142.1	35.0	—	—	634.1
Subtotal	552.0	30.0	220.6	573.3	207.4	400.0	—	132.0	—	142.1	286.0	8.0	90.0	2,641.4
South Asia														
India	210.3	150.0	—	604.5	300.0	—	—	—	—	—	—	—	—	1,264.8
Pakistan	—	—	—	—	38.5	60.0	—	—	—	40.0	—	—	—	138.5
Sri Lanka	—	—	—	42.7	—	—	—	—	—	—	—	—	—	42.7
Subtotal	210.3	150.0	—	647.2	338.5	60.0	—	—	—	40.0	—	—	—	1,446.0
Europe, the Middle East and North Africa														
Cyprus	—	—	—	—	—	—	—	—	—	—	12.2	—	—	12.2
Egypt	—	120.0	—	90.0	—	—	—	—	—	64.0	132.0	59.0	—	465.0
Jordan	—	—	25.0	35.0	—	—	—	—	—	—	—	—	—	60.0
Morocco	56.5	70.0	50.0	—	29.5	—	—	70.0	—	—	—	—	—	276.0
Oman	—	—	—	—	—	—	—	—	—	—	15.0	—	—	15.0
Portugal	51.0	—	—	—	30.0	—	—	—	—	—	—	—	—	81.0
Romania	95.0	—	—	101.5	—	—	—	—	—	—	125.0	—	—	321.5
Syrian Arab Republic	22.0	—	—	—	—	—	—	—	—	—	—	—	—	22.0
Tunisia	64.0	—	—	—	30.5	—	—	—	—	—	35.5	—	30.5	160.5
Turkey	40.0	100.0	—	—	44.1	304.5	—	—	—	—	71.1	—	88.1	647.8
Yugoslavia	149.6	66.0	—	—	—	—	—	—	—	—	—	—	41.0	256.6
Subtotal	478.1	356.0	75.0	226.5	134.1	304.5	—	70.0	—	64.0	390.8	59.0	159.6	2,317.6
Latin America and the Caribbean														
Argentina	—	100.0	—	100.0	200.0	—	—	—	—	—	—	—	—	400.0
Bahamas	—	—	—	—	—	—	—	—	—	—	—	5.8	—	5.8
Barbados	—	—	—	—	—	—	—	2.7	—	—	—	—	—	2.7
Brazil	162.5	—	—	182.7	—	—	13.0	—	—	—	240.0	123.9	—	722.1
Colombia	62.0	—	—	—	—	—	—	—	—	—	229.3	—	—	291.3
Dominican Republic	—	—	—	—	—	—	—	—	—	—	—	25.4	—	25.4
Ecuador	17.0	60.0	16.0	100.0	—	—	—	—	—	—	—	35.7	—	228.7

REGION/COUNTRY	Agriculture and rural development	Development finance companies	Education	Energy	Industry	Non-project	Population, health and nutrition	Small-scale enterprises	Technical assistance	Telecommunications	Transportation	Urbanization	Water supply and sewerage	Total
Latin America and the Caribbean (cont.)														
Honduras	—	30.0	—	—	—	—	—	—	—	—	—	—	—	30.0
Jamaica	—	13.5	6.8	30.5	—	76.2	—	—	6.1	—	—	—	—	133.1
Mexico	355.0	212.3	90.0	—	—	—	—	—	—	—	—	—	—	657.3
Nicaragua	—	—	—	—	—	—	—	—	—	—	—	16.0	—	16.0
Panama	—	—	—	—	—	—	—	—	—	—	24.4	—	—	24.4
Paraguay	53.4	—	—	—	—	—	—	—	—	—	46.0	—	—	99.4
Peru	40.6	—	—	81.2	5.3	—	—	26.0	—	—	93.0	—	40.6	286.7
Uruguay	—	—	—	—	—	—	—	—	—	40.0	—	—	—	40.0
Subtotal	690.5	415.8	112.8	494.4	205.3	76.2	13.0	26.0	8.8	40.0	632.7	206.8	40.6	2,962.9
Total	2,180.2	957.8	428.4	2,153.5	910.4	990.7	13.0	228.0	24.8	338.3	1,379.5	324.8	400.2	10,329.6
NUMBER OF LOANS	41	13	10	21	14	6	1	3	3	6	17	8	7	150

Development finance companies

The Bank made 13 loans in fiscal 1982 totalling $957.8 million to assist development finance companies in 12 countries. The largest borrowers were Mexico with two loans totalling $212.3 million for a capital goods industries development programme and for pollution-control investments, India ($150 million for industrial projects and the Industrial Credit and Investment Corporation of India), Egypt ($120 million to the Development Industrial Bank) and Argentina ($100 million for the Banco National de Desarrollo).

Education

During fiscal 1982, the Bank granted 10 loans totalling $428.4 million for education projects in nine countries. Indonesia received a total of $105 million, of which $80 million was for a teacher-training project to improve the effectiveness of educational staff in primary and secondary education. A $90 million loan to Mexico was for the construction or remodelling of 99 technical training centres to benefit 800 teachers and 20,000 skilled workers each year.

Other purposes for which loans were committed included projects to improve access to, and quality of, primary/secondary education, and construction of technical and vocational educational facilities.

Energy

Twenty-one projects in the energy field—oil, gas, coal and power—were assisted in 18 countries during fiscal 1982 at a total cost of $2,153.5 million.

Of two loans totalling $604.5 million made to India, one was for the expanding and improving rural electrification in about 14 States. Indonesia received loans totalling $380 million, of which $185 million was for the development of a three million tons-per-year coal mine and related infrastructure.

A $182.7 million loan was made to Brazil to finance five small or medium-sized state utility companies in the country's less-developed regions.

Other purposes for which loans were committed included energy resources evaluation or exploration, training and construction of facilities.

Industry

The Bank made 14 loans amounting to $910.4 million to 12 countries during the fiscal year. India received a total of $300 million, of which $200 million was to remedy the imbalance between domestic demand for, and supply of, petroleum products and to improve energy efficiency in the sector. Argentina received $200 million to improve conversion capacity at two major oil refineries and to improve plant operations and financial planning. A $157.4 million loan to the Philippines was for the physical rehabilitation and modernization of some textile factories and for technical assistance and training.

In other countries, loans were provided for improving the efficiency of various industries, including mining or refinery operations, research, technical assistance and training.

Non-project

Six non-project loans totalling $990.7 million were made to six countries in fiscal 1982. Turkey received $304.5 million for its stabilization and structural-adjustment programme for macro-economic liberalization, rationalized public investment and reformed state enterprises. A $250 million loan was made to the Republic of Korea to provide foreign exchange for essential imports, while $150 million each went to the Ivory Coast to improve economic management and planning, and to Thailand for programmes aimed at restoring a sustainable balance-of-payments position and maintaining the economic growth momentum.

In other countries, loans were committed for financing of high-priority imports and assisting other structural-adjustment programmes.

Population, health and nutrition

In fiscal 1982, Brazil received $13 million for a project forming part of an integrated development programme for its northwest region. It included a malaria-control programme, implementation of basic health infrastructure and services, and training and research.

Small-scale enterprises

Three loans totalling $228 million were granted to three nations for small-scale enterprises. The Philippines received $132 million to finance cottage, small- and medium-scale industries, develop financing institutions and expand a programme to assist that sector. Morocco received $70 million for relending—through the Banque Nationale pour le Développement Economique and local commercial banks—to about 600 small industries, thereby creating some 15,000 jobs. A $26 million loan was made to Peru to help finance the foreign-exchange cost of up to 1,500 sub-projects for small-scale enterprise development.

Technical assistance

Three countries received loans amounting to $24.8 million for technical assistance projects. The Ivory Coast received $16 million to strengthen its agricultural/industrial policy planning and project preparation, to devise a research strategy for the Ministry of Scientific Research, and to improve the management of eight public enterprises. A $6.1 million loan was made to Jamaica to develop local management capabilities in order to assist the government in implementing its structural-adjustment programme. Barbados received $2.7 million to help diversify and increase agricultural production as well as promote and implement an energy-conservation programme.

As in previous years, the Bank also served as executing agency for projects financed by the United Nations Development Programme (UNDP). Projects in progress at the end of fiscal 1982 stood at 132—down from 138 a year earlier—while 37 new projects involving commitments of $41.8 million were approved during the fiscal year.

Although the projects related to several sectors, energy was particularly prominent. Funding was approved for a $1.25 million project to test and demonstrate renewable energy technologies in several developing countries and UNDP agreed to co-finance the first of a series of power and energy-sector courses to be organized by the Bank's Economic Development Institute, for officials of Eu-

ropean, Middle Eastern and North African countries. In the Caribbean, the Bank was designated executing agency of a newly-established Caribbean Project Development Facility, with funds from UNDP and other sources. Further, the Bank was to head a mission to be established in Antigua—in the framework provided by UNDP—to assist seven less-developed Eastern Caribbean countries in economic management and investment rationalization.

Telecommunications

Six countries received six loans totalling $338.3 million for telecommunications projects in fiscal 1982. Thailand received $142.1 million towards expanding telephone facilities in Bangkok and the provinces, and extending service to about 330 additional rural communities. Kenya received $44.7 million to finance the highest-priority items on its Posts and Telecommunications Corporation's 1982-1986 development programme.

Other purposes for which loans were committed included improvement of domestic and international post and telecommunications services, and provision of technical assistance.

Transportation

Fourteen countries received 17 loans amounting to $1,379.5 million in fiscal 1982 to help develop their transportation systems.

Indonesia received three loans totalling $251 million, of which $100 million was for improving rural road infrastructure in selected provinces. Brazil received $240 million for a project—one of three forming an integrated development programme in the north-west region—that included the reconstruction of highways, construction of bridges, installation of traffic control equipment and technical assistance and staff training. Of two credits totalling $229.3 million given to Colombia, one of $152.3 million went to the government's highway development programme.

Other loans were for construction or improvement of highway and other road networks, railway systems and ports; technical assistance; and equipment and training.

Urbanization

Eight loans totalling $324.8 million were made to eight countries in fiscal 1982 to aid the urban poor.

Brazil received $123.9 million to benefit several low-income settlements and poor neighborhoods in the Recife metropolitan region, including installation of urban infrastructure and employment centres and provision of assistance to agencies responsible for project implementation. A $59 million loan to Egypt was to improve Cairo's public-transport system and strengthen institutional capabilities for urban planning. The Ivory Coast received $51 million to improve the standards of living for more than 1 million people by developing an urban-transport system in Abidjan and providing urban infrastructure, equipment, materials and technical assistance for two secondary cities.

Other loans also went for provision of basic infrastructure, and housing and community facilities to benefit residents in low-income urban areas.

Water supply and sewerage

The Bank made seven loans amounting to $400.2 million for water supply and sewerage projects in seven countries during fiscal 1982.

A $90 million loan made to the Republic of Korea was to improve water supply and sewerage services in five cities, benefiting 3.4 million people. Turkey received $88.1 million for improvement of sewage services and environmental conditions in Istanbul. Nigeria received $67 million to improve the water supply and sanitation system in Onitsha, providing 260,000 people with safe water for the first time. Peru received $40.6 million to extend water supply and sewerage systems to low-income areas, develop groundwater resources and strengthen the Lima Water and Sewerage Services, increasing its population coverage by some 900,000 people.

Loans to other countries also went for the improvement of their water supply and sewerage systems.

Economic Development Institute

The fiscal 1982 programme of the Economic Development Institute, designed to train senior officials of the Bank's member developing countries in economic management and investment, included nine courses and ten seminars at Washington, D.C. (United States) for 450 participants, and 29 regional and 26 national courses and seminars in other countries for 1,300 participants. Three courses held at Washington, D.C.—on urban finance, on regional development planning and on irrigation projects—were given for the first time.

In Africa the Institute co-sponsored four regional courses for French-speaking African countries, a regional seminar, a national seminar in Niger on rural development project management and several structural-adjustment policy seminars. In Asia, it co-sponsored 11 regional courses, a regional seminar and a series of national training activities in Bangladesh, China, India, Pakistan, Philippines and Thailand. Other regional courses and seminars co-sponsored by the Institute included: an agro-industrial project course in Tunisia for Middle East and North African countries, with the Arab Planning Institute;

a first course for Latin American countries on improving the urban habitat, held in Colombia, with the United Nations Centre for Human Settlements; and a regional seminar on water-supply and sanitation projects, with the Instituto Nacional de Fomento Municipal and the Universidad de los Andes.

During the fiscal year, requests for the Institute's training materials, such as case studies and course notes, increased by 10 per cent over the previous year, and approximately 45,000 items were distributed. The training materials were translated into French and Spanish, and some in Chinese; the Institute initiated an Arabic translation programme to benefit training institutions in the Middle East.

Financing activities

During fiscal 1982, the World Bank borrowed the equivalent of $8,520.5 million: $3,459 million in United States dollars; $1,565.4 in Swiss francs; $1,381.1 million in Japanese yen; $1,030.5 million in deutsche mark; $650.9 million in Netherlands guilders; and $310.5 million in pounds sterling. $1,500 million was accounted for by public offerings in the United States market from which the Bank had been absent since July 1977.

Of the 81 borrowing operations conducted by the Bank, 64 were public issues or private placements throughout the world and accounted for $6,535.5 million, or 77 per cent of total funds borrowed. The other 17 issues, totalling $1,966.9 million, or 23 per cent of the funds raised, were placed with official sources such as member Governments of the Bank, central banks and government institutions.

During fiscal 1982, the Bank executed, in markets outside the United States, its first US dollar/Swiss franc-linked bond issue, thus broadening the base of the Swiss franc market for its borrowings. The year was also marked by the Bank's first Eurokrone bond issue; the equivalent of $17.2 million was placed with non-residents of Norway by an international syndicate headed by Den Norske Creditbank.

As at 30 June 1982, the Bank's outstanding obligations amounted to $31,839.8 million, denominated in 18 different currencies placed with investors in over 100 countries. Estimates indicated that 20.7 per cent was held in the Federal Republic of Germany, 17.9 per cent in the United States, 15.6 per cent in Japan, 14.1 per cent in Switzerland, 13.6 per cent by countries belonging to the Organization of Petroleum Exporting Countries, and the remaining 18.1 per cent in other countries.

Capitalization

In the Bank's Articles of Agreement, the institution's capital stock is expressed in terms of 1944 dollars—the United States dollar of the weight and fineness in effect on 1 July 1944. On 1 April 1978, when the Second Amendment of the Articles of Agreement of the International Monetary Fund (IMF) became effective, currencies no longer had par values, and the basis for translating the 1944 dollar into current United States dollars no longer existed.

Thus, for the fiscal year ended 30 June 1982, the value of the Bank's capital stock was expressed on the basis of special drawing rights (SDRs) in terms of the United States dollar as computed by IMF on 30 June. On that date, the value of the SDR was set at $1.09224.

The subscribed capital of the Bank, as at 30 June, totalled SDR 39,519.4 million.

Income, expenditures and reserves

The Bank's gross revenues, generated primarily from its loans and investments, increased by $373 million in fiscal 1982 to a total of $3,372 million. Net income was $598 million, down $12 million from the previous fiscal year.

Total expenses amounted to $2,775 million, up 16.2 per cent from fiscal 1981. Administrative costs totalled $290 million, up $35 million.

The General Reserve of the Bank amounted to $2,831 million at the end of fiscal 1982.

STATEMENT OF INCOME AND EXPENSES
(for the fiscal year ended 30 June 1982)

	Amount (in thousands of US dollars)
Income	
Income from investments*	954,463
Income from loans	
Interest	2,160,688
Commitment charges	191,579
Front-end fees†	39,079
Other income‡	26,510
Total income	3,372,319
Expenses	
Administrative expenses§	290,060
Interest on borrowings	2,456,074
Bond issuance and other financial expenses	5,833
Contributions to special programmes	22,700
Total expenses	2,774,667
Net income	597,652

*Includes net losses of $102,228,000 resulting from sales of investments.
†For loans negotiated after 5 January 1982, a fee of 1 1/2 per cent of the principal amount of the loan is payable when the loan becomes effective.
‡Includes net gains of $24,021,000 resulting from repurchases of obligations of the Bank prior to maturity pursuant to the terms of the respective borrowing agreements.
§All administrative expenses of the Bank and IDA and a portion of those of the International Finance Corporation (IFC) are paid by the Bank. The administrative expenses are net of a management fee of $193 million charged to IDA and of a service and support fee of $3,844,000 charged to IFC.

Secretariat

As at 30 June 1982, the staff of the World Bank numbered over 5,000, of which 2,689 were in Professional or higher categories, drawn from 104 nationalities.

Annex I. MEMBERS OF THE WORLD BANK, SUBSCRIPTIONS AND VOTING POWER

(As at 30 June 1982)

	SUBSCRIPTION		VOTING POWER			SUBSCRIPTION		VOTING POWER	
MEMBER	Amount (in SDRs)	Percentage of total	Number of votes	Percentage of total	MEMBER	Amount (in SDRs)	Percentage of total	Number of votes	Percentage of total
Afghanistan	30,000	0.08	550	0.13	Cyprus	27,800	0.07	528	0.12
Algeria*	110,900	0.28	1,359	0.32	Democratic Kampuchea	21,400	0.05	464	0.11
Argentina	470,100	1.19	4,951	1.15	Democratic Yemen	24,800	0.06	498	0.12
Australia*	645,000	1.63	6,700	1.56	Denmark	513,600	1.30	5,386	1.25
Austria	521,900	1.32	5,469	1.27	Djibouti	3,100	0.01	281	0.07
Bahamas	17,100	0.04	421	0.10	Dominica	1,600	†	266	0.06
Bahrain	56,600	0.14	816	0.19	Dominican Republic	58,900	0.15	839	0.19
Bangladesh*	124,200	0.31	1,492	0.35	Ecuador	36,800	0.09	618	0.14
Barbados	13,900	0.04	389	0.09	Egypt	165,000	0.42	1,900	0.44
Belgium	726,800	1.84	7,518	1.75	El Salvador	12,000	0.03	370	0.09
Belize	3,900	0.01	289	0.07	Equatorial Guinea	6,400	0.02	314	0.07
Benin	10,000	0.03	350	0.08	Ethiopia	11,400	0.03	364	0.08
Bhutan	900	†	259	0.06	Fiji	14,700	0.04	397	0.09
Bolivia	26,400	0.07	514	0.12	Finland	247,400	0.63	2,724	0.63
Botswana	4,300	0.01	293	0.07	France	1,756,700	4.45	17,817	4.14
Brazil	1,070,600	2.71	10,956	2.54	Gabon	12,000	0.03	370	0.09
Burma*	59,100	0.15	841	0.20	Gambia	5,300	0.01	303	0.07
Burundi	15,000	0.04	400	0.09	Germany, Federal Republic of	1,761,200	4.46	17,862	4.15
Canada	1,112,200	2.81	11,372	2.64	Ghana	85,600	0.22	1,106	0.26
Cape Verde	1,600	†	266	0.06	Greece	94,500	0.24	1,195	0.28
Central African Republic	10,000	0.03	350	0.08	Grenada	1,700	†	267	0.06
Chad	10,000	0.03	350	0.08	Guatemala	16,700	0.04	417	0.10
Chile	124,000	0.31	1,490	0.35	Guinea	20,000	0.05	450	0.10
China	1,200,000	3.04	12,250	2.84	Guinea-Bissau	2,700	0.01	277	0.06
Colombia	117,500	0.30	1,425	0.33	Guyana*	17,100	0.04	421	0.10
Comoros	1,600	†	266	0.06	Haiti	15,000	0.04	400	0.09
Congo	10,000	0.03	350	0.08	Honduras	8,400	0.02	334	0.08
Costa Rica	13,100	0.03	381	0.09	Iceland	22,200	0.06	472	0.11

MEMBER	SUBSCRIPTION Amount (in SDRs)	Percentage of total	VOTING POWER Number of votes	Percentage of total	MEMBER	SUBSCRIPTION Amount (in SDRs)	Percentage of total	VOTING POWER Number of votes	Percentage of total
India	2,263,300	5.73	22,883	5.31	Republic of Korea	294,700	0.75	3,197	0.74
Indonesia	388,800	0.98	4,138	0.96	Romania	162,100	0.41	1,871	0.43
Iran	158,000	0.40	1,830	0.42	Rwanda*	15,000	0.04	400	0.09
Iraq	69,800	0.18	948	0.22	Saint Lucia	2,900	0.01	279	0.06
Ireland	126,600	0.32	1,516	0.35	Samoa	1,700	†	267	0.06
Israel	110,800	0.28	1,358	0.32	Sao Tome and Principe	1,400	†	264	0.06
Italy	1,959,200	4.96	19,842	4.61	Saudi Arabia	489,900	1.24	5,149	1.20
Ivory Coast*	43,800	0.11	688	0.16	Senegal	36,200	0.09	612	0.14
Jamaica	44,600	0.11	696	0.16	Seychelles	1,100	†	261	0.06
Japan	3,420,600	8.66	34,456	8.00	Sierra Leone	15,000	0.04	400	0.09
Jordan*	18,700	0.05	437	0.10	Singapore	32,000	0.08	570	0.13
Kenya*	40,000	0.10	650	0.15	Solomon Islands*	1,700	†	267	0.06
Kuwait	320,300	0.81	3,453	0.80	Somalia	18,900	0.05	439	0.10
Lao People's Democratic Republic	10,000	0.03	350	0.08	South Africa	346,300	0.88	3,713	0.86
Lebanon	9,000	0.02	340	0.08	Spain	455,100	1.15	4,801	1.11
Lesotho*	4,300	0.01	293	0.07	Sri Lanka*	96,100	0.24	1,211	0.28
Liberia	21,300	0.05	463	0.11	Sudan	60,000	0.15	850	0.20
Libyan Arab Jamahiriya	158,700	0.40	1,837	0.43	Suriname	16,200	0.04	412	0.10
Luxembourg	65,800	0.17	908	0.21	Swaziland*	6,800	0.02	318	0.07
Madagascar	21,900	0.06	469	0.11	Sweden	736,700	1.86	7,617	1.77
Malawi*	15,000	0.04	400	0.09	Syrian Arab Republic	50,800	0.13	758	0.18
Malaysia	206,600	0.52	2,316	0.54	Thailand	147,800	0.37	1,728	0.40
Maldives	600	†	256	0.06	Togo	15,000	0.04	400	0.09
Mali	17,300	0.04	423	0.10	Trinidad and Tobago	53,500	0.14	785	0.18
Mauritania	10,000	0.03	350	0.08	Tunisia	37,300	0.09	623	0.14
Mauritius	22,100	0.06	471	0.11	Turkey	340,800	0.86	3,658	0.85
Mexico	315,600	0.80	3,406	0.79	Uganda	33,300	0.08	583	0.14
Morocco	122,000	0.31	1,470	0.34	United Arab Emirates	98,000	0.25	1,230	0.29
Nepal	14,600	0.04	396	0.09	United Kingdom	2,600,000	6.58	26,250	6.09
Netherlands	767,900	1.94	7,929	1.84	United Republic of Cameroon	20,000	0.05	450	0.10
New Zealand	243,100	0.62	2,681	0.62	United Republic of Tanzania*	35,000	0.09	600	0.14
Nicaragua	9,100	0.02	341	0.08	United States	8,850,900	22.40	88,759	20.61
Niger	10,000	0.03	350	0.08	Upper Volta	10,000	0.03	350	0.08
Nigeria	294,100	0.74	3,191	0.74	Uruguay	41,100	0.10	661	0.15
Norway	241,000	0.61	2,660	0.62	Vanuatu	3,800	.01	288	0.07
Oman	19,200	0.05	442	0.10	Venezuela	197,200	0.50	2,222	0.52
Pakistan	251,900	0.64	2,769	0.64	Viet Nam	54,300	0.14	793	0.18
Panama	21,600	0.05	466	0.11	Yemen	10,600	0.03	356	0.08
Papua New Guinea	24,600	0.06	496	0.12	Yugoslavia*	117,800	0.30	1,428	0.33
Paraguay*	7,000	0.02	320	0.07	Zaire	96,000	0.24	1,210	0.28
Peru	93,800	0.24	1,188	0.28	Zambia*	64,800	0.16	898	0.21
Philippines	171,500	0.43	1,965	0.46	Zimbabwe	81,700	0.21	1,067	0.25
Portugal	132,400	0.34	1,574	0.37					
Qatar	32,700	0.08	577	0.13	Total	39,519,400	100.00‡	430,694	100.00§

NOTE: Belize became a member on 19 March 1982.

*Amounts aggregating the equivalent of $65,152,000 in current United States dollars had been received from members on account of increases in subscriptions, which were in process of completion: Algeria $3,440,000, Australia $47,985,000, Bangladesh $211,000, Burma $951,000, Guyana $1,737,000, Ivory Coast $176,000, Jordan $498,000, Kenya $1,192,000, Lesotho $566,000, Malawi $228,000, Paraguay $597,000, Rwanda $1,765,000, Solomon Islands $140,000, Sri Lanka $2,047,000, Swaziland $932,000, United Republic of Tanzania $130,000, Yugoslavia $1,781,000 and Zambia $776,000.

†Less than 0.005 per cent.

‡May differ from the sum of the individual percentages because of rounding.

Annex II. EXECUTIVE DIRECTORS AND ALTERNATES OF THE WORLD BANK
(As at 30 June 1982)

Appointed Director	Appointed Alternate	Casting the vote of
Vacant*	Vacant	United States
John Anson	Derek F. Smith	United Kingdom
Reinhard Münzberg	Norbert Schmidt-Gerritzen	Germany, Federal Republic of
Bruno de Maulde	Robert Hudry	France
Kenji Yamaguchi	Kimiaki Nakajima†	Japan

Elected Director	Elected Alternate	Casting the votes of
Said E. El-Naggar (Egypt)	Abdulrahman A. Sehaibani (Saudi Arabia)	Bahrain, Egypt, Iraq, Jordan, Kuwait, Lebanon, Maldives, Pakistan, Qatar, Saudi Arabia, Syrian Arab Republic, United Arab Emirates, Yemen
Earl G. Drake (Canada)	Reno J. Brown (Bahamas)	Bahamas, Barbados, Canada, Dominica, Grenada, Guyana, Ireland, Jamaica, Saint Lucia
H. N. Ray (India)	M. Syeduz-Zaman (Bangladesh)	Bangladesh, India, Sri Lanka
Giorgio Ragazzi (Italy)	Rodrigo M. Guimarães (Portugal)	Greece, Italy, Portugal
Anthony IJ. A. Looijen (Netherlands)	Miodrag M. Stojiljkovic (Yugoslavia)	Cyprus, Israel, Netherlands, Romania, Yugoslavia

Elected Director	Elected Alternate	Casting the votes of
Jacques de Groote (Belgium)	Turan S. Kivanç (Turkey)	Austria, Belgium, Luxembourg, Turkey
Joaquín Muns (Spain)	Roberto Mayorga-Cortés (Nicaragua)	Costa Rica, El Salvador, Guatemala, Honduras, Mexico, Nicaragua, Panama, Spain, Suriname, Venezuela
Wang Liansheng (China)	Chen Hui (China)	China
Hans Lundström (Sweden)	Ole L. Poulsen (Denmark)	Denmark, Finland, Iceland, Norway, Sweden
Zain Azraai (Malaysia)	Aung Pe (Burma)	Burma, Fiji, Indonesia, Lao People's Democratic Republic, Malaysia, Nepal, Singapore, Thailand, Viet Nam
S. A. McLeod (New Zealand)	Anthony S. Cole (Australia)	Australia, New Zealand, Papua New Guinea, Republic of Korea, Samoa, Solomon Islands
Y. S. M. Abdulai (Nigeria)	William Smith (Liberia)	Botswana, Burundi, Equatorial Guinea, Ethiopia, Gambia, Guinea, Kenya, Lesotho, Liberia, Malawi, Nigeria, Seychelles, Sierra Leone, Sudan, Swaziland, Trinidad and Tobago, Uganda, United Republic of Tanzania, Zambia, Zimbabwe
Jaime García-Parra (Colombia)	José-Germán Cárdenas (Ecuador)	Brazil, Colombia, Dominican Republic, Ecuador, Haiti, Philippines
Armand Razafindrabe (Madagascar)	Nicéphore Soglo (Benin)	Benin, Cape Verde, Central African Republic, Chad, Comoros, Congo, Djibouti, Gabon, Guinea-Bissau, Ivory Coast, Madagascar, Mali, Mauritania, Mauritius, Niger, Rwanda, Sao Tome and Principe, Senegal, Somalia, Togo, United Republic of Cameroon, Upper Volta, Zaire
David Blanco (Bolivia)	Alberto Sola (Argentina)	Argentina, Bolivia, Chile, Paraguay, Peru, Uruguay
Ismail Khelil (Tunisia)	Saad M. Zerhouni (Algeria)	Afghanistan, Algeria, Democratic Yemen, Ghana, Iran, Libyan Arab Jamahiriya, Morocco, Oman, Tunisia

NOTE: Democratic Kampuchea and South Africa did not participate in the 1980 regular election of Executive Directors. Belize, Bhutan and Vanuatu became members after that election.

*James B. Burnham was appointed by the United States as its Director effective 2 July.

†Resigned effective 13 July; succeeded by Toshihiro Yamakawa.

Annex III. PRINCIPAL OFFICERS AND OFFICES OF THE WORLD BANK

(As at 1 July 1982)

PRINCIPAL OFFICERS*

President: A. W. Clausen.
Senior Vice-President, Finance: Moeen A. Qureshi.
Senior Vice-President, Operations: Ernest Stern.
Regional Vice-President, Latin America and the Caribbean: Nicolás Ardito Barletta.
Vice-President, Operations Policy: Warren C. Baum.
Vice-President, External Relations: Munir P. Benjenk.
Regional Vice-President, Europe, Middle East and North Africa: Roger Chaufournier.
Vice-President, Economics and Research: Hollis B. Chenery.
Vice-President, Programming and Budgeting, and Vice-President, Pension Fund: K. Georg Gabriel.

Vice-President and General Counsel: Heribert Golsong.
Vice-President and Controller: Masaya Hattori.
Regional Vice-President, South Asia: W. David Hopper.
Regional Vice-President, East Asia and Pacific: S. Shahid Husain.
Regional Vice-President, Western Africa: A. David Knox.
Vice-President, Personnel and Administration: Martijn J. W. M. Paijmans.
Vice-President and Treasurer: Eugene H. Rotberg.
Vice-President and Secretary: Timothy T. Thahane.
Regional Vice-President, Eastern Africa: Willi A. Wapenhans.
Director-General, Operations Evaluation: Mervyn L. Weiner.

*The World Bank and IDA had the same officers and staff.

HEADQUARTERS AND OTHER OFFICES

HEADQUARTERS
The World Bank
1818 H Street, N. W.
Washington, D. C. 20433, United States
Cable address: INTBAFRAD WASHINGTONDC
Telephone: (202) 477-1234
Telex: RCA 248423 WORLDBK,
WUI 64145 WORLDBANK

NEW YORK OFFICE
The World Bank Mission to the United Nations
747 Third Avenue, 26th floor
New York, N. Y. 10017, United States
Cable address: INTBAFRAD NEWYORK
Telephone: (212) 754-6008

REGIONAL MISSION IN EASTERN AFRICA
The World Bank
Reinsurance Plaza, 5th and 6th floors
Taifa Road
(P. O. Box 30577)
Nairobi, Kenya
Cable address: INTBAFRAD NAIROBI
Telephone: 24391
Telex: 22022

EUROPEAN OFFICE
The World Bank
66 Avenue d'Iéna
75116 Paris, France
Cable address: INTBAFRAD PARIS
Telephone: (1) 723-54-21
Telex: 620628

LONDON OFFICE
The World Bank
New Zealand House, 15th floor
Haymarket
London SW1 Y4TE, England
Cable address: INTBAFRAD LONDON
Telephone: (01) 930-3886
Telex: 919462

REGIONAL MISSION IN WESTERN AFRICA
The World Bank
Immeuble Shell, 64 Aveue Lamblin
(Boîte Postale 1850)
Abidjan 01, Ivory Coast
Cable address: INTBAFRAD ABIDJAN
Telephone: 32-24-01, 32-42-40
Telex: 3533

GENEVA OFFICE
The World Bank
ITC Building
54 Rue de Montbrillant
(P. O. Box 104)
1211 Geneva 20 CIC, Switzerland
Telephone: 33 21 20
Telex: 28883

TOKYO OFFICE
The World Bank
Kokusai Building, Room 916
1-1 Marunouchi 3-chome, Chiyoda-ku
Tokyo 100, Japan
Cable address: INTBAFRAD TOKYO
Telephone: (03) 214-5001, 5002
Telex: 26838

REGIONAL MISSION IN THAILAND
The World Bank
Udom Vidhya Building, 956 Rama IV Road
Sala Daeng
Bangkok 5, Thailand
Cable address: INTBAFRAD BANGKOK
Telephone: 235-9115-9
Telex: 82817

Chapter VII

International Finance Corporation (IFC)

The International Finance Corporation (IFC) was established in 1956 as an affiliate of the International Bank for Reconstruction and Development (World Bank) to assist developing member countries by helping them to promote the private sector of their economies. The principal objectives of IFC are: to provide risk capital for productive private enterprise, in association with private investors and management; to encourage the development of local capital markets; and to stimulate the international flow of private capital.

In the fiscal year ending on 30 June 1982, the IFC Board of Directors approved 65 projects with an equity and loan commitment value of about $612 million, as compared with 56 projects valued at $810 million in 1981; few larger projects were undertaken in fiscal 1982 due to the unattractive investment climate in many developing countries. Operating income for fiscal 1982 was $126.5 million, an increase of $26.2 million over 1981. Net income was $21.6 million, compared with the previous year's $19.5 million. Syndications, in which IFC was joined in financing projects by commercial banks and other financial institutions, reached $187.6 million, which was lower than the previous year's $374.4 million due to fewer large projects suitable for syndication. The Corporation signed participation agreements during the year with 30 financial institutions.

The total cost of approved investment was about $2,900 million—of which IFC provided $612 million—as compared with $3,300 for 1981. Fifty-one per cent of project financing was raised from domestic sources. Suppliers' credits or government funding made up most of the funds from foreign sources. Of the $279.4 million provided by foreign commercial banks, over 67 per cent was raised through syndication of IFC loans.

Of the total approvals, some $580 million was for loans, including a $12.5 million subordinated loan, and about $32 million in the form of equity, invested in 39 ventures. Four stand-by loans and underwritings were also approved.

Reflecting the Corporation's efforts to diversify its activities, manufacturing sector investments were below 50 per cent of the total, while agribusiness investments continued to increase, receiving about $392 million for 13 projects in 1982. Investments in new types of businesses included $30.5 million in loan and equity to an agricultural equipment leasing company in Brazil, $16 million for

a rehabilitation hospital in Yugoslavia, $1.6 million for a cold storage plant in Colombia, $300,000 for a petroleum promotion company in Sudan and some $710,000 for a company commercializing technical research and development in the Republic of Korea. Among the 65 businesses funded were seven cement plants, five leasing companies, five pulp and paper mills and five mining operations.

Projects were located in 31 countries; in five of them (Cyprus, Mali, Nepal, Niger and Tunisia), IFC either had not undertaken investments during the previous three years or it did so for the first time. About half of the 1982 investments were in countries with a per capita income of less than $760 per year, a reflection of the Corporation's increasing emphasis on smaller, low-income countries. Eighteen investments were in Africa, 16 in Asia, 21 in Latin America and the Caribbean and 10 in the Middle East and Europe.

IFC membership rose to 122, following the admission of Belize and Saint Lucia.

TOTAL IFC COMMITMENTS BY TYPE OF BUSINESS
(as at 30 June 1982)

Sector	Amount *(in millions of US dollars)*
Cement and construction materials	807.2
Mining	448.0
General manufacturing	400.5
Iron and steel	357.7
Pulp and paper products	318.4
Chemicals and petrochemicals	311.6
Textiles and fibres	282.1
Motor vehicles and accessories	216.5
Development financing	215.4
Food and food processing	207.6
Fertilizer	196.8
Money and capital markets	185.0
Tourism	119.2
Non-ferrous metals	46.9
Utilities	36.0
Machinery	33.5
Others	35.5

IFC INVESTMENTS
(1 July 1981—30 June 1982)

Recipient	Sector	Amount *(in thousands of US dollars)*
Argentina	Chemicals and petrochemicals	10,000
Brazil	Pulp and paper products	61,000
	Cement and construction materials	45,000
	Fertilizer	45,000
	Money and capital markets	31,450
	Food products	22,100
	Motor vehicles and accessories	2,000
Chile	Mining	10,000
	Money and capital markets	200

Recipient	Sector	Amount (in thousands of US dollars)
Colombia	Mining	12,540
	Food and food processing	1,600
	Chemicals and petrochemicals	440
Congo	Pulp and paper	200
Cyprus	Tourism	2,290
	Money and capital markets	230
Ecuador	Money and capital markets	9,200
	Development financing	80
	Cement and construction materials	60
Egypt	Food and food processing	9,910
	Ceramics	2,300
India	Motor vehicles and accessories	28,000
	Cement and construction materials	25,190
	Chemical and petrochemicals	19,100
	Iron and steel	16,900
Indonesia	Money and capital markets	4,300
Jamaica	Food and food processing	11,400
Jordan	Fertilizer	10,250
Kenya	Cement and construction materials	5,000
	Pulp and paper products	2,640
	Money and capital markets	1,840
Malawi	Textiles and fibres	4,970
	Chemicals and petrochemicals	550
Mali	Food and food processing	2,610
Mexico	Food and food processing	10,500
Morocco	Cement and construction materials	2,250
Nepal	Mining	6,230
Niger	Food and food processing	2,550
Pakistan	Pulp and paper products	15,630
	Cement and construction materials	3,950
	Chemicals and petrochemicals	230
Paraguay	Food and food processing	7,000
	Tourism	3,380
Peru	Food and food processing	15,000
	Money and capital markets	3,150
Philippines	Food and food processing	11,000
	Money and capital markets	10,000
Republic of Korea	Money and capital markets	1,720
Sri Lanka	Tourism	2,000
Sudan	Chemicals and petrochemicals	300
Tunisia	Tourism	40,000
Turkey	Motor vehicles and accessories	10,340
	Food and food processing	2,500
	Glass manufacturing	1,130
	Development financing	610
	Pulp and paper products	170
United Republic of Cameroon	Food and food processing	1,500
Yugoslavia	Health services	16,000
	Motor vehicles and accessories	12,000
Zambia	Mining	30,000
	Chemicals and petrochemicals	4,350
Total		611,840

Financial operations

The Corporation's total operating income in fiscal year 1982 was $126.5 million, including $98.2 million in interest from loan and equity investments and $12.5 million in dividend income. Gains realized on equity sales amounted to $5.9 million as compared with $1.9 million for the previous year. After administrative expenses and financial charges on borrowings of $82.5 million, income from operations amounted to $44 million. Net income was $21.6 million compared with $19.5 million for the previous year.

STATEMENT OF INCOME AND EXPENDITURE
(for fiscal year ending 30 June 1982)

	Amount (in US dollars)
Income	
Income from obligations of Governments	3,602,189
Income from loan and equity investments and underwriting commitments:	
Interest	98,189,076
Dividends and profit participations	12,513,818
Commitment charges	4,791,422
Realized gain on equity sales	5,926,239
Commissions	1,229,582
Other operating income	272,473
Total income	126,524,799
Expenditure	
Charges on borrowings	43,296,596
Administrative expenses*	39,254,654
Total expenditure	82,551,250
Income from operations	43,973,549
Provision for losses	(22,400,000)
Net income—transferred to accumulated earnings	21,573,549

*The World Bank charges IFC an annual service and support fee which for the year ending 30 June 1982 was fixed at $3,344,000.

Capital and reserves

The terminal payment date for subscriptions to IFC's capital increase—approved by its Board of Governors in November 1977—was 1 August 1982. Of the $468.8 million allocated to 106 member States, $412.5 million (88 per cent) had been subscribed by 80 countries. Payments of $105.3 million for subscribed shares were received during the year.

At the end of the year, total Capital and General Reserve of IFC amounted to $678.1 million, up from $551.3 million at the end of fiscal 1981. Accumulated earnings amounted to $180.7 million, including the $21.6 million net income. Reserve against losses was increased to $84 million, largely due to a provision for losses of $22.4 million charged to 1982 income.

Technical assistance

The Corporation continued to focus its technical assistance efforts in developing capital markets. In fiscal 1982, assistance was provided in 14 countries, including advice on stimulating securities markets and on leasing regulations. It also assisted Egypt in its ongoing efforts to revise the financial system, worked with a Kenyan bank to strengthen its project appraisal/supervision and business advisory services, advised Korean authorities on access to international securities markets, and assisted a Sri Lankan bank to improve its medium-scale enterprises credit facility and business advisory services.

In other activities, IFC participated in World Bank financial sector reviews for Nigeria and Thailand, and prepared seven studies on topics in developing capital markets.

Secretariat

As at 30 June 1982, IFC staff numbered 406, drawn from 64 nationalities.

Annex I. MEMBERS OF THE INTERNATIONAL FINANCE CORPORATION, SUBSCRIPTIONS AND VOTING POWER

(As at 30 June 1982)

MEMBER	SUBSCRIPTION Amount (in thousands of US dollars)	SUBSCRIPTION Percentage of total	VOTING POWER Number of votes	VOTING POWER Percentage of total	MEMBER	SUBSCRIPTION Amount (in thousands of US dollars)	SUBSCRIPTION Percentage of total	VOTING POWER Number of votes	VOTING POWER Percentage of total
Afghanistan	111	0.02	361	0.07	Malaysia	3,921	0.79	4,171	0.79
Argentina	8,190	1.65	8,440	1.60	Mali	116	0.02	366	0.07
Australia	10,195	2.05	10,445	1.98	Mauritania	55	0.01	305	0.06
Austria	4,179	0.84	4,429	0.84	Mauritius	363	0.07	613	0.12
Bangladesh	2,005	0.40	2,255	0.43	Mexico	6,004	1.21	6,254	1.18
Barbados	93	0.02	343	0.06	Morocco	1,940	0.39	2,190	0.41
Belgium	13,723	2.76	13,973	2.65	Nepal	256	0.05	506	0.10
Belize	26	0.01	276	0.05	Netherlands	12,176	2.45	12,426	2.35
Bolivia	407	0.08	657	0.12	New Zealand	923	0.19	1,173	0.22
Botswana	29	0.01	279	0.05	Nicaragua	149	0.03	399	0.08
Brazil	8,367	1.68	8,617	1.63	Niger	67	0.01	317	0.06
Burma	666	0.13	916	0.17	Nigeria	5,575	1.12	5,825	1.10
Burundi	100	0.02	350	0.07	Norway	4,533	0.91	4,783	0.91
Canada	20,952	4.21	21,202	4.02	Oman	252	0.05	502	0.10
Chile	1,940	0.39	2,190	0.41	Pakistan	4,411	0.89	4,661	0.88
China	4,154	0.84	4,404	0.83	Panama	344	0.07	594	0.11
Colombia	1,744	0.35	1,994	0.38	Papua New Guinea	490	0.10	740	0.14
Congo	67	0.01	317	0.06	Paraguay	123	0.02	373	0.07
Costa Rica	245	0.05	495	0.09	Peru	1,461	0.29	1,711	0.32
Cyprus	457	0.09	707	0.13	Philippines	3,247	0.65	3,497	0.66
Denmark	4,779	0.96	5,029	0.95	Portugal	2,144	0.43	2,394	0.45
Djibouti	21	*	271	0.05	Republic of Korea	2,450	0.49	2,700	0.51
Dominica	11	*	261	0.05	Rwanda	265	0.05	515	0.10
Dominican Republic	306	0.06	556	0.11	Saint Lucia	19	*	269	0.05
Ecuador	674	0.14	924	0.18	Samoa	9	*	259	0.05
Egypt	3,124	0.63	3,374	0.64	Saudi Arabia	9,251	1.86	9,501	1.80
El Salvador	11	*	261	0.05	Senegal	184	0.04	434	0.08
Ethiopia	33	0.01	283	0.05	Seychelles	7	*	257	0.05
Fiji	74	0.01	324	0.06	Sierra Leone	83	0.02	333	0.06
Finland	3,319	0.67	3,569	0.68	Singapore	177	0.04	427	0.08
France	20,579	4.14	20,829	3.95	Solomon Islands	11	*	261	0.05
Gabon	55	0.01	305	0.06	Somalia	83	0.02	333	0.06
Germany, Federal Republic of	33,204	6.68	33,454	6.34	South Africa	3,108	0.63	3,358	0.64
Ghana	1,306	0.26	1,556	0.29	Spain	5,025	1.01	5,275	1.00
Greece	1,477	0.30	1,727	0.33	Sri Lanka	1,838	0.37	2,088	0.40
Grenada	21	*	271	0.05	Sudan	111	0.02	361	0.07
Guatemala	306	0.06	556	0.11	Swaziland	184	0.04	434	0.08
Guinea-Bissau	18	*	268	0.05	Sweden	1,108	0.22	1,358	0.26
Guyana	368	0.07	618	0.12	Syrian Arab Republic	72	0.01	322	0.06
Haiti	306	0.06	556	0.11	Thailand	2,818	0.57	3,068	0.58
Honduras	149	0.03	399	0.08	Togo	368	0.07	618	0.12
Iceland	11	*	261	0.05	Trinidad and Tobago	1,059	0.21	1,309	0.25
India	16,717	3.36	16,967	3.21	Tunisia	133	0.03	383	0.07
Indonesia	7,351	1.48	7,601	1.44	Turkey	3,063	0.62	3,313	0.63
Iran	372	0.07	622	0.12	Uganda	184	0.04	434	0.08
Iraq	67	0.01	317	0.06	United Arab Emirates	1,838	0.37	2,088	0.40
Ireland	332	0.07	582	0.11	United Kingdom	37,900	7.62	38,150	7.23
Israel	450	0.09	700	0.13	United Republic of Cameroon	414	0.08	664	0.13
Italy	15,689	3.16	15,939	3.02	United Republic of Tanzania	724	0.15	974	0.18
Ivory Coast	459	0.09	709	0.13	United States	146,661	29.49	146,911	27.84
Jamaica	1,103	0.22	1,353	0.26	Upper Volta	167	0.03	417	0.08
Japan	25,546	5.14	25,796	4.89	Uruguay	919	0.18	1,169	0.22
Jordan	350	0.07	600	0.11	Vanuatu	25	0.01	275	0.05
Kenya	1,041	0.21	1,291	0.24	Venezuela	116	0.02	366	0.07
Kuwait	3,700	0.74	3,950	0.75	Viet Nam	166	0.03	416	0.08
Lebanon	50	0.01	300	0.06	Yemen	184	0.04	434	0.08
Lesotho	18	*	268	0.05	Yugoslavia	2,422	0.49	2,672	0.51
Liberia	83	0.02	333	0.06	Zaire	1,530	0.31	1,780	0.34
Libyan Arab Jamahiriya	55	0.01	305	0.06	Zambia	1,286	0.26	1,536	0.29
Luxembourg	551	0.11	801	0.15	Zimbabwe	546	0.11	796	0.15
Madagascar	111	0.02	361	0.07					
Malawi	368	0.07	618	0.12	Total	497,273	100.00†	527,773	100.00†

*Less than 0.005 per cent.

†May differ from the sum of the individual percentages because of rounding.

Annex II. DIRECTORS AND ALTERNATES
OF THE INTERNATIONAL FINANCE CORPORATION
(As at 30 June 1982)

Appointed Director	Appointed Alternate	Casting the vote of
James E. Burnham*	Vacant	United States
John Anson	Derek F. Smith	United Kingdom
Reinhard Münzberg	Norbert Schmidt-Gerritzen	Germany, Federal Republic of
Kenji Yamaguchi	Kimiaki Nakajima†	Japan
Bruno de Maulde	Robert Hudry	France

Elected Director	Elected Alternate	Casting the votes of
Said E. El-Naggar (Egypt)	Abdulrahman A. Sehaibani (Saudi Arabia)	Egypt, Iraq, Jordan, Kuwait, Lebanon, Pakistan, Saudi Arabia, Syrian Arab Republic, United Arab Emirates, Yemen
Earl G. Drake (Canada)	Reno J. Brown (Bahamas)	Barbados, Canada, Dominica, Grenada, Guyana, Ireland, Jamaica, Saint Lucia
Giorgio Ragazzi (Italy)	Rodrigo M. Guimarães (Portugal)	Greece, Italy, Portugal
Jacques de Groote (Belgium)	Turan Kivanç (Turkey)	Austria, Belgium, Luxembourg, Turkey
H. N. Ray (India)	M. Syeduz-Zaman (Bangladesh)	Bangladesh, India, Sri Lanka
Zain Azraai (Malaysia)	Aung Pe (Burma)	Burma, Fiji, Indonesia, Malaysia, Nepal, Singapore, Thailand, Viet Nam
Jaime García-Parra‡ (Colombia)	José-Germán Cárdenas (Ecuador)	Brazil, Colombia, Dominican Republic, Ecuador, Haiti, Philippines
Anthony IJ. A. Looijen (Netherlands)	Miodrag M. Stojiljkoviç (Yugoslavia)	Cyprus, Israel, Netherlands, Yugoslavia
David Blanco (Bolivia)	Alberto Sola (Argentina)	Argentina, Bolivia, Chile, Paraguay, Peru, Uruguay
Hans Lundström§ (Sweden)	Ole L. Poulsen (Denmark)	Denmark, Finland, Iceland, Norway, Sweden
Y. S. M. Abdulai (Nigeria)	William Smith (Liberia)	Botswana, Burundi, Ethiopia, Kenya, Lesotho, Liberia, Malawi, Nigeria, Seychelles, Sierra Leone, Sudan, Swaziland, Trinidad and Tobago, Uganda, United Republic of Tanzania, Zambia, Zimbabwe
Armand Razafindrabe (Madagascar)	Nicéphore Soglo (Benin)	Congo, Djibouti, Gabon, Guinea-Bissau, Ivory Coast, Madagascar, Mali, Mauritania, Mauritius, Niger, Rwanda, Senegal, Somalia, Togo, United Republic of Cameroon, Upper Volta, Zaire
Joaquín Muns (Spain)	Roberto Mayorga-Cortés (Nicaragua)	Costa Rica, El Salvador, Guatemala, Honduras, Mexico, Nicaragua, Panama, Spain, Venezuela
S. A. McLeod (New Zealand)	Anthony S. Cole (Australia)	Australia, New Zealand, Papua New Guinea, Republic of Korea, Samoa, Solomon Islands
Ismail Khelil (Tunisia)	Saad Zerhouni (Algeria)	Afghanistan, Ghana, Iran, Libyan Arab Jamahiriya, Morocco, Oman, Tunisia
Wang Liansheng (China)	Chen Hui (China)	China

NOTE: South Africa did not participate in the 1980 regular election of Executive Directors. Belize and Vanuatu became members after that election.
*Appointed effective 2 July 1982.
†Resigned 31 July 1982; succeeded by Toshihiro Yamakawa.
‡Resigned 31 July 1982; succeeded by Antonio V. Romualdez (Philippines).
§Resigned 31 July 1982; succeeded by Pekka Korpinen (Finland).

Annex III. PRINCIPAL OFFICERS AND OFFICES
OF THE INTERNATIONAL FINANCE CORPORATION
(As at 1 July 1982)
PRINCIPAL OFFICERS

President: A. W. Clausen.*
Executive Vice-President: Hans A. Wuttke.
Vice-President, Asia, Europe and Middle East: Judhvir Parmar.
  Director, Department of Investments, Asia: Torstein Stephansen.
  Director, Department of Investments, Europe and Middle East: Douglas Gustafson.
Vice-President, Latin America and the Caribbean: Jose M. Ruisanchez.
  Director, Department of Investments, Latin America and Caribbean I: Giovanni Vacchelli.
  Director, Department of Investments, Latin America and Caribbean II: Daniel F. Adams.
Vice-President, Africa (acting): Judhvir Parmar.
  Director, Department of Investments, Africa I: Gunter H. Kreuter.
  Director, Department of Investments, Africa II: M. Azam K. Alizai.
Vice-President and General Counsel: Jose E. Camacho.
  Deputy General Counsel: Walter F. Norris.
  Director, Capital Markets Department: David Gill.
  Deputy Director, Capital Markets Department: Richard H. Frank.
  Director of Syndications: Rolf Th. Lundberg.
Vice-President, Engineering and Technical Assistance: Makarand V. Dehejia.
  Deputy Director: Robert D. King.
Secretary: Timothy T. Thahane.*

Director-General, Operations Evaluation: Mervyn L. Weiner.*
  Director, Corporate Planning Department: Richard W. Richardson.
  Director, Finance and Management Department: Marshall Burkes.
  Chief, Information Office: Carl T. Bell.
  Director, Compensation Department: R. A. Clarke.*
  Director, Personnel Management Department: Gautam S. Kaji.*
  Director, Internal Auditing Department: Lawrence N. Rapley.*
  Director, Administrative Services Department: James E. Twining, Jr.*
  Director, Programming and Budgeting Department: Heinz Vergin.*
  Special Representative, Middle East: Cherif Hassan.
  Special Representative, Far East: Naokado Nishihara.
  Special Representative, Europe: Hans Pollan.
  Regional Mission in East Asia: Sakdiyiam Kupasrimonkol.
  Regional Mission in Eastern Africa: V. S. Raghavan.
  Regional Mission in Western Africa: Guy C. Antoine.
  Special Adviser for African Affairs: Pierre C. Damiba.
  Special Adviser: James M. Kearns.
  Senior Adviser, Portfolio: Fawzi Habib.
  Senior Adviser, Technical: H. Geoffrey Hilton.†

*Held the same position in the World Bank.
†Retired 31 May 1982.

HEADQUARTERS AND OTHER OFFICES

HEADQUARTERS
International Finance Corporation
1818 H Street, N. W.
Washington, D. C. 20433, United States
Cable address: CORINTFIN
　　　　　　　　WASHINGTONDC
Telephone: (202) 477-1234
Telex: ITT 440098, RCA 248423, WU 64145

NEW YORK OFFICE
International Finance Corporation
747 Third Avenue, 26th floor
New York, N. Y. 10017, United States
Cable address: CORINTFIN NEWYORK
Telephone: (212) 754-6008

LONDON OFFICE
International Finance Corporation
New Zealand House, 15th floor
Haymarket
London SW1 Y4TE, England
Cable address: CORINTFIN LONDON
Telephone: (01) 930-8741
Telex: 851-919462

EUROPEAN OFFICE
International Finance Corporation
66 Avenue d'Iéna
75116 Paris, France
Cable address: CORINTFIN PARIS
Telephone: (1) 723-54-21
Telex: 842-620628

TOKYO OFFICE
International Finance Corporation
5-1 Nibancho, Chiyoda-ku
Tokyo 102, Japan
Cable address: SPCORINTFIN TOKYO
Telephone: (03) 261-3626, (03) 408-0634
Telex: 781-26554

REGIONAL MISSION IN EAST ASIA
World Bank Group
Central Bank of the Philippines
Manila, Philippines
Cable address: CORINTFIN MANILA
Telephone: 58-93-12
Telex: 742-40541

REGIONAL MISSION IN EASTERN AFRICA
International Finance Corporation
Reinsurance Plaza, 5th floor
Taifa Road
(P. O. Box 30577)
Nairobi, Kenya
Cable address: CORINTFIN NAIROBI
Telephone: 24726, 520842
Telex: 963-22022

REGIONAL MISSION IN THE MIDDLE EAST
International Finance Corporation
3 Elbergas Street, Garden City
Cairo, Egypt
Cable address: IFCAI CAIRO
Telephone: 23923, 25045, 982914
Telex: 927-93110

REGIONAL MISSION IN WESTERN AFRICA
International Finance Corporation
Immeuble Alpha 2000, Rue Gourgas
01-P. O. Box 1748
Abidjan, Ivory Coast
Cable address: CORINTFIN ABIDJAN
Telephone: 32-65-97, 33-11-51
Telex: 969-3533

Chapter VIII

International Development Association (IDA)

Established in 1960 as an affiliate of the International Bank for Reconstruction and Development (World Bank), the International Development Association (IDA) promotes economic development by supporting productive, high-priority projects in developing member countries.

The Association lends for the same purposes as the World Bank, using the same staff and appraisal criteria, but its capital and assets are entirely separate from those of the Bank.

The Bank obtains the larger part of its funds, called credits to distinguish them from Bank loans, in the capital markets and lends on roughly conventional terms. The bulk of the resources of IDA are contributed by member Governments, enabling it to lend to the poorest countries on more flexible terms that bear less heavily on their balance of payments.

In general, a country eligible to receive IDA credits must have an annual per capita gross national product of less than $731 (in 1980 dollars); in the fiscal year ending on 30 June 1982 over 50 countries were eligible under this criterion.

The Association's credits are interest-free, with a service charge of 0.75 per cent on disbursed and outstanding credit balances. In January 1982 the service charge was extended to the entire credit—

0.75 per cent on disbursed balances and 0.5 per cent on undisbursed balances. The credits are repayable over 50 years, with an initial grace period of 10 years before repayment begins.

Unlike the Bank, which may lend to public and private entities with Government guarantees, IDA lends only to Governments. In the case of revenue-producing projects, IDA credits are re-lent by the Governments on terms reflecting the local cost of capital. Thus, IDA terms help Governments to finance economic development without distorting the local credit structure.

At the end of fiscal 1982, IDA's resources totalled the equivalent of $26,119 million, including $1,723 million approved but not yet effective and $485 million from exchange adjustments.

The bulk of IDA funds for lending is provided by its Part I (richer) member countries and several Part II (developing) countries under a series of replenishment agreements. In fiscal 1982, the sixth replenishment of IDA, covering fiscal years 1981-1983 and providing the equivalent of $12 billion at October 1979 exchange rates, became effective on receipt of the United States formal notification of participation with a total contribution of $3.24 billion. Thus the effectiveness condition was satisfied by twelve Part I members having committed

$9.6 billion or 80 per cent of the replenishment's total. Prior to the sixth replenishment becoming effective, IDA had made credit commitments against advance contributions amounting to some $2.5 billion provided by 24 countries.

Due to a reduced first payment by the United States and the sixth replenishment's pro-rata provisions whereby resources from other donors could be committed only in the same proportion as unqualified commitments from the United States, IDA exhausted its commitment authority at the beginning of fiscal 1982. To avoid interruptions or reductions in its commitment authority, IDA waived the pro-rata rule for the first installment, making available about $2.6 billion as commitment authority for the fiscal year.

Membership of IDA rose to 130 during the year, with the admission of Belize on 19 March and Saint Lucia on 28 April.

Lending operations

By 30 June 1982, IDA had made cumulative net commitments totalling $26,738.2 million. Commitments in fiscal 1982 amounted to $2,686.3 million, of which $1,678 million went to six countries in South Asia and $606.7 million went to 14 countries in East Africa. India, with 5 credits amounting to $900 million, was the largest borrower from IDA during the year, followed by Bangladesh with 8 credits of $391 million and Pakistan with 4 credits of $171 million.

The table below summarizes IDA lending in the fiscal year 1982 by area and by purpose.

Agriculture and rural development

As in previous years, credits for agriculture and rural development accounted for the largest portion of IDA lending in fiscal 1982. Thirty credits totalling the equivalent of $898.2 million were committed to 21 countries. Of credits totalling $475 million made to India, one of $220 million funded construction work on 6 dams, expanding and remodelling of 217 kilometres of canal systems and constructing or improving 671 kilometres of rural road, thereby helping to increase agricultural production.

To benefit about 280,000 farm families, China's first IDA-assisted agriculture project provided $60 million for drainage and irrigation in nine northern counties, including agricultural inputs, rural electrification, rural roads, technical assistance and training.

Other purposes for which credits were committed included: agricultural credit, agro-industry, area development, forestry, fisheries, livestock, irrigation and drainage systems, and research and extension.

Development finance companies

Of five credits totalling $135.5 million granted in fiscal 1982, Uganda's $35 million was to finance capital expenditures to replace industrial equipment. Ethiopia received $30 million for industrial enterprises and an experimental programme for small-scale contractors and $30 million went to Pakistan to invest in small and medium-sized enterprises in the private sector, especially for export-oriented, agro-based and labour-intensive projects.

(continued on p. 1559)

IDA CREDITS APPROVED BY REGION/COUNTRY AND PURPOSE, 1 JULY 1981–30 JUNE 1982

(including IDA share of joint Bank/IDA operations; in millions of US dollars)

REGION/COUNTRY	Agriculture and rural development	Development finance companies	Education	Energy	Industry	Non-project	Population, health and nutrition	Small-scale enterprises	Technical assistance	Telecommunications	Transportation	Urbanization	Water supply and sewerage	Total
Eastern Africa														
Burundi	16.0	—	—	—	—	—	—	5.2	—	—	—	—	—	21.2
Comoros	—	—	6.0	—	—	—	—	—	—	—	6.3	—	—	12.3
Djibouti	—	—	—	—	—	—	—	—	3.0	—	—	—	—	3.0
Ethiopia	—	30.0	—	—	—	—	—	—	—	—	—	—	—	30.0
Kenya	38.0	—	—	—	—	—	23.0	—	—	—	—	—	—	61.0
Madagascar	15.0	—	—	—	—	—	—	—	5.7	—	—	—	—	20.7
Malawi	7.3	—	—	—	—	—	—	—	—	—	—	—	4.0	11.3
Rwanda	—	—	10.0	—	—	—	—	—	5.0	—	25.9	—	—	40.9
Somalia	—	—	—	—	—	—	—	—	—	—	—	—	15.0	15.0
Sudan	31.0	—	—	—	—	—	—	—	—	—	25.0	—	—	56.0
Uganda	—	35.0	—	—	4.0	70.0	—	—	—	—	—	—	—	109.0
United Republic of Tanzania	12.0	—	—	20.0	—	—	—	—	12.0	27.0	—	—	4.0	75.0
Zaire	11.3	21.5	—	19.0	—	—	—	—	5.0	—	26.0	—	18.0	100.8
Zambia	25.5	—	25.0	—	—	—	—	—	—	—	—	—	—	50.5
Subtotal	156.1	86.5	41.0	39.0	4.0	70.0	23.0	5.2	30.7	27.0	83.2	—	41.0	606.7

REGION/COUNTRY	Agriculture and rural development	Development finance companies	Education	Energy	Industry	Non-project	Population, health and nutrition	Small-scale enterprises	Technical assistance	Telecommunications	Transportation	Urbanization	Water supply and sewerage	Total
Western Africa														
Benin	—	—	14.0	9.8	—	—	—	—	—	—	—	—	—	23.8
Central African Republic	—	—	—	—	—	—	—	—	—	—	18.0	—	—	18.0
Congo	—	—	—	—	—	—	—	—	—	—	17.0	—	—	17.0
Gambia	—	—	—	1.5	—	—	—	—	—	—	6.5	—	—	8.0
Guinea	—	19.0	—	—	—	—	—	—	—	—	—	—	—	19.0
Liberia	15.5	—	—	—	—	—	—	—	—	—	—	10.0	—	25.5
Mali	—	—	—	—	—	—	—	—	6.5	13.5	—	—	—	20.0
Mauritania	—	—	5.7	3.0	—	—	—	—	—	—	4.0	—	—	12.7
Niger	10.1	—	—	—	—	—	—	16.0	—	—	—	—	—	26.1
Senegal	19.5	—	—	—	—	—	—	—	—	—	—	—	—	19.5
Sierra Leone	—	—	—	5.0	—	—	—	—	—	—	—	—	—	5.0
Togo	—	—	—	2.0	—	—	—	—	3.5	—	—	—	—	5.5
Upper Volta	16.0	—	—	—	—	—	—	—	—	17.0	—	—	—	33.0
Subtotal	61.1	19.0	19.7	21.3	—	—	—	16.0	10.0	30.5	45.5	10.0	—	233.1
East Asia and Pacific														
China	60.0	—	—	—	—	—	—	—	—	—	—	—	—	60.0
Lao People's Democratic Republic	—	—	—	15.0	—	—	—	—	—	—	—	—	—	15.0
Papua New Guinea	2.0	—	—	—	—	—	—	—	—	—	—	—	—	2.0
Solomon Islands	—	—	5.0	—	—	—	—	—	—	—	—	—	—	5.0
Subtotal	62.0	—	5.0	15.0	—	—	—	—	—	—	—	—	—	82.0
South Asia														
Bangladesh	54.0	—	—	132.0	45.0	100.0	—	—	—	—	60.0	—	—	391.0
Burma	—	—	—	80.0	—	—	—	—	—	—	20.0	—	—	100.0
India	475.0	—	—	400.0	—	—	—	—	—	—	—	25.0	—	900.0
Nepal	—	—	14.3	9.2	—	—	—	6.5	—	—	—	—	—	30.0
Pakistan	54.0	30.0	—	—	—	80.0	—	—	7.0	—	—	—	—	171.0
Sri Lanka	20.0	—	—	36.0	—	—	—	30.0	—	—	—	—	—	86.0
Subtotal	603.0	30.0	14.3	657.2	45.0	180.0	—	36.5	7.0	—	80.0	25.0	—	1,678.0
Europe, the Middle East and North Africa														
Democratic Yemen	6.0	—	6.0	7.5	—	—	—	—	—	—	—	—	—	19.5
Yemen	6.0	—	12.0	2.0	—	—	—	—	—	—	7.0	15.0	—	42.0
Subtotal	12.0	—	18.0	9.5	—	—	—	—	—	—	7.0	15.0	—	61.5
Latin America and the Caribbean														
Dominica	—	—	—	—	—	—	—	—	—	—	5.0	—	—	5.0
Guyana	—	—	—	2.0	—	—	—	—	—	—	—	—	—	2.0
Haiti	4.0	—	—	—	—	—	—	—	—	—	14.0	—	—	18.0
Subtotal	4.0	—	—	2.0	—	—	—	—	—	—	19.0	—	—	25.0
Total	898.2	135.5	98.0	744.0	49.0	250.0	23.0	57.7	47.7	57.5	234.7	50.0	41.0	2,686.3
NUMBER OF CREDITS	30	5	9	18	3	3	1	4	8	3	13	3	4	104

Zaire was allotted $21.5 million to finance subprojects in key sectors of the economy and $19 million went to Guinea to strengthen the industrial sector.

Education

Nine credits totalling $98 million were granted to nine countries for educational projects during fiscal 1982.

A $25 million credit went to Zambia to construct and equip eight rural junior secondary schools and to strengthen a programme to arrest the decline in students progressing from primary to junior secondary levels. Nepal received $14.3 million to expand technical and vocational training programmes for civil, electrical and mechanical-engineering technicians needed to implement development programmes.

Other loans went for: teacher, agricultural and health training; primary education; vocational and maritime training centres; expanded secondary-school facilities for commerce, nursing and primary education; educational administration; and educational materials.

Energy

Sixteen countries received 18 credits totalling $744 million for energy-related projects. India received $400 million to construct three generating units and associated transmission lines in its western region. Burma received $80 million to install single-circuit transmission lines for power transmission from generation facilities, to construct and expand eight substations and to provide load-dispatch-centre and meter-testing equipment.

In other countries credits were committed for: electrification programmes, petroleum and geo-thermal research and exploration, hydroelectric and irrigation projects and evaluation of hydrocarbon potential.

Industry

Three credits amounting to $49 million were made to two countries for industrial development during fiscal 1982. Of credits totalling $45 million made to Bangladesh, one of $30 million was to improve the textile industry by implementing new pricing, distribution and employment policies and rehabilitating 15 mills, and one of $15 million was to increase domestic fertilizer production. Uganda received $4 million for an engineering study on phosphate deposits to determine the economic viability of full-scale development.

Non-project

In the non-project sector, three credits totalling $250 million were made during the 1982 fiscal year. Bangladesh received $100 million for foreign exchange to import raw materials, chemicals and equipment for industry, construction and agriculture. A credit of $80 million was made to Pakistan for a structural-adjustment programme to improve development planning and agricultural, water, energy and industrial sector policies. Uganda received $70 million to finance the importation of agricultural inputs, spare parts and raw materials for industry and transport.

Population, health and nutrition

Kenya received $23 million to reduce fertility, mortality and morbidity in rural areas by establishing an inter-agency information and education programme for population and family planning and by improving the accessibility and quality of rural health and family-planning services.

Small-scale enterprises

A total of $57.7 million was granted to four countries for small-scale enterprises.

Sri Lanka received $30 million to help small and medium industries become more efficient and increase output, employment and exports. Niger received $16 million for small-scale enterprise development and to promote and train local businessmen. A $6.5 million credit to Nepal financed a lending programme to cottage industries which, by expanded production and export of carpets, fabrics and metal, would generate employment, raise incomes and increase foreign-exchange earnings. Burundi received $5.2 million to develop the production of local construction materials and the small-construction sector by supporting small and medium-sized construction contractors, brickmakers and lime producers.

Technical assistance

Eight nations received credits of $47.7 million for technical assistance during fiscal 1982. The United Republic of Tanzania received $12 million to support its export-rehabilitation programme by eliminating manpower bottlenecks in the agricultural sector and assisting in the preparation of a comprehensive energy plan. Pakistan received $7 million for technical assistance in macro-economic planning, agricultural pricing, project preparation, industrial planning and incentives, monitoring of public enterprises, exploration and development of hydrocarbon energy resources and national power planning.

Other credits went to assist government efforts to formulate and implement development strategy and economic policies, co-ordinate development efforts, assist agricultural reform, redefine sector investment programmes and policies and strengthen local project preparation.

Telecommunications

Three credits totalling $57.5 million were made for telecommunications projects during fiscal 1982. The United Republic of Tanzania received $27 million to extend domestic telecommunication services and to meet part of the country's posts and telecommunications corporation's investment programme. A $17 million credit went to Upper Volta to extend local and long-distance telephone and telecommunications services. Mali received $13.5 million to construct an automatic telephone exchange, cable networks in eight provincial cities, a microwave-radio relay link, a new telex exchange and to expand existing telephone and cable facilities.

Transportation

Thirteen credits totalling $234.7 million were made for transportation projects in 13 countries during fiscal 1982.

Bangladesh received $60 million to improve existing port facilities at Chittagong. Zaire received $26 million to replace its river-transport fleet and rehabilitate 65 kilometres of railway line.

Credits approved for other countries went to improve highways and road maintenance, river transport services and ports.

Urbanization

Three credits totalling $50 million were made for urban development in fiscal 1982. India received $25 million to support the reorientation of shelter and infrastructure investments. Yemen received $15 million for its first urbanization project aimed at establishing a basic model for urban development schemes. It also focused on providing basic services to the lowest-income groups. A $10 million credit was made to Liberia to improve living conditions for some 100,000 people in Monrovia.

Water supply and sewerage

Four credits totalling $41 million were made for water supply and sewerage projects during fiscal 1982. Zaire received $18 million to strengthen and expand production and distribution systems in three cities, reducing mortality and disease and providing safe water to more than 500,000 people. A $15 million credit to Somalia was to provide Mogadishu with a reliable supply of safe water, eliminate current shortages in low-income areas and help satisfy the city's water demand through 1986. Malawi received $4 million to develop a master plan for a long-term programme for water supply and sewerage and sanitation development, and to identify a water-supply project for the programme's first phase. A supplemental credit of $4 million was approved for the United Republic of Tanzania to assist completion of an urban water-supply project funded by the World Bank.

Secretariat

The principal officers, staff, headquarters and other offices of IDA are the same as those of the World Bank.

STATEMENT OF INCOME AND EXPENSES
(for the fiscal year ending 30 June 1982)

	Amount (in thousands of US dollars)
Income	
From development credits	
Service charges	105,085
Commitment charges	5
From investments	24,558
Exchange adjustments	(1,466)
Total income	128,182
Expenses	
Management fee to World Bank	193,375
Operating loss (income less expenses)	(65,193)
Translation adjustments as a result of currency fluctuations	(17,014)
Net loss	(82,207)

Annex I. MEMBERS OF THE INTERNATIONAL DEVELOPMENT ASSOCIATION, SUBSCRIPTIONS, VOTING POWER AND SUPPLEMENTARY RESOURCES

(As at 30 June 1982)

MEMBER	TOTAL SUBSCRIPTIONS AND SUPPLEMENTARY RESOURCES (in thousands of US dollars) Amount (in current US dollars)*	Percentage of total	VOTING POWER Number of votes	Percentage of total	MEMBER	TOTAL SUBSCRIPTIONS AND SUPPLEMENTARY RESOURCES (in thousands of US dollars) Amount (in current US dollars)*	Percentage of total	VOTING POWER Number of votes	Percentage of total
Part I countries					*Part I countries* (cont.)				
Australia	566,187	1.98	64,494	1.46	Germany, Federal Republic of	3,268,741	11.42	308,201	6.99
Austria	189,517	0.66	27,912	0.63	Iceland	2,779	0.01	10,573	0.24
Belgium	411,011	1.44	53,716	1.22	Ireland	32,043	0.11	13,466	0.31
Canada	1,458,304	5.10	157,028	3.56	Italy	837,480	2.93	113,934	2.58
Denmark	292,674	1.02	42,936	0.97	Japan	3,381,351	11.82	293,863	6.67
Finland	142,423	0.50	24,294	0.55	Kuwait	451,912	1.58	49,418	1.12
France	1,407,024	4.92	166,855	3.79					

MEMBER	TOTAL SUBSCRIPTIONS AND SUPPLEMENTARY RESOURCES (in thousands of US dollars) Amount (in current US dollars)*	Percentage of total	VOTING POWER Number of votes	Percentage of total
Part I countries (cont.)				
Luxembourg	12,767	0.04	11,269	0.26
Netherlands	797,630	2.79	88,326	2.00
New Zealand	28,470	0.10	13,278	0.30
Norway	300,392	1.05	39,527	0.90
South Africa	46,797	0.16	15,058	0.34
Sweden	888,891	3.11	108,610	2.46
United Arab Emirates	136,464	0.48	15,942	0.36
United Kingdom	3,087,620	10.79	313,019	7.10
United States	9,643,055	33.70	836,056	18.97
Subtotal	27,383,532	95.71	2,767,775	62.79‡
Part II countries				
Afghanistan	1,233	0.01	13,266	0.30
Algeria	4,798	0.02	18,481	0.42
Argentina	47,083	0.16	74,787	1.70
Bangladesh	6,377	0.02	27,961	0.63
Belize	220	†	540	0.01
Benin	552	†	600	0.01
Bhutan	55	†	510	0.01
Bolivia	1,251	0.01	13,442	0.30
Botswana	191	†	10,440	0.24
Brazil	52,718	0.18	75,082	1.70
Burma	2,428	0.01	16,697	0.38
Burundi	924	†	12,447	0.28
Cape Verde	88	†	516	0.01
Central African Republic	591	†	9,575	0.22
Chad	573	†	2,093	0.05
Chile	4,069	0.02	17,113	0.39
China	35,884	0.13	91,311	2.07
Colombia	11,826	0.04	21,787	0.49
Comoros	94	†	5,774	0.13
Congo	585	†	6,685	0.15
Costa Rica	234	†	7,844	0.18
Cyprus	913	†	12,447	0.28
Democratic Kampuchea	1,175	0.01	7,826	0.18
Democratic Yemen	1,415	0.01	10,591	0.24
Djibouti	178	†	532	0.01
Dominica	89	†	516	0.01
Dominican Republic	557	†	11,261	0.26
Ecuador	913	†	12,084	0.27
Egypt	6,079	0.02	26,950	0.61
El Salvador	376	†	6,244	0.14
Equatorial Guinea	367	†	1,967	0.04
Ethiopia	632	†	11,582	0.26
Fiji	641	†	2,130	0.05
Gabon	576	†	2,093	0.05
Gambia	322	†	10,799	0.24
Ghana	2,793	0.01	14,678	0.33
Greece	6,670	0.02	18,733	0.42
Grenada	109	†	10,186	0.23
Guatemala	488	†	11,250	0.26
Guinea	1,223	0.01	13,266	0.30
Guinea-Bissau	155	†	528	0.01
Guyana	976	†	12,624	0.29
Haiti	927	†	12,447	0.28
Honduras	368	†	10,896	0.25
India	51,209	0.18	145,397	3.30
Indonesia	13,318	0.05	47,171	1.07
Iran	5,824	0.02	15,455	0.35
Iraq	911	†	9,407	0.21
Israel	2,394	0.01	9,386	0.21
Ivory Coast	1,180	0.01	7,771	0.18
Jordan	394	†	10,896	0.25

MEMBER	TOTAL SUBSCRIPTIONS AND SUPPLEMENTARY RESOURCES (in thousands of US dollars) Amount (in current US dollars)*	Percentage of total	VOTING POWER Number of votes	Percentage of total
Part II countries (cont.)				
Kenya	2,016	0.01	15,534	0.35
Lao People's Democratic Republic	579	†	11,578	0.26
Lebanon	528	†	8,562	0.19
Lesotho	191	†	10,440	0.24
Liberia	927	†	12,447	0.28
Libyan Arab Jamahiriya	1,194	0.01	7,771	0.18
Madagascar	1,115	0.01	702	0.02
Malawi	914	†	12,447	0.28
Malaysia	3,070	0.01	18,349	0.42
Maldives	35	†	9,999	0.23
Mali	1,028	†	12,810	0.29
Mauritania	590	†	6,685	0.15
Mauritius	1,056	†	12,804	0.29
Mexico	19,526	0.07	18,212	0.41
Morocco	4,221	0.02	21,764	0.49
Nepal	605	†	11,578	0.26
Nicaragua	396	†	10,896	0.25
Niger	693	†	11,578	0.26
Nigeria	3,901	0.01	4,057	0.09
Oman	390	†	10,899	0.25
Pakistan	12,281	0.04	43,818	0.99
Panama	26	†	5,657	0.13
Papua New Guinea	1,048	†	12,799	0.29
Paraguay	359	†	8,124	0.18
Peru	1,953	0.01	854	0.02
Philippines	6,082	0.02	16,583	0.38
Republic of Korea	4,134	0.02	14,483	0.33
Rwanda	924	†	12,447	0.28
Saint Lucia	170	†	10,402	0.24
Samoa	106	†	7,537	0.17
Sao Tome and Principe	77	†	514	0.01
Saudi Arabia	774,084	2.71	88,413	2.01
Senegal	2,004	0.01	15,534	0.35
Sierra Leone	915	†	12,447	0.28
Solomon Islands	100	†	518	0.01
Somalia	894	†	10,286	0.23
Spain	39,519	0.14	40,084	0.91
Sri Lanka	3,573	0.01	20,062	0.46
Sudan	1,203	0.01	13,266	0.30
Swaziland	382	†	10,980	0.25
Syrian Arab Republic	1,123	0.01	7,651	0.17
Thailand	3,669	0.01	20,062	0.46
Togo	898	†	10,286	0.23
Trinidad and Tobago	1,490	0.01	770	0.02
Tunisia	1,731	0.01	2,793	0.06
Turkey	6,750	0.02	23,450	0.53
Uganda	1,933	0.01	11,960	0.27
United Republic of Cameroon	1,184	0.01	7,771	0.18
United Republic of Tanzania	2,027	0.01	15,534	0.35
Upper Volta	591	†	9,575	0.22
Vanuatu	209	†	538	0.01
Viet Nam	1,737	0.01	8,889	0.20
Yemen	525	†	11,343	0.26
Yugoslavia	25,315	0.09	27,401	0.62
Zaire	3,471	0.01	12,164	0.28
Zambia	2,969	0.01	1,038	0.02
Zimbabwe	4,596	0.02	1,324	0.03
Subtotal	1,227,873	4.29	1,640,533	37.21‡
Total	28,611,405	100.00	4,408,308	100.00

*Includes amounts aggregating $5,202,591,000 equivalent in current United States dollars receivable from members, of which at 30 June 1982 $390,171,000 equivalent was past due and $4,812,420,000 equivalent was not yet due.

†Less than 0.005 per cent.

‡Differs from the sum of the individual percentages because of rounding.

Annex II. EXECUTIVE DIRECTORS AND ALTERNATES OF THE INTERNATIONAL DEVELOPMENT ASSOCIATION

(As at 30 June 1982)

Appointed Director	*Appointed Alternate*	*Casting the vote of*
Vacant*	Vacant	United States
John Anson	Derek F. Smith	United Kingdom
Reinhard Münzberg	Norbert Schmidt-Gerritzen	Germany, Federal Republic of
Bruno de Maulde	Robert Hudry	France
Kenji Yamaguchi	Kimiaki Nakajima†	Japan

Elected Director	*Elected Alternate*	*Casting the votes of*
Said E. El-Naggar (Egypt)	Abdulrahman A. Sehaibani (Saudi Arabia)	Egypt, Iraq, Jordan, Kuwait, Lebanon, Maldives, Pakistan, Saudi Arabia, Syrian Arab Republic, United Arab Emirates, Yemen
Earl G. Drake (Canada)	Reno J. Brown (Bahamas)	Canada, Dominica, Grenada, Guyana, Ireland, Saint Lucia
H. N. Ray (India)	M. Syeduz-Zaman (Bangladesh)	Bangladesh, India, Sri Lanka
Giorgio Ragazzi (Italy)	Rodrigo M. Guimarães (Portugal)	Greece, Italy
Anthony IJ. A. Looijen (Netherlands)	Miodrag M. Stojiljkovic (Yugoslavia)	Cyprus, Israel, Netherlands, Yugoslavia
Jacques de Groote (Belgium)	Turan S. Kivanç (Turkey)	Austria, Belgium, Luxembourg, Turkey
Joaquín Muns (Spain)	Roberto Mayorga-Cortés (Nicaragua)	Costa Rica, El Salvador, Guatemala, Honduras, Mexico, Nicaragua, Panama, Spain
Wang Liansheng (China)	Chen Hui (China)	China
Hans Lundström (Sweden)	Ole L. Poulsen (Denmark)	Denmark, Finland, Iceland, Norway, Sweden
Zain Azraai (Malaysia)	Aung Pe (Burma)	Burma, Fiji, Indonesia, Lao People's Democratic Republic, Malaysia, Nepal, Thailand, Viet Nam
S. A. McLeod (New Zealand)	Anthony S. Cole (Australia)	Australia, New Zealand, Papua New Guinea, Republic of Korea, Samoa, Solomon Islands
Y. S. M. Abdulai (Nigeria)	William Smith (Liberia)	Botswana, Burundi, Equatorial Guinea, Ethiopia, Gambia, Guinea, Kenya, Lesotho, Liberia, Malawi, Nigeria, Sierra Leone, Sudan, Swaziland, Trinidad and Tobago, Uganda, United Republic of Tanzania, Zambia, Zimbabwe
Jaime García-Parra (Colombia)	José-Germán Cárdenas (Ecuador)	Brazil, Colombia, Dominican Republic, Ecuador, Haiti, Philippines
Armand Razafindrabe (Madagascar)	Nicéphore Soglo (Benin)	Benin, Cape Verde, Central African Republic, Chad, Comoros, Congo, Djibouti, Gabon, Guinea-Bissau, Ivory Coast, Madagascar, Mali, Mauritania, Mauritius, Niger, Rwanda, Sao Tome and Principe, Senegal, Somalia, Togo, United Republic of Cameroon, Upper Volta, Zaire
David Blanco (Bolivia)	Alberto Sola (Argentina)	Argentina, Bolivia, Chile, Paraguay, Peru
Ismail Khelil (Tunisia)	Saad M. Zerhouni (Algeria)	Afghanistan, Algeria, Democratic Yemen, Ghana, Iran, Libyan Arab Jamahiriya, Morocco, Oman, Tunisia

NOTE: Democratic Kampuchea and South Africa did not participate in the 1980 regular election of Executive Directors. Belize, Bhutan and Vanuatu became members after that election.

*James B. Burnham was appointed by the United States as its Director effective 2 July.

†Resigned effective 13 July; succeeded by Toshihiro Yamakawa.

Annex III. PRINCIPAL OFFICERS AND OFFICES OF THE INTERNATIONAL DEVELOPMENT ASSOCIATION

(As at 1 July 1982)

PRINCIPAL OFFICERS*

President: A. W. Clausen.
Senior Vice-President, Finance: Moeen A. Qureshi.
Senior Vice-President, Operations: Ernest Stern.
Regional Vice-President, Latin America and the Caribbean: Nicolás Ardito Barletta.
Vice-President, Operations Policy: Warren C. Baum.
Vice-President, External Relations: Munir P. Benjenk.
Regional Vice-President, Europe, Middle East and North Africa: Roger Chaufournier.
Vice-President, Economics and Research: Hollis B. Chenery.
Vice-President, Programming and Budgeting, and Vice-President, Pension Fund: K. Georg Gabriel.

Vice-President and General Counsel: Heribert Golsong.
Vice-President and Controller: Masaya Hattori.
Regional Vice-President, South Asia: W. David Hopper.
Regional Vice-President, East Asia and Pacific: S. Shahid Husain.
Regional Vice-President, Western Africa: A. David Knox.
Vice-President, Personnel and Administration: Martijn J. W. M. Paijmans.
Vice-President and Treasurer: Eugene H. Rotberg.
Vice-President and Secretary: Timothy T. Thahane.
Regional Vice-President, Eastern Africa: Willi A. Wapenhans.
Director-General, Operations Evaluation: Mervyn L. Weiner.

*The World Bank and IDA had the same officers and staff.

HEADQUARTERS AND OTHER OFFICES

Chapter IX

International Monetary Fund (IMF)

In light of the deep international economic recession and its impact on world trade and payments positions, the International Monetary Fund (IMF) increased its financial assistance to members substantially in 1982. Measured in special drawing rights (SDRs)—the Fund-created international reserve asset—members' purchases (drawings) from the Fund in 1982 reached a record level of SDR 7.4 billion, while repurchases (repayments) by members totalled SDR 1.8 billion, down from SDR 2.1 billion in 1981 and marking their lowest annual level since 1976. The net use of IMF credit by members amounted to SDR 5.9 billion in 1982, surpassing the previous record of SDR 4.9 billion in 1981.

Of the SDR 7.4 billion in IMF member drawings in 1982, SDR 2.6 billion, or 35 per cent of the total, represented the compensatory financing facility, which entailed relatively low Fund conditionality, reflecting the severe drop in the commodity export earnings of developing countries. Of the remaining drawings, SDR 2.3 billion were under stand-by arrangements; SDR 2.1 billion under extended arrangements; and record-high purchases of SDR 144 million under the buffer stock financing facility.

New loan commitments under stand-by and extended arrangements declined to SDR 2.4 billion in 1982 from SDR 12.1 billion in 1981, due, in part, to cancellations of arrangements totalling SDR 4.1 billion. At year's end, there were 25 stand-by ar-

rangements in effect and seven extended arrangements with an undrawn balance totalling SDR 11.1 billion.

Reserve tranche drawings, or drawings by members on unconditional reserve assets deposited with the Fund, totalling SDR 1.3 billion in 1982 as against SDR 359 million in 1981, marked their highest annual level since 1978. Industrial country purchases, other than reserve tranche, amounted to SDR 54 million in 1982—the first year of such purchases since 1979.

The use of SDRs in 1982, with total transfers amounting to SDR 12.2 billion, reached a record high since the SDR facility was established in 1970, and topped the previous high of SDR 11.1 billion set in 1980; this was a threefold increase over 1980 in transfers among participants and "prescribed holders", amounting to SDR 5.3 billion. The year also marked the first full year in effect of the new SDR interest rate, set in May 1981 at 100 per cent of the SDR's combined market rate—a weighted basket of prime domestic debt instruments reflecting the currency composition of the SDR valuation basket. Reflecting market rates, the SDR interest rate, calculated quarterly, dropped from 11.63 to 8.9 per cent between the first and final quarters of the year.

IMF continued to administer as a Trustee the oil facility subsidy and the supplementary financing facility subsidy accounts. The oil facility subsidy account, established in 1975 to assist Fund members most seriously affected by oil price increases, completed in June the seventh annual payments totalling SDR 9.3 million to 23 members, bringing the total payments under the subsidy account to SDR 172.5 million.

Under the supplementary financing facility's subsidy account, established in December 1980 to reduce the cost of using the supplementary financing facility for low-income developing member countries, SDR 44.3 million in payments were made in August 1982 to 23 eligible members, bringing total payments under the subsidy account to SDR 67.2 million.

Although a third account, the Trust Fund, was terminated in April 1981, IMF remained responsible for unfinished business and in June and December 1982 collected two installments of semi-annual interest payments for a total of SDR 15 million. Trust Fund loan repayment commenced in July.

In January, the Fund's Executive Board adopted borrowing guidelines to be reviewed when the Eighth General Review of Quotas (scheduled in 1983) was completed, or in the event of major developments in the world economy. The Board also decided in January to review regularly the Fund's liquidity, taking into account such factors as the need to foster and maintain the confidence of creditors to the Fund in its policies and operations. The first such comprehensive review was completed in April.

Among other actions taken by the Board during the year were: a review of the Fund's surveillance over members' exchange rate policies, and endorsement of the Managing Director's efforts to strengthen that function; the increase, effective 1 May, of the Fund's rate of charge from 6.25 to 6.6 per cent on members' use of the Fund's ordinary resources; and a decision, in November, to permit the use of the Fund's buffer stock financing facility to finance eligible members' compulsory contributions to the buffer stocks of the 1979 International Natural Rubber Agreement and the Sixth International Tin Agreement.

The Interim Committee of the IMF Board of Governors, at its 1982 meetings (Helsinki, Finland, 12-13 May; Toronto, Canada, 4-5 September), stressed the importance of IMF's role in promoting balance of payments adjustment, and emphasized that the Fund's surveillance over the balance-of-payments and exchange-rate policies of members should be exercised even-handedly.

The Interim Committee reiterated that quotas must remain the primary source of financing for the Fund's operations, and that the Eighth General Review of Quotas should result in an increase large enough to enable the Fund to perform its functions in the 1980s. It reaffirmed that the Review should serve to bring members' quotas more in line with their relative positions in the world economy, taking account of the need to maintain a proper balance between different groups of countries. The Committee asked the Executive Board to strive for a convergence of views to permit the Fund's Managing Director to propose new SDR allocations in the fourth basic period, which began on 1 January 1982. It also asked the Board to assess the existing arrangements to deal with major strains in the international financial system, including a United States suggestion to establish an additional permanent borrowing arrangement for use in emergencies.

In 1982, the Joint Ministerial Committee of the Boards of Governors of the World Bank and IMF on the Transfer of Real Resources to Developing Countries (Development Committee) met at Helsinki, Finland (13-14 May), and at Toronto, Canada (5 September).

In the face of a growing problem of international indebtedness, the Fund expanded its technical assistance for external debt management and for collecting external debt statistics. Among Fund seminars and courses was a July seminar offered for the first time on central banking, attended by senior officials of central banks of member countries.

SUMMARY OF TRANSACTIONS, 1982
(in billions of SDRs)

Total purchases	7.4
Reserve tranche purchases	1.3
Credit tranche purchases	2.5
Compensatory financing purchases	2.6
Extended facility purchases	2.1
Buffer stock purchases	0.1
Total repurchases	1.8

Membership

Membership of the Fund rose to 146 in 1982, with the admission of Antigua and Barbuda on 25 February, Belize on 16 March, and Hungary on 6 May.

Publications

Publications issued by IMF in 1982 included the *Annual Report*, the *Annual Report on Exchange Arrangements and Exchange Restrictions, Balance of Payments Statistics* (monthly and *Yearbook*), *Direction of Trade Statistics* (monthly and *Yearbook*), *Government Finance Statistics Yearbook, International Financial Statistics* (monthly, *Yearbook* and two supplements) and *World Economic Outlook*. Periodicals included the quarterlies *Staff Papers* and *Finance and Development* (published jointly with the World Bank), the *IMF Survey* (published 23 times a year) and the monthly *IMF Memorandum*.

Also published were explanatory pamphlets on the working of the Fund.

Secretariat

As at 21 December 1982, the total full-time staff of IMF under permanent, fixed-term and short-term appointments was 1,673, drawn from 100 nationalities.

DRAWINGS AND REPAYMENTS BY REPURCHASE IN 1982
(in millions of SDRs)

	Drawings	Repurchases
World	8,783.9	1,637.1
Industrial countries	341.8*	471.3*
Australia	283.7	—
Finland	—	37.7
Iceland	30.6	5.1
New Zealand	27.6	30.8
Spain	—	136.9
United Kingdom	—	261.0
Developing countries		
Oil-exporting countries	308.7	—
Nigeria	308.7	—
Non-oil developing countries	8,133.3	1,165.7
Africa	2,312.0*	273.0*
Central African Republic	2.4	0.6
Equatorial Guinea	1.3	1.3
Ethiopia	23.5	2.3
Gabon	—	2.0
Gambia	16.9	2.2
Ghana	8.5	4.8
Guinea	15.9	1.6
Guinea-Bissau	—	0.3
Ivory Coast	115.4	—
Kenya	150.4	16.9
Lesotho	2.0	—
Liberia	64.4	—
Madagascar	57.7	5.4
Malawi	14.7	12.6
Mali	25.4	1.1
Mauritania	18.8	3.7
Mauritius	28.0	5.5
Morocco	433.3	32.5
Senegal	53.2	13.3
Sierra Leone	5.1	5.3
Somalia	37.0	4.8
South Africa	902.2	—
Sudan	71.8	30.2
Swaziland	4.3	—
Uganda	85.0	1.5
United Republic of Cameroon	—	3.0
United Republic of Tanzania	1.7	11.1
Zaire	131.6	22.1
Zambia	41.5	86.2
Asia	2,395.5	334.3
Bangladesh	131.2	33.9
Burma	25.6	6.9
Fiji	13.5	—
India	1,500.0	—
Malaysia	58.5	—
Nepal	—	4.8
Pakistan	455.2	84.7
Philippines	—	67.7
Republic of Korea	106.2	35.1
Samoa	0.1	0.7
Solomon Islands	1.6	—
Sri Lanka	39.2	44.6
Thailand	64.4	34.4
Viet Nam	—	21.5
Europe	1,485.2	276.8
Cyprus	—	9.3
Greece	—	13.9
Hungary	295.9	—
Portugal	14.0	51.7
Romania	321.3	46.3
Turkey	300.0	116.4
Yugoslavia	554.0	39.2
Middle East	84.6*	119.7*
Democratic Yemen	17.9	2.9
Egypt	47.0	43.9
Israel	—	60.4
Syrian Arab Republic	19.6	12.5

	Drawings	Repurchases
Western Hemisphere	1,856.1*	161.9*
Antigua and Barbuda	0.7	—
Argentina	137.4	—
Barbados	27.2	0.8
Bolivia	24.5	7.5
Brazil	498.8	—
Chile	—	36.1
Costa Rica	—	4.0
Dominica	2.8	—
Dominican Republic	54.1	9.8
Ecuador	24.8	—
El Salvador	59.8	—
Grenada	—	0.8
Guyana	5.9	2.2
Haiti	12.0	1.0
Honduras	61.7	—
Jamaica	170.1	46.5
Mexico	361.7	—
Nicaragua	—	3.6
Panama	—	4.3
Peru	299.9	43.9
Saint Lucia	—	1.5
Uruguay	114.9	—

*Differs from sum of individual figures because of rounding.

CURRENCIES DRAWN AND REPURCHASES BY CURRENCY OF REPURCHASE IN 1982
(in millions of SDRs)

	Currencies drawn	Repurchases by currency of repurchase
World	8,783.9*	1,762.2*
Industrial countries	4,378.7*	850.2*
Austrian schillings	44.7	9.2
Belgian francs	—	15.3
Canadian dollars	—	15.2
Danish kroner	—	5.5
Deutsche marks	492.9	160.5
French francs	—	15.0
Japanese yen	633.2	76.9
Netherlands guilders	96.0	29.5
Norwegian kroner	68.8	9.5
Pounds sterling	171.7	—
Swedish kronor	—	5.3
United States dollars	2,871.5	508.4
Developing countries		
Oil-exporting countries	1,388.8*	112.2*
Algerian dinars	10.8	2.0
Indonesian rupiahs	26.8	2.1
Kuwaiti dinars	127.8	6.1
Nigerian naira	—	4.0
Omani rials	3.9	—
Qatar riyals	1.3	—
Saudi Arabian riyals	1,032.4	84.8
United Arab Emirates dirhams	18.1	1.4
Venezuelan bolívares	167.9	11.7
Non-oil developing countries	120.5	39.6
Asia	6.5	2.2
Indian rupees	—	—
Malaysian ringgits	—	—
Singapore dollars	6.5	2.2
Europe	2.5	0.1
Malta pounds	2.5	0.1
Middle East	2.9	—
Bahrain dinars	2.9	—
Western Hemisphere	108.5*	37.3*
Argentine pesos	—	10.8
Brazilian cruzeiros	47.0	13.9
Chilean pesos	6.3	—
Colombian pesos	34.1	9.3
Paraguayan guaranies	3.3	0.8
Trinidad and Tobago dollars	17.9	2.5
SDRs	2,895.9	750.2

*Differs from sum of individual figures because of rounding.

Annex I. MEMBERSHIP OF THE INTERNATIONAL MONETARY FUND, QUOTAS AND VOTING POWER (As at 31 December 1982)

MEMBER	QUOTA Amount (in millions of SDRs)	QUOTA General and SDR Departments percentage of total*	VOTING POWER Number of votes†	VOTING POWER General and SDR Departments percentage of total
Afghanistan	67.50	0.11	925	0.14
Algeria	427.50	0.70	4,525	0.70
Antigua and Barbuda	3.60	0.01	286	0.04
Argentina	802.50	1.31	8,275	1.28
Australia	1,185.00	1.94	12,100	1.87
Austria	495.00	0.81	5,200	0.80
Bahamas	49.50	0.08	745	0.12
Bahrain	30.00	0.05	550	0.08
Bangladesh	228.00	0.37	2,530	0.39
Barbados	25.50	0.04	505	0.08
Belgium	1,335.00	2.19	13,600	2.10
Belize	7.20	0.01	322	0.05
Benin	24.00	0.04	490	0.08
Bhutan	1.70	0.003	267	0.04
Bolivia	67.50	0.11	925	0.14
Botswana	13.50	0.02	385	0.06
Brazil	997.50	1.63	10,225	1.58
Burma	109.50	0.18	1,345	0.21
Burundi	34.50	0.06	595	0.09
Canada	2,035.50	3.33	20,605	3.18
Cape Verde	3.00	0.005	280	0.04
Central African Republic	24.00	0.04	490	0.08
Chad	24.00	0.04	490	0.08
Chile	325.50	0.53	3,505	0.54
China	1,800.00	2.95	18,250	2.82
Colombia	289.50	0.47	3,145	0.49
Comoros	3.50	0.01	285	0.04
Congo	25.50	0.04	505	0.08
Costa Rica	61.50	0.10	865	0.13
Cyprus	51.00	0.08	760	0.12
Democratic Kampuchea	25.00	0.04	500	0.08
Democratic Yemen	61.50	0.10	865	0.13
Denmark	465.00	0.76	4,900	0.76
Djibouti	5.70	0.01	307	0.05
Dominica	2.90	0.005	279	0.04
Dominican Republic	82.50	0.14	1,075	0.17
Ecuador	105.00	0.17	1,300	0.20
Egypt	342.00	0.56	3,670	0.57
El Salvador	64.50	0.11	895	0.14
Equatorial Guinea	15.00	0.02	400	0.06
Ethiopia	54.00	0.09	790	0.12
Fiji	27.00	0.04	520	0.08
Finland	393.00	0.64	4,180	0.65
France	2,878.50	4.71	29,035	4.49
Gabon	45.00	0.07	700	0.11
Gambia	13.50	0.02	385	0.06
Germany, Federal Republic of	3,234.00	5.30	32,590	5.04
Ghana	159.00	0.26	1,840	0.28
Greece	277.50	0.45	3,025	0.47
Grenada	4.50	0.01	295	0.05
Guatemala	76.50	0.13	1,015	0.16
Guinea	45.00	0.07	700	0.11
Guinea-Bissau	5.90	0.01	309	0.05
Guyana	37.50	0.06	625	0.10
Haiti	34.50	0.06	595	0.09
Honduras	51.00	0.08	760	0.12
Hungary	375.00	0.61	4,000	0.62
Iceland	43.50	0.07	685	0.11
India	1,717.50	2.81	17,425	2.69
Indonesia	720.00	1.18	7,450	1.15
Iran	660.00	1.08	6,850	1.06
Iraq	234.10	0.38	2,591	0.40
Ireland	232.50	0.38	2,575	0.40
Israel	307.50	0.50	3,325	0.51
Italy	1,860.00	3.05	18,850	2.91
Ivory Coast	114.00	0.19	1,390	0.21
Jamaica	111.00	0.18	1,360	0.21
Japan	2,488.50	4.08	25,135	3.88
Jordan	45.00	0.07	700	0.11
Kenya	103.50	0.17	1,285	0.20
Kuwait	393.30	0.64	4,183	0.65
Lao People's Democratic Republic	24.00	0.04	490	0.08
Lebanon	27.90	0.05	529	0.08
Lesotho	10.50	0.02	355	0.05
Liberia	55.50	0.09	805	0.12
Libyan Arab Jamahiriya	298.40	0.49	3,234	0.50
Luxembourg	46.50	0.08	715	0.11
Madagascar	51.00	0.08	760	0.12
Malawi	28.50	0.05	535	0.08
Malaysia	379.50	0.62	4,045	0.63
Maldives	1.40	0.002	264	0.04
Mali	40.50	0.07	655	0.10
Malta	30.00	0.05	550	0.08
Mauritania	25.50	0.04	505	0.08
Mauritius	40.50	0.07	655	0.10
Mexico	802.50	1.31	8,275	1.28
Morocco	225.00	0.37	2,500	0.39
Nepal	28.50	0.05	535	0.08
Netherlands	1,422.00	2.33	14,470	2.24
New Zealand	348.00	0.57	3,730	0.58
Nicaragua	51.00	0.08	760	0.12
Niger	24.00	0.04	490	0.08
Nigeria	540.00	0.88	5,650	0.87
Norway	442.50	0.72	4,675	0.72
Oman	30.00	0.05	550	0.08
Pakistan	427.50	0.70	4,525	0.70
Panama	67.50	0.11	925	0.14
Papua New Guinea	45.00	0.07	700	0.11
Paraguay	34.50	0.06	595	0.09
Peru	246.00	0.40	2,710	0.42
Philippines	315.00	0.52	3,400	0.53
Portugal	258.00	0.42	2,830	0.44
Qatar	66.20	0.11	912	0.14
Republic of Korea	255.90	0.42	2,809	0.43
Romania	367.50	0.60	3,925	0.61
Rwanda	34.50	0.06	595	0.09
Saint Lucia	5.40	0.01	304	0.05
Saint Vincent and the Grenadines	2.60	0.004	276	0.04
Samoa	4.50	0.01	295	0.05
Sao Tome and Principe	3.00	0.005	280	0.04
Saudi Arabia	2,100.00	3.44	21,250	3.28
Senegal	63.00	0.10	880	0.14
Seychelles	2.00	0.003	270	0.04
Sierra Leone	46.50	0.08	715	0.11
Singapore	92.40	0.15	1,174	0.18
Solomon Islands	3.20	0.005	282	0.04
Somalia	34.50	0.06	595	0.09
South Africa	636.00	1.04	6,610	1.02
Spain	835.50	1.37	8,605	1.33
Sri Lanka	178.50	0.29	2,035	0.31
Sudan	132.00	0.22	1,570	0.24
Suriname	37.50	0.06	625	0.10
Swaziland	18.00	0.03	430	0.07
Sweden	675.00	1.11	7,000	1.08
Syrian Arab Republic	94.50	0.15	1,195	0.18
Thailand	271.50	0.44	2,965	0.46
Togo	28.50	0.05	535	0.08
Trinidad and Tobago	123.00	0.20	1,480	0.23
Tunisia	94.50	0.15	1,195	0.18
Turkey	300.00	0.49	3,250	0.50
Uganda	75.00	0.12	1,000	0.15
United Arab Emirates	202.60	0.33	2,276	0.35
United Kingdom	4,387.50	7.19	44,125	6.82
United Republic of Cameroon	67.50	0.11	925	0.14
United Republic of Tanzania	82.50	0.14	1,075	0.17
United States	12,607.50	20.65	126,325	19.52
Upper Volta	24.00	0.04	490	0.08

MEMBER	QUOTA		VOTING POWER		MEMBER	QUOTA		VOTING POWER	
	Amount (in millions of SDRs)	General and SDR Departments percentage of total*	Number of votes†	General and SDR Departments percentage of total		Amount (in millions of SDRs)	General and SDR Departments percentage of total*	Number of votes†	General and SDR Departments percentage of total
Uruguay	126.00	0.21	1,510	0.23	Zaire	228.00	0.37	2,530	0.39
Vanuatu	6.90	0.01	319	0.05	Zambia	211.50	0.35	2,365	0.37
Venezuela	990.00	1.62	10,150	1.57	Zimbabwe	150.00	0.25	1,750	0.27
Viet Nam	135.00	0.22	1,600	0.25					
Yemen	19.50	0.03	445	0.07					
Yugoslavia	415.50	0.68	4,405	0.68	Total	61,059.80	100.00†	647,098	100.00‡

*All members were participants in the SDR Department.

†Voting power varies on certain matters pertaining to the General Department with use of the Fund's resources in that Department, which comprised four accounts: the General Resources Account, the Borrowed Resources Suspense Account, the Special Disbursement Account and the Investment Account.

‡May differ from the sum of individual percentages because of rounding.

Annex II. EXECUTIVE DIRECTORS AND ALTERNATES OF THE INTERNATIONAL MONETARY FUND (As at 31 December 1982)

Appointed Director	Appointed Alternate	Casting the vote of
Richard D. Erb	Charles H. Dallara	United States
John Anson	Christopher T. Taylor	United Kingdom
Gerhard Laske	Guenter Grosche	Germany, Federal Republic of
Bruno de Maulde	Anne Le Lorier	France
Teruo Hirao	Tadaie Yamashita	Japan
Yusuf A. Nimatallah	Jobarah E. Suraisry	Saudi Arabia

Elected Director	Elected Alternate	Casting the vote of
Miguel A. Senior (Venezuela)	José L. Feito (Spain)	Costa Rica, El Salvador, Guatemala, Honduras, Mexico, Nicaragua, Spain, Venezuela
Robert K. Joyce (Canada)	Michael Casey (Ireland)	Antigua and Barbuda, Bahamas, Barbados, Belize, Canada, Dominica, Grenada, Ireland, Jamaica, Saint Lucia, Saint Vincent and the Grenadines
J. J. Polak (Netherlands)	Tom de Vries (Netherlands)	Cyprus, Israel, Netherlands, Romania, Yugoslavia
Jacques de Groote (Belgium)	Heinrich G. Schneider (Austria)	Austria, Belgium, Hungary, Luxembourg, Turkey
Giovanni Lovato (Italy)	Costa P. Caranicas (Greece)	Greece, Italy, Malta, Portugal
A. R. G. Prowse (Australia)	Kerry G. Morrell (New Zealand)	Australia, New Zealand, Papua New Guinea, Philippines, Republic of Korea, Samoa, Seychelles, Solomon Islands, Vanuatu
Mohamed Finaish (Libyan Arab Jamahiriya)	Tariq Alhaimus (Iraq)	Bahrain, Democratic Yemen, Iraq, Jordan, Kuwait, Lebanon, Libyan Arab Jamahiriya, Maldives, Oman, Pakistan, Qatar, Somalia, Syrian Arab Republic, United Arab Emirates, Yemen
R. N. Malhotra (India)	A. S. Jayawardena (Sri Lanka)	Bangladesh, Bhutan, India, Sri Lanka
Jón Sigurdsson (Iceland)	Leiv Vidvei (Norway)	Denmark, Finland, Iceland, Norway, Sweden
N'Faly Sangare (Guinea)	E. I. M. Mtei (United Republic of Tanzania)	Botswana, Burundi, Ethiopia, Gambia, Guinea, Kenya, Lesotho, Liberia, Malawi, Nigeria, Sierra Leone, Sudan, Swaziland, Uganda, United Republic of Tanzania, Zambia, Zimbabwe
A. Hasnan Habib (Indonesia)	Vijit Supinit (Thailand)	Burma, Fiji, Indonesia, Lao People's Democratic Republic, Malaysia, Nepal, Singapore, Thailand, Viet Nam
Alexandre Kafka (Brazil)	José Gabriel-Peña (Dominican Republic)	Brazil, Colombia, Dominican Republic, Ecuador, Guyana, Haiti, Panama, Suriname, Trinidad and Tobago
Zhang Zicun (China)	Tai Qianding (China)	China
Ghassem Salehkhou (Iran)	Omar Kabbaj (Morocco)	Afghanistan, Algeria, Ghana, Iran, Morocco, Tunisia
Alvaro Donoso (Chile)	Mario Teijeiro (Argentina)	Argentina, Bolivia, Chile, Paraguay, Peru, Uruguay
Abderrahmane Alfidja (Niger)	Vacant	Benin, Cape Verde, Central African Republic, Chad, Comoros, Congo, Djibouti, Equatorial Guinea, Gabon, Guinea-Bissau, Ivory Coast, Madagascar, Mali, Mauritania, Mauritius, Niger, Rwanda, Sao Tome and Principe, Senegal, Togo, United Republic of Cameroon, Upper Volta, Zaire

NOTE: Democratic Kampuchea, Egypt and South Africa did not participate in the 1982 regular election of Executive Directors.

Annex III. PRINCIPAL OFFICERS AND OFFICES OF THE INTERNATIONAL MONETARY FUND

(As at 31 December 1982)

PRINCIPAL OFFICERS

Managing Director: J. de Larosière.
Deputy Managing Director: William B. Dale.
Counsellor: Walter O. Habermeier.*
Economic Counsellor: William C. Hood.*
Counsellor: L. A. Whittome.*
Director, Adjustment Studies: Charles F. Schwartz.
Director, Administration Department: Roland Tenconi.
Director, African Department: J. B. Zulu.
Director, Asian Department: Tun Thin.
Director, Central Banking Department: P. N. Kaul.
Director, European Department: L. A. Whittome.
Director, Exchange and Trade Relations Department: C. David Finch.
Director, External Relations Department: Azizali F. Mohammed.
Director, Fiscal Affairs Department: Vito Tanzi.

   *Alphabetical listing.

Director, IMF Institute: Gérard M. Teyssier.
Director, Legal Department: George Nicoletopoulos.
Director, Middle Eastern Department: A. Shakour Shaalan.
Director, Research Department: William C. Hood.
Secretary, Secretary's Department: Leo Van Houtven.
Treasurer, Treasurer's Department: Walter O. Habermeier.
Director, Western Hemisphere Department: Eduardo Wiesner.
Director, Bureau of Computing Services: Warren N. Minami.
Director, Bureau of Language Services: Andrew J. Beith.
Director, Bureau of Statistics: Werner Dannemann.
Director, Office in Europe (Paris): Aldo Guetta.
Acting Director, Office in Geneva: Jack P. Barnouin.
Internal Auditor: Peter A. Whipple.
Special Representative to the United Nations: Jan-Maarten Zegers.

HEADQUARTERS AND OTHER OFFICES

HEADQUARTERS

International Monetary Fund
700 19th Street N. W.
Washington, D. C. 20431, United States
  Cable address: INTERFUND WASHINGTONDC
  Telephone: (202) 477-7000
  Telex: (RCA) 248331 IMF, (ITT) 440040 UI,
    (TRT) 197677 FUND UT, (WU) 89524,
    (WUI) 64111 INTERFUND WSH

OTHER OFFICES

International Monetary Fund
European Office
64-66 Avenue d'Iéna
75116 Paris, France
  Cable address: INTERFUND PARIS
  Telephone: 723-54-21
  Telex: 610712 INTERFUND

International Monetary Fund
58, Rue de Moillebeau
1209 Geneva, Switzerland
  Cable address: INTERFUND GENEVA
  Telephone: 34-30-00
  Telex: 23503 IMF CH

International Monetary Fund Office
United Nations Headquarters, Room DC-1145
New York, N. Y. 10017, United States
  Telephone: (212) 754-6009

Chapter X

International Civil Aviation Organization (ICAO)

The International Civil Aviation Organization (ICAO) estimated total traffic of the world's scheduled airlines to be over 138 million tonne-kilometres during 1982, an increase of about 2.4 per cent over 1981. Airlines carried over 750 million passengers at a load factor of 64 per cent, the same as for the previous year. Air freight increased by a little over 1 per cent, the lowest rate recorded during the past decade, to some 31 billion tonne-kilometres. Airmail traffic amounted to 3.9 billion tonne-kilometres, an increase of about 2 per cent, below the average rate of increase in 10 years.

During 1982, membership of ICAO remained unchanged at 150.

Activities in 1982

Air navigation

During 1982, the main efforts of ICAO in the air navigation field continued to be directed towards updating and implementing ICAO Specifications and Regional Plans. The Specifications consisted of International Standards and Recommended Practices contained in 17 technical annexes to the Convention on International Civil Aviation (Chicago, United States, 1944), and of Procedures for Air Navigation Services (PANS) contained in three PANS documents. The Regional Plans set forth air navigation facilities and services required for international air navigation in the nine ICAO regions.

The Specifications in 11 annexes and in the three PANS documents were amended. Amendments were also made to Regional Plans.

Five air navigation meetings were held in 1982; they covered a wide range of subjects and made recommendations for changes to ICAO Specifications. To promote uniform application of the Specifications, ICAO made available guidance material in the form of 10 new and revised technical manuals and ICAO circulars.

The regional offices of ICAO assisted States in implementing Regional Plans. This work was supplemented by that of experts sent to advise States on the installation of new facilities and services and the operation of existing ones.

Special attention was given to: aircraft operations, noise, and accident investigation and prevention; aerodromes; air traffic control; aeronautical charts, communications, information services and meteorology; personnel licensing and training; aviation medicine and security; and transport of dangerous goods.

Air transport

In the air transport field during 1982, ICAO continued its programmes of economic studies, collecting and publishing air transport statistics and promoting greater facilitation in international air transport.

The sixth meeting of the expert panel on regulating air transport services, held in March, considered the regulation of non-scheduled air transport and the feasibility of amending certain articles of the Convention on International Civil Aviation. Another panel of experts, on machinery for establishing international fares and rates, held its sixth meeting in October. It examined and made recommendations on rules and practices concerning denied boarding compensation, baggage allowances and charges, and airline conditions of carriage. It also gave preliminary consideration to conditions attached to different types of fares.

Informal regional workshop meetings were held during 1982 to study aviation forecasting and economic planning (Amman, Jordan, June), airport and route facility economics (Lima, Peru, April; Helsinki, Finland, September), international fares and rates (Mexico City, March) and facilitation (Mexico City, June).

A study of air passenger and freight transport for Latin America and the Caribbean was completed for publication in 1983. Other 1982 publications included the regular series of digests of civil aviation statistics, the yearbook on world civil aviation statistics, a manual of airport and air navigation facility tariffs and a survey of international air transport fares and rates in 1981.

ICAO continued secretariat services to three independent regional civil aviation bodies—the African Civil Aviation Commission, the European Civil Aviation Conference and the Latin American Civil Aviation Commission.

A 1956 joint financing agreement for air navigation services in Greenland and the Faeroe Islands, and another in Iceland, continued to be administered by ICAO. In February 1982, a conference adopted recommendations to amend the agreements and their annexes. The necessary protocols were adopted in November for implementation as of 1 January 1983.

Legal matters

The ICAO Council, during its March 1982 session, decided to convene the twenty-fifth session of the Legal Committee at Montreal, Canada, from 12 to 27 April 1983. It did so bearing in mind a decision of the twenty-third (1980) session of the ICAO Assembly that the Committee should meet to consider any revisions necessary to its general work programme to reflect the needs of civil aviation in the 1980s. As a result of a decision of the Legal Commission, approved by the Assembly in 1980, the Committee's work programme currently included the legal status of the aircraft commander, the liability of air traffic control agencies, aerial collisions, the study of the status of the legal instruments of the "Warsaw System" (the 1929 Warsaw Convention for the Unification of Certain Rules relating to International Carriage by Air, as amended by Protocols dated 1955, 1971 and 1975), and liability for damage caused by noise and sonic boom.

The Council also gave preliminary consideration to a study of the Legal Bureau on the liability of air traffic control agencies and the status of the legal instruments of the Warsaw System, items which an expert panel, meeting at Montreal in June 1981 to make recommendations to the Council on the general work programme of the Legal Committee, had recommended should remain in the programme. The study, together with a questionnaire, was sent to contracting States and international organizations for comment.

The Committee on Unlawful Interference with International Civil Aviation and its Facilities held eight meetings during the year. The Committee made recommendations to the Council concerning implementation of a 1980 Assembly resolution on the refusal to allow unlawfully seized aircraft to land. The Council, on 30 June, adopted a resolution in which it urged contracting States to provide assistance to aircraft subjected to acts of unlawful seizure, including the provision of navigational aids, air traffic services and permission to land.

In response to a recommendation of the United Nations Security Council Commission of Inquiry, set up to investigate a 1981 mercenary aggression against Seychelles,[a] the Committee considered

---

[a]See YUN 1981, p. 226.

measures to prevent clandestine transportation of weapons and munition in checked baggage.

The following conventions on international air law concluded under ICAO auspices were ratified or adhered to during 1982:

International Air Services Transit Agreement of the Convention on International Civil Aviation (Chicago, 1944)
  Panama

Convention on International Recognition of Rights in Aircraft (Geneva, 1948)
  Congo

Convention on Damage Caused by Foreign Aircraft to Third Parties on the Surface (Rome, 1952)
  USSR, Vanuatu

Convention, Supplementary to the Warsaw Convention, for the Unification of Certain Rules relating to International Carriage by Air Performed by a Person other than the Contracting Carrier (Guadalajara, 1961)
  Zimbabwe

Convention on Offences and Certain other Acts Committed on Board Aircraft (Tokyo, 1963)
  Solomon Islands, Uganda

Convention for the Suppression of Unlawful Seizure of Aircraft (The Hague, 1970)
  India, Liberia, United Arab Emirates

Convention for the Suppression of Unlawful Acts against the Safety of Civil Aviation (Montreal, 1971)
  India, Liberia, Luxembourg, Solomon Islands, Uganda

Technical assistance

During 1982, ICAO provided technical assistance to 102 States; in 63 of these, there were resident missions of one or more experts. In addition to resident expertise, assistance was provided in the form of equipment, fellowships and scholarships, and through short missions by experts.

Thirty-three new large-scale projects, each costing more than $500,000, for which ICAO was to be the executing agency, were approved by the Administrator of the United Nations Development Programme (UNDP). Three other large-scale projects were financed under trust fund assistance.

ICAO employed 697 experts from 55 countries during all or part of 1982, 370 on assignments under UNDP and 327 on trust fund projects (including 13 under the associate experts programme). There were also 13 United Nations Volunteers. The number of experts in the field at the end of 1982 was 411 as compared with 415 at the end of 1981.

A total of 1,014 fellowships were awarded in 1982 (compared with 1,180 for 1981), of which 962 were implemented.

Equipment purchases and sub-contracts were a substantial proportion of the technical assistance programme in 1982; the total sum committed was $16.6 million. Thirty-one Governments or organizations had registered with ICAO under the Civil Aviation Purchasing Service.

The following countries and territories were aided:

Africa: Angola, Benin, Botswana, Cape Verde, Central African Republic, Chad, Ethiopia, Gabon, Ghana, Guinea, Guinea-Bissau, Ivory Coast, Kenya, Lesotho, Liberia, Madagascar, Malawi, Mali, Mauritania, Mauritius, Mozambique, Niger, Nigeria, Senegal, Seychelles, Sierra Leone, Somalia, Swaziland, Togo, Uganda, United Republic of Cameroon, United Republic of Tanzania, Zaire, Zambia, Zimbabwe.

Americas: Antigua, Argentina, Bahamas, Bolivia, Brazil, Cayman Islands, Chile, Colombia, Ecuador, El Salvador, Guatemala, Haiti, Honduras, multiple islands (Caribbean), Netherlands Antilles, Panama, Peru, St. Kitts–Nevis–Anguilla, Saint Lucia, Suriname, Trinidad and Tobago, Turks and Caicos Islands, Uruguay, Venezuela.

Asia/Pacific: Afghanistan, Bangladesh, Burma, China, Cook Islands, Democratic People's Republic of Korea, India, Indonesia, Lao People's Democratic Republic, Malaysia, Maldives, Nepal, Pakistan, Philippines, Samoa, Singapore, Sri Lanka, Thailand, Viet Nam.

Europe, Mediterranean and Middle East: Algeria, Cyprus, Democratic Yemen, Djibouti, Egypt, Greece, Iraq, Jordan, Kuwait, Lebanon, Libyan Arab Jamahiriya, Morocco, Oman, Poland, Qatar, Romania, Saudi Arabia, Sudan, Syrian Arab Republic, Turkey, Yemen.

Included in the above were the following, aided during the year under trust fund arrangements: Argentina, Bolivia, Cape Verde, Ecuador, Iraq, Ivory Coast, Jordan, Libyan Arab Jamahiriya, Nigeria, Panama, Peru, Qatar, Saudi Arabia, Suriname, Trinidad and Tobago, Yemen.

Secretariat

As at 31 December 1982, the total number of staff members employed in the ICAO secretariat stood at 900; 325 in the Professional and higher categories drawn from 66 nationalities, and 575 in the General Service and related categories. Among them were 197 persons employed at regional offices. In addition, there were 182 in the Professional category serving as technical experts on UNDP projects in the field.

Budget

The revised appropriations for the 1982 financial year totalled $29,473,000. Modifications were approved by the ICAO Council and are reflected below (in United States dollars):

	Appropriations*	Revised appropriations	Actual obligations
Meetings	678,000	203,000	202,440
Secretariat	21,435,000	25,015,000	25,014,570
General service	3,365,000	3,804,000	3,803,737
Equipment	195,000	413,000	412,323
Other budgetary provisions	226,000	38,000	37,411
Contingencies	3,903,000	—	—
Establishment of new regional office	80,000	—	—
Total	29,882,000	29,473,000	29,470,481

*Includes carry-over of $500,000 from 1981.

Annex I. MEMBERSHIP OF THE INTERNATIONAL CIVIL AVIATION ORGANIZATION AND CONTRIBUTIONS

(Membership as at 31 December 1982; contributions as assessed for 1982)

MEMBER	CONTRIBUTION Percentage	Net amount (in US dollars)	MEMBER	CONTRIBUTION Percentage	Net amount (in US dollars)	MEMBER	CONTRIBUTION Percentage	Net amount (in US dollars)
Afghanistan	0.06	13,392	Grenada	0.06	13,392	Panama	0.06	13,392
Algeria	0.16	35,712	Guatemala	0.06	13,392	Papua New Guinea	0.06	13,392
Angola	0.06	13,392	Guinea	0.06	13,392	Paraguay	0.06	13,392
Antigua and Barbuda	0.06	13,392	Guinea-Bissau	0.06	13,392	Peru	0.10	22,320
Argentina	0.83	185,256	Guyana	0.06	13,392	Philippines	0.22	49,104
Australia	1.92	428,544	Haiti	0.06	13,392	Poland	1.02	227,664
Austria	0.55	122,760	Honduras	0.06	13,392	Portugal	0.33	73,656
Bahamas	0.06	13,392	Hungary	0.30	66,960	Qatar	0.06	13,392
Bahrain	0.06	13,392	Iceland	0.08	17,856	Republic of Korea	0.53	118,296
Bangladesh	0.07	15,624	India	0.71	158,472	Romania	0.24	53,568
Barbados	0.06	13,392	Indonesia	0.26	58,032	Rwanda	0.06	13,392
Belgium	1.13	252,216	Iran	0.56	124,992	Saint Lucia	0.06	13,392
Benin	0.06	13,392	Iraq	0.19	42,408	Sao Tome and Principe	0.06	13,392
Bolivia	0.06	13,392	Ireland	0.19	42,408	Saudi Arabia	0.43	95,976
Botswana	0.06	13,392	Israel	0.37	82,584	Senegal	0.06	13,392
Brazil	1.51	337,032	Italy	2.97	662,904	Seychelles	0.06	13,392
Bulgaria	0.16	35,712	Ivory Coast	0.06	13,392	Sierra Leone	0.06	13,392
Burma	0.06	13,392	Jamaica	0.07	15,624	Singapore	0.47	104,904
Burundi	0.06	13,392	Japan	8.14	1,816,848	Somalia	0.06	13,392
Canada	3.21	716,472	Jordan	0.09	20,088	South Africa	0.58	129,456
Cape Verde	0.06	13,392	Kenya	0.06	13,392	Spain	1.85	412,920
Central African Republic	0.06	13,392	Kiribati	0.06	13,392	Sri Lanka	0.06	13,392
Chad	0.06	13,392	Kuwait	0.23	51,336	Sudan	0.06	13,392
Chile	0.13	29,016	Lao People's Democratic			Suriname	0.06	13,392
China	0.83	185,256	Republic	0.06	13,392	Swaziland	0.06	13,392
Colombia	0.23	51,336	Lebanon	0.26	58,032	Sweden	1.13	252,216
Congo	0.06	13,392	Lesotho	0.06	13,392	Switzerland	1.21	270,072
Costa Rica	0.06	13,392	Liberia	0.06	13,392	Syrian Arab Republic	0.08	17,856
Cuba	0.12	26,784	Libyan Arab Jamahiriya	0.19	42,408	Thailand	0.24	53,568
Cyprus	0.06	13,392	Luxembourg	0.06	13,392	Togo	0.06	13,392
Czechoslovakia	0.63	140,616	Madagascar	0.06	13,392	Trinidad and Tobago	0.06	13,392
Democratic Kampuchea	0.06	13,392	Malawi	0.06	13,392	Tunisia	0.06	13,392
Democratic People's			Malaysia	0.15	33,480	Turkey	0.33	73,656
Republic of Korea	0.06	13,392	Maldives	0.06	13,392	Uganda	0.06	13,392
Democratic Yemen	0.06	13,392	Mali	0.06	13,392	USSR	10.64	2,374,848
Denmark	0.67	149,544	Malta	0.06	13,392	United Arab Emirates	0.10	22,320
Djibouti	0.06	13,392	Mauritania	0.06	13,392	United Kingdom	4.92	1,098,144
Dominican Republic	0.06	13,392	Mauritius	0.06	13,392	United Republic of		
Ecuador	0.06	13,392	Mexico	0.86	191,952	Cameroon	0.06	13,392
Egypt	0.17	37,944	Monaco	0.06	13,392	United Republic of		
El Salvador	0.06	13,392	Morocco	0.12	26,784	Tanzania	0.06	13,392
Equatorial Guinea	0.06	13,392	Mozambique	0.06	13,392	United States	25.00	5,580,000
Ethiopia	0.06	13,392	Nauru	0.06	13,392	Upper Volta	0.06	13,392
Fiji	0.06	13,392	Nepal	0.06	13,392	Uruguay	0.06	13,392
Finland	0.41	91,512	Netherlands	1.84	410,688	Venezuela	0.54	120,528
France	5.77	1,287,864	New Zealand	0.37	82,584	Viet Nam	0.06	13,392
Gabon	0.06	13,392	Nicaragua	0.06	13,392	Yemen	0.06	13,392
Gambia	0.06	13,392	Niger	0.06	13,392	Yugoslavia	0.45	100,440
Germany, Federal			Nigeria	0.16	35,712	Zaire	0.06	13,392
Republic of	6.81	1,519,992	Norway	0.50	111,600	Zambia	0.06	13,392
Ghana	0.06	13,392	Oman	0.06	13,392	Zimbabwe	0.06	13,392
Greece	0.47	104,904	Pakistan	0.28	62,496	Total*	100.24	22,373,568

*Includes assessments for Antigua and Barbuda, Grenada, Kiribati and Zimbabwe which became contracting States after current assessment rates were set.

Annex II. OFFICERS AND OFFICES OF THE INTERNATIONAL CIVIL AVIATION ORGANIZATION

(As at 31 December 1982)

ICAO COUNCIL

OFFICERS

President: Assad Kotaite (Lebanon).
First Vice-President: L. Mesón (Spain).
Second Vice-President: E. F. De Araujo Cortes (Brazil).
Third Vice-President: E. M. K. Wakida (Uganda).
Secretary: Yves Lambert (France).

MEMBERS

Algeria, Argentina, Australia, Brazil, Canada, China, Colombia, Czechoslovakia, Denmark, Egypt, El Salvador, France, Germany, Federal Republic of, India, Indonesia, Iraq, Italy, Jamaica, Japan, Lebanon, Madagascar, Mexico, Netherlands, Nigeria, Pakistan, Senegal, Spain, Uganda, USSR, United Kingdom, United Republic of Cameroon, United States, Venezuela.

PRINCIPAL OFFICERS OF THE SECRETARIAT

Secretary-General: Yves Lambert.
Director, Air Navigation Bureau: D. W. Freer.
Director, Air Transport Bureau: R. A. Bickley.

Director, Legal Bureau: B. S. Gidwani.
Director, Technical Assistance Bureau: M. J. Challons.
Chief, Public Information Office: Eugene Sochor.

OFFICES

HEADQUARTERS

International Civil Aviation Organization
P. O. Box 400, Succursale: Place de
L'Aviation Internationale
1000 Sherbrooke Street West, Suite 400
Montreal, Quebec, Canada H3A 2R2
Cable address: ICAO MONTREAL
Telephone: (514) 285-8219
Telex: 05-24513

REGIONAL OFFICES

International Civil Aviation Organization
African Office
P. O. Box 2356
Dakar, Senegal
Cable address: ICAOREP DAKAR
Telephone: 22-47-86, 21-42-13
Telex: 3348 ICAO/SG

International Civil Aviation Organization
European Office
3 bis, Villa Emile-Bergerat
92522 Neuilly-sur-Seine (Cedex)
France
Cable address: ICAOREP PARIS
Telephone: 745-13-26
Telex: 610075

International Civil Aviation Organization
North American and Caribbean Office
Apartado postal 5-377
Mexico 5, D. F., Mexico
Cable address: ICAOREP MEXICO
Telephone: 250-32-11
Telex: 1777598

International Civil Aviation Organization
Asia and Pacific Office
P. O. Box 614
Bangkok, Thailand
Cable address: ICAOREP BANGKOK
Telephone: 281-5366, 281-5571,
281-0138
Telex: 87969 ICAOBKK TH

International Civil Aviation Organization
South American Office
Apartado postal 4127
Lima 100, Peru
Cable address: ICAOREP LIMA
Telephone: 51-5414, 51-5325, 51-5497
Telex: 25689PEICAO

International Civil Aviation Organization
Middle East and Eastern African Office
16 Hassan Sabri
Zamalek
Cairo, Egypt
Cable address: ICAOREP CAIRO
Telephone: 650163, 650344, 650463, 650532
Telex: 92459 ICAOR UN

Chapter XI

Universal Postal Union (UPU)

The Universal Postal Union (UPU), established at Berne, Switzerland, in 1874 for the reciprocal exchange of postal services between nations, is one of the oldest international intergovernmental organizations. Its aim is to promote the organization and improvement of postal services and to further the development of international collaboration in this sphere. It also participates in various forms of postal technical assistance requested by its member States.

In 1982, the number of UPU members increased to 166, following the admission of Vanuatu (16 July) and Belize (1 October).

Activities of UPU organs in 1982

Universal Postal Congress

The Universal Postal Congress, composed of all UPU member States, is the supreme legislative authority of UPU. Normally meeting every five years, the most recent Congress—the eighteenth—took place at Rio de Janeiro, Brazil, in 1979 and the next was scheduled to meet at Hamburg, Federal Republic of Germany, in 1984.

Executive Council

At its 1982 session, held at Berne from 29 April to 13 May, the 40-member Executive Council—responsible for carrying out the work of UPU between sessions of the Congress—considered administrative matters and studies concerning international mail which had been referred to it by the 1979 Congress.

Among other matters taken up by the Council were: technical assistance for developing countries; relations with the United Nations and other international organizations; UPU finances; international high-speed mail (Datapost, Express Mail, Postadex, etc.); transit charges and terminal dues; customs treatment of postal items; revision of rates and supplementary charges for parcel post; various matters relating to airmail such as basic rates, calculating internal dues, maximizing air conveyance and shipment of biological substances and of radioactive materials, and settlement of accounts; and preparations for the 1984 UPU Congress.

The Council also examined the progress of work by UPU relating to World Communications Year:

Development of Communications Infrastructures (1983), proclaimed by the General Assembly in 1981.[a]

Consultative Council for Postal Studies

The 35-member Consultative Council for Postal Studies, which celebrated its twenty-fifth anniversary in 1982, continued to study problems in the technical, operational and economic fields and technical co-operation problems of the postal administrations of UPU member States, including matters of particular interest to new and developing countries.

During its annual session, held at Berne from 8 to 18 November, the Council continued to examine the future of postal services, particularly new electronic communication technologies. The Council also discussed the development of postal needs and forecasting techniques; improving postal operations; postal mechanization, buildings and motor transport; financial services and accounting; personnel; postal management; and international post. It called the attention of Governments to the importance of reaffirming the postal monopoly and developing measures to combat competition.

International Bureau

Under the general supervision of the Government of the Swiss Confederation, the International Bureau—the secretariat of UPU—continued to serve member States' postal administrations as an organ for liaison, information and consultation.

The Bureau remained responsible for collecting, co-ordinating, publishing and disseminating international postal service information, continued conducting inquiries requested by postal administrations and acted as a clearing-house for the settlement of certain accounts between them.

In connection with the Transport and Communications Decade in Africa (1978-1988), the Bureau examined achievements of the first phase (1980-1983) and prepared its programme for the second phase (1984-1988). At the end of 1982, only 12 postal projects had been implemented; the balance of 61 first-phase projects were to be transferred to the second phase and 79 new projects added, making a total of 140 projects with an estimated total cost of $478 million. The majority of the projects involved the construction of sorting and transit centres and other postal establishments, with the remaining projects concerned with extending and equipping the postal network, training and organization of services.

With regard to the 1983 World Communications Year, the Bureau provided postal administrations with information concerning the Year and invited them to implement activities to increase public awareness, including the issuance of postage stamps commemorating it. The Bureau also asked postal administrations to name representatives for the Year's national committees to implement national programmes and co-operate in regional and international programmes.

As at 31 December 1982, the total number of permanent and temporary staff members employed at the Bureau was 138, of whom 56 were in the Professional and higher categories (drawn from 47 countries) and 82 in the General Service category. Also, 14 officials were employed in the Arabic, English, Portuguese, Spanish and Russian translation services.

Technical co-operation

In 1982, UPU technical co-operation was financed mainly by the United Nations Development Programme (UNDP) with expenditure amounting to some $2.6 million, including approximately $90,000 for consultative services to developing countries. Also, under a new system, UNDP was to reimburse the support costs of its executed projects to UPU at the rate of 22 per cent of the projects' cost—$444,000 for 1982.

Assistance was also provided through the UPU Special Fund and the regular budget. Total expenditures from these two sources in 1982 amounted to approximately $900,000. In addition, the postal administrations provided assistance on a bilateral basis.

Training of postal instructors continued to be given priority: several training courses were organized in Belgium, France, Switzerland, the United Kingdom and other regional training centres; interregional courses were organized in developing countries, including Kenya, Malawi and Senegal.

Forty-three national and regional projects concerning postal services were carried out under UNDP. Fifty-five expert missions were undertaken and 108 scholarships were awarded, two thirds of which were for study courses. Several projects received assistance in the form of equipment. Projects dealt with all main branches of postal service, including national or regional training centres.

The Special Fund, with voluntary contributions in cash and kind from member States, funded various projects including missions by experts and consultants, scholarships for training, instruction materials and equipment. Projects financed under the Special Fund and the regular budget accounted for 30 consultants (one financed by the World Bank) whose missions were made in response to 37 postal administrations, and 177 scholarships, the majority for participation in training courses or technical meetings. In addition, the Special Fund included a contribution by Belgium to con-

[a]See YUN 1981, p. 573, resolution 36/40 of 19 November 1981.

tinue a project assisting the drought-stricken Sahelian region of Africa. Several countries offered contributions in kind in the framework of the Special Fund, largely in the form of scholarships and the organization of workshops.

The Union continued its programme of technical assistance subject to payment, under which member States could finance assistance themselves by funds on deposit, and efforts to promote technical co-operation among developing countries.

Budget

The 1982 financial year was the second year of the self-financing system introduced by the 1979 Universal Postal Congress, by which member countries were to pay in advance on the basis of the following year's budget, instead of on the basis of actual expenditure. At its 1982 April/May session, the Executive Council approved a budget of 20,778,200 Swiss francs for 1983 (see table).

Each member State of UPU chooses its class of contribution, on a scale of 1 to 50 units. For 1983, the Executive Council fixed the amount of the contributory unit at 17,500 Swiss francs on the basis of a total of 1,063 units. The table opposite gives assessments in Swiss francs by class of contribution.

Income	Amount (in Swiss francs)
Contributions from member States	18,602,500
Taken out of reserve funds	429,000
Contributions allocated by UNDP for support of technical co-operation projects	792,000
Sale of publications	191,000
Other	763,700
Total	20,778,200*

Expenditures	
Staff	16,001,100
General expenses	4,777,100
Total	20,778,200*

*Equal to $9,755,023 on the basis of Swiss francs 2.13 = US $1.00.

	ASSESSMENTS	
CLASS OF CONTRIBUTION	Swiss francs	US dollar equivalents*
50 units	875,000	410,798
25 units	437,500	205,399
20 units	350,000	164,319
15 units	262,500	123,239
10 units	175,000	82,160
5 units	87,500	41,080
3 units	52,500	24,648
1 unit	17,500	8,216

*Calculated on the basis of Swiss francs 2.13 = US $1.00.

Annex I. MEMBERSHIP OF THE UNIVERSAL POSTAL UNION AND CLASS OF CONTRIBUTION

(Membership as at 31 December 1982; contributions as assessed for 1983)

Member	Class of contribution;* no. of units	Member	Class of contribution;* no. of units	Member	Class of contribution;* no. of units	Member	Class of contribution;* no. of units	Member	Class of contribution;* no. of units	Member	Class of contribution;* no. of units
Afghanistan	1	Congo	1	Germany,		Libyan Arab		Peru	3	Togo	1
Albania	1	Costa Rica	1	Federal		Jamahiriya	5	Philippines	1	Tonga	1
Algeria	5	Cuba	3	Republic of	50	Liechtenstein	1	Poland	10	Trinidad and	
Angola	1	Cyprus	1	Ghana	3	Luxembourg	3	Portugal	5	Tobago	1
Argentina	20	Czecho-		Greece	3	Madagascar	3	Qatar	5	Tunisia	5
Australia	25	slovakia	10	Grenada	1	Malawi	1	Republic of		Turkey	5
Austria	5	Democratic		Guatemala	3	Malaysia	3	Korea	1	Tuvalu	1
Bahamas	1	Kampuchea	1	Guinea	1	Maldives	1	Romania	5	Uganda	1
Bahrain	1	Democratic		Guinea-Bissau	1	Mali	1	Rwanda	1	Ukrainian SSR	10
Bangladesh	15	People's		Guyana	1	Malta	1	Saint Lucia	1	USSR	25
Barbados	1	Republic		Haiti	3	Mauritania	1	Saint Vincent		United Arab	
Belgium	15	of Korea	5	Honduras	1	Mauritius	1	and the		Emirates	1
Belize	1	Democratic		Hungary	10	Mexico	15	Grenadines	1	United	
Benin	1	Yemen	1	Iceland	1	Monaco	1	San Marino	1	Kingdom	50
Bhutan	1	Denmark	10	India	25	Mongolia	1	Sao Tome		United Kingdom	
Bolivia	1	Djibouti	1	Indonesia	10	Morocco	5	and Principe	1	Overseas	
Botswana	1	Dominica	1	Iran	5	Mozambique	1	Saudi Arabia	25	Territories	5
Brazil	25	Dominican		Iraq	5	Nauru	1	Senegal	1	United Republic	
Bulgaria	3	Republic	3	Ireland	10	Nepal	3	Seychelles	1	of Cameroon	1
Burma	3	Ecuador	3	Israel	3	Netherlands	15	Sierra Leone	1	United Republic	
Burundi	1	Egypt	15	Italy	25	Netherlands		Singapore	1	of Tanzania	1
Byelorussian		El Salvador	1	Ivory Coast	3	Antilles	1	Somalia	1	United States	50
SSR	3	Equatorial		Jamaica	1	New Zealand	20	South Africa	1	Upper Volta	1
Canada	50	Guinea	3	Japan	50	Nicaragua	1	Spain	25	Uruguay	3
Cape Verde	1	Ethiopia	1	Jordan	1	Niger	1	Sri Lanka	5	Vanuatu	1
Central		Fiji	1	Kenya	3	Nigeria	10	Sudan	1	Vatican	1
African		Finland	10	Kuwait	10	Norway	10	Suriname	1	Venezuela	3
Republic	1	France	50	Lao People's		Oman	1	Swaziland	1	Viet Nam	1
Chad	1	Gabon	1	Democratic		Pakistan	15	Sweden	15	Yemen	1
Chile	5	Gambia	1	Republic	1	Panama	1	Switzerland	15	Yugoslavia	5
China	50	German		Lebanon	1	Papua New		Syrian Arab		Zaire	3
Colombia	3	Democratic		Lesotho	1	Guinea	1	Republic	1	Zambia	3
Comoros	1	Republic	15	Liberia	1	Paraguay	1	Thailand	3	Zimbabwe	3

NOTE: The UPU official nomenclature differs from that of the United Nations.
*For amount of contributions from members, see table under BUDGET above.

Annex II.   ORGANS, OFFICERS AND OFFICES OF THE UNIVERSAL POSTAL UNION

EXECUTIVE COUNCIL

(Elected to hold office until the nineteenth (1984) Universal Postal Congress)

Chairman: Brazil.
Vice-Chairmen: China, Liberia, Spain, USSR.
Secretary-General: Mohamed I. Sobhi, Director-General of the International Bureau.
Members: Algeria, Argentina, Bangladesh, Barbados, Brazil, Canada, Chile, China, Cuba, Czechoslovakia, Denmark, Egypt, France, Gabon, Germany, Federal Repub-

lic of, Guinea, Honduras, India, Iraq, Ireland, Ivory Coast, Jordan, Kenya, Liberia, Libyan Arab Jamahiriya, Malaysia, Mali, Mexico, Mongolia, Saudi Arabia, Senegal, Spain, Sri Lanka, Sudan, Syrian Arab Republic, Thailand, USSR, United Kingdom, United States, Yugoslavia.

CONSULTATIVE COUNCIL FOR POSTAL STUDIES

(Elected to hold office until the nineteenth (1984) Universal Postal Congress)

Chairman: United Kingdom.
Vice-Chairman: Tunisia.
Secretary-General: Mohamed I. Sobhi, Director-General of the International Bureau.
Members: Algeria, Argentina, Australia, Austria, Bangladesh, Belgium, Brazil, China,

Colombia, Egypt, France, German Democratic Republic, Germany, Federal Republic of, India, Indonesia, Iraq, Italy, Japan, Mexico, Morocco, Netherlands, New Zealand, Nigeria, Pakistan, Poland, Romania, Spain, Sweden, Switzerland, Thailand, Tunisia, USSR, United Kingdom, United Republic of Cameroon, United States.

INTERNATIONAL BUREAU

OFFICERS

Director-General: Mohamed I. Sobhi.
Deputy Director-General a.i.: Félix Cicéron.
Assistant Directors-General: Félix Cicéron, Abdel Kader Baghdadi, El Mostafa Gharbi.
Assistant Director-General a.i.: Sven Bäckström.

HEADQUARTERS

Bureau international de l'Union postale universelle
Weltpoststrasse 4
Berne, Switzerland
  Postal address: Union postale universelle
        Case postale
        3000 Berne 15 (Suisse)
  Cable address: UPU BERNE
  Telephone: (031) 43 22 11
  Telex: 32 842 UPU CH

Chapter XII

International Telecommunication Union (ITU)

As at 31 December 1982, 157 countries were members of the International Telecommunication Union (ITU).

Administrative Council

The thirty-seventh session of the Administrative Council of ITU was held from 19 May to 7 June 1982 at ITU headquarters, Geneva. It reviewed administrative matters, approved a revised schedule of conferences, and drew up a report for the Plenipotentiary Conference of ITU, the organization's supreme organ.

Plenipotentiary Conference

The Plenipotentiary Conference of ITU was held at Nairobi, Kenya, from 28 September to 6 November 1982. The Conference increased the number of members of the Administrative Council from 36 to 41, and elected Richard E. Butler, Secretary-General, and Jean Jipguep, Deputy Secretary-General of ITU, to take office on 1 January 1983, and members of the International Frequency Registration Board (IFRB).

The Conference also revised basic provisions and general regulations of the 1973 International Telecommunication Convention.[a] The main changes made by the Conference, which emphasized the Union's principles of universality, rotation and geographic distribution of high-level posts, and the problems of technical co-operation and assistance, included: adopting Arabic as an official language of ITU; election of directors of the International Consultative Committees to be by the Conference rather than by the Committees' plenary assemblies; promoting technical co-operation and assistance; and extending the table of classes of members' contributory units both upwards and downwards.

To increase the scope and effectiveness of ITU's technical co-operation activities, the Conference set up a special voluntary programme for developing countries, recognized the need to give higher priority to telecommunications investment and aid programmes, invited the United Nations Development Programme (UNDP) to consider increasing

[a] See YUN 1973, p. 954.

funds for telecommunications projects, and issued guidelines which included training fellowships, recruitment of experts, special facilities for the least developed countries, ITU participation in UNDP, the training of refugees, the organization of seminars, and ITU research on the interrelation between telecommunication infrastructure and development.

In addition, the Conference established an Independent International Commission for World-Wide Telecommunications Development, to be composed of representatives of various administrations and operating agencies as well as industry, financial institutions and other bodies.

The Conference adopted a resolution on the observance of World Communications Year in 1983, recognizing that the basic objectives laid down by the United Nations General Assembly[b] were to provide an opportunity for countries to review their communications policies and to facilitate the development of communications infrastructures.

Administrative radio conferences

The radio regulations adopted by the 1979 World Administrative Radio Conference[c] entered into force on 1 January 1982.

The first session of the Regional Administrative Conference for FM (frequency modulation) sound broadcasting in the VHF (very high frequency) band (Region 1 and certain countries in Region 3) was held from 23 August to 17 September 1982 at Geneva. The Conference prepared a technical report to be forwarded to the second session which was to draw up a frequency plan and agreement.

International consultative committees

The two ITU international consultative committees—the International Radio Consultative Committee (CCIR) and the International Telegraph and Telephone Consultative Committee (CCITT)—held a number of meetings during 1982.

From 15 to 26 February, the fifteenth plenary assembly of CCIR met in Geneva. Action taken included: adoption of a recommendation on a standard concerning the coding parameters for digital television studio equipment; a report on teletext systems—for transmitting textual or graphical information by television; recommendations concerning a digital selective-calling system and automated radiotelephone systems for maritime communications; a series of reports on maritime satellite services; texts on utilizing satellites for broadcasting and other communication purposes; a report on low-capacity earth stations and associated satellite systems; and studies on radio-frequency sharing.

The CCIR also carried out preparatory work for forthcoming administrative radio conferences. No CCIR study group meetings were held during 1982.

The study groups of CCITT concentrated on preparing the final versions of recommendations and replies to questions assigned to them by the 1980 CCITT plenary assembly. These included transmission systems; telephone operation and quality of service; data transmission over the public telephone network; public data networks; digital networks; switching and signalling; maintenance; and general tariff principles.

CCITT's regional plan committee for Asia and Oceania met to co-ordinate development of telecommunications facilities and drew up a plan for 1982-1986 and forecasts for 1990.

International Frequency Registration Board

In 1982, the International Frequency Registration Board (IFRB) continued to implement the decisions of the 1979 World Administrative Radio Conference, including a review of the Master International Frequency Register, developing a method for placing a large number of frequency assignments currently in the fixed service to appropriate bands, developing a method for conversion of designation of emissions, and preparing a handbook on procedures.

IFRB also undertook to adapt its working methods to increased use of the computer; prepared for the Regional FM sound broadcasting conference; assisted member administrations in applying the Radio Regulations, and examined and recorded in the Master Register some 67,000 frequency assignment notices received from member countries.

Technical co-operation

Under various ITU programmes of technical co-operation in developing countries during 1982, 612 expert missions were carried out, 739 fellows underwent training abroad and equipment valued at $5,541,585 was delivered, mainly to telecommunication training centres. The amount of assistance totalled $31,859,857, a reduction of 21 per cent from the previous year. Countries and territories aided were the following:

Africa—Algeria, Angola, Burundi, Botswana, Cape Verde, Central African Republic, Chad, Congo, Djibouti, Egypt, Equatorial Guinea, Ethiopia, Gambia, Ghana, Guinea, Ivory Coast, Malawi, Mauritius, Morocco, Mozambique, Namibia, Nigeria, Rwanda, Senegal, Somalia, Sudan, Swaziland, Tunisia, Uganda, United Republic of Cameroon, Zaire.

The Americas—Argentina, Belize, Brazil, Colombia, Cuba, Ecuador, El Salvador, Guatemala, Guyana, Haiti, Honduras, Jamaica, Nicaragua, Panama, St. Christopher/Nevis, Trinidad and Tobago, Uruguay.

Asia and the Pacific—Afghanistan, Bangladesh, Burma, China, India, Indonesia, Lao People's

Democratic Republic, Malaysia, Nepal, Pakistan, Papua New Guinea, Philippines, Republic of Korea, Singapore, Sri Lanka, Tonga, Western Samoa.

Europe and the Middle East—Albania, Bulgaria, Czechoslovakia, Democratic Yemen, Greece, Jordan, Kuwait, Lebanon, Oman, Poland, Romania, Saudi Arabia, Turkey, United Arab Emirates, Yemen.

The three main objectives of ITU technical co-operation activity continued to be: developing regional telecommunication networks in Africa, the Americas, Asia, the Pacific, the Middle East and the Mediterranean Basin; strengthening telecommunication technical and administrative services in developing countries; and vocational training.

ITU continued its efforts to promote development of regional telecommunication networks and their integration into the world-wide telecommunication system, in accordance with objectives established by its World Plan Committee and regional plan committees. In this connection, 113 expert missions were carried out during the year.

Progress continued to be made in implementing the Pan-African Telecommunications Network comprising high-grade, large-capacity terrestrial, submarine and space systems. The bringing into service of the North/South route in Tanzania between the Kenya border and the Zambia border bridged the gap in the main artery of eastern Africa thus permitting communication from Ethiopia/Djibouti down to Zambia/Zimbabwe.

In west Africa, further sections of the inland backbone, linking Senegal through Mali, Upper Volta and Niger to Benin were tested and brought into service at the end of the year. The PANAFTEL implementation team, stationed in west Africa, assisted the Economic Community of West African States (ECOWAS), the Western African Development Bank and the Liptako-Gourma Authority to further plans for developing the telecommunication network. Pre-investment surveys carried out at the request of ECOWAS were completed during the year, and assistance was given in evaluating offers received in response to the ECOWAS invitation to tender. In central Africa, the microwave system linking Brazzaville, Congo to Pointe Noire, Congo was brought into service.

The Union continued to collaborate with the Central American Telecommunication Commission, particularly in connection with the third phase of developing a regional network, and with the Inter-American Telecommunications Conference in its programme for development and integration of telecommunications.

Following an ITU study, the Asia-Pacific Telecommunity prepared proposals for integrating telecommunication networks at regional and sub-regional levels. It was foreseen that these proposals would lead to an agreement to standardize on one signalling system for the South Asian sub-region.

Two main factors slowed the development of telecommunication networks in Asia—resource constraints both internal and external and the geopolitical situation which hampered implementation of some of the inter-country terrestrial links.

In the sub-region encompassing Kampuchea, the Lao People's Democratic Republic and Viet Nam, no progress was reported on implementing terrestrial intercountry links. However, in the west Asian sub-region comprising India, Iran and Pakistan, preliminary discussions on the upgrading of the microwave route between Iran and Pakistan were initiated.

Under a UNDP/ITU regional project—developing telecommunications in the South Pacific—the ITU provided assistance for a study of rural communications. The study made recommendations on upgrading and developing telecommunication services in Pacific island countries, particularly in the outer islands.

The European Economic Community (EEC) approved, under LOME II—the 1979 Lomé (Togo) Convention between the EEC and the Asian-Caribbean-Pacific countries—a grant and loan to finance satellite earth stations in Papua New Guinea and Kiribati, an extension to the telex exchange in Fiji, and equipment to upgrade facilities in Tuvalu.

In the Middle East and Mediterranean Basin, ITU continued to assist in establishing the components of the 1978 Middle East and Mediterranean telecommunication master plan. Among the principal activities were assistance in negotiations on a sub-regional microwave network and on the international switching centres in Aden and Djibouti; a field survey of the microwave links to extend telephone and television services in Yemen; and preparations for installing earth stations in Democratic Yemen, Djibouti, Mauritania, Somalia and Sudan.

The Union continued to advise developing countries on administrative and technical measures; 272 expert missions were devoted to assistance of this type.

About two-thirds of the total ITU field expenditure in 1982 was spent on training telecommunications personnel in developing countries.

Publications

ITU publications are issued in separate English, French and Spanish editions or a single trilingual edition. Those issued in 1982 included:

Report on the Activities of the Union, 1981
Financial Operating Report for 1981

Twenty-first Report by the International Telecommunication Union on Telecommunication and the Peaceful Uses of Outer Space, Information Booklet No. 30

Mobile Services Terminology, GLOS/3, 1982

Financial and Administrative Terms, GLOS/4, 1982

Table of International Telex Relations and Traffic, 1982

List of Ship Stations, 22nd ed., 1982 and Supplements Nos. 1 to 3

Manual for Use by the Maritime Mobile and Maritime Mobile-Satellite Services, 1982

Documents of the XVth Plenary Assembly of the CCIR, 1982, Geneva

Economic Studies at the National Level in the Field of Telecommunications (GAS 5), 1 - *Market Factors Affecting Telecommunication Demand*

Case Study on a Rural Network (GAS 9)

Jointing of Telecommunication Cable Conductors, 1st ed., 1982

Secretariat

As at 31 December 1982, the total staff of ITU numbered 721 officials (excluding staff on short-term contracts). Of these, nine were elected officials, 530 had permanent contracts and 182 had fixed-term contracts; 53 nationalities were represented in posts subject to geographical distribution.

Budget

The following budget for 1982 was adopted by the Administrative Council's session in 1981.

	Amount (in Swiss francs)
Income	
Contribution by members and private operating agencies	78,206,000
Contribution by UNDP for technical co-operation administrative expenses	9,845,000
Sales of publications	11,930,000
Miscellaneous	110,000
Total	100,091,000
Expenditures	
Administrative Council	790,000
Common headquarters expenditure	62,130,000
Miscellaneous	110,000
Conferences and meetings	13,851,000
Other expenses	1,435,000
Total general expenses	78,316,000
Technical co-operation	9,845,000
Publications	11,930,000
Total	100,091,000

Each member of ITU chooses the class of contribution in which it wishes to be included and pays in advance its annual contributory share to the budget on the basis of the budgetary provision. The classes of contribution for 1983 for members are listed in ANNEX I below.

At the end of 1982, the total of units for members was 429 1/2.

The amount of the contributory unit for 1982 was 161,800 Swiss francs and the contributory unit for 1983 was to be 176,600 Swiss francs.

Annex I. MEMBERSHIP OF THE INTERNATIONAL TELECOMMUNICATION UNION AND CONTRIBUTIONS

(Membership as at 31 December 1982; contributions as assessed for 1983)

MEMBER	CONTRIBUTION Class of contribution; no. of units	In Swiss francs*	MEMBER	CONTRIBUTION Class of contribution; no. of units	In Swiss francs*	MEMBER	CONTRIBUTION Class of contribution; no. of units	In Swiss francs*
Afghanistan	1/2	88,300	Colombia	3	529,800	Ghana	1	176,600
Albania	1/2	88,300	Comoros	1/2	88,300	Greece	1	176,600
Algeria	1	176,600	Congo	1/2	88,300	Grenada	1/8	22,075
Angola	1/2	88,300	Costa Rica	1/2	88,300	Guatemala	1/2	88,300
Argentina	3	529,800	Cuba	1	176,600	Guinea	1/2	88,300
Australia	18	3,178,800	Cyprus	1/2	88,300	Guinea-Bissau	1/2	88,300
Austria	1	176,600	Czechoslovakia	3	529,800	Guyana	1/2	88,300
Bahamas	1/2	88,300	Democratic Kampuchea	1/2	88,300	Haiti	1/2	88,300
Bahrain	1/2	88,300	Democratic People's Republic of Korea	1/2	88,300	Honduras	1/2	88,300
Bangladesh	1	176,600	Democratic Yemen	1/2	88,300	Hungary	1	176,600
Barbados	1/2	88,300	Denmark	5	883,000	Iceland	1/2	88,300
Belgium	5	883,000	Djibouti	1/2	88,300	India	13	2,295,800
Belize	1/8	22,075	Dominican Republic	1/2	88,300	Indonesia	1	176,600
Benin	1/2	88,300	Ecuador	1	176,600	Iran	1	176,600
Bolivia	1/2	88,300	Egypt	2	353,200	Iraq	1/2	88,300
Botswana	1/2	88,300	El Salvador	1/2	88,300	Ireland	2	353,200
Brazil	5	883,000	Equatorial Guinea	1/2	88,300	Israel	1	176,600
Bulgaria	1	176,600	Ethiopia	1	176,600	Italy	10	1,766,000
Burma	1/2	88,300	Fiji	1/2	88,300	Ivory Coast	1	176,600
Burundi	1/2	88,300	Finland	3	529,800	Jamaica	1/2	88,300
Byelorussian SSR	1	176,600	France	30	5,298,000	Japan	20	3,532,000
Canada	18	3,178,800	Gabon	1/2	88,300	Jordan	1/2	88,300
Cape Verde	1/2	88,300	Gambia	1/2	88,300	Kenya	1/2	88,300
Central African Republic	1/2	88,300	German Democratic Republic	3	529,800	Kuwait	1	176,600
Chad	1/2	88,300	Germany, Federal Republic of	25	4,415,000	Lao People's Democratic Republic	1/2	88,300
Chile	1	176,600				Lebanon	1	176,600
China	20	3,532,000						

MEMBER	Class of contribution; no. of units	In Swiss francs*	MEMBER	Class of contribution; no. of units	In Swiss francs*	MEMBER	Class of contribution; no. of units	In Swiss francs*
	CONTRIBUTION			CONTRIBUTION			CONTRIBUTION	
Lesotho	1/2	88,300	Panama	1/2	88,300	Syrian Arab Republic	1/2	88,300
Liberia	1	176,600	Papua New Guinea	1/2	88,300	Thailand	1 1/2	264,900
Libyan Arab			Paraguay	1/2	88,300	Togo	1/2	88,300
Jamahiriya	1 1/2	264,900	Peru	1/2	88,300	Tonga	1/8	22,075
Liechtenstein	1/2	88,300	Philippines	1	176,600	Trinidad and Tobago	1	176,600
Luxembourg	1/2	88,300	Poland	3	529,800	Tunisia	2	353,200
Madagascar	1	176,600	Portugal	1/2	88,300	Turkey	2	353,200
Malawi	1/2	88,300	Qatar	1/2	88,300	Uganda	1/2	88,300
Malaysia	3	529,800	Republic of Korea	1	176,600	Ukrainian SSR	3	529,800
Maldives	1/2	88,300	Romania	1	176,600	USSR	30	5,298,000
Mali	1/2	88,300	Rwanda	1/2	88,300	United Arab Emirates	1	176,600
Malta	1/2	88,300	Saint Vincent and the			United Kingdom	30	5,298,000
Mauritania	1/2	88,300	Grenadines†	1/8	18,395	United Republic of		
Mauritius	1/2	88,300	San Marino	1/2	88,300	Cameroon	1/2	88,300
Mexico	3	529,800	Sao Tome and			United Republic of		
Monaco	1/2	88,300	Principe	1/2	88,300	Tanzania	1/2	88,300
Mongolia	1/2	88,300	Saudi Arabia	1	176,600	United States	30	5,298,000
Morocco	1	176,600	Senegal	1	176,600	Upper Volta	1/2	88,300
Mozambique	1/2	88,300	Sierra Leone	1/2	88,300	Uruguay	1/2	88,300
Nauru	1/8	22,075	Singapore	1	176,600	Vatican City State	1/2	88,300
Nepal	1/2	88,300	Somalia	1/2	88,300	Venezuela	3	529,800
Netherlands	10	1,766,000	South Africa	8	1,412,800	Viet Nam	1/2	88,300
New Zealand	3	529,800	Spain	3	529,800	Yemen	1/2	88,300
Nicaragua	1	176,600	Sri Lanka	1/2	88,300	Yugoslavia	1	176,600
Niger	1/2	88,300	Sudan	1	176,600	Zaïre	1	176,600
Nigeria	2	353,200	Suriname	1/2	88,300	Zambia	1/2	88,300
Norway	5	883,000	Swaziland	1/2	88,300	Zimbabwe	1	176,600
Oman	1/2	88,300	Sweden	10	1,766,000			
Pakistan	2	353,200	Switzerland	10	1,766,000	Total	427 5/8	75,514,895

NOTE: The nomenclature of ITU differs from that of the United Nations.

*For the equivalent amounts in United States dollars, the rate of exchange to be applicable on 1 January 1983 was Swiss francs 1.99 = US $1.00.

†Assessment in anticipation of Saint Vincent and the Grenadines becoming a member on 25 March 1983.

Annex II. OFFICERS AND OFFICES OF THE INTERNATIONAL TELECOMMUNICATION UNION

ADMINISTRATIVE COUNCIL, INTERNATIONAL FREQUENCY REGISTRATION BOARD AND PRINCIPAL OFFICERS

PRINCIPAL OFFICERS OF THE UNION
Secretary-General: Mohamed Mili.
Deputy Secretary-General: Richard E. Butler.

ITU ADMINISTRATIVE COUNCIL
Algeria, Argentina, Australia, Benin, Brazil, Canada, China, Colombia, Egypt, Ethiopia, France, German Democratic Republic, Germany, Federal Republic of, India, Indonesia, Italy, Japan, Kenya, Kuwait, Lebanon, Mexico (Chairman), Morocco, Nigeria, Pakistan, Peru, Philippines, Romania, Saudi Arabia, Senegal, Spain (Vice-Chairman), Sweden, Switzerland, Thailand, USSR, United Kingdom, United Republic of Cameroon, United Republic of Tanzania, United States, Venezuela, Yugoslavia, Zambia.

INTERNATIONAL FREQUENCY REGISTRATION BOARD
Chairman: Petr Sergeevich Kurakov (USSR).
Vice-Chairmen: W. H. Bellchambers (United Kingdom), Abderrazak Berrada (Morocco), G. C. Brooks (Canada), Y. Kurihara (Japan).

OFFICERS OF THE
INTERNATIONAL CONSULTATIVE COMMITTEES
Director, International Radio Consultative Committee (CCIR): Richard C. Kirby (United States).
Director, International Telegraph and Telephone Consultative Committee (CCITT): Léon Burtz (France).

HEADQUARTERS

General Secretariat of the International Telecommunication Union
Place des Nations
1211 Geneva 20, Switzerland
Cable address: BURINTERNA GENEVA
Telephone: 99 51 11
Telex: 421000

Chapter XIII

World Meteorological Organization (WMO)

Membership of the World Meteorological Organization (WMO) increased to 157 in 1982—152 States and five territories. New members admitted in 1982 were Belize (24 June), Vanuatu (24 July) and Swaziland (2 December).

The programme and financial resources of WMO for 1980-1983 had been adopted by the Eighth (1979) Meteorological Congress, the highest body of WMO, which meets at least once every four years.

The 29-member Executive Committee, which supervises Congress resolutions and regulations, held its thirty-fourth session at Geneva from 7 to 24 June 1982.

The twenty-seventh International Meteorological Organization Prize was awarded to William James Gibbs (Australia) for outstanding contributions to the science of the atmosphere and his services to the cause of international collaboration in meteorology.

Activities in 1982

World Weather Watch

The World Weather Watch (WWW), the basic programme of WMO, continued as an integrated global system making observational data and processed information available to member States for their operational and research purposes. Its essential elements were: the Global Observing System (GOS), which obtains observational data; the Global Data-Processing System (GDPS), which provides for processing, storage and retrieval of observational data and making available processed information; and the Global Telecommunication System (GTS), which offers telecommunication facilities and arrangements for rapid, reliable collection, exchange and distribution of observational data and processed information.

During 1982, activities to maintain and improve GOS operations continued under its two subsystems—one surface-based and the other space-based. The surface-based sub-system provided conventional basic data from regional basic synoptic networks, other operational networks of stations on land and at sea, and aircraft meteorological observations required for operation and research. Meteorological satellites for the space-based sub-system—in both near-polar orbiting and geostationary systems—took direct observations, accomplishing data collection and dissemination missions. These satellite systems contributed greatly to operations and research in meteorology, hydrology and other related environmental activities by providing member States with additional quantitative data and qualitative information such as: vertical profiles of temperature and humidity; temperatures of sea, land and cloud top surfaces; wind field derived from cloud displacements; cloud amounts, type and height of cloud tops; snow and ice cover; and radiance balance data.

With regard to GDPS, a new international code for surface observations from different types of surface stations was introduced in January. A number of WWW processing centres installed new-generation electronic computers, improving their capability for global and regional exchange of analysis and forecast products in real time. Upgrading to high-speed data transmission was accomplished on some additional GTS circuits during 1982 and a number of high-frequency point-to-point circuits were converted to satellite communications, making the system more reliable.

Ocean affairs

In 1982, WMO, through its Commission for Marine Meteorology (CMM), continued to promote the improvement of data coverage of the world's oceans using the latest advances in marine telecommunications, satellite systems and automation techniques. In a consultative meeting held in London (14-16 September), it discussed with the International Maritime Satellite Organization, which was established in 1982, requirements for the collection and distribution of marine meteorological and oceanographic information.

Other activities during the year included formulation of standard symbols and map specifications for facsimile marine charts, publication of an annual volume of marine climatological summaries, and development of procedures for a complete global sea-ice data bank using the general format for gridded sea-ice information.

The joint WMO/International Oceanographic Commission (IOC) Integrated Global Ocean Services System continued efforts to increase and improve its global collection and exchange of oceanic data for operational and research activities.

Aviation

The WMO Commission for Aeronautical Meteorology met in 1982 (seventh session, Montreal, Canada, 14 April–7 May) to plan programme activities in aeronautical meteorology, including greater support to general aviation. Part of the session was held with the International Civil Aviation Organization (ICAO). With ICAO, the Commission recommended the use of its Global Telecommunications System to support the new World Area Forecast System. A WMO/ICAO training seminar (Mexico City, 8-12 November) met to discuss the provision of meteorological service to general aviation.

World Climate Programme

The World Climate Programme continued to focus on research, applications, impact studies and data, in an effort to apply climatic data and knowledge to the planning and management of all aspects of human activities. Technical and expert meetings in individual problem areas were held to analyse the latest developments and direct future activities.

In 1982, the WMO/International Council of Scientific Unions (ICSU) Joint Scientific Committee (third session) agreed on a revised plan for the research programme, to give clearer distinction to the areas of study and understanding of climate on different time-scales of concern. Work continued on a proposed Climate Applications Referral System to promote the use of climatology to benefit a wide range of human activities, including food production, energy, and urban and economic planning. The United Nations Environment Programme continued to implement the World Climate Impact Studies Programme, designed to reduce food systems' vulnerability to climate, to anticipate impacts of man-induced climatic changes and to identify climate-sensitive sectors of human activity. A draft plan for the World Climate Data Programme, developed at a November meeting of experts on data management for formal adoption in May 1983, identified goals, activities and executing organizations. The Commission for Climatology and Applications of Meteorology (eighth session, Washington, D.C., 19-30 April) discussed its role in the implementation of the World Climate Programme.

Research and development

The research and development programme continued to focus on weather prediction, weather modification, tropical meteorology and environmental prediction. The WMO Commission for Atmospheric Sciences (eighth session, Melbourne, Australia, 8-19 February) established numerous groups and appointed rapporteurs to keep abreast of the latest developments in atmospheric research, including weather prediction. An expert study meeting on long-range forecasting formulated in December an international research programme on the feasibility of monthly and seasonal forecasting.

In the weather modification programme, the Executive Committee's Panel of Experts on Cloud Physics and Weather Modification, meeting twice in 1982, focused on a precipitation enhancement project and reported that no conclusion could be drawn as to the suitability of the site in Spain for a demonstration project. At a conference organized by the Cercle International Grêle and hosted by the Hydrometeorological Services of Bulgaria, WMO helped organize a session in which scientists reviewed the uncertainties in hail suppression and the progress being made in narrowing the gap between theory and operations. The seventh annual register of national weather modification projects, containing information for 1981, was issued.

Research continued in tropical meteorology, and WMO co-sponsored with the Meteorological Society of Japan in October the Regional Scientific Conference on Tropical Meteorology. The data-management activity for the Monsoon Experiment was concluded, and the work of the International Management Centres for both the winter and summer Monsoon Experiments (Kuala Lumpur, Malaysia; New Dehli, India) was successfully completed. A Monsoon Climate Programme was being developed, aiming at a ten-year study of monsoons on various scales and their inter-annual variability. The Scientific and Management Regional Committee (Cairo, Egypt, November-December) developed plans for encouraging research related to the West African Monsoon Experiment.

Under the environmental prediction research programme, efforts continued to upgrade and standardize the observing network for a global ozone research and monitoring project, upon which most of the activities in the World Plan of Action on the Ozone Layer depended. In April, WMO co-organized a meeting of experts on sources of errors in detecting ozone trends (Toronto, Canada), and a meeting was held in September on the radiative properties of ozone and other minor constituents (Boulder, United States).

Several years of planning culminated in 1982 with implementation of a special observing period (1 March–30 April) for the Alpine Experiment, the last in a series of co-operative field experiments undertaken in the Global Atmospheric Research Programme. The observations, which led to new views regarding the flow of air masses around and over mountains, began to be assembled in data sets.

Meteorological applications and environment

The meteorological applications and environment programme included activities with implications to such fields of human activity as agriculture, aviation, marine activities, atmospheric and marine pollution, energy problems, urban and regional land-use planning, human settlements, engineering and building, and human health and welfare. In April, the Commission for Climatology and Applications of Meteorology (eighth session, Washington, D.C., 19-30 April) allocated to its new working groups and rapporteurs tasks in these fields, and endeavoured to structure its work for the coming four years in harmony with the plans and objectives of the World Climate Programme.

Projects relating to agriculture included short-term missions, training courses on application of remote sensing techniques to agrometeorology, working group meetings on such topics as the effects of meteorological factors on maize development and yield and on animal health, and symposia on meteorology and plant protection, and on sorghum and millet production. A Task Force on Crop-Weather Models (Geneva, September) drafted a guide that included examples on application of land-use evaluation, crop monitoring and yield forecasting, management, risk and disease assessment.

With regard to energy, the WMO Executive Committee updated its action plan to reflect progress in solar-energy assessment methods and the Programme of Action adopted at the 1981 United Nations Conference on New and Renewable Sources of Energy. Missions to developing countries assisted in applying climatological/meteorological information to various activities including energy problems.

In the environmental pollution field, the Executive Committee's panel of experts (fourth session, Geneva, September) discussed new approaches and procedures for quality control of observations and data. During 1982, the total number of stations involved in the WMO Background Air Pollution Monitoring Network increased to 134, and another 57 stations were being considered or prepared. WMO continued participation, along with the Economic Commission for Europe and the United Nations Environment Programme (UNEP), in a programme on monitoring and evaluating long-range transmission of air pollution in Europe. It monitored for a UNEP project the deposit of pollutants from the atmosphere in the Mediterranean Sea.

Under the WMO Tropical Cyclone Programme, the first Typhoon Operational Experiment was successfully conducted from August to October by the Economic and Social Commission for Asia and the Pacific (ESCAP)/WMO Typhoon Committee, with the Committee members from eight countries guiding the experiment from the International Experiment Centre in Tokyo. A draft Tropical Cyclone Operational Plan for the South-west Indian Ocean was submitted to the eighth session of Regional Association I (Cairo, Egypt, November) for adoption.

WMO also co-operated with other international bodies in such areas as desertification control and in disaster prevention and preparedness.

Work continued on the publication of the second volume of the *Climatic Atlas of Europe* and the first volume of the *Climatic Atlas of Africa*.

Hydrology and water resources development

The hydrology and water resources programme focused on the operational hydrology programme (OHP), whose objectives included the improvement of the quantity and quality of hydrological data and an international and systematic framework of the integration of techniques and procedures for the collection and processing of hydrological data.

The first phase of the hydrological operational multipurpose subprogramme was fully implemented in 1982 with promising prospects, and the number of national reference centres for the subprogramme rose from 48 to 58 during the year. Preparations were under way for its second phase, entailing systematic operational applications of its components.

The programme for hydrology in environmental management and development included technical support for the hydrological components of other WMO activities dealing with environmental problems such as the tropical cyclone programme, the world climate programme, and drought and desertification control.

Education and training

The main activities of the education and training programme for 1982 were the awarding of fellowships, strengthening of regional meteorological training centres, organization and co-sponsorship of courses, seminars and workshops, preparation of training publications and other aids, studies and surveys of training needs, information education and training, and collaboration with other organizations.

The WMO Executive Committee's Panel of Experts on Education and Training (tenth session, Barbados, February) reviewed proposals for programme development, with attention to problems experienced at the WMO Regional Meteorological Training Centres.

Eight training events were organized by WMO during 1982 on the following subjects: tropical meteorology and hurricane forecasting (United States), application of satellite data to tropical cyclone forecasting (Thailand), background air pollution measurements (Hungary), radar meteorology (Italy), agrometeorological observations and their utilization (Philippines), a course for hydrometeorological instruments technicians (Colombia), a seminar for national meteorological instructors (Sri Lanka), and a symposium on training in meteorology emphasizing climatic change and variability (Costa Rica).

In addition, WMO co-sponsored 13 training events dealing with: water resources technology in developing countries (United Kingdom), monsoon dynamics (Bangladesh), agrometeorology (Belgium, Colombia), hydrology (Hungary, India), operational and applied hydrology (Switzerland), hydrological techniques (United States), techniques for regionalizing and transferring hydrological variables (United Kingdom), agricultural meteorology (Israel), urban hydrology (Canada), meteorological service to general aviation (Mexico) and application of satellite remote sensing to desert locust survey and forecasting (Italy).

Over 500 participants, mainly from developing countries, benefited from the training events organized by WMO, and a further 310 were granted training awards under fellowship funds administered by WMO from various sources.

Technical co-operation

In 1982, under the WHO technical co-operation programme, assistance was provided to 119 countries through the United Nations Development Programme (UNDP), the Voluntary Co-operation Programme, trust-fund arrangements and from the WMO regular budget.

Under UNDP, assistance for meteorological and hydrological services development and for personnel training was provided to 93 countries at an estimated value of $11 million, compared to $12.4 million in 1981.

Under the Voluntary Co-operation Programme, 37 projects were completed and 74 projects were under implementation in 1982, including 36 new projects which were begun during the year in 29 countries. The Programme supported the implementation of the World Weather Watch, fellowships for training, agrometeorological activities, and the establishment of facilities needed for the World Climate Programme. In 1982, cash contributions to the Voluntary Co-operation Fund amounted to some $350,000, and contributions to the Equipment and Services Programme, including fellowships, totalled nearly $5 million.

Twenty-four fellowships were awarded from the regular budget of WMO and financial support was given for participation in group training, technical conferences and study tours.

To help meet the need of the meteorological and hydrological services of developing countries, a total of 482 fellowships were granted in 1982 for training in meteorology or hydrology; the number of those awarded fellowships under UNDP was 218; under the Voluntary Co-operation Programme, 200; under trust funds, 30; and under the regular budget, 34.

Seven trust-fund projects were under implementation in 1982—four funded by countries receiving assistance and three by various countries.

Secretariat

As at 31 December 1982, the total number of full-time staff employed by WMO (excluding professionals on technical assistance projects) on permanent and fixed-term contracts stood at 301, drawn from 57 nationalities: 129 in the Professional and higher categories and 172 in the General Service and related categories.

Budget

The year 1982 was the third year of the eighth financial period (1980-1983), for which the 1979 World Meteorological Congress had established a maximum expenditure of $74,400,000, and authorized additional expenditures of not more than $1 million to provide for such circumstances as losses from currency exchange rate changes or urgent unforeseen programme activities.

The regular budget for 1982 amounted to $18,414,000; the budget for technical co-operation activities, financed from overhead allocations and other extrabudgetary sources, amounted to an additional $2,537,000.

At its June 1982 session, the Executive Committee approved the following regular budget of $18,108,200 for 1983:

	Amount (in US dollars)
Income	
Contributions	14,075,100
As for General Fund	4,033,100
	18,108,200
Expenditure	
Policy-making organs	1,031,500
Executive management	910,000
Scientific and technical programmmes	
World Weather Watch	2,475,400
Meteorligcal applications and environment	1,434,600
Research and development	951,400
World Climate Programme	1,294,900
Hydrology and water resources	824,900
Supporting programmes	
Technical co-operation	209,500
Regional	1,087,700
Education and training	959,700
Programme supporting activities	3,489,000
Administration and common services	2,968,500
Other budgetary provisions	471,100
Total	18,108,200

Annex I.　MEMBERSHIP OF WMO AND CONTRIBUTIONS

(Membership as at 31 December 1982; contributions as assessed for 1983)

STATE	CONTRIBUTION Unit*	CONTRIBUTION Net amount (in US dollars)	STATE	CONTRIBUTION Unit*	CONTRIBUTION Net amount (in US dollars)	STATE	CONTRIBUTION Unit*	CONTRIBUTION Net amount (in US dollars)
Afghanistan	1	6,708	Ghana	3	20,124	Philippines	9	60,374
Albania	1	6,708	Greece	6	40,249	Poland	29	194,538
Algeria	2	13,417	Guatemala	2	13,417	Portugal	6	40,249
Angola	2	13,417	Guinea	1	6,708	Qatar	2	13,417
Argentina	30	201,247	Guinea-Bissau	1	6,708	Republic of Korea	4	26,832
Australia	40	268,328	Guyana	1	6,708	Romania	9	60,374
Austria	13	87,207	Haiti	1	6,708	Rwanda	1	6,708
Bahamas	1	6,708	Honduras	1	6,708	Saint Lucia	1	6,708
Bahrain	1	6,708	Hungary	12	80,499	Sao Tome and Principe	1	6,708
Bangladesh	1	6,708	Iceland	2	13,417	Saudi Arabia	4	26,832
Barbados	1	6,708	India	41	275,036	Senegal	1	6,708
Belgium	28	187,829	Indonesia	14	93,915	Seychelles	1	6,708
Belize	1	6,306	Iran	9	60,374	Sierra Leone	1	6,708
Benin	1	6,708	Iraq	2	13,417	Singapore	2	13,417
Bolivia	5	33,541	Ireland	6	40,249	Somalia	1	6,708
Botswana	1	6,708	Israel	6	40,249	South Africa†	18	120,748
Brazil	30	201,247	Italy	50	335,411	Spain	28	187,829
Bulgaria	8	53,665	Ivory Coast	2	13,417	Sri Lanka	5	33,541
Burma	4	26,832	Jamaica	2	13,417	Sudan	3	20,124
Burundi	1	6,708	Japan	57	382,368	Suriname	1	6,708
Byelorussian SSR	11	73,791	Jordan	1	6,708	Swaziland	1	6,483
Canada	59	395,784	Kenya	1	6,708	Sweden	31	207,955
Cape Verde	1	6,708	Kuwait	3	20,124	Switzerland	26	174,413
Central African Republic	1	6,708	Lao People's Democratic			Syrian Arab Republic	4	26,832
Chad	1	6,708	Republic	1	6,708	Thailand	7	46,957
Chile	8	53,665	Lebanon	2	13,417	Togo	1	6,708
China	86	576,905	Lesotho	1	6,708	Trinidad and Tobago	2	13,417
Colombia	7	46,957	Liberia	1	6,708	Tunisia	2	13,417
Comoros	1	6,708	Libyan Arab Jamahiriya	2	13,417	Turkey	12	80,499
Congo	1	6,708	Luxembourg	2	13,417	Uganda	1	6,708
Costa Rica	2	13,417	Madagascar	1	6,708	Ukrainian SSR	36	241,495
Cuba	6	40,249	Malawi	1	6,708	USSR	231	1,549,595
Cyprus	1	6,708	Malaysia	8	53,665	United Kingdom	128	858,649
Czechoslovakia	21	140,872	Maldives	1	6,708	United Republic of		
Democratic Kampuchea	1	6,708	Mali	1	6,708	Cameroon	1	6,708
Democratic People's			Malta	1	6,708	United Republic of Tanzania	1	6,708
Republic of Korea	2	13,417	Mauritania	1	6,708	United States	548	3,676,093
Democratic Yemen	1	6,708	Mauritius	1	6,708	Upper Volta	1	6,708
Denmark	16	107,331	Mexico	19	127,456	Uruguay	7	46,957
Djibouti	1	6,708	Mongolia	1	6,708	Vanuatu	1	6,339
Dominica	1	6,708	Morocco	4	26,832	Venezuela	12	80,499
Dominican Republic	2	13,417	Mozambique	2	13,417	Viet Nam	2	13,417
Ecuador	2	13,417	Nepal	1	6,708	Yemen	1	6,708
Egypt	10	67,083	Netherlands	25	167,705	Yugoslavia	12	80,499
El Salvador	1	6,708	New Zealand	12	80,499	Zaire	4	26,832
Ethiopia	1	6,708	Nicaragua	1	6,708	Zambia	2	13,417
Fiji	1	6,708	Niger	1	6,708	Zimbabwe	1	6,708
Finland	12	80,499	Nigeria	6	40,249			
France	104	697,653	Norway	14	93,915	British Caribbean Territories	1	6,708
Gabon	1	6,708	Oman	1	6,708	French Polynesia	1	6,708
Gambia	1	6,708	Pakistan	5	33,541	Hong Kong	1	6,708
German Democratic			Panama	2	13,417	Netherlands Antilles	1	6,708
Republic	31	207,955	Papua New Guinea	1	6,708	New Caledonia	1	6,708
Germany, Federal			Paraguay	1	6,708			
Republic of	110	737,903	Peru	7	46,957	Total	2,234	14,985,122

*Exact unit value was $6,708.20.

†Suspended by the seventh (1975) WMO Congress from exercising the rights and privileges of a member.

Annex II.　OFFICERS AND OFFICES OF WMO

MEMBERS OF THE WMO EXECUTIVE COMMITEE

President: R. L. Kintanar (Philippines).
First Vice-President: C. A. Abayomi (Nigeria).
Second Vice-President: Ju. A. Izrael (USSR).
Third Vice-President: J. E. Echeveste (Argentina).
Members: S. Aguilar Anguiano* (Mexico), M. A. Badran (Egypt) (acting), F. Bermudez Gomez (Colombia), J. P. Bruce (Canada) (acting), P. K. Das (India), Workineh Degefu* (Ethiopia), J. Djigbenou (Ivory Coast) (acting), C. A. Grezzi* (Uruguay), R. E. Hallgren (United States) (acting), Ho Tong Yuen* (Malaysia), A. W. Kabakibo* (Syrian Arab Republic), J. Labrousse (France) (acting), K. Langlo (Norway), E. Lingelbach (Germany, Federal Republic of), G. Mankedi (Congo) (acting), Sir John Mason (United Kingdom), J. Masuzawa (Japan) (acting), J. K. Murithi (Kenya), C. Padilha (Brazil), M. Rahmatullah (Pakistan), V. Richter (Czechoslovakia) (acting), M. Seck (Senegal), U Thu Ta* (Burma), J. W. Zillman (Australia), Zou Jingmeng (China) (acting).

NOTE: The Executive Committee is composed of four elected officers; the six Presidents of the regional associations (indicated by an asterisk), who are *ex-officio* members; and 19 elected members. Members serve in their personal capacities, not as representatives of Governments.

SENIOR MEMBERS OF THE WMO SECRETARIAT

Secretary-General: A. C. Wiin-Nielsen.
Deputy Secretary-General: R. List.
Director, Scientific and Technical Programmes: R. Czelnai.
Director, World Weather Watch Department: G. K. Weiss.
Director, Research and Development Department: A. Zaitsev.
Director, Hydrology and Water Resources Department: J. Nemec.
Director, Technical Co-operation Department: G. Gosset.
Director, Education and Training Department: G. O. P. Obasi.

Director, Administration Department: M. J. Connaughton.
Director, Languages, Publications and Conferences Department: H. Tabatabay.
Director, World Climate Programme Department: T. D. Potter.
Director, World Climate Research Programme: P. Morel.
Regional Director for Africa: S. Mbele-Mbong.
Regional Director for Latin America: I. G. Meira-Filho.
Regional Director for Asia: K. Rajendram.
Special Assistant for Regional Affairs: A. K. Elamly.

PRESIDENTS OF REGIONAL ASSOCIATIONS AND TECHNICAL COMMISSIONS

REGIONAL ASSOCIATIONS

I. Africa: W. Degefu (Ethiopia).
II. Asia: U Thu Ta (Burma).
III. South America: C. A. Grezzi (Uruguay).

IV. North and Central America: S. Aguilar Anguiano (Mexico).
V. South-West Pacific: Ho Tong Yuen (Malaysia).
VI. Europe: A. W. Kabakibo (Syrian Arab Republic).

TECHNICAL COMMISSIONS

Aeronautical Meteorology: J. Kastelein (Netherlands).
Agricultural Meteorology: M. N. Gerbier (France).
Atmospheric Sciences: F. Mesinger (Yugoslavia).
Basic Systems: J. R. Neilon (USA)

Climatology and Applications of Meteorology: J. Rasmussen (USA)
Hydrology: R. H. Clark (Canada)
Instruments and Methods of Observation: S. Huovila (Finland)
Marine Meteorology: K. P. Vasiliev (USSR)

HEADQUARTERS

World Meteorological Organization
41, Avenue Guiseppe-Motta
Case Postale No. 5
1211 Geneva 20, Switzerland
Cable address: METEOMOND GENEVA
Telephone: 34 64 00
Telex: 23260

Chapter XIV

International Maritime Organization (IMO)

On 22 May 1982, the Inter-Governmental Maritime Consultative Organization changed its name to the International Maritime Organization (IMO). The change resulted from the entry into force of amendments, adopted in November 1975, to the organization's basic Convention.

The 1975 amendments also expanded article I of the Convention (Purposes of the organization) to include functions concerning "the prevention and control of marine pollution from ships" and "legal matters related to the purposes set out in this article". In addition, the amendments provided for the institutionalization of the Legal Committee and the Marine Environment Protection Committee in the IMO constitution. Previously the only committee so institutionalized was the Maritime Safety Committee.

As at 31 December 1982, IMO membership stood at 122 with one associate member. Nicaragua was admitted on 17 March.

Activities in 1982

Convention on Tonnage Measurement

On 18 July 1982, the International Convention on Tonnage Measurement of Ships, 1969, entered

into force, two years after being accepted by 25 countries whose combined merchant fleets represented 65 per cent of world gross tonnage.[a] At the time of entry into force, the Convention had been accepted by 49 countries accounting for 75 per cent. Although existing tonnage measuring systems might continue to be used for several years, it was intended that the uniform system of the Convention would become the only method used for measuring tonnage, thereby eliminating such anomalies as sister ships being allocated varying tonnages because they operated under different national systems.

Safe containers

Another landmark occurred on 6 September 1982 when the five-year period during which owners of existing containers could apply for approvals under the 1972 International Convention for Safe Containers expired. The purpose of the Convention, which had entered into force in 1977, was to establish international standards for the construction and maintenance of containers. The five-year period had been agreed because the huge

[a]See YUN 1980, p. 1330.

number of existing containers meant that the task of approval and plating them would take several years. In 1981, the IMO Maritime Safety Committee had adopted amendments to the Convention extending the deadline for examination and plating of existing containers to 1 January 1985, although the deadline for application remained unchanged.

International Maritime Prize

The International Maritime Prize, awarded annually for the most significant contribution to the work and objectives of IMO, was awarded in 1982 to Rear Admiral Roderick Y. Edwards, formerly of the United States Coast Guard. The recipient was a member of the United States delegation to IMO for many years and served as Chairman of the IMO Council for a record four consecutive terms. He was also elected President of the IMO Assembly's 1979 session and of the 1974 International Conference on the Safety of Life at Sea.

Prevention of pollution

On 1 October 1982, the International Convention for the Prevention of Pollution from Ships, 1973, as modified by its Protocol of 1978, received the requisite number of acceptances (15) for entry into force. The Convention was to enter into force on 2 October 1983.

World Maritime University

A new major project launched in October 1982 was the World Maritime University, which was to be located at Malmö, Sweden. Under an agreement with the City of Malmö and with the assistance of the Swedish Government, the University was to provide an international centre for advanced study for high-level specialized training for maritime administrators, surveyors and inspectors, accident investigators, maritime lecturers and others holding key positions in the administrations of developing countries.

New headquarters

On 1 November 1982, IMO moved to new headquarters in London at 4 Albert Embankment, on the south bank of the River Thames near to Lambeth Bridge. Built for IMO by the United Kingdom Government, the building provides under one roof all the accommodation necessary for the secretariat, together with meetings facilities which were not available at its previous offices in Piccadilly. The new premises were to be formally opened by Her Majesty Queen Elizabeth II in 1983.

Publications

New IMO publications issued in 1982 included: *Emergency Procedures for Ships Carrying Dangerous Goods—Group Emergency Schedules;* the *Convention on the International Maritime Organization;* a new edition of *Crude Oil Washing Systems; Guidelines on Surveys under the 1978 SOLAS Protocol;* amendment no. 3 to *Ships' Routeing; Noise Levels on Board Ships; Performance Standards for Navigational Equipment; Dedicated Clean Ballast Tanks; Guidelines for the Design and Construction of Offshore Supply Vessels;* a new version of *Procedures for the Control of Ships; Oily-Water Separating and Monitoring Equipment; Inert Gas Systems for Ships Carrying Petroleum Products in Bulk;* the *Code of Safety for Nuclear Merchant Ships; Amendments to the International Convention for the Safety of Life at Sea, 1974;* and amendment 19-80 to the *International Maritime Dangerous Goods Code.*

Secretariat

As at 31 December 1982, IMO employed 238 full-time staff members (excluding those on technical assistance projects). Of these, 81 were in the Professional and higher categories (drawn from 34 nationalities) and 157 were in the General Service and related categories. There were 71 Professionnal staff employed on technical assistance projects in the field.

Budget

In November 1981, the IMO Assembly had adopted a budget of $25.7 million for the 1982-1983 biennium ($11.4 million for 1982 and $14.3 million for 1983). In November 1982, the IMO Council adopted a revised budget of $12.7 million for 1983.

Annex I.   MEMBERSHIP OF THE INTERNATIONAL MARITIME ORGANIZATION AND CONTRIBUTIONS

(Membership as at 31 December 1982; contributions as assessed for 1982)

MEMBER	CONTRIBUTION Percentage of total	CONTRIBUTION Net amount (in US dollars)	MEMBER	CONTRIBUTION Percentage of total	CONTRIBUTION Net amount (in US dollars)	MEMBER	CONTRIBUTION Percentage of total	CONTRIBUTION Net amount (in US dollars)
Algeria	0.32	34,689	Barbados	0.02	2,127	Chile	0.15	16,314
Angola	0.04	4,030	Belgium	0.47	50,653	China	1.82	196,230
Argentina	0.56	60,551	Benin	0.02	2,127	Colombia	0.09	9,538
Australia	0.43	46,871	Brazil	1.22	132,273	Congo	0.02	2,203
Austria	0.03	3,574	Bulgaria	0.30	32,303	Costa Rica	0.02	2,508
Bahamas	0.06	7,000	Burma	0.04	4,157	Cuba	0.23	25,349
Bahrain	0.02	2,431	Canada	0.78	84,174	Cyprus	0.45	48,166
Bangladesh	0.11	12,177	Cape Verde	0.02	2,279	Czechoslovakia	0.06	6,695

MEMBER	CONTRIBUTION Percent-age of total	Net amount (in US dollars)	MEMBER	CONTRIBUTION Percent-age of total	Net amount (in US dollars)	MEMBER	CONTRIBUTION Percent-age of total	Net amount (in US dollars)
Democratic Kampuchea	0.02	2,102	Japan	9.63	1,040,401	Senegal	0.03	2,964
Democratic Yemen	0.02	2,355	Jordan	0.02	2,025	Seychelles	0.02	2,076
Denmark	1.20	130,116	Kenya	0.02	2,127	Sierra Leone	0.02	2,102
Djibouti	0.02	2,076	Kuwait	0.56	60,805	Singapore	1.64	176,815
Dominica	0.02	2,000	Lebanon	0.09	10,121	Somalia	0.03	2,888
Dominican Republic	0.03	2,736	Liberia	17.61	1,903,084	Spain	1.93	208,438
Ecuador	0.09	9,589	Libyan Arab Jamahiriya	0.23	24,562	Sri Lanka	0.04	4,665
Egypt	0.16	17,202	Madagascar	0.04	3,878	Sudan	0.04	4,360
El Salvador	0.02	2,076	Malaysia	0.22	24,309	Suriname	0.02	2,381
Equatorial Guinea	0.02	2,152	Maldives	0.06	6,594	Sweden	0.97	104,381
Ethiopia	0.02	2,634	Malta	0.07	7,863	Switzerland	0.09	9,995
Finland	0.59	64,053	Mauritania	0.02	2,076	Syrian Arab Republic	0.03	3,066
France	2.73	294,723	Mauritius	0.03	2,964	Thailand	0.11	12,228
Gabon	0.04	3,980	Mexico	0.28	30,806	Trinidad and Tobago	0.02	2,431
Gambia	0.02	2,076	Morocco	0.11	11,492	Tunisia	0.05	5,452
German Democratic Republic	0.39	41,846	Mozambique	0.03	3,015	Turkey	0.41	44,232
			Nepal	0.02	2,000	USSR	5.61	606,243
Germany, Federal Republic of	1.85	199,626	Netherlands	1.30	140,750	United Arab Emirates	0.06	6,492
Ghana	0.08	8,472	New Zealand	0.08	8,193	United Kingdom	6.01	649,124
Greece	9.88	1,068,070	Nicaragua*	—	—	United Republic of Cameroon	0.03	3,015
Guinea	0.02	2,127	Nigeria	0.13	14,081	United Republic of Tanzania	0.03	3,472
Guinea-Bissau	0.02	2,051	Norway	5.11	552,103	United States	4.53	489,877
Guyana	0.02	2,402	Oman	0.02	2,203	Uruguay	0.07	7,076
Haiti	0.02	2,076	Pakistan	0.14	14,867	Venezuela	0.19	20,832
Honduras	0.07	7,101	Panama	6.51	703,923	Yemen	0.02	2,076
Hungary	0.04	4,107	Papua New Guinea	0.02	2,711	Yugoslavia	0.62	66,490
Iceland	0.06	6,644	Peru	0.21	22,964	Zaire	0.04	4,335
India	1.43	154,785	Philippines	0.61	66,464			
Indonesia	0.43	46,287	Poland	0.86	92,834			
Iran	0.30	32,506	Portugal	0.34	36,948	*Associate member*		
Iraq	0.37	39,841	Qatar	0.04	4,639	Hong Kong	0.31	33,740
Ireland	0.08	8,802	Republic of Korea	1.23	132,502			
Israel	0.15	16,746	Romania	0.50	53,571	Total	100.00	10,808,100
Italy	2.54	274,064	Saint Lucia	0.02	2,051			
Ivory Coast	0.05	5,858	Saint Vincent and the Grenadines	0.02	2,634			
Jamaica	0.02	2,279	Saudi Arabia	0.75	81,235			

*Became a member on 17 March 1982.

Annex II. OFFICERS AND OFFICES OF THE INTERNATIONAL MARITIME ORGANIZATION

(As at 31 December 1982)

IMO COUNCIL AND MARITIME SAFETY COMMITTEE

IMO COUNCIL
Chairman: W. A. O'Neill (Canada).
Members: Bangladesh, Brazil, Canada, Egypt, France, Germany, Federal Republic of, Greece, India, Italy, Jamaica, Japan, Kuwait, Lebanon, Liberia, Mexico, Nigeria, Norway, Panama, Poland, Saudi Arabia, Spain, USSR, United Kingdom, United States.

MARITIME SAFETY COMMITTEE
Chairman: Per Eriksson (Sweden).

Membership in the Maritime Safety Committee was opened to all member States with effect from 1 April 1978.

OFFICERS AND OFFICES

PRINCIPAL OFFICERS OF IMO SECRETARIAT
Secretary-General: Chandrika Prasad Srivastava.
Assistant Secretary-General: Thomas A. Mensah.
Secretary, Maritime Safety Committee: G. P. Kostylev.

HEADQUARTERS
International Maritime Organization
4 Albert Embankment
London SE1 7SR, England
  Cable address: INTERMAR LONDON, SE1
  Telephone: 01-735-7611
  Telex: 23588

Chapter XV

World Intellectual Property Organization (WIPO)

During 1982, membership of the World Intellectual Property Organization (WIPO) rose to 100 with the admission of Mali, Saudi Arabia and Somalia. Mali acceded to the Paris Convention for the Protection of Industrial Property, bringing membership of the Paris Union to 92. Berne Union membership increased to 74 as a result of Venezuela's accession to the Berne Convention for the Protection of Literary and Artistic Works. At the end of the year, total membership in WIPO and its various Unions, taken together, was 121.

The Nairobi Treaty on the Protection of the Olympic Symbol entered into force on 25 September 1982. Brazil, Chile, New Zealand and Zambia signed the Treaty in 1982, bringing the number of signatory States to 26.

Sixteen intergovernmental Unions in the two main fields of intellectual property were administered by WIPO in 1982. They were founded on the multilateral treaties, conventions and agreements listed below in order of adoption:

Industrial property: Paris Convention for the Protection of Industrial Property; Madrid Agreement for the Repression of False or Deceptive Indications of Source on Goods; Madrid Agreement Concerning the International Registration of Marks; The Hague Agreement Concerning the International Deposit of Industrial Designs; Nice Agreement Concerning the International Classification of Goods and Services for the Purpose of the Registration of Marks; Lisbon Agreement for the Protection of Appellations of Origin and Their International Registration; Locarno Agreement Establishing an International Classification for Industrial Designs; Patent Co-operation Treaty; International Patent Classification Agreement; Trademark Registration Treaty; Budapest Treaty on the International Recognition of the Deposit of Microorganisms for the Purposes of Patent Procedure; Nairobi Treaty on the Protection of the Olympic Symbol.

Copyright and neighbouring rights: Berne Convention for the Protection of Literary and Artistic Works; Rome Convention for the Protection of Performers, Producers of Phonograms and Broadcasting Organizations; Geneva Convention for the Protection of Producers of Phonograms Against Unauthorized Duplication of Their Phonograms; Brussels Convention Relating to the Distribution of Programme-Carrying Signals Transmitted by Satellite.

At the thirteenth series of meetings, held at Geneva in November 1982, the governing bodies of WIPO and the Unions administered by it reviewed and noted with approval the activities of the International Bureau, WIPO's secretariat, and reports on the accounts for 1981.

Activities in 1982

Development co-operation activities

Two WIPO permanent programmes, supervised by intergovernmental permanent committees, provided the framework for development co-operation relating to industrial property and to copyright and neighbouring rights.

In the field of industrial property, WIPO organized or participated in the meetings of an Asian and Pacific Symposium on the Use and Usefulness of Trademarks in Developing Countries, at Colombo, Sri Lanka; a Working Group on the Establishment of a Guide on the Organization of Industrial Property Activities of Enterprises in Developing Countries, at Geneva; and a Training Seminar for Industrial Property Lawyers and Agents, at Dakar, Senegal.

Medals and prizes for inventors were awarded by WIPO at exhibitions and competitions held in India, Japan, Morocco, the Philippines, the USSR and at Geneva.

Continuing a programme initiated in 1975, 274 state-of-the-art search reports on technology disclosed in patent documents and related literature were furnished to developing countries, free of charge, under agreements concluded between WIPO and contributing industrial property offices in developed countries.

Development co-operation activities in copyright and neighbouring rights included the convening, jointly with the United Nations Educational, Scientific and Cultural Organization (UNESCO), of working groups and committees of experts on model provisions for national legislation on the protection of folklore, on the system of licences for developing countries under copyright conventions, and on model contracts concerning co-publishing and commissioned works.

WIPO training programmes in industrial property and in copyright continued to grow, with 181 fellowships granted in 1982 to nationals of 74 developing countries. Twenty-six countries, including nine developing countries, and three intergovernmental organizations provided individual training, in addition to study opportunities and courses for groups organized in Budapest (Hungary), Geneva (Switzerland), The Hague (Netherlands), Madrid (Spain), Moscow (USSR), Rio de

Janeiro (Brazil), Stockholm (Sweden), Strasbourg (France), Vienna (Austria) and Zurich (Switzerland). Regional and national meetings and seminars were organized by WIPO in Algeria, Brazil, China, India, Indonesia, Malaysia, Panama, Singapore, Sri Lanka, the United Republic of Cameroon and Zimbabwe.

During 1982, WIPO co-operated with Governments of 76 developing countries and with six intergovernmental organizations in development projects relating to intellectual property, by providing assistance in the preparation of legislation, or establishment or modernization of national or regional institutions, including patent documentation and information services.

Industrial property

The third session of the Diplomatic Conference on the Revision of the Paris Convention was held at Geneva from 4 to 30 October and from 23 to 27 November 1982; it requested the Paris Assembly to take the measures necessary to continue the Conference on dates to be fixed between October 1983 and March 1984. The objective of the revision was to introduce special provisions to meet the needs of developing countries more effectively, and to incorporate new provisions giving full recognition to inventors' certificates, a form of protection of inventions existing in some socialist countries.

Work continued on keeping up to date the International Patent Classification and other classifications relating to industrial designs or registration of trade marks and service marks. As in the past, WIPO assisted the International Patent Documentation Centre and remained on its Supervisory Board, while efforts continued towards early conclusion of the Computerized Administration of Patent Documents Reclassified According to the International Patent Classification.

At the end of 1982, thirty-two States were party to the Patent Co-operation Treaty (PCT). During the year, 4,713 international applications were filed in 20 receiving offices. Thirty issues of the *PCT Gazette* were published during the year, containing information on 4,519 published international applications.

The International Association for the Advancement of Teaching and Research in Intellectual Property held its second annual Assembly at Geneva in September 1982. A study on the role of industrial property in the protection of consumers was published.

Publications in the industrial property field included those on industrial property statistics, industrial property laws and treaties, the monthly review *Industrial Property* (special issues were devoted to anti-piracy measures and to public disclosure of an invention prior to filing a patent application), and the second volume of the *WIPO Handbook on Patent Information and Documentation*.

Copyright and neighbouring rights

At joint WIPO/UNESCO meetings, recommendations were made on the use of computers for access to or the creation of (copyright) works; on the "domaine public payant"; on questions concerning employed authors; on access by the handicapped to works protected by copyright; and on the impact of cable television in the sphere of copyright and neighbouring rights.

Publications in the copyright field included the *WIPO Guide to the Rome Convention and the Phonograms Convention* (in Spanish), and the monthly periodical *Copyright*; special issues of the latter were devoted to private copying of recordings, broadcasts and printed matter.

Secretariat

As at 31 December 1982, WIPO employed 264 full-time staff members. Of these, 85 were in the Professional and higher categories (drawn from 35 member States); 179 were in the General Service category. In addition, 49 experts were employed during 1982.

Budget

The principal sources of the budget of WIPO—expected to approximate Swiss francs 72 million for the biennium 1982-1983—are ordinary and special contributions from member States and income derived from international registration services.

Ordinary contributions are paid on the basis of a class-and-unit system by members of the Paris, Berne, Nice and Locarno Unions and by member States of WIPO that are not members of any of the Unions.

States members of those four Unions were placed in seven classes (I to VII) to determine the amounts of their ordinary contributions. States members of WIPO not members of any of the Unions were placed in three classes (A, B or C) for the same purpose. States in Class I or A pay the highest contributions of their group and those in Class VII or C the lowest. The class in which a State is placed is solely a matter for the State itself to decide. The rights of each State are the same, irrespective of class chosen.

The contribution class for each member State of WIPO and of the Paris or Berne Unions, together with the amount of the ordinary contribution of each State, is given in Annex I to this chapter (the class indicated for the Paris Union also applies to the Nice, Locarno and International Patent Classification Unions). The members of one or more Unions do not pay separate contributions to WIPO; the Unions themselves contribute towards the costs of WIPO's International Bureau.

The amounts of ordinary contributions payable for 1982 are given in the table below.

Income and expenditure

Summary figures for income and expenditure for 1982 are shown in the table opposite.

Income	In thousands of Swiss francs	Equivalent in thousands of US dollars*
Contributions	18,639	8,751
Income from registration services	15,070	7,075
Publications and miscellaneous	2,894	1,358
Total	36,603	17,184
Expenditure		
Staff	21,879	10,272
Travel	789	370
Meetings	578	271
Publications	2,186	1,026
Buildings†	4,270	2,005
Other	4,769	2,239
Total	34,471	16,183

*At the United Nations rate of exchange for December 1982; 2.13 Swiss francs = US $1.00.

†Includes maintenance, rental and amortization of the building loan.

CONTRIBUTION SCALES FOR 1983

(Swiss francs 2.13 = US$1.00: United Nations rate as at 31 December 1982)

	In Swiss francs	Equivalent in US dollars		In Swiss francs	Equivalent in US dollars
WIPO*			**IPC UNION**		
Class			*Class*		
A	62,500	29,343	I	199,757	93,782
B	18,750	8,803	II	†	†
C	6,250	2,934	III	119,853	56,269
			IV	79,903	37,513
PARIS UNION			V	†	†
Class			VI	23,970	11,253
I	410,025	192,500	VII	7,990	3,751
II	†	†	**PCT UNION**		
III	246,016	115,500	*Countries*		
IV	164,011	77,000	Australia	63,300	29,718
V	82,006	38,500	Austria	27,150	12,747
VI	49,203	23,100	Belgium	31,650	14,859
VII	16,402	7,700	Brazil	29,100	13,662
			Central African Republic‡	—	—
NICE UNION			Chad‡	—	—
Class			Congo‡	—	—
I	40,257	18,900	Democratic People's Republic of Korea‡	—	—
II	†	†	Denmark	36,300	17,042
III	24,154	11,339	Finland	26,250	12,324
IV	16,104	7,560	France	100,050	46,972
V	8,050	3,779	Gabon‡	—	—
VI	4,831	2,268	Germany, Federal Republic of	149,850	70,352
VII	1,610	756	Hungary	19,650	9,225
			Japan	181,200	85,070
LOCARNO UNION			Liechtenstein	§	§
Class			Luxembourg‡	—	—
I	16,025	7,523	Madagascar‡	—	—
II	†	†	Malawi‡	—	—
III	9,616	4,515	Monaco‡	—	—
IV	6,410	3,009	Netherlands	43,050	20,212
V	3,205	1,505	Norway	25,950	12,183
VI	†	†	Romania‡	—	—
VII	†	†	Senegal‡	—	—
			Soviet Union	80,850	37,958
BERNE UNION			Sri Lanka‡	—	—
Class			Sweden	104,100	48,873
I	236,043	110,818	Switzerland	60,000	28,169
II	188,834	88,654	Togo‡	—	—
III	141,626	66,491	United Kingdom	124,950	58,662
IV	94,418	44,328	United Republic of Cameroon‡	—	—
V	47,210	22,164	United States	396,600	186,197
VI	28,325	13,298	Total	1,500,000	704,225
VII	9,441	4,432			

*The amounts indicated are payable by those States members of WIPO which are not members of any of the Unions (see Annex I).

†No State currently belonged to this class.

‡No contributions are paid by States which, while members of the PCT Union, have fewer than ten international applications filed in a year.

§Liechtenstein accepted to pay a voluntary contribution of 2,500 Swiss francs = US $1,174.

Annex I. MEMBERSHIP OF THE WORLD INTELLECTUAL PROPERTY ORGANIZATION AND UNIONS ADMINISTERED TO WHICH CONTRIBUTIONS ARE PAYABLE

(As at 31 December 1982; ordinary contributions payable in 1983)

STATE	MEMBER							CLASS W	CLASS P	CLASS B	CONTRIBUTION* In Swiss francs	CONTRIBUTION* Equivalent in US dollars†
Algeria	W	P	—	N	—	—	—	—	VI	—	62,048	29,130
Argentina	W	P	B	—	—	—	—	—	III	IV	391,256	183,688
Australia	W	P	B	N	—	IPC	PCT	—	III	III	656,512	308,221
Austria	W	P	B	N	—	IPC	PCT	—	IV	VI	346,510	162,680
Bahamas	W	P	B	—	—	—	—	—	VII	VII	29,708	13,947
Barbados	W	—	—	—	—	—	—	C	—	—	6,250	2,934
Belgium	W	P	B	N	—	IPC	PCT	—	III	III	624,862	293,362
Benin	W	P	B	N	—	—	—	—	VII	VII	31,318	14,703
Brazil	W	P	B	—	—	IPC	PCT	—	III	III	594,577	279,144
Bulgaria	W	P	B	—	—	—	—	—	VI	VI	89,124	41,842
Burundi	W	P	—	—	—	—	—	—	VII	—	16,402	7,700
Byelorussian SSR	W	—	—	—	—	—	—	C	—	—	6,250	2,934
Canada	W	P	B	—	—	—	—	—	III	III	445,624	209,213
Central African Republic	W	P	B	—	—	—	PCT	—	VII	VII	28,276	13,275
Chad	W	P	B	—	—	—	PCT	—	VII	VII	29,708	13,947
Chile	W	—	B	—	—	—	—	—	—	VI	32,622	15,315
China	W	—	—	—	—	—	—	B	—	—	18,750	8,802
Colombia	W	—	—	—	—	—	—	C	—	—	6,250	2,934
Congo	W	P	B	—	—	—	PCT	—	VII	VII	29,708	13,947
Costa Rica	W	—	B	—	—	—	—	—	—	VII	9,441	4,432
Cuba	W	P	—	—	—	—	—	—	VI	—	56,502	26,526
Cyprus	—	P	B	—	—	—	—	—	VI	VI	89,124	41,842
Czechoslovakia	W	P	B	N	LO	IPC	—	—	IV	IV	401,890	188,680
Democratic People's Republic of Korea	W	P	—	—	—	—	PCT	—	VII	—	16,402	7,700
Denmark	W	P	B	N	LO	IPC	PCT	—	IV	IV	438,190	205,722
Dominican Republic	—	P	—	—	—	—	—	—	VI	—	56,502	26,526
Egypt	W	P	B	—	—	IPC	—	—	VI	VII	89,913	42,212
El Salvador	W	—	—	—	—	—	—	C	—	—	6,250	2,934
Fiji	W	—	B	—	—	—	—	—	—	VII	10,873	5,104
Finland	W	P	B	N	LO	IPC	PCT	—	IV	IV	428,140	201,004
France	W	P	B	N	LO	IPC	PCT	—	I	I	1,104,764	518,668
Gabon	W	P	B	—	—	—	PCT	—	VII	VII	29,708	13,947
Gambia	W	—	—	—	—	—	—	C	—	—	6,250	2,934
German Democratic Republic	W	P	B	N	LO	IPC	—	—	III	IV	548,460	257,492
Germany, Federal Republic of	W	P	B	N	—	IPC	PCT	—	I	I	1,138,539	534,525
Ghana	W	P	—	—	—	—	—	—	VII	—	18,835	8,842
Greece	W	P	B	—	—	—	—	—	V	VI	126,794	59,527
Guinea	W	P	B	—	—	—	—	—	VII	VII	25,843	12,132
Haiti	—	P	—	—	—	—	—	—	VI	—	56,502	26,526
Holy See	W	P	B	—	—	—	—	—	VII	VII	29,708	13,947
Hungary	W	P	B	N	LO	—	PCT	—	V	VI	158,893	74,597
Iceland	—	P	B	—	—	—	—	—	VI	VI	89,124	41,842
India	W	—	B	—	—	—	—	—	—	IV	108,742	51,052
Indonesia	W	P	—	—	—	—	—	—	VI	—	56,502	26,526
Iran	—	P	—	—	—	—	—	—	VI	—	56,597	26,571
Iraq	W	P	—	—	—	—	—	—	VI	—	56,502	26,526
Ireland	W	P	B	N	LO	IPC	—	—	IV	IV	401,890	188,680
Israel	W	P	B	N	—	IPC	—	—	VI	VI	118,640	55,699
Italy	W	P	B	N	LO	IPC	—	—	III	III	602,828	283,017
Ivory Coast	W	P	B	—	—	—	—	—	VII	VI	51,457	24,158
Jamaica	W	—	—	—	—	—	—	C	—	—	6,250	2,934
Japan	W	P	B	—	—	IPC	PCT	—	I	II	1,069,293	502,015
Jordan	W	P	—	—	—	—	—	—	VII	—	18,835	8,842
Kenya	W	P	—	—	—	—	—	—	VI	—	56,502	26,526
Lebanon	—	P	B	N	—	—	—	—	VI	VI	94,670	44,446
Libyan Arab Jamahiriya	W	P	B	—	—	—	—	—	VI	VI	89,124	41,842

STATE	MEMBER							CLASS			CONTRIBUTION*	
								W	P	B	In Swiss francs	Equivalent in US dollars†
Liechtenstein	W	P	B	N	—	—	PCT	—	VII	VII	34,058	15,989
Luxembourg	W	P	B	N	—	IPC	PCT	—	VII	VII	39,548	18,567
Madagascar	—	P	B	—	—	—	PCT	—	VII	VI	51,457	24,158
Malawi	W	P	—	—	—	—	PCT	—	VII	—	18,835	8,842
Mali	W	P	B	—	—	—	—	—	VII	VII	10,873	5,104
Malta	W	P	B	—	—	—	—	—	VII	VII	29,708	13,947
Mauritania	W	P	B	—	—	—	—	—	VII	VII	29,708	13,947
Mauritius	W	P	—	—	—	—	—	—	VII	—	18,835	8,842
Mexico	W	P	B	—	—	—	—	—	IV	IV	297,086	139,476
Monaco	W	P	B	N	—	IPC	PCT	—	VII	VII	39,548	18,567
Mongolia	W	—	—	—	—	—	—	C	—	—	6,250	2,934
Morocco	W	P	B	N	—	—	—	—	VI	VI	94,670	44,446
Netherlands	W	P	B	N	LO	IPC	PCT	—	III	III	645,878	303,229
New Zealand	—	P	B	—	—	—	—	—	V	V	148,544	69,738
Niger	W	P	B	—	—	—	—	—	VII	VII	29,708	13,947
Nigeria	—	P	—	—	—	—	—	—	VI	—	56,502	26,526
Norway	W	P	B	N	LO	IPC	PCT	—	IV	IV	427,840	200,863
Pakistan	W	—	B	—	—	—	—	—	—	VI	32,622	15,315
Peru	W	—	—	—	—	—	—	C	—	—	6,250	2,934
Philippines	W	P	B	—	—	—	—	—	VI	VI	89,124	41,842
Poland	W	P	B	—	—	—	—	—	V	VI	127,988	60,088
Portugal	W	P	B	N	—	IPC	—	—	IV	V	341,110	160,145
Qatar	W	—	—	—	—	—	—	B	—	—	18,750	8,802
Republic of Korea	W	P	—	—	—	—	—	—	VI	—	49,203	23,100
Romania	W	P	B	—	—	—	PCT	—	V	VI	126,794	59,527
San Marino	—	P	—	—	—	—	—	—	VI	—	56,502	26,526
Saudi Arabia	W	—	—	—	—	—	—	A	—	—	62,500	29,342
Senegal	W	P	B	—	—	—	PCT	—	VII	VI	51,457	24,158
Somalia	W	—	—	—	—	—	—	C	—	—	6,250	2,934
South Africa	W	P	B	—	—	—	—	—	IV	IV	297,086	139,476
Spain	W	P	B	N	LO	IPC	—	—	IV	II	510,629	239,731
Sri Lanka	W	P	B	—	—	—	PCT	—	VII	VII	29,708	13,947
Sudan	W	—	—	—	—	—	—	C	—	—	6,250	2,934
Suriname	W	P	B	N	—	IPC	—	—	VII	VII	37,876	17,782
Sweden	W	P	B	N	LO	IPC	PCT	—	III	III	706,928	331,891
Switzerland	W	P	B	N	LO	IPC	PCT	—	III	III	662,828	311,186
Syrian Arab Republic	—	P	—	—	—	—	—	—	VI	—	56,502	26,526
Thailand	—	—	B	—	—	—	—	—	—	VII	10,873	5,104
Togo	W	P	B	—	—	—	PCT	—	VII	VII	29,708	13,947
Trinidad and Tobago	—	P	—	—	—	—	—	—	VI	—	56,502	26,526
Tunisia	W	P	B	N	—	—	—	—	VI	VI	94,670	44,446
Turkey	W	P	B	—	—	—	—	—	VI	VI	89,124	41,842
Uganda	W	P	—	—	—	—	—	—	VII	—	18,835	8,842
Ukrainian SSR	W	—	—	—	—	—	—	C	—	—	6,250	2,934
USSR	W	P	—	N	LO	IPC	PCT	—	I	—	813,713	382,024
United Arab Emirates	W	—	—	—	—	—	—	B	—	—	18,750	8,802
United Kingdom	W	P	B	N	—	IPC	PCT	—	I	I	1,113,639	522,835
United Republic of Cameroon	W	P	B	—	—	—	PCT	—	VII	VI	51,457	24,158
United Republic of Tanzania	—	P	—	—	—	—	—	—	VI	—	56,502	26,526
United States	W	P	—	N	LO	IPC	PCT	—	I	—	1,113,438	522,740
Upper Volta	W	P	B	—	—	—	—	—	VII	VII	29,708	13,947
Uruguay	W	P	B	—	—	—	—	—	VII	VII	29,708	13,947
Venezuela	—	—	B	—	—	—	—	—	—	V	47,210	22,164
Viet Nam	W	P	—	—	—	—	—	—	VII	—	18,835	8,842
Yemen	W	—	—	—	—	—	PCT	C	—	—	6,250	2,934
Yugoslavia	W	P	B	N	LO	—	—	—	V	V	160,993	75,583
Zaire	W	P	B	—	—	—	—	—	VI	VI	89,124	41,842
Zambia	W	P	—	—	—	—	—	—	VII	—	18,835	8,842
Zimbabwe	W	P	B	—	—	—	—	—	VII	VII	25,843	12,132
Total	100	92	74	32	16	27	32				20,325,606	9,542,480

NOTE: Membership in WIPO is indicated by "W"; in the Paris Union by "P"; in the Berne Union by "B"; in the Nice Union by "N"; in the Locarno Union by "LO"; in the Strasbourg (IPC) Union by "IPC"; in the Patent Co-operation Treaty Union by "PCT". The class indicated for the Paris Union applies equally to the Nice, Locarno and IPC Unions.

*The amount of ordinary contributions of each member State includes—where applicable—15 per cent of the contributions for 1982 and 100 per cent of the contributions for 1983 to the Paris, Berne and Nice Unions. In addition, it includes ordinary contributions payable in 1983 to the other Unions and the supplementary contribution to the PCT Union for 1982, payable in 1983.

†Calculated on the basis of the United Nations rate of exchange for December 1982; Swiss francs 2.13 = US $1.00.

Annex II. OFFICERS AND OFFICES OF THE WORLD INTELLECTUAL PROPERTY ORGANIZATION

(As at 31 December 1982)

CO-ORDINATION COMMITTEE

OFFICERS
Chairman: Otto Leberl (Austria).
First Vice-Chairman: Mohamed Ben Slama (Tunisia).
Second Vice-Chairman: Lev Evgenyevich Komarov (USSR).
MEMBERS
Algeria, Argentina, Australia, Austria, Belgium, Brazil, Bulgaria, Canada, Chile, China,*

Congo, Cuba, Czechoslovakia, Egypt, Finland, France, German Democratic Republic, Germany, Federal Republic of, Ghana, Hungary, India, Italy, Ivory Coast, Japan, Kenya, Lebanon, Mexico, Mongolia, Nigeria, Philippines, Poland, Portugal, Qatar, Senegal, Sri Lanka, Sudan, Switzerland, Tunisia, Turkey, Uganda, USSR, United Kingdom, United Republic of Cameroon†, United Republic of Tanzania, United States, Uruguay.

*With effect from the date on which the number of members of WIPO, not members of any of the Unions, becomes 16.
†With effect from the date on which the number of members of the Berne Union Assembly becomes 68.

SENIOR OFFICERS OF THE INTERNATIONAL BUREAU

Director General: Arpad Bogsch.
Deputy Directors General: Lev Kostikov, Klaus Pfanner, Marino Porzio.
Director, Public Information and Copyright Department: Claude Masouyé.
Director, Developing Countries Division (Copyright): Shahid Alikhan.
Director, Public Information Division: Roger Harben.

Director, Industrial Property Division: Ludwig Baeumer.
Director, Classifications and Patent Information Division: Paul Claus.
Director, Patent Co-operation Treaty Division: François Curchod.
Director, Administrative Division: Thomas Keefer.
Legal Counsel: Gust Ledakis.

HEADQUARTERS AND OTHER OFFICE

HEADQUARTERS
World Intellectual Property Organization
34 Chemin des Colombettes
1211 Geneva 20, Switzerland
 Cable address: WIPO GENEVA or OMPI GENÈVE
 Telephone: 99 91 11
 Telex: 22376

LIAISON OFFICE WITH THE UNITED NATIONS IN NEW YORK
World Intellectual Property Organization
2 United Nations Plaza, Room 560
New York, N. Y. 10017, United States
 Telephone: (212) 867-0029, (212) 754-6813
 Telex: 420544

Chapter XVI

International Fund for Agricultural Development (IFAD)

The International Fund for Agricultural Development (IFAD), created in 1977 to provide concessional-term resources for the agricultural development and reduction of rural poverty in its developing member States, completed its fifth year of operation in 1982. The Fund's lending policies continued to reflect its conviction that food problems could be solved only if the rural poor were enabled to participate in the development process.

Membership of IFAD rose to 139 in 1982, when its Governing Council (fifth and sixth sessions, Rome, Italy, 19-22 January and 13-15 December) approved the admission of Belize, Saint Vincent and the Grenadines, Suriname and Tonga. Of these, 20 were in Category I (developed countries), 12 in Category II (oil-exporting developing countries) and 107 in Category III (other developing countries).

With the approval of 25 additional projects in 1982, total assistance provided by the Fund to 80 member countries since 1978 amounted to some $1,474 million, with about $1,415 million committed for 114 projects and $59 million provided as tech-

nical assistance grants. Special attention was paid to the needs of the poorest developing countries: of the total loan commitments of $1,415 million, 69 per cent were provided to low-income countries with per capita gross national product of less than $300, and about 31 per cent of the total commitment went to the least developed countries. Of the 114 loans approved, 35 were for projects in Africa, 35 in Asia, 25 in Latin America and 19 in the Near East and North Africa.

Most (67 per cent) of the loans were provided on highly concessional terms, with a service charge of one per cent per annum, a 50-year maturity period and a 10-year grace period. Another 28 per cent of the loans were made available on intermediate terms (at 4 per cent, 20 years maturity and a five-year grace period) and the remaining 5 per cent were made on ordinary terms (8 per cent, 15-18 years maturity and a three-year grace period).

Since 1979, approved loans were denominated in special drawing rights (SDRs), an international unit of account. Dollar figures in this chapter are based on the SDR/United States dollar conversion rate at 31 December 1982 (SDR 1 = US $1.10311).

Resources

The first replenishment of IFAD resources, providing it with additional funds of about $1,100 million for 1981/1983, became effective on 18 June 1982 when instruments totalling 50 per cent of contributions pledged by member States in Categories I and II were received. Norway provided an additional contribution of $4.3 million in 1982 to the amount originally pledged. Under the terms of the replenishment resolution adopted by the Governing Council in 1981, all contributions are to be paid before the end of 1983. Since actual payments were slower than expected, the size of IFAD lending operations was somewhat smaller in 1982 than in 1981.

In December 1982, the Governing Council decided to initiate discussions on a second replenishment of the Fund's resources, while taking into account the necessity of completing the first replenishment as well as all payments due under the initial contributions to the Fund.

Investments

Investments of the Fund's liquid assets, which totalled $559 million at the end of 1982, continued to be restricted to obligations (bonds) issued or fully guaranteed by Governments and to time deposits with major banks. While 49 per cent ($273 million) of those assets was held on deposit with, or in obligations issued by, commercial banks, 33 per cent ($185 million) of the total was deposited with banks from developing countries or in bonds and similar securities issued by developing country Governments and international development institutions.

Despite the sharp decline of interest rates during the last months of the year, the average rate of return earned on these assets for 1982 was 12.4 per cent, compared to the 12.8 per cent rate for 1981.

Activities in 1982

During 1982, IFAD approved financial assistance totalling some $315 million for 25 new projects and a supplementary loan of $6 million for one ongoing project in Sri Lanka—compared with 30 projects in 1981, 27 in 1980, 22 in 1979 and 10 in 1978. Of these 25 projects, seven were in Africa, seven in Asia, five in Latin America and six in the Near East and North Africa. Thirteen of them were initiated by IFAD and 12 were co-financed with other financing institutions. Eight projects related to member countries which had not previously received any IFAD loans.

The Fund continued to concentrate on increasing food-crop production, raising the living conditions of the poor, and strengthening the institutional base for alleviating rural poverty. Lending was diversified among projects for agricultural productivity, irrigation, rural development, credit, livestock and fisheries development, research and training.

In addition, the Fund approved in 1982 over $18 million for technical assistance in project preparation, institutional development and training, and agricultural research, including $2.8 million in support of project preparation activities to assist 14 member States. Grant financing continued to be provided, in appropriate cases, for certain elements of technical assistance forming part of a project such as training, agricultural extension and special studies. Mauritania received such grants, totalling $1 million.

The tables below show the technical assistance grants approved during 1982 for project preparation and those for research.

Also in 1982, four special missions—to Burundi, Guyana, Lao People's Democratic Republic and Morocco—analysed the food production and nutrition situation, explored the nature and extent of rural poverty and identified specific assistance programmes suitable for IFAD financing.

Income and expenditures

Total revenue for 1982 was $66.5 million, mainly income from investments but including about $3 million from interest and service charges on loans. Expenses for the year amounted to $16.6 million compared with a budget of $20.5 million approved by the Governing Council at its fifth session (Rome, Italy, 19-22 January). The excess of revenue over expenses for 1982 was $50 million.

Secretariat

As at December 1982, the secretariat of IFAD totalled 164, of whom 72 were executive or technical staff (Professional category and above), drawn from 41 countries, and 92 were support staff (General Service category).

PROJECT PREPARATION GRANTS

Country	Amount (in thousands of US dollars)
Bangladesh	300
Bhutan	250
Central African Republic	200
Comoros	300
Dominican Republic	150
Haiti	320
Ivory Coast	200
Madagascar	130
Nicaragua	150
Pakistan	250
Philippines	200
Senegal	80
Syrian Arab Republic	150
Zambia	135
Total	2,815

RESEARCH GRANTS

Recipient	Amount (in thousands of US dollars)
Arab Centre for the Study of Arid Zones and Dry Lands, Damascus, Syrian Arab Republic	1,690
Centro Agronómico Tropical de Investigación y Enseñanza, Turrialba, Costa Rica	1,400
Centro Internacional de Agricultura Tropical, Cali, Colombia	1,000
International Centre for Agricultural Research in the Dry Areas, Aleppo, Syrian Arab Republic	1,850
International Centre for Insect Physiology and Ecology, Nairobi, Kenya	2,060
International Crops Research Institute for the Semi-Arid Tropics, Hyderabad, India	300
International Fertilizer Development Centre, Alabama, United States	1,000
International Food Policy Research Institute, Washington, D.C., United States	200
International Institute for Tropical Agriculture, Ibadan, Nigeria	1,800
International Livestock Centre for Africa, Addis Ababa, Ethiopia	600
International Potato Centre, Lima, Peru	600
International Rice Research Institute, Los Baños, Philippines	1,600
West African Rice Development Association, Monrovia, Liberia	400
Total	14,500

PROJECT LOANS APPROVED DURING 1982

Country	Purpose	Amount (in thousands of US dollars)
Bangladesh	Rural development in north-western region	15,100
Benin	Rural development in Atacora province	9,100
China*	Agricultural development in Hebei province	25,300
Costa Rica†	Agricultural credit	4,900
Democratic Yemen	Fisheries development	4,900
Dominican Rep.*	Small-scale food producers development	9,900
Egypt	Agricultural development, Minya	26,000
Honduras*	Rural development in Santa Barbara region	12,000
Indonesia*	Irrigation in East Java province	24,000
Jamaica*	Small farmers' credit	9,800
Jordan*	Small farmers' credit	12,500
Madagascar	Livestock and rural development	7,700
Maldives	Fisheries	2,100
Mali	Village development fund	9,000
Mauritania‡	Farmers' training in Gorgol region	1,300
Mozambique	National programme for food production in the co-operative and family sector	19,500
Papua New Guinea*	Artisanal fisheries	10,000
Peru*	Rural development in Alto Mayo Valley	19,800
Philippines*	Communal irrigation	11,900
Sri Lanka	Rural development in Badulla district	14,300
Syrian Arab Rep.*	Agricultural development in southern region	17,300
Turkey†	Rural development in Erzurum province	19,000
Upper Volta	Agricultural development in Hauts Bassins/Volta Noire	10,900
Yemen	Agricultural research and development	5,800
Zambia	Area development in north-western province	13,200
Total		315,300

NOTE: Loans are on highly concessional terms except for those marked (*), which are on intermediate terms, and (†), which are on ordinary terms.

‡Also received 880,000 SDRs for technical assistance; as at 31 December 1982, the SDR/United States dollar conversion rate stood at SDR 1 = US $1.10311.

Annex I. MEMBERSHIP OF THE INTERNATIONAL FUND FOR AGRICULTURAL DEVELOPMENT AND CONTRIBUTIONS PLEDGED AND PAID

(As at 31 December 1982)

MEMBER	INITIAL CONTRIBUTIONS (in US dollar equivalents)		FIRST REPLENISHMENT CONTRIBUTIONS (in US dollar equivalents)	
	Pledged	Paid	Pledged	Paid
Category I				
Australia	7,843,137	7,843,137	8,789,216	8,789,216
Austria	4,800,000	4,800,000	4,461,400	4,461,400
Belgium	11,656,437	11,656,437	9,915,601	—
Canada	26,829,268	26,829,268	34,146,341	11,382,114
Denmark	7,500,000	7,500,000	7,159,905	4,773,270
Finland	2,268,431	2,268,431	4,536,862	3,024,575
France	18,916,914	18,916,914	34,041,543	17,020,772
Germany, Federal Republic of	55,000,000	55,000,000	49,084,034	24,542,017
Ireland	920,840	920,840	886,872	674,986
Italy	25,000,000	25,000,000	38,700,000	38,700,000
Japan	55,000,000	55,000,000	54,086,515	18,028,838
Luxembourg	352,995	352,995	—	—
Netherlands	41,167,939	41,167,939	—	—
New Zealand	1,459,854	1,459,854	1,521,022	760,511
Norway	18,439,717	18,439,717	25,721,631	16,938,830
Spain	2,000,000	2,000,000	2,000,000	1,000,000
Sweden	15,731,874	15,731,874	20,284,542	14,128,591
Switzerland	11,055,276	11,055,276	14,291,457	7,035,176
United Kingdom	29,079,160	29,079,160	20,841,885	6,947,296
United States	200,000,000	200,000,000		
Subtotal	535,021,842	535,021,842	330,468,826	178,207,592
Category II				
Algeria	10,000,000	10,000,000	15,580,000	15,580,000
Gabon	500,000	500,000	801,000	—
Indonesia	1,250,000	1,250,000	1,909,000	636,333
Iran	124,750,000	41,583,333	—	—
Iraq	20,000,000	20,000,000	31,099,000	—
Kuwait	36,000,000	36,000,000	56,041,000	56,041,000

MEMBER	INITIAL CONTRIBUTIONS (in US dollar equivalents)		FIRST REPLENISHMENT CONTRIBUTIONS (in US dollar equivalents)	
	Pledged	Paid	Pledged	Paid
Category II (cont.)				
Libyan Arab Jamahiriya	20,000,000	20,000,000	—	—
Nigeria	26,000,000	26,000,000	40,459,000	13,498,333
Qatar	9,000,000	9,000,000	13,980,000	13,980,000
Saudi Arabia	105,500,000	105,500,000	155,618,000	51,872,666
United Arab Emirates	16,500,000	16,500,000	25,680,000	25,680,000
Venezuela	66,000,000	66,000,000	—	—
Subtotal	435,500,000	352,333,333	341,167,000	177,288,332
Category III				
Afghanistan	5,238	5,238	—	—
Angola*	—	—	—	—
Argentina	4,944	4,944	900,000	900,000
Bangladesh	308,642	308,642	750,000	480,000
Barbados	1,000	1,000	—	—
Belize	—	—	—	—
Benin	—	—	10,000	—
Bhutan	—	—	1,000	1,000
Bolivia	—	—	50,000	—
Botswana	—	—	15,000	15,000
Brazil	—	—	9,972,791	9,972,791
Burundi	—	—	111,111	—
Cape Verde	1,000	1,000	—	—
Central African Republic	2,967	2,967	—	—
Chad	—	—	—	—
Chile	50,000	50,000	—	—
China	912,500	912,500	1,300,000	700,000
Colombia	—	—	—	—
Comoros	29,740	14,870	—	—
Congo	—	—	54,291	54,291

MEMBER	INITIAL CONTRIBUTIONS (in US dollar equivalents)		FIRST REPLENISHMENT CONTRIBUTIONS (in US dollar equivalents)		MEMBER	INITIAL CONTRIBUTIONS (in US dollar equivalents)		FIRST REPLENISHMENT CONTRIBUTIONS (in US dollar equivalents)	
	Pledged	Paid	Pledged	Paid		Pledged	Paid	Pledged	Paid
Category III (cont.)					*Category III* (cont.)				
Costa Rica	—	—	—	—	Panama	—	—	25,000	25,000
Cuba	—	—	100,000	—	Papua New Guinea	20,000	20,000	—	—
Cyprus	25,000	25,000	12,000	12,000	Paraguay	—	—	—	—
Democratic Yemen	—	—	50,000	50,000	Peru	—	—	60,000	60,000
Djibouti	—	—	3,000	3,000	Philippines	250,000	250,000	—	—
Dominica	—	—	7,361	7,361	Portugal	—	—	—	—
Dominican Republic	25,000	25,000	—	—	Republic of Korea	169,814	169,814	300,000	184,000
Ecuador	25,047	25,047	42,050	42,050	Romania	331,333	331,333	—	—
Egypt	171,429	171,429	—	—	Rwanda	—	—	—	—
El Salvador	40,000	40,000	—	—	Saint Lucia	—	—	—	—
Equatorial Guinea	—	—	—	—	Saint Vincent and the Grenadines*	—	—	—	—
Ethiopia	23,623	23,623	23,623	—	Samoa	10,000	10,000	—	—
Fiji	10,000	10,000	10,000	10,000	Sao Tome and Principe	—	—	—	—
Gambia	—	—	—	—	Senegal	10,000	10,000	14,870	—
Ghana	100,000	100,000	—	—	Seychelles	5,000	1,667	—	—
Greece	150,000	150,000	200,000	197,183	Sierra Leone	18,296	18,296	18,430	18,430
Grenada	—	—	—	—	Solomon Islands	—	—	10,000	—
Guatemala	—	—	—	—	Somalia	10,000	10,000	—	—
Guinea	1,190,476	1,190,476	60,000	—	Sri Lanka	864,447	864,447	—	—
Guinea-Bissau	—	—	10,000	—	Sudan	10,000	10,000	10,000	—
Guyana	—	—	30,000	—	Suriname	—	—	—	—
Haiti	60,000	—	—	—	Swaziland	—	—	—	—
Honduras	25,000	25,000	—	—	Syrian Arab Republic	127,226	42,409	—	—
India	4,609,711	4,609,711	6,500,000	4,333,000	Thailand	100,000	100,000	200,000	—
Israel	150,000	150,000	150,000	—	Togo	8,902	8,902	—	—
Ivory Coast	—	—	—	—	Tonga	—	—	—	—
Jamaica	4,820	4,820	15,000	15,000	Tunisia	81,169	81,169	300,000	—
Jordan	30,000	30,000	75,000	75,000	Turkey	16,956	16,956	100,000	100,000
Kenya	621,069	621,069	1,070,277	1,070,277	Uganda	840	840	70,999	70,999
Lao People's Democratic Republic	10,000	10,000	—	—	United Republic of Cameroon	50,000	50,000	59,480	29,849
Lebanon	—	—	25,000	25,000	United Republic of Tanzania	31,348	31,348	39,185	—
Lesotho	15,000	15,000	50,000	10,000	Upper Volta	10,000	10,000	—	—
Liberia	10,000	10,000	—	—	Uruguay	—	—	—	—
Madagascar	—	—	—	—	Viet Nam	51,230	51,230	—	—
Malawi	5,000	5,000	9,761	9,761	Yemen	50,000	50,000	—	—
Maldives	—	—	—	—	Yugoslavia	87,977	87,977	227,908	138,954
Mali	—	—	10,000	10,000	Zaire	30,000	—	—	—
Malta	—	—	—	—	Zambia	39,374	39,374	56,077	56,077
Mauritania	—	—	—	—	Zimbabwe	—	—	—	—
Mauritius	—	—	—	—					
Mexico	5,000,000	5,000,000	7,000,000	4,219,006	Subtotal	17,344,245	17,151,225	31,507,551	23,651,044
Morocco	344,829	344,829	—	—					
Mozambique	31,112	31,112	93,337	93,337	Total	987,866,087	904,506,400	703,143,377	379,146,968
Nepal	5,000	5,000	5,000	5,000					
Nicaragua	28,571	28,571	—	—	Special contributions				
Niger	44,510	44,510	—	—	OPEC Fund	—	—	20,000,000	20,000,000
Oman*	—	—	—	—	Other	101,157	101,157		
Pakistan	889,105	889,105	1,300,000	657,678					

NOTE: According to article 4, section 2 *(c)*, of the Agreement establishing IFAD, members' initial contributions are payable in cash or promissory notes, either in a single sum or in three annual instalments. Contributions have been translated on the basis of International Monetary Fund exchange rates as at 31 December 1982.

*Had not completed the required membership formalities.

Annex II.   OFFICERS AND OFFICES OF THE INTERNATIONAL FUND FOR AGRICULTURAL DEVELOPMENT

EXECUTIVE BOARD

Chairman: Abdelmuhsin M. Al-Sudeary.

MEMBERS

Category I: France, Germany, Federal Republic of, Japan, Netherlands, Sweden, United States. *Alternates:* Austria, Canada, Denmark, Switzerland, United Kingdom.

Category II: Iran, Kuwait, Libyan Arab Jamahiriya, Nigeria, Saudi Arabia, Venezuela. *Alternates:* Algeria, Gabon, Indonesia, Iraq, Qatar, United Arab Emirates.

*Category III:** Bangladesh, Brazil, Jamaica, Kenya, Tunisia, Thailand. *Alternates:* Colombia, Ghana, Lesotho, Panama, Republic of Korea, Turkey.

*As of 14 December 1982, following the election at the sixth session of the Governing Council.

SENIOR SECRETARIAT OFFICERS

President: Abdelmuhsin M. Al-Sudeary.

Vice-President: Philip Birnbaum.

Assistant President, Head of Economic and Planning Department: Sartaj Aziz.

Assistant President, Head of Project Management Department: Moise Mensah.

Assistant President, Head of General Affairs Department: Abbas Ordoobadi.

Director, Personnel Services Division: John Sykes.

Director, Legal Services Division: Mohammed Nawaz.

HEADQUARTERS AND OTHER OFFICE

HEADQUARTERS
International Fund for Agricultural Development
107 Via del Serafico
00142 Rome, Italy
  Cable address: IFAD ROME
  Telephone: 54591
  Telex: 614160, 614162

ACTING LIAISON OFFICE WITH UNITED NATIONS IN NEW YORK
International Fund for Agricultural Development
Room S-2955
United Nations Headquarters
New York, N. Y. 10017, United States
  Telephone: (212) 754-4245, 4246, 4248

Chapter XVII

Interim Commission for the International Trade Organization (ICITO) and the General Agreement on Tariffs and Trade (GATT)

The United Nations Conference on Trade and Employment, held at Havana, Cuba, between November 1947 and March 1948, drew up a charter for an International Trade Organization (ITO) and established an Interim Commission for the International Trade Organization (ICITO). Since the charter itself was never accepted, ITO was not established. However, while drawing up the charter, the Preparatory Committee's members negotiated on tariffs among themselves, and also drew up the General Agreement on Tariffs and Trade (GATT). The Agreement—a multilateral treaty embodying reciprocal rights and obligations—is the only multilateral instrument that lays down agreed rules for international trade. It entered into force on 1 January 1948 with 23 contracting parties. Since then, ICITO has provided the GATT secretariat.

By the end of 1982, the number of contracting parties to GATT had risen to 88 with the addition of Zambia (10 February) and Thailand (20 November). One other country, Tunisia, had acceded provisionally. The contracting parties conducted about 85 per cent of all international trade while 30 other countries applied the rules of GATT.

Multilateral trade negotiations

Implementation of the Tokyo Round agreements

By 1982 there had been seven "rounds" of multilateral trade negotiations in the 35-year history of GATT, the latest being the Tokyo Round, concluded in 1979.[a] The agreements provided an improved framework for the conduct of world trade and were adopted as an integral part of the rules of GATT.

On 1 January 1982, the industrialized participants in the Tokyo Round made the third of a series of eight annual agreed tariff cuts which, when completed, were to reduce the average duties they imposed on imports of manufactured goods by about one third, a cut comparable to that achieved in the 1964-1967 Kennedy Round. Cuts were also being made in duties on agricultural products. A number of countries were following faster schedules for reducing import tariffs for developing countries while many of those countries were themselves making tariff concessions.

By 1982 all the non-tariff agreements were a part of normal international co-operation in trade relations, and the various supervisory bodies had in a number of cases formally reviewed their operation. The review of the customs valuation agreement indicated that the new valuation procedures were being applied by virtually all developed countries and also by a number of developing ones, resulting in a considerable reduction in trade difficulties. The codes of anti-dumping measures, standards and licensing procedures, the agreement on civil aircraft, and the arrangements on dairy products and bovine meat all appeared to be working well. The agreement on subsidies and countervailing measures, acknowledged as a particularly difficult sector of trade relations, was being tested by a number of dispute settlement cases which were being considered during 1982 by independent expert panels. The practical effects on international trade of the agreement on government procurement, the only other Tokyo Round agreement whose dispute settlement procedures had been activated by 1982, had not been assessed by year's end.

[a]See YUN 1979, p. 1328.

Other GATT activities

1982 ministerial session

The 1982 session of GATT member States was held at Geneva from 22 to 30 November at ministerial level to examine the implementation of the results of the multilateral trade negotiations, problems affecting the trading system, the position of developing countries in world trade, and future prospects for the development of trade, and to determine future priorities for co-operation among contracting parties. Attended by some 70 Ministers from the 88 GATT member countries, the ministerial session resulted in the adoption by consensus of a declaration diagnosing the problems of the world trading system. It affirmed a basic commitment against protectionism and for a renewed consensus in support of the GATT system. The declaration set out undertakings on which contracting parties had agreed in drawing up their work programme and priorities for the 1980s. The practical consequences of these political commitments for the future work of GATT were outlined in separate decisions, dealing with such issues as safeguards, GATT rules and activities relating to developing countries, dispute settlement and trade in agriculture. Other decisions included tropical products, quantitative restrictions and other non-tariff measures, tariffs, structural adjustment and trade policy, trade in counterfeit goods, exports of domestically prohibited goods, textiles and services.

Regarding safeguards, the need for an improved and more efficient system was reaffirmed and the Council of Representatives, the highest body of GATT, was instructed to draw up an understanding to preserve the results of trade liberalization and avoid the proliferation of restrictive measures.

Particular attention was given to the problems of developing countries. The declaration strengthened the role of the Committee on Trade and Development, requiring it to examine prospects for increasing trade between developed and developing countries. The technical co-operation programme of GATT was also strengthened.

Recognizing the urgent need to find lasting solutions to the problems of trade in agricultural products, it was decided to establish a committee to examine, in the light of the provisions of the General Agreement and also taking into account the effects of national agricultural policies, measures affecting trade, market access and competition as well as supply of agricultural products, including subsidies and other forms of assistance.

In deciding to set up a group to review quantitative restrictions and other non-tariff measures, the contracting parties set the objective of eliminating restrictions inconsistent with the General Agreement or bringing them into conformity with that instrument. The group was also to give attention to restrictions affecting products of particular export interest to developing countries.

On the GATT work programme and priorities for the 1980s, while agreeing that no major change was required in the dispute settlement arrangements negotiated during the Tokyo Round, the declaration underlined that there was scope for more effective use of the existing mechanism and for improvements to that end, particularly in respect of the role of the Director-General of GATT, the time frame and recommendations aimed at achieving settlement of any dispute.

Council of Representatives

The Council of Representatives, which meets about nine times a year between sessions of the contracting parties, in 1982 acted on various international trade policy issues, including reports of independent expert panels set up to examine and make recommendations on trade disputes between GATT member States.

Consultative Group of Eighteen

In 1982, the Consultative Group of Eighteen, the GATT forum for discussing international trade problems, examined three closely related subjects: preparations for the 1982 ministerial session, the current international economic situation and its implications for trade policies, and improving co-operation in GATT on world trade in farm products.

Committee on Trade and Development

During its three 1982 meetings, the Committee on Trade and Development reviewed progress in consultations on trade liberalization in the areas of tropical products and quantitative restrictions, discussed its contribution to the preparations for the ministerial session and reviewed the implementation of the part of the Tokyo Round agreement on improving the legal framework for the conduct of world trade. Discussions on the problems of least developed countries and on protective measures continued in the Committee's two subcommittees, established in 1980.

Preferential arrangements among developing countries

The possibilities for expansion of trade among developing countries through a further round of negotiations continued to be examined in 1982 by the 18 developing countries party to the 1973 Protocol relating to Trade Negotiations among Developing Countries.

Balance-of-payments restrictions

Consultations with countries whose balance-of-payments difficulties had led them to restrict imports were held in 1982 with Bangladesh, Ghana, India, Israel, Pakistan, the Philippines and Portugal.

Textiles Arrangement

Originally negotiated in 1973 under GATT auspices, the Arrangement regarding International Trade in Textiles, known as the Multifibre Arrangement, regulating most of world trade in textiles and clothing, had been extended in December 1981.[b] The renewed Arrangement, whose signatories accounted for about four fifths of world trade in textiles and clothing, was extended from 1 January 1982 until 31 July 1986. In December 1982, the Textile Committee made its first annual review of the extended Arrangement.

Technical assistance

In 1982, the GATT secretariat's Technical Co-operation Division organized missions to developing countries and GATT officials participated in seminars and training courses on GATT and the Tokyo Round agreements held in Bolivia, Chile, Colombia, Indonesia, the Ivory Coast, Pakistan, Romania and Singapore. Technical missions related to accession, subsidies, anti-dumping, customs valuation and preparatory work for future seminars visited Benin, Burundi, the Philippines, Rwanda, Senegal and Thailand.

Training programme

The biannual commercial policy courses continued in 1982 at Geneva with 23 developing country officials attending a March-June course and 19 participating in an August-December course. The 1982 ministerial declaration (see above) included a decision to increase participation in the courses, and to include a regular Spanish-language course in the training programme.

International Trade Centre

In 1964, GATT established the International Trade Centre to provide trade information and trade promotion advisory services for developing countries. Since 1968, the Centre had been jointly operated with the United Nations Conference on Trade and Development. The Centre continued to support developing countries' trade promotion programmes and activities, and to help them become progressively self-reliant. The value of its technical co-operation programme in 1982 was estimated at $16 million.

Publications

Publications issued in 1982 included the annual volumes of *GATT Activities* and *International Trade*, and the monthly newsletter *GATT Focus*.

Secretariat

As at 31 December 1982, the GATT secretariat employed 275 staff members; of these, 118 were in the Professional and higher categories and 157 were in the General Service category. They were drawn from 42 nationalities.

Financial arrangements

Member countries of GATT contribute to the budget in accordance with a scale assessed on the basis of each country's share in the total trade of the contracting parties and associated Governments. The budget for 1982 was 45,501,000 Swiss francs.

[b]See YUN 1981, p. 1484.

Annex I. CONTRACTING PARTIES TO THE GENERAL AGREEMENT ON TARIFFS AND TRADE AND SCALE OF CONTRIBUTIONS FOR 1982

(As at 31 December 1982)

Contracting party	Net contribution (in Swiss francs)	Contracting party	Net contribution (in Swiss francs)	Contracting party	Net contribution (in Swiss francs)
Argentina	181,670	Egypt	106,350	Kuwait	345,620
Australia	580,460	Finland	358,910	Luxembourg	146,230
Austria	553,880	France	3,292,230	Madagascar	53,170
Bangladesh	53,170	Gabon	53,170	Malawi	53,170
Barbados	53,170	Gambia	53,170	Malaysia	292,450
Belgium	1,670,490	Germany, Federal Republic of	5,113,380	Malta	53,170
Benin	53,170	Ghana	53,170	Mauritania	53,170
Brazil	562,740	Greece	181,670	Mauritius	53,170
Burma	53,170	Guyana	53,170	Netherlands	2,118,020
Burundi	53,170	Haiti	53,170	New Zealand	141,790
Canada	1,781,260	Hungary	257,000	Nicaragua	53,170
Central African Republic	53,170	Iceland	53,170	Niger	53,170
Chad	53,170	India	257,000	Nigeria	496,270
Chile	124,070	Indonesia	305,740	Norway	443,100
Colombia	110,780	Ireland	261,430	Pakistan	97,480
Congo	53,170	Israel	186,100	Peru	66,470
Cuba	128,500	Italy	2,304,120	Philippines	177,240
Cyprus	53,170	Ivory Coast	70,900	Poland	545,020
Czechoslovakia	447,530	Jamaica	53,170	Portugal	137,360
Denmark	505,140	Japan	3,465,040	Republic of Korea	540,580
Dominican Republic	53,170	Kenya	53,170	Romania	283,590

Contracting party	Net contribution (in Swiss francs)	Contracting party	Net contribution (in Swiss francs)	Contracting party	Net contribution (in Swiss francs)
Rwanda	53,170	Thailand	22,430	Uruguay	53,170
Senegal	53,170	Togo	53,170	Yugoslavia	310,170
Sierra Leone	53,170	Trinidad and Tobago	84,190	Zaire	53,170
Singapore	354,480	Turkey	115,210	Zambia	53,170
South Africa	283,590	Uganda	53,170	Zimbabwe	53,170
Spain	682,380	United Kingdom	3,597,970	*Associated Governments*	
Sri Lanka	53,170	United Republic of Cameroon	53,170		
Suriname	53,170	United Republic of Tanzania	53,170	Democratic Kampuchea	53,170
Sweden	855,180	United States	6,358,490	Tunisia	70,900
Switzerland	886,200	Upper Volta	53,170	Total	44,385,600

Annex II. OFFICERS AND OFFICES OF THE GENERAL AGREEMENT ON TARIFFS AND TRADE
(As at 31 December 1982)

OFFICERS

OFFICERS OF THE CONTRACTING PARTIES*

Chairman of the Contracting Parties: Bhagirath Lal Das (India).

Vice-Chairmen of the Contracting Parties: Peter Field (Australia), F. Grunwaldt Ramasso (Uruguay), Janos Nyerges (Hungary).
Chairman of the Council of Representatives: Hans Ewerlof (Sweden).
Chairman of the Committee on Trade and Development: Kazimir Vidas (Yugoslavia).

*Elected at the end of the November 1982 session, to hold office until the end of the next session.

SENIOR OFFICERS OF THE SECRETARIAT
Director-General: Arthur Dunkel.
Deputy Directors-General: Madan G. Mathur, William B. Kelly, Jr.

SENIOR OFFICERS OF THE
INTERNATIONAL TRADE CENTRE UNCTAD/GATT
Executive Director: Goran M. Engblom.
Deputy Executive Director: Said T. Harb.

HEADQUARTERS

GATT Secretariat
Centre William Rappard
Rue de Lausanne 154
1211 Geneva 21, Switzerland
  Cable address: GATT GENEVA
  Telephone: 31 02 31
  Telex: 28787

Appendices

Appendix I

Roster of the United Nations

(As at 31 December 1982)

MEMBER	DATE OF ADMISSION	MEMBER	DATE OF ADMISSION	MEMBER	DATE OF ADMISSION
Afghanistan	19 Nov. 1946	Ghana	8 Mar. 1957	Philippines	24 Oct. 1945
Albania	14 Dec. 1955	Greece	25 Oct. 1945	Poland	24 Oct. 1945
Algeria	8 Oct. 1962	Grenada	17 Sep. 1974	Portugal	14 Dec. 1955
Angola	1 Dec. 1976	Guatemala	21 Nov. 1945	Qatar	21 Sep. 1971
Antigua and Barbuda	11 Nov. 1981	Guinea	12 Dec. 1958	Romania	14 Dec. 1955
Argentina	24 Oct. 1945	Guinea-Bissau	17 Sep. 1974	Rwanda	18 Sep. 1962
Australia	1 Nov. 1945	Guyana	20 Sep. 1966	Saint Lucia	18 Sep. 1979
Austria	14 Dec. 1955	Haiti	24 Oct. 1945	Saint Vincent and	
Bahamas	18 Sep. 1973	Honduras	17 Dec. 1945	the Grenadines	16 Sep. 1980
Bahrain	21 Sep. 1971	Hungary	14 Dec. 1955	Samoa	15 Dec. 1976
Bangladesh	17 Sep. 1974	Iceland	19 Nov. 1946	Sao Tome and	
Barbados	9 Dec. 1966	India	30 Oct. 1945	Principe	16 Sep. 1975
Belgium	27 Dec. 1945	Indonesia[2]	28 Sep. 1950	Saudi Arabia	24 Oct. 1945
Belize	25 Sep. 1981	Iran (Islamic		Senegal	28 Sep. 1960
Benin	20 Sep. 1960	Republic of)	24 Oct. 1945	Seychelles	21 Sep. 1976
Bhutan	21 Sep. 1971	Iraq	21 Dec. 1945	Sierra Leone	27 Sep. 1961
Bolivia	14 Nov. 1945	Ireland	14 Dec. 1955	Singapore[3]	21 Sep. 1965
Botswana	17 Oct. 1966	Israel	11 May 1949	Solomon Islands	19 Sep. 1978
Brazil	24 Oct. 1945	Italy	14 Dec. 1955	Somalia	20 Sep. 1960
Bulgaria	14 Dec. 1955	Ivory Coast	20 Sep. 1960	South Africa	7 Nov. 1945
Burma	19 Apr. 1948	Jamaica	18 Sep. 1962	Spain	14 Dec. 1955
Burundi	18 Sep. 1962	Japan	18 Dec. 1956	Sri Lanka	14 Dec. 1955
Byelorussian Soviet		Jordan	14 Dec. 1955	Sudan	12 Nov. 1956
Socialist Republic	24 Oct. 1945	Kenya	16 Dec. 1963	Suriname	4 Dec. 1975
Canada	9 Nov. 1945	Kuwait	14 May 1963	Swaziland	24 Sep. 1968
Cape Verde	16 Sep. 1975	Lao People's		Sweden	19 Nov. 1946
Central African		Democratic Republic	14 Dec. 1955	Syrian Arab Republic[1]	24 Oct. 1945
Republic	20 Sep. 1960	Lebanon	24 Oct. 1945	Thailand	16 Dec. 1946
Chad	20 Sep. 1960	Lesotho	17 Oct. 1966	Togo	20 Sep. 1960
Chile	24 Oct. 1945	Liberia	2 Nov. 1945	Trinidad and	
China	24 Oct. 1945	Libyan Arab		Tobago	18 Sep. 1962
Colombia	5 Nov. 1945	Jamahiriya	14 Dec. 1955	Tunisia	12 Nov. 1956
Comoros	12 Nov. 1975	Luxembourg	24 Oct. 1945	Turkey	24 Oct. 1945
Congo	20 Sep. 1960	Madagascar	20 Sep. 1960	Uganda	25 Oct. 1962
Costa Rica	2 Nov. 1945	Malawi	1 Dec. 1964	Ukrainian Soviet	
Cuba	24 Oct. 1945	Malaysia[3]	17 Sep. 1957	Socialist Republic	24 Oct. 1945
Cyprus	20 Sep. 1960	Maldives	21 Sep. 1965	Union of Soviet	
Czechoslovakia	24 Oct. 1945	Mali	28 Sep. 1960	Socialist Republics	24 Oct. 1945
Democratic Kampuchea	14 Dec. 1955	Malta	1 Dec. 1964	United Arab Emirates	9 Dec. 1971
Democratic Yemen	14 Dec. 1967	Mauritania	27 Oct. 1961	United Kingdom of	
Denmark	24 Oct. 1945	Mauritius	24 Apr. 1968	Great Britain and	
Djibouti	20 Sep. 1977	Mexico	7 Nov. 1945	Northern Ireland	24 Oct. 1945
Dominica	18 Dec. 1978	Mongolia	27 Oct. 1961	United Republic	
Dominican Republic	24 Oct. 1945	Morocco	12 Nov. 1956	of Cameroon	20 Sep. 1960
Ecuador	21 Dec. 1945	Mozambique	16 Sep. 1975	United Republic	
Egypt[1]	24 Oct. 1945	Nepal	14 Dec. 1955	of Tanzania[4]	14 Dec. 1961
El Salvador	24 Oct. 1945	Netherlands	10 Dec. 1945	United States	
Equatorial Guinea	12 Nov. 1968	New Zealand	24 Oct. 1945	of America	24 Oct. 1945
Ethiopia	13 Nov. 1945	Nicaragua	24 Oct. 1945	Upper Volta	20 Sep. 1960
Fiji	13 Oct. 1970	Niger	20 Sep. 1960	Uruguay	18 Dec. 1945
Finland	14 Dec. 1955	Nigeria	7 Oct. 1960	Vanuatu	15 Sep. 1981
France	24 Oct. 1945	Norway	27 Nov. 1945	Venezuela	15 Nov. 1945
Gabon	20 Sep. 1960	Oman	7 Oct. 1971	Viet Nam	20 Sep. 1977
Gambia	21 Sep. 1965	Pakistan	30 Sep. 1947	Yemen	30 Sep. 1947
German Democratic		Panama	13 Nov. 1945	Yugoslavia	24 Oct. 1945
Republic	18 Sep. 1973	Papua New Guinea	10 Oct. 1975	Zaire	20 Sep. 1960
Germany, Federal		Paraguay	24 Oct. 1945	Zambia	1 Dec. 1964
Republic of	18 Sep. 1973	Peru	31 Oct. 1945	Zimbabwe	25 Aug. 1980

(footnotes on next page)

(footnotes for preceding page)

[1]Egypt and Syria, both of which became Members of the United Nations on 24 October 1945, joined together—following a plebiscite held in those countries on 21 February 1958—to form the United Arab Republic. On 13 October 1961, Syria, having resumed its status as an independent State, also resumed its separate membership in the United Nations; it changed its name to the Syrian Arab Republic on 14 September 1971. The United Arab Republic continued as a Member of the United Nations and reverted to the name of Egypt on 2 September 1971.

[2]By a letter of 20 January 1965, Indonesia informed the Secretary-General that it had decided to withdraw from the United Nations. By a telegram of 19 September 1966, it notified the Secretary-General of its decision to resume participation in the activities of the United Nations. On 28 September 1966, the General Assembly took note of that decision and the President invited the representatives of Indonesia to take their seats in the Assembly.

[3]On 16 September 1963, Sabah (North Borneo), Sarawak and Singapore joined with the Federation of Malaya (which became a United Nations Member on 17 September 1957) to form Malaysia. On 9 August 1965, Singapore became an independent State and on 21 September 1965 it became a Member of the United Nations.

[4]Tanganyika was admitted to the United Nations on 14 December 1961, and Zanzibar, on 16 December 1963. Following ratification, on 26 April 1964, of the Articles of Union between Tanganyika and Zanzibar, the two States became represented as a single Member: the United Republic of Tanganyika and Zanzibar; it changed its name to the United Republic of Tanzania on 1 November 1964.

Appendix II

Charter of the United Nations and Statute of the International Court of Justice

Charter of the United Nations

NOTE: The Charter of the United Nations was signed on 26 June 1945, in San Francisco, at the conclusion of the United Nations Conference on International Organization, and came into force on 24 October 1945. The Statute of the International Court of Justice is an integral part of the Charter.

Amendments to Articles 23, 27 and 61 of the Charter were adopted by the General Assembly on 17 December 1963 and came into force on 31 August 1965. A further amendment to Article 61 was adopted by the General Assembly on 20 December 1971, and came into force on 24 September 1973. An amendment to Article 109, adopted by the General Assembly on 20 December 1965, came into force on 12 June 1968.

The amendment to Article 23 enlarges the membership of the Security Council from 11 to 15. The amended Article 27 provides that decisions of the Security Council on procedural matters shall be made by an affirmative vote of nine members (formerly seven) and on all other matters by an affirmative vote of nine members (formerly seven), in-cluding the concurring votes of the five permanent members of the Security Council.

The amendment to Article 61, which entered into force on 31 August 1965, enlarged the membership of the Economic and Social Council from 18 to 27. The subsequent amendment to that Article, which entered into force on 24 September 1973, further increased the membership of the Council from 27 to 54.

The amendment to Article 109, which relates to the first paragraph of that Article, provides that a General Conference of Member States for the purpose of reviewing the Charter may be held at a date and place to be fixed by a two-thirds vote of the members of the General Assembly and by a vote of any nine members (formerly seven) of the Security Council. Paragraph 3 of Article 109, which deals with the consideration of a possible review conference during the tenth regular session of the General Assembly, has been retained in its original form in its reference to a "vote of any seven members of the Security Council," the paragraph having been acted upon in 1955 by the General Assembly, at its tenth regular session, and by the Security Council.

WE THE PEOPLES
OF THE UNITED NATIONS
DETERMINED
to save succeeding generations from the scourge of war, which twice in our lifetime has brought untold sorrow to mankind, and
to reaffirm faith in fundamental human rights, in the dignity and worth of the human person, in the equal rights of men and women and of nations large and small, and
to establish conditions under which justice and respect for the obligations arising from treaties and other sources of international law can be maintained, and
to promote social progress and better standards of life in larger freedom,

AND FOR THESE ENDS
to practice tolerance and live together in peace with one another as good neighbours, and
to unite our strength to maintain international peace and security, and
to ensure, by the acceptance of principles and the institution of methods, that armed force shall not be used, save in the common interest, and
to employ international machinery for the promotion of the economic and social advancement of all peoples,

HAVE RESOLVED TO
COMBINE OUR EFFORTS TO
ACCOMPLISH THESE AIMS
Accordingly, our respective Governments, through representatives assembled in the city of San Francisco, who have exhibited their full powers found to be in good and due form, have agreed to the present Charter of the United Nations and do hereby establish an international organization to be known as the United Nations.

Chapter I
PURPOSES AND PRINCIPLES

Article 1
The Purposes of the United Nations are:
1. To maintain international peace and security, and to that end: to take effective collective measures for the prevention and removal of threats to the peace, and for the suppression of acts of aggression or other breaches of the peace, and to bring about by peaceful means, and in conformity with the principles of justice and international law, adjustment or settlement of international disputes or situations which might lead to a breach of the peace;
2. To develop friendly relations among nations based on respect for the principle of equal rights and self-determination of peoples, and to take other appropriate measures to strengthen universal peace;
3. To achieve international co-operation in solving international problems of an economic, social, cultural, or humanitarian character, and in promoting and encouraging respect for human rights and for fundamental freedoms for all without distinction as to race, sex, language, or religion; and
4. To be a centre for harmonizing the actions of nations in the attainment of these common ends.

Article 2
The Organization and its Members, in pursuit of the Purposes stated in Article 1, shall act in accordance with the following Principles.
1. The Organization is based on the principle of the sovereign equality of all its Members.
2. All Members, in order to ensure to all of them the rights and benefits resulting from membership, shall fulfil in good faith the obligations assumed by them in accordance with the present Charter.

3. All Members shall settle their international disputes by peaceful means in such a manner that international peace and security, and justice, are not endangered.

4. All Members shall refrain in their international relations from the threat or use of force against the territorial integrity or political independence of any state, or in any other manner inconsistent with the Purposes of the United Nations.

5. All Members shall give the United Nations every assistance in any action it takes in accordance with the present Charter, and shall refrain from giving assistance to any state against which the United Nations is taking preventive or enforcement action.

6. The Organization shall ensure that states which are not Members of the United Nations act in accordance with these Principles so far as may be necessary for the maintenance of international peace and security.

7. Nothing contained in the present Charter shall authorize the United Nations to intervene in matters which are essentially within the domestic jurisdiction of any state or shall require the Members to submit such matters to settlement under the present Charter; but this principle shall not prejudice the application of enforcement measures under Chapter VII.

Chapter II
MEMBERSHIP

Article 3

The original Members of the United Nations shall be the states which, having participated in the United Nations Conference on International Organization at San Francisco, or having previously signed the Declaration by United Nations of 1 January 1942, sign the present Charter and ratify it in accordance with Article 110.

Article 4

1. Membership in the United Nations is open to all other peace-loving states which accept the obligations contained in the present Charter and, in the judgment of the Organization, are able and willing to carry out these obligations.

2. The admission of any such state to membership in the United Nations will be effected by a decision of the General Assembly upon the recommendation of the Security Council.

Article 5

A Member of the United Nations against which preventive or enforcement action has been taken by the Security Council may be suspended from the exercise of the rights and privileges of membership by the General Assembly upon the recommendation of the Security Council. The exercise of these rights and privileges may be restored by the Security Council.

Article 6

A Member of the United Nations which has persistently violated the Principles contained in the present Charter may be expelled from the Organization by the General Assembly upon the recommendation of the Security Council.

Chapter III
ORGANS

Article 7

1. There are established as the principal organs of the United Nations: a General Assembly, a Security Council, an Economic and Social Council, a Trusteeship Council, an International Court of Justice, and a Secretariat.

2. Such subsidiary organs as may be found necessary may be established in accordance with the present Charter.

Article 8

The United Nations shall place no restrictions on the eligibility of men and women to participate in any capacity and under conditions of equality in its principal and subsidiary organs.

Chapter IV
THE GENERAL ASSEMBLY

Composition

Article 9

1. The General Assembly shall consist of all the Members of the United Nations.

2. Each Member shall have not more than five representatives in the General Assembly.

Functions and powers

Article 10

The General Assembly may discuss any questions or any matters within the scope of the present Charter or relating to the powers and functions of any organs provided for in the present Charter, and, except as provided in Article 12, may make recommendations to the Members of the United Nations or to the Security Council or to both on any such questions or matters.

Article 11

1. The General Assembly may consider the general principles of co-operation in the maintenance of international peace and security, including the principles governing disarmament and the regulation of armaments, and may make recommendations with regard to such principles to the Members or to the Security Council or to both.

2. The General Assembly may discuss any questions relating to the maintenance of international peace and security brought before it by any Member of the United Nations, or by the Security Council, or by a state which is not a Member of the United Nations in accordance with Article 35, paragraph 2, and, except as provided in Article 12, may make recommendations with regard to any such questions to the state or states concerned or to the Security Council or to both. Any such question on which action is necessary shall be referred to the Security Council by the General Assembly either before or after discussion.

3. The General Assembly may call the attention of the Security Council to situations which are likely to endanger international peace and security.

4. The powers of the General Assembly set forth in this Article shall not limit the general scope of Article 10.

Article 12

1. While the Security Council is exercising in respect of any dispute or situation the functions assigned to it in the present Charter, the General Assembly shall not make any recommendation with regard to that dispute or situation unless the Security Council so requests.

2. The Secretary-General, with the consent of the Security Council, shall notify the General Assembly at each session of any matters relative to the maintenance of international peace and security which are being dealt with by the Security Council and shall similarly notify the General Assembly, or the Members of the United Nations if the General Assembly is not in session, immediately the Security Council ceases to deal with such matters.

Article 13

1. The General Assembly shall initiate studies and make recommendations for the purpose of:
   a. promoting international co-operation in the political field and encouraging the progressive development of international law and its codification;
   b. promoting international co-operation in the economic, social, cultural, educational, and health fields, and assisting in the realization of human rights and fundamental freedoms for all without distinction as to race, sex, language, or religion.

2. The further responsibilities, functions and powers of the General Assembly with respect to matters mentioned in paragraph 1(b) above are set forth in Chapters IX and X.

Article 14

Subject to the provisions of Article 12, the General Assembly may recommend measures for the peaceful adjustment of any situation, regardless of origin, which it deems likely to impair the general welfare or friendly relations among nations, including situations resulting from a violation of the provisions of the present Charter setting forth the Purposes and Principles of the United Nations.

Article 15

1. The General Assembly shall receive and consider annual and special reports from the Security Council; these reports shall include an account of the measures that the Security Council has decided upon or taken to maintain international peace and security.

2. The General Assembly shall receive and consider reports from the other organs of the United Nations.

Article 16

The General Assembly shall perform such functions with respect to the international trusteeship system as are assigned to it under Chapters XII and XIII, including the approval of the trusteeship agreements for areas not designated as strategic.

Article 17

1. The General Assembly shall consider and approve the budget of the Organization.

2. The expenses of the Organization shall be borne by the Members as apportioned by the General Assembly.

3. The General Assembly shall consider and approve any financial and budgetary arrangements with specialized agencies referred to in Article 57 and shall examine the administrative budgets of such specialized agencies with a view to making recommendations to the agencies concerned.

Voting

Article 18

1. Each member of the General Assembly shall have one vote.

2. Decisions of the General Assembly on important questions shall be made by a two-thirds majority of the members present and voting. These questions shall include: recommendations with respect to the maintenance of international peace and security, the election of the non-permanent members of the Security Council, the election of the members of the Economic and Social Council, the election of members of the Trusteeship Council in accordance with paragraph 1(c) of Article 86, the admission of new Members to the United Nations, the suspension of the rights and privileges of membership, the expulsion of Members, questions relating to the operation of the trusteeship system, and budgetary questions.

3. Decisions on other questions, including the determination of additional categories of questions to be decided by a two thirds majority, shall be made by a majority of the members present and voting.

Article 19

A Member of the United Nations which is in arrears in the payment of its financial contributions to the Organization shall have no vote in the General Assembly if the amount of its arrears equals or exceeds the amount of the contributions due from it for the preceding two full years. The General Assembly may, nevertheless, permit such a Member to vote if it is satisfied that the failure to pay is due to conditions beyond the control of the Member.

Procedure

Article 20

The General Assembly shall meet in regular annual sessions and in such special sessions as occasion may require. Special sessions shall be convoked by the Secretary-General at the request of the Security Council or of a majority of the Members of the United Nations.

Article 21

The General Assembly shall adopt its own rules of procedure. It shall elect its President for each session.

Article 22

The General Assembly may establish such subsidiary organs as it deems necessary for the performance of its functions.

Chapter V
THE SECURITY COUNCIL

Composition

Article 23[1]

1. The Security Council shall consist of fifteen Members of the United Nations. The Republic of China, France, the Union of Soviet Socialist Republics, the United Kingdom of Great Britain and Northern Ireland, and the United States of America shall be permanent members of the Security Council. The General Assembly shall elect ten other Members of the United Nations to be non-permanent members of the Security Council, due regard being specially paid, in the first instance to the contribution of Members of the United Nations to the maintenance of international peace and security and to the other purposes of the Organization, and also to equitable geographical distribution.

2. The non-permanent members of the Security Council shall be elected for a term of two years. In the first election of the non-permanent members after the increase of the membership of the Security Council from eleven to fifteen, two of the four additional members shall be chosen for a term of one year. A retiring member shall not be eligible for immediate re-election.

3. Each member of the Security Council shall have one representative.

Functions and powers

Article 24

1. In order to ensure prompt and effective action by the United Nations, its Members confer on the Security Council primary responsibility for the maintenance of international peace and security, and agree that in carrying out its duties under this responsibility the Security Council acts on their behalf.

2. In discharging these duties the Security Council shall act in accordance with the Purposes and Principles of the United Nations. The specific powers granted to the Security Council for the discharge of these duties are laid down in Chapters VI, VII, VIII, and XII.

3. The Security Council shall submit annual and, when necessary, special reports to the General Assembly for its consideration.

Article 25

The Members of the United Nations agree to accept and carry out the decisions of the Security Council in accordance with the present Charter.

Article 26

In order to promote the establishment and maintenance of international peace and security with the least diversion for armaments of the world's human and economic resources, the Security Council shall be responsible for formulating, with the assistance of the Military Staff Committee referred to in Article 47, plans to be submitted to the Members of the United Nations for the establishment of a system for the regulation of armaments.

---

[1] Amended text of Article 23 which came into force on 31 August 1965. (The text of Article 23 before it was amended read as follows:

1. The Security Council shall consist of eleven Members of the United Nations. The Republic of China, France, the Union of Soviet Socialist Republics, the United Kingdom of Great Britain and Northern Ireland, and the United States of America shall be permanent members of the Security Council. The General Assembly shall elect six other Members of the United Nations to be non-permanent members of the Security Council, due regard being specially paid, in the first instance to the contribution of Members of the United Nations to the maintenance of international peace and security and to the other purposes of the Organization, and also to equitable geographical distribution.

2. The non-permanent members of the Security Council shall be elected for a term of two years. In the first election of non-permanent members, however, three shall be chosen for a term of one year. A retiring member shall not be eligible for immediate re-election.

3. Each member of the Security Council shall have one representative.)

Voting

Article 27[2]

1. Each member of the Security Council shall have one vote.
2. Decisions of the Security Council on procedural matters shall be made by an affirmative vote of nine members.
3. Decisions of the Security Council on all other matters shall be made by an affirmative vote of nine members including the concurring votes of the permanent members; provided that, in decisions under Chapter VI, and under paragraph 3 of Article 52, a party to a dispute shall abstain from voting.

Procedure

Article 28

1. The Security Council shall be so organized as to be able to function continuously. Each member of the Security Council shall for this purpose be represented at all times at the seat of the Organization.
2. The Security Council shall hold periodic meetings at which each of its members may, if it so desires, be represented by a member of the government or by some other specially designated representative.
3. The Security Council may hold meetings at such places other than the seat of the Organization as in its judgment will best facilitate its work.

Article 29

The Security Council may establish such subsidiary organs as it deems necessary for the performance of its functions.

Article 30

The Security Council shall adopt its own rules of procedure, including the method of selecting its President.

Article 31

Any Member of the United Nations which is not a member of the Security Council may participate, without vote, in the discussion of any question brought before the Security Council whenever the latter considers that the interests of that Member are specially affected.

Article 32

Any Member of the United Nations which is not a member of the Security Council or any state which is not a Member of the United Nations, if it is a party to a dispute under consideration by the Security Council, shall be invited to participate, without vote, in the discussion relating to the dispute. The Security Council shall lay down such conditions as it deems just for the participation of a state which is not a Member of the United Nations.

Chapter VI
PACIFIC SETTLEMENT OF DISPUTES

Article 33

1. The parties to any dispute, the continuance of which is likely to endanger the maintenance of international peace and security, shall, first of all, seek a solution by negotiation, enquiry, mediation, conciliation, arbitration, judicial settlement, resort to regional agencies or arrangements, or other peaceful means of their own choice.
2. The Security Council shall, when it deems necessary, call upon the parties to settle their dispute by such means.

Article 34

The Security Council may investigate any dispute or any situation which might lead to international friction or give rise to a dispute, in order to determine whether the continuance of the dispute or situation is likely to endanger the maintenance of international peace and security.

Article 35

1. Any Member of the United Nations may bring any dispute, or any situation of the nature referred to in Article 34, to the attention of the Security Council or of the General Assembly.
2. A state which is not a Member of the United Nations may bring to the attention of the Security Council or of the General Assembly any dispute to which it is a party if it accepts in advance, for the purposes of the dispute, the obligations of pacific settlement provided in the present Charter.
3. The proceedings of the General Assembly in respect of matters brought to its attention under this Article will be subject to the provisions of Articles 11 and 12.

Article 36

1. The Security Council may, at any stage of a dispute of the nature referred to in Article 33 or of a situation of like nature, recommend appropriate procedures or methods of adjustment.
2. The Security Council should take into consideration any procedures for the settlement of the dispute which have already been adopted by the parties.
3. In making recommendations under this Article the Security Council should also take into consideration that legal disputes should as a general rule be referred by the parties to the International Court of Justice in accordance with the provisions of the Statute of the Court.

Article 37

1. Should the parties to a dispute of the nature referred to in Article 33 fail to settle it by the means indicated in that Article, they shall refer it to the Security Council.
2. If the Security Council deems that the continuance of the dispute is in fact likely to endanger the maintenance of international peace and security, it shall decide whether to take action under Article 36 or to recommend such terms of settlement as it may consider appropriate.

Article 38

Without prejudice to the provisions of Articles 33 to 37, the Security Council may, if all the parties to any dispute so request, make recommendations to the parties with a view to a pacific settlement of the dispute.

Chapter VII
ACTION WITH RESPECT TO THREATS TO THE PEACE, BREACHES OF THE PEACE, AND ACTS OF AGGRESSION

Article 39

The Security Council shall determine the existence of any threat to the peace, breach of the peace, or act of aggression and shall make recommendations, or decide what measures shall be taken in accordance with Articles 41 and 42, to maintain or restore international peace and security.

Article 40

In order to prevent an aggravation of the situation, the Security Council may, before making the recommendations or deciding upon the measures provided for in Article 39, call upon the parties concerned to comply with such provisional measures as it deems necessary or desirable. Such provisional measures shall be without prejudice to the rights, claims, or position of the parties concerned. The Security Council shall duly take account of failure to comply with such provisional measures.

Article 41

The Security Council may decide what measures not involving the use of armed force are to be employed to give effect to its decisions, and it may call upon the Members of the United Nations to apply such measures. These may include complete or partial interruption of economic relations and of rail, sea, air, postal, telegraphic, radio, and other means of communication, and the severance of diplomatic relations.

---

[2]Amended text of Article 27 which came into force on 31 August 1965. (The text of Article 27 before it was amended read as follows:
1. Each member of the Security Council shall have one vote.
2. Decisions of the Security Council on procedural matters shall be made by an affirmative vote of seven members.
3. Decisions of the Security Council on all other matters shall be made by an affirmative vote of seven members including the concurring votes of the permanent members; provided that, in decisions under Chapter VI, and under paragraph 3 of Article 52, a party to a dispute shall abstain from voting.)

Article 42

Should the Security Council consider that measures provided for in Article 41 would be inadequate or have proved to be inadequate, it may take such action by air, sea, or land forces as may be necessary to maintain or restore international peace and security. Such action may include demonstrations, blockade, and other operations by air, sea, or land forces of Members of the United Nations.

Article 43

1. All Members of the United Nations, in order to contribute to the maintenance of international peace and security, undertake to make available to the Security Council, on its call and in accordance with a special agreement or agreements, armed forces, assistance, and facilities, including rights of passage, necessary for the purpose of maintaining international peace and security.

2. Such agreement or agreements shall govern the numbers and types of forces, their degree of readiness and general location, and the nature of the facilities and assistance to be provided.

3. The agreement or agreements shall be negotiated as soon as possible on the initiative of the Security Council. They shall be concluded between the Security Council and Members or between the Security Council and groups of Members and shall be subject to ratification by the signatory states in accordance with their respective constitutional processes.

Article 44

When the Security Council has decided to use force it shall, before calling upon a Member not represented on it to provide armed forces in fulfilment of the obligations assumed under Article 43, invite that Member, if the Member so desires, to participate in the decisions of the Security Council concerning the employment of contingents of that Member's armed forces.

Article 45

In order to enable the United Nations to take urgent military measures, Members shall hold immediately available national air-force contingents for combined international enforcement action. The strength and degree of readiness of these contingents and plans for their combined action shall be determined, within the limits laid down in the special agreement or agreements referred to in Article 43, by the Security Council with the assistance of the Military Staff Committee.

Article 46

Plans for the application of armed force shall be made by the Security Council with the assistance of the Military Staff Committee.

Article 47

1. There shall be established a Military Staff Committee to advise and assist the Security Council on all questions relating to the Security Council's military requirements for the maintenance of international peace and security, the employment and command of forces placed at its disposal, the regulation of armaments, and possible disarmament.

2. The Military Staff Committee shall consist of the Chiefs of Staff of the permanent members of the Security Council or their representatives. Any Member of the United Nations not permanently represented on the Committee shall be invited by the Committee to be associated with it when the efficient discharge of the Committee's responsibilities requires the participation of that Member in its work.

3. The Military Staff Committee shall be responsible under the Security Council for the strategic direction of any armed forces placed at the disposal of the Security Council. Questions relating to the command of such forces shall be worked out subsequently.

4. The Military Staff Committee, with the authorization of the Security Council and after consultation with appropriate regional agencies, may establish regional sub-committees.

Article 48

1. The action required to carry out the decisions of the Security Council for the maintenance of international peace and security shall be taken by all the Members of the United Nations or by some of them, as the Security Council may determine.

2. Such decisions shall be carried out by the Members of the United Nations directly and through their action in the appropriate international agencies of which they are members.

Article 49

The Members of the United Nations shall join in affording mutual assistance in carrying out the measures decided upon by the Security Council.

Article 50

If preventive or enforcement measures against any state are taken by the Security Council, any other state, whether a Member of the United Nations or not, which finds itself confronted with special economic problems arising from the carrying out of those measures shall have the right to consult the Security Council with regard to a solution of those problems.

Article 51

Nothing in the present Charter shall impair the inherent right of individual or collective self-defence if an armed attack occurs against a Member of the United Nations, until the Security Council has taken measures necessary to maintain international peace and security. Measures taken by Members in the exercise of this right of self-defence shall be immediately reported to the Security Council and shall not in any way affect the authority and responsibility of the Security Council under the present Charter to take at any time such action as it deems necessary in order to maintain or restore international peace and security.

Chapter VIII
REGIONAL ARRANGEMENTS

Article 52

1. Nothing in the present Charter precludes the existence of regional arrangements or agencies for dealing with such matters relating to the maintenance of international peace and security as are appropriate for regional action, provided that such arrangements or agencies and their activities are consistent with the Purposes and Principles of the United Nations.

2. The Members of the United Nations entering into such arrangements or constituting such agencies shall make every effort to achieve pacific settlement of local disputes through such regional arrangements or by such regional agencies before referring them to the Security Council.

3. The Security Council shall encourage the development of pacific settlement of local disputes through such regional arrangements or by such regional agencies either on the initiative of the states concerned or by reference from the Security Council.

4. This Article in no way impairs the application of Articles 34 and 35.

Article 53

1. The Security Council shall, where appropriate, utilize such regional arrangements or agencies for enforcement action under its authority. But no enforcement action shall be taken under regional arrangements or by regional agencies without the authorization of the Security Council, with the exception of measures against any enemy state, as defined in paragraph 2 of this Article, provided for pursuant to Article 107 or in regional arrangements directed against renewal of aggressive policy on the part of any such state, until such time as the Organization may, on request of the Governments concerned, be charged with the responsibility for preventing further aggression by such a state.

2. The term enemy state as used in paragraph 1 of this Article applies to any state which during the Second World War has been an enemy of any signatory of the present Charter.

Article 54

The Security Council shall at all times be kept fully informed of activities undertaken or in contemplation under regional arrangements or by regional agencies for the maintenance of international peace and security.

Chapter IX
INTERNATIONAL ECONOMIC
AND SOCIAL CO-OPERATION

Article 55

With a view to the creation of conditions of stability and well-being which are necessary for peaceful and friendly relations among nations based on respect for the principle of equal rights and self-determination of peoples, the United Nations shall promote:

a. higher standards of living, full employment, and conditions of economic and social progress and de-velopment;
b. solutions of international economic, social, health, and related problems; and international cultural and educational co-operation; and
c. universal respect for, and observance of, human rights and fundamental freedoms for all without distinction as to race, sex, language, or religion.

Article 56

All Members pledge themselves to take joint and separate action in co-operation with the Organization for the achievement of the purposes set forth in Article 55.

Article 57

1. The various specialized agencies, established by intergovernmental agreement and having wide international responsibilities, as defined in their basic instruments, in economic, social, cultural, educational, health, and related fields, shall be brought into relationship with the United Nations in accordance with the provisions of Article 63.
2. Such agencies thus brought into relationship with the United Nations are hereinafter referred to as specialized agencies.

Article 58

The Organization shall make recommendations for the co-ordination of the policies and activities of the specialized agencies.

Article 59

The Organization shall, where appropriate, initiate negotiations among the states concerned for the creation of any new specialized agencies required for the accomplishment of the purposes set forth in Article 55.

Article 60

Responsibility for the discharge of the functions of the Organization set forth in this Chapter shall be vested in the General Assembly and, under the authority of the General Assembly, in the Economic and Social Council, which shall have for this purpose the powers set forth in Chapter X.

Chapter X
THE ECONOMIC AND SOCIAL COUNCIL

Composition

Article 61[3]

1. The Economic and Social Council shall consist of fifty-four Members of the United Nations elected by the General Assembly.
2. Subject to the provisions of paragraph 3, eighteen members of the Economic and Social Council shall be elected each year for a term of three years. A retiring member shall be eligible for immediate re-election.
3. At the first election after the increase in the membership of the Economic and Social Council from twenty-seven to fifty-four members, in addition to the members elected in place of the nine members whose term of office expires at the end of that year, twenty-seven additional members shall be elected. Of these twenty-seven additional members, the term of office of nine members so elected shall expire at the end of one year, and of nine other members at the end of two years, in accordance with arrangements made by the General Assembly.
4. Each member of the Economic and Social Council shall have one representative.

Functions and powers

Article 62

1. The Economic and Social Council may make or initiate studies and reports with respect to international economic, social, cultural, educational, health, and related matters and may make recommendations with respect to any such matters to the General Assembly, to the Members of the United Nations, and to the specialized agencies concerned.
2. It may make recommendations for the purpose of promoting respect for, and observance of, human rights and fundamental freedoms for all.

3. It may prepare draft conventions for submission to the General Assembly, with respect to matters falling within its competence.
4. It may call, in accordance with the rules prescribed by the United Nations, international conferences on matters falling within its competence.

Article 63

1. The Economic and Social Council may enter into agreements with any of the agencies referred to in Article 57, defining the terms on which the agency concerned shall be brought into relationship with the United Nations. Such agreements shall be subject to approval by the General Assembly.
2. It may co-ordinate the activities of the specialized agencies through consultation with and recommendations to such agencies and through recommendations to the General Assembly and to the Members of the United Nations.

Article 64

1. The Economic and Social Council may take appropriate steps to obtain regular reports from the specialized agencies. It may make arrangements with the Members of the United Nations and with the specialized agencies to obtain reports on the steps taken to give effect to its own recommendations and to recommendations on matters falling within its competence made by the General Assembly.
2. It may communicate its observations on these reports to the General Assembly.

Article 65

The Economic and Social Council may furnish information to the Security Council and shall assist the Security Council upon its request.

Article 66

1. The Economic and Social Council shall perform such functions as fall within its competence in connexion with the carrying out of the recommendations of the General Assembly.
2. It may, with the approval of the General Assembly, perform services at the request of Members of the United Nations and at the request of specialized agencies.
3. It shall perform such other functions as are specified elsewhere in the present Charter or as may be assigned to it by the General Assembly.

Voting

Article 67

1. Each member of the Economic and Social Council shall have one vote.
2. Decisions of the Economic and Social Council shall be made by a majority of the members present and voting.

Procedure

Article 68

The Economic and Social Council shall set up commissions in economic and social fields and for the promotion of human rights, and such other commissions as may be required for the performance of its functions.

---

[3]Amended text of Article 61, which came into force on 24 September 1973. (The text of Article 61 as previously amended on 31 August 1965 read as follows:

1. The Economic and Social Council shall consist of twenty-seven Members of the United Nations elected by the General Assembly.
2. Subject to the provisions of paragraph 3, nine members of the Economic and Social Council shall be elected each year for a term of three years. A retiring member shall be eligible for immediate re-election.
3. At the first election after the increase in the membership of the Economic and Social Council from eighteen to twenty-seven members, in addition to the members elected in place of the six members whose term of office expires at the end of that year, nine additional members shall be elected. Of these nine additional members, the term of office of three members so elected shall expire at the end of one year, and of three other members at the end of two years, in accordance with arrangements made by the General Assembly.
4. Each member of the Economic and Social Council shall have one representative.)

Article 69

The Economic and Social Council shall invite any Member of the United Nations to participate, without vote, in its deliberations on any matter of particular concern to that Member.

Article 70

The Economic and Social Council may make arrangements for representatives of the specialized agencies to participate, without vote, in its deliberations and in those of the commissions established by it, and for its representatives to participate in the deliberations of the specialized agencies.

Article 71

The Economic and Social Council may make suitable arrangements for consultation with non-governmental organizations which are concerned with matters within its competence. Such arrangements may be made with international organizations and, where appropriate, with national organizations after consultation with the Member of the United Nations concerned.

Article 72

1.   The Economic and Social Council shall adopt its own rules of procedure, including the method of selecting its President.

2.   The Economic and Social Council shall meet as required in accordance with its rules, which shall include provision for the convening of meetings on the request of a majority of its members.

Chapter XI
DECLARATION REGARDING
NON-SELF-GOVERNING TERRITORIES

Article 73

Members of the United Nations which have or assume responsibilities for the administration of territories whose peoples have not yet attained a full measure of self-government recognize the principle that the interests of the inhabitants of these territories are paramount, and accept as a sacred trust the obligation to promote to the utmost, within the system of international peace and security established by the present Charter, the well-being of the inhabitants of these territories, and, to this end:

a.   to ensure, with due respect for the culture of the peoples concerned, their political, economic, social, and educational advancement, their just treatment, and their protection against abuses;

b.   to develop self-government, to take due account of the political aspirations of the peoples, and to assist them in the progressive development of their free political institutions, according to the particular circumstances of each territory and its peoples and their varying stages of advancement;

c.   to further international peace and security;

d.   to promote constructive measures of development, to encourage research, and to co-operate with one another and, when and where appropriate, with specialized international bodies with a view to the practical achievement of the social, economic, and scientific purposes set forth in this Article; and

e.   to transmit regularly to the Secretary-General for information purposes, subject to such limitation as security and constitutional considerations may require, statistical and other information of a technical nature relating to economic, social, and educational conditions in the territories for which they are respectively responsible other than those territories to which Chapters XII and XIII apply.

Article 74

Members of the United Nations also agree that their policy in respect of the territories to which this Chapter applies, no less than in respect of their metropolitan areas, must be based on the general principle of good-neighbourliness, due account being taken of the interests and well-being of the rest of the world, in social, economic, and commercial matters.

Chapter XII
INTERNATIONAL TRUSTEESHIP SYSTEM

Article 75

The United Nations shall establish under its authority an international trusteeship system for the administration and supervision of such territories as may be placed thereunder by subsequent individual agreements. These territories are hereinafter referred to as trust territories.

Article 76

The basic objectives of the trusteeship system, in accordance with the Purposes of the United Nations laid down in Article 1 of the present Charter, shall be:

a.   to further international peace and security;

b.   to promote the political, economic, social, and educational advancement of the inhabitants of the trust territories, and their progressive development towards self-government or independence as may be appropriate to the particular circumstances of each territory and its peoples and the freely expressed wishes of the peoples concerned, and as may be provided by the terms of each trusteeship agreement;

c.   to encourage respect for human rights and for fundamental freedoms for all without distinction as to race, sex, language, or religion, and to encourage recognition of the interdependence of the peoples of the world; and

d.   to ensure equal treatment in social, economic, and commercial matters for all Members of the United Nations and their nationals, and also equal treatment for the latter in the administration of justice, without prejudice to the attainment of the foregoing objectives and subject to the provisions of Article 80.

Article 77

1.   The trusteeship system shall apply to such territories in the following categories as may be placed thereunder by means of trusteeship agreements:

a.   territories now held under mandate;

b.   territories which may be detached from enemy states as a result of the Second World War; and

c.   territories voluntarily placed under the system by states responsible for their administration.

2.   It will be a matter for subsequent agreement as to which territories in the foregoing categories will be brought under the trusteeship system and upon what terms.

Article 78

The trusteeship system shall not apply to territories which have become Members of the United Nations, relationship among which shall be based on respect for the principle of sovereign equality.

Article 79

The terms of trusteeship for each territory to be placed under the trusteeship system, including any alteration or amendment, shall be agreed upon by the states directly concerned, including the mandatory power in the case of territories held under mandate by a Member of the United Nations, and shall be approved as provided for in Articles 83 and 85.

Article 80

1.   Except as may be agreed upon in individual trusteeship agreements, made under Articles 77, 79, and 81, placing each territory under the trusteeship system, and until such agreements have been concluded, nothing in this Chapter shall be construed in or of itself to alter in any manner the rights whatsoever of any states or any peoples or the terms of existing international instruments to which Members of the United Nations may respectively be parties.

2.   Paragraph 1 of this Article shall not be interpreted as giving grounds for delay or postponement of the negotiation and conclusion of agreements for placing mandated and other territories under the trusteeship system as provided for in Article 77.

Article 81

The trusteeship agreement shall in each case include the terms under which the trust territory will be administered and designate the authority which will exercise the administration of the trust territory. Such authority, hereinafter called the administering authority, may be one or more states or the Organization itself.

Article 82

There may be designated, in any trusteeship agreement, a strategic area or areas which may include part or all of the trust territory to which the agreement applies, without prejudice to any special agreement or agreements made under Article 43.

Article 83

1. All functions of the United Nations relating to strategic areas, including the approval of the terms of the trusteeship agreements and of their alteration or amendments, shall be exercised by the Security Council.

2. The basic objectives set forth in Article 76 shall be applicable to the people of each strategic area.

3. The Security Council shall, subject to the provisions of the trusteeship agreements and without prejudice to security considerations, avail itself of the assistance of the Trusteeship Council to perform those functions of the United Nations under the trusteeship system relating to political, economic, social, and educational matters in the strategic areas.

Article 84

It shall be the duty of the administering authority to ensure that the trust territory shall play its part in the maintenance of international peace and security. To this end the administering authority may make use of volunteer forces, facilities, and assistance from the trust territory in carrying out the obligations towards the Security Council undertaken in this regard by the administering authority, as well as for local defence and the maintenance of law and order within the trust territory.

Article 85

1. The functions of the United Nations with regard to trusteeship agreements for all areas not designated as strategic, including the approval of the terms of the trusteeship agreements and of their alteration or amendment, shall be exercised by the General Assembly.

2. The Trusteeship Council, operating under the authority of the General Assembly, shall assist the General Assembly in carrying out these functions.

Chapter XIII
THE TRUSTEESHIP COUNCIL

Composition

Article 86

1. The Trusteeship Council shall consist of the following Members of the United Nations:
   a. those Members administering trust territories;
   b. such of those Members mentioned by name in Article 23 as are not administering trust territories; and
   c. as many other Members elected for three-year terms by the General Assembly as may be necessary to ensure that the total number of members of the Trusteeship Council is equally divided between those Members of the United Nations which administer trust territories and those which do not.

2. Each member of the Trusteeship Council shall designate one specially qualified person to represent it therein.

Functions and powers

Article 87

The General Assembly and, under its authority, the Trusteeship Council, in carrying out their functions, may:
   a. consider reports submitted by the administering authority;
   b. accept petitions and examine them in consultation with the administering authority;
   c. provide for periodic visits to the respective trust territories at times agreed upon with the administering authority; and
   d. take these and other actions in conformity with the terms of the trusteeship agreements.

Article 88

The Trusteeship Council shall formulate a questionnaire on the political, economic, social, and educational advancement of the inhabitants of each trust territory, and the administering authority for each trust territory within the competence of the General Assembly shall make an annual report to the General Assembly upon the basis of such questionnaire.

Voting

Article 89

1. Each member of the Trusteeship Council shall have one vote.

2. Decisions of the Trusteeship Council shall be made by a majority of the members present and voting.

Procedure

Article 90

1. The Trusteeship Council shall adopt its own rules of procedure, including the method of selecting its President.

2. The Trusteeship Council shall meet as required in accordance with its rules, which shall include provision for the convening of meetings on the request of a majority of its members.

Article 91

The Trusteeship Council shall, when appropriate, avail itself of the assistance of the Economic and Social Council and of the specialized agencies in regard to matters with which they are respectively concerned.

Chapter XIV
THE INTERNATIONAL COURT OF JUSTICE

Article 92

The International Court of Justice shall be the principal judicial organ of the United Nations. It shall function in accordance with the annexed Statute, which is based upon the Statute of the Permanent Court of International Justice and forms an integral part of the present Charter.

Article 93

1. All Members of the United Nations are *ipso facto* parties to the Statute of the International Court of Justice.

2. A state which is not a Member of the United Nations may become a party to the Statute of the International Court of Justice on conditions to be determined in each case by the General Assembly upon the recommendation of the Security Council.

Article 94

1. Each Member of the United Nations undertakes to comply with the decision of the International Court of Justice in any case to which it is a party.

2. If any party to a case fails to perform the obligations incumbent upon it under a judgment rendered by the Court, the other party may have recourse to the Security Council, which may, if it deems necessary, make recommendations or decide upon measures to be taken to give effect to the judgment.

Article 95

Nothing in the present Charter shall prevent Members of the United Nations from entrusting the solution of their differences to other tribunals by virtue of agreements already in existence or which may be concluded in the future.

Article 96

1. The General Assembly or the Security Council may request the International Court of Justice to give an advisory opinion on any legal question.

2. Other organs of the United Nations and specialized agencies, which may at any time be so authorized by the General Assembly, may also request advisory opinions of the Court on legal questions arising within the scope of their activities.

Chapter XV
THE SECRETARIAT

Article 97

The Secretariat shall comprise a Secretary-General and such staff as the Organization may require. The Secretary-General shall be appointed by the General Assembly upon the recommendation of the Security Council. He shall be the chief administrative officer of the Organization.

Article 98

The Secretary-General shall act in that capacity in all meetings of the General Assembly, of the Security Council, of the Economic and Social Council, and of the Trusteeship Council, and shall perform such other functions as are entrusted to him by these organs. The Secretary-General shall make an annual report to the General Assembly on the work of the Organization.

Article 99

The Secretary-General may bring to the attention of the Security Council any matter which in his opinion may threaten the maintenance of international peace and security.

Article 100

1. In the performance of their duties the Secretary-General and the staff shall not seek or receive instructions from any government or from any other authority external to the Organization. They shall refrain from any action which might reflect on their position as international officials responsible only to the Organization.

2. Each Member of the United Nations undertakes to respect the exclusively international character of the responsibilities of the Secretary-General and the staff and not to seek to influence them in the discharge of their responsibilities.

Article 101

1. The staff shall be appointed by the Secretary-General under regulations established by the General Assembly.

2. Appropriate staffs shall be permanently assigned to the Economic and Social Council, the Trusteeship Council, and, as required, to other organs of the United Nations. These staffs shall form a part of the Secretariat.

3. The paramount consideration in the employment of the staff and in the determination of the conditions of service shall be the necessity of securing the highest standards of efficiency, competence, and integrity. Due regard shall be paid to the importance of recruiting the staff on as wide a geographical basis as possible.

Chapter XVI
MISCELLANEOUS PROVISIONS

Article 102

1. Every treaty and every international agreement entered into by any Member of the United Nations after the present Charter comes into force shall as soon as possible be registered with the Secretariat and published by it.

2. No party to any such treaty or international agreement which has not been registered in accordance with the provisions of paragraph 1 of this Article may invoke that treaty or agreement before any organ of the United Nations.

Article 103

In the event of a conflict between the obligations of the Members of the United Nations under the present Charter and their obligations under any other international agreement, their obligations under the present Charter shall prevail.

Article 104

The Organization shall enjoy in the territory of each of its Members such legal capacity as may be necessary for the exercise of its functions and the fulfilment of its purposes.

Article 105

1. The Organization shall enjoy in the territory of each of its Members such privileges and immunities as are necessary for the fulfilment of its purposes.

2. Representatives of the Members of the United Nations and officials of the Organization shall similarly enjoy such privileges and immunities as are necessary for the independent exercise of their functions in connexion with the Organization.

3. The General Assembly may make recommendations with a view to determining the details of the application of paragraphs 1 and 2 of this Article or may propose conventions to the Members of the United Nations for this purpose.

Chapter XVII
TRANSITIONAL SECURITY ARRANGEMENTS

Article 106

Pending the coming into force of such special agreements referred to in Article 43 as in the opinion of the Security Council enable it to begin the exercise of its responsibilities under Article 42, the parties to the Four-Nation Declaration, signed at Moscow, 30 October 1943, and France, shall, in accordance with the provisions of paragraph 5 of that Declaration, consult with one another and as occasion requires with other Members of the United Nations with a view to such joint action on behalf of the Organization as may be necessary for the purpose of maintaining international peace and security.

Article 107

Nothing in the present Charter shall invalidate or preclude action, in relation to any state which during the Second World War has been an enemy of any signatory to the present Charter, taken or authorized as a result of that war by the Governments having responsibility for such action.

Chapter XVIII
AMENDMENTS

Article 108

Amendments to the present Charter shall come into force for all Members of the United Nations when they have been adopted by a vote of two thirds of the members of the General Assembly and ratified in accordance with their respective constitutional processes by two thirds of the Members of the United Nations, including all the permanent members of the Security Council.

Article 109[4]

1. A General Conference of the Members of the United Nations for the purpose of reviewing the present Charter may be held at a date and place to be fixed by a two-thirds vote of the members of the General Assembly and by a vote of any nine members of the Security Council. Each Member of the United Nations shall have one vote in the conference.

2. Any alteration of the present Charter recommended by a two-thirds vote of the conference shall take effect when ratified in accordance with their respective constitutional processes by two thirds of the Members of the United Nations including all the permanent members of the Security Council.

3. If such a conference has not been held before the tenth annual session of the General Assembly following the coming into force of the present Charter, the proposal to call such a conference shall be

---

[4]Amended text of Article 109 which came into force on 12 June 1968.
(The text of Article 109 before it was amended read as follows:

1. A General Conference of the Members of the United Nations for the purpose of reviewing the present Charter may be held at a date and place to be fixed by a two-thirds vote of the members of the General Assembly and by a vote of any seven members of the Security Council. Each Member of the United Nations shall have one vote in the conference.

2. Any alteration of the present Charter recommended by a two-thirds vote of the conference shall take effect when ratified in accordance with their respective constitutional processes by two thirds of the Members of the United Nations including all the permanent members of the Security Council.

3. If such a conference has not been held before the tenth annual session of the General Assembly following the coming into force of the present Charter, the proposal to call such a conference shall be placed on the agenda of that session of the General Assembly, and the conference shall be held if so decided by a majority vote of the members of the General Assembly and by a vote of any seven members of the Security Council.)

placed on the agenda of that session of the General Assembly, and the conference shall be held if so decided by a majority vote of the members of the General Assembly and by a vote of any seven members of the Security Council.

Chapter XIX
RATIFICATION AND SIGNATURE

Article 110

1. The present Charter shall be ratified by the signatory states in accordance with their respective constitutional processes.

2. The ratifications shall be deposited with the Government of the United States of America, which shall notify all the signatory states of each deposit as well as the Secretary-General of the Organization when he has been appointed.

3. The present Charter shall come into force upon the deposit of ratifications by the Republic of China, France, the Union of Soviet Socialist Republics, the United Kingdom of Great Britain and Northern Ireland, and the United States of America, and by a majority of the other signatory states. A protocol of the ratifications deposited shall thereupon be drawn up by the Government of the United States of America which shall communicate copies thereof to all the signatory states.

4. The states signatory to the present Charter which ratify it after it has come into force will become original Members of the United Nations on the date of the deposit of their respective ratifications.

Article 111

The present Charter, of which the Chinese, French, Russian, English, and Spanish texts are equally authentic, shall remain deposited in the archives of the Government of the United States of America. Duly certified copies thereof shall be transmitted by that Government to the Governments of the other signatory states.

IN FAITH WHEREOF the representatives of the Governments of the United Nations have signed the present Charter.

DONE at the city of San Francisco the twenty-sixth day of June, one thousand nine hundred and forty-five.

Statute of the International Court of Justice

Article 1

THE INTERNATIONAL COURT OF JUSTICE established by the Charter of the United Nations as the principal judicial organ of the United Nations shall be constituted and shall function in accordance with the provisions of the present Statute.

Chapter I
ORGANIZATION OF THE COURT

Article 2

The Court shall be composed of a body of independent judges, elected regardless of their nationality from among persons of high moral character, who possess the qualifications required in their respective countries for appointment to the highest judicial offices, or are jurisconsults of recognized competence in international law.

Article 3

1. The Court shall consist of fifteen members, no two of whom may be nationals of the same state.

2. A person who for the purposes of membership in the Court could be regarded as a national of more than one state shall be deemed to be a national of the one in which he ordinarily exercises civil and political rights.

Article 4

1. The members of the Court shall be elected by the General Assembly and by the Security Council from a list of persons nominated by the national groups in the Permanent Court of Arbitration, in accordance with the following provisions.

2. In the case of Members of the United Nations not represented in the Permanent Court of Arbitration, candidates shall be nominated by national groups appointed for this purpose by their governments under the same conditions as those prescribed for members of the Permanent Court of Arbitration by Article 44 of the Convention of The Hague of 1907 for the pacific settlement of international disputes.

3. The conditions under which a state which is a party to the present Statute but is not a Member of the United Nations may participate in electing the members of the Court shall, in the absence of a special agreement, be laid down by the General Assembly upon recommendation of the Security Council.

Article 5

1. At least three months before the date of the election, the Secretary-General of the United Nations shall address a written request to the members of the Permanent Court of Arbitration belonging to the states which are parties to the present Statute, and to the members of the national groups appointed under Article 4, paragraph 2, inviting them to undertake, within a given time, by national groups, the nomination of persons in a position to accept the duties of a member of the Court.

2. No group may nominate more than four persons, not more than two of whom shall be of their own nationality. In no case may the number of candidates nominated by a group be more than double the number of seats to be filled.

Article 6

Before making these nominations, each national group is recommended to consult its highest court of justice, its legal faculties and schools of law, and its national academies and national sections of international academies devoted to the study of law.

Article 7

1. The Secretary-General shall prepare a list in alphabetical order of all the persons thus nominated. Save as provided in Article 12, paragraph 2, these shall be the only persons eligible.

2. The Secretary-General shall submit this list to the General Assembly and to the Security Council.

Article 8

The General Assembly and the Security Council shall proceed independently of one another to elect the members of the Court.

Article 9

At every election, the electors shall bear in mind not only that the persons to be elected should individually possess the qualifications required, but also that in the body as a whole the representation of the main forms of civilization and of the principal legal systems of the world should be assured.

Article 10

1. Those candidates who obtain an absolute majority of votes in the General Assembly and in the Security Council shall be considered as elected.

2. Any vote of the Security Council, whether for the election of judges or for the appointment of members of the conference envisaged in Article 12, shall be taken without any distinction between permanent and non-permanent members of the Security Council.

3. In the event of more than one national of the same state obtaining an absolute majority of the votes both of the General Assembly and of the Security Council, the eldest of these only shall be considered as elected.

Article 11

If, after the first meeting held for the purpose of the election, one or more seats remain to be filled, a second and, if necessary, a third meeting shall take place.

Article 12

1. If, after the third meeting, one or more seats still remain unfilled, a joint conference consisting of six members, three appointed by the General Assembly and three by the Security Council, may be formed at any time at the request of either the General Assembly or the Security Council, for the purpose of choosing by the vote of an absolute majority one name for each seat still vacant, to submit to the General Assembly and the Security Council for their respective acceptance.

2. If the joint conference is unanimously agreed upon any person who fulfils the required conditions, he may be included in its list, even though he was not included in the list of nominations referred to in Article 7.

3. If the joint conference is satisfied that it will not be successful in procuring an election, those members of the Court who have already been elected shall, within a period to be fixed by the Security Council, proceed to fill the vacant seats by selection from among those candidates who have obtained votes either in the General Assembly or in the Security Council.

4. In the event of an equality of votes among the judges, the eldest judge shall have a casting vote.

Article 13

1. The members of the Court shall be elected for nine years and may be re-elected; provided, however, that of the judges elected at the first election, the terms of five judges shall expire at the end of three years and the terms of five more judges shall expire at the end of six years.

2. The judges whose terms are to expire at the end of the above-mentioned initial periods of three and six years shall be chosen by lot to be drawn by the Secretary-General immediately after the first election has been completed.

3. The members of the Court shall continue to discharge their duties until their places have been filled. Though replaced, they shall finish any cases which they may have begun.

4. In the case of the resignation of a member of the Court, the resignation shall be addressed to the President of the Court for transmission to the Secretary-General. This last notification makes the place vacant.

Article 14

Vacancies shall be filled by the same method as that laid down for the first election, subject to the following provision: the Secretary-General shall, within one month of the occurrence of the vacancy, proceed to issue the invitations provided for in Article 5, and the date of the election shall be fixed by the Security Council.

Article 15

A member of the Court elected to replace a member whose term of office has not expired shall hold office for the remainder of his predecessor's term.

Article 16

1. No member of the Court may exercise any political or administrative function, or engage in any other occupation of a professional nature.

2. Any doubt on this point shall be settled by the decision of the Court.

Article 17

1. No member of the Court may act as agent, counsel, or advocate in any case.

2. No member may participate in the decision of any case in which he has previously taken part as agent, counsel, or advocate for one of the parties, or as a member of a national or international court, or of a commission of enquiry, or in any other capacity.

3. Any doubt on this point shall be settled by the decision of the Court.

Article 18

1. No member of the Court can be dismissed unless, in the unanimous opinion of the other members, he has ceased to fulfil the required conditions.

2. Formal notification thereof shall be made to the Secretary-General by the Registrar.

3. This notification makes the place vacant.

Article 19

The members of the Court, when engaged on the business of the Court, shall enjoy diplomatic privileges and immunities.

Article 20

Every member of the Court shall, before taking up his duties, make a solemn declaration in open court that he will exercise his powers impartially and conscientiously.

Article 21

1. The Court shall elect its President and Vice-President for three years; they may be re-elected.

2. The Court shall appoint its Registrar and may provide for the appointment of such other officers as may be necessary.

Article 22

1. The seat of the Court shall be established at The Hague. This, however, shall not prevent the Court from sitting and exercising its functions elsewhere whenever the Court considers it desirable.

2. The President and the Registrar shall reside at the seat of the Court.

Article 23

1. The Court shall remain permanently in session, except during the judicial vacations, the dates and duration of which shall be fixed by the Court.

2. Members of the Court are entitled to periodic leave, the dates and duration of which shall be fixed by the Court, having in mind the distance between The Hague and the home of each judge.

3. Members of the Court shall be bound, unless they are on leave or prevented from attending by illness or other serious reasons duly explained to the President, to hold themselves permanently at the disposal of the Court.

Article 24

1. If, for some special reason, a member of the Court considers that he should not take part in the decision of a particular case, he shall so inform the President.

2. If the President considers that for some special reason one of the members of the Court should not sit in a particular case, he shall give him notice accordingly.

3. If in any such case the member of the Court and the President disagree, the matter shall be settled by the decision of the Court.

Article 25

1. The full Court shall sit except when it is expressly provided otherwise in the present Statute.

2. Subject to the condition that the number of judges available to constitute the Court is not thereby reduced below eleven, the Rules of the Court may provide for allowing one or more judges, according to circumstances and in rotation, to be dispensed from sitting.

3. A quorum of nine judges shall suffice to constitute the Court.

Article 26

1. The Court may from time to time form one or more chambers, composed of three or more judges as the Court may determine, for dealing with particular categories of cases; for example, labour cases and cases relating to transit and communications.

2. The Court may at any time form a chamber for dealing with a particular case. The number of judges to constitute such a chamber shall be determined by the Court with the approval of the parties.

3. Cases shall be heard and determined by the chambers provided for in this Article if the parties so request.

Article 27

A judgment given by any of the chambers provided for in Articles 26 and 29 shall be considered as rendered by the Court.

Article 28

The chambers provided for in Articles 26 and 29 may, with the consent of the parties, sit and exercise their functions elsewhere than at The Hague.

Article 29

With a view to the speedy dispatch of business, the Court shall form annually a chamber composed of five judges which, at the request of the parties, may hear and determine cases by summary procedure. In addition, two judges shall be selected for the purpose of replacing judges who find it impossible to sit.

Article 30

1. The Court shall frame rules for carrying out its functions. In particular, it shall lay down rules of procedure.

2. The Rules of the Court may provide for assessors to sit with the Court or with any of its chambers, without the right to vote.

Article 31

1. Judges of the nationality of each of the parties shall retain their right to sit in the case before the Court.

2. If the Court includes upon the Bench a judge of the nationality of one of the parties, any other party may choose a person to sit as judge. Such person shall be chosen preferably from among those persons who have been nominated as candidates as provided in Articles 4 and 5.

3. If the Court includes upon the Bench no judge of the nationality of the parties, each of these parties may proceed to choose a judge as provided in paragraph 2 of this Article.

4. The provisions of this Article shall apply to the case of Articles 26 and 29. In such cases, the President shall request one or, if necessary, two of the members of the Court forming the chamber to give place to the members of the Court of the nationality of the parties concerned, and, failing such, or if they are unable to be present, to the judges specially chosen by the parties.

5. Should there be several parties in the same interest, they shall, for the purpose of the preceding provisions, be reckoned as one party only. Any doubt upon this point shall be settled by the decision of the Court.

6. Judges chosen as laid down in paragraphs 2, 3 and 4 of this Article shall fulfil the conditions required by Articles 2, 17 (paragraph 2), 20, and 24 of the present Statute. They shall take part in the decision on terms of complete equality with their colleagues.

Article 32

1. Each member of the Court shall receive an annual salary.

2. The President shall receive a special annual allowance.

3. The Vice-President shall receive a special allowance for every day on which he acts as President.

4. The judges chosen under Article 31, other than members of the Court, shall receive compensation for each day on which they exercise their functions.

5. These salaries, allowances, and compensation shall be fixed by the General Assembly. They may not be decreased during the term of office.

6. The salary of the Registrar shall be fixed by the General Assembly on the proposal of the Court.

7. Regulations made by the General Assembly shall fix the conditions under which retirement pensions may be given to members of the Court and to the Registrar, and the conditions under which members of the Court and the Registrar shall have their travelling expenses refunded.

8. The above salaries, allowances, and compensation shall be free of all taxation.

Article 33

The expenses of the Court shall be borne by the United Nations in such a manner as shall be decided by the General Assembly.

Chapter II
COMPETENCE OF THE COURT

Article 34

1. Only states may be parties in cases before the Court.

2. The Court, subject to and in conformity with its Rules, may request of public international organizations information relevant to cases before it, and shall receive such information presented by such organizations on their own initiative.

3. Whenever the construction of the constituent instrument of a public international organization or of an international convention adopted thereunder is in question in a case before the Court, the Registrar shall so notify the public international organization concerned and shall communicate to it copies of all the written proceedings.

Article 35

1. The Court shall be open to the states parties to the present Statute.

2. The conditions under which the Court shall be open to other states shall, subject to the special provisions contained in treaties in force, be laid down by the Security Council, but in no case shall such conditions place the parties in a position of inequality before the Court.

3. When a state which is not a Member of the United Nations is a party to a case, the Court shall fix the amount which that party is to contribute towards the expenses of the Court. This provision shall not apply if such state is bearing a share of the expenses of the Court.

Article 36

1. The jurisdiction of the Court comprises all cases which the parties refer to it and all matters specially provided for in the Charter of the United Nations or in treaties and conventions in force.

2. The states parties to the present Statute may at any time declare that they recognize as compulsory *ipso facto* and without special agreement, in relation to any other state accepting the same obligation, the jurisdiction of the Court in all legal disputes concerning:

   a. the interpretation of a treaty;

   b. any question of international law;

   c. the existence of any fact which, if established, would constitute a breach of an international obligation;

   d. the nature or extent of the reparation to be made for the breach of an international obligation.

3. The declarations referred to above may be made unconditionally or on condition of reciprocity on the part of several or certain states, or for a certain time.

4. Such declarations shall be deposited with the Secretary-General of the United Nations, who shall transmit copies thereof to the parties to the Statute and to the Registrar of the Court.

5. Declarations made under Article 36 of the Statute of the Permanent Court of International Justice and which are still in force shall be deemed, as between the parties to the present Statute, to be acceptances of the compulsory jurisdiction of the International Court of Justice for the period which they still have to run and in accordance with their terms.

6. In the event of a dispute as to whether the Court has jurisdiction, the matter shall be settled by the decision of the Court.

Article 37

Whenever a treaty or convention in force provides for reference of a matter to a tribunal to have been instituted by the League of Nations, or to the Permanent Court of International Justice, the matter shall, as between the parties to the present Statute, be referred to the International Court of Justice.

Article 38

1. The Court, whose function is to decide in accordance with international law such disputes as are submitted to it, shall apply:

   a. international conventions, whether general or particular, establishing rules expressly recognized by the contesting states;

   b. international custom, as evidence of a general practice accepted as law;

   c. the general principles of law recognized by civilized nations;

   d. subject to the provisions of Article 59, judicial decisions and the teachings of the most highly qualified publicists of the various nations, as subsidiary means for the determination of rules of law.

2. This provision shall not prejudice the power of the Court to decide a case *ex aequo et bono*, if the parties agree thereto.

Chapter III
PROCEDURE

Article 39

1. The official languages of the Court shall be French and English. If the parties agree that the case shall be conducted in French, the

judgment shall be delivered in French. If the parties agree that the case shall be conducted in English, the judgment shall be delivered in English.

2. In the absence of an agreement as to which language shall be employed, each party may, in the pleadings, use the language which it prefers; the decision of the Court shall be given in French and English. In this case the Court shall at the same time determine which of the two texts shall be considered as authoritative.

3. The Court shall, at the request of any party, authorize a language other than French or English to be used by that party.

Article 40

1. Cases are brought before the Court, as the case may be, either by the notification of the special agreement or by a written application addressed to the Registrar. In either case the subject of the dispute and the parties shall be indicated.

2. The Registrar shall forthwith communicate the application to all concerned.

3. He shall also notify the Members of the United Nations through the Secretary-General, and also any other states entitled to appear before the Court.

Article 41

1. The Court shall have the power to indicate, if it considers that circumstances so require, any provisional measures which ought to be taken to preserve the respective rights of either party.

2. Pending the final decision, notice of the measures suggested shall forthwith be given to the parties and to the Security Council.

Article 42

1. The parties shall be represented by agents.

2. They may have the assistance of counsel or advocates before the Court.

3. The agents, counsel, and advocates of parties before the Court shall enjoy the privileges and immunities necessary to the independent exercise of their duties.

Article 43

1. The procedure shall consist of two parts: written and oral.

2. The written proceedings shall consist of the communication to the Court and to the parties of memorials, counter-memorials and, if necessary, replies; also all papers and documents in support.

3. These communications shall be made through the Registrar, in the order and within the time fixed by the Court.

4. A certified copy of every document produced by one party shall be communicated to the other party.

5. The oral proceedings shall consist of the hearing by the Court of witnesses, experts, agents, counsel, and advocates.

Article 44

1. For the service of all notices upon persons other than the agents, counsel, and advocates, the Court shall apply direct to the government of the state upon whose territory the notice has to be served.

2. The same provision shall apply whenever steps are to be taken to procure evidence on the spot.

Article 45

The hearing shall be under the control of the President or, if he is unable to preside, of the Vice-President; if neither is able to preside, the senior judge present shall preside.

Article 46

The hearing in Court shall be public, unless the Court shall decide otherwise, or unless the parties demand that the public be not admitted.

Article 47

1. Minutes shall be made at each hearing and signed by the Registrar and the President.

2. These minutes alone shall be authentic.

Article 48

The Court shall make orders for the conduct of the case, shall decide the form and time in which each party must conclude its arguments, and make all arrangements connected with the taking of evidence.

Article 49

The Court may, even before the hearing begins, call upon the agents to produce any document or to supply any explanations. Formal note shall be taken of any refusal.

Article 50

The Court may, at any time, entrust any individual, body, bureau, commission, or other organization that it may select, with the task of carrying out an enquiry or giving an expert opinion.

Article 51

During the hearing any relevant questions are to be put to the witnesses and experts under the conditions laid down by the Court in the rules of procedure referred to in Article 30.

Article 52

After the Court has received the proofs and evidence within the time specified for the purpose, it may refuse to accept any further oral or written evidence that one party may desire to present unless the other side consents.

Article 53

1. Whenever one of the parties does not appear before the Court, or fails to defend its case, the other party may call upon the Court to decide in favour of its claim.

2. The Court must, before doing so, satisfy itself, not only that it has jurisdiction in accordance with Articles 36 and 37, but also that the claim is well founded in fact and law.

Article 54

1. When, subject to the control of the Court, the agents, counsel, and advocates have completed their presentation of the case, the President shall declare the hearing closed.

2. The Court shall withdraw to consider the judgment.

3. The deliberations of the Court shall take place in private and remain secret.

Article 55

1. All questions shall be decided by a majority of the judges present.

2. In the event of an equality of votes, the President or the judge who acts in his place shall have a casting vote.

Article 56

1. The judgment shall state the reasons on which it is based.

2. It shall contain the names of the judges who have taken part in the decision.

Article 57

If the judgment does not represent in whole or in part the unanimous opinion of the judges, any judge shall be entitled to deliver a separate opinion.

Article 58

The judgment shall be signed by the President and by the Registrar. It shall be read in open court, due notice having been given to the agents.

Article 59

The decision of the Court has no binding force except between the parties and in respect of that particular case.

Article 60

The judgment is final and without appeal. In the event of dispute as to the meaning or scope of the judgment, the Court shall construe it upon the request of any party.

Article 61

1. An application for revision of a judgment may be made only when it is based upon the discovery of some fact of such a nature as to be a decisive factor, which fact was, when the judgment was given, unknown to the Court and also to the party claiming revision, always provided that such ignorance was not due to negligence.

2. The proceedings for revision shall be opened by a judgment of the Court expressly recording the existence of the new fact, recognizing

that it has such a character as to lay the case open to revision, and declaring the application admissible on this ground.

3. The Court may require previous compliance with the terms of the judgment before it admits proceedings in revision.

4. The application for revision must be made at latest within six months of the discovery of the new fact.

5. No application for revision may be made after the lapse of ten years from the date of the judgment.

Article 62

1. Should a state consider that it has an interest of a legal nature which may be affected by the decision in the case, it may submit a request to the Court to be permitted to intervene.

2. It shall be for the Court to decide upon this request.

Article 63

1. Whenever the construction of a convention to which states other than those concerned in the case are parties is in question, the Registrar shall notify all such states forthwith.

2. Every state so notified has the right to intervene in the proceedings; but if it uses this right, the construction given by the judgment will be equally binding upon it.

Article 64

Unless otherwise decided by the Court, each party shall bear its own costs.

Chapter IV
ADVISORY OPINIONS

Article 65

1. The Court may give an advisory opinion on any legal question at the request of whatever body may be authorized by or in accordance with the Charter of the United Nations to make such a request.

2. Questions upon which the advisory opinion of the Court is asked shall be laid before the Court by means of a written request containing an exact statement of the question upon which an opinion is required, and accompanied by all documents likely to throw light upon the question.

Article 66

1. The Registrar shall forthwith give notice of the request for an advisory opinion to all states entitled to appear before the Court.

2. The Registrar shall also, by means of a special and direct communication, notify any state entitled to appear before the Court or international organization considered by the Court, or, should it not be sitting, by the President, as likely to be able to furnish information on the question, that the Court will be prepared to receive, within a time limit to be fixed by the President, written statements, or to hear, at a public sitting to be held for the purpose, oral statements relating to the question.

3. Should any such state entitled to appear before the Court have failed to receive the special communication referred to in paragraph 2 of this Article, such state may express a desire to submit a written statement or to be heard; and the Court will decide.

4. States and organizations having presented written or oral statements or both shall be permitted to comment on the statements made by other states or organizations in the form, to the extent, and within the time limits which the Court, or, should it not be sitting, the President, shall decide in each particular case. Accordingly, the Registrar shall in due time communicate any such written statements to states and organizations having submitted similar statements.

Article 67

The Court shall deliver its advisory opinions in open court, notice having been given to the Secretary-General and to the representatives of Members of the United Nations, of other states and of international organizations immediately concerned.

Article 68

In the exercise of its advisory functions the Court shall further be guided by the provisions of the present Statute which apply in contentious cases to the extent to which it recognizes them to be applicable.

Chapter V
AMENDMENT

Article 69

Amendments to the present Statute shall be effected by the same procedure as is provided by the Charter of the United Nations for amendments to that Charter, subject however to any provisions which the General Assembly upon recommendation of the Security Council may adopt concerning the participation of states which are parties to the present Statute but are not Members of the United Nations.

Article 70

The Court shall have power to propose such amendments to the present Statute as it may deem necessary, through written communications to the Secretary-General, for consideration in conformity with the provisions of Article 69.

Appendix III

Structure of the United Nations

General Assembly

The General Assembly is composed of all the Members of the United Nations.

SESSIONS
Ninth emergency special session: 29 January–5 February 1982.
Resumed thirty-sixth session: 16-29 March, 28 April and 20 September 1982.
Resumed seventh emergency special session: 20-28 April, 25 and 26 June, 16-19 August and 24 September 1982 (suspended).
Twelfth special session: 7 June–10 July 1982.
Thirty-seventh session:[1] 21 September–21 December 1982 (suspended).

OFFICERS
Ninth emergency special, resumed thirty-sixth, resumed seventh emergency special (April-August) and twelfth special sessions
President: Ismat T. Kittani (Iraq).[a]
Vice-Presidents:[b] Australia, Benin, Botswana, China, Cuba, Cyprus, France, Indonesia, Mexico, Morocco, Pakistan, Panama, Papua New Guinea, Rwanda, Seychelles, Sweden, Togo, Ukrainian SSR, USSR, United Kingdom, United States.

Thirty-seventh session and resumed seventh emergency special session (September)
President: Imre Hollai (Hungary).[c]
Vice-Presidents:[d] Austria, China, Congo, Cyprus, Democratic Yemen, France, Haiti, Jamaica, Kuwait, Libyan Arab Jamahiriya, Mali, Nicaragua, Philippines, Qatar, Turkey, Uganda, USSR, United Kingdom, United States, Upper Volta, Zambia.

[a]On 7 June 1982, the Assembly decided that the President at its thirty-sixth session would serve in the same capacity at the twelfth special session (decision S-12/12).
[b]On 20 April and 7 June 1982, the Assembly decided that the Vice-Presidents of the thirty-sixth session would serve in the same capacity at the seventh emergency special and twelfth special sessions (decisions ES-7/22 A and S-12/14), respectively.
[c]Elected on 21 September 1982 (decision 37/302).
[d]Elected on 21 September 1982 (decision 37/304); on 24 September, the Assembly decided that the Vice-Presidents of the thirty-seventh session would serve in the same capacity at the seventh emergency special session (decision ES-7/22 B).

The Assembly has four types of committees: (1) Main Committees; (2) procedural committees; (3) standing committees; (4) subsidiary and *ad hoc* bodies. In addition, it convenes conferences to deal with specific subjects.

Main Committees

Seven Main Committees have been established as follows:

Political and Security Committee (disarmament and related international security questions) (First Committee)
Special Political Committee
Economic and Financial Committee (Second Committee)
Social, Humanitarian and Cultural Committee (Third Committee)
Trusteeship Committee (including Non-Self-Governing Territories) (Fourth Committee)
Administrative and Budgetary Committee (Fifth Committee)
Legal Committee (Sixth Committee)

The General Assembly may constitute other committees, on which all Members of the United Nations have the right to be represented.

OFFICERS OF THE MAIN COMMITTEES

Resumed thirty-sixth session

Fifth Committee[a]
Chairman: Abdel-Rahman Abdalla (Sudan).
Vice-Chairmen: Soemadi Djoko Moerdjono Brotodiningrat (Indonesia), Michael F. Godfrey (New Zealand).
Rapporteur: Mario Martorell (Peru).

[a]The only Main Committee which met at the resumed thirty-sixth session.

Twelfth special session[a]

Ad Hoc Committee of the Twelfth Special Session[b]
Chairman: Oluyemi Adeniji (Nigeria).
Vice-Chairmen: Mario Alessi (Italy), Juan José Calle y Calle (Peru), Alfonso García Robles (Mexico), Baruch Grinberg (Bulgaria), Guy Hazoumé (Benin), Davidson L. Hepburn (Bahamas), Gerhard Herder (German Democratic Republic), Miljan Komatina (Yugoslavia), Mehdi Mrani Zentar (Morocco), Yoshio Okawa (Japan), Waliur Rahman (Bangladesh), David Marshall Sadleir (Australia), Ayilam Panchapakesa Venkataswaran (India).
Rapporteur: Omer Ersun (Turkey).

[a]On 7 June 1982, the Assembly decided that the Chairmen of the Main Committees of the thirty-sixth session (YUN 1981, p. 1506) would serve in the same capacity at the twelfth special session (decision S-12/13).
[b]Chairman elected by the Assembly on 7 June 1982; other officers elected by the *Ad Hoc* Committee on 8 June (decision S-12/15).

Thirty-seventh session[a]

[a]Chairmen elected by the Main Committees; announced by the Assembly President on 21 September 1982 (decision 37/303).

First Committee
Chairman: James Victor Gbeho (Ghana).
Vice-Chairmen: Julio César Carasales (Argentina), Tom Eric Vraalsen (Norway).
Rapporteur: Luvsangiin Erdenechuluun (Mongolia).

Special Political Committee
Chairman: Abduldayem M. Mubarez (Yemen).
Vice-Chairmen: Turkia Ould Daddah (Mauritania), Ernesto Rodríguez-Medina (Colombia).
Rapporteur: Osman Faruk Logoglu (Turkey).

Second Committee
Chairman: Oladapo Olusola Fafowora (Nigeria).
Vice-Chairmen: Qazi Shaukat Fareed (Pakistan), George Papadatos (Greece).
Rapporteur: Stoyan Bakalov (Bulgaria).

Third Committee
Chairman: Carlos Calero Rodrigues (Brazil).
Vice-Chairmen: Dharar Abdul Razzak Razzooqi (Kuwait), Willi Schlegel (German Democratic Republic).
Rapporteur: Karl Borchard (Federal Republic of Germany).

[1]The thirty-seventh session of the General Assembly resumed in 1983 from 10 to 13 May and on 19 September.

Fourth Committee
Chairman: Raúl Roa Kouri (Cuba).
Vice-Chairmen: Essam Sadek Ramadan (Egypt), Jukka Valtasaari (Finland).
Rapporteur: Victor G. Garcia III (Philippines).

Fifth Committee
Chairman: Andrzej Abraszewski (Poland).
Vice-Chairmen: Sumihiro Kuyama (Japan), Ernest Besley Maycock (Barbados).
Rapporteur: Mohamed Adel El-Safty (Egypt).

Sixth Committee
Chairman: Philippe Kirsch (Canada).
Vice-Chairmen: Ion Diaconu (Romania), Peter D. Maynard (Bahamas).
Rapporteur: Salwa Gabriel Berberi (Sudan).

Procedural committees

General Committee
The General Committee consists of the President of the General Assembly, as Chairman, the 21 Vice-Presidents and the Chairmen of the seven Main Committees.

Credentials Committee
The Credentials Committee consists of nine members appointed by the General Assembly on the proposal of the President.

Ninth emergency special, resumed thirty-sixth, resumed seventh emergency special (April-August) and twelfth special sessions
China, Ghana, Netherlands, Niger *(Chairman)*, Panama, Papua New Guinea, Paraguay, USSR, United States.[a]

Thirty-seventh session and resumed seventh emergency special session (September)
Bahamas *(Chairman)*, China, Dominican Republic, Nepal, New Zealand, Nigeria, Seychelles, USSR, United States.[b]

[a]On 29 January, 20 April and 7 June 1982, the Assembly decided that the Committee for the ninth emergency, seventh emergency and twelfth special sessions would have the same composition as that for the thirty-sixth session (decisions ES-9/11, ES-7/11 B and S-12/11), respectively.
[b]Appointed on 21 September 1982 (decision 37/301); on 24 September, the Assembly decided that the Committee for the seventh emergency special session would have the same composition as that for the thirty-seventh session (decision ES-7/11 C).

Standing committees

The two standing committees consist of experts appointed in their individual capacity for three-year terms.

Advisory Committee on Administrative and Budgetary Questions
Members:
To serve until 31 December 1982: Andrzej Abraszewski (Poland); Mohamed Malloum Fall (Mauritania); Anwar Kemal (Pakistan); C. S. M. Mselle, *Chairman* (United Republic of Tanzania); Christopher R. Thomas (Trinidad and Tobago).
To serve until 31 December 1983: Henrik Amneus (Sweden); Michel Brochard (France); Ernesto C. Garrido (Philippines); Sumihiro Kuyama (Japan); Tang Jianwen (China); Norman Williams (Panama).[a]
To serve until 31 December 1984: Lucio García del Solar (Argentina);[b] A. V. Grodsky (USSR); Virginia C. Housholder (United States); Rachid Lahlou (Morocco); Carl C. Pedersen (Canada).

[a]Resigned with effect from 1 January 1983; Samuel Pinheiro-Guimarães (Brazil) was appointed by the General Assembly on 16 November 1982 (decision 37/305 B) to fill the resultant vacancy.
[b]Resigned on 20 September 1982; Enrique Ferrer Vieyra (Argentina) was appointed by the General Assembly on 4 October (decision 37/305 A) to fill the resultant vacancy.

On 16 November 1982 (decision 37/305 B), the General Assembly appointed the following five members for a three-year term beginning on 1 January 1983 to fill the vacancies occurring on 31 December 1982:

Traian Chebeleu (Romania), Mohamed Malloum Fall (Mauritania), Mohammad Samir Mansouri (Syrian Arab Republic), C. S. M. Mselle (United Republic of Tanzania), Christopher R. Thomas (Trinidad and Tobago).

Committee on Contributions
Members:
To serve until 31 December 1982: Mohammed Sadiq Al-Mahdi (Iraq); Fathih Khaouane Bouayad-Agha (Algeria); Richard Vognild Hennes (United States); Katsumi Sezaki (Japan); Ladislav Smid (Czechoslovakia); Jozsef Tardos (Hungary).
To serve until 31 December 1983: Hélio de Burgos Cabal (Brazil); Leoncio Fernández Maroto (Spain); Lance Louis E. Joseph (Australia); Japhet Gideon Kiti, *Vice-Chairman* (Kenya); Rachid Lahlou (Morocco); Atilio Norberto Molteni (Argentina).
To serve until 31 December 1984: Syed Amjad Ali, *Chairman* (Pakistan); A. S. Chistyakov (USSR); Miguel Angel Dávila Mendoza (Mexico); Wilfried Koschorreck (Federal Republic of Germany); Yang Hushan (China); Philippe Zeller (France).

On 16 November 1982 (decision 37/309), the General Assembly appointed the following six members for a three-year term beginning on 1 January 1983 to fill the vacancies occurring on 31 December 1982: Andrzej Abraszewski (Poland), Nobutoshi Akao (Japan), Mohammed Sadiq Al-Mahdi (Iraq), Hamed Arabi El-Houderi (Libyan Arab Jamahiriya), Richard Vognild Hennes (United States), Zoran Lazarevic (Yugoslavia).

Subsidiary, *ad hoc* and related bodies

The following subsidiary, *ad hoc* and related bodies were in existence or functioning in 1982, or were established during the General Assembly's thirty-seventh session, held from 21 September to 21 December 1982.

Ad Hoc Committee of the General Assembly for the Announcement of Voluntary Contributions to the 1983 Programme of the United Nations High Commissioner for Refugees
As soon as practicable after the opening of each regular session of the General Assembly, an *ad hoc* committee of the whole of the Assembly meets, under the chairmanship of the President of the session, to enable Governments to announce pledges of voluntary contributions to the programme of UNHCR for the following year. Also invited to announce their pledges are States which are members of specialized agencies but not Members of the United Nations. In 1982, the *Ad Hoc* Committee met on 19 November.

Ad Hoc Committee of the General Assembly for the Announcement of Voluntary Contributions to the United Nations Relief and Works Agency for Palestine Refugees in the Near East
As soon as practicable after the opening of each regular session of the General Assembly, an *ad hoc* committee of the whole of the Assembly meets, under the chairmanship of the President of the session, to enable Governments to announce pledges of voluntary contributions to the programme of UNRWA for the following year. Also invited to announce their pledges are States which are members of specialized agencies but not Members of the United Nations. In 1982, the *Ad Hoc* Committee met on 22 November.

Ad Hoc Committee of the International Conference on Kampuchea
In 1982, the membership of the *Ad Hoc* Committee of the International Conference on Kampuchea rose from 7 to 10 with the appointment to the Committee of Belgium, Nepal and Peru by the Conference President, pursuant to a 1981 Conference resolution authorizing the inclusion of additional members.
The *Ad Hoc* Committee held seven meetings during the year, at United Nations Headquarters, between 11 January and 21 September.

Members: Belgium, Japan, Malaysia, Nepal, Nigeria, Peru, Senegal, Sri Lanka, Sudan, Thailand.

Chairman: Massamba Sarré (Senegal).
Vice-Chairman: Edmonde Dever (Belgium).
Rapporteur: Zainal Abidin bin Sulong (Malaysia).

Ad Hoc Committee on the Drafting of an International Convention against *Apartheid* in Sports

The *Ad Hoc* Committee on the Drafting of an International Convention against *Apartheid* in Sports, which was to consist of 25 members, had a membership of 24 in 1982. It held three meetings during the year, at United Nations Headquarters: on 17 February, 12 May and 27 August.

Members: Algeria, Barbados, Canada, Congo, German Democratic Republic, Ghana, Guinea, Haiti, Hungary, India, Indonesia, Jamaica, Malaysia, Nepal, Nigeria, Peru, Philippines, Somalia, Sudan, Syrian Arab Republic, Trinidad and Tobago, Ukrainian SSR, United Republic of Tanzania, Yugoslavia.

Chairman: Ernest Besley Maycock (Barbados).
Vice-Chairmen: Keshav Raj Jha (Nepal), Janos Matus (Hungary), George K. Mwanjabala (United Republic of Tanzania).
Rapporteur: Stafford Oliver Neil (Jamaica).

Ad Hoc Committee on the Drafting of an International Convention against the Recruitment, Use, Financing and Training of Mercenaries

The *Ad Hoc* Committee on the Drafting of an International Convention against the Recruitment, Use, Financing and Training of Mercenaries, which was to be composed of 35 members, had a membership of 34 in 1982. It held its second session at United Nations Headquarters from 25 January to 19 February.

Members: Algeria, Angola, Bahamas, Bangladesh, Barbados, Benin, Bulgaria, Canada, Democratic Yemen, Ethiopia, France, German Democratic Republic, Germany, Federal Republic of, Guyana, India, Italy, Jamaica, Japan, Mongolia, Nigeria, Portugal, Senegal,[a] Seychelles, Spain, Suriname, Turkey, Ukrainian SSR, USSR, United Kingdom, United States, Uruguay, Yugoslavia, Zaire, Zambia.

[a]Until 31 December 1982, when it withdrew in accordance with a schedule of rotation agreed on by the Group of African States. On 16 December 1982 (decision 37/315), the General Assembly took note of the appointment by its President of Togo, effective 1 January 1983, to fill the resultant vacancy.

Chairman: Mohammed Bedjaoui (Algeria).
Vice-Chairmen: Luigi Ferrari Bravo (Italy), Y. K. Kachurenko (Ukrainian SSR), Harley S. L. Moseley (Barbados).
Rapporteur: Waliur Rahman (Bangladesh).

Ad Hoc Committee on the Indian Ocean

The *Ad Hoc* Committee on the Indian Ocean, which undertook among other tasks the preparatory work for the Conference on the Indian Ocean (scheduled for 1984 at Colombo, Sri Lanka), held the following series of meetings in 1982: between 1 and 12 March and between 20 and 28 May, at United Nations Headquarters; between 3 and 20 August, at Geneva; and on 23 November, at Headquarters.

Members: Australia, Bangladesh, Bulgaria, Canada, China, Democratic Yemen, Djibouti, Egypt, Ethiopia, France, German Democratic Republic, Germany, Federal Republic of, Greece, India, Indonesia, Iran, Iraq, Italy, Japan, Kenya, Liberia, Madagascar, Malaysia, Maldives, Mauritius, Mozambique, Netherlands, Norway, Oman, Pakistan, Panama, Poland, Romania, Seychelles, Singapore, Somalia, Sri Lanka, Sudan, Thailand, USSR, United Kingdom, United Republic of Tanzania, United States, Yemen, Yugoslavia, Zambia. Sweden, a major maritime user of the Indian Ocean, continued to participate in the meetings as an observer.

Chairman: Ignatius Benedict Fonseka (Sri Lanka).
Vice-Chairmen: Susan Jennifer Boyd (Australia); Siegfried Kahn (German Democratic Republic); José Carlos Lobo (Mozambique); Wirjono Sastrohandojo (Indonesia) (until 20 May), Izhar Ibrahim (Indonesia) (from 20 May).
Rapporteur: Henri Rasolondraibe (Madagascar).

Ad Hoc Committee on the World Disarmament Conference

The 40-member *Ad Hoc* Committee on the World Disarmament Conference held two sessions in 1982, at United Nations Headquarters: the first from 5 to 8 April; and the second from 23 to 27 August.

Members: Algeria, Argentina, Austria, Belgium, Brazil, Bulgaria, Burundi, Canada, Chile, Colombia, Czechoslovakia, Egypt, Ethiopia, Hungary, India, Indonesia, Iran, Italy, Japan, Lebanon, Liberia, Mexico, Mongolia, Morocco, Netherlands, Nigeria, Pakistan, Peru, Philippines, Poland, Romania, Spain, Sri Lanka, Sweden, Tunisia, Turkey, Venezuela, Yugoslavia, Zaire, Zambia.

The USSR participated in the work of the *Ad Hoc* Committee, while China, France, the United Kingdom and the United States maintained contact with it through its Chairman, pursuant to a 1973 General Assembly resolution.[2]

Chairman: Ignatius Benedict Fonseka (Sri Lanka).
Vice-Chairmen: Juan José Calle y Calle (Peru), Ryszard Krystosik (Poland).
Rapporteur: Fermín Zelada (Spain) (until 23 August), Arturo Laclaustra (Spain) (from 23 August).

WORKING GROUP
Members: Burundi, Egypt, Hungary, India, Iran, Italy, Mexico, Peru, Poland, Spain *(Chairman)*, Sri Lanka.

Ad Hoc Intergovernmental Group on the United Nations Financing System for Science and Technology for Development

The *Ad Hoc* Intergovernmental Group on the United Nations Financing System for Science and Technology for Development, open to the participation of all States as full members, held the following sessions in 1982, at United Nations Headquarters: its first from 1 to 5 March; its second from 12 to 20 April; and its resumed second and final session from 24 to 26 May. Represented at the sessions were:

Algeria, Argentina, Australia, Austria, Bahrain, Bangladesh, Belgium, Bhutan, Bolivia, Brazil, Canada, Chile, China, Colombia, Congo, Cuba, Denmark, Ecuador, Egypt, Ethiopia, Finland, France, Germany, Federal Republic of, Ghana, Greece, Guinea, Holy See, India, Indonesia, Iran, Ireland, Italy, Ivory Coast, Jamaica, Japan, Kenya, Lesotho, Malaysia, Malta, Mexico, Morocco, Nepal, Netherlands, Nigeria, Norway, Pakistan, Panama, Peru, Philippines, Poland, Portugal, Republic of Korea, Romania, Sierra Leone, Spain, Sri Lanka, Sudan, Sweden, Switzerland, Thailand, Togo, Trinidad and Tobago, Tunisia, Turkey, Uganda, United Kingdom, United States, Upper Volta, Uruguay, Venezuela, Yemen, Yugoslavia, Zambia, Zimbabwe.

Chairman: Paolo Bruni (Italy).
Vice-Chairmen: Mirko Bunc (Yugoslavia), Awad Mohamed Elhassan (Sudan), Enrique Martín del Campo (Mexico).

Advisory Committee for the International Year of Disabled Persons

The 23-member Advisory Committee for the International Year of Disabled Persons held its fourth and final session at Vienna, Austria, from 5 to 14 July 1982.

Members: Algeria, Argentina, Bangladesh,[a] Barbados,[a] Belgium, Byelorussian SSR, Canada, German Democratic Republic, India, Kenya,[a] Libyan Arab Jamahiriya, Morocco, Nigeria, Oman, Panama,[a] Philippines, Sweden, United Kingdom, United States, Uruguay,[a] Viet Nam,[a] Yugoslavia, Zaire.

[a]Not represented at the fourth session.

Chairman: Ali Sunni Muntasser (Libyan Arab Jamahiriya).
Vice-Chairmen: K. P. Becker (German Democratic Republic), Alicia Amate de Esquivel (Argentina), Antonio O. Periquet (Philippines).
Rapporteur: André LeBlanc (Canada).

---

[2]Resolution 3183(XXVIII), 18 December 1973 (YUN 1973, p. 18).

Advisory Committee for the International Youth Year

The 24-member Advisory Committee for the International Youth Year held its second session at Vienna, Austria, from 14 to 23 June 1982.

Members: Algeria, Chile, Costa Rica, Democratic Yemen, Germany, Federal Republic of, Guatemala, Guinea, Indonesia, Ireland, Jamaica, Japan, Lebanon, Morocco, Mozambique,[a] Netherlands, Nigeria, Norway, Poland, Romania, Rwanda, Sri Lanka, USSR, United States, Venezuela.

[a]Not represented at the second session.

Chairman: Nicu Ceausescu (Romania).
Vice-Chairmen: Oumar Diarso (Guinea), J. F. Gonzales Morales (Guatemala), Mr. Soenaryo (Indonesia).
Rapporteur: Frans L. Schlingemann (Netherlands).

Advisory Committee for the World Assembly on Aging

During 1982, the 22-member Advisory Committee for the World Assembly on Aging (p. 1637) held its second session at United Nations Headquarters from 16 to 22 February and its third and final session at Vienna, Austria, from 3 to 7 May.

Members: Benin,[a] Byelorussian SSR, Chile, Costa Rica,[a] Dominican Republic, France, Hungary, India, Indonesia, Japan, Lebanon, Malta, Morocco, Nigeria, Philippines, Spain, Suriname, Sweden, Togo, USSR, United States, Venezuela.

[a]Not represented at the third session.

Chairman: Anthony H. B. de Bono (Malta).
Vice-Chairmen: Ryoko Akamatsu (Japan); M. Lantzev (USSR); Olajumoke Oladayo Obafemi (Nigeria) (second session), Lasisi Adetuyi (Nigeria) (third session).
Rapporteur: Lucien Johan Henar (Suriname).

Advisory Committee on the United Nations Educational and Training Programme for Southern Africa

Members: Byelorussian SSR, Canada, Denmark, India, Japan, Liberia, Nigeria, Norway, United Republic of Tanzania, United States, Venezuela, Zaire, Zambia.

Chairman: Gérard Pelletier (Canada).
Vice-Chairman: Alhaji Yusuff Maitama-Sule (Nigeria).

Advisory Committee on the United Nations Programme of Assistance in the Teaching, Study, Dissemination and Wider Appreciation of International Law

The Advisory Committee on the United Nations Programme of Assistance in the Teaching, Study, Dissemination and Wider Appreciation of International Law did not meet in 1982.

Members (until 31 December 1983): Barbados, Cyprus, Egypt, El Salvador, France, Ghana, Hungary, Netherlands, Sierra Leone, Syrian Arab Republic, Turkey, USSR, United Kingdom.

Board of Auditors

The Board of Auditors consists of three members appointed by the General Assembly for three-year terms.

Members:
To serve until 30 June 1983: Senior President of the Audit Office of Belgium.
To serve until 30 June 1984: Comptroller and Auditor-General of Bangladesh.
To serve until 30 June 1985: Auditor-General of Ghana.

On 16 November 1982 (decision 37/310), the General Assembly reappointed the Senior President of the Audit Office of Belgium for a three-year term beginning on 1 July 1983.

Collective Measures Committee

Established in 1950 under the General Assembly's "Uniting for Peace" resolution,[3] the Collective Measures Committee reported three times to the Assembly. In noting the third report, to its ninth (1954) session,

the Assembly directed the Committee to remain in a position to pursue such further studies as it may deem desirable to strengthen the capability of the United Nations to maintain peace and to report to the Security Council and to the Assembly as appropriate.[4]

Members: Australia, Belgium, Brazil, Burma, Canada, Egypt, France, Mexico, Philippines, Turkey, United Kingdom, United States, Venezuela, Yugoslavia.

Commission on Human Settlements

The Commission on Human Settlements reports to the General Assembly through the Economic and Social Council.

For details of the Commission's membership and session in 1982, see p. 1643.

Committee for Programme and Co-ordination

The Committee for Programme and Co-ordination is the main subsidiary organ of the Economic and Social Council and of the General Assembly for planning, programming and co-ordination; it reports to both.

For details of the Committee's membership and session in 1982, see p. 1644.

Committee for the United Nations Population Award

The Committee for the United Nations Population Award, which did not meet in 1982, was to be composed of:

Ten representatives of United Nations Member States elected by the Economic and Social Council for a three-year period, with due regard for equitable geographical representation and the need to include Member States that had made contributions for the Award;
The Secretary-General and the UNFPA Executive Director, to serve *ex officio;*
Five individuals eminent for their significant contributions to population-related activities, selected by the Committee, to serve as honorary members in an advisory capacity for a renewable three-year term.

On 11 November 1982 (decision 1982/188), the Economic and Social Council elected the following 10 members to serve for a three-year term beginning on 1 January 1983: Australia, Bangladesh, Burundi, China, Colombia, Egypt, Japan, Mexico, Tunisia, Yugoslavia.

The five honorary members had not been selected by the end of 1982.

Committee of Governmental Experts to Evaluate the Present Structure of the Secretariat in the Administrative, Finance and Personnel Areas

The 17-member Committee of Governmental Experts to Evaluate the Present Structure of the Secretariat in the Administrative, Finance and Personnel Areas completed its work at two series of meetings held at United Nations Headquarters between 15 and 20 September and between 18 and 22 October 1982.

Members: Abdel-Rahman Abdalla (Sudan);[a] Michael F. Gepp (Brazil); Teresa Ivars Benalcazar (Colombia); Kamanda wa Kamanda (Zaire);[a] Anwar Kemal (Pakistan); E. V. Kudryavtsev (USSR); Sumihiro Kuyama (Japan); Harald Löschner (Federal Republic of Germany); Antoine Mérieux (France); Ousmane Mounirou (Benin);[b] Love Kunda M'tesa (Zambia);[b] Satyabrata Pal (India); Leif Skare, *Vice-Chairman* (Norway); Henryk J. Sokalski (Poland); Winthrop M. Southworth (United States); Tang Jianwen (China); Christopher R. Thomas, *Chairman/Rapporteur* (Trinidad and Tobago).

[a]Did not attend the 1982 meetings.

[b]Appointed by the Secretary-General on 15 September 1982 to replace, respectively, Apollinaire Hachème, *Vice-Chairman* (Benin), and Humphrey B. Kunda (Zambia), who had resigned.

---

[3]Resolution 377(V), part A, para. 11, 3 November 1950 (YUN 1950, p. 194).
[4]Resolution 809(IX), 4 November 1954 (YUN 1954, p. 23).

Committee of Trustees of the United Nations Trust Fund for South Africa
Members: Chile, Morocco, Nigeria, Pakistan, Sweden.

Chairman: Anders I. Thunborg (Sweden).
Vice-Chairman: Alhaji Yusuff Maitama-Sule (Nigeria).

Committee on Applications for Review of Administrative Tribunal Judgements
The Committee on Applications for Review of Administrative Tribunal Judgements held two sessions in 1982, at United Nations Headquarters: its twenty-first on 30 June; and the first part of its twenty-second on 14 December.

Members (until 20 September 1982) (based on the composition of the General Committee at the General Assembly's thirty-sixth session): Australia, Benin, Botswana, China, Cuba, Cyprus, France, Indonesia, Iraq, Ireland, Mexico, Morocco, Pakistan, Panama, Papua New Guinea, Peru, Philippines, Qatar, Rwanda, Seychelles, Sudan, Sweden, Togo, Uganda, Ukrainian SSR, USSR, United Kingdom, United States, Yugoslavia.

Chairman: Juan José Calle y Calle (Peru).
Vice-Chairman: Soemadi Djoko Moerdjono Brotodiningrat (Indonesia).
Rapporteur: David H. Anderson (United Kingdom).

Members (from 21 September 1982) (based on the composition of the General Committee at the General Assembly's thirty-seventh session): Austria, Brazil, Canada, China, Congo, Cuba, Cyprus, Democratic Yemen, France, Ghana, Haiti, Hungary, Jamaica, Kuwait, Libyan Arab Jamahiriya, Mali, Nicaragua, Nigeria, Philippines, Poland, Qatar, Turkey, Uganda, USSR, United Kingdom, United States, Upper Volta, Yemen, Zambia.

Chairman: Philippe Kirsch (Canada).
Rapporteur: Franklin D. Berman (United Kingdom).

Committee on Arrangements for a Conference for the Purpose of Reviewing the Charter
All Members of the United Nations are members of the Committee on Arrangements for a Conference for the Purpose of Reviewing the Charter.
The Committee did not meet in 1982.

Committee on Conferences
The Committee on Conferences consists of 22 Member States appointed by the President of the General Assembly on the basis of equitable geographical balance, to serve for a three-year term.

Members (until 31 December 1983): Algeria, Austria, Chile, Cyprus, France, Germany, Federal Republic of, Honduras, Hungary, Indonesia, Japan, Kenya, Mexico, New Zealand, Nigeria, Peru, Senegal, Sri Lanka, Tunisia, USSR, United Kingdom, United States, Yugoslavia.

Chairman: Michael G. Okeyo (Kenya).
Vice-Chairmen: Bernard A. B. Goonetilleke (Sri Lanka), Tibor Gubcsi (Hungary), Mario Martorell (Peru).
Rapporteur: Richard J. Martin (New Zealand).

Committee on Information
In 1982, the 67-member Committee on Information held, at United Nations Headquarters, an organizational session on 15 March and its fourth session from 21 June to 9 July.

Members: Algeria, Argentina, Bangladesh, Belgium, Benin, Brazil, Bulgaria, Burundi, Chile, Colombia, Congo, Costa Rica, Cuba, Cyprus, Denmark, Ecuador, Egypt, El Salvador, Ethiopia, Finland, France, German Democratic Republic, Germany, Federal Republic of, Ghana, Greece, Guatemala, Guinea, Guyana, India, Indonesia, Italy, Ivory Coast, Japan, Jordan, Kenya, Lebanon, Mongolia, Morocco, Netherlands, Niger, Nigeria, Pakistan, Peru, Philippines, Poland, Portugal, Romania, Singapore, Somalia, Spain, Sri Lanka, Sudan, Syrian Arab Republic, Togo, Trinidad and Tobago, Tunisia, Turkey, Ukrainian SSR, USSR, United Kingdom, United Republic of Tanzania, United States, Venezuela, Viet Nam, Yemen, Yugoslavia, Zaire.

Chairman: Miguel A. Albornoz (Ecuador).
Vice-Chairmen: Monique P. A. Frank (Netherlands), Rachid Lahlou (Morocco), Willi Schlegel (German Democratic Republic).
Rapporteur: Vasant Vishnu Nevrekar (India).

Committee on Relations with the Host Country
Members: Bulgaria, Canada, China, Costa Rica, Cyprus, France, Honduras, Iraq, Ivory Coast, Mali, Senegal, Spain, USSR, United Kingdom, United States (host country).

Chairman: Andreas V. Mavrommatis (Cyprus) (until 11 March), Constantine Moushoutas (Cyprus) (from 11 March).
Vice-Chairmen: Bulgaria, Canada, Ivory Coast.
Rapporteur: Emilia Castro de Barish (Costa Rica).

Committee on the Review and Appraisal of the Implementation of the International Development Strategy for the Third United Nations Development Decade
On 20 December 1982, the General Assembly established a committee of universal membership (i.e. open to the participation of all States as full members) to carry out in 1984 a review and appraisal of the implementation of the International Development Strategy for the Third United Nations Development Decade.[5] The Committee was to report to the Assembly at its thirty-ninth (1984) session through the Economic and Social Council.

Committee on the Development and Utilization of New and Renewable Sources of Energy
On 21 December 1982, the General Assembly established an intergovernmental committee to assist it in, *inter alia*, recommending policy guidelines for United Nations bodies concerned with implementing the Nairobi Programme of Action for the Development and Utilization of New and Renewable Sources of Energy[6] and with financing this implementation; formulating plans for carrying out the Programme according to its priorities, modifying these as necessary; monitoring and reviewing the implementation to ensure co-ordination of activities and, where applicable, making recommendations on adapting the Programme; and co-operating with appropriate governmental and other intergovernmental institutions and drawing upon their expertise.

The Committee was to be open to the participation of all States as full members. It was to meet once every two years in even years, but was to hold its first session during 1983. It was to report to the Assembly through the Economic and Social Council.

Committee on the Exercise of the Inalienable Rights of the Palestinian People
Members: Afghanistan, Cuba, Cyprus, German Democratic Republic, Guinea, Guyana, Hungary, India, Indonesia, Lao People's Democratic Republic, Madagascar, Malaysia, Mali, Malta, Nigeria, Pakistan, Romania, Senegal, Sierra Leone, Tunisia, Turkey, Ukrainian SSR, Yugoslavia.

Chairman: Massamba Sarré (Senegal).
Vice-Chairmen: Raúl Roa Kouri (Cuba), Mohammad Farid Zarif (Afghanistan).
Rapporteur: Victor J. Gauci (Malta).

WORKING GROUP
Members: Afghanistan, Cuba, German Democratic Republic, Guinea, Guyana, India, Malta *(Chairman)*, Pakistan,[a] Senegal, Tunisia, Turkey,[a] Ukrainian SSR; Palestine Liberation Organization.

[a]Members from 21 January and 30 March 1982, respectively.

Committee on the Peaceful Uses of Outer Space
The 53-member Committee on the Peaceful Uses of Outer Space held its twenty-fifth session at United Nations Headquarters from 22 March to 1 April 1982.

---

[5]General Assembly resolution 35/56, annex, 5 December 1980 (YUN 1980, p. 503).
[6]YUN 1981, p. 689.

Members: Albania,[a] Argentina, Australia, Austria, Belgium, Benin, Brazil, Bulgaria, Canada, Chad, Chile, China, Colombia, Czechoslovakia, Ecuador, Egypt, France, German Democratic Republic, Germany, Federal Republic of, Greece, Hungary, India, Indonesia, Iran, Iraq, Italy, Japan, Kenya, Lebanon, Mexico, Mongolia, Morocco, Netherlands, Niger, Nigeria, Pakistan, Philippines, Poland, Romania, Sierra Leone, Spain, Sudan, Sweden, Syrian Arab Republic, USSR, United Kingdom, United Republic of Cameroon, United States, Upper Volta, Uruguay, Venezuela, Viet Nam, Yugoslavia.

[a]Not represented at the twenty-fifth session.

Chairman: Peter Jankowitsch (Austria).
Vice-Chairman: Teodor Marinescu (Romania).
Rapporteur: Carlos Antonio Bettencourt Bueno (Brazil).

LEGAL SUB-COMMITTEE
The Legal Sub-Committee, a committee of the whole, held its twenty-first session at Geneva from 1 to 19 February 1982.

Chairman: Eugeniusz Wyzner (Poland).

SCIENTIFIC AND TECHNICAL SUB-COMMITTEE
The Scientific and Technical Sub-Committee, a committee of the whole, held its nineteenth session at United Nations Headquarters from 11 to 22 January 1982.

Chairman: J. H. Carver (Australia).

Disarmament Commission

In 1982, the Disarmament Commission, composed of all the Members of the United Nations, held a series of meetings between 17 and 28 May, one meeting on 14 October and organizational meetings on 13 and 15 December, all at United Nations Headquarters.

Chairman: Eugeniusz Wyzner (Poland) (until 16 July), Wlodzimierz Natorf (Poland) (from 14 October).
Vice-Chairmen: Bahamas, Belgium, Czechoslovakia, Iraq, Liberia, Pakistan, Sweden, Zaire.
Rapporteur: Max de la Fuente (Peru).

High-level Committee on the Review of Technical Co-operation among Developing Countries

The High-level Committee on the Review of Technical Co-operation among Developing Countries, composed of all States participating in UNDP, did not meet in 1982.

Intergovernmental Committee on Science and Technology for Development

During 1982, the Intergovernmental Committee on Science and Technology for Development, open to the participation of all States as full members, held its fourth session at United Nations Headquarters in two parts: from 24 May to 4 June; and from 8 to 10 September. Represented at the session were:

Algeria, Australia, Austria, Bangladesh, Belgium, Brazil, Bulgaria, Byelorussian SSR, Canada, Cape Verde, Chile, China, Colombia, Congo, Cuba, Czechoslovakia, Denmark, Ecuador, Egypt, El Salvador,[a] Ethiopia, Fiji,[a] Finland, France, German Democratic Republic, Germany, Federal Republic of, Ghana, Greece, Guatemala,[a] Holy See, Hungary, India, Indonesia, Iran, Ireland, Italy, Ivory Coast,[a] Jamaica, Japan, Kenya, Lesotho, Madagascar,[a] Mexico, Nepal,[a] Netherlands, New Zealand, Nicaragua, Nigeria, Norway, Oman, Pakistan, Peru, Philippines,[a] Poland, Portugal, Qatar, Republic of Korea, Romania, Saint Vincent and the Grenadines,[a] Sierra Leone, Spain, Sri Lanka, Sudan,[a] Swaziland,[a] Sweden, Switzerland, Thailand, Togo, Trinidad and Tobago, Tunisia, Turkey, Ukrainian SSR, USSR, United Kingdom, United Republic of Tanzania,[a] United States, Upper Volta, Uruguay, Venezuela, Yemen,[a] Yugoslavia, Zambia, Zimbabwe.

[a]Represented at the resumed fourth session only.

Chairman: Mohamed Baha-Eldin Fayez (Egypt).
Vice-Chairmen: Slawomir Cytrycki (Poland), Jesper Knudsen (Denmark), Alfredo Ramírez Araiza (Mexico).
Rapporteur: Tadamichi Yamamoto (Japan) (first part), Minoru Shibuya (Japan) (second part).

ADVISORY COMMITTEE ON SCIENCE
AND TECHNOLOGY FOR DEVELOPMENT
The 28-member Advisory Committee on Science and Technology for Development held its second session at United Nations Headquarters from 9 to 19 February 1982.

Members:
To serve until 31 December 1982: Daniel Adzei Bekoe (Ghana); Umberto Colombo, *Vice-Chairman* (Italy); Bernard M. J. Delapalme (France); Jan Gabel (Czechoslovakia); Henri Hogbe-Nlend, *Vice-Chairman* (United Republic of Cameroon); Jorge Katz (Argentina); Abdelsalam Majali (Jordan); Cyril Agodi Onwumechili (Nigeria); Keichi Oshima (Japan); Armando Samper (Colombia); Sitali Mundia Silangwa (Zambia);[a] M. S. Swaminathan, *Chairman* (India); José Israel Vargas (Brazil);[a] Rudolf Wittenzellner (Federal Republic of Germany).
To serve until 31 December 1983: Sadak Ben Jamaa, *Vice-Chairman* (Tunisia);[a] Just Faaland (Norway); Edmundo Flores (Mexico); Peter Gacii (Kenya); Radouane Hamida (Algeria); Dennis Irvine (Jamaica); Lin Hua (China);[a,b] Loretta Makasiar-Sicat (Philippines); Rodney W. Nichols (United States); V. I. Popkov (USSR); Bachtiar Rifai (Indonesia); Leopold Schmetterer (Austria); Adnan Shihab-Eldin (Kuwait); Klaus Stubenrauch, *Vice-Chairman* (German Democratic Republic).

[a]Did not attend the second session.
[b]Resigned by a letter of 10 February 1982; replaced by Lu Jing-ting (China), who was appointed by the Intergovernmental Committee on 4 June.

On 4 June 1982, the Intergovernmental Committee decided as an exception to extend the terms of office of the current members of the Advisory Committee for one year, until 31 December 1983 and 31 December 1984, respectively. Members were normally to be appointed for three-year terms.

Interim Committee of the General Assembly

The Interim Committee of the General Assembly, on which each Member of the United Nations has the right to appoint one representative, was originally established by the General Assembly in 1947[7] to function between the Assembly's regular sessions. It was re-established in 1948[8] for a further year and in 1949[9] for an indefinite period. The Committee has not met since 29 June 1961.[10]

Interim Committee of the United Nations Conference on an International Code of Conduct on the Transfer of Technology

The Interim Committee of the United Nations Conference on an International Code of Conduct on the Transfer of Technology, open to the participation of all States members of UNCTAD, held three sessions in 1982, at Geneva: its first from 1 to 5 March; its second from 17 to 21 May; and its third and final session from 20 September to 1 October.

Chairman: Miroslav Pravda (Czechoslovakia).
Vice-Chairmen: A. M. Plate (Netherlands), José Ramón Sanchis Muñoz (Argentina).

Interim Committee on New and Renewable Sources of Energy

The Interim Committee on New and Renewable Sources of Energy, open to the participation of all States as full members, held its only session at Rome, Italy, from 7 to 18 June 1982. Represented at the session were:

Afghanistan, Algeria, Angola, Argentina, Australia, Austria, Bangladesh, Belgium, Benin, Bhutan, Brazil, Bulgaria, Burundi, Canada, Cape Verde, Central African Republic, Chile, China, Colombia, Comoros, Costa Rica, Czechoslovakia, Democratic People's Republic of Korea, Denmark, Dominican Republic, Ecuador, Egypt, El Salvador, Finland, France, German Democratic Republic, Germany, Federal Republic of, Ghana, Greece, Guinea, Guinea-Bissau, Haiti, Hungary, India, Indonesia, Iran, Iraq, Ireland,

[7]Resolution 111(II), 13 November 1947 (YUN 1947-48, p. 80).
[8]Resolution 196(III), 3 December 1948 (YUN 1948-49, p. 407).
[9]Resolution 295(IV), 21 November 1949 (*ibid.*, p. 411).
[10]YUN 1961, p. 705.

Israel, Italy, Ivory Coast, Jamaica, Japan, Jordan, Kenya, Lao People's Democratic Republic, Lebanon, Lesotho, Malawi, Malaysia, Mali, Mexico, Morocco, Nepal, Netherlands, New Zealand, Nicaragua, Niger, Norway, Pakistan, Panama, Paraguay, Peru, Philippines, Poland, Portugal, Romania, Rwanda, Somalia, Spain, Sri Lanka, Sudan, Sweden, Switzerland, Thailand, Tunisia, Turkey, Uganda, USSR, United Arab Emirates, United Kingdom, United Republic of Cameroon, United Republic of Tanzania, United States, Uruguay, Venezuela, Yemen, Yugoslavia, Zambia.

Chairman: Sergio Cattani (Italy).
Vice-Chairmen: Marcelo Didier (Brazil), Erten Kayalibay (Turkey), Andrew Ligale (Kenya).
Rapporteur: Ion Margineanu (Romania).

International Civil Service Commission

The International Civil Service Commission consists of 15 members who serve in their personal capacity as individuals of recognized competence in public administration or related fields, particularly in personnel management. They are appointed by the General Assembly, with due regard for equitable geographical distribution, for four-year terms.

The Commission held two sessions in 1982: its fifteenth at Geneva from 1 to 19 March; and its sixteenth at United Nations Headquarters from 12 to 30 July.

Members:
To serve until 31 December 1982: Richard M. Akwei, *Chairman* (Ghana); Gastón de Prat Gay, *Vice-Chairman* (Argentina); Moulaye El Hassen (Mauritania); Pascal Frochaux (Switzerland); Jiri Nosek (Czechoslovakia).
To serve until 31 December 1984: Syed Amjad Ali (Pakistan); Michael O. Ani (Nigeria); A. S. Chistyakov (USSR); M. A. Vellodi (India); Halima Embarek Warzazi (Morocco).
To serve until 31 December 1985: Ralph Enckell (Finland); Jean-Claude Fortuit (France); Helmut Kitschenberg (Federal Republic of Germany); Akira Matsui (Japan);[a] António Fonseca Pimentel (Brazil).

[a]Resigned with effect from 31 December 1982; Masao Kanazawa (Japan) was appointed by the General Assembly on 21 December (decision 37/325) for a three-year term beginning on 1 January 1983 to fill the resultant vacancy.

On 21 December 1982 (decision 37/325), the General Assembly appointed the following members for a four-year term beginning on 1 January 1983 to fill the vacancies occurring on 31 December 1982: Richard M. Akwei (Ghana), Gastón de Prat Gay (Argentina), Moulaye El Hassen (Mauritania), Dayton W. Hull (United States), Jiri Nosek (Czechoslovakia). By the same decision, the Assembly designated Richard M. Akwei as *Chairman* and Gastón de Prat Gay as *Vice-Chairman* for the same term.

ADVISORY COMMITTEE ON
POST ADJUSTMENT QUESTIONS
The Advisory Committee on Post Adjustment Questions consists of six members, of whom five are chosen from the geographical regions of Africa, Asia, Latin America, Eastern Europe, and Western Europe and other States; and one, from ICSC, who serves *ex officio* as Chairman. Members are appointed by the ICSC Chairman to serve for four-year terms.

The Advisory Committee held its seventh session at Vienna, Austria, from 17 to 28 May 1982.

Members:
To serve until 31 December 1982: Stephen Van Dyke Baer (United States).
To serve until 31 December 1983: A. F. Revenko (USSR).
To serve until 31 December 1984: G. K. Nair (Malaysia).
To serve until 31 December 1985: Nana Wereko Ampem II (also known as Emmanuel Noi Omaboe) (Ghana);[a] Janes A. de Souza (Brazil).[a]
Ex-officio member: Pascal Frochaux, *Chairman* (Switzerland).

[a]Reappointed in January 1982.

International Law Commission

The International Law Commission consists of 34 persons of recognized competence in international law, elected by the General Assem-

bly to serve in their individual capacity for a five-year term. Vacancies occurring within the five-year period are filled by the Commission.

The Commission held its thirty-fourth session at Geneva from 3 May to 23 July 1982.

Members (until 31 December 1986): Richard Osuolale A. Akinjide (Nigeria); Riyadh Mahmoud Sami Al-Qaysi (Iraq); Balanda Mikuin Leliel (Zaire); Julio Barboza (Argentina); Boutros Boutros-Ghali (Egypt); Carlos Calero Rodrigues (Brazil); Jorge Castañeda (Mexico); Leonardo Díaz-González, *First Vice-Chairman* (Venezuela); Khalafalla El Rasheed Mohamed-Ahmed (Sudan); Jens Evensen (Norway); Constantin Flitan, *Second Vice-Chairman* (Romania); Laurel B. Francis (Jamaica); Jorge Enrique Illueca (Panama); Andreas J. Jacovides (Cyprus); S. P. Jagota (India); Abdul G. Koroma (Sierra Leone); José Manuel Lacleta Muñoz (Spain); Ahmed Mahiou (Algeria);[a] Chafic Malek (Lebanon); Stephen C. McCaffrey (United States); Ni Zhengyu (China); Frank X. J. C. Njenga, *Rapporteur* (Kenya); Motoo Ogiso (Japan); Syed Sharifuddin Pirzada (Pakistan); Robert Q. Quentin-Baxter (New Zealand); Edilbert Razafindralambo (Madagascar); Paul Reuter, *Chairman* (France); Willem Riphagen (Netherlands); Sir Ian Sinclair (United Kingdom); Constantin A. Stavropoulos (Greece); Sompong Sucharitkul (Thailand); Doudou Thiam (Senegal); N. A. Ushakov (USSR); Alexander Yankov (Bulgaria).

[a]Elected by the Commission on 6 May 1982 to fill the vacancy created by the resignation of Mohammed Bedjaoui (Algeria) upon his election to the International Court of Justice on 19 March.

Investments Committee

The Investments Committee consists of nine members appointed by the Secretary-General, after consultation with the United Nations Joint Staff Pension Board and ACABQ, subject to confirmation by the General Assembly. Members serve for three-year terms.

Members:
To serve until 31 December 1982: Aloysio de Andrade Faria; Braj Kumar Nehru, *Chairman;* Stanislaw Raczkowski.
To serve until 31 December 1983: David Montagu; Yves Oltramare; Emmanuel Noi Omaboe (also known as Nana Wereko Ampem II).
To serve until 31 December 1984: Jean Guyot; George Johnston; Michiya Matsukawa.

In addition, during 1982, Juergen Reimnitz served in an *ad hoc* consultative capacity.

On 17 December 1982 (decision 37/316), the General Assembly confirmed the appointment by the Secretary-General of Aloysio de Andrade Faria, Braj Kumar Nehru and Stanislaw Raczkowski as members for a three-year term beginning on 1 January 1983.

Joint Advisory Group on the International
Trade Centre UNCTAD/GATT

The Joint Advisory Group was established in accordance with an agreement between UNCTAD and GATT with effect from 1 January 1968, the date on which under their joint sponsorship the International Trade Centre commenced operations.

Participation in the Group is open to all States members of UNCTAD and to all Contracting Parties to GATT.

The Group, which normally meets annually, held two sessions in 1982, at Geneva: its resumed fourteenth on 21 January; and its fifteenth from 22 to 26 March.

Resumed fourteenth session
Chairman: Plácido García Reynoso (Mexico).[a]
Vice-Chairman: Wiebo J. Rijpma (Netherlands).
Rapporteur: Antal Szentfulopi (Hungary).

[a]Did not attend the resumed fourteenth session; in his absence, the Vice-Chairman presided.

Fifteenth session
Chairman: Wiebo J. Rijpma (Netherlands).
Vice-Chairman: Sukon Kanchanalai (Thailand).
Rapporteur: Andrzej S. Horoszkiewicz (Poland).

TECHNICAL COMMITTEE

The Technical Committee of the Joint Advisory Group on the International Trade Centre UNCTAD/GATT meets annually to review the Centre's work programme and organizational structure and reports to the Group.

The Committee, which is open to the participation of experts, as well as officials responsible for national trade promotion activities, from any country represented in the Joint Advisory Group, held its eleventh session at Geneva from 18 to 22 January 1982.

Chairman: Arvind Govind Barvé (Kenya).

Joint Inspection Unit

The Joint Inspection Unit consists of not more than 11 Inspectors appointed by the General Assembly from candidates nominated by Member States following appropriate consultations, including consultations with the President of the Economic and Social Council and with the Chairman of ACC. The Inspectors, chosen for their special experience in national or international administrative and financial matters, with due regard for equitable geographical distribution and reasonable rotation, serve in their personal capacity for five-year terms.

Members:
To serve until 31 December 1982:[a] Mark E. Allen (United Kingdom); A. S. Bryntsev (USSR); Toman Hutagalung (Indonesia); Julio C. Rodríguez Arias (Argentina); Joseph Adolph Sawe (United Republic of Tanzania); Zakaria Sibahi (Syrian Arab Republic).
To serve until 31 December 1985: Maurice Bertrand, *Chairman* (France); Alfred Nathaniel Forde (Barbados); Moustapha Ould Khalifa (Mauritania); Earl D. Sohm (United States); Miljenko Vukovic, *Vice-Chairman* (Yugoslavia).

[a]Members to fill the vacancies occurring on 31 December 1982 were appointed by the General Assembly on 17 December 1981 (YUN 1981, p. 1514).

Negotiating Committee on the Financial Emergency of the United Nations

Established in 1975 by the General Assembly[11] to consist of 54 Member States appointed by its President on the basis of equitable geographical balance, the Negotiating Committee on the Financial Emergency of the United Nations has a membership of 48. It has not met since 1976.[12]

Members: Argentina, Austria, Bangladesh, Bolivia, Canada, Chad, Colombia, Cuba, Ecuador, Egypt, Finland, France, Gabon, German Democratic Republic, Germany, Federal Republic of, Ghana, Greece, Grenada, India, Indonesia, Iran, Ireland, Italy, Jamaica, Japan, Jordan, Kenya, Kuwait, Libyan Arab Jamahiriya, Malawi, Mexico, Morocco, Nigeria, Pakistan, Philippines, Poland, Spain, Sudan, Swaziland, Sweden, Trinidad and Tobago, Tunisia, Turkey, USSR, United Kingdom, United States, Upper Volta, Venezuela.

Office of the United Nations High Commissioner for Refugees (UNHCR)

EXECUTIVE COMMITTEE OF THE HIGH COMMISSIONER'S PROGRAMME

The Executive Committee's membership rose from 40 to 41 on 16 April 1982, when the Economic and Social Council, responding to a 1981 General Assembly request,[13] granted membership to Namibia, represented by the United Nations Council for Namibia (decision 1982/110).

The Executive Committee held its thirty-third session at Geneva from 11 to 20 October 1982.

Members: Algeria, Argentina, Australia, Austria, Belgium, Brazil, Canada, China, Colombia, Denmark, Finland, France, Germany, Federal Republic of, Greece, Holy See, Iran, Israel, Italy, Japan, Lebanon, Lesotho, Madagascar, Morocco, Netherlands, Nicaragua, Nigeria, Norway, Sudan, Sweden, Switzerland, Thailand, Tunisia, Turkey, Uganda, United Kingdom, United Republic of Tanzania, United States, Venezuela, Yugoslavia, Zaire; Namibia (represented by the United Nations Council for Namibia).

Chairman: Ibrahim Kharma (Lebanon).
Vice-Chairman: Hans V. Ewerlof (Sweden).
Rapporteur: I. Lejri (Tunisia).

United Nations High Commissioner for Refugees: Poul Hartling.[a]
Deputy High Commissioner: William Richard Smyser.

[a]Re-elected by the General Assembly on 18 December 1982 (decision 37/319) for a further three-year term beginning on 1 January 1983.

SUB-COMMITTEE OF THE WHOLE ON INTERNATIONAL PROTECTION

The Sub-Committee of the Whole on International Protection held its seventh meeting at Geneva on 7, 8 and 12 October 1982.

Chairman: Peter H. R. Marshall (United Kingdom).

SUB-COMMITTEE ON ADMINISTRATIVE AND FINANCIAL MATTERS

The Sub-Committee on Administrative and Financial Matters, which is composed of all members of the Executive Committee, held its second meeting at Geneva concurrently with the seventh meeting of the Sub-Committee of the Whole on International Protection.

Chairman: Ibrahim Kharma (Lebanon).

Panel for Inquiry and Conciliation

The Panel for Inquiry and Conciliation was created by the General Assembly in 1949[14] to consist of qualified persons, designated by United Nations Member States, each to serve for a term of five years. Information concerning the Panel's composition had from time to time been communicated to the Assembly and the Security Council; the last consolidated list was issued by the Secretary-General in a note of 20 January 1961.

Panel of External Auditors

The Panel of External Auditors consists of the members of the United Nations Board of Auditors and the appointed external auditors of the specialized agencies and IAEA.

Panel of Military Experts

The General Assembly's "Uniting for Peace" resolution[15] called for the appointment of military experts to be available, on request, to United Nations Member States wishing to obtain technical advice on the organization, training and equipment of elements within their national armed forces which could be made available, in accordance with national constitutional processes, for service as a unit or units of the United Nations upon the recommendation of the Security Council or the Assembly.

Peace Observation Commission

The Peace Observation Commission did not meet in 1982. On 27 April, the Committee for Programme and Co-ordination, in reviewing the proposed medium-term plan for 1984-1989, recommended termination of the Commission's mandate and hence deletion of reference to the Commission from the plan. The General Assembly adopted the revised plan on 21 December, but without specific reference to the recommendation.

Members (until 31 December 1983): Czechoslovakia, France, Honduras, India, Maldives, New Zealand, Pakistan, Sweden, USSR, United Kingdom, United States, Uruguay.

Preparatory Committee for the International Conference on the Question of Palestine

The Committee on the Exercise of the Inalienable Rights of the Palestinian People (p. 1623) was designated by the General Assembly as the Preparatory Committee for the International Conference on the Question of Palestine, to be convened under United Nations auspices in 1983.

---

[11]Resolution 3538(XXX), 17 December 1975 (YUN 1975, p. 957).
[12]YUN 1976, pp. 889 and 1064.
[13]Resolution 36/121 D, para. 7, 10 December 1981 (YUN 1981, p. 1165).
[14]Resolution 268 D (III), 28 April 1949 (YUN 1948-49, p. 416).
[15]Resolution 377(V), part A, para. 10, 3 November 1950 (YUN 1950, p. 194).

The Preparatory Committee held its first session at United Nations Headquarters from 31 March to 22 October 1982.

Chairman: Massamba Sarré (Senegal).
Vice-Chairmen: Raúl Roa Kouri (Cuba), Mohammad Farid Zarif (Afghanistan).
Rapporteur: Victor J. Gauci (Malta).

Preparatory Committee for the Second Special Session of the General Assembly Devoted to Disarmament

The 78-member Preparatory Committee for the Second Special Session of the General Assembly Devoted to Disarmament (the twelfth special session, held from 7 June to 10 July 1982), held its fourth and final session at United Nations Headquarters from 26 April to 14 May 1982.

Members: Algeria, Argentina, Australia, Austria, Bahamas, Bangladesh, Belgium, Benin, Brazil, Bulgaria, Burundi, Byelorussian SSR, Canada, China, Colombia, Congo, Costa Rica, Cuba, Cyprus, Czechoslovakia, Denmark, Ecuador, Egypt, Ethiopia, Fiji, Finland, France, German Democratic Republic, Germany, Federal Republic of, Greece, Guyana, Honduras, Hungary, India, Indonesia, Iran, Iraq, Italy, Jamaica, Japan, Kenya, Lebanon, Liberia, Libyan Arab Jamahiriya, Malaysia, Mauritius, Mexico, Mongolia, Morocco, Nepal, Netherlands, New Zealand, Nigeria, Norway, Pakistan, Panama, Peru, Philippines, Poland, Romania, Senegal, Sierra Leone, Spain, Sri Lanka, Sudan, Suriname, Sweden, Tunisia, Turkey, Ukrainian SSR, USSR, United Kingdom, United Republic of Tanzania, United States, Venezuela, Yugoslavia, Zaire, Zambia.

Chairman: Oluyemi Adeniji (Nigeria).
Vice-Chairmen: Australia, Bahamas, Bangladesh, Benin, Bulgaria, German Democratic Republic, India, Italy, Japan, Mexico, Morocco, Peru, Yugoslavia.
Rapporteur: Omer Ersun (Turkey).

Preparatory Committee for the Second United Nations Conference on the Exploration and Peaceful Uses of Outer Space

The Committee on the Peaceful Uses of Outer Space was designated by the General Assembly as the Preparatory Committee for the Second United Nations Conference on the Exploration and Peaceful Uses of Outer Space (p. 1636).

The Preparatory Committee held its fourth and final session during the twenty-fifth session of the Committee on the Peaceful Uses of Outer Space (p. 1623) and on 6 April.

Chairman: Peter Jankowitsch (Austria).
Vice-Chairman: Teodor Marinescu (Romania).
Rapporteur: Carlos Antonio Bettencourt Bueno (Brazil).

ADVISORY COMMITTEE TO THE PREPARATORY COMMITTEE
FOR THE SECOND UNITED NATIONS CONFERENCE ON
THE EXPLORATION AND PEACEFUL USES OF OUTER SPACE

The Scientific and Technical Sub-Committee of the Committee on the Peaceful Uses of Outer Space was designated by the General Assembly as the Advisory Committee to the Preparatory Committee for the Second United Nations Conference on the Exploration and Peaceful Uses of Outer Space.

The Advisory Committee held its third and final session during the nineteenth session of the Scientific and Technical Sub-Committee.

Chairman: J. H. Carver (Australia).

Preparatory Committee for the United Nations Conference for the Promotion of International Co-operation in the Peaceful Uses of Nuclear Energy

In 1982, the Preparatory Committee for the United Nations Conference for the Promotion of International Co-operation in the Peaceful Uses of Nuclear Energy (scheduled for 1983), which was to be composed of 70 Member States and, on an equal footing, other Member States which might express interest in participating in the Committee's work, had a membership of 64. It held two sessions during the year,

at Vienna, Austria: its second from 21 to 30 June; and its third from 27 October to 2 November.

Members: Algeria, Argentina, Australia, Austria, Belgium, Brazil, Bulgaria, Byelorussian SSR, Canada, Chile, China, Colombia, Costa Rica,[a] Cuba, Czechoslovakia, Denmark, Ecuador,[b] Egypt, Finland, France, German Democratic Republic, Germany, Federal Republic of, Ghana,[a] Greece, Guatemala,[a,b] Hungary, India, Indonesia, Iraq, Ireland,[c] Italy, Ivory Coast,[a,c] Japan, Libyan Arab Jamahiriya, Malaysia, Mauritania,[a,b] Mexico, Morocco,[b] Netherlands, Niger,[a,b,c] Nigeria,[b,c] Norway, Pakistan, Peru, Philippines,[b] Poland, Romania, Senegal,[a,b,c] Spain, Sri Lanka,[a,b] Sweden, Syrian Arab Republic,[b] Thailand, Turkey, Ukrainian SSR, USSR, United Arab Emirates, United Kingdom, United Republic of Cameroon,[a,b,c] United States, Uruguay, Venezuela, Yugoslavia, Zaire.

[a]Not represented at the third session.
[b]Not represented at the second session.
[c]Appointed by the President of the General Assembly's thirty-sixth session on 16 June 1982.

Chairman: Novak Pribicevic (Yugoslavia).
Vice-Chairmen: F. K. A. Allotey (Ghana); Essam El-Din Hawas (Egypt); Suror Merza Mahmoud (Iraq); L. A. Olivieri (Argentina); Miroslav Oplt (Czechoslovakia); Alvaro Salcedo Rubio (Peru) (until 30 June); Augusto Arzubiaga Rospigliosi (Peru) (from 30 June); B. Skala (Sweden); Frans J. A. Terwisscha van Scheltinga (Netherlands).
Rapporteur: Dalindra Aman (Indonesia).

Special Committee against *Apartheid*

The Special Committee against *Apartheid* has a membership of 18. Additional members remained to be appointed by the end of 1982 in pursuance of a 1979 General Assembly request[16] to increase that number.

Members: Algeria, German Democratic Republic, Ghana, Guinea, Haiti, Hungary, India, Indonesia, Malaysia, Nepal, Nigeria, Peru, Philippines, Somalia, Sudan, Syrian Arab Republic, Trinidad and Tobago, Ukrainian SSR.

Chairman: Alhaji Yusuff Maitama-Sule (Nigeria).
Vice-Chairmen: Uddhav Deo Bhatt (Nepal), V. A. Kravets (Ukrainian SSR).
Rapporteur: Gervais Charles (Haiti).

SUB-COMMITTEE ON PETITIONS AND INFORMATION
Members: Algeria *(Chairman)*, German Democratic Republic, Nepal, Somalia, Trinidad and Tobago.

SUB-COMMITTEE ON THE IMPLEMENTATION
OF UNITED NATIONS RESOLUTIONS
AND COLLABORATION WITH SOUTH AFRICA
Members: Ghana *(Chairman)*, Hungary, India, Peru, Sudan.

Special Committee on Enhancing the Effectiveness of the Principle of Non-Use of Force in International Relations

The 35-member Special Committee on Enhancing the Effectiveness of the Principle of Non-Use of Force in International Relations held one series of meetings at United Nations Headquarters between 29 March and 23 April 1982.

Members: Belgium, Benin, Bulgaria, Cuba, Cyprus, Ecuador, Egypt, Finland, France, Germany, Federal Republic of, Greece, Guinea, Hungary, India, Iraq, Italy, Japan, Mexico, Mongolia, Morocco, Nepal, Nicaragua,[a] Panama,[a] Peru,[a] Poland, Romania, Senegal, Somalia, Spain, Togo, Turkey, Uganda, USSR, United Kingdom, United States.

[a]Replaced Argentina, Brazil and Chile in accordance with a system of rotation agreed upon by the Latin American States when the Special Committee was constituted.

---

[16]Resolution 34/93 R, 17 December 1979 (YUN 1979, p. 201).

Chairman: Nabil A. Elaraby (Egypt).
Vice-Chairmen: Mohammed Al-Haj Hammond (Iraq), Ryszard Krystosik (Poland), Olga Valdés Pérez (Cuba).
Rapporteur: Antonio Viñal (Spain).

Special Committee on Peace-keeping Operations

The 33-member Special Committee on Peace-keeping Operations did not meet in 1982.

Members: Afghanistan, Algeria, Argentina, Australia, Austria, Canada, Denmark, Egypt, El Salvador, Ethiopia, France, German Democratic Republic, Guatemala, Hungary, India, Iraq, Italy, Japan, Mauritania, Mexico, Netherlands, Nigeria, Pakistan, Poland, Romania, Sierra Leone, Spain, Thailand, USSR, United Kingdom, United States, Venezuela, Yugoslavia.

WORKING GROUP
Members: France, India, Mexico, Pakistan, USSR, United Kingdom, United States, and the officers of the Special Committee.

Special Committee on the Charter of the United Nations and on the Strengthening of the Role of the Organization

The 47-member Special Committee on the Charter of the United Nations and on the Strengthening of the Role of the Organization held a series of meetings at Geneva between 22 February and 19 March 1982.

Members: Algeria, Argentina, Barbados, Belgium, Brazil, China, Colombia, Congo, Cyprus, Czechoslovakia, Ecuador, Egypt, El Salvador, Finland, France, German Democratic Republic, Germany, Federal Republic of, Ghana, Greece, Guyana, India, Indonesia, Iran, Iraq, Italy, Japan, Kenya, Liberia, Mexico, Nepal, New Zealand, Nigeria, Pakistan, Philippines, Poland, Romania, Rwanda, Sierra Leone, Spain, Tunisia, Turkey, USSR, United Kingdom, United States, Venezuela, Yugoslavia, Zambia.

Chairman: Siegfried Zachmann (German Democratic Republic).
Vice-Chairmen: Mario Alemán (Ecuador), Bengt H. G. A. Broms (Finland), Ignace Karuhije (Rwanda).
Rapporteur: María Lourdes Ramiro Lopez (Philippines).

Special Committee on the Situation with regard to the Implementation of the Declaration on the Granting of Independence to Colonial Countries and Peoples

Members: Afghanistan, Australia, Bulgaria, Chile, China, Congo, Cuba, Czechoslovakia, Ethiopia, Fiji, India, Indonesia, Iran, Iraq, Ivory Coast, Mali, Norway, Sierra Leone, Syrian Arab Republic, Trinidad and Tobago, Tunisia, USSR, United Republic of Tanzania, Venezuela, Yugoslavia.

Chairman: Frank Owen Abdulah (Trinidad and Tobago).
Vice-Chairmen: Stefan Kalina (Czechoslovakia), Ole Peter Kolby (Norway), Abdul G. Koroma (Sierra Leone).
Rapporteur: Mohamed Farouk Adhami (Syrian Arab Republic).

SUB-COMMITTEE ON PETITIONS, INFORMATION AND ASSISTANCE
Members: Bulgaria, Congo, Cuba, Czechoslovakia *(Chairman)*, Indonesia, Iran, Iraq, Mali, Norway, Sierra Leone, Syrian Arab Republic, Tunisia, United Republic of Tanzania.

SUB-COMMITTEE ON SMALL TERRITORIES
Members: Afghanistan, Australia *(Rapporteur)*, Bulgaria, Chile, Cuba, Czechoslovakia, Ethiopia, Fiji, India, Indonesia, Iran, Iraq, Ivory Coast *(Chairman)*, Mali, Norway, Trinidad and Tobago, United Republic of Tanzania, Venezuela, Yugoslavia.

WORKING GROUP
In 1982, the Working Group of the Special Committee, which functions as a steering committee, consisted of: Congo, Cuba, Iran, Tunisia; the five officers of the Special Committee; and the Chairman and the Rapporteur of the Sub-Committee on Small Territories.

Special Committee to Investigate Israeli Practices Affecting the Human Rights of the Population of the Occupied Territories

Members: Senegal, Sri Lanka *(Chairman)*, Yugoslavia.

Special Committee to Select the Winners of the United Nations Human Rights Prize

The Special Committee to Select the Winners of the United Nations Human Rights Prize was established pursuant to a 1966 resolution of the General Assembly[17] recommending that a prize or prizes in the field of human rights be awarded not more often than at five-year intervals. Prizes were awarded for the third time on 11 December 1978.[18]

Members: The President of the General Assembly, the President of the Economic and Social Council, the Chairman of the Commission on Human Rights, the Chairman of the Commission on the Status of Women and the Chairman of the Sub-Commission on Prevention of Discrimination and Protection of Minorities.

United Nations Administrative Tribunal

Members:
To serve until 31 December 1982: Mrs. Paul Bastid, *First Vice-President* (France); Mutuale Tshikankie (Zaire); Samarendranath Sen, *Second Vice-President* (India).
To serve until 31 December 1983: Arnold Wilfred Geoffrey Kean (United Kingdom); Herbert K. Reis (United States).
To serve until 31 December 1984: Luis María de Posadas Montero (Uruguay); Endre Ustor, *President* (Hungary).

On 17 December 1982 (decision 37/317), the General Assembly appointed Mutuale Tshikankie (Zaire), Roger Pinto (France) and Samarendranath Sen (India) for a three-year term beginning on 1 January 1983 to fill the vacancies occurring on 31 December 1982.

United Nations Capital Development Fund

The United Nations Capital Development Fund was set up as an organ of the General Assembly to function as an autonomous organization within the United Nations framework, with the control of its policies and operations to be exercised by a 24-member Executive Board elected by the General Assembly from Members of the United Nations or members of the specialized agencies or of IAEA. The chief executive officer of the Fund, the Managing Director, exercises his functions under the general direction of the Executive Board. The Executive Board reports to the General Assembly through the Economic and Social Council.

EXECUTIVE BOARD
The UNDP Governing Council (p. 1648) acts as the Executive Board of the Fund—and the UNDP Administrator as its Managing Director (see below)—in conformity with measures the General Assembly adopted provisionally in 1967[19] and reconfirmed yearly until 1980.[20] In 1981 the Assembly decided that UNDP would continue to provide the Fund with, among other things, all headquarters administrative support services;[21] the Fund thus continued to operate under the same arrangements, which remained unchanged in 1982.

Managing Director: F. Bradford Morse (UNDP Administrator).

United Nations Children's Fund (UNICEF)

EXECUTIVE BOARD
The Executive Board of UNICEF (p. 1647) reports to the Economic and Social Council and, as appropriate, to the General Assembly.

United Nations Commission on International Trade Law (UNCITRAL)

The United Nations Commission on International Trade Law consists of 36 members elected by the General Assembly, in accordance with a

---

[17]Resolution 2217 A (XXI), annex, recommendation C, 19 December 1966 (YUN 1966, p. 458).
[18]YUN 1978, p. 721.
[19]Resolution 2321(XXII), para. 1 *(a)* & *(b)*, 15 December 1967 (YUN 1967, p. 372).
[20]Decision 35/422, para. *(c)*, 5 December 1980 (YUN 1980, p. 607).
[21]Resolution 36/196, para. 6, 17 December 1981 (YUN 1981, p. 469).

formula providing equitable geographical representation and adequate representation of the principal economic and legal systems of the world. Members serve for six-year terms.

The Commission held its fifteenth session at United Nations Headquarters from 26 July to 6 August 1982.

Members:

To serve until the day preceding the Commission's regular annual session in 1983 (23 May): Australia, Austria, Burundi,[a] Chile, Colombia, Egypt, Finland, France, German Democratic Republic, Ghana, Indonesia, Japan, Nigeria, Singapore, USSR, United Kingdom, United Republic of Tanzania.

To serve until the day preceding the Commission's regular annual session in 1986: Cuba, Cyprus,[a] Czechoslovakia, Germany, Federal Republic of, Guatemala, Hungary, India, Iraq, Italy, Kenya, Peru, Philippines, Senegal,[a] Sierra Leone, Spain, Trinidad and Tobago, Uganda, United States, Yugoslavia.

[a]Not represented at the fifteenth session.

Chairman: Rafael Eyzaguirre (Chile).
Vice-Chairmen: Alfred Duchek (Austria), Fawzi M. Sami (Iraq), H. M. Joko Smart (Sierra Leone).
Rapporteur: Fritz Enderlein (German Democratic Republic).

On 15 November 1982 (decision 37/308), the General Assembly elected the following for a six-year term beginning on the first day of the regular annual session in 1983 (24 May) to fill the vacancies occurring the day before: Algeria, Australia, Austria, Brazil, Central African Republic, China, Egypt, France, German Democratic Republic, Japan, Mexico, Nigeria, Singapore, Sweden, USSR, United Kingdom, United Republic of Tanzania.

WORKING GROUP ON
INTERNATIONAL CONTRACT PRACTICES
The Working Group on International Contract Practices held two sessions in 1982: its third at United Nations Headquarters from 16 to 26 February; and its fourth at Vienna, Austria, from 4 to 15 October.

Members: Austria, Czechoslovakia, France, Ghana,[a,b] Guatemala,[b] Hungary, India,[b] Japan, Kenya, Philippines, Sierra Leone,[b] Trinidad and Tobago,[b] USSR, United Kingdom, United States.

[a]Not represented at the third session.
[b]Not represented at the fourth session.

Chairman: I. Szasz (Hungary).
Rapporteur: Jorge Skinner-Klee (Guatemala) (third session), Stephen K. Muchui (Kenya) (fourth session).

WORKING GROUP ON
INTERNATIONAL NEGOTIABLE INSTRUMENTS
The Working Group on International Negotiable Instruments held its twelfth and final session at Vienna, Austria, from 4 to 12 January 1982.

Members: Chile, Egypt, France, India, Nigeria,[a] USSR, United Kingdom, United States.

[a]Not represented at the twelfth session.

Chairman: Joë Galby (France).
Rapporteur: Malena Saavedra (Chile).

WORKING GROUP ON THE
NEW INTERNATIONAL ECONOMIC ORDER
The Working Group on the New International Economic Order, which is composed of all States members of UNCITRAL, held its third session at United Nations Headquarters from 12 to 23 July 1982. All the members were represented except Burundi, Cuba, Cyprus, Hungary, Senegal, Singapore, Spain and the United Republic of Tanzania.

Chairman: Leif Sevon (Finland).
Rapporteur: Peter Kihara Mathanjuki (Kenya).

United Nations Conciliation Commission for Palestine
Members: France, Turkey, United States.

**United Nations Conference on Trade
and Development (UNCTAD)**
Members of UNCTAD are Members of the United Nations or members of the specialized agencies or of IAEA.

TRADE AND DEVELOPMENT BOARD
The Trade and Development Board is a permanent organ of UNCTAD. Its membership is drawn from the following list of UNCTAD members.

Part A. Afghanistan, Algeria, Angola, Bahrain, Bangladesh, Benin, Bhutan, Botswana, Burma, Burundi, Cape Verde, Central African Republic, Chad, China, Comoros, Congo, Democratic Kampuchea, Democratic People's Republic of Korea, Democratic Yemen, Djibouti, Egypt, Equatorial Guinea, Ethiopia, Fiji, Gabon, Gambia, Ghana, Guinea, Guinea-Bissau, India, Indonesia, Iran, Iraq, Israel, Ivory Coast, Jordan, Kenya, Kuwait, Lao People's Democratic Republic, Lebanon, Lesotho, Liberia, Libyan Arab Jamahiriya, Madagascar, Malawi, Malaysia, Maldives, Mali, Mauritania, Mauritius, Mongolia, Morocco, Mozambique, Nepal, Niger, Nigeria, Oman, Pakistan, Papua New Guinea, Philippines, Qatar, Republic of Korea, Rwanda, Samoa, Sao Tome and Principe, Saudi Arabia, Senegal, Seychelles, Sierra Leone, Singapore, Solomon Islands, Somalia, South Africa, Sri Lanka, Sudan, Swaziland, Syrian Arab Republic, Thailand, Togo, Tonga, Tunisia, Uganda, United Arab Emirates, United Republic of Cameroon, United Republic of Tanzania, Upper Volta, Vanuatu,[a] Viet Nam, Yemen, Yugoslavia, Zaire, Zambia, Zimbabwe;[a] Namibia.[a]

Part B. Australia, Austria, Belgium, Canada, Cyprus, Denmark, Finland, France, Germany, Federal Republic of, Greece, Holy See, Iceland, Ireland, Italy, Japan, Liechtenstein, Luxembourg, Malta, Monaco, Netherlands, New Zealand, Norway, Portugal, San Marino, Spain, Sweden, Switzerland, Turkey, United Kingdom, United States.

Part C. Antigua and Barbuda,[b] Argentina, Bahamas, Barbados, Belize,[a] Bolivia, Brazil, Chile, Colombia, Costa Rica, Cuba, Dominica, Dominican Republic, Ecuador, El Salvador, Grenada, Guatemala, Guyana, Haiti, Honduras, Jamaica, Mexico, Nicaragua, Panama, Paraguay, Peru, Saint Lucia,[a] Saint Vincent and the Grenadines,[a] Suriname, Trinidad and Tobago, Uruguay, Venezuela.

Part D. Albania, Bulgaria, Byelorussian SSR, Czechoslovakia, German Democratic Republic, Hungary, Poland, Romania, Ukrainian SSR, USSR.

[a]Became members of UNCTAD after the fifth (1979) session of the Conference. By decision of the Board, they were subsequently included in Parts A (Namibia, Vanuatu and Zimbabwe) and C (Belize, Saint Lucia, and Saint Vincent and the Grenadines) for the purpose of elections, pending approval by the Conference at its sixth (1983) session.
[b]Became a member of UNCTAD after the fifth (1979) session of the Conference. On 8 March 1982, the Board decided that it should be associated with the countries listed in Part C for the purpose of elections, pending approval by the Conference at its sixth (1983) session.

BOARD MEMBERS AND SESSIONS
The membership of the Board is open to all UNCTAD members. Those wishing to become members of the Board communicate their intention to the Secretary-General of UNCTAD for transmittal to the Board President, who announces the membership on the basis of such notifications.

The Trade and Development Board held two sessions in 1982, at Geneva: its twenty-fourth from 8 to 24 March (first part), from 11 to 18 May (second part) and from 30 June to 2 July (third part); and its twenty-fifth from 6 to 23 September (first part) and from 19 to 28 October (second part).

Members: Afghanistan,[a,b,c,d] Algeria, Angola,[a,b,c] Argentina, Australia, Austria, Bahrain,[e] Bangladesh, Barbados,[b,c,d] Belgium, Benin, Bolivia, Brazil, Bulgaria, Burma, Burundi, Byelorussian SSR, Canada, Central African Republic,[a,b,c] Chad,[a,b,c,d] Chile, China, Colombia, Costa Rica,[c] Cuba, Cyprus, Czechoslovakia, Democratic People's Republic of Korea, Democratic Yemen, Denmark, Dominican Republic, Ecuador, Egypt, El Salvador, Ethiopia, Finland, France, Gabon, German Democratic Republic, Germany, Federal Republic of, Ghana, Greece, Grenada,[a,b,c,d] Guatemala, Guinea,[a,b,c,d] Guyana,[a,b,c,d] Haiti,[a,b,c]

Honduras,[a,b] Hungary, India, Indonesia, Iran,[a] Iraq, Ireland, Israel, Italy, Ivory Coast, Jamaica, Japan, Jordan, Kenya, Kuwait, Lebanon,[c] Liberia,[a,b,c] Libyan Arab Jamahiriya, Liechtenstein,[b,c,d] Luxembourg, Madagascar, Malaysia, Mali,[a,b,c,d] Malta, Mauritania,[a,b,c,d] Mauritius,[a,b,c,d] Mexico, Mongolia,[c] Morocco, Netherlands, New Zealand, Nicaragua, Nigeria, Norway, Oman, Pakistan, Panama,[a] Papua New Guinea,[a,b,c,d] Peru, Philippines, Poland, Portugal, Qatar, Republic of Korea, Romania, Saudi Arabia, Senegal, Sierra Leone,[a,b,c,d] Singapore, Somalia, Spain, Sri Lanka, Sudan, Suriname,[a,b,c,d] Sweden, Switzerland, Syrian Arab Republic, Thailand, Togo,[b,c,d] Trinidad and Tobago, Tunisia, Turkey, Uganda,[a,b,c,d] Ukrainian SSR, USSR, United Arab Emirates, United Kingdom, United Republic of Cameroon, United Republic of Tanzania, United States, Upper Volta,[a,b,c,d] Uruguay, Venezuela, Viet Nam, Yemen, Yugoslavia, Zaire, Zambia.[a,b,c,d]

[a]Not represented at the first part of the twenty-fourth session.
[b]Not represented at the second part of the twenty-fourth session.
[c]Not represented at the third part of the twenty-fourth session.
[d]Not represented at the second part of the twenty-fifth session.
[e]Became a member on 19 October 1982.

OFFICERS (BUREAU) OF THE BOARD
Twenty-fourth session
President: Gabriel O. Martínez (Argentina).
Vice-Presidents: Franz Blankart (Switzerland), Hans V. Ewerlof (Sweden), Richard Hlavaty (Czechoslovakia), Gabriel O. Ijewere (Nigeria), Alexander Tissa Jayakoddy (Sri Lanka), Frans J. C. Klinkenbergh (Netherlands), Dominique Laloux (Belgium), Fouad Mebazza (Tunisia), Janos Nyerges (Hungary), Agustín Saavedra Weise (Bolivia).
Rapporteur: Borisa Micevic (Yugoslavia).

Twenty-fifth session
President: Franz Blankart (Switzerland).
Vice-Presidents: Abd-el-Latif Al Maimani (Saudi Arabia), Salah Fellah (Algeria), William Friis-Moller (Denmark), Maung Maung Gyi (Burma), Richard Hlavaty (Czechoslovakia), Martin J. Huslid (Norway), Charles F. Meissner (United States), Eduardo Ponce (Peru), Gustavo Adolfo Vargas (Nicaragua), G. K. Zhuravlev (USSR).
Rapporteur: Kwasi Yeboah-Konadu (Ghana).

SUBSIDIARY ORGANS OF THE
TRADE AND DEVELOPMENT BOARD
The main committees of the Board are open to the participation of all interested UNCTAD members, on the understanding that those wishing to attend a particular session of one or more of the main committees communicate their intention to the Secretary-General of UNCTAD during the preceding regular session of the Board. On the basis of such notifications, the Board determines the membership of the main committees.

COMMITTEE ON COMMODITIES
The Committee on Commodities held its first special session at Geneva from 8 to 12 February 1982.

Members: Algeria, Argentina, Australia, Austria, Bangladesh, Belgium, Bolivia, Brazil, Bulgaria, Burma,[a] Burundi,[b] Canada, Central African Republic, Chad,[b] Chile, China, Colombia, Costa Rica, Cuba,[b] Czechoslovakia, Democratic People's Republic of Korea,[b] Democratic Yemen,[b] Denmark, Dominican Republic,[b] Ecuador, Egypt, El Salvador, Ethiopia, Finland, France, Gabon, German Democratic Republic, Germany, Federal Republic of, Ghana, Greece, Guatemala, Guinea,[b] Honduras, Hungary, India, Indonesia, Iran,[b] Iraq, Ireland, Israel, Italy, Ivory Coast, Jamaica, Japan, Jordan, Kenya, Liberia,[b] Libyan Arab Jamahiriya, Madagascar, Malaysia, Malta, Mauritius,[b] Mexico, Morocco, Netherlands, New Zealand, Nicaragua,[b] Nigeria, Norway, Pakistan, Panama,[b] Peru, Philippines, Poland, Qatar, Republic of Korea, Romania, Rwanda, Saudi Arabia, Senegal, Somalia,[a] Spain, Sri Lanka, Sudan, Sweden, Switzerland, Syrian Arab Republic, Thailand, Togo,[b] Trinidad and Tobago, Tunisia, Turkey, Uganda,[b] USSR, United Kingdom, United Republic of Cameroon, United Republic of Tanzania, United States, Upper Volta,[b] Uruguay, Venezuela, Viet Nam,[b] Yemen,[b] Yugoslavia, Zaire.

[a]Declared elected by the Trade and Development Board on 9 and 8 March 1982, respectively, raising the Committee's membership to 100.
[b]Not represented at the first special session.

Chairman: Witold Jozwiak (Poland).
Vice-Chairmen: Choophong Angpiroj (Thailand), D. Browne (Canada), Tatsuro Kunugi (Japan), Youssef Mokaddem (Tunisia), Carlos E. Paes de Carvalho (Brazil).
Rapporteur: Morella Ferrero (Venezuela).

COMMITTEE ON TUNGSTEN
The Committee on Tungsten held its fourteenth session at Geneva from 25 to 29 October 1982.

Members: Argentina, Australia, Austria,[a] Belgium, Bolivia, Brazil, Canada, China, Cyprus,[a] France, Gabon,[a] Germany, Federal Republic of, Italy, Japan, Mexico, Netherlands, Peru, Poland, Portugal, Republic of Korea, Romania,[a] Rwanda, Spain, Sweden, Thailand, Turkey, USSR, United Kingdom, United States.

[a]Not represented at the fourteenth session.

Chairman: B. F. Meere (Australia).
Vice-Chairman/Rapporteur: Roger P. Taylor (United Kingdom).

PERMANENT GROUP ON SYNTHETICS AND SUBSTITUTES
The Permanent Group on Synthetics and Substitutes did not meet in 1982.

Members: Argentina, Brazil, Canada, Chad, Egypt, France, Germany, Federal Republic of, Indonesia, Italy, Japan, Malaysia, Mexico, Netherlands, Nigeria, Philippines, Poland, Senegal, Sri Lanka, Sudan, Uganda, USSR, United Kingdom, United States, Viet Nam.

PERMANENT SUB-COMMITTEE ON COMMODITIES
Pursuant to a 1980 decision of the Committee on Commodities,[22] its Permanent Sub-Committee on Commodities, which had last met in 1967[23] and whose membership is identical to that of the Committee, reconvened in a second session at Geneva from 1 to 8 February 1982. All members were represented except:
Bolivia, Burundi, Central African Republic, Chad, China, Cuba, Democratic People's Republic of Korea, Democratic Yemen, Dominican Republic, Guinea, Honduras, Iran, Israel, Liberia, Libyan Arab Jamahiriya, Mauritius, Nicaragua, Panama, Qatar, Togo, Uganda, United Republic of Cameroon, Upper Volta, Viet Nam, Yemen.

Chairman: John J. Noble (Canada).
Vice-Chairmen: Jahid Rabah Ahmad (Iraq), Tatsuro Kunugi (Japan), Carlos E. Paes de Carvalho (Brazil), V. N. Polezhaev (USSR), Kifle Shenkoru (Ethiopia).
Rapporteur: Morella Ferrero (Venezuela).

COMMITTEE ON ECONOMIC CO-OPERATION
AMONG DEVELOPING COUNTRIES
The Committee on Economic Co-operation among Developing Countries did not meet in 1982.

Members: Algeria, Argentina, Australia, Austria, Bangladesh, Belgium, Bolivia, Brazil, Bulgaria, Burma,[a] Canada, Central African Republic, Chile, China, Colombia, Costa Rica, Cuba, Czechoslovakia, Democratic People's Republic of Korea, Democratic Yemen, Denmark, Ecuador, Egypt, El Salvador, Ethiopia, Finland, France, Gabon, German Democratic Republic, Germany, Federal Republic of, Ghana, Greece, Guatemala, Guyana, Honduras, India, Indonesia, Iran, Iraq, Ireland, Israel, Italy, Jamaica, Japan, Jordan, Kenya, Kuwait, Lebanon, Liberia, Libyan Arab Jamahiriya, Madagascar, Malaysia, Malta, Mauritius, Mexico, Morocco, Netherlands, New Zealand, Nicaragua, Nigeria, Norway, Oman, Pakistan, Panama, Peru, Philippines, Poland, Qatar, Republic of Korea, Romania, Saudi Arabia, Senegal, Somalia, Spain, Sri Lanka, Sudan, Suriname, Sweden, Switzerland, Syrian Arab Republic, Thailand, Togo, Trinidad and Tobago, Tunisia, Turkey, Uganda, USSR, United Arab Emirates, United Kingdom, United Republic of Cameroon, United Republic of Tanzania, United States, Uruguay, Venezuela, Viet Nam, Yemen, Yugoslavia, Zaire, Zambia.

[a]Declared elected by the Trade and Development Board on 9 March 1982, raising the Committee's membership to 99.

---

[22]YUN 1980, p. 622.
[23]YUN 1967, p. 963.

COMMITTEE ON INVISIBLES AND FINANCING RELATED TO TRADE

The Committee on Invisibles and Financing related to Trade held the first part of its tenth session at Geneva from 13 to 17 December 1982.

Members: Algeria, Argentina, Australia, Austria, Bangladesh, Belgium, Bolivia, Brazil, Bulgaria, Burundi,[a] Canada, Central African Republic, Chad,[a] Chile, China, Colombia, Costa Rica, Cuba,[a] Czechoslovakia, Democratic People's Republic of Korea,[a] Democratic Yemen, Denmark,[a] Dominican Republic, Ecuador, Egypt, El Salvador, Ethiopia, Finland, France, German Democratic Republic,[a] Germany, Federal Republic of, Ghana, Greece, Guatemala, Guinea,[a] Honduras, Hungary,[a] India, Indonesia, Iran, Iraq,[a] Ireland,[a] Israel, Italy, Ivory Coast, Jamaica, Japan, Jordan,[a] Kenya,[a] Kuwait, Lebanon, Liberia,[a] Libyan Arab Jamahiriya, Madagascar, Malaysia, Mali, Malta, Mexico, Morocco, Netherlands, New Zealand,[a] Nicaragua,[a] Nigeria, Norway, Pakistan, Panama,[a] Peru,[a] Philippines, Poland,[a] Qatar, Republic of Korea, Romania, Saudi Arabia,[a] Senegal, Somalia,[b] Spain, Sri Lanka,[a] Sudan, Sweden, Switzerland, Syrian Arab Republic, Thailand, Trinidad and Tobago, Tunisia, Turkey, Uganda,[a] USSR, United Kingdom, United Republic of Cameroon, United Republic of Tanzania, United States, Upper Volta,[a] Uruguay,[a] Venezuela, Viet Nam,[a] Yemen,[a] Yugoslavia, Zaire.

[a]Not represented at the first part of the tenth session.
[b]Declared elected by the Trade and Development Board on 8 March 1982, raising the Committee's membership to 98.

Chairman: Mario Alemán (Ecuador).
Vice-Chairmen: A. Goenka (India), H. Helps (United Kingdom), D. Popov (Bulgaria), Raymond Raoelina (Madagascar), Paulina Reiss (Chile).
Rapporteur: Christian du Plessis (Switzerland).

COMMITTEE ON MANUFACTURES

The Committee on Manufactures did not meet in 1982.

Members: Algeria, Argentina, Australia, Austria, Bangladesh, Belgium, Bolivia, Brazil, Bulgaria, Canada, Central African Republic, Chile, China, Colombia, Costa Rica, Cuba, Czechoslovakia, Democratic People's Republic of Korea, Democratic Yemen, Denmark, Dominican Republic, Ecuador, Egypt, El Salvador, Ethiopia, Finland, France, German Democratic Republic, Germany, Federal Republic of, Ghana, Greece, Guatemala, Honduras, Hungary, India, Indonesia, Iran, Iraq, Ireland, Israel, Italy, Ivory Coast, Jamaica, Japan, Jordan, Kenya, Liberia, Libyan Arab Jamahiriya, Madagascar, Malaysia, Mali, Malta, Mauritius, Mexico, Morocco, Netherlands, New Zealand, Nicaragua, Nigeria, Norway, Pakistan, Panama, Peru, Philippines, Poland, Qatar, Republic of Korea, Romania, Saudi Arabia, Senegal, Singapore, Somalia,[a] Spain, Sri Lanka, Sudan, Sweden, Switzerland, Syrian Arab Republic, Thailand, Trinidad and Tobago, Tunisia, Turkey, USSR, United Kingdom, United Republic of Cameroon, United Republic of Tanzania, United States, Upper Volta, Uruguay, Venezuela, Viet Nam, Yemen, Yugoslavia, Zaire.

[a]Declared elected by the Trade and Development Board on 8 March 1982, raising the Committee's membership to 94.

COMMITTEE ON SHIPPING

The Committee on Shipping held its tenth session at Geneva from 14 to 25 June 1982.

Members: Algeria, Argentina, Australia, Bangladesh,[a] Belgium, Benin,[a,b] Bolivia,[a] Brazil, Bulgaria, Canada, Central African Republic,[a] Chile, China, Colombia, Costa Rica,[a] Cuba, Cyprus, Czechoslovakia, Democratic People's Republic of Korea,[a] Democratic Yemen, Denmark, Dominican Republic,[a] Ecuador, Egypt, El Salvador,[a] Ethiopia,[a] Finland, France, Gabon, German Democratic Republic, Germany, Federal Republic of, Ghana, Greece, Guatemala,[a] Guinea, Honduras,[a] Hungary,[a] India, Indonesia, Iran, Iraq, Israel, Italy, Ivory Coast, Jamaica,[a] Japan, Jordan,[a] Kenya, Kuwait, Lebanon, Liberia, Libyan Arab Jamahiriya,[a] Madagascar, Malaysia, Malta, Mauritius,[a] Mexico, Morocco, Netherlands, New Zealand, Nicaragua,[a] Nigeria, Norway, Pakistan, Panama, Peru, Philippines, Poland, Portugal,[a] Qatar, Republic of Korea, Romania, Saudi Arabia, Senegal, Somalia,[a,b] Spain, Sri Lanka, Sudan,[a] Sweden, Switzerland, Syrian Arab

Republic, Thailand, Trinidad and Tobago, Tunisia, Turkey, Uganda,[a] USSR, United Kingdom, United Republic of Cameroon, United Republic of Tanzania, United States, Upper Volta, Uruguay,[a] Venezuela, Viet Nam,[a] Yemen,[a] Yugoslavia, Zaire.

[a]Not represented at the tenth session.
[b]Declared elected by the Trade and Development Board on 6 September and 8 March 1982, respectively, raising the Committee's membership to 98.

Chairman: I. Averin (USSR).
Vice-Chairmen: María Chen Su (Panama), Ibrahim Kharma (Lebanon), Gérard Mihindou (Gabon), R. Okken (Netherlands), D. Turner (Australia).
Rapporteur: Moncef Baati (Tunisia).

WORKING GROUP ON INTERNATIONAL SHIPPING LEGISLATION

The Working Group on International Shipping Legislation, whose membership is identical to that of the Committee on Shipping, did not meet in 1982.

COMMITTEE ON TRANSFER OF TECHNOLOGY

The Committee on Transfer of Technology held its fourth session at Geneva from 29 November to 10 December 1982.

Members: Algeria, Argentina, Australia, Austria, Belgium, Bolivia, Brazil, Bulgaria, Canada, Chile, China, Colombia, Costa Rica,[a] Cuba, Czechoslovakia, Democratic People's Republic of Korea,[a] Democratic Yemen, Denmark, Ecuador, Egypt, El Salvador, Ethiopia, Finland, France, German Democratic Republic, Germany, Federal Republic of, Ghana, Greece, Guatemala, Honduras, Hungary, India, Indonesia, Iran,[a] Iraq, Ireland, Israel, Italy, Ivory Coast, Jamaica, Japan, Jordan, Kenya,[a] Kuwait, Liberia,[a] Libyan Arab Jamahiriya, Madagascar, Malaysia, Malta, Mauritius,[a] Mexico, Morocco, Netherlands, New Zealand,[a] Nicaragua, Nigeria, Norway, Pakistan, Panama, Peru, Philippines, Poland, Qatar, Republic of Korea, Romania, Saudi Arabia, Senegal, Sierra Leone,[a] Somalia, Spain, Sri Lanka,[a] Sudan, Sweden, Switzerland, Syrian Arab Republic, Thailand, Trinidad and Tobago, Tunisia, Turkey, USSR, United Arab Emirates, United Kingdom, United Republic of Cameroon, United Republic of Tanzania, United States, Upper Volta,[a] Venezuela, Viet Nam, Yemen, Yugoslavia, Zaire.

[a]Not represented at the fourth session.

Chairman: Mohamed Baha-Eldin Fayez (Egypt).
Vice-Chairmen: Khalil Abdul-Rahim (Jordan), A. Akopyan (USSR), Jean de Breucker (Belgium), Marcel Namfua (United Republic of Tanzania), Germán Pérez Castillo (Venezuela).
Rapporteur: John J. Harter (United States).

SPECIAL COMMITTEE ON PREFERENCES

The Special Committee on Preferences, which is open to the participation of all UNCTAD members, held its eleventh session at Geneva from 3 to 11 May 1982. Represented at the session were:

Algeria, Argentina, Australia, Austria, Bangladesh, Belgium, Bolivia, Brazil, Bulgaria, Burundi, Canada, Chile, China, Colombia, Cuba, Czechoslovakia, Denmark, Dominican Republic, Ecuador, Egypt, El Salvador, Finland, France, German Democratic Republic, Germany, Federal Republic of, Ghana, Greece, Hungary, India, Indonesia, Iran, Iraq, Ireland, Israel, Italy, Ivory Coast, Japan, Jordan, Kenya, Kuwait, Lebanon, Madagascar, Malaysia, Malta, Mexico, Morocco, Netherlands, New Zealand, Nicaragua, Nigeria, Norway, Pakistan, Peru, Philippines, Poland, Qatar, Republic of Korea, Romania, Saudi Arabia, Senegal, Singapore, Spain, Sri Lanka, Sudan, Sweden, Switzerland, Syrian Arab Republic, Thailand, Trinidad and Tobago, Tunisia, Turkey, USSR, United Arab Emirates, United Kingdom, United Republic of Tanzania, United States, Uruguay, Venezuela, Yemen, Yugoslavia, Zaire.

Chairman: Federico Grünwaldt Ramasso (Uruguay).
Vice-Chairmen: Romuald Daniel (Poland), J. N. Goodman (New Zealand), Douglas M. Jayasekera (Sri Lanka), Gottfried Mazal (Austria), Ibrahim Sy (Senegal).
Rapporteur: Abdulaziz Al-Duaij (Kuwait).

INTERGOVERNMENTAL PREPARATORY GROUP ON CONDITIONS FOR REGISTRATION OF SHIPS

The Intergovernmental Preparatory Group on Conditions for Registration of Ships, open to the participation of all UNCTAD members, held two sessions in 1982, at Geneva: its first from 13 to 30 April; and its second and final session from 8 to 26 November. Represented at the sessions were:

Algeria, Argentina, Australia, Austria,[a] Bangladesh,[b] Belgium, Benin,[b] Bolivia,[a] Brazil, Bulgaria, Canada, Chile, China, Colombia, Congo,[b] Costa Rica,[a] Cuba, Cyprus, Czechoslovakia, Democratic Yemen,[a] Denmark, Dominican Republic, Ecuador,[a] Egypt, El Salvador,[a] Ethiopia, Finland, France, Gabon, German Democratic Republic, Germany, Federal Republic of, Ghana, Greece, Guatemala,[a] Honduras,[a] Hungary, India, Indonesia, Iran,[b] Iraq, Italy, Ivory Coast, Japan, Kuwait, Lebanon, Libyan Arab Jamahiriya, Madagascar, Malaysia, Malta, Mexico, Morocco, Netherlands, New Zealand, Nigeria, Norway, Oman,[b] Pakistan,[a] Philippines, Poland, Portugal,[b] Qatar, Republic of Korea, Romania, Saudi Arabia, Senegal, Singapore, Somalia,[a] Spain, Sri Lanka, Sudan, Sweden, Switzerland, Syrian Arab Republic,[a] Trinidad and Tobago, Tunisia, Turkey, USSR, United Kingdom, United Republic of Cameroon, United Republic of Tanzania, Venezuela,[a] Yugoslavia,[a] Zaire.

[a]Not represented at the first session.
[b]Not represented at the second session.

Chairman: Misbah Ibrahim Oreibi (Libyan Arab Jamahiriya).
Vice-Chairmen: A. Denekew (Ethiopia); B. El-Rami (Lebanon) (first session), Sergios Sergiou (Cyprus) (second session); J. Lebhar (France); Tadeusz Lodykowski (Poland); A. C. Roca (Mexico) (first session), Alberto Székely (Mexico) (second session).
Rapporteur: James O. Lynch (Canada) (first session), Steinar Kringlebotten (Norway) (second session).

United Nations Council for Namibia

Members: Algeria, Angola, Australia, Bangladesh, Belgium, Botswana, Bulgaria, Burundi, Chile, China, Colombia, Cyprus, Egypt, Finland, Guyana, Haiti, India, Indonesia, Liberia, Mexico, Nigeria, Pakistan, Poland, Romania, Senegal, Turkey, USSR, United Republic of Cameroon, Venezuela, Yugoslavia, Zambia.

President: Paul John Firmino Lusaka (Zambia).
Vice-Presidents: Mohammed Bedjaoui (Algeria) (until 29 September), Mohamed Sahnoun (Algeria) (from 29 September); A. Coskun Kirca (Turkey); Miljan Komatina (Yugoslavia) (until 29 September), Ignac Golob (Yugoslavia) (from 29 September); Natarajan Krishnan (India); Noel G. Sinclair (Guyana).

United Nations Commissioner for Namibia: Brajesh Chandra Mishra.[a]

[a]Appointed by the General Assembly on 29 March 1982 (decision 36/325) for a nine-month term beginning on 1 April 1982; reappointed on 20 December (decision 37/324) for a further year beginning on 1 January 1983.

COMMITTEE ON THE UNITED NATIONS FUND FOR NAMIBIA
Members: Australia, Finland, India, Nigeria, Romania, Senegal, Turkey, Venezuela *(Vice-Chairman/Rapporteur)*, Yugoslavia, Zambia; the President of the Council *(ex-officio Chairman)*.

STANDING COMMITTEE I
Members: Algeria, Belgium,[a] China, Colombia, Finland, Haiti, Indonesia, Nigeria, Poland, Senegal, Turkey *(Vice-Chairman)*, USSR, United Republic of Cameroon *(Chairman)*, Venezuela, Zambia.

[a]Resigned as of 1 January 1983.

STANDING COMMITTEE II
Members: Angola, Australia, Bangladesh, Botswana, Bulgaria, Chile, Colombia, Cyprus, Finland, Guyana, Liberia *(Vice-Chairman)*, Mexico, Pakistan *(Chairman)*, Romania, Zambia.

STANDING COMMITTEE III
Members: Algeria, Angola, Australia, Belgium, Bulgaria *(Chairman)*, Burundi, Colombia, Cyprus, Egypt, India, Mexico *(Vice-Chairman)*, Nigeria, Pakistan, Romania, Venezuela, Yugoslavia, Zambia.

STEERING COMMITTEE
In 1982, the Steering Committee consisted of the Council's President and five Vice-Presidents, the chairmen of its three standing committees and the Vice-Chairman/Rapporteur of the Committee on the United Nations Fund for Namibia.

United Nations Development Programme (UNDP)

GOVERNING COUNCIL
The Governing Council of UNDP reports to the Economic and Social Council and through it to the General Assembly.

United Nations Environment Programme (UNEP)

GOVERNING COUNCIL
The Governing Council of UNEP consists of 58 members elected by the General Assembly for three-year terms.

Seats on the Governing Council are allocated as follows: 16 to African States, 13 to Asian States, 6 to Eastern European States, 10 to Latin American States, and 13 to Western European and other States.

The Governing Council, which reports to the Assembly through the Economic and Social Council, held two sessions in 1982, at Nairobi, Kenya: a session of a special character, open to all States, from 10 to 18 May; and its tenth session from 20 to 31 May.

Members:
To serve until 31 December 1982: Argentina, Bangladesh, Belgium, Bulgaria, Chile, China, Ethiopia, France, Gabon, Indonesia, Mauritania,[a] New Zealand, Peru, Saudi Arabia, Sierra Leone,[a] Sudan, Sweden, United Arab Emirates, Yugoslavia.
To serve until 31 December 1983: Brazil, Egypt, Germany, Federal Republic of, Ghana, Haiti,[a] Iceland, Japan, Kenya, Libyan Arab Jamahiriya, Malaysia, Netherlands, Pakistan, Sri Lanka, Switzerland, Ukrainian SSR, USSR, United States, Venezuela, Zaire.
To serve until 31 December 1984: Afghanistan,[a] Botswana, Burundi, Byelorussian SSR, Canada, Colombia, Greece, Guinea, India, Jamaica, Mexico, Morocco, Oman, Poland, Senegal, Spain, Thailand, United Kingdom, United Republic of Tanzania, Uruguay.

[a]Not represented at the tenth session.

Session of a special character
President: Peter Oloo-Aringo (Kenya).
Vice-Presidents: Abdul Rehaman Abdallah Al-Awadi (Kuwait), Jaroslav Sobisek (Czechoslovakia), Gote Svensson (Sweden).
Rapporteur: Sálvano Briceño (Venezuela).

Tenth session
President: V. Kozlov (Byelorussian SSR).
Vice-Presidents: Saad Ahmed Abbadi (Sudan), L. S. Clark (Canada), Luis Felipe Guerrero (Venezuela).
Rapporteur: S. T. Sundram (Malaysia).

Executive Director of UNEP: Mostafa Kamal Tolba.
Deputy Executive Director: Peter Shaw Thacher.

On 16 November 1982 (decision 37/312), the General Assembly elected the following 19 members for a three-year term beginning on 1 January 1983 to fill the vacancies occurring on 31 December 1982: Argentina, Australia, Chile, China, Finland, France, Hungary, Indonesia, Italy, Ivory Coast, Lesotho, Nigeria, Papua New Guinea, Peru, Philippines, Saudi Arabia, Uganda, United Republic of Cameroon, Yugoslavia.

United Nations Financing System for Science and Technology for Development

The United Nations Financing System for Science and Technology for Development, established by a 1979 General Assembly resolution,[24] became operational on 1 January 1982, with the Intergovernmental Committee on Science and Technology for Development (p. 1624) as its directing and policy-making body. It finances at the request of Governments a broad range of activities intended to strengthen the endogenous scientific and technological capacities of developing countries.

[24]Resolution 34/218, sect. VI, 19 December 1979 (YUN 1979, p. 646).

Under the institutional arrangements set up by the Assembly on 21 December 1982, the Intergovernmental Committee was to continue as the policy-making body of the Financing System, an Executive Board was to be responsible for its operation and conduct, and the overall supervision of its management was to be entrusted to the UNDP Administrator, who was to be accountable to the Board in the exercise of this responsibility. The Administrator, in consultation with the Director-General for Development and International Economic Cooperation, was to report annually to the Intergovernmental Committee.

EXECUTIVE BOARD

The Executive Board was to be composed of 21 directors elected by the Intergovernmental Committee on Science and Technology for Development for three-year terms, one third to be drawn from developed countries and two thirds from developing countries reflecting an appropriate balance between donors and recipients.

The Board had not been constituted by the end of 1982.

United Nations Fund for Population Activities (UNFPA)

The United Nations Fund for Population Activities, a subsidiary organ of the General Assembly, plays a leading role within the United Nations system in promoting population programmes and in providing assistance to developing countries at their request in dealing with their population problems. It operates under the overall policy guidance of the Economic and Social Council and under the financial and administrative policy guidance of the Governing Council of UNDP.

Executive Director: Rafael M. Salas.
Deputy Executive Director: Halvor Gille (until 15 January), Heino E. Wittrin (from 15 January).

United Nations Industrial Development Organization (UNIDO)

INDUSTRIAL DEVELOPMENT BOARD

The Industrial Development Board, the principal organ of UNIDO, consists of 45 States elected by the General Assembly, on the basis of equitable geographical distribution, to serve for three-year terms. States eligible for election to the Board are those which are Members of the United Nations or members of the specialized agencies or of IAEA.

The Board reports annually to the Assembly through the Economic and Social Council.

The Board's membership is drawn from the following four groups of States:

List A. 18 of the following States: Afghanistan, Algeria, Angola, Bahrain, Bangladesh, Benin, Bhutan, Botswana, Burma, Burundi, Cape Verde, Central African Republic, Chad, China, Comoros, Congo, Democratic Kampuchea, Democratic People's Republic of Korea, Democratic Yemen, Djibouti, Egypt, Equatorial Guinea, Ethiopia, Fiji, Gabon, Gambia, Ghana, Guinea, Guinea-Bissau, India, Indonesia, Iran, Iraq, Israel, Ivory Coast, Jordan, Kenya, Kuwait, Lao People's Democratic Republic, Lebanon, Lesotho, Liberia, Libyan Arab Jamahiriya, Madagascar, Malawi, Malaysia, Maldives, Mali, Mauritania, Mauritius, Mongolia, Morocco, Mozambique, Nepal, Niger, Nigeria, Oman, Pakistan, Papua New Guinea, Philippines, Qatar, Republic of Korea, Rwanda, Sao Tome and Principe, Saudi Arabia, Senegal, Seychelles, Sierra Leone, Singapore, Solomon Islands, Somalia, South Africa, Sri Lanka, Sudan, Swaziland, Syrian Arab Republic, Thailand, Togo, Tunisia, Uganda, United Arab Emirates, United Republic of Cameroon, United Republic of Tanzania, Upper Volta, Vanuatu, Viet Nam, Yemen, Yugoslavia, Zaire, Zambia, Zimbabwe.
List B. 15 of the following States: Australia, Austria, Belgium, Canada, Cyprus, Denmark, Finland, France, Germany, Federal Republic of, Greece, Iceland, Ireland, Italy, Japan, Liechtenstein, Luxembourg, Malta, Monaco, Netherlands, New Zealand, Norway, Portugal, Spain, Sweden, Switzerland, Turkey, United Kingdom, United States.
List C. 7 of the following States: Antigua and Barbuda, Argentina, Bahamas, Barbados, Belize, Bolivia, Brazil, Chile, Colombia, Costa Rica, Cuba, Dominica, Dominican Republic, Ecuador, El Salvador, Grenada, Guatemala, Guyana, Haiti, Honduras, Jamaica, Mexico, Nicaragua, Panama, Paraguay, Peru, Saint Lucia, Saint Vincent and the Grenadines, Suriname, Trinidad and Tobago, Uruguay, Venezuela.

List D. 5 of the following States: Albania, Bulgaria, Byelorussian SSR, Czechoslovakia, German Democratic Republic, Hungary, Poland, Romania, Ukrainian SSR, USSR.

The Industrial Development Board held its sixteenth session at Vienna, Austria, from 11 to 28 May 1982.

BOARD MEMBERS
To serve until 31 December 1982: Argentina, Austria, Belgium, Central African Republic,[a] Czechoslovakia, Gabon, Indonesia, Italy, Kenya, Madagascar, Morocco, Sweden, Switzerland, Trinidad and Tobago, USSR.
To serve until 31 December 1983: Brazil, Denmark, Ecuador, France, German Democratic Republic, Guinea, India, Japan, Mongolia, Netherlands, Pakistan, Romania, Sri Lanka, United States, Zambia.
To serve until 31 December 1984: Australia, China, Germany, Federal Republic of, Iraq, Lesotho, Liberia, Malaysia, Mexico, Panama, Sierra Leone,[a] Spain, Turkey, Ukrainian SSR, United Kingdom, Venezuela.

[a]Not represented at the sixteenth session.

President: Standwell C. I. Mapara (Zambia).
Vice-Presidents: Ferhang Jalal (Iraq), Erich M. Schmid (Austria), Adolfo R. Taylhardat (Venezuela).
Rapporteur: N. T. Reshetniak (Ukrainian SSR).

Executive Director of UNIDO: Abd El Rahman Khane.
Deputy Executive Director: Philippe Jacques Farlan Carré.

On 16 November 1982 (decision 37/311), the General Assembly elected the following 15 members of the Industrial Development Board for a three-year term beginning on 1 January 1983 to fill the vacancies occurring on 31 December 1982: Austria, Belgium, Bulgaria, Chad, Chile, Finland, Indonesia, Italy, Libyan Arab Jamahiriya, Peru, Rwanda, Sudan, Switzerland, Uganda, USSR.

PERMANENT COMMITTEE

The Permanent Committee has the same membership as the Industrial Development Board and normally meets twice a year.

During 1982, the Committee held its seventeenth session on 10, 11 and 14 May and its eighteenth from 15 to 19 November, both at Vienna, Austria. All members attended, except the Central African Republic, Gabon and Sierra Leone, which were not represented at either session; and Guinea, Liberia and Sri Lanka, which were not represented at the eighteenth session.

Chairman: Standwell C. I. Mapara (Zambia).[a]
Vice-Chairmen: H. Alshawi (Iraq) (seventeenth session), Ferhang Jalal (Iraq) (eighteenth session); Erich M. Schmid (Austria); Adolfo R. Taylhardat (Venezuela).
Rapporteur: N. T. Reshetniak (Ukrainian SSR).

[a]Did not attend the eighteenth session; each of the three Vice-Chairmen served in rotation as Acting Chairman.

United Nations Institute for Disarmament Research (UNIDIR)

The United Nations Institute for Disarmament Research was established at Geneva in 1980[25] pursuant to a 1979 General Assembly resolution.[26] Set up within the framework of UNITAR as an interim arrangement until the Assembly's second (1982) special session devoted to disarmament, the Institute carried out its mandate under the guidance of a 17-member Advisory Council that held two sessions in 1981.[27]

On 13 December 1982, the Assembly decided that the Institute should function as an autonomous institution in close relationship with the Secretariat's Department for Disarmament Affairs; that it be organized to ensure participation on an equitable political and geographical basis; and that it continue independent research on disarmament and related security issues. The Secretary-General's Advisory Board on Disarmament Studies was to function as the Board of Trustees of the Institute; its Director was to report to the Assembly.

---

[25]YUN 1980, p. 113.
[26]Resolution 34/83 M, 11 December 1979 (YUN 1979, p. 101).
[27]YUN 1981, p. 107.

BOARD OF TRUSTEES

The Advisory Board on Disarmament Studies, to function as the Institute's Board of Trustees, is a board of eminent persons appointed by the Secretary-General on the basis of their personal expertise with due regard for the principle of equitable geographical representation. The terms of office of its members expired at the end of 1981 and a new Board was not appointed in 1982.

Director of UNIDIR: Liviu Bota.

United Nations Institute for Training and Research (UNITAR)

The Executive Director of UNITAR, in consultation with the Board of Trustees of the Institute, reports through the Secretary-General to the General Assembly and, as appropriate, to the Economic and Social Council and other United Nations bodies.

BOARD OF TRUSTEES

The Board of Trustees of UNITAR consists of: *(a)* up to 24 members, which may include one or more officials of the United Nations Secretariat, appointed on a broad geographical basis by the Secretary-General, in consultation with the Presidents of the General Assembly and the Economic and Social Council; and *(b)* four *ex-officio* members. The Board held its twenty-first session (with its composition as of 1 July 1982) at United Nations Headquarters from 14 to 17 September 1982.

Members (until 30 June 1982):

To serve until 30 June 1982: Ole Algard (Norway), Abdalla Yaccoub Bishara (Kuwait), Louis de Guiringaud (France),[a] Johan Kaufmann (Netherlands), Gwendoline Chomba Konie (Zambia), Missoum Sbih (Algeria), Inga Thorsson (Sweden), B. S. Vaganov (USSR).

To serve until 30 June 1983: Wahbi El-Bouri (Libyan Arab Jamahiriya), Lai Ya-li (China), Donald O. Mills (Jamaica), Bibiano F. Osorio-Tafall (Mexico), Agha Shahi (Pakistan), Victor Umbricht (Switzerland), Brian E. Urquhart (Secretariat),[b] Anton Vratusa (Yugoslavia).

To serve until 30 June 1984:[c] Siméon Aké (Ivory Coast), William H. Barton (Canada), Ademar M. A. d'Alcantara (Belgium), Roberto E. Guyer (Argentina), K. Natwar-Singh (India), Shizuo Saito (Japan), Rüdiger von Wechmar (Federal Republic of Germany).

[a]Died on 15 April 1982; the resultant vacancy was not filled.
[b]Resigned with effect from 30 June 1982; Margaret Joan Anstee (Secretariat) was appointed on 2 September for the remainder of the term.
[c]One seat remained vacant.

On 30 June 1982, the Secretary-General appointed the following members for a three-year term beginning on 1 July 1982 to fill six of the eight vacancies occurring on 30 June: Ole Algard (Norway), Stephane Hessel (France), Johan Kaufmann (Netherlands), Olara Otunnu (Uganda), Taieb Slim (Tunisia), B. S. Vaganov (USSR).

Members (from 1 July 1982):

To serve until 30 June 1983: Margaret Joan Anstee (Secretariat); Wahbi El-Bouri (Libyan Arab Jamahiriya); Lai Ya-li (China); Donald O. Mills (Jamaica); Bibiano F. Osorio-Tafall (Mexico); Agha Shahi, *Chairman* (Pakistan); Victor Umbricht (Switzerland); Anton Vratusa (Yugoslavia).

To serve until 30 June 1984: Siméon Aké (Ivory Coast); William H. Barton, *Vice-Chairman* (Canada); Ademar M. A. d'Alcantara (Belgium); Roberto E. Guyer (Argentina); K. Natwar-Singh (India); Shizuo Saito (Japan); Joel Segall (United States);[a] Rüdiger von Wechmar (Federal Republic of Germany).

To serve until 30 June 1985:[b] Ole Algard (Norway); Stephane Hessel (France); Johan Kaufmann (Netherlands); Olara Otunnu (Uganda); Taieb Slim (Tunisia); Anders I. Thunborg (Sweden);[a] B. S. Vaganov (USSR).

[a]Appointed on 2 September and 31 August 1982, respectively.
[b]One seat remained vacant.

Ex-officio members: The Secretary-General, the President of the General Assembly, the President of the Economic and Social Council and the Executive Director of UNITAR.

Executive Director of UNITAR: Davidson S. H. W. Nicol.

United Nations Joint Staff Pension Board

The United Nations Joint Staff Pension Board is composed of 21 members, as follows:

Six appointed by the United Nations Staff Pension Committee (two from members elected by the General Assembly, two from those appointed by the Secretary-General, two from those elected by participants).

Fifteen appointed by Staff Pension Committees of other member organizations of the United Nations Joint Staff Pension Fund, as follows: two each by WHO, FAO, UNESCO; and one each by ILO, ICAO, IAEA, WMO, IMO, ITU, ICITO/GATT, WIPO, IFAD.

In addition to these organizations and the International Centre for the Study of the Preservation and the Restoration of Cultural Property, the European and Mediterranean Plant Protection Organization was admitted to membership in the Fund with effect from 1 January 1983 by decision of the General Assembly on 17 December 1982.

The Board held its thirtieth session at Geneva from 9 to 20 August 1982.

Members:

United Nations

Representing the General Assembly: Representatives: Mario Majoli (Italy); Sol Kuttner (United States). Alternates: Michael G. Okeyo (Kenya); Jobst Holborn (Federal Republic of Germany); Ernesto C. Garrido (Philippines); Enrique Buj-Flores (Mexico).

Representing the Secretary-General: Representatives: Patricio Ruedas (Spain); Leila H. Doss (Egypt). Alternates: Clayton C. Timbrell (United States); J. Richard Foran (Canada); Raymond Gieri (United States); V. Elissejev (USSR).

Representing the Participants: Representatives: Angel Antonio García, *Rapporteur* (United States); Anders Tholle (Denmark). Alternates: Rosa Maria Vicien-Milburn (Argentina); Sergio Zampetti (Italy); Bruce C. Hillis (Canada).

International Labour Organisation

Representing the Executive Head: Representative: Amjad Ali, *Chairman* (India). Alternates: Niall MacCabe (Ireland); Franz von Mutius (Federal Republic of Germany); Jean Paul Picard (Canada).

World Health Organization

Representing the Governing Body: Representative: Dr. Arnold Sauter (Switzerland). Alternate: Dr. A. Tanaka (Japan).

Representing the Executive Head: Representative: Robert L. Munteanu (Romania). Alternates: Alistair J. S. Taylor (United Kingdom); Warren W. Furth (United States); Dr. Sahib Djazzar (Syrian Arab Republic); Dr. Jean Jacques Guilbert (France); John Morgan (Australia).

Food and Agriculture Organization of the United Nations

Representing the Governing Body: Representative: Shri Ramadhar (India). Alternate: Horatio Mends (Ghana).

Representing the Participants: Representative: Aurelio Marcucci (Italy). Alternate: Pietro E. Buttinelli (Italy).

United Nations Educational, Scientific and Cultural Organization

Representing the Governing Body: Representative: G. H. Dumont (Belgium). Alternate: Francis Briquet (France).

Representing the Executive Head: Representative: Gilles de Leiris (United States). Alternate: Serge Vieux (Haiti).

International Civil Aviation Organization

Representing the Executive Head: Representative: Daniel E. Conway (United States). Alternate: Shelton E. Jayasekera (Sri Lanka).

International Atomic Energy Agency

Representing the Participants: Representative: William E. Price (United States).

World Meteorological Organization

Representing the Participants: Representative: Robin M. Perry (United Kingdom). Alternate: M. Favre (Switzerland).

International Maritime Organization

Representing the Governing Body: Representative: G. S. Santa-Cruz, *First Vice-Chairman* (Chile). Alternate: M. Bley (Federal Republic of Germany).

International Telecommunication Union

Representing the Executive Head: Representative: Michel Bardoux (France). Alternate: Jean-Patrick Baré (France).

Interim Commission for the International Trade Organization/General Agreement on Tariffs and Trade
   Representing the Participants: Representative: Peter Williams, *Second Vice-Chairman* (United Kingdom). Alternate: Lothar Huehne (Federal Republic of Germany).
World Intellectual Property Organization
   Representing the Governing Body: Representative: Henry Oladele Ajomale (Nigeria).
International Fund for Agricultural Development
   Representing the Participants: Representative: John McGhie (United Kingdom).

STANDING COMMITTEE OF THE PENSION BOARD
Members (elected at the Board's thirtieth session):

United Nations (Group I)
   Representing the General Assembly: Representative: Mario Majoli. Alternates: Sol Kuttner, Michael G. Okeyo, Jobst Holborn, Ernesto C. Garrido, Enrique Buj-Flores.
   Representing the Secretary-General: Representative: Patricio Ruedas. Alternates: Leila H. Doss, Clayton C. Timbrell, J. Richard Foran, Raymond Gieri, V. Elissejev.
   Representing the Participants: Representative: Angel Antonio García. Alternates: Anders Tholle, Rosa Maria Vicien-Milburn, Sergio Zampetti, Bruce C. Hillis.
Specialized agencies (Group II)
   Representing the Governing Body: Representative: William M. Yoffee (ILO). Alternates: R. M. Schibli (ILO), G. M. J. Veldkamp (ILO), J. Mainwaring (ILO).
   Representing the Executive Head: Representative: Robert L. Munteanu (WHO). Alternates: Alistair J. S. Taylor (WHO), Warren W. Furth (WHO), Dr. Sahib Djazzar (WHO), Dr. Jean Jacques Guilbert (WHO), John Morgan (WHO).
   Representing the Participants: Representative: William E. Price (IAEA). Alternates: Robin M. Perry (WMO), Lorentz Goll (IMO), Jean Balfroid (ITU).
Specialized agencies (Group III)
   Representing the Governing Body: Representative: Shri Ramadhar (FAO). Alternates: Horatio Mends (FAO), Milan Zjalic (FAO), R. de Meira (FAO), Sayed A. A. Khalil (FAO), C. Palmer (FAO).
   Representing the Executive Head: Representative: Gilles de Leiris (UNESCO). Alternate: Serge Vieux (UNESCO).
   Representing the Participants: Representative: Gilles Frammery (WIPO). Alternates: John McGhie (IFAD), Francis X. Byrne (ICAO), Peter Williams (ICITO/GATT).

COMMITTEE OF ACTUARIES
The Committee of Actuaries consists of five members, each representing one of the five geographical regions of the United Nations.

Members: Ajibola O. Ogunshola (Nigeria), *Region I* (African States); Kunio Takeuchi (Japan), *Region II* (Asian States); E. M. Chetyrkin (USSR), *Region III* (Eastern European States); Gonzalo Arroba (Ecuador), *Region IV* (Latin American States); Robert J. Myers (United States), *Region V* (Western European and other States).

United Nations Relief and Works Agency for Palestine Refugees in the Near East (UNRWA)

ADVISORY COMMISSION OF UNRWA
The Advisory Commission of UNRWA met at Vienna, Austria, on 26 August 1982.

Members: Belgium, Egypt, France *(Chairman)*, Japan, Jordan, Lebanon, Syrian Arab Republic, Turkey, United Kingdom, United States.

WORKING GROUP ON THE FINANCING OF UNRWA
Members: France, Ghana *(Vice-Chairman)*, Japan, Lebanon, Norway *(Rapporteur)*, Trinidad and Tobago, Turkey *(Chairman)*, United Kingdom, United States.

Commissioner-General of UNRWA: Olof Rydbeck.
Deputy Commissioner-General: Alan J. Brown.

United Nations Scientific Advisory Committee

Established by the General Assembly in 1954[28] as a seven-member advisory committee on the International Conference on the Peaceful Uses of Atomic Energy (1955), the United Nations Scientific Advisory Committee was so renamed and its mandate revised by the Assembly in 1958,[29] retaining its original composition. The Committee has not met since 1956.[30]

Members: Brazil, Canada, France, India, USSR, United Kingdom, United States.

United Nations Scientific Committee on the Effects of Atomic Radiation

The 20-member United Nations Scientific Committee on the Effects of Atomic Radiation held its thirty-first session at Vienna, Austria, from 15 to 26 March 1982.

Members: Argentina, Australia, Belgium, Brazil, Canada, Czechoslovakia, Egypt, France, Germany, Federal Republic of, India, Indonesia, Japan, Mexico, Peru, Poland, Sudan, Sweden, USSR, United Kingdom, United States.

Chairman: Z. Jaworowski (Poland).
Vice-Chairman: D. Beninson (Argentina).
Rapporteur: T. Kumatori (Japan).

United Nations Special Fund
(to provide emergency relief and development assistance)

BOARD OF GOVERNORS
The activities of the United Nations Special Fund were suspended, *ad interim*, in 1978 by the General Assembly, which assumed the functions of the Board of Governors of the Fund. In 1981,[31] the Assembly decided to continue performing those functions, within the context of its consideration of the item on development and international economic co-operation, pending consideration of the question at its thirty-eighth (1983) session.

United Nations Special Fund for Land-locked Developing Countries

The General Assembly established the United Nations Special Fund for Land-locked Developing Countries in 1975[32] and approved its statute in 1976.[33] The Special Fund was to operate as an organ of the Assembly, with its policies and procedures to be formulated by a Board of Governors.

The chief executive officer of the Special Fund, the Executive Director, to be appointed by the Secretary-General subject to the confirmation of the Assembly, was to discharge his functions under the guidance and supervision of the Board of Governors and an Executive Committee, if established.

Pending appointment of the Executive Director, the Administrator of UNDP, in close collaboration with the Secretary-General of UNCTAD, manages the Fund.

BOARD OF GOVERNORS
A 36-member Board of Governors of the United Nations Special Fund for Land-locked Developing Countries was to be elected by the General Assembly from among Members of the United Nations or members of the specialized agencies or of IAEA, keeping in view the need for a balanced representation of the beneficiary land-locked developing countries and their transit neighbours, on the one hand, and potential donor countries on the other.

Members were to serve three-year terms, except that at the first election the terms of one third of the members were to be for one year and those of a further third for two years.

The Board was to report annually to the Assembly through the Economic and Social Council.

---

[28]Resolution 810(IX), sect. B, para. 5, 4 December 1954 (YUN 1954, p. 10).
[29]Resolution 1344(XIII), 13 December 1958 (YUN 1958, p. 31).
[30]YUN 1956, p. 108.
[31]Decision 36/424, 4 December 1981 (YUN 1981, p. 418).
[32]Resolution 3504(XXX), 15 December 1975 (YUN 1975, p. 387).
[33]Resolution 31/177, annex, 21 December 1976 (YUN 1976, p. 356).

On 20 December 1982 (decision 37/320), the Assembly deferred election of the Board to its thirty-eighth (1983) session.

United Nations Staff Pension Committee

The United Nations Staff Pension Committee consists of three members elected by the General Assembly, three appointed by the Secretary-General and three elected by the participants in the United Nations Joint Staff Pension Fund. The term of office of the elected members is three years.

Members:
Elected by Assembly (to serve until 31 December 1982): *Members:* Ernesto C. Garrido; Sol Kuttner, *Chairman*; Mario Majoli. *Alternates:* Enrique Buj-Flores; Jobst Holborn; Michael G. Okeyo.
Appointed by Secretary-General (to serve until further notice): *Members:* Helmut F. Debatin; James O. C. Jonah; Clayton C. Timbrell. *Alternates:* Raymond Gieri; V. Elissejev.
Elected by Participants (to serve until 31 December 1982 or until the election of their successors): *Members:* Angel Antonio García; Eduardo Albertal; Anders Tholle. *Alternates:* Rosa Maria Vicien-Milburn; Sergio Zampetti; Bruce C. Hillis.

On 17 December 1982 (decision 37/318), the General Assembly elected the following for a three-year term beginning on 1 January 1983 to fill the vacancies occurring on 31 December 1982: *Members:* Sol Kuttner, Mario Majoli, Michael G. Okeyo. *Alternates:* Eduardo César Añón Noceti, Jobst Holborn, Yukio Takasu.

By the end of 1982, the participants in the Fund had not elected the members and alternates to fill the vacancies occurring on 31 December.

United Nations University

COUNCIL OF THE UNITED NATIONS UNIVERSITY

The Council of the United Nations University, the governing board of the University, consists of: *(a)* 24 members appointed jointly by the Secretary-General and the Director-General of UNESCO, in consultation with the agencies and programmes concerned including UNITAR, who serve in their personal capacity for six-year terms; *(b)* the Secretary-General, the Director-General of UNESCO and the Executive Director of UNITAR, who are *ex-officio* members; and *(c)* the Rector of the University, who is normally appointed for a five-year term.

The Council held two sessions in 1982, at Tokyo, Japan: its nineteenth from 21 to 25 June; and its twentieth from 6 to 10 December.

Members:
To serve until 2 May 1983: Estefania Aldaba-Lim (Philippines); Pawel Bozyk (Poland); Carlos Chagas (Brazil);[a,b] Wilbert Kumalija Chagula (United Republic of Tanzania); Jean Coulomb (France);[a] Shams E. El-Wakil (Egypt); Father Felipe E. MacGregor, *Vice-Chairman* (Peru); Abdelsalam Majali, *Chairman* (Jordan); Malu wa Kalenga (Zaire); Stephan Verosta (Austria);[b] Ines Wesley Tanaskovic (Yugoslavia).
To serve until 2 May 1986: Ungku Abdul Aziz (Malaysia);[a] Daniel Adzei Bekoe (Ghana); Elise M. Boulding, *Vice-Chairman* (United States); Satish Chandra (India); Valy Charles Diarrassouba (Ivory Coast); Dennis H. Irvine, *Vice-Chairman* (Guyana); André Louis Jaumotte (Belgium); Reimut Jochimsen, *Vice-Chairman* (Federal Republic of Germany);[b] F. S. C. P. Kalpage (Sri Lanka); Sir John Kendrew (United Kingdom);[a] Karl Eric Knutsson (Sweden); Shizuo Saito, *Vice-Chairman* (Japan); Víctor Luis Urquidi (Mexico).
Ex-officio members: The Secretary-General, the Director-General of UNESCO and the Executive Director of UNITAR.
Rector of the United Nations University: Mr. Soedjatmoko.

[a]Did not attend the nineteenth session.
[b]Did not attend the twentieth session.

The Council maintained two standing committees during 1982: the Committee on Finance and Budget; and the Committee on Institutional and Programmatic Development. It also appointed an *Ad Hoc* Committee on Statutes and Rules.

United Nations Voluntary Fund for Victims of Torture

BOARD OF TRUSTEES

The Board of Trustees to advise the Secretary-General in his administration of the United Nations Voluntary Fund for Victims of Torture was to consist of five members with wide experience in the field of human rights, appointed in their personal capacity by the Secretary-General with due regard for equitable geographical distribution and in consultation with their Governments.

In 1982 only four members were appointed, on 11 November, to serve for a three-year term. The Board did not meet during the year.

Members: Hans Danelius (Sweden), Elizabeth Odio Benito (Costa Rica), Waleed M. Sadi (Jordan), Amos Wako (Kenya).

World Food Council

The World Food Council, at the ministerial or plenipotentiary level, functions as an organ of the United Nations and reports to the General Assembly through the Economic and Social Council. It consists of 36 members, nominated by the Economic and Social Council and elected by the Assembly according to the following pattern: nine members from African States, eight from Asian States, seven from Latin American States, four from socialist States of Eastern Europe and eight from Western European and other States. Members serve for three-year terms.

During 1982, the World Food Council held its eighth session at Acapulco, Mexico, from 21 to 24 June. It was preceded by a series of preparatory meetings held at Rome, Italy, from 10 to 13 May.

Members:
To serve until 31 December 1982: Australia, Bangladesh, Barbados, Germany, Federal Republic of, Ghana, Honduras, Nicaragua, Philippines, Romania, Senegal, Sudan, USSR.
To serve until 31 December 1983: Argentina, Egypt, France, Haiti, Hungary, Indonesia, Italy, Japan, Norway, Pakistan, Rwanda, Zaire.
To serve until 31 December 1984: Botswana, Canada, China, Colombia, Gambia, Greece, India, Mexico, Thailand, United Republic of Tanzania, United States, Yugoslavia.

President: Francisco Merino Rábago (Mexico).
Vice-Presidents: Soedarsono Hadisapoetro (Indonesia), Robert Sagna (Senegal), Dumitru Vsiliu (Romania).[a]
Rapporteur: Aage Bothner (Norway).

[a]Did not attend the eighth session.

Executive Director: Maurice J. Williams.
Deputy Executive Director: Salahuddin Ahmed (until 30 November), Diogo A. N. de Gaspar (from 1 December).

On 10 November 1982 (decision 1982/187), the Economic and Social Council nominated the following 12 States for election by the General Assembly for a three-year term beginning on 1 January 1983 to fill the vacancies occurring on 31 December 1982: Australia, Bangladesh, Ecuador, Ethiopia, German Democratic Republic, Germany, Federal Republic of, Ghana, Nicaragua, Nigeria, USSR, United Arab Emirates, Venezuela. They were elected by the Assembly on 16 November 1982 (decision 37/313).

Conferences

Second United Nations Conference on the Exploration and Peaceful Uses of Outer Space

The Second United Nations Conference on the Exploration and Peaceful Uses of Outer Space was held at Vienna, Austria, from 9 to 21 August 1982. Participating were the following 93 States and the United Nations Council for Namibia:

Albania, Algeria, Angola, Argentina, Australia, Austria, Bangladesh, Belgium, Benin, Bolivia, Brazil, Bulgaria, Byelorussian SSR, Canada, Chile, China, Colombia, Costa Rica, Cuba, Cyprus, Czechoslovakia, Democratic Yemen, Denmark, Ecuador, Egypt, Finland, France, Gabon, German Democratic Republic, Germany, Federal Republic of, Greece, Guatemala, Holy See, Hungary, India, Indonesia, Iran, Iraq, Ireland, Israel, Italy, Japan, Kenya, Kuwait, Lebanon, Lesotho, Libyan Arab

Jamahiriya, Luxembourg, Malaysia, Mali, Mexico, Morocco, Netherlands, New Zealand, Nigeria, Norway, Pakistan, Panama, Peru, Philippines, Poland, Portugal, Qatar, Republic of Korea, Romania, Rwanda, San Marino, Saudi Arabia, Senegal, Somalia, Spain, Sri Lanka, Sudan, Sweden, Switzerland, Syrian Arab Republic, Thailand, Tunisia, Turkey, Uganda, Ukrainian SSR, USSR, United Kingdom, United Republic of Cameroon, United Republic of Tanzania, United States, Upper Volta, Uruguay, Venezuela, Viet Nam, Yugoslavia, Zaire, Zimbabwe.

President: Willibald Pahr (Austria).
Vice-Presidents: Australia, Bulgaria, Canada, China, Colombia, Ecuador, Egypt, Germany, Federal Republic of, Indonesia, Iraq, Nigeria, Pakistan, Peru, Romania, Senegal, Uganda, Upper Volta.
Rapporteur-General: Carlos Antonio Bettencourt Bueno (Brazil).

Chairmen of committees:
First Committee: Robert Knuth (German Democratic Republic).
Second Committee: Minoru Oda (Japan).
Third Committee: David K. Andere (Kenya).
Credentials Committee: Domingo L. Siazon (Philippines).

Third United Nations Conference on the Law of the Sea
Participation in the Third United Nations Conference on the Law of the Sea was open to all Member States of the United Nations and members of the specialized agencies and IAEA.

During 1982, the Conference held its eleventh and final session, in three parts: from 8 March to 30 April and from 22 to 24 September at United Nations Headquarters, and from 6 to 10 December at Montego Bay, Jamaica. Participating were the following 160 States and the United Nations Council for Namibia:[a]

Afghanistan,[b] Albania,[b] Algeria, Angola, Antigua and Barbuda,[b] Argentina,[b] Australia, Austria, Bahamas, Bahrain, Bangladesh, Barbados, Belgium, Belize,[c] Benin, Bhutan, Bolivia,[b] Botswana, Brazil, Bulgaria, Burma, Burundi, Byelorussian SSR, Canada, Cape Verde, Central African Republic,[b] Chad, Chile, China, Colombia, Congo, Costa Rica, Cuba, Cyprus, Czechoslovakia, Democratic Kampuchea,[b] Democratic People's Republic of Korea, Democratic Yemen, Denmark, Djibouti, Dominican Republic, Ecuador, Egypt, El Salvador, Equatorial Guinea,[c] Ethiopia, Fiji, Finland, France, Gabon, Gambia,[c] German Democratic Republic, Germany, Federal Republic of, Ghana, Greece, Grenada, Guatemala,[b] Guinea-Bissau, Guyana, Haiti, Holy See, Honduras, Hungary, Iceland, India, Indonesia, Iran, Iraq, Ireland, Israel, Italy, Ivory Coast, Jamaica, Japan, Jordan, Kenya, Kuwait, Lao People's Democratic Republic, Lebanon,[b] Lesotho, Liberia, Libyan Arab Jamahiriya, Liechtenstein,[b] Luxembourg, Madagascar, Malawi, Malaysia, Maldives, Mali,[b] Malta, Mauritania, Mauritius, Mexico, Monaco, Mongolia, Morocco, Mozambique, Nauru, Nepal, Netherlands, New Zealand, Niger, Nigeria, Norway, Oman, Pakistan, Panama, Papua New Guinea, Paraguay, Peru, Philippines, Poland, Portugal, Qatar, Republic of Korea, Romania, Rwanda, Saint Lucia, Saint Vincent and the Grenadines,[b] Samoa, San Marino,[b] Sao Tome and Principe,[b] Saudi Arabia,[b] Senegal, Seychelles, Sierra Leone, Singapore, Solomon Islands, Somalia, Spain, Sri Lanka, Sudan, Suriname, Swaziland,[b] Sweden, Switzerland, Syrian Arab Republic,[b] Thailand, Togo, Trinidad and Tobago, Tunisia, Turkey, Uganda, Ukrainian SSR, USSR, United Arab Emirates, United Kingdom, United Republic of Cameroon, United Republic of Tanzania, United States, Upper Volta, Uruguay, Vanuatu,[c] Venezuela, Viet Nam, Yemen, Yugoslavia, Zaire, Zambia, Zimbabwe.

The Cook Islands,[c] the Netherlands Antilles and the Trust Territory of the Pacific Islands were represented by observers.

[a]Information on participation at the second part of the eleventh session was not available.
[b]Not represented at the third part of the eleventh session.
[c]Not represented at the first part of the eleventh session.

President: Tommy T. B. Koh (Singapore).
Vice-Presidents: Algeria, Bolivia, Chile, China, Dominican Republic, Egypt, France, Iceland, Indonesia, Iran, Iraq, Ireland, Kuwait, Liberia, Madagascar, Nepal, Nigeria, Norway, Pakistan, Peru, Poland, Sri Lanka, Trinidad and Tobago, Tunisia, Uganda, USSR, United Kingdom, United States, Yugoslavia, Zaire, Zambia.
Rapporteur-General: Kenneth O. Rattray (Jamaica).

Chairmen of committees:
First Committee: Paul Bamela Engo (United Republic of Cameroon).
Second Committee: Andrés Aguilar (Venezuela).
Third Committee: Alexander Yankov (Bulgaria).
General Committee: President of the Conference.
Drafting Committee: J. Alan Beesley (Canada).
Credentials Committee: Karl Wolf (Austria).

World Assembly on Aging
The World Assembly on Aging was held at Vienna, Austria, from 26 July to 6 August 1982. Participating were the following 124 States and the United Nations Council for Namibia:

Afghanistan, Algeria, Angola, Argentina, Australia, Austria, Bahrain, Bangladesh, Belgium, Benin, Botswana, Brazil, Bulgaria, Burundi, Byelorussian SSR, Canada, Cape Verde, Central African Republic, Chad, Chile, China, Colombia, Congo, Costa Rica, Cuba, Cyprus, Czechoslovakia, Democratic Kampuchea, Democratic Yemen, Denmark, Djibouti, Dominican Republic, Ecuador, Egypt, El Salvador, Ethiopia, Finland, France, Gabon, Gambia, German Democratic Republic, Germany, Federal Republic of, Greece, Guatemala, Guinea, Guinea-Bissau, Haiti, Holy See, Hungary, Iceland, India, Indonesia, Iran, Iraq, Ireland, Israel, Italy, Ivory Coast, Jamaica, Japan, Jordan, Kenya, Kuwait, Lebanon, Lesotho, Liberia, Libyan Arab Jamahiriya, Luxembourg, Malawi, Malaysia, Maldives, Mali, Malta, Mauritius, Mexico, Morocco, Mozambique, Netherlands, Nicaragua, Niger, Nigeria, Norway, Pakistan, Panama, Peru, Philippines, Poland, Portugal, Republic of Korea, Romania, Rwanda, San Marino, Saudi Arabia, Senegal, Seychelles, Spain, Sri Lanka, Sudan, Suriname, Swaziland, Sweden, Switzerland, Syrian Arab Republic, Thailand, Togo, Trinidad and Tobago, Tunisia, Turkey, Ukrainian SSR, USSR, United Arab Emirates, United Kingdom, United Republic of Cameroon, United Republic of Tanzania, United States, Upper Volta, Uruguay, Venezuela, Viet Nam, Yemen, Yugoslavia, Zaire, Zambia.

President: Hertha Firnberg (Austria).
Vice-Presidents for Co-ordination: Babacar Diagne (Senegal), Sylvia P. Montes (Philippines), Janos Szentagothai (Hungary).
Vice-Presidents: Algeria, Bulgaria, Chile, China, Djibouti, Dominican Republic, France, Indonesia, Jamaica, Japan, Kuwait, Lesotho, Liberia, Morocco, Romania, Sri Lanka, Sweden, USSR, United Republic of Tanzania, United States, Venezuela.
Rapporteur-General: Lucien Johan Henar (Suriname).

Chairmen of committees:
Main Committee: Anthony H. B. de Bono (Malta).
Credentials Committee: Djibo Doufray (Niger).

Security Council

The Security Council consists of 15 Member States of the United Nations, in accordance with the provisions of Article 23 of the United Nations Charter as amended in 1965.

MEMBERS
Permanent members: China, France, USSR, United Kingdom, United States.
Non-permanent members: Guyana, Ireland, Japan, Jordan, Panama, Poland, Spain, Togo, Uganda, Zaire.

On 19 October 1982 (decision 37/306), the General Assembly elected Malta, the Netherlands, Nicaragua, Pakistan and Zimbabwe for a two-year term beginning on 1 January 1983, to replace Ireland, Japan, Panama, Spain and Uganda, whose terms of office were to expire on 31 December 1982.

PRESIDENTS
The presidency of the Council rotates monthly, according to the English alphabetical listing of its member States. The following served as Presidents during 1982:

Month	Member	Representative
January	USSR	O. A. Troyanovsky
February	United Kingdom	Sir Anthony Parsons
March	United States	Jeane J. Kirkpatrick
April	Zaire	Kamanda wa Kamanda
May	China	Ling Qing
June	France	Luc de La Barre de Nanteuil
July	Guyana	Noel G. Sinclair
August	Ireland	Noel Dorr
September	Japan	Masahiro Nisibori
October	Jordan	Hazem Nuseibeh
November	Panama	Carlos Ozores Typaldos
December	Poland	Wlodzimierz Natorf

Collective Measures Committee

The Collective Measures Committee reports to both the General Assembly and the Security Council.

Military Staff Committee

The Military Staff Committee consists of the chiefs of staff of the permanent members of the Security Council or their representatives. It met fortnightly throughout 1982; the first meeting was held on 28 January and the last on 30 December.

Standing committees

Each of the two standing committees of the Security Council is composed of representatives of all Council members:

Committee of Experts (to examine the provisional rules of procedure of the Council and any other matters entrusted to it by the Council)
Committee on the Admission of New Members

In addition the Council maintains an *ad hoc* Committee on Council Meetings Away from Headquarters.

Ad hoc bodies

Ad Hoc Committee established under resolution 507(1982)

On 28 May 1982, the Security Council established a special fund to be supplied by voluntary contributions, through which assistance would be channelled for the economic reconstruction of Seychelles. At the same time it established an *ad hoc* committee of four Council members, chaired by France, to co-ordinate and mobilize resources for the Special Fund for immediate disbursement to Seychelles. In a note, also of 28 May, the Council President announced that, following consultations with Council members, the other three members would be as given below.

Members: France *(Chairman)*, Guyana, Jordan, Uganda.

Ad Hoc Sub-Committee on Namibia

The *Ad Hoc* Sub-Committee on Namibia consists of all the members of the Security Council. It did not meet in 1982.

Committee of Experts established by the Security Council at its 1506th meeting
(on the question of micro-States)

The Committee of Experts consists of all the members of the Security Council. The chairmanship is rotated monthly in the English alphabetical order of the member States.

The Committee did not meet in 1982.

Committee on the Exercise of the Inalienable Rights of the Palestinian People

The Committee reports to the General Assembly, which has also drawn the attention of the Security Council to the need for urgent action on the recommendations of the Committee.

Security Council Commission established under resolution 446(1979)
(to examine the situation relating to settlements in the Arab territories occupied since 1967, including Jerusalem)

Members:[a] Bolivia, Portugal *(Chairman)*, Zambia.

[a]Not Council members in 1982.

Security Council Commission of Inquiry established under resolution 496(1981)

Members: Ireland, Japan, Panama *(Chairman)*.

Security Council Committee established by resolution 421(1977) concerning the question of South Africa

The Committee consists of all the members of the Security Council.

Special Committee against *Apartheid*

The Special Committee against *Apartheid* reports to both the General Assembly and the Security Council.

PEACE-KEEPING OPERATIONS AND SPECIAL MISSIONS

United Nations Truce Supervision Organization (UNTSO)
Chief of Staff: Lieutenant-General Emmanuel Alexander Erskine.

United Nations Disengagement Observer Force (UNDOF)
Force Commander: Major-General Erkki Rainer Kaira (until 31 May), Major-General Carl-Gustav Stahl (from 1 June).

United Nations Interim Force in Lebanon (UNIFIL)
Force Commander: Lieutenant-General William Callaghan.

United Nations Peace-keeping Force in Cyprus (UNFICYP)
Special Representative of the Secretary-General in Cyprus: Hugo J. Gobbi.
Force Commander: Major-General Günther G. Greindl.

United Nations Military Observer Group in India and Pakistan (UNMOGIP)
Chief Military Observer: Brigadier-General Stig Waldenstrom (until 31 May), Brigadier-General Thor A. Johnsen (from 1 June).

United Nations Transition Assistance Group (UNTAG)
Authorized by the Security Council in 1978,[34] the United Nations Transition Assistance Group had not been emplaced in Namibia by the end of 1982.

Special Representative of the Secretary-General: Martti Ahtisaari.
Commander-designate: Lieutenant-General Dewan Prem Chand.

---

[34]Resolution 435(1978), 29 September 1978 (YUN 1978, p. 915).

Economic and Social Council

The Economic and Social Council consists of 54 Member States of the United Nations, elected by the General Assembly, each for a three-year term, in accordance with the provisions of Article 61 of the United Nations Charter as amended in 1965 and 1973.

MEMBERS
To serve until 31 December 1982: Australia, Bahamas, Belgium, Bulgaria, Chile, Ethiopia, Iraq, Italy, Jordan, Libyan Arab Jamahiriya, Malawi, Mexico, Nepal, Nigeria, Thailand, United States, Yugoslavia, Zaire.

To serve until 31 December 1983: Argentina, Bangladesh, Burundi, Byelorussian SSR, Canada, China, Denmark, Fiji, India, Kenya, Nicaragua, Norway, Peru, Poland, Sudan, USSR, United Kingdom, United Republic of Cameroon.

To serve until 31 December 1984: Austria, Benin, Brazil, Colombia, France, Germany, Federal Republic of, Greece, Japan, Liberia, Mali, Pakistan, Portugal, Qatar, Romania, Saint Lucia, Swaziland, Tunisia, Venezuela.

On 20 October 1982 (decision 37/307), the General Assembly elected the following 18 States for a three-year term beginning on 1 January 1983 to fill the vacancies occurring on 31 December 1982: Algeria, Botswana, Bulgaria, Congo, Djibouti, Ecuador, German Democratic Republic, Lebanon, Luxembourg, Malaysia, Mexico, Netherlands, New Zealand, Saudi Arabia, Sierra Leone, Suriname, Thailand, United States.

SESSIONS

Organizational session for 1982: United Nations Headquarters, 2-5 February.

First regular session of 1982: United Nations Headquarters, 13 April–7 May.

Second regular session of 1982: Geneva, 7-30 July.

Resumed second regular session of 1982: United Nations Headquarters, 25-27 October and 9-11 November.

On 10 November 1982 (decision 1982/189), the Economic and Social Council decided to discontinue its practice of holding resumed second regular sessions as from 1983.

OFFICERS

President: Miljan Komatina (Yugoslavia).

Vice-Presidents: Uddhav Deo Bhatt (Nepal); Kamanda wa Kamanda (Zaire), John Reid Morden (Canada), Gilberto Coutinho Paranhos Velloso (Brazil).

Subsidiary and other related organs

SUBSIDIARY ORGANS

In addition to three regular sessional committees, the Economic and Social Council may, at each session, set up other committees or working groups, of the whole or of limited membership, and refer to them any items on the agenda for study and report.

Other subsidiary organs reporting to the Council are the functional commissions, regional commissions, standing committees, expert bodies and *ad hoc* bodies.

The inter-agency Administrative Committee on Co-ordination also reports to the Council.

Sessional bodies

SESSIONAL COMMITTEES

Each of the sessional committees of the Economic and Social Council consists of the 54 members of the Council.

First (Economic) Committee. Chairman: Gilberto Coutinho Paranhos Velloso (Brazil). *Vice-Chairmen:* Anwarul Karim Chowdhury (Bangladesh), Habib Kaabachi (Tunisia).

Second (Social) Committee. Chairman: John Reid Morden (Canada). *Vice-Chairmen:* Alfredo Corti (Argentina), N. N. Komissarov (Byelorussian SSR).

Third (Programme and Co-ordination) Committee. Chairman: Uddhav Deo Bhatt (Nepal). *Vice-Chairmen:* Awad Mohamed Elhassan (Sudan), António Martins da Cruz (Portugal).

SESSIONAL WORKING GROUP (OF GOVERNMENTAL EXPERTS)
ON THE IMPLEMENTATION OF THE INTERNATIONAL
COVENANT ON ECONOMIC, SOCIAL AND CULTURAL RIGHTS

In 1982 the Working Group had 13 members, the two seats allocated to Asian States having remained vacant.

Members: Bulgaria, Byelorussian SSR, France, Germany, Federal Republic of, Japan, Kenya, Libyan Arab Jamahiriya, Mexico, Norway, Peru, Tunisia, USSR, Venezuela.

Chairman: Awad S. Burwin (Libyan Arab Jamahiriya).

Vice-Chairmen: Nobutoshi Akao (Japan), Karl Borchard (Federal Republic of Germany), Carmen Silva de Arana (Peru).

Rapporteur: Ljudmila Boshkova (Bulgaria).

On 6 May 1982, the Economic and Social Council renamed the Group the Sessional Working Group of Governmental Experts on the Implementation of the International Covenant on Economic, Social and Cultural Rights. It also decided to elect the Group's 15 members from

among the States parties to the Covenant, three from each of the five geographical regions. Members were to be elected for three-year terms, one third of them (each third comprising one member from each region) to be renewed each year. At the first election, however, one third of the members, to be chosen by lot, were to serve for one year and another third for two years. Each elected State was to designate, in consultation with the Secretary-General and subject to Council confirmation, a representative qualified as an expert of recognized competence in human rights. The Group was to meet yearly, to precede the Council's first regular session.

By an earlier Council decision (1982/119), of 3 May, the Group's 1983 Bureau was to be constituted as follows: Chairman—Asian States; Vice-Chairmen—African States, Eastern European States, Latin American States; Rapporteur—Western European and other States.

On 11 November (decision 1982/188), the Council elected 13 members for terms all beginning on 1 January 1983 and expiring on 31 December of the years indicated: 1983—Colombia, Denmark, German Democratic Republic, Japan, Tunisia; 1984—Bulgaria, Jordan, Libyan Arab Jamahiriya, Spain; and 1985—France, Kenya, Peru, USSR.

No further elections were held in 1982 for the seats allocated to one member from Asian States and to another from Latin American States for terms to expire, respectively, on 31 December 1985 and on 31 December 1984.

Functional commissions and subsidiaries

Commission for Social Development

The Commission for Social Development consists of 32 members, elected for four-year terms by the Economic and Social Council according to a specific pattern of equitable geographical distribution. The Commission did not meet in 1982.

Members:

To serve until 31 December 1982: Bolivia, Chad, Cyprus, India, Lesotho, Nicaragua, Norway, Romania, Senegal, Togo, United Kingdom.

To serve until 31 December 1983: Costa Rica, El Salvador, France, Indonesia, Kenya, Mongolia, Morocco, Netherlands, Ukrainian SSR, USSR, United States.

To serve until 31 December 1984: Chile, Italy, Madagascar, Panama, Philippines, Poland, Sudan, Sweden, Thailand, Turkey.

On 6 May 1982 (decision 1982/126) and (with respect to Argentina and Ecuador) on 10 November (decision 1982/188), the Economic and Social Council elected the following 11 members for a four-year term beginning on 1 January 1983 to fill the vacancies occurring on 31 December 1982: Argentina, Austria, Byelorussian SSR, Central African Republic, Cyprus, Ecuador, Finland, Ghana, India, Liberia, Togo.

Commission on Human Rights

The Commission on Human Rights consists of 43 members, elected for three-year terms by the Economic and Social Council according to a specific pattern of equitable geographical distribution.

Members:

To serve until 31 December 1982: Algeria, Byelorussian SSR, Costa Rica, Cyprus, Denmark, Ethiopia, Greece, India, Netherlands, Panama, Peru, Syrian Arab Republic, USSR, Zambia.

To serve until 31 December 1983: Australia, Brazil, Fiji, France, Ghana, Jordan, Mexico, Philippines, Poland, Senegal, Uganda, United States, Yugoslavia, Zaire.

To serve until 31 December 1984: Argentina, Bulgaria, Canada, China, Cuba, Gambia, Germany, Federal Republic of, Italy, Japan, Pakistan, Rwanda, Togo, United Kingdom, Uruguay, Zimbabwe.

The Commission held its thirty-eighth session at Geneva from 1 February to 12 March 1982. The members were represented as follows:
Algeria: Anisse Salah-Bey, *Vice-Chairman.* Argentina: Gabriel O. Martínez; Alberto Luis Davérède (alternate), *Rapporteur.* Australia: Pierre Hutton. Brazil: Carlos Calero Rodrigues. Bulgaria: Ivan Garvalov, *Chairman.* Byelorussian SSR: L. I. Maksimov. Canada: Yvon Beaulne. China: Gu Yijie. Costa Rica: Elizabeth Odio Benito (until 19 February), Luis Alberto Varela Quirós (from 22 February). Cuba: Luis Solá Vila. Cyprus: Andreas C. Pouyouros, *Vice-Chairman.* Denmark: Niels Boel. Ethiopia: Tadesse Terrefe. Fiji: Ross I. V. Ligairi. France: Claude-Albert Colliard.

Gambia: Ousman Ahmadou Sallah. Germany, Federal Republic of: Gerhard Jahn. Ghana: Jonas Kwami Dotse Foli. Greece: Emmanuel Roucounas. India: B. R. Bhagat. Italy: Emilio Bettini. Japan: Sadako Ogata. Jordan: Ghaleb Z. Barakat. Mexico: Antonio González de León. Netherlands: Peter H. Kooijmans, *Vice-Chairman*. Pakistan: Agha Hilaly. Panama: Octavio Ferrer Anguizola. Peru: Juan Alvarez Vita. Philippines: Luis Moreno-Salcedo. Poland: Adam Lopatka. Rwanda: François Habiyakare. Senegal: Alioune Sène. Syrian Arab Republic: Adib Daoudy. Togo: Atsu-Koffi Amega;[a] Koffi Adjoyi (alternate). Uganda: Olara Otunnu. USSR: V. A. Zorin. United Kingdom: Viscount Colville of Culross. United States: Michael Novak. Uruguay: Carlos Giambruno. Yugoslavia: Ivan Tosevski. Zaire: Bagbeni Adeito Nzengeya. Zambia: Chama L. C. Mubanga-Chipoya. Zimbabwe: Galilee Jess Jani.

[a]Did not attend the thirty-eighth session.

On 6 May 1982 (decision 1982/126), the Economic and Social Council elected the following 14 members for a three-year term beginning on 1 January 1983 to fill the vacancies occurring on 31 December 1982: Bangladesh, Colombia, Costa Rica, Cyprus, Finland, India, Ireland, Libyan Arab Jamahiriya, Mozambique, Netherlands, Nicaragua, Ukrainian SSR, USSR, United Republic of Tanzania.

AD HOC WORKING GROUP OF EXPERTS
(established by Commission on Human Rights resolution 2(XXIII) of 6 March 1967)
Members: Balanda Mikuin Leliel (Zaire);[a] Annan Arkyin Cato, *Chairman/Rapporteur* (from 12 March) (Ghana); Humberto Díaz-Casanueva (Chile); Felix Ermacora (Austria); Branimir M. Jankovic, *Vice-Chairman* (Yugoslavia); Mulka Govinda Reddy (India).

[a]Appointed by the Commission on Human Rights at its thirty-eighth session to replace Kéba M'Baye (Senegal), who resigned upon his election to the International Court of Justice on 6 February 1982.

GROUP OF THREE ESTABLISHED UNDER THE INTERNATIONAL CONVENTION ON THE SUPPRESSION AND PUNISHMENT OF THE CRIME OF *APARTHEID*
Members: Bulgaria, Mexico, Zaire.

The Group of Three held its fifth session at Geneva from 25 to 29 January 1982. The members were represented as follows:
Bulgaria: Roumiana Dermendjieva, *Chairman/Rapporteur*. Mexico: Orpha Garrido-Ruiz. Zaire: Moyila Ngonda Bempu.

SUB-COMMISSION ON PREVENTION OF DISCRIMINATION AND PROTECTION OF MINORITIES
The Sub-Commission consists of 26 members elected by the Commission on Human Rights from candidates nominated by Member States of the United Nations, in accordance with a scheme to ensure equitable geographical distribution. Members serve in their individual capacity as experts, rather than as governmental representatives, each for a three-year term.

Members (until March 1984): Marc Bossuyt (Belgium), W. Beverly Carter, Jr. (United States),[a] Dumitru Ceausu (Romania), Abu Sayeed Chowdhury (Bangladesh), Erica-Irene A. Daes (Greece), Asbjorn Eide (Norway), Raúl Ferrero Costa (Peru), Jonas Kwami Dotse Foli (Ghana), Riyadh Aziz Hadi (Iraq), Ibrahim Sulaiman Jimeta (Nigeria), Louis Joinet (France),[b] Nasser Kaddour (Syrian Arab Republic), Ahmed Mohamed Khalifa (Egypt), Antonio Martínez-Báez (Mexico), Syed S. A. Masud (India), Chama L. C. Mubanga-Chipoya (Zambia), Mohamed Yousif Mudawi (Sudan), Elizabeth Odio Benito (Costa Rica), Julio Oyhanarte (Argentina), Syed Sharifuddin Pirzada (Pakistan), Jorge Eduardo Ritter (Panama), V. N. Sofinsky (USSR), Ivan Tosevski (Yugoslavia), Halima Embarek Warzazi (Morocco), Benjamin Charles George Whitaker (United Kingdom), Fisseha Yimer (Ethiopia).

[a]Died on 9 May 1982; the resultant vacancy was not filled in 1982.
[b]Elected on 12 March 1982 to replace Nicole Questiaux (France), who resigned on 22 January.

The Sub-Commission held its thirty-fifth session at Geneva from 16 August to 10 September 1982, with the following members and alternates:

Marc Bossuyt (Belgium). John Carey (alternate) (United States). Dumitru Ceausu (Romania). Abu Sayeed Chowdhury, *Chairman* (Bangladesh). Erica-Irene A. Daes (Greece). Asbjorn Eide, *Vice-Chairman* (Norway). Raúl Ferrero Costa (Peru). Jonas Kwami Dotse Foli (Ghana). Riyadh Aziz Hadi (Iraq). Ibrahim Sulaiman Jimeta (Nigeria). Louis Joinet (France). Nasser Kaddour;[a] Ahmed Saker (alternate) (Syrian Arab Republic). Ahmed Mohamed Khalifa (Egypt). Antonio Martínez-Báez (Mexico).[a] Syed S. A. Masud (India). Chama L. C. Mubanga-Chipoya, *Vice-Chairman* (Zambia). Mohamed Yousif Mudawi (Sudan). Elizabeth Odio Benito, *Vice-Chairman* (Costa Rica). Julio Oyhanarte;[a] Mario Pena (alternate) (Argentina). Syed Sharifuddin Pirzada;[a] Munir Akram (alternate) (Pakistan). Jorge Eduardo Ritter;[a] Mary Perdomo de Sousa (alternate) (Panama). V. N. Sofinsky (USSR). Ivan Tosevski, *Rapporteur* (Yugoslavia). Halima Embarek Warzazi (Morocco). Benjamin Charles George Whitaker (United Kingdom). Fisseha Yimer (Ethiopia).

[a]Did not attend the thirty-fifth session.

Working Group
(established by resolution 2(XXIV) of 16 August 1971 of the Sub-Commission on Prevention of Discrimination and Protection of Minorities pursuant to Economic and Social Council resolution 1503(XLVIII))
The Working Group on Communications concerning human rights held its eleventh session at Geneva from 2 to 13 August 1982.

Members:[a] Raúl Ferrero Costa (Peru); Syed S. A. Masud, *Chairman/Rapporteur* (India); V. N. Sofinsky (USSR); Fisseha Yimer (Ethiopia).

[a]W. Beverly Carter, Jr. (United States) died on 9 May 1982; no replacement was appointed for the eleventh session.

Working Group
(established on 21 August 1974 by resolution 11(XXVII) of the Sub-Commission on Prevention of Discrimination and Protection of Minorities)
The Working Group on Slavery held its eighth session at Geneva from 9 to 12 August 1982.

Members: Dumitru Ceausu (Romania);[a] Abu Sayeed Chowdhury, *Chairman/Rapporteur* (Bangladesh); Chama L. C. Mubanga-Chipoya (Zambia); Julio Oyhanarte (Argentina);[a] Benjamin Charles George Whitaker (United Kingdom).

[a]Did not attend the eighth session.

Working Group on Indigenous Populations
On the recommendation of the Sub-Commission on Prevention of Discrimination and Protection of Minorities, as endorsed by the Commission on Human Rights, the Economic and Social Council, on 7 May 1982, authorized the Sub-Commission to establish yearly a working group to meet before the Sub-Commission's annual session to review developments on the promotion and protection of the human rights of indigenous populations. The Group was to give special attention to the evolution of standards concerning these rights, taking account of both similarities and differences in the situations and aspirations of such populations throughout the world.
The Working Group held its first session at Geneva from 9 to 13 August 1982.

Members: Asbjorn Eide, *Chairman/Rapporteur* (Norway); Nasser Kaddour (Syrian Arab Republic);[a] Mohamed Yousif Mudawi, *Vice-Chairman* (Sudan); Jorge Eduardo Ritter (Panama);[a] Ivan Tosevski (Yugoslavia).

[a]Did not attend the first session.

WORKING GROUP OF GOVERNMENTAL EXPERTS ON THE RIGHT TO DEVELOPMENT
The Working Group of Governmental Experts on the Right to Development held three sessions in 1982, at Geneva: its third from 18 to 22 January; its fourth from 28 June to 9 July; and its fifth from 22 November to 3 December.

Members: Peter L. Berger (United States);[a] D. V. Bykov (USSR);[a,b] Juan Carlos Capunay (Peru);[b,c] Gilles Chouraqui, *Rapporteur* (France); Paul J. I. M. de Waart (Netherlands); Salah Fellah (Algeria);[b] Riyadh Aziz Hadi (Iraq); Julio Heredia Pérez, *Vice-Chairman* (Cuba); Luis Enrique Martínez Cruz (Panama); Viswanathan Ramachandran, *Vice-Chairman* (India);[c] Ahmed Saker (Syrian Arab Republic); Alioune Sène, *Chairman* (Senegal); Kongit Sinegiorgis (Ethiopia);[b] Henryk J. Sokalski (Poland);[b,c] Danilo Turk, *Vice-Chairman* (Yugoslavia).

[a]Did not attend the third session.
[b]Did not attend the fifth session.
[c]Did not attend the fourth session.

WORKING GROUP ON ENFORCED
OR INVOLUNTARY DISAPPEARANCES

During 1982, the mandate of the Working Group on Enforced or Involuntary Disappearances was extended for one year by a Commission on Human Rights resolution of 10 March, as approved by the Economic and Social Council on 7 May (decision 1982/131).

The Working Group held three sessions during the year, at Geneva: its seventh from 24 to 28 May; its eighth from 27 September to 1 October; and its ninth from 6 to 10 December.

Members: Viscount Colville of Culross, *Chairman/Rapporteur* (United Kingdom); Jonas Kwami Dotse Foli (Ghana); Agha Hilaly (Pakistan); Ivan Tosevski (Yugoslavia); Luis Alberto Varela Quirós (Costa Rica).

WORKING GROUPS
(to study situations revealing a consistent
pattern of gross violations of human rights)

Working Group established by Commission on
Human Rights decision 4(XXXVII) of 6 March 1981:
Members: Niels Boel (Denmark); Octavio Ferrer Anguizola (Panama); Andreas C. Pouyouros, *Chairman/Rapporteur* (Cyprus); Anisse Salah-Bey (Algeria); Ivan Tosevski (Yugoslavia).

Working Group established by Commission on
Human Rights decision 1982/103 of 5 March 1982:
Members: Yvon Beaulne (Canada), Borislav Konstantinov (Bulgaria), E. E. E. Mtango (United Republic of Tanzania), Andreas C. Pouyouros (Cyprus), Luis Solá Vila (Cuba).

WORKING GROUPS (OPEN-ENDED)

Working Group established by Commission on
Human Rights resolution 21(XXXVII) of 10 March 1981
(to continue consideration of a revised draft
declaration on the rights of minorities):
Chairman/Rapporteur: Ivan Tosevski (Yugoslavia).

Working Group established by Commission on
Human Rights resolution 23(XXXVII) of 10 March 1981
(to undertake an overall analysis of alternative
approaches for effective enjoyment of human rights):
Chairman/Rapporteur: T. C. A. Rangachari (India).

Working Group established by Commission on
Human Rights resolution 25(XXXVII) of 10 March 1981
(to draft a convention against torture and other
cruel, inhuman or degrading treatment or punishment):
Chairman/Rapporteur: Jan Herman Burgers (Netherlands).

Working Group established by Commission on
Human Rights resolution 26(XXXVII) of 10 March 1981
(to draft a convention on the rights of the child):
Chairman/Rapporteur: Adam Lopatka (Poland).

Commission on Narcotic Drugs

The Commission on Narcotic Drugs consists of 30 members, elected for four-year terms by the Economic and Social Council from among the Members of the United Nations and members of the specialized agencies and the parties to the Single Convention on Narcotic Drugs, 1961, with due regard for the adequate representation of *(a)* countries which are important producers of opium or coca leaves, *(b)* countries which are important in the manufacture of narcotic drugs, and *(c)* countries in which drug addiction or the illicit traffic in narcotic drugs constitutes an important problem, as well as taking into account the principle of equitable geographical distribution.

Members:
To serve until 31 December 1983: Argentina, Colombia, France, Germany, Federal Republic of, Hungary, India, Italy, Madagascar, Malawi, Norway, Pakistan, Spain, Thailand, United States, Yugoslavia.
To serve until 31 December 1985: Australia, Bahamas, Belgium, Bulgaria, Japan, Malaysia, Mexico, Nigeria, Panama, Republic of Korea, Senegal, Turkey, USSR, United Kingdom, Zaire.

The Commission held its seventh special session at Vienna, Austria, from 2 to 8 February 1982. The members were represented as follows:

Argentina: Juan Carlos García Fernández, *First Vice-Chairman.* Australia: Duncan Campbell. Bahamas: Missouri A. Sherman-Peter. Belgium: B. J. A. Huyghe-Braeckmans. Bulgaria: Alexandrina Nentcheva. Colombia: Guillermo González-Charry. France: François Colcombet. Germany, Federal Republic of: Oskar Schroeder. Hungary: Istvan Bayer, *Second Vice-Chairman.* India: B. B. Gujral. Italy: Giuseppe di Gennaro, *Chairman.* Japan: Hisateru Ichihara. Madagascar: Maurice Randrianame, *Rapporteur.* Malawi: F. G. Chalira. Malaysia: Dato Haji Rozan bin Haji Kuntom. Mexico: Fernando Baeza Melendez. Nigeria: T. A. A. Ajayi. Norway: Torbjorn Mork. Pakistan: Mairaj Husain. Panama: Laura Torres de Rodríguez. Republic of Korea: Myung Won Shim. Senegal: Mounirou Ciss. Spain: Enrique Suárez de Puga y Villegas. Thailand: Chavalit Yodmani. Turkey: Ecmel Barutcu. USSR: E. A. Babayan. United Kingdom: Brian Oliver Bubbear. United States: Dominick L. DiCarlo. Yugoslavia: Petar Dzundev. Zaire: Bintou-a Tshiabola.

SUB-COMMISSION ON ILLICIT DRUG TRAFFIC AND
RELATED MATTERS IN THE NEAR AND MIDDLE EAST
Members: Afghanistan, Iran, Pakistan, Sweden, Turkey.

The Sub-Commission met at Vienna, Austria, on 1 February and from 4 to 6 October 1982, with the following members and their representatives:

Afghanistan: Hadi Abawi, Abdullah Hamkar (February meeting); Kabir Katawazi, Enayatullah Nabiel (October meetings). Iran: Sayed Hossein Fakhr. Pakistan: Mairaj Husain, *Vice-Chairman.* Sweden: Lars Hultstrand. Turkey: Ecmel Barutcu, *Chairman.*

MEETING OF OPERATIONAL HEADS
OF NATIONAL NARCOTICS LAW ENFORCEMENT
AGENCIES, FAR EAST REGION

A meeting to co-ordinate regional activities directed against illicit drug traffic has been convened annually following endorsement on 15 May 1974 by the Economic and Social Council of a recommendation by the *Ad Hoc* Committee on Illicit Traffic in the Far East Region to hold such a meeting.[35] It is usually held in any one of the region's capitals close to the centre of trafficking routes.

The meeting is open to any country in the region approved by the Commission, as well as to observers from the Customs Co-operation Council, the International Criminal Police Organization and the International Narcotics Control Board. Any interested Government outside the region may be invited by the Secretary-General to send an observer at its own expense.

Commission on the Status of Women

The Commission on the Status of Women consists of 32 members, elected for four-year terms by the Economic and Social Council according to a specific pattern of equitable geographical distribution.

Members:
To serve until 31 December 1982: Czechoslovakia, Finland, Ghana, Iraq, Malaysia, Panama, Senegal, Uganda, USSR, United Kingdom, United States.
To serve until 31 December 1983: China, Cuba, France, German Democratic Republic, Guatemala, Honduras, Lesotho, Nigeria, Norway, Pakistan.

---

[35]Resolution 1845(LVI) (YUN 1974, p. 615).

To serve until 31 December 1984: Canada, Egypt, India, Italy, Japan, Spain, Sudan, Trinidad and Tobago, Ukrainian SSR, Venezuela, Zaire.

The Commission held its twenty-ninth session at Vienna, Austria, from 24 February to 5 March 1982. The members were represented as follows:

Canada: Maureen O'Neil. China: Guan Minqian. Cuba: Olga Finlay Saavedra. Czechoslovakia: Dagmar Molkova, *Vice-Chairman.* Egypt: Nihad Abou Zikry. Finland: Marjatta Rasi, *Vice-Chairman.* France: Marcelle Devaud. German Democratic Republic: Helga Hoerz. Ghana: Florence Dolphyne.[a] Guatemala: Edna Haydee León Menéndez. Honduras: Martha Luz Mejía. India: P. Patil, *Vice-Chairman.* Iraq: Adnan Assif. Italy: Paola Gaiotti de Biase. Japan: Yoko Nuita. Lesotho: Mahlape Theresia Qoane. Malaysia: Nik Safiah Abdul Karim. Nigeria: Olajumoke Oladayo Obafemi. Norway: Grethe Vaernoe. Pakistan: Attiya Inayatullah. Panama: Ernesto Koref. Senegal: Amadou Ba. Spain: María Isabel Pérez Serrano Jauregui. Sudan: Fatima Talib Ismael.[a] Trinidad and Tobago: Elmina Clarke-Allen. Uganda: Marjorie Dungu.[a] Ukrainian SSR: N. K. Kovalskaia. USSR: T. N. Nikolaeva. United Kingdom: R. T. Gardner of Parkes. United States: Nancy Clark Reynolds. Venezuela: Hanna Binstock, *Rapporteur.* Zaire: Bolie Nonkwa.

[a]Did not attend the twenty-ninth session.

On 6 May 1982 (decision 1982/126), the Economic and Social Council elected the following 11 members for a four-year term beginning on 1 January 1983 to fill the vacancies occurring on 31 December 1982: Australia, Czechoslovakia, Indonesia, Kenya, Liberia, Mexico, Philippines, Sierra Leone, USSR, United Kingdom, United States.

On 4 May 1982, the Council decided that the Commission was to be the preparatory body for the World Conference to Review and Appraise the Achievements of the United Nations Decade for Women (scheduled for 1985). The Commission, acting as the preparatory body, was to meet in extraordinary session in 1983 and 1985; its 1984 regular session was to be extended to allow additional time for conference preparations.

Population Commission

The Population Commission consists of 27 members, elected for four-year terms by the Economic and Social Council according to a specific pattern of equitable geographical distribution.

The Commission was designated by the Council as the Preparatory Committee for the International Conference on Population, scheduled for 1984.

The Commission did not meet in 1982.

Members:

To serve until 31 December 1983: Ecuador, Finland, France, Indonesia, Morocco, Nigeria, Sierra Leone, Sri Lanka, Ukrainian SSR.

To serve until 31 December 1984: Greece, Honduras, Hungary, Netherlands, Norway, Peru, Rwanda, Thailand, Zaire.

To serve until 31 December 1985: Bolivia, China, Japan, Mexico, Sudan, USSR, United Kingdom, United States, Zambia.

Statistical Commission

The Statistical Commission consists of 24 members, elected for four-year terms by the Economic and Social Council according to a specific pattern of equitable geographical distribution.

The Commission did not meet in 1982.

Members:

To serve until 31 December 1983: Austria, Czechoslovakia, Ecuador, Ghana, Hungary, India, Iraq, Kenya.

To serve until 31 December 1984: Australia, Brazil, Finland, Japan, Malaysia, Mexico, Ukrainian SSR, United Kingdom.

To serve until 31 December 1985: Argentina, France, Ireland, Libyan Arab Jamahiriya, Nigeria, Spain, Togo, USSR.

WORKING GROUP ON INTERNATIONAL
STATISTICAL PROGRAMMES AND CO-ORDINATION

The Working Group consists of the Bureau of the Statistical Commission; the representatives to the Commission of the two major contributors to the United Nations budget, unless these are already

represented in the Bureau; and one representative to the Commission from a developing country from among members of each of the following: ECA, ECLA, ECWA and ESCAP, unless these are also already represented in the Bureau. Members serve two-year terms.

The Working Group did not meet in 1982.

Regional commissions

Economic and Social Commission for Asia and the Pacific (ESCAP)

The Economic and Social Commission for Asia and the Pacific held its thirty-eighth session at Bangkok, Thailand, from 23 March to 2 April 1982.

Members: Afghanistan, Australia, Bangladesh, Bhutan, Burma, China, Democratic Kampuchea, Fiji,[a] France, India, Indonesia, Iran, Japan, Lao People's Democratic Republic, Malaysia, Maldives, Mongolia, Nauru, Nepal, Netherlands, New Zealand, Pakistan, Papua New Guinea, Philippines, Republic of Korea, Samoa, Singapore, Solomon Islands, Sri Lanka, Thailand, Tonga,[a] USSR, United Kingdom, United States, Viet Nam.

Associate members: Brunei,[a] Cook Islands,[a] Guam, Hong Kong, Kiribati, Niue, Trust Territory of the Pacific Islands, Tuvalu,[a] Vanuatu.[b]

Switzerland, not a Member of the United Nations, participates in a consultative capacity in the work of the Commission.

[a]Not represented at the thirty-eighth session.
[b]Retained associate membership in 1982 although admitted to the United Nations on 15 September 1981.

Chairman: Conrado F. Estrella (Philippines).
Vice-Chairmen: Datuk Abdullah bin Haji Ahmad Badawi (Malaysia), Jambalyn Banzar (Mongolia), He Ying (China), Toshio Kimura (Japan), Mochtar Kusumaatmadja (Indonesia), Fasihuddin Mahtab (Bangladesh), M. H. M. Naina Marikkar (Sri Lanka), Shivraj V. Patil (India), Soulivong Phasithideth (Lao People's Democratic Republic), Siddhi Savetsila (Thailand), Ian J. Shearer (New Zealand).

Following are the main subsidiary bodies of the Commission:

For advice on policy and direction: Advisory Committee of Permanent Representatives and Other Representatives Designated by Members of the Commission.
For sectoral review and project formulation and programming: Committee on Agricultural Development; Committee on Development Planning; Committee on Industry, Technology, Human Settlements and the Environment; Committee on Natural Resources; Committee on Population; Committee on Shipping, and Transport and Communications; Committee on Social Development; Committee on Statistics; Committee on Trade; Special Body on Land-locked Countries. *Ad hoc* conferences are convened for issues not dealt with by these committees.
For project implementation: Advisory Council, Statistical Institute for Asia and the Pacific; Committee for Co-ordination of Joint Prospecting for Mineral Resources in Asian Offshore Areas; Committee for Co-ordination of Joint Prospecting for Mineral Resources in South Pacific Offshore Areas; Governing Board, Regional Co-ordination Centre for Research and Development of Coarse Grains, Pulses, Roots and Tuber Crops in the Humid Tropics of Asia and the Pacific;[a] Governing Council, Regional Mineral Resources Development Centre; Interim Committee for Co-ordination of Investigations of the Lower Mekong Basin; Management Board, Asian and Pacific Development Centre; Typhoon Committee.

[a]The Centre's Statute was adopted by ESCAP on 1 April 1982.

Economic Commission for Africa (ECA)

The Economic Commission for Africa meets in annual session at the ministerial level known as the Conference of Ministers.

The Commission held its seventeenth session (eighth meeting of the Conference of Ministers) at Tripoli, Libyan Arab Jamahiriya, from 27 to 30 April 1982.

Members: Algeria, Angola, Benin, Botswana,[a] Burundi, Cape Verde,[a] Central African Republic,[a] Chad, Comoros, Congo, Djibouti, Egypt,[a] Equatorial Guinea,[a] Ethiopia, Gabon, Gambia,[a] Ghana, Guinea, Guinea-Bissau, Ivory Coast, Kenya, Lesotho, Liberia,[a] Libyan Arab Jamahiriya, Madagascar,[a] Malawi,[a] Mali, Mauritania, Mauritius,[a] Morocco, Mozambique,[a] Niger, Nigeria, Rwanda, Sao Tome and Principe, Senegal, Seychelles,[a] Sierra Leone, Somalia,[a] South Africa,[b] Sudan,[a] Swaziland,[a] Togo, Tunisia, Uganda, United Republic of Cameroon, United Republic of Tanzania, Upper Volta, Zaire, Zambia, Zimbabwe.

Switzerland, not a Member of the United Nations, participates in a consultative capacity in the work of the Commission.

[a]Not represented at the seventeenth session.
[b]On 30 July 1963, the Economic and Social Council decided that South Africa should not take part in the work of ECA until conditions for constructive co-operation had been restored by a change in South Africa's racial policy (resolution 974 D IV (XXXVI), YUN 1963, p. 274).

Chairman: Fauzi Ahmed Elshakshouki (Libyan Arab Jamahiriya).
First Vice-Chairman: Boubacar Diallo (Guinea).
Second Vice-Chairman: Henry S. Meebelo (Zambia).
Rapporteur: Bieme Ngalisame Mokelo (Zaire).

The Commission has established the following principal legislative organs:

Conference of Ministers; sectoral ministerial conferences, each assisted by an appropriate committee of technical officials; Council of Ministers of each Multinational Programming and Operational Centre, assisted by its committee of officials; Governing Council, African Institute for Economic Development and Planning.

The Commission has also established the following subsidiary bodies:

Joint Conference of African Planners, Statisticians and Demographers, and Technical Preparatory Committee of the Whole (two standing technical bodies); Intergovernmental Committee of Experts on Science and Technology Development; Joint Intergovernmental Regional Committee on Human Settlements and Environment.

Economic Commission for Europe (ECE)
The Economic Commission for Europe held its thirty-seventh session at Geneva from 23 March to 2 April 1982.

Members: Albania, Austria, Belgium, Bulgaria, Byelorussian SSR, Canada, Cyprus, Czechoslovakia, Denmark, Finland, France, German Democratic Republic, Germany, Federal Republic of, Greece, Hungary, Iceland, Ireland, Italy, Luxembourg, Malta, Netherlands, Norway, Poland, Portugal, Romania, Spain, Sweden, Switzerland, Turkey, Ukrainian SSR, USSR, United Kingdom, United States, Yugoslavia.

The Holy See, Liechtenstein and San Marino,[a] which are not Members of the United Nations, participate in a consultative capacity in the work of the Commission.

[a]Not represented at the thirty-seventh session.

Chairman: Ferenc Bartha (Hungary).
Vice-Chairman: Fernando Reino (Portugal).
Rapporteurs: Sacho Spassov (Bulgaria), Johann Wenzl (Federal Republic of Germany).

Following are the principal subsidiary bodies of the Commission:

Chemical Industry Committee; Coal Committee; Committee on Agricultural Problems; Committee on Electric Power; Committee on Gas; Committee on Housing, Building and Planning; Committee on the Development of Trade; Committee on Water Problems; Conference of European Statisticians; Inland Transport Committee; Senior Advisers to ECE Governments on Environmental Problems; Senior Advisers to ECE Governments on Science and Technology; Senior Economic Advisers to ECE Governments; Steel Committee; Timber Committee.

Other subsidiary bodies are: Senior Advisers to ECE Governments on Energy; Working Party on Engineering Industries and Automation.

Ad hoc meetings of experts are convened for sectors of activity not dealt with by these principal bodies.

Economic Commission for Latin America (ECLA)
The Economic Commission for Latin America did not meet in 1982. The Committee of the Whole of ECLA held two sessions in 1982, at United Nations Headquarters: its fifteenth special session on 22 and 23 July; and its sixteenth session on 2 and 3 December.

Members: Antigua and Barbuda,[a] Argentina, Bahamas,[b] Barbados, Belize,[a,b] Bolivia, Brazil, Canada, Chile, Colombia, Costa Rica, Cuba, Dominica,[b] Dominican Republic, Ecuador, El Salvador, France, Grenada,[a] Guatemala, Guyana, Haiti,[a] Honduras, Jamaica, Mexico, Netherlands, Nicaragua, Panama, Paraguay,[b] Peru, Saint Lucia,[b] Saint Vincent and the Grenadines, Spain, Suriname, Trinidad and Tobago, United Kingdom, United States,[b] Uruguay, Venezuela.
Associate members: Netherlands Antilles, West Indies Associated States[a,b] (St. Kitts–Nevis–Anguilla and the Territory of Montserrat—collectively as a single member).

Switzerland,[a,b] not a Member of the United Nations, participates in a consultative capacity in the work of the Commission.

[a]Not represented at the sixteenth session.
[b]Not represented at the fifteenth special session.

Chairman: Juan Carlos Blanco (Uruguay).
First Vice-Chairman: Harold Peter Bartlett (Jamaica) (fifteenth special session), Douglas A. C. Saunders (Jamaica) (sixteenth session).
Second Vice-Chairman: Carlos Ozores Typaldos (Panama) (fifteenth special session), Luis M. Martínez (Panama) (sixteenth session).
Third Vice-Chairman: Nicolás Martínez Fresno (Spain) (fifteenth special session), Francisco Monforte (Spain) (sixteenth session).
Rapporteur: Gustavo García Moreno (Colombia).

The Commission has established the following principal subsidiary bodies:

Caribbean Development and Co-operation Committee; Central American Economic Co-operation Committee and its Inter-agency Committee; Committee of High-level Government Experts; Committee of the Whole; Technical Committee, Latin American Institute for Economic and Social Planning; Trade Committee.

Economic Commission for Western Asia (ECWA)
The Economic Commission for Western Asia held its ninth session at Baghdad, Iraq, from 8 to 12 May 1982.

Members: Bahrain, Democratic Yemen, Egypt, Iraq, Jordan, Kuwait, Lebanon, Oman, Qatar, Saudi Arabia, Syrian Arab Republic,[a] United Arab Emirates, Yemen; Palestine Liberation Organization.

[a]Not represented at the ninth session.

Chairman: Thamer Razuki (Iraq).
Vice-Chairmen: Khaled Jumblatt (Lebanon), Yassin Said Na'aman (Democratic Yemen).
Rapporteur: Ahmed Salim Ahmed (Qatar).

On 30 July 1982, the Economic and Social Council, on the recommendation of ECWA at its ninth session, established a Standing Committee for the Programme, composed of all ECWA members, as the main subsidiary organ of the Commission to assist it in programme planning and review.

Standing committees

Commission on Human Settlements
The Commission on Human Settlements consists of 58 members elected by the Economic and Social Council for three-year terms according to a specific pattern of equitable geographical distribution; it reports to the General Assembly through the Council.

The Commission held its fifth session at Nairobi, Kenya, from 26 April to 7 May 1982.

Members:
To serve until 31 December 1982: Belgium, Canada, Colombia, Cuba,[a] Egypt, France, German Democratic Republic, Hungary, Indonesia, Iraq, Lesotho, Malaysia, Netherlands, Nigeria, Norway, Papua New Guinea, Peru,[a] Sierra Leone,[a] Uganda.

To serve until 31 December 1983: Argentina, Barbados, Bulgaria, Burundi, Denmark, Finland, Guinea,[a] Jamaica, Japan, Mexico, Pakistan, Philippines, Somalia,[a] Spain, Swaziland, Syrian Arab Republic,[a] USSR, United Republic of Tanzania, United States, Zambia.

To serve until 31 December 1984: Bangladesh, Bolivia,[a] Byelorussian SSR,[a] Chile, Cyprus, El Salvador,[a] Germany, Federal Republic of, Greece, India, Italy, Jordan,[a] Kenya, Liberia, Morocco, New Zealand, Romania,[a] Sri Lanka, Sudan, Zimbabwe.

[a]Not represented at the fifth session.

Chairman: Y. N. Sokolov (USSR).
Vice-Chairmen: Bruce Golding (Jamaica), David Miller (Canada), Ramalingam Paskaralingam (Sri Lanka).
Rapporteur: Salah R. El-Ashry (Egypt).

On 6 May 1982 (decision 1982/126), the Economic and Social Council elected the following for a three-year term beginning on 1 January 1983 to fill 17 of the 19 vacancies occurring on 31 December 1982: Algeria, Canada, Colombia, Cuba, France, German Democratic Republic, Hungary, Indonesia, Libyan Arab Jamahiriya, Netherlands, Nigeria, Norway, Papua New Guinea, Peru, Sierra Leone, Sweden, Uganda. No further elections were held during the year for the remaining vacancies.

On 20 December 1982, the General Assembly designated the Commission, in the framework of its regular sessions, as the United Nations intergovernmental body responsible for organizing the International Year of Shelter for the Homeless (1987).

Commission on Transnational Corporations

The Commission on Transnational Corporations consists of 48 members, elected from all States for three-year terms by the Economic and Social Council according to a specific pattern of geographical distribution.

The Commission held its eighth session at Manila, Philippines, from 30 August to 10 September 1982.

Members:
To serve until 31 December 1982:[a] Brazil, Cuba,[b] Kenya,[b] Mexico, Netherlands, Panama,[b] Philippines, Somalia,[b] Sweden, Thailand, Uganda,[b] USSR, United Kingdom, United States, Zaire.[b]

To serve until 31 December 1983:[c] Argentina, China, Costa Rica,[b] Egypt, France, German Democratic Republic, Germany, Federal Republic of, Guatemala,[b] Guinea,[b] Japan, Libyan Arab Jamahiriya,[b] Romania, Sierra Leone,[b] Switzerland.

To serve until 31 December 1984: Algeria, Canada, Congo, Ghana,[b] India, Iran, Italy, Jamaica, Pakistan, Peru, Republic of Korea,[d] Swaziland,[b] Turkey,[b] Ukrainian SSR, Venezuela, Yugoslavia.

Expert advisers (to serve through the eighth session): Michael A. Ajomo (Nigeria),[e] James Dennis Akumu (Kenya), S. Babar Ali (Pakistan), José A. Encinas del Pando (Peru), Johan M. Goudswaard (Netherlands), Elizabeth R. Jager (United States), Kiyoshi Kojima (Japan), David Lea (United Kingdom), Carlos Omar Navarro Carrasco (Venezuela),[e] Jones Santos Neves (Brazil),[e] Samuel Paul (India), Mario Joel Ramos da Silva (Portugal),[e,f] Bogdan Sosnowski (Poland),[e] Louis von Planta (Switzerland),[e] Branko Vukmir (Yugoslavia),[e] Ralph A. Weller (United States).[e]

[a]One seat allocated to a member from Asian States remained unfilled in 1982.
[b]Not represented at the eighth session.
[c]Two seats allocated to members from Asian States remained unfilled in 1982.
[d]Elected on 5 February 1982 (decision 1982/108).
[e]Reappointed by the Commission on 9 September 1982 to serve for a further two years, up to and including the tenth (1984) session. Appointed on the same date for the same term were: Friedrich Dribbusch (Federal Republic of Germany), Wim Kok (Netherlands), Elias Mashasi (United Republic of Tanzania), Charles Albert Michalet (France), Zuhayr Mikdashi (Lebanon), David Sycip (Philippines), Nat Weinberg (United States), Eduardo White (Argentina).
[f]Appointment effective 1 March 1982, the date of voluntary resignation of Gianandrea Sandri (Italy).

Chairman: Edgardo Tordesillas (Philippines).
Vice-Chairmen: Eugenio Anguiano (Mexico), Eugene Berg (France), Hassan Gadel Hak (Egypt).
Rapporteur: Horst Heininger (German Democratic Republic).

On 6 May 1982 (decision 1982/126) and (with respect to Cyprus) on 10 November (decision 1982/188), the Economic and Social Council elected the following 16 members for a three-year term beginning on 1 January 1983 to fill the vacancies occurring on 31 December 1982: Bahamas, Brazil, Central African Republic, Cuba, Cyprus, Indonesia, Kenya, Mexico, Netherlands, Nigeria, Norway, Thailand, Uganda, USSR, United Kingdom, United States.

INTERGOVERNMENTAL WORKING GROUP
OF EXPERTS ON INTERNATIONAL
STANDARDS OF ACCOUNTING AND REPORTING
On 27 October 1982, the Economic and Social Council established an Intergovernmental Working Group of Experts on International Standards of Accounting and Reporting, which was to report to the Commission on Transnational Corporations.

INTERGOVERNMENTAL WORKING
GROUP ON A CODE OF CONDUCT
The Intergovernmental Working Group on a Code of Conduct, a working group of the whole of the Commission, held three sessions in 1982, at United Nations Headquarters: its fifteenth from 4 to 15 January; its sixteenth from 1 to 12 March; and its seventeenth and final session from 10 to 21 May.

Chairman: Sten Niklasson (Sweden).
Vice-Chairmen: Hassan Gadel Hak (Egypt), Horst Heininger (German Democratic Republic), Nitish Kumar Sengupta (India).
Rapporteur: Luzmila Zanabria (Peru).

Committee for Programme and Co-ordination

The Committee for Programme and Co-ordination is the main subsidiary organ of the Economic and Social Council and of the General Assembly for planning, programming and co-ordination and reports directly to both. It consists of 21 members nominated by the Council and elected by the Assembly for three-year terms according to a specific pattern of equitable geographical distribution.

The Committee held an organizational meeting on 9 March and its twenty-second session from 19 April to 29 May 1982, both at United Nations Headquarters.

Members:
To serve until 31 December 1982: Argentina, Costa Rica, France, Sudan, USSR, United Republic of Tanzania, United States.
To serve until 31 December 1983: Brazil, India, Japan, Morocco, Philippines, Senegal, United Republic of Cameroon.
To serve until 31 December 1984: Germany, Federal Republic of, Netherlands, Pakistan, Romania, Trinidad and Tobago, United Kingdom, Yugoslavia.

Chairman: Shri Vatsa Purushottam (India).
Vice-Chairmen: Adhemar Gabriel Bahadian (Brazil), Mirko Bunc (Yugoslavia), Tommo Monthe (United Republic of Cameroon).
Rapporteur: Jan Berteling (Netherlands).

On 6 May 1982 (decision 1982/126), the Economic and Social Council nominated the following seven Member States of the United Nations, for election by the General Assembly, for a three-year term beginning on 1 January 1983 to fill the vacancies occurring on 31 December 1982: Argentina, Chile, Ethiopia, France, Nigeria, USSR, United States. They were elected by the Assembly on 16 November 1982 (decision 37/314).

Committee on Natural Resources

The Committee on Natural Resources consists of 54 members, elected by the Economic and Social Council for four-year terms in accordance with the geographical distribution of seats in the Council. The Committee did not meet in 1982.

Members:
To serve until 31 December 1982:[a] Argentina, Australia, Bhutan, Bulgaria, Chad, Finland, France, German Democratic Republic, Iran, Iraq, Italy, Ivory Coast, Netherlands, Nigeria, Pakistan, Poland, Senegal, Spain, Sweden, Togo, Trinidad and Tobago, Turkey, Uganda, United States, Yugoslavia.

To serve until 31 December 1984:[a] Bangladesh, Belgium, Botswana, Brazil, Canada, Colombia, Dominican Republic, Greece, Guinea, India, Jamaica, Japan, Kenya, Morocco, Niger, Paraguay, Peru, Sierra Leone, Sudan, Ukrainian SSR, USSR, United Kingdom, Uruguay, Venezuela, Zaire.

[a]Two seats allocated to members from Asian States remained unfilled in 1982.

On 6 May 1982 (decision 1982/126), the Economic and Social Council elected the following for a four-year term beginning on 1 January 1983 to fill 20 of the 27 vacancies occurring on 31 December 1982: Algeria, Australia, Bolivia, Central African Republic, Denmark, France, German Democratic Republic, Germany, Federal Republic of, Italy, Liberia, Mexico, Norway, Pakistan, Spain, Turkey, Uganda, United States, Upper Volta, Yugoslavia, Zimbabwe. On 10 November, the Council elected Thailand and on 11 November, the Philippines, for the same term (decision 1982/188).

No further elections were held during the year for the remaining five vacancies.

Committee on Negotiations with Intergovernmental Agencies

The Committee on Negotiations with Intergovernmental Agencies, established by the Economic and Social Council on 16 February 1946, was reconstituted by the Council on 13 May 1976 for the purpose of negotiating a relationship agreement between the United Nations and IFAD.

The Committee adjourned *sine die* on 11 May 1977 upon completion of its report on the negotiations.

Committee on Non-Governmental Organizations

Pursuant to a 1981 Council decision,[36] the membership of the Committee on Non-Governmental Organizations was increased in 1982 from 13 to 19 Members of the United Nations. Members are elected for a term of four years by the Council according to a specific pattern of equitable geographical representation.

The Committee met during the year at United Nations Headquarters between 14 and 16 April and on 7 July.

Members (until 31 December 1982): Chile, Costa Rica,[a] Cuba, Cyprus,[a] France, Ghana, India, Iraq, Kenya, Libyan Arab Jamahiriya,[a] Nicaragua,[a] Nigeria,[a] Pakistan, Sweden, Ukrainian SSR, USSR, United Kingdom, United States, Zaire.[a]

[a]Elected on 13 April 1982 (decision 1982/126) and (with respect to Cyprus and Nicaragua) on 5 February (decision 1982/108).

Chairman: Sajjad Ali (Pakistan).
Rapporteur: Richard H. O. Okwaro (Kenya).

On 6 May 1982 (decision 1982/126), the Economic and Social Council elected the following 19 members for a four-year term beginning on 1 January 1983 to fill the vacancies occurring on 31 December 1982: Chile, Costa Rica, Cuba, Cyprus, France, Ghana, India, Kenya, Libyan Arab Jamahiriya, Nicaragua, Nigeria, Pakistan, Rwanda, Sweden, Thailand, USSR, United Kingdom, United States, Yugoslavia.

Expert bodies

Ad Hoc Group of Experts on International Co-operation in Tax Matters

The membership of the *Ad Hoc* Group of Experts on International Co-operation in Tax Matters—to consist of 25 members drawn from 15 developing and 10 developed countries, appointed by the Secretary-General to serve in their individual capacity—remained at 24 in 1982, with one member from a developing country still to be appointed.

The *Ad Hoc* Group, which meets every two years, did not meet in 1982.

Members: Maurice Hugh Collins (United Kingdom), Jean François Court (France), T. Dekker (Netherlands), Francisco O. N. Dornelles (Brazil), Hussein M. El Baroudi (Egypt), Mordecai S. Feinberg (United States), José Ramón Fernández Pérez (Spain), Antonio H. Figueroa (Argentina), Mayer Gabay (Israel), Yasuyuki Kawahara (Japan), R. R. Khosla (India), Marwan Koudsi (Syrian Arab Republic), Felipe Lamarca (Chile), Daniel Luthi (Switzerland), Thomas Menck (Federal Republic of Germany), Canute R. Miller (Jamaica), Medaghri Alaoui

Mohamed (Morocco), Alberto Navarro Rodríguez (Mexico), I. O. Oni (Nigeria), Alfred Philipp (Austria), Rainer Söderholm (Finland), Sutadi Sukarya (Indonesia), André Titty (United Republic of Cameroon), Abdul Waheed (Pakistan).

Committee for Development Planning

The Committee for Development Planning is composed of 24 experts representing different planning systems. They are appointed by the Economic and Social Council, on nomination by the Secretary-General, to serve in their personal capacity for a term of three years.

The Committee held its eighteenth session at United Nations Headquarters from 19 to 28 April 1982.

Members (until 31 December 1983): Ismail-Sabri Abdalla (Egypt); Khatijah Ahmad (Malaysia); Abdlatif Y. Al-Hamad (Kuwait);[a] Maria Augusztinovics, *Vice-Chairman* (Hungary); Hendricus Cornelis Bos (Netherlands); Robert Cassen (United Kingdom);[b] William Gilbert Demas, *Chairman* (Trinidad and Tobago); José Encarnacion, Jr. (Philippines); Gerhard Fels (Federal Republic of Germany);[c] Celso Furtado (Brazil); Robert K. A. Gardiner (Ghana);[a] Shinichi Ichimura (Japan); V. N. Kirichenko (USSR); John P. Lewis (United States); Li Zong (China); Gabriel Mignot (France); J. M. Mwanza (Zambia);[a] Joseph Elenga Ngaporo (Congo);[a] G. O. Nwankwo (Nigeria);[a] Goran Ohlin, *Rapporteur* (Sweden); Jozef Pajestka (Poland); I. G. Patel (India); Germánico Salgado (Ecuador); Leopoldo Solís (Mexico).[a]

[a]Did not attend the eighteenth session.
[b]Appointed on 5 February 1982 (decision 1982/108) to fill the vacancy created by the resignation on 1 January of Richard Jolly (United Kingdom).
[c]Resigned on 2 August 1982; no replacement was appointed in 1982.

Committee of Experts on the Transport of Dangerous Goods

The Committee of Experts on the Transport of Dangerous Goods is composed of experts from countries interested in the international transport of dangerous goods. The experts are made available by their Governments at the request of the Secretary-General. The membership, to be increased to 15 in accordance with a 1975 resolution of the Economic and Social Council,[37] remained at 13 in 1982.

Members: Canada, France, Germany, Federal Republic of, Iran,[a] Iraq,[a] Italy, Japan, Norway, Poland, Thailand,[a] USSR, United Kingdom, United States.

[a]Inactive member.

The Committee held its twelfth session at Geneva from 6 to 15 December 1982. The experts who attended the session were:

L. P. Andronov (USSR); T. Austerheim (Norway); T. D. Ellison (Canada); J. Engeland (Federal Republic of Germany); L. Grainger (United Kingdom); K. Kumagai (Japan); P. Marrec (France); T. Pusty (Poland); A. I. Roberts, *Chairman* (United States); M. Santarella (Italy).

The Committee may alter, as required, the composition of its subsidiary bodies. In addition, any Committee member may participate in the work of and vote in those bodies provided such member notify the United Nations Secretariat of the intention to do so.

GROUP OF EXPERTS ON EXPLOSIVES

The Group of Experts on Explosives held its twenty-second session at Geneva from 2 to 6 August 1982. The experts who attended the session were:

L. P. Andronov (USSR); E. Becarelli (Italy); J. des Rivières (Canada); J. Engeland (Federal Republic of Germany); O. Hakenstad (Norway); K. Kumagai (Japan); P. Marrec (France); A. I. Roberts (United States); R. R. Watson, *Chairman* (United Kingdom).

GROUP OF RAPPORTEURS OF THE COMMITTEE OF EXPERTS ON THE TRANSPORT OF DANGEROUS GOODS

The Group of Rapporteurs of the Committee of Experts on the Transport of Dangerous Goods held two sessions during 1982, at Geneva:

[36]Resolution 1981/50, 20 July 1981 (YUN 1981, p. 1088).
[37]Resolution 1973(LIX), 30 July 1975 (YUN 1975, p. 734).

its twenty-eighth from 8 to 12 March; and its twenty-ninth from 9 to 13 August. The experts who attended the sessions were:

L. P. Andronov, *Chairman* (twenty-ninth session) (USSR);[a] T. Austerheim (Norway); J. Engeland, *Vice-Chairman* (Federal Republic of Germany); L Grainger (United Kingdom); K. Kumagai (Japan); P. Marrec (France); A. I. Roberts (United States); M. Santarella (Italy);[b] D. Wiwczaruk, *Chairman* (twenty-eighth session), *Vice-Chairman* (twenty-ninth session) (Canada).

[a]Did not attend the twenty-eighth session.
[b]Did not attend the twenty-ninth session.

Committee on Crime Prevention and Control
The Committee on Crime Prevention and Control consists of 27 members elected for four-year terms by the Economic and Social Council, according to a specific pattern of equitable geographical representation, from among experts nominated by Member States.

The Committee held its seventh session at Vienna, Austria, from 15 to 24 March 1982.

Members:
To serve until 31 December 1982: S. V. Borodin (USSR); Dusan Cotic, *Vice-Chairman* (Yugoslavia); Ahmed Mohamed Khalifa (Egypt); Manuel López-Rey y Arrojo (Bolivia); Francis Joseph Mahony, *Rapporteur* (Australia); Mustafa Abdul Majid-Karah (Libyan Arab Jamahiriya); Jorge Arturo Montero-Castro (Costa Rica); Chadly Mohamed Ahmed Nefzaoui (Tunisia);[a] John Olden (Ireland); P. R. Rajagopal (India);[a] Simone Andrée Rozes (France); Saladh El-Din Salhadar (Syrian Arab Republic);[a] Silvino Julián Sorhegui Mato (Cuba);[a] Yoshio Suzuki (Japan).[a]
To serve until 31 December 1984: A. Adeyemi (Nigeria); Anthony John Edward Brennan (United Kingdom); Giuseppe di Gennaro (Italy);[b] Ronald L. Gainer (United States); Jozsef Godony (Hungary);[a] Aura Guerra de Villaláz, *Vice-Chairman* (Panama); Ds. Hudioro (Indonesia); Abdul Meguid Ibrahim Kharbit (Kuwait); Mawik-Ndi-Muyeng (Zaire);[a] Juan Manuel Mayorca (Venezuela);[a] Albert Metzger (Sierra Leone); Abdel Aziz Abdalla Shiddo, *Chairman* (Sudan); Ramananda Prasad Singh, *Vice-Chairman* (Nepal).

[a]Did not attend the seventh session.
[b]Resigned before the seventh session; replaced by Gioacchino Polimeni (Italy), who was elected on 6 May 1982 (decision 1982/126).

On 6 May 1982 (decision 1982/126), the Economic and Social Council elected the following 14 members for a four-year term beginning on 1 January 1983 to fill the vacancies occurring on 31 December 1982: André Bissonnette (Canada), S. V. Borodin (USSR), Dusan Cotic (Yugoslavia), Ahmed Mohamed Khalifa (Egypt), Robert Linke (Austria), Manuel López-Rey y Arrojo (Bolivia), Charles Alfred Lunn (Barbados), Jorge Arturo Montero-Castro (Costa Rica), Mphanza Patrick Mvunga (Zambia), Amadou Racine Ba (Mauritania), Simone Andrée Rozes (France), Yoshio Suzuki (Japan), Mervyn Patrick Wijesinha (Sri Lanka), Wu Han (China).

United Nations Group of Experts on Geographical Names
The United Nations Group of Experts on Geographical Names held its tenth session at Geneva on 23 August and 15 September 1982. Attending the session were the chairmen or chief representatives of 13 of the 17 geographical/linguistic divisions, as follows:

Africa Central Division: Not represented.
Africa East Division: Not represented.
Africa West Division: Not represented.
Arabic Division: Abdelhadi Tazi (Morocco).
Asia East Division (other than China): Hiroyuki Matsuda (Japan).
Asia South-East and Pacific South-West Division: Abdul Majid Mohamed (Malaysia).
Asia South-West Division (other than Arabic): Mohammad Jafar Mahallati (Iran).
China Division: Wang Jitong (China).
Dutch- and German-speaking Division: Dirk P. Blok, *Chairman* (15 September) (Netherlands).
East Central and South-East Europe Division: Dusan Ficor (Czechoslovakia).
India Division: Not represented.

Latin America Division: Ydelis R. Velázquez García, *Vice-Chairman* (15 September) (Cuba).
Norden Division: Allan Rostvik (Sweden).
Romano-Hellenic Division: Jean Ramondou (France).
Union of Soviet Socialist Republics Division: E. Arjanov (USSR).
United Kingdom Division: H. A. G. Lewis (United Kingdom).
United States of America and Canada Division: Alan Rayburn, *Rapporteur* (Canada).[a]

[a]Acted as Chairman at the August meeting in the absence of both the Chairman, Joseph Breu (Austria), and the Vice-Chairman, W. J. Absaloms (Kenya); Rudolph Knöpfli (Switzerland) then served as Rapporteur.

Ad hoc bodies

Ad Hoc Committee on the Preparations for the Public Hearings on the Activities of Transnational Corporations in South Africa
On 27 October 1982, the Economic and Social Council decided that the Commission on Transnational Corporations (p. 1644) should conduct public hearings on the activities of transnational corporations in South Africa and Namibia, with a view to identifying concrete measures that could be taken by Governments and by intergovernmental and non-governmental bodies to bring about the eradication of *apartheid*.

At the same time, the Council decided to establish an *ad hoc* committee of five States to prepare, with the assistance of the United Nations Centre on Transnational Corporations, guidelines for the organization of the hearings, for adoption by the Commission.

The *Ad Hoc* Committee had not been constituted by the end of 1982.

Ad Hoc Intergovernmental Working Group of Experts on International Standards of Accounting and Reporting
The *Ad Hoc* Intergovernmental Working Group of Experts on International Standards of Accounting and Reporting held two sessions in 1982, at United Nations Headquarters: its fifth from 18 to 29 January; and its sixth and final session from 29 March to 9 April.

The Group, created to consist of 34 members elected by the Economic and Social Council according to a specific pattern of equitable geographical distribution, had only 32 members, two seats allocated to Eastern European States having remained vacant.

Members: Algeria, Argentina, Brazil, Canada, China, Cyprus, Dominican Republic, Egypt, France, Germany, Federal Republic of, India, Iran, Italy, Japan, Liberia, Libyan Arab Jamahiriya, Mexico, Morocco, Netherlands, Nigeria, Norway, Pakistan, Panama, Peru, Philippines, Poland, Swaziland, Switzerland, Tunisia, Uganda, United Kingdom, United States.

Chairman: Jaime C. Laya (Philippines).
Vice-Chairmen: Mohamed Adel El-Safty (Egypt), Pieter A. Wessel (Netherlands).
Rapporteur: Ricardo J. Fox (Argentina).

Intergovernmental Working Group of Experts on International Standards of Accounting and Reporting
On 27 October 1982, the Economic and Social Council established an Intergovernmental Working Group of Experts on International Standards of Accounting and Reporting, to be composed of 34 members elected by the Council, as follows: nine from African States; seven from Asian States; three from Eastern European States; six from Latin American States; and nine from Western European and other States. Each State elected was to appoint an expert with appropriate experience in accounting and reporting. The term of office was for three years, except that at the first election the term of one half of the members, chosen by lot, was to be for two years.

The Group was to meet for a two-week period not more than once a year and report to the Commission on Transnational Corporations (p. 1644).

Members:[a]
To serve until 31 December 1984:[b] Argentina, Brazil, Canada, China, Egypt, France, Grenada, Liberia, Netherlands, Nigeria, Norway, Pakistan, Philippines, Spain, Swaziland, Zaire.

To serve until 31 December 1985:[c] Algeria, Cyprus, Ecuador, Germany, Federal Republic of, India, Italy, Japan, Morocco, Panama, Saint Lucia, Tunisia, Uganda, United Kingdom, United States.

[a]Thirty members, elected by the Council on 11 November 1982 (decision 1982/188) for terms beginning on 1 January 1983.
[b]One seat allocated to a member from Eastern European States remained unfilled.
[c]The seats allocated to one member from Asian States and two members from Eastern European States remained unfilled.

Preparatory Committee for the International Conference on Population

The Population Commission (p. 1642) was designated by the Economic and Social Council as the Preparatory Committee for the International Conference on Population, scheduled for 1984.

The Preparatory Committee, to convene in open-ended session with the participation of any other State, did not meet in 1982.

Preparatory Sub-Committee for the Second World Conference to Combat Racism and Racial Discrimination

The Preparatory Sub-Committee for the Second World Conference to Combat Racism and Racial Discrimination (scheduled for 1983), to consist of 23 members appointed by the Economic and Social Council President on the basis of equitable geographical distribution, had a membership of 19 in 1982. It held its first session at United Nations Headquarters from 15 to 26 March.

Members: Bulgaria, Congo, Costa Rica, Cuba, Egypt, German Democratic Republic, Ghana, India, Iraq, Mexico, Nigeria, Pakistan, Philippines, Sudan, Syrian Arab Republic, USSR, Venezuela, Yugoslavia, Zimbabwe.

Chairman: Eubert Paul Mashaire (Zimbabwe).
Vice-Chairmen: Javid Husain (Pakistan), Willi Schlegel (German Democratic Republic).
Rapporteur: Miguel Ruíz Cabañas (Mexico).

Administrative Committee on Co-ordination

The Administrative Committee on Co-ordination held three sessions in 1982: its first at Rome, Italy, on 5 and 6 April; its second at Geneva on 5 July; and its third at United Nations Headquarters from 1 to 3 November.

The membership of ACC includes, under the chairmanship of the Secretary-General of the United Nations, also the executive heads of ILO, FAO, UNESCO, WHO, the World Bank, IMF, ICAO, UPU, ITU, WMO, IMO, WIPO, IFAD, IAEA and the secretariat of the Contracting Parties to GATT.

Also taking part in the work of ACC are the United Nations Director-General for Development and International Economic Co-operation; the Under-Secretaries-General for International Economic and Social Affairs, for Administration, Finance and Management, for Technical Co-operation for Development, and for Legal Affairs; and the executive heads of UNCTAD, UNDP, UNEP, UNFPA, UNHCR, UNICEF, UNIDO, UNITAR, UNRWA and WFP.

ACC has established subsidiary bodies on organizational, administrative and substantive questions.

Other related bodies

Human Rights Committee

The Human Rights Committee reports annually to the General Assembly through the Economic and Social Council.

Intergovernmental Committee on Science and Technology for Development

The Intergovernmental Committee on Science and Technology for Development reports annually to the General Assembly through the Economic and Social Council.

Interim Committee on New and Renewable Sources of Energy

The Interim Committee on New and Renewable Sources of Energy reported to the General Assembly at its thirty-seventh (1982) session through the Economic and Social Council.

International Research and Training Institute for the Advancement of Women (INSTRAW)

The International Research and Training Institute for the Advancement of Women, a body of the United Nations financed through voluntary contributions, functions under the authority of a Board of Trustees. The Institute continued to operate from United Nations Headquarters in 1982, pending completion of its headquarters premises at Santo Domingo, Dominican Republic.

BOARD OF TRUSTEES

The Board of Trustees of INSTRAW is composed of a President appointed by the Secretary-General; 10 members serving in their individual capacity, appointed by the Economic and Social Council on the nomination of the Secretary-General; and *ex-officio* members. Members serve for three-year terms, with a maximum of two terms.

The Board, which reports annually to the Council, held its second session at United Nations Headquarters from 25 to 29 January 1982.

Members (until 30 June 1982):
To serve until 30 June 1982: Gulzar Bano (Pakistan); Ester Boserup (Denmark); Vilma Espín de Castro (Cuba);[a] Vida Tomsic (Yugoslavia).
To serve until 30 June 1983: Emmanuel T. Esquea-Guerrero (Dominican Republic); Lily Monze (Zambia); Irene Tinker (United States).
To serve until 30 June 1984: Marcelle Devaud (France); Aziza Hussein, *Rapporteur* (Egypt); Nobuko Takahashi, *Vice-President* (Japan).

[a]Did not attend the second session.

On 6 May 1982 (decision 1982/126), the Economic and Social Council reappointed Gulzar Bano (Pakistan), Ester Boserup (Denmark), Vilma Espín de Castro (Cuba) and Vida Tomsic (Yugoslavia) for a three-year term beginning on 1 July 1982 to fill the vacancies occurring on 30 June.

Members (from 1 July 1982):
To serve until 30 June 1983: Emmanuel T. Esquea-Guerrero (Dominican Republic), Lily Monze (Zambia), Irene Tinker (United States).
To serve until 30 June 1984: Marcelle Devaud (France), Aziza Hussein (Egypt), Nobuko Takahashi (Japan).
To serve until 30 June 1985: Gulzar Bano (Pakistan), Ester Boserup (Denmark), Vilma Espín de Castro (Cuba), Vida Tomsic (Yugoslavia).

President: Delphine Tsanga (United Republic of Cameroon).
Ex-officio members: The representative of the Secretary-General, the Director of the Institute and the directors of the centres and programmes for women of the regional commissions.

Director of the Institute: Dunja Pastizzi-Ferencic.

Office of the United Nations High Commissioner for Refugees (UNHCR)

The United Nations High Commissioner for Refugees reports annually to the General Assembly through the Economic and Social Council.

United Nations Capital Development Fund

EXECUTIVE BOARD

The Executive Board of the United Nations Capital Development Fund reports annually to the General Assembly through the Economic and Social Council.

United Nations Children's Fund (UNICEF)

EXECUTIVE BOARD

The UNICEF Executive Board is elected by the Economic and Social Council from Members of the United Nations or members of the specialized agencies or of IAEA, for three-year terms. Its membership rose from 30 to 41 in 1982, pursuant to a General Assembly decision of 28 April, the seats on the enlarged Board distributed as follows: nine each for African States and Asian States; four for Eastern European States; six for Latin American States; 12 for Western European and other States; and one to be rotated among African States, Latin American States, Asian States, Western European and other States, and Eastern European States, in that order.

During the year the Executive Board (with its composition until 31 July) held a special session on 16 April, a series of meetings between 10 and 21 May, and (with its composition from 1 August) an organizational meeting on 28 June, all at United Nations Headquarters.

Members (until 31 July 1982):
To serve until 31 July 1982: Australia, Burundi, France, Hungary, Japan, Libyan Arab Jamahiriya, Mexico, Somalia, USSR, United States.
To serve until 31 July 1983: Barbados, Belgium, Botswana, Brazil, Canada, China, Germany, Federal Republic of, Norway, Thailand, Yugoslavia.
To serve until 31 July 1984: Austria, German Democratic Republic, India, Ivory Coast, Pakistan, Sweden, Switzerland, Togo, United Arab Emirates, Venezuela.

Chairman: Dragan Mateljak (Yugoslavia).
First Vice-Chairman: Suleiman Mohamoud Aden (Somalia).
Second Vice-Chairman: Mihaly Simai (Hungary).
Third Vice-Chairman: A. S. Gill (India).
Fourth Vice-Chairman: François Nordmann (Switzerland).

On 6 May 1982 (decision 1982/126), the Economic and Social Council elected the following 21 members for a three-year term beginning on 1 August 1982 to fill the vacancies occurring on 31 July and the 11 additional seats: Algeria, Bahrain, Bangladesh, Central African Republic, Chad, Chile, France, Hungary, Italy, Japan, Madagascar, Mexico, Nepal, Netherlands, Panama, Somalia, Swaziland, USSR, United Kingdom, United States, Upper Volta.

Members (from 1 August 1982):
To serve until 31 July 1983: Barbados, Belgium, Botswana, Brazil, Canada, China, Germany, Federal Republic of, Norway, Thailand, Yugoslavia.
To serve until 31 July 1984: Austria, German Democratic Republic, India, Ivory Coast, Pakistan, Sweden, Switzerland, Togo, United Arab Emirates, Venezuela.
To serve until 31 July 1985: Algeria, Bahrain, Bangladesh, Central African Republic, Chad, Chile, France, Hungary, Italy, Japan, Madagascar, Mexico, Nepal, Netherlands, Panama, Somalia, Swaziland, USSR, United Kingdom, United States, Upper Volta.

Chairman: Hugo Scheltema (Netherlands).
First Vice-Chairman: Dr. Haydee Martínez de Osorio (Venezuela).
Second Vice-Chairman: Mihaly Simai (Hungary).
Third Vice-Chairman: Amara Essy (Ivory Coast).
Fourth Vice-Chairman: Basharat Jazbi (Pakistan).

Executive Director of UNICEF: James P. Grant.

COMMITTEE ON ADMINISTRATION AND FINANCE
The Committee on Administration and Finance is a committee of the whole of the UNICEF Executive Board.

Chairman: Richard Manning (Australia) (until 31 July), François Nordmann (Switzerland) (from 1 August).

PROGRAMME COMMITTEE
The Programme Committee is a committee of the whole of the UNICEF Executive Board.

Chairman: Dr. Haydee Martínez de Osorio (Venezuela) (until 31 July), Serla Grewal (India) (from 1 August).

UNICEF/WHO Joint Committee on Health Policy
The UNICEF/WHO Joint Committee on Health Policy consists of: six members of the UNICEF Executive Board, among whom are the chairmen of the Executive Board and the Programme Committee who serve *ex officio;* and six members of the WHO Executive Board.
The Joint Committee did not meet in 1982.

United Nations Conference on Trade
and Development (UNCTAD)

TRADE AND DEVELOPMENT BOARD
The Trade and Development Board reports to UNCTAD; it also reports annually to the General Assembly through the Economic and Social Council.

United Nations Development Programme (UNDP)

GOVERNING COUNCIL
The Governing Council of UNDP consists of 48 members, elected by the Economic and Social Council from Member States of the United Nations or members of the specialized agencies or of IAEA.

Twenty-seven seats are allocated to developing countries as follows: 11 to African countries, 9 to Asian countries and Yugoslavia, and 7 to Latin American countries.

Twenty-one seats are allocated to economically more advanced countries as follows: 17 to Western European and other countries, and 4 to Eastern European countries.

The term of office is three years, one third of the members being elected each year.

During 1982, the Governing Council held an organizational meeting on 25 February at United Nations Headquarters, and a special meeting from 24 to 28 May (continued during the twenty-ninth session on 4 and 18 June) and its twenty-ninth session from 1 to 18 June at Geneva.

Members:
To serve until 31 December 1982: Belgium, Brazil, Canada, Denmark, France, Gabon, Kuwait, Liberia, Malawi, Malaysia, New Zealand, Norway, Romania, Rwanda, Sri Lanka, Uganda.
To serve until 31 December 1983: Argentina, Bulgaria, Germany, Federal Republic of, Guinea, India, Netherlands, Niger, Pakistan, Poland, Somalia, Sweden, Switzerland, Trinidad and Tobago, Turkey, Venezuela, Yemen.
To serve until 31 December 1984: Austria, Barbados, Bhutan, China, Ecuador, Fiji, Italy, Japan, Mali, Mexico, Spain, Tunisia, USSR, United Kingdom, United States, Zambia.

President: Douglas P. Lindores (Canada).
First Vice-President: Mohamed Memmi (Tunisia).
Second Vice-President: B. M. Oza (India).
Third Vice-President: Anton Baramov (Bulgaria).
Fourth Vice-President: Miguel A. Albornoz (Ecuador).

On 6 May 1982 (decision 1982/126), the Economic and Social Council elected the following 16 members for a three-year term beginning on 1 January 1983 to fill the vacancies occurring on 31 December 1982: Australia, Belgium, Brazil, Canada, Central African Republic, Chad, Denmark, Finland, France, German Democratic Republic, Lesotho, Mauritania, Nepal, Philippines, United Republic of Tanzania, Yugoslavia.

Administrator of UNDP: F. Bradford Morse.
Deputy Administrator: G. Arthur Brown.

BUDGETARY AND FINANCE COMMITTEE
The Budgetary and Finance Committee, a committee of the whole, held one series of meetings in 1982, at Geneva, between 24 May and 18 June.

Chairman: Mohamed Memmi (Tunisia).
Rapporteur: Finn Norman Christensen (Denmark).

INTER-SESSIONAL COMMITTEE OF THE WHOLE
On 18 June 1982, the Governing Council established an Inter-sessional Committee of the Whole to study the longer-term financing of UNDP and ways to strengthen the effectiveness of the work of the Governing Council.
The Inter-sessional Committee held its first session at United Nations Headquarters from 13 to 15 September 1982.

Chairman: Douglas P. Lindores (Canada).
First Vice-Chairman: Taieb Slim (Tunisia).
Second Vice-Chairman: Shri Vatsa Purushottam (India).
Third Vice-Chairman: None.
Fourth Vice-Chairman: Miguel A. Albornoz (Ecuador).
Rapporteur: Qazi Shaukat Fareed (Pakistan).

United Nations Environment Programme (UNEP)

GOVERNING COUNCIL
The Governing Council of UNEP reports to the General Assembly through the Economic and Social Council.

United Nations Industrial Development Organization (UNIDO)

INDUSTRIAL DEVELOPMENT BOARD

The Industrial Development Board, the principal organ of UNIDO, reports annually to the General Assembly through the Economic and Social Council.

United Nations Institute for Training and Research (UNITAR)

The Executive Director of UNITAR reports to the General Assembly and, as appropriate, to the Economic and Social Council.

United Nations Research Institute for Social Development (UNRISD)

BOARD OF DIRECTORS

The Board of Directors of UNRISD reports to the Economic and Social Council through the Commission for Social Development.

The Board consists of:

The Chairman, appointed by the Secretary-General: Mohamed Diawara (Ivory Coast);

Seven members, nominated by the Commission for Social Development and confirmed by the Economic and Social Council (to serve until 30 June 1983): Paul-Marc Henry (France), Karl Eric Knutsson (Sweden), Vera Nyitrai (Hungary), Achola Pala Okeyo (Kenya), K. N. Raj (India), Eugene B. Skolnikoff (United States); (to serve until 30 June 1985): Gustavo Esteva (Mexico);

Eight other members, as follows: a representative of the Secretary-General, the Director of the Latin American Institute for Economic and Social Planning, the Director of the Asian and Pacific Development Centre, the Director of the African Institute for Economic Development and Planning, the Executive Secretary of ECWA, the Director of UNRISD *(ex officio)*, and the representatives of two of the following specialized agencies appointed as members and observers in annual rotation: ILO and FAO (observers); UNESCO and WHO (members).

United Nations Special Fund

BOARD OF GOVERNORS

The Board of Governors of the United Nations Special Fund reports annually to the General Assembly through the Economic and Social Council.

United Nations Special Fund for Land-locked Developing Countries

BOARD OF GOVERNORS

A Board of Governors of the United Nations Special Fund for Land-locked Developing Countries, when constituted, was to report to the General Assembly through the Economic and Social Council.

United Nations University

COUNCIL OF THE UNITED NATIONS UNIVERSITY

The Council of the United Nations University, the governing board of the University, reports annually to the General Assembly, to the Economic and Social Council and to the UNESCO Executive Board through the Secretary-General and the UNESCO Director-General.

World Food Council

The World Food Council, an organ of the United Nations at the ministerial or plenipotentiary level, reports to the General Assembly through the Economic and Social Council.

World Food Programme

COMMITTEE ON FOOD AID POLICIES AND PROGRAMMES

The Committee on Food Aid Policies and Programmes, the governing body of WFP, consists of 30 members, of which 15 are elected by the Economic and Social Council and 15 by the FAO Council, from Member States of the United Nations or from members of FAO. Members serve for three-year terms.

The Committee reports annually to the Economic and Social Council, the FAO Council and the World Food Council.

The Committee held two sessions during 1982, at Rome, Italy: its thirteenth from 19 to 29 April; and its fourteenth from 11 to 18 October.

Members:
To serve until 31 December 1982:
    Elected by Economic and Social Council: Argentina, Ireland, Lesotho *(Second Vice-Chairman)*, Mexico, United Kingdom.
    Elected by FAO Council: Cuba, Egypt, France, Germany, Federal Republic of, Sierra Leone.
To serve until 31 December 1983:
    Elected by Economic and Social Council: Denmark, Greece, Hungary, India, Morocco.
    Elected by FAO Council: Australia, Bangladesh, Canada, Saudi Arabia *(Chairman)*, United States.
To serve until 31 December 1984:
    Elected by Economic and Social Council: Belgium, Finland, Japan, Pakistan, Somalia.[a,b]
    Elected by FAO Council: Brazil, Congo, Mali,[b] Netherlands *(First Vice-Chairman)*, Thailand.

[a]Not represented at the thirteenth session.
[b]Not represented at the fourteenth session.

On 6 May 1982 (decision 1982/126), the Economic and Social Council elected Colombia, Mexico, Sweden, United Kingdom and Upper Volta; and, on 29 November, the FAO Council elected Cuba, France, Germany, Federal Republic of, Nigeria and Zambia, all for a three-year term beginning on 1 January 1983 to fill the vacancies occurring on 31 December 1982.

Executive Director of WFP: Bernardo de Azevedo Brito (acting, until 31 March), James Charles Ingram (from 1 April).
Deputy Executive Director: Juan Felipe Yriart *(ad interim,* until 17 October), Salahuddin Ahmed (from 18 October).

Conference

Fourth United Nations Conference on the Standardization of Geographical Names

The Fourth United Nations Conference on the Standardization of Geographical Names was held at Geneva from 24 August to 14 September 1982. Participating were the following 62 States:

Algeria, Angola, Argentina, Australia, Bahrain, Belgium, Brazil, Bulgaria, Canada, China, Costa Rica, Cuba, Cyprus, Czechoslovakia, Denmark, Egypt, Finland, France, German Democratic Republic, Germany, Federal Republic of, Greece, Holy See, Hungary, India, Indonesia, Iran, Iraq, Ireland, Israel, Italy, Japan, Kuwait, Libyan Arab Jamahiriya, Malaysia, Mexico, Morocco, Netherlands, Nigeria, Pakistan, Peru, Philippines, Poland, Portugal, Republic of Korea, Romania, Saudi Arabia, Senegal, Spain, Sudan, Sweden, Switzerland, Syrian Arab Republic, Togo, Trinidad and Tobago, Tunisia, Turkey, Ukrainian SSR, USSR, United Kingdom, United States, Venezuela, Yugoslavia.

President: Dirk P. Blok (Netherlands).
Vice-Presidents: Jean Ramondou (France), Abdelhadi Tazi (Morocco), Ydelis R. Velázquez García (Cuba).
Rapporteur: Alan Rayburn (Canada).
Editor-in-Chief: R. R. Randall (United States).

Chairmen of committees:
    Technical Committee I: E. Arjanov (USSR).
    Technical Committee II: H. A. G. Lewis (United Kingdom).
    Technical Committee III: Jean Ramondou (France).
    Technical Committee IV: Y. L. Khular (India).
    Technical Committee V: O. Adebekun (Nigeria).
    Editorial Committee: R. R. Randall (United States).
    Credentials Committee: The President of the Conference.

Trusteeship Council

Article 86 of the United Nations Charter lays down that the Trusteeship Council shall consist of the following:

Members of the United Nations administering Trust Territories;

Permanent members of the Security Council which do not administer Trust Territories;

As many other members elected for a three-year term by the General Assembly as will ensure that the membership of the Council is equally divided between United Nations Members which administer Trust Territories and those which do not.[a]

[a]During 1982, only one Member of the United Nations was an administering member of the Trusteeship Council, while four permanent members of the Security Council continued as non-administering members. Therefore, the parity called for by Article 86 of the Charter was not maintained.

MEMBERS
Member administering a Trust Territory: United States.

Non-administering members: China, France, USSR, United Kingdom.

SESSIONS
Forty-ninth session: United Nations Headquarters, 17 May–11 June 1982.
Fifteenth special session: United Nations Headquarters, 16-20 December 1982.

OFFICERS
President: Paul Poudade (France).
Vice-President: Marrack I. Goulding (United Kingdom).

**United Nations Visiting Mission to the
Trust Territory of the Pacific Islands, 1982**
Members: Sheila E. Harden (United Kingdom); Paul Poudade, *Chairman* (France).

International Court of Justice

Judges of the Court

The International Court of Justice consists of 15 Judges elected for nine-year terms by the General Assembly and the Security Council, each voting independently.

The following were the Judges of the Court serving in 1982, listed in the order of precedence:

Judge	Country of nationality	End of term[a]
Taslim Olawale Elias, *President*	Nigeria	1985
José Sette Câmara, *Vice-President*	Brazil	1988
Manfred Lachs	Poland	1985
Platon D. Morozov	USSR	1988
Nagendra Singh	India	1991
José María Ruda	Argentina	1991
Hermann Mosler	Federal Republic of Germany	1985
Shigeru Oda	Japan	1985
Roberto Ago	Italy	1988
Abdullah Fikri El-Khani	Syrian Arab Republic	1985
Stephen M. Schwebel	United States	1988
Sir Robert Y. Jennings	United Kingdom	1991
Guy Ladreit de Lacharrière	France	1991
Kéba M'Baye	Senegal	1991
Mohammed Bedjaoui[b]	Algeria	1988

[a]Term expires on 5 February of the year indicated.
[b]Elected by the General Assembly (decision 36/309 B) and the Security Council on 19 March 1982 to fill the vacancy created by the death of Abdullah Ali El-Erian (Egypt) in 1981.

In 1982, Judges Isaac Forster (Senegal) and André Gros (France) continued to discharge their duties beyond the date of expiry of their term (5 February 1982). They sat until judgement was rendered on 24 February in the case concerning *Continental shelf (Tunisia/Libyan Arab Jamahiriya)*. This was the first time that the relevant provision of the Court's Statute (Article 13, paragraph 3) had been applied.

Registrar: Santiago Torres Bernárdez.
Deputy Registrar: Alain Pillepich.

Chamber formed in the case concerning *Delimitation of the maritime boundary in the Gulf of Maine area*

By an Order of 20 January 1982, the Court, at the request of the parties and pursuant to Article 26, paragraph 2, of the Court's Statute, formed a Chamber to deal with the case concerning *Delimitation of the maritime boundary in the Gulf of Maine area*.

Members: Roberto Ago *(President)*, André Gros,[a] Hermann Mosler, Stephen M. Schwebel.
Ad hoc member: Maxwell Cohen.[b]

[a]Member of the Court whose term of office expired on 5 February 1982, but who continued to sit as a member of the Chamber in accordance with Article 13, paragraph 3, of the Statute.
[b]As the Court noted in its Order constituting the Chamber, one of the members of the Court elected to the Chamber gave place to the Judge *ad hoc* chosen by one of the parties (Canada) in accordance with Article 31, paragraph 4, of the Statute.

Chamber of Summary Procedure
(as constituted by the Court on 25 February 1982)

Members: Taslim Olawale Elias *(ex officio)*, José Sette Câmara *(ex officio)*, Platon D. Morozov, Nagendra Singh, Abdullah Fikri El-Khani.
Substitute members: Guy Ladreit de Lacharrière, Kéba M'Baye.

Parties to the Court's Statute

All Members of the United Nations are *ipso facto* parties to the Statute of the International Court of Justice. Also parties to it are the following non-members: Liechtenstein, San Marino, Switzerland.

States accepting the compulsory jurisdiction of the Court

Declarations made by the following States accepting the Court's compulsory jurisdiction (or made under the Statute of the Permanent Court of International Justice and deemed to be an acceptance of the jurisdiction of the International Court) were in force at the end of 1982:

Australia, Austria, Barbados, Belgium, Botswana, Canada, Colombia, Costa Rica, Democratic Kampuchea, Denmark, Dominican Republic, Egypt, El Salvador, Finland, Gambia, Haiti, Honduras, India, Israel, Japan, Kenya, Liberia, Liechtenstein, Luxembourg, Malawi, Malta, Mauritius, Mexico, Netherlands, New Zealand, Nicaragua, Nigeria, Norway, Pakistan, Panama, Philippines, Portugal, Somalia, Sudan, Swaziland, Sweden, Switzerland, Togo, Uganda, United Kingdom, United States, Uruguay.

United Nations organs and specialized and related agencies authorized to request advisory opinions from the Court

Authorized by the United Nations Charter to request opinions on any legal question: General Assembly, Security Council.
Authorized by the General Assembly in accordance with the Charter to request opinions on legal questions arising within the scope of their activities: Economic and Social Council, Trusteeship Council, Interim Committee of the General Assembly, Committee on Applications for Review of Administrative Tribunal Judgements, ILO, FAO, UNESCO, WHO, World Bank, IFC, IDA, IMF, ICAO, ITU, WMO, IMO, WIPO, IFAD, IAEA.

Committees of the Court

BUDGETARY AND ADMINISTRATIVE COMMITTEE
Members: Taslim Olawale Elias *(ex officio)*, José Sette Câmara *(ex officio)*, Manfred Lachs, Nagendra Singh, Stephen M. Schwebel.

COMMITTEE ON RELATIONS
Members: Platon D. Morozov, Guy Ladreit de Lacharrière, Kéba M'Baye.

LIBRARY COMMITTEE
Members: José María Ruda, Hermann Mosler, Shigeru Oda, Sir Robert Y. Jennings.

RULES COMMITTEE
Members: Manfred Lachs, Platon D. Morozov, Hermann Mosler, José María Ruda, Shigeru Oda, Roberto Ago, Sir Robert Y. Jennings.

Other United Nations-related bodies

The following bodies are not subsidiary to any principal organ of the United Nations but were established by an international treaty instrument or arrangement sponsored by the United Nations and are thus related to the Organization and its work. These bodies, often referred to as "treaty organs", are serviced by the United Nations Secretariat and may be financed in part or wholly from the Organization's regular budget, as authorized by the General Assembly, to which most of them report annually.

Committee on Disarmament

The Committee on Disarmament, the multilateral negotiating forum on disarmament, reports annually to the General Assembly and is serviced by the United Nations Secretariat. It was composed of 40 members in 1982.

The Committee met at Geneva in 1982 from 2 February to 23 April and from 3 August to 17 September.

Members: Algeria, Argentina, Australia, Belgium, Brazil, Bulgaria, Burma, Canada, China, Cuba, Czechoslovakia, Egypt, Ethiopia, France, German Democratic Republic, Germany, Federal Republic of, Hungary, India, Indonesia, Iran, Italy, Japan, Kenya, Mexico, Mongolia, Morocco, Netherlands, Nigeria, Pakistan, Peru, Poland, Romania, Sri Lanka, Sweden, USSR, United Kingdom, United States, Venezuela, Yugoslavia, Zaire.

The chairmanship, which rotates in English alphabetical order among the members, was held by the following in 1982: February, Iran; March, Italy; April and the recess between the first and second parts of the 1982 session, Japan; August, Kenya; September and the recess until the 1983 session, Mexico.

Committee on the Elimination of Discrimination against Women

The Committee on the Elimination of Discrimination against Women was established under the Convention on the Elimination of All Forms of Discrimination against Women.[38] It consists of 23 experts elected by the States parties to the Convention to serve in their personal capacity, with due regard for equitable geographical distribution and for representation of the different forms of civilization and principal legal systems.

Members serve for four-year terms; at the first election, however, 11 members, chosen by lot by the Committee Chairman, were to serve for two years.

The Committee, which reports annually to the General Assembly through the Economic and Social Council, held its first session at Vienna, Austria, from 18 to 22 October 1982.

Members:[a]
To serve until 15 April 1984: Desirée P. Bernard, *Rapporteur* (Guyana);[b] Marie Caron, *Vice-Chairman* (Canada); Graciela Escudero-Moscoso (Ecuador); Aida Gonzalez Martínez (Mexico); Vanda Lamm (Hungary); Maria Margarida de Rego da Costa Salema Moura Ribeiro (Portugal); Nguyen Ngoc Dung (Viet Nam); Johan Nordenfelt (Sweden); Edith Oeser (German Democratic Republic); Lia Patiño de Martínez (Panama); Esther Véliz Díaz de Villalvilla (Cuba).
To serve until 15 April 1986: A. P. Biryukova (USSR); Irene R. Cortes (Philippines); Guan Minqian (China); Luvsandanzangyn Ider, *Chairman* (Mongolia); Zagorka Ilic, *Vice-Chairman* (Yugoslavia); Vinitha Jayasinghe (Sri Lanka); Raquel Macedo de Sheppard (Uruguay); Landrada Mukayiranga, *Vice-Chairman* (Rwanda); Vesselina Peytcheva (Bulgaria); Maria Regent-Lechowicz (Poland); Rakel Surlien (Norway).

[a]Elected on 16 April 1982. Mervat Tallawy (Egypt) was also elected on that date but, having become a United Nations staff member since her election, became ineligible for Committee membership; no replacement was appointed during 1982.
[b]Appointment approved by the Committee on 18 October 1982 to fill the vacancy created by the death of Shirley Field-Ridley (Guyana) in June.

Committee on the Elimination of Racial Discrimination

The Committee on the Elimination of Racial Discrimination was established under the International Convention on the Elimination of All Forms of Racial Discrimination.[39] It consists of 18 experts elected by the States parties to the Convention to serve in their personal capacity, with due regard for equitable geographical distribution and for representation of the different forms of civilization and principal legal systems. Members serve for four-year terms.

The Committee held two sessions in 1982: its twenty-fifth from 1 to 19 March at Geneva; and its twenty-sixth from 2 to 20 August at United Nations Headquarters.

Members:
To serve until 19 January 1984: Eugenio Carlos José Aramburu (Argentina);[a] Yuli Bahnev (Bulgaria); Pedro Brin Martínez (Panama); André Dechezelles (France); Silvo Devetak (Yugoslavia); José D. Ingles, *Chairman* (Philippines); Erik Nettel (Austria); Shanti Sadiq Ali (India); G. B. Starushenko, *Vice-Chairman* (USSR).
To serve until 19 January 1986:[b] Jean-Marie Apiou (Upper Volta); Dimitrios J. Evrigenis (Greece); Abdel Moneim M. Ghoneim (Egypt); George O. Lamptey, *Vice-Chairman* (Ghana); Karl Josef Partsch, *Rapporteur* (Federal Republic of Germany); Agha Shahi (Pakistan); Michael E. Sherifis (Cyprus); Luis Valencia Rodríguez, *Vice-Chairman* (Ecuador); Shuaib Uthman Yolah (Nigeria).[c]

[a]Appointment approved by the Committee on 1 March 1982 to replace Manuel V. Ordóñez (Argentina), who resigned by a letter of 12 February.
[b]Elected on 15 January 1982.
[c]Did not attend the twenty-fifth session. Resigned in June 1982; replaced by Oladapo Olusola Fafowora (Nigeria), whose appointment was approved by the Committee on 2 August.

Human Rights Committee

The Human Rights Committee was established under the International Covenant on Civil and Political Rights.[40] It consists of 18 experts elected by the States parties to the Covenant to serve in their personal capacity for four-year terms.

The Committee, which reports annually to the General Assembly through the Economic and Social Council, held three sessions in 1982: its fifteenth at United Nations Headquarters from 22 March to 8 April; and its sixteenth and seventeenth at Geneva from 12 to 30 July and from 11 to 29 October, respectively.

Members:
To serve until 31 December 1982: Néjib Bouziri (Tunisia); Abdoulaye Diéye (Senegal);[a] Bernhard Graefrath, *Vice-Chairman* (German Democratic Republic); Dejan Janca (Yugoslavia); Rajsoomer Lallah, *Rapporteur* (Mauritius); Torkel Opsahl (Norway); Julio Prado Vallejo, *Vice-Chairman* (Ecuador); Waleed M. Sadi (Jordan); Christian Tomuschat, *Vice-Chairman* (Federal Republic of Germany).

---

[38]General Assembly resolution 34/180, annex, article 17, 18 December 1979 (YUN 1979, p. 898).
[39]General Assembly resolution 2106 A (XX), annex, article 8, 21 December 1965 (YUN 1965, p. 443).
[40]General Assembly resolution 2200 A (XXI), annex, part IV, 16 December 1966 (YUN 1966, p. 427).

To serve until 31 December 1984: Andrés Aguilar (Venezuela); Mohammed Abdullah Ahmed Al Douri (Iraq); Felix Ermacora (Austria); Sir Vincent Evans (United Kingdom); Vladimir Hanga (Romania); Leonte Herdocia Ortega (Nicaragua); Andreas V. Mavrommatis, *Chairman* (Cyprus); A. P. Movchan (USSR);[b] Walter Surma Tarnopolsky (Canada).

[a]Did not attend the seventeenth session.
[b]Did not attend the fifteenth session.

On 17 September 1982, the States parties to the International Covenant on Civil and Political Rights elected the following nine members for a four-year term beginning on 1 January 1983 to fill the vacancies occurring on 31 December 1982: Néjib Bouziri (Tunisia), Joseph A. L. Cooray (Sri Lanka), Abdoulaye Diéye (Senegal), Vojin Dimitrijevic (Yugoslavia), Roger Errera (France), Bernhard Graefrath (German Democratic Republic), Torkel Opsahl (Norway), Julio Prado Vallejo (Ecuador), Christian Tomuschat (Federal Republic of Germany).

International Narcotics Control Board (INCB)

The International Narcotics Control Board, established under the Single Convention on Narcotic Drugs, 1961, as amended by the 1972 Protocol, consists of 13 members, elected by the Economic and Social Council for five-year terms, three from candidates nominated by WHO and 10 from candidates nominated by Members of the United Nations and parties to the Single Convention.

The Board held two sessions in 1982, at Vienna, Austria: its thirty-first from 17 to 28 May; and its thirty-second from 5 to 22 October.

Members:
To serve until 1 March 1985: Dr. Bela Bolcs (Hungary); Dr. John C. Ebie (Nigeria)[a,b] Dr. Diego Garcés-Giraldo (Colombia); Dr. Mohsen Kchouk, *Rapporteur* (Tunisia); Dr. Victorio V. Olguín, *First Vice-President* (Argentina); Jasjit Singh (India).
To serve until 1 March 1987: Dr. Ramón de la Fuente Muñiz (Mexico);[a] Betty C. Gough (United States); Dr. Sukru Kaymakcalan, *Second Vice-President* (Turkey);[a] Paul Reuter, *President* (France); Dr. Bror Anders Rexed (Sweden); Adolf-Heinrich von Arnim (Federal Republic of Germany); Edward Williams (Australia).

[a]Elected from candidates nominated by WHO.
[b]Elected on 5 February 1982 (decision 1982/108).

Preparatory Commission for the International Sea-Bed Authority and for the International Tribunal for the Law of the Sea

The Preparatory Commission for the International Sea-Bed Authority and for the International Tribunal for the Law of the Sea was established under resolution 1 of the Third United Nations Conference on the Law of the Sea, adopted on 30 April 1982. As at 31 December 1982, it consisted of the 119 signatories of the United Nations Convention on the Law of the Sea.

The Commission was to be convened between 60 and 90 days after 10 December 1982, the date on which the Convention was opened for signature.

Members: Algeria, Angola, Australia, Austria, Bahamas, Bahrain, Bangladesh, Barbados, Belize, Bhutan, Brazil, Bulgaria, Burma, Burundi, Byelorussian SSR, Canada, Cape Verde, Chad, Chile, China, Colombia, Congo, Cook Islands, Costa Rica, Cuba, Cyprus, Czechoslovakia, Democratic People's Republic of Korea, Democratic Yemen, Denmark, Djibouti, Dominican Republic, Egypt, Ethiopia, Fiji, Finland, France, Gabon, Gambia, German Democratic Republic, Ghana, Greece, Grenada, Guinea-Bissau, Guyana, Haiti, Honduras, Hungary, Iceland, India, Indonesia, Iran, Iraq, Ireland, Ivory Coast, Jamaica, Kenya, Kuwait, Lao People's Democratic Republic, Lesotho, Liberia, Malaysia, Maldives, Malta, Mauritania, Mauritius, Mexico, Monaco, Mongolia, Morocco, Mozambique, Namibia (United Nations Council for), Nauru, Nepal, Netherlands, New Zealand, Niger, Nigeria, Norway, Pakistan, Panama, Papua New Guinea, Paraguay, Philippines, Poland, Portugal, Romania, Rwanda, Saint Lucia, Saint Vincent and the Grenadines, Senegal, Seychelles, Sierra Leone, Singapore, Solomon Islands, Somalia, Sri Lanka, Sudan, Suriname, Sweden, Thailand, Togo, Trinidad and Tobago, Tunisia, Tuvalu, Uganda, Ukrainian SSR, USSR, United Arab Emirates, United Republic of Cameroon, United Republic of Tanzania, Upper Volta, Uruguay, Vanuatu, Viet Nam, Yemen, Yugoslavia, Zambia, Zimbabwe.

Principal members of the United Nations Secretariat

(as at 31 December 1982)

Secretariat

The Secretary-General: Javier Pérez de Cuéllar

Executive Office of the Secretary-General
Under-Secretary-General, Chef de Cabinet: Virendra Dayal

Office of the Director-General for Development and International Economic Co-operation
Director-General: Jean L. Ripert

Office of the Under-Secretaries-General for Special Political Affairs
Under-Secretaries-General: Diego Cordovez, Brian E. Urquhart

Office for Special Political Questions
Under-Secretary-General, Co-ordinator, Special Economic Assistance Programmes: Abdulrahim Abby Farah
Assistant Secretary-General, Joint Co-ordinator, Unit for Special Economic Assistance Programmes: Sotirios Mousouris

Office of the Under-Secretary-General for Political and General Assembly Affairs
Under-Secretary-General: William B. Buffum

Office of Secretariat Services for Economic and Social Matters
Assistant Secretary-General: Robert Muller

Office for Field Operational and External Support Activities
Assistant Secretary-General: James O. C. Jonah

Office of Legal Affairs
Under-Secretary-General, the Legal Counsel: Erik Suy

Department of Political and Security Council Affairs
Under-Secretary-General: Viacheslav A. Ustinov
Assistant Secretary-General, Centre for Disarmament: Jan Martenson

Department of Political Affairs, Trusteeship and Decolonization
Under-Secretary-General: Issoufou Saidou Djermakoye

Department of International Economic and Social Affairs
Under-Secretary-General: Shuaib Uthman Yolah
Assistant Secretary-General for Development Research and Policy Analysis: P. N. Dhar
Assistant Secretary-General for Programme Planning and Co-ordination: Peter Hansen
Assistant Secretary-General for Social Development and Humanitarian Affairs: Leticia R. Shahani

Department of Technical Co-operation for Development
Under-Secretary-General: Bi Jilong
Assistant Secretary-General: Margaret J. Anstee

Economic Commission for Europe
Under-Secretary-General, Executive Secretary: Janez I. Stanovnik

Economic and Social Commission for Asia and the Pacific
Assistant Secretary-General, Executive Secretary: Shah A. M. S. Kibria

Economic Commission for Latin America
Under-Secretary-General, Executive Secretary: Enrique V. Iglesias

Economic Commission for Africa
Under-Secretary-General, Executive Secretary: Adebayo Adedeji

Economic Commission for Western Asia
Under-Secretary-General, Executive Secretary: Mohamed-Said Al-Attar

Centre for Science and Technology for Development
Assistant Secretary-General, Executive Director: Amilcar F. Ferrari

United Nations Centre for Human Settlements
Under-Secretary-General, Executive Director: Arcot Ramachandran

United Nations Centre on Transnational Corporations
Assistant Secretary-General, Executive Director: Klaus Aksel Sahlgren

Department of Administration and Management
Under-Secretary-General: Patricio Ruedas

OFFICE OF FINANCIAL SERVICES
Assistant Secretary-General: J. Richard Foran

OFFICE OF PERSONNEL SERVICES
Assistant Secretary-General: Leila H. Doss

OFFICE OF GENERAL SERVICES
Assistant Secretary-General: Clayton C. Timbrell

Department of Conference Services
Under-Secretary-General for Conference Services and Special Assignments: Eugeniusz Wyzner

Department of Public Information
Under-Secretary-General: Yasushi Akashi

United Nations Office at Geneva
Under-Secretary-General, Director-General of the United Nations Office at Geneva: Luigi Cottafavi
Assistant Secretary-General, Personal Representative of the Secretary-General, Secretary of the Committee on Disarmament: Rikhi Jaipal

United Nations Office at Vienna
Assistant Secretary-General, Director-General: Mowaffak Allaf

International Court of Justice Registry
Registrar: Santiago Torres Bernárdez

Secretariats of subsidiary organs, special representatives and other related bodies

Office of the Under-Secretary-General for Special Assignments
Under-Secretary-General: Helmut F. Debatin

Office of the Special Representative of the Secretary-General for Namibia
Under-Secretary-General, Special Representative of the Secretary-General: Martti Ahtisaari

Office of the Special Representative of the Secretary-General for Humanitarian Affairs in South-East Asia
Under-Secretary-General: Rafeeuddin Ahmed

Office of the United Nations Disaster Relief Co-ordinator
Under-Secretary-General, Disaster Relief Co-ordinator: M'Hamed Essaafi

Office of the United Nations High Commissioner for Refugees
High Commissioner: Poul Hartling
Deputy High Commissioner: William Richard Smyser

International Conference on the Question of Palestine
Under-Secretary-General, Secretary-General of the Conference: Lucille M. Mair

United Nations Conference for the Promotion of International Co-operation in the Peaceful Uses of Nuclear Energy
Assistant Secretary-General, Secretary-General of the Conference: Amrik S. Mehta

Office of the Special Representative of the Secretary-General for the Law of the Sea
Under-Secretary-General, Special Representative of the Secretary-General: Bernardo Zuleta

Office of the United Nations Co-ordinator of Assistance for the Reconstruction and Development of Lebanon
Assistant Secretary-General, Co-ordinator: Iqbal A. Akhund

Office of the United Nations Commissioner for Namibia
Assistant Secretary-General, Commissioner for Namibia: Brajesh Chandra Mishra

United Nations Children's Fund
Under-Secretary-General, Executive Director: James P. Grant
Assistant Secretary-General, Deputy Executive Director: Margaret Yvonne Catley-Carlson
Assistant Secretary-General, Deputy Executive Director, Programmes: Richard Jolly
Assistant Secretary-General, Deputy Executive Director, External Affairs: Varindra T. Vittachi

United Nations Conference on Trade and Development
Under-Secretary-General, Secretary-General of the Conference: Gamani Corea
Assistant Secretaries-General, Deputy Secretaries-General of the Conference: Alister McIntyre, Johannes Pronk

United Nations Development Programme
Administrator: F. Bradford Morse
Deputy Administrator: G. Arthur Brown
Assistant Administrator, Bureau for Finance and Administration: Pierre Vinde
Assistant Administrator, Bureau for Special Activities: Paul Thyness
Assistant Administrator and Director, Bureau for Programme Policy and Evaluation: Horst Wiesebach
Executive Director, United Nations Fund for Population Activities: Rafael M. Salas
Deputy Executive Director, United Nations Fund for Population Activities: Heino E. Wittrin
Assistant Administrator and Regional Director, Regional Bureau for Africa: Michel Doo Kingué
Assistant Administrator and Regional Director, Regional Bureau for Arab States: Mustapha Zaanouni
Assistant Administrator and Regional Director, Regional Bureau for Asia and the Pacific: Andrew J. Joseph
Assistant Administrator and Regional Director, Regional Bureau for Latin America: Carlos S. Vegega

United Nations Disengagement Observer Force
Force Commander: Major-General Carl-Gustav Stahl

United Nations Environment Programme
Executive Director: Mostafa Kamal Tolba
Assistant Secretary-General, Deputy Executive Director: Peter Shaw Thacher

Assistant Secretary-General, Assistant Executive Director, Office of the Environment Programme: Gennady N. Golubev
Assistant Secretary-General, Assistant Executive Director, Office of the Environment Fund and Administration: Rudolf Schmidt

United Nations Fund for Drug Abuse Control
Assistant Secretary-General, Executive Director: Giuseppe di Gennaro

United Nations Industrial Development Organization
Under-Secretary-General, Executive Director: Abd-El Rahman Khane
Assistant Secretary-General, Deputy Executive Director: Philippe Jacques Farlan Carré

United Nations Institute for Training and Research
Under-Secretary-General, Executive Director: Davidson S. H. W. Nicol

United Nations Interim Force in Lebanon
Force Commander: Lieutenant-General William Callaghan

United Nations Peace-keeping Force in Cyprus
Force Commander: Major-General Günther G. Greindl
Special Representative of the Secretary-General: Hugo J. Gobbi

United Nations Relief and Works Agency for Palestine Refugees in the Near East
Commissioner-General: Olof Rydbeck

United Nations Truce Supervision Organization
Assistant Secretary-General, Chief of Staff: Lieutenant-General Emmanuel Alexander Erskine

United Nations University
Rector: Mr. Soedjatmoko

World Food Council
Assistant Secretary-General, Executive Director: Maurice J. Williams

---

On 31 December 1982, the total number of staff of the United Nations holding permanent, probationary and fixed-term appointments with service or expected service of a year or more was 26,681. Of these, 8,885 were in the Professional and higher categories and 17,796 were in the General Service, Manual Worker and Field Service categories. Of the same total, 23,285 were regular staff serving at Headquarters or other established offices and 3,396 were assigned as project personnel to technical co-operation projects. In addition, UNRWA had some 16,500 local area staff.

Appendix IV

Agenda of United Nations principal organs in 1982

This appendix lists the items on the agenda of the General Assembly, the Security Council, the Economic and Social Council and the Trusteeship Council during 1982. The column headed "Page" shows the page of the present volume on which a summary of the main treatment of each item begins. For the Assembly and the Economic and Social Council, the column headed "Allocation" indicates the assignment of each item to plenary meetings or committees.

Agenda item titles have been shortened by omitting mention of reports following the subject of the item. Thus, "Question of Cyprus: report of the Secretary-General" has been shortened to "Question of Cyprus". Where the subject-matter of the item is not apparent from its title, the subject is identified in square brackets; this is not part of the title.

As treatment of topics in the *Yearbook* does not always correspond to agenda items, the page number cited in the last column does not necessarily refer to the treatment of all resolutions or decisions adopted under that item. Thus, under item 12, "Report of the Economic and Social Council", the reference is to a page in the *Yearbook* describing the Assembly's treatment of that report; no reference is given to the resolutions on specific topics adopted under that item. These may be found by resolution or decision number in the INDEX OF RESOLUTIONS AND DECISIONS.

General Assembly

Agenda of the ninth emergency special session
(29 January–5 February 1982)

Item No.	*Title*	*Allocation*	*Page*
1.	Opening of the session by the President of the General Assembly.	Plenary	—
2.	Minute of silent prayer or meditation.	Plenary	—
3.	Credentials of representatives to the ninth emergency special session of the General Assembly:		
	(a) Appointment of the members of the Credentials Committee;	Plenary	1620
	(b) Report of the Credentials Committee.	Plenary	—
4.	Adoption of the agenda.	Plenary	—
5.	The situation in the occupied Arab territories.	Plenary	502

Agenda items considered at the resumed thirty-sixth session
(16-29 March, 28 April and 20 September 1982)

Item No.	*Title*	*Allocation*	*Page*
15.	Elections to fill vacancies in principal organs:		
	(c) Election of a member of the International Court of Justice.	Plenary	1650
18.	Appointments to fill vacancies in subsidiary organs and other appointments:		
	(i) Appointment of the United Nations Commissioner for Namibia.	Plenary	1310
35.	Question of Cyprus.	Plenary	376
37.	Launching of global negotiations on international economic co-operation for development.	Plenary	595
60.	United Nations Relief and Works Agency for Palestine Refugees in the Near East.	SPC	548
70.	Operational activities for development:		
	(h) United Nations Children's Fund.	2nd	1164
100.	Proposed programme budget for the biennium 1982-1983.	5th	1409
110.	Financing of the United Nations peace-keeping forces in the Middle East:		
	(b) United Nations Interim Force in Lebanon.	5th	489

Agenda items considered at the resumed seventh emergency special session
(20-28 April, 25 and 26 June, 16-19 August and 24 September 1982)

Item No.	*Title*	*Allocation*	*Page*
3.	Credentials of representatives to the seventh emergency special session of the General Assembly.	Plenary	1620
5.	Question of Palestine.	Plenary	396

Agenda of the twelfth special session
(7 June–10 July 1982)

Item No.	Title	Allocation	Page
1.	Opening of the session by the Chairman of the delegation of Iraq.	Plenary	—
2.	Minute of silent prayer or meditation.	Plenary	—
3.	Credentials of representatives to the twelfth special session of the General Assembly:		
	(a) Appointment of the members of the Credentials Committee;	Plenary	1620
	(b) Report of the Credentials Committee.	Plenary	584
4.	Election of the President of the General Assembly.	Plenary	1619
5.	Organization of the session.	Plenary	12
6.	Report of the Preparatory Committee for the Second Special Session of the General Assembly Devoted to Disarmament.	Plenary	11
7.	Adoption of the agenda.	Plenary	583
8.	General debate (including review and appraisal of the present international situation in the light of the pressing need for specific, generally agreed measures to eliminate the danger of war, in particular nuclear war, to halt and reverse the arms race and to achieve substantial progress in the field of disarmament, especially in its nuclear aspects, taking due account of the close interrelationship between disarmament and international peace and security, as well as between disarmament and economic and social development, particularly of the developing countries).	Plenary	—
9.	Review of the implementation of the recommendations and decisions adopted by the General Assembly at its tenth special session:		
	(a) Status of negotiations on disarmament as contained in the Programme of Action and bearing in mind the priorities set out in the Programme;	Plenary	12
	(b) Consideration of the report of the Committee on Disarmament, in particular of any draft instruments transmitted by the Committee;	Plenary	21
	(c) Consideration of the report of the Disarmament Commission;	Plenary	24
	(d) Consideration of the implementation of resolutions of the General Assembly on specific tasks, in particular studies, aimed at the realization of the Final Document and their follow-up.	Plenary	12
10.	Consideration and adoption of the Comprehensive Programme of Disarmament.	Plenary	19
11.	Implementation of the Declaration of the 1980s as the Second Disarmament Decade and consideration of initiatives and proposals of Member States.	Plenary	12
12.	Enhancement of the effectiveness of machinery in the field of disarmament and strengthening of the role of the United Nations in this field, including the possible convening of a World Disarmament Conference.	Plenary	12
13.	Measures to mobilize world public opinion in favour of disarmament:		
	(a) Disarmament education, seminars and training (United Nations programme of fellowships on disarmament);	Plenary	12
	(b) World Disarmament Campaign;	Plenary	31
	(c) Other public information activities.	Plenary	12
14.	Adoption, in an appropriate format, of the documents of the twelfth special session of the General Assembly.	Plenary	12

Agenda of the thirty-seventh session
(first part, 21 September–21 December 1982)

Item No.	Title	Allocation	Page
1.	Opening of the session by the Chairman of the delegation of Iraq.	Plenary	—
2.	Minute of silent prayer or meditation.	Plenary	—
3.	Credentials of representatives to the thirty-seventh session of the General Assembly:		
	(a) Appointment of the members of the Credentials Committee;	Plenary	1620
	(b) Report of the Credentials Committee.	Plenary	584
4.	Election of the President of the General Assembly.	Plenary	1619
5.	Election of the officers of the Main Committees.	Plenary	1619
6.	Election of the Vice-Presidents of the General Assembly.	Plenary	1619
7.	Notification by the Secretary-General under Article 12, paragraph 2, of the Charter of the United Nations.	Plenary	581
8.	Adoption of the agenda and organization of work:		
	(a) Report of the General Committee;	Plenary	583
	(b) Subsidiary organs of the General Assembly.	5th	1495
9.	General debate.	Plenary	—
10.	Report of the Secretary-General on the work of the Organization.	Plenary	3

---

[1] Hearings of organizations.

---

[2]Hearings of Cypriot representatives.

[3]Hearings of bodies and individuals.

Security Council

Agenda items considered during 1982[4]

[4]Numbers indicate the order in which items were taken up in 1982.

Economic and Social Council

Agenda of the organizational session for 1982
(2-5 February 1982)

Agenda of the first regular session of 1982
(13 April–7 May 1982)

Agenda of the second regular session of 1982
(7-30 July 1982; resumed 25-27 October and 9-11 November)

[5]Item considered at the resumed second regular session only, at plenary meetings.

Trusteeship Council
Agenda of the forty-ninth session
(17 May–11 June 1982)

Appendix V

United Nations Information Centres and Services

(As at 31 December 1982)

ACCRA. United Nations Information Centre
Liberia and Maxwell Roads
(P. O. Box 2339)
Accra, Ghana

> *Serving:* Ghana, Sierra Leone

ADDIS ABABA. United Nations Information
Service, Economic Commission for Africa
Africa Hall
(P. O. Box 3001)
Addis Ababa, Ethiopia

> *Serving:* Ethiopia

ALGIERS. United Nations Information Centre
19 Avenue Chahid El Waly Mustapha Sayed
Algiers, Algeria

> *Serving:* Algeria

ANKARA. United Nations Information Centre
197 Ataturk Bulvari
(P. K. 407)
Ankara, Turkey

> *Serving:* Turkey

ANTANANARIVO. United Nations Information
Centre
22 Rue Rainitovo
Antsahavola
(Boîte Postale 1348)
Antananarivo, Madagascar

> *Serving:* Madagascar

ASUNCION. United Nations Information
Centre
Calle Estrella y Chile
Edificio City (3er piso)
(Casilla de Correo 1107)
Asunción, Paraguay

> *Serving:* Paraguay

ATHENS. United Nations Information Centre
36 Amalia Avenue
Athens 119, Greece

> *Serving:* Cyprus, Greece, Israel

BAGHDAD. United Nations Information
Service, Economic Commission for
Western Asia
Khairat Building, Saadoun Street
near Unknown Soldier Square
(P. O. Box 27)
Baghdad, Iraq

> *Serving:* Iraq

BANGKOK. United Nations Information
Service, Economic and Social Commission
for Asia and the Pacific
United Nations Building
Rajdamnern Avenue
Bangkok 2, Thailand

> *Serving:* Brunei, Democratic Kampuchea, Hong Kong, Lao People's Democratic Republic, Malaysia, Singapore, Thailand, Viet Nam

BEIRUT. United Nations Information Centre
Apt. No. 1, Fakhoury Building
Montée Baim Militaire
(P. O. Box 4656)
Beirut, Lebanon

> *Serving:* Jordan, Kuwait, Lebanon, Syrian Arab Republic

BELGRADE. United Nations Information
Centre
Svetozara Markovica 58
(P. O. Box 157)
Belgrade, Yugoslavia YU-11001

> *Serving:* Albania, Yugoslavia

BOGOTA. United Nations Information Centre
Calle 61 No. 13-23 (piso 5)
(Apartado Aéreo 058964)
Bogotá 2, Colombia

> *Serving:* Colombia, Ecuador, Venezuela

BRUSSELS. United Nations Information
Centre and Liaison Office
108 Rue d'Arlon
1040 Brussels, Belgium

> *Serving:* Belgium, Luxembourg, Netherlands; liaison with European Communities

BUCHAREST. United Nations Information
Centre
16 Aurel Vlaicu Street
(P. O. Box 1-701)
Bucharest, Romania

> *Serving:* Romania

BUENOS AIRES. United Nations Information
Centre
Ugarteche 3069
1425 Buenos Aires, Argentina

> *Serving:* Argentina, Uruguay

BUJUMBURA. United Nations Information
Centre
Avenue de la Poste 7
Place de l'Indépendance
(Boîte Postale 2160)
Bujumbura, Burundi

> *Serving:* Burundi

CAIRO. United Nations Information Centre
1 Osiris Street
Tagher Building (Garden City)
(Boîte Postale 262)
Cairo, Egypt

> *Serving:* Egypt, Saudi Arabia, Yemen

COLOMBO. United Nations Information
Centre
202-204 Bauddhaloka Mawatha
(P. O. Box 1505)
Colombo 7, Sri Lanka

> *Serving:* Sri Lanka

COPENHAGEN. United Nations Information
Centre
37 H. C. Andersen Boulevard
DK 1553 Copenhagen V, Denmark

> *Serving:* Denmark, Finland, Iceland, Norway, Sweden

DAKAR. United Nations Information Centre
9 Allée Robert Delmas
(Boîte Postale 154)
Dakar, Senegal

> *Serving:* Cape Verde, Gambia, Guinea, Guinea-Bissau, Ivory Coast, Mauritania, Senegal

DAR ES SALAAM. United Nations Information Centre
Samora Machel Avenue
Matasalamat Building (1st floor)
(P. O. Box 9224)
Dar es Salaam, United Republic of Tanzania

> *Serving:* United Republic of Tanzania

DHAKA. United Nations Information Centre
House 12, Road 6
Dhanmondi
(G. P. O. Box 3658)
Dhaka, Bangladesh

> *Serving:* Bangladesh

GENEVA. United Nations Information Service,
United Nations Office at Geneva
Palais des Nations
1211 Geneva 10, Switzerland

> *Serving:* Bulgaria, Holy See, Hungary, Poland, Spain, Switzerland

HARARE. United Nations Information Centre
Lenbern House, Moffat Street
(P. O. Box 4408)
Harare, Zimbabwe

> *Serving:* Zimbabwe

ISLAMABAD. United Nations Information Centre
House No. 26
88th Street, Ramna 6/3
(P. O. Box 1107)
Islamabad, Pakistan

Serving: Pakistan

KABUL. United Nations Information Centre
Shah Mahmoud Ghazi Watt
(P. O. Box 5)
Kabul, Afghanistan

Serving: Afghanistan

KATHMANDU. United Nations Information Centre
Lazimpat
(P. O. Box 107)
Kathmandu, Nepal

Serving: Nepal

KHARTOUM. United Nations Information Centre
Al Qasr Avenue, Street No. 15
Block 3, House 3 East
Khartoum East
(P. O. Box 1992)
Khartoum, Sudan

Serving: Somalia, Sudan

KINSHASA. United Nations Information Centre
Bâtiment Deuxième République
Boulevard du 30 Juin
(Boîte Postale 7248)
Kinshasa, Zaire

Serving: Zaire

LAGOS. United Nations Information Centre
17 Kingsway, Ikoyi
(P. O. Box 1068)
Lagos, Nigeria

Serving: Nigeria

LA PAZ. United Nations Information Centre
Avenida Arce No. 2529
Edificio Santa Isabel
Bloque C, 2° Mezzanine
(Apartado Postal 686)
La Paz, Bolivia

Serving: Bolivia

LIMA. United Nations Information Centre
Av. Los Incas 580, San Isidro
Bosque El Olivar
(Apartado Postal 11199)
Lima, Peru

Serving: Peru

LISBON. United Nations Information Centre
Rua Latino Coelho No. 1
Edificio Aviz, Bloco A1-10°
1000 Lisbon, Portugal

Serving: Portugal

LOME. United Nations Information Centre
Rue Albert Sarraut
coin Avenue de Gaulle
(Boîte Postale 911)
Lomé, Togo

Serving: Benin, Togo

LONDON. United Nations Information Centre
14/15 Stratford Place
London, W1N 9AF, England

Serving: Ireland, United Kingdom

LUSAKA. United Nations Information Centre
P. O. Box 32905
Lusaka, Zambia

Serving: Botswana, Malawi, Namibia, Swaziland, Zambia

MANAMA. United Nations Information Centre
King Faisal Road, Gufool
(P. O. Box 26004)
Manama, Bahrain

Serving: Bahrain, Qatar, United Arab Emirates

MANILA. United Nations Information Centre
NEDA Building (ground floor)
106 Amorsolo Street
Legaspi Village, Makati
(P. O. Box 7285 (ADC), MIA Road, Pasay City)
Metro Manila, Philippines

Serving: Philippines

MASERU. United Nations Information Centre
Corner Hilton Road
opposite Sanlam Centre
Kingsway
(P. O. Box 301)
Maseru 100, Lesotho

Serving: Lesotho

MEXICO CITY. United Nations Information Centre
Presidente Masaryk 29 (7° piso)
México 5, D. F., Mexico

Serving: Cuba, Dominican Republic, Mexico

MONROVIA. United Nations Information Centre
LBDI Building
Main Road, Congotown
(P. O. Box 274)
Monrovia, Liberia

Serving: Liberia

MOSCOW. United Nations Information Centre
4/16 Ulitsa Lunacharskogo
Moscow 121002, USSR

Serving: Byelorussian SSR, Ukrainian SSR, USSR

NAIROBI. United Nations Information Centre
P. O. Box 30218
Nairobi, Kenya

Serving: Kenya, Seychelles, Uganda

NEW DELHI. United Nations Information Centre
55 Lodi Estate
New Delhi 110003, India

Serving: Bhutan, India

OUAGADOUGOU. United Nations Information Centre
218 Rue de la Gare
(Boîte Postale 135)
Ouagadougou, Upper Volta

Serving: Chad, Mali, Niger, Upper Volta

PARIS. United Nations Information Centre
4 et 6 Avenue de Saxe
75700 Paris, France

Serving: France

PORT MORESBY. United Nations Information Centre
Towers Building (ground floor)
Musgrave Street, Ela Beach
(P. O. Box 472)
Port Moresby, Papua New Guinea

Serving: Papua New Guinea, Solomon Islands

PORT OF SPAIN. United Nations Information Centre
15 Keate Street
(P. O. Box 130)
Port of Spain, Trinidad

Serving: Bahamas, Barbados, Belize, Dominica, Grenada, Guyana, Jamaica, Netherlands Antilles, Saint Lucia, Saint Vincent and the Grenadines, Suriname, Trinidad and Tobago

PRAGUE. United Nations Information Centre
Panska 5
11000 Prague 1, Czechoslovakia

Serving: Czechoslovakia, German Democratic Republic

RABAT. United Nations Information Centre
Angle Charia Moulay Hassan et Zankat Assafi
(Casier ONU)
Rabat-Chellah, Morocco

Serving: Morocco

RANGOON. United Nations Information Centre
18A Manawhari Road
(P. O. Box 230)
Rangoon, Burma

Serving: Burma

RIO DE JANEIRO. United Nations Information Centre
Rua Cruz Lima 19, Grupo 201
22230 Rio de Janeiro, Brazil RJ

Serving: Brazil

ROME. United Nations Information Centre
Palazzetto Venezia
Piazza San Marco 50
Rome, Italy

Serving: Italy, Malta

SAN SALVADOR. United Nations Information
Centre
Edificio Escalón (2° piso)
Paseo General Escalón y 87 Avenida Norte
Colonia Escalón
(Apartado Postal 2157)
San Salvador, El Salvador

    Serving: Costa Rica, El Salvador,
Guatemala, Honduras, Nicaragua, Panama

SANTIAGO. United Nations Information
Service, Economic Commission for Latin
America
Edificio Naciones Unidas
Avenida Dag Hammarskjold
(Casilla 179-D)
Santiago, Chile

    Serving: Chile

SYDNEY. United Nations Information Centre
National Mutual Centre
44 Market Street (16th floor)
(P. O. Box 4045, Sydney 2001, N. S. W.)
Sydney 2000, N. S. W., Australia

    Serving: Australia, Fiji, Kiribati, Nauru,
New Zealand, Samoa, Tonga, Tuvalu,
Vanuatu

TEHERAN. United Nations Information Centre
Avenue Gandhi
43 Street No. 3
(P. O. Box 1555)
Teheran, Iran

    Serving: Iran

TOKYO. United Nations Information Centre
Shin Aoyama Building Nishikan (22nd floor)
1-1 Minami Aoyama 1-chome, Minato-ku
Tokyo 107, Japan

    Serving: Japan, Trust Territory of the Pa-
cific Islands

TRIPOLI. United Nations Information Centre
67-71 Turkiya Street
(P. O. Box 286)
Tripoli, Libyan Arab Jamahiriya

    Serving: Libyan Arab Jamahiriya

TUNIS. United Nations Information Centre
61 Boulevard Bab-Benat
(Boîte Postale 863)
Tunis, Tunisia

    Serving: Tunisia

VIENNA. United Nations Information Service
Vienna International Centre
(P. O. Box 500)
A-1400 Vienna, Austria

    Serving: Austria, Federal Republic of
Germany

WASHINGTON, D. C. United Nations Information Centre
2101 L Street, N. W.
Washington, D. C. 20037, United States

    Serving: United States

YAOUNDE. United Nations Information Centre
Immeuble Kamden
Rue Joseph Clerc
(Boîte Postale 836)
Yaoundé, United Republic of Cameroon

    Serving: Central African Republic,
Gabon, United Republic of Cameroon

Indexes

USING THE SUBJECT INDEX

The subject index to the *Yearbook of the United Nations 1982* is designed to assist the reader to find information on specific subjects. The designations employed and the presentation of entries in the index do not imply the expression of any opinion by the Department of Public Information of the United Nations. The subject index contains four types of entries:

Subject terms, including geographical names, are in bold face and are based on the subject descriptors used in the United Nations Bibliographical Information System (UNBIS), published in the *UNBIS Thesaurus* (United Nations Publication: Sales No. E.81.I.17). In order to minimize subentries, the index lists broad and narrow terms in their separate alphabetical positions; for example, "human rights", "racial discrimination" and "right to development". Subjects pertaining to the United Nations or the system as a whole, such as "contributions (UN)", "finances (UN)" and "staff (UN/UN system)", are indexed separately, with cross-references under "United Nations".

NAMES of organizations and subsidiary bodies, conferences, United Nations Secretariat departments and offices, programmes, and special decades and observances, are given in full in capitals and small capitals and are alphabetized in either of two ways: (1) Names of bodies, units and programmes that are part of the United Nations, names of subsidiary bodies of specialized agencies and of their affiliated institutions, and titles of special decades and observances, are indexed under their key word: APARTHEID, SPEC. CT. AGAINST; DEVELOPMENT DECADE, 3RD UN; LAW OF THE SEA, 3RD UN CF. ON THE; MARITIME DAY, WORLD; TECHNICAL CO-OPERATION FOR DEVELOPMENT, DEPARTMENT OF. (2) Names of specialized agencies and of non–United Nations organizations are alphabetized under the first word of their title: INTER-AMERICAN CS. ON HUMAN RIGHTS; WORLD METEOROLOGICAL ORGANIZATION.

Names of publications are italicized, with only those receiving relatively extensive treatment in *Yearbook* articles, such as *Development Forum* and the *World Economic Survey 1981-1982*, being listed.

Cross-references are not given to entries in close proximity; for example, there is a cross-reference to "Information, Ct. on" under "public information" but not under "information"; and to "economic development" but not "development assistance" under "development".

Entries are alphabetized word by word. Examples: **human rights**; HUMAN RIGHTS, CS. ON; **humanitarian assistance**.

Within most entries, the organization, body or unit dealing with the subject is indicated (by abbreviation or short title) in parentheses, preceded or followed by the appropriate page number(s). Bold-face numbers refer to resolution or decision texts. Thus, the entry

agrometeorology, 1582 (WMO)

indicates that WMO activities relating to agrometeorology are described on the page cited. The entry

American Samoa, 1353-54 (Colonial Countries Ct., 1353; GA, 1353, **1353-54**)

indicates that information on American Samoa appears on pages 1353 to 1354 and that, on this topic, the activities of the Special Committee on the Situation with regard to the Implementation of the Declaration on the Granting of Independence to Colonial Countries and Peoples are described on page 1353; the activities of the General Assembly are described on page 1353 and the text of one or more resolution(s)/decision(s) (or provision(s) thereof) adopted by the Assembly is on pages 1353 and 1354.

Abbreviations

In addition to the abbreviations contained in the list on pp. xii-xiii, the subject index uses the following:

CD	Committee on Disarmament
cf(s).	conference(s)
cl(s).	council(s)
cs(s).	commission(s)
ct(s).	committee(s)
DC	Disarmament Commission
DG	Director-General
mtg(s).	meeting(s)
sess.	session
spec.	special
UNCLS	United Nations Conference on the Law of the Sea
UNJSPB	United Nations Joint Staff Pension Board

Subject index

Page numbers in boldface type indicate resolutions and decisions

order; radio broadcasting; television broadcasting; *and under* apartheid *and other topics*

PUBLIC INFORMATION, DEPARTMENT OF (DPI), 570-75 (GA, **568-69**; Information Ct./SG, 570); co-operation with news agencies, 571-72 (GA, **570**, 571-72; Information Ct./SG, 571); & developing countries, 574-75 (Information Ct.); evaluation, 574 (Information Ct./SG); liaison services 578 (ACC/Information Ct.); & OAU, 330; staff, geographical distribution, 574 (GA, **569**, 574; Information Ct./SG, 574); Under-SG, 1653; *see also* Radio and Visual Services Division; television broadcasting

Puerto Rico, 1275-76 (Colonial Countries Ct., 1275-76; GA, 1276); & trade union rights, 1093, **1093** (ESC/ILO)

pulp and paper industry, 779 (UNIDO), 1553 (IFC)

racial discrimination, elimination of, 1050-62; International Day for, observance, 1050 (*Apartheid* Ct.); *see also apartheid*; discrimination; fascism; indigenous peoples; minorities; nazism

RACIAL DISCRIMINATION, CONVENTION ON THE ELIMINATION OF ALL FORMS OF *(1965)*: accessions/ratifications, 1061-62 (GA, 1061, **1061**; SG, 1062); implementation, 1058-61 (CERD, 1058-59; GA, 1059-60, **1060-61**); reports from governments, 1061, **1061** (CERD/GA)

RACIAL DISCRIMINATION, CT. ON THE ELIMINATION OF (CERD), 1058-59 (GA, 1059, **1060-61**); members, 1651; & 2nd World Cf., 1050, 1058; & TC, 1290

RACIAL DISCRIMINATION, DECADE FOR ACTION TO COMBAT RACISM AND *(1973-1983)*: implementation, 1050-53 (CERD/Human Rights Ct./SG, 1050; ESC, 1050, **1051-52**; GA, 1050-51, **1052-53**); & NGOs, **304**, 1053 (ESC); Seminar for ESCAP, 1053, **1053** (ESC)

RACIAL DISCRIMINATION, 2ND WORLD CF. TO COMBAT RACISM AND *(1983)*, 1053-58 (ESC, 1054, **1055-56**; GA, 1054-55, **1057-58**, **1060**, **1115**; Human Rights Cs., 1054; Preparatory Sub-Ct., 1053-54); dates/location, 1054, 1056 (ESC), 1054, **1057** (GA); financing, 1054, **1056** (ESC), 1055, 1058, **1058** (ACABQ/GA), 1059 (CERD); observers/participants, 1054, **1055-56** (ESC), 1054, **1056** (GA); provisional agenda, 1054, 1055 (ESC), 1057-58

RACIAL DISCRIMINATION, 2D WORLD CF. TO COMBAT RACISM AND *(1983)*, Preparatory Sub-Ct., 1053-54 (ESC, 1054, **1056**; GA, **1053**, 1055); members/officers, 1647

RADIATION, UN SCIENTIFIC CT. ON THE EFFECTS OF ATOMIC (UNSCEAR), 578-80 (GA, 579, **579-80**); co-operation with UNEP, 579, **579** (GA); & IAEA, 579, **580** (GA); members/officers, 1635

radiation dosimetry, *see under* dosimetry

radiation effects: UNSCEAR report, 578-79 (GA, 579, **579-80**)

RADIATION PROTECTION, BASIC SAFETY STANDARDS FOR (IAEA), publication, 1515

RADIO AND VISUAL SERVICES DIVISION (DPI): regional units, 573-74 (Information Ct./SG)

radioactive waste management, *see under* nuclear power; Trust Territory of the Pacific Islands

radio broadcasting, **569**, 572-73 (GA/Information Ct./SG); frequency allocation, 1576 (ITU)

RADIO CONSULTATIVE CT., INTERNATIONAL (CCIR), 1576 (ITU)

RADIOLOGICAL PROTECTION, INTERNATIONAL CS. ON, 1515

radiological weapons, 107-8 (CD, 107; GA, June/July, 107; GA, Dec., 107-8, **108**)

RADIOLOGICAL WEAPONS, *AD HOC* WORKING GROUP ON (CD), 107

RAIL TRANSPORT, WORKING PARTY ON (ECE), 854

railway transport, 810 (ECA), 842 (ESCAP), 854 (ECE)

Red Cross, International Ct. of the, *see* International Ct. of the Red Cross

Red Sea: regional seas programme (UNEP), 1022

refugees, 1194-1220

aging, 1219 (World Assembly on Aging/UNHCR)

assistance, 1200-2 (UNHCR); expenditures by country, 1201 *(table)*; *Handbook on Emergencies*, 1200

asylum-seekers at sea, Working Group on, 1218

attacks on camps, **1195**, 1218 (GA)

documentation, 1218

food aid operations, 917, 918-19 (WFP)

handicapped, Trust Fund for, 1200; regional activities, 1200

human rights of, **1195**, 1218 (GA)

international co-operation to avert new flows of, 1219-20 (GA, **1072**, **1134**, 1219-20, **1220**; SG, 1220)

international instruments, accessions/ratifications, 1218-19

programme policy, 1194-95 (GA, 1194, **1194-95**; UNHCR, 1194)

protection, 1217-18 (GA, **1195**, 1218; Sub-ct. of the Whole, 1218; UNHCR, 1217-18); seminar (Institute of Humanitarian Law), 1219

resettlement, 1194, **1195** (GA/UNHCR), 1200, 1205 (Tripartite Cs./UNHCR)

see also country names and regional entries

REFUGEES, *AD HOC* CT. OF THE GA FOR ANNOUNCEMENT OF VOLUNTARY CONTRIBUTIONS TO *1983* PROGRAMME OF UN HIGH COMMISSIONER FOR, 1196, 1197 *(table)*; chairman/members, 1620

REFUGEES, CONVENTION *(1951)*, and PROTOCOL *(1967)*, RELATING TO THE STATUS OF, ratifications/accessions, 1215, 1218-19

REFUGEES, EXECUTIVE CT. OF THE PROGRAMME OF UN HIGH COMMISSIONER FOR, 1196; proposed enlargement, 1199, **1199** (ESC); representation of Namibia, 1198-99, **1199** (ESC)

REFUGEES, GROUP OF GOVERNMENTAL EXPERTS ON INTERNATIONAL CO-OPERATION TO AVERT NEW FLOWS OF, 1219-20 (GA, 1219-20, **1220**)

REFUGEES, OFFICE OF THE UN HIGH COMMISSIONER FOR (UNHCR), 1194-95; administrative costs, 1196-98 (ACABQ, 1196-97; GA, 1197-98, **1198**; SG, 1196; UNHCR, 1197); continuation, 1195, **1195-96** (GA); contributions, 1196 *(Ad Hoc* Ct./Auditors Board/ UNHCR), 1197 *(table)*; expenditures/income, 1196; programme, 1194, **1194-95** (GA); public information, 1199-1200; Social Services Section, establishment, 1219; Sub-cts., members/officers, 1626; voluntary funds, accounts *(1981)*, 1198 (ACABQ/Auditors Board, 1198; GA, 1198, **1428**)

REFUGEES, UN HIGH COMMISSIONER FOR, 1653; extension of term, 1199, **1199** (GA); Deputy, 1653; report, **1194-95** (GA)

REFUGEES IN AFRICA, INTERNATIONAL CF. ON ASSISTANCE TO *(1981)*: follow-up, 1202-4 (ESC, **674**, 1202; GA, **1195**, 1203, **1203-4**; SG, 1202-3; Steering Ct., 1202); 2nd international cf. (proposed), 1203, **1204** (GA); Steering Ct., members/mtgs., 1202

refugee seamen, Agreement *(1957)* and Protocol *(1973)* relating to, 1219

regional co-operation, 795-96, **796** (ESC/Cs. secretaries)

regional css., *see under* Economic and Social Council

REGIONAL MARINE PROGRAMMES, MTG. OF GOVERNMENTAL EXPERTS (Nairobi, Kenya), 1023 (UNEP Cl.)

regional seas programme: action plans, 1022-23 (GA, **1004**, 1023; Experts Mtg., 1023; UNEP Cl., 1022-23); & South Asia seas, proposed programme, 849 (ESCAP/UNEP); trust funds, 1023 (UNEP Cl.)

REGIONAL AND SUBREGIONAL INSTITUTIONS, CF. OF CHIEF EXECUTIVES OF (ECA), 835

religious intolerance, Declaration *(1981)*, 1064-65 (ESC, 1064, **1064**; GA, 1064, **1064-65**; SCPDPM, 1064)

remote sensing: & agriculture, 1529 (FAO); cartographic applications, 171, 885 (FAO); legal principles (draft), 175 (COPUOS/Outer Space Cf., 175; GA, **161**, 175); natural resources exploration, 843 (ESCAP); technical aspects, 168 (COPUOS/Outer Space Cf., 168; GA, **161**, 168)

REMOTE SENSING CENTRE (FAO), 165, 168 (Outer Space Cf.), 1529

REMOTE SENSING LABORATORIES, EUROPEAN ASSOCIATION OF (EARSEL): co-operation with UN Programme, 166 (COPUOS)

Repertoire of the Practice of the Security Council/Repertory of Practice of United Nations Organs, publication, 1390 (SG)

resources, *see* energy resources; human resources; natural resources

restrictive business practices, 733 (TDB); *see also* protectionism

RESTRICTIVE BUSINESS PRACTICES, INTERGOVERNMENTAL GROUP OF EXPERTS ON, 733

reverse transfer of technology, *see* brain drain

Index of names

Index of resolutions and decisions

[a]Adopted on 21 September to appoint the members of the Credentials Committee.
[b]Adopted on 21 September to elect the Chairmen of the Main Committees.
[c]Adopted on 20 December to confirm the appointment of the Secretary-General of UNCTAD.
[d]Adopted on 21 December to take note of the appointment by the General Assembly President of the members of the Consultative Committee on the Voluntary Fund for the United Nations Decade for Women.
[e]Adopted on 24 September in regard to the organization of the thirty-seventh session on the recommendations of the General Committee.

[f]Adopted on 20 December to keep the item on "launching of global negotiations on international economic co-operation for development" open in order to allow for the continuation of informal consultations after suspension of the thirty-seventh session.
[g]Adopted on 5 February to approve the basic programme of work of the Economic and Social Council for 1982 and 1983.
[h]Adopted on 7 July to transmit without debate the report of the United Nations High Commissioner for Refugees to the General Assembly at its thirty-seventh session.

How to obtain previous volumes of the *Yearbook*

Volumes of the *Yearbook of the United Nations* published previously may be obtained in many bookstores throughout the world and also from the Sales Section, United Nations, New York, N. Y. 10017, or from United Nations Publications, Palais des Nations, 1211 Geneva 10, Switzerland. Volumes listed below with an asterisk (*) are special reprints of editions out of print.

Yearbook of the United Nations, 1981
Vol. 35. Sales No. E.84.I.1 $75.

Yearbook of the United Nations, 1980
Vol. 34. Sales No. E.83.I.1 $72.

Yearbook of the United Nations, 1979
Vol. 33. Sales No. E.82.I.1 $72.

Yearbook of the United Nations, 1978
Vol. 32. Sales No. E.80.I.1 $60.

Yearbook of the United Nations, 1977
Vol. 31. Sales No. E.79.I.1 $50.

Yearbook of the United Nations, 1976
Vol. 30. Sales No. E.78.I.1 $42.

Yearbook of the United Nations, 1975
Vol. 29. Sales No. E.77.I.1 $35.

Yearbook of the United Nations, 1974
Vol. 28. Sales No. E.76.I.1 $35.

Yearbook of the United Nations, 1973
Vol. 27. Sales No. E.75.I.1 $35.

Yearbook of the United Nations, 1972
Vol. 26. Sales No. E.74.I.1 $35.

Yearbook of the United Nations, 1971
Vol. 25. Sales No. E.73.I.1 $35.

Yearbook of the United Nations, 1970*
Vol. 24. Sales No. E.72.I.1 $35.

Yearbook of the United Nations, 1969
Vol. 23. Sales No. E.71.I.1 $35.

Yearbook of the United Nations, 1968
Vol. 22. Sales No. E.70.I.1 $35.

Yearbook of the United Nations, 1967
Vol. 21. Sales No. E.68.I.1 $35.

Yearbook of the United Nations, 1966*
Vol. 20. Sales No. E.67.I.1 $50.

Yearbook of the United Nations, 1965*
Vol. 19. Sales No. 66.I.1 $50.

Yearbook of the United Nations, 1964*
Vol. 18. Sales No. 65.I.1 $58.

Yearbook of the United Nations, 1963
Vol. 17. Sales No. 64.I.1 $35.

Yearbook of the United Nations, 1962
Vol. 16. Sales No. 63.I.1 $35.

Yearbook of the United Nations, 1961
Vol. 15. Sales No. 62.I.1 $35.

Yearbook of the United Nations, 1960
Vol. 14. Sales No. 61.I.1 $35.

Yearbook of the United Nations, 1959*
Vol. 13. Sales No. 60.I.1 $58.

Yearbook of the United Nations, 1958
Vol. 12. Sales No. 59.I.1 $35.

Yearbook of the United Nations, 1957*
Vol. 11. Sales No. 58.I.1 $58.

Yearbook of the United Nations, 1956*
Vol. 10. Sales No. 57.I.1 $40.

Yearbook of the United Nations, 1955*
Vol. 9. Sales No. 56.I.20 $40.

Yearbook of the United Nations, 1954*
Vol. 8. Sales No. 55.I.25 $46.

Yearbook of the United Nations, 1953*
Vol. 7. Sales No. 54.I.15 $50.

Yearbook of the United Nations, 1952*
Vol. 6. Sales No. 53.I.30 $50.

Yearbook of the United Nations, 1951*
Vol. 5. Sales No. 52.I.30 $50.

Yearbook of the United Nations, 1950*
Vol. 4. Sales No. 1951.I.24 $75.

Yearbook of the United Nations, 1948-49*
Vol. 3. Sales No. 1950.I.11 $75.

Yearbook of the United Nations, 1947-48
Vol. 2. Sales No. 1949.I.13 $35.

Yearbook of the United Nations, 1946-47*
Vol. 1. Sales No. 1947.I.18 $75.

Yearbook Volumes 1-34 (1946-1980) are now also available in microfiche at the cost of US$ 1,198.90 for silver halide or US$ 1,041.15 for diazo duplication. Orders for microfiche sets should be sent either to the Sales Section, United Nations, New York, N. Y. 10017, or to United Nations Publications, Palais des Nations, 1211 Geneva 10, Switzerland.

NOTES

NOTES

NOTES

NOTES

NOTES

NOTES